2012
STANDARD POSTAGE
STAMP CATALOGUE

ONE HUNDRED AND SIXTY-EIGHTH EDITION IN SIX VOLUMES

VOLUME 3
COUNTRIES OF THE WORLD
G-I

EDITOR	James E. Kloetzel
ASSISTANT EDITOR	Charles Snee
ASSISTANT EDITOR /NEW ISSUES & VALUING	Martin J. Frankevicz
ASSOCIATE EDITORS	David Akin, Donna Houseman
VALUING ANALYST	Steven R. Myers
ADMINISTRATIVE ASSISTANT/CATALOGUE LAYOUT	Eric Wiessinger
PRINTING AND IMAGE COORDINATOR	Stacey Mahan
CREATIVE DIRECTOR	Mark Potter
ADVERTISING	Angela Nolte
CIRCULATION/PRODUCT PROMOTION MANAGER	Tim Wagner
VICE PRESIDENT/EDITORIAL AND PRODUCTION	Steve Collins
PRESIDENT	William Fay

Released June 2011
Includes New Stamp Listings through the April 2011 *Linn's Stamp News Special Edition* Catalogue Update

Copyright© 2011 by

Scott Publishing Co.

911 Vandemark Road, Sidney, OH 45365-0828
A division of AMOS PRESS, INC., publishers of *Linn's Stamp News, Linn's Stamp News Special Edition, Coin World* and *Coin World Special Edition.*

Table of Contents

See Volume 1 for United States, United Nations and Countries of the World A-B
See Volume 2, 4 through 6 for Countries of the World, C-F, J-Z.

Volume 2: C-F
Volume 4: J-M
Volume 5: N-Sam
Volume 6: San-Z

Scott Publishing Mission Statement

The Scott Publishing Team exists to serve the recreational,
educational and commercial hobby needs of stamp collectors and dealers.

We strive to set the industry standard for philatelic information and products by developing and
providing goods that help collectors identify, value, organize and present their collections.

Quality customer service is, and will continue to be, our highest priority.
We aspire toward achieving total customer satisfaction.

Scott Publishing Co.

SCOTT   911 VANDEMARK ROAD, SIDNEY, OHIO 45365   937-498-0802

Dear Scott Catalogue User:

Where are the value changes in the 2012 Volume 3?

Almost 18,000 value changes appear in the 2012 edition of Volume 3 of the *Scott Standard Postage Stamp Catalogue*. This volume covers countries of the world alphabetically G through I. This is very much in line with the average number of changes seen each year for about the past decade. The changes are well spread throughout all of the countries in the volume.

The country with the most value changes in the Volume 3 Standard catalogue is Indonesia, with almost 2,800 changes. Other areas with a large number of changes are Italy, Italian Offices Abroad, Aegean Islands and Trieste Zone A, with more than 2,400 value changes combined; German States (1,402), Iran (1,375), Guyana (1,157), Hong Kong (1,048), Ghana (843) and Great Britain (838).

Value changes in Indonesia occur throughout the country's listings, with the overwhelming majority of the changes being modest increases. Occasional slight decreases can be found in some issues in the earlier period. Value increases in the most modern period are the largest. Fairly typical of the modern value increases is Scott 1916, the 2000 souvenir sheet for Olymphilex 2000, which rises to $4.50 mint, never hinged and $2.25 used, from $2.75 mint, never hinged and $1.25 used in the 2011 Volume 3.

In Italy, value changes are sporadic through the 1930s, with more modern issues showing no changes. Most early changes are to slightly higher values, while an occasional stamp shows a value decrease. The very first Italian stamp, Scott 17, the 10-centesimo bister King Victor Emmanuel II, shows healthy increases both unused and used, jumping to $9,500 unused and $360 used, from $8,000 unused and $325 used last year. On the other hand, the value of the 1879 5c to 2-lire King Humbert I set, Scott 45-51, takes a bit of a tumble unused, to $1,999, from $2,312 in 2011. In used condition, however, the set rises to $3,242 from just $2,785 last year.

In Italian Offices Abroad, there are frequent changes throughout. General issues fall somewhat in value, while values for Offices in China are significantly higher, as are values for Offices in Turkish Empire. Changes to the Aegean Islands values show mixed results, but with more increases than decreases. Trieste Zone A shows value increases throughout.

A thorough review of German States results in ubiquitous higher values for very fine stamps. What is true throughout the catalogue bears repeating here. The values are for stamps in the grade of very fine, which can be difficult to locate for many German States issues. Stamps in lower grades, as always, will sell for lower to much lower prices.

A big winner in German States stamps is Bavaria Scott J14, the 1895 2-pfennig-on-3pf gray postage due surcharged in red in each corner. It has been established that only six examples of this stamp exist, all used. There are two covers, each bearing two examples, and only two loose stamps off cover available to collectors. The value of this key stamp jumps to $150,000, from $100,000 in the 2011 Volume 3.

The general weakness in worldwide economies has continued throughout the past year, and that certainly has dampened most upward pressure on values. The results of a weak United States economy, from the perspective of U.S. catalogue editors, are threefold. First, economic weakness harms hobby-related fields generally because it is relatively easy to put hobby expenses on hold for a period of time, whereas it is not possible to put necessities such as food and housing on hold. It follows that the more common philatelic material in the marketplace would be expected to show a pretty lethargic sales pattern, and that is what we have

been seeing. Nothing terribly upsetting, but also very little showing strength in the market.

Second, as usual during such uncertain periods, true rarities and condition rarities show strength.

The third pattern we see often during difficult economic times is a swing in the relative value for different currencies. If all countries experienced the same weakness, currencies could be expected to remain relatively stable in relation to each other. That pattern, however, is seldom the case. There are strong currencies and there are weak currencies, and with Scott being a retail-value catalogue, these relative shifts have an impact on values. If an important country experiences a stronger currency in relation to the United States dollar's value, it will tend to cause prices to rise in the United States, because more dollars are needed to compete with the stronger home-country currency.

Some interesting editorial changes.

As announced last year, we are in the midst of a project to convert previous footnotes concerning like designs with different dated inscriptions into lettered minor listings, because such stamps often have different catalogue values. This year, the affected stamps in Guernsey, Jersey and Isle of Man have been added to the listings, including values.

In Hong Kong, the postage dues of 1976-86 have been relisted to be more consistent with Scott listing practices. This results in some previous lettered minors becoming major numbers, plus the addition of new lettered minors and majors for stamps on chalk-surfaced paper. A comparison of last year's listings with the 2012 listings will show the details, but we can say here that the 1978 dues with watermark 373 have been made major listings rather than minor, the chalk-surfaced stamps of 1976 with the same watermark have been made lettered minors, and the two 1986 chalk-surfaced stamps that are unwatermarked (previous numbers J21b and J22a) have been added as majors in their own right, Scott J22D and J22E.

To see these and all other listing changes that have been made this year, consult the 2012 Volume 3 Number Additions, Deletions & Changes list. In this volume, it is on page 1402.

Final thoughts.

Dr. Hsien-Ming Meng, a great Scott friend and benefactor, passed away Feb. 8, 2011, at age 84. Longtime catalogue users might recognize his name. When Scott began digitally scanning stamps for our catalogue images in 2001, we began by scanning all of the stamps in our own reference collection. But this left a huge number of earlier stamps in the old black and white velox format, often fuzzy in appearance. Recognizing the benefit of Scott's scanning project, Dr. Meng stepped forward with an offer to loan us his massive collection of unused stamps for scanning purposes. The time and effort saved by having this immense resource made available proved invaluable, and the Scott catalogues began appearing in full color much sooner than they otherwise would have. We will forever remember the kindness and generosity shown by this wonderful Ohio collector.

And speaking of our color project, there are only 57 images in this Volume 3 remaining to be converted to color. Most of these are stamps with overprints of one kind or another. Other volumes have more or fewer images remaining to be found. We still have staff and outside contributors on the lookout for the stamps not currently shown in color.

A hobby is a great gift. Happy collecting.

James E Kloetzel

James E. Kloetzel/Catalogue Editor

Acknowledgments

Our appreciation and gratitude go to the following individuals who have assisted us in preparing information included in this year's Scott Catalogues. Some helpers prefer anonymity. These individuals have generously shared their stamp knowledge with others through the medium of the Scott Catalogue.

Those who follow provided information that is in addition to the hundreds of dealer price lists and advertisements and scores of auction catalogues and realizations that were used in producing the catalogue values. It is from those noted here that we have been able to obtain information on items not normally seen in published lists and advertisements. Support from these people goes beyond data leading to catalogue values, for they also are key to editorial changes.

A special acknowledgment to Liane and Sergio Sismondo of The Classic Collector for their extraordinary assistance and knowledge sharing that has aided in the preparation of this year's Standard and Classic Specialized Catalogues.

A. R. Allison (Orange Free State Study Circle)
Roland Austin
Robert Ausubel (Great Britain Collectors Club)
Jack Hagop Barsoumian (International Stamp Co.)
George G. Birdsall
John Birkinbine II
Roger S. Brody
Keith & Margie Brown
Mahdi Bseiso
Paul Buchsbayew
Bernard Bujnak
Timothy Bryan Burgess
Mike Bush (Joseph V. Bush, Inc.)
Tina & John Carlson (JET Stamps)
Richard A. Champagne (Richard A. Champagne, Inc.)
Henry Chlanda
Bob Coale
Leroy P. Collins III (United Postal Stationery Society)
Frank D. Correl
Tom Cossaboom
Francis J. Crown, Jr.
Tony L. Crumbley (Carolina Coin & Stamp, Inc.)
Stephen R. Datz
Tony Davis
Kenneth E. Diehl
Bob Dumaine
Sister Theresa Durand
Mark Eastzer (Markest Stamp Co.)
Esi Ebrani (Iran Philatelic Study Circle)
Paul G. Eckman
George Epstein
Mehdi Esmaili
Leon Finik
Robert A. Fisher
Geoffrey Flack
Jeffrey M. Forster
Ken Fowler
Ernest E. Fricks (France & Colonies Philatelic Society)
Phillip F. Gallagher
Bob Genisol (Sultan Stamp Center)
Stan Goldfarb
Daniel E. Grau
Jan E. Gronwall
Bruce Hecht (Bruce L. Hecht Co.)
Robert R. Hegland
Clifford O. Herrick (Fidelity Trading Co.)
Peter Hoffman

Armen Hovsepian
Philip J. Hughes
Doug Iams
Thomas Jackson (Stamp Parlor)
N. M. Janoowalla
Peter Jeannopoulos
Stephen Joe (International Stamp Service)
Richard A. Johnson
Allan Katz (Ventura Stamp Co.)
Stanford M. Katz
Lewis Kaufman
Patricia A. Kaufmann
William V. Kriebel
Dr. Ingert (Ihor) Kuzych-Berlzovsky
Frederick P. Lawrence
John R. Lewis (The William Henry Stamp Co.)
Ulf Lindahl
Pedro Llach (Filatelia Llach S.L.)
George Luzitano
Dennis Lynch
Robert L. Markovits (Quality Investors, Ltd.)
Marilyn R. Mattke
William K. McDaniel
Gary McLean
Mark S. Miller (India Study Circle)
Allen Mintz (United Postal Stationery Society)
Gary Morris (Pacific Midwest Co.)
Peter Mosiondz, Jr.
Bruce M. Moyer (Moyer Stamps & Collectibles)
Richard H. Muller
Gregg Nelson
Robert Odenweller
Marc Parren
John E. Pearson (Pittwater Philatelic Service)
Donald J. Peterson (International Philippine Philatelic Society)
Stanley M. Piller (Stanley M. Piller & Associates)
Todor Drumev Popov
Peter W. W. Powell
Stephen Radin (Albany Stamp Co.)
Siddique Mahmudur Rahman
Dr. Reuben A. Ramkissoon
Ghassan D. Riachi
Eric Roberts
Omar Rodriguez
Michael Rogers (Michael Rogers, Inc.)
Robert G. Rufe
Michael Ruggiero
Andrew Sader
Mehrdad Sadri (Persiphila)
Alex Schauss (Schauss Philatelics)

Jacques C. Schiff, Jr. (Jacques C. Schiff, Jr., Inc.)
Bernard Seckler (Fine Arts Philatelists)
Guy Shaw
Jeff Siddiqui
Sergio & Liane Sismondo (The Classic Collector)
Jay Smith
Frank J. Stanley, III
Alfred E. Staubus
Scott R. Trepel (Siegel Auction Galleries)
Philip T. Wall
Giana Wayman
William R. Weiss, Jr. (Weiss Expertizing)
Ed Wener (Indigo)
Don White (Dunedin Stamp Centre)
Kirk Wolford (Kirk's Stamp Company)
Robert F. Yacano (K-Line Philippines)
Ralph Yorio
Val Zabijaka
Michal Zika
Alfonso G. Zulueta, Jr.

Addresses, Telephone Numbers, Web Sites, E-Mail Addresses of General & Specialized Philatelic Societies

Collectors can contact the following groups for information about the philately of the areas within the scope of these societies, or inquire about membership in these groups. Aside from the general societies, we limit this list to groups that specialize in particular fields of philately, particular areas covered by the Scott Standard Postage Stamp Catalogue, and topical groups. Many more specialized philatelic society exist than those listed below. These addresses are updated yearly, and they are, to the best of our knowledge, correct and current. Groups should inform the editors of address changes whenever they occur. The editors also want to hear from other such specialized groups not listed.

Unless otherwise noted all website addresses begin with http://

American Philatelic Society
100 Match Factory Place
Bellefonte PA 16823-1367
Ph: (814) 933-3803
www.stamps.org
E-mail: apsinfo@stamps.org

American Stamp Dealers
Association, Inc.
Joe Savarese
217-14 Northern Blvd.
Bayside NY 11361
Ph: (718) 224-2500
www.asdaonline.com
E-mail: asda@erols.com

National Stamp Dealers Association
Dick Keiser, president
2916 NW Bucklin Hill Rd #136
Silverdale WA 98383-8514
Ph: (800) 875-6633
www.nsdainc.org
E-mail: gail@nsdainc.org

International Society of Worldwide
Stamp Collectors
Joanne Berkowitz, MD
P.O. Box 19006
Sacramento CA 95819
www.iswsc.org
E-mail: executivedirector@iswsc.org

Royal Philatelic Society
41 Devonshire Place
London, W1G 6JY
UNITED KINGDOM
www.rpsl.org.uk
E-mail: secretary@rpsl.org.uk

Royal Philatelic Society of Canada
P.O. Box 929, Station Q
Toronto, ON, M4T 2P1
CANADA
Ph: (888) 285-4143
www.rpsc.org
E-mail: info@rpsc.org

Young Stamp Collectors of America
Janet Houser
100 Match Factory Place
Bellefonte PA 16823-1367
Ph: (814) 933-3820
www.stamps.org/ysca/intro.htm
E-mail: ysca@stamps.org

Philatelic Research Resources

(Scott editors are encouraging any additional research organizations to submit data for inclusion in this new listing category)

The Western Philatelic Library
P.O. Box 2219
1500 Partridge Avenue
Sunnyvale CA 94087
Ph: (408) 733-0336
www.fwpf.org

Groups focusing on fields or aspects found in worldwide philately (some may cover U.S. area only)

American Air Mail Society
Stephen Reinhard
P.O. Box 110
Mineola NY 11501
www.americanairmailsociety.org
E-mail: sreinhard1@optonline.net

American First Day Cover Society
Douglas Kelsey
P.O. Box 16277
Tucson AZ 85732-6277
Ph: (520) 321-0880
www.afdcs.org
E-mail: afdcs@aol.com

American Revenue Association
Eric Jackson
P.O. Box 728
Leesport PA 19533-0728
Ph: (610) 926-6200
www.revenuer.org
E-mail: eric@revenuer.com

American Topical Association
Vera Felts
P.O. Box 8
Carterville IL 62918-0008
Ph: (618) 985-5100
www.americantopicalassn.org
E-mail: americantopical@msn.com

Christmas Seal & Charity Stamp
Society
John Denune
234 East Broadway
Granville OH 43023
Ph: (740) 587-0276
http://www.charityseals.org
E-mail: jdenune@roadrunner.com

Errors, Freaks and Oddities
Collectors Club
Don David Price
5320 Eastchester Drive
Sarasota FL 34134-2711
Ph: (717) 445-9420 Nor. Am. Phone No.
www.efocc.org
E-mail: ddprice98@hotmail.com

First Issues Collectors Club
Clark Buchi
P.O. Box 453
Brentwood TN 37024-0453
www.firstissues.org
E-mail: orders@firstissues.org

International Society of Reply
Coupon Collectors
Peter Robin
P.O. Box 353
Bala Cynwyd PA 19004
E-mail: peterrobin@verizon.net

The Joint Stamp Issues Society
Richard Zimmermann
124, Avenue Guy de Coubertin
Saint Remy Les Chevreuse, F-78470
FRANCE
www.jointstampissues.net
E-mail: contact@jointstampissues.net

National Duck Stamp Collectors
Society
Anthony J. Monico
P.O. Box 43
Harleysville PA 19438-0043
www.ndscs.org
E-mail: ndscs@ndscs.org

No Value Identified Club
Albert Sauvanet
Le Clos Royal B, Boulevard des Pas
Enchantes
St. Sebastien-sur Loire, 44230
FRANCE
E-mail: alain.vailly@irin.univ nantes.fr

The Perfins Club
Jerry Hejduk
P.O. Box 490450.
Leesburg FL 34749-0450
Ph: (352) 326-2117
E-mail: flprepers@comcast.net

Postage Due Mail Study Group
John Rawlins
13, Longacre
Chelmsford, CM1 3BJ
UNITED KINGDOM
E-mail: john.rawlins2@ukonline.co.uk.

Post Mark Collectors Club
Beverly Proulx
7629 Homestead Drive
Baldwinsville NY 13027
Ph: (315) 638-0532
www.postmarks.org
E-mail: stampdance@yahoo.com

Postal History Society
Kalman V. Illyefalvi
869 Bridgewater Drive
New Oxford PA 17350-8206
Ph: (717) 624-5941
www.stampclubs.com
E-mail: kalphyl@juno.com

Precancel Stamp Society
Jerry Hejduk
P.O. Box 490450.
Leesburg FL 34749-0450
Ph: (352) 326-2117
www.precancels.com
E-mail: psspromosec@comcast.net

United Postal Stationery Society
Stuart Leven
P.O. Box 24764
San Jose CA 95154-4764
www.upss.org
E-mail: poststat@gmail.com

United States Possessions Philatelic
Society
Geoffrey Brewster
6453 E. Stallion Rd.
Paradise Valley AZ 85253
Ph: (480) 607-7184
www.uspps.com
E-mail: patlabb@aol.com

Groups focusing on U.S. area philately as covered in the Standard Catalogue

Canal Zone Study Group
Richard H. Salz
60 27th Ave.
San Francisco CA 94121-1026

Carriers and Locals Society
Martin Richardson
P.O. Box 74
Grosse Ile MI 48138
www.pennypost.org
E-mail: martinr362@aol.com

Confederate Stamp Alliance
Patricia A. Kaufmann
10194 N. Old State Road
Lincoln DE 19960
Ph. (302) 422-2656
www.csalliance.org
E-mail: csaas@comcast.net

Hawaiian Philatelic Society
Kay H. Hoke
P.O. Box 10115
Honolulu HI 96816-0115
Ph: (808) 521-5721

Plate Number Coil Collectors Club
Gene Trinks
16415 W. Desert Wren Ct.
Surprise AZ 85374
Ph: (623) 322-4619
www.pnc3.org
E-mail: gctrinks@cox.net

Ryukyu Philatelic Specialist Society
Laura Edmonds, Secy.
P.O. Box 240177
Charlotte NC 28224-0177
Ph: (704) 519-5157
www.ryukyustamps.org
E-mail: secretary@ryukyustamps.org

United Nations Philatelists
Blanton Clement, Jr.
P.O. Box 146
Morrisville PA 19067-0146
www.unpi.com
E-mail: bclemjr@yahoo.com

United States Stamp Society
Executive Secretary
P.O. Box 6634
Katy TX 77491-6631
www.usstamps.org
E-mail: webmaster@usstamps.org

U.S. Cancellation Club
Roger Rhoads
6160 Brownstone Ct.
Mentor OH 44060
http://bob.trachimowicz.org/indfk.html
E-mail: rrrhoads@aol.com

U.S. Philatelic Classics Society
Rob Lund
2913 Fulton
Everett WA 98201-3733
www.uspcs.org
E-mail: membershipchairman@uspcs.org

Groups focusing on philately of foreign countries or regions

Aden & Somaliland Study Group
Gary Brown
P.O. Box 106
Briar Hill, Victoria, 3088
AUSTRALIA
E-mail: garyjohn951@optushome.com.au

American Society of Polar Philatelists (Antarctic areas)
Alan Warren
P.O. Box 39
Exton PA 19341-0039
www.polarphilatelists.org
E-mail: alanwar@att.net

Andorran Philatelic Study Circle
D. Hope
17 Hawthorn Dr.
Stalybridge, Cheshire, SK15 1UE
UNITED KINGDOM
apsc.free.fr
E-mail: apsc@free.fr

Australian States Study Circle of The Royal Sydney Philatelic Club
Ben Palmer
GPO 1751
Sydney, N.S.W., 2001
AUSTRALIA

Austria Philatelic Society
Ralph Schneider
P.O. Box 23049
Belleville IL 62223
Ph: (618) 277-6152
www.austriaphilatelicsociety.com
E-mail: rschneider39@charter.net

American Belgian Philatelic Society
Edward de Bary
11 Wakefield Dr. Apt. 2105
Asheville NC 28803
E-mail: belgam@charter.net

Bechuanalands and Botswana Society
Neville Midwood
69 Porlock Lane
Furzton, Milton Keynes, MK4 1JY
UNITED KINGDOM
www.nevsoft.com
E-mail: bbsoc@nevsoft.com

Bermuda Collectors Society
Thomas J. McMahon
P.O. Box 1949
Stuart FL 34995
www.bermudacollectorssociety.org
E-mail: science29@comcast.net

Brazil Philatelic Association
William V. Kriebel
1923 Manning St.
Philadelphia PA 19103-5728
Ph: (215) 735-3697
E-mail: kriebewv@drexel.edu

British Caribbean Philatelic Study Group
Dr. Reuben A. Ramkissoon
11075 Benton Street #236
Loma Linda CA 92354-3182
www.bcpsg.org
E-mail: rramkissoon@juno.com

The King George VI Collectors Society (British Commonwealth)
Brian Livingstone
21 York Mansions, Prince of Wales Drive
London, SW11 4DL
UNITED KINGDOM
www.kg6.info
E-mail: livingstone484@btinternet.com

British North America Philatelic Society (Canada & Provinces)
David G. Jones
184 Larkin Dr.
Nepean, ON, K2J 1H9
CANADA
www.bnaps.org
E-mail: shibumi.management@gmail.com

British West Indies Study Circle
John Seidl
4324 Granby Way
Marietta GA 30062
Ph: (770) 642-6424
www.bwisc.org
E-mail: jseidl@mindspring.com

Burma Philatelic Study Circle
Michael Whittaker
1, Ecton Leys, Hillside
Rugby, Warwickshire, CV22 5SL
UNITED KINGDOM
www.burmastamps.homecall.co.uk
E-mail: whittaker2004@btinternet.com

Cape and Natal Study Circle
Dr. Guy Dillaway
P.O. Box 181
Weston MA 02493
www.nzsc.demon.co.uk

Ceylon Study Group
R. W. P. Frost
42 Lonsdale Road, Cannington
Bridgewater, Somerset, TA5 2JS
UNITED KINGDOM
E-mail: rodney.frost@tiscali.co.uk

Channel Islands Specialists Society
Moira Edwards
86, Hall Lane, Sandon,
Chelmsford, Essex, CM2 7RQ
UNITED KINGDOM
www.ciss1950.org.uk
E-mail: membership@ciss1950.org.uk

China Stamp Society
Paul H. Gault
P.O. Box 20711
Columbus OH 43220
www.chinastampsociety.org
E-mail: secretary@chinastampsociety.org

Colombia/Panama Philatelic Study Group (COPAPHIL)
Thomas P. Myers
P.O. Box 522
Gordonsville VA 22942
www.copaphil.org
E-mail: tpmphil@hotmail.com

Association Filatelic de Costa Rica
Giana Wayman
c/o Interlink 102, P.O. Box 52-6770
Miami, FL 33152
E-mail: scotland@racsa.co.cr

Society for Costa Rica Collectors
Dr. Hector R. Mena
P.O. Box 14831
Baton Rouge LA 70808
www.socorico.org
E-mail: hrmena@aol.com

International Cuban Philatelic Society
Ernesto Cuesta
P.O. Box 34434
Bethesda MD 20827
www.cubafil.org
E-mail: ecuesta@philat.com

Cuban Philatelic Society of America
P.O. Box 141656
Coral Gables FL 33114-1656
www.cubapsa.com
E-mail: cpsa.usa@gmail.com

Cyprus Study Circle
Colin Dear
10 Marne Close, Wem
Shropshire, SY4 5YE
UNITED KINGDOM
www.cyprusstudycircle.org/index.htm
E-mail: colindear@talktalk.net.

Society for Czechoslovak Philately
Phil Rhoade
905 E. Oakside St.
South Bend IN 46614
www.csphilately.org
E-mail: philip.rhoade@mnsu.edu

Danish West Indies Study Unit of the Scandinavian Collectors Club
Arnold Sorensen
7666 Edgedale Drive
Newburgh IN 47630
Ph: (812) 480-6532
www.scc-online.org
E-mail: valbydwi@hotmail.com

East Africa Study Circle
Jonathan Smalley
1 Lincoln Close
Tweeksbury, B91 1AE
UNITED KINGDOM
easc.org.uk
E-mail: jpasmalley@tiscali.co.uk

Egypt Study Circle
Mike Murphy
109 Chadwick Road
London, SE15 4PY
UNITED KINGDOM
Dick Wilson: North American Agent
egyptstudycircle.org.uk
E-mail: egyptstudycircle@hotmail.com

Estonian Philatelic Society
Juri Kirsimagi
29 Clifford Ave.
Pelham NY 10803
Ph: (914) 738-3713

Ethiopian Philatelic Society
Ulf Lindahl
21 Westview Place
Riverside CT 06878
Ph: (203) 866-3540
home.comcast.net/~fbheiser/ethiopia5.htm
E-mail: ulindahl@optonline.net

Falkland Islands Philatelic Study Group
Carl J. Faulkner
Williams Inn, On-the-Green
Williamstown MA 01267-2620
www.fipsg.org.uk
Ph: (413) 458-9371

Faroe Islands Study Circle
Norman Hudson
40 Queenís Road, Vicarís Cross
Chester, CH3 5HB
UNITED KINGDOM
www.faroeislandssc.org.
E-mail: jntropics@hotmail.com

Former French Colonies Specialist Society
BP 628
75367 Paris, Cedex 08
FRANCE
www.colfra.com
E-mail: clubcolfra@aol.com

France & Colonies Philatelic Society
Edward Grabowski
111 Prospect St., 4C
Westfield NJ 07090
www.franceandcolonies.org
E-mail: edjjg@alum.mit.edu

Germany Philatelic Society
P.O. Box 6547
Chesterfield MO 63006
www.gps.nu

Gibraltar Study Circle
David R. Stirrups
34 Glamis Drive
Dundee, DD2 1QP
UNITED KINGDOM
E-mail: drstirrups@dundee.ac.uk

Great Britain Collectors Club
Steve McGill
10309 Brookhollow Circle
Highlands Ranch CO 80129
www.gbstamps.com/gbcc
E-mail: steve.mcgill@comcast.net

International Society of Guatemala Collectors
Jaime Marckwordt
449 St. Francis Blvd.
Daly City CA 94015-2136
www.guatemalastamps.com

Haiti Philatelic Society
Ubaldo Del Toro
5709 Marble Archway
Alexandria VA 22315
www.haitiphilately.org
E-mail: u007ubi@aol.com

Hong Kong Stamp Society
Ming W. Tsang
P.O. Box 206
Glenside PA 19038

Society for Hungarian Philately
Robert Morgan
2201 Roscomare Rd.
Los Angeles CA 90077-2222
www.hungarianphilately.org
E-mail: bwilson1951@aol.com

India Study Circle
John Warren
P.O. Box 7326
Washington DC 20044
Ph: (202) 564-6876
www.indiastudycircle.org
E-mail: warren.john@epa.gov

Indian Ocean Study Circle
Mrs. S. Hopson
Field Acre, Hoe Benham
Newbury, Berkshire, RG20 8PD
UNITED KINGDOM

Society of Indo-China Philatelists
Ron Bentley
2600 North 24th Street
Arlington VA 22207
www.sicp-online.org
E-mail: ron.bentley@verizon.net

Iran Philatelic Study Circle
Mehdi Esmaili
P.O. Box 750096
Forest Hills NY 11375
www.iranphilatelic.org
E-mail: m.esmaili@earthlink.net

Eire Philatelic Association (Ireland)
David J. Brennan
P.O. Box 704
Bernardsville NJ 07924
eirephilatelicassoc.org
E-mail: brennan704@aol.com

Society of Israel Philatelists
Michael Bass
P.O. Box 507
Northfield OH 44067
www.israelstamps.com
israelstamps@gmail.com

Italy and Colonies Study Circle
Andrew DíAnneo
1085 Dunweal Lane
Calistoga CA 94515
www.icsc.pwp.blueyonder.co.uk
E-mail: audanneo@napanet.net

International Society for Japanese
    Philately
William Eisenhauer
P.O. Box 230462
Tigard OR 97281
www.isjp.org
E-mail: secretary@isjp.org

Korea Stamp Society
John E. Talmage
P.O. Box 6889
Oak Ridge TN 37831
www.pennfamily.org/KSS-USA
E-mail: jtalmage@usit.net

Latin American Philatelic Society
Jules K. Beck
30 1/2 Street #209
St. Louis Park MN 55426-3551

Liberian Philatelic Society
William Thomas Lockard
P.O. Box 106
Wellston OH 45692
Ph: (740) 384-2020
E-mail: tlockard@zoomnet.net

Liechtenstudy USA (Liechtenstein)
Paul Tremaine
410 S. W. Ninth St.
Dundee OR 97115
Ph: (503) 538-4500
www.liechtenstudy.org
E-mail: editor@liechtenstudy.org

Lithuania Philatelic Society
John Variakojis
3715 W. 68th St.
Chicago IL 60629
Ph: (773) 585-8649
http://lithuanianphilately.com/lps
E-mail: variakojis@sbcglobal.net

Luxembourg Collectors Club
Gary B. Little
7319 Beau Road
Sechelt, BC, VON 3A8
CANADA
lcc.luxcentral.com
E-mail: gary@luxcentral.com

Malaya Study Group
David Tett
P.O. Box 34
Wheathampstead, Herts, AL4 8JY
UNITED KINGDOM
www.m-s-g/org/uk
E-mail: davidtett@aol.com

Malta Study Circle
Alec Webster
50 Worcester Road
Sutton, Surrey, SM2 6QB
UNITED KINGDOM
E-mail: alecwebster50@hotmail.com

Mexico-Elmhurst Philatelic Society
    International
David Pietsch
P.O. Box 50997
Irvine CA 92619-0997
E-mail: mepsi@msn.com

Asociacion Mexicana de Filatelia
AMEXFIL
Ave. 16 de Septiembre #6-401, Col.
Centro
Mexico City DF, 06000
MEXICO
www.amexfil.org.mx
E-mail: carlosfet@prodigy.net.mx

Society for Moroccan and Tunisian
    Philately
206, bld. Pereire
75017 Paris
FRANCE
members.aol.com/Jhaik5814
E-mail: splm206@aol.com

Nepal & Tibet Philatelic Study Group
Roger D. Skinner
1020 Covington Road
Los Altos CA 94024-5003
Ph: (650) 968-4163
fuchs-online.com/ntpsc/
E-mail: colinhepper@hotmail.co.uk

American Society for Netherlands
    Philately
Hans Kremer
50 Rockport Ct.
Danville CA 94526
Ph: (925) 820-5841
www.angelfire.com/ca2/asnp
E-mail: hkremer@usa.net

New Zealand Society of Great Britain
Keith C. Collins
13 Briton Crescent
Sanderstead, Surrey, CR2 0JN
UNITED KINGDOM
www.cs.stir.ac.uk/~rgc/nzsgb
E-mail: rgc@cs.stir.ac.uk

Nicaragua Study Group
Erick Rodriguez
11817 S.W. 11th St.
Miami FL 33184-2501
clubs.yahoo.com/clubs/nicara-
guastudygroup
E-mail: nsgsec@yahoo.com

Society of Australasian Specialists/
    Oceania
Stuart Leven
P.O. Box 24764
San Jose CA 95154-4764
Ph: (408) 978-0193
www.sasoceania.org
E-mail: sas_oceania@yahoo.com

Orange Free State Study Circle
J. R. Stroud
28 Oxford St.
Burnham-on-sea, Somerset, TA8 1LQ
UNITED KINGDOM
orangefreestatephilately.org.uk
E-mail: richardstroudph@gofast.co.uk

Pacific Islands Study Circle
John Ray
24 Woodvale Avenue
London, SE25 4AE
UNITED KINGDOM
www.pisc.org.uk
E-mail: info@pisc.org.uk

Pakistan Philatelic Study Circle
Jeff Siddiqui
P.O. Box 7002
Lynnwood WA 98046
E-mail: jeffsiddiqui@msn.com

Centro de Filatelistas
    Independientes de Panama
Vladimir Berrio-Lemm
Apartado 0823-02748
Plaza Concordia Panama,
PANAMA
E-mail: panahistoria@gmail.com

Papuan Philatelic Society
Steven Zirinsky
P.O. Box 49, Ansonia Station
New York NY 10023
Ph: (718) 706-0616
www.communigate.co.uk/york/pps
E-mail: szirinsky@cs.com

International Philippine Philatelic
    Society
Donald J. Peterson
7408 Alaska Ave., NW
Washington DC 20012
Ph: (202) 291-6229
www.theipps.info
E-mail: dpeterson@comcast.net

Pitcairn Islands Study Group
Dr. Everett L. Parker
249 NW Live Oak Place
Lake City FL 32055-8906
Ph: (386) 754-8524
www.pisg.net
E-mail: eparker@hughes.net

Polonus Philatelic Society (Poland)
Chris Kulpinski
9350 E. Palm Tree Dr.
Scottsdale AZ 85255
Ph: (480) 585-7114
www.polonus.org
E-mail: ctk@kulpinski.net

International Society for
    Portuguese Philately
Clyde Homen
1491 Bonnie View Rd.
Hollister CA 95023-5117
www.portugalstamps.com
E-mail: cjh1491@sbcglobal.net

Rhodesian Study Circle
William R. Wallace
P.O. Box 16381
San Francisco CA 94116
www.rhodesianstudycircle.org.uk
E-mail: bwall8rscr@earthlink.net

Rossica Society of Russian Philately
Edward J. Laveroni
P.O. Box 320997
Los Gatos CA 95032-0116
www.rossica.org
E-mail: ed.laveroni@rossica.org

St. Helena, Ascension & Tristan Da
    Cunha Philatelic Society
Dr. Everett L. Parker
249 NW Live Oak Place
Lake City FL 32055-8906
Ph: (386) 754-8524
www.atlanticislands.org
E-mail: eparker@hughes.net

St. Pierre & Miquelon Philatelic
    Society
James R. (Jim) Taylor
2335 Paliswood Rd. SW
Calgary, AB, T2V 3P6
CANADA

Associated Collectors of El Salvador
Joseph D. Hahn
1015 Old Boalsburg Rd. Apt G-5
State College PA 16801-6149
www.elsalvadorphilately.org
E-mail: joehahn2@yahoo.com

Fellowship of Samoa Specialists
Donald Mee
23 Leo Street
Christchurch, 8051
NEW ZEALAND
www.samoaexpress.org
E-mail: donanm@xtra.co.nz

Sarawak Specialists' Society
Stu Leven
P.O. Box 24764
San Jose CA 95154-4764
Ph: (408) 978-0193
www.britborneostamps.org.uk
www.s-s-s.org.uk
E-mail: stulev@ix.netcom.com

Scandinavian Collectors Club
Donald B. Brent
P.O. Box 13196
El Cajon CA 92020
www.scc-online.org
E-mail: dbrent47@sprynet.com

Slovakia Stamp Society
Jack Benchik
P.O. Box 555
Notre Dame IN 46556

Philatelic Society for Greater
    Southern Africa
Alan Hanks
34 Seaton Drive
Aurora, ON, L4G 2KI
CANADA
Ph: (905) 727-6993
www.psgsa.thestampweb.com
Email: alan.hanks@sympatico.ca

Spanish Philatelic Society
Robert H. Penn
1108 Walnut Drive
Danielsville PA 18038
Ph: (610) 767-6793
E-mail: roberthpenn@aol.com

Sudan Study Group
c/o North American Agent
Richard S. Wilson
53 Middle Patent Road
Bedford NY 10506
www.sudanstamps.org
E-mail: dadu1@verizon.net

American Helvetia Philatelic
    Society (Switzerland,
    Liechtenstein)
Richard T. Hall
P.O. Box 15053
Asheville NC 28813-0053
www.swiss-stamps.org
E-mail: secretary2@swiss-stamps.org

Tannu Tuva Collectors Society
Ken Simon
513 Sixth Ave. So.
Lake Worth FL 33460-4507
Ph: (561) 588-5954
www.tuva.tk
E-mail: yurttuva@yahoo.com

Society for Thai Philately
H. R. Blakeney
P.O. Box 25644
Oklahoma City OK 73125
E-mail: HRBlakeney@aol.com

Transvaal Study Circle
J. Woolgar
P.O. Box 379
Gravesend, DA11 9EW
UNITED KINGDOM
www.transvaal.org.uk

Ottoman and Near East Philatelic
    Society (Turkey and related areas)
Bob Stuchell
193 Valley Stream Lane
Wayne PA 19087
www.oneps.org
E-mail: rstuchell@msn.com

Ukrainian Philatelic & Numismatic
    Society
George Slusarczuk
P.O. Box 303
Southfields NY 10975-0303
www.upns.org
E-mail: Yurko@frontiernet.net

Vatican Philatelic Society
Sal Quinones
1 Aldersgate, Apt. 1002
Riverhead NY 11901-1830
Ph: (516) 727-6426
www.vaticanphilately.org

British Virgin Islands Philatelic
    Society
Giorgio Migliavacca
P.O. Box 7007
St. Thomas VI 00801-0007
www.islandsun.com/FEATURES/
bviphil9198.html
E-mail: issun@candwbvi.net

West Africa Study Circle
Dr. Peter Newroth
Suite 603
5332 Sayward Hill Crescent
Victoria, BC, V8Y 3H8
CANADA
www.wasc.org.uk/

Western Australia Study Group
Brian Pope
P.O. Box 423
Claremont, Western Australia, 6910
AUSTRALIA
www.wastudygroup.com
E-mail: black5swan@yahoo.com.au

Yugoslavia Study Group of the
Croatian Philatelic Society
Michael Lenard
1514 North 3rd Ave.
Wausau WI 54401
Ph: (715) 675-2833
E-mail: mjlenard@aol.com

Topical Groups

Americana Unit
Dennis Dengel
17 Peckham Rd.
Poughkeepsie NY 12603-2018
www.americanaunit.org
E-mail: info@americanaunit.org

Astronomy Study Unit
John W. G. Budd
29203 Coharie Loop
San Antonio FL 33576-4643
Ph: (352) 588-4706
www.astronomystudyunit.com
E-mail: jwgbudd@earthlink.net

Bicycle Stamp Club
Tony Teideman
P.O. Box 90
Baulkham Hills, NSW, 1755
AUSTRALIA
members.tripod.com/~bicyclestamps
E-mail: tonimaur@bigpond.com

Biology Unit
Alan Hanks
34 Seaton Dr.
Aurora, ON, L4G 2K1
CANADA
Ph: (905) 727-6993

Bird Stamp Society
Graham Horsman
23 A East Main Street
Blackburn West Lothian
Scotland, EH47 7QR
UNITED KINGDOM
www.bird-stamps.org/bss
E-mail: graham_horsman7@msn.com

Canadiana Study Unit
John Peebles
P.O. Box 3262, Station ìBî
London, ON, N6A 4K3
CANADA
E-mail: c.s.u@sympatico.ca

Captain Cook Study Unit
Brian P. Sandford
173 Minuteman Dr.
Concord MA 01742-1923
www.captaincooksociety.com
E-mail: US@captaincooksociety.com

Casey Jones Railroad Unit
Dr. Roy Menninger
85 SW Pepper Tree Lane
Topeka KS 66611-2072
www.uqp.de/cjr/index.htm
E-mail: roymenn@sbcglobal.net

Cats on Stamps Study Unit
Mary Ann Brown
3006 Wade Rd.
Durham NC 27705
www.catsonstamps.org
E-mail: mabrown@nc.rr.com

Chemistry & Physics on Stamps
Study Unit
Dr. Roland Hirsch
20458 Water Point Lane
Germantown MD 20874
www.cpossu.org
E-mail: rfhirsch@cpossu.org

Chess on Stamps Study Unit
Ray C. Alexis
608 Emery St.
Longmont CO 80501
E-mail: chessstuff911459@aol.

Christmas Philatelic Club
Linda Lawrence
312 Northwood Drive
Lexington KY 40505
www.web.295.ca/cpc/
E-mail: stamplinda@aol.com

Christopher Columbus Philatelic
Society
Donald R. Ager
P.O. Box 71
Hillsboro NH 03244-0071
ccps.maphist.nl/
Ph: (603) 464-5379
E-mail: meganddon@tds.net

Collectors of Religion on Stamps
Verna Shackleton
425 North Linwood Avenue #110
Appleton WI 54914
www://my.vbe.com/~cmfourl/
coros1.htm
E-mail: corosec@sbcglobal.net

Dogs on Stamps Study Unit
Morris Raskin
202A Newport Rd.
Monroe Township NJ 08831
Ph: (609) 655-7411
www.dossu.org
E-mail: mraskin@cellurian.com

Earth's Physical Features Study Group
Fred Klein
515 Magdalena Ave.
Los Altos CA 94024
epfsu.jeffhayward.com

Ebony Society of Philatelic Events
and Reflections, Inc (African-
American topicals)
Manuel Gilyard
800 Riverside Drive, Ste 4H
New York NY 10032-7412
www.esperstamps.org
E-mail: gilyardmani@aol.com

Europa Study Unit
Donald W. Smith
P.O. Box 576
Johnstown PA 15907-0576
www.europastudyunit.org/
E-mail: eunity@aol.com or
donsmith65@msn.com

Fine & Performing Arts
Deborah L. Washington
6922 So. Jeffery Boulevard
#7 - North
Chicago IL 60649
E-mail: brasslady@comcast.net

Fire Service in Philately
Brian R. Engler, Sr.
726 1/2 W. Tilghman St.
Allentown PA 18102-2324
Ph: (610) 433-2782
www.firestamps.com

Gay & Lesbian History on Stamps Club
Joe Petronie
P.O. Box 190842
Dallas TX 75219-0842
www.glhsc.org
E-mail: glhsc@aol.com

Gems, Minerals & Jewelry Study
Unit
George Young
P.O. Box 632
Tewksbury MA 01876-0632
Ph: (978) 851-8283
www.rockhounds.com/rockshop/
gmjsuapp.txt
E-mail: george-young@msn.com

Graphics Philately Association
Mark H Winnegrad
P.O. Box 380
Bronx NY 10462-0380
www.graphics-stamps.org
E-mail: indybruce1@yahoo.com

Journalists, Authors & Poets on Stamps
Ms. Lee Straayer
P.O. Box 6808
Champaign IL 61826
E-mail: lstraayer@dcbnet.com

Lighthouse Stamp Society
Dalene Thomas
8612 West Warren Lane
Lakewood CO 80227-2352
Ph: (303) 986-6620
www.lighthousestampsociety.org
E-mail: dalene@lighthousestampsociety.org

Lions International Stamp Club
John Bargus
108-2777 Barry Rd. RR 2
Mill Bay, BC, V0R 2P2
CANADA
Ph: (250) 743-5782

Mahatma Gandhi On Stamps
Study Circle
Pramod Shivagunde
Pratik Clinic, Akluj
Solapur, Maharashtra, 413101
INDIA
E-mail: drnanda@bom6.vsnl.net.in

Mask Study Unit
Carolyn Weber
1220 Johnson Drive, Villa 104
Ventura CA 93003-0540
E-mail: cweber@venturalink.net

Masonic Study Unit
Stanley R. Longenecker
930 Wood St.
Mount Joy PA 17552-1926
Ph: (717) 669-9094
E-mail: natsco@usa.net

Mathematical Study Unit
Estelle Buccino
5615 Glenwood Rd.
Bethesda MD 20817-6727
Ph: (301) 718-8898
www.math.ttu.edu/msu/
E-mail: montystrauss@gmail.com

Medical Subjects Unit
Dr. Frederick C. Skvara
P.O. Box 6228
Bridgewater NJ 08807
E-mail: fcskvara@optonline.net

Military Postal History Society
Ed Dubin
One South Wacker Drive, Suite 3500
Chicago IL 60606
www.militaryPHS.org
E-mail: dubine@comcast.net

Mourning Stamps and Covers Club
James Bailey, Jr.
P.O. Box 937
Brownwood TX 76804
E-mail: jfbailey238@earthlink.net

Napoleonic Age Philatelists
Ken Berry
7513 Clayton Dr.
Oklahoma City OK 73132-5636
Ph: (405) 721-0044
www.nap-stamps.org
E-mail: krb2@earthlink.net

Old World Archeological Study Unit
Caroline Scannel
11 Dawn Drive
Smithtown NY 11787-1761
www.owasu.org
E-mail: editor@owasu.org

Petroleum Philatelic Society
International
Dr. Chris Coggins
174 Old Bedford Road
Luton, England, LU2 7HW
UNITED KINGDOM
E-mail: WAMTECH@Luton174.fsnet.co.uk

Philatelic Computing Study Group
Robert de Violini
P.O. Box 5025
Oxnard CA 93031-5025
www.pcsg.org
E-mail: dviolini@adelphia.net

Philatelic Lepidopterists' Association
Alan Hanks
34 Seaton Dr.
Aurora, ON, L4G 2K1
CANADA
Ph: (905) 727-6933
E-mail: alan.hanks@sympatico.ca

Rotary on Stamps Unit
Gerald L. Fitzsimmons
105 Calla Ricardo
Victoria TX 77904
rotaryonstamps.org
E-mail: glfitz@suddenlink.net

Scouts on Stamps Society
International
Lawrence Clay
P.O. Box 6228
Kennewick WA 99336
Ph: (509) 735-3731
www.sossi.org
E-mail: lclay3731@charter.net

Ships on Stamps Unit
Les Smith
302 Conklin Avenue
Penticton, BC, V2A 2T4
CANADA
Ph: (250) 493-7486
www.shipsonstamps.org
E-mail: lessmith440@shaw.ca

Space Unit
Carmine Torrisi
P.O. Box 780241
Maspeth NY 11378
Ph: (917) 620-5687
stargate.1usa.com/stamps/
E-mail: ctorrisi1@nyc.rr.com

Sports Philatelists International
Margaret Jones
705 S Laclede Station Rd S, Apt 163.
St. Louis MO 63119-4969
www.sportstamps.org

Stamps on Stamps Collectors Club
Alf Jordan
156 West Elm Street
Yarmouth ME 04096
www.stampsonstamps.org
E-mail: ajordan1@maine.rr.com

Windmill Study Unit
Walter J. Hollien
P.O. Box 346
Long Valley NJ 07853-0346
Ph: (862) 812-0030
E-mail: whollien@earthlink.net

Wine On Stamps Study Unit
Bruce L. Johnson
115 Raintree Drive
Zionsville IN 46077
www.wine-on-stamps.org
E-mail: indybruce@yahoo.com

Women on Stamps Study Unit
Hugh Gottfried
2232 26th St.
Santa Monica CA 90405-1902
E-mail: hgottfried@adelphia.net

Zeppelin Collectors Club
Cheryl Ganz
P.O. Box 77196
Washington DC 20013
www.americanairmailsociety.org

Expertizing Services

The following organizations will, for a fee, provide expert opinions about stamps submitted to them. Collectors should contact these organizations to find out about their fees and requirements before submiting philatelic material to them. The listing of these groups here is not intended as an endorsement by Scott Publishing Co.

General Expertizing Services

American Philatelic Expertizing
  Service (a service of the
  American Philatelic Society)
100 Match Factory Place
Bellefonte PA 16823-1367
Ph: (814) 237-3803
Fax: (814) 237-6128
www.stamps.org
E-mail: ambristo@stamps.org
Areas of Expertise: Worldwide

B. P. A. Expertising, Ltd.
P.O. Box 137
Leatherhead, Surrey, KT22 0RG
UNITED KINGDOM
E-mail: sec.bpa@tcom.co.uk
Areas of Expertise: British
Commonwealth, Great Britain,
Classics of Europe, South America and
the Far East

Philatelic Foundation
70 West 40th St., 15th Floor
New York NY 10018
Ph: (212) 221-6555
Fax: (212) 221-6208
www.philatelicfoundation.org
E-mail:philatelicfoundation@verizon.net
Areas of Expertise: U.S. & Worldwide

Philatelic Stamp Authentication
  and Grading, Inc.
P.O. Box 56-2111
Miami FL 33256-2111
Customer Service: (305) 345-9864
www.stampauthentication.com
E-mail: info@stampauthentication.com

Professional Stamp Experts
P.O. Box 6170
Newport Beach CA 92658
Ph: (877) STAMP-88
Fax: (949) 833-7955
www.collectors.com/pse
E-mail: pseinfo@collectors.com
Areas of Expertise: Stamps and
covers of U.S., U.S. Possessions,
British Commonwealth

Royal Philatelic Society Expert
  Committee
41 Devonshire Place
London, W1N 1PE
UNITED KINGDOM
www.rpsl.org.uk/experts.html
E-mail: experts@rpsl.org.uk
Areas of Expertise: All

Expertizing Services Covering Specific Fields Or Countries

China Stamp Society Expertizing
  Service
1050 West Blue Ridge Blvd
Kansas City MO 64145
Ph: (816) 942-6300
E-mail: hjmesq@aol.com
Areas of Expertise: China

Confederate Stamp Alliance
  Authentication Service
Gen. Frank Crown, Jr.
P.O. Box 278
Capshaw AL 35742-0396
Ph: (302) 422-2656
Fax: (302) 424-1990
www.csalliance.org
E-mail: csaas@knology.net
Areas of Expertise: Confederate stamps
and postal history

Errors, Freaks and Oddities
  Collectors Club
  Expertizing Service
138 East Lakemont Dr.
Kingsland GA 31548
Ph: (912) 729-1573
Areas of Expertise: U.S. errors, freaks
and oddities

Estonian Philatelic Society
  Expertizing Service
39 Clafford Lane
Melville NY 11747
Ph: (516) 421-2078
E-mail: esto4@aol.com
Areas of Expertise: Estonia

Hawaiian Philatelic Society
  Expertizing Service
P.O. Box 10115
Honolulu HI 96816-0115
Areas of Expertise: Hawaii

Hong Kong Stamp Society
  Expertizing Service
P.O. Box 206
Glenside PA 19038
Fax: (215) 576-6850
Areas of Expertise: Hong Kong

International Association of
  Philatelic Experts
United States Associate members:
  Paul Buchsbayew
  119 W. 57th St.
  New York NY 10019
  Ph: (212) 977-7734
  Fax: (212) 977-8653
  Areas of Expertise: Russia, Soviet
  Union

  William T. Crowe
  P.O. Box 2090
  Danbury CT 06813-2090
  E-mail: wtcrowe@aol.com
  Areas of Expertise: United States

  John Lievsay
  (see American Philatelic Expertizing
  Service and Philatelic Foundation)
  Areas of Expertise: France

  Robert W. Lyman
  P.O. Box 348
  Irvington on Hudson NY 10533
  Ph and Fax: (914) 591-6937
  Areas of Expertise: British North
  America, New Zealand

  Robert Odenweller
  P.O. Box 401
  Bernardsville NJ 07924-0401
  Ph and Fax: (908) 766-5460
  Areas of Expertise: New Zealand,
  Samoa to 1900

  Sergio Sismondo
  10035 Carousel Center Dr.
  Syracuse NY 13290-0001
  Ph: (315) 422-2331
  Fax: (315) 422-2956
  Areas of Expertise: British East
  Africa, Camerouns,
  Cape of Good Hope, Canada, British
  North America

International Society for Japanese
  Philately Expertizing Committee
132 North Pine Terrace
Staten Island NY 10312-4052
Ph: (718) 227-5229
Areas of Expertise: Japan and related
areas, except WWII Japanese
Occupation issues

International Society for
  Portuguese Philately
  Expertizing Service
P.O. Box 43146
Philadelphia PA 19129-3146
Ph: (215) 843-2106
Fax: (215) 843-2106
E-mail: s.s.washburne@worldnet.att.
net
Areas of Expertise: Portugal and
Colonies

Mexico-Elmhurst Philatelic
  Society International Expert
  Committee
P.O. Box 1133
West Covina CA 91793
Areas of Expertise: Mexico

Ukrainian Philatelic &
  Numismatic Society
  Expertizing Service
30552 Dell Lane
Warren MI 48092-1862
Areas of Expertise: Ukraine, Western
Ukraine

V. G. Greene Philatelic Research
  Foundation
P.O. Box 204, Station Q
Toronto, ON, M4T 2M1
CANADA
Ph: (416) 921-2073
Fax: (416) 921-1282
E-mail: vggfoundation@on.aibn.com
www.greenefoundation.ca
Areas of Expertise: British North
America

Information on Catalogue Values, Grade and Condition

Catalogue Value

The Scott Catalogue value is a retail value; that is, an amount you could expect to pay for a stamp in the grade of Very Fine with no faults. Any exceptions to the grade valued will be noted in the text. The general introduction on the following pages and the individual section introductions further explain the type of material that is valued. The value listed for any given stamp is a reference that reflects recent actual dealer selling prices for that item.

Dealer retail price lists, public auction results, published prices in advertising and individual solicitation of retail prices from dealers, collectors and specialty organizations have been used in establishing the values found in this catalogue. Scott Publishing Co. values stamps, but Scott is not a company engaged in the business of buying and selling stamps as a dealer.

Use this catalogue as a guide for buying and selling. The actual price you pay for a stamp may be higher or lower than the catalogue value because of many different factors, including the amount of personal service a dealer offers, or increased or decreased interest in the country or topic represented by a stamp or set. An item may occasionally be offered at a lower price as a "loss leader," or as part of a special sale. You also may obtain an item inexpensively at public auction because of little interest at that time or as part of a large lot.

Stamps that are of a lesser grade than Very Fine, or those with condition problems, generally trade at lower prices than those given in this catalogue. Stamps of exceptional quality in both grade and condition often command higher prices than those listed.

Values for pre-1900 unused issues are for stamps with approximately half or more of their original gum. Stamps with most or all of their original gum may be expected to sell for more, and stamps with less than half of their original gum may be expected to sell for somewhat less than the values listed. On rarer stamps, it may be expected that the original gum will be somewhat more disturbed than it will be on more common issues. Post-1900 unused issues are assumed to have full original gum. From breakpoints in most countries' listings, stamps are valued as never hinged, due to the wide availability of stamps in that condition. These notations are prominently placed in the listings and in the country information preceding the listings. Some countries also feature listings with dual values for hinged and never-hinged stamps.

Grade

A stamp's grade and condition are crucial to its value. The accompanying illustrations show examples of Very Fine stamps from different time periods, along with examples of stamps in Fine to Very Fine and Extremely Fine grades as points of reference. When a stamp seller offers a stamp in any grade from fine to superb without further qualifying statements, that stamp should not only have the centering grade as defined, but it also should be free of faults or other condition problems.

FINE stamps (illustrations not shown) have designs that are quite off center, with the perforations on one or two sides very close to the design but not quite touching it. There is white space between the perforations and the design that is minimal but evident to the unaided eye. Imperforate stamps may have small margins, and earlier issues may show the design just touching one edge of the stamp design. Very early perforated issues normally will have the perforations slightly cutting into the design. Used stamps may have heavier than usual cancellations.

FINE-VERY FINE stamps will be somewhat off center on one side, or slightly off center on two sides. Imperforate stamps will have two margins of at least normal size, and the design will not touch any edge. For perforated stamps, the perfs are well clear of the design, but are still noticeably off center. *However, early issues of a country may be printed in such a way that the design naturally is very close to the edges. In these cases, the perforations may cut into the design very slightly.* Used stamps will not have a cancellation that detracts from the design.

VERY FINE stamps will be just slightly off center on one or two sides, but the design will be well clear of the edge. The stamp will present a nice, balanced appearance. Imperforate stamps will be well centered within normal-sized margins. *However, early issues of many countries may be printed in such a way that the perforations may touch the design on one or more sides. Where this is the case, a boxed note will be found defining the centering and margins of the stamps being valued.* Used stamps will have light or otherwise neat cancellations. This is the grade used to establish Scott Catalogue values.

EXTREMELY FINE stamps are close to being perfectly centered. Imperforate stamps will have even margins that are slightly larger than normal. Even the earliest perforated issues will have perforations clear of the design on all sides.

Scott Publishing Co. recognizes that there is no formally enforced grading scheme for postage stamps, and that the final price you pay or obtain for a stamp will be determined by individual agreement at the time of transaction.

Condition

Grade addresses only centering and (for used stamps) cancellation. *Condition* refers to factors other than grade that affect a stamp's desirability.

Factors that can increase the value of a stamp include exceptionally wide margins, particularly fresh color, the presence of selvage, and plate or die varieties. Unusual cancels on used stamps (particularly those of the 19th century) can greatly enhance their value as well.

Factors other than faults that decrease the value of a stamp include loss of original gum, regumming, a hinge remnant or foreign object adhering to the gum, natural inclusions, straight edges, and markings or notations applied by collectors or dealers.

Faults include missing pieces, tears, pin or other holes, surface scuffs, thin spots, creases, toning, short or pulled perforations, clipped perforations, oxidation or other forms of color changelings, soiling, stains, and such man-made changes as reperforations or the chemical removal or lightening of a cancellation.

Grading Illustrations

On the following two pages are illustrations of various stamps from countries appearing in this volume. These stamps are arranged by country, and they represent early or important issues that are often found in widely different grades in the marketplace. The editors believe the illustrations will prove useful in showing the margin size and centering that will be seen on the various issues.

In addition to the matters of margin size and centering, collectors are reminded that the very fine stamps valued in the Scott catalogues also will possess fresh color and intact perforations, and they will be free from defects.

Examples shown are computer-manipulated images made from single digitized master illustrations.

Stamp Illustrations Used in the Catalogue

It is important to note that the stamp images used for identification purposes in this catalogue may not be indicative of the grade of stamp being valued. Refer to the written discussion of grades on this page and to the grading illustrations on the following two pages for grading information.

Fine-Very Fine →

SCOTT
CATALOGUES
VALUE
STAMPS IN
THIS GRADE

Very Fine →

Extremely Fine →

Fine-Very Fine →

SCOTT
CATALOGUES
VALUE
STAMPS IN
THIS GRADE

Very Fine →

Extremely Fine →

Fine-Very Fine ⟶

SCOTT
CATALOGUES
VALUE
STAMPS IN
THIS GRADE

Very Fine ⟶

Extremely Fine ⟶

Fine-Very Fine ⟶

SCOTT
CATALOGUES
VALUE
STAMPS IN
THIS GRADE

Very Fine ⟶

Extremely Fine ⟶

For purposes of helping to determine the gum condition and value of an unused stamp, Scott Publishing Co. presents the following chart which details different gum conditions and indicates how the conditions correlate with the Scott values for unused stamps. Used together, the Illustrated Grading Chart on the previous pages and this Illustrated Gum Chart should allow catalogue users to better understand the grade and gum condition of stamps valued in the Scott catalogues.

Gum Categories:	MINT N.H.	ORIGINAL GUM (O.G.)					NO GUM
	Mint Never Hinged *Free from any disturbance*	**Lightly Hinged** *Faint impression of a removed hinge over a small area*	**Hinge Mark or Remnant** *Prominent hinged spot with part or all of the hinge remaining*	**Large part o.g.** *Approximately half or more of the gum intact*	**Small part o.g.** *Approximately less than half of the gum intact*		**No gum** *Only if issued with gum*
Commonly Used Symbol:	★★	★	★	★	★		(★)
Pre-1900 Issues (Pre-1881 for U.S.)	*Very fine pre-1900 stamps in these categories trade at a premium over Scott value*			Scott Value for "Unused"			Scott "No Gum" listings for selected unused classic stamps
From 1900 to breakpoints for listings of never-hinged stamps	Scott "Never Hinged" listings for selected unused stamps	Scott Value for "Unused" (Actual value will be affected by the degree of hinging of the full o.g.)					
From breakpoints noted for many countries	Scott Value for "Unused"						

Never Hinged (NH; ★★): A never-hinged stamp will have full original gum that will have no hinge mark or disturbance. The presence of an expertizer's mark does not disqualify a stamp from this designation.

Original Gum (OG; ★): Pre-1900 stamps should have approximately half or more of their original gum. On rarer stamps, it may be expected that the original gum will be somewhat more disturbed than it will be on more common issues. Post-1900 stamps should have full original gum. Original gum will show some disturbance caused by a previous hinge(s) which may be present or entirely removed. The actual value of a post-1900 stamp will be affected by the degree of hinging of the full original gum.

Disturbed Original Gum: Gum showing noticeable effects of humidity, climate or hinging over more than half of the gum. The significance of gum disturbance in valuing a stamp in any of the Original Gum categories depends on the degree of disturbance, the rarity and normal gum condition of the issue and other variables affecting quality.

Regummed (RG; (★)): A regummed stamp is a stamp without gum that has had some type of gum privately applied at a time after it was issued. This normally is done to deceive collectors and/or dealers into thinking that the stamp has original gum and therefore has a higher value. A regummed stamp is considered the same as a stamp with none of its original gum for purposes of grading.

Understanding the Listings

On the opposite page is an enlarged "typical" listing from this catalogue. Below are detailed explanations of each of the highlighted parts of the listing.

1 **Scott number** — Scott catalogue numbers are used to identify specific items when buying, selling or trading stamps. Each listed postage stamp from every country has a unique Scott catalogue number. Therefore, Germany Scott 99, for example, can only refer to a single stamp. Although the Scott catalogue usually lists stamps in chronological order by date of issue, there are exceptions. When a country has issued a set of stamps over a period of time, those stamps within the set are kept together without regard to date of issue. This follows the normal collecting approach of keeping stamps in their natural sets.

When a country issues a set of stamps over a period of time, a group of consecutive catalogue numbers is reserved for the stamps in that set, as issued. If that group of numbers proves to be too few, capital-letter suffixes, such as "A" or "B," may be added to existing numbers to create enough catalogue numbers to cover all items in the set. A capital-letter suffix indicates a major Scott catalogue number listing. Scott generally uses a suffix letter only once. Therefore, a catalogue number listing with a capital-letter suffix will seldom be found with the same letter (lower case) used as a minor-letter listing. If there is a Scott 16A in a set, for example, there will seldom be a Scott 16a. However, a minor-letter "a" listing may be added to a major number containing an "A" suffix (Scott 16Aa, for example).

Suffix letters are cumulative. A minor "b" variety of Scott 16A would be Scott 16Ab, not Scott 16b.

There are times when a reserved block of Scott catalogue numbers is too large for a set, leaving some numbers unused. Such gaps in the numbering sequence also occur when the catalogue editors move an item's listing elsewhere or have removed it entirely from the catalogue. Scott does not attempt to account for every possible number, but rather attempts to assure that each stamp is assigned its own number.

Scott numbers designating regular postage normally are only numerals. Scott numbers for other types of stamps, such as air post, semipostal, postal tax, postage due, occupation and others have a prefix consisting of one or more capital letters or a combination of numerals and capital letters.

2 **Illustration number** — Illustration or design-type numbers are used to identify each catalogue illustration. For most sets, the lowest face-value stamp is shown. It then serves as an example of the basic design approach for other stamps not illustrated. Where more than one stamp use the same illustration number, but have differences in design, the design paragraph or the description line clearly indicates the design on each stamp not illustrated. Where there are both vertical and horizontal designs in a set, a single illustration may be used, with the exceptions noted in the design paragraph or description line.

When an illustration is followed by a lower-case letter in parentheses, such as "A2(b)," the trailing letter indicates which overprint or surcharge illustration applies.

Illustrations normally are 70 percent of the original size of the stamp. Oversized stamps, blocks and souvenir sheets are reduced even more. Overprints and surcharges are shown at 100 percent of their original size if shown alone, but are 70 percent of original size if shown on stamps. In some cases, the illustration will be placed above the set, between listings or omitted completely. Overprint and surcharge illustrations are not placed in this catalogue for purposes of expertizing stamps.

3 **Paper color** — The color of a stamp's paper is noted in italic type when the paper used is not white.

4 **Listing styles** — There are two principal types of catalogue listings: major and minor.

Major listings are in a larger type style than minor listings. The catalogue number is a numeral that can be found with or without a capital-letter suffix, and with or without a prefix.

Minor listings are in a smaller type style and have a small-letter suffix or (if the listing immediately follows that of the major number) may show only the letter. These listings identify a variety of the major item. Examples include perforation and shade differences, multiples (some souvenir sheets, booklet panes and se-tenant combinations), and singles of multiples.

Examples of major number listings include 16, 28A, B97, C13A, 10N5, and 10N6A. Examples of minor numbers are 16a and C13Ab.

5 **Basic information about a stamp or set** — Introducing each stamp issue is a small section (usually a line listing) of basic information about a stamp or set. This section normally includes the date of issue, method of printing, perforation, watermark and, sometimes, some additional information of note. *Printing method, perforation and watermark apply to the following sets until a change is noted.* Stamps created by overprinting or surcharging previous issues are assumed to have the same perforation, watermark, printing method and other production characteristics as the original. Dates of issue are as precise as Scott is able to confirm and often reflect the dates on first-day covers, rather than the actual date of release.

6 **Denomination** — This normally refers to the face value of the stamp; that is, the cost of the unused stamp at the post office at the time of issue. When a denomination is shown in parentheses, it does not appear on the stamp. This includes the non-denominated stamps of the United States, Brazil and Great Britain, for example.

7 **Color or other description** — This area provides information to solidify identification of a stamp. In many recent cases, a description of the stamp design appears in this space, rather than a listing of colors.

8 **Year of issue** — In stamp sets that have been released in a period that spans more than a year, the number shown in parentheses is the year that stamp first appeared. Stamps without a date appeared during the first year of the issue. Dates are not always given for minor varieties.

9 **Value unused and Value used** — The Scott catalogue values are based on stamps that are in a grade of Very Fine unless stated otherwise. Unused values refer to items that have not seen postal, revenue or any other duty for which they were intended. Pre-1900 unused stamps that were issued with gum must have at least most of their original gum. Later issues are assumed to have full original gum. From breakpoints specified in most countries' listings, stamps are valued as never hinged. Stamps issued without gum are noted. Modern issues with PVA or other synthetic adhesives may appear ungummed. Unused self-adhesive stamps are valued as appearing undisturbed on their original backing paper. Values for used self-adhesive stamps are for examples either on piece or off piece. For a more detailed explanation of these values, please see the "Catalogue Value," "Condition" and "Understanding Valuing Notations" sections elsewhere in this introduction.

In some cases, where used stamps are more valuable than unused stamps, the value is for an example with a contemporaneous cancel, rather than a modern cancel or a smudge or other unclear marking. For those stamps that were released for postal and fiscal purposes, the used value represents a postally used stamp. Stamps with revenue cancels generally sell for less.

Stamps separated from a complete se-tenant multiple usually will be worth less than a pro-rated portion of the se-tenant multiple, and stamps lacking the attached labels that are noted in the listings will be worth less than the values shown.

10 **Changes in basic set information** — Bold type is used to show any changes in the basic data given for a set of stamps. These basic data categories include perforation gauge measurement, paper type, printing method and watermark.

11 **Total value of a set** — The total value of sets of three or more stamps issued after 1900 are shown. The set line also notes the range of Scott numbers and total number of stamps included in the grouping. The actual value of a set consisting predominantly of stamps having the minimum value of twenty cents may be less than the total value shown. Similary, the actual value or catalogue value of se-tenant pairs or of blocks consisting of stamps having the minimum value of twenty cents may be less than the catalogue values of the component parts.

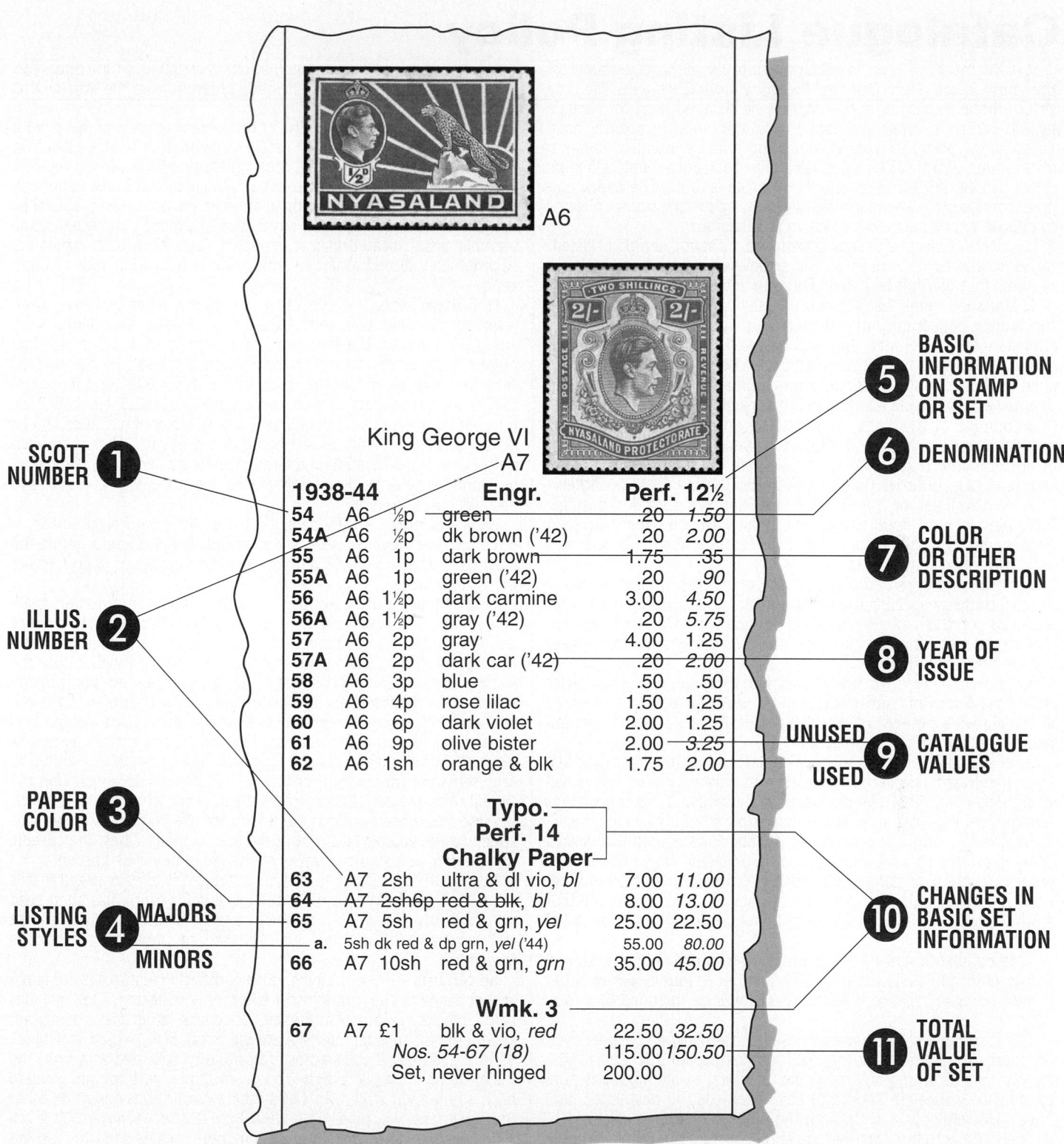

SCOTT NUMBER ❶

ILLUS. NUMBER ❷

PAPER COLOR ❸

LISTING STYLES ❹

MAJORS

MINORS

King George VI
A7

BASIC INFORMATION ON STAMP OR SET ❺

DENOMINATION ❻

COLOR OR OTHER DESCRIPTION ❼

YEAR OF ISSUE ❽

CATALOGUE VALUES ❾

UNUSED

USED

CHANGES IN BASIC SET INFORMATION ❿

TOTAL VALUE OF SET ⓫

A6

1938-44			Engr.	Perf. 12½	
54	A6	½p	green	.20	*1.50*
54A	A6	½p	dk brown ('42)	.20	*2.00*
55	A6	1p	dark brown	1.75	.35
55A	A6	1p	green ('42)	.20	.90
56	A6	1½p	dark carmine	3.00	*4.50*
56A	A6	1½p	gray ('42)	.20	*5.75*
57	A6	2p	gray	4.00	1.25
57A	A6	2p	dark car ('42)	.20	*2.00*
58	A6	3p	blue	.50	.50
59	A6	4p	rose lilac	1.50	1.25
60	A6	6p	dark violet	2.00	1.25
61	A6	9p	olive bister	2.00	*3.25*
62	A6	1sh	orange & blk	1.75	*2.00*

Typo.
Perf. 14
Chalky Paper

63	A7	2sh	ultra & dl vio, *bl*	7.00	*11.00*
64	A7	2sh6p	red & blk, *bl*	8.00	*13.00*
65	A7	5sh	red & grn, *yel*	25.00	22.50
a.		5sh dk red & dp grn, *yel* ('44)		55.00	*80.00*
66	A7	10sh	red & grn, *grn*	35.00	*45.00*

Wmk. 3

67	A7	£1	blk & vio, *red*	22.50	*32.50*
			Nos. 54-67 (18)	115.00	*150.50*
			Set, never hinged	200.00	

Catalogue Listing Policy

It is the intent of Scott Publishing Co. to list all postage stamps of the world in the *Scott Standard Postage Stamp Catalogue*. The only strict criteria for listing is that stamps be decreed legal for postage by the issuing country and that the issuing country actually have an operating postal system. Whether the primary intent of issuing a given stamp or set was for sale to postal patrons or to stamp collectors is not part of our listing criteria. Scott's role is to provide basic comprehensive postage stamp information. It is up to each stamp collector to choose which items to include in a collection.

It is Scott's objective to seek reasons why a stamp should be listed, rather than why it should not. Nevertheless, there are certain types of items that will not be listed. These include the following:

1. Unissued items that are not officially distributed or released by the issuing postal authority. If such items are officially issued at a later date by the country, they will be listed. Unissued items consist of those that have been printed and then held from sale for reasons such as change in government, errors found on stamps or something deemed objectionable about a stamp subject or design.

2. Stamps "issued" by non-existent postal entities or fantasy countries, such as Nagaland, Occusi-Ambeno, Staffa, Sedang, Torres Straits and others. Also, stamps "issued" in the names of legitimate, stamp-issuing countries that are not authorized by those countries.

3. Semi-official or unofficial items not required for postage. Examples include items issued by private agencies for their own express services. When such items are required for delivery, or are valid as prepayment of postage, they are listed.

4. Local stamps issued for local use only. Postage stamps issued by governments specifically for "domestic" use, such as Haiti Scott 219-228, or the United States non-denominated stamps, are not considered to be locals, since they are valid for postage throughout the country of origin.

5. Items not valid for postal use. For example, a few countries have issued souvenir sheets that are not valid for postage. This area also includes a number of worldwide charity labels (some denominated) that do not pay postage.

6. Intentional varieties, such as imperforate stamps that look like their perforated counterparts and are usually issued in very small quantities. Also, other egregiously exploitative issues such as stamps sold for far more than face value, stamps purposefully issued in artificially small quantities or only against advance orders, stamps awarded only to a selected audience such as a philatelic bureau's standing order customers, or stamps sold only in conjunction with other products. All of these kinds of items are usually controlled issues and/or are intended for speculation. These items normally will be included in a footnote.

7. Items distributed by the issuing government only to a limited group, club, philatelic exhibition or a single stamp dealer or other private company. These items normally will be included in a footnote.

The fact that a stamp has been used successfully as postage, even on international mail, is not in itself sufficient proof that it was legitimately issued. Numerous examples of so-called stamps from non-existent countries are known to have been used to post letters that have successfully passed through the international mail system.

There are certain items that are subject to interpretation. When a stamp falls outside our specifications, it may be listed along with a cautionary footnote.

A number of factors are considered in our approach to analyzing how a stamp is listed. The following list of factors is presented to share with you, the catalogue user, the complexity of the listing process.

Additional printings — "Additional printings" of a previously issued stamp may range from an item that is totally different to cases where it is impossible to differentiate from the original. At least a minor number (a small-letter suffix) is assigned if there is a distinct change in stamp shade, noticeably redrawn design, or a significantly different perforation measurement. A major number (numeral or capital-letter combination) is assigned if the editors feel the "additional printing" is sufficiently different from the original that it constitutes a different issue.

Commemoratives — Where practical, commemoratives with the same theme are placed in a set. For example, the U.S. Civil War Centennial set of 1961-65 and the Constitution Bicentennial series of 1989-90 appear as sets. Countries such as Japan and Korea issue such material on a regular basis, with an announced, or at least predictable, number of stamps known in advance. Occasionally, however, stamp sets that were released over a period of years have been separated. Appropriately placed footnotes will guide you to each set's continuation.

Definitive sets — Blocks of numbers generally have been reserved for definitive sets, based on previous experience with any given country. If a few more stamps were issued in a set than originally expected, they often have been inserted into the original set with a capital-letter suffix, such as U.S. Scott 1059A. If it appears that many more stamps than the originally allotted block will be released before the set is completed, a new block of numbers will be reserved, with the original one being closed off. In some cases, such as the U.S. Transportation and Great Americans series, several blocks of numbers exist. Appropriately placed footnotes will guide you to each set's continuation.

New country — Membership in the Universal Postal Union is not a consideration for listing status or order of placement within the catalogue. The index will tell you in what volume or page number the listings begin.

"No release date" items — The amount of information available for any given stamp issue varies greatly from country to country and even from time to time. Extremely comprehensive information about new stamps is available from some countries well before the stamps are released. By contrast some countries do not provide information about stamps or release dates. Most countries, however, fall between these extremes. A country may provide denominations or subjects of stamps from upcoming issues that are not issued as planned. Sometimes, philatelic agencies, those private firms hired to represent countries, add these later-issued items to sets well after the formal release date. This time period can range from weeks to years. If these items were officially released by the country, they will be added to the appropriate spot in the set. In many cases, the specific release date of a stamp or set of stamps may never be known.

Overprints — The color of an overprint is always noted if it is other than black. Where more than one color of ink has been used on overprints of a single set, the color used is noted. Early overprint and surcharge illustrations were altered to prevent their use by forgers.

Se-tenants — Connected stamps of differing features (se-tenants) will be listed in the format most commonly collected. This includes pairs, blocks or larger multiples. Se-tenant units are not always symmetrical. An example is Australia Scott 508, which is a block of seven stamps. If the stamps are primarily collected as a unit, the major number may be assigned to the multiple, with minors going to each component stamp. In cases where continuous-design or other unit se-tenants will receive significant postal use, each stamp is given a major Scott number listing. This includes issues from the United States, Canada, Germany and Great Britain, for example.

Special Notices

Classification of stamps

The *Scott Standard Postage Stamp Catalogue* lists stamps by country of issue. The next level of organization is a listing by section on the basis of the function of the stamps. The principal sections cover regular postage, semi-postal, air post, special delivery, registration, postage due and other categories. Except for regular postage, catalogue numbers for all sections include a prefix letter (or number-letter combination) denoting the class to which a given stamp belongs. When some countries issue sets containing stamps from more than one category, the catalogue will at times list all of the stamps in one category (such as air post stamps listed as part of a postage set).

The following is a listing of the most commonly used catalogue prefixes.

Prefix... Category
C ....Air Post
M........Military
P ....Newspaper
N ....Occupation - Regular Issues
O ....Official
Q ....Parcel Post
J ....Postage Due
RA .....Postal Tax
B ....Semi-Postal
E ....Special Delivery
MR ....War Tax

Other prefixes used by more than one country include the following:
H ....Acknowledgment of Receipt
I ....Late Fee
CO.....Air Post Official
CQ.....Air Post Parcel Post
RAC...Air Post Postal Tax
CF......Air Post Registration
CB .....Air Post Semi-Postal
CBO...Air Post Semi-Postal Official
CE .....Air Post Special Delivery
EY......Authorized Delivery
S ....Franchise
G ....Insured Letter
GY .....Marine Insurance
MC ....Military Air Post
MQ....Military Parcel Post
NC.....Occupation - Air Post
NO.....Occupation - Official
NJ ......Occupation - Postage Due
NRA...Occupation - Postal Tax
NB .....Occupation - Semi-Postal
NE .....Occupation - Special Delivery
QY .....Parcel Post Authorized Delivery
AR .....Postal-fiscal
RAJ ....Postal Tax Due
RAB ...Postal Tax Semi-Postal
F ....Registration
EB......Semi-Postal Special Delivery
EO .....Special Delivery Official
QE .....Special Handling

New issue listings

Updates to this catalogue appear each month in the *Scott Stamp Monthly* magazine. Included in this update are additions to the listings of countries found in the *Scott Standard Postage Stamp Catalogue* and the *Specialized Catalogue of United States Stamps*, as well as corrections and updates to current editions of this catalogue.

From time to time there will be changes in the final listings of stamps from the *Scott Stamp Monthly* to the next edition of the catalogue. This occurs as more information about certain stamps or sets becomes available.

The catalogue update section of the *Scott Stamp Monthly* is the most timely presentation of this material available. Annual subscriptions to the *Scott Stamp Monthly* are available from Scott Publishing Co., Box 828, Sidney, OH 45365-0828.

Number additions, deletions & changes

A listing of catalogue number additions, deletions and changes from the previous edition of the catalogue appears in each volume. See Catalogue Number Additions, Deletions & Changes in the table of contents for the location of this list.

Understanding valuing notations

The *minimum catalogue value* of an individual stamp or set is 20 cents. This represents a portion of the cost incurred by a dealer when he prepares an individual stamp for resale. As a point of philatelic-economic fact, the lower the value shown for an item in this catalogue, the greater the percentage of that value is attributed to dealer mark up and profit margin. In many cases, such as the 20-cent minimum value, that price does not cover the labor or other costs involved with stocking it as an individual stamp. The sum of minimum values in a set does not properly represent the value of a complete set primarily composed of a number of minimum-value stamps, nor does the sum represent the actual value of a packet made up of minimum-value stamps. Thus a packet of 1,000 different common stamps — each of which has a catalogue value of 20-cents — normally sells for considerably less than 200 dollars!

The *absence of a retail value* for a stamp does not necessarily suggest that a stamp is scarce or rare. A dash in the value column means that the stamp is known in a stated form or variety, but information is either lacking or insufficient for purposes of establishing a usable catalogue value.

Stamp values in *italics* generally refer to items that are difficult to value accurately. For expensive items, such as those priced at $1,000 or higher, a value in italics indicates that the affected item trades very seldom. For inexpensive items, a value in italics represents a warning. One example is a "blocked" issue where the issuing postal administration may have controlled one stamp in a set in an attempt to make the whole set more valuable. Another example is an item that sold at an extreme multiple of face value in the marketplace at the time of its issue.

One type of warning to collectors that appears in the catalogue is illustrated by a stamp that is valued considerably higher in used condition than it is as unused. In this case, collectors are cautioned to be certain the used version has a genuine and contemporaneous cancellation. The type of cancellation on a stamp can be an important factor in determining its sale price. Catalogue values do not apply to fiscal, telegraph or non-contemporaneous postal cancels, unless otherwise noted.

Some countries have released back issues of stamps in canceled-to-order form, sometimes covering as much as a 10-year period. The Scott Catalogue values for used stamps reflect canceled-to-order material when such stamps are found to predominate in the marketplace for the issue involved. Notes frequently appear in the stamp listings to specify which items are valued as canceled-to-order, or if there is a premium for postally used examples.

Many countries sell canceled-to-order stamps at a marked reduction of face value. Countries that sell or have sold canceled-to-order stamps at *full* face value include United Nations, Australia, Netherlands, France and Switzerland. It may be almost impossible to identify such stamps if the gum has been removed, because official government canceling devices are used. Postally used copies of these items on cover, however, are usually worth more than the canceled-to-order stamps with original gum.

Abbreviations

Scott Publishing Co. uses a consistent set of abbreviations throughout this catalogue to conserve space, while still providing necessary information.

COLOR ABBREVIATIONS

amb	amber	crim	crimson	ol	olive
anil	aniline	cr	cream	olvn	olivine
ap	apple	dk	dark	org	orange
aqua	aquamarine	dl	dull	pck	peacock
az	azure	dp	deep	pnksh	pinkish
bis	bister	db	drab	Prus	Prussian
bl	blue	emer	emerald	pur	purple
bld	blood	gldn	golden	redsh	reddish
blk	black	grysh	grayish	res	reseda
bril	brilliant	grn	green	ros	rosine
brn	brown	grnsh	greenish	ryl	royal
brnsh	brownish	hel	heliotrope	sal	salmon
brnz	bronze	hn	henna	saph	sapphire
brt	bright	ind	indigo	scar	scarlet
brnt	burnt	int	intense	sep	sepia
car	carmine	lav	lavender	sien	sienna
cer	cerise	lem	lemon	sil	silver
chlky	chalky	lil	lilac	sl	slate
cham	chamois	lt	light	stl	steel
chnt	chestnut	mag	magenta	turq	turquoise
choc	chocolate	man	manila	ultra	ultramarine
chr	chrome	mar	maroon	Ven	Venetian
cit	citron	mv	mauve	ver	vermilion
cl	claret	multi	multicolored	vio	violet
cob	cobalt	mlky	milky	yel	yellow
cop	copper	myr	myrtle	yelsh	yellowish

When no color is given for an overprint or surcharge, black is the color used. Abbreviations for colors used for overprints and surcharges include: "(B)" or "(Blk)," black; "(Bl)," blue; "(R)," red; and "(G)," green.

Additional abbreviations in this catalogue are shown below:

Adm	Administration
AFL	American Federation of Labor
Anniv.	Anniversary
APS	American Philatelic Society
Assoc.	Association
ASSR	Autonomous Soviet Socialist Republic
b.	Born
BEP	Bureau of Engraving and Printing
Bicent.	Bicentennial
Bklt.	Booklet
Brit.	British
btwn.	Between
Bur.	Bureau
c. or ca.	Circa
Cat.	Catalogue
Cent.	Centennial, century, centenary
CIO	Congress of Industrial Organizations
Conf.	Conference
Cong.	Congress
Cpl.	Corporal
CTO	Canceled to order
d.	Died
Dbl.	Double
EDU	Earliest documented use
Engr.	Engraved
Exhib.	Exhibition
Expo.	Exposition
Fed.	Federation
GB	Great Britain
Gen.	General
GPO	General post office
Horiz.	Horizontal
Imperf.	Imperforate
Impt.	Imprint

Intl.	International
Invtd.	Inverted
L	Left
Lieut., lt.	Lieutenant
Litho.	Lithographed
LL	Lower left
LR	Lower right
mm	Millimeter
Ms.	Manuscript
Natl.	National
No.	Number
NY	New York
NYC	New York City
Ovpt.	Overprint
Ovptd	Overprinted
P	Plate number
Perf.	Perforated, perforation
Phil.	Philatelic
Photo.	Photogravure
PO	Post office
Pr.	Pair
P.R.	Puerto Rico
Prec.	Precancel, precanceled
Pres.	President
PTT	Post, Telephone and Telegraph
Rio	Rio de Janeiro
Sgt.	Sergeant
Soc.	Society
Souv.	Souvenir
SSR	Soviet Socialist Republic, see ASSR
St.	Saint, street
Surch.	Surcharge
Typo.	Typographed
UL	Upper left
Unwmkd	Unwatermarked
UPU	Universal Postal Union
UR	Upper Right
US	United States
USPOD	United States Post Office Department
USSR	Union of Soviet Socialist Republics
Vert.	Vertical
VP	Vice president
Wmk.	Watermark
Wmkd	Watermarked
WWI	World War I
WWII	World War II

Examination

Scott Publishing Co. will not comment upon the genuineness, grade or condition of stamps, because of the time and responsibility involved. Rather, there are several expertizing groups that undertake this work for both collectors and dealers. Neither will Scott Publishing Co. appraise or identify philatelic material. The company cannot take responsibility for unsolicited stamps or covers sent by individuals.

All letters, E-mails, etc. are read attentively, but they are not always answered due to time considerations.

How to order from your dealer

When ordering stamps from a dealer, it is not necessary to write the full description of a stamp as listed in this catalogue. All you need is the name of the country, the Scott catalogue number and whether the desired item is unused or used. For example, "Japan Scott 422 unused" is sufficient to identify the unused stamp of Japan listed as "422 A206 5y brown."

Basic Stamp Information

A stamp collector's knowledge of the combined elements that make a given stamp issue unique determines his or her ability to identify stamps. These elements include paper, watermark, method of separation, printing, design and gum. On the following pages each of these important areas is briefly described.

Paper

Paper is an organic material composed of a compacted weave of cellulose fibers and generally formed into sheets. Paper used to print stamps may be manufactured in sheets, or it may have been part of a large roll (called a web) before being cut to size. The fibers most often used to create paper on which stamps are printed include bark, wood, straw and certain grasses. In many cases, linen or cotton rags have been added for greater strength and durability. Grinding, bleaching, cooking and rinsing these raw fibers reduces them to a slushy pulp, referred to by paper makers as "stuff." Sizing and, sometimes, coloring matter is added to the pulp to make different types of finished paper.

After the stuff is prepared, it is poured onto sieve-like frames that allow the water to run off, while retaining the matted pulp. As fibers fall onto the screen and are held by gravity, they form a natural weave that will later hold the paper together. If the screen has metal bits that are formed into letters or images attached, it leaves slightly thinned areas on the paper. These are called watermarks.

When the stuff is almost dry, it is passed under pressure through smooth or engraved rollers - dandy rolls - or placed between cloth in a press to be flattened and dried.

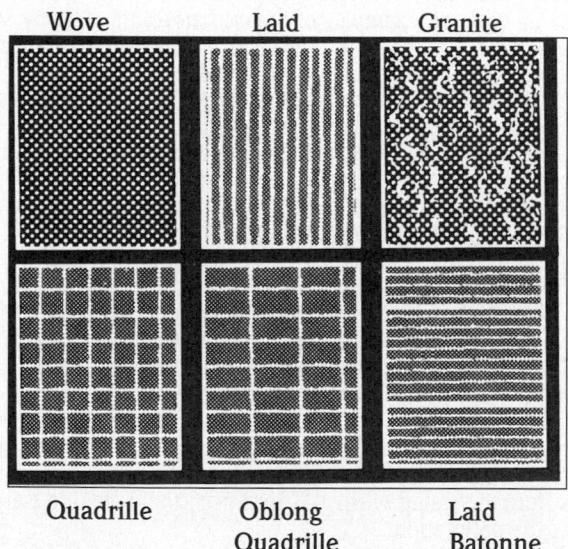

| Wove | Laid | Granite |

| Quadrille | Oblong Quadrille | Laid Batonne |

Stamp paper falls broadly into two types: wove and laid. The nature of the surface of the frame onto which the pulp is first deposited causes the differences in appearance between the two. If the surface is smooth and even, the paper will be of fairly uniform texture throughout. This is known as *wove paper*. Early papermaking machines poured the pulp onto a continuously circulating web of felt, but modern machines feed the pulp onto a cloth-like screen made of closely interwoven fine wires. This paper, when held to a light, will show little dots or points very close together. The proper name for this is "wire wove," but the type is still considered wove. Any U.S. or British stamp printed after 1880 will serve as an example of wire wove paper.

Closely spaced parallel wires, with cross wires at wider intervals, make up the frames used for what is known as *laid paper*. A greater thickness of the pulp will settle between the wires. The paper, when held to a light, will show alternate light and dark lines. The spacing and the thickness of the lines may vary, but on any one sheet of paper they are all alike. See Russia Scott 31-38 for examples of laid paper.

Batonne, from the French word meaning "a staff," is a term used if the lines in the paper are spaced quite far apart, like the printed ruling on a writing tablet. Batonne paper may be either wove or laid. If laid, fine laid lines can be seen between the batons.

Quadrille is the term used when the lines in the paper form little squares. *Oblong quadrille* is the term used when rectangles, rather than squares, are formed. See Mexico-Guadalajara Scott 35-37 for examples of oblong quadrille paper.

Paper also is classified as thick or thin, hard or soft, and by color if dye is added during manufacture. Such colors may include yellowish, greenish, bluish and reddish.

Brief explanations of other types of paper used for printing stamps, as well as examples, follow.

Pelure — Pelure paper is a very thin, hard and often brittle paper that is sometimes bluish or grayish in appearance. See Serbia Scott 169-170.

Native — This is a term applied to handmade papers used to produce some of the early stamps of the Indian states. Stamps printed on native paper may be expected to display various natural inclusions that are normal and do not negatively affect value. Japanese paper, originally made of mulberry fibers and rice flour, is part of this group. See Japan Scott 1-18.

Manila — This type of paper is often used to make stamped envelopes and wrappers. It is a coarse-textured stock, usually smooth on one side and rough on the other. A variety of colors of manila paper exist, but the most common range is yellowish-brown.

Silk — Introduced by the British in 1847 as a safeguard against counterfeiting, silk paper contains bits of colored silk thread scattered throughout. The density of these fibers varies greatly and can include as few as one fiber per stamp or hundreds. U.S. revenue Scott R152 is a good example of an easy-to-identify silk paper stamp.

Silk-thread paper has uninterrupted threads of colored silk arranged so that one or more threads run through the stamp or postal stationery. See Great Britain Scott 5-6 and Switzerland Scott 14-19.

Granite — Filled with minute cloth or colored paper fibers of various colors and lengths, granite paper should not be confused with either type of silk paper. Austria Scott 172-175 and a number of Swiss stamps are examples of granite paper.

Chalky — A chalk-like substance coats the surface of chalky paper to discourage the cleaning and reuse of canceled stamps, as well as to provide a smoother, more acceptable printing surface. Because the designs of stamps printed on chalky paper are imprinted on what is often a water-soluble coating, any attempt to remove a cancellation will destroy the stamp. *Do not soak these stamps in any fluid.* To remove a stamp printed on chalky paper from an envelope, wet the paper from underneath the stamp until the gum dissolves enough to release the stamp from the paper. See St. Kitts-Nevis Scott 89-90 for examples of stamps printed on this type of chalky paper.

India — Another name for this paper, originally introduced from China about 1750, is "China Paper." It is a thin, opaque paper often used for plate and die proofs by many countries.

Double — In philately, the term double paper has two distinct meanings. The first is a two-ply paper, usually a combination of a thick and a thin sheet, joined during manufacture. This type was used experimentally as a means to discourage the reuse of stamps.

The design is printed on the thin paper. Any attempt to remove a cancellation would destroy the design. U.S. Scott 158 and other Banknote-era stamps exist on this form of double paper.

The second type of double paper occurs on a rotary press, when the end of one paper roll, or web, is affixed to the next roll to save time feeding the paper through the press. Stamp designs are printed over the joined paper and, if overlooked by inspectors, may get into post office stocks.

Goldbeater's Skin — This type of paper was used for the 1866 issue of Prussia, and was a tough, translucent paper. The design was printed in reverse on the back of the stamp, and the gum applied over the printing. It is impossible to remove stamps printed on this type of paper from the paper to which they are affixed without destroying the design.

Ribbed — Ribbed paper has an uneven, corrugated surface made by passing the paper through ridged rollers. This type exists on some copies of U.S. Scott 156-165.

Various other substances, or substrates, have been used for stamp manufacture, including wood, aluminum, copper, silver and gold foil, plastic, and silk and cotton fabrics.

Watermarks

Watermarks are an integral part of some papers. They are formed in the process of paper manufacture. Watermarks consist of small designs, formed of wire or cut from metal and soldered to the surface of the mold or, sometimes, on the dandy roll. The designs may be in the form of crowns, stars, anchors, letters or other characters or symbols. These pieces of metal - known in the paper-making industry as "bits" - impress a design into the paper. The design sometimes may be seen by holding the stamp to the light. Some are more easily seen with a watermark detector. This important tool is a small black tray into which a stamp is placed face down and dampened with a fast-evaporating watermark detection fluid that brings up the watermark image in the form of dark lines against a lighter background. These dark lines are the thinner areas of the paper known as the watermark. Some watermarks are extremely difficult to locate, due to either a faint impression, watermark location or the color of the stamp. There also are electric watermark detectors that come with plastic filter disks of various colors. The disks neutralize the color of the stamp, permitting the watermark to be seen more easily.

Multiple watermarks of Crown Agents and Burma

Watermarks of Uruguay, Vatican City and Jamaica

WARNING: Some inks used in the photogravure process dissolve in watermark fluids (Please see the section on Soluble Printing Inks). Also, see "chalky paper."

Watermarks may be found normal, reversed, inverted, reversed and inverted, sideways or diagonal, as seen from the back of the stamp. The relationship of watermark to stamp design depends on the position of the printing plates or how paper is fed through the press. On machine-made paper, watermarks normally are read from right to left. The design is repeated closely throughout the sheet in a "multiple-watermark design." In a "sheet watermark," the design appears only once on the sheet, but extends over many stamps. Individual stamps may carry only a small fraction or none of the watermark.

"Marginal watermarks" occur in the margins of sheets or panes of stamps. They occur on the outside border of paper (ostensibly outside the area where stamps are to be printed). A large row of letters may spell the name of the country or the manufacturer of the paper, or a border of lines may appear. Careless press feeding may cause parts of these letters and/or lines to show on stamps of the outer row of a pane.

Soluble Printing Inks

WARNING: Most stamp colors are permanent; that is, they are not seriously affected by short-term exposure to light or water. Many colors, especially of modern inks, fade from excessive exposure to light. There are stamps printed with inks that dissolve easily in water or in fluids used to detect watermarks. Use of these inks was intentional to prevent the removal of cancellations. Water affects all aniline inks, those on so-called safety paper and some photogravure printings - all such inks are known as *fugitive colors. Removal from paper of such stamps requires care and alternatives to traditional soaking.*

Separation

"Separation" is the general term used to describe methods used to separate stamps. The three standard forms currently in use are perforating, rouletting and die-cutting. These methods are done during the stamp production process, after printing. Sometimes these methods are done on-press or sometimes as a separate step. The earliest issues, such as the 1840 Penny Black of Great Britain (Scott 1), did not have any means provided for separation. It was expected the stamps would be cut apart with scissors or folded and torn. These are examples of imperforate stamps. Many stamps were first issued in imperforate formats and were later issued with perforations. Therefore, care must be observed in buying single imperforate stamps to be certain they were issued imperforate and are not perforated copies that have been altered by having the perforations trimmed away. Stamps issued imperforate usually are valued as singles. However, imperforate varieties of normally perforated stamps should be collected in pairs or larger pieces as indisputable evidence of their imperforate character.

PERFORATION

The chief style of separation of stamps, and the one that is in almost universal use today, is perforating. By this process, paper between the stamps is cut away in a line of holes, usually round, leaving little bridges of paper between the stamps to hold them together. Some types of perforation, such as hyphen-hole perfs, can be confused with roulettes, but a close visual inspection reveals that paper has been removed. The little perforation bridges, which project from the stamp when it is torn from the pane, are called the teeth of the perforation.

As the size of the perforation is sometimes the only way to differentiate between two otherwise identical stamps, it is necessary to be able to accurately measure and describe them. This is done with a perforation gauge, usually a ruler-like device that has dots or graduated lines to show how many perforations may be counted in the space of two centimeters. Two centimeters is the space universally adopted in which to measure perforations.

Perforation gauge

perce en arc   perce en lignes

perce en points   oblique roulette

perce en scie   perce serpentin

To measure a stamp, run it along the gauge until the dots on it fit exactly into the perforations of the stamp. If you are using a graduated-line perforation gauge, simply slide the stamp along the surface until the lines on the gauge perfectly project from the center of the bridges or holes. The number to the side of the line of dots or lines that fit the stamp's perforation is the measurement. For example, an "11" means that 11 perforations fit between two centimeters. The description of the stamp therefore is "perf. 11." If the gauge of the perforations on the top and bottom of a stamp differs from that on the sides, the result is what is known as *compound perforations*. In measuring compound perforations, the gauge at top and bottom is always given first, then the sides. Thus, a stamp that measures 11 at top and bottom and 10 1/2 at the sides is "perf. 11 x 10 1/2." See U.S. Scott 632-642 for examples of compound perforations.

Stamps also are known with perforations different on three or all four sides. Descriptions of such items are clockwise, beginning with the top of the stamp.

A perforation with small holes and teeth close together is a "fine perforation." One with large holes and teeth far apart is a "coarse perforation." Holes that are jagged, rather than clean-cut, are "rough perforations." *Blind perforations* are the slight impressions left by the perforating pins if they fail to puncture the paper. Multiples of stamps showing blind perforations may command a slight premium over normally perforated stamps.

The term *syncopated perfs* describes intentional irregularities in the perforations. The earliest form was used by the Netherlands from 1925-33, where holes were omitted to create distinctive patterns. Beginning in 1992, Great Britain has used an oval perforation to help prevent counterfeiting. Several other countries have started using the oval perfs or other syncopated perf patterns.

A new type of perforation, still primarily used for postal stationery, is known as microperfs. Microperfs are tiny perforations (in some cases hundreds of holes per two centimeters) that allows items to be intentionally separated very easily, while not accidentally breaking apart as easily as standard perforations. These are not currently measured or differentiated by size, as are standard perforations.

ROULETTING

In rouletting, the stamp paper is cut partly or wholly through, with no paper removed. In perforating, some paper is removed. Rouletting derives its name from the French roulette, a spur-like wheel. As the wheel is rolled over the paper, each point makes a small cut. The number of cuts made in a two-centimeter space determines the gauge of the roulette, just as the number of perforations in two centimeters determines the gauge of the perforation.

The shape and arrangement of the teeth on the wheels varies. Various roulette types generally carry French names:

Perce en lignes - rouletted in lines. The paper receives short, straight cuts in lines. This is the most common type of rouletting. See Mexico Scott 500.

Perce en points - pin-rouletted or pin-perfed. This differs from a small perforation because no paper is removed, although round, equidistant holes are pricked through the paper. See Mexico Scott 242-256.

Perce en arc and *perce en scie* - pierced in an arc or saw-toothed designs, forming half circles or small triangles. See Hanover (German States) Scott 25-29.

Perce en serpentin - serpentine roulettes. The cuts form a serpentine or wavy line. See Brunswick (German States) Scott 13-18.

Once again, no paper is removed by these processes, leaving the stamps easily separated, but closely attached.

DIE-CUTTING

The third major form of stamp separation is die-cutting. This is a method where a die in the pattern of separation is created that later cuts the stamp paper in a stroke motion. Although some standard stamps bear die-cut perforations, this process is primarily used for self-adhesive postage stamps. Die-cutting can appear in straight lines, such as U.S. Scott 2522, shapes, such as U.S. Scott 1551, or imitating the appearance of perforations, such as New Zealand Scott 935A and 935B.

Printing Processes

ENGRAVING (Intaglio, Line-engraving, Etching)

Master die — The initial operation in the process of line engraving is making the master die. The die is a small, flat block of softened steel upon which the stamp design is recess engraved in reverse.

Master die

Photographic reduction of the original art is made to the appropriate size. It then serves as a tracing guide for the initial outline of the design. The engraver lightly traces the design on the steel with his graver, then slowly works the design until it is completed. At various points during the engraving process, the engraver hand-inks the die and makes an impression to check his progress. These are known as progressive die proofs. After completion of the engraving, the die is hardened to withstand the stress and pressures of later transfer operations.

Transfer roll

Transfer roll — Next is production of the transfer roll that, as the name implies, is the medium used to transfer the subject from the master die to the printing plate. A blank roll of soft steel, mounted on a mandrel, is placed under the bearers of the transfer press to allow it to roll freely on its axis. The hardened die is placed on the bed of the press and the face of the transfer roll is applied to the die, under pressure. The bed or the roll is then rocked back and forth under increasing pressure, until the soft steel of the roll is forced into every engraved line of the die. The resulting impression on the roll is known as a "relief" or a "relief transfer." The engraved image is now positive in appearance and stands out from the steel. After the required number of reliefs are "rocked in," the soft steel transfer roll is hardened.

Different flaws may occur during the relief process. A defective relief may occur during the rocking in process because of a minute piece of foreign material lodging on the die, or some other cause. Imperfections in the steel of the transfer roll may result in a breaking away of parts of the design. This is known as a relief break, which will show up on finished stamps as small, unprinted areas. If a damaged relief remains in use, it will transfer a repeating defect to the plate. Deliberate alterations of reliefs sometimes occur. "Altered reliefs" designate these changed conditions.

Plate — The final step in pre-printing production is the making of the printing plate. A flat piece of soft steel replaces the die on the bed of the transfer press. One of the reliefs on the transfer roll is positioned over this soft steel. Position, or layout, dots determine the correct position on the plate. The dots have been lightly marked on

the plate in advance. After the correct position of the relief is determined, the design is rocked in by following the same method used in making the transfer roll. The difference is that this time the image is being transferred from the transfer roll, rather than to it. Once the design is entered on the plate, it appears in reverse and is recessed. There are as many transfers entered on the plate as there are subjects printed on the sheet of stamps. It is during this process that double and shifted transfers occur, as well as re-entries. These are the result of improperly entered images that have not been properly burnished out prior to rocking in a new image.

Modern siderography processes, such as those used by the U.S. Bureau of Engraving and Printing, involve an automated form of rocking designs in on preformed cylindrical printing sleeves. The same process also allows for easier removal and re-entry of worn images right on the sleeve.

Transferring the design to the plate

Following the entering of the required transfers on the plate, the position dots, layout dots and lines, scratches and other markings generally are burnished out. Added at this time by the siderographer are any required *guide lines, plate numbers* or other *marginal markings.* The plate is then hand-inked and a proof impression is taken. This is known as a plate proof. If the impression is approved, the plate is machined for fitting onto the press, is hardened and sent to the plate vault ready for use.

On press, the plate is inked and the surface is automatically wiped clean, leaving ink only in the recessed lines. Paper is then forced under pressure into the engraved recessed lines, thereby receiving the ink. Thus, the ink lines on engraved stamps are slightly raised, and slight depressions (debossing) occur on the back of the stamp. Prior to the advent of modern high-speed presses and more advanced ink formulations, paper had to be dampened before receiving the ink. This sometimes led to uneven shrinkage by the time the stamps were perforated, resulting in improperly perforated stamps, or misperfs. Newer presses use drier paper, thus both *wet* and *dry printings* exist on some stamps.

Rotary Press — Until 1914, only flat plates were used to print engraved stamps. Rotary press printing was introduced in 1914, and slowly spread. Some countries still use flat-plate printing.

After approval of the plate proof, older *rotary press plates* require additional machining. They are curved to fit the press cylinder. "Gripper slots" are cut into the back of each plate to receive the "grippers," which hold the plate securely on the press. The plate is then hardened. Stamps printed from these bent rotary press plates are longer or wider than the same stamps printed from flat-plate presses. The stretching of the plate during the curving process is what causes this distortion.

Re-entry — To execute a re-entry on a flat plate, the transfer roll is re-applied to the plate, often at some time after its first use on the press. Worn-out designs can be resharpened by carefully burnishing out the original image and re-entering it from the transfer roll. If the original impression has not been sufficiently removed and the transfer roll is not precisely in line with the remaining impression, the resulting double transfer will make the re-entry obvious. If the registration is true, a re-entry may be difficult or impossible to distinguish. Sometimes a stamp printed from a successful re-entry is identified by having a much sharper and clearer impression than its neighbors. With the advent of rotary presses, post-press re-entries were not possible. After a plate was curved for the rotary press, it was impossible to make a re-entry. This is because the plate had already been bent once (with the design distorted).

However, with the introduction of the previously mentioned modern-style siderography machines, entries are made to the preformed cylindrical printing sleeve. Such sleeves are dechromed and softened. This allows individual images to be burnished out and re-entered on the curved sleeve. The sleeve is then rechromed, resulting in longer press life.

Double Transfer — This is a description of the condition of a transfer on a plate that shows evidence of a duplication of all, or a portion of the design. It usually is the result of the changing of the registration between the transfer roll and the plate during the rocking in of the original entry. Double transfers also occur when only a portion of the design has been rocked in and improper positioning is noted. If the worker elected not to burnish out the partial or completed design, a strong double transfer will occur for part or all of the design.

It sometimes is necessary to remove the original transfer from a plate and repeat the process a second time. If the finished re-worked image shows traces of the original impression, attributable to incomplete burnishing, the result is a partial double transfer.

With the modern automatic machines mentioned previously, double transfers are all but impossible to create. Those partially doubled images on stamps printed from such sleeves are more than likely re-entries, rather than true double transfers.

Re-engraved — Alterations to a stamp design are sometimes necessary after some stamps have been printed. In some cases, either the original die or the actual printing plate may have its "temper" drawn (softened), and the design will be re-cut. The resulting impressions from such a re-engraved die or plate may differ slightly from the original issue, and are known as "re-engraved." If the alteration was made to the master die, all future printings will be consistently different from the original. If alterations were made to the printing plate, each altered stamp on the plate will be slightly different from each other, allowing specialists to reconstruct a complete printing plate.

Dropped Transfers — If an impression from the transfer roll has not been properly placed, a dropped transfer may occur. The final stamp image will appear obviously out of line with its neighbors.

Short Transfer — Sometimes a transfer roll is not rocked its entire length when entering a transfer onto a plate. As a result, the finished transfer on the plate fails to show the complete design, and the finished stamp will have an incomplete design printed. This is known as a "short transfer." U.S. Scott No. 8 is a good example of a short transfer.

TYPOGRAPHY (Letterpress, Surface Printing, Flexography, Dry Offset, High Etch)

Although the word "Typography" is obsolete as a term describing a printing method, it was the accepted term throughout the first century of postage stamps. Therefore, appropriate Scott listings in this catalogue refer to typographed stamps. The current term for this form of printing, however, is "letterpress."

As it relates to the production of postage stamps, letterpress printing is the reverse of engraving. Rather than having recessed areas trap the ink and deposit it on paper, only the raised areas of the design are inked. This is comparable to the type of printing seen by inking and using an ordinary rubber stamp. Letterpress includes all printing where the design is above the surface area, whether it is wood, metal or, in some instances, hardened rubber or polymer plastic.

For most letterpress-printed stamps, the engraved master is made in much the same manner as for engraved stamps. In this instance, however, an additional step is needed. The design is transferred to another surface before being transferred to the transfer roll. In this way, the transfer roll has a recessed stamp design, rather than one done in relief. This makes the printing areas on the final plate raised, or relief areas.

For less-detailed stamps of the 19th century, the area on the die not used as a printing surface was cut away, leaving the surface area raised. The original die was then reproduced by stereotyping or electrotyping. The resulting electrotypes were assembled in the required number and format of the desired sheet of stamps. The plate used in printing the stamps was an electroplate of these assembled electrotypes.

Once the final letterpress plates are created, ink is applied to the raised surface and the pressure of the press transfers the ink impression to the paper. In contrast to engraving, the fine lines of letterpress are impressed on the surface of the stamp, leaving a debossed surface. When viewed from the back (as on a typewritten page), the corresponding line work on the stamp will be raised slightly (embossed) above the surface.

PHOTOGRAVURE (Gravure, Rotogravure, Heliogravure)

In this process, the basic principles of photography are applied to a chemically sensitized metal plate, rather than photographic paper. The design is transferred photographically to the plate through a halftone, or dot-matrix screen, breaking the reproduction into tiny dots. The plate is treated chemically and the dots form depressions, called cells, of varying depths and diameters, depending on the degrees of shade in the design. Then, like engraving, ink is applied to the plate and the surface is wiped clean. This leaves ink in the tiny cells that is lifted out and deposited on the paper when it is pressed against the plate.

Gravure is most often used for multicolored stamps, generally using the three primary colors (red, yellow and blue) and black. By varying the dot matrix pattern and density of these colors, virtually any color can be reproduced. A typical full-color gravure stamp will be created from four printing cylinders (one for each color). The original multicolored image will have been photographically separated into its component colors.

Modern gravure printing may use computer-generated dot-matrix screens, and modern plates may be of various types including metal-coated plastic. The catalogue designation of Photogravure (or "Photo") covers any of these older and more modern gravure methods of printing.

For examples of the first photogravure stamps printed (1914), see Bavaria Scott 94-114.

LITHOGRAPHY (Offset Lithography, Stone Lithography, Dilitho, Planography, Collotype)

The principle that oil and water do not mix is the basis for lithography. The stamp design is drawn by hand or transferred from engraving to the surface of a lithographic stone or metal plate in a greasy (oily) substance. This oily substance holds the ink, which will later be transferred to the paper. The stone (or plate) is wet with an acid fluid, causing it to repel the printing ink in all areas not covered by the greasy substance.

Transfer paper is used to transfer the design from the original stone or plate. A series of duplicate transfers are grouped and, in turn, transferred to the final printing plate.

Photolithography — The application of photographic processes to lithography. This process allows greater flexibility of design, related to use of halftone screens combined with line work. Unlike photogravure or engraving, this process can allow large, solid areas to be printed.

Offset — A refinement of the lithographic process. A rubber-covered blanket cylinder takes the impression from the inked lithographic plate. From the "blanket" the impression is *offset* or transferred to the paper. Greater flexibility and speed are the principal reasons offset printing has largely displaced lithography. The term "lithography" covers both processes, and results are almost identical.

EMBOSSED (Relief) Printing

Embossing, not considered one of the four main printing types, is a method in which the design first is sunk into the metal of the die. Printing is done against a yielding platen, such as leather or linoleum. The platen is forced into the depression of the die, thus forming the design on the paper in relief. This process is often used for metallic inks.

Embossing may be done without color (see Sardinia Scott 4-6); with color printed around the embossed area (see Great Britain Scott 5 and most U.S. envelopes); and with color in exact registration with the embossed subject (see Canada Scott 656-657).

HOLOGRAMS

For objects to appear as holograms on stamps, a model exactly the same size as it is to appear on the hologram must be created. Rather than using photographic film to capture the image, holography records an image on a photoresist material. In processing, chemicals eat away at certain exposed areas, leaving a pattern of constructive and destructive interference. When the phororesist is developed, the result is a pattern of uneven ridges that acts as a mold. This mold is then coated with metal, and the resulting form is used to press copies in much the same way phonograph records are produced.

A typical reflective hologram used for stamps consists of a reproduction of the uneven patterns on a plastic film that is applied to a reflective background, usually a silver or gold foil. Light is reflected off the background through the film, making the pattern present on the film visible. Because of the uneven pattern of the film, the viewer will perceive the objects in their proper three-dimensional relationships with appropriate brightness.

The first hologram on a stamp was produced by Austria in 1988 (Scott 1441).

FOIL APPLICATION

A modern tecnique of applying color to stamps involves the application of metallic foil to the stamp paper. A pattern of foil is applied to the stamp paper by use of a stamping die. The foil usually is flat, but it may be textured. Canada Scott 1735 has three different foil applications in pearl, bronze and gold. The gold foil was textured using a chemical-etch copper embossing die. The printing of this stamp also involved two-color offset lithography plus embossing.

COMBINATION PRINTINGS

Sometimes two or even three printing methods are combined in producing stamps. In these cases, such as Austria Scott 933 or Canada 1735 (described in the preceding paragraph), the multiple-printing technique can be determined by studying the individual characteristics of each printing type. A few stamps, such as Singapore Scott 684-684A, combine as many as three of the four major printing types (lithography, engraving and typography). When this is done it often indicates the incorporation of security devices against counterfeiting.

INK COLORS

Inks or colored papers used in stamp printing often are of mineral origin, although there are numerous examples of organic-based pigments. As a general rule, organic-based pigments are far more subject to varieties and change than those of mineral-based origin.

The appearance of any given color on a stamp may be affected by many aspects, including printing variations, light, color of paper, aging and chemical alterations.

Numerous printing variations may be observed. Heavier pressure or inking will cause a more intense color, while slight interruptions in the ink feed or lighter impressions will cause a lighter appearance. Stamps printed in the same color by water-based and solvent-based inks can differ significantly in appearance. This affects several stamps in the U.S. Prominent Americans series. Hand-mixed ink formulas (primarily from the 19th century) produced under different conditions (humidity and temperature) account for notable color variations in early printings of the same stamp (see U.S. Scott 248-250, 279B, for example). Different sources of pigment can also result in significant differences in color.

Light exposure and aging are closely related in the way they affect stamp color. Both eventually break down the ink and fade colors, so that a carefully kept stamp may differ significantly in color from an identical copy that has been exposed to light. If stamps are exposed to light either intentionally or accidentally, their colors can be faded or completely changed in some cases.

Papers of different quality and consistency used for the same stamp printing may affect color appearance. Most pelure papers, for example, show a richer color when compared with wove or laid papers. See Russia Scott 181a, for an example of this effect.

The very nature of the printing processes can cause a variety of differences in shades or hues of the same stamp. Some of these shades are scarcer than others, and are of particular interest to the advanced collector.

Luminescence

All forms of tagged stamps fall under the general category of luminescence. Within this broad category is fluorescence, dealing with forms of tagging visible under longwave ultraviolet light, and phosphorescence, which deals with tagging visible only under shortwave light. Phosphorescence leaves an afterglow and fluorescence does not. These treated stamps show up in a range of different colors when exposed to UV light. The differing wavelengths of the light activates the tagging material, making it glow in various colors that usually serve different mail processing purposes.

Intentional tagging is a post-World War II phenomenon, brought about by the increased literacy rate and rapidly growing mail volume. It was one of several answers to the problem of the need for more automated mail processes. Early tagged stamps served the purpose of triggering machines to separate different types of mail. A natural outgrowth was to also use the signal to trigger machines that faced all envelopes the same way and canceled them.

Tagged stamps come in many different forms. Some tagged stamps have luminescent shapes or images imprinted on them as a form of security device. Others have blocks (United States), stripes, frames (South Africa and Canada), overall coatings (United States), bars (Great Britain and Canada) and many other types. Some types of tagging are even mixed in with the pigmented printing ink (Australia Scott 366, Netherlands Scott 478 and U.S. Scott 1359 and 2443).

The means of applying taggant to stamps differs as much as the intended purposes for the stamps. The most common form of tagging is a coating applied to the surface of the printed stamp. Since the taggant ink is frequently invisible except under UV light, it does not interfere with the appearance of the stamp. Another common application is the use of phosphored papers. In this case the paper itself either has a coating of taggant applied before the stamp is printed, has taggant applied during the papermaking process (incorporating it into the fibers), or has the taggant mixed into the coating of the paper. The latter method, among others, is currently in use in the United States.

Many countries now use tagging in various forms to either expedite mail handling or to serve as a printing security device against counterfeiting. Following the introduction of tagged stamps for public use in 1959 by Great Britain, other countries have steadily joined the parade. Among those are Germany (1961); Canada and Denmark (1962); United States, Australia, France and Switzerland (1963); Belgium and Japan (1966); Sweden and Norway (1967); Italy (1968); and Russia (1969). Since then, many other countries have begun using forms of tagging, including Brazil, China, Czechoslovakia, Hong Kong, Guatemala, Indonesia, Israel, Lithuania, Luxembourg, Netherlands, Penrhyn Islands, Portugal, St. Vincent, Singapore, South Africa, Spain and Sweden to name a few.

In some cases, including United States, Canada, Great Britain and Switzerland, stamps were released both with and without tagging. Many of these were released during each country's experimental period. Tagged and untagged versions are listed for the aforementioned countries and are noted in some other countries' listings. For at least a few stamps, the experimentally tagged version is worth far more than its untagged counterpart, such as the 1963 experimental tagged version of France Scott 1024.

In some cases, luminescent varieties of stamps were inadvertently created. Several Russian stamps, for example, sport highly fluorescent ink that was not intended as a form of tagging. Older stamps, such as early U.S. postage dues, can be positively identified by the use of UV light, since the organic ink used has become slightly fluorescent over time. Other stamps, such as Austria Scott 70a-82a (varnish bars) and Obock Scott 46-64 (printed quadrille lines), have become fluorescent over time.

Various fluorescent substances have been added to paper to make it appear brighter. These optical brighteners, as they are known, greatly affect the appearance of the stamp under UV light. The brightest of these is known as Hi-Brite paper. These paper varieties are beyond the scope of the Scott Catalogue.

Shortwave UV light also is used extensively in expertizing, since each form of paper has its own fluorescent characteristics that are impossible to perfectly match. It is therefore a simple matter to detect filled thins, added perforation teeth and other alterations that involve the addition of paper. UV light also is used to examine stamps that have had cancels chemically removed and for other purposes as well.

Gum

The Illustrated Gum Chart in the first part of this introduction shows and defines various types of gum condition. Because gum condition has an important impact on the value of unused stamps, we recommend studying this chart and the accompanying text carefully.

The gum on the back of a stamp may be shiny, dull, smooth, rough, dark, white, colored or tinted. Most stamp gumming adhesives use gum arabic or dextrine as a base. Certain polymers such as polyvinyl alcohol (PVA) have been used extensively since World War II.

The *Scott Standard Postage Stamp Catalogue* does not list items by types of gum. The *Scott Specialized Catalogue of United States Stamps* does differentiate among some types of gum for certain issues.

Reprints of stamps may have gum differing from the original issues. In addition, some countries have used different gum formulas for different seasons. These adhesives have different properties that may become more apparent over time.

Many stamps have been issued without gum, and the catalogue will note this fact. See, for example, United States Scott 40-47. Sometimes, gum may have been removed to preserve the stamp. Germany Scott B68, for example, has a highly acidic gum that eventually destroys the stamps. This item is valued in the catalogue with gum removed.

Reprints and Reissues

These are impressions of stamps (usually obsolete) made from the original plates or stones. If they are valid for postage and reproduce obsolete issues (such as U.S. Scott 102-111), the stamps are *reissues*. If they are from current issues, they are designated as *second, third,* etc., *printing*. If designated for a particular purpose, they are called *special printings*.

When special printings are not valid for postage, but are made from original dies and plates by authorized persons, they are *official reprints*. *Private reprints* are made from the original plates and dies by private hands. An example of a private reprint is that of the 1871-1932 reprints made from the original die of the 1845 New Haven, Conn., postmaster's provisional. *Official reproductions* or imitations are made from new dies and plates by government authorization. Scott will list those reissues that are valid for postage if they differ significantly from the original printing.

The U.S. government made special printings of its first postage stamps in 1875. Produced were official imitations of the first two stamps (listed as Scott 3-4), reprints of the demonetized pre-1861 issues (Scott 40-47) and reissues of the 1861 stamps, the 1869 stamps and the then-current 1875 denominations. Even though the official imitations and the reprints were not valid for postage, Scott lists all of these U.S. special printings.

Most reprints or reissues differ slightly from the original stamp in some characteristic, such as gum, paper, perforation, color or watermark. Sometimes the details are followed so meticulously that only a student of that specific stamp is able to distinguish the reprint or reissue from the original.

Remainders and Canceled to Order

Some countries sell their stock of old stamps when a new issue replaces them. To avoid postal use, the *remainders* usually are canceled with a punch hole, a heavy line or bar, or a more-or-less regular-looking cancellation. The most famous merchant of remainders was Nicholas F. Seebeck. In the 1880s and 1890s, he arranged printing contracts between the Hamilton Bank Note Co., of which he was a director, and several Central and South American countries. The contracts provided that the plates and all remainders of the yearly issues became the property of Hamilton. Seebeck saw to it that ample stock remained. The "Seebecks," both remainders and reprints, were standard packet fillers for decades.

Some countries also issue stamps *canceled-to-order (CTO),* either in sheets with original gum or stuck onto pieces of paper or envelopes and canceled. Such CTO items generally are worth less than postally used stamps. In cases where the CTO material is far more prevalent in the marketplace than postally used examples, the catalogue value relates to the CTO examples, with postally used examples noted as premium items. Most CTOs can be detected by the presence of gum. However, as the CTO practice goes back at least to 1885, the gum inevitably has been soaked off some stamps so they could pass as postally used. The normally applied postmarks usually differ slightly from standard postmarks, and specialists are able to tell the difference. When applied individually to envelopes by philatelically minded persons, CTO material is known as *favor canceled* and generally sells at large discounts.

Cinderellas and Facsimiles

Cinderella is a catch-all term used by stamp collectors to describe phantoms, fantasies, bogus items, municipal issues, exhibition seals, local revenues, transportation stamps, labels, poster stamps and many other types of items. Some cinderella collectors include in their collections local postage issues, telegraph stamps, essays and proofs, forgeries and counterfeits.

A *fantasy* is an adhesive created for a nonexistent stamp-issuing authority. Fantasy items range from imaginary countries (Occusi-Ambeno, Kingdom of Sedang, Principality of Trinidad or Torres

Straits), to non-existent locals (Winans City Post), or nonexistent transportation lines (McRobish & Co.'s Acapulco-San Francisco Line).

On the other hand, if the entity exists and could have issued stamps (but did not) or was known to have issued other stamps, the items are considered *bogus* stamps. These would include the Mormon postage stamps of Utah, S. Allan Taylor's Guatemala and Paraguay inventions, the propaganda issues for the South Moluccas and the adhesives of the Page & Keyes local post of Boston.

Phantoms is another term for both fantasy and bogus issues.

Facsimiles are copies or imitations made to represent original stamps, but which do not pretend to be originals. A catalogue illustration is such a facsimile. Illustrations from the Moens catalogue of the last century were occasionally colored and passed off as stamps. Since the beginning of stamp collecting, facsimiles have been made for collectors as space fillers or for reference. They often carry the word "facsimile," "falsch" (German), "sanko" or "mozo" (Japanese), or "faux" (French) overprinted on the face or stamped on the back. Unfortunately, over the years a number of these items have had fake cancels applied over the facsimile notation and have been passed off as genuine.

Forgeries and Counterfeits

Forgeries and counterfeits have been with philately virtually from the beginning of stamp production. Over time, the terminology for the two has been used interchangeably. Although both forgeries and counterfeits are reproductions of stamps, the purposes behind their creation differ considerably.

Among specialists there is an increasing movement to more specifically define such items. Although there is no universally accepted terminology, we feel the following definitions most closely mirror the items and their purposes as they are currently defined.

Forgeries (also often referred to as *Counterfeits*) are reproductions of genuine stamps that have been created to defraud collectors. Such spurious items first appeared on the market around 1860, and most old-time collections contain one or more. Many are crude and easily spotted, but some can deceive experts.

An important supplier of these early philatelic forgeries was the Hamburg printer Gebruder Spiro. Many others with reputations in this craft included S. Allan Taylor, George Hussey, James Chute, George Forune, Benjamin & Sarpy, Julius Goldner, E. Oneglia and L.H. Mercier. Among the noted 20th-century forgers were Francois Fournier, Jean Sperati and the prolific Raoul DeThuin.

Forgeries may be complete replications, or they may be genuine stamps altered to resemble a scarcer (and more valuable) type. Most forgeries, particularly those of rare stamps, are worth only a small fraction of the value of a genuine example, but a few types, created by some of the most notable forgers, such as Sperati, can be worth as much or more than the genuine. Fraudulently produced copies are known of most classic rarities and many medium-priced stamps.

In addition to rare stamps, large numbers of common 19th- and early 20th-century stamps were forged to supply stamps to the early packet trade. Many can still be easily found. Few new philatelic forgeries have appeared in recent decades. Successful imitation of well-engraved work is virtually impossible. It has proven far easier to produce a fake by altering a genuine stamp than to duplicate a stamp completely.

Counterfeit (also often referred to as *Postal Counterfeit* or *Postal Forgery*) is the term generally applied to reproductions of stamps that have been created to defraud the government of revenue. Such items usually are created at the time a stamp is current and, in some cases, are hard to detect. Because most counterfeits are seized when the perpetrator is captured, postal counterfeits, particularly used on cover, are usually worth much more than a genuine example to specialists. The first postal counterfeit was of Spain's 4-cuarto carmine of 1854 (the real one is Scott 25). Apparently, the counterfeiters were not satisfied with their first version, which is now very scarce,

and they soon created an engraved counterfeit, which is common. Postal counterfeits quickly followed in Austria, Naples, Sardinia and the Roman States. They have since been created in many other countries as well, including the United States.

An infamous counterfeit to defraud the government is the 1-shilling Great Britain "Stock Exchange" forgery of 1872, used on telegraph forms at the exchange that year. The stamp escaped detection until a stamp dealer noticed it in 1898.

Fakes

Fakes are genuine stamps altered in some way to make them more desirable. One student of this part of stamp collecting has estimated that by the 1950s more than 30,000 varieties of fakes were known. That number has grown greatly since then. The widespread existence of fakes makes it important for stamp collectors to study their philatelic holdings and use relevant literature. Likewise, collectors should buy from reputable dealers who guarantee their stamps and make full and prompt refunds should a purchased item be declared faked or altered by some mutually agreed-upon authority. Because fakes always have some genuine characteristics, it is not always possible to obtain unanimous agreement among experts regarding specific items. These students may change their opinions as philatelic knowledge increases. More than 80 percent of all fakes on the philatelic market today are regummed, reperforated (or perforated for the first time), or bear forged overprints, surcharges or cancellations.

Stamps can be chemically treated to alter or eliminate colors. For example, a pale rose stamp can be re-colored to resemble a blue shade of high market value. In other cases, treated stamps can be made to resemble missing color varieties. Designs may be changed by painting, or a stroke or a dot added or bleached out to turn an ordinary variety into a seemingly scarcer stamp. Part of a stamp can be bleached and reprinted in a different version, achieving an inverted center or frame. Margins can be added or repairs done so deceptively that the stamps move from the "repaired" into the "fake" category.

Fakers have not left the backs of the stamps untouched either. They may create false watermarks, add fake grills or press out genuine grills. A thin India paper proof may be glued onto a thicker backing to create the appearance an issued stamp, or a proof printed on cardboard may be shaved down and perforated to resemble a stamp. Silk threads are impressed into paper and stamps have been split so that a rare paper variety is added to an otherwise inexpensive stamp. The most common treatment to the back of a stamp, however, is regumming.

Some in the business of faking stamps have openly advertised foolproof application of "original gum" to stamps that lack it, although most publications now ban such ads from their pages. It is believed that very few early stamps have survived without being hinged. The large number of never-hinged examples of such earlier material offered for sale thus suggests the widespread extent of regumming activity. Regumming also may be used to hide repairs or thin spots. Dipping the stamp into watermark fluid, or examining it under long-wave ultraviolet light often will reveal these flaws.

Fakers also tamper with separations. Ingenious ways to add margins are known. Perforated wide-margin stamps may be falsely represented as imperforate when trimmed. Reperforating is commonly done to create scarce coil or perforation varieties, and to eliminate the naturally occurring straight-edge stamps found in sheet margin positions of many earlier issues. Custom has made straight-edged stamps less desirable. Fakers have obliged by perforating straight-edged stamps so that many are now uncommon, if not rare.

Another fertile field for the faker is that of overprints, surcharges and cancellations. The forging of rare surcharges or overprints began in the 1880s or 1890s. These forgeries are sometimes difficult to detect, but experts have identified almost all. Occasionally, overprints or cancellations are removed to create non-overprinted stamps or seemingly unused items. This is most commonly done by removing a manuscript cancel to make a stamp resemble an unused example. "SPECIMEN" overprints may be removed by scraping and repainting to create non-overprinted varieties. Fakers use inexpensive revenues or pen-canceled stamps to generate unused stamps for further faking by adding other markings. The quartz lamp or UV lamp and a high-powered magnifying glass help to easily detect removed cancellations.

The bigger problem, however, is the addition of overprints, surcharges or cancellations - many with such precision that they are very difficult to ascertain. Plating of the stamps or the overprint can be an important method of detection.

Fake postmarks may range from many spurious fancy cancellations to a host of markings applied to transatlantic covers, to adding normally appearing postmarks to definitives of some countries with stamps that are valued far higher used than unused. With the increased popularity of cover collecting, and the widespread interest in postal history, a fertile new field for fakers has come about. Some have tried to create entire covers. Others specialize in adding stamps, tied by fake cancellations, to genuine stampless covers, or replacing less expensive or damaged stamps with more valuable ones. Detailed study of postal rates in effect at the time a cover in question was mailed, including the analysis of each handstamp used during the period, ink analysis and similar techniques, usually will unmask the fraud.

Restoration and Repairs

Scott Publishing Co. bases its catalogue values on stamps that are free of defects and otherwise meet the standards set forth earlier in this introduction. Most stamp collectors desire to have the finest copy of an item possible. Even within given grading categories there are variances. This leads to a controversial practice that is not defined in any universal manner: stamp *restoration.*

There are broad differences of opinion about what is permissible when it comes to restoration. Carefully applying a soft eraser to a stamp or cover to remove light soiling is one form of restoration, as is washing a stamp in mild soap and water to clean it. These are fairly accepted forms of restoration. More severe forms of restoration include pressing out creases or removing stains caused by tape. To what degree each of these is acceptable is dependent upon the individual situation. Further along the spectrum is the freshening of a stamp's color by removing oxide build-up or the effects of wax paper left next to stamps shipped to the tropics.

At some point in this spectrum the concept of *repair* replaces that of restoration. Repairs include filling thin spots, mending tears by reweaving or adding a missing perforation tooth. Regumming stamps may have been acceptable as a restoration or repair technique many decades ago, but today it is considered a form of fakery.

Restored stamps may or may not sell at a discount, and it is possible that the value of individual restored items may be enhanced over that of their pre-restoration state. Specific situations dictate the resultant value of such an item. Repaired stamps sell at substantial discounts from the value of sound stamps.

Terminology

Booklets — Many countries have issued stamps in small booklets for the convenience of users. This idea continues to become increasingly popular in many countries. Booklets have been issued in many sizes and forms, often with advertising on the covers, the panes of stamps or on the interleaving.

The panes used in booklets may be printed from special plates or made from regular sheets. All panes from booklets issued by the United States and many from those of other countries contain stamps that are straight edged on the sides, but perforated between. Others are distinguished by orientation of watermark or other identifying features. Any stamp-like unit in the pane, either printed or blank, that is not a postage stamp, is considered to be a *label* in the catalogue listings.

Scott lists and values booklet panes. Modern complete booklets also are listed and valued. Individual booklet panes are listed only when they are not fashioned from existing sheet stamps and, therefore, are identifiable from their sheet stamp counterparts.

Panes usually do not have a used value assigned to them because there is little market activity for used booklet panes, even though many exist used and there is some demand for them.

Cancellations — The marks or obliterations put on stamps by postal authorities to show that they have performed service and to prevent their reuse are known as cancellations. If the marking is made with a pen, it is considered a "pen cancel." When the location of the post office appears in the marking, it is a "town cancellation." A "postmark" is technically any postal marking, but in practice the term generally is applied to a town cancellation with a date. When calling attention to a cause or celebration, the marking is known as a "slogan cancellation." Many other types and styles of cancellations exist, such as duplex, numerals, targets, fancy and others. See also "precancels," below.

Coil Stamps — These are stamps that are issued in rolls for use in dispensers, affixing and vending machines. Those coils of the United States, Canada, Sweden and some other countries are perforated horizontally or vertically only, with the outer edges imperforate. Coil stamps of some countries, such as Great Britain and Germany, are perforated on all four sides and may in some cases be distinguished from their sheet stamp counterparts by watermarks, counting numbers on the reverse or other means.

Covers — Entire envelopes, with or without adhesive postage stamps, that have passed through the mail and bear postal or other markings of philatelic interest are known as covers. Before the introduction of envelopes in about 1840, people folded letters and wrote the address on the outside. Some people covered their letters with an extra sheet of paper on the outside for the address, producing the term "cover." Used airletter sheets, stamped envelopes and other items of postal stationery also are considered covers.

Errors — Stamps that have some major, consistent, unintentional deviation from the normal are considered errors. Errors include, but are not limited to, missing or wrong colors, wrong paper, wrong watermarks, inverted centers or frames on multicolor printing, inverted or missing surcharges or overprints, double impressions, missing perforations, unintentionally omitted tagging and others. Factually wrong or misspelled information, if it appears on all examples of a stamp, are not considered errors in the true sense of the word. They are errors of design. Inconsistent or randomly appearing items, such as misperfs or color shifts, are classified as freaks.

Color-Omitted Errors — This term refers to stamps where a missing color is caused by the complete failure of the printing plate to deliver ink to the stamp paper or any other paper. Generally, this is caused by the printing plate not being engaged on the press or the ink station running dry of ink during printing.

Color-Missing Errors — This term refers to stamps where a color or colors were printed somewhere but do not appear on the finished stamp. There are four different classes of color-missing errors, and the catalog indicates with a two-letter code appended to each such listing what caused the color to be missing. These codes are used only for the United States' color-missing error listings.

FO = A *foldover* of the stamp sheet during printing may block ink from appearing on a stamp. Instead, the color will appear on the back of the foldover (where it might fall on the back of the selvage or perhaps on the back of the stamp or another stamp). FO also will be used in the case of foldunders, where the paper may fold underneath the other stamp paper and the color will print on the platen.

EP = A piece of *extraneous paper* falling across the plate or stamp paper will receive the printed ink. When the extraneous paper is removed, an unprinted portion of stamp paper remains and shows partially or totally missing colors.

CM = A misregistration of the printing plates during printing will result in a *color misregistration*, and such a misregistraion may result in a color not appearing on the finished stamp.

PS = A *perforation shift* after printing may remove a color from the finished stamp. Normally, this will occur on a row of stamps at the edge of the stamp pane.

Measurements – When measurements are given in the Scott catalogues for stamp size, grill size or any other reason, the first measurement given is always for the top and bottom dimension, while the second measurement will be for the sides (just as perforation gauges are measured). Thus, a stamp size of 15mm x 21mm will indicate a vertically oriented stamp 15mm wide at top and bottom, and 21mm tall at the sides. The same principle holds for measuring or counting items such as U.S. grills. A grill count of 22x18 points (B grill) indicates that there are 22 grill points across by 18 grill points down.

Overprints and Surcharges — Overprinting involves applying wording or design elements over an already existing stamp. Overprints can be used to alter the place of use (such as "Canal Zone" on U.S. stamps), to adapt them for a special purpose ("Porto" on Denmark's 1913-20 regular issues for use as postage due stamps, Scott J1-J7) or to commemorate a special occasion (United States Scott 647-648).

A *surcharge* is a form of overprint that changes or restates the face value of a stamp or piece of postal stationery.

Surcharges and overprints may be handstamped, typeset or, occasionally, lithographed or engraved. A few hand-written overprints and surcharges are known.

Personalized Stamps — In 1999, Australia issued stamps with se-tenant labels that could be personalized with pictures of the customer's choice. Other countries quickly followed suit, with some offering to print the selected picture on the stamp itself within a frame that was used exclusively for personalized issues. As the picture used on these stamps or labels vary, listings for such stamps are for *any* picture within the common frame (or any picture on a se-tenant label), be it a "generic" image or one produced especially for a customer, almost invariably at a premium price.

Precancels — Stamps that are canceled before they are placed in the mail are known as precancels. Precanceling usually is done to expedite the handling of large mailings and generally allow the affected mail pieces to skip certain phases of mail handling.

In the United States, precancellations generally identified the point of origin; that is, the city and state. This information appeared across the face of the stamp, usually centered between parallel lines. More recently, bureau precancels retained the parallel lines, but the city and state designations were dropped. Recent coils have a service inscription that is present on the original printing plate. These show the mail service paid for by the stamp. Since these stamps are not intended to receive further cancellations when used as intended, they are considered precancels. Such items often do not have parallel lines as part of the precancellation.

In France, the abbreviation *Affranchts* in a semicircle together with the word *Postes* is the general form of precancel in use. Belgian precancellations usually appear in a box in which the name of the city appears. Netherlands precancels have the name of the city enclosed between concentric circles, sometimes called a "lifesaver." Precancellations of other countries usually follow these patterns, but may be any arrangement of bars, boxes and city names.

Precancels are listed in the Scott catalogues only if the precancel changes the denomination (Belgium Scott 477-478); if the precanceled stamp is different from the non-precanceled version (such as untagged U.S. precancels); or if the stamp exists only precanceled (France Scott 1096-1099, U.S. Scott 2265).

Proofs and Essays — Proofs are impressions taken from an approved die, plate or stone in which the design and color are the same as the stamp issued to the public. Trial color proofs are impressions taken from approved dies, plates or stones in colors that vary from the final version. An essay is the impression of a design that differs in some way from the issued stamp. "Progressive die proofs" generally are considered to be essays.

Provisionals — These are stamps that are issued on short notice and intended for temporary use pending the arrival of regular issues. They usually are issued to meet such contingencies as changes in government or currency, shortage of necessary postage values or military occupation.

During the 1840s, postmasters in certain American cities issued stamps that were valid only at specific post offices. In 1861, postmasters of the Confederate States also issued stamps with limited validity. Both of these examples are known as "postmaster's provisionals."

Se-tenant — This term refers to an unsevered pair, strip or block of stamps that differ in design, denomination or overprint.

Unless the se-tenant item has a continuous design (see U.S. Scott 1451a, 1694a) the stamps do not have to be in the same order as shown in the catalogue (see U.S. Scott 2158a).

Specimens — The Universal Postal Union required member nations to send samples of all stamps they released into service to the International Bureau in Switzerland. Member nations of the UPU received these specimens as samples of what stamps were valid for postage. Many are overprinted, handstamped or initial-perforated "Specimen," "Canceled" or "Muestra." Some are marked with bars across the denominations (China-Taiwan), punched holes (Czechoslovakia) or back inscriptions (Mongolia).

Stamps distributed to government officials or for publicity purposes, and stamps submitted by private security printers for official approval, also may receive such defacements.

The previously described defacement markings prevent postal use, and all such items generally are known as "specimens."

Tete Beche — This term describes a pair of stamps in which one is upside down in relation to the other. Some of these are the result of intentional sheet arrangements, such as Morocco Scott B10-B11. Others occurred when one or more electrotypes accidentally were placed upside down on the plate, such as Colombia Scott 57a. Separation of the tete-beche stamps, of course, destroys the tete beche variety.

Pronunciation Symbols

ə .... banana, collide, abut

'ə, ˌə .... humdrum, abut

ə .... immediately preceding \l\, \n\, \m\, \ŋ\, as in battle, mitten, eaten, and sometimes open \'ō-pᵊm\, lock and key \-ᵊŋ-\; immediately following \l\, \m\, \r\, as often in French table, prisme, titre

ər .... further, merger, bird

'ər-
'ə-r .... as in two different pronunciations of hurry \'hər-ē, 'hə-rē\

a .... mat, map, mad, gag, snap, patch

ā .... day, fade, date, aorta, drape, cape

ä .... bother, cot, and, with most American speakers, father, cart

à .... father as pronunced by speakers who do not rhyme it with bother; French patte

aù .... now, loud, out

b .... baby, rib

ch .... chin, nature \'nā-chər\

d .... did, adder

e .... bet, bed, peck

'ē, ˌē .... beat, nosebleed, evenly, easy

ē .... easy, mealy

f .... fifty, cuff

g .... go, big, gift

h .... hat, ahead

hw .... whale as pronounced by those who do not have the same pronunciation for both whale and wail

i .... tip, banish, active

ī .... site, side, buy, tripe

j .... job, gem, edge, join, judge

k .... kin, cook, ache

ḵ .... German ich, Buch; one pronunciation of loch

l .... lily, pool

m .... murmur, dim, nymph

n .... no, own

ⁿ .... indicates that a preceding vowel or diphthong is pronounced with the nasal passages open, as in French un bon vin blanc \œⁿ -bōⁿ -vaⁿ -blä̃ⁿ\

ŋ .... sing \'siŋ\, singer \'siŋ-ər\, finger \'fiŋ-gər\, ink \'iŋk\

ō .... bone, know, beau

ȯ .... saw, all, gnaw, caught

œ .... French boeuf, German Hölle

œ̄ .... French feu, German Höhle

ȯi .... coin, destroy

p .... pepper, lip

r .... red, car, rarity

s .... source, less

sh .... as in shy, mission, machine, special (actually, this is a single sound, not two); with a hyphen between, two sounds as in grasshopper \'gras-ˌhä-pər\

t .... tie, attack, late, later, latter

th .... as in thin, ether (actually, this is a single sound, not two); with a hyphen between, two sounds as in knighthood \'nit-ˌhud\

th̲ .... then, either, this (actually, this is a single sound, not two)

ü .... rule, youth, union \'yün-yən\, few \'fyü\

u̇ .... pull, wood, book, curable \'kyu̇r-ə-bəl\, fury \'fyu̇r-ē\

ue .... German füllen, hübsch

u̅e̅ .... French rue, German fühlen

v .... vivid, give

w .... we, away

y .... yard, young, cue \'kyü\, mute \'myüt\, union \'yün-yən\

ʸ .... indicates that during the articulation of the sound represented by the preceding character the front of the tongue has substantially the position it has for the articulation of the first sound of yard, as in French digne \dēnʸ\

z .... zone, raise

zh .... as in vision, azure \'a-zhər\ (actually, this is a single sound, not two); with a hyphen between, two sounds as in hogshead \'hȯgz-ˌhed, 'hägz-\

\ .... slant line used in pairs to mark the beginning and end of a transcription: \'pen\

' .... mark preceding a syllable with primary (strongest) stress: \'pen-mən-ˌship\

ˌ .... mark preceding a syllable with secondary (medium) stress: \'pen-mən-ˌship\

- .... mark of syllable division

( ) .... indicate that what is symbolized between is present in some utterances but not in others: factory \'fak-t(ə-)rē\

÷ .... indicates that many regard as unacceptable the pronunciation variant immediately following: cupola \'kyü-pə-lə, ÷-ˌlō\

Currency Conversion

Country	Dollar	Pound	S Franc	Yen	HK $	Euro	Cdn $	Aus $
Australia	1.0102	1.6168	1.0540	0.0122	0.1297	1.3754	1.0151	—
Canada	0.9952	1.5928	1.0384	0.0121	0.1277	1.3549	—	0.9852
European Union	0.7345	1.1756	0.7664	0.0089	0.0943	—	0.7380	0.7271
Hong Kong	7.7908	12.469	8.1290	0.0944	—	10.607	7.8284	7.7121
Japan	82.563	132.14	86.147	—	10.597	112.41	82.961	81.729
Switzerland	0.9584	1.5339	—	0.0116	0.1230	1.3048	0.9630	0.9487
United Kingdom	0.6248	—	0.6519	0.0076	0.0802	0.8507	0.6278	0.6185
United States	—	1.6005	1.0434	0.0121	0.1284	1.3615	1.0048	0.9899

Country	Currency	U.S. $ Equiv.
Gabon	Community of French Africa (CFA) franc	.0021
Gambia	dalasy	.0354
Georgia	lari	.5533
Germany	euro	1.3615
Ghana	cedi	.6612
Gibraltar	pound	1.6005
Great Britain	pound	1.6005
Alderney	pound	1.6005
Guernsey	pound	1.6005
Jersey	pound	1.6005
Isle of Man	pound	1.6005
Greece	euro	1.3615
Greenland	Danish krone	.1826
Grenada	East Caribbean dollar	.3724
Grenada Grenadines	East Caribbean dollar	.3724
Guatemala	quetzal	.1257
Guinea	franc	.0001
Guinea-Bissau	CFA franc	.0021
Guyana	dollar	.0049
Haiti	gourde	.0252
Honduras	lempira	.0529
Hong Kong	dollar	.1284
Hungary	forint	.0050
Iceland	krona	.0085
India	rupee	.0219
Indonesia	rupiah	.0001
Iraq	dinar	.0008
Ireland	euro	1.3615
Israel	shekel	.2756
Italy	euro	1.3615
Ivory Coast	CFA franc	.0021

*Source: **Wall Street Journal** Jan. 22, 2011. Figures reflect values as of Jan. 21, 2011.*

COMMON DESIGN TYPES

Pictured in this section are issues where one illustration has been used for a number of countries in the Catalogue. Not included in this section are over-printed stamps or those issues which are illustrated in each country.

EUROPA
Europa, 1956

The design symbolizing the cooperation among the six countries comprising the Coal and Steel Community is illustrated in each country.

Belgium	496-497
France	805-806
Germany	748-749
Italy	715-716
Luxembourg	318-320
Netherlands	368-369

Europa, 1958

"E" and Dove — CD1

European Postal Union at the service of European integration.

1958, Sept. 13

Belgium	527-528
France	889-890
Germany	790-791
Italy	750-751
Luxembourg	341-343
Netherlands	375-376
Saar	317-318

Europa, 1959

6-Link Enless Chain — CD2

1959, Sept. 19

Belgium	536-537
France	929-930
Germany	805-806
Italy	791-792
Luxembourg	354-355
Netherlands	379-380

Europa, 1960

19-Spoke Wheel CD3

First anniverary of the establishment of C.E.P.T. (Conference Europeenne des Administrations des Postes et des Telecommunications.) The spokes symbolize the 19 founding members of the Conference.

1960, Sept.

Belgium	553-554
Denmark	379
Finland	376-377
France	970-971
Germany	818-820
Great Britain	377-378
Greece	688
Iceland	327-328

Ireland	175-176
Italy	809-810
Luxembourg	374-375
Netherlands	385-386
Norway	387
Portugal	866-867
Spain	941-942
Sweden	562-563
Switzerland	400-401
Turkey	1493-1494

Europa, 1961

19 Doves Flying as One — CD4

The 19 doves represent the 19 members of the Conference of European Postal and Tele-communications Administrations C.E.P.T.

1961-62

Belgium	572-573
Cyprus	201-203
France	1005-1006
Germany	844-845
Great Britain	383-384
Greece	718-719
Iceland	340-341
Italy	845-846
Luxembourg	382-383
Netherlands	387-388
Spain	1010-1011
Switzerland	410-411
Turkey	1518-1520

Europa, 1962

Young Tree with 19 Leaves CD5

The 19 leaves represent the 19 original members of C.E.P.T.

1962-63

Belgium	582-583
Cyprus	219-221
France	1045-1046
Germany	852-853
Greece	739-740
Iceland	348-349
Ireland	184-185
Italy	860-861
Luxembourg	386-387
Netherlands	394-395
Norway	414-415
Switzerland	416-417
Turkey	1553-1555

Europa, 1963

Stylized Links, Symbolizing Unity — CD6

1963, Sept.

Belgium	598-599
Cyprus	229-231
Finland	419
France	1074-1075
Germany	867-868
Greece	768-769
Iceland	357-358
Ireland	188-189
Italy	880-881
Luxembourg	403-404
Netherlands	416-417
Norway	441-442
Switzerland	429
Turkey	1602-1603

Europa, 1964

Symbolic Daisy — CD7

5th anniversary of the establishment of C.E.P.T. The 22 petals of the flower symbolize the 22 members of the Conference.

1964, Sept.

Austria	738
Belgium	614-615
Cyprus	244-246
France	1109-1110
Germany	897-898
Greece	801-802
Iceland	367-368
Ireland	196-197
Italy	894-895
Luxembourg	411-412
Monaco	590-591
Netherlands	428-429
Norway	458
Portugal	931-933
Spain	1262-1263
Switzerland	438-439
Turkey	1628-1629

Europa, 1965

Leaves and "Fruit" CD8

1965

Belgium	636-637
Cyprus	262-264
Finland	437
France	1131-1132
Germany	934-935
Greece	833-834
Iceland	375-376
Ireland	204-205
Italy	915-916
Luxembourg	432-433
Monaco	616-617
Netherlands	438-439
Norway	475-476
Portugal	958-960
Switzerland	469
Turkey	1665-1666

Europa, 1966

Symbolic Sailboat — CD9

1966, Sept.

Andorra, French	172
Belgium	675-676
Cyprus	275-277
France	1163-1164
Germany	963-964
Greece	862-863
Iceland	384-385
Ireland	216-217
Italy	942-943
Liechtenstein	415
Luxembourg	440-441
Monaco	639-640
Netherlands	441-442
Norway	496-497
Portugal	980-982
Switzerland	477-478
Turkey	1718-1719

Europa, 1967

Cogwheels CD10

1967

Andorra, French	174-175
Belgium	688-689
Cyprus	297-299
France	1178-1179
Germany	969-970
Greece	891-892
Iceland	389-390
Ireland	232-233
Italy	951-952
Liechtenstein	420
Luxembourg	449-450
Monaco	669-670
Netherlands	444-447
Norway	504-505
Portugal	994-996
Spain	1465-1466
Switzerland	482
Turkey	B120-B121

Europa, 1968

Golden Key with C.E.P.T. Emblem CD11

1968

Andorra, French	182-183
Belgium	705-706
Cyprus	314-316
France	1209-1210
Germany	983-984
Greece	916-917
Iceland	395-396
Ireland	242-243
Italy	979-980
Liechtenstein	442
Luxembourg	466-467
Monaco	689-691
Netherlands	452-453
Portugal	1019-1021
San Marino	687
Spain	1526
Turkey	1775-1776

Europa, 1969

"EUROPA" and "CEPT" CD12

Tenth anniversary of C.E.P.T.

1969

Andorra, French	188-189
Austria	837
Belgium	718-719
Cyprus	326-328
Denmark	458
Finland	483
France	1245-1246
Germany	996-997
Great Britain	585
Greece	947-948
Iceland	406-407
Ireland	270-271
Italy	1000-1001
Liechtenstein	453
Luxembourg	475-476
Monaco	722-724
Netherlands	475-476
Norway	533-534
Portugal	1038-1040
San Marino	701-702
Spain	1567
Sweden	814-816

Switzerland.............................500-501
Turkey....................................1799-1800
Vatican....................................470-472
Yugoslavia 1003-1004

Europa, 1970

Interwoven Threads CD13

1970

Andorra, French 196-197
Belgium..................................741-742
Cyprus....................................340-342
France.....................................1271-1272
Germany.................................1018-1019
Greece....................................985, 987
Iceland....................................420-421
Ireland....................................279-281
Italy..1013-1014
Liechtenstein.........................470
Luxembourg...........................489-490
Monaco...................................768-770
Netherlands...........................483-484
Portugal..................................1060-1062
San Marino.............................729-730
Spain......................................1607
Switzerland............................515-516
Turkey....................................1848-1849
Yugoslavia 1024-1025

Europa, 1971

"Fraternity, Cooperation, Common Effort" CD14

1971

Andorra, French 205-206
Belgium..................................803-804
Cyprus....................................365-367
Finland....................................504
France.....................................1304
Germany.................................1064-1065
Greece....................................1029-1030
Iceland....................................429-430
Ireland....................................305-306
Italy..1038-1039
Liechtenstein.........................485
Luxembourg...........................500-501
Malta......................................425-427
Monaco...................................797-799
Netherlands...........................488-489
Portugal..................................1094-1096
San Marino.............................749-750
Spain......................................1675-1676
Switzerland............................531-532
Turkey....................................1876-1877
Yugoslavia 1052-1053

Europa, 1972

Sparkles, Symbolic of Communications CD15

1972

Andorra, French 210-211
Andorra, Spanish 62
Belgium..................................825-826
Cyprus....................................380-382
Finland....................................512-513
France.....................................1341
Germany.................................1089-1090
Greece....................................1049-1050
Iceland....................................439-440
Ireland....................................316-317
Italy..1065-1066
Liechtenstein.........................504
Luxembourg...........................512-513
Malta......................................450-453
Monaco...................................831-832

Netherlands...........................494-495
Portugal..................................1141-1143
San Marino.............................771-772
Spain......................................1718
Switzerland............................544-545
Turkey....................................1907-1908
Yugoslavia 1100-1101

Europa, 1973

Post Horn and Arrows CD16

1973

Andorra, French 219-220
Andorra, Spanish 76
Belgium..................................839-840
Cyprus....................................396-398
Finland....................................526
France.....................................1367
Germany.................................1114-1115
Greece....................................1090-1092
Iceland....................................447-448
Ireland....................................329-330
Italy..1108-1109
Liechtenstein.........................528-529
Luxembourg...........................523-524
Malta......................................469-471
Monaco...................................866-867
Netherlands...........................504-505
Norway...................................604-605
Portugal..................................1170-1172
San Marino.............................802-803
Spain......................................1753
Switzerland............................580-581
Turkey....................................1935-1936
Yugoslavia 1138-1139

Europa, 2000

CD17

2000

Albania...................................2621-2622
Andorra, French 522
Andorra, Spanish 262
Armenia..................................610-611
Austria 1814
Azerbaijan..............................698-699
Belarus...................................350
Belgium..................................1818
Bosnia & Herzegovina (Moslem) 358
Bosnia & Herzegovina (Serb) 111-112
Croatia....................................428-429
Cyprus....................................959
Czech Republic 3120
Denmark.................................1189
Estonia....................................394
Faroe Islands.........................376
Finland....................................1129
Aland Islands.........................166
France.....................................2771
Georgia...................................228-229
Germany.................................2086-2087
Gibraltar.................................837-840
Great Britain (Guernsey).......805-809
Great Britain (Jersey).............935-936
Great Britain (Isle of Man) 883
Greece....................................1959
Greenland...............................363
Hungary..................................3699-3700
Iceland....................................910
Ireland....................................1230-1231
Italy..2349
Latvia......................................504
Liechtenstein.........................1178
Lithuania................................668
Luxembourg...........................1035
Macedonia..............................187
Malta......................................1011-1012
Moldova..................................358
Monaco...................................2161-2162
Poland.....................................3519
Portugal..................................2358
Portugal (Azores)...................455
Portugal (Madeira).................208

Romania.................................4370
Russia.....................................6589
San Marino.............................1480
Slovakia..................................355
Slovenia..................................424
Spain......................................3036
Sweden...................................2394
Switzerland............................1074
Turkey....................................2762
Turkish Rep. of Northern Cyprus....500
Ukraine...................................379
Vatican City............................1152

    The Gibraltar stamps are similar to the stamp illustrated, but none have the design shown above. All other sets listed above include at least one stamp with the design shown, but some include stamps with entirely different designs. Bulgaria Nos. 4131-4132 and Yugoslavia Nos. 2485-2486 are Europa stamps with completely different designs.

PORTUGAL & COLONIES
Vasco da Gama

Fleet Departing CD20

Fleet Arriving at Calicut — CD21

Embarking at Rastello CD22

Muse of History CD23

San Gabriel, da Gama and Camoens CD24

Archangel Gabriel, the Patron Saint CD25

Flagship San Gabriel — CD26

Vasco da Gama — CD27

    Fourth centenary of Vasco da Gama's discovery of the route to India.

1898

Azores 93-100
Macao.....................................67-74
Madeira...................................37-44
Portugal..................................147-154
Port. Africa.............................1-8
Port. Congo............................75-98
Port. India..............................189-196
St. Thomas & Prince Islands 170-193
Timor......................................45-52

Pombal
POSTAL TAX
POSTAL TAX DUES

Marquis de Pombal — CD28

Planning Reconstruction of Lisbon, 1755 — CD29

Pombal Monument, Lisbon — CD30

    Sebastiao Jose de Carvalho e Mello, Marquis de Pombal (1699-1782), statesman, rebuilt Lisbon after earthquake of 1755. Tax was for the erection of Pombal monument. Obligatory on all mail on certain days throughout the year. Postal Tax Dues are inscribed "Multa."

1925

Angola RA1-RA3, RAJ1-RAJ3
Azores RA9-RA11, RAJ2-RAJ4
Cape Verde RA1-RA3, RAJ1-RAJ3
Macao.............. RA1-RA3, RAJ1-RAJ3
Madeira............ RA1-RA3, RAJ1-RAJ3
Mozambique..... RA1-RA3, RAJ1-RAJ3
Nyassa............. RA1-RA3, RAJ1-RAJ3
Portugal RA11-RA13, RAJ2-RAJ4
Port. Guinea RA1-RA3, RAJ1-RAJ3
Port. India RA1-RA3, RAJ1-RAJ3
St. Thomas & Prince
  Islands RA1-RA3, RAJ1-RAJ3
Timor RA1-RA3, RAJ1-RAJ3

Vasco da Gama CD34

Mousinho de Albuquerque CD35

Dam CD36

Prince Henry the Navigator CD37

Affonso de Albuquerque CD38

Plane over Globe CD39

1938-39

Angola 274-291, C1-C9
Cape Verde 234-251, C1-C9
Macao......................289-305, C7-C15
Mozambique.............270-287, C1-C9
Port. Guinea.............233-250, C1-C9
Port. India.................439-453, C1-C8
St. Thomas & Prince
  Islands ... 302-319, 323-340, C1-C18
Timor 223-239, C1-C9

Lady of Fatima

Our Lady of the Rosary, Fatima, Portugal — CD40

1948-49

Angola 315-318
Cape Verde 266
Macao 336
Mozambique 325-328
Port. Guinea 271
Port. India 480
St. Thomas & Prince Islands 351
Timor 254

A souvenir sheet of 9 stamps was issued in 1951 to mark the extension of the 1950 Holy Year. The sheet contains: Angola No. 316, Cape Verde No. 266, Macao No. 336, Mozambique No. 325, Portuguese Guinea No. 271, Portuguese India Nos. 480, 485, St. Thomas & Prince Islands No. 351, Timor No. 254. The sheet also contains a portrait of Pope Pius XII and is inscribed "Encerramento do Ano Santo, Fatima 1951." It was sold for 11 escudos.

Holy Year

Church Bells and Dove
CD41

Angel Holding Candelabra
CD42

Holy Year, 1950.

1950-51

Angola 331-332
Cape Verde 268-269
Macao 339-340
Mozambique 330-331
Port. Guinea 273-274
Port. India 490-491, 496-503
St. Thomas & Prince Islands ...353-354
Timor 258-259

A souvenir sheet of 8 stamps was issued in 1951 to mark the extension of the Holy Year. The sheet contains: Angola No. 331, Cape Verde No. 269, Macao No. 340, Mozambique No. 331, Portuguese Guinea No. 275, Portuguese India No. 490, St. Thomas & Prince Islands No. 354, Timor No. 258, some with colors changed. The sheet contains doves and is inscribed 'Encerramento do Ano Santo, Fatima 1951.' It was sold for 17 escudos.

Holy Year Conclusion

Our Lady of Fatima — CD43

Conclusion of Holy Year. Sheets contain alternate vertical rows of stamps and labels bearing quotation from Pope Pius XII, different for each colony.

1951

Angola 357
Cape Verde 270
Macao 352
Mozambique 356
Port. Guinea 275
Port. India 506
St. Thomas & Prince Islands 355
Timor 270

Medical Congress

CD44

First National Congress of Tropical Medicine, Lisbon, 1952. Each stamp has a different design.

1952

Angola 358
Cape Verde 287
Macao 364
Mozambique 359
Port. Guinea 276
Port. India 516
St. Thomas & Prince Islands 356
Timor 271

Postage Due Stamps

CD45

1952

Angola J37-J42
Cape Verde J31-J36
Macao J53-J58
Mozambique J51-J56
Port. Guinea J40-J45
Port. India J47-J52
St. Thomas & Prince Islands ...J52-J57
Timor J31-J36

Sao Paulo

Father Manuel da Nobrega and View of Sao Paulo — CD46

Founding of Sao Paulo, Brazil, 400th anniv.

1954

Angola 385
Cape Verde 297
Macao 382
Mozambique 395
Port. Guinea 291
Port. India 530
St. Thomas & Prince Islands 369
Timor 279

Tropical Medicine Congress

CD47

Sixth International Congress for Tropical Medicine and Malaria, Lisbon, Sept. 1958. Each stamp shows a different plant.

1958

Angola 409
Cape Verde 303
Macao 392
Mozambique 404
Port. Guinea 295
Port. India 569
St. Thomas & Prince Islands 371
Timor 289

Sports

CD48

Each stamp shows a different sport.

1962

Angola 433-438
Cape Verde 320-325
Macao 394-399
Mozambique 424-429
Port. Guinea 299-304
St. Thomas & Prince Islands ...374-379
Timor 313-318

Anti-Malaria

Anopheles Funestus and Malaria Eradication Symbol — CD49

World Health Organization drive to eradicate malaria.

1962

Angola 439
Cape Verde 326
Macao 400
Mozambique 430
Port. Guinea 305
St. Thomas & Prince Islands 380
Timor 319

Airline Anniversary

Map of Africa, Super Constellation and Jet Liner — CD50

Tenth anniversary of Transportes Aereos Portugueses (TAP).

1963

Angola 490
Cape Verde 327
Mozambique 434
Port. Guinea 318
St. Thomas & Prince Islands 381

National Overseas Bank

Antonio Teixeira de Sousa — CD51

Centenary of the National Overseas Bank of Portugal.

1964, May 16

Angola 509
Cape Verde 328
Port. Guinea 319
St. Thomas & Prince Islands 382
Timor 320

ITU

ITU Emblem and the Archangel Gabriel — CD52

International Communications Union, Cent.

1965, May 17

Angola 511
Cape Verde 329
Macao 402
Mozambique 464
Port. Guinea 320
St. Thomas & Prince Islands 383
Timor 321

National Revolution

CD53

40th anniv. of the National Revolution. Different buildings on each stamp.

1966, May 28

Angola 525
Cape Verde 338
Macao 403
Mozambique 465
Port. Guinea 329
St. Thomas & Prince Islands 392
Timor 322

Navy Club

CD54

Centenary of Portugal's Navy Club. Each stamp has a different design.

1967, Jan. 31

Angola 527-528
Cape Verde 339-340
Macao 412-413
Mozambique 478-479
Port. Guinea 330-331
St. Thomas & Prince Islands ...393-394
Timor 323-324

Admiral Coutinho

CD55

Centenary of the birth of Admiral Carlos Viegas Gago Coutinho (1869-1959), explorer and aviation pioneer. Each stamp has a different design.

1969, Feb. 17

Angola 547
Cape Verde 355
Macao 417
Mozambique 484
Port. Guinea 335
St. Thomas & Prince Islands 397
Timor 335

Administration Reform

Luiz Augusto Rebello da Silva — CD56

Centenary of the administration reforms of the overseas territories.

1969, Sept. 25

Angola 549
Cape Verde 357
Macao 419
Mozambique 491
Port. Guinea 337
St. Thomas & Prince Islands 399
Timor 338

Marshal Carmona

CD57

Birth centenary of Marshal Antonio Oscar Carmona de Fragoso (1869-1951), President of Portugal. Each stamp has a different design.

1970, Nov. 15

Angola 563
Cape Verde 359
Macao 422
Mozambique 493
Port. Guinea 340
St. Thomas & Prince Islands 403
Timor 341

Olympic Games

CD59

20th Olympic Games, Munich, Aug. 26-Sept. 11. Each stamp shows a different sport.

1972, June 20

Angola 569
Cape Verde 361
Macao 426
Mozambique 504
Port. Guinea 342
St. Thomas & Prince Islands 408
Timor 343

Lisbon-Rio de Janeiro Flight

CD60

50th anniversary of the Lisbon to Rio de Janeiro flight by Arturo de Sacadura and Coutinho, March 30-June 5, 1922. Each stamp shows a different stage of the flight.

1972, Sept. 20

Angola 570
Cape Verde 362
Macao 427
Mozambique 505
Port. Guinea 343
St. Thomas & Prince Islands 409
Timor 344

WMO Centenary

WMO Emblem — CD61

Centenary of international meterological cooperation.

1973, Dec. 15

Angola 571
Cape Verde 363
Macao 429
Mozambique 509
Port. Guinea 344
St. Thomas & Prince Islands 410
Timor 345

FRENCH COMMUNITY

Upper Volta can be found under Burkina Faso in Vol. 1
Madagascar can be found under Malagasy in Vol. 3
Colonial Exposition

People of French Empire CD70

Women's Heads CD71

France Showing Way to Civilization CD72

"Colonial Commerce" CD73

International Colonial Exposition, Paris.

1931

Cameroun 213-216
Chad 60-63
Dahomey 97-100
Fr. Guiana 152-155
Fr. Guinea 116-119
Fr. India 100-103
Fr. Polynesia 76-79
Fr. Sudan 102-105
Gabon 120-123
Guadeloupe 138-141
Indo-China 140-142
Ivory Coast 92-95
Madagascar 169-172
Martinique 129-132
Mauritania 65-68
Middle Congo 61-64
New Caledonia 176-179
Niger 73-76
Reunion 122-125
St. Pierre & Miquelon 132-135
Senegal 138-141
Somali Coast 135-138
Togo 254-257
Ubangi-Shari 82-85
Upper Volta 66-69
Wallis & Futuna Isls. 85-88

Paris International Exposition
Colonial Arts Exposition

"Colonial Resources"
CD74   CD77

Overseas Commerce CD75

Exposition Building and Women CD76

"France and the Empire" CD78

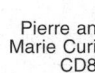

Cultural Treasures of the Colonies CD79

Souvenir sheets contain one imperf. stamp.

1937

Cameroun 217-222A
Dahomey 101-107
Fr. Equatorial Africa 27-32, 73
Fr. Guiana 162-168
Fr. Guinea 120-126
Fr. India 104-110
Fr. Polynesia 117-123
Fr. Sudan 106-112
Guadeloupe 148-154
Indo-China 193-199
Inini 41
Ivory Coast 152-158
Kwangchowan 132
Madagascar 191-197
Martinique 179-185
Mauritania 69-75
New Caledonia 208-214
Niger 72-83
Reunion 167-173
St. Pierre & Miquelon 165-171
Senegal 172-178
Somali Coast 139-145
Togo 258-264
Wallis & Futuna Isls. 89

Curie

Pierre and Marie Curie CD80

40th anniversary of the discovery of radium. The surtax was for the benefit of the Intl. Union for the Control of Cancer.

1938

Cameroun B1
Cuba B1-B2
Dahomey B2
France B76
Fr. Equatorial Africa B1
Fr. Guiana B3
Fr. Guinea B2
Fr. India B6
Fr. Polynesia B5
Fr. Sudan B1
Guadeloupe B3

Indo-China B14
Ivory Coast B2
Madagascar B2
Martinique B2
Mauritania B3
New Caledonia B4
Niger B1
Reunion B4
St. Pierre & Miquelon B3
Senegal B3
Somali Coast B2
Togo B1

Caillie

Rene Caillie and Map of Northwestern Africa — CD81

Death centenary of Rene Caillie (1799-1838), French explorer. All three denominations exist with colony name omitted.

1939

Dahomey 108-110
Fr. Guinea 161-163
Fr. Sudan 113-115
Ivory Coast 160-162
Mauritania 109-111
Niger 84-86
Senegal 188-190
Togo 265-267

New York World's Fair

Natives and New York Skyline CD82

1939

Cameroun 223-224
Dahomey 111-112
Fr. Equatorial Africa 78-79
Fr. Guiana 169-170
Fr. Guinea 164-165
Fr. India 111-112
Fr. Polynesia 124-125
Fr. Sudan 116-117
Guadeloupe 155-156
Indo-China 203-204
Inini 42-43
Ivory Coast 163-164
Kwangchowan 121-122
Madagascar 209-210
Martinique 186-187
Mauritania 112-113
New Caledonia 215-216
Niger 87-88
Reunion 174-175
St. Pierre & Miquelon 205-206
Senegal 191-192
Somali Coast 179-180
Togo 268-269
Wallis & Futuna Isls. 90-91

French Revolution

Storming of the Bastille CD83

French Revolution, 150th anniv. The surtax was for the defense of the colonies.

1939

Cameroun B2-B6
Dahomey B3-B7
Fr. Equatorial Africa B4-B8, CB1
Fr. Guiana B4-B8, CB1
Fr. Guinea B3-B7
Fr. India B7-B11
Fr. Polynesia B6-B10, CB1
Fr. Sudan B2-B6
Guadeloupe B4-B8
Indo-China B15-B19, CB1
Inini B1-B5
Ivory Coast B3-B7

Kwangchowan B1-B5
Madagascar....................B3-B7, CB1
Martinique.............................B3-B7
Mauritania B4-B8
New Caledonia B5-B9, CB1
Niger.....................................B2-B6
Reunion B5-B9, CB1
St. Pierre & Miquelon.............B4-B8
Senegal B4-B8, CB1
Somali Coast.........................B3-B7
Togo.....................................B2-B6
Wallis & Futuna Isls. B1-B5

Plane over
Coastal
Area
CD85

All five denominations exist with colony
name omitted.

1940

Dahomey C1-C5
Fr. Guinea C1-C5
Fr. Sudan..............................C1-C5
Ivory Coast C1-C5
Mauritania C1-C5
Niger....................................C1-C5
Senegal C12-C16
Togo.....................................C1-C5

Defense of the Empire

Colonial
Infantryman — CD86

1941

Cameroun...............................B13B
Dahomey B13
Fr. Equatorial Africa B8B
Fr. Guiana B10
Fr. Guinea B13
Fr. India B13
Fr. Polynesia...........................B12
Fr. Sudan...............................B12
Guadeloupe B10
Indo-China B19B
Inini B7
Ivory Coast B13
Kwangchowan B7
Madagascar..............................B9
Martinique................................B9
Mauritania B14
New Caledonia B11
Niger.....................................B12
Reunion B11
St. Pierre & Miquelon.................B8B
Senegal B14
Somali Coast.............................B9
Togo.....................................B10B
Wallis & Futuna Isls. B7

Colonial Education Fund

CD86a

1942

Cameroun.................................CB3
Dahomey CB4
Fr. Equatorial Africa CB5
Fr. Guiana CB4
Fr. Guinea CB4

Fr. India CB3
Fr. Polynesia............................CB4
Fr. Sudan................................CB4
Guadeloupe CB3
Indo-China CB5
Inini CB3
Ivory Coast CB4
Kwangchowan CB4
Malagasy CB5
Martinique...............................CB3
Mauritania CB4
New Caledonia CB4
Niger.....................................CB4
Reunion CB4
St. Pierre & Miquelon.................CB3
Senegal CB5
Somali Coast............................CB3
Togo.....................................CB3
Wallis & Futuna CB3

Cross of
Lorraine &
Four-motor
Plane
CD87

1941-5

Cameroun C1-C7
Fr. Equatorial Africa C17-C23
Fr. Guiana C9-C10
Fr. India C1-C6
Fr. Polynesia...........................C3-C9
Fr. West Africa C1-C3
Guadeloupe C1-C2
Madagascar............................C37-C43
Martinique...............................C1-C2
New Caledonia C7-C13
Reunion C18-C24
St. Pierre & Miquelon................C1-C7
Somali Coast...........................C1-C7

Transport
Plane
CD88

Caravan
and Plane
CD89

1942

Dahomey C6-C13
Fr. Guinea C6-C13
Fr. Sudan..............................C6-C13
Ivory Coast C6-C13
Mauritania C6-C13
Niger....................................C6-C13
Senegal C17-C25
Togo.....................................C6-C13

Red Cross

Marianne
CD90

The surtax was for the French Red Cross
and national relief.

1944

Cameroun.................................B28
Fr. Equatorial Africa B38
Fr. Guiana B12
Fr. India B14
Fr. Polynesia.............................B13
Fr. West Africa B1
Guadeloupe B12
Madagascar...............................B15
Martinique................................B11
New Caledonia B13
Reunion B15
St. Pierre & Miquelon...................B13
Somali Coast.............................B13

Wallis & Futuna Isls. B9

Eboue

CD91

Felix Eboue, first French colonial administrator to proclaim resistance to Germany after
French surrender in World War II.

1945

Cameroun...........................296-297
Fr. Equatorial Africa 156-157
Fr. Guiana 171-172
Fr. India 210-211
Fr. Polynesia.......................150-151
Fr. West Africa 15-16
Guadeloupe 187-188
Madagascar.......................259-260
Martinique.........................196-197
New Caledonia 274-275
Reunion 238-239
St. Pierre & Miquelon............322-323
Somali Coast......................238-239

Victory

Victory — CD92

European victory of the Allied Nations in
World War II.

1946, May 8

Cameroun....................................C8
Fr. Equatorial Africa C24
Fr. Guiana C11
Fr. India C7
Fr. Polynesia................................C10
Fr. West Africa C4
Guadeloupe C3
Indo-China C19
Madagascar.................................C44
Martinique.....................................C3
New Caledonia C14
Reunion C25
St. Pierre & Miquelon.......................C8
Somali Coast..................................C8
Wallis & Futuna Isls. C1

Chad to Rhine

Leclerc's Departure from
Chad — CD93

Battle at Cufra Oasis — CD94

Tanks in Action, Mareth — CD95

Normandy Invasion — CD96

Entering Paris — CD97

Liberation of Strasbourg — CD98

"Chad to the Rhine" march, 1942-44, by
Gen. Jacques Leclerc's column, later French
2nd Armored Division.

1946, June 6

Cameroun...............................C9-C14
Fr. Equatorial Africa C25-C30
Fr. Guiana C12-C17
Fr. India C8-C13
Fr. Polynesia.......................C11-C16
Fr. West Africa C5-C10
Guadeloupe C4-C9
Indo-China C20-C25
Madagascar.........................C45-C50
Martinique..............................C4-C9
New Caledonia C15-C20
Reunion C26-C31
St. Pierre & Miquelon.............C9-C14
Somali Coast.......................C9-C14
Wallis & Futuna Isls. C2-C7

UPU

French Colonials, Globe and
Plane — CD99

Universal Postal Union, 75th anniv.

1949, July 4

Cameroun.................................C29
Fr. Equatorial Africa C34
Fr. India C17
Fr. Polynesia.............................C20
Fr. West Africa C15
Indo-China C26
Madagascar...............................C55
New Caledonia C24
St. Pierre & Miquelon...................C18
Somali Coast.............................C18
Togo.......................................C18
Wallis & Futuna Isls. C10

Tropical Medicine

Doctor Treating Infant CD100

The surtax was for charitable work.

1950

Cameroun	B29
Fr. Equatorial Africa	B39
Fr. India	B15
Fr. Polynesia	B14
Fr. West Africa	B3
Madagascar	B17
New Caledonia	B14
St. Pierre & Miquelon	B14
Somali Coast	B14
Togo	B11

Military Medal

Medal, Early Marine and Colonial Soldier — CD101

Centenary of the creation of the French Military Medal.

1952

Cameroun	322
Comoro Isls.	39
Fr. Equatorial Africa	186
Fr. India	233
Fr. Polynesia	179
Fr. West Africa	57
Madagascar	286
New Caledonia	295
St. Pierre & Miquelon	345
Somali Coast	267
Togo	327
Wallis & Futuna Isls.	149

Liberation

Allied Landing, Victory Sign and Cross of Lorraine — CD102

Liberation of France, 10th anniv.

1954, June 6

Cameroun	C32
Comoro Isls.	C4
Fr. Equatorial Africa	C38
Fr. India	C18
Fr. Polynesia	C22
Fr. West Africa	C17
Madagascar	C57
New Caledonia	C25
St. Pierre & Miquelon	C19
Somali Coast	C19
Togo	C19
Wallis & Futuna Isls.	C11

FIDES

Plowmen CD103

Efforts of FIDES, the Economic and Social Development Fund for Overseas Possessions

(Fonds d' Investissement pour le Developpement Economique et Social). Each stamp has a different design.

1956

Cameroun	326-329
Comoro Isls.	43
Fr. Equatorial Africa	189-192
Fr. Polynesia	181
Fr. West Africa	65-72
Madagascar	292-295
New Caledonia	303
St. Pierre & Miquelon	350
Somali Coast	268
Togo	331

Flower

CD104

Each stamp shows a different flower.

1958-9

Cameroun	333
Comoro Isls.	45
Fr. Equatorial Africa	200-201
Fr. Polynesia	192
Fr. So. & Antarctic Terr.	11
Fr. West Africa	79-83
Madagascar	301-302
New Caledonia	304-305
St. Pierre & Miquelon	357
Somali Coast	270
Togo	348-349
Wallis & Futuna Isls.	152

Human Rights

Sun, Dove and U.N. Emblem CD105

10th anniversary of the signing of the Universal Declaration of Human Rights.

1958

Comoro Isls.	44
Fr. Equatorial Africa	202
Fr. Polynesia	191
Fr. West Africa	85
Madagascar	300
New Caledonia	306
St. Pierre & Miquelon	356
Somali Coast	274
Wallis & Futuna Isls.	153

C.C.T.A.

CD106

Commission for Technical Cooperation in Africa south of the Sahara, 10th anniv.

1960

Cameroun	339
Cent. Africa	3
Chad	66
Congo, P.R.	90
Dahomey	138
Gabon	150
Ivory Coast	180
Madagascar	317
Mali	9
Mauritania	117
Niger	104
Upper Volta	89

Air Afrique, 1961

Modern and Ancient Africa, Map and Planes — CD107

Founding of Air Afrique (African Airlines).

1961-62

Cameroun	C37
Cent. Africa	C5
Chad	C7
Congo, P.R.	C5
Dahomey	C17
Gabon	C5
Ivory Coast	C18
Mauritania	C17
Niger	C22
Senegal	C31
Upper Volta	C4

Anti-Malaria

CD108

World Health Organization drive to eradicate malaria.

1962, Apr. 7

Cameroun	B36
Cent. Africa	B1
Chad	B1
Comoro Isls.	B1
Congo, P.R.	B3
Dahomey	B15
Gabon	B4
Ivory Coast	B15
Madagascar	B19
Mali	B1
Mauritania	B16
Niger	B14
Senegal	B16
Somali Coast	B15
Upper Volta	B1

Abidjan Games

CD109

Abidjan Games, Ivory Coast, Dec. 24-31, 1961. Each stamp shows a different sport.

1962

Chad	83-84
Cent. Africa	19-20
Congo, P.R.	103-104
Gabon	163-164, C6
Niger	109-111
Upper Volta	103-105

African and Malagasy Union

Flag of Union CD110

First anniversary of the Union.

1962, Sept. 8

Cameroun	373
Cent. Africa	21

Chad	85
Congo, P.R.	105
Dahomey	155
Gabon	165
Ivory Coast	198
Madagascar	332
Mauritania	170
Niger	112
Senegal	211
Upper Volta	106

Telstar

Telstar and Globe Showing Andover and Pleumeur-Bodou — CD111

First television connection of the United States and Europe through the Telstar satellite, July 11-12, 1962.

1962-63

Andorra, French	154
Comoro Isls.	C7
Fr. Polynesia	C29
Fr. So. & Antarctic Terr.	C5
New Caledonia	C33
Somali Coast	C31
St. Pierre & Miquelon	C26
Wallis & Futuna Isls.	C17

Freedom From Hunger

World Map and Wheat Emblem CD112

U.N. Food and Agriculture Organization's "Freedom from Hunger" campaign.

1963, Mar. 21

Cameroun	B37-B38
Cent. Africa	B2
Chad	B2
Congo, P.R.	B4
Dahomey	B16
Gabon	B5
Ivory Coast	B16
Madagascar	B21
Mauritania	B17
Niger	B15
Senegal	B17
Upper Volta	B2

Red Cross Centenary

CD113

Centenary of the International Red Cross.

1963, Sept. 2

Comoro Isls.	55
Fr. Polynesia	205
New Caledonia	328
St. Pierre & Miquelon	367
Somali Coast	297
Wallis & Futuna Isls.	165

African Postal Union, 1963

UAMPT Emblem, Radio Masts, Plane and Mail CD114

Establishment of the African and Malagasy Posts and Telecommunications Union.

1963, Sept. 8

Cameroun	C47
Cent. Africa	C10
Chad	C9
Congo, P.R.	C13
Dahomey	C19
Gabon	C13
Ivory Coast	C25
Madagascar	C75
Mauritania	C22
Niger	C27
Rwanda	36
Senegal	C32
Upper Volta	C9

Air Afrique, 1963

Symbols of Flight — CD115

First anniversary of Air Afrique and inauguration of DC-8 service.

1963, Nov. 19

Cameroun	C48
Chad	C10
Congo, P.R.	C14
Gabon	C18
Ivory Coast	C26
Mauritania	C26
Niger	C35
Senegal	C33

Europafrica

Europe and Africa Linked — CD116

Signing of an economic agreement between the European Economic Community and the African and Malagasy Union, Yaounde, Cameroun, July 20, 1963.

1963-64

Cameroun	402
Chad	C11
Cent. Africa	C12
Congo, P.R.	C16
Gabon	C19
Ivory Coast	217
Niger	C43
Upper Volta	C11

Human Rights

Scales of Justice and Globe CD117

15th anniversary of the Universal Declaration of Human Rights.

1963, Dec. 10

Comoro Isls.	58
Fr. Polynesia	206
New Caledonia	329
St. Pierre & Miquelon	368
Somali Coast	300
Wallis & Futuna Isls.	166

PHILATEC

Stamp Album, Champs Elysees Palace and Horses of Marly CD118

Intl. Philatelic and Postal Techniques Exhibition, Paris, June 5-21, 1964.

1963-64

Comoro Isls.	60
France	1078
Fr. Polynesia	207
New Caledonia	341
St. Pierre & Miquelon	369
Somali Coast	301
Wallis & Futuna Isls.	167

Cooperation

CD119

Cooperation between France and the French-speaking countries of Africa and Madagascar.

1964

Cameroun	409-410
Cent. Africa	39
Chad	103
Congo, P.R.	121
Dahomey	193
France	1111
Gabon	175
Ivory Coast	221
Madagascar	360
Mauritania	181
Niger	143
Senegal	236
Togo	495

ITU

Telegraph, Syncom Satellite and ITU Emblem CD120

Intl. Telecommunication Union, Cent.

1965, May 17

Comoro Isls.	C14
Fr. Polynesia	C33
Fr. So. & Antarctic Terr.	C8
New Caledonia	C40
New Hebrides	124-125
St. Pierre & Miquelon	C29
Somali Coast	C36
Wallis & Futuna Isls.	C20

French Satellite A-1

Diamant Rocket and Launching Installation — CD121

Launching of France's first satellite, Nov. 26, 1965.

1965-66

Comoro Isls.	C15-C16
France	1137-1138
Fr. Polynesia	C40-C41
Fr. So. & Antarctic Terr.	C9-C10
New Caledonia	C44-C45
St. Pierre & Miquelon	C30-C31
Somali Coast	C39-C40
Wallis & Futuna Isls.	C22-C23

French Satellite D-1

D-1 Satellite in Orbit — CD122

Launching of the D-1 satellite at Hammaguir, Algeria, Feb. 17, 1966.

1966

Comoro Isls.	C17
France	1148
Fr. Polynesia	C42
Fr. So. & Antarctic Terr.	C11
New Caledonia	C46
St. Pierre & Miquelon	C32
Somali Coast	C49
Wallis & Futuna Isls.	C24

Air Afrique, 1966

Planes and Air Afrique Emblem — CD123

Introduction of DC-8F planes by Air Afrique.

1966

Cameroun	C79
Cent. Africa	C35
Chad	C26
Congo, P.R.	C42
Dahomey	C42
Gabon	C47
Ivory Coast	C32
Mauritania	C57
Niger	C63
Senegal	C47
Togo	C54
Upper Volta	C31

African Postal Union, 1967

Telecommunications Symbols and Map of Africa — CD124

Fifth anniversary of the establishment of the African and Malagasy Union of Posts and Telecommunications, UAMPT.

1967

Cameroun	C90
Cent. Africa	C46
Chad	C37
Congo, P.R.	C57
Dahomey	C61
Gabon	C58
Ivory Coast	C34
Madagascar	C85
Mauritania	C65
Niger	C75
Rwanda	C1-C3
Senegal	C60
Togo	C81
Upper Volta	C50

Monetary Union

Gold Token of the Ashantis, 17-18th Centuries — CD125

West African Monetary Union, 5th anniv.

1967, Nov. 4

Dahomey	244
Ivory Coast	259
Mauritania	238
Niger	204
Senegal	294
Togo	623
Upper Volta	181

WHO Anniversary

Sun, Flowers and WHO Emblem CD126

World Health Organization, 20th anniv.

1968, May 4

Afars & Issas	317
Comoro Isls.	73
Fr. Polynesia	241-242
Fr. So. & Antarctic Terr.	31
New Caledonia	367
St. Pierre & Miquelon	377
Wallis & Futuna Isls.	169

Human Rights Year

Human Rights Flame — CD127

1968, Aug. 10

Afars & Issas	322-323

Comoro Isls.	76
Fr. Polynesia	243-244
Fr. So. & Antarctic Terr.	32
New Caledonia	369
St. Pierre & Miquelon	382
Wallis & Futuna Isls.	170

2nd PHILEXAFRIQUE

CD128

Opening of PHILEXAFRIQUE, Abidjan, Feb. 14. Each stamp shows a local scene and stamp.

1969, Feb. 14

Cameroun	C118
Cent. Africa	C65
Chad	C48
Congo, P.R.	C77
Dahomey	C94
Gabon	C82
Ivory Coast	C38-C40
Madagascar	C92
Mali	C65
Mauritania	C80
Niger	C104
Senegal	C68
Togo	C104
Upper Volta	C62

Concorde

Concorde in Flight CD129

First flight of the prototype Concorde supersonic plane at Toulouse, Mar. 1, 1969.

1969

Afars & Issas	C56
Comoro Isls.	C29
France	C42
Fr. Polynesia	C50
Fr. So. & Antarctic Terr.	C18
New Caledonia	C63
St. Pierre & Miquelon	C40
Wallis & Futuna Isls.	C30

Development Bank

Bank Emblem — CD130

African Development Bank, fifth anniv.

1969

Cameroun	499
Chad	217
Congo, P.R.	181-182
Ivory Coast	281
Mali	127-128
Mauritania	267
Niger	220
Senegal	317-318
Upper Volta	201

ILO

ILO Headquarters, Geneva, and Emblem — CD131

Intl. Labor Organization, 50th anniv.

1969-70

Afars & Issas	337
Comoro Isls.	83
Fr. Polynesia	251-252
Fr. So. & Antarctic Terr.	35
New Caledonia	379
St. Pierre & Miquelon	396
Wallis & Futuna Isls.	172

ASECNA

Map of Africa, Plane and Airport CD132

10th anniversary of the Agency for the Security of Aerial Navigation in Africa and Madagascar (ASECNA, Agence pour la Securite de la Navigation Aerienne en Afrique et a Madagascar).

1969-70

Cameroun	500
Cent. Africa	119
Chad	222
Congo, P.R.	197
Dahomey	269
Gabon	260
Ivory Coast	287
Mali	130
Niger	221
Senegal	321
Upper Volta	204

U.P.U. Headquarters

CD133

New Universal Postal Union headquarters, Bern, Switzerland.

1970

Afars & Issas	342
Algeria	443
Cameroun	503-504
Cent. Africa	125
Chad	225
Comoro Isls.	84
Congo, P.R.	216
Fr. Polynesia	261-262
Fr. So. & Antarctic Terr.	36
Gabon	258
Ivory Coast	295
Madagascar	444
Mali	134-135
Mauritania	283
New Caledonia	382
Niger	231-232
St. Pierre & Miquelon	397-398
Senegal	328-329
Tunisia	535
Wallis & Futuna Isls.	173

De Gaulle

CD134

First anniversary of the death of Charles de Gaulle, (1890-1970), President of France.

1971-72

Afars & Issas	356-357
Comoro Isls.	104-105
France	1322-1325
Fr. Polynesia	270-271
Fr. So. & Antarctic Terr.	52-53
New Caledonia	393-394
Reunion	377, 380
St. Pierre & Miquelon	417-418
Wallis & Futuna Isls.	177-178

African Postal Union, 1971

UAMPT Building, Brazzaville, Congo — CD135

10th anniversary of the establishment of the African and Malagasy Posts and Telecommunications Union, UAMPT. Each stamp has a different native design.

1971, Nov. 13

Cameroun	C177
Cent. Africa	C89
Chad	C94
Congo, P.R.	C136
Dahomey	C146
Gabon	C120
Ivory Coast	C47
Mauritania	C113
Niger	C164
Rwanda	C8
Senegal	C105
Togo	C166
Upper Volta	C97

West African Monetary Union

African Couple, City, Village and Commemorative Coin — CD136

West African Monetary Union, 10th anniv.

1972, Nov. 2

Dahomey	300
Ivory Coast	331
Mauritania	299
Niger	258
Senegal	374
Togo	825
Upper Volta	280

African Postal Union, 1973

Telecommunications Symbols and Map of Africa — CD137

11th anniversary of the African and Malagasy Posts and Telecommunications Union (UAMPT).

1973, Sept. 12

Cameroun	574
Cent. Africa	194
Chad	294
Congo, P.R.	289
Dahomey	311
Gabon	320
Ivory Coast	361
Madagascar	500
Mauritania	304
Niger	287

Rwanda	540
Senegal	393
Togo	849
Upper Volta	297

Philexafrique II — Essen

CD138

CD139

Designs: Indigenous fauna, local and German stamps. Types CD138-CD139 printed horizontally and vertically se-tenant in sheets of 10 (2x5). Label between horizontal pairs alternately commemorates Philexafrique II, Libreville, Gabon, June 1978, and 2nd International Stamp Fair, Essen, Germany, Nov. 1-5.

1978-1979

Benin	C285-C286
Central Africa	C200-C201
Chad	C238-C239
Congo Republic	C245-C246
Djibouti	C121-C122
Gabon	C215-C216
Ivory Coast	C64-C65
Mali	C356-C357
Mauritania	C185-C186
Niger	C291-C292
Rwanda	C12-C13
Senegal	C146-C147
Togo	C363-C364

BRITISH COMMONWEALTH OF NATIONS

The listings follow established trade practices when these issues are offered as units by dealers. The Peace issue, for example, includes only one stamp from the Indian state of Hyderabad. The U.P.U. issue includes the Egypt set. Pairs are included for those varieties issued with bilingual designs se-tenant.

Silver Jubilee

Windsor Castle and King George V CD301

Reign of King George V, 25th anniv.

1935

Antigua	77-80
Ascension	33-36
Bahamas	92-95
Barbados	186-189
Basutoland	11-14
Bechuanaland Protectorate	117-120
Bermuda	100-103
British Guiana	223-226
British Honduras	108-111
Cayman Islands	81-84
Ceylon	260-263
Cyprus	136-139
Dominica	90-93
Falkland Islands	77-80
Fiji	110-113
Gambia	125-128

Coronation

Queen Elizabeth and King George VI CD302

1937

Peace

King George VI and Parliament Buildings, London CD303

Return to peace at the close of World War II.

1945-46

Silver Wedding

King George VI and Queen Elizabeth

CD304   CD305

1948-49

U.P.U.

Mercury and Symbols of Communications — CD306

Plane, Ship and Hemispheres — CD307

Mercury Scattering Letters over Globe CD308

U.P.U. Monument, Bern CD309

Universal Postal Union, 75th anniversary.

1949

Sarawak..............................176-179
Seychelles..........................153-156
Sierra Leone.......................190-193
Singapore.............................23-26
Solomon Islands....................84-87
Somaliland Protectorate.........112-115
Southern Rhodesia................71-72
Swaziland.............................50-53
Tonga..................................87-90
Trinidad & Tobago.................66-69
Turks & Caicos Islands..........101-104
Virgin Islands.......................92-95
Zanzibar.............................226-229

The following have different designs but are included in the omnibus set:

Great Britain.......................276-279
  Offices in Morocco..............546-549
Australia..............................223
Bahrain...............................68-71
Burma.................................116-121
Ceylon...............................304-306
Egypt.................................281-283
India..................................223-226
Kuwait.................................89-92
Oman..................................31-34
Pakistan-Bahawalpur 26-29, O25-O28
South Africa.........................109-111
South-West Africa 160-162

319 stamps

University

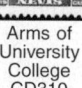

Arms of   Alice, Princess
University   of Athlone
College   CD311
CD310

1948 opening of University College of the West Indies at Jamaica.

1951

Antigua 104-105
Barbados............................228-229
British Guiana.......................250-251
British Honduras....................141-142
Dominica.............................120-121
Grenada..............................164-165
Jamaica..............................146-147
Leeward Islands....................130-131
Montserrat...........................112-113
St. Kitts-Nevis......................105-106
St. Lucia.............................149-150
St. Vincent...........................174-175
Trinidad & Tobago 70-71
Virgin Islands........................96-97

28 stamps

Coronation

Queen Elizabeth
II — CD312

1953

Aden....................................47
  Kathiri State of Seiyun..............28
  Qu'aiti State of Shihr and Mukalla .....
....28
Antigua 106
Ascension.............................61
Bahamas..............................157
Barbados.............................234
Basutoland............................45
Bechuanaland Protectorate.........153
Bermuda..............................142
British Guiana........................252
British Honduras.....................143
Cayman Islands......................150

Cyprus................................167
Dominica.............................141
Falkland Islands.....................121
Falkland Islands Dependencies 1L18
Fiji.....................................145
Gambia...............................152
Gibraltar..............................131
Gilbert & Ellice Islands...............60
Gold Coast............................160
Grenada...............................170
Hong Kong............................184
Jamaica...............................153
Kenya, Uganda, Tanganyika........101
Leeward Islands......................132
Malaya
  Johore...............................155
  Kedah.................................82
  Kelantan..............................71
  Malacca...............................27
  Negri Sembilan........................63
  Pahang................................71
  Penang................................27
  Perak.................................126
  Perlis..................................28
  Selangor.............................101
  Trengganu............................74
Malta..................................241
Mauritius..............................250
Montserrat............................127
New Hebrides, British.................77
Nigeria.................................79
North Borneo.........................260
Northern Rhodesia....................60
Nyasaland Protectorate...............96
Pitcairn.................................19
St. Helena............................139
St. Kitts-Nevis.......................119
St. Lucia..............................156
St. Vincent...........................185
Sarawak..............................196
Seychelles............................172
Sierra Leone..........................194
Singapore..............................27
Solomon Islands.......................88
Somaliland Protectorate.............127
Swaziland..............................54
Trinidad & Tobago.....................84
Tristan da Cunha.......................13
Turks & Caicos Islands 118
Virgin Islands.........................114

The following have different designs but are included in the omnibus set:

Great Britain.........................313-316
  Offices in Morocco................579-582
Australia..............................259-261
Bahrain................................92-95
Canada.................................330
Ceylon.................................317
Cook Islands 145-146
Kuwait.................................113-116
New Zealand...........................280-284
Niue....................................104-105
Oman....................................52-55
Samoa.................................214-215
South Africa............................192
Southern Rhodesia 80
South-West Africa 244-248
Tokelau Islands 4

106 stamps

Royal Visit 1953

Separate designs for each country for the visit of Queen Elizabeth II and the Duke of Edinburgh.

1953

Aden....................................62
Australia..............................267-269
Bermuda...............................163
Ceylon.................................318
Fiji.....................................146
Gibraltar..............................146
Jamaica...............................154
Kenya, Uganda, Tanganyika........102
Malta..................................242
New Zealand..........................286-287

13 stamps

West Indies Federation

Map of the
Caribbean
CD313

Federation of the West Indies, April 22, 1958.

1958

Antigua...............................122-124
Barbados.............................248-250
Dominica.............................161-163
Grenada..............................184-186
Jamaica..............................175-177
Montserrat...........................143-145
St. Kitts-Nevis.......................136-138
St. Lucia..............................170-172
St. Vincent...........................198-200
Trinidad & Tobago.....................86-88

30 stamps

Freedom from Hunger

Protein Food
CD314

U.N. Food and Agricultural Organization's "Freedom from Hunger" campaign.

1963

Aden....................................65
Antigua 133
Ascension.............................89
Bahamas..............................180
Basutoland.............................83
Bechuanaland Protectorate...........194
Bermuda..............................192
British Guiana.........................271
British Honduras......................179
Brunei.................................100
Cayman Islands.......................168
Dominica..............................181
Falkland Islands......................146
Fiji.....................................198
Gambia...............................172
Gibraltar..............................161
Gilbert & Ellice Islands................76
Grenada...............................190
Hong Kong............................218
Malta..................................291
Mauritius..............................270
Montserrat............................150
New Hebrides, British 93
North Borneo.........................296
Pitcairn.................................35
St. Helena............................173
St. Lucia..............................179
St. Vincent............................201
Sarawak..............................212
Seychelles............................213
Solomon Islands......................109
Swaziland.............................108
Tonga.................................127
Tristan da Cunha.......................68
Turks & Caicos Islands 138
Virgin Islands.........................140
Zanzibar...............................280

37 stamps

Red Cross Centenary

Red Cross
and
Elizabeth
II
CD315

1963

Antigua 134-135
Ascension.............................90-91
Bahamas..............................183-184
Basutoland.............................84-85
Bechuanaland Protectorate.........195-196
Bermuda..............................193-194
British Guiana........................272-273
British Honduras......................180-181
Cayman Islands......................169-170
Dominica..............................182-183
Falkland Islands......................147-148
Fiji.....................................203-204
Gambia...............................173-174
Gibraltar..............................162-163
Gilbert & Ellice Islands...............77-78
Grenada...............................191-192
Hong Kong............................219-220
Jamaica...............................203-204

Malta..................................292-293
Mauritius..............................271-272
Montserrat............................151-152
New Hebrides, British................94-95
Pitcairn Islands.......................36-37
St. Helena............................174-175
St. Kitts-Nevis.......................143-144
St. Lucia..............................180-181
St. Vincent............................202-203
Seychelles............................214-215
Solomon Islands......................110-111
South Arabia...........................1-2
Swaziland.............................109-110
Tonga.................................134-135
Tristan da Cunha.......................69-70
Turks & Caicos Islands 139-140
Virgin Islands.........................141-142

70 stamps

Shakespeare

Shakespeare Memorial Theatre,
Stratford-on-Avon — CD316

400th anniversary of the birth of William Shakespeare.

1964

Antigua 151
Bahamas..............................201
Bechuanaland Protectorate...........197
Cayman Islands......................171
Dominica..............................184
Falkland Islands......................149
Gambia...............................192
Gibraltar..............................164
Montserrat............................153
St. Lucia..............................196
Turks & Caicos Islands 141
Virgin Islands.........................143

12 stamps

ITU

ITU
Emblem
CD317

Intl. Telecommunication Union, cent.

1965

Antigua 153-154
Ascension.............................92-93
Bahamas..............................219-220
Barbados.............................265-266
Basutoland............................101-102
Bechuanaland Protectorate......202-203
Bermuda..............................196-197
British Guiana.........................293-294
British Honduras......................187-188
Brunei.................................116-117
Cayman Islands......................172-173
Dominica..............................185-186
Falkland Islands......................154-155
Fiji.....................................211-212
Gibraltar..............................167-168
Gilbert & Ellice Islands...............87-88
Grenada...............................205-206
Hong Kong............................221-222
Mauritius..............................291-292
Montserrat............................157-158
New Hebrides, British................108-109
Pitcairn Islands.......................52-53
St. Helena............................180-181
St. Kitts-Nevis.......................163-164
St. Lucia..............................197-198
St. Vincent............................224-225
Seychelles............................218-219
Solomon Islands......................126-127
Swaziland.............................115-116
Tristan da Cunha.......................85-86
Turks & Caicos Islands 142-143
Virgin Islands.........................159-160

64 stamps

Intl. Cooperation Year

ICY Emblem CD318

1965

Antigua	155-156
Ascension	94-95
Bahamas	222-223
Basutoland	103-104
Bechuanaland Protectorate	204-205
Bermuda	199-200
British Guiana	295-296
British Honduras	189-190
Brunei	118-119
Cayman Islands	174-175
Dominica	187-188
Falkland Islands	156-157
Fiji	213-214
Gibraltar	169-170
Gilbert & Ellice Islands	104-105
Grenada	207-208
Hong Kong	223-224
Mauritius	293-294
Montserrat	176-177
New Hebrides, British	110-111
New Hebrides, French	126-127
Pitcairn Islands	54-55
St. Helena	182-183
St. Kitts-Nevis	165-166
St. Lucia	199-200
Seychelles	220-221
Solomon Islands	143-144
South Arabia	17-18
Swaziland	117-118
Tristan da Cunha	87-88
Turks & Caicos Islands	144-145
Virgin Islands	161-162

64 stamps

Churchill Memorial

Winston Churchill and St. Paul's, London, During Air Attack CD319

1966

Antigua	157-160
Ascension	96-99
Bahamas	224-227
Barbados	281-284
Basutoland	105-108
Bechuanaland Protectorate	206-209
Bermuda	201-204
British Antarctic Territory	16-19
British Honduras	191-194
Brunei	120-123
Cayman Islands	176-179
Dominica	189-192
Falkland Islands	158-161
Fiji	215-218
Gibraltar	171-174
Gilbert & Ellice Islands	106-109
Grenada	209-212
Hong Kong	225-228
Mauritius	295-298
Montserrat	178-181
New Hebrides, British	112-115
New Hebrides, French	128-131
Pitcairn Islands	56-59
St. Helena	184-187
St. Kitts-Nevis	167-170
St. Lucia	201-204
St. Vincent	241-244
Seychelles	222-225
Solomon Islands	145-148
South Arabia	19-22
Swaziland	119-122
Tristan da Cunha	89-92
Turks & Caicos Islands	146-149
Virgin Islands	163-166

136 stamps

Royal Visit, 1966

Queen Elizabeth II and Prince Philip CD320

Caribbean visit, Feb. 4 - Mar. 6, 1966.

1966

Antigua	161-162
Bahamas	228-229
Barbados	285-286
British Guiana	299-300
Cayman Islands	180-181
Dominica	193-194
Grenada	213-214
Montserrat	182-183
St. Kitts-Nevis	171-172
St. Lucia	205-206
St. Vincent	245-246
Turks & Caicos Islands	150-151
Virgin Islands	167-168

26 stamps

World Cup Soccer

Soccer Player and Jules Rimet Cup CD321

World Cup Soccer Championship, Wembley, England, July 11-30.

1966

Antigua	163-164
Ascension	100-101
Bahamas	245-246
Bermuda	205-206
Brunei	124-125
Cayman Islands	182-183
Dominica	195-196
Fiji	219-220
Gibraltar	175-176
Gilbert & Ellice Islands	125-126
Grenada	230-231
New Hebrides, British	116-117
New Hebrides, French	132-133
Pitcairn Islands	60-61
St. Helena	188-189
St. Kitts-Nevis	173-174
St. Lucia	207-208
Seychelles	226-227
Solomon Islands	167-168
South Arabia	23-24
Tristan da Cunha	93-94

42 stamps

WHO Headquarters

World Health Organization Headquarters, Geneva — CD322

1966

Antigua	165-166
Ascension	102-103
Bahamas	247-248
Brunei	126-127
Cayman Islands	184-185
Dominica	197-198
Fiji	224-225
Gibraltar	180-181
Gilbert & Ellice Islands	127-128
Grenada	232-233
Hong Kong	229-230
Montserrat	184-185
New Hebrides, British	118-119
New Hebrides, French	134-135
Pitcairn Islands	62-63
St. Helena	190-191
St. Kitts-Nevis	177-178
St. Lucia	209-210

St. Vincent	247-248
Seychelles	228-229
Solomon Islands	169-170
South Arabia	25-26
Tristan da Cunha	99-100

46 stamps

UNESCO Anniversary

"Education" — CD323

"Science" (Wheat ears & flask enclosing globe). "Culture" (lyre & columns). 20th anniversary of the UNESCO.

1966-67

Antigua	183-185
Ascension	108-110
Bahamas	249-251
Barbados	287-289
Bermuda	207-209
Brunei	128-130
Cayman Islands	186-188
Dominica	199-201
Gibraltar	183-185
Gilbert & Ellice Islands	129-131
Grenada	234-236
Hong Kong	231-233
Mauritius	299-301
Montserrat	186-188
New Hebrides, British	120-122
New Hebrides, French	136-138
Pitcairn Islands	64-66
St. Helena	192-194
St. Kitts-Nevis	179-181
St. Lucia	211-213
St. Vincent	249-251
Seychelles	230-232
Solomon Islands	171-173
South Arabia	27-29
Swaziland	123-125
Tristan da Cunha	101-103
Turks & Caicos Islands	155-157
Virgin Islands	176-178

84 stamps

Silver Wedding, 1972

Queen Elizabeth II and Prince Philip — CD324

Designs: borders differ for each country.

1972

Anguilla	161-162
Antigua	295-296
Ascension	164-165
Bahamas	344-345
Bermuda	296-297
British Antarctic Territory	43-44
British Honduras	306-307
British Indian Ocean Territory	48-49
Brunei	186-187
Cayman Islands	304-305
Dominica	352-353
Falkland Islands	223-224
Fiji	328-329
Gibraltar	292-293
Gilbert & Ellice Islands	206-207
Grenada	466-467
Hong Kong	271-272
Montserrat	286-287
New Hebrides, British	169-170
Pitcairn Islands	127-128
St. Helena	271-272
St. Kitts-Nevis	257-258
St. Lucia	328-329
St. Vincent	344-345
Seychelles	309-310
Solomon Islands	248-249
South Georgia	35-36

Tristan da Cunha	178-179
Turks & Caicos Islands	257-258
Virgin Islands	241-242

60 stamps

Princess Anne's Wedding

Princess Anne and Mark Phillips — CD325

Wedding of Princess Anne and Mark Phillips, Nov. 14, 1973.

1973

Anguilla	179-180
Ascension	177-178
Belize	325-326
Bermuda	302-303
British Antarctic Territory	60-61
Cayman Islands	320-321
Falkland Islands	225-226
Gibraltar	305-306
Gilbert & Ellice Islands	216-217
Hong Kong	289-290
Montserrat	300-301
Pitcairn Island	135-136
St. Helena	277-278
St. Kitts-Nevis	274-275
St. Lucia	349-350
St. Vincent	358-359
St. Vincent Grenadines	1-2
Seychelles	311-312
Solomon Islands	259-260
South Georgia	37-38
Tristan da Cunha	189-190
Turks & Caicos Islands	286-287
Virgin Islands	260-261

44 stamps

Elizabeth II Coronation Anniv.

CD326 CD327

CD328

Designs: Royal and local beasts in heraldic form and simulated stonework. Portrait of Elizabeth II by Peter Grugeon. 25th anniversary of coronation of Queen Elizabeth II.

1978

Ascension	229
Barbados	474
Belize	397
British Antarctic Territory	71
Cayman Islands	404
Christmas Island	87
Falkland Islands	275
Fiji	384
Gambia	380
Gilbert Islands	312
Mauritius	464
New Hebrides, British	258
St. Helena	317
St. Kitts-Nevis	354
Samoa	472

Solomon Islands	368
South Georgia	51
Swaziland	302
Tristan da Cunha	238
Virgin Islands	337

20 sheets

Queen Mother Elizabeth's 80th Birthday

CD330

Designs: Photographs of Queen Mother Elizabeth. Falkland Islands issued in sheets of 50; others in sheets of 9.

1980

Ascension	261
Bermuda	401
Cayman Islands	443
Falkland Islands	305
Gambia	412
Gibraltar	393
Hong Kong	364
Pitcairn Islands	193
St. Helena	341
Samoa	532
Solomon Islands	426
Tristan da Cunha	277

12 stamps

Royal Wedding, 1981

Prince Charles and Lady Diana — CD331

CD331a

Wedding of Charles, Prince of Wales, and Lady Diana Spencer, St. Paul's Cathedral, London, July 29, 1981.

1981

Antigua	623-625
Ascension	294-296
Barbados	547-549
Barbuda	497-499
Bermuda	412-414
Brunei	268-270
Cayman Islands	471-473
Dominica	701-703
Falkland Islands	324-326
Falkland Islands Dep	1L59-1L61
Fiji	442-444
Gambia	426-428
Ghana	759-761
Grenada	1051-1053
Grenada Grenadines	440-443
Hong Kong	373-375
Jamaica	500-503
Lesotho	335-337
Maldive Islands	906-908
Mauritius	520-522
Norfolk Island	280-282
Pitcairn Islands	206-208
St. Helena	353-355
St. Lucia	543-545
Samoa	558-560
Sierra Leone	509-517
Solomon Islands	450-452
Swaziland	382-384
Tristan da Cunha	294-296
Turks & Caicos Islands	486-488
Caicos Island	8-10
Uganda	314-316
Vanuatu	308-310
Virgin Islands	406-408

Princess Diana

CD332

CD333

Designs: Photographs and portrait of Princess Diana, wedding or honeymoon photographs, royal residences, arms of issuing country. Portrait photograph by Clive Friend. Souvenir sheet margins show family tree, various people related to the princess. 21st birthday of Princess Diana of Wales, July 1.

1982

Antigua	663-666
Ascension	313-316
Bahamas	510-513
Barbados	585-588
Barbuda	544-546
British Antarctic Territory	92-95
Cayman Islands	486-489
Dominica	773-776
Falkland Islands	348-351
Falkland Islands Dep	1L72-1L75
Fiji	470-473
Gambia	447-450
Grenada	1101A-1105
Grenada Grenadines	485-491
Lesotho	372-375
Maldive Islands	952-955
Mauritius	548-551
Pitcairn Islands	213-216
St. Helena	372-375
St. Lucia	591-594
Sierra Leone	531-534
Solomon Islands	471-474
Swaziland	406-409
Tristan da Cunha	310-313
Turks and Caicos Islands	530A-534
Virgin Islands	430-433

250th anniv. of first edition of Lloyd's List (shipping news publication) & of Lloyd's marine insurance.

CD335

Designs: First page of early edition of the list; historical ships, modern transportation or harbor scenes.

1984

Ascension	351-354
Bahamas	555-558
Barbados	627-630
Cayes of Belize	10-13
Cayman Islands	522-525
Falkland Islands	404-407
Fiji	509-512
Gambia	519-522
Mauritius	587-590
Nauru	280-283
St. Helena	412-415
Samoa	624-627
Seychelles	538-541
Solomon Islands	521-524
Vanuatu	368-371
Virgin Islands	466-469

Queen Mother 85th Birthday

CD336

Designs: Photographs tracing the life of the Queen Mother, Elizabeth. The high value in each set pictures the same photograph taken of the Queen Mother holding the infant Prince Henry.

1985

Ascension	372-376
Bahamas	580-584
Barbados	660-664
Bermuda	469-473
Falkland Islands	420-424
Falkland Islands Dep	1L92-1L96
Fiji	531-535
Hong Kong	447-450
Jamaica	599-603
Mauritius	604-608
Norfolk Island	364-368
Pitcairn Islands	253-257
St. Helena	428-432
Samoa	649-653
Seychelles	567-571
Solomon Islands	543-547
Swaziland	476-480
Tristan da Cunha	372-376
Vanuatu	392-396
Zil Elwannyen Sesel	101-105

Queen Elizabeth II, 60th Birthday

CD337

1986, April 21

Ascension	389-393
Bahamas	592-596
Barbados	675-679
Bermuda	499-503
Cayman Islands	555-559
Falkland Islands	441-445
Fiji	544-548
Hong Kong	465-469
Jamaica	620-624
Kiribati	470-474
Mauritius	629-633
Papua New Guinea	640-644
Pitcairn Islands	270-274
St. Helena	451-455
Samoa	670-674
Seychelles	592-596
Solomon Islands	562-566
South Georgia	101-105
Swaziland	490-494
Tristan da Cunha	388-392
Vanuatu	414-418
Zambia	343-347
Zil Elwannyen Sesel	114-118

Royal Wedding

Marriage of Prince Andrew and Sarah Ferguson CD338

1986, July 23

Ascension	399-400
Bahamas	602-603
Barbados	687-688
Cayman Islands	560-561
Jamaica	629-630
Pitcairn Islands	275-276
St. Helena	460-461
St. Kitts	181-182

Seychelles	602-603
Solomon Islands	567-568
Tristan da Cunha	397-398
Zambia	348-349
Zil Elwannyen Sesel	119-120

Queen Elizabeth II, 60th Birthday

Queen Elizabeth II & Prince Philip, 1947 Wedding Portrait — CD339

Designs: Photographs tracing the life of Queen Elizabeth II.

1986

Anguilla	674-677
Antigua	925-928
Barbuda	783-786
Dominica	950-953
Gambia	611-614
Grenada	1371-1374
Grenada Grenadines	749-752
Lesotho	531-534
Maldive Islands	1172-1175
Sierra Leone	760-763
Uganda	495-498

Royal Wedding, 1986

CD340

Designs: Photographs of Prince Andrew and Sarah Ferguson during courtship, engagement and marriage.

1986

Antigua	939-942
Barbuda	809-812
Dominica	970-973
Gambia	635-638
Grenada	1385-1388
Grenada Grenadines	758-761
Lesotho	545-548
Maldive Islands	1181-1184
Sierra Leone	769-772
Uganda	510-513

Lloyds of London, 300th Anniv.

CD341

Designs: 17th century aspects of Lloyds, representations of each country's individual connections with Lloyds and publicized disasters insured by the organization.

1986

Ascension	454-457
Bahamas	655-658
Barbados	731-734
Bermuda	541-544
Falkland Islands	481-484
Liberia	1101-1104
Malawi	534-537
Nevis	571-574
St. Helena	501-504
St. Lucia	923-926
Seychelles	649-652
Solomon Islands	627-630

South Georgia 131-134
Trinidad & Tobago 484-487
Tristan da Cunha.....................439-442
Vanuatu 485-488
Zil Elwannyen Sesel.................146-149

Moon Landing, 20th Anniv.

CD342

Designs: Equipment, crew photographs, spacecraft, official emblems and report profiles created for the Apollo Missions. Two stamps in each set are square in format rather than like the stamp shown; see individual country listings for more information.

1989

Ascension Is.............................468-472
Bahamas 674-678
Belize......................................916-920
Kiribati 517-521
Liberia 1125-1129
Nevis 586-590
St. Kitts 248-252
Samoa 760-764
Seychelles 676-680
Solomon Islands.....................643-647
Vanuatu 507-511
Zil Elwannyen Sesel.................154-158

Queen Mother, 90th Birthday

CD343   CD344

Designs: Portraits of Queen Elizabeth, the Queen Mother. See individual country listings for more information.

1990

Ascension Is.............................491-492
Bahamas 698-699
Barbados 782-783
British Antarctic Territory..........170-171
British Indian Ocean Territory 106-107
Cayman Islands.......................622-623
Falkland Islands 524-525
Kenya......................................527-528
Kiribati 555-556
Liberia 1145-1146
Pitcairn Islands.......................336-337
St. Helena 532-533
St. Lucia 969-970
Seychelles 710-711
Solomon Islands.....................671-672
South Georgia 143-144
Swaziland 565-566
Tristan da Cunha....................480-481
Zil Elwannyen Sesel.................171-172

Queen Elizabeth II, 65th Birthday, and Prince Philip, 70th Birthday

CD345

CD346

Designs: Portraits of Queen Elizabeth II and Prince Philip differ for each country. Printed in sheets of 10 + 5 labels (3 different) between. Stamps alternate, producing 5 different triptychs.

1991

Ascension Is. 505-506
Bahamas 730-731
Belize......................................969-970
Bermuda 617-618
Kiribati 571-572
Mauritius.................................733-734
Pitcairn Islands.......................348-349
St. Helena 554-555
St. Kitts 318-319
Samoa 790-791
Seychelles 723-724
Solomon Islands.....................688-689
South Georgia 149-150
Swaziland 586-587
Vanuatu 540-541
Zil Elwannyen Sesel.................177-178

Royal Family Birthday, Anniversary

CD347

Queen Elizabeth II, 65th birthday, Charles and Diana, 10th wedding anniversary: Various photographs of Queen Elizabeth II, Prince Philip, Prince Charles, Princess Diana and their sons William and Henry.

1991

Antigua 1446-1455
Barbuda 1229-1238
Dominica 1328-1337
Gambia 1080-1089
Grenada................................2006-2015
Grenada Grenadines............1331-1340
Guyana 2440-2451
Lesotho 871-875
Maldive Islands...................1533-1542
Nevis 666-675
St. Vincent.........................1485-1494
St. Vincent Grenadines 769-778
Sierra Leone 1387-1396
Turks & Caicos Islands 913-922
Uganda 918-927

Queen Elizabeth II's Accession to the Throne, 40th Anniv.

CD348

CD349

Various photographs of Queen Elizabeth II with local Scenes.

1992 - CD348

Antigua 1513-1518
Barbuda 1306-1309
Dominica 1414-1419
Gambia 1172-1177
Grenada................................2047-2052
Grenada Grenadines............1368-1373

Lesotho...................................881-885
Maldive Islands...................1637-1642
Nevis 702-707
St. Vincent.........................1582-1587
St. Vincent Grenadines 829-834
Sierra Leone 1482-1487
Turks and Caicos Islands.........978-987
Uganda 990-995
Virgin Islands 742-746

1992 - CD349

Ascension Islands 531-535
Bahamas 744-748
Bermuda 623-627
British Indian Ocean Territory 119-123
Cayman Islands.......................648-652
Falkland Islands 549-553
Gibraltar..................................605-609
Hong Kong 619-623
Kenya......................................563-567
Kiribati 582-586
Pitcairn Islands.......................362-366
St. Helena 570-574
St. Kitts 332-336
Samoa 805-809
Seychelles 734-738
Solomon Islands.....................708-712
South Georgia 157-161
Tristan da Cunha....................508-512
Vanuatu 555-559
Zambia 561-565
Zil Elwannyen Sesel.................183-187

Royal Air Force, 75th Anniversary

CD350   15P FALKLAND ISLANDS

1993

Ascension 557-561
Bahamas 771-775
Barbados 842-846
Belize..................................1003-1008
Bermuda 648-651
British Indian Ocean Territory 136-140
Falkland Is. 573-577
Fiji..687-691
Montserrat 830-834
St. Kitts 351-355

Royal Air Force, 80th Anniv.

Design CD350 Re-inscribed

1998

Ascension 697-701
Bahamas 907-911
British Indian Ocean Terr 198-202
Cayman Islands.......................754-758
Fiji..814-818
Gibraltar..................................755-759
Samoa 957-961
Turks & Caicos Islands 1258-1265
Tuvalu 763-767
Virgin Islands 879-883

End of World War II, 50th Anniv.

CD351

CD352

1995

Ascension................................613-617
Bahamas 824-828
Barbados 891-895
Belize..................................1047-1050
British Indian Ocean Territory 163-167
Cayman Islands.......................704-708
Falkland Islands 634-638
Fiji..720-724
Kiribati 662-668
Liberia 1175-1179
Mauritius.................................803-805
St. Helena 646-654
St. Kitts 389-393
St. Lucia 1018-1022
Samoa 890-894
Solomon Islands.....................799-803
South Georgia & S. Sandwich Is..........198-200
Tristan da Cunha....................562-566

UN, 50th Anniv.

CD353   BRITISH VIRGIN ISLANDS

1995

Bahamas 839-842
Barbados 901-904
Belize..................................1055-1058
Jamaica 847-851
Liberia 1187-1190
Mauritius.................................813-816
Pitcairn Islands.......................436-439
St. Kitts 398-401
St. Lucia 1023-1026
Samoa 900-903
Tristan da Cunha....................568-571
Virgin Islands 807-810

Queen Elizabeth, 70th Birthday

CD354

1996

Ascension 632-635
British Antarctic Territory..........240-243
British Indian Ocean Territory 176-180
Falkland Islands 653-657
Pitcairn Islands.......................446-449
St. Helena 672-676
Samoa 912-916
Tokelau 223-227
Tristan da Cunha....................576-579
Virgin Islands 824-828

Diana, Princess of Wales (1961-97)

CD355

1998

Ascension	696
Bahamas	901A-902
Barbados	950
Belize	1091
Bermuda	753
Botswana	659-663
British Antarctic Territory	258
British Indian Ocean Terr.	197
Cayman Islands	752A-753
Falkland Islands	694
Fiji	819-820
Gibraltar	754
Kiribati	719A-720
Namibia	909
Niue	706
Norfolk Island	644-645
Papua New Guinea	937
Pitcairn Islands	487
St. Helena	711
St. Kitts	437A-438
Samoa	955A-956
Seycelles	802
Solomon Islands	866-867
South Georgia & S. Sandwich Islands	220
Tokelau	252B-253
Tonga	980
Niuafo'ou	201
Tristan da Cunha	618
Tuvalu	762
Vanuatu	719
Virgin Islands	878

Wedding of Prince Edward and Sophie Rhys-Jones

CD356

1999

Ascension	729-730
Cayman Islands	775-776
Falkland Islands	729-730
Pitcairn Islands	505-506
St. Helena	733-734
Samoa	971-972
Tristan da Cunha	636-637
Virgin Islands	908-909

1st Manned Moon Landing, 30th Anniv.

CD357

1999

Ascension	731-735
Bahamas	942-946
Barbados	967-971
Bermuda	778
Cayman Islands	777-781

Fiji	853-857
Jamaica	889-893
Kirbati	746-750
Nauru	465-469
St. Kitts	460-464
Samoa	973-977
Solomon Islands	875-879
Tuvalu	800-804
Virgin Islands	910-914

Queen Mother's Century

CD358

1999

Ascension	736-740
Bahamas	951-955
Cayman Islands	782-786
Falkland Islands	734-738
Fiji	858-862
Norfolk Island	688-692
St. Helena	740-744
Samoa	978-982
Solomon Islands	880-884
South Georgia & South Sandwich Islands	231-235
Tristan da Cunha	638-642
Tuvalu	805-809

Prince William, 18th Birthday

CD359

2000

Ascension	755-759
Cayman Islands	797-801
Falkland Islands	762-766
Fiji	889-893
South Georgia and South Sandwich Islands	257-261
Tristan da Cunha	664-668
Virgin Islands	925-929

Reign of Queen Elizabeth II, 50th Anniv.

CD360

2002

Ascension	790-794
Bahamas	1033-1037
Barbados	1019-1023
Belize	1152-1156
Bermuda	822-826
British Antarctic Territory	307-311
British Indian Ocean Territory	239-243
Cayman Islands	844-848
Falkland Islands	804-808
Gibraltar	896-900
Jamaica	952-956
Nauru	491-495
Norfolk Island	758-762
Papua New Guinea	1019-1023
Pitcairn Islands	552
St. Helena	788-792
St. Lucia	1146-1150
Solomon Islands	931-935
South Georgia & So. Sandwich Is.	274-278
Swaziland	706-710
Tokelau	302-306
Tonga	1059

Niuafo'ou	239
Tristan da Cunha	706-710
Virgin Islands	967-971

Queen Mother Elizabeth (1900-2002)

CD361

2002

Ascension	799-801
Bahamas	1044-1046
Bermuda	834-836
British Antarctic Territory	312-314
British Indian Ocean Territory	245-247
Cayman Islands	857-861
Falkland Islands	812-816
Nauru	499-501
Pitcairn Islands	561-565
St. Helena	808-812
St. Lucia	1155-1159
Seychelles	830
Solomon Islands	945-947
South Georgia & So. Sandwich Isls.	281-285
Tokelau	312-314
Tristan da Cunha	715-717
Virgin Islands	979-983

Head of Queen Elizabeth II

CD362

2003

Ascension	822
Bermuda	865
British Antarctic Territory	322
British Indian Ocean Territory	261
Cayman Islands	878
Falkland Islands	828
St. Helena	820
South Georgia & South Sandwich Islands	294
Tristan da Cunha	731
Virgin Islands	1003

Coronation of Queen Elizabeth II, 50th Anniv.

CD363

2003

Ascension	823-825
Bahamas	1073-1075
Bermuda	866-868
British Antarctic Territory	323-325
British Indian Ocean Territory	262-264
Cayman Islands	879-881
Jamaica	970-972
Kiribati	825-827
Pitcairn Islands	577-581
St. Helena	821-823
St. Lucia	1171-1173
Tokelau	320-322
Tristan da Cunha	732-734
Virgin Islands	1004-1006

Prince William, 21st Birthday

CD364

2003

Ascension	826
British Indian Ocean Territory	265
Cayman Islands	882-884
Falkland Islands	829
South Georgia & South Sandwich Islands	295
Tokelau	323
Tristan da Cunha	735
Virgin Islands	1007-1009

British Commonwealth of Nations

Dominions, Colonies, Territories, Offices and Independent Members

Comprising stamps of the British Commonwealth and associated nations.

A strict observance of technicalities would bar some or all of the stamps listed under Burma, Ireland, Kuwait, Nepal, New Republic, Orange Free State, Samoa, South Africa, South-West Africa, Stellaland, Sudan, Swaziland, the two Transvaal Republics and others but these are included for the convenience of collectors.

1. Great Britain

Great Britain: Including England, Scotland, Wales and Northern Ireland.

2. The Dominions, Present and Past

AUSTRALIA

The Commonwealth of Australia was proclaimed on January 1, 1901. It consists of six former colonies as follows:

New South Wales	Victoria
Queensland	Tasmania
South Australia	Western Australia

The following islands and territories are, or have been, administered by Australia: Australian Antarctic Territory, Christmas Island, Cocos (Keeling) Islands, Nauru, New Guinea, Norfolk Island, Papua.

CANADA

The Dominion of Canada was created by the British North America Act in 1867. The following provinces were former separate colonies and issued postage stamps:

British Columbia and Vancouver Island	Newfoundland
	Nova Scotia
New Brunswick	Prince Edward Island

FIJI

The colony of Fiji became an independent nation with dominion status on Oct. 10, 1970.

GHANA

This state came into existence Mar. 6, 1957, with dominion status. It consists of the former colony of the Gold Coast and the Trusteeship Territory of Togoland. Ghana became a republic July 1, 1960.

INDIA

The Republic of India was inaugurated on January 26, 1950. It succeeded the Dominion of India which was proclaimed August 15, 1947, when the former Empire of India was divided into Pakistan and the Union of India. The Republic is composed of about 40 predominantly Hindu states of three classes: governor's provinces, chief commissioner's provinces and princely states. India also has various territories, such as the Andaman and Nicobar Islands.

The old Empire of India was a federation of British India and the native states. The more important princely states were autonomous. Of the more than 700 Indian states, these 43 are familiar names to philatelists because of their postage stamps.

CONVENTION STATES

Chamba	Jhind
Faridkot	Nabha
Gwalior	Patiala

FEUDATORY STATES

Alwar	Jammu and Kashmir
Bahawalpur	Jasdan
Bamra	Jhalawar
Barwani	Jhind (1875-76)
Bhopal	Kashmir
Bhor	Kishangarh
Bijawar	Kotah
Bundi	Las Bela
Bussahir	Morvi
Charkhari	Nandgaon
Cochin	Nowanuggur
Dhar	Orchha
Dungarpur	Poonch
Duttia	Rajasthan
Faridkot (1879-85)	Rajpeepla
Hyderabad	Sirmur
Idar	Soruth
Indore	Tonk
Jaipur	Travancore
Jammu	Wadhwan

NEW ZEALAND

Became a dominion on September 26, 1907. The following islands and territories are, or have been, administered by New Zealand:

Aitutaki	Ross Dependency
Cook Islands (Rarotonga)	Samoa (Western Samoa)
Niue	Tokelau Islands
Penrhyn	

PAKISTAN

The Republic of Pakistan was proclaimed March 23, 1956. It succeeded the Dominion which was proclaimed August 15, 1947. It is made up of all or part of several Moslem provinces and various districts of the former Empire of India, including Bahawalpur and Las Bela. Pakistan withdrew from the Commonwealth in 1972.

SOUTH AFRICA

Under the terms of the South African Act (1909) the self-governing colonies of Cape of Good Hope, Natal, Orange River Colony and Transvaal united on May 31, 1910, to form the Union of South Africa. It became an independent republic May 3, 1961.

Under the terms of the Treaty of Versailles, South-West Africa, formerly German South-West Africa, was mandated to the Union of South Africa.

SRI LANKA (CEYLON)

The Dominion of Ceylon was proclaimed February 4, 1948. The island had been a Crown Colony from 1802 until then. On May 22, 1972, Ceylon became the Republic of Sri Lanka.

3. Colonies, Past and Present; ControlledTerritory and Independent Members of the Commonwealth

Aden	Bechuanaland
Aitutaki	Bechuanaland Prot.
Antigua	Belize
Ascension	Bermuda
Bahamas	Botswana
Bahrain	British Antarctic Territory
Bangladesh	British Central Africa
Barbados	British Columbia and
Barbuda	Vancouver Island
Basutoland	British East Africa
Batum	British Guiana

British Honduras
British Indian Ocean Territory
British New Guinea
British Solomon Islands
British Somaliland
Brunei
Burma
Bushire
Cameroons
Cape of Good Hope
Cayman Islands
Christmas Island
Cocos (Keeling) Islands
Cook Islands
Crete,
  British Administration
Cyprus
Dominica
East Africa & Uganda
  Protectorates
Egypt
Falkland Islands
Fiji
Gambia
German East Africa
Gibraltar
Gilbert Islands
Gilbert & Ellice Islands
Gold Coast
Grenada
Griqualand West
Guernsey
Guyana
Heligoland
Hong Kong
Indian Native States
  (see India)
Ionian Islands
Jamaica
Jersey

Kenya
Kenya, Uganda & Tanzania
Kuwait
Labuan
Lagos
Leeward Islands
Lesotho
Madagascar
Malawi
Malaya
  Federated Malay States
  Johore
  Kedah
  Kelantan
  Malacca
  Negri Sembilan
  Pahang
  Penang
  Perak
  Perlis
  Selangor
  Singapore
  Sungei Ujong
  Trengganu
Malaysia
Maldive Islands
Malta
Man, Isle of
Mauritius
Mesopotamia
Montserrat
Muscat
Namibia
Natal
Nauru
Nevis
New Britain
New Brunswick
Newfoundland
New Guinea

New Hebrides
New Republic
New South Wales
Niger Coast Protectorate
Nigeria
Niue
Norfolk Island
North Borneo
Northern Nigeria
Northern Rhodesia
North West Pacific Islands
Nova Scotia
Nyasaland Protectorate
Oman
Orange River Colony
Palestine
Papua New Guinea
Penrhyn Island
Pitcairn Islands
Prince Edward Island
Queensland
Rhodesia
Rhodesia & Nyasaland
Ross Dependency
Sabah
St. Christopher
St. Helena
St. Kitts
St. Kitts-Nevis-Anguilla
St. Lucia
St. Vincent
Samoa
Sarawak
Seychelles
Sierra Leone
Solomon Islands
Somaliland Protectorate
South Arabia
South Australia
South Georgia

Southern Nigeria
Southern Rhodesia
South-West Africa
Stellaland
Straits Settlements
Sudan
Swaziland
Tanganyika
Tanzania
Tasmania
Tobago
Togo
Tokelau Islands
Tonga
Transvaal
Trinidad
Trinidad and Tobago
Tristan da Cunha
Trucial States
Turks and Caicos
Turks Islands
Tuvalu
Uganda
United Arab Emirates
Victoria
Virgin Islands
Western Australia
Zambia
Zanzibar
Zululand

**POST OFFICES IN
FOREIGN COUNTRIES**
Africa
  East Africa Forces
  Middle East Forces
Bangkok
China
Morocco
Turkish Empire

Colonies, Former Colonies, Offices, Territories Controlled by Parent States

Belgium
Belgian Congo
Ruanda-Urundi

Denmark
Danish West Indies
Faroe Islands
Greenland
Iceland

Finland
Aland Islands

France

COLONIES PAST AND PRESENT, CONTROLLED TERRITORIES
Afars & Issas, Territory of
Alaouites
Alexandretta
Algeria
Alsace & Lorraine
Anjouan
Annam & Tonkin
Benin
Cambodia (Khmer)
Cameroun
Castellorizo
Chad
Cilicia
Cochin China
Comoro Islands
Dahomey
Diego Suarez
Djibouti (Somali Coast)
Fezzan
French Congo
French Equatorial Africa
French Guiana
French Guinea
French India
French Morocco
French Polynesia (Oceania)
French Southern & Antarctic Territories
French Sudan
French West Africa
Gabon
Germany
Ghadames
Grand Comoro
Guadeloupe
Indo-China
Inini
Ivory Coast
Laos
Latakia
Lebanon
Madagascar
Martinique
Mauritania
Mayotte
Memel
Middle Congo
Moheli
New Caledonia
New Hebrides
Niger Territory
Nossi-Be
Obock
Reunion
Rouad, Ile
Ste.-Marie de Madagascar
St. Pierre & Miquelon
Senegal
Senegambia & Niger
Somali Coast
Syria
Tahiti
Togo
Tunisia
Ubangi-Shari
Upper Senegal & Niger
Upper Volta
Viet Nam
Wallis & Futuna Islands

POST OFFICES IN FOREIGN COUNTRIES
China
Crete
Egypt
Turkish Empire
Zanzibar

Germany

EARLY STATES
Baden
Bavaria
Bergedorf
Bremen
Brunswick
Hamburg
Hanover
Lubeck
Mecklenburg-Schwerin
Mecklenburg-Strelitz
Oldenburg
Prussia
Saxony
Schleswig-Holstein
Wurttemberg

FORMER COLONIES
Cameroun (Kamerun)
Caroline Islands
German East Africa
German New Guinea
German South-West Africa
Kiauchau
Mariana Islands
Marshall Islands
Samoa
Togo

Italy

EARLY STATES
Modena
Parma
Romagna
Roman States
Sardinia
Tuscany
Two Sicilies
  Naples
  Neapolitan Provinces
  Sicily

FORMER COLONIES, CONTROLLED TERRITORIES, OCCUPATION AREAS
Aegean Islands
  Calimno (Calino)
  Caso
  Cos (Coo)
  Karki (Carchi)
  Leros (Lero)
  Lipso
  Nisiros (Nisiro)
  Patmos (Patmo)
  Piscopi
  Rodi (Rhodes)
  Scarpanto
  Simi
  Stampalia
Castellorizo
Corfu
Cyrenaica
Eritrea
Ethiopia (Abyssinia)
Fiume
Ionian Islands
  Cephalonia
  Ithaca
  Paxos
Italian East Africa
Libya
Oltre Giuba
Saseno
Somalia (Italian Somaliland)
Tripolitania

POST OFFICES IN FOREIGN COUNTRIES
"ESTERO"*
Austria
China
  Peking
  Tientsin
Crete
Tripoli
Turkish Empire
  Constantinople
  Durazzo
  Janina
Jerusalem
Salonika
Scutari
Smyrna
Valona
*Stamps overprinted "ESTERO" were used in various parts of the world.

Netherlands
Aruba
Netherlands Antilles (Curacao)
Netherlands Indies
Netherlands New Guinea
Surinam (Dutch Guiana)

Portugal

COLONIES PAST AND PRESENT, CONTROLLED TERRITORIES
Angola
Angra
Azores
Cape Verde
Funchal
Horta
Inhambane
Kionga
Lourenco Marques
Macao
Madeira
Mozambique
Mozambique Co.
Nyassa
Ponta Delgada
Portuguese Africa
Portuguese Congo
Portuguese Guinea
Portuguese India
Quelimane
St. Thomas & Prince Islands
Tete
Timor
Zambezia

Russia

ALLIED TERRITORIES AND REPUBLICS, OCCUPATION AREAS
Armenia
Aunus (Olonets)
Azerbaijan
Batum
Estonia
Far Eastern Republic
Georgia
Karelia
Latvia
Lithuania
North Ingermanland
Ostland
Russian Turkestan
Siberia
South Russia
Tannu Tuva
Transcaucasian Fed. Republics
Ukraine
Wenden (Livonia)
Western Ukraine

Spain

COLONIES PAST AND PRESENT, CONTROLLED TERRITORIES
Aguera, La
Cape Juby
Cuba
Elobey, Annobon & Corisco
Fernando Po
Ifni
Mariana Islands
Philippines
Puerto Rico
Rio de Oro
Rio Muni
Spanish Guinea
Spanish Morocco
Spanish Sahara
Spanish West Africa

POST OFFICES IN FOREIGN COUNTRIES
Morocco
Tangier
Tetuan

Dies of British Colonial Stamps

DIE A

DIE B

DIE I

DIE II

DIE A:
1. The lines in the groundwork vary in thickness and are not uniformly straight.
2. The seventh and eighth lines from the top, in the groundwork, converge where they meet the head.
3. There is a small dash in the upper part of the second jewel in the band of the crown.
4. The vertical color line in front of the throat stops at the sixth line of shading on the neck.

DIE B:
1. The lines in the groundwork are all thin and straight.
2. All the lines of the background are parallel.
3. There is no dash in the upper part of the second jewel in the band of the crown.
4. The vertical color line in front of the throat stops at the eighth line of shading on the neck.

DIE I:
1. The base of the crown is well below the level of the inner white line around the vignette.
2. The labels inscribed "POSTAGE" and "REVENUE" are cut square at the top.
3. There is a white "bud" on the outer side of the main stem of the curved ornaments in each lower corner.
4. The second (thick) line below the country name has the ends next to the crown cut diagonally.

DIE Ia.	DIE Ib.
1 as die II.	1 and 3 as die II.
2 and 3 as die I.	2 as die I.

DIE II:
1. The base of the crown is aligned with the underside of the white line around the vignette.
2. The labels curve inward at the top inner corners.
3. The "bud" has been removed from the outer curve of the ornaments in each corner.
4. The second line below the country name has the ends next to the crown cut vertically.

Wmk. 1
Crown and C C

Wmk. 2
Crown and C A

Wmk. 3
Multiple Crown
and C A

Wmk. 4
Multiple Crown
and Script C A

Wmk. 4a

Wmk. 314
St. Edward's Crown
and C A Multiple

Wmk. 373

Wmk. 384

Wmk. 406

British Colonial and Crown Agents Watermarks

Watermarks 1 to 4, 314, 373, 384 and 406, common to many British territories, are illustrated here to avoid duplication.

The letters "CC" of Wmk. 1 identify the paper as having been made for the use of the Crown Colonies, while the letters "CA" of the others stand for "Crown Agents." Both Wmks. 1 and 2 were used on stamps printed by De La Rue & Co.

Wmk. 3 was adopted in 1904; Wmk. 4 in 1921; Wmk. 314 in 1957; Wmk. 373 in 1974; Wmk. 384 in 1985; Wmk 406 in 2008.

In Wmk. 4a, a non-matching crown of the general St. Edwards type (bulging on both sides at top) was substituted for one of the Wmk. 4 crowns which fell off the dandy roll. The non-matching crown occurs in 1950-52 printings in a horizontal row of crowns on certain regular stamps of Johore and Seychelles, and on various postage due stamps of Barbados, Basutoland, British Guiana, Gold Coast, Grenada, Northern Rhodesia, St. Lucia, Swaziland and Trinidad and Tobago. A variation of Wmk. 4a, with the non-matching crown in a horizontal row of crown-CA-crown, occurs on regular stamps of Bahamas, St. Kitts-Nevis and Singapore.

Wmk. 314 was intentionally used sideways, starting in 1966. When a stamp was issued with Wmk. 314 both upright and sideways, the sideways varieties usually are listed also – with minor numbers. In many of the later issues, Wmk. 314 is slightly visible.

Wmk. 373 is usually only faintly visible.

GABON

ga-'bōⁿ

LOCATION — West coast of Africa, at the equator
GOVT. — Republic
AREA — 102,089 sq. mi.
POP. — 1,225,853 (1999 est.)
CAPITAL — Libreville

Gabon originally was under the control of French West Africa. In 1886, it was united with French Congo. In 1904, Gabon was granted a certain degree of colonial autonomy which prevailed until 1934, when it merged with French Equatorial Africa. Gabon Republic was proclaimed November 28, 1958.

100 Centimes = 1 Franc

Catalogue values for unused stamps in this country are for Never Hinged items, beginning with Scott 148 in the regular postage section, Scott B4 in the semipostal section, Scott C1 in the airpost section, Scott CB1 in the airpost semi-postal section, Scott J34 in the postage due section, and Scott O1 in the officials section.

Watermark

Wmk. 385

For detailed listings of overprint and surcharge varieties of Gabon Nos. 1-15, see the *Scott Classic Specialized Catalogue of Stamps and Covers.*

Stamps of French Colonies of 1881-86 Handstamp Surcharged in Black:

a

b

1886		Unwmk.	Perf. 14x13½	
1	A9 (a)	5c on 20c red, grn	550.00	600.00
2	A9 (b)	10c on 20c red, grn	525.00	550.00
3	A9 (b)	25c on 20c red, grn	100.00	72.50
e.		56-dot diamond grid around "GAB"	6,400.	1,900.
4	A9 (b)	50c on 15c bl	1,500.	2,100.
5	A9 (b)	75c on 15c bl	1,900.	2,300.

Nos. 1-3 exist with double surcharge of numeral; No. 3 with "GAB" double or inverted, or with "25" double.
On Nos. 3 and 5 the surcharge slants down; on No. 4 it slants up. The number of dots varies.
Counterfeits of Nos. 1-15 exist.

Handstamp Surcharged in Black

c

1888-89

6	A9	15c on 10c blk, lav	5,800.	1,500.
7	A9	15c on 1fr brnz grn, straw	2,400.	1,200.
8	A9	25c on 5c grn, grnsh	1,500.	300.00
a.		Double surcharge	4,000.	4,000.
9	A9	25c on 10c blk, lav	5,900.	1,900.
10	A9	25c on 75c car, rose	3,600.	1,900.

Official reprints exist.

Postage Due Stamps of French Colonies Handstamp Surcharged in Black — d

1889			Imperf.	
11	D1	15c on 5c black	300.00	275.00
12	D1	15c on 30c black	5,000.	3,800.
13	D1	25c on 20c black	140.00	120.00

Nos. 11 and 13 exist with "GABON," "TIMBRE" or "25" double; "TIMBRE" or "15" omitted, etc.

A8

1889			Typeset	
14	A8	15c blk, rose	1,900.	1,200.
15	A8	25c blk, green	1,200.	950.

Ten varieties of each. Nos. 14-15 exist with "GAB" inverted or omitted, and with small "f" in "Francaise."

Navigation and Commerce — A9

1904-07		Typo.	Perf. 14x13½	
Name of Colony in Blue or Carmine				
16	A9	1c blk, lil bl	1.20	1.20
a.		"GABON" double	360.00	360.00
17	A9	2c brn, buff	1.60	1.60
18	A9	4c claret, lav	2.75	2.00
19	A9	5c yellow green	3.25	2.40
20	A9	10c rose	10.50	7.50
21	A9	15c gray	11.00	7.50
22	A9	20c red, grn	15.00	14.00
23	A9	25c blue	14.00	7.50
24	A9	30c yel brn	16.00	15.00
25	A9	35c blk, yel ('06)	24.00	24.00
26	A9	40c red, straw	25.00	20.00
27	A9	45c blk, gray grn ('07)	37.50	32.50
28	A9	50c brn, az	16.00	14.00
29	A9	75c dp vio, org	25.00	25.00
30	A9	1fr brnz grn, straw	40.00	40.00
31	A9	2fr vio, rose	80.00	80.00
32	A9	5fr lil, lav	125.00	125.00
		Nos. 16-32 (17)	447.80	419.20

Perf. 13½x14 stamps are counterfeits.
For surcharges see Nos. 72-84.

Fang Warrior — A10   Fang Woman — A12

Libreville A11

Inscribed: "Congo Français"

1910			Perf. 13½x14	
33	A10	1c choc & org	2.00	2.00
34	A10	2c black & choc	2.75	2.75
35	A10	4c vio & dp bl	2.50	2.50
36	A10	5c ol gray & grn	4.00	4.00
37	A10	10c red & car	5.75	5.75
38	A10	20c choc & dk vio	8.00	8.00
39	A11	25c dp bl & choc	8.00	8.00
40	A11	30c gray blk & red	40.00	40.00
41	A11	35c dk vio & grn	24.00	24.00
42	A11	40c choc & ultra	32.50	32.50
43	A11	45c carmine & vio	52.50	52.50
44	A11	50c bl grn & gray	75.00	75.00
45	A11	75c org & choc	130.00	130.00
46	A12	1fr dk brn & bis	130.00	130.00
47	A12	2fr carmine & brn	325.00	325.00
48	A12	5fr blue & choc	325.00	325.00
		Nos. 33-48 (16)	1,167.	1,167.

Inscribed: "Afrique Equatoriale"

1910-22				
On Dull Cream Paper				
49	A10	1c choc & org	.30	.40
50	A10	2c black & choc	.30	.40
b.		2c gray black & deep olive	.65	.80
51	A10	4c vio & dp bl	.50	.55
52	A10	5c ol gray & grn	.95	.55
53	A10	5c gray blk & ocher ('22)	1.25	1.25
54	A10	10c red & car	1.40	1.00
55	A10	10c yel grn & bl grn ('22)	1.25	1.25
56	A10	15c brn vio & rose ('18)	1.25	.80
57	A10	20c ol brn & dk vio	6.50	5.50
58	A11	25c dp bl & choc	1.40	1.00
59	A11	25c Prus bl & blk ('22)	1.60	1.60
60	A11	30c gray blk & red	1.60	1.60
61	A11	30c rose & red ('22)	2.00	2.40
62	A11	35c dk vio & grn	1.25	1.25
63	A11	40c choc & ultra	1.60	1.60
64	A11	45c carmine & vio	1.60	1.60
65	A11	45c blk & red ('22)	2.75	3.25
66	A11	50c bl grn & gray	2.00	2.00
67	A11	50c dk bl & bl ('22)	1.60	1.60
68	A11	75c org & choc	6.50	6.50
69	A12	1fr dk brn & bis	3.25	3.25
70	A12	2fr car & brn	6.50	7.25
71	A12	5fr blue & choc	8.75	9.50
		Nos. 49-71 (23)	56.10	56.10

Nos. 49-51, 54, 62, 64 and 66 also exist on white paper. See the *Scott Classic Specialized Catalogue of Stamps and Covers* for listings.
For overprints and surcharges, see Nos 85-119, B1-B3.

Stamps of 1904-07 Surcharged in Black or Carmine

1912				
Spacing between figures of surcharge 1.5mm (5c), 2mm (10c)				
72	A9	5c on 2c brn, buff	1.60	2.00
73	A9	5c on 4c cl, lav (C)	1.60	2.00
74	A9	5c on 15c gray (C)	1.25	1.25
75	A9	5c on 20c red, grn	1.25	1.60
76	A9	5c on 25c bl (C)	1.25	1.60
77	A9	5c on 30c pale brn (C)	1.60	2.00
78	A9	10c on 40c red, straw	1.25	1.60
a.		Double surcharge	2,000.	
79	A9	10c on 45c blk, gray grn (C)	1.25	1.60
80	A9	10c on 50c brn, az (C)	1.60	2.00
81	A9	10c on 75c dp vio, org	1.60	2.00
82	A9	10c on 1fr brnz grn, straw	1.60	2.00
83	A9	10c on 2fr vio, rose	1.60	2.00
a.		Inverted surcharge	340.00	340.00
84	A9	10c on 5fr lil, lav	4.50	4.75
		Nos. 72-84 (13)	21.95	26.40

Two spacings between the surcharged numerals are found on Nos. 72 to 84. For detailed listings, see the *Scott Classic Specialized Catalogue of Stamps and Covers.*

Stamps of 1910-22 Overprinted in Black, Blue or Carmine

On A10, A12

On A11

1924-31				
85	A10	1c brown & org	.30	.40
86	A10	2c blk & choc (Bl)	.50	.60
87	A10	4c violet & ind	.30	.40
88	A10	5c gray blk & ocher	.45	.55
89	A10	10c yel grn & bl grn	1.00	1.00
a.		Double overprint (Bk & Bl)	175.00	
90	A10	10c dk bl & brn ('26) (C)	.40	.40
a.		Overprint omitted	350.00	350.00
b.		Double overprint	475.00	
91	A10	15c brn vio & rose (Bl)	1.00	1.00
92	A10	15c rose & brn vio ('31) (Bl)	1.25	1.25
a.		Overprint omitted	250.00	
93	A10	20c ol brn & dk vio (C)	1.00	1.00
a.		Inverted overprint	180.00	180.00
b.		Double overprint	400.00	
c.		Double overprint, both inverted	525.00	
94	A11	25c Prus bl & blk (C)	.95	.95
95	A11	30c rose & red (Bl)	.90	1.00
96	A11	30c blk & org ('26)	1.00	1.00
a.		Overprint omitted	10,000.	
97	A11	30c dk grn & bl grn ('28)	1.25	1.25
a.		Overprint omitted	1,800.	
98	A11	35c dk vio & grn (Bl)	.80	.95
99	A11	40c choc & ultra (C)	.75	.90
100	A11	45c blk & red (Bl)	1.50	1.50
101	A11	50c dk bl & bl (C)	1.00	1.00
102	A11	50c car & grn ('26)	1.10	1.10
103	A11	65c dp bl & red org ('27)	4.50	4.00
104	A11	75c org & brn (Bl)	2.25	2.25
105	A11	90c brn red & rose ('30)	2.75	2.75
106	A12	1fr dk brn & bis	1.90	1.90
107	A12	1.10fr dl grn & rose red ('28)	6.00	7.50
108	A12	1.50fr pale bl & dk bl ('30)	1.25	1.25
a.		Overprint omitted	290.00	
109	A12	2fr rose & brn	2.25	2.50
110	A12	3fr red vio ('30)	10.50	8.25
a.		Overprint omitted	275.00	
111	A12	5fr dp bl & choc	5.50	6.50
		Nos. 85-111 (27)	52.35	53.15

Types of 1924-31 Issues Surcharged with New Values in Black or Carmine

1925-28				
112	A12	65c on 1fr ol grn & brn	1.25	1.25
113	A12	85c on 1fr ol grn & brn	1.25	1.25
114	A11	90c on 75c brn red & cer ('27)	1.60	1.60
a.		"90" omitted	240.00	
115	A12	1.25fr on 1fr dk bl & ultra (C)	1.25	1.25
116	A12	1.50fr on 1fr lt bl & dk bl ('27)	2.00	2.00
117	A12	3fr on 5fr mag & ol brn	9.25	8.75
118	A12	10fr on 5fr org brn & grn ('27)	13.00	14.00

119 A12   20fr on 5fr red vio
      & org red
      ('27)   16.00   17.50
Nos. 112-119 (8)   45.60   47.60

Bars cover the old denominations on #114-119.

Common Design Types
pictured following the introduction.

Colonial Exposition Issue
Common Design Types

1931   *Perf. 12½*

Name of Country in Black

120 CD70   40c dp green   4.00   4.00
121 CD71   50c violet   4.00   4.00
122 CD72   90c red orange   4.00   4.00
123 CD73   1.50fr dull blue   5.50   5.50
    Nos. 120-123 (4)   17.50   17.50

Timber Raft
on Ogowe
River
A16

Count Savorgnan de
Brazza — A17

Village of
Setta
Kemma
A18

1932-33   **Photo.**   *Perf. 13x13½*

124 A16   1c brown violet   .25   .25
125 A16   2c blk, *rose*   .25   .25
126 A16   4c green   .30   .30
127 A16   5c grnsh blue   .55   .55
128 A16   10c red, *yel*   .55   .55
129 A16   15c red, *grn*   .70   .65
130 A16   20c deep red   .70   .65
131 A16   25c brown red   .70   .50
132 A17   30c yellow grn   2.00   1.60
133 A17   40c brown vio   2.25   1.10
134 A17   45c blk, *dl grn*   3.25   2.40
135 A17   50c red brown   1.60   1.25
136 A17   65c Prus blue   6.50   6.50
137 A17   75c blk, *red org*   4.00   3.25
138 A17   90c rose red   4.00   3.25
139 A17   1fr yel grn, *bl*   27.50   24.00
140 A18   1.25fr dp vio ('33)   2.25   2.00
141 A18   1.50fr dull blue   11.00   7.25
142 A18   1.75fr dp green
         ('33)   2.50   2.00
143 A18   2fr brn red   52.50   45.00
144 A18   3fr yel grn, *bl*   6.00   4.50
145 A18   5fr red brown   15.00   13.50
146 A18   10fr blk, *red org*   32.50   27.50
147 A18   20fr dk violet   47.50   40.00
    Nos. 124-147 (24)   224.35   188.80

See French Equatorial Africa No. 192 for stamp inscribed "Gabon" and "Afrique Equatoriale Francaise."

Catalogue values for all unused stamps in this section, from this point to the end of the section, are for Never Hinged items.

Republic

Prime Minister
Leon
Mba — A19

Flag & Map of
Gabon & UN
Emblem — A20

Unwmk.

1959, Nov. 28   **Engr.**   *Perf. 13*
148 A19   15fr shown   .40   .20
149 A19   25fr Mba, profile   .40   .20
    Proclamation of the Republic, 1st anniv.

Imperforates
Most Gabon stamps from 1959 onward exist imperforate in issued and trial colors, and also in small presentation sheets in issued colors.

C.C.T.A. Issue
Common Design Type

1960, May 21   **Engr.**   *Perf. 13*
150 CD106   50fr vio brn & Prus bl   1.10   1.10

1961, Feb. 9
151 A20   15fr multi   .35   .20
152 A20   25fr multi   .55   .20
153 A20   85fr multi   1.90   1.10
    Nos. 151-153 (3)   2.80   1.50
    Gabon's admission to United Nations.

Combretum
A21

1fr, 5fr, Tulip tree, vert. 2fr, 3fr, Yellow cassia.

1961, July 4   **Unwmk.**   *Perf. 13*
154 A21   50c rose red & grn   .20   .20
155 A21   1fr sl grn, red & bis   .20   .20
156 A21   2fr dk grn & yel   .40   .20
157 A21   3fr ol grn & yel   .60   .55
158 A21   5fr multi   .75   .60
159 A21   10fr grn & rose red   .80   .60
    Nos. 154-159 (6)   2.95   2.35

President Leon
Mba — A22

1962   **Engr.**
160 A22   15fr indigo, car & grn   .30   .20
161 A22   20fr brn blk, car & grn   .50   .20
162 A22   25fr brn, car & grn   .55   .20
    Nos. 160-162 (3)   1.35   .60

Abidjan Games Issue
Common Design Type

1962, July 21   **Photo.**   *Perf. 12½x12*
163 CD109   20fr Foot race, start   .75   .50
164 CD109   50fr Soccer   1.25   1.00
    Nos. 163-164,C6 (3)   5.75   3.75

African-Malgache Union Issue
Common Design Type

1962, Sept. 8   *Perf. 12½x12*
165 CD110   30fr emer, bluish grn,
          red & gold   1.60   1.25

Captain
Ntchorere
and Flags
of France
and
Gabon
A23

1962, Nov. 23   *Perf. 12*
166 A23   80fr multi   1.60   1.10
    Capt. Ntchorere, who died for France, 6/7/40.

Waves
Around
Globe
A23a

Design: 100fr, Orbit patterns around globe.

1963, Sept. 19   **Photo.**   *Perf. 12½*
167 A23a   25fr ultra, grn & org   .55   .55
168 A23a   100fr grn, ultra & red
          brn   2.10   1.75
    Issued to publicize space communications.

UNESCO
Emblem,
Scales and
Tree
A23b

1963, Dec. 10   **Engr.**   *Perf. 13*
169 A23b   25fr grn, dk gray & red
           brn   .60   .20
    15th anniv. of the Universal Declaration of Human Rights.

Barograph
and WMO
Emblem
A23c

1964, Mar. 23   **Unwmk.**   *Perf. 13*
170 A23c   25fr ol brn, sl grn & ul-
         tra   .90   .60
    UN's 4th World Meteorological Day, Mar. 23.

Arms of
Gabon — A24

1964, June 15   **Photo.**   *Perf. 13x12½*
171 A24   25fr ocher & multi   .90   .45

Tarpon
A25

Designs: 60fr, Gorilla, vert. 80fr, Buffalo.

1964, July 15   **Engr.**   *Perf. 13*
172 A25   30fr brn red, bl & blk   1.25   .70
173 A25   60fr brn, grn & brn red   2.25   .90
174 A25   80fr dk bl, grn & red brn   2.40   1.25
    Nos. 172-174 (3)   5.90   2.85

Cooperation Issue
Common Design Type

1964, Nov. 7
175 CD119   25fr gray, dk brn & lt
          bl   .90   .60

Dissotis
Rotundifolia — A26

5fr, Gloriosa superba. 15fr, Eulophia horsfallii.

1964, Nov. 16   **Photo.**   *Perf. 12x12½*

Flowers in Natural Colors
176 A26   3fr deep grn   .40   .25
177 A26   5fr green   .75   .40
178 A26   15fr dark brn   1.20   .80
    Nos. 176-178 (3)   2.35   1.45

Sun and
IQSY
Emblem
A27

1965, Feb. 25   *Perf. 12½x12*
179 A27   85fr multi   1.75   .80
    International Quiet Sun Year, 1964-65.

Morse
Telegraph
A28

1965, May 17   **Engr.**   *Perf. 13*
180 A28   30fr multi   1.10   .60
    Cent. of the ITU.

Manganese
Crusher,
Moanda
A29

Design: 60fr, Uranium mining, Mounana.

1965, June 15   **Unwmk.**   *Perf. 13*
181 A29   15fr brt bl, pur & red   .55   .30
182 A29   60fr brn, brt bl & red   1.90   .90
    Issued to publicize Gabon's mineral wealth.

Field Ball — A30   Okoukoue
                    Dance — A31

1965, July 15   **Engr.**   *Perf. 13*
183 A30   25fr brt grn, blk & red   .90   .60
    1st African Games, Brazzaville, 7/18-25.
    See #C35.

1965, Sept. 15   *Perf. 13*
    Design: 60fr, Mukudji dance.
184 A31   25fr brn, grn & yel   .55   .20
185 A31   60fr blk, dk red & brn   1.75   .90

Abraham Lincoln A32

1965, Sept. 28 Photo. Perf. 12½x13
186 A32 50fr vio bl, blk, gold & buff   1.00 .50

Centenary of death of Abraham Lincoln.

Old & New Post Offices and Mail Transport A33

1965, Dec. 18 Engr. Perf. 13
187 A33 30fr bl, brt grn & choc   .90 .70

Issued for Stamp Day, 1965.

Balumbu Mask — A34

Intl. Negro Arts Festival, Dakar, Senegal, Apr. 1-24:
10fr, Fang ancestral figure, Byeri. 25fr, Fang mask. 30fr, Okuyi mask, Myene. 85fr, Bakota leather mask.

1966, Apr. 18 Photo. Perf. 12x12½
188 A34 5fr red, brn, blk & buff   .30 .20
189 A34 10fr brt grnsh bl, dk brn & yel   .35 .30
190 A34 25fr multicolored   1.00 .35
191 A34 30fr mar, yel & blk   1.25 .70
192 A34 85fr multicolored   3.00 1.60
   Nos. 188-192 (5)   5.90 3.15

WHO Headquarters, Geneva — A35

1966, May 3 Photo. Perf. 12½x13
193 A35 50fr org yel, ultra & blk   1.40 .60

Inauguration of the WHO Headquarters, Geneva.

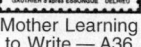

Mother Learning to Write — A36   Soccer Player — A37

1966, June 22 Photo. Perf. 12x12½
194 A36 30fr multi   .90 .45

UNESCO literacy campaign.

1966, July 15 Engr. Perf. 13
Design: 90fr, Player facing left.
195 A37 25fr brn, grn & ultra   .80 .20
196 A37 90fr ultra & dk pur   2.50 1.25
   Nos. 195-196,C45 (3)   6.30 2.70

8th World Cup Soccer Championship, Wembley, England, July 11-30.

Timber Industry — A38

Economic development: 85fr, Offshore oil rigs.

1966, Aug. 17 Perf. 13
197 A38 20fr red brn, lil & dk grn   .80 .50
198 A38 85fr dk brn, brt bl & brt grn   4.00 1.60

Woman with Children at Bank Window A39

1966, Sept. 23 Engr. Perf. 13
199 A39 25fr brt bl, vio brn & sl grn   1.00 .50

Issued to publicize Savings Banks.

Scouts Around Campfire A40

50fr, Boy Scout pledging ceremony, vert.

1966, Oct. 17 Engr. Perf. 13
200 A40 30fr sl bl, car & dk brn   1.00 .60
201 A40 50fr Prus bl, brn red & dk brn   1.60 .70

Issued to honor Gabon's Boy Scouts.

Sikorsky S-43 Hydroplane and Map of West Africa A41

1966, Dec. 17 Photo. Perf. 12½x12
202 A41 30fr multi   2.10 1.25

Stamp Day and for the 30th anniv. of the 1st air-mail service from Libreville to Port Gentil.

Hippopotami — A42

Animals: 2fr, African crocodiles. 3fr, Water chevrotain. 5fr, Chimpanzees. 10fr, Elephants. 20fr, Leopards.

1967, Jan. 5 Photo. Perf. 13x14
203 A42 1fr multi   .20 .20
204 A42 2fr multi   .45 .20
205 A42 3fr multi   .45 .20
206 A42 5fr multi   .50 .20
207 A42 10fr multi   2.25 .80
208 A42 20fr multi   5.00 .80
   Nos. 203-208 (6)   8.85 2.40

Lions International Emblem — A43

50fr, Lions emblem, map of Gabon and globe.

1967, Jan. 14 Perf. 12½x13
209 A43 30fr multicolored   .80 .20
210 A43 50fr blue & multi   1.40 .80
   a. Strip of 2, #209-210 + label   3.25 1.75

50th anniv. of Lions Intl.

Carnival Masks — A44

1967, Feb. 4 Photo. Perf. 12x12½
211 A44 30fr brn, yel bis & bl   1.10 .45

Libreville Carnival, Feb. 4-7.

"Transportation" and Tourist Year Emblem — A45

1967, Feb. 15 Perf. 12½x13
212 A45 30fr multi   1.10 .45

International Tourist Year, 1967.

Olympic Diving Tower, Mexico City — A46   Symbolic of Atomic Energy Agency — A47

1968 Olympic Games: 30fr, Sun, snow crystals and Olympic rings. 50fr, Ice skating rink and view of Grenoble.

1967, Mar. 18 Engr. Perf. 13
213 A46 25fr dk vio, grnsh bl & ultra   .75 .40
214 A46 30fr grn, red lil & mar   1.10 .50
215 A46 50fr ultra, grn & brn   1.75 1.10
   Nos. 213-215 (3)   3.60 2.00

1967, Apr. 15 Engr. Perf. 13
216 A47 30fr red brn, dk grn & ultra   1.00 .20

International Atomic Energy Agency.

Pope Paul VI, Papal Arms and Libreville Cathedral A48

1967, June 1 Engr. Perf. 13
217 A48 30fr ultra, grn & blk   1.10 .50

"Populorum progressio" encyclical by Pope Paul VI concerning underdeveloped countries.

Flags, Tree, Logger, Map of Gabon and Mask — A49

1967, June 24 Engr. Perf. 13
218 A49 30fr multi   1.00 .50

EXPO '67, International Exhibition, Montreal, Apr. 28-Oct. 27, 1967.

Europafrica Issue, 1967

Map of Europe and Africa and Products A50

1967, July 18 Photo. Perf. 12½x12
219 A50 50fr multi   1.50 .60

UN Emblem, Women and Child A51

1967, Aug. 10 Engr. Perf. 13
220 A51 75fr brt blue, dk brn & emer   1.90 .80

United Nations Commission for Women.

19th Century Mail Ships — A52

Design: No. 222, Modern mail ships.

1967, Nov. 17 Photo. Perf. 12½
221 A52 30fr multi   1.90 .95
222 A52 30fr multi   1.90 .95
   a. Pair, #221-222   5.00 5.00

Stamp Day. No. 222a has continuous design.

Draconea Fragrans — A53

Trees: 10fr, Pycnanthus angolensis. 20fr, Disthemonanthus benthamianus.

1967, Dec. 5 Engr. Perf. 13
Size: 22x36mm
223 A53 5fr bl, emer & brn   1.00 .35
224 A53 10fr grn, dk grn & bl   1.10 .55
225 A53 20fr rose red, grn & ol   1.60 .90
   Nos. 223-225,C61-C62 (5)   9.30 4.80

For booklet pane see No. C62a.

WHO
Regional
Office
A54

1968, Apr. 8   Engr.   *Perf. 13*
226 A54 20fr multi   1.00 .50
20th anniv. of the WHO.

Dam, Power
Station and
UNESCO
Emblem
A55

1968, June 18   Engr.   *Perf. 13*
227 A55 15fr lake, org & Prus bl   .70 .40
Hydrological Decade (UNESCO), 1965-74.

Pres. Albert Bernard
Bongo — A56

30fr, Pres. Bongo & arms of Gabon in
background.

1968, June 24   Photo.   *Perf. 12x12½*
228 A56 25fr grn, buff & blk   .65 .20
229 A56 30fr rose lil, lt bl & blk   .75 .20

Tanker, Refinery, and Map of Area
Served — A56a

1968, July 30   Photo.   *Perf. 12½*
230 A56a 30fr multi   1.00 .50
Port Gentil (Gabon) Refinery opening,
6/12/68.

Open Book,
Child and
UNESCO
Emblem
A57

1968, Sept. 10   Engr.   *Perf. 13*
231 A57 25fr vio bl, dl red & brn   1.60 .20
Issued for International Literacy Day.

A58   A60

A59

1968, Oct. 15   Engr.   *Perf. 13*
232 A58 20fr Coffee   1.60 .75
233 A58 40fr Cacao   2.50 1.10

1968, Nov. 23   Engr.   *Perf. 13*
234 A59 30fr "La Junon"   2.00 .70
Issued for Stamp Day.

1968, Dec. 10
Lawyer, globe and human rights flame.
235 A60 20fr blk, bl grn & car   .70 .45
International Human Rights Year.

Okanda
Gap — A61

Designs: 15fr, Barracuda. 25fr, Kinguele
Waterfall, vert. 30fr, Sitatunga trophies, vert.

1969, Mar. 28   Engr.   *Perf. 13*
236 A61 10fr brn, bl & sl grn   .35 .20
237 A61 15fr brn red, emer & ind   2.50 .50
238 A61 25fr bl, pur & ol   .75 .35
239 A61 30fr multi   1.60 .70
   Nos. 236-239 (4)   5.20 1.75
Year of African Tourism, 1969.

Mvet
(Musical
Instrument)
A62

Musical Instruments: 30fr, Ngombi harp.
50fr, Ebele and Mbe drums. 100fr, Medzang
xylophone.

1969, June 6   Engr.   *Perf. 13*
240 A62 25fr plum, ol & dp car   .50 .20
241 A62 30fr red brn, ol & dk
             brn   .50 .20
242 A62 50fr plum, ol & dp car   1.10 .65
243 A62 100fr red brn, ol & dk
             brn   2.40 1.00
   a.   Min. sheet of 4, #240-243   6.50 6.50
   Nos. 240-243 (4)   4.50 2.05

Aframomum   Tree of Life
Polyanthum   A64
(Zingiberaceae)
A63

African Plants: 2fr, Chlamydocola
chlamydantha (Sterculiaceae). 5fr, Costus din-
klagei (Zingiberaceae). 10fr, Cola rostrata
(Sterculiaceae). 20fr, Dischistocalyx
grandifolius (Acanthaceae).

1969, July 15   Photo.   *Perf. 12x12½*
244 A63 1fr multi   .20 .20
245 A63 2fr lt ol & multi   .20 .20
246 A63 5fr multi   .20 .20
247 A63 10fr slate & multi   1.10 .20
248 A63 20fr yel & multi   1.75 .70
   Nos. 244-248 (5)   3.45 1.50

1969, Aug. 17   Photo.
249 A64 25fr multi   .60 .50
National renovation.

Drilling for Oil on   Workers and
Land — A65   ILO
                           Emblem — A66

Design: 50fr, Offshore drilling station.

1969, Sept. 13   *Perf. 12x12½*
250 A65 25fr multi   .20 .20
251 A65 50fr multi   2.10 .20
   a.   Strip of 2, #250-251 + label 3.00 3.00
20th anniv. of the ELF-SPAFE oil operations
in Gabon.

1969, Oct. 29   Engr.   *Perf. 13*
252 A66 30fr bl, sl grn & dp car   .90 .45
50th anniv. of the ILO.

Arms of Port
Gentil — A67

Coats of Arms: 20fr, Lambarene. 30fr,
Libreville.

1969, Nov. 19   Photo.   *Perf. 12*
253 A67 20fr red, gold, sil & blk   1.00 .20
254 A67 25fr bl, blk & gold   1.40 .20
255 A67 30fr bl & multi   1.60 .80
   Nos. 253-255 (3)   4.00 1.20
See Nos. 267-269, 291-293, 321-326, 340-
348, 409-417, 492-501.

Canoe Mail
Transport
A68

1969, Dec. 18   Engr.   *Perf. 13*
256 A68 30fr brt grn, grnsh bl &
             red brn   1.25 .80
Issued for Stamp Day 1969.

Satellite,
Globe, TV
Screen and
ITU
Emblem
A69

1970, May 17   Engr.   *Perf. 13*
257 A69 25fr dk bl, dk red brn & blk .90 .60
International Telecommunications Day.

UPU Headquarters Issue
Common Design Type
1970, May 20   Engr.   *Perf. 13*
258 CD133 30fr brt grn, brt rose lil
             & brn   1.10 .55

Geisha and
African
Drummer
A70

1970, May 27   Photo.   *Perf. 12½x12*
259 A70 30fr ultra & multi   1.25 .60
EXPO '70 Intl. Exhibition, Osaka, Japan,
3/15-9/13.

ASECNA Issue
Common Design Type
1970, Aug. 26   Engr.   *Perf. 13*
260 CD132 100fr brt grn & bl grn 2.00 .95

UN
Emblem,
Globe,
Dove and
Charts
A71

1970, Oct. 24   Photo.   *Perf. 12½x12*
261 A71 30fr Prus bl & multi   .90 .60
25th anniversary of the United Nations.

Bushbucks
A72

Designs: 15fr, Pels scaly-tailed flying squirrel. 25fr, Gray-cheeked monkey, vert. 40fr,
African golden cat. 60fr, Sevaline genet.

1970, Dec. 14   Photo.   *Perf. 12½x13*
262 A72 5fr yel grn & multi   .60 .40
263 A72 15fr red org & blk   .95 .55
264 A72 25fr vio & multi   1.75 .80
265 A72 40fr red & multi   2.75 1.10
266 A72 60fr bl & multi   4.75 2.10
   Nos. 262-266 (5)   10.80 4.95

Coats of Arms Type of 1969
20fr, Mouila. 25fr, Bitam. 30fr, Oyem.

1971, Feb. 16   Photo.   *Perf. 12*
267 A67 20fr ver, bl, sil & gold   .90 .20
268 A67 25fr emer, gold & blk   1.00 .20
269 A67 30fr emer, gold, blk & red   1.25 .20
   Nos. 267-269 (3)   3.15 .60

Men of Four Races
and Emblem — A73

1971, Mar. 21   Engr.   *Perf. 13*
270 A73 40fr multi   .90 .45
Intl. year against racial discrimination.

Map of Africa and Telecommunications
System — A74

1971, Apr. 30   Photo.   *Perf. 13*
271 A74 30fr org & multi   .90 .45
Pan-African telecommunications system.

Charaxes
Smaragdalis — A75

Butterflies: 10fr, Euxanthe crossleyi. 15fr,
Epiphora rectifascia. 25fr, Imbrasia bouvieri.

1971, May 26 Photo. *Perf. 13*

272	A75	5fr yel & multi	2.40 .80
273	A75	10fr bl & multi	5.00 1.00
274	A75	15fr grn & multi	9.00 1.10
275	A75	25fr ol & multi	11.50 2.00
		Nos. 272-275 (4)	27.90 4.90

Hertzian Center, Nkol Ogoum A76

1971, June 17 Engr. *Perf. 13*

276	A76	40fr grn, blk & dk car	1.10 .70

3rd World Telecommunications Day.

Mother Nursing Child A77

1971, Aug. 17 Engr. *Perf. 13*

277	A77	30fr lil rose, sep & ocher	.90 .45

Gabonese social security system, 15th anniv.

UN Headquarters and Emblem — A78

1971, Sept. 30 Photo. *Perf. 13*

278	A78	30fr red & multi	.90 .45

10th anniv. of Gabon's admission to the UN.

Large Egret — A79

Birds: 40fr, African gray parrot. 50fr, Woodland Kingfisher. 75fr, Cameroon bareheaded rock-fowl. 100fr, Gold Coast touraco.

1971, Oct. 12 Litho. *Perf. 13*

279	A79	30fr multi	2.25 1.10
280	A79	40fr multi	3.00 1.50
281	A79	50fr multi	3.25 1.60
282	A79	75fr multi	4.50 2.10
283	A79	100fr multi	6.25 2.50
		Nos. 279-283 (5)	19.25 8.80

Asystasia Volgeliana A80

Designs: Flowers of Acanthus Family after paintings by Noel Hallé.

1972, Apr. 4 Photo. *Perf. 13*

284	A80	5fr pale cit & multi	.20 .20
285	A80	10fr multi	.50 .20
286	A80	20fr multi	.75 .60
287	A80	30fr lil rose & multi	1.10 .70
288	A80	40fr dk grn & multi	1.90 1.00
289	A80	65fr red & multi	3.25 1.40
		Nos. 284-289 (6)	7.70 4.00

Louis Pasteur — A81

1972, May 15 Engr. *Perf. 13*

290	A81	80fr dp org, pur & grn	1.25 .60

Sesquicentennial of the birth of Louis Pasteur (1822-1895), scientist and bacteriologist.

Arms Type of 1969

30fr, Franceville. 40fr, Makokou. 60fr, Tchibanga.

1972, June 2 Photo. *Perf. 12*

291	A67	30fr sil & multi	.75 .20
292	A67	40fr grn & multi	.75 .50
293	A67	60fr blk, grn & sil	1.60 .75
		Nos. 291-293 (3)	3.10 1.45

Globe and Telecommunications Symbols — A81a

1972, July 25 *Perf. 13x12½*

294	A81a	40fr blk, yel & org	.90 .45

4th World Telecommunications Day.

Nat King Cole — A82

Black American Jazz Musicians: 60fr, Sidney Bechet. 100fr, Louis Armstrong.

1972, Sept. 1 Photo. *Perf. 13x13½*

295	A82	40fr bl & multi	1.60 .35
296	A82	60fr org & multi	2.40 .70
297	A82	100fr multi	4.00 1.10
		Nos. 295-297 (3)	8.00 2.15

Blanding's Rear-fanged Snake — A83

Designs: 2fr, Beauty snake. 3fr, Eggeating snake. 15fr, Striped ground snake. 25fr, Jameson's mamba. 50fr, Gabon viper.

1972, Oct. 2 Litho. *Perf. 13*

298	A83	1fr lem & multi	.20 .20
299	A83	2fr red brn & multi	.20 .20
300	A83	3fr brn org & multi	.50 .20
301	A83	15fr multi	1.90 .50
302	A83	25fr grn & multi	3.75 .55
303	A83	50fr multi	5.75 1.00
		Nos. 298-303 (6)	12.30 2.65

See Nos. 330-332, 354-357.

Dr. Armauer G. Hansen, Lambarene Leprosarium — A84

1973, Jan. 28 Engr. *Perf. 13*

304	A84	30fr Prus grn, sl grn & brn	1.25 .55

Centenary of the discovery of the Hansen bacillus, the cause of leprosy.

Charaxes Candiope — A85

Designs: Various butterflies.

1973, Feb. 23 Litho. *Perf. 13*

305	A85	10fr *shown*	2.50 .40
306	A85	15fr *Eunica pechueli*	3.00 .40
307	A85	20fr *Cyrestis camillus*	5.00 .85
308	A85	30fr *Charaxes castor*	6.75 1.25
309	A85	40fr *Charaxes ameliae*	8.00 1.75
310	A85	50fr *Pseudacrea boisduvali*	8.75 2.10
		Nos. 305-310 (6)	34.00 6.75

Balloon of Santos-Dumont, 1901 — A86

History of Aviation: 1fr, Montgolfier's balloon, 1783, vert. 3fr, Octave Chanute's biplane, 1896. 4fr, Clement Ader's Plane III, 1897. 5fr, Louis Bleriot crossing the Channel, 1909. 10fr, Fabre's hydroplane, 1910.

1973, May 3 Engr. *Perf. 13*

311	A86	1fr grn, sl grn & dk red	.20 .20
312	A86	2fr sl grn & brt bl	.20 .20
313	A86	3fr bl, sl & org	.20 .20
314	A86	4fr lil & dk pur	.75 .20
315	A86	5fr slate grn & org	1.10 .35
316	A86	10fr rose lil & Prus bl	2.10 .50
		Nos. 311-316 (6)	4.55 1.65

1977 Coil Stamp

316A	A86	10fr aqua	3.50 .20

No. 316A has red control numbers on back of every 10th stamp.

INTERPOL Emblem — A87

1973, June 26 Engr. *Perf. 13*

317	A87	40fr magenta & ultra	.90 .40

50th anniversary of the International Criminal Police Organization (INTERPOL).

Earth Station "2 Decembre" A88

1973, July 2 Engr. *Perf. 13*

318	A88	40fr slate grn, bl & brn	.90 .40

Party Headquarters, Libreville — A89

1973, Aug. 17 Photo.

319	A89	30fr multi	.90 .20

African Postal Union Issue
Common Design Type

1973, Sept. 12 Engr. *Perf. 13*

320	CD137	100fr red lil, pur & bl	1.25 .75

Arms Type of 1969

5fr, Gamba. 10fr, Ogowe-Lolo. 15fr, Fougamou. 30fr, Kango. 40fr, Booue. 60fr, Koula-Moutou.

1973-74 Photo. *Perf. 12*

321	A67	5fr bl & multi ('74)	.65 .20
322	A67	10fr blk, red & gold ('74)	.65 .20
323	A67	15fr grn & multi ('74)	.90 .20
324	A67	30fr red & multi	1.60 .50
325	A67	40fr red & multi	1.90 .55
326	A67	60fr emer & multi	3.00 .70
		Nos. 321-326 (6)	8.70 2.20

Issued #321-323, 2/13; #324-326, 10/4.

St. Teresa of Lisieux — A90

40fr, St. Teresa and Jesus carrying cross.

1973, Dec. 4 Photo. *Perf. 13*

327	A90	30fr blk & multi	.90 .20
328	A90	40fr blk & multi	1.10 .35

St. Teresa of the Infant Jesus (Thérèse Martin, 1873-97), Carmelite nun.

Human Rights Flame — A91

1973, Dec. 10 Engr.

329	A91	20fr grn, red & ultra	.60 .20

25th anniversary of the Universal Declaration of Human Rights.

Wildlife Type of 1972

Monkeys: 40fr, Mangabey. 60fr, Cercopithecus cephus. 80fr, Mona monkey.

1974, Mar. 20 Litho. *Perf. 14*

330	A83	40fr gray grn & multi	1.50 .65
331	A83	60fr lt bl & multi	2.50 .80
332	A83	80fr lil rose & multi	4.00 1.25
		Nos. 330-332 (3)	8.00 2.70

Ogowe River at Lambarene A93

50fr, Cape Estérias. 75fr, Poubara rope bridge.

1974, July 30   Photo.   Perf. 13x13½
333	A93	30fr multi	.60	.20
334	A93	50fr multi	.80	.20
335	A93	75fr multi	1.75	.90
		Nos. 333-335 (3)	3.15	1.30

Manioc
A94

Design: 50fr, Palms and dates.

1974, Nov. 13   Photo.   Perf. 13x12½
336	A94	40fr org red & multi	.90	.30
337	A94	50fr bister & multi	1.10	.30

UDEAC Issue

Presidents and Flags of Cameroun,
CAR, Congo, Gabon and Meeting
Center — A95

1974, Dec. 8   Photo.   Perf. 13
338	A95	40fr multi	.70	.30

See No. C156.

Hôtel du Dialogue — A96

1975, Jan. 20   Photo.   Perf. 13
339	A96	50fr multi	.90	.45

Opening of Hôtel du Dialogue.

Arms Type of 1969

5fr, Ogowe-Ivindo. 10fr, Moabi. #342, Moanda. #343, Nyanga. 25fr, Mandji. #345, Mekambo. #346, Omboué. 60fr, Minvoul. 90fr, Mayumba.

1975-77   Photo.   Perf. 12
340	A67	5fr red & multi	.20	.20
341	A67	10fr gold & multi	.20	.20
342	A67	15fr red, sil & blk	.45	.20
343	A67	15fr bl & multi	.35	.20
344	A67	25fr grn & multi	.45	.20
345	A67	50fr blk, gold & red	1.40	.35
346	A67	50fr multi	1.50	.60
347	A67	60fr multi	1.40	.60
348	A67	90fr multi	1.90	.75
		Nos. 340-348 (9)	7.85	3.30

Issued: #340-342, Jan. 21, 1975; #343-345, Aug. 17, 1976; #346-348, July 12, 1977.

Map of Africa with Lion's Head, and
Lions Emblem — A97

1975, May 2   Typo.   Perf. 13
349	A97	50fr grn & multi	.90	.30

Lions Club 17th congress, District 403, Libreville.

Hertzian
Wave
Transmitter
Network,
Map of
Gabon
A98

1975, July 8   Engr.   Perf. 13
350	A98	40fr multi	.90	.60

City and Rural Women, Car, Train and
Building — A99

1975, July 22   Engr.   Perf. 13
351	A99	50fr car, bl & brn	2.10	.80

International Women's Year 1975.

Scoutmaster Ange Mba, Emblems and
Rope — A100

Design: 50fr, Hand holding rope, Scout, camp, Boy Scout and Nordjamb 75 emblems.

1975, July 29
352	A100	40fr multi	.60	.30
353	A100	50fr grn, red & dk brn	.90	.40

Nordjamb 75, 14th Boy Scout Jamboree, Lillehammer, Norway, July 29-Aug. 7.

Wildlife Type of 1972

Fish: 30fr, Lutjanus goreensis. 40fr, Galeoides decadactylus. 50fr, Sardinella aurita. 120fr, Scarus hoefleri.

1975, Sept. 22   Litho.   Perf. 14
354	A83	30fr multi	.75	.30
355	A83	40fr multi	1.25	.50
356	A83	50fr multi	1.75	.50
357	A83	120fr multi	3.25	1.25
		Nos. 354-357 (4)	7.00	2.55

Agro-Industrial Complex — A102

1975, Dec. 15   Litho.   Perf. 12½
358	A102	60fr multi	1.00	.50

Inauguration of Agro-Industrial Complex, Franceville.

Tchibanga Bridge — A103

Bridges of Gabon: 10fr, Mouila. 40fr, Kango. 50fr, Lambaréné, vert.

1976, Jan. 30   Engr.   Perf. 13
359	A103	5fr multi	.20	.20
360	A103	10fr multi	.35	.20
361	A103	40fr multi	.80	.30
362	A103	50fr multi	1.10	.45
		Nos. 359-362 (4)	2.45	1.15

Telephones 1876 and 1976, Satellite,
A. G. Bell — A104

1976, Mar. 10   Engr.   Perf. 13
363	A104	60fr dk bl, grn & sl grn	.90	.40

Centenary of first telephone call by Alexander Graham Bell, Mar. 10, 1876.

Msgr. Jean Remy Bessieux — A105

1976, Apr. 30   Engr.   Perf. 13
364	A105	50fr grn, bl & sepia	.90	.45

Death centenary of Msgr. Bessieux.

Athletes, Torch, Map of Africa, Games
Emblem — A106

1976, June 25   Photo.   Perf. 13x12½
365	A106	50fr multi	.70	.20
366	A106	60fr org & multi	.90	.30

First Central African Games (Zone 5), Libreville, June-July.

Motobécane, France — A107

Motorcycles: 5fr, Bultaco, Spain. 10fr, Suzuki, Japan. 20fr, Kawasaki, Japan. 100fr, Harley-Davidson, US.

1976, July 20   Litho.   Perf. 12½
367	A107	3fr multi	.40	.25
368	A107	5fr org & multi	.40	.25
369	A107	10fr bl & multi	.70	.30
370	A107	20fr multi	1.25	.30
371	A107	100fr car & multi	4.50	1.00
		Nos. 367-371 (5)	7.25	2.10

Rice
A108

1976, Oct. 15   Litho.   Perf. 13x13½
372	A108	50fr shown	.90	.35
373	A108	60fr Pepper plants	1.10	.55

1977, Apr. 22   Litho.   Perf. 13x13½

50fr, Banana plantation. 60fr, Peanut market.

374	A108	50fr multi	.90	.35
375	A108	60fr multi	1.10	.55

Telecommunications Emblem and
Telephone — A109

1977, May 17   Perf. 13
376	A109	60fr multi	.90	.50

World Telecommunications Day.

View of
Oyem
A110

50fr, Cape Lopez. 70fr, Lebamba Cave.

1977, June 9   Litho.   Perf. 12½
377	A110	50fr multi	.70	.30
378	A110	60fr multi	.75	.40
379	A110	70fr multi	.85	.45
		Nos. 377-379 (3)	2.30	1.15

Conference Hall — A111

1977, June 23   Photo.   Perf. 13x12½
380	A111	100fr multi	1.40	.75

Meeting of the OAU, Libreville.

Arms of
Gabon — A112

1977   Engr.   Perf. 13

Size: 23x36mm
381	A112	50fr blue	1.25	.50

Size: 17x23mm
382	A112	60fr orange	1.10	.50
a.		Booklet pane of 5	6.00	
383	A112	80fr red	1.60	.65
		Nos. 381-383 (3)	3.95	1.65

#381 issued in coils, #382 in booklets only.
Issued: #381-382, June 23; #383, Sept.

Modern Buildings, Libreville — A113

1977, Aug. 17   Litho.   Perf. 12
387	A113	50fr multi	.90	.20

National Festival 1977.

Paris to Vienna, 1902 — A114

Renault Automobiles: 10fr, Coupé 1 2 CV, 1921. 30fr, Torpédo Scaphandrier, 1925. 40fr, Reinastella 40 CV, 1929. 100fr, Nerva Grand Sport, 1937. 150fr, Voiturette 1 CV, 1899. 200fr, Alpine Renault V6, 1977.

1977, Aug 30   **Engr.**   *Perf. 13*
388 A114   5fr multi   .50   .35
389 A114   10fr multi   .50   .35
390 A114   30fr multi   1.25   .50
391 A114   40fr multi   2.10   .60
392 A114   100fr multi   5.25   2.25
    Nos. 388-392 (5)   9.60   4.05

Miniature Sheet
393   Sheet of 2 + label   18.00   18.00
  a.   A114 150fr multi   5.25   5.25
  b.   A114 200fr multi   7.00   7.00

Louis Renault, French automobile pioneer, birth centenary. Nos. 383a-393b are perf. on 3 sides, without perforation between stamps and center label showing dark brown portrait of Renault.
See Nos. 395-400.

Globe
A115

1978, Feb. 21   **Engr.**   *Perf. 13x12½*
394 A115 80fr multi   .90   .60

World Leprosy Day.

Automobile Type of 1977

Citroen Cars: 10fr, Cabriolet, 1922. 50fr, Taxi, 1927. 60fr, Berline, 1932. 80fr, Berline, 1934. 150fr, Torpedo, 1919. 200fr, Berline, 1948. 250fr, Pallas, 1975.

1978, May 9   **Engr.**   *Perf. 13*
395 A114   10fr multi   .80   .35
396 A114   50fr multi   1.50   .45
397 A114   60fr multi   2.50   .95
398 A114   80fr multi   2.50   .95
399 A114   200fr multi   6.75   2.25
    Nos. 395-399 (5)   14.05   4.95

Miniature Sheet
400   Sheet of 2   18.00   18.00
  a.   A114 150fr multi   5.25   5.25
  b.   A114 250fr multi   7.00   7.00

Andre Citroen (1878-1935), automobile designer and manufacturer.

Ndjole on Ogowe River — A116

Views: 40fr, Lambarene lake district. 50fr, Owendo Harbor.

1978, May 17   **Litho.**   *Perf. 12½*
401 A116   30fr multi   .40   .20
402 A116   40fr multi   .70   .20
403 A116   50fr multi   .90   .35
    Nos. 401-403 (3)   2.00   .75

Sternotomis
Mirabilis — A117

Anti-Apartheid
Emblem — A118

Various Coleopteras.

1978, June 21   **Photo.**   *Perf. 12½x13*
404 A117   20fr multi   .75   .30
405 A117   60fr multi   3.00   .65
406 A117   75fr multi   3.75   .75
407 A117   80fr multi   4.50   1.25
    Nos. 404-407 (4)   12.00   2.95

1978, July 25   **Engr.**   *Perf. 13*
408 A118 80fr multi   .90   .60

Arms Type of 1969
1978-80   **Photo.**   *Perf. 12*
409 A67   5fr Oyem   .20   .20
410 A67   5fr Ogowe-Maritime
    ('79)   .20   .20
411 A67   10fr Lastoursville ('79)   .20   .20
412 A67   10fr Haut-Ogooue ('80)   .20   .20
413 A67   15fr M'Bigou ('79)   .20   .20
414 A67   20fr Estuaire ('80)   .20   .20
415 A67   30fr Bitam ('80)   .20   .20
416 A67   40fr Okondja   1.10   .20
417 A67   60fr Mimongo   1.60   .40
    Nos. 409-417 (9)   4.10   2.00

A119

1978, Oct. 24   **Engr.**   *Perf. 13*
419 A119 80fr multi   1.10   .65

UNESCO campaign to save the Acropolis.

Penicillin Formula, — A120

1978, Nov. 21   **Engr.**   *Perf. 13*
420 A120 90fr multi   2.40   1.10

Alexander Fleming's discovery of antibiotics, 50th anniversary.

The
Visitation — A121

80fr, Massacre of the Innocents. Woodcarvings from St. Michael's Church, Libreville.

1978, Dec. 15   **Photo.**
421 A121   60fr gold & multi   .90   .40
422 A121   80fr gold & multi   1.10   .50

Christmas 1978. See Nos. 437-438.

Train and
Map
A122

1978, Dec. 27   **Litho.**   *Perf. 12½*
423 A122 60fr multi   1.50   .60

Inauguration of Trans-Gabon Railroad, Libreville to Njolé.

A123

Pre-Olympic Year (Kremlin Towers, Olympic Emblem, Ancestral Figure and): 80fr, Long jump, vert. 100fr, Yachts.

1979, May 15   **Engr.**   *Perf. 13*
424 A123   60fr multi   .60   .30
425 A123   80fr multi   .75   .40
426 A123   100fr multi   .95   .55
  a.   Miniature sheet of 3, #424-426   3.75   3.75
    Nos. 424-426 (3)   2.30   1.25

Rowland Hill, Messenger and Gabon
No. O9 — A124

Allamanda
Schottii
A125

Designs: 80fr, Bakota mask and tulip tree flowers, vert. 150fr, Pigeon, UPU emblem, truck and canoe. No. 430b, Gloriosa superba. No. 430c, Phaeomeria magnifica, vert. No. 430d, Berlinia bracteosa, vert.

1979, June 8   **Photo.**   *Perf. 13*
427 A124   50fr multi   1.10   1.10
428 A124   80fr multi   2.00   1.25

Engr.
429 A124   150fr multi   3.25   2.00
    Nos. 427-429 (3)   6.35   4.35

Souvenir Sheet
    Photo.   *Perf. 14*
430   Sheet of 4   11.00   11.00
  a.   A125 100fr multicolored   2.00
  b.   A125 100fr multicolored   2.00
  c.   A125 100fr multicolored   2.00
  d.   A125 100fr multicolored   2.00

Philexafrique II, Libreville, June 8-17. Nos. 427-429 each printed in sheets of 10 with 5 labels showing exhibition emblem. No. 427 also commemorates Sir Rowland Hill (1795-1879), originator of penny postage. No. 430 has label with exhibition emblem.

IYC Emblem,
Globe, Child with
Bird — A126

1979, June 15   **Engr.**   *Perf. 13*
431 A126 100fr multi   1.40   .70

International Year of the Child.

"TELECOM
79" — A127

1979, Sept. 18   **Litho.**   *Perf. 13x12½*
432 A127 80fr multi   1.00   .40

3rd World Telecommunications Exhibition, Geneva, Sept. 20-26.

Sugar Cane
Harvest — A128

1979, Oct. 9   **Photo.**   *Perf. 12½x13*
433 A128   25fr shown   .45   .20
434 A128   30fr Yams   .65   .20

Judo
Throw — A129

1979, Oct. 23   **Engr.**   *Perf. 13*
435 A129 40fr multi   1.60   .55

World Judo Championships, Paris, Dec.

Mother and Child, Map of Congo River
Basin — A130

1979, Dec. 2   **Litho.**   *Perf. 12*
436 A130 200fr multi   2.50   .80

Medical Week, Dec. 2-9.

Christmas Type of 1978

Wood Carvings, St. Michael's Church, Libreville: 60fr, Flight into Egypt. 80fr, The Circumcision.

1979, Dec. 12   Photo.   Perf. 13
437   A121   60fr multi   .90   .40
438   A121   80fr multi   1.10   .40

Pres. Omar
Bongo — A131

1979-80   Litho.   Perf. 12½
439   A131   60fr multi   .90   .40
440   A131   80fr multi   2.50   1.25

Bongo's 44th birthday (#439); re-election and inauguration (#440).
Issued: 60fr, 12/30/79; 80fr, 2/27/80.

OPEC, 20th
Anniv. — A132

1980, Mar. 27   Litho.   Perf. 13½x13
441   A132   50fr multi   1.10   .35

Donguila Church — A133

1980 Apr. 3   Litho.   Perf. 12½
442   A133   60fr shown   .65   .30
443   A133   80fr Bizengobibere
         Church   .85   .35

Easter 1980.

De Brazza
(1852-1905),
Map of Gabon
with Franceville
A134

1980, June 30   Litho.   Perf. 12½
444   A134   165fr multi   2.50   1.10

Franceville Foundation centenary, founded by Savorgnan De Brazza.

20th Anniversary of
Independence — A135

1980, Aug. 17   Photo.   Perf. 13
445   A135   60fr Leon Mba and
         Omar Bongo   .90   .25

World Tourism Conference, Manila,
Sept. 27 — A136

1980, Sept. 10   Engr.
446   A136   80fr multi   .90   .35

20th
Anniversary
of OPEC
A137

1980, Sept. 15   Litho.   Perf. 12½
447   A137   90fr shown   1.00   .40
448   A137   120fr Men Holding
         OPEC emblem,
         vert.   1.50   .60

Pseudochelidon
Eurystomina
A138

1980, Oct. 15   Photo.   Perf. 14x14½
449   A138   50fr shown   3.00   .80
450   A138   60fr Merops nubicus   3.50   1.10
451   A138   80fr Pitta angolensis   4.75   1.60
452   A138   150fr Scotopelia peli   7.50   2.75
         Nos. 449-452 (4)   18.75   6.25

Statue of Bull,
Bizengobibere
Church — A139

1980, Dec. 10   Photo.   Perf. 14x14½
453   A139   60fr shown   .75   .35
454   A139   80fr Male statue   1.25   .55

Christmas 1980.

Heinrich von
Stephan — A140

1981, Jan. 7   Engr.   Perf. 13
455   A140   90fr brn & dk brn   .90   .35

Von Stephan (1831-97), UPU founder.

13th Anniversary of National
Renovation Movement — A141

1981, Mar. 12   Litho.   Perf. 13x12½
456   A141   60fr multi   .70   .25

Lion Statue,
Bizangobibere
A142

1981, Apr. 12   Photo.   Perf. 14x14½
457   A142   75fr multi   .90   .40
458   A142   100fr multi   1.10   .55

Easter 1981.

Port Gentil Lions
Club
Banner — A143

1981, May 1   Litho.   Perf. 12½
459   A143   60fr shown   .75   .25
460   A143   75fr District 403   .85   .30
461   A143   80fr Libreville Coco-
         tiers   1.10   .35
462   A143   100fr Libreville Hibis-
         cus   1.40   .40
463   A143   165fr Ekwata   2.10   .70
464   A143   200fr Haut-Ogooue   2.40   .90
         Nos. 459-464 (6)   8.60   2.90

Lions International, 23rd Congress of District 403, Libreville, May 1-3.

13th World Telecommunications
Day — A144

1981, May 17   Photo.   Perf. 13
465   A144   125fr multi   1.60   .55

Unity, Work
and Justice
A145

R.P. Klaine
(Missionary), 70th
Death Anniv.
A146

1981-96?   Photo.   Perf. 13
466   A145   5fr beige & blk   .20   .20
467   A145   10fr pale lil & blk   .20   .20
468   A145   15fr brt yel grn &
         blk   .20   .20
469   A145   20fr pink & blk   .20   .20
470   A145   25fr vio & blk   .20   .20
471   A145   40fr red org & blk   .45   .20
472   A145   50fr bluish grn & blk   .55   .20
473   A145   75fr bis brn & blk   .70   .25
473A   A145   90fr lt bl & blk ('83)   .70   .25
474   A145   100fr yel & blk   1.00   .40
474A   A145   125fr grn & blk ('83)   1.10   .35
474B   A145   150fr brt pink & blk
         ('86)   1.25   .40
474C   A145   175fr grnish bl & blk
         ('96)   .55   .55
         Nos. 466-474B (12)   6.75   3.05

See Nos. 862-871.

1981, July 2   Litho.

90fr, Archbishop Walker, 110th birth anniv.
475   A146   70fr multi   .80   .30
476   A146   90fr multi   1.25   .35

Map of Gabon
and Scout
Sign — A147

Intl. Year of the
Disabled — A148

1981, July 16   Perf. 12½
477   A147   75fr multi   1.00   .35

4th Pan-African Scouting Congress, Abidjan, Aug.

No. 477 Overprinted: DAKAR / 28e
CONFERENCE / MONDIALE DU /
SCOUTISME

1981, July 23
478   A147   75fr multi   1.50   .45

28th World Scouting Conf., Dakar, Aug.

1981, Aug. 6   Engr.   Perf. 13
479   A148   100fr multi   1.10   .45

Hypolimnas
Salmacis
A149

1981, Sept. 10 Litho. Perf. 14½x14
480 A149 75fr shown   2.00 .70
481 A149 100fr Euphaedra
                  themis   2.50 1.00
482 A149 150fr Amauris niavi-
                  us   3.50 1.50
483 A149 250fr Cymothoe lu-
                  casi   6.00 2.25
    Nos. 480-483 (4)   14.00 5.45

Paul as
Harlequin, by
Pablo Picasso
(1881-1973)
A150

1981, Sept. 25   Perf. 14½x13½
484 A150 500fr multi   7.00 2.50

World Food Day — A151

1981, Oct. 16   Engr.   Perf. 13
485 A151 350fr multi   4.00 1.60

Traditional
Hairstyle — A152

Designs: Various hairstyles.

1981, Nov. 12 Litho. Perf. 14½x15
486 A152 75fr multi   1.10 .55
487 A152 100fr multi   1.25 .50
488 A152 125fr multi   1.90 .80
489 A152 200fr multi   3.00 1.10
 a. Souvenir sheet of 4, #486-489   7.50 7.50
    Nos. 486-489 (4)   7.25 2.95
    See Nos. 609A-609B, 676.

Christmas
1981
A153

Designs: Children's drawings.

1981, Dec. 10   Perf. 14½x14
490 A153 75fr Girls dancing .90 .35
491 A153 100fr Dinner   1.25 .50

Arms Type of 1969
Perf. 12, 13 (#495-497)
1982-92   Photo.
492 A67 75fr Moyen-Ogooue   .70 .20
493 A67 90fr Cocobeach   .90 .25
494 A67 100fr Woleu-N'tem   1.00 .25
495 A67 100fr Lambarene   .90 .30
496 A67 100fr Port Gentil Dis-
                  trict   .90 .35
497 A67 100fr Medoueneu   .90 .35
498 A67 125fr Mouila   1.25 .35
499 A67 135fr N'Djole   1.40 .40
500 A67 150fr N'Gounie   1.50 .40
501 A67 160fr Leconi   1.40 .60
    Nos. 492-501 (10)   10.85 3.45

Issued: #492, 494, 500, 1/13/82; #493, 498, 499, 8/7/84; #496, 4/17/91; #497, 8/12/82.

A154

1982, Feb. 16   Litho.   Perf. 13
502 A154 100fr multi   2.40 1.10
    Visit of Pope John Paul II, Feb. 17-19.

A155

1982, Mar. 31   Engr.   Perf. 13
503 A155 75fr black   .80 .30
    Alfred de Musset (1810-1857), writer.

Merchant
Navy Ships
A156

1982, Apr. 7   Litho.   Perf. 14½x14
504 A156 75fr Timber carrier .75 .30
505 A156 100fr Freighter   1.00 .40
506 A156 200fr Oil tanker   2.00 .85
    Nos. 504-506 (3)   3.75 1.55
    See Nos. 588, 599.

TB Bacillus Centenary — A157

1982, Apr. 24   Litho.   Perf. 13
507 A157 100fr multi   1.60 .50

PHILEXFRANCE
'82 Stamp
Exhibition, Paris,
June 11-
21 — A158

1982, Apr. 28   Perf. 12½
508 A158 100fr Rope bridge   .85 .40
509 A158 200fr Sculptured head 1.90 .55
 a. Pair, #508-509 + label   4.00 2.75

14th World Telecommunications
Day — A159

1982, May 17   Perf. 13
510 A159 75fr multi   .90 .40

1982 World
Cup — A160

Designs: Various soccer players.

1982, May 19   Perf. 14x14½
511 A160 100fr multi   1.00 .40
512 A160 125fr multi   1.10 .45
513 A160 200fr multi   2.10 .75
 a. Souvenir sheet of 3, #511-513,
      perf. 14½   5.00 5.00
    Nos. 511-513 (3)   4.20 1.00
    For overprints see Nos. 516-518.

2nd UN Conf. on Peaceful Uses of
Outer Space, Vienna, Aug. 9-
21 — A161

1982, July 7   Engr.   Perf. 13
514 A161 250fr Satellites   2.75 1.25

White
Carnations
A162

Designs: Various carnations.

1982, June 9 Photo. Perf. 14½x14
515   Strip of 3   5.00 4.25
 a. A162 75fr multi   .90 .45
 b. A162 100fr multi   1.10 .50
 c. A162 175fr multi   2.25 1.00

Nos. 511-513a Overprinted in Red
with Semi-Finalists or Finalists

1982, Aug. 19 Litho. Perf. 14x14½
516 A160 100fr multi   1.00 .35
517 A160 125fr multi   1.10 .45
518 A160 200fr multi   2.10 .75
 a. Souvenir sheet of 3   5.00 5.00
    Nos. 516-518 (3)   4.20 1.55

Italy's victory in 1982 World Cup.

Phyllonotus
Duplex
A163

1982, Sept. 22   Perf. 14½x14
519 A163 75fr shown   1.40 .50
520 A163 100fr Chama crenulata 1.75 .65
521 A163 125fr Cardium hians 2.50 1.25
    Nos. 519-521 (3)   5.65 2.40

Okouyi
Mask — A164

1982, Oct. 13   Litho.   Perf. 14x14½
522 A164 75fr shown   .65 .30
523 A164 100fr Ondoumbo reli-
                  quary   1.10 .40
524 A164 150fr Tsogho statuette 1.90 .55
525 A164 250fr Fang bellows 2.75 .95
    Nos. 522-525 (4)   6.40 2.20

Christmas
1982 — A165

1983, Dec. 15   Litho.   Perf. 14x14½
526 A165 100fr St. Francis Xavier
                  Church   .90 .35

Trans-Gabon Railroad
Inauguration — A166

1983, Jan. 18   Perf. 12½
527 A166 75fr multi   2.00 .50

5th African Highway Conference,
Libreville, Feb. 6-11 — A167

1983, Feb. 2   Perf. 13
528 A167 100fr multi   .90 .35

15th Anniv. of Natl.
Renewal — A168

Provincial Symbols: a. Bakota mask, Ogowe Ivindo. b. Butterfly, Ogowe Lolo. c. Buffalo, Nyanga. d. Isogho hairdo, Ngounie. e. Tarpon, Ogowe Maritime. f. Manganese, Haut Ogowe. g. Crocodiles, Moyen Ogowe. h. Coffee plant. i. Epitorium trochiformis.

1983, Mar. 12   Litho.   Perf. 13x13½
529   Strip of 9 + label 17.50 15.00
 a. A168 75fr multi   1.00 .45
 b. A168 90fr multi   1.25 .50
 c. A168 90fr multi   1.25 .50
 d. A168 100fr multi   1.40 .60
 e. A168 125fr multi   1.60 .75
 f. A168 125fr multi   1.60 .75
 g. A168 125fr multi   1.60 .75
 h. A168 135fr multi   1.90 .85
 i. A168 135fr multi   1.90 .85

25th Anniv. of Intl. Maritime
Org. — A169

1983, Mar. 17   *Perf. 13*
530 A169 125fr multi   1.40 .50

Pelican
A170

1983, Apr. 20   **Litho.**   *Perf. 15x14½*
531 A170 90fr Water musk
       deer   .90 .35
532 A170 125fr shown   1.25 .45
533 A170 225fr Elephant   3.25 .85
534 A170 400fr Iguana   4.50 1.50
   a. Souv. sheet of 4, #531-534   16.00 16.00
     Nos. 531-534 (4)   9.90 3.15

25th Anniv.
of UN
Economic
Commission
for Africa
A171

1983, Apr. 29   **Litho.**   *Perf. 12½*
535 A171 125fr multi   1.25 .50

15th World Telecommunications
Day — A172

1983, May 17   **Litho.**   *Perf. 13*
536 A172 90fr multi   1.40 .55
537 A172 90fr multi   1.40 .55
   a. Pair, #536-537   4.00 4.00

Denomination of No. 536 in lower right, No.
537, upper left.

Nkoltang Earth Satellite
Station — A173

1983, July 2
538 A173 125fr multi   1.25 .50
    10th anniv. of station; WCY.

Ivindo River Rapids — A174

1983, Sept. 7   **Engr.**   *Perf. 13*
539 A174 90fr shown   .85 .35
540 A174 125fr Ogooue River   1.40 .60
541 A174 185fr Wonga Wongue
       Preserve   2.00 .80
542 A174 350fr Coastal view   3.75 1.50
     Nos. 539-542 (4)   8.00 3.25

Hand Drum,
Mahongwe
A175

Harmful
Insects — A176

1983, Oct. 12   **Litho.**   *Perf. 14x14½*
543 A175 90fr shown   .90 .35
544 A175 125fr Okoukoue dancer 1.40 .45
545 A175 135fr Four-stringed fid-
       dle   1.50 .60
546 A175 260fr Ndoumou dancer 3.00 1.10
     Nos. 543-546 (4)   6.80 2.50

1983, Nov. 9
547 A176 90fr Glossinidae   1.60 .80
548 A176 125fr Belonogaster
       junceus   2.00 1.10
549 A176 300fr Aedes aegypti   4.25 1.60
550 A176 350fr Mylabris   5.25 2.10
     Nos. 547-550 (4)   13.10 5.60

Christmas
1983 — A177

Wood Carvings, St. Michael's Church,
Libreville.

      Perf. 14½x13½
1983, Dec. 14   **Litho.**
551 A177 90fr Adultress   .80 .35
552 A177 125fr Good Samaritan 1.40 .65

Boeing 737, No. 202 — A178

1984, Jan. 12   *Perf. 13x12½*
553 A178 125fr shown   1.50 .40
554 A178 225fr Lufthansa jet,
       Germany No.
       C2   3.00 .70
   a. Pair, #553-554 + label   5.50 4.75

    19th World UPU Congress, Hamburg, June
19-26.

3rd Anniv. of Africa 1 Radio
Transmitter — A179

1984, Feb. 7   **Litho.**   *Perf. 12½*
555 A179 125fr multi   1.25 .35

Local
Flowers — A180

Various flowers.

1984, Apr. 18   **Litho.**   *Perf. 14x15*
556 A180 90fr multi   1.40 .45
557 A180 125fr multi   1.60 .55
558 A180 135fr multi   2.10 .65
559 A180 350fr multi   4.50 1.60
     Nos. 556-559 (4)   9.60 3.25

Fruit Trees
A181

1984, Mar. 1   **Litho.**   *Perf. 14½x14*
560 A181 90fr Coconut   1.40 .45
561 A181 100fr Papaya   1.40 .55
562 A181 125fr Mango   1.90 .65
563 A181 250fr Banana   3.75 .85
     Nos. 560-563 (4)   8.45 2.50

World Telecommunications
Day — A182

1984, May 17   *Perf. 13x13½*
564 A182 125fr multi   1.25 .45

Black Jazz
Musicians
A183

1984, July 5   *Perf. 12½*
565 A183 90fr Lionel Hampton 1.75 .70
566 A183 125fr Charlie Parker   2.40 .70
567 A183 260fr Erroll Garner   3.75 1.75
     Nos. 565-567 (3)   7.90 3.15

View of Medouneu — A184

1984, Sept. 1   **Litho.**   *Perf. 13*
568 A184 90fr shown   .95 .40
569 A184 125fr Canoes, Ogooue
       River   1.50 .55
570 A184 165fr Railroad   2.50 1.25
     Nos. 568-570 (3)   4.95 2.20

15th World UPU
Day — A185

1984, Oct. 9   **Litho.**   *Perf. 13½*
571 A185 125fr UPU emblem,
       globe, mail   1.40 .50

40th Anniv., International Civil Aviation
Organization — A186

1984, Dec. 1   **Litho.**   *Perf. 13½*
572 A186 125fr Icarus   1.40 .50

Masks — A186a

1984, Oct. 30   **Litho.**   *Perf. 14x15*
572A A186a 90fr Kouele   — —
572B A186a 125fr Eventail Pou-
       nou   — —
572C A186a 150fr Reliquaire
       Mahongoue   — —
572D A186a 250fr Kota du Sud   — —

Christmas — A187

1984, Dec. 14   **Litho.**   *Perf. 12½*
573 A187 90fr St. Michael's
       Church Libreville .90 .45
574 A187 125fr St. Michael's, diff. 1.40 .65
   a. Pair, #573-574   3.00 2.50

World Leprosy Day — A188

1985, Jan. 27   **Litho.**   *Perf. 12½*
575 A188 125fr Hospital, Libreville 1.50 .55

International Youth Year — A189

1985, Feb. 6　Litho.　Perf. 13x12½
576　A189　125fr　Silhouttes, wreath　1.40　.50

Birds
A190

1984　Litho.　Perf. 15x14
577　A190　90fr　Crowned crane　1.25　.75
578　A190　125fr　Hummingbird　2.00　1.00
579　A190　150fr　Toucan　2.50　1.25
　　　Nos. 577-579 (3)　5.75　3.00

Silhouettes,
Emblem — A191

1985, Mar. 20　Perf. 12½
580　A191　125fr　brt ultra, red & bl　1.40　.50

Cultural and Technical Cooperation Agency, 15th anniv.

Wildlife
A192

1985, Apr. 17　Perf. 15x14
581　A192　90fr　Aulacode　1.75　.60
582　A192　100fr　Porcupine　1.75　.60
583　A192　125fr　Giant pangolin　2.25　1.25
584　A192　350fr　Antelope　5.75　2.25
　a.　Souvenir sheet of 4, #581-584　13.00　13.00
　　　Nos. 581-584 (4)　11.50　4.70

Georges
Damas
Aleka,
Composer
A193

1985, Apr. 30　Perf. 13
585　A193　90fr　Portrait, La Concorde score　1.10　.35

A194

A195

1985, May 17　Perf. 13½
586　A194　125fr　multi　1.40　.50

World Telecommunications Day. ITU, 120th anniv.

1985, June 9
587　A195　90fr　Emblem　1.10　.60

J.O.C., 30th anniv.

Merchant Navy Ships Type of 1982

1985, July 1　Perf. 15x14
588　A156　185fr　Freighter Mpassa　2.10　.80

Posts and Telecommunications
Administration, 20th Anniv. — A196

1985, July 25　Perf. 13
589　A196　90fr　Headquarters　1.10　.50

President
Bongo — A197

1985, Aug. 17　Perf. 14
590　A197　250fr　multi　3.50　1.60
591　A197　500fr　multi　7.75　4.00
　a.　Pair, #590-591 + 3 labels　14.00　14.00

Imperf
Size: 120x90mm
592　A197　1000fr　View of Libreville　14.00　14.00
　　　Nos. 590-592 (3)　25.25　19.60

Natl. Independence, 25th anniv.
No. 592 has non-denominated vignettes of Nos. 590-591.

Org. of Petroleum
Exporting
Countries, 25th
Anniv. — A198

1985, Sept. 25　Perf. 13½
593　A198　350fr　multi　4.00　1.90

Intl. Center of the Bantu
Civilizations — A199

1985, Nov. 16　Litho.　Perf. 15x14
594　A199　185fr　multi　2.00　.95

St. Andrew's
Church, Libreville
— A199a

Design: 125fr, Church interior, horiz.

Perf. 14x15, 15x14
1985, Dec.　Litho.
594A　A199a　90fr　multicolored　—　—
594B　A199a　125fr　multicolored　—　—
　　Christmas.

UNESCO, 25th Anniv. — A200

1986, Jan. 5　Litho.　Perf. 12½
595　A200　100fr　multi　1.10　.45

A201

1986, May 1　Litho.　Perf. 13½
596　A201　150fr　multi　1.75　.60

Rotary Intl. District 915, 4th conf.

A202

1986, June 16　Litho.　Perf. 12½
597　A202　150fr　multi　1.75　.60

Natl. Week of Cartography, Libreville, June 16-20.

Coffee Flowers, Berries,
Beans — A203

1986, Aug. 27　Litho.　Perf. 12½
598　A203　125fr　multi　2.00　.90

Organization of African and Madagascar Coffee Producers, 25th anniv.

Merchant Navy Ships Type of 1982
1986, June 24　Litho.　Perf. 15x14
599　A156　250fr　Merchantman L'Abanga　3.00　1.25

Natl. Postage Stamp, Cent. — A205

1986, July 10　Perf. 13½x14½
600　A205　500fr　Boats, No. 4　7.00　3.50

Flowering
Plants — A206

1986, July 23　Perf. 14½x15
601　A206　100fr　Allamanda neri-ifolia　1.25　.50
602　A206　150fr　Musa cultivar　1.90　.80
603　A206　160fr　Dissotis decumbens　2.10　.85
604　A206　350fr　Campylospermum laeve　4.75　2.10
　　　Nos. 601-604 (4)　10.00　4.25

Butterflies
A207

1986, Sept. 18　Litho.　Perf. 15x14
605　A207　150fr　Machaon　2.50　1.00
606　A207　290fr　Urania　5.00　1.75

St. Pierre
Church,
Libreville
A208

1986, Dec. 23　Litho.　Perf. 15x14½
607　A208　500fr　multi　5.00　2.10

Christmas.

Trans-Gabon Railway from Owendo to
Franceville, Inauguration — A209

1986, Dec. 30　Perf. 13
608　A209　90fr　multi　1.40　.50

Souvenir Sheet
609　A209　250fr　multi　4.50　4.50

Traditional Hairstyles Type of 1981
1986　Litho.　Perf. 14x15
609A　A152　100fr　black, gray & yellow　150.00　7.50
609B　A152　150fr　tan, black & red brown　5.00　1.50

Fish
A210

1987, Jan. 15 *Perf. 15x14½*
610 A210 90fr Adioryx bas-
tatus 1.40 .60
611 A210 125fr Scarus boefleri 2.00 .85
612 A210 225fr Cephala-
canthus
volitans 2.50 1.25
613 A210 350fr Dasyatis
marmorata 3.75 1.90
a. Souv. sheet of 4, Nos. 610-
613 13.00 13.00
Nos. 610-613 (4) 9.65 4.60

No. 613a issued Oct. 1987.

Raoul Follereau
(1903-1977)
A211

1987, Jan. 23 *Perf. 12½*
614 A211 125fr multi 1.75 .85

World Leprosy Day.

Pres. Bongo Accepting the 1986 Dag
Hammarskjold Peace Prize — A212

1987, Mar. 31 Litho. *Perf. 13*
615 A212 125fr multi 1.25 .60

World Telecommunications
Day — A213

1987, May 17 Litho. *Perf. 13½*
616 A213 90fr multi 1.10 .40

Lions Club of
Gabon, 30th
Anniv. — A214

1987, July 18 Litho. *Perf. 12x12½*
617 A214 90fr multi 1.10 .40

Pierre de
Coubertin, Father
of the Modern
Olympics
A215

1987, Aug. 29
618 A215 200fr multi 2.00 .85

Lions Club Intl.,
70th
Anniv. — A216

1987, Oct. 1
619 A216 165fr multi 1.75 .65

World Post
Day — A217

1987, Oct. 9 Litho. *Perf. 13½*
620 A217 125fr multi 1.25 .50

Seashells
A218

1987, Oct. *Perf. 15x14*
621 A218 90fr Natica fanel .90 .30
622 A218 125fr Natica fulminea
cruentata 1.25 .45
a. Souv. sheet of 2, Nos. 621-622 6.00 6.00

Intl. Year of Shelter for the
Homeless — A219

1987, Oct. 5 *Perf. 12½*
623 A219 90fr multi 1.10 .40

Solidarity with the
South West
African Peoples'
Organization
(SWAPO) — A220

St. Anna of
Odimba
Mission — A221

1987, Sept. 15 Litho. *Perf. 14½x15*
624 A220 225fr Pres. Bongo,
SWAPO leader 2.10 .95

1987, Nov. 2 *Perf. 13½*
625 A221 90fr multi 1.00 .30

Universal Child Immunization — A222

1987, Nov. 16 *Perf. 15x14½*
626 A222 100fr multi 1.25 .40

20th Anniv. of
the
Presidency of
Omar Bongo
A223

1987, Dec. 2 *Perf. 14½x13½*
627 A223 1000fr multi 10.00 5.50

Christmas
A224

1987, Dec. 15 *Perf. 15x14½*
628 A224 90fr St. Therese
Church, Oyem 1.00 .30

1988 Winter Olympics,
Calgary — A225

1987, Dec. 30 *Perf. 13½x14½*
629 A225 125fr multi 1.25 .50

Medicinal
Plants — A226

1988, Jan. 26 Litho. *Perf. 14x15*
630 A226 90fr Cassia oc-
cidentalis 1.10 .55
631 A226 125fr Tabernanthe
iboga 1.60 .55
632 A226 225fr Cassia alata 2.75 1.10
633 A226 350fr Anthocleista
schweinfurthii 5.50 2.75
a. Miniature sheet of 4, #630-
633 12.00 12.00
Nos. 630-633 (4) 10.95 4.95

World Wildlife Fund — A227

African forest elephant, *Loxodonta africana
cyclotis*.

1988, Feb. 29 Litho. *Perf. 13½*
634 A227 25fr multi 2.50 .90
635 A227 40fr multi, diff. 3.25 1.75
636 A227 50fr multi, diff. 5.25 2.00
637 A227 100fr multi, diff. 8.75 3.50
Nos. 634-637 (4) 19.75 8.15

Traditional Musical
Instruments — A228

1988, Feb. 17 *Perf. 14*
638 A228 90fr Obamba
hochet 1.25 .70
639 A228 100fr Fang sanza,
vert. 1.50 .70
640 A228 125fr Mitsogho harp,
vert. 1.75 .90
641 A228 165fr Fang xylo-
phone 2.75 1.00
a. Souv. sheet of 4, Nos. 638-
641 7.50 7.50
Nos. 638-641 (4) 7.25 3.30

World Cup Rugby — A229

Perf. 13½x14½
1987, June 10 Litho.
642 A229 350fr multi 4.25 1.90

Delta Post Office Inauguration — A230

1988, Mar. 9
643 A230 90fr multi 1.00 .30

World Telecommunications
Day — A231

1988, May 17   *Perf. 13½*
644 A231 125fr multi   1.25 .45

Storming of the Bastille, July 14,
1789 — A232

1988, May 30   **Litho.**   *Perf. 13*
645 A232 125fr multi   1.60 .50

PHILEXFRANCE '89.

Intl. Fund for Agricultural Development
(IFAD), 10th Anniv. — A233

1988, June 20   *Perf. 13½*
646 A233 350fr multi   4.25 1.60

Intl. Red Cross and Red Crescent
Organizations, 125th Annivs. — A234

1988, July 15   **Litho.**   *Perf. 12½*
647 A234 125fr multi   1.25 .45

1988
Summer
Olympics,
Seoul
A235

1988, Sept. 17   **Litho.**   *Perf. 15x14*
648 A235 90fr Tennis   1.00 .35
649 A235 100fr Swimming   1.00 .45
650 A235 350fr Running   3.75 1.60
651 A235 500fr Hurdles   5.75 2.00
  a.   Souv. sheet of 4, #648-651   13.00 13.00
     Nos. 648-651 (4)   11.50 4.40

World
Post
Day
A236

1988, Oct. 9   *Perf. 13½*
652 A236 125fr blk, brt yel & brt
     blue   1.25 .45

Christmas
A237

1988, Dec. 20   **Litho.**   *Perf. 15x14*
653 A237 200fr Medouneu
     Church   2.00 .70

Natica
Fanel —
A237a

1988   **Litho.**   *Perf. 15x14*
653A A237a 90fr shown   *25.00 5.00*
653B A237a 125fr Natica sp.   *30.00 7.50*
  c.   Souv. sheet of 2, #653A-
     653B   — —

A238

1989, Feb. 21   *Perf. 13½*
654 A238 175fr multi   1.50 .60

Chaine des Rotisseurs in Gabon, 10th anniv.

A239

1989, Mar. 6   **Litho.**   *Perf. 13½*
655 A239 125fr multi   1.40 .55

Rabi Kounga oil field. See No. 707.

Traditional Games — A240

     Perf. 13½x14½
1989, Mar. 20   **Litho.**
656 A240 90fr multicolored   1.10 .55

Birds — A241

1989, Apr. 17   **Litho.**   *Perf. 14x15*
657 A241 100fr White-tufted
     bittern   1.00 .35
658 A241 175fr Gabon gray
     parakeet   1.50 .65
659 A241 200fr Pygmy hornbill   1.90 .70

660 A241 500fr Pope's martin   4.75 2.10
  a.   Souv. sheet of 4, Nos. 657-
     660   12.00 12.00
     Nos. 657-660 (4)   9.15 3.80
     See Nos. 750-753.

A242

1989, Apr. 27   *Perf. 13*
661 A242 125fr multi   1.25 .45

8th Convention of Lions Intl. District 403,
Libreville, Apr. 27-29.

World Telecommunications
Day — A243

1989, May 17   **Wmk. 385**   *Perf. 13½*
662 A243 300fr multi   3.25 1.10

PHILEXFRANCE '89 — A244

Symbols of the French revolution, 1789.

     Wmk. 385
1989, July 7   **Litho.**   *Perf. 13*
663 A244 175fr multi   2.10 .80

French Revolution, Bicent. — A245

1989, July 14
664 A245 500fr multi   6.50 3.25

Fruit — A246

     Perf. 14½x15
1989, May 30   **Litho.**   **Unwmk.**
665 A246 90fr Coconuts   1.00 .45
666 A246 125fr Cabosse   1.50 .50
667 A246 175fr Pineapple   2.25 .80
668 A246 250fr Breadfruit   2.75 1.25
  a.   Souv. sheet of 4, #665-668   8.50 8.50
     Nos. 665-668 (4)   7.50 3.00

AIMF, 10th Anniv. — A247

1989, July 27   **Litho.**   *Perf. 13*
669 A247 100fr multi   1.25 .50

African
Development
Bank, 25th
Anniv. — A248

1989, Aug. 2   **Litho.**   *Perf. 13*
670 A248 100fr multi   1.00 .40

Apples and Oranges, by Cezanne
(1839-1906) — A249

     Perf. 13½x14½
1989, June 22   **Litho.**
671 A249 500fr multicolored   6.00 3.25

1990 World Cup Soccer
Championships, Italy — A250

Various athletes.

     Perf. 15x14½
1989, Aug. 23   **Litho.**   **Unwmk.**
672 A250 100fr shown   .95 .35
673 A250 175fr multi, diff.   1.75 .65
674 A250 300fr multi, diff.   3.00 1.25
675 A250 500fr multi, diff.   4.75 1.90
  a.   Souv. sheet of 4, #672-675   11.00 11.00
     Nos. 672-675 (4)   10.45 4.15

Traditional Hair Style Type of 1981

1989, Sept. 16   *Perf. 14½x15*
676 A152 175fr gray, black & vio   2.00 .85

Post Day — A252

1989, Sept. 10   **Litho.**   *Perf. 12*
     Granite Paper
677 A252 175fr multicolored   1.75 .80

Postal Service, 125th Anniv. (in
1987) — A255

Perf. 13½x14½
1989   Litho.   Unwmk.
681 A255 90fr multicolored   11.00 2.75
Dated 1988.

St. Louis
Church,
Port Gentil
A256

1989, Dec. 15   Litho.   Perf. 15x14
682 A256 100fr multicolored   1.00   .40
Christmas. See Nos. 725-726, 757.

L'Ogooue',
N'Gomo

1989   Litho.   Perf. 15x14
682A A256a 100fr multicolored

Libreville Coat of
Arms — A257

Wmk. 385
1990, Mar. 12   Litho.   Perf. 13½
683 A257 100fr multicolored   1.10   .55

World Health
Day — A258

1990, Apr. 7   Litho.   Perf. 13
684 A258 400fr multicolored   4.50 2.10

Souvenir Sheet

Prehistoric
Tools
A259

1990, Feb. 14   Litho.   Perf. 15x14
685   Sheet of 4   30.00 30.00
a. A259 100fr Hand axe   1.25   .60
b. A259 175fr Knife blade   2.10 1.40

---

c. A259 300fr Arrowhead   3.75 1.50
d. A259 400fr Double bladed hand
    axe   6.25 4.50
See Nos. 727-730.

Souvenir Sheet

Fauna — A260

Illustration reduced.

1990, Apr. 13   Perf. 14
686 A260 Sheet of 4   15.00 15.00
a.   100fr Cercopitheque   1.40   .70
b.   175fr Potamocherus Porcus 2.40 1.60
c.   200fr Antelope   3.00 1.75
d.   500fr Mandrill   7.50 4.25

First Postage Stamps, 150th
Anniv. — A261

1991, Jan. 9 Litho. Perf. 13½x14½
687 A261 500fr multicolored   7.00 3.50

Independence, 30th Anniv. — A263

1990, Aug. 17   Litho.   Perf. 13
693 A263 100fr multicolored   1.10   .50

Mushrooms — A263a

Various mushrooms.

1990   Litho.   Perf. 15x14
693A A263a 100fr multicolored   6.00 1.10
693B A263a 175fr multicolored   12.00 2.25
693C A263a 300fr multicolored   17.50 4.25
693D A263a 500fr multicolored   24.50 6.50
     Nos. 693A-693D (4)   60.00 14.10

Organization of
Petroleum
Exporting
Countries
(OPEC), 30th
anniv. — A264

1990, Sept. 19   Litho.   Perf. 13
694 A264 200fr multicolored   2.00 1.00

1990 World Cup Soccer
Championships, Italy — A264a

1990, June 8   Litho.   Perf. 15x14
694A A264a 100fr Goalie making
                   save   1.00   .50
694B A264a 175fr Four players,
                   ball   1.75   .80
694D A264a 500fr Player cele-
                   brating   4.75 2.25

A 300fr stamp and a souvenir sheet containing 694A-694D, with the 300fr value, exist.
The editors would like to examine examples.

A265

1990, Oct. 9   Perf. 13½
695 A265 175fr blue, yel & blk   2.00 1.00
World Post Day.

Traditional
Bwiti Dancer
A265a

1990   Litho.   Perf. 15x14
695A A265a 100fr Ndjembe
                   dancers   —
695B A265a 175fr shown   —

Flowers
A266

1991, Jan. 9   Litho.   Perf. 15x14
696 A266 100fr Frangipanier   1.25   .60
697 A266 175fr Boule de feu   2.10 1.00
698 A266 200fr Flamboyant   2.40 1.10
699 A266 300fr Rose de
                 porcelaine   3.75 1.75
a. Souvenir sheet of 4, #696-
    699   10.00 10.00
     Nos. 696-699 (4)   9.50 4.45

Petroglyphs — A267

1991, Feb. 26   Litho.   Perf. 15x14
700 A267 100fr Lizard figure   1.25   .60
701 A267 175fr Triangular fig-
                  ure   2.00 1.25
702 A267 300fr Incused lines   3.50 1.50
703 A267 500fr Concentric cir-
                  cles, circles in
                  lines   5.75 3.00
a. Souvenir sheet of 4, #700-
    703   75.00 75.00
     Nos. 700-703 (4)   12.50 6.35

Rubber
Trees — A268

1991, Mar. 20   Litho.   Perf. 14x15
705 A268 100fr multicolored   1.00   .45

World Telecommunications
Day — A269

1991, May 17   Litho.   Perf. 13½
706 A269 175fr multicolored   1.90   .95

Rabi Kounga Oil Field Type of 1989
1991   Litho.   Perf. 13½
707 A239 175fr multicolored   150.00

Ngounie
Women
Washing
Clothes
A271

1991, July 17   Litho.   Perf. 13½
708 A271 100fr multicolored   1.00   .45

A272

A273

Designs: Craftsmen.

1991, June 19   **Perf. 14x15**
709 A272 100fr Basket maker   1.10   .55
710 A272 175fr Wood carver   1.90   .95
711 A272 200fr Weaver   2.25 1.10
712 A272 500fr Thatch maker   5.75 2.75
   Nos. 709-712 (4)   11.00 5.35

1991, Aug. 18   Litho.   Perf. 14x15
Gabonese Medals: 100fr, Equatorial
Knight's Star. 175fr, Equatorial Officer's Star.
200fr, Equatorial Commander's Star.

Gray Background
713 A273 100fr multicolored   1.00   .50
714 A273 175fr multicolored   1.75   .90
715 A273 200fr multicolored   2.00 1.00
   Nos. 713-715 (3)   4.75 2.40

See Nos. 735-737.

Fishing in
Gabon
A274

1991, Sept. 18   **Perf. 15x14**
716 A274 100fr Bow-net fishing 1.25   .55
717 A274 175fr Trammel fishing 1.60   .95
718 A274 200fr Net fishing   2.25 1.10
719 A274 300fr Seine fishing   3.25 1.75
a.   Souvenir sheet of 4, #716-719 9.50 9.50
   Nos. 716-719 (4)   8.35 4.35

World Post
Day — A275

Termite
Mounds — A276

1991, Oct. 9   **Perf. 13½**
720 A275 175fr blue & multi   2.00   .95
See Nos. 749, 786.

1991, Nov. 6   **Perf. 14x15**
721 A276 100fr Phallic   1.50   .60
722 A276 175fr Cathedral   2.50 1.00
723 A276 200fr Mushroom   3.00 1.10
724 A276 300fr Arboreal   4.00 1.75
   Nos. 721-724 (4)   11.00 4.45

Church Type of 1989
1991, Dec. 18   Litho.   Perf. 15x14
725 A256 100fr Church of
             Makokou   1.00   .40
726 A256 100fr Church of
             Dibwangui   1.00   .40

Christmas. No. 725 inscribed 1990.

Prehistoric Tools Type of 1990
Pottery: 100fr, Neolithic pot. 175fr, Bottle,
8th cent. 200fr, Vase, 8th cent. 300fr, Vase,
8th cent, diff.

1992, Jan. 9   Litho.   Perf. 14x15
727 A259 100fr multi, vert.   1.10   .40
728 A259 175fr multi, vert.   1.90   .75
729 A259 200fr multi, vert.   2.50   .85
730 A259 300fr multi, vert.   3.00 1.25
a.   Sheet of 4, #727-730   9.50 9.50
   Nos. 727-730 (4)   8.50 3.25

Occupations
A277

1992, Feb. 5
731 A277 100fr Basket maker   1.10   .55
732 A277 175fr Blacksmith   1.90   .95
733 A277 200fr Boat builder   2.10 1.10
734 A277 300fr Hairdresser   3.25 1.75
a.   Souvenir sheet of 4, #731-734 9.50 9.50
   Nos. 731-734 (4)   8.35 4.35

No. 734a issued Feb. 9.

Gabonese Medals Type of 1991
Designs: 100fr, Equatorial Grand Officer's
Star. 175fr, Grand Cross of Dignity and Equa-
torial Star. 200fr, Order of Merit.

1992, Mar. 18   Litho.   Perf. 14x15
Aquamarine Background
735 A273 100fr multicolored   .95   .50
736 A273 175fr multicolored   1.90   .90
737 A273 200fr multicolored   2.25 1.00
   Nos. 735-737 (3)   5.10 2.40

A278

A279

1992, Apr. 19   **Perf. 13**
738 A278 500fr multicolored   6.00 3.00
Konrad Adenauer (1876-1967), German
Statesman.

1992, May 17   **Perf. 13½**
739 A279 175fr multicolored   2.00   .95
World Telecommunications Day.

Butterflies
A280

1992, June 10   Litho.   Perf. 15x14
740 A280 100fr Graphium
             policenes   2.00 1.00
741 A280 175fr Acraea egina   3.00 1.50

A281

A282

1992, July 25   **Perf. 14x15**
742 A281 100fr Cycling   1.10   .55
743 A281 175fr Boxing   2.00 1.00
744 A281 200fr Pole vault   2.25 1.10
   Nos. 742-744 (3)   5.35 2.65

1992 Summer Olympics, Barcelona.

1992, Sept. 16   Litho.   Perf. 14x15
Tribal masks.
745 A282 100fr Fang   1.00   .50
746 A282 175fr Mpongwe   1.90   .95
747 A282 200fr Kwele   2.10 1.00
748 A282 300fr Pounou   3.25 1.60
a.   Souvenir sheet of 4, #745-748 9.50 9.50
   Nos. 745-748 (4)   8.25 4.05

World Post Day Type of 1991
Inscribed 1992
1992, Oct. 9   Litho.   Perf. 13½
749 A275 175fr bl grn & multi   2.00   .95

Bird Type of 1989
1992, Nov. 4   Litho.   Perf. 14x15
750 A241 100fr African owl   2.50   .90
751 A241 175fr Coliou strie   4.00 1.50
752 A241 200fr Vulture   5.00 2.10
753 A241 300fr Giant kingfish-
             er   9.00 2.75
a.   Souvenir sheet of 4, #750-
      753   27.50 27.50
   Nos. 750-753 (4)   20.50 7.25

Cattle
A283

Various scenes of cattle in pasture.

1992, Dec. 10   **Perf. 15x14**
754 A283 100fr multicolored   1.00   .50
755 A283 175fr multicolored   1.75   .90
756 A283 200fr multicolored   2.00 1.00
   Nos. 754-756 (3)   4.75 2.40

Church Type of 1989
1992, Dec. 16
757 A256 100fr Tchibanga
             Church   1.00   .40

Christmas.

Intl. Conference
on Nutrition,
Rome — A284

1992, Dec. 20   **Perf. 13½**
758 A284 100fr multicolored   1.00   .40

Shells
A285

1993, Jan. 6   Litho.   Perf. 15x14
759 A285 100fr Pugilina   .90   .40
760 A285 175fr Conus pulcher   1.90   .70
761 A285 200fr Fusinus   2.25   .80
762 A285 300fr Cymatium   3.50 1.25
a.   Souvenir sheet, #759-762 14.00 14.00
   Nos. 759-762 (4)   8.55 3.15

World
Leprosy
Day
A286

1993, Jan. 28   **Perf. 13½**
763 A286 175fr multicolored   2.00   .95

Fernan-Vaz
Mission
A287

1993, Feb. 3   **Perf. 15x14**
764 A287 175fr multicolored   3.00 1.25

Chappe's
Semaphore
Telegraph,
Bicent. — A288

Designs: 100fr, Claude Chappe (1763-
1805), engineer and inventor. 175fr, Chappe's
signaling device and code. 200fr, Emile
Baudot (1845-1903), devising telegraph code,
early telegraph equipment. 300fr, Modern satellite, electronic chip and fiber optics.

1993, Mar. 10   Litho.   Perf. 13½
765 A288 100fr multicolored   1.00   .50
766 A288 175fr multicolored   1.75   .90
767 A288 200fr multicolored   2.00 1.10
768 A288 300fr multicolored   3.25 1.60
a.   Souvenir sheet of 4, #765-768 9.50 9.50
   Nos. 765-768 (4)   8.00 4.10

Albert Schweitzer's Arrival in
Lambarene, 80th Anniv. — A289

1993, Apr. 6   Litho.   Perf. 13
769 A289 500fr multicolored   6.00 2.75
a.   Booklet pane of 1   6.50

Booklet Stamps
Size: 26x37mm
Perf. 13½
770 A289 250fr Feeding chick-
             ens   2.75 1.40
a.   Booklet pane of 4   16.00
771 A289 250fr Holding babies   2.75 1.40
a.   Booklet pane of 4   16.00
   Nos. 769-771 (3)   11.50 5.55

Booklet containing one of each pane sold
for 3000fr. Value $40.

Nicolaus
Copernicus,
Heliocentric
Solar System
A290

1993, May 5   Litho.   Perf. 15x14
772 A290 175fr multicolored   1.60   .75

Polska '93.

A291

A292

1993, May 17 Perf. 13½
773 A291 175fr multicolored 1.60 .75
World Telecommunications Day.

1993, June 9 Litho. Perf. 14
Traditional Wine Making: 100fr, Still. 175fr, Extracting juice from palm roots. 200fr, Man in palm tree.
774 A292 100fr multicolored 1.00 .45
775 A292 175fr multicolored 1.60 .80
776 A292 200fr multicolored 1.90 .95
a. Souvenir sheet of 3, #774-776 6.00 6.00
Nos. 774-776 (3) 4.50 2.20

Crustaceans — A293

1993, July 21 Litho. Perf. 15x14
777 A293 100fr Spiny lobster 1.10 .60
778 A293 175fr Violin crab 1.75 .95
779 A293 200fr Crayfish 2.25 1.10
780 A293 300fr Spider crab 3.25 1.60
Nos. 777-780 (4) 8.35 4.25

Paris '94 — A294

1993, Aug. 10 Litho. Perf. 13
781 A294 100fr multicolored 1.10 .50

Animal Traps A295

1993, Sept. 15 Litho. Perf. 15x14
782 A295 100fr Squirrel 1.10 .20
783 A295 175fr Small game 1.75 .55
784 A295 200fr Large game 1.90 .90
785 A295 300fr Palm rat 3.25 1.40
a. Souvenir sheet of 4, #782-785 6.00 6.00
Nos. 782-785 (4) 8.00 3.05

World Post Day Type of 1991
Inscribed 1993

1993, Oct. 9 Perf. 13½
786 A275 175fr yellow & multi 1.60 .75

Making Bamboo Toys — A296

1993, Oct. 20 Perf. 11½
787 A296 100fr multicolored 1.10 .55

Tourism A297

1993, Nov. 16
788 A297 100fr Leconi Canyon 1.00 .20
789 A297 175fr La Lope Valley 1.60 .50

Christmas A298

1993, Dec. 20 Perf. 15x14
790 A298 100fr Catholic Mission, Mandji 1.10 .55

Provincial Map — A299

1994 Litho. Perf. 14½
791 A299 5fr yellow & multi .20 .20
792 A299 10fr multicolored .20 .20
793 A299 25fr multi .20 .20
795 A299 75fr violet & multi .40 .25
796 A299 100fr pink & multi .70 .30
797 A299 175fr blue & multi 1.00 .45

Issued: 5fr, 75fr, 100fr, 1/28/94.

Numbers have been reserved for 2 additional values in this set released between 1993 and 1994. The editors would like to examine the other stamps.

Vision of Gabon's Future — A300

1994, Oct. 5 Litho. Perf. 14½
798 A300 500fr multicolored 3.00 1.50

1994 World Cup Soccer Championships, US — A301

Designs: a, 100fr, Hands on soccer ball. b, 175fr, Two players, ball in air. c, 200fr, Legs of players. d, 300fr, Player, ball.

1994, Apr. 5 Perf. 15x14
799 A301 Sheet of 4, #a.-d. 30.00 15.00

UN, 50th Anniv. — A301a

1995, July 5 Litho. Perf. 11¾x11½
799E A301a 500fr multi 2.00 2.00

Prehistoric Wildlife — A302

No. 800: a, Sordes. b, Diplodocus (d-e, g-h). c, Eudimorphodon (b). d, Dimetrodon (a). e, Anuroenathus. f, Deinonychus, pachycephalosaurus (e). g, Triceratops (j). h, Hadrosaur (i, k-l). i, Genus Meganeura. j, Longisquama. k, Oviraptor. l, Monoclonius.

No. 801: a, Pistosaurus (d-e, h). b, Pteranodon (c). c, Coelophysis. d, Xenacanthus (g). e, Ischyodus (f, h-i). f, Placochelys. g, Dunkleosteus (j). h, Cymbospondylus (i). i, Enchodus. j, Paracybeloides (k). k, Nautiliod (h). l, Palaeospondylus.

No. 802: a, Tyrannosaurus rex (d). b, Apatosaurus (a, d-e). c, Dimorphodon. d, Stegasaurus (a, e). e, Archaeopteryx. f, Protoceratops. g, Ichthyosaur. h, Phobosuchus, deltoptychius. i, Parasaurolophus (f). j, Scapanorhynchus (g). k, Spathobathis, plesiosaurus (j, l). l, Cladoselacho.

1995, Sept. 4 Litho. Perf. 14
800 A302 125fr Sheet of 12, #a.-l. 9.00 4.50
801 A302 225fr Sheet of 12, #a.-l. 15.00 7.50
802 A302 260fr Sheet of 12, #a.-l. 17.50 8.75
Nos. 800-802 (3) 41.50 20.75

Singapore '95 (#800).

Nobel Prize Fund Established, Cent. — A303

No. 803 — Nobel Prize recipients: a, Walter H. Brattain, physics, 1956. b, Carl F. Cori, medicine, 1947. c, Gerty T. Cori, medicine, 1947. d, Owen Chamberlain, physics, 1959. e, Christian Anfinsen, chemistry, 1972. f, George de Hevesy, chemistry, 1943. g, Kenichi Fukui, chemistry, 1981. h, Elie Wiesel, peace, 1986. i, Carl F. Braun, physics, 1909.

No. 804: a, Georg Wittig, chemistry, 1979. b, Charles Dawes, peace, 1925. c, Frederic Mistral, literature, 1904. d, Juan Jimenez, literature, 1956. e, Michael S. Brown, medicine, 1985. f, Guglielmo Marconi, physics, 1909. g, Werner Forssmann, medicine, 1956. h, Francis W. Aston, chemistry, 1922. i, Martin Ryle, physics, 1974.

No. 805: a, Leon Jouhaux, peace, 1951. b, Rudolf L. Mossbauer, physics, 1961. c, George Seferis, literature, 1963. d, James Chadwick, physics, 1935. e, Aung San Suu Kyi, peace, 1991. f, John H. Nothrop, chemistry, 1946. g, Eduard Buchner, chemistry, 1907. h, Hans A. Bethe, physics, 1967. i, Nils Dalen, physics, 1912.

No. 806, 1500fr, Hermann Hesse, literature, 1946. No. 807, 1500fr, Albert Schweitzer, peace, 1952. No. 808, 1500fr, Nelson Mandela, peace, 1993.

1995, Oct. 18 Litho. Perf. 14
803 A303 125fr Sheet of 9, #a.-i. 6.75 3.25
804 A303 225fr Sheet of 9, #a.-i. 9.00 6.00
805 A303 260fr Sheet of 9, #a.-i. 14.00 7.00
Nos. 803-805 (3) 29.75 16.25
Souvenir Sheets
806-808 A303 Set of 3 27.00 27.00

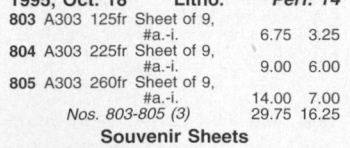

Monseigneur Bessieux (1803-76), Evangelist A306

1995, Dec. 25 Litho. Perf. 13
811 A306 500fr multicolored 2.75 1.40

Louis Pasteur (1822-95), Microbiologist — A306a

1995 Litho. Perf. 14¼x14¾
811A A306a 500fr multi — —

Food and Agriculture Organization, 50th Anniv. — A306b

1995 Litho. Perf. 11¾
811B A306b 500fr multi — —

Mbigou Rock Sculptor — A306c

1995 Litho. Perf. 14¼x14¾
811C A306c 500fr multi 2.40 2.40

Miniature Sheet of 8

World War II, 50th Anniv. A307

No. 812: a, German generals planning attack. b, Afrika Korps troops ride tanks into El Agheila. c, German artillary fires on British positions in Tobruk. d, British soldiers surrender. e, British soldiers break siege of Tobruk. f, Allies advancing though barbed wire, El Alamein. g, German tanks retreat to Tunis. h, German tank surrenders.

1996, Jan. 29 Perf. 14
812 A307 125fr Sheet of 8, #a.-h. + label 6.50 2.75

World War II, 50th Anniv. A308

No. 813: a, Pres. Franklin D. Roosevelt. b, Pres. Harry S Truman. c, Gen. George Marshall.
1000fr, Flags of US, Great Britain, USSR.

1996, Jan. 26   Litho.   Perf. 14
813 A308 225fr Strip of 3, #a.-c. 4.50 4.50

Souvenir Sheet
814 A308 1000fr multicolored   6.50 6.50
No. 813 was issued in sheets of 9 stamps.

Dogs — A309

No. 815: a, Dalmatian. b, Basset hound. c, Harrier. d, German Shepherd. e, Bernese bouvier. f, Pug. g, West highland white terrier. h, Akita.

1996, May 13   Litho.   Perf. 14
815 A309 125fr Sheet of 8, #a.-h. 6.00 6.00
China '96 Philatelic Exhibition.

St. Pius X Catholic Mission, 10th Anniv. A310

Mgr. Marcel Lefebvre, interior of mission.

1996, Mar. 4   Perf. 13½
816 A310 100fr yellow & multi   .75 .20
817 A310 125fr blue & multi   .95 .45

Rotary, Intl. A311

Rotary emblem and: 125fr, UN flag. 225fr, Natl. flag of Gabon. 260fr, Rotary, Intl. flag. 1500fr, Olympic flag.

1996, July 3   Litho.   Perf. 14
818-820 A311 Set of 3   4.00 3.00

Souvenir Sheet
821 A311 1500fr multicolored   9.00 9.00

Boy Scouts — A312

Designs: 125fr, Scout sign. 225fr, Constructing a lean-to. 260fr, Camping. 1500fr, Lord Baden-Powell.

1996, July 15
822-824 A312 Set of 3   4.00 3.25

Souvenir Sheet
825 A312 1500fr multicolored   9.00 9.00

Cercopithecus Solatus — A313

1996, Mar. 6   Perf. 13½x13
826 A313 500fr multicolored   3.25 1.75

Fight Against AIDS — A314

1996, Apr. 3   Perf. 13½x13
827 A314 500fr multicolored   3.25 1.75

Shells — A315

Designs: 100fr, Fusinus caparti. 260fr, Hexaplex rosarium. 500fr, Conus pulcher, horiz.

1996   Perf. 13½x13, 13x13½
828-830 A315 Set of 3   5.00 3.50

1996 Summer Olympic Games, Atlanta A316

1996, May 8   Perf. 11½
831 A316 225fr Boxing   1.25 .75
832 A316 500fr Relay race   2.50 1.60

Campaign Against Use of Illegal Drugs A317

1996, Aug. 6   Litho.   Perf. 11½
833 A317 500fr multicolored   2.75 1.25

Contemporary Paintings, by H. Moundounga — A318

1996, Sept. 10
834 A318 100fr Girl   .65 .20
835 A318 125fr Three faces   .85 .40
836 A318 225fr Eyes   1.50 .75
a.   Souvenir sheet, #834-836   3.25 3.25
Nos. 834-836 (3)   3.00 1.35

Souvenir Sheet

Temple in Winter — A319

1996, May 13   Litho.   Perf. 14
837 A319 500fr multicolored   4.50 2.25
China '96 Philatelic Exhibition, No. 837 was not available until March 1997.

Environmental Protection — A320

Endangered species: 100fr, Galago alleni, vert. 125fr, Perodicticus potto. 225fr, Orycteropus afer. 260fr, Manis gigantea.

1996, June 5   Perf. 13½
838-841 A320 Set of 4   5.00 3.25

Children's Paintings A321

Designs: 100fr, Woman's arms encircling world, vert. 125fr, People forming circle around animals. 225fr, Slaughtering of elephants, vert.

1996, Dec. 25   Litho.   Perf. 11½
842-844 A321 Set of 3   1.75 1.25
Dated 1996.

Traditional Houses A322

Designs: 100fr, Mud & stick cabin. 125fr, Pygmy hut. 225fr, Bark-sided cabins. 260fr, Wood-sided cabins.

1996, Nov. 6
845-848 A322 Set of 4   4.50 2.75
a.   Souvenir sheet, #845-848   5.00 5.00

A323   A324

1996, Oct. 10
849 A323 500fr multicolored   2.00 1.25
Investiture of Pres. Nelson Mandela, 3rd anniv.

1997, Apr. 9   Litho.   Perf. 14
UNICEF, 50th Anniv.: No. 850: a, Boy holding cup. b, Girl holding cup. c, Boy eating.

1500fr, Boy holding plate.
850 A324 260fr Sheet of 3, #a.-
c.   4.00 4.00
Souvenir Sheet
851 A324 1500fr multicolored   8.50 8.50

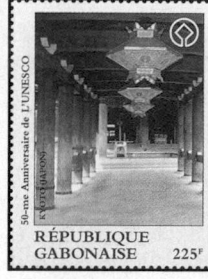

UNESCO, 50th Anniv. A325

No. 852, 225fr: a, Kyoto, Japan. b, Puma, Los Katios Natl. Park, Colombia. c, Abu Simbel Monument, Egypt. d, Old Rauma, Finland. e, Rotunda, City of Vicenza, Italy. f, Homes, China. g, Port of Salvador, Brazil. h, Delos Ruins, Greece.
No. 853, 225fr: a, Fasil Ghebbi Monument, Gondar Region, Ethiopia. b, Victoria Falls, Zambia. c, Zambezi Plains, Chewore Safari Areas, Zimbabwe. d, Nature Reserve, Niger. e, Banc D'Arguin Natl. Park, Mauritania. f, Gorée Island, Senegal. g, Djémila Ruins, Algeria. h, Mosque, Medina of Fez, Morocco.
1000fr, Terracotta warriors, Mausoleum of first Qin Emperor, China.

1997, Apr. 16
Sheets of 8, #a-h, + Label
852-853 A325 Set of 2   19.50 19.50
Souvenir Sheet
854 A325 1000fr multicolored   7.50 7.50

City Arms — A326

1997, Mar. 12   Litho.   Perf. 11½x12
855 A326 100fr N'Dendé   .65 .20
856 A326 125fr Libreville   .85 .35
857 A326 225fr Mitzic   1.50 .80
Nos. 855-857 (3)   3.00 1.35

Return of Hong Kong to China — A327

Designs: 125fr, Skyline. 225fr, Skyline, diff. 260fr, Skyline at night, horiz. 500fr, Skyline at night, Deng Xiaoping (1904-97), horiz.

1997, July 1   Perf. 14
858-861 A327 Set of 4   6.00 4.00
Nos. 858-859 were each issued in sheets of 4. Nos. 860-861 are 59x28mm and were issued in sheets of 3.

Unity, Work and Justice Type of 1981
1994-95   Litho.   Perf. 11¾
Granite Paper
862 A145 5fr green blue & black   .20 .20
863 A145 10fr orange & black   .20 .20
864 A145 25fr grey lilac & black   .20 .20
865 A145 50fr salmon & black   .20 .20
866 A145 75fr tan & blk   .20 .20
867 A145 100fr pink & black   .20 .20
868 A145 125fr yellow green & black   .45 .35
869 A145 175fr yellow & black   .55 .40

870	A145	225fr green & black	.70 .55
871	A145	260fr lt blue & black	.80 .60
		Nos. 862-871 (10)	3.70 3.10

Issued: 50fr, 125fr, 9/30/95; others, 9/20/94.

Paintings — A328

1995, Oct. 10   **Litho.**   **Perf. 14**

872	A328	100fr Woman	1.00 .45
873	A328	125fr Stylized women	1.50 .65
873A	A328	225fr Masked Face	2.00 1.10

Raponda Walker,
25th Death
Anniv. — A329

Masks — A330

1995, June 7   **Perf. 13½**

874	A329	500fr multicolored	7.50 —

1995

875	A330	100fr Bateke	2.50 —
876	A330	125fr Bavili	2.50 —
877	A330	225fr Fang	2.50 —
878	A330	260fr Bandjabi	2.50 —

Shells
A331

1995

879	A331	100fr Cymbium glans	—
880	A331	125fr Muricidae murey	—
880A	A331	225fr Siliquaria	— —
881	A331	260fr Strombus latus	— —

The editors suspect that additional stamps may have been issued in this set and would like to examine any examples.

Saint-Exupery French Cultural
Center — A332

1996   **Perf. 13x13½**

883	A332	100fr black & multi	—
884	A332	125fr blue & multi	—
885	A332	225fr red & multi	—

Inter-Continental Hotel, 50th
Anniv. — A333

1996   **Perf. 13½**

886	A333	125fr creme & blue	
886A	A333	225fr lt yel & blue	1.00 —

Early Post
Offices —
A333a

1996, July 20   **Litho.**   **Perf. 12x11½**

886B	A333a	100fr Port Gentil, 1917	1.00 .50
886C	A333a	125fr Cap-Lopez, 1888	1.00 .65
886D	A333a	225fr Libreville, 1862	1.45 1.10

The editors would like to examine any examples of stamps from this set heretofore unlisted.

Flowers,
Butterflies,
Moths,
Insects
A334

Designs, vert: 125fr, Rubra tigridia pauonia, pieridae. 225fr, Acraeidae, strelitzia reginae. 260fr, Zautedeschia aethiopica, zonabris oculata. 500fr, Bee orchid, iron prominent moth caterpillar.

No. 891, 260fr: a, Liliaceae. b, Macrophylla, phoebis philea. c, Theaceae amugashita. d, Lilium american cultivars, vanessa atalanta. e, Hybrids, hippodamia convergens. f, Sibine stimulea, iridaceae.

No. 892, 260fr: a, Kalmialati. b, G. gandavensis, calopteryx maculata. c, Narcissus pseudonarcisus. d, Ipheton uniflorum, Tlemaris thysbe. e, Rudbackia hirta. f, Tritida grandiflora, danaus plexippus.

No. 893, 1500fr, Papilion zellicaon, geranium pelargonium, vert. No. 894, 1500fr, Anax jumus, gladstoniana, vert.

1997, Aug. 11   **Litho.**   **Perf. 14**

887-890	A334	Set of 4	7.25 5.00

Sheets of 6, #a-f

891-892	A334	Set of 2	22.00 22.00

Souvenir Sheets

893-894	A334	Set of 2	19.00 19.00

Protection of
Indigenous
Animals — A335

Designs: 100fr, Dendrohyrax arboreus. 125fr, Galago elegantulus. 225fr, Stephanoaetus coronatus.

1997, June 5   **Perf. 13½x13**

895-897	A335	Set of 3	3.00 2.00
897a		Souvenir sheet of 3, #895-897	1.75 1.75

Gabonese
Art — A336

Designs: 100fr, Droits de Creatures, vert. 125fr, Ambassadeur, vert. 225fr, Hallucinations.

1997, May 8   **Perf. 13½x13, 13x13½**

898-900	A336	Set of 3	1.50 1.00
900a		Souvenir sheet of 1, #900	.80 .80

Air Gabon,
20th Anniv.
A337

1997, June 1   **Perf. 13x13½**

901	A337	125fr multicolored	.90 .50
902	A337	225fr multicolored	1.60 .80

First ACP
Summit,
Libreville — A338

1997   **Litho.**   **Perf. 13½x13**

903	A338	225fr multicolored	1.40 .70

Lions Club in
Gabon, 40th
Anniv. — A339

1997, Oct. 8   **Perf. 13½x13**

904	A339	225fr multicolored	1.40 .70

AIPLF,
30th Anniv.
A340

1997, Oct. 30   **Perf. 12x11½**

905	A340	260fr multicolored	1.40 .65

Paul Gondjout, 1st
Pres. of the Natl.
Assembly — A341

1997, Nov. 11   **Perf. 14x14½**

906	A341	500fr multicolored	2.75 1.25

Heinrich von
Stephan (1831-
97) — A342

1997, Nov. 17   **Perf. 11½x12**

907	A342	500fr multicolored	2.75 1.25

Princess Diana
(1961-97) — A343

No. 908: a, 500fr. b, 300fr. c, 260fr. d, 225fr. e, f, 125fr.
3000fr, Diana in white dress.

1998, Feb. 10   **Litho.**   **Perf. 13½**

908	A343	Sheet of 6, #a-f.	10.00 10.00

Souvenir Sheet

909	A343	3000fr multicolored	15.00 15.00

District
Arms — A344

Designs: 100fr, Akieni. 125fr, Pana. 225fr, Lebamba.

1998, June 4   **Litho.**   **Perf. 13½x13**

910-912	A344	Set of 3	3.00 1.50

Traditional
Tools
A345

Designs: 100fr, Yanghe. 125fr, Ikanga. 225fr, Ivedili.

1997, Nov. 5   **Litho.**   **Perf. 14**

913-915	A345	Set of 3	3.00 1.90

New
Horizons
Foundation
A346

1998   **Litho.**   **Perf. 13x13½**

916	A346	225fr multicolored	1.40 .70

Protected
Animals — A347

Designs: 100fr, Hippopotamus amphibius. 125fr, Sylvicapra grimmia. 225fr, Pelecanus rufescens.

1998   **Perf. 13½x13**

917	A347	100fr multicolored	.65 .35
918	A347	125fr multicolored	.95 .65
919	A347	225fr multicolored	1.25 .75
a.		Souvenir sheet, #917-919	3.25 3.25

1998 World Cup Soccer Championships, France — A348

Various soccer plays, country flags in background: 100fr, 125fr, 225fr, 260fr.

1998, July 10 Litho. Perf. 13½x13
920-923 A348 Set of 4   4.75 2.75
923a   Sheet of 4, #920-923   5.00 5.00

ACCT, 26th Anniv. — A349

1998
924 A349 260fr multicolored   1.40 .65

Elimination of Land Mines — A350

1998 Litho. Perf. 11½x12
925 A350 260fr multicolored   1.60 .80

Gandhi — A351

1998
926 A351 260fr multicolored   1.60 .80

Mother Teresa (1910-97) — A352

1998
927 A352 500fr multicolored   2.75 1.40

Deng Xiaoping (1904-97) — A353

1998
928 A353 500fr multicolored   2.75 1.40

Intl. Year of the Ocean A354

1999 Litho. Perf. 11½
929 A354 125fr multicolored   1.60 .85
   Dated 1998.

Wooden Tools — A355

1999
930 A355 100fr Mortier   .70 .55
931 A355 125fr Pilon   1.00 .80
   Dated 1998.

Universal Declaration of Human Rights A356

1999
932 A356 225fr multicolored   1.40 .80
   Dated 1998.

Space Exploration — A357

Designs: No. 933, 225fr, Gemini 7. No. 934, 225fr, Skylab. No. 935, 225fr, Atlas Moon Explorer. No. 936, 225fr, Space Shuttle.
No. 937: a, Venera 4. b, TDRS. c, Sputnik II. d, Zond II. e, Untethered walk. f, Intelsat 6. g, Luna 16. h, Sputnik III. i, Vostok V. j, Lunar explorer. k, 2nd lunar landing. l, Conrad and Surveyor.
No. 938: a, Sputnik. b, Mariner 2. c, Apollo 11 Lunar Module. d, Gemini 7. e, Mir. f, Atlas Moon Explorer. g, Space Shuttle Orbit. h, Hubbell. i, Soyuz. j, Apollo 11 re-entry. k, Skylab. l, Venture Star.
No. 939: a, Lunar landing II. b, Gemini 7. c, Venture Star. d, Hubbell.
No. 940, 1500fr, Shuttle launch. No. 941, 1500fr, Untethered walk. No. 942, 1500fr, Apollo II. No. 943, 1500fr, Lunar landing module.

1999, Apr. 30 Litho. Perf. 14
933-936 A357 Set of 4   3.75 2.00
937 A357 100fr Sheet of 12,   6.00 6.00
   #a.-l.
938 A357 125fr Sheet of 12,   8.50 8.50
   #a.-l.
   Sheet of 4
939 A357 225fr Sheet of 4,   4.00 4.00
   #a.-d.
   Souvenir Sheets
940-943 A357 Set of 4   35.00 35.00
   Moon landing, 30th anniv.

Traditional Weapons — A358

Designs: 100fr, Sagaie. 125fr, Arbalète. 225fr, Couteau et jet.

1999 Perf. 13
944-946 A358 Set of 3   3.00 1.60

Folklore — A358a

Designs: 125fr, Mitsogho reliquary. 225fr, Bwèri Fang sculpture.

1999 Litho. Perf. 13¼
946A A358a 125fr multi
946B A358a 225fr multi
   The editors suspect that additional stamps may have been issued in this set and would like to examine any examples.

Democracy A359

1999 Litho. Perf. 11¾
947 A359 100fr multicolored   1.00 .50

UPU, 125th Anniv. A360

Designs: 100fr, People, map. 225fr, Emblem, letters, vert. 260fr, Great Wall of China, vert.

1999
948 A360 100fr multicolored   .60 .40
949 A360 225fr multicolored   1.00 .75
950 A360 260fr multicolored   1.50 1.00
   Nos. 948-950 (3)   3.10 2.15

Manufacture of Aspirin, Cent. — A361

1999
951 A361 225fr multicolored   1.40 .70

Mushrooms — A361a

Designs: 100fr, Amanite panthère. 125fr, Basidiomycetes, horiz. 225fr, Basidiomycetes, diff., horiz. 260fr, Amanite tue-mouches.

1999 Litho. Perf. 13¼x13, 13x13¼
951A-951D A361a Set of 4   5.50 5.50

PhilexFrance '99 — A362

1999, July 2 Litho. Perf. 13
952 A362 225fr multi   2.00 1.40
   No. 952 has a holographic image. Soaking in water may affect hologram.

Central African Economic and Monetary Community Days — A364

Map of Africa and: 125fr, Circle of member's flags. 225fr, Rows of member's flags.

1999 Litho. Perf. 14½
954-955 A364 Set of 2   2.40 2.40

Pope John XXIII, St. Peter's Basilica A365

1999 Litho. Perf. 11¾
956 A365 100fr multi   .75 .75
   Announcement of 2nd Vatican Council, 40th anniv., Christmas.

Unity, Work and Justice Type of 1981

1999 Litho. Perf. 11¾
Granite Paper
959 A145 40fr lil & blk   .20 .20
960 A145 90fr olive grn & blk   — —

Shells A365a

Designs: 100fr, Harpa doris. 125fr, Thais haemastoma. 225fr, Cassis tessellata.

1999, June 25 Litho. Perf. 13x13½
964-966 A365a Set of 3   4.00 4.00

Fish A365b

Designs: 100fr, Epinephelus marginatus, mugil cephalus. 125fr, Brycinus macrolepidotus. 225fr, Oreochromis schwebischi. 260fr, Pomadasys peroteti, caranx hippos, ethmalosa fimbriata.

1999
967-970 A365b Set of 4   5.50 5.50

Expo 2000, Hanover
A366

Perf. 11¾x11½

2000, Feb. 16   **Litho.**
971 A366 225fr multi   1.60 1.60

Protected Animals
A367

Designs: 125fr, Haliaetus vocifer. 225fr, Panthera pardus. 260fr, Panthera leo.

2000, June 5
972-974 A367   Set of 3   4.00 4.00

Events of the 20th Century
A368

Designs: 100fr, Universal Declaration of Human Rights, vert. 125fr, World War II. 225fr, First man on the moon.

Perf. 11½x11¾, 11¾x11½

2000, July 20
975-977 A368   Set of 3   3.00 3.00

Scientific Achievements of the 20th Century — A369

Designs: 100fr, Microprocessor, 1971. 125fr, Nuclear reactor, 1942. 225fr, Structure of DNA, 1953.

2000   *Perf. 11¾x11½*
978-980 A369   Set of 3   3.00 3.00
    See Nos. 1040-1042.

Tourism
A370

100fr, Pygmy village. 125fr, Lake region. 225fr, Poubara Waterfall. 260fr, Mt. Brazza.

2000   *Perf. 13x13½*
981-984 A370   Set of 4   4.75 4.75
984a   Miniature sheet of 4, #981-984   — —

Y2K Bug — A371

2000, Dec. 11   *Perf. 11½x11¾*
985 A371 225fr multi   1.40 1.40

Dr. Albert Schweitzer (1875-1965)
A372

2000, Jan. 14   *Perf. 13¼x13*
986 A372 260fr multi   1.60 1.60

A373

Trains — A374

Designs: No. 987, 100fr, Japanese Hikari trains. 125fr, Hungarian Bo-Bo electric locomotive. No. 989, 500fr, Pakistani electric locomotive. No. 990, 500fr, Belgian locomotive.

No. 991: a, 100fr, Korean Bo-Bo locomotive. b, 100fr, Moroccan electric locomotive. c, 100fr, Spanish electric locomotive. d, 500fr, Yugoslavian Type J2-441. e, 500fr, Chinese electric locomotive. f, 500fr, Norwegian Type E115.

No. 992: a, 100fr, Portuguese Diesel-electric locomotive. b, 100fr, Japanese mag-lev train. c, 100fr, Long Island Railroad diesel car. d, 500fr, German Type 103. e, 500fr, Romanian Co-Co locomotive. f, 500fr, English HST.

No. 993, 1500fr, English train "The Advanced." No. 994, 1500fr, French TGV 001. No. 995, 1500fr, Austrian Transalpine train. No. 996, 1500fr, Stourbridge Lion. No. 997, 1500fr, Puffing Billy, vert. No. 998, 1500fr, Union Pacific 4-8-8-4 Big Boy, vert. No. 999, French TGV, vert.

Illustration A374 reduced.

Perf. 13¼x13¾, 13¾x13¼

2000, Dec. 10   **Litho.**
987-990 A373   Set of 4   6.00 6.00
   Sheets of 6, #a-f
991-992 A373   Set of 2   20.00 20.00
   Souvenir Sheets
993-995 A373   Set of 3   24.00 24.00
996-999 A374   Set of 4   30.00 30.00
   See Nos. 1024-1027, 1032-1033, 1036-1037.

A375

Prehistoric Animals — A376

Designs: No. 1000, 100fr, Archaeopteryx. No. 1001, 100fr, Velociraptor, vert. No. 1002, 125fr, Torosaurus. No. 1003, 125fr, Corythosaurus. No. 1004, 225fr, Pachycephalosaurus, vert. No. 1005, 500fr, Parasaurolophus.

No. 1006, 100fr, Pterodactylus. No. 1007, 125fr, Allosaurus. No. 1008, 125fr, Struthiomimus, vert. No. 1009, 225fr, Psittacosaurus, vert. No. 1010, 260fr, Parasauraolophus, vert. No. 1011, 500fr, Acanthostega.

No. 1012: a, 125fr, Camarasaurus. b, 125fr, Rhamphorhynchus. c, 125fr, Saltasaurus. d, 225fr, Camptosaurus. e, 225fr, Megalosaurus. f, 225fr, Allosaurus. g, 260fr, Anchisaurus. h, 260fr, Dilophosaurus. i, 260fr, Massospondylus.

No. 1013: a, 100fr, Stegosaurus. b, 100fr, Pteranodon. c, 100fr, Carnotaurus. d, 125fr, Iguanodon. e, 125fr, Pentaceratops. f, 125fr, Styracosaurus. g, 500fr, Deinonychus. h, 500fr, Stegoceras. i, 500fr, Struthiomimus.

No. 1014: a, 125fr, Volcano. b, 125fr, Pterodactylus. c, 125fr, Dimorphodon. d, 125fr, Alamosaurus. e, 225fr, Psittacosaurus. f, 225fr, Deinonychus. g, 225fr, Dromiceiomimus. h, 225fr, Yangchuanosaurus. i, 260fr, Protorosaurus. j, 260fr, Triceratops. k, 260fr, Daspletosaurus. l, 260fr, Pentaceratops.

No. 1015: a, 125fr, Brachiosaurus. b, 125fr, Scaphognathus. c, Mountain and sun. d, 125fr, Pteranodon. e, 225fr, Tyrannosaurus. f, 225fr, Ichthyosaurus. g, 225fr, Macroplata. h, 225fr, Dilophosaurus. i, 500fr, Stegosaurus. j, 500fr, Thecodontosaurus. k, 500fr, Saltosaurus. l, 500fr, Pachyrhinosaurus.

No. 1016, 225fr: a, Tyrannosaurus. b, Criorhynchus. c, Pterodactylus. d, Albertosaurus. e, Dromiceiomimus. f, Opisthocoelicaudia. g, Brachiosaurus. h, Pachycephalosaurus. i, Parasaurolophus. j, Edmontosaurus. k, Pentaceratops. l, Corythosaurus.

No. 1017, 260fr: a, Peteinosaurus. b, Volcanoes. c, Acanthostega. d, Ceresiosaurus. e, Pliosaur. f, Stethacanthus. g, Ichthyosaur. h, Pholidogaster. i, Gerrothorax. j, Diplocaulus. k, Mixosaurus. l, Echinoceras raricostatum.

No. 1018, 1500fr, Tyrannosaurus Rex. No. 1019, 1500fr, Arrhinoceratops. No. 1020, 1500fr, Argentinosaurus, vert. No. 1021, 1500fr, Cetiosaurus, vert. No. 1022, 1500fr, Archaeopteryx. No. 1023, Saltasaurus, vert.

2000, Dec. 20
1000-1005 A375   Set of 6   8.00 8.00
1006-1011 A376   Set of 6   8.00 8.00
   Sheets of 9, #a-i
1012-1013 A375   Set of 2   20.00 20.00
   Sheets of 12, #a-l
1014-1015 A375   Set of 2   30.00 30.00
1016-1017 A375   Set of 2   30.00 30.00
   Souvenir Sheets
1018-1021 A375   Set of 4   30.00 30.00
1022-1023 A376   Set of 2   16.00 16.00
   No. 1021 contains one 42x56mm stamp.

Train Type of 2000 and

A377

Designs: 100fr, German Type 201. No. 1025, 225fr, German Type 112. No. 1026, 225fr, ICT. No. 1027, 260fr, ICE.
No. 1028, 260fr, French Electric BB9004. No. 1029, 260fr, French Type 232U 4-8-2. No. 1030, 500fr, French Type 241C 4-8-2 "Mountain." No. 1031, 500fr, German TEE.
No. 1032: a, 125fr, German Type 41. b, 125fr, Type 39. c, 125fr, German Type 10. d, 500fr, German Type 99. e, 500fr, German Type 58. f, 500fr, German Type 44.
No. 1033: a, 225fr, German Type 229. b, 225fr, Type 152. c, 225fr, German Type 101. d, 500fr, German Type 250. e, 500fr, German Type 232. f, 500fr, Type 216.
No. 1034: a, 125fr, Prussian Type P8 4-6-0. b, 125fr, Bavarian Type S3/6 4-6-2. c, 125fr, German Type 01 4-6-2. d, 500fr, German Electric "Crocodile." e, 500fr, Swiss Electric Type Be 4/6. f, 500fr, Swiss Electric Type Ae 6/6.
No. 1035: a, 125fr, Stirling 8ft Single 4-2-2 "No. 1," UK. b, 125fr, Greeley Pacific Type A3 4-6-2 "Flying Scotsman," UK. c, 125fr, Stanier Coronation Type 4-6-2 "Coronation Scot," UK. d, 500fr, Baldwin 4-4-0 "The General," US. e, Class J1 Hudson 4-8-4, US. f, "Super Chief" Diesel-electric, US.
No. 1036, 1500fr, Type 91. No. 1037, 1500fr, Type 57. No. 1038, Greeley Pacific Type A4 4-6-2 "Silver Link," UK. No. 1039, J Type 4-8-4, US.

Perf. 13¼x13½, 13½x13¼

2000?   **Litho.**
1024-1027 A374   Set of 4   4.00 4.00
1028-1031 A377   Set of 4   8.00 8.00
   Sheets of 6, #a-f
1032-1033 A374   Set of 2   20.00 20.00
1034-1035 A377   Set of 2   19.00 19.00
   Souvenir Sheets
1036-1037 A374   Set of 2   16.00 16.00
1038-1039 A377   Set of 2   16.00 16.00
   Nos. 1038-1039 each contain one 56x42mm stamp.

Raponda Walker Foundation
A378

2000   **Litho.**   *Perf. 11½*
1039A A378 225fr multi   1.10 1.10

End of the Millennium
A379

2000
1039B A379 225fr multi   1.20 1.20

Scientific Achievements of the 20th Century Type of 2000

Designs: 100fr, Isolation of insulin, 1921. 125fr, Invention of television, 1921. 225fr, Invention of the calculator, 1951.

Perf. 11¾x11½

2000, Nov. 28   **Litho.**
1040-1042 A369   Set of 3   3.00 3.00

Mengane Dancers
A380

2001   **Litho.**   *Perf. 11¾*
1043 A380 100fr multi   .30 .30
   Souvenir Sheet
   No. 1045: a, 100fr, Mengane. b, 130fr, Maghouba. c, 225fr, Ndjobi.

1045 A380   Sheet of 3, #a-c   2.25 2.25

Two additional stamps may have been issued in this set. The editors would like to examine any examples.

Flowers — A381

Design: 100fr, Pseudogardenia kallreyeri. 125fr, Ouratea turnerae. 225fr, Strophantus gratus. 260fr, Spathodea campanulata.

2001   **Litho.**   *Perf. 11¾*
1046-1049 A381   Set of 4   — —
1049a   Miniature sheet of 4, #1046-1049   — —

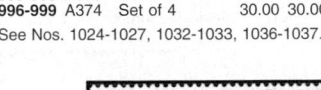

Gabon Poste Emblem
A382

Color of denomination: 125fr, Green. 225fr, Blue.

2003, Apr. 5   **Litho.**   *Perf. 13x13¼*
1050-1051 A382   Set of 2   1.75 1.75

Orchids — A383

Designs: 100fr, Plectrelmintus caudatus. 125fr, Eulophia. 225fr, Jacinthe d'eau.

2004, Feb. 20   **Perf. 13¼x13**
1052-1054 A383   Set of 3   2.25 2.25
1054a   Souvenir sheet, #1052-1054   2.75 2.75

Cooperation Between Gabon and People's Republic of China, 30th Anniv. — A384

No. 1055: a, 125fr, Chinese Prime Minister Wen Jiabao, Gabon Pres. Omar Bongo and flags. b, 225fr, Coats of arms of People's Republic of China and Gabon. No. 1056, 2500fr, Like #1055a. No. 1057, 2500fr, Like #1055b.
Illustration reduced.

2004, Apr. 20   **Perf. 12**
1055 A384   Horiz. pair, #a-b   1.75 1.75
Souvenir Sheets
Printed on Wood Veneer
Self-Adhesive
1056-1057 A384   Set of 2   — —

Nos. 1056 and 1057 are airmail and each contains one 90x50mm stamp.

FIFA (Fédération Internationale de Football Association), Cent. — A385

Background color: 125fr, Blue. 225fr, Green.

2004, Apr. 24   Litho.   Perf. 13x13¼
1058-1059 A385   Set of 2   1.75 1.75

Biodiversity — A386

Designs: 100fr, Hyperolius kuligae. 125fr, Chameleon, vert. 225fr, Merops malimbicus. 260fr, Owl.

2004, June 5   Perf. 13x13¼, 13¼x13
1060-1063 A386   Set of 4   3.50 3.50

Rotary International, Cent. — A387

2005, Feb. 23   Litho.   Perf. 13x13¼
1064 A387   125fr multi   .60 .60
Souvenir Sheet
1065 A387   2500fr multi   — —

Souvenir Sheet

Lake Evaro — A388

Illustration reduced.

2005   Litho.   Perf. 13¾x13½
1066 A388   225fr multi   .85 .85
Souvenir Sheet
1067 A388   500fr multi   1.90 1.90

Soccer Players and Flag A390

2005   Litho.   Perf. 13x13¼
1069 A390   225fr multi   .85 .85
No. 1069 issued in sheets of 4.

Central African Network of Protected Areas — A391

2007, July   Litho.   Perf. 13¼
1070 A391   500fr multi   2.10 2.10

Petroleum Exploration in Gabon, 80th Anniv. A392

Designs: No. 1071, 250fr, Ship and offshore drilling platform. No. 1072, 250fr, Oil drilling complex in jungle. No. 1073, 250fr, Oil workers. No. 1074, 500fr, Oil tanker at dock. No. 1075, 500fr, Elephants and oil drilling complex in jungle, vert. No. 1076, 500fr, Oil workers, vert.

Perf. 13x13¼, 13¼x13
2008, May 5   Litho.
1071-1076 A392   Set of 6   11.00 11.00
1076a   Sheet of 6, #1071-1076   11.00 11.00
Souvenir Sheet

Children's Drawings of Petroleum Industry — A393

No. 1077: a, Workers at Shell Gabon Terminal. b, Petroleum and Biodiversity.

2008, Sept. 25   Litho.   Perf. 13x13¼
1077 A393   250fr Sheet of 2, #a-b   2.75 2.75

Rule of Pres. Omar Bongo, 41st Anniv. A394

Litho. & Embossed
2008, Dec. 5   Perf. 13½x13
1078 A394   500fr multi   2.25 2.25
Litho. & Embossed With Foil Application
1079 A394   5000fr gold & multi   22.50 22.50
Nos. 1078-1079 each were printed in sheets of 4.

SEMI-POSTAL STAMPS

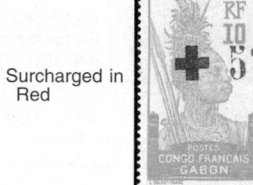

No. 37 Surcharged in Red

1916   Unwmk.   Perf. 13½x14
B1 A10   10c + 5c red & car   30.00 30.00
a.   Double surcharge   200.00 225.00
d.   In pair with unsurcharged stamp   550.00

Same Surcharge on No. 54 in Red
B2 A10   10c + 5c red & car   37.50 37.50
a.   Double surcharge   200.00 225.00
b.   Inverted surcharge   175.00
c.   Double surcharge, one inverted   175.00 200.00
d.   In pair with unsurcharged stamp   550.00

No. 54 Surcharged in Red

1917
B3 A10   10c + 5c red & car   2.40 2.40

Catalogue values for unused stamps in this section, from this point to the end of the section, are for Never Hinged items.

Republic
Anti-Malaria Issue
Common Design Type
1962, Apr. 7   Engr.   Perf. 12½x12
B4 CD108   25c + 5fr yel grn   1.00 1.00
WHO drive to eradicate malaria.

Freedom from Hunger Issue
Common Design Type
1963, Mar. 21   Unwmk.   Perf. 13
B5 CD112   25c + 5fr dk red, grn & brn   1.00 1.00

Red Cross — SP1

1997, May 8   Litho.   Perf. 13½x13
B6 SP1   150fr +75fr multi   1.40 1.10

AIR POST STAMPS

Catalogue values for unused stamps in this section are for Never Hinged items.

Dr. Albert Schweitzer — AP1

Unwmk.
1960, July 23   Engr.   Perf. 13
C1 AP1   200fr grn, dl red brn & ultra   7.50 3.75
For surcharge see No. C11.

Workmen Felling Tree — AP2

1960, Oct. 8
C2 AP2   100fr red brn, grn & blk   4.50 1.90
5th World Forestry Cong., Seattle, WA, Aug. 29-Sept. 10.

Olympic Games Issue
French Equatorial Africa No. C37 Surcharged in Red Like Chad No. C1

AP2a

1960, Dec. 15
C3 AP2a   250fr on 500fr grnsh blk, blk & slate   10.00 10.00
17th Olympic Games, Rome, 8/25-9/11.

Lyre-tailed Honey Guide — AP3

1961, May 30   Perf. 13
C4 AP3   50fr sl grn, red brn & ultra   4.75 1.60
See Nos. C14-C17.

Air Afrique Issue
Common Design Type

1962, Feb. 17 Engr. Perf. 13
C5 CD107 500fr sl grn, blk &
bis 13.00 7.00

Long
Jump — AP3a

1962, July 21 Photo. Perf. 12x12½
C6 AP3a 100fr dk & lt bl, brn &
blk 3.75 2.25
Issued to publicize the Abidjan Games.

Breguet 14, 1928 — AP4

Development of air transport: 20fr, Dragon
biplane transport. 60fr, Caravelle jet. 85fr,
Rocket-propelled aircraft.

1962, Sept. 4 Engr. Perf. 13
C7 AP4 10fr dl red brn & sl .75 .20
C8 AP4 20fr dk bl, sl & ocher 1.10 .45
C9 AP4 60fr dk sl grn, blk &
brn 2.75 1.00
C10 AP4 85fr dk bl, blk & org 2.75 1.60
a. Souv. sheet of 4, #C7-C10 11.00 11.00
Nos. C7-C10 (4) 7.35 3.25
Gabon's 1st phil. exhib., Libreville, Sept. 2-9.

No. C1 Surcharged in Red:
"100F/JUBILE GABONAIS/1913-1963"
1963, Apr. 18
C11 AP1 100fr on 200fr 4.00 2.10
50th anniv. of Dr. Albert Schweitzer's arrival
in Gabon.

Post Office, Libreville — AP5

1963, Apr. 28 Photo. Perf. 13x12
C12 AP5 100fr multi 1.90 1.00

African Postal Union Issue
Common Design Type

1963, Sept. 8 Unwmk. Perf. 12½
C13 CD114 85fr brt car, ocher &
red 1.90 .80

Bird Type of 1961

Birds: 100fr, Johanna's sunbird. 200fr,
Blue-headed bee-eater, vert. 250fr, Crowned
hawk-eagle, vert. 500fr, Narina trogon, vert.

1963-64 Engr. Perf. 13
C14 AP3 100fr dk grn, vio bl &
car 3.75 1.25
C15 AP3 200fr ol, vio bl & red 8.00 3.00
C16 AP3 250fr grn, blk & dk
brn ('64) 15.00 4.00
C17 AP3 500fr multi 15.00 7.00
Nos. C14-C17 (4) 41.75 15.25

1963 Air Afrique Issue
Common Design Type

1963, Nov. 19 Photo. Perf. 13x12
C18 CD115 50fr lt vio, gray, blk &
grn 1.60 .65

Europafrica Issue
Common Design Type

1963, Nov. 30 Perf. 12x13
C19 CD116 50fr vio, yel & dk brn 1.60 .75

Chiefs of State Issue

Map and
Presidents
of Chad,
Congo,
Gabon and
CAR
AP5a

1964, June 23 Perf. 12½
C20 AP5a 100fr multi 2.10 .90
See note after Central African Republic No.
C19.

Europafrica Issue, 1964

Globe and
Emblems of
Industry and
Agriculture — AP6

1964, July 20 Perf. 12x13
C21 AP6 50fr red, olive & blue 1.60 .75
See note after Cameroun No. 402.

Start of Race — AP7

Athletes (Greek): 50fr, Massage at gymnasium, vert. 100fr, Anointing with oil before
game, vert. 200fr, Four athletes.

1964, July 30 Engr. Perf. 13
C22 AP7 25fr sl grn, dk brn &
org 1.00 .45
C23 AP7 50fr dk brn, sl grn &
org brn 1.60 .60
C24 AP7 100fr vio bl, ol grn &
dk brn 3.00 1.10
C25 AP7 200fr dk brn, mag &
org red 5.25 3.00
a. Min. sheet of 4, #C22-C25 14.00 14.00
Nos. C22-C25 (4) 10.85 5.15
18th Olympic Games, Tokyo, Oct. 10-25.

Communications Symbols — AP7a

1964, Nov. 2 Litho. Perf. 12½x13
C26 AP7a 25fr lt grn, dk brn & lt
red brn .90 .20
See note after Chad No. C19.

John F. Kennedy
(1917-63) — AP8

1964, Nov. 23 Photo. Perf. 12½
C27 AP8 100fr grn, org & blk 2.25 1.50
a. Souv. sheet of 4 11.00 11.00

Telephone Operator, Nurse and Police
Woman — AP9

1964, Dec. 5 Engr. Perf. 13
C28 AP9 50fr car, bl & chocolate 1.40 .40
Social evolution of Gabonese women.

World Map and ICY Emblem — AP10

1965, Mar. 25 Unwmk. Perf. 13
C29 AP10 50fr org, Prus bl &
grnsh bl 1.40 .70
International Cooperation Year.

Merchant Ship, 17th Century — AP11

25fr, Galleon, 16th cent., vert. 85fr, Frigate,
18th cent., vert. 100fr, Brig, 19th cent.

1965, Apr. 22 Photo. Perf. 13
C30 AP11 25fr lilac & multi 1.25 .55
C31 AP11 50fr yellow & multi 2.75 .80
C32 AP11 85fr multi 4.75 1.75
C33 AP11 100fr multi 6.25 2.10
Nos. C30-C33 (4) 15.00 5.20

Red Cross Nurse Carrying Sick
Child — AP12

1965, June 25 Engr. Perf. 13
C34 AP12 100fr brn, slate grn &
red 2.25 .75
Issued for the Gabonese Red Cross.

Women's
Basketball
AP13

1965, July 15 Unwmk.
C35 AP13 100fr sep, red org &
brt lil 2.75 .90
African Games, Brazzaville, July 18-25.

Maps of Europe and Africa — AP14

1965, July 26 Photo. Perf. 13x12
C36 AP14 50fr multi 1.90 .65
See note after Cameroun No. 421.

Pres.
Leon
Mba
AP15

1965, Aug. 17 Perf. 12½
C37 AP15 25fr multi .90 .50
Fifth anniversary of independence.

Sir Winston Churchill and
Microphones — AP16

1965, Sept. 28 Photo. Perf. 12½
C38 AP16 100fr gold, blk & bl 2.50 1.10
Sir Winston Spencer Churchill (1874-1965),
statesman and World War II leader.

Dr. Albert Schweitzer — AP17

Embossed on Gold Foil
Die-cut Perf. 14½, Approx.
1965, Dec. 4
C39 AP17 1000fr gold 75.00 75.00
Dr. Albert Schweitzer (1875-1965), medical
missionary, theologian and musician.

Pope John XXIII and St. Peter's — AP18

1965, Dec. 10   Photo.   Perf. 13x12½
C40 AP18 85fr multi   1.75 1.10
Issued in memory of Pope John XXIII.

Anti-Malaria Treatment AP19

1966, Apr. 8   Photo.   Perf. 12½
C41 AP19 50fr shown   1.25   .75
  a.   Min. sheet of 4   8.75 8.75
C42 AP19 100fr First aid   2.75 1.10
  a.   Min. sheet of 4   14.00 14.00
Issued for the Red Cross.

Diamant Rocket, A-1 Satellite and Map of Africa — AP20

90fr, FR-1 satellite, Diamant rocket and earth.

1966, May 18   Engr.   Perf. 13
C43 AP20 30fr dk pur, brt bl &
             red brn   .85   .45
C44 AP20 90fr brt lil, red & pur 2.00   .80
French achievements in space.

Soccer and World Map — AP21

1966, July 15   Engr.   Perf. 13
C45 AP21 100fr slate & brn red   3.00 1.25
8th World Soccer Cup Championship, Wembley, England, July 11-30.

Symbols of Industry and Transportation AP22

1966, July 26   Photo.   Perf. 12x13
C46 AP22 50fr multi   1.50   .65
3rd anniv. of the economic agreement between the European Economic Community and the African and Malgache Union.

Air Afrique Issue, 1966
Common Design Type
1966, Aug. 31   Photo.   Perf. 13
C47 CD123 30fr org, blk & gray   1.00   .60

Student and UNESCO Emblem — AP23

1966, Nov. 4   Engr.   Perf. 13
C48 AP23 100fr dl bl, ocher & blk 2.25   .85
20th anniv. of UNESCO.

Libreville Airport — AP24

1966, Nov. 21   Engr.   Perf. 13
C49 AP24 200fr dp bl & red brn   5.00 1.50
Inauguration of Libreville Airport.

Farman 190 — AP25

Planes: 300fr, De Havilland Heron. 500fr, Potez 56.

1967, Apr. 1   Engr.   Perf. 13
C50 AP25 200fr ultra, lil & bl grn 5.25 1.75
C51 AP25 300fr brn, lil & brt bl   8.75 2.10
C52 AP25 500fr brn car, dk grn
             & indigo   14.00 4.75
        Nos. C50-C52 (3)   28.00 8.60
For surcharge see No. C128.

Planes, Runways and ICAO Emblem — AP26

1967, May 19   Engr.   Perf. 13
C53 AP26 100fr plum, brt bl &
             yel grn   2.50 1.10
International Civil Aviation Organization.

Blood Donor and Bottles — AP27

100fr, Human heart and transfusion apparatus.

1967, June 26   Photo.   Perf. 12½
C54 AP27   50fr ocher, red &
             sl   1.75   .65
  a.   Souvenir sheet of 4   9.75 9.75
C55 AP27 100fr yel grn, red &
             gray   3.50 1.25
  a.   Souvenir sheet of 4   15.00 15.00
Issued for the Red Cross. Nos. C54a, C55a each contain 2 vertical tête bêche pairs.

Jamboree Emblem and Symbols of Orientation AP28

1967, Aug. 1   Engr.   Perf. 13
Design: 100fr, Jamboree emblem, maps and Scouts of Africa and America.
C56 AP28   50fr multi   1.60   .80
C57 AP28 100fr brt grn, dp car &
             bl   2.40 1.60
12th Boy Scout World Jamboree, Farragut State Park, Idaho, Aug. 1-9.

African Postal Union Issue, 1967
Common Design Type
1967, Sept. 9   Engr.   Perf. 13
C58 CD124 100fr dl bl, ol & red
             brn   2.25   .95

Mission Church — AP29

1967, Oct. 18   Engr.   Perf. 13
C59 AP29 100fr brt bl, dk grn &
             blk   2.75 1.25
125th anniv. of the arrival of American Protestant missionaries in Baraka-Libreville.

UN Emblem, Sword, Book and People — AP30

1967, Nov. 7   Photo.   Perf. 13
C60 AP30 60fr dk red, vio bl & bis 1.10   .65
UN Commission on Human Rights.

Tree Type of Regular Issue

Designs: 50fr, Baillonella toxisperma. 100fr, Aucoumea klaineana.

1967, Dec. 5   Engr.   Perf. 13
Size: 26½x47½mm
C61 A53   50fr grn, brt bl & brn   2.10 1.10
C62 A53 100fr multi   3.50 1.90
  a.   Bklt. pane of 5, #223-225,
        C61-C62 with gutter btwn.   10.00 10.00

Konrad Adenauer AP31

1968, Feb. 20   Photo.   Perf. 12½
C63 AP31 100fr blk, dl org &
             red   3.25 1.10
  a.   Souvenir sheet of 4   13.00 13.00
Issued in memory of Konrad Adenauer (1876-1967), chancellor of West Germany (1949-63). No. C63a includes 1967 CEPT (Europa) emblem.

Madonna of the Rosary by Murillo AP32

90fr, Christ in Bonds, by Luis de Morales. 100fr, St. John on Patmos, by Juan Mates.

1968, July 9   Photo.   Perf. 12½x12
C64 AP32   60fr multi   1.40   .55
C65 AP32   90fr multi   2.00   .95
C66 AP32 100fr multi, horiz.   2.25 1.10
        Nos. C64-C66 (3)   5.65 2.60
See #C77, C102-C104, C132-C133, C146-C148.

Europafrica Issue

Stylized Knot — AP32a

1968, July 23   Photo.   Perf. 13
C67 AP32a 50fr yel brn, emer &
             lt ultra   1.10   .45
See note after Congo Republic No. C69.

Support for Red Cross — AP33

50fr, Distribution of Red Cross gifts.

1968, Aug. 13
C68	AP33	50fr multi	1.40	.65
C69	AP33	100fr multi	3.25	1.40
a.		Bklt. pane of 2, #C68, C69 with gutter btwn.	7.50	7.50

Issued for the Red Cross.

High Jump — AP34

1968, Sept. 3   **Engr.**
C70	AP34	25fr shown	.85	.50
C71	AP34	30fr Bicycling, vert.	1.00	.55
C72	AP34	100fr Judo, vert.	2.75	1.25
C73	AP34	200fr Boxing	5.00	2.10
a.		Bklt. pane of 4, #C70-C71, C72-C73 with gutter btwn.	13.00	13.00
		Nos. C70-C73 (4)	9.60	4.40

Issued to publicize the 19th Summer Olympic Games, Mexico City, Oct. 12-27.

Pres. Mba, Flag and Arms of Gabon — AP35

Embossed on Gold Foil

1968, Nov. 28   **Perf. 14½**
C74	AP35	1000fr gold, grn, yel & dk bl	30.00 30.00

Death of Pres. Léon Mba (1902-67), 1st anniv.

Pres. Bongo, Maps of Gabon and Owendo Harbor — AP36

1968, Dec. 16   Photo.   Perf. 12½
C75	AP36	25fr shown	1.60	.20
C76	AP36	30fr Owendo Harbor	1.60	.20
a.		Strip of 2, #C75-C76 + label	3.75	3.75

Laying of the foundation stone for Owendo Harbor, June 24, 1968.

PHILEXAFRIQUE Issue
Painting Type of 1968

Design: 100fr, The Convent of St. Mary of the Angels, by Francois Marius Granet.

1969, Jan. 8   Photo.   Perf. 12½x12
C77	AP32	100fr multi	4.75 4.75

Issued to publicize PHILEXAFRIQUE Philatelic Exhibition in Abidjan, Feb. 14-23. Printed with alternating brown label.

Mahatma Gandhi — AP37

Portraits: 30fr, John F. Kennedy. 50fr, Robert F. Kennedy. 100fr, Martin Luther King, Jr.

1969, Jan. 15   **Perf. 12½**
C78	AP37	25fr pink & blk	.75	.45
C79	AP37	30fr lt yel grn & blk	.75	.45
C80	AP37	50fr lt bl & blk	1.10	.45
C81	AP37	100fr brt rose lil & blk	2.25	.90
a.		Souv. sheet of 4, #C78-C81	6.00	6.00
		Nos. C78-C81 (4)	4.85	2.25

Issued to honor exponents of non-violence.

2nd PHILEXAFRIQUE Issue
Common Design Type

1969, Feb. 14   Engr.   Perf. 13
C82	CD128	50fr grn, ind & red brn	2.25 2.25

Battle of Rivoli, by Henri Philippoteaux — AP39

100fr, The Oath of the Army, by Jacques Louis David. 250fr, Napoleon with the Children on the Terrace in St. Cloud, by Louis Ducis.

1969, Apr. 23   Photo.   Perf. 12½x12
C83	AP39	50fr brn & multi	2.25	1.10
C84	AP39	100fr grn & multi	2.75	2.40
C85	AP39	250fr lil & multi	12.00	7.00
		Nos. C83-C85 (3)	17.00	10.50

Birth bicentenary of Napoleon I.

Red Cross Plane, Nurse and Biafran Children — AP40

20fr, Dispensary, ambulance & supplies. 25fr, Physician & nurse in children's ward. 30fr, Dispensary & playing children.

1969, June 20   Photo.   Perf. 14x13½
C86	AP40	15fr lt ultra, dk brn & red	.80	.20
C87	AP40	20fr emer, blk, brn & red	.75	.45
C88	AP40	25fr grnsh bl, dk brn & red	.75	.45
C89	AP40	30fr org yel, dk brn & red	1.10	.45
		Nos. C86-C89 (4)	3.40	1.55

Red Cross help for Biafra.
A souvenir sheet contains four stamps similar to Nos. C86-C89, but lithographed and rouletted 13x13½. Gray margin with red inscription and Red Cross. Size: 118x75mm. Sold in cardboard folder. Value $4.

Astronauts and Lunar Landing Module, Apollo 11 — AP41

Embossed on Gold Foil

1969, July 25   Die-cut Perf. 10½x10
C90	AP41	1000fr gold	26.00 26.00

See note after Algeria No. 427.

African and European Heads and Symbols — AP42

Icarus and Sun — AP43

Europafrica Issue, 1970

1970, June 5   Photo.   Perf. 12x13
C91	AP42	50fr multi	1.25 .50

1970, June 10   Engr.   Perf. 13

Designs: 100fr, Leonardo da Vinci's flying man, 1519. 200fr, Jules Verne's space shell approaching moon, 1865.
C92	AP43	25fr ultra, red & org	.85	.50
C93	AP43	100fr ocher, plum & sl grn	2.00	1.00
C94	AP43	200fr gray, ultra & dk car	4.75	2.00
a.		Min. sheet of 3, #C92-C94	8.50	8.50
		Nos. C92-C94 (3)	7.60	3.50

UAMPT Emblem AP44

Embossed on Gold Foil

1970, June 18   Die-cut Perf. 12½
C95	AP44	200fr gold, yel grn & bl	4.25 2.40

Meeting of the Afro-Malagasy Union of Posts & Telecommuncations (UAMPT), Libreville, 6/17-23.

Throwing Knives AP45

Gabonese Weapons: 30fr, Assegai and crossbow, vert. 50fr, War knives, vert. 90fr, Dagger and sheath.

1970, July 10   Engr.   Perf. 13
C96	AP45	25fr multi	.60	.35
C97	AP45	30fr multi	.80	.40
C98	AP45	50fr multi	1.00	.50
C99	AP45	90fr multi	2.40	.90
a.		Min. sheet of 4, #C96-C99	6.50	6.50
		Nos. C96-C99 (4)	4.80	2.15

Japanese Masks, Mt. Fuji and Torii at Miyajima — AP46

Embossed on Gold Foil

1970, July 31   Die-cut Perf. 10
C100	AP46	1000fr multi	25.00 25.00

Issued to publicize EXPO '70 International Exhibition, Osaka, Japan, Mar. 15-Sept. 13.

Pres. Albert Bernard Bongo — AP47

Lithographed; Gold Embossed
1970, Aug. 17   **Perf. 12½**
C101	AP47	200fr multi	5.00 2.25

10th anniversary of independence.

Painting Type of 1968

Paintings: 50fr, Portrait of a Young Man, School of Raphael. 100fr, Portrait of Jeanne d'Aragon, by Raphael. 200fr, Madonna with Blue Diadem, by Raphael.

1970, Oct. 16   Photo.   Perf. 12½x12
C102	AP32	50fr multi	1.10	.50
C102A	AP32	100fr blue & multi	2.40	.95
C102B	AP32	200fr brown & multi	4.75	2.50
		Nos. C102-C102B (3)	8.25	3.95

Raphael (1483-1520).

Miniature Sheets

Sikorsky S-32 — AP47a

Hugo Junkers — AP47b

1970, Dec. 5   Litho.   Perf. 12
C103		Sheet of 8	11.00 11.00
a.		AP47a 15fr shown	
b.		AP47a 25fr Fokker "Southern Cross"	
c.		AP47a 40fr Dornier DO-18	
d.		AP47a 60fr Dornier DO-X	
e.		AP47a 80fr Breguet "Bizerte"	
f.		AP47a 125fr Douglas "Cloudster"	

g. AP47a 150fr De Havilland DH-2
h. AP47a 200fr Vickers "Vimi"
C104 Sheet of 4   18.50 18.50
a. AP47b 200fr shown
b. AP47b 300fr Claude Dornier
c. AP47b 400fr Anthony Fokker
d. AP47b 500fr Igor Sikorsky

Imperf

C105 Sheet of 8   11.00 11.00
a. AP47a 10fr Dornier "Spatz"
b. AP47a 20fr Douglas DC-3
c. AP47a 30fr Dornier DO-7 "Wal"
d. AP47a 50fr Sikorsky S-38
e. AP47a 75fr De Havilland "Moth"
f. AP47a 100fr Supermarine "Spitfire"
g. AP47a 125fr Breguet XIX
h. AP47a 150fr Fokker "Universal"

Size: 80x90mm

C106 AP47b 1000fr Claude Dornier   18.50 18.50

Claude Dornier (1884-1969), aviation pioneer. No. C104 exists imperf. Value $17.

Presidents Bongo and Pompidou — AP48

1971, Feb. 11   Photo.   Perf. 13
C107 AP48 50fr multi   2.25 1.10
Visit of Georges Pompidou, Pres. of France.

Apollo 14 — AP48a

1971, Feb. 19   Perf. 14
Yellow Inscriptions
C108 15fr Lift off   .20 .20
C108A 25fr Achieving orbit   .45 .30
C108B 40fr Lunar module descent   .80 .60
C108C 55fr Lunar landing   1.00 .65
C108D 75fr Lunar liftoff   1.50 1.00
C108E 120fr Earth re-entry   2.50 1.50
   Nos. C108-C108E (6)   6.45 4.25

Souvenir Sheet
C108F Sheet of 2   7.50 4.25
g. AP48a 100fr Modules attached   3.00 1.75
h. AP48a 100fr like #C108E   3.00 1.75

Nos. C108-C108F exist imperf. with white inscriptions. Same values.

Flowers and Plane — AP49

25fr, Carnations. 40fr, Roses. 55fr, Daffodils. 75fr, Orchids. 120fr, Tulips.

1971, May 7   Litho.   Perf. 13½x14
C109 AP49 15fr yellow & multi   .45 .20
C109A AP49 25fr multi   .70 .20
C109B AP49 40fr pink & multi   1.10 .40
C109C AP49 55fr blue & multi   1.40 .45
C110 AP49 75fr multi   2.40 .60

C111 AP49 120fr green & multi   3.00 .85
a. Souv. sheet of 2, #C110-C111   6.00 6.00
   Nos. C109-C111 (6)   9.05 2.70
"Flowers by air."

Napoleon's Death Mask AP50

Designs: 200fr, Longwood, St. Helena, by Jacques Marchand, horiz. 500fr, Sarcophagus in Les Invalides, Paris.

1971, May 12   Photo.   Perf. 13
C112 AP50 100fr gold & multi   3.00 .70
C113 AP50 200fr gold & multi   5.00 .80
C114 AP50 500fr gold & multi   12.00 3.25
   Nos. C112-C114 (3)   20.00 4.75
Napoleon Bonaparte (1769-1821).

Souvenir Sheet

Charles de Gaulle — AP51

Designs: 40fr, President de Gaulle. 80fr, General de Gaulle. 100fr, Quotation.

1971, June 18   Photo.   Perf. 12½
C115 AP51 Sheet of 5   11.00 11.00
a. 40fr dark red & multi   .95 .95
b. 80fr dark green & multi   .95 .95
c. 100fr green, brown & yel   2.50 2.50

In memory of Gen. Charles de Gaulle (1890-1970), Pres. of France.
For surcharge see No. C126.

Red Crosses AP52

1971, June 29
C116 AP52 50fr multicolored   1.40 .40
For the Red Cross of Gabon.
For surcharge see No. C143.

Uranium — AP53

1971, July 20   Photo.   Perf. 13x12½
C117 AP53 85fr shown   7.00 3.50
C118 AP53 90fr Manganese   8.00 4.00

Landing Module over Moon — AP54

Embossed on Gold Foil

1971, July 30   Die-cut Perf. 10
C119 AP54 1500fr multi   30.00 30.00
Apollo 11 and 15 US moon missions.

African Postal Union Issue, 1971
Common Design Type

Design: 100fr, Bakota copper mask and UAMPT building, Brazzaville, Congo.

1971, Nov. 13   Photo.   Perf. 13x13½
C120 CD135 100fr bl & multi   2.00 .70

Ski Jump and Miyajima Torii AP55

130fr, Speed skating and Japanese temple.

1972, Jan. 31   Engr.   Perf. 13
C121 AP55 40fr hn brn, sl grn & vio bl   1.25 .35
C122 AP55 130fr hn brn, sl grn & vio bl   3.25 .75
a. Souvenir sheet of 2, #C121-C122 + label   5.00 5.00

11th Winter Olympic Games, Sapporo, Japan, Feb. 3-13.

The Basin and Grand Canal, by Vanvitelli — AP56

Paintings: 70fr, Rialto Bridge, by Canaletto (erroneously inscribed Caffi), vert. 140fr, Santa Maria della Salute, by Vanvitelli, vert.

1972, Feb. 7   Photo.   Perf. 13
C123 AP56 60fr gold & multi   2.50 .70
C124 AP56 70fr gold & multi   3.75 1.00
C125 AP56 140fr gold & multi   7.25 1.50
   Nos. C123-C125 (3)   13.50 3.20
UNESCO campaign to save Venice.

No. C115 Surcharged in Brown and Gold
Souvenir Sheet

1972, Feb. 11   Perf. 12½
C126 AP51 Sheet of 5   20.00 20.00
a. 60fr on 40fr multi   2.75 2.75
b. 120fr on 80fr multi   4.00 4.00
c. 180fr on 100fr multi   8.25 8.25

Publicity for the erection of a memorial for Charles de Gaulle. Nos. C126a-C126b have surcharge and Cross of Lorraine in gold, 2 bars obliterating old denomination in brown; No. C126c has surcharge, cross and bars in brown. Two Lorraine Crosses and inscription (MEMORIAL DU GENERAL DE GAULLE) in brown added in margin.

Hotel Inter-Continental, Libreville — AP57

1972, Feb. 26   Engr.   Perf. 13
C127 AP57 40fr bl, sl grn & org brn   1.10 .35

No. C51 Surcharged

1972, Mar. 3
C128 AP25 50fr on 300fr multi   1.00 .30
Official visit of the Grand Master of the Knights of Malta, March 3.

Discobolus, by Alcamenes AP58

Designs: 100fr, Doryphoros, by Polycletus. 140fr, Borghese gladiator, by Agasias.

1972, May 10   Engr.   Perf. 13
C129 AP58 30fr rose cl & gray   .90 .40
C130 AP58 100fr rose cl & gray   1.90 .50
C131 AP58 140fr rose cl & gray   2.50 .70
a. Min. of sheet of 3, #C129-C131   6.50 6.50
   Nos. C129-C131 (3)   5.30 1.60
20th Olympic Games, Munich, 8/26-9/10.
For surcharges see Nos. C134-C136.

Painting Type of 1968

Paintings: 30fr, Adoration of the Magi, by Peter Brueghel, the Elder, horiz. 40fr, Madonna and Child, by Marco Basaiti.

1972, Oct. 30   Photo.   Perf. 13
C132 AP32 30fr gold & multi   1.10 .20
C133 AP32 40fr gold & multi   1.60 .20

Christmas 1972.

Nos. C129-C131 Surcharged with New Value, Two Bars and Names of Athletes.

1972, Dec. 5   Engr.   Perf. 13
C134 AP58 40fr on 30fr   1.10 .35
C135 AP58 120fr on 100fr   2.00 .65
C136 AP58 170fr on 140fr   3.25 1.00
   Nos. C134-C136 (3)   6.35 2.00

Gold medal winners in 20th Olympic Games: Daniel Morelon, France, Bicycling (C134); Kipchoge Keino, Kenya, steeplechase (C135); Mark Spitz, US, swimming (C136).

Globe with Space Orbits, Simulated
Stamps — AP59

1973, Feb. 20   Photo.   *Perf. 13*
C137 AP59 100fr multi   2.25   .50
  a. Souv. sheet of 4, perf.
      12x12½   25.00 25.00
PHILEXGABON 1973, Phil. Exhib., Libreville, Feb. 19-26. No. C137a exists imperf.

DC10-30 "Libreville" over Libreville
Airport — AP60

1973, Mar. 19   Typo.   *Perf. 13*
C138 AP60 40fr blue & multi   2.25   .50

Kinguélé Hydroelectric Station — AP61

Design: 40fr, Kinguélé Dam.

1973, June 19   Engr.   *Perf. 13*
C139 AP61 30fr slate grn & dk ol   .80   .20
C140 AP61 40fr slate grn, dk ol
         & bl   1.10   .20
  a. Strip of 2, #C139-C140 + label 2.75 1.25
Hydroelectric installations at Kinguélé.

M'Bigou Stone
Sculpture,
Woman's
Head — AP62

Design: 200fr, Sculpture, man's head.

1973, July 5
C141 AP62 100fr blk, bl & grn   3.25   .70
C142 AP62 200fr grn, sep & sl
         grn   3.75 1.25

No. C116 Surcharged with New Value,
2 Bars, and Overprinted in
Ultramarine: "SECHERESSE
SOLIDARITE AFRICAINE"

1973, Aug. 16   Photo.   *Perf. 12½*
C143 AP52 100fr on 50fr multi   2.25   .65

African solidarity in drought emergency.

Astronauts and Lunar Rover on
Moon — AP63

1973, Sept. 6   Engr.   *Perf. 13*
C144 AP63 500fr multi   10.00 4.00
Apollo 17 US moon mission, 12/7-19/73.

Presidents Houphouet Boigny (Ivory
Coast) and De Gaulle — AP64

1974, Apr. 30   Engr.   *Perf. 13*
C145 AP64 40fr rose lilac & indigo 2.25   .55
30th anniv. of the Conf. of Brazzaville.

Painting Type of 1968

Impressionist Paintings: 40fr, Pleasure
Boats, by Claude Monet, horiz. 50fr, Ballet
Dancer, by Edgar Degas. 130fr, Young Girl
with Flowers, by Auguste Renoir.

1974, June 11   Photo.   *Perf. 13*
C146 AP32 40fr gold & multi   3.50   .50
C147 AP32 50fr gold & multi   5.50   .70
C148 AP32 130fr gold & multi   8.75 1.10
    Nos. C146-C148 (3)   17.75 2.30

Astronaut on
Moon, Eagle and
Emblems
AP65

1974, July 20   Engr.   *Perf. 13*
C149 AP65 200fr multi   3.00   .90
First men on the moon, 5th anniversary.

UPU
Emblem,
Letters,
Pigeon
AP66

UPU cent.: 300fr, UPU emblem, letters,
pigeons, diff.

1974, Oct. 9   Engr.   *Perf. 13*
C150 AP66 150fr lt bl & Prus bl   2.50   .90
C151 AP66 300fr org & claret   5.00 1.75

Space
Docking,
US and
USSR
Crafts
AP67

1974, Oct. 23   Engr.   *Perf. 13*
C152 AP67 1000fr grn, red & sl   11.00 5.25
Russo-American space cooperation.
For overprint see No. C169.

Soccer and Games Emblem — AP68

Designs: Soccer actions.

1974, Oct. 25
C153 AP68 40fr grn, red & brn   .70   .20
C154 AP68 65fr red, brn & grn   1.00   .35
C155 AP68 100fr grn, red & brn   1.50   .60
  a. Souv. sheet of 3, #C153-C155
      + 3 labels   4.50 4.50
    Nos. C153-C155 (3)   3.20 1.15
World Cup Soccer Championship, Munich,
June 13-July 7.

UDEAC Issue

Presidents and Flags of Cameroun,
CAR, Gabon and Congo — AP68a

1974, Dec. 8   Photo.   *Perf. 13*
C156 AP68a 100fr gold & multi   1.25   .45

Annunciation, Tapestry, 15th
Century — AP69

Christmas: 40fr, Visitation from 15th century tapestry, Notre Dame de Beaune, vert.

1974, Dec. 11
C157 AP69 40fr gold & multi   1.10   .30
C158 AP69 50fr gold & multi   1.25   .35

Dr. Schweitzer and Lambarene
Hospital — AP70

1975, Jan. 14   Engr.   *Perf. 13*
C159 AP70 500fr multi   9.00 3.00
Dr. Albert Schweitzer (1875-1965), medical
missionary, birth centenary.

Crucifixion, by
Bellini — AP71

Paintings: 150fr, Resurrection, Burgundian
School, c. 1500.

1975, Apr. 8   Photo.   *Perf. 13½*
      Size: 26x45mm
C160 AP71 140fr gold & multi   2.10   .60
      Size: 36x48mm
      Perf. 13
C161 AP71 150fr gold & multi   2.50   .70
Easter 1975.

Marc Seguin Locomotive,
1829 — AP72

Locomotives: 25fr, The Iron Duke, 1847.
40fr, Thomas Rogers, 1895. 50fr, The Soviet
272, 1934.

1975, Apr. 8   Engr.   *Perf. 13*
C162 AP72 20fr multi   1.60   .40
C163 AP72 25fr multi   2.25   .40
C164 AP72 40fr multi   2.75   .65
C165 AP72 50fr lil & multi   3.50   .75
    Nos. C162-C165 (4)   10.10 2.20

Swimming Pool, Montreal Olympic
Games' Emblem — AP73

Designs: 150fr, Boxing ring and emblem.
300fr, Stadium, aerial view, and emblem.

1975, Sept. 30   Litho.   *Perf. 13x12½*
C166 AP73 100fr multi   1.50   .30
C167 AP73 150fr multi   1.90   .60
C168 AP73 300fr multi   3.75 1.10
  a. Min. sheet of 3, #C166-C168 8.00 8.00
    Nos. C166-C168 (3)   7.15 2.00
Pre-Olympic Year 1975.

No. C152 Surcharged in Violet Blue:
"JONCTION / 17 Juillet 1975"

1975, Oct. 20   Engr.   *Perf. 13*
C169 AP67 1000fr multi   11.00 4.50
Apollo-Soyuz link-up in space, July 17, 1975.

Annunciation, by Maurice
Denis — AP74

Painting: 50fr, Virgin and Child with Two
Saints, by Fra Filippo Lippi.

1975, Dec. 9   Photo.   *Perf. 13*
C170 AP74 40fr gold & multi   1.25   .40
C171 AP74 50fr gold & multi   1.60   .55
Christmas 1975.

Concorde and Globe — AP75

1975, Dec. 29   Engr.   Perf. 13
C172 AP75 500fr bl, vio bl & red 11.00 3.75
For overprint see No. C198.

No. C172 Surcharged

1976, Jan. 21
C173 AP75 1000fr on 500fr 20.00 8.00
Nos. C172-C173 for the 1st commercial flight of supersonic jet Concorde from Paris to Rio, Jan. 21.

Slalom and Olympic Games Emblem — AP76

Design: 250fr, Speed skating and Winter Olympic Games emblem.

1976, Apr. 22   Engr.   Perf. 13
C174 AP76 100fr blk, bl & red 1.50 .40
C175 AP76 250fr blk, bl & red 3.25 1.40
  a. Souvenir sheet 6.50 6.50
12th Winter Olympic Games, Innsbruck, Austria, Feb. 4-15. No. C175a contains 100fr and 250fr stamps in continuous design with additional inscription and skier between, but without perforations between the design elements.
Size of perforated area: 125x27mm; size of sheet: 169x90mm.

Jesus Between the Thieves AP77

Design: 130fr, St. Thomas putting finger into wounds of Jesus. Both designs after wood carvings in Church of St. Michael, Libreville.

1976, Apr. 28   Litho.   Perf. 12½x13
C176 AP77 120fr multi 1.60 .65
C177 AP77 130fr multi 2.25 .95
Easter 1976. See #C188-C189, C220-C221.

Boston Tea Party — AP78

Designs: 150fr, Battle of New York. 200fr, Demolition of statue of George III.

1976, May 3   Engr.   Perf. 13
C178 AP78 100fr multi 1.25 .50
C179 AP78 150fr multi 2.25 .70
C180 AP78 200fr multi 2.75 .80
  a. Triptych, #C178-C180 + 2 labels 9.50 6.50
American Bicentennial.

Nos. C178-C180 Overprinted: "4 JUILLET 1976"

1976, July 4   Engr.   Perf. 13
C181 AP78 100fr multi 1.25 .50
C182 AP78 150fr multi 2.25 .70
C183 AP78 200fr multi 2.75 .80
  a. Triptych, #C181-C183 + 2 labels 9.50 6.50
Independence Day.

Running — AP79

200fr, Soccer. 260fr, High jump.

1976, July 27   Litho.   Perf. 12½
C184 AP79 100fr multi 1.10 .35
C185 AP79 200fr multi 2.50 .65
C186 AP79 260fr multi 3.25 .90
  a. Souv. sheet of 3, #C184-C186, perf. 13 8.00 3.75
  Nos. C184-C186 (3) 6.85 1.90
21st Olympic Games, Montreal, Canada, July 17-Aug. 1.

Presidents Giscard d'Estaing and Bongo — AP80

1976, Aug. 5   Photo.   Perf. 13
C187 AP80 60fr blue & multi 1.25 .30
Visit of Pres. Valèrie Giscard d'Estaing of France.

Sculpture Type of 1976

Christmas: 50fr, Presentation at the Temple. 60fr, Nativity. Designs after wood Carvings in Church of St. Michael, Libreville.

1976, Dec. 6   Litho.   Perf. 12½x13
C188 AP77 50fr multi 1.00 .20
C189 AP77 60fr multi 1.10 .35

Oklo Fossil Reactor — AP81

1976, Dec. 15   Litho.   Perf. 13
C190 AP81 60fr red & multi 1.10 .30

The Last Supper, by Juste de Gand — AP82

100fr, The Deposition, by Nicolas Poussin.

1977, Mar. 25   Litho.   Perf. 12½
C191 AP82 50fr gold & multi 1.10 .20
C192 AP82 100fr gold & multi 2.25 .65
Easter 1977.

Air Gabon Plane and Insigne — AP83

1977, June 3   Litho.   Perf. 12½
C193 AP83 60fr multi 1.10 .30
Air Gabon's first intercontinental route.

Beethoven, Piano and Score — AP84

1977, June 15   Engr.   Perf. 13
C194 AP84 260fr slate 3.50 .95
Ludwig van Beethoven (1770-1827).

Lindbergh and Spirit of St. Louis — AP85

1977, Sept. 13   Engr.   Perf. 13
C195 AP85 500fr multi 8.50 2.75
Charles A. Lindbergh's solo transatlantic flight from NY to Paris, 50th anniv.

Soccer — AP86

1977, Oct. 18   Photo.   Perf. 13x12½
C196 AP86 250fr multi 3.25 1.10
Elimination games, World Soccer Cup, Buenos Aires, 1978.

Viking on Mars AP87

1977, Nov. 17   Engr.   Perf. 13
C197 AP87 1000fr multi 13.00 3.50
Viking, US space probe.

No. C172 Overprinted: "PARIS NEW-YORK / PREMIER VOL / 22.11.77"

1977, Nov. 22   Engr.   Perf. 13
C198 AP75 500fr multi 11.00 2.50
Concorde, 1st commercial flight, Paris to NYC.

Lion Hunt, by Rubens — AP88

Rubens Paintings: 80fr, Hippopotamus Hunt. 200fr, Head of Black Man, vert.

1977, Nov. 24   Litho.   Perf. 13
C199 AP88 60fr gold & multi 1.10 .35
C200 AP88 80fr gold & multi 1.25 .45
C201 AP88 200fr gold & multi 3.50 1.10
  a. Souv. sheet of 3, #C199-C201 8.00 4.00
  Nos. C199-C201 (3) 5.85 1.90
Peter Paul Rubens (1577-1640).

Adoration of the Kings, by Rubens — AP89

Design: 80fr, Flight into Egypt, by Rubens.

1977, Dec. 15   Litho.   Perf. 12½
C202 AP89 60fr gold & multi 1.10 .30
C203 AP89 80fr gold & multi 1.25 .45
Christmas 1977; Peter Paul Rubens.

Paul Gauguin, Self-Portrait AP90

150fr, Flowers in vase and Maori statuette.

1978, Feb. 8   Litho.   Perf. 12½x12
C204 AP90 150fr multi 3.00 .60
C205 AP90 300fr multi 5.50 1.10
Paul Gauguin (1848-1903), French painter.

Pres. Bongo, Map of Gabon, Plane and Train AP91

Lithographed; Gold Embossed
1978, Mar. 12   *Perf. 12½*
C206 AP91 500fr multi   7.00 1.75

10th anniversary of national renewal.

Soccer and Argentina '78 Emblem — AP92

Argentina '78 Emblem and: 120fr, Three soccer players. 200fr, Jules Rimet Cup, vert.

1978, July 18   **Engr.**   *Perf. 13*
C207 AP92 100fr red, grn & brn   1.10   .20
C208 AP92 120fr grn, red & brn   1.25   .40
C209 AP92 200fr brn & red   2.40   .55
  a.   Min. sheet of 3, #C207-C209   6.50 3.00
       Nos. C207-C209 (3)   4.75 1.15

11th World Cup Soccer Championship, Argentina, June 1-25.

Nos. C207-C209a Overprinted in Ultramarine or Black:
a. ARGENTINE / HOLLANDE / 3-1
b. BRESIL / ITALIE / 2-1
c. CHAMPION / DU MONDE 1978 / ARGENTINE

1978, July 21   **Engr.**   *Perf. 13*
C210 AP92(a) 100fr multi   1.00   .30
C211 AP92(b) 120fr multi   1.25   .40
C212 AP92(c) 200fr multi   2.10   .65
  a.   Min. sheet of 3 (Bk)   6.00 6.00
       Nos. C210-C212 (3)   4.35 1.35

Argentina's World Cup victory.

Albrecht Dürer (age 13), Self-portrait AP93

Design: 250fr, Lucas de Leyde, by Dürer.

1978, Sept. 15   **Engr.**   *Perf. 13*
C213 AP93 100fr red brn & slate   1.40   .30
C214 AP93 250fr blk & red brn   3.75   .80

Dürer (1474-1528), German painter.

Philexafrique II-Essen Issue
Common Design Types

Designs: No. C215, Gorilla and Gabon No. 280. No. C216, Stork and Saxony No. 1.

1978, Nov. 1   **Litho.**   *Perf. 13x12½*
C215 CD138 100fr multi   2.75 1.40
C216 CD139 100fr multi   2.75 1.40
  a.   Pair, #C215-C216 + label   9.00 5.00

#C216a exists with two different labels: one for PHILEXAFRIQUE II and one for ESSEN '78.

Wright Brothers and Flyer AP94

1978, Dec. 19   **Engr.**   *Perf. 13*
C217 AP94 380fr multi   5.00 1.10

75th anniversary of 1st powered flight.

Pope John Paul II AP95

Design: 200fr, Popes Paul VI and John Paul I, St. Peter's Basilica and Square, horiz.

1979, Jan. 24   **Litho.**   *Perf. 12½*
C218 AP95 100fr multi   2.50   .35
C219 AP95 200fr multi   5.50   .80

Sculpture Type of 1976

Easter: 100fr, Disciples recognizing Jesus in the breaking of the bread. 150fr, Jesus appearing to Mary Magdalene. Designs after wood carvings in Church of St. Michael, Libreville.

1979, Apr. 10   **Litho.**   *Perf. 12½x13*
C220 AP77 100fr multi   1.25   .45
C221 AP77 150fr multi   2.25   .65

Capt. Cook and Ships AP96

1979, July 10   **Engr.**   *Perf. 13*
C222 AP96 500fr multi   7.00 2.00

Capt. James Cook (1728-1779), explorer, death bicentenary.

Flags and Map of England and France, Bleriot, Bleriot XI — AP97

Aviation Retrospect: 1000fr, Astronauts walking on moon (gold embossed inset).

Perf. 12½x12, 12
1979, Aug. 8   **Litho.**
C223 AP97 250fr multi   3.25 1.00
C224 AP97 1000fr multi   11.00 3.75

1st flight over English Channel, 70th anniv.; Apollo 11 moon landing, 10th anniv.

Rotary Emblem, Map of Africa, Head — AP98

1979, Sept. 25   **Photo.**   *Perf. 13*
C225 AP98 80fr multi   1.10   .35

Rotary International, 75th anniversary.

Eugene Jamot, Tsetse Fly — AP99

1979, Nov. 23   **Engr.**   *Perf. 13*
C226 AP99 300fr multi   5.00 1.50

Eugene Jamot (1879-1937), discoverer of sleeping sickness cure.

Bobsledding, Lake Placid '80 Emblem AP100

1980, Feb. 25   **Litho.**   *Perf. 12½*
C227 AP100 100fr shown   1.00   .40
C228 AP100 200fr Ski jump   2.10   .75
  a.   Souv. sheet of 2, #C227-C228   4.00 1.90

13th Winter Olympic Games, Lake Placid, NY, Feb. 12-24.

Jean Ingres AP101

1980, May 14   **Engr.**   *Perf. 13*
C229 AP101 100fr shown   1.50   .50
C230 AP101 200fr Jacques Of-
            fenbach   3.00   .95
C231 AP101 360fr Gustave
            Flaubert   4.50 1.75
       Nos. C229-C231 (3)   9.00 3.20

12th World Telecommunications Day — AP102

1980, May 17   **Litho.**   *Perf. 12½*
C232 AP102 80fr multi   1.10   .35

Costes, Bellonte and Plane — AP103

Design: 1000fr, Mermoz, sea plane.

1980, July 16   **Engr.**   *Perf. 13*
C233 AP103 165fr multi   1.60   .70
C234 AP103 1000fr multi   11.00 4.50

1st North Atlantic crossing, 50th anniv.; 1st South Atlantic air mail service, 50th anniv.

Running, Moscow '80 Emblem AP104

1980, July 25   **Litho.**
C235 AP104 50fr shown   .55   .20
C236 AP104 100fr Pole vault   1.10   .45
C237 AP104 250fr Boxing   2.90 1.00
  a.   Souv. sheet of 3, #C235-C237   8.50 4.00
       Nos. C235-C237 (3)   4.55 1.65

22nd Summer Olympic Games, Moscow, July 19-Aug. 3.

Nos. C235-C237a Overprinted in Red, Brown, Ultramarine or Black

50fr: YIFTER (Eth.) / NYAMBUI (Tanz.) / MAANINKA (Finl.) / 5000 Metres
100fr: KOZIAKIEWICZ (Pol.) / (record du monde) / VOLKOV (Urss) et / SLUSARSKI (Pol.)
250fr: WELTERS / ALDAMA (Cuba) / MUGABI (Oug.) / KRUBER (Rda) / et SZCZERDA (Pol.)

1980, Sept. 25   **Litho.**   *Perf. 13*
C238 AP104 50fr (R, vert. &
            horiz.)   .50   .20
C239 AP104 100fr (Br)   .95   .40
C240 AP104 250fr (U)   2.50   .85
  a.   Souv. sheet of 3 (Blk)   8.50 4.00
       Nos. C238-C240 (3)   3.95 1.45

Pres. Charles de Gaulle AP105

1980, Nov. 9   **Photo.**   *Perf. 13*
C241 AP105 100fr shown   1.25   .35
C242 AP105 200fr Pres. & Mrs.
            de Gaulle   2.40   .70
  a.   Souv. sheet of 2, #C241-C242   6.50 3.25

Pres. Charles de Gaulle (1890-1970).

AP106

1981, Feb. 19   Litho.   Perf. 13
C243 AP106 60fr Soccer Play-
ers   .65   .20
C244 AP106 190fr Soccer player 2.10 .75
ESPANA '82 World Cup Soccer
Championship.

AP107

1981, Mar. 26   Litho.   Perf. 13
Spacecraft and Astronauts: 250fr, Yuri
Gagarin. 500fr, Alan B. Shepard.
C245 AP107 150fr multi   1.40   .55
C246 AP107 250fr multi   2.40   .85
C247 AP107 500fr multi   4.75 1.75
  a.   Souv. sheet of 3, #C245-
        C247, perf. 12½   9.00 4.50
  Nos. C245-C247 (3)   8.55 3.15
200th anniv. of discovery of Uranus by Wil-
liam Herschel (1738-1822).

Map of Africa
and Emblems
AP108

1981, June 1   Litho.   Perf. 12½
C248 AP108 100fr multi   1.00   .40
Electric Power Distribution Union, 7th Con-
gress, Libreville, June 1-5.

D-51 Steam Locomotive, Japan, and
SNCF Turbotrain TGV-001,
France — AP109

200th Birth Anniv. of George Stephenson:
100fr, B&O Mallet 7100, US, Prussian T3
steam locomotive. 350fr, Stephenson and his
Rocket, BB Alsthom electric locomotive, Central Africa.

1981, June 4   Engr.   Perf. 13
C249 AP109 75fr multi   .95   .35
C250 AP109 100fr multi   1.40   .45
C251 AP109 350fr multi   4.50 1.50
  a.   Souvenir sheet of 3   6.50 3.25
  Nos. C249-C251 (3)   6.85 2.30
#C251a contains #C249-C251 in changed
colors.

No. C251a Overprinted in 1 line
across 3 stamps: 26 février 1981-
Record du monde de vitesse 380 km
a l'heure
Souvenir Sheet
1981, June 13   Engr.   Perf. 13
C252 AP109   Sheet of 3   6.50 3.25
New world railroad speed record, set Feb.
26.

Intl. Letter Writing
Week, Oct. 9-
16 — AP110

1981, Oct. 9   Photo.   Perf. 13
C253 AP110 200fr multi   2.25   .90

Souvenir Sheet

22nd Anniv. of Independence —
AP110a

Illustration reduced.

1982   Typo.   Perf. 13x12½
Self-Adhesive
C253A AP110a 2000fr multi   40.00 40.00
Printed on wood.

Still Life with a Mandolin, by George
Braque (1882-1963) — AP111

Design: 350fr, Boy Blowing Bubbles, by
Edouard Manet (1832-1883), vert.

Perf. 13x12½, 12½x13
1982, Oct. 5   Litho.
C254 AP111 300fr multi   3.75 1.10
C255 AP111 350fr multi   6.00 1.25

Pre-olympic
Year — AP112

Manned Flight
Bicentenary
AP113

1983, Feb. 16   Litho.   Perf. 13
C256 AP112 90fr Gymnast   .70   .30
C257 AP112 350fr Wind surfing 4.00 1.10

1983, June 1   Engr.   Perf. 13
Balloons.
C258 AP113 100fr Transatlantic
flight, 5th an-
niv.   1.10   .40
C259 AP113 125fr Montgolfiere,
1783   1.25   .45
C260 AP113 350fr Rozier's bal-
loon, 1783   4.00 1.50
  Nos. C258-C260 (3)   6.35 2.35

Lady with
Unicorn, by
Raphael
(1483-1520)
AP114

1983, June 19   Perf. 12½x13
C261 AP114 1000fr multi   12.00 5.25

1984 Winter Olympics — AP115

1984, Feb. 8   Litho.   Perf. 12½
C262 AP115 125fr Hockey   1.40   .20
C263 AP115 350fr Figure skaters 3.75 .70
See No. C268.

Paris-Libreville-Paris Air Race, Mar.
15-28 — AP116

1984, Mar. 15   Litho.   Perf. 13x12½
C264 AP116 500fr Planes, emblem   5.00   .85

The Racetrack, by Edgar
Degas — AP117

1984, Mar. 21   Perf. 13
C265 AP117 500fr multi   8.00 1.25

1984 Summer
Olympics
AP118

Hamburg '84 Philatelic
Exhibition — AP119

Illustration AP119 reduced.

1984, May 31   Litho.   Perf. 12½
C266 AP118 90fr Basketball   .80   .20
C267 AP118 125fr Running   1.25   .20

Souvenir Sheet
Nos. C262-C263, C266-C267 with
Added Inscriptions
1984, Oct. 3   Litho.   Perf. 13
C268   Sheet of 4   7.50 3.50
  a.   AP118 90fr MEDAILLE D'OR:
        U.S.A.   .65   .20
  b.   AP118 125fr MEDAILLE D'OR:
        KORIR   .95   .20
  c.   AP115 125fr Hockey sur glace:
        U.R.S.S.   .95   .20
  d.   AP115 350fr Danse couple: J.
        Torvill-C. Dean   2.75   .55

Souvenir Sheet
1984   Typo.   Perf. 13x12½
Self-Adhesive
C268A AP119 1000fr multi   21.00 21.00
Printed on wood.

Dr. Albert
Schweitzer
(1875-1965) —
AP119a

1985, Sept. 5   Litho.   Perf. 12½
C269 AP119a 350fr multi   4.75 .70

Flags of Gabon, UN AP120

1985, Sept. 20
C270 AP120 225fr multi   2.50 .40
Admission of Gabon to UN, 25th anniv.

Central Post Office, Libreville, UPU and Gabon Postal Emblems — AP121

1985, Oct. 9
C271 AP121 300fr multi   3.50 .60
World Post Day.

UN, 40th Anniv. — AP122

1985, Oct. 24   Litho.   Perf. 12½
C272 AP122 350fr multi   4.25 .70

PHILEXAFRICA '85, Lome, Togo — AP123

1985, Oct. 30   Perf. 13
C273 AP123 100fr Scout camp-
     site   2.00 .20
C274 AP123 150fr Telecommuni-
     cations,
     transporta-
     tion   3.50 .50
   a.   Pair, #C273-C274 + label   6.50 2.00

Gabon's Gift to the UN — AP124

Design: Mother and Child, carved wood statue, and UN emblem.

1986, Mar. 15   Litho.   Perf. 13½
C275 AP124 350fr multi   4.25 1.10

Lastour Arriving in Gabon — AP125

1986, Mar. 25   Litho.   Perf. 12½
C276 AP125 100fr multi   1.50 .45
Lastoursville, cent.

World Telecommunications Day — AP126

1986, May 17   Perf. 13½
C277 AP126 300fr multi   3.00 .95

1986 World Cup Soccer Championships, Mexico — AP127

1986, May 31   Perf. 12½
C278 AP127 100fr Goal   1.00 .35
C279 AP127 150fr Dribbling, re-
     ligious carv-
     ing   1.50 .45
C280 AP127 250fr Players,
     map, soccer
     cup   2.50 .80
C281 AP127 350fr Stadium,
     flags   3.25 1.10
   a.   Souv. sheet of 4, #C278-
     C281   10.00 4.75
     Nos. C278-C281 (4)   8.25 2.70
For overprints see Nos. C283-C286.

World Post Day — AP128

1986, Oct. 9   Litho.   Perf. 12½
C282 AP128 500fr multi   5.00 1.50

Nos. C278-C281 Ovptd. "ARGENTINA 3 -R.F.A 2" in One or Two Lines in Red

1986, Oct. 23   Litho.   Perf. 12½
C283 AP127 100fr multi   1.00 .35
C284 AP127 150fr multi   1.50 .45
C285 AP127 250fr multi   2.50 .80
C286 AP127 350fr multi   3.25 1.10
     Nos. C283-C286 (4)   8.25 2.70

The Renewal, 19th Anniv. AP129

1987, Mar. 12   Litho.   Perf. 13
C287 AP129 500fr multi   6.50 2.00

Konrad Adenauer (1876-1967), West German Chancellor AP130

1987, Apr. 15   Perf. 12x12½
C288 AP130 300fr mar, chlky bl
     & blk   4.50 1.25

Schweitzer and Medical Settlement — AP131

1988, Apr. 17   Litho.   Perf. 12½x12
C289 AP131 500fr multi   6.50 2.25
Dr. Albert Schweitzer (1875-1965), missionary physician and founder of the hospital and medical settlement, Lambarene, Gabon.

Port Gentil Refinery, 20th Anniv. — AP132

1988, Sept. 1   Litho.   Perf. 13½
C290 AP132 350fr multi   4.00 1.75

De Gaulle's Call for French Resistance, 50th Anniv. — AP133

1990, June 18   Litho.   Perf. 13
C291 AP133 500fr multicolored   7.50 2.50

Port of Marseilles by J. B. Jongkind (1819-1891) — AP134

1991, Feb. 9   Litho.   Perf. 13
C292 AP134 500fr multicolored   6.00 2.75

Discovery of America, 500th Anniv. — AP135

1992, Oct. 12   Litho.   Perf. 13
C293 AP135 500fr multicolored   5.50 2.50

Antoine de Saint-Exupery (1900-44) — AP136

1994   Litho.   Perf. 13
C294 AP136 500fr multicolored   3.25 1.60

Opening of the Channel Tunnel — AP137

1994
C295 AP137 500fr multicolored   3.00 1.50

AIR POST SEMI-POSTAL STAMPS

Catalogue values for unused stamps in this section are for Never Hinged items.

Ramses II Paying Homage to Four Gods, Wadi-es-Sabua — SPAP1

Unwmk.
1964, Mar. 9   Engr.   Perf. 13
CB1 SPAP1 10fr + 5fr dk bl & bis
     brn   1.00 1.00
CB2 SPAP1 25fr + 5fr dk car
     rose & vio bl   1.25 1.25
CB3 SPAP1 50fr + 5fr sl grn &
     claret   2.10 2.10
     Nos. CB1-CB3 (3)   4.35 4.35

UNESCO world campaign to save historic monuments in Nubia.

POSTAGE DUE STAMPS

Postage Due Stamps of France Overprinted

1928		**Unwmk.**	**Perf. 14x13½**	
J1	D2	5c light blue	.40	.55
J2	D2	10c gray brown	.40	.65
J3	D2	20c olive green	1.25	1.60
J4	D2	25c bright rose	1.25	1.60
J5	D2	30c light red	1.60	2.00
J6	D2	45c blue green	2.00	2.40
J7	D2	50c brown violet	3.00	3.25
J8	D2	60c yellow brown	3.00	3.25
J9	D2	1fr red brown	3.00	3.25
J10	D2	2fr orange red	4.75	4.75
J11	D2	3fr bright violet	5.50	5.50
		Nos. J1-J11 (11)	26.15	28.80

Chief Makoko, de Brazza's Aide — D3
Count Savorgnan de Brazza — D4

1930		**Typo.**	**Perf. 13½x14**	
J12	D3	5c dk bl & olive	1.25	1.25
J13	D3	10c dk red & brn	1.40	1.40
J14	D3	20c green & brn	1.90	1.90
J15	D3	25c lt bl & brn	1.90	1.90
J16	D3	30c bis brn & Prus bl	2.75	2.75
J17	D3	45c Prus bl & ol	4.50	4.50
J18	D3	50c red vio & brn	4.75	4.75
J19	D3	60c gray lil & bl blk	9.00	9.00
J20	D4	1fr bis brn & bl blk	12.50	12.50
J21	D4	2fr violet & brn	16.00	16.00
J22	D4	3fr dp red & brn	18.00	18.00
		Nos. J12-J22 (11)	73.95	73.95

Fang Woman — D5

1932		**Photo.**	**Perf. 13x13½**	
J23	D5	5c dk bl, *bl*	.95	.95
J24	D5	10c red brown	1.10	1.10
J25	D5	20c chocolate	1.75	1.75
J26	D5	25c yel grn, *bl*	1.75	1.75
J27	D5	30c car rose	2.10	2.10
J28	D5	45c red org, *yel*	7.75	7.75
J29	D5	50c dk violet	2.50	2.50
J30	D5	60c dull blue	3.75	3.75
J31	D5	1fr blk, *red org*	9.00	9.00
J32	D5	2fr dark green	10.00	10.00
J33	D5	3fr rose lake	9.25	9.25
		Nos. J23-J33 (11)	49.90	49.90

Catalogue values for unused stamps in this section, from this point to the end of the section, are for Never Hinged items.

Republic

Pineapple — D6

1962, Dec. 10		**Unwmk. Engr.**	**Perf. 11**	
J34	D6	50c shown	.20	.20
J35	D6	50c Mangoes	.20	.20
a.		Pair, #J34-J35		.35

J36	D6	1fr Avocados	.20	.20
J37	D6	1fr Tangerines	.20	.20
a.		Pair, #J36-J37	.50	
J38	D6	2fr Coconuts	.20	.20
J39	D6	2fr Grapefruit	.20	.20
a.		Pair, #J38-J39	.50	
J40	D6	5fr Oranges	.35	.35
J41	D6	5fr Papaya	.35	.35
a.		Pair, #J40-J41	1.00	
J42	D6	10fr Breadfruit	.75	.75
J43	D6	10fr Guavas	.75	.75
a.		Pair, #J42-J43	2.25	
J44	D6	25fr Lemons	1.00	1.00
J45	D6	25fr Bananas	1.00	1.00
a.		Pair, #J44-J45	3.50	
		Nos. J34-J45 (12)	5.40	5.40

Pairs se-tenant at the base.

Charaxes Candiope — D7

Butterflies: 10fr, Charaxes ameliae. 25fr, Cyrestis camillus. 50fr, Charaxes castor. 100fr, Pseudacrea boisduvali.

1978, July 4		**Litho.**	**Perf. 13**	
J46	D7	5fr multi	.30	.20
J47	D7	10fr multi	.30	.20
J48	D7	25fr multi	.65	.30
J49	D7	50fr multi	1.25	.50
J50	D7	100fr multi	2.00	.95
		Nos. J46-J50 (5)	4.50	2.15

OFFICIAL STAMPS

Catalogue values for unused stamps in this section are for Never Hinged items.

Map of Gabon — O1
Flag of Gabon — O2

Designs: 25fr, 30fr, Flag of Gabon. 50fr, 85fr, 100fr, 200fr, Coat of Arms.

1968		**Unwmk. Photo.**	**Perf. 14**	
O1	O1	1fr olive & multi	.20	.20
O2	O1	2fr multi	.20	.20
O3	O1	5fr lilac & multi	.20	.20
O4	O1	10fr emer & multi	.20	.20
O5	O1	25fr brn & multi	.50	.20
O6	O1	30fr org & multi	.50	.20
O7	O1	50fr multi	.95	.20
O8	O1	85fr multi	1.75	.35
O9	O1	100fr yel & multi	2.10	.45
O10	O1	200fr gray & multi	4.00	1.10
		Nos. O1-O10 (10)	10.60	3.30

1971-84		**Typo.**	**Perf. 13x14**	
O11	O2	5fr multi ('81)	.20	.20
O12	O2	10fr multi	.20	.20
O13	O2	20fr multi ('81)	.20	.20
O14	O2	25fr multi ('84)	.25	.20
O15	O2	30fr multi ('78)	.40	.20
O16	O2	40fr multi ('72)	.75	.25
O17	O2	50fr multi ('76)	.85	.20
O18	O2	60fr multi ('77)	1.10	.20
O19	O2	75fr multi ('81)	.75	.20
O20	O2	80fr multi ('77)	1.50	.40
O21	O2	100fr multi ('78)	1.25	.20
O22	O2	500fr multi ('78)	6.25	1.25
		Nos. O11-O22 (12)	13.70	3.80

GAMBIA

ˈgam-bē-ə

LOCATION — Extending inland from the mouth of the Gambia River on the west coast of Africa
GOVT. — Republic in British Commonwealth
AREA — 4,068 sq. mi.
POP. — 1,087,000 (1995 est.)
CAPITAL — Banjul

The British Crown Colony and Protectorate of Gambia became independent in 1965 and a republic in 1970.

12 Pence = 1 Shilling
100 Bututs = 1 Dalasy (1971)

Catalogue values for unused stamps in this country are for Never Hinged items, beginning with Scott 144.

Queen Victoria
A1   A2

Typographed and Embossed

1869, Jan.		**Unwmk.**	**Imperf.**	
1	A1	4p pale brown	525.	225.
a.		4p brown	575.	210.
2	A1	6p deep blue	550.	225.
a.		6p blue	625.	210.
b.		6p pale blue	3,000.	1,250.

1874, Aug.			**Wmk. 1**	
3	A1	4p brown	450.	225.
a.		4p pale brown	425.	210.
4	A1	6p blue	375.	210.
a.		6p deep blue	375.	225.
b.		Panel sloping down from left to right	700.	400.

The name panel sloping down variety is from a top right corner position. A top left corner position exists with a less noticeable sloping of the panel down from right to left; it is worth less.

1880, June			**Perf. 14**	
5	A1	½p orange	13.00	20.00
6	A1	1p maroon	7.00	7.00
7	A1	2p rose	40.00	12.50
8	A1	3p ultra	75.00	37.50
9	A1	4p pale brown	300.00	18.50
a.		4p brown	300.00	17.50
10	A1	6p blue	120.00	52.50
a.		Panel sloping down from left to right	325.00	175.00
11	A1	1sh green	275.00	150.00
a.		1sh deep green	325.00	160.00
		Nos. 5-11 (7)	830.00	298.00

The watermark on Nos. 5-11 exists both upright and sideways.
See footnote following No. 4.

1886-93			**Wmk. 2 Sideways**	
12	A1	½p gray grn	4.75	3.25
13	A1	1p rose car ('87)	6.50	9.00
a.		1p maroon		17,250.
14		2p deep orange	2.25	9.50
b.		2p orange	13.00	5.75
15	A1	2½p dp br blue	8.00	1.40
16	A1	3p gray	8.50	17.00
17	A1	4p dp brown	12.00	2.25
18	A1	6p slate green ('93)	15.00	62.50
a.		6p pale olive green ('86)	82.50	70.00
b.		6p bronze green ('89)	37.50	65.00
c.		As "a," panel sloping down from left to right	225.00	175.00
d.		As "b," panel sloping down from left to right	85.00	150.00
19	A1	1sh violet	6.25	20.00
a.		1sh purple	7.50	22.50
		Nos. 12-19 (8)	63.25	124.90

See footnote following No. 4.

1898, Jan.		**Typo.**	**Wmk. 2**	
20	A2	½p gray green	3.25	2.00
21	A2	1p carmine rose	2.50	.85
22	A2	2p brn org & pur	7.00	4.00
23	A2	2½p ultramarine	.25	2.75
24	A2	3p red vio & ultra	35.00	14.00
25	A2	4p brown & ultra	14.00	35.00
26	A2	6p ol grn & car rose	12.00	37.50
27	A2	1sh vio & green	37.50	77.50
		Nos. 20-27 (8)	113.50	173.60

King Edward VII — A3

1902-05			**Perf. 14**	
28	A3	½p green	3.75	2.75
29	A3	1p car rose	9.00	1.10
30	A3	2p org & pur	3.75	2.25
31	A3	2½p ultramarine	32.50	20.00
32	A3	3p red vio & ultra	14.00	4.00
33	A3	4p brn & ultra	4.00	30.00
34	A3	6p ol grn & rose	9.50	14.00
35	A3	1sh bluish vio & green	47.50	92.50
36	A3	1sh6p grn & red, *yel*	8.00	22.00
37	A3	2sh black & org	55.00	70.00
38	A3	2sh6p pur & brn, *yel*	17.50	70.00
39	A3	3sh red & grn, *yel*	22.50	70.00
		Nos. 28-39 (12)	227.00	398.60

Numerals of 5p, 7½p, 10p, 1sh6p, 2sh, 2sh6p and 3sh of type A3 are in color on plain tablet.

Issue dates: 1p, Mar. 13. ½p, 3p, Apr. 19. 2p, 2½p, 4p, 6p, 1sh, 2sh, June 14. 1sh6p, 2sh6p, 3sh, Apr. 6, 1905.

For surcharges, see Nos. 65-66.

1904-09			**Wmk. 3**	
41	A3	½p green	5.25	.35
42	A3	1p car rose	5.25	.20
a.		1p carmine ('09)	12.00	.20
43	A3	2p org & pur ('06)	14.00	2.50
44	A3	2p gray ('09)	2.00	12.50
45	A3	2½p br blue ('05)	9.00	5.50
46	A3	3p red vio & ultra	11.00	2.25
47	A3	3p vio, *yel* ('09)	5.00	1.10
48	A3	4p brn & ultra ('06)	20.00	45.00
49	A3	4p blk & red, *yel* ('09)	1.75	.75
50	A3	5p gray & black	16.00	25.00
51	A3	5p org & vio ('09)	1.75	1.40
52	A3	6p ol grn & rose ('06)	20.00	62.50
53	A3	6p dull vio ('09)	2.50	2.50
54	A3	7½p blue grn & red	14.00	55.00
55	A3	7½p brn & ultra ('09)	2.75	2.75
56	A3	10p ol bis & red	24.00	35.00
57	A3	10p ol grn & car rose ('09)	4.00	8.00
58	A3	1sh violet & grn	29.00	55.00
59	A3	1sh blk, *grn* ('09)	4.00	20.00
60	A3	1sh 6p vio & grn ('09)	22.50	70.00
61	A3	2sh black & org	85.00	120.00
62	A3	2sh vio & bl, *bl* ('09)	16.00	22.50
63	A3	2sh 6p blk & red, *bl* ('09)	24.00	22.50
64	A3	3sh yel & grn ('09)	26.00	55.00
		Nos. 41-64 (24)	364.75	627.30

Nos. 38-39 Surcharged in Black:

a   b

Type a (I) — The word "PENNY" is 5mm from the horizontal bars.
Type a (II) — "PENNY" is 4mm from the bars.

1906, Apr.			**Wmk. 2**	
65	A3	½p on 2sh6p, type I	57.50	70.00
a.		Type II	62.50	75.00
66	A3	1p on 3sh	62.50	35.00
a.		Double surcharge	2,150.	5,750.

King George V — A4

1912-22			**Wmk. 3**	
70	A4	½p dp green	2.25	1.75
71	A4	1p carmine	2.75	2.00
a.		1p scarlet ('16)	5.50	1.00
72	A4	1½p ol brn & grn	.60	.35
73	A4	2p gray	.60	3.25
74	A4	2½p dp br blue	4.50	3.50
75	A4	3p violet	.60	.35
76	A4	4p blk & red, *yel*	1.10	11.50
77	A4	5p orange & vio	1.10	2.25
78	A4	6p dl vio & red violet	1.10	2.75
79	A4	7½p brn & ultra	3.00	19.00
80	A4	10p ol grn & car rose	3.25	20.00
81	A4	1sh blk, *green*	2.25	1.10
a.		1sh black, *emerald*	1.10	22.50
82	A4	1sh6p vio & green	14.00	11.50
83	A4	2sh vio & bl, *bl*	4.75	7.00
84	A4	2sh6p blk & red, *bl*	5.00	16.00
85	A4	3sh vel & green	11.00	37.50
86	A4	5sh grn & red, *yel* ('22)	110.00	175.00
		Nos. 70-86 (17)	167.85	304.80

Numerals of 1½p, 5p, 7½p, 10p, 1sh6p, 2sh, 2sh6p, 3sh, 4sh and 5sh of type A3 are in color on colorless tablet. No. 86 is on chalky paper.

1921-22　　　　　　　　　**Wmk. 4**
87	A4	½p green	.35	20.00
88	A4	1p carmine	1.10	7.50
89	A4	1½p ol grn & bl grn	1.40	15.00
90	A4	2p gray	1.10	2.50
91	A4	2½p ultramarine	.60	9.00
92	A4	5p org & violet	2.00	18.00
93	A4	6p dl vio & red vio	2.00	20.00
94	A4	7½p brn & ultra	2.25	42.50
95	A4	10p yel grn & car rose	8.00	24.00
96	A4	4sh gray & red ('22)	85.00	175.00
		Nos. 87-96 (10)	103.80	333.50

No. 96 is on chalky paper.

George V and Elephant — A5

George V — A6

1922-27　　　　**Engr.**　　　**Wmk. 4**
Head and Shield in Black
102	A5	½p green	.65	.65
103	A5	1p brown	1.00	.25
104	A5	1½p carmine	1.00	.25
105	A5	2p gray	1.10	4.25
106	A5	2½p orange	1.10	12.50
107	A5	3p ultramarine	1.10	.20
108	A5	4p car, *org* ('27)	15.00	24.00
109	A5	5p yellow green	3.50	11.50
110	A5	6p claret	1.50	.35
111	A5	7½p vio, *yel* ('27)	16.00	82.50
112	A5	10p blue	5.50	20.00
113	A5	1sh vio, *org* ('24)	2.75	1.90
114	A6	1sh3p blue	16.00	16.00
115	A6	2sh vio, *blue*	9.00	7.00
116	A6	2sh6p dark green	9.00	11.00
117	A6	3sh aniline vio	20.00	72.50
a.		3sh black purple	240.00	475.00
118	A6	4sh brown	13.00	19.00
119	A6	5sh dk grn, *yel* ('26)	25.00	55.00
120	A6	10sh yellow green	80.00	125.00
		Nos. 102-120 (19)	222.20	463.85

♦ **1922, Sept. 1**　　　　　　**Wmk. 3**
Head & Shield in Black
121	A5	4p carmine, *yel*	4.25	4.75
122	A5	7½p violet, *yel*	6.75	8.00
123	A6	1sh violet, *orange*	24.00	35.00
124	A6	5sh dk green, *yel*	55.00	175.00
		Nos. 121-124 (4)	90.00	222.75

Common Design Types pictured following the introduction.

Silver Jubilee Issue
Common Design Type
1935, May 6　**Wmk. 4**　*Perf. 11x12*
125	CD301	1½p carmine & bl	.75	1.00
126	CD301	3p ultra & brn	1.00	1.60
127	CD301	6p ol grn & lt bl	1.75	6.00
128	CD301	1sh brn vio & ind	6.00	11.00
		Nos. 125-128 (4)	9.50	18.60
		Set, never hinged	20.00	

Coronation Issue
Common Design Type
1937, May 12　　　　*Perf. 11x11½*
129	CD302	1p brown	.20	.80
130	CD302	1½p dark carmine	.20	.40
131	CD302	3p deep ultra	.50	1.10
		Nos. 129-131 (3)	.90	2.30
		Set, never hinged	1.60	

King George VI and Elephant Badge of Gambia — A7

1938-46　　　　　　　　　*Perf. 12*
132	A7	½p bl grn & blk	.20	.80
133	A7	1p brn & red vio	.20	.55
134	A7	1½p rose red & brn lake	.25	2.25
134A	A7	1½p gray black & ultra ('44)	.20	1.75
135	A7	2p gray black & ultra	3.00	3.75

135A	A7	2p rose red & brn lake ('43)	.65	2.50
136	A7	3p blue & brt bl	.40	.20
136A	A7	5p dk vio brn & olive ('41)	.45	.60
137	A7	6p plum & ol grn	1.25	.40
138	A7	1sh vio & sl blk	1.60	.20
138A	A7	1sh3p bl & choc ('46)	2.00	2.75
139	A7	2sh bl & dp rose	5.00	3.75
140	A7	2sh6p sl grn & sep	10.00	2.75
141	A7	4sh dk vio & red orange	17.50	2.75
142	A7	5sh org red & dk blue	17.50	4.50
143	A7	10sh blk & yel org	17.00	18.00
		Nos. 132-143 (16)	77.20	37.50
		Set, never hinged	129.00	

Issued: 5p, Mar. 13; #135A, Oct. 1; #134A, Jan. 2; 1sh3p, Nov. 28; others, Apr. 1.

Catalogue values for unused stamps in this section, from this point to the end of the section, are for Never Hinged items.

Peace Issue
Common Design Type
1946, Aug. 6　　**Engr.**　　*Perf. 13½*
144	CD303	1½p black	.20	.20
145	CD303	3p deep blue	.20	.20

Silver Wedding Issue
Common Design Types
1948, Dec. 24　**Photo.**　*Perf. 14x14½*
146	CD304	1½p black	.25	.20

Perf. 11½x11
Engr.; Name Typo.
147	CD305	£1 purple	19.00	19.00

UPU Issue
Common Design Types
Engr.; Name Typo. on 3p, 6p
Perf. 13½, 11x11½
1949, Oct. 10　　　　　　**Wmk. 4**
148	CD306	1½p slate	.40	1.40
149	CD307	3p indigo	1.90	2.00
150	CD308	6p red lilac	.75	1.10
151	CD309	1sh violet	.55	.45
		Nos. 148-151 (4)	3.60	4.95

Coronation Issue
Common Design Type
1953, June 2　**Engr.**　*Perf. 13½x13*
152	CD312	1½p dk blue & black	.40	.40

Palm Wine Tapping — A8

Palm Leaf and Elizabeth II, by Annigoni — A9

Designs: 1p, 1sh3p, Cutter. 1½p, 5sh, Wollof woman. 2½p, 2sh, Barra canoe. 3p, 10sh, "Lady Wright." 4p, 4sh, James Island. 1sh, 2sh6p, Woman farming. £1, Elephant badge of Gambia.

1953, Nov. 2　　　　　　*Perf. 13½*
153	A8	½p dk green & car	.40	.20
154	A8	1p dk brn & ultra	.35	.35
155	A8	1½p gray & dk brn	.20	.45
156	A8	2½p car & black	.40	.75
157	A8	3p pur & indigo	.35	.20
158	A8	4p dp blue & blk	.60	2.25
159	A8	6p dp plum & brn	.30	.20
160	A8	1sh green & yel brn	.60	.50
161	A8	1sh3p blue & vio bl	11.00	.95
162	A8	2sh car & indigo	7.50	3.25
163	A8	2sh6p brn & bl grn	5.00	2.00
164	A8	4sh brn org & dp bl	12.50	3.50
165	A8	5sh ultra & red brn	3.50	2.50
166	A8	10sh dk yel green & ultra	22.50	11.00
167	A8	£1 black & bl grn	25.00	11.00
		Nos. 153-167 (15)	90.20	38.70

Wmk. 314
1961, Dec. 2　**Engr.**　*Perf. 11½*
Design: 3p, 6p, Map of West Africa.
168	A9	2p lilac & green	.20	.40
169	A9	3p brown & Prus grn	1.00	.20
170	A9	6p car rose & dk blue	1.00	.65
171	A9	1sh3p green & violet	1.00	2.25
		Nos. 168-171 (4)	3.20	3.50

Visit of Elizabeth II to Gambia, Dec., 1961.

Freedom from Hunger Issue
Common Design Type
1963, June 4　**Photo.**　*Perf. 14x14½*
172	CD314	1sh3p car rose	.55	.20

Red Cross Centenary Issue
Common Design Type
1963, Sept. 2　**Litho.**　*Perf. 13*
173	CD315	2p black & red	.20	.20
174	CD315	1sh3p ultra & red	.65	.65

Beautiful Long-tailed Sunbird — A10

Birds: 1p, Yellow-mantled whydah. 1½p, Cattle egret. 2p, Yellow-bellied parrot. 3p, Ring-necked parakeet. 4p, Amethyst starling. 6p, Village weaver. 1sh, Rufous-crowned roller. 1sh3p, Red-eyed turtle dove. 2sh6p, Double-spurred francolin. 5sh, Palm-nut vulture. 10sh, Orange-cheeked waxbill. £1, Emerald cuckoo.

Perf. 12½x13
1963, Nov. 4　**Photo.**　**Wmk. 314**
Multicolored Design & Inscription
175	A10	½p rose buff	.55	.90
176	A10	1p gray green	.75	.25
177	A10	1½p pale violet	2.25	.90
178	A10	2p buff	2.25	.90
179	A10	3p light gray	2.25	.95
180	A10	4p lt yel green	2.25	.95
181	A10	6p light blue	2.25	.20
182	A10	1sh pale grysh grn	2.25	.20
183	A10	1sh3p light blue	13.50	1.75
184	A10	2sh6p pale green	9.00	3.25
185	A10	5sh blue	9.00	3.75
186	A10	10sh tan	14.00	10.00
187	A10	£1 pale rose	29.00	17.50
		Nos. 175-187 (13)	89.30	41.50

For overprints see Nos. 188-191, 193-205.

Nos. 176, 179, 182 and 183 Overprinted: "SELF GOVERNMENT/1963"

1963, Nov. 7
188	A10	1p multicolored	.25	.35
189	A10	3p multicolored	.35	.25
190	A10	1sh multicolored	.35	.35
191	A10	1sh3p multicolored	.45	.45
		Nos. 188-191 (4)	1.40	1.40

Shakespeare Issue
Common Design Type
1964, Apr. 23　**Photo.**　*Perf. 14x14½*
192	CD316	6p ultramarine	.25	.20

Nos. 175-187 Overprinted: "INDEPENDENCE / 1965"
Perf. 12½x13
1965, Feb. 18　**Photo.**　**Wmk. 314**
Multicolored Design & Inscription
193	A10	½p rose buff	.40	.85
194	A10	1p gray green	.40	.25
195	A10	1½ pale violet	.65	.85
196	A10	2p buff	.90	.30
197	A10	3p light gray	.90	.25
198	A10	4p lt yel green	.90	1.50
199	A10	6p light blue	.90	.25
200	A10	1sh pale grysh grn	.90	.25
201	A10	1sh3p light blue	.90	.25
202	A10	2sh6p pale green	.90	.65
203	A10	5sh blue	.90	.85
204	A10	10sh tan	1.75	4.00
205	A10	£1 pale rose	9.00	10.00
		Nos. 193-205 (13)	19.40	20.25

In the overprint, "1965" is flush at left side under "Independence" on the ½p, 1½p, 6p, 1sh3p and 2sh6p; it is centered on the others.

Flag of Gambia over Gambia River — A11

Design: 2p, 1sh6p, Coat of arms.

1965, Feb. 18　**Unwmk.**　*Perf. 14*
206	A11	½p slate & multi	.25	.25
207	A11	2p lt brown & multi	.25	.25
208	A11	7½p dk brown & multi	.45	.40
209	A11	1sh6p lt green & multi	.60	.30
		Nos. 206-209 (4)	1.55	1.20

Gambia's Independence.

ITU Emblem, Old and New Communication Equipment — A12

1965, May 17　**Photo.**　*Perf. 14½x14*
210	A12	1p dull blue & silver	.40	.20
211	A12	1sh6p violet & gold	1.25	.30

Cent. of the ITU.

Winston Churchill and Parliament — A13

1966, Jan. 24　　　　*Perf. 14x14½*
212	A13	1p multicolored	.20	.20
213	A13	6p multicolored	.40	.20
214	A13	1sh6p multicolored	.60	.60
		Nos. 212-214 (3)	1.20	1.00

Sir Winston Leonard Spencer Churchill, statesman and WWII leader.

Red-cheeked Cordon Bleu and Emblem — A14

Birds: 1p, White-faced tree duck. 1½p, Red-throated bee eater. 2p, Pied kingfisher. 3p, Yellow-crowned bishop. 4p, Fish eagle. 6p, Bruce's green pigeon. 1sh, Blue-bellied roller. 1sh6p, African pigmy kingfisher. 2sh6p, Spur-winged goose. 5sh, Little woodpecker. 10sh, Violet plantain eater. £1, Pintailed whydah, vert.

Perf. 12½x13
1966, Feb. 18　**Photo.**　**Unwmk.**
Size: 29x25mm
Multicolored Design & Inscription
215	A14	½p gray	.75	.30
216	A14	1p bluish green	.25	.45
217	A14	1½p yel green	.25	.35
218	A14	2p rose lilac	4.00	.70
219	A14	3p lilac	.25	.20
220	A14	4p blue	.40	.30
221	A14	6p gray	.30	.20
222	A14	1sh light green	.30	.20
223	A14	1sh6p bright blue	.75	.25
224	A14	2sh6p tan	.75	.60
225	A14	5sh gray green	.75	.75
226	A14	10sh ocher	.75	2.50

Perf. 14x14½
Size: 25x39mm
227	A14	£1 pink	1.00	6.00
		Nos. 215-227 (13)	10.50	12.80

Coat of Arms, Old and New Views of Bathurst — A15

Photo.; Silver Impressed (Arms)
1966, June 24   Perf. 14½x14
228	A15	1p orange & dk brn	.20	.20
229	A15	2p lt ultra & dk brn	.20	.20
230	A15	6p emer & dk brown	.20	.20
231	A15	1sh6p brt pink & dk brn	.25	.25
		Nos. 228-231 (4)	.85	.85

150th anniv. of the founding of Bathurst.

Adonis and Atlantic Hotels and ITY Emblem — A16

Photo.; Silver Impressed (Emblem)
1967, Dec. 20   Perf. 14½x14
232	A16	2p lt yel green & brn	.20	.20
233	A16	1sh orange & brown	.20	.20
234	A16	1sh6p lilac rose & brn.	.20	.20
		Nos. 232-234 (3)	.60	.60

International Tourist Year.

Handcuffs and Human Rights Flame A17

Intl. Human Rights Year: 1sh, Fort Bullen. 5sh, Methodist Church.

1968, July 15   **Photo.**   Perf. 14x13
235	A17	1p gold & multi	.20	.20
236	A17	1sh gold & multi	.20	.20
237	A17	5sh gold & multi	.40	.75
		Nos. 235-237 (3)	.80	1.15

Gambia #1, Victoria and Elizabeth II — A18

Designs: 6p, Gambia #2, Victoria & Elizabeth II. 2sh6p, Gambia #1-2, Elizabeth II.

Photo. and Embossed
Perf. 14x13½
1969, Jan. 20   Wmk. 314
238	A18	4p dull yel & dk brn	.40	.20
239	A18	6p dp yel grn & bl	.40	.20
240	A18	2sh6p dk bl gray, brn & bl	1.10	1.10
		Nos. 238-240 (3)	1.90	1.50

Centenary of Gambian postage stamps.

Dornier Wal, Route Gambia to Brazil and Lufthansa Emblem — A19

2p, Plane & ship Westfalen, route Gambia to Brazil & Lufthansa emblem. 1sh6p, Zeppelin, route Gambia to Brazil & Lufthansa emblem.

Perf. 13½x14
1969, Dec. 15   **Litho.**   Unwmk.
241	A19	2p pink, org red & blk	.85	.20
242	A19	1sh buff, dl yel & blk	.85	.20
243	A19	1sh6p lt bl, ultra & blk	1.00	1.25
		Nos. 241-243 (3)	2.70	1.65

35th anniversary of pioneer air services.

Runner, Flag and Arms of Gambia A20

1970, July 16   Perf. 14½x14
Flag in Red, Blue & Green
244	A20	1p pink & brown	.20	.20
245	A20	1sh ultra & brown	.20	.20
246	A20	5sh green & brown	.40	.40
		Nos. 244-246 (3)	.80	.80

9th Commonwealth Games, Edinburgh, Scotland, July 16-25.

Pres. Jawara and State House A21

Republic Day, Apr. 24, 1970: 1sh, Pres. Sir Dauda Kairaba Jawara, vert. 1sh6p, Pres. Jawara and Gambia flag, vert.

1970, Nov. 2   **Litho.**   Perf. 14
247	A21	2p gray & multi	.20	.20
248	A21	1sh multicolored	.20	.20
249	A21	1sh6p pink & multi	.70	.70
		Nos. 247-249 (3)	1.10	1.10

Methodist Church, Georgetown — A22

Designs: 1sh, Map of Africa and cross, vert. 1sh6p, John Wesley.

1971, Apr. 16   **Unwmk.**   Perf. 14
250	A22	2p multicolored	.20	.20
251	A22	1sh vio blue & multi	.20	.20
252	A22	1sh6p green & multi	.60	.60
		Nos. 250-252 (3)	1.00	1.00

Establishment of Methodist Mission, 150th anniv.

Yellowfin Tuna A23

Fish from Gambian Waters: 4b, Peters' mormyrid. 6b, Tropical two-wing flying fish. 8b, African sleeper goby. 10b, Yellowtail snapper. 13b, Rock hind. 25b, West African eel cat. 38b, Tiger shark. 50b, Electric catfish. 63b, Swamp eel. 1.25d, Smalltooth sawfish. 2.50d, Barracuda. 5d, Brown bullhead.

1971, July 1   **Litho.**   Perf. 14
Fish in Natural Colors
253	A23	2b blue	.20	.20
254	A23	4b lemon	.20	.20
255	A23	6b lt blue green	.20	.20
256	A23	8b orange brown	.20	.20
257	A23	10b lt Prus blue	.20	.20
258	A23	13b orange yel	.20	.20
259	A23	25b green	.35	.50
260	A23	38b brick red	.40	.50
261	A23	50b Prus blue	.70	.80
262	A23	63b bister	.85	1.60
263	A23	1.25d yel green	1.50	3.25
264	A23	2.50d deep rose	2.50	4.50
265	A23	5d ultramarine	4.50	7.50
		Nos. 253-265 (13)	12.00	19.90

Mungo Park, Scottish Landscape, Map of Gambia Basin — A24

Map of Gambia River Basin and: 25b, Park traveling in dugout canoe. 37b, Park's death under attack at Busa Rapids.

Perf. 13½x14
1971, Sept. 10   **Litho.**   Unwmk.
270	A24	4b ultra & multi	.35	.20
271	A24	25b yel green & multi	1.10	.45
272	A24	37b brick red & multi	1.75	2.00
		Nos. 270-272 (3)	3.20	2.65

Mungo Park (1771-1806), Scottish explorer of the Gambia and Niger Rivers.

Radio Gambia and Pres. Jawara A25

Designs: 25b, Map showing area reached by Radio Gambia. 37b, Like 4b.

1972, July 1   Perf. 14
273	A25	4b black & dull yel	.20	.20
274	A25	25b black, blue & red	.20	.25
275	A25	37b black & yel green	.40	.75
		Nos. 273-275 (3)	.80	1.20

Radio Gambia, 10th anniv., May 1.

High Jump A26

1972, Aug. 31   Perf. 13½
276	A26	4b emerald & multi	.20	.20
277	A26	25b lt ultra & multi	.20	.20
278	A26	37b red & multi	.60	.60
		Nos. 276-278 (3)	1.00	1.00

20th Olympic Games, Munich, 8/26-9/11.

Mandingo Woman — A27

Designs: 25b, Musician playing Mandingo 21-stringed lute (kora). 37b, Map of Mali empire and area of Mandingo language.

1972, Oct. 18   **Litho.**   Perf. 14x14½
279	A27	2b rose red & multi	.20	.20
280	A27	25b lt ultra & multi	.30	.30
281	A27	37b emerald & multi	.50	.50
		Nos. 279-281 (3)	1.00	1.00

International Conference on Mandingo Studies, London, June 30-July 3.

Ship Model with Lanterns A28

Christmas: 2b, Lighted ship (lantern) carried by boys.

1972, Dec. 1   **Litho.**   Perf. 13x13½
282	A28	2b violet & multi	.20	.20
283	A28	1.25d blue & multi	.80	.80

Peanuts, FAO Emblem — A29

1973, Mar. 31   **Litho.**   Perf. 14½x14
284	A29	2b red & multi	.20	.20
285	A29	25b lt blue & multi	.25	.25
286	A29	37b emerald & multi	.40	.40
		Nos. 284-286 (3)	.85	.85

Freedom from Hunger, 2nd UN development campaign.

Planting and Drying Rice — A30   Oil Palms — A31

Cassava A32

1973, Apr. 30   Perf. 14½x14
287	A30	2b shown	.20	.20
288	A30	25b Sorghum (Guinea corn)	.20	.20
289	A30	37b Rice crop	.40	.30

1973, July 16
290	A31	2b shown	.20	.20
291	A31	25b Limes	.25	.25
292	A31	37b Oil palm fruits	.55	.45

1973, Oct. 15
293	A32	2b shown	.20	.20
294	A32	50b Cotton	.55	.45
		Nos. 287-294 (8)	2.55	2.25

Gambian agriculture.

OAU Emblem — A33

1973, Nov. 1   **Unwmk.**   Perf. 13½x13
295	A33	4b green, yel & black	.20	.20
296	A33	25b dp mag, yel & black	.25	.25
297	A33	37b blue, yel & black	.25	.25
		Nos. 295-297 (3)	.70	.70

10th anniv. of the OAU.

Red Cross — A34

Perf. 14½x14

1973, Nov. 30   **Wmk. 314**
298	A34	4b red & black	.20	.20
299	A34	25b ultra, red & black	.25	.25
300	A34	37b emer, red & black	.30	.30
		Nos. 298-300 (3)	.75	.75

25th anniv. of Gambia Red Cross Soc.

Flag of Gambia and Arms of Banjul — A35

Perf. 13½x13

1973, Dec. 17   **Litho.**   **Unwmk.**
301	A35	4b yel green & multi	.20	.20
302	A35	25b ver & multi	.25	.25
303	A35	37b lt ultra & multi	.25	.25
		Nos. 301-303 (3)	.70	.70

Change of name of Bathurst to Banjul and of St. Mary's Island to Banjul Island.

UPU Emblem — A36

1974, Aug. 24   **Litho.**   **Perf. 13½x13**
304	A36	4b multi & multi	.20	.20
305	A36	37b blue & multi	.55	.55

Centenary of Universal Postal Union.

Churchill at Harrow — A37   Churchill in Uniform of 4th Hussars — A38

Designs: 50b, Churchill as Prime Minister.

1974, Nov. 30   **Litho.**   **Perf. 13½**
306	A37	4b multicolored	.20	.20
307	A38	37b multicolored	.30	.25
308	A38	50b multicolored	.50	.65
		Nos. 306-308 (3)	1.00	1.10

Sir Winston Churchill (1874-1965).

WPY Emblem, Races of Man A39

Symbolic Designs and WPY Emblem: 37b, Races multiplying and dividing like atom. 50b, World population.

1974, Dec. 16   **Litho.**   **Perf. 14**
309	A39	4b multicolored	.20	.20
310	A39	10b multicolored	.20	.20
311	A39	50b multicolored	.25	.25
		Nos. 309-311 (3)	.65	.65

World Population Year.

Dr. Schweitzer and Hospital, Lambarene — A40

50b, Dr. Schweitzer examining patient. 1.25d, Dr. Schweitzer in boat on Ogowe River.

1975, Jan. 14   **Litho.**   **Perf. 14**
312	A40	10b multicolored	.20	.20
313	A40	50b multicolored	.65	.25
314	A40	1.25d multicolored	1.40	.75
		Nos. 312-314 (3)	2.25	1.20

Dr. Albert Schweitzer (1875-1965), medical missionary, birth centenary.

Peace Dove A41

10b, Gambia flag. 50b, Gambia coat of arms. 1.25d, Map of Gambia & Gambia River.

1975, Feb. 18   **Perf. 13**
315	A41	4b multicolored	.20	.20
316	A41	10b multicolored	.20	.20
317	A41	50b multicolored	.20	.20
318	A41	1.25d multicolored	.30	.30
		Nos. 315-318 (4)	.90	.90

10th anniversary of independence.

Public Services Graph, A.D.B. Emblem A42   David, by Michelangelo A43

African Development Bank Emblem and: 50b, Plant symbolizing growth of Africa, fed by Development Bank. 1.25d, A.D.B. emblem surrounded by symbols of water, education, roads and hospitals.

1975, Mar. 31   **Litho.**   **Perf. 14**
319	A42	10b multicolored	.20	.20
320	A42	50b multicolored	.25	.25
321	A42	1.25d multicolored	.45	.45
		Nos. 319-321 (3)	.90	.90

African Development Bank, 10th anniv.

1975, Nov. 14   **Perf. 14½**

Bas-reliefs by Michelangelo: 50b, Madonna of the Steps. 1.25d, Battle of the Centaurs, horiz.
322	A43	10b dull blue & multi	.20	.20
323	A43	50b sepia & multi	.35	.35
324	A43	1.25d green & multi	.90	.90
		Nos. 322-324 (3)	1.45	1.45

Michelangelo Buonarroti (1475-1564), Italian painter, sculptor and architect.

Gambia High School A44

Designs: 50b, Pupil in laboratory and school emblem. 1.50d, School emblem.

1975, Nov. 17
325	A44	10b multicolored	.20	.20
326	A44	50b multicolored	.20	.20
327	A44	1.50d multicolored	.50	.50
		Nos. 325-327 (3)	.90	.90

Gambia High School, centenary.

Teacher and IWY Emblem A45

IWY: 10b, Women planting rice. 50b, Nurse holding baby. 1.50d, Woman traffic officer.

1975, Dec. 15   **Litho.**   **Perf. 14½**
328	A45	4b yellow & multi	.20	.20
329	A45	10b multicolored	.20	.20
330	A45	50b multicolored	.35	.20
331	A45	1.50d blue & multi	.60	.30
		Nos. 328-331 (4)	1.35	.90

Woman Golfer A46

Designs: 50b, Golfer addressing ball. 1.50d, Golfer finishing iron shot.

1976, Feb. 18   **Litho.**   **Perf. 14½**
332	A46	10b multicolored	1.25	.20
333	A46	50b multicolored	2.50	.35
334	A46	1.50d multicolored	3.75	1.40
		Nos. 332-334 (3)	7.50	1.95

11th anniversary of independence.

American Militiaman — A47

American Bicent.: 50b, Continental Army soldier. 1.25d, Declaration of Independence.

1976, May 15   **Litho.**   **Perf. 14x13½**
335	A47	25b multicolored	.25	.20
336	A47	50b multicolored	.50	.40
337	A47	1.25d multicolored	.90	.90
a.		Souvenir sheet of 3, #335-337	2.50	4.00
		Nos. 335-337 (3)	1.65	1.50

Mother and Child, Christmas Decoration — A48

1976, Oct. 28   **Litho.**   **Perf. 14**
338	A48	10b lt ultra & multi	.20	.20
339	A48	50b rose & multi	.20	.20
340	A48	1.25d yel grn & multi	.50	.40
		Nos. 338-340 (3)	.90	.80

Christmas.

Serval Cat and Wildlife Fund Emblem — A49

Designs: 25b, Harnessed antelope. 50b, Sitatunga. 1.25d, Leopard.

1976, Nov. 29   **Perf. 13½x14**
341	A49	10b multicolored	10.50	.50
342	A49	25b multicolored	13.50	.50
343	A49	50b multicolored	25.00	1.00
344	A49	1.25d multicolored	45.00	10.00
a.		Souvenir sheet of 4, #341-344	125.00	20.00
		Nos. 341-344 (4)	94.00	12.00

Abuko Nature Reserve.

Queen's Visit, 1961 — A50

Designs: 50b, The spurs and jeweled sword. 1.25d, The oblation of the sword.

1977, Feb. 7   **Litho.**   **Perf. 13½x14**
345	A50	25b multicolored	.20	.20
346	A50	50b multicolored	.20	.20
347	A50	1.25d multicolored	.50	.50
		Nos. 345-347 (3)	.90	.90

25th anniv. of the reign of Elizabeth II.

Festival Emblem and Weaver A51

1977, Jan. 12   **Litho.**   **Perf. 14**
348	A51	25b multicolored	.20	.20
349	A51	50b multicolored	.30	.30
350	A51	1.25d multicolored	.75	.75
a.		Souvenir sheet of 3, #348-350	2.75	3.50
		Nos. 348-350 (3)	1.25	1.25

2nd World Black and African Festival, Lagos, Nigeria, Jan. 15-Feb. 12.

Stone Circles, near Kuntaur A52

Tourism: 50b, Ruins of Fort on James Island. 1.25d, Mungo Park Monument.

1977, Feb. 18   **Litho.**   **Perf. 14½**
351	A52	25b multicolored	.20	.20
352	A52	50b multicolored	.30	.30
353	A52	1.25d multicolored	.75	.75
		Nos. 351-353 (3)	1.25	1.25

Clerodendrum Splendens — A53

Flowers and Shrubs: 4b, White water lily. 6b, Fireball lily. 8b, Mussaenda elegans. 10b, Broad-leaved ground orchid. 13b, Fiber plant. 25b, False kapok. 38b, Baobab. 50b, Coral tree. 63b, Gloriosa lily. 1.25d, Bell-flowered mimosa. 2.50d, Kindin dolo. 5d, African tulip tree. 6b, 8b, 10b, 13b, 25b, 38b, 1.25d, 2.50d, vertical.

1977, July 1   Litho.   Perf. 14½

354	A53	2b multicolored	.20	.20
355	A53	4b multicolored	.20	.25
356	A53	6b multicolored	.20	.25
357	A53	8b multicolored	.20	.25
358	A53	10b multicolored	2.25	.25
359	A53	13b yellow & multi	1.75	1.75
a.		Pale olive background	3.50	4.50
360	A53	25b multicolored	.20	.20
361	A53	38b multicolored	.25	.70
362	A53	50b multicolored	.40	.55
363	A53	63b multicolored	.45	.75
364	A53	1.25d multicolored	.70	1.90
365	A53	2.50d multicolored	.75	1.90
366	A53	5d multicolored	1.10	3.00
	Nos. 354-366 (13)		*8.65*	*11.90*

For surcharges see Nos. 390A-390C.

Crowned Crane, Nile Crocodile, Bush Buck — A54   Madonna, Flight into Egypt, by Rubens — A55

Designs: 25b, Banjul Declaration, excerpt, flag colors. 50b, Banjul Declaration. 1.25d, Climbing lily, butterfly and moth.

1977, Oct. 15   Litho.   Perf. 14

367	A54	10b lt blue & black	.20	.20
368	A54	25b multicolored	.50	.20
369	A54	50b multicolored	.95	.25
370	A54	1.25d red & black	3.00	.75
	Nos. 367-370 (4)		*4.65*	*1.40*

Banjul Declaration, for the conservation of flora and fauna, Feb. 18, 1977.

1977, Dec. 15   Litho.   Perf. 14x13½

Rubens Paintings: 25b, Education of Mary by St. Ann. 50b, Child's head. 1d, Madonna surrounded by saints.

371	A55	10b multicolored	.20	.20
372	A55	25b multicolored	.25	.25
373	A55	50b multicolored	.55	.35
374	A55	1d multicolored	1.00	1.00
	Nos. 371-374 (4)		*2.00*	*1.80*

Peter Paul Rubens (1577-1640). Nos. 371-374 printed in sheets of 5 stamps and decorative label.

Dome of the Rock, Jerusalem — A56

1978, Jan. 3   Litho.   Perf. 14½

375	A56	8b olive green & multi	1.25	.60
376	A56	25b red & multi	5.00	2.50

Palestinian fighters and their families.

Walking on Greased Pole — A57

Verreaux's Eagle Owl — A58

Designs: 50b, Pillow fight on greased pole. 1.25d, Rowers in long boat.

1978, Feb. 18   Perf. 14

377	A57	10b multicolored	.20	.20
378	A57	50b multicolored	.30	.20
379	A57	1.25d multicolored	.50	.50
	Nos. 377-379 (3)		*1.00*	*.90*

Independence Regatta celebrating 13th anniversary of independence.

Elizabeth II Coronation Anniversary Issue
Souvenir Sheet
Common Design Types

1978, Apr. 15   Litho.   Perf. 15

380		Sheet of 6	1.50	1.50
a.		CD326 1d White grayhound of Richmond	.30	.30
b.		CD327 1d Elizabeth II	.30	.30
c.		CD328 1d Lion	.30	.30

No. 380 contains 2 se-tenant strips of Nos. 380a-380c, separated by horizontal gutter with commemorative and descriptive inscriptions.

1978, Oct. 28   Litho.   Perf. 14x13½

Birds of Prey and Wildlife Fund Emblem: 25b, Lizard buzzard. 50b, West African harrier hawk. 1.25d, Long-crested hawk eagle.

381	A58	20b multicolored	20.00	.75
382	A58	20b multicolored	20.00	.75
383	A58	50b multicolored	30.00	3.00
384	A58	1.25d multicolored	45.00	11.00
	Nos. 381-384 (4)		*115.00*	*15.50*

Abuko Nature Reserve.

MV Lady Wright A59

New river vessels: 25b, River vessel Lady Chilel Jawara. 1d, Cross section of Lady Chilel Jawara.

1978, Dec. 1   Litho.   Perf. 14½

385	A59	8b multicolored	.20	.20
386	A59	25b multicolored	.40	.30
387	A59	1d multicolored	1.40	1.25
	Nos. 385-387 (3)		*2.00*	*1.75*

Motorized Police A60

1979, Feb. 18   Litho.   Perf. 14

388	A60	10b shown	.90	.20
389	A60	50b Fire engine	1.60	.30
390	A60	1.25d Ambulance	2.50	1.00
	Nos. 388-390 (3)		*5.00*	*1.50*

14th anniversary of independence.

Nos. 359, 363-364 Surcharged

1979   Litho.   Perf. 14½

390A	A53	25b on 13b multi	.25	.35
390B	A53	25b on 63b multi	.20	.20
390C	A53	25b on 1.25d multi	.20	.20
	Nos. 390A-390C (3)		*.65*	*.75*

Issued: #390A, 3/5; others, 3/26.

Ramsgate Sands, by William P. Frith — A61

Designs: 10b, 25b, IYC emblem and details from painting shown on 1d. 25b, vert.

1979, May 25   Litho.   Perf. 14
Size: 38x21mm, 21x38mm

391	A61	10b multicolored	.20	.20
392	A61	25b multicolored	.20	.20

Size: 56x21mm

393	A61	1d multicolored	.85	.85
	Nos. 391-393 (3)		*1.25*	*1.25*

International Year of the Child.

Gambia No. 15, Maltese Cross Postmark A62

Gambian Stamps and Maltese Cross Postmark: 25b, #1. 50b, #208. 1.25d, #125.

1979, Aug. 16   Litho.   Perf. 14½

394	A62	10h multicolored	.20	.20
395	A62	25b multicolored	.20	.20
396	A62	50b multicolored	.20	.30
397	A62	1.25d multicolored	.50	.70
a.		Souvenir sheet of 1	1.25	1.40
	Nos. 394-397 (4)		*1.10*	*1.40*

Sir Rowland Hill (1795-1879), originator of penny postage.

Abuko Earth Station, Construction — A63

Telecommunications: 50b, Newly opened station. 1d, Intelsat satellites orbiting earth.

1979, Sept. 20   Litho.   Perf. 14

398	A63	25b multicolored	.20	.20
399	A63	50b multicolored	.30	.30
400	A63	1d multicolored	.50	.50
	Nos. 398-400 (3)		*1.00*	*1.00*

Apollo 11 Lift-off — A64

1979, Oct. 17   Litho.   Perf. 14

401	A64	25b shown	.20	.20
402	A64	38b Orbiting moon	.25	.25
403	A64	50b Splashdown	.55	.55
a.		Souvenir booklet	5.00	
b.		Pane, 2 each 25b, 38b, 50b	1.90	
c.		Pane of 1 (2d Lunar module)	1.75	
	Nos. 401-403 (3)		*1.00*	*1.00*

Apollo 11 moon landing, 10th anniversary. No. 403a contains Nos. 403b-403c printed on peelable, self-adhesive paper backing with Apollo 11 emblems on back. Stamps and panes are die-cut and have 1 to 3 sides rouletted 9½.

Large Spotted Acraea, Wildlife Fund Emblem — A65

Wildlife Fund Emblem and Butterflies: 50b, Yellow pansy. 1d, Veined swallowtail. 1.25d, Foxy charaxes.

1980, Jan. 3   Litho.   Perf. 13½x14

404	A65	25b multicolored	15.00	.50
405	A65	50b multicolored	20.00	1.00
406	A65	1d multicolored	32.50	2.50
407	A65	1.25d multicolored	35.00	3.00
a.		Souvenir sheet of 4, #404-407	125.00	20.00
	Nos. 404-407 (4)		*102.50*	*7.00*

Abuko Nature Reserve.

Steam Launch "Vampire" — A66

1980, May 6   Litho.   Perf. 14½

408	A66	10b shown	.20	.20
409	A66	25b "Lady Denham"	.40	.20

Perf. 13½x14½
Size: 49x21mm

410	A66	50b "Mansa Kila Ba"	.60	.50
411	A66	1.25d "Prince of Wales"	.80	.85
	Nos. 408-411 (4)		*2.00*	*1.75*

London 80 Intl. Stamp Exhib., May 6-14.
For surcharge see No. 497A.

Queen Mother Elizabeth Birthday Issue
Common Design Type

1980, Aug. 4   Litho.   Perf. 14

412	CD330	67b multicolored	.40	.50

Phoenician Trading Vessel — A67

1980, Oct. 2   Litho.   Perf. 14½

413	A67	8b shown	.20	.20
414	A67	67b Egyptian seagoing ship	.80	.60
415	A67	75b Portuguese caravel	.90	.70
416	A67	1d Spanish galleon	1.10	.90
	Nos. 413-416 (4)		*3.00*	*2.40*

Virgin and Child, by Francesco de Mura — A68

Christmas: 67b, Praying Virgin with Crown of Stars, by Correggio. 75b, Rest on the Flight, after Correggio.

1980, Dec. 18   Litho.   Perf. 14

417	A68	8b multicolored	.20	.20
418	A68	67b multicolored	.25	.25
419	A68	75b multicolored	.40	.40
	Nos. 417-419 (3)		*.85*	*.85*

New Atlantic Hotel, Conference
Emblem — A69

1981, Feb. 18   Litho.   Perf. 14
420 A69 25b shown   .25   .25
421 A69 75b Ancient stone circle   .45   .45
422 A69 85b Conference emblem   .60   .60
  Nos. 420-422 (3)   1.30 1.30

World Tourism Conference, Manila, Sept. 27
and 16th anniversary of independence.

13th World Telecomunications
Day — A70

1981, May 17   Litho.   Perf. 14
423 A70 50b No. 399   .50   .35
424 A70 50b No. 313   .50   .35
425 A70 85b ITU, WHO emblems   .85   .60
  Nos. 423-425 (3)   1.85 1.30

Royal Wedding Issue
Common Design Type
1981, July 22   Litho.   Perf. 13½x13
426 CD331 75b Bouquet   .25   .25
427 CD331 1d Charles   .35   .35
428 CD331 1.25d Charles, Diana   .40   .40
  Nos. 426-428 (3)   1.00 1.00

For surcharges see Nos. 439, 497C.

Planting
Rice
Seedlings
A71

1981, Sept. 4   Litho.   Perf. 14
429 A71 10b shown   .20   .20
430 A71 50b Spraying   .30   .35
431 A71 85b Winnowing and dry-
            ing   .50   .55
  Nos. 429-431 (3)   1.00 1.10

West African Rice Development Assoc.,
10th anniv.

Abuko
Nature
Reserve
A72

Designs: Wildlife Fund emblem and reptiles.

1981, Nov. 17   Litho.   Perf. 14
432 A72 40b Bosc's monitor   30.00   .75
433 A72 60b Dwarf crocodile   22.50 1.50
434 A72 80b Royal python   40.00 2.50
435 A72 85b Chameleon   45.00 3.00
  Nos. 432-435 (4)   137.50 7.75

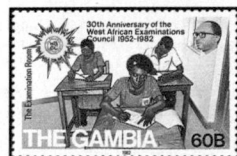

30th Anniv. of West African
Examinations Council — A73

1982, Mar. 16   Litho.   Perf. 14
436 A73 60b Test room   .60   .40
437 A73 85b 1st high school   .75   .55
438 A73 1.10d Council office   1.00   .75
  Nos. 436-438 (3)   2.35 1.70

No. 426 Surcharged
1982, Apr. 19   Litho.   Perf. 13½x13
439 CD331 60b on 75b multi   5.00 3.00

Scouting
Year
A74

1982, May   Perf. 14
440 A74 85b Tree planting   2.75 1.25
441 A74 1.25d Woodworking   3.00 2.50
442 A74 1.27d Baden-Powell   3.50 3.25
  Nos. 440-442 (3)   9.25 7.00

1982
World
Cup
A75

1982, June 13   Litho.   Perf. 14
443 A75 10b Team   .20   .20
444 A75 1.10d Players   1.75   .75
445 A75 1.25d Stadium   1.75   .80
446 A75 1.55d Cup   2.00 1.00
  a. Souvenir sheet of 4, #443-446 6.75 6.75
  Nos. 443-446 (4)   5.70 2.75

For surcharge see No. 497B.

Princess Diana Issue
Common Design Type
1982, July 1   Perf. 14½x14
447 CD333 10b Arms   .20   .20
448 CD333 85b Diana   .65   .65
449 CD333 1.10d Wedding   .85   .85
450 CD333 2.50d Portrait   1.75 1.75
  Nos. 447-450 (4)   3.45 3.45

For surcharge see No. 479D.

Economic
Community
of West
African
States
Development
A76

Designs: 10b, Yundum Experimental Farm.
60b, Banjul/Kaolack Microwave Tower. 90b,
Soap Factory, Denton Bridge Banjul. 1.25d,
Control Tower, Yundum.

1982, Nov. 5   Litho.   Perf. 14x14½
451 A76 10b multicolored   .35   .20
452 A76 60b multicolored   2.40 2.40
453 A76 90b multicolored   2.40 3.25
454 A76 1.25d multicolored   3.25 3.75
  Nos. 451-454 (4)   8.40 9.60

Kassina Cassinoides — A77

1982, Dec.   Litho.   Perf. 14
455 A77 10b shown   2.50   .20
456 A77 20b Hylarana
            galamensis   4.50   .45
457 A77 85b Euphlyctis occip-
            italis   7.50 4.50
458 A77 2d Kassina sene-
            galensis   10.00 12.00
  Nos. 455-458 (4)   24.50 17.15

A78

1983, Mar. 14   Wmk. 373   Perf. 12
459 A78 10b Globe showing
            Gambia   .20   .20
460 A78 60b Batik cloth   .25   .35
461 A78 1.10d Bagging peanuts   .45   .60
462 A78 2.10d Flag   .70 1.25
  Nos. 459-462 (4)   1.60 2.40

Commonwealth Day.

Sisters of St. Joseph of Cluny
Centenary — A79

1983, Apr. 8   Litho.   Perf. 14
463 A79 10b Founder Anne Marie
            Javouhey, vert.   .20   .20
464 A79 85b Javouhey with chil-
            dren, house   .50   .50

River
Boats
A80

1983, July 11   Litho.   Perf. 14
465 A80 1b Canoes   .20   .20
466 A80 2b Upstream ferry   .20   .20
467 A80 3b Dredging vessel   .20   .20
468 A80 4b Harbor launch   .30   .30
469 A80 5b Freighter   .30   .30
470 A80 10b 60-foot launch   .30   .30
471 A80 20b Multi-purpose
            vessel   .40   .40
472 A80 30b Large sailing
            canoe   .40   .40
473 A80 40b Passenger-car-
            go ferry   .40   .40
474 A80 50b Cargo liner, diff.   .45   .45
475 A80 75b Fishing boats   .60   .50
476 A80 1d Peanut river
            train   .95   .60
477 A80 1.25d Groundnutter   1.00 1.25
478 A80 2.50d Banjul-Barra
            ferry   1.75 2.25
479 A80 5d Binlang Bolong   3.25 4.75
480 A80 10d Passenger-car-
            go ferry, diff.   6.50 8.50
  Nos. 465-480 (16)   17.20 21.00

For overprints see Nos. 523-524.

World Communications Year — A81

1983, Oct. 10
481 A81 10b Local ferry   .20   .20
482 A81 85b GPO telex, Banjul   .95   .80
483 A81 90b Radio Gambia   1.10   .90
484 A81 1.10d Loading mail,
            Yundum Airport   1.25 1.10
  Nos. 481-484 (4)   3.50 3.00

Osprey,
Breeding
Range
A82

Designs: Birds, Maps of Europe and Africa.

1983, Sept. 12   Litho.   Perf. 14
485 A82 10b multicolored   3.00   .65
486 A82 60b multicolored   5.00 4.25
487 A82 85b multicolored   5.75 4.75
488 A82 1.10d multicolored   6.50 7.25
  Nos. 485-488 (4)   20.25 16.90

Raphael,
500th
Birth
Anniv.
A83

Details from St. Paul Preaching at Athens.

1983, Nov. 1   Litho.   Perf. 14
489 A83 60b multicolored   .65   .65
490 A83 85b multicolored   .85   .85
491 A83 1d multicolored   .90   .90
  Nos. 489-491 (3)   2.40 2.40

Souvenir Sheet
492 A83 2d multi, vert.   2.00 1.50

Manned
Flight,
200th
Anniv.
A84

Flown covers and: 60b, Montgolfier Balloon.
85b, British Caledonian Aircraft. 96b, Junkers
Airplane. 1.25d, Lunar module. 4d, Zeppelin.

1983, Dec. 12   Litho.   Perf. 14
493 A84 60b multicolored   .35   .35
494 A84 85b multicolored   .45   .45
  a. Bklt. pane, 2 each #493, 494   2.75
495 A84 90b multicolored   .45   .45
496 A84 1.25d multicolored   .50   .50
  a. Bklt. pane, 2 each #495, 496   4.50
  Nos. 493-496 (4)   1.75 1.75

Souvenir Sheet
497 A84 4d multicolored   10.00 10.00

No. 497 issued in booklet containing Nos.
497, 494a, 496a.

Nos. 411, 445, 428 and 449
Surcharged with Black Bars and New
Value
Perfs. as before
1983, Dec. 14   Litho.
497A A66 1.50d on 1.25d,
            #411   40.00
497B A75 1.50d on 1.25d,
            #445   40.00
497C CD331 2d on 1.25d,
            #428   40.00
497D CD333 2d on 1.10d,
            #449   40.00

The status of Nos. 497A-497D is questioned.

Easter
A85

Various Disney characters painting Easter
eggs.

1984, Apr. 15   Litho.   Perf. 11
498 A85 1b multicolored   .25   .20
499 A85 2b multicolored   .25   .20
500 A85 3b multicolored   .25   .20
501 A85 4b multicolored   .25   .20
502 A85 5b multicolored   .25   .20
503 A85 10b multicolored   .25   .20
504 A85 60b multicolored   .55   .45
505 A85 90b multicolored   .85   .70
506 A85 5d multicolored   3.50 3.00
  Nos. 498-506 (9)   6.40 5.35

Souvenir Sheet
Perf. 14
507 A85 5d multicolored   6.75 6.75

1984 Summer Olympics A86

1984, Mar. 30   Litho.   Perf. 14
508 A86   60b Shot put, vert.   .30   .30
509 A86   85b High jump   .45   .45
510 A86   90b Wrestling, vert.   .45   .45
511 A86   1d Gymnastics, vert.   .50   .50
512 A86   1.25d Swimming   .60   .60
513 A86   2d Diving   1.00   1.00
    Nos. 508-513 (6)   3.30   3.30

Souvenir Sheet
514 A86   5d Yachting, vert.   3.75   3.75

For overprints see Nos. 570-576.

Nile Crododile A87

1984, May 23
515 A87   4b Young hatching   4.00   .75
516 A87   6b Adult carrying young   4.00   .75
517 A87   90b Adult   27.50   5.00
518 A87   1.50d Adult, diff.   32.50   6.00
    Nos. 515-518 (4)   68.00   12.50

Souvenir Sheet
As Nos. 515-518, without WWF emblem.

518A A87   Sheet of 4   9.50   6.00
    b.-e.   each single   2.25   1.50

Lloyd's List Issue
Common Design Type

1984, June 1   Litho.   Perf. 14
519 CD335   60b Banjul Port   .90   .60
520 CD335   85b Bulk cargo carrier   1.10   .90
521 CD335   90b Sinking of the Dagomba   1.10   1.10
522 CD335   1.25d 19th-cent. frigate   2.00   1.90
    Nos. 519-522 (4)   5.10   4.50

Nos. 478-479 Overprinted: "19th UPU / CONGRESS HAMBURG"

1984, June 19   Litho.   Perf. 14
523 A80   2.50d multicolored   1.60   1.75
524 A80   5d multicolored   3.00   3.50

1984 Summer Olympics A88

1984, July 28   Litho.   Perf. 14
525 A88   60b Running   .50   .40
526 A88   85b Long jump   .65   .55
527 A88   90b Running, diff.   .65   .55
528 A88   1.25d Long jump, diff.   .85   .70
    Nos. 525-528 (4)   2.65   2.20

Gambia-South America Transatlantic Flight, 50th Anniv. — A89

1984, Nov. 1   Litho.   Perf. 14
529 A89   60b Graf Zeppelin D-LZ127   1.60   1.10
530 A89   85b Dornier Wal on S.S. Westfalen   2.40   1.90
531 A89   90b Dornier DO-18 D-ABYM   2.75   2.75
532 A89   1.25d Dornier Wal D-2069   2.75   3.00
    Nos. 529-532 (4)   9.50   8.75

Butterflies A90

1984, Nov. 27
533 A90   10b Antanartia hippomene   .40   .25
534 A90   85b Pseudacraea eurytus   1.10   1.00
535 A90   90b Charaxes lactitinctus   1.10   1.00
536 A90   3d Graphium pylades   3.00   4.25
    Nos. 533-536 (4)   5.60   6.50

Souvenir Sheet
537 A90   5d Eurema hapale   14.50   14.50

Marine Life — A90a

1984, Nov. 27
538 A90a   55b Penaeus duorarum   .50   .35
539 A90a   75b Caretta caretta   .75   .50
540 A90a   1.50d Physalia   1.10   1.00
541 A90a   2.35d Uca pugilator   2.10   1.90
    Nos. 538-541 (4)   4.45   3.75

Souvenir Sheets
542 A90a   5d Cowrie snail   6.50   6.50

UN Child Survival Campaign A91

1985, Feb. 27
543 A91   10b Oral rehydration therapy   .20   .20
544 A91   85b Growth monitoring   .50   .50
545 A91   1.10d Breast-feeding   .65   .65
546 A91   1.50d Universal immunization   .75   .75
    Nos. 543-546 (4)   2.10   2.10

UN Decade for Women A92

Design: 1d, 1.25d, Woman working in office.

1985, Mar. 11
547 A92   60b multicolored   .35   .35
548 A92   85b multicolored   .50   .50
549 A92   1d multicolored   .65   .65
550 A92   1.25d multicolored   .70   .70
    Nos. 547-550 (4)   2.20   2.20

Audubon Birth Bicent. — A93   Queen Mother, 85th Birthday — A94

Illustrations of North American bird species by John J. Audubon (1785-1851).

1985, July 15
551 A93   60b Cathartes aura   2.10   1.00
552 A93   85b Anhinga anhinga   2.50   1.75

553 A93   1.50d Butoroides striatus   2.75   3.75
554 A93   5d Aix sponsa   4.75   6.25
    Nos. 551-554 (4)   12.10   12.75

Souvenir Sheet
555 A93   10d Gavia immer   10.50   10.50

1985, July 24
556 A94   85b Inspecting troops   .50   .50
557 A94   3d Portrait   1.50   1.50
558 A94   5d Portrait, diff.   2.75   2.75
    Nos. 556-558 (3)   4.75   4.75

Souvenir Sheet
559 A94   10d On parade with Prince Charles   5.75   5.75

Life on the Mississippi, by Mark Twain (1835-1910) — A95

Walt Disney characters. The 60b, 85b, 2.35d, 5d and No. 569 show scenes from "Faithful John" by the brothers Grimm.

1985, Oct. 30
560 A95   60b Portrait   .85   .85
561 A95   85b Treasure   1.10   1.10
562 A95   1.50d Helm of Calamity Jane   2.25   2.25
563 A95   2d Antebellum Mansion, Missouri Shore   2.50   2.50
564 A95   2.35d Music   2.50   2.50
565 A95   2.50d Measuring Channel Depth, Natchez   3.00   3.00
566 A95   3d Card Game aboard the Gold Dust   3.25   3.25
567 A95   5d Statue   4.25   4.25
    Nos. 560-567 (8)   19.70   19.70

Souvenir Sheet
568 A95   10d Landing, St. Louis   11.00   11.00
569 A95   10d Goofy   11.00   11.00

Nos. 508-514 Ovptd. "GOLD MEDALIST" or "GOLD MEDAL," Name of Winner and Country

60b, Claudia Losch, West Germany, women's shot put. 85b, Ulrike Meyfarth, West Germany, women's high jump. 90b, Pasquale Passarelli, West Germany, 126-pound Greco-Roman wrestling. 1d, Li Ning, China, men's gymnastic floor exercises. 1.25d, Michael Gross, West Germany, men's 100-meter butterfly and 200-meter freestyle swimming. 2d, Sylvie Bernier, Canada, women's springboard diving. 5d, US, Star Class yachting.

1985, Nov. 11   Perf. 14
570 A86   60b multicolored   .65   .30
571 A86   85b multicolored   .85   .40
572 A86   90b multicolored   .85   .45
573 A86   1d multicolored   .85   .50
574 A86   1.25d multicolored   1.25   .65
575 A86   2d multicolored   1.60   1.00
    Nos. 570-575 (6)   6.05   3.30

Souvenir Sheet
576 A86   5d multicolored   3.00   3.00

UN 40th Anniv. A97

Views of Banjul.

1985, Nov. 15
577 A97   85b Independence Stadium   1.00   1.00
578 A97   2d Central Bank   2.40   2.40
579 A97   4d Port   5.00   5.00
580 A97   6d Oyster Creek Bridge   7.50   7.50
    Nos. 577-580 (4)   15.90   15.90

Natl. independence, 20th anniv.

UN FAO, 40th Anniv. A98

1985, Nov. 15
581 A98   60b Corn   .95   .95
582 A98   1.10d Paddy   1.90   1.90
583 A98   3d Cow, calf   5.50   5.50
584 A98   5d Fruit   8.50   8.50
    Nos. 581-584 (4)   16.85   16.85

Diocese of Gambia and Guinea, 50th Anniv. A99

Designs: 60b, Fishermen, Fotoba, Guinea. 85b, St. Mary's Primary School, Banjul. 1.10d, St. Mary's Cathedral, Banjul. 1.50d, Mobile Dispensary at Christy, Kunda, 1935-45.

1985, Dec. 24
585 A99   60b multicolored   .40   .30
586 A99   85b multicolored   .65   .45
587 A99   1.10d multicolored   .70   .60
588 A99   1.50d multicolored   1.25   .90
    Nos. 585-588 (4)   3.00   2.25

Girl Guides, 75th Anniv. — A100   Christmas — A101

1985, Dec. 27
589 A100   60b Application, horiz.   .40   .40
590 A100   85b 2nd Bathurst, horiz.   .60   .60
591 A100   1.50d Lady Baden-Powell   1.25   1.25
592 A100   5d Rosamond Fowlis, leader   4.00   4.00
    Nos. 589-592 (4)   6.25   6.25

Souvenir Sheet
593 A100   10d Guides   7.75   7.75

1985, Dec. 27   Perf. 15
Painting details: 60b, Virgin and Child, by Dirck Bouts (c. 1400-1475). 85b, The Annunciation, by Robert Campin (c. 1378-1444). 1.50d, Adoration of the Shepherds, by Gerard David (c. 1460-1523). 5d, The Nativity, by Gerard David. 10d, Adoration of the Magi, by Hieronymus Bosch (1450-1516).

594 A101   60b multicolored   .30   .30
595 A101   85b multicolored   .45   .45
596 A101   1.50d multicolored   .90   .90
597 A101   5d multicolored   1.75   1.75
    Nos. 594-597 (4)   3.40   3.40

Souvenir Sheet
598 A101   10d multicolored   6.00   6.00

Intl. Youth Year A102

1985, Dec. 31   Perf. 14
599 A102   60b Mother's helper   .30   .30
600 A102   85b Wrestling   .45   .45
601 A102   1.10d Griot storyteller   .60   1.00
602 A102   1.50d Crocodile pool   1.00   1.25
    Nos. 599-602 (4)   2.35   3.00

Souvenir Sheet
603 A102   5d Cow herder   3.25   3.25

A103

Halley's Comet — A104

Designs: 10b, Maria Mitchell (1818-1889), American astronomer, Kitt Peak Natl. Observatory, Papago Indian Reservation, Arizona. 20b, Apollo 11, Neil Armstrong steps on moon, 1969. 75b, Skylab 4, Kohoutek Comet, 1973. 1d, NASA Infrared Astronomical Satellite, 1983. 2d, Comet sighting, 1577, Turkish art. No. 609, NASA Intl. Cometary Explorer satellite. No. 610, Comet.

1986, Mar.
604	A103	10b multicolored	.40	.20
605	A103	20b multicolored	.75	.20
606	A103	75b multicolored	1.10	.55
607	A103	1d multicolored	1.40	.80
608	A103	2d multicolored	2.10	1.40
609	A103	10d multicolored	5.75	5.00
		Nos. 604-609 (6)	11.50	8.15

Souvenir Sheet
610	A104	10d multicolored	9.00	9.00

For overprints see Nos. 650-656.

Queen Elizabeth II, 60th Birthday
Common Design Type

Designs: 1d, Royal family at Royal Tournament, 1936. 2.50d, Christening, 1983. No. 613, State visit to West Germany, 1978. No. 614, At Balmoral, 1935.

1986, Apr. 21
611	CD339	1d lt yel bis & blk	.55	.40
612	CD339	2.50d pale green & multi	1.10	.75
613	CD339	10d dl lil & multi	3.50	3.00
		Nos. 611-613 (3)	5.15	4.15

Souvenir Sheet
614	CD339	10d tan & black	4.25	4.25

1986 World Cup Soccer Championships, Mexico — A105

1986, May 2
615	A105	75b Block	.65	.60
616	A105	1d Kneeing the ball	.90	.85
617	A105	2.50d Kick	2.75	2.50
618	A105	10d Heading the ball	7.00	7.00
		Nos. 615-618 (4)	11.30	10.95

Souvenir Sheet
619	A105	10d Goalie catching ball	11.50	11.50

For overprints see Nos. 639-643.

AMERIPEX '86 — A106

Exhibition emblem, automobiles and flags: 25b, 1986 Mercedes 500, Germany. 75b, 1935 Cord 810, US. 1d, 1957 Borgward Isabella Coupe, Germany. 1.25d, 1985-6 Lamborghini Countach, Italy. 2d, 1955 Ford

Thunderbird, US. 2.25d, 1956 Citroen DS19, France. 5d, 1936 Bugatti Atlante, France. 10d, 1936 Horch 853, Germany. No. 628, 1913 Benz 8/20, Germany. No. 629, 1924 Steiger 10/50, Germany.

1986, May 22 — **Perf. 15**
620	A106	25b multi	.20	.20
621	A106	75b multi	.45	.35
622	A106	1d multi	.70	.55
623	A106	1.25d multi	.75	.65
624	A106	2d multi	.90	1.00
625	A106	2.25d multi	.90	1.10
626	A106	5d multi	1.75	2.50
627	A106	10d multi	3.75	4.25
		Nos. 620-627 (8)	9.40	10.60

Souvenir Sheets
628	A106	12d multi	8.25	8.25
629	A106	12d multi	8.25	8.25

Karl Benz automobile cent.

Statue of Liberty, Cent. A107

Statue and famous emigrants: 20b, John Jacob Astor (1763-1848), financier. 1d, Jacob Riis (1849-1914), journalist. 1.25d, Igor Sikorsky (1889-1972), aeronautics engineer. 5d, Charles Boyer (1899-1978), actor. 10d, Statue, vert.

1986, June 10 — **Perf. 14**
630	A107	20b multicolored	.20	.20
631	A107	1d multicolored	.70	.70
632	A107	1.25d multicolored	.80	.80
633	A107	5d multicolored	3.25	3.25
		Nos. 630-633 (4)	4.95	4.95

Souvenir Sheet
634	A107	10d multicolored	6.25	6.25

Royal Wedding Issue, 1986
Common Design Type

1d, Engagement of Prince Andrew and Sarah Ferguson. 2.50d, Andrew. 4d, Andrew in flight uniform, other helicopter pilot. 7d, Couple, diff.

1986, July 23
635	CD340	1d multi	.60	.60
636	CD340	2.50d multi	1.40	1.40
637	CD340	4d multi	2.25	2.25
		Nos. 635-637 (3)	4.25	4.25

Souvenir Sheet
638	CD340	7d multi	5.00	5.00

Nos. 615-619 Overprinted "WINNERS / Argentina 3 / W. Germany 2" in Gold

1986, Sept. 16 — **Litho.** — **Perf. 14**
639	A105	75b multicolored	.40	.40
640	A105	1d multicolored	.60	.60
641	A105	2.50d multicolored	1.50	1.50
642	A105	10d multicolored	5.50	5.50
		Nos. 639-642 (4)	8.00	8.00

Souvenir Sheet
643	A105	10d multicolored	7.25	7.25

Christmas, STOCKHOLMIA '86 — A108

Disney characters mailing letters in various countries.

1986, Nov. 4 — **Perf. 11**
644	A108	1d Great Britain	1.25	.50
645	A108	1.25d United States	1.40	.70
646	A108	2d France	2.25	1.25
647	A108	2.35d Australia	2.50	1.40
648	A108	5d Germany	3.25	2.00
		Nos. 644-648 (5)	10.65	5.85

Souvenir Sheet
649	A108	10d Sweden	10.00	10.00

Nos. 604-610 Ovptd. in Silver

1986, Oct. 21 — **Litho.** — **Perf. 14**
650	A103	10b multicolored	.25	.20
651	A103	20b multicolored	.70	.20
652	A103	75b multicolored	1.10	.50
653	A103	1d multicolored	1.25	.60
654	A103	2d multicolored	1.60	1.50
655	A103	10d multicolored	4.75	4.50
		Nos. 650-655 (6)	9.65	7.50

Souvenir Sheet
656	A104	10d multicolored	5.75	5.75

Marc Chagall (1887-1985), Artist A109

Paintings, ceramicware, sculpture: 75b, Snowing. 85b, The Boat, 1957. 1d, Maternity, 1913. 1.25d, The Flute Player. 2.35d, Lovers and the Beast, 1957. 4d, Fishes at Saint Jean. 5d, Entering the Ring, 1968. 10d, Three Acrobats, 1956. No. 665, The Sabbath. No. 666, The Cattle Driver.

1987, Feb. 6 — **Litho.**
657	A109	75b multi	.50	.25
658	A109	85b multi	.60	.30
659	A109	1d multi	.70	.40
660	A109	1.25d multi	.90	.50
661	A109	2.35d multi	1.50	.80
662	A109	4d multi	2.25	1.25
663	A109	5d multi	2.75	1.50
664	A109	10d multi	4.50	2.50

Sizes: 110x95mm, 110x68mm
Imperf
665	A109	12d multi	7.00	7.00
666	A109	12d multi	7.00	7.00
		Nos. 657-666 (10)	27.70	21.50

Musical Instruments — A110

Various instruments from the Mandingo Empire.

1987, Jan. 21 — **Litho.** — **Perf. 15**
667	A110	75b Bugarab, tabala	.20	.20
668	A110	1d Balaphong, fiddle	.40	.30
669	A110	1.25d Bolongbato, konting	.50	.35
670	A110	10d Koras	2.50	2.50
		Nos. 667-670 (4)	3.60	3.35

Souvenir Sheet
671	A110	12d Sabarrs	3.75	3.75

Nos. 669-670 vert.
For overprints see Nos. 750, 856-860.

America's Cup A111

1987, Apr. 3 — **Perf. 14**
672	A111	20b America, 1851	.20	.20
673	A111	1d Courageous, 1974	.45	.45

674	A111	2.50d Volunteer, 1887	1.10	1.10
675	A111	10d Intrepid, 1967	4.50	4.50
		Nos. 672-675 (4)	6.25	6.25

Souvenir Sheet
676	A111	12d Australia II, 1983	6.50	6.50

For overprint see No. 751.

Statue of Liberty, Cent. A112

Photographs of restoration and unveiling in 1986.

1987, Apr. 9 — **Litho.**
677	A112	1b Shoulder, torch	.20	.20
678	A112	2b Operation Sail flotilla	.20	.20
679	A112	3b Tall ship, ships	.20	.20
680	A112	5b Luxury liner, aircraft carrier	.20	.20
681	A112	50b Statue's coiffure	.55	.55
682	A112	75b Coiffure, diff.	.80	.80
683	A112	1d Workmen scaling statue	.95	.95
684	A112	1.25d Back of statue	1.10	1.10
685	A112	10d Front of Statue	5.75	5.75
686	A112	12d Side of statue	6.00	6.00
		Nos. 677-686 (10)	15.95	15.95

Nos. 677, 681-686 vert.

Flowers from Abuko Nature Reserve — A113

75b, Lantana camara. 1d, Clerodendrum thomsoniae. 1.50d, Haemanthus multiflorus. 1.70d, Gloriosa simplex. 1.75d, Combretum microphyllum. 2.25d, Eulophia guineensis. 5d, Erythrina senegalensis. 15d, Dichrostachys glomerata.
#691, Costus spectabilis. #691A, Strophanthus preussii.

1987, May 25
687	A113	75b multi	.20	.20
687A	A113	1d multi	.25	.25
688	A113	1.50d multi	.45	.40
688A	A113	1.70d multi	.50	.45
689	A113	1.75d multi	.50	.45
689A	A113	2.25d multi	.70	.60
689B	A113	5d multi	1.60	1.40
690	A113	15d multi	3.75	3.75
		Nos. 687-690 (8)	7.95	7.50

Souvenir Sheets
691	A113	15d shown	3.75	3.75
691A	A113	15d multi	3.75	3.75

#691-691A are continuous designs.
For overprint see No. 752.

CAPEX '87 A115

Various buses.

1987, June 15
692	A115	20b multi, vert.	.60	.20
693	A115	75b multi	.80	.25
694	A115	1d multi	2.10	.75
695	A115	10d multi, vert.	4.25	2.00
		Nos. 692-695 (4)	7.75	3.20

Souvenir Sheet
696	A115	12d multi	7.75	7.75

For overprint see No. 749.

1988
Summer
Olympics,
Seoul
A116

1987, July 3

697	A116	50b	Women's basket-ball	.20 .20
698	A116	1d	Volleyball	.65 .30
699	A116	3d	Field hockey	1.25 .90
700	A116	10d	Handball	4.00 3.00
			Nos. 697-700 (4)	6.10 4.40

Souvenir Sheet

701	A116	15d	Soccer	5.75 5.75

Nos. 697-698 vert.

A117

The Twelve Days of Christmas,
Medieval Counting Song — A118

Designs: 20b, Partridge in a pear tree. 40b, 2 turtle doves. 60b, 3 French hens. 75b, 4 calling birds. 1d, 5 golden rings. 1.25d, 6 geese a-laying. 1.50d, 7 swans a-swimming. 2d, 8 maids a-milking. 3d, 9 ladies dancing. 5d, 10 lords a-leaping. 10d, 11 pipers piping. 12d, 12 drummers drumming.

Miniature Sheet

1987, Nov. 2   Litho.   Perf. 14

702			Sheet of 12	16.00 16.00
a.	A117	20b	multicolored	.20 .20
b.	A117	40b	multicolored	.20 .20
c.	A117	60b	multicolored	.20 .20
d.	A117	75b	multicolored	.20 .20
e.	A117	1d	multicolored	.40 .40
f.	A117	1.25d	multicolored	.45 .45
g.	A117	1.50d	multicolored	.70 .60
h.	A117	2d	multicolored	.90 .75
i.	A117	3d	multicolored	1.50 1.25
j.	A117	5d	multicolored	2.25 1.90
k.	A117	10d	multicolored	4.00 3.50
l.	A117	12d	multicolored	5.00 4.25

Souvenir Sheet

703	A118	15d	multi	5.75 5.75

16th Boy
Scout
Jamboree,
Australia,
1987-88
A119

1987, Nov. 9

704	A119	75b	Singing around campfire	.20 .20
705	A119	1d	Nature study, African katydid	.70 .30
706	A119	1.25d	Bird watching, red-tailed tropicbird	.95 .40
707	A119	12d	Boarding bus	6.75 3.50
			Nos. 704-707 (4)	8.60 4.40

Souvenir Sheet

708	A119	15d	Nature study	8.75 8.75

Mickey Mouse, 60th Anniv. — A120

Disney animated characters and historic locomotives: 60b, Richard Trevithick's locomotive, 1804. 75b, Empire State Express 999, 1893. 1d, George Stephenson's Rocket, 1829. 1.25d, Santa Fe Mountain 2-10-2, 1920. 2d, Class GG-1 Pennsylvania, 1933. 5d, Stourbridge Lion, 1829. 10d, Best Friend of Charleston, 1830. 12d, M10001 Union Pacific, 1934. No. 717, Tres Grande Vitesse-SNCF, 1981, France. No. 718, The General, Western & Atlantic, 1855.

1987, Dec. 9   Litho.   Perf. 14x13½

709	A120	60b	multicolored	.20 .20
710	A120	75b	multicolored	.25 .25
711	A120	1d	multicolored	.50 .30
712	A120	1.25d	multicolored	.60 .40
713	A120	2d	multicolored	.90 .60
714	A120	5d	multicolored	2.25 1.50
715	A120	10d	multicolored	4.50 3.00
716	A120	12d	multicolored	5.00 3.50
			Nos. 709-716 (8)	14.20 9.75

Souvenir Sheets

717	A120	15d	multicolored	7.25 7.25
718	A120	15d	multicolored	7.25 7.25

Fauna and
Flora
A121

1988, Feb. 9   Litho.   Perf. 15

719	A121	50b	Duiker, acacia	.20 .20
720	A121	75b	Red-billed hornbill, casuarina	.20 .20
721	A121	90b	West African dwarf crocodile, rice	.25 .25
722	A121	1d	Leopard, papyrus	.25 .25
723	A121	1.25d	Crested cranes, millet	.35 .35
724	A121	2d	Waterbuck, baobab tree	.55 .55
725	A121	3d	Oribi, Senegal palm	.80 .80
726	A121	5d	Hippopotamus, papaya	1.40 1.40
			Nos. 719-726 (8)	4.00 4.00

Souvenir Sheets

727	A121	12d	Great white pelican	2.50 2.50
728	A121	12d	Red-throated bee-eater	2.50 2.50

Nos. 720, 722, 724, 726 and 728 vert.

40th Wedding
Anniv. of Queen
Elizabeth II and
Prince
Philip — A122

1988, Mar. 15   Perf. 14

729	A122	75b	Wedding portrait, 1947	.20 .20
730	A122	1d	Couple at leisure	.25 .25
731	A122	3d	Couple, c. 1987 diff.	1.00 1.00
732	A122	10d	Couple, c. 1987	3.50 3.50
			Nos. 729-732 (4)	4.95 4.95

Souvenir Sheet

733	A122	15d	Wedding party	3.50 3.50

1988
Summer
Olympics,
Seoul
A123

1988, May 3   Litho.   Perf. 14

734	A123	1d	Archery, vert.	.20 .20
735	A123	1.25d	Boxing, vert.	.20 .20
736	A123	5d	Gymnastics, vert.	1.50 1.25
737	A123	10d	100-Meter sprint	3.50 2.50
			Nos. 734-737 (4)	5.40 4.15

Souvenir Sheet

738	A123	15d	Award ceremony, Olympic stadium	4.00 4.00

Anniversaries & Events — A124

Designs: 50b, Red Cross flag. 75b, Friendship 7, piloted by John Glenn, 1963. 1d, British Airways Concorde jet. 1.25d, Spirit of St. Louis, piloted by Charles Lindbergh, 1927. 2d, X-15, piloted by Major William Knight, 1967. 3d, Bell X-1, piloted by Capt. Charles Yeager, 1947. 10d, Spanish galleon, British warship, 1588. 12d, The Titanic. No. 747, Kangaroo and joey. No. 748, Cathedral, modern church, vert.

1988, May 15

739	A124	50b	multicolored	.75 .75
740	A124	75b	multicolored	.75 .75
741	A124	1d	multicolored	1.25 1.25
742	A124	1.25d	multicolored	1.25 1.25
743	A124	2d	multicolored	1.75 1.75
744	A124	3d	multicolored	2.25 2.25
745	A124	10d	multicolored	5.50 5.50
746	A124	12d	multicolored	6.50 6.50
			Nos. 739-746 (8)	20.00 20.00

Souvenir Sheets

747	A124	15d	multicolored	4.75 4.75
748	A124	15d	multicolored	4.75 4.75

Intl. Red Cross, 125th anniv. (50b); first American in space, 25th anniv. in 1987 (75b); 1st London-New York scheduled Concorde flight, 10th anniv. in 1987 (1d); first solo transatlantic flight, 60th anniv. in 1987 (1.25d); fastest speed flown, 6.72 Mach, 20th anniv. in 1987 (2d); 1st supersonic flight, 40th anniv. in 1987 (3d); defeat of the Spanish Armada, 400th anniv. (10d); maiden voyage of the Titanic, 75th anniv. in 1987 (12d); founding of Australia, bicentennial (No. 747); and founding of Berlin, 750th anniv. in 1987 (No. 748).

Nos. 694, 670, 675 and 690 Ovptd. for
Philatelic Exhibitions

a

b

c

d

1988, Apr. 19   Litho.   Perf. 14, 15

749	A115(a)	1d	multi	.50 .50
750	A110(b)	10d	multi	3.50 3.50
751	A111(c)	10d	multi	3.50 3.50
752	A113(d)	15d	multi	4.50 4.50
			Nos. 749-752 (4)	12.00 12.00

Paintings by
Titian
A125

Designs: 25b, Emperor Charles V, 1549. 50b, St. Margaret and the Dragon, 1565. 60b, Ranuccio Farnese, 1542. 75b, Tarquin and Lucretia, 1570. 1d, The Knight of Malta, c. 1550. 5d, Spain Succouring Faith, 1571. 10d, Doge Francesco Venier, 1555. 12d, Doge Grimani Before the Faith, c. 1555-1576. No. 761, Jealous Husband, 1511. No. 762, Venus Blindfolding Cupid, 1560.

1988, July 7   Litho.   Perf. 13½x14

753	A125	25b	multicolored	.20 .20
754	A125	50b	multicolored	.50 .50
755	A125	60b	multicolored	.55 .55
756	A125	75b	multicolored	.80 .80
757	A125	1d	multicolored	.90 .90
758	A125	5d	multicolored	3.00 3.00
759	A125	10d	multicolored	5.00 5.00
760	A125	12d	multicolored	5.75 5.75
			Nos. 753-760 (8)	16.70 16.70

Souvenir Sheets

761	A125	15d	multicolored	4.25 4.25
762	A125	15d	multicolored	4.25 4.25

Tribute to
John F.
Kennedy
A126

1988, Sept. 1   Litho.   Perf. 14

763	A126	75b	Sailing	.20 .20
764	A126	1d	Peace Corps enactment	.35 .35
765	A126	1.25d	Public address, vert.	.45 .45
766	A126	12d	Grave, Arlington Natl. Cemetery	3.25 3.25
			Nos. 763-766 (4)	4.25 4.25

Souvenir Sheet

767	A126	15d	Kennedy, vert.	4.75 4.75

Entertainers — A127

20b, Emmett Lee Kelly (1898-1979), clown. 1d, Gambia Natl. Ensemble. 1.25d, Jackie Gleason (1916-87), comedian, & The Honeymooners cast. 1.50d, Stan Laurel (1890-1965) & Oliver Hardy (1892-1957), film comedy team. 2.50d, Yul Brynner (c. 1920-85), actor. 3d, Cary Grant (1904-86), actor. 10d, Danny Kaye (1918-87), comedian, actor. 20d, Charlie Chaplin (1889-1977), comedian, actor. #776,

Harpo (1893-1964), Chico (1891-1961), Zeppo (1901-79) & Groucho (1890-1977) Marx, comedy team. #777, Fred Astaire (1899-1987) & Rita Hayworth (1918-87), dancers & film stars. #768-775 vert.

1988, Nov. 9   Litho.

768	A127	20b multi	.20	.20
769	A127	1d multi	.50	.50
770	A127	1.25d multi	.60	.60
771	A127	1.50d multi	.65	.65
772	A127	2.50d multi	1.10	1.10
773	A127	3d multi	1.40	1.40
774	A127	10d multi	4.50	4.50
775	A127	20d multi	8.00	8.00
		Nos. 768-775 (8)	16.95	16.95

Souvenir Sheets

776	A127	15d multi	7.75	7.75
777	A127	15d multi	7.75	7.75

Kelly's name is spelled incorrectly; Brynner's and Grant's dates are incorrect.

Zeppelin LZ7 Deutschland, 1910 — A128

Transportation innovations: 50b, Stephenson's Locomotion, 1825. 75b, General Motors Sun Racer, 1987. 1d, Sprague's Premiere, 1888. 1.25d, Gold Rush bicycle, 1986. 2.50d, 1st Liquid-fuel rocket, invented by Robert Goddard, 1925. 10d, Orukter Amphibolos, 1805. 12d, Sovereign of the Seas, 1988. No. 786, USS Nautilus, 1954, vert. No. 787, Fulton's Nautilus, early 19th cent.

1988, Nov. 21   Litho.   *Perf. 14*

778	A128	25b multi	.65	.25
779	A128	50b multi	1.10	.40
780	A128	75b multi	1.25	.55
781	A128	1d multi	1.75	.70
782	A128	1.25d multi	1.75	.75
783	A128	2.50d multi	2.75	1.25
784	A128	10d multi	6.75	3.50
785	A128	12d multi	7.75	4.00
		Nos. 778-785 (8)	23.75	11.40

Souvenir Sheets

786	A128	15d multi	6.00	6.00
787	A128	15d multi	6.00	6.00

Discovery of America, 500th Anniv. (in 1992) A129

Designs: 50b, Caravel, Henry the Navigator (1394-1460), Prince of Portugal, and coat of arms, vert. 75b, Jesse Ramsden's sextant, map of Africa, arms, vert. 1d, Hour glass, 15th cent., and map, vert. 1.25d, Henry and Vasco da Gama, vert. 2.50d, Da Gama and 15th cent. caravel, vert. 5d, Mungo Park (1771-1806), Scottish explorer, arms and map of Gambia River. 10d, Map of west African coast, 1563. 12d, Portuguese caravel, arms. No. 796, Caravel off the Gambian coast, 15th cent., vert. No. 797, European ship off Gambian coast, 15th cent., vert.

1988, Dec. 1   Litho.   *Perf. 14*

788	A129	50b multi	.95	.95
789	A129	75b multi	1.10	1.10
790	A129	1d multi	1.50	1.50
791	A129	1.25d multi	1.75	1.75
792	A129	2.50d multi	2.25	2.25
793	A129	5d shown	3.75	3.75
794	A129	10d multi	6.25	6.25
795	A129	12d multi	6.50	6.50
		Nos. 788-795 (8)	24.05	24.05

Souvenir Sheets

796	A129	15d multi	6.00	6.00
797	A129	15d multi	6.00	6.00

Space Achievements — A130

Galileo and: 50b, Futuristic aerospace plane and Ernst Mach (1838-1916), Austrian physicist, vert. 75b, OAO III astronomical satellite and Niels Bohr (1885-1962), Danish physicist and Nobel laurate in 1922, vert. 1d, NASA space shuttle, future space station and Robert Goddard (1882-1945), American rocket scientist. 1.25d, Flyby of probe past Jupiter, 1979, and Edward Barnard (1857-1923), American astronomer who discovered Jupiter's 5th satellite in 1892. 2d, Hubble Space Telescope and George Hale (1868-1938), American astronomer, vert. 3d, Precision measurement of the distance between the Earth and the Moon by laser and Albert A. Michelson (1852-1931), Nobel laurate in 1907 for research on the speed of light. 10d, HEAO-2 Einstein orbital satellite and Albert Einstein, vert. 20d, Voyager, 1st circumnavigation of the world without refueling, 1987, and the Wright Brothers. No. 806, Moon Ganymede passing the Great Red Spot on Jupiter. No. 807, Apollo and Neil Armstrong, 1st man on the Moon, July 20, 1969, vert.

1988, Dec. 12   *Perf. 14*

798	A130	50b multi	.50	.30
799	A130	75b multi	.60	.40
800	A130	1d multi	.75	.55
801	A130	1.25d multi	.90	.75
802	A130	2d multi	1.50	1.10
803	A130	3d multi	1.75	1.75
804	A130	10d multi	4.50	4.50
805	A130	20d multi	8.00	8.00
		Nos. 798-805 (8)	18.50	17.35

Souvenir Sheets

806	A130	15d multi	5.50	5.50
807	A130	15d multi	5.50	5.50

350th anniv. of the publication of Discourses, by Galileo.

Army Day A131

1989, Feb. 10   Litho.   *Perf. 14*

808	A131	75b Troops on parade	.20	.20
809	A131	1d Regimental flags	.30	.30
810	A131	1.25d Drummer, vert.	.45	.45
811	A131	10d Atlantic Shooting Cup winner, vert.	2.75	2.75
812	A131	15d Assault course, vert.	4.50	4.50
813	A131	20d 105-mm gun	5.00	5.00
		Nos. 808-813 (6)	13.20	13.20

Miniature Sheet

Mickey Mouse, 60th Anniv. (in 1988) — A132

Mickey Mouse through the years: a, 1928. b, 1931. c, 1936. d, 1955. e, 1947. f, 1940. g, 1960. h, 1976. i, 1988. 15d, Birthday party.

1989, Apr. 6   Litho.   *Perf. 13x13½*

814	A132	Sheet of 9	17.50	17.50
a.-i.		2d any single	1.50	1.40

Size: 139x110mm

Imperf

815	A132	15d multi	8.00	8.00

Easter A133

Paintings by Rubens: 50b, Le Coup de Lance, 1620. 75b, The Flagellation of Christ, 1617. 1d, The Lamentation for Christ, 1617. 1.25d, Descent from the Cross, c. 1611. 2d, The Holy Trinity, c. 1617. 5d, The Doubting Thomas. 10d, Lamentation over Christ, 1614. 12d, Lamentation over Christ with the Virgin and St. John, c. 1613. No. 824, The Last Supper, c. 1631. No. 825, The Raising of the Cross, c. 1610.

1989, Apr. 14   *Perf. 13½x14*

816	A133	50b multi	.45	.25
817	A133	75b multi	.55	.35
818	A133	1d multi	.55	.35
819	A133	1.25d multi	.60	.50
820	A133	2d multi	1.00	.80
821	A133	5d multi	2.00	1.75
822	A133	10d multi	3.00	3.00
823	A133	12d multi	3.50	3.50
		Nos. 816-823 (8)	11.65	10.50

Souvenir Sheets

824	A133	15d multi	4.25	4.25
825	A133	15d multi	4.25	4.25

Indigenous Birds — A134

1989, Apr. 24   *Perf. 14*

826	A134	20b African emerald cuckoo	.80	.25
827	A134	60b Gray-headed bush shrike	1.10	.50
828	A134	75b Crowned crane	1.10	.55
829	A134	1d Secretary bird	1.25	.60
830	A134	2d Red-billed hornbill	1.50	.90
831	A134	5d Superb sunbird	2.75	2.50
832	A134	10d Little owl	6.00	3.75
833	A134	12d Bateleur eagle	6.75	4.50
		Nos. 826-833 (8)	21.25	13.55

Souvenir Sheets

834	A134	15d Red-billed fire finch	6.00	6.00
835	A134	15d Ostriches	6.00	6.00

Indigenous Butterflies — A135

1989, May 15

836	A135	50b Papilio antimachus	.60	.25
837	A135	75b Euphaedra neophron	.75	.45
838	A135	1d Aterica rabena	.75	.45
839	A135	1.25d Salamis parhassus	.90	.90
840	A135	5d Precis rhadama	2.75	2.75
841	A135	10d Papilio demodocus	5.00	5.00
842	A135	12d Charaxes etesippe	5.75	5.75
843	A135	15d Danaus formosa	7.25	7.25
		Nos. 836-843 (8)	23.75	22.80

Souvenir Sheets

844	A135	15d Euphaedra ceres	8.75	8.75
845	A135	15d Cymothoe pluto	8.75	8.75

Trains of Africa A136

Designs: 50b, Nigerian coal train, 1959. 75b, 14A Class 2-6-6-2 Garratt. 1d, British (Pacific) in Sudan. 1.25d, American 0-8-0, 1925. 5d, Scottish 4-8-2, 1955. 7d, Scottish 4-8-2, 1926. 10d, British 4-6-0. 12d, American-made 2-6-0 in Ghana. No. 854, British 2-8-2 Class 25 facing forward, vert. No. 855, Class 25 facing left, vert.

1989, June 15   Litho.   *Perf. 14*

846	A136	50b multi	.60	.30
847	A136	75b multi	.75	.45
848	A136	1d multi	.80	.65
849	A136	1.25d multi	.95	.90
850	A136	5d multi	2.75	2.75
851	A136	7d multi	3.00	3.00
852	A136	10d multi	5.25	5.25
853	A136	12d multi	6.00	6.00
		Nos. 846-853 (8)	20.10	19.30

Souvenir Sheets

854	A136	15d multi	6.75	6.75
855	A136	15d multi	6.75	6.75

Nos. 667-671 Ovptd. "PHILEXFRANCE / '89"

1989, June 23   Litho.   *Perf. 15*

856	A110	75b multi	.25	.25
857	A110	1d multi	.30	.30
858	A110	1.25d multi	.45	.45
859	A110	10d multi	2.00	2.00
		Nos. 856-859 (4)	3.00	3.00

Souvenir Sheet

860	A110	12d multi	3.50	3.50

Paintings by Japanese Artists A137

Paintings by Hiroshige unless noted otherwise: 50b, Sparrow and Bamboo. 75b, Peonies and a Canary, by Hokusai. 1d, Crane and Marsh Grasses. 1.25d, Crossbill and Thistle, by Hokusai. 2d, Cuckoo and Azalea, by Hokusai. 5d, Parrot on a Pine Branch. 10d, Mandarin Ducks in a Stream. 12d, Bullfinch and Drooping Cherry, by Hokusai. No. 869, Tit and Peony, horiz. No. 870, Peony and Butterfly, by Shigenobu, horiz.

1989, July 7   *Perf. 13½x14, 14x13½*

861	A137	50b multi	.55	.30
862	A137	75b multi	.75	.40
863	A137	1d multi	.90	.55
864	A137	1.25d multi	1.00	.65
865	A137	2d multi	1.50	1.00
866	A137	5d multi	2.50	2.50
867	A137	10d multi	5.00	5.00
868	A137	12d multi	5.50	5.50
		Nos. 861-868 (8)	17.70	15.90

Souvenir Sheets

869	A137	15d multi	6.25	6.25
870	A137	15d multi	6.25	6.25

1990 World Cup Soccer Championships, Italy — A138

Various athletes and Italian landmarks: 75b, Rialto Bridge, Venice. 1.25d, The Baptistery, Pisa. 7d, Casino San Remo. 12d, The Colosseum, Rome. No. 875, St. Mark's Cathedral, Venice. No. 876, Piazza Colonna, Rome.

1989, Aug 25   **Perf. 14**

871	A138	75b multi	.55	.55
872	A138	1.25b multi	.70	.70
873	A138	7d multi	3.25	3.25
874	A138	12d multi	5.50	5.50
		Nos. 871-874 (4)	10.00	10.00

Souvenir Sheets

875	A138	15d multi	6.50	6.50
876	A138	15d multi	6.50	6.50

Medicinal Plants — A139

1989, Sept. 18   **Litho.**   **Perf. 14**

877	A139	20b Vitex doniana	.20	.20
878	A139	50b Ricinus communis	.30	.30
879	A139	75b Palisota hirsuta	.45	.45
880	A139	1d Smilax kraussiana	.55	.55
881	A139	1.25d Aspilia africana	.65	.65
882	A139	5d Newbouldia laevis	2.25	2.25
883	A139	8d Monodora tenuifolia	3.50	3.50
884	A139	10d Gossypium arboreum	4.25	4.25
		Nos. 877-884 (8)	12.15	12.15

Souvenir Sheets

885	A139	15d Kigelia africana	6.75	6.75
886	A139	15d Spathodea campanulata	6.75	6.75

Fish A140

1989, Oct. 19   **Litho.**   **Perf.**

887	A140	20b Lookdown	.25	.25
888	A140	75b Boarfish	.70	.70
889	A140	1d Gray triggerfish	.75	.75
890	A140	1.25d Skipjack tuna	.90	.90
891	A140	2d Bermuda chub	1.25	1.25
892	A140	4d Atlantic manta	2.40	2.40
893	A140	5d Striped mullet	3.00	3.00
894	A140	10d Ladyfish	4.25	4.25
		Nos. 887-894 (8)	13.50	13.50

Souvenir Sheet

895	A140	15d Porcupinefish	8.25	8.25
896	A140	15d Shortfin makos	8.25	8.25

Souvenir Sheet

The White House, Washington, D.C. — A141

1989, Nov. 17   **Litho.**   **Perf. 14**

897	A141	10d multicolored	3.50	3.50

World Stamp Expo '89.

World Stamp Expo '89, Washington, D.C. — A142

Disney characters riding carousel horses: 20b, Daniel Muller Indian pony. 50b, Herschell-Spillman steed. 75b, Gustav Dentzel stander. 1d, Muller armored stander. 1.25d, Jumper from the Smithsonian Collection. 2d, Illion "American Beauty." 8d, Zalar jumper. 10d, Parker buckling. No. 906, Philadelphia Tobaggan Co. Carousel, Elitch Gardens, Denver, CO. No. 907, PTC Roman chariot.

1989, Nov. 29   **Litho.**   **Perf. 14x13½**

898	A142	20b multicolored	.70	.20
899	A142	50b multicolored	1.10	.30
900	A142	75b multicolored	1.25	.40
901	A142	1d multicolored	1.25	.50
902	A142	1.25d multicolored	1.40	.75
903	A142	2d multicolored	1.90	1.00
904	A142	8d multicolored	5.50	3.00
905	A142	10d multicolored	5.50	3.25
		Nos. 898-905 (8)	18.60	9.40

Souvenir Sheets

906	A142	12d multicolored	7.75	7.75
907	A142	12d multicolored	7.75	7.75

Nobel Prize Winners for Physiology and Great Medical Pioneers — A143

20b, Charles Nicolle (1866-1936), France, 1928 Prize, discovered transmission of typhus by body lice. 50b, Paul Ehrlich (1854-1915), Germany, 1908 Prize, immunology research. 75b, Selman Waksman (1888-1973), Russian-American, 1952 Prize, discovered antibiotic streptomycin, used to treat tuberculosis. 1d, Edward Jenner (1749-1823), Great Britain, discovered smallpox vaccine. 1.25d, Robert Koch (1843-1910), 1905 Prize, isolated the tubercle bacillus. 5d, Sir Alexander Fleming (1881-1955), Scotland, 1945 Prize, developed penicillin. 8d, Max Theiler (1899-1972), US, 1951 Prize, developed yellow fever vaccine. 10d, Louis Pasteur (1822-95), France, proved the germ theory of infection.

#916, C-9 Nightingale Aeromedical Airlift. #917, Hughes Vicking helicopter used in airlift.

1989, Dec. 12   **Perf. 14**

908	A143	20b multicolored	1.00	.30
909	A143	50b multicolored	1.10	.40
910	A143	75b multicolored	1.25	.50
911	A143	1d multicolored	1.40	.60
912	A143	1.25d multicolored	1.50	.70
913	A143	5d multicolored	2.75	1.60
914	A143	8d multicolored	4.25	2.50
915	A143	10d multicolored	5.50	3.25
		Nos. 908-915 (8)	18.75	9.85

Souvenir Sheets

916	A143	15d multicolored	6.25	6.25
917	A143	15d multicolored	6.25	6.25

Orchids — A144

1989, Dec. 18   **Perf. 14**

918	A144	20b Bulbophyllum lepidum	.45	.30
919	A144	75b Tridactyle tridactylites	.75	.75
920	A144	1d Vanilla imperialis	1.10	1.10
921	A144	1.25d Oeceoclades maculata	1.25	1.25
922	A144	2d Polystachya affinis	1.75	1.75

923	A144	4d Ancistrochilus rothschildianus	3.00	3.00
924	A144	5d Angraecum distichum	3.50	3.50
925	A144	10d Liparis guineensis	5.50	5.50
		Nos. 918-925 (8)	17.30	17.15

Souvenir Sheets

926	A144	15d Eulophia guineensis	7.75	7.75
927	A144	15d Plectrelminthus caudatus	7.75	7.75

Christmas — A145

Disney characters and classic automobiles: 20b, 1922 Pierce-Arrow. 50b, 1919 Spyker. 75b, 1929 Packard. 1d, 1920 Daimler. 1.25d, 1924 Hispano Suiza. 2d, Opel Laubfrosch, 1924-27. 10d, 1927 Vauxhall 30/98. 12d, 1923 Peerless. No. 936, 1930 Bentley Supercharged, Santa Claus. No. 937, 1928 Stutz Blackhawk Speedster, picnic.

1989, Dec. 19   **Litho.**   **Perf. 14**

928	A145	20b multicolored	.75	.25
929	A145	50b multicolored	1.00	.40
930	A145	75b multicolored	1.10	.55
931	A145	1d multicolored	1.25	.65
932	A145	1.25d multicolored	1.40	.90
933	A145	2d multicolored	1.50	1.25
934	A145	10d multicolored	5.00	3.00
935	A145	12d multicolored	5.50	3.25
		Nos. 928-935 (8)	17.50	10.25

Souvenir Sheets

936	A145	15d multicolored	8.75	8.75
937	A145	15d multicolored	8.75	8.75

Wimbledon Tennis Champions A146   1st Moon Landing, 20th Anniv. (in 1989) A147

1990, Jan. 2   **Litho.**   **Perf. 15x14½**

938	A146	20b John Newcombe	.20	.20
939	A146	20b G.W. Hillyard	.20	.20
a.		Pair, #938-939	.40	.40
940	A146	50b Roy Emerson	.30	.30
941	A146	50b Dorothy Chambers	.30	.30
a.		Pair, #940-941	.65	.65
942	A146	75b Donald Budge	.40	.40
943	A146	75b Suzanne Lenglen	.40	.40
a.		Pair, #942-943	.85	.85
944	A146	1d Laurence Doherty	.45	.45
945	A146	1d Helen Wills Moody	.45	.45
a.		Pair, #944-945	.95	.95
946	A146	1.25d Bjorn Borg	.50	.50
947	A146	1.25d Maureen Connolly	.50	.50
a.		Pair, #946-947	1.10	1.10
948	A146	4d Jean Borotra	1.25	1.25
949	A146	4d Maria Bueno	1.25	1.25
a.		Pair, #948-949	2.75	2.75
950	A146	5d Anthony Wilding	1.50	1.50
951	A146	5d Louise Brough	1.50	1.50
a.		Pair, #950-951	3.25	3.25
952	A146	7d Fred Perry	2.00	2.00
953	A146	7d Margaret Court	2.00	2.00
a.		Pair, #952-953	4.50	4.50
954	A146	10d Bill Tilden	2.75	2.75
955	A146	10d Billie Jean King	2.75	2.75
a.		Pair, #954-955	6.25	6.25

956	A146	12d Rod Laver	3.00	3.00
957	A146	12d Martina Navratilova	3.00	3.00
a.		Pair, #956-957	6.75	6.75
		Nos. 938-957 (20)	24.70	24.70

Souvenir Sheets

958	A146	15d Rod Laver, diff.	7.25	7.25
959	A146	15d Martina Navratilova, diff.	7.25	7.25

1990, Feb. 16   **Perf. 14**

Designs: 20b, Eagle lunar module descending. 50b, Apollo 11 liftoff. 75b, Astronaut descending ladder, horiz. 1d, Astronaut, US flag over Sea of Tranquillity, horiz. 1.25d, Mission emblem. 1.75d, Crew, horiz. 8d, Lunar module, Sea of Tranquillity, horiz. 12d, Recovery of command module Columbia after splashdown. No. 968, Neil Armstrong returning to Eagle. No. 969, View of Earth.

960	A147	20b multicolored	.75	.25
961	A147	50b multicolored	1.00	.30
962	A147	75b multicolored	1.25	.45
963	A147	1d multicolored	1.40	.55
964	A147	1.25d multicolored	1.50	.60
965	A147	1.75d multicolored	1.60	1.00
966	A147	8d multicolored	4.75	2.25
967	A147	12d multicolored	6.00	2.75
		Nos. 960-967 (8)	18.25	8.15

Souvenir Sheets

968	A147	15d multicolored	5.75	5.75
969	A147	15d multicolored	5.75	5.75

Miniature Sheet

Birds of Africa A148

No. 970: a, White-faced owl. b, Village weaver. c, Red-throated bee eater. d, Brown harrier eagle. e, Red bishop. f, Scarlet-chested sunbird. g, Red-billed hornbill. h, Mosque swallow. i, White-faced tree duck. j, African fish eagle. k, Great white pelican. l, Carmine bee eater. m, Hadada ibis. n, Crocodile plover. o, Yellow-bellied sunbird. p, African skimmer. q, Woodland kingfisher. r, Jacana. s, Pygmy goose. t, Hamerkop.

1990, Apr. 12   **Litho.**   **Perf. 14**

970		Sheet of 20	21.00	21.00
a.-t.		A148 1.25d any single	1.00	1.00

RAF World War II Fighter Planes A149

Designs: 10b, Bristol Blenheim Mk-1. 20b, Battle. 50b, Blenheim 4. 60b, Wellington 1C. 75b, Whitley 5. 1d, Hampden Mk-1. 1.25d, Spitfire 1A and Hurricane 1. 2d, Avro Manchester. 3d, Stirling. 5d, Handley Page Halifax B-2. 10d, Lancaster B-3. 12d, Mosquito B-4. No. 983, Lancaster B-3 over Hamburg. No. 984, Spitfire 1, Battle of Britain.

1990, Apr. 18   **Perf. 14**

971	A149	10b multicolored	.75	.50
972	A149	20b multicolored	1.00	.50
973	A149	50b multicolored	1.10	.50
974	A149	60b multicolored	1.25	.50
975	A149	75b multicolored	1.25	.50
976	A149	1d multicolored	1.40	.50
977	A149	1.25d multicolored	1.50	.50
978	A149	2d multicolored	1.75	.55
979	A149	3d multicolored	2.10	.90
980	A149	5d multicolored	2.75	1.40
981	A149	10d multicolored	5.00	2.50
982	A149	12d multicolored	6.25	3.00
		Nos. 971-982 (12)	26.10	11.85

Souvenir Sheets

983	A149	15d multicolored	7.00	7.00
984	A149	15d multicolored	7.00	7.00

Independence, 25th Anniv. — A150

Designs: 3d, Sir Dawda Jawara, President. 12d, Jet and map showing airport. 18d, National arms.

1990, June 5   Litho.   Perf. 14
985	A150	1d multicolored	.20	.20
986	A150	3d multicolored	1.10	1.10
987	A150	12d multicolored	5.75	5.75
		Nos. 985-987 (3)	7.05	7.05

Souvenir Sheet
988	A150	18d multicolored	6.25	6.25

Baobab Tree A151

1990, June 14   Litho.   Perf. 14
989	A151	5b shown	.60	.60
990	A151	10b Woodcarving	.20	.20
991	A151	20b Pres. Jawara	.20	.20
992	A151	50b Map	.40	.25
993	A151	75b Batik fabric	.20	.20
994	A151	1d Bakau Beach Resort	.25	.25
995	A151	1.25d Tendaba Camp	.30	.30
996	A151	2d Shrimp industry	.45	.45
997	A151	5d Peanut oil mill	.75	1.25
998	A151	10d Pottery, kora	1.50	1.50
999	A151	15d Ansellia Africana orchid	6.00	6.00
1000	A151	30d Ancient stone rings, Euryphene gambiae	8.00	8.00
		Nos. 989-1000 (12)	18.85	19.20

Nos. 990, 999 vert.

Penny Black, 150th Anniv. A152

1990, June 18
1001	A152	1.25d brt bl & blk	.90	.35
1002	A152	12d dark red & blk	6.00	3.50

Souvenir Sheet
1003	A152	15d sil, bis & blk	7.75	7.75

Mickey Visits England — A153

Walt Disney characters at: 20b, 10 Downing Street. 50b, Trafalgar Square. 75b, Cliffs of Dover. 1d, Tower of London. 5d, Hampton Court Palace. 8d, Magdalen Tower, Oxford University. 10d, Old London Bridge. 12d, Rosetta Stone, British Museum. No. 1012, Picadilly Circus. No. 1013, Houses of Parliament and Big Ben on the River Thames.

1990, June 19   Perf. 14x13½
1004	A153	20b multicolored	.50	.30
1005	A153	50b multicolored	.75	.35
1006	A153	75b multicolored	1.00	.40
1007	A153	1d multicolored	1.25	.45
1008	A153	5d multicolored	3.00	3.00
1009	A153	8d multicolored	3.50	3.50

1010	A153	10d multicolored	4.50	4.50
1011	A153	12d multicolored	5.50	5.50
		Nos. 1004-1011 (8)	20.00	18.00

Souvenir Sheets
1012	A153	18d multicolored	9.50	9.50
1013	A153	18d multicolored	9.50	9.50

Stamp World London '90. Nos. 1004-1005, 1007, 1009 vert.

A154

1990, July 19   Perf. 14
1014	A156	6d Girl facing left	1.75	1.75
1015	A156	6d Young girl, diff.	1.75	1.75
1016	A156	6d Seated in chair	1.75	1.75
a.		A154 Strip of 3, #1014-1016	6.25	6.25

Souvenir Sheet
1017	A154	18d like No. 1014	5.75	5.75

A156   A157

Players from participating countries.

1990, Sept. 24   Litho.   Perf. 14
1018	A156	1d Italy	.45	.45
1019	A156	1.25d Argentina	.55	.55
1020	A156	3d Costa Rica	1.25	1.25
1021	A156	5d UAE	2.00	2.00
		Nos. 1018-1021 (4)	4.25	4.25

Souvenir Sheets
1022	A156	18d Holland	8.75	8.75
1023	A156	18d Romania	8.75	8.75

World Cup Soccer Championships, Italy.

1990, Nov. 1   Litho.   Perf. 14
1024	A157	20b Men's discus	.40	.20
1025	A157	50b Men's 100-meter race	.45	.20
1026	A157	75b Women's 400-meter race	.50	.30
1027	A157	1d Men's 200-meter race	.55	.55
1028	A157	1.25d Rhythmic gymnastics	.45	.45
1029	A157	3d Soccer	1.60	1.60
1030	A157	10d Men's marathon	5.25	5.25
1031	A157	12d Tornado class sailing	6.25	6.25
		Nos. 1024-1031 (8)	15.45	14.80

Souvenir Sheets
1032	A157	15d Parade of flags	7.50	7.50
1033	A157	15d Stadium, card section	7.50	7.50

1992 Summer Olympics, Barcelona.

Christmas A158

Entire paintings or different details from: 20b, 7d, The Annunciation with St. Emidius by Crivelli. 50b, The Annunciation by Campin. 75b, The Solly Madonna by Raphael. 1.25d, The Tempi Madonna by Raphael. 2d, Madonna of the Linen Window by Raphael. 10d, The Orleans Madonna by Raphael. 15d,

Madonna and Child by Crivelli. No. 1042, The Niccolini-Cowper Madonna by Raphael.

1990, Dec. 24   Litho.   Perf. 13½x14
1034	A158	20b multicolored	.45	.20
1035	A158	50b multicolored	.55	.20
1036	A158	75b multicolored	.75	.25
1037	A158	1.25d multicolored	.90	.65
1038	A158	2d multicolored	1.00	1.00
1039	A158	7d multicolored	3.25	3.25
1040	A158	10d multicolored	4.00	4.00
1041	A158	15d multicolored	5.75	5.75
		Nos. 1034-1041 (8)	16.65	15.30

Souvenir Sheet
1042	A158	15d multicolored	9.00	9.00

Peter Paul Rubens (1577-1640), Painter — A159

Entire paintings or different details from: 20b, 75b, 10d, No. 1054, The Lion Hunt. 1d, 1.25d, 3d, 15d, The Tiger Hunt. 5d, No. 1055, The Boar Hunt. No. 1056, The Crocodile and Hippopotamus Hunt. No. 1057, Saint George Slays the Dragon, vert.

1990, Dec. 24   Litho.   Perf. 14x13½
1046	A159	20b multicolored	.20	.20
1047	A159	75b multicolored	.35	.25
1048	A159	1d multicolored	.40	.40
1049	A159	1.25d multicolored	.55	.55
1050	A159	3d multicolored	1.25	1.25
1051	A159	5d multicolored	1.90	1.90
1052	A159	10d multicolored	3.25	3.25
1053	A159	15d multicolored	4.50	4.50
		Nos. 1046-1053 (8)	12.40	12.30

Souvenir Sheets
1054	A159	15d multicolored	5.25	5.25
1055	A159	15d multicolored	5.25	5.25
1056	A159	15d multicolored	5.25	5.25
1057	A159	15d multicolored	5.25	5.25

World Summit for Children A160

1991, Jan. 7   Litho.   Perf. 14
1058	A160	1d multicolored	.80	.80

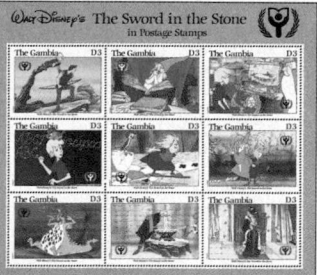

Intl. Literacy Year — A161

Walt Disney characters in "The Sword in the Stone": No. 1059a, Wart and Sir Kay. b, Merlin reading book. c, Wart learning geography. d, Wart writing on blackboard. e, Wart as bird, Madam Mim. f, Merlin and Madam Mim. g, Mim as dragon. h, Wart pulling sword from stone. i, Wart as King of England. No. 1060, Merlin, Wart in forest, vert. No. 1061, Knight trying to remove sword from stone, vert.

1991, Feb. 14   Litho.   Perf. 14x13½
1059	A161	3d Sheet of 9, #a-i	16.00	16.00

Souvenir Sheets
1060	A161	20d multicolored	10.50	10.50
1061	A161	20d multicolored	10.50	10.50

Miniature Sheets

Wildlife A162

No. 1062: a, Bebearia senegalensis. b, Graphium ridleyanus. c, Precis antilope. d, Charaxes ameliae. e, Addax. f, Sassaby. g, Civet. h, Green monkey. i, Spurwing goose. j, Red-billed hornbill. k, Osprey. l, Glossy ibis. m, Egyptian plover. n, Golden-tailed woodpecker. o, Green woodhoopoe. p, Gaboon viper.

No. 1063: a, Red-billed firefinch. b, Leaflove. c, Piacpiac. d, Emerald cuckoo. e, Red colobus monkey. f, African elephant. g, Duiker. h, Giant eland. i, Oribi. j, West African dwarf crocodile. k, Crowned crane. l, Jackal. m, Yellow-throated longclaw. n, Abyssinian ground hornbill. o, Papilio hesperus. p, Papilio antimachus.

No. 1064: a, Martial eagle. b, Red-cheeked cordon-bleu. c, Red bishop. d, Great white pelican. e, Patas monkey. f, Vervet monkey. g, Roan antelope. h, Western hartebeest. i, Waterbuck. j, Warthog. k, Spotted hyena. l, Olive baboon. m, Palla decius. n, Acraea pharsalus. o, Neptidopsis ophione. p, Acraea caecilia.

No. 1065, African spoonbill, vert. No. 1066, Lion, vert. No. 1067, Buffalo weaver, vert.

1991, May 31   Litho.   Perf. 14
1062	A162	1d Sheet of 16, #a.-p.	6.50	6.50
1063	A162	1.50d Sheet of 16, #a.-p.	9.50	9.50
1064	A162	5d Sheet of 16, #a.-p.	30.00	30.00
		Nos. 1062-1064 (3)	46.00	46.00

Souvenir Sheets
1065	A162	18d multicolored	6.50	6.50
1066	A162	18d multicolored	6.50	6.50
1067	A162	18d multicolored	6.50	6.50

Butterflies — A163

Designs: 20b, Papilio dardanus. 50b, Bematistes poggei. 1d, Vanessa cardui. 1.50d, Amphicallia tigris. 3d, Hypolimnes dexithea. 8d, Acraea egina. 10d, Salmis temora. 15d, Precis octavia. No. 1076, Danaus chrysippus. No. 1077, Charaxes jasius. No. 1078, Papilio demodocus. No. 1079, Papilio nireus.

1991, June 1   Litho.   Perf. 14
1068	A163	20b multicolored	.40	.40
1069	A163	50b multicolored	.50	.50
1070	A163	1d multicolored	.60	.60
1071	A163	1.50d multicolored	.70	.70
1072	A163	3d multicolored	1.40	1.40
1073	A163	8d multicolored	3.50	3.50
1074	A163	10d multicolored	4.25	4.25
1075	A163	15d multicolored	6.50	6.50
		Nos. 1068-1075 (8)	17.85	17.85

Souvenir Sheets
1076	A163	18d multicolored	6.50	6.50
1077	A163	18d multicolored	6.50	6.50
1078	A163	18d multicolored	6.50	6.50
1079	A163	18d multicolored	6.50	6.50

While Nos. 1078-1079 have same release date as Nos. 1068-1077, the dollar value of Nos. 1078-1079 were lower when they were released.

Royal Family Birthday, Anniversary
Common Design Type

1991, Aug. 12   Litho.   Perf. 14
1080	CD347	20b multi	.35	.25
1081	CD347	50b multi	.40	.30
1082	CD347	75b multi	.45	.40
1083	CD347	1d multi	.50	.50
1084	CD347	1.25d multi	.65	.65
1085	CD347	1.50d multi	.80	.80
1086	CD347	12d multi	6.00	6.00
1087	CD347	15d multi	7.50	7.50
		Nos. 1080-1087 (8)	16.65	16.40

Souvenir Sheets

1088	CD347	18d Elizabeth, Philip	5.25	5.25
1089	CD347	18d Diana, sons, Charles	7.50	7.50

20b, 75b, 1.50d, 15d, No. 1089, Charles and Diana, 10th wedding anniversary. Others, Queen Elizabeth II, 65th birthday.

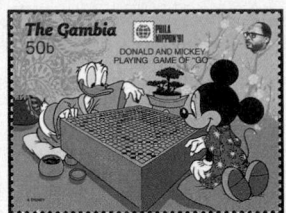

Phila Nippon '91 — A164

Walt Disney characters playing Japanese games and sports: 50b, Donald Duck and Mickey Mouse playing Go. 75b, Morty, Ferdie and Pete sumo wrestling. 1d, Minnie Mouse, Clarabelle, Daisy Duck playing battledore and shuttlecock. 1.25d, Goofy, Mickey at Okinawa bullfight, vert. 5d, Mickey as a Hawk Hunter Tagari, vert. 7d, Mickey, Minnie, and Donald play Jan-Ken-Pon, vert. 10d, Goofy as archer. 15d, Morty, Ferdie fly Japanese kites, vert. No. 1098, Goofy batting in Japanese baseball game, vert. No. 1099, Mickey, Scrooge McDuck playing Japanese football, vert. No. 1100, Mickey fly fishing, vert. No. 1101, Mickey climbing Mt. Fuji, vert.

Perf. 14x13½, 13½x14
1991, Aug. 22   **Litho.**

1090	A164	50b multicolored	.50	.30
1091	A164	75b multicolored	.60	.40
1092	A164	1d multicolored	.70	.45
1093	A164	1.25d multicolored	.80	.55
1094	A164	5d multicolored	2.25	2.25
1095	A164	7d multicolored	3.00	3.00
1096	A164	10d multicolored	4.50	4.50
1097	A164	15d multicolored	6.50	6.50
		Nos. 1090-1097 (8)	18.85	17.95

Souvenir Sheets

1098	A164	20d multicolored	5.75	5.75
1099	A164	20d multicolored	5.75	5.75
1100	A164	20d multicolored	5.75	5.75
1101	A164	20d multicolored	5.75	5.75

Intl. Literacy Year — A165

Walt Disney characters in scenes from Rudyard Kipling's "Just So Stories": 50b, How the Whale Got His Throat. 75b, How the Camel Got His Hump. 1d, How the Leopard Got His Spots. 1.25d, The Elephant's Child. 1.50d, Singsong of Old Man Kangaroo. 7d, The Crab that Played with the Sea. 10d, The Cat that Walked by Himself. 15d, The Butterfly that Stamped. No. 1110, How the Alphabet was Made, vert. No. 1111, The Beginning of the Armadillos. No. 1112, How the First Letter was Written, vert. No. 1113, How the Rhinoceros Got His Skin.

1991, Aug. 28   **Litho.**   **Perf. 14x13½**

1102	A165	50b multicolored	.75	.30
1103	A165	75b multicolored	.80	.40
1104	A165	1d multicolored	.85	.45
1105	A165	1.25d multicolored	.90	.55
1106	A165	1.50d multicolored	1.00	.90
1107	A165	7d multicolored	3.50	3.50
1108	A165	10d multicolored	5.00	5.00
1109	A165	15d multicolored	7.50	7.00
		Nos. 1102-1109 (8)	20.30	18.60

Souvenir Sheets
Perf. 13½x14, 14x13½

1110	A165	20d multicolored	7.00	7.00
1111	A165	20d multicolored	7.00	7.00
1112	A165	20d multicolored	7.00	7.00
1113	A165	20d multicolored	7.00	7.00

Train Cabooses — A166

No. 1114: a, Steel cupola, Canadian Pacific. b, Four-wheel, Cumberland and Pennsylvania. c, Mexican slim gauge. d, All steel cupola, Northern Pacific. e, Four-wheel, Morristown & Erie. f, Streamlined cupola, Burlington Northern. g, Caboose coach, McCloud River. h, Wide vision, Santa Fe. i, Wide vision, Frisco.
No. 1115: a, Narrow gauge, Oahu Railway. b, Standard brake-van, British Railways. c, Wide view steel, Union Pacific. d, Four-wheel, Belt Railway of Chicago. e, Four-wheel, McCloud River. f, Logging, Angelina County Lumber Co. g, Narrow gauge, Coahuila & Zacatecas. h, Three-foot gauge, United Railways of Yucatan. i, Steel cupola, Rio Grande.
No. 1116: a, Four-wheel, Colorado & Southern. b, Transfer, Santa Fe. c, Wooden cupola, Canadian National. d, Transfer steel, Union Pacific. e, Caboose coach, Virginia & Truckee. f, Standard brake-van, British. g, Narrow gauge, Intl. Railways of Central America. h, Steel cupola, Northern Pacific. i, Wood, Burlington Northern.
No. 1117, Pennsylvania electric, vert. No. 1118, Unidentified caboose, trainman with flag, vert. No. 1119, Unidentified green wooden caboose behind yellow freight car.

1991, Sept. 12   **Litho.**   **Perf. 14x13½**
Sheets of 9

1114	A166	1d Sheet of 9, #a.-i.	4.75	4.75
1115	A166	2d Sheet of 9, #a.-i.	6.00	6.00
1116	A166	1.50d Sheet of 9, #a.-i.	4.75	4.75
		Nos. 1114-1116 (3)	15.50	15.50

Souvenir Sheets
Perf. 12x13, 13x12

1117	A166	20d multicolored	6.00	6.00
1118	A166	20d multicolored	6.00	6.00
1119	A166	20d multicolored	6.00	6.00

While Nos. 1115-1116 and 1118-1119 have the same issue date as Nos. 1114 and 1117, the dollar value of Nos. 1115-1116 and 1118-1119 was lower when they were released.

Fish — A167

1991, Oct. 28   **Litho.**   **Perf. 14x14½**

1120	A167	20b Tiger shark	.25	.25
1121	A167	25b Common jewel fish	.25	.25
1122	A167	50b Five spot fish	.45	.45
1123	A167	75b Smalltooth sawfish	.45	.45
1124	A167	1d Five spot tilapia	.45	.45
1125	A167	1.25d Dwarf jewel fish	.55	.55
1126	A167	1.50d Five spot jewel fish	.65	.65
1127	A167	3d Bumphead	1.00	1.00
1128	A167	10d Egyptian mouthbrooder	3.25	3.25
1129	A167	15d Burton's mouthbrooder	4.50	4.50
		Nos. 1120-1129 (10)	11.80	11.80

Souvenir Sheets

1130	A167	18d Great barracuda	10.50	10.50
1131	A167	18d Yellowtail snapper	10.50	10.50

While Nos. 1120-1122, 1125, 1129-1131 have the same issue date as Nos. 1123-1124, 1126-1128 the dollar value of Nos. 1120-1122, 1125, 1129-1130 was lower when they were released.

Hummel Figurines — A168

20b, #1141a, Girl and boy waving handkerchiefs. 75b, #1140a, Boy and girl under umbrella. 1d, #1140b, Two girls wearing scarfs. 1.50d, #1140c, Girl and boy in window with flower box. 2.50d, #1141b, Two girls with basket. 5d, #1141c, Boy wearing long pants, boy wearing shorts. 10d, #1141d, Two girls on fence. 15d, #1140d, Boy with stick, girl with bag.

1991, Nov. 4   **Litho.**   **Perf. 14**

1132	A168	20b multicolored	.20	.20
1133	A168	75b multicolored	.20	.20
1134	A168	1d multicolored	.25	.25
1135	A168	1.50d multicolored	.50	.50
1136	A168	2.50d multicolored	.70	.70
1137	A168	5d multicolored	1.50	1.50
1138	A168	10d multicolored	3.00	3.00
1139	A168	15d multicolored	4.50	4.50
		Nos. 1132-1139 (8)	10.85	10.85

Souvenir Sheets

1140	A168	4d Sheet of 4, #a.-d.	5.00	5.00
1141	A168	5d Sheet of 4, #a.-d.	6.25	6.25

Paintings by Vincent Van Gogh A169

Designs: 20b, The Old Cemetery Tower at Nuenen in the Snow, horiz. 25b, Head of a Peasant Woman with White Cap. 50b, The Green Parrot. 75b, Vase with Carnations. 1d, Vase with Red Gladioli. 1.25b, Beach at Scheveningen in Calm Weather, horiz. 1.50d, Boy Cutting Grass with a Sickle, horiz. 2d, Coleus Plant in a Flowerpot. 3d, Self-portrait, spring-summer 1887. 4d, Self-portrait. 5d, Self-portrait, diff. 6d, Self-portrait, spring 1887. 8d, Still Life with a Bottle, Two Glasses, Cheese and Bread. 10d, Still Life with Cabbage, Clogs and Potatoes, horiz. 12d, Montmartre: The Street Lamps. 15d, Head of a Peasant Woman with Brownish Cap. No. 1158, Arles: View From the Wheat Fields. No. 1159, Autumn Landscape. No. 1160, Montmartre: Quarry, The Mills, horiz. No. 1161, The Potato Eaters, horiz.

Perf. 13½x14, 14x13½
1991, Dec. 5   **Litho.**

1142	A169	20b multicolored	.40	.25
1143	A169	25b multicolored	.45	.25
1144	A169	50b multicolored	.50	.25
1145	A169	75b multicolored	.55	.30
1146	A169	1d multicolored	.60	.35
1147	A169	1.25d multicolored	.65	.45
1148	A169	1.50d multicolored	.70	.55
1149	A169	2d multicolored	.75	.65
1150	A169	3d multicolored	.90	.90
1151	A169	4d multicolored	1.25	1.25
1152	A169	5d multicolored	1.50	1.50
1153	A169	6d multicolored	2.00	2.00
1154	A169	8d multicolored	2.75	2.75
1155	A169	10d multicolored	3.25	3.25
1156	A169	12d multicolored	4.25	4.25
1157	A169	15d multicolored	4.50	4.50

Size: 127x102mm
Imperf

1158	A169	20d multicolored	6.25	6.25
1159	A169	20d multicolored	6.25	6.25
1160	A169	20d multicolored	6.25	6.25
1161	A169	20d multicolored	6.25	6.25
		Nos. 1142-1161 (20)	50.00	48.45

While Nos. 1142-1143, 1146, 1148, 1150, 1153, 1155-1156, 1160-1161 have the same issue date as Nos. 1144-1145, 1147, 1149, 1151-1152, 1154, 1157-1159, the dollar value of Nos. 1142-1143, 1146, 1148, 1150, 1153, 1155-1156, 1160-1161 was lower when they were released.

Christmas A170

Paintings by Fra Angelico: 20b, The Madonna of Humility. 50b, Madonna and Child with Angels. 75b, The Virgin and Child with Angels. 1d, Annunciation. 1.25d, Presentation in the Temple. 5d, Annunciation, diff. 10d, Madonna della Stella. 15d, Naming of St. John the Baptist. No. 1170, Annunciation and Adoration of the Magi. No. 1171, Coronation of the Virgin.

1991, Dec. 23   **Perf. 12**

1162	A170	20b multicolored	.20	.20
1163	A170	50b multicolored	.25	.20
1164	A170	75b multicolored	.30	.25
1165	A170	1d multicolored	.35	.30
1166	A170	1.25d multicolored	.45	.45
1167	A170	5d multicolored	1.60	1.60
1168	A170	10d multicolored	3.00	3.00
1169	A170	15d multicolored	4.50	4.50
		Nos. 1162-1169 (8)	10.65	10.50

Souvenir Sheets
Perf. 14½

1170	A170	20d multicolored	6.25	6.25
1171	A170	20d multicolored	6.25	6.25

Queen Elizabeth II's Accession to the Throne, 40th Anniv.
Common Design Type
1992, Feb. 6   **Litho.**   **Perf. 14**

1172	CD348	20b multicolored	.20	.20
1173	CD348	50b multicolored	.35	.35
1174	CD348	1d multicolored	.50	.35
1175	CD348	15d multicolored	6.25	6.25
		Nos. 1172-1175 (4)	7.30	7.00

Souvenir Sheets

1176	CD348	20d Queen at left, yacht	6.25	6.25
1177	CD348	20d Queen at right, boat	6.25	6.25

Famous Blues Musicians — A171

1992, Feb. 12   **Perf. 14**

1178	A171	20b Son House	.25	.25
1179	A171	25b W. C. Handy	.25	.25
1180	A171	50b Muddy Waters	.45	.45
1181	A171	75b Lightnin Hopkins	.65	.65
1182	A171	1d Ma Rainey	.70	.70
1183	A171	1.25d Mance Lipscomb	.80	.80
1184	A171	1.50d Mahalia Jackson	.90	.90
1185	A171	2d Ella Fitzgerald	1.00	1.00
1186	A171	3d Howlin Wolf	1.25	1.25
1187	A171	5d Bessie Smith	2.00	2.00
1188	A171	7d Leadbelly	2.75	2.75
1189	A171	10d Joe Willie Wilkins	4.25	4.25
		Nos. 1178-1189 (12)	15.25	15.25

Souvenir Sheets

1190	A171	20d Gambian string drummer	7.50	7.50
1191	A171	20d Elvis Presley	7.50	7.50
1192	A171	20d Billie Holiday	7.50	7.50

While all stamps have the same issue date the dollar value of some was lower when they actually were released.

A172

Papal Visit, 1992 — A172a

Designs: 1d, Pope John Paul II. 1.25d, Pope, Pres. Dwada Jawara. 20d, Flags, Papal arms. 25d, Pope at Mass.
Illustration A172a reduced.

1992, Feb. 23   Litho.   Perf. 14
1193	A172	1d multicolored	.65	.65
1194	A172	1.25d multicolored	.80	.80
1195	A172	20d multicolored	7.25	7.25
		Nos. 1193-1195 (3)	8.70	8.70

Souvenir Sheet
1196	A172	25d multicolored	11.00	11.00

Embossed
Perf. 12
Without Gum
Size: 65x43mm
1196A	A172a 50d gold		35.00

No. 1196A was not available until late 1993, exists imperf on large card.

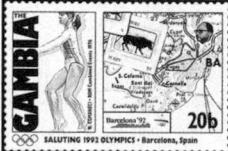

1992 Summer Olympics, Barcelona A173

20b, Map & Nadia Comaneci, gymnastics, Romania, 1976. 50b, D. Moorcraft, 5000 meters, Great Britain, 1984. 75b, M. Nemeth, javelin, Hungary, 1976. 1d, J. Pedraza, 20k walking, Mexico, 1968. 1.25d, Map, Spanish Arms & flag, Yachting soling class, Brazil, 1984. 1.50d, Spanish building, Field hockey, East Germany, 1984. 12d, Map & Michael Jordan, basketball, US, 1984. 15d, V. Borzov, 100 meters, USSR, 1972. #1205, Flamenco dancer, vert. #1206, Map & Bull.

1992, Mar. 6   Litho.   Perf. 14
1197	A173	20b multicolored	.30	.20
1198	A173	50b multicolored	.40	.30
1199	A173	75b multicolored	.45	.40
1200	A173	1d multicolored	.50	.50
1201	A173	1.25d multicolored	.70	.70
1202	A173	1.50d multicolored	.75	.75
1203	A173	12d multicolored	4.00	4.00
1204	A173	15d multicolored	6.00	6.00
		Nos. 1197-1204 (8)	13.10	12.85

Souvenir Sheet
1205	A173	20d multicolored	7.25	7.25
1206	A173	20d multicolored	7.25	7.25

While Nos. 1197, 1201-1203, 1206 have the same issue date as Nos. 1198-1200, 1204-1205, the value of Nos. 1197, 1201-1203, 1206 was lower when they were released.

Easter A174

Paintings: 20b, Christ Presented to the People, by Rembrandt. 50b, Christ Carrying the Cross, by Mathias Grunewald. 75b, The Crucifixion, by Mathias Grunewald. 1d, The Crucifixion, by Rubens. 1.25d, The Road to Calvary

(detail), by Tintoretto. 1.50d, The Road to Calvary (entire), by Tintoretto. 15d, The Crucifixion, by Masaccio. 20d, Descent from the Cross (detail), by Rembrandt. No. 1215, Crowning with Thorns (detail), by Titian. No. 1216, Crowning with Thorns, by Anthony Van Dyck.

1992, Apr. 16   Litho.   Perf. 13½
1207	A174	20b multicolored	.20	.20
1208	A174	50b multicolored	.25	.20
1209	A174	75b multicolored	.25	.20
1210	A174	1d multicolored	.35	.35
1211	A174	1.25d multicolored	.55	.35
1212	A174	1.50d multicolored	.65	.40
1213	A174	15d multicolored	4.50	4.50
1214	A174	5.75d multicolored	5.75	5.75
		Nos. 1207-1214 (8)	12.50	11.85

Souvenir Sheets
1215	A174	25d multicolored	7.50	7.50
1216	A174	25d multicolored	7.50	7.50

World Columbian Stamp Expo, Chicago A175

Walt Disney characters in Chicago: 50b, Mickey at Navy pier. 1d, Mickey floats by Wrigley Building. 1.25d, Donald graduates from University of Chicago. 12d, Goofy at Chicago's Adler Planetarium. No. 1221, Goofy above Chicago at the Hancock Center, horiz.

1992, Apr. 8   Litho.   Perf. 13½x14
1217	A175	50b multicolored	.50	.25
1218	A175	1d multicolored	.65	.50
1219	A175	1.25d multicolored	.80	.75
1220	A175	12d multicolored	6.00	6.00
		Nos. 1217-1220 (4)	7.95	7.50

Souvenir Sheet
Perf. 14x13½
1221	A175	18d multicolored	9.00	9.00

No. 1220 has name spelled "Alder."

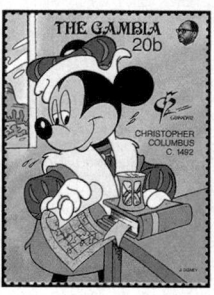

Granada '92 — A176

Mickey Mouse as Columbus: 20b, With map. 75b, Ideas rejected. 1.50d, Explores America. 15d, Returns to Spain. No. 1231, Embarks for America.

1992, Apr. 8   Perf. 13½x14
1227	A176	20b multicolored	.60	.60
1228	A176	75b multicolored	.90	.90
1229	A176	1.50d multicolored	1.25	1.25
1230	A176	12d multicolored	6.25	6.25
		Nos. 1227-1230 (4)	9.00	9.00

Souvenir Sheet
1231	A176	18d multicolored	9.00	9.00

Flowers — A177

1992, July 21   Litho.   Perf. 14
1237	A177	20b Hibiscus	.20	.20
1238	A177	50b Calabash nutmeg	.25	.25
1239	A177	75b Silk cotton tree	.35	.35
1240	A177	1d Oncoba	.45	.45
1241	A177	1.25d Paintbrush plant	.55	.55
1242	A177	1.50d Tree gardenia	.65	.65
1243	A177	2d Glory bower	.80	.80
1244	A177	5d Ashanti blood	1.50	1.50
1245	A177	10d African peach	2.50	2.50
1246	A177	12d Butterfly bush	2.75	2.75
1247	A177	15d Crepe ginger	3.50	3.50
1248	A177	18d Spider tresses	3.75	3.75
		Nos. 1237-1248 (12)	17.25	17.25

Souvenir Sheets
1249	A177	20d Water lily	4.75	4.75
1250	A177	20d Bougainvillea	4.75	4.75
1251	A177	20d Baobab tree	4.75	4.75
1252	A177	20d Climbing pea	4.75	4.75

While Nos. 1240, 1242, 1244, 1247, 1250 have the same release date as Nos. 1237, 1241, 1243, 1248-1249, their values in relation to the dollar were higher when they were released.

Riverboats — A178

Riverboat and waterway: 20b, Joven Antonia, Gambia River. 50b, Dresden, Elbe River. 75b, Medway Queen, Medway River. 1d, Lady Wright, Gambia River. 1.25d, Devin, Vltava River. 1.50d, Lady Chilel, Gambia River. 5d, Robert Fulton, Hudson River. 10d, Coonawarra, Murray River. 12d, Nakusp, Columbia River. 15d, Lucy Ashton, Firth of Clyde. No. 1263, Rudesheim, Rhine River. No. 1264, City of Cairo, Mississippi River.

1992, Aug. 3   Litho.   Perf. 14
1253	A178	20b multicolored	.20	.20
1254	A178	50b multicolored	.25	.25
1255	A178	75b multicolored	.35	.35
1256	A178	1d multicolored	.45	.45
1257	A178	1.25d multicolored	.60	.60
1258	A178	1.50d multicolored	.75	.75
1259	A178	5d multicolored	1.90	1.90
1260	A178	10d multicolored	3.00	3.00
1261	A178	12d multicolored	3.25	3.25
1262	A178	15d multicolored	4.25	4.25
		Nos. 1253-1262 (10)	15.00	15.00

Souvenir Sheets
1263	A178	20d multicolored	7.50	7.50
1264	A178	20d multicolored	7.50	7.50

Miniature Sheet

World War II in the Pacific — A179

Designs: a, USS Pennsylvania. b, Japanese attack begins. c, USS Ward sinking Japanese submarine. d, Ford Naval Air Station under attack. e, News bulletin announcing attack. f, Front page of Honolulu Star-Bulletin. g, Japanese invade Guam. h, US recovers Wake Island. i, Doolittle raids Japan from USS Hornet. j, Battle of Midway.

1992   Litho.   Perf. 14½x15
1265	A179	2d Sheet of 10, #a.-j.	19.00	19.00

1992 Summer Olympics, Barcelona A180

Designs: 20b, Women's double sculls. 50b, Kayak, vert. 75b, Women's precision rapid-fire shooting. 1d, Judo, vert. 1.25d, Javelin, vert.

1.50d, Gymnastics, vault, vert. 3d, Windsurfing, vert. 5d, High jump. No. 1274, Women's 200-meter backstroke. No. 1275, Table tennis.

1992, Aug. 10   Litho.   Perf. 14
1266	A180	20b multicolored	.25	.25
1267	A180	50b multicolored	.45	.45
1268	A180	75b multicolored	.65	.65
1269	A180	1d multicolored	.70	.70
1270	A180	1.25d multicolored	.80	.80
1271	A180	1.50d multicolored	1.00	1.00
1272	A180	3d multicolored	1.50	1.50
1273	A180	5d multicolored	2.25	2.25
		Nos. 1266-1273 (8)	7.60	7.60

Souvenir Sheets
1274	A180	18d multicolored	5.00	5.00
1275	A180	18d multicolored	5.00	5.00

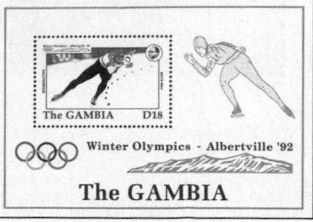

1992 Winter Olympics, Albertville — A181

Designs: 2d, Downhill skiing, vert. 10d, Four-man bobsled, vert. 12d, Ski jumping, vert. 15d, Slalom skiing.
No. 1280, 18d, Men's 500-meter speedskating. No. 1281, 18d, Pairs figure skating, vert.

1992, Aug. 10   Litho.   Perf. 14
1276-1279	A181	Set of 4	20.00	20.00

Souvenir Sheets
1280-1281	A181	Set of 2	11.50	11.50

Dinosaurs — A182

20b, Dryosaurus. 25b, Saurolophus. 50b, #1291, Allosaurus. 75b, Fabrosaurus. 1d, Deinonychus. 1.25d, #1292A, Cetiosaurus. 1.50d, Camptosaurus. 2d, #1292, Ornithosuchus. 3d, Spinosaurus. 5d, Ornithomimus. 10d, Kentrosaurus. 12d, Schlermochus.

1992, Sept. 21   Litho.   Perf. 14
1283	A182	20b multi	.45	.45
1284	A182	25b multi	.45	.45
1284A	A182	50b multi	.55	.55
1284B	A182	75b multi	.65	.65
1284C	A182	1d multi	.65	.65
1285	A182	1.25d multi	.80	.80
1286	A182	1.50d multi	.80	.80
1286A	A182	2d multi	.80	.80
1287	A182	3d multi	.90	.90
1288	A182	5d multi	1.50	1.50
1289	A182	10d multi	2.75	2.75
1290	A182	12d multi	3.25	3.25
		Nos. 1283-1290 (12)	13.55	13.55

Souvenir Sheets
1291	A182	25d multi	8.00	8.00
1292	A182	25d multi	8.00	8.00
1292A	A182	25d multi	8.00	8.00

Genoa '92.

Walt Disney's Goofy, 60th Anniv. — A183

Scenes from Disney cartoon films: 50b, Orphan's Benefit, 1934, 1941. 75b, Moose Hunters, 1937. 1d, Mickey's Amateurs, 1937. 1.25d, Lonesome Ghosts, 1937. 5d, Boat Builders, 1938. 7d, The Whalers, 1938. 10d, Goofy and Wilbur, 1939. 15d, Saludos

Amigos, 1941. No. 1301, The Band Concert, 1935, vert. No. 1302, Goofy today, vert.

1992		Litho.		Perf. 14x13½	
1293	A183	50b multicolored		.45	.45
1294	A183	75b multicolored		.65	.65
1295	A183	1d multicolored		.80	.80
1296	A183	1.25d multicolored		.80	.80
1297	A183	5d multicolored		2.10	2.10
1298	A183	7d multicolored		2.75	2.75
1299	A183	10d multicolored		3.00	3.00
1300	A183	15d multicolored		3.75	3.75
	Nos. 1293-1300 (8)			14.30	14.30

Souvenir Sheets
Perf. 13½x14

1301	A183	20d multicolored	9.00	9.00
1302	A183	20d multicolored	9.00	9.00

Discovery of America, 500th Anniv. A184

5d, Santa Maria. 12d, Pinta, Santa Maria, and Nina. 18d, Tree branch, green-winged macaw.

1992, Oct.		Litho.	Perf. 14	
1303	A184	5d multi	2.00	2.00
1304	A184	12d multi	3.25	3.25

Souvenir Sheet

1305	A184	18d multi, vert.	6.50	6.50

Golf — A186

Pres. Jarwara playing golf and: 20b, Map, flag of Australia. 1d, Trophy, Gambian flag. 1.50d, Gambian flag. 2d, Map, flag of Japan. 3d, Map, flag of US. 5d, Trophy, 1985, Gambian flag (small portrait only). #1312, Map, flag of Scotland. 12d, Map, flag of Italy. #1312B, Pres. Jawara about to tee off. #1312C, Gambian flag (small portrait).

1992		Litho.	Perf. 14	
1306	A186	20b multi	.65	.45
1307	A186	1d multi	1.00	1.00
1308	A186	1.50d multi	1.25	1.25
1309	A186	2d multi	1.50	1.50
1310	A186	3d multi	2.00	2.00
1311	A186	5d multi	2.75	2.75
1312	A186	10d multi	4.00	4.00
1312A	A186	12d multi	4.75	4.75
	Nos. 1306-1312A (8)		17.90	17.70

Souvenir Sheets

1312B	A186	10d multi	8.00	8.00
1312C	A186	18d multi, horiz.	8.00	8.00

No. 1306, Royal Melbourne Golf Course, Australia. No. 1309, Shinonoseki Golf Course, Japan. No. 1310, US Open, Pebble Beach. No. 1312, St. Andrew's Golf Course, Scotland. No. 1312A, Italian Open, Monticello, Milan.
Issued: 20b, 2d, 5d, #1312, 1312B, Dec. 8; others, Oct.

Souvenir Sheet

Ellis Island, New York City — A187

1992, Oct. 28		Litho.	Perf. 14	
1313	A187	18d multicolored	6.50	6.50

Postage Stamp Mega Event '92, New York City.

Christmas A188

Details or entire paintings: 50b, The Holy Family, by Raphael. 75b, Madonna and Child with St. Elizabeth and the Infant St. John (Small Holy Family), by Raphael. 1d, The Holy Family as the Little Holy Family, by Raphael. 1.25d, Escape to Egypt, by Broederlam. 1.50d, Flight Into Egypt, by Isenbrant. No. 1319, The Flight into Egypt, by Cosimo Tura. No. 1320, Flight into Egypt, by Master of Hoogstraelen. No. 1321, Flight into Egypt, by El Greco. 4d, The Holy Family, by Bernard Van Orley. 5d, Holy Family with Infant Jesus Sleeping, by Charles Le Brun. 10d, Rest on the Flight to Egypt, by Gentileschi. 12d, Rest on the Flight to Egypt, by Orazio Gentileschi. No. 1326, The Holy Family, by Giorgione. No. 1327, Rest on the Flight to Egypt, by Simone Cantarino. No. 1328, The Flight to Egypt, by Vittore Carpaccio.

1992, Nov. 3		Litho.	Perf. 13½x14	
1314	A188	50b multicolored	.25	.25
1315	A188	75b multicolored	.35	.35
1316	A188	1d multicolored	.45	.45
1317	A188	1.25d multicolored	.60	.60
1318	A188	1.50d multicolored	.60	.60
1319	A188	2d multicolored	.85	.85
1320	A188	2d multicolored	.85	.85
1321	A188	2d multicolored	.85	.85
1322	A188	4d multicolored	1.50	1.50
1323	A188	5d multicolored	1.90	1.90
1324	A188	10d multicolored	3.25	3.25
1325	A188	12d multicolored	3.50	3.50
	Nos. 1314-1325 (12)		14.95	14.95

Souvenir Sheets

1326	A188	25d multicolored	5.25	5.25
1327	A188	25d multicolored	5.25	5.25
1328	A188	25d multicolored	5.25	5.25

A189

A190

A191

A192

A193

Anniversaries and Events — A195

A194

Designs: No. 1329, Ariane 4 rocket. No. 1330, Berlin airlift, Konrad Adenauer. No. 1331, LZ127 Graf Zeppelin. 6d, Jentink's duiker. 7d, World map. 9d, Wolfgang Amadeus Mozart. No. 1335, America's Cup yacht Enterprise, 1930. No. 1336, Imperial parrot. No. 1337, Lions Intl. emblem. No. 1338, American Space shuttle. 15d, Prisoners of war returning home, Adenauer. 18d, First rigid airship, LZ1. No. 1341, European Space Agency's Hermes space shuttle. No. 1342, Scene from "The Marriage of Figaro." No. 1343, Face of Adenauer. No. 1344, Count Ferdinand von Zeppelin. No. 1345, Earth as seen from space.

1992-93		Litho.	Perf. 14	
1329	A189	2d multicolored	.80	.80
1330	A191	2d multicolored	.90	.90
1331	A191	2d multicolored	.80	.80
1332	A192	6d multicolored	2.50	2.50
1333	A193	7d multicolored	3.00	3.00
1334	A190	9d multicolored	5.00	5.00
1335	A194	10d multicolored	3.75	3.75
1336	A192	10d multicolored	3.25	3.25
1337	A195	10d multicolored	2.75	2.75
1338	A191	12d multicolored	3.00	3.00
1339	A191	15d multicolored	4.50	4.50
1340	A191	18d multicolored	4.50	4.50
	Nos. 1329-1340 (12)		34.75	34.75

Souvenir Sheets

1341	A189	18d multicolored	7.00	7.00
1342	A190	18d multicolored	7.00	7.00
1343	A191	18d multicolored	7.00	7.00
1344	A191	18d multicolored	7.00	7.00
1345	A192	18d multicolored	7.00	7.00

Intl. Space Year (#1329, 1338, 1341). Wolfgang Amadeus Mozart, bicent. of death (#1334, 1342). Konrad Adenauer, 25th anniv. of death (#1330, 1339, 1343). Count Zeppelin, 75th anniv. of death (#1331, 1340, 1344). Earth Summit, Rio de Janeiro (#1332, 1336, 1345). Intl. Conf. on Nutrition, Rome (#1333). America's Cup yacht race (#1335). Lions Intl., 75th anniv. (#1337).
Issued: #1333, 1335, 1339, 1343, 1/93; others, 12/92.

Peace Corps, 25th Anniv. A196

1993, Feb.
1346	A196	2d multicolored	1.50	1.50

Elvis Presley, 15th Anniv. of Death (in 1992) — A197

No. 1347: a, Portrait. b, With guitar. c, Holding microphone.

1993
1347	A197	3d Strip of 3, #a.-c.	3.25	3.25

Miniature Sheets

Baseball Films — A198

No. 1348 — Movie and stars: a, Casey at the Bat, Wallace Beery, 1927, Elliott Gould, 1986. b, Babe Comes Home, Anna Q. Nilsson, Babe Ruth, 1927. c, Elmer the Great, Joe E. Brown, 1933. d, The Naughty Nineties, Bud Abbott and Lou Costello, 1945. e, Take Me Out to the Ball Game, Frank Sinatra, Gene Kelly, Esther Williams, 1949. f, Damn Yankees, Tab Hunter, Gwen Verdon, 1958. g, The Pride of St. Louis, Dan Dailey, 1952. h, Brewster's Millions, John Candy, Richard Pryor, 1985.
No. 1349: a, The Jackie Robinson Story, Jackie Robinson, Ruby Dee, 1950. b, Bang the Drum Slowly, Robert DeNiro, 1973. c, The Bingo Long Traveling All-Stars & Motor Kings, James Earl Jones, Billy Dee Williams, 1976. d, Bull Durham, Kevin Costner, Susan Sarandon, 1988. e, Eight Men Out, eight actors, 1988. f, Field of Dreams, Ray Liotta, 1989. g, Major League, Charlie Sheen, 1989. h, Mr. Baseball, Tom Selleck, 1992.
No. 1350, The Babe, John Goodman, 1992. No. 1351, The Natural, Robert Redford. No. 1351A, The Winning Team, Ronald Reagan. No. 351B, A League of Their Own, Tom Hanks, Madonna.

1993, Mar. 25		Litho.	Perf. 13	
1348	A198	3d Sheet of 8, #a.-h.	8.50	8.50
1349	A198	3d Sheet of 8, #a.-h.	8.50	8.50

Souvenir Sheet

1350	A198	20d multi	5.75	5.75
1351	A198	20d multi, vert.	5.75	5.75
1351A	A198	20d multi	5.75	5.75
1351B	A198	20d multi, vert.	5.75	5.75

Miniature Sheets

Louvre Museum, Bicent. — A199

Details from paintings, by Jacques-Louis David (1748-1825): Nos. 1352a-b, Oath of the Horatii (diff. details). c, The Love of Paris & Helen. d, Rape of the Sabine Women. e, Leonidas of Thermopylae. f-h, Napoleon Crowning Josephine (left, center, right).
Details from paintings, by Antoine (c. 1588-1648) and Louis (1593-1648) Le Nain: No. 1353a, Inside Home of Peasants. b-c, The Tobacco Smokers (diff. details). d, The Cart. e, Peasants' Meal. f-g, Interior Portraits (diff. details). h, The Forge.
Details or entire paintings, by Leonardo Da Vinci: No. 1354a, St. John the Baptist. b, Virgin of the Rocks. c, Bacchus. d, Woman from the Court of Milan. e, The Virgin of the Rocks

(detail). f, Mona Lisa. g, Mona Lisa (detail of hands). h, Two Horsemen, Study of the Horse.
No. 1355, Allegory of Victory, by Mathieu Le Nain (1607-1677). No. 1356, The Artist and Her Daughter, by Elisabeth Vigee-Lebrun (1755-1842).

1993, Jan. 7　　Litho.　　Perf. 12

1352	A199	3d Sheet of 8,		
		#a.-h.	8.00	8.00
1353	A199	3d Sheet of 8,		
		#a.-h.	8.00	8.00
1354	A199	3d Sheet of 8,		
		#a.-h.	8.00	8.00

Souvenir Sheets
Perf. 14½

1355	A199	20d multicolored	8.75	8.75
1356	A199	20d multicolored	8.75	8.75

#1355-1356 each contain one 55x88mm stamp.

Miniature Sheet

Animals of West Africa — A200

No. 1358: a, Giraffe. b, Baboon. c, Caracal. d, Large-spotted genet. e, Bushbuck. f, Red-fronted gazelle. g, Red-flanked duiker. h, Cape buffalo. i, African civet. j, Side-striped jackal. k, Ratel. l, Striped polecat.
No. 1359: a, Vervet. b, Blackish-green guenon. c, Long-tailed pangolin. d, Leopard. e, Elephant. f, Hunting dog. g, Spotted hyena. h, Lion. i, Hippopotamus. j, Nile crocodile. k, Aardvark. l, Warthog.

1993, Apr. 5　　Litho.　　Perf. 14

1358	A200	2d Sheet of 12,		
		#a.-l.	10.50	10.50
1359	A200	5d Sheet of 12,		
		#a.-l.	15.00	15.00

Souvenir Sheet

1360	A200	20d like #1359b	9.00	9.00

No. 1360 printed in continuous design with black frameline around stamp. A number has been reserved for an additional value in this set.

Long-Tailed Pangolin — A201

Pangolin in various positions on tree limb.

1993, Apr. 5

1362	A201	1.25d multicolored	.75	.75
1363	A201	1.50d multicolored	1.00	1.00
1364	A201	2d multicolored	1.25	1.25
1365	A201	5d multicolored	3.00	3.00
		Nos. 1362-1365 (4)	6.00	6.00

Souvenir Sheet

1366	A201	20d like #1363	7.50	7.50

World Wildlife Federation.

Birds

A202　　　　　　　A203

Designs: 1.25d, Osprey. 1.50d, Egyptian vulture, horiz. 2d, Martial eagle. 3d, Ruppell's griffon vulture, horiz. 5d, Auger buzzard. 8d,

Greater kestrel. 10d, Secretary bird. 15d, Bateleur eagle, horiz.
No. 1375a, Rose-ringed parakeet. b, Variable sunbird. c, Red-billed hornbill. d, Red-billed fire-finch. e, Common go-away bird. f, Crimson-breasted shrike. g, Gray-headed bush-shrike. h, Nicator. i, Egyptian plover. j, Congo peacock. k, Greater painted snipe. l, Crowned crane.
#1376, Verreaux's eagle. #1377, Tawny owl.

1993, Apr. 15　　Litho.　　Perf. 14

1367	A202	1.25d multicolored	1.00	1.00
1368	A202	1.50d multicolored	1.25	1.25
1369	A202	2d multicolored	1.50	1.50
1370	A202	3d multicolored	2.00	2.00
1371	A202	5d multicolored	2.25	2.25
1372	A202	8d multicolored	3.00	3.00
1373	A202	10d multicolored	3.00	3.00
1374	A202	15d multicolored	4.25	4.25
		Nos. 1367-1374 (8)	18.25	18.25
1375	A203	2d Sheet of 12,		
		#a.-l.	21.00	21.00

Souvenir Sheets

1376	A202	20d multicolored	9.00	9.00
1377	A202	20d multicolored	9.00	9.00

#1376-1377 each contain 1 56x42mm stamp.

Aviation Anniversaries — A204

Designs: No. 1379, Guyot balloon, 1785, vert. No. 1380, Dr. Hugo Eckener, zeppelin LZ3 in flight. No. 1381, Sopwith Snipe. No. 1382, Eckener, LZ3 moored to ground. 8d, Eckener, Graf Zeppelin. 10d, Balloon, Comte D'Artois, 1785, vert. 15d, Royal Aircraft Factory S.E.5. No. 1386, Avro 504K. No. 1387, Eckener, LZ3 in flight, diff. No. 1388, Blanchard's flying ship, 1785, vert.

1993, May　　Litho.　　Perf. 14

1379	A204	2d multicolored	.80	.80
1380	A204	2d multicolored	.80	.80
1381	A204	5d multicolored	1.50	1.50
1382	A204	5d multicolored	1.50	1.50
1383	A204	8d multicolored	2.50	2.50
1384	A204	10d multicolored	2.75	2.75
1385	A204	15d multicolored	3.75	3.75
		Nos. 1379-1385 (7)	13.60	13.60

Souvenir Sheets

1386	A204	20d multicolored	8.50	8.50
1387	A204	20d multicolored	8.50	8.50
1388	A204	20d multicolored	8.50	8.50

Dr. Hugo Eckener, 125th birth anniv. (#1380, 1382, 1383, 1387). Royal Air Force, 75th anniv. (#1381, 1385, 1386).
Nos. 1379, 1384, 1388 are airmail.

Miniature Sheet

Coronation of Queen Elizabeth II, 40th Anniv. A205

Designs: a, 2d, Official coronation photograph. b, 5d, Orb and Scepter. c, 8d, Winston Churchill. d, 10d, Queen during Trooping of the Color.
20d, Portrait, by Joe King, 1972.

1993, June 2　　Perf. 13½x14

1389	A205	Sheet of 8, 2 each		
		#a.-d.	18.00	18.00

Souvenir Sheet
Perf. 14

1390	A205	20d multicolored	9.50	9.50

No. 1390 contains one 28x42mm stamp.

Miniature Sheet

A206

No. 1391 — Benz Automobiles: a, 1894 Benz Velo. b, 1894 Benz. c, 1885 Benz. d, 1905 Benz Mannheim. e, 1892 Benz. f, 1900 Benz, blue. g, 1911 Benz. h, 1893 Benz Velo. i, 1900 Benz, black. j, 1900 Benz, red. k, 1911 Benz, front view. l, 1885 Benz, rear view.
No. 1393, 20d, 1900 Benz, diff.
No. 1392 — Ford automobiles: a, Henry Ford, age 30, 1910 Model T. b, 1896, green seat. c, Henry Ford with Barney Oldfield and 1902 racing car, 999. d, 1896, Henry Ford with bicycle. e, 1903 Model A. f, 1908 Model T, top down. g, 1908 Model T, top up. h, 1906 Model K. i, 1931 Model A. j, 1906 Model A. k, 1906 Model N. l, 1905 Model F.
No. 1393, 1900 Benz, diff. No. 1394, 1896 Ford with red seat.

1993, June 7　　　　Perf. 14

1391	A206	2d Sheet of 12, #a.-l.	8.50	8.50
1392	A206	2d Sheet of 12, #a.-l.	8.50	8.50

Souvenir Sheets

1393	A206	20d multicolored	7.00	7.00
1394	A206	20d multicolored	7.00	7.00

1st Benz 4-wheel automobile, cent. (#1391, 1393).
1st engine by Henry Ford, cent. (#1392, 1394).

Miniature Sheets

Entertainers — A207

No. 1395: a, Buddy Holly. b, Otis Redding. c, Bill Haley. d, Dinah Washington. e, Musical instruments. f, Ritchie Valens. g, Clyde McPhatter. h, Elvis Presley.
No. 1396: a-i, Various pictures of Madonna.
No. 1397: a-i, Various pictures of Elvis Presley.
No. 1398: a-i, Various pictures of Marilyn Monroe.

1993, July 26　　Litho.　　Perf. 14

1395	A207	3d Sheet of 8, #a.-h.	14.00	14.00
1396	A207	3d Sheet of 9, #a.-i.	14.00	14.00
1397	A207	3d Sheet of 9, #a,-i.	14.00	14.00
1398	A207	3d Sheet of 9, #a.-i.	14.00	14.00
		Nos. 1395-1398 (4)	56.00	56.00

Cats and Dogs
A208

No. 1399 — Cats, Siamese. b, Colorpoint longhair. c, Burmese. d, Birman. e, Snowshoe. f, Tonkinese. g, Foreign shorthair. h, Balinese. i, Oriental shorthair. j, Foreign shorthair, diff. k, Colorpoint longhair, diff. l, Colorpoint longhair, diff.
Dogs: No. 1400a, Shih tzu. b, Skye terrier. c, Berner laufhund. d, Boxer. e, Welsh corgi (Queen Elizabeth II). f, Dumfrieshire. g, Lurcher. h, Welsh corgi (Princess Anne). i, Pekinese. j, Papillon. k, Otterhound. l, Pug.
No. 1401, Colorpoint shorthair, vert. No. 1402, Burmese, vert. No. 1403, Long-haired dachshund. No. 1404, Cairn terrier.

Miniature Sheet

Taipei '93 — A209

1993, Sept. 13　　Litho.　　Perf. 14

1399	A208	2d Sheet of 12,		
		#a.-l.	16.00	16.00
1400	A208	2d Sheet of 12,		
		#a.-i.	15.00	15.00

Souvenir Sheets

1401	A208	20d multicolored	7.50	7.50
1402	A208	20d multicolored	7.50	7.50
1403	A208	20d multicolored	7.50	7.50
1404	A208	20d multicolored	7.50	7.50

Designs: No. 1405, Fawang Si Pagoda, Song Shan Mt., Henan. No. 1406, Wanshoubao Pagoda, Shashi. No. 1407, Red Pavilion, Shibaozhai. No. 1408, Songyue Si Pagoda, Song Shan Mt., Henan. No. 1409, Bond Center, Hong Kong. No. 1410, Tianning Si Pagoda, Beijing. No. 1411, Xuanzhuang Pagoda, Xian, Shenxi. No. 1412, Forbidden City, Beijing.
No. 1413 — Tang Dynasty funerary objects: a, Camel. b, Horse and female rider. c, Camel, diff. d, Yellow-glazed horse. e, Camel, diff. f, Horse with saddle.
No. 1414 — Pottery: a, Vase. b, Small wine cup. c, Fahua type Mei-ping vase. d, Urn vase, export ware. e, Tureen. f, Lidded Potiche.
No. 1415, Standing Buddhas, Hallway of Upper Huayan Si Temple, Datong, horiz. No. 1416, Seated Buddha, Main Hall, Shanhua Si Temple, Datong.

1993, Sept. 27　　Litho.　　Perf. 14

1405	A209	20b multicolored	.25	.25
1406	A209	20b multicolored	.25	.25
1407	A209	2d multicolored	.90	.90
1408	A209	2d multicolored	.90	.90
1409	A209	5d multicolored	2.00	2.00
1410	A209	5d multicolored	2.00	2.00
1411	A209	15d multicolored	4.00	4.00
1412	A209	15d multicolored	4.00	4.00
		Nos. 1405-1412 (8)	14.30	14.30

Miniature Sheets

1413	A209	5d Sheet of 6,		
		#a.-f.	17.00	17.00
1414	A209	5d Sheet of 6,		
		#a.-f.	17.00	17.00

Souvenir Sheets

1415	A209	18d multicolored	7.00	7.00
1416	A209	18d multicolored	7.00	7.00

With Bangkok '93 Emblem

No. 1417, Sanctuary of Prasat Phanom Wan. No. 1418, Lai Kham Vihan, Chiang Mai. No. 1419, Spirit Shrine, Bangkok. No. 1420, Walking Buddha, Wat Phra Si Ratana Mahathat. No. 1421, Buddha, Sukhothai's Wat Mahathat. No. 1422, Gopura of Prasat Phanom Rung. No. 1423, Prang of Prasat Hin Phimai. No. 1424, Slender Chedis, Wat Yai Chai, Mongkon.
No. 1425 — Thai painting: a, Early Fruit Stand. b, Scene in Chinese Style, Wat Bovornivet. c, Buddha Descends from Tauatimsa. d, Sang Thong Tales, Lai Kham Vihan. e, The Damned in Hell, Wah Suthat. f, King Sanjaya Travels on Elephant, Wat Suwannaram.
No. 1426 — Thai Buddha sculpture: a, U Thong C, 14th-15th cent. b, Adorned Seated, 17th cent. c, Phra Chai, 19th cent. d, Bronze, 14th cent. e, U Thong A, bronze. f, Crowned, 14th-15th cent.
No. 1427, Ceramics, horiz. No. 1428, Character in Khon, dance drama.

1993

1417	A209	20b multicolored	.25	.25
1418	A209	20b multicolored	.25	.25
1419	A209	2d multicolored	.90	.90
1420	A209	2d multicolored	.90	.90
1421	A209	5d multicolored	2.00	2.00
1422	A209	5d multicolored	2.00	2.00
1423	A209	15d multicolored	4.00	4.00
1424	A209	15d multicolored	4.00	4.00
		Nos. 1417-1424 (8)	14.30	14.30

Miniature Sheets

1425	A209	5d Sheet of 6,		
		#a.-f.	17.00	17.00
1426	A209	5d Sheet of 6,		
		#a.-f.	17.00	17.00

Souvenir Sheets

1427	A209	18d multicolored	7.00	7.00
1428	A209	18d multicolored	7.00	7.00

With Indopex '93 Emblem

Designs: No. 1429, Pura Taman Ayun (garden temple), Mengwi, Bali. No. 1430, Natl. monument with statue of Prince Diponegoro, Jakarta. No. 1431, Candi Jawi, East Java. No. 1432, Guardian at Singosari Palace, East Java. No. 1433, Monument of Irian Jaya, (liberation), Jakarta. No. 1434, Central Temple, Prambanan complex, Lara Djonggrang. No. 1435, "Date of the Year Temple," Panataran complex, East Java. No. 1436, Brahma & Siva Temples, Loro Jonggrang, Java.

No. 1437 — Masks: a, Telek Luh. b, Jero Gde. c, Barong Macan. d, Monkey. e, Mata Gde. f, Jauk Kras.

No. 1438 — Paintings: a, Tree Mask, Soedibio, 1978. b, Dry Lizard, Hendra Gunawan, 1977. c, The Corn Eater, Sudjana Kerton, 1988. d, Night Watchman, Djoko Pekik, 1988. e, Hunger, Kerton, 1984. f, Arje Player, Soedjojono, 1971.

No. 1439, Stone carving, Brahma & Gods, Borobudur, Java, horiz. No. 1440, Effigies of the Dead, Torajaland, horiz.

1993, Sept. 27	Litho.	Perf. 14	
1429	A209	20b multicolored	.25	.25
1430	A209	20b multicolored	.25	.25
1431	A209	2d multicolored	.90	.90
1432	A209	2d multicolored	.90	.90
1433	A209	5d multicolored	2.00	2.00
1434	A209	5d multicolored	2.00	2.00
1435	A209	15d multicolored	4.00	4.00
1436	A209	15d multicolored	4.00	4.00
Nos. 1429-1436 (8)			14.30	14.30

Miniature Sheets

1437	A209	5d Sheet of 6, #a.-f.	16.00	16.00
1438	A209	5d Sheet of 6, #a.-f.	16.00	16.00

Souvenir Sheets

1439	A209	18d multicolored	7.00	7.00
1440	A209	18d multicolored	7.00	7.00

Miniature Sheet

Casey at the Bat — A210

Nos. 1441-1443: Characters and scenes from Disney's animated film Casey at the Bat.

1993, Oct. 25	Litho.	Perf. 14x13½
1441	A210	2d Sheet of 9, #a.-i.	12.00	12.00

Souvenir Sheets

1442	A210	20d multicolored	8.00	8.00

Perf. 13½x14

1443	A210	20d multi, vert.	8.00	8.00

Picasso — A211

Paintings: 2d, Woman with a Comb, 1906. 5d, The Mirror, 1932. 7d, Woman on a Pillow, 1969. 18d, The Three Dancers, 1925.

1993, Oct. 7	Litho.	Perf. 14
1444-1446	A211	Set of 3	5.25	5.25

Souvenir Sheet

1447	A211	18d multicolored	7.00	7.00

Copernicus
A212

5d, Early astronomical instrument. 10d, Telescope.

1993, Oct. 7		Perf. 14
1448-1449	A212	Set of 2	5.00	5.00

Souvenir Sheet

Perf. 12x13

1450	A212	18d Copernicus	7.00	7.00

Polska '93
A213

Paintings: 2d, Pont-Neuf, Paris, by Rudzka-Cybisowa, 1932. No. 1452, 10d, Honegger's Liturgical Symphony, by Bogusz, 1973. No. 1453, 10d, Niedzica castle. 18d, When You Enter Here, Whisper My Name Soundlessly, by Waniek, 1973.

1993, Oct. 7		Perf. 14
1451-1453	A213	Set of 3	7.25	7.25

Souvenir Sheet

1454	A213	18d multicolored	7.00	7.00

1994 World Cup Soccer Championships, US — A214

Players, country: 1.25d, Hannich, Hungary; Stopyra, France. 1.50d, Labd, Morocco; Lineker, England. 2d, Segota, Canada; Morozov, Russia. 3d, Roger Milla, Cameroun. 5d, Rodax, Australia; Weiss, Czech Republic. 10d, Claesen, Belgium; Bossis & Amoros, France. 12d, Candida, Brazil; Ramirez, Costa Rica. 15d, Silva, Brazil; Platini, France. No. 1463, Muller, Brazil; McDonald, Ireland, horiz. No. 1463A, Buchwald and Matthaeus, Germany; Maradona, Argentina, horiz.

1993, Nov. 22		Perf. 13½x14
1455	A214	1.25d multi	.65	.65
1456	A214	1.50d multi	.70	.70
1457	A214	2d multi	1.00	1.00
1458	A214	3d multi	1.75	1.75
1459	A214	5d multi	2.50	2.50
1460	A214	10d multi	3.75	3.75
1461	A214	12d multi	4.00	4.00
1462	A214	15d multi	5.00	5.00
Nos. 1455-1462 (8)			19.35	19.35

Souvenir Sheets

Perf. 13

1463	A214	25d multi	9.00	9.00
1463A	A214	25d multi	9.00	9.00

Christmas
A215

Designs: No. 1464, 25b, No. 1467, 2d, No. 1471, 15d, Details or entire painting, Adoration of the Magi, by Rubens.

Details or entire woodcut by Durer: No. 1465, 1d, Holy Family with Joachim & Anna. No. 1466, 1.50d, The Annunciation, Life of the Virgin. No. 1468, 2d, The Virgin Mary Worshipped by Albrecht Bonstetten. No. 1469, 7d, Virgin on a Throne, Crowned by an Angel. No. 1470, 10d, The Holy Family with Two Angels in a Portico (detail).

No. 1472, 20d, Adoration of the Magi, by Rubens. No. 1473, 20d, The Holy Family with Two Angels in a Portico, (entire), by Durer, horiz.

1993, Dec. 1	Perf. 13½x14, 14x13½
1464-1471	A215	Set of 8	16.00	16.00

Souvenir Sheets

1472-1473	A215	Set of 2	14.00	14.00

Fine Art — A216

Paintings by Rembrandt: 50b, A Man in a Cap. No. 1476, Man with a Gold Helmet. 7d, A Franciscan Monk. 15d, The Apostle Paul. 20d, Dr. Tulp Demonstrating the Anatomy of the Arm, horiz.

Paintings by Matisse: 1.50d, Portrait of Pierre Matisse. No. 1477, Portrait of Auguste Pellerin (II). 5d, Andre Derain. 12d, The Young Sailor (II). No. 1483, Pianist and Checker Players, horiz.

1993, Dec. 15		Perf. 13½x14
1474	A216	50b multicolored	.70	.70
1475	A216	1.50d multicolored	1.10	1.10
1476	A216	2d multicolored	1.25	1.25
1477	A216	2d multicolored	1.25	1.25
1478	A216	5d multicolored	2.50	2.50
1479	A216	7d multicolored	3.25	3.25
1480	A216	12d multicolored	4.00	4.00
1481	A216	15d multicolored	4.00	4.00
Nos. 1474-1481 (8)			19.05	19.05

Souvenir Sheets

Perf. 14x13½

1482	A216	20d multicolored	8.50	8.50
1483	A216	20d multicolored	8.50	8.50

Winter Sports A217

Disney characters portraying sports: 50b, Ski ballet. 75b, Pairs figure skating. 1d, Speed skating. 1.25d, Biathlon. 4d, 4-Man bobsled. 5d, Luge. 7d, Figure skating. 10d, Downhill skiing. 15d, Ice hockey.

No. 1493, 20d, Cross country skiing. No. 1494, 20d, Mogul skiing.

1993, Dec. 20		Perf. 13½x14
1484-1492	A217	Set of 9	18.00	18.00

Souvenir Sheets

1493-1494	A217	20d Set of 2	15.00	15.00

Hong Kong '94 — A219

Stamps, painting, Spring Garden-1846, by M. Bruce: No. 1495, Hong Kong #357, left detail. No. 1496, Right detail, #1000.

No. 1497 — Museum of Qin Figures, Shaanxi Province, Tomb of First Emperor: a, Qin warriors, horses. b, Warrior in battle dress. c, Armor clad warrior. d, Chariot driver. e, Dog. f, Qin warriors.

No. 1498, Show emblem, Hong Kong #253, vert.

1994, Feb. 18	Litho.	Perf. 14
1495	A218	1.50d multicolored	.80	.40
1496	A218	1.50d multicolored	.80	.40
a.	Pair, #1495-1496		2.00	1.50
1497	A219	1.50d Sheet of 6, #a.-f.	5.00	5.00

Souvenir Sheet

1498	A218	20d multicolored	5.75	5.75

Nos. 1495-1496 issued in sheets of 5 pairs. No. 1496a is a continuous design.

New Year 1994 (Year of the Dog) (#1497e, #1498).

New Year 1994 (Year of the Dog) A220

Disney characters: 25b, Pluto the Racer. 50b, Fifi. 75b, Pluto, Jr. 1.25d, Goofy and Bowser. 1.50d, Butch. 2d, Toliver. 3d, Ronnie. 5d, Primo. 8d, Pluto's kid brother. 10d, Army mascot. 12d, Pluto and Dinah's pups. 18d, Bent Tail, Junior.

#1511, Pluto, Dinah. #1512, Eega Beeva, Dog Pflip, Goofy, horiz. #1513, Dinah's pups, Pluto.

1994, Apr. 11	Litho.	Perf. 13½x14
1499-1510	A220	Set of 12	22.50	22.50

Souvenir Sheets

1511	A220	20d multicolored	6.50	6.50

Perf. 14x13½, 13½x14

1512	A220	20d multicolored	6.50	6.50
1513	A220	20d multicolored	6.50	6.50

Orchids A221

Designs: 1d, Oeceoclades maculata. 1.25d, Angraecum distichum. 2d, Plectrelminthus caudatus. 5d, Tridactyle tridactylites. 8d, Bulbophyllum lepidum. 10d, Angraecum eburneum. 12d, Eulophia guineensis. 15d, Angraecum eichleranum.

No. 1522, Ancistrochilus rothschildianus. No. 1523, Vanilla imperialis.

1994, May 1		Perf. 14
1514	A221	1d multicolored	.30	.30
1515	A221	1.25d multicolored	.30	.30
1516	A221	2d multicolored	.50	.50
1517	A221	5d multicolored	1.25	1.25
1518	A221	8d multicolored	2.10	2.10
1519	A221	10d multicolored	2.50	2.50

1520	A221	12d multicolored	3.00	3.00
1521	A221	15d multicolored	3.75	3.75
		Nos. 1514-1521 (8)	13.70	13.70

Souvenir Sheets

1522	A221	25d multicolored	7.50	7.50
1523	A221	25d multicolored	7.50	7.50

Easter
A222

Disney characters celebrate Easter: No. 1524, 25b, No. 1527, 4d, No. 1529, 8d, No. 1531, 12d, Ludwig von Drake. No. 1525, 50b, Minnie Mouse, Daisy Duck. No. 1526, 3d, Mickey Mouse. No. 1528, 5d, Donald Duck. No. 1530, 10d, Goofy.
No. 1532, 20d, Von Drake. No. 1533, 20d, Mickey, Minnie.

1994, Apr. 11   Litho.   Perf. 13½x14

1524-1531	A222	Set of 8	19.00	19.00

Souvenir Sheets

1532-1533	A222	Set of 2	15.00	15.00

Miniature Sheets of 6 or 8

Sierra Club, Cent. A223

No. 1534, 5d — Various views of: a-b, Prince William Sound. c-d, The Serengeti. e-f, Ross Island.
No. 1535, 5d: a-c, Briksdal Fjord, vert. d-f, Yosemite, vert.
No. 1536, 5d: a-b, Tibetan Plateau, vert. c-d, Yellowstone, vert. e, Ross Island, vert. f, The Serengeti, vert. g, Mount Erebus, vert. h, Ansel Adams Wilderness, vert.
No. 1537, 5d: a-b, Ansel Adams Wilderness. c-d, Mount Erebus. e, Prince William Sound. f, Yellowstone. g, Tibetan Plateau. h, Sierra Club emblem.

1994, Apr. 25   Perf. 14
Sheets of 6, #a-f

1534-1535	A223	Set of 2	24.00	24.00

Sheets of 8, #a-h

1536-1537	A223	Set of 2	30.00	30.00

Paintings of Cats
A224

No. 1538, 5d: a, The Arena, by Harold Weston. b, Cat Killing a Bird, by Picasso. c, Cat and Butterfly, by Hokusai. d, Winter: Cat on a Cushion, by Steinlen. e, Rattown Tigers, by Prang. f, Cat on the Floor, by Steinlen. g, Cat and Kittens. h, Cats Looking Over a Fence, by Prang. i, Little White Kittens into Mischief, by Ives. j, Cat Bathing, by Hiroshige. k, Playtime, by Tuck. l, Summer: Cat on a Balustrade, by Steinlen.
No. 1539, 5d, vert.: a, Girl with a Kitten, by Perronneau. b, Still Life with Cat and Fish, by Chardin. c, Tinkle a Cat. d, Naughty Puss! e, Cats, by Steinlen. f, Girl in Red with Cat and Dog, by Phillips. g, Cat, Butterfly and Begonia, by Haronobu. h, Cat and Kitten, by Higgins. i, Woman with a Cat, by Renoir. j, Minnie from Outskirts of Village, by Thrall. k, The Fisher, by Tuck. l, Artist and His Family, by Vaenius.
No. 1540, 20d, The Morning Rising, by Lepicie. No. 1541, 20d, The Graham Children, by Hogarth, vert.

1994, July 11   Litho.   Perf. 14
Sheets of 12, #a-l

1538-1539	A224	Set of 2	50.00	50.00

Souvenir Sheets

1540-1541	A224	Set of 2	14.50	14.50

Monkeys — A225

Designs: 1d, Patas. 1.50d, Collared mangabey. 2d, Black and white colobus. 5d, Mona. 8d, Kirk's colobus. 10d, Vervet. 12d, Red colobus. 15d, Guinea baboon.
Heads of: No. 1550, 2d, Collared mangabey. No. 1551, 25d, Guinea baboon.

1994, Aug. 1   Litho.   Perf. 14

1542-1549	A225	Set of 8	17.50	17.50

Souvenir Sheets

1550-1551	A225	25d Set of 2	19.00	19.00

D-Day, 50th Anniv.
A226

Designs: 50b, Free Dutch sloop Soema joins attack. 75b, HMS Belfast fires on beach defenses. 1d, USS Texas hits Point Du Hoc. 2d, Free French cruiser George Leygues. 20d, HMS Ramillies.

1994, Aug. 16

1552-1555	A226	Set of 4	4.50	4.50

Souvenir Sheet

1556	A226	20d multicolored	7.00	7.00

First Manned Moon Landing, 25th Anniv.
A227

No. 1557: a, Yuri Gagarin. b, Valentina Tereshkova. c, Ham (chimpanzee). d, Alexei Leonov. e, Neil Armstrong. f, Svetlana Y. Savitskaya. g, Marc Garneau. h, Vladimir Komarov. i, Ulf Merbold.
30d, Neil Armstrong, Edwin "Buzz" Aldrin, Michael Collins at press conference.

1994, Aug. 16

1557	A227	2d Sheet of 9, #a-i.	9.00	9.00

Souvenir Sheet

1558	A227	30d multicolored	11.00	11.00

A228

PHILAKOREA '94 — A229

Designs: 50b, Kungnakchon Hall, Naejangsa. 2d, Kettle of Popchusa. 3d, Pomun Tourist Resort.
Paper screen panels, episode from Sanguozhi, 18th cent. Choson Dynasty: a, Warriors on horseback. b, Soldiers atop fort. c, Shooting with bows and arrows. d, Bowing before horse & rider. e, Fight on horseback. f,

h, Charging on horses. g, Trudging through valley. i, j, Living peacefully.
20d, Traditional tombstone guardian, Taenung, vert.

1994, Aug. 16   Perf. 14, 13½ (#1562)

1559-1561	A228	Set of 3	2.00	2.00
1562	A229	1d Sheet of 10, #a.-		
		j.	6.75	6.75

Souvenir Sheet

1563	A228	20d multicolored	8.00	8.00

A230

Intl. Olympic Committee, Cent. — A231

Designs: 1.50d, Daley Thompson, Great Britain, decathlon, 1980, 1984. 5d, Heide Marie Rosendohl, Germany, long jump, 1972. 20d, Team Sweden, ice hockey, 1994.

1994, Aug. 16   Perf. 14

1564	A230	1.50d multicolored	.65	.65
1565	A230	5d multicolored	2.00	2.00

Souvenir Sheet

1566	A231	20d multicolored	7.75	7.75

Butterflies
A232

Designs: 1d, Mylothris rhodope. 1.25d, Iolaphilus menas. 2d, Neptis nemetes. 5d, Antanartia delius. 8d, Acraea caecilia. 10d, Papilio nireus. 12d, Pipilio menestheus. 15d, Iolaphilus julus.
No. 1575, 25d, Colotis evippe. No. 1576, 25d, Bematistes epaea.

1994, Aug. 18   Perf. 14

1567-1574	A232	Set of 8	16.00	16.00

Souvenir Sheets

1575-1576	A232	Set of 2	17.00	17.00

1994 World Cup Soccer Championships, US — A233

Designs: 50b, Bobby Charlton, England. 75b, Ferenc Puskas, Hungary. 1d, Paolo Rossi, Italy. 2d, Biri Biri, Gambian playing for Spain. 3d, Diego Maradona, Argentina. 8d, Johan Cruyff, Netherlands. 10d, Franz Beckenbauer, Germany. 15d, Thomas Dooley, US. No. 1585, 25d, Pele, Brazil. No. 1586, 25d, Gordon Banks, England.

1994, Sept. 1

1577-1584	A233	Set of 8	15.00	15.00

Souvenir Sheets

1585-1586	A233	Set of 2	18.00	18.00

Mushrooms
A234

No. 1587, 5d: a, Agaricus campestris. b, Lepista nuda. c, Podaxis pistillaris. d, Oudemansiella radicata. e, Schizophyllum commune. f, Chlorophyllum molybdites. g, Hypholoma fasciculare. h, Mycena pura. i, Ganoderma lucidum.
No. 1588, 5d: a, Suillus luteus. b, Bolbitius vitellinus. c, Clitocybe nebularis. d, Omphalotus olearius. e, Auricularia auricula. f, Macrolepiota rhacodes. g, Volvariella volvacea. h, Psilocybe coprophila. i, Suillus granulatus.
No. 1589, 20d, Cyathus striatus. No. 1590, 20d, Leucoagaricus naucina.

1994, Sept. 30
Sheets of 9, #a-i

1587-1588	A234	Set of 2	25.00	25.00

Souvenir Sheets

1589-1590	A234	Set of 2	16.00	16.00

Christmas
A235

French paintings: 50b, Expectant Madonna with St. Joseph, by unknown artist. 75b, Rest of the Holy Family, by Louis Le Nain. 1d, Rest on the Flight into Egypt, by Antoine Watteau. No. 1594, 2d, Noon, by Claude Lorrain. No. 1595, 2d, Rest on the Flight into Egypt, by Francois Boucher. No. 1596, 2d, Rest on the Flight into Egypt, by Jean-Honore Fragonard. 10d, The Holy Family, by Nicolas Poussin. 12d, Mystical Marriage of St. Catherine, by Pierre-Francois Mignard.
No. 1599, 25d, The Nativity by Torchlight, by Louis Le Nain. No. 1600, 25d, Adoration of the Shepherds, by Mathieu Le Nain.

1994, Dec. 5   Litho.   Perf. 13½x14

1591-1598	A235	Set of 8	13.00	13.00

Souvenir Sheets

1599-1600	A235	Set of 2	16.00	16.00

Marilyn Monroe (1926-62), Actress — A236

No. 1601: a-i, Various portraits.
No. 1602, 25d, Wearing red dress. No. 1603, 25d, Wearing long, dangling earrings.

1995, Jan. 8   Litho.   Perf. 14

1601	A236	4d Sheet of 9, #a.-		
		i.	12.00	12.00

Souvenir Sheets

1602-1603	A236	Set of 2	13.00	13.00

Elvis Presley (1935-77), Entertainer A237

No. 1604: a, As child. b, Singing, later years. c, With mother. d, With wife, Priscilla. e, With gold medallion. f, Wearing army uniform. g, Singing, younger years. h, Wearing hat. i, With daughter, Lisa Marie.

1995, Jan. 8
1604 A237 4d Sheet of 9, #a.-
　　　i.　　　　　　　10.50 10.50

Dinosaurs A238

No. 1605: a, Pteranodon. b, Archaeopteryx. c, Rhamphorhynchus. d, Ornithomimus. e, Stegosaurus. f, Heterodontosaurus. g, Lystrosaurus. h, Euoplocephalus. i, Coelophysis. j, Staurilosaurus. k, Giantoperis. l, Diarthrognathus.
No. 1606: a, Archaeopteryx, diff. b, Vangehuanosaurus. c, Ceolophysis, diff. d, Plateosaurus. e, Baryonyx. f, Ornitholestes. g, Dryosaurus. h, Estemmenosuchus. i, Macroplata. j, Shonisaurus. k, Muraeonosaurus. l, Archelon.
20d, Bactrosaurus. 22d, Tyrannosaurus, vert. No. 1609, 25d, Triceratops, vert. No. 1610, 25d, Spinosaurus.

1995 **Litho.** **Perf. 14**
1605 A238 2d Sheet of 12,
　　　#a.-l.　　　　　11.00 11.00
1606 A238 3d Sheet of 12,
　　　#a.-l.　　　　　11.00 11.00
　　Souvenir Sheets
1607 A238 20d multi　　　7.50 7.50
1608 A238 22d multi　　　7.50 7.50
1609-1610 A238 Set of 2　15.00 15.00

New Year 1995 (Year of the Boar) — A239

No. 1611: Stylized boars with Chinese inscriptions in: a, Green. b, Blue violet. c, White. d, Black.
10d, Three boars.

1995, May 4 **Perf. 14½**
1611 A239 3d Sheet of 4, #a.-d. 3.50 3.50
　　Souvenir Sheet
1612 A239 10d multicolored　3.50 3.50

Water Birds A240

Designs: 2d, Great white egret. 8d, Hammerkop. 10d, Shoveler. 12d, Crowned crane.
No. 1617: a, Pintail. b, Fulvous tree duck (a). c, Garganey. d, White-faced tree duck. e, White-backed duck. f, Egyptian goose. g, Pigmy goose. h, Little bittern (k). i, Redshank. j, Ringed plover. k, Black-winged stilt. l, Squacco heron (k).
No. 1618, 25d, Ferruginous duck. No. 1619, 25d, Moorhen.

1995, May 8 **Perf. 14**
1613-1616 A240 Set of 4　10.00 10.00

1617 A240 3d Sheet of 12,
　　　#a.-l.　　　　　11.00 11.00
　　Souvenir Sheets
1618-1619 A240 Set of 2　16.50 16.50

ECOWAS — A241

Designs: 2d, Free movement of people in Gambia. 5d, Captain Yaya AJJ Jammeh, Chairman of Arm Force Provisional Ruling Council, Head of State.

1995, May 30 **Litho.** **Perf. 14**
1620 A241 2d multicolored　　.60 .60
1621 A241 5d multicolored　1.50 1.50

Marine Life A242

No. 1622, vert: a, Multicolored parrot fish. b, Sparisoma viride. c, Queen parrot fish. d, Bicolor parrot fish.
No. 1623: a, Leatherback turtle. b, Tiger shark. c, Surgeon fish. d, Emperor angelfish. e, Blue parro fish. f, Triggerfish. g, Sea horse. h, Lionfish. i, Moray eel. j, Red fin butterflyfish. k, Octopus. l, Ray.
No. 1624, 25d, Holacanthus ciliaris. No. 1625, 25d, Angelichthys isabelita.

1995, June 20
1622 A242 8d Strip of 4, #a.-d. 10.00 10.00
1623 A242 3d Sheet of 12,
　　　#a.-l.　　　　　10.00 10.00
　　Souvenir Sheets
1624-1625 A242 Set of 2　19.00 19.00

UN, 50th Anniv. — A243

No. 1626: a, 3d, Girls. b, 5d, Woman helping girl at blackboard. c, 8d, Girl writing on blackboard.
25d, Nurse holding baby on scales.

1995, July 6
1626 A243 Strip of 3, #a.-c.　3.50 3.50
　　Souvenir Sheet
1627 A243 25d multicolored　6.50 6.50

World War II Motion Pictures A244

No. 1628 — Movie stars: a, Peter Lawford. b, Gene Tierney, Dana Andrews. c, Groucho, Gummo Marx. d, James Stewart. e, Chico, Harpo Marx. f, Tyrone Power. g, Cary Grant, Ingrid Bergman. h, Veronica Lake.
Motion pictures: No. 1629, 25d, A Lady Fights Back. No. 1630, 25d, Desert Victory.

1995, July 6
1628 A244 3d Sheet of 8, #a.-
　　　h. + label　　　　12.00 12.00
　　Souvenir Sheets
1629-1630 A244 Set of 2　14.50 14.50

VJ Day, 50th Anniv. A245

No. 1631: a, Fairey Firefly. b, Fairey Barracuda II. c, Vickers Supermarine Seafire II. d, HMS Repulse. e, HMS Illustrious. f, HMS Exeter.
25d, Bomber being shot down by 3-stack cruiser.

1995, Aug. 1
1631 A245 5d Sheet of 6,
　　　#a.-f. + label　　11.00 11.00
　　Souvenir Sheet
1632 A245 25d multicolored　9.00 9.00

A246　　　　　A247

Carrying sacks of grain: No. 1633a, 3d, Woman in pink. b, 5d, Two people. c, 8d, Man. 25d, Fisherman with net.

1995, Aug. 1 **Litho.** **Perf. 14**
1633 A246 Strip of 3, #a.-c.　3.75 3.75
　　Souvenir Sheet
1634 A246 25d multicolored　6.50 6.50

FAO, 50th Anniv. No. 1633 is a continuous design.

1995, Aug. 1

Nobel Prize Winners: 2d, Kenichi Fukui, chemistry, 1981. 3d, Gustav Stresemann, peace, 1929. 5d, Thomas Mann, literature, 1929. 8d, Albert Schweitzer, peace, 1952. 12d, Leo Esaki, physics, 1973. 15d, Lech Walsea, peace, 1983.
No. 1635: a, Marie Curie, chemistry, 1911. b, Adolf Butenandt, chemistry, 1939. c, Tonegawa Susumu, medicine, 1987. d, Nelly Sachs, literature, 1966. e, Kawabata Yasunari, literature, 1968. f, Yukawa Hideki, physics, 1949. g, Paul Ehrlich, medicine, 1908. h, Sato Eisaku, peace, 1974. i, Carl von Ossietzky, peace, 1935.
25d, Willy Brandt, peace, 1971.

1634A-1634F A247 Set of 6　11.00 11.00
1635 A247 5d Sheet of 9,
　　　#a.-i.　　　　　12.50 12.50
　　Souvenir Sheet
1636 A247 25d multicolored　7.00 7.00

Rotary Intl., 90th Anniv. A248

Designs: 15d, Paul Haris, Rotary emblem. 20d, Natl. flag, Rotary emblem.

1995, Aug. 1
1637 A248 15d multicolored　3.50 3.50
　　Souvenir Sheet
1638 A248 20d multicolored　5.75 5.75

Miniature Sheets of 3

1995 Boy Scout Jamboree, Holland — A249

No. 1639 — How to tie the lariat: a, First step. b, Second step. c, Completed.
No. 1640 — How to tie bowline: a, 12d, First step. b, 10d, Second step. c, 5d, Completed.
No. 1641, 25d, Bowline used to lift injured scout. No. 1642, 25d, Hitch used in lifesaving lift.

1995, Aug. 1
1639 A249 2d Sheet of 3, #a.-
　　　c.　　　　　　　2.00 2.00
1640 A249　Sheet of 3, #a.-
　　　c.　　　　　　　8.50 8.50
　　Souvenir Sheets
1641-1642 A249 Set of 2　13.00 13.00

Queen Mother, 95th Birthday A250

No. 1643: a, Drawing. b, Bright blue hat, dress. c, Formal portrait. d, Green hat, dress. 25d, Pale blue & white dress, blue hat.

1995, Aug. 1 **Perf. 13½×14**
1643 A250 5d Strip or block of
　　　4, #a.-d.　　　　5.00 5.00
　　Souvenir Sheet
1644 A250 25d multicolored　6.25 6.25

No. 1643 was issued in sheets of 8 stamps.
Nos. 1643-1644 exist with black frame and overprint in sheet margin "In Memoriam 1900-2002" in one or two lines.

1996 Summer Olympics, Atlanta A251

Designs: 1d, Bruce Jenner, US, decathlon. 1.25d, Greg Louganis, US, diving. 1.50d, Michael Gross, Germany 50-meter butterfly. 2d, Vasily Alexeev, USSR, weight lifting. 3d, Patrick Ewing, US, Juan Antonio Corbalan, Spain, basketball. 5d, Men's volleyball, US v. Brazil. 10d, John Svenden, West Germany, Armando Fernandez, US, water polo. 15d, Pertti Karppinen, Finland, single sculls.
No. 1653, vert: a, Stefano Cerioni, Italy, fencing. b, Alberto Covo, Italy, 10,000-meter run. c, Mary Lou Retton, US, women's gymnastics. d, Vladimir Artemov, USSR, men's gymnastics. e, Florence Griffith-Joyner, US, 400-meter relay. f, Brazil, soccer. g, Nelson Valis, US, 1000-meter sprint cycling. h, Cheryl Miller, US, women's basketball.
No. 1654, 25d, Karen Stives, US, equestrian. No. 1655, 25d, Edwin Moses, US, 400-meter hurdles, vert.

1995, Aug. 17
1645-1652 A251 Set of 8　11.00 11.00
1653 A251 3d Sheet of 8, #a.-
　　　h.　　　　　　　7.00 7.00
　　Souvenir Sheets
1654-1655 A251 Set of 2　15.50 15.50
Volleyball, cent. (#1650).

Rotary, Intl., 90th Anniv., 1995 Boy Scout Jamboree, Holland — A252

Designs: 2d, Gambia Rotary contributing to education. No. 1657, 5d, Wood Badge course, Yundum, 1980. No. 1658, 5d, M.J.E. Sambou, organizing scout commissioner, vert.

1995, Sept. 5
1656-1658 A252 Set of 3　4.00 4.00

Flowers — A253

Designs: 2d, Zantedeschia rehmannii. 5d, Euadenia eminens. 10d, Passiflora vitifolia. 15d, Dietes grandiflora.

No. 1663, 3d: a, Canarina abyssinica. b, Nerine bowdenii. c, Zantedeschia aethiopica. d, Aframomum sceptrum. e, Schotia brachypetala. f, Catharanthus roseus. g, Protea grandiceps. h, Plumbago capensis. i, Uncarina grandidieri.

No. 1664, 3d: a, Kigelia africana. b, Hibiscus schizopetalus. c, Dombeya mastersii. d, Agapanthus orientalis. e, Strelitzia reginae. f, Spathodea campanulata. g, Rhodolaena bakeriana. h, Gazania rigens. i, Ixianthes retzioides.

No. 1665, 25d, Eulophia quartiniana. No. 1666, 25d, Gloriosa simplex.

1995, Oct. 2   Litho.   Perf. 14
1659-1662 A253   Set of 4   8.00   8.00
Sheets of 9, #a-i
1663-1664 A253   Set of 2   14.50 14.50
Souvenir Sheets
1665-1666 A253   Set of 2   15.00 15.00

SOS Children's Villages A254

Designs: No. 1667, 2d, Children playing near houses. No. 1668, 2d, Aid worker with child, vert. 5d, Children.

1995, Oct. 9   Litho.   Perf. 14
1667-1669 A254   Set of 3   2.75   2.75

Entertainers A255

No. 1670: a, Roy Orbison. b, Mick Jagger. c, Bruce Springsteen. d, Jimi Hendrix. e, Bill Haley. f, Gene Vincent. g, Buddy Holly. h, Jerry Lee Lewis. i, Chuck Berry.

No. 1671: a-i, Various pictures of James Dean.

No. 1672, 25d, James Dean. No. 1673, 25d, Elvis Presley.

1995, Dec. 1   Litho.   Perf. 13½x14
1670   A255   3d Sheet of 9, #a.-
        i.   10.00 10.00
1671   A255   3d Sheet of 9, #a.-
        i.   9.00   9.00
Souvenir Sheets
1672-1673 A255   Set of 2   19.00 19.00
Motion pictures, cent. (#1671-1672).

Christmas
A256

Details or entire paintings: 75b, Madonna of the, Valley. 1d, Madonna, by Giotto. 2d, The Flight into Egypt, by Luca Giordano. 5d, The Epiphany, by Bondone. 8d, Virgin & Child, by Burgkmair. 12d, Madonna, by Bellini.

No. 1680, 25d, Mother and Child, by Rubens. No. 1681, 25d, The Christ, by Carpaccio.

1995, Dec. 18
1674-1679 A256   Set of 6   11.00 11.00
Souvenir Sheets
1680-1681 A256   Set of 2   18.00 18.00

Banjul Intl. Airport A257

Denominations: 1d, 2d, 3d, 5d.

1995, Dec. 21   Litho.   Perf. 14
1682-1685 A257   Set of 4   4.00   4.00

UPU, 121st Anniv. — A258

Denominations: 1d, 2d, 3d, 7d.

1995, Dec. 21
1686-1689 A258   Set of 4   4.00   4.00

Marine Life A259

Designs: 2d, Commerson's dolphin. 5d, Narwhal. 8d, True's beaked whale. 10d, Rough-toothed dolphin.

No. 1694, 3d — Dolphins:a, Northern rightwhale. b, Spotted. c, Common. d, Pacific white-sided. e, Atlantic humpbacked. f, Atlantic white-sided. g, White-beaked. h, Striped. i, Risso's.

No. 1695, 3d — Whales: a, Bryde's. b, Sperm. c, Humpback. d, Sei. e, Blue. f, Gray. g, Fin. h, Killer. i, Right.

No. 1696, 25d, Beluga, clymene dolphin. No. 1697, 25d, Bowhead whale, dall's porpoise, blue shark.

1995, Dec. 22
1690-1693 A259   Set of 4   6.75   6.75
Sheets of 9, #a-i
1694-1695 A259   Set of 2   14.50 14.50
Souvenir Sheets
1696-1697 A259   Set of 2   15.50 15.50

Cowboys and American Indians — A260

Disney characters portraying Amerian Indians or in western scenes: 15b, Pete, Seminole. 20b, Donald, Chinook. 25b, Huey, Dewey, Louie, Blackfoot. 30b, Sharp shooter Minnie. 40b, Bull-riding Donald. 50b, Cattle-branding Mickey. 2d, Donald, Tlingit. 3d, Bronco-busting Mickey. 12d, Trick-roping Grandma Duck. No. 1707, 15d, Goofy the ranch hand. No. 1708, 15d, Mickey, Pomo. 20d, Minnie, Goofy, Navaho.

No. 1710, 25d, Minnie, Massachusetts Tribe. No. 1711, 25d, Pluto singing, vert. No.

1712, 25d, Donald with rope around neck, vert. No. 1712, 25d, Minnie, Shoshoni, vert.

1995, Dec. 22   Perf. 14x13½
1698-1709 A260   Set of 12   21.00 21.00
Souvenir Sheets
1710-1713 A260   Set of 4   32.50 32.50

New Year 1996 (Year of the Rat) — A261

No. 1714 — Various stylized rats: a, 63b. b, 75b. c, 1.50d. d, 4d.
No. 1715a, Like #1714a. b, Like #1714d. c, Like #1714c. d, Like #1714b.
No. 1716, Two rats.

1996, Jan. 2   Perf. 14½
1714   A261   Strip of 4, #a.-d.   1.50   1.50
1715   A261   3d Sheet of 4, #a.-d. 2.75   2.75
Souvenir Sheet
1716   A261   10d multicolored   5.00   5.00
#1714 issued in sheets of 16 stamps.

Paintings from Metropolitan Museum of Art — A262

No. 1717, 4d: a, Don Tiburcio Pérez y Cuervo, by Goya. b, Jean Antoine Moltedo, by J.A.D. Ingres. c, The Letter, by Corot. d, General Etienne Maurice Gerard, by J.L. David. e, Portrait of the Artist, by Van Gogh. f, Joseph Henri Altés, by Degas. g, Princess de Broglie, by Ingres. h, Lady at the Table, by Cassatt.

No. 1718, 4d: a, Broken Eggs, by Greuze. b, Johann Joachim Winckelmann, by Mengs. c, Col. George K.H. Coussmaker, by Reynolds. d, Self Portrait with Pupils, by Labille-Guiard. e, Courtesan Holding a Fan, by Utamaro. f, The Woodgatherers, by Gainsborough. g, Mr. Grace D. Elliott, by Gainsborough. h, The Drummond Children, by Raeburn.

No. 1719, 4d: a, Sunflowers, by Monet. b, Still Life with Pansies, by Fantin-Latour. c, Parisians Enjoying the Park, by Monet. d, La Mére Larchevêque, by Pissarro. e, Rue de L'Epicerie, Rouen, by Pissarro. f, The Abduction of Rebecca, by Delacroix. g, Daughter, Abraham-Ben-Chimol, by Delacroix. h, Christ on Lake of Gennesaret, by Delacroix.

No. 1720, 4d: a, Henry Frederick, Prince of Wales, by Peake. b, Saints Peter, Martha, Mary & Leonard, by Correggio. c, Marriage Feast at Cana, by Juan de Flandes. d, Portrait of one of Wedigh Family, by Holbein. e, Guilluame Budé, by Clouet. f, Portrait of a Cardinal, by El Greco. g, St. Jerome as a Cardinal, by El Greco. h, Portrait of a Man, by Titian.

No. 1721, 25d, The Harvesters, by Bruegel. No. 1722, 25d, The Creation of the World and the Expulsion from Paradise, by Giovanni de Paolo. No. 1723, 25d, Henry IV at the Battle of Ivry, by Rubens. No. 1724, 25d, The Israelites Gathering Manna in the Desert, by Rubens.

1996, Jan. 29   Litho.   Perf. 13½x14
Sheets of 8, #a-h
1717-1720 A262   Set of 4   40.00 40.00
Souvenir Sheets
Perf. 14
1721-1724 A262   Set of 4   29.00 29.00

Nos. 1721-1724 each contain one 85x57mm stamp.

No. 1723 is actually in the Uffizi Gallery in Florence; No. 1724 in the Los Angeles County Museum of Art.

Traditional Fire Dance A263

Designs: 1d, Blowing fire from mouth, vert. 2d, Like 1d, diff. 3d, Holding sticks of fire at leg, vert. 7d, Holding out two sticks of fire.

1996, Jan. 29   Litho.   Perf. 14
1725-1728 A263   Set of 4   3.50   3.50

Disney Characters Performing Good Deeds — A264

Designs: 1d, Community blood drive. 4d, Adopt-a-pet. 5d, Christmas giving for the needy. 10d, Teaching outdoor skills. 15d, Teaching reading. 20d, Volunteer fire fighters. No. 1735, 25d, Highway volunteers. No. 1736, 25d, Counting whales.

1996, Apr. 12   Litho.   Perf. 13½x14
1729-1734 A264   Set of 6   14.00 12.00
Souvenir Sheets
1735-1736 A264   Set of 2   13.00 11.00

Bruce Lee (1940-73), Martial Arts Expert — A265

No. 1737: Various portraits. 25d, In fighting stance.

1996, Apr. 1   Litho.   Perf. 14
1737   A265   3d Sheet of 9, #a.-i. 7.50   7.50
Souvenir Sheet
1738   A265   25d multicolored   6.25   6.25

China '96, 9th Asian Intl. Philatelic Exhibition (#1737).

African Wildlife A266

15d, African civet.
No. 1740: a, Roan antelope. b, Lesser bush baby. c, Leopard. d, Guinea forest red colobus. e, Kob. f, Common eland.
No. 1741: a, African buffalo. b, Topi. c, Vervet. d, Hippopotamus. e, Waterbuck. f, Senegal chameleon. g, Western green mamba. h, Slender snouted crocodile (i). i, Adanson's mud turtle.
No. 1742, 25d, Lion. No. 1743, 25d, Chimpanzee.

1996, Apr. 15   Litho.   Perf. 14
1739   A266   15d multicolored   3.50   3.50
1740   A266   3d Block of 6, #a.-
        f.   4.25   4.25
1741   A266   4d Sheet of 9,
        #a.-i.   7.25   7.25
Souvenir Sheets
1742-1743 A266   Set of 2   13.50 13.50
No. 1740 issued in sheets of 12 stamps.

Queen Elizabeth II, 70th Birthday A267

No. 1744: a, Portrait wearing blue dress. b, Wearing white dress, crown. c, Younger picture, crown.
25d, Buckingham Palace, horiz.

1996, May 9   Litho.   Perf. 13½x14
1744 A267   8d Strip of 3, #a.-c.   5.25 5.25
Souvenir Sheet
Perf. 14x13½
1745 A267   25d multicolored   6.50 6.50
No. 1744 was issued in sheets of 9 stamps with each strip in a different order.

Classic Cars and Fire Engines A268

No. 1746, 4d — Classic cars: a, 1912 Fiat Tipo 510, Italy. b, 1936 Toyota Model 4B Phaeton, Japan. c, 1924 NAG C4B, Germany. d, 1903 Cadillac, US. e, 1925 Bentley, Great Britain. f, 1909 Renault Model AX, France.
No. 1747, 4d — Fire engines: a, 1850 Pumper Hose Cart, US. b, 1891 Steam Fire Engine, US. c, 1864 Lausitzer, Germany. d, 1902 Chemical Engine, Great Britain. e, 1904 Motor Fire Engine, Great Britain. f, 1860 Colonia No. 5, Germany.
No. 1748, 25d, 1917 Mitsubishi Model A, Japan. No. 1749, 25d, 1865 Amoskeag steamer, US.

1996, May 27   Perf. 14
Sheets of 6, #a-f
1746-1747 A268   Set of 2   12.00 12.00
Souvenir Sheets
1748-1749 A268   Set of 2   13.00 13.00

Euro '96, 1996 European Soccer Championships, England — A269

Team pictures: No. 1750, 2d, Bulgaria. No. 1751, 2d, Croatia. No. 1752, 2d, Czech Republic. No. 1753, 2d, Denmark. No. 1754, 2d, England. No. 1755, 2d, France. No. 1756, 2d, Germany. No. 1757, 2d, Holland. No. 1758, 2d, Italy. No. 1759, 2d, Portugal. No. 1760, 2d, Romania. No. 1761, 2d, Russia. No. 1762, 2d, Scotland. No. 1763, 2d, Spain. No. 1764, 2d, Switzerland. No. 1765, 2d, Turkey.
No. 1766, 25d, Hristo Stoitchkov, Bulgaria, vert. No. 1767, 25d, Davor Suker, Croatia, vert. No. 1768, 25d, Pavel Hapal, Czech Republic. No. 1769, 25d, 1992 Denmark team, European championship winners. No. 1770, 25d, Bryan Robson, England, vert. No. 1771, 25d, 1984 Championship cup won by French team, vert. No. 1772, 25d, Jüegen Klinsmann, Germany. No. 1773, 25d, Ruud Gullit, Holland, vert. No. 1774, 25d, Roberto Baggio, Italy, vert. No. 1775, 25d, Eusebio, Portugal, vert. No. 1776, 25d, Gheorge Hagi, Romania, vert. No. 1777, 25d, Oleg Salenko, Russia, vert. No. 1778, 25d, Gary McAllister, Scotland, vert. No. 1779, 25d, Juan Goikoetxea, Spain, vert. No. 1780, 25d, Christophe Ohrel, Switzerland, vert. No. 1781, 25d, Hami Mandirali, Turkey, vert.

1996, June 8   Litho.   Perf. 14
1750-1765 A269   Set of 16   12.50 12.50
Souvenir Sheets
1766-1781 A269   Set of 16   120.00 120.00
Nos. 1750-1765 each exist in miniature sheets of 8 + 1 label.
See Nos. 1808-1819.

1996 Summer Olympic Games, Atlanta — A270

1912 Olympics, Stockholm: 1d, Ray Ewry, standing high jump. 2d, Fanny Durack, freestyle swimming. 5d, Stadium, scenes in Stocholm. 10d, Jim Thorpe, decathlon, pentathlon.
No. 1786, 3d — Winners in past Olympics: a, Japanese volleyball team, 1964. b, Li Neng, floor exercises, 1984. c, Sergei Bubka, pole vault, 1988. d, Nadia Comaneci, all around gymnastics, 1976. e, Edwin Moses, 400-meter hurdles, 1984. f, Vitaly Shcherbo, all around gymnastics, 1984. g, Evelyn Ashford, 100-meters, 1984. h, Muhammad Ali, light heavyweight boxing, 1960. i, Carl Lewis, C. Smith, 400-meters relay, 1984.
No. 1787, 3d — 1992 Olympians: a, Fu Mingxia, platform diving. b, Heike Henkel, high jump. c, Spanish soccer team. d, Jackie Joyner-Kersee, heptathlon. e, Tatiana Gutsu, all around gymnastics. f, Michael Johnson, 400-meters. g, Lin Li, 200-meter individual medley. h, Gail Devers, 100-meters. i, Mike Powell, long jump.
No. 1788, 25d, Michael Gross, swimming, 1984, 1988, horiz. No. 1789, 25d, Ulrike Meyfarth, high jump, 1972, 1984.

1996, July 18   Litho.   Perf. 14
1782-1785 A270   Set of 4   3.50 3.50
Sheets of 9, #a-i
1786-1787 A270   Set of 2   10.00 10.00
Souvenir Sheets
1788-1789 A270   Set of 2   11.00 11.00

Jerusalem, 3000th Anniv. — A271

Designs: 1.50d, Roman costume, Pillar of Absalem. 2d, Turkish costume, Gate of Mercy. 3d, Greek costume, Church of the Holy Sepulcher. 10d, Western Wall of the Temple Mount, Hasidic costume.
25d, Emblem, King David Tower, vert.

1996, July 25
1790-1793 A271   Set of 4   3.75 3.75
Souvenir Sheet
1794 A271   25d multicolored   5.50 5.50

Radio, Cent. A272

Designs: 1d, Glenn Miller. 4d, Louis Armstrong. 5d, Nat King Cole. 10d, Andrews Sisters.
25d, Harry S Truman.

1996, July 25   Perf. 13½x14
1795-1798 A272   Set of 4   5.25 5.25
Souvenir Sheet
1799 A272   25d multicolored   5.75 5.75

UNICEF, 50th Anniv. — A273

Designs: 63b, Boy holding shoes. 3d, Girl receiving vaccination. 8d, Boy with soup ladle. 10d, Girl with blanket.
25d, Boy receiving vaccination, horiz.

1996, July 25   Perf. 14
1800-1803 A273   Set of 4   4.50 4.50
Souvenir Sheet
1804 A273   25d multicolored   5.50 5.50

A274   A275

No. 1805: a, John F. Kennedy. b, Jacqueline Kennedy Onassis. c, Willy Brandt. d, Marilyn Monroe. e, Mao Tse Tung. f, Sung Ching Ling. g, Charles de Gaulle. h, Marlene Dietrich.
Nos. 1806-1807: Various portraits of Jacqueline Kennedy Onassis (1929-94).

1996, Aug. 22
1805 A274   5d Sheet of 8, #a-h.   11.00 11.00
1806 A275   5d Sheet of 9, #a.-i.   13.00 13.00
Souvenir Sheet
1807 A274   25d multicolored   6.25 6.25

Nos. 1751-1752, 1754, 1756, 1758, 1761, 1767-1768, 1770, 1772, 1774, 1777 With Added Inscriptions
1996, Aug. 26
1808-1813 A269   Set of 6   3.50 3.50
Souvenir Sheets
1814-1819 A269   Set of 6   37.50 37.50
Nos. 1808-1813, each of which are 2d stamps, were issued in sheets of 8 + 1 label. Inscriptions on Nos. 1808-1813 and in sheet margins of Nos. 1814-1819, each of which are 25d stamps, show date of game, teams competing, and final score. Margin of the miniature sheets show additional information about individual games, and name of Germany as winner.
Team or team player shown as follows: Croatia (#1808, 1814), Czech Republic (#1809, 1815), England (#1810, 1816), Germany (#1811, 1817), Italy (#1812, 1818), Russia (#1813, 1819).

Richard Petty, NASCAR Driving Champion A276

No. 1820: a, 1969 Ford. b, Richard Petty. c, 1978 Dodge Magnum. d, 1987 Pontiac. e, 1989 Pontiac. f, 1975 Dodge Daytona.
25d, 1972 Plymouth.

1996, Aug. 27
1820 A276   5d Sheet of 6, #a.-f.   7.75 7.75
Souvenir Sheet
1821 A276   25d multicolored   5.50 5.50
No. 1821 contains one 85x28mm stamp.

Elvis Presley's 1st "Hit" Year, 40th Anniv. A277

Designs: Various portraits.

1996, Sept. 8   Litho.   Perf. 13½x14
1822 A277   5d Sheet of 6, #a.-f.   7.50 7.50

Supermarine S6B's Schneider Trophy Victory, 65th Anniv. — A278

No. 1823 — Spitfire aircraft: a, PR XIX, Royal Swedish Air Force. b, MK VB, US Army Air. c, MK VC, French Air Force. d, MK VB, Soviet Air Force. e, MK IXE, Netherlands East Indies Air Force. f, MK IXE, Israeli Defense Force. g, MK VIII, Royal Australian Air Force. h, MK VB, Turkish Air Force. i, PR XI, Royal Danish Air Force.
No. 1823J: k, K5054, first prototype aircraft. l, K9787, first production aircraft. m, MK 1A, "Battle of Britain." n, LF MK IXE, D-Day invasion markings. o, MK XII, first "Griffon" engined model. p, MK XIVC, SEAC markings. q, PR XIX, Royal Swedish Air Force. r, PR MK XIX. s, FMK 22/24 final variant.
No. 1824, The Supermarine S.6B S1595. No. 1824A, Supermarine S.6B S1595 seaplane.

1996, Sept. 13   Litho.   Perf. 14
1823 A278   4d Sheet of 9, #a.-i.   8.00 8.00
1823J A278   4d Sheet of 9, #k.-s.   8.00 8.00
Souvenir Sheets
1824 A278   25d multicolored   5.50 5.50
1824A A278   25d multicolored   5.50 5.50

Bob Dylan, Singer — A279

1996, Sept. 8   Litho.   Perf. 14
1825 A279   5d multicolored   1.75 1.75
Issued in sheets of 16.

Birds — A280

Designs: 50b, Egyptian plover. 63b, Painted snipe. 75b, Golden-breasted bunting. 1d, Bateleur. 1.50d, Didric cuckoo. 2d, European turtle dove. 3d, Village weaver. 4d, European roller. 5d, Cut-throat. 10d, Hoopoe. 15d, White-faced scops-owl. 20d, Narina trogan. 25d, Pied kingfisher. 30d, Common kestrel.

1996, Oct. 22   Litho.   Perf. 14
1826 A280   50b multicolored   .20 .20
1827 A280   63b multicolored   .20 .20
1828 A280   75b multicolored   .20 .20
1829 A280   1d multicolored   .25 .25
1830 A280   1.50d multicolored   .30 .30
1831 A280   2d multicolored   .45 .45

1832	A280	3d multicolored		.65	.65
1833	A280	4d multicolored		.90	.90
1834	A280	5d multicolored		1.10	1.10
1835	A280	10d multicolored		2.25	2.25
1836	A280	15d multicolored		3.25	3.25
1837	A280	20d multicolored		4.50	4.50
1838	A280	25d multicolored		5.50	5.50
1839	A280	30d multicolored		6.50	6.50
	Nos. 1826-1839 (14)			26.25	26.25

See Nos. 1898-1900.

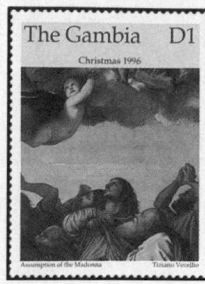

Christmas
A281

Details of painting, Assumption of the Madonna, by Titian: 1d, Watching assumption, cherub, clouds. 1.50d, Cherubs. 2d, Cherub. 3d, Cherub holding up cloud, outstretched arms below. 10d, People watching assumption. 15d, Cherubs pointing.

No. 1846, 25d, Madonna and Child with Two Angels, by Filippo Lippi, horiz. No. 1847, 25d, Virgin and Child with Infant St. John, by Raphael.

1996, Nov. 18   **Perf. 13½x14**
1840-1845 A281 Set of 6   7.25 7.25

Souvenir Sheets
1846-1847 A281 Set of 2   11.00 11.00

Sylvester Stallone in Movie, "Rocky" — A282

1996, Nov. 21   **Litho.**   **Perf. 14**
1848 A282 10d multicolored   2.25 2.25

Issued in sheets of 3.

Development Projects — A283

Designs: No. 1849, 63b, No. 1852, 2d, Arch 22, vert. 1d, Tractor, rice development project. 1.50d, Worker in rice paddy, vert. 3d, Banjul Intl. Airport Terminal Building. 5d, Chamoi Bridge.

20d, Workers in rice paddy. 25d, Statue in front of Arch 22, vert.

1996   **Litho.**   **Perf. 14**
1849-1854 A283 Set of 6   3.00 3.00

Souvenir Sheets
1855 A283 20d multicolored   4.50 4.50
1856 A283 25d multicolored   5.50 5.50

New Year 1997
(Year of the
Ox) — A284

Nos. 1857-1858 — Various stylized oxen, background color: a, 63b, orange. b, 75b, purple. c, 1.50d, blue green. d, 4d, yellow orange. All stamps in No. 1858 are 3d.
10d, Ox with baby lying on its back.

1997, Jan. 16   **Perf. 15**
1857 A284   Strip of 4, #a.-d.   1.50 1.50
1858 A284 3d Sheet of 4, #a.-d. 2.75 2.75

Souvenir Sheet
Perf. 14
1859 A284 10d multicolored   3.00 3.00

No. 1859 contains one 43x29mm stamp.

Mickey's Journey to the West — A285

Nos. 1860-1861: a-f, Scenes from Disney's "Monkey King."

No. 1862, Donald, Mickey, vert. No. 1863, Wu-Kong Sun (The Monkey King), monkeys, Mickey. No. 1864, Mickey, Intelligent Tortoise, Master San Tang. No. 1865, Mickey, Minnie obtaining Buddhist scriptures.

1997, Jan. 28   **Perf. 14x13½**
1860 A285 2d Sheet of 6, #a.-f. 5.50 5.50
   g. No. 1860 overprinted   5.50 5.50
1861 A285 3d Sheet of 6, #a.-f. 6.25 6.25
   g. No. 1861 overprinted   7.00 7.00

Souvenir Sheets
1862 A285 2d Sheet of 6 multi   5.00 5.00
   a. With marginal overprint   5.00 5.00
1863 A285 10d multi   5.00 5.00
   a. With marginal overprint   5.00 5.00
1864 A285 10d multi   5.00 5.00
   a. With marginal overprint   5.00 5.00
1865 A285 15d multi   5.00 5.00
   a. With marginal overprint   5.00 5.00

Nos. 1860g, 1861g are overprinted in red in sheet margin: "70TH ANNIVERSARY OF MICKEY & MINNIE," and in black with "Happy Birthday," Mickey Mouse, and "1998" in emblem. Nos. 1862a, 1863a, 1864a, 1865a are overprinted in black in sheet margin with just "Happy Birthday" emblem.

Souvenir Sheet

Deng Xiaoping — A286

No. 1867, Like #1866.

1996, May 13   **Litho.**   **Perf. 13**
1866 A286 5d shown   5.25 5.25

Litho. & Embossed
Die Cut Perf. 9
Size: 95x56mm

1867 A286 300d gold

China '96. Nos. 1866-1867 were not available until March 1997.

Jackie Chan,
Action Film
Actor — A287

A287a

Various portraits.

1997, Feb. 12   **Perf. 14**
1868 A287 4d Sheet of 8, #a.-h.   8.00 8.00

Souvenir Sheet
1869 A287 25d multi, horiz.   7.00 7.00

Litho. & Embossed
Die Cut Perf. 9
Without Gum
1869A A287a 300d gold & multi

Endangered Species — A288

No. 1870, 1.50d: a, Clouded leopard. b, Audouin's gull. c, Leatherback turtle. d, White-eared pheasant. e, Kakapo. f, Right whale. g, Black-footed ferret. h, Dwarf lemur. i, Peacock pheasant. j, Brown hyena. k, Cougar. l, Gharial. m, Monk seal. n, Mountain gorilla. o, Blyth's tragopan. p, Malayan tapir. q, Black rhinoceros. r, Polar bear. s, Red colobus. t, Tiger.

No. 1871, 1.50d: a, Arabian oryx. b, Baiji. c, Ruffed lemur. d, California condor. e, Blue-headed quail-dove. f, Numbat. g, Congo peacock. h, White uakari. i, Eskimo curlew. j, Gouldian finch. k, Coelacanth. l, Toucan barbet. m, Snow leopard. n, Queen Alexandra's birdwing. o, Dalmatian pelican. p, Chaco tortoise. q, Medong catfish. r, Helmeted hornbill. s, White-eyed river martin. t, Fluminense swallowtail.

No. 1872, 25d, Giant panda. No. 1873, 25d, Humpback whale. No. 1874, 25d, Japanese crane.

1997, Feb. 24
Sheets of 20, #a-t
1870-1871 A288 Set of 2   17.50 17.50

Souvenir Sheets
1872-1874 A288 Set of 3   19.00 19.00

Hong Kong '97 (Nos. 1870-1871).

Jungle
Book — A289

No. 1875: a, Monkey facing right. b, Bear. c, Elephant. d, Monkey facing left. e, Panther, butterfly. f, Buffalo. g, Mandrill. h, Tiger. i, Wolf. j, Cobra. k, Mongoose. l, Child's face, flower.

1997
1875 A289 3d Sheet of 12, #a.-l. 8.75 8.75

Mushrooms — A290

Designs: 1d, Polyporus squamosus. 3d, Armillaria tabescens. 5d, Collybia velutipes. 10d, Sarcoscypha coccinea.

No. 1880, vert: a, Amanita caesarea. b, Lepiota procera. c, Hygophorus psittacinus. d, Russula xerampelina. e, Laccaria amethystina. f, Coprinus micaceus. g, Boletus edulis. h, Morchella esculenta. i, Otidea auricula.

25d, Volvariella bombycina.

1997, Mar. 10   **Litho.**   **Perf. 14**
1876-1879 A290 Set of 4   4.75 4.75
1880 A290 4d Sheet of 9, #a.-i. 8.00 8.00

Souvenir Sheet
1881 A290 25d multicolored   7.00 7.00

UNESCO, 50th Anniv. — A291

World Heritage sites: 1d, Horyu-Ji, Japan. 2d, Great Wall, China. 3d, City of Ayutthaya, Thailand. 4d, Ascension Convent, Santa Maria, Philippines. 10d, Dragons, Komodo Natl. Park, Indonesia. 15d, Timbuktu, Mali.

No. 1888, 4d, vert. — Various sites in Japan: a, g, h. Kyoto. b, Himeji-Jo. c, d, Horyu-Ji. e, f, Yakushima.

No. 1889, 4d, vert. — Various sites in China: a, b, c, Mogao Caves. d, e, Great Wall. f, g, h, Imperial Palace.

No. 1890, 4d, vert. — Various sites: a, Mt. Nimba Strict Nature Reserve, Guinea. b, Banc D'Argun Natl. Park, Mauritania. c, Marrakesh, Morocco. d, Ichkeul Natl. Park, Tunisia. e, Algeria. h, Benin.

No. 1891, 5d — Various sites in Germany: a, b, c, Bamberg. d, e, Maulbronn.

No. 1892, 5d — Various sites in Greece: a, d, e, Ruins in Delphi. b, c, City of Rhodes.

No. 1893, 5d — Various sites in Japan: a, b, Shirakami-Sanchi. c, d, e, Himeji-Jo.

No. 1894, 25d, Cloisters, Santa Maria de Alcobaca, Portugal, No. 1895, 25d, Kyoto, Japan. No. 1896, 25d, Ruins of Kilwa Kisiwani, Tanzania. No. 1897, 25d, Plitvice Lakes Natl. Park, Croatia.

1997, Mar. 24
1882-1887 A291 Set of 6   7.75 7.75

Sheets of 8, #a-h, + Label
1888-1890 A291 Set of 3   21.00 21.00

Sheets of 5, #a-e, + Label
1891-1893 A291 Set of 3   16.50 16.50

Souvenir Sheets
1894-1897 A291 each   22.00 22.00

Bird Type of 1996

Designs: 40d, Temminck's courser. 50d, European bee-eater. 100d, Green-winged teal.

1997, Mar. 25   **Litho.**   **Perf. 14**
1898 A280 40d multicolored   8.00 8.00
1899 A280 50d multicolored   10.00 10.00
1900 A280 100d multicolored   20.00 20.00
   Nos. 1898-1900 (3)   38.00 38.00

Disney's 101 Dalmatians — A293

No. 190, vert.1: a, Dipstick. b, Fidget. c, Jewel. d, Lucky. e, Two-Tone. f, Wizzer.
No. 1902: a-i, Various "Playful Puppies."
No. 1903: a-i, Various "Mischievous puppies."
No. 1904, 25d, Hiding under sheep. No. 1905, 25d, Cruella. No. 1906, 25d, Looking at picture. No. 1907, 25d, Distributing mail, vert. No. 1908, 25d, Into paint. No. 1909, 25d, Playing video game.

1997, May 1   **Perf. 13½x14, 14x13½**
1901 A293 50b Sheet of 6, #a.-f. 2.75 2.75
1902 A293 2d Sheet of 9, #a.-i. 4.75 4.75
1903 A293 3d Sheet of 9, #a.-i. 7.50 7.50

Souvenir Sheets
1904-1909 A293 Set of 6   45.00 45.00

MINNIE THRU THE YEARS

Minnie Thru the Years — A294

No. 1910 — Minnie in various scenes dated: a, 1928. b, 1933. c, 1934. d, 1937. e, 1938. f, 1941. g, 1950. h, 1990. i, 1997. 25d, 1987.

1997, May 1   **Perf. 13½x14**
1910 A294   4d Sheet of 9,   #a.-i.   12.00 12.00
Souvenir Sheet
1911 A294 25d multicolored   9.75 9.75

Juventus (World Club Soccer Champions), Cent. — A295

No. 1912: a, Juventus, 1897. b, Player from early years, emblems. c, Giampiero Boniperti. d, Roberto Bettega. e, European/ South American Cup, 1996. f, Drawing in celebration of cent.

1997, May 9   **Litho.**   **Perf. 14x13½**
1912 A295   5d Sheet of 6, #a.-f.   6.25 6.25

Queen Elizabeth II, Prince Philip, 50th Wedding Anniv. A296

No. 1913: a, Queen. b, Royal Arms. c, Queen, Prince Philip. d, Queen holding flowers, Prince saluting. e, Royal Yacht Britannia. f, Prince Philip.
20d, Queen in red hat.

1997, May 20   **Perf. 14**
1913 A296   4d Sheet of 6, #a.-f.   5.25 5.25
Souvenir Sheet
1914 A296 20d multicolored   4.25 4.25

Paul P. Harris (1868-1947), Founder of Rotary Intl. — A297

Rotary emblem, portrait of Harris and: 10d, Tree of friendship planted by Sydney W. Pascall, Rotary Pres. 1931-32.
25d, Emblem, preserve planet earth.

1997, May 20   **Litho.**   **Perf. 14**
1915 A297 10d multicolored   2.00 2.00
Souvenir Sheet
1916 A297 25d multicolored   5.25 5.25

Heinrich von Stephan (1831-97), Founder of UPU A298

No. 1917 — Portrait of von Stephan and: a, Otto von Bismarck. b, UPU emblem. c, Two-horse team and wagon, Boston, 1900. 25d, Hamburg-Lübeck postilion, 1828.

1997, May 20
1917 A298   5d Sheet of 3, #a.-c.   3.50 3.50
Souvenir Sheet
1918 A298 25d multicolored   5.75 5.75
PACIFIC 97.

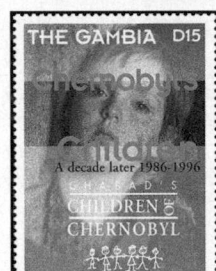

Chernobyl Disaster, 10th Anniv. A299

Designs: No. 1919, Chabad's Children of Chernobyl. No. 1920, UNESCO.

1997, May 20   **Litho.**   **Perf. 13½x14**
1919 A299 15d multicolored   3.00 3.00
1920 A299 15d multicolored   3.00 3.00

Grimm's Fairy Tales A300

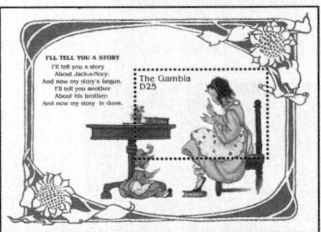

Mother Goose — A301

No. 1921 — Scenes from "Little Red Riding Hood": a, Grandmother's house. b, Little Red Riding Hood. c, Wolf.
No. 1922, Little Red Riding Hood, wolf, horiz. No. 1923, Girl seated on chair from "I'll Tell You a Story."

1997, May 20   **Perf. 13½x14**
1921 A300 10d Sheet of 3, #a.-c.   6.00 6.00
Souvenir Sheets
Perf. 14x13½
1922 A300 10d multicolored   4.50 4.50
Perf. 14
1923 A301 25d multicolored   5.25 5.25

Paintings, by Hiroshige (1797-1858) A302

No. 1924, 4d: a, Morning Glory and Cricket. b, Dragonfly and Begonia. c, Two Ducks Swimming among Reeds. d, A Black-Naped Oriole Perched on a Stem of Rose Mallow. e, A Pheasant on a Snow-covered Pine. f, A Cuckoo Flying through the Rain.
No. 1925, 4d: a, An Egret among Rushes. b, Peacock and Peonies. c, Three Wild Geese Flying across the Moon. d, A Cock in the Snow. e, A Pheasant and Bracken. f, Peonies.
No. 1926, 4d: a, Sparrow and Bamboo. b, Mandarin Ducks on an Icy Pond with Brown Leaves Falling. c, Blossoming Plum Tree. d, Java Sparrow and Magnolia. e, Chinese Bellflowers and Miscanthus. f, A Small Black Bird Clinging to a Tendril of Ivy.
No. 1927, 5d: a, Sparrows and Camellia in Snow. b, Parrot on a Branch of Pine. c, A Long-tailed Blue Bird on a Branch of Flowering Plum. d, Sparrow and Bamboo. e, Bird in a Tree. f, A Wild Duck Swimming beneath Snow-laden Reeds.
No. 1928, 5d: a, Kingfisher above a Yellow-flowered Water Plant. b, Wagtail and Roses. c, A Mandarin Duck on a Snowy Bank. d, A Japanese White-eye on a Persimmon Branch. e, Sparrows and Camellia in Snow. f, Kingfisher and Moon above a Yellow-flowered Water Plant.
No. 1929, 5d: a, Sparrow and Bamboo. b, Birds Flying over Waves. c, Blossoming Plum Tree with Full Moon. d, Kingfisher and Iris. e, A Blue-and-white Flycatcher on a Hibiscus Flower. f, Mandarin Ducks in Snowfall.
Unidentified paintings of: No. 1930, 25d, Falcon on perch. No. 1931, 25d, Two birds seated on branch. No. 1932, 25d, Kingfisher above Iris. No. 1933, 25d, Like #1925c. No. 1934, 25d, Bird on grapevine. No. 1935, 25d, Small bird in flowering tree.

1997, May 20   **Perf. 14**
Sheets of 6, #a-f
1924-1926 A302   Set of 3   15.00 15.00
1927-1929 A302   Set of 3   19.00 19.00
Souvenir Sheets
1930-1935 A302   Set of 6   33.00 33.00

Return of Hong Kong & Macao to China — A303

No. 1936: a, Signing of joint declaration on question of Macao, 1987. b, Deng Xiaoping sharing toast with Portugal's Prime Minister Anibal Cavaco Silva after signing declaration. c, Deng Xiaoping, Britain's Prime Minister Margaret Thatcher sharing toast after signing Sino-British Declaration, 1984. d, Signing of the Sino-British Joint Declaration on question of Hong Kong, 1984.
No. 1937: a, Sir Henry Pottinger, 1st governor of Hong Kong, 1841-44, Hong Kong Island ceded to Britain, 1843. b, Sir Hercules Robinson, governor 1859-65, Kowloon ceded to Britain, 1860. c, Sir Henry Blake, governor 1898-1903, New Territories leased to Britain, 1899.
No. 1938: a, Ships in harbor, Sir Henry Pottinger. b, Suspension bridge, Chris Patten, governor of Hong Kong, 1992-1997. c, Skyline at night, C.H. Tung, first Chinese chief executive, 1997.
No. 1939: a, Signing of Treaty of Nanking, 1842. b, Signing of Japanese surrender document, 1945. c, Signing of Sino-British Joint Declaration on question of Hong Kong, 1984, diff.

1997, July 1
1936 A303   3d Sheet of 4, #a.-d.   2.75 2.75
1937 A303   4d Sheet of 3, #a.-c.   2.75 2.75
1938 A303   5d Sheet of 3, #a.-c.   3.25 3.25
1939 A303   6d Sheet of 3, #a.-c.   3.75 3.75

Wonders of the World — A304

Designs: 63b, Great Mosque at Samarra, Iraq, vert. (24x38mm). 75b, Moai stone faces, Easter Island. 1d, Golden Gate Bridge, San Francisco. 1.50d, Statue of Liberty, New York, vert. (24x38mm). 2d, Parthenon, Greece. 3d, Pyramid of the Sun, Teotihuacán, Mexico.
No. 1946, 5d: a, Rock of Gibraltar. b, St. Peter's Basilica, Vatican City. c, Santa Sophia, Istanbul. d, Gateway Arch, St. Louis. e, Great Wall of China. f, Carcassonne, France.
No. 1947, 5d: a, Stonehenge, England. b, Hughes HK-1 Hercules "Spruce Goose" airplane. c, Hoverspeed catamaran, Great Britain. d, Jet powered "Thrust 2." e, Djoser Step Pyramid, Egypt. f, Mallard steam locomotive.
No. 1948, 25d, Grand Canyon of the Colorado River, Arizona. No. 1949, 25d, Mt. Everest, Nepal. No. 1950, 25d, Washington Monument, Washington, DC.

1997, July 15
1940-1945 A304   Set of 6   3.75 3.75
Sheets of 6, #a-f
1946-1947 A304   Set of 4   12.50 12.50
Souvenir Sheets
1948-1950 A304   Set of 3   15.00 15.00

1993 Winter Olympics, Nagano A305

Designs: 5d, Downhill skiing. 10d, Luge. 15d, Speed skating. 20d, Ice hockey.
No. 1955, 5d: a, Luge, diff. b, Ice hockey (goalie). c, 4-man bobsled. d, Ski jumping. e, Curling. f, Women's figure skating. g, Speed skating, diff. h, Biathlon. i, Downhill skiing, diff.
No. 1956, 5d, vert: a, 2-man bobsled. b, Free-style skiing. c, Speed skating, diff. d, Downhill skiing, diff. e, Women's figure skating, diff. f, Slalom skiing. g, Pairs figure skating. h, Cross-country skiing. i, Ski jumping, diff.
No. 1957, 25d, Female figure skater, vert. No. 1958, 25d, 2-man bobsled, diff.

1997, July 21   **Litho.**   **Perf. 14**
1951-1954 A305   Set of 4   11.00 11.00
Sheets of 9, #a-i
1955-1956 A305   Set of 2   21.00 21.00
Souvenir Sheets
1957-1958 A305   Set of 2   12.00 12.00

Cats A306

Designs: 63b, Scottish fold. 1.50d, American curl. 2d, British bi-color. 3d, Devon rex. 6d, Silver tabby 20d, Abyssinian.
No. 1965: a, Burmilla. b, Blue Burmese. c, Korat. d, British tabby. e, Foreign white. f, Somali.
No. 1966, 25d, Cornish rex. No. 1967, 25d, Siamese.

1997, Aug. 12
1959-1964 A306   Set of 6   8.75 8.75
1965 A306   5d Sheet of 6, #a.-   f.   8.00 8.00
Souvenir Sheets
1966-1967 A306   Set of 2   12.50 12.50

Dinosaurs
A307

Designs: 50b, Coelophysis, ornitholestes. 63b, Spinosaurus. 75b, Kentrosaurus. 1d, Ceratosaurus. 1.50d, Stygimoloch. 2d, Troodon. 3d, Velociraptor. 4d, Triceratops. 5d, Protoceratops. 10d, Ornithomimus. 15d, Stegosaurus. 20d, Ankylosaurus saichania.

No. 1980, 4d: a, Anurognathus. b, Pteranodon. c, Pterosaurus. d, Saltasaurus. e, Agathaumus. f, Stegosaurus. g, Albertosaurus libratus. h, 4 Lesothosaurus. i, 7 Lesothosaurus.

No. 1981, 4d: a, Tarbosaurus bataar. b, Brachiosaurus. c, Styracosasaurus. d, Baryonyx. e, Coelophysis. f, Carnotaurus. g, Compsognathus longipes. h, Compsognathuselegant jaw. i, Stenonychosaurus.

No. 1982, 25d, Deinonychus. No. 1983, 25d, Seismosaurus.

1997, June 23   Litho.   Perf. 14
1968-1979 A307   Set of 12   17.50 17.50
Sheets of 9, #a-i
1980-1981 A307   Set of 2   13.50 13.50
Souvenir Sheets
1982-1983 A307   Set of 2   13.00 13.00
No. 1982 contains one 50x38mm stamp. No. 1983 contains one 89x28mm stamp.

Dogs
A308

Designs: 75b, Dalmatian. 1d, Rottweiler. 3d, Newfoundland. 4d, Great Dane. 10d, Old English sheepdog. 15d, Queensland heeler.

No. 1990: a, Akita. b, Welsh corgi. c, German shepherd. d, St. Bernard. e, Bullmastiff. f, Malamute.

No. 1991, 25d, Doberman pinscher. No. 1992, 25d, Boxer.

1997, Aug. 12
1984-1989 A308   Set of 6   8.75 8.75
1990 A308 5d Sheet of 6, #a-f.   8.00 8.00
Souvenir Sheets
1991-1992 A308   Set of 2   12.50 12.50

1998 World Cup Soccer Championships, France — A309

Winning teams: 1d, Uruguay, 1950. 1.50d, W. Germany, 1954. 2d, Brazil, 1970. 3d, Brazil, 1962. 5d, Italy, 1938. 10d, Uruguay, 1930.

No. 1999, 4d: a, Brazil, 1994. b, Argentina, 1986. c, Brazil, 1970. d, Italy, 1934. e, Uruguay, 1958. f, England, 1966. g, Brazil, 1962. h, W. Germany, 1990.

No. 2000, 4d: a, Mario Kempes, Argentina, 1978. b, Ademir, Brazil, 1950. c, Muller, W. Germany, 1970. d, Lineker, England, 1986. e, Eusebio, Portugal, 1966. f, Schillaci, Italy, 1990. g, Lata, Poland, 1974. h, Rossi, Italy, 1982.

No. 2001, 4d, vert: a, Kinkladze, Georgia. b, Shearer, England. c, Dani, Portugal. d, Weah, Liberia. e, Ravanelli, Italy. f, Raducioiu, Romania. g, Peter Schmeichel, Denmark. h, Bergkamp, Holland.

No. 2002, 4d, vert: a, Moore, England, 1966. b, Fritzwalter, W. Germany, 1954. c, Beckenbauer, W. Germany, 1974. d, Zoff, Italy, 1982. e, Maradona, Argentina, 1986. f, Passarella, Argentina, 1978. g, Matthäus, W. Germany, 1990. h, Dunga, Brazil, 1994.

No. 2003, Pele, Brazil. No. 2004, 25d, Eusebio, Portugal. No. 2005, 25d, Juninho, Brazil. No. 2006, 25d, Philippe Albert, Belgium.

1997, Sept. 4   Perf. 14x13½, 13½x14
1993-1998 A309   Set of 6   5.00 5.00
Sheets of 8, #a-h, + Label
1999-2002 A309   Set of 4   30.00 30.00
Souvenir Sheets
2003-2006 A309   Set of 4   25.00 25.00

Sea Birds
A310

Designs: 5d, Red-legged cormorant. 10d, Roseate tern. 15d, Blue-footed booby. 20d, Sanderling.

No. 2011: a, Brown pelican. b, Galapagos penguin. c, Red billed tropic bird. d, Little tern. e, Dunlin. f, Kittiwake. g, Atlantic puffin. h, Wandering albatross. i, Masked booby. j, Glaucous winged gull. k, Artic tern. l, Piping plover.

No. 2012, 23d, Osprey. No. 2013, 23d, Long-tailed skua.

1997, Aug. 4   Litho.   Perf. 14
2007-2010 A310   Set of 4   11.00 11.00
2011 A310 3d Sheet of 12, #a-l.   9.50 9.50
Souvenir Sheets
2012-2013 A310   Set of 2   9.00 9.00

A311

Diana, Princess of Wales (1961-97) — A312

Various portraits.

1997, Nov. 26   Litho.   Perf. 14
2014 A311 10d Sheet of 4, #a.-d. 8.50 8.50
Souvenir Sheet
2015 A312 25d multicolored   5.75 5.75

Christmas
A313

Entire paintings or details: 1d, Angel, by Rembrandt. 1.50d, Initiation into the Rites of Dionysus, in Villa dei Misteri, Pompeii. 2d, Pair of Erotes with Purple Cloaks. 3d, The Ecstasy of Saint Teresa, by Gianlorenzo Bernini (carving). 5d, Annunciation, by Mathias Grunewald. 10d, Angel Playing the Organ, by Stefan Lochner.

No. 2022, 25d, The Rest on the Flight into Egypt, by Caravaggio. No. 2023, 25d, Education of Cupid, by Titian.

1997, Dec. 8
2016-2021 A313   Set of 6   8.25 8.25
Souvenir Sheets
2022-2023 A313   Set of 2   10.50 10.50

New Year 1998 (Year of the Tiger) — A314

No. 2024 — Various stylized tigers with: a, Yellow brown background. b, Purple background. c, Brown background. d, Orange background.
10d, Tiger, landscape.

1998, Jan. 5   Litho.   Perf. 14½
2024 A314   3d Sheet of 4, #a.-d. 2.75 2.75
Souvenir Sheet
Perf. 14
2025 A314 10d multicolored   2.75 2.75
No. 2025 contains one 38x24mm stamp.

Trains
A315

No. 2026, 5d: a, Electric Train, Scotland. b, Beaconsfield, China. c, TGV, France. d, People Mover, England. e, ICE train, Germany. f, Montmartre Funicular, France.

No. 2027, 5d: a, SD70 Burlington Northern, US. b, Mallard, England. c, Baldwin 4-8-0, Peru. d, Sweden Rail. e, Rack Train, Amberawa-Java. f, Beyer-Peacock, Pakistan.

No. 2028, 25d, Monorail, England. No. 2029, 25d, Southern Pacific, US.

1998, May 19   Litho.   Perf. 14
Sheets of 6, #a-f
2026-2027 A315   Set of 2   14.00 14.00
Souvenir Sheets
2028-2029 A315   Set of 2   10.50 10.50

Flowers
A316

Designs, vert: 75b, Daffodil. 1.50d, Transvaal daisy. 3d, Torchlily. 4d, Ancistrochilus rothschildianus. 10d, Polystachya vulcanica. 15d, Gladiolus.

No. 2036: a, Adenium multiflorum. b, Huernia namaquensis. c, Gloriosa superba. d, Strelitzia reginae. e, Passiflora mollissima. f, Bauhinia variegata.

No. 2037, 25d, Aerangis rhodosticta, vert. No. 2038, 25d, Ansella gigantea, vert.

1998, June 2   Litho.   Perf. 14
2030-2035 A316   Set of 6   8.50 8.50
2036 A316 5d Sheet of 6, #a.-f.   7.50 7.50
Souvenir Sheets
2037-2038 A316   Set of 2   12.00 12.00

Historical Aircraft A317

No. 2039, 5d: a, Short Type 38, 1913. b, Fokker F.VII B 3m, 1925. c, Junkers F-13, 1919. d, Pitcairn "Mailwing," 1927. e, Douglas, 1920. f, Curtiss "Condor," 1934.

No. 2040, 5d: a, Wright Brothers, 1903. b, Curtiss, 1910. c, Farman, 1907. d, Bristol, 1911. e, Antoinette, 1908. f, Sopwith "Bat Boat," 1912.

No. 2041, 25d, Albatross, 1913. No. 2042, 25d, Boeing 247, 1932.

1998, June 10
Sheets of 6, #a-f
2039-2040 A317   Set of 2   15.00 15.00
Souvenir Sheets
2041-2042 A317   Set of 2   12.00 12.00
Nos. 2041-2042 each contain one 85x28mm stamp.

Disney's "Mulan" A318

Characters from the animated movie — No. 2043: a, Mulan. b, Mushu. c, Little Brother. d, Cri-Kee. e, Grandmother Fa. f, Fa Li. g, Fa Zhou. h, Mulan and Khan.

No. 2044: a, Mulan riding Khan. b, Shang. c, Chi Fu. d, Chien-Po. e, Yao. f, Ling. g, Shan-Yu. h, Mulan, Shang & Mushu.

No. 2045, 25d, Mulan. No. 2046, 25d, Mulan riding Khan, diff. No. 2047, 25d, Mulan jumping in air. No. 2048, 25d, Mulan looking at Shang (in margin).

1998, July 1   Litho.   Perf. 13½x14
2043 A318 4d Sheet of 8, #a.-h.   11.00 11.00
2044 A318 5d Sheet of 8, #a.-h.   11.50 11.50
Souvenir Sheets
2045-2048 A318   Set of 4   30.00 30.00

Ferrari Automobiles — A318a

No. 2048A: c, 365 GTB/4. d, Daytona. e, 1966 275 GTB.
25d, 365 GTB/4, diff.

1998, Oct. 29   Litho.   Perf. 14
2048A A318a 10d Sheet of 3, #c-e   5.75 5.75
Souvenir Sheet
Perf. 13¾x14¼
2048B A318a 25d multi   5.00 5.00
No. 2048A contains three 39x25mm stamps.

Famous People — A319

Sinking of the Titanic — A320

No. 2049, 4d — Jazz musicians: a, Sidney Bechet (1897-1959). b, Bechet playing clarinet. c, "Duke" Ellington conducting band. d, Ellington (1899-1974). e, Louis Armstrong (1900-71). f, Armstrong playing trumpet. g, Charlie "Bird" Parker playing saxophone. h, Parker (1920-55).

No. 2050, 4d —2:49 PM 12/6/2007 Composers: a, Cole Porter (1893-1964). b, "Born to Dance," by Porter. c, "Porgy and Bess," by George Gershwin (1898-1937). d, Gershwin (1898-1937). e, Richard Rodgers (1902-79) & Oscar Hammerstein II (1895-1960). f, "The King and I," by Rodgers & Hammerstein. g, "West Side Story," by Leonard Bernstein. h, Bernstein (1918-90).

No. 2051, 25d, Ella Fitzgerald (1917-96). No. 2052, 25d, Irving Berlin (1888-1989), "Oh How I Hate to Get Up in the Morning."

1998, Oct. 12   Litho.   Perf. 14
Sheets of 8, #a-h
2049-2050 A319 Set of 2   15.00 15.00
Souvenir Sheets
2051-2052 A319 Set of 2   14.00 14.00

Nos. 2049b-2049c, 2049f-2049g, 2050b-2050c, 2050f-2050g are 53x38mm.

1998, Oct. 25

No. 2053: a, Capt. Edward J. Smith. b, Molly Brown. c, News of the disaster breaks. d, Benjamin Guggenheim. e, Isidor Strauss. f, Ida Strauss.

No. 2054, 25d, Picture of ship on postcard. No. 2055, 25d, Ship sinking. No. 2056, 25d, Remains of ship lying on bottom of ocean years later.

2053 A320 5d Sheet of 6, #a.-
        f.   8.25 8.25
Souvenir Sheets
2054-2056 A320 Set of 3   19.00 19.00

Diana, Princess of Wales (1961-97) — A321

1998, Oct. 29   Perf. 14½x14
2057 A321 10d multicolored   2.00 2.00
Issued in sheets of 6.

Pablo Picasso (1881-1973) — A322

Paintings: 3d, Death of Casagemas, 1901. 5d, Seated Woman, 1920, vert. 10d, Mother and Child, 1907, vert.

25d, Child Playing with a Toy Truck, 1953, vert.

1998, Oct. 29   Perf. 14½
2058-2060 A322 Set of 3   3.50 3.50
Souvenir Sheet
2061 A322 25d multicolored   5.00 5.00

A323   A324

No. 2062 — Mahatma Gandhi (1869-1948): a, Age 62, 1932. b, Age 60, 1930, with Sarojini Naidu. c, Age 61, 1931, spinning yarn. d, Age 47, 1916.
25d, Age 61, 1931.

1998, Oct. 29   Perf. 14
2062 A323 10d Sheet of 4, #a.-d. 7.50 7.50
Souvenir Sheet
2063 A323 25d multicolored   5.00 5.00
Nos. 2062b-2062c are 53x39mm.

1998

Ships: 2d, Chinese Junk. 3d, HMS Victory. 10d, County Class Destroyer. 15d, Viking Longboat.

No. 2068, 5d, horiz: a, HMS Dreadnought. b, Truxton Class Cruiser. c, Queen Mary. d, Canberra. e, Queen Elizabeth. f, Queen Elizabeth 2.

No. 2069, 5d: a, Santa Maria. b, Mary Rose. c, Mayflower. d, Ark Royal. e, HMS Beagle. f, HMS Bounty.

No. 2070, 25d, Cutty Sark. No. 2071, 25d, Sovereign of the Seas.

2064-2067 A324 Set of 4   6.00 6.00
Sheets of 6, #a-f
2068-2069 A324 Set of 2   12.00 12.00
Souvenir Sheets
2070-2071 A324 Set of 2   10.00 10.00

No. 2070 contains one 42x56mm stamp; No. 2071, one 56x42mm stamp.

1998 World Scouting Jamboree, Chile — A325

No. 2072: a, Scout handclasp. b, Small boat sailing. c, Scout salute.
No. 2073, Lord Robert Baden-Powell.

1998, Oct. 29   Litho.   Perf. 14
2072 A325 10d Sheet of 3, #a.-c. 6.00 6.00
Souvenir Sheet
2073 A325 25d multicolored   5.00 5.00

Royal Air Force, 80th Anniv. A326

No. 2074, 5d: a, Sepecat Jaguar GR1. b, BAe Harrier GR7. c, Panavia Tornado GR1 firing Sidewinder AIM 9-L missle. d, Panavia Tornado GR1 on afterburner.

No. 2075, 5d: a, Sepecat Jaguar GR1A in low visibility gray finish. b, Panavia Tornado GR1A. c, Sepecat Jaguar GR1A in Bosnia theater camouflage finish. d, BAe Hawk 200.

No. 2076, 5d: a, Panavia Tornado GR1 flying left. b, BAe Hawk TIA. c, Sepecat Jaguar GR1A. d, Panavia Tornado GR1 flying right.

No. 2077, 20d, Eurofighters. No. 2078, 25d, Biplane, hawk's head. No. 2079, 25d, Lightning, Eurofighter. No. 2080, 25d, Biplane, hawk in flight. No. 2081, 25d, Lancaster, Eurofighter. No. 2082, 25d, Biplane, hawk perched.

1998, Oct. 29
Sheets of 4, #a-d
2074-2076 A326 Set of 3   13.50 13.50
Souvenir Sheets
2077-2082 A326 Set of 6   29.00 29.00

Paintings by Eugène Delacroix (1798-1863) — A327

No. 2083, 4d: a, Mule Drivers from Tetuan. b, Encampment of Arab Mule Drivers. c, An Orange Seller. d, The Banks of the River. e, View of Tangier from the Seashore. f, Arab Horses Fighting in a Stable. g, Horses at the Trough. h, The Combat of the Giaour and Hassan.

No. 2084, 4d, vert: a, Moroccan from Tangier Standing. b, A Man of Tangier. c, Young Arab Standing with a Rifle. d, Moroccan Chieftain. e, Jewish Bride of Tangiers. f, Seated Jewess from Morocco. g, A seated Arab. h, Young Arab Seated by a Wall.

No. 2085, 4d: a, Turk Seated on a Sofa Smoking. b, View of Tangier from North African and Spanish Album. c, The Spanish Coast at Salobrena from North African and Spanish Album. d, The Aissaouas. e, Sea View from the Heights of Dieppe. f, An Arab Fantasy. g, Arab Comic Fantasy. h, An Arab Camp at Night.

Details: No. 2086, 25d, Self-portrait, vert. No. 2087, 25d, Two Women of Algiers in Their Apartment. No. 2088, 25d, Massacre of Chios.

1998, Oct. 29
Sheets of 8, #a-h
2083-2085 A327 Set of 3   19.50 19.50
Souvenir Sheets
2086-2088 A327 Set of 3   15.00 15.00

Christmas — A328

Designs: 1d, Beagle in sock. 2d, Giraffe, wreath. 3d, Rainbow bee eater, ribbon, ornament. 4d, Adult deer. 5d, Fawn. 10d, Irish red and white setter in package.

No. 2095, 25d, Brown classic tabby kitten. No. 2096, 25d, Basset hound, rough collie.

1998, Nov. 23
2089-2094 A328 Set of 6   5.00 5.00
Souvenir Sheets
2095-2096 A328 Set of 2   10.00 10.00

New Year 1999 (Year of the Rabbit) — A329

No. 2097 — Stylized rabbits, background color: a, Olive brown. b, Green blue. c, Red brown. d, Pale orange.

1999, Jan. 4   Litho.   Perf. 14½
2097 A329 3d Sheet of 4, #a.-d. 2.40 2.40
Souvenir Sheet
2098 A329 10d multicolored   2.00 2.00
No. 2098 contains one 39x24mm stamp.

Disney's Jungle Book A330

No. 2099: a, Mowgli, King Louie (bear). b, Mowgli, snake. c, Flunky Monkey. d, Monkey singing. e, Girl. f, Mowgli, Flunky Monkey. g, Mowgli, buzzards. h, Shere Khan (tiger).

No. 2100, 25d, Baby elephant, horiz. No. 2101, 25d, King Louie, horiz.

1999, Mar. 11   Litho.   Perf. 13½x14
2099 A330 5d Sheet of 8, #a.-
         h.   10.00 10.00
Souvenir Sheets
2100-2101 A330 Set of 2   10.00 10.00

Australia '99, World Stamp Expo A331

No. 2102, 6d — African butterflies: a, Golden piper. b, Citrus swallowtail. c, Azure hairstreak. d, Two-tailed pasha. e, Blue pansy. f, African leaf butterfly.

No. 2103, 6d: a, Plain tiger. b, Blue swallowtail. c, Papilio mnesheus. d, Common opal. e, Forest green. f, Boisduval's false acraea.

No. 2104, 25d, Pirate butterfly, vert. No. 2105, 25d, Two-tailed pasha.

1999, Apr. 12   Litho.   Perf. 14
Sheets of 6, #a-f
2102-2103 A331 Set of 2   13.00 13.00
Souvenir Sheets
2104-2105 A331 Set of 2   10.00 10.00

Wedding of Prince Edward and Sophie Rhys-Jones A332

No. 2106 — Various portraits of couple showing Sophie with: a, Blue collar. b, Long hair. c, Red collar.
25d, Couple, horiz.

1999, June 19   Litho.   Perf. 13½
2106 A332 10d Sheet of 3, #a.-c. 5.50 5.50
Souvenir Sheet
2107 A332 25d multicolored   5.00 5.00

IBRA '99, World Philatelic Exhibition, Nuremberg — A333

Exhibition emblem, Adler 2-3-2 steam engine and: 4d, Samoa #104d. 5d, Samoa #55.

Emblem, sailing ship Friedrech August and: 10d, Samoa #64, #65. 15d, Samoa #67.
25d, Cover with Samoa #67 (part), 68.

1999, July 6   Perf. 14x14¼
2108-2111 A333 Set of 4   6.75 6.75
Souvenir Sheet
2112 A333 25d multicolored   5.00 5.00
No. 2112 contains one 60x40mm stamp.

Apollo 11 Moon Landing, 30th Anniv. — A334

No. 2113: a, Bell X-14A VTOL aircraft. b, Lunar landing practice rig. c, Early prototype lander. d, Zero gravity training. e, Jet pack training. f, Lunar lander pilot training.

No. 2114, 25d, Apollo 11 Eagle, horiz. No. 2115, 25d, Apollo 11 splash down, horiz.

1999, July 6   Perf. 14
2113 A334 6d Sheet of 6, #a.-
         f.   6.50 6.50
Souvenir Sheets
2114-2115 A334 Set of 2   10.00 10.00

Souvenir Sheets

PhilexFrance '99, World Philatelic
Exhibition — A335

Early railroads: No. 2116, 25d, Road-railer
carriage. No. 2117, 25d, 2-2-2 Passenger
locomotive, 1846.

1999, July 6			Perf. 13¾	
2116-2117	A335	Set of 2	10.00	10.00

Roots Homecoming Festival — A336

Designs: 1d, Cannon, Freedom Post, Juf-
fureh. 2d, Fort Bullen, Barra. 3d, James Fort
Island.

1999, June 21	Litho.		Perf. 14	
2118-2120	A336	Set of 3	1.10	1.10

UN Rights of the Child, 10th
Anniv. — A337

No. 2121 — Children: a, With head down on
table.-b, Drinking from cup. c, Drawing on
paper.
25d, Child smiling under umbrella.

1999, July 6				
2121	A337	10d Sheet of 3, #a.-c.	5.75	5.75

Souvenir Sheet

2122	A337	25d multicolored	5.00	5.00

Johann Wolfgang von Goethe (1749-
1832), Poet — A338

No. 2123: a, Faust quaffs the spirit's nectar.
b, Portraits of Goethe and Friedrich von Schiller (1759-1805). c, Faust contemplates
mortality.
25d, Portrait of Goethe, vert.

1999, July 6				
2123	A338	15d Sheet of 3, #a.-c.	8.50	8.50

Souvenir Sheet

2124	A338	25d multicolored	5.00	5.00

Paintings by
Hokusai
(1760-1849)
A339

No. 2125, 5d — Details or entire paintings:
a, Bunshosei. b, Overthrower of Castles,
Overthrower of Nations. c, Bee on Wild Rose.
d, Sei Shonagon. e, Kuan-Yu. f, The Fifth
Month.
No. 2126, 5d: a, Exotic Beauty. b, Wind (2
people). c, Dancing Monkey. d, Lady and
Maiden on an Outing. e, Wind (3 people). f,
Courtesan with Fan.
No. 2127, 25d, People on the Balcony of
Sazaido. No. 2128, 25d, Caocao before the
Battle of Chibi.

1999, July 6			Perf. 13¾	
Sheets of 6, #a-f				
2125-2126	A339	Set of 2	12.00	12.00
Souvenir Sheets				
2127-2128	A339	Set of 2	10.00	10.00

Sea Birds
A340

Designs: 2d, American oystercatcher. 3d,
Blue-footed booby. 10d, Western gull. 15d,
Brown pelican.
No. 2133, 4d: a, Atlantic puffin. b, Red-tailed
tropicbird. c, Reddish egret. d, Laughing gull.
e, Great white egret. f, Northern gannet. g,
Forster's tern. h, Great cormorant. i, Razor bill.
No. 2134, 4d: a, Adélie penguin. b, Black
skimmer. c, Erect-crested penguin. d, Heer-
man's gull. e, Glaucous-winged gull. f, Layson
albatross. g, White pelican. h, Tufted puffin. i,
Black guillemot.
No. 2135: a, Razor bill. b, Shelduck. c,
Sandwich tern. d, Arctic skua. e, Gannet. f,
Common gull.
No. 2136, 25d, Pelicans. No. 2137, 25d,
California gull. No. 2138, 25d, Gentoo
penguin.

1999, Aug. 1			Perf. 14	
2129-2132	A340	Set of 4	5.50	5.50
Sheets of 9, #a-i				
2133-2134	A340	Set of 2	14.50	14.50
2135	A340	5d Sheet of 6, #a.-f.	9.75	9.75
Souvenir Sheets				
2136-2138	A340	Set of 3	15.00	15.00

Nos. 2135-2138 have continuous designs.

Prehistoric Amimals — A341

No. 2139, 3d: a, Diatryma. b, Pteranodon. c,
Stegodon. d, Icaronycteris. e, Archaeopteryx.
f, Chasmatosaurus. g, Tytthostonyx. h, Hyae-
nodon. i, Uintatherium. j, Hesperocyon. k,
Ambelodon. l, Indricotherium.
No. 2140, 3d: a, Carnotaurus. b,
Quetzalcoatlus. c, Peteinosaurus. d, Pre-
nocephale. e, Hesperornis. f, Coelophysis. g,
Camptosaurus. h, Panderichthys. i,
Garudimimus. j, Cacops. k, Ichthyostega. l,
Scutellosaurus.
No. 2141, 25d, Lepisosteus. No. 2142, 25d,
Sabertooth cat. No. 2143, 25d, Deinonychus.
No. 2144, 25d, Microceratops.

1999, Aug. 1				
Sheets of 12, #a-l				
2139-2140	A341	Set of 2	13.00	13.00
Souvenir Sheets				
2141-2144	A341	Set of 4	20.00	20.00

Queen Mother,
100th Birthday (in
2000) — A342

No. 2145: a, Duchess of York, Princess Elizabeth, 1928. b, Lady Elizabeth Bowles-Lyon,
1923. c, Queen Elizabeth, 1946. d, Queen
Mother, Prince Harry.
25d, Queen Mother celebrating 89th birthday, 1989.

1999, Aug. 4				
2145	A342	10d Sheet of 4, #a.-d. + label	7.25	7.25
Souvenir Sheet				
Perf. 13¾				
2146	A342	25d multicolored	5.00	5.00

No. 2146 contains one 38x51mm stamp.
Margins of sheets are embossed.
See Nos. 2555-2556.

Orchids — A343

Designs: 2d, Sophrocattleya. 3d, Cattleya.
4d, Brassolaeliocattleya. 5d, Brassoepiden-
drum. 10d, Sophrolaeliocattleya. 15d,
Iwanagaara.
No. 2153, 6d: a, Brassolaeliocattleya (yellow). b, Cattleytonia. c, Laeliocattleya (yellow).
d, Miltonia. e, Cattleya forbesii. f, Odontoglossum cervantesii.
No. 2154, 6d: a, Lycaste macrobulbon. b,
Laeliocattleya (red). c, Brassocattleya (pink).
d, Cattleya, diff. e, Brassocattleya (speckled).
f, Brassolaeliocattleya (yellow & red).
No. 2155, 25d, Unnamed. No. 2156, 25d,
Brassolaeliocattleya (white & red).

1999, Aug. 1	Litho.		Perf. 14	
2147-2152	A343	Set of 6	7.25	7.25
Sheets of 6, #a-f				
2153-2154	A343	Set of 2	14.00	14.00
Souvenir Sheets				
2155-2156	A343	Set of 2	10.00	10.00

Marine
Fauna
A344

Designs: 1d, Sea gull. 1.50d, Portuguese
man-of-war. 5d, Walrus. 10d, Manatee.
No. 2161, 3d: a, Anglefish. b, Leafy sea
dragon. c, Hawksbill turtle. d, Mandarin fish. e,
Candy cane sea star. f, Plate coral. g, Butter-
lyfish. h, Coral polyp. i, Hermit crab. j, Strawberry shrimp. k, Giant blue clam. l, Sea
cucumber.
No. 2162, 3d: a, Whale shark. b, Gray reef
shark. c, New ZEngland octopus. d, Puffer
fish. e, Lionfish. f, Squid. g, Chambered nautilus. h, Clown fish. i, Moray eel. j, Spiny lobster.
k, Sotted ray. l, Clown anemone.
25d, Common dolphin.

1999, Aug. 1				
2157-2160	A344	Set of 4	3.50	3.50
Sheets of 12, #a-l				
2161-2162	A344	Set of 2	13.00	13.00
2163	A343	25d multicolored	5.00	5.00

Galapagos Islands Marine
Fauna — A345

No. 2164: a, Swallow-tailed gull. b, Frigate
bird. c, Red-footed booby. d, Galapagos hawk.
e, Great blue heron. f, Masked booby. g, Bottlenose dolphins. h, Black grunts. i, Surgeonfish. j, Stingray. k, Pilot whales. l, Pacific
green sea turtle. m, Shark. n, Sea lion. o,
Marine iguana. p, Pacific manta ray. q, Moorish idol. r, Galapagos penguin. s, Silver grunts.
t, Sea urchin. u, Wrasse. v, Almaco
amberjack. w, Blue-chin parrotfish. x, Yellow
sea urchin. y, Lobster. z, Grouper. aa, Scorpionfish. ab, Squirrelfish. ac, Octopus. ad,
King angelfish. ae, Horned shark. af,
Galapagos hogfish. ag, Puffer fish. ah, Moray
eel. ai, Orange tube corals. aj, Whitestripe
chromis. ak, Longnose hawkfish. al, Sea
cucumber. am, Spotted hawkfish. an, Zebra
moray eel.
25d, Emperor penguins.

1999, Aug. 1				
2164	A345	1.50d Sheet of 40, #a.-an.	14.00	14.00
Souvenir Sheet				
2165	A345	25d multicolored	5.00	5.00

Souvenir Sheet

1999 Return of Macao to People's
Republic of China — A346

No. 2166: a, Temple of A-ma. b, Border
gate. c, Ruins of St. Paul's Cathedral.

1999, Aug. 20	Litho.		Perf. 14	
2166	A346	7d Sheet of 3, #a-c	4.00	4.00

Space Exploration
A347

Designs: 1d, Telstar I, horiz. 1.50d, Skylab.
2d, Mars 3 orbiter and lander. 3d, COBE. 10d,
Astronaut Bruce McCandless. 15d, Apollo 13.
No. 2173, 6d: a, German V-2 rocket. b,
Delta Straight 8. c, Ariane 4. d, Mercury on
Atlas rocket. e, Saturn 1B. f, Cassini.
No. 2174, 6d, horiz.: a, Mariner 4. b, Viking
Mars orbiter and lander. c, Giotto. d, Luna 9. e,
Voyager. f, Galileo.
No. 2175, 6d, horiz.: a, Soviet Vostok 1. b,
Apollo command and service modules. c,
Mecury capsule. d, Apollo 16 lunar module. e,
Gemini 8. f, Soviet Soyuz.
No. 2176, 25d, Apollo-Soyuz, horiz. No.
2177, 25d, Mars Pathfinder, horiz.

1999				
2167-2172	A347	Set of 6	6.25	6.25
Sheets of 6, #a-f				
2173-2175	A347	Set of 3	19.50	19.50
2176-2177	A347	Set of 2	10.00	10.00

#2176-2177 contain one 57x43mm stamp.

John F. Kennedy, Jr. (1960-99) A348

No. 2178: a, In 1961. b, In 1970s. c, In 1997.

1999, Dec. 7
2178 A348 15d Sheet of 3, #a.-c. 7.75 7.75

Flowers — A349

Various flower photographs making up a photomosaic of Princess Diana.

1999, Dec. 31   Litho.   Perf. 13¾
2179 A349 3d Sheet of 8, #a.-h.   5.00 5.00
See No. 2290.

Millennium A350

No. 2180, 3d — Highlights of 1450-1500: a, Da Vinci designs 1st flying machine. b, Gutenberg prints the Bible. c, 1st book in color printed. d, Ivan III becomes Grand Prince of Moscow. e, Ottomans capture Constantinople. f, Ming emperors rebuild Great Wall of China. g, Lorenzo de Medici begins rule in Florence. h, Henry VII becomes first Tudor king of England. i, Vasco da Gama sails to India. j, Aragon and Castile unite. k, Birth of Desiderius Erasmus. l, Cabot explores No. America. m, Henry VI wages War of the Roses. n, Bartholomeu Dias discovers Cape of Good Hope. o, Matthias Corvinus (Hunyadi) becomes king of Hungary. p, Columbus sails to America (60x40mm). q, Girolamo Savonarola burned at stake.
No. 2181, 3d — Highlights of 1900-1910: a, Max Planck develops quantum theory. b, Graf Ferdinand von Zeppelin constructs first airship. c, Marconi sends 1st transatlantic message. d, Queen Victoria dies. e, 1st Nobel Prize. f, Boer War ends. g, Wright Brothers' 1st flight. h, 1st teddy bears made in Germany. i, Work begins on Panama Canal. j, Einstein develops theory of relativity. k, 1905 revolution in Russia. l, San Francisco earthquake. m, Color photography developed by Louis Lumière. n, Picasso paints "Les Demoiselles d'Avignon." o, Peary reaches North Pole. p, Model T appears (60x40mm). q, 1st kibbutz founded in Holy Land.

2000, Feb. 1   Perf. 12¾x12½
Sheets of 17, #a-q
2180-2181 A350   Set of 2   23.00 23.00
Inscriptions are misspelled on several stamps on No. 2181.

New Year 2000 (Year of the Dragon) A351

No. 2182 — Various dragons and Chinese characters with background colors: a, Blue

green. b, Brownish gray. c, Red orange (purple dragon). d, Orange.
15d, Dull orange.

2000, Feb. 5   Perf. 14x14½
2182 A351 5d Sheet of 4, #a.-d. 4.25 4.25
Souvenir Sheet
Perf. 14
2183 A351 15d multi   3.00 3.00
No. 2183 contains one 42x28mm stamp.

African Wildlife A352

Designs: 50b, Indri. 75b, Nubian ibex. 1d, Grevy's zebra, vert. 2d, Bongo, vert. 3d, White rhinoceros. 4d, Lesser galago. 5d, Okapi, vert. 10d, Mhorr gazelle, vert.
No. 2192, 5d: a, Giant sable antelope. b, Greater kudu. c, Somali wild ass. d, Dorcas gazelle. e, Addax. f, Pelzeln's gazelle.
No. 2193, 6d: a, Cheetah. b, Chimpanzee. c, Angwantibo. d, Black rhinoceros. e, Bontebok. f, Giant eland.
No. 2194, 7d: a, Mountain gorilla. b, Black-faced impala. c, Crowned lemur. d, Long-tailed ground roller. e, Brown hyena. f, Mountain zebra.
No. 2195, 7d: a, Sacred ibis. b, Mauritius kestrel. c, Barbary leopard. d, Radiated tortoise. e, Pygmy hippopotamus. f, Bald ibis.
No. 2196, 25d, Aye-aye. No. 2197, 25d, Black lechwe, vert. No. 2198, 25d, Nile crocodile. No. 2199, 25d, African elephant.

2000, Feb. 18   Perf. 14
2184-2191 A352   4.50 4.50
Sheets of 6, #a.-f.
2192-2195 A352   Set of 4   29.00 29.00
Souvenir Sheets
2196-2199 A352   Set of 4   23.00 23.00
AmeriStamp Expo, Portland, Ore. (#2194).

The Three Stooges — A353

No. 2200: a, Curly pulling Moe's hair. b, Curly caught in wringer. c, Curly, Moe with drill. d, Moe pulling Larry's hair. e, Moe. f, Moe sticking finger in Curly's nose. g, Stooges pointing. h, Skull biting Curly's nose. i, Shemp.
No. 2201, 25d, Larry with crown. No. 2202, 25d, Curly on telephone, vert.

2000, Jan. 14   Litho.   Perf. 13¼
2200 A353 5d Sheet of 9, #a.-
    i.   11.50 11.50
Souvenir Sheets
2201-2202   Set of 2   10.50 10.50
See Nos. 2446-2448.

I Love Lucy — A354

No. 2203: a, Lucy on sofa. b, Lucy, Ricky. c, Fred, Lucy, and Ethel. d, Lucy standing. e, Lucy, Ricky embracing. f, Lucy looking in mirror. g, Lucy with fists clenched. h, Lucy, Ricky on sofa. i, Lucy and Ethel.
No. 2204, 25d, Lucy, Ricky embracing, vert. No. 2205, 25d, Lucy looking in mirror, vert.

2000, Jan. 14   Litho.   Perf. 13¼
2203 A354 5d Sheet of 9, #a.-
    i.   11.50 11.50
Souvenir Sheets
2204-2205 A354   Set of 2   10.50 10.50
See Nos. 2440-2442, 2449-2451.

Betty Boop A355

No. 2206: a, In green and yellow outfit. b, In red dress. c, In red shirt and blue jeans. d, In green and brown outfit. e, Seated in chair. f, In orange shirt and blue jeans. g, In fur coat. h, In pink dress. i, With dumbbell and water bottle.
No. 2207, 25d, In yellow flowered dress. No. 2208, 25d, In bathtub.

2000, Jan. 14   Litho.   Perf. 13¼
2206 A355 5d Sheet of 9, #a.-
    i.   11.50 11.50
Souvenir Sheets
2207-2208 A355   Set of 2   10.50 10.50

Paintings of Anthony Van Dyck — A356

No. 2209: a, Samson and Delilah, c. 1619-20. b, Samson and Delilah sketch, 1618-20. c, Samson and Delilah, c. 1628-30.
No. 2210, 5d: a, The Adoration of the Shepherds. b, The Rest on the Flight to Egypt, The Virgin of the Partridges. c, Suffer the Little Children to Come Unto Me. d, Christ and the Moneychangers. e, Feast at the House of Simon the Pharisee. f, The Lamentation Over the Dead Christ.
No. 2211, 5d, vert.: a, Anton Giulo Brignole-Sale. b, Paolina Adorno Brignole-Sale. c, Battina Balbi Durazzo. d, Portrait of a Man of the Cattaneo Family. e, Portrait of a Woman. f, Elena Grimaldi Cattaneo.
No. 2212, 5d, vert.: a, A Genoese Senator. b, A Seated Gentlewoman. c, The Senator's Wife. d, A Genoese Lady, The Marchesa Balbi. e, Polyxena Spinola, Marchesa de Legones. f, Agostino Pallavicini.
No. 2213, 5d, vert.: a, Prince Rupert of the Palatinate. b, William II of Nassau and Orange. c, Prince Charles Louis of the Palatinate. d, Prince Rupert, Count Palatine. e, The Princess Mary. f, Prince Charles Louis, Count Palatine.
No. 2214, 5d, vert.: a, Sir George Villiers and Lady Katherine Manners as Adonis and Venus. b, Lady Mary Villiers with Lord Arran. c, Rachel de Ruvigny, Countess Southampton as Fortune. d, Venus at Forge of Vulcan. e, Daedalus and Icarus. f, The Clipping of Cupid's Wing.
No. 2215, 25d, A Man with His Son. No. 2216, 25d, Prince Charles Louis, Elector Palatine and His Brother, Prince Rupert of the Palatinate, vert. No. 2217, 25d, Venetia, Lady Digby, as Prudence, vert. No. 2218, 25d, Drunken Silenus, vert. No. 2219, 25d, Portrait of a Genoese Lady, vert. No. 2220, 25d, Charles II as Prince of Wales, vert. No. 2221, 25d, William II, Prince of Orange, and His Bride, Mary, Princess Royal of England, vert. No. 2222, 25d, The Three Eldest Children of Charles I, vert.

2000, May 1   Perf. 13¾
2209 A356 5d Sheet of 3, #a.-
    c.   3.00 3.00
Sheets of 6, #a.-f.
2210-2214 A356   Set of 5   30.00 30.00
Souvenir Sheets
2215-2222 A356   Set of 8   47.50 47.50

Papal Visits — A357

No. 2223, 6d — 1991-92 Visits: a, Portugal. b, Poland. c, Hungary. d, Brazil. e, Senegal. f, Gambia. g, Guinea. h, Angola. i, Sao Tomé. j, Dominican Republic.
No. 2224, 6d — 1993 Visits: a, Benin. b, Uganda. c, Sudan. d, Albania. e, Spain. f, Jamaica. g, Mexico. h, United States. i, Lithuania. j, Latvia.
No. 2225, 6d — 1993-95 Visits: a, Estonia. b, Croatia. c, Philippines. d, Papua New Guinea. e, Australia. f, Sri Lanka. g, Czech Republic. h, Belgium. i, Slovakia. j, Cameroon.
No. 2226, 6d — 1995-96 Visits: a, South Africa. b, Kenya. c, United States. d, United Nations. e, Guatemala. f, Nicaragua. g, El Salvador. h, Venezuela. i, Tunisia. j, Slovenia.
No. 2227, 6d — 1996-98 Visits: a, Germany. b, Hungary. c, France, 1996. d, Bosnia. e, Czech Republic. f, Lebanon. g, Poland. h, France, 1997. i, Brazil. j, Cuba.
No. 2228, 6d — 1998-99 Visits: a, Nigeria. b, Austria. c, Croatia. d, Mexico. e, United States. f, Romania. g, Poland. h, Slovenia. i, India. j, Georgia.
No. 2229, 25d, Pope rekindles Eternal Flame. No. 2230, 25d, Pope blesses Holy Land. No. 2231, 25d, Pope places prayer on Western Wall. No. 2232, 25d, Pope assisted by Israeli president and prime minister. No. 2233, 25d, Pope prays at Western Wall. No. 2234, 25d, Pope receives Bible from chief rabbis. No. 2235, 25d, Pope touches bowl of soil. No. 2236, 25d, Pope at Yad Vashem, horiz.

2000, May 15   Litho.   Perf. 13¾
Sheets of 10, #a.-j, + 2 labels
2223-2228 A357   Set of 6   63.00 63.00
Souvenir Sheets
Perf. 14½x14¾, 14¾x14½ (#2236)
2229-2236 A357   Set of 8   36.00 36.00
Stamps from Nos. 2223-2228 are 28x47mm.

Mushrooms A358

Designs: 4d, Morel. 5d, Chanterelle. 15d, Knight cap. 20d, Spindle.
No. 2241, 7d: a, Yellow parasol. b, Mottlegill. c, Poplar field cap. d, Caesar's. e, Flame shield-cap. f, Lilac bonnet.
No. 2242, 7d: a, Common puffball. b, Earth star. c, Silky volvar. d, Stump puffball. e, Spindle-stemmed bolete. f, Fox-orange cort.
No. 2243, 25d, Red-stemmed tough shank. No. 2244, 25d, St. George's.

2000, May 15   Perf. 14
2237-2240 A358   Set of 4   7.75 7.75
Sheets of 6, #a.-f.
2241-2242 A358   Set of 2   15.00 15.00
Souvenir Sheets
2243-2244 A358   Set of 2   9.00 9.00

First Zeppelin Flight, Cent. — A359

No. 2245: a, LZ-10. b. LZ-127. c, LZ-129.
25d, LZ-130.

2000, May 1   Litho.   Perf. 14
2245 A359 15d Sheet of 3, #a-c   7.75 7.75
Souvenir Sheet
2246 A359 25d multi   4.50 4.50
No. 2246 contains one 50x38mm stamp.

Prince William, 18th Birthday — A360

No. 2247: a, As child. b, In sweater. c, In
suit, with flowers. d, In suit.
25d, With Prince Harry.

2000, May 1   Perf. 14
2247 A360 7d Sheet of 4, #a-d   5.00 5.00
Souvenir Sheet
Perf. 13¾
2248 A360 25d multi   4.50 4.50
No. 2248 contains one 38x50mm stamp.

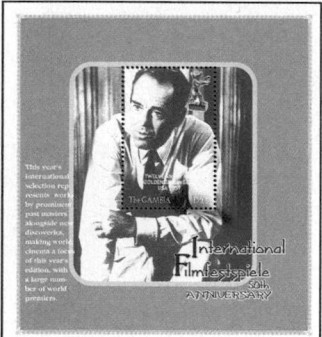

Berlin Film Festival, 50th
Anniv. — A361

No. 2249: a, Pane. Amore e Fantasia. b,
Richard III. c, Smultronstället (Wild Strawberries). d, The Defiant Ones. e, The Living
Desert. f, A Bout de Souffle.
25d, Twelve Angry Men.

2000, May 1   Perf. 14
2249 A361 7d Sheet of 6, #a-f   7.25 7.25
Souvenir Sheet
2250 A361 25d multi   4.50 4.50

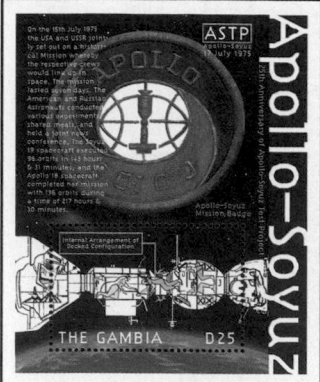

Apollo-Soyuz Mission, 25th
Anniv. — A362

No. 2251: a, Donald K. Slayton. b, Thomas
P. Stafford. c, Vance D. Brand.
25d, Diagram of docked spacecraft.

2000, May 1
2251 A362 15d Sheet of 3, #a-c   7.75 7.75
Souvenir Sheet
2252 A362 25d multi   4.50 4.50

Souvenir Sheet

2000 Summer Olympics,
Sydney — A363

No. 2253: a, Paavo Nurmi. b, Basketball. c,
Panathenian Stadium, Athens and Greek flag.
d, Ancient Greek chariot racing.

2000, May 1
2253 A363 6d Sheet of 4, #a-d   4.25 4.25

Public Railways, 175th Anniv. — A364

No. 2254: a, Locomotion No. 1, George Stephenson. b, Chesapeake.

2000, May 1
2254 A364 15d Sheet of 2, #a-b   5.25 5.25

Souvenir Sheet

Johann Sebastian Bach (1685-
1750) — A365

2000, May 1
2255 A365 25d multi   4.50 4.50

Popes — A366

No. 2256, 7d: a, Pope Felix IV, 526-30. b,
Gelasius I, 492-96. c, Gregory I, 590-604. d,
Gregory IX, 1227-41. e, Gregory XII, 1406-15.
f, Honorius III, 1216-27.
No. 2257, 7d: a, Gregory XIII, 1572-85. b,
Urban II, 1088-99. c, Sixtus I, 115-125. d, Pius
IX, 1846-78. e, Pius IV, 1559-65. f, Paschal I,
817-24.
No. 2258, 7d: a, Alexander VII, 1655-67. b,
Benedict XI, 1303-04. c, Calixtus III, 1455-58.
d, Celestine V, 1294. e, Clement IX, 1667-69.
f, Fabian, 236-50.
No. 2259, 25d, Peter, 33-64. No. 2260, 25d,
Damasus I, 366-384. No. 2261, 25d, John I,
523-526.

2000, July 26   Litho.   Perf. 13¾
Sheets of 6, #a-f
2256-2258 A366 Set of 3   21.00 21.00
Souvenir Sheets
2259-2261 A366 Set of 3   13.00 13.00

Butterflies — A367

Designs: 1.50d, Amphicalia tigris. 2d,
Myrina silenus. 3d, Chrysiridia madagas-
carensis. 5d, Papilionidae. 10d, Dasiothia
medea.

2000, Aug. 7   Perf. 14¾x14
2262 A367 1.50d multi   .20   .20
2263 A367 2d multi   .35   .35
2264 A367 3d multi   .50   .50
2265 A367 5d multi   .80   .80
2266 A367 10d multi   1.60 1.60
    Nos. 2262-2266 (5)   3.45 3.45
Nos. 2264-2266 exist dated 2003.
See Nos. 2436-2439, 2452-2452B, 2699.

Souvenir Sheet

Albert Einstein (1879-1955) — A368

2000, May 1   Litho.   Perf. 14¼
2267 A368 25d multi   4.00 4.00

Space — A369

No. 2268, 7d: a, Uhuru. b, Rosat. c, I.U.E. d,
Astro E. e, Exosat. f, Chandra.
No. 2269, 7d, vert.: a, Helios. b, Solar Max.
c, SOHO. d, O.S.O. e, Special rocket launch. f,
I.M.P.
No. 2270, 25d, XMM. No. 2271, 25d, Cas-
sini Huygens.

2000, May 1   Perf. 14
Sheets of 6, #a-f
2268-2269 A369 Set of 2   12.50 12.50
Souvenir Sheets
2270-2271 A369 Set of 2   7.50   7.50
The Stamp Show 2000, London; World
Stamp Expo 2000, Anaheim.

Monarchs — A370

No. 2272: a, Charles I of Great Britain,
1625-49. b, Clovis III, king of the Franks (691-
95).
No. 2273, 7d: a, Charles II of France, 885-
887. b, Catherine de Medici of France, 1547-
59. c, Boris Godunov of Russia, 1598-1605. d,
Basil III of Russia, 1505-33. e, Anne of Great
Britain, 1702-14. f, Charles IX of France,
1560-74.
No. 2274, 7d: a, James IV of Scotland,
1488-1513. b, James V of Scotland, 1513-42.
c, James VI of Scotland, 1567-1625. d, Mary
of Scotland, 1542-67. e, Mary of Great Britain,
1689-94. f, Elizabeth II, of Great Britain, 1952-
present.
No. 2275, 25d, James Francis Edward Stuart. No. 2276, 25d, James IV of Scotland. No.
2277, 25d, Bahadur Shah of India, 1837-57.
Illustration reduced.

2000, July 26   Perf. 13¾
2272 A370 7d Sheet of 2, #a-b   2.10 2.10
Sheets of 6, #a-f
2273-2274 A370 Set of 2   12.50 12.50
Souvenir Sheets
2275-2277 A370 Set of 3   11.00 11.00

Puppies — A371

Designs: 1d, West Highland terrier. 1.50d, Bernese mountain dog. 3d, Yorkshire terrier. 4d, West Highland terrrier, diff. 10d, Chow chow. 15d, Poodle.

No. 2284: a, Border collie (brown and white). b, Border collie (black, brown and white). c, Yorkshire terrier. d, German shepherd. e, Beagle. f, Spaniel.

2000, Aug. 7   *Perf. 14¼*
2278-2283 A371 Set of 6   5.25 5.25
2284 A371 7d Sheet of 6, #a-f   6.25 6.25

Souvenir Sheet
2285 A371 25d Boxer   3.50 3.50

The Stamp Show 2000, London (Nos. 2284-2285).

Cats — A372

No. 2286, 4d: a, Egyptian mau. b, Singapura. c, American shorthair. d, Cornish rex. e, Birman. f, Scottish fold. g, Turkish angora. h, Turkish van.

No. 2287, 5d: a, Ragdoll. b, Bombay. c, Korat. d, Somali. e, British shorthair. f, American curl. g, Maine coon cat. h, Like No. 2286h.

No. 2288, 25d, Cat and kitten. No. 2289, 25d, Cat.

2000, Aug. 7
Sheets of 8, #a-h
2286-2287 A372 Set of 2   10.50 10.50

Souvenir Sheets
2288-2289 A372 Set of 2   7.50 7.50

The Stamp Show 2000, London.

Flower Photomosaic Type of 1999 and

Queen Mother, 100th Birthday — A373

Designs: No. 2090, Various flower photographs making up a photomosaic of the Queen Mother. No. 2290I: Various photos of religious scenes making up a photomosaic of Pope John Paul II.

2000, Aug. 7   **Litho.**   *Perf. 13¾*
2290 A349 5d Sheet of 8, #a-h   6.00 6.00
2290I A349 6d Sheet of 8, #j-q   7.50 7.50

Litho. & Embossed
Without Gum
Die Cut 9x8¾

2291 A373 85d multi

Issued: Nos. 2290, 2291 8/7. No. 2290I, 8/8.

European Soccer
Championships — A374

No. 2292, horiz. — Czech Republic: a, Nedved. b, Team photo. c, Maier. d, Antonin Panenka. e, Selessin Stadium, Liege. f, Patrik Berger.

No. 2293, horiz. — England: a, Alan Shearer. b, Team photo. c, David Seaman. d, Sol Campbell. e, Philips Stadium, Eindhoven. f, Southgate.

No. 2294, horiz. — Norway: a, Leonardsen. b, Team photo. c, Mykland. d, Solbakken. e, Rekdal.

No. 2295, horiz. — Slovenia: a, Aleksander Knavs. b, Team photo. c, Zlatko Zahovic. d, Ales Ceh. e, Stade Communal, Charleroi. f, Miran Pavlin.

No. 2296, horiz. — Sweden: a, Ljungberg. b, Team photo. c, Andersson. d, Nilsson. e, Schwarz.

No. 2297, horiz. — Turkey: a, Yalcin. b, Team photo. c, Buruk. d, Erdem. e, King Baudouin Stadium, f, Korkut.

No. 2298, 25d, Czech Republic coach, Jozef Chovanec. No. 2299, 25d, England coach Kevin Keegan. No. 2300, 25d, Norway coach Nils-Johan Semb. No. 2301, 25d, Slovenia coach Srecko Katanec. No. 2302, 25d, Sweden coaches, Söderberg and Lagerbäck. No. 2303, 25d, Turkey coach Mustafa Denizli. Illustration reduced.

2000, Aug. 7   **Litho.**   *Perf. 13¾*
2292 A374 7d Sheet of 6, #a-f   6.25 6.25
2293 A374 7d Sheet of 6, #a-f   6.25 6.25
2294 A374 7d Sheet of 6, #a-
     e, 2292e   6.25 6.25
2295 A374 7d Sheet of 6, #a-f   6.25 6.25
2296 A374 7d Sheet of 6, #a-
     e, 2293e   6.25 6.25
2297 A374 7d Sheet of 6, #a-f   6.25 6.25
   Nos. 2292-2297 (6)   37.50 37.50

Souvenir Sheets
2298-2303 A374 Set of 6   22.50 22.50

Paintings of
Birds — A375

Designs: 1.50d, A White Pheasant and Other Fowl in a Classical Landscape, by Abraham Bisschop. 3d, Salmon-crested Cockatoo, by Bartolomeo Bimbi. 4d, A Great Bustard Cock and Other Birds, by Ludger Tom Ring. 15d, A Great Black-backed Gull and Other Birds, by Jokob Bogdani.

No. 2308, 5d: a, Peacocks, Hens and Mouse, by Tobias Stranover. b, Lady in a Red Jacket Feeding a Parrot, by Frans van Mieris. c, Birds by a Pool, by Melchior de Hondecoeter. d, Ganymede and the Eagle, by Peter Paul Rubens. e, Leda and the Swan, by Cesare de Sesto. f, Ducks and Ducklings at the Foot of a Tree in a Mediterranean Landscape, by Adriaen van Oolen. g, Portrait of the Falconer Robert Cheseman Carrying a Hooded Falcon, by Hans Holbein. h, A Golden Pheasant on a Stone Plinth, with Other Birds, by Jacobus Vonck.

No. 2309, 5d, horiz.: a, Still Life of Birds, by Caravaggio (hanging dead birds, basket). b, Turkeys with Young and Rock Doves, by Johan Wenzel Peter. c, The Threatened Swan, by Jan Asselyn. d, Still Life of Fruit and Birds in a Landscape, by Jakab Bogdany. e, Mobbing the Owl, by Tobias Stranover (owl at right, other birds). f, A Concert of Birds, by Hondecoeter (owl, cockatoo at center). g, Owls and Young Ones, by William Tomkins. h, Birds by a Stream, by Jean Baptiste Oudry.

No. 2310, 25d, The King Eagle Pursued to the Sun, by Philip Reinagle. No. 2311, 25d, Still Life of Birds, by Georg Flegl, horiz.

2000, Oct. 2   *Perf. 13½*
2304-2307 A375 Set of 4   3.50 3.50

Sheets of 8, #a-h
2308-2309 A375 Set of 2   12.00 12.00
Souvenir Sheets
2310-2311 A375 Set of 2   7.50 7.50

Descriptions of paintings are in margins on Nos. 2308-2311.

Paintings from the Prado — A376

No. 2312, 6d: a, The Madonna of the Fish, by Raphael. b, The Holy Family with a Lamb, by Raphael. c, The Madonna of the Stair, by Andrea del Sarto. d, Moneychanger from The Moneychanger and his Wife, by Marinus van Reymerswaele. e, Madonna and Child by Jan Gossaert. f, Wife from The Moneychanger and his Wife.

No. 2313, 6d: a, Bearded man from St. Benedict's Supper, by Juan Andres Ricci. b, Our Lady of the Immaculate Conception, by Francisco de Zurbarán. c, Monk with candle from St. Benedict's Supper. d, The Penitent Magdalen, by José de Ribera. e, Christ as Man of Sorrows, by Antonion de Pereda. f, St. Jerome, by Pereda.

No. 2314, 6d: a, Children with a Shell, by Bartolomé Esteban Murillo. b, Our Lady of the Immaculate Conception, by Murillo. c, The Good Shepherd, by Murillo. d, Woman with red headdress from The Parasol, by Francisco de Goya. e, A Rural Gift, by Ramon Bayeu. f, Woman with blue headdress from The Parasol.

No. 2315, 6d: a, Queen Isabella Farnese, by Jean Ranc. b, Young Woman Seen from the Back, by Jean-Baptiste Greuze. c, Charles III as a Child, by Ranc. d, James Bourdieu, by Sir Joshua Reynolds. e, Dr. Isaac Henrique Sequeira, by Thomas Gainsbourough. f, Portrait of a Clergyman, by Reynolds.

No. 2316, 6d: a, Portrait of a Young Woman, by Zacarias González Velázquez. b, The Painter Francisco de Goya, by Vicente Lopez Portaña. c, Portrait of a Girl, by Rafael Tejeo Diaz. d, Mary, from The Nativity, by Federico Barocci. e, Madonna and Child with St. John, by Correggio. f, Jesus, from The Nativity.

No. 2317, 6d: a, St. Andrew, by Francisco Rizi. b, Christ Crucified, by Diego Velázquez. c, St. Onuphrius, by Francisco Collantes. d, Charles II, by Juan Carreño de Miranda. e, St. Sebastian, by Carreño de Miranda. f, Peter Ivanovich Potemkin, by Carreño de Miranda.

No. 2318, 25d, The Defense of Cádiz Against the English, by Zurbarán. No. 2319, 25d, The Surrender of Juliers, by Jusepe Leonardo. No. 2320, 25d, The Holy Family with a Bird, by Murillo. No. 2321, 25d, Danäe, by Titian, horiz. No. 2322, 25d, Venus and Adonis, by Paolo Veronese, horiz. No. 2323, 25d, Jacob's Dream, by Ribera.

2000, Oct. 6   *Perf. 12x12¼, 12¼x12*
Sheets of 6, #a-f
2312-2317 A376 Set of 6   32.50 32.50
Souvenir Sheets
2318-2323 A376 Set of 6   22.50 22.50

Espana 2000, Intl. Philatelic Exhibition.

Battle of Britain, 60th Anniv. — A377

No. 2324, 5d, horiz.: a, Hurricane downing German BF109. b, Spitfire over River Thames. c, Flight Lt. Denys E. Gilliam attacking German Dornier 217 planes. d, Hurricanes heading to intercept Luftwaffe bombers. e, Hurricanes returning to Croydon. f, G.A. Langley in combat with BF109. g, Bristol Blenheim IV

over English Channel. h, Spitfires taking off from Hornchurch.

No. 2325, 5d, horiz.: a, Plane from 29th Blenheim Squadron heading to Norwegian coast. b, Luftwaffe pilot Helmut Wick downs RAF pilot John Cock. c, Spitfire downs Dornier 217 off Dover. d, Bristol Beaufighter IIF on patrol. e, Bolton-Paul Defiants intercept Luftwaffe bombers. f, Spitfire in dogfite with German Stuka JU-87 divebomber. g, Spitfire and Hurricane fly over London and River Thames. h, Gloster Gladiator.

No. 2326, 25d, Group Captain Frank Carey. No. 2327, 25d, German Commander Adolf Joseph Ferdinand Galland.

2000, Oct. 16   *Perf. 14*
Sheets of 8, #a-h
2324-2325 A377 Set of 2   12.00 12.00
Souvenir Sheets
2326-2327 A377 Set of 2   7.50 7.50

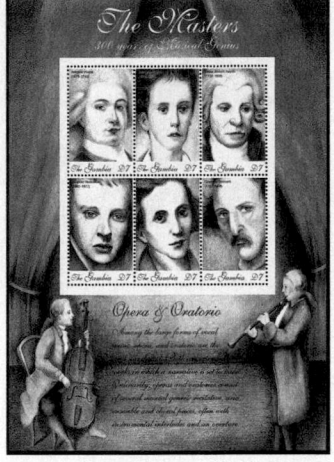

Composers — A378

No. 2328, 7d: a, Antonio Vivaldi. b, Giacomo Puccini. c, Franz Joseph Haydn. d, Leopold Stokowski. e, Felix Mendelssohn. f, Gaetano Donizetti.

No. 2329, 7d: a, Witold Lutoslawski. b, William Sterndale Bennett. c, Wolfgang Amadeus Mozart. d, Ludwig van Beethoven. e, Sergei Rachmaninoff. f, Peter Ilich Tchaikovsky.

No. 2330, 7d: a, Manuel de Falla. No. 2331, 25d, Fréderic Chopin.

2000, Oct. 2   **Litho.**   *Perf. 13¾x13¼*
Sheets of 6, #a-f
2328-2329 A378 Set of 2   12.50 12.50
Souvenir Sheets
2330-2331 A378 Set of 2   7.50 7.50

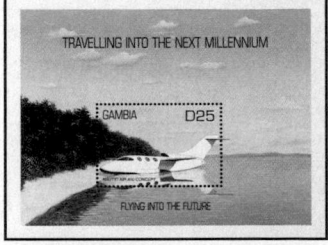

Transportation of the Future — A379

No. 2332 — Automobiles: b, Mazda RX-Evolv. c, Isuzu Kai. d, Ford 021C. e, Pontiac GTO. f, Chevrolet CERV III. g, Toyota Will VI.

No. 2333 — Aircraft: a, Blended wing body, BWB-1. b, Boeing 767-400 ERX. c, Lockheed concept. d, Boeing X. e, American National Aerospace plane X-30 concept. f, Hotol taking off from Russian AN-225.

No. 2334 — Trains: a, Maglev train MLU-002. b, Magnetic rail car. c, Monorail above ground concept. d, Seattle Monorail. e, Monorail above cabin concept. f, Monorail concept boat.

No. 2335 — Watercraft: h, Pendolare concept boat. i, Planesail boat. j, Airfoil concept. k, Ferry Sea Coaster concept. l, Shinaitoku Matu new sail technology. m, Supersport luxury yacht concept.

No. 2335G, 25d, Nautic Air 400 concept. No. 2335H, 25d, Maglev train. No. 2335I, 25d, Honda Sprocket concept. No. 2335J, 25d, Triton, US Coast Guard concept. Illustration reduced.

2000, Oct. 2 *Perf. 14*
Sheets of 6, #a-f

2332	A379	7d Sheet of 6, #b-g	6.25	6.25
2333	A379	7d Sheet of 6, #a-f	6.25	6.25
2334	A379	8d Sheet of 6, #a-f	6.50	6.50
2335	A379	8d Sheet of 6, #h-m	7.50	7.50

Souvenir Sheets

| 2335G-2335J | A379 | Set of 4 | 15.00 | 15.00 |

Nos. 2335 and 2335A contain one 56x41mm stamp.

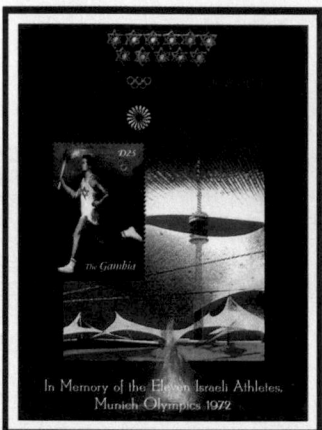

Massacre of Israeli Olympic Athletes, 1972 — A380

No. 2336, horiz.: a, Moshe Weinberg. b, Eliezer Halffin. c, Mark Slavin. d, Ze'ev Friedman. e, Joseph Romano. f, Kahat Shor. g, David Berger. h, Joseph Gottfreund. i, Andrei Schpitzer. j, Amitsur Shapira. k, Yaakov Springer. l, Olympic poster.

2000, Nov. 9

| 2336 | A380 | 4d Sheet of 12, #a-l | 7.25 | 7.25 |

Souvenir Sheet

| 2337 | A380 | 25d Torchbearer | 4.00 | 4.00 |

Ships A381

Designs: 5d, Spanish Armada. 10d, Brazilian river gunboat Colombo. 15d, Russian Navy mine carrier Jenissel. 20d, Japanese battleship Yamato.

No. 2342, 7d: a, British first-rate battleship, 18th cent. b, Spanish galleon, 16th cent. c, Russian four-masted barque, 20th cent. d, Henri Grace à Dieu with flag on stern, 16th cent. e, Frontispiece of John Dee's Arte of Navigation, 16th cent. f, British ironclad, 19th cent.

No. 2343, 7d: a, Chinese junk, 18th cent. b, Two-masted cog, 15th cent. c, Henri Grace à Dieu, no flag on stern, 16th cent. d, St. Brendan and monks at sea, 6th cent. e, Figurehead. f, British carrack, 16th cent.

No. 2344, 25d, Challenger, 19th cent. No. 2345, 25d, Golden Hind, 16th cent.

2000, Oct. 2 *Litho.* *Perf. 14*

| 2338-2341 | A381 | Set of 4 | 7.25 | 7.25 |

Sheets of 6, #a-f

| 2342-2343 | A381 | Set of 2 | 12.00 | 12.00 |

Souvenir Sheets

| 2344-2345 | A381 | Set of 2 | 7.25 | 7.25 |

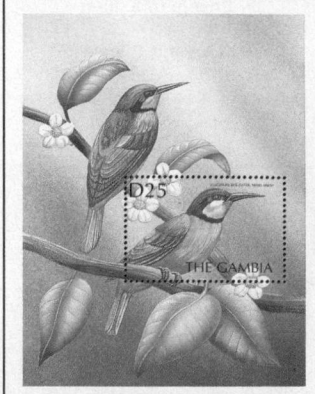

Birds — A382

No. 2346, 7d, vert.: a, Pied flycatcher. b, Blackcap. c, Stonechat. d, Nightingale. e, Black-headed tchagra. f, Yellow wagtail.

No. 2347, 7d, vert.: a, Gray parrot. b, Great spotted cuckoo. c, Bar-tailed trogon. d, African hobby. e, Green turaco. f, Trumpeter hornbill.

No. 2348, 7d, vert.: a, Yellow-rumped tinkerbird. b, Greater honeyguide. c, Hoopoe. d, European roller. e, Carmine bee-eater. f, White-throated bee-eater.

#2349, 25d, European bee-eater. #2350, 25d, Bateleur. #2351, 25d, Secretary bird. Illustration reduced.

2000, Oct. 2 *Perf. 13¾x13¼*
Sheets of 6, #a-f

| 2346-2348 | A382 | Set of 3 | 17.50 | 17.50 |

Souvenir Sheets

| 2349-2351 | A382 | Set of 3 | 10.50 | 10.50 |

Ferrari Automobiles — A383

Designs: 4d, 3335P. 5d, 5125. 10d, 312P. 25d, 330P4.

2000, Nov. 15 *Perf. 14*

| 2352-2355 | A383 | Set of 4 | 6.25 | 6.25 |

12th Classic Automobile Marathon — A384

No. 2356, 5d: a, Morgan. b, Rover. c, Marmon. d, Rolls Royce Silver Cloud. e, Rolls Royce Phantom. f, Mercedes 680S. g, Mercedes 74. h, Invicta.

No. 2357, 5d: a, Allard. b, Ford coupe. c, Citroen Pilot. d, Packard (white). e, Austin A90. f, Bentley. g, Packard (red). h, Aston Martin.

No. 2358, 25d, Cadillac. No. 2359, 25d, Morris Minor.

2000, Nov. 15
Sheets of 8, #a-h

| 2356-2357 | A384 | Set of 2 | 11.50 | 11.50 |

Souvenir Sheets

| 2358-2359 | A384 | Set of 2 | 7.25 | 7.25 |

Queen Mother, 100th Birthday — A385

2000, Aug. 7 *Litho.* *Perf. 14*

| 2360 | A385 | 7d multi | 1.00 | 1.00 |

Printed in sheets of 6.

The Horse in Art A386

Designs: 4d, At Full Stretch, by John Skeaping. 5d, The Burton, by Lionel Edwards. 10d, A Game of Polo, by Li Lin. 15d, St. George and the Dragon, by Raphael, vert.

No. 2365, 7d: a, Horses Emerging From the Sea, by Eugène Delacroix. b, The Ninth Duke of Marlborough on a Grey Horse, by Sir Alfred Munnings. c, Ovid in Exile Amongst the Scythians, by Delacroix. d, Early Morning Gallop, by Skeaping. e, Mare and Foal, by Munnings. f, Detail from Three-a-side Polo at Simla, by Edwards.

No. 2366, 7d, vert.: a, A Lady Hawking, by E. J. H. Vernet. b, Captain Robert Orme, by Sir Joshua Reynolds. c, Napoleon Crossing the Alps, by Jacques-Louis David. d, Nobby Gray, by Munnings. e, Amateur Jockeys Near a Carriage, by Edgar Degas. f, Detail from Three-a-side Polo at Simla, diff.

No. 2367, 25d, The Reckoning, by George Morland. No. 2368, 25d, One of the Family, by Frederic G. Cotman.

2000, Oct. 2

| 2361-2364 | A386 | Set of 4 | 5.00 | 5.00 |

Sheets of 6, #a-f

| 2365-2366 | A386 | Set of 2 | 12.00 | 12.00 |

Souvenir Sheets

| 2367-2368 | A386 | Set of 2 | 7.25 | 7.25 |

New Year 2001 (Year of the Snake) — A387

No. 2369: a, Vermilion background. b, Purple background. c, Dark blue background. d, Light green background.

2001, Jan. 2

| 2369 | A387 | 4d Sheet of 4, #a-d | 2.40 | 2.40 |

Souvenir Sheet

| 2370 | A387 | 15d Snake | 2.25 | 2.25 |

Rijksmuseum, Amsterdam, Bicent. (in 2000) — A388

No. 2371, 7d, vert.: a, Vessels in a Strong wind, by Jan Porcellis. b, Seascape in the Morning, by Simon de Vlieger. c, Travelers at a Country Inn, by Isaack van Ostade. d, Orpheus with Animals in a Landscape, by Aelbert Cuyp. e, Italian With a Mountain Plateau, by Cornelis van Poelenburch. f, Boatmen and hill from Boatman Moored on a Lake Shore, by Adam Pynacker.

No. 2372, 7d, vert.: a, Cow, boatmen and sailboat from Boatmen Moored on a Lake Shore. b, The Ford in the River, by Jan Baptist Weenix. c, Two Horses Near a Gate in a Meadow, by Paulus Potter. d, Cows and Sheep at a Stream, by Cornelis Saftleven. f, Lute player from The Duet.

No. 2373, 7d, vert.: a, Teapot from Still Life With Turkey Pie, by Pieter Claesz. b, Bouquet of Flowers in a Vase, by Ambrosius Bosschaert. c, Vase from Still Life With Flowers, Fruit and Shells, by Balthasar van der Ast. d, Flowers and fruit from Still Life With Flowers, Fruit and Shells. e, Tulips in a Vase, by Hans Boulenger. f, Laid Table With Cheese and Fruit, by Floris van Dijck.

No. 2374, 7d, vert.: a, Turkey, from Still Life With Turkey Pie. b, Still Life With Gilt Goblet, by Willem Claesz Heda. c, Still Life With Lobster and Nautilus Cup, by Jan Davidsz de Heem. d, Bacchanal, by Moses van Uyttenbroeck. e, The Anatomy Lesson of Dr. Nicolaes Tulp, by Rembrandt. f, Johannes Lutma, by Jacob Backer.

No. 2375, 7d, vert.: a, The Meagre Company, by Frans Hals and Pieter Codde. b, The Twins Clara and Aelbert de Bray, by Salomon de Bray. c, Self-portrait, by Ferdinand Bol. d, Ambulatory of the New Church in Delft, with the Tomb of Willem the Silent, by Gerard Houckgeest. e, View of the Tomb of Willem in the New Church in Delft, by Emanuel de Witte. f, Mountainous Landscape, by Hercules Segers.

No. 2376, 7d, vert.: a, Lute player from Gallant Company by Codde. b, Men and archway from Gallant Company. c, Man on bended knee from The Marriage of Willem van Loon and Margaretha Bas, by Jan Miense Molenaer. d, Crowd from The Marriage of Willen van Loon and Margaretha Bas. e, Woman in black robe from The Marriage of Willem van Loon and Margaretha Bas. f, Johanna Le Maire, by Nicolaes Eliasz Pickenoy.

No. 2377, 25d, The Fall of Man, by Cornelis van Haarlem. No. 2378, 25d, The Art Gallery of Jan Gildemeester Jansz, by Jan Ekels II. No. 2379, 25d, View of the Nieuwe Kerk and the Rear of the Town Hall in Amsterdam, by Isaak Outwater. No. 2380, 25d, The Spendthrift, by Cornelis Troost. No. 2381, 25d, Morning Ride on the Beach, by Anton Mauve. No. 2382, 25d, Meadow Landscape With Cattle, by Willen Roelofs.

2001, Jan. 15 *Perf. 13¾*
Sheets of 6, #a-f

| 2371-2376 | A388 | Set of 6 | 35.00 | 35.00 |

Souvenir Sheets

| 2377-2382 | A388 | Set of 6 | 22.50 | 22.50 |

The Wizard of Oz, Cent. (in 2000) — A389

No. 2383, 7d: a, Witch of the North. b, Poppies. c, Dorothy's house. d, Witch of the East. e, Dorothy. f, The Wizard.
No. 2384, 7d: a, Witch's wolf. b, Witch's forest. c, Witch's monkeys. d, Dorothy in poppies. e, Queen Mouse. f, Witch and evil bees.
No. 2385, 7d: a, Cowardly Lion. b, Land of Oz. c, Tin Man. d, Scarecrow. e, Toto. f, Munchkins.
No. 2386, 27d, Green Maiden. No. 2387, 27d, Gate keeper. No. 2388, 27d, Dorothy at crossroads, horiz.

2001, Jan. 30
Sheets of 6, #a-f
2383-2385 A389   Set of 3   17.50 17.50
Souvenir Sheets
2386-2388 A389   Set of 3   11.50 11.50

History of the Theater — A390

No. 2389, 6d: a, Terra cotta statue. b, Tragic masks of King Priam. c, Euripides. d, Terra cotta statues of actors portraying drunks. e, Scene from Chinese play. f, Indian actors. g, Scene from Noh play, Japan. h, Scene from Clytemnestra.
No. 2390, 6d: a, William Shakespeare. b, Johann Wolfgang von Goethe. c, Moliere. d, Henrik Ibsen. e, George Bernard Shaw. f, Anton Chekhov. g, Sholom Aleichem. h, Tennessee Williams.
No. 2391, 25d, Sarah Bernhardt, vert. No. 2392, 25d, John Barrymore, vert.

2001, Jan. 30   **Perf. 14**
Sheets of 8, #a-h
2389-2390 A390   Set of 2   14.00 14.00
Souvenir Sheet
2391-2392 A390   Set of 2   7.25 7.25

Pokémon — A391

No. 2393: a, Beedrill. b, Arbok. c, Machop. d, Vileplume. e, Clefairy. f, Poliwhirl.

2001, Feb. 1   **Perf. 13¾**
2393 A391   7d Sheet of 6, #a-f   6.00 6.00
Souvenir Sheet
2394 A391   25d Articuno   3.50 3.50

Orchids — A392

Designs: 1.50d, Encyclia alata. 2d, Dendrobium lasiantherum. 3d, Cymbidiella pardalina. No. 2398, 4d, Cymbidium lowianum. 5d, Cypripedium irapeanum. 15d, Doritas pulcherrima.
No. 2401: a, Epidendrum pseudepidendrum. b, Eriopsis biloba. c, Masdevallia coccinea. d, Odontoglossum lindleyanum. e, Oerstedella wallisii. f, Paphiopedilum acmodontum. g, Laelia rubescens. h, Huntleya wallisii. i, Lycaste longiscapa. j, Maxillaria variabilis. k, Mexicoa ghiesbrechtiana. l, Miltoniopsis phalaenopsis.
No. 2402: a, Sobralia candida. b, Phragmipedium basseae. c, Phaius tankervilleae. d, Vanda rothchildiana. e, Telipogon pulchera. f, Rossioglossum insleayi.
No. 2403, 25d, Chaubardia heteroclita. No. 2404, 25d, Cychnoches loddigesii. No. 2405, 25d, Cattleya dowiana.

2001, Feb. 1   Litho.   Perf. 14
2395-2400 A392   Set of 6   6.00 6.00
2401 A392 4d Sheet of 12, #a-l 9.25 9.25
2402 A392 7d Sheet of 6, #a-f   8.25 8.25
Souvenir Sheets
2403-2405 A392   Set of 3   15.00 15.00
Hong Kong 2001 Stamp Exhibition (Nos. 2401-2405).

Medicinal Plants — A393

Designs: 3d, Pokeweed. 5d, Bay laurel. 10d, Coltsfoot. 15d, Marshmallow.
No. 2410, 8d, vert.: a, Restharrow. b, White willow. c, Sweet serge. d, Passion flower. e, Rosemary. f, Pepper.
No. 2411, 8d, vert.: a, Succory. b, Dandelion. c, Garlic. d, Hemp agrimony. e, Star thistle. f, Cypress.
No. 2412, 25d, Arbutus, vert. No. 2413, 25d, Olive, vert.

2001, Mar. 1
2406-2409 A393   Set of 4   6.25 6.25
Sheets of 6, #a-f
2410-2411 A393   Set of 2   19.00 19.00
Souvenir Sheets
2412-2413 A393   Set of 2   9.50 9.50

Japanese Art — A394

Designs: 1d, Mount Fuji and Tea Fields, by Matsuoka Eikyu. 2d, One heron from Herons and Flowers, by Okamoto Shuki. No. 2416, 3d, Two herons from Herons and Flowers. No. 2417, 3d, The Realm of Gods in Yingzhou, by Tomioka Tessai. No. 2418, 4d, Peach Blossom Spring in Wuling, by Tessai. No. 2419, 4d, Egret, by Takeuchi Seiho. No. 2420, 5d, Spring Colors of the Lake and Mountains, by Shoda Gyokan. No. 2421, 5d, Sparrows, by Seiho. No. 2422, 10d, Red Lotus and White Goose, by Goun Saku. No. 2423, 10d, Portrait of Ushiwakamaru, by Kano Osanobu. 15d, Woman Selling Flowers, by Ito Shoha. 20d, The Sound of the Ocean, by Matsumoto Ichiyo.
No. 2426, 5d — Birds and Flowers of the Twelve Months, by Sakai Hoitsu: a, Red and white flowers, bird on branch. b, Yellow flowers, bird flying. c, White flowers, bird on branch. d, Blue flowers. e, Sun, white and blue flowers. f, Red and white flowers.
No. 2427, 5d — Birds and Flowers of the Twelve Months, by Hoitsu: a, Insect in sky, red pink and white flowers. b, Blue irises. c, Red, white light blue flowers. d, Fruit on tree. e, Bird standing in water. f, Snow-covered tree.
No. 2428, 7d — Birds and Flowers, by Soga Chokuan: a, White flowers. b, Rooster at R. c, Roosters at L, red flower at R. d, Rooster at R, white flowers. e, Birds in sky. f, Roosters at L and R, white and red flowers. g, Roosters at L and R. Rooster at L, tree and red flowers.
No. 2429, 7d — The Four Accomplishments, by Kaiho Yusho: a, Table. b, Two people near tree. c, Rock and hill. d, Two people. e, Rock and tree. f, One person. g, Three people. h, Three people, table.
No. 2430 — Book of Lacquer Paintings, by Shibata Zeshin: a, Flower. b, Birds. c, Butterfly on flower. d, Lobster.
No. 2431, 30d, Untitled painting (Yanagibashi at Ryogoku), by Utagawa Kuniyoshi, horiz. No. 2432, 30d, Poppies, by Tsuchida Bakusen, horiz. No. 2433, 30d, Puppies and Morning Glories, by Yamaguchi Soken, horiz. No. 2434, 30d, Deep Pool, by Nishimura Goun, horiz. No. 2435, 30d, Spring Farming Near a Riverside Village, by Mori Getsujo, horiz.

2001, Apr. 17
2414-2425 A394   Set of 12   16.00 16.00
Sheets of 6, #a-f
2426-2427 A394   Set of 2   11.50 11.50
Sheets of 8, #a-h
2428-2429 A394   Set of 2   22.50 22.50
2430 A394 10d Sheet of 4, #a-d 7.75 7.75
Imperf.
Size: 118x88mm
2431-2435 A394   Set of 5   29.00 29.00
Nos. 2428-2430 contain 28x42mm stamps. Phila Nippon '01, Japan.

Butterflies Type of 2000

Designs: 7d, Salamis temora. 8d, Cyrestus camillus. 20d, Papilio demodocus. 25d, Danaus chrysippus.

2001   **Perf. 14¾x14**
2436-2439 A367   Set of 4   11.50 11.50
No. 2439 exists dated 2003.

I Love Lucy Type of 2000

No. 2440: a, Lucy singing. b, Lucy with tambourine. c, Lucy with Ricky and Ethel. d, Lucy. e, Ethel and Ricky at piano. f, Ethel and Ricky on bench. g, Lucy at typewriter. h, Ethel singing. i, Lucy on bench.
No. 2441, 25d, Like #2440a, vert. No. 2442, 25d, Like #2440d, vert.

2001   **Perf. 13¾**
2440 A354 5d Sheet of 9, #a-i   8.75 8.75
Souvenir Sheets
2441-2442 A354   Set of 2   9.50 9.50

Horses — A395

No. 2443, 7d, Head of: a, Akhal-Teke. b, Palomino. c, Kladruber. d, Paint Horse. e, Pinto. f, Kabardin.
No. 2444, 7d, horiz: a, Akhal-Teke. b, Kladruber. c, Palomino. d, Pinto. e, Paint Horse. f, Kabardin.

2001   Litho.   Perf. 14
Sheets of 6, #a-f
2443-2444 A395   Set of 2   11.50 11.50
Souvenir Sheet
2445 A395   25d Palomino   3.50 3.50

Three Stooges Type of 2000

No. 2446: a, Shemp as angel. b, Larry, Moe, Shemp, wearing feathered hats. c, Moe, Shemp and Larry wearing hospital uniforms. d, Larry with hammer, Shemp with gun, Moe. e, Moe, Larry with woman. f, Moe and Shemp wearing tams. g, Moe, Larry, wagon wheel. h, Shemp, Moe, Larry in bus driver uniforms. i, Shemp hitting Larry and Moe.
No. 2447, 25d, Curly with telephone, skull, vert. No. 2448, 25d, Shemp on Moe's back, vert.

2001   **Perf. 13¾**
2446 A353 5d Sheet of 9, #a-i   6.25 6.25
Souvenir Sheets
2447-2448 A353   Set of 2   7.00 7.00

I Love Lucy Type of 2000

No. 2449: a, Lucy crawling on building ledge. b, Lucy standing against wall, arms outstretched. c, Lucy in apartment. d, Lucy reclining on ledge. e, Lucy with hand on forehead. f, Lucy reclining against wall. g, Ricky, bound and gagged Lucy. h, Lucy on sofa. i, Lucy, robber.
No. 2450, 25d, Lucy, robber, vert. No. 2451, 25d, Bound and gagged Lucy, seated Ethel, vert.

2001
2449 A354 5d Sheet of 9, #a-i   6.25 6.25
Souvenir Sheets
2450-2451 A354   Set of 2   7.00 7.00

Butterfly Type of 2000

2001   **Perf. 14¾x14**
2452   A367 50d Coeliades
                forestan   7.00 7.00
2452A A367 75d Ornithoptera
                alexandrae   10.00 10.00
2452B A367 100d Morpho
                cypris   14.00 14.00

Queen Victoria (1819-1901) — A396

No. 2453, horiz.: a, Reading speech from throne. b, Benjamin Disraeli. c, Riding in procession from Parliament.

2001, Apr. 26   **Perf. 14**
2453 A396 15d Sheet of 3, #a-c   6.25 6.25
Souvenir Sheet
2454 A396 25d Portrait   3.50 3.50

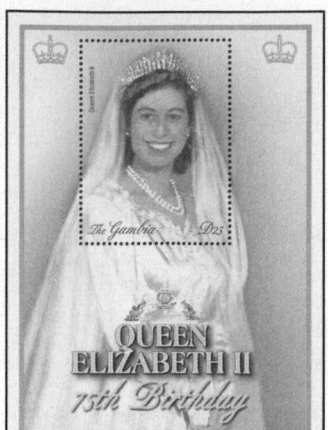

Queen Elizabeth II, 75th Birthday — A397

No. 2456: a, In uniform. b, In pink hat. c, Wearing crown, facing R. d, Wearing crown, facing L.

2001, Apr. 26   **Perf. 14**
2455 A397 15d Sheet of 4, #a-d   8.25 8.25
Souvenir Sheet
2456 A397 25d In wedding dress   3.50 3.50

Flowers — A398

Designs: 1d, Disa unifloria. 4d, Monodora myristica. 6d, Clappertonia ficifolia. 20d, Calanthe rosea.
No. 2461, 7d: a, Vanilla planifolia. b, Strelitzia reginae. c, Gladiolus cardinalis. d, Arctotis venusta. e, Protea obtusifolia. f, Geissorhiza rochensis.
No. 2462, 7d: a, Canarina abyssinica. b, Amorphophallus abyssinicus. c, Calanthe rosea, diff. d, Gloriosa simplex. e, Clappertonia ficifolia, diff. f, Ansellia gigantea.
No. 2463, 25d, Arctoris venusta, diff. No. 2464, 25d, Geissorhiza rochensis, horiz.

2001, Mar. 1   **Litho.**   **Perf. 14**
2457-2460 A398   Set of 4   4.75 4.75
Sheets of 6, #a-f
2461-2462 A398   Set of 2   12.50 12.50
Souvenir Sheets
2463-2464 A398   Set of 2   7.50 7.50

Photomosaic of Queen Elizabeth II — A399

2001, Apr. 26
2465 A399 8d multi   1.10 1.10
Printed in sheets of 8, with and without marginal inscription "In Celebration of the 50th Anniversary of H. M. Queen Elizabeth II's Accession to the Throne.'

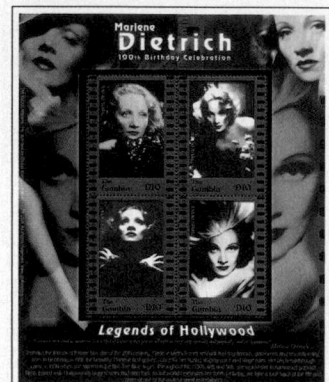

Marlene Dietrich — A400

No. 2466: a, With head on forearm. b, With bare shoulder. c, With arms crossed. d, Wearing hat.

2001, Apr. 26   **Perf. 13¾**
2466 A400 10d Sheet of 4, #a-d   5.75 5.75

Mao Zedong (1893-1976) — A401

No. 2467: a, In 1935. b, In 1949. c, In 1951. 25d, In 1928.

2001, Apr. 26   **Perf. 14**
2467 A401 15d Sheet of 3, #a-c   6.25 6.25
Souvenir Sheet
2468 A401 25d multi   3.50 3.50

Giuseppe Verdi (1813-1901), Opera Composer — A402

No. 2469: a, Verdi with gray hair. b, Score and perfromers from La Traviata. c, Score and performer from Aida. d, Verdi with brown hair. 25d, Verdi and scores of Don Carlos and Rigoletto.

2001, Apr. 26
2469 A402 10d Sheet of 4, #a-d   5.75 5.75
Souvenir Sheet
2470 A402 25d multi   3.50 3.50

Monet Paintings — A403

No. 2471, horiz.: a, Madame Monet on the Sofa. b, The Picnic. c, The Luncheon. d, Jean Monet on His Mechanical Horse. 25d, La Japonaise.

2001, Apr. 26   **Perf. 13¾**
2471 A403 10d Sheet of 4, #a-d   5.75 5.75
Souvenir Sheet
2472 A403 25d multi   3.50 3.50

Toulouse-Lautrec Paintings — A404

No. 2473: a, At Le Rat Mort. b, The Milliner. c, Messaline. 25d, Napoleon.

2001, Apr. 26
2473 A404   7d Sheet of 3, #a-c   3.00 3.00
Souvenir Sheet
2474 A404 25d multi   3.50 3.50

Orchids — A405

Designs: 3d, Orchis morio. 4d, Fulophia speciosa. 5d, Angraecum leonis. 15d, Oeceoclades maculata.
No. 2479, 8d: a, Ceratostylis retisquama. b, Rangaeris rhipsalisocia. c, Phaius hybrid. d, Disa hybrid. e, Disa uniflora. f, Angraecum leonis.
No. 2480, 8d, horiz.: a, Satyrium erectum. b, Aeranthes grandiose. c, Aerangis somasticta. d, Polystachya bella. e, Eulophia guineensis. f, Disa blackii.
No. 2482, 25d, Disa kirstenbosch pride.

2001, June 15   **Perf. 14**
2475-2478 A405   Set of 4   4.00 4.00

Sheets of 6, #a-f
2479-2480 A405   Set of 2   13.00 13.00
Souvenir Sheets
2482 A405 multi   3.50 3.50
Belgica 2001 Intl. Stamp Exhibition, Brussels (#2479-2480).
A 25d souvenir sheet, similar to No. 2482, depicting Aerangis curnowiana, was prepared but not issued.

SOS Children's Village A406

2001, July 2
2483 A406 10d multi   1.40 1.40

Flora & Fauna A407

Designs: 2d, Hoopoe. 3d, Great spotted cuckoo. 4d, Plain tiger butterfly. 5d, Zebra duiker. 10d, Sooty managbey. 20d, Greater kudu.
No. 2490, 8d: a, Hippopotamus. b, Elephant. c, Parusta simplex. d, Gray heron. e, Charaxes imperialis. f, Gloriosa simplex.
No. 2491, 8d: a, Alpine swift. b, Blotched genet. c, Thomas' galago. d, Carmine beeeater. e, Tree pangolin. f, Campbell's monkey.
No. 2492, 8d: a, Gray parrot. b, Rachel's weaver. c, European bee-eater. d, River kingfisher. e, Red river hog. f, Bushbuck.
No. 2493, 8d: a, Blue diadem butterfly. b, Fire-footed rope squirrel. c, Clappertonia ficifolia. d, Costus spectabilis. e, African migrant butterfly. f, Giant African snail.
No. 2494, 25d, Long-tailed pangolin, vert. No. 2495, 25d, Eurasian kestrel, vert.

2001, July 16
2484-2489 A407   Set of 6   6.00 6.00
Sheets of 6, #a-f
2490-2493 A407   Set of 4   26.00 26.00
Souvenir Sheets
2494-2495 A407   Set of 2   7.00 7.00

A408

Ducks and Geese — A409

Designs: 2d, Blue-winged teal. No. 2497, 3d, Red-crested pochard. No. 2498, 4d, Falcated teal. No. 2499, 5d, Mandarin duck. No. 2500, 10d, King eider. 15d, Hooded merganser.
No. 2502, 8d, Wood duck. No. 2503, 4d, Mallard. No. 2504, 5d, Barrow's goldeneye. No. 2505, 10d, Bufflehead.
No. 2506, 7d, horiz.: a, Barrow's goldeneye. b, Harlequin duck. c, Pintail. d, Black-bellied whistling duck. e, Cinnamon teal. f, Surf scoter.
No. 2507, 7d, horiz.: a, Black scoter. b, Black duck. c, Green-winged teal. d, Bufflehead. e, Red-breasted merganser. f, Fulvous whistling duck.
No. 2508, 8d: a, European wigeon. b, Mallard. c, Garganey. d, Pintail, diff. e, Shoveler. f, Green-winged teal.
No. 2509, 8d: a, Black duck. b, Bufflehead. c, Cinnamon teal, diff. d, Goldeneye. e, Ruddy shelduck. f, Ferruginous duck.
No. 2510, 8d: a, Masked duck. b, Old squaw. c, Ring-necked duck. d, Harlequin duck, diff. e, Redhead. f, Canvasback.

No. 2511, 25d, American wigeon. No. 2512, 25d, Wood duck. No. 2513, 25d, Baikal teal. No. 2514, 25d, Green-winged teal, horiz. No. 2515, 25d, Canada geese, horiz.

2001, July 16
| 2496-2501 | A408 | Set of 6 | 5.25 | 5.25 |
| 2502-2505 | A409 | Set of 4 | 3.00 | 3.00 |

Sheets of 6, #a-f
| 2506-2507 | A409 | Set of 2 | 11.00 | 11.00 |
| 2508-2510 | A409 | Set of 3 | 19.00 | 19.00 |

Souvenir Sheets
| 2511-2513 | A408 | Set of 3 | 10.00 | 10.00 |
| 2514-2515 | A409 | Set of 2 | 6.50 | 6.50 |

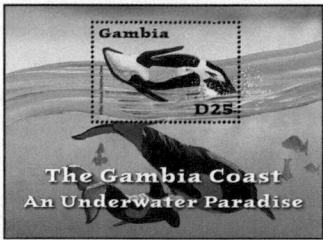

Cetaceans — A410

No. 2516, 7d: a, Killer whale (denomination at UR). b, Sperm whale (denomination at UR). c, Strap-toothed whale. d, Humpback whale. e, Southern right whale. f, Beluga.
No. 2517, 7d: a, Killer whale (denomination at LR). b, Sperm whale (denomination at LR). c, Narwhal. d, Gray whale. e, Blue whale. f, Northern right whale.
No. 2518, 25d, Killer whale. No. 2519, 25d, Humpback whale.

2001, July 16   Sheets of 6, #a-f
| 2516-2517 | A410 | Set of 2 | 11.00 | 11.00 |

Souvenir Sheets
| 2518-2519 | A410 | Set of 2 | 6.50 | 6.50 |

A411

Trains
A412

Designs: 2d, Rheingold Express. No. 2521, 10d, Amtrak train. No. 2522, 15d, The Blue Train. 20d, Cisalpino.
4d, Eurostar. No. 2525, 7d, Mallard. No. 2526, 10d, Rocket. No. 2527, TGV.
No. 2528, 7d: a, Eurostar, diff. b, Flying Hamburger. c, Coast Starlight. d, Tres Grande Vitesse. e, Golden Arrow. f, Shinkanzen "Max."
No. 2529, 7d: a, Siliguri to Darjeeling, India train. b, California Zephyr. c, Flying Scotsman. d, Trans-Siberian Express. e, Indian-Pacific. f, Thunersee.
No. 2530, 8d: a, Le Shuttle. b, Nord Express. c, 2-6-0, Switzerland. d, Duchess. e, Balkan Express. f, Class 44 2-10-0, Germany.
No. 2531, 8d: a, 7029 Clun Castle. b, Puffing Billy. c, ICE Electric. d, 4-4-2 S, Belgium. e, 2-8-2, Germany. f, PLM Coupe-Vents.
No. 2532, 25d, Cape Town to Victoria Falls train. No. 2533, 25d, The Southerner.
No. 2534, 25d, Stanier Class 5 4-6-0. No. 2535, 25d, Flying Scotsman, diff.

2001, July 31   Perf. 14
| 2520-2523 | A411 | Set of 4 | 6.25 | 6.25 |
| 2524-2527 | A412 | Set of 4 | 5.00 | 5.00 |

Sheets of 6, #a-f
| 2528-2529 | A411 | Set of 2 | 11.00 | 11.00 |
| 2530-2531 | A412 | Set of 2 | 13.00 | 13.00 |

Souvenir Sheets
| 2532-2533 | A411 | Set of 2 | 6.50 | 6.50 |
| 2534-2535 | A412 | Set of 2 | 6.50 | 6.50 |

British Royal Navy — A413

Designs: 3d, St. Andrew, 1600s. 4d, Fleet maneuvers, 1914. 10d, HMS Illustrious, 1899. 15d, Battle of North Foreland, 1666.
No. 2540, 7d, horiz.: a, Mary Rose, 1512. b, Attack off Quebec, 1759. c, Armada campaign, 1588. d, Battle of Scheveningen, 1653. e, Blanche captures La Pique, 1795. f, Embarkation at Dover, 1520.
No. 2541, 7d, horiz. — Battles: a, Quiberon Bay, 1759. b, Barfleur, 1692. c, Nile, 1798. d, Trafalgar, 1805. e, Jutland, 1916. f, Camperdown, 1797.
No. 2542, 7d, horiz.: a, Battle of Navarino, 1827. b, Sinking of Eurydice, 1878. c, HMS Pantaloon captures Borboleta, 1845. d, Dardanelles, 1915. e, HMS Pickle captures Bolodora, 1829. f, HMS Invincible and Inflexible, Battle of the Falklands, 1914.
No. 2543, 25d, Ark Royal, 1582, horiz. No. 2544, 25d, Sovereign of the Seas, 1637, horiz.

2001, Sept. 6   Litho.
| 2536-2539 | A413 | Set of 4 | 4.25 | 4.25 |

Sheets of 6, #a-f
| 2540-2542 | A413 | Set of 3 | 17.00 | 17.00 |

Souvenir Sheets
| 2543-2544 | A413 | Set of 2 | 6.50 | 6.50 |

2002 World Cup Soccer Championships, Japan and Korea — A414

Jules Rimet Trophy and: 2d, Netherlands flag and player. 3d, Argentina flag and player. 4d, Ibaraki Kashima Stadium, Japan, horiz. 5d, George Best and Northern Ireland flag. 10d, Dino Zoff and Italian flag. 15d, Poster for 1938 tournament, France.
25d, Pat Bonner making save for Ireland.

2001, Sept. 6
| 2545-2550 | A414 | Set of 6 | 5.25 | 5.25 |

Souvenir Sheet
| 2551 | A414 | 25d multi | | 3.25 | 3.25 |

No. 2551 contains one 56x42mm stamp.

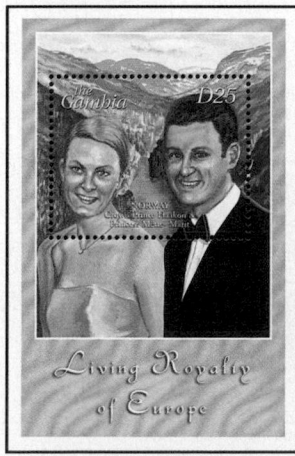

European Royalty — A415

No. 2552: a, King Harald V, Queen Sonja, Norway. b, Queen Margrethe II, Denmark. c, King Carl XVI Gustaf and Queen Silvia, Sweden. d, King Juan Carlos, Queen Sofia, Spain. e, Queen Beatrix, Netherlands. f, King Albert II, Queen Paola, Belgium.
No. 2553, 25d, Crown Prince Haakon, Princess Mette-Marit, Norway. No. 2554, 25d, King Juan Carlos, Spain, vert.

Perf. 14¼x14½, 14½x14¼
2001, Nov. 15
| 2552 | A415 | 7d Sheet of 6, #a-f | 5.50 | 5.50 |

Souvenir Sheets
| 2553-2554 | A415 | Set of 2 | 6.25 | 6.25 |

Queen Mother Type of 1999

No. 2555: a, Duchess of York, Princess Elizabeth, 1928. b, Lady Elizabeth Bowes-Lyon, 1923. c, Queen Elizabeth, 1946. d, Queen Mother, Prince Harry.
40d, Queen Mother celebrating 89th birthday, 1989.

2001, Dec. 13   Perf. 14
| 2555 | A342 | 15d Sheet of 4, #a-d + label | 7.75 | 7.75 |

Souvenir Sheet
Perf. 13¾
| 2556 | A342 | 40d multi | 5.00 | 5.00 |

No. 2556 contains one 38x50mm stamp.

Oriental Actors and Actresses — A416

No. 2557, 15d: a, Alex Fong. b, William So. c, Flora Chan. d, Rain Li.
No. 2558, 15d — Kelly Chen: a, Close-up. b, As child, with cherry. c, On swing. d, As child, with hand above eyes.
No. 2559, 15d — Jacky Cheung: a, At L, laughing, looking to R. b, Looking forward, mouth open. c, At R, laughing, looking L. d, Looking forward, mouth closed.
No. 2560, 15d — Andy Hui, and Chinese characters at: a, L (pink suit). b, R (yellow suit). c, L (yellow suit). d, R (pink suit).
No. 2561, 15d — Miriam Yeung, with roses and petals at: a, LR. b, LL. c, UR. d, UL.

2001, Nov. 5   Litho.   Perf. 13¾x13¼
Sheets of 4, #a-d
| 2557-2561 | A416 | Set of 5 | 37.50 | 37.50 |

New Year 2002 (Year of the Horse) — A417

No. 2562 — Denomination at: a, UR. b, UL. c, LR. d, LL.
20d, African zebra.

2001, Dec. 26   Perf. 13
| 2562 | A417 | 6d Miniature sheet of 4, #a-d | 3.00 | 3.00 |

Souvenir Sheet
Perf. 12½x13
| 2563 | A417 | 20d multi | 2.25 | 2.25 |

No. 2563 contains one 68x31mm triangular stamp.

Jacqueline Kennedy Onassis (1929-94) — A418

No. 2564: a, As baby. b, At age 6. c, Engagement to J.F.K. d, In wedding gown, 1955. e, In 1960. f, In 1980.
30d, At wedding to Aristotle Onassis.

2002, Jan. 24   Perf. 14
| 2564 | A418 | 7d Sheet of 6, #a-f | 5.50 | 5.50 |

Souvenir Sheet
| 2565 | A418 | 30d multi | 4.00 | 4.00 |

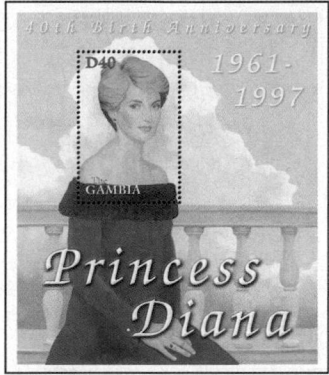

Princess Diana (1961-97) — A419

No. 2566 — Diana and: a, Coral rose. b, White rose. c, Yellow rose. d, Purple rose.
40d, Portrait.

2002, Jan. 24
| 2566 | A419 | 15d Sheet of 4, #a-d | 7.75 | 7.75 |

Souvenir Sheet
| 2567 | A419 | 40d multi | 5.25 | 5.25 |

Moths
A420

Designs: 2d, Tiger moth. 3d, Hawk moth. No. 2570, 10d, Pericopid moth. 15d, Spurge hawk.
No. 2572, 10d (50x38mm): a, Sloane's urania. b, Saturniid moth. c, Black witch moth. d, Burnet moth on plant. e, Day-flying moth. f, Lime hawk moth.
No. 2573, 10d (50x38mm): a, Emperor moth. b, Millar's tiger. c, Hawk moth, diff. d, Phrygionis privignara. e, Burnet moth, waterfall. f, Urania leilus.
No. 2574, 40d, Emerald moth. No. 2575, 40d, Red under-wing moth, vert.

Perf. 14, 13¾ (#2572-2573)
2002, Jan. 24
| 2568-2571 | A420 | Set of 4 | 4.00 | 4.00 |

Sheets of 6, #a-f
| 2572-2573 | A420 | Set of 2 | 15.00 | 15.00 |

Souvenir Sheets
| 2574-2575 | A420 | Set of 2 | 10.00 | 10.00 |

United We Stand — A421

2002, Feb. 6   *Perf. 13¾x13¼*
2576 A421 20d multi   2.50 2.50
    Issued in sheets of 4.

Reign of Queen Elizabeth II, 50th Anniv. — A422

No. 2577: a, With beige hat. b, With red hat. c, With blue hat. d, Near vehicle. 40d, Wearing uniform.

2002, Feb. 6   *Perf. 14½*
2577 A422 15d Sheet of 4, #a-d   7.50 7.50
Souvenir Sheet
2578 A422 40d multi   5.00 5.00

A423

Orchids — A424

No. 2579, vert.: a, Machu piechu. b, Masdevallia copper angel. c, Masdevallia hirtzi. d, Tuakau canoy.
No. 2580: a, Eriopsis sceptrum. b, Sarcanthopsis muellem. c, Bougainville white. d, Telipogon klotzchianus.
No. 2581, 7d: a, Richard Mueller. b, Colmanara wildcat. c, Cycnoches chlorochilon. d, Vanda coerylea. e, Disa blackii. f, Unnamed.
No. 2582, 7d: a, Seagulls beaulu queen. b, Hazel Boyd. c, Costa Rica. d, Dendrobium infudibulum. e, Disa hybrid. f, Chysis.
No. 2583, 6d, horiz.: a, Spathoglottis portusfinschii. b, Dendrobium macrophyllum. c, Grammaneis ellisii. d, Stanhopea wardii. e,

Dendrobium nindi. f, Dendrobium williamsianum.
No. 2584, 7d: a, Seutieama steeli. b, Dendrobium inaequale. c, Dendrobium lasiathera. d, Calypso bulbosa. e, Vanda hindsii. f, Dendrobium violaceoflavens.
No. 2585, 8d, horiz.: a, Phaleonopsis rosenstomii. b, Cypripedium guttatum. c, Cypripedium reginae. d, Dendrobium engae. e, Diplocaulobium hydrophilum. f, Dendrobium cuthbertsonii.
No. 2586, 25d, Dendrobium nobile. No. 2587, 25d, Ancidium alliance, vert.
No. 2588, 25d, Menadenium labiosum. No. 2589, 25d, Dendrobium spectabile. No. 2590, 25d, Dendrobium canaliculatum, horiz.

2001, June 15   Litho.   *Perf. 14*
2579 A423 7d Sheet of 4, #a-d   2.75 2.75
2580 A424 10d Sheet of 4, #a-d   4.00 4.00
Sheets of 6, #a-f
2581-2582 A423 Set of 2   8.50 8.50
2583-2585 A424 Set of 3   12.50 12.50
Souvenir Sheets
2586-2587 A423 Set of 2   5.00 5.00
2588-2590 A424 Set of 3   7.50 7.50

Nos. 2579-2590 were not available until 2002. Belgica 2001 Intl. Stamp Exhibition (#2579).

Wildlife A425

Designs: 2d, Martial eagle. 4d, Lion. 5d, Aardvark. 10d, Lion cub, vert.
No. 2595, 7d: a, Lion cub. b, Water buffalo. c, Topi. d, Hyena. e, Secretary bird. f, Genet.
No. 2596, 7d: a, Reedbuck. b, Hippopotamus. c, Waterbuck and malachite kingfisher. d, Hoopoe. e, White pelican. f, Waterbuck.
No. 2597, 25d, Hippopotamus. No. 2598, 25d, Crocodile.

2001, July 16
2591-2594 A425 Set of 4   2.10 2.10
Sheets of 6, #a-f
2595-2596 A425 Set of 2   8.50 8.50
Souvenir Sheets
2597-2598 A425 Set of 2   5.00 5.00

Nos. 2591-2598 were not available until 2002.

Pres. Theodore Roosevelt (1858-1919) — A426

No. 2599: a, Wearing hat and uniform. b, Close-up. c, With hand on chair. d, Wearing hat and neckerchief. 40d, Close-up, diff.

2002, Jan. 24
2599 A426 15d Sheet of 4, #a-d   7.75 7.75
Souvenir Sheet
2600 A426 40d multi   5.25 5.25

Betty Boop — A427

No. 2602, 40d, With gray ribbon in hair, horiz. No. 2603, 40d, With ice cream sundae.

2002, Feb. 13   *Perf. 13¾*
2601 A427 7d shown   .90 .90
Souvenir Sheets
2602-2603 A427 Set of 2   10.00 10.00
No. 2601 was issued in sheets of 9.

Shirley Temple in "Little Miss Broadway" — A428

No. 2604, horiz.: a, With man and old woman. b, Close-up. c, Waving. d, Holding man's tie. e, At hotel desk with men. f, Woman watching Temple point to tooth.
No. 2605: a, Dancing with young man. b, Dancing with old man with hat. c, Sitting with boy. d, Holding hands with old man. 30d, Wearing tiara and dancing with young man.

2002, Feb. 13
2604 A428 8d Sheet of 6, #a-f   6.00 6.00
2605 A428 10d Sheet of 4, #a-d   5.00 5.00
Souvenir Sheet
2606 A428 30d multi   4.00 4.00

2002 Winter Olympics, Salt Lake City — A429

Designs: No. 2607, 20d, Curling. No. 2608, 20d, Ski jumping.

2002, Mar. 18   *Perf. 14*
2607-2608 A429 Set of 2   5.00 5.00
   a. Souvenir sheet, #2607-2608   5.00 5.00

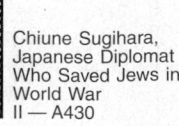

Chiune Sugihara, Japanese Diplomat Who Saved Jews in World War II — A430

2002, Apr. 29   *Perf. 13½x13¼*
2609 A430 10d multi   1.25 1.25
   Printed in sheets of 4.

Intl. Year of Mountains — A431

No. 2610: a, Winkler Tower, Italy. b, Mt. Huanstan Chico, Peru. c, Hodaka Mountains, Japan. d, Mustagh Ata, Kashmir. 40d, Mt. Myoko, Japan.

2002, July 1   *Perf. 13¼x13½*
2610 A431 15d Sheet of 4, #a-d   7.25 7.25
Souvenir Sheet
2611 A431 40d multi   4.75 4.75

2002 World Cup Soccer Championships, Japan and Korea — A432

Players, dates and locations of matches —
No. 2612, 9d: a, France v. Senegal. b, Uruguay v. Denmark. c, France v. Uruguay. d, Denmark v. Senegal. e, Denmark v. France. f, Senegal v. Uruguay.
No. 2613, 9d: a, Paraguay v. South Africa. b, Spain v. Slovenia. c, Spain v. Paraguay. d, South Africa v. Slovenia. e, South Africa v. Spain. f, Slovenia v. Paraguay.
No. 2614, 9d: a, Brazil v. Turkey. b, China v. Costa Rica. c, Brazil v. China. d, Costa Rica v. Turkey. e, Costa Rica v. Brazil. f, Turkey v. China.
No. 2615, 9d: a, South Korea v. Poland. b, US v. Portugal. c, South Korea v. US. d, Portugal v. Poland. e, Portugal v. South Korea. f, Poland v. US.
No. 2616, 9d: a, Germany v. Saudi Arabia. b, Ireland v. Cameroun. c, Germany v. Ireland. d, Cameroun v. Saudi Arabia. e, Cameroun v. Germany. f, Saudi Arabia v. Ireland.
No. 2617, 9d: a, England v. Sweden. b, Argentina v. Nigeria. c, Sweden v. Nigeria. d, Argentina v. England. e, Sweden v. Argentina. f, Nigeria v. England.
No. 2618, 9d: a, Croatia v. Mexico. b, Italy v. Ecuador. c, Italy v. Croatia. d, Mexico v. Ecuador. e, Mexico v. Italy. f, Ecuador v. Croatia.
No. 2619, 9d: a, Japan v. Belgium. b, Russia v. Tunisia. c, Japan v. Russia. d, Tunisia v. Belgium. e, Tunisia v. Japan. f, Belgium v. Russia.
Stadia and dates of matches between —
No. 2620, 20d: a, France v. Senegal. b, Uruguay v. Denmark.
No. 2621, 20d: a, France v. Uruguay. b, Denmark v. Senegal.
No. 2622, 20d: a, Denmark v. France. b, Senegal v. Uruguay.
No. 2623, 20d: a, Paraguay v. South Africa. b, Spain v. Slovenia.
No. 2624, 20d: a, Spain v. Paraguay. b, South Africa v. Slovenia.
No. 2625, 20d: a, South Africa v. Spain. b, Slovenia v. Paraguay.
No. 2626, 20d: a, Brazil v. Turkey. b, China v. Costa Rica.
No. 2627, 20d: a, Brazil v. China. b, Costa Rica v. Turkey.
No. 2628, 20d: a, Costa Rica v. Brazil. b, Turkey v. China.
No. 2629, 20d: a, South Korea v. Poland. b, US v. Portugal.
No. 2630, 20d: a, South Korea v. US. b, Portugal v. Poland.
No. 2631, 20d: a, Portugal v. South Korea. b, Poland v. US.
No. 2632, 20d: a, Germany v. Saudi Arabia. b, Ireland v. Cameroun.
No. 2633, 20d: a, Germany v. Ireland. b, Cameroun v. Saudi Arabia.
No. 2634, 20d: a, Cameroun v. Germany. b, Saudi Arabia v. Ireland.

No. 2635, 20d: a, England v. Sweden. b, Argentina v. Nigeria.
No. 2636, 20d: a, Sweden v. Nigeria. b, Argentina v. England.
No. 2637, 20d: a, Sweden v. Argentina. b, Nigeria v. England.
No. 2638, 20d: a, Croatia v. Mexico. b, Italy v. Ecuador.
No. 2639, 20d: a, Italy v. Croatia. b, Mexico v. Ecuador.
No. 2640, 20d: a, Mexico v. Italy. b, Ecuador v. Croatia.
No. 2641, 20d: a, Japan v. Belgium. b, Russia v. Tunisia.
No. 2642, 20d: a, Japan v. Russia. b, Tunisia v. Belgium.
No. 2643, 20d: a, Tunisia v. Japan. b, Belgium v. Russia.

2002, July 1   **Perf. 13¼**
Sheets of 6, #a-f
2612-2619 A432   Set of 8   52.50 52.50
Souvenir Sheets
2620-2643 A432   Set of 24   110.00 110.00
  See Nos. 2654-2656 for sheets with match results.

Popeye — A433

No. 2644, 10d: a, Popeye on cross-country skis. b, Popeye ski jumping. c, Popeye slaloming. d, Popeye snowboarding.
No. 2645, 10d: a, Swee'Pea on sled. b, Olive Oyl on skis. c, Brutus. d, Wimpy on ice skates.
No. 2646, 25d, Popeye and Olive in bobsled. No. 2647, 25d, Brutus playing hockey. No. 2648, 25d, Olive on ice skates. No. 2649, 25d, Popeye speed skating, horiz.

2002, June 17   **Litho.**   **Perf. 14**
Sheets of 6, #a-f
2644-2645 A433   Set of 2   9.25 9.25
Souvenir Sheets
2646-2649 A433   Set of 4   12.00 12.00

20th World Scout Jamboree, Thailand — A434

No. 2650: a, Scout with bugle. b, Scout making fire. c, Scout fishing.
40d, Scout tying knot.

2002, July 1   **Perf. 13½x13¼**
2650 A434 15d Sheet of 3, #a-c   5.25 5.25
Souvenir Sheet
2651 A434 40d multi   4.75 4.75

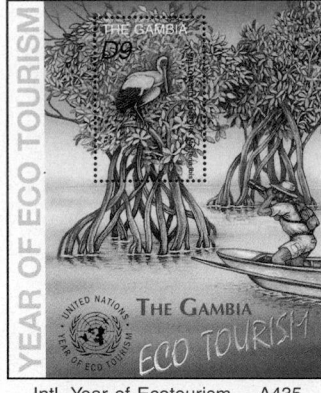

Intl. Year of Ecotourism — A435

No. 2652: a, Bird-of-Paradise flower. b, Goliath heron. c, Baobab tree. d, Roan antelope. e, Red tip butterfly. f, Egyptian cobra.
No. 2653, Yellow-billed stork.

2002, July 1
2652 A435 9d Sheet of 6, #a-d   6.25 6.25
Souvenir Sheet
2653 A435 9d multi   1.00 1.00

Nos. 2616, 2617 and 2619 Redrawn With Match Scores

No. 2654, 9d: a, Germany 8, Saudi Arabia 0. b, Ireland 1, Cameroun 1. c, Germany 1, Ireland 1. d, Cameroun 1, Saudi Arabia 0. e, Cameroun 0, Germany 2. f, Saudi Arabia 0, Ireland 3.
No. 2655, 9d: a, England 1, Sweden 1. b, Argentina 1, Nigeria 0. c, Sweden 2, Nigeria 1. d, Argentina 0, England 1. e, Sweden 1, Argentina 1. f, Nigeria 0, England 0.
No. 2656, 9d: a, Japan 2, Belgium 2. b, Russia 2, Tunisia 0. c, Japan 1, Russia 0. d, Tunisia 1, Belgium 1. e, Japan 2, Tunisia 0. f, Belgium 3, Russia 2.

2002, July 15   **Perf. 13¼**
Sheets of 6, #a-f
2654-2656 A432   Set of 3   19.00 19.00

Elvis Presley (1935-77) A436

2002, Aug. 19   **Perf. 13½x13¾**
2657 A436 5d multi   .55 .55

Things from the Netherlands — A437

Netherlands Lighthouses — A438

Netherlands Postage Stamps, 150th Anniv. — A439

Women's Traditional Costumes of the Netherlands — A440

No. 2658: a, Farm. b, Porcelain. c, Building. d, Ice skaters. e, Cheese, flowers and wooden shoes. f, Prince Willem-Alexander and his bride.
No. 2659: a, Den Helder. b, Terschelling. c, Maasvlakte. d, Ijmuiden. e, Westkapelle. f, Breskens.
No. 2660: a, Netherlands #1. b, Netherlands #B72. c, Netherlands #279. d, Netherlands #586. e, Netherlands #620. f, Netherlands #1108a.
No. 2661: a, Woman from Friesland (plaid headdress). b, Back of woman from Utrecht. c, Woman and child from Noord-Holland.

2002, Aug. 30   **Perf. 13½x13¼**
2658 A437 10d Sheet of 6, #a-f   6.50 6.50
2659 A438 10d Sheet of 6, #a-f   6.50 6.50
Perf. 13¼x13½
2660 A439 10d Sheet of 6, #a-f   6.50 6.50
Perf. 13¼
2661 A440 20d Sheet of 3, #a-c   6.50 6.50
  Amphilex 2002 Intl. Stamp Exhibition, Amsterdam.

Marine Mammals and Flowers — A441

No. 2662, 10d: a, Blue whale. b, Pan-tropical spotted dolphin. c, Killer whale. d, Minke whale. e, Sperm whale. f, Pilot whale.

No. 2663, 10d: a, Juba-jamba. b, Devil's tongue. c, Rattle box. d, Vernonia purpurea. e, Seaside purslane. f, Fireball lily.
No. 2664, 50d, Humpback whale. No. 2665, 50d, Cape weed, swamp arum, vert.

2002, Sept. 23   **Perf. 14**
Sheets of 6, #a-f
2662-2663 A441   Set of 2   11.50 11.50
Souvenir Sheets
2664-2665 A441   Set of 2   10.00 10.00
  See Nos. 2763-2764.

A442

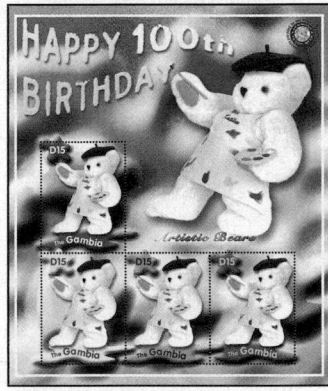

Teddy Bears, Cent. — A443

No. 2666: a, Bear with green feathered cap. b, Bear with beer stein. c, Bear with flower bouquet. d, Bear with mountain hat.
No. 2667 — Color of denomination and country name: a, White. b, Red violet. c, Blue violet. d, Green.

2002, Oct. 21   **Perf. 14**
2666 A442 15d Sheet of 4, #a-d   6.00 6.00
Perf. 14¼
2667 A443 15d Sheet of 4, #a-d   6.00 6.00

Christmas — A444

  Designs: 3d, Madonna of Loreto, by Perugino. 5d, Madonna della Consolazione, by Perugino. 7d, Adoration of the Shepherds, by Perugino. 15d, Transfiguration of Christ, by Giovanni Bellini. 35d, Adoration of the Magi, by Perugino.
45d, Christ Blessing, by Bellini.

2002, Nov. 4   **Perf. 14**
2668-2672 A444   Set of 5   6.25 6.25
Souvenir Sheet
2673 A444 45d multi   4.50 4.50

Princess Diana (1961-97) — A445

No. 2674, 15d — With red panel at bottom: a, As child. b, Wearing tiara. c, Holding baby. d, With children.

No. 2675, 15d: a, Wearing red hat. b, Wearing red and white hat. c, Wearing white gown. d, Wearing black gown and choker.

2002, Nov. 18
Sheets of 4, #a-d

2674-2675 A445 Set of 2   11.50 11.50

Souvenir Sheet

Gold-banded Forester Butterfly — A446

2002   Litho.   Perf. 14
2676 A446 60d multi   5.75 5.75

Birds — A447

No. 2677: a, Black-crowned crane. b, Barn owl. c, African pygmy kingfisher. d, Audouin's gull. e, Royal tern. f, Blue-bellied roller.

2002
2677 A447 7d Sheet of 6, #a-f   4.25 4.25

Pres. John F. Kennedy (1917-63) — A448

No. 2678, 15d: a, With daughter Caroline. b, At typewriter. c, At wedding to Jacqueline. d, With Jacqueline.

No. 2679, 15d, vert: a, In naval uniform. b, As child. c, Wearing shirt with open collar. d, At microphone.

2002, Nov. 8
Sheets of 4, #a-d

2678-2679 A448 Set of 2   11.50 11.50

A449

Trains
A450

Designs: 2d, Paris, Lyon & Mediterranean Railway. 3d, Zugspitz rack train, Germany. No. 2682, 10d, Austrian State Railway Class 210. 15d, State Railway of Saxony.

4d, 1922 Great Britain Class A1 4-6-2. 5d, 1957 Tee four car train. No. 2686, 7d, 1928 German Rheingold Mitropa car. 8d, 1900 German Gerda 4-4-0.

No. 2688, 7d: a, French Natl. Railway Series 68. b, French Natl. Railway Mistral. c, Prussian State Railway. d, Austrian Southern Railway. e, Paris-Orleans Railway. f, German Federal Railway E10.

No. 2689, 7d: a, Royal Prussian Union Railway. b, Austrian Federal Railway. c, German Rugen steam locomotive. d, Rh B Ge 2/4 electric locomotive. e, Panoramic Express, Switzerland. f, Brunig steam engine, Swiss Natl. Railway.

No. 2690, 10d: a, 1813 Puffing Billy, Great Britain. b, Adler, Germany, 1836. c, 1906 German 4-6-0. d, Class 132 Co-Co, Germany.

No. 2691, 10d: a, 1832 Brother Jonathan 4-2-0, US. b, Medoc Class 2-4-0, Germany and Switzerland, 1857. c, 1908 German Class S 3/6 4-6-2. d, 1959 German Class VT 11.5.

No. 2692, 10d: a, 1843 Beuth 2-2-2, Germany. b, 1852 Crampton 4-2-0, France. c, 1932 Sut 877 Flying Hamburger, Germany. d, 1970 Class 103.1 Co-Co, Germany.

No. 2693, 25d, German Federal Railway V200. No. 2694, 25d, German Federal Railway Trans-Europe Express.

No. 2695, 25d, 1953 VT10.5, Germany. No. 2696, 25d,1973 Class ET 403 four-car electric, Germany.

2002
2680-2683 A449 Set of 4   2.75 2.75
2684-2687 A450 Set of 4   2.40 2.40

Sheets of 6, #a-f
2688-2689 A449 Set of 2   8.00 8.00

Sheets of 4, #a-d
2690-2692 A450 Set of 3   11.50 11.50

Souvenir Sheets
2693-2694 A449 Set of 2   5.00 5.00
2695-2696 A450 Set of 2   5.00 5.00

Charles A. Lindbergh (1902-74), Aviator — A451

No. 2697, 15d: a, As child, with dog. b, As young man, brown violet background. c, With aviator goggles. d, Anne Morrow Lindbergh.

No. 2698, 15d: a, As child. b, As young man, blue background. c, Wearing uniform. d, Wearing suit and tie.

2002, Nov. 18   Litho.   Perf. 14
Sheets of 4, #a-d

2697-2698 A451 Set of 2   11.50 11.50

Butterfly Type of 2000

Designs: 4d, Amphicalia tigris.

2003, Jan. 14   Perf. 14¾x14
2699 A367 4d multi   .40 .40

New Year 2003 (Year of the Ram) — A452

No. 2697: a, Tan background, brown ram. b, Purple background. c, Brown background, orange ram. d, Orange background, purple and red ram.

2003, Jan. 27   Perf. 13¾
2701 A452 10d Sheet of 4, #a-d   3.50 3.50

A453

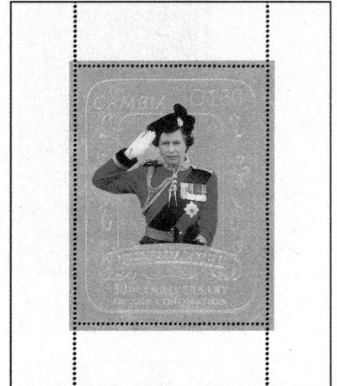

Coronation of Queen Elizabeth II, 50th Anniv. — A454

No. 2702: a, Wearing tiara. b, Wearing blue hat. c, Wearing cape and hat.

2003   Litho.   Perf. 14
2702 A453 20d Sheet of 3,
     #a-c   5.50 5.50

Souvenir Sheet
2703 A453 45d shown   4.25 4.25

Miniature Sheet
Litho. & Embossed
Perf. 13¼x13

2704 A454 130d shown   10.50 10.50
Issued: Nos. 2702-2703, 5/13; 130d, 2/24.

Art by Yoshitoshi Taiso (1839-92) A455

Designs: 5d, Concubine Washing Her Hands Under an Ornate Faucet. 10d, Housewife in an Inner Chamber Fanning a Fire. 15d, Geisha Catching a Firefly. 25d, A Young Geisha Dressed as an Elegant Young Man While Taking Part in the Niwaka Celebration.

No. 2709: a, Music Teacher Playing on a Samisen. b, An "Okamisan," or Proprietress of a Tea House, at Work. c, A City Merchant's Widow Absorbed in a Novelette. d, Busy Young Waitress Preoccupied With Her Responsibilities.

45d, A "Saikun," or Wife of a Government Official, Lighting an Oil Lamp.

2003, Mar. 10   Litho.   Perf. 14¼
2705-2708 A455 Set of 4   4.75 4.75
2709 A455 20d Sheet of 4, #a-d   6.50 6.50

Souvenir Sheet
2710 A455 45d multi   4.00 4.00

Paintings by the Cranachs A456

Paintings by Lucas Cranach the Elder (1472-1553) or Lucas Cranach the Younger (1515-86) (Y): 5d, Portrait of Johannes Scheyring. 7d, Rudolph Agricola. 10d, Portrait Head of a Gentleman (Y). 20d, Hans von Lindau (Y).

No. 2715: a, Margravine Elizabeth von Ansbach (Y). b, Elector Joachim II of Brandenburg (Y). c, Portrait of a Nobleman (Y). d, Portrait of a Noblewoman (Y).

40d, The Ill-matched Couple.

2003, Mar. 10
2711-2714 A456 Set of 4   3.50 3.50
2715 A456 15d Sheet of 4, #a-d   5.00 5.00

Souvenir Sheet
2716 A456 40d multi   3.25 3.25

Paintings by Wassily Kandinsky (1866-1944) — A457

Designs: 2d, Composition X. 4d, Arrow Towards the Circle. 5d, Yellow-Red-Blue. 7d, Accompanied Middle. 10d, In Blue. 20d, Round and Pointed.

No. 2723, vert.: a, Picture with Archer. b, Light. c, Picture in the Picture. d, White Stroke.

No. 2724, 45d, Improvisation XIX. No. 2725, 45d, On the Points.

2003, Mar. 10   Perf. 14¼
2717-2722 A457 Set of 6   4.25 4.25
2723 A457 15d Sheet of 4, #a-d   5.00 5.00
Size: 97x78mm
Imperf

2724-2725 A457 Set of 2   7.50 7.50

Astronauts Killed In Space Shuttle
Columbia Accident — A459

No. 2726, 15d — Michael P. Anderson: a,
Columbia crew, brown background, country
name at UL. b, Anderson and jet. c, Shuttle
lifting off. d, Shuttle in orbit, Space Station.
No. 2727, 15d — Kalpana Chawla: a, Like
No. 2726a, country name at LL. b, Shuttle
being transported by jet. c, Shuttle glowing in
re-entry. d, Chawla, astronaut spacewalking.
No. 2728, 15d — Laurel Blair Salton Clark:
a, Like No. 2727a, green and red background.
b, Shuttle in orbit, moon in background. c,
Shuttle on launch pad. d, Clark and jet.
No. 2729, 15d — Ilan Ramon: a, Columbia
crew, purple and yellow background. b,
Ramon in jet. c, Shuttle with engines firing at
launch pad. d, Shuttle in orbit.
No. 2730: a, Mission Specialist David M.
Brown. b, Commander Rick D. Husband. c,
Mission Specialist 4 Laurel Blair Salton Clark.
d, Mission Specialist 4 Kalpana Chawla. e,
Payload Commander, Michael P. Anderson. f,
Pilot William C. McCool. g, Payload Specialist
4 Ilan Ramon.

2003, Apr. 7		Perf. 14¼
Sheets of 4, #a-d		
2726-2729 A458	Set of 4	21.00 21.00
Souvenir Sheet		
2730 A459 10d Sheet of 7, #a-g		6.00 6.00

A460

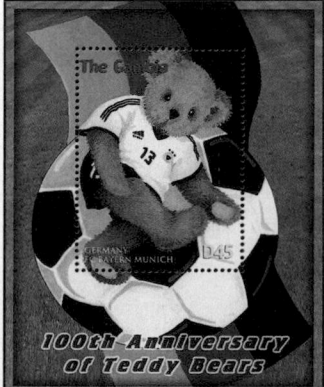

Teddy Bears — A461

No. 2732, 15d — Bears with flags and soccer uniforms of: a, England. b, Brazil. c, Germany. d, Spain.
No. 2733, 15d — Bears with soccer
uniforms of German teams: a, Schalke 04. b,
FC Bayern Munich. c, Bayer Leaerkusen. d,
Hertha Berlin.
No. 2734, 45d, FC Bayern Munich, white
uniform. No. 2735, 45d, FC Bayern Munich
red uniform, horiz.

2003	**Embroidered**	**Imperf.**
	Self-Adhesive (#2731)	
2731 A460 150d shown		14.00 14.00
Sheets of 4, #a-d		
Litho.		
Perf. 13¼		
2732-2733 A461	Set of 2	11.00 11.00
Souvenir Sheets		
2734-2735 A461	Set of 2	8.25 8.25

Issued: No. 2731, Apr.; Nos. 2732-2735, 7/1.
No. 2731 was issued in sheets of 4.

Prince William, 21st Birthday — A462

No. 2736: a, Wearing suit, no tie. b, Wearing
suit and tie. c, Wearing blue shirt, no suit.
45d, Wearing polo uniform.

2003, May 13	**Litho.**	**Perf. 14**
2736 A462 20d Sheet of 3, #a-c		5.50 5.50
Souvenir Sheet		
2737 A462 45d multi		4.25 4.25

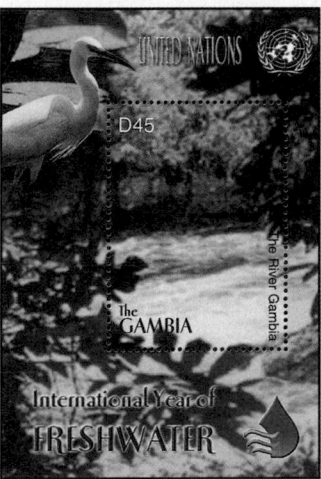

Intl. Year of Fresh Water — A463

No. 2738 — Gambia River: a, Foliage at top.
b, Foliage at top, silhouette of far shore at
center. c, Trees at right.
45d, Gambia River rapids.

2003, July 1		Perf. 13¼
2738 A463 20d Sheet of 3, #a-c		5.50 5.50
Souvenir Sheet		
2739 A463 45d multi		4.25 4.25

Tour de France Bicycle Race,
Cent. — A464

No. 2740, 15d: a, Henri Pelissier, 1923. b,
Ottavio Bottecchia, 1924. c, Bottecchia, 1925.
d, Lucien Buysse, 1926.
No. 2741, 15d: a, Nicholas Frantz, 1927. b,
Frantz, 1928. c, Maurice de Waele, 1929. d,
André Leducq, 1930.
No. 2742, 15d: a, Antonin Magne, 1931. b,
Leducq, 1932. c, Georges Speicher, 1933. d,
Magne, 1934.

2003, July 1		Perf. 13¼
Sheets of 4, #a-d		
2740-2742 A464	Set of 3	17.00 17.00

General Motors Automobiles — A465

No. 2743, 15d — Cadillacs: a, 1937 Series
60. b, 1927 La Salle. c, 1930 V-16. d, 1931 V-
16 Convertible.
No. 2744, 15d — Corvettes: a, 1960 Shark.
b, 1964 Sting Ray Convertible. c, 1956 Convertible. d, 1967.
No. 2745, 45d, 1954 Cadillac Eldorado. No.
2746, 45d, 1964 Corvette Sting Ray.

2003, July 1		Perf. 13¼x13½
Sheets of 4, #a-d		
2743-2744 A465	Set of 2	11.00 11.00
Souvenir Sheets		
2745-2746 A465	Set of 2	8.25 8.25

History of Aviation — A466

No. 2747, 15d: a, First powered flight by
Wright Brothers, 1903. b, Goupy I, first full-
size triplane, 1908. c, Deutschland LZ-7, first
commercial airship, 1909. d, Lt. Col. Richard
Byrd's flight over North Pole, 1926.
No. 2748, 15d: a, Granville Gee Bee, world
speed record, 1932. b, Boeing 247D with all-
metal construction retractable landing gear,
1933. c, Douglas DC-3, 1935. d, Amelia Earhart's solo flight from Hawaii to California,
1935.
No. 2749, 15d: a, First solar powered flight,
by MacCready Solar Challenger, 1981. b, Voyager 2 space probe explores Saturn, 1981. c,
Space Shuttle Columbia, 1981. d, First non-
stop non-refueled around the world flight, by
Voyager, 1986.
No. 2750, 40d, Vought V-173 Short Takeoff
and Landing research airplane, 1942. No,
2751, 40d, Pioneer 10 space probe, 1972. No.
2752, 40d, AD-1 scissors-wing SST, 1979.

2003, July 14		Perf. 14
Sheets of 4, #a-d		
2747-2749 A466	Set of 3	17.00 17.00
Souvenir Sheets		
2750-2752 A466	Set of 3	11.00 11.00

Ferrari Race Cars — A467

Designs: 2d, 126 C2. 3d, 312 T2. 5d, 312
T4. 7d, 126 C3. 10d, F399. 15d, F1-2000. 20d,
F2001. 25d, F2002.

2003, July 28		Perf. 14¼
2753-2760 A467	Set of 8	6.50 6.50

Circus Performers — A468

No. 2761, 15d: a, Francesco Caroli. b, Lou
Jacobs. c, Frankie Saluto. d, Gingernut.
No. 2762, 15d: a, Evgeny Maranogli. b,
Saby. c, Colonel Joe. d, Puma.

2003, Sept. 1		Perf. 14
Sheets of 4, #a-d		
2761-2762 A468	Set of 2	10.00 10.00

**Marine Mammals and Flowers Type
of 2002**

No. 2763 — Insects and flowers: a, Colored
shield-backed bug, Waltheria indica. b, Dragonfly, Red mangrove. c, Cotton stainer bug,
Baissea multiflora. d, Harpagomantis. Mimosa
pigra. e, Katydid, Coia cordifolia. f, African
grasshopper, Urena labata.
50d, Giant swallowtail butterfly, Ipomoea
cairica.

2003		Perf. 14
2763 A441 10d Sheet of 6, #a-f		4.50 4.50
Souvenir Sheet		
2764 A441 50d multi		4.00 4.00

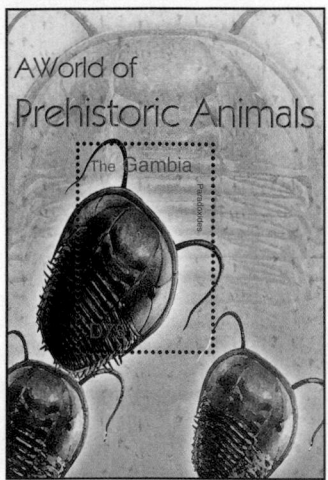

Prehistoric Animals — A469

No. 2765, 30d: a, Peteinosaurus. b, Pachycephalosaurus. c, Ichthyosaur. d, Anomalocaris.
No. 2766, 30d, horiz.: a, Criorhynchus. b, Seismosaurus. c, Triceratops. d, Stegosaurus.
No. 2767, 75d, Paradoxides. No. 2768, 75d, Edmontosaurus, horiz.

2003, Nov. 4   Litho.   Perf. 14
Sheets of 4, #a-d
2765-2766 A469 Set of 2   17.00 17.00
Souvenir Sheets
2767-2768 A469 Set of 2   10.50 10.50

Christmas A470

Paintings: 3d, Madonna of the Grand Duke, by Raphael. 5d, Madonna della Impannata, by Raphael. 7d, Adoration of the Magi, by Filippo Lippi. 60d, Adoration in the Woods, by Lippi. 75d, Madonna del Carmelo, by Giambattista Tiepolo.

2003, Nov. 17   Perf. 14¼
2769-2772 A470 Set of 4   5.50 5.50
Souvenir Sheet
2773 A470 75d multi   5.50 5.50

Leo Diamond A471

2003, Nov. 18   Perf. 13¼x13½
2774 A471 15d multi   1.10 1.10
Souvenir Sheet
2775 A471 60d multi   4.50 4.50
No. 2774 issued in sheets of six.

Pearls — A472

No. 2776: a, South Sea pearls. b, Mabe pearls. c, Pinctada maxima. d, Australian pearls. e, Pearls on ocean floor. f, South Sea white pearls.
60d, Champagne pearls.

2003, Nov. 18
2776 A472 15d Sheet of 6, #a-f   6.50 6.50
Souvenir Sheet
2777 A472 60d multi   4.50 4.50

James Cagney (1899-1986) — A473

No. 2778: a, With solid tie. b, With hat. c, With gun. d, With lapel handkerchief. e, With plaid tie. f, With woman.

2003   Perf. 14
2778 A473 10d Sheet of 6, #a-d   4.50 4.50

Clark Gable (1901-60) — A474

No. 2779: a, Wearing tuxedo and bow tie, hand showing. b, Wearing suit and tie, no mustache, no hand showing. c, Wearing tuxedo and bow tie, no hand showing. d, Wearing suit and tie, hand showing. e, Wearing suit and solid tie, with mustache. f, Wearing suit and striped tie, with mustache.

2003
2779 A474 10d Sheet of 6, #a-f   4.50 4.50

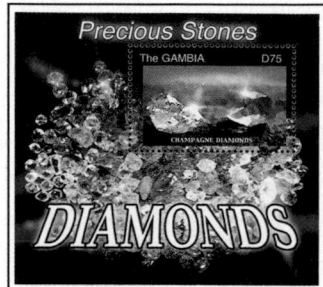

Diamonds — A475

No. 2780: a, Rough diamonds. b, Yellow diamonds. c, Pink diamonds. d, Blue diamonds. e, White diamonds. f, Green diamonds.
75d, Champagne diamonds.

Perf. 13¼x13½
2003, Nov. 18   Litho.
2780 A475 20d Sheet of 6, #a-f   8.00 8.00
Souvenir Sheet
2781 A475 75d multi   5.00 5.00

Minerals — A476

No. 2782: a, Stilbite. b, Smoky quartz. c, Lapis lazuli. d, Amethyst. e, Black opals. f, Rubies.
60d, Quartz.

2003, Nov. 18
2782 A476 15d Sheet of 6, #a-f   6.00 6.00
Souvenir Sheet
2783 A476 60d multi   4.00 4.00

New Year 2004 (Year of the Monkey) — A477

No. 2784: a, Monkey with white and brown face, white ears. b, Monkey with white and blue gray face. c, Monkey with white and brown face. d, Monkey with orange and white face.

2004, Jan. 5   Perf. 13¼
2784 A477 15d Sheet of 4, #a-d   4.50 4.50

Paintings by Xu Beihong (1895-1953) — A478

No. 2785, vert.: a, Four Magpies. b, Cormorants. c, Under the Banyan Tree. d, Citrus Tree. e, Double Happiness. f, Rooster in Bamboo Garden.
No. 2786: a, Bird on the Kapok Tree. b, Twin Pines.

2004, Jan. 21 Litho. Perf. 13½x13¼
2785 A478 10d Sheet of 6, #a-f   4.00 4.00
Perf. 13¼
2786 A478 25d Sheet of 2, #a-b   3.50 3.50
2004 Hong Kong Stamp Expo. No. 2785 contains six 28x42mm stamps.

FIFA (Fédération Internationale de Football Association), Cent. — A479

FIFA cups: No. 2787, 10d, World Cup. No. 2788, 10d, Jules Rimet Cup. No. 2789, 10d, Women's World Cup. No. 2790, 10d, Under 17 World Championship Cup. No. 2791, 10d, Under 19 Women's World Championship Cup. No. 2792, 10d, Club World Championship Cup. No. 2793, 10d, Confederations Cup. No. 2794, 10d, World Youth Championship Cup. No. 2795, 10d, Fustal (Indoor Soccer) World Championship Cup.

2004, Feb. 16   Perf. 13¼
2787-2795 A479 Set of 9   6.25 6.25

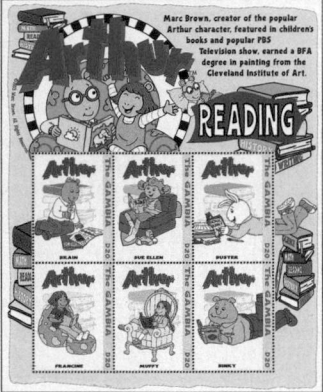

Arthur and Friends — A480

No. 2796 — Characters reading: a, Brain. b, Sue Ellen. c, Buster. d, Francine. e, Muffy. f, Binky.
No. 2797, 30d: a, Brain playing clarinet. b, Francine playing banjo. c, Buster playing flute. d, Sue Ellen playing violin.
No. 2798, 30d: a, Brain playing bass. b, Francine playing drum. c, Buster playing tuba. d, Sue Ellen playing saxophone.

2004, Feb. 16
2796 A480 20d Sheet of 6,
#a-f   8.25 8.25
Sheets of 4, #a-d
2797-2798 A480 Set of 2   16.50 16.50

Concorde and Queen Elizabeth 2 — A481

Concorde — A482

No. 2800, 25d — Concorde 216 G-BOAF and: a, British flag, with dots of blue at UR. b, British flag, no dots at UR. c, Clouds.
No. 2801, 25d — Concorde 216 G-BOAF and: a, Statue of Liberty. b, Field of US flag. c, Stripes of US flag.
No. 2802, 25d — Concorde 213 F-BTSD and: a, Top of Eiffel Tower. b, French flag, middle part of Eiffel Tower. c, French flag, first and second landings of Eiffel Tower.

2004, Feb. 17　　　**Perf. 14**
2799 A481 60d multi　　　4.25　4.25
Sheets of 3, #a-c
Perf. 13¼x13½
2800-2802 A482　Set of 3　15.50 15.50

Paintings in the Hermitage, St. Petersburg, Russia — A483

No. 2803, vert.: a, Portrait of a Gentleman, by Domenico Capriolo. b, Sybil, by Dosso Dossi. c, A Woman in a Turban, by Anne-Louis Girodet-Trioson. d, Portrait of a Gentleman, by Ambrosius Holbein.
75d, Husband and Wife, by Lorenzo Lotto.

2004, Feb. 17　　　**Perf. 13¼**
2803 A483 30d Sheet of 4, #a-d　8.25 8.25
Imperf
2804 A483 75d multi　　　5.25 5.25
St. Petersburg, 300th anniv. No. 2803 contains four 37x50mm stamps.

Paintings by Pablo Picasso — A484

No. 2805, vert.: a, Girl in Chemise. b, Portrait of Jacinto Salvadó as Harlequin. c, Tumblers. d, Woman with a Crow.
75d, The Siesta.

2004, Feb. 17　　　**Perf. 13¼**
2805 A484 30d Sheet of 4, #a-d　8.25 8.25
Imperf
2806 A484 75d multi　　　5.25 5.25
No. 2805 contains four 37x50mm stamps.

Paintings by Norman Rockwell — A485

No. 2807: a, Detail of 1957 Saturday Evening Post Illustration. b, Girl at Mirror. c, After the Prom. d, The Prom Dress.
75d, Losing the Game.

2004, Feb. 17　　　**Perf. 13¼**
2807 A485 30d Sheet of 4, #a-d　8.25 8.25
Souvenir Sheet
2808 A485 75d multi　　　5.25 5.25

Paintings by Kunichika Toyohara (1835-1900) A486

Designs: 10d, The Actor Kikugoro Onoe V as Moronao with the Late Sojuro Nakamura I as Hangan Enya. 15d, The Actor Kikugoro Onoe V as Kunimoto Shinohara with Danjuro Ichikawa IX as Takamori. 20d, The Actor Kikugoro Onoe V as Kansuke Yamamoto with Sadanji Ichikawa I as Daizo Ushikubo. 35d, The Actor Kikugoro Onoe V as the Ghost Seigen with Fukusuke Nakamura IV as Sakurahime.
No. 2813: a, The Actor Sadanji Ichikawa I as the Fishmonger Fukashichi. b, The Actor Sadanji Ichikawa I as Umeomaru. c, The Actor Kuzo Ichikawa III as Shihei Fujiwara. d, The Actor Shikan Nakamura IV as Motome.
75d, The Actor Udanji Ichikawa as Saihei Koya (Ozawa Keifu Tomofusa), horiz.

2004, Feb. 17
2809-2812 A486　Set of 4　5.50 5.50
2813 A486 30d Sheet of 4, #a-d　8.25 8.25
Souvenir Sheet
2814 A486 75d multi　　　5.25 5.25

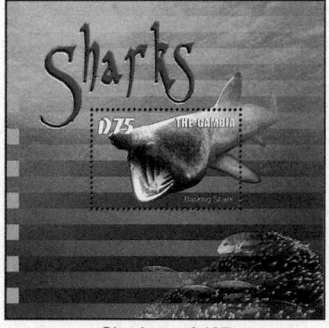

Sharks — A487

No. 2815: a, Lemon shark. b, Nurse shark. c, Leopard shark. d, Starry smoothhound sharks.
75d, Basking shark.

2004, Mar. 8　　　**Perf. 13¼x13½**
2815 A487 30d Sheet of 4, #a-d　8.25 8.25
Souvenir Sheet
2816 A487 75d multi　　　5.25 5.25

Cats — A488

No. 2817, vert.: a, Black and white bicolor American shorthair. b, Brown and white Sphinx. c, Copper-eyed white Persian. d, Blue mackerel tabby Oriental longhair.
75d, Copper-eyed cameo Persian.

2004, Mar. 8　　　**Perf. 13½x13¼**
2817 A488 30d Sheet of 4, #a-d　8.25 8.25
Souvenir Sheet
Perf. 13¼x13½
2818 A488 75d multi　　　5.25 5.25

Dogs — A489

No. 2819, vert.: a, Bracco. b, Shih tzu. c, Boston terrier. d, Chihuahua.
75d, Borzoi.

2004, Mar. 8　　　**Perf. 13½x13¼**
2819 A489 30d Sheet of 4, #a-d　8.25 8.25
Souvenir Sheet
Perf. 13¼x13½
2820 A489 75d multi　　　5.25 5.25

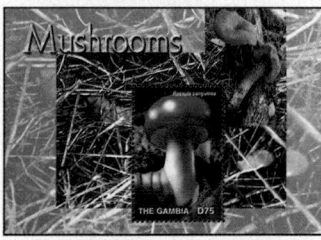

Mushrooms — A490

No. 2821, 30d: a, Hydrocybe conica. b, Laccaria fraterna. c, Gomphus clavatus. d, Hydrocybe psittacina.
No. 2822, 30d, horiz.: a, Steel blue entoloma. b, Caged stinkhorn. c, Flowerpot depiota. d, Singeri dodge.
75d, Russula sanguinea.

Perf. 13½x13¼, 13¼x13½
2004, Mar. 8
2821-2822 A490　Set of 2　16.50 16.50
Souvenir Sheet
2823 A490 75d multi　　　5.25 5.25

Orchid Cacti — A491

No. 2824, 30d: a, Echinocerus. b, Harrisia. c, Stapelia. d, Matucana.
No. 2825, 30d: a, Epiphyllum crenatum. b, Isopogon latifolius. c, Banksia ericifolia. d, Echinopsis.
75d, Epiphyllum.

2004, Mar. 8　　　**Perf. 13¼x13½**
Sheets of 4, #a-d
2824-2825 A491　Set of 2　16.50 16.50
Souvenir Sheet
2826 A491 75d multi　　　5.25 5.25

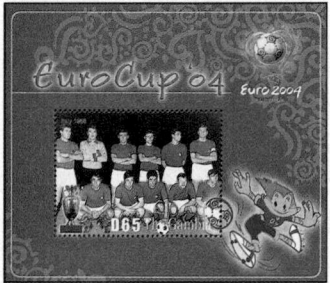

European Soccer Championships, Portugal — A492

No. 2827 — Teams from: a, Bulgaria. b, Croatia. c, Czech Republic. d, Denmark. e, England. f, France. g, Germany. h, Greece. i, Italy. j, Latvia. k, Netherlands. l, Portugal (no country name). m, Russia. n, Spain. o, Sweden. p, Switzerland.
No. 2828, vert.: a, Angelo Domenghini. b, Dragan Dzajic. c, Luigi Riva. d, Stadio Olimpico.
65d, 1968 champions, Italy.

Perf. 13¼, 13½x13¼ (#2828)
2004, Mar. 26
2827 A492　6d Sheet of 16, #a-p 6.75 6.75
2828 A492 25d Sheet of 4, #a-d　7.00 7.00
Souvenir Sheet
2829 A492 65d multi　　　4.50 4.50
No. 2828 contains four 28x42mm stamps.

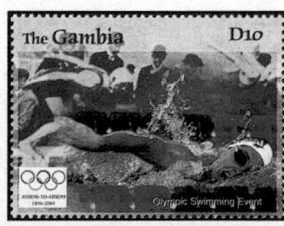

2004 Summer Olympics, Athens — A493

Designs: 10d, Swimming. 15d, Henri de Baillet-Latour (1876-1942), Intl. Olympic Committee President, vert. 20d, Gold medal of 1896 Olympics, vert. 30d, Pentathlon.

2004, Apr. 19　　　**Perf. 13¼**
2830-2833 A493　Set of 4　5.25 5.25

Trains, Bridges, Tunnels and Stations — A494

No. 2834, 12d: a, Mallard locomotive. b, North British 4-8-2T locomotive. c, Russian P36 4-8-4 locomotive. d, Forth Rail Bridge. e, Lune Viaduct. f, Lambley Viaduct. g, Alston Arches Viaduct. h, Royal Albert Bridge. i, Blackfriar's Bridge.

No. 2835, 12d: a, City of Truro train. b, Sharp Stewart 4-4-0 locomotive. c, Indian Railways WT Class locomotive. d, Charing Cross Station. e, Linlithgow Station. f, Hellifield Station. g, Kings Cross Station. h, Paddington Station. i, Victoria Station.

No. 2836, 12d: a, Virgin Pendolino train. b, Mountain Class Garratt locomotive. c, 2-8-8-4 No. 227 locomotive. d, Kilsby Tunnel. e, Box Tunnel. f, Willersley Tunnel. g, Stansted Airport Tunnel. h, Clayton Tunnel. i, Severn Tunnel.

No. 2837, 65d, West Highland Line train. No. 2838, 65d, Darjeeling-Himalaya train. No. 2839, 65d, Eurostar.

2004, Apr. 19   *Perf. 13¼x13½*
Sheets of 9, #a-i
2834-2836   A494   Set of 3   22.50 22.50
Souvenir Sheets
2837-2839   A494   Set of 3   13.50 13.50

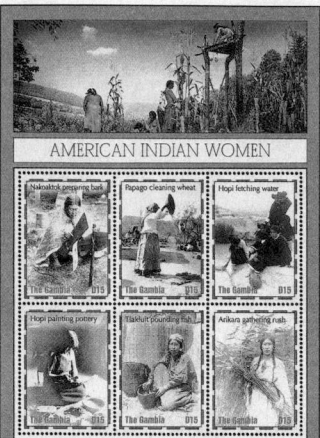

American Indians — A495

No. 2840: a, Nakoaktok preparing bark. b, Papago cleaning wheat. c, Hopi fetching water. d, Hopi painting pottery. e, Tlakluit pounding fish. f, Arikara gathering rush.

No. 2841, horiz.: a, Apsaroke Indians and teepee. b, Pigean Indians. c, Apsaroke Indians. d, Sioux chiefs.

2004, May 3   *Perf. 14¼x14¾*
2840   A495   15d Sheet of 6, #a-f   6.25 6.25
             Perf. 13¾
2841   A495   30d Sheet of 4, #a-d   8.25 8.25
No. 2841 contains four 38x30mm stamps.

History of Aviation — A496

No. 2842: a, Leonardo da Vinci. b, Count Ferdinand von Zeppelin. c, William E. Boeing. d, Capt. John Cunningham. e, Capt. Edwin C. Musick. f, Capt. Jock Lowe. g, William Lear. h, Jenny Murray.

60d, Mars Rover mission.

2004, May 3   *Perf. 14*
2842   A496   12d Sheet of 8, #a-h   6.75 6.75
Souvenir Sheet
2843   A496   60d multi   4.25 4.25

A497

Marilyn Monroe (1926-62) — A498

No. 2844: a, Wearing necklace. b, No necklace.

No. 2845 — Background color: a, Orange. b, Green. c, Bright lilac rose. d, Bright yellow. e, Bright blue. f, Bright red. g, Dull blue. h, Bright yellow green. i, Blue green. j, Yellow. k, Red orange. l, Purple. m, Red lilac. n, Light blue. o, Dark blue. p, Rose pink.

No. 2846 — Black background and: a, Hand on face. b, Wearing necklace. c, Wearng red dress. d, Wearing blouse with collar.

2004, May 3   *Perf. 14*
2844   A497   25d Pair, #a-b   3.50 3.50
2845   A498   7d Sheet of 16, #a-p   7.75 7.75
2846   A498   25d Sheet of 4, #a-d   7.00 7.00
No. 2844 was printed in sheets containing two pairs.

D-Day, 60th Anniv. A499

Designs: 7d, Jim Wallwork, 6th Airborne Division. 10d, Major Gen. Richard Gale. 15d, Winston Churchill. 30d, J.K. "Paddy" Byrne, 197th Typhoon Squadron.

No. 2851, 25d: a, Bombers over coast of Normandy. b, RAF Mitchell bomber dropping bombs. c, British Horsa gliders behind enemy lines. d, Paratroopers dropping into Normandy.

No. 2852, 25d: a, British paratroopers prepare for mission. b, British paratroopers secure Pegasus Bridge. c, American paratroopers drop into Sainte-Mère-Eglise area. d, American paratroopers enter town of Sainte-Mère-Eglise.

No. 2853, 60d, RAF bombers under construction. No. 2854, 60d, Troops disembarking from landing craft.

2004, May 3   *Litho.*
2847-2850   A499   Set of 4 + labels   4.25 4.25
Sheets of 4, #a-d
2851-2852   A499   Set of 2   14.00 14.00
Souvenir Sheets
2853-2854   A499   Set of 2   8.25 8.25

Election of Pope John Paul II, 25th Anniv. (in 2003) — A500

No. 2855 — Pope in: a, 1988. b, 1989. c, 1990. d, 1991. e, 1992. f, 1993. g, 1994. h, 1995. i, 1996. j, 1997. k, 1998. l, 1999. m, 2000. n, 2001. o, 2002.

No. 2856 — Pope in: a, 1978. b, 1979. c, 1980. d, 1981. e, 1982. f, 1983. g, 1984. h, 1985. i, 1986. j, 1987.

2004, May 13   *Perf. 13½x13¼*
2855   A500   7d Sheet of 15, #a-o   7.25 7.25
2856   A500   10d Sheet of 10, #a-j   6.75 6.75

American Lighthouses A501

Designs: 25d, Tybee Island, Georgia. 30d, Old Cape Henry, Virginia. 35d, Morris Island, South Carolina. 40d, Hillsboro Inlet, Florida. 50d, Cape Lookout, North Carolina.

2004, May 27   *Perf. 14¾x14¼*
2857-2861   A501   Set of 5   12.50 12.50

Gambian postal authorities have declared the following items as "illegal:"

Sheet of nine 25d stamps: Oceans;

Sheets of six 25d stamps: Birds of Prey with Rotary emblem, Orchids with Rotary emblem, New Cinema, Vincent van Gogh Paintings, Monuments of Egypt, Fire Engines;

Sheets of four 25d stamps: Pope John Paul II, Nude Art, Great Composers, Lighthouses with Rotary emblem, Aircraft with Rotary emblem, Actresses, Pin-up Art;

Sheet of three 25d stamps: Polar Birds with Rotary emblem;

Sheets of two 25d stamps: Prehistoric World, Chinese New Year, Looney Tunes, Games and Sports.

Paintings by Joan Miró A502

Designs: 20d, Woman, 1934, pastel on paper. 25d, Woman, 1934, pastel and pencil on emery paper. 35d, Self-portrait. No. 2865, 75d, Man with Pipe.

No. 2866: a, Portrait IV. b, Seated Woman. c, Painting on Ingres Paper. d, Portrait II.

No. 2867, 75d, Composition with Personages in the Burning Forest, horiz. No. 2868, 75d, Bird, horiz.

2004, Feb. 17   *Litho.*   *Perf. 13¼*
2862-2865   A502   Set of 4   11.00 11.00
2866   A502   30d Sheet of 4, #a-d   8.25 8.25

Size: 100x80mm
Imperf
2867-2868   A502   Set of 2   10.50 10.50

Souvenir Sheet

Deng Xiaoping (1904-97), Chinese Leader — A503

2004, May 3   *Perf. 13½*
2869   A503   75d multi   5.25 5.25

Miniature Sheet

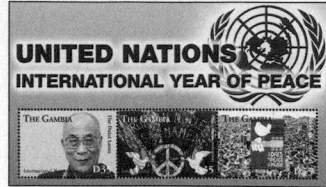

Intl. Year of Peace — A504

No. 2870: a, Dalai Lama. b, European nuclear disarmament banner. c, Woodstock music festival.

2004, May 3   *Perf. 14*
2870   A504   35d Sheet of 3, #a-c   7.25 7.25

Miniature Sheet

Rare and Famous Postage Stamps — A505

No. 2871: a, British Guiana #13. b, Great Britain #1. c, United States #85A. d, United States #C3a. e, United States #1.

2004, June 24   *Perf. 13*
2871   A505   20d Sheet of 5, #a-e, + label   6.75 6.75

Flowers — A506

Designs: 1d, Babiana rubrocyanaea. 2d, Protea. 3d, Lithops bromfieldii. 5d, Saintpaulia ionantha. 6d, Monopsis lutea. 7d, Dudleya lanceolata. 9d, Euphorbia punicea. 10d, Oxalis violacea. 25d, Helichrysum bracteatum. 50d, Senecio obovatus. 75d, Mesembryanthemum acinaciforme. 100d, Montbretia crocosmiiflora. 200d, Gladiolus colvillei.

2004, July 1   *Perf. 14¾x14*

2872	A506	1d multi	.20	.20
2873	A506	2d multi	.20	.20
2874	A506	3d multi	.20	.20
2875	A506	5d multi	.35	.35
2876	A506	6d multi	.40	.40
2877	A506	7d multi	.50	.50
2878	A506	9d multi	.60	.60
2879	A506	10d multi	.70	.70
2880	A506	25d multi	1.75	1.75
2881	A506	50d multi	3.50	3.50
2882	A506	75d multi	5.00	5.00
2883	A506	100d multi	6.75	6.75
2884	A506	200d multi	13.50	13.50
Nos. 2872-2884 (13)			33.65	33.65

A507

First Elvis Presley Record, 50th Anniv. — A508

Various portraits of Elvis Presley.

2004, Aug. 2   **Perf. 13¼**
2885 A507 12d Sheet of 9, #a-i   7.50 7.50
2886 A508 12d Sheet of 9, #a-i   7.50 7.50

Miniature Sheet

George Herman "Babe" Ruth (1895-1948), Baseball Player — A509

No. 2887: a, Swinging, legs spread apart. b, Standing. c, Swinging, legs together. d, Holding bat.

2004, Sept. 3   **Perf. 13½**
2887 A509 25d Sheet of 4, #a-d   6.75 6.75

Pres. Ronald Reagan (1911-2004) — A510

No. 2888: a, With wife, Nancy and Pope John Paul II. b, With Israeli Prime Minister Shimon Peres.
No. 2889: a, With window in background. b, Before microphones. c, Holding glass.

2004, Oct. 13
2888 A510 15d Pair, #a-b   2.10 2.10
2889 A510 15d Vert. strip of 3,   #a-c   3.25 3.25

No. 2888 was printed in sheets of three pairs. No. 2889 was printed in sheets of two strips.

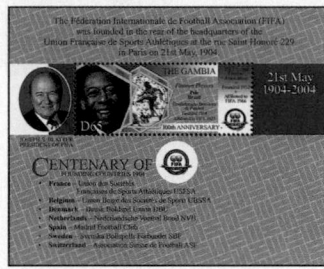

FIFA (Fédération Internationale de Football Association), Cent. — A511

No. 2890: a, Dixie Dean. b, Ruud Gullit. c, Karl-Heinz Rummenigge. d, Luis Enrique Martinez.
65d, Pele.

2004, Oct. 27   **Perf. 12¾x12½**
2890 A511 25d Sheet of 4, #a-d   7.00 7.00

Souvenir Sheet
2891 A511 65d multi   4.50 4.50

National Basketball Association Players — A512

Designs: No. 2892, 10d, Darko Milicic, Detroit Pistons. No. 2893, 10d, Chris Kaman, Los Angeles Clippers. No. 2894, 10d, Andrei Kirilenko, Utah Jazz. No. 2895, 10d, T. J. Ford, Milwaukee Bucks.

2004   **Perf. 14**
2892-2895 A512   Set of 4   2.75 2.75

Issued: No. 2892, 11/2; Nos. 2893-2894, 11/3; No. 2895, 11/6. Each stamp printed in sheets of 12.

Ocean Liners — A513

Designs: 7d, Bremen. 10d, RMS Queen Mary. 15d, Queen Mary II. 20d, RMS Queen Elizabeth 2. 25d, Britannic. 35d, RMS Majestic.
90d, RMS Aquitania.

2004, Nov. 5   **Perf. 14¼**
2896-2901 A513   Set of 6   7.75 7.75

Souvenir Sheet
2902 A513 90d multi   6.25 6.25

Miniature Sheet

Elvis Presley and Teddy Bears — A514

No. 2903: a, Presley in dark red suit. b, Teddy bear, plaid sleeve in background. c, Presley with guitar. d, Teddy bear, dark red suit in background. e, Presley in pink suit and tie. f, Teddy bear, guitar in background.

2004, Nov. 29   **Perf. 14**
2903 A514 20d Sheet of 6, #a-f   8.25 8.25

Christmas A515

Designs: 7d, Greek Madonna, by Giovanni Bellini. 10d, Madonna in the Church, by Jan van Eyck. 20d, Conestabile Madonna, by Raphael. 25d, Madonna and Child, by Sandro Botticelli.
65d, Madonna and Child with Chancellor Rolin, by van Eyck.

2004, Dec. 13   **Perf. 12**
2904-2907 A515   Set of 4   4.25 4.25

Souvenir Sheet
2908 A515 65d multi   4.50 4.50

Pres. Ronald Reagan (1911-2004) — A516

No. 2909, 25d: a, With Margaret Thatcher, 1986. b, With Pope John Paul II, 1982. c, Signing Missing Children's Act and Victim Witness Protection Act, 1992. d, With wife, Nancy, 1987.
No. 2910, 25d, horiz.: a, First Family, 1982. b, Signing treaty with Mikhail Gorbachev, 1987. c, Assassination attempt, 1981. d, With Deng Xiaoping, 1984.
60d, Portrait.

2004, Oct. 13   **Litho.**   **Perf. 14**
Sheets of 4, #a-d
2909-2910 A516   Set of 2   14.00 14.00
Souvenir Sheet
2911 A516 60d multi   4.25   4.25

Lighthouse Type of 2004

Designs: 5d, Isla de Flores Lighthouse, Uruguay. 7d, Punta Brava Lighthouse, Uruguay. 15d, Boston Lighthouse, US. No. 2911D, 20d, Cabo Polonio Lighthouse, Uruguay. No. 2911E, 20d, Bass Harbor Head Lighthouse, US. 45d, Punta del Este Lighthouse, Uruguay. 60d, Portland Head Lighthouse, US.

2004   **Litho.**   **Perf. 14¾x14**
2911A-2911G A501   Set of 7   12.00 12.00

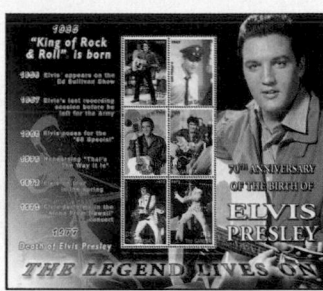

Elvis Presley (1935-77) — A517

No. 2912, 15d: a, Standing, with guitar, 1956. b, Wearing army hat, 1957. c, Holding guitar, 1968. d, Holding guitar, 1970. e, Playing guitar, 1972. f, Singing, 1973.
No. 2913, 15d: a, Seated, with guitar, 1956. b, With guitar, 1958. c, Playing guitar, 1964. d, Playing drums, 1966. e, On horse, 1968. f, Playing guitar, 1969.

2005, Jan. 8
Sheets of 6, #a-f
2912-2913 A517   Set of 2   12.50 12.50

New Year 2005 (Year of the Rooster) A518

Paintings by Xu Beihong: 10d, Rooster. 40d, Black Rooster, horiz.

2005, Jan.   **Perf. 11½**
2914 A518 10d multi   .70   .70

Souvenir Sheet
2915 A518 40d multi   2.75 2.75

No. 2914 printed in sheets of 4. No. 2915 contains one 46x36mm stamp.

Basketball Players Type of 2004

Designs: No. 2916, 25d, Steve Nash, Dallas Mavericks. No. 2917, 25d, Shaquille O'Neal, Los Angeles Lakers.

2005, Feb. 10   **Perf. 14**
2916-2917 A512   Set of 2   3.50 3.50

Both players were on different teams when stamps were released.

Intl. Year of Rice (in 2004) — A519

No. 2918, vert.: a, Rice terraces. b, Woman holding rice plants. c, Two people holding rice plants.
60d, Rice farmers.

2005, Feb. 10
2918 A519 30d Sheet of 3, #a-c   6.25 6.25
Souvenir Sheet
2919 A519 60d multi   4.25 4.25

Butterflies — A520

Designs: 1d, Belenois solilucis. 2d, Colotis evippe. 3d, Acraea cepheus. 5d, Bebearia senegalensis. 6d, Danaus chrysippus. 7d, Papilio dardanus. 10d, Graphium agamedes. 15d, Papilio hesperus. 25d, Charaxes boueti. 30d, Cymothoe egesta. 50d, Amauris albimaculata. 75d, Charaxes lucretius. 100d, Papilio zalmoxis. 200d, Papilio antimachus.

Perf. 13¼x13½, 14¾x14¼ (7d, 30d)

2005, Apr. 4

2920	A520	1d multi	.20	.20
2921	A520	2d multi	.20	.20
2922	A520	3d multi	.20	.20
2923	A520	5d multi	.35	.35
2924	A520	6d multi	.40	.40
2924A	A520	7d multi	.50	.50
2925	A520	10d multi	.70	.70
2926	A520	15d multi	1.00	1.00
2927	A520	25d multi	1.75	1.75
2927A	A520	30d multi	2.10	2.10
2928	A520	50d multi	3.50	3.50
2929	A520	75d multi	5.25	5.25
2929A	A520	100d multi	7.00	7.00
2929B	A520	200d multi	14.00	14.00
	Nos. 2920-2929B (14)		37.15	37.15

Battle of Trafalgar, Bicent. — A521

Designs: 5d, Santisima Trinidad. 10d, Victory firing at French flagship Bucentaure, horiz. 15d, Lord Horatio Nelson. 30d, French sailors from the Redoubtable boarding Victory. 60d, Vice-admiral Horatio Nelson.

2005, Apr. 4   **Perf. 14**

2930-2933 A521   Set of 4   4.25   4.25

Souvenir Sheet

2934 A521   60d multi   4.25   4.25

Souvenir Sheet

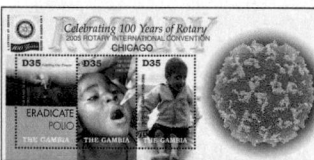

Rotary International, Cent. — A522

No. 2935: a, "Eradicate Polio," child receiving polio vaccine. b, Child receiving polio vaccine, diff. c, Child seated.

2005, Apr. 4

2935 A522   35d Sheet of 3, #a-c   7.25   7.25

Blondie, by Dean Young and Denis LeBrun — A523

No. 2936, 40d: a, "I have a date with Cookie." b, "Wait one second, please." c, "Wow, Cookie! I didn't know your family was wealth enough to have a chauffeur!"

No. 2937, 40d: a, "Listen up, everybody. . ." b, "Then after he leaves you can get back to normal." c, "I want to see this place humming with activity and enthusiasm!"

2005, Apr. 4   **Perf. 13¼**

Sheets of 3, #a-c

2936-2937 A523   Set of 2   17.00   17.00

World Cup Soccer Championships, 75th Anniv. — A524

No. 2938 — Brazilian flag and scenes from 1950 World Cup: a, 1950 Uruguay team. b, Goal from Uruguay-Brazil championship game. c, Maracaná Municipal Stadium, Brazil. d, Alcide Edgardo Ghiggia. 60d, 1950 Uruguay team, diff.

2005, Apr. 4   **Perf. 14¼**

2938 A524   25d Sheet of 4, #a-d   7.00   7.00

Souvenir Sheet

2939 A524   60d multi   4.25   4.25

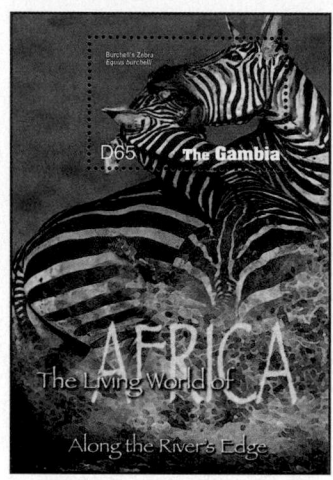

African Fauna — A525

No. 2940, 25d: a, African fish eagle. b, Hummingbird hawkmoth. c, Nile crocodile. d, Blue wildebeest.

No. 2941, 25d: a, Bateleur eagle. b, Green mamba. c, Chimpanzee. d, Yellow pansy butterfly.

No. 2942, 25d: a, Jackass penguins. b, Leatherback turtle. c, Scaevola thunbergii. d, Cancrid crab.

No. 2943, 25d: a, Mediterranean monk seal. b, Horned boxfish. c, Scorpion fish. d, Cnidarians.

No. 2944, Burchell's zebra. No. 2945, 65d, Greater galago. No. 2946, 65d, Bottlenose dolphin, vert. No. 2947, 65d, Gerbera daisies, vert.

2005, Apr. 4   **Perf. 13¼x13½**

Sheets of 4, #a-d

2940-2943 A525   Set of 4   28.00   28.00

Souvenir Sheets

2944-2947 A525   Set of 4   18.00   18.00

Hans Christian Andersen (1805-75), Author — A526

No. 2942, horiz.: a, The Ugly Duckling. b, The Little Match Girl. c, The Rose Tree Regiment. 60d, The Emperor's New Clothes.

2005, Apr. 4   **Perf. 14**

2948 A526   35d Sheet of 3, #a-c   7.25   7.25

Souvenir Sheet

2949 A526   60d multi   4.25   4.25

Wedding of Prince Charles and Camilla Parker Bowles — A527

Various photos of couple with oval color of: No. 2950, 2d, Brown. No. 2951, 2d, Purple. No. 2952, 2d, Red brown.

2005, Apr. 9   **Perf. 13½**

2950-2952 A527   Set of 3   .45   .45

Each stamp printed in sheets of 4.

Friedrich von Schiller (1759-1805), Writer — A528

No. 2953: a, Statue of Schiller. b, Painting of Schiller. c, Bust of Schiller. 60d, Cameo of Schiller.

2005, Apr. 4   **Litho.**   **Perf. 14**

2953 A528   35d Sheet of 3, #a-c   7.25   7.25

Souvenir Sheet

2954 A528   60d multi   4.25   4.25

Miniature Sheet

End of World War II, 60th Anniv. — A529

No. 2955 — Prince Bernhard of the Netherlands: a, And Prime Minister Pieter Gerbrandy. b, And Queen Wilhelmina. c, And Generals Bernard Montgomery and Hendrik Kruls. d, And people of Nimwegen. e, At German surrender. f, Returning home with family.

2005, Apr. 14   **Litho.**   **Perf. 12¾**

2955 A529   12d Sheet of 6, #a-f   5.00   5.00

End of World War II, 60th Anniv. — A530

No. 2956, 20d — Dunkirk: a, Germans advance across France. b, Anthony C. Bartley. c, Ships and boats. d, Rescued soldiers.

No. 2957, 20d — D-Day: a, Allied troops hit the beaches of Normandy. b, Germans blast Sword Beach. c, Allied troops advance inland. d, Germans begin to surrender.

No. 2958, 80d, Operation Dynamo. No. 2959, 80d, Royal Navy lands on Gold Beach.

2005, May 9   **Perf. 13¼x13½**

Sheets of 4, #a-d

2956-2957 A530   Set of 2   11.50   11.50

Souvenir Sheets

2958-2959 A530   Set of 2   11.50   11.50

Souvenir Sheet

Expo 2005, Aichi, Japan — A531

No. 2960: a, Mt. Kilimanjaro. b, Lion. c, Splitting of the Red Sea. d, Astronaut on Moon.

2005, May 16   **Perf. 12**

2960 A531   15d Sheet of 4, #a-d   4.25   4.25

Pope John Paul II (1920-2005) and Mother Teresa (1910-97) — A532

2005, June 1   **Perf. 14**

2961 A532   30d multi   2.10   2.10

Printed in sheets of 6.

Maimonides (1135-1204) — A533

No. 2962: a, Denomination in white. b, Denomination in red.

2005, July 12   **Perf. 12**

2962 A533   25d Pair, #a-b   3.75   3.75

Printed in sheets of 2 pairs.

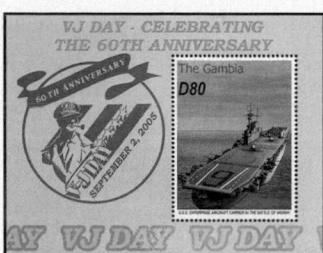

VJ Day, 60th Anniv. — A534

No. 2963, horiz. — Paintings by Jean Masterly: a, B-29 Flies Over the Missouri. b, Enola Gay Over Hiroshima. c, Dogfight Over the Pacific. d, Hellcat Fury Engages the Enemy.
80d, USS Enterprise Aircraft Carrier in the Battle of Midway.

2005, July 12   **Perf. 12¾**
2963 A534 25d Sheet of 4, #a-d   7.25 7.25
     Souvenir Sheet
2964 A534 80d multi   5.75 5.75
   No. 2963 contains four 40x31mm stamps.

Jules Verne (1828-1905), Writer — A535

No. 2965, horiz.: a, Hungary #C287. b, Monaco #1100. c, France #770.
80d, Scene from "From the Earth to the Moon."

2005, July 12
2965 A535 35d Sheet of 3, #a-c   7.75 7.75
     Souvenir Sheet
2966 A535 80d multi   5.75 5.75

     Souvenir Sheet

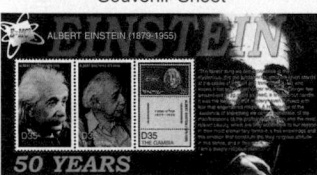

Albert Einstein (1879-1955), Physicist — A536

No. 2967: a, Einstein, country name in red. b, Einstein, country name in white. c, Israel #117.

2005, July 28
2967 A536 35d Sheet of 3, #a-c   7.75 7.75

American First Day Cover Society, 50th Anniv. A537

2005, July 29
2968 A537 25d multi   1.90 1.90

     Souvenir Sheet

Taipei 2005 Stamp Exhibition — A538

No. 2969: a, Presidential Palace, Taipei. b, Chiang Kai-Shek Memorial, Taipei. c, Queen's Head, Yehliu. d, National Palace Museum, Taipei.

2005, Aug. 19   **Perf. 14**
2969 A538 35d Sheet of 4, #a-d   10.00 10.00

First Europa Stamps, 50th Anniv. (in 2006) A539

Designs: 35d, Mailman, Luxembourg #318. 40d, Stars, "50," France #806. 50d, Map of Europe, France #805.

2005, Oct. 20
2970-2972 A539   Set of 3   9.00 9.00
2972a   Souvenir sheet, #2970-2972 + label   9.00 9.00

Election of Pope Benedict XVI — A540

2005, Nov. 15   **Perf. 13½**
2973 A540 35d multi   2.50 2.50
     Printed in sheets of 4.

Pope John Paul II (1920-2005) A541

Pope John Paul II: No. 2974, 40d, Looking right. No. 2975, 40d, With arm raised. No. 2976, 40d, With hand to face. No. 2977, 40d, Praying with four men at side. No. 2978, 40d, Surrounded by praying clergymen. No. 2979, With praying hands of other people. No. 2980, 40d, Wearing miter, with crowd. No. 2981, 40d, Praying at church. No. 2982, 40d, With arms outstretched at church. No. 2983, 40d, Praying with rosary. No. 2984, 40d, Holding crucifix, round globe. No. 2985, 40d, Holding crucifix, oval world map. No. 2986, 40d, Holding crucifix, at doorway. No. 2987, 40d, With crucifix at side of face. No. 2988, 40d, Holding crucifix in front of his face. No. 2989, 40d, Holding crucifix, with other arm raised. No. 2990, 40d, With crucifix, Papal arms. No. 2991, 40d, With Good Shepherd. No. 2992, 40d, Holding child. No. 2993, 40d, With UN emblem. No. 2994, 40d, Being assisted.
No. 2995, 80d, Bowing with crucifix. No. 2996, 80d, Wearing miter in front of church. No. 2997, 80d, With kneeling bishop. No. 2998, 80d, Holding microphone. No. 2999, 80d, With raised hands, Papal arms. No. 3000, 80d, With Virgin Mary.

     Embossed on Metal
2005   **Die Cut Perf. 12½**
     Self-Adhesive
     Silver-Colored Metal
2974-2994 A541   Set of 21   60.00 60.00
     Gold-Colored Metal
2995-3000 A541   Set of 6   35.00 35.00

     Miniature Sheet

American Indian Chiefs — A542

No. 3001: a, Hiawatha. b, Chief Joseph. c, Sitting Bull. d, Red Cloud. e, Powhatan. f, Sequoyah. g, Crazy Horse. h, Cochise. i, Geronimo. j, Tecumseh.

2005, Nov. 15   **Litho.**   **Perf. 13½**
3001 A542 12d Sheet of 10, #a-j   8.50 8.50

Christmas — A543

Designs: 7d, The Annunciation, by Lorenzo di Credi. 10d, The Holy Family, by di Credi. 25d, The Adoration of the Magi, by Filippo Lippi. 30d, Marriage of St. Catherine, by Lippi. 65d, The Annunciation, by Fra Angelico.

2005, Dec. 19   **Perf. 13½x¼**
3002-3005 A543   Set of 4   5.00 5.00
     Souvenir Sheet
3006 A543 65d multi   4.50 4.50

New Year 2006 (Year of the Dog) A544

2006, Jan. 3   **Perf. 13¼**
3007 A544 15d multi   1.10 1.10
     Printed in sheets of 4.

Elvis Presley (1935-77) — A545

     Serpentine Die Cut 7¾
2006, Jan. 24   **Litho. & Embossed**
3008 A545 200d multi   14.50 14.50

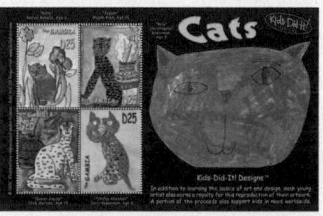

Children's Drawings — A546

No. 3009, 25d — Cats: a, Kitty, by Raquel Bobolia. b, Jaguar, by Megan Albe. c, Quazy Jaguar, by Nick Abrams. d, Chelsy Cheetah, by Carly Bowerman.

No. 3010, 25d — Reptiles: a, Stripey, by Christopher Bowerman. b, Sea Turtle, by Tyler Overton. c, Hungry Lizard, by Jessica Shutt. d, Frogs, by Elyse Bobczynski.
No. 3011, 25d — Flowers: a, Three Flowers, by Lauren Van Way. b, Blossoms, by Michelle Malachowsky. c, Flower Pot, by Van Way. d, Red Flower Pot, by Anne Wilks.

2006, Jan. 24   **Litho.**   **Perf. 13¼**
     Sheets of 4, #a-d
3009-3011 A546   Set of 3   22.00 22.00

Queen Elizabeth II, 80th Birthday — A547

No. 3012: a, Wearing military uniform. b, At coronation. c, On Time Magazine cover. d, Wearing wedding gown.
65d, Wearing robe and crown.

2006, Feb. 27   **Perf. 13¼**
3012 A547 30d Sheet of 4, #a-d   8.50 8.50
     Souvenir Sheet
     Perf. 12
3013 A547 65d multi   4.75 4.75

Worldwide Fund for Nature (WWF) — A548

No. 3014 — Black-crowned crane: a, Head. b, Standing on one leg. c, Birds in wild. d, Chick.

2006, Feb. 27   **Perf. 12¾**
3014 A548 30d Block or strip of 4, #a-d   8.50 8.50
   e.   Souvenir sheet, 2 each #3014a-3014d   17.00 17.00

2006 Winter Olympics, Turin A549

Designs: No. 3015, Norway #1048. No. 3015A, Poster for 1992 Albertville Winter Olympics. 15d, Norway #1047. No. 3017,

Poster for 2002 Salt Lake City Winter Olympics. No. 3017A, France #B611, horiz. 25d, Poster for 1994 Lillehammer Winter Olympics.

2006, Mar. 23   *Perf. 13¼*
3015	A549	10d multicolored	.75	.75
3015A	A549	10d multi	.75	.75
3016	A549	15d multicolored	1.10	1.10
3017	A549	20d multicolored	1.40	1.40
3017A	A549	20d multi	1.40	1.40
3018	A549	25d multicolored	1.75	1.75
		Nos. 3015-3018 (6)	7.15	7.15

Marilyn Monroe (1926-62), Actress — A550

2006, Apr. 6
3019   A550   30d multi   2.10 2.10
Printed in sheets of 4.

Dr. Martin Luther King, Jr. (1929-68), Civil Rights Activist — A551

2006, May 27   *Perf. 11½x12*
3020   A551   40d multi   3.00 3.00
Printed in sheets of 3.

Miniature Sheet

American Philatelic Society, 120th Anniv. — A552

No. 3021 — United States stamps: a, #1120. b, #E14. c, #114. d, #C3. e, #894. f, #E2. g, #294. h, #Q2.

2006, May 27   *Perf. 13¼*
3021   A552   17d Sheet of 8, #a-h   9.75 9.75
Washington 2006 World Philatelic Exhibition.

Souvenir Sheet

Ludwig Durr (1878-1956), Engineer, and Zeppelins — A553

No. 3022 — Durr and: a, Zeppelin NT. b, Zeppelin ZR-3 (U.S.S. Los Angeles). c, Zeppelin ZRS (U.S.S. Macon)

2006, June 22   *Perf. 12¾*
3022   A553   40d Sheet of 3, #a-c   8.75 8.75

Souvenir Sheet

Wolfgang Amadeus Mozart (1756-91), Composer — A554

No. 3023: a, Mozart's Memorial, Vienna. b, Portrait of Mozart, by Barbara Kraft. c, Portrait of Mozart by unknown artist. d, Mozart family graves, Salzburg.

2006, June 22
3023   A554   30d Sheet of 4, #a-d   8.75 8.75

Rembrandt (1606-69), Painter A555

Details from paintings: 10d, Jacob Blessing the Sons of Joseph. 12d, Jacob Blessing the Sons of Joseph, diff. 15d, Jacob Blessing the Sons of Joseph, diff. No. 3027, 25d, Jacob Wrestling with the Angel.
No. 3028, 25d — The Staalmeesters: a, Man wearing hat, leaning to right, "Rembrandt" in white. b, Man wearing hat, "Rembrandt" in white. c, Man without hat. d, Man wearing hat, "Rembrandt" in black.
No. 3029, 25d: a, Young Girl at Open Half-Door. b, Self-portrait, 1632-39. c, Self-portrait, 1640. d, Portrait of a Young Woman.
No. 3030, 25d — A Married Couple with Their Children: a, Man. b, Child, "Rembrandt" in white. c, Child, "Rembrandt" in black. d, Woman.
No. 3031, 65d — A Polish Nobleman. No. 3032, 65d, The Knight with the Falcon. No. 3033, 65d, A Young Woman in Fancy Dress. No. 3034, 65d, Portrait of a Lady with a Lap Dog.

2006, Aug. 23   Litho.   *Perf. 14¼*
3024-3027   A555   Set of 4   4.50 4.50
Sheets of 4, #a-d
3028-3030   A555   Set of 3   22.00 22.00
Imperf
Size: 76x106mm
3031-3034   A555   Set of 4   18.50 18.50

Queen Juliana of the Netherlands A556

2006, July 24   Litho.   *Perf. 13¼*
3035   A556   15d multi   1.10 1.10
Printed in sheets of 6.

Princess Maxima of the Netherlands — A557

No. 3036: a, Head. b, Head and torso.

2006, Dec. 6
3036   A557   30d Pair, #a-b   4.50 4.50
Printed in sheets containing 3 of each stamp.

Christmas — A558

Designs: No. 3037, 25d, Gingerbread man. 30d, Christmas tree. 45d, Bell. 50d, Mittens.
No. 3041: a, 15d, Gingerbread man. b, 18d, Christmas tree. c, 25d, Bell.

2006, Dec. 8   *Perf. 14*
3037-3040   A558   Set of 4   11.00 11.00
Souvenir Sheet
3041   A558   Sheet of 4,
     #3041a-3041c,
     3040   7.75 7.75

Miniature Sheet

2006 World Cup Soccer Championships, Germany — A559

No. 3042 — World Cup and soccer ball with flag of: a, 10d, Australia. b, 20d, Germany. c, 25d, Sweden. d, 30d, Brazil.

2006, Dec. 20   *Perf. 13¼*
3042   A559   Sheet of 4, #a-d   6.25 6.25

Concorde A560

No. 3043, 15d: a, Concorde arriving at Filton. b, Concorde G-BOAF in flight.
No. 3044, 15d: a, Concorde taking off from Toulouse. b, Concorde test pilot Andre Turcat.

2006, Dec. 20   *Perf. 13¼x13½*
Pairs, #a-b
3043-3044   A560   Set of 2   4.50 4.50
Nos. 3043-3044 were each printed in sheets containing three pairs.

Space Achievements — A561

No. 3045, 20d — Various views of Mars Reconnaissance Orbiter.
No. 3046, 20d — Space Shuttle Columbia: a, Columbia attached to rocket boosters in flight. b, Lift-off of Columbia. c, Shuttle mission simulator. d, Mission control. e, Capt. John W. Young. f, Capt. Robert L. Crippen.
No. 3047, 25d — Giotto Comet Probe: a, Halley's Comet. b, Giotto Comet Probe, green and orange lines. c, Giotto Comet Probe. d, Comet and Giotto Comet Probe.
No. 3048, 25d — Viking 1: a, Viking 1 in flight. b, Viking 1 on Mars, text in black, denomination at UL. c, Viking 1 on Mars, text in black, denomination at UR. d, Viking 1 on Mars, "Viking 1" in white.
No. 3049, 65d, Venus Express. No. 3050, 65d, Hayabusa spacecraft. No. 3051, 65d, Luna 9, vert. No. 3052, 65d, Space Shuttle Discovery returns to space, vert.

2006, Dec. 20   *Perf. 14*
Sheets of 6, #a-f
3045-3046   A561   Set of 2   17.50 17.50
Sheets of 4, #a-d
3047-3048   A561   Set of 2   14.50 14.50
Souvenir Sheets
3049-3052   A561   Set of 4   19.00 19.00

New Year 2007 (Year of the Pig) A562

2007, Feb. 15   *Perf. 13x13½*
3053   A562   20d multi   1.50 1.50
Printed in sheets of 4.

Scouting, Cent. A563

Knot in: 30d, Green. 65d, Orange.

2007, Feb. 15   *Perf. 13¼*
3054   A563   30d multi   2.25 2.25
Souvenir Sheet
3055   A563   65d multi   4.75 4.75
No. 3054 printed in sheets of 4.

Miniature Sheets

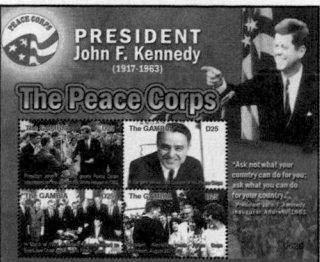

Programs of Pres. John F. Kennedy — A564

No. 3056, 25d — Peace Corps: a, Kennedy greeting Peace Corps volunteers at White House. b, R. Sargent Shriver, first director of Peace Corps. c, Kennedy signing executive order creating Peace Corps. d, Kennedy greeting Peace Corps volunteers.

No. 3057, 25d — Alliance for Progress: a, Kennedy in rocking chair. b, Kennedy and Cabinet. c, Volunteer Ida Shoatz in Peru. d, Kennedy speaking at University of Michigan.

2007, Feb. 15   *Perf. 12¾*
Sheets of 4, #a-d
3056-3057 A564 Set of 2   14.50 14.50

Betty Boop — A565

No. 3058 — Betty Boop: a, With hands at side. b, Holding flowers. c, With dog biting swimsuit. d, Wearing long red dress. e, With hands clasped. f, Holding top hat and cane.

No. 3059 — Betty Boop in: a, Red. b, Purple.

2007, Feb. 15   *Litho.*
3058 A565 15d Sheet of 6, #a-f   6.50 6.50
Souvenir Sheet
3059 A565 40d Sheet of 2, #a-b   6.00 6.00

Pope Benedict XVI — A566

2007, May 1   *Perf. 13¼*
3060 A566 12d multi   .90 .90
Printed in sheets of 8.

Intl. Polar Year — A567

No. 3061 — Penguin: a, At bongo drums. b, With lei and grass skirt. c, At drum set. d, With purple guitar. e, At microphone. f, With yellow and orange guitar.
65d, Penguin in chair at table.

2007, May 1   *Litho.*
3061 A567 15d Sheet of 6, #a-f   6.75 6.75
Souvenir Sheet
3062 A567 65d multi   4.75 4.75

Wedding of Queen Elizabeth II and Prince Philip, 60th Anniv. — A568

No. 3063, vert. — Photos of Queen and Prince: a, On wedding day, gray brown frame. b, As older couple, gray brown frame. c, As older couple, pink frame. d, On wedding day, pink frame. e, On wedding day, blue gray frame. f, As older couple, blue gray frame.
65d, Queen and Prince, diff.

2007, May 1
3063 A568 15d Sheet of 6, #a-f   6.75 6.75
Souvenir Sheet
3064 A568 65d multi   4.75 4.75

Princess Diana (1961-97) — A569

No. 3065, vert. — Diana wearing: a, Tiara, close-up. b, Light blue dress, close-up. c, Maroon dress, close-up. d, Tiara, from distance. e, Light blue dress, from distance. f, Maroon dress, from distance.

No. 3066, vert. — Diana wearing: a, Blue and white hat. b, Lilac and purple hat. c, Black dress. d, Red and white hat.
65d, Painting of Diana.

2007, May 1
3065 A569 15d Sheet of 6, #a-f   6.75 6.75
3066 A569 25d Sheet of 4, #a-d   7.50 7.50
Souvenir Sheet
3067 A569 65d multi   4.75 4.75

1986 Halley's Comet Merchandising Emblem — A570

No. 3068: a, Light olive green frame. b, Light blue frame. c, Violet black frame. d, Brown frame.
65d, Black background.

2007, June 20   *Perf. 13¼*
3068 A570 20d Sheet of 4, #a-d   6.00 6.00
Souvenir Sheet
3069 A570 65d black   5.00 5.00

Ferrari Automobiles, 60th Anniv. — A571

No. 3070: a, 1970 512 S. b, 1996 F 310. c, 1950 195 S. d, 1965 275 P2. e, 1980 Mondial 8. f, 1975 312 T. g, 1952 500 F2. h, 1986 GTB Turbo.

2007, June 20   *Perf. 13½x13¼*
3070 A571 12d Sheet of 8, #a-h   7.25 7.25

Paintings by Qi Baishi (1864-1957) — A572

No. 3071: a, Autumn Leaves and Magpie. b, Camellias. c, Pomegranates. d, Mynahs and Amaranthus.
65d, Magpie and Plum Blossoms.

2007, July 16   *Perf. 12½*
3071 A572 25d Sheet of 4, #a-d   8.25 8.25
Souvenir Sheet
Perf. 11¼x11½
3072 A572 65d multi   5.50 5.50

First Helicopter Flight, Cent. — A573

No. 3073: a, UH-1B/C. b, S-65/RH-53B. c, UH-1. d, BK 117. e, Autogyro. f, AS-61.
65d, AH-1 Huey Cobra.

2007, July 16   *Perf. 13¼*
3073 A573 15d Sheet of 6, #a-f   7.50 7.50
Souvenir Sheet
3074 A573 65d multi   5.50 5.50

Wives of United States Presidents and First Ladies — A574

No. 3075: a, Martha Washington. b, Abigail Adams. c, Dolley Madison. d, Elizabeth Monroe. e, Louisa Adams. f, Emily Donelson. g, Angelica Van Buren. h, Anna Harrison. i, Letitia Tyler. j, Julia Iyler. k, Sarah Polk. l, Margaret Taylor. m, Abigail Fillmore. n, Jane Pierce. o, Eagle, flags, White House.

No. 3076: a, Harriet Johnston. b, Mary Lincoln. c, Eliza Johnson. d, Julia Grant. e, Lucy Hayes. f, Lucretia Garfield. g, Mary Arthur McElroy. h, Frances Cleveland. i, Caroline Harrison. j, Ida McKinley. k, Edith Roosevelt. l, Helen Taft. m, Ellen Wilson. n, Edith Wilson.

No. 3077: a, Florence Harding. b, Grace Coolidge. c, Lou Hoover. d, Eleanor Roosevelt. e, Bess Truman. f, Mamie Eisenhower. g, Jacqueline Kennedy. h, Lady Bird Johnson. i, Pat Nixon. j, Betty Ford. k, Rosalynn Carter. l, Nancy Reagan. m, Barbara Bush. n, Hillary Clinton. o, Laura Bush.

No. 3078, 65d, Martha Washington. No. 3079, 65d, Abigail Adams. No. 3080, 65d, Martha Jefferson. No. 3081, 65d, Martha Washington Jefferson Randolph. No. 3082, 65d, Dolley Madison. No. 3083, 65d, Elizabeth Monroe. No. 3084, 65d, Louisa Adams. No. 3085, 65d, Rachael Jackson. No. 3086, 65d, Emily Donelson. No. 3087, 65d, Hannah Van Buren. No. 3088, 65d, Angelica Van Buren. No. 3089, 65d, Anna Harrison. No. 3090, 65d, Letitia Tyler. No. 3091, 65d, Priscilla Tyler. No. 3092, 65d, Julia Tyler. No. 3093, 65d, Sarah Polk. No. 3094, 65d, Margaret Taylor. No. 3095, 65d, Mary Taylor. No. 3096, 65d, Abigail Fillmore. No. 3097, 65d, Jane Pierce. No. 3098, 65d, Harriet Johnston. No. 3099, 65d, Mary Lincoln. No. 3100, 65d, Eliza Johnson. No. 3101, 65d, Julia Grant. No. 3102, 65d, Lucy Hayes. No. 3103, 65d, Lucretia Garfield. No. 3104, 65d, Ellen Arthur. No. 3105, 65d, Mary Arthur McElroy. No. 3106, 65d, Frances Cleveland. No. 3107, 65d, Caroline Harrison. No. 3108, 65d, Mary Lord Harrison. No. 3109, 65d, Ida McKinley. No. 3110, 65d, Edith Roosevelt. No. 3111, 65d, Helen Taft. No. 3112, 65d, Ellen Wilson. No. 3113, 65d, Edith Wilson. No. 3114, 65d, Florence Harding. No. 3115, 65d, Grace Coolidge. No. 3116, 65d, Lou Hoover. No. 3117, 65d, Eleanor Roosevelt. No. 3118, 65d, Bess Truman. No. 3119, 65d, Mamie Eisenhower. No. 3120, 65d, Jacqueline Kennedy. No. 3121, 65d, Lady Bird Johnson. No. 3122, 65d, Pat Nixon. No. 3123, 65d, Betty Ford. No. 3124, 65d, Rosalynn Carter. No. 3125, 65d, Nancy Reagan. No. 3126, 65d, Barbara Bush. No. 3127, 65d, Hillary Clinton. No. 3128, 65d, Laura Bush.

2007   *Perf. 13¼*
3075 A574 10d Sheet of 15, #a-o   12.50 12.50
3076 A574 10d Sheet of 15, #a-n, 3075o   12.50 12.50
3077 A574 10d Sheet of 15, #a-o   12.50 12.50
   Nos. 3075-3077 (3)   37.50 37.50
Souvenir Sheets
3078-3128 A574   Set of 51   350.00 350.00
3078a   Perf. 14¼   6.75 6.75

Issued: Nos. 3075-3077, 7/31. Nos. 3078-3128, 10/24. Nos. 3075-3077 each contain fifteen 25x37mm stamps.

No. 3078a was not issued in a souvenir sheet.

See No. 3293.

Miniature Sheet

Pres. Gerald R. Ford (1913-
2006) — A575

No. 3129 — Ford: a, With wife, Betty. b, At
Presidential inauguration ceremony. c, With
Betty, Pres. Richard Nixon and Pat Nixon. d,
At 90th birthday celebration.

2007, Aug. 9　　Litho.　　Perf. 13¼
3129 A575 25d Sheet of 4, #a-d　8.25 8.25

Miniature Sheet

Elvis Presley (1935-77) — A576

No. 3130 — Presley, guitar and background
color of: a, Green. b, Tan. c, Orange. d, Black
(white suit). e, Brown. f, Black (black jacket).

2007, Sept. 6
3130 A576 15d Sheet of 6, #a-f　7.75 7.75

Miniature Sheets

Intl. Holocaust Remembrance
Day — A577

No. 3131, 14d — United Nations diplomats
and delegates: a, Ronaldo Mota Sardenberg,
Brazil. b, Alisher Vohidov, Uzbekistan. c, Mar-
tin Belinga-Eboutou, Cameroun. d, Fernand
Poukre-Kono, Central African Republic. e,
Heraldo Muñoz, Chile. f, Wang Guangya,
China. g, Elbio O. Rosselli, Uruguay. h, Shashi
Tharoor, Undersecretary General.
No. 3132, 14d: a, Basile Ikouebe, Republic
of the Congo. b, Saul Weisleder, Costa Rica.
c, Alcicle Djedje, Ivory Coast. d, Andreas D.
Mavroiannis, Cyprus. e, Martin Palous, Czech
Republic. f, Atoki Ileka, Democratic Republic
of the Congo. g, Crispin S. Gregoire, Domi-
nica. h, Parfait Onanga-Anyanga, Ambassador
and Special Advisor of the 61st UN General
Assembly.
No. 3133, 14d: a, Hoya Rashed Al-Khalifa,
President of 61st UN General Assembly. b,
Denis Dangue Rewaka, Gabon. c, Crispin
Grey-Johnson, Gambia. d, Irakli Alasania,
Georgia. e, Nana Effah-Apenteng, Ghana. f,
Adamantios Vassilakis, Greece. g, Jorge Skin-
ner-Klee Arenales, Guatemala. h, Jean-Mau-
rice Ripert, France.
No. 3134, 14d: a, Hilari G. Davide, Jr., Phil-
ippines. b, Andrzej Towpik, Poland. c, Joao
Manuel Guerra Salgueiro, Portugal. d, Alexei
Tulbure, Moldova. e, Mihnea I. Motoc,
Romania. f, Vitaly I. Churkin, Russia. g,
Joseph Nsengimana, Rwanda. h, Augustine P.
Mahiga, Tanzania.

2007, Nov. 28　　Litho.　　Perf. 13½
Sheets of 8, #a-h
3131-3134 A577　Set of 4　41.00 41.00

2008 Summer Olympics,
Beijing — A578

Die Cut Perf. 8½x8¼
2007, Nov. 29　　Litho. & Embossed
Without Gum
3135 A578 40d multi　　3.75 3.75

Christmas
A579

Designs: 25d, Girl at manger scene. 30d,
Children eating holiday dishes. 45d, Boy with
Madonna and Child sculptures. 50d, Christ-
mas celebrations with music.

2007, Dec. 3　　Litho.　　Perf. 12
3136-3139 A579　Set of 4　　14.00 14.00

Souvenir Sheet

Breast Cancer Prevention — A580

2007, Dec. 10　　　　Perf. 14
3140 A580 65d multi　　6.00 6.00

America's
Cup Yacht
Races
A581

No. 3141 — Various yachts with wide
panels in: a, Blue. b, Yellow orange. c, Red. d,
Orange.

2007, Dec. 28　　　　Perf. 13¼
3141　　Strip of 4　　6.75 6.75
  a. A581 10d multi　　.85 .85
  b. A581 15d multi　　1.40 1.40
  c. A581 20d multi　　1.75 1.75
  d. A581 30d multi　　2.75 2.75

Miniature Sheet

National Basketball Association
Players — A582

No. 3142: a, Carmelo Anthony, Denver Nug-
gets. b, Kobe Bryant, Los Angeles Lakers. c,
Vince Carter, New Jersey Nets. d, Allen Iver-
son, Denver Nuggets. e, LeBron James,
Cleveland Cavaliers. f, Yao Ming, Houston
Rockets. g, Steve Nash, Phoenix Suns. h,
Shaquille O'Neal, Miami Heat. i, Dwayne
Wade, Miami Heat.

2007, Dec. 28　　　　Perf. 13¼
3142 A582 10d Sheet of 9, #a-i　8.25 8.25

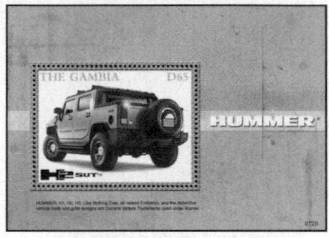

Hummer Vehicles — A583

No. 3143: a, H2 on road, denomination in
white. b, H2 on road, denomination in black. c,
H2, white background. d, H2 on rocks.
65d, H2 SUT.

2007, Dec. 28　　　　Perf. 13½
3143 A583 25d Sheet of 4, #a-d　9.00 9.00
Souvenir Sheet
3144 A583 65d multi　　6.00 6.00

New Year
2008 (Year
of the Rat)
A584

2008, Jan. 28　　Litho.　　Perf. 12
3145 A584 30d multi　　2.75 2.75
Printed in sheets of 4.

2008 Taipei Intl. Stamp
Exhibition — A585

No. 3146, horiz. — Taipei landmarks: a,
Temple and garden. b, Dr. Sun Yat-sen Memorial Hall. c, Natl. Opera House. d, Temple.
45d, Lover's Bridge, Tamsui.

2008, Apr. 11　　　　Perf. 13¼
3146 A585 12d Sheet of 4, #a-d　5.00 5.00
Souvenir Sheet
Perf. 13¼x13½
3147 A585 45d multi　　4.50 4.50
No. 3146 contains four 42x28mm stamps.

Pioneer Satellites — A586

No. 3148: a, Pioneer 1 in orbit, Moon in
background. b, Pioneer 1 in nose cone. c, Pio-
neer 1.
No. 3149, horiz.: a, Technicians and Pioneer
3. b, Pioneer 3 in orbit. c, Pioneer 3 on launch
pad.
No. 3150: a, Pioneer 1 on launch pad. b,
Pioneer 1 in orbit, diff.
No. 3151: a, Pioneer 3. b, Pioneer 3 in orbit,
Moon in background.
No. 3152, Pioneer 1, horiz. No. 3153, Pio-
neer 3, horiz.

2008, Apr. 11　　　　Perf. 13¼
3148 A586 15d Horiz. strip of 3,
　　#a-c　　4.50 4.50
3149 A586 15d Vert. strip of 3,
　　#a-c　　4.50 4.50
3150 A586 20d Pair, #a-b　4.00 4.00
3151 A586 20d Pair, #a-b　4.00 4.00
Souvenir Sheets
3152 A586 65d multi　　6.50 6.50
Perf. 13¼x13½
3153 A586 65d multi　　6.50 6.50
No. 3153 contains one 51x38mm stamp.
Nos. 3148-3151 were issued in sheets containing two strips or pairs.

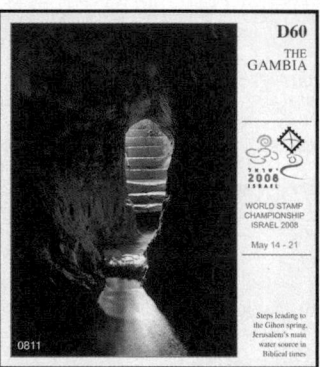

2008 World Stamp Championship,
Israel — A587

2008, May 14　　　　Imperf.
3154 A587 60d multi　　5.75 5.75

Miniature Sheet

Seven Wonders of the Ancient
World — A588

No. 3155: a, Mausoleum of Maussollos,
Halicarnassus. b, Colossus of Rhodes. c, Tip
of Giant Pyramid, Giza. d, Hanging Gardens of
Babylon. e, Sphinx and Giant Pyramid. f,
Lighthouse of Alexandria. g, Statue of Zeus,
Olympia. h, Temple of Artemis, Ephesus.

2008, May 16   *Perf. 13¼*
3155 A588 12d Sheet of 8, #a-h   9.25 9.25

Miniature Sheet

Elvis Presley (1935-77) — A589

No. 3156 — Presley: a, Wearing striped
jacket. b, With acoustic guitar. c, With arms on
knee. d, With electric guitar.

2008, May 16
3156 A589 25d Sheet of 4, #a-d   9.50 9.50

Miniature Sheet

Sir Edmund Hillary (1919-2008),
Mountaineer — A590

No. 3157: a, Hillary and flag. b, Mt. Everest.
c, Statue of Hillary. d, Hillary as young man.

2008, May 16
3157 A590 25d Sheet of 4, #a-d   9.50 9.50

Miniature Sheet

2008 Summer Olympics,
Beijing — A591

No. 3158: a, Suzanne Lenglen, 1920 Tennis
gold medalist. b, Duke Kahanamoku, 1920

Swimming gold medalist. c, Nedo Nadi, 1920
Fencing gold medalist. d, Olympic rings and
text "Olympex 2008."

2008, May 28   *Perf. 12*
3158 A591 10d Sheet of 4, #a-d   4.00 4.00

Visit of Pope Benedict XVI to United
States — A592

2008, June 12   *Perf. 13¼*
3159 A592 25d multi   2.40 2.40
   Printed in sheets of 4.

United States Landmarks — A593

No. 3160, vert.: a, Grant's Tomb, New York.
b, Jefferson Memorial, Washington, DC. c,
Kennedy Eternal Flame, Arlington, Virginia. d,
Capitol, Washington, DC. e, Lincoln Memorial,
Washington, DC. f, Washington Monument,
Washington, DC.
   65d, Mount Rushmore, South Dakota.

2008, June 12
3160 A593 15d Sheet of 6, #a-f   8.50 8.50
   Souvenir Sheet
3161 A593 65d multi   6.25 6.25

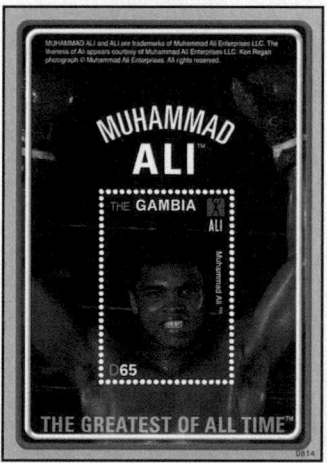

Muhammad Ali, Boxer — A594

No. 3162, 25d — Ali : a, With white trunks,
fists in front of chest. b, Seated. c, With white
trunks, arm extended. d, Wearing drawstring
shorts.
   No. 3163, 25d, horiz. — Ali: a, Behind
microphone. b, With hand on chin. c, With fist
raised. d, Running.
   No. 3164, 65d, Head of Ali in color. No.
3165, 65d, Head of Ali in black and white.

2008, July 21   *Perf. 11½*
   Sheets of 4, #a-d
3162-3163 A594 Set of 2   19.00 19.00
   Souvenir Sheets
          Perf. 13¼
3164-3165 A594 Set of 2   12.50 12.50
   No. 3162 contains four 30x40mm stamps.
No. 3163 contains four 40x30mm stamps.

Gambia Coat of Arms — A595

2008, Sept. 15 Litho.   Perf. 14x15
3166 A595 40d blk & mar + label 3.50 3.50
   Printed in sheets of 8 stamps + 8 labels.

Miniature Sheet

Marilyn Monroe (1926-62),
Actress — A596

No. 3167 — Monroe: a, Facing forward,
eyes open. b, Facing left. c, Facing right. d,
Facing forward, eyes shut.

2008, Sept. 22   *Perf. 13¼*
3167 A596 25d Sheet of 4, #a-d   8.50 8.50

Miniature Sheets

A597

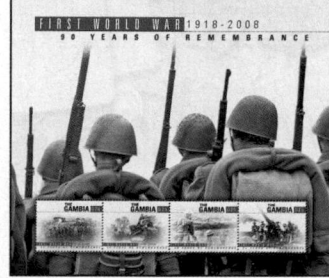

End of World War I, 90th
Anniv. — A598

No. 3168: a, Generals talking. b, Soldier and
trench. c, Pilot. d, Pilot and propeller. e, Soldier wearing helmet. f, Officers standing in
row.
   No. 3169: a, Soldiers at air field. b, Tanks. c,
Two soldiers. d, Soldiers at cannon.

2008, Nov. 11 Litho.   Perf. 11½x12
3168 A597 15d Sheet of 6, #a-f   6.75 6.75
3169 A598 25d Sheet of 4, #a-d   7.50 7.50

Miniature Sheet

Prince Charles, 60th Birthday — A599

No. 3170: a, Wearing black suit. b, Wearing
top hat. c, Wearing gray suit. d, Wearing military uniform.

2008, Nov. 14   *Perf. 11¼x11½*
3170 A599 25d Sheet of 4, #a-d   7.50 7.50

Christmas
A600

   Designs: 25d, Map of West Africa, ribbon
and bow. 30d, Red, blue and green bows. 45d,
Woman carrying gift on head, flag, vert. 50d,
Gifts, flag.

2008, Dec. 1   Perf. 14¾x14, 14x14¾
3171-3174 A600 Set of 4   11.50 11.50

Miniature Sheet

Signing of Limited Nuclear Test Ban
Treaty — A601

No. 3175: a, Pres. John F. Kennedy. b, Kennedy and Soviet Premier Nikita Khrushchev. c,
Kennedy at American University commence-
ment. d, Atomic bomb test, Bikini Atoll, 1946.

2008, Dec. 4   *Perf. 11½x12*
3175 A601 25d Sheet of 4, #a-d   7.50 7.50

Miniature Sheet

Pres. Abraham Lincoln (1809-
65) — A602

No. 3176: a, Lincoln with son, Tad. b, Lincoln with beard in profile. c, Lincoln without
beard. d, Lincoln with beard.

2008, Dec. 4   *Perf. 13¼*
3176 A602 25d Sheet of 4, #a-d   7.50 7.50

A603

Flowers of the Gambia

A604

A605

Flowers — A606

No. 3177: a, Calotropis procera. b, Callian-dra surinamensis. c, Plumeria alba. d, Quis-qualis indica.

No. 3178: a, Adansonia digitata. b, Comme-lina benghalensis. c, Heliconia psittacorum. d, Tabebuia rosea.

2008, Dec. 31   *Perf. 12½*
3177 A603 25d Sheet of 4, #a-d   7.50 7.50
            Perf. 12
3178 A604 25d Sheet of 4, #a-d   7.50 7.50
       Souvenir Sheets
3179 A605 65d multi   5.00 5.00
3180 A606 65d multi   5.00 5.00

New Year 2009 (Year of the Ox) A607

2009, Jan. 5   *Perf. 12*
3181 A607 25d multi   1.90 1.90
      Printed in sheets of 4.

Inauguration of US Pres. Barack Obama — A608

No. 3183: a, Pres. Obama. b, Vice-presi-dent Joseph Biden.

2009, Jan. 20   *Perf. 14x14¾*
3182 A608 16d shown   1.25 1.25
       Souvenir Sheet
3183 A608 60d Sheet of 2, #a-b   9.00 9.00
    No. 3182 was printed in sheets of 9.

        Miniature Sheet

Pope John Paul II (1920-2005) — A609

No. 3184 — Pope John Paul II at: a, Inaugu-ral Mass, 1978. b, United Nations, 1979. c, Warsaw, 1983. d, Denver, Colorado, 1993.

2009, Feb. 4   *Perf. 13¼*
3184 A609 25d Sheet of 4, #a-d   7.75 7.75

A610

A611

A612

A613

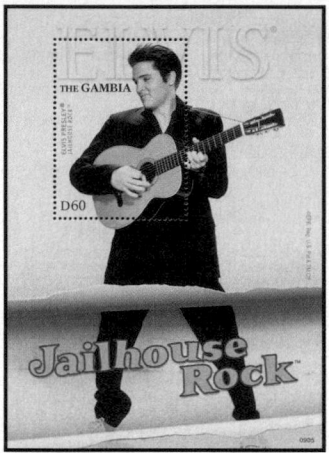

Elvis Presley (1935-77) — A614

No. 3185 — Presley wearing: a, Black suit and tie, white shirt. b, Black suit and shirt, no tie. c, Red sweater. d, Brown shirt and gray tie. e, Blue shirt. f, Gray sweater and white shirt.

2009   *Perf. 13¼*
3185 A610 20d Sheet of 6, #a-f   9.00 9.00
       Souvenir Sheets
3186 A611 60d multi   4.75 4.75
3187 A612 60d multi   4.75 4.75
3188 A613 60d multi   4.75 4.75
3189 A614 60d multi   4.75 4.75
    Issued: No. 3185, 4/30; others, 2/25.

        Miniature Sheet

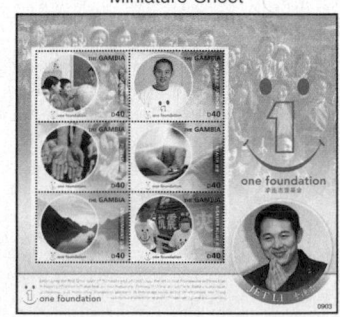

Jet Li One Foundation — A615

No. 3190: a, Education. b, Jet Li. c, Poverty. d, Health. e, Environment. f, Disaster relief.

2009, Apr. 1   *Perf. 12¾*
3190 A615 40d Sheet of 6, #a-
      f   18.00 18.00

        Souvenir Sheet

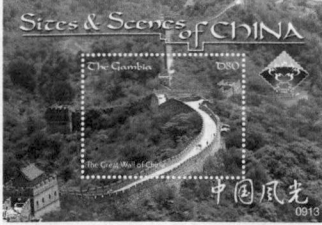

Great Wall of China — A616

2009, Apr. 10   *Perf. 12*
3191 A616 80d multi   6.00 6.00
    China 2009 Intl. Philatelic Exhibition.

Visit to Cameroun of Pope Benedict XVI A617

2009, Apr. 30   *Perf. 11½x11¼*
3192 A617 25d multi   1.90 1.90
      Printed in sheets of 4.

        Miniature Sheet

Whistle-stop Inaugural Journeys of US Presidents Abraham Lincoln and Barack Obama — A618

No. 3193: a, Inaugural speech of Pres. Obama. b, Inaugural speech of Pres. Lincoln. c, Lincoln, map of train route. d, Pres. Obama and Vice-president Joseph Biden on train in Wilmington, Delaware.

2009, Apr. 30   *Perf. 14¾x14*
3193 A618 25d Sheet of 4, #a-d   7.50 7.50

American Military Aviation, Cent. — A619

No. 3194, horiz.: a, B-17 and P-51 Escort. b, Doolittle's B-25. c, B-24. d, P-47D. e, F-86F. f, AT-6. g, F-80. h, F-15. i, T-38 and F-117. 80d, P-38 and ME-262.

2009, June 12   **Perf. 11½x11¼**
3194 A619 15d Sheet of 9, #a-
i   10.50 10.50

Souvenir Sheet
Perf. 13¼

3195 A619 80d multi   6.00 6.00
No. 3194 contains nine 40x30mm stamps. National Topical Stamp Show, Dayton, Ohio.

Miniature Sheets

Michael Jackson (1958-2009), Singer — A620

No. 3196: a, 20d, Holding microphone. b, 20d, Wearing white jacket and hat. c, 30d, As "b." d, 30d, As "a."
No. 3197, horiz.: a, 20d, Wearing black jacket and hat. b, 20d, Wearing white jacket. c, 30d, As "a." d, 30d, As "b."

Perf. 12x11½, 11½ (#3197)
2009, July 7   **Litho.**
Sheets of 4, #a-d
3196-3197 A620   Set of 2   15.00 15.00

Miniature Sheet

First Man on the Moon, 40th Anniv. — A621

No. 3198: a, Obverse and reverse of US Susan B. Anthony dollar coin. b, Apollo 11 Lunar Module. c, Neil Armstrong. d, Apollo 11. e, Statue of Armstrong. f, Apollo 11 Command Module.

2009, July 20   **Perf. 13¼**
3198 A621 20d Sheet of 6, #a-f   9.00 9.00

Miniature Sheets

Dogs — A622

No. 3199, 25d — Pembroke Welsh corgi: a, Jumping. b, Sitting in leaves. c, Sitting in front of flower basket. d, Sitting on lawn.
No. 3200, 25d — West Highland white terrier and: a, Upright basket. b, Beach ball. c, Gift boxes. d, Yellow flowers and basket on side.

2009, Aug. 29   **Perf. 12**
Sheets of 4, #a-d
3199-3200 A622   Set of 2   15.00 15.00

Birds
A623

Designs: 15d, Hamerkop. 20d, Pied kingfisher. No. 3203, 25d, Black-capped babbler. No. 3204, 40d, African darter.
No. 3205, 25d, vert.: a, Malachite kingfisher. b, Common bulbul. c, Black-crowned night heron. d, Wire-tailed swallow.
No. 3206, 40d: a, Sacred ibis. b, Little grebe.

2009, Aug. 29   **Perf. 11½**
3201-3204 A623   Set of 4   7.50 7.50
3205 A623   25d Sheet of 4, #a-d   7.50 7.50

Souvenir Sheet
3206 A623   40d Sheet of 2, #a-b   6.00 6.00

Miniature Sheet

Teenage Mutant Ninja Turtles, 25th Anniv. — A624

No. 3207: a, Raphael. b, Leonardo. c, Michelangelo. d, Donatello.

2009, Aug. 29   **Perf. 13¼**
3207 A624 25d Sheet of 4, #a-d   7.50 7.50

Pres. Barack Obama and Queen Elizabeth II — A625

No. 3208, horiz.: a, Pres. Obama. b, Queen Elizabeth II. c, Michelle Obama.
80d, Pres. Obama and Queen Elizabeth II at G20 World Leader Reception.

2009, Aug. 29   **Perf. 11½x12**
3208 A625 25d Sheet of 3, #a-c   5.75 5.75
Souvenir Sheet
Perf. 11½
3209 A625 80d multi   6.00 6.00

Pres. Barack Obama in Germany — A626

No. 3210: a, Obama, Bishop Jochen Bohl, German Chancellor Angela Merkel. b, Obama. c, Merkel. d, Obama and Merkel.
65d, Obama, Merkel, Elie Wiesel and Bertrand Herz at Buchenwald Concentration Camp.

2009, Oct. 22   **Perf. 11½**
3210 A626 25d Sheet of 4, #a-d   7.50 7.50
Souvenir Sheet
Perf. 13¼
3211 A626 65d multi   4.75 4.75
No. 3210 contains four 30x40mm stamps.

Methodist Church Conference — A627

Cross and map of: 25d, The Gambia. 35d, Africa, vert.

2009   **Perf. 11½**
3212-3213 A627   Set of 2   4.50 4.50

Miniature Sheet

The Three Stooges — A628

No. 3214 — Scenes from: a, Rockin' Thru the Rockies. b, The Sitter Downers. c, Violent is the Word for Curly. d, We Want Our Mummy.

2009   **Perf. 13¼**
3214 A628 25d Sheet of 4, #a-d   7.50 7.50

Miniature Sheet

Pres. Barack Obama, 2009 Nobel Peace Laureate — A629

No. 3215 — Pres. Obama with: a, Microphones at LR. b, Microphones at LL. c, Foliage at right. d, Flag at right.

2009, Dec. 30   **Litho.**   **Perf. 13x13¼**
3215 A629 25d Sheet of 4, #a-d   7.50 7.50

Mushrooms
A630

Designs: 10d, Panaeolus bispora. No. 3217, 15d, Panaeolus tropicalis. 25d, Psilocybe mairei. 30d, Gymnopilus aeruginosus.
No. 3220, 15d, horiz.: a, Panaeolus retirugis. b, Gymnopilus junioninus. c, Psilocybe natalensis. d, Panaeolus africanus. e, Panaeolus cinctulus. f, Panaeolus subbalteatus.

2009, Dec. 30   **Perf. 14x14¾**
3216-3219 A630   Set of 4   6.00 6.00
Perf. 14¾x14
3220 A630   15d Sheet of 6, #a-f   6.75 6.75

Butterflies
A631

Designs: 10d, Elegant acraea. No. 3222, 15d, Bamboo charaxes. 25d, Green-veined charaxes. 30d, Pink acraea.
No. 3225, 15d, horiz.: a, Abadima acraea. b, African common white. c, Cream-bordered charaxes. d, African caper white. e, Large spotted acraea. f, Tiny orange tip.

2009, Dec. 30   **Perf. 14x14¾**
3221-3224 A631   Set of 4   6.00 6.00
Perf. 14¾x14
3225 A631   15d Sheet of 6, #a-f   6.75 6.75

Christmas — A632

Designs: 10d, Map of Africa with stocking cap. 15d, Cane-shaped cookies. 25d, Christmas light display. 30d, Candle and poinsettia.

2009, Dec. 30   **Perf. 14x14¾**
3226-3229 A632   Set of 4   6.00 6.00

Ferraris and Their Parts
A633

No. 3230, 12d: a, Chassis of 1999 360 Modena. b, 1999 360 Modena.
No. 3231, 12d: a, Engine and drive train of 2003 F2003-GA. b, 2003 F2003-GA.
No.3232, 12d: a, Convertible roof of 2005 Superamerica. b, 2005 Superamerica.
No. 3233, 12d: a, Engine of 2008 California. b, 2008 California.

2010, Feb. 24   **Perf. 12**
Vert. Pairs, #a-b
3230-3233 A633   Set of 4   7.25 7.25

Whales and Dolphins
A634

Designs: 10d, Common dolphin. 15d, Pygmy killer whale. No. 3236, 25d, Short-finned pilot whale. 30d, Clymene dolphin.
No. 3228, 25d: a, Southern bottlenose whale. b, Fraser's dolphin. c, Atlantic humpbacked dolphin. d, Ginkgo-toothed beaked whale.

No. 3239, 35d: a, Blainville's beaked whalen. b, Atlantic spotted dolphin.

2010, Feb. 24   **Perf. 11½x11¼**
3234-3237 A634   Set of 4   6.00 6.00
Perf. 11½x12
3238 A634   25d Sheet of 4,
     #a-d   7.50 7.50
Souvenir Sheet
Perf. 11½x11¼
3239 A634   35d Sheet of 2,
     #a-b   5.25 5.25

Miniature Sheet

Charles Darwin (1809-82), Naturalist — A635

No. 3240 — Birds: a, Warbler finch. b, Common cactus finch. c, Large cactus finch. d, Small ground finch.

2010, Feb. 24   **Perf. 13¼**
3240 A635 25d Sheet of 4, #a-d   7.50 7.50

Miniature Sheet

Pres. John F. Kennedy (1917-63) — A636

No. 3241 — Kennedy: a, Curtain in background at left. b, At inauguration ceremony. c, With flag in background at right. d, With family.

2010, Apr. 15   **Perf. 12x11½**
3241 A636 30d Sheet of 4, #a-d   9.00 9.00

Miniature Sheets

Pres. Abraham Lincoln (1809-65) — A637

No. 3242, 25d — Lincoln and: a, Peter Cooper, Cooper Union. b, Mathew Brady, Brady Gallery. c, William Cullen Bryant, Great Hall, Cooper Union. d, Horace Greeley, Astor House.
No. 3243, 25d — Lincoln and: a, Brady, photograph of Lincoln by Brady. b, Alexander Gardner, photographs of Lincoln by Gardner. c, Victor David Brenner, Lincoln cent, Pres. Theodore Roosevelt. d, Daniel Chester French, statue of Lincoln in Lincoln Memorial.

2010, Apr. 15   **Perf. 11½x12**
Sheets of 4, #a-d
3242-3243 A637   Set of 2   15.00 15.00

Miniature Sheets

A638

Elvis Presley (1935-77) — A639

No. 3244 — Presley: a, Holding microphone, facing right, cape and microphone cord visible. b, Holding microphone, leaning. c, Holding microphone, no cord visible. d, Standing with arms akimbo.
No. 3245 — Presley: a, With guitar. b, With microphone near mouth. c, With guitar, pointing, and holding microphone on stand. d, Holding microphone on stand, with guitar strap on shoulder.

2010, Apr. 15   **Perf. 11¼x11½**
3244 A638 25d Sheet of 4, #a-d   7.50 7.50
Perf. 13¼
3245 A639 30d Sheet of 4, #a-d   9.00 9.00

2010 World Cup Soccer Championships, South Africa — A640

Soccer ball with flag of participating nations: No. 3246, 20d, Algeria. No. 3247, 20d, Argentina. No. 3248, 20d, Australia. No. 3249, 20d, Brazil. No. 3250, 20d, Cameroon. No. 3251, 20d, Chile. No. 3252, 20d, Denmark. No. 3253, 20d, England. No. 3254, 20d, France. No. 3255, 20d, Germany. No. 3256, 20d, Ghana. No. 3257, 20d, Greece. No. 3258, 20d, Honduras. No. 3259, 20d, Italy. No. 3260, 20d, Ivory Coast (Côte d'Ivoire). No. 3261, 20d, Japan. No. 3262, 20d, Korea DPR (North Korea). No. 3263, 20d, Korea Republic (South Korea). No. 3264, 20d, Mexico. No. 3265, 20d, Netherlands. No. 3266, 20d, New Zealand. No. 3267, 20d, Nigeria. No. 3268, 20d, Paraguay. No. 3269, 20d, Portugal. No. 3270, 20d, Serbia. No. 3271, 20d, Slovakia. No. 3272, 20d, Slovenia. No. 3273, 20d, South Africa. No. 3274, 20d, Spain. No. 3275, 20d, Switzerland. No. 3276, 20d, United States. No. 3277, 20d, Uruguay.

2010, May 24   **Perf. 14x14¾**
3246-3277 A640   Set of 32   45.00 45.00
Nos. 3246-3277 each were printed in sheets of 6.

Traditional Musical Instruments A641

Designs: 2d, 25d, Wollof tabala. 3d, 30d, Jola bugarab. 5d, 35d, Fula rilty. 6d, 50d, Mandinka kontingo. 7d, 65d, Mandinka bolongbato. 10d, 100d, Mandinka kora. 15d, 200d, Mandinka kora, diff. 18d, Mandinka balafongo, horiz.

Perf. 11¼x11½, 11½x11¼
2010, June 8
3278	A641	2d multi	.20	.20
3279	A641	3d multi	.20	.20
3280	A641	5d multi	.35	.35
3281	A641	6d multi	.40	.40
3282	A641	7d multi	.50	.50
3283	A641	10d multi	.70	.70
3284	A641	15d multi	1.00	1.00
3285	A641	18d multi	1.25	1.25
3286	A641	25d multi	1.75	1.75
3287	A641	30d multi	2.00	2.00
3288	A641	35d multi	2.40	2.40
3289	A641	50d multi	3.50	3.50
3290	A641	65d multi	4.50	4.50
3291	A641	100d multi	6.75	6.75
3292	A641	200d multi	13.50	13.50
	Nos. 3278-3292 (15)		39.00	39.00

US First Ladies Type of 2007
Souvenir Sheet
No. 3293, Michelle Obama.

2010, June 8   **Perf. 13¼**
3293 A574 65d multi   4.50 4.50

Miniature Sheet

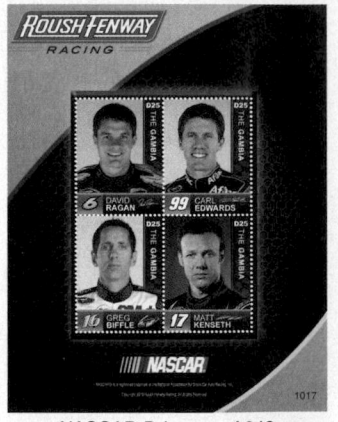

NASCAR Drivers — A642

No. 3294: a, David Ragan. b, Carl Edwards. c, Greg Biffle. d, Matt Kenseth.

2010, June 8   **Perf. 13¼x13**
3294 A642 25d Sheet of 4, #a-d   6.75 6.75

Souvenir Sheet

Elvis Presley (1935-77) — A643

No. 3295 — Presley wearing: a, Black jacket. b, White jacket.

2010, June 11   **Imperf.**
3295 A643 140d Sheet of 2,
     #a-b   19.00 19.00

Miniature Sheet

Elvis Presley (1935-77) — A644

No. 3296 — Presley wearing: a, Checked shirt. b, Jacket and tie. c, Sweater. d, White shirt with open collar.

2010, Apr. 15   **Litho.**   **Perf. 13¼**
3296 A644 30d Sheet of 4, #a-d   9.00 9.00

Lech Kaczynski (1949-2010), President of Poland — A645

2010, July 14   **Perf. 12x11½**
3297 A645 30d multi   2.25 2.25
Printed in sheets of 4.

Miniature Sheet

Accession to the Throne by King George V, Cent. — A646

No. 3298: a, 1917 cartoon of King George V. b, King George V. c, King Edward VIII. d, Badge of the House of Windsor. e, King George VI. f, Queen Elizabeth II.

2010, July 14 Litho.   Perf. 11¼x11½
3298 A646 20d Sheet of 6, #a-f   8.75 8.75

Visit of Pope Benedict XVI to Malta A647

Pope Benedict XVI wearing: No. 3299, 30d, Miter. No. 3300, 30d, Zucchetto.

2010, Aug. 26   **Perf. 13¼**
3299-3300 A647   Set of 2   4.25 4.25
Nos. 3299-3300 each were printed in sheets of 5.

Miniature Sheet

Paintings by Sandro Botticelli (1445-1510) — A648

No. 3301: a, Lamentation. b, Madonna del Magnificat. c, The Return of Judith to Bethulia. d, Venus from Venus and Mars. e, Mars from Venus and Mars. f, The Punishment of Korah.

2010, Aug. 26   Perf. 11¼x11½
3301 A648 20d Sheet of 6, #a-f   8.25 8.25

Miniature Sheets

Mother Teresa (1910-97), Humanitarian — A649

No. 3302, 30d — Mother Teresa at left, Princess Diana at right, with: a, Princess Diana bending to talk to Mother Teresa. b, Princess Diana with hands clasped at waist and Mother Teresa with hands clasped below chin. c, Mother Teresa and Princess Diana holding hands, Mother Teresa's arm at side. d, Mother Teresa and Princess Diana holding hands, Mother Teresa's arm extended.
No. 3303, 30d — Mother Teresa with: a, Pres. Ronald Reagan. b, Archbishop Desmond Tutu. c, Pope John Paul II. d, Queen Elizabeth II.

2010, Aug. 26   Perf. 11½x12
Sheets of 4, #a-d
3302-3303 A649   Set of 2   16.50 16.50

Robert Schumann (1810-56), Composer — A650

No. 3304, horiz. — Schumann and: a, Birthplace. b, His wife, Clara. c, Schumann Monument, Zwickau, Germany. d, Grave marker, Bonn, Germany.
65d, Robert and Clara Schumann.

2010, Aug. 26   Perf. 11½x12
3304 A650 30d Sheet of 4, #a-d   8.25 8.25
Souvenir Sheet
Perf. 11¼x11½
3305 A650 65d multi   4.50 4.50

Posters for Films Directed by Akira Kurosawa (1910-98) — A651

No. 3306, 30d, vert.: a, Nora Inu (Stray Dog). b, Zoku Sugata Sanshiro (Sanshiro Sugata Part II). c, Shichinin no Samurai (Seven Samurai). d, Shizukanaru Ketto (The Quiet Duel).
No. 3307, 30d, vert.: a, Donzoko (The Lower Depths). b, Hakuchi (The Idiot). c, Ikimono no Kiroku (I Live in Fear). d, Ikiru.
80d, Ichiban Utsukushiku (The Most Beautiful).

2010, Aug. 26   Perf. 13¼
Sheets of 4, #a-d
3306-3307 A651   Set of 2   16.50 16.50
Souvenir Sheet
3308 A651 80d multi   5.50 5.50

Girl Guides, Cent. — A652

No. 3309 — Girl Guides emblem, centenary emblem and: a, Four Girl Guides in green uniforms. b, Four Girl Guides not wearing uniforms. c, Two Girl Guides. d, Three Girl Guides.
80d, Two Girl Guides with backpacks, vert.

2010, Oct. 15   Perf. 11½x12
3309 A652 30d Sheet of 4, #a-d   8.50 8.50
Souvenir Sheet
Perf. 11¼x11½
3310 A652 80d multi   5.75 5.75

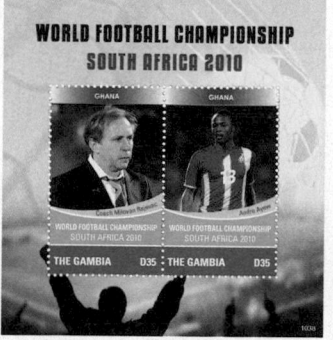

Players and Coaches in Second Round Matches of 2010 World Cup Soccer Championships — A653

No. 3311, 15d — United States vs. Ghana: a, Jay Demerit. b, Asamoah Gyan. c, Robbie Findley. d, Samuel Inkoom. e, Ricardo Clark. f, Stephen Appiah.
No. 3312, 15d — Uruguay vs. South Korea: a, Fernando Musiera. b, Lee Chung-Yong. c, Jorge Fucile. d, Cha Du-Ri. e, Maximiliano Pereira. f, Park Chu-Young.
No. 3313, 15d — Argentina vs. Mexico: a, Gabriel Heinze. b, Efrain Juarez. c, Carlos Tevez. d, Carlos Salcida. e, Lionel Messi. f, Andres Guardado.
No. 3314, 15d — Germany vs. England: a, Sami Khedira. b, Steven Gerrard. c, Philipp

Lahm. d, Joe Cole. e, Lukas Podolski. f, Ashley Cole.
No. 3315, 35d — Ghana: a, Coach Milovan Rajevac. b, Andre Ayew.
No. 3316, 35d — Uruguay: a, Coach Oscar Tabarez. b, Diego Forlan.
No. 3317, 35d — Argentina: a, Coach Diego Maradona. b, Nicolas Otramendi.
No. 3318, 35d — Germany: a, Coach Joachim Loew. b, Thomas Mueller.

2010, Oct. 15   Perf. 12
Sheets of 6, #a-f
3311-3314 A653   Set of 4   26.00 26.00
Souvenir Sheets of 2, #a-b
3315-3318 A653   Set of 4   20.00 20.00

GEORGIA

ˈjor-jə

LOCATION — South of Russia, bordering on the Black Sea and occupying the entire western part of Trans-Caucasia
GOVT. — Republic
AREA — 26,900 sq. mi.
POP. — 5,066,499 (1999 est.)
CAPITAL — Tbilisi (Tiflis)

Georgia was formerly a province of the Russian Empire and later a part of the Transcaucasian Federation of Soviet Republics. Stamps of Georgia were replaced in 1923 by those of Transcaucasian Federated Republics.
On Mar. 1, 1994, Georgia joined the Commonwealth of Independent States.

100 Kopecks = 1 Ruble
100 Kopecks = 1 Coupon (1993)
100 Tetri = 1 Lari (Sept. 25, 1995)

> Catalogue values for unused stamps in this country are for Never Hinged items, beginning with Scott 75 in the regular postage section, and Scott B10 in the semi-postal section.

Tiflis

A 6k local stamp, imperforate and embossed without color on white paper, was issued in November, 1857, at Tiflis by authority of the viceroy. The square design shows a coat of arms.

National Republic

St. George
A1   A2
Perf. 11½, Imperf.

1919		Litho.	Unwmk.	
12	A1	10k blue	.80	.80
13	A1	40k red orange	.80	.80
a.		Tête bêche pair	50.00	50.00
14	A1	50k emerald	.80	.80
15	A1	60k red	.80	.80
16	A1	70k claret	.80	.80
17	A2	1r orange brown	.80	.80
		Nos. 12-17 (6)	4.80	4.80

Queen Thamar — A3

1920		Perf. 11½, Imperf.		
18	A3	2r red brown	.65	.90
19	A3	3r gray blue	.65	.95
20	A3	5r orange	.65	1.25
		Nos. 18-20 (3)	1.95	3.10

Nos. 12-20 with parts of design inverted, sideways or omitted are fraudulent varieties.
Overprints meaning "Day of the National Guard, 12, 12, 1920" (5 lines) and "Recognition of Independence, 27, 1, 1921" (4 lines) were applied, probably in Italy, to remainders taken by government officials who fled when Russian forces occupied Georgia.
"Constantinople" and new values were unofficially surcharged on stamps of 1919-20 by a consul in Turkey.

Soviet Socialist Republic

Soldier with Flag — A5   Peasant Sowing Grain — A6

Industry and Agriculture — A7

1922		Unwmk.	Perf. 11½	
26	A5	500r rose	8.00	3.25
27	A6	1000r bister brown	8.00	3.25
28	A7	2000r slate	11.50	6.00
29	A7	3000r brown	11.50	6.00
30	A7	5000r green	11.50	6.00
		Nos. 26-30 (5)	50.50	24.50

Forgeries exist of Nos. 26-30.
Nos. 26 to 30 exist imperforate but were not so issued. Value for set, $100.

Nos. 26-30 Handstamped with New Values in Violet

1923				
36	A6	10,000r on 1000r	6.50	6.50
a.		Black surcharge	20.00	25.00
b.		20,000r on 1000r	200.00	
37	A7	15,000r on 2000r, blk surch.	7.75	8.50
a.		Violet surcharge	30.00	30.00
38	A5	20,000r on 500r	7.75	8.50
a.		Black surcharge	15.00	7.50
39	A7	40,000r on 5000r	5.50	5.50
a.		Black surcharge	15.00	15.00
40	A7	80,000r on 3000r	7.75	8.50
a.		Black surcharge	15.00	17.50
		Nos. 36-40 (5)	35.25	37.50

There were two types of the handstamped surcharges, with the numerals 5½mm and 6½mm high. The impressions are often too indistinct to measure or even to distinguish the numerals.
Double and inverted surcharges exist, as is usual with handstamps.

Printed Surcharge in Black

43	A6	10,000r on 1000r	6.00	6.25
44	A7	15,000r on 2000r	4.00	4.00
45	A5	20,000r on 500r	2.00	2.00
46	A7	40,000r on 5000r	4.00	3.75
47	A7	80,000r on 3000r	4.00	4.00
		Nos. 43-47 (5)	20.00	20.00

Nos. 43, 45, 46 and 47 exist imperforate but were not so issued. Value $25 each.

Russian Stamps of 1909-
18 Handstamp
Surcharged

Type I. Surcharge 20x5½mm.
Type II. Surcharge 22x7¼mm.

1923   *Perf. 14½x15*
48 A14 10,000r on 7k lt bl   150.00 150.00
49 A11 15,000r on 15k red
         brn & bl
         (I)   15.00 15.00
  a.   Type II   10.00 10.00

**Type I Surcharge Handstamped on
Armenia No. 141**

50 A11 15,000r on 5r on
         15k red
         brn & bl   200.00 *500.00*
  a.   Type II
         Nos. 48-50 (3)   365.00 *665.00*

Russian Stamps and
Types of 1909-18
Surcharged in Dark Blue
or Black

1923   *Perf. 11½, 14½x15*
51 A14 75,000r on 1k org   3.00   4.25
  a.   Imperf.   150.00 150.00
52 A14 200,000r on 5k cl   4.00   5.00
53 A8   300,000r on 20k bl
         & car
         (Bk)   4.00   5.00
  a.   Dark blue surcharge   70.00 100.00
54 A14 350,000r on 3k red   7.00   8.00
  a.   Imperf.   7.00   7.25
                   Imperf
55 A14 700,000r on 2k grn   7.00 10.00
  a.   Perf. 14½x15   27.50 32.50
         Nos. 51-55 (5)   25.00 32.25

> **Catalogue values for unused
> stamps in this section, from this
> point to the end of the section, are
> for Never Hinged items.**

Republic

Admission
to UN, 1st
Anniv.
A20

Map, flag, UN emblem.

1993, July 31   Litho.   *Perf. 13¼*
73 A20 25r green & multi   .75   .75
74 A20 50r brown & multi   1.10 1.10
75 A20 100r violet & multi   1.75 1.75
  a.   Souvenir sheet of 3, #73-75 +
         label   4.00 4.00
         Nos. 73-75 (3)   3.60 3.60

For overprint, see Nos. 327-328.

Natl. Arms,
Flag — A21

Fresco, 18th
Cent. — A22

Apostle
Simon, 11th
Cent. — A23

Three
Women, by
Lado
Gudiashvili
A24

1993, Oct. 11   Photo.   *Perf. 12x11½*
76 A21 50k multicolored   .50   .50

Litho.
Perf. 12x12½
77 A22 50k multicolored   1.10 1.10
78 A23 1c multicolored   .90   .90
79 A24 1c multicolored   1.40 1.40
         Nos. 76-79 (4)   3.90 3.90

Nos. 76, 78-79 dated 1992.
For surcharges see Nos. 80-83, 93-95.

Surcharged in Claret, Black, or Blue

1994, May 31   Photo.   *Perf. 12x11½*
80 A21 5000c on 50k #76 (C)   .45   .45

Litho.
Perf. 12x12½
81 A22 5000c on 50k #77
         (Blk)   .45   .45
82 A23 10,000c on 1c #78 (Bl)   .65   .65
83 A24 10,000c on 1c #79 (C)   .65   .65
         Nos. 80-83 (4)   2.20 2.20

Size and location of surcharge varies.

Places of
Worship — A25

30c, Mtskheta Church. 40c, Gelati Church.
50c, Nikortsminda Church. 60c, Ikorta Church.
70c, Samtavisi Church. 80c, Bolnisi Zion Synagogue. 90c, Gremi Citadel Church.

1993, Oct. 11   Litho.   *Perf. 13½*
84 A25 30c blue   .45   .45
85 A25 40c red brown   .55   .55
86 A25 50c olive brown   .65   .65
87 A25 60c rose carmine   .85   .85
88 A25 70c rose lake   .95   .95
89 A25 80c green   1.10 1.10
90 A25 90c slate   1.25 1.25
         Nos. 84-90 (7)   5.80 5.80

See Nos. 111-120.

Niko Nikoladze (1843-1928) — A26

1994, May 31   Litho.   *Perf. 13½*
91 A26 150c black & gold   1.00 1.00

UPU,
120th
Anniv.
A27

1994, May 30
92 A27 200c multicolored   1.10 1.10

Nos. 77-79 Surcharged in Green or
Red

1994   Litho.   *Perf. 12x12½*
93 A22 200c on 50k #77   .50   .50
94 A23 300c on 1c #78 (R)   .55   .55
95 A24 500c on 1c #79   1.25 1.25
         Nos. 93-95 (3)   2.30 2.30

Set exists with inverted surcharges. Value
$10.

A27a

A28

1994, Oct. 9   Litho.   *Perf. 14*
95A A27a 100c shown   2.75 2.75
95B A27a 200c Monument   5.00 5.00

All Georgian Congress.

1995, Mar. 28   Litho.   *Perf. 14½*
Georgia Natl. Olympic Committee: 10c, Intl.
year of sport & Olympic ideal. 15c, Olympic
congress, cent. 20c, Intl. Olympic Committee,
cent. 25c, Olympic truce.
96-99 A28 Set of 4   5.50 5.50

Dated 1994.

Paintings by Niko Piromanashvili
(1862-1918) — A29

#100, Three Princes Carousing on the
Grass. #101, Still life. #102, Georgian Woman
with a Tambourine, vert. #103, Bear on a
Moonlit Night, vert. #104, Woman with a Tankard of Beer, vert. #105, Deer, vert. #106, Fisherman, vert. #107, Giraffe, vert. #108, Boy on
a Donkey, vert. #109, Brooder with Chicks.
#110, Family Picnicking.

1995, Mar. 29   Litho.   *Perf. 14*
100-109 A29 20c Set of 10   11.50 11.50
         Souvenir Sheet
110 A29 100c multicolored   6.25 6.25

Churches Type of 1993

10c   20c

400c

1c, #120, Metechi, 1278-1289. 2c, #117,
Alaverdi, 11th cent. 3c, #116, Dranda, 8th
cent. #114, Sveti-Zchoveli, 1010-1019. #115,
Kumurdo, 964. #118, Anauri, 17th cent. #119,
Bitschvinta, 10th cent.

1995   Litho.   *Perf. 14*
         Size: 25½x39mm
111 A25 1c black & violet   1.60 1.60
112 A25 2c black & sepia   1.60 1.60
113 A25 3c black & red brn   1.60 1.60
114 A25 10c black & violet   1.60 1.60
115 A25 10c black & sepia   1.60 1.60
116 A25 10c black & grn blue   1.60 1.60
117 A25 20c black & slate   1.60 1.60
118 A25 20c black & olive grn   1.60 1.60
119 A25 400c black & org brn   1.60 1.60
120 A25 400c black & red brn   1.60 1.60
         Nos. 111-120 (10)   16.00 16.00

Paolo Iashvili (1894-1937) — A30

1995, Apr. 1
125 A30 300c multicolored   1.25 1.25

Prehistoric Animals — A31

#126, Brontosaurus. #127, Saurolophus. #128, Scolosaurus. #129, Triceratops. #130, Parasaurolophus. #131, Ceratosaurus. #132, Deinonichus. #133, Tyrannosaurus. #134, Stegosaurus.

#135: a, Pterodactylus (d). b, Rhamphophynghus (c, e). c, Pteranodon. d, Spinosaurus. e, Tyrannosaurus (f, h, i). f, Velociraptor. g, Monoklonius. h, Ornithomimus. i, Mastodon.

100c, Deinonychus.

1995   **Litho.**   **Perf. 14**
126-134 A31 15c Set of 9   6.25 6.25

Miniature Sheet of 9
135 A31 15c #a.-i.   7.25 7.25

Souvenir Sheet
136 A31 100c multicolored   5.25 5.25

Issued: #126-134, 5/12.

UNESCO
World
Heritage
Sites
A32

100c, Bagrati Cathedral. 500c, Jvari of Mtskhetha.

1995, Aug. 30   **Litho.**   **Perf. 14**
137 A32 100c multi   1.10 1.10

Souvenir Sheet
138 A32 500c multi, vert.   5.75 5.75

Miniature Sheet

Wildlife
Painting
A33

Design: #a.-p., Various animals and birds.

1995, Aug. 4
139 A33 15c Sheet of 16, #a.-p.   9.75 9.75

Miniature Sheets of 16

Birds
A34

Designs: Each 15t: Nos. 140a-140p, Various songbirds. Nos. 141a-141p, Various raptors.

Each 100t: No. 142, Songbird. No. 143, Owl.

1996, Feb. 26   **Litho.**   **Perf. 14**
140-141 A34 Set of 2   22.50 22.50

Souvenir Sheets
142-143 A34 Set of 2   12.50 12.50

Miniature Sheet

Fauna
and Flora
A35

a, Stork's head. b, Stork's body (a, f), berries. c, Snake (d, g, h). d, Moth. e, Lizard. f, Songbirds. g, Insect, flowers. h, Bee on flower. i, Butterfly, flower. j, Frog, lily (f). k, Snail. l, Turtle (p). m. Lobster. n, Sea plant, eel (o). o, Fish. p, Salamander.

1996, Mar. 14   **Litho.**   **Perf. 14**
144 A35 10t Sheet of 16, #a.-p.   12.00 12.00

Dinosaurs — A36

1996, Apr. 24   **Litho.**   **Perf. 14**
145 A36 10t Sheet of 9, #a.-i.   7.25 7.25

Intl. Olympic Committee, Cent. — A37

Georgian Olympians, landmarks from earlier Summer Olympic Games: 1t, Helsinki, 1952. 2t, Melbourne, 1956. 3t, Rome, 1960. 4t, Tokyo, 1964. 5t, Mexico City, 1968. 6t, Munich, 1972. 7t, Montreal, 1976. 8t, Moscow, 1980. 9t, Seoul, 1988. 10t, Barcelona, 1992. Early Greek: 50t, Wrestlers. 70t, Runner.

1996, Aug. 16   **Litho.**   **Perf. 14**
146-155 A37 Set of 10   8.25 8.25

Souvenir Sheets
156 A37 50t multicolored   7.50 7.50
157 A37 70t multicolored   8.75 8.75

Olymphilex '96 (#157).

Paintings — A38

Designs: 10t, Citizens of Paris, by Lado Gudiashvili. 20t, Abstract, by Wassily Kandinsky. 30t, Still Life, by David Kakabadze. 50t, Three Painters, by Shalva Kikodze. 80t, Portrait of Niko Pirosmani, by Pablo Picasso.

1996, Aug. 2   **Litho.**   **Perf. 14**
158 A38 10t multicolored   .40 .40
159 A38 20t multicolored   .70 .70
160 A38 30t multicolored   1.00 1.00
161 A38 50t multicolored   1.40 1.40

Size: 72x90mm

Imperf
162 A38 80t multicolored   3.00 3.00
Nos. 158-162 (5)   6.50 6.50

A39

1996, Dec. 25   **Litho.**   **Perf. 13x14**
163 A39 30t Anton I (1720-88)   1.25 1.25

Ivan Javakhishvili (1876-1940),
Writer — A40

1997, Mar. 6   **Perf. 14**
164 A40 50t multicolored   1.50 1.50

UN, 50th
Anniv.
A41

1997, Mar. 5   **Litho.**   **Perf. 14**
165 A41 30t purple & blue   1.50 1.50
166 A41 125t red & blue   4.00 4.00

Dogs — A42

Designs: 10t, Rottweiler. 30t, Gordon setter. 50t, St. Bernard. 60t, English bulldog. 70t, Caucasian sheep dog.

125t, Caucasian sheep dog, diff.

1997, June 2   **Litho.**   **Perf. 14**
167 A42 10t multicolored   .35 .35
168 A42 30t multicolored   .85 .85
169 A42 50t multicolored   1.40 1.40
170 A42 60t multicolored   1.60 1.60
171 A42 70t multicolored   2.00 2.00
a.   Sheet of 6, #167-172   9.50
Nos. 167-171 (5)   6.20 6.20

Souvenir Sheet
172 A42 125t multicolored   3.75 3.75

No. 171a contains stamp from No. 172 without the continuous design. Issued: 2/27/98.

Animated Film Characters — A43

Designs: a, 20t, Two mice talking. b, 30t, Man in bed. c, 40t, Balloons, bear, girl on cloud. d, 50t, Animals dancing, tree. e, 60t, Duck dressed as woman, tree.

1997, July 15   **Litho.**   **Perf. 14**
173 A43 Strip of 5, #a.-e.   9.00 9.00

Georgian Women's Team, Winners of
1996 World Chess Olympiad — A44

No. 174: a, Maia Chiburdanidze, Nona Gaprindashvili, Nana Ioseliani, Nino Gurieli, 1992 winners. b, Chiburdanidze, Ioseliani, Ketevan Arakhamia, Gurieli, 1994 winners. c, Chiburdanidze, Ioseliani, Arakhamia, Gurieli, 1996 winners.

No. 175: a, 20t, Vice-Champion Nana Alexandria, 1975, 1981. b, 40t, Chiburdanidze, 1978, 1981 (Vice-Champion), 1984, 1986, 1991. c, 20t, Ioseliani, 1988, 1993. d, 50t, Gaprindashvili, 1962, 1965, 1969, 1972, 1975 (Vice-Champion).

1997, July 21   **Litho.**   **Imperf.**
174 A44 30t Sheet of 3, #a.-d.+ label   3.25 3.25
175 A44 Sheet of 4, #a.-d.   4.25 4.25

Nos. 174-175 have simulated perforations.

A45

1998
Winter
Olympic
Games,
Nagano
A46

Stylized skier — #176: a, 20t. b, 30t. c, 40t. d, 50t.

Early hand-made winter apparel, equipment — No. 177: a, 20t, Snow shoe, hat, gloves. b, 30t, Scarf, snow shoe. c, 40t, Sled, gloves. d, 50t, Scarf, snow shoe.

No. 178, Stylized skier, diff. No. 179, Man's feet with snow shoes.

1998, Feb. 8   **Litho.**   **Perf. 14**
176 A45 Sheet of 4, #a.-d.   4.00 4.00
177 A46 Sheet of 4, #a.-d.   4.00 4.00

Souvenir Sheets
178 A45 70t multicolored   2.75 2.75
179 A46 70t multicolored   2.75 2.75

Moscow
'97 — A47

Tiflis local postage stamp of 1857.

1997, Oct. 17   **Litho.**   **Perf. 13x14**
180 A47 80t multicolored   2.25 2.25

Souvenir Sheet
181 A47 1 l multicolored   3.00 3.00

Prince Vakhushti Bagrationi (1696-
1758) — A48

40t, Map of Georgia, 1745, portrait. 80t, Portrait.

1997, Oct. 9
182 A48 40t multi   1.00 1.00
183 A48 80t multi, vert.   2.25 2.25

World Delphic Congress — A49

40t, Symbols of education, art & music, 1st World Junior Delphics. 80t, Building on mountaintop, 2nd World Delphic Cong.

1997, Nov. 24   Litho.   Perf. 14
184 A49 40t multicolored   1.10 1.10
185 A49 80t multicolored   2.10 2.10

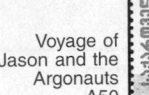

Voyage of Jason and the Argonauts A50

Plate and Vase Paintings: a, 30t, Greek galley from Rhodes, terracotta plate, 700-650BC. b, 40t, Preparation for Battle, vase painting, 460BC. c, 50t, Boreades, Phineus & Harpy, vase painting, 6th cent. d, 60t, Punishment of King Amicus, vase painting, 420-400BC. e, 70t, Argonauts in Colchis, vase painting, 4th cent. BC. f, 80t, The Dragon Vomiting Jason, vase painting, 490-485BC.

1998, June 23   Litho.   Perf. 13x13½
186 A50 Sheet of 6, #a.-f.   9.00 9.00

Independence, 80th Anniv. — A51

1998, Dec. 25   Litho.   Perf. 14
187 A51 80t multicolored   2.50 2.50

Horses A52

Various breeds.

1998, Dec. 22
188 A52 10t multicolored   .55   .55
189 A52 40t multicolored   1.60 1.60
190 A52 70t multicolored   2.75 2.75
191 A52 80t multicolored   3.25 3.25
    Nos. 188-191 (4)   8.15 8.15
Souvenir Sheet
Imperf
192 A52 100t multicolored   4.50 4.50

No. 192 has simulated perfs.

Locomotives — A53

Various locomotives built at Tbilisi Locomotives Works.

1998, Dec. 24
193 A53 10t multicolored   .40   .40
194 A53 30t multicolored   1.10 1.10
195 A53 40t multicolored   1.40 1.40

196 A53 50t multicolored   1.60 1.60
197 A53 80t multicolored   2.75 2.75
    Nos. 193-197 (5)   7.25 7.25
Souvenir Sheet
198 A53 100t multicolored   4.00 4.00

Europa A54

1998, Dec. 31   Litho.   Perf. 13x12¾
199 A54 (80t) Berikaoba   1.60 1.60
200 A54 (100t) Chiakokonoba   2.10 2.10

Wildlife A55

10t, Vormela peregusna guld. 40t, Hyaena hyaena. 80t, Ursus arctos syriacus. 100t, Capra aegagrus erxleber.

1999, Feb.   Litho.   Perf. 14x13½
201 A55 10t multicolored   .40   .40
202 A55 40t multicolored   1.25 1.25
203 A55 80t multicolored   2.50 2.50
    Nos. 201-203 (3)   4.15 4.15
Souvenir Sheet
Imperf
204 A55 100t multicolored   3.25 3.25

Dated 1998. No. 204 has simulated perfs.

Ancient and Modern Bridges of Tbilisi A56

Bridges: a, 10t, Michael. b, 40t, Saarbruken. c, 50t, N. Baratashvili. d, 60t, Mukhrani. e, 70t, Avlabari. f, 80t, Metekhi.

1999, Feb.   Perf. 13½x14
205 A56 Sheet of 6, #a.-f.   12.00 12.00

Mustela Lutreola, Worldwide Fund for Wildlife A57

1999, Apr. 27   Litho.   Perf. 13x12¾
206 A57 (10t) Standing in water   1.60 1.60
207 A57 (20t) Feeding   1.60 1.60
208 A57 (30t) Two standing   1.60 1.60
209 A57 (60t) In burrow   1.60 1.60
    b.   Strip of 4, #206-209   13.00 13.00

Nos. 206-209 were issued in sheets of 10 of each denomination and as se-tenant blocks of 4 in sheets of 20. The stamps from the se-tenant sheets have thicker lettering in the country and Latin names. Singles from the se-tenant sheets of 20 and from the individual sheetlets of 10 are of equal value.

Europa — A58

(80t), Batsara-Babaneury Reserve. (100t), Lagodekhy Reserve.

Council of Europe, 50th Anniv. — A59

1999, Apr. 28   Litho.   Perf. 12¾x13
210 A58 (80t) multi   2.50 2.50
211 A58 (100t) multi   3.00 3.00

1999, Nov.   Litho.   Perf. 12¾
212 A59 50t shown   1.00 1.00
213 A59 80t Latin letters   1.40 1.40

Georgian Olympic Committee, 10th Anniv. A60

1999, Nov.   Perf. 13¾
214 A60 20t multi   .90   .90
215 A60 50t multi   2.00 2.00

Butterflies A61

Designs: 10t, Iphiclides podalirius. 20t, Parnassius apollo. 50t, Colias aurorina herrich-schaffer. 80t, Tomares romanovi.

1999, Nov.
216 A61 10t multi   .60   .60
217 A61 20t multi   1.00 1.00
218 A61 50t multi   1.90 1.90
219 A61 80t multi   4.00 4.00
    Nos. 216-219 (4)   7.50 7.50

UPU, 125th Anniv. — A62

1999, Nov.   Perf. 13¼x13½
220 A62 20t shown   .75   .75
221 A62 80t Letter writer   2.75 2.75

Trucks A63

1999, Dec.   Perf. 13¾
Color of Truck
222 A63 20t green   .65   .65
223 A63 40t red & yellow   1.25 1.25
224 A63 50t blue & white   1.60 1.60
225 A63 80t red & white   2.50 2.50
    Nos. 222-225 (4)   6.00 6.00
Souvenir Sheet
226 A63 100t red   4.25 4.25

Souvenir Sheet

Svaneti, World Heritage Site — A64

1999, Dec.   Perf. 12¾
227 A64 100t multi   3.50 3.50

Europa, 2000
Common Design Type
Denominations: 80t, 100t.

2000, Mar. 31   Litho.   Perf. 12¾x13
228-229 CD17 Set of 2   9.00 9.00

Scenes from "The Knight in a Tiger's Skin," by Shota Rustaveli A65

Denominations: 10t, 20t, 30t, 50t, 60t.

2000, May 8   Perf. 14¼x13¾
230-234 A65 Set of 5   5.50 5.50
Souvenir Sheet
235 A65 80t multi + label   4.25 4.25

Nos. 230-235 also issued imperf. Value, set $10.

Christianity, 2000th Anniv. — A66

Icons: 20t, St. Nino the Preacher. 50t, The Savior. 80t, The Virgin Hodigitria.

2000, May 10   Perf. 13¾
236-238 A66 Set of 3   5.50 5.50

Souvenir Sheet

Georgian State System, 3000th Anniv. — A67

2000, May 11   Perf. 13
239 A67 100t multi   4.50 4.50

Fish — A68

Various fish: 10t, 20t, 30t, 50t, 80t.

2000, May 12 **Perf. 13¾x13¼**
240-244 A68 Set of 5 7.75 7.75

David Saradjishvili (1848-1911), Brandy Maker A69

2000, Sept. 20 Litho. Perf. 14¼x14
245 A69 80t multi 2.25 2.25

2000 Summer Olympics, Sydney — A70

No. 246: a, 20t, Runner at left. b, 50t, Runner at center. c, 80t, Runner at right.

2000 Sept. 20 Perf. 13¾
246 A70 Strip of 3, #a-c 6.50 6.50

Millennium — A71

No. 247: a, 20t, "1999." b, 50t, "2000." c, 80t, "2001."

2000, Sept. 20
247 A71 Strip of 3, #a-c 6.50 6.50

Joint Georgia-Russia Space Reflector Project — A72

Designs: 20t, Astronauts at work. 80t, Reflector.

2000, Dec. 11 Litho. Perf. 13¾
248-249 A72 Set of 2 4.00 4.00

Human Rights in Europe, 50th Anniv. A73

Denomination colors: 50t, Orange brown. 80t, Blue.

2000, Dec. 12 Perf. 14¼x14
250-251 A73 Set of 2 3.75 3.75

Mushrooms A74

Designs: 10t, Cantharellus cibarius. 20t, Agaricus campestris. 30t, Armillariella mella. 50t, Russula adusta. 80t, Cortinarus violaceus.

2000, Dec. 14 Perf. 13¼x13½
252-256 A74 Set of 5 7.75 7.75

UN High Commissioner for Refugees, 50th Anniv. — A75

2000, Dec. 14 Perf. 13½x14
257 A75 50t multi 1.50 1.50

Houses of Worship Type of 1993

Unidentified buildings. Colors: 10t, Brown. 50t, Blue.

2000, Dec. 18 Perf. 13¼x13
Size: 24x32mm
258-259 A25 Set of 2 2.25 2.25

Writers — A76

Designs: 30t, Alexander Kazbegi (1848-93). 40t, Jakob Gogebashvili (1840-1912). 50t, Vadja Pshavela (1861-1915). 70t, Akaki Tsereteli (1840-1915). 80t, Ilia Chavchavadze (1837-1907).

2000, Dec. 19 Perf. 13¼x13¾
260-264 A76 Set of 5 6.50 6.50

Alexander Kartveli (1896-1977), Aircraft Designer — A77

Designs: 10t, P-47D Thunderbolt. 20t, F-84. 80t, F-105D Thunderchief.

2000, Dec. 20 Perf. 13¾x14
265-267 A77 Set of 3 4.00 4.00
Souvenir Sheet
Perf. 13
268 A77 100t Portrait, vert. 3.50 3.50

Fire Fighting Service, 175th Anniv. — A78

2000, Dec. 24 Perf. 13¾x14
269 A78 50t multi 2.25 2.25

Europa — A79

Designs: 40t, Ritsa Lake. 80t, Borjomi Park.

2001, Sept. 10 Litho. Perf. 12½x13
270-271 A79 Set of 2 5.75 5.75
  a. Booklet pane, 2 each #270-271,
    perf. 12½x13 on 3 sides 11.00
    Booklet, #271a 12.00

Great Silk Route A80

2001, Sept. 20 Perf. 13x12½
272 A80 20t shown .75 .75
Souvenir Sheet
273 A80 80t Like 20t, no emblem 3.00 3.00

Kutaisi Synagogue — A81

2001, Sept. 13 Litho. Perf. 13x14
274 A81 140t multi 4.50 4.50

First Europe-Asia Chess Match — A82

2001, Sept. 18 Litho. Perf. 13¾
275 A82 1 l multi 4.50 4.50

Poets — A83

No. 276: a, Taras Shevchenko (1814-61), Ukrainian poet. b, Akaki Tsereteli (1840-1915), Georgian poet.

2001, Dec. 19 Perf. 13
276 A83 50t Horiz. pair, #a-b 3.75 3.75
See Ukraine No. 445.

Georgian National Ballet — A84

Designs: 30t, Dancers Iliko Sukhishvili (1907-85) and Nino Ramishvili (1910-2000), sketch for dance "Mtiuluri." 50t, Dancers, sketch for dance "Samaya." 80t, Sukhishvili, Ramishvili, and sketch for dance "Jeirani."

2002, Feb. 11 Perf. 13½x13¼
277-279 A84 Set of 3 5.25 5.25

Port of Poti, 140th Anniv. — A85

No. 280: a, Map, ship (black and white photograph). b, Mobile container crane, containers. c, Ship and tugboat, cargo hauler. d, Cargo hauler, small boat, container crane lifting container (black and white photograph). e, Ship, cargo hauler (black and white photograph). f, Cargo hauler, large ship.

2002, Feb. 11 Perf. 13¼x13½
280 A85 30t Sheet of 6, #a-f 6.50 6.50

A86

Ashot Kurapatl Opiza — A87

2002, Feb. 11 Perf. 13¼x13½
281 A86 100t blue 3.00 3.00
Perf. 13¼
282 A87 5 l brown 11.00 11.00

Europa — A88

Designs: 40t, Georgian Circus. 80t, Tbilisi Circus.

2002, Mar. 22 Perf. 13½x13¼
283-284 A88 Set of 2 3.75 3.75
  a. Booklet pane, 2 each #283-284,
    perf. 13½x13¼ on 3 sides 8.75
    Booklet, #284a 9.75

Convention on Status of Refugees, 50th Anniv. — A89

2002, May 15　　Litho.　　Perf. 13¼
285　A89　50t multi　　　　　1.25　1.25

Dinamo Tbilisi, Winner of 1981 European Soccer Cup — A90

2002, Sept. 23　　　　Perf. 13¾
286　A90　20t multi　　　　　2.50　2.50

Year of Dialogue Among Civilizations A91

2002, Sept. 23　　Perf. 13x13¾
287　A91　40t multi　　　　　1.25　1.25

Intl. Federation of Stamp Dealers Associations, 50th Anniv. — A92

2002, Sept. 23　　Perf. 13¼x13
288　A92　100t No. 12　　　　3.00　3.00

Fighter Aircraft A93

Designs: 30t, SU-25 Scorpio. 80t, MiG 21U.

2002, Sept. 23　　Perf. 13¾x13
289-290　A93　Set of 2　　　　3.25　3.25

Traditional Costumes A94

Men and women in various costumes: 20t, 30t, 50t.

2002, Sept. 23　　　　Perf. 13¾
291-293　A94　Set of 3　　　　3.25　3.25

Church Murals A95

Murals from: 10t, 14th cent., vert. 30t, 16th-17th cent. 80t, 18th cent., vert.

Perf. 13½x13, 13x13½
2002, Sept. 23
294-296　A95　Set of 3　　　　4.00　4.00

Pectoral Crosses A96

Designs: 10t, Crucifixion, 10th cent. 20t, Cross from Martvili, 7th-9th cent. 50t, Cross from Martvili, 10th cent. 80t, Cross of King Tamari, 12th cent.

2002, Sept. 23　　Perf. 14¼x14
297-300　A96　Set of 4　　　　5.00　5.00

Flowers — A97

Designs: 20t, Bellflower. 30t, Caucasia rhododendron. 50t, Anemone. 80t, Marsh marigold.

2003, Sept. 23　　Perf. 13x13¾
301-304　A97　Set of 4　　　　5.50　5.50

Souvenir Sheet

Alexandre Dumas (Père) (1802-70), French Novelist — A98

2002, Sept. 23　　Perf. 14x13¾
305　A98　120t multi　　　　　4.25　4.25

Europa — A99

Poster art: 40t, Three men and donkey. 80t, Four people.

2003, Mar. 10　　Perf. 13½x13¼
306-307　A99　Set of 2　　　　4.50　4.50
307a　Booklet pane, 2 each #306-
　　　307, perf. 13½x13¼ on 3
　　　sides　　　　　　　　　8.75
　　Complete booklet, #307a　　9.75

Souvenir Sheet

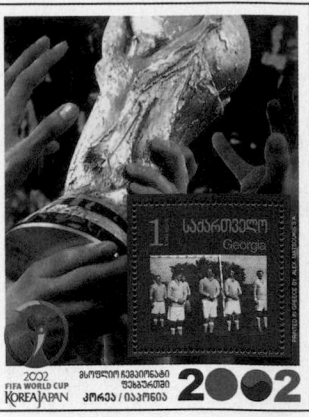

2002 World Cup Soccer Championships, Japan and Korea — A100

2003, Apr. 25　　　　Perf. 13¾
308　A100　1 l multi　　　　　3.25　3.25

Souvenir Sheet

Paleontology — A101

No. 309: a, Stylized drawing of ancient European man. b, Skull.

2003, Apr. 25　　　　Perf. 12¾
309　A101　60t Sheet of 2, #a-b　4.00　4.00

Margin of No. 309 has "1700000 YEARS OLD" overprinted in red brown on silver oval that is an overprint over an inscription that reads "17000000 YEARS OLD". Examples exist without the red brown overprint.

Youth — A102

2003, June 20　　Litho.　　Perf. 14x14¼
310　A102　50t multi　　　　　1.50　1.50

Women for Peace A103

2003, June 20　　Perf. 13¾x13
311　A103　50t multi　　　　　1.50　1.50

Zoo Animals — A104　　Minerals — A105

Animals at Tbilisi Zoo: 20t, Elephant. 30t, Wolf. 40t, Ostrich. 50t, Bear.

2003, Aug. 25　　　　Perf. 14x13¾
312-315　A104　Set of 4　　　4.75　4.75
315a　Miniature sheet, 2 each
　　　#312-315　　　　　　10.00　10.00

No. 315a was sold in a booklet cover but unattached, and is comprised of two tete-beche blocks of Nos. 312-315.

2003, Aug. 25　　Perf. 13¼x13

Minerals: 10t, Rock crystal. 20t, Agate with amethyst. 30t, Orpiment rose. 50t, Realgar with orpiment.

316-319　A105　Set of 4　　　3.75　3.75
319a　Miniature sheet, 2 each #316-
　　　319　　　　　　　　　8.00　8.00

No. 319a was sold in a booklet cover but unattached, and is composed of two tete-beche blocks of Nos. 316-319.

Fruit — A106

Designs: 10t, Prunus spinosa. 20t, Laurocerasus officinalis. 30t, Cydonia oblonga. 50t, Punica granatum. 80t, Pyrus caucasica.

2003, Aug. 25　　Perf. 14x13¾
320-324　A106　Set of 5　　　6.00　6.00

Souvenir Sheet

Old Tbilisi, by Elene Akhvlediani (1901-75) — A107

2003, Aug. 25
325　A107　80t multi　　　　　3.00　3.00

Souvenir Sheet

Self-portrait, by Vincent van Gogh (1853-90) — A108

2003, Aug. 25　　Perf. 13x12¾
326　A108　100t multi　　　　4.00　4.00

Nos. 73, 75a Overprinted

2003, Oct. 6   **Litho.**   *Perf. 13¼*
327   A20   25t green & multi   .85   .85

Souvenir Sheet
328   Sheet, #327, 328a, 328b   6.00   6.00
   a.   A20 50t brown & multi   1.60   1.60
   b.   A20 100t violet & multi   3.50   3.50
   First postage stamps, 10th anniv.

Intl. Association of Academies of Science, 10th Anniv. — A109

2003, Nov. 28   *Perf. 13¾x13¼*
329   A109   30t multi   1.10   1.10

East-West Energy Corridor — A110

2003, Nov. 28   *Perf. 13¼x13¾*
330   A110   80t multi   2.50   2.50

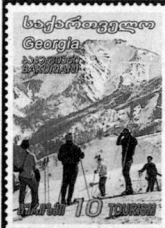

Tourism — A111

Designs: 10t, Skiers, Bakuriani. 20t, Caves, Vardzia. 30t, Harbor, Batum. 50t, Lake Ritsa.

2003, Nov. 28   *Perf. 13¾x13¼*
331-334   A111   Set of 4   3.50   3.50
334a   Booklet pane, 2 each #331-
     334   7.00   —
   Complete booket, #334a   7.50
No. 334a is composed of two tete-beche blocks of Nos. 331-334.

Grapes A112

Designs: 10t, Aladasturi. 20t, Rkhatsiteli. 30t, Ojaleshi. 50t, Goruli Mtsvane. 80t, Aleksandrouli (Khvanchkhara).

2003, Nov. 28
335-339   A112   Set of 5   7.00   7.00

Europa A113

Designs: 40t, Merry Christmas. 80t, Happy Easter.

2004, Jan. 28   **Litho.**   *Perf. 13¼x13½*
340-341   A113   Set of 2   5.00   5.00
341a   Booklet pane, 4 each #340-
     341, perf. 13¼x13½ on 2
     or 3 sides   17.50   —
   Complete booklet, #341a   20.00

Georgi Tsereteli (1904-73), Direcetor of Institute of Oriental Studies A114

2004, Nov. 5   **Litho.**   *Perf. 13¼x13¾*
342   A114   30t multi   1.10   1.10

Souvenir Sheet

Rose Revolution, 1st Anniv. — A115

No. 343: a, Crowd with flags. b, Protestors with flag sprayed with water.

2004, Nov. 5   *Perf. 13¼x13*
343   A115   50t Sheet of 2, #a-b   3.75   3.75

FIFA (Fédération Internationale de Football Association), Cent. — A116

Caricatures of soccer players: 20t, Boris Paichadze. 30t, Avtandil Gogoberidze. 50t, Mikheil Meskhi. 80t, David Kipiani.

2004, Nov. 5   *Perf. 13¾x13¼*
344-347   A116   Set of 4   5.50   5.50

2004 Summer Olympics, Athens — A117

Sculptures of athletes by: 20t, B. Skhulukhia. 30t, V. Cherkezishvili. 50t, N. Jikia. 80t, L. Vardosanidze.

2004, Nov. 5   *Perf. 13¼x13¾*
348-351   A117   Set of 4   6.75   6.75

Ancient Jewelry — A118

Designs: 20t, Belt and buckle, 3rd-4th cent. 30t, Necklace and belt buckle, 3rd-4th cent. 40t, Necklace and pins, 2000-1500 B.C. 80t, Necklace, 5th cent. B.C., double-voluted pins, 3rd millennium B.C.

2004, Nov. 5
352-355   A118   Set of 4   5.50   5.50

UNESCO World Heritage Sites A119

Designs: 20t, Ushguli. 30t, Bagrati. 50t, Gelati. 60t, Samtavro. 70t, Svetitskhoveli. 80t, Jvari.

2004, Nov. 5   **Litho.**   *Perf. 14x13¼*
356-361   A119   Set of 6   9.50   9.50

Flag of Georgia A120

2005, Feb. 11   **Litho.**   *Perf. 14x13¼*
362   A120   50t multi   1.75   1.75

Europa — A121

Loaves of bread and: 20t, Girl. 80t, Bakers.

2005, May 27   *Perf. 14x13¾*
363   A121   20t multi   1.25   1.25
364   A121   80t multi   4.75   4.75

Booklet Stamps
Size: 29x41mm
Perf. 13¾ on 2, 3 or 4 Sides
365   A121   20t multi   1.25   1.25
366   A121   80t multi   4.75   4.75
   a.   Booklet pane, 2 each #365-
     366   12.50   —
   b.   Booklet pane, 3 each #365-
     366   19.00   —
   Complete booklet, #366a, 366b   32.50

Rabbi Abraam Khvoles — A122

2005, June 1   *Perf. 12*
367   A122   1 l multi   3.00   3.00

2008 Summer Olympics, Beijing A123

2005, Dec. 28   **Litho.**   *Perf. 12*
368   A123   80t multi   2.40   2.40

2006 World Cup Soccer Championships, Germany — A124

2005, Dec. 28
369   A124   100t multi   3.00   3.00

Georgian Ballet — A125

Designs: 40t, V. Tsiguadze. 50t, V. Chabukiani.

2005, Dec. 28
370-371   A125   Set of 2   3.00   3.00

Orchids — A126

Designs: 20t, Dactylorhiza euxina. 40t, Dactylorhiza iberica. 50t, Oprys caucasica. 80t, Orchis caucasica.

2005, Dec. 28
372-375   A126   Set of 4   6.00   6.00

Theaters — A127

Designs: No. 376, 30t, Georgian Drama Theater, Batumi. No. 377, 30t, Georgian Drama Theater, Kutaisi. No. 378, 30t, Abkhazian Drama Theater, Sukhumi. No. 379, 30t, Georgian Academic Theater, Tbilisi. No. 380, 30t, Georgian Drama Theater, Tbilisi. No. 381, 30t, Georgian Opera and Ballet Theater, Tbilisi. No. 382, 30t, Armenian Drama Theater, Tbilisi. No. 383, 30t, Ossetian Drama Theater, Tskhinvali.

2005, Dec. 28
376-383   A127   Set of 8   7.50   7.50

2006 Winter Olympics, Turin
A128

Designs: 10t, Speed skating. 20t, Biathlon. 30t, Ski jumping. 40t, Figure skating. 80t, Downhill skiing.

2005, Dec. 29
384-388 A128 Set of 5   5.50 5.50

Souvenir Sheet

Tbilisi Funicular, Cent. — A129

2005, Dec. 30
389 A129 100t multi   3.00 3.00

Europa Stamps, 50th Anniv.
A130

Designs: 10t, Various Georgian Europa stamps. 20t, Person inserting postcard in mail slot. 30t, France #805, Germany #748, magnifying glass, newspaper. 40t, Earth in ripped newspaper wrapper.
No. 394, 80t, Like 10t. No. 395, 80t, Like 20t. No. 396, 80t, Like 30t. No. 397, 80t, Like 40t.

2006, Jan. 30   **Perf. 12¾x13**
390-393 A130 Set of 4   3.75 3.75

Souvenir Sheets
394-397 A130 Set of 4   12.50 12.50

Europa — A131

Stars and: 20t, People holding flags. 80t, Earth, Georgian flag.

Perf. 13½x13¼
2006, June 30   **Litho.**
398-399 A131 Set of 2   4.50 4.50
399a   Booklet pane, 4 each #398-399, perf. 13½x13¼ on 3 sides   22.00 —
   Complete booklet, #399a   23.00
No. 399a contains two tete-beche pairs of Nos. 398-399.

Nos. 365-366 Overprinted

Perf. 13¾ on 2, 3 or 4 Sides
2006, Oct. 23   **Litho.**
402 A121 20t multi   .90 .90
403 A121 80t multi   3.75 3.75
  a.   Sheet of 4, 2 each #402-403   9.50 9.50
  b.   Sheet of 6, 3 each #402-403   14.50 14.50
Europa stamps, 50th anniv. Nos. 403a and 403b are Nos. 366a and 366b removed from the booklet and overprinted on the stamps and margin.

No. 79 Surcharged in Gray and Silver

Method and Perf. As Before
2006, Nov. 2
404 A24 10t on 1c #79   .40 .40

Nikola Tesla (1856-1943), Electrical Engineer, and Wireless Transmission Tower — A132

2006, Nov. 15   **Litho.**   **Perf. 12x12¼**
405 A132 50t multi   1.50 1.50

Souvenir Sheet

Georgian Wild West Show Horsemen — A133

2007, Jan. 25   **Litho.**   **Perf. 12¼**
406 A133 100t multi   3.00 3.00

Tbilisi State University, Cent.
A134

2007, Jan. 25   **Litho.**   **Perf. 12¼x12**
407 A134 40t multi   1.10 1.10

Prince David Guramishvili (1705-92), Poet
A135

2007, July 11   **Perf. 13¾x13¼**
408 A135 50t multi   1.40 1.40

2006 Chess Olympics, Turin
A136

2007, July 11
409 A136 200t multi   5.50 5.50

Famous Men
A137

Designs: No. 410, Rembrandt (1606-69), painter. No. 411, Wolfgang Amadeus Mozart (1756-91), composer.

2007, July 11   **Perf. 13¾x13¼**
410 A137 100t multi   2.75 2.75

Perf. 13¾x14
Size: 39x27mm
411 A137 100t multi   2.75 2.75

Worldwide Fund for Nature (WWF) — A138

Aquila clanga: 30t, In flight. 40t, On branch. 50t, With prey. 60t, Head.

2007, July 11   **Perf. 13¼x13¾**
412-415 A138 Set of 4   5.00 5.00

Eagles — A139

Designs: 10t, Aquila rapax. 30t, Haliaeetus albicilla. 50t, Circaetus gallicus. 70t, Aquila chryaetus.

2007, July 11
416-419 A139 Set of 4   4.50 4.50

Georgian Military
A140

Designs: 20t, Tanks. 30t, Soldiers. 40t, Ship. 50t, Helicopters.

2007, July 11   **Perf. 14¼x14**
420-423 A140 Set of 4   3.75 3.75

Ancient Ships
A141

Various ships: 20t, 30t, 50t, 70t.

2007, July 11
424-427 A141 Set of 4   4.75 4.75

Souvenir Sheets

Guns from National Museum — A142

Sculpture from National Museum — A143

No. 428 — Various guns with background color of: a, Yellow. b, Buff. c, Light blue. d, Light green.

2007, July 11   **Perf. 13x13¼**
428 A142 50t Sheet of 4, #a-d   5.00 5.00
429 A143 100t multi   2.75 2.75

Souvenir Sheet

Magician, Cards and Dove — A144

Perf. 13¼x13¾
2008, Mar. 14   **Litho.**
430 A144 1 l multi   3.50 3.50

Europa — A145

Designs: 90t, Scouts in boat and near tent. 1 l, Scouts around campfire.

2008, Mar. 14   **Perf. 14x13¾**
431-432 A145 Set of 2   6.75 6.75
432a   Booklet pane, 4 each #431-432   27.00
   Complete booklet, #432a   27.00
Scouting, cent. (in 2007). No. 432a contains two tete-beche pairs of Nos. 431-432.

Diplomatic Relations Between Georgia and Japan, 15th Anniv. (in 2007) — A146

2008, Mar. 14   Litho.   Perf. 13¾
433   A146   1 l multi   3.25 3.25
Dated 2007.

Mountains A147

Designs: 20t, Mt. Ushba. 30t, Mt. Ushba, diff. 50t, Mt. Kazbeg. 70t, Mt. Shkhara.

2008   Litho.   Perf. 13¼x13¾
434-437   A147   Set of 4   6.25 6.25

Issued. 30l, 6/1; others, 3/14. Bottom panel with mountain name on No. 435 was overprinted in silver and black to correct inscription. No. 435 was not issued without overprint.

King David IV (1073-1125) A148

2008, Dec. 5   Litho.   Perf. 13¾x14¼
438   A148   50t multi   1.75 1.75

Europa A149

Dove and: 90t, Georgia #398, cover with Georgia #213. 1 l, Letter, pencil, eyeglasses, Georgia #399.

2008, Dec. 5   Perf. 13¾x14
439-440   A149   Set of 2   7.00 7.00
440a   Booklet pane of 8, 4 each
        #439-440, perf. 13¾x13¼
        on 3 sides   28.00

No. 440a was sold with but not attached to a booklet cover.

2008 Summer Olympics, Beijing A150

Designs: 10t, Shooting. 30t, Wrestling. 60t, Weight lifting. 80t, Judo.

2008, Dec. 5   Perf. 14¼x14
441-444   A150   Set of 4   6.25 6.25

Prince Sulkhan-Saba Orbeliani (1658-1725), Monk — A151

2009, Mar. 20   Perf. 13¼
445   A151   60t multi   1.75 1.75

Kakutsa Cholokhashvili (1888-1930), Military Leader — A152

2009, Mar. 20
446   A152   80t multi   2.10 2.10

Port of Poti, 150th Anniv. A153

2009, Mar. 20
447   A153   1 l multi   2.75 2.75

Grape Varieties A154

Designs: 10t, Chkhaveri. 20t, Aleksandrouli. 30t, Rkatsiteli. 40t, Ojaleshi. 50t, Tsolikouri. 70t, Tavkveri. 90t, Saperavi.

2009, Mar. 20
448-454   A154   Set of 7   8.00 8.00

Souvenir Sheet

Anti-war Movement in Georgia — A155

No. 455: a, 30t, Flowers. b, 50t, Hands, Georgian flags. c, 70t, Demonstrators.

2009, Mar. 20
455   A155   Sheet of 3, #a-c   4.00 4.00

European Court of Human Rights, 50th Anniv. A156

Council of Europe, 60th Anniv. A157

2009, Aug. 10   Litho.   Perf. 13¼
456   A156   1 l multi   2.50 2.50
457   A157   2 l multi   5.00 5.00

SEMI-POSTAL STAMPS

SP1   SP2

SP3   SP4

Surcharge in Red or Black

1922   Unwmk.   Perf. 11½
B1   SP1   1000r on 50r vio (R)   .50   3.00
B2   SP2   3000r on 100r brn
            red   .50   3.00
B3   SP3   5000r on 250r gray
            grn   .50   3.00
B4   SP4   10,000r on 25r blue
            (R)   .50   3.00
    Nos. B1-B4 (4)   2.00 12.00

Nos. B1-B4 exist imperf but were not so issued. Value slightly more than perforated examples.

Georgian Natl. Olympic Committee SP10

1994, May 27   Litho.   Perf. 13½
B10   SP10   100c +50c multi   1.10 1.10

UNICEF, 50th Anniv. SP11

Children's paintings: 20t+5t, People on ladder above rainbow, vert. 30t+10t, Animal character.

Perf. 13x14, 14x13
1996, Dec. 20   Litho.
B11   SP11   20t +5t multi   1.40 1.40
B12   SP11   30t +10t multi   1.90 1.90

In Remembrance of Sept. 11, 2001 Terrorist Attacks — SP12

2001, Dec. 31   Litho.   Perf. 13x13¼
B13   SP12   30t +10t multi   1.60 1.60
Souvenir Sheet
B14   SP12   120t +10t multi   5.50 5.50

GERMAN EAST AFRICA

ˈjər-mən ˈēst ˈa-fri-kə

LOCATION — In East Africa, bordering on the Indian Ocean
GOVT. — German Colony
AREA — 384,180 sq. mi.
POP. — 7,680,132 (1913)
CAPITAL — Dar-es Salaam

Following World War I, the greater part of this German Colonial possession was mandated to Great Britain. The British ceded to the Belgians the provinces of Ruanda and Urundi (Belgian East Africa). The Kionga triangle was awarded to the Portuguese and became part of the Mozambique Colony. The remaining area became the British Mandated Territory of Tanganyika.

64 Pesa = 1 Rupee
100 Heller = 1 Rupee (1905)
100 Centimes = 1 Franc (1916)
12 Pence = 1 Shilling (1916)
100 Cents = 1 Rupee (1917)
12 Pence = 1 Shilling 100 Cents = 1 Rupee (1917)

Stamps of Germany Surcharged in Black

Nos. 1-5   Nos. 6-10

1893   Unwmk.   Perf. 13½x14½
Surcharge 15¼mm long
1   A9   2pes on 3pf brown   45.00 57.50
2   A9   3pes on 5pf green   52.50 57.50
3   A10   5pes on 10pf car   45.00 29.00
Surcharge 16¼mm long
4   A10   10pes on 20pf ultra   32.50 16.00
Surcharge 16¾mm long
5   A10   25pes on 50pf red
           brn   45.00 32.50
    Nos. 1-5 (5)   220.00 192.50

The surcharge also comes 16¾mm on #1; 14¼ or 16¼mm on #2-3; 17½mm on #5. See the *Scott Classic Catalogue* for listings of these spacings.

1896
6   A9   2pes on 3pf dk brn   2.00   37.50
 a.   2pes on 3pf light brown   28.00 45.00
 b.   2pes on 3pf grayish brown 11.50 11.50
 c.   2pes on 3pf reddish brown 105.00 200.00
7   A9   3pes on 5pf green   2.50   4.50
8   A10   5pes on 10pf car   4.75   4.50
9   A10   10pes on 20pf ultra   5.25   5.25
10   A10   25pes on 50pf red
           brn   23.00 28.00
    Nos. 6-10 (5)   37.50 79.75

A5

Kaiser's Yacht "Hohenzollern" — A6

1900		Typo.	Perf. 14	
11	A5	2p brown	2.75	1.60
12	A5	3p green	2.75	2.00
13	A5	5p carmine	3.25	2.50
14	A5	10p ultra	5.25	5.00
15	A5	15p org & blk, sal	5.25	6.50
16	A5	20p lake & blk	7.50	15.00
17	A5	25p pur & blk, sal	7.50	15.00
18	A5	40p lake & blk, rose	9.00	23.00

		Engr.		
		Perf. 14½x14		
19	A6	1r claret	20.00	57.50
20	A6	2r yel green	10.00	90.00
21a	A6	3r 3r red & slate	120.00	200.00
		Nos. 11-21a (11)	193.25	418.10

Value in Heller

1905		Typo.	Perf. 14	
22	A5	2½h brown	4.00	1.75
23	A5	4h dk olive green	16.50	5.75
a.		4h green	15.00	2.00
b.		4h dark yellowish green	29.00	20.00
24	A5	7½h carmine	15.00	1.60
25	A5	15h ultra	24.00	6.00
a.		15h violet blue	50.00	16.00
26	A5	20h org & blk, yel	15.00	16.00
27	A5	30h lake & blk	15.00	6.00
28	A5	45h pur & blk	29.00	37.50
29	A5	60h lake & blk, rose	37.50	100.00
		Nos. 22-29 (8)	156.00	174.60

1905-16		Wmk. Lozenges (125)		
31	A5	2½h brn ('06)	1.00	1.00
32	A5	4h grn ('06)	1.00	.65
b.		Booklet pane of 4 + 2 labels	45.00	
c.		Booklet pane of 5 + label	400.00	
33	A5	7½h car ('06)	1.10	1.60
b.		Booklet pane of 4 + 2 labels	45.00	
c.		Booklet pane of 5 + label	400.00	
34	A5	15h dk blue ('08)	2.25	1.50
35	A5	20h org & blk, yel ('11)	2.50	20.00
36	A5	30h lake & blk ('09)	2.60	8.25
37	A5	45h pur & blk ('06)	5.75	57.50
38	A5	60h lake & blk, rose	30.00	200.00

		Engr.		
		Perf. 14½x14		
39	A6	1r red ('16)	15.00	25,000.
40	A6	2r yel grn	50.00	
41	A6	3r car & sl ('08)	50.00	250.00
a.		3r red & blackish green ('08)	160.00	400.00
		Nos. 31-41 (11)	161.20	

No. 40 was never placed in use.

The frame of No. 41a fluoresces bright orange under ultra-violet light.

Forged cancellations are found on #35-39, 41.

In early 1916, German East African authorities ordered supplies of provisional stamps, printed by the press of the Evangelical Mission in Wuga. Three values in denominations most urgently needed were produced in March, but before they could be issued, new stocks of regular stamps were received from Germany. To prevent their capture by the British, the provisionals were buried until 1922, when they were retrieved by the German government and sold at auction. Because of their long storage in the tropical climate, 90-95% of the stamps were destroyed and those surviving are usually brittle and somewhat faded.

Values: 2½h violet brown, $57.50; 7½h, carmine, $25; 1r pink, $1,400.

OCCUPATION STAMPS

Issued Under Belgian Occupation

Stamps of Belgian Congo, 1915, Handstamped "RUANDA" in Black, Blue or Red Violet

1916		Unwmk.	Perf. 13½ to 15	
N1	A29	5c green & blk	25.00	
N2	A30	10c carmine & blk	25.00	
N3	A21	15c blue grn & blk	50.00	
N4	A31	25c blue & blk	25.00	
N5	A23	40c brown red & blk	25.00	

N6	A24	50c brown lake & blk	35.00	
N7	A25	1fr olive bis & blk	180.00	
N8	A27	5fr ocher & blk	2,750.	
		Nos. N1-N7 (7)	365.00	

Stamps of Belgian Congo, 1915, Handstamped "URUNDI" in Black, Blue or Red Violet

N9	A29	5c green & blk	25.00	
N10	A30	10c carmine & blk	25.00	
N11	A21	15c bl grn & blk	50.00	
N12	A31	25c blue & blk	25.00	
N13	A23	40c brn red & blk	25.00	
N14	A24	50c brn lake & blk	35.00	
N15	A25	1fr ol bis & blk	180.00	
N16	A27	5fr ocher & blk	2,750.	
		Nos. N9-N15 (7)	365.00	

Stamps of Belgian Congo overprinted "Karema," "Kigoma" and "Tabora" were not officially authorized.

Nos. N1-N16 exist with forged overprint.

Stamps of Belgian Congo, 1915, Overprinted in Dark Blue

1916			Perf. 12½ to 15	
N17	A29	5c green & blk	.75	.25
b.		Inverted overprint	175.00	—
N18	A30	10c carmine & blk	1.00	.40
N19	A21	15c bl grn & blk	.75	.25
N20	A31	25c blue & blk	6.50	1.50
N21	A23	40c brn red & blk	14.00	5.50
N22	A24	50c brn lake & blk	17.50	5.50
N23	A25	1fr olive bis & blk	3.00	.65
N24	A27	5fr ocher & blk	3.00	1.40
		Nos. N17-N24 (8)	46.50	15.45

Nos. N17-N18, N20-N22 Surcharged in Black or Red

1922				
N25	A24	5c on 50c brn lake & blk	.50	.40
N26	A29	10c on 5c grn & blk (R)	.50	.35
N27	A23	25c on 40c brn red & blk (R)	3.00	1.75
N28	A30	30c on 10c car & blk	.50	.25
N29	A31	50c on 25c bl & blk (R)	.50	.25
		Nos. N25-N29 (5)	5.00	3.00

No. N25 has the surcharge at each side.

ISSUED UNDER BRITISH OCCUPATION

Stamps of Nyasaland Protectorate, 1913-15 Overprinted

1916		Wmk. 3	Perf. 14	
N101	A3	½p green	1.75	9.50
a.		Double overprint (R & Bk)		
N102	A3	1p carmine	1.75	3.75
N103	A3	3p violet, yel	14.00	20.00
a.		Double overprint		26,000.
N104	A3	4p scar & blk, yel	37.50	47.50
N105	A3	1sh black, green	50.00	60.00
		Nos. N101-N105 (5)	105.00	140.75

"N.F." stands for "Nyasaland Force."

Stamps of East Africa and Uganda, 1912-14, Overprinted in Black or Red

1917				
N106	A3	1c black (R)	.20	.95
N107	A3	3c blue green	.20	.20
N108	A3	6c carmine	.20	.20
N109	A3	10c brown orange	.60	.70
N110	A3	12c gray	.60	2.50
N111	A3	15c ultramarine	1.20	3.50
N112	A3	25c scar & blk, yel	.90	4.00
N113	A3	50c violet & blk	1.20	3.75
N114	A3	75c blk, bl grn, olive back (R)	1.20	5.25
a.		75c black, emerald (R)	3.75	52.50

Overprinted

N115	A4	1r blk, green(R)	3.50	8.00
a.		1r black, emerald (R)	9.50	65.00
N116	A4	2r blk & red, bl	13.00	52.50
N117	A4	3r gray grn & vio	15.00	95.00
N118	A4	4r grn & red, yel	20.00	105.00
N119	A4	5r dl vio & ultra	45.00	105.00
N120	A4	10r grn & red, grn	105.00	375.00
a.		10r grn & red, emerald	130.00	450.00
N121	A3	20r vio & blk, red	225.00	475.00
N122	A3	50r gray grn & blk	575.00	950.00
		Nos. N106-N120 (15)	207.80	761.55

See Tanganyika for "G.E.A." overprints on stamps inscribed "East Africa and Uganda Protectorates" with watermark 4.

SEMI-POSTAL STAMPS

Issued under Belgian Occupation

Semi-Postal Stamps of Belgian Congo, 1918, Overprinted

1918		Unwmk.	Perf. 14, 15	
NB1	A29	5c + 10c grn & bl	.50	.50
NB2	A30	10c + 15c car & bl	.50	.50
NB3	A21	15c + 20c bl grn & bl	.50	.50
NB4	A31	25c + 25c dp & pale bl	.50	.50
NB5	A23	40c + 40c brn red & bl	.75	.75
NB6	A24	50c + 50c brn lake & bl	1.00	1.00
NB7	A25	1fr + 1fr ol bis & bl	2.75	2.75
NB8	A27	5fr + 5fr ocher & bl	8.50	8.50
NB9	A28	10fr + 10fr grn & bl	70.00	70.00
		Nos. NB1-NB9 (9)	85.00	85.00

The letters "A.O." are the initials of "Afrique Orientale" (East Africa).

GERMAN NEW GUINEA

ˈjər-mən ˈnü ˈgi-nē

LOCATION — A group of islands in the west Pacific Ocean, including a part of New Guinea and adjacent islands of the Bismarck Archipelago.

GOVT. — German Protectorate

AREA — 93,000 sq. mi.

POP. — 601,427 (1913)

CAPITAL — Herbertshöhe (later Kokopo)

The islands were occupied by Australian troops during World War I and renamed "New Britain." By covenant of the League of Nations they were made a mandated territory of Australia in 1920. The old name of "New Guinea" has since been restored. Postage stamps were issued under all regimes. For other listings see New Britain (1914-15), North West Pacific Islands (1915-22) and New Guinea in Vol. 4.

100 Pfennig = 1 Mark

Stamps of Germany Overprinted in Black

1897-99		Unwmk.	Perf. 13½x14½	
1	A9	3pf brown	8.25	11.00
a.		3pf reddish brown ('99)	115.00	200.00
b.		3pf yellow brown ('99)	31.00	57.50
2	A9	5pf green	4.00	5.75
3	A10	10pf carmine	6.50	9.00
4	A10	20pf ultra	9.00	14.00
5	A10	25pf orange ('98)	29.00	52.50
a.		Inverted overprint	2,750.	
6	A10	50pf red brown	32.50	50.00
		Nos. 1-6 (6)	89.25	142.25

Kaiser's Yacht "Hohenzollern"
A3　　　　A4

1901		Typo.	Perf. 14	
7	A3	3pf brown	1.25	1.25
8	A3	5pf green	7.50	1.25
9	A3	10pf carmine	25.00	2.75
10	A3	20pf ultra	1.50	2.75
11	A3	25pf org & blk, yel	1.75	16.00
12	A3	30pf org & blk, sal	1.75	20.00
13	A3	40pf lake & blk	1.75	23.00
14	A3	50pf pur & blk, sal	2.00	20.00
15	A3	80pf lake & blk, rose	3.75	27.50

Engr.
Perf. 14½x14

16	A4	1m carmine	8.00	52.50
17	A4	2m blue	8.00	77.50
18	A4	3m blk vio	11.00	150.00
19	A4	5m slate & car	190.00	500.00
		Nos. 7-19 (13)	263.25	894.50

Fake cancellations exist on Nos. 10-19.
The stamps of German New Guinea overprinted 'G.R.I.' and new values in British currency were all used in New Britain and are listed under that country as Nos. 1-29C, O1-2.

A5

A6

Wmk. Lozenges (125)

			Typo.	Perf. 14
1914-19				
20	A3	3pf brown ('19)		.80
21	A5	5pf green		1.60
22	A5	10pf carmine		1.60

Engr.
Perf. 14½x14

23	A6	5m slate & carmine		32.50
		Nos. 20-23 (4)		36.50

Nos. 20-23 were never placed in use.
Nos. 21-23 have "NEUGUINEA" as one word without a hyphen.

GERMAN SOUTH WEST AFRICA

ˈjər-mən ˈsauth ˈwest ˈa-fri-kə

LOCATION — In southwest Africa, bordering on the South Atlantic
GOVT. — German Colony
AREA — 322,450 sq. mi. (1913)
POP. — 94,372 (1913)
CAPITAL — Windhoek

The Colony was occupied by South African troops during World War I and in 1920 was mandated to the Union of South Africa by the League of Nations. See South West Africa in Vol. 6.

100 Pfennig = 1 Mark

Stamps of Germany Overprinted

1897			Unwmk.	Perf. 13½x14½
1	A9	3pf dark brown	8.25	12.00
a.		3pf yellow brown	50.00	2,800.
2	A9	5pf green	4.50	4.75
3	A10	10pf carmine	21.00	20.00
4	A10	20pf ultra	5.75	5.25
5	A10	25pf orange	225.00	29,000.
6	A10	50pf red brown	225.00	29,000.
		Nos. 1-4 (4)	39.50	42.00

Nos. 5 and 6 were prepared for issue but were not sent to the Colony.

Overprinted "Deutsch-Südwestafrika"

1899				
7	A9	3pf dark brown	4.00	12.00
a.		3pf reddish brown	52.50	160.00
b.		3pf yellow brown	7.00	12.00
8	A9	5pf green	3.25	2.60
9	A10	10pf carmine	3.25	4.00
10	A10	20pf ultra	11.50	15.00
11	A10	25pf orange	350.00	400.00
12	A10	50pf red brown	11.50	10.50

Kaiser's Yacht "Hohenzollern"
A3   A4

1900			Typo.	Perf. 14
13	A3	3pf brown	4.00	1.50
14	A3	5pf green	20.00	1.50
15	A3	10pf carmine	14.00	.80
16	A3	20pf ultra	30.00	1.50
17	A3	25pf org & blk, yel	1.50	5.50
18	A3	30pf org & blk, sal	72.50	2.75
19	A3	40pf lake & blk	1.75	3.25
20	A3	50pf pur & blk, sal	2.10	2.10
21	A3	80pf lake & blk, rose	2.10	9.00

Engr.
Perf. 14½x14

22	A4	1m carmine	110.00	30.00
23	A4	2m blue	30.00	37.50
24	A4	3m blk vio	32.50	50.00
25	A4	5m slate & car	200.00	160.00
		Nos. 13-25 (13)	520.45	305.40

Wmk. Lozenges (125)

1906-19			Typo.	Perf. 14
26	A3	3pf dk brn ('07)	.80	3.75
27	A3	5pf green	.80	1.40
b.		Bklt. pane of 6 (2 #27, 4 #28)	40.00	
c.		Booklet pane of 5 + label	160.00	
28	A3	10pf lt rose	1.00	1.40
b.		Booklet pane of 5 + label	400.00	
29	A3	20pf ultra ('11)	1.00	3.75
30	A3	30pf org & blk, pale yellow ('11)	6.00	52.50

Engr.
Perf. 14½x14

31	A4	1m carmine ('12)	12.50	75.00
32	A4	2m blue ('11)	12.50	75.00
33	A4	3m blk vio ('19)	14.00	
a.		3m gray violet	40.00	
34	A4	5m slate & car	32.50	300.00
a.		5m slate & rose red	55.00	
		Nos. 26-34 (9)	81.10	512.80

Nos. 33, 33a, 34a were never placed in use.
Forged cancellations are found on #30-32, 34.

GERMAN STATES

ˈjər-mən ˈstāts

Watermarks

Wmk. 92 —   Wmk. 93 —
17mm wide   14mm wide

Wmk. 94 — Horiz. Wavy Lines Wide Apart

Wmk. 95v — Vert. Wavy Lines Close Together

Wmk. 95h —   Wmk. 102 — Post
Horiz. Wavy Lines   Horn
Close Together

Wmk. 116 — Crosses and Circles

Wmk. 128 — Wavy Lines

Wmk. 130 —   Wmk. 148 —
Wreath of Oak   Small Flowers
Leaves

Wmk. 162 —   Wmk. 192 —
Laurel Wreath   Circles

BADEN

LOCATION — In southwestern Germany
GOVT. — Former Grand Duchy
AREA — 5,817 sq. mi.
POP. — 1,432,000 (1864)
CAPITAL — Karlsruhe (Principal city)

Baden was a member of the German Confederation. In 1870 it became part of the German Empire.

60 Kreuzer = 1 Gulden

Values for unused stamps are for examples with original gum as defined in the catalogue introduction except for Nos. 1-9 which are valued without gum. Very fine examples of Nos. 1-9 will have one or two margins touching the framelines due to the very narrow spacing of the stamps on the plates. Stamps with margins clear of the framelines on all four sides are scarce and sell for considerably more.

A1

1851-52			Unwmk.	Typo.	Imperf.
1	A1	1kr blk, dk buff		275.00	250.00
2	A1	3kr blk, yellow		140.00	16.00
3	A1	6kr blk, yel grn		440.00	45.00
4	A1	9kr blk, lil rose		90.00	24.00
		Nos. 1-4 (4)		945.00	335.00

Thin Paper (First Printing, 1851)

1a	A1	1kr black, buff		2,000.	800.00
2a	A1	3kr black, orange		675.00	35.00
3a	A1	6kr black, blue green		2,250.	90.00
4a	A1	9kr black, deep rose		2,800.	160.00

No. 4b

4b	A1	9kr black, bl grn (error)		1,300,000.

1853-58					
6	A1	1kr black		160.00	25.00
a.		Tête bêche gutter pair			45,000.
7	A1	3kr black, green		160.00	16.00
8	A1	3kr black, bl ('58)		675.00	30.00
a.		Printed on both sides			
9	A1	6kr black, yellow		250.00	25.00
		Nos. 6-9 (4)		1,245.	96.00

Reissues (1865) of Nos. 1, 2, 3, 6, 7 and 8 exist on thick paper and No. 9 on thin paper; the color of the last is brighter than that of the original.

Coat of Arms
A2   A3

1860-62				Perf. 13½
10	A2	1kr black		80.00	30.00
12	A2	3kr ultra ('61)		90.00	20.00
a.		3kr Prussian blue		290.00	50.00
13	A2	6kr red org ('61)		100.00	72.50
a.		6kr yellow orange ('62)		175.00	80.00
14	A2	9kr rose ('61)		250.00	190.00
		Nos. 10-14 (4)		520.00	312.50

Examples of Nos. 10-14 and 18 with all perforations intact sell for considerably more.

1862				Perf. 10
15	A2	1kr black		65.00	80.00
a.		1kr silver gray			6,600.
16	A2	6kr Prus bl ('62)		140.00	72.50
17	A2	9kr brown		90.00	72.50
a.		9kr dark brown		350.00	275.00

Perf. 13½

18	A3	3kr rose		2,500.	375.00

1862-65				Perf. 10
19	A3	1kr black ('64)		50.00	15.00
a.		1kr silver gray			2,100.
20	A3	3kr rose		50.00	4.00
a.		Imperf.		100,000.	40,000.

22	A3	6kr ultra ('65)	11.00	*25.00*
a.		6kr Prussian blue ('64)	*575.00*	*65.00*
23	A3	9kr brn ('64)	16.00	30.00
a.		9kr bister	*375.00*	*90.00*
b.		Printed on both sides		*6,500.*
24	A3	18kr green	400.00	*575.00*
25	A3	30kr deep orange	32.50	*2,250.*
a.		30kr yellow orange	*140.00*	*2,200.*

Forged cancellations are known on #25.

A4

1868

26	A4	1kr green	4.00	*9.00*
27	A4	3kr rose	2.50	*4.00*
28	A4	7kr dull blue	20.00	35.00
a.		7kr sky blue	42.50	*92.50*
		Nos. 26-28 (3)	26.50	48.00

Forged cancellations are known on #28a.
The postage stamps of Baden were superseded by those of the German Empire on Jan. 1, 1872, but Official stamps were used during the year 1905.

Stamps of the Baden sector of the French Occupation Zone of Germany, issued in 1947-49, are listed under Germany, Occupation Issues.

RURAL POSTAGE DUE STAMPS

RU1

1862   Unwmk.   Perf. 10
Thin Paper

LJ1	RU1	1kr blk, *yellow*	5.00	*325.00*
a.		Thick paper	*140.00*	*600.00*
LJ2	RU1	3kr blk, *yellow*	2.75	*125.00*
a.		Thick paper	*110.00*	*400.00*
LJ3	RU1	12kr blk, *yellow*	35.00	*20,000.*
a.		Half used as 6kr on cover		*25,000.*
b.		Quarter used as 3kr on cover		
		Nos. LJ1-LJ3 (3)	42.75	20,450.

On #LJ3, "LAND-POST" is a straight line.
Paper of #LJ1a, LJ2a is darker yellow.
Forged cancellations abound on #LJ1-LJ3.

OFFICIAL STAMPS
See Germany Nos. OL16-OL21.

BAVARIA

LOCATION — In southern Germany
GOVT. — Kingdom
AREA — 30,562 sq. mi. (1920)
POP. — 7,150,146 (1919)
CAPITAL — Munich

Bavaria was a member of the German Confederation and became part of the German Empire in 1870. After World War I, it declared itself a republic. It lost its postal autonomy on Mar. 31, 1920.

60 Kreuzer = 1 Gulden
100 Pfennig = 1 Mark (1874)

Values for unused stamps are for examples with original gum as defined in the catalogue introduction. Unused examples of the 1849-78 issues without gum sell for about 50-60% of the figures quoted.

A1   Broken Circle — A1a

1849   Unwmk.   Typo.   *Imperf.*

1	A1	1kr black	1,000.	*2,000.*
a.		deep black	2,800.	*2,900.*
b.		Tête bêche pair	*125,000.*	

With Silk Thread

2	A1a	3kr blue	60.00	3.50
a.		3kr greenish blue	60.00	3.50
b.		3kr deep blue	60.00	3.50
3	A1a	6kr brown	7,000.	240.00

No. 1 exists with silk thread, from a single proof sheet, value about $4,000.

Complete circle — A2   Coat of Arms — A3

1850-58   With Silk Thread

4	A2	1kr pink	95.00	22.50
5	A2	6kr brown	50.00	6.50
a.		Half used as 6kr on cover		*15,750.*
6	A2	9kr yellow green	65.00	16.00
a.		9kr blue green ('53)	11,000.	*150.00*
7	A2	12kr red ('58)	150.00	140.00
8	A2	18kr yel ('54)	140.00	*190.00*
		Nos. 4-8 (5)	500.00	375.00

1862

9	A2	1kr yellow	70.00	20.00
10	A1a	3kr rose	140.00	2.25
a.		3kr carmine	45.00	4.75
11	A2	6kr blue	70.00	12.00
a.		6kr ultra	*1,750.*	*9,000.*
b.		Half used as 3kr on cover		10,000.
12	A2	9kr bister	110.00	16.00
13	A2	12kr yel grn	95.00	65.00
a.		Half used as 6kr on cover		*32,000.*
14	A2	18kr ver red	875.00	140.00
a.		18kr pale red	190.00	*450.00*
		Nos. 9-14 (6)	1,360.	255.25

No. 11a was not put in use.

1867-68   Embossed

15	A3	1kr yel grn	75.00	12.00
a.		1kr dark blue green	300.00	44.00
16	A3	3kr rose	70.00	2.40
a.		Printed on both sides		*5,000.*
17	A3	6kr ultra	45.00	19.00
a.		Half used as 3kr on cover		*75,000.*
18	A3	6kr bis ('68)	80.00	50.00
a.		Half used as 3kr on cover		*32,000.*
19	A3	7kr ultra ('68)	400.00	16.00
20	A3	9kr bister	45.00	35.00
21	A3	12kr lilac	350.00	95.00
22	A3	18kr red	140.00	175.00
		Nos. 15-22 (8)	1,205.	404.40

The paper of the 1867-68 issues often shows ribbed or laid lines.

1870-72   Wmk. 92   *Perf. 11½*
Without Silk Thread

23	A3	1kr green	11.00	1.60
24	A3	3kr rose	24.00	1.25
25	A3	6kr bister	30.00	27.50
26	A3	7kr ultra	3.50	*4.50*
a.		7kr Prussian blue	19.00	11.00
27	A3	9kr pale brn ('72)	4.50	4.00
28	A3	10kr yellow	5.50	*13.50*
29	A3	12kr lilac	1,200.	*4,800.*
30	A3	18kr dull brick red	12.00	*14.50*
b.		18kr dark brick red	225.00	62.50

The paper of the 1870-75 issues frequently appears to be laid with the lines either close or wide apart.
See Nos. 33-37.
Reprints exist.

Wmk. 93

23a	A3	1kr green	100.00	9.50
24a	A3	3kr rose	95.00	2.40
25a	A3	6kr bister	175.00	70.00
26b	A3	7kr ultra	140.00	35.00
27a	A3	9kr pale brown	290.00	*475.00*
28a	A3	10kr yellow	240.00	*360.00*
29a	A3	12kr lilac	360.00	*1,125.*
30a	A3	18kr dull brick red	300.00	*190.00*
c.		18kr dark brick red	250.00	225.00

A4   A5

1874-75   Wmk. 92   *Imperf.*

31	A4	1m violet	640.00	80.00

Perf. 11½

32	A4	1m violet ('75)	200.00	50.00

See Nos. 46-47, 54-57, 73-76.

1875   Wmk. 94

33	A3	1kr green	.80	24.00
34	A3	3kr rose	.80	8.00
35	A3	7kr ultra	5.25	275.00
36	A3	10kr yellow	30.00	250.00
37	A3	18kr red	24.00	60.00
		Nos. 33-37 (5)	60.85	617.00

1876-78   Embossed   *Perf. 11½*

38	A5	3pf lt grn	35.00	1.60
39	A5	5pf dk grn	90.00	13.00
40	A5	5pf lilac ('78)	160.00	20.00
41	A5	10pf rose	190.00	1.25
42	A5	20pf ultra	190.00	3.25
43	A5	25pf yel brn	175.00	6.50
44	A5	50pf scarlet	55.00	7.25
45	A5	50pf brn ('78)	800.00	27.50
46	A4	1m violet	1,925.	90.00
47	A4	2m orange	24.00	9.50

The paper of the 1876-78 issue often shows ribbed lines.
See Nos. 48-53, 58-72. For overprints and surcharge see Nos. 237, O1-O5.

1881-1906   Wmk. 95v   *Perf. 11½*

48	A5	3pf green	12.00	.80
a.		Imperf.	400.00	*2,000.*
49	A5	5pf lilac	17.50	1.25
50	A5	10pf carmine	12.50	.65
a.		Imperf.	400.00	*2,000.*
51	A5	20pf ultramarine	13.00	.80
52	A5	25pf yellow brown	125.00	3.50
53	A5	50pf deep brown	145.00	3.25
54	A4	1m rose lil ('00)	225.00	1.40
a.		1m brownish lilac, toned paper	62.50	3.00
55	A4	2m orange ('01)	5.50	*8.00*
a.		Toned paper ('90)	72.50	10.00
56	A4	3m olive gray ('00)	24.00	*30.00*
a.		White paper ('06)	140.00	*500.00*
57	A4	5m yellow green ('00)	24.00	*30.00*
a.		White paper ('06)	140.00	*375.00*

Nos. 54-55 are on white paper. Nos. 56-57 are on toned paper. A 2m lilac was not regularly issued.

1888-1900   Wmk. 95h   *Perf. 14½*

58	A5	2pf gray ('00)	2.40	.55
59	A5	3pf green	9.25	2.10
60	A5	3pf brown ('00)	.30	.65
61	A5	5pf lilac	22.50	3.25
62	A5	5pf dk grn ('00)	.30	.65
63	A5	10pf carmine	.40	.80
64	A5	20pf ultra	.40	.40
65	A5	25pf yel brn	27.50	6.00
66	A5	25pf orange ('00)	.50	.95
67	A5	30pf ol grn ('00)	.80	1.40
68	A5	40pf yellow ('00)	.80	1.10
69	A5	50pf dp brn	57.50	3.25
70	A5	50pf maroon ('00)	.50	1.60
71	A5	80pf lilac ('00)	3.25	4.00
		Nos. 58-71 (14)	126.40	27.10

Nos. 59, 61, 65, 69 and 70 are on toned paper; Nos. 67-68 on white.

Toned Paper
1888-99

58a	A5	2pf gray ('99)	11.00	3.50
60a	A5	3pf dk ocher brn ('90)	9.25	.40
62a	A5	5pf dk green ('90)	9.25	.40
63a	A5	10pf car red	6.00	.40
b.		Imperf.	72.50	*175.00*
64a	A5	20pf ultra	8.75	1.25
66a	A5	25pf org ('90)	15.00	1.50
70a	A5	50pf mar ('90)	45.00	2.10
71a	A5	80pf lilac ('99)	27.50	8.25

1911, Jan. 23   Wmk. 95v

72	A5	5pf dark green	.65	13.50

1911, Jan.   Wmk. 95h   *Perf. 11½*

73	A4	1m rose lilac	4.00	27.50
74	A4	2m orange	17.00	37.50
75	A4	3m olive gray	17.00	57.50
76	A4	5m pale yel grn	17.00	57.50
		Nos. 73-76 (4)	55.00	180.00

See note after No. 91 concerning used values.

A6   A7

A8

Prince Regent Luitpold
Perf. 14x14½

1911   Wmk. 95h   Litho.

77	A6	3pf brn, *gray brn*	.30	.30
a.		"911" for "1911"	275.00	275.00
78	A6	5pf dk grn, *grn*	.30	.30
a.		Tête bêche pair	4.50	10.50
b.		Booklet pane of 4 + 2 labels	100.00	*150.00*
c.		Bklt. pane of 5 + label	225.00	*375.00*
d.		Bklt. pane of 6	35.00	
79	A6	10pf scar, *buff*	.30	.30
a.		Tête bêche pair	5.75	62.50
b.		"911" for "1911"	15.00	15.00
c.		Booklet pane of 5 + label	65.00	30.00
80	A6	20pf dp bl, *bl*	2.00	.75
81	A6	25pf vio brn, *buff*	3.25	1.25

Perf. 11½
Wmk. 95v

82	A7	30pf org buff, *buff*	2.00	1.25
83	A7	40pf ol grn, *buff*	3.25	1.25
84	A7	50pf cl, *gray brn*	3.25	*3.25*
84A	A7	60pf dk grn, *buff*	3.25	*3.25*
85	A7	80pf vio, *gray brn*	7.00	10.00
86	A8	1m brn, *gray brn*	3.25	*4.00*
87	A8	2m dk grn, *grn*	4.75	12.00
88	A8	3m lake, *buff*	13.00	55.00
89	A8	5m dk bl, *buff*	13.00	45.00
90	A8	10m org, *yel*	45.00	65.00
91	A8	20m blk brn, *yel*	25.00	*32.50*
		Nos. 77-91 (16)	128.90	235.40

90th birthday of Prince Regent Luitpold.
All values exist in 2 types except No. 84A. Nos. 77-84, 85-91 exist imperf.
Used values: Nos. 73-76 and 77-91 often were canceled en masse for accounting purposes. These cancels are perfectly clear, and used values are for stamps canceled thus. Postally used examples are worth about twice as much.

Prince Regent Luitpold — A9

1911, June 10   Unwmk.

92	A9	5pf grn, yel & blk	.80	*1.40*
b.		Horiz. pair, imperf. btwn.	140.00	225.00
93	A9	10pf rose, yel & blk	1.25	*2.40*
b.		Pair, imperf. between	140.00	225.00

Silver Jubilee of Prince Regent Luitpold.

Used values given for Nos. 94-275, B1-B3 are for postally used. Canceled-to-order stamps, which abound, sell for same prices as unused.

A10   A11

King Ludwig III
A12   A13

Perf. 14x14½

				Photo.
1914-20		**Wmk. 95h**		
94	A10	2pf gray ('18)	.20	2.00
95	A10	3pf brown	.20	2.00
96	A10	5pf yellow grn	1.10	2.00
a.		5pf dark green	1.10	2.00
b.		Tête bêche pair	3.00	14.00
c.		Booklet pane of 5 + 1 label	13.00	50.00
97	A10	7½pf dp green ('16)	.20	2.00
a.		Tête bêche pair	1.90	8.50
b.		Booklet pane of 6	12.50	
98	A10	10pf vermilion	1.40	2.00
a.		Tête bêche pair	3.00	14.00
b.		Booklet pane of 5 + 1 label	13.00	50.00
99	A10	10pf car rose ('16)	.20	2.00
100	A10	15pf ver ('16)	.20	2.00
a.		Tête bêche pair	1.90	8.50
b.		Booklet pane of 5 + 1 label	5.50	19.00
101	A10	15pf car ('20)	1.50	27.50
102	A10	20pf blue	.20	2.00
103	A10	25pf gray	.20	2.00
104	A10	30pf orange	.80	2.00
105	A10	40pf olive grn	.20	2.00
106	A10	50pf red brn	.20	2.00
107	A10	60pf blue grn	.80	2.00
108	A10	80pf violet	.20	2.00

Perf. 11½
Wmk. 95v

109	A11	1m brown	.20	2.00
110	A11	2m violet	.20	2.75
111	A11	3m scarlet	.30	5.50

Wmk. 95h

112	A12	5m deep blue	.55	20.00
113	A12	10m yellow grn	1.75	55.00
114	A12	20m brown	3.25	100.00
		Nos. 94-114 (21)	13.85	240.75

No. 94 Surcharged

			Perf. 14x14½
1916		**Wmk. 95h**	
115	A13	2½pf on 2pf gray	.20 2.00
a.		Double surcharge	

Ludwig III Types of 1914-20

				Imperf.
1916-20				
117	A10	2pf gray	.20	13.50
118	A10	3pf brown	.20	14.50
119	A10	5pf pale yel grn	.20	14.50
120	A10	7½pf dp green	.20	14.50
a.		Tête bêche pair	3.25	25.00
121	A10	10pf car rose	.20	14.50
122	A10	15pf vermilion	.20	14.50
a.		Tête bêche pair	3.25	25.00
123	A10	20pf blue	.20	14.50
124	A10	25pf gray	.20	14.50
125	A10	30pf orange	.20	14.50
126	A10	40pf olive grn	.20	14.50
127	A10	50pf red brown	.20	14.50
128	A10	60pf dark green	.20	16.00
129	A10	80pf violet	.20	16.00
130	A11	1m brown	.35	16.00
131	A11	2m violet	.35	20.00
132	A11	3m scarlet	.50	27.50
133	A12	5m deep blue	.95	45.00
134	A12	10m yellow green	1.60	65.00
135	A12	20m brown	2.25	110.00
		Nos. 117-135 (19)	8.60	474.00

Stamps and Type of 1914-20 Overprinted:

a   b

Wmk. 95h or 95v

			Perf. 14x14½
1919			
		Overprint "a"	
136	A10	3pf brown	.20 2.00
137	A10	5pf yellow grn	.20 2.00
138	A10	7½pf deep green	.20 2.00
139	A10	10pf car rose	.20 2.00
140	A10	15pf vermilion	.20 2.00

141	A10	20pf blue	.20	2.00
142	A10	25pf gray	.20	2.00
143	A10	30pf orange	.20	2.00
144	A10	35pf orange	.20	2.50
a.		Without overprint	100.00	
145	A10	40pf olive grn	.20	2.00
146	A10	50pf red brown	.20	2.00
147	A10	60pf dark green	.20	2.00
148	A10	75pf red brown	.20	2.00
a.		Without overprint	22.50	225.00
149	A10	80pf violet	.20	2.00

Perf. 11½
Overprint "a"

150	A11	1m brown	.20	2.00
151	A11	2m violet	.20	2.00
152	A11	3m scarlet	.40	4.75

Overprint "b"

153	A12	5m deep blue	.90	12.00
154	A12	10m yellow green	.95	50.00
155	A12	20m dk brown	2.50	50.00
		Nos. 136-155 (20)	7.95	149.25

Inverted overprints exist on Nos. 137-143, 145-147, 149. Value, each $15.
Double overprints exist on Nos. 137, 139, 143, 145, 150. Values, $30-$75.

Imperf
Overprint "a"

156	A10	3pf brown	.20	20.00
157	A10	5pf pale yel grn	.20	20.00
158	A10	7½pf dp green	.20	20.00
159	A10	10pf car rose	.20	20.00
160	A10	15pf vermilion	.20	20.00
161	A10	20pf blue	.20	20.00
162	A10	25pf gray	.20	20.00
163	A10	30pf orange	.20	20.00
164	A10	35pf orange	.20	20.00
a.		Without overprint	13.00	
165	A10	40pf olive grn	.20	20.00
166	A10	50pf red brown	.20	20.00
167	A10	60pf dk green	.20	20.00
168	A10	75pf red brown	.20	20.00
a.		Without overprint	190.00	
169	A10	80pf violet	.20	20.00
170	A11	1m brown	.20	24.00
171	A11	2m violet	.50	27.50
172	A11	3m scarlet	.70	45.00

Overprint "b"

173	A12	5m deep blue	.95	55.00
174	A12	10m yellow green	1.40	80.00
175	A12	20m brown	2.75	80.00
		Nos. 156-175 (20)	9.30	591.50

Stamps of Germany 1906-19 Overprinted

Wmk. 125

				Perf. 14, 14½
1919				
176	A22	2½pf gray	.20	2.00
177	A16	3pf brown	.20	2.00
178	A16	5pf green	.20	2.00
179	A22	7½pf orange	.20	2.00
180	A16	10pf carmine	.20	2.00
181	A16	15pf dk violet	.20	2.00
a.		Double overprint	375.00	1,050.
182	A16	20pf ultra	.20	2.00
183	A16	25pf org & blk, yel	.20	2.00
184	A22	35pf red brown	.20	2.00
185	A16	40pf lake & blk	.40	2.00
186	A16	75pf green & blk	.55	2.40
187	A16	80pf lake & blk, rose	.55	3.25
188	A17	1m car rose	1.25	4.75
189	A21	2m dull blue	1.60	11.00
190	A19	3m gray violet	1.60	13.00
191	A20	5m slate & car	1.60	13.00
a.		Inverted overprint	3,575.	
		Nos. 176-191 (16)	9.35	67.40

Bavarian Stamps of 1914-16 Overprinted:

c   d

Wmk. 95h or 95v

			Perf. 14x14½
1919-20			
		Overprint "c"	
193	A10	3pf brown	.20 2.00
194	A10	5pf yellow grn	.20 2.00
195	A10	7½pf dp green	.20 16.00
196	A10	10pf car rose	.20 2.00
197	A10	15pf vermilion	.20 2.00
198	A10	20pf blue	.20 2.00

199	A10	25pf gray	.20	2.00
200	A10	30pf orange	.20	2.00
201	A10	40pf olive grn	.20	14.50
202	A10	50pf red brown	.20	14.50
203	A10	60pf dk green	.20	14.50
204	A10	75pf olive bister	.40	14.50
205	A10	80pf violet	.20	3.50

Perf. 11½
Overprint "c"

206	A11	1m brown	.20	3.50
207	A11	2m violet	.20	4.25
208	A11	3m scarlet	.35	6.00

Overprint "d"

209	A12	5m deep blue	1.10	17.50
210	A12	10m yellow grn	2.00	35.00
211	A12	20m dk brown	2.40	60.00
		Nos. 193-211 (19)	9.05	205.25

Imperf
Overprint "c"

212	A10	3pf brown	.20	12.00
213	A10	5pf pale yel grn	.20	12.00
214	A10	7½pf deep green	.20	22.50
215	A10	10pf car rose	.20	12.00
216	A10	15pf vermilion	.20	12.00
217	A10	20pf blue	.20	12.00
a.		Double overprint	50.00	
218	A10	25pf gray	.20	12.00
219	A10	30pf orange	.20	13.50
220	A10	40pf olive grn	.20	14.50
221	A10	50pf red brn	.20	14.50
222	A10	60pf dk green	.20	14.50
223	A10	75pf olive bis	.20	35.00
a.		Without overprint	5.00	
224	A10	80pf violet	.20	14.50
225	A11	1m brown	.20	22.50
226	A11	2m violet	.20	22.50
227	A11	3m scarlet	.65	27.50

Overprint "d"

228	A12	5m deep blue	1.10	40.00
229	A12	10m yellow grn	2.00	70.00
230	A12	20m brown	2.40	110.00
		Nos. 212-230 (19)	9.15	493.50

Ludwig Type of 1914, Printed in Various Colors and Surcharged

			Perf. 11½
1919			
231	A11	1.25m on 1m yel grn	.20 2.40
232	A11	1.50m on 1m orange	.20 3.25
233	A11	2.50m on 1m gray	.35 6.50
		Nos. 231-233 (3)	.75 12.15

			Imperf.
1920			
234	A11	1.25m on 1m yel grn	.20 35.00
a.		Without surcharge	325.00
235	A11	1.50m on 1m org	.20 35.00
a.		Without surcharge	6.50
236	A11	2.50m on 1m gray	.35 35.00
a.		Without surcharge	6.50
		Nos. 234-236 (3)	.75 105.00

No. 60 Surcharged in Dark Blue

			Perf. 14½
1920			
237	A5	20pf on 3pf brown	.20 1.25
a.		Inverted surcharge	6.50 26.00
b.		Double surcharge	80.00 190.00

Plowman
A14

"Electricity"
Harnessing Light to a Water Wheel
A15

Sower — A16   Madonna and Child — A17

---

von Kaulbach's "Genius" — A18

TWENTY PFENNIG
Type I — Foot of "2" turns downward.
Type II — Foot of "2" turns upward.

Perf. 14x14½

				Typo.
1920		**Wmk. 95h**		
238	A14	5pf yellow grn	.20	2.40
239	A14	10pf orange	.20	2.40
240	A14	15pf carmine	.20	2.40
241	A14	20pf violet (I)	.20	2.40
a.		20pf violet (II)	8.00	1,150.
242	A15	30pf dp blue	.20	3.25
243	A15	40pf brown	.20	2.40
244	A16	50pf vermilion	.20	2.40
245	A16	60pf blue green	.20	2.40
246	A16	75pf lilac rose	.20	2.40

Perf. 12x11½
Wmk. 95v

247	A17	1m car & gray	.35	2.40
248	A17	1¼m ultra & ol bis	.20	2.40
249	A17	1½m dk grn & gray	.20	3.25
250	A17	2½m blk & gray	.20	32.50

Perf. 11½x12
Wmk. 95h

251	A18	3m pale blue	.55	14.50
252	A18	5m orange	.55	14.50
253	A18	10m deep green	.95	25.00
254	A18	20m black	1.40	32.50
		Nos. 238-254 (17)	6.20	149.50

Imperf. Pairs

238a	A14	5pf yellow grn	55.00	350.00
239a	A14	10pf orange	125.00	
241b	A15	20pf violet (I)	55.00	
243a	A15	40pf brown	110.00	
244a	A16	50pf vermilion	32.50	
245a	A16	60pf blue green	37.50	
246a	A16	75pf lilac rose	37.50	
247a	A17	1m car & gray	6.50	26.00
248a	A17	1¼m ultra & ol bis	6.50	26.00
249a	A17	1½m dk grn & gray	6.50	26.00
250a	A17	2½m blk & gray	11.50	80.00
251a	A18	3m pale blue	11.50	65.00
252a	A18	5m orange	11.50	65.00
253a	A18	10m deep green	11.50	65.00
254a	A18	20m black	11.50	65.00

Perf. 12x11½

			Litho.	Wmk. 95v
1920				
255	A17	2½m black & gray	.50	65.00

On No. 255 the background dots are small, hazy and irregularly spaced. On No. 250 they are large, clear, round, white and regularly spaced in rows. The backs of the typo. stamps usually show a raised impression of parts of the design.

Stamps and Types of Preceding Issue Overprinted

1920				
256	A14	5pf yellow green	.20	1.60
a.		Inverted overprint	26.00	
b.		Imperf., pair	37.50	375.00
257	A14	10pf orange	.20	1.60
a.		Imperf., pair	37.50	375.00
258	A14	15pf carmine	.20	1.60
259	A15	20pf violet	.20	1.60
a.		Inverted overprint	26.00	650.00
b.		Double overprint	13.00	
c.		Imperf., pair	50.00	
260	A15	30pf deep blue	.20	1.60
a.		Inverted overprint	26.00	
b.		Imperf., pair	50.00	375.00
261	A15	40pf brown	.20	1.60
a.		Inverted overprint	26.00	450.00
b.		Imperf., pair	50.00	
262	A16	50pf vermilion	.20	2.40
263	A16	60pf blue green	.50	1.40
264	A16	75pf lilac rose	.40	5.25
265	A16	80pf dark blue	.40	2.75
a.		Without overprint	100.00	
b.		Imperf., pair	50.00	

Overprinted in Black
or Red

266	A17	1m car & gray	.50	2.75
a.		Imperf., pair	50.00	375.00
b.		Inverted overprint	47.50	
267	A17	1¼m ultra & ol bis	.50	2.75
a.		Imperf., pair	47.50	
268	A17	1½m dk grn & gray	.50	3.50
a.		Imperf., pair	47.50	
269	A17	2m vio & ol bis	.80	4.00
a.		Without overprint	32.50	
b.		Imperf., pair	50.00	
270	A17	2½m (#250) (R)	.20	2.75
c.		Imperf., pair	50.00	
270A	A17	2½m (#255) (R)	.95	95.00
b.		Imperf., pair	50.00	

Overprinted

271	A18	3m pale blue	2.75	8.75
272	A18	4m dull red	3.25	10.00
a.		Without overprint	47.50	
273	A18	5m orange	2.75	6.50
274	A18	10m dp green	3.25	16.00
275	A18	20m black	6.00	13.00
		Nos. 256-275 (21)	24.15	186.40

Nos. 256-275 were available for postage through all Germany, but were used almost exclusively in Bavaria.

SEMI-POSTAL STAMPS

Regular Issue of 1914-20 Surcharged in Black

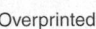

1919		Wmk. 95h	Perf. 14x14½	
B1	A10	10pf + 5pf car rose	.40	2.00
a.		Inverted surcharge	26.00	65.00
b.		Surcharge on back	50.00	
c.		Imperf., pair	325.00	
B2	A10	15pf + 5pf ver	.40	2.00
a.		Inverted surcharge	26.00	65.00
b.		Imperf., pair	190.00	
B3	A10	20pf + 5pf blue	.40	2.40
a.		Inverted surcharge	26.00	65.00
b.		Imperf., pair	375.00	
		Nos. B1-B3 (3)	1.20	6.40

Surtax was for wounded war veterans.

POSTAGE DUE STAMPS

D1   D2

With Silk Thread

1862	Typeset	Unwmk.	Imperf.	
J1	D1	3kr black	125.00	325.00
a.		"Empfange"	375.00	1,000.

Without Silk Thread

1870	Typo.	Wmk. 93	Perf. 11½	
J2	D1	3kr black	12.00	800.00
a.		Wmk. 92	55.00	1,750.
J3	D1	3kr black	12.00	475.00
a.		Wmk. 92	55.00	960.00

Type of 1876 Regular Issue
Overprinted in Red
"Vom Empfänger zahlbar"

1876			Wmk. 94	
J4	D2	3pf gray	16.00	40.00
J5	D2	5pf gray	10.00	17.00
J6	D2	10pf gray	3.25	1.25
a.		Vert. half used as 5pf on cover		2,800.
		Nos. J4-J6 (3)	29.25	58.25

1883			Wmk. 95v	
J7	D2	3pf gray	90.00	100.00
J8	D2	5pf gray	55.00	70.00
J9	D2	10pf gray	2.40	.80
a.		"Empfanper"	140.00	140.00
b.		"zahlhar"	72.50	72.50
c.		Imperf.	87.50	
		Nos. J7-J9 (3)	147.40	170.80

1895-1903		Wmk. 95h	Perf. 14½	
J10	D2	2pf gray	.80	2.40
J11	D2	3pf gray ('03)	.80	2.50
J12	D2	5pf gray ('03)	1.00	1.75
J13	D2	10pf gray ('03)	.60	.90
		Nos. J10-J13 (4)	3.20	7.55

1888		Rose-toned Paper		
J10a	D2	2pf gray	1.90	4.50
J11a	D2	3pf gray	2.50	2.25
b.		Inverted overprint		2,200.
J12a	D2	5pf gray	2.50	2.50
J13a	D2	10pf gray	2.50	1.10
b.		As "a," double overprint		2,200.
		Nos. J10a-J13a (4)	9.40	10.35

No. J13b was used at Pirmasens.

Surcharged in Red in Each Corner

1895				
J14	D2	2pf on 3pf gray		150,000.

Six used examples of No. J14 exist, all used in Aichach. There are two covers (each bearing two examples) and two loose stamps.

OFFICIAL STAMPS

Nos. 77-81, 84, 95-96, 98-99, 102 perforated with a large E were issued for official use in 1912-16.

Regular Issue of 1888-1900
Overprinted

1908		Wmk. 95h	Perf. 14½	
O1	A5	3pf dk brown (R)	.75	3.25
O2	A5	5pf dk green (R)	.20	.40
O3	A5	10pf carmine (G)	.20	.40
O4	A5	20pf ultra (R)	.50	.80
O5	A5	50pf maroon	4.50	7.25
		Nos. O1-O5 (5)	6.15	12.10

Nos. O1-O5 were issued for the use of railway officials. "E" stands for "Eisenbahn."

Coat of
Arms — O1

1916-17		Typo.	Perf. 11½	
O6	O1	3pf bister brn	.20	.80
O7	O1	5pf yellow grn	.20	.80
O8	O1	7½pf grn, grn	.20	.50
O9	O1	7½pf grn ('17)	.20	.80
O10	O1	10pf deep rose	.20	.65
O11	O1	15pf red, buff	.30	.50
O12	O1	15pf red ('17)	.20	.80
O13	O1	20pf dp bl, bl	2.00	2.00
O14	O1	20pf dp blue ('17)	.20	.65
O15	O1	25pf gray	.20	.65
O16	O1	30pf orange	.20	.65
O17	O1	60pf dark green	.20	1.25
O18	O1	1m dl vio, gray	.95	2.75
O19	O1	1m maroon ('17)	2.75	4.75
		Nos. O6-O19 (14)	8.00	17.55

Used values of Nos. O6-O69 are for postally used stamps. Canceled-to-order stamps, which abound, sell for same prices as unused.

Official Stamps
and Type of 1916-17 Overprinted

1918				
O20	O1	3pf bister brn	.20	13.50
O21	O1	5pf yellow green	.20	2.00
O22	O1	7½pf gray green	.20	13.00
O23	O1	10pf deep rose	.20	2.25
O24	O1	15pf red	.20	2.25
O25	O1	20pf blue	.20	2.25
O26	O1	25pf gray	.20	2.25
O27	O1	30pf orange	.20	2.25
O28	O1	35pf orange	.20	2.25
O29	O1	50pf olive gray	.20	2.50
O30	O1	60pf dark green	.30	13.50
O31	O1	75pf red brown	.35	3.50
O32	O1	1m dl vio, gray	1.10	14.50
O33	O1	1m maroon	4.00	375.00
		Nos. O20-O33 (14)	7.75	451.00

O2   O3

O4

1920		Typo.	Perf. 14x14½	
O34	O2	5pf yellow grn	.20	6.50
O35	O2	10pf orange	.20	6.50
O36	O2	15pf carmine	.20	6.50
O37	O2	20pf violet	.20	6.50
O38	O2	30pf dark blue	.20	7.25
O39	O2	40pf bister	.20	7.25
			Perf. 14½x14	
			Wmk. 95v	
O40	O3	50pf vermilion	.20	22.50
O41	O3	60pf blue green	.20	9.50
O42	O3	70pf dk violet	.20	27.50
a.		Imperf., pair	26.00	
O43	O3	75pf deep rose	.20	35.00
O44	O3	80pf dull blue	.20	35.00
O45	O3	90pf olive green	.20	55.00
O46	O4	1m dark brown	.20	50.00
a.		Imperf., pair	72.50	
O47	O4	1¼m green	.20	65.00
O48	O4	1½m vermilion	.20	65.00
a.		Imperf. pair	25.00	
O49	O4	2½m deep blue	.20	70.00
a.		Imperf., pair	72.50	
O50	O4	3m dark red	.20	100.00
a.		Imperf., pair	20.00	
O51	O4	5m black	1.50	125.00
a.		Imperf., pair	72.50	
		Nos. O34-O51 (18)	4.90	700.00

Stamps of Preceding
Issue Overprinted

1920, Apr. 1				
O52	O2	5pf yellow green	.20	3.25
a.		Imperf., pair	26.00	
O53	O2	10pf orange	.20	1.90
O54	O2	15pf carmine	.20	2.00
O55	O2	20pf violet	.20	1.60
O56	O2	30pf dark blue	.20	1.60
O57	O2	40pf bister	.20	1.60
O58	O3	50pf vermilion	.20	2.00
a.		Imperf., pair	26.00	
O59	O3	60pf blue green	.20	1.60
O60	O3	70pf dark violet	2.00	2.75
O61	O3	75pf deep rose	.35	1.40
O62	O3	80pf dull blue	.20	1.40
O63	O3	90pf olive green	1.60	3.50
	Similar Ovpt., Words 8mm apart			
O64	O4	1m dark brown	.20	2.00
a.		Imperf., pair	26.00	
O65	O4	1¼m green	.20	2.00
O66	O4	1½m vermilion	.20	2.00
O67	O4	2½m deep blue	.20	2.00
a.		Imperf., pair	37.50	
O68	O4	3m dark red	.20	2.00
O69	O4	5m black	8.75	24.00
		Nos. O52-O69 (18)	15.50	59.60

Nos. O52-O69 could be used in all parts of Germany, but were almost exclusively used in Bavaria.

BERGEDORF

LOCATION — A town in northern Germany.
POP. — 2,989 (1861)

Originally Bergedorf belonged jointly to the Free City of Hamburg and the Free City of Lübeck. In 1867 it was purchased by Hamburg.

16 Schillings = 1 Mark

Values for unused stamps are for examples with original gum as defined in the catalogue introduction. Copies without gum sell for about 40% of the figures quoted. Values for used stamps are for examples canceled with parallel bars. Copies bearing dated town postmarks sell for more.

Combined Arms of Lübeck and
Hamburg

A1   A2   A3

A4   A5

1861-67	Unwmk.	Litho.	Imperf.	
1	A1	½s blk, pale bl	45.00	725.00
a.		½s black, blue ('67)	125.00	4,750.
2	A3	1s blk, white	45.00	375.00
a.		Tête bêche pair, vert.	225.00	
b.		Tête bêche pair, horiz.	300.00	
3	A4	1½s blk, yellow	20.00	1,350.
a.		Tête bêche pair	125.00	
4	A2	3s blue, pink	25.00	2,000.
5	A5	4s blk, brown	25.00	2,250.
		Nos. 1-5 (5)	160.00	6,700.

Counterfeit cancellations are plentiful.
No. 3 exists in a tête bêche gutter pair. Value, unused $325.

The ½s on violet and 3s on rose, listed previously, as well as a 1s and 1½s on thick paper and 4s on light rose brown, come from proof sheets and were never placed in use. A 1½ "SCHILLINGE" (instead of SCHILLING) also exists only as a proof.

REPRINTS
½ SCHILLING
There is a dot in the upper part of the right branch of "N" of "EIN." The upper part of the shield is blank or almost blank. The horizontal bar of "H" in "HALBER" is generally defective.
1 SCHILLING
The "1" in the corners is generally with foot. The central horizontal bar of the "E" of "EIN" is separated from the vertical branch by a black line. The "A" of "POSTMARKE" has the horizontal bar incomplete or missing. The horizontal bar of the "H" of "SCHILLING" is separated from the vertical branches by a dark line at each side, sometimes the bar is missing.
1½ SCHILLINGE
There is a small triangle under the right side of the tower, exactly over the "R" of "POSTMARKE."
3 SCHILLINGE
The head of the eagle is not shaded. The horizontal bar of the second "E" of "BERGEDORF" is separated from the vertical branch by a thin line. There is generally a colored dot in the lower half of the "S" of "POSTMARKE."
4 SCHILLINGE
The upper part of the shield is blank or has two or three small dashes. In most of the reprints there is a diagonal dash across the wavy lines of the groundwork at the right of "I" and "E" of "VIER."
Reprints, value $1 each.

These stamps were superseded by those of the North German Confederation in 1868.

BREMEN

LOCATION — In northwestern Germany
AREA — 99 sq. mi.
POP. — 122,402 (1871)

Bremen was a Free City and member of the German Confederation. In 1870 it became part of the German Empire.

22 Grote = 10 Silbergroschen.

Values for unused stamps are for examples with original gum as defined in the catalogue introduction. Stamps without gum sell for about 50-60% the figures quoted.

Coat of Arms — A1

Type I. The central part of the scroll below the word Bremen is crossed by one vertical line.
Type II. The center of the scroll is crossed by two vertical lines.
Type III. The center of the scroll is crossed by three vertical lines.

1855	Unwmk.	Litho.	*Imperf.*	
Horizontally Laid Paper				
1	A1	3gr black, *blue*	200.00	290.00
Vertically Laid Paper				
1A	A1	3gr black, *blue*	350.00	550.00

No. 1 can be found with parts of a papermaker's watermark, consisting of lilies. Value: unused $650; unused, no gum, $375; used $950.
See Nos. 9-10.

A2   A3

FIVE GROTE
Type I. The shading at the left of the ribbon containing "funf Grote" runs downward from the shield.
Type II. The shading at the left of the ribbon containing "funf Grote" runs upward.

1856-60			**Wove Paper**	
2	A2	5gr blk, *rose*	150.00	300.00
a.	Printed on both sides			
b.	"Marken" (not issued)		11.00	
3	A2	7gr blk, *yel* ('60)	240.00	725.00
4	A3	5sgr green ('59)	275.00	300.00
a.	Chalky paper		50.00	1,500.
b.	5sgr yellow green		125.00	300.00

See Nos. 6, 8, 12-13, 15.

A4   A5

1861-63			*Serpentine Roulette*	
5	A4	2gr orange ('63)	400.00	2,000.
a.	2gr red orange		700.00	3,000.
b.	Chalky paper		350.00	2,800.
c.	as "a," chalky paper		700.00	4,000.
6	A2	5gr blk, *rose* ('62)	200.00	175.00
a.	Horiz. pair, imperf between			
7	A5	10gr black	700.00	850.00
8	A3	5sgr yellow green ('63)	1,100.	175.00
a.	Chalky paper		600.00	425.00
b.	5sgr green		925.00	210.00

See Nos. 11, 14.

Horizontally (H) or Vertically (V) Laid Paper

1863				
9	A1	3gr blk, *blue* (V)	650.00	725.00
a.	3gr black, *blue* (H)		2,250.	4,000.

1866-67			*Perf. 13*	
10	A1	3gr black, *blue*	80.00	325.00
Wove Paper				
11	A4	2gr orange	95.00	325.00
a.	2gr red orange		275.00	500.00
b.	Horiz. pair, imperf. btwn.		2,800.	
12	A2	5gr blk, *rose*	125.00	325.00
a.	Horiz. pair, imperf. btwn.		1,250.	
13	A2	7gr blk, *yel* ('67)	150.00	4,500.
14	A5	10gr black ('67)	190.00	1,125.
15	A3	5sgr green	140.00	3,750.
a.	5sgr yellow green		450.00	175.00
b.	As "a," chalky paper		450.00	275.00

The stamps of Bremen were superseded by those of the North German Confederation on Jan. 1, 1868.

BRUNSWICK

LOCATION — In northern Germany
GOVT. — Former duchy
AREA — 1,417 sq. mi.
POP. — 349,367 (1880)
CAPITAL — Brunswick

Brunswick was a member of the German Confederation and, in 1870 became part of the German Empire.

12 Pfennigs = 1 Gutegroschen

30 Silbergroschen (Groschen) = 24 Gutegroschen = 1 Thaler

Values for unused stamps are for examples with original gum as defined in the catalogue introduction except for Nos. 1-3 which are valued without gum. Nos. 1-3 with original gum sell for much higher prices, and Nos. 4-26 without gum sell for about 50-60% of the figures quoted.

The "Leaping Saxon Horse" — A1

The ½gr has white denomination and "Gr" in right oval.

1852	Unwmk.	Typo.	*Imperf.*	
1	A1	1sgr rose	2,000.	300.00
2	A1	2sgr blue	1,450.	250.00
a.	Half used as 1sgr on cover			
3	A1	3sgr vermilion	1,450.	250.00

See Nos. 4-11, 13-22.

1853-63			**Wmk. 102**	
4	A1	¼ggr blk, *brn* ('56)	800.00	250.00
5	A1	⅓sgr black ('56)	140.00	325.00
6	A1	½gr blk, *grn* ('63)	25.00	240.00
7	A1	1sgr blk, *orange*	400.00	55.00
a.	1sgr black, orange buff		400.00	57.50
8	A1	1sgr blk, *yel* ('61)	400.00	50.00
a.	Diagonal half used as ½sgr on cover			18,000.
9	A1	2sgr blk, *blue*	325.00	65.00
a.	Diagonal half used as 1sgr on cover			8,750.
b.	Vertical half used as 1sgr on cover			18,000.
10	A1	3sgr blk, *rose*	475.00	72.50
11	A1	3sgr rose ('62)	600.00	200.00

A3   A4

1857				
12	A3	Four ¼ggr blk, *brn* ('57)	40.00	95.00
a.	Four ¼ggr blk, *yel brown*			210.00

1864			*Serpentine Roulette 16*	
13	A1	⅓sgr black	475.00	2,250.
14	A1	½gr blk, *green*	190.00	3,000.
15	A1	1sgr blk, *yellow*	2,850.	1,425.
16	A1	1sgr yellow	400.00	145.00
17	A1	2sgr blk, *blue*	400.00	340.00
a.	Half used as 1sgr on cover			12,000.
18	A1	3sgr rose	800.00	525.00

Rouletted 12

20	A1	1sgr blk, *yellow*		11,000.
21	A1	1sgr yellow	600.00	325.00
22	A1	3sgr rose		2,500.

Nos. 13, 16, 18, 21-22 are on white paper.
Faked roulettes of Nos. 13-22 exist.

Serpentine Roulette

1865	**Embossed**		**Unwmk.**	
23	A4	½gr black	27.50	350.00
24	A4	1gr carmine	2.50	50.00
25	A4	2gr ultra	8.75	125.00
a.	2gr gray blue		8.75	125.00
c.	Half used as 1sgr on cover			17,600.
26	A4	3gr brown	7.25	160.00
		Nos. 23-26 (4)	46.00	685.00

Faked cancellations of Nos. 5-26 exist.

Imperf., Pairs

23a	A4	½gr	100.00
24a	A4	1gr	30.00
25b	A4	2gr	85.00
26a	A4	3gr	100.00

Stamps of Brunswick were superseded by those of the North German Confederation on Jan. 1, 1868.

HAMBURG

LOCATION — Northern Germany
GOVT. — A former Free City
AREA — 160 sq. mi.
POP. — 453,869 (1880)
CAPITAL — Hamburg

Hamburg was a member of the German Confederation and became part of the German Empire in 1870.

16 Schillings = 1 Mark

Values for unused stamps are for examples with original gum as defined in the catalogue introduction. Stamps without gum sell for about 50-60% of the figures quoted.

Value Numeral on Arms — A1

1859	Typo.	Wmk. 128	*Imperf.*	
1	A1	½s black	125.00	600.00
2	A1	1s brown	125.00	95.00
3	A1	2s red	125.00	100.00
4	A1	3s blue	125.00	125.00
5	A1	4s yellow green	50.00	1,450.
a.	4s green		110.00	1,150.
b.	Double impression			
6	A1	7s orange	55.00	40.00
7	A1	9s yellow	125.00	2,000.

See Nos. 13-21.

A2   A3

1864			**Litho.**	
9	A2	1¼s gray	90.00	80.00
a.	1¼s lilac		150.00	85.00
b.	1¼s red lilac		125.00	72.50
c.	1¼s blue		425.00	850.00
d.	1¼s greenish gray		110.00	200.00
12	A3	2½s green	140.00	140.00

See Nos. 22-23.
The 1¼s and 2½s have been reprinted on watermarked and unwatermarked paper.

1864-65	**Typo.**		**Perf. 13½**	
13	A1	½s black	6.50	12.00
a.	Horiz. pair, imperf between		65.00	
14	A1	1s brown	13.00	17.50
a.	Half used as ½s on cover			16,000.
b.	Horiz. pair, imperf between		450.00	650.00
15	A1	2s red	16.00	20.00
17	A1	3s blue	40.00	40.00
a.	Imperf., pair		140.00	
b.	Horiz. pair, imperf. vert.			
c.	3s blue		42.50	29.00
18	A1	4s green	10.00	20.00
19	A1	7s orange	160.00	125.00

20	A1	7s vio ('65)	11.50	16.00
a.	Imperf, pair		275.00	
21	A1	9s yellow	25.00	2,000.
a.	Vert. pair, imperf btwn.		375.00	

Litho.

22	A2	1¼s lilac	125.00	20.00
a.	1¼s red lilac		125.00	20.00
b.	1¼s violet		125.00	15.00
23	A3	2½s yel grn, blurred printing	190.00	45.00
a.	2½s blue green		190.00	47.50

The 1¼s has been reprinted on watermarked and unwatermarked paper; the 2½s on unwatermarked paper.

A4   A5

Rouletted 10

1866	**Unwmk.**		**Embossed**	
24	A4	1¼s violet	40.00	35.00
a.	1¼s red violet		72.50	72.50
25	A5	1½s rose	9.50	125.00

Reprints:
1¼s: The rosettes between the words of the inscription have a well-defined open circle in the center of the originals, while in the reprints this circle is filled up.
In the upper part of the top of the "g" of "Schilling", there is a thin vertical line which is missing in the reprints.
The two lower lines of the triangle in the upper left corner are of different thicknesses in the originals while in the reprints they are of equal thickness.
The labels at the right and left containing the inscriptions are 2¾mm in width in the originals while they are 2½mm in reprints.
1½s: The originals are printed on thinner paper than the reprints. This is easily seen by turning the stamps over, when on the originals the color and impression will clearly show through, which is not the case in the reprints.
The vertical stroke of the upper part of the "g" in Schilling is very short on the originals, scarcely crossing the top line, while in the reprints it almost touches the center of the "g."
The lower part of the "g" of Schilling in the originals, barely touches the inner line of the frame, in some stamps it does not touch it at all, while in the reprints the whole stroke runs into the inner line of the frame.

A6

1867	**Typo.**	**Wmk. 128**	**Perf. 13½**	
26	A6	2½s dull green	12.50	80.00
a.	2½s dark green		65.00	100.00
b.	Imperf., pair		225.00	
c.	Horiz. pair, imperf between		92.50	

Forged cancellations exist on almost all stamps of Hamburg, especially on Nos. 4, 7, 21 and 25.
Nos. 1-23 and 26 exist without watermark, but they come from the same sheets as the watermarked stamps.
The stamps of Hamburg were superseded by those of the North German Confederation on Jan. 1, 1868.

HANOVER

LOCATION — Northern Germany
GOVT. — A former Kingdom
AREA — 14,893 sq. mi.
POP. — 3,191,000
CAPITAL — Hanover

Hanover was a member of the German Confederation and became in 1866 a province of Prussia.

10 Pfennigs = 1 Groschen

24 Gute Groschen = 1 Thaler

30 Silbergroschen = 1 Thaler (1858)

Values for unused stamps are for examples with original gum as defined in the catalogue introduction. Examples without gum sell for about 50-60% of the figures quoted.

Coat of Arms
A1   A2

Wmk. Square Frame

1850		Rose Gum	Typo.	*Imperf.*
1	A1	1 g g blk, *gray bl*	4,000.	60.00

See Nos. 2, 11.
The reprints have white gum and no watermark.

1851-55			**Wmk. 130**	
2	A1	1g g blk, *gray grn*	95.00	9.00
a.		1g g black, *yellow green*	950.00	32.50
3	A2	1⁄30th blk, *salmon*	125.00	50.00
a.		1⁄30th black, *crimson* ('55)	125.00	50.00
b.		Bisect on cover		—
5	A2	1⁄15th blk, *gray bl*	190.00	80.00
a.		Bisect on cover		—
6	A2	1⁄10th blk, *yellow*	240.00	70.00
a.		1⁄10th black, *orange*	240.00	65.00
		Nos. 2-6 (4)	650.00	209.00

Bisects Nos. 3b, 5a, 12a and 13a were used for 1⁄2g.
See Nos. 8, 12-13.
The 1⁄10th has been reprinted on unwatermarked paper, with white gum.

Crown and
Numeral — A3

1853			**Wmk. 130**	
7	A3	3pf rose	475.00	325.00

See Nos. 9, 16-17, 25.
The reprints of No. 7 have white gum.

Fine Network in Second Color

1855				**Unwmk.**
8	A2	1⁄10th blk & org	240.00	160.00
a.		1⁄10th black & yellow	400.00	240.00

No. 8 with olive yellow network and other values with fine network are essays.

Large Network in Second Color

1856-57				
9	A3	3pf rose & blk	325.00	275.00
a.		3pf rose & gray	425.00	360.00
11	A1	1g g blk & grn	80.00	12.00
12	A1	1⁄30th blk & rose	160.00	32.50
a.		Bisect on cover		13,500.
13	A2	1⁄15th blk & bl	125.00	72.50
a.		Bisect on cover		6,500.
14	A2	1⁄10th blk & org ('57)	800.00	55.00

The reprints have white gum, and the network does not cover all the outer margin.

Without Network

1859-63				
16	A3	3pf pink	140.00	100.00
a.		3pf carmine rose	80.00	90.00
17	A3	3pf grn (Drei Zehntel) ('63)	325.00	775.00

Examples of No. 25 with rouletting trimmed off are sometimes offered as No. 17. Minimum size of No. 17 acknowledged as genuine: 21 1⁄2 x24 1⁄2mm.
The reprints of No. 16 have pink gum instead of red; the extremities of the banderol point downward instead of outward.

Crown and   King George
Post   V — A8
Horn — A7

1859-61				*Imperf.*
18	A7	1⁄2g black ('60)	175.00	200.00
a.		Rose gum	325.00	275.00
19	A8	1g rose	4.00	4.50
a.		1g vio rose	20.00	20.00
b.		1g carmine	65.00	26.00
c.		Half used as 1⁄2g on cover		10,000.
20	A8	2g ultra	16.00	40.00
a.		Half used as 1g on cover		7,000.
22	A8	3g yellow	200.00	60.00
a.		3g orange yellow	110.00	120.00

23	A8	3g brown ('61)	27.50	50.00
a.		One third used as 1g on cover		—
24	A8	10g green ('61)	240.00	875.00

Reprints of 1⁄2g are on thick toned paper with yellowish gum. Originals are on white paper with rose or white gum. Reprints exist tête bêche.
Reprints of 3g yellow and 3g brown have white or pinkish gum. Originals have rose or orange gum.

1864		White Gum		**Perce en Arc 16**
25	A3	3pf grn (Drei Zehntel)	30.00	60.00
26	A7	1⁄2g black	275.00	275.00
27	A8	1g rose	12.00	8.00
28	A8	2g ultra	125.00	60.00
a.		Half used as 1g on cover		—
29	A8	3g brown	70.00	70.00
		Nos. 25-29 (5)	512.00	473.00

Reprints of 3g are percé en arc 13 1⁄2.

		Rose Gum		
25a	A3	3pf green	80.00	80.00
26a	A7	1⁄2g black	475.00	450.00
27a	A8	1g rose	40.00	25.00
29a	A8	3g brown	1,200.	1,200.

Used examples of Nos. 25a-29a retain the rose color on the reverse after the gum has been removed.

The stamps of Prussia superseded those of Hanover on Oct. 1, 1866.

LUBECK

LOCATION — Situated on an arm of the Baltic Sea between the former German States of Holstein and Mecklenburg.
GOVT. — Former Free City and State
AREA — 115 sq. mi.
POP. — 136,413
CAPITAL — Lubeck

Lubeck was a member of the German Confederation and became part of the German Empire in 1870.

16 Schillings = 1 Mark

Values for Nos. 1-7 unused are for stamps without gum. Nos. 6 and 7 with gum sell for about twice the figures quoted. Values for Nos. 8-14 unused are for examples with original gum as defined in the catalogue introduction. Nos. 8-14 without gum sell for about 50-60% of the figures quoted.

Coat of Arms — A1

1859		Litho.	**Wmk. 148**	*Imperf.*
1	A1	1⁄2g gray lilac	475.00	2,000.
2	A1	1s orange	475.00	2,000.
3	A1	2s brown	25.00	240.00
a.		Value in words reads "ZWEI EIN HALB"	400.00	7,200.
4	A1	2 1⁄2s rose	50.00	800.00
5	A1	4s green	25.00	600.00

1862				**Unwmk.**
6	A1	1⁄2s lilac	17.50	1,600.
7	A1	1s yellow orange	27.50	1,600.

The reprints of the 1859-62 issues are unwatermarked and printed in bright colors.

A2   A3

1863				**Rouletted 11 1⁄2**
		Eagle embossed		
8	A2	1⁄2s green	50.00	72.50
9	A2	1s orange	125.00	160.00
a.		Rouletted 10	200.00	475.00

10	A2	2s rose	27.50	65.00
11	A2	2 1⁄2s ultra	125.00	400.00
12	A2	4s bister	55.00	100.00
		Nos. 8-12 (5)	382.50	797.50

The reprints are imperforate and without embossing.

1864		Litho.		*Imperf.*
13	A3	1 1⁄4s dark brown	32.50	72.50
a.		1 1⁄4s reddish brown	21.00	125.00

A4

1865				**Rouletted 11 1⁄2**
		Eagle embossed		
14	A4	1 1⁄2s red lilac	30.00	80.00

The reprints are imperforate and without embossing.
Counterfeit cancellations are found on #1-14.
The stamps of Lübeck were superseded by those of the North German Confederation on Jan. 1, 1868.

MECKLENBURG-SCHWERIN

LOCATION — In northern Germany, bordering on the Baltic Sea.
GOVT. — Grand Duchy
AREA — 5,065 sq. mi. (approx.)
POP. — 674,000 (approx.)
CAPITAL — Schwerin

Mecklenburg-Schwerin was a member of the German Confederation and became part of the German Empire in 1870.

48 Schillings = 1 Thaler

Values for unused stamps are for examples with original gum as defined in the catalogue introduction. Examples without gum sell for about 70% of the figures quoted.

Coat of Arms
A1   A2

1856		Unwmk.	Typo.	*Imperf.*
1	A1	Four 1⁄4s red	140.00	125.00
a.		1⁄4s red	14.50	12.00
2	A2	3s yellow	82.50	50.00
3	A2	5s blue	225.00	275.00
		Nos. 1-3 (3)	447.50	450.00

See Nos. 4, 6-8.

A3

1864-67				**Rouletted 11 1⁄2**
4	A1	Four 1⁄4s red	2,800.	1,750.
a.		1⁄4s red	175.00	240.00
5	A3	Four 1⁄4s red	65.00	50.00
a.		1⁄4s red	9.50	9.50
6	A2	2s gray lil ('67)	140.00	1,600.
a.		2s red violet ('66)	240.00	240.00
7	A2	3s org yel, wide margin ('67)	40.00	300.00
a.		Narrow margin ('65)	160.00	125.00
8	A2	5s bister brn	160.00	240.00
a.		Thick paper	240.00	340.00

The overall size of #7, including margin, is 24 1⁄2 x24 1⁄2mm. That of #7a is 23 1⁄2 x23mm.
The bister on white paper was not issued. Value $12.

Counterfeit cancellations exist on those stamps valued higher used than unused.

These stamps were superseded by those of the North German Confederation on Jan. 1, 1868.

MECKLENBURG-STRELITZ

LOCATION — In northern Germany, divided by Mecklenburg-Schwerin.
GOVT. — Grand Duchy
AREA — 1,131 sq. mi.
POP. — 106,347
CAPITAL — Neustrelitz

Mecklenburg-Strelitz was a member of the German Confederation and became part of the German Empire in 1870.

30 Silbergroschen = 48 Schillings = 1 Thaler

Values for unused stamps are for examples with original gum as defined in the catalogue introduction. Examples without gum sell for about 50% of the figures quoted.

Coat of Arms
A1   A2

1864		**Rouletted 11 1⁄2**		
		Unwmk.		**Embossed**
1	A1	1⁄4sg orange	175.00	2,400.
a.		1⁄4sg yellow orange	340.00	4,000.
2	A1	1⁄3sg green	80.00	1,350.
a.		1⁄3sg dark green	140.00	2,400.
3	A1	1sch violet	275.00	3,200.
4	A2	1sg rose	140.00	190.00
5	A2	2sg ultra	40.00	800.00
6	A2	3sg bister	32.50	1,275.

Counterfeit cancellations abound.

These stamps were superseded by those of the North German Confederation in 1868.

OLDENBURG

LOCATION — In northwestern Germany, bordering on the North Sea.
GOVT. — Grand Duchy
AREA — 2,482 sq. mi.
POP. — 483,042 (1910)
CAPITAL — Oldenburg

Oldenburg was a member of the German Confederation and became part of the German Empire in 1870.

30 Silbergroschen = 1 Thaler
30 Groschen = 1 Thaler

Values for unused stamps are for examples with original gum as defined in the catalogue introduction. Examples without gum sell for about 50% of the figures quoted.

A1   A2

1852-55		Unwmk.	Litho.	*Imperf.*
1	A1	1⁄30th blk, *blue*	350.00	27.50
2	A1	1⁄15th blk, *rose*	800.00	80.00
3	A1	1⁄10th blk, *yellow*	800.00	95.00
4	A2	1⁄3sgr blk, *grn* ('55)	1,275.	950.00

There are three types of Nos. 1 and 2.

A3   A4

1859

5	A3	⅓g blk, *green*	2,400.	2,900.
6	A3	1g blk, *blue*	725.00	45.00
7	A3	2g blk, *rose*	950.00	600.00
8	A3	3g blk, *yellow*	950.00	600.00
a.		"OLBENBURG"	1,200.	1,000.

See Nos. 10, 13-15.

1861

9	A4	¼g orange	300.00	3,600.
10	A3	⅓g green	475.00	875.00
a.		⅓g bluish green	475.00	875.00
b.		⅓g moss green	1,400.	2,300.
c.		"OLDEIBURG"	600.00	1,000.
d.		"Dritto"	600.00	1,000.
e.		"Dritt"	600.00	1,000.
f.		Printed on both sides		5,000.
12	A4	½g redsh brn	400.00	525.00
a.		½g dark brown	400.00	525.00
13	A3	1g blue	240.00	160.00
a.		1g gray blue	375.00	200.00
b.		Printed on both sides		3,750.
14	A3	2g red	450.00	450.00
15	A3	3g yellow	450.00	450.00
a.		"OLDEIBURG"	600.00	600.00
b.		Printed on both sides		5,000.

Forged cancellations are found on Nos. 9,. 10, 12 and their minor varieties.

Coat of Arms — A5

1862   Embossed   Rouletted 11½

16	A5	⅓g green	200.00	190.00
17	A5	½g orange	200.00	95.00
a.		½g orange red	250.00	150.00
18	A5	1g rose	75.00	16.00
19	A5	2g ultra	200.00	50.00
20	A5	3g bister	210.00	52.50

1867   Rouletted 10

21	A5	⅓g green	32.50	725.00
22	A5	½g orange	32.50	360.00
23	A5	1g rose	20.00	55.00
a.		Half used as ½g on cover		—
24	A5	2g ultra	20.00	475.00
25	A5	3g bister	45.00	400.00
		Nos. 21-25 (5)	150.00	2,015.

Forged cancellations are found on #21-25.
The stamps of Oldenburg were replaced by those of the North German Confederation on Jan. 1, 1868.

PRUSSIA

LOCATION — The greater part of northern Germany.
GOVT. — Independent Kingdom
AREA — 134,650 sq. mi.
POP. — 40,165,219 (1910)
CAPITAL — Berlin

Prussia was a member of the German Confederation and became part of the German Empire in 1870.

12 Pfennigs = 1 Silbergroschen
60 Kreuzer = 1 Gulden (1867)

Values for unused stamps are for examples with original gum as defined in the catalogue introduction. Examples without gum sell for about 50% of the figures quoted.

King Frederick William IV
A1   A2

1850-56   Engr.   Wmk. 162   *Imperf.*
Background of Crossed Lines

1	A1	4pf yel grn ('56)	110.00	72.50
a.		4pf dark green	160.00	125.00
2	A1	6pf (½sg) red org	90.00	52.50
3	A2	1sg black, *rose*	80.00	12.00
a.		1sg black, *bright red*	18,750.	400.00
4	A2	2sg black, *blue*	110.00	16.00
a.		Half used as 1sg on cover		—
5	A2	3sg black, *yellow*	110.00	16.00
a.		3sg black, *orange buff*	390.00	37.50
		Nos. 1-5 (5)	500.00	169.00

See Nos. 10-13.

Reprints exist on watermarked and unwatermarked paper.

A3   A4

Solid Background

1857   Typo.   Unwmk.

6	A3	1sg rose	325.00	35.00
a.		1sg carmine rose	360.00	50.00
7	A3	2sg blue	1,280.	90.00
a.		2sg dark blue	1,795.	125.00
b.		Half used as 1sg on cover		—
8	A3	3sg orange	160.00	40.00
a.		3sg yellow	1,625.	100.00
b.		3sg deep orange	800.00	125.00
		Nos. 6-8 (3)	1,765.	165.00

The reprints of Nos. 6-8 have a period instead of a colon after "SILBERGR."

Background of Crossed Lines

1858-60   Typo.

9	A4	4pf green	72.50	35.00

Engr.

10	A1	6pf (½sg) org ('59)	190.00	160.00
a.		6pf (½sg) brick red	290.00	200.00

Typo.

11	A2	1sg rose	32.50	4.00
12	A2	2sg blue	110.00	17.50
a.		2sg dark blue	160.00	42.50
b.		Half used as 1sg on cover		—
13	A2	3sg orange	95.00	16.00
a.		3sg yellow	140.00	17.50
		Nos. 9-13 (5)	500.00	232.50

Coat of Arms
A6   A7

1861-67   Embossed   Rouletted 11½

14	A6	3pf red lilac ('67)	27.50	45.00
a.		3pf red violet ('65)	340.00	275.00
15	A6	4pf yellow green	12.00	12.00
a.		4pf green	42.50	55.00
16	A6	6pf orange	12.00	14.50
a.		6pf vermilion	125.00	67.50
17	A7	1sg rose	3.25	1.60
18	A7	2sg ultra	12.00	1.60
a.		2sg blue	425.00	30.00
20	A7	3sg bister	8.75	2.00
a.		3sg gray brown ('65)	—	30.00
		Nos. 14-20 (6)	75.50	76.70

A8   A9

Typographed in Reverse on Paper Resembling Goldbeater's Skin

1866   Rouletted 10

21	A8	10sg rose	95.00	105.00
22	A9	30sg blue	110.00	225.00

Perfect examples of Nos. 21-22 are extremely rare.

A10

1867   Embossed   Rouletted 16

23	A10	1kr green	25.00	45.00
24	A10	2kr orange	40.00	95.00
25	A10	3kr rose	20.00	27.50
26	A10	6kr ultra	20.00	45.00
27	A10	9kr bister brown	25.00	47.50
		Nos. 23-27 (5)	130.00	260.00

Imperforate stamps of the above sets are proofs.

The stamps of Prussia were superseded by those of the North German Confederation on Jan. 1, 1868.

OFFICIAL STAMPS
See Germany Nos. OL1-OL15.

SAXONY

LOCATION — In central Germany
GOVT. — Kingdom
AREA — 5,787 sq. mi.
POP. — 2,500,000 (approx.)
CAPITAL — Dresden

Saxony was a member of the German Confederation and became a part of the German Empire in 1870.

10 Pfennings = 1 Neu-Groschen
30 Neu-Groschen = 1 Thaler

Values for unused stamps are for examples with original gum as defined in the catalogue introduction. Examples without gum sell for about 50-60% of the figures quoted.

A1

1850   Unwmk.   Typo.   *Imperf.*

1	A1	3pf brick red	6,400.	6,400.
a.		3pf cherry red	10,675.	16,150.
b.		3pf brown red	10,675.	11,575.

There are vertical dividing lines between stamps.

Coat of   Frederick
Arms — A2   Augustus II — A3

1851

2	A2	3pf green	125.00	95.00
a.		3pf yellow green	1,350.	600.00

Nos. 2 and 2a are valued with the margin just touching the design in one or two places. Stamps with margins all around sell for considerably more.
Stamps with very fine impressions, from the first printing, command substantial premiums.

1851-52   Engr.

3	A3	½ng black, *gray*	72.50	12.00
a.		½ng black, *pale blue* (error)	19,000.	
5	A3	1ng black, *rose*	95.00	9.50
6	A3	2ng black, *pale bl*	250.00	65.00
7	A3	2ng blk, *dk bl* ('52)	725.00	55.00
8	A3	3ng black, *yellow*	160.00	25.00
		Nos. 3-8 (5)	1,302.	166.50

The error No. 3a occurred when paper meant for printing No. 6 was inadvertently placed in the stack of paper for printing No. 3.

King John I — A4

1855-60

9	A4	½ng black, *gray*	9.50	4.00
a.		"1½" at left or right		

10	A4	1ng black, *rose*	9.50	4.00
11	A4	2ng black, *dark blue*	20.00	16.00
a.		2ng black, *blue*	65.00	30.00
12	A4	3ng black, *yellow*	21.00	12.00
13	A4	5ng ver ('56)	90.00	55.00
a.		5ng orange brown ('60)	225.00	300.00
b.		5ng deep brown ('57)	650.00	175.00
14	A4	10ng milky blue ('56)	225.00	225.00

A5   A6

Typo.; Arms Embossed

1863   Perf. 13

15	A5	3pf blue green	2.00	40.00
a.		3pf yellow green	55.00	72.50
16	A5	½ng orange	2.00	2.75
a.		½ng red orange	22.50	4.50
17	A6	1ng rose	1.25	2.40
a.		Vert. pair, imperf. between	225.00	
b.		Horiz. pair, imperf. between	375.00	
18	A6	2ng blue	2.75	6.50
a.		2ng dark blue	11.00	25.00
19	A6	3ng red brown	4.00	8.75
a.		3ng bister brown	22.50	7.25
20	A6	5ng dull violet	30.00	47.50
a.		5ng gray violet	10.00	450.00
b.		5ng gray blue	30.00	72.50
c.		5ng slate	22.50	250.00

The stamps of Saxony were superseded on Jan. 1, 1868, by those of the North German Confederation.

SCHLESWIG-HOLSTEIN

LOCATION — In northern Germany.
GOVT. — Duchies
AREA — 7,338 sq. mi.
POP. — 1,519,000 (approx.)
CAPITAL — Schleswig

Schleswig-Holstein was an autonomous territory from 1848 to 1851 when it came under Danish rule. In 1864, it was occupied by Prussia and Austria, and in 1866 it became a province of Prussia.

16 Schillings = 1 Mark

Values for unused stamps are for examples with original gum as defined in the catalogue introduction. Stamps without gum sell for about 50% of the figures quoted.

Coat of Arms — A1

Typographed; Arms Embossed

1850   Unwmk.   *Imperf.*
With Silk Threads

1	A1	1s dl bl & grnsh bl	325.00	5,600.
a.		1s Prussian blue	725.00	
2	A1	2s rose & pink	560.00	5,325.
a.		2s deep pink & rose	725.00	
b.		Double embossing	2,900.	

Forged cancellations are found on Nos. 1-2, 5-7, 9, 16 and 19.

A2   A3

1865   Typo.   Rouletted 11½

3	A2	½s rose	35.00	45.00
4	A2	1¼s green	17.50	20.00
5	A3	1⅓s red lilac	45.00	125.00
6	A2	2s ultra	50.00	240.00
7	A3	4s bister	65.00	1,300.
		Nos. 3-7 (5)	212.50	1,730.

Schleswig

A4

A5

1864		Typo.	Rouletted 11½	
8	A4	1¼s green	40.00	18.50
9	A4	4s carmine	87.50	450.00

1865			Rouletted 10, 11½	
10	A4	½s green	32.50	55.00
11	A4	1¼s red lilac	55.00	25.00
a.	1¼s gray lilac ('67)		225.00	67.50
b.	Half of #11a used as ½s on cover			30,000.
12	A5	1⅓s rose	27.50	60.00
13	A4	2s ultra	27.50	60.00
14	A4	4s bister	32.50	80.00
	Nos. 10-14 (5)		175.00	280.00

Holstein

A6

A7

Type I — Small lettering in frame. Wavy lines in spandrels close together.
Type II — Small lettering in frame. Wavy lines wider apart.
Type III — Larger lettering in frame and no periods after "H R Z G." Wavy lines as II.

1864		Litho.	Imperf.	
15	A6	1¼s bl & gray, I	52.50	55.00
a.	Half used as ½s on cover			9,250.
16	A6	1¼s bl & gray, II	800.00	2,400.
a.	Half used as ½s on cover			23,000.
17	A6	1¼s bl & gray, III	45.00	55.00
a.	Half used as ½s on cover			7,750.

1864			Rouletted 8	
18	A7	1¼s blue & rose	40.00	20.00
a.	Half used as ½s on cover			1,900.

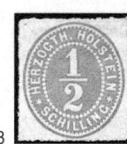
A8

1865			Rouletted 8	
19	A8	½s green	65.00	95.00
20	A8	1¼s red lilac	47.50	25.00
21	A8	2s blue	52.50	47.50
	Nos. 19-21 (3)		165.00	167.50

A9

A10

1865-66			Rouletted 7 and 8	
22	A9	1¼s red lilac ('66)	72.50	25.00
a.	Half used as ½s on cover			23,000.
23	A10	1⅓s carmine	60.00	45.00
24	A9	2s blue ('66)	145.00	160.00
25	A10	4s bister	55.00	80.00
	Nos. 22-25 (4)		332.50	310.00

These stamps were superseded by those of North German Confederation on Jan. 1, 1868.

THURN AND TAXIS

A princely house which, prior to the formation of the German Empire, enjoyed the privilege of a postal monopoly. These stamps were superseded on July 1, 1867, by those of Prussia, followed by those of the North German Postal District on Jan. 1, 1868, and later by stamps of the German Empire on Jan. 1, 1872.

Values are for stamps with four complete margins just clear of the framelines. Stamps with margins just touching the framelines on one or two sides are worth approximately 60% of the values quoted. Stamps with four large margins are rare and command premiums of up to 500% over the values quoted.

Values for unused stamps are for examples with original gum as defined in the catalogue introduction. Stamps without gum sell for about 50% of the figures quoted.

NORTHERN DISTRICT
30 Silbergroschen or Groschen = 1 Thaler

A1

A2

1852-58		Unwmk. Typo.	Imperf.	
1	A1	¼sgr blk, red brn ('54)	275.00	67.50
2	A1	½sgr blk, buff ('58)	125.00	275.00
3	A1	½sgr blk, green	750.00	42.50
4	A1	1sgr blk, dk bl	1,375.	160.00
5	A1	1sgr blk, lt bl ('53)	825.00	25.00
6	A1	2sgr blk, rose	875.00	37.50
a.	Half used as 1sgr on cover			6,000.
7	A1	3sgr blk, brownish yellow	1,000.	32.50
a.	3sgr blk, pale orange yellow	875.00	100.00

Reprints of Nos. 1-12, 15-20, 23-24, were made in 1910. They have "ND" in script on the back. Value, $6.50 each.

1859-60				
8	A1	¼sgr red ('60)	72.50	82.50
9	A1	½gr green	300.00	125.00
10	A1	1sgr blue	300.00	57.50
11	A1	2sgr rose ('60)	160.00	110.00
12	A1	3sgr red brn ('60)	160.00	140.00
13	A2	5sgr lilac	1.90	400.00
14	A2	10sgr orange	2.75	1,000.

Excellent forged cancellations exist on Nos. 13 and 14. For reprints, see note after No. 7.

1862-63				
15	A1	¼sgr black ('63)	35.00	82.50
16	A1	½sgr green ('63)	50.00	275.00
17	A1	½sgr org yel	110.00	65.00
18	A1	1sgr rose ('63)	72.50	45.00
19	A1	2sgr blue ('63)	57.50	125.00
20	A1	3sgr bister ('63)	27.50	65.00
	Nos. 15-20 (6)		352.50	657.50

For reprints, see note after No. 7.

1865			Rouletted	
21	A1	¼sgr black	8.00	400.00
22	A1	½sgr green	12.00	275.00
23	A1	½sgr yellow	24.00	37.50
24	A1	1sgr rose	24.00	27.50
25	A1	2sgr blue	1.60	75.00
26	A1	3sgr bister	2.75	30.00
	Nos. 21-26 (6)		72.35	845.00

For reprints, see note after No. 7.

1866			Rouletted in Colored Lines	
27	A1	¼sgr black	2.00	2,600.
28	A1	½sgr green	2.00	1,300.
29	A1	½sgr yellow	2.00	275.00
30	A1	1sgr rose	2.00	125.00
a.	Horizontal pair without rouletting between		140.00	1,450.
b.	Half used as ½sgr on cover			50,000.
31	A1	2sgr blue	2.00	1,300.
32	A1	3sgr bister	2.00	375.00
	Nos. 27-32 (6)		12.00	5,975.

Forged cancellations on Nos. 2, 13-14, 15-16, 21-22, 25-32 are plentiful.

SOUTHERN DISTRICT
60 Kreuzer = 1 Gulden

A1

A2

1852-53		Unwmk.	Imperf.	
42	A1	1kr blk	250.00	21.00
43	A1	3kr blk, dk bl	950.00	65.00
44	A1	3kr blk, bl ('53)	825.00	21.00
45	A1	6kr blk, rose	1,325.	14.50
46	A1	9kr blk, brnish yell	875.00	21.00
a.	9kr blk, pale orange yellow	850.00	55.00

Reprints of Nos. 42-50, 53-56 were made in 1910. Each has "ND" in script on the back. Value, each $6.50.

1859				
47	A1	1kr green	25.00	17.50
48	A1	3kr blue	600.00	32.50
49	A1	6kr rose	600.00	87.50
50	A1	9kr yellow	600.00	125.00
51	A2	15kr lilac	2.75	210.00
52	A2	30kr orange	2.75	575.00

Forged cancellations exist on Nos. 51 and 52. For reprints, see note after No. 46.

1862				
53	A1	3kr rose	14.50	45.00
54	A1	6kr blue	14.50	45.00
55	A1	9kr bister	14.50	45.00
	Nos. 53-55 (3)		43.50	135.00

For reprints, see note after No. 46.

1865			Rouletted	
56	A1	1kr green	12.50	15.00
57	A1	3kr rose	18.50	7.50
58	A1	6kr blue	1.50	20.00
59	A1	9kr bister	2.25	22.50
	Nos. 56-59 (4)		34.75	65.00

For reprint of No. 56, see note after No. 46.

1866			Rouletted in Colored Lines	
60	A1	1kr green	1.50	22.50
61	A1	3kr rose	1.50	20.00
62	A1	6kr blue	1.50	37.50
63	A1	9kr bister	1.50	32.50
	Nos. 60-63 (4)		6.00	112.50

Forged cancellations exist on Nos. 51-52, 58-63.

The Thurn & Taxis Stamps, Northern and Southern Districts, were replaced on July 1, 1867, by those of Prussia.

WURTTEMBERG

LOCATION — In southern Germany
GOVT. — Kingdom
AREA — 7,530 sq. mi.
POP. — 2,580,000 (approx.)
CAPITAL — Stuttgart

Württemberg was a member of the German Confederation and became a part of the German Empire in 1870. It gave up its postal autonomy on March 31, 1902, but official stamps were issued until 1923.

16 Kreuzer = 1 Gulden
100 Pfennigs = 1 Mark (1875)

Values for unused stamps are for examples with original gum as defined in the catalogue introduction. Unused stamps without gum of Nos. 1-46 sell for about 60-70% of the figures quoted. Unused stamps without gum of Nos. 47-54 sell for about 50% of the figures quoted.

A1

A1a

1851-52		Unwmk. Typo.	Imperf.	
1	A1	1kr blk, buff	1,125.	95.00
a.	1kr black, straw		3,500.	500.00
2	A1	3kr blk, yellow	275.00	7.25
a.	3kr black, orange		3,000.	300.00
4	A1	6kr blk, yel grn	1,450.	32.50
a.	6kr black, blue green		2,600.	50.00
5	A1	9kr blk, rose	4,800.	32.50
6	A1a	18kr blk, dl vio ('52)	1,450.	725.00

On the "reprints" the letters of "Württemberg" are smaller, especially the first "e"; the right branch of the "r's" of Württemberg runs

---

upward in the reprints and downward in the originals.

Coat of Arms — A2

With Orange Silk Threads
Typographed and Embossed

1857				
7	A2	1kr yel brn	800.00	80.00
a.	1kr dark brown		1,000.	225.00
9	A2	3kr yel org	400.00	11.00
10	A2	6kr green	800.00	65.00
11	A2	9kr car rose	1,925.	70.00
12	A2	18kr blue	3,350.	1,350.

Very fine examples of Nos. 7-12 with have one or two margins touching, but not cutting, the frameline.
See Nos. 13-46, 53.
The reprints have red or yellow silk threads and are printed 2mm apart, while the originals are ¾mm apart.

1859			Without Silk Threads	
13	A2	1kr brown	650.00	100.00
a.	1kr dark brown		1,900.	675.00
15	A2	3kr yel org	275.00	13.00
16	A2	6kr green	9,600.	125.00
17	A2	9kr car rose	1,275.	70.00
18	A2	18kr dark blue	2,900.	1,700.

The colors of the reprints are brighter; they are also printed 2mm apart instead of 1¼mm.

1860			Perf. 13½	
19	A2	1kr brown	1,125.	125.00
20	A2	3kr yel org	325.00	9.50
21	A2	6kr green	3,000.	110.00
22	A2	9kr carmine	1,200.	125.00

1861			Thin Paper	
23	A2	1kr brown	950.00	250.00
a.	1kr black brown		950.00	250.00
25	A2	3kr yel org	200.00	65.00
26	A2	6kr green	400.00	110.00
27	A2	9kr rose	1,275.	300.00
a.	9kr claret		1,160.	325.00
29	A2	18kr dark blue	3,000.	2,250.

Examples of Nos. 23-29 with all perforations intact sell for considerably more.

1862			Perf. 10	
30	A2	1kr blk brn	650.00	440.00
31	A2	3kr yel org	800.00	47.50
32	A2	6kr green	525.00	200.00
33	A2	9kr claret	4,000.	800.00

1863				
34	A2	1kr yel grn	45.00	13.50
a.	1kr green		375.00	87.50
36	A2	3kr rose	325.00	4.75
a.	3kr dark claret		1,500.	250.00
37	A2	6kr blue	160.00	52.50
39	A2	9kr yel brn	750.00	160.00
a.	9kr red brown		260.00	52.50
b.	9kr black brown		1,125.	175.00
40	A2	18kr orange	1,200.	400.00

1865-68			Rouletted 10	
41	A2	1kr yel grn	45.00	12.00
a.	1kr dark green		575.00	300.00
42	A2	3kr rose	45.00	3.25
a.	3kr claret		1,900.	2,250.
43	A2	6kr blue	275.00	52.50
44	A2	7kr slate bl ('68)	960.00	125.00
45	A2	9kr bis brn	1,500.	110.00
a.	9kr red brown		1,150.	100.00
46	A2	18kr orange ('67)	1,750.	1,000.

A3

1869-73			Typo. & Embossed	
47	A3	1kr yel grn	32.50	2.40
48	A3	2kr orange	175.00	140.00
49	A3	3kr rose	16.00	1.60
50	A3	7kr blue	67.50	17.50
51	A3	9kr lt brn ('73)	80.00	40.00
52	A3	14kr orange	88.00	45.00
a.	14kr lemon yellow		1,400.	1,400.
	Nos. 47-52 (6)		459.00	246.50

See No. 54.

1873   **Imperf.**

53	A2	70kr red violet	1,750.	4,000.
a.		70kr violet	2,900.	5,250.

Nos. 53 and 53a have single or double lines of fine black dots printed in the gutters between the stamps.

1874   **Perf. 11½x11**

54	A3	1kr yellow green	110.00	40.00

A4   A5

1875-1900   **Typo.**

55	A4	2pf sl gray ('93)	2.00	.95
56	A4	3pf green	20.00	1.60
57	A4	3pf brn ('90)	.80	.55
a.		Imperf., pair	125.00	
58	A4	5pf violet	9.50	.80
59	A4	5pf grn ('90)	1.60	.55
a.		5pf blue green	250.00	24.00
b.		Imperf., pair	125.00	
60	A4	10pf carmine	1.25	.80
a.		10pf rose	67.50	.75
b.		Imperf., pair	67.50	
61	A4	20pf ultra	1.25	.80
a.		20pf dull blue	1.00	.65
b.		Imperf., pair	125.00	
62	A4	25pf red brn	125.00	9.50
63	A4	25pf org ('90)	2.75	1.60
a.		Imperf., pair	125.00	
64	A5	30pf org & blk ('00)	3.25	4.75
65	A5	40pf dp rose & blk ('00)	4.00	5.50
66	A4	50pf gray	725.00	40.00
67	A4	50pf gray grn	65.00	6.50
68	A4	50pf pur brn ('90)	2.75	.95
a.		50pf red brown	640.00	65.00
b.		Imperf., pair	125.00	
69	A4	2m yellow	800.00	260.00
70	A4	2m ver, buff ('79)	2,800.	125.00
71	A5	2m org & blk ('86)	8.00	9.50
		Telegraph cancel		3.00
a.		2m yellow & black	350.00	47.50
b.		Imperf., pair	125.00	
72	A5	5m bl & blk ('81)	45.00	160.00
		Telegraph cancel		67.50
a.		Double impression of figure of value	160.00	

No. 70 has "Unverkäuflich" (not for sale) printed on its back to remind postal clerks that it, like No. 69, was for their use and not to be sold to the public.

The regular postage stamps of Württemberg were superseded by those of the German Empire in 1902. Official stamps were in use until 1923.

WURTTEMBERG OFFICIAL STAMPS

For the Communal Authorities

O1

Perf. 11½x11

1875-1900   **Typo.**   **Unwmk.**

O1	O1	2pf sl gray ('00)	2.40	1.60
O2	O1	3pf brn ('96)	2.40	1.60
O3	O1	5pf violet	45.00	2.40
a.		Imperf., pair		3,750.
O4	O1	5pf bl grn ('90)	1.60	1.45
a.		Imperf., pair	47.50	
O5	O1	10pf rose	9.50	2.25
a.		Imperf., pair	82.50	
O6	O1	25pf org ('00)	25.00	8.00
		Nos. O1-O6 (6)	85.90	17.30

See Nos. O12-O32. For overprints and surcharges see Nos. O7-O11, O40-O52, O59-O93.

Used Values

When italicized, used values for Nos. O7-O183 are for favor-canceled stamps. Postally used stamps command a premium.

Stamps of Previous Issues Overprinted in Black

1906, Jan. 30

O7	O1	2pf slate gray	45.00	80.00
O8	O1	3pf dk brown	14.00	10.00
O9	O1	5pf green	4.75	5.50
O10	O1	10pf deep rose	4.75	5.25
O11	O1	25pf orange	55.00	75.00
		Nos. O7-O11 (5)	123.50	175.75
		Set, C.T.O.		40.00

Centenary of Kingdom of Württemberg.
Nos. O7-O11 also exist imperf but it is doubtful if they were ever issued in that condition.

1906-21   **Wmk. 116**

O12	O1	2pf slate gray	4.00	.40
O13	O1	2½pf gray blk ('16)	.80	.20
O14	O1	3pf dk brown	.95	.40
O15	O1	5pf green	.80	.40
O16	O1	7½pf orange ('16)	.80	.40
O17	O1	10pf dp rose	.80	.40
O18	O1	10pf orange ('21)	.30	.20
O19	O1	15pf yellow brn ('16)	2.00	.20
O20	O1	15pf purple ('17)	1.25	.20
O21	O1	20pf dp ultra ('11)	1.60	.40
O22	O1	20pf dp green ('21)	.30	.20
O23	O1	25pf orange	.95	.40
O24	O1	25pf brn & blk ('17)	1.25	.20
O25	O1	35pf brown ('19)	1.60	.95
O26	O1	40pf rose red ('21)	.30	.20
O27	O1	50pf rose lake ('11)	14.50	.40
O28	O1	50pf vio brn ('21)	.30	.20
O29	O1	60pf olive grn ('21)	.55	.20
O30	O1	1.25m emerald ('21)	.30	.20
O31	O1	2m gray ('21)	.80	.20
O32	O1	3m brown ('21)	.30	.20
		Nos. O12-O32 (21)	34.65	6.35

No. O24 contains solid black numerals.
Nos. O12-O32 exist imperf. Value, each pair, $6.50-$17.50.

O3

Perf. 14½x14

1916, Oct. 6   **Typo.**   **Unwmk.**

O33	O3	2½pf slate	1.60	1.25
O34	O3	7½pf orange	1.25	1.25
O35	O3	10pf car rose	1.25	1.25
O36	O3	15pf yellow brn	1.25	1.25
O37	O3	20pf blue	1.25	1.25
O38	O3	25pf gray blk	4.00	1.25
O39	O3	50pf red brown	8.00	1.25
		Nos. O33-O39 (7)	18.60	8.75

25th year of the reign of King Wilhelm II.

Stamps of 1900-06 Surcharged

Perf. 11½x11

1916, Sept. 10   **Wmk. 116**

O40	O1	25pf on 25pf orange	4.00	.95
a.		Without wmk.	32.50	

No. O13 Surcharged in Blue

1919   **Wmk. 116**

O42	O1	2pf on 2½pf gray blk	.80	.55

Official Stamps of 1906-19 Overpriented

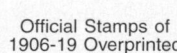

1919

O43	O1	2½pf gray blk	.40	.55
O44	O1	3pf dk brown	12.00	.55
O45	O1	5pf green	.35	.55
O46	O1	7½pf orange	1.00	.55
O47	O1	10pf rose	.35	.55
O48	O1	15pf purple	.35	.55
O49	O1	20pf ultra	.35	.55
O50	O1	25pf brown & blk	.40	.55
O51	O1	35pf brown	4.00	.55
O52	O1	50pf red brown	5.50	.55
		Nos. O43-O52 (10)	24.70	5.50

Stag — O4

Wmk. 192

1920, Mar. 19   **Litho.**   **Perf. 14½**

O53	O4	10pf maroon	1.45	1.25
O54	O4	15pf brown	1.45	1.25
O55	O4	20pf indigo	1.45	1.25
O56	O4	30pf deep green	1.45	1.25
O57	O4	50pf yellow	1.60	1.25
O58	O4	75pf bister	3.25	1.25
		Nos. O53-O58 (6)	10.65	7.50

Official Stamps of 1906-19 Overprinted

Perf. 11½x11

1920, Apr. 1   **Wmk. 116**

O59	O1	5pf green	4.00	10.00
O60	O1	10pf deep rose	2.40	4.75
O61	O1	15pf dp violet	2.40	5.25
O62	O1	20pf ultra	4.00	8.75
a.		Wmk. 192	4.75	8.75
O63	O1	50pf red brown	4.75	17.50
		Nos. O59-O63 (5)	17.55	46.25

Nos. O59 to O63 were available for official postage throughout all Germany but were used almost exclusively in Württemberg.

Stamps of 1917-21 Surcharged in Black, Red or Blue

1923

O64	O1	5m on 10pf orange	.20	.55
O65	O1	10m on 15pf dp violet	.20	.55
O66	O1	12m on 40pf rose red	.20	.55
O67	O1	20m on 10pf orange	.80	.55
O68	O1	25m on 20pf green	.20	.55
O69	O1	40m on 20pf green	.20	.55
O70	O1	50m on 60pf olive grn	.20	.55

Surcharged

O71	O1	60m on 1.25m emerald	.20	.55
O72	O1	100m on 40pf rose red	.20	.55
O73	O1	200m on 2m gray (R)	.20	.55
O74	O1	300m on 50pf red brn (Bl)	.20	.55
O75	O1	400m on 3m brn (Bl)	.20	.55
O76	O1	1000m on 60pf ol grn	.20	.55
O77	O1	2000m on 1.25m emerald	.20	.55
		Nos. O64-O77 (14)	3.40	7.70

Abbreviations:
Th = (Tausend) Thousand
Mil = (Million) Million
Mlrd = (Milliarde) Billion

Surcharged

1923

O78	O1	5th m on 10pf orange	.20	.50
O79	O1	20th m on 40pf rose red	.20	.50
O80	O1	50th m on 15pf violet	.80	.50
O81	O1	75th m on 2m gray	1.60	.50
O82	O1	100th m on 20pf green	.20	.50
O83	O1	250th m on 3m brown	.20	.50

Surcharged

O84	O1	1mil m on 60pf ol grn	1.25	.50
O85	O1	2mil m on 50pf red brn	.20	.50
O86	O1	5mil m on 1.25m emer	.20	.50

Surcharged

O87	O1	4 mlrd m on 50pf red brn	3.25	.50
O88	O1	10 mlrd m on 3m brn	3.25	.50
		Nos. O78-O88 (11)	11.35	5.50

No. O23 Surcharged with New Values in Rentenpfennig as

1923, Dec.

O89	O1	3pf on 25pf orange	.50	.35
O90	O1	5pf on 25pf orange	.50	.35
O91	O1	10pf on 25pf orange	.40	.35
O92	O1	20pf on 25pf orange	.40	.35
O93	O1	50pf on 25pf orange	.65	.35
		Nos. O89-O93 (5)	2.45	1.75

For the State Authorities

O6

Perf. 11½x11

1881-1902   **Typo.**   **Unwmk.**

O94	O6	2pf sl gray ('96)	1.60	1.60
O95	O6	3pf green	25.00	4.50
O96	O6	3pf dk brown ('90)	1.60	.80
O97	O6	5pf violet	8.00	1.90
O98	O6	5pf green ('90)	2.40	.80
O99	O6	10pf rose	8.00	1.90
O100	O6	20pf ultra	1.00	1.60
O101	O6	25pf brown	35.00	6.50
O102	O6	25pf orange ('90)	5.25	1.40
O103	O6	30pf org & blk ('02)	2.00	2.75
O104	O6	40pf dp rose & blk ('02)	2.00	2.75
O105	O6	50pf gray grn	7.00	8.75
O106	O6	50pf maroon ('91)	1.60	4.00
a.		50pf red brown ('90)	240.00	1,750.
O107	O6	1m yellow	72.50	200.00
O108	O6	1m violet ('90)	6.25	16.00
		Nos. O94-O108 (15)	179.20	255.25

See #O119-O135. For overprints & surcharges see #O109-O118, O146-O164, O176-O183.

Overprinted in Black

1906

O109	O6	2pf slate gray	27.50	5.25
O110	O6	3pf dk brown	5.25	5.25
O111	O6	5pf green	4.75	5.25
O112	O6	10pf dp rose	4.50	5.25
O113	O6	20pf ultra	4.75	5.25
O114	O6	25pf orange	11.00	5.25
O115	O6	30pf org & blk	9.50	5.25
O116	O6	40pf dp rose & blk	32.50	5.25

O117	O6	50pf red brown	32.50	*5.25*
O118	O6	1m purple	65.00	*5.25*
		Nos. O109-O118 (10)	197.25	*52.50*

Cent. of the kingdom of Wüttemberg. Nos. O109 to O118 are also found imperforate, but it is doubtful if they were ever issued in that condition.

1906-19   **Wmk. 116**

O119	O6	2pf slate gray	.50	*.20*
O120	O6	2½pf gray blk ('16)	.50	*.20*
O121	O6	3pf dk brown	.50	*.20*
O122	O6	5pf green	.50	*.20*
O123	O6	7½pf orange ('16)	.55	*.20*
O124	O6	10pf deep rose	.50	*.20*
O125	O6	15pf yel brn ('16)	.55	*.20*
O126	O6	15pf purple ('17)	1.25	*.30*
O127	O6	20pf ultra	.65	*.20*
O128	O6	25pf orange	.50	*.20*
O129	O6	25pf brn & blk ('17)	.40	*.20*
O130	O6	30pf org & blk	.50	*.20*
O131	O6	35pf brown ('19)	1.60	*3.25*
O132	O6	40pf dp rose & blk	.65	*.20*
O133	O6	50pf red brown	.65	*.20*
O134	O6	1m purple	2.40	*.20*
O135	O6	1m sl & blk ('17)	2.40	*.65*
		Nos. O119-O135 (17)	14.45	*7.00*

King Wilhelm II — O8

1916   **Unwmk.**   **Typo.**   **Perf. 14**

O136	O8	2½pf slate	.80	*.60*
O137	O8	7½pf orange	.80	*.60*
O138	O8	10pf carmine	.80	*.60*
O139	O8	15pf yellow brn	.80	*.60*
O140	O8	20pf blue	.80	*.60*
O141	O8	25pf gray blk	1.60	*.60*
O142	O8	30pf green	1.60	*.60*
O143	O8	40pf claret	2.40	*.60*
O144	O8	50pf red brn	3.25	*.60*
O145	O8	1m violet	3.25	*.60*
		Nos. O136-O145 (10)	16.10	*6.00*

25th year of the reign of King Wilhelm II.

Stamps of 1890-1906 Surcharged

1916-19   **Wmk. 116**   **Perf. 11½x11**

O146	O6	25pf on 25pf orange	3.00	*.80*
a.		Without watermark	35.00	*14,400.*
O147	O6	50pf on 50pf red brn	1.60	*1.10*
a.		Inverted surcharge	32.50	

Beware of fake cancels on No. O146a.

No. O120 Surcharged in Blue

1919   **Wmk. 116**

O149	O6	2pf on 2½pf gray blk	1.45	*1.60*

Official Stamps of 1890-1919 Overprinted

1919

O150	O6	2½pf gray blk	.55	*.40*
O151	O6	3pf dk brown	7.25	*.80*
a.		Without watermark	52.50	
O152	O6	5pf green	.40	*.40*
O153	O6	7½pf orange	.40	*.40*
O154	O6	10pf rose	.40	*.40*
O155	O6	15pf purple	.40	*.40*
O156	O6	20pf ultra	.40	*.40*
O157	O6	25pf brn & blk	.40	*.40*
a.		Inverted overprint	82.50	*160.00*
O158	O6	30pf org & blk	.80	*.40*
a.		Inverted overprint	225.00	*350.00*
O159	O6	35pf brown	.55	*.40*
O160	O6	40pf rose & blk	.55	*.40*
O161	O6	50pf claret	.80	*.65*
O162	O6	1m slate & blk	.80	*.80*
		Nos. O150-O162 (13)	13.70	*6.25*

Nos. O151, O151a Surcharged in Carmine

1920   **Wmk. 116**

O164	O6	75pf on 3pf dk brn	1.25	*1.25*
a.		Without watermark	80.00	*20.00*

View of Stuttgart O9

10pf, 50pf, 2.50m, 3m, View of Stuttgart. 15pf, 75pf, View of Ulm. 20pf, 1m, View of Tubingen. 30pf, 1.25m, View of Ellwangen.

Wmk. 192

1920, Mar. 25   **Typo.**   **Perf. 14½**

O166	O9	10pf maroon	.55	*1.00*
O167	O9	15pf brown	.55	*1.00*
O168	O9	20pf indigo	.55	*1.00*
O169	O9	30pf blue grn	.55	*1.00*
O170	O9	50pf yellow	.55	*1.00*
O171	O9	75pf bister	.55	*1.00*
O172	O9	1m orange red	.80	*1.00*
O173	O9	1.25m dp violet	.80	*1.00*
O174	O9	2.50m dark ultra	2.00	*1.00*
O175	O9	3m yellow grn	2.40	*1.00*
		Nos. O166-O175 (10)	9.30	*10.00*

Official Stamps of 1906-19 Overprinted

1920   **Wmk. 116**   **Perf. 11½x11**

O176	O6	5pf green	2.40	*3.25*
O177	O6	10pf deep rose	1.60	*2.75*
O178	O6	15pf purple	1.60	*2.75*
O179	O6	20pf ultra	1.60	*1.25*
a.		Wmk. 192	125.00	*275.00*
O180	O6	30pf orange & blk	1.60	*3.25*
O181	O6	40pf dp rose & blk	1.60	*2.75*
O182	O6	50pf red brown	1.60	*3.25*
O183	O6	1m slate & blk	2.40	*7.00*
		Nos. O176-O183 (8)	14.40	*26.25*

The note after No. O63 will also apply to Nos. O176-O183.

NORTH GERMAN CONFEDERATION

Northern District
30 Groschen = 1 Thaler
Southern District
60 Kreuzer = 1 Gulden
Hamburg
16 Schillings = 1 Mark

Values for unused stamps are for examples with original gum as defined in the catalogue introduction. Stamps without gum sell for about 50% of the figures quoted.

A1   A2

Rouletted 8½ to 10, 11 to 12½ and Compound

1868		**Typo.**		**Unwmk.**
1	A1	¼gr violet	25.00	15.00
2	A1	⅓gr green	30.00	4.00
3	A1	½gr orange	30.00	2.50
4	A1	1gr rose	20.00	1.60
b.		Half used as ½gr on cover		
5	A1	2gr ultra	80.00	3.25
6	A1	5gr bister	80.00	9.50
7	A2	1kr green	35.00	8.00
8	A2	2kr orange	55.00	55.00
9	A2	3kr rose	35.00	3.25

10	A2	7kr ultra	160.00	11.00
11	A2	18kr bister	35.00	65.00
		Nos. 1-11 (11)	585.00	178.10

See Nos. 13-23.

Imperf

1a	A1	¼gr red lilac	190.00	—
2a	A1	⅓gr green	90.00	—
3a	A1	½gr orange	140.00	—
4a	A1	1gr rose	75.00	—
5a	A1	2gr ultra	250.00	—
6a	A1	5gr bister	250.00	—
7a	A2	1kr green	67.50	110.00
8a	A2	2kr orange	190.00	90.00
9a	A2	3kr rose	75.00	95.00
10a	A2	7kr ultra	325.00	625.00
11a	A2	18kr bister	325.00	625.00

A3

1868

12	A3	(½s) lilac brown	110.00	55.00
d.		Imperf	200.00	

See No. 24.

1869   **Perf. 13½x14**

13	A1	¼gr lilac	14.50	16.00
a.		¼gr red violet	25.00	20.00
14	A1	⅓gr green	5.25	2.75
15	A1	½gr orange	5.25	2.75
16	A1	1gr rose	4.00	1.60
17	A1	2gr ultra	7.25	2.00
18	A1	5gr bister	8.75	10.00
19	A2	1kr green	12.75	10.00
20	A2	2kr orange	40.00	110.00
21	A2	3kr rose	7.25	3.25
22	A2	7kr ultra	11.00	12.00
23	A2	18kr bister	150.00	1,750.
		Nos. 13-23 (11)	266.00	1,920.

Counterfeit cancels exist on No. 23.

1869

24	A3	(½s) dull violet brown	4.75	8.75

A4   A5

Perf. 14x13½

25	A4	10gr gray	325.00	400.00
		Pen cancellation		200.00
26	A5	30gr blue	240.00	960.00
		Pen cancellation		300.00

Counterfeit cancels exist on No. 26. See Germany designs A2, A3 and A8 for similar stamps.

OFFICIAL STAMPS

O1

1870   **Unwmk.**   **Typo.**   **Perf. 14½x14**

O1	O1	¼gr black & buff	27.50	45.00
O2	O1	⅓gr black & buff	9.50	20.00
O3	O1	½gr black & buff	2.75	4.00
O4	O1	1gr black & buff	2.75	2.00
O5	O1	2gr black & buff	7.25	4.75
O6	O1	1kr black & gray	32.50	250.00
O7	O1	2kr black & gray	80.00	1,250.
O8	O1	3kr black & gray	25.00	47.50
O9	O1	7kr black & gray	45.00	275.00
		Nos. O1-O9 (9)	232.25	1,898.

Counterfeit cancels exist on Nos. O6-O9. The stamps of the North German Confederation were replaced by those of the German Empire on Jan. 1, 1872.

GERMANY

ˈjər-mə-nē

LOCATION — In northern Europe bordering on the Baltic and North Seas
AREA — 182,104 sq. mi. (until 1945)
POP. — 67,032,242 (1946)
CAPITAL — Berlin

In 1949 the Russian occupied areas became a separate country, the German Democratic Republic. The country was reunified Oct. 3, 1990.

30 Silbergroschen or Groschen = 1 Thaler
60 Kreuzer = 1 Gulden
100 Pfennigs = 1 Mark (1875)
100 Pfennigs = 1 Deutsche Mark (1948)
100 Cents = 1 Euro (2002)

Catalogue values for unused stamps in this country are for Never Hinged items, beginning with Scott 722 in the regular postage section, Scott B338 in the semi-postal section, Scott C61 in the airpost section, Scott 9N103 in the Berlin regular postage section and Scott 9NB12 in the Berlin semi-postal section.

Watermarks

Wmk. 48 —
Diagonal
Zigzag Lines

Wmk. 116 —
Crosses and
Circles

Wmk. 125 —
Lozenges

Wmk. 126 —
Network

Wmk. 127 —
Quatrefoils

Wmk. 192 —
Circles

Wmk. 223 —
Eagle

Wmk. 237 —
Swastikas

Wmk. 241 —
Cross

Wmk. 284 —
"DEUTSCHE
POST" Multiple

Wmk. 285 — Marbleized Pattern

Wmk. 286 — D P Multiple

Wmk. 292 —
Flowers,
Multiple

Wmk. 295 —
B P and
Zigzag Lines

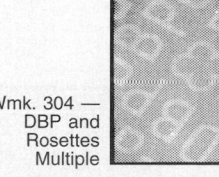
Wmk. 304 —
DBP and
Rosettes
Multiple

Empire

Values for unused stamps are for examples with original gum as defined in the catalogue introduction. Any exceptions are specifically mentioned.

Imperial Eagle — A1

Typographed, Center Embossed
1872   Unwmk.   Perf. 13½x14½
Eagle with small shield

1	A1	¼gr violet	190.00	87.50
2	A1	⅓gr green	450.00	37.50
a.		Imperf.		—
3	A1	½gr red orange	950.00	37.50
a.		½gr orange yellow	1,100.	45.00
4	A1	1gr rose	300.00	5.25
a.		Imperf.		—
b.		Half used as ½gr on cover		47,500.
5	A1	2gr ultra	1,600.	14.50
a.		Imperf.		8,750.
6	A1	5gr bister	875.00	87.50
a.		Imperf.		10,000.
7	A1	1kr green	650.00	52.50
8	A1	2kr orange	37.50	160.00
a.		2kr red orange	600.00	300.00
9	A1	3kr rose	1,750.	12.50
10	A1	7kr ultra	2,350.	87.50
11	A1	18kr bister	475.00	375.00

Values for imperforates are for copies postmarked at Leipzig (⅓gr), Coblenz (1gr), Hoengen (2gr) and Leutersdorf (5gr).

A2   A3

1872	**Typo.**	**Perf. 14½x13½**	
12	A2 10gr gray	52.50	2,400.
	Pen cancellation		150.00
13	A3 30gr blue	105.00	2,500.
	Pen cancellation		525.00

For similar designs see A8, North German Confederation A4, A5.

A4

A5

Center Embossed
1872   Perf. 13½x14½
Eagle with large shield

14	A4	¼gr violet	72.50	95.00
15	A4	⅓gr yellow green	32.50	14.50
a.		⅓gr blue green	125.00	110.00
16	A4	½gr orange	37.50	8.00
		Imperf.		
17	A4	1gr rose	42.50	1.90
a.		Imperf.		16,000.
b.		Half used as ½gr on cover		50,000.
18	A4	2gr ultra	19.00	4.25
19	A4	2½gr orange brn	1,800.	55.00
a.		2½gr lilac brown	4,750.	375.00
20	A4	5gr bister	29.00	29.00
a.		Imperf.		6,500.
21	A4	1kr yel grn	32.50	25.00
a.		1kr blue green	365.00	440.00
22	A4	2kr orange	475.00	2,350.
23	A4	3kr rose	22.50	5.00
24	A4	7kr ultra	30.00	67.50
25	A4	9kr red brown	440.00	400.00
a.		9kr lilac brown	1,400.	450.00
26	A4	18kr bister	35.00	2,000.

Values for Nos. 17a and 20a are for copies postmarked at Potsdam (1gr), Damgarten or Anklam (5gr).
Nos. 14-26 with embossing inverted are fraudulent.

1874

Brown Surcharge

27	A5 2½gr on 2½gr brn	37.50	40.00
28	A5 9kr on 9kr brown	65.00	450.00

A6   A7

"Pfennige"

1875-77		**Typo.**
29	A6 3pf blue green	55.00	5.25
30	A6 5pf violet	97.50	3.75

Center Embossed

31	A7 10pf rose	40.00	1.50
32	A7 20pf ultra	450.00	1.50
33	A7 25pf red brown	475.00	18.00
34	A7 50pf gray	1,500.	11.00
35	A7 50pf ol gray ('77)	1,650.	12.50
	Nos. 29-35 (7)	4,267.	53.50

See Nos. 37-42. For surcharges see Offices in Turkey Nos. 1-6.

A8

1875-90   Typo.   Perf. 14½x13½

36	A8	2m brownish pur ('90)	65.00	3.50
a.		2m purple ('75)	375.00	125.00
b.		2m dull vio pur ('89)	1,500.	60.00

No. 36a used is valued as a stamp with cds cancel dated between Jan. 1875 and November 17, 1884.

Types of 1875-77, "Pfennig" without final "e"

1880-83   Perf. 13½x14½

37	A6	3pf yel green	3.00	1.25
a.		Imperf.	—	
38	A6	5pf violet	1.50	1.25

Center Embossed

39	A7	10pf red	8.00	1.25
a.		Imperf.	325.00	
40	A7	20pf brt ultra	6.00	1.25
41	A7	25pf dull rose brn	15.00	5.25
a.		25pf red brown, thick paper	190.00	6.00
42	A7	50pf dp grayish ol grn	7.50	1.25
a.		50pf olive green	210.00	1.25
		Nos. 37-42 (6)	41.00	11.50

Values for Nos. 37-42 are for stamps on thin paper. Those on thick paper sell for considerably more.

A9

A10

1889-1900   Perf. 13½x14½

45	A9	2pf gray ('00)	.50	.75
a.		"REIGHPOST"	55.00	140.00
		Never hinged	190.00	
46	A9	3pf brown	2.25	1.10
a.		3pf yellow brown	9.00	3.75
b.		Imperf.	600.00	
		Never hinged	1,800.	
c.		3pf reddish brown	110.00	8.00
47	A9	5pf blue green	1.40	1.10
48	A10	10pf carmine	1.75	1.10
a.		Imperf.	225.00	
		Never hinged	650.00	
49	A10	20pf ultra	7.50	1.10
a.		20pf Prus blue	2,250.	110.00
50	A10	25pf orange ('90)	30.00	1.50
a.		Imperf.	190.00	
		Never hinged	625.00	
51	A10	50pf chocolate	26.00	1.10
a.		50pf copper brown	375.00	9.75
b.		Imperf.	325.00	
		Never hinged	425.00	
		Nos. 45-51 (7)	69.40	7.75
		Set, never hinged	320.00	

For surcharges and overprints see Offices in China Nos. 1-6, 16, Offices in Morocco 1-6, Offices in Turkey 8-12.

Germania — A11

1900, Jan. 1   Perf. 14

52	A11	2pf gray	.85	.50
a.		Imperf.	350.00	
		Never hinged	1,600.	
53	A11	3pf brown	.85	1.00
a.		Imperf.	350.00	
		Never hinged	1,600.	
54	A11	5pf green	1.60	.60
55	A11	10pf carmine	2.40	.75
a.		Imperf.	52.50	
		Never hinged	150.00	
56	A11	20pf ultra	8.00	.60
57	A11	25pf orange & blk, *yel*	14.50	4.50
58	A11	30pf orange & blk, *sal*	18.50	.85
59	A11	40pf lake & black	22.50	1.25
60	A11	50pf pur & blk, *sal*	22.50	1.00
61	A11	80pf lake & blk, *rose*	37.50	2.25
		Nos. 52-61 (10)	129.20	13.30
		Set, never hinged	795.00	

Early printings of Nos. 57-61 had "REICHSPOST" in taller and thicker letters than on the ordinary stamps.

For surcharges see Offices in China 17-32, Offices in Morocco 7-15, 32A, Offices in Turkey 13-20, 25-27.

"REICHSPOST" Larger

57a	A11	25pf	1,800.	6,750.
58a	A11	30pf	1,800.	4,500.
59a	A11	40pf	1,800.	4,500.
60a	A11	50pf	1,800.	4,500.
61a	A11	80pf	1,800.	4,500.

General Post Office in Berlin — A12

"Union of North and South Germany" A13

Unveiling Kaiser Wilhelm I Memorial, Berlin — A14

Wilhelm II Speaking at Empire's 25th Anniversary Celebration A15

Type I

Type II

Two types of 5m:
I — "5" is thick; "M" has slight serifs.
II — "5" thinner; "M" has distinct serifs.

Engr.   Perf. 14½x14

62	A12	1m carmine rose	110.00	2.75
		Never hinged	400.00	
a.		Imperf.	2,600.	
63	A13	2m gray blue	75.00	6.75
		Never hinged	450.00	
64	A14	3m black violet	110.00	50.00
		Never hinged	600.00	
65	A15	5m slate & car, I	1,350.	2,250.
		Never hinged	4,500.	
d.		Red and white retouched	325.00	375.00
		Never hinged	1,350.	
e.		White only retouched	600.00	600.00
		Never hinged	1,650.	
65A	A15	5m slate & car, II	350.00	400.00
		Never hinged	1,350.	

Nos. 62-65 exist perf. 11½.

The vignette and frame of No. 65 usually did not align perfectly during printing. Red paint was used to retouch the vignette and/or white paint was used to retouch the inner frame.

No. 62a is without gum.

For surcharges see Offices in China Nos. 33-36A, Offices in Morocco 16-19A, Offices in Turkey 21-24B, 28-30.

Half of No. 54 Handstamp Surcharged in Violet

3PF

1901   Perf. 14

65B	A11	3pf on half of 5pf	9,750.	7,500.
		Never hinged	26,500.	

This provisional was produced aboard the German cruiser Vineta. The purser, with the ship commander's approval, surcharged and bisected 300 5pf stamps so the ship's post office could meet the need for a 3pf (printed matter rate). The crew wanted to send home U.S. newspapers reporting celebrations of the Kaiser's birthday.

Forgeries exist and improper usages as well.

A16

1902   Typo.

65C	A16	2pf gray	1.50	.60
66	A16	3pf brown	.75	1.00
a.		"DFUTSCHES"	9.75	40.00
67	A16	5pf green	2.25	1.00
68	A16	10pf carmine	7.25	1.00
69	A16	20pf ultra	30.00	1.00
70	A16	25pf org & blk, *yel*	45.00	2.10
71	A16	30pf org & blk, *sal*	52.50	.60
72	A16	40pf lake & blk	67.50	1.00
73	A16	50pf pur & blk, *buff*	67.50	1.10
74	A16	80pf lake & blk, *rose*	150.00	2.75
		Nos. 65C-74 (10)	424.25	12.15
		Set, never hinged	1,900.	

Nos. 65C-74 exist imperf. Value, set $2,000.
See Nos. 80-91, 118-119, 121-132, 169, 174, 210. For surcharges see Nos. 133-136, B1, Offices in China 37-42, 47-52, Offices in Morocco 20-28, 33-41, 45-53, Offices in Turkey 31-38, 43-50, 55-59.

A17

A18

A19

A20

Perf. 14¼-14½ (26x17 holes)

Engr.

75	A17	1m carmine rose	240.00	2.75
a.		Imperf.	900.00	
76	A18	2m gray blue	82.50	97.50
77	A19	3m black violet	225.00	18.00
a.		Imperf.	900.00	
78	A20	5m slate & car	210.00	18.00
a.		Imperf.	900.00	

See Nos. 92, 94-95, 102, 111-113. For surcharges see Nos. 115-116, Offices in China 43, 45-46, 53, 55-56, Offices in Morocco 29, 31-32, 42, 44, 54, 56-57, Offices in Turkey 39, 41-42, 51, 53-54.

A21

79	A21	2m gray blue	120.00	5.00
a.		Imperf.	900.00	—
		Never hinged	2,600.	
		Nos. 75-79 (5)	877.50	141.25
		Set, never hinged	3,125.	

See Nos. 93, 114. For surcharges see Nos. 117, Offices in China 44, 54, Offices in Morocco 30, 43, 55, Offices in Turkey 40, 52.

1905-19   Typo.   Wmk. 125   Perf. 14

80	A16	2pf gray ('05)	1.60	2.60
81	A16	3pf brown ('15)	.60	1.40
82	A16	5pf green (shades)	.60	1.40
b.		Bklt. pane of 5 + label ('11)	250.00	500.00
		Never hinged	500.00	
c.		Bklt. pane of 4 + 2 labels ('10)	400.00	800.00
		Never hinged	800.00	
d.		Bklt. pane of 2 + 4 labels ('12)	250.00	500.00
		Never hinged	500.00	
e.		Bklt. pane, #82 + 5 #83 ('17)	75.00	190.00
		Never hinged	190.00	
f.		Bklt. pane, 2 #82 + 4 #83 ('20)	21.00	50.00
		Never hinged	50.00	
g.		Bklt. pane, 4 #82 + 2 #83 ('19)	21.00	50.00
		Never hinged	50.00	
83	A16	10pf red	.60	1.40
b.		Bklt. pane of 5 + label ('10)	325.00	650.00
		Never hinged	650.00	
c.		Bklt. pane of 4 + 2 labels ('12)	300.00	625.00
		Never hinged	625.00	
d.		10pf carmine red	2.00	1.50
84	A16	20pf blue vio ('18)	.75	1.40
a.		20pf light blue	13.00	3.75
		Never hinged	52.50	
b.		20pf ultramarine	8.00	1.50
		Never hinged	42.50	
c.		Imperf.	625.00	2,750.
		Never hinged	1,750.	
d.		Half used as 10pf on cover		700.00
85	A16	25pf org & blk, *yel*	.60	1.40
86	A16	30pf org & blk, *buff*	.60	1.40
a.		30pf org & blk, *cr*	26.00	90.00
87	A16	40pf lake & black	1.00	1.40
88	A16	50pf pur & blk, *buff*	.60	1.40
89	A16	60pf magenta	1.50	1.40
a.		60pf red violet	22.50	13.50
90	A16	75pf green & blk ('19)	.25	2.25
91	A16	80pf lake & blk, *rose*	1.10	1.90

Perf. 14½ (25x17 holes)

Engr.

92	A17	1m car rose	2.25	2.25
93	A21	2m brt blue	5.25	4.75
a.		2m gray blue ('16)	42.50	52.50
94	A19	3m violet gray	2.25	4.25
b.		3m blk violet	11.50	26.00
95	A20	5m slate & car	1.90	4.75
a.		Center inverted	45,000.	65,000.
		Nos. 80-95 (16)	21.45	35.35
		Set, Never Hinged	52.50	

Pre-war printings of Nos. 80-91 have brighter colors and white instead of yellow gum. They sell for considerably more than the wartime printings which are valued here. No. 80 exists only from a pre-war printing.

Nos. 92-95 exist only from a wartime printing. The 1m-5m also exist perf 14¼-14¾ (26x17 holes) in both pre-war and wartime printings. Both of these printings are much more expensive than Nos. 92-95. See the *Scott Classic Specialized Catalogue* for detailed listings.

Labels on No. 82c contain an "X." The version with advertising is worth 3 times as much. No. 82f has three 10pf stamps in the top row. The version with 3 on the bottom row is worth 4 times as much.

No. 84d was used at Field Post Office No. 107 in 1915, and at Field Post Office No. 766 during 1917.

Surcharged and overprinted stamps of designs A16-A22 are listed under Allenstein, Belgium, Danzig, France, Latvia, Lithuania, Marienwerder, Memel, Poland, Romania, Saar and Upper Silesia.

A22

1916-19   Typo.

96	A22	2pf lt gray ('18)	.25	3.25
97	A22	2½pf lt gray	.25	1.90
98	A22	7½pf red orange	.30	2.25
b.		Bklt. pane, 4 #98 + 2 #100	110.00	275.00
		Never hinged	275.00	
c.		Bklt. pane, 2 #98 + 4 #99	125.00	300.00
		Never hinged	300.00	
d.		Bklt. pane, 2 #98 + 4 #100	110.00	275.00
		Never hinged	275.00	
e.		Bklt. pane, 2 #82 + 4 #98	37.50	90.00
		Never hinged	90.00	
f.		7½pf yellow orange	3.25	2.25

99	A22	15pf yellow brown	3.00	2.25
100	A22	15pf dk violet ('17)	.20	1.90
b.		Bklt. pane, 4 #82 + 2 #100	110.00	275.00
		Never hinged	275.00	
c.		Bklt. pane, 2 #83 + 4 #100	82.50	210.00
		Never hinged	210.00	
101	A22	35pf red brown ('19)	.20	2.25
		Nos. 96-101 (6)	4.20	13.80
		Set, never hinged	13.50	

See No. 120. For surcharge see No. B2.
Nos. 98e and 100c have the 2 stamps first in the bottom row.

Type of 1902

1920 Engr. Wmk. 192 Perf. 14½

102	A19	3m black violet	1,875.	3,750.
		Never hinged	4,500.	

Republic
National Assembly Issue

A23   A24

Rebuilding
Germany — A25

Designs: A23, Live Stump of Tree Symbolizing that Germany will Survive her Difficulties. A24, New Shoots from Oak Stump Symbolical of New Government.

Perf. 13x13½

1919-20		**Unwmk.**		**Typo.**
105	A23	10pf carmine rose	.20	1.50
106	A24	15pf choc & blue	.20	1.50
107	A25	25pf green & red	.20	1.50
108	A25	30pf red vio & red ('20)	.20	1.50
		Nos. 105-108 (4)	.80	6.00
		Set, never hinged	2.65	

Types of 1902
Perf. 15x14½

1920		**Wmk. 125**		**Offset**
111	A17	1m red	2.00	2.50
a.		Double impression	120.00	600.00
112	A17	1.25m green	1.60	1.90
a.		Double impression	1,200.	
113	A17	1.50m yellow brown	.50	1.90
c.		As "a," double impression	100.00	725.00
114	A21	2.50m lilac rose	.50	2.50
a.		2.50m magenta	1.50	12.00
b.		2.50m brown lilac	.60	2.75
c.		Double impression	100.00	725.00
d.		As "a," double impression		650.00
e.		As "b," double impression		650.00
		Nos. 111-114 (4)	4.60	8.80
		Set, never hinged	14.00	

Nos. 111, 112 and 113 differ from the illustration in many minor respects. The numerals of Nos. 75 and 92 are outlined, with shaded background. Those of No. 111 are plain, with solid background and flags have been added to the top of the building, at right and left.

Types of 1902 Surcharged

1920		**Engr.**		**Perf. 14½**
115	A17	1.25m on 1m green	.40	6.00
116	A17	1.50m on 1m org brn	.40	7.25
117	A21	2.50m on 2m lilac rose	8.75	200.00
		Nos. 115-117 (3)	9.55	213.25
		Set, never hinged	25.00	

Germania Types of 1902-16

1920		**Typo.**		**Perf. 14, 14½**
118	A16	5pf brown	.20	2.00
119	A16	10pf orange	.20	1.50
a.		Tête bêche pair	.90	5.75
		Never hinged	2.25	

d.		Bklt. pane, 4 #119 + 2 #123	2.40	13.00
		Never hinged	6.00	
120	A22	15pf violet brn	.20	1.90
a.		Imperf.	67.50	
		Never hinged	190.00	
c.		Bklt. pane, 4 #84 + 2 #120	7.25	17.00
		Never hinged	17.00	
121	A16	20pf green	.20	2.25
a.		Imperf.		1,200.
123	A16	30pf dull blue	.20	2.50
a.		Tête bêche pair	.90	6.75
		Never hinged	2.25	
b.		Bklt. pane, 2 #123 + 4 #124	2.40	13.00
		Never hinged	6.00	
124	A16	40pf carmine rose	.20	1.90
a.		Tête bêche pair	.90	6.75
		Never hinged	2.25	
b.		Imperf.	150.00	900.00
		Never hinged	375.00	
d.		Bklt. pane, 2 #124 + 4 #126	4.50	42.50
		Never hinged	11.50	
125	A16	50pf red lilac	.60	1.90
126	A16	60pf olive green	.20	1.60
a.		Tête bêche pair	.70	9.75
		Never hinged	1.75	
c.		Imperf.	160.00	
		Never hinged	425.00	
127	A16	75pf red violet	.60	1.90
128	A16	80pf blue violet	.20	2.25
a.		Imperf.	190.00	
		Never hinged	450.00	
129	A16	1m violet & grn	.20	2.25
a.		Imperf.	77.50	
		Never hinged	190.00	
130	A16	1¼m ver & mag	.20	1.90
131	A16	2m carmine & bl	.60	1.50
132	A16	4m black & rose	.20	2.25
		Nos. 118-132 (14)	4.00	27.60
		Set, never hinged	10.50	

Stamps of 1920 Surcharged:

No. 133   No. 135

Nos. 134, 136

1921, Aug.				
133	A16	1.60m on 5pf	.20	2.25
134	A16	3m on 1¼m	.20	2.25
135	A16	5m on 75pf (G)	.20	2.25
136	A16	10m on 75pf	.40	2.25
		Nos. 133-136 (4)	1.00	9.00
		Set, never hinged	3.50	

In 1920 the current stamps of Bavaria were overprinted "Deutsches Reich". These stamps were available for postage throughout Germany, but because they were used almost exclusively in Bavaria, they are listed among the issues of that state.

A26

Iron Workers
A27

Farmers
A29

Miners
A28

Post Horn
A30

Numeral of
Value — A31

Plowing
A32

Wmk. Lozenges (125)

1921		**Typo.**		**Perf. 14**
137	A26	5pf claret	.20	1.75
138	A26	10pf olive green	.20	1.90
a.		Tête bêche pair	.85	21.00
		Never hinged	2.10	
b.		Bklt. pane, 5 #138 + 1 #141	4.50	60.00
		Never hinged	11.50	
139	A26	15pf grnsh blue	.20	1.60
140	A26	25pf dark brown	.20	1.60
141	A26	30pf blue green	.20	1.60
a.		Tête bêche pair	.70	19.00
		Never hinged	1.75	
b.		Bklt. pane, 2 #124 + 4 #141	5.00	42.50
		Never hinged	12.00	
142	A26	40pf red orange	.20	1.40
143	A26	50pf violet	.30	1.60
144	A27	60pf red violet	.20	1.40
145	A27	80pf carmine rose	.20	5.25
146	A28	100pf yellow grn	.30	1.90
147	A28	120pf ultra	.20	1.60
148	A29	150pf orange	.20	1.90
149	A29	100pf slate grn	.20	8.25
150	A30	2m dp vio & rose	.40	3.50
151	A30	3m red & yel	.40	15.00
152	A30	4m dp grn & yel grn	.20	3.50

Engr.

153	A31	5m orange	.30	2.25
154	A31	10m carmine rose	.50	2.50
155	A32	20m indigo & grn	1.10	2.75
a.		Green background inverted	190.00	900.00
		Never hinged	675.00	
		Nos. 137-155 (19)	5.70	61.25
		Set, never hinged	16.00	

See Nos. 156-209, 211, 222-223, 225, 227. For surcharges and overprints see Nos. 241-245, 247-248, 261-262, 273-276, B6-B7, O24.

1922		**Litho.**		**Perf. 14½x14**
156	A31	100m brown vio, *buff*	.20	1.40
157	A31	200m rose, *buff*	.20	1.40
158	A31	300m green, *buff*	.20	1.40
159	A31	400m bis brn, *buff*	.50	2.25
160	A31	500m orange, *buff*	.20	1.40
		Nos. 156-160 (5)	1.30	7.85
		Set, never hinged	3.40	

Postally Used vs. CTO

Values quoted for canceled stamps of the 1921-1923 issues are for postally used stamps. These bring higher prices than the plentiful canceled-to-order stamps made by applying genuine handstamps to remainders. C.T.O. examples sell for about the same price as unused stamps. Certification of postal usage by competent authorities is necessary.

Perf. 14, 14½

1921-22		**Typo.**		**Wmk. 126**
161	A26	5pf claret	.75	200.00
162	A26	10pf olive grn	6.75	175.00
163	A26	15pf grnsh blue	.55	210.00
164	A26	25pf dark brown	.20	3.00
165	A26	30pf blue green	.85	300.00
166	A26	40pf red orange	.20	3.75
167	A26	50pf violet ('21)	.20	1.50
168	A27	60pf red violet	.20	20.00
169	A16	75pf red violet	.35	2.25
170	A26	75pf deep ultra	.20	3.00
171	A27	80pf car rose	.40	55.00
172	A28	100pf olive green	.20	1.50
a.		Imperf.	60.00	1,500.
		Never hinged	150.00	
173	A28	120pf ultra	.70	110.00
174	A16	1¼m ver & mag	.20	1.50
175	A29	150pf orange	.20	1.40
a.		Imperf.	37.50	
		Never hinged	110.00	
176	A29	160pf slate green	.70	160.00
177	A30	2m violet & rose	.20	1.40
178	A30	3m red & yel ('21)	.20	1.40
a.		Imperf.	37.50	375.00
		Never hinged	110.00	
179	A30	4m dp grn & yel grn	.20	1.40
180	A30	5m org & yel	.30	1.90
a.		Imperf.	140.00	
181	A30	10m car & pale rose	.30	1.50
a.		Pale rose (background) omitted	45.00	975.00
182	A30	20m violet & org	.20	2.50
183	A30	30m brown & yel	.20	1.50
184	A30	50m dk grn & vio	.20	1.50
		Nos. 161-184 (24)	14.45	1,261.
		Set, never hinged	37.50	

1922-23

SIX MARKS:
Type I — Numerals upright.
Type II — Numerals leaning toward the right and slightly thinner.

EIGHT MARKS:
Type I — Numerals 2½mm wide with thick strokes.
Type II — Numerals 2mm wide with thinner strokes.

185	A30	2m blue violet	.20	1.50
a.		Imperf.	140.00	
186	A30	3m red	.20	1.50
187	A30	4m dark green	.20	1.50
a.		Imperf.	30.00	
b.		4m deep blue green	1.50	5.25
188	A30	5m orange	.20	1.50
a.		Imperf.	110.00	
189	A30	6m dark blue (II)	.20	1.50
a.		Type I	110.00	1.90
b.		Imperf.		
190	A30	8m olive green (I)	.20	1.50
a.		Type II	.40	37.50
191	A30	20m dk violet ('23)	.20	1.50
192	A30	30m pur brn ('23)	.20	7.25
193	A30	40m lt green	.20	1.90

Engr.

194	A31	5m orange	.25	1.50
a.		Imperf.	140.00	2,100.
195	A31	10m carmine rose	.55	2.25
196	A32	20m indigo & grn	.20	3.50
a.		Imperf.	175.00	2,100.
b.		Green background inverted	32.50	675.00
		Nos. 185-196 (12)	2.80	26.90
		Set, never hinged	8.85	

1922-23   Litho.   Perf. 14½x14

198	A31	50m indigo	.20	1.50
199	A31	100m brn vio, buff ('23)	.20	1.40
200	A31	200m rose, buff ('23)	.20	1.90
201	A31	300m grn, buff ('23)	.20	1.50
202	A31	400m bis brn, buff ('23)	.20	1.50
203	A31	500m org, buff ('23)	.20	1.50
204	A31	1000m gray ('23)	.20	1.50
205	A31	2000m bl ('23)	.35	1.90
206	A31	3000m brn ('23)	.20	2.75
207	A31	4000m vio ('23)	.20	1.50
a.		Imperf.	37.50	190.00
		Never hinged	110.00	
208	A31	5000m gray grn ('23)	.30	1.50
a.		Imperf.	52.50	225.00
		Never hinged	150.00	
209	A31	100,000m ver ('23)	.20	1.40
a.		Imperf.	52.50	225.00
		Never hinged	150.00	
		Nos. 198-209 (12)	2.65	19.85
		Set, never hinged	5.35	

1920-22   Wmk. 127   Typo.

210	A16	1¼m ver & mag	450.00	975.00
		Never hinged	1,350.	
211	A30	50m grn & vio ('22)	2.25	825.00
		Never hinged	5.25	

Wmk. 127 was intended for use only in printing revenue stamps.

Arms of Munich — A33

Wmk. Network (126)
1922, Apr. 22   Typo.   Perf. 13x13½

212	A33	1¼m claret	.20	1.90
213	A33	2m dark violet	.20	1.90
214	A33	3m vermilion	.20	1.90
215	A33	4m deep blue	.20	1.90

Wmk. Lozenges (125)

216	A33	10m brown, buff	.55	2.75
217	A33	20m lilac rose, pink	3.25	11.50
		Nos. 212-217 (6)	4.60	21.85
		Set, never hinged	14.70	

Munich Industrial Fair.

Type of 1921 and

Miners — A34   A35

1922-23   Wmk. 126   Perf. 14

221	A34	5m orange	.20	13.00
222	A29	10m dull blue ('22)	.20	1.50
223	A29	12m vermilion ('22)	.20	1.50
224	A34	20m red lilac	.20	1.50
225	A29	25m olive brown	.20	1.50
226	A34	30m olive green	.20	2.25
227	A29	40m green	.20	1.50
228	A34	50m grnsh blue	.35	125.00
229	A35	100m violet	.20	1.50
230	A35	200m carmine rose	.20	1.50
231	A35	300m green	.20	1.40
232	A35	400m dark brown	.20	5.75
233	A35	500m red orange	.20	6.50
234	A35	1000m slate	.20	1.40
		Nos. 221-234 (14)	2.95	165.80
		Set, never hinged	7.00	

The 50m was issued only in vertical coils.
Nos. 222-223 exist imperf.
For surcharges and overprints see Nos. 246, 249-260, 263-271, 277, 310, B5, O22-O23, O25-O28.

Wartburg Castle — A36

Cathedral of Cologne — A37

1923   Engr.

237	A36	5000m deep blue	.30	3.25
a.		Imperf.	300.00	1,100.
		Never hinged	750.00	
238	A37	10,000m brn ol	.30	4.00
		Set, never hinged	1.80	

Abbreviations:
Th = (Tausend) Thousand
Mil = (Million) Million
Mlrd = (Milliarde) Billion

A38

1923   Typo.

238A	A38	5th m grnsh blue	.20	17.00
b.		Imperf.	90.00	
		Never hinged	240.00	
239	A38	50th m bister	.20	1.50
a.		Imperf.	22.50	3,750.
		Never hinged	60.00	
240	A38	75th m dark violet	.20	11.00
		Nos. 238A-240 (3)	.60	29.50
		Set, never hinged	1.10	

For surcharges see Nos. 272, 278.

Stamps and Types of 1922-23 Surcharged in Black, Blue, Green or Brown with Bars over Original Value

Wmk. Lozenges (125)
1923   Perf. 14

241	A26	8th m on 30pf	.20	1.50
a.		"8" inverted	21.00	325.00
		Never hinged	60.00	

Wmk. Network (126)

242	A26	5th m on 40pf	.20	1.60
242A	A26	8th m on 30pf	16.00	6,000.
243	A29	15th m on 40m	.20	1.50

244	A29	20th m on 12m	.20	1.50
a.		Inverted surcharge	110.00	1,000.
245	A29	20th m on 25m	.20	2.25
246	A35	20th m on 200m	.20	2.25
a.		Inverted surcharge	57.50	750.00
		Never hinged	150.00	
247	A29	25th m on 25m	.20	14.50
248	A29	30th m on 10m dp bl	.20	1.40
a.		Inverted surcharge	67.50	175.00
		Never hinged	175.00	
249	A35	30th m on 200m pale bl (Bl)	.20	1.50
a.		Without surcharge	110.00	
		Never hinged	225.00	
250	A35	75th m on 300m yel grn	.20	14.50
a.		Imperf.	45.00	
		Never hinged	125.00	
251	A35	75th m on 400m yel grn	.20	1.50
252	A35	75th m on 1000m yel grn	.20	1.90
a.		Without surcharge	110.00	
		Never hinged	225.00	
253	A35	100th m on 100m	.20	2.25
a.		Double surcharge	37.50	450.00
		Never hinged	97.50	
b.		Inverted surcharge	14.50	
		Never hinged	37.50	
254	A35	100th m on 400m bluish grn (G)	.20	1.40
a.		Imperf.	50.00	525.00
		Never hinged	110.00	
b.		Without surcharge	110.00	
		Never hinged	225.00	
255	A35	125th m on 1000m sal	.20	1.90
256	A35	250th m on 200m	.20	5.25
a.		Inverted surcharge	35.00	
		Never hinged	90.00	
b.		Double surcharge	52.50	
		Never hinged	140.00	
257	A35	250th m on 300m dp grn	.20	17.00
a.		Inverted surcharge	35.00	
		Never hinged	90.00	
258	A35	250th m on 400m	.20	19.00
a.		Inverted surcharge	26.00	
		Never hinged	75.00	
259	A35	250th m on 500m pink	.20	1.50
a.		Imperf.	52.50	675.00
		Never hinged	125.00	
260	A35	250th m on 500m red org	.20	19.00
a.		Double surcharge	30.00	975.00
		Never hinged	75.00	
b.		Inverted surcharge	30.00	
		Never hinged	82.50	
261	A26	800th m on 5pf lt grn (G)	.20	4.25
a.		Imperf.	35.00	150.00
		Never hinged	90.00	
262	A26	800th m on 10pf lt grn (G)	.20	5.00
a.		Imperf.	30.00	
		Never hinged	90.00	
263	A35	800th m on 200m	.20	75.00
a.		Double surcharge	75.00	975.00
		Never hinged	190.00	
b.		Inverted surcharge	37.50	
		Never hinged	110.00	
264	A35	800th m on 300m lt grn (G)	.20	5.00
a.		Black surcharge	47.50	
265	A35	800th m on 400m dk brn	.20	14.50
a.		Inverted surcharge	42.50	
		Never hinged	110.00	
b.		Double surcharge	75.00	
		Never hinged	190.00	
266	A35	800th m on 400m lt grn (G)	.20	3.75
267	A35	800th m on 500m lt grn (G)	.20	1,500.
a.		800th m on 500m red org (Bk)	37.50	
268	A35	800th m on 1000m lt grn (G)	.20	1.50
269	A35	2mil m on 200m rose red	.20	2.25
b.		2mil m on 200m car rose (#230)	1,500.	
		Never hinged	3,400.	
270	A35	2mil m on 300m dp grn	.20	2.25
a.		Inverted surcharge	42.50	
		Never hinged	110.00	
b.		Double surcharge	75.00	
		Never hinged	190.00	
271	A35	2mil m on 500m dl rose	.20	6.50

272	A38	2mil m on 5th m dl rose	.20	1.50
b.		Imperf.	42.50	125.00

Nos. 264a, 267a were not put in use.

Serrate Roulette 13½

273	A26	400th m on 15pf bis (Br)	.20	4.50
a.		Imperf.	52.50	275.00
		Never hinged	125.00	
274	A26	400th m on 25pf bis (Br)	.20	4.50
a.		Imperf.	90.00	275.00
		Never hinged	225.00	
275	A26	400th m on 30pf bis (Br)	.20	4.50
a.		Imperf.	45.00	
		Never hinged	110.00	
b.		Double surcharge	90.00	
		Never hinged	175.00	
276	A26	400th m on 40pf bis (Br)	.20	4.50
a.		Imperf.	45.00	—
		Never hinged	110.00	
b.		Double surcharge	90.00	
		Never hinged	175.00	
277	A35	2mil m on 200m rose red	.45	150.00
278	A38	2mil m on 5th m dull rose	.20	9.00
		Nos. 241-278 (39)	23.85	7,911.
		Set, never hinged	51.00	

Nos. 272-276 exist without surcharge. Value each, $150 unused, $375 never hinged.

A39   A39a

The stamps of types A39 and A39a usually have the value darker than the rest of the design.

1923   Wmk. 126   Perf. 14

280	A39	500th m brown	.20	2.75
281	A39	1mil m grnsh bl	.20	1.60
a.		Imperf.	52.50	350.00
		Never hinged	110.00	
282	A39	2mil m dull vio	.20	20.00
284	A39	4mil m yel grn	.20	1.50
a.		Value double	57.50	
		Never hinged	140.00	
b.		Imperf.	42.50	
		Never hinged	97.50	
285	A39	5mil m rose	.20	1.50
286	A39	10mil m red	.20	1.50
a.		Value double	50.00	3,750.
		Never hinged	125.00	
287	A39	20mil m ultra	.20	1.90
288	A39	30mil m red brn	.20	9.25
289	A39	50mil m dull ol grn	.20	1.90
a.		Imperf.	52.50	350.00
		Never hinged	125.00	
b.		Value inverted	45.00	
		Never hinged	120.00	
290	A39	100mil m gray	.20	1.50
291	A39	200mil m bis brn	.20	1.50
a.		Imperf.	42.50	
		Never hinged	97.50	
293	A39	500mil m ol grn	.20	1.40
294	A39a	1mlrd m choc	.30	1.90
295	A39a	2mlrd m pale brn & grn	.20	1.90
296	A39a	5mlrd m yellow & brn	.20	1.90
297	A39a	10mlrd m ap grn & grn	.20	1.50
a.		Imperf.	45.00	275.00
		Never hinged	110.00	
298	A39a	20mlrd m bluish grn & brn	.20	1.90
299	A39a	50mlrd m bl & dp bl	.20	35.00
		Nos. 280-299 (18)	3.70	90.00
		Set, never hinged	11.50	

The variety "value omitted" exists on Nos. 280-281, 284-287, 290-291, 293-294, 296 and 298-299. Values $37.50 to $100 hinged, $75 to $190 never hinged.
See Nos. 301-309. For surcharges and overprints see Nos. 311-321, O40-O46.

Serrate Roulette 13½

301	A39	10mil m red	.55	45.00
302	A39	20mil m ultra	.55	300.00
303	A39	50mil m dull grn	.55	6.00
304	A39	200mil m bis brn	.55	11.50
305	A39a	1mlrd m choc	.55	7.50
306	A39a	2mlrd m pale brn & grn	.55	3.50
307	A39a	5mlrd m yel & brn	.75	2.25
308	A39a	20mlrd m bluish grn & brn	.75	11.00
309	A39a	50mlrd m bl & dp bl	1.90	675.00
		Nos. 301-309 (9)	6.70	1,061.
		Set, never hinged	18.50	

**Stamps and Types of 1923
Surcharged with New Values**

1923 — Perf. 14

Design Type A35

310	1mlrd m on 100m vio		.20	29.00
a.	Inverted surcharge		110.00	
	Never hinged		300.00	
b.	Deep reddish purple		60.00	3,600.
	Never hinged		150.00	

Design Type A39

311	5mlrd m on 2mil m		.20	125.00
a.	Inverted surcharge		19.00	
	Never hinged		57.50	
b.	Double surcharge		45.00	
	Never hinged		110.00	
312	5mlrd m on 4mil m		.20	22.50
a.	Inverted surcharge		37.50	1,200.
	Never hinged		110.00	
b.	Double surcharge		37.50	
	Never hinged		97.50	
313	5mlrd m on 10mil m		.20	2.75
a.	Inverted surcharge		19.00	1,100.
	Never hinged		57.50	
b.	Double surcharge		37.50	
	Never hinged		97.50	
314	10mlrd m on 20mil m		.20	4.50
a.	Double surcharge		45.00	
	Never hinged		125.00	
b.	Inverted surcharge		26.00	
	Never hinged		75.00	
315	10mlrd m on 50mil m		.20	4.50
a.	Inverted surcharge		19.00	900.00
	Never hinged		57.50	
b.	Double surcharge		45.00	
	Never hinged		125.00	
316	10mlrd m on 100mil m		.20	7.50
a.	Inverted surcharge		26.00	1,500.
	Never hinged		75.00	
b.	Double surcharge		45.00	
	Never hinged		125.00	
	Nos. 310-316 (7)		1.40	195.75
	Set, never hinged		5.00	

No. 310b was issued in Bavaria only and is known as the Hitler provisional. Excellent forgeries exist.

Serrate Roulette 13½

Design Type A39

319	5mlrd m on 10mil m		1.90	190.00
a.	Inverted surcharge		26.00	1,100.
	Never hinged		67.50	
b.	Double surcharge		45.00	
	Never hinged		110.00	
320	10mlrd m on 20mil m		5.00	110.00
321	10mlrd m on 50mil m		1.90	37.50
a.	Inverted surcharge		26.00	1,100.
	Never hinged		67.50	
	Nos. 319-321 (3)		8.80	337.50
	Set, never hinged		22.50	

A40

German Eagle — A41

1923 — Perf. 14

323	A40	3pf brown	.35	.20
324	A40	5pf dark green	.35	.20
325	A40	10pf carmine	.35	.20
326	A40	20pf deep ultra	.95	.35
327	A40	50pf orange	2.75	1.00
328	A40	100pf brn vio	8.25	1.10
	Nos. 323-328 (6)		13.00	3.05
	Set, never hinged		80.00	

For overprints see Nos. O47-O52.

Imperf

323a	A40	3pf	125.00	275.00
324a	A40	5pf	110.00	
325a	A40	10pf	110.00	190.00
326a	A40	20pf	140.00	225.00
327a	A40	50pf	800.00	—
328a	A40	100pf	175.00	—
	Nos. 323a-328a (6)		1,460.00	690.00
	Set, never hinged		3,100.	

Value Omitted

323b	A40	3pf	160.00	300.00
324b	A40	5pf	160.00	300.00
325b	A40	10pf	160.00	
326b	A40	20pf	160.00	
327b	A40	50pf	160.00	
328b	A40	100pf	160.00	
	Nos. 323b-328b (6)		960.00	
	Set, never hinged		2,250.	

1924 — Wmk. 126

330	A41	3pf lt brown	.30	.35
331	A41	5pf lt green	.30	.35
332	A41	10pf vermilion	.35	.35
333	A41	20pf dull blue	1.90	.35
334	A41	30pf rose lilac	1.90	.45
335	A41	40pf olive green	13.00	.75
336	A41	50pf orange	13.50	1.00
	Nos. 330-336 (7)		31.25	3.70
	Set, never hinged		275.00	

The values above 5pf have "Pf" in the upper right corner.
For overprints see Nos. O53-O61.

Imperf.

330a	A41	3pf	140.00	375.00
331a	A41	5pf	175.00	375.00
332a	A41	10pf	225.00	
333a	A41	20pf	160.00	
334a	A41	30pf	160.00	
335a	A41	40pf	190.00	
	Nos. 330a-335a (6)		1,050.	
	Set, never hinged		2,475.	

Rheinstein Castle — A43

View of Cologne A44

Marienburg Castle — A45

1924 — Engr. — Wmk. 126

337	A43	1m green	10.50	2.25
338	A44	2m blue	18.00	2.25
339	A45	3m claret	21.00	5.25
	Nos. 337-339 (3)		49.50	9.50
	Set, never hinged		153.75	

See No. 387.

Dr. Heinrich von Stephan
A46   A47

1924-28 — Typo.

340	A46	10pf dark green	.55	.30
a.	Imperf		325.00	
341	A46	20pf dark blue	1.25	.60
342	A46	60pf red brown	3.75	.75
a.	Chalky paper ('28)		21.00	13.50
343	A47	80pf slate	9.75	1.50
	Nos. 340-343 (4)		15.30	3.15
	Set, never hinged		77.75	

Universal Postal Union, 50th anniversary.

Traffic Wheel — A48

German Eagle Watching Rhine Valley — A49

1925, May 30 — Perf. 13½x13

345	A48	5pf deep green	3.00	5.25
346	A48	10pf vermilion	3.75	9.75
	Set, never hinged		38.00	

German Traffic Exhibition, Munich, May 30-Oct. 11, 1925.

1925 — Perf. 14

347	A49	5pf green	.45	.35
348	A49	10pf vermilion	1.10	.35
349	A49	20pf deep blue	4.50	1.00
	Nos. 347-349 (3)		6.05	1.70
	Set, never hinged		35.00	

1000 years' union of the Rhineland with Germany.

Speyer Cathedral
A50

1925, Sept. 11 — Engr.

350	A50	5m dull green	32.50	14.50
	Never hinged		125.00	

Johann Wolfgang von Goethe — A51

Designs: 3pf, 25pf, Goethe. 5pf, Friedrich von Schiller. 8pf, 20pf, Ludwig van Beethoven. 10pf, Frederick the Great. 15pf, Immanuel Kant. 30pf, Gotthold Ephraim Lessing. 40pf, Gottfried Wilhelm Leibnitz. 50pf, Johann Sebastian Bach. 80pf, Albrecht Durer.

1926-27 — Typo. — Perf. 14

351	A51	3pf olive brown	1.25	.30
352	A51	3pf bister ('27)	1.25	.30
353	A51	5pf dark green	1.25	.30
b.	5pf light green ('27)		1.10	.30
	Never hinged		9.50	
354	A51	8pf blue grn ('27)	1.60	.30
355	A51	10pf carmine	1.60	.30
356	A51	15pf vermilion	2.40	.30
a.	Booklet pane of 8 + 2 labels		275.00	
	Never hinged		675.00	
357	A51	20pf myrtle grn	11.00	1.10
358	A51	25pf blue	3.50	.90
359	A51	30pf olive grn	6.50	.50
360	A51	40pf dp violet	12.00	.55
361	A51	50pf brown	15.00	7.50
362	A51	80pf chocolate	30.00	4.75
	Nos. 351-362 (12)		87.35	17.10
	Set, never hinged		865.00	

Nos. 351-354, 356 and 357 exist imperf. See *Scott Classic Specialized Catalogue of Stamps & Covers* for detailed listing.

Nos. 354, 356 and 358 Overprinted

1927, Oct. 10

363	A51	8pf blue green	17.00	62.50
364	A51	15pf vermilion	17.00	62.50
365	A51	25pf blue	17.00	62.50
	Nos. 363-365 (3)		51.00	187.50
	Set, never hinged		180.00	

"I.A.A." stands for "Internationales Arbeitsamt," (Intl. Labor Bureau), an agency of the League of Nations. Issued in connection with a meeting of the I.A.A. in Berlin, Oct. 10-15, 1927, they were on sale to the public.

Pres. Friedrich Ebert
A60

Pres. Paul von Hindenburg
A61

1928-32 — Typo. — Perf. 14

366	A60	3pf bister	.20	.60
367	A61	4pf lt blue ('31)	.75	1.25
a.	Tête bêche pair		4.75	9.00
b.	Bklt. pane of 9 + label		35.00	90.00
	Never hinged		90.00	
368	A61	5pf lt green	.40	.60
a.	Tête bêche pair		4.25	9.00
	Never hinged		9.00	
b.	Imperf.		125.00	
	Never hinged		250.00	
c.	Bklt. pane of 6 + 4 labels		22.50	60.00
	Never hinged		60.00	
d.	Bklt. pane, 4 #368 + 6 #369		35.00	90.00
	Never hinged		90.00	
369	A60	6pf lt olive grn ('32)	.75	.65
a.	Bklt. pane, 2 #369 + 8 #373		55.00	135.00
	Never hinged		135.00	
370	A60	8pf dark green	.20	.60
a.	Tête bêche pair		3.75	7.50
	Never hinged		7.50	
371	A60	10pf vermilion	2.00	2.25
372	A60	10pf red violet ('30)	.95	.75
373	A61	12pf orange ('32)	1.10	.65
a.	Tête bêche pair		11.00	22.50
	Never hinged		22.50	
374	A61	15pf car rose	.60	.60
a.	Tête bêche pair		7.75	15.00
	Never hinged		30.00	
b.	Bklt. pane 6 + 4 labels		27.50	67.50
	Never hinged		67.50	
375	A60	20pf Prus green	6.25	3.75
a.	Imperf.		300.00	
	Never hinged		600.00	
376	A60	20pf gray ('30)	6.00	.75
377	A60	25pf blue	7.50	.90
378	A60	30pf olive green	5.00	.90
379	A61	40pf violet	13.00	.90
380	A61	45pf orange	9.00	3.00
381	A61	50pf brown	9.00	2.50
382	A60	60pf orange brn	11.50	3.00
383	A61	80pf chocolate	21.00	6.75
384	A61	80pf yel bis ('30)	9.00	2.25
	Nos. 366-384 (19)		104.20	32.65
	Set, never hinged		1,080.	

Stamps of 1928 Overprinted

1930, June 30

385	A60	8pf dark green	1.10	.90
386	A61	15pf carmine rose	1.10	.90
	Set, never hinged		15.00	

Issued in commemoration of the final evacuation of the Rhineland by the Allied forces.

View of
Cologne
A63

1930　　　　Engr.　　　Wmk. 126
Inscribed: "Reichsmark"

387　A63　2m dark blue　　　　29.00　14.00
　　　Never hinged　　　　　　100.00

A type of design A43 in green exists with "Reichsmark" instead of "Mark." It was not issued, though some examples are known in private hands. Value $15,000.

Pres. von　　　　Frederick the
Hindenburg　　　　　Great
A64　　　　　　　　A65

1932, Oct. 1　　Typo.　　Wmk. 126
391　A64　4pf blue　　　　　　.55　.60
392　A64　5pf brt green　　　　.75　.60
393　A64　12pf dp orange　　　4.50　.60
394　A64　15pf dk red　　　　3.75　9.75
395　A64　25pf ultra　　　　　1.10　.75
396　A64　40pf violet　　　　18.00　1.50
397　A64　50pf dk brown　　　6.00　11.00
　　Nos. 391-397 (7)　　　34.65　24.80
　　Set, never hinged　　　129.00

85th birthday of von Hindenburg.
See Nos. 401-431, 436-441. For surcharges and overprints see France N27-N58, Luxembourg N1-N16 and Poland N17-N29.

1933, Apr. 12　　　　　　Photo.
398　A65　6pf dk green　　　　.60　.90
　a.　Tête bêche pair　　　　5.25　13.50
　　　Never hinged　　　　　10.50
399　A65　12pf carmine　　　　.60　.90
　a.　Tête bêche pair　　　　5.25　13.50
　　　Never hinged　　　　　10.50
　b.　Bklt. pane of 5 + label　19.00　45.00
　　　Never hinged　　　　　45.00
400　A65　12pf ultra　　　　37.50　21.00
　　Nos. 398-400 (3)　　　38.70　22.80
　　Set, never hinged　　　249.00

Celebration of Potsdam Day.

Hindenburg Type of 1932

1933　　　　　　　　　Typo.
401　A64　3pf olive bister　　13.50　.75
402　A64　4pf dull blue　　　3.75　.75
403　A64　6pf dk green　　　1.90　.75
404　A64　8pf dp orange　　　6.00　.75
　a.　Bklt. pane, 3 #404 + 5 #406　75.00　180.00
　　　Never hinged　　　　　180.00
　b.　Open "D"　　　　　　19.00　3.75
　　　Never hinged　　　　　37.50
405　A64　10pf chocolate　　3.75　.75
406　A64　12pf dp carmine　2.25　.75
　a.　Bklt. pane, 4 #392 + 4 #406　40.00　97.50
　　　Never hinged　　　　　97.50
407　A64　15pf maroon　　　5.25　26.00
408　A64　20pf brt blue　　6.75　1.50
409　A64　30pf olive grn　6.75　1.40
410　A64　40pf red violet　27.50　2.75
411　A64　50pf dk grn & blk　15.00　2.25
412　A64　60pf claret & blk　27.50　.95
413　A64　80pf dk blue & blk　9.00　1.10
414　A64　100pf orange & blk　24.00　12.50
　　Nos. 401-414 (14)　　152.90　52.95
　　Set, never hinged

Hindenburg Type of 1932

1933-36　　Wmk. 237　　Perf. 14
415　A64　1pf black　　　　　.20　.35
　a.　Bklt. pane, 4 #415, 3 #417, label　4.00　10.50
　　　Never hinged　　　　　10.50
　b.　Bklt. pane, 3 #415, 3 #416 + 2 #418　6.00　15.00
　　　Never hinged　　　　　15.00
　c.　Bklt. pane, 2 #415, 5 #420, label　9.00　22.50
　　　Never hinged　　　　　22.50
　d.　Bklt. pane, 4 #415 + 4 #422　3.25　7.50
　　　Never hinged　　　　　7.50
416　A64　3pf olive bis ('34)　.20　.35
　a.　Bklt. pane, 4 #416 + 4 #418　3.00　7.50
　　　Never hinged　　　　　7.50
　b.　Bklt. pane, 4 #416 + 4 #419　3.00　7.50
　　　Never hinged　　　　　7.50
　c.　Bklt. pane, 6 #416, 1 #422, label　2.50　6.00
　　　Never hinged　　　　　6.00
417　A64　4pf dull blue ('34)　.20　.35
　a.　Bklt. pane, 4 #417, 4 #422, label　7.50　19.00
　　　Never hinged　　　　　19.00
418　A64　5pf brt green ('34)　.20　.35
　a.　Bklt. pane, 2 #418, 5 #419, label　5.25　13.50
　　　Never hinged　　　　　13.50

　b.　Bklt. pane, 2 #418, 3 #419 + 3 #420　4.50　11.00
　　　Never hinged　　　　　11.00
　c.　Bklt. pane, 4 #418 + 4 #420　5.25　13.50
　　　Never hinged　　　　　13.50
419　A64　6pf dk green ('34)　.20　.35
　b.　Bklt. pane of 7 + label　9.00　22.50
　　　Never hinged　　　　　22.50
　c.　Bklt. pane, 1 #419, 6 #422, label　25.00　67.50
　　　Never hinged　　　　　67.50
420　A64　8pf dp orange ('34)　.20　.35
　a.　Bklt. pane, 3 #420, 4 #422, label　5.25　13.50
　　　Never hinged　　　　　13.50
　b.　Open "D"　　　　　　4.50　4.50
　　　Never hinged　　　　　13.00
421　A64　10pf choc ('34)　.20　.35
422　A64　12pf dp car ('34)　.20　.35
　a.　Bklt. pane of 7 + label　9.00　22.50
　　　Never hinged　　　　　22.50
423　A64　15pf maroon ('34)　.30　.35
424　A64　20pf brt blue ('34)　.45　.35
425　A64　25pf ultra ('34)　.45　.35
426　A64　30pf olive grn ('34)　.75　.35
427　A64　40pf red violet ('34)　.75　.35
428　A64　50pf dk grn & blk ('34)　3.00　.35
429　A64　60pf claret & blk ('34)　.75　.35
430　A64　80pf dk bl & blk ('36)　2.25　1.25
431　A64　100pf orange & blk ('34)　3.00　1.10
　　Nos. 415-431 (17)　　13.30　7.60
　　Set, never hinged　　100.00

Karl
Peters — A66

Swastika, Sun
and
Nuremberg
Castle — A70

Designs: 3pf, Franz Adolf E. Lüderitz. 6pf, Dr. Gustav Nachtigal. 12pf, Karl Peters. 25pf, Hermann von Wissmann.

1934, June 30　　　Perf. 13x13½
432　A66　3pf brown & choc　2.25　6.00
433　A66　6pf dk grn & choc　1.10　1.50
434　A66　12pf dk car & choc　1.75　1.50
435　A66　25pf brt blue & choc　9.00　20.00
　　Nos. 432-435 (4)　　14.10　29.00
　　Set, never hinged　　149.00

Issued in remembrance of the lost colonies of Germany.

**Hindenburg Memorial Issue
Type of 1932
With Black Border**

1934, Sept. 4　　　　Perf. 14
436　A64　3pf olive bister　.75　.45
437　A64　5pf brt green　.75　.55
438　A64　6pf dk green　1.40　.45
439　A64　8pf vermilion　2.25　.45
440　A64　12pf deep carmine　2.25　.45
441　A64　25pf ultra　6.75　8.25
　　Nos. 436-441 (6)　　14.15　10.60
　　Set, never hinged　　120.00

1934, Sept. 1　　　　Photo.
442　A64　6pf dark green　3.00　.60
443　A70　12pf dark carmine　3.75　.60
　　Set, never hinged　　63.50

Nazi Congress at Nuremberg.
Imperfs exist. Value never hinged, each $750.

Allegory　　　　German
"Saar Belongs　　Eagle
to Germany"　　　A72
A71

1934, Aug. 26　　Typo.　　Wmk. 237
444　A71　6pf dark green　3.00　.60
445　A72　12pf dark carmine　3.25　.60
　　Set, never hinged　　63.50

Issued to mark the Saar Plebiscite.

Friedrich von　　　Germania
Schiller　　　　Welcoming
A73　　　　　Home the
　　　　　　　Saar
　　　　　　　A74

1934, Nov. 5
446　A73　6pf green　　　　2.50　.60
447　A73　12pf carmine　　　4.50　.60
　　Set, never hinged　　82.50

175th anniv. of the birth of von Schiller.

1935, Jan. 16　　　　Photo.
448　A74　3pf brown　　　　.35　1.10
449　A74　6pf dark green　　.35　.75
450　A74　12pf lake　　　　1.75　.75
451　A74　25pf dark blue　　7.25　8.25
　　Nos. 448-451 (4)　　9.70　10.85
　　Set, never hinged　　92.50

Return of the Saar to Germany.

German　　　　Wreath and
Soldier　　　　Swastika
A75　　　　　　A76

1935, Mar. 15
452　A75　6pf dark green　　.75　1.50
453　A75　12pf copper red　　.75　1.50
　　Set, never hinged　　15.75

Issued to commemorate War Heroes' Day.

1935, Apr. 26　　　　Unwmk.
454　A76　6pf dark green　　.75　1.40
455　A76　12pf crimson　　.90　1.40
　　Set, never hinged　　18.50

Young Workers' Professional Competitions.

Heinrich　　　　"The
Schütz — A77　　Eagle" — A80

Wmk. Swastikas (237)

1935, June 21　　Engr.　　Perf. 14
456　A77　6pf shown　　　　.45　.50
457　A77　12pf Bach　　　　.65　.50
458　A77　25pf Handel　　1.10　.90
　　Nos. 456-458 (3)　　2.20　1.90
　　Set, never hinged　　24.00

Schutz-Bach-Handel celebration.

1935, July 10　　　　Perf. 14
Designs: 12pf, Modern express train. 25pf, "The Hamburg Flyer." 40pf, Streamlined locomotive.

459　A80　6pf dark green　　.90　.60
460　A80　12pf copper red　　.90　.60
461　A80　25pf ultra　　　5.00　1.75
462　A80　40pf red violet　8.25　1.75
　　Nos. 459-462 (4)　　15.05　4.70
　　Set, never hinged　　102.00

Centenary of railroad in Germany.
Exist imperf. Values: Nos. 459-460, $900 each; Nos. 461-462, $1,100 each.

Bugler of Hitler　　Eagle and
Youth Movement　Swastika over
A84　　　　Nuremberg
　　　　　　A85

1935, July 25　　　　　Photo.
463　A84　6pf deep green　　1.10　2.25
464　A84　15pf brown lake　　1.50　2.50
　　Set, never hinged　　18.75

Hitler Youth Meeting.

1935, Aug. 30　　　　Engr.
465　A85　6pf gray green　　.75　.35
466　A85　12pf dark carmine　1.90　.35
　　Set, never hinged　　15.00

1935 Nazi Congress at Nuremberg.

Nazi Flag　　　Airplane — A87
Bearer and
Feldherrnhalle
at
Munich — A86

1935, Nov. 5　Photo.　Perf. 13½
467　A86　3pf brown　　　　.30　.60
468　A86　12pf dark carmine　.45　.60
　　Set, never hinged　　11.25

12th anniv. of the 1st Hitler "Putsch" at Munich, Nov. 9, 1923.

1936, Jan. 6
469　A87　40pf sapphire　　6.40　3.25
　　Never hinged　　　　45.00

10th anniv. of the Lufthansa air service.

Gottlieb　　　　Carl
Daimler — A88　Benz — A89

1936, Feb. 15　　　　Perf. 14
470　A88　6pf dark green　　.50　.75
471　A89　12pf copper red　　.50　.75
　　Set, never hinged　　12.00

The 50th anniv. of the automobile; Intl. Automobile and Motorcycle Show, Berlin.

Otto von　　　Symbolical of
Guericke　　Municipalities
A90　　　　　A91

1936, May 4
472　A90　6pf dark green　　.30　.45
　　Never hinged　　　　1.20

250th anniv. of the death of the German inventor, Otto von Guericke, May 11, 1686.

1936, June 3
473　A91　3pf dark brown　　.65　.30
474　A91　5pf deep green　　.65　.30
475　A91　12pf lake　　　　1.00　.50
476　A91　25pf dark ultra　1.60　1.00
　　Nos. 473-476 (4)　　3.90　2.10
　　Set, never hinged　　15.00

6th Intl. Cong. of Municipalities, June 7-13.

Allegory of Recreation Congress A92

Salute to Swastika A93

1936, June 30
477	A92	6pf dark green	.35	.50
478	A92	15pf deep claret	.55	.95
		Set, never hinged	13.50	

World Congress for Vacation and Recreation held at Hamburg.

1936, Sept. 3 *Perf. 14*
479	A93	6pf deep green	.45	.50
480	A93	12pf copper red	.55	1.00
		Set, never hinged	14.00	

The 1936 Nazi Congress.

Shield Bearer — A94

German and Austrian Carrying Nazi Flag — A95

1937, Mar. 3 **Engr.** **Unwmk.**
481	A94	3pf brown	.55	.30
482	A94	6pf green	.55	.30
483	A94	12pf carmine	1.25	.60
		Nos. 481-483 (3)	2.35	1.20
		Set, never hinged	12.00	

The Reich's Air Protection League.

Wmk. Swastikas (237)
1938, Apr. 8 **Photo.** *Perf. 14x13½*
Size: 23x28mm
484	A95	6pf dark green	.80	.65
		Never hinged	2.00	

Unwmk. *Perf. 12½*
Size: 21½x26mm
485	A95	6pf deep green	.80	1.40
		Never hinged	2.00	

Union of Austria and Germany.

Cathedral Island A96

Hermann Goering Stadium A97

Town Hall, Breslau — A98

Centennial Hall, Breslau — A99

1938, June 21 **Engr.** *Perf. 14*
486	A96	3pf dark brown	.50	.55
487	A97	6pf deep green	.50	.55
488	A98	12pf copper red	.75	.55
489	A99	15pf violet brown	1.50	.80
		Nos. 486-489 (4)	3.25	2.45
		Set, never hinged	12.00	

16th German Gymnastic and Sports Festival held at Breslau, July 23-31, 1938.

Nazi Emblem — A100

1939, Apr. 4 **Photo.** **Wmk. 237**
490	A100	6pf dark green	1.90	4.00
491	A100	12pf deep carmine	2.50	4.00
		Set, never hinged	20.00	

Young Workers' Professional Competitions.

St. Mary's Church — A101

The Krantor, Danzig — A102

1939, Sept. 18
492	A101	6pf dark green	.45	.80
493	A102	12pf orange red	.65	.80
		Set, never hinged	4.00	

Unification of Danzig with the Reich.

Johannes Gutenberg and Library at Leipzig — A103

Designs: 6pf, "High House," Leipzig. 12pf, Old Town Hall, Leipzig. 25pf, View of Leipzig Fair.

Inscribed "Leipziger Messe"
Perf. 10½
1940, Mar. 3 **Photo.** **Unwmk.**
494	A103	3pf dark brown	.45	.50
495	A103	6pf dk gray green	.45	.50
496	A103	12pf henna brown	.45	.50
497	A103	25pf ultra	1.10	1.25
		Nos. 494-497 (4)	2.45	2.75
		Set, never hinged	8.00	

Leipzig Fair.

House of Nations, Leipzig — A107

6pf, Concert Hall, Leipzig. 12pf, Leipzig Fair Office. 25pf, Railroad Terminal, Leipzig.

Inscribed: "Reichsmesse Leipzig, 1941"
1941, Mar. 1 *Perf. 14x13½*
498	A107	3pf brown	.25	1.00
499	A107	6pf green	.25	1.00
500	A107	12pf dark red	.35	1.25
501	A107	25pf bright blue	.80	1.60
		Nos. 498-501 (4)	1.65	4.85
		Set, never hinged	10.00	

Leipzig Fair.

Fashion Allegory — A111

Vienna Fair Hall — A112

"Burgtheater" A113

Monument to Prince Eugene A114

1941, Mar. 8 *Perf. 13½x14*
502	A111	3pf dark red brown	.40	.55
503	A112	6pf brt blue grn	.40	.55
504	A113	12pf scarlet	.40	.65
505	A114	25pf bright blue	1.10	1.60
		Nos. 502-505 (4)	2.30	3.35
		Set, never hinged	10.00	

Vienna Fair.

A115

Adolf Hitler — A116

1941-44 **Typo.** *Perf. 14*
Size: 18½x22½mm
506	A115	1pf gray black	.20	.30
a.		Bklt. pane, 4 #506 + 4 #509	1.10	2.50
		Never hinged	2.50	
507	A115	3pf lt brown	.20	.30
a.		Bklt. pane, 6 #507 + 2 #510	1.20	3.00
		Never hinged	3.00	
508	A115	4pf slate	.20	.30
a.		Bklt. pane, 4 #508, 2 #511 + 2 labels	1.00	2.50
		Never hinged	2.50	
509	A115	5pf dp yellow grn	.20	.30
510	A115	6pf purple	.20	.30
a.		Bklt. pane of 7 + label	7.75	19.00
		Never hinged	19.00	
511	A115	8pf red	.20	.30
511A	A115	10pf dk brown ('42)	.20	.45
511B	A115	12pf carmine ('42)	.20	.45

Engr.
512	A115	10pf dark brown	.35	.30
513	A115	12pf brt carmine	.35	.30
a.		Bklt. pane of 6 + 2 labels	3.25	7.50
		Never hinged	7.50	
514	A115	15pf brown lake	.20	.35
515	A115	16pf peacock green	.20	1.50
516	A115	20pf blue	.20	.35
517	A115	24pf orange brown	.20	1.50

Size: 21½x26mm
518	A115	25pf brt ultra	.20	.45
519	A115	30pf olive green	.20	.45
520	A115	40pf brt red vio	.20	.45
521	A115	50pf myrtle green	.20	.45
522	A115	60pf dk red brown	.20	.45
523	A115	80pf indigo	.20	.45
524	A116	1m dk slate grn ('44)	.40	5.25
a.		Perf. 12½ ('42)	1.25	6.00
525	A116	2m violet ('44)	.90	5.25
a.		Perf. 12½ ('42)	1.40	6.00

Perf. 12½
526	A116	3m cop red ('42)	1.25	15.00
a.		Perf. 14 ('44)	2.00	9.00
527	A116	5m dark blue ('42)	2.25	47.50
a.		Perf. 14 ('44)	3.50	13.00
		Nos. 506-527 (24)	9.10	82.70
		Set, #506-527, never hinged	23.00	
		Set, #524a-527a, never hinged	40.00	

Nos. 507, 510, 511, 511A, 511B, 520, 524-526 exist imperf.
For surcharge see No. MQ3. For overprints see Russia Nos. N9-N48.

Storm Trooper Emblem A117

Adolf Hitler A118

1942, Aug. 8 **Photo.** *Perf. 14*
528	A117	6pf purple	.20	.75
		Never hinged		.75

War Effort Day of the Storm Troopers.

1944 **Engr.**
529	A118	42pf bright green	.20	2.00
		Never hinged		.30

Exists imperf. Value $375.

A119

1946 **Typo.** **Wmk. 284** *Perf. 14*
Size: 18x22mm
530	A119	1pf black	.20	3.00
531	A119	2pf black	.20	.20
532	A119	3pf yellow brn	.20	3.25
533	A119	4pf slate	.20	4.50
534	A119	5pf yellow grn	.20	.60
535	A119	6pf purple	.20	.20
536	A119	8pf dp ver	.20	.20
537	A119	10pf chocolate	.20	.20
538	A119	12pf bright red	.20	.20
539	A119	12pf slate gray	.20	.20
a.		Bklt. pane, 5 #539 + 3 #542	9.00	90.00
		Never hinged	18.00	
540	A119	15pf violet brn	.20	6.75
541	A119	15pf lt yel grn	.20	.20
542	A119	16pf slate green	.20	.20
543	A119	20pf lt blue	.20	.20
544	A119	24pf orange brn	.20	.20
545	A119	25pf brt ultra	.20	6.00
546	A119	25pf orange yel	.20	1.20
547	A119	30pf olive	.20	.20
548	A119	40pf red violet	.20	.20
549	A119	42pf emerald	.75	30.00
550	A119	45pf brt red	.20	.30
551	A119	50pf dk ol grn	.20	.20
552	A119	60pf brown red	.20	.20
553	A119	75pf deep ultra	.20	.20
554	A119	80pf dark blue	.20	.20
555	A119	84pf emerald	.20	.20

Size: 24½x29½mm
556	A119	1m olive green	.20	.20
		Nos. 530-556 (27)		59.20
		Set, never hinged	5.25	

Imperf. examples of Nos. 543, 544 and 548 are usually from the souvenir sheet No. B295. Most other denominations exist imperf.
For overprints see Nos. 585A-599, 9N64, 10N17-10N21.

Planting Olive A120

Sower A121

Laborer A122

Reaping Wheat A123

Germany Reaching for Peace — A124

Heinrich von Stephan — A125

1947-48 *Perf. 14*
557	A120	2pf brown blk	.20	.35
558	A120	6pf purple	.20	.20
559	A121	8pf red	.20	.35
560	A121	10pf yel grn ('48)	.20	.20
561	A122	12pf gray	.20	.20
562	A120	15pf choc ('48)	.20	3.75
563	A123	16pf dk bl grn	.20	.35
564	A121	20pf blue	.20	1.10
565	A123	24pf brown org	.20	.35

566	A120	25pf orange yel	.20 *1.10*
567	A122	30pf red ('48)	.20 *3.00*
568	A121	40pf red vio	.20 *.35*
569	A123	50pf ultra ('48)	.20 *2.00*
571	A122	60pf red brn ('48)	.20 *.75*
a.		60pf brown red	.20 *.35*
572	A122	80pf dark blue	.20 *1.10*
573	A123	84pf emerald	.20 *1.90*

Engr.

574	A124	1m olive	.20 *.35*
575	A124	2m dk brown vio	.20 *1.10*
576	A124	3m copper red	.20 *10.00*
577	A124	5m dk blue ('48)	.75 *40.00*
		Nos. 557-577 (20)	68.65
		Set, never hinged	5.25

Used examples of Nos. 576-577 with expertized postal cancellations sell for much more.

For overprints see Nos. 600-633, 9N1-9N34, 9N65-9N67, 10N1-10N16.

1947, May 15   **Litho.**

578	A125	24pf orange brown	.20 *1.50*
579	A125	75pf dark blue	.20 *1.50*
		Set, never hinged	.45

50th anniv. of the death of Heinrich von Stephan, 1st postmaster general of the German Empire.

Leipzig Fair Issues
Type of Semi-Postal Stamp of 1947

12pf, Maximilian I granting charter, 1497.
75pf, Estimating and collecting taxes, 1365.

Perf. 13½x13

1947, Sept. 2   **Litho.**   **Wmk. 284**

580	SP252	12pf carmine	.20 *1.90*
581	SP252	75pf dk vio blue	.20 *2.50*
		Set, never hinged	.45

Type of Semi-Postal Stamp of 1947, Dated 1948

50pf, Merchants at customs barrier, 1388.
84pf, Arranging stocks of merchandise, 1433.

1948, Mar. 2   **Engr.**

582	SP252	50pf deep blue	.20 *1.50*
583	SP252	84pf green	.20 *2.25*
		Set, never hinged	.45

Exist imperf. Value, each, $450.

Hanover Fair Issue

Weighing Goods for Export — A126

1948, May 22   **Typo.**   **Perf. 14**

584	A126	24pf deep carmine	.20 *1.50*
585	A126	50pf ultra	.20 *2.25*
c.		Pair, #584-585	2.10 *15.00*
		Pair, never hinged	5.50
		Set, never hinged	.45

For Use in the United States and British Zones
Stamps of Germany 1946-47
Overprinted in Black

a	b

Overprint Type "a" on 1946 Numeral Issue

1948   **Wmk. 284**   **Perf. 14**

585A	A119	2pf black	2.25 *32.50*
585B	A119	8pf dp ver	5.25 *62.50*
586	A119	10pf chocolate	.30 *4.75*
586A	A119	12pf bright red	3.75 *52.50*
586B	A119	12pf slate gray	67.50 *550.00*
586C	A119	15pf violet brn	3.75 *52.50*
587	A119	15pf lt yel grn	1.25 *16.00*
587A	A119	16pf slate green	21.00 *200.00*
587B	A119	24pf orange brn	37.50 *210.00*
587C	A119	25pf brt ultra	7.50 *62.50*
588	A119	25pf orange yel	.60 *8.25*
589	A119	30pf olive	.60 *8.25*
589A	A119	40pf red violet	27.50 *210.00*
590	A119	42pf brt red	.90 *8.25*
591	A119	50pf dk olive grn	.90 *8.25*
592	A119	75pf dp ultra	2.25 *24.00*
593	A119	84pf emerald	2.25 *24.00*
		Nos. 585A-593 (17)	185.05
		Nos. 585A-593 (17)	185.05
		Set, never hinged	375.00

Same, Overprinted Type "b"

593A	A119	2pf black	10.50 *67.50*
593B	A119	8pf dp ver	18.00 *140.00*
593C	A119	10pf chocolate	16.50 *140.00*
593D	A119	12pf bright red	5.25 *67.50*
593E	A119	12pf slate gray	140.00 *1,000.*
593F	A119	15pf violet brown	5.25 *47.50*
594	A119	15pf lt yel grn	.35 *8.25*
594A	A119	16pf slate grn	20.00 *160.00*
594B	A119	24pf org brn	21.00 *210.00*
594C	A119	25pf brt ultra	6.00 *62.50*
594D	A119	25pf orange yel	19.00 *200.00*
595	A119	30pf olive	.60 *6.75*
595A	A119	40pf red violet	27.50 *250.00*
596	A119	42pf bright red	1.25 *12.00*
597	A119	50pf dk ol grn	1.25 *12.00*
598	A119	75pf dp ultra	1.40 *12.00*
599	A119	84pf emerald	1.40 *13.00*
		Nos. 593A-599 (17)	295.25
		Nos. 593A-599 (17)	295.25
		Set, never hinged	600.00

Nine other denominations of type A119 (1, 3, 4, 5, 6, 20, 42, 60 and 80pf) were also overprinted with types "a" and "b." These overprints were not authorized, but the stamps were sold at post offices and tolerated for postal use. Forgeries exist.

The overprints on Nos. 585A-599 have been extensively counterfeited.

Overprint Type "a" on Stamps and Types of 1947 Pictorial Issue

600	A120	2pf brown black	.20 *.45*
601	A120	6pf purple	.20 *.45*
602	A121	8pf dp vermilion	.20 *.45*
603	A121	10pf yellow green	.20 *.45*
604	A122	12pf slate gray	.20 *.45*
605	A120	15pf chocolate	3.00 *15.00*
606	A123	16pf dk blue green	.60 *2.25*
607	A121	20pf blue	.20 *.90*
608	A123	24pf brown orange	.20 *.45*
609	A120	25pf orange yellow	.20 *.45*
610	A122	30pf red	1.10 *4.50*
611	A121	40pf red violet	.30 *1.10*
612	A123	50pf ultra	.35 *.90*
614	A122	60pf red brown	.35 *.90*
a.		60pf brown red	22.50 *225.00*
		Never hinged	60.00
615	A122	80pf dark blue	.60 *2.25*
616	A123	84pf emerald	1.90 *6.00*
		Nos. 600-616 (16)	9.80 *36.95*
		Set, never hinged	22.50

Same, Overprinted Type "b"

617	A120	2pf brown black	.35 *1.40*
618	A120	6pf purple	.35 *1.40*
619	A121	8pf red	.35 *1.40*
620	A121	10pf yellow green	.20 *.45*
621	A122	12pf gray	.35 *1.50*
622	A120	15pf chocolate	.20 *.65*
623	A123	16pf dk blue green	.65 *2.25*
624	A121	20pf blue	.20 *.45*
625	A123	24pf brown orange	.30 *1.50*
626	A120	25pf orange yel	3.50 *15.00*
627	A122	30pf red	.20 *.65*
628	A121	40pf red violet	.20 *.65*
629	A123	50pf ultra	.20 *.60*
631	A122	60pf red brown	.20 *.65*
a.		60pf brown red	1.10 *3.75*
		Never hinged	2.25
632	A122	80pf dark blue	.20 *.65*
633	A123	84pf emerald	.45 *1.40*
		Nos. 617-633 (16)	7.90 *30.55*
		Set, never hinged	18.00

Most of Nos. 585A-633 exist with inverted and double overprints.

Frankfurt Town Hall A127

Our Lady's Church, Munich A128

Cologne Cathedral A129

Brandenburg Gate, Berlin A130

Holsten Gate, Lübeck — A131

Two types of mark values:
Type I — Four horiz. lines in stairs.
Type II — Seven horizontal lines.

Perf. 11½x11, 11

1948-51   **Litho.**   **Wmk. 286**

634	A127	2pf black	.20 *.45*
a.		Perf. 14	1.10 *4.75*
635	A128	4pf orange brown	.20 *.45*
a.		Perf. 14	2.75 *.90*
636	A129	5pf blue	.20 *.45*
a.		Perf. 14	.75 *.45*
637	A128	6pf orange brown	.20 *.60*
638	A128	6pf orange	.20 *.45*
a.		Perf. 14	6.00 *4.50*
639	A127	8pf orange yel	.20 *.45*
640	A128	8pf dk slate blue	.20 *.45*
641	A129	10pf green	.20 *.45*
a.		Perf. 14	.75 *.45*
642	A129	15pf orange	.90 *4.50*
643	A127	15pf violet	.50 *.45*
a.		Perf. 14	4.50 *.45*
644	A127	16pf bluish green	.30 *.60*
645	A127	20pf blue	.45 *3.00*
646	A130	20pf carmine	.30 *.60*
a.		Perf. 14	1.90 *.45*
647	A130	24pf carmine	.20 *.45*
648	A129	25pf vermilion	.45 *.45*
a.		Perf. 14	27.50 *160.00*
649	A130	30pf blue	.60 *.45*
a.		Perf. 14	11.00 *.45*
650	A128	30pf scarlet	1.10 *5.25*
651	A129	40pf rose lilac	.75 *.45*
a.		Perf. 14	7.50 *.45*
652	A130	50pf ultra	.60 *1.90*
653	A129	50pf bluish green	.75 *.45*
a.		Perf. 14	67.50 *.45*
654	A129	60pf violet brn	30.00 *.45*
a.		Perf. 14	1.10 *.45*
655	A130	80pf red violet	1.25 *.45*
a.		Perf. 14	45.00 *.45*
656	A128	84pf rose violet	.75 *6.00*
657	A129	90pf rose lilac	1.25 *.45*
a.		Perf. 14	65.00 *.50*

Perf. 11, 11x11½

658	A131	1m yellow grn (I)	15.00 *.60*
a.		Perf. 14 (II) ('51)	60.00 *.45*
b.		Perf. 11 (II)	19.00 *.45*
659	A131	2m violet (I)	13.50 *.45*
a.		Type II	22.50 *.45*
660	A131	3m car rose (I)	15.00 *2.50*
a.		Type II	75.00 *1.00*
661	A131	5m blue (I)	22.50 *21.00*
a.		Type II	90.00 *3.25*
		Nos. 634-661 (28)	107.75 *54.35*
		Set, never hinged	260.00
		Set, 634a-658a, never hinged	550.00
		Set, 658b-661a, never hinged	375.00

Imperforates of many values exist.
Specialists collect Nos. 634-661 with watermark in four positions: upright, D's facing left; upright, D's facing right; sideways, D's facing up; sideways, D's facing down.

Two types of perforation: line and comb. Nos. 634-657 are found both perf. 11 and 11½x11.

Herman Hildebrant Wedigh — A132

Wmk. 116

1949, Apr. 22   **Engr.**   **Perf. 14**

662	A132	10pf green	1.10 *2.25*
663	A132	20pf carmine rose	1.10 *2.25*
664	A132	30pf blue	1.50 *3.00*
a.		Sheet of 3, #662-664	32.50 *180.00*
		Sheet, never hinged	82.50
		Nos. 662-664 (3)	3.70 *7.50*
		Set, never hinged	8.50

Hanover Export Fair, 1949.
No. 664a sold for 1 mark.

Federal Republic
AREA — 95,520 sq. mi.
POP. — 62,040,000 (1974 est.)
CAPITAL — Bonn

"Reconstruction" A133	Bavaria Stamp A134

1949, Sept. 7   **Litho.**   **Wmk. 286**

665	A133	10pf blue green	15.00 *21.00*
666	A133	20pf rose carmine	17.50 *24.00*
		Set, never hinged	90.00

Opening of the first Federal Assembly.
Exist imperf. Value, each $475.

Wmk. 285

1949, Sept. 30   **Litho.**   **Perf. 14**

Design: 30pf, Bavaria 6kr.

667	A134	20pf red & dull blue	19.00 *37.50*
668	A134	30pf dull blue & choc	32.50 *60.00*
		Set, never hinged	90.00

Cent. of German postage stamps. See No. B309.

Heinrich von Stephan, General Post Office and Guild House, Bern A135

1949, Oct. 9   **Wmk. 286**

669	A135	30pf ultra	21.00 *37.50*
		Never hinged	60.00

75th anniv. of the UPU.

Numeral and Post Horn — A136

1951-52   **Typo.**   **Wmk. 295**

670	A136	2pf yellow grn	.35 *.95*
671	A136	4pf yellow brn	.35 *.30*
a.		Booklet pane, 4 #671 + 3 #673 + 4 #677	110.00 *450.00*
		Never hinged	450.00
672	A136	5pf dp rose vio	1.90 *.30*
673	A136	6pf orange	4.50 *3.00*
674	A136	8pf gray	5.25 *7.50*
675	A136	10pf dk green	.75 *.30*
a.		Booklet pane, 4 #675 + 5 #677 + label	110.00 *450.00*
		Never hinged	450.00
676	A136	15pf purple	10.00 *.95*
677	A136	20pf carmine	.75 *.30*
678	A136	25pf dk rose lake	22.50 *4.75*

Engr.

Size: 20x24½mm

679	A136	30pf blue	13.00 *.45*
680	A136	40pf rose lilac ('52)	32.50 *.45*
681	A136	50pf blue gray ('52)	45.00 *.45*
682	A136	60pf brown ('52)	32.50 *.45*
683	A136	70pf dp yel ('52)	135.00 *14.00*
684	A136	80pf carmine ('52)	150.00 *1.90*
685	A136	90pf yel grn ('52)	150.00 *2.25*
		Nos. 670-685 (16)	604.35 *38.30*
		Set, never hinged	1,875.

Imperfs. exist of #671, 673, 675, 681 & 684.

W. K.
Roentgen
A137

Mona Lisa
A138

1951, Dec. 10
686 A137 30pf blue 30.00 18.00
Never hinged 72.50

50th anniv. of the awarding of the Nobel prize in physics to Wilhelm K. Roentgen.

Wmk. 285
1952, Apr. 15 Litho. Perf. 13½
687 A138 5pf multicolored .75 1.10
Never hinged 2.00

500th anniv. of the birth of Leonardo da Vinci.

N. A.
Otto — A139

Martin
Luther — A140

Wmk. 295
1952, July 25 Engr. Perf. 14
688 A139 30pf deep blue 15.00 15.00
Never hinged 29.00

75th anniv. of the four-cycle gas engine.

1952, July 25
689 A140 10pf green 4.00 4.75
Never hinged 13.50

Issued to publicize the Lutheran World Federation Assembly, Hanover, 1952.

Freighter Off
Heligoland
A141

Carl Schurz
A142

1952, Sept. 6
690 A141 20pf red 6.25 5.75
Never hinged 15.00

Return of Heligoland, Mar. 1, 1952.

Wmk. 285
1952, Sept. 17 Litho. Perf. 13½
691 A142 20pf blue, blk & brn
org 6.25 7.50
Never hinged 19.00

Centenary of Carl Schurz's arrival in America.

Thurn and Taxis
Postilion
A143

Philipp
Reis — A144

1952, Oct. 25
692 A143 10pf multicolored 3.00 2.00
Never hinged 7.50

1st Thurn and Taxis stamp, cent.

1952, Oct. 27 Photo. Perf. 14
693 A144 30pf blue 18.00 15.00
Never hinged 45.00

75 years of telephone service in Germany.

"Prevent Traffic
Accidents" — A145

1953, Mar. 30 Litho. Wmk. 285
694 A145 20pf blk, red & bl grn 6.25 4.50
Never hinged 16.50

Justus von
Liebig — A146

Red Cross and
Compass — A147

1953, May 12 Engr. Wmk. 295
695 A146 30pf dark blue 14.50 22.50
Never hinged 45.00

150th anniv. of the birth of Justus von Liebig, chemist.

Perf. 14x13½
1953, May 8 Litho. Wmk. 285
696 A147 10pf dp ol grn & red 4.50 6.75
Never hinged 20.00

125th anniv. of the birth of Henri Dunant, founder of the Red Cross.

War Prisoner and
Barbed
Wire — A148

Train and
Hand
Signal — A149

Typographed and Embossed
1953, May 9 Unwmk. Perf. 14
697 A148 10pf gray & black 1.90 .35
Never hinged 6.00

Issued in memory of the prisoners of war.

Wmk. 295
1953, June 20 Engr. Perf. 14

Designs: 10pf, Pigeon and planes. 20pf, Automobiles and traffic signal. 30pf, Ship, barges and buoy.

698 A149 4pf brown 2.25 3.75
699 A149 10pf deep green 4.50 6.00
700 A149 20pf red 5.75 9.75
701 A149 30pf deep ultra 17.50 22.50
Nos. 698-701 (4) 30.00 42.00
Set, never hinged 77.50

Exhibition of Transport and Communications, Munich, 1953.

Pres. Theodor
Heuss — A150

1954-60 Typo. Perf. 14
Size: 18½x22mm
702 A150 2pf citron .20 .20
  a. Booklet pane, 5 #702, 4
     #704 + label ('55) 22.50 110.00
     Never hinged 42.50
  b. Booklet pane, 3 #702, 6
     #704 + label ('55) 3.75 60.00
     Never hinged 7.50
  c. Booklet pane, 3 #702, 1
     #707, 5 #708 + label ('56) 7.50 75.00
     Never hinged 16.50
703 A150 4pf orange brn .20 .20
704 A150 5pf rose lilac .20 .20
  a. Booklet pane, 2 #704, 7
     #708 + label ('55) 22.50 110.00
     Never hinged 42.50
705 A150 6pf lt brown .20 .75
706 A150 7pf bluish green .20 .30
707 A150 8pf gray .20 .60
708 A150 10pf green .20 .20
  a. Booklet pane, 4 #708, 5
     #710 + label ('55) 22.50 110.00
     Never hinged 42.50
709 A150 15pf ultra .20 .45
710 A150 20pf dk car rose .20 .20
711 A150 25pf red brown .30 .60

Engr.
Size: 19½x24mm
712 A150 30pf blue 4.50 4.50
713 A150 40pf red violet 1.90 .30
714 A150 50pf gray 67.50 .45
715 A150 60pf red brown 15.00 .60
716 A150 70pf olive 4.50 1.90
717 A150 80pf deep rose .75 4.50
718 A150 90pf deep green 4.50 2.25

Size: 24½x29½mm
719 A150 1m olive green .50 .30
720 A150 2m lt vio blue .75 1.10
721 A150 3m deep plum 1.90 2.25
Nos. 702-721 (20) 103.90 21.85
Set, never hinged 275.00

Coils and sheets of 100 were issued of the 5, 7, 10, 15, 20, 25, 40 and 70pf. Every fifth coil stamp has a control number on the back.
Printings of Nos. 704, 706, 708-711 and 708b were made on fluorescent paper beginning in 1960.
Nos. 702, 709, 714 exist imperf. Value about $425 each.
See Nos. 737Ab, 755-761.

Catalogue values for unused stamps in this section, from this point to the end of the section, are for Never Hinged items.

Paul Ehrlich and
Emil von
Behring — A151

15th Century
Printer — A152

Wmk. 285
1954, Mar. 13 Litho. Perf. 13½
722 A151 10pf dark green 11.00 3.75

Centenary of the births of Paul Ehrlich and Emil von Behring, medical researchers. Exists imperf. Value $1,000.

1954, May 5 Typo. Wmk. 295
723 A152 4pf chocolate 1.10 .60

500th anniversary of the publication of Gutenberg's 42-line Bible. Design from woodcut by Jost Amman.

Bishop's Miter
and
Sword — A153

Carl F.
Gauss — A154

Engraved; Center Embossed
1954, June 5 Unwmk. Perf. 13½x14
724 A153 20pf gray & red 8.00 4.50

Martyrdom of Saint Boniface, 1200th anniv.

Wmk. 295
1955, Feb. 23 Engr. Perf. 14
725 A154 10pf deep green 5.00 .60

Cent. of the death of Carl Friedrich Gauss, mathematician.

A155

A156

Wmk. 304
1955, May 7 Litho. Perf. 13½
726 A155 10pf green 5.00 1.50

Cent. of the birth of Oskar von Miller, electrical engineer.

Engraved and Embossed
1955, May 9 Unwmk. Perf. 13½x14
727 A156 40pf blue 16.50 5.50

Friedrich von Schiller, poet, 150th death anniv.

1906
Automobile
A157

Wmk. 304

1955, June 1   Typo.   Perf. 13½
728 A157 20pf red & black   10.50 5.00
German postal motor-bus service, 50th anniv.

Arms of Baden-Württemberg A158

Globe and Atomic Symbol A159

Perf. 13x13½
1955, June 15   Litho.   Wmk. 295
729 A158 7pf lemon, blk & brn red   4.00 4.50
730 A158 10pf lemon, blk & grn   6.50 6.50
a.   Value omitted   475.00 450.00
Baden-Wurttemberg Exhibition, Stuttgart, 1955.

1955, June 24 Photo. Perf. 13½x14
731 A159 20pf rose brown   10.50 1.10
Issued to encourage scientific research.

Orb and Symbols of Battle — A160

Photogravure and Embossed
Perf. 14x13½
1955, Aug. 10   Unwmk.
732 A160 20pf red lilac   9.00 3.75
Issued in honor of Augsburg and the millenium of the Battle on the Lechfeld.

Family in Flight — A161

Railroad Signal, Tracks — A162

1955, Aug. 2   Engr.   Wmk. 304
733 A161 20pf brown lake   3.75 .50
Ten years of German expatriation. See No. 930.

Perf. 13½x14
1955, Oct. 5   Litho.   Wmk. 304
734 A162 20pf red & black   10.00 2.50
European Timetable conf. at Wiesbaden, Oct. 5-15, 1955.

A163

A164
Stifter monument and sylized Trees.

1955, Oct. 22   Engr.
735 A163 10pf dark green   3.75 2.50
150th anniv. of the birth of Adalbert Stifter, poet.

Lithographed and Embossed
Perf. 14x13½
1955, Oct. 24   Unwmk.
736 A164 10pf UN emblem   3.75 4.50
United Nations Day, Oct. 24, 1955.

Numeral A165

Numeral and Signature A166

1955-58 Wmk. 304 Typo. Perf. 14
737 A165 1pf gray   .20 .20
Wmk. 295
737A A165 1pf gray ('58)   7.75 19.00
b.   Bklt. pane of 10 (#707, 2 each #737A, #704, #708, 3 #710)   22.50 52.50
No. 737A was issued only in the booklet pane, No. 737b. No. 737 was issued on fluorescent paper in 1963.

1956, Jan. 7   Engr.   Wmk. 304
738 A166 20pf dark red   6.75 2.75
125th anniv. of the birth of Heinrich von Stephan, co-founder of the UPU.

Clavichord A167

1956, Jan. 27   Litho.
739 A167 10pf dull lilac   .75 .35
200th anniv. of the birth of Wolfgang Amadeus Mozart, composer.

Heinrich Heine, Poet, Death Cent. — A168

Perf. 13x13½
1956, Feb. 17   Wmk. 295
740 A168 10pf ol grn & blk   2.75 3.00

Old Buildings, Lüneburg A169

Wmk. 304
1956, May 2   Engr.   Perf. 14
741 A169 20pf dull red   7.50 8.25
Millenary of Lüneburg.

Olympic Rings A170

Robert Schumann A171

1956, June 9   Perf. 13½x14
742 A170 10pf slate green   .80 .60
Issued to publicize the Olympic year, 1956.

1956, July 28   Litho.   Unwmk.
743 A171 10pf citron, blk & red   .65 .45
Schumann, composer, death cent.

Synod Emblem — A172

Thomas Mann — A173

Perf. 13½x13
1956, Aug. 8   Wmk. 304
744 A172 10pf green   3.50 3.75
745 A172 20pf brown carmine   4.00 5.25
Meeting of German Protestants (Evangelical Synod), Frankfurt-on-Main, Aug. 8-12.

1956, Aug. 11 Engr. Perf. 13½x14
746 A173 20pf pale rose vio   3.00 2.10
1st anniv. of the death of Thomas Mann, novelist.

Maria Laach Abbey — A174

"Rebuilding Europe" — A175

1956, Aug. 24 Photo. Perf. 13½x13½
747 A174 20pf brn lake & gray   2.25 2.00
800th anniv. of the dedication of the Maria Laach Abbey.

Europa Issue, 1956
1956, Sept. 15   Engr.   Perf. 14
748 A175 10pf green   1.00 .20
749 A175 40pf blue   6.00 .95
Issued to symbolize the cooperation among the six countries comprising the Coal and Steel Community.

Plan of Cologne Cathedral and Hand — A176

1956, Aug. 29 Litho. Perf. 13x13½
750 A176 10pf gray grn & red brn   2.75 2.50
77th meeting of German Catholics, Cologne, Aug. 29.

Map of the World and Policeman's Hand — A177

1956, Sept. 1   Perf. 13½x13
751 A177 20pf red org, grn & blk   3.00 2.50
Issued on the occasion of the International Police Show, Essen, Sept. 1-23.

Pigeon Holding Letter — A178

1956, Oct. 27   Engr.   Perf. 14
752 A178 10pf green   1.50 .65
Issued to publicize the Day of the Stamp.

Cemetery Crosses — A179

1956, Nov. 17   Perf. 14x13½
753 A179 10pf slate   1.50 .65
Issued to commemorate the people of Germany who died during WWII and to promote the Society for the Care of Military Cemeteries.

Saar Coat of Arms — A180

1957, Jan. 2   Litho.   Perf. 13x13½
754 A180 10pf bluish grn & brn   .45 .45
Return of the Saar to Germany. See Saar #262.

Heuss Type of 1954
1956-57 Wmk. 304 Engr. Perf. 14
Size: 18½x22mm
755 A150 30pf slate green   .40 .60
756 A150 40pf lt ultra   1.90 .30
757 A150 50pf olive   .95 .30
758 A150 60pf lt brown   3.25 .45
759 A150 70pf violet   10.00 .45
760 A150 80pf red orange   5.25 1.90
761 A150 90pf bluish green   16.50 .95
    Nos. 755-761 (7)   38.25 4.95
Nos. 755-756 were printed on both ordinary and fluorescent paper; Nos. 757-761 only on ordinary paper. Issue dates: 40pf, 1956. Others, 1957.
The 40pf and 70pf were also issued in coils. Every fifth coil stamp has control number on back.

Heinrich Hertz — A181

1957, Feb. 22   Litho.   Perf. 14
762 A181 10pf lt green & blk   1.25 .50
Heinrich Hertz, physicist, birth cent.

Paul Gerhardt — A182

1957, May 18   **Engr.**
763 A182 20pf carmine lake   .50   .50
350th anniv. of the birth of Paul Gerhardt, Lutheran clergyman and hymn writer.

Tulip and Post Horn — A183

1957, June 8
764 A183 20pf red orange   .50   .50
Flora & Philately Exhib., Cologne, June 8-10.

Arms of Aschaffenburg, 1332 — A184

      Perf. 13x13½
1957, June 15   **Wmk. 304**
765 A184 20pf dp salmon & blk   .50   .50
1000th anniv. of the founding of the Abbey and town of Aschaffenburg.

Scholars (Sapiens Manuscript) A185

1957, June 24   **Perf. 13½x13**
766 A185 10pf blk, bl grn & red org   .40   .40
Founding of Freiburg University, 500th anniv.

Modern Passenger Freighter — A186

1957, June 25   **Perf. 13½x14**
767 A186 15pf brt blue, blk & red   1.10   1.00
Merchant Marine Day, June 25.

Liebig Laboratory A187

1957, July 3   **Engr.**   **Perf. 14x13½**
768 A187 10pf dark green   .40   .40
350th anniv. of the Justus Liebig School at Ludwig University, Giessen.

Albert Ballin — A188

      Perf. 13½x14
1957, Aug. 15   **Litho.**   **Wmk. 304**
769 A188 20pf dk car rose & blk   1.25   .45
Cent. of the birth of Albert Ballin, founder of the Hamburg-America Steamship Line.

Television Screen — A189

1957, Aug. 23   **Engr.**   **Perf. 14x13½**
770 A189 10pf blue vio & grn   .40   .40
Issued to publicize the television industry.

Europa Issue, 1957

"United Europe" A190

Lithographed; Tree Embossed
1957-58   **Unwmk.**   **Perf. 14x13½**
771   A190 10pf yel grn & lt bl   .35   .20
   a.   Imperf.   300.00   300.00
772   A190 40pf dk bl & lt bl   3.75   .35
      Wmk. 304
772A A190 10pf yel grn & lt bl   5.50   8.25
   Nos. 771-772A (3)   9.60   8.80
A united Europe for peace and prosperity. Issued: #771-772, 9/16; #772A, 8/1958.

Water Lily — A191

European Robin — A192

      Wmk. 304
1957, Oct. 4   **Litho.**   **Perf. 14**
773 A191 10pf yel grn & org yel   .35   .45
774 A192 20pf multicolored   .55   .45
Protection of wild animals and plants.

Carrier Pigeons — A193

Baron vom Stein — A194

1957, Oct. 5
775 A193 20pf dp car & blk   .85   .50
Intl. Letter Writing Week, Oct. 6-12.

1957, Oct. 26   **Engr.**   **Perf. 13½x14**
776 A194 20pf red   1.50   .60
200th anniv. of the birth of Baron Heinrich Friedrich vom und zum Stein, Prussian statesman.

Leo Baeck — A195

Landschaft Building, Stuttgart — A196

1957, Nov. 2
777 A195 20pf dark red   1.50   .60
1st anniv. of the death of Rabbi Leo Baeck of Berlin.

      Perf. 13x13½
1957, Nov. 16   **Litho.**   **Wmk. 304**
778 A196 10pf dk grn & yel grn   .80   .50
500th anniversary of the Wurttemberg Landtag (Assembly).

Coach — A197

"Max and Moritz" — A198

1957, Nov. 26   **Engr.**   **Perf. 14**
779 A197 10pf olive green   .75   .50
Centenary of the death of Joseph V. Eichendorff, poet.

1958, Jan. 9   **Litho.**   **Perf. 13½x13**
Design: 20pf, Wilhelm Busch.
780 A198 10pf lt ol grn & blk   .20   .20
781 A198 20pf red & black   .75   .60
50th anniv. of the death of Wilhelm Busch, humorist.

"Prevent Forest Fires" — A199

1958, Mar. 5   **Perf. 14**
782 A199 20pf brt red & blk   .65   .50

Rudolf Diesel A200

1958, Mar. 18   **Engr.**   **Perf. 14**
783 A200 10pf dk blue grn   .40   .40
Centenary of the birth of Rudolf Diesel, inventor.

Giraffe and Lion — A201

View of Old Munich — A202

      Perf. 13x13½
1958, May 7   **Litho.**   **Wmk. 304**
784 A201 10pf brt yel grn & blk   .50   .40
Zoo at Frankfort on the Main, cent.
Exists imperf. Value $225.

1958, May 22   **Engr.**   **Perf. 14x13½**
785 A202 20pf dark red   .50   .40
800th anniversary of Munich.

Market Cross, Trier — A203

Heraldic Eagle 5m Coin — A204

1958, June 3
786 A203 20pf dark red & black   .50   .50
Millennium of the market of Trier (Treves).

1958, June 20   **Litho.**   **Perf. 13x13½**
787 A204 20pf red & black   .60   1.40
10th anniv. of the German currency reform.
Exists imperf. Value $300.

Turner Emblem and Oak Leaf A205

Schulze-Delitzsch A206

Perf. 13½x14
1958, July 21   Wmk. 304
788 A205 10pf gray, blk & dl grn   .35   .45
150 years of German Turners and on the occasion of the 1958 Turner festival.

1958, Aug. 29   Engr.   Perf. 13½x14
789 A206 10pf yellow green   .45   .35
150th anniv. of the birth of Hermann Schulze-Delitzsch, founder of German trade organizations.

Common Design Types pictured following the introduction.

Europa Issue, 1958
Common Design Type
1958, Sept. 13   Litho.
Size: 24½x30mm
790 CD1 10pf yel grn & blue   .35   .20
791 CD1 40pf lt blue & red   3.00   .35

Nicolaus Cusanus   Pres. Theodor
(Nikolaus Krebs)   Heuss
A207   A208

1958, Dec. 3   Litho.   Perf. 14x13½
792 A207 20pf dk car rose & blk   .45   .35
500th anniv. of the Cusanus Hospice at Kues, founded by Cardinal Nicolaus (1401-64).
Exists imperf. Value $300.

1959   Wmk. 304   Perf. 14
793 A208   7pf blue green   .20   .20
794 A208 10pf green   .40   .20
795 A208 20pf dk car rose   .40   .20
Engr.
796 A208 40pf blue   12.00   .90
797 A208 70pf deep purple   3.50   .75
    Nos. 793-797 (5)   16.50   2.25

Nos. 793-795 were issued in sheets of 100 and in coils. Every fifth coil stamp has a control number on the back.
An experimental booklet containing one pane of 10 of No. 794 was sold at Darmstadt in 1960. Value $750.

Jakob
Fugger — A209

Adam
Riese — A210

1959, Mar. 6   Perf. 13x13½
798 A209 20pf dk red & black   .40   .45
500th anniversary of the birth of Jakob Fugger the Rich, businessman and banker.

1959, Mar. 28   Perf. 13½x13
799 A210 10pf ol grn & blk   .40   .45
Adam Riese (c. 1492-1559), arithmetic teacher, 400th death anniversary.

Alexander von
Humboldt — A211

Buildings,
Buxtehude
A212

1959, May 6   Engr.   Perf. 13½x14
800 A211 40pf blue   1.60   1.25
Alexander von Humboldt (1769-1859), naturalist and geographer, death centenary.

1959, June 20   Litho.   Perf. 14
801 A212 20pf lt blue, ver & blk   .40   .40
Millennium of town of Buxtehude.

Holy Coat of
Trier — A213

Lithographed; Coat Embossed
1959, July 18   Wmk. 304   Perf. 14
802 A213 20pf dull cl, buff & blk   .40   .40
Showing of the seamless robe of Christ at the Cathedral of Trier, July 19-Sept. 20.

Synod
Emblem — A214

1959, Aug. 12   Litho.
803 A214 10pf grn, brt vio & blk   .30   .30
Meeting of German Protestants (Evangelical Synod), Munich, Aug. 12-16.

Souvenir Sheet

A215

Portraits: 10pf, George Friedrich Handel. 15pf, Louis Spohr. 20pf, Ludwig van Beethoven. 25pf, Joseph Haydn. 40pf, Felix Mendelssohn-Bartholdy.

Perf. 14x13½
1959, Sept. 8   Engr.   Wmk. 304
804 A215 Sheet of 5   24.00   50.00
  a.   10pf deep green   3.00   5.50
  b.   15pf blue   3.00   5.50
  c.   20pf dark carmine   3.00   3.75
  d.   25pf brown   3.00   7.50
  e.   40pf dark blue   3.00   5.50
Opening of Beethoven Hall in Bonn and to honor various anniversaries of German composers.

Europa Issue, 1959
Common Design Type
1959, Sept. 19   Litho.   Perf. 13½x14
Size: 24x29½mm
805 CD2 10pf olive green   .30   .20
806 CD2 40pf dark blue   1.60   .40

Uprooted Oak
Emblem — A216

1960, Apr. 7   Perf. 13½x13
807 A216 10pf grn, blk & lil   .20   .20
808 A216 40pf bl, blk & org   2.10   2.10
World Refugee Year, 7/1/59-6/30/60.

Philipp
Melanchthon
A217

Symbols of
Christ's
Sufferings
A218

1960, Apr. 19   Perf. 13½x14
809 A217 20pf dk car rose & blk   1.25   1.10
400th anniversary of the death of Philipp Melanchthon, co-worker of Martin Luther in the German Reformation.

1960, May 17   Perf. 14x13½
810 A218 10pf Prus grn, gray & ocher   .30   .30
1960 Passion Play, Oberammergau, Bavaria.

Dove, Chalice
and
Crucifix — A219

1960, July 30   Engr.   Perf. 14x13½
811 A219 10pf dull green   .55   .45
812 A219 20pf maroon   .75   .75
37th Eucharistic World Congress, Munich.

Wrestlers and
Olympic
Rings — A220

Sport scenes from Greek urns: 10pf, Sprinters. 20pf, Discus and Javelin throwers. 40pf, Chariot race.

1960, Aug. 8   Wmk. 304
813 A220   7pf red brown   .20   .20
814 A220 10pf olive green   .40   .20
815 A220 20pf vermilion   .40   .20
816 A220 40pf dark blue   1.25   1.25
    Nos. 813-816 (4)   2.25   1.85
17th Olympic Games, Rome, 8/25-9/11.

Hildesheim
Cathedral, Miters,
Cross and
Crosier — A221

1960, Sept. 6   Engr.   Perf. 13½x14
817 A221 20pf claret   .75   .45
St. Bernward (960-1022) and St. Godehard (960-1038), bishops.

Europa Issue, 1960
Common Design Type
1960, Sept. 19   Wmk. 304
Size: 30x25mm
818 CD3 10pf ol grn & yel grn   .20   .20
819 CD3 20pf brt red & lt red   .75   .20
820 CD3 40pf bl & lt bl   1.25   .75
    Nos. 818-820 (3)   2.20   1.15

George C.   Steam
Marshall   Locomotive
A222   A223

1960, Oct. 15   Litho.   Perf. 13x13½
821 A222 40pf dp blue & blk   2.50   2.10
Issued to honor George C. Marshall, US general and statesman.

1960, Dec. 7   Perf. 13½x14
822 A223 10pf ol bis & blk   .30   .35
125th anniversary of German railroads.

St.
George — A224

Wmk. 304
1961, Apr. 23   Engr.   Perf. 14
823 A224 10pf green   .20   .30
Honoring Boy Scouts of the world on St. George's Day (patron saint of Boy Scouts).

Albrecht Dürer — A225

Portraits: 5pf, Albertus Magnus. 7pf, St. Elizabeth of Thuringia. 8pf, Johann Gutenberg. 15pf, Martin Luther. 20pf, Johann Sebastian Bach. 25pf, Balthasar Neumann. 30pf, Immanuel Kant. 40pf, Gotthold Ephraim Lessing. 50pf, Johann Wolfgang von Goethe. 60pf, Friedrich von Schiller. 70pf, Ludwig van Beethoven. 80pf, Heinrich von Kleist. 90pf, Prof. Franz Oppenheimer. 1m, Annette von Droste-Hülshoff. 2m, Gerhart Hauptmann.

1961-64   Typo.   Perf. 14
Fluorescent or Ordinary Paper
824 A225   5pf olive   .20   .20
  b.   Tête bêche pair ('63)   .50   .90
825 A225   7pf dark bister   .20   .20
826 A225   8pf lilac   .20   .35
827 A225 10pf olive green   .20   .20
  b.   Tête bêche pair   .50   1.50
828 A225 15pf blue   .35   .75
  b.   Tête bêche pair ('63)   .90   2.10
829 A225 20pf dk red   .35   .30
  b.   Tête bêche pair ('63)   .60   1.90
830 A225 25pf orange brn   .20   .20

Engr.
831 A225 30pf gray   .20   .20
832 A225 40pf blue   .20   .20
833 A225 50pf red brown   .35   .20
834 A225 60pf dk car rose ('62)   .35   .20
835 A225 70pf grnsh black   .20   .20
  a.   70pf deep green   .60   .20
836 A225 80pf brown   .40   .40
837 A225 90pf yel ol ('64)   .35   .30
838 A225   1m violet blue   .50   .20
839 A225   2m yel grn ('62)   3.00   .50
    Nos. 824-839 (16)   7.25   4.60

Nos. 824-825, 827-830, 832, 834-835, 835a were issued in coils as well as in sheets. Every fifth coil stamp has a black control number on the back.
Nos. 824-839, including booklet panes and tête bêche pairs, were printed on fluorescent paper. Nos. 824-829 and 832 were also printed on ordinary paper.

Gottlieb
Daimler's Car of
1886 and
Signature
A226

Design: 20pf, Carl Benz's 3-wheel car of 1886 and signature.

1961, July 3   **Litho.**
840 A226 10pf green & blk   .20 .20
841 A226 20pf brick red & blk   .35 .30
75 years of motorized traffic.

Messenger, Nuremberg, 18th Century — A227

Cathedral, Speyer — A228

Photogravure and Engraved
1961, Aug. 31   **Wmk. 304**   *Perf. 14*
842 A227 7pf brown red & blk   .20 .30
Issued to publicize the exhibition "The Letter in Five Centuries," Nuremberg.

1961, Sept. 2   **Engr.**
843 A228 20pf vermilion   .30 .45
900th anniversary of Speyer Cathedral.

Europa Issue, 1961
Common Design Type
1961, Sept. 18   **Litho.**
Size: 28½x18½mm
844 CD4 10pf olive green   .20 .20
845 CD4 40pf violet blue   .35 .50
No. 844 was printed on both ordinary and fluorescent paper.

Reis Telephone A229

Wmk. 304
1961, Oct. 26   **Engr.**   *Perf. 14*
846 A229 10pf green   .30 .35
Cent. of the demonstration of the 1st telephone by Philipp Reis.

Wilhelm Emanuel von Ketteler — A230

1961, Dec. 22   **Litho.**
847 A230 10pf olive grn & blk   .30 .35
Sesquicentennial of the birth of von Ketteler, Bishop of Mainz and pioneer in social development.

Fluorescent Paper
was introduced for all stamps, starting with No. 848. Of the stamps before No. 848, those issued on both ordinary and fluorescent paper include Nos. 704, 706, 708-711, 737, 755-756, 824-829, 832, 844. Those issued only on fluorescent paper (up to No. 848) include Nos. 708b, 830-831, 833-839 and 842.

Drusus Stone and Old View of Mainz — A231

Notes and Tuning Fork — A232

1962, May 10   **Engr.**   **Wmk. 304**
848 A231 20pf deep claret   .30 .35
The 2000th anniversary of Mainz.

1962, July 12   **Litho.**   *Perf. 14*
849 A232 20pf red & black   .30 .45
Issued to show appreciation of choral singing. The music is from the choral movement for three voices "In dulci jubilo" from "Musae Sioniae" by Michael Praetorius.

"Faith, Thanksgiving, Service" A233

1962, Aug. 22   **Engr.**   **Unwmk.**
850 A233 20pf magenta   .30 .45
79th meeting of German Catholics, Hanover, Aug. 22-29.

Open Bible, Chrismon and Chalice — A234

1962, Sept. 11   **Litho.**   **Wmk. 304**
851 A234 20pf vermilion & blk   .30 .45
Württemberg Bible Society, 150th anniv.

Europa Issue, 1962
Common Design Type
1962, Sept. 17   **Engr.**
Size: 28x23mm
852 CD5 10pf green   .20 .20
853 CD5 40pf blue   .40 .35

"Bread for the World" — A235

Lithographed and Embossed
1962, Nov. 23   *Perf. 14*
854 A235 20pf brown red & blk   .30 .45
Issued in connection with the Advent Collection of the Protestant Church in Germany.

Mother and Child Receiving Gift Parcel — A236

1963, Feb. 9   **Engr.**
855 A236 20pf dark carmine   .20 .35
Issued to express gratitude to the American organizations, CRALOG (Council of Relief Agencies Licensed to Operate in Germany) and CARE (Cooperative for American Remittances to Everywhere), for help during 1946-1962.

Globe, Cross, Seeds and Stalks of Wheat — A237

Checkered Lily — A238

Lithographed and Engraved
1963, Feb. 27   **Wmk. 304**   *Perf. 14*
856 A237 20pf gray, blk & red   .20 .35
German Catholic "Misereor" (I have compassion) campaign against hunger and illness.

1963, Apr. 28   **Litho.**   **Unwmk.**
Flowers: 15pf, Lady's slipper. 20pf, Columbine. 40pf, Beach thistle.
857 A238 10pf multicolored   .20 .20
858 A238 15pf multicolored   .20 .20
859 A238 20pf multicolored   .20 .20
860 A238 40pf multicolored   .35 .35
Nos. 857-860 (4)   .95 .95
Flora and Philately Exhibition, Hamburg.

Heidelberg Catechism — A239

1963, May 2   **Litho. & Engr.**
861 A239 20pf dp org, brn org & blk   .30 .35
400th anniv. of the Heidelberg Catechism, containing the doctrine of the reformed church.

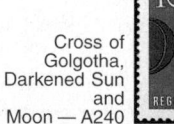

Cross of Golgotha, Darkened Sun and Moon — A240

1963, May 4   **Litho.**   **Wmk. 304**
862 A240 10pf grn, dp car, blk & vio   .20 .30
Consecration of the Regina Martyrum Church, Berlin-Plötzensee, in memory of the victims of Nazism.

Arms of 18 Participating Countries, Paris Conference, 1863 — A241

1963, May 7   **Engr.**
863 A241 40pf violet blue   .40 .50
1st Intl. Postal Conf., Paris, 1863, cent.

Map Showing New Railroad Link, German and Danish Flags — A242

1963, May 14   **Litho.**   **Unwmk.**
864 A242 20pf multi   .30 .30
Inauguration of the "Bird Flight Line" railroad link between Germany and Denmark.

Cross — A243

Lithographed and Embossed
1963, May 24   **Unwmk.**   *Perf. 14*
865 A243 20pf magenta, red & yel   .20 .30
Cent. of the founding of the Intl. Red Cross in connection with the German Red Cross cent. celebrations, Munster, May 24-26.

Synod Emblem and Crown of Barbed Wire — A244

Perf. 13½x13
1963, July 24   **Litho.**   **Wmk. 304**
866 A244 20pf dp orange & blk   .30 .35
Meeting of German Protestants (Evangelical Synod), Dortmund, July 24-28.

Europa Issue, 1963
Common Design Type
1963, Sept. 14   **Engr.**   *Perf. 14*
Size: 28x23½mm
867 CD6 15pf green   .25 .30
868 CD6 20pf red   .20 .20

Old Town Hall, Hanover A245

State Capitals: #870, Hamburg harbor, 775th anniv. #871, North Ferry pier, Kiel. #872, National Theater, Munich. #873, Fountain & building, Wiesbaden. #874, Reichstag Building, Berlin. #875, Gutenberg Museum, Mainz. #876, Jan Wellem (Johann Wilhelm II, 1658-1716) statue, Dusseldorf. #877, City Hall, Bonn. #878, City Hall, Bremen. #879, View of Stuttgart. #879A, Ludwig's Church, Saarbrucken.

1964-65   **Litho.**   **Unwmk.**   *Perf. 14*
869 A245 20pf gray, blk & red   .20 .30
870 A245 20pf multicolored   .20 .30
871 A245 20pf multicolored   .20 .30
872 A245 20pf multicolored   .20 .30
873 A245 20pf multicolored   .20 .30
874 A245 20pf blue, blk, & grn   .20 .30
875 A245 20pf multicolored   .20 .30
876 A245 20pf multicolored   .20 .30
877 A245 20pf multi ('65)   .20 .30
878 A245 20pf multi ('65)   .20 .30
879 A245 20pf multi ('65)   .20 .30
879A A245 20pf multi ('65)   .20 .30
Nos. 869-879A (12)   2.40 3.60

View of Ottobeuren Abbey — A246

Lithographed and Engraved
1964, May 29   *Perf. 14*
880 A246 20pf pink, red & blk   .20 .30
Ottobeuren Benedictine Abbey, 1200th anniv.

Pres. Heinrich Lübke — A247

Sophie Scholl — A248

1964, July 1   Litho.   Perf. 14
881 A247 20pf carmine   .20 .20
882 A247 40pf ultra   .20 .30

Lübke's re-election. See Nos. 974-975.

1964, July 20   Litho. & Engr.
Designs: No. 884, Ludwig Beck. No. 885, Dietrich Bonhoeffer. No. 886, Alfred Delp. No. 887, Karl Friedrich Goerdeler. No. 888, Wilhelm Leuschner. No. 889, Count James von Moltke. No. 890, Count Claus Schenk von Stauffenberg.

883 A248 20pf blue gray & blk .60 1.10
884 A248 20pf blue gray & blk .60 1.10
885 A248 20pf blue gray & blk .60 1.10
886 A248 20pf blue gray & blk .60 1.10
887 A248 20pf blue gray & blk .60 1.10
888 A248 20pf blue gray & blk .60 1.10
889 A248 20pf blue gray & blk .60 1.10
890 A248 20pf blue gray & blk .60 1.10
    Nos. 883-890 (8)   4.80 8.80

Issued to honor the German resistance to the Nazis, 1943-45. Printed in sheet of eight, containing one each of Nos. 883-890, se-tenant. Size: 148x105mm. The stamps were valid; the sheet was not, though widely used.

John Calvin — A249

Benzene Ring, Kekulé's Formula — A250

1964, Aug. 3   Litho.   Perf. 14
891 A249 20pf red & black   .20 .30

Issued to honor the meeting of the International Union of the Reformed Churches in Germany, Frankfort on the Main, Aug. 3-13.

1964, Aug. 14   Unwmk.   Perf. 14
Designs: 15pf, Cerenkov radiation, reactor in operation. 20pf, German gas engine.

892 A250 10pf dk brn, brt grn & blk .20 .20
893 A250 15pf brt grn, ultra & blk   .20 .20
894 A250 20pf red, grn & blk   .20 .20
    Nos. 892-894 (3)   .60 .60

Progress in science and technology: 10pf, centenary of benzene formula by August Friedrich Kekulé; 15pf, 25 years of nuclear fission, Hahn and Strassmann; 20pf, centenary of German internal combustion engine, Nikolaus August Otto and Eugen Langen.

Ferdinand Lasalle — A251

Radiating Sun — A252

1964, Aug. 31   Litho.
895 A251 20pf slate bl & blk   .20 .30

Cent. of the death of Ferdinand Lasalle, a founder of the German Labor Movement.

1964, Sept. 2   Engr.   Wmk. 304
896 A252 20pf gray & red   .20 .30

80th meeting of German Catholics, Stuttgart, Sept. 2-6. The inscription from Romans

12:2: ". . . be ye transformed through the renewing of your mind."

Europa Issue, 1964
Common Design Type
1964, Sept. 14   Litho.   Unwmk.
Size: 23x29mm
897 CD7 15pf yellow grn & lil .20 .20
898 CD7 20pf rose & lilac   .20 .20

Judo — A253

1964, Oct. 10
899 A253 20pf multicolored   .20 .30

18th Olympic Games, Tokyo, Oct. 10-25.

Prussian Eagle — A254

Lithographed and Embossed
1964, Oct. 30   Unwmk.   Perf. 14
900 A254 20pf brown org & blk .20 .30

250 years of the Court of Accounts in Germany, founded as the Royal Prussian Upper Chamber of Accounts.

John F. Kennedy (1917-63) A255

Castle Gate, Ellwangen A256

1964, Nov. 21   Engr.   Wmk. 304
901 A255 40pf dark blue   .30 .30

1964-66   Typo.   Unwmk.
Designs: (German buildings through 12 centuries): 10pf, Wall pavilion, Zwinger, Dresden. 15pf, Tegel Castle, Berlin. 20pf, Portico, Lorsch. 40pf, Trifels Fortress, Palatinate. 60pf, Treptow Gate, Neubrandenburg. 70pf, Osthofen Gate, Soest. 80pf, Elling Gate, Weissenburg.

903 A256 10pf brown ('65)   .20 .20
904 A256 15pf dk green ('65)   .20 .20
  b.   Tête bêche pair ('65) 1.10 1.25
905 A256 20pf brown red ('65) .20 .20
  b.   Tête bêche pair ('66) 1.10 1.50

Engr.
908 A256 40pf violet bl ('65) .20 .20
909 A256 50pf olive bister   .40 .20
910 A256 60pf rose red   .95 .35
911 A256 70pf dark green ('65) 1.25 .35
912 A256 80pf chocolate   .95 .35
    Nos. 903-912 (8)   4.35 2.05

Nos. 903-905, 908, 910-912 were issued in sheets of 100 and in coils. Every fifth coil stamp has a black control number on the back.

Illustrations from the Works of Matthias Claudius A257

Otto von Bismarck by Franz von Lenbach — A258

1965, Jan. 21   Engr.   Perf. 14
917 A257 20pf black & red   .20 .30

150th anniv. of the death of Matthias Claudius, poet and editor of the "Wandsbecker Bothe." Exists imperf. Value $225.

1965, Apr. 1   Litho.   Perf. 14
918 A258 20pf black & dull red .20 .30

Prince Otto von Bismarck (1815-1898), Prussian statesman and 1st chancellor of the German Empire.
Exists imperf. Value $750.

Jet Plane and Space Capsule — A259

Bouquet of Flowers — A260

Designs: 5pf, Traffic lights and signs. 10pf, Communications satellite and ground station. 15pf, Old and new post buses. 20pf, Semaphore telegraph and telecommunication tower. 40pf, Old and new railroad engines. 70pf, Sailing ship and ocean liner.

1965
919 A259 5pf gray & multi   .20 .30
920 A259 10pf multicolored   .20 .30
921 A259 15pf multicolored   .20 .30
922 A259 20pf maroon & multi   .20 .30
923 A259 40pf dk blue & multi .20 .30
924 A259 60pf dull vio, yel & lt bl .20 .30
925 A259 70pf multicolored   .30 .30
    Nos. 919-925 (7)   1.50 2.10

Intl. Transport and Communications Exhib., Munich, June 25-Oct. 30. No. 924 also for the 10th anniv. of the reopening of air service by Lufthansa. Issued: 60pf, 4/1; others, 6/25.
No. 919 exists imperf. Value $225.

1965, May 1   Litho.
926 A260 15pf multicolored   .20 .20

75th anniv. of May Day celebration in Germany.

ITU Emblem — A261

Adolph Kolping — A262

1965, May 17   Unwmk.   Perf. 14
927 A261 40pf dp blue & blk   .30 .35

Cent. of the ITU.

1965, May 26   Typo.
928 A262 20pf black, gray & red .20 .30

Kolping (1813-65). founder of the Catholic Unions of Journeymen, the Kolpingwork.

Rescue Ship — A263

1965, May 29   Litho. & Engr.
929 A263 20pf red & black   .20 .30

Cent. of the German Sea Rescue Service.

Type of 1955 dated "1945-1965"
Perf. 14x13½
1965, July 28   Engr.   Wmk. 304
930 A161 20pf gray   .20 .30

20 years of German expatriation.

Synod Emblem and Labyrinth — A264

Lithographed and Engraved
Perf. 13½x14
1965, July 28   Unwmk.
931 A264 20pf dp bl, grnsh bl & blk .20 .30

12th meeting of German Protestants (Evangelical Synod), Cologne, July 28-Aug. 1.

Waves and Stuttgart Television Tower — A265

1965, July 28   Litho.   Perf. 13½x13
932 A265 20pf dp bl, blk & brt pink .20 .30

Issued to publicize the German Radio Exhibition, Stuttgart, Aug. 27-Sept. 5.

Stamps of Thurn and Taxis, 1852-59 A266

1965, Aug. 28   Perf. 14
933 A266 20pf multicolored   .20 .30

125th anniv. of the introduction of postage stamps in Great Britain.

Europa Issue, 1965
Common Design Type
Perf. 14x13½
1965, Sept. 27   Engr.   Wmk. 304
Size: 28x23mm
934 CD8 15pf green   .20 .20
935 CD8 20pf dull red   .20 .20

Nordertor, Flensburg A267

Brandenburg Gate A268

Designs: 5pf, Berlin Gate, Stettin. 10pf, Wall Pavilion, Zwinger, Dresden. 20pf, Portico, Lorsch. 40pf, Trifels Fortress, Palatinate. 50pf, Castle Gate, Ellwangen. 60pf, Treptow Gate, Neubrandenburg. 70pf, Osthofen Gate, Soest. 80pf, Elling Gate, Weissenburg. 90pf, Zschocke Ladies' Home, Königsberg. 1m, Melanchthon House, Wittenberg. 1.10m, Trinity Hospital, Hildesheim. 1.30m, Tegel Castle,

Berlin. 2m, Löwenberg, Town Hall, interior view.

1966-69		Unwmk.	Engr.	Perf.	14
936	A267	5pf olive		.20	.20
937	A267	10pf dk brn ('67)		.20	.20
939	A267	20pf dk grn ('67)		.20	.20
940	A267	30pf yellow green		.20	.20
941	A267	30pf red ('67)		.20	.20
942	A267	40pf olive bis ('67)		.30	.30
943	A267	50pf blue ('67)		.40	.20
944	A267	60pf dp org ('67)		2.50	1.50
945	A267	70pf slate grn ('67)		1.10	.20
946	A267	80pf red brown ('67)		2.10	1.50
947	A267	90pf black		.75	.20
948	A267	1m dull blue		.75	.20
949	A267	1.10m red brown		.75	.35
950	A267	1.30m green ('69)		2.10	1.40
951	A267	2m purple		2.10	.60
		Nos. 936-951 (15)		13.85	7.55

1966-68		Typo.		Perf.	14
952	A268	10pf chocolate		.20	.20
a.		Bklt. pane, 4 #952, 2 #953, 4 #954 ('67)		3.75	15.00
b.		Tête bêche pair		.65	.75
c.		Bklt. pane, 2 #952, 4 #953		2.25	7.50
953	A268	20pf deep green		.30	.20
a.		Tête bêche pair ('68)		.90	1.25
b.		Bklt. pane, 2 #953, 4 #954 ('68)		1.50	6.00
954	A268	30pf red		.30	.20
a.		Tête bêche pair ('68)		.95	1.40
955	A268	50pf dark blue		1.25	.35
956	A268	100pf dark blue ('67)		9.75	.60
		Nos. 952-956 (5)		11.80	1.55

Nos. 952-956 were issued in sheets of 100 and in coils. Every fifth coil stamp has a black control number on the back.

Nathan Söderblom
A269

Cardinal von Galen
A270

1966, Jan. 15   Litho.   Perf. 13x13½
959 A269 20pf dull lilac & blk   .20   .30

Soderblom (1866-1931), Swedish Protestant theologian, who worked for the union of Christian churches and received 1930 Nobel Peace Prize.

1966, Mar. 22   Litho.   Perf. 14
960 A270 20pf dp lil rose, sal pink & blk   .20   .30

Clemens August Cardinal Count von Galen (1878-1946), anti-Nazi Bishop of Munster.

"The Miraculous Draught" — A271

G. W. Leibniz — A272

1966, July 13   Litho.   Perf. 14
961 A271 30pf dp orange & blk   .20   .30

81st meeting of German Catholics, Bamberg, July 13-17.

1966, Aug. 24   Unwmk.   Perf. 14
962 A272 30pf rose car, pink & blk   .20   .30

Gottfried Wilhelm Leibniz (1646-1716), philosopher and mathematician.

Europa Issue, 1966
Common Design Type
1966, Sept. 24   Perf. 14
Size: 23x28½mm
963 CD9 20pf multicolored   .25   .30
964 CD9 30pf multicolored   .20   .20

Diagram of Three-Phase Transmission
A273

UNICEF Emblem
A274

1966, Sept. 28   Litho.
965 A273 20pf shown   .20   .20
966 A273 30pf Dynamo   .20   .20

Progress in science and technology: 20pf, 75th anniv. of three-phase power transmission; 30pf, cent.y of discovery by Werner von Siemens of the dynamoelectric principle.

1966, Oct. 24   Litho.   Perf. 14
967 A274 30pf red, blk & gray   .20   .30

Awarding of the 1965 Nobel Peace Prize to UNICEF.

Werner von Siemens (1816-92), Electrical Engineer and Inventor — A275

1966, Dec. 13   Engr.   Perf. 14
968 A275 30pf maroon   .20   .30

Europa Issue, 1967
Common Design Type
1967, May 2   Photo.   Perf. 14
Size: 23x28mm
969 CD10 20pf multi   .30   .30
970 CD10 30pf multi   .20   .25

Franz von Taxis — A276

"Peace Is Among Us" — A277

Lithographed and Engraved
1967, June 3   Perf. 14
971 A276 30pf dp orange & blk   .20   .30

450th anniv. of the death of Franz von Taxis, founder of the Taxis (Thurn and Taxis) postal system.

1967, June 21
972 A277 30pf brt pink & blk   .20   .30

13th meeting of German Protestants (Evangelical Synod), Hanover, June 21-25.

Friedrich von Bodelschwingh
A278

Perf. 13½x13
1967, July 1   Litho.   Unwmk.
973 A278 30pf redsh brown & blk   .20   .30

Cent. of Bethel Institution (for the incurable). Friedrich von Bodelschwingh (1877-1946), manager of Bethel (1910-46) & son of the founder.

Lübke Type of 1964
1967, Oct. 14   Litho.   Perf. 14
974 A247 30pf carmine   .20   .20
975 A247 50pf ultra   .35   .35

Re-election of President Heinrich Lübke.

The Wartburg, Eisenach
A279

1967, Oct. 31   Engr.   Perf. 14
976 A279 30pf red   .30   .35

450th anniversary of the Reformation.

Cross and Map of South America — A280

Koenig Printing Press — A281

1967, Nov. 17   Photo.   Perf. 14
977 A280 30pf multicolored   .20   .30

"Adveniat," aid movement of German Catholics for the Latin American church.

1968, Jan. 12   Litho.   Perf. 14

Designs: 20pf, Zinc sulfide and lead sulfide crystals. 30pf, Schematic diagram of a microscope.

978 A281 10pf multicolored   .20   .20
979 A281 20pf multicolored   .20   .20
980 A281 30pf multicolored   .20   .20
     Nos. 978-980 (3)   .60   .60

Progress in science and technology: 10pf, 150th anniv. of the Koenig printing press; 20pf, 1000th anniv. of mining in the Harz Mountains; 30pf, cent. of scientific microscope construction.

Symbols of Various Crafts
A282

1968, Mar. 8   Litho.   Perf. 14
981 A282 30pf multicolored   .30   .35

Traditions and progress of the crafts. Exists imperf. Value $250.

Souvenir Sheet

Adenauer, Churchill, de Gasperi and Schuman — A283

Portraits: 10pf, Winston S. Churchill. 20pf, Alcide de Gasperi. 30pf, Robert Schuman. 50pf, Konrad Adenauer.

1968, Apr. 19   Litho.   Perf. 14
Black Inscriptions
982 A283 Sheet of 4   2.25   2.25
a. 10pf dark red brown   .50   .30
b. 20pf green   .50   .35
c. 30pf dark red   .50   .50
d. 50pf bright blue   .50   .75

1st anniv. of the death of Konrad Adenauer (1876-1967), chancellor of West Germany (1949-63), and honoring leaders in building a united Europe.

Europa Issue, 1968
Common Design Type
1968, Apr. 29   Photo.
Size: 29x24½mm
983 CD11 20pf green, yel & brn   .25   .30
984 CD11 30pf car, yel & brn   .20   .30

Karl Marx (1818-83)
A284

Lithographed and Engraved
1968, Apr. 29   Perf. 14
985 A284 30pf red, black & gray   .20   .20

Pierre de Coubertin — A285

1968, June 6   Unwmk.   Perf. 14
986 A285 30pf lilac & dk pur   .30   .30
     Nos. 986,B434-B437 (5)   2.20   2.30

19th Olympic Games, Mexico City, 10/12-27.

Opening Bars, "Die Meistersinger von Nurnberg," by Wagner — A286

Lithographed and Photogravure
1968, June 21
987 A286 30pf gray, blk & fawn   .20   .30

Cent. of the 1st performance of Richard Wagner's "Die Meistersinger von Nurnberg."

Konrad Adenauer (1876-1967)
A287

1968, July 19   Litho.   Perf. 14
988 A287 30pf dp orange & blk   .30   .30

Cross and Dove in Center of Universe
A288

1968, July 19   Litho. & Engr.
989 A288 20pf brt grn, bl blk & yel   .20   .30

Issued to publicize the 82nd meeting of German Catholics, Essen, Sept. 4-8.

North German Confederation Nos. 4 and 10 — A289

1968, Sept. 5   Engr.   Perf. 14
990 A289 30pf cop red, gray vio & blk   .20   .20

Cent. of the stamps of the North German Confederation.

Arrows Symbolizing Determination A290

Human Rights Flame A291

1968, Sept. 26   Photo.   Perf. 14
991 A290 30pf multi   .20   .30

Centenary of the German trade unions.

1968, Dec. 10   Photo.   Perf. 14
992 A291 30pf multicolored   .20   .30

International Human Rights Year.

Junkers 52 A292

Design: 30pf, Boeing 707.

1969, Feb. 6   Litho.   Perf. 14
993 A292 20pf green & multi   .40   .20
994 A292 30pf red & multi   .60   .20

50th anniv. of German airmail service.

Five-pointed Star — A293

1969, Apr. 28   Litho.   Perf. 13½x13
995 A293 30pf red & multi   .45   .30

50th anniv. of the ILO.

Europa Issue, 1969
Common Design Type

1969, Apr. 28   Photo.   Perf. 14
Size: 29x23mm

996 CD12 20pf green, blue & yel   .30   .20
997 CD12 30pf red brn, yel & blk   .35   .20

Heraldic Eagles of Federal and Weimar Republics A294

1969, May 23   Photo.   Perf. 14
998 A294 30pf red, black & gold   .90   .45

German Basic Law, 20th anniv., and the proclamation of the Weimar Constitution, 50th anniv.

Crosses — A295

1969, June 4   Litho. & Engr.
999 A295 30pf dk violet bl &
          cream   .45   .30

German War Graves Commission, 50th anniv.

Seashore A296

1969, June 4   Perf. 14
1000 A296 10pf shown   .20   .20
1001 A296 20pf Foothills   .60   .35
1002 A296 30pf Mountains   .30   .20
1003 A296 50pf Riverbed   .90   .50
     Nos. 1000-1003 (4)   2.00 1.25

Issued to publicize Nature Protection.

"Hungry for Justice" — A297

1969, July 7   Litho.   Perf. 14
1004 A297 30pf multicolored   .45   .30

14th meeting of German Protestants (Evangelical Synod), Stuttgart, July 16-20.

Electromagnetic Field — A298

1969, Aug. 11   Litho.   Perf. 14
1005 A298 30pf red & multi   .45   .30

Issued to publicize the German Radio Exhibition, Stuttgart, Aug. 29-Sept. 7.

Maltese Cross — A299

1969, Aug. 11   Perf. 13x13½
1006 A299 30pf red & black   .45   .30

Maltese Relief Service, founded 1955, world-wide activities in social services, first aid and disaster assistance.

Souvenir Sheet

Marie Juchacz, Marie-Elisabeth Lüders and Helene Weber — A300

1969, Aug. 11   Engr.   Perf. 14
1007 A300   Sheet of 3   .90   .65
   a.   10pf olive   .20   .20
   b.   20pf dark green   .20   .20
   c.   30pf lake   .20   .20

50th anniv. of universal women's suffrage. Marie Juchacz (1879-1956), Marie-Elisabeth Lüders (1878-1966) and Helene Weber (1881-1962) were members of the German Reichstag.

Bavaria No. 16 — A301

Brine Pipe Line — A302

1969, Sept. 4   Litho. & Embossed
1008 A301 30pf gray & rose   .45   .30

23rd meeting of the Federation of German Philatelists, Sept. 6, the 70th Philatelists' Day, Sept. 7, and the phil. exhib. "120 Years of Bavarian Stamps" in Garmish-Partenkirchen, Sept. 4-7.

1969, Sept. 4   Litho.   Perf. 13½x13
1009 A302 20pf multicolored   .45   .30

350th anniversary of the Brine Pipe Line from Traunstein to Bad Reichenhall.

Rothenburg ob der Tauber — A303

Lithographed and Engraved
1969, Sept. 4   Perf. 14
1010 A303 30pf dark red & blk   .45   .30

See #1047-1049, 1067-1069A, 1106-1110.

Pope John XXIII (1881-1963) A304

Mahatma Gandhi (1869-1948) A305

1969, Oct. 2   Engr.   Perf. 13½x14
1011 A304 30pf dark red   .35   .30

1969, Oct. 2   Litho.
1012 A305 20pf yellow grn & blk   .30   .30

Ernst Moritz Arndt A306

Ludwig van Beethoven A307

1969, Nov. 13   Litho. & Engr.
1013 A306 30pf gray & maroon   .35   .30

Arndt (1769-1860), historian, poet and member of German National Assembly.

1970, Mar. 20   Perf. 13½x14

Portraits: 20pf, Georg Wilhelm Hegel (1770-1831), philosopher. 30pf, Friedrich Hölderlin (1770-1843), poet.

1014 A307 10pf pale vio & blk   .75   .20
1015 A307 20pf olive & blk   .35   .20
1016 A307 30pf rose & blk   .35   .20
     Nos. 1014-1016 (3)   1.45   .60

Saar No. 171 A308

1970, Apr. 29   Photo.   Perf. 14x13½
1017 A308 30pf blk, red & gray
             grn   .35   .30

Issued to publicize the SABRIA National Stamp Exhibition, Saarbrucken, Apr. 29-May 4. No. 1017 was issued Apr. 29 at the SABRIA post office in Saarbrucken, on May 4 throughout Germany.

Europa Issue, 1970
Common Design Type

1970, May 4   Engr.   Perf. 14x13½
Size: 28x23mm
1018 CD13 20pf green   .30   .20
1019 CD13 30pf red   .35   .20

Münchhausen on His Severed Horse — A309

1970, May 11   Litho.   Perf. 13½x13
1020 A309 20pf multicolored   .35   .30

Soldier and storyteller Count Hieronymus C. F. von Münchhausen (1720-97).

Seagoing Vessel and Underpass A310

1970, June 18   Litho.   Perf. 14
1021 A310 20pf multicolored   .35   .30

North Sea-Baltic Sea Canal, 75th anniv.

Nurse Assisting Elderly Woman — A311

1970   Photo.

5pf, Welder (industrial protection). 10pf, Mountain climbers (rescuer bringing down casualty). 30pf, Fireman. 50pf, Stretcher bearer, casualty & ambulance. 70pf, Rescuer & drowning boy.

1022 A311 5pf dull blue & multi   .20   .20
1023 A311 10pf brown & multi   .20   .20
1024 A311 20pf green & multi   .30   .20
1025 A311 30pf red & multi   .75   .20
1026 A311 50pf blue & multi   .75   .35
1027 A311 70pf green & multi   .90   .75
     Nos. 1022-1027 (6)   3.10 1.90

Honoring various voluntary services. Issued: 20pf, 30pf, 6/18; others, 9/21.

Pres. Gustav Heinemann A312

Cross Seen through Glass A313

1970-73   Engr.   Perf. 14
1028 A312 5pf dark gray   .20   .20
1029 A312 10pf brown   .20   .20
1030 A312 20pf green   .20   .20
1030A A312 25pf dp yellow
             grn   .30   .20

1031	A312	30pf red brown	.30	.20
1032	A312	40pf brown org	.30	.20
1033	A312	50pf dark blue	1.40	.20
1034	A312	60pf blue	.50	.20
1035	A312	70pf dark brown	.65	.30
1036	A312	80pf slate grn	.65	.30
1037	A312	90pf magenta	1.25	1.10
1038	A312	1m olive	.90	.30
1038A	A312	110pf olive gray	1.00	.60
1039	A312	120pf ocher	1.10	.75
1040	A312	130pf ocher	1.25	.75
1040A	A312	140pf dk blue grn	1.40	.90
1041	A312	150pf purple	1.40	.60
1042	A312	160pf orange	2.00	1.00
1042A	A312	170pf orange	1.60	.60
1043	A312	190pf deep claret	2.25	.75
1044	A312	2m deep violet	1.75	.35
		Nos. 1028-1044 (21)	20.60	9.90

Issued: 5pf, 1m, 7/23/70; 10, 20pf, 10/23/70; 30, 90pf, 2m, 1/7/71; 40, 50, 70, 80pf, 4/8/71; 60pf, 6/25/71; 25pf, 8/27/71; 120, 160pf, 3/8/72; 130pf, 6/20/72; 150pf, 7/5/72; 170pf, 9/11/72; 110, 140, 190pf, 1/16/73.

1970, Aug. 25   **Litho.**
| 1045 | A313 | 20pf emerald & yellow | .30 | .20 |

Issued to publicize the world mission of Catholic missionaries who bring the Gospel to all peoples.

Cross A314   Comenius A315

1970, Sept. 4   **Perf. 13x13½**
| 1046 | A314 | 20pf multicolored | .30 | .30 |

Issued to publicize the 83rd meeting of German Catholics, Trier, Sept. 9-13.

Town Type of 1969

Designs: No. 1047, View of Cochem and Moselle River. No. 1048, Cathedral and view of Freiburg im Breisgau. No. 1049, View of Oberammergau.

1970   **Litho.**   **Perf. 14**
1047	A303	20pf apple grn & blk	.45	.30
1048	A303	20pf green & dk brn	.45	.30
1049	A303	30pf dp orange & blk	.45	.30
		Nos. 1047-1049 (3)	1.35	.90

Issued: #1047, 9/21; #1048, 11/4; #1049, 5/11.

1970, Nov. 12   **Perf. 13½x14**
| 1050 | A315 | 30pf dark red & blk | .45 | .30 |

John Amos Comenius (1592-1670), theologian and educator.

Friedrich Engels — A316

Imperial Eagle, 1872 — A317

1970, Nov. 27   **Litho.**   **Perf. 14**
| 1051 | A316 | 50pf red & vio blue | 1.40 | .75 |

Engels (1820-95), socialist, collaborator with Marx.

1971, Jan. 18   **Litho.**   **Perf. 13½x14**
| 1052 | A317 | 30pf multicolored | 1.40 | .30 |

Centenary of the German Empire.

Friedrich Ebert (Germany No. 378) — A318

Molecule Diagram Textile Pattern — A319

1971, Jan. 18   **Perf. 13**
| 1053 | A318 | 30pf red brn, ol & blk | 1.40 | .30 |

Ebert (1871-1925), 1st Pres. of the German Republic.

1971, Feb. 18   **Litho.**   **Perf. 13½x13**
| 1054 | A319 | 20pf brt grn, red & blk | .30 | .20 |

Synthetic textile fiber research, 125th anniversary.

School Crossing — A320

Signal to Pass — A321

Traffic Signs: 20pf, Proceed with caution. 30pf, Stop. 50pf, Pedestrian crossing.

1971, Feb. 18   **Perf. 14**
1055	A320	10pf black, ultra & red	.20	.20
1056	A320	20pf black, red & grn	.30	.20
1057	A320	30pf black, gray & red	.45	.20
1058	A320	50pf black, ultra & red	.75	.45
		Nos. 1055-1058 (4)	1.70	1.05

New traffic rules, effective Mar. 1, 1971.

1971, Apr. 16   **Photo.**   **Perf. 14**
Traffic Signs: 10pf, Warning signal. 20pf, Drive at right. 30pf, "Observe pedestrian crossings."
1059	A321	5pf blue, blk & car	.20	.20
1060	A321	10pf multicolored	.20	.20
1061	A321	20pf brt grn, blk & car	.35	.20
1062	A321	30pf carmine & multi	.65	.20
		Nos. 1059-1062 (4)	1.40	.80

New traffic rules, effective Mar. 1, 1971.

Luther Facing Charles V, Woodcut by Rabus — A322

Thomas à Kempis — A323

1971, Mar. 18   **Perf. 14**
| 1063 | A322 | 30pf red & black | .60 | .30 |

450th anniversary of the Diet of Worms.

Europa Issue, 1971
Common Design Type

1971, May 3   **Photo.**   **Perf. 14**
Size: 28½x23mm
| 1064 | CD14 | 20pf green, gold & blk | .30 | .20 |
| 1065 | CD14 | 30pf dp car, gold & blk | .30 | .20 |

1971, May 3   **Engr.**
| 1066 | A323 | 30pf red & black | .50 | .30 |

500th anniversary of the death of Thomas à Kempis (1379-1471), Augustinian monk, author of "The Imitation of Christ."

Town Type of 1969

20pf, View of Goslar. #1068, View of Nuremberg. #1069, Heligoland. 40pf, Heidelberg.

1971-72   **Litho. & Engr.**   **Perf. 14**
1067	A303	20pf brt green & blk	.45	.35
1068	A303	30pf vermilion & blk	.45	.30
1069	A303	30pf lt grn & blk ('72)	.45	.20
1069A	A303	40pf orange & blk ('72)	.50	.20
		Nos. 1067-1069A (4)	1.85	1.05

Issued: 20pf, 9/15; #1068, 5/21; #1069, 1069A, 10/20.

Dürer's Signature A324

1971, May 21   **Engr.**
| 1070 | A324 | 30pf copper red & blk | 1.25 | .30 |

500th anniversary of the birth of Albrecht Dürer (1471-1528), painter and engraver.

Congress Emblem — A325

Illustration from New Astronomy, by Kepler — A326

1971, May 28   **Litho.**   **Perf. 13½x13**
| 1071 | A325 | 30pf red, orange & blk | .45 | .30 |

Ecumenical Meeting at Pentecost of the German Evangelical and Catholic Churches, Augsburg, June 2-5.

1971, June 25   **Photo.**   **Perf. 14**
| 1072 | A326 | 30pf brt car, gold & blk | .50 | .30 |

Johannes Kepler (1571-1630), astronomer.

Dante Alighieri — A327

"Matches Cause Fires" — A328

1971, Sept. 3   **Engr.**   **Perf. 14**
| 1073 | A327 | 10pf black | .20 | .20 |

650th anniversary of the death of Dante Alighieri (1265-1321), poet.

1971-74   **Typo.**   **Perf. 14**

Designs: 10pf, Broken ladder. 20pf, Hand and circular saw. 25pf, "Alcohol and automobile." 30pf, Safety helmets prevent injury. 40pf, Defective plug. 50pf, Nail sticking from board. 60pf, 70pf, Traffic safety (ball rolling before car). 1m, Hoisted cargo. 1.50m, Fenced-in open manhole.

1074	A328	5pf orange	.20	.20
a.		Bklt. pane, 2 each #1074, 1077-1079 ('74)	5.25	11.00
1075	A328	10pf dark brown	.20	.20
a.		Bklt. pane, 4 #1075, 2 #1078	3.00	3.00
b.		Bklt. pane, 2 each #1075-1076, 1078-1079 ('75)	5.25	11.00
c.		Bklt. pane, 2 each #1079, 1075, 1078, 1076	13.50	16.50
1076	A328	20pf purple	.30	.20
1077	A328	25pf green	.40	.20
1078	A328	30pf dark red	.35	.20
1079	A328	40pf rose claret	.35	.20
1080	A328	50pf Prus blue	1.90	.20
1081	A328	60pf violet blue	1.10	.45
1082	A328	70pf green & vio bl	1.10	.30
1083	A328	100pf olive	1.60	.20
1085	A328	150pf red brown	5.00	1.10
		Nos. 1074-1085 (11)	12.50	3.45

Accident prevention.
Issued in sheets of 100 and in coils. Every fifth coil stamp has a control number on the back.
Issued: 25pf, 60pf, 9/10; 5pf, 10/29; 10pf, 30pf, 3/8/72; 40pf, 6/20/72; 20pf, 100pf, 7/5/72; 150pf, 9/11/72; 50pf, 1/16/73; 70pf, 6/5/73.

Deaconesses A329

Senefelder's Lithography Press — A330

1972, Jan. 20   **Litho.**   **Perf. 13x13½**
| 1087 | A329 | 25pf green, blk & gray | .45 | .30 |

Wilhelm Löhe (1808-1872), founder of the Deaconesses Training Institute at Neuendettelsau.

1972, Apr. 14   **Litho.**   **Perf. 13½x13**
| 1088 | A330 | 25pf multicolored | .45 | .30 |

175th anniv. of the invention of the lithographic printing process by Alois Senefelder in 1796.

Europa Issue 1972
Common Design Type

1972, May 2   **Photo.**   **Perf. 13½x14**
Size: 23x29mm
| 1089 | CD15 | 25pf yel grn, dk bl & yel | .35 | .20 |
| 1090 | CD15 | 30pf pale rose, dk & lt bl | .50 | .25 |

Lucas Cranach, by Dürer A331

Archer in Wheelchair A332

Lithographed and Engraved
1972, May 18 _Perf. 14_
1091 A331 25pf green, buff & blk .50 .30
Cranach (1472-1553), painter and engraver.

1972, July 18 _Litho._ _Perf. 14_
1092 A332 40pf yel, blk & red brn .60 .30
21st Stoke-Mandeville Games for the Paralyzed, Heidelberg, Aug. 1-10.

Kurt Schumacher A333

1972, Aug. 18 _Litho. & Engr._
1093 A333 40pf red & black 1.25 .30
Schumacher (1895-1952), 1st chairman of the German Social Democratic Party.

Post Horn and Decree — A334

1972, Aug. 18 _Photo._
1094 A334 40pf gold, car & blk .80 .30
Centenary of the German Postal Museum, Berlin. Design shows page from Heinrich von Stephan's decree establishing the museum.

Open Book — A335

1972, Sept. 11 Photo. _Perf. 13x13½_
1095 A335 40pf red & multi .60 .30
International Book Year 1972.

Lithographed and Engraved
1972, Sept. 29 _Perf. 14_
1096 A336 40pf multicolored .75 .30
300th anniversary of the death of Heinrich Schütz (1585-1672), composer.

Music by Heinrich Schütz — A336

Carnival Dancers A337

1972, Nov. 10 _Litho._ _Perf. 14_
1097 A337 40pf red & multi .90 .30
Cologne Carnival sesquicentennial.

Heinrich Heine (1797-1856), Poet — A338

1972, Dec. 13 _Litho._ _Perf. 14_
1098 A338 40pf rose, blk & red .90 .30

"Bread for the World" A339

1972, Dec. 13 _Photo._ _Perf. 14_
1099 A339 30pf green & red .45 .45
14th "Bread for the World-Developing Peace" campaign of the Protestant Church in Germany.

Würzburg Cathedral, 13th Century Seal — A340

1972, Dec. 13 _Litho._
1100 A340 40pf dp car, lil rose & blk .50 .30
Synod 72, meeting of Catholic bishoprics, Würzburg.

Colors of France and Germany Interlaced — A340a

1973, Jan. 22 _Litho._ _Perf. 14_
Size: 51x28mm
1101 A340a 40pf multicolored 1.25 .30
10th anniversary of the Franco-German Cooperation Treaty.

Meteorological Map — A341

1973, Feb. 19 _Litho._ _Perf. 14_
1102 A341 30pf multicolored .35 .30
Cent. of intl. meteorological cooperation.

Radio Tower and "Interpol" A342

1973, Feb. 19 _Perf. 13½x13_
1103 A342 40pf blk & red .45 .30
50th anniversary of International Criminal Police Organization (INTERPOL).

Nicolaus Copernicus and Solar System — A343

1973, Feb. 19 _Perf. 14_
1104 A343 40pf blk & red 1.25 .30

Festival Poster — A344

1973, Mar. 15 _Photo._ _Perf. 14_
1105 A344 40pf multicolored .45 .30
German Turner Festival, Stuttgart, 6/12-17.

Maximilian Kolbe — A345

Town Type of 1969
Designs: 30pf, Saarbrücken. No. 1107, Ship in Hamburg Harbor. No. 1108, Rüdesheim. No. 1109, Aachen. No. 1110, Ships, Bremen Harbor.

1973 **Lithographed and Engraved**
1106 A303 30pf yel grn & blk .60 .20
1107 A303 30pf red & blk .90 .20
1108 A303 40pf org & blk .75 .20
1109 A303 40pf brn red & blk .60 .20
1110 A303 40pf red & blk .60 .20
  Nos. 1106-1110 (5) 3.45 1.00
Issued: #1107-1108, 3/15; others 10/19.

Europa Issue 1973
Common Design Type
1973, Apr. 30 _Photo._ _Perf. 13½x14_
Size: 38½x21mm
1114 CD16 30pf grn, lt grn & yel .35 .20
1115 CD16 40pf dp mag, lil & yel .50 .20

1973, May 25 _Litho._ _Perf. 14_
1116 A345 40pf red, blk & brn .50 .30
Maximilian Kolbe (1894-1941), Polish priest who died in Auschwitz and was beatified in 1971.

"R" for Roswitha — A346

"Not by Bread Alone" — A347

1973, May 25
1117 A346 40pf red, blk & yel .50 .30
Millenary of the death of Roswitha of Gandersheim, Germany's first poetess.

1973, May 25 _Photo._
1118 A347 30pf multicolored .35 .20
15th meeting of German Protestants (Evangelical Synod), Dusseldorf, June 27-July 1.

Environment Emblem and "Waste" — A348

30pf, "Water." 40pf, "Noise." 70pf, "Air."
1973, June 5 _Litho._
1119 A348 25pf multicolored .35 .20
1120 A348 30pf multicolored .40 .20
1121 A348 40pf org & multi .75 .20
1122 A348 70pf ultra & multi 1.25 .65
  Nos. 1119-1122 (4) 2.75 1.25
International environment protection and Environment Day, June 5.

Reconstructed Model of Schickard's Calculator A349

1973, June 12
1123 A349 40pf org & multi .45 .40
350th anniv. of the calculator built by Prof. Wilhelm Shickard, University of Tubingen.

Otto Wels (1873-1939), Leader of German Social Democratic Party — A350

1973, Sept. 14 _Litho._ _Perf. 14_
1124 A350 40pf magenta & lilac .50 .30

Lubeck Cathedral — A351

1973, Sept. 14 _Litho. & Engr._
1125 A351 40pf blk & multi .90 .30
800th anniversary of Lubeck Cathedral.

Emblems from UN and German Flags A352

1973, Sept. 21 _Litho._
1126 A352 40pf multicolored 1.25 .30
Germany's admission to the UN.

Radio and Speaker, 1923 — A353

1973, Oct. 19 _Photo._ _Perf. 14_
1127 A353 30pf brt grn & multi .35 .20
50 years of German broadcasting.

Luise Otto-Peters A354

1974, Jan. 15 _Litho. & Engr._
1128 A354 40pf shown .60 .45
1129 A354 40pf Helene Lange .60 .45
1130 A354 40pf Gertrud Bäumer .60 .45
1131 A354 40pf Rosa Luxemburg .60 .45
  Nos. 1128-1131 (4) 2.40 1.80
Honoring German women writers and leaders in political and women's movements.

Drop of Blood and Police Car Light A355

1974, Feb. 15   Photo.   Perf. 14
1132 A355 40pf carmine & ultra   .80 .30
Blood donor service in conjunction with accident emergency service.

Handicapped People — A356

1974, Feb. 15   Litho.   Perf. 14
1133 A356 40pf red & blk   .80 .30
Rehabilitation of the handicapped.

Thomas Aquinas Teaching A357

1974, Feb. 15
1134 A357 40pf blk & red   .50 .30
St. Thomas Aquinas (1225-1274), scholastic philosopher.

Girls under Trees, by August Macke — A358

Paintings: No. 1135, Deer in Red, by Franz Marc. 40pf, Portrait in Blue, by Alexej von Jawlensky, vert. 50pf, Pechstein (man) Asleep, by Erich Heckel, vert. 70pf, "Big Still-life," by Max Beckmann. 120pf, Old Farmer, by Ernst Ludwig Kirchner, vert.

1974   Photo.
1135 A358   30pf multicolored   .50 .20
1136 A358   30pf multicolored   .60 .20
1137 A358   40pf multicolored   .60 .20
1138 A358   50pf multicolored   .65 .20
1139 A358   70pf multicolored   .90 .75
1140 A358   120pf multicolored   1.75 1.50
        Nos. 1135-1140 (6)   5.00 3.05
German expressionist painters.
Issued: #1135, 1137, Feb. 15; #1136, 1138, Aug. 16; #1139-1140, Oct. 29.

Young Man, by Lehmbruck A359

Immanuel Kant A360

Europa: 40pf, Kneeling Woman, by Wilhelm Lehmbruck.

1974, Apr. 17   Litho.   Perf. 14
1141 A359   30pf multicolored   .35 .20
1142 A359   40pf multicolored   .50 .25

1974   Litho. and Engr.   Perf. 14
1143 A360 40pf Klopstock   .50 .20
Engr.
1144 A360 90pf shown   1.90 .45
Friedrich Gottlieb Klopstock (1724-1803), poet, and Immanuel Kant (1724-1804), philosopher.
Issue dates: 40pf, May 15; 90pf, Apr. 17.

Souvenir Sheet

Federal Eagle and Flag — A361

1974, May 15   Litho. & Embossed
1145 A361 40pf gray & multi   1.25 1.90
Federal Republic of Germany, 25th anniv.

Soccer and Games Emblem A362

Design: 40pf, Three soccer players.

1974, May 15   Litho.
1146 A362 30pf grn & multi   .80 .20
1147 A362 40pf org & multi   1.60 .20
World Cup Soccer Championship, Munich, June 13-July 7.

Crowned Cross Emblem of Diaconate A363

Landscape A364

1974, May 15
1148 A363 40pf multicolored   .45 .30
125th anniversary of the Diaconal Association of the German Protestant Church.

1974, May 15
1149 A364 30pf multicolored   .35 .30
To promote hiking and youth hostels.

Broken Bars of Prison Window — A365

1974, July 16   Litho.   Perf. 14x13½
1150 A365 70pf violet bl & blk   .95 .45
"Amnesty International," an organization for the protection of the rights of political, non-violent, prisoners.

Hans Holbein, Self-portrait A366

Lithographed and Engraved
1974, July 16   Perf. 13½x14
1151 A366 50pf multicolored   .75 .30
Hans Holbein the Elder (c. 1470-1524), painter.

Man and Woman Looking at Moon, by Friedrich — A367

1974, Aug. 16   Photo.   Perf. 14
1152 A367 50pf multicolored   .95 .30
Caspar David Friedrich (1774-1840), German Romantic painter.

Swiss and German 19th Century Mail Boxes — A368

1974, Oct. 29   Litho.   Perf. 14
1153 A368 50pf red & multi   1.25 .35
Centenary of Universal Postal Union.

Mothers and Foundation Emblem — A369

1975, Jan. 15   Litho.   Perf. 13
1154 A369 50pf multicolored   .65 .30
Convalescent Mothers' Foundation, 25th anniversary.

Annette Kolb (1875-1967), Writer — A370

German women writers: 40pf, Ricarda Huch (1864-1947), writer. 50pf, Else Lasker-Schüler (1869-1945), poetess. 70pf, Gertrud von Le Fort (1876-1971), writer.

Lithographed and Engraved
1975, Jan. 15   Perf. 14
1155 A370 30pf brown & multi   .60 .30
1156 A370 40pf multicolored   .50 .30
1157 A370 50pf claret & multi   .50 .30
1158 A370 70pf blue & multi   .90 .90
        Nos. 1155-1158 (4)   2.50 1.80

Dr. Albert Schweitzer — A371

Design: 40pf, Hans Böckler.

1975   Engr.
1159 A371 40pf grn & blk   .65 .30
1160 A371 70pf bl & blk   1.90 .75
Böckler (1875-1951), German Workers' Union leader, and of Dr. Albert Schweitzer (1875-1965), medical missionary. Issued: 40pf, Feb. 14; 70pf, Jan. 15.

Head, by Michelangelo A372

Plan of St. Peter's, Rome A373

1975, Feb. 14   Photo.   Perf. 14
1161 A372 70pf vio bl & blk   1.40 1.25
Michelangelo Buonarroti (1475-1564), Italian sculptor, painter and architect.

1975, Feb. 14
1162 A373 50pf red & multi   .65 .30
Holy Year 1975, the "Year of Reconciliation."

Ice Hockey A374

1975, Feb. 14   Litho.   Perf. 14
1163 A374 50pf bl & multi   .95 .30
Ice Hockey World Championship, Munich and Düsseldorf, Apr. 3-19.

Concentric Group, by Oskar Schlemmer — A375

Europa: 50pf, Bauhaus Staircase, painting by Oskar Schlemmer (1888-1943) and CEPT emblem.

1975, Apr. 15   Litho. & Engr.
1164 A375 40pf gray & multi   .45 .20
1165 A375 50pf gray & multi   .70 .20

Eduard Mörike, Weather Vane, Quill and Signature A376

1975, May 15
1166 A376 40pf multicolored   .40 .20
Eduard Mörike (1804-75), pastor and poet.

Joust, from Jousting Book of William IV A377

1975, May 15   Photo.   Perf. 14
1167 A377 50pf multicolored   .90 .30
500th anniv. of the Wedding of Landshut, (last Duke of Landshut married the daughter of King of Poland, now a yearly local festival).

Cathedral of Mainz
A378

1975, May 15　　　　Litho. & Engr.
1168 A378 40pf multicolored　　　　.90 .30
Millennium of the Cathedral of Mainz.

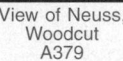

View of Neuss, Woodcut
A379

Satellite
A380

1975, May 15
1169 A379 50pf multicolored　　　　.60 .30
500th anniv. of the unsuccessful siege of Neuss by Duke Charles the Bold of Burgundy.

1975-82　　　　Engr.　　　　Perf. 14
1170 A380 5pf Shown　　　　　　.20 .20
1171 A380 10pf Electric train　　　.20 .20
1172 A380 20pf Old Weser lighthouse　　　　　.20 .20
1173 A380 30pf Rescue helicopter　　　　　.20 .20
1174 A380 40pf Space shuttle　　　　　.30 .20
1175 A380 50pf Radar station　　　.40 .20
1176 A380 60pf X-ray machine　　　　　.50 .20
1177 A380 70pf Shipbuilding　　　.60 .20
1178 A380 80pf Tractor　　　　　.65 .20
1179 A380 100pf Bituminous coal excavator　　　.75 .20
1180 A380 110pf Color TV camera　　　1.50 .60
1181 A380 120pf Chemical plant　　　　.95 .30
1182 A380 130pf Brewery　　　1.90 .60
1183 A380 140pf Heating plant, Licterfelde　　　1.10 .40
1184 A380 150pf Power shovel　　2.40 .75
1185 A380 160pf Blast furnace　　1.50 .60
1186 A380 180pf Payloader　　1.90 .75
1187 A380 190pf As #1184　　2.25 .60
1188 A380 200pf Oil drilling　　1.60 .30
1189 A380 230pf Frankfurt Airport　　　2.75 .90
1190 A380 250pf Airport　　3.25 1.40
1191 A380 300pf Electro. RR　　3.75 1.40
1192 A380 500pf Effelsberg radio telescope　　　4.00 1.10
Nos. 1170-1192 (23)　32.85 11.70

Issued: 40, 50, 100pf, 5/15; 10, 30, 70pf, 8/14; 80, 120, 160pf, 10/15; 5, 140, 200pf, 11/14; 20, 500pf, 2/17/76; 60pf, 11/16/78; 230pf, 5/17/79; 150, 180pf, 7/12/79; 110, 130, 300pf, 6/16/82; 190, 250pf, 7/15/82.

Market and Town Hall, Alsfeld
A381

#1197, Plönlein Corner, Siebers Tower and Kobolzeller Gate, Rothenburg. #1198, Town Hall (Steipe), Trier. #1199, View of Xanten.

1975, July 15　　　　Litho. & Engr.
1196 A381 50pf multicolored　　　.75 .50
1197 A381 50pf multicolored　　　.75 .50
1198 A381 50pf multicolored　　　.75 .50
1199 A381 50pf multicolored　　　.75 .50
Nos. 1196-1199 (4)　　3.00 2.00
European Architectural Heritage Year.

Three Stages of Drug Addiction
A382

1975, Aug. 14　　　　Photo.　　　　Perf. 14
1200 A382 40pf multicolored　　　.40 .30
Fight against drug abuse.

Matthias Erzberger
A383

1975, Aug. 14　　　　Engr.
1201 A383 50pf red & black　　　.60 .30
Erzberger (1875-1921), statesman, signer of Compiègne Armistice (1918) at end of World War I.

Sign of Royal Prussian Post, 1776 — A384

1975, Aug. 14　　　　Litho.
1202 A384 10pf blue & multi　　　.35 .20
Stamp Day, 1975, and 76th German Philatelists' Day, Sept. 21.

Souvenir Sheet

Gustav Stresemann, Ludwig Quidde, Carl von Ossietzky — A385

1975, Nov. 14　　　　Engr.　　　　Perf. 14
1203 A385 Sheet of 3　　　1.90 1.90
a.-c.　　50pf, single stamp　　.60 .50
German winners of Nobel Peace Prize. No. 1203 has litho. marginal inscription.

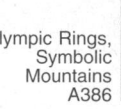

Olympic Rings, Symbolic Mountains
A386

1976, Jan. 5　　　　Litho. & Engr.
1204 A386 50pf red & multi　　　.90 .30
12th Winter Olympic Games, Innsbruck, Austria, Feb. 4-15.

Konrad Adenauer — A387

1976, Jan. 5　　　　Engr.
1205 A387 50pf dark slate green 1.75 .30
Konrad Adenauer (1876-1967), Chancellor (1949-63).

Books by Hans Sachs — A388

1976, Jan. 5　　　　Litho.
1206 A388 40pf multicolored　　　.60 .30
Hans Sachs (1494-1576), poet (meistersinger), 400th death anniversary.

Junkers F 13, 1926 — A389

1976, Jan. 5
1207 A389 50pf multicolored　　　.90 .30
Lufthansa, 50th anniversary.

German Eagle — A390

1976, Feb. 17　　Photo.　　Perf. 14
1208 A390 50pf red, blk & gold　　.75 .30
Federal Constitutional Court, 25th anniv.

"EG"
A391

1976, Apr. 6　　Photo.　　Perf. 14
1209 A391 40pf red & multi　　　.75 .30
European Coal and Steel Community, 25th anniversary.

Wuppertal Suspension Train — A392

1976, Apr. 6　　　　Litho.
1210 A392 50pf multicolored　　　.75 .30
Wuppertal suspension railroad, 75th anniv.

Girl Selling Trinkets and Prints — A393

Europa: 50pf, Boy selling copperplate prints, and CEPT emblem. Ludwigsburg china figurines, c. 1765.

1976, May 13　　　　Photo.
1211 A393 40pf olive & multi　　　.40 .20
1212 A393 50pf scarlet & multi　　.60 .20

Dr. Carl Sonnenschein
A394

1976, May 13　　　　Litho.
1213 A394 50pf carmine & multi　　.60 .30
Sonnenschein (1876-1929), Roman Catholic clergyman and social reformer.

Weber Conducting "Freischutz" in Covent Garden — A395

1976, May 13
1214 A395 50pf red brown & blk　　.75 .30
Carl Maria von Weber (1786-1826), composer, 150th death anniversary.

Hymn, by Paul Gerhardt
A396

1976, May 13　　　　Engr. & Litho.
1215 A396 40pf multicolored　　　.40 .20
Gerhardt (1607-76), Lutheran hymn writer.

Carl Schurz, American Flag, Capitol
A397

1976, May 13　　　　Litho.
1216 A397 70pf multicolored　　　.95 .35
American Bicentennial.

Modern Stage
A398

1976, July 14　　　　Litho.　　　　Perf. 14
1217 A398 50pf multicolored　　　1.25 .30
Bayreuth Festival, centenary.

Bronze Ritual Chariot c. 1000 B.C. A399

Archaeological Treasures: 40pf, Celtic gold vessel, 5th-4th centuries B.C. 50pf, Celtic silver torque, 2nd-1st centuries B.C. 120pf, Roman cup with masks, 1st century A.D.

1976, July 14
1218	A399	30pf multicolored	.35	.30
1219	A399	40pf multicolored	.50	.30
1220	A399	50pf multicolored	.75	.45
1221	A399	120pf multicolored	1.60	1.60
		Nos. 1218-1221 (4)	3.20	2.65

Golden Plover A400 — "Simplicissimus Teutsch" A401

1976, Aug. 17
1222	A400	50pf multicolored	1.00	.30

Protection of birds.

1976, Aug. 17
1223	A401	40pf multicolored	1.00	.30

Johann Jacob Christoph von Grimmelshausen, 300th birth anniversary; author of the "Adventures of Simplicissimus Teutsch."

Imperial Post Emblem, Höchst am Main, 18th Cent. — A402 — Caroline Neuber as Medea — A403

1976, Oct. 14   Litho.   Perf. 14
1224	A402	10pf brown & multi	.30	.20

Stamp Day.

1976, Nov. 16   Photo.
German Actresses: 40pf, Sophie Schröder (1781-1868) as Sappho. 50pf, Louise Dumont (1862-1932) as Hedda Gabler. 70pf, Hermine Körner (1878-1960) as Lady Macbeth.

1225	A403	30pf multicolored	.40	.20
1226	A403	40pf multicolored	.40	.20
1227	A403	50pf multicolored	.60	.30
1228	A403	70pf multicolored	1.00	.90
		Nos. 1225-1228 (4)	2.40	1.60

Palais de l'Europe, Strasbourg — A404

1977, Jan. 13   Engr.   Perf. 14
1229	A404	140pf green & blk	1.60	.50

Inauguration of the new Council of Europe Headquarters, Jan. 28.

Scenes from Till Eulenspiegel A405 — Pfaueninsel Castle A406

1977, Jan. 13   Litho.
1230	A405	50pf multicolored	.50	.30

Till Eulenspiegel (d. 1350), roguish fool and hero, his adventures reported in book of same name.

1977-79   Typo.   Perf. 14
1231	A406	10pf Glucksburg	.20	.20
a.		Bklt. pane, 4 #1231, 2 each #1234, 1236	4.00	6.75
b.		Bklt. pane, 4 #1231, 2 #1234, 2 #1310	2.50	3.00
c.		Bklt. pane, 4 #1231, 2 #1310, 2 #1312	6.00	6.25
d.		Bklt. pane, 2 each #1231, 1234, 1310-1311	9.00	13.50
1232	A406	20pf Shown	.20	.20
1233	A406	25pf Gemen	.35	.20
1234	A406	30pf Ludwigstein	.30	.20
1235	A406	40pf Eltz	.50	.20
1236	A406	50pf Neuschwanstein	.55	.20
1237	A406	60pf Marksburg	.75	.20
1238	A406	70pf Mespelbrunn	.75	.20
1239	A406	90pf Vischerenburg	1.10	.35
1240	A406	190pf Pfaueninsel	1.90	.75
1240A	A406	200pf Burresheim	2.25	.75
1241	A406	210pf Schwanenburg	3.00	1.10
1242	A406	230pf Lichtenberg	3.00	1.10
		Nos. 1231-1242 (13)	14.85	5.65

See Nos. 1308-1315.
Issued in sheets of 100 and in coils. Every fifth coil stamp has control number on the back.
Issued: 60, 200pf, 1/13; 40, 190pf, 2/16; 10, 30pf, 4/14; 50, 70pf, 5/17; 230pf, 11/16/78; 25, 90pf, 1/11/79; 20, 210pf, 2/14/79.

Souvenir Sheet

German Art Nouveau — A407

Designs: 30pf, Floral ornament. 70pf, Athena, poster by Franz von Stuck. 90pf, Chair, c. 1902.

1977, Feb. 16   Litho.   Perf. 14
1243	A407	Sheet of 3	2.00	1.50
a.		30pf multicolored	.30	.20
b.		70pf multicolored	.55	.50
c.		90pf multicolored	.90	.70

1st German Art Nouveau Exhib., 75th anniv.

Jean Monnet A408

1977, Feb. 16
1244	A408	50pf black & yellow	.60	.30

Jean Monnet (1888-1979), French proponent of unification of Europe, became first Honorary Citizen of Europe in Apr. 1976.

Flower Show Emblem A409 — Gauss Plane of Complex Numbers A410

1977, Apr. 14
1245	A409	50pf green & multi	.80	.30

25th Federal Horticultural Show, Stuttgart, Apr. 29-Oct. 23.

1977, Apr. 14
1246	A410	40pf silver & multi	1.25	.30

Carl Friedrich Gauss (1777-1855), mathematician, 200th birth anniversary.

Barbarossa Head, Cappenberg Reliquary — A411

1977, Apr. 14
1247	A411	40pf multicolored	1.25	.30

Staufer Year 1977. "Time of the Hohenstaufen" Exhibition, Stuttgart, Mar. 25-June 5, in connection with the 25th anniversary of Baden-Wurttemberg.

Rhön Highway A412

Europa: 50pf, Rhine, Siebengebirge and train.

1977, May 7   Litho. & Engr.
1248	A412	40pf brt green & blk	.70	.25
1249	A412	50pf brt red & blk	.70	.25

Rubens, Self-portrait A413 — Ulm Cathedral A414

1977, May 17   Engr.
1250	A413	30pf brown black	.80	.30

Peter Paul Rubens (1577-1640), Flemish painter, 400th birth anniversary.

1977, May 17   Litho. & Engr.
1251	A414	40pf blue & sepia	.50	.30

600th anniversary of Ulm Cathedral.

Madonna, Oldest Rector's Seal A415 — Landgrave Philipp, Great Seal of University A416

1977, May 17   Photo.
1252	A415	50pf indigo & org red	.75	.30
1253	A416	50pf indigo & org red	.75	.30

Mainz University, 500th anniv. (No. 1252); Marburg University, 450th anniv. (No. 1253).

Morning, by Runge — A417

1977, July 13   Litho.   Perf. 14
1254	A417	60pf blue & multi	.75	.35

Philipp Otto Runge (1777-1810), painter.

Bishop Ketteler's Coat of Arms — A418

1977, July 13
1255	A418	50pf multicolored	.60	.30

Wilhelm Emmanuel von Ketteler (1811-1877), Bishop of Mainz, Reichstag member and social reformer, death centenary.

Fritz von Bodelschwingh A419

1977, July 13   Litho. & Engr.
1256	A419	50pf multicolored	.75	.30

Pastor Fritz von Bodelschwingh (1877-1946), manager of Bethel Institute (for the incurable sick), birth centenary.

Jesus as Teacher, Great Seal of University — A420

1977, Aug. 16   Photo.
1257	A420	50pf multicolored	.90	.30

Tübingen University, 500th anniversary.

Golden Hat, Schifferstadt, Bronze Age — A421

1977, Aug. 16 Litho.

Archaeological heritage: 120pf, Gilt helmet, from Prince's Tomb, Krefeld-Gellep. 200pf, Bronze Centaur's head, Schwarzenacker.

1258	A421	30pf multicolored	.40	.30
1259	A421	120pf multicolored	1.50	1.10
1260	A421	200pf multicolored	2.00	1.60
	Nos. 1258-1260 (3)		3.90	3.00

Telephone Operator and Switchboard, 1881 — A422

1977, Oct. 13 Litho. *Perf. 14*

1261 A422 50pf multicolored 1.00 .30

German telephone centenary.

Arms of Hamburg, Post Emblem, c. 1861 — A423

Wilhelm Hauff — A424

1977, Oct. 13

1262 A423 10pf multicolored .35 .20

Stamp Day.

1977, Nov. 10 Photo. *Perf. 14*

1263 A424 40pf multicolored .40 .20

Wilhelm Hauff (1802-1827), writer and fabulist, 150th death anniversary.

Traveling Surgeon A425

Book Cover, by Alexander Schröder A426

1977, Nov. 10 Litho.

1264 A425 50pf multicolored .75 .30

Dr. Johann Andreas Eisenbarth (1663-1727), traveling surgeon and adventurer.

1978, Jan. 12 Litho. *Perf. 14*

1265 A426 50pf multicolored .60 .30

Rudolf Alexander Schröder (1878-1962), writer, designer, Lutheran minister.

"Refugees" — A427

1978, Jan. 12 Photo.

1266 A427 50pf multicolored .60 .30

Friedland Aid Society for displaced Germans, 20th anniversary.

Souvenir Sheet

Gerhart Hauptmann, Hermann Hesse, Thomas Mann — A428

1978, Feb. 16 Litho. *Perf. 14*

1267	A428	Sheet of 3	1.75	1.40
a.		30pf multicolored	.35	.25
b.		50pf multicolored	.50	.50
c.		70pf multicolored	.70	.50

German winners of Nobel Literature Prize.

Martin Buber (1878-1965), Writer and Philosopher A429

1978, Feb. 16

1268 A429 50pf multicolored .60 .30

Museum Tower and Observatory — A430

1978, Apr. 13 Litho. *Perf. 14*

1269 A430 50pf multicolored .60 .30

German Museum for Natural Sciences and Technology, Munich, 75th anniversary.

Old City Halls A431

Europa: 40pf, Bamberg. 50pf, Regensburg. 70pf, Esslingen on Neckar.

Lithographed and Engraved

1978, May 22 *Perf. 14*

1270	A431	40pf multicolored	.50	.20
1271	A431	50pf multicolored	.85	.20
1272	A431	70pf multicolored	.95	.45
	Nos. 1270-1272 (3)		2.30	.85

Pied Piper of Hamelin A432

1978, May 22 Litho.

1273 A432 50pf multicolored .75 .30

The Pied Piper led 130 children of Hamelin away never to be seen again.

Janusz Korczak — A433

Fossil Bat — A434

1978, July 13 Litho. *Perf. 14*

1274 A433 90pf multicolored 1.00 .50

Dr. Janusz Korczak (1878-1942), physician, educator, proponent of children's rights.

1978, July 13

200pf, Eohippus (primitive horse), horiz.

1275	A434	80pf multicolored	1.40	1.40
1276	A434	200pf multicolored	1.50	1.50

Archaeological heritage from Messel open-cast mine, c. 50 million years old.

Parliament, Bonn — A435

1978, Aug. 17 Litho. *Perf. 14*

1277 A435 70pf multicolored 1.10 .35

65th Interparliamentary Conf., Bonn, Sept. 3-14.

A436

Rose Window, Freiburg Cathedral.

1978, Aug. 17

1278 A436 40pf multicolored .40 .30

85th Congress of German Catholics, Freiburg, Sept. 13-17.

A437

1978, Aug. 17

Brentano as Butterfly, by Luise Duttenhofer.

1279 A437 30pf multicolored .40 .30

Clemens Brentano (1778-1842), poet.

A438

1978, Aug. 17

1280 A438 50pf multicolored .75 .30

European Human Rights Convention, 25th anniversary.

Baden Posthouse Sign, c. 1825 — A439

Saxony No. 1 with "World Philatelic Movement" Cancel — A440

1978, Oct. 12 Litho. *Perf. 14*

1281	A439	40pf multicolored	.40	.40
1282	A440	50pf multicolored	.40	.40
a.		Pair, #1281-1282	1.10	1.25

Stamp Day and German Philatelists' Meeting, Frankfurt am Main, Oct. 12-15.

Easter at Walchensee, by Lovis Corinth — A441

Impressionist Paintings: 70pf, Horseman on Shore, by Max Liebermann, vert. 120pf, Lady with Cat, by Max Slevogt, vert.

1978, Nov. 16 Photo. *Perf. 14*

1283	A441	50pf multicolored	.55	.45
1284	A441	70pf multicolored	.85	.60
1285	A441	120pf multicolored	1.50	1.40
	Nos. 1283-1285 (3)		2.90	2.45

Child and Building A442

1979, Jan. 11 Photo.

1286 A442 60pf black & rose .90 .30

International Year of the Child and 20th anniv. of Declaration of Children's Rights.

Agnes Miegel — A443

Film — A444

1979, Feb. 14 Photo. *Perf. 14*

1287 A443 60pf multicolored .60 .30

Agnes Miegel (1879-1964), poet.

1979, Feb. 14 Litho.

1288 A444 50pf black & green .75 .30

25th German Short-Film Festival, Oberhausen, Apr. 23-28.

Parliament Benches in Flag Colors of Members — A445

1979, Feb. 14
1289 A445 50pf multicolored   .90 .30
European Parliament, first direct elections, June 7-10, 1979.

Emblems of Road Rescue Services A446

1979, Feb. 14
1290 A446 50pf multicolored   .75 .30

A447

Europa: 50pf, Telegraph office, 1863. 60pf, Post Office window, 1854.

1979, May 17   Litho.   Perf. 14
1291 A447 50pf multicolored   .60 .20
1292 A447 60pf multicolored   .75 .20

A448

1979, May 17   Photo.
1293 A448 60pf red & black   .85 .30
Anne Frank (1929-45), author, Nazi victim.

First Electric Train, 1879 Berlin Exhibition A449

1979, May 17   Litho.
1294 A449 60pf multicolored   .90 .30
Intl. Transportation Exhib., Hamburg.

Hand Setting Radio Dial A450

1979, July 12   Litho.   Perf. 14
1295 A450 60pf multicolored   .85 .30
World Administrative Radio Conference, Geneva, Sept. 24-Dec. 1.

Moses Receiving Tablets of the Law, by Lucas Cranach — A451

1979, July 12   Litho. & Engr.
1296 A451 50pf black & blue grn   .90 .30
450th anniv. of Martin Luther's Catechism.

Cross and Charlemagne's Emblem — A452

1979, July 12   Litho. & Embossed
1297 A452 50pf multicolored   .60 .30
1979 pilgrimage to Aachen.

Hildegard von Bingen with Manuscript A453

1979, Aug. 9   Litho.
1298 A453 110pf multicolored   1.10 .50
Hildegard von Bingen, Benedictine nun, mystic and writer, 800th death anniversary.

Diagram of Einstein's Photoelectric Effect — A454

Designs: No. 1300, Otto Hahn's diagram of the splitting of the uranium nucleus. No. 1301, Max von Laue's atom arrangement in crystals.

1979, Aug. 9   Photo.
1299 A454 60pf multicolored   .75 .35
1300 A454 60pf multicolored   1.50 .35
1301 A454 60pf multicolored   .75 .35
    Nos. 1299-1301 (3)   3.00 1.05
Birth centenaries of German Nobel Prize winners: Albert Einstein, physics, 1921; Otto Hahn, chemistry, 1944; Max von Laue, physics, 1914.

Pilot on Board — A455

Lithographed and Engraved
1979, Oct. 11   Perf. 14
1302 A455 60pf multicolored   .60 .30
Three centuries of pilots' regulations.

Birds in Garden, by Paul Klee — A456

1979, Nov. 14   Photo.
1303 A456 90pf multicolored   .90 .50
Paul Klee (1879-1940), Swiss artist.

Mephistopheles and Faust — A457

1979, Nov. 14   Litho.
1304 A457 60pf multicolored   1.10 .30
Doctor Johannes Faust.

Energy Conservation A458

1979, Nov. 14   Perf. 13x13½
1305 A458 40pf multicolored   .60 .30

Castle Type A406 of 1977-79
1979-82   Typo.   Perf. 14
1308 35pf Lichtenstein   .50 .30
1309 40pf Wolfsburg   .45 .20
1310 50pf Inzlingen   .60 .20
1311 60pf Rheydt   .65 .30
1312 80pf Wilhelmsthal   .95 .20
1313 120pf Charlottenburg   1.50 .50
1314 280pf Ahrensburg   3.25 .50
1315 300pf Herrenhausen   3.75 .35
    Nos. 1308-1315 (8)   11.65 2.55
Issued: 60pf, 11/14; 40pf, 50pf, 2/14/80; 35pf, 80pf, 300pf, 6/16/82; 120pf, 280pf, 7/15/82.

Iphigenia, by Anselm Feuerbach — A459

1980, Jan. 10   Litho.
1321 A459 50pf multicolored   1.00 .30
Anselm Feuerbach (1829-1880), historical and portrait painter.

Flags of NATO and Members A460

1980, Jan. 10
1322 A460 100pf multicolored   1.60 .75
Germany's membership in NATO, 25th anniv.

Osnabruck, 1,200th Anniversary — A461

1980, Jan. 10   Litho. & Engr.
1323 A461 60pf multicolored   .75 .30

Götz von Berlichingen, Painting on Glass — A462

1980, Jan. 10   Litho.
1324 A462 60pf multicolored   .75 .30
Götz von Berlichingen (1480-1562), knight.

Duden Dictionary, Old and New Editions — A463

1980, Jan. 14
1325 A463 60pf multicolored   .75 .30
Konrad Duden's German Language Dictionary, centenary of publication.

German Association for Public and Private Social Welfare Centenary — A464

1980, Apr. 10
1326 A464 60pf multicolored   .75 .30

A465

Emperor Frederick I (Barbarossa) and Sons, Welf Chronicles, 12th century.

1980, Apr. 10
1327 A465 60pf multicolored   1.00 .30
Imperial Diet of Geinhausen, 800th anniv.

A466

1980, May 8   Litho.   Perf. 14
Europa: 50pf, Albertus Magnus (1193-1280), saint and doctor of the Church. 60pf, Gottfried Wilhelm Leibniz (1646-1716), philosopher.

1328 A466 50pf multicolored   .75 .25
1329 A466 60pf multicolored   .75 .25

Confession of
Augsburg,
Engraving,
1630 — A467

1980, May 8
1330 A467 50pf multicolored　.60　.30
Reading of Confession of Augsburg to
Charles V (first official creed of Lutheran
Church), 450th anniversary.

Nature
Preserves
A468

1980, May 8　　　　　　　　　**Photo.**
1331 A468 40pf multicolored　1.00　.30

Oscillogram Pulses and Ear — A469

Lithographed and Embossed
1980, July 10　　　　　　　**Perf. 14**
1332 A469 90pf multicolored　1.10　.35
16th Intl. Cong. for the Training and Education of the Hard of Hearing, Hamburg, 8/4-8.

Book of Daily Bible Readings, Title
Page, 1731
A470

1980, July 10　　　　　　　**Litho.**
1333 A470 50pf multicolored　.60　.30
Moravian Brethren's Book of Daily Bible
Readings, 250th edition.

St. Benedict of
Nursia, 1500th
Birth
Anniv. — A471

1980, July 10　　　**Perf. 13x13½**
1334 A471 50pf multicolored　.60　.30

Helping
Hand — A472

1980, Aug. 14　　　**Litho. & Engr.**
1335 A472 60pf multicolored　.75　.30
Dr. Friedrich Joseph Haass (1780-1853),
physician and philanthropist.

Marie von Ebner-
Eschenbach (1830-
1916),
Writer — A473

1980, Aug. 14　　　　　　　**Photo.**
1336 A473 60pf multicolored　.75　.30

Ship's
Rigging
A474

1980, Aug. 14　　　　　　　**Litho.**
1337 A474 60pf multicolored　1.50　.30
Gorch Fock (pen name of Johan Kinau)
(1880-1916), poet and dramatist.

Hoeing, Pressing Grapes, Wine Cellar,
14th Century Woodcuts
A475

1980, Oct. 9　　　**Litho.**　　**Perf. 14**
1338 A475 50pf multicolored　.75　.30
Wine production in Central Europe, 2000th
anniversary.

Setting Final Stone
in South Tower,
Cologne
Cathedral — A476

1980, Oct. 9
1339 A476 60pf multicolored　1.50　.30
Completion of Cologne Cathedral, cent.

Landscape with Fir Trees, by
Altdorfer — A477

Lithographed and Engraved
1980, Nov. 13　　　　　　**Perf. 14**
1340 A477 40pf multicolored　.60　.30
Albrecht Altdorfer (1480-1538), painter and
engraver.

Elly Heuss-Knapp
A478

1981, Jan. 15　　　　　　　**Photo.**
1341 A478 60pf multicolored　.75　.30
Elly Heuss-Knapp (1881-1951), founded
Elly Heuss-Knapp Foundation (Rest and
Recuperation for Mothers).

International Year of the
Disabled — A479

1981, Jan. 15　　　　　　　**Litho.**
1342 A479 60pf multicolored　.75　.30

European Urban Renaissance — A480

1981, Jan. 15　　　**Litho. & Engr.**
1343 A480 60pf multicolored　.85　.30

Georg Philipp
Telemann, Title
Page of "Singet
dem Herrn"
Cantata — A481

1981, Feb. 12　　　　　　　**Photo.**
1344 A481 60pf multicolored　.75　.30
Georg Telemann (1681-1767), composer.

Foreign Guest Worker
Integration — A482

1981, Feb. 12　　　　　　　**Litho.**
1345 A482 50pf multicolored　.85　.30

Preservation
of the
Environment
A483

1981, Feb. 12
1346 A483 60pf multicolored　1.25　.30

European
Patent
Office
Centenary
A484

1981, Feb. 12
1347 A484 60pf multicolored　.75　.30

A485

1981, Feb. 12　　　**Perf. 13x13½**
1348 A485 40pf Chest scintigram　.60　.30
Early examination for the prevention of
cancer.

A486

1981, May 7　　**Litho.**　　**Perf. 14**
50pf, South German couple dancing in
regional costumes. 60pf, Northern couple.

1349 A486 50pf multicolored　.60　.20
1350 A486 60pf multicolored　.70　.20
　　Europa.

19th German Protestant Convention,
Hamburg, June 17-21 — A487

1981, May 7　　　　　　　**Photo.**
1351 A487 50pf multicolored　.75　.30

A488

1981, May 7　　　　　　　**Litho.**
1352 A488 60pf Altar figures　.75　.30
Tilman Riemenschneider (1460-1531),
sculptor, 450th death anniversary.

A489

1981, July 16　　**Litho.**　　**Perf. 14**
1353 A489 110pf multicolored　1.60　.50
Georg von Neumayer polar research station.

Energy Conservation
Research — A490

1981, July 16
1354 A490 50pf Solar generator　.95　.30

Wildlife
Protection
A491

1981, July 16
1355 A491 60pf Baby coot　1.25　.30

Cooperation in Third World
Development — A492

1981, July 16
1356 A492 90pf multicolored   1.25 .45

Wilhelm Raabe
(1831-1910),
Poet — A493

1981, Aug. 13   Litho. & Engr.
1357 A493 50pf dk green & green   .75 .30

Statement of Constitutional Freedom
(Fundamental Concept of
Democracy) — A494

1981, Aug. 13   Litho.   Perf. 14
1358 A494 40pf shown   .85 .20
1359 A494 50pf Separation of
     powers   .85 .20
1360 A494 60pf Sovereignty of
     the people   1.25 .20
   Nos. 1358-1360 (3)   2.95 .60

A495

People by Mailcoach, lithograph, 1855.

1981, Oct. 8   Litho.
1361 A495 60pf multicolored   1.25 .30
   Stamp Day, Oct. 25.

A496

1981, Nov. 12   Litho.   Perf. 14
1362 A496 100pf multicolored   1.40 .45
   Antarctic Treaty, 20th anniv.

St. Elizabeth
of Thuringia,
750th Anniv.
of
Death — A497

1981, Nov. 12
1363 A497 50pf multicolored   1.00 .30

Karl von
Clausewitz, by W.
Wach — A498

1981, Nov. 12   Photo.
1364 A498 60pf multicolored   1.00 .30
Prussian general and writer, (1780-1831).

Social Insurance Centenary — A499

1981, Nov. 12
1365 A499 60pf multicolored   .85 .30

Pear-shaped Pot
with Lid,
1715 — A500

1982, Jan. 13   Litho.
1366 A500 60pf multicolored   .85 .30
   Johann Friedrich Bottger (1682-1719), originator of Dresden china, 300th birth anniv.

Energy Conservation — A501

1982, Jan. 13
1367 A501 60pf multicolored   .85 .30

A502

Illustration from The Town Band of Bremen
(folktale).

1982, Jan. 13
1368 A502 40pf red & black   .60 .30

A503

1982, Feb. 18   Photo.
1369 A503 60pf multicolored   2.25 .30
   Johann Wolfgang von Goethe (1749-1832),
by Georg Melchior Kraus, 1776.

Robert Koch (1843-1910), Discoverer
of Tubercle Bacillus, (1882) — A504

1982, Feb. 18
1370 A504 50pf multicolored   2.50 .30

Die Fromme
Helene, by Wilhelm
Busch (1832-1908)
A505

1982, Apr. 15   Litho.   Perf. 13½x14
1371 A505 50pf multicolored   1.00 .30

Europa
1982
A506

1982, May 5   Litho.   Perf. 14
1372 A506 50pf Hambach Meeting
     sesquicentennial   .90 .25
1373 A506 60pf Treaties of Rome,
     1957-1982   1.10 .25

Kiel Regatta Week Centenary — A507

1982, May 5
1374 A507 60pf multicolored   1.00 .30

Young Men's Christian Assoc. (YMCA)
Centenary — A508

1982, May 5
1375 A508 50pf multicolored   .75 .30

"Don't
Drink and
Drive"
A509

1982, July 15   Photo.
1376 A509 80pf red & black   1.00 .30

25th Anniv. of
German Lepers'
Org. — A510

1982, July 15   Photo.
1377 A510 80pf multicolored   1.00 .30

Prevent
Water
Pollution
A511

1982, July 15
1378 A511 120pf multicolored   2.50 .35

Urea
Model
and
Synthesis
Formula
A512

1982, Aug. 12   Photo.
1379 A512 50pf multicolored   .90 .30
   Friedrich Wohler (1800-1882), chemist, discoverer of organic chemistry.

St. Francis
Preaching to the
Birds, by
Giotto — A513

1982, Aug. 12   Litho.
1380 A513 60pf multicolored   .90 .30
   800th birth anniv. of St. Francis of Assisi
and 87th German Catholics Cong., Dusseldorf, 9/1-5.

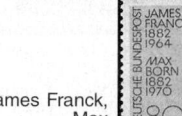

James Franck,
Max
Born — A514

1982, Aug. 12   Litho. & Engr.
1381 A514 80pf multicolored   1.25 .30
   James Franck (1882-1964) and Max Born
(1882-1970), Nobel Prize physicists, developed quantum theory.

Stamp
Day, Oct.
24
A515

1982, Oct. 14   Photo.   Perf. 14
1382 A515 80pf Poster   1.40 .30

400th Anniv. of the
Gregorian
Calendar — A516

   Design: Calendar illumination, by Johannes
Rasch, 1586.

1982, Oct. 14   Litho.
1383 A516 60pf multicolored   .90 .30

A517

Presidents: a, Theodor Heuss, 1949-59. b, Heinrich Lubke, 1959-69. c, Gustav Heinemann, 1969-74. d, Walter Scheel, 1974-79. e, Karl Carstens, 1979-84.

1982, Nov. 10
| 1384 | | Sheet of 5 | 5.00 | 4.50 |
| a.-e. | A517 | 80pf, single stamp | .75 | .75 |

A518

1983, Jan. 13   **Litho.**   ***Perf. 14***
| 1385 | A518 | 80pf gray & black | 1.50 | .45 |

Edith Stein (d. 1942), philospher and Carmelite Nun.

Persecution and Resistance, 1933-1945 — A519

1983, Jan. 13
| 1386 | A519 | .80pf multicolored | 1.50 | .45 |

Light Space Modulator, 1930 — A520

Walter Gropius (1883-1969), Founder of Bauhaus Architecture: 60pf, Sanctuary, zinc lithograph, 1942. 80pf, Bauhaus Archives, Berlin, 1979.

1983, Feb. 8
1387	A520	50pf multicolored	.75	.30
1388	A520	60pf multicolored	1.10	.30
1389	A520	80pf multicolored	1.25	.30
		Nos. 1387-1389 (3)	3.10	.90

Federahannes, Swabian-Alemannic Carnival — A521

1983, Feb. 8
| 1390 | A521 | 60pf multicolored | 1.00 | .30 |

4th Intl. Horticultural Show, Munich, Apr. 28-Oct. 9 — A522

1983, Apr. 12   **Litho.**   ***Perf. 14***
| 1391 | A522 | 60pf multicolored | 1.00 | .30 |

Europa 1983 A523

Discoveries: 60pf, Printing press by Johannes Guttenburg. 80pf, Electromagnetic waves by Heinrich Hertz.

1983, May 5   **Litho.**   ***Perf. 14***
| 1392 | A523 | 60pf | Movable type | *1.90* | *.35* |
| 1393 | A523 | 80pf | Resonant circuit, electric flux lines | *1.10* | *.35* |

Johannes Brahms (1833-1897), Composer A524

1983, May 5   **Photo.**
| 1394 | A524 | 80pf multicolored | 1.50 | .45 |

Franz Kafka (1883-1924), Writer — A525

1983, May 5
| 1395 | A525 | 80pf Signature, Tyn Church, Prague | 1.50 | .45 |

Beer Pureness Law, 450th Anniv. A526

1983, May 5   **Litho.**
| 1396 | A526 | 80pf Brewers, engraving, 1677 | 1.50 | .45 |

300th Anniv. of Immigration to US — A527

1983, May 5   **Litho. & Engr.**
| 1397 | A527 | 80pf Concord | 1.60 | .45 |

See US No. 2040.

Children and Road Safety A528

1983, July 14   **Litho.**   ***Perf. 14***
| 1398 | A528 | 80pf multicolored | 1.50 | .45 |

50th Intl. Auto Show, Frankfurt, Sept. 15-25 A529

1983, July 14
| 1399 | A529 | 60pf multicolored | .75 | .30 |

Otto Warburg — A530

1983, Aug. 11   **Photo.**   ***Perf. 14***
| 1400 | A530 | 50pf multicolored | .90 | .45 |

Warburg (1883-1970), pioneer of modern biochemistry, 1931 Nobel prize winner in medicine.

Christoph Martin Wieland (1733-1813), Poet — A531

1983, Aug. 11   **Litho.**
| 1401 | A531 | 80pf multicolored | 1.25 | .45 |

10th Anniv. of UN Membership — A532

1983, Aug. 11   **Photo.**
| 1402 | A532 | 80pf multicolored | 1.60 | .45 |

Rauhe Haus Orphanage Sesquicentennial — A533

1983, Aug. 11   **Litho.**
| 1403 | A533 | 80pf multicolored | 1.25 | .45 |

Survey and Measuring Maps — A534

1983, Aug. 11
| 1404 | A534 | 120pf multicolored | 1.60 | .50 |

Intl. Union of Geodesy and Geophysics Gen. Assembly, Hamburg, Aug. 15-26.

Stamp Day — A535

1983, Oct. 13   **Litho.**   ***Perf. 13½***
| 1405 | A535 | 80pf Postrider | 1.40 | .45 |

Martin Luther (1483-1546) A536

1983, Oct. 13   ***Perf. 14***
| 1406 | A536 | 80pf Engraving by G. Konig | 2.25 | .45 |

Customs Union Sesquicentennial — A537

1983, Nov. 10
| 1407 | A537 | 60pf multicolored | 1.60 | .30 |

Territorial Authorities (Federation, Land, Communities) — A538

1983, Nov. 10   **Litho.**
| 1408 | A538 | 80pf multicolored | 1.60 | .45 |

Trier, 2000th Anniv. A539

1984, Jan. 12   **Litho. & Engr.**
| 1409 | A539 | 80pf Black Gate, 175 A.D. | 1.60 | .45 |

Philipp Reis (1834-1874) Physicist and Inventor — A540

1984, Jan. 12   **Litho.**
| 1410 | A540 | 80pf multicolored | 1.60 | .45 |

Gregor Mendel (1822-1884), Basic Laws of Heredity — A541

1984, Jan. 12   **Litho.**
| 1411 | A541 | 50pf multicolored | 1.00 | .30 |

500th Anniv. of Michelstadt Town Hall — A542

1984, Feb. 16   **Litho.**
| 1412 | A542 | 60pf multicolored | 1.00 | .30 |

350th Anniv. of Oberammergau Passion Play — A543

1984, Feb. 16   **Photo.**
| 1413 | A543 | 60pf multicolored | 1.00 | .30 |

Second Election of Parliament, June 17 — A544

1984, Apr. 12   Litho.   Perf. 13½
1414 A544 80pf multicolored   1.75 .50

Europa (1959-1984) A545

1984, May 8   Photo.   Perf. 14
1415 A545 60pf multicolored   1.25 .35
1416 A545 80pf multicolored   1.25 .35

A546

1984, May 8   Engr.
1417 A546 60pf multicolored   .75 .30
Nursery Rhyme Illustration, by Ludwig Richter (1803-84).

A547

1984, May 8
1418 A547 80pf Statue, 1693   1.25 .45
St. Norbert von Xanten (1080-1134).

Barmer Theological Declaration, 50th Anniv. — A548

1984, May 8   Litho.
1419 A548 80pf Cross, text   1.25 .45

Souvenir Sheet

1984 UPU Congress A549

1984, June 19   Litho.   Perf. 14
1420   Sheet of 3   3.50 2.75
  a. A549 60pf Letter sorting, 19th cent.   .60 .50
  b. A549 80pf Scanner   .90 .75
  c. A549 120pf H. von Stephan, founder   1.50 1.40

City of Neuss Bimillenium A550

1984, June 19   Litho. & Engr.
1421 A550 80pf Tomb of Oclatius 1.25 .45

Friedrich Wilhelm Bessel (1784-1846), Astronomer A551

1984, June 19
1422 A551 80pf Bessel function diagram   1.25 .45

88th German Catholic Convention, Munich, July 4-8 — A552

1984, June 19   Photo.
1423 A552 60pf Pope Pius XII   1.00 .30

Town Hall, Duderstadt — A553

1984, Aug. 21   Litho.   Perf. 14
1424 A553 60pf multicolored   .90 .30

Medieval Document, Computer — A554

1984, Aug. 21
1425 A554 70pf multicolored   1.25 .45
10th Intl. Archives Congress, Bonn.

German Electron Synchrotron (DESY) Research Center, Hamburg — A555

1984, Aug. 21   Photo.
1426 A555 80pf multicolored   1.60 .45

Schleswig-Holstein Canal Bicentenary — A556

1984, Aug. 21   Litho.
1427 A556 80pf Knoop lock   1.50 .45

Stamp Day A557

1984, Oct. 18   Litho.   Perf. 14
1428 A557 80pf Imperial Taxis Posthouse, Augsburg   1.60 .45

Anti-smoking Campaign — A558

1984, Nov. 8   Litho.
1429 A558 60pf Match, text   1.00 .30

Equal Rights for Men and Women — A559

1984, Nov. 8
1430 A559 80pf Male & female symbols   1.50 .45

Peace and Understanding — A560

1984, Nov. 8
1431 A560 80pf Text   1.25 .45

Augsburg, 2000th Anniv. — A561

1985, Jan. 10   Litho.
1432 A561 80pf Roman Emperor Augustus, Augsburg buildings   1.50 .35

Philipp Jakob Spener, Religious Leader (1635-1705) A562

1985, Jan. 10   Litho.
1433 A562 80pf multicolored   1.25 .45

Deutches Wortebuch — A563

1985, Jan. 10   Litho.
1434 A563 80pf Bros. Grimm, text 1.60 .45

Romano Guardini, Theologist (1885-1968) A564

1985, Jan. 10   Litho.
1435 A564 80pf multicolored   1.25 .45

Market and Coinage Rights in Verden, 1000th Anniv. A565

1985, Feb. 21   Litho.
1436 A565 60pf multicolored   1.60 .30

German-Danish Border Areas and Flags — A566

1985, Feb. 21
1437 A566 80pf multicolored   1.75 .60
Bonn-Copenhagen declarations on mutual minorities, 30th anniv.

Johann Peter Hebel (1760-1826), Poet — A567

1985, Apr. 16   Litho.
1438 A567 80pf multicolored   1.25 .45

Egon Erwin Kisch (1885-1948), Journalist A568

1985, Apr. 16   Litho.
1439 A568 60pf Kisch using telephone   1.00 .30

Europa 1985 — A569

European Music Year: 60pf, Georg Friedrich Handel. 80pf, Johann Sebastian Bach.

1985, May 7   Photo.
1440 A569 60pf Portrait of Handel   1.50 .35
1441 A569 80pf Portrait of Bach   1.50 .35

Dominikus Zimmermann (1685-1766), Architect — A570

1985, May 7   Photo.
1442 A570 70pf Stucco column   1.10 .45

St. George's Cathedral, 750th Anniv. — A571

1985, May 7 **Litho.** **Perf. 14**
1443 A571 60pf Cathedral, Limburg .90 .45

Father Josef Kentenich (1885-1968) — A572

1985, May 7 **Litho.**
1444 A572 80pf Portrait 1.25 .45

Forest Conservation A573

1985, July 16 **Litho.** **Perf. 14**
1445 A573 80pf Clock, forest 1.75 .45

Intl. Youth Year A574

1985, July 16 **Perf. 14**
1446 A574 60pf Scouts, scouting and IYY emblems 1.00 .45
30th World Scouting Conf., Munich, 7/15-19.

Frankfurt Stock Exchange, 400th Anniv. — A575

Design: Bourse, est. 1879, and Frankfurt Eagle, the exchange emblem.

1985, Aug. 13 **Perf. 14x14½**
1447 A575 80pf multicolored 1.50 .45

The Sunday Walk, by Carl Spitzweg (1808-85) A576

1985, Aug. 13
1448 A576 60pf multicolored 1.60 .45

Fritz Reuter (1810-1874), Dialect Author — A577

1985, Oct. 15 **Litho.** **Perf. 14**
1449 A577 80pf Portrait, manuscript 1.75 .45

Departure of the 1st Train from Nuremberg to Furth, 1835 — A578

1985, Nov. 12 **Litho.** **Perf. 14x14½**
1450 A578 80pf Adler locomotive 1.75 .45
Founder Johannes Scharrer (1785-1844), German Railways 150th anniv.

Reintegration of German World War II Refugees, 40th Anniv. — A579

1985, Nov. 12 **Perf. 14**
1451 A579 80pf multicolored 1.75 .45

Natl. Armed Forces, 30th Anniv. A580

1985, Nov. 12 **Perf. 14x14½**
1452 A580 80pf Iron Cross, natl. colors 2.50 .45

Benz Tricycle, Saloon Car, 1912, and Modern Automobile — A581

1986, Jan. 16 **Litho.** **Perf. 14**
1453 A581 80pf multicolored 1.75 .45
Automobile cent.

Bad Hersfeld, 1250th Anniv. A582

1986, Feb. 13 **Litho.** **Perf. 14**
1454 A582 60pf multicolored 1.25 .45

Bach Contata, Detail, by Oskar Kokoschka (1886-1980) A583

1986, Feb. 13
1455 A583 80pf Self portrait 1.25 .45

Halley's Comet A584

1986, Feb. 13
1456 A584 80pf multicolored 1.75 .50

Europa 1986 A585

Details from Michelangelo's David: 60pf, Mouth (pure water). 80pf, Nose, (pure air).

1986, May 5 **Photo.** **Perf. 14**
1457 A585 60pf multicolored 1.25 .35
1458 A585 80pf multicolored 1.25 .35

St. Johannis Monastery, Walsrode — A586

1986, May 5 **Litho. & Engr.**
1459 A586 60pf multicolored 1.25 .45
Monastery millennium and town of Walsrode, 603rd anniv.

King Ludwig II of Bavaria (1845-1886), Neuschwanstein Castle — A587

1986, May 5 **Litho.**
1460 A587 60pf multicolored 2.10 .45

Karl Barth (1886-1968), Protestant Theologian A588

1986, May 5 **Engr.**
1461 A588 80pf blk, dk red & red lil 1.40 .45

Religion, Science, Friendship and Fatherland — A589

1986, May 5 **Litho.**
1462 A589 80pf multicolored 1.40 .45
Union of German Catholic Students, 100th assembly, Frankfurt, June 12-15.

Carl Maria von Weber (1786-1826), Mass in E-flat Major — A590

1986, June 20 **Litho.** **Perf. 14**
1463 A590 80pf multicolored 1.75 .45

Franz Liszt and Signature A591

1986, June 20
1464 A591 80pf dk blue & dk org 1.75 .45

Intl. Peace Year A592

1986, June 20
1465 A592 80pf multicolored 1.60 .45

Souvenir Sheet

Reichstag, Berlin — A593

Historic buildings: b, Koening Museum, Bonn. c, Parliament, Bonn.

1986, June 20
1466 Sheet of 3 3.75 3.25
a.-c. A593 80pf, any single 1.00 1.00

European Satellite Technology — A594

Design: TV-SAT/TDF-1 over Europe.

1986, June 20
1467 A594 80pf multicolored 1.90 .50

Augsburg Cathedral Stained Glass Window A595

1986, Aug. 14 **Perf. 14**
1468 A595 80pf multicolored 1.90 .45
Monuments protection.

King Frederick the Great (1712-1786) A596

1986, Aug. 14
1469 A596 80pf multicolored 2.50 .45

German Skat Congress, Cent. — A597

1986, Aug. 14
1470 A597 80pf Tournament card 1.75 .45

Organization for Economic Cooperation and Development, 25th Anniv. — A598

1986, Aug. 14
1471 A598 80pf multicolored 1.40 .45

Heidelberg University, 600th Anniv. — A599

1986, Oct. 16 **Litho.**
1472 A599 80pf multicolored 1.60 .45

Stagecoach, Stamps from 1975-1984 — A600

1986, Oct. 16
1473 A600 80pf multicolored 1.60 .45
Stamp Day, 50th Anniv.

A601   A602

1986, Nov. 13 **Litho.** **Perf. 14**
1474 A601 70pf multicolored 1.00 .45
Mary Wigman (1886-1973), dancer.

1986-91 **Engr.** **Perf. 14**
Famous Women: 5pf, Emma Ihrer (1857-1911), politician, labor leader. 10pf, Paula Modersohn-Becker (1876-1907), painter. 20pf, Cilly Aussem (1909-63), tennis champion. 30pf, Kathe Kollwitz (1867-1945), painter, graphic artist. 40pf, Maria Sibylla Merian (1647-1717), naturalist, painter. 50pf, Christine Teusch (1888-1968), minister of education and cultural affairs. 60pf, Dorothea Erxleben (1715-62), physician. 70pf, Elisabet Boehm (1859-1943), social organizer. 80pf, Clara Schumann (1819-96), pianist, composer. 100pf, Therese Giehse (1898-1975), actress. 120pf, Elisabeth Selbert (1896-1986), politician. 130pf, Lise Meitner (1878-1968), physicist. 140pf, Cecile Vogt (1875-1962), neurologist. 150pf, Sophie Scholl (1921-43), member of anti-Nazi resistance. 170pf, Hannah Arendt (1906-75), American political scientist. 180pf, Lotte Lehmann (1888-1976), soprano. 200pf, Bertha von Suttner (1843-1914), 1905 Nobel Peace Prize winner. 240pf, Mathilde Franziska Anneke, (1817-84), American author. 250pf, Queen Louise of Prussia (1776-1810). 300pf, Fanny Hensel (1805-47), composer-conductor. 350pf, Hedwig Dransfeld (1871-1925), women's rights activist. 500pf, Alice Salomon (1872-1948), feminist and social activist.

1475	A602	5pf multi	.20	.20
1476	A602	10pf multi	.20	.20
1477	A602	20pf multi	.75	.35
1478	A602	30pf multi	.35	.30
1479	A602	40pf multi	.75	.20
1480	A602	50pf multi	.75	.20
1481	A602	60pf multi	.90	.20
1482	A602	70pf multi	1.10	.60
1483	A602	80pf multi	.90	.20
1484	A602	100pf multi	1.10	.35
1485	A602	120pf multi	1.50	.90
1486	A602	130pf multi	2.25	.75
1487	A602	140pf multi	2.60	1.40
1488	A602	150pf multi	3.00	1.40
1489	A602	170pf multi	1.90	1.10
1490	A602	180pf multi	2.25	1.10
1491	A602	200pf multi	1.90	.75
1492	A602	240pf multi	2.60	1.90
1493	A602	250pf multi	3.75	1.90
1493A	A602	300pf multi	2.25	1.10
1494	A602	350pf multi	4.00	2.25
1494A	A602	500pf multi	5.00	3.00
	Nos. 1475-1494A (22)		40.00	20.35

Issued: 50pf, 80pf, 11/18; 40pf, 60pf, 9/17/87; 120pf, 11/7/87; 10pf, 4/14/88; 130pf, 5/5/88; 100pf, 170pf, 240pf, 350pf, 11/10/88; 500pf, 1/12/89; 5pf, 2/9/89; 180pf, 250pf, 7/13/89; 140pf, 300pf, 8/10/89; 30pf, 70pf, 1/8/91; 150pf, 200pf, 2/14/91.

See #1723/1735, 2185-2188, Berlin #9N516-9N532.

Advent Collection for Church Projects in Latin America, 25th Anniv. A603

1986, Nov. 13 **Litho.** **Perf. 14**
1495 A603 80pf multicolored 1.00 .45

Berlin, 750th Anniv. — A604

1987, Jan. 15 **Litho.**
1496 A604 80pf multicolored 2.00 .60

Archbishop's Residence at Wurzburg, 1719-44 A605

1987, Jan. 15 **Photo.**
1497 A605 80pf multicolored 1.50 .45
Balthasar Neumann (1687-1753), Baroque architect.

Ludwig Erhard (1897-1977), Economist, Chancellor 1963-66 A606

1987, Jan. 15
1498 A606 80pf multicolored 1.75 .35

1987 Census — A607

1987, Jan. 15 **Litho.**
1499 A607 80pf Federal Eagle 1.60 .45

Clemenswerth Hunting Castle, 250th Anniv. — A608

1987, Feb. 12 **Litho.**
1500 A608 60pf multicolored 1.25 .45

Joseph von Fraunhofer (1787-1826), Optician, Physicist — A609

1987, Feb. 12 **Litho. & Engr.**
1501 A609 80pf Light spectrum diagram 1.25 .45

Karl May (1842-1912), Novelist — A610

1987, Feb. 12 **Photo.**
1502 A610 80pf Apache Chief Winnetou 1.40 .45

Papal Arms, Madonna and Child, Buildings in Kevelaer — A611

1987, Apr. 9 **Litho.**
1503 A611 80pf multicolored 1.60 .45
State visit of Pope John Paul II, Apr. 30-May 4; 17th Marian and 10th Mariological World Congress, Kevelaer, Sept. 11-20.

German Choral Soc., 125th Anniv. A612

1987, Apr. 9
1504 A612 80pf multicolored 1.40 .45

Europa 1987 A613

Modern architecture: 60pf, German Pavilion, designed by Ludwig Mies van der Rohe, 1928 World's Fair, Barcelona. 80pf, Kohlbrand Bridge, 1974, Hamburg, designed by Thyssen Engineering.

1987, May 5 **Litho.**
1505 A613 60pf multicolored *1.25* *.35*
1506 A613 80pf multicolored *1.50* *.35*

Organ Pipes, Signature A614

1987, May 5
1507 A614 80pf multicolored 1.00 .45
Dietrich Buxtehude (c. 1637-1707), composer.

Wilhelm Kaisen (1887-1979), Bremen City Senate President — A615

1987, May 5
1508 A615 80pf multicolored 1.40 .45

Johann Albrecht Bengel (1687-1752), Lutheran Theologian — A616

1987, May 5 **Photo.** **Perf. 14**
1509 A616 80pf multicolored 1.25 .45

Kurt Schwitters (1887-1948), Artist — A617

1987, May 5 **Litho.**
1510 A617 80pf multicolored 1.25 .45

Rotary Intl. Convention, Munich, June 7-10 — A618

1987, May 5 **Photo.**
1511 A618 70pf multicolored 1.40 .45

Dulmen's Wild Horses, Merfelder Bruch Nature Reserve A619

1987, May 5
1512 A619 60pf multicolored 1.60 .45
European Environmental Conservation Year.

Bishopric of Bremen, 1200th Anniv. A620

Design: Charlemagne, Bremen Cathedral, city arms, Bishop Willehad.

1987, July 16 **Litho.** **Perf. 14**
1513 A620 80pf multicolored 1.25 .45

7th European Rifleman's Festival, Lippstadt, Sept. 12-13 — A621

1987, Aug. 20 **Litho.** **Perf. 14**
1514 A621 80pf multicolored 1.25 .45

Stamp Day — A622

1987, Oct. 15   Litho.
1515 A622 80pf Postmen, 1897   1.25   .85

Historic Sites and Objects — A623

Designs: 5pf, Brunswick Lion. 10pf, Frankfurt Airport. 20pf, No. 1526, Queen Nefertiti of Egypt, bust, Egyptian Museum, Berlin. 30pf, Corner tower, Celle Castle, 14th cent. 33pf, 120pf, Schleswig Cathedral. 38pf, 280pf, Statue of Roland, Bremen. 40pf, Chile House, Hamburg. 41pf, 170pf, Russian church, Wiesbaden. 45pf, Rastatt Castle. 50pf, Filigree tracery on spires, Freiburg Cathedral. 60pf, Bavaria Munich, bronze statue above the Theresienwiese, Hall of Fame. No. 1527, Heligoland. 80pf, Entrance to Zollern II coal mine, Dortmund. 90pf, 140pf, Bronze flagon from Reinheim. 100pf, Altotting Chapel, Bavaria. 200pf, Magdeburg Cathedral. 300pf, Hambach Castle. 350pf, Externsteine Bridge near Horn-Bad Meinberg. 400pf, Opera House, Dresden. 450pf, New Gate, Neubrandenburg. 500pf, State Theatre, Cottbus. 700pf, German Theater, Berlin.

1987-96		Typo.	Perf. 14	
1515A	A623	5pf multi	.20	.20
1516	A623	10pf multi	.20	.20
1517	A623	20pf multi	.30	.20
1518	A623	30pf multi	.50	.20
1519	A623	33pf tmulti	.45	.30
1520	A623	38pf multi	.75	.45
1521	A623	40pf multi	.30	.30
1522	A623	41pf multi	.50	.35
1523	A623	45pf multi	.45	.35
1524	A623	50pf multi	.50	.20
1525	A623	60pf multi	.75	.20
1526	A623	70pf multi	.70	.20
1527	A623	70pf multi	.45	.30
1528	A623	80pf multi	.75	.20
a.		Bklt. pane, 4 10pf, 2 50pf, 2 80pf ('89)	3.75	4.00
b.		Bklt. pane, 2 each 20pf, 80pf	4.00	5.50
1529	A623	90pf multi	1.25	1.50
1530	A623	100pf multi	1.50	.30
a.		Bklt. pane, 2 each 10, 60, 80, 100pf	7.50	9.00
b.		Bklt. pane, 2 each 20, 50, 80, 100pf	5.75	9.75
c.		Booklet pane, 10 #1530	19.00	16.00
		Complete booklet, #1530c	22.50	
d.		Booklet pane, 4 #1516, 2 each #1524, 1528, 1530	6.00	7.50
		Complete booklet, #1530d	7.00	
1531	A623	120pf multi	1.50	.50
1532	A623	140pf multi	1.75	.60
1533	A623	170pf multi	2.50	.75
1534	A623	200pf lmulti	2.25	.65
1535	A623	280pf multi	3.75	1.90
1536	A623	300pf multi	2.60	.45
1537	A623	350pf multi	3.00	.60
1538	A623	400pf multi	3.75	.60
1539	A623	450pf multi	5.00	.50
1540	A623	500pf multi	5.00	1.40
1540A	A623	700pf multi	8.00	3.00
	Nos. 1515A-1540A (27)		48.65	16.40

Issued: 30, 50, 60, 80pf, 11/6/87; 10, 300pf, 1/14/88; 120pf, #1526, 7/14/88; 40, 90, 280pf, 8/11/88; 20, 33, 38, 140pf, 1/12/89; 100, 350pf, 2/9/89; 5pf, 2/15/90; 45p, #1527, 6/21/90; 170pf, 6/4/91; 400pf, 10/10/91; 450pf, 8/13/92; 200pf, 4/15/93; 500pf, 6/17/93; 41pf, 8/12/93; 700pf, 9/16/93; #1530b, 11/9/94; #1530d, 8/14/96.
See #1655-1663, 1838-60, 2199-2216, Berlin #9N543-9N557.

Christoph Willibald Gluck (1714-1787), Composer, and Score from the Opera Armide — A624

1987, Nov. 6   Perf. 14
1541 A624 60pf car lake & dk gray   1.00   .35

Gerhart Hauptmann (1862-1946), Playwright — A625

1987, Nov. 6   Litho.
1542 A625 80pf black & brick red   1.50   .45

German Agro Action Organization, 125th Anniv. — A626

1987, Nov. 6   Photo.
1543 A626 80pf Rice field   1.50   .45

Mainz Carnival, 150th Anniv. — A627

1988, Jan. 14   Litho.   Perf. 14
1544 A627 60pf Jester   1.00   .45

Jacob Kaiser (1888-1961), Labor Leader — A628

1988, Jan. 14   Litho. & Engr.
1545 A628 80pf black   1.00   .45

Franco-German Cooperation Treaty, 25th Anniv. — A629

1988, Jan. 14
1546 A629 80pf Adenauer, De Gaulle   1.60   .60

See France No. 2086.

Beatification of Edith Stein and Rupert Mayer by Pope John Paul II in 1987 — A630

1988, Jan. 14   Photo.
1547 A630 80pf brown, blk & ver   1.25   .45

A631

Woodcut (detail) by Ludwig Richter.

1988, Feb. 18   Litho.
1548 A631 60pf multicolored   1.25   .45

Woodcut inspired by poem Solitude of the Green Woods, by Baron Joseph von Eichendorff (1788-1857).

A632

1988, Feb. 18   Photo.
1549 A632 80pf dk red & brn blk   1.50   .45

Arthur Schopenhauer (1788-1860), philosopher.

Friedrich Wilhelm Raiffeisen (1818-1888), Economist — A633

1988, Feb. 18   Litho.
1550 A633 80pf black & brt yel grn   1.60   .45

The German Raiffeisen Assoc., an agricultural cooperative credit soc., was founded by Raiffeisen.

Ulrich Reichsritter von Hutten (1488-1523), Humanist — A634

Design: Detail from an engraving published with Hutten's Conquestiones.

1988, Apr. 14   Litho. & Engr.
1551 A634 80pf multicolored   1.25   .50

Europa 1988 A635

Transport and communication: 60pf, Airbus A320. 80pf, Integrated Services Digital Network (ISDN) system.

1988, May 5   Litho.
1552 A635 60pf multicolored   1.00   .35
1553 A635 80pf multicolored   1.00   .35

City of Dusseldorf, 700th Anniv. — A636

1988, May 5
1554 A636 60pf multicolored   1.25   .45

Cologne University, 600th Anniv. — A637

1988, May 5
1555 A637 80pf multicolored   1.25   .45

Jean Monnet (1888-1979), French Statesman A638

1988, May 5
1556 A638 80pf multicolored   1.25   .45

Theodor Storm (1817-1888), Poet, Novelist — A639

1988, May 5
1557 A639 80pf multicolored   1.25   .45

German Volunteer Service, 25th Anniv. — A640

1988, May 5
1558 A640 80pf multicolored   1.25   .45

Town of Meersburg, Millennium — A641

1988, July 14   Litho.   Perf. 14
1559 A641 60pf multicolored   .90   .45

Leopold Gmelin (1788-1853), Chemist A642

1988, July 14   Litho. & Engr.
1560 A642 80pf multicolored   1.00   .45

Vernier Scale as a Symbol of Precision and Quality — A643

1988, July 14   Litho.
1561 A643 140pf multicolored   1.90   .90

Made in Germany.

August Bebel (1840-1913), Founder of the Social Democratic Party — A644

1988, Aug. 11   Photo.
1562 A644 80pf multicolored   1.40   .45

Intl. Red Cross, 125th Anniv. — A645

1988, Oct. 13   **Litho. & Engr.**
1563 A645 80pf scarlet & black   1.40   .45

Stamp Day — A646

1988, Oct. 13   **Litho.**
1564 A646 20pf Carrier pigeon   .60   .35

1st Nazi Pogrom, Nov. 9, 1938 A647

1988, Oct. 13   **Photo.**
1565 A647 80pf dull pale pur & blk   1.00   .45

Star, "Remembering is the secret of redemption," & burning synagogue in Baden-Baden.

Postage Stamps for Bethel, Cent. A648

1988, Nov. 10   **Litho.**
1566 A648 60pf multicolored   1.10   .45

The Postage Stamps for Bethel program was founded by Pastor Friedrich V. Bodelschwingh to employ disabled residents of Bethel.

Samaritan Association of Workers (ASB) Rescue Service, Cent. — A649

1988, Nov. 10
1567 A649 80pf multicolored   1.10   .45

Bonn Bimillennium — A650

1989, Jan. 12   **Litho.**
1568 A650 80pf multicolored   1.50   .65

Bonn as capital of the federal republic, 40th anniv.

Bluxao I, 1955, by Willi Baumeister (1889-1955) — A651

1989, Jan. 12
1569 A651 60pf multicolored   1.00   .45

Misereor and Brot fur die Welt, 30th Annivs. A652

1989, Jan. 12   **Photo.**
1570 A652 80pf Barren and verdant soil   1.10   .45

Church organizations helping Third World nations to become self-sufficient in food production.

Cats in the Attic, Woodcut by Gerhard Marcks (1889-1981) — A653

1989, Feb. 9   **Litho.**   **Perf. 14**
1571 A653 60pf multicolored   1.00   .45

European Parliament 3rd Elections, June 18 — A654

1989, Apr. 20   **Litho.**
1572 A654 100pf multicolored   1.90   .90

Flags of member nations.

Europa 1989 A655

1989, May 5
1573 A655   60pf Kites   *1.00*   *.30*
1574 A655 100pf Puppets   *1.50*   *.35*

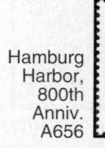

Hamburg Harbor, 800th Anniv. A656

1989, May 5
1575 A656 60pf multicolored   1.40   .45

Cosmas Damian Asam (1686-1739), Painter, Architect A657

1989, May 5   **Litho. & Engr.**
1576 A657 60pf Fresco   .75   .45

Federal Republic of Germany, 40th Anniv. — A658

1989, May 5   **Photo.**
1577 A658 100pf Natl. crest, flag, presidents' signatures   1.75   .65

Council of Europe, 40th Anniv. — A659

1989, May 5   **Perf. 14**
1578 A659 100pf Parliamentary Assembly, stars   1.60   .75

Franz Xaver Gabelsberger (1789-1849), Inventor of a German Shorthand — A660

1989, May 5   **Litho.**
1579 A660 100pf multicolored   1.60   .60

Sts. Kilian, Colman and Totnan (d. 689), Martyred Missionaries, and Clover — A661

1989, June 15   **Litho.**
1580 A661 100pf multicolored   1.50   .60

See Ireland No. 748.

Friedrich Silcher (1789-1860), Composer, and *Lorelai* Score — A662

1989, June 15
1581 A662 80pf multicolored   1.00   .45

Social Security Pension Insurance, Cent. — A663

1989, June 15
1582 A663 100pf dull ultra, bl & ver   1.50   .50

Friedrich List (1789-1846), Economist — A664

1989, July 13   **Engr.**   *Perf. 14*
1583 A664 170pf black & dark red   2.25   .90

Summer Evening, 1905, by Heinrich Vogler — A665

1989, July 13   **Litho.**
1584 A665 60pf multicolored   .85   .45

Worpswede Artists' Village, cent.

A666

1989, July 13   **Photo.**
1585 A666 100pf slate grn, blk & gray   1.10   .50

Reverend Paul Schneider (d. 1939), martyr of Buchenwald concentration camp.

A667

1989, Aug. 10   **Litho.**
1586 A667 60pf multicolored   1.25   .45

Frankfurt Cathedral, 750th anniv.

Child Welfare A668

1989, Aug. 10   **Perf. 14**
1587 A668 100pf multicolored   1.40   .50

Trade Union of the Mining and Power Industries, Cent. — A669

1989, Aug. 10   **Perf. 14**
1588 A669 100pf multicolored   1.25   .50

Reinhold Maier
(1889-1971),
Politician
A670

1989, Oct. 12   **Litho.**
1589 A670 100pf multicolored   1.40   .50

Restoration of St. James Church
Organ, Constructed by Arp Schnitger,
1689 — A671

1989, Nov. 16
1590 A671 60pf multicolored   1.25   .45

Speyer,
2000th
Anniv.
A672

1990, Jan. 12   **Litho.**   **Perf. 14x14½**
1591 A672 60pf multicolored   1.25   .45

A673

Design: *The Young Post Rider,* an Engraving by Albrecht Durer.

Litho. & Engr.
1990, Jan. 12   **Perf. 14**
1592 A673 100pf buff, vio brn & gray   2.00   .60

Postal communications in Europe, 500th anniv. See Austria No. 1486, Belgium No. 1332, Berlin 9N584, and DDR No. 2791.

A674

1990, Jan. 12   **Litho.**
1593 A674 100pf multicolored   1.25   .60

Riesling Vineyards, 500th anniv.

Addition of Lubeck to the UNESCO
World Heritage List, 1987
A675

1990, Jan. 12   **Litho. & Engr.**
1594 A675 100pf multicolored   1.25   .60

Seal of Col.
Spittler, 1400,
and Teutonic
Order Heraldic
Emblem
A676

1990, Feb. 15   **Litho.**
1595 A676 100pf multicolored   1.50   .60

Teutonic Order, 800th anniv.

Seal of Frederick II and Galleria
Reception Hall at the Frankfurt Fair
A677

1990, Feb. 15
1596 A677 100pf multicolored   1.50   .60

Granting of fair privileges to Frankfurt by
Frederick II, 750th anniv.

Youth Science and Technology
Competition, 25th Anniv. — A678

1990, Feb. 15
1597 A678 100pf multicolored   1.50   .60

Nature and Environmental
Protection — A679

1990, Feb. 15
1598 A679 100pf North Sea   1.60   .60

Labor
Day,
Cent.
A680

1990, Apr. 19   **Photo.**   **Perf. 14**
1599 A680 100pf dark red & blk   1.25   .60

German Assoc. of Housewives, 75th
Anniv. — A681

1990, Apr. 19   **Litho.**
1600 A681 100pf multicolored   1.25   .60

Europa
A682

Post offices in Frankfurt am Main: 60pf,
Thurn and Taxis Palace. 100pf, Modern Giro
office.

1990, May 3   **Litho.**
1601 A682 60pf multicolored   *1.10*   .50
1602 A682 100pf multicolored   *1.50*   .50

German Students' Fraternity, 175th
Anniv. — A683

1990, May 3   **Litho. & Engr.**
1603 A683 100pf multicolored   1.60   .60

Intl. Telecommunication Union, 125th
Anniv. — A684

1990, May 3   **Litho.**
1604 A684 100pf multicolored   1.25   .60

German Life Boat Institution, 125th
Anniv. — A685

1990, May 3
1605 A685 60pf multicolored   1.25   .50

Wilhelm
Leuschner
(1890-1944),
Politician
A686

1990, May 3   **Litho. & Engr.**
1606 A686 100pf lt gray violet   1.50   .60

Rummelsberg Diaconal Institution,
Cent. — A687

1990, May 3   **Litho.**
1607 A687 100pf multicolored   1.25   .60

Charter of German Expellees, 40th
Anniv. — A688

1990, June 21   **Photo.**
1608 A688 100pf multicolored   1.50   .50

Intl. Chamber of Commerce, 30th
Universal Congress — A689

1990, June 21   **Litho.**
1609 A689 80pf multicolored   1.25   .75

Matthias
Claudius
(1740-1815),
Writer — A691

1990, Aug. 9   **Litho.**
1611 A691 100pf multicolored   1.40   .45

Reunified Germany
AREA — 137,179 sq. mi.
POP. — 82,087,361 (1999 est.)
CAPITAL — Berlin

German Reunification — A692

1990, Oct. 3   **Litho.**   **Perf. 14**
1612 A692 50pf black, red & yel   1.10   .35
1613 A692 100pf black, red & yel   1.50   .50

First Postage Stamps, 150th
Anniv. — A693

1990, Oct. 11   **Litho.**
1614 A693 100pf multicolored   1.40   .45

Heinrich Schliemann (1822-1890),
Archaeologist — A694

1990, Oct. 11
1615 A694 60pf multicolored   1.25   .45
     See Greece No. 1705.

Kathe Dorsch
(1912-1957),
Actress — A695

1990, Nov. 6   **Photo.**
1616 A695 100pf red & violet   1.40   .60

Opening of Berlin
Wall, 1st
Anniv. — A696

1990, Nov. 6   Photo.   *Perf. 14*
1617 A696 50pf shown   1.10 .70
1618 A696 100pf Brandenburg
Gate   1.50 .70

Souvenir Sheet
1619   Sheet of 2   3.00 3.25
a.   A696 50pf like No. 1617   1.10 .90
b.   A696 100pf like No. 1618   1.50 1.10
Rainbow continuous on stamps from #1619.

Pharmacy
Profession,
750th
Anniv. — A697

1991, Jan. 8   Litho.
1620 A697 100pf multicolored   1.50 .60

Hanover,
750th
Anniv. — A698

1991, Jan. 8
1621 A698 60pf multicolored   1.25 .45

Brandenburg Gate,
Bicentennial — A699

1991, Jan. 8   Litho. & Engr.
1622 A699 100pf gray, dk bl &
red   1.75 .45

A700

1991, Jan. 8   Photo.
1623 A700 60pf multicolored   1.00 .45
Erich Buchholz (1891-1972), painter and
architect.

A701

1991, Jan. 8   Litho.
1624 A701 100pf multicolored   1.25 .60
Walter Eucken (1891-1950), economist.

25th Intl.
Tourism
Exchange,
Berlin — A702

1991, Jan. 8
1625 A702 100pf multicolored   1.40 .45

Souvenir Sheet

World Bobsled Championships,
Altenberg — A703

1991, Jan. 8   *Perf. 12½x13*
1626 A703 100pf multicolored   1.75 2.00

Friedrich Spee von Langenfeld (1591-
1635), Poet — A704

1991, Feb. 14   Litho.   *Perf. 14*
1627 A704 100pf multicolored   1.40 .45

A705

1991, Feb. 14
1628 A705 100pf multicolored   1.40 .45
Ludwig Windthorst (1812-1891), politician.

A706

1991, Mar. 12
1629 A706 60pf multicolored   1.00 .45
Jan von Werth (1591-1652), general.

Flowers
A707

1991, Mar. 12   *Perf. 13*
1630 A707 30pf Schweizer
mannschild   .40 .30
1631 A707 50pf Wulfens primel
(primula)   .55 .50
1632 A707 80pf Sommerenzian
(gentian)   .90 .35
1633 A707 100pf Preiselbeere
(cranberry)   1.25 .35
1634 A707 350pf Alpenedelweiss   4.00 3.00
Nos. 1630-1634 (5)   7.10 4.50

Battle of
Legnica,
750th
Anniv.
A708

Litho. & Engr.
1991, Apr. 9   *Perf. 14*
1635 A708 100pf multicolored   1.50 .90
See Poland No. 3019.

Choral
Singing
Academy
of Berlin,
Bicent.
A709

1991, Apr. 9
1636 A709 100pf multicolored   1.40 .60

Lette Foundation, 125th
Anniv. — A710

1991, Apr. 9   Photo.
1637 A710 100pf multicolored   1.40 .45

Historic
Aircraft
A711

1991, Apr. 9
1638 A711 30pf Junkers F13,
1930   .35 .35
1639 A711 50pf Grade Eindeck-
er, 1909   .55 .30
1640 A711 100pf Fokker FIII,
1922   1.50 .35
1641 A711 165pf Graf Zeppelin
LZ 127, 1928   2.25 2.00
Nos. 1638-1641 (4)   4.65 3.00

Europa
A712

Satellites: 60pf, ERS-1. 100pf, Copernicus.

1991, May 2   Litho.   *Perf. 14*
1642 A712 60pf multicolored   *1.10 .45*
1643 A712 100pf multicolored   2.00 .45

Town
Charters,
700th
Anniv. — A713

Design: Arms of Bernkastel, Mayen,
Montabaur, Saarburg, Welschbillig, and
Wittlich.

1991, May 2
1644 A713 60pf multicolored   1.00 .45

Max Reger (1873-1916),
Composer — A714

1991, May 2
1645 A714 100pf multicolored   1.50 .45

Inter-City
Express
Railway
A715

1991, May 2
1646 A715 60pf multicolored   1.00 .45

18th World Gas Congress,
Berlin — A716

Designs: 60pf, Wilhelm August Lampadius
(1772-1842), chemist. 100pf, Gas street lamp.

1991, June 4   Litho.   *Perf. 13x12½*
1647 A716 60pf lt blue & black   .75 .30
1648 A716 100pf lt blue & black   1.10 .45
a.   Pair, #1647-1648 + label   2.40 2.40

Sea Birds — A717

Designs: 60pf, Kampflaufer, Philomachus
pugnax. 80pf, Zwergseeschwalbe, Sterna
albifrons. 100pf, Ringelgans, Branta bernicla.
140pf, Seeadler, Haliaeetus albicilla.

1991, June 4   Litho.   *Perf. 14*
1649 A717 60pf multicolored   .75 .45
1650 A717 80pf multicolored   1.10 .75
1651 A717 100of multicolored   1.10 .75
1652 A717 140pf multicolored   2.10 1.50
Nos. 1649-1652 (4)   5.05 3.45

Paul Wallot (1841-1912),
Architect — A718

Litho. & Engr.
1991, June 4   *Perf. 14*
1653 A718 100pf multicolored   1.50 .45

Historic Sites Type of 1987

Designs: No. 1655, Frankfurt Airport. No.
1656, Wernigerode Town Hall. 60pf, Munich,
Bavaria. 80pf, Zech Zollern II Dortmund. No.
1663, Wallfahrtskapelle Alloting. No. 1664,
Schwerin Castle. 110pf, Regensburg Stone
Bridge.

Die Cut perf 10¼x10¾ on 3 sides
(#1656, 1664, 1666), Die Cut Imperf
1991-2001   Litho.

Self-Adhesive
1655 A623 10pf multi   1.00 1.40
1656 A623 10pf multi   2.25 1.90
1659 A623 60pf multi   1.00 1.40
1661 A623 80pf multi   1.00 1.00
1663 A623 100pf multi   1.25 1.25
a.   Bklt. pane, 2 each #1655,
1659, 1661, 1663   8.25 8.25

1664 A623 100pf multi 2.25 2.25
1666 A623 110pf multi 2.25 2.25
   a.   Booklet, 2 each #1656,
       1664, 8 #1666 25.00 25.00
      Nos. 1655-1666 (7) 11.00 11.45
Issued: #1655, 1659, 1661, 1663, June 4.
Nos. 1656, 1664, 110pf, 5/25/01.
Nos. 1655, 1659, 1661, 1663 issued on
peelable paper backing serving as booklet
cover.

Dragonflies
A719

50pf, #1671, Libellula depressa. #1672,
70pf, Sympetrum sanguineum. #1673, 80pf,
Cordulegaster boltonii. #1674, 100pf, Aeshna
viridis.

1991, July 9   **Photo.**   *Perf. 14*
1670 A719 50pf multicolored .65 .30
1671 A719 60pf multicolored 1.25 .60
1672 A719 60pf multicolored 1.25 .60
1673 A719 60pf multicolored 1.25 .60
1674 A719 60pf multicolored 1.25 .60
   a.   Block of 4, #1671-1674 5.50 5.50
1675 A719 70pf multicolored 1.00 .75
1676 A719 80pf multicolored 1.10 .75
1677 A719 100pf multicolored 1.25 .75
      Nos. 1670-1677 (8) 9.00 4.95

Traffic
Safety
A720

1991, July 9   **Litho.**
1678 A720 100pf multicolored 1.50 .60

Geneva Convention
on Refugees, 40th
Anniv. — A721

1991, July 9
1679 A721 100pf blk, gray & pink 1.40 .45

Intl. Radio Exhibition, Berlin — A722

1991, July 9
1680 A722 100pf multicolored 1.40 .45

Reinold von Thadden-Trieglaff (1891-
1976), Founder of German Protestant
Convention — A723

1991, Aug. 8   **Litho.**   *Perf. 14*
1681 A723 100pf multicolored 1.40 .45

August Heinrich Hoffman von
Fallersleben (1798-1874), Poet and
Philologist — A724

1991, Aug. 8
1682 A724 100pf multicolored 1.40 .45
German national anthem, 150th anniv.

3-Phase Energy Transmission,
Cent. — A725

1991, Aug. 8
1683 A725 170pf multicolored 2.25 1.10

Rhine-Ruhr Harbor, Duisburg, 275th
Anniv. — A726

1991, Sept. 12   **Litho.**   *Perf. 14*
1684 A726 100pf multicolored 1.40 .45

Souvenir Sheet

Theodor Korner (1791-1813),
Poet — A727

1991, Sept. 12   *Perf. 13x12½*
1685 A727 Sheet of 2 2.25 2.25
   a.   60pf Sword and pen 1.10 1.10
   b.   100pf Portrait 1.10 1.10

Hans Albers
(1891-1960),
Actor — A728

1991, Sept. 12   **Photo.**   *Perf. 14*
1686 A728 100pf multicolored 1.75 .45

Postman,
Spreewald
Region
A729

1991, Oct. 10   **Litho.**   *Perf. 14*
1687 A729 100pf multicolored 1.40 .45
Stamp Day.

Bird
Monument by
Max
Ernst — A730

1991, Oct. 10
1688 A730 100pf multicolored 1.40 .45

Sorbian
Legends
A731

1991, Nov. 5   *Perf. 13*
1689 A731 60pf Fiddler, water
       sprite .90 .45
1690 A731 100pf Midday woman,
       woman from
       Nochten 1.40 .45

Souvenir Sheet

Wolfgang Amadeus Mozart, Death
Bicent. — A732

1991, Nov. 5   **Litho.**   *Perf. 14*
1691 A732 100pf multicolored 2.25 2.25

Otto Dix (1891-
1969),
Painter — A733

Designs: 60pf, Portrait of the Dancer Anita
Berber. 100pf, Self-portrait.

1991, Nov. 5   **Photo.**   *Perf. 14*
1692 A733 60pf multicolored .75 .45
1693 A733 100pf multicolored 1.50 .45

Julius Leber
(1891-1945),
Politician
A734

1991, Nov. 5   **Litho.**
1694 A734 100pf black & red 1.40 .45

Nelly Sachs (1891-
1970),
Writer — A735

1991, Nov. 5
1695 A735 100pf violet 1.40 .45

City of
Koblenz,
2000th
Anniv.
A736

1992, Jan. 9   *Perf. 13x12½*
1696 A736 60pf multicolored 1.50 .50

Terre Des
Hommes Child
Welfare
Organization,
25th
Anniv. — A737

1992, Jan. 9   **Litho.**   *Perf. 14*
1697 A737 100pf multicolored 1.50 .60

Martin
Niemoller
(1892-1984),
Theologian
A738

1992, Jan. 9
1698 A738 100pf multicolored 1.10 .45

Coats of Arms
of States of
the Federal
Republic of
Germany
A739

1992-94   *Perf. 13½*
1699 100pf Baden-Wurttem-
      berg 1.40 .65
1700 100pf Bavaria 1.40 .65
1701 100pf Berlin 1.40 .65
1702 100pf Brandenburg 1.40 .65
1703 100pf Bremen 1.40 .65
1704 100pf Hamburg 1.40 .65
1705 100pf Hesse 1.40 .65
1706 100pf Mecklenburg-
      Western Pomera-
      nia 1.40 .65
1707 100pf Lower Saxony 1.40 .65
1708 100pf North Rhine -
      Westphalia 1.40 .65
1709 100pf Rhineland-Palati-
      nate 1.40 .65
1710 100pf Saar 1.40 .65
1711 100pf Saxony 1.40 .65
1712 100pf Saxony-Anhalt 1.40 .65
1713 100pf Schleswig-Holstein 1.40 .65
1714 100pf Thuringia 1.40 .65
      Nos. 1699-1714 (16) 22.40 10.40
See #B818.
Issued: #1699, 1/9/92; #1700, 3/12/92;
#1701, 6/11/92; #1702, 7/16/92; #1703,
8/13/92; #1704, 9/10/92; #1705. 3/11/93;
#1706, 6/17/93; #1707, 7/15/93; #1708,
8/12/93; #1709, 9/16/93; #1710, 1/13/94;
#1711, 3/10/94; #1712, 6/16/94; #1713,
7/14/94; #1714, 9/8/94.

Famous Women Type of 1986

80pf, Rahel Varnhagen von Ense (1771-
1833), pioneer in women's movement. No.
1724, Elisabeth Schwarzhaupt (1901-86), politician. No. 1725, Louise Henriette of Orange
(1627-67), mother of Frederick, King of Prussia. No. 1726, Grethe Weiser (1903-70),
actress. No. 1727, Marlene Dietrich (1901-92),
actress. No. 1728, Käte Strobel (1907-96),
government minister. No. 1729, Marie-Elisabeth Lüders (1878-1966), politician. No. 1730,

Marieluise Fleisser (1901-74), writer. No. 1731, Maria Probst (1902-67), politician. No. 1732, Nelly Sachs (1891-1970), writer. 400pf, Charlotte von Stein (1742-1827), confidant of Goethe. 440pf, Gret Palucca (1902-93), dancer. 450pf, Hedwig Courths-Mahler (1867-1950), novelist.

1992-2000		Engr.		Perf. 14
1723	A602	80pf blue & brown	.85	.45
1724	A602	100pf green & org brown	1.00	.75
1725	A602	100pf violet & bister	.85	.45
1726	A602	100pf ol bis & bl grn	.85	.75
1727	A602	110pf vio & dk brn	1.00	.60
1728	A602	110pf ol & red brn	.90	.75
1729	A602	220pf grn bl & vio bl	1.90	1.75
1730	A602	220pf grn & brn	1.60	1.60
1731	A602	300pf deep blue & brown	2.25	1.90
1732	A602	300pf brn & vio	2.10	2.10
1733	A602	400pf lake & blk	4.50	3.25
1734	A602	440pf dp vio & dk car	4.25	5.00
1735	A602	450pf brt blue & blue	5.00	3.75
	Nos. 1723-1735 (13)		27.05	23.10

Issued: 400pf, 1/9/92; 450pf, 6/11/92; 80pf, #1725, 10/13/94; #1727, 8/14/97; #1729, 8/28/97; #1724, #1731, 10/16/97; 440pf, 10/8/98; #1726, 1728, 11/9/00; Nos. 1730, 1732, 1/11/01.

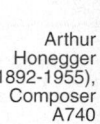

Arthur Honegger (1892-1955), Composer A740

1992, Feb. 6 Photo. Perf. 14
1736 A740 100pf sepia & black 1.50 .65

Ferdinand von Zeppelin (1838-1917), Airship Builder — A741

1992, Feb. 6 Litho.
1737 A741 165pf multicolored 2.25 1.25

City of Kiel, 750th Anniv. A742

1992, Mar. 12
1738 A742 60pf multicolored 1.00 .50

Konrad Adenauer A743

1992, Mar. 12 Photo.
1739 A743 100pf black & dull org 1.75 .50

Ernst Jakob Renz (1815-1892), Circus Director — A744

1992, Mar. 12 Litho.
1740 A744 100pf multicolored 1.40 .50

Berlin Sugar Institute, 125th Anniv. A745

1992, Mar. 12 Perf. 13x12½
1741 A745 100pf multicolored 1.40 .65

Johann Adam Schall von Bell (1592-1666), Astronomer and Missionary — A746

1992, Apr. 9 Litho. Perf. 13x12½
1742 A746 140pf multicolored 2.00 1.00

Erfurt, Capital of Thuringia, 1250th Anniv. — A747

1992, May 7 Litho. Perf. 14
1743 A747 60pf multicolored 1.00 .50

Discovery of America, 500th Anniv. — A748

Europa: 60pf, Woodcut illustrating letters from Columbus, 1493. 100pf, Rene de Laudonniere and Chief Athore by Jacques le Moyne de Morgues, 1564.

1992, May 7 Perf. 13½
1744 A748 60pf multicolored .85 .40
1745 A748 100pf multicolored 1.50 .45

1992, May 7 Perf. 13
1746 A749 100pf multicolored 1.40 .50
Order of Merit, 150th anniv.

A750

1992, May 7 Litho. Perf. 14
1747 A750 100pf multicolored 1.40 .60
St. Ludgerus, 1250th birth anniv.

Adam Riese (1492-1559), Mathematician — A751

1992, May 7
1748 A751 100pf multicolored 1.40 .60

Georg Christoph Lichtenberg (1742-1799), Physicist A752

1992, June 11 Litho. Perf. 14
1749 A752 100pf multicolored 1.40 .60

20th Century Paintings — A753

Designs: 60pf, Landscape with a Horse, by Franz Marc (1880-1916). 100pf, Fashion Shop, by August Macke (1887-1914). 170pf, Murnau with a Rainbow, by Vassily Kandinsky (1866-1944).

1992, June 11 Litho. Perf. 14
1750 A753 60pf multicolored .75 .60
1751 A753 100pf multicolored 1.25 .60
1752 A753 170pf multicolored 2.00 1.60
Nos. 1750-1752 (3) 4.00 2.80

See Nos. 1878-1880.

Leipzig Botanical Garden A754

1992, July 16 Litho. Perf. 13x12½
1753 A754 60pf multicolored 1.00 .50

Family Living — A755

1992, July 16 Perf. 13½
1754 A755 100pf multicolored 1.50 .50

17th World Congress on Home Economics, Hanover — A756

1992, July 16 Photo. Perf. 14
1755 A756 100pf multicolored 1.50 .60

Egid Quirin Asam (1692-1750), Architect and Sculptor — A757

1992, Aug. 13 Litho. Perf. 14
1756 A757 60pf multicolored 1.00 .50

German State Opera, Berlin, 250th Anniv. A758

1992, Aug. 13
1757 A758 80pf multicolored 1.25 .50

Federation of German Amateur Theaters, Cent. — A759

1992, Aug. 13
1758 A759 100pf multicolored 1.50 .50

Construction of First Globe by Martin Behaim, 500th Anniv. — A760

1992, Sept. 10 Perf. 13½
1759 A760 60pf multicolored 1.25 .50

Opening of Main-Danube Canal — A761

1992, Sept. 10 Perf. 14
1760 A761 100pf multicolored 1.25 .50

Werner Bergengruen (1892-1964), Writer — A762

1992, Sept. 10
1761 A762 100pf blk, bl & gray 1.25 .50

Jewelry & Watch Industries in Pforzheim, 225th Anniv. — A763

1992, Sept. 10
1762 A763 100pf multicolored 1.25 .50

Balloon
Post — A764

1992, Oct. 15　　Litho.　　Perf. 14
1763 A764 100pf multicolored　　1.50　.60
　　　　Stamp Day.

Hugo Distler
(1908-1942),
Composer
A765

1992, Oct. 15
1764 A765 100pf violet & black　　1.50　.50

Association of German Plant and
Machine Builders, Cent. — A766

1992, Oct. 15　　Litho. & Engr.
1765 A766 170pf multicolored　　2.00　1.00

Single
European
Market
A767

1992, Nov. 5　　Litho.　　Perf. 14
1766 A767 100pf multicolored　　1.60　.60

Jochen Klepper
(1903-1942),
Writer — A768

Litho. & Engr.
1992, Nov. 5　　　　　Perf. 14
1767 A768 100pf multicolored　　1.50　.50

A769

1992, Nov. 5　　　　　Photo.
1768 A769 100pf sepia & black　　1.50　.50
　　Werner von Siemens (1816-1892), electrical
engineer.

A770

1992, Nov. 5　　　　　Litho.
1769 A770 100pf multicolored　　1.50　.50
　　Gebhard Leberecht von Blucher (1742-
1819), Commander of Prussian Army.

City of Munster,
1200th
Anniv. — A771

1993, Jan. 14　　Litho.　　Perf. 14
1770 A771 60pf multicolored　　1.00　.50

Sir Isaac
Newton,
Scientist
A772

1993, Jan. 14　　Litho. & Engr.
1771 A772 100pf multicolored　　1.25　.50

North German Naval Observatory,
Hamburg, 125th Anniv. — A773

1993, Jan. 14　　Litho.　　Perf. 13x12½
1772 A773 100pf multicolored　　1.25　.50

Health and Safety
in
Workplace — A774

1993, Jan. 14　　Photo.　　Perf. 14
1773 A774 100pf blk, yel & bl　　1.25　.50

Association of
German
Electrical
Engineers,
Cent. — A775

1993, Jan. 14
1774 A775 170pf multicolored　　1.90　1.00

Leipzig Gewandhaus Orchestra, 250th
Anniv. — A776

1993, Feb. 11　　Litho.　　Perf. 13x12½
1775 A776 100pf black & gold　　1.25　.50

St. John of Nepomuk, 600th Death
Anniv. — A777

1993, Mar. 11
1776 A777 100pf multicolored　　1.25　.50

New
Postal
Codes
A778

1993, Mar. 11　　　　　Perf. 14
1777 A778 100pf multicolored　　1.50　.50

20th Century German
Paintings — A779

　　Designs: No. 1778, Cafe, by George Grosz
(1893-1959). No. 1779, Sea and Sun, by Otto
Pankok (1893-1966). No. 1780, Audience, by
A. Paul Weber (1893-1980).

1993, Mar. 11
1778 A779 100pf multicolored　　1.25　.75
1779 A779 100pf multicolored　　1.25　.75
1780 A779 100pf multicolored　　1.25　.75
　　　Nos. 1778-1780 (3)　　3.75　2.25
　　See Nos. 1863-1865, 1922-1924.

Benedictine Abbeys of Maria Laach
and Bursfelde, 900th Anniv. — A780

Litho. & Engr.
1993, Apr. 15　　　　　Perf. 14
1781 A780 80pf multicolored　　1.25　.50

5th Intl. Horticultural Show,
Stuttgart — A781

1993, Apr. 15　　Litho.　　Perf. 13x12½
1782 A781 100pf multicolored　　1.25　.50

Contemporary Art — A782

　　Europa: 80pf, Storage Place, by Joseph
Beuys (1921-1986). 100pf, Homage to the
Square, by Joseph Albers (1888-1976).
1993, May 5　　Litho.　　Perf. 13½x14
1783 A782 80pf multicolored　　1.25　.60
1784 A782 100pf multicolored　　1.25　.60

Dahlwitz Hoppegarten (Hippodrome),
Berlin, 125th Anniv. — A783

1993, May 5　　Litho.　　Perf. 14
1785 A783 80pf multicolored　　1.00　.60

Lake Constance Steamer
Hohentwiel — A784

1993, May 5　　　　　Photo.
1786 A784 100pf multicolored　　1.25　.50
　　See Austria No. 1618, Switzerland No. 931.

Schulpforta School
for Boys, 450th
Anniv. — A785

1993, May 5　　　　　Litho.
1787 A785 100pf multicolored　　1.25　.50

Coburger
Convent,
125th
Anniv.
A786

1993, May 5　　Litho. & Engr.
1788 A786 100pf black, green &
　　　　　red　　1.25　.50

City of
Potsdam,
1000th
Anniv.
A787

1993, June 17　　Litho.　　Perf. 13x12½
1789 A787 80pf multicolored　　1.25　.50

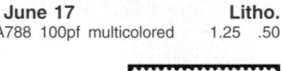

German UNICEF Committee, 40th
Anniv. — A788

1993, June 17　　　　　Litho.
1790 A788 100pf multicolored　　1.25　.50

Friedrich Holderlin
(1770-1843),
Writer — A789

1993, June 17　　Photo.　　Perf. 14
1791 A789 100pf multicolored　　1.25　.50

Hans Fallada
(1893-1947),
Novelist — A790

1993, July 15
1792 A790 100pf multicolored　　1.25　.50

Scenic Regions in Germany — A791

1993-96   Litho.   Perf. 14
Denominations 100pf
1793	A791	Rugen Island	1.10	.65
1794	A791	Harz Mountains	1.10	.65
1795	A791	Rhon Mountains	1.10	.65
1796	A791	Bavarian Alps	1.10	.75
1797	A791	Ore Mountains	1.10	.75
1798	A791	Main River Valley	1.10	.75
1799	A791	Mecklenburg lake district	1.10	.75
1800	A791	Franconian Switzerland	1.00	.75
1801	A791	Upper Lusatia	1.00	.75
1802	A791	Sauerland	1.00	.75
1803	A791	Havel River, Berlin	1.00	.75
1804	A791	Holstein Switzerland	1.00	.75
1805	A791	Saale	1.00	.75
1806	A791	Spreewald	1.00	.75
1807	A791	Eifel	1.00	.75
Nos. 1793-1807 (15)			15.70	10.95

Issued: #1793-1795, 7/15/93; #1796-1799, 7/14/94; #1800-1803, 7/6/95; #1804-1807, 4/11/96.
See #1938, 1974-1976, 2072-2073.

Mathias Klotz (1653-1743), Violin Maker — A792

1993, Aug. 12   Litho.   Perf. 13x12½
1808 A792 80pf multicolored   1.00 .45

Heinrich George (1893-1946), Actor — A793

1993, Aug. 12   Perf. 14
1809 A793 100pf multicolored   1.25 .50

Intl. Radio Exhibition, Berlin — A794

1993, Aug. 12
1810 A794 100pf multicolored   1.25 .50

Hans Leip (1893-1983), Poet and Painter A795

1993, Sept. 16   Litho.   Perf. 13
1811 A795 100pf red, black & blue   1.50 .50

Birger Forell (1893-1958), Swedish Priest — A796

1993, Sept. 16   Perf. 14
1812 A796 100pf multicolored   1.50 .70

Souvenir Sheet

For the Children — A797

1993, Sept. 16
1813 A797 100pf multicolored   1.50 1.50

Peter I. Tchaikovsky (1840-93), Composer — A798

1993, Oct. 14
1814 A798 80pf multicolored   1.25 .50

Max Reinhardt (1873-1943), Theatrical Director — A799

1993, Oct. 14
1815 A799 100pf buff, black & red   1.50 .50

St. Hedwig of Silesia, 750th Death Anniv. — A800

1993, Oct. 14
1816 A800 100pf multicolored   1.50 .50
See Poland No. 3176.

Paracelsus (1493-1541), Physician, Teacher — A801

Litho. & Engr.
1993, Nov. 10   Perf. 14
1817 A801 100pf multicolored   1.50 .50

Claudio Monteverdi (1567-1643), Composer — A802

1993, Nov. 10   Litho.   Perf. 13x12½
1818 A802 100pf multicolored   1.50 .50

Willy Brandt (1913-92), Statesman A803

1993, Nov. 10   Perf. 14
1819 A803 100pf multicolored   1.75 .90

Staade, 1000th Anniv. A804

Litho. & Engr.
1994, Jan. 13.   Perf. 14
1820 A804 80pf multicolored   1.00 .50

Intl. Year of the Family A805

1994, Jan. 13   Litho.
1821 A805 100pf multicolored   1.25 .65

Heinrich Hertz (1857-94), Physicist — A806

1994, Jan. 13   Perf. 13x12½
1822 A806 200pf multicolored   2.25 1.00

Frankfurt Am Main, 1200th Anniv. A807

1994, Feb. 10
1823 A807 80pf multicolored   1.00 .50

Fulda, 1250th Anniv. A808

1994, Mar. 10   Perf. 14
1824 A808 80pf multicolored   1.00 .50

German Women's Associations, German Women's Council, Cent. — A809

1994, Mar. 10   Perf. 13x12½
1825 A809 100pf black, red & yellow   1.25 .60

Fourth European Parliamentary Elections — A810

1994, Mar. 10   Perf. 14
1826 A810 100pf multicolored   1.50 .65

Foreigners in Germany: Living Together — A811

1994, Mar. 10
1827 A811 100pf multicolored   1.25 .65

Church of Our Lady, Munich, 500th Anniv. A812

1994, Apr. 14   Litho.   Perf. 14
1828 A812 100pf multicolored   1.50 .75

Europa A813

Designs: 80pf, Ohm's Law, by Georg Simon Ohm. 100pf, Quantum theory, by Max Planck.

1994, May 5   Photo.
1829 A813 80pf multicolored   1.00 .45
1830 A813 100pf multicolored   1.00 .45

Souvenir Sheet

Carl Hagenbeck (1844-1913), Circus Director, Animal Trainer, and Berlin Zoo, 150th Anniv. — A814

Designs: a, Hagenbeck, circus animals, zoo entrance. b, Zoo entrance, animals.

1994, May 5   **Litho.**

1831	A814	Sheet of 2	3.25	4.00
a.		100pf multicolored	1.00	.95
b.		200pf multicolored	2.00	2.00

Hans Pfitzner (1869-1949), Composer, Conductor — A815

1994, May 5

1832	A815	100pf multicolored	1.25	.60

Spandau Fortress, 400th Anniv. A816

1994, June 16   **Litho.**   **Perf. 14**

1833	A816	80pf multicolored	1.00	.50

Herzogsagmuhle, Social Welfare Organization, Cent. — A817

1994, June 16   **Perf. 13**

1834	A817	100pf blue, yel & blk	1.25	.60

Emperor Frederick II (1194-1250) A818

1994, June 16   **Perf. 13½x14**

1835	A818	400pf multicolored	4.25	3.25

Souvenir Sheet

Attempt to Assassinate Hitler, 50th Anniv. — A819

1994, July 20   **Litho.**   **Perf. 14**

1836	A819	100pf multicolored	1.50	1.50

Historic Sites Type of 1987

No. 1838, Wernigerode Town Hall. No. 1839, Böttcherstrasse, Bremen. No. 1840, Berus Monument, Uberherrn. No. 1841, Wilhelmshöhe Hillside Park, Kassel. No. 1842, Kirchheim Castle. No. 1843, St. Reinoldi Church, Dortmund. No. 1844, Goethe-Schiller Monument. No. 1845, Schwerin Castle, Weimar. No. 1846, Bellevue Castle, Berlin. No. 1847, EXPO 2000, Hanover. No. 1848, Regensburg Stone Bridge. No. 1849, Brühl's Terrace, Dresden. No. 1850, St. Nikolai Cathedral, Greifswald. No. 1851, Grimma Town Hall. No. 1852, Wartburg Castle, Eisenach. No. 1853, Town hall, Bremen. No. 1854, Cologne Cathedral. No. 1855, Holsten Gate, Lübeck. No. 1856, Heidelberg Castle. No. 1857, Town Hall, Suhl-Heinrichs. No. 1858, Speyer Cathedral. No. 1859, St. Michael's Church, Hamburg. No. 1860, Hildesheim Town Hall.

1994-2001   **Typo.**   **Perf. 14**

1838	A623	10pf multi	.45	.20
1839	A623	20pf dk bl & brn org	.35	.35
1840	A623	47pf green & gray	.55	.45
1841	A623	47pf dk grn & gray	.45	.45
1842	A623	50pf vio brn & beige	.75	.50
1843	A623	80pf dull grn & sepia	.75	.60
1844	A623	100pf blue & black	.80	.75
a.		Booklet pane of 10	9.00	9.00
		Complete booklet, #1844a	9.00	9.00
1845	A623	100pf multi	1.10	1.10
1846	A623	110pf dark gray & buff	1.00	.35
a.		Booklet pane of 10	11.50	11.50
		Complete booklet, #1846a	11.50	
1847	A623	110pf org & bl	1.10	.50
a.		Booklet pane of 10	13.50	13.50
		Complete booklet, #1847a	13.50	
1848	A623	110pf multi	1.10	.75
a.		Booklet pane of 10	12.50	12.50
		Booklet, #1848a	13.50	
1849	A623	220pf grn & blk	1.60	.75
1850	A623	220pf multi	2.25	1.90
1851	A623	300pf brn & ind	2.25	2.00
1852	A623	400pf vio brn & beige	4.50	3.00
1853	A623	440pf multicolored	4.25	3.25
1854	A623	440pf blk & gray	5.00	3.25
1855	A623	510pf red brn & ind	5.00	3.75
1856	A623	510pf brn & bis brn	5.50	4.25
1857	A623	550pf multicolored	5.25	2.10
1858	A623	640pf rose brn & gray bl	6.75	2.25
1859	A623	690pf blk & grn	7.25	2.50
1860	A623	720pf dk gray & lil	7.50	5.50
		Nos. 1838-1860 (23)	65.50	40.50

Issued: 550pf, 8/11/94; 640pf, 8/10/95; 690pf, 6/13/96; 47pf, 7/17/97; #1846, #1849, #1853, 8/14/97; #1844, #1855, 8/28/97; #1847, 9/10/98; 10pf, #1848, 300pf, 9/28/00; #1845, 1/11/01. #1841, 80pf, 4/5/01. 720pf, 7/2/01. #1850, #1854, 8/9/01. 50pf, #1852, 9/5/01. 20pf, #1856, 11/8/01.

Johann Gottfried Herder (1744-1803), Theologian A820

1994, Aug. 11   **Photo.**   **Perf. 14**

1862	A820	80pf multicolored	1.00	.50

Paintings Type of 1993

Designs: 100pf, Maika, by Christian Schad. 200pf, Landscape, by Erich Heckel. 300pf, Couple Lying on Grass, by Gabriele Munter.

1994, Aug. 11   **Litho.**   **Perf. 14**

1863	A779	100pf multicolored	1.00	.60
1864	A779	200pf multicolored	2.00	1.50
1865	A779	300pf multicolored	3.00	2.40
		Nos. 1863-1865 (3)	6.00	4.50

Ethnological Museum, Leipzig, 125th Anniv. — A821

1994, Sept. 8   **Litho.**   **Perf. 13x12½**

1866	A821	80pf multicolored	1.00	.50

Hermann von Helmholtz (1821-94), Scientist — A822

Litho. & Engr.

1994, Sept. 8   **Perf. 13½x14**

1867	A822	100pf multicolored	1.40	.50

Willi Richter (1894-1972), Politician, Labor Leader — A823

1994, Sept. 8   **Litho.**

1868	A823	100pf multicolored	1.25	.50

Souvenir Sheet

For the Children — A824

1994, Sept. 8   **Perf. 14**

1869	A824	100pf multicolored	1.50	1.50

Hans Sachs (1494-1576), Singer & Poet — A825

1994, Oct. 13   **Engr.**   **Perf. 13½x14**

1870	A825	100pf olive & maroon	1.25	.60

St. Wolfgang (924-94), Bishop of Regensburg A826

1994, Oct. 13   **Litho.**   **Perf. 14**

1871	A826	100pf multicolored	1.25	.60

Mail Delivery, Spreewald Region, c. 1900 — A827

1994, Oct. 13

1872	A827	100pf multicolored	1.25	.60

Stamp Day.

Quedlinburg, 1000th Anniv. — A828

Litho. & Engr.

1994, Nov. 9   **Perf. 14**

1873	A828	80pf multicolored	1.00	.50

Opening of the Berlin Wall, 5th Anniv. A829

1994, Nov. 9   **Litho.**   **Perf. 13x12½**

1874	A829	100pf black, org & yel	1.25	.60

Natl. Assoc. for Preservation of German Graves Abroad, 75th Anniv. — A830

1994, Nov. 9   **Perf. 14**

1875	A830	100pf black & red	1.25	.60

Theodore Fontane (1819-98), Poet — A831

1994, Nov. 9   **Perf. 13½x14**

1876	A831	100pf multicolored	1.25	.60

Baron Friedrich von Steuben (1730-94) A832

1994, Nov. 9   **Perf. 14**

1877	A832	100pf multicolored	1.25	.60

Paintings Type of 1992

Designs: 100pf, The Water Tower in Bremen, by Franz Radziwill. 200pf, Still Life with a Cat, by Georg Schrimpf. 300pf, An Estate in Dangast, by Karl Schmidt-Rottluff.

1995, Jan. 12   **Litho.**   **Perf. 14**

1878	A753	100pf multicolored	1.00	.50
1879	A753	200pf multicolored	2.00	1.50
1880	A753	300pf multicolored	3.00	2.25
		Nos. 1878-1880 (3)	6.00	4.25

Province of Gera, 1000th Anniv. — A833

1995, Jan. 12   **Perf. 13½x13**

1881	A833	80pf multicolored	.90	.50

Diet of Worms, 500th Anniv. A834

1995, Jan. 12   **Perf. 13x12½**

1882	A834	100pf multicolored	1.00	.60

Frederick William of Brandenburg, the Great Elector (1620-88) A835

1995, Feb. 9   **Litho.**   **Perf. 14**

1883	A835	300pf multicolored	3.25	2.10

Conf. of General Convention on Climate, Berlin — A836

1995, Mar. 9   Litho.   Perf. 14
1884 A836 100pf multicolored   1.00   .60

W.K. Roentgen (1845-1923) — A837

1995, Mar. 9
1885 A837 100pf multicolored   1.00   .60

Carolo-Wilhelmina Technical University, Braunschweig, 250th Anniv. — A838

1995, Mar. 9
1886 A838 100pf multicolored   1.00   .60

Former State of Mecklenburg, 1000th Anniv. — A839

1995, Mar. 9
1887 A839 100pf multicolored   1.00   .60

City of Regensburg, 750th Anniv. — A840

1995, Apr. 6   Litho.   Perf. 14
1888 A840 80pf multicolored   .90   .50

Freedom of Expression A841

1995, Apr. 6   Photo.
1889 A841 100pf multicolored   1.00   .60

Dietrich Bonhoeffer (1906-45), Protestant Theologian — A842

1995, Apr. 6
1890 A842 100pf multicolored   1.00   .60

Johann Conrad Schlaun (1695-1773), Architect A843

1995, Apr. 6   Litho.   Perf. 13
1891 A843 200pf multicolored   2.00 1.60

Vincent Conferences in Germany, 150th Anniv. — A844

1995, May 5   Litho.   Perf. 14
1892 A844 100pf multicolored   1.00   .65

Schiller Society, Cent. — A845

1995, May 5   Photo.
1893 A845 100pf multicolored   1.00   .60

End of World War II, 50th Anniv. — A846

Designs: No. 1894, End of the war. 200pf, Moving towards United Europe. No. 1896, Liberation of concentration camps. No. 1897: a, Destruction of buildings. b, Refugees.

1995, May 5   Litho.   Perf. 14
1894 A846 100pf red & black   1.00   .55
1895 A846 200pf bl, gray, yel & blk   2.00 1.00
Souvenir Sheets
1896 A846 100pf multicolored   1.10 1.50
1897   Sheet of 2   2.25 2.50
a.-b. A846 100pf any single   1.10 1.10
Europa (#1894-1895).

Kiel Canal, Cent. — A847

1995, June 8   Litho.   Perf. 14
1898 A847 80pf multicolored   .90   .50

UN, 50th Anniv. — A848

1995, June 8
1899 A848 100pf gold, lil & gray   1.00   .60

Radio, Cent. A849

1995, June 8
1900 A849 100pf Marconi, wireless apparatus   1.25   .80
See Ireland Nos. 973-974, Italy 2038-2039, San Marino Nos. 1336-1337, Vatican City Nos. 978-979.

Carl Orff (1895-1982), Composer — A850

1995, July 6   Litho.   Perf. 13x13½
1901 A850 100pf multicolored   1.00   .60

Henry the Lion, Duke of Bavaria (1129-95) A851

1995, July 6   Perf. 14
1902 A851 400pf multicolored   3.75 3.00

Kaiser Wilhelm Memorial Church, Berlin, Cent. — A852

1995, Aug. 10   Photo.   Perf. 14
1903 A852 100pf multicolored   1.00   .60

Franz Werfel (1890-1945), Author — A853

1995, Aug. 10   Litho.
1904 A853 100pf multicolored   1.00   .60

Franz Josef Strauss (1915-88), Politician A854

1995, Sept. 6   Photo.   Perf. 14x13½
1905 A854 100pf multicolored   1.10   .75

German Film, Cent. — A855

Illustration reduced.

1995, Sept. 6   Perf. 14
1906 A855 Sheet of 3   4.00 4.75
a.   80pf Metropolis   .75   .75
b.   100pf Little Superman   .90   .90
c.   200pf The Sky Over Berlin   2.10 2.10

Kurt Schumacher (1895-1952), Politician A856

1995, Oct. 12   Litho.   Perf. 13
1907 A856 100pf multicolored   1.00   .60

Souvenir Sheet

For the Children — A857

Illustration reduced.

1995, Oct. 12   Perf. 14
1908 A857 100pf multicolored   1.25 1.50

Leopold von Ranke (1795-1886), Historian A858

1995, Nov. 9   Litho.   Perf. 14
1909 A858 80pf multicolored   .85   .50

Paul Hindemith (1895-1963), Composer A859

1995, Nov. 9
1910 A859 100pf multicolored   1.00   .60

Nobel Prize Fund Established,
Cent. — A860

1995, Nov. 9   **Litho. & Engr.**
1911 A860 100pf Nobel, last will   1.25   .90
See Sweden Nos. 2155-2158.

CARE,
50th
Anniv.
A861

1995, Nov. 9   **Litho.**   **Perf. 13x12½**
1912 A861 100pf multicolored   1.00   .60

Victims of a
Divided
Germany,
1945-89
A862

1995, Nov. 9   **Perf. 14**
1913 A862 100pf Berlin Wall   1.00   .60

Borussia Dortmund, Soccer
Champions — A863

1995, Dec. 6   **Photo.**   **Perf. 14**
1914 A863 100pf multicolored   1.25   .75

Children's Missionary Work in
Germany, Cent. — A864

1996, Jan. 11   **Litho.**   **Perf. 14**
1915 A864 100pf multicolored   .95   .65

Friedrich von
Bodelschwingh
(1877-1946),
Protestant
Theologian
A865

1996, Jan. 11   **Perf. 13½**
1916 A865 100pf black & red   .95   .65

Martin Luther
(1483-1546),
Theologian
A866

1996, Feb. 8   **Litho.**   **Perf. 14**
1917 A866 100pf multicolored   1.00   .80

Philipp Franz von Siebold (1796-1866),
Physician and Diplomat — A867

1996, Feb. 17   **Perf. 13x12½**
1918 A867 100pf multicolored   1.00   .80

Cathedral
Square,
Halberstadt,
1000th
Anniv. — A868

1996, Mar. 7   **Litho.**   **Perf. 13**
1919 A868 80pf multicolored   .80   .45

August
Cardinal Graf
von Galen
(1878-1946)
A869

1996, Mar. 7   **Perf. 13½**
1920 A869 100pf bl, gray & bis   .95   .60

Giovanni Battista Tiepolo (1696-1770),
Painter — A870

1996, Mar. 7   **Perf. 13**
1921 A870 200pf multicolored   2.00 1.40

20th Century German Paintings Type of 1993

Designs: 100pf, Sitting Female Nude, by
Max Pechstein (1881-1955). 200pf, Abstract
For Wilhelm Runge, by Georg Muche (1895-
1987). 300pf, Still Life with Guitar, Book and
Vase, by Helmut Kolle (1899-1931).

1996, Mar. 7   **Perf. 14**
1922 A779 100pf multicolored   1.10   .90
1923 A779 200pf multicolored   2.40 1.75
1924 A779 300pf multicolored   2.50 2.50
    Nos. 1922-1924 (3)   6.00 5.15

Souvenir Sheet

For the Children — A871

Illustration reduced.

1996, Apr. 11   **Litho.**   **Perf. 14**
1925 A871 100pf Racing mes-
senger   1.10 1.40

Famous
Women — A872

Europa: 80pf, Self-portrait, by Paula Modersohn-Becker (1876-1907). 100pf, Self-portrait,
by Käthe Kollwitz (1867-1945).

1996, May 3
1926 A872 80pf multicolored   *1.00*   *.35*
1927 A872 100pf red & black   *1.00*   *.75*

Freising's
Right to
Hold
Markets,
1000th
Anniv.
A873

1996, May 3   **Perf. 13**
1928 A873 100pf multicolored   1.00   .65

Wolfgang Borchert (1921-47),
Writer — A874

1996, May 3   **Perf. 13**
1929 A874 100pf multicolored   1.00   .65

Ruhr Festival, Recklinghausen, 50th
Anniv. — A875

1996, May 3
1930 A875 100pf multicolored   1.00   .65

German
Theater
Assoc., 150th
Anniv. — A876

1996, May 3   **Photo.**   **Perf. 14**
1931 A876 200pf multicolored   2.00 1.10

Academy of
Arts in Berlin,
300th Anniv.
A877

1996, June 13   **Litho.**   **Perf. 13**
1932 A877 100pf multicolored   1.00   .65

Gottfried Wilhelm Leibniz (1646-1716),
Mathematician, Philosopher — A878

1996, June 13   **Perf. 14**
1933 A878 100pf multicolored   1.00   .65

City of
Heidelberg,
800th
Anniv. — A879

1996, July 18   **Litho.**   **Perf. 14**
1934 A879 100pf multicolored   1.00   .65
   Complete booklet, 10 #1934   10.00

UNICEF,
50th
Anniv.
A880

1996, July 18
1935 A880 100pf multicolored   1.00   .65

Ludwig Thoma
(1867-1921),
Satirist
A881

1996, July 18   **Perf. 13x13½**
1936 A881 100pf multicolored   1.00   .65

Souvenir Sheet

German
Natl.
Parks
A882

1996, July 18   **Perf. 14**
1937   Sheet of 3   6.50 6.50
   a. A882 100pf Coastal   1.00 1.00
   b. A882 200pf Mudflat   1.75 1.75
   c. A882 300pf Sea-inlet   2.75 2.75

Scenic Regions Type of 1993

"Gendarmenmarkt," central district of Berlin.

1996, Aug. 14   **Litho.**   **Perf. 14**
1938 A791 100pf multicolored   1.00   .65

Assoc. of German Philatelists, 50th
Anniv. — A883

1996, Aug. 14   **Photo.**   **Perf. 14**
1939 A883 100pf multicolored   1.00   .65

Paul Lincke (1866-1946), Musician, Composer A884

1996, Aug. 14   Litho.   *Perf. 13*
1940 A884 100pf multicolored   1.00 .65

UNESCO World Cultural Heritage A885

Design: Closed blast furnace, Völklingen.

1996, Aug. 14   *Perf. 13½*
1941 A885 100pf multicolored   1.00 .65

German Civil Code, Cent. — A886

1996, Aug. 14
1942 A886 300pf multicolored   3.00 2.25

Borussia Dortmund, Champion Soccer Club — A887

1996, Aug. 27
1943 A887 100pf multicolored   1.00 .65

Life Without Drugs A888

1996, Sept. 12   Photo.   *Perf. 14*
1944 A888 100pf multicolored   1.00 .65

UNESCO World Cultural Heritage A889

Design: Old Town, Bamberg

1996, Sept. 12   Litho.   *Perf. 14*
1945 A889 100pf multicolored   1.00 .65

Homeopathic Medicine, Bicent. — A890

Samuel Hahnemann (1755-1843), physician.

1996, Sept. 12   Litho.   *Perf. 14*
1946 A890 400pf multicolored   4.00 3.00

Anton Bruckner (1824-96), Composer A891

1996, Oct. 9   Litho.   *Perf. 13*
1947 A891 100pf multicolored   1.00 .65

Donaueschingen Music Festival, 75th Anniv. — A892

1996, Oct. 18   Litho.   *Perf. 13½*
1948 A892 100pf multicolored   1.00 .65

Baron Ferdinand von Mueller (1825-96), Botanist — A893

Litho. & Engr.   *Perf. 14*
1949 A893 100pf multicolored   1.00 .65
See Australia No. 1566.

Carl Zuckmayer (1896-1977), Playwright A894

1996, Nov. 14   Litho.   *Perf. 13*
1950 A894 100pf red, gray & blue 1.00 .65

Carlo Schmid (1896-1979), Politician, Scholar & Writer — A895

1996, Dec. 3   Photo.   *Perf. 14*
1951 A895 100pf multicolored   1.00 .65

Franz Schubert (1797-1828), Composer A896

1997, Jan. 16   Litho.   *Perf. 14*
1952 A896 100pf multicolored   1.00 .65

Sepp Herberger (1897-1977), Soccer Coach — A897

1997, Jan. 16
1953 A897 100pf multicolored   1.00 .65

Traffic Safety for Children A898

1997, Jan. 16
1954 A898 100pf multicolored   1.00 .65
See No. 1979.

Philipp Melanchthon (1497-1560), Protestant Reformer A899

1997, Feb. 4   Litho.   *Perf. 14*
1955 A899 100pf multicolored   1.00 .65

Cologne Carnival, 175th Anniv. — A900

1997, Feb. 4
1956 A900 100pf multicolored   1.00 .65

Chancellor Ludwig Erhard (1897-1977) A901

1997, Feb. 4   Photo.
1957 A901 100pf multicolored   1.00 .65

Leipzig Fair, 500th Anniv. A902

1997, Mar. 6   *Perf. 13x12½*
1958 A902 100pf red, sil & blue   1.00 .65

German Architecture after 1945 — A903

Building, architect: a, Berlin Philharmonic, by Hans Scharoun. b, New National Gallery, Berlin, by Ludwig Mies van der Rohe. c, St. Mary, Queen of Peace Church, Neviges, by Gottfried Böhm. d, German Pavilion, 1967 World's Fair, Montreal, by Frei Otto.

1997, Mar. 6   Litho.   *Perf. 14*
1959 A903 Sheet of 4   4.50 4.50
a.-d. 100pf any single   1.00 1.00

City of Straubing, 1100th Anniv. — A904

1997, Mar. 10   *Perf. 13x12½*
1960 A904 100pf multicolored   1.00 .65

Heinrich von Stephan (1831-97) — A905

1997, Apr. 8   Litho.   *Perf. 14*
1961 A905 100pf multicolored   1.00 .65

Augustusburg and Falkenlust Castles, UNESCO World Heritage Sites — A906

1997, Apr. 8
1962 A906 100pf multicolored   1.00 .65

Idar-Oberstein Gem & Jewelry Industry, 500th Anniv. — A907

1997, Apr. 8   *Perf. 13½*
1963 A907 300pf multicolored   3.25 2.25

St. Adalbert (956-997) — A908

1997, Apr. 23   Engr.   *Perf. 14*
1964 A908 100pf deep violet   1.00 .65
See Poland #3337, Czech Republic #3012, Hungary #3569, Vatican City #1040.

Stories and Legends A909

Europa: 80pf, Fisherman and his Wife. 100pf, Rübezahl of Riesengebirge (Giant Mountains).

1997, May 5   Litho.   Perf. 14
1965 A909 80pf multicolored   1.00 .60
1966 A909 100pf multicolored   1.00 .75

Sister Cities Movement, 50th Anniv. — A910

1997, May 5
1967 A910 100pf multicolored   1.10 .65

Souvenir Sheet

Society for Protection of German Forests, 50th Anniv. — A911

1997, May 5
1968 A911 Sheet of 2   3.25 3.25
 a.   100pf multicolored   1.10 1.10
 b.   200pf multicolored   2.00 2.00

Fr. Sebastian Kneipp (1821-97), Hydrotherapist A912

1997, June 9   Perf. 13
1969 A912 100pf multicolored   1.00 .65

Marshall Plan, 50th Anniv. A913

1997, June 9   Perf. 13
1970 A913 100pf multicolored   1.10 .65

"Documenta" Intl. Exhibition of Modern Art, Kassel — A914

Designs: a, Composition, by Fritz Winter, 1956. b, Mouth No. 15, by Tom Wesselmann, 1968. c, Quathlamba, by Frank Stella, 1964. d, Video sculpture, Beuys/Bois, by Nam June Paik.

1997, June 20   Litho.   Perf. 14
1971 A914 100pf Sheet of 4, #a.-
           d.   4.25 4.25

Müngsten Bridge, Cent. — A915

1997, June 20   Litho.   Perf. 13½
1972 A915 100pf multicolored   1.00 .65

Souvenir Sheet

For the Children — A916

Illustration reduced.

1997, July 17   Photo.   Perf. 13½
1973 A916 100pf multicolored   1.10 1.40

Scenic Regions Type of 1993

#1974, Bavarian Forest. #1975, Lüneburg Heath. #1976, North German Moorland.

1997, Aug. 28   Litho.   Perf. 14
1974 A791 110pf multicolored   1.10 .90
1975 A791 110pf multicolored   1.10 .90
1976 A791 110pf multicolored   1.10 .90
       Nos. 1974-1976 (3)   3.30 2.70

Centenary of Rudolf Diesel's Engine A917

1997, Aug. 28   Perf. 13
1977 A917 300pf blue & gray   3.00 2.25

Cultivation of Potatoes in Germany, 350th Anniv. — A918

1997, Sept. 17   Litho.   Perf. 13
1978 A918 300pf multicolored   3.00 2.25

Traffic Safety for Children Type

1997, Oct. 9   Litho.   Perf. 14
1979 A898 10pf like #1954   .20 .20

Felix Mendelssohn-Bartholdy (1809-47), Composer — A919

1997, Oct. 9   Perf. 13x13½
1980 A919 110pf multicolored   1.10 .75

FC Bayern Munchen, 1997 German Soccer Champions — A920

1997, Oct. 16   Photo.   Perf. 14
1981 A920 110pf multicolored   1.10 .75

Third Saar-Lorraine-Luxembourg Summit — A921

1997, Oct. 16   Litho.
1982 A921 110pf multicolored   1.10 .75
    See Luxembourg #972, France #2613.

Charitable Assoc. of the German Catholic Church, Cent. — A922

1997, Nov. 6   Photo.   Perf. 14
1983 A922 110pf multicolored   1.10 .75

Heinrich Heine (1797-1856), Poet — A923

1997, Nov. 6   Litho.   Perf. 13
1984 A923 110pf multicolored   1.25 .75

No. 1984 was sold in sheets of 10. It was withdrawn from sale 11/18/97, because runes associated with Nazi Germany were printed on the decorative selvage of the sheet. Value of withdrawn sheet of 10, $35. It was again placed on sale in sheets with runes removed.

Gerhard Tersteegen (1697-1769), Author of Religious Hymns, Booklets A924

1997, Nov. 6   Perf. 14
1985 A924 110pf multicolored   1.10 .75

Thomas Dehler (1897-1967), Politician — A925

1997, Nov. 6
1986 A925 110pf multicolored   1.10 .75

Cistercian Monastery Maulbronn, UNESCO World Heritage Site — A926

1998, Jan. 22   Litho.   Perf. 14
1987 A926 100pf multicolored   1.10 .75

Glienicke Bridge, Berlin — A927

1998, Jan. 22
1988 A927 110pf multicolored   1.10 .75

City of Nördlingen, 1100th Anniv. — A928

1998, Jan. 22
1989 A928 110pf multicolored   1.10 .75
 a.   Booklet pane of 10   11.50
       Complete booklet, #1989a +
       20 self-adhesive labels   12.00

Bertolt Brecht (1898-1956), Playwright A929

1998, Feb. 5
1990 A929 110pf multicolored   1.10 .75

Max Planck Society for Advancement of Science, 50th Anniv. — A930

1998, Feb. 5
1991 A930 110pf multicolored   1.10 .75

Town of Bad Frankenhausen, 1000th Anniv. — A931

1998, Mar. 12   Litho.   *Perf. 13*
1992 A931 110pf multicolored   1.10 .75

Peace of Westphalia, End of Thirty Years' War, 350th Anniv. — A932

1998, Mar. 12   *Perf. 14*
1993 A932 110pf black & red   1.10 .75

German State Parliament Buildings — A933

Designs: No. 1994, Baden-Württemberg. No. 1995, Bavaria. No. 1996, Chamber of Deputies, Berlin. No. 1997, Brandenburg.

1998, Mar. 12
1994 A933 110pf multicolored   1.25 .75
1995 A933 110pf multicolored   1.25 .75
1996 A933 110pf multicolored   1.25 .75
1997 A933 110pf multicolored   1.25 .75
    Nos. 1994-1997 (4)   5.00 3.00

See Nos 2027, 2029-2031, 2074-2076, 2113-2116.

Hildegard von Bingen (1098-1179), Christian Mystic — A934

1998, Apr. 16
1998 A934 100pf multicolored   1.00 .75

Cistercian Abbey of St. Marienstern, Panschwitz-Kuckau, 750th Anniv. — A935

1998, Apr. 16   *Perf. 13x12½*
1999 A935 110pf multicolored   1.10 .75

Souvenir Sheet

For the Children — A936

1998, Apr. 16   *Perf. 14*
2000 A936 110pf multicolored   1.25 1.25

Bayreuth Opera, 250th Anniv. — A937

1998, Apr. 16   *Perf. 13½*
2001 A937 300pf multicolored   3.25 2.40

Ernst Jünger (1895-1998), Writer — A938

1998, Apr. 22   *Perf. 14*
2002 A938 110pf multicolored   1.10 .75

German Rural Women's Assoc. A939

1998, May 7   Litho.   *Perf. 13*
2003 A939 110pf multicolored   1.10 .75

Europa and German Reunification Day — A940

1998, May 7   *Perf. 14½x14*
2004 A940 110pf multicolored   1.10 .75

Souvenir Sheet

German Constitution — A941

Designs: a, Parliamentary Council, Bonn, 1948, convening to draw up constitution. b, Natl. Assembly, St. Paul's Church, Frankfurt, 1848, electing pan-German constitutional Parliament.

1998, May 7   *Perf. 14*
2005 A941 Sheet of 2   3.50 3.50
a.   110pf multicolored   1.00 1.00
b.   220pf multicolored   2.00 2.00

Congress of German Catholics, 150th Anniv. — A942

1998, June 10   Litho.   *Perf. 13x13½*
2006 A942 110pf multicolored   1.25 .70

Deutsche Mark, 50th Anniv. — A943

1998, June 19   *Perf. 13*
2007 A943 110pf multicolored   1.25 .90

German Cultivation of Hops — A944

1998, July 16   Litho.   *Perf. 13*
2008 A944 110pf multicolored   1.10 .75

Founding of the European Central Bank, Frankfurt am Main — A945

1998, July 16   Photo.   *Perf. 14*
2009 A945 110pf multicolored   1.10 .70

Souvenir Sheet

Saxon Switzerland Natl. Park — A945a

1998, July 16   Litho.   *Perf. 14*
2009A A945a Sheet of 2   3.50 3.50
b.   110pf multicolored   1.00 1.00
c.   220pf multicolored   2.00 2.00

1998 Intl. Congress of Mathematicians, Berlin — A946

1998, Aug. 20   Photo.   *Perf. 14x13½*
2010 A946 110pf multicolored   1.10 .75

Grube Messel Fossil Beds A947

Würzburg Palace, Germany — A948

UNESCO World Heritage Sites: No. 2013, Puning Temple, Chengde, People's Republic of China.

1998, Aug. 20   Litho.   *Perf. 13x12½*
2011 A947 100pf multicolored   1.00 .65

**   *Perf. 13½x14***
2012 A948 110pf multicolored   1.10 .70
2013 A948 110pf multicolored   1.10 .70

See China People's Republic #2887-2888.

Souvenir Sheet

20th Cent. German Design — A949

Designs: a, Glassware, by Peter Behrens, 1910. b, Teapot, by Marianne Brandt, 1924. c, Desk lamp, by Wilhelm Wagenfeld, 1924. d, "Wassily" chair, by Marcel Breuer, 1926.

1998, Aug. 20   *Perf. 14*
2014   Sheet of 4   4.75 4.75
a.-d. A949 110pf any single   1.10 1.10
    See No. 2051.

Manfred Hausmann (1898-1986), Author — A950

1998, Sept. 10   Litho.   *Perf. 14*
2015 A950 110pf multicolored   1.10 .75

A951

1998, Sept. 10
2016 A951 110pf multicolored   1.10 .75

Team 1 FC Kaiserslautern, 1998 German soccer champions.

Prevent Child Abuse — A952

1998, Sept. 10
2017 A952 110pf black & red   1.10 .75

Francke Charitable Institutions, Halle, 300th Anniv. — A953

1998, Sept. 10   *Perf. 13*
2018 A953 110pf Building   1.10 .75

Mail Boat, "Hiorten" A954

1998, Oct. 8   *Litho.*   *Perf. 14*
2019 A954 110pf multicolored   1.10 .75
Stamp Day.

Telephone Help Lines for People in Distress — A955

1998, Oct. 8   *Perf. 13x12½*
2020 A955 110pf multicolored   1.10 .75

Günther Ramin (1898-1956), Organist, Choir Leader — A956

1998, Oct. 8   *Photo.*   *Perf. 14x14½*
2021 A956 300pf multicolored   3.00 2.25

Saxony State Orchestra, Dresden, 450th Anniv. — A957

1998, Nov. 12   *Litho.*   *Perf. 14*
2022 A957 300pf multicolored   3.00 2.25

Universal Delcaration of Human Rights, 50th Anniv. — A958

1998, Nov. 12   *Perf. 13x12½*
2023 A958 110pf multicolored   1.10 .75
See No. B848.

Weimar, 1999 European City of Culture, 1100th Anniv. — A959

1999, Jan. 14   *Litho.*   *Perf. 14*
2024 A959 100pf multicolored   1.10 .80
   a.   Booklet pane of 10   12.50 12.50
     Complete booklet, #2024a + 20 labels   12.50

The self-adhesive labels are part of the booklet cover.

International Year of the Elderly A960

1999, Jan. 14   *Perf. 13*
2025 A960 110pf multicolored   1.10 .80

Katharina von Bora (1499-1552), Wife of Martin Luther, from Painting by Lucas Cranach A961

1999, Jan. 14   *Perf. 14*
2026 A961 110pf multicolored   1.10 .80

State Parliaments Type of 1998
The Hessian Parliament.

1999, Jan. 14
2027 A933 110pf multicolored   1.10 .80

Erich Kästner (1899-1974), Writer — A963

1999, Feb. 18   *Litho.*   *Perf. 13*
2028 A963 300pf multicolored   3.00 2.40

State Parliaments Type of 1998
Buildings: No. 2029, Hamburg. No. 2030, Mecklenburg-Western Pomerania. No. 2031, Bremen City Parliament.

1999   *Litho.*   *Perf. 14*
2029 A933 110pf multicolored   1.10 .80
2030 A933 110pf multicolored   1.10 .80
2031 A933 110pf multicolored   1.10 .80
   Nos. 2029-2031 (3)   3.30 2.40

Issued: #2029-2030, 3/11; #2031, 4/27.

NATO, 50th Anniv. A963a

1999, Mar. 11   *Photo.*
2032 A963a 110pf multicolored   1.10 .80

Fraunhofer Society, 50th Anniv. — A964

1999, Mar. 11   *Litho.*   *Perf. 13*
2033 A964 110pf multicolored   1.10 .80

Expo 2000, Hanover A965

1999, Apr. 27
2034 A965 110pf multicolored   1.10 .80
See No. 2083.

German Automobile Club, Cent. — A966

1999, Apr. 27   *Photo.*
2035 A966 110pf multicolored   1.10 .80

German Cancer Relief Organization, 25th Anniv. — A967

1999, Apr. 27   *Litho.*   *Perf. 13*
2036 A967 110pf multicolored   1.10 .80

Knights of St. John of Jerusalem and Knights of Malta, 900th Anniv. — A968

1999, May 4
2037 A968 110pf multicolored   1.10 .80

Berlin Airlift, 1948-49 A969

1999, May 4   *Photo.*   *Perf. 14*
2038 A969 110pf multicolored   1.10 .80

Council of Europe, 50th Anniv. — A970

1999, May 4   *Litho.*   *Perf. 13*
2039 A970 110pf multicolored   1.10 .80

Souvenir Sheet

Berchtesgaden Natl. Park — A971

1999, May 4   *Perf. 14*
2040 A971 110pf multicolored   *1.40 1.60*
Europa.

Souvenir Sheet

Basic Law, 50th Anniv. — A972

1999, May 21   *Litho.*   *Perf. 14*
2041 A972 110pf multicolored   1.25 1.25

Souvenir Sheet

Federal Republic of Germany, 50th Anniv. — A973

Scenes from 1949, 1999: a, Leaders gathering, session of Parliament. b, Child carrying wood, child picking flower. c, Building "The Wall," people walking where "The Wall" has been removed. d, Soldiers, government assembly.

1999, May 21
2042   Sheet of 4   4.50 4.50
   a.-d.   A973 110pf any single   1.10 1.10

SOS Children's Village, 50th Anniv. — A974

1999, June 10   *Litho.*   *Perf. 13¾x14*
2043 A974 110pf multicolored   1.10 .75

Paderborn Bishopric, 1200th Anniv. — A975

1999, June 10 **Perf. 14**
2044 A975 110pf multicolored 1.10 .75

Johann Strauss, the Younger (1825-99) A976

1999, June 10 **Photo.** **Perf. 13¾**
2045 A976 300pf multicolored 3.25 2.25

Dominikus-Ringeisen Institution, Ursberg, 115th Anniv. — A977

1999, July 15 **Litho.**
2046 A977 110pf multicolored 1.10 .75

Pres. Gustav Heinemann (1899-1976) A978

1999, July 15
2047 A978 110pf multicolored 1.10 .75

Cultural Foundation of the Federal States — A979

Sculpture: 110pf, Old Woman Smiling, by Ernst Barlach (1870-1938). 220pf, Bust of a Thinker, by Wilhelm Lehmbruck (1881-1919).

1999, July 15 **Photo.** **Perf. 14**
2048 A979 110pf multicolored 1.25 .80
2049 A979 220pf multicolored 2.10 1.50

First Peace Conference in The Hague, Cent. — A980

1999, July 15 **Litho.** **Perf. 13¼x13**
2050 A980 300pf multicolored 3.25 2.10

20th Cent. German Design Type of 1998
Souvenir Sheet

Designs: a, HF1 Television set, by Herbert Hirche, 1958. b, Knife, fork, spoon and tea- spoon, by Peter Raacke, 1959. c, Pearl bottle, by Günter Kupetz, 1969. d, "Transrapid," Maglev train, by Alexander Neumeister, 1982.

1999, Aug. 12 **Litho.** **Perf. 14**
Souvenir Sheet
2051 Sheet of 4 4.50 4.50
a.-d. A949 110pf any single 1.10 1.10

Johann Wolfgang von Goethe (1749- 1832), Poet — A981

1999, Aug. 12 **Perf. 13¾**
2052 A981 110pf multicolored 1.10 .80

Souvenir Sheet

For the Children — A982

1999, Aug. 12 **Perf. 13¼**
2053 A982 110pf multicolored 1.10 1.10

Bayern München, 1999 German Soccer Champions — A983

1999, Sept. 16 **Litho.** **Perf. 14**
2054 A983 110pf multicolored 1.10 .80

Federal Association of German Book Traders Peace Prize, 50th Anniv. — A984

1999, Sept. 16 **Photo.** **Perf. 13¾**
2055 A984 110pf multicolored 1.10 .80

Richard Strauss (1864- 1949), Composer A985

1999, Sept. 16 **Litho.** **Perf. 13¼**
2056 A985 300pf multicolored 3.25 2.40

Göltzsch Valley Bridge A986

1999, Oct. 14 **Litho.** **Perf. 14**
2057 A986 110pf multicolored 1.10 .80

German Federation of Trade Unions, 50th Anniv. — A987

1999, Oct. 14
2058 A987 110pf red & black 1.10 .80

Endangered Species A988

1999, Nov. 4 **Litho.** **Perf. 13¾**
2059 A988 100pf Large horse- shoe bat 1.00 .80

EXPO 2000, Hanover A989

2000, Jan. 13 **Litho.** **Perf. 14x14¼**
2060 A989 100pf multi 1.10 .80
See No. 2094.

Holy Year 2000 — A990

2000, Jan. 13 **Perf. 13¾**
2061 A990 110pf multi 1.10 .80

Completion of Aachen Cathedral, 1200th Anniv. — A991

2000, Jan. 13
2062 A991 110pf Charlemagne 1.10 .80

German Soccer Assoc., Cent. — A992

2000, Jan. 13 **Photo.**
2063 A992 110pf multi 1.10 .80
Value is for stamp with surrounding selvage.

Herbert Wehner (1906- 90), Politician A993

2000, Jan. 13
2064 A993 110pf multi 1.10 .80

Albert Schweitzer (1875-1965), Humanitarian A994

2000, Jan. 13 **Litho.** **Perf. 14x13¾**
2065 A994 110pf multi 1.10 .80

Prevention of Violence Against Women — A995

2000, Jan. 13 **Perf. 14**
2066 A995 110pf multi 1.10 .80

Berlin Intl. Film Festival, 50th Anniv. A996

2000, Feb. 17 **Litho.** **Perf. 14**
2067 A996 100pf multi 1.00 .80

Johannes Gutenberg (c. 1400-1468) A997

2000, Feb. 17 **Perf. 13¾**
2068 A997 110pf red & black 1.10 .80

Friedrich Ebert (1871-1925), President of German Reich — A998

2000, Feb. 17 **Photo.**
2069 A998 110pf multi 1.25 .80

Düsseldorf Carnival, 175th Anniv. — A999

2000, Feb. 17 **Litho.** **Perf. 13x13½**
2070 A999 110pf multi 1.10 .80

Kurt Weill (1900-50),
Composer — A1000

2000, Feb. 17   *Perf. 14*
2071 A1000 300pf multi   3.25 2.40

Scenic Regions Type of 1993

Design: #2072, Passau. #2073, Saar River
bend, Mettlach.

2000   **Litho.**   *Perf. 13¾x14*
2072 A791 110pf multi   1.25 .80
2073 A791 110pf multi   1.25 .80

Issued: No. 2072, 3/16.

State Parliament Building Type

#2074, Lower Saxony. #2075, North Rhine-
Westphalia. #2076, Rhineland-Palatinate.
#2077, Saarland.

2000   **Litho.**   *Perf. 13¾x14*
2074 A933 110pf multi   1.10 .80
2075 A933 110pf multi   1.10 .80
2076 A933 110pf multi   1.10 .80
           Perf. 14
2077 A933 110pf multi   1.10 .80
    Nos. 2074-2077 (4)   4.40 3.20

Issued: #2074, 3/16; #2075, 4/13; #2076,
8/14; #2077, 11/9.

Pinwheel
A1001

2000, Mar. 16   **Litho.**   *Perf. 13¾*
2078 A1001 110pf multi   1.25 .80

Souvenir Sheet

Hainich National Park — A1002

2000, Mar. 16   *Perf. 13¼*
2079 A1002 110pf multi   1.25 1.25

Blue Wonder
Bridge,
Dresden
A1003

2000, Apr. 13   **Litho.**   *Perf. 13¼*
2080 A1003 100pf multi   1.10 .75

Cultural Foundation Type of 1999

Designs: 110pf, The Expulsion from Paradise, sculpture by Leonhard Kern. 220pf, Silver table fountain, 1652-53, by Melchior Gelb.

2000, Apr. 13   *Perf. 14x14¼*
2081 A979 110pf multi   1.25 .75
2082 A979 220pf multi   2.10 1.60

Expo 2000 Type of 1999
2000, Apr. 13   *Die Cut Perf. 11*
Booklet Stamp
Self-Adhesive
2083 A965 110pf multi   4.00 3.75
   a.   Booklet pane of 10   42.50

No. 2083a is a complete booklet.

Griefswald, 750th Anniv. — A1004

Litho. & Engr.
2000, Apr. 13   *Perf. 14x14¼*
2084 A1004 110pf multi   1.10 .80

Nikolaus
Ludwig von
Zinzendorf
(1700-60),
Religious
Leader
A1005

2000, May 12   **Photo.**   *Perf. 13¾*
2085 A1005 110pf multi   1.10 .75

Europa, 2000
Common Design Type

2000, May 12   **Litho.**   *Perf. 13¾*
2086 CD17 110pf multi   *1.40 .80*
Booklet Stamp
Self-Adhesive
Die Cut Perf. 10¾
2087 CD17 110pf multi   *1.50 1.25*
   a.   Complete booklet of 10   17.50

Einkommende Zeitungen, First Daily
Newspaper, 350th Anniv. — A1006

2000, June 8   **Litho.**   *Perf. 13¾x14*
2088 A1006 110pf multi   1.10 .80

Chambers of Handicrafts in Germany,
Cent. — A1007

2000, June 8   *Perf. 14*
2089 A1007 300pf gray & org   3.25 2.40

Zugspitze Weather Station,
Cent. — A1008

2000, July 13   **Litho.**   *Perf. 13¾x14*
2090 A1008 100pf multi   1.10 .80

Federal Disaster Relief Organization,
50th Anniv. — A1009

2000, July 13   *Perf. 14*
2091 A1009 110pf multi   1.25 .80

Johann
Sebastian
Bach (1685-
1750)
A1010

2000, July 13   *Perf. 13¼*
2092 A1010 110pf multi   1.10 .80

First Zeppelin
Flight,
Cent. — A1011

2000, July 13   *Perf. 13¼*
2093 A1011 110pf multi   1.25 .80

Expo 2000 Type of 2000
110pf, Expo emblem, Earth, fingerprint.

2000, Aug. 14   **Litho.**   *Perf. 14x14¼*
2094 A989 110pf multi   1.25 .80

Friedrich
Nietzsche
(1844-1900),
Philosopher
A1012

2000, Aug. 14   *Perf. 13¼*
2095 A1012 110pf multi   1.25 .80

Ernst Wiechert
(1887-1950),
Writer
A1013

2000, Aug. 14   *Perf. 13¾*
2096 A1013 110pf multi   1.25 .80

"For You" — A1014

2000, Sept. 14   **Litho.**   *Perf. 13x13¼*
2097 A1014 100pf multi   1.00 .80

Souvenir Sheet

For the Children — A1015

2000, Sept. 14   *Perf. 13¾x14*
2098 A1015 110pf multi   1.25 1.25

Adolph
Kolping (1813-
65)
A1016

2000, Sept. 14   *Perf. 13¼*
2099 A1016 110pf multi   1.25 .80

Kolping Society, 150th anniv.

Federal
Court of
Justice,
50th
Anniv.
A1017

Litho. & Engr.
2000, Sept. 14   *Perf. 14x14¼*
2100 A1017 110pf multi   1.25 .80

Bernhard Nocht Institute for Tropical
Medicine, Cent. — A1018

2000, Sept. 14   **Litho.**   *Perf. 13¾x14*
2101 A1018 300pf multi   3.25 2.50

Reunification
of Germany,
10th Anniv.
A1019

2000, Sept. 28   *Perf. 13¼*
2102 A1019 110pf multi   1.10 .80

Stamp Day — A1020

2000, Oct. 12 **Litho.** **Perf. 13x13¼**
2103 A1020 110pf multi 1.10 .80

Rainer Maria Rilke (1875-1926), Poet — A1021

2000, Nov. 9 **Litho.** **Perf. 13¼x13½**
2104 A1021 110pf multi 1.10 .80

Arnold Bode (1900-77), Artist — A1022

2000, Nov. 9 **Perf. 13¼**
2105 A1022 110pf red & black 1.10 .80

Leonhart Fuchs (1501-66), Botanist A1023

2001, Jan. 11 **Litho.** **Perf. 13¾**
2106 A1023 100pf multi 1.25 .70

Kingdom of Prussia, 300th Anniv. A1024

2001, Jan. 11 **Perf. 14**
2107 A1024 110pf multi 1.40 1.00

Association of Disabled War Veterans, 50th Anniv. — A1025

2001, Jan. 11 **Photo.** **Perf. 14**
2108 A1025 110pf multi 1.40 1.00

Youth Helpline Federation — A1026

2001, Jan. 11 **Litho.** **Perf. 13¾x14**
2109 A1026 110pf multi 1.40 1.00

Albert Lortzing (1801-51), Opera Composer A1027

2001, Jan. 11 **Perf. 13¾**
2110 A1027 110pf multi 1.40 1.00

Martin Bucer (1491-1551), Theologian A1028

2001, Feb. 8 **Litho.** **Perf. 13¾**
2111 A1028 110pf multi 1.40 1.00

Johann Heinrich Voss (1751-1826), Translator of Greek Classics A1029

2001, Feb. 8 **Perf. 13¼**
2112 A1029 300pf multi 3.75 2.75
See No. 2157.

State Parliament Type of 1998
Design: No. 2113, Saxony. No. 2114, Saxony-Anhalt. No. 2115, Schleswig-Holstein. No. 2116, Thuringia.

2001 **Litho.** **Perf. 13¾x14**
2113 A933 110pf multi 1.40 1.00
2114 A933 110pf multi 1.40 1.00
2115 A933 110pf multi 1.40 1.00
2116 A933 110pf multi 1.40 1.00
Nos. 2113-2116 (4) 5.60 4.00

Issued: No. 2113, 3/8/01. No. 2114, 5/10. No. 2115, 7/12. No. 2116, 9/5.

Erich Ollenhauer (1901-63), Politician — A1030

2001, Mar. 8 **Perf. 14**
2117 A1030 110pf multi 1.40 1.00

Karl Arnold (1901-58), Politician A1031

2001, Mar. 8 **Perf. 13¼**
2118 A1031 110pf multi 1.40 1.00

Federal Border Police, 50th Anniv. A1032

2001, Mar. 8 **Litho.** **Perf. 13¾**
2119 A1032 110pf multi 1.40 1.00

Rendsburg Railway Bridge — A1033

2001, Apr. 5 **Litho.** **Perf. 14**
2120 A1033 100pf multi 1.25 .95

Folk Music — A1034

2001, Apr. 5 **Perf. 13x13½**
2121 A1034 110pf multi 1.40 1.00

"Post!" A1035

2001, Apr. 5 **Photo.** **Perf. 14**
2122 A1035 110pf multi 1.40 1.00

Goethe Institute, 50th Anniv. — A1036

2001, Apr. 5 **Litho.**
2123 A1036 300pf multi 3.75 2.75

Endangered Species — A1037

Designs: No. 2124, Mountain gorilla. No. 2125, Indian rhinoceros.

2001, May 10 **Litho.** **Perf. 14**
2124 A1037 110pf multi 1.40 1.00
2125 A1037 110pf multi 1.40 1.00
See Nos. 2132-2133.

Europa A1038

2001, May 10 **Perf. 13¾**
2126 A1038 110pf multi 1.25 1.00

Werner Egk (1901-83), Composer — A1039

2001, May 10 **Perf. 14**
2127 A1039 110pf multi 1.40 1.00

St. Catherine's Monastery, 750th Anniv., Oceanographic Museum, 50th Anniv. — A1040

2001, June 13 **Litho.** **Perf. 13x13¼**
2128 A1040 110pf multi 1.40 1.00

Catholic Court Church, Dresden, 250th Anniv. A1041

2001, June 13 **Perf. 13¼**
2129 A1041 110pf multi 1.40 1.00

Canzow Village Church A1042

2001, July 12 **Photo.** **Perf. 14x14¼**
2130 A1042 110pf multi 1.40 1.00
Conservation of sacred monuments.

Souvenir Sheet

Health — A1043

No. 2131: a, Hand (circulatory diseases). b, Chest (cancer). c, Abdomen (infectious diseases). d, Head (depression).

2001, July 12 **Litho.** **Perf. 13x13½**
2131 A1043 Sheet of 4 5.00 5.00
a.-d. 110pf Any single 1.25 1.25

Endangered Species Type of 2001
Die Cut Perf. 11¼x11
2001, July 12   Litho.
Booklet Stamps
Self-Adhesive
2132 A1037 110pf Like #2124   1.40 1.40
2133 A1037 110pf Like #2125   1.40 1.40
  a.   Booklet, 5 each #2132-2133   20.00

Furth Dragon Lancing Festival A1044

2001, Aug. 9   Litho.   *Perf. 13¼*
2134 A1044 100pf multi   1.25 .95

Himmelsberg Lime Tree Natural Monument — A1045

2001   *Perf. 13¾x14*
2135   A1045 110pf multi   1.40 1.00
Die Cut Perf. 9¾x10½
2135A A1045 110pf multi   2.25 1.10
  b.   Booklet of 20   47.50

Issued: No. 2135, 8/9; No. 2135A, 9/13.

Lifelong Learning A1046

2001, Aug. 9   *Perf. 14*
2136 A1046 110pf multi   1.40 1.00

Federal Constitutional Court, 50th Anniv. — A1047

2001, Sept. 5
2137 A1047 110pf multi   1.40 1.00

First World Congress of Union Network International — A1048

2001, Sept. 5   *Perf. 13x13½*
2138 A1048 110pf multi   1.40 1.00

Opening of Jewish Museum, Berlin — A1049

2001, Sept. 5   Photo.   *Perf. 13¾*
2139 A1049 110pf multi   1.40 1.00

Souvenir Sheet

For Children — A1050

2001, Sept. 5   Litho.   *Perf. 13¾x14*
2140 A1050 110pf multi   1.40 1.00

"For You" — A1051

2001, Oct. 11   *Perf. 13x13¼*
2141 A1051 110pf multi   1.40 1.00

Werner Heisenberg (1901-76), Physicist A1052

2001, Nov. 8   Litho.   *Perf. 13¾*
2142 A1052 300pf multi   3.75 2.75

Souvenir Sheet

German Antarctic Expeditions, Cent. — A1053

Expedition vessels: a, Gauss. b, Polarstern.

2001, Nov. 8   *Perf. 13¾x14*
2143 A1053   Sheet of 2, #a-b   3.75 3.75
  a.   110pf multi   1.25 1.25
  b.   220pf multi   2.50 2.50

Introduction of the Euro, Jan. 1 — A1054

2002, Jan. 10   Litho.   *Perf. 13¾*
2144   A1054 56c multi   1.50 .50

Coil Stamp
Self-Adhesive
2144A A1054 56c multi   3.25 2.40

Hans von Dohnanyi (1902-45), Documenter of Nazi Atrocities A1055

2002, Jan. 10   Photo.
2145   A1055 56c multi   1.75 1.40
2145A A1055 56c multi   *900.00*

No. 2145A has "2002" in upper right corner and colored face and name. Approximately 320 small panes of 10 of No. 2145A were accidentally mixed in with approved stock of No. 2145 and sold over post office counters.

Bautzen, 1000th Anniv. A1056

2002, Jan. 10   Litho.
2146   A1056 56c multi   1.50 .80
Die Cut Perf. 11
Litho.
Booklet Stamp
Self-Adhesive
2146A A1056 56c multi   2.40 1.90
  b.   Booklet of 10   24.00

More Tolerance — A1057

2002, Jan. 10   *Perf. 13¾x14*
2147 A1057 56c multi   1.50 .80

Adolph Freiherr Knigge (1762-96), Writer — A1058

2002, Feb. 7   Litho.   *Perf. 13¾*
2148 A1058 56c multi   1.50 .80

Berlin Subway System, Cent. — A1059

2002, Feb. 7   *Perf. 13¼*
2149 A1059 56c multi   1.50 .80

Johann Christoph Schuster's Mechanical Calculator — A1060

2002, Mar. 7   Litho.   *Perf. 14*
2150 A1060 56c multi   1.50 .80

Cultural Foundation of the Federal States.

Deggendorf, 1000th Anniv. — A1061

2002, Mar. 7
2151 A1061 56c multi   1.50 .80

Ecksberg Foundation for the Mentally Handicapped, 150th Anniv. — A1062

Litho. & Engr.
2002, Apr. 4   *Perf. 14x13¾*
2152 A1062 56c multi   1.50 .80

Freemason's Museum, Cent. — A1063

2002, Apr. 4   Litho.   *Perf. 14*
2153 A1063 56c multi   1.50 .80

Baden-Württemberg, 50th Anniv. — A1064

2002, Apr. 4   *Perf. 13¼*
2154 A1064 56c multi   1.50 .80

"Post" — A1065

2002, Apr. 4   *Perf. 13x13½*
2155 A1065 56c multi   1.50 .80

Federal Employment Services, 50th Anniv. — A1066

2002, Apr. 4   *Perf. 14*
2156 A1066 153c black & red   4.25 2.40

Voss Type of 2001
Die Cut Perf. 10¼
2002, Apr. 4   **Litho.**
Coil Stamp
Self-Adhesive
2157 A1029 €1.53 multi   4.25 2.75
Dated 2001. No. 2157 was sold only for euro currency.

Europa
A1067

2002   **Litho.**   *Perf. 13¼*
2158 A1067 56c multi   1.50 .80
Self-Adhesive Coil Stamp
Die Cut Perf. 10¼
2158A A1067 56c multi   2.40 2.00
Issued: No. 2158, 5/2; No. 2158A, 7/4.

Garden Kingdom of Dessau-Wörlitz, UNESCO World Heritage Site — A1068

2002   *Perf. 13¾x14*
2159 A1068 56c multi   1.50 .80
Booklet Stamp
Self-Adhesive
2159A A1068 56c multi   1.50 .80
   b.   Booklet of 20   30.00
Issued: No. 2159, 5/2; No. 2159A, 8/8.

Halle-Wittenberg University, 500th Anniv. — A1069

2002, May 2   *Perf. 14*
2160 A1069 56c multi   1.50 .80

Children's Church, 150th Anniv. A1070

2002, May 2   *Perf. 13¼*
2161 A1070 56c multi   1.50 .80

Souvenir Sheet

Documenta 11 Art Exhibition — A1071

2002, May 2   *Perf. 13¾x14*
2162 A1071 56c multi   1.50 .80

2002 World Cup Soccer Championships, Japan and Korea — A1072

No. 2163: a, Flags, soccer ball and field (28mm diameter). b, Soccer players, years of German championships. Illustration reduced.

2002, May 2   *Perf. 13¾*
2163 A1072   Horiz. pair   3.00 2.25
   a.-b.   56c Any single   1.50 .95
See Argentina No. 2184, Brazil No. 2840, France No. 2891, Italy No. 2526 and Uruguay No. 1946.

Albrecht Daniel Thaer (1752-1828), Agronomist — A1073

2002, May 2   *Perf. 13x13½*
2164 A1073 225c multi   6.25 3.50

Yellow Feather in Red, by Ernst Wilhelm Nay (1902-68) — A1074

2002, June 6   **Litho.**   *Perf. 13¾x14*
2165 A1074 56c multi   1.50 .80

Endangered Species — A1075

Designs: 51c, Desmoulins whorl snail. 56c, Freshwater pearl mussel.

2002, June 6   *Perf. 14x14¼*
2166 A1075 51c multi   1.40 .80
2167 A1075 56c multi   1.50 .80
See Czech Republic No. 3173.

World Hunger Help — A1076

2002, July 4   **Litho.**   *Perf. 13¾x14*
2168 A1076 51c multi   1.40 .80

Natl. Germanic Museum, 150th Anniv. — A1077

2002, July 4
2169 A1077 56c multi   1.50 .80

Hermann Hesse (1877-1962), Writer — A1078

2002, July 4   *Perf. 14*
2170 A1078 56c multi   1.50 .80

Souvenir Sheet

Hochharz Natl. Park — A1079

2002, July 4   *Perf. 13¾x14*
2171 A1079 56c multi   1.60 1.00

Josef Felder (1900-2000), Politician, Journalist A1080

2002, Aug. 8   **Litho.**   *Perf. 13*
2172 A1080 56c multi   1.50 .80

Volunteer Fire Brigades A1081

2002, Aug. 8   *Perf. 14*
2173 A1081 56c multi   1.50 .80

Museum Island, Berlin, UNESCO World Heritage Site A1082

Litho. & Engr.
2002, Aug. 8   *Perf. 13¾x14*
2174 A1082 56c blk & Prus blue   1.50 .80

Communications Museum, Berlin — A1083

2002, Aug. 8   **Litho.**   *Perf. 14*
2175 A1083 153c multi   4.25 2.40

Foundation Walls of Roman Villa Bathhouse, Wurmlingen — A1084

2002, Sept. 5   **Litho.**   *Perf. 13¾x14*
2176 A1084 51c multi   1.40 .70

Rotes Elisabeth-Ufer, by Ernst Ludwig Kirchner (1880-1938) — A1085

2002, Sept. 5
2177 A1085 112c multi   3.25 1.60

Souvenir Sheet

For Children — A1086

2002, Sept. 5   *Perf. 13x13½*
2178 A1086 56c multi   1.50 1.00

Heinrich von Kleist (1777-1811), Writer — A1087

2002, Oct. 10   **Litho.**   *Perf. 13*
2179 A1087 56c multi   1.50 .80

Eugen Jochum (1902-87), Conductor A1088

2002, Oct. 10   *Perf. 14x14¼*
2180 A1088 56c multi   1.50 .80

Otto von Guericke (1602-86), Physicist — A1089

2002, Oct. 10   *Perf. 14*
2181 A1089 153c multi   4.25 2.25

Federal Agency for Civic Education, 50th Anniv. A1090

2002, Nov. 7   *Litho.*   *Perf. 13¼*
2182 A1090 56c blk, red & org   1.50 .80

German Television, 50th Anniv. — A1091

2002, Nov. 7   *Perf. 14*
2183 A1091 56c multi   1.50 .80

Halle Market Church, by Lyonel Feininger (1871-1956) — A1092

2002, Dec. 5   *Litho.*   *Perf. 13¾x14*
2184 A1092 55c multi   1.50 .80

Famous Women Type of 1986 With Euro Denominations Only

Designs: 45c, Annette von Droste-Hülshoff (1797-1848), poet. 55c, Hildegard Knef (1925-2002), actress. €1, Marie Juchacz (1879-1956), politician. €1.44, Esther von Kirchbach (1894-1946), writer.

2002-03   *Engr.*   *Perf. 14*
2185 A602   45c ol grn & Prus bl   1.25 .65
2186 A602   55c car & blk   1.50 .80
2187 A602   €1 dk bl & claret   2.75 1.40
2188 A602   €1.44 dk bl & ocher   4.00 2.10
   Nos. 2185-2188 (4)   9.50 4.95

Issued: 45c, 55c, €1.44, 12/27/02; €1, 1/16/03.

Historic Sites Type of 1987 With Euro Denominations Only

Designs: 25c, Prince's Residence, Arolsen. 40c, Bach Statue, Leipzig. 44c, Berlin Philharmonic Hall. 45c, Tönninger Packhaus (Warehouse, Tönning). 55c, Old Opera House, Frankfurt. €1, Porta Nigra, Trier. €1.44, Birthplace of Ludwig van Beethoven, Bonn. €1.60, Bauhaus, Dessau. €1.80, Stuttgart Staatsgalerie. €2, Equestrian statue, Bamberg. €2.20, Monument to Theodor Fontane, Neuruppin. €2.60, Barque "Seute Deern," Bremerhaven. €4.10, Gabled houses, Wismar.

Typo., Litho. (#2209, 2213)
2002-04   *Perf. 14*
2199 A623   5c olive & turq   .20 .20
2200 A623   25c multi   .70 .35
2201 A623   40c pur & grn   1.10 .60
2202 A623   44c blk & yel   1.25 .60
2203 A623   45c gray blk & brick red   1.25 .60
2204 A623   55c blk & yel   1.50 .75
2205 A623   €1 blk & greenish gray   2.75 1.40
2206 A623   €1.44 gray grn & pink   4.00 2.00
2207 A623   €1.60 slate & org   4.50 2.25

2208 A623   €1.80 dull grn & brn   5.00 2.50
2209 A623   €2 brn blk & lake   5.50 2.75
2210 A623   €2.20 blue blk & gray bl   6.25 3.50
2211 A623   €2.60 blue & red   7.25 3.75
2212 A623   €4.10 bl grn & red vio   11.50 6.00

Self-Adhesive
Die Cut Perf. 10¼x11
Photo.
2213 A623 €1.44 Like #2206   4.00 2.00
Coil Stamp
Litho.
2214 A623 55c blk & yel   2.00 1.00
Booklet Stamps
Die Cut Perf. 10¼x11 on 3 Sides
2215 A623   45c gray blk & brick red   1.60 .80
2216 A623   55c blk & yel   2.00 1.00
   a.   Booklet 4 #2215, 8 #2216   20.00
   Nos. 2199-2216 (18)   62.35 32.05

Issued: 44c, 45c, 55c, €1, €1.60, 12/27/02; €1.44, €2.20, 1/16/03; €1.80, €2, 2/13/03; €2.60, €4.10, 3/6/03; No. 2213, June 2003. 25c, 40c, 1/8/04; 5c, 2/5/04.

Kronach, 1000th Anniv. — A1093

2003, Jan. 16   *Litho.*   *Perf. 14*
2222 A1093 45c multi   1.25 .65

Georg Elser (1903-45), Failed Assassin of Hitler — A1094

2003, Jan. 16   *Perf. 13¼*
2223 A1094 55c multi   1.50 .80

Treaty for German-French Cooperation, 40th Anniv. A1095

2003, Jan. 16   *Perf. 13¾*
2224 A1095 55c multi   1.50 .80

Bible Year A1096

2003, Jan. 16   *Perf. 14x14¼*
2225 A1096 55c multi   1.50 .80

Proun 30t, by El Lissitzky (1890-1941) — A1097

2003, Jan. 16
2226 A1097 144c multi   4.00 2.10
Cultural Foundation of the Federal States.

Rose A1098

2003, Feb. 13   *Litho.*   *Perf. 14*
2227 A1098 55c multi   1.50 .80
Booklet Stamp
Self-Adhesive
Die Cut Perf. 10x10¼
2228 A1098 55c multi   1.50 .80
   a.   Booklet pane of 10   15.00

Junger Argentinier, by Max Beckmann — A1099

Composition, by Adolf Hölzel — A1100

2003, Feb. 13   *Perf. 13¾x14*
2229 A1099 55c multi   1.50 .80
2230 A1100 100c multi   2.75 1.40

Souvenir Sheet

Boys' Choirs — A1101

No. 2231: a, Thomanerchor Leipzig. b, Dredner Kreuzchor. c, Regensburger Domspatzen.

2003, Feb. 13   *Perf. 14x14¼*
2231 A1101   Sheet of 3   5.50 3.25
   a.   45c multi   1.25 .80
   b.   55c multi   1.50 .80
   c.   100c multi   2.75 1.40

Cologne Cathedral, UNESCO World Heritage Site — A1102

2003, Mar. 6   *Perf. 13¼*
2232 A1102 55c multi   1.50 .80
Self-Adhesive
Coil Stamp
2233 A1102 55c multi   1.50 .80

Intl. Horticultural Exhibition 2003, Rostock A1103

2003, Apr. 10   *Litho.*   *Perf. 13¼*
2234 A1103 45c multi   1.25 .70

German Museum, Munich, Cent. A1104

2003, Apr. 10   *Photo.*   *Perf. 14x14¼*
2235 A1104 55c multi   1.50 .80

Deutsche Welle Radio, 50th Anniv. — A1105

2003, Apr. 10   *Litho.*   *Perf. 14*
2236 A1105 55c multi   1.50 .80

German Society for the Protection of Children, 50th Anniv. A1106

2003, Apr. 10   *Perf. 13¼*
2237 A1106 55c multi   1.50 .80

Reinhold Schneider (1903-58), Writer — A1107

2003, May 8   *Litho.*   *Perf. 13¼*
2238 A1107 55c multi   1.50 .80

Ecumenical Church Conference, Berlin — A1108

2003, May 8   *Perf. 14*
2239 A1108 55c multi   1.50 .80

Justus von Liebig (1803-73), Chemist — A1109

2003, May 8
2240 A1109 55c multi   1.50 .80

German General Automobile Club, Cent. — A1110

2003, May 8   *Perf. 13¼x13½*
2241 A1110 55c multi   1.50 .80

Europa — A1111

2003, May 8
2242 A1111 55c multi   1.50   .80

Hans Jonas (1903-93),
Philosopher — A1112

2003, May 8   *Perf. 13¾x14*
2243 A1112 220c multi   6.25 3.25

Five
Digit
Postal
Codes,
10th
Anniv.
A1113

2003, June 12   Litho.   *Perf. 14*
2244 A1113 55c multi   1.50   .80

Salzach River Bridge, Laufen,
Germany - Oberndorf, Austria,
Cent. — A1114

2003, June 12
2245   A1114 55c multi   1.50   .80
Booklet Stamp
Self-Adhesive
2245A A1114 55c multi   1.50   .80
   b.   Booklet pane of 20   30.00
See Austria No. 1922.

Souvenir Sheet

Unteres Odertal National
Park — A1115

2003, June 12   *Perf. 13x13½*
2246 A1115 55c multi   1.50 1.00

German
Music
Council,
50th
Anniv.
A1116

2003, June 12   *Perf. 14*
2247 A1116 144c multi   4.00 2.10
Self-Adhesive
Booklet Stamp
Die Cut Perf. 11¼x11
2247A A1116 144c multi   4.00 2.10
   b.   Booklet pane of 10   40.00
Issued: No. 2247, 6/12/03; No. 2247A,
1/8/04.

Scenic Regions in Germany — A1117

2003   Litho.   *Perf. 13x13½*
2248 A1117 55c Ruhr Region   1.50   .80
   Issued: No. 2248, 7/10. This is an
expanding set. Numbers have been reserved
for additional items.

Andreas Hermes (1878-1964),
Politician — A1118

2003, July 10   Photo.   *Perf. 14x14¼*
2258 A1118 55c multi   1.50   .80

Petrified Forest,
Chemnitz
A1119

2003, Aug. 7   Litho.   *Perf. 13¼*
2259 A1119 144c multi   4.00 2.10
City Views

Market, Munich
A1120

Buildings in Old City, Görlitz — A1121

2003, Aug. 7   Litho.   *Perf. 13¼*
2260   A1120 45c multi   1.25   .65
              Perf. 13x13½
2261   A1121 55c multi   1.50   .80
Self-Adhesive
Booklet Stamp
Die Cut Perf. 11x 10¾
2261A A1120 45c multi   1.40   .55
   b.   Booklet pane of 10   14.00
Issued: Nos. 2260, 2261, 8/7/03; No.
2261A, 1/8/04.

Theodor W. Adorno (1903-69),
Philosopher — A1122

2003, Sept. 11   *Perf. 14*
2262 A1122 55c multi   1.50   .80

Bietigheim Enzviadukt, 150th
Anniv. — A1123

2003, Sept. 11   *Perf. 13x13½*
2263 A1123 55c multi   1.50   .80

Souvenir Sheet

For Children — A1124

2003, Sept. 11   *Perf. 13¾x14*
2264 A1124 55c multi   1.50   .80

Mailbox
A1125

2003, Oct. 9   Litho.   *Perf. 13¼*
2265 A1125 55c multi   1.50   .80

German Lifesaving
Association — A1126

2003, Oct. 9   *Perf. 13¾*
2266 A1126 144c multi   4.00 2.10

Opera House, Dresden, by Gottfried
Semper (1803-79), Architect — A1127

2003, Nov. 13   Litho.   *Perf. 13x13½*
2267 A1127 55c multi   1.50   .80

German Catholic Women's
Organization, Cent. — A1128

2003, Nov. 13   *Perf. 14*
2268 A1128 55c multi   1.50   .80

Ratification of Maastricht Treaty, 10th
Anniv. — A1129

2003, Nov. 13
2269 A1129 55c multi   1.50   .80

Landshut, 800th Anniv. — A1130

2004, Jan. 8   Litho.   *Perf. 14*
2270 A1130 45c multi   1.25   .65

Schleswig,
1200th Anniv.
A1131

2004, Jan. 8   *Perf. 13¼*
2271 A1131 55c multi   1.50   .80

Arnstadt,
1300th Anniv.
A1132

2004, Feb. 5   Litho.   *Perf. 13¼*
2272 A1132 55c multi   1.50   .80

Greetings — A1133

2004, Feb. 5   *Perf. 14*
2273 A1133 55c multi   1.50   .80

Joseph Schmidt (1904-42),
Singer — A1134

2004, Mar. 11   Litho.   *Perf. 14*
2274 A1134 55c multi   1.50   .80

Paul Ehrlich (1854-1915) and Emil von
Behring (1854-1917),
Physicians — A1135

2004, Mar. 11
2275 A1135 144c multi   4.00 2.10

Souvenir Sheet

Classical Theater — A1136

No. 2276: a, Premiere of *William Tell*, by Friedrich von Schiller, bicent. b, Premiere of *Faust*, by Johann Wolfgang von Goethe, 150th anniv.

2004, Mar. 11   **Perf. 13¾**
2276 A1136   Sheet of 2   4.00 2.10
  a.   45c multi   1.25   .65
  b.   100c multi   2.75 1.40

Bauhaus World Heritage Sites, Weimar and Dessau — A1137

2004, Apr. 7   Litho.   Perf. 14
2277 A1137 55c multi   1.50   .80

White Stork A1138

2004, Apr. 7
2278 A1138 55c multi   1.50   .80

Kurt Georg Kiesinger (1904-88), Chancellor A1139

2004, Apr. 7   Perf. 13¾
2279 A1139 55c multi   1.50   .80

Electric Light Bulb of Heinrich Göbel, 150th Anniv. A1140

2004, Apr. 7
2280 A1140 220c red & blue   6.25 3.25

Europa A1141

2004, May 6   Litho.   Perf. 13¼
2281 A1141 45c multi   1.25   .65

Expansion of the European Union A1142

2004, May 6
2282 A1142 55c multi   1.50   .80

St. Boniface of Mainz (c. 675-754) A1143

2004, May 6   Perf. 13¾
2283 A1143 55c multi   1.50   .80

Reinhard Schwarz-Schilling (1904-85), Composer — A1144

2004, May 6   Perf. 14
2284 A1144 55c multi   1.50   .80

Ludwigsburg Castle, 300th Anniv. — A1145

2004, May 6
2285 A1145 144c multi   4.00 2.10

Wattenmeer National Park — A1146

2004, June 3   Litho.   Perf. 13
2286 A1146 55c multi   1.50   .80

German - Russian Youth Meeting A1147

2004, June 3   Perf. 13¾
2287 A1147 55c multi   1.50   .80
See Russia No. 6845.

Transatlantic Speed Record-Breaking Voyage of the Steamship "Bremen," 75th Anniv. — A1148

2004, July 8   Litho.   Perf. 14
2288 A1148 55c multi   1.50   .80
Booklet Stamp
Self-Adhesive
2288A A1148 55c multi   1.50   .80
  b.   Booklet pane of 20   30.00

Ludwig Feuerbach (1804-72), Philosopher A1149

2004, July 8   Perf. 13¾
2289 A1149 144c multi   4.00 2.10

Lighthouses A1150

2004, July 8
2290 A1150 45c Griefswalder
                    Oie   1.25   .65
2291 A1150 55c Roter Sand   1.50   .80
Die Cut Perf. 10¼
Coil Stamp
Self-Adhesive
2291A A1150 55c Roter Sand   1.50   .80
See Nos. 2344-2345B, 2447-2448, 2491-2494.

Memorial Church, Speyer, Cent. A1151

2004, Aug. 12   Litho.   Perf. 13¾
2292 A1151 55c multi   1.50   .80

Camellia — A1152

2004, Aug. 12   Perf. 14
2293 A1152 55c multi   1.50   .80
Booklet Stamp
Self-Adhesive
Die Cut Perf. 10x10¼
2294 A1152 55c multi   1.50   .80
  a.   Booklet pane, 5 each #2228,
                    2294   15.00

Engelbert Humperdinck (1854-1921), Composer — A1153

2004, Sept. 9   Litho.   Perf. 14
2295 A1153 45c multi   1.25   .65

Eduard Mörike (1804-75), Poet — A1154

2004, Sept. 9
2296 A1154 55c multi   1.50   .80

For Children A1155

2004, Sept. 9   Perf. 13¾
2297 A1155 55c multi   1.50   .80

Egon Eiermann (1904-70), Architect — A1156

2004, Sept. 9   Perf. 14
2298 A1156 100c multi   2.75 1.40

Federal Social Court, 50th Anniv. A1157

Litho. & Embossed
2004, Sept. 9   Perf. 13¾
2299 A1157 144c multi   4.00 2.10

Dornier Do X A1158

2004, Oct. 7   Litho.   Perf. 14
2300 A1158 55c multi   1.50   .80
Stamp Day.

Winter Scene A1159

2004, Nov. 4
2301 A1159 55c multi   1.50 .80

International Space Station — A1160

2004, Nov. 4
2302 A1160 55c multi   1.50 .80

The Secret, by Felix Nussbaum (1904-44) — A1161

2004, Nov. 4
2303 A1161 55c multi   1.50 .80

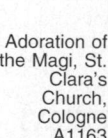

Forchheim, 1200th Anniv. A1162

2005, Jan. 3   Litho.   Perf. 13¼
2304 A1162 45c multi   1.25 .65

Adoration of the Magi, St. Clara's Church, Cologne A1163

2005, Jan. 3
2305 A1163 55c multi   1.50 .80
See No. 2509.

Sculpture of Celtic Prince Found in Glauberg A1164

2005, Jan. 3   Perf. 13¾
2306 A1164 144c multi   4.00 2.10

Flowers — A1165

Designs: 5c, Krokus (crocus) 10c, Tulpe (tulip). 20c, Tagetes (marigold). 25c, Malve (mallow). 35c, Dahlie (dahlia). 40c, Leber-blümchen (hepatica). 45c, Margerite (daisy). 50c, Aster. 55c, Klatschmohn (red poppy). 65c, Sonnenhut (rudbeckia). 70c, Kartaüsernelke (clusterhead pink). 90c, Narzisse (narcissus). 95c, Sonnenblume (sun-flower). 100c, Tränendes herz (Bleeding heart). 145c, Schwertlilie (iris). 220c, Edel-weiss. 390c, Feuerlilie (tiger lily). 430c, Ritter-sporn (larkspur).

2005-06   Litho.   Perf. 14
2307 A1165 5c multi   .20 .20
2308 A1165 10c multi   .30 .20
2309 A1165 20c multi   .55 .30
  a. Miniature sheet, 4 each
      #2307-2308, 2 each
      #2309   2.75 2.75
2310 A1165 25c multi   .70 .40
2311 A1165 35c multi   1.00 .50
2312 A1165 40c multi   1.10 .55
2313 A1165 45c multi   1.25 .65
2314 A1165 50c multi   1.40 .70
2315 A1165 55c multi   1.50 .80
2316 A1165 65c multi   1.75 .90
2317 A1165 70c multi   2.00 .95
2318 A1165 90c multi   2.50 1.25
2319 A1165 95c multi   2.75 1.40
2320 A1165 100c multi   2.75 1.40
2321 A1165 145c multi   4.00 2.10
2322 A1165 220c multi   6.25 3.00
2323 A1165 390c multi   11.00 5.50
2324 A1165 430c multi   12.00 6.25
Nos. 2307-2324 (18)   53.00 27.05

Coil Stamp
Self-Adhesive
Die Cut Perf. 10¼x10
2325 A1165 25c multi   .70 .40
2326 A1165 35c multi   1.00 .55
2326A A1165 55c multi   1.50 .80
2326B A1165 90c multi   2.50 1.40
  a. Booklet pane of 10   25.00

Issued: 95c, 430c, 1/3. 45c, 4/7. #2310, 50c, 6/2. 20c, #2315, 7/7. 5c, 8/11.10c, 40c, 9/8; #2326A, 7/7. #2325, 35c, 90c, 145c, 1/2/06. 65c, 3/2/06. 70c, 220c, 4/13/06. 390c, 5/4/06. 100c, 7/13/06. #2309a, 3/1/07.
See Nos. 2405-2422.

Advertising Pillars, 150th Anniv. A1166

2005, Feb. 10   Litho.   Perf. 13¾
2327 A1166 55c multi   1.50 .80

Berlin Cathedral, Cent. A1167

2005, Feb. 10   Perf. 13
2328 A1167 95c multi   2.75 1.40

Booklet Stamp
Self-Adhesive
Die Cut Perf. 11
2329 A1167 95c multi   2.75 1.40
  a. Booklet pane of 10   27.50

Bonn-Copenhagen Declaration, 50th Anniv. — A1168

2005, Mar. 3   Perf. 14
2330 A1168 55c multi   1.50 .80
See Denmark No. 1322.

Resumption of Regulated Civil Aviation, 50th Anniv. — A1169

2005, Mar. 3
2331 A1169 155c multi   4.25 2.25

Postal Workers A1170

Designs: No. 2332, Postman on bicycle. No. 2333, Postman on snowy hillside.

2005, Mar. 3   Perf. 13¾
2332 A1170 55c multi   1.50 .80
2333 A1170 55c multi   1.50 .80
See Nos. 2348-2349.

Mittelland Canal, Cent. — A1171

2005, Apr. 7   Litho.   Perf. 14
2334 A1171 45c multi   1.25 .80

Bavarian Forest National Park — A1172

2005, Apr. 7   Perf. 13¾
2335 A1172 55c multi   1.50 .80

Hans Christian Andersen (1805-75), Author — A1173

2005, Apr. 7   Perf. 14
2336 A1173 144c multi   4.00 2.10

Coil Stamp
Self-Adhesive
Die Cut Perf. 10¼
2336A A1173 144c multi   4.00 2.10

Founding of Die Brücke Expressionist Group, Cent. A1174

2005, May 12   Litho.   Perf. 13¾
2337 A1174 55c buff, blk & red   1.50 .80

Paris Treaty, 50th Anniv. A1175

2005, May 12
2338 A1175 55c black & red   1.50 .80

Friedrich von Schiller Year — A1176

2005, May 12   Perf. 14
2339 A1176 55c multi   1.50 .80

Pope John Paul II (1920-2005) — A1177

2005, May 12
2340 A1177 55c multi   1.50 .80

Europa A1178

2005, May 12
2341 A1178 55c multi   1.50 .80

Sixth Congress of European Organization of Supreme Audit Institutions, Bonn A1179

2005, June 2   Litho.   Perf. 13¾
2342 A1179 55c multi   1.50 .80

20th World Youth Day A1180

2005, June 2   Perf. 14
2343 A1180 55c multi   1.50 .80
See Vatican City No. 1298.

Lighthouse Type of 2004
Designs: Nos. 2344, 2345B, Brunsbüttel, Jetty 1. No. 2345A, Griefswalde Oie. 55c, Westerheversand.

2005, July 7   Litho.   Perf. 13¾
2344 A1150 45c multi   1.25 .65
2345 A1150 55c multi   1.50 .80

Booklet Stamps
Self-Adhesive
Die Cut Perf. 10¾
2345A A1150 45c multi   1.25 .65
2345B A1150 45c multi   1.25 .65
  c. Booklet pane, 5 each
      #2345A-2345B   12.50

Albert Einstein's Theory of Relativity, Cent. — A1181

2005, July 7 Perf. 14
2346 A1181 55c multi 1.50 .80

Souvenir Sheet

Prussian Castles and Gardens — A1182

2005, July 7 Perf. 13x13½
2347 A1182 220c multi 6.25 3.25

Self-Adhesive
Booklet Stamp
Die Cut Perf. 11

2347A A1182 220c multi 6.25 3.25
b. Booklet pane of 10 57.50 —
Issued: #2347, 7/7. #2347A, 11/3.

Postal Workers Type of 2005

Designs: No. 2348, Postman on punt. No. 2349, Postman with handcart.

2005, Aug. 11 Litho. Perf. 13¾
2348 A1170 55c multi 1.50 .80
2349 A1170 55c multi 1.50 .80

German Friends of Nature, Cent. A1183

2005, Aug. 11 Perf. 13¼
2350 A1183 144c multi 4.00 2.10

Magdeburg, 1200th Anniv. — A1184

2005, Sept. 8 Litho. Perf. 14
2351 A1184 55c multi 1.50 .80

For Children — A1185

2005, Sept. 8
2352 A1185 55c multi 1.50 .80

Peace of Augsburg, 450th Anniv. A1186

2005, Sept. 8 Perf. 13¾
2353 A1186 55c multi 1.50 .80
See No. 2508.

Max Schmeling (1905-2005), Boxer — A1187

2005, Sept. 8 Perf. 14
2354 A1187 55c multi 1.50 .80

Dedication of Rebuilt Church of Our Lady, Dresden — A1188

2005, Oct. 13 Litho. Perf. 14
2355 A1188 55c multi 1.50 .80

Adalbert Stifter (1805-68), Writer A1189

2005, Oct. 13 Perf. 13¾
2356 A1189 95c multi 2.75 1.40

St. Leonhard's Day Procession, Bad Tölz — A1190

2005, Nov. 3 Litho. Perf. 13¼
2357 A1190 45c multi 1.25 .65

Federal Armed Forces, 50th Anniv. A1191

2005, Nov. 3 Perf. 13¾
2358 A1191 55c multi 1.50 .80

Diplomatic Relations With Israel, 40th Anniv. A1192

2005, Nov. 3
2359 A1192 55c multi 1.50 .80
See Israel No. 1619.

Awarding of Nobel Peace Prize to Bertha von Suttner, Cent. — A1193

2005, Nov. 3 Perf. 14
2360 A1193 55c multi 1.50 .80

Awarding of Nobel Physiology or Medicine Prize to Robert Koch, Cent. — A1194

2005, Nov. 3 Perf. 13¼
2361 A1194 144c multi 4.00 2.10

Halle, 1200th Anniv. A1195

2006, Jan. 2 Litho. Perf. 14
2362 A1195 45c multi 1.25 .65

Winter A1196

2006, Jan. 2 Litho. Perf. 14
2363 A1196 55c multi 1.50 .80
See No. 2400.

Spring A1197

2006, Apr. 13 Litho. Perf. 14
2364 A1197 55c multi 1.50 .80
See No. 2397.

Summer — A1198

2006, July 13 Litho. Perf. 14
2365 A1198 55c multi 1.50 .80
See no. 2398.

Autumn — A1199

2006, Oct. 5 Litho. Perf. 14
2366 A1199 55c multi 1.50 .80
See No. 2399.

Wolfgang Amadeus Mozart (1756-91), Composer A1200

2006, Jan. 2 Litho. Perf. 13¼
2367 A1200 55c multi 1.50 .80

Golden Bull of Emperor Charles IV — A1201

2006, Jan. 2 Perf. 14
2368 A1201 145c multi 4.00 2.10

Self-Adhesive
Booklet Stamp
Die Cut Perf. 10

2369 A1201 145c multi 4.00 2.10
a. Booklet pane of 10 40.00

St. Michael's Church, Schwäbisch Hall, 850th Anniv. — A1202

2006, Feb. 9 Litho. Perf. 14
2370 A1202 55c multi 1.50 .80

Frisian Council, 50th Anniv. A1203

2006, Feb. 9
2371 A1203 90c multi 2.50 1.40

Ingolstadt, 1200th Anniv. A1204

2006, Mar. 2   Litho.   Perf. 13¼
2372 A1204 55c multi   1.50   .80

Karl Friedrich Schinkel (1781-1841), Architect — A1205

2006   Perf. 14
2373 A1205 55c multi   1.50   .80

Coil Stamp
Self-Adhesive
Die Cut Perf. 10x10¼
2373A A1205 55c multi   1.50   .80
Issued: No. 2373, 3/2. No. 2373A, 7/13.

Care for the Blind — A1206

Litho. & Embossed
2006, Mar. 2   Perf. 13x13½
2374 A1206 55c black & gray   1.50   .80
Berlin School for the Blind, 200th Anniv., Nikolaus Care Foundation, 150th Anniv.

Pres. Johannes Rau (1931-2006) — A1207

2006, Mar. 2   Litho.   Perf. 14
2375 A1207 55c multi   1.50   .80

Viadrina Universtiy, Frankfurt an der Oder, 500th Anniv. A1208

Litho. & Embossed
2006, Apr. 13   Perf. 13¾
2376 A1208 55c multi   1.50   .80

Self-Portrait in Fur Coat, by Albrecht Dürer A1209

2006, Apr. 13   Litho.
2377 A1209 145c multi   4.00 2.10

Upper Middle Rhine Valley UNESCO World Heritage Site — A1210

2006, May 4   Litho.   Perf. 13¾
2378 A1210 55c multi   1.50   .80

Self-Adhesive
Booklet Stamp
Die Cut Perf. 11
2379 A1210 55c multi   1.50   .80
a.   Booklet pane of 10   15.00

Europa A1211

2006, May 4   Perf. 14
2380 A1211 55c multi   1.50   .80

Gerd Bucerius (1906-95), Publisher and Politician — A1212

2006, May 4
2381 A1212 85c multi   2.40 1.25

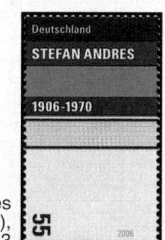

Stefan Andres (1906-70), Writer — A1213

2006, June 8
2382 A1213 55c multi   1.50   .80

John Augustus Roebling (1806-69), Bridge Designer — A1214

2006, June 8   Perf. 14
2383 A1214 145c multi   4.00 2.10

Self-Adhesive
Coil Stamp
Die Cut Perf. 11
2384 A1214 145c multi   4.00 2.10

Standardized Motor Vehicle Identification, Cent. — A1215

2006, July 13   Litho.   Perf. 14
2385 A1215 45c multi   1.25   .65

Burghausen Castle, Burghausen — A1216

2006, July 13
2386 A1216 55c multi   1.50   .80

Saskia van Uylenburgh, by Rembrandt (1606-69) A1217

2006, July 13   Perf. 13¾
2387 A1217 70c multi   2.00 1.00
See Netherlands No. 1253. The design of No. 2387 was reproduced without the permission of the German authorities in a Netherlands booklet pane that also contains a similar Netherlands stamp.

Discovery of Neanderthal Man Bones, 150th Anniv. — A1218

2006, Aug. 10   Litho.   Perf. 14
2388 A1218 220c multi   6.00 3.25

Souvenir Sheet

Black Forest — A1219

2006, Aug. 10   Perf. 13¾
2389 A1219 55c multi   1.50   .80

Lighthouses Type of 2004
Designs: 45c, Neuland. 55c, Hohe Weg.

2006, Aug. 10   Perf. 13¾
2390 A1150 45c multi   1.25   .65
2391 A1150 55c multi   1.50   .80

"Captain of Köpenick" A1220

2006, Sept. 7   Litho.   Perf. 13¼
2392 A1220 55c multi   1.50   .80
Theft of town funds and arrest of mayor in Köpenick by petty thief Friedrich Wilhelm Voigt, who masqueraded as an army officer, cent.

For Children A1221

2006, Sept. 7
2393 A1221 55c multi   1.50   .80

Hanseatic League, 650th Anniv. — A1222

Litho. & Engr.
2006, Sept. 7   Perf. 14
2394 A1222 70c multi   2.00 1.00
See Sweden No. 2541

Stamp Day A1223

2006, Oct. 5   Litho.   Perf. 14
2395 A1223 55c multi   1.50   .80

Hannah Arendt (1906-75), Political Scientist — A1224

2006, Oct. 5   Perf. 13¾x14
2396 A1224 145c multi   4.00 2.10

Seasons Types of 2006
Die Cut Perf. 14
2006, Nov. 9   Litho.
Booklet Stamps
Self-Adhesive
2397 A1197 55c Spring   1.50   .80
2398 A1198 55c Summer   1.50   .80
2399 A1199 55c Autumn   1.50   .80
2400 A1196 55c Winter   1.50   .80
a.   Booklet pane, 5 each #2397-
       2400   30.00

Eugen Bolz (1881-1945), Politician A1225

2006, Nov. 9   Perf. 13¾
2401 A1225 45c multi   1.25   .65

Joseph Cardinal Höffner (1906-87) A1226

2006, Nov. 9   **Perf. 13¼**
2402 A1226 55c multi   1.50   .80

Werner Forssmann (1904-79), 1956 Physiology or Medicine Nobel Laureate — A1227

2006, Nov. 9   **Perf. 14**
2403 A1227 90c multi   2.50 1.40

Flowers Type of 2005

Designs: 25c, Gartennelke (carnation). 45c, Maiglöckchen (lily of the valley). 55c, Gartenrose (rose). 65c, Sonnenhut (rudbeckia). 70c, Kartäusernelke (clusterhead pink). 75c, Ballonblume (balloon flower). 200c, Goldmohn (California poppy) 410c, Frauenschuh (lady's slipper).

2006-11   **Litho.**   **Perf. 14**
2405 A1165 25c multi   .70   .35
2406 A1165 45c multi   1.25   .60
2407 A1165 55c multi   1.75   .85
2408 A1165 75c multi   2.00 1.00
2416 A1165 200c multi   5.50 2.75
2417 A1165 410c multi   12.00 6.00
   Nos. 2405-2417 (6)   23.20 11.55

Self-Adhesive
Coil Stamps
Die Cut Perf. 10¼x10
2419 A1165 25c multi   .70   .35
2420 A1165 55c multi   1.75   .85
   a.   Booklet pane of 10   17.50

Booklet Stamps
2421 A1165 65c multi   1.75   .85
   a.   Booklet pane of 5 + 5 etiquettes   8.75
2422 A1165 70c multi   1.90   .95
   a.   Booklet pane of 5 + 5 etiquettes   9.50
   b.   Booklet pane of 10   19.00

Issued: 200c, 11/9/06; 55c, 6/12/08. 25c, 10/9/08. No. 2419, 10/9/08; No. 2420, 6/12/08, No. 2420a, 3/11/10; Nos. 2421-2422, 1/2/09. No. 2417, 1/2/10. 45c, 5/6/10; No. 2422b, 6/10/2010; 75c, 1/3/11.

Fürth, 1000th Anniv. A1228

2007, Jan. 2   **Litho.**   **Perf. 13¼**
2424 A1228 45c multi   1.25   .65

Booklet Stamp
Self-Adhesive
Die Cut Perf. 11
2425 A1228 45c multi   1.25   .65
   a.   Booklet pane of 10   12.50

Germany, 2007 President of the European Union A1229

Litho. & Embossed
2007, Jan. 2   **Perf. 13¾**
2426 A1229 55c multi   1.50   .80

Bamberg Bishopric, 1000th Anniv. A1230

2007, Jan. 2   **Litho.**   **Perf. 13¼**
2427 A1230 55c multi   1.50   .80

Admission of Saarland into Federal Republic, 50th Anniv. — A1231

2007, Jan. 2   **Perf. 14**
2428 A1231 55c multi   1.50   .80

Booklet Stamp
Self-Adhesive
Die Cut Perf. 10x10¼
2428A A1231 55c multi   1.50   .80
   b.   Booklet pane of 10   15.00

Wankel Rotary Engine, 50th Anniv. — A1232

2007, Jan. 2
2429 A1232 145c multi   4.00 2.10

Johann Christian Senckenberg (1707-72), Founder of Hospital, Frankfurt am Main — A1233

2007, Feb. 8   **Litho.**   **Perf. 14**
2430 A1233 90c multi   2.50 1.40

Munich Jewish Center A1234

2007, Mar. 1   **Litho.**   **Perf. 14**
2431 A1234 55c multi   1.50   .80

Paul Gerhardt (1607-76), Hymn Writer — A1235

2007, Mar. 1
2432 A1235 55c multi   1.50   .80

The Unearthing of the Cross, by Adam Elsheimer A1236

2007, Mar. 1   **Perf. 13¼**
2433 A1236 55c multi   1.50   .80

Rome Treaty, 50th Anniv. A1237

2007, Mar. 1   **Perf. 13¾**
2434 A1237 55c multi   1.50   .80

Leaders of Anti-Nazi Resistance Movement — A1238

2007, Mar. 1   **Perf. 13¾x14**
2435 A1238 55c multi   1.50   .80

Claus Schenk Graf von Stauffenberg (1907-44), Hitler assassination plotter, and Helmuth James Graf von Moltke (1907-45), founding member of Kreisau Circle resistance group.

Pope Benedict XVI, 80th Birthday — A1239

2007, Apr. 12   **Litho.**   **Perf. 14**
2436 A1239 55c multi   1.50   .80

Letter Writing A1240

2007, Apr. 12   **Perf. 13¾**
2437 A1240 55c Boy writing letter   1.50   .80
2438 A1240 55c Boy mailing letter   1.50   .80
   See Nos. 2454-2455.

Publication of World Map of Martin Waldseemuller, 500th Anniv. — A1241

Litho. & Engr.
2007, Apr. 12   **Perf. 14**
2439 A1241 220c multi   6.00 3.25

Europa A1242

2007, May 3   **Litho.**   **Perf. 14**
2440 A1242 45c multi   1.25   .65
   Scouting, cent.

Bellevue Palace, Presidential Residence — A1243

2007, May 3
2441 A1243 55c multi   1.50   .80

Coil Stamp
Self-Adhesive
Die Cut Perf. 10x10¼
2441A A1243 55c multi   1.50   .80

Moyland Castle, 700th Anniv. — A1244

2007, May 3
2442 A1244 85c multi   2.40 1.25

Hambacher Fest, 175th Anniv. — A1245

2007, May 3   **Perf. 14**
2443 A1245 145c multi   4.00 2.00

Booklet Stamp
Self-Adhesive
Die Cut Perf. 10x10¼
2444 A1245 145c multi   4.00 2.00
   a.   Booklet pane of 10   40.00

Karl Valentin (1882-1948), Writer A1246

2007, June 14   **Litho.**   **Perf. 13¾**
2445 A1246 45c multi   1.25   .65

Paul Klinger (1907-71), Film Actor A1247

2007, June 14
2446 A1247 55c multi   1.50   .80

Lighthouses Type of 2004

Designs: 45c, Bremerhaven Oberfeuer. 55c, Hörnum.

2007, July 12   **Perf. 13¾**
2447 A1150 45c multi   1.25 .65
2448 A1150 55c multi   1.50 .80

UNESCO World Heritage Sites — A1248

Designs: 65c, Historic Center of Riga, Latvia. 70c, Historic Centers of Straslund and Wismar, Germany.

2007, July 12   **Perf. 14**
2449 A1248 65c multi   1.90 .95
2450 A1248 70c multi   2.00 1.00

See Latvia Nos. 679-680.

Saale Valley Dam and Lake Bleiloch, 75th Anniv. — A1249

2007, Aug. 9   **Litho.**   **Perf. 14**
2451 A1249 55c multi   1.50 .80

German Federal Bank, 50th Anniv. A1250

2007, Aug. 9
2452 A1250 55c multi   1.50 .80

Kaiser Wilhelm Bridge, Wilhelmshaven, Cent. — A1251

2007, Aug. 9   **Litho. & Engr.**
2453 A1251 145c multi   4.00 2.00

Letter Writing Type of 2007

Designs: No. 2454, Postman delivering letter to woman. No. 2455, Woman reading letter.

2007, Sept. 20   **Litho.**   **Perf. 13¾**
2454 A1240 55c multi   1.60 .80
2455 A1240 55c multi   1.60 .80

For Children — A1252

2007, Sept. 20   **Perf. 14**
2456 A1252 55c multi   1.60 .80

Science Advisory Committee, 50th Anniv. — A1253

2007, Sept. 20
2457 A1253 90c multi   2.60 1.40

German Work Federation (Architecture Group), Cent. A1254

2007, Oct. 11   **Litho.**   **Perf. 13¼**
2458 A1254 55c multi   1.60 .80

Souvenir Sheet

Frontiers of the Roman Empire UNESCO World Heritage Site — A1255

2007, Oct. 11   **Perf. 14**
2459 A1255 55c multi   1.60 .80

Heinrich Friedrich Carl Freiherr vom und zum Stein (1757-1831), Prussian Statesman — A1256

2007, Oct. 11   **Perf. 13¾x14**
2460 A1256 145c multi   4.00 2.10

St. Elizabeth of Hungary (1207-31) A1257

2007, Nov. 8   **Litho.**   **Perf. 13¾**
2461 A1257 55c multi   1.60 .80

Astrid Lindgren (1907-2002), Writer — A1258

Litho. & Engr.
2007, Nov. 8   **Perf. 13¾x14**
2462 A1258 100c multi   2.75 1.40

See Sweden No. 2572.

Brandenburg Gate, Designed by Carl Gotthard Langhans (1732-1808) — A1259

2007, Dec. 27   **Litho.**   **Perf. 14**
2463 A1259 55c multi   1.60 .80

Self-Adhesive
Booklet Stamp
Die Cut Perf. 10x10¼
2464 A1259 55c multi   1.60 .80
   a.   Booklet pane of 10   16.00

Reichenau Monastic Island UNESCO World Heritage Site — A1260

2008, Jan. 2   **Litho.**   **Perf. 13**
2465 A1260 45c multi   1.40 .70

Booklet Stamp
Self-Adhesive
Die Cut Perf. 10¾
2466 A1260 45c multi   1.40 .70
   a.   Booklet pane of 10   14.00

Heinrich Zille (1858-1929), Illustrator A1261

2008, Jan. 2   **Perf. 13¾**
2467 A1261 55c multi   1.60 .80

Federal Cartel Office, 50th Anniv. A1262

2008   **Perf. 14**
2468   A1262 90c multi   2.50 1.40

Booklet Stamp
Self-Adhesive
Die Cut Perf. 11¼x11
2468A A1262 90c multi   3.00 1.50
   b.   Booklet pane of 10   30.00

Issued: No. 2468, 1/2; No. 2468A, 3/13.

Eichstätt, 1100th Anniv. A1263

2008, Jan. 2   **Perf. 13¾**
2469   A1263 145c multi   4.00 2.10

Coil Stamp
Self-Adhesive
Die Cut Perf. 10¼
2469A A1263 145c multi   4.25 2.10

Wenzel Jamnitzer (1508-85), Goldsmith — A1264

2008, Jan. 2   **Perf. 13¾x14**
2470 A1264 220c multi   6.00 3.25

"Congratulations" — A1265

"All the Best" A1266

2008, Feb. 7   **Perf. 14**
2471 A1265 55c multi   1.60 .80
2472 A1266 55c multi   1.60 .80

Carl Spitzweg (1808-85), Painter A1267

2008, Feb. 7   **Litho.**   **Perf. 13¾**
2473 A1267 55c multi   1.60 .80

Coil Stamp
Self-Adhesive
Die Cut Perf. 10¼
2474 A1267 55c multi   1.60 .80

Village Church, Bochum-Stiepel, 1000th Anniv. — A1268

2008, Feb. 7   **Litho.**   **Perf. 13¾**
2475 A1268 145c multi   4.00 2.10

Helmut Käutner (1908-80), Film Director — A1269

2008, Mar. 13   **Litho.**   **Perf. 14**
2476 A1269 55c multi   1.75 .85

Frankfurt Zoo, 150th Anniv. A1270

2008, Mar. 13   *Perf. 13¼*
2477 A1270 65c multi   2.10 1.10

Seebach Bird Sanctuary, Cent. — A1271

2008, Apr. 10   *Litho. Perf. 14*
2478 A1271 45c multi   1.50 .75

Johann Hinrich Wichern (1808-81), Theologian — A1272

2008, Apr. 10
2479 A1272 55c multi   1.75 .85

Max Planck (1858-1947), Physicist A1273

2008, Apr. 10   *Perf. 13¾*
2480 A1273 55c multi   1.75 .85

Oskar Schindler (1908-74), Industrialist Who Saved Jews From Holocaust — A1274

2008, Apr. 10   *Perf. 14x14¼*
2481 A1274 145c multi   4.75 2.40

First International Match of German Soccer Team, Cent. A1275

2008, Apr. 10   *Perf. 13¾*
2482 A1275 170c multi   5.50 2.75

Christoffel Blind Mission, Cent. — A1276

2008, May 8   *Litho. Perf. 13x13½*
2483 A1276 55c multi   1.75 .85

Greetings Types of 2008 and

"Kind Regards" — A1277

"Thank You" A1278

2008, May 8   *Perf. 14*
2484 A1277 55c multi   1.75 .85
2485 A1278 55c multi   1.75 .85

Booklet Stamps
Self-Adhesive
Die Cut Perf. 14
2486 A1277 55c multi   1.75 .85
2487 A1265 55c multi   1.75 .85
2488 A1266 55c multi   1.75 .85
2489 A1278 55c multi   1.75 .85
  a.   Booklet pane of 20, 5 each   35.00
     #2486-2489
    Nos. 2486-2489 (4)   7.00 3.40

Europa (#2484, 2486).

Honorary Offices — A1279

2008, June 12   *Litho. Perf. 14*
2490 A1279 55c multi   1.75 .85

Lighthouses Type of 2004
Designs: No. 2491, 45c, Warnemünde. Nos. 2492, 2494, 55c, Amrum. No. 2493, 55c, Hörnum.

2008, July 3   *Litho. Perf. 13¾*
2491 A1150 45c multi   1.40 .70
2492 A1150 55c multi   1.75 .85

Booklet Stamps
Self-Adhesive
Die Cut Perf. 11
2493 A1150 55c multi   1.75 .85
2494 A1150 55c multi   1.75 .85
  a.   Booklet pane of 10, 5 each   17.50
     #2493-2494

Drachenfels Railway, 125th Anniv. — A1280

2008, July 3   *Perf. 14*
2495 A1280 45c multi   1.40 .70

Franz Kafka (1883-1924), Writer — A1281

2008, July 3
2496 A1281 55c black   1.75 .85

Self-portrait With Model, by Lovis Corinth (1858-1925) — A1282

2008, July 3   *Perf. 13x13½*
2497 A1282 145c multi   4.75 2.40

Training Ship Gorch Fock, 50th Anniv. A1283

2008, Aug. 7   *Litho. Perf. 13¼*
2498 A1283 55c multi   1.75 .85

Joachim Ringelnatz (1883-1934), Writer and Painter A1284

2008, Aug. 7   *Perf. 13¾*
2499 A1284 85c pur & black   2.60 1.40

Hermann Schulze-Delitzsch (1808-83), Economist — A1285

2008, Aug. 7   *Perf. 14*
2500 A1285 90c multi   2.75 1.40

Stamp Day — A1286

2008, Sept. 4   *Litho. Perf. 13¼*
2501 A1286 55c multi   1.60 .80

For Children A1287

2008, Sept. 4   *Perf. 14*
2502 A1287 55c multi   1.60 .80

Old Rhine Bridge, Bad Sackingen, Germany - Stein, Switzerland — A1288

2008, Sept. 4
2503 A1288 70c multi   2.00 1.00

See Switzerland No. 1319.

Gallimarkt (Livestock Market) of Leer, 500th Anniv. — A1289

2008, Oct. 9   *Litho. Perf. 14*
2504 A1289 45c multi   1.25 .60

Nebra Sky Disk A1290

2008, Oct. 9
2505 A1290 55c multi   1.50 .75

Lorenz Werthmann (1858-1921), Founder of Caritas Charity A1291

2008, Oct. 9   *Perf. 13¾*
2506 A1291 55c multi   1.50 .75

First Powered Flight Over Germany, by Hans Grade, Cent. — A1292

2008, Oct. 9   *Perf. 14*
2507 A1292 145c multi   4.00 2.00

Peace of Augsburg and Adoration of the Magi Types of 2005
Die Cut Perf. 11¼
2008, Nov. 1   *Litho.*
Booklet Stamps
Self-Adhesive
2508 A1186 55c multi   1.40 .70
2509 A1163 55c multi   1.40 .70
  a.   Booklet pane of 10, 5 each   14.00
     #2508-2509

Lebenshilfe (Organization for the Mentally Handicapped), 50th Anniv. — A1293

2008, Nov. 13 *Perf. 14*
2510 A1293 55c multi 1.40 .70

A Heart for Children Charity, 30th Anniv. A1294

2008, Nov. 13 *Perf. 13¼*
2511 A1294 55c black & red 1.40 .70

Nils Holgersson on Goose A1295

2008, Nov. 13 *Perf. 13¾*
2512 A1295 100c multi 2.60 1.25

Selma Lagerlöf (1858-1940), author of *Nils Holgersson's Wonderful Journey Through Sweden.*

Frankenberg City Hall, 500th Anniv. A1296

2009, Jan. 2 *Litho.* *Perf. 13¾*
2513 A1296 45c multi 1.25 .60

Booklet Stamp
Self-Adhesive
Die Cut Perf. 10¾
2514 A1296 45c multi 1.25 .60
a. Booklet pane of 10 12.50

Misereor and Bread for the World Charities, 50th Anniv. — A1297

2009, Jan. 2 *Perf. 14*
2515 A1297 55c multi 1.50 .75

Tangermünde, 1000th Anniv. — A1298

2009, Jan. 2
2516 A1298 90c multi 2.40 1.25

Pres. Theodor Heuss (1884-1963) A1299

2009, Jan. 2 *Perf. 13¾*
2517 A1299 145c multi 4.00 2.00

Heinz Erhardt (1909-79), Comedian A1300

2009, Feb. 12 *Litho.* *Perf. 13¾*
2518 A1300 55c multi 1.40 .70

Felix Mendelssohn Bartholdy (1809-47), Composer A1301

2009, Feb. 12 *Perf. 13¼*
2519 A1301 65c multi 1.75 .85

Munich Propylaea, by Architect Leo von Klenze (1784-1864) A1302

2009, Feb. 12 *Perf. 13¾*
2520 A1302 70c multi 1.90 .95

Der Feuervogel (Firebird), Woodcut by Helmut Andreas Paul Grieshaber (1909-81) A1303

2009, Feb. 12 *Perf. 13¼*
2521 A1303 165c multi 4.25 2.10

Golo Mann (1909-94), Historian A1304

2009, Mar. 12 *Litho.* *Perf. 13¾*
2522 A1304 45c multi 1.25 .60

1889 Daimler Automobile A1305

2009, Mar. 12 *Perf. 13¾x14*
2523 A1305 170c multi 4.75 2.40

Gottlieb Daimler (1834-1900), automobile engineer and manufacturer.

The Post — A1306

Designs: No. 2524, Hand affixing stamp on letter. No. 2525, Postal clerk serving customer. No. 2526, Postal truck. No. 2527, Postman carrying mail.

2009 *Perf. 13*
2524 A1306 55c multi 1.50 .75
2525 A1306 55c multi 1.50 .75
2526 A1306 55c multi 1.50 .75
2527 A1306 55c multi 1.50 .75

Issued: Nos. 2524-2525, 3/12. Nos. 2526-2527, 5/7.

Bernhard Grzimek (1909-87), Zoologist A1307

2009, Apr. 9
2528 A1307 55c multi 1.50 .75

Europa A1308

2009, May 7 *Perf. 14*
2529 A1308 55c multi 1.50 .75

Intl. Year of Astronomy.

Luther Memorials in Eisleben and Wittenberg UNESCO World Heritage Sites — A1309

2009, May 7 *Perf. 13¾x14*
2530 A1309 145c multi 4.00 2.00

Battle of the Teutoberg Forset, 2000th Anniv. A1310

2009, June 4 *Perf. 13¼*
2531 A1310 55c multi 1.60 .80

Booklet Stamp
Self-Adhesive
Serpentine Die Cut 10¾
2532 A1310 55c multi 1.60 .80
a. Booklet pane of 20 32.50

Frankfurt Intl. Aeronautical Exposition, Cent. A1311

2009, June 4 *Perf. 13¾*
2533 A1311 55c multi 1.60 .80

Coil Stamp
Self-Adhesive
Die Cut Perf. 10¼
2534 A1311 55c multi 1.60 .80

Heinrich Hoffmann (1809-94), Writer — A1312

2009, June 4 *Perf. 13¼*
2535 A1312 85c multi 2.40 1.25

Souvenir Sheet

Eifel National Park — A1313

2009, June 4 *Perf. 13¾*
2536 A1313 220c multi 6.25 3.25

Lighthouses Type of 2004
Designs: 45c, Norderney. 55c, Dornbusch.

2009, July 2
2537 A1150 45c multi 1.25 .65
2538 A1150 55c multi 1.60 .80

Leipzig University, 600th Anniv. — A1314

2009, July 2 *Perf. 14*
2539 A1314 55c multi 1.60 .80

Booklet Stamp
Self-Adhesive
Size: 39x22mm
Die Cut Perf. 10
2540 A1314 55c multi 1.60 .80
a. Booklet pane of 10 16.00

John Calvin (1509-64), Theologian and Religious Reformer A1315

2009, July 2 *Perf. 13¼*
2541 A1315 70c black 2.00 1.00

Rail Ferry From Sassnitz to Trelleborg, Sweden, Cent. — A1316

2009, July 2   *Perf. 13¾x14*
2542 A1316 145c multi   4.25 2.10

Youth Hostels in Germany, Cent. — A1317

2009, Aug. 13   *Perf. 14*
2543 A1317 55c multi   1.60 .80

Consecration of Mainz Cathedral, 1000th Anniv. A1318

2009, Aug. 13   *Perf. 13¾*
2544 A1318 90c multi   2.60 1.40

Souvenir Sheet

Historical Motor Sports — A1319

2009, Aug. 13   *Perf. 14*
2545 A1319 85c multi   2.40 1.25

For Children — A1320

2009, Sept. 3
2546 A1320 55c multi   1.60 .80

People Waving German Flags — A1321

2009, Sept. 3
2547 A1321 55c multi   1.60 .80

Opening of Border Between Austria and Hungary, 20th Anniv. A1322

2009, Sept. 3   *Perf. 13¾*
2548 A1322 70c multi   2.00 1.00
See Austria No. 2219, Hungary No. 4136.

Souvenir Sheet

Federal Government Buildings, Berlin — A1323

2009, Sept. 3   *Perf. 14*
2549 A1323   Sheet of 2   4.25 2.10
    a.   55c Bundestag   1.60 .80
    b.   90c Bundesrat   2.60 1.25

Still Life with Cheese and Cherries, by Georg Flegel A1324

2009, Oct. 8   *Perf. 13¼*
2550 A1324 45c multi   1.40 .70

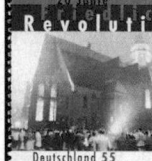

Crowd at St. Nicholas' Church, Leipzig A1325

2009, Oct. 8
2551 A1325 55c multi   1.60 .80
Peaceful political protest in East Germany, 20th anniv.

Marion Gräfin Dönhoff (1909-2002), Journalist — A1326

2009, Nov. 12   *Perf. 14*
2552 A1326 55c multi   1.75 .85

Badger A1327

2009, Nov. 12   *Perf. 13¾*
2553 A1327 55c multi   1.75 .85

Friedrich von Schiller (1759-1805), Writer A1328

2009, Nov. 12
2554 A1328 145c multi   4.50 2.25

Berlin Natural History Museum, 200th Anniv. — A1329

2010, Jan. 2 Litho.   *Perf. 13½x13¾*
2555 A1329 45c multi   1.40 .70

Booklet Stamp
Self-Adhesive
Die Cut Perf. 10

2556 A1329 45c multi   1.40 .70
    a.   Booklet pane of 10   14.00

Ruhr Valley, 2010 European Cultural Capital — A1330

2010, Jan. 2   *Perf. 13½x13¾*
2557 A1330 55c multi   1.60 .80

Limburg an der Lahn, 1100th Anniv. A1331

2010, Jan. 2   *Perf. 13½x13¾*
2558 A1331 145c multi   4.25 2.10

Booklet Stamp
Self-Adhesive
Die Cut Perf. 10

2559 A1331 145c multi   4.25 2.10
    a.   Booklet pane of 10   42.50

St. Michael's Church, Hildesheim UNESCO World Heritage Site — A1332

2010, Jan. 2   *Perf. 13¼*
2560 A1332 220c multi   6.25 3.00

Booklet Stamp
Self-Adhesive
Die Cut Perf. 10¾

2561 A1332 220c multi   6.25 3.00
    a.   Booklet pane of 10   62.50

Mensch Argere Dich Nicht Board Game A1333

     Perf. 13½x13¾
2010, Feb. 11   **Litho.**
2562 A1333 55c multi   1.50 .75

Jewish Wedding Ring — A1334

2010, Feb. 11   *Perf. 13¼*
2563 A1334 90c multi   2.50 1.25

Ariadne Abandoned by Theseus, by Angelica Kauffmann (1741-1807) A1335

2010, Mar. 11 Litho.   *Perf. 13¾*
2564 A1335 260c multi   7.00 3.50

Greetings — A1336

2010   **Litho.**   *Perf. 13¾*
2565 A1336 55c Rainbow   1.50 .75
2566 A1336 55c Ship   1.50 .75
2567 A1336 55c Dove   1.50 .75
2568 A1336 55c Angel with heart   1.50 .75
    Nos. 2565-2568 (4)   6.00 3.00

    Issued: Nos. 2565-2566, 3/11; Nos. 2567-2568, 4/8. See Nos. 2596-2597, 2605-2606.

Souvenir Sheet

Heligoland Bird Station, Cent. — A1337

2010, Apr. 8   *Perf. 14*
2569 A1337 145c multi   4.00 2.00

Coil Stamp
Die Cut Perf. 11
Self-Adhesive

2570 A1337 145c multi   4.00 2.00

Robert Schumann (1810-56), Composer — A1338

2010, May 6 Litho.   *Perf. 13½x13¾*
2571 A1338 55c multi   1.40 .70

Bee on Flower A1339

2010, May 6   *Perf. 13¾*
2572   A1339   55c multi   1.40   .70

Coil Stamp
Self-Adhesive
Die Cut Perf. 10¼
2572A   A1339   55c multi   1.40   .70

Europa
A1340

2010, May 6   *Perf. 13¼*
2573   A1340   55c multi   1.40   .70

Lighthouses Type of 2004
Designs: 45c, Neuwerk. 55c, Falshöft.

2010, June 10   *Litho.*   *Perf. 13¾*
2574   A1150   45c multi   1.10   .55
2575   A1150   55c multi   1.40   .70

Konrad Zuse (1910-95), Computer
Engineer — A1341

2010, June 10   *Perf. 13½x13¾*
2576   A1341   55c multi   1.40   .70

Porcelain Manufacturing in Germany,
300th Anniv. — A1342

2010, July 1   *Litho.*   *Perf. 13½x13¾*
2577   A1342   55c multi   1.40   .70
Booklet Stamp
Self-Adhesive
Die Cut Perf. 9¾x10
2577A   A1342   55c multi   1.40   .70
   b.   Booklet pane of 20   28.00

Four-seat Mail
Coach,
1858 — A1343

2010, July 1   *Perf. 13¾*
2578   A1343   145c multi   3.75   1.90

Andrea
Doria
A1344

Pankow
Special
Train
A1345

2010, July 1   *Perf. 13½x13¾*
2579   A1344   45c multi   1.10   .55
2580   A1345   55c multi   1.40   .70

Booklet Stamps
Self-Adhesive
Die Cut Perf. 10
2581   A1344   45c multi   1.10   .55
   a.   Booklet pane of 10   11.00
2582   A1345   55c multi   1.40   .70
   a.   Booklet pane of 10   14.00
Drawings on stamps are subjects of songs
by the stamp designer, Udo Lindenberg.

Elly Beinhorn (1907-2007),
Pilot — A1346

       Perf. 13½x13¾
2010, Aug. 12   *Litho.*
2583   A1346   55c multi   1.50   .75

Mother Teresa
(1910-97),
Humanitarian
A1347

2010, Aug. 12   *Perf. 13¼*
2584   A1347   70c multi   1.90   .95

Jorge Luis Borges
(1899-1986),
Writer — A1348

2010, Aug. 12   *Perf. 13¾x13½*
2585   A1348   170c multi   4.50   2.25
2010 Frankfurt Book Fair. See Argentina
No. 2585.

For Children
A1349

2010, Sept. 9   *Litho.*   *Perf. 13¾*
2586   A1349   55c multi   1.40   .70

Octoberfest,
200th Anniv.
A1350

2010, Sept. 9   *Perf. 13¼*
2587   A1350   55c multi   1.40   .70

Stamp
Day — A1351

2010, Sept. 9
2588   A1351   55c multi   1.40   .70

Reunification
of Germany,
20th Anniv.
A1352

2010, Sept. 9   *Litho.*   *Perf. 13¾*
2589   A1352   55c multi   1.40   .70

Coil Stamp
Self-Adhesive
Die Cut Perf. 10¼
2590   A1352   55c multi   1.50   .75

St. John's
Foundation,
150th Anniv.
A1353

2010, Sept. 9   *Litho.*   *Perf. 13¾*
2591   A1353   90c multi   2.40   1.25

Old Buildings
A1354

Buildings in: 45c, Eppingen, 1582. 55c,
Trebel-Dänsche, 1734.

2010, Oct. 7   *Litho.*   *Perf. 13¾*
2592   A1354   45c multi   1.25   .65
2593   A1354   55c multi   1.60   .80

Thanksgiving
A1355

2010, Oct. 7
2594   A1355   55c multi   1.60   .80

Friedrich Loeffler (1852-1915),
Bacteriologist, Virus and
Microscope — A1356

2010, Oct. 7   *Perf. 13½x13¾*
2595   A1356   85c multi   2.40   1.25
Friedrich Loeffler Institute, Cent.

Greetings Type of 2010
Die Cut Perf. 10
2010, Nov. 11   *Litho.*
Booklet Stamps
Self-Adhesive
2596   A1336   55c Dove   1.50   .75
2597   A1336   55c Angel with
                 heart   1.50   .75
   a.   Booklet pane of 10, 5 each
       #2596-2597   15.00

Railroads in
Germany,
175th Anniv.
A1357

Litho. & Engr.
2010, Nov. 11   *Perf. 13¾*
2598   A1357   55c multi   1.50   .75

2010 World Alpine Skiing
Championships, Garmisch-
Partenkirchen — A1358

Perf. 13½x13¾

2010, Nov. 11		Litho.	
2599	A1358	55c multi	1.50 .75

Fritz Reuter (1810-74), Writer
A1359

2010, Nov. 11		Perf. 13¼	
2600	A1359	100c multi	2.75 1.40

German Miners' Guild, 750th Anniv. A1360

2010, Nov. 11		Perf. 13½x13¾	
2601	A1360	145c black & red	4.00 2.00

Glider Flights from Wasserkuppe, Cent. — A1361

2011, Jan. 3	Litho.	Perf. 13½x13¾	
2602	A1361	45c multi	1.25 .60

The Wanderer Above the Mists, by Caspar David Friedrich A1362

2011, Jan. 3		Perf. 13¾	
2603	A1362	55c multi	1.50 .75

Kellerwald-Edersee National Park — A1363

2011, Jan. 3		Perf. 13½x13¾	
2604	A1363	145c multi	4.00 2.00

Greetings Type of 2010
Die Cut Perf. 10

2011, Feb. 3			Litho.

Booklet Stamps
Self-Adhesive

2605	A1336	55c Ship	1.50 .75
2606	A1336	55c Rainbow	1.50 .75
a.		Booklet pane of 10, 5 each #2605-2606	15.00

Franz Liszt (1811-86), Composer — A1364

2011, Feb. 3		Perf. 13½x13¾	
2607	A1364	55c multi	1.50 .75

Werra Valley View of Ludwigstein Castle and Ruins of Hanstein Castle — A1365

2011, Feb. 3		Perf. 13½x13¾	
2608	A1365	90c multi	2.50 1.25

Booklet Stamp
Self-Adhesive
Die Cut Perf. 9¾

2609	A1365	90c multi	2.50 1.25
a.		Booklet pane of 10	25.00

UNESCO World Heritage Sites — A1366

Designs: 55c, Historic Monuments of Ancient Nara, Japan. 75c, Old Town, Regensburg, Germany.

2011, Feb. 3		Perf. 13½x13¾	
2610	A1366	55c multi	1.50 .75
2611	A1366	75c multi	2.10 1.10

Booklet Stamp
Self-Adhesive
Die Cut Perf. 10

2612	A1366	75c multi	2.10 1.10
a.		Booklet pane of 10	21.00

See Japan Nos.

The Four Elements — A1367

Designs: No. 2613, Earth (sand dune). No. 2614, Wind (clouds). No. 2615, Fire (volcano). No. 2616, Water (droplets on leaf).

2011, Mar. 3		Perf. 13½x13¾	
2613	A1367	55c multi	1.60 .80
2614	A1367	55c multi	1.60 .80
2615	A1367	55c multi	1.60 .80
2616	A1367	55c multi	1.60 .80
		Nos. 2613-2616 (4)	6.40 3.20

SEMI-POSTAL STAMPS

Issues of the Republic

Nos. 83, 83d, 100, 100a, 100d Surcharged

1919, May 1	Wmk. 125	Perf. 14	
B1	A16	10pf + 5pf on #83d	.45 4.50
B2	A22	15pf + 5pf on #100	.45 4.50
		Set, never hinged	2.75

The surtax was for the war wounded.

"Planting Charity" — SP1   Feeding the Hungry — SP2

1922, Dec. 11	Litho.	Wmk. 126	
B3	SP1	6m + 4m ultra & brn	.20 22.50
B4	SP1	12m + 8m red org & bl gray	.20 22.50
		Set, never hinged	1.50

Nos. 221, 225 and 196 Surcharged

1923, Feb. 19			
B5	A34	5m + 100m	.20 9.00
B6	A29	25m + 500m	.20 22.50
a.		Inverted surcharge	95.00
		Never hinged	190.00
B7	A32	20m + 1000m	2.10 87.50
a.		Inverted surcharge	975.00 3,750.
		Never hinged	2,100.
b.		Green background inverted	260.00 1,200.
		Never hinged	400.00
		Nos. B5-B7 (3)	2.50 119.00
		Set, never hinged	5.50

Note following No. 160 applies to #B1-B7.

1924, Feb. 25	Typo.	Perf. 14½x15	

Designs: 10pf+30pf, Giving drink to the thirsty. 20pf+60pf, Clothing the naked. 50pf+1.50m, Healing the sick.

B8	SP2	5pf + 15pf dk grn	1.10 2.60
B9	SP2	10pf + 30pf ver	1.10 2.60
B10	SP2	20pf + 60pf dk blue	6.00 7.50
B11	SP2	50pf + 1.50m red brn	22.50 60.00
		Nos. B8-B11 (4)	30.70 72.70
		Set, never hinged	126.00

The surtax was used for emergency aid. See No. B58.

Prussia — SP6

1925, Dec. 15		Perf. 14	

Inscribed: "1925"

B12	SP6	5pf + 5pf shown	.50 1.90
B13	SP6	10pf + 10pf Bavaria	1.90 1.90
B14	SP6	20pf + 20pf Saxony	9.00 13.50
a.		Bklt. pane of 2 + 2 labels	190.00 600.00
		Never hinged	500.00
		Nos. B12-B14 (3)	11.40 17.30
		Set, never hinged	33.40

1926, Dec. 1			

Inscribed: "1926"

B15	SP6	5pf + 5pf Wurttemberg	1.00 2.25
B16	SP6	10pf + 10pf Baden	1.75 3.00
a.		Bklt. pane of 6 + 2 labels	77.50 190.00
		Never hinged	190.00
B17	SP6	25pf + 25pf Thuringia	11.00 19.00
B18	SP6	50pf + 50pf Hesse	40.00 95.00
		Nos. B15-B18 (4)	53.75 119.25
		Set, never hinged	170.00

See Nos. B23-B32.

Pres. Paul von Hindenburg — SP13

1927, Sept. 26		Photo.	
B19	SP13	8pf dark green	2.25 1.50
a.		Bklt. pane, 4 #B19, 3 #B20 + label	45.00 110.00
		Never hinged	110.00

B20	SP13	15pf scarlet	1.90	2.25
B21	SP13	25pf deep blue	9.00	21.00
B22	SP13	50pf bister brown	11.25	24.00
		Nos. B19-B22 (4)	24.40	48.75
		Set, never hinged	81.00	

80th birthday of Pres. Hindenburg. The stamps were sold at double face value. The surtax was given to a fund for War Invalids.

Arms Type of 1925

Design: 8pf+7pf, Mecklenberg-Schwerin.

1928, Nov. 15   Typo.
SP6
Inscribed: "1928"

B23	5pf + 5pf Hamburg	.50	3.75
B24	8pf + 7pf multi	.50	3.75
a.	Bklt. pane, 4 #B24, 3 #B25 + label	110.00	275.00
	Never hinged	275.00	
B25	15pf + 15pf Oldenburg	.75	3.75
B26	25pf + 25pf Brunswick	9.00	47.50
B27	50pf + 50pf Anhalt	45.00	90.00
	Nos. B23-B27 (5)	55.75	148.75
	Set, never hinged	178.00	

1929, Nov. 4

Coats of Arms: 8pf+4pf, Lippe-Detmold. 25pf+10pf, Mecklenburg-Strelitz. 50pf+40pf, Schaumburg-Lippe.

Inscribed: "1929"

B28	SP6	5pf + 2pf Bremen	.75	1.50
a.	Bklt. pane of 6 + 2 labels	12.50	32.50
	Never hinged	32.50	
B29	SP6	8pf + 4pf multi	1.40	1.50
a.	Bklt. pane, 4 #B29, 3 #B30 + label	40.00	100.00
	Never hinged	100.00	
B30	SP6	15pf + 5pf Lubeck	1.50	1.50
B31	SP6	25pf + 10pf multi	11.00	45.00
B32	SP6	50pf + 40pf choc, ocher & red	40.00	90.00
a.	"PE" for "PF"	150.00	400.00
	Never hinged	450.00	
	Nos. B28-B32 (5)	54.65	139.50
	Set, never hinged	180.00	

Cathedral of Aachen — SP24

Brandenburg Gate, Berlin — SP25

Castle of Marienwerder SP26

Statue of St. Kilian and Marienburg Fortress at Würzburg SP27

Souvenir Sheet
Wmk. 223

1930, Sept. 12   Engr.   Perf. 14

B33	Sheet of 4	375.00	1,500.
	Never hinged	1,200.	
a.	SP24 8pf + 4pf dark green	26.00	90.00
	Never hinged	67.50	
b.	SP25 15pf + 5pf carmine	26.00	90.00
	Never hinged	67.50	
c.	SP26 25pf + 10p dark blue	26.00	90.00
	Never hinged	67.50	
d.	SP27 50pf + 40pf dark brown	26.00	90.00
	Never hinged	67.50	

Intl. Phil. Exhib., Berlin, Sept. 12-21, 1930.
No. B33 is watermarked Eagle on each stamp and "IPOSTA"-"1930" in the margins. Size: approximately 105x150. Each holder of an admission ticket was entitled to purchase one sheet. The ticket cost 1m and the sheet 1.70m (face value 98pf, charity 59pf, special paper 13pf).
The margin of the souvenir sheet is ungummed.

Types of International Philatelic Exhibition Issue

1930, Nov. 1   Wmk. 126

B34	SP24	8 + 4pf dp green	.75	.75
a.	Bklt. pane of 7 + label	19.00	50.00
	Never hinged	50.00	
b.	Bklt. pane, 3 #B34, 4 #B35 + label	25.00	60.00
	Never hinged	60.00	

B35	SP25	15 + 5pf car	.75	1.10
B36	SP26	25 + 10pf dk blue	9.00	22.50
B37	SP27	50 + 40pf dp brn	21.00	82.50
		Nos. B34-B37 (4)	31.50	106.85
		Set, never hinged	105.00	

The surtax was for charity.

The Zwinger at Dresden SP28

Breslau City Hall SP29

Heidelberg Castle SP30

Holsten Gate, Lübeck SP31

1931, Nov. 1

B38	SP28	8 + 4pf dk grn	.60	1.00
a.	Bklt. pane of 7 + label	15.00	35.00
	Never hinged	40.00	
b.	Bklt. pane, 3 #B38, 4 #B39 + label	25.00	57.50
	Never hinged	57.50	
B39	SP29	15 + 5pf carmine	.60	1.00
B40	SP30	25 + 10pf dk blue	7.50	22.50
B41	SP31	50 + 40pf dp brown	32.50	75.00
		Nos. B38-B41 (4)	41.20	99.50
		Set, never hinged	165.00	

The surtax was for charity.

Nos. B38-B39 Surcharged

1932, Feb. 2

B42	SP28	6 + 4pf on 8+4pf	4.50	9.75
B43	SP29	12 + 3pf on 15+5pf	5.00	11.00
		Set, never hinged	41.50	

Wartburg Castle — SP32

Stolzenfels Castle — SP33

Nuremberg Castle — SP34

Lichtenstein Castle — SP35

Marburg Castle — SP36

1932, Nov. 1   Engr.

B44	SP32	4 + 2pf lt blue	.90	.50
a.	Bklt. pane, 5 #B44, 5 #B45	11.00	27.50
	Never hinged	27.50	
B45	SP33	6 + 4pf olive grn	.90	.50
B46	SP34	12 + 3pf lt red	.90	1.00
b.	Bklt. pane of 8 + 2 labels	11.00	27.50
	Never hinged	27.50	
B47	SP35	25 + 10pf dp blue	7.50	17.00
B48	SP36	40 + 40pf brn vio	27.50	60.00
		Nos. B44-B48 (5)	37.70	79.00
		Set, never hinged	140.25	

The surtax was for charity.

"Tannhäuser" SP37

Designs: 4pf+2pf, "Der Fliegende Hollander." 5pf+2pf, "Das Rheingold." 6pf+4pf, "Die Meistersinger." 8pf+4pf, "Die Walkure." 12pf+3pf, "Siegfried." 20pf+10pf, "Tristan und Isolde." 25pf+15pf, "Lohengrin." 40pf+35pf, "Parsifal."

Wmk. Swastikas (237)

1933, Nov. 1   Perf. 13½x13

B49	SP37	3 + 2pf bis brn	4.50	5.50
B50	SP37	4 + 2pf dk blue	1.90	2.25
b.	Bklt. pane, 5 #B50, 5 #B52	65.00	160.00
	Never hinged	160.00	
B51	SP37	5 + 2pf brt grn	6.00	6.75
B52	SP37	6 + 4pf gray grn	1.50	2.25
B53	SP37	8 + 4pf dp org	3.75	3.75
b.	Bklt. pane, 5 #B53, 4 #B54 + label	77.50	190.00
	Never hinged	190.00	
B54	SP37	12 + 3pf brn red	3.25	2.60
B55	SP37	20 + 10pf blue	150.00	190.00
B56	SP37	25 + 15pf ultra	24.00	37.50
B57	SP37	40 + 35pf mag	110.00	125.00
		Nos. B49-B57 (9)	304.90	375.60
		Set, never hinged	2,205.	

Perf. 13½x14

B50a	SP37	4 + 2pf dark blue	1.90	3.00
B52a	SP37	6 + 4pf gray grn	1.50	4.75
B53a	SP37	8 + 4pf dp org	3.25	4.00
B54a	SP37	12 + 3pf brn red	3.25	6.25
B55a	SP37	20 + 10pf blue	110.00	97.50
		Nos. B50a-B55a (6)	119.90	115.50
		Set, never hinged	765.00	

Types of Semi-Postal Stamps of 1924 Issue Overprinted Souvenir Sheet

1933, Nov. 29   Typo.   Perf. 14½

B58	Sheet of 4	1,350.	9,750.
	Never hinged	5,250.	
a.	SP2 5 + 15pf dark green	75.00	300.00
b.	SP2 10 + 30pf vermilion	75.00	300.00
c.	SP2 20 + 60pf dark blue	75.00	300.00
d.	SP2 50pf + 1.50m dk brown	75.00	300.00
	Any single, never hinged	190.00	

The Swastika watermark covers the four stamps and above them appears a further watermark "10 Jahre Deutsche Nothilfe" and "1923-1933" below. Sheet size: 208x148mm. The margin of the souvenir sheet is ungummed.

Businessman SP46

Judge SP54

Designs: 4pf+2pf, Blacksmith. 5pf+2pf, Mason. 6pf+4f, Miner. 8pf+4pf, Architect. 12pf+3pf, Farmer. 20pf+10pf, Agricultural Chemist. 25pf+15pf, Sculptor.

1934, Nov. 5   Engr.   Perf. 13x13½

B59	SP46	3 + 2pf brown	.75	1.50
B60	SP46	4 + 2pf black	.75	1.50
a.	Bklt. pane, 5 #B60, 5 #B62	18.00	45.00
	Never hinged	45.00	
B61	SP46	5 + 2pf green	6.00	7.50
B62	SP46	6 + 4pf dull grn	.45	.50
B63	SP46	8 + 4pf org brn	.75	1.90
a.	Bklt. pane, 5 #B63, 4 #B64 + label	30.00	75.00
	Never hinged	75.00	
B64	SP46	12 + 3pf hn brn	.45	.50
B65	SP46	20 + 10pf Prus bl	15.00	21.00
B66	SP46	25 + 15pf ultra	15.00	21.00
B67	SP54	40 + 35pf plum	45.00	67.50
		Nos. B59-B67 (9)	84.15	122.90
		Set, never hinged	420.00	

Souvenir Sheet

SP55

1935, June 23   Wmk. 241   Perf. 14

B68	SP55	Sheet of 4	825.00	700.00
a.	3pf red brown	32.50	37.50
b.	6pf dark green	32.50	37.50
c.	12pf dark carmine	32.50	37.50
d.	25pf dark blue	32.50	37.50

Watermarked cross on each stamp and "OSTROPA 1935" in the margins of the sheet. Size: 148x104mm. 1.70m was the price of a ticket of admission to the Intl. Exhib., Königsberg, June 23-July 3, 1935.
Because the gum on No. B68 contains sulphuric acid and tends to damage the sheet, most collectors prefer to remove it. **Catalogue unused values are for sheet and singles without gum.**

East Prussia
SP59

Skating
SP69

Designs (Costumes of Various Sections of Germany): 4pf+3pf, Silesia. 5pf+3pf, Rhineland. 6pf+4pf, Lower Saxony. 8pf+4pf, Brandenburg. 12pf+6pf, Black Forest. 15pf+10pf, Hesse. 25pf+15pf, Upper Bavaria. 30pf+20pf, Friesland. 40pf+35pf, Franconia.

Wmk. Swastikas (237)

1935, Oct. 4   **Perf. 14x13½**

B69	SP59	3 + 2pf dk brown	.30	.35
a.		Bklt. pane, 4 #B69, 5 #B74 + label	15.00	37.50
		Never hinged	37.50	
B70	SP59	4 + 3pf gray	1.20	1.50
B71	SP59	5 + 3pf emerald	.30	1.00
a.		Bklt. pane, 5 #B71, 5 #B72	4.75	11.00
		Never hinged	11.00	
B72	SP59	6 + 4pf dk green	.20	.35
B73	SP59	8 + 4pf yel brn	1.75	1.50
B74	SP59	12 + 6pf dk car	.20	.35
B75	SP59	15 + 10pf red brn	4.25	5.50
B76	SP59	25 + 15pf ultra	7.50	6.00
B77	SP59	30 + 20pf olive brn	9.00	19.50
B78	SP59	40 + 35pf plum	8.25	14.00
		Nos. B69-B78 (10)	32.95	50.05
		Set, never hinged	160.00	

1935, Nov. 25   **Perf. 13½**

12+6pf, Ski jump. 25+15pf, Bobsledding.

B79	SP69	6 + 4pf green	.70	1.40
B80	SP69	12 + 6pf carmine	1.40	1.20
B81	SP69	25 + 15pf ultra	6.00	7.50
		Nos. B79-B81 (3)	8.10	10.10
		Set, never hinged	51.00	

Winter Olympic Games held in Bavaria, Feb. 6-16, 1936.

1936, May 8

Designs: 3pf+2pf, Horizontal bar. 4pf+3pf, Diving. 6pf+4pf, Soccer. 8pf+4pf, Throwing javelin. 12pf+6pf, Torch runner. 15pf+10pf, Fencing. 25pf+15pf, Sculling. 40pf+35pf, Equestrian.

B82	SP69	3 + 2pf brown	.30	.45
a.		Bklt. pane, 5 #B82, 5 #B86	8.00	20.00
		Never hinged	20.00	
B83	SP69	4 + 3pf indigo	.25	.75
a.		Bklt. pane, 5 #B83, 5 #B84	8.00	20.00
		Never hinged	20.00	
B84	SP69	6 + 4pf green	.25	.45
B85	SP69	8 + 4pf red org	3.00	1.25
B86	SP69	12 + 6pf carmine	.30	.45
B87	SP69	15 + 10pf brn vio	5.00	3.00
B88	SP69	25 + 15pf ultra	3.00	3.75
B89	SP69	40 + 35pf violet	5.25	7.50
		Nos. B82-B89 (8)	17.35	17.60
		Set, never hinged	110.00	

Summer Olympic Games, Berlin, 8/1-16/36. See Nos. B91-B92.

Souvenir Sheet

Horse Race — SP80

1936, June 22   **Wmk. 237**   **Perf. 14**

B90	SP80	42pf brown	7.50	13.50
		Never hinged	24.00	

A surtax of 1.08m was to provide a 100,000m sweepstakes prize. Wmk. 237 appears on the stamp, with "Munchen Riem 1936" watermarked on sheet margin. For overprint see No. B105.

Types of 1936
Souvenir Sheets

1936, Aug. 1   **Perf. 14x13½**

B91	SP69	Sheet of 4	30.00	47.50
B92	SP69	Sheet of 4	30.00	47.50
		Set, never hinged	180.00	

11th Olympic Games, Berlin. No. B91 contains Nos. B82-B84, B89. No. B92 contains Nos. B85-B88.
Wmk. 237 appears on each stamp with "XI Olympische Spiele-Berlin 1936" watermarked on sheet margin. Sold for 1m each.

Frontier Highway, Munich — SP81

Designs: 4pf+3pf, Ministry of Aviation. 5pf+3pf, Nuremberg Memorial. 6pf+4pf, Bridge over the Saale, Saxony. 8pf+4pf, German Alpine highway. 15pf+10pf, Fuhrer House, Munich. 25pf+15pf, Bridge over the Mangfall. 40pf+35pf, Museum of German Art, Munich.

Perf. 13½x14

1936, Sept. 21   **Unwmk.**

B93	SP81	3pf + 2pf blk brn	.20	.35
a.		Bklt. pane, 4 #B93 + 5 #B98 + label	10.00	24.00
		Never hinged	24.00	
B94	SP81	4pf + 3pf black	.20	.55
B95	SP81	5pf + 3pf brt grn	.20	.35
a.		Bklt. pane, 5 #B95, 5 #B96	3.75	9.75
		Never hinged	9.75	
B96	SP81	6pf + 4pf dk grn	.20	.35
B97	SP81	8pf + 4pf brown	.80	1.25
B98	SP81	12pf + 6pf brn car	.20	.35
B99	SP81	15pf + 10pf vio brn	2.75	3.25
B100	SP81	25pf + 15pf indigo	1.90	3.75
B101	SP81	40pf + 35pf rose vio	3.00	5.50
		Nos. B93-B101 (9)	9.45	15.70
		Set, never hinged	62.50	

Souvenir Sheets

WER EIN VOLK RETTEN WILL KANN NUR HEROISCH DENKEN

Adolf Hitler — SP90

Wmk. 237

1937, Apr. 5   **Photo.**   **Perf. 14**

B102	SP90	Sheet of 4	18.00	12.00
		Never hinged	52.50	
a.		6pf dark green	1.10	1.50
		Never hinged	4.00	

48th birthday of Adolf Hitler. Sold for 1m. See #B103-B104. For overprint see #B106.

1937, Apr. 16   **Imperf.**

B103	SP90	Sheet of 4	37.50	22.50
		Never hinged	165.00	
a.		6pf dark green	2.25	3.00
		Never hinged	7.50	

German Natl. Phil. Exhib., Berlin, June 16-18, 1937 and the Phil. Exhib. of the Stamp Collectors Group of the Strength Through Joy Organization at Hamburg, Apr. 17-20, 1937. Sold at the Exhib. post offices for 1.50m.

No. B102 with Marginal Inscriptions
Perf. 14 and Rouletted

1937, June 10   **Wmk. 237**

B104	SP90	Sheet of 4	37.50	67.50
		Never hinged	240.00	
a.		6pf dark grn + 25pf label	3.00	6.75
		Never hinged	9.75	

No. B104 inscribed in the margin beside each stamp "25 Rpf. einschliesslich Kulturspende" in three lines.
The sheets were rouletted to allow for separation of each stamp with its component label. Sold at the post office as individual stamps with labels attached or in complete sheets.

Souvenir Sheet No. B90 Overprinted in Red

1937, Aug. 1   **Perf. 14**

B105	SP80	42pf brown	60.00	97.50
		Never hinged	150.00	

4th running of the "Brown Ribbon" horse race at the Munich-Riem Race Course, Aug. 1, 1937.

Souvenir Sheet No. B104 Overprinted in Black on Each Stamp

Perf. 14 and Rouletted

1937, Sept. 3   **Wmk. 237**

B106	SP90	Sheet of 4	75.00	45.00
		Never hinged	250.00	
a.		6pf dark grn + 25pf label	4.50	5.50
		Never hinged	13.50	

1937 Nazi Congress at Nuremburg.

Lifeboat — SP91

Designs: 4pf+3pf, Lightship "Elbe I." 5pf+3pf, Fishing smacks. 6pf+4pf, Steamer. 8pf+4pf, Sailing vessel. 12pf+6pf, The "Tannenberg." 15pf+10pf, Sea-Train "Schwerin." 25pf+15pf, S. S. Hamburg. 40pf+35pf, S. S. Bremen.

Perf. 13½

1937, Nov. 4   **Engr.**   **Unwmk.**

B107	SP91	3pf + 2pf dk brwn	.20	.35
a.		Bklt. pane, 4 #B107 + 5 #B112 + label	25.00	
		Never hinged	47.50	
B108	SP91	4pf + 3pf black	1.00	1.10
B109	SP91	5pf + 3pf yel grn	.20	.35
a.		Bklt. pane, 5 #B109, 5 #B110	14.00	
		Never hinged	24.00	
B110	SP91	6pf + 4pf bl grn	.20	.35
B111	SP91	8pf + 4pf orange	.60	1.25
B112	SP91	12pf + 6pf car lake	.20	.35
B113	SP91	15pf + 10pf vio brn	1.25	3.75
B114	SP91	25pf + 15pf ultra	3.00	3.75
B115	SP91	40pf + 35pf red vio	5.00	7.50
		Nos. B107-B115 (9)	11.65	18.75
		Set, never hinged	83.55	

No. B115 actually pictures the S.S. Europa.

Youth Carrying Torch and Laurel — SP100

Adolf Hitler — SP101

Wmk. 237

1938, Jan. 28   **Photo.**   **Perf. 14**

B116	SP100	6 + 4pf dk green	.90	1.90
B117	SP100	12 + 8pf brt car	.90	1.90
		Set, never hinged	15.00	

Assumption of power by the Nazis, 5th anniv.

1938, Apr. 13   **Engr.**   **Unwmk.**

B118	SP101	12 + 38pf copper red	1.90	2.25
		Never hinged	9.75	

Hitler's 49th birthday.

Horsewoman SP102

1938, July 20

B119	SP102	42 + 108pf dp brn	21.00	45.00
		Never hinged	125.00	

5th "Brown Ribbon" at Munich.

Adolf Hitler
SP103

Theater at Saarbrücken
SP104

1938, Sept. 1

B120	SP103	6 + 19pf deep grn	2.25	4.00
		Never hinged	15.00	

1938 Nazi Congress at Nuremberg. The surtax was for Hitler's National Culture Fund.

1938, Oct. 9   **Photo.**   **Wmk. 237**

B121	SP104	6 + 4pf blue grn	.90	1.90
B122	SP104	12 + 8pf dk car	1.90	2.60
		Set, never hinged	20.00	

Inauguration of the theater of the District of Saarpfalz at Saarbrücken. The surtax was for Hitler's National Culture Fund.

Castle of Forchtenstein
SP105

Designs (scenes in Austria and various flowers): 4pf+3pf, Flexenstrasse in Vorarlberg. 5pf+3pf, Zell am See, Salzburg. 6pf+4pf, Grossglockner. 8pf+4pf, Ruins of Aggstein. 12pf+6pf, Prince Eugene Monument, Vienna. 15pf+10pf, Erzberg. 25pf+15pf, Hall, Tyrol. 40pf+35pf, Braunau.

Unwmk.

1938, Nov. 18   **Engr.**   **Perf. 14**

B123	SP105	3 + 2pf olive brn	.20	.45
a.		Bklt. pane, 4 #B123, 5 #B128 + label	9.25	24.00
		Never hinged	24.00	
B124	SP105	4 + 3pf indigo	1.60	1.25
B125	SP105	5 + 3pf emerald	.20	.45
a.		Bklt. pane, 5 #B125, 5 #B126	3.25	7.50
		Never hinged	7.50	
B126	SP105	6 + 4pf dk grn	.20	.35
B127	SP105	8 + 4pf red org	1.60	1.25
B128	SP105	12 + 6pf dk car	.20	.45
B129	SP105	15 + 10pf dp cl	3.00	4.50
B130	SP105	25 + 15pf dk blue	2.50	4.50
B131	SP105	40 + 35pf plum	6.00	7.50
		Nos. B123-B131 (9)	15.50	20.70
		Set, never hinged	76.00	

The surtax was for "Winter Help."

Sudeten Couple — SP114

Early Types of Automobiles
SP115

1938, Dec. 2   **Photo.**   **Wmk. 237**

B132	SP114	6 + 4pf blue grn	1.10	3.00
B133	SP114	12 + 8pf dk car	2.25	3.00
		Set, never hinged	30.00	

Annexation of the Sudeten Territory. The surtax was for Hitler's National Culture Fund.

1939

Designs: 12pf+8pf, Racing cars. 25pf+10pf, Modern automobile.

B134	SP115 6 + 4pf dk grn	3.50	3.50
B135	SP115 12 + 8pf brt car	3.50	3.50
B136	SP115 25 + 10pf dp blue	5.75	6.00
	Nos. B134-B136 (3)	12.75	13.00
	Set, never hinged	82.50	

Berlin Automobile and Motorcycle Exhibition. The surtax was for Hitler's National Culture Fund. For overprints see #B141-B143.

Adolf Hitler
SP118

Exhibition
Building
SP119

Unwmk.
1939, Apr. 13   Engr.   Perf. 14

B137	SP118 12 + 38pf carmine	1.50	4.50
	Never hinged	8.25	

Hitler's 50th birthday. The surtax was for Hitler's National Culture Fund.

1939, Apr. 22   Photo.   Perf. 12½

B138	SP119 6 + 4pf dk green	1.00	3.00
B139	SP119 15 + 5pf dp plum	1.00	3.00
	Set, never hinged	12.75	

Horticultural Exhib. held at Stuttgart. Surtax for Hitler's National Culture Fund.

Adolf
Hitler — SP120

Perf. 14x13½
1939, Apr. 28   Wmk. 237

B140	SP120 6 + 19pf black brn	2.25	5.00
	Never hinged	12.00	

Day of National Labor. The surtax was for Hitler's National Culture Fund.
See No. B147.

Nos. B134-B136
Overprinted in
Black

1939, May 18   Perf. 14

B141	SP115 6 + 4pf dk green	18.00	26.00
B142	SP115 12 + 8pf brt car	18.00	26.00
B143	SP115 25 + 10pf dp blue	18.00	26.00
	Nos. B141-B143 (3)	54.00	78.00
	Set, never hinged	210.00	

Nurburgring Auto Races, 5/21, 7/23/39.

Racehorse
"Investment"
and Jockey
SP121

1939, June 18   Engr.   Unwmk.

B144	SP121 25 + 50pf ultra	15.00	15.00
	Never hinged	60.00	

70th anniv. of the German Derby. The surtax was divided between Hitler's National Culture Fund and the race promoters.

Man Holding
Rearing
Horse — SP122

"Venetian Woman"
by Albrecht
Dürer — SP123

1939, July 12

B145	SP122 42 + 108pf dp brown	15.00	24.00
	Never hinged	60.00	

6th "Brown Ribbon" at Munich.

1939, July 12   Photo.   Wmk. 237

B146	SP123 6 + 19pf dk grn	5.25	9.75
	Never hinged	26.00	

Day of German Art. The surtax was used for Hitler's National Culture Fund.

Hitler Type of 1939
Inscribed "Reichsparteitag 1939"
1939, Aug. 25   Perf. 14x13½

B147	SP120 6 + 19pf blk brn	3.50	9.00
	Never hinged	18.00	

1939 Nazi Congress at Nuremberg.

Meeting in
German
Hall, Berlin
SP124

Designs: 4pf+3pf, Meeting of postal and telegraph employees. 5pf+3pf, Professional competitions. 6pf+4pf, 6pf+9pf, Professional camp. 8pf+4pf, 8pf+12pf, Gold flag competitions. 10pf+5pf, Awarding prizes. 12&f+6pf, 12pf+18pf, Automobile race. 15pf+10pf, Sports. 16pf+10pf, 16pf+24pf, Postal police. 20pf+10pf, 20pf+30pf, Glider workshops. 24pf+10pf, 24pf+36pf, Mail coach. 25pf+15pf, Convalescent home, Konigstein.

Perf. 13½x14
1939-41   Unwmk.   Photo.

B148	3 + 2pf bister brn	2.25	5.25
B149	4 + 3pf slate blue	2.00	5.25
B150	5 + 3pf brt bl grn	.55	1.50
B151	6 + 4pf myrtle grn	.70	1.50
B151A	6 + 9pf dk grn ('41)	.70	2.25
B152	8 + 4pf dp org	.70	1.50
B152A	8 + 12pf hn brn ('41)	1.00	1.50
B153	10 + 5pf dk brown	.70	2.00
B154	12 + 6pf rose brown	.85	2.00
B154A	12 + 18pf dk car rose ('41)	1.00	1.90
B155	15 + 10pf dp red lilac	.70	2.25
B156	16 + 10pf slate grn	.70	2.25
B156A	16 + 24pf black ('41)	1.00	3.75
B157	20 + 10pf ultra	.70	2.00
B157A	20 + 30pf ultra ('41)	1.50	3.75
B158	24 + 10pf ol grn	2.00	3.75
B158A	24 + 36pf pur ('41)	3.50	11.25
B159	25 + 15pf dk blue	1.80	3.00
	Nos. B148-B159 (18)	22.35	56.65
	Set, never hinged	120.00	

The surtax was used for Hitler's National Culture Fund and the Postal Employees' Fund. See Nos. B273, B275-B277.

Elbogen
Castle — SP136

Buildings: 4pf+3pf, Drachenfels on the Rhine. 5pf+3pf, Kaiserpfalz at Goslar. 6pf+4pf, Clocktower at Graz. 8pf+4pf, Town Hall, Frankfurt. 12pf+6pf, Guild House, Klagenfurt. 15pf+10pf, Ruins of Schreckenstein Castle. 25pf+15pf, Fortress of Salzburg. 40pf+35pf, Castle of Hohentwiel.

1939   Unwmk.   Engr.   Perf. 14

B160	SP136 3 + 2pf dk brn	.20	.45
a.	Bklt. pane, 4 #B160, 5 #B165 + label	9.25	24.00
B161	SP136 4 + 3pf gray blk	1.75	1.90
B162	SP136 5 + 3pf emerald	.30	.50
a.	Bklt. pane, 5 #B162, 5 #B163	4.00	9.75
B163	SP136 6 + 4pf slate grn	.20	.35
B164	SP136 8 + 4pf red org	1.40	1.60
B165	SP136 12 + 6pf dk car	.30	.75
B166	SP136 15 + 10pf brn vio	2.25	4.50
B167	SP136 25 + 15pf ultra	1.75	4.50
B168	SP136 40 + 35pf rose vio	2.40	6.00
	Nos. B160-B168 (9)	10.55	20.55
	Set, never hinged	47.50	

Hall of Honor at
Chancellery,
Berlin — SP145

Child Greeting
Hitler — SP146

1940, Mar. 28

B169	SP145 24 + 76pf dk grn	6.00	17.00
	Never hinged	27.50	

2nd National Stamp Exposition, Berlin.

Perf. 14x13½
1940, Apr. 10   Photo.   Wmk. 237

B170	SP146 12 + 38pf cop red	1.50	6.00
	Never hinged	12.00	

51st birthday of Adolf Hitler.

Armed Warrior
SP147

Horseman
SP148

1940, Apr. 30   Unwmk.   Perf. 14

B171	SP147 6 + 4pf sl grn & lt grn	.30	1.25
	Never hinged	1.40	

Issued to commemorate May Day.

Perf. 14x13½
1940, June 22   Wmk. 237

B172	SP148 25 + 100pf dp ultra	3.50	11.00
	Never hinged	20.00	

Blue Ribbon race, Hamburg, June 30, 1940. Surtax for Hitler's National Culture Fund.

Chariot
SP149

Unwmk.
1940, July 20   Engr.   Perf. 14

B173	SP149 42 + 108pf brown	22.50	26.00

7th "Brown Ribbon" at Munich.
The surtax was for Hitler's National Culture Fund and the promoters of the race.

View of
Malmedy
SP150

Design: 12pf+8pf, View of Eupen.

Perf. 14x13½
1940, July 25   Photo.   Wmk. 237

B174	SP150 6 + 4pf dk green	.65	2.90
B175	SP150 12 + 8pf org red	.65	2.90
	Set, never hinged	9.50	

Issued on the occasion of the reunion of Eupen-Malmedy with the Reich.

Rocky Cliffs of
Heligoland
SP152

Artushof in
Danzig — SP153

1940, Aug. 9   Unwmk.

B176	SP152 6 + 94pf brt bl grn & red org	4.00	11.00
	Never hinged	22.50	

Heligoland's 50th year as part of Germany.

1940, Nov. 5   Engr.   Perf. 14

Buildings: 4pf+3pf, Town Hall, Thorn. 5pf+3pf, Castle at Kaub. 6pf+4pf, City Theater, Poznan. 8pf+4pf, Castle at Heidelberg. 12pf+6pf, Porta Nigra Trier. 15pf+10pf, New German Theater, Prague. 25pf+15pf, Town Hall, Bremen. 40pf+35pf, Town Hall, Munster.

B177	SP153 3 + 2pf dk brn	.20	.45
a.	Bklt. pane, 4 #B177 + 5 #B182 + label	7.50	19.00
	Never hinged	19.00	
B178	SP153 4 + 3pf bluish blk	.65	.80
B179	SP153 5 + 3pf yel grn	.20	.50
a.	Bklt. pane, 5 #B179, 5 #B180	3.75	9.25
	Never hinged	9.25	
B180	SP153 6 + 4pf dk grn	.20	.45
B181	SP153 8 + 4pf dp org	1.00	.80
B182	SP153 12 + 6pf carmine	.25	.45
B183	SP153 15 + 10pf dk vio brn	1.00	2.60
B184	SP153 25 + 15pf dp ultra	1.40	2.60
B185	SP153 40 + 35pf red lil	2.50	4.50
	Nos. B177-B185 (9)	7.40	14.65
	Set, never hinged	35.00	

von
Behring — SP162

1940, Nov. 26   Photo.

B186	SP162 6 + 4pf dp green	.45	2.25
B187	SP162 25 + 10pf brt ultra	.90	2.25
	Set, never hinged	11.00	

Dr. Emil von Behring (1854-1917), bacteriologist.

Postilion — SP163

1941, Jan. 12   *Perf. 14x13½*
B188 SP163 6 +24pf dp green   1.25   *3.25*
   Never hinged   5.25

Postage Stamp Day. The surtax was for Hitler's National Culture Fund.

Benito Mussolini and Adolf Hitler SP164

Perf. 13½x14
1941, Jan. 30   **Wmk. 237**
B189 SP164 12 + 38pf rose brn   1.25   *4.50*
   Never hinged   6.75

Issued as propaganda for the Rome-Berlin Axis. The surtax was for Hitler's National Culture Fund.

Adolf Hitler — SP165   Race Horse — SP166

1941, Apr. 17   *Perf. 14x13½*
B190 SP165 12 + 38pf dk red   1.25   *3.25*
   Never hinged   8.00

52nd birthday of Adolf Hitler. The surtax was for Hitler's National Culture Fund.

Perf. 13½x14
1941, June 20   **Unwmk.**
B191 SP166 25 + 100pf sapphire   2.75   *7.50*
   Never hinged   13.00

Issued in commemoration of the Blue Ribbon race held at Hamburg, June 29, 1941.

Amazons SP167

1941, July 20   *Perf. 14*
B192 SP167 42 + 108pf brown   2.00   *5.25*
   Never hinged   9.50

8th "Brown Ribbon" at Munich.

Brandenburg Gate, Berlin — SP168

1941, Sept. 9
B193 SP168 25 + 50pf dp ultra   2.75   *7.25*
   Never hinged   11.00

Issued in honor of the Berlin races.

Marburg SP169   Veldes SP170

Pettau — SP171   Triglav — SP172

1941, Sept. 29   **Photo.**
B194 SP169 3 + 7pf brown   .70   *2.00*
B195 SP170 6 + 9pf purple   .55   *2.00*
B196 SP171 12 + 13pf rose brn   .70   *2.40*
B197 SP172 25 + 15pf dk blue   1.40   *1.75*
   Nos. B194-B197 (4)   3.35   *8.15*
   Set, never hinged   16.00

Annexation of Styria and Carinthia.

View from Belvedere Palace, Vienna — SP173

Belvedere Gardens, Vienna SP174

1941, Sept. 16   **Engr.**
B198 SP173 12 + 8pf dp red   1.40   *3.25*
B199 SP174 15 + 10pf violet   1.40   *3.25*
   Set, never hinged   11.00

Issued to commemorate the Vienna Fair.

Mozart — SP175

1941, Nov. 28
B200 SP175 6 + 4pf dk rose vio   .20   *.60*
   Never hinged   .75

Wolfgang Amadeus Mozart (1756-91).

Philatelist SP176

1942, Jan. 11   **Photo.**
B201 SP176 6 + 24pf dp purple   .50   *2.75*
   Never hinged   3.00

To commemorate Stamp Day.

Soldier's Head — SP177

1942, Mar. 10   *Perf. 14x13½*
B202 SP177 12 + 38pf slate blk   .30   *1.50*
             1.60

To commemorate Hero Memorial Day.

Adolf Hitler — SP178

1942, Apr. 13
B203 SP178 12 + 38pf lake   1.50   *6.00*
   Never hinged   11.00

To commemorate Hitler's 53rd birthday.

Racing Three-year-old SP179

1942, June 16   **Engr.**   *Perf. 14*
B204 SP179 25 + 100pf dk bl   4.50   *11.00*
   Never hinged   16.50

73rd Hamburg Derby.

Race Horses SP180

1942, July 14
B205 SP180 42 + 108pf brown   1.50   *5.25*
   Never hinged   7.50

9th "Brown Ribbon" at Munich.

Lüneburg Lion and Nuremberg Betrothal Cup — SP181

1942, Aug. 8   **Photo.**   *Perf. 14x13½*
B206 SP181 6 + 4pf copper red   .20   *1.50*
B207 SP181 12 + 88pf green   .50   *2.25*
   Set, never hinged   3.00

10th anniv. of the German Goldsmiths' Society and the 1st Goldsmiths' Day in Germany.

Henlein Monument, Nuremberg — SP182

1942, Aug. 29   *Perf. 14*
B208 SP182 6 + 24pf rose vio   .45   *1.50*
             1.60

400th anniversary of the death of Peter Henlein, inventor of the pocket watch.

Postilion and Map of Europe SP183

Postilion and Globe — SP184

Postilion SP185

Perf. 13½x14, 14x13½
1942, Oct. 12   **Photo.**
B209 SP183 3 + 7pf dull blue   .25   *1.50*
         Engr.
B210 SP184 6 + 14pf ultra & dp brn   .35   *1.50*
B211 SP185 12 + 38pf rose red & dp brn   .50   *2.50*
   Nos. B209-B211 (3)   1.10   *5.50*
   Set, never hinged   3.75

European Postal Congress, Vienna.

Nos. B209 to B211 Overprinted in Black

1942, Oct. 19
B212 SP183 3 + 7pf   .65   *2.50*
B213 SP184 6 + 14pf   .65   *2.50*
B214 SP185 12 + 38pf   .90   *4.50*
   Nos. B212-B214 (3)   2.20   *9.50*
   Set, never hinged   7.50

To commemorate the signing of the European postal-telegraph agreement at Vienna.

Mail Coach SP186

1943, Jan. 10   **Engr.**
B215 SP186 6 + 24pf gray, brn & yel   .20   *.90*
   Never hinged   .75

To commemorate Stamp Day. The surtax went to Hitler's National Culture Fund.

Brandenburg Gate SP187   Nazi Emblem SP188

1943, Jan. 26   **Photo.**
B216 SP187 54 + 96pf cop red   .45   *2.25*
   Never hinged   1.90

10th anniversary of the assumption of power by the Nazis.

1943, Jan. 26
B217 SP188 3 + 2pf olive bister   .20   *.90*
   Never hinged   .60

Used to secure special philatelic cancellations.

Submarine
SP189

Designs: 4pf+3pf, Schutz-Staffel Troops. 5pf+4pf, Motorized marksmen. 6pf+9pf, Signal Corps. 8pf+7pf, Engineer Corps. 12pf+8pf, Grenade assault. 15pf+10pf, Heavy artillery. 20pf+14pf, Anti-aircraft units in action. 25pf+15pf, Dive bombers. 30pf+30pf, Paratroops. 40pf+40pf, Tank. 50pf+50pf, Speed boat.

1943, Mar. 21   Engr.
B218	SP189	3 + 2pf dk brn	.35	1.25
B219	SP189	4 + 3pf brown	.35	1.25
B220	SP189	5 + 4pf dk grn	.35	1.25
B221	SP189	6 + 9pf dp violet	.35	1.25
B222	SP189	8 + 7pf brn org	.35	1.25
B223	SP189	12 + 8pf car lake	.35	1.25
B224	SP189	15 + 10pf vio brn	.35	1.25
B225	SP189	20 + 14pf slate bl	.35	1.25
B226	SP189	25 + 15pf indigo	.35	1.25
B227	SP189	30 + 30pf green	.55	1.90
B228	SP189	40 + 40pf red lil	.55	1.90
B229	SP189	50 + 50pf grnsh blk	.80	3.00
	Nos. B218-B229 (12)		5.05	18.05
	Set, never hinged		17.00	

Army Day and Hero Memorial Day.
Nos. B220 and B224 exist imperf. Value, each $75.

Nazi Flag and Children
SP201

1943, Mar. 26   Photo.
B230	SP201	6 + 4pf dk green	.20	.90
	Never hinged			.85

To commemorate the Day of Youth Obligation when all German boys and girls had to take an oath of allegiance to Hitler.

Adolf Hitler
SP202

1943, Apr. 13
B231	SP202	3 + 7pf brown blk	.45	1.50
B232	SP202	6 + 14pf dk grn	.45	1.50
B233	SP202	8 + 22pf dk chlky bl	.45	1.50
B234	SP202	12 + 38pf cop red	.45	1.50
B235	SP202	24 + 76pf vio brn	.95	3.50
B236	SP202	40 + 160pf dk ol grn	.95	3.50
	Nos. B231-B236 (6)		3.70	13.00
	Set, never hinged		9.75	

Hitler's 54th birthday. No. B231 exists imperf. Value $100.

Reich Labor Service Corpsmen
SP203   SP204

Designs: 6pf+14pf, Corpsman chopping. 12pf+18pf, Corpsman with implements.

1943, June 26   Engr.
B237	SP203	3 + 7pf bis brn	.20	.75
B238	SP204	5 + 10pf pale ol grn	.20	.60
B239	SP204	6 + 14pf dp blue	.20	.50
B240	SP204	12 + 18pf dk red	.35	1.40
	Nos. B237-B240 (4)		.95	3.15
	Set, never hinged		2.40	

Anniversary of Reich Labor Service.
Nos. B237-B238, B240 exist imperf. Values: Nos. B237-B238, $45 each; No. B240, $60.

Rosegger's Birthplace, Upper Styria — SP207

Peter Rosegger
SP208

Perf. 13½x14, 14x13½
1943, July 27   Photo.
B241	SP207	6 + 4pf green	.20	.90
B242	SP208	12 + 8pf copper red	.20	.90
	Set, never hinged		1.50	

Centenary of the birth of Peter Rosegger, Austrian writer.

Hunter
SP209

1943, July 27   Engr.
B243	SP209	42 + 108pf brown	.20	1.25
	Never hinged			.90

10th "Brown Ribbon" at Munich.
No. B243 exists imperf. Value $200.

Race Horse — SP210

1943, Aug. 14
B244	SP210	6 + 4pf vio blk	.20	1.25
B245	SP210	12 + 88pf dk car	.20	1.25
	Set, never hinged		1.60	

Grand Prize of the Freudenau, the Vienna race track, Aug. 15, 1943.

Mother and Children — SP211

1943, Sept. 1
B246	SP211	12 + 38pf dark red	.20	1.25
	Never hinged			.80

10th anniversary of Winter Relief.

St. George in Gold — SP212

1943, Oct. 1
B247	SP212	6 + 4pf dk ol grn	.20	.75
B248	SP212	12 + 88pf vio brn	.20	1.10
	Set, never hinged		1.10	

German Goldsmiths' Society.

Ancient Lübeck — SP213

1943, Oct. 24   Photo.
B249	SP213	12 + 8pf copper red	.20	1.10
	Never hinged			.65

Hanseatic town of Lubeck, 800th anniv.
No. B249 exists imperf. Value, $110.

"And Despite All, You Were Victorious"
SP214

1943, Nov. 5
B250	SP214	24 + 26pf henna	.20	1.10
	Never hinged			.80

20th anniv. of the Nazis' Munich beer-hall putsch and to honor those who died for the Nazi movement. No. B250 exists imperf; value, $100.

Dr. Robert Koch — SP215

1944, Jan. 25   Engr.   Unwmk.
B251	SP215	12 + 38pf sepia	.20	1.10
	Never hinged			.75

Centenary of the birth of the bacteriologist, Robert Koch (1843-1910).

Hitler and Nazi Emblems
SP216

1944, Jan. 29   Photo.
B252	SP216	54 + 96pf yel brn	.25	1.25
	Never hinged			.80

Assumption of power by the Nazis, 11th anniv.

Airport Scene — SP217

Seaplane
SP218

Plane Seen from Above — SP219

Perf. 14x13½, 13½x14
1944, Feb. 11   Photo.   Unwmk.
B252A	SP217	6 + 4pf dk grn	.20	1.10
B252B	SP218	12 + 8pf maroon	.20	1.10
B252C	SP219	42 + 108pf dp slate bl	.30	2.25
	Nos. B252A-B252C (3)		.70	4.45
	Set, never hinged		2.40	

25th anniv. of German air mail. The surtax was for the National Culture Fund.

Infant's Crib — SP220

6pf+4pf, Public nurse. 12pf+8pf, "Mother & Child" clinic. 15pf+10pf, Expectant mothers.

1944, Mar. 2
B253	SP220	3 + 2pf dk brn	.20	.50
B254	SP220	6 + 4pf dk grn	.20	.50
B255	SP220	12 + 8pf dk car	.20	.50
B256	SP220	15 + 10pf vio brn	.20	.65
	Nos. B253-B256 (4)		.80	2.15
	Set, never hinged		1.25	

10th anniv. of "Mother and Child" aid.

Assault Boat — SP221

1944, Mar. 11

Designs: 4pf+3pf, Chain-wheel vehicle. 5pf+3pf, Paratroops. 6pf+4pf, Submarine officer. 8pf+4pf, Schutz-Staffel grenade throwers. 10pf+5pf, Searchlight. 12pf+6pf, Infantry. 15pf+10pf, Self-propelled gun. 16pf+10pf, Speed boat. 20pf+10pf, Sea raider. 24pf+10pf, Railway artillery. 25pf+15pf, Rockets. 30pf+20pf, Mountain trooper.

Inscribed: "Grossdeutsches Reich"
B257	SP221	3 + 2pf yel brn	.20	1.25
B258	SP221	4 + 3pf royal bl	.20	.70
B259	SP221	5 + 3pf dp yel grn	.20	.60
B260	SP221	6 + 4pf dp vio	.20	.60
B261	SP221	8 + 4pf org ver	.20	.70
B262	SP221	10 + 5pf chocolate	.20	.60
B263	SP221	12 + 6pf carmine	.20	.60
B264	SP221	15 + 10pf dp claret	.20	.70
B265	SP221	16 + 10pf dk bl grn	.20	1.25
B266	SP221	20 + 10pf brt bl	.20	1.50
B267	SP221	24 + 10pf dl org brn	.20	1.60
B268	SP221	25 + 15pf vio bl	.80	4.00
B269	SP221	30 + 20pf olive grn	.80	4.00
	Nos. B257-B269 (13)		3.80	18.00
	Set, never hinged		14.00	

To commemorate Hero Memorial Day.

Flora Statue in Fulda's Schloss Garden — SP234

1944, Mar. 11
B270	SP234	12 + 38pf dp brown	.20	.90
	Never hinged			.60

1,200th anniversary of town of Fulda.

Adolf Hitler — SP235

1944, Apr. 14   Engr.   Unwmk.
B271 SP235 54 + 96pf rose car   .30   1.75
   Never hinged   1.25

To commemorate Hitler's 55th birthday.

Type of 1939-41 and

Woman Mail Carrier SP236

Field Post in the East — SP237

Designs: 8pf+12pf, Mail coach. 16pf+24pf, Automobile race. 20pf+30pf, Postal police. 24pf+36pf, Glider workshops.

1944, May 3   Photo.
Designs measure 29½x24½mm
B272 SP236 6 + 9pf vio bl   .20   .75
B273 SP124 8 + 12pf gray blk   .20   .75
B274 SP237 12 + 18pf dp plum   .20   .75
B275 SP124 16 + 24pf dk grn   .20   .75
B276 SP124 20 + 30pf blue   .20   1.40
B277 SP124 24 + 36pf dk pur   .20   1.40
   Nos. B272-B277 (6)   1.20   5.80
   Set, never hinged   2.50

Surtax for the Postal Employees' Fund.

Soldier and Tirolese Rifleman — SP238

1944, July
B278 SP238 6 + 4pf dp grn   .20   .80
B279 SP238 12 + 8pf brn lake   .20   .80
   Set, never hinged   .75

7th National Shooting Matches at Innsbruck.

Albert I, Duke of Prussia — SP239

1944, July
B280 SP239 6 + 4pf dk bl grn   .25   1.25
   Never hinged   .75

400th anniv. of Albert University, Königsberg.

Labor Corps Girl SP240   Labor Corpsman SP241

1944, June   Engr.
B281 SP240 6 + 4pf green   .20   .60
B282 SP241 12 + 8pf carmine   .20   .65
   Set, never hinged   .80

Issued to honor an exhibit of the Reich Labor Service.

Race Horse and Foal — SP242

1944, July 23   Perf. 14x13½
B283 SP242 42 + 108pf brown   .25   2.00
   Never hinged   1.10

11th "Brown Ribbon" at Munich.

Race Horse's Head in Oak Wreath — SP243

1944, Aug.   Photo.   Perf. 14
B284 SP243 6 + 4pf Prus green   .20   1.10
B285 SP243 12 + 88pf car lake   .20   1.10
   Set, never hinged   1.10

Vienna Grand Prize Race.

Nautilus Cup in Green Vault, Dresden — SP244

1944, Sept. 11
B286 SP244 6 + 4pf dk
           green   .20   1.10
B287 SP244 12 + 88pf car
           brn   .20   1.10
   Set, never hinged   1.10

German Goldsmiths' Society. No. B287 exists imperf. Value $175.

Post Horn and Letter — SP245

1944, Oct. 2
B288 SP245 6 + 24pf dk green   .20   1.25
   Never hinged   .65

To commemorate Stamp Day.

Eagle and Serpent — SP246

1944, Nov. 9
B289 SP246 12 + 8pf rose red   .20   1.25
   Never hinged   .75

21st anniv. of the Munich putsch.

Count Anton Günther — SP247

1945, Jan. 6   Typo.   Perf. 13½x14
B290 SP247 6 + 14pf brown vio   .20   1.25
   Never hinged   .75

600th anniv. of municipal law in Oldenburg. Exists imperf. Value, $75.

People's Army — SP248

1945, Feb.   Photo.   Perf. 14x13½
B291 SP248 12 + 8pf rose car   .30   2.25
   Never hinged   1.25

Proclamation of the People's Army (Volksturm) in East Prussia to fight the Russians.

Elite Storm Trooper (S. S.) — SP249   Storm Trooper (S. A.) — SP250

1945, Apr. 21   Perf. 13½x14
B292 SP249 12 + 38pf brt
           car   7.50   900.00
B293 SP250 12 + 38pf brt
           car   7.50   900.00
   Set, never hinged   65.00

12th anniv. of the assumption of power by the Nazis. Nos. B292-B293 were on sale in Berlin briefly before the collapse of that city. Exist imperf unused. Value same as perf. Forged cancels abound. Certificates of authenticity mandatory for used examples.

Souvenir Sheets

SP251

Wmk. 284
1946, Dec. 8   Typo.   Perf. 14
B294 SP251 Sheet of 3   19.00   140.00
   Never hinged   45.00

Imperf
B295 SP251 Sheet of 3   19.00   175.00
   Never hinged   45.00
  a.   A119 20pf light blue   3.75   19.00
  b.   A119 24pf orange brown   3.75   19.00
  c.   A119 40pf red violet   3.75   19.00

No. B294 contains Nos. 543, 544 and 548. Nos. B294-B295 sold for 5m each. Surtax for refugees and the aged.

Leipzig Proclaimed Market Place, 1160 — SP252

Design: 60pf+40pf, Foreign merchants displaying their wares, 1268.

Wmk. 48
1947, Mar. 5   Engr.   Perf. 13
B296 SP252 24 +26pf chestnut
           brn   .20   4.75
B297 SP252 60 + 40pf dp vio
           blue   .20   4.75
   Set, never hinged   1.50

1947 Leipzig Fairs. No. B296 exists imperf. Value $150.

See Nos. 580-583, 10NB1-10NB2, 10NB4-10NB5, 10NB12-10NB13 and German Democratic Republic Nos. B15-B16.

Madonna SP254   Cathedral Towers SP255

Designs: 12pf+8pf, Three Kings. 24pf+16pf, Cologne Cathedral.

Wmk. 286
1948, Aug. 15   Typo.   Perf. 11
B298 SP254 6 + 4pf org brn   .30   .75
  a.   "1948-1248"   4.75   19.00
   Never hinged   11.50
B299 SP254 12 + 8pf grnsh
           blue   .70   1.90
  a.   "1948-1948"   6.25   22.50
   Never hinged   15.00
B300 SP254 24 + 16pf car   1.40   3.50
B301 SP255 50 + 50pf blue   3.25   9.00
   Nos. B298-B301 (4)   5.65   15.15
   Set, never hinged   10.50

700th anniv. of the laying of the cornerstone of Cologne Cathedral. The surtax was to aid in its reconstruction.

Specialists collect Nos. B298-B301 with watermark in four positions: upright, D's facing left; upright, D's facing right; sideways, D's facing up; sideways, D's facing down. Two types of perforation: line and comb.

Brandenburg Gate, Berlin SP256   Bicycle Racers SP257

Perf. 10½x11½, 11
1948, Dec.   Litho.
B302 SP256 10 + 5pf green   3.00   7.50
B303 SP256 20 + 10pf rose car   3.00   7.50
   Set, never hinged   11.50

The surtax was for aid to Berlin.

Wmk. 116
1949, May 15   Engr.   Perf. 14
B304 SP257 10 + 5pf green   1.90   6.00
B305 SP257 20 + 10pf brn org   4.50   16.50
   Set, never hinged   16.50

1949 Bicycle Tour of Germany.

Goethe at Rome — SP258

Goethe — SP259

30pf+15pf, Goethe portrait facing left.

1949, Aug. 15

B306	SP258	10 + 5pf green	.90	3.00
B307	SP259	20 + 10pf red	1.40	5.25
B308	SP259	30 + 15pf blue	7.50	24.00
	Nos. B306-B308 (3)		9.80	32.25
	Set, never hinged		32.50	

Bicentenary of the birth of Johann Wolfgang von Goethe.
The surtax was for the reconstruction of Goethe House, Frankfurt-on-Main.

Federal Republic

Bavaria Stamp of 1849
SP260

St. Elisabeth
SP261

1949, Sept. 30   Litho.   Wmk. 285

B309	SP260	10 + 2pf grn & blk	7.25	22.50
	Never hinged		13.00	

Centenary of German postage stamps.

1949, Dec. 14   Engr.   Wmk. 286

Designs: 10pf+5pf, Paracelsus. 20pf+10pf, F. W. A. Froebel. 30pf+15pf, J. H. Wichern.

B310	SP261	8 + 2pf brn vio	8.50	22.50
B311	SP261	10 + 5pf yel grn	6.25	11.50
B312	SP261	20 + 10pf red	6.25	11.50
B313	SP261	30 + 15pf vio bl	32.50	100.00
	Nos. B310-B313 (4)		53.50	145.50
	Set, never hinged		125.00	

The surtax was for welfare organizations.

Seal of Johann Sebastian Bach — SP262

Frescoes from Marienkirche
SP263

1950, July 28   Perf. 14

B314	SP262	10 + 2pf dk grn	22.50	42.50
B315	SP262	20 + 3pf dk car	26.00	50.00
	Set, never hinged		120.00	

Bicentenary of the death of Bach.

1951, Aug. 30   Photo.   Wmk. 286
Center in Gray

B316	SP263	10 + 5pf green	27.50	67.50
B317	SP263	20 + 5pf brn lake	32.50	75.00
	Set, never hinged		180.00	

Construction of Marienkirche, Lübeck, 700th anniv.
The surtax aided in its reconstruction.

Stamps Under Magnifying Glass — SP264

St. Vincent de Paul — SP265

Wmk. 295
1951, Sept. 14   Typo.   Perf. 14

B318	SP264	10 + 2pf multi	15.00	45.00
B319	SP264	20 + 3pf multi	15.00	45.00
	Set, never hinged		82.50	

Natl. Philatelic Exposition, Wuppertal, 1951.

1951, Oct. 23   Engr.

Portraits: 10pf+3pf, Friedrich von Bodelschwingh. 20pf+5pf, Elsa Brandstrom. 30pf+10pf, Johann Heinrich Pestalozzi.

B320	SP265	4 + 2pf brown	4.25	9.00
B321	SP265	10 + 3pf green	6.25	7.50
B322	SP265	20 + 5pf rose red	6.25	7.50
B323	SP265	30 + 10pf dp blue	47.50	110.00
	Nos. B320-B323 (4)		64.25	134.00
	Set, never hinged		130.00	

The surtax was for charitable purposes.

Nuremberg Madonna
SP266

Boy Hikers and Youth Hostel
SP267

1952, Aug. 9

B324	SP266	10 + 5pf green	7.50	18.00
	Never hinged		15.00	

Centenary of the founding of the Germanic National Museum, Nuremberg. The surtax was for the museum.

1952, Sept. 17   Perf. 13½x14

Design: 20pf+3pf, Girls and Hostel.

B325	SP267	10 + 2pf green	9.25	20.00
B326	SP267	20 + 3pf dp car	9.25	20.00
	Set, never hinged		37.50	

The surtax was to aid the youth program of the Federal Republic.

Elizabeth Fry
SP268

Owl and Cogwheel
SP269

10pf+5pf, Dr. Carl Sonnenschein. 20pf+10pf, Theodor Fliedner. 30pf+10pf, Henri Dunant.

1952, Oct. 1

B327	SP268	4 + 2pf org brn	3.25	6.00
B328	SP268	10 + 5pf green	3.25	6.00
B329	SP268	20 + 10pf brn car	6.75	12.00
B330	SP268	30 + 10pf dp blue	35.00	82.50
	Nos. B327-B330 (4)		48.25	106.50
	Set, never hinged		120.00	

The surtax was for welfare organizations.

1953, May 7   Wmk. 295   Perf. 14

B331	SP269	10 + 5pf dp grn	13.00	30.00
	Never hinged		27.50	

50th anniv. of the founding of the German Museum in Munich.

Thurn and Taxis Palace Gate — SP270

August Hermann Francke — SP271

Design: 20pf+3pf, Telecommunications Bldg., Frankfurt-on-Main.

Wmk. 285
1953, July 29   Litho.   Perf. 13½

B332	SP270	10 + 2pf yel grn, bl & fawn	8.25	25.00
B333	SP270	20 + 3pf fawn, blk & gray	8.25	25.00
	Set, never hinged		47.50	

The surtax was for the International Stamp Exhibition, Frankfurt-on-Main, 1953.

Wmk. 295
1953, Nov. 2   Engr.   Perf. 14

Designs: 10pf+5pf, Sebastian Kneipp. 20pf+10pf, Dr. Johann Christian Senckenberg. 30pf+10pf, Fridtjof Nansen.

B334	SP271	4 + 2pf choc	1.75	7.50
B335	SP271	10 + 5pf bl grn	3.00	7.50
B336	SP271	20 + 10pf red	5.00	11.00
B337	SP271	30 + 10pf blue	20.00	67.50
	Nos. B334-B337 (4)		29.75	93.50
	Set, never hinged		77.50	

The surtax was for welfare organizations.

> **Catalogue values for unused stamps in this section, from this point to the end of the section, are for Never Hinged items.**

Käthe Kollwitz — SP272

Carrier Pigeon and Magnifying Glass — SP273

Portraits: 10pf+5pf, Lorenz Werthmann. 20pf+10pf, Johann Friedrich Oberlin. 40pf+10pf, Bertha Pappenheim.

1954, Dec. 28   Perf. 13½x14

B338	SP272	7 + 3pf brown	3.00	3.00
B339	SP272	10 + 5pf green	1.50	1.50
B340	SP272	20 + 10pf red	7.50	4.50
B341	SP272	40 + 10pf blue	32.50	40.00
	Nos. B338-B341 (4)		44.50	49.00

The surtax was for welfare organizations.

1955, Sept. 14   Wmk. 304   Perf. 14

20pf+3pf, Post horn and stamp tongs.

B342	SP273	10 + 2pf green	4.50	5.75
B343	SP273	20 + 3pf red	10.50	13.50

WESTROPA, 1955, philatelic exhibition at Dusseldorf. The surtax aided the Society of German Philatelists.

Amalie Sieveking — SP274

Portraits: 10pf+5pf, Adolph Kolping. 20pf+10pf, Dr. Samuel Hahnemann. 40pf+10pf, Florence Nightingale.

1955, Nov. 15   Photo. & Litho.

B344	SP274	7 + 3pf olive bis	3.00	3.00
B345	SP274	10 + 5pf dk green	2.25	1.50
B346	SP274	20 + 10pf red org	2.25	1.50
B347	SP274	40 + 10pf grnsh blue	30.00	37.50
	Nos. B344-B347 (4)		37.50	43.50

Surtax for independent welfare organizations.

Boy and Geometrical Designs
SP275

Design: 10pf+5pf, Girl playing flute.

Unwmk.
1956, July 21   Litho.   Perf. 14

B348	SP275	7pf + 3pf multi	1.90	3.00
B349	SP275	10pf + 5pf multi	6.50	7.50

The surtax was for the Youth Hostel Organization.

The Midwife
SP276

10+5pf, Ignaz Philipp Semmelweis. 20+10pf, The mother. 40+10pf, The children's nurse.

1956, Oct. 1   Photo.
Design and Inscription in Black

B350	SP276	7pf + 3pf org brn	1.50	2.25
B351	SP276	10pf + 5pf green	1.10	.75
B352	SP276	20pf + 10pf brt red	1.10	.75
B353	SP276	40pf + 10pf brt blue	15.00	15.00
	Nos. B350-B353 (4)		18.70	18.75

Issued to honor Ignaz Philipp Semmelweis, the discoverer of the cause of puerperal fever. Surtax for independent welfare organizations.

Children Leaving
SP277

Design: 20pf+10pf, Child arriving.

1957, Feb. 1   Litho.   Perf. 13½x13

B354	SP277	10pf + 5pf gray grn & red org	1.10	1.90
B355	SP277	20pf + 10pf red org & lt bl	2.75	3.75

The surtax was for vacations for the children of Berlin.

Young Miner — SP278

"A Hunter from the Palatinate."
SP279

10+5pf, Miner with drill. 20+10pf, Miner & conveyor. 40+10pf, Miner & coal elevator.

1957, Oct. 1   Wmk. 304   Perf. 14

B356	SP278	7pf + 3pf bis brn & blk	1.10	1.50
B357	SP278	10pf + 5pf blk & yel grn	.75	.75
B358	SP278	20pf + 10pf black & red	1.10	.75
B359	SP278	40pf + 10pf black & blue	16.50	18.00
	Nos. B356-B359 (4)		19.45	21.00

Surtax for independent welfare organizations.

1958, Apr. 1   Litho.

10pf + 5pf, "The Fox who Stole the Goose"

B360	SP279	10pf + 5pf brn red, grn & blk	1.50	1.90
B361	SP279	20pf + 10pf multi	3.00	3.50

The surtax was to finance young peoples' study trips to Berlin.

Friedrich Wilhelm
Raiffeisen
SP280

Dairy Maid
SP281

Designs: 20pf+10pf, Girl picking grapes.
40pf+10pf, Farmer with pitchfork.

1958, Oct. 1   Wmk. 304   Perf. 14

B362	SP280	7pf + 3pf gldn brn & dk brn	.45 .45
B363	SP281	10pf + 5pf grn, red & yel	.45 .45
B364	SP281	20pf + 10pf red, yel & bl	.45 .45
B365	SP281	40pf + 10pf blue & ocher	6.00 7.25
	Nos. B362-B365 (4)		7.35 8.60

Surtax for independent welfare organizations.

Stamp of Hamburg,
1859 — SP282

Design: 20pf+10pf, Stamp of Lübeck, 1859.

1959   Engr.   Wmk. 304

B366	SP282	10pf + 5pf yel green & brown	.25 .60
a.		10pf + 5pf green & brown	.75 2.10
B367	SP282	20pf + 10pf red org & red brn	.25 .65
a.		20pf + 10pf maroon & red brown	1.10 2.10

"Interposta" Philatelic Exhibition, Hamburg,
May 22-31, 1959 for the cent. of the 1st
stamps of Hamburg and Lübeck.
The surtax on #B366, B367 was for vacations for the children of Berlin.
Issued: #B366-B367, 8/22; #B366a-B367a,
5/22.

Girl Giving
Bread to Beggar
SP283

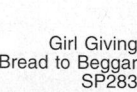

Jacob and
Wilhelm Grimm
SP284

Designs (from "Star Dollars" fairy tale):
10pf+5pf, Girl giving coat to boy, 20pf+10pf,
Star-Money from Heaven.

1959, Oct. 1   Litho.   Perf. 14

B368	SP283	7pf + 3pf brown & yel	.25 .35
B369	SP283	10pf + 5pf green & yel	.25 .35
B370	SP283	20pf + 10pf brick red & yel	.30 .35
B371	SP284	40pf + 10pf bl, blk, ocher & emer	3.00 4.50
	Nos. B368-B371 (4)		3.80 5.55

Surtax for independent welfare organizations.

Little Red
Riding Hood
and the
Wolf — SP285

Various Scenes from Little Red Riding
Hood.

1960, Oct. 1   Wmk. 304   Perf. 14

B372	SP285	7pf + 3pf brn ol, red & blk	.45 .45
B373	SP285	10pf + 5pf grn, red & blk	.45 .35
B374	SP285	20pf + 10pf brick red, emer & blk	.45 .35
B375	SP285	40pf + 20pf brt bl, red & blk	2.25 3.75
	Nos. B372-B375 (4)		3.60 4.90

Surtax for independent welfare organizations.

1961, Oct. 2

Various Scenes from Hansel and Gretel.

B376	SP285	7pf + 3pf multi	.20 .30
B377	SP285	10pf + 5pf multi	.20 .30
B378	SP285	20pf + 10pf multi	.20 .30
B379	SP285	40pf + 20pf multi	1.00 1.75
	Nos. B376-B379 (4)		1.60 2.65

Surtax for independent welfare organizations.
See B384-B387, B392-B395, B400-B403.

Fluorescent Paper
was introduced for semipostal
stamps, starting with No. B380.

Apollo — SP286

Hoopoe — SP287

10pf+5pf, Camberwell beauty. 20pf+10pf,
Tortoise-shell. 40pf+20pf, Tiger swallowtail.

Wmk. 304
1962, May 25   Litho.   Perf. 14
**Butterflies in Natural Colors, Black
Inscriptions**

B380	SP286	7pf + 3pf bis brn	.35 .60
B381	SP286	10pf + 5pf brt green	.35 .60
B382	SP286	20pf + 10pf dp crim	.75 1.10
B383	SP286	40pf + 20pf brt blue	1.10 1.90
	Nos. B380-B383 (4)		2.55 4.20

Issued for the benefit of young people.
Nos. B381-B383 exist without watermark.
Value, each $900 unused, $975 used.

Fairy Tale Type of 1960

Scenes from Snow White (Schneewittchen).

1962, Oct. 10   Perf. 14

B384	SP285	7pf + 3pf multi	.20 .25
B385	SP285	10pf + 5pf multi	.20 .25
B386	SP285	20pf + 10pf multi	.20 .25
B387	SP285	40pf + 20pf multi	.80 1.25
	Nos. B384-B387 (4)		1.40 2.00

Surtax for independent welfare organizations.

1963, June 12   Unwmk.   Perf. 14

Birds: 15pf+5pf, European golden oriole.
20pf+10pf, Bullfinch. 40pf+20pf, European
kingfisher.

B388	SP287	10pf + 5pf multi	.45 .60
B389	SP287	15pf + 5pf multi	.35 .60
B390	SP287	20pf + 10pf multi	.35 .60
B391	SP287	40pf + 20pf multi	1.60 2.40
	Nos. B388-B391 (4)		2.75 4.20

Issued for the benefit of young people.

Fairy Tale Type of 1960

Various Scenes from the Grimm Brothers'
"The Wolf and the Seven Kids."

1963, Sept. 23   Litho.

B392	SP285	10pf + 5pf multi	.20 .25
B393	SP285	15pf + 5pf multi	.20 .25
B394	SP285	20pf + 10pf multi	.20 .25
B395	SP285	40pf + 20pf multi	.60 1.10
	Nos. B392-B395 (4)		1.20 1.85

Surtax for independent welfare organizations.

Herring
SP288

Fish: 15pf+5pf, Rosefish. 20pf+10pf, Carp.
40pf+20pf, Cod.

1964, Apr. 10   Unwmk.   Perf. 14

B396	SP288	10pf + 5pf multi	.20 .30
B397	SP288	15pf + 5pf multi	.20 .30
B398	SP288	20pf + 10pf multi	.35 .45
B399	SP288	40pf + 20pf multi	.95 1.90
	Nos. B396-B399 (4)		1.70 2.95

Issued for the benefit of young people.

Fairy Tale Type of 1960

Various Scenes from Sleeping Beauty
(Dornroschen).

1964, Oct. 6   Litho.   Perf. 14

B400	SP285	10pf + 5pf multi	.20 .25
B401	SP285	15pf + 5pf multi	.20 .25
B402	SP285	20pf + 10pf multi	.20 .25
B403	SP285	40pf + 20pf multi	.35 .90
	Nos. B400-B403 (4)		.95 1.65

Surtax for independent welfare organizations.

Woodcock
SP289

1965, Apr. 1   Unwmk.   Perf. 14

Birds: 15pf+5pf, Ring-necked pheasant.
20pf+10pf, Black grouse. 40pf+20pf,
Capercaillie.

B404	SP289	10pf + 5pf multi	.20 .30
B405	SP289	15pf + 5pf multi	.20 .30
B406	SP289	20pf + 10pf multi	.20 .30
B407	SP289	40pf + 20pf multi	.30 .90
	Nos. B404-B407 (4)		.90 1.80

Issued for the benefit of young people.

Cinderella
Feeding
Pigeons
SP290

Various Scenes from Cinderella.

1965, Oct. 6   Litho.   Perf. 14

B408	SP290	10pf + 5pf multi	.20 .25
B409	SP290	15pf + 5pf multi	.20 .25
B410	SP290	20pf + 10pf multi	.20 .25
B411	SP290	40pf + 20pf multi	.45 .65
	Nos. B408-B411 (4)		1.05 1.40

Surtax for independent welfare organizations.
See Nos. B418-B421, B426-B429.

Roe
Deer — SP291

1966, Apr. 22   Litho.   Perf. 14

Designs: 20pf+10pf, Chamois. 30pf+15pf,
Fallow deer. 50pf+25pf, Red deer.

B412	SP291	10pf + 5pf multi	.25 .25
B413	SP291	20pf + 10pf multi	.25 .25
B414	SP291	30pf + 15pf multi	.25 .30
B415	SP291	50pf + 25pf multi	.60 .90
	Nos. B412-B415 (4)		1.35 1.70

Issued for the benefit of young people.
See Nos. B422-B425.

Prussian Letter
Carrier — SP292

Design: 30pf+15pf, Bavarian mail coach.

1966   Litho.   Perf. 14

B416	SP292	30pf + 15pf multi	.35 .65
B417	SP292	50pf + 25pf multi	.50 .65

Meeting of the Federation Internationale de
Philatélie (FIP), Munich, Sept. 26-29, and
stamp exhibition, Municipal Museum, Sept.
24-Oct. 1. The surcharge was for the Foundation for the Promotion of Philately and Postal
History.
Issued: #B416, 9/24; #B417, 7/13.

Fairy Tale Type of 1965

Various Scenes from The Princess and the
Frog.

1966, Oct. 5   Litho.   Perf. 14

B418	SP290	10pf + 5pf multi	.20 .25
B419	SP290	20pf + 10pf multi	.20 .25
B420	SP290	30pf + 15pf multi	.20 .25
B421	SP290	50pf + 25pf multi	.45 .90
	Nos. B418-B421 (4)		1.05 1.65

Surtax for independent welfare organizations.

Animal Type of 1966

10pf+5pf, Rabbit. 20pf+10pf, Ermine.
30pf+15pf, Hamster. 50pf+25pf, Red fox.

1967, Apr. 4   Litho.   Perf. 14

B422	SP291	10pf + 5pf multi	.20 .30
B423	SP291	20pf + 10pf multi	.25 .30
B424	SP291	30pf + 15pf multi	.45 .60
B425	SP291	50pf + 25pf multi	.95 1.50
	Nos. B422-B425 (4)		1.85 2.70

Issued for the benefit of young people.

Fairy Tale Type of 1965

Various Scenes from Frau Holle.

1967, Oct. 3   Litho.   Perf. 14

B426	SP290	10pf + 5pf multi	.20 .25
B427	SP290	20pf + 10pf multi	.20 .25
B428	SP290	30pf + 15pf multi	.20 .25
B429	SP290	50pf + 25pf multi	.60 1.10
	Nos. B426-B429 (4)		1.20 1.85

Surtax for independent welfare organizations.

Wildcat
SP293

Animals: 20pf+10pf, Otter. 30pf+15pf,
Badger. 50pf+25pf, Beaver.

1968, Feb. 2   Photo.   Unwmk.

B430	SP293	10pf + 5pf multi	.25 .45
B431	SP293	20pf + 15pf multi	.35 .75
B432	SP293	30pf + 15pf multi	.50 1.00
B433	SP293	50pf + 25pf multi	1.90 3.00
	Nos. B430-B433 (4)		3.00 5.20

The surtax was for the benefit of young
people.

Olympic Games Type of Regular Issue

10pf+5pf, Karl-Friedrich Freiherr von
Langen, equestrian. 20pf+10pf, Rudolf Harbig,
runner. 30pf+15pf, Helene Mayer, fencer.
50pf+25pf, Carl Diem, sports organizer.

Lithographed and Engraved
1968, June 6   Unwmk.   Perf. 14

B434	A285	10 + 5pf olive & dk brn	.30 .30
B435	A285	20 + 10pf dp emer & dk grn	.30 .30
B436	A285	30 + 15pf dp rose & dk red	.50 .50
B437	A285	50 + 25pf brt bl & dk bl	.80 .90
	Nos. B434-B437 (4)		1.90 2.00

The surtax was for the Foundation for the
Promotion of the 1972 Olympic Games in
Munich.

Doll, c.
1878 — SP294

Pony — SP295

Various 19th Cent. Dolls. #B438-B440 are from Germanic Natl. Museum, Nuremberg; #B441 is from Altona Museum, Hamburg.

1968, Oct. 3   Litho.   Perf. 14
B438 SP294 10pf + 5pf multi .20 .25
B439 SP294 20pf + 10pf multi .20 .25
B440 SP294 30pf + 15pf multi .25 .25
B441 SP294 50pf + 25pf multi .60 .90
    Nos. B438-B441 (4) 1.25 1.65

Surtax for independent welfare organizations.

1969, Feb. 6   Litho.   Perf. 14
Horses: 20pf+10pf, Work horse. 30pf+15pf, Hotblood. 50pf+25pf, Thoroughbred.

B442 SP295 10pf + 5pf multi .30 .45
B443 SP295 20pf + 10pf multi .30 .45
B444 SP295 30pf + 15pf multi .50 .75
B445 SP295 50pf + 25pf multi 1.60 1.50
    Nos. B442-B445 (4) 2.70 3.15

Surtax for the benefit of young people.

SP296   SP297

Olympic Rings and: 10pf+5pf, Track. 20pf+10pf, Hockey. 30pf+15pf, Archery. 50pf+25pf, Sailing.

1969, June 4   Photo.   Perf. 14
B446 SP296 10pf + 5pf dk brn &
    lem .20 .20
B447 SP296 20pf + 10pf bl grn &
    emer .35 .30
B448 SP296 30pf + 15pf mag &
    dp lil rose .50 .45
B449 SP296 50pf + 25pf dp bl &
    brt bl 1.10 .90
    Nos. B446-B449 (4) 2.15 1.85

1972 Olympic Games in Munich. The surtax was for the German Olympic Committee.

1969, Oct. 2   Litho.   Perf. 13½x14
Tin Toys: 10pf+5pf, Locomotive. 20pf+10pf, Gardener. 30pf+15pf, Bird seller. 50pf+25pf, Knight on horseback.

B450 SP297 10pf + 5pf multi .20 .20
B451 SP297 20pf + 10pf multi .25 .25
B452 SP297 30pf + 15pf multi .30 .30
B453 SP297 50pf + 25pf multi .85 1.10
    Nos. B450-B453 (4) 1.60 1.85

Surtax for independent welfare organizations.

Tin Toy Type of 1969 Inscribed: "Weihnachtsmarke 1969"
Christmas: 10pf+5pf, Jesus in Manger.

1969, Nov. 13   Perf. 13½x14
B454 SP297 10pf + 5pf multi .30 .30

Heinrich von
Rugge — SP298

Minnesingers: 20pf+10pf, Wolfram von Eschenbach. 30pf+15pf, Walther von Metz. 50pf+25pf, Walther von der Vogelweide.

1970, Feb. 5   Photo.   Perf. 13½x14
B455 SP298 10pf + 5pf multi .35 .30
B456 SP298 20pf + 10pf multi .60 .35
B457 SP298 30pf + 15pf multi .75 .60
B458 SP298 50pf + 25pf multi 1.60 1.50
    Nos. B455-B458 (4) 3.30 2.75

Surtax was for benefit of young people.

Residenz
(Palace),
Munich
SP299

Munich Buildings: 20pf+10pf, Propylaea. 30pf+15pf, Glyptothek. 50pf+25pf, Bavaria Statue and Colonnade.

1970, June 5   Engr.   Perf. 14
B459 SP299 10pf + 5pf olive bis .20 .20
B460 SP299 20pf + 10pf dk bl
    grn .45 .30
B461 SP299 30pf + 15pf carmine .60 .45
B462 SP299 50pf + 25pf dk blue 1.00 .90
    Nos. B459-B462 (4) 2.25 1.85

The surtax was for the Foundation for the Promotion of the 1972 Olympic Games in Munich.

Jester — SP300   King
                  Caspar — SP301

Puppets: 20pf+10pf, "Hanswurst." 30pf+15pf, Clown. 50pf+25pf, Harlequin.

1970, Oct. 6   Litho.   Perf. 13½x14
B463 SP300 10pf + 5pf multi .25 .25
B464 SP300 20pf + 10pf multi .25 .30
B465 SP300 30pf + 15pf multi .35 .35
B466 SP300 50pf + 25pf multi .90 .95
    Nos. B463-B466 (4) 1.75 1.85

Surtax for independent welfare organizations.

1970, Nov. 12
Christmas: 10pf+5pf, Rococo Angel, from Ursuline Sisters' Convent, Innsbruck.

B467 SP300 10pf + 5pf multi .30 .25

1971, Feb. 5   Litho.   Perf. 14
Children's Drawings: 20pf+10pf, Flea. 30pf+15pf, Puss-in-Boots. 50pf+25pf, Snake.

B468 SP301 10pf + 5pf multi .30 .30
B469 SP301 20pf + 10pf multi .35 .35
B470 SP301 30pf + 15pf multi .60 .60
B471 SP301 50pf + 25pf multi 1.00 1.00
    Nos. B468-B471 (4) 2.25 2.25

Surtax for the benefit of young people.

Ski   Women Churning
Jump — SP302   Butter — SP303

20pf+10pf, Figure skating. 30pf+15pf, Downhill skiing. 50pf+25pf, Ice hockey.

"1971" at Lower Right
1971, June 4   Litho.   Perf. 14
B472 SP302 10pf + 5pf brn org &
    blk .25 .20
B473 SP302 20pf + 10pf green &
    blk .45 .30
B474 SP302 30pf + 15pf rose red
    & blk .60 .60

B475 SP302 50pf + 25pf blue &
    blk 1.50 1.50
a.   Souvenir sheet of 4 3.00 2.50
b.   10pf + 5pf brown org & blk .25 .20
c.   20pf + 10pf green & black .45 .30
d.   30pf + 15pf rose red & black .80 .60
e.   50pf + 25pf blue & black 1.50 1.25
    Nos. B472-B475 (4) 2.80 2.60
Olympic Games 1972.
#B475a contains #B475b-B475e which lack the small date ("1971") at lower right.

1971, Oct. 5   Litho.   Perf. 14
Wooden Toys: 25pf+10pf, Horseback rider. 30pf+15pf, Nutcracker. 60pf+30pf, Dovecot.

B476 SP303 20pf + 10pf multi .20 .20
B477 SP303 25pf + 10pf multi .20 .20
B478 SP303 30pf + 15pf multi .45 .45
B479 SP303 60pf + 30pf multi 1.25 1.25
    Nos. B476-B479 (4) 2.10 2.10

Surtax for independent welfare organizations.

1971, Nov. 11
Christmas: Christmas angel with lights.
B480 SP303 20pf + 10pf multi .45 .35

Ducks Crossing
Road — SP304

Olympic Rings and
Wrestling — SP305

Designs: 25pf+10pf, Hunter chasing deer and rabbits. 30pf+15pf, Girl protecting birds from cat. 60pf+30pf, Boy annoying swans.

1972, Feb. 4   Litho.   Perf. 14
B481 SP304 20pf + 10pf multi .50 .45
B482 SP304 25pf + 10pf multi .40 .30
B483 SP304 30pf + 15pf multi .75 .75
B484 SP304 60pf + 30pf multi 1.50 1.50
    Nos. B481-B484 (4) 3.15 3.00

Animal protection. Surtax for the benefit of young people.

1972, June 5   Photo.   Perf. 14
25pf+10pf, Sailing. 30pf+15pf, Gymnastics. 60pf+30pf, Swimming.

B485 SP305 20pf + 10pf multi .45 .35
B486 SP305 25pf + 10pf multi .45 .35
B487 SP305 30pf + 15pf multi .45 .35
B488 SP305 60pf + 30pf multi 1.60 1.50
    Nos. B485-B488 (4) 2.95 2.55

20th Olympic Games, Munich, Aug. 26 Sept. 10. See No. B490.

Souvenir Sheet

Olympic Games Site,
Munich — SP306

1972, July 5   Litho.   Perf. 14
B489 SP306   Sheet of 4 5.00 5.00
a.   25pf + 10pf Gymnastics
    stadium 1.10 1.10
b.   30pf + 15pf Soccer stadi-
    um 1.10 1.10
c.   40pf + 20pf Tent and lake 1.10 1.10
d.   70pf + 35pf Television tow-
    er, vert. 1.10 1.10

20th Olympic Games, Munich. Surcharge was for the Foundation for the Promotion of the Munich Olympic Games.

**Olympic Games Type of 1972
Souvenir Sheet**
1972, Aug. 18   Litho.   Perf. 14
B490   Sheet of 4 4.50 4.50
a.   SP305 25pf + 5pf Long jump,
    women's .45 .45
b.   SP305 30pf + 10pf Basketball 1.25 1.25
c.   SP305 40pf + 10pf Discus, wo-
    men's 1.60 1.60
d.   SP305 70pf + 10pf Canoeing .80 .80
e.   Bklt. pane of 4, #B490a-B490d 8.00 8.00

20th Olympic Games, Munich.

Knight — SP307

Adoration of the
Kings — SP308

1972, Oct. 5
B491 SP307 25pf + 10pf shown .30 .30
B492 SP307 30pf + 15pf Rook .30 .25
B493 SP307 40pf + 20pf Queen .50 .25
B494 SP307 70pf + 35pf King 1.90 1.75
    Nos. B491-B494 (4) 3.00 2.55

19th cent. chess pieces made by Faience Works, Gien, France; now in Hamburg Museum. Surtax for independent welfare organizations.

1972, Nov. 10   Litho.
B495 SP308 30pf + 15pf multi .65 .45

Christmas 1972.

Osprey   Hesse-Kassel
SP309   SP310

Birds of Prey: 30pf+15pf, Buzzard. 40pf+20pf, Red kite. 70pf+35pf, Montagu's harrier.

1973, Feb. 6   Photo.   Perf. 14
B496 SP309 25pf + 10pf multi .90 .75
B497 SP309 30pf + 15pf multi 1.10 1.10
B498 SP309 40pf + 20pf multi 1.50 1.40
B499 SP309 70pf + 35pf multi 3.50 3.50
    Nos. B496-B499 (4) 7.00 6.55

Surtax was for benefit of young people.

1973, Apr. 5   Litho.   Perf. 14
Posthouse Signs: No. B501, Prussia. No. B502a, Württemberg. No. B502b, Bavaria.

B500 SP310 40pf + 20pf multi .65 .65
B501 SP310 70pf + 35pf multi 1.25 1.25

Souvenir Sheet
B502   Sheet of 2 4.25 4.25
a.   SP310 40pf + 20pf multi .90 .90
b.   SP310 70pf + 35pf multi 1.50 1.50

IBRA München 1973 International Philatelic Exhibition, Munich, May 11-20. No. B502 sold for 2.20 mark.

French Horn, 19th   Christmas
Century — SP311   Star — SP312

Musical Instruments: 30pf+15pf, Pedal piano, 18th century. 40pf+20pf, Violin, 18th century. 70pf+35pf, Pedal harp, 18th century.

1973, Oct. 5   Litho.   Perf. 14
B503 SP311 25pf + 10pf multi   .50   .30
B504 SP311 30pf + 15pf multi   .60   .30
B505 SP311 40pf + 20pf multi   .75   .45
B506 SP311 70pf + 35pf multi   1.90   1.50
      Nos. B503-B506 (4)   3.75   2.55

Surtax was for independent welfare organizations.

1973, Nov. 9   Litho. & Engr.
B507 SP312 30pf + 15pf multi   .60   .45

Christmas 1973.

Young Builder — SP313

30+15pf, Girl in national costume. 40+20pf, Boy studying. 70+35pf, Girl with microscope.

1974, Apr. 17   Photo.   Perf. 14
B508 SP313 25pf + 10pf multi   .50   .45
B509 SP313 30pf + 15pf multi   .90   .75
B510 SP313 40pf + 20pf multi   1.50   1.40
B511 SP313 70pf + 35pf multi   2.75   2.25
      Nos. B508-B511 (4)   5.65   4.85

Surtax was for benefit of young people.

Campion — SP314

1974, Oct. 15   Litho.   Perf. 14

Flowers: 40pf+20pf, Foxglove. 50pf+25pf, Mallow. 70pf+35pf, Bellflower.

B512 SP314 30pf + 15pf multi   .30   .30
B513 SP314 40pf + 20pf multi   .40   .30
B514 SP314 50pf + 25pf multi   .45   .40
B515 SP314 70pf + 35pf multi   1.25   1.25
      Nos. B512-B515 (4)   2.40   2.25

Surtax was for independent welfare organizations.

1974, Oct. 29

Christmas: 40pf+20pf, Advent decoration.

B516 SP314 40pf + 20pf multi   .75   .50

Diesel Locomotive Class 218 — SP315

Locomotives: 40pf+20pf, Electric engine Class 103. 50pf+25pf, Electric rail motor train Class 403. 70pf+35pf, Magnetic suspension train "Transrapid" (model).

1975, Apr. 15   Litho.   Perf. 14
B517 SP315 30pf + 15pf multi   .45   .40
B518 SP315 40pf + 20pf multi   .70   .60
B519 SP315 50pf + 25pf multi   .95   .90
B520 SP315 70pf + 35pf multi   1.60   1.50
      Nos. B517-B520 (4)   3.70   3.40

Surtax was for benefit of young people.

Edelweiss   Basketball
SP316   SP317

Alpine Flowers: 40pf+20pf, Trollflower. 50pf+25pf, Alpine rose. 70pf+35pf, Pasqueflower.

1975, Oct. 15   Litho.   Perf. 14
B521 SP316 30pf + 15pf multi   .35   .30
B522 SP316 40pf + 20pf multi   .35   .30
B523 SP316 60pf + 25pf multi   .60   .45
B524 SP316 70pf + 35pf multi   1.40   1.40
      Nos. B521-B524 (4)   2.70   2.45

Surtax was for independent welfare organizations.

1975, Nov. 14

Christmas: Snow rose.

B525 SP316 40pf + 20pf multi   .75   .75

1976, Apr. 6   Litho.   Perf. 14

Designs: 40pf+20pf, Rowing. 50pf+25pf, Gymnastics, women's. 70pf+35pf, Volleyball.

B526 SP317 30pf + 15pf multi   .45   .35
B527 SP317 40pf + 20pf multi   .80   .60
B528 SP317 50pf + 25pf multi   1.00   .90
B529 SP317 70pf + 35pf multi   1.40   1.25
      Nos. B526-B529 (4)   3.65   3.10

Youth training for Olympic Games. Surtax was for benefit of young people.

Swimmer and Olympic Rings — SP318

30pf+15pf, Hockey. 50pf+25pf, High jump. 70pf+35pf, Rowing, coxed four.

1976, Apr. 6
B530 SP318 40pf + 20pf multi   .75   .45
B531 SP318 50pf + 25pf multi   1.00   .75

Souvenir Sheet
B532   Sheet of 2   2.00   2.00
    a.   SP318 30pf + 15pf multi   .75   .50
    b.   SP318 70pf + 35pf multi   1.00   .85

21st Olympic Games, Montreal, Canada, July 17-Aug. 1. The surtax was for the German Sports Aid Foundation.

Phlox
SP319

Flowers: 40pf+20pf, Marigolds. 50pf+25pf, Dahlias. 70pf+35pf, Pansies.

1976, Oct. 14   Litho.   Perf. 14
B533 SP319 30pf + 15pf multi   .45   .35
B534 SP319 40pf + 20pf multi   .60   .50
B535 SP319 50pf + 25pf multi   .65   .60
B536 SP319 70pf + 35pf multi   1.10   1.10
      Nos. B533-B536 (4)   2.80   2.55

Surtax was for independent welfare organizations.

Souvenir Sheet

Nativity, Window, Frauenkirche, Esslingen — SP320

1976, Nov. 16   Litho. & Engr.
B537 SP320 50pf + 25pf multi   .90   .75

Christmas 1976.

Wapen von Hamburg, c. 1730 SP321

Historic Ships: 40pf+20pf, Preussen, 5-master, 1902. 50pf+25pf, Bremen, 1929. 70pf+35pf, Freighter Sturmfels, 1972.

1977, Apr. 14   Litho.   Perf. 14
B538 SP321 30pf + 15pf multi   .50   .50
B539 SP321 40pf + 20pf multi   .65   .60
B540 SP321 50pf + 25pf multi   .90   .80
B541 SP321 70pf + 35pf multi   1.25   1.25
      Nos. B538-B541 (4)   3.30   3.15

Surtax was for benefit of young people.

Caraway — SP322

Meadow Flowers: 40pf+20pf, Dandelion. 50pf+25pf, Red clover. 70pf+35pf, Meadow sage.

1977, Oct. 13   Litho.   Perf. 14
B542 SP322 30pf + 15pf multi   .35   .30
B543 SP322 40pf + 20pf multi   .45   .35
B544 SP322 50pf + 25pf multi   .50   .45
B545 SP322 70pf + 35pf multi   1.00   *1.10*
      Nos. B542-B545 (4)   2.30   *2.20*

Surtax was for independent welfare organizations.
See Nos. B553-B556.

Souvenir Sheet

King Caspar Offering Gold, Window, St. Gereon's, Cologne — SP323

1977, Nov. 10
B546 SP323 50pf + 25pf multi   .80   .75

Christmas 1977.

Giant Slalom SP324

Design: No. B548, Steeplechase.

1978   Litho.   Perf. 14
B547 SP324 50pf + 25pf multi   1.40   1.10
B548 SP324 70pf + 35pf multi   3.00   2.75

Issued: #B547, Jan. 12, #B548, Apr. 13. Surtax was for the German Sports Foundation.

Balloon Ascent, Oktoberfest, Munich, 1820 — SP325

Designs: 40pf+20pf, Airship LZ 1, 1900. 50pf+25pf, Bleriot monoplane, 1909. 70pf+35pf, Grade monoplane, 1909.

1978, Apr. 13   Litho.   Perf. 14
B549 SP325 30pf + 15pf multi   .50   .45
B550 SP325 40pf + 20pf multi   .70   .60
B551 SP325 50pf + 25pf multi   .90   .80
B552 SP325 70pf + 35pf multi   1.10   1.10
      Nos. B549-B552 (4)   3.20   2.95

Surtax was for benefit of young people.

Flower Type of 1977

Woodland Flowers: 30pf+15pf, Arum. 40pf+20pf, Weaselsnout. 50pf+25pf, Turk's-cap lily. 70pf+35pf, Liverwort.

1978, Oct. 12   Litho.   Perf. 14
B553 SP322 30pf + 15pf multi   .35   .30
B554 SP322 40pf + 20pf multi   .50   .40
B555 SP322 50pf + 25pf multi   .75   .65
B556 SP322 70pf + 35pf multi   1.00   1.00
      Nos. B553-B556 (4)   2.60   2.35

Surtax was for independent welfare organizations.

Souvenir Sheet

Christ Child, Window, Frauenkirche, Munich — SP326

1978, Nov. 16   Litho.   Perf. 14
B557 SP326 50pf + 25pf multi   .75 .75
Christmas 1978.

Dornier Wal, 1922 SP327

Airplanes: 50pf+25pf, Heinkel HE70, 1932. 60pf+30pf, Junkers W33 Bremen, 1928. 90pf+45pf, Focke-Wulf FW61, 1936.

1979, Apr. 5   Litho.   Perf. 14
B558 SP327 40pf + 20pf multi   .50 .50
B559 SP327 50pf + 25pf multi   .75 .75
B560 SP327 60pf + 30pf multi   .90 .90
B561 SP327 90pf + 45pf multi   1.25 1.25
    Nos. B558-B561 (4)   3.40 3.40
Surtax was for benefit of young people.
See Nos. B570-B573.

Handball SP328

Design: 90pf+45pf, Canoeing.

1979, Apr. 5
B562 SP328 60pf + 30pf multi   .90 .80
B563 SP328 90pf + 45pf multi   1.40 1.25
Surtax was for German Sports Foundation.

Post House Sign, Altheim, Saar, 1754 — SP329

1979, Oct. 11   Litho.   Perf. 14
B564 SP329 60pf + 30pf multi   1.10 1.10
Stamp Day. Surtax was for Foundation of Promotion of Philately and Postal History. Issued in sheet of 10.

Red Beech SP330

Woodland Plants: 50pf+25pf, English oak. 60pf+30pf, Hawthorn. 90pf+45pf, Mountain pine.

1979, Oct. 11   Litho.   Perf. 14
B565 SP330 40pf + 20pf multi   .45 .45
B566 SP330 50pf + 25pf multi   .60 .60
B567 SP330 60pf + 30pf multi   .70 .70
B568 SP330 90pf + 45pf multi   1.25 1.25
    Nos. B565-B568 (4)   3.00 3.00
Surtax was for independent welfare organizations.

Nativity, Medieval Manuscript SP331

1979, Nov. 14   Litho.   Perf. 13½
B569 SP331 60pf + 30pf multi   .90 .90
Christmas 1979.

Aviation Type of 1979

40+20pf, FS 24 Phoenix, 1957. 50+25pf, Lockheed Super Constellation, 1950. 60+30pf, Airbus A300, 1972. 90+45pf, Boeing 747, 1969.

1980, Apr. 10   Litho.   Perf. 14
B570 SP327 40 + 20pf multi   .35 .35
B571 SP327 50 + 25pf multi   .60 .60
B572 SP327 60 + 30pf multi   .80 .80
B573 SP327 90 + 45pf multi   1.25 1.25
    Nos. B570-B573 (4)   3.00 3.00
Surtax was for benefit of young people.

Soccer SP332

Designs: 60pf+30pf, Equestrian. 90pf+45pf, Cross-country skiing.

1980, May 8   Photo.   Perf. 14
B574 SP332 50 + 25pf multi   .50 .45
B575 SP332 60 + 30pf multi   .75 .60
B576 SP332 90 + 45pf multi   1.40 1.40
    Nos. B574-B576 (3)   2.65 2.45
Surtax was for German Sports Foundation.

Ceratocephalus — SP333

Wildflowers: 50pf+25pf, Climbing meadow pea. 60pf+30pf, Corn cockle. 90pf+45pf, Grape hyacinth.

1980, Oct. 9   Litho.   Perf. 14
B577 SP333 40 + 20pf multi   .50 .45
B578 SP333 50 + 25pf multi   .65 .60
B579 SP333 60 + 30pf multi   .75 .75
B580 SP333 90 + 45pf multi   1.25 1.25
    Nos. B577-B580 (4)   3.15 3.05
Surtax was for independent welfare organizations.

Post House Sign, 1754, Altheim, Saar — SP334

1980, Nov. 13   Litho.   Perf. 14
B581 SP334 60 + 30pf multi   .75 .65
49th FIP Congress (Federation Internationale de Philatelie), Essen, Nov. 12-13.

Nativity, Altomunster Manuscript, 12th Century SP335

1980, Nov. 13   Perf. 14x13½
B582 SP335 60 + 30pf multi   1.00 .90
Christmas 1980.

Borda Circle, 1800 — SP336

Historic Optical Instruments: 50pf+25pf, Reflecting telescope, 1770. 60pf+30pf, Binocular microscope, 1860. 90pf+45pf, Octant, 1775.

1981, Apr. 10   Litho.   Perf. 13½
B583 SP336 40 + 20pf multi   .50 .35
B584 SP336 50 + 25pf multi   .90 .75
B585 SP336 60 + 30pf multi   .90 .75
B586 SP336 90 + 45pf multi   1.25 1.25
    Nos. B583-B586 (4)   3.55 3.10
Surtax was for benefit of young people.

Rowing SP337

1981, Apr. 10   Perf. 14
B587 SP337 60 + 30pf shown   .90 .75
B588 SP337 90 + 45pf Gliding   1.40 1.25
Surtax was for the German Sports Foundation.

Water Nut — SP338

Endangered Species: 50pf+25pf, Floating heart. 60pf+30pf, Water gillyflower. 90pf+45pf, Water lobelia.

1981, Oct. 8   Litho.
B589 SP338 40 + 20pf multi   .45 .35
B590 SP338 50 + 25pf multi   .60 .50
B591 SP338 60 + 30pf multi   .75 .75
B592 SP338 90 + 45pf multi   1.40 1.40
    Nos. B589-B592 (4)   3.20 3.00
Surtax was for independent welfare organizations.

Nativity, 19th Cent. Painting SP339

1981, Nov. 12   Litho.
B593 SP339 60 + 30pf multi   1.00 .85
Christmas 1981.

Antique Cars SP340

Designs: 40+20pf, Benz, 1886. 50+25pf, Mercedes, 1913. 60+30pf, Hanomag, 1925. 90+45pf, Opel Olympia, 1937.

1982, Apr. 15   Litho.
B594 SP340 40 + 20pf multi   .50 .45
B595 SP340 50 + 25pf multi   .65 .60
B596 SP340 60 + 30pf multi   .90 .75
B597 SP340 90 + 45pf multi   1.50 1.60
    Nos. B594-B597 (4)   3.55 3.40
Surtax was for benefit of young people.

Jogging SP341

1982, Apr. 15   Litho.
B598 SP341 60 + 30pf shown   .90 .80
B599 SP341 90 + 45pf Archery   1.40 1.25
Surtax was for the German Sports Foundation.

Tea-rose Hybrid — SP342

60+30pf, Floribunda. 80f+40pf, Bourbon rose. 120+60pf, Polyantha hybrid.

1982, Oct. 14   Litho.   Perf. 14
B600 SP342 50 + 20pf multi   .50 .45
B601 SP342 60 + 30pf multi   .65 .60
B602 SP342 80 + 40pf multi   1.10 1.00
B603 SP342 120 + 60pf multi   1.50 1.50
    Nos. B600-B603 (4)   3.75 3.55
Surtax was for independent welfare organizations.

Christmas SP343

1982, Nov. 10
Designs: Nativity, Oak altar, St. Peter's Church, Hamburg, 1380.

B604 SP343 80 + 40pf multi   1.50 1.00

Historic Motorcycles — SP344

Designs: 50pf+20pf, Daimler-Maybach, 1885. 60pf+30pf, NSU, 1901. 80pf+40pf, Megola-Sport, 1922. 120pf+60pf, BMW, 1936.

1983, Apr. 12   Litho.   Perf. 14
B605 SP344 50 + 20pf multi   .50 .45
B606 SP344 60 + 30pf multi   .65 .60
B607 SP344 80 + 40pf multi   1.25 1.10
B608 SP344 120 + 60pf multi   1.75 1.60
    Nos. B605-B608 (4)   4.15 3.75
Surtax was for benefit of young people.

1983 Sports Championships — SP345

80+40pf, Gymnastics Festival. 120+60pf, Modern Pentathlon World Championships.

1983, Apr. 12
B609 SP345 80 + 40pf multi   1.10 .95
B610 SP345 120 + 60pf multi   1.75 1.60

Surtax was for German Sports Foundation.

Swiss Androsace SP346

60+30pf, Krain groundsel. 80+40pf, Fleischer's willow herb. 120+60pf, Alpine sow-thistle.

1983, Oct. 13   Litho.   Perf. 14
B611 SP346 50 + 20pf multi   .50 .45
B612 SP346 60 + 30pf multi   .65 .60
B613 SP346 80 + 40pf multi   1.25 1.10
B614 SP346 120 + 60pf multi   1.75 1.60
   Nos. B611-B614 (4)   4.15 3.75

Surtax was for welfare organizations.

Christmas SP347

1983, Nov. 10   Litho.
B615 SP347 80 + 40pf Carolers   1.60 1.25

Surtax was for free welfare work.

Insects — SP348

1984, Apr. 12   Litho.
Designs: 50pf+20pf, Trichodes apoarius. 60pf+30pf, Vanessa atalanta. 80pf+40pf, Apis mellifera. 120pf+60pf, Chrysotoxum festivum.

B616 SP348 50 + 20pf multi   .60 .50
B617 SP348 60 + 30pf multi   1.10 1.00
B618 SP348 80 + 40pf multi   1.50 1.40
B619 SP348 120 + 60pf multi   2.10 2.10
   Nos. B616-B619 (4)   5.30 5.00

Surtax was for German Youth Stamp Foundation.

Women's Discus SP349

Olympic Sports: 80pf+40pf, Rhythmic gymnastics. 120pf+60pf, Wind surfing.

1984, Apr. 12
B620 SP349 60 + 30pf multi   1.00 .75
B621 SP349 80 + 40pf multi   1.40 1.25
B622 SP349 120 + 60pf multi   2.75 2.50
   Nos. B620-B622 (3)   5.15 4.50

Surtax was for German Sports Foundation.

Orchids SP350

Designs: 50pf+20pf, Aceras anthropophorum. 60pf+30pf, Orchis ustulata. 80pf+40pf, Limodorum abortivum. 120pf+60pf, Dactylorhiza sambucina.

1984, Oct. 18   Litho.   Perf. 14
B623 SP350 50 + 20pf multi   .75 .65
B624 SP350 60 + 30pf multi   .75 .65
B625 SP350 80 + 40pf multi   1.10 1.00
B626 SP350 120 + 60pf multi   2.25 2.25
   Nos. B623-B626 (4)   4.85 4.55

Surtax was for welfare organizations.

Christmas 1984 — SP351

1984, Nov. 8   Litho.
B627 SP351 80pf + 40pf St. Martin   1.40 1.25

Surtax was for welfare organizations.

Bowling SP352

1985, Feb. 21   Photo.
B628 SP352 80pf + 40pf multi   1.25 1.00
B629 SP352 120pf + 60pf Kayaking   2.00 1.75

Surtax was for German Sports Foundation.

Antique Bicycles SP353

50pf+20pf, Draisienne, 1817. 60pf+30pf, NSU Germania, 1886. 80pf+40pf, Cross-frame, 1887. 120pf+60pf, Adler tricycle, 1888.

1985, Apr. 16   Litho.
B630 SP353 50 + 20pf multi   .75 .75
B631 SP353 60 + 30pf multi   .90 .90
B632 SP353 80 + 40pf multi   1.25 1.25
B633 SP353 120 + 60pf multi   2.40 2.40
   Nos. B630-B633 (4)   5.30 5.30

Surtax was for benefit of young people. Each stamp shows the Intl. Youth Year emblem.

MOPHILA '85, Hamburg, Sept. 11-15 SP354

1985, Aug. 13   Litho.   Perf. 14x14½
B634 SP354 60 + 20pf Coachman, horses   2.25 1.90
B635 SP354 80 + 20pf Stagecoach   2.25 1.90
   a.   Pair, #B634-B635   6.00 5.25

Surtax for the benefit of the Philatelic & Postal History Foundation. No. B635a has continuous design.

SP355

Various ornamental borders, medieval prayer book, Prussian State Library, Berlin.

1985, Oct. 15   Litho.   Perf. 14
B636 SP355 50pf + 20pf multi   .70 .60
B637 SP355 60pf + 30pf multi   .85 .75
B638 SP355 80pf + 40pf multi   1.10 1.00
B639 SP355 120pf + 60pf multi   1.90 1.90
   Nos. B636-B639 (4)   4.55 4.25

Surtax for welfare organizations.

Christmas 1985 — SP356

Woodcut: The Birth of Christ, by Hans Baldung Grien (1485-1545), Freiburg Cathedral High Altar.

1985, Nov. 12   Litho.   Perf. 14
B640 SP356 80pf + 40pf multi   1.40 1.40

Surtax for welfare organizations.

European World Sports Championships — SP357

1986, Feb. 13   Litho.   Perf. 14
B641 SP357 80 + 40pf Running   1.50 1.50
B642 SP357 120 + 55pf Bobsledding   2.25 2.25

Surtax for the Natl. Sports Promotion Foundation.

Vocational Training — SP358

1986, Apr. 10
B643 SP358 50 + 25pf Optician   1.00 .90
B644 SP358 60 + 30pf Mason   1.10 1.00
B645 SP358 70 + 35pf Beautician   1.40 1.25
B646 SP358 80 + 40pf Baker   1.90 1.75
   Nos. B643-B646 (4)   5.40 4.90

Surtax for German Youth Stamp Foundation.

Glassware in German Museums — SP359

1986, Oct. 16   Litho.
B647 SP359 50 + 25pf Ornamental flask, c. 300   .70 .60
B648 SP359 60 + 30pf Goblet, c. 1650   .90 .80
B649 SP359 70 + 35pf Imperial eagle tankard, c. 1662   1.00 .90
B650 SP359 80 + 40pf Engraved goblet, c. 1720   1.25 1.10
   Nos. B647-B650 (4)   3.85 3.40

Surtax for public welfare organizations.

Christmas SP360

Adoration of the Infant Jesus, Ortenberg Altarpiece, c. 1430, Hesse Museum, Darmstadt.

1986, Nov. 13   Litho.   Perf. 14
B651 SP360 80 + 40pf multi   1.40 1.25

Surtax for public welfare organizations.

World Championships — SP361

1987, Feb. 12   Litho.
B652 SP361 80 + 40pf Sailing   1.25 1.25
B653 SP361 120 + 55pf Cross-country skiing   2.10 2.10

Surtax for the benefit of the national Sports Promotion Foundation.

Youth in Industry SP362

1987, Apr. 9   Litho.
B654 SP362 50 + 25pf Plumber   1.10 1.10
B655 SP362 60 + 30pf Dental technician   1.40 1.40
B656 SP362 70 + 35pf Butcher   1.50 1.50
B657 SP362 80 + 40pf Bookbinder   2.00 2.00
   Nos. B654-B657 (4)   6.00 6.00

Surtax for youth organizations.

Gold and Silver Artifacts SP363

1987, Oct. 15
B658 SP363 50 + 25pf Roman bracelet, 4th cent.   1.10 1.10
B659 SP363 60 + 30pf Gothic buckle, 6th cent.   1.10 1.10
B660 SP363 70 + 35pf Merovingian disk fibula, 7th cent.   1.10 1.10
B661 SP363 80 + 40pf Purse-shaped reliquary, 8th cent.   1.50 1.50
   Nos. B658-B661 (4)   4.80 4.80

Surtax for welfare organizations sponsoring free museum exhibitions.

Christmas SP364

Illustration from Book of Psalms, 13th cent., Bavarian Natl. Museum: Birth of Christ.

1987, Nov. 6
B662 SP364 80 + 40pf multi   1.50 1.25

Surtax for public welfare organizations.

Sports
SP365

1988, Feb. 18   Litho.
B663 SP365   60 + 30pf Soccer   1.10 1.10
B664 SP365   80 + 40pf Tennis   1.90 1.90
B665 SP365   120 + 55pf Diving   2.25 2.25
   Nos. B663-B665 (3)   5.25 5.25

Surtax for Stiftung Deutsche Sporthilfe, a foundation for the promotion of sports in Germany.

Rock
Stars
SP366

#B666, Buddy Holly (1936-59). #B667, Elvis Presley (1935-77). #B668, Jim Morrison (1943-71). #B669, John Lennon (1940-80).

1988, Apr. 14   Litho.   Perf. 14
B666 SP366   50 + 25pf multi   1.10 1.10
B667 SP366   60 + 30pf multi   2.75 2.75
B668 SP366   70 + 35pf multi   1.50 1.50
B669 SP366   80 + 40pf multi   2.40 2.40
   Nos. B666-B669 (4)   7.75 7.75

Surtax for German Youth Stamp Foundation.

Gold and Rock
Crystal
Reliquary, c.
1200,
Schnutgen
Museum,
Cologne
SP367

Gold and silver artifacts: No. B671, Bust of Charlemagne, 14th cent., Aachen cathedral. No. B672, Crown of Otto III, 10th cent., Essen cathedral. No. B673, Flower bouquet, c. 1620, Schmuck Museum, Pforzheim.

1988, Oct. 13   Litho.
B670 SP367   50 + 25pf multi   .60 .60
B671 SP367   60 + 30pf multi   .95 .95
B672 SP367   70 + 35pf multi   .95 .95
B673 SP367   80 + 40pf multi   1.40 1.40
   Nos. B670-B673 (4)   3.90 3.90

Surtax for welfare organizations.

Christmas
SP368

Illumination from The Gospel Book of Henry the Lion, Helmarshausen, 1188, Prussian Cultural Museum, Bavaria: Adoration of the Magi.

1988, Nov. 10   Litho.
B674 SP368   80 + 40pf multi   1.40 1.25

Surtax for public welfare organizations.

World Championship Sporting Events
Hosted by Germany — SP369

1989, Feb. 9   Litho.
B675 SP369   100pf + 50pf Table
           tennis   2.00 2.00
B676 SP369   140pf + 60pf Gym-
           nastics   3.00 3.00

Surtax for the Natl. Sports Promotion Foundation.

IPHLA Philatelic Literature Exhibition,
Frankfurt, Apr. 19-23 — SP370

1989, Apr. 20   Litho.
B677 SP370   100 + 50pf multi   2.75 2.75

Surtax benefited the Foundation for the Promotion of Philately and Postal History.

Circus
SP371

1989, Apr. 20
B678 SP371   60 + 30pf Ele-
           phants   1.75 1.75
B679 SP371   70 + 30pf Bare-
           back rider   2.10 2.10
B680 SP371   80 + 35pf Clown   3.00 3.00
B681 SP371   100 + 50pf Cara-
           vans, big
           top   4.50 4.50
   Nos. B678-B681 (4)   11.35 11.35

Surtax for natl. youth welfare organizations.

Mounted
Courier of
Thurn and
Taxis, 18th
Cent.
SP372

History of mail carrying: No. B683, Hamburg postal service messenger, 1808. No. B684, Bavarian mail coach, c. 1900.

1989, Oct. 12   Litho.
B682 SP372   60 + 30pf multi   1.10 1.10
B683 SP372   80 + 35pf multi   1.90 1.90
B684 SP372   100 + 50pf multi   2.50 2.50
   Nos. B682-B684 (3)   5.50 5.50

Surtax for the benefit of Free Welfare Work.

Christmas
SP373

Wood carvings by Veit Stoss in St. Lawrence's Church, Nuremburg, 1517-18.

1989, Nov. 16   Litho.
B685 SP373   60 + 30pf Angel   1.25 1.10
B686 SP373   100 + 50pf Adora-
           tion of the
           Kings   1.60 1.50

Surtax for benefit of the Federal Working Assoc. of Free Welfare Work.

Popular
Sports
SP374

1990, Feb. 15   Litho.
B687 SP374   100 + 50pf Handball   2.50 2.50
B688 SP374   140 + 60pf Physical
           fitness   3.00 3.00

Surtax for the Natl. Sports Promotion Foundation.

Max and
Moritz, by
Wilhelm
Busch,
125th
Anniv.
SP375

1990, Apr. 19   Litho.
B689 SP375   60 + 30pf Widow
           Bolte   .80 .80
B690 SP375   70 + 30pf Max   1.25 1.25
B691 SP375   80 + 35pf Max and
           Moritz   1.60 1.60
B692 SP375   100 + 50pf Max and
           Moritz, diff.   2.00 2.00
   Nos. B689-B692 (4)   5.65 5.65

Surcharge for the German Youth Stamp Foundation.

Souvenir Sheet

Dusseldorf '90 — SP376

1990, June 21   Litho.
B693 SP376   Sheet of 6   17.00 19.00
  a.   100pf + 50pf multi   2.75 2.75

Surtax for the Foundation for Promotion of Philately and Postal History. 10th Intl. Philatelic Exhibition of Youth and 11th Natl. Philatelic Exhibition of Youth.

Post and
Telecommunications — SP377

Designs: 60pf+30pf, Postal vehicle, 1900. 80pf+35pf, Telephone exchange, 1890. 100pf+50pf, Post office, 1900.

1990, Sept. 27   Litho.   Perf. 13½x14
B694 SP377   60pf + 30pf multi   .90 .90
B695 SP377   80pf + 35pf multi   1.40 1.40
B696 SP377   100pf + 50pf multi   2.00 2.00
   Nos. B694-B696 (3)   4.30 4.30

Surtax for welfare organizations.

Christmas
SP378

1990, Nov. 6   Litho.   Perf. 14
B697 SP378   50pf + 20pf shown   .90 .90
B698 SP378   60pf + 30pf Smok-
           ing manikin   1.00 1.00
B699 SP378   70pf + 30pf Nut-
           cracker   1.40 1.40
B700 SP378   100pf + 50pf Angel,
           diff.   2.25 2.25
   Nos. B697-B700 (4)   5.55 5.55

Surtax for welfare organizations.

Sports
SP379

1991, Feb. 14   Litho.   Perf. 14
B701 SP379   70 + 30pf Weight
           lifting   1.50 1.50
B702 SP379   100 + 50pf Cycling   1.50 1.50
B703 SP379   140 + 60pf Basket-
           ball   2.25 2.25
B704 SP379   170 + 80pf Wrestling   2.25 2.25
   Nos. B701-B704 (4)   7.50 7.50

Surtax for the Foundation for the Promotion of Sports.

Endangered
Butterflies
SP380

#B705, Alpen gelbling, alpine sulphur. #B706, Grosser eisvogel, Viceroy. #B707, Grosser schillerfalter, purple emperor. #B708, Blauschillernder beuerfalter, bluish copper. #B709, Schwalben-schwanz, swallowtail. #B710, Alpen apollo, alpine apollo. #B711, Hochmoor gelbling, moor sulphur. #B712, Grosser feuerfalter, large copper.

1991, Apr. 9   Litho.   Perf. 13½
B705 SP380   30 + 15pf multi   .50 .50
B706 SP380   50 + 25pf multi   .60 .60
B707 SP380   60 + 30pf multi   1.10 1.10
B708 SP380   70 + 30pf multi   1.25 1.25
B709 SP380   80 + 35pf multi   1.50 1.50
B710 SP380   90 + 45pf multi   2.00 2.00
B711 SP380   100 + 50pf multi   2.50 2.50
B712 SP380   140 + 60pf multi   3.00 3.00
   Nos. B705-B712 (8)   12.45 12.45

Surtax for German Youth Stamp Foundation. See Nos. B728-B732.

Souvenir Sheet

Otto Lilienthal's First Glider Flight,
Cent. — SP381

1991, July 9   Litho.   Perf. 14
B713 SP381   100pf + 50pf multi   3.00 3.00

Surtax benefited Foundation of Philately and Postal History.

Post Offices
SP382

30pf+15pf, Bethel. 60pf+30pf, Budingen postal station. 70pf+30pf, Stralsund. 80pf+35pf, Lauscha. 100pf+50pf, Bonn. 140pf+60pf, Weilburg.

1991, Oct. 10   Litho.   Perf. 14
B714 SP382   30pf + 15pf multi   .50 .50
B715 SP382   60pf + 30pf multi   1.00 1.00
B716 SP382   70pf + 30pf multi   1.25 1.25
B717 SP382   80pf + 35pf multi   1.50 1.50
B718 SP382   100pf + 50pf multi   2.00 2.00
B719 SP382   140pf + 60pf multi   2.50 2.50
   Nos. B714-B719 (6)   8.75 8.75

Christmas
SP383

Paintings by Martin Schongauer (c. 1450-1491): 60pf+30pf, Angel of the Annunciation. 70pf+30pf, The Annunciation. 80pf+35pf, Angel. 100pf+50pf, Nativity.

1991, Nov. 5	Litho.		Perf. 14	
B720	SP383	60pf +30pf multi	1.00	1.00
B721	SP383	70pf +30pf multi	1.25	1.25
B722	SP383	80pf +35pf multi	2.25	2.25
B723	SP383	100pf +50pf multi	3.00	3.00
		Nos. B720-B723 (4)	7.50	7.50

Surtax for Federal Working Association of Free Welfare Work.

Olympic
Sports
SP384

1992, Feb. 6	Litho.		Perf. 14	
B724	SP384	60pf +30pf Women's fencing	.90	.90
B725	SP384	80pf +40pf Rowing coxed eights	1.10	1.10
B726	SP384	100pf +50pf Dressage	2.25	2.25
B727	SP384	170pf +80pf Men's slalom skiing	3.50	3.50
		Nos. B724-B727 (4)	7.75	7.75

Endangered Butterfly Type of 1991

60+30pf, Purpurbar. 70+30pf, Labkraut schwarmer. 80+40pf, Silbermonch. 100+50pf, Schwarzer bar. 170+80pf, Rauschbeeren-fleckenspanner.

1992, Apr. 9	Litho.		Perf. 13½	
B728	SP380	60pf +30pf multi	1.50	1.50
B729	SP380	70pf +30pf multi	1.75	1.75
B730	SP380	80pf +40pf multi	2.25	2.25
B731	SP380	100pf +50pf multi	2.50	2.50
B732	SP380	170pf +80pf multi	2.75	2.75
		Nos. B728-B732 (5)	10.75	10.75

Surtax for German Youth Stamp Foundation.

Preservation
of Tropical
Rain Forests
SP385

1992, June 11	Litho.		Perf. 13	
B733	SP385	100pf +50pf multi	1.75	1.75

Antique Clocks
SP386

Antique clocks: 60pf+30pf, Turret, c. 1400. 70pf+30pf, Astronomical geographical mantelpiece, 1738. 80pf+40pf, Fluted, c. 1790. 100fpf+50pf, Figurine, c. 1580. 170pf+80pf, Table, c. 1550.

1992, Oct. 15	Litho.		Perf. 14	
B734	SP386	60pf +30pf multi	1.10	1.10
B735	SP386	70pf +30pf multi	1.40	1.40
B736	SP386	80pf +40pf multi	1.40	1.40
B737	SP386	100pf +50pf multi	1.75	1.75
B738	SP386	170pf +80pf multi	2.50	2.50
		Nos. B734-B738 (5)	8.15	8.15

Surtax for welfare organizations.

Christmas
SP387

Carvings from Church of St. Anne, Annaberg-Buchholz, by Franz Maidburg: 60pf + 30pf, Adoration of the Magi. 100pf + 50pf, The Nativity.

1992, Nov. 5				
B739	SP387	60pf +30pf multi	1.00	.90
B740	SP387	100pf +50pf multi	1.75	1.50

Surtax for benefit of free welfare work.

Sports
SP388

Designs: 60pf+30pf, Olympic ski jump, Garmisch-Partenkirchen. 80pf+40pf, Olympic Park, Munich. 100pf+50pf, Olympic Stadium, Berlin. 170pf+80pf, Olympic harbor, Kiel.

1993, Feb. 11	Litho.		Perf. 13½	
B741	SP388	60pf +30pf multi	1.50	1.50
B742	SP388	80pf +40pf multi	2.00	2.00
B743	SP388	100pf +50pf multi	2.50	2.50
B744	SP388	170pf +80pf multi	3.00	3.00
		Nos. B741-B744 (4)	9.00	9.00

Surtax for Natl. Sports Promotion Foundation.

Beetles
SP389

Designs: No. B745, Alpenbock (Alpine sawyer). No. B746, Rosenkafer (rose chafer). No. B747, Hirschkafer (stag beetle). No. B748, Sandlaufkafer (tiger beetle). 200pf + 50pf, Maikafer (cockchafer).

1993, Apr. 15	Litho.		Perf. 14	
B745	SP389	80pf +40pf multi	1.60	1.60
B746	SP389	80pf +40pf multi	1.60	1.60
B747	SP389	100pf +50pf multi	2.00	2.00
B748	SP389	100pf +50pf multi	2.00	2.00
B749	SP389	200pf +50pf multi	3.25	3.25
		Nos. B745-B749 (5)	10.45	10.45

Surtax for German Youth Stamp Foundation.

Stamp
Day — SP390

1993, Sept. 16	Litho.		Perf. 13½x14	
B750	SP390	100pf +50pf multi	1.60	1.60

Surtax for the Foundation for Promotion of Philately and Postal History.

Traditional
Costumes
SP391

Costumes from: No. B751, Rugen, Mecklenburg, Western Pomerania. No. B752, Fohr, Schleswig-Holstein. No. B753, Schwalm, Hesse. No. B754, Oberndorf, Bavaria. 200pf + 40pf, Ernstroda, Thuringia.

1993, Oct. 14			Perf. 14	
B751	SP391	80pf +40pf multi	1.50	1.50
B752	SP391	80pf +40pf multi	1.50	1.50
B753	SP391	100pf +50pf multi	1.75	1.75
B754	SP391	100pf +50pf multi	1.75	1.75
B755	SP391	200pf +40pf multi	3.00	3.00
		Nos. B751-B755 (5)	9.50	9.50

Surtax for welfare organizations. See Nos. B768-B772.

Christmas
SP392

Wings of high altar in choir of Blaubeuren Monastery: 80pf+40pf, Adoraration of Magi. 100pf+50pf, Nativity.

1993, Nov. 10	Litho.		Perf. 14	
B756	SP392	80pf +40pf multi	1.00	.90
B757	SP392	100pf +50pf multi	1.90	1.75

Surtax for welfare organizations.

Figure Skating
SP393

Sports: #B759, Olympic Flame. #B760, Soccer ball, World Cup Trophy. 200pf+80pf, Skiier.

1994, Feb. 10	Litho.		Perf. 14x13½	
B758	SP393	80pf +40pf multi	1.40	1.40
B759	SP393	100pf +50pf multi	1.60	1.60
B760	SP393	100pf +50pf multi	1.60	1.60
B761	SP393	200pf +80pf multi	2.75	2.75
		Nos. B758-B761 (4)	7.35	7.35

1994 Winter Olympics, Lillehammer (#B758). Intl. Olympic Committee, Cent. (#B759). 1994 World Cup Soccer Championships, US (#B760). 1994 Paralympics, Lillehammer (#B761).

Heinrich Hoffmann (1809-94), Physician, Writer of Children's Books
SP394

Characters from "Slovenly Peter:" No. B762, Little Pauline. No. B763, Johnny Head-in-the-air. No. B764, Slovenly Peter. No. B765, Naughty Frederick. 200pf+80pf, The Fidget.

1994, Apr. 14	Litho.		Perf. 13½	
B762	SP394	80pf +40pf multi	1.25	1.25
B763	SP394	80pf +40pf multi	1.25	1.25
B764	SP394	100pf +50pf multi	1.50	1.50
B765	SP394	100pf +50pf multi	1.50	1.50
B766	SP394	200pf +80pf multi	2.75	2.75
		Nos. B762-B766 (5)	8.25	8.25

Surtax for German Youth Stamp Foundation.

Environmental
Protection
SP395

1994, June 16	Litho.		Perf. 13	
B767	SP395	100pf +50pf blk & grn	1.60	1.60

Traditional Costume Type 1993

Costumes from: No. B768, Buckeburg. No. B769, Halle an der Saale. No. B770, Hoyerswerda. No. B771, Minden. 200pf+70pf, Betzingen.

1994, Oct. 13	Litho.		Perf. 13½	
B768	SP391	80pf +40pf multi	1.25	1.25
B769	SP391	80pf +40pf multi	1.25	1.25
B770	SP391	100pf +50pf multi	1.75	1.75
B771	SP391	100pf +50pf multi	1.75	1.75
B772	SP391	200pf +70pf multi	2.75	2.75
		Nos. B768-B772 (5)	8.75	8.75

Surtax for welfare organizations.

Christmas
SP396

Paintings by Hans Memling: 80pf+40pf, Adoration of the Magi. 100pf+50pf, Nativity Scene.

1994, Nov. 9	Litho.		Perf. 13½	
B773	SP396	80pf +40pf multi	1.25	1.10
B774	SP396	100pf +50pf multi	1.75	1.60

Sports
SP397

1995, Feb. 9	Photo.		Perf. 13½	
B775	SP397	80pf +40pf Rowing	1.25	1.25
B776	SP397	100pf +50pf Gymnastics	1.50	1.50
B777	SP397	100pf +50pf Boxing	1.50	1.50
B778	SP397	200pf +80pf Volleyball	3.00	3.00
		Nos. B775-B778 (4)	7.25	7.25

World Kayaking Championships, Duisburg (#B775). Intl. Gymnastics Festival, Berlin (#B776). World Amateur Boxing Championships, Berlin (#B777). Volleyball, cent. (#B778).

Dogs
SP398

#B779, Munsterlander. #B780, Schnauzer. #B781, German shepherd. #B782, Wire haired dachshund. 200pf+80pf, Wolf spitz.

1995, June 8	Litho.		Perf. 13½	
B779	SP398	80pf +40pf multi	1.25	1.25
B780	SP398	80pf +40pf multi	1.25	1.25
B781	SP398	100pf +50pf multi	1.60	1.60
B782	SP398	100pf +50pf multi	1.60	1.60
B783	SP398	200pf +80pf multi	2.75	2.75
		Nos. B779-B783 (5)	8.45	8.45

Surtax for benefit of German Youth Stamp Foundation.
See Nos. B792-B796.

Stamp
Day — SP399

1995, Sept. 6 Litho. *Perf. 13*
B784 SP399 200pf +100pf multi 3.00 3.00
Surtax for Foundation for Promotion of Philately and Postal History.

Farmhouses — SP400

#B785, Eifel region. #B786, Saxony. #B787, Lower Germany. #B788, Upper Bavaria. 200pf+70pf, Mecklenburg.

1995, Oct. 12 Litho. *Perf. 14*
B785 SP400 80pf +40pf multi 1.25 1.25
B786 SP400 80pf +40pf multi 1.25 1.25
B787 SP400 100pf +50pf multi 1.60 1.60
B788 SP400 100pf +50pf multi 1.60 1.60
B789 SP400 200pf +70pf multi 2.75 2.75
Nos. B785-B789 (5) 8.45 8.45
Surtax for welfare organizations.
See Nos. B802-B806.

Christmas
SP401

Stained glass windows, Augsburg Cathedral: 80pf+40pf, Annunciation. 100pf+50pf, Nativity.

1995, Nov. 9 Litho. *Perf. 14*
B790 SP401 80pf +40pf multi 1.25 1.10
B791 SP401 100pf +50pf multi 1.75 1.60
Surtax for welfare organizations.

Dog Type of 1995
#B792, Borzoi. #B793, Chow chow. #B794, St. Bernard. #B795, Collie. 200pf+80pf, Briard.

1996, Feb. 8 Litho. *Perf. 13½*
B792 SP398 80pf +40pf multi 1.25 1.25
B793 SP398 80pf +40pf multi 1.25 1.25
B794 SP398 100pf +50pf multi 1.60 1.60
B795 SP398 100pf +50pf multi 1.60 1.60
B796 SP398 200pf +80pf multi 2.50 2.50
Nos. B792-B796 (5) 8.20 8.20
Surtax for benefit of German Youth Stamp Foundation.

Modern
Olympic
Games, Cent.
SP402

Olympic champions: 80pf+40pf, Carl Schuhmann (1869-1946), pommel horse. No. B798, Annie Hübler Horn (1885-1976), pairs figure skating. No. B799, Josef Neckermann (1912-92), equestrian. 200pf+80pf, Alfred Flatow (1869-1945), Gustav Felix Flatow (1875-1945), gymnastics.

1996, June 13 Photo. *Perf. 13½*
B797 SP402 80pf +40pf multi 1.25 1.25
B798 SP402 100pf +50pf multi 1.60 1.60
B799 SP402 100pf +50pf multi 1.60 1.60
B800 SP402 200pf +80pf multi 2.75 2.75
Nos. B797-B800 (4) 7.20 7.20

Preservation of Tropical
Habitats — SP403

1996, July 18 Photo. *Perf. 14*
B801 SP403 100pf +50pf multi 1.50 1.50

Farmhouse Type of 1995
Location: No. B802, Spree Forest. No. B803, Thuringia. No. B804, Black Forest. No. B805, Westphalia. 200pf+70pf, Schleswig-Holstein.

1996, Oct. 9 Litho. *Perf. 14*
B802 SP400 80pf +40pf multi 1.25 1.25
B803 SP400 80pf +40pf multi 1.25 1.25
B804 SP400 100pf +50pf multi 1.50 1.50
B805 SP400 100pf +50pf multi 1.50 1.50
B806 SP400 200pf +70pf multi 2.50 2.50
Nos. B802-B806 (5) 8.00 8.00

Christmas
SP404

Illuminated pages from Henry II's book of pericopes (Gospels), 11th cent.: 80pf+40pf, Adoration of the Magi. 100pf+50pf, Nativity.

1996, Nov. 14 Litho. *Perf. 14*
B807 SP404 80pf +40pf multi 1.25 1.10
B808 SP404 100pf +50pf multi 1.50 1.40
Surtax for welfare organizations.

Sports
SP405

1997, Feb. 4 Litho. *Perf. 14x13½*
B809 SP405 80pf +40pf Aerobics 1.25 1.25
B810 SP405 100pf +50pf Inline skating 1.60 1.60
B811 SP405 100pf +50pf Streetball 1.60 1.60
B812 SP405 200pf +80pf Free climbing 2.50 2.50
Nos. B809-B812 (4) 6.95 6.95

Horses
SP406

1997, June 9 Litho. *Perf. 14*
B813 SP406 80pf + 40pf Rheno-German draft 1.25 1.25
B814 SP406 80pf + 40pf Shetland pony 1.25 1.25
B815 SP406 100pf + 50pf Friesian 1.50 1.50
B816 SP406 100pf + 50pf Haflinger 1.50 1.50
B817 SP406 200pf + 80pf Hanoverian 3.00 3.00
Nos. B813-B817 (5) 8.50 8.50

Arms Type of 1992 Redrawn and
Inscribed
"Hochwasserhilfe 1997" and
"DEUTSCHLAND"

1997, Aug. 19 Litho. *Perf. 13½*
B818 A739 110pf +90pf like
#1702 2.00 2.00

Souvenir Sheet

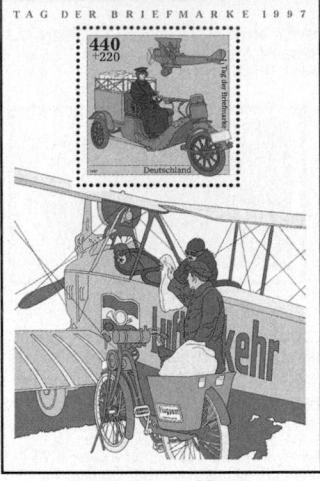

Stamp Day — SP407

1997, Sept. 17 Litho. *Perf. 14*
B819 SP407 440pf +220pf multi 6.75 6.75

Mills — SP408

Designs: 100pf+50pf, Black Forest. No. B821, Hesse. No. B822, Windmill, lower Rhine. No. B823, Scoop windmill, Schleswig-Holstein. 220pf+80pf, Dutch windmill.

1997, Oct. 9 Litho. *Perf. 13½x14*
Background Color
B820 SP408 100pf +50pf grn 1.75 1.75
B821 SP409 110pf +50pf brn 1.75 1.75
B822 SP408 110pf +50pf blue 1.75 1.75
B823 SP408 110pf +50pf yel 1.75 1.75
B824 SP408 220pf +80pf pink 3.00 3.00
Nos. B820-B824 (5) 10.00 10.00

Christmas
SP409

1997, Nov. 6 Litho. *Perf. 14*
B825 SP409 100pf +50pf Magi 1.40 1.40
B826 SP409 110pf +50pf Nativity 1.60 1.50
Surtax for Federal Assoc. of Free Welfare Work in Bonn.

Sports
SP410

1998 Sporting events: 100pf+50pf, World Cup Soccer Championships, France. No. B828, Winter Olympic Games, Nagano. No. B829, Rowing Championships, Cologne. 300pf+100pf, Winter Paralympics, Nagano.

1998, Feb. 5 Photo. *Perf. 14*
B827 SP410 100pf +50pf multi 1.50 1.50
B828 SP410 110pf +50pf multi 1.75 1.75
B829 SP410 110pf +50pf multi 1.75 1.75

B830 SP410 300pf +100pf multi 4.25 4.25
Nos. B827-B830 (4) 9.25 9.25

Environmental Protection — SP411

1998, May 7 Litho. *Perf. 14*
B831 SP411 110pf +50pf multi 1.60 1.60

Cartoon
Figures
SP412

#B832, Mouse, Little Yellow Duck, Elephant. #833, Sandman. #834, Maja the Bee. #835, Captain Bluebear. #836, Pumuckl.

1998, June 10 Litho. *Perf. 14*
B832 SP412 100pf +50pf multi 1.50 1.50
B833 SP412 100pf +50pf multi 1.50 1.50
B834 SP412 110pf +50pf multi 1.75 1.75
B835 SP412 110pf +50pf multi 1.75 1.75
B836 SP412 220pf +50pf multi 3.50 3.50
Nos. B832-B836 (5) 10.00 10.00
Surtax for the German Youth Stamp Foundation.

Welfare
Stamps
SP413

Birds: 100pf+50pf, Hen-harrier. No. B838, Great bustard. No. B839, White-eyed duck. No. B840, Sedge warbler. 220pf+80pf, Woodchat shrike.

1998, Oct. 8 Litho. *Perf. 14*
Background Colors
B837 SP413 100pf +50pf tan 1.50 1.50
B838 SP413 110pf +50pf gray grn 1.75 1.75
B839 SP413 110pf +50pf gray blue 1.75 1.75
B840 SP413 110pf +50pf blue grn 1.75 1.75
B841 SP413 220pf +80pf lilac 3.50 3.50
Nos. B837-B841 (5) 10.25 10.25

Christmas
SP414

1998, Nov. 12
B842 SP414 100pf +50pf Shepherds 1.50 1.40
B843 SP414 110pf +50pf Holy Child 1.75 1.60

Racing
Sports
SP415

1999, Feb. 18 Photo. *Perf. 14*
B844 SP415 100pf +50pf Bicycles 1.75 1.75
B845 SP415 110pf +50pf Cars 1.75 1.75

B846 SP415 110pf +50pf Hor-
ses 1.75 1.75
B847 SP415 300pf +100pf
Motorcycles 3.75 3.75
Nos. B844-B847 (4) 9.00 9.00

**Declaration of Human Rights Type
of 1998**
Inscribed "KOSOVO-HILFE 1999"

1999, Apr. 27 Litho. Perf. 14
B848 A958 110pf +100pf multi 2.25 2.25

Sutax for aid to refugees from Kosovo.

Souvenir Sheet

IBRA '99, Intl. Stamp Exhibition,
Nuremberg — SP416

Design: Bavaria #1 & Saxony #1.

1999, Apr. 27 Perf. 13½
B849 SP416 300pf +110pf multi 4.50 4.50

German postage stamps, 150th anniv.

Cartoons
SP417

#B850, The Little Polar Bear. #B851, Rudi
the Crow. #B852, Mecki (hedgehog). #B853,
Twipsy, mascot of Expo 2000, Hanover.
220pf+80pf, Tabaluga (green dragon).

1999, June 10 Litho. Perf. 13¾
B850 SP417 100pf +50pf multi 1.75 1.75
B851 SP417 100pf +50pf multi 1.75 1.75
B852 SP417 110pf +50pf multi 2.00 2.00
B853 SP417 110pf +50pf multi 2.00 2.00
B854 SP417 220pf +80pf multi 2.50 2.50
Nos. B850-B854 (5) 10.00 10.00

Surtax for the German Youth Stamp
Foundation.

The Cosmos — SP418

#B855, Andromeda galaxy. #B856, Cygnus
constellation. #B857, X-ray image of exploding
star. #B858, Collision of Comet Shoemaker-
Levy 9 and Jupiter. 300pf + 100pf, Gamma ray
image of entire sky, satellite.

1999, Oct. 14 Litho. Perf. 14
B855 SP418 100pf +50pf multi 1.50 1.50
B856 SP418 100pf +50pf multi 1.50 1.50
B857 SP418 110pf +50pf multi 1.75 1.75
B858 SP418 110pf +50pf multi 1.75 1.75
B859 SP418 300pf +100pf
multi 3.50 3.50
Nos. B855-B859 (5) 10.00 10.00

Surtax for the Federal Association of Free
Welfare Work. Nos. B858-B859 have a
holographic image. Soaking in water may
affect hologram.

Christmas
SP419

1999, Nov. 4 Litho. Perf. 13¾
B860 SP419 100pf +50pf Angel 1.60 1.40
B861 SP419 110pf +50pf Manger 1.75 1.50

Sports — SP420

Ancient art and: 100pf + 50pf, Swimmer.
No. B863, Gymnast. No. B864, Sprinters.
300pf + 100pf; Hands.

2000, Feb. 17 Litho. Perf. 13¾x14
B862 SP420 100pf + 50pf multi 1.60 1.60
B863 SP420 110pf + 50pf multi 1.75 1.75
B864 SP420 110pf + 50pf multi 1.75 1.75
B865 SP420 300pf + 100pf multi 4.25 4.25
Nos. B862-B865 (4) 9.35 9.35

Surtax was for German Sports Federation.

Environmental Protection — SP421

2000, May 12 Litho. Perf. 13¾x14
B866 SP421 110pf +50pf multi 1.75 1.75

Expo 2000, Hanover — SP422

#B867, 4 backpackers. #B868, Crowd.
#B869, Map of Africa, words "see, come, hear,
feel." #B870, Eye. #B871, Abstract with Chinese characters. #B872, Abstract.

2000, June 8 Litho. Perf. 13¾x14
B867 SP422 100pf +50pf multi 1.50 1.50
B868 SP422 100pf +50pf multi 1.50 1.50
B869 SP422 110pf +50pf multi 1.60 1.60
B870 SP422 110pf +50pf multi 1.60 1.60
B871 SP422 110pf +50pf multi 1.60 1.60
B872 SP422 300pf +100pf
multi 4.25 4.25
Nos. B867-B872 (6) 12.05 12.05

Surtax for German Youth Stamp Foundation.

Actors and Actresses — SP423

#B873, Curd Jürgens (1915-82). #B874, Lilli
Palmer (1914-86). #B875, Heinz Rühmann
(1902-94). #B876, Romy Schneider (1938-82).
#B877, Gert Fröbe (1913-88).

2000, Oct. 12 Litho. Perf. 14
B873 SP423 100pf +50pf multi 1.50 1.50
B874 SP423 100pf +50pf multi 1.50 1.50
B875 SP423 110pf +50pf multi 1.75 1.75
B876 SP423 110pf +50pf multi 1.75 1.75

B877 SP423 300pf +100pf
multi 4.00 4.00
Nos. B873-B877 (5) 10.50 10.50

Surtax was for Federal Association of Welfare Work.

Christmas
SP424

Designs: 100pf+50pf, Birth of Christ, by
Conrad von Soest. 110pf+50pf, Nativity scene.

2000, Nov. 9 Litho. Perf. 13¾
B878 SP424 100pf +50pf multi 1.50 1.40
B879 SP424 110pf +50pf multi 1.75 1.60

Surtax for the Federal Association of Voluntary Welfare Work.
See Spain Nos. 3071-3072.

Sports — SP425

Designs: 100pf+50pf, Sports for schools.
No. B881, Sports for the disabled. No. B882,
Popular and leisure sports. 300pf+100pf,
Sports for senior citizens.

2001, Feb. 8 Litho. Perf. 13¾x14
B880 SP425 100pf +50pf multi 1.90 1.90
B881 SP425 110pf +50pf multi 2.00 2.00
B882 SP425 110pf +50pf multi 2.00 2.00
B883 SP425 300pf +100pf
multi 4.75 4.75
Nos. B880-B883 (4) 10.65 10.65

Surtax for German Sports Federation.

Wuppertal Suspension
Railway — SP426

2001, Mar. 8
B884 SP426 110pf +50pf multi 2.00 2.00

Surtax for the Foundation for Promotion of
Philately and Postal History.

Characters
from
Children's
Stories
SP427

Designs: No. B885, Pinocchio. No. B886,
Pippi Longstockings. No. B887, Jim Knopf.
No. B888, Heidi. 300pf +100pf, Tom Sawyer
and Huckleberry Finn.

2001, June 13 Litho. Perf. 13¾
B885 SP427 100pf +50pf multi 1.90 1.90
B886 SP427 100pf +50pf multi 1.90 1.90
B887 SP427 110pf +50pf multi 2.00 2.00
B888 SP427 110pf +50pf multi 2.00 2.00
B889 SP427 300pf +100pf
multi 4.75 4.75
Nos. B885-B889 (5) 12.55 12.55

Surtax for the German Youth Stamp
Foundation.

Film
Stars
SP428

Designs: No. B890, Marilyn Monroe. No.
B891, Charlie Chaplin. No. B892, Film reel.
No. B893, Greta Garbo. 300pf+100pf, Jean
Gabin.

2001, Oct. 11 Litho. Perf. 14
B890 SP428 100pf +50pf multi 1.90 1.90
  a. Perf. 13x13¼x13x13¼ 1.90 1.90
B891 SP428 100pf +50pf multi 1.90 1.90
  a. Perf. 13½x13¼ 1.90 1.90
B892 SP428 110pf +50pf multi 2.00 2.00
  a. Perf. 13½x13¼ 2.00 2.00
B893 SP428 110pf +50pf multi 2.00 2.00
  a. Perf. 13x13¼ 2.00 2.00
B894 SP428 300pf +100pf
multi 4.75 4.75
  a. Perf. 13x13¼ 4.75 4.75
  b. Booklet pane, #B890a-
B894a 11.50 11.50
  Booklet, #B894b 11.50
Nos. B890-B894 (5) 12.55 12.55

Surtax for the Federal Association of Voluntary Welfare Work.

A stamp picturing Audrey Hepburn
originally was to have been included in
this set but was withdrawn. It was never
officially issued, nor were any examples
sold over post office counters. However,
30 examples from the original printing
were not recovered and destroyed as
ordered by the post office. Four of the
stamps have been found used on German mail.

Christmas
SP429

Designs: 100pf+50pf, Madonna and Child,
by Alfredo Roldán. 110pf+50pf, Adoration of
the Shepherds, by José de Ribera.

2001, Nov. 8 Litho. Perf. 13¼
B895 SP429 100pf +50pf multi 1.90 1.90
B896 SP429 110pf +50pf multi 2.00 2.00
  a. Souvenir sheet (see footnote) 5.50 5.50

No. B896a contains Nos. B895-B896 and
lithographed and perf. 13¼ examples of Spain
Nos. 3123-3124. No. B896a sold for 4.45m.
See Spain Nos. 3123-3124.

Intl. Year of Mountains — SP430

2002, Jan. 10 Litho. Perf. 14
B897 SP430 56c +26c multi 2.00 2.00

Winter Olympic Sports — SP431

Designs: 51c+26c, Biathlon. No. B899, 56c+26c, Ski jumping. No. B900, 56c+26c, Speed skating. 153c+51c, Luge.

2002, Feb. 7   Litho.   Perf. 13¾x14

B898	SP431	51c +26c multi	1.90	1.90
B899	SP431	56c +26c multi	2.00	2.00
B900	SP431	56c +26c multi	2.00	2.00
B901	SP431	153c +51c multi	4.75	4.75
a.	Booklet pane, #B898-B901		10.50	10.50
	Booklet, #B901a		10.50	
	Nos. B898-B901 (4)		10.65	10.65

Surtax for German Sports Promotion Foundation.

Toys and Games SP432

Designs: No. B902, Chess pieces. No. B903, Toy truck. No. B904, Doll. No. B905, Teddy bear. 153c+51c, Toy train.

2002, June 6   Litho.   Perf. 13¾

B902	SP432	51c +26c multi	1.90	1.90
B903	SP432	51c +26c multi	1.90	1.90
B904	SP432	56c +26c multi	2.00	2.00
B905	SP432	56c +26c multi	2.00	2.00
B906	SP432	153c +51c multi	4.75	4.75
	Nos. B902-B906 (5)		12.55	12.55

Surtax for German Youth Stamp Foundation.

Environmental Protection Type of 1998 Inscribed "Hochwasserhilfe 2002"

2002, Aug. 30   Litho.   Perf. 13x13½

B907	SP411	56c +44c multi	2.40	2.40

Surtax for flood victims relief.

Christmas SP433

Details from paintings by Rogier van der Weyden: 51c+26c, Annunciation to the Virgin. 56c+26c, Miraflores Altarpiece.

2002, Nov. 7   Litho.   Perf. 13¾

B908	SP433	51c +26c multi	2.00	2.00
B909	SP433	56c +26c multi	2.00	2.00

Surtax for Federal Working Party on Independent Welfare.

Automobiles — SP434

Designs: 45c+20c, 1960 BMW Isetta 300. No. B911, 55c+25c, 1961 VEB Sachsenring Trabant P50. No. B912, 55c+25c, 1949 Volkswagen Beetle. No. B913, 55c+25c, 1954 Mercedes-Benz 300 SL. 144c+56c, 1957 Borgward Isabella Coupe.

2002, Dec. 5   Litho.   Perf. 14

B910	SP434	45c +20c multi	1.60	1.60
B911	SP434	55c +25c multi	1.90	1.90
B912	SP434	55c +25c multi	1.90	1.90
B913	SP434	55c +25c multi	1.90	1.90
B914	SP434	144c +56c multi	5.00	5.00
	Nos. B910-B914 (5)		12.30	12.30

Surtax for Federal Working Party on Independent Welfare.

2006 World Cup Soccer Championships, Germany — SP435

Designs: 45c+20c, Player kicking ball. No. B916, Player heading ball. No. B917, Four children playing soccer. No. B918, Fan celebrating. 144c+56c, Child and adult playing soccer.

2003, Mar. 6   Litho.   Perf. 13x13½

B915	SP435	45c +20c multi	1.40	1.40
B916	SP435	55c +25c multi	1.75	1.75
B917	SP435	55c +25c multi	1.75	1.75
B918	SP435	55c +25c multi	1.75	1.75
B919	SP435	144c +56c multi	4.50	4.50
	Nos. B915-B919 (5)		11.15	11.15

Surtax for German Sports Promotion Foundation.

First East-to-West Non-Stop Transatlantic Flight, 75th Anniv. SP436

2003, Apr. 10   Perf. 13¾

B920	SP436	144c +56c multi	4.25	4.25

Surtax for German Organization for the Enhancement of Philately and Postal History.

June 17, 1953 Uprising in East Germany, 50th Anniv. SP437

2003, June 12   Photo.   Perf. 14x14¼

B921	SP437	55c +25c multi	1.90	1.90

Souvenir Sheet

Father and Son, Cartoons by Ehrich Ohser — SP438

No. B922: a, Father and son running in same direction. b, Father and son falling. c, Son running, father seated. d, Father and son running in different directions. e, Father and son with arms extended.

2003, July 10   Litho.   Perf. 13x13½

B922	SP438	Sheet of 5	11.50	11.50
a.		45c +20c multi	1.50	1.50
b.-d.		55c +25c any single	1.75	1.75
e.		144c +56c multi	4.50	4.50

Automobile Type of 2002

Designs: 45c+20c, Wartburg 311 Coupe. No. B924, Olympia Rekord P1. No. B925, 356 B Coupe. No. B926, 55c+25c, Taunus 17 M P3. 144c+56c, Auto Union 1000 S.

2003, Oct. 9   Litho.   Perf. 14

B923	SP434	45c +20c multi	1.50	1.50
B924	SP434	55c +25c multi	1.90	1.90
B925	SP434	55c +25c multi	1.90	1.90
B926	SP434	55c +25c multi	1.90	1.90
B927	SP434	144c +56c multi	4.50	4.50
	Nos. B923-B927 (5)		11.70	11.70

Christmas SP439

Designs: 45c+20c, Adoration of the Shepherds. 55c+25c, Holy Family.

2003, Nov. 13   Litho.   Perf. 13¾

B928	SP439	45c +20c multi	1.50	1.50
B929	SP439	55c +25c multi	1.90	1.90

Wind Energy SP440

2004, Jan. 8   Litho.   Perf. 13¾

B930	SP440	55c +25c multi	2.10	2.10

Sporting Events and Anniversaries — SP441

Designs: 45c+20c, European Soccer Championships, June 12-July 4, 2004. No. B932, Summer Olympic Games, Athens, Greece. No. B933, Paralympics, Athens, Greece. No. B934, First German World Cup Championship, 50th anniv. 144c+56c, FIFA (Fédération Internationale de Football Association), cent.

2004, Feb. 5   Litho.   Perf. 13x13½

B931	SP441	45c +20c multi	1.75	1.75
B932	SP441	55c +25c multi	2.10	2.10
B933	SP441	55c +25c multi	2.10	2.10
B934	SP441	55c +25c multi	2.10	2.10
B935	SP441	144c +56c multi	5.25	5.25
	Nos. B931-B935 (5)		13.30	13.30

Cats — SP442

Designs: 45c+20c, Two cats playing with ball of string. No. B937, Cat, two kittens playing with ball. No. B938, Kitten on cat. No. B939, Cat licking paw. 144c+56c, Two cats sleeping.

2004, June 3   Litho.   Perf. 13¾x14

B936	SP442	45c +20c multi	1.60	1.60
B937	SP442	55c +25c multi	1.90	1.90
B938	SP442	55c +25c multi	1.90	1.90
B939	SP442	55c +25c multi	1.90	1.90
B940	SP442	144c +56c multi	4.75	4.75
	Nos. B936-B940 (5)		12.05	12.05

Landscapes — SP443

Designs: 45c+20c, Iceberg and pack ice. No. B942, Mountains and clouds. No. B943, Islands. No. B944, Sand dunes. 144c+56c, Tree tops.

2004, Oct. 7   Litho.   Perf. 14

B941	SP443	45c +20c multi	1.60	1.60
B942	SP443	55c +25c multi	2.00	2.00
B943	SP443	55c +25c multi	2.00	2.00
B944	SP443	55c +25c multi	2.00	2.00
B945	SP443	144c +56c multi	5.00	5.00
	Nos. B941-B945 (5)		12.60	12.60

Christmas SP444

Paintings by Peter Paul Rubens: 45c+20c, The Flight Into Egypt. 55c+25c, Adoration of the Magi.

2004, Nov. 4   Perf. 13¾

B946	SP444	45c +20c multi	1.75	1.75
B947	SP444	55c +25c multi	2.10	2.10

See Belgium Nos. 2051-2053.

Sports — SP445

Designs: 45c+20c, Soccer fans, mascot of 2006 World Cup Soccer Championships. No. B949, Soccer players, soccer ball globe. No. B950, Gymnasts, Brandenburg Gate, Berlin. No. B951, Ski jumper and ski jump. 144c+56c, Fencers, Leipzig Arena.

2005, Feb. 10   Litho.   Perf. 13¾x14

B948	SP445	45c +20c multi	1.75	1.75
B949	SP445	55c +25c multi	2.10	2.10
B950	SP445	55c +25c multi	2.10	2.10
B951	SP445	55c +25c multi	2.10	2.10
B952	SP445	144c +56c multi	5.25	5.25
	Nos. B948-B952 (5)		13.30	13.30

2006 World Cup Soccer Championships (Nos. B948-B949), Intl. Gymnastics Exhibition, Berlin (No. B950), Nordic Skiing World Championships, Oberstdorf (No. B951), Fencing World Championships, Leipzig (No. B952).

Stamp Day SP446

2005, May 12   Litho.   Perf. 14

B953	SP446	55c +25c multi	2.10	2.10

Sailing Ships — SP447

Designs: 45c+20c, Greif. No. B955, Rickmer Rickmers. No. B956, Passat. No. B957, Grossherzogin Elisabeth. 144c+56c, Deutschland.

2005, June 2   Litho.   Perf. 13¾x14

B954	SP447	45c +20c multi	1.60	1.60
B955	SP447	55c +25c multi	2.00	2.00
B956	SP447	55c +25c multi	2.00	2.00
B957	SP447	55c +25c multi	2.00	2.00
B958	SP447	144c +56c multi	5.00	5.00
	Nos. B954-B958 (5)		12.60	12.60

Christmas
SP448

Paintings by Stefan Lochner: 45c+20c, Adoration of the Child. 55c+25c, Madonna and Child in Rose Garden.

2005, Nov. 3   Litho.   Perf. 13¾

B959	SP448	45c +20c multi	1.60	1.60
B960	SP448	55c +25c multi	1.90	1.90

Butterflies — SP449

Designs: 45c+20c, Zitronenfalter. No. B962, Russischer Bär. Nos. B963, B965, Tagpfauenauge. 145c+55c, Weisser Waldportier.

2005, Dec. 1   Litho.   Perf. 14

B961	SP449	45c +20c multi	1.60	1.60
B962	SP449	55c +25c multi	1.90	1.90
B963	SP449	55c +25c multi	1.90	1.90
B964	SP449	145c +55c multi	4.75	4.75
	Nos. B961-B964 (4)		10.15	10.15

Self-Adhesive
Booklet Stamp
Die Cut Perf. 11

B965	SP449	55c +25c multi	2.25	2.25
a.	Booklet pane of 10		22.50	

Protection of the Ozone
Layer — SP450

2006, Jan. 2   Perf. 14

B966	SP450	55c +25c multi	2.50	2.50

Sports — SP451

Designs: 45c+20c, Crowd waving German flags, stadium lights. No. B968, Stadium exterior, blurred athlete. No. B969, Stadium interior, players holding World Cup. No. B970, Horse and rider, rider's leg. 145c+55c, Emblem of 2006 World Cup Soccer Championships, blurred picture of soccer player kicking ball.

2006, Feb. 9   Litho.   Perf. 13x13½

B967	SP451	45c +20c multi	1.60	1.60
B968	SP451	55c +25c multi	1.90	1.90
B969	SP451	55c +25c multi	1.90	1.90
B970	SP451	55c +25c multi	1.90	1.90

B971	SP451	145c +55c multi	4.75	4.75
a.	Souvenir sheet, #B967-B969, B971		12.00	12.00
	Nos. B967-B971 (5)		12.05	12.05

2006 World Cup Soccer Championships (Nos. B967-B969, B971), World Equestrian Championships, Aachen (No. B970). No. B971a issued 5/4.

Mammals — SP452

Designs: 45c+20c, Pine marten. No. B973, Doe and fawn. No. B974, Hares. No. B975, Squirrel. 145c+55c, Wild pig and piglets.

2006, June 8   Litho.   Perf. 14

B972	SP452	45c +20c multi	1.75	1.75
B973	SP452	55c +25c multi	2.10	2.10
B974	SP452	55c +25c multi	2.10	2.10
B975	SP452	55c +25c multi	2.10	2.10
B976	SP452	145c +55c multi	5.25	5.25
	Nos. B972-B976 (5)		13.30	13.30

Surtax for the German Youth Stamp Foundation.

Trains — SP453

Designs: 45c+20c, Fliegender Hamburger (VT 877). No. B978, Trans Europ Express (VT 11.5). Nos. B979, B981, InterCityExpress (ET403). 145c+55c, Henschel-Wegmann train (61 001).

2006, Oct. 5   Litho.   Perf. 13¾x14

B977	SP453	45c +20c multi	1.75	1.75
B978	SP453	55c +25c multi	2.00	2.00
B979	SP453	55c +25c multi	2.00	2.00
B980	SP453	145c +55c multi	5.00	5.00
	Nos. B977-B980 (4)		10.75	10.75

Booklet Stamp
Self-Adhesive
Die Cut Perf. 11

B981	SP453	55c +25c multi	2.50	2.50
a.	Booklet pane of 10		25.00	

Christmas — SP454

15th Cent. altarpiece art by Meister Francke: 45c+20c, Nativity. 55c+25c, Adoration of the Magi.

2006, Nov. 9   Litho.   Perf. 14

B982	SP454	45c +20c multi	1.75	1.75
B983	SP454	55c +25c multi	2.00	2.00

SP455

Designs: 45c+20c, Canoe World Championships. No. B985, Handball World Championships. No. B986, Gymnastics World Championships. 145c+55c, Modern Pentathlon World Championships.

2007   Litho.   Perf. 13x13½

B984	SP455	45c +20c multi	1.75	1.75
B985	SP455	55c +25c multi	2.10	2.10
B986	SP455	55c +25c multi	2.10	2.10
B987	SP455	145c +55c multi	5.25	5.25
a.	Souvenir sheet, #B984-B987		12.00	12.00
	Nos. B985-B987 (3)		9.45	9.45

Issued: B985, 1/2. B984, B986-B987, 2/8. B987a, 5/3.

Souvenir Sheet

Graf Zeppelin and Itinerary of Flight to South America — SP456

Litho. & Engr.

B988	SP456	170c +70c multi	6.50	6.50

Stamp Day.

Souvenir Sheet

Hans Huckelbein, der Unglücksrabe, by Wilhelm Busch — SP457

No. B989: a, Bird eating berry jam. b, Bird standing in jam. c, Bird tipping pan of jam. d, Bird dirtying clean laundry.

2007, June 14   Litho.   Perf. 13¼

B989	SP457	Sheet of 4	12.00	12.00
a.	45c +20c multi		1.75	1.75
b.-c.	55c +25c either single		2.10	2.10
d.	145c +55c multi		5.50	5.50

Christmas
SP458

Designs: 45c+20c, Magi. 55c+25c, Madonna and Child, donkey and bull.

2007, Nov. 8   Litho.   Perf. 13¼

B990	SP458	45c +20c multi	1.90	1.90
B991	SP458	55c +25c multi	2.40	2.40

Adult and Juvenile Animals — SP459

Designs: 45c+20c, Guinea pigs. Nos. B993, B996, Horses. No. B994, Dogs. 145c+55c, Rabbits.

2007, Dec. 27   Photo.   Perf. 13¾x14

B992	SP459	45c +20c multi	1.90	1.90
B993	SP459	55c +25c multi	2.40	2.40
B994	SP459	55c +25c multi	2.40	2.40
B995	SP459	145c +55c multi	6.00	6.00
	Nos. B992-B995 (4)		12.70	12.70

Self-Adhesive
Booklet Stamp
Die Cut Perf. 11

B996	SP459	55c +25c multi	2.50	2.50
a.	Booklet pane of 10		25.00	

Sports Championships — SP460

Designs: 45c+20c, World Gliding Championships, Berlin. No. B998, Chess Olympiad, Dresden. No. B999, European Soccer Championships, Austria and Switzerland. 145c+55c, 2008 Summer Olympics, Beijing.

Perf. 13¼x13½

2008, Mar. 13   Litho.

B997	SP460	45c +20c multi	2.10	2.10
B998	SP460	55c +25c multi	2.50	2.50
B999	SP460	55c +25c multi	2.50	2.50
B1000	SP460	145c +55c multi	6.25	6.25
	Nos. B997-B1000 (4)		13.35	13.35

Knut, Polar Bear Cub in Berlin Zoo
SP461

2008, Apr. 10   Litho.   Perf. 14

B1001	SP461	55c +25c multi	2.60	2.60

Aircraft — SP462

Designs: 45c+20c, Dornier Do J Wal. No. B1003, Junkers Ju 52. Nos. B1004, B1006, Airbus A380. 145c+55c, Messerschmitt-Bölkow-Blohm BO 105 helicopter.

2008, June 12   Litho.   Perf. 14

B1002	SP462	45c +20c multi	2.00	2.00
B1003	SP462	55c +25c multi	2.50	2.50
B1004	SP462	55c +25c multi	2.50	2.50
B1005	SP462	145c +55c multi	6.25	6.25
	Nos. B1002-B1005 (4)		13.25	13.25

Self-Adhesive
Die Cut Perf. 11

B1006	SP462	55c +25c multi	2.50	2.50
a.	Booklet pane of 10		25.00	

Miniature Sheet

Dinosaurs — SP463

No. B1007: a, Triceratops. b, Diplodocus. c, Tyrannosaurus rex. d, Plateosaurus.

2008, Sept. 4   Litho.   Perf. 13x13½

B1007	SP463	Sheet of 4	12.50	12.50
a.	45c +20c multi		1.90	1.90
b.-c.	55c +25c Either single		2.40	2.40
d.	145c +55c multi		5.75	5.75

Christmas
SP464

Designs: 45c+20c, Nativity, by Albrecht Dürer. 55c+25c, Adoration of the Magi, by Raphael, horiz.

2008, Nov. 13   **Litho.**   *Perf. 14*
B1008 SP464 45c +20c multi   1.75   1.75
B1009 SP464 55c +25c multi   2.10   2.10
    See Vatican City Nos. 1399-1401.

Atmospheric Phenomena — SP465

Designs: 45c+20c, Rainbow. Nos. B1011, B1014, Clouds. No. B1012, Aurora borealis. 145c+55c, Lightning.

2009, Jan. 2   **Litho.**   *Perf. 14*
B1010 SP465 45c +20c multi   1.75   1.75
B1011 SP465 55c +25c multi   2.25   2.25
B1012 SP465 55c +25c multi   2.25   2.25
B1013 SP465 145c +55c multi   5.50   5.50
    Nos. B1010-B1013 (4)   11.75   11.75

Booklet Stamp
Self-Adhesive
Die Cut Perf. 11
B1014 SP465 55c +25c multi   2.25   2.25
   a.   Booklet pane of 10   22.50

2009 World Track and Field Championships, Berlin — SP466

Designs: 45c+20c, Hurdles. No. B1016, Pole vault. No. B1017, Runners. 145c+55c, Discus.

2009, Apr. 9   *Perf. 13x13½*
B1015 SP466 45c +20c multi   1.75   1.75
B1016 SP466 55c +25c multi   2.10   2.10
   a.   Booklet pane of 8, 4 each
      #B1015-B1016   15.50
      Complete booklet,
      #B1016a   15.50
B1017 SP466 55c +25c multi   2.10   2.10
B1018 SP466 145c +55c multi   5.25   5.25
    Nos. B1015-B1018 (4)   11.20   11.20

Stamp Day — SP467

2009, May 7   *Perf. 13¾ Syncopated*
B1019 SP467 55c +25c multi   2.25   2.25

"Our Sandman" Children's Television Show, 50th Anniv. SP468

Sandman: 45c+20c, On beach with boy. No. B1021, In flying suitcase. No. B1022, On train. 145c+55c, In spaceship.

2009, Aug. 13   *Perf. 13¼*
B1020 SP468 45c +20c multi   1.90   1.90
B1021 SP468 55c +25c multi   2.25   2.25
B1022 SP468 55c +25c multi   2.25   2.25
B1023 SP468 145c +55c multi   5.75   5.75
    Nos. B1020-B1023 (4)   12.15   12.15

Christmas — SP469

Illuminated manuscripts depicting: 45c+20c, Adoration of the Magi. 55c+25c, Nativity.

2009, Nov. 12   *Perf. 14*
B1024 SP469 45c +20c multi   2.00   2.00
B1025 SP469 55c +25c multi   2.40   2.40

Fruit — SP470

Blossom and fruit (whole and halved): 45c+20c, Apple (Malus domestica). No. B1027, Lemon (Citrus limon). Nos. B1028, B1030, Strawberry (Fragaria ananassa). 145c+55c, Blueberry (vaccinium myrtillus).

2010, Jan. 2   **Litho.**   *Perf. 14*
B1026 SP470 45c +20c multi   1.90   1.90
B1027 SP470 55c +25c multi   2.40   2.40
B1028 SP470 55c +25c multi   2.40   2.40
B1029 SP470 145c +55c multi   5.75   5.75
    Nos. B1026-B1029 (4)   12.45   12.45

Self-Adhesive
Die Cut Perf. 10¾
B1030 SP470 55c +25c multi   2.40   2.40
   a.   Booklet pane of 10   24.00

Nos. B1026-B1030 have a scratch-and-sniff coating on the whole and halved fruit parts of the vignette having the scent of the fruit shown.

Athletes — SP471

Designs: 45c+20c, Skier at Winter Paralympics, Vancouver. No B1032, Skier at 2010 Winter Olympics, Vancouver. Designs: No. B1033, Soccer players, 2010 World Cup Soccer Championships, South Africa. 145c+55c, Ice hockey players, 2010 World Ice Hockey Championships, Germany.

2010   **Litho.**   *Perf. 14*
B1031 SP471 45c +20c multi   1.75   1.75
B1032 SP471 55c +25c multi   2.25   2.25
B1033 SP471 55c +25c multi   2.25   2.25
B1034 SP471 145c+55c multi   5.50   5.50
    Issued: Nos. B1031-B1032, 2/11. Nos. B1033-B1034, 4/8.

Protection of the Seas — SP472

2010, May 6   **Litho.**   *Perf. 13x13½*
B1035 SP472 55c +25c multi   2.10   2.10

Steamers — SP473

Designs: 45c+20c, Deutschland. No. B1037, Aller. No. B1038, Imperator. 145c+55c, Columbus.

2010, Aug. 12   **Litho.**   *Perf. 13x13¼*
B1036 SP473 45c +20c multi   1.75   1.75
B1037 SP473 55c +25c multi   2.10   2.10
B1038 SP473 55c +25c multi   2.10   2.10
B1039 SP473 145c +55c multi   5.50   5.50
    Nos. B1036-B1039 (4)   11.45   11.45

Christmas — SP474

Creche figures: 45c+20c, Nativity. 55c+25c, Adoration of the Magi.

2010, Nov. 11   **Litho.**   *Perf. 13x13½*
B1040 SP474 45c +20c multi   1.75   1.75
B1041 SP474 55c +25c multi   2.25   2.25

Cartoons by Loriot (Bernhard-Viktor von Bülow) — SP475

Designs: 45c+20c, Two men and talking dog. Nos. B1043, B1046, Two men at race-track fence. No. B1044, Two naked men standing in bathtub. 145c+55c, Man and woman at breakfast table.

2011, Jan. 3   **Litho.**   *Perf. 13¾x14*
B1042 SP475 45c +20c multi   1.75   1.75
B1043 SP475 55c +25c multi   2.25   2.25
B1044 SP475 55c +25c multi   2.25   2.25
B1045 SP475 145c +55c multi   5.50   5.50
    Nos. B1042-B1045 (4)   11.75   11.75

Booklet Stamp
Self-Adhesive
Die Cut Perf. 11
B1046 SP475 55c +25c multi   2.25   2.25
   a.   Booklet pane of 10   22.50

AIR POST STAMPS

Issues of the Republic

Post Horn with Wings — AP1

Biplane AP2

Perf. 15x14½
1919, Nov. 10   **Typo.**   **Unwmk.**
C1   AP1 10pf orange   .20   2.50
C2   AP2 40pf dark green   .20   3.00
   a.   Imperf.   1,875.
    Set, never hinged   1.30
    No. C2a is ungummed.

Carrier Pigeon AP3

German Eagle AP4

1922-23   **Wmk. 126**   *Perf. 14, 14½*
Size: 19x23mm
C3   AP3 25(pf) chocolate   .45   18.00
C4   AP3 40(pf) orange   .35   24.00
C5   AP3 50(pf) violet   .20   8.25
C6   AP3 60(pf) carmine   .50   20.00
C7   AP3 80(pf) blue grn   .35   20.00
    Perf. 13x13½
    Size: 22x28mm
C8   AP3   1m dk grn & pale
      grn   .20   3.75
C9   AP3   2m lake & gray   .20   3.75
C10 AP3   3m dk blue &
      gray   .20   4.50
C11 AP3   5m red org & yel   .20   3.75
C12 AP3   10m vio & rose
      ('23)   .20   10.50
C13 AP3   25m brn & yel
      ('23)   .20   8.50
C14 AP3   100m ol grn & rose
      ('23)   .20   7.25
    Nos. C3-C14 (12)   3.25   132.25
    Set, never hinged   11.50

1923
C15 AP3   5m vermilion   .20   45.00
C16 AP3   10m violet   .20   10.50
C17 AP3   25m dark brown   .20   10.50
C18 AP3   100m olive grn   .20   11.00
C19 AP3   200m deep blue   .20   32.50
   a.   Imperf.   60.00
    Nos. C15-C19 (5)   1.00   109.50
    Set, never hinged   2.25
    Issued: #C15-C18, June 1. #C19, July 25. Note following #160 applies to #C1-C19.

1924, Jan. 11   *Perf. 14*
Size: 19x23mm
C20 AP3   5(pf) yellow grn   1.25   2.25
C21 AP3   10(pf) carmine   1.25   1.90
C22 AP3   20(pf) violet blue   6.75   5.25
C23 AP3   50(pf) orange   11.00   24.00
C24 AP3   100(pf) dull violet   30.00   55.00
C25 AP3   200(pf) grnsh
      blue   55.00   75.00
C26 AP3   300(pf) gray   97.50   100.00
   a.   Imperf.   1,425.
    Nos. C20-C26 (7)   202.75   263.40
    Set, never hinged   1,130.

1926-27
C27 AP4   5pf green   1.10   1.10
C28 AP4   10pf rose red   1.90   1.10
   b.   Tête bêche pair   92.50   200.00
      Never hinged   200.00
   d.   Bklt. pane 10 (6 No. C28
      + 4 No. C29)   55.00   150.00
      Never hinged   150.00
C29 AP4   15pf lilac rose
      ('27)   1.90   1.90
   a.   Double impression   1,375.
C30 AP4   20pf dull blue   1.90   1.90
   a.   Tête bêche pair   92.50   200.00
      Never hinged   200.00
   b.   Bklt. pane 4 (4 No. C30
      + 6 labels)   62.50   150.00
      Never hinged   150.00
   c.   Bklt. pane 5 (5 No. C30
      + 5 labels)   200.00   500.00
      Never hinged   500.00
C31 AP4   50pf brown org   18.00   5.25
C32 AP4   1m black &
      salmon   18.00   6.00
C33 AP4   2m black & blue   18.00   22.50
C34 AP4   3m black & ol
      grn   52.50   90.00
    Nos. C27-C34 (8)   113.30   129.75
    Set, never hinged   935.00

"Graf Zeppelin" Crossing Ocean — AP5

1928-31   **Photo.**
C35 AP5   1m carmine ('31)   25.00   32.50
C36 AP5   2m ultra   37.50   52.50
C37 AP5   4m black brown   27.50   35.00
    Nos. C35-C37 (3)   90.00   120.00
    Set, never hinged   400.00

    Issued: 2m, 4m, Sept. 20. 1m, May 8. For overprints see Nos. C40-C45.

AP6

1930, Apr. 19   **Wmk. 126**
C38 AP6 2m ultra   240.00 *300.00*
C39 AP6 4m black brown   240.00 *300.00*
Set, never hinged   2,625.

First flight of Graf Zeppelin to South America. Nos. C38-C39 exist with watermark vertical or horizontal.
Counterfeits exist of Nos. C38-C45.

Nos. C35-C37 Overprinted in Brown

1931, July 15
C40 AP5 1m carmine   110.00 110.00
C41 AP5 2m ultra   160.00 *200.00*
C42 AP5 4m black brown   400.00 *675.00*
Nos. C40-C42 (3)   670.00 *985.00*
Set, never hinged   3,050.

Polar flight of Graf Zeppelin.

Nos. C35-C37 Overprinted

1933, Sept. 25
C43 AP5 1m carmine   750.00 *375.00*
C44 AP5 2m ultra   75.00 *190.00*
C45 AP5 4m black brown   75.00 *190.00*
Nos. C43-C45 (3)   900.00 *755.00*
Set, never hinged   3,000.

Graf Zeppelin flight to Century of Progress International Exhibition, Chicago.

Swastika Sun, Globe and Eagle — AP7   Otto Lilienthal — AP8

Design: 3m, Count Ferdinand von Zeppelin.

Perf. 14, 13½x13
1934, Jan. 21   **Typo.**   **Wmk. 237**
C46 AP7   5(pf) brt green   1.10 .90
C47 AP7   10(pf) brt carmine   1.10 .90
C48 AP7   15(pf) ultra   1.80 1.25
C49 AP7   20(pf) dull blue   3.25 1.60
C50 AP7   25(pf) brown   3.50 1.90
C51 AP7   40(pf) red violet   6.75 1.10
C52 AP7   50(pf) dk green   12.00 .90
C53 AP7   80(pf) orange yel   3.75 3.75
C54 AP7   100(pf) black   7.50 2.75
C55 AP8   2m green & blk   16.50 *19.00*
C56 AP8   3m blue & blk   30.00 *42.50*
Nos. C46-C56 (11)   87.25 76.55
Set, never hinged   535.00

"Hindenburg" — AP10

Perf. 14, 14½x14
1936, Mar. 16   **Engr.**
C57 AP10 50pf dark blue   18.00 .75
C58 AP10 75pf dull green   19.00 1.10

The note concerning gum after No. B68 also applies to Nos. C57-C58.
Unused values are for stamps without gum.

Count Zeppelin — AP11

Airship Gondola — AP12

1938, July 5   **Unwmk.**   **Perf. 13½**
C59 AP11 25pf dull blue   2.25 1.50
C60 AP12 50pf green   3.50 1.50
Set, never hinged   42.00

Count Ferdinand von Zeppelin (1838-1917), airship inventor and builder.

> **Catalogue values for unused stamps in this section, from this point to the end of the section, are for Never Hinged items.**

Federal Republic

Lufthansa Emblem AP13

Perf. 13½x13
1955, Mar. 31   **Litho.**   **Wmk. 295**
C61 AP13   5pf lilac rose & blk   1.00 .75
C62 AP13   10pf green & blk   1.25 1.25
C63 AP13   15pf blue & blk   7.50 5.75
C64 AP13   20pf red & blk   21.00 7.50
Nos. C61-C64 (4)   30.75 15.25

Re-opening of German air service, Apr. 1.

MILITARY AIR POST STAMP

Junkers 52 Transport MAP1

1942   **Unwmk.**   **Typo.**   **Perf. 13½**
MC1   MAP1   ultramarine   .20 *.30*
    Never hinged   .45
a.   Rouletted   .20 *.60*
    Never hinged   .45

MILITARY PARCEL POST STAMPS

Nazi Emblem — MPP1

1942   **Unwmk.**   **Typo.**   **Perf. 13½**
    Size: 28x23mm
MQ1 MPP1   red brown   .20 *.45*
    Never hinged   .45
a.   Rouletted   .20 *.45*
    Never hinged   .45

1944   **Size: 22½x18mm**   **Perf. 14**
MQ2 MPP1   bright green   .45 *2.25*
    Never hinged   1.10

No. 520 Overprinted in Black

1944   **Engr.**
MQ3 A115   on 40pf brt red vio   .45 *3.50*
    Never hinged   1.10

Forged surcharges exist.
Used values for Nos. MQ1-MQ3 are for CTO examples. Postally used stamps are scarce and sell for much more.

OFFICIAL STAMPS

Issues of the Republic

In 1920 the Official Stamps of Bavaria and Wurttemberg then current were overprinted "Deutsches Reich" and made available for official use in all parts of Germany. They were, however, used almost exclusively in the two states where they originated and we have listed them among the issues of those states.

O1   O2

O3   O4

O5   O6

O7   O8

O9   O10

O11   O12

1920-21   **Typo.**   **Wmk. 125**   **Perf. 14**
O1   O1   5pf deep green   .90 13.50
O2   O2   10pf car rose   .20 1.60
O3   O2   10pf orange ('21)   .50 450.00
O4   O3   15pf violet brn   .20 2.25
a.   Imperf. ('21)   750.00 750.00
O5   O4   20pf deep ultra   .20 1.90
O6   O5   30pf org, *buff*   .20 1.90
O7   O6   40pf carmine   .20 1.90
O8   O7   50pf violet, *buff*   .20 1.90
O9   O8   60pf red brown ('21)   .20 1.90
O10   O9   1m red, *buff*   .20 1.90

O11	O10	1.25m dk bl, *ycl*	.20	2.25
O12	O11	2m dark blue	4.25	3.00
O13	O12	5m brown, *yel*	.20	3.00
		Nos. O1-O13 (13)	7.65	487.00
		Set, never hinged	34.00	

The value of No. O4a is for a stamp post-marked at Bautzen.
See No. O15. For surcharges see Nos. O29-O33, O35-O36, O38.

Postally Used vs. CTO

Values quoted for canceled examples of Nos. O1-O46 are for postally used stamps. See note after No. 160.

O13   O14

O15

Wmk. 126, 125 (#O16-O17)

1922-23

O14	O13	75pf dark blue	.20	7.50
O15	O11	2m dark blue	.25	1.50
a.		Imperf.	97.50	
O16	O14	3m brown, *rose*	.20	1.50
O17	O15	10m dk grn, *rose*	.20	1.50
O18	O15	10m dk grn, *rose*	.20	9.00
O19	O15	20m dk bl, *rose*	.20	1.50
O20	O15	50m vio, *rose*	.20	1.50
a.		Imperf	97.50	
O21	O15	100m rose red, *rose*	.20	1.50
a.		Imperf	110.00	750.00
		Nos. O14-O21 (8)	1.60	25.50
		Set, never hinged	4.50	

Issue date: #O18-O21, 1923.
Nos. O20-O21 exist imperf.
For surcharges see Nos. O34, O37, O39.

Regular Issue of 1923 Overprinted

a

1923

O22	A34	20m red lilac	.30	7.50
O23	A34	30m olive grn	.20	32.50
O24	A29	40m green	.20	3.00
O25	A35	200m car rose	.20	1.50
O26	A35	300m green	.20	1.50
O27	A35	400m dk brn	.20	1.50
O28	A35	500m red orange	.20	1.50
		Nos. O22-O28 (7)	1.50	49.00
		Set, never hinged	4.50	

Official Stamps of 1920-23 Surcharged with New Values

Abbreviations:
Th=(Tausend) Thousand
Mil=(Million) Million
Mlrd=(Milliarde) Billion

1923   **Wmk. 125**

O29	O12	5th m on 5m	.20	3.00
a.		Inverted surcharge	50.00	
		Never hinged	110.00	
O30	O5	20th m on 30pf	.20	3.00
a.		Inverted surcharge	55.00	
		Never hinged	125.00	
b.		Imperf.	60.00	
O31	O2	100th m on 15pf	.20	3.00
a.		Imperf.	60.00	
		Never hinged	150.00	
b.		Inverted surcharge	50.00	
		Never hinged	110.00	
O32	O2	500th m on 10pf car rose	.20	3.00
a.		Double surcharge	37.50	
		Never hinged	90.00	
O33	O5	800th m on 30pf	.20	300.00

Official Stamps and Types of 1920-23 Surcharged with New Values

Wmk. 126

O34	O15	75th m on 50m	.20	3.00
a.		Inverted surcharge	50.00	
		Never hinged	110.00	
O35	O3	400th m on 15pf brn	.20	27.50

O36	O5	800th m on 30pf org, *buff*	.20	4.50
O37	O13	1 mil m on 75pf	.20	37.50
O38	O2	2 mil m on 10m car rose	.30	3.75
a.		Imperf.	90.00	
		Never hinged	210.00	
O39	O15	5 mil m on 100m	.20	5.75
		Nos. O29-O39 (11)	2.70	394.00
		Set, never hinged	5.90	

The 10, 15 and 30 pfennig are not known with this watermark and without surcharge.

#290-291, 295-299 Overprinted Type "a"

1923

O40	A39	100 mil m	.20	150.00
O41	A39	200 mil m	.20	150.00
O42	A39a	2 mlrd m	.20	110.00
O43	A39a	5 mlrd m	.20	82.50
O44	A39a	10 mlrd m	3.00	140.00
O45	A39a	20 mlrd m	3.75	150.00
O46	A39a	50 mlrd m	1.90	200.00
		Nos. O40-O46 (7)	9.45	982.50
		Set, never hinged	32.50	

Same Overprint on Nos, 323-328, Values in Rentenpfennig

1923

O47	A40	3pf brown	.20	.75
O48	A40	5pf dk green	.20	.75
a.		Inverted overprint	92.50	175.00
		Never hinged	175.00	
O49	A40	10pf carmine	.20	.75
a.		Inverted overprint	80.00	175.00
		Never hinged	150.00	
b.		Imperf.	60.00	
		Never hinged	150.00	
O50	A40	20pf dp ultra	.60	1.10
O51	A40	50pf orange	.60	1.50
O52	A40	100pf brown vio	3.75	7.50
		Nos. O47-O52 (6)	5.55	12.35
		Set, never hinged	26.25	

Same Overprint On Issues of 1924

1924

O53	A41	3pf lt brown	.35	2.25
a.		Inverted overprint	60.00	300.00
		Never hinged	300.00	
O54	A41	5pf lt green	.20	.75
a.		Imperf.	75.00	
		Never hinged	225.00	
b.		Inverted overprint	110.00	
		Never hinged	300.00	
O55	A41	10pf vermilion	.20	.75
O56	A41	20pf blue	.20	.75
O57	A41	30pf rose lilac	.75	.75
O58	A41	40pf olive green	.75	.75
O59	A41	50pf orange	6.75	3.75
O60	A47	60pf red brown	1.50	3.75
O61	A47	80pf slate	6.75	32.50
		Nos. O53-O61 (9)	17.45	46.00
		Set, never hinged	60.00	

O16

Swastika — O17

1927-33   **Perf. 14**

O62	O16	3pf bister	.30	.75
O63	O16	4pf lt bl ('31)	.50	.90
O64	O16	4pf blue ('33)	6.75	13.50
O65	O16	5pf green	.20	.75
O66	O16	6pf pale ol grn ('32)	.75	.90
O67	O16	8pf dk grn	.30	.75
O68	O16	10pf carmine	7.50	6.00
O69	O16	10pf ver ('29), wmk. upright	15.00	19.00
O70	O16	10pf red vio ('30)	.45	.90
a.		Imperf.	150.00	
		Never hinged	375.00	
O71	O16	10pf choc ('33)	3.00	9.00
O72	O16	12pf org ('32)	.50	.90
O73	O16	15pf vermilion	1.75	.90
O74	O16	15pf car ('29)	.45	.90
O75	O16	20pf Prus grn, wmk. upright	7.50	3.00
O76	O16	20pf gray ('30), wmk. upright	2.25	1.10
O77	O16	30pf olive grn	.90	.90
O78	O16	40pf violet, wmk up-right	.75	.90
O79	O16	60pf red brn ('28)	1.10	1.90
		Nos. O62-O79 (18)	49.95	62.95
		Set, never hinged	275.00	

1934, Jan. 18   **Wmk. 237**

O80	O17	3pf bister	.75	1.10
O81	O17	4pf dull blue	.30	.90
O82	O17	5pf brt green	.20	1.10
O83	O17	6pf dk green	.20	.90
a.		Imperf.	150.00	
		Never hinged	375.00	
O84	O17	8pf vermilion	2.25	.90
O85	O17	10pf chocolate	.30	7.50
O86	O17	12pf brt carmine	2.25	1.50
a.		Unwmkd.	5.00	7.00
O87	O17	15pf claret	.90	9.00
O88	O17	20pf light blue	.45	1.50
O89	O17	30pf olive grn	.90	1.50
O90	O17	40pf red violet	.90	1.50
O91	O17	50pf orange yel	1.40	3.75
		Nos. O80-O91 (12)	10.80	31.15
		Set, never hinged	40.00	

1942   **Unwmk.**   **Perf. 14**

O92	O17	3pf bister brn	.30	.65
O93	O17	4pf dull blue	.30	.65
O94	O17	5pf deep olive	.30	3.00
O95	O17	6pf deep violet	.30	.65
O96	O17	8pf vermilion	.30	.65
O97	O17	10pf chocolate	.30	.60
O98	O17	12pf rose car	.30	1.25
a.		Wmk. 237	1.50	13.50
O99	O17	15pf brown car	2.40	12.00
O100	O17	20pf light blue	.30	1.30
O101	O17	30pf olive grn	.30	1.30
O102	O17	40pf red violet	.30	1.30
O103	O17	50pf dk green	2.25	7.25
		Nos. O92-O103 (12)	7.65	30.60
		Set, never hinged	35.00	

LOCAL OFFICIAL STAMPS

For Use in Prussia

("Nr. 21" refers to the district of Prussia) — LO1

1903 Unwmk. Typo. Perf. 14, 14½

OL1	LO1	2pf slate	.90	3.75
OL2	LO1	3pf bister brn	.90	3.75
OL3	LO1	5pf green	.30	.50
OL4	LO1	5pf carmine	.30	.50
OL5	LO1	20pf ultra	.30	.50
OL6	LO1	25pf org & blk, *yel*	.30	1.60
OL7	LO1	40pf lake & blk	.35	1.90
OL8	LO1	80pf pur & blk, *sal*	.35	1.90
		Nos. OL1-OL8 (8)	3.70	14.40
		Set, never hinged	11.65	

LO2   LO3

LO4   LO5

LO6   LO7

LO8

1920 Typo. Wmk. 125 Perf. 14

OL9	LO2	5pf green	.20	3.00
OL10	LO3	10pf carmine	.70	1.50
OL11	LO4	15pf vio brn	.20	1.50
OL12	LO5	20pf dp ultra	.20	1.40
OL13	LO6	30pf org, *buff*	.20	1.40

OL14	LO7	50pf brn lil, *buff*	.30	1.50
OL15	LO8	1m red, *buff*	8.25	3.75
		Nos. OL9-OL15 (7)	10.05	14.05
		Set, never hinged	35.00	

For Use in Baden

LO9

1905 Unwmk. Typo. Perf. 14, 14½

OL16	LO9	2pf gray blue	52.50	75.00
OL17	LO9	3pf brown	6.00	10.50
OL18	LO9	5pf green	4.25	7.50
OL19	LO9	10pf rose	.75	2.10
OL20	LO9	20pf blue	1.50	3.00
OL21	LO9	25pf org & blk, *yel*	35.00	52.50
		Nos. OL16-OL21 (6)	100.00	150.60
		Set, never hinged	883.00	

NEWSPAPER STAMPS

Newsboy and Globe — N1

Wmk. Swastikas (237)

1939, Nov. 1   Photo.   Perf. 14

P1	N1	5pf green	.60	5.25
P2	N1	10pf red brown	.60	5.25
		Set, never hinged	4.50	

POSTAL TAX STAMPS

On November 28, 1948, the "Notopfer Berlin" ("Berlin emergency levy") was enacted by the West German authorities to raise funds to subsidize civilian operations in West Berlin. Part of this levy was a 2pf surtax on virtually all types of internal mail in West Germany, except that of the military governments and foreign consulates and surface mail to Berlin. Initially applied to the Bizone (American and British administration), this levy was later extended to the French zone of occupation, and was continued by the Federal Republic of Germany after its formation in Sept. 1949.

From Dec. 1, 1948, until the expiration of the levy on March 31, 1956, most mail was required to carry one of the "Notopfer" tax stamps.

PT1

1948   Wmk. 286   Typo.
Imperf

RA1	PT1	2pf dk blue	.25	.25
		Never hinged	.55	

Compound Perf 12 and 14

RA2	PT1	2pf dk blue	.30	.30
		Never hinged	1.25	

No. RA2 also exists perf 9-10, 11, 11¼x11, 11½, compund 11½ and 12, 12x11½, 13½x11½ and rouletted, some of which were produced by local post offices or by private parties.
Issued: RA1, 12/1; RA2, 12/15.
Illustration PT1 actual size.

1948-50   Wmk. 285   Typo.
Imperf

RA3	PT1	2pf dk blue	15.00	1.50
		Never hinged	50.00	

Compound Perf 12 and 14

RA4	PT1	2pf dk blue ('49)	.60	.25
		Never hinged	2.25	

No. RA4 also exists perf 9½, 11, 11¼x11, 11½, 12, 12x11, 12x13½, 12¼ and rouletted, some of which were produced by local post offices or by private parties.

Wmk. 285

1950, June 10   Litho.   Perf. 14

RA5	PT1	2pf dk blue	.25	.25
		Never hinged		.45

1955, Aug. 8   Wmk. 295

RA6	PT1	2pf dk blue	.25	.25
		Never hinged		.45

FRANCHISE STAMPS

For use by the National Socialist German Workers' Party

Party Emblem — F1

1938   Typo.   Wmk. 237   Perf. 14

S1	F1	1pf black	.70	3.00
S2	F1	3pf bister	.70	1.90
S3	F1	4pf dull blue	.70	1.50
S4	F1	5pf brt green	.40	1.50
S5	F1	6pf dk green	.40	1.50
S6	F1	8pf vermilion	2.75	1.50
S7	F1	12pf brt car	4.50	1.50
S8	F1	16pf gray	.65	9.00
S9	F1	24pf citron	1.00	4.75
S10	F1	30pf olive	1.00	7.50
S11	F1	40pf red violet	1.00	11.00
		Nos. S1-S11 (11)	13.80	44.65
		Set, never hinged	120.00	

1942   Unwmk.

S12	F1	1pf gray blk	.70	3.50
S13	F1	3pf bister brn	.30	.55
S14	F1	4pf dk gray blue	.30	.55
S15	F1	5pf gray green	.30	3.50
S16	F1	6pf violet	.30	.55
S17	F1	8pf deep orange	.30	.55
	a.	Imperf.	95.00	
		Never hinged	190.00	
S18	F1	12pf carmine	.30	.55
S19	F1	16pf blue green	3.25	16.00
S20	F1	24pf yellow brn	.50	1.00
S21	F1	30pf dp olive grn	.50	1.75
S22	F1	40pf light rose vio	.55	2.25
		Nos. S12-S22 (11)	7.30	30.75
		Set, never hinged	25.00	

GERMAN OCCUPATION STAMPS

100 Centimes = 1 Franc
100 Pfennig = 1 Mark

Issued under Belgian Occupation

Belgian Stamps of 1915-1920 Overprinted

Perf. 11½, 14, 14½

1919-21   Unwmk.

1N1	A46	1c orange	.30	.45
1N2	A46	2c chocolate	.30	.45
1N3	A46	3c gray blk ('21)	.30	1.90
1N4	A46	5c green	.60	.90
1N5	A46	10c carmine	1.25	1.90
1N6	A46	15c purple	.60	.90
1N7	A46	20c red violet	.90	1.25
1N8	A46	25c blue	1.10	1.50
1N9	A54	25c dp blue ('21)	3.75	8.25

Overprinted

1N10	A47	35c brn org & blk	1.10	1.25
1N11	A48	40c green & blk	1.10	1.90
1N12	A49	50c car rose & blk	5.50	9.00
1N13	A56	65c cl & blk ('21)	3.00	10.50
1N14	A50	1fr violet	21.00	19.00
1N15	A51	2fr slate	35.00	37.50
1N16	A52	5fr deep blue	8.25	10.00

1N17	A53	10fr brown	55.00	55.00
		On cover		
		Nos. 1N1-1N17 (17)	139.05	161.65
		Set, never hinged	450.00	

Nos. 1N14-1N17 exist with two overprint types: spacing between "Allemagne" and "Duitshland" 2mm (1919) and 1mm (1920).

Belgian Stamps of 1915 Surcharged

Nos. 1N18-1N22   Nos. 1N23-1N24

Black Surcharge

1920

1N18	A46	5pf on 5c green	.40	.35
1N19	A46	10pf on 10c car	.50	.45
1N20	A46	15pf on 15c pur	.70	.70
1N21	A46	20pf on 20c red vio	.70	1.00
1N22	A46	30pf on 25c blue	1.10	1.25

Red Surcharge

1N23	A49	75pf on 50c car rose & blk	15.00	15.00
1N24	A50	1m25pf on 1fr violet	21.00	21.00
		Nos. 1N18-1N24 (7)	39.40	39.75
		Set, never hinged	110.00	

EUPEN ISSUE
Belgian Stamps of 1915-20 Overprinted

Nos. 1N25-1N36   Nos. 1N37-1N41

1920-21   Perf. 11½, 14, 14½

1N25	A46	1c orange	.30	.40
		Never hinged	.75	
1N26	A46	2c chocolate	.30	.40
1N27	A46	3c gray blk ('21)	.45	1.40
1N28	A46	5c green	.45	.90
1N29	A46	10c carmine	.75	1.25
1N30	A46	15c purple	1.10	1.40
1N31	A46	20c red violet	1.25	1.40
1N32	A46	25c blue	1.10	1.90
1N33	A54	25c dp blue ('21)	3.50	9.50
1N34	A47	35c brn org & blk	1.40	1.90
1N35	A48	40c green & blk	1.75	2.25
1N36	49	50c car rose & blk	5.00	7.25
1N37	A56	65c cl & blk ('21)	2.75	11.00
1N38	A50	1fr violet	20.00	19.00
1N39	A51	2fr slate	32.50	30.00
1N40	A52	5fr deep blue	10.50	11.00
1N41	A53	10fr brown	45.00	50.00
		Nos. 1N25-1N41 (17)	128.10	150.80
		Set, never hinged	325.00	

MALMEDY ISSUE
Belgian Stamps of 1915-20 Overprinted

Nos. 1N42-1N50   Nos. 1N51-1N53

Nos. 1N54-1N58

1920-21

1N42	A46	1c orange	.25	.40
1N43	A46	2c chocolate	.25	.40
1N44	A46	3c gray blk ('21)	.35	1.60

1N45	A46	5c green	.45	.90
1N46	A46	10c carmine	.70	1.25
1N47	A46	15c purple	1.10	1.40
1N48	A46	20c red violet	1.50	1.90
1N49	A46	25c blue	1.25	1.90
1N50	A54	25c dp blue ('21)	3.50	8.75
1N51	A47	35c brn org & blk	1.25	2.25
1N52	A48	40c green & blk	1.50	2.25
1N53	A49	50c car rose & blk	6.00	7.25
1N54	A56	65c cl & blk ('21)	2.75	11.00
1N55	A50	1fr violet	20.00	17.00
1N56	A51	2fr slate	32.50	30.00
1N57	A52	5fr deep blue	10.50	17.00
1N58	A53	10fr brown	45.00	50.00
		Nos. 1N42-1N58 (17)	128.85	155.25
		Set, never hinged	325.00	

OCCUPATION POSTAGE DUE STAMPS

Belgian Postage Due Stamps of 1919-20, Overprinted

1920   Unwmk.   Perf. 14½

1NJ1	D3	5c green	.75	1.10
1NJ2	D3	10c carmine	1.50	1.90
1NJ3	D3	20c gray green	3.00	4.50
1NJ4	D3	30c bright blue	3.00	4.50
1NJ5	D3	50c gray	15.00	15.00
		Nos. 1NJ1-1NJ5 (5)	23.25	27.00
		Set, never hinged	57.50	

Belgian Postage Due Stamps of 1919-20, Overprinted

Unwmk.

1NJ6	D3	5c green	1.50	1.10
1NJ7	D3	10c carmine	3.00	1.90
	a.	Inverted overprint	100.00	90.00
1NJ8	D3	20c gray green	10.50	11.50
1NJ9	D3	30c bright blue	6.00	8.50
1NJ10	D3	50c gray	12.00	11.00
		Nos. 1NJ6-1NJ10 (5)	33.00	34.00
		Set, never hinged	82.50	

A. M. G. ISSUE

Issued jointly by the Allied Military Government of the US and Great Britain, for civilian use in areas under Allied occupation.

OS1

Type I. Thick paper, white gum.
Type II. Medium paper, yellow gum.
Type III. Medium paper, white gum.

Perf. 11, 11½ and Compound

1945-46   Litho.   Unwmk.

Type III, Brunswick Printing
Size: 19-19½x22-22½mm

3N1	OS1	1pf slate gray	.20	5.00
3N2	OS1	3pf dull lilac	.20	1.10
3N3	OS1	4pf lt gray	.20	1.50
3N4	OS1	5pf emerald	.20	4.00
3N5	OS1	6pf yellow	.20	1.10
3N6	OS1	8pf orange	2.00	37.50
3N7	OS1	10pf yel brn	.20	1.50
3N8	OS1	12pf rose vio	.20	.90
3N9	OS1	15pf rose car	.20	3.00
3N10	OS1	16pf dp Prus grn	.20	13.50
3N11	OS1	20pf blue	.20	3.00
3N12	OS1	24pf chocolate	.20	13.50
3N13	OS1	25pf brt ultra	.20	13.50

Size: 21½x25mm

3N14	OS1	30pf olive	.20	1.90
3N15	OS1	40pf dp mag	.20	2.50
3N16	OS1	42pf green	.20	2.25
3N17	OS1	50pf slate grn	.20	15.00
3N18	OS1	60pf vio brn	.50	19.00
3N19	OS1	80pf bl blk	15.00	300.00

Size: 25x29½mm

3N20	OS1	1m dk ol grn ('46)	2.50	500.00
		Nos. 3N1-3N20 (20)	23.20	939.75
		Set, never hinged	50.00	

Most of Nos. 3N1-3N20 exist imperforate and part-perforate.

Type I, Washington Printing
Size: 19-19½x22-22½mm
Perf. 11

3N2a	OS1	3pf lilac	.20	1.90
3N3a	OS1	4pf light gray	.20	1.50
3N4a	OS1	5pf emerald	.20	.35
3N5a	OS1	6pf yellow	.20	.35
3N6a	OS1	8pf deep orange	.20	.35
3N7a	OS1	10pf brown	.20	.35
3N8a	OS1	12pf rose violet	.25	.35
3N9a	OS1	15pf cerise	.20	1.50
3N13a	OS1	25pf bright ultra	.20	1.50
		Nos. 3N2a-3N13a (9)	1.85	8.15
		Set, never hinged	2.50	

Type II, London Printing
Size: 19-19½x22-22½mm
Perf. 14, 14½ and Compound
Photo.

3N2b	OS1	3pf lilac	.20	.60
3N3b	OS1	4pf light gray	.20	.60
3N4b	OS1	5pf deep emerald	.20	15.00
3N5b	OS1	6pf orange yellow	.20	.60
3N6b	OS1	8pf dark orange	.20	3.75
3N8b	OS1	12pf rose violet	.20	.60
		Nos. 3N2b-3N8b (6)	1.20	21.15
		Set, never hinged	2.00	

ISSUED UNDER FRENCH OCCUPATION

Coats of Arms

Rhine Province OS3   Palatinate District OS4

Saarland OS5   Württemberg OS6

Baden OS7   Johann Wolfgang von Goethe OS8

Friedrich von Schiller — OS9   Heinrich Heine — OS10

Perf. 14x13½

1945-46   Unwmk.   Typo.

4N1	OS3	1pf blk, grn & lem	.20	.25
4N2	OS4	3pf dk red, blk & dl yel	.20	.25
4N3	OS6	5pf brn, blk & org yel	.20	.20

4N4	OS7	8pf brn, yel & red	.20	.20
4N5	OS3	10pf brn, grn & lem	6.50	52.50
4N6	OS4	12pf red, blk & org yel	.20	.20
4N7	OS5	15pf blk, ultra & red ('46)	.20	.25
4N8	OS6	20pf blk, org yel & blk	.20	.25
4N9	OS5	24pf blk, dp ultra & red ('46)	.20	.20
4N10	OS7	30pf blk, org yel & red	.20	.25

Perf. 13
Engr.

4N11	OS8	1m lilac brn	.70	18.00
4N12	OS9	2m dp bl ('46)	.45	52.50
4N13	OS10	5m dl red brn ('46)	.55	67.50
		Nos. 4N1-4N13 (13)	10.00	192.50
		Set, never hinged	20.00	

Exist imperf. Value for set of 13, $475 mint never hinged.

BADEN

Johann Peter Hebel OS1

Girl of Constance OS2

Hans Baldung Grien — OS3
Rastatt Castle — OS4

Black Forest Scene OS5

Cathedral of Freiburg — OS6

1947 Unwmk. Photo. Perf. 14

5N1	OS1	2pf gray	.20	.30
5N2	OS2	3pf brown	.20	.30
5N3	OS3	10pf slate blue	.20	.30
5N4	OS2	12pf dk green	.20	.30
5N5	OS2	15pf purple	.20	.35
5N6	OS4	16pf olive green	.20	1.50
5N7	OS3	20pf blue	.20	.35
5N8	OS4	24pf crimson	.20	.30
5N9	OS2	45pf cerise	.20	.90
5N10	OS1	60pf deep orange	.20	.90
5N11	OS5	75pf brt blue	.20	1.90
5N12	OS5	84pf blue green	.20	1.90
5N13	OS6	1m dark brown	.20	.75
		Nos. 5N1-5N13 (13)		9.45
		Set, never hinged		2.25

Festival Headdress OS7

Grand Duchess Stephanie OS8

1948

5N14	OS1	2pf dp orange	.20	.30
5N15	OS7	6pf violet brn	.20	.30
5N16	OS7	8pf blue green	.25	1.10
5N17	OS3	10pf dark brown	.20	.30
5N18	OS1	12pf crimson	.20	.30
5N19	OS2	15pf blue	.25	.60
5N20	OS4	16pf violet	.35	1.90
5N21	OS3	20pf brown	1.50	.95
5N22	OS4	24pf dark green	.25	.30
5N23	OS8	30pf cerise	.55	1.10
5N24	OS8	50pf brt blue	.55	.30
5N25	OS1	60pf gray	1.90	.60
5N26	OS5	84pf rose brn	2.75	4.50
5N27	OS6	1dm brt blue	2.75	4.50
		Nos. 5N14-5N27 (14)	11.90	17.05
		Set, never hinged	26.50	

Without "PF"

1948-49

5N28	OS1	2(pf) dp orange	.35	.55
5N29	OS4	4(pf) violet	.25	.45
5N30	OS2	5(pf) blue	.35	.60
5N31	OS2	6(pf) violet brn	11.50	13.50
5N32	OS7	8(pf) rose brn	.35	1.00
5N33	OS3	10(pf) dark green	1.60	.55
5N37	OS3	20(pf) cerise	.65	.35
5N38	OS4	40(pf) brown	30.00	75.00
5N39	OS4	80(pf) red	3.75	6.00
5N40	OS5	90(pf) rose brn	29.00	75.00
		Nos. 5N28-5N40 (10)	77.80	173.00
		Set, never hinged	150.00	

Constance Cathedral and Insel Hotel — OS9

Type I. Frameline thick and straight. Inscriptions thick. Shading dark. Upper part of "B" narrow.
Type II. Frameline thin and zigzag. Inscriptions fine. Shading light. Upper part of "B" wide.

1949, June 22

5N41	OS9	30pf dark blue (I)	9.00	65.00
		Never hinged	20.00	
a.		Type II	250.00	1,450.
		Never hinged	475.00	

Issued to publicize the International Engineering Congress, Constance, 1949.

Conradin Kreutzer — OS10

1949, Aug. 27

5N42	OS10	10pf dark green	1.50	7.50
		Never hinged	3.00	

Conradin Kreutzer (1780-1849), composer.

Stagecoach — OS11

Design: 20pf, Post bus, trailer and plane.

1949, Sept. 17

5N43	OS11	10pf green	2.25	10.50
5N44	OS11	20pf red brown	2.25	10.50
		Set, never hinged	9.00	

Centenary of German postage stamps.

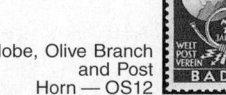
Globe, Olive Branch and Post Horn — OS12

1949, Oct. 4

5N45	OS12	20pf dark red	2.75	10.50
5N46	OS12	30pf deep blue	2.75	9.00
		Set, never hinged	10.00	

75th anniv. of the UPU.

OCCUPATION SEMI-POSTAL STAMPS

Arms of Baden OSP1

Cornhouse, Freiburg OSP2

Perf. 13½x14
1949, Feb. 25 Photo. Unwmk.
Cross in Red

5NB1	OSP1	10 + 20pf green	8.50	75.00
5NB2	OSP1	20 + 40pf lilac	8.50	75.00
5NB3	OSP1	30 + 60pf blue	8.50	75.00
5NB4	OSP1	40 + 80pf gray	8.50	75.00
a.		Sheet of 4, #5NB1-5NB4, imperf.	110.00	1,350.
		Nos. 5NB1-5NB4 (4)	34.00	300.00
		Set, never hinged	75.00	

The surtax was for the Red Cross.
No. 5NB4a measures 90x101mm. and has no gum.

1949, Feb. 24 Perf. 14

10pf+20pf, Cathedral tower. 20pf+30pf, Trumpeting angel. 30pf+50pf, Fish pool.

5NB5	OSP2	4 + 16pf dk vio	5.25	35.00
5NB6	OSP2	10 + 20pf dk grn	5.25	35.00
5NB7	OSP2	20 + 30pf car	5.25	35.00
5NB8	OSP2	30 + 50pf blue	6.75	45.00
a.		Sheet of 4, #5NB5-5NB8	26.00	210.00
		Never hinged	52.50	
b.		As "a," imperf.	26.00	210.00
		Never hinged	52.50	
		Nos. 5NB5-5NB8 (4)	22.50	150.00
		Set, never hinged	55.00	

The surtax was for the reconstruction of historical monuments in Freiburg.

Carl Schurz at Rastatt OSP3

Goethe OSP4

1949, Aug. 23

5NB9	OSP3	10 + 5pf green	4.75	29.00
5NB10	OSP3	20 + 10pf cer	4.75	29.00
5NB11	OSP3	30 + 15pf blue	5.50	29.00
		Nos. 5NB9-5NB11 (3)	15.00	87.00
		Set, never hinged	29.00	

Centenary of the surrender of Rastatt.

1949, Aug. 12

Various Portraits.

5NB12	OSP4	10 + 5pf green	3.50	19.00
5NB13	OSP4	20 + 10pf cer	3.50	19.00
5NB14	OSP4	30 + 15pf blue	5.25	45.00
		Nos. 5NB12-5NB14 (3)	12.25	83.00
		Set, never hinged	26.00	

Johann Wolfgang von Goethe (1749-1832).

RHINE PALATINATE

Beethoven OS1

Wilhelm E. F. von Ketteler OS2

Girl Carrying Grapes OS3

Porta Nigra, Trier OS4

Karl Marx OS5

"Devil's Table", Near Pirmasens OS6

Street Corner, St. Martin OS7

Cathedral of Worms OS8

Cathedral of Mainz OS9

Statue of Johann Gutenberg OS10

Gutenfels and Pfalzgrafenstein Castles on Rhine — OS11

Statue of Charlemagne OS12

1947-48 Unwmk. Photo. Perf. 14

6N1	OS1	2pf gray	.20	.30
6N2	OS2	3pf dk brown	.20	.30
6N3	OS3	10pf slate blue	.20	.30
6N4	OS4	12pf green	.20	.30
6N5	OS5	15pf purple	.20	.30
6N6	OS6	16pf lt ol grn	.20	1.10
6N7	OS7	20pf brt blue	.20	.30
6N8	OS8	24pf crimson	.20	.30
6N9	OS10	30pf cerise ('48)	.20	2.25
6N10	OS9	45pf cerise	.20	.60
6N11	OS9	50pf blue ('48)	.20	2.25
6N12	OS1	60pf dp orange	.20	.30
6N13	OS10	75pf blue	.20	.60

6N14 OS11 84pf green .20 *1.40*
6N15 OS12 1m brown .20 *.75*
 Nos. 6N1-6N15 (15)   *11.35*
 Set, never hinged 2.25
 Exist imperf. Value for set, $525 mint never hinged.

1948
6N16 OS1 2pf dp orange .20 *.30*
6N17 OS2 6pf violet brn .20 *.30*
6N18 OS4 8dpf blue green .25 *1.10*
6N19 OS3 10pf dk brown .25 *.30*
6N20 OS4 12pf crim rose .25 *.30*
6N21 OS5 15pf blue .60 *.60*
6N22 OS6 16dpf dk violet .30 *1.40*
6N23 OS7 20dpf brown 1.40 *.60*
6N24 OS8 24pf green .25 *.30*
6N25 OS9 30pf cerise .45 *.35*
6N26 OS10 50pf brt blue .75 *.35*
6N27 OS1 60dpf gray 3.75 *.35*
6N28 OS11 84dpf rose brown 1.90 *5.50*
6N29 OS12 1dm red blue 3.00 *5.75*
 Nos. 6N16-6N29 (14) 13.55 *17.50*
 Set, never hinged 26.00
 Exist imperf. Value for set, $500 mint never hinged.

Types of 1947 Without "PF"
1948-49
6N30 OS1 2(pf) dp org .30 *.35*
6N31 OS6 4(pf) vio ('49) .30 *.35*
6N32 OS5 5(pf) blue
 ('49) .35 *.60*
6N33 OS2 6(pf) vio brn 13.50 *15.00*
6N33A OS4 8(pf) rose brn
 ('49) 30.00 *375.00*
6N34 OS3 10(pf) dk grn .35 *.35*
 a. Imperf. 55.00 *190.00*
 Never hinged 110.00
6N35 OS7 20(pf) cerise .35 *.35*
6N36 OS8 40(pf) brn ('49) 1.40 *3.75*
6N37 OS11 80(pf) red ('49) 1.50 *5.00*
6N38 OS11 90(pf) rose brn
 ('49) 2.25 *15.00*
 Nos. 6N30-6N38 (10) 50.30 *415.75*
 Set, never hinged 110.00

Type of Baden, 1949
Designs as in Baden.
1949, Sept. 17
6N39 OS11 10pf green 4.25 *19.00*
6N40 OS11 20pf red brown 4.25 *19.00*
 Set, never hinged 16.50

UPU Type of Baden, 1949
1949, Oct. 4
6N41 OS12 20pf dark red 3.00 *11.50*
6N42 OS12 30pf deep blue 3.00 *9.75*
 Set, never hinged 10.50

OCCUPATION SEMI-POSTAL STAMPS

St. Martin — OSP1

Design: 30pf+50pf, St. Christopher.

1948 Unwmk. Photo. Perf. 14
6NB1 OSP1 20pf + 30pf dp cl .60 *57.50*
6NB2 OSP1 30pf + 50pf dp bl .60 *57.50*
 Set, never hinged 3.00
 The surtax was to aid victims of an explosion at Ludwigshafen.

Type of Baden, 1949, Showing Arms of Rhine Palatinate
1949, Feb. 25 Perf. 13½x14
Cross in Red
6NB3 OSP1 10pf + 20pf grn 7.75 *82.50*
6NB4 OSP1 20pf + 40pf lil 7.75 *82.50*
6NB5 OSP1 30pf + 60pf bl 7.75 *82.50*
6NB6 OSP1 40pf + 80pf
 gray 7.75 *82.50*
 a. Sheet of 4, #6NB3-
 6NB6, imperf. 82.50 *1,050.*
 Nos. 6NB3-6NB6 (4) 31.00 *330.00*
 Set, never hinged 65.00
 The surtax was for the Red Cross. #6NB6a measures 90x100mm and has no gum.

Goethe Type of Baden, 1949
Various Portraits.
1949, Aug. 12
6NB7 OSP4 10pf + 5pf green 2.25 *18.00*
6NB8 OSP4 20pf + 10pf cerise 2.25 *18.00*
6NB9 OSP4 30pf + 15pf blue 4.50 *42.50*
 Nos. 6NB7-6NB9 (3) 9.00 *78.50*
 Set, never hinged 22.50

WURTTEMBERG

Friedrich von Schiller OS1   Castle of Bebenhausen OS2

Friedrich Hölderlin OS3   Town Gate of Wangen (Allgäu) OS4

Lichtenstein Castle — OS5   Zwiefalten Church — OS6

1947-48 Unwmk. Photo. Perf. 14
8N1 OS1 2pf gray ('48) .20 *.60*
8N2 OS3 3pf brown ('48) .20 *.30*
8N3 OS4 10pf slate bl ('48) .20 *.35*
8N4 OS1 12pf dk green .20 *.25*
8N5 OS3 15pf purple ('48) .20 *.45*
8N6 OS2 16pf ol grn ('48) .20 *1.00*
8N7 OS2 20pf blue ('48) .20 *1.00*
8N8 OS2 24pf crimson .20 *.30*
8N9 OS3 45pf cerise .20 *1.00*
8N10 OS1 60pf dp org ('48) .20 *.75*
8N11 OS4 75pf brt blue .20 *1.10*
8N12 OS5 84pf blue grn .20 *1.40*
8N13 OS6 1m dk brown .20 *1.10*
 Nos. 8N1-8N13 (13)   *9.60*
 Set, never hinged 2.25
 Nos. 8N4 and 8N10 exist imperf. Value, each $37.50, mint never hinged.

Waldsee OS7   Ludwig Uhland OS8

1948
8N14 OS1 2pf dp orange .20 *.35*
8N15 OS3 6pf violet brn .20 *.30*
8N16 OS7 8dpf blue grn .35 *1.75*
8N17 OS4 10pf dk brown .20 *.35*
8N18 OS1 12pf crimson .20 *.30*
8N19 OS3 15pf blue .30 *.35*
8N20 OS2 16dpf dk violet .35 *1.60*
8N21 OS4 20dpf brown .75 *.75*
8N22 OS2 24pf dk green .45 *.60*
8N23 OS7 30pf cerise .60 *.60*
8N24 OS8 50pf dull blue .95 *.60*
8N25 OS1 60dpf gray 5.75 *.60*

8N26 OS5 84dpf rose brn 1.50 *3.75*
8N27 OS6 1dm brt blue 1.50 *3.75*
 Nos. 8N14-8N27 (14) 13.30 *15.65*
 Set, never hinged 26.00
 Nos. 8N14, 8N17, 8N22-8N23 exist imperf. Value, each $35, mint never hinged.

Without "PF"
1948-49
8N28 OS1 2(pf) dp orange .35 *.60*
8N29 OS2 4(pf) violet 1.10 *.35*
8N30 OS3 5(pf) blue 3.00 *2.25*
8N31 OS3 6(pf) vio brown 3.00 *5.75*
8N32 OS7 8(pf) rose brn 3.00 *2.25*
8N33 OS4 10(pf) dk green 3.00 *.35*
8N34 OS2 20(pf) cerise 3.00 *.35*
8N35 OS2 40(pf) brown 9.75 *37.50*
8N36 OS1 80(pf) red 19.00 *37.50*
8N37 OS5 90(pf) rose brn 30.00 *97.50*
 Nos. 8N28-8N37 (10) 75.20 *184.40*
 Set, never hinged 150.00
 Nos. 8N29 and 8N31 exist imperf. Value, respectively $75 and $57.50, mint never hinged.

Type of Baden, 1949
Designs as in Baden.
1949, Sept. 17
8N38 OS11 10pf green 3.50 *12.00*
8N39 OS11 20pf red brown 3.50 *12.00*
 Set, never hinged 11.50

UPU Type of Baden, 1949
1949, Oct. 4
8N40 OS12 20pf dark red 2.25 *9.75*
8N41 OS12 30pf deep blue 2.25 *9.00*
 Set, never hinged 9.75

OCCUPATION SEMI-POSTAL STAMPS

Type of Baden, 1949
Design: Arms of Württemberg.

Perf. 13½x14
1949, Feb. 25 Photo. Unwmk.
Cross in Red
8NB1 OSP1 10 + 20pf grn 16.00 *90.00*
8NB2 OSP1 20 + 40pf lilac 16.00 *90.00*
8NB3 OSP1 30 + 60pf blue 16.00 *90.00*
8NB4 OSP1 40 + 80pf gray 16.00 *90.00*
 a. Sheet of 4, imperf. 110.00 *1,350.*
 Nos. 8NB1-8NB4 (4) 64.00 *360.00*
 Set, never hinged 120.00
 The surtax was for the Red Cross. No. 8NB4a measures 90x100mm and contains one each of Nos. 8NB1 to 8NB4, with red inscription in upper margin and no gum.

View of Isny OSP1

Design: 20pf+6pf, Skier and village.

Wmk. 116
1949, Feb. 11 Typo. Perf. 14
8NB5 OSP1 10 + 4pf dull
 green 2.75 *19.00*
8NB6 OSP1 20 + 6pf red
 brown 2.75 *19.00*
 Set, never hinged 11.00
 Issued to commemorate the 1948-49 German Ski Championship at Isny im Allgau.

Gustav Werner — OSP2

1949, Sept. 4
8NB7 OSP2 10 + 5pf bl grn 2.25 *12.00*
8NB8 OSP2 20 + 10pf claret 2.25 *12.00*
 Set, never hinged 9.00
 Cent. of the founding of Gustav Werner's "Christianity in Action" and "House of Brotherhood."

Goethe Type of Baden, 1949
Various Portraits.

1949, Aug. 12
8NB9 OSP4 10 + 5pf green 3.75 *19.00*
8NB10 OSP4 20 + 10pf cerise 5.50 *26.00*
8NB11 OSP4 30 + 15pf blue 5.50 *37.50*
 Nos. 8NB9-8NB11 (3) 14.75 *82.50*
 Set, never hinged 26.00

OCCUPATION POSTAL TAX STAMPS

Wohnungsbau Issues
During July 1-December 31, 1949, a postal tax was levied on most categories of mail, with proceeds going to the 'Social Housing' (*Socialen Wohnungsbau*) program, which provided interest-free loans for housing construction and renovation intended to provide housing for economically-disadvantaged families.

Germany Nos. RA1, RA2, RA4
Overprinted in Red

Illustration actual size.

Overprint 18.7mm wide
Wmk. 286
1949, July 1 Typo. *Imperf.*
8NRA1 PT1 2pf dk blue 225.00 *425.00*
 Never hinged 550.00
Compound Perf 12, 14
8NRA2 PT1 2pf dk blue 15.00 *2.75*
 Never hinged 37.50
Overprint 16.5 mm wide
1949, July 22 Wmk. 285 *Perf. 12¼*
8NRA3 PT1 2pf dk blue 3.75 *1.75*
 Never hinged 9.00

OSPT1

1949 *Perf. 12¼*
8NRA4 OSPT1 2pf yellow .20 *1.00*
 Never hinged .50
 a. 2pf yellow orange 13.50 *15.00*
 Never hinged 30.00
 b. 2pf orange .20 *1.00*
 Never hinged .50
 Issued: No. 4a, 8/19; No. 4, 8/22. No. 4b, 8/25. No. 4c, 10/4.
 Illustration OSPT1 actual size.

BERLIN

Issued for Use in the American, British and French Occupation Sectors of Berlin
Germany Nos. 557-569, 571-573
Overprinted Diagonally in Black

a

Wmk. 284
1948, Sept. 1 Typo. *Perf. 14*
9N1 A120 2pf brown blk .45 *4.50*
9N2 A120 6pf purple .30 *4.50*
9N3 A121 8pf red .30 *4.50*
9N4 A122 10pf yellow grn .25 *1.10*
9N5 A122 12pf gray .25 *1.10*
9N6 A122 15pf chocolate 4.75 *67.50*
9N7 A123 16pf dk blue grn .35 *1.60*
9N8 A121 20pf blue 2.25 *6.75*
9N9 A123 24pf brown org .25 *.45*
9N10 A120 25pf orange yel 6.75 *52.50*
9N11 A122 30pf red 1.00 *7.50*
9N12 A121 40pf red violet 1.10 *7.50*
9N13 A123 50pf ultra 2.50 *30.00*
9N14 A122 60pf red brown .75 *.45*
9N15 A122 80pf dark blue 2.00 *26.00*
9N16 A123 84pf emerald 5.25 *97.50*

Germany Nos. 574-577 Overprinted Diagonally in Black

b

Engr.

9N17	A124	1m olive	20.00	150.00
9N18	A124	2m dk brown vio	22.50	475.00
9N19	A124	3m copper red	26.00	675.00
9N20	A124	5m dark blue	30.00	675.00
	Nos. 9N1-9N20 (20)		127.00	2,288.
	Set, never hinged		350.00	

Forged overprints and cancellations are found on Nos. 9N1-9N20.

Stamps of Germany 1947-48 with "a" Overprint in Red

1948-49		Wmk. 284	Typo.	Perf. 14
9N21	A120	2pf brn blk ('49)	.75	1.90
9N22	A120	6pf purple ('49)	4.50	1.90
9N23	A121	8pf red ('49)	19.00	4.50
9N24	A121	10pf yellow grn	.75	.60
9N25	A120	15pf chocolate	1.60	1.90
9N26	A120	20pf blue	.75	.75
9N27	A120	25pf org yel ('49)	32.50	45.00
9N28	A122	30pf red ('49)	30.00	4.75
9N29	A121	40pf red vio ('49)	30.00	13.50
9N30	A123	50pt ultra ('49)	30.00	7.50
9N31	A122	60pf red brown	3.75	.60
9N32	A122	80pf dk bl ('49)	42.50	9.00

With "b" Overprint in Red
Engr.

9N33	A124	1m olive	225.00	450.00
9N34	A124	2m dk brn vio	100.00	225.00
	Nos. 9N21-9N34 (14)		521.10	766.90
	Set, never hinged		1,300.	

Forgeries exist of the overprints on Nos. 9N21-9N34. No. 9N33 exists imperf.

A1

Statue of Heinrich von Stephan — A2

1949, Apr. 9		Litho.	Perf. 14
9N35	A1	12pf gray	5.75	9.00
9N36	A1	16pf blue green	11.00	19.00
9N37	A1	24pf orange brn	7.50	.75
9N38	A1	50pf brown olive	55.00	45.00
9N39	A1	60pf brown red	65.00	37.50
9N40	A2	1m olive	30.00	140.00
9N41	A2	2m brown violet	37.50	90.00
	Nos. 9N35-9N41 (7)		211.75	341.25
	Set, never hinged		750.00	

75th anniv. of the UPU.

Brandenburg Gate, Berlin — A3

Tempelhof Airport — A4

Designs: 4pf, 8pf, 40pf, Schoeneberg, Rudolf Wilde Square. 5pf, 25pf, 5m, Tegel Castle. 6pf, 50pf, Reichstag Building. 10pf, 30pf, Cloisters, Kleist Park. 15pf, Tempelhof Airport. 20pf, 80pf, 90pf, Polytechnic College, Charlottenburg. 60pf, National Gallery. 2m, Gendarmen Square. 3m, Brandenburg Gate.

1949		Typo.	Wmk. 284

Size: 22x18mm

9N42	A3	1pf black	.20	.35
a.	Bklt. pane 5 + label		9.00	22.50
	Never hinged		22.50	
b.	Tête bêche		.35	1.25
	Never hinged		1.00	
9N43	A3	4pf yellow brn	.20	.35
a.	Bklt. pane 5 + label		9.00	22.50
	Never hinged		22.50	
b.	Tête bêche		.95	2.40
	Never hinged		1.90	
9N44	A3	5pf blue green	.20	.35
9N45	A3	6pf red violet	.35	1.50
9N46	A3	8pf red orange	.35	1.50
9N47	A3	10pf yellow grn	.35	.35
a.	Bklt. pane 5 + label		65.00	175.00
	Never hinged		140.00	
9N48	A4	15pf chocolate	3.75	.90
9N49	A3	20pf red	1.50	.35
a.	Bklt. pane 5 + label		65.00	175.00
	Never hinged		140.00	
9N50	A3	25pf orange	7.50	1.10
9N51	A3	30pf violet bl	3.50	1.25
a.	Imperf.		675.00	
	Never hinged		1,350.	
9N52	A3	40pf lake	4.50	1.10
9N53	A3	50pf olive	4.50	.35
9N54	A3	60pf red brown	15.00	.35
9N55	A3	80pf dark blue	3.00	1.10
9N56	A3	90pf emerald	3.00	1.50

Engr.
Size: 29¼-29¾x24-24½mm

9N57	A4	1m olive	5.50	1.10
9N58	A4	2m brown vio	15.00	1.50
9N59	A4	3m henna brn	67.50	15.00
9N60	A4	5m deep blue	45.00	15.00
	Nos. 9N42-9N60 (19)		180.90	45.00
	Set, never hinged		700.00	

See Nos. 9N101-9N102, 9N108-9N110.

Goethe and "Iphigenie" — A5

Statue of Atlas, New York — A6

Designs (Goethe and scenes from his works): 20pf, "Reineke Fuchs." 30pf, "Faust."

1949, July 29		Litho.	Perf. 14
9N61	A5	10pf green	42.50	65.00
9N62	A5	20pf carmine	42.50	75.00
9N63	A5	30pf ultra	7.50	50.00
	Nos. 9N61-9N63 (3)		92.50	190.00
	Set, never hinged		300.00	

Bicentenary of the birth of Johann Wolfgang von Goethe.

Germany Nos. 550, 565, 572 and 576 Surcharged "BERLIN" and New Value in Dark Green

1949, Aug. 1			Typo.
9N64	A119	5pf on 45pf	1.10	.35
9N65	A123	10pf on 24pf	3.25	.35
9N66	A122	20pf on 80pf	19.00	16.50
9N67	A124	1m on 3m	45.00	17.00
	Nos. 9N64-9N67 (4)		68.35	34.20
	Set, never hinged		250.00	

1950, Oct. 1		Engr.	Wmk. 116
9N68	A6	20pf dk carmine	35.00	40.00
	Never hinged		90.00	

European Recovery Plan.

Albert Lortzing — A7

Freedom Bell, Berlin — A8

1951, Apr. 22			
9N69	A7	20pf red brown	20.00	52.50
	Never hinged		52.50	

Centenary of the death of Albert Lortzing, composer.

1951			Perf. 14
9N70	A8	5pf chocolate	.75	7.50
9N71	A8	10pf deep green	3.75	22.50
9N72	A8	20pf rose red	2.25	19.00
9N73	A8	30pf blue	19.00	67.50
9N74	A8	40pf rose violet	5.50	37.50
	Nos. 9N70-9N74 (5)		31.25	154.00
	Set, never hinged		87.50	

Re-engraved

1951-52			
9N75	A8	5pf olive bis ('52)	.75	1.90
9N76	A8	10pf yellow grn	2.25	3.75
9N77	A8	20pf brt red	10.50	16.50
9N78	A8	30pf blue ('52)	24.00	50.00
9N79	A8	40pf dp car ('52)	10.50	15.00
	Nos. 9N75-9N79 (5)		48.00	87.15
	Set, never hinged		110.00	

Bell clapper moved from left to right. Imprint "L. Schnell" in lower margin.

No. 9N76 exists imperf. Value, $575 unused, $1,100 mint never hinged.

See Nos. 9N94-9N98.

Ludwig van Beethoven — A9

Olympic Symbols — A10

1952, Mar. 26		Engr.	Unwmk.
9N80	A9	30pf blue	16.00	30.00
	Never hinged		42.50	

125th anniversary of the death of Ludwig van Beethoven.

1952, June 20		Litho.	Wmk. 116
9N81	A10	4pf yellow brown	.35	1.90
9N82	A10	10pf green	3.75	15.00
9N83	A10	20pf rose red	6.75	26.00
	Nos. 9N81-9N83 (3)		10.85	42.90
	Set, never hinged		27.50	

Pre-Olympic Festival Day, June 20, 1952.

Carl Friedrich Zelter — A11

Arms Breaking Chains — A12

Portraits: 5pf, Otto Lilienthal. 6pf, Walter Rathenau. 8pf, Theodor Fontane. 10pf, Adolph von Menzel. 15pf, Rudolf Virchow. 20pf, Werner von Siemens. 25pf, Karl Friedrich Schinkel. 30pf, Max Planck. 40pf, Wilhelm von Humboldt.

1952-53		Engr.	Wmk. 284
9N84	A11	4pf brown	.20	.55
9N85	A11	5pf dp blue ('53)	.35	.55
9N86	A11	6pf choc ('53)	2.00	9.75
9N87	A11	8pf henna brn ('53)	.75	2.25
9N88	A11	10pf deep green	1.10	.55
9N89	A11	15pf purple ('53)	5.25	15.00
9N90	A11	20pf brown red	.75	.75
9N91	A11	25pf dp olive ('53)	16.00	6.75
9N92	A11	30pf brn vio ('53)	5.50	9.75
9N93	A11	40pf black ('53)	6.75	3.00
	Nos. 9N84-9N93 (10)		38.65	48.90
	Set, never hinged		140.00	

Bell Type of 1951-1952
Second Re-engraving

1953		Wmk. 284	Perf. 14
9N94	A8	5pf brown	.35	1.00
9N95	A8	10pf deep green	1.10	1.50
9N96	A8	20pf brt red	3.00	3.00
9N97	A8	30pf blue	5.00	12.00
9N98	A8	40pf rose violet	21.00	37.50
	Nos. 9N94-9N98 (5)		30.45	55.00
	Set, never hinged		77.50	

Bell clapper hangs straight down. Marginal imprint omitted.

For overprint & surcharge see #9N106, 9NB17.

1953, Aug. 17			Typo.

Design: 30pf, Brandenburg Gate.

9N99	A12	20pf black	1.25	1.50
9N100	A12	30pf dp carmine	9.00	30.00
	Set, never hinged		37.50	

Strike of East German workers, 6/17/53.

Similar to Type of 1949

Designs: 4pf, Exposition halls. 20pf, Olympic Stadium, Berlin.

1953-54		Wmk. 284	Perf. 14
9N101	A3	4pf yellow brn ('54)	1.75	5.00
9N102	A3	20pf red	22.50	2.50
	Set, never hinged		70.00	

> **Catalogue values for unused stamps in this section, from this point to the end of the section, are for Never Hinged items.**

Allied Council Building — A13

1954, Jan. 25			Litho.
9N103	A13	20pf red	8.25	4.50

Four Power Conference, Berlin, 1954.

Prof. Ernst Reuter (1889-1953), Mayor of Berlin (1948-53) A14

1954, Jan. 18		Engr.	Wmk. 284
9N104	A14	20pf chocolate	8.25	1.90

See No. 9N174.

Ottmar Mergenthaler and Linotype — A15

1954, May 11			
9N105	A15	10pf dk blue grn	2.75	2.75

Cent. of the birth of Ottmar Mergenthaler.

No. 9N96 Overprinted in Black

1954, July 17			Perf. 13½x14
9N106	A8	20pf bright red	4.25	5.25

Issued to publicize the West German presidential election held in Berlin July 17, 1954.

Germany in
Bondage — A16

Richard
Strauss — A17

1954, July 20   Typo.
9N107 A16 20pf car & gray   5.25 5.25

10th anniv. of the attempted assassination of Adolf Hitler.

Similar to Type of 1949

Designs: 7pf, Exposition halls. 40pf, Memorial library. 70pf, Hunting lodge, Grunewald.

1954   Wmk. 284   Perf. 14
9N108 A3   7pf aqua   5.50   1.50
9N109 A3 40pf rose lilac   9.00   3.00
9N110 A3 70pf olive green 105.00 21.00
Nos. 9N108-9N110 (3)   119.50 25.50
Set, hinged   50.00

1954, Sept. 18   Engr.
9N111 A17 40pf violet blue   11.00 3.75

5th anniv. of the death of Richard Strauss, composer.

Early
Forge — A18

1954, Sept. 25
9N112 A18 20pf reddish brown   7.50 1.90

Centenary of the death of August Borsig, industrial leader.

M. S. Berlin and
Arms of
Berlin — A19

1955, Mar. 12   Wmk. 284
9N113 A19 10pf Prus green   1.10 .75
9N114 A19 25pf violet blue   7.25 4.25

Issued to publicize the resumption of shipping under West German ownership.

Wilhelm
Furtwängler — A20

Perf. 13½x14
1955, Sept. 17   Unwmk.
9N115 A20 40pf ultra   21.00 21.00

Issued to honor the conductor Wilhelm Furtwängler and to publicize the Berlin Music Festival, September 1955.

Arms of Berlin
A21   A22

1955, Oct. 17   Litho.   Wmk. 304
9N116 A21 10pf red, org yel &
                  blk   .35   .75
9N117 A21 20pf red, org yel &
                  blk   5.25 9.00

Meeting of the German Bundestag in Berlin, Oct. 17-22, 1955.

1956, Mar. 16
9N118 A22 10pf red, ocher & blk 1.10 .75
9N119 A22 25pf red, ocher & blk 4.50 4.50

Meeting of the German Bundesrat in Berlin Mar. 16, 1956.

Radio Station, Berlin (A23
has no top inscription. A24
has top inscription.)
A23   A24

Free University
A25

Monument of the
Great Elector
Frederick William
A26

Designs: 1pf, 3pf, Brandenburg Gate. 5pf, General Post Office. 8pf, City Hall, Neukölln. 10pf, Kaiser Wilhelm Memorial Church. 15pf, Airlift memorial. 25pf, Lilienthal Monument. 30pf, Pfaueninsel Castle. 40pf, Charlottenburg Castle. 50pf, Reuter power plant. 60pf, Chamber of Commerce and Industry and Stock Exchange. 70pf, Schiller Theater. 3m, Congress Hall.

Typo.; Litho. (3pf, #9N122)
1956-63   Wmk. 304   Perf. 14
9N120 A25 1pf gray ('57)   .25   .20
9N120A A25 3pf brt pur ('63) .25   .20
9N121 A25 5pf rose lil ('57) .25   .20
9N122 A23 7pf blue green   8.25 2.40
9N123 A24 7pf blue green   .25   .20
9N124 A24 8pf gray   .45   .35
9N125 A24 8pf red org ('59) .30   .30
9N126 A24 10pf emerald   .25   .20
9N127 A24 15pf chlky blue   .45   .25
9N128 A25 20pf rose car   .45   .20
9N129 A24 25pf dull red brn   .45   .45

Engr.
9N130 A24 30pf gray grn
                  ('57)   .90   .90
9N131 A25 40pf lt ultra ('57) 9.00 7.50
9N132 A24 50pf olive   .90   .90
9N133 A25 60pf lt brn ('57)   .90   .90
9N134 A25 70pf violet   24.00 13.50
9N135 A26 1m olive   1.90 2.25

Size: 29x24½mm
9N136 A25 3m rose cl ('58) 5.25 22.50
Nos. 9N120-9N136 (18)   54.45 53.40

No. 9N120 exists on both ordinary and fluorescent paper; No. 9N120A on fluorescent paper only; others on ordinary paper.

Engineers' Society
Emblem — A27

Paul
Lincke — A28

1956, May 12   Engr.   Perf. 14
9N140 A27 10pf dark green   1.90 1.50
9N141 A27 20pf dark red   4.25 5.00

Cent. of Soc. of German Civil Engineers.

1956, Sept. 3
9N142 A28 20pf dark red   2.50 2.75

Death of Paul Lincke, composer, 10th anniv.

Radio Station,
Berlin-Nikolassee
A29

Spandau,
1850 — A30

1956, Sept. 15
9N143 A29 25pf brown   6.00 9.00

German Industrial Fair, Berlin, Sept. 15-30.

1957, Mar. 7
9N144 A30 20pf gray ol & brn
                  red   .60   .75

725th anniversary of Spandau.

Hansa Model
Town and
"B" — A31

Designs: 20pf, View of exposition grounds and "B." 40pf, Auditorium and "B."

1957   Engr.
9N145 A31 7pf violet brown   .20   .20
9N146 A31 10pf carmine   .75   .75
9N147 A31 40pf violet blue   1.90 2.25
Nos. 9N145-9N147 (3)   2.85 3.20

Intl. Building Show, Berlin, 7/6-9/29/57.

Friedrich Karl von
Savigny, Law
Teacher — A32

Uta Statue,
Naumburg
Cathedral — A33

Portraits: 7pf, Theodor Mommsen, historian. 8pf, Heinrich Zille, painter. 10pf, Ernst Reuter, mayor of Berlin. 15pf, Fritz Haber, chemist. 20pf, Friedrich Schleiermacher, theologian. 25pf, Max Reinhardt, theatrical director. 40pf, Alexander von Humboldt, naturalist and geographer. 50pf, Christian Daniel Rauch, sculptor.

1957-59   Wmk. 304   Perf. 14
Portraits in Brown
9N148 A32 7pf blue grn ('58) .20   .25
9N149 A32 8pf gray ('58)   .20   .25
9N150 A32 10pf green ('58)   .20   .25
9N151 A32 15pf dark blue   .35   .75
9N152 A32 20pf carmine ('58)   .20   .25
9N153 A32 25pf magenta   .80 1.00
9N154 A32 30pf olive green   2.10 2.50
9N155 A32 40pf blue ('59)   .80 1.00
9N156 A32 50pf olive   3.75 6.50
Nos. 9N148-9N156 (9)   8.60 12.75

Issued to honor famous men of Berlin.

See No. 9NB19.

1957, Aug. 6
9N157 A33 25pf brown red   .90 1.10

Issued to publicize the annual meeting of the East German Culture Society in Berlin.

"Unity and
Justice and
Liberty" — A34

Postilion 1897-
1925 — A35

1957, Oct. 15   Litho.
9N158 A34 10pf multicolored   .30   .75
9N159 A34 20pf multicolored   2.25 3.00

1st meeting of the 3rd German Bundesrat, Berlin, 10/15.

1957, Oct. 23   Wmk. 304   Perf. 14
9N160 A35 20pf multicolored   .75   .90

Issued for Stamp Day and BEPHILA stamp exhibition, Berlin, Oct. 23-27.

World Veterans'
Federation
Emblem — A36

Christ and the
Cosmos — A37

1957, Oct. 28
9N161 A36 20pf bl grn, ol grn &
                  yel   .90   .75

7th General Assembly of the World Veterans' Federation, Berlin, Oct. 24-Nov. 1.

1958, Aug. 13
9N162 A37 10pf lt bl grn & blk .35   .60
9N163 A37 20pf rose lilac & blk 1.00 1.50

Issued in honor of the 78th German Catholics Meeting, Berlin, Aug. 13-17.

Prof. Otto Suhr
(1894-1957),
Mayor of Berlin
(1955-57)
A38

1958, Aug. 30   Engr.   Perf. 14
9N164 A38 20pf rose red   1.10 2.00

Pres. Heuss Type of Germany, 1959
Litho., Engraved (40pf, 70pf)
1959
9N165 A208 7pf blue green   .20   .35
9N166 A208 10pf green   .25   .35
9N167 A208 20pf dk car rose   .50   .35
9N168 A208 40pf blue   2.25 4.50
9N169 A208 70pf dull purple 8.25 10.50
Nos. 9N165-9N169 (5)   11.45 16.05

Nos. 9N168-9N169 were issued in sheets of 100 and in coils. Every fifth coil stamp has a control number on the back.

Aerial Bridge to Berlin — A39

1959, May 12   **Engr.**
9N170 A39 25pf maroon & blk   .60   .45

10th anniversary of Berlin Airlift.

Globe and Brandenburg Gate — A40

1959, June 18   **Litho.**   **Perf. 14**
9N171 A40 20pf lt blue & red   .85   .45

Issued to publicize the 14th International Municipal Congress, Berlin, June 18-23.

Friedrich von Schiller (1759-1805), Poet — A41

1959, Nov. 10   **Engr.**   **Wmk. 304**
9N172 A41 20pf dull red & brn   .35   .45

Dr. Robert Koch (1843-1910), Bacteriologist A42

Hans Böckler (1875-1951), Labor Leader — A43

1960, May 27   **Perf. 14**
9N173 A42 20pf rose lake   .35   .45

Mayor Type of 1954

Portrait: Dr. Walther Carl Rudolf Schreiber, Mayor of Berlin, 1953-54.

1960, June 30   **Wmk. 304**   **Perf. 14**
9N174 A14 20pf brown car   .50   .65

1961, Feb. 16   **Litho.**   **Perf. 14**
9N175 A43 20pf dk brick red & blk   .30   .35

Hans Böckler (1875-1951), labor leader.

Fluorescent Paper was introduced for all stamps, starting with No. 9N176, and including Nos. 9N120 and 9N120A.

Albrecht Dürer — A44

Portraits: 5pf, Albertus Magnus. 7pf, St. Elizabeth of Thuringia. 8pf, Johann Gutenberg. 15pf, Martin Luther. 20pf, Johann Sebastian Bach. 25pf, Balthasar Neumann. 30pf, Immanuel Kant. 40pf, Gotthold Ephraim Lessing. 50pf, Johann Wolfgang von Goethe. 60pf, Friedrich von Schiller. 70pf, Ludwig van Beethoven. 80pf, Heinrich von Kleist. 1m,

Annette von Droste-Hülshoff. 2m, Gerhart Hauptmann.

1961-62   **Typo.**   **Wmk. 304**
9N176	A44	5pf olive	.20	.25
9N177	A44	7pf dk bister	.20	.35
9N178	A44	8pf lilac	.20	.35
9N179	A44	10pf olive green	.20	.25
b.		Tête bêche pair	1.10	2.25
9N180	A44	15pf blue	.20	.35
9N181	A44	20pf dark red	.20	.25
9N182	A44	25pf orange brn	.20	.35

Engr.
9N183	A44	30pf gray	.25	.50
9N184	A44	40pf blue	.50	.95
9N185	A44	50pf red brown	.35	.95
9N186	A44	60pf dk car rose ('62)	.35	1.10
9N187	A44	70pf green	.50	1.10
9N188	A44	80pf brown	3.00	7.50
9N189	A44	1m violet blue	1.40	3.50
9N190	A44	2m yel grn ('62)	1.75	5.00
		Nos. 9N176-9N190 (15)	9.50	22.75

Nos. 9N176-9N182, 9N184 and 9N187 were issued in sheets and in coils. Every fifth coil stamp has a black control number on the back.

Louise Schroeder A45

1961, June 3   **Engr.**   **Perf. 14**
9N192 A45 20pf dark brown   .35   .35

Issued to honor Louise Schroeder, acting mayor of Berlin (1947-1948).

Synod Emblem & St. Mary's Church — A46

Design: 20pf, Emblem and Kaiser Wilhelm Memorial Church.

1961, July 19   **Litho.**   **Wmk. 304**
9N193 A46 10pf green & vio   .25   .25
9N194 A46 20pf rose claret & vio   .25   .25

10th meeting of German Protestants (Evangelical Synod), Berlin, July 19-23.

Berlin Bear with Record, TV Set & Radio Tower — A47

1961, Aug. 3   **Engr.**
9N195 A47 20pf brn red & dk brn   .30   .30

German Radio, Television and Phonograph Exhibition, Berlin, Aug. 25-Sept. 3.

Berlin, 1650 — A48

Views of Old Berlin: 10pf, Spree and Waisenbrücke (Orphans' Bridge). 15pf, Mauer Street, 1780. 20pf, Berlin Palace, 1703. 25pf, Potsdam Square, 1825. 40pf, Bellevue Palace, 1800. 50pf, Fischer Bridge, 1830. 60pf, Halle Gate, 1880. 70pf, Parochial Church, 1780. 80pf, University, 1825. 90pf, Opera House, 1780. 1m, Grunewald Lake, 1790.

1962-63   **Wmk. 304**   **Perf. 14**
9N196 A48 7pf dk gray & gldn brn   .20   .20
9N197 A48 10pf grn & dk gray   .20   .20

9N198	A48	15pf bluish gray & dk bl ('63)	.20	.20
9N199	A48	20pf org brn & sep	.20	.20
9N200	A48	25pf ol & gray ('63)	.20	.25
9N201	A48	40pf bluish gray & ultra	.25	.40
9N202	A48	50pf gray & dk brn ('63)	.40	.40
9N203	A48	60pf gray & car rose ('63)	.45	.45
9N204	A48	70pf dk gray & lilac	.45	.45
9N205	A48	80pf dk gray & dk red ('63)	.55	.70
9N206	A48	90pf sep & brn org ('63)	.60	.75
9N207	A48	1m ol gray & dp grn	.70	1.10
		Nos. 9N196-9N207 (12)	4.40	5.30

Gelber Hund, 1912, and Boeing 707 — A49

1962, Sept. 12   **Litho.**
9N208 A49 60pf brt blue & blk   .55   .55

50th anniv. of German airmail service.

Berlin Bear and Radio Tower — A50

1963, July 24   **Unwmk.**   **Perf. 14**
9N209 A50 20pf bl, vio bl & gray   .30   .30

German Radio, Television and Phonograph Exhibition, Berlin, Aug. 30-Sept. 8.

Schöneberg City Hall, John F. Kennedy Place, Berlin — A51

1964, May 30   **Engr.**   **Wmk. 304**
9N210 A51 20pf dk brn, cr   .30   .30

700th anniv. of the Schöneberg district of Berlin. The Senate and House of Representatives of West Berlin meet at Schöneberg City Hall.

Lübke Type of Germany, 1964

1964, July 1   **Litho.**   **Unwmk.**
9N211 A247 20pf carmine   .20   .20
9N212 A247 40pf ultra   .35   .35

See Nos. 9N263-9N264.

Capitals Type of Germany

Design: Reichstag Building, Berlin.

1964, Sept. 14   **Litho.**   **Perf. 14**
9N213 A245 20pf blue, blk & grn   .35   .35

Kennedy Type of Germany

1964, Nov. 21   **Engr.**   **Wmk. 304**
9N214 A255 40pf dark blue   .45   .55

Castle Gate, Ellwangen — A52

Designs (German buildings through 12 centuries): 10pf, Wall pavilion, Zwinger, Dresden. 15pf, Tegel Castle, Berlin. 20pf, Portico, Lorsch. 40pf, Trifels Fortress, Palatinate. 60pf, Treptow Gate, Neubrandenburg. 70pf, Osthofen Gate, Soest. 80pf, Elling Gate, Weissenburg.

1964-65   **Typo.**   **Unwmk.**
9N215 A52 10pf brown ('65)   .20   .20
   b.   Tête bêche pair   .45   2.00
9N216 A52 15pf dk green ('65)   .20   .25

9N217 A52 20pf brn red ('65)   .20   .25

Engr.
9N218	A52	40pf vio bl ('65)	.60	1.10
9N219	A52	50pf olive bis	1.40	1.50
9N220	A52	60pf rose red	.95	1.10
9N221	A52	70pf dk green ('65)	1.90	3.50
9N222	A52	80pf chocolate	1.90	1.50
		Nos. 9N215-9N222 (8)	7.35	9.45

Nos. 9N215-9N218, 9N221 were issued in sheets of 100 and in coils. Every fifth coil stamp has a black control number on the back.

Kaiser Wilhelm Memorial Church A53

Nordertor, Flensburg A54

The New Berlin: 15pf, German Opera House, horiz. 20pf, Philharmonic Hall, horiz. 30pf, Jewish Community Center, horiz. 40pf, Regina Martyrum Memorial, horiz. 50pf, Ernst Reuter Square, horiz. 60pf, Europa Center. 70pf, School of Engineering, horiz. 80pf, City Highway. 90pf, Planetarium and observatory, horiz. 1m, Schaeferberg radio tower, Wannsee. 1.10m, University clinic, Steglitz, horiz.

Engraved and Lithographed
1965-66   **Unwmk.**   **Perf. 14**
9N223	A53	10pf multi	.20	.20
9N224	A53	15pf multi	.20	.20
9N225	A53	20pf multi	.20	.20
9N226	A53	30pf multi ('66)	.20	.20
9N227	A53	40pf multi ('66)	.25	.25
9N228	A53	50pf multi	.25	.30
9N229	A53	60pf multi ('66)	.30	.35
9N230	A53	70pf multi ('66)	.45	.45
9N231	A53	80pf multi	.45	.45
9N232	A53	90pf multi ('66)	.55	.75
9N233	A53	1m multi ('66)	.55	.90
9N234	A53	1.10m multi ('66)	.55	.95
		Nos. 9N223-9N234 (12)	4.15	5.20

1966-69   **Engr.**   **Perf. 14**

5pf, Berlin Gate, Stettin. 8pf, Castle, Kaub on the Rhine. 10pf, Wall Pavilion, Zwinger, Dresden. 20pf, Portico, Lorsch. 40pf, Trifels Fortress, Palatinate. 50pf, Castle Gate, Ellwangen. 60pf, Treptow Gate, Neubrandenburg. 70pf, Osthofen Gate, Soest. 80pf, Elling Gate, Weissenburg. 90pf, Zschocke Ladies' Home, Königsberg. 1m, Melanchthon House, Wittenberg. 1.10m, Trinity Hospital, Hildesheim. 1.30m, Tegel Castle, Berlin. 2m, Löwenberg Town Hall, interior view.

9N235	A54	5pf olive	.20	.20
9N236	A54	8pf car rose	.20	.20
9N237	A54	10pf dk brn ('67)	.20	.20
9N238	A54	20pf dk grn ('67)	.20	.20
9N239	A54	30pf yellow grn	.25	.25
9N240	A54	30pf red ('67)	.25	.20
9N241	A54	40pf ol bis ('67)	.55	.75
9N242	A54	50pf blue ('67)	.35	.45
9N243	A54	60pf dp org ('67)	1.50	1.90
9N244	A54	70pf sl grn ('67)	.75	.75
9N245	A54	80pf red brn ('67)	.95	1.60
9N246	A54	90pf black	.50	.75
9N247	A54	1m dull blue	.50	.75
9N248	A54	1.10m red brn	1.40	1.40
9N249	A54	1.30m green ('69)	2.25	2.25
9N250	A54	2m purple	2.25	1.90
		Nos. 9N235-9N250 (16)	12.30	13.75

Brandenburg Gate Type of Germany

1966-70   **Typo.**   **Perf. 14**
9N251	A268	10pf chocolate	.20	.20
a.		Bklt. pane of 10 (4 #9N251, 2 #9N252, 4 #9N253)	6.75	12.00
b.		Tête bêche pair	.90	1.10
c.		Bklt. pane of 6 (4 #9N251, 2 #9N253) ('70)	3.00	4.50
9N252	A268	20pf dp green	.20	.20
a.		Bklt. pane of 4 (2 #9N252, 2 #9N253) ('70)	2.25	3.00
9N253	A268	30pf red	.20	.20
a.		Tête bêche pair	1.10	2.40
9N254	A268	50pf dk blue	.55	.35
9N255	A268	100pf dk blue ('67)	4.25	4.25
		Nos. 9N251-9N255 (5)	5.40	5.20

Nos. 9N251-9N255 were issued in sheets of 100 and in coils. Every fifth coil stamp has a black control number on the back.

A55   A56

Designs: 10pf, Young Man, by Conrat Meit, 1520. 20pf, The Great Elector Friedrich Wilhelm (1640-88), head from monument by Andreas Schlüter. 30pf, The Evangelist Mark, by Tilman Riemenschneider. 50pf, Head of "Victory" from Brandenburg Gate, by Gottfried Schadow, 1793. 1m, Madonna, by Joseph Anton Feuchtmayer. 1.10m, Jesus and John, wood sculpture, anonymous, c. 1320.

1967   **Engr.**   **Perf. 14**
9N256 A55 10pf sepia & lemon   .20   .20
9N257 A55 20pf sl grn & bluish
              gray   .20   .20
9N258 A55 30pf brown & olive   .20   .20
9N259 A55 50pf black & gray   .35   .35
9N260 A55 1m blue & chlky
              blue   .75   .75

Size: 22x40mm

9N261 A55 1.10m brown & buff   1.10 1.50
  Nos. 9N256-9N261 (6)   2.80 3.20

Issued to publicize Berlin art treasures.

1967, July 19   Litho. and Engr.

Berlin Radio Tower and Television Screens

9N262 A56 30pf multicolored   .30   .35

25th German Radio, Television and Phonograph Exhibition, Berlin, Aug. 25-Sept. 3.

Lübke Type of Germany, 1964

1967, Oct. 14   Litho.
9N263 A247 30pf carmine   .20   .25
9N264 A247 50pf ultra   .35   .45

Old Court   Turners'
Building (Berlin   Emblem — A58
Museum) — A57

1968, Mar. 16   Engr.   Perf. 14
9N265 A57 30pf black   .30   .35

500th anniv. of the Berlin Court of Appeal.

1968, Apr. 29   Litho.   Perf. 14
9N266 A58 20pf gray, blk & red   .30   .35

Issued to publicize the German Turner Festival, Berlin, May 28-June 3.

Newspaper Vendor by Christian Wilhelm Allers — A59

19th Century Berliners: 5pf, Hack, by Heinrich Zille, horiz. No. 9N269, Horse omnibus, coachman and passengers, 1890, by C. W. Allers. No. 9N270, Cobbler's apprentice, by Franz Kruger. No. 9N271, Cobbler, by Adolph von Menzel. No. 9N272, Blacksmiths, by Paul Meyerheim. No. 9N273, Three Ladies, by Franz Kruger. 50pf, Strollers at Brandenburg Gate, by Christian W. Allers.

1969   **Engr.**   **Perf. 14**
9N267 A59 5pf black   .20   .20
9N268 A59 10pf dp brown   .20   .20
9N269 A59 10pf brown   .20   .20
9N270 A59 20pf dk olive grn   .20   .20
9N271 A59 20pf green   .20   .20
9N272 A59 30pf dk red brown   .60   .45
9N273 A59 30pf red brown   .60   .45
9N274 A59 50pf ultra   1.50 1.75
  Nos. 9N267-9N274 (8)   3.70 3.65

Berlin Zoo Animals — A60

Designs: 10pf, Orangutan family. 20pf, White pelicans. 30pf, Gaur and calf. 50pf, Zebra and foal.

Engraved and Lithographed
1969, June 4   Perf. 14
9N275 A60   Sheet of 4   1.90 1.90
  a.   10pf bister & black   .45   .45
  b.   20pf light green & black   .45   .45
  c.   30pf lilac rose & black   .45   .45
  d.   50pf blue & black   .45   .45

125th anniversary of the Berlin Zoo. The sheet was sold with a 20pf surtax for the benefit of the Zoo.

Australian   Joseph
Postman — A61   Joachim — A62

Designs: 20pf, African telephone operator. 30pf, Middle East telecommunications engineer. 50pf, Loading mail on plane.

1969, July 21   Litho.   Perf. 14
9N276 A61 10pf olive & apple
              grn   .20   .20
9N277 A61 20pf dk brn, bis &
              brn   .25   .25
9N278 A61 30pf vio blk & bis   .55   .60
9N279 A61 50pf dk blue & blue   1.25 1.25
  Nos. 9N276-9N279 (4)   2.25 2.30

20th Congress of the Post Office Trade Union Federation, Berlin, July 7-11.

1969, Sept. 12   Photo.   Perf. 14

Design: 50pf, Alexander von Humboldt, painting by Joseph Stieler.

9N280 A62 30pf multicolored   .55   .45
9N281 A62 50pf multicolored   .90   1.25

Cent. of the Berlin Music School and honoring its 1st director, Joseph Joachim (1831-1907), violinist, conductor and composer; Alexander von Humboldt (1769-1859), naturalist and explorer.

1970, Jan. 7

Theodor Fontane, painting by Hanns Fechner.

9N282 A62 20pf multicolored   .35   .30

150th anniv. of the birth of Theodor Fontane (1819-1898), poet and writer.
See No. 9N303.

Film   Symbols of
Frame — A63   Dance, Theater &
                   Art — A64

1970, June 18   Photo.   Perf. 14
9N283 A63 30pf multicolored   .45   .55

20th International Film Festival.

1970-73   **Engr.**   **Perf. 14**
9N284 A312 5pf dk gray   .20   .20
9N285 A312 8pf olive bis   .70   .90
9N286 A312 10pf brown   .20   .20
9N286A A312 15pf olive   .20   .25
9N287 A312 20pf green   .20   .20
9N288 A312 25pf dp yel grn   .90   .55
9N289 A312 30pf red brown   .95   .25
9N290 A312 40pf brown org   .55   .25
9N291 A312 50pf dark blue   .55   .20
9N292 A312 60pf blue   .90   .55
9N293 A312 70pf dk brown   .70   .60
9N294 A312 80pf slate grn   .90   .90
9N295 A312 90pf magenta   1.75 2.25
9N296 A312 1m olive   .90   .70
9N297 A312 110pf olive gray   1.10 1.10
9N296A A312 120pf ocher   1.10 .90
9N298 A312 130pf ocher   1.60 1.50
9N298A A312 140pf dk blue
              grn   1.60 1.50
9N299 A312 150pf purple   1.60 .75
9N300 A312 160pf orange   2.25 1.90
9N300A A312 170pf orange   1.60 1.60
9N300B A312 190pf dp claret   1.90 2.75
9N301 A312 2m dp violet   1.90 1.40
  Nos. 9N284-9N301 (23)   24.25 21.70

Issued: 5pf, 1m, 7/23; 10, 20pf, 10/23; 30, 90pf, 2m, 1/7/71; 8, 40, 50, 70, 80pf, 4/8/71; 60pf, 6/25/71; 25pf, 8/27/71; 120, 160pf, 3/8/72; 15, 130pf, 6/20/72; 150pf, 7/5/72; 170pf, 9/11/72; 110, 140, 190pf, 1/16/73.

1970, Sept. 4   Litho.   Perf. 13½x14
9N302 A64 30pf gray & multi   .55   .55

20th Berlin Festival Weeks.

Portrait Type of 1969

30pf, Leopold von Ranke, by Julius Schrage.

1970, Oct. 23   Photo.   Perf. 13½x14
9N303 A62 30pf multicolored   .45   .35

175th anniversary of the birth of Leopold von Ranke (1795-1886), historian.

Imperial Eagle Type of Germany
1971, Jan. 18   Litho.   Perf. 13½x14
9N304 A317 30pf org, red, gray &
              blk   .55   .55

Metropolitan Train, 1932 — A65

5pf, Suburban train, 1925. 10pf, Street cars, 1890. 20pf, Horsedrawn trolley. 50pf, Street car, 1950. 1m, Subway train, 1971.

1971   **Litho.**   **Perf. 14**
9N305 A65 5pf multicolored   .20   .20
9N306 A65 10pf multicolored   .20   .20
9N307 A65 20pf multicolored   .25   .25
9N308 A65 30pf multicolored   .45   .35
9N309 A65 50pf multicolored   1.60 1.40
9N310 A65 1m multicolored   1.90 1.90
  Nos. 9N305-9N310 (6)   4.60 4.30

Issued: 30pf, 1m, Jan. 18; others, May 3.

Bagpipe Player, by Dürer — A66

1971, May 21   Engr.   Perf. 14
9N311 A66 10pf black & brown   .45   .30

500th anniversary of the birth of Albrecht Dürer (1471-1528), painter and engraver.

Score from 2nd Brandenburg Concerto and Bach — A67

1971, July 14   Litho.   Perf. 14
9N312 A67 30pf buff, brn & slate   .70   .60

250th anniv. of 1st performance of Johann Sebastian Bach's 2nd Brandenburg Concerto.

A68   A69

1971, July 14   Photo.

Telecommunications tower, Berlin.

9N313 A68 30pf dk blue, blk &
              car   .75   .60

Intl. Broadcasting Exhibition, Berlin.

1971, Aug. 27

9N314 A69 25pf multicolored   .55   .40

Hermann von Helmholtz (1821-94), scientist. See Nos. 9N332-9N333, 9N341.

Souvenir Sheet

Racing Cars — A70

1971, Aug. 27   Litho.   Perf. 14
9N315 A70   Sheet of 4   1.50 1.50
  a.   10pf Opel racer   .20   .20
  b.   25pf Auto Union racer   .25   .20
  c.   30pf Mercedes-Benz SSKL,
          1931   .35   .20
  d.   60pf Mercedes and Auto
          Union cars racing on North
          embankment   .60   .60

50th anniversary of Avus Race Track.

Accident Prevention Type of Germany

5pf, "Matches cause fires." 10pf, Broken ladder. 20pf, Hand & circular saw. 25pf, "Alcohol & automobile." 30pf, Safety helmets prevent injury. 40pf, Defective plug. 50pf, Nail sticking from board. 60pf, 70pf, Traffic safety (ball rolling before car). 100pf, Hoisted cargo. 150pf, Fenced-in open manhole.

1971-73   **Typo.**   **Perf. 14**
9N316 A328 5pf orange   .25   .30
9N317 A328 10pf dk
              brown   .20   .20
  a.   Bklt. pane, 2 each
          #9N317-9N318,
          9N320-9N321 ('74)   7.00 7.50
9N318 A328 20pf purple   .25   .25
9N319 A328 25pf green   .35   .60
9N320 A328 30pf dark
              red   .35   .30
9N321 A328 40pf rose cl   .35   .40
9N322 A328 50pf Prus
              blue   1.90 1.10
9N323 A328 60pf violet
              blue   1.90 2.25
9N323A A328 70pf green &
              vio bl   1.40 1.00
9N324 A328 100pf olive   1.90 1.10
9N325 A328 150pf red
              brown   5.75 6.75
  Nos. 9N316-9N325 (11)   14.60 14.25

Issued in sheets of 100 and coils. Every fifth coil stamp has a control number on the back. Issued: 25pf, 60pf, 9/10; 5pf, 10/29; 10pf, 30pf, 3/8/72; 40pf, 6/20/72; 20pf, 100pf, 7/5/72; 150pf, 9/11/72; 50pf, 1/16/73; 70pf, 6/5/73.

Microscope and Metal Slide — A71

Friedrich Gilly, by Gottfried Schadow — A72

1971, Oct. 26　Photo.　Perf. 14
9N326　A71 30pf multicolored　.45　.35

Materials Testing Laboratory centenary.

1972, Feb. 4　Engr.　Perf. 14
9N327　A72 30pf black & blue　.55　.35

Friedrich Gilly (1772-1800), sculptor.

Grunewaldsee, by Alexander von Riesen — A73

Paintings of Berlin Lakes: 25pf, Wannsee, by Max Liebermann. 30pf, Schlachtensee, by Walter Leistikow.

1972, Apr. 14　Photo.　Perf. 14
9N328　A73 10pf blue & multi　.20　.20
9N329　A73 25pf green & multi　.55　.55
9N330　A73 30pf black & multi　.95　.60
　Nos. 9N328-9N330 (3)　1.70　1.35

A74　　A75

1972, May 18
9N331　A74 60pf violet & blk　1.00　1.00

E. T. A. Hoffmann (1776-1822), writer and composer. (Portrait by Wilhelm Hensel.)

Portrait Type of 1971

Designs: No. 9N332, Max Liebermann (1847-1935), self-portrait. No. 9N333, Karl August, Duke of Hardenberg (1750-1822), Prussian statesman, by J. H. W. Tischbein.

1972　Photo.　Perf. 14
9N332　A69 40pf multicolored　.70　.45
9N333　A69 40pf multicolored　.60　.45

Issued: #9N332, July 18; #9N333, Nov. 10.

1972, Oct. 20　Engr. & Litho.
9N334　A75 20pf Stamp-printing
　　　press　.45　.30

Stamp Day 1972, and for the 5th National Youth Philatelic Exhib., Berlin, Oct. 26-29.

Streetcar, 1907 A76

#9N336, Double-decker bus, 1919. #9N337, Double-decker bus, 1925. #9N338, Electrobus, 1933. #9N339, Double-decker bus, 1970. #9N340, Elongated bus, 1973.

1973, Apr. 30　Litho.　Perf. 14
9N335　A76 20pf gray & multi　.35　.30
9N336　A76 30pf gray & multi　.75　.45
9N337　A76 40pf gray & multi　1.10　.70

1973, Sept. 14
9N338　A76 20pf gray & multi　.35　.30
9N339　A76 30pf gray & multi　1.10　.45
9N340　A76 40pf gray & multi　1.10　.70
　Nos. 9N335-9N340 (6)　4.75　2.90

Public transportation in Berlin.

Portrait Type of 1971

Design: 40pf, Ludwig Tieck (1773-1853), poet and writer, by Carl Christian Vogel von Vogelstein.

1973, May 25　Photo.　Perf. 14
9N341　A69 40pf multicolored　.70　.40

Johann Joachim Quantz (1697-1773), Flutist and Composer — A77

1973, June 12　Engr.　Perf. 14
9N342　A77 40pf black　.75　.60

Souvenir Sheet

50 Years of Broadcasting — A78

1973, Aug. 23　Litho.　Perf. 14
9N343　A78　Sheet of 4　3.75　3.75
　a.　A78 20pf Speaker, set, 1926　.90　.60
　b.　A78 30pf Hans Bredow　.90　.90
　c.　A78 40pf Girl, TV, tape re-
　　　corder　.90　.90
　d.　A78 70pf TV camera　.90　1.25

50 years of German broadcasting. Sold for 1.80m.

Georg W. von Knobelsdorff A79

Gustav R. Kirchhoff — A80

1974, Feb. 15　Engr.　Perf. 14
9N344　A79 20pf chocolate　.45　.30

275th anniversary of the birth of Georg Wenzelslaus von Knobelsdorff (1699-1753), architect.

1974, Feb. 15　Litho. & Engr.
9N345　A80 30pf gray & dk grn　.35　.35

Sesquicentennial of the birth of Gustav Robert Kirchhoff (1824-1887), physicist.

Airlift Memorial, Allied Flags — A81

1974, Apr. 17　Photo.　Perf. 14
9N346　A81 90pf multicolored　2.25　1.50

End of the Allied airlift into Berlin, 25th anniv.

Adolf Slaby and Waves — A82

1974, Apr. 17　Litho.　Perf. 14
9N347　A82 40pf black & red　.55　.40

125th anniversary of the birth of Adolf Slaby (1849-1913), radio pioneer.

School Seal Showing Athena and Hermes — A83

1974, July 13　Photo.　Perf. 14
9N348　A83 50pf multicolored　.70　.45

400th anniversary of the Gray Brothers' School, a secondary Franciscan school.

Berlin-Tegel Airport — A84

Lithographed and Engraved
1974, Oct. 15　Perf. 14
9N349　A84 50pf multicolored　1.00　.60

Opening of Berlin-Tegel Airport and Terminal, Nov. 1, 1974.

Venus, by F. E. Meyer, c. 1775 — A85

Gottfried Schadow — A86

Berlin Porcelain: 40pf, "Astronomy," by W. C. Meyer, c. 1772. 50pf, "Justice," by J. G. Müller, c. 1785.

1974, Oct. 29　Litho.　Perf. 14
9N350　A85 30pf carmine & multi　.55　.45
9N351　A85 40pf carmine & multi　.60　.55
9N352　A85 50pf carmine & multi　.70　.70
　Nos. 9N350-9N352 (3)　1.85　1.70

1975, Jan. 15　Engr.
9N353　A86 50pf maroon　.75　.55

Johann Gottfried Schadow (1764-1850), sculptor.

S.S. Princess Charlotte A87

Ships: 40pf, S.S. Siegfried. 50pf, S.S. Sperber. 60pf, M.S. Vaterland. 70pf, M.S. Moby Dick.

1975, Feb. 14　Litho.　Perf. 14
9N354　A87 30pf gray & multi　.60　.30
9N355　A87 40pf olive & multi　.60　.30
9N356　A87 50pf ultra & multi　1.10　.70
9N357　A87 60pf red brn & multi　1.10　.70
9N358　A87 70pf dk blue & multi　1.50　1.40
　Nos. 9N354-9N358 (5)　4.90　3.40

Berlin passenger ships

Industry Type of Germany
1975-82　Engr.　Perf. 14
Design A380
9N359　5pf Symphonie sat-
　　　ellite　.20　.20
9N360　10pf Electric train　.20　.20
9N361　20pf Old Weser
　　　lighthouse　.20　.20
9N362　30pf Rescue heli-
　　　copter　.35　.20
9N363　40pf Space shuttle　.50　.25
9N364　50pf Radar station　.50　.20
9N365　60pf X-ray machine　.80　.35
9N366　70pf Shipbuilding　.90　.45
9N367　80pf Tractor　.90　.25
9N368　100pf Coal excavator　.90　.45
9N368A　110pf TV camera　1.40　1.10
9N369　120pf Chemical plant　1.25　.90
9N369A　130pf Brewery　2.25　1.10
9N370　140pf Heating plant　1.25　1.25
9N371　150pf Power shovel　3.00　1.10
9N372　160pf Blast furnace　2.90　1.25
9N373　180pf Payloader　3.00　1.90
9N373A　190pf As #9N371　3.00　2.10
9N374　200pf Oil drill plat-
　　　form　1.60　.45
9N375　230pf Frankfurt air-
　　　port　2.40　1.90
9N375A　250pf Airport　4.00　2.10
9N375B　300pf Electric railroad　4.00　2.10
9N376　500pf Radio tele-
　　　scope　5.75　3.75
　Nos. 9N359-9N376 (23)　41.25　23.75

Issued: 40, 50, 100pf, 5/15; 10, 30, 70pf, 8/14; 80, 120, 160pf, 10/15; 5, 140, 200pf, 11/14; 20, 500pf, 2/17/76; 60pf, 11/16/78; 230pf, 5/17/79; 150, 180pf, 7/12/79; 110, 130, 300pf, 6/16/82; 190, 250pf, 7/15/82.

Ferdinand Sauerbruch — A88

Lithographed and Engraved
1975, May 15　Perf. 13½x14
9N379　A88 50pf dull red & dk brn　.75　.55

Ferdinand Sauerbruch (1875-1951) surgeon, birth centenary.

Gymnasts' Emblem — A89

1975, May 15　Photo.　Perf. 14
9N380　A89 40pf green, gold &
　　　blk　.55　.35

6th Gymnaestrada, Berlin, July 1-5.

Lovis Corinth (1858-1925), Self-portrait, 1900 — A90

1975, July 15   Photo.   Perf. 14
9N381 A90 50pf multicolored   .75 .55

Architecture Type of Germany

Houses, Naunynstrasse, Berlin-Kreuzberg.

1975, July 15   Litho. & Engr.
9N382 A381 50pf multicolored   .75 .60

European Architectural Heritage Year.

Paul Löbe and Reichstag A92

1975, Nov. 14   Engr.   Perf. 14
9N383 A92 50pf copper red   .75 .55

Paul Löbe (1875-1967), president of German Parliament 1920-1932, birth centenary.

Grain — A93

1976, Jan. 5   Photo.   Perf. 14
9N384 A93 70pf green & yellow   .75 .60

Green Week International Agricultural Exhibition, Berlin, 50th anniversary.

Hockey A94

1976, May 13   Engr.   Perf. 14
9N385 A94 30pf green   .70 .35

Women's World Hockey Championships.

Treble Clef — A95

1976, May 13   Photo.
9N386 A95 40pf multicolored   .75 .45

German Choir Festival.

Berlin Fire Brigade Emblem — A96

1976, May 13   Litho.
9N387 A96 50pf red & multi   1.25 .75

Berlin Fire Brigade, 125th anniversary.

Sailboat on Havel River — A97

Berlin Views: 40pf, Spandau Castle. 50pf, Tiergarten.

1976, Nov. 16   Engr.   Perf. 14
9N388 A97 30pf blue & blk   .55 .35
9N389 A97 40pf brown & blk   .75 .35
9N390 A97 50pf green & blk   .85 .35
    Nos. 9N388-9N390 (3)   2.15 1.05

See Nos. 9N422-9N424.

Castle Type of Germany

1977-79   Typo.   Perf. 14

10pf, Glücksburg. 20pf, 190pf, Pfaueninsel. 25pf, Gemen. 30pf, Ludwigstein. 40pf, Eltz. 50pf, Neuschwanstein. 60pf, Marksburg. 70pf, Mespelbrunn. 90pf, Vischering. 200pf, Bürresheim. 210pf, Schwanenburg. 230pf, Lichtenberg.

9N391 A406 10pf gray blue   .20 .20
    a.   Bklt. pane, 4 #9N391, 2
          each #9N394, 9N396   8.00 10.50
    b.   Bklt. pane, 4 #9N391, 2
          #9N394, 2 #9N440   4.00 6.75
    c.   Bklt. pane, 4 #9N391, 2
          #9N440, 2 #9N442   8.75 15.00
    d.   Bklt. pane, 2 each
          #9N391, 9N394, 9N440-
          9N441   15.00 22.50
9N392 A406 20pf orange   .20 .20
9N393 A406 25pf crimson   .35 .35
9N394 A406 30pf olive   .25 .20
9N395 A406 40pf blue green   .30 .20
9N396 A406 50pf rose car   .55 .25
9N397 A406 60pf brown   .95 .45
9N398 A406 70pf blue   .95 .45
9N399 A406 90pf dark blue   .85 .75
9N400 A406 190pf red brown   1.40 1.40
9N401 A406 200pf green   1.40 1.40
9N402 A406 210pf red brown   2.00 1.50
9N403 A406 230pf dark green   2.00 1.50
    Nos. 9N391-9N403 (13)   11.40 8.85

Issued in sheets of 100 and coils. Every fifth coil stamp has a control number on the back. Issued: 60pf, 200pf, 1/13; 40pf, 190pf, 2/16; 10pf, 20pf, 30pf, 4/14; 50pf, 70pf, 5/17; 230pf, 11/16/78; 25pf, 90pf, 1/11/79; 210pf, 2/14/79. See Nos. 9N438-9N445.

Eugenie d'Alton, by Rausch — A98

1977, Jan. 13   Photo.   Perf. 14
9N404 A98 50pf violet black   .75 .55

Christian Daniel Rausch (1777-1857), sculptor, birth bicentenary.

Eduard Gaertner (1801-77), Painter — A99

1977, Feb. 16   Litho. & Engr.
9N405 A99 40pf lt grn, grn & blk   .55 .35

Fountain, by Georg Kolbe — A100

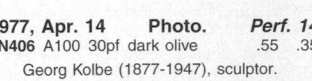

1977, Apr. 14   Photo.   Perf. 14
9N406 A100 30pf dark olive   .55 .35

Georg Kolbe (1877-1947), sculptor.

"Bear each other's burdens" A101

1977, May 17   Litho.   Perf. 14
9N407 A101 40pf green blk & yel   .55 .35

17th meeting of German Protestants (Evangelical Synod), Berlin.

Patent Office, Berlin-Kreuzberg — A102

1977, July 13   Litho. & Engr.
9N408 A102 60pf gray & red   1.50 .65

Centenary of German patent laws.

Telephones, 1905 and 1977 A103

Painting by George Grosz (1893-1959) A104

1977, July 13   Litho.
9N409 A103 50pf multicolored   1.75 1.00

International Broadcasting Exhibition, Berlin, Aug. 26-Sept. 4, and centenary of telephone in Germany.

1977, July 13
9N410 A104 70pf multicolored   .90 .90

15th European Art Exhibition, Berlin, Aug. 14-Oct. 16.

Rhinecanthus Aculeatus — A105

Designs: 30pf, Paddlefish. 40pf, Tortoise. 50pf, Rhinoceros iguana. Designs include statue of iguanodon from Aquarium entrance.

1977, Aug. 16   Photo.   Perf. 14
9N411 A105 20pf multicolored   .45 .45
9N412 A105 30pf multicolored   .70 .60
9N413 A105 40pf multicolored   .95 .75
9N414 A105 50pf multicolored   1.40 .90
    Nos. 9N411-9N414 (4)   3.50 2.70

25th anniv. of the reopening of Berlin Aquarium.

Walter Kollo (1878-1940), Composer — A106

1978, Jan. 12   Engr.   Perf. 14
9N415 A106 50pf brn, red & dk brn   1.00 .65

Chamber of Commerce Emblem — A107

1978, Apr. 13   Engr.   Perf. 14
9N416 A107 90pf dk blue & red   1.25 1.25

American Chamber of Commerce in Germany, 75th anniversary.

Albrecht von Graefe — A108

1978, May 22   Engr.   Perf. 14
9N417 A108 30pf red brn & blk   .55 .35

Dr. von Graefe (1828-70) ophthalmologist.

Friedrich Ludwig Jahn — A109

1978, July 13   Engr.   Perf. 14
9N418 A109 50pf dk carmine   .75 .55

Friedrich Ludwig Jahn (1778-1852), founder of organized gymnastics.

Swimmers — A110

1978, Aug. 17   Litho.   Perf. 14
9N419 A110 40pf multicolored   1.00 .80

3rd World Swimming Championships, Berlin, Aug. 18-28.

The Boat, by Karl Hofer — A111

1978, Oct. 12   Photo.   Perf. 14
9N420 A111 50pf multicolored   .75 .60

Karl Hofer (1878-1955), painter.

National Library A112

1978, Nov. 16   Engr.   Perf. 14
9N421 A112 90pf red & olive   1.40 .95

Opening of new National Library building.

Views Type of 1976

Berlin Views: 40pf, Belvedere, Charlottenburg Castle. 50pf, Shell House on Landwehr Canal. 60pf, Village Church, Alt-Lichtenrade.

1978, Nov. 16
9N422 A97 40pf green & blk .60 .35
9N423 A97 50pf lilac & blk .75 .60
9N424 A97 60pf brown & blk .90 .70
Nos. 9N422-9N424 (3) 2.25 1.65

International Conference Center — A113

Photogravure and Engraved
1979, Feb. 14   **Perf. 14**
9N425 A113 60pf multicolored 1.10 .65
Opening of Intl. Conference Center in Berlin.

A114   A115

1979, May 17   Litho.   Perf. 14
9N426 A114 60pf German eagles 1.40 1.00
Cent. of German Natl. Printing Bureau.

1979, July 12   Photo.   Perf. 14
9N427 A115 60pf TV screen, emblem 1.00 .75
Intl. Broadcasting Exhibition, Berlin.

Target and Arrows A116

1979, July 12
9N428 A116 50pf multicolored .75 .55
World Archery Championships, Berlin.

Moses Mendelssohn A117

1979, Aug. 9   Engr.   Perf. 14
9N429 A117 90pf black 1.25 .75
Mendelssohn (1729-86), philosopher.

Gas Lamp — A118

Historic Street Lanterns: 40pf, Carbon arc lamp. 50pf, Hanging gas lamps. 60pf, 5-armed candelabra.

1979, Aug. 9   Litho.
9N430 A118 10pf multicolored .35 .20
9N431 A118 40pf multicolored .75 .60
9N432 A118 50pf multicolored 1.10 .60
9N433 A118 60pf multicolored 1.10 1.00
Nos. 9N430-9N433 (4) 3.30 2.40
300 years of street lighting in Berlin.

Orchid A119

1979, Aug. 9
9N434 A119 50pf multicolored .85 .55
Botanical Gardens, Berlin, 300th anniv.

Berlin Poster Columns, 125th Anniversary A120

Lithographed and Engraved
1979, Nov. 14   **Perf. 14**
9N435 A120 50pf multicolored 1.40 .75

Castle Type of Germany

1979-82   Typo.   Perf. 14
9N438 A406 35pf Lichtenstein .30 .30
9N439 A406 40pf Wolfsburg .55 .30
9N440 A406 50pf Inzlingen .60 .30
9N441 A406 60pf Rheydt .90 .45
9N442 A406 80pf Wilhelmsthal .60 .30
9N443 A406 120pf Charlottenburg 1.00 .90
9N444 A406 280pf Ahrensburg 3.50 2.25
9N445 A406 300pf Herrenhausen 3.50 2.25
Nos. 9N438-9N445 (8) 10.95 7.05

Issued: 60pf, 11/14; 40pf, 50pf, 2/14/80; 35pf, 80pf, 30pf, 6/16/82; 120pf, 280pf, 7/15/82.

World Map Showing Continental Drift — A121

1980, Feb. 14   Litho.   Perf. 14
9N451 A121 60pf multicolored 1.40 1.00
Alfred Wegener (1880-1930), geophysicist and meteorologist; founded theory of continental drift.

German Catholics Day — A122

1980, May 8   Engr.   Perf. 14
9N452 A122 50pf blk & car rose .75 .55

Cardinal Count Preysing (1880-1950).

Prussian Museum, Berlin, 150th Anniv. — A123

Designs: 40pf, Angel, enamel medallion, 12th cent. 60pf, Monks Reading, oak sculpture, by Ernest Barlach (1870-1938).

1980, July 10   Litho.   Perf. 14
9N453 A123 40pf multicolored .75 .45
9N454 A123 60pf multicolored 1.00 .60

Von Steuben Leading Troops — A124

1980, Aug. 14   Litho.   Perf. 14
9N455 A124 40pf multicolored 1.00 .55
Friedrich Wilhelm von Steuben (1730-94).

Robert Stolz (1880-1975), Composer A125

1980, Aug. 14
9N456 A125 60pf dk blue & bis 1.00 .75

Lilienthal Memorial — A126

Designs: 50pf, Grosse Neugierde Memorial, 1835. 60pf, Lookout tower, Grunewald Memorial to Kaiser Wilhelm I.

1980, Nov. 13   Engr.   Perf. 14
9N457 A126 40pf dk green & blk .75 .35
9N458 A126 50pf brown & blk .80 .75
9N459 A126 60pf dk blue & blk 1.25 .75
Nos. 9N457-9N459 (3) 2.80 1.85

Von Gontard and Kleist Park Colonnades, Berlin — A127

1981, Jan. 15   Litho.   Perf. 14
9N460 A127 50pf multicolored .90 .60
Karl Philipp von Gontard (1731-91), architect.

Achim von Arnim (1781-1831), Poet — A128

1981, Jan. 15   Engr.
9N461 A128 60pf dark green .90 .60

Adelbert von Chamisso (1781-1838), Poet — A129

1981, Jan. 15   Litho.
9N462 A129 60pf brn & gldn brn .90 .60

Berlin-Kreuzberg, Liberation Monument, 1813 — A130

1981, Feb. 12   Engr.   Perf. 14
9N463 A130 40pf brown 1.10 .75
Karl Friedrich Schinkel (1781-1841), architect, 400th anniversary of birth.

Robert Stolz (1880-1975), Composer A125

Arts and Science Medal, Awarded 1842-1933 — A131

1981, July 16   Litho.   Perf. 14
9N464 A131 40pf multicolored .75 .55
"Prussia—an attempt at a balance" exhibition.

Amor and Psyche, by Reinhold Begas (1831-1911) A132

1981, July 16   Photo.
9N465 A132 50pf multicolored .75 .55

Intl. Telecommunications Exhibition — A133

1981, July 16   Litho.
9N466 A133 60pf multicolored 1.25 .75

Peter Beuth (1781-1853), Constitutional Law Expert — A134

Lithographed and Engraved
1981, Nov. 12   **Perf. 14**
9N467 A134 60pf gold & black .75 .60

Nijinsky, by Georg Kolbe, 1914 — A135

20th Century Sculptures: 60pf, Mother Earth II, by Ernst Barlach, 1920. 90pf, Flora Kneeling, by Richard Scheibe, 1930.

1981, Nov. 12   Photo.
9N468 A135 40pf multicolored .55 .35
9N469 A135 60pf multicolored .90 .60
9N470 A135 90pf multicolored 1.25 1.00
Nos. 9N468-9N470 (3) 2.70 1.95

750th Anniv. of Spandau A136

Lithographed and Engraved
1982, Feb. 18   **Perf. 14**
9N471 A136 60pf multicolored   1.25 .90

Berlin Philharmonic Centenary — A137

Lithographed and Embossed
1982, Apr. 15   **Perf. 14**
9N472 A137 60pf multicolored   1.10 .60

Salzburg Emigration to Prussia, 250th Anniv. — A138

& 1982, May 5   **Litho.**   **Engr.**
9N473 A138 50pf multicolored   .75 .55

Italian Stone Carriers, by Max Pechstein — A139

80pf, Two Girls Bathing, by Otto Mueller.

1982, July 15   **Litho.**   **Perf. 14**
9N474 A139 50pf multicolored   .90 .70
9N475 A139 80pf multicolored   1.40 1.00

Villa Borsig — A140

1982, Nov. 10   **Engr.**   **Perf. 14**
9N476 A140 50pf shown   1.10 .70
9N477 A140 60pf Sts. Peter and Paul Church   1.10 .80
9N478 A140 80pf Villa von der Heydt   1.50 .90
   Nos. 9N476-9N478 (3)   3.70 2.40

State Theater, Charlottenburg, 1790 — A141

1982, Nov. 10   **Litho. & Engr.**
9N479 A141 80pf multicolored   1.60 1.10
   Carl Gotthard Langhans (1732-1808), architect.

A142   A142a

Various street pumps and fire hydrants, 1900.

1983, Jan. 13   **Litho.**   **Perf. 14**
9N480 A142 50pf multi   1.10 .75
9N481 A142 60pf multi   1.40 .75
9N482 A142 80pf multi   1.60 1.25
9N483 A142 120pf multi   2.25 2.00
   Nos. 9N480-9N483 (4)   6.35 4.75

1983, Feb. 8   **Engr.**   **Perf. 14**
9N484 A142a 80pf dark brown   1.75 1.40
   Berlin-Koblenz Telegraph Service sesquicentennial.

Portrait of Barbara Campanini, 1745, by Antoine Pesne (1683-1757) A143

1983, May 5   **Photo.**   **Perf. 14**
9N485 A143 50pf multicolored   .90 .65

Joachim Ringelnatz (1883-1934), Painter and Writer — A144

1983, July 14   **Litho.**   **Perf. 14**
9N486 A144 50pf Silhouette   1.00 .75

Intl. Radio Exhibition, Sept. 2-11 — A145

1983, July 14
9N487 A145 80pf Nipkow's phototelegraphy diagram   1.60 1.25

Ancient Artwork, Berlin Museum A146

   30pf, Bust of Queen Cleopatra VII, 69-30 B.C. 50pf, Statue of Egyptian Couple, Giza, 2400 B.C. 60pf, Stone God with Beaded Turban, Mexico, 300 B.C. 80pf, Enamel Plate, 16th cent.

1984, Jan. 12   **Litho.**   **Perf. 14**
9N488 A146 30pf multicolored   1.00 .75
9N489 A146 50pf multicolored   1.40 1.00
9N490 A146 60pf multicolored   1.75 1.40
9N491 A146 80pf multicolored   2.25 1.60
   Nos. 9N488-9N491 (4)   6.40 4.75

Electricity Centenary — A147

Design: Allegorical figure holding light bulb (symbol of electric power).

1984, May 8   **Litho.**   **Perf. 14**
9N492 A147 50pf black & org   .90 .65

Conference Emblem — A148

1984, May 8
9N493 A148 60pf multicolored   1.10 .75
   European Ministers of Culture, 4th Conf.

Erich Klausener (1885-1934), Chairman of Catholic Action — A149

1984, May 8   **Engr.**   **Perf. 14x13½**
9N494 A149 80pf dark green   1.10 .75

Alfred Brehm (1829-1884), Zoologist — A150

Lithographed and Engraved
1984, Apr. 18   **Perf. 14**
9N495 A150 80pf Brehm, white stork   1.90 1.25

Ernst Ludwig Heim (1747-1834), Botanist — A151

1984, Aug. 21   **Engr.**   **Perf. 14**
9N496 A151 50pf brown & blk   1.10 .75

Sunflowers, by Karl Schmidt-Rottluff (1884-1976) A152

1984, Nov. 8   **Litho.**   **Perf. 14**
9N497 A152 60pf multi   1.10 .75

Bettina von Arnim (1785-1859), Writer — A153

1985, Feb. 21   **Litho. & Engr.**
9N498 A153 50pf multicolored   1.00 .80

Wilhelm von Humboldt (1767-1835), Statesman A154

1985, Feb. 21   **Engr.**
9N499 A154 80pf blue, blk & red   1.50 1.25

1985 Berlin Horticultural Show — A155

1985, Apr. 16   **Litho.**   **Perf. 14**
9N500 A155 80pf Symbolic flower   1.40 1.10

Berlin Bourse, 300th Anniv. A156

1985, May 7   **Litho. & Engr.**
9N501 A156 50pf multicolored   1.10 .80

Otto Klemperer (1885-1973), Conductor — A157

1985, May 7   **Engr.**
9N502 A157 60pf dp blue violet   1.40 1.10

Telefunken Camera, 1936 — A158

1985, July 16   **Litho.**   **Perf. 14**
9N503 A158 80pf multicolored   1.90 1.50
   German Television, 50th anniv., Intl. Telecommunications Exhibition, Berlin.

9th World Gynecological Congress — A159

Design: Emblem of the Intl. Federation for Gynecology and birth aid.

1985, July 16   **Photo.**   **Perf. 13½x14**
9N504 A159 60pf pale yel, ap grn & dp grn   1.10 .80

Edict of Potsdam, 300th Anniv. A160

Lithographed and Engraved

1985, Oct. 15   **Perf. 14**
9N505 A160 50pf dk bluish lilac   .90 .70

Kurt Tucholsky (1890-1935), Novelist, Journalist — A161

1985, Nov. 12   **Litho.**   **Perf. 14**
9N506 A161 80pf multi   1.75 1.10

Wilhelm Furtwangler (1886-1954), Composer — A162

Score from Sonata in D Sharp.

Lithographed and Engraved

1986, Jan. 16   **Perf. 14**
9N507 A162 80pf multi   1.90 1.60

Ludwig Mies van der Rohe (1886-1969), Architect — A163

1986, Feb. 13
9N508 A163 50pf multi   1.10 1.25

New Natl. Gallery, Berlin.

16th European Communities Day — A164

1986, Apr. 10   **Litho.**   **Perf. 14**
9N509 A164 60pf Flags   .95 1.00

Leopold von Ranke (1795-1886), Historian — A165   Gottfried Benn (1886-1956), Writer and Physician — A166

1986, May 5   **Litho.**
9N510 A165 80pf brn blk & tan   1.75 1.40

Engr.
9N511 A166 80pf brt blue   1.75 1.40

Portals and Gateways A167

1986, June 20   **Litho. & Engr.**
9N512 A167 50pf Charlotteburg Gate   1.50 1.25
9N513 A167 60pf Gryphon Gate, Glienicke Castle   1.50 1.25
9N514 A167 80pf Elephant Gate, Berlin Zoo   1.75 1.75
   Nos. 9N512-9N514 (3)   4.75 4.25

King Frederick the Great — A168

Painting: The Flute Concert (detail), by Adolph von Menzel.

1986, Aug. 14   **Litho.**   **Perf. 14**
9N515 A168 80pf multicolored   1.75 1.40

Famous Women Type of Germany

Designs: 5pf, Emma Ihrer (1857-1911), politician, labor leader. 10pf, Paula Modersohn-Becker (1876-1907), painter. 20pf, Cilly Aussem (1909-63), tennis champion. 40pf, Maria Sibylla Merian. 50pf, Christine Teusch. 60pf, Dorothea Erxleben (1715-62), physician. 80pf, Clara Schumann. 100pf, Therese Giehse (1898-1975), actress. 130pf, Lise Meitner (1878-1968), physicist. 140pf, Cecile Vogt (1875-1962), neurologist. 170pf, Hannah Arendt (1906-75), American political scientist. 180pf, Lotte Lehmann (1888-1976), soprano. 240pf, Mathilde Franziska Anneke, (1817-84), American author. 250pf, Queen Louise of Prussia (1776-1810). 300pf, Fanny Hensel (1805-1847), composer-conductor. 350pf, Hedwig Dransfeld (1871-1925), women's rights activist. 500pf, Alice Salomon (1872-1948), feminist and social activist.

1986-89   **Engr.**   **Perf. 14**
Type A602
9N516   5pf bluish gray & org brn   .35   1.50
9N517   10pf vio & yel brn   .35   1.40
9N518   20pf lake & Prus bl   1.50   3.75
9N519   40pf dp bl & dk lil rose   1.25   3.75
9N520   50pf gray ol & Prus bl   1.90   2.50
9N521   60pf dp vio & grnsh blk   .75   3.75
9N522   80pf dk grn & lt red brn   1.10   2.25
9N523   100pf dk red & grnsh blk   1.50   1.50
9N524   130pf Prus bl & dk vio   3.50   11.00
9N525   140pf blk & dk ol bis   3.75   11.00
9N526   170pf gray grn & dk brn   2.25   9.00
9N527   180pf bl & brn vio   3.50   11.00
9N528   240pf Prus bl & yel brn   3.00   13.00
9N529   250pf dp lil rose & dp bl   7.25   19.00
9N530   300pf dk vio & sage grn   7.50   19.00
9N531   350pf gray grn & lake   5.25   15.00
9N532   500pf slate grn & brt ver   8.25   32.50
   Nos. 9N516-9N532 (17)   52.95 160.90

Issued: 50pf, 80pf, 11/1/86; 40pf, 9/17/87; 10pf, 4/4/88; 20pf, 130pf, 5/5/88; 60pf, 100pf, 170pf, 240pf, 350pf, 11/10/88; 500pf, 1/12/89; 5pf, 2/9/89; 180pf, 250pf, 7/13/89; 140pf, 300pf, 8/10/89.

Berlin 750th Anniv. Type of Germany

Designs: a, Berlin, 1650, engraving by Caspar Merian. b, Charlottenburg Castle, c. 1830. c, AEG Company turbine construction building, by architect Walter Behrens, 1909. d, Philharmonic Concert Hall and Chamber Music Rooms on the Kemperplatz, 1987.

1987, Jan. 15   **Litho.**   **Perf. 14**
9N536 A604 80pf like #1496   1.90 1.50

Souvenir Sheet
Perf. 14x14½
9N537   Sheet of 4   4.25 4.25
a.   A604 40pf multicolored   .90 .75
b.   A604 50pf multicolored   .90 .75
c.   A604 60pf multicolored   .90 .90
d.   A604 80pf multicolored   1.00 1.25

No. 9N537 contains four 43x25mm stamps.

Louise Schroeder (1887-1957), Politican — A169

1987, Feb. 12   **Engr.**   **Perf. 14**
9N538 A169 50pf sep & dk red   1.10 1.10

Settlement of Bohemians at Rixdorf, 250th Anniv. — A170

Bohemian refugees, bas-relief detail from monument to King Friedrich Wilhelm I of Prussia, 1912.

1987, May 5   **Litho. & Engr.**
9N539 A170 50pf sep & pale gray grn   .80 .90

1987 Intl. Architecture Exhibition — A171

1987, May 5   **Litho.**   **Perf. 14x14½**
9N540 A171 80pf lt ultra, sil & blk 1.40 1.10

14th Int'l. Botanical Congress — A172

1987, July 16   **Litho.**   **Perf. 14**
9N541 A172 60pf multicolored   .90 1.00

Int'l. Radio Exhibition A173

1987, Aug. 20
9N542 A173 80pf Gramophone, compact disc 1.25 .95

Historic Sites and Objects Type of Germany

Designs: 5pf, Brunswick Lion. 10pf, Frankfurt Airport. 20pf, No. 9N550, Queen Nefertiti, bust, Egyptian Museum, Berlin. 30pf, Corner tower, Celle Castle, 14th cent. 40pf, Chile House, Hamburg. 50pf, Filigree tracery on spires, Freiburg Cathedral. 60pf, Bavaria Munich, bronze statue above the Theresienwiese, Hall of Fame. No. 9N551, Heligoland. 80pf, Entrance to Zollern II, coal mine, Dortmund. 100pf, Altotting Chapel, Bavaria. 120pf, Schleswig Cathedral. 140pf, Bronze flagon from Reinheim. 300pf, Hambach Castle. 350pf, Externsteine Bridge near Horn-Bad Meinberg.

1987-90   **Typo.**   **Perf. 14**
Type A623
9N543   5pf Prus bl & gray   .30   .45
9N544   10pf lt chalky bl & slate bl   .35   .35

9N545   20pf dull blue & tan   .35   .75
9N546   30pf aqua & org brn   .95   .95
9N547   40pf ultra, dk red brn & org red   1.25   2.10
9N548   50pf ultra & yel brn   1.50   1.10
9N549   60pf cob & pale gray   1.50   1.10
9N550   70pf dull bl & fawn   1.50   2.50
9N551   70pf vio bl & henna brn   2.10   4.50
9N552   80pf cob & pale gray   1.50   1.10
a.   Bklt. pane of 8 (4 10pf, 2 50pf, 2 80pf) ('89)   22.50   52.50
9N553   100pf brt bluish grn & olive bis   1.10   1.50
a.   Bklt. pane of 8 (2 each 10pf, 60pf, 80pf, 100pf)   45.00   90.00
9N554   120pf brn org & lt grnsh bl   2.25   3.50
9N555   140pf tan & lt grn   2.25   4.25
9N556   300pf dk red brn & tan   4.50   4.50
9N557   350pf brt ultra & ol bis   4.50   7.50
   Nos. 9N543-9N557 (15)   25.90 36.15

Issued: 30pf, 50pf, 60pf, 80pf, 11/6/87; 10pf, 300pf, 1/14/88; #9N550, 120pf, 7/14/88; 20pf, 140pf, 1/12/89; 100pf, 350pf, 2/9/89; 5pf, 2/15/90; #9N551, 6/21/90.

European Culture — A175

1988, Jan. 14   **Litho.**   **Perf. 14**
9N568 A175 80pf Berlin Bear   1.90 1.90

Urania Science Museum, Cent. A176

1988, Feb. 18
9N569 A176 50pf multicolored   1.40 1.25

A177

Design: Thoroughbred Foal, bronze sculpture by Renee Sintenis (1888-1965).

1988, Feb. 18
9N570 A177 60pf multicolored   .90 .90

A178

Design: The Great Elector with Family in Berlin Castle Gardens.

1988, May 5   **Litho. & Engr.**
9N571 A178 50pf multicolored   1.10 1.10
The Great Elector of Brandenburg (d. 1688).

Intl. Monetary Fund and World Bank Congress, Berlin — A179

1988, Aug. 11   **Litho.**
9N572 A179 70pf multicolored   1.10 1.00

Berlin-Potsdam Railway, 150th Anniv. — A180

1988, Oct. 13 **Litho.**
9N573 A180 10pf multicolored   .65   .45

The Collector, 1913, by Ernst Barlach (1870-1938) A181

1988, Oct. 13
9N574 A181 40pf multicolored   .70   .55

Berlin Airlift, 40th Anniv. — A182

1989, May 5 **Photo.** **Perf. 14**
9N575 A182 60pf multicolored   1.10 1.25

13th Intl. Congress of the Supreme Audit Office, Berlin — A183

1989, May 5 **Litho.**
9N576 A183 80pf multicolored   1.40 1.40

Ernst Reuter (1889-1953), Mayor of Berlin — A184

Litho. & Engr.
1989, July 13 **Perf. 14x14½**
9N577 A184 100pf multicolored   1.90 1.60

Intl. Radio Exhibition, Berlin — A185

1989, July 13 **Litho.**
9N578 A185 100pf multicolored   1.60 1.50

Plans of the Zoological Gardens, Berlin, and Designer Peter Joseph Lenne (1789-1866) — A186

Litho. & Engr.
1989, Aug. 10 **Perf. 14**
9N579 A186 60pf multicolored   1.50 1.25

Carl von Ossietzky (1889-1938), Awarded Nobel Peace Prize of 1935 — A187

1989, Aug. 10 **Photo.**
9N580 A187 100pf multicolored   1.75 1.60

450th Anniv. of the Reformation A188

Design: Nikolai Church, Spandau District.

1989, Oct. 12 **Litho.**
9N581 A188 60pf multicolored   .95   .85

French Gymnasium, 300th Anniv. — A189

School from 1701 to 1873 and frontispiece of *Leges Gymnasie Gallici,* published in 1689.

1989, Oct. 12 **Litho. & Engr.**
9N582 A189 40pf multicolored   .95   .85

Journalists, 1925, by Hannah Hoch (1889-1978) A190

1989, Oct. 12 **Litho.** **Perf. 13½**
9N583 A190 100pf multicolored   1.90 1.50

European Postal Service 500th Anniv. Type
Litho. & Engr.
1990, Jan. 12 **Perf. 14**
9N584 A673 100pf *The Young Post Rider*   2.50 2.10

See Austria No. 1486, Belgium No. 1332, Germany No. 1592, and DDR No. 2791.

Public Transportation, 250th Anniv. — A191

1990, Jan. 12 **Litho.**
9N585 A191 60pf multicolored   1.90 1.50

Ernst Rudorff (1840-1916), Conservationist — A192

1990, Jan. 12
9N586 A192 60pf multicolored   1.90 1.50

People's Free Theater Organization, Cent. — A193

1990, Feb. 15 **Perf. 13½**
9N587 A193 100pf multicolored   2.00 1.90

Parliament House, 40th Anniv. — A194

1990, Feb. 15 **Perf. 14x14½**
9N588 A194 100pf multicolored   2.75 1.90

Bicent. of the Invention of the Barrel Organ — A195

1990, May 3 **Litho.** **Perf. 14**
9N589 A195 100pf multicolored   2.00 1.75

90th German Catholics Day — A196

1990, May 3
9N590 A196 60pf multicolored   1.75 1.60

German Pharmaceutical Society, Cent. — A197

1990, Aug. 9 **Litho.** **Perf. 14**
9N591 A197 100pf multicolored   3.75 3.00

Adolph Diesterweg (1790-1866), Educator — A198

1990, Sept. 27
9N592 A198 60pf multicolored   2.75 2.75

Stamps for Berlin were discontinued Oct. 3, 1990, when Germany and the German Democratic Republic merged. The stamps remained valid until Dec. 31, 1991.

OCCUPATION SEMI-POSTAL STAMPS

Offering Plate and Berlin Bear — SP1

Wmk. 284
1949, Dec. 1 **Litho.** **Perf. 14**
9NB1 SP1 10 + 5pf grn   35.00 160.00
9NB2 SP1 20 + 5pf car   35.00 160.00
9NB3 SP1 30 + 5pf blue   37.50 225.00
  a. Souv. sheet of 3,
    #9NB1-9NB3   500.00 2,100.
    Never hinged   900.00
  Nos. 9NB1-9NB3 (3)   107.50 545.00
  Set, never hinged   375.00

The surtax was for Berlin victims of currency devaluation.

Harp and Laurel Branch — SP2   "Singing Angels" — SP3

1950, Oct. 29 **Engr.** **Wmk. 116**
9NB4 SP2 10 + 5pf grn   16.00 35.00
9NB5 SP3 30 + 5pf dk sl bl   32.50 90.00
  Set, never hinged   140.00

The surtax was to aid in reestablishing the Berlin Philharmonic Orchestra.

Young Stamp Collectors — SP4   Kaiser Wilhelm Memorial Church — SP5

1951, Oct. 7 **Perf. 14**
9NB6 SP4 10 + 3pf grn   10.50 30.00
9NB7 SP4 20 + 2pf brn red   13.50 37.50
  Set, never hinged   52.50

Stamp Day, Berlin, Oct. 7, 1951.

1953, Aug. 9 **Wmk. 284**

Design: 20pf+10pf, 30pf+15pf, Ruins of Kaiser Wilhelm Memorial Church.

9NB8 SP5 4 + 1pf choc   .20   15.00
9NB9 SP5 10 + 5pf green   .75   42.50
9NB10 SP5 20 + 10pf car   1.40 42.50
9NB11 SP5 30 + 15pf dp bl   6.00 97.50
  Nos. 9NB8-9NB11 (4)   8.35 197.50
  Set, never hinged   22.50

The surtax was to aid in reconstructing the church.

Catalogue values for unused stamps in this section, from this point to the end of the section, are for Never Hinged items.

Prussian Postilion — SP6   Prussian Field Postilion — SP7

1954, Aug. 4   Litho.   Wmk. 284
9NB12 SP6 20 + 10pf multi   15.00 30.00
National Stamp Exhibition, Berlin, Aug. 4-8.

Perf. 13½x14
1955, Oct. 27   Wmk. 304
9NB13 SP7 25 + 10pf multi   6.00 13.50
The surtax was for the benefit of philately.

St. Otto, Bishop of Bamberg — SP8

Statues: 10pf+5pf, St. Hedwig, Duchess of Silesia. 20pf+10pf, St. Peter.

1955, Nov. 26   Engr.   Perf. 14
9NB14 SP8 7 + 3pf brown   .75 2.75
9NB15 SP8 10 + 5pf gray grn   1.40 3.00
9NB16 SP8 20 + 10pf rose lil   1.90 3.75
    Nos. 9NB14-9NB16 (3)   4.05 9.50
25th anniv. of the Bishopric of Berlin.
The surtax was for the reconstruction of destroyed churches throughout the bishopric.

Bell Type of 1951 Surcharged

Perf. 13½x14
1956, Aug. 9   Wmk. 284
9NB17 OS8 20pf + 10pf citron   2.50 3.00
The surtax was for help for flood victims.

Postrider of Brandenburg, 1700 — SP9   Ludwig Heck — SP10

Wmk. 304
1956, Oct. 26   Litho.   Perf. 14
9NB18 SP9 25pf + 10pf multi   2.50 3.50
The surtax was for the benefit of philately.

1957, Sept. 7   Engr.   Perf. 13½x14
9NB19 SP10 20pf + 10pf red & dk brn   .75 .90
Dr. Ludwig Heck, zoologist and long-time director of the Berlin Zoo. The surtax was for the Zoo.

Elly Heuss-Knapp and Relaxing Mothers SP11

Boy at Window — SP12

1957, Nov. 30   Perf. 14
9NB20 SP11 20pf + 10pf dk red   1.40 2.40
The surtax was for welfare work among mothers.

1960, Sept. 15   Litho.   Wmk. 304
Designs: 10pf+5pf, Girl going to school. 20pf+10pf, Girl with flower and mountains. 40pf+20pf, Boy at seashore.
9NB21 SP12 7pf + 3pf dk brn & brn   .20 .30
9NB22 SP12 10pf + 5pf ol grn & slate grn   .20 .30
9NB23 SP12 20pf + 10pf dk car & brn blk   .55 .55
9NB24 SP12 40pf + 20pf bl & ind   1.25 3.75
    Nos. 9NB21-9NB24 (4)   2.20 4.90
The surtax was for vacations for the children of Berlin.

Fluorescent Paper was introduced for semipostal stamps, starting with Nos. 9NB25-9NB28.

Fairy Tale Type of 1960
Various Scenes from Sleeping Beauty.

1964, Oct. 6   Unwmk.   Perf. 14
9NB25 SP285 10pf + 5pf multi   .20 .20
9NB26 SP285 15pf + 5pf multi   .20 .20
9NB27 SP285 20pf + 10pf multi   .40 .20
9NB28 SP285 40pf + 20pf multi   .55 .90
    Nos. 9NB25-9NB28 (4)   1.35 1.50
The surtax was for independent welfare organizations.

Beginning with 9NB25-9NB28 semipostals are types of Germany inscribed "Berlin" except Nos. 9NB129-9NB131.

Bird Type of 1965
Birds: 10pf+5pf, Woodcock. 15pf+5pf, Ring-necked pheasant. 20pf+10pf, Black grouse. 40pf+20pf, Capercaillie.

1965, Apr. 1   Litho.   Perf. 14
9NB29 SP289 10pf + 5pf multi   .20 .20
9NB30 SP289 15pf + 5pf multi   .20 .20
9NB31 SP289 20pf + 10pf multi   .20 .20
9NB32 SP289 40pf + 20pf multi   .50 .75
    Nos. 9NB29-9NB32 (4)   1.10 1.35
Issued for the benefit of young people.

Fairy Tale Type of 1965
Various Scenes from Cinderella.

1965, Oct. 6   Litho.   Perf. 14
9NB33 SP290 10pf + 5pf multi   .20 .20
9NB34 SP290 15pf + 5pf multi   .20 .20
9NB35 SP290 20pf + 10pf multi   .20 .20
9NB36 SP290 40pf + 20pf multi   .50 .75
    Nos. 9NB33-9NB36 (4)   1.10 1.35
The surtax was for independent welfare organizations.

Animal Type of 1966
10pf+5pf, Roe deer. 20pf+10pf, Chamois. 30pf+15pf, Fallow deer. 50pf+25pf, Red deer.

1966, Apr. 22   Litho.   Perf. 14
9NB37 SP291 10pf + 5pf multi   .20 .20
9NB38 SP291 20pf + 10pf multi   .20 .20
9NB39 SP291 30pf + 15pf multi   .25 .25
9NB40 SP291 50pf + 25pf multi   .55 .75
    Nos. 9NB37-9NB40 (4)   1.20 1.40
Issued for the benefit of young people.

Fairy Tale Type of 1965
Various Scenes from The Princess and the Frog.

1966, Oct. 5   Litho.   Perf. 14
9NB41 SP290 10pf + 5pf multi   .20 .20
9NB42 SP290 20pf + 10pf multi   .20 .20
9NB43 SP290 30pf + 15pf multi   .35 .20
9NB44 SP290 50pf + 25pf multi   .45 .70
    Nos. 9NB41-9NB44 (4)   1.20 1.30
Surtax for independent welfare organizations.

Animal Type of 1966
10pf+5pf, Rabbit. 20pf+10pf, Ermine. 30pf+15pf, Hamster. 50pf+25pf, Red fox.

1967, Apr. 4   Unwmk.
9NB45 SP291 10pf + 5pf multi   .20 .25
9NB46 SP291 20pf + 10pf multi   .20 .25
9NB47 SP291 30pf + 15pf multi   .35 .30
9NB48 SP291 50pf + 25pf multi   1.00 1.40
    Nos. 9NB45-9NB48 (4)   1.75 2.20
Issued for the benefit of young people.

Fairy Tale Type of 1965
Various Scenes from Frau Holle.

1967, Oct. 3   Litho.   Perf. 14
9NB49 SP290 10pf + 5pf multi   .20 .25
9NB50 SP290 20pf + 10pf multi   .20 .25
9NB51 SP290 30pf + 15pf multi   .20 .35
9NB52 SP290 50pf + 25pf multi   .55 .75
    Nos. 9NB49-9NB52 (4)   1.15 1.60
The surtax was for independent welfare organizations.

Animal Type of 1968
Animals: 10pf+5pf, Wildcat. 20pf+10pf, Otter. 30pf+15pf, Badger. 50pf+25pf, Beaver.

1968, Feb. 2   Photo.   Perf. 14
9NB53 SP293 10pf + 5pf multi   .25 .45
9NB54 SP293 20pf + 10pf multi   .30 .45
9NB55 SP293 30pf + 15pf multi   .55 .90
9NB56 SP293 50pf + 25pf multi   1.60 2.10
    Nos. 9NB53-9NB56 (4)   2.70 3.90
Surtax for benefit of young people.

Doll Type of 1968
Various 19th century dolls in sitting position.

1968, Oct. 3   Litho.   Perf. 14
9NB57 SP294 10pf + 5pf multi   .20 .25
9NB58 SP294 20pf + 10pf multi   .20 .25
9NB59 SP294 30pf + 15pf multi   .20 .35
9NB60 SP294 50pf + 25pf multi   .60 .75
    Nos. 9NB57-9NB60 (4)   1.20 1.60
The surtax was for independent welfare organizations.

Horse Type of 1969
Horses: 10pf+5pf, Pony. 20pf+10pf, Work horse. 30pf+15pf, Hotblood. 50pf+25pf, Thoroughbred.

1969, Feb. 6   Litho.   Perf. 14
9NB61 SP295 10pf + 5pf multi   .20 .30
9NB62 SP295 20pf + 10pf multi   .30 .55
9NB63 SP295 30pf + 15pf multi   .45 .75
9NB64 SP295 50pf + 25pf multi   1.25 1.50
    Nos. 9NB61-9NB64 (4)   2.20 3.10
Surtax for benefit of young people.

Tin Toy Type of 1969
Tin Toys: 10pf+5pf, Coach. 20pf+10pf, Woman feeding chickens. 30pf+15pf, Woman grocer. 50pf+25pf, Postilion on horseback.

1969, Oct. 2   Litho.   Perf. 13½x14
9NB65 SP297 10pf + 5pf multi   .20 .20
9NB66 SP297 20pf + 10pf multi   .20 .20
9NB67 SP297 30pf + 15pf multi   .35 .35
9NB68 SP297 50pf + 25pf multi   1.00 1.00
    Nos. 9NB65-9NB68 (4)   1.75 1.75
The surtax was for independent welfare organizations.

1969, Nov. 13   Litho.   Perf. 13½x14
Christmas: 10pf+5pf, The Three Kings.
9NB69 SP297 10pf + 5pf multi   .35 .30

Minnesinger Type of 1970
Minnesingers (and their Ladies): 10pf+5pf, Heinrich von Stretlingen. 20pf+10pf, Meinloh von Sevelingen. 30pf+15pf, Burkhart von Hohenfels. 50pf+25pf, Albrecht von Johansdorf.

1970, Feb. 5   Photo.   Perf. 13½x14
9NB70 SP298 10pf + 5pf multi   .20 .25
9NB71 SP298 20pf + 10pf multi   .35 .45
9NB72 SP298 30pf + 15pf multi   .55 .60
9NB73 SP298 50pf + 25pf multi   1.25 1.40
    Nos. 9NB70-9NB73 (4)   2.35 2.70
Surtax for benefit of young people.

Puppet Type of 1970
10pf+5pf, "Kasperl." 20pf+10pf, Polichinelle. 30pf+5pf, Punch. 50pf+25pf, Pulcinella.

1970, Oct. 6   Litho.   Perf. 13½x14
9NB74 SP300 10pf + 5pf multi   .20 .20
9NB75 SP300 20pf + 10pf multi   .25 .25
9NB76 SP300 30pf + 15pf multi   .55 .45
9NB77 SP300 50pf + 25pf multi   .90 1.10
    Nos. 9NB74-9NB77 (4)   1.90 2.00
Surtax for independent welfare organizations.

1970, Nov. 12
Christmas: 10pf+5pf, Rococo angel, from Ursuline Sisters' Convent, Innsbruck.
9NB78 SP300 10pf + 5pf multi   .30 .30

Drawings Type of 1971
Children's Drawings: 10pf+5pf, Fly. 20pf+10pf, Fish. 30pf+15pf, Porcupine. 50pf+25pf, Cock. All stamps horizontal.

1971, Feb. 5   Litho.   Perf. 14
9NB79 SP301 10pf + 5pf multi   .30 .30
9NB80 SP301 20pf + 10pf multi   .30 .30
9NB81 SP301 30pf + 15pf multi   .45 .50
9NB82 SP301 50pf + 25pf multi   1.25 1.40
    Nos. 9NB79-9NB82 (4)   2.30 2.50
Surtax for the benefit of young people.

Wooden Toy Type of 1971
Wooden Toys: 10pf+5pf, Movable dolls in box. 25pf+10pf, Knight on horseback. 30pf+15pf, Jumping jack. 60pf+30pf, Nurse rocking babies.

1971, Oct. 5
9NB83 SP303 10pf + 5pf multi   .20 .25
9NB84 SP303 25pf + 10pf multi   .25 .35
9NB85 SP303 30pf + 15pf multi   .55 .55
9NB86 SP303 60pf + 30pf multi   1.00 1.10
    Nos. 9NB83-9NB86 (4)   2.00 2.25

1971, Nov. 11
Christmas: Christmas angel with candles.
9NB87 SP303 10pf + 5pf multi   .35 .35

Animal Protection Type of 1972
10pf+5pf, Boy trying to rob bird's nest. 25pf+10pf, Girl with kittens to be drowned. 30pf+15pf, Watch dog & man with whip. 60pf+30pf, Hedgehog & deer passing before car at night.

1972, Feb. 4
9NB88 SP304 10pf + 5pf multi   .20 .20
9NB89 SP304 25pf + 10pf multi   .30 .30
9NB90 SP304 30pf + 15pf multi   .55 .55
9NB91 SP304 60pf + 30pf multi   1.25 1.25
    Nos. 9NB88-9NB91 (4)   2.30 2.30
Surtax for the benefit of young people.

Chess Type of 1972
1972, Oct. 5   Litho.   Perf. 14
9NB92 SP307 20pf + 10 Knight   .30 .30
9NB93 SP307 30pf + 15 Rook   .45 .45
9NB94 SP307 40pf + 20 Queen   1.25 1.25
9NB95 SP307 70pf + 35 King   1.75 1.75
    Nos. 9NB92-9NB95 (4)   3.75 3.75
Surtax for independent welfare organizations.

Christmas Type of 1972
Design: 20pf+10pf, Holy Family.

1972, Nov. 10   Litho.   Perf. 14
9NB96 SP308 20pf + 10pf multi   .55 .45

Bird Type of 1973
Birds of Prey: 20pf+10pf, Goshawk. 30pf+15pf, Peregrine falcon. 40pf+20pf, Sparrow hawk. 70pf+35pf, Golden eagle.

1973, Feb. 6   Photo.   Perf. 14
9NB97 SP309 20pf + 10pf multi   .50 .50
9NB98 SP309 30pf + 15pf multi   .75 .75
9NB99 SP309 40pf + 20pf multi   1.00 1.00
9NB100 SP309 70pf + 35pf multi   1.75 1.75
    Nos. 9NB97-9NB100 (4)   4.00 4.00
Surtax was for benefit of young people.

Instrument Type of 1973
Musical Instruments: 20+10pf, Hurdy-gurdy, 17th cent. 30+15pf, Drum, 16th cent. 40+20pf,

Archlute, 18th cent. 70+35pf, Organ, 16th cent.

1973, Oct. 5   Litho.   Perf. 14
9NB101 SP311 20pf + 10pf multi   .35   .35
9NB102 SP311 30pf + 15pf multi   .75   .75
9NB103 SP311 40pf + 20pf multi   .90   .90
9NB104 SP311 70pf + 35pf multi   1.25   1.25
 Nos. 9NB101-9NB104 (4)   3.25   3.25

Surtax was for independent welfare organizations.

Star Type of 1973

Christmas: 20pf+10pf, Christmas star.

1973, Nov. 9   Litho. & Engr.
9NB105 SP312 20pf + 10pf multi   .55   .55

Youth Type of 1974

Designs: 20pf+10pf, Boy photographing. 30pf+15pf, Boy athlete. 40pf+20pf, Girl violinist. 70pf+35pf, Nurse's aid.

1974, Apr. 17   Photo.   Perf. 14
9NB106 SP313 20pf + 10pf multi   .35   .45
9NB107 SP313 30pf + 15pf multi   .40   .45
9NB108 SP313 40pf + 20pf multi   .90   1.00
9NB109 SP313 70pf + 35pf multi   1.25 1.40
 Nos. 9NB106-9NB109 (4)   2.90   3.30

Surtax was for benefit of young people.

Flower Type of 1974

Designs: 30pf+15pf, Spring bouquet. 40pf+20pf, Autumn bouquet. 50pf+25pf, Roses. 70pf+35pf, Winter flowers. All horiz.

1974, Oct. 15   Litho.   Perf. 14
9NB110 SP314 30pf + 15pf multi   .40   .40
9NB111 SP314 40pf + 20pf multi   .85   .85
9NB112 SP314 50pf + 25pf multi   .85   .85
9NB113 SP314 70pf + 35pf multi   1.25 1.25
 Nos. 9NB110-9NB113 (4)   3.35   3.35

Surtax was for independent welfare organizations.

1974, Oct. 29

Christmas: Christmas bouquet, horiz.

9NB114 SP314 30pf + 15pf multi   .75   .85

Locomotive Type of 1975

Steam Locomotives: 30pf+15pf, Dragon. 40pf+20pf, Class 89 (70-75). 50pf+25pf, Class O50. 70pf+35pf, Class O10.

1975, Apr. 15   Litho.   Perf. 14
9NB115 SP315 30pf + 15pf multi   .75   .60
9NB116 SP315 40pf + 20pf multi   .75   .75
9NB117 SP315 50pf + 25pf multi   1.50 1.25
9NB118 SP315 70pf + 35pf multi   2.25 2.25
 Nos. 9NB115-9NB118 (4)   5.25   4.85

Surtax was for benefit of young people.

Flower Type of 1975

Alpine Flowers: 30pf+15pf, Yellow gentian. 40pf+20pf, Arnica. 50pf+25pf, Cyclamen. 70pf+35pf, Blue gentian.

1975, Oct. 15   Litho.   Perf. 14
9NB119 SP316 30pf + 15pf multi   .55   .55
9NB120 SP316 40pf + 20pf multi   .45   .45
9NB121 SP316 50pf + 25pf multi   .60   .60
9NB122 SP316 70pf + 35pf multi   1.00 1.00
 Nos. 9NB119-9NB122 (4)   2.60   2.60

Surtax was for independent welfare organizations.

1975, Nov. 14

Christmas: 30pf+15pf, Snow heather.

9NB123 SP316 30pf + 15pf multi   .75   .75

Sports Type of 1976

30+15pf, Shot put, women's. 40+20pf, Hockey. 50+25pf, Handball. 70+35pf, Swimming.

1976, Apr. 6   Litho.   Perf. 14
9NB124 SP317 30pf + 15pf multi   .75   .70
9NB125 SP317 40pf + 20pf multi   .75   .70
9NB126 SP317 50pf + 25pf multi   .75   .80
9NB127 SP317 70pf + 35pf multi   1.50 1.60
 Nos. 9NB124-9NB127 (4)   3.75   3.80

Youth training for Olympic Games. The surtax was for the benefit of young people.

Iris — SP13

Flowers: 40pf+20pf, Wallflower. 50pf+25pf, Dahlia. 70pf+35pf, Larkspur.

1976, Oct. 14   Litho.   Perf. 14
9NB128 SP13 30pf + 15pf   .35   .35
9NB129 SP13 40pf + 20pf   .40   .40
9NB130 SP13 50pf + 25pf   .75   .75
9NB131 SP13 70pf + 35pf   1.00   1.00
 Nos. 9NB128-9NB131 (4)   2.50   2.50

Surtax was for independent welfare organizations.

Souvenir Sheet
Christmas Type of 1976

Christmas: 30pf+15pf, Annunciation to the Shepherds, stained-glass window, Frauenkirche, Esslingen.

1976, Nov. 16   Litho. & Engr.
9NB132 SP320 30pf + 15pf multi   .75   .65

Ship Type of 1977

Historic Ships: 30pf+15pf, Bremer Kogge, c. 1380. 40pf+20pf, Helena Sloman, 1850. 50pf+25pf, Passenger ship, Cap Polonio, 1914. 70pf+35pf, Freighter Widar, 1971.

1977, Apr. 14   Litho.   Perf. 14
9NB133 SP321 30pf + 15pf   .45   .45
9NB134 SP321 40pf + 20pf   .70   .70
9NB135 SP321 50pf + 25pf   .95   .95
9NB136 SP321 70pf + 35pf   1.40   1.40
 Nos. 9NB133-9NB136 (4)   3.50   3.50

Surtax was for benefit of young people.

Flower Type of 1977

Meadow Flowers: 30pf+15pf, Daisy. 40pf+20pf, Cowslip. 50pf+25pf, Sainfoin. 70pf+35pf, Forget-me-not.

1977, Oct. 13   Litho.   Perf. 14
9NB137 SP322 30pf + 15pf   .30   .30
9NB138 SP322 40pf + 20pf   .55   .55
9NB139 SP322 50pf + 25pf   .75   .75
9NB140 SP322 70pf + 35pf   1.10   1.10
 Nos. 9NB137-9NB140 (4)   2.70   2.70

Surtax was for independent welfare organizations.
See Nos. 9NB148-9NB151.

Souvenir Sheet
Christmas Type of 1977

30pf+15pf, Virgin and Child, stained-glass window, Sacristy of St. Gereon Basilica, Cologne.

1977, Nov. 10
9NB141 SP323 30pf + 15pf multi   .75   .75

Aviation Type of 1978

Designs: 30pf+15pf, Montgolfier balloon, 1783. 40pf+20pf, Lilienthal's glider, 1891. 50pf+25pf, Wright brothers' plane, 1909. 70pf+35pf, Etrich/Rumpler Taube, 1910.

1978, Apr. 13   Litho.   Perf. 14
9NB142 SP325 30pf + 15pf   .35   .45
9NB143 SP325 40pf + 20pf   .55   .60
9NB144 SP325 50pf + 25pf   .70   .75
9NB145 SP325 70pf + 35pf   1.25   1.25
 Nos. 9NB142-9NB145 (4)   2.85   3.05

Surtax was for benefit of young people.

Sports Type of 1978

50+25pf, Bicycling. 70+35pf, Fencing.

1978, Apr. 13   Litho.   Perf. 14
9NB146 SP324 50pf + 25pf   .90   .60
9NB147 SP324 70pf + 35pf   1.25   1.00

Surtax was for German Sports Foundation.

Flower Type of 1977

Woodland Flowers: 30pf+15pf, Solomon's-seal. 40pf+20pf, Wood primrose. 50pf+25pf, Cephalanthera rubra (orchid). 70pf+35pf, Bugle.

1978, Oct. 12   Litho.   Perf. 14
9NB148 SP322 30pf + 15pf   .45   .45
9NB149 SP322 40pf + 20pf   .55   .55
9NB150 SP322 50pf + 25pf   .75   .75
9NB151 SP322 70pf + 35pf   1.10   1.10
 Nos. 9NB148-9NB151 (4)   2.85   2.85

Surtax was for independent welfare organizations.

Souvenir Sheet
Christmas Type of 1978

Christmas: 30pf+15pf, Adoration of the Kings, stained glass window, Frauenkirche, Munich.

1978, Nov. 16   Litho.   Perf. 14
9NB152 SP326 30pf + 15pf multi   .75   .75

Aviation Type of 1979

Airplanes: 40pf+20pf, Vampyr, 1921. 50pf+25pf, Junkers JU52/3M, 1932. 60pf+30pf, Messerschmitt BF/ME 108, 1934. 90pf+45pf, Douglas DC3, 1935.

1979, Apr. 5   Litho.   Perf. 14
9NB153 SP327 40pf + 20pf   .55   .55
9NB154 SP327 50pf + 25pf   .75   .75
9NB155 SP327 60pf + 30pf   .95   .95
9NB156 SP327 90pf + 45pf   1.50   1.50
 Nos. 9NB153-9NB156 (4)   3.75   3.75

Surtax was for benefit of young people.

Sports Type of 1979

60pf+30pf, Runners. 90pf+45pf, Archers.

1979, Apr. 5
9NB157 SP328 60pf + 30pf   .90   .95
9NB158 SP328 90pf + 45pf   1.25   1.25

Surtax was for German Sports Foundation.

Plant Type of 1979

Woodland Plants: 40pf+20pf, Larch. 50pf+25pf, Hazelnut. 60pf+30pf, Horse chestnut. 90pf+45pf, Blackthorn.

1979, Oct. 11   Litho.   Perf. 14
9NB159 SP330 40pf + 20pf   .60   .45
9NB160 SP330 50pf + 25pf   .75   .70
9NB161 SP330 60pf + 30pf   1.00   .95
9NB162 SP330 90pf + 45pf   1.40   1.25
 Nos. 9NB159-9NB162 (4)   3.75   3.35

Surtax was for independent welfare organizations.

Christmas Type of 1979

Christmas: Nativity, medieval manuscript, Cistercian Abby, Altenberg.

1979, Nov. 14   Litho.   Perf. 13½
9NB163 SP331 40pf + 20pf multi   .90   .75

Aviation Type of 1979

Designs: 40pf+20pf, Vickers Viscount, 1950. 50pf+25pf, Fokker 27 Friendship, 1955. 60pf+30pf, Sud Aviation Caravelle, 1955. 90pf+45pf, Sikorsky-55, 1949.

1980, Apr. 10   Litho.   Perf. 14
9NB164 SP327 40 + 20pf multi   .75   .75
9NB165 SP327 50 + 25pf multi   .80   .80
9NB166 SP327 60 + 30pf multi   1.00   1.00
9NB167 SP327 90 + 45pf multi   1.50   1.50
 Nos. 9NB164-9NB167 (4)   4.05   4.05

Surtax was for benefit of young people.

Sports Type of 1980

Designs: 50pf+25pf, Javelin. 60pf+30pf, Weight lifting. 90pf+45pf, Water polo.

1980, May 8   Photo.   Perf. 14
9NB168 SP332 50 + 25pf multi   .75   .75
9NB169 SP332 60 + 30pf multi   .75   .75
9NB170 SP332 90 + 45pf multi   1.10   1.10
 Nos. 9NB168-9NB170 (3)   2.60   2.60

Surtax was for German Sports Foundation.

Wildflower Type of 1980

Wildflowers: 40pf+20pf, Orlaya. 50pf+25pf, Yellow gagea. 60pf+30pf, Summer pheasant's eye. 90pf+45pf, Small-flowered Venus' looking-glass.

1980, Oct. 9   Litho.   Perf. 14
9NB171 SP333 40 + 20pf multi   .80   .80
9NB172 SP333 50 + 25pf multi   .90   .90
9NB173 SP333 60 + 30pf multi   .90   .90
9NB174 SP333 90 + 45pf multi   1.50   1.50
 Nos. 9NB171-9NB174 (4)   4.10   4.10

Surtax was for independent welfare organizations.

Christmas Type of 1980

Christmas: 40pf+20pf, Annunciation to the Shepherds, from Altomunster manuscript, 12th century.

1980, Nov. 13   Litho.   Perf. 14x13½
9NB175 SP335 40 + 20pf multi   .90   .80

Optical Instrument Type of 1981

40pf+20pf, Theodolite, 1810. 50pf+25pf, Equatorial telescope, 1820. 60pf+30pf, Microscope, 1790. 90pf+45pf, Sextant, 1830.

1981, Apr. 10   Litho.   Perf. 13½
9NB176 SP336 40 + 20pf multi   .60   .60
9NB177 SP336 50 + 25pf multi   .80   .80
9NB178 SP336 60 + 30pf multi   1.00   1.00
9NB179 SP336 90 + 45pf multi   1.60   1.60
 Nos. 9NB176-9NB179 (4)   4.00   4.00

Surtax for benefit of young people.

Sports Type of 1981

Designs: 60pf+30pf, Women's gymnastics. 90pf+45pf, Cross-county running.

1981, Apr. 10   Perf. 14
9NB180 SP337 60 + 30pf multi   .90   .75
9NB181 SP337 90 + 45pf multi   1.40   1.10

Surtax for the German Sports Foundation.

Plant Type of 1981

40pf+20pf, Common bistort. 50pf+25pf, Pedicularis sceptrum-carolinum. 60pf+30pf, Gladiolus palustris. 90pf+45pf, Iris sibirica.

1981, Oct. 8   Litho.
9NB182 SP338 40 + 20pf multi   .75   .75
9NB183 SP338 50 + 25pf multi   .80   .75
9NB184 SP338 60 + 30pf multi   .90   .75
9NB185 SP338 90 + 45pf multi   1.75   1.50
 Nos. 9NB182-9NB185 (4)   4.20   3.75

Surtax was for independent welfare organizations.

Christmas Type of 1981

Adoration of the Kings, 19th cent. painting.

1981, Nov. 12   Litho.
9NB186 SP339 40 + 20pf multi   .90   .60

Antique Car Type of 1982

Designs: 40pf+20pf, Daimler, 1889. 50pf+25pf, Wanderer, 1911. 60pf+30pf, Adler limousine, 1913. 90pf+45pf, DKW-F, 1931.

1982, Apr. 15   Litho.
9NB187 SP340 40 + 20pf multi   .75   .75
9NB188 SP340 50 + 25pf multi   .80   .80
9NB189 SP340 60 + 30pf multi   1.00   1.00
9NB190 SP340 90 + 45pf multi   1.60   1.60
 Nos. 9NB187-9NB190 (4)   4.15   4.15

Surtax was for benefit of young people.

Sports Type of 1982

60pf+30pf, Sprinting. 90pf+45pf, Volleyball.

1982, Apr. 15   Litho.
9NB191 SP341 60 + 30pf multi   .95   .75
9NB192 SP341 90 + 45pf multi   1.40   1.00

Surtax was for the German Sports Foundation.

Flower Type of 1982

Designs: 50pf+20pf, Floribunda grandiflora. 60pf+30pf, Tea-rose hybrid, diff. 80pf+40pf, Floribunda, diff. 120pf+60pf, Miniature rose.

1982, Oct. 14   Litho.   Perf. 14
9NB193 SP342 50 + 20pf multi   1.00   .90
9NB194 SP342 60 + 30pf multi   1.10   .90
9NB195 SP342 80 + 40pf multi   1.50   1.50
9NB196 SP342 120 + 60pf multi 2.40   2.40
 Nos. 9NB193-9NB196 (4)   6.00   5.70

Surtax was for independent welfare organizations.

Christmas Type of 1982

Christmas: Adoration of the Kings, Oak altar, St. Peter's Church, Hamburg, 1380.

1982, Nov. 10
9NB197 SP343 50 + 20pf multi   .90   .75

Motorcycle Type of 1983

Designs: 50pf+20pf, Hildebrand & Wolfmuller, 1894. 60pf+30pf, Wanderer, 1908. 80pf+40pf, DKW-Lomos, 1922. 120pf+60pf, Mars, 1925.

1983, Apr. 12 Litho. *Perf. 14*
9NB198	SP344	50 + 20pf multi	.75	.55
9NB199	SP344	60 + 30pf multi	1.10	.95
9NB200	SP344	80 + 40pf multi	1.25	.95
9NB201	SP344	120 + 60pf multi	3.00	2.50
Nos. 9NB198-9NB201 (4)			6.10	4.95

Surtax was for benefit of young people.

Sports Type of 1983

Designs: 80pf+40pf, European Latin American Dance Championship. 120pf+60pf, World Hockey Championship.

1983, Apr. 12
9NB202	SP345	80 + 40pf multi	1.50	1.10
9NB203	SP345	120 + 60pf multi	2.25	1.90

Surtax was for German Sports Foundation.

Flower Type of Germany

Designs: 50pf+20pf, Mountain wildflower. 60pf+30pf, Alpine auricula. 80pf+40pf, Little primrose. 120pf+60pf, Einsele's aquilegia.

1983, Oct. 13 Litho. *Perf. 14*
9NB204	SP346	50 + 20pf multi	.70	.70
9NB205	SP346	60 + 30pf multi	1.00	1.00
9NB206	SP346	80 + 40pf multi	1.75	1.75
9NB207	SP346	120 + 60pf multi	2.75	2.75
Nos. 9NB204-9NB207 (4)			6.20	6.20

Surtax was for welfare organizations.

Christmas Type of Germany

1983, Nov. 10 Litho.
9NB208	SP347	50 + 20pf Nativity	.90	.80

Surtax was for free welfare work.

Insect Type of 1984

Designs: 50pf+20pf, Trichius fasciatus. 60pf+30pf, Agrumenia carnioloa. 80pf+40pf, Bombus terrestris. 120pf+60pf, Eristalis tenax.

1984, Apr. 12 Litho.
9NB209	SP348	50 + 20pf multi	1.00	.65
9NB210	SP348	60 + 30pf multi	1.00	.80
9NB211	SP348	80 + 40pf multi	2.10	1.25
9NB212	SP348	120 + 60pf multi	2.50	2.50
Nos. 9NB209-9NB212 (4)			6.60	5.20

Surtax was for German Youth Stamp Foundation.

Olympic Type of 1984

Women's Events: 60pf+30pf, Hurdles. 80pf+40pf, Cycling. 120pf+60pf, Kayak.

1984, Apr. 12
9NB213	SP349	60 + 30pf multi	1.50	1.00
9NB214	SP349	80 + 40pf multi	1.90	1.00
9NB215	SP349	120 + 60pf multi	2.75	2.75
Nos. 9NB213-9NB215 (3)			6.15	4.75

Surtax was for German Sports Foundation.

Orchid Type of 1984

50+20pf, Listera cordata. 60pf+30pf, Ophrys insectifera. 80pf+40pf, Epipactis palustris. 120pf+60pf, Ophrys coriophora.

1984, Oct. 18 Litho. *Perf. 14*
9NB216	SP350	50 + 20pf multi	1.25	1.10
9NB217	SP350	60 + 30pf multi	1.75	1.10
9NB218	SP350	80 + 40pf multi	3.00	2.50
9NB219	SP350	120 + 60pf multi	4.50	4.00
Nos. 9NB216-9NB219 (4)			10.50	8.70

Surtax was for welfare organizations.

Christmas Type of 1984

1984, Nov. 8 Litho.
9NB220	SP351	50 + 20pf St. Nicholas	1.10	1.10

Surtax was for welfare organizations.

Sport Type of 1985

1985, Feb. 21 Photo.
9NB221	SP352	80 + 40pf Basketball	1.40	1.40
9NB222	SP352	120 + 60pf Table Tennis	2.25	2.25

Surtax was for German Sport Foundation.

Bicycle Type of 1985

50pf+20pf, Bussing bicycle, 1868. 60pf+30pf, Child's tricycle, 1885. 80pf+40pf, Jaray bicycle, 1925. 120pf+60pf, Opel racer, 1925.

1985, Apr. 16 Litho.
9NB223	SP353	50 + 20pf multi	1.10	1.10
9NB224	SP353	60 + 30pf multi	1.10	1.10
9NB225	SP353	80 + 40pf multi	1.50	1.50
9NB226	SP353	120 + 60pf multi	3.50	3.50
Nos. 9NB223-9NB226 (4)			7.20	7.20

Surtax for benefit of young people. Each stamp also shows the International Youth Year emblem.

Prayer Book Type of 1985

1985, Oct. 15 Litho. *Perf. 14*
9NB227	SP355	50 + 20pf multi	1.10	1.10
9NB228	SP355	60 + 30pf multi	1.50	1.50
9NB229	SP355	80 + 40pf multi	1.50	1.50
9NB230	SP355	120 + 60pf multi	2.25	2.25
Nos. 9NB227-9NB230 (4)			6.35	6.35

Surtax for welfare organizations.

Christmas Type of 1985

Woodcut: Worship of the Kings, Epiphany Altar, Frieburg Cathedral, by Hans Baldung Grien (1485-1545).

1985, Nov. 12 Litho. *Perf. 14*
9NB231	SP356	50 + 20pf multi	1.25	1.00

Surtax for welfare organizations.

European Sports Championships Type of 1986

1986, Feb. 13 Litho. *Perf. 14*
9NB232	SP357	80 + 40pf Swimming	1.60	1.60
9NB233	SP357	120 + 55pf Show jumping	2.25	2.25

Surtax for the Natl. Sports Promotion Foundation.

Vocational Training Type of 1986

1986, Apr. 10
9NB234	SP358	50 + 25pf Glazier	1.10	1.25
9NB235	SP358	60 + 30pf Mechanic	1.50	1.60
9NB236	SP358	70 + 35pf Tailor	1.50	1.60
9NB237	SP358	80 + 40pf Carpenter	1.90	1.90
Nos. 9NB234-9NB237 (4)			6.00	6.35

Surtax for German Youth Stamp Foundation.

Glassware Type of 1986

1986, Oct. 16 Litho. *Perf. 13x13½*
9NB238	SP359	50 + 25pf Cantharus, 1st cent.	1.10	1.10
9NB239	SP359	60 + 30pf Tumbler, c. 200	1.50	1.50
9NB240	SP359	70 + 35pf Jug, 3rd cent.	1.50	1.50
9NB241	SP359	80 + 40pf Diatreta, 4th cent.	1.90	1.90
Nos. 9NB238-9NB241 (4)			6.00	6.00

Surtax for public welfare organizations.

Christmas Type of 1986

Christmas: Adoration of the Magi, Ortenberg Altarpiece, c. 1420.

1986, Nov. 13 Litho. *Perf. 14*
9NB242	SP360	50 + 25pf multi	.90	.80

Surtax for public welfare organizations.

Sports Championships Type of 1987

1987, Feb. 12 Litho.
9NB243	SP361	80 + 40pf Gymnastics	1.50	1.50
9NB244	SP361	120 + 55pf Judo	2.25	2.25

Surtax for the benefit of the national Sports Promotion Foundation.

Industry Type of 1987

1987, Apr. 9 Litho.
9NB245	SP362	50 + 25pf Cooper	1.10	1.10
9NB246	SP362	60 + 30pf Stonemason	1.10	1.10
9NB247	SP362	70 + 35pf Furrier	1.50	1.50
9NB248	SP362	80 + 40pf Painter	1.50	1.50
Nos. 9NB245-9NB248 (4)			5.20	5.20

Surtax for youth organizations.

Gold and Silver Artifacts Type of 1987

1987, Oct. 15
9NB249	SP363	50 + 25pf Bonnet ornament, 5th cent.	.75	.90
9NB250	SP363	60 + 30pf Athena plate, 1st cent. B.C.	1.10	1.25
9NB251	SP363	70 + 35pf Armilla armlet, c. 1180	1.40	1.50
9NB252	SP363	80 + 40pf Snake bracelet, 300 B.C.	1.60	1.75
Nos. 9NB249-9NB252 (4)			4.85	5.40

Surtax for welfare organizations sponsoring free museum exhibitions.

Christmas Type of 1987

Illustration from Book of Psalms, 13th cent., Bavarian Natl. Museum: Adoration of the Magi.

1987, Nov. 6
9NB253	SP364	50 + 25pf multi	.90	.80

Surtax for public welfare ogranizations.

Sports Type of 1988

1988, Feb. 18 Litho.
9NB254	SP365	60 + 30pf Trapshooting	1.60	1.50
9NB255	SP365	80 + 40pf Figure skating	1.60	1.50
9NB256	SP365	120 + 55pf Hammer throw	2.10	2.10
Nos. 9NB254-9NB256 (3)			5.30	5.10

Music Type of 1988

No. 9NB257, Piano terzet. No. 9NB258, Wind quintet. No. 9NB259, Guitar, mandolin, recorder. No. 9NB260, Children's choir.

1988, Apr. 14 Litho. *Perf. 14*
9NB257	SP366	50 +25pf multi	1.25	1.25
9NB258	SP366	60 +30pf multi	1.60	1.60
9NB259	SP366	70 +35pf multi	1.60	1.60
9NB260	SP366	80 i 40pf multi	2.50	2.50
Nos. 9NB257-9NB260 (4)			6.95	6.95

Surtax for German Youth Stamp Foundation.

Artifacts Type of 1988

#9NB261, Brooch, c. 1700, Schmuck Jewelry Museum, Pforzheim. #9NB262, Lion, 1540, Kunstgewerbe Museum, Berlin. #9NB263, Lidded goblet, 1536, Kunstgewerbe Museum. #9NB264, Cope clasp, c. 1400, Aachen cathedral.

1988, Oct. 13 Litho.
9NB261	SP367	50 +25pf multi	1.10	1.25
9NB262	SP367	60 +30pf multi	1.25	1.40
9NB263	SP367	70 +35pf multi	1.40	1.50
9NB264	SP367	80 +40pf multi	1.60	1.75
Nos. 9NB261-9NB264 (4)			5.35	5.90

Surtax for welfare organizations.

Christmas Type of 1988

Illumination from *The Gospel Book of Henry the Lion*, Helmarshausen, 1188, Prussian Cultural Museum, Bavaria: Angels announce the birth of Christ to the shepherds.

1988, Nov. 10 Litho.
9NB265	SP368	50 +25pf multi	1.40	1.25

Surtax for public welfare organizations.

Sports Type of 1989

1989, Feb. 9 Litho.
9NB266	SP369	100 +50pf Volleyball	2.50	2.50
9NB267	SP369	140 +60pf Hockey	3.25	3.25

Surtax for the Natl. Sports Promotion Foundation.

Circus Type of 1989

1989, Apr. 20 Litho.
9NB268	SP371	60 +30pf Tamer and tigers	1.60	1.60
9NB269	SP371	70 +30pf Trapeze artists	2.10	2.10
9NB270	SP371	80 +35pf Seals	3.00	3.00
9NB271	SP371	100 +50pf Jugglers	3.25	3.25
Nos. 9NB268-9NB271 (4)			9.95	9.95

Surtax for natl. youth welfare organizations.

Mail Carrying Type of 1989

#9NB272, Messenger, 15th cent. #9NB273, Brandenburg mail wagon, c. 1700. #9NB274, Prussian postal workers, 19th cent.

1989, Oct. 12 Litho.
9NB272	SP372	60 +30pf multi	2.50	2.50
9NB273	SP372	80 +35pf multi	3.25	3.00
9NB274	SP372	100 +50pf multi	4.00	4.00
Nos. 9NB272-9NB274 (3)			9.75	9.50

Surtax for the benefit of Free Welfare Work.

Christmas Type of 1989

1989, Nov. 16 Litho.
9NB275	SP373	40 +20pf Angel	1.25	1.25
9NB276	SP373	60 +30pf Nativity	2.10	2.10

Surtax for the benefit of the Federal Working Assoc. of Free Welfare Work.

Sports Type of 1990

Designs: No. 9NB277, Water polo. No. 9NB278, Wheelchair basketball.

1990, Feb. 15 Litho.
9NB277	SP374	100 +50pf multi	3.25	3.25
9NB278	SP374	140 +60pf multi	5.50	6.25

Surtax for the Natl. Sports Promotion Foundation.

Max and Moritz Type of 1990

1990, Apr. 19 Litho.
9NB279	SP375	60 +30pf Max, Moritz	1.60	*1.90*
9NB280	SP375	70 +30pf Max, Moritz, diff.	2.50	*2.75*
9NB281	SP375	80 +35pf Moritz	2.50	*2.75*
9NB282	SP375	100 +50pf Bug, Uncle	2.50	*2.75*
Nos. 9NB279-9NB282 (4)			9.10	10.15

Surcharge for the German Youth Stamp Foundation.

Post and Telecommunications Type

Designs: 60pf + 30pf, Railway mail car, 1900. 80pf + 35pf, Telephone installation, 1900. 100pf + 50pf, Mail truck, 1900.

1990, Sept. 27 Litho. *Perf. 13½x14*
9NB283	SP377	60 +30pf multi	2.10	2.10
9NB284	SP377	80 +35pf multi	3.00	3.00
9NB285	SP377	100 +50pf multi	4.00	4.00
Nos. 9NB283-9NB285 (3)			9.10	9.10

Surtax for welfare organizations.

GERMAN OFFICES ABROAD

OFFICES IN CHINA

100 Pfennings = 1 Mark
100 Cents = 1 Dollar (1905)

Stamps of Germany, 1889-90, Overprinted in Black at 56 degree Angle

1898   **Unwmk.**   *Perf. 13½x14½*

1	A9	3pf dark brown	5.25	5.00
a.		3pf yellow brown	9.00	12.00
b.		3pf reddish ocher	37.50	125.00
2	A9	5pf green	2.75	2.25
3	A10	10pf carmine	5.75	6.25
4	A10	20pf ultramarine	17.00	16.00
5	A10	25pf orange	32.50	30.00
6	A10	50pf red brown	16.00	12.50
		Nos. 1-6 (6)	79.25	72.00

Overprinted at 45 degree Angle

1c	A9	3pf yellow brown	125.00	23,000.
1d	A9	3pf reddish ocher	175.00	
e.		3pf gray brown	1,400.	
2a	A9	5pf green	11.50	12.50
3a	A10	10pf carmine	14.00	10.50
4a	A10	20pf ultramarine	12.50	10.50
5a	A10	25pf orange	50.00	60.00
6a	A10	50pf red brown	20.00	18.00

Value for No. 1c used is for a stamp with small 1898 Shanghai cancel. Examples with other cancellations or later Shanghai cancels sell for about half the value quoted.

Foochow Issue

Nos. 3 and 3a Handstamp Surcharged

1900

16	A10	5pf on 10pf, #3	525.00	900.00
a.		On No. 3a	600.00	850.00

For similar 5pf surcharges on 10pf carmine, see Tsingtau Issue, Kiauchau.

Tientsin Issue
German Stamps of 1900 Issue Handstamped

1900

17	A11	3pf brown	575.00	750.00
18	A11	5pf green	375.00	350.00
19	A11	10pf carmine	900.00	850.00
20	A11	20pf ultra	750.00	900.00
21	A11	30pf org & blk, sal	6,500.	6,500.
22	A11	50pf pur & blk, sal	30,000.	16,000.
23	A11	80pf lake & blk, rose	4,500.	4,500.

This handstamp is known inverted and double on most values.
Excellent faked handstamps are plentiful.

Regular Issue

German Stamps of 1900 Overprinted

A14

A15

Overprinted Horizontally in Black

1901   *Perf. 14, 14½*

24	A11	3pf brown	1.50	1.50
a.		3pf light red brown	35.00	35.00
25	A11	5pf green	1.50	1.10
26	A11	10pf carmine	2.50	1.10
27	A11	20pf ultra	3.25	1.75
28	A11	25pf org & blk, yel	9.00	16.00
29	A11	30pf org & blk, sal	9.00	13.00
30	A11	40pf lake & blk	9.00	8.50
31	A11	50pf pur & blk, sal	9.00	8.50
32	A11	80pf lake & blk, rose	11.00	11.00

Overprinted in Black or Red

33	A12	1m car rose	26.00	32.50
34	A13	2m gray blue	27.50	30.00
35	A14	3m blk vio (R)	45.00	65.00
36	A15	5m slate & car, I	450.00	600.00
b.		Red and/or white retouched	210.00	300.00
36A	A15	5m slate & car, II	210.00	300.00
		Nos. 24-36A (14)	814.25	1,089.

See note after Germany No. 65A for information on retouches on No. 36. For description of the 5m Type I and Type II, see note above Germany No. 62.

Surcharged on German Stamps of 1902 in Black or Red

a

b

c

1905

37	A16(a)	1c on 3pf	2.90	3.25
38	A16(a)	2c on 5pf	2.90	1.40
39	A16(a)	4c on 10pf	5.00	1.40
40	A16(a)	10c on 20pf	2.90	1.75
41	A16(a)	20c on 40pf	20.00	7.50
42	A16(a)	40c on 80pf	32.50	13.00
43	A17(b)	½d on 1m	15.00	19.00
44	A21(b)	1d on 2m	17.50	21.00
45	A19(c)	1½d on 3m (R)	15.00	45.00
46	A20(b)	2½d on 5m	110.00	300.00
		Nos. 37-46 (10)	223.70	413.30

Surcharged on German Stamps of 1905 in Black or Red

1906-13   **Wmk. 125**

47	A16(a)	1c on 3pf	.40	1.25
48	A16(a)	2c on 5pf	.40	1.25
49	A16(a)	4c on 10pf	.40	1.25
50	A16(a)	10c on 20pf	.85	5.75
51	A16(a)	20c on 40pf	.90	3.50
52	A16(a)	40c on 80pf	1.10	50.00
53	A17(b)	½d on 1m	6.00	37.50
54	A21(b)	1d on 2m	7.50	37.50
55	A19(c)	1½d on 3m (R)	7.50	110.00
56	A20(b)	2½d on 5m	29.00	65.00
		Nos. 47-56 (10)	54.05	313.00

Forged cancellations exist.

OFFICES IN MOROCCO

100 Centimos = 1 Peseta

Stamps of Germany Surcharged in Black

1899   **Unwmk.**   *Perf. 13½x14½*

1	A9	3c on 3pf dk brn	3.00	2.10
2	A9	5c on 5pf green	3.00	2.40
3	A10	10c on 10pf car	7.50	6.25
4	A10	25c on 20pf ultra	18.00	15.00
5	A10	30c on 25pf orange	26.00	32.50
6	A10	60c on 50pf red brn	22.50	37.50
		Nos. 1-6 (6)	80.00	95.75

Before Nos. 1-6 were issued, the same six basic stamps of Germany's 1889-1900 issue were overprinted "Marocco" diagonally without the currency-changing surcharge line, but were not issued. Value, $750.

German Stamps of 1900 Surcharged

A12

A13

A14

A15

Black or Red Surcharge

1900   *Perf. 14, 14½*

7	A11	3c on 3pf brn	1.25	1.75
8	A11	5c on 5pf grn	1.50	1.10
9	A11	10c on 10pf car	2.00	1.10
10	A11	25c on 20pf ultra	2.75	2.75
11	A11	30c on 25pf org & blk, yel	9.00	15.00
12	A11	35c on 30pf org & blk, sal	6.75	6.25
13	A11	50c on 40pf lake & blk	6.75	6.25
14	A11	60c on 50pf pur & blk, blk	14.00	32.50
15	A11	1p on 80pf lake & blk, rose	11.00	11.00
16	A12	1p25c on 1m car rose	32.50	45.00
17	A13	2p50c on 2m gray bl	37.50	57.50
18	A14	3p75c on 3m blk vio (R)	45.00	65.00
19	A15	6p25c on 5m sl & car, type I	375.00	500.00
b.		Red and/or white retouched	200.00	325.00
19A	A15	6p25c on 5m sl & car, type II	210.00	275.00
		Nos. 7-19A (14)	755.00	1,020.

A 1903 printing of Nos. 8, 16-18 and 19A differs in the "M" and "t" of the surcharge. Values are for 1900 printing: Nos. 8, 16-18. 1903 printing: No. 19A.

See note after Germany No. 65A for information on retouches on No. 19. For description of the 5m Type I and Type II, see note above Germany No. 62.

German Stamps of 1902 Surcharged in Black or Red

a

b

c

1905

20	A16(a)	3c on 3pf	2.75	2.75
21	A16(a)	5c on 5pf	4.75	1.10
22	A16(a)	10c on 10pf	8.25	1.10
23	A16(a)	25c on 20pf	19.00	3.00
24	A16(a)	30c on 25pf	6.75	5.50
25	A16(a)	35c on 30pf	10.00	5.50
26	A16(a)	50c on 40pf	9.50	7.75
27	A16(a)	60c on 50pf	21.00	24.00
28	A16(a)	1p on 80pf	21.00	19.00
		On cover		45.00
29	A17(b)	1p25c on 1m	52.50	37.50
30	A21(b)	2p50c on 2m	95.00	150.00
31	A19(c)	3p75c on 3m (R)	42.50	55.00
32	A20(b)	6p25c on 5m	150.00	210.00
		Nos. 20-32 (13)	443.00	522.20

Surcharged on Germany No. 54

32A	A11(a)	5c on 5pf	8.00	24.00

German Stamps of 1905 Surcharged

1906-11			**Wmk. 125**	
33	A16(a)	3c on 3pf	8.75	2.10
34	A16(a)	5c on 5pf	6.50	1.10
35	A16(a)	10c on 10pf	6.50	1.10
36	A16(a)	25c on 20pf	16.00	6.00
37	A16(a)	30c on 25pf	19.00	8.75
38	A16(a)	35c on 30pf	16.00	9.75
39	A16(a)	50c on 40pf	32.50	150.00
40	A16(a)	60c on 50pf	25.00	17.00
41	A16(a)	1p on 80pf	140.00	275.00
42	A17(b)	1p25c on 1m	62.50	175.00
43	A21(b)	2p50c on 2m	62.50	175.00
44	A20(b)	6p25c on 5m	125.00	325.00
		Nos. 33-44 (12)	520.25	1,145.

Excellent forgeries exist of No. 41.

Surcharge Spelled "Marokko" in Black or Red

1911				
45	A16(a)	3c on 3pf	.55	.70
46	A16(a)	5c on 5pf	.55	1.00
47	A16(a)	10c on 10pf	.55	1.10
48	A16(a)	25c on 20pf	.65	1.40
49	A16(a)	30c on 25pf	1.50	16.00
50	A16(a)	35c on 30pf	1.50	8.75
51	A16(a)	50c on 40pf	1.25	5.25
52	A16(a)	60c on 50pf	1.50	37.50
53	A16(a)	1p on 80pf	1.60	24.00
54	A17(b)	1p25c on 1m	2.75	65.00
55	A21(b)	2p50c on 2m	5.25	47.50
56	A19(c)	3p75c on 3m (R)	7.00	225.00
57	A20(b)	6p25c on 5m	19.00	325.00
		On cover		575.00
		Nos. 45-57 (13)	43.65	758.20

Forged cancellations exist.

OFFICES IN THE TURKISH EMPIRE

Unused values for Nos. 1-6 are for stamps with original gum. Stamps without gum sell for about one-third of the figures quoted.

40 Paras = 1 Piaster

A1

A2

German Stamps of 1880-83 Surcharged in Black or Blue

1884		**Unwmk.**	**Perf. 13½x14½**	
1	A1	10pa on 5pf dull vio	55.00	32.50
2	A2	20pa on 10pf rose	80.00	80.00
3	A2	1pi on 20pf ultra (Bk)	65.00	5.25
4	A2	1pi on 20pf ultra (Bl)	2,250.	72.50
5	A2	1¼pi on 25pf brn	190.00	250.00
6	A2	2½pi on 50pf gray grn	100.00	80.00
a.		2½pi on 50pf deep olive grn	275.00	210.00
		Nos. 1-6 (6)	2,740.	520.25

There are two types of the surcharge on the 1¼pi and 2½pi stamps, the difference being in the spacing between the figures and the word "PIASTER."

Covers: There are re-issues of these stamps which vary only slightly from the originals in overprint measurements.

A3

A4

A5

German Stamps of 1889-1900 Surcharged in Black

1889				
8	A3	10pa on 5pf grn	3.75	4.00
9	A4	20pa on 10pf car	8.00	2.75
10	A4	1pi on 20pf ultra	5.50	2.40
11	A5	1¼pi on 25pf org	24.00	20.00
12	A5	2½pi on 50pf choc	37.50	24.00
a.		2½pi on 50pf copper brown	200.00	125.00
		Nos. 8-12 (5)	78.75	53.15

German Stamps of 1900 Surcharged

A12

A13

A14

A15

1900			**Perf. 14, 14½**	
		Black or Red Surcharge		
13	A11	10pa on 5pf grn	1.75	1.75
14	A11	20pa on 10pf car	2.25	2.10
15	A11	1pi on 20pf ultra	4.75	1.90
16	A11	1¼pi on 25pf org & blk, yel	6.50	3.50
17	A11	1½pi on 30pf org & blk, sal	6.50	4.75
18	A11	2pi on 40pf lake & blk	6.50	4.75
19	A11	2½pi on 50pf pur & blk, sal	11.00	13.50
20	A11	4pi on 80pf lake & blk, rose	14.00	13.50
21	A12	5pi on 1m car rose	40.00	40.00
22	A13	10pi on 2m gray bl	35.00	45.00
23	A14	15pi on 3m blk vio (R)	50.00	110.00
24	A15	25pi on 5m sl & car, type I	350.00	675.00
a.		Double surcharge		11,000.
d.		Red and/or white re-touched	175.00	250.00
24B	A15	25pi on 5m sl & car, type II	210.00	375.00
c.		Double surcharge	9,750.	—
		Nos. 13-24B (13)	738.25	1,290.

See note after Germany #65A for information on retouches on #24. For description of the 5m Type I & Type II, see note above Germany #62.

German Stamps of 1900 Surcharged in Black

1903-05				
25	A11	10pa on 5pf green	9.50	13.50
		On cover		75.00
26	A11	20pa on 10pf car	30.00	19.00
27	A11	1pi on 20pf ultra	8.75	7.25

28	A12	5pi on 1m car rose	140.00	95.00
29	A13	10pi on 2m bl ('05)	160.00	275.00
30	A15	25pi on 5m sl & car	190.00	550.00
a.		Double surcharge	9,000.	
		Nos. 25-30 (6)	538.25	959.75

The 1903-05 surcharges may be easily distinguished from those of 1900 by the added bar at the top of the letter "A."

German Stamps of 1902 Surcharged in Black or Red

a

b

1905			**Unwmk.**	
31	A16(a)	10pa on 5pf	3.50	2.50
32	A16(a)	20pa on 10pf	8.00	3.25
33	A16(a)	1pi on 20pf	19.00	2.00
34	A16(a)	1¼pi on 25pf	9.50	8.00
35	A16(a)	1½pi on 30pf	14.00	16.00
36	A16(a)	2pi on 40pf	22.50	16.00
37	A16(a)	2½pi on 50pf	9.50	22.50
38	A16(a)	4pi on 80pf	27.50	17.50
39	A17(b)	5pi on 1m	47.50	40.00
40	A21(b)	10pi on 2m	40.00	47.50
		On cover		110.00
41	A19(b)	15pi on 3m (R)	47.50	55.00
42	A20(b)	25pi on 5m	240.00	550.00
		Nos. 31-42 (12)	488.50	780.25

German Stamps of 1905 Surcharged in Black or Red

1906-12			**Wmk. 125**	
43	A16(a)	10pa on 5pf	2.40	.65
44	A16(a)	20pa on 10pf	4.75	.75
45	A16(a)	1pi on 20pf	6.50	.75
46	A16(a)	1¼pi on 25pf	13.00	13.00
47	A16(a)	1½pi on 30pf	13.00	10.00
48	A16(a)	2pi on 40pf	5.25	1.75
49	A16(a)	2½pi on 50pf	9.50	17.50
50	A16(a)	4pi on 80pf	15.00	22.50
51	A17(b)	5pi on 1m	35.00	32.50
52	A21(b)	10pi on 2m	35.00	47.50
53	A19(b)	15pi on 3m (R)	40.00	475.00
54	A20(b)	25pi on 5m	32.50	80.00
		Nos. 43-54 (12)	211.90	701.90

German Stamps of 1905 Surcharged Diagonally in Black

1908				
55	A16	5c on 5pf	1.60	2.75
56	A16	10c on 10pf	2.75	4.75
57	A16	25c on 20pf	6.50	25.00
58	A16	50c on 40pf	27.50	60.00
59	A16	100c on 80pf	50.00	65.00
		On cover		210.00
		Nos. 55-59 (5)	88.35	157.50

Forged cancellations exist on #37, 53-54, 57-59.

GERMAN DEMOCRATIC REPUBLIC

LOCATION — Eastern Germany
GOVT. — Republic
AREA — 41,659 sq. mi.
POP. — 16,701,500 (1983)
CAPITAL — Berlin (Soviet sector)

100 Pfennigs = 1 Deutsche Mark (East)

100 Pfennigs = 1 Mark of the Deutsche Notenbank (MDN) (1965)

100 Pfennigs = 1 Mark of the National Bank (M) (1969)

100 Pfennigs = 1 Deutsche Mark (West) (1990)

Catalogue values for unused stamps in this country are for Never Hinged items, beginning with Scott 48 in the regular postage section, Scott B14 in the semipostal section, Scott C1 in the airpost section, and Scott O1 official section.

Watermarks

Watermark 292, see Germany.

Wmk. 297 — DDR and Post Horn

Wmk. 313 — Quatrefoil and DDR

FOR USE IN ALL PROVINCES IN THE RUSSIAN ZONE

When the mark was revalued in June, 1948, a provisional overprint, consisting of various city and town names and post office or zone numerals, was applied by hand in black, violet or blue at innumerable post offices to their stocks.

Germany Nos. 557 to 573 Overprinted in Black

1948, July 3		Wmk. 284	Perf. 14	
10N1	A120	2pf brown blk	.20	.20
10N2	A120	6pf purple	.20	.30
10N3	A121	8pf red	.20	.30
10N4	A121	10pf yellow grn	.20	.30
10N5	A122	12pf gray	.20	.30

10N6	A120	15pf chocolate	.20	.30
10N7	A123	16pf dk blue grn	.20	.50
10N8	A121	20pf blue	.20	.30
10N9	A123	24pf brown org	.20	.25
10N10	A120	25pf orange yel	.20	.25
10N11	A122	30pf red	.25	.30
10N12	A121	40pf red violet	.20	.30
10N13	A123	50pf ultra	.20	.65
10N14	A122	60pf red brown	.25	.65
a.		60pf brown red	30.00	100.00
10N15	A122	80pf dark blue	.65	.80
10N16	A122	84pf emerald	.65	1.10
Nos. 10N1-10N16 (16)			4.20	6.80
Set, never hinged			10.00	

Same Overprint on Numeral Stamps of Germany, 1946

1948, Sept.				
10N17	A119	5pf yellow grn	.20	.70
10N18	A119	30pf olive	.40	2.00
10N19	A119	45pf brt red	.20	.80
10N20	A119	75pf deep ultra	.20	.80
10N21	A119	84pf emerald	.40	1.60
Nos. 10N17-10N21 (5)			1.40	5.90
Set, never hinged			3.50	

Nos 10N1-10N21 all exist with inverted overprint, and majority with double overprint.

Same Overprint on Berlin-Brandenburg Nos. 11N1-11N7

Unwmk.

1948, Sept.		Litho.	Perf. 14	
10N22	OS1	5pf green	.20	.65
a.		Serrate roulette	.20	.65
10N23	OS1	6pf violet	.20	.65
10N24	OS1	8pf red	.20	.65
10N25	OS1	10pf brown	.20	.65
10N26	OS1	12pf rose	.20	1.20
10N27	OS1	20pf blue	.20	1.00
10N28	OS1	30pf olive	.20	1.20
Nos. 10N22-10N28 (7)			1.40	6.00
Set, never hinged			2.75	

The overprint made #10N22-10N28 valid for postage throughout the Russian Zone.

Gerhard Hauptmann — OS2

Designs: 2pf, 20pf, Käthe Kollwitz. 40pf, Gerhard Hauptmann. 8pf, 50pf, Karl Marx. 10pf, 84pf, August Bebel. 12pf, 30pf, Friedrich Engels. 15pf, 60pf, G. W. F. Hegel. 16pf, 25pf, Rudolf Virchow. 24pf, 80pf, Ernst Thälmann.

		Perf. 13x12½		
1948		Typo.	Wmk. 292	
10N29	OS2	2pf gray	.25	.80
10N30	OS2	6pf violet	.25	.80
10N31	OS2	8pf red brn	.25	.80
10N32	OS2	10pf blue grn	.20	.80
10N33	OS2	12pf blue	1.60	.80
10N34	OS2	15pf brown	.20	1.60
10N35	OS2	16pf turquoise	.20	.80
10N36	OS2	20pf maroon	.20	1.00
10N37	OS2	24pf carmine	1.60	.80
10N38	OS2	25pf olive grn	.40	1.60
10N39	OS2	30pf red	1.25	1.60
10N40	OS2	40pf red violet	1.25	1.60
10N41	OS2	50pf dk ultra	.25	1.60
10N42	OS2	60pf dull green	1.60	1.60
10N43	OS2	80pf dark blue	.50	1.00
10N44	OS2	84pf brown lake	1.10	2.75
Nos. 10N29-10N44 (16)			11.10	19.95
Set, never hinged			35.00	

See German Democratic Republic #122-136.

Karl Liebknecht and Rosa Luxemburg OS3

		Perf. 13½x13		
1949, Jan. 15		Litho.	Wmk. 292	
10N45	OS3	24pf rose	.20	.70
		Never hinged	.40	

30th anniv. of the death of Karl Liebknecht and Rosa Luxemburg, German socialists.

Dove and Laurel — OS4

1949				
10N46	OS4	24pf carmine rose	.50	2.00
		Never hinged	1.00	

Overprinted in Black: "3. Deutscher Volkskongress 29.-30. Mai 1949"

1949, May 29				
10N47	OS4	24pf carmine rose	.65	3.00
		Never hinged	2.00	

Nos. 10N46 and 10N47 were issued for the 3rd German People's Congress.

GERMAN DEMOCRATIC REPUBLIC

Catalogue values for unused stamps in this section, from this point to the end of the section, are for Never Hinged items.

Canceled to Order

The government stamp agency started in 1949 to sell canceled sets of new issues.

Used values are for CTO's for Nos. 48-2831, except for souvenir sheets, which are valued as postally used.

Pigeon, Letter and Globe A5

		Wmk. Flowers Multiple (292)		
1949, Oct. 9		Litho.	Perf. 13½	
48	A5	50pf lt blue & dk blue	12.00	10.50

75th anniv. of the UPU.

Letter Carriers — A6

Skier — A7

1949, Oct. 27			Perf. 13	
49	A6	12pf blue	8.50	10.00
50	A6	30pf red	12.50	17.50

"Day of the International Postal Workers' Trade Union," October 27-29, 1949.

1950, Mar. 2			Perf. 13	
51	A7	12pf shown	6.50	4.00
52	A7	24pf Skater	8.00	6.50

1st German Winter Sport Championship Matches, Schierke, 1950.

Globe and Sun — A8

1950, May 1			Typo.	
53	A8	30pf deep carmine	20.00	16.00

60th anniv. of Labor Day.

A9   Pres. Wilhelm Pieck — A10

1950-51		Wmk. 292	Perf. 13x12½	
54	A9	12pf dark blue	22.50	1.75
55	A9	24pf red brown	32.50	1.00
			Perf. 13x13½	
56	A10	1m olive green	32.50	5.75
		Litho.		
57	A10	2m red brown	19.00	4.25
		Engr.		
57A	A10	5m deep blue ('51)	7.00	1.50
Nos. 54-57A (5)			113.50	14.25

See Nos. 113-117, 120-121.

Leonhard Euler — A11   Miner — A12

Portraits: 5pf, Alexander von Humboldt. 6pf, Theodor Mommsen. 8pf, Wilhelm von Humboldt. 10pf, H. L. F. von Helmholtz. 12pf, Max Planck. 16pf, Jacob Grimm. 20pf, W. H. Nernst. 24pf, Gottfried von Leibnitz. 50pf, Adolf von Harnack.

		Wmk. 292		
1950, July 10		Litho.	Perf. 12½	
58	A11	1pf gray	5.00	1.60
59	A11	5pf dp green	5.75	5.00
60	A11	6pf purple	11.50	5.00
61	A11	8pf orange brn	18.00	11.50
62	A11	10pf dk gray grn	16.00	11.50
63	A11	12pf dk blue	15.00	3.25
64	A11	16pf Prus blue	20.00	20.00
65	A11	20pf violet brn	18.00	16.50
66	A11	24pf red	20.00	3.25
67	A11	50pf dp ultra	30.00	21.00
Nos. 58-67 (10)			159.25	98.60
Set, hinged			60.00	

250th anniv. of the founding of the Academy of Science, Berlin.
See Nos. 352-354.

1950, Sept. 1			Perf. 13	

Design: 24pf, Smelting copper.

68	A12	12pf blue	6.00	7.50
69	A12	24pf dark red	9.00	8.25

750th anniv. of the opening of the Mannsfeld copper mines.

Symbols of a Democratic Vote — A13

Hand Between Dove and Tank — A14

1950, Sept. 28				
70	A13	24pf brown red	16.00	6.00

Publicizing the election of Oct. 15, 1950.

1950, Dec. 15 Litho. Perf. 13

Designs show hand shielding dove from: 8pf, Exploding shell. 12pf, Atomic explosion. 24pf, Cemetery.

71	A14	6pf violet blue	4.00	3.25
72	A14	8pf brown	4.00	1.50
73	A14	12pf blue	5.75	3.25
74	A14	24pf red	5.75	1.50
		Nos. 71-74 (4)	19.50	9.50

Issued to publicize the "Fight for Peace."

Tobogganing A15

Design: 24pf, Ski jump.

1951, Feb. 3 Litho. Perf. 13

76	A15	12pf blue	8.25	7.50
77	A15	24pf rose	10.50	9.00

Issued to publicize the second Winter Sports Championship Matches at Oberhof.

A16

1951, Mar. 4 Wmk. 292 Perf. 13

78	A16	24pf rose carmine	17.50	14.00
79	A16	50pf violet blue	17.50	14.00

Issued to publicize the 1951 Leipzig Fair.

Pres. Wilhelm Pieck and Pres. Boleslaw Bierut Shaking Hands Across Oder-Neisse Frontier — A17

1951, Apr. 22 Perf. 13

80	A17	24pf scarlet	21.00	19.00
81	A17	50pf blue	21.00	19.00

Visit of Pres. Boleslaw Bierut of Poland to the Russian Zone of Germany.

Mao Tse-tung A18

Redistribution of Chinese Land — A19

1951, June 27 Perf. 13

82	A18	12pf dark green	100.00	27.50
83	A19	24pf deep carmine	125.00	35.00
84	A18	50pf violet blue	100.00	35.00
		Nos. 82-84 (3)	325.00	97.50
		Set, hinged	150.00	

Issued to publicize East Germany's friendship toward Communist China.

Boy Raising Flag A20

5-Year Plan Symbolism A21

Design: 24pf, 50pf, Girls dancing.

1951, Aug. 3
Grayish Paper, Except 30pf

85	A20	12pf choc & org brn	12.00	8.00
86	A20	24pf dk car & yel grn	12.00	5.00
87	A20	30pf dk bl grn & org brn, cit	14.50	10.00
88	A20	50pf vio bl & dk car	14.50	10.00
		Nos. 85-88 (4)	53.00	33.00

3rd World Youth Festival, Berlin, 1951.

1951, Sept. 2 Typo. Wmk. 292

89	A21	24pf multicolored	5.00	3.00

East Germany's Five-Year Plan.

Karl Liebknecht — A22

Father and Children with Stamp Collection A23

1951, Oct. 7 Litho. Perf. 13½x13

90	A22	24pf red & blue gray	5.00	2.50

Karl Liebknecht, socialist, 80th birth anniv.

1951, Oct. 28 Perf. 13

91	A23	12pf deep blue	5.50	3.00

Stamp Day, Oct. 28, 1951.

Stalin and Wilhelm Pieck A24

Design: 12pf, Pavel Bykov and Erich Wirth.

1951

92	A24	12pf deep blue	5.00	4.00
93	A24	24pf red	5.00	5.50

Month of East German-Soviet friendship. Issue dates: 12pf, Dec. 15, 24pf, Dec. 1.

Winter Sports Championship Matches, Oberhof, 1952 — A25

Design: 12pf, Skier. 24pf, Ski jump.

1952, Jan. 12 Wmk. 292

94	A25	12pf blue green	4.50	3.00
95	A25	24pf deep blue	4.50	3.00

Ludwig van Beethoven, 125th Death Anniv. — A26

1952, Mar. 26 Perf. 13½

Design: 12pf, Beethoven full face.

96	A26	12pf bl gray & vio bl	2.00	.75
97	A26	24pf gray & red brn	2.75	1.00

See Nos. 100-102.

Cyclists — A27

Klement Gottwald — A28

1952, May 5 Photo. Perf. 13x13½

98	A27	12pf blue	3.75	1.80

5th International Bicycle Peace Race, Warsaw-Berlin-Prague.

1952, May 1

99	A28	24pf violet blue	3.00	2.50

Friendship between German Democratic Republic and Czechoslovakia.

Type of 1952

Portraits: 6pf, G. F. Handel. 8pf, Albert Lortzing. 50pf, C. M. von Weber.

1952, July 5 Litho. Wmk. 297

100	A26	6pf brn buff & choc	2.25	1.50
101	A26	8pf pink & dp rose pink	3.00	2.75
102	A26	50pf bl gray & dp bl	3.00	3.00
		Nos. 100-102 (3)	8.25	7.25

Victor Hugo — A29

Portraits: 20pf, Leonardo da Vinci. 24pf, Nicolai Gogol. 35pf, Avicenna.

Wmk. 292

1952, Aug. 11 Photo. Perf. 13

103	A29	12pf brown	3.25	4.75
104	A29	20pf green	3.25	4.75
105	A29	24pf rose	3.25	4.75
106	A29	35pf blue	4.75	6.50
		Nos. 103-106 (4)	14.50	20.75

Machine, Globe and Dove — A30

1952, Sept. 7 Wmk. 297 Perf. 13

108	A30	24pf red	2.25	1.00
109	A30	35pf deep blue	2.25	2.00

Issued to publicize the 1952 Leipzig Fair.

Friedrich Ludwig Jahn — A31

1952, Oct. 15 Litho.

110	A31	12pf blue	2.10	1.25

Jahn (1778-1852), introduced gymnastics to Germany, and was a politician.

Halle University — A32

1952, Oct. 18 Photo.

111	A32	24pf green	2.25	1.00

450th anniv. of the founding of Halle University, Wittenberg.

Stamp, Flags, Wreath, Dove and Hammer — A33

1952, Oct. 26

112	A33	24pf red brown	2.50	1.25

Stamp Day, Oct. 26, 1952.

Pieck Types of 1950
Perf. 13x12½

1952-53 Wmk. 297 Typo.

113	A9	5pf blue green	10.00	2.75
114	A9	8pf dark blue	26.00	1.50
115	A9	24pf red brown	24.00	1.25

Perf. 13x13½

116	A10	1m olive green	32.50	16.00

Litho. Perf. 13

117	A10	2m red brown ('53)	27.50	3.25
		Nos. 113-117 (5)	120.00	24.75
		Set, hinged	35.00	

Globe, Dove and St. Stephen's Cathedral — A34

Pres. Wilhelm Pieck — A35

1952, Dec. 8 Photo. Perf. 13

118	A34	24pf brt carmine	1.60	2.50
119	A34	35pf deep blue	1.60	4.00

Issued to publicize the Congress of Nations for Peace, Vienna, Dec. 12-19, 1952.

1953 Perf. 13x13½

120	A35	1m olive	14.00	.50
a.		1m dark olive	22.50	2.50
121	A35	2m red brown	10.00	.50

See Nos. 339-340, 532.

Portrait Types of Russian Occupation, 1948

Designs as before.

Perf. 13x12½

			Typo.		**Wmk. 297**
1953					
122	OS2	2pf	gray	2.50	*3.00*
123	OS2	6pf	purple	2.50	1.75
124	OS2	8pf	red brown	1.75	1.75
125	OS2	10pf	blue grn	3.50	3.00
126	OS2	15pf	brown	11.50	11.50
127	OS2	16pf	turquoise	4.25	3.00
128	OS2	20pf	maroon	7.50	1.50
129	OS2	25pf	olive grn	180.00	200.00
130	OS2	30pf	red	13.00	7.50
131	OS2	40pf	red violet	3.50	2.50
132	OS2	50pf	dk ultra	22.00	16.00
133	OS2	60pf	dull green	4.25	2.50
134	OS2	80pf	dark blue	6.00	1.75
a.			Varnish coating, dark ultramarine	11.00	7.50
135	OS2	80pf	crimson	11.00	7.50
136	OS2	84pf	brown lake	50.00	*65.00*
			Nos. 122-136 (15)	323.25	328.25
			Set, hinged	100.00	

"Industry" and Red Flag — A36

Marx and Engels — A37

Karl Marx Speaking — A38

Karl Marx Medallion — A39

Designs: 12pf, Spasski tower and communist flag. 16pf, Marching workers. 24pf, Portrait of Karl Marx. 35pf, Marx addressing audience. 48pf, Karl Marx and Friedrich Engels. 60pf, Red banner above heads and shoulders of workers.

1953			**Photo.**		**Perf. 13**
137	A36	6pf	grnsh gray & red	1.50	.35
138	A37	10pf	grnsh gray & dk brn	4.00	.75
139	A36	12pf	grn, dp plum & dk grn	1.10	.50
140	A37	16pf	vio bl & dk car	3.00	1.75
141	A38	20pf	brown & buff	1.50	.75
142	A38	24pf	brown & red	3.00	.75
143	A36	35pf	dp pur & cr	3.00	2.50
144	A36	48pf	dk ol grn & red brn	2.25	.75
a.			Souvenir sheet of 6	100.00	*150.00*
			Hinged	35.00	
145	A37	60pf	vio brn & red	3.75	2.50
146	A39	84pf	blue & brown	3.25	1.75
a.			Souvenir sheet of 4	100.00	*150.00*
			Hinged	35.00	
			Nos. 137-146 (10)	26.35	12.35

No. 144a contains one each of the denominations in types A36 and A38. Perf. and imperf.

No. 146a contains one each of the denominations in types A37 and A39. Perf. and imperf.

Maxim Gorky — A40

Bicycle Racers — A41

1953, Mar. 28

147	A40	35pf	brown	.35	.25

1953, May 2　　Wmk. 297　　Perf. 13

24pf, 60pf, Different views of bicycle race.

148	A41	24pf	bluish green	2.50	2.00
149	A41	35pf	deep ultra	1.25	1.25
150	A41	60pf	chocolate	1.60	1.60
			Nos. 148-150 (3)	5.35	4.85

6th International Bicycle Peace Race.

Heinrich von Kleist A42

Woman Mariner A43

20pf, Evangelical Marienkirche. 24pf, Sailboat on Oder River. 35pf, City Hall, Frankfurt-on-Oder.

1953, July 6　　　　　　　　Litho.

151	A42	16pf	chocolate	1.60	*2.00*
152	A42	20pf	blue green	1.00	*1.60*
153	A42	24pf	rose red	1.60	*2.00*
154	A42	35pf	violet blue	1.60	*2.50*
			Set, 151-154 (4)	5.80	8.10

700th anniversary of the founding of Frankfurt-on-Oder.

1953　　　Litho.　　Perf. 13x12½

Designs: 1pf, Coal miner. 6pf, German and Soviet workers. 8pf, Mother teaching Marxist principles. 10pf, Machinists. 12pf, Worker, peasant and intellectual. 15pf, Teletype operator. 16pf, Steel worker. 20pf, Bad Elster. 24pf, Stalin Boulevard. 25pf, Locomotive building. 30pf, Dancing couple. 35pf, Sports Hall, Berlin. 40pf, Laboratory worker. 48pf, Zwinger Castle, Dresden. 60pf, Launching ship. 80pf, Agricultural workers. 84pf, Dove and East German family.

155	A43	1pf	black brown	1.60	.20
156	A43	5pf	emerald	2.00	.20
157	A43	6pf	violet	2.00	.20
158	A43	8pf	orange brn	2.75	.20
159	A43	10pf	blue green	2.00	.20
160	A43	12pf	blue	2.00	.20
161	A43	15pf	purple	3.25	.20
162	A43	17pf	dk violet	5.00	.20
163	A43	20pf	olive	4.75	.20
163A	A43	24pf	carmine	8.75	.20
164	A43	25pf	dk green	6.25	.20
165	A43	30pf	dp car	6.25	.20
166	A43	35pf	violet bl	19.00	.20
167	A43	40pf	rose red	16.00	.20
168	A43	48pf	rose red	16.00	.20
169	A43	60pf	deep blue	16.00	.20
170	A43	80pf	aqua	17.50	.20
171	A43	84pf	chocolate	16.00	.20
			Nos. 155-171 (18)	147.10	3.60
			Set, hinged	40.00	

See Nos. 187-204, 227-230A, 330-338, 476-482. For surcharges see #216-223A.

Used values of Nos. 155-171 are for cto reprints with printed cancellations. The reprints differ slightly from originals in design and shade.

Power Shovel — A44

Design: 35pf, Road-building machine.

1953, Aug. 29　　Photo.　　Perf. 13

172	A44	24pf	red brown	2.25	2.00
173	A44	35pf	deep green	3.25	2.50

The 1953 Leipzig Fair.

G. W. von Knobelsdorff and Berlin State Opera House — A45

Design: 35pf, Balthasar Neumann and Wurzburg bishop's palace.

1953, Sept. 16　　　　Perf. 13x12½

174	A45	24pf	cerise	1.50	.90
175	A45	35pf	dk slate blue	2.00	1.50

200th anniv. of the deaths of G. W. von Knobelsdorff and Balthasar Neumann, architects.

Lucas Cranach — A46

1953, Oct. 16　　　　Perf. 13x13½

176	A46	24pf	brown	3.25	1.50

400th anniversary of the death of Lucas Cranach (1472-1553), painter.

Nurse Applying Bandage — A47

Perf. 13½x13

1953, Oct. 23　　　　　　Wmk. 297

177	A47	24pf	brown & red	2.50	1.50

Issued to honor the Red Cross.

Mail Delivery — A48

1953, Oct. 25　　　　　　Photo.

178	A48	24pf	blue gray	3.25	.60

Stamp Day, Oct. 24, 1953.

Lion and Lioness — A49

1953, Nov. 2　　　　Perf. 13x13½

179	A49	24pf	olive brown	1.75	.50

75th anniversary of Leipzig Zoo.

Thomas Muntzer and Attackers A50

16pf, H. F. K. vom Stein. 20pf, Ferdinand von Schill leading cavalry. 24pf, G. L. Blucher and battle scene. 35pf, Students fighting for National Unity. 48pf, Revolution of 1848.

1953, Nov.　　Photo.　　Perf. 13x12½

180	A50	12pf	red brown	1.50	.60
181	A50	16pf	dp brown	1.50	.60
182	A50	20pf	dk car rose	1.50	.40
183	A50	24pf	deep blue	1.50	.40

184	A50	35pf	dk green	2.50	1.60
185	A50	48pf	dk brown	2.50	1.25
			Nos. 180-185 (6)	11.00	4.85

Issued to honor German patriots.

Franz Schubert — A51

Gotthold E. Lessing — A52

1953, Nov. 13　　　　Perf. 13½x13

186	A51	48pf	brt orange brn	2.75	1.50

Death of Franz Schubert, 125th anniv.

Types of 1953 Redrawn

Designs as before.

1953-54　　Typo.　　Perf. 13x12½

187	A43	1pf	black brn	.80	.20
188	A43	5pf	emerald	3.50	.20
a.			Bklt. pane, 3 #188 + 3 #227	24.00	24.00
b.			Bklt. pane, 3 #188 + 3 #228	24.00	24.00
189	A43	6pf	purple	4.00	.20
190	A43	8pf	orange brn	5.00	.20
191	A43	10pf	blue grn	32.50	.20
192	A43	12pf	grnsh blue	5.50	.20
193	A43	15pf	brt vio ('54)	20.00	.20
194	A43	16pf	dk purple	6.00	.20
195	A43	20pf	olive ('54)	85.00	.20
196	A43	24pf	carmine	6.25	.20
197	A43	25pf	dk bl grn	4.00	.20
198	A43	30pf	dp carmine	5.00	.20
199	A43	35pf	dp vio bl	5.50	.20
200	A43	40pf	rose red ('54)	12.00	.20
201	A43	48pf	rose vio	11.00	.20
202	A43	60pf	blue	17.50	.20
203	A43	80pf	aqua	4.00	.20
204	A43	84pf	chocolate	20.00	.20
			Nos. 187-204 (18)	247.55	3.60
			Set, hinged	60.00	

Nos. 155-171 were printed from screened halftones, and shading consists of dots. Shading in lines without screen on Nos. 187-204. Designers' and engravers' names added below design on all values except 6, 12, 16 and 35pf. There are many other minor differences.

See note on used values after No. 171.

1954, Jan. 20　　Photo.　　Perf. 13

205	A52	20pf	dark green	2.00	.90

225th anniversary of the birth of G. E. Lessing, dramatist.

Dove Over Conference Table — A53

Joseph V. Stalin — A54

1954, Jan. 25　　　　Perf. 12½x13

206	A53	12pf	blue	1.75	.75

Four Power Conference, Berlin, 1954.

1954, Mar. 5　　Typo.　　Perf. 13x12½

207	A54	20pf	gray, dk brn & red org	2.50	.75

1st anniv. of the death of Joseph V. Stalin.

Cyclists A55

Design: 24pf, Cyclists passing farm.

1954, Apr. 30   **Photo.**
208 A55 12pf brown   1.20   .75
209 A55 24pf dull green   2.00 1.20

7th International Bicycle Peace Race.

Dancers — A56

Fritz
Reuter — A57

Design: 24pf, Boy, two girls and flag.

1954, June 3   **Perf. 13**
210 A56 12pf emerald   1.00   .75
211 A56 24pf rose brown   1.00   .75

Issued to publicize the 2nd German youth meeting for peace, unity and freedom.

1954, July 12
212 A57 24pf sepia   1.75 1.00

Death of Fritz Reuter, writer, 80th anniv.

Ernst
Thälmann — A58

1954, Aug. 18   **Perf. 13½x13**
213 A58 24pf red org & indigo   1.00   .65

10th anniv. of the death of Ernst Thälmann (1886-1944), Communist leader.

Hall of
Commerce,
Leipzig
Fair — A59

1954, Sept. 4   **Perf. 13x13½**
214 A59 24pf dark red   .85   .45
215 A59 35pf gray blue   .85   .60

Issued to publicize the 1954 Leipzig Fair.

Redrawn Types of 1953-54
Surcharged with New Value and "X" in Black

1954		Typo.	Perf. 13x12½	
216	A43	5pf on 6pf purple	1.00	.20
217	A43	5pf on 8pf org brn	1.40	.20
218	A43	10pf on 12pf grnsh bl	1.00	.20
219	A43	15pf on 16pf dk pur	1.00	.20
220	A43	20pf on 24pf car	1.10	.20
221	A43	40pf on 48pf rose vio	3.00	.20
222	A43	50pf on 60pf blue	3.00	.20
223	A43	70pf on 84pf choc	10.00	.20
		Nos. 216-223 (8)	21.50	1.60

See note on used values after No. 171.

No. 163A Surcharged with New Value and "X" in Black

1955		Litho.		
223A	A43	20pf on 24pf car	.80	.25

Counterfeit surcharges exist on other values of the lithographed set (Nos. 155-171).

Pres.
Wilhelm
Pieck and
Flags
A60

1954, Oct. 6   **Photo.**
224 A60 20pf brown   2.25   .90
225 A60 35pf greenish blue   2.25 1.00

5th anniv. of the founding of the German Democratic Republic.

Cologne
Cathedral,
Leipzig
Monument and
Unissued Stamp
Design — A61

1954, Oct. 23   **Perf. 13x13½**
226 A61 20pf brt car rose   1.50   .75
    a.   Souvenir sheet, imperf.   50.00 40.00

Stamp Day. No. 226a has frame and inscription in blue. Size: 60x80mm.

Redrawn Types of 1953-54

Designs: 10pf, Worker, peasant and intellectual. 15pf, Steelworker. 20pf, Stalin Boulevard. 40pf, Zwinger Castle, Dresden. 50pf, Launching ship. 70pf, Dove and East German family.

1955		Typo.	Perf. 13x12½	
227	A43	10pf blue	2.00	.20
	a.	Bklt. pane, 4 #227 + 2 #228		
227B	A43	15pf violet	2.40	.20
228	A43	20pf carmine	1.75	.20
229	A43	40pf rose violet	3.75	.20
230	A43	50pf deep blue	6.25	.20
230A	A43	70pf chocolate	8.50	.20
		Nos. 227-230A (6)	24.65	1.20

See note on used values after No. 171.

Soviet Pavilion,
Leipzig Spring
Fair — A62

Women of
Three
Nations — A63

Design: 35pf, Chinese pavilion.

1955, Feb. 21   **Photo.**   **Wmk. 297**
231 A62 20pf rose violet   1.20   .75
232 A62 35pf violet blue   1.40   .75

Issued to publicize the Leipzig Spring Fair.

1955, Mar. 1   **Perf. 13x13½**
233 A63 10pf green   1.00   .35
234 A63 20pf red   1.00   .35

International Women's Day, 45th year.

Workers' Demonstration — A64

1955, Mar. 15   **Perf. 13x12½**
235 A64 10pf black & red   1.00   .75

Intl. Trade Union Conference, Apr., 1955.

A65   A66

Monument to the Victims of Fascism.

1955, Apr. 9   **Perf. 13½x13**
236 A65 10pf violet blue   .80   .75
237 A65 20pf cerise   1.10 1.20
   a.   Souv. sheet of 2, #236-237, imperf.   15.00 19.00

No. 237a sold for 50pf.

1955, Apr. 15   **Perf. 12½x13**
Russian War Memorial, Berlin.
238 A66 20pf lilac rose   1.25   .75

Nos. 236-238 issued for 10th anniv. of liberation, No. 237a for reconstruction of natl. memorial sites.

Cyclists — A67   Friedrich von
                 Schiller — A68

1955   **Wmk. 297**   **Perf. 13½x13**
239 A67 10pf blue green   1.00   .45
240 A67 20pf car rose   1.25   .50

8th International Bicycle Peace Race, Prague-Berlin-Warsaw.

Starting with the 1955 issues, commemorative stamps which are valued in italics were sold on a restricted basis.

1955, Apr. 20
Various Portraits of Schiller.
241 A68 5pf dk gray grn   *2.75*   *2.25*
242 A68 10pf brt blue   *.40*   *.20*
243 A68 20pf chocolate   *.40*   *.20*
   a.   Souv. sheet, #241-243, imperf.   24.00 24.00
    Nos. 241-243 (3)   *3.55* *2.65*

150th anniv. of the death of Friedrich von Schiller, poet.
No. 243a sold for 50pf.

Karl Liebknecht — A69

Portraits: 10pf, August Bebel. 15pf, Franz Mehring. 20pf, Ernst Thalmann. 25pf, Clara Zetkin. 40pf, Wilhelm Liebknecht. 60pf, Rosa Luxemburg.

1955, June 20   **Photo.**   **Perf. 13x12½**
244 A69 5pf blue green   .30   .20
245 A69 10pf deep blue   .40   .20
246 A69 15pf violet   5.50 2.25
247 A69 20pf red   .40   .20
248 A69 25pf slate   .40   .20
249 A69 40pf rose carmine   2.10   .20
250 A69 60pf dk brown   .40   .20
    Nos. 244-250 (7)   9.50 3.45

Issued to honor German communists.

Optical
Goods — A70

Design: 20pf, Pottery and china.

1955, Aug. 29   **Photo.**   **Perf. 13x13½**
253 A70 10pf dark blue   .50   .25
254 A70 20pf slate green   .50   .25

Issued to publicize the 1955 Leipzig Fair.

Farmer Receiving
Deed — A71

Harvesters
A72

10pf, Construction of new farm community.

1955, Sept. 3   **Perf. 13½x13, 13x13½**
255 A71 5pf dull green   4.75 3.50
256 A71 10pf ultra   .65   .20
257 A72 20pf lake   .65   .20
    Nos. 255-257 (3)   6.05 3.90

10th anniv. of the Land-Reform Program.

Man Holding   Engels at "First
Badge of   International,"
Peoples'   1864 — A74
Solidarity — A73

Perf. 13½x13

1955, Oct. 10   **Wmk. 297**
258 A73 10pf dark blue   .60   .25

10th anniv. of the "Peoples' Solidarity."

1955, Nov. 7   **Perf. 13½x13**
Designs: 10pf, Marx and Engels writing the Communist Manifesto. 15pf, Engels as newspaper editor. 20pf, Friedrich Engels. 30pf, Friedrich Engels. 70pf, Engels on the barricades in 1848.
259 A74 5pf Prus blue & olive   .35   .20
260 A74 10pf dk blue & yel   .70   .20
261 A74 15pf dk green & ol   .70   .20
262 A74 20pf brn vio & org   1.40   .20
263 A74 30pf org brn & lt bl   8.50 6.50
264 A74 70pf gray grn & rose car   2.50   .25
   a.   Souvenir sheet of 6, #259-264   62.50 75.00
    Nos. 259-264 (6)   14.15 7.55

Friedrich Engels, 135th birth anniv.

Cathedral at   Georgius
Magdeburg   Agricola
A75   A76

German Buildings: 10pf, German State Opera. 15pf, Old City Hall, Leipzig. 20pf, City Hall, Berlin. 30pf, Cathedral at Erfurt. 40pf, Zwinger at Dresden.

1955, Nov. 14
265 A75 5pf black brown   .75   .30
266 A75 10pf gray green   .75   .30
267 A75 15pf purple   .75   .30
268 A75 20pf carmine   .75   .75
269 A75 30pf dk red brown   10.00 10.00
270 A75 40pf indigo   1.50   .75
    Nos. 265-270 (6)   14.50 12.40

For surcharges see Nos. B29-B30.

1955, Nov. 21   **Wmk. 297**
271 A76 10pf brown   .60   .35

400th anniv. of the death of Georgius Agricola, mineralogist and scholar.

Paintings in
Dresden
Gallery — A77

Mozart — A78

Famous Paintings: 5pf, Portrait of a Young
Man, by Dürer. 10pf, Chocolate Girl, by
Liotard. 15pf, Portrait of a Boy, by Pinturicchio.
20pf, Self-portrait with Saskia, by Rembrandt.
40pf, Girl with Letter, by Vermeer. 70pf, Sistine
Madonna, by Raphael.

1955, Dec. 15   **Perf. 13½x13**
272 A77 5pf dk red brown   .65   .20
273 A77 10pf chestnut   .65   .20
274 A77 15pf pale purple   29.00 16.00
275 A77 20pf brown   .65   .20
276 A77 40pf olive green   .65   .25
277 A77 70pf deep blue   1.60   .50
       Nos. 272-277 (6)   33.20 17.35

Issued to publicize the return of famous art
works to the Dresden Art Gallery.
See Nos. 355-360, 439-443.

1956, Jan. 27   **Photo.**
Designs: 20pf, Portrait facing left.
278 A78 10pf gray green   10.00 6.00
279 A78 20pf copper brown   3.50 1.00

200th anniv. of the birth of Wolfgang
Amadeus Mozart, composer.

Flag and Schoenefeld Airport,
Berlin — A79

Lufthansa
Plane
A80

Designs: 15pf, Plane facing right. 20pf,
Plane facing down and left.

1956, Feb. 1   **Perf. 13x12½**
280 A79 5pf multicolored   12.00 6.25
281 A80 10pf gray green   .70   .20
282 A80 15pf dull blue   .70   .20
283 A80 20pf brown red   .70   .20
       Nos. 280-283 (4)   14.10 6.85

Issued to commemorate the opening of passenger service of the German Lufthansa.

Heinrich
Heine — A81

Railroad
Cranes — A82

Design: 20pf, Heine (different portrait.)

1956, Feb. 17   **Perf. 13½x13**
284 A81 10pf Prus green   11.50 4.25
285 A81 20pf dark red   2.50   .40

Cent. of the death of Heinrich Heine, poet.

1956, Feb. 26   **Perf. 13x13½**
286 A82 20pf brown red   .50   .25
287 A82 35pf violet blue   .75   .45

Issued to publicize the Leipzig Spring Fair.

Ernst Thälmann
A83

1956, Apr. 16   Litho.   Perf. 13x13½
288 A83 20pf black olive &
               red   .60   .35
  a. Souvenir sheet of 1, imperf 10.00 18.00

Birth of Ernst Thälmann, 70th anniv.
No. 288a was sold at double face value. The
proceeds were used for national memorials at
former concentration camps.

Wheel, Hand and
Olive
Branch — A84

City Hall and Old
Market — A85

Design: 20pf, Wheel and coats of arms of
Warsaw, Berlin, Prague.

Perf. 13½x13
1956, Apr. 30   **Wmk. 297**
289 A84 10pf lt green   .60   .25
290 A84 20pf brt carmine   .60   .25

9th International Bicycle Peace Race, Warsaw-Berlin-Prague, May 1-15, 1956.

1956, June 1
Designs: 20pf, Hofkirche and Elbe Bridge.
40pf, Technical College.
291 A85 10pf green   .25   .20
292 A85 20pf carmine rose   .25   .20
293 A85 40pf brt purple   1.75 1.75
       Nos. 291-293 (3)   2.25 2.15

750th anniversary of Dresden.

Worker Holding
Cogwheel
Emblem — A86

1956, June 30   **Perf. 13½x13**
294 A86 20pf rose red   .45   .20

10th anniversary of nationalized industry.

Robert
Schumann
(Music by
Schubert)
A87

1956, July 20   **Perf. 13x13½**
295 A87 10pf brt green   1.75   .95
296 A87 20pf rose red   1.10   .20

Centenary of the death of Robert Schumann, composer. See Nos. 303-304.

Soccer
Players — A88

Thomas
Mann — A89

Designs: 10pf, Javelin Thrower. 15pf,
Women Hurdlers. 20pf, Gymnast.

1956, July 25   **Perf. 13½x13**
297 A88 5pf green   .20   .20
298 A88 10pf dk vio blue   .20   .20
299 A88 15pf red violet   2.10   .70
300 A88 20pf rose red   .20   .20
       Nos. 297-300 (4)   2.70 1.30

Second Sports Festival, Leipzig, Aug. 2-5.

1956, Aug. 13   **Wmk. 297**
301 A89 20pf bluish black   1.00   .40

Death of Thomas Mann, novelist, 1st anniv.

Jakub Bart
Cisinski — A90

Robert
Schumann
(Music by
Schumann)
A91

1956, Aug. 20   **Photo.**
302 A90 50pf claret   1.00   .40

Birth centenary of Jakub Bart Cisinski, poet.

1956, Oct. 8   **Perf. 13x13½**
303 A91 10pf brt green   4.50 1.75
304 A91 20pf rose red   2.50   .25

See Nos. 295, 296.

Lace — A92

Olympic Rings,
Laurel and
Torch — A93

Design: 20pf, Sailboat.

1956, Sept. 1   Typo.   Perf. 13½x13
305 A92 10pf green & blk   .30   .25
306 A92 20pf rose red & blk   .30   .25

Leipzig Fair, Sept. 2-9.

1956, Sept. 28   **Litho.**
Design: 35pf, Classic javelin thrower.
307 A93 20pf brown red   .40   .20
308 A93 35pf slate blue   .60   .25

16th Olympic Games at Melbourne, Nov.
22-Dec. 8, 1956.

Post Runner of
1450 — A94

Greifswald
University
Seal — A95

1956, Oct. 27
309 A94 20pf red   .45   .20

Issued to publicize the Day of the Stamp.

1956, Oct. 17   **Perf. 13x13½**
310 A95 20pf magenta   .45   .20

500th anniv. of Greifswald University.

Ernst Abbe — A96

Zeiss
Works,
Jena
A97

Portrait: 25pf, Carl Zeiss.

Perf. 12½x13, 13x12½
1956, Nov. 9   Photo.   Wmk. 297
311 A96 10pf dark green   .20   .20
312 A97 20pf brown red   .20   .20
313 A96 25pf bluish black   .35   .25
       Nos. 311-313 (3)   .75   .65

Carl Zeiss Optical Works, Jena, 110th anniv.

Chinese Girl with
Flowers — A98

Designs: 10pf, Negro woman and child.
25pf, European man and dove.

1956, Dec. 10   Litho.   Perf. 13
314 A98 5pf ol, *pale lem*   1.25   .70
315 A98 10pf brown, *pink*   .20   .20
316 A98 25pf vio bl, *pale vio bl* .20 .25
       Nos. 314-316 (3)   1.65 1.10

Issued for Human Rights Day.

Elephants
A99

1956, Dec. 14   Photo.   Perf. 13x12½
Design in Gray
317 A99 5pf shown   .20   .20
318 A99 10pf Flamingoes   .20   .20
319 A99 15pf White rhinoceros 4.25 2.25
320 A99 20pf Mouflon   .20   .20
321 A99 25pf Bison   .20   .20
322 A99 30pf Polar bear   .20   .20
       Nos. 317-322 (6)   5.25 3.25

Issued to publicize the Berlin Zoo.

Freighter
A100

Design: 25pf, Electric Locomotive.

1957, Mar. 1   Litho.   Wmk. 313
323 A100 20pf rose red   .25   .20
324 A100 25pf bright blue   .25   .20

Leipzig Spring Fair.

Silver
Thistle
A101

10pf, Emerald lizard. 20pf, Lady's-slipper.

1957, Apr. 12 Photo. Wmk. 313
325 A101 5pf chocolate .20 .20
326 A101 10pf dk slate grn 2.25 2.00
327 A101 20pf red brown .20 .20
Nos. 325-327 (3) 2.65 2.40
Nature Conservation Week, Apr. 14-20.

Children at Play — A102

20pf, Friedrich Froebel and Children.

1957, Apr. 18 Litho. Perf. 13
328 A102 10pf dk slate grn & ol 1.20 .80
329 A102 20pf black & brown red .20 .20
175th anniv. of the birth of Friedrich Froebel, educator.

Redrawn Types of 1953

Designs: 5pf, Woman mariner. 10pf, Worker, peasant and intellectual. 15pf, Steel worker. 20pf, Stalin Boulevard. 25pf, Locomotive building. 30pf, Dancing couple. 40pf, Zwinger Castle, Dresden. 50pf, Launching ship. 70pf, Dove and East German family.

Imprint: "E. Gruner K. Wolf"
No imprint on 10pf, 15pf

Perf. 13x12½, 14

1957-58 Typo. Wmk. 313
330 A43 5pf emerald .20 .20
  a. Bklt. pane, 3 #330 + 3 #331b 25.00
  b. Bklt. pane, 3 #330 + 3 #333 25.00
  c. Booklet pane of 6 2.00
331 A43 10pf blue ('58) .20 .20
  a. Bklt. pane, 4 #331b + 2 #333 40.00
  b. Perf. 13x12½ 5.00 .20
332 A43 15pf violet ('58) .20 .20
  a. Perf. 13x12½ .30 .20
333 A43 20pf carmine .30 .20
  a. Bklt. pane, 5 #333 + 1 #477 2.00
334 A43 25pf bluish green .30 .20
335 A43 30pf dull red .75 .20
336 A43 40pf rose violet 1.10 .20
337 A43 50pf bright blue 1.40 .20
338 A43 70pf chocolate 1.60 .20
See Nos. 476-482.

Pieck Type of 1953
Photo. Perf. 13x13½
339 A35 1m dk olive grn ('58) 2.25 .25
340 A35 2m red brown ('58) 4.50 .30
Nos. 330-340 (11) 12.80 2.35

No. 334 comes only perf 13x12½. Nos 330-333 and 335-338 come both perf 13x12½ and perf 14.

Bicycle Race Route — A103

Perf. 13x13½
1957, Apr. 30 Litho. Wmk. 313
346 A103 5pf orange .30 .20
Issued to publicize the 10th International Bicycle Peace Race, Prague-Berlin-Warsaw.

Steam Shovel A104

Miner — A105

Design: 20pf, Coal conveyor.

Perf. 13x12½, 13½x13 (25pf)
1957, May 3
347 A104 10pf green .20 .20
348 A104 20pf redsh brown .20 .20
349 A105 25pf blue violet 2.25 .75
Nos. 347-349 (3) 2.65 1.15
Issued in honor of the coal mining industry.

Henri Dunant and Globe A106

25pf, Henri Dunant facing right and globe.

1957, May 7 Photo. Perf. 13x12½
350 A106 10pf green, red & blk .25 .20
351 A106 25pf brt blue, red & blk .25 .20
Tenth Red Cross world conference.

Portrait Type of 1950, Redrawn

Portraits: 5pf, Joachim Jungius. 10pf, Leonhard Euler. 20pf, Heinrich Hertz.

1957, June 7 Litho.
352 A11 5pf brown 1.50 .50
353 A11 10pf green .20 .20
354 A11 20pf henna brown .20 .20
Nos. 352-354 (3) 1.90 .90
Issued to honor famous German scientists.

Painting Type of 1955.

Famous Paintings: 5pf, Holy Family, by Mantegna. 10pf, The Dancer Campani, by Carriera. 15pf, Portrait of Morette, by Holbein. 20pf, The Tribute Money, by Titian. 25pf, Saskia with Red Flower, by Rembrandt. 40pf, Young Standard Bearer, by Piazetta.

Perf. 13½x13
1957, June 26 Photo. Wmk. 313
355 A77 5pf dk brown .30 .20
356 A77 10pf lt yellow grn .30 .20
357 A77 15pf brown olive .30 .20
358 A77 20pf rose brown .30 .20
359 A77 25pf deep claret .30 .20
360 A77 40pf dk blue gray 4.50 1.50
Nos. 355-360 (6) 6.00 2.50

Clara Zetkin — A107

Bertolt Brecht — A108

1957, July 5 Perf. 13x13½
361 A107 10pf dk green & red .60 .25
Centenary of the birth of Clara Zetkin, politician and founder of the socialist women's movement.

1957, Aug. 14 Perf. 13½x13
362 A108 10pf dark green .30 .20
363 A108 25pf deep blue .40 .20
Brecht (1898-1956), playwright and poet.

Congress Emblem — A109

Fair Emblem — A110

1957, Aug. 23 Litho.
364 A109 20pf brt red & black .50 .25
4th Intl. Trade Union Congress, Leipzig, Oct. 4-15.

1957, Aug. 30 Wmk. 313
365 A110 20pf crimson & ver .25 .20
366 A110 25pf brt blue & lt blue .30 .20
Issued to publicize the 1957 Leipzig Fair.

Savings Book — A111

Postrider, 1563 — A112

1957, Oct. 10 Perf. 13½x13
367 A111 10pf grn & blk, gray .75 .45
368 A111 20pf rose car & blk, gray .30 .30
Issued to publicize "Savings Weeks."

1957, Oct. 25 Wmk. 313
369 A112 5pf black, pale sepia .50 .20
Issued for the Day of the Stamp.

Sputnik I A113

Storming of the Winter Palace A114

20pf, Stratospheric balloon above clouds. 25pf, Ship with plumb line exploring deep sea.

1957-58 Perf. 12½x13
370 A113 10pf blue black .35 .20
371 A113 20pf car rose ('58) .50 .20
372 A113 25pf brt blue ('58) 1.90 .95
Nos. 370-372 (3) 2.75 1.35
IGY. The 10pf also for the launching of 1st artificial satellite.

1957, Nov. 7 Photo.
373 A114 10pf yellow grn & red .25 .20
374 A114 25pf brt blue & red .25 .20
40th anniv. of the Russian Revolution.

Guenther Ramin — A115

Dove and Globe — A116

Portrait: 20pf, Hermann Abendroth.

Perf. 13½x13
1957, Nov. 22 Litho. Wmk. 313
375 A115 10pf yellow grn & blk 1.00 .60
376 A115 20pf red orange & blk .20 .20
Ramin (1898-1956) and Abendroth (1883-1956), musicians, on the 1st anniv. of their death.

1958, Feb. 27 Perf. 13x13½
377 A116 20pf rose red .25 .20
378 A116 25pf blue .30 .20
Issued to publicize the 1958 Leipzig Fair.

Radio Tower, Morse Code and Post Horn A117

Design: 20pf, Radio tower and small post horn.

1958, Mar. 6 Perf. 13x12½
379 A117 5pf gray & blk .75 .45
380 A117 20pf crim rose & dk red .35 .20
Conf. of Postal Ministers of Communist countries, Moscow, Dec. 3-17, 1957.

Sketch by Zille — A118

Symbolizing Quantum Theory — A119

Design: 20pf, Self-portrait of Zille.

1958, Mar. 20 Perf. 13½x13
381 A118 10pf green & gray 2.40 1.00
382 A118 20pf dp car & gray .55 .20
Centenary of the birth of Heinrich Zille, artist.

1958, Apr. 23 Litho.
Design: 20pf, Max Planck.
383 A119 10pf gray green 1.10 .75
384 A119 20pf magenta .35 .20
Centenary of the birth of Max Planck, physicist.

Prize Cow — A120

10pf, Mowing machine. 20pf, Beet harvester.

Perf. 13x13½
1958, June 4 Wmk. 313
Size: 28x23mm
385 A120 5pf gray & blk 2.25 1.00
Size: 39x22mm
Perf. 13x12½
386 A120 10pf brt green .35 .20
387 A120 20pf rose red .35 .20
Nos. 385-387 (3) 2.95 1.40
6th Agricultural Show, Markkleeberg.

Charles Darwin — A121

1958, June 19 Perf. 13x13½
Portrait: 20pf, Carl von Linné.
388 A121 10pf green & black 1.25 .75
389 A121 20pf dk red & black .20 .20
Cent. of Darwin's theory of evolution and the bicent. of Linné's botanical system.

Seven Towers of Rostock and Ships — A122

Congress Emblem — A123

10pf, Ship at pier. 25pf, Ships in harbor.

1958   **Perf. 13½x13**
390	A122	10pf emerald	.20	.20
391	A122	20pf red orange	.40	.25
392	A122	25pf lt blue	1.00	1.00
		Nos. 390-392 (3)	1.60	1.45

Establishment of Rostock as a seaport. Issue dates: 20pf, July 5; 10pf and 25pf, Nov. 24.
For overprint see No. 500.

1958, June 25   **Perf. 13x13½**
393	A123	10pf rose red	.35	.20

5th congress of the Socialist Party of the German Democratic Republic (SED).

Mare and Foal A124

Designs: 10pf, Trotter. 20pf, Horse race.

1958, July 22   **Photo.**   **Perf. 13x12½**
394	A124	5pf black brown	2.25	1.75
395	A124	10pf dark olive green	.20	.20
396	A124	20pf dark red brown	.20	.20
		Nos. 394-396 (3)	2.65	2.15

Grand Prize of the DDR, 1958.

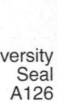

Jan Amos Komensky (Comenius) A125

Design: 20pf, Teacher and pupils, 17th cent.

1958, Aug. 7   **Litho.**   **Perf. 13x13½**
397	A125	10pf brt bl grn & blk	1.50	.75
398	A125	20pf org brn & blk	.20	.20

University Seal A126

Design: 20pf, Schiller University, Jena.

1958, Aug. 19   **Perf. 13x12½**
399	A126	5pf gray & black	1.25	.75
400	A126	20pf dark red & gray	.30	.20

Friedrich Schiller University in Jena, 400th anniv.

Soldier on Obstacle Course — A127

Arms Breaking A-Bomb — A128

Design: 20pf, Spartacist emblem. 25pf, Marching athletes, map and flag.

      Perf. 13½x13

1958, Sept. 19   **Litho.**   **Wmk. 313**
401	A127	10pf emerald & brn	1.50	.70
402	A127	20pf brown red & yel	.20	.20
403	A127	25pf lt blue & red	.20	.20
		Nos. 401-403 (3)	1.90	1.10

1st Spartacist Sports Meet of Friendly Armies, Leipzig, Sept. 20-28.

1958, Sept. 19   **Perf. 13x13½**
404	A128	20pf rose red	.20	.20
405	A128	25pf blue	.40	.20

People's fight against atomic death.

Woman and Leipzig Railroad Station A129

Design: 25pf, Woman in Persian lamb coat and old City Hall, Leipzig.

1958, Aug. 29   **Perf. 13x12½**
406	A129	10pf green, brn & blk	.20	.20
407	A129	25pf blue & black	.30	.20

Issued to publicize the 1958 Leipzig Fair.

Post Wagon, 17th Century A130

Design: 20pf, Mail train and plane.

1958, Oct. 23   **Wmk. 313**
408	A130	10pf green	1.75	.80
409	A130	20pf lake	.35	.20

Issued for the Day of the Stamp.

Brandenburg Gate, Berlin — A131

Head from Greek Tomb — A132

1958, Nov. 29   **Perf. 13x13½**
410	A131	20pf rose red	.35	.20
411	A131	25pf dark blue	2.50	1.50

Issued to commemorate 10 years of democratic city administration of Berlin.

1958, Dec. 2   **Perf. 13½x13**

20pf, Giant's head from Pergamum frieze.
412	A132	10pf blue grn & blk	1.25	.70
413	A132	20pf dp rose & black	.20	.20

Return of art treasures from Russia. See #484-486.

Negro and Caucasian Men — A133

Design: 25pf, Chinese and Caucasian girls.

1958, Dec. 10   **Perf. 13x12½**
414	A133	10pf brt blue grn & blk	.20	.20
415	A133	25pf blue & black	1.75	.80

10th anniv. of the signing of the Universal Declaration of Human Rights.

Worker and Soldier — A134

Otto Nuschke — A135

1958, Nov. 7   **Perf. 12½x13**
416	A134	20pf blk, ver & dl pur	10.00	14.00

40th anniv. of the Revolution of Nov. 7. (Stamp inscribed Nov. 9.) Withdrawn from sale on day of issue.

     Perf. 13½x13

1958, Dec. 27   **Wmk. 313**
417	A135	20pf red	.30	.20

First anniversary of the death of Otto Nuschke, vice president of the republic.

Communist Newspaper, "The Red Flag" — A136

1958, Dec. 30   **Perf. 13x12½**
418	A136	20pf red	.35	.25

German Communist Party, 40th anniv.

Rosa Luxemburg Addressing Crowd — A137

20pf, Karl Liebknecht addressing crowd.

     Perf. 13x13½

1959, Jan. 15   **Wmk. 313**
419	A137	10pf blue green	2.00	.90
420	A137	20pf henna brn & blk	.20	.20

40th anniversary of the death of Rosa Luxemburg and Karl Liebknecht.

Gewandhaus, Leipzig — A138

President Wilhelm Pieck — A139

Design: 25pf, Opening theme of Mendelssohn's A Major symphony.

1959, Feb. 28   **Engr.**   **Perf. 14**
421	A138	10pf green, grnsh	.35	.25
422	A138	25pf blue, bluish	1.50	2.00

150th anniversary of the birth of Felix Mendelssohn-Bartholdy, composer.

1959, Jan. 3   **Photo.**   **Perf. 13½x13**
423	A139	20pf henna brown	.45	.20

83rd birthday of President Wilhelm Pieck. See No. 511.

"Black Pump" Plant A140

Design: 25pf, Photographic equipment.

1959, Feb. 28   **Litho.**   **Perf. 13x12½**
424	A140	20pf carmine rose	.20	.20
425	A140	25pf lt ultra	.35	.20

1959 Leipzig Spring Fair.

Boy and Girl — A141

Statue of Handel, Halle — A142

1959, Apr. 2   **Perf. 13½x13**
426	A141	10pf blk, lt grn	1.50	.75
427	A141	20pf blk, salmon	.20	.20

5 years of the Youth Consecration ceremony.

1959, Apr. 27   **Wmk. 313**

20pf, Handel by Thomas Hudson, 1749.
428	A142	10pf bluish grn & blk	1.60	.80
429	A142	20pf rose & blk	.20	.20

Bicentenary of the death of George Frederick Handel, composer.

Alexander von Humboldt and Central American View — A143

Post Horn — A144

Design: 20pf, Portrait and Siberian view.

1959, May 6
430	A143	10pf bluish grn	1.25	.75
431	A143	20pf rose	.30	.20

Centenary of the death of Alexander von Humboldt, naturalist and geographer.

1959, May 30   **Perf. 13½x13**
432	A144	20pf scar, yel & blk	.20	.20
433	A144	25pf lt bl, yel & blk	.75	.60

Conference of socialist postal ministers.

Gray Heron A145

10pf, Bittern. 20pf, Lily of the valley & butterfly. 25pf, Beaver. 40pf, Pussy willows and bee.

1959, June 26   **Perf. 13x12½**
434	A145	5pf lt bl, blk & lil	.20	.20
435	A145	10pf grnsh bl, dk brn & org	.20	.20
436	A145	20pf org red, grn & vio	.20	.20
437	A145	25pf lilac, yel & blk	.35	.20
438	A145	40pf gray bl, yel & blk	5.50	2.50
		Nos. 434-438 (5)	6.45	3.30

Issued to publicize wildlife protection.

Painting Type of 1955.

Famous Paintings: 5pf, Portrait, by Angelica Kauffmann. 10pf, The Lady Lace Maker, by Gabriel Metsu. 20pf, Mademoiselle Lavergne, by Liotard. 25pf, Old Woman with Brazier, by Rubens. 40pf, Young Man in Black Coat, by Hals.

1959, June 29 Photo. *Perf. 13½x13*

439	A77	5pf olive	.20	.20
440	A77	10pf green	.20	.20
441	A77	20pf dp org	.20	.20
442	A77	25pf chestnut	.35	.20
443	A77	40pf dp magenta	5.50	1.90
		Nos. 439-443 (5)	6.45	2.70

Great
Cormoran — A146

Youths of Three
Races — A147

Birds: 10pf, Black Stork. 15pf, Eagle owl. 20pf, Black grouse. 25pf, Hoopoe. 40pf, Peregrine falcon.

Perf. 13x13½

1959, July 2 Litho. Wmk. 313
Designs in Black

444	A146	5pf yellow	.20	.20
445	A146	10pf lt green	.20	.20
446	A146	15pf pale violet	4.75	2.10
447	A146	20pf deep pink	.20	.20
448	A146	25pf blue	.20	.20
449	A146	40pf vermilion	.20	.20
		Nos. 444-449 (6)	5.75	3.10

Protection of native birds.

1959, July 25 *Perf. 12½x13, 13x12½*

25pf, Swedish girl kissing African girl, horiz.

450	A147	20pf crimson	.20	.20
451	A147	25pf bright blue	.75	.45

7th World Youth Festival, Vienna, 7/26-8/14.

Glass
Tea
Service
A148

Design: 25pf, Distilling apparatus, vert.

1959, Sept. 1 *Perf. 13x12½, 12½x13*
452	A148	10pf bluish green	.20	.20
453	A148	25pf bright blue	1.75	.75

75 years of Jena glassware.

Lunik 2 Hitting Moon — A149

1959, Sept. 21 *Perf. 13½x13*
| 454 | A149 | 20pf rose red | .60 | .30 |

Landing of the Soviet rocket Lunik 2 on the moon, Sept. 13, 1959.

New
Buildings,
Leipzig,
Globe
and Fair
Emblem
A150

1959, Aug. 17 *Perf. 13x12½*
| 455 | A150 | 20pf gray & rose | .35 | .25 |

1959 Leipzig Fall Fair.

Flag and
Harvester — A151

Johannes R.
Becher — A152

10pf, Fritz Heckert rest home. 15pf, Zwinger, Dresden. 20pf, Steelworker. 25pf, Chemist. 40pf, Central Stadium, Leipzig. 50pf, Woman tractor driver. 60pf, Airplane. 70pf, Merchant ship. 1m, 1st atomic reactor of the DDR.

1959, Oct. 6 *Perf. 13½x13*
Flag in Black, Red & Orange Yellow
Inscription and Design in Black &
Red

456	A151	5pf yellow	.20	.20
457	A151	10pf gray	.20	.20
458	A151	15pf citron	.20	.20
459	A151	20pf gray	.20	.20
460	A151	25pf lt gray olive	.20	.20
461	A151	40pf citron	.20	.20
462	A151	50pf salmon	.20	.20
463	A151	60pf pale bluish grn	.20	.20
464	A151	70pf pale grnsh yel	.20	.20
465	A151	1m bister brn	.30	.25
		Nos. 456-465 (10)	2.10	2.05

German Democratic Republic, 10th anniv.

1959, Oct. 28 Litho. *Perf. 13½x13*
| 466 | A152 | 20pf red & slate | 1.20 | .20 |

1st anniversary of the death of Johannes R. Becher, writer.

Printed with alternating yellow labels. The label carries in blue a verse from the national anthem and Becher's signature.

Schiller's Home,
Weimar — A153

Post Rider and Mile
Stone, 18th
Century — A154

Design: 20pf, Friedrich von Schiller.

1959, Nov. 10 Engr. *Perf. 14*
467	A153	10pf dull green, grnsh	1.40	.75
468	A153	20pf lake, *pink*	.50	.20

Birth of Friedrich von Schiller, 200th anniv.

1959, Nov. 17 Litho. *Perf. 13½x13*
Design: 20pf, Motorized mailman.
469	A154	10pf green	1.25	.70
470	A154	20pf dk car rose	.20	.20

Issued for the Day of the Stamp.

Red
Squirrels
A155

1959, Nov. 27 *Perf. 13x12½*
471	A155	5pf shown	.35	.20
472	A155	10pf Hares	.45	.20
473	A155	20pf Roe deer	.45	.20
474	A155	25pf Red deer	.50	.20
475	A155	40pf Lynx	9.50	2.50
		Nos. 471-475 (5)	11.25	3.30

Redrawn Types of 1953
Without Imprint
Perf. 14, 13x12½ (#477)

1959-60			**Wmk. 313**	**Typo.**
476	A43	5pf emerald	.20	.20
477	A43	10pf lt bl grn (Machinists)	.20	.20
a.		Perf. 14	1.00	.20
b.		Bklt. pane of 6 #477a	6.00	
478	A43	20pf carmine	.25	.20
a.		Se-tenant with DEBRIA label	.95	.20
479	A43	30pf dull red	.20	.20
480	A43	40pf rose violet	.20	.20
481	A43	50pf brt blue	.25	.20
482	A43	70pf choc ('60)	.25	.20
		Nos. 476-482 (7)	1.55	1.40

No. 478a was issued Sept. 3, 1959, to commemorate the 2nd German Stamp Exhibition, Berlin. Sheet contains 60 stamps, 40 labels.
Two other stamps without imprint are Nos. 331-332.

Type of 1958 and

Pergamum Altar of Zeus — A156

Designs: 5pf, Head of an Attic goddess, 580 B.C. 10pf, Head of a princess from Tell el Amarna, 1360 B.C. 20pf, Bronze figure from Toprak-Kale (Armenia), 7th century B.C.

1959, Dec. 29 Litho. *Perf. 13½x13*
484	A132	5pf yellow & black	.20	.20
485	A132	10pf bluish grn & blk	.20	.20
486	A132	20pf rose & black	.20	.20
487	A156	25pf lt blue & blk	.80	.55
		Nos. 484-487 (4)	1.40	1.15

Boxing — A157

10pf, Sprinters. 20pf, Ski jump. 25pf, Sailboat.

Perf. 13x13½
1960, Jan. 27			**Wmk. 313**
488	A157	5pf brown & ocher	4.50	1.75
489	A157	10pf green & ocher	.20	.20
490	A157	20pf car & ocher	.20	.20
491	A157	25pf ultra & ocher	.20	.20
		Nos. 488-491 (4)	5.10	2.35

1960 Winter and Summer Olympic Games.

Technical
Fair,
North
Entrance
A158

Design: 25pf, "Ring" Fair building.

1960, Feb. 17 *Perf. 13x12½*
492	A158	20pf red & gray	.20	.20
493	A158	25pf lt blue & gray	.20	.20

1960 Leipzig Spring Fair.

Purple Foxglove
A159

Lenin
A160

Medicinal Plants: 10pf, Camomile. 15pf, Peppermint. 20pf, Poppy. 40pf, Dog rose.

1960, Apr. 7 *Perf. 12½x13*
494	A159	5pf grn, gray & car rose	.25	.20
495	A159	10pf citron, gray & grn	.25	.20
496	A159	15pf fawn, gray & grn	.25	.20
497	A159	20pf grnsh bl, gray & vio	.25	.20
498	A159	40pf brn, gray, grn & red	4.50	1.75
		Nos. 494-498 (5)	5.50	2.55

1960, Apr. 22 Engr. *Perf. 14*
| 499 | A160 | 20pf lake | .35 | .20 |

90th anniversary of the birth of Lenin.

No. 390 Overprinted:
"Inbetriebnahme des
Hochseehafens 1.Mai 1960"

1960, Apr. 28 Litho. *Perf. 13½x13*
| 500 | A122 | 10pf emerald | .40 | .30 |

Inauguration of the seaport Rostock.

Russian Soldier
and Liberated
Prisoner — A161

1960, May 5 Litho. *Perf. 13x13½*
| 501 | A161 | 20pf rose red | .35 | .25 |

15th anniv. of Germany's liberation from fascism.

Model of Vacation Ship — A162

Designs: 25pf, Ship before Leningrad.

Perf. 13½x13
1960, June 23			**Wmk. 313**
502	A162	5pf slate, cit & blk	.20	.20
503	A162	25pf blk, yel & ultra	4.00	4.00
		Nos. 502-503,B58-B59 (4)	4.65	4.60

Launching of the trade union (FDGB) vacation ship, June 25, 1960.

Masked Dancer
in Porcelain
A163

Lenin Monument,
Eisleben
A164

Meissen porcelain: 10pf, Plate with Meissen mark and date. 15pf, Otter. 20pf, Potter. 25pf, Coffee pot.

1960, July 28 *Perf. 12½x13*
504	A163	5pf blue & orange	.25	.20
505	A163	10pf blue & emerald	.25	.20
506	A163	15pf blue & purple	3.25	3.25
507	A163	20pf blue & orange red	.25	.20
508	A163	25pf blue & apple grn	.25	.20
		Nos. 504-508 (5)	4.25	4.05

Meissen porcelain works, 250th anniv.

Perf. 13x13½

1960, July 2   **Wmk. 313**

Design: 20pf, Thälmann monument, gift for Pushkin, USSR.

509	A164	10pf dark green	.25	.20
510	A164	20pf bright red	.25	.20

Pieck Type of 1959

1960, Sept. 10   **Litho.**   **Perf. 13½x13**

511	A139	20pf black	.40	.25
a.		Souv. sheet of 1, imperf.	1.25	1.50

Pres. Wilhelm Pieck (1876-1960).

Modern Postal Trucks A165

Design: 25pf, Railroad mail car, 19th cent.

1960, Oct. 6   **Perf. 13x12½**

512	A165	20pf car rose, blk & yel	.25	.20
513	A165	25pf blue, gray & blk	2.75	1.20

Issued for the Day of the Stamp, 1960.

New Opera House, Leipzig A166

Design: 25pf, Car, sailboat, tent, campers.

1960, Aug. 29   **Wmk. 313**

514	A166	20pf rose brn & gray	.25	.20
515	A166	25pf blue & grysh brn	.30	.25

1960 Leipzig Fall Fair.

Hans Burkmair Medal, 1518 A167

Neidhardt von Gneisenau A168

25pf, Dancing Peasants by Albrecht Dürer.

1960, Oct. 20   **Litho.**   **Perf. 12½x13**

516	A167	20pf buff, grn & ocher	.20	.20
517	A167	25pf lt blue & blk	1.50	1.50

400th anniv. of the Dresden Art Gallery.

1960, Oct. 27   **Perf. 13x12½, 12½x13**

20pf, Neidhardt von Gneisenau, horiz.

518	A168	20pf dk car & blk	.20	.20
519	A168	25pf ultra	1.25	1.25

200th anniversary of the birth of Count August Neidhardt von Gneisenau, Prussian Field Marshal.

Rudolf Virchow A169

Humboldt University, Berlin — A170

10pf, Robert Koch. 25pf, Wilhelm & Alexander von Humboldt medal. 40pf, Wilhelm Griesinger.

1960, Nov. 4   **Litho.**   **Perf. 13x12½**

520	A169	5pf ocher & blk	.20	.20
521	A169	10pf green & blk	.20	.20
522	A170	20pf cop red, gray & blk	.20	.20
523	A170	25pf brt blue & blk	.20	.20
524	A169	40pf car rose & blk	2.25	1.20
		Nos. 520-524 (5)	3.05	2.00

Nos. 520, 521, 524 for the 250th anniv. of the Charité (hospital), Berlin; Nos. 522-523 the 150th anniv. of Humboldt University, Berlin. Nos. 520 and 523, and Nos. 521 and 522 are printed se-tenant.

Scientist and Chemical Formula — A171

Designs: 10pf, Chemistry worker (fertilizer). 20pf, Woman worker (automobile). 25pf, Laboratory assistant (synthetic fabrics).

Perf. 13x13½

1960, Nov. 10   **Wmk. 313**

525	A171	5pf dk red & gray	.20	.20
526	A171	10pf orange & brt grn	.20	.20
527	A171	20pf blue & red	.20	.20
528	A171	25pf yellow & ultra	1.60	1.60
		Nos. 525-528 (4)	2.20	2.20

Day of the Chemistry Worker.

"Young Socialists' Express" A172

20pf, Sassnitz Harbor station & ferry. 25pf, Diesel locomotive & 1835 "Adler."

Perf. 13x13½; 13x12½ (20pf)

1960, Dec. 5

Sizes: 10pf, 25pf, 28x23mm; 20pf, 38½x22mm

529	A172	10pf emerald & blk	.25	.20
530	A172	20pf red & blk	.25	.20
531	A172	25pf blue & blk	4.50	2.75
		Nos. 529-531 (3)	5.00	3.15

125th anniv. of German railroads. No. 530 exists imperf. Value $3.50.

Pieck Type of 1953 with Dates Added

1961, Jan. 3   **Photo.**   **Perf. 13x13½**

532	A35	20pf henna brn & blk	.35	.25

Issued on the 85th anniversary of the birth of Pres. Wilhelm Pieck (1876-1960).

380 Kilovolt Switch A173

Lilienstein A174

Design: 25pf, Leipzig Press Center.

1961, Mar. 3   **Litho.**   **Perf. 13½x13**

533	A173	10pf brt grn & dk gray	.30	.20
534	A173	25pf vio blue & dk gray	.30	.20

Leipzig Spring Fair of 1961.

1961   **Typo.**   **Perf. 14**

Designs: 5pf, Rudelsburg on Saale. 10pf, Wartburg. No. 538, City Hall, Wernigerode. 25pf, Brocken, Harz Mts., horiz.

535	A174	5pf gray	.20	.20
536	A174	10pf blue green	.20	.20
537	A174	20pf red brown	.20	.20

538	A174	20pf dull red	.20	.20
539	A174	25pf dark blue	.20	.20
		Nos. 535-539 (5)	1.00	1.00

Issued: #538, 25pf, 3/14; 5pf, 10pf, #537, 6/22.

Trawler — A176

Designs: 20pf, Fishermen. 25pf, S.S. Robert Koch. 40pf, Cannery worker.

1961, Apr. 4   **Engr.**   **Wmk. 313**

545	A176	10pf gray green	.20	.20
546	A176	20pf claret	.20	.20
547	A176	25pf slate	.20	.20
548	A176	40pf dull violet	2.00	1.20
		Nos. 545-548 (4)	2.60	1.80

Deep-sea fishing industry.

Vostok 1 Leaving Earth A177

Designs: 20pf, Cosmonaut in capsule. 25pf, Parachute landing of capsule.

1961, Apr.   **Litho.**   **Perf. 13x12½**

549	A177	10pf lt blue grn & red	1.00	.60
550	A177	20pf red	1.00	.60
551	A177	25pf lt blue	4.00	4.00
		Nos. 549-551 (3)	6.00	5.20

1st man in space, Yuri A. Gagarin, 4/12/61. Issue dates: 10pf, Apr. 18; others, Apr. 20.

Zebra A178

Dresden Zoo cent.: 20pf, Black-and-white colobus monkeys.

1961, May 9

552	A178	10pf green & blk	4.50	4.50
553	A178	20pf lilac rose & blk	.75	.25

Engels, Marx, Lenin and Crowd — A179

1961, Apr. 20   **Litho.**   **Perf. 13½x13**

554	A179	20pf red	.45	.25

15th anniversary of Socialist Unity Party of Germany (SED).

Stag Leap — A180

Designs: 20pf, Arabesque. 25pf, Exercise on parallel bars, horiz.

1961, June 3   **Perf. 13½x13, 13x13½**

555	A180	10pf blue green	.20	.20
556	A180	20pf rose pink	.20	.20
557	A180	25pf brt blue	5.00	3.50
		Nos. 555-557 (3)	5.40	3.90

3rd Europa Cup for Women's Gymnastics.

Salt Miners and Castle Giebichenstein — A181

20pf, Chemist and "Five Towers" of Halle.

1961, June 22   **Perf. 13x12½**

558	A181	10pf blk, grn & yel	2.40	1.00
559	A181	20pf blk, dk red & yel	.20	.20

1000th anniv. of the founding of Halle.

Kayak Slalom A182

10pf, Canoe. 20pf, Two seater canoe.

1961, July 6   **Litho.**   **Wmk. 313**

560	A182	5pf gray & Prus bl	2.75	2.00
561	A182	10pf gray & slate grn	.20	.20
562	A182	20pf gray & dk car rose	.20	.20
		Nos. 560-562 (3)	3.15	2.40

Canoe Slalom and Rapids World Championships.

Target Line Casting A183

Design: 20pf, River fishing.

1961, July 21

563	A183	10pf green & blue	2.25	1.50
564	A183	20pf dk red brn & blue	.35	.20

World Fishing Championships, Dresden.

Tulip — A184

"Alte Waage," Historical Building, Leipzig — A185

1961, Sept. 13   **Photo.**   **Perf. 14**

565	A184	10pf shown	.35	.20
566	A184	20pf Dahlia	.35	.20
567	A184	40pf Rose	8.00	8.00
		Nos. 565-567 (3)	8.70	8.40

Intl. Horticulture Exhibition, Erfurt.

Perf. 13½x14

1961, Aug. 23   **Litho.**   **Wmk. 313**

Design: 25pf, Old Exchange Building.

568	A185	10pf citron & bl grn	.20	.20
569	A185	25pf lt blue & ultra	1.00	.25

1961 Leipzig Fall Fair. See Nos. 595-597.

Liszt's Hand, French Sculpture — A186

Television Camera and Screen — A187

Designs: 5pf, Liszt and Hector Berlioz. 20pf, Franz Liszt, medallion by Ernst Rietschel, 1852. 25pf, Liszt and Frederic Chopin.

1961, Oct.-Nov.   Engr.   Perf. 14
570	A186	5pf gray	.25	.20
571	A186	10pf blue green	1.75	1.75
572	A186	20pf dull red	.25	.20
573	A186	25pf chalky blue	2.25	2.25
		Nos. 570-573 (4)	4.50	4.40

150th anniversary of the birth of Franz Liszt, composer.

1961, Oct. 25   Perf. 13x13½

Design: 20pf, Microphone and radio dial.
574	A187	10pf brt green & blk	1.50	1.50
575	A187	20pf brick red & blk	.20	.20

Issued for Stamp Day, 1961.

Maj. Gherman Titov and Young Pioneers — A188

10pf, Titov in Leipzig, vert. 15pf, Titov in spaceship. 20pf, Titov & Walter Ulbricht. 25pf, Spaceship Vostok 2. 40pf, Titov & Ulbricht in Berlin.

1961, Dec. 11   Litho.   Perf. 13½
576	A188	5pf carmine & vio	.25	.20
577	A188	10pf olive grn & car	.25	.20
578	A188	15pf blue & lilac	7.50	7.50
579	A188	20pf blue & car rose	.25	.20
580	A188	25pf carmine & blue	.25	.20
581	A188	40pf car & dk blue	1.25	.30
		Nos. 576-581 (6)	9.75	8.60

Visit of Russian Maj. Gherman Titov to the German Democratic Republic.

Chairman Walter Ulbricht — A189

1961-67   Wmk. 313   Typo.   Perf. 14
Size: 17x21mm
582	A189	5pf slate	.20	.20
a.		Booklet pane of 8	9.25	13.00
583	A189	10pf brt green	.20	.20
a.		Booklet pane of 8	5.25	8.75
584	A189	15pf red lilac	.25	.20
585	A189	20pf dark red	.30	.20
586	A189	25pf dull bl ('63)	.30	.20
587	A189	30pf car rose ('63)	.20	.20
588	A189	40pf brt vio ('63)	.20	.20
589	A189	50pf ultra ('63)	.20	.20
589A	A189	60pf dp yel grn ('64)	.30	.20
590	A189	70pf red brn ('63)	.30	.20
590A	A189	80pf brt blue ('67)	.40	.40

Engr.
Size: 24x28½mm
590B	A189	1dm dull grn ('63)	.75	.35
590C	A189	2dm brown ('63)	1.50	.50
		Nos. 582-590C (13)	5.10	3.25

See #751-752, 1112A-1114A, 1483. Currency abbreviation is "DM" on #590B-590C, "MDN" on #751-752, "M" on #1113-1114A.

Red Ants A190

1962, Feb. 16   Photo.
591	A190	5pf shown	3.25	4.00
592	A190	10pf Weasels	.20	.20
593	A190	20pf Shrews	.20	.20
594	A190	40pf Bat	.50	.30
		Nos. 591-594 (4)	4.15	4.70

See Nos. 663-667.

Type of 1961
Buildings: 10pf, "Coffee Tree House." 20pf, Gohlis Castle. 25pf, Romanus House.

1962, Feb. 22   Litho.   Perf. 13x13½
595	A185	10pf olive grn & brn	.20	.20
596	A185	20pf orange red & blk	.30	.20
597	A185	25pf brt blue & brn	.75	.50
		Nos. 595-597 (3)	1.25	.90

Leipzig Spring Fair of 1962.

Air Defense A191

Designs: 10pf, Motorized infantry. 20pf, Soldier and worker as protectors. 25pf, Sailor and destroyer escort. 40pf, Tank and tankman.

1962, Mar. 1   Perf. 13x12½
598	A191	5pf light blue	.20	.20
599	A191	10pf bright green	.20	.20
600	A191	20pf red	.20	.20
601	A191	25pf ultra	.25	.25
602	A191	40pf brown	1.50	1.00
		Nos. 598-602 (5)	2.35	1.85

National People's Army, 6th anniv.

Cyclists and Hradcany, Prague — A192

25pf, Cyclist, East Berlin City Hall and dove.

1962, Apr. 26   Litho.   Wmk. 313
603	A192	10pf multicolored	.20	.20
604	A192	25pf multicolored	1.25	1.00
		Nos. 603-604,B89 (3)	1.65	1.40

15th International Bicycle Peace Race, Berlin-Warsaw-Prague.

Johann Gottlieb Fichte — A193

10pf, Fichte's birthplace in Rammenau.

1962, May 17   Perf. 13x13½
605	A193	10pf brt green & blk	1.25	1.25
606	A193	20pf vermilion & blk	.20	.20

Bicentenary of the birth of Johann Gottlieb Fichte, philosopher.

Cross, Crown of Thorns and Rose — A194

George Dimitrov at Reichstag Trial, Leipzig — A195

1962, June 7   Perf. 12½x13
607	A194	20pf red & black	.20	.20
608	A194	25pf brt blue & blk	1.10	.65

20th anniversary of the destruction of Lidice in Czechoslovakia by the Nazis.

1962, June 18   Photo.   Perf. 14

20pf, Dimitrov as Premier of Bulgaria.
609	A195	5pf blue grn & blk	.50	.30
610	A195	20pf car rose & blk	.20	.20
a.		Pair, #609-610, + label	5.00	30.00

George Dimitrov, (1882-1949), communist leader and premier of the Bulgarian Peoples' Republic.
Nos. 609-610 also printed se-tenant, divided by a label inscribed with a Dimitrov quotation.

Corn Planter A196

20pf, Milking machine. 40pf, Combine harvester.

1962, June 26   Litho.   Perf. 13x12½
611	A196	10pf multicolored	.20	.20
612	A196	20pf multicolored	.20	.20
613	A196	40pf yel, grn & dk red	1.50	1.25
		Nos. 611-613 (3)	1.90	1.65

10th Agricultural Exhibition, Markkleeberg.

Map of Baltic Sea and Emblem — A197

Designs: 20pf, Hotel, Rostock, vert. 25pf, Cargo ship "Frieden" in Rostock harbor.

Perf. 13x13½, 13½x13 (20pf)
1962, July 2   Wmk. 313
614	A197	10pf bluish grn & ultra	.20	.20
615	A197	20pf dk red & yellow	.20	.20
616	A197	25pf blue & bister	2.25	2.25
		Nos. 614-616 (3)	2.65	2.65

5th Baltic Sea Week, Rostock, July 7-15.

Brandenburg Gate, Berlin — A198

1962, July 17   Perf. 13½x13

#618 Heads of youths of three races. #619, Peace dove. #620, National Theater, Helsinki.
617	A198	5pf multicolored	2.25	2.25
618	A198	5pf multicolored	2.25	2.25
619	A198	20pf multicolored	2.25	2.25
620	A198	25pf multicolored	2.25	2.25
a.		Block of 4, #617-620	13.00	13.00
		Nos. 617-620 (4)	9.00	9.00

8th Youth Festival for Peace and Friendship, Helsinki, July 28-Aug. 6, 1962.
No. 620a forms the festival flower emblem.

Free Style Swimming A199

Designs: 10pf, Back stroke. 25pf, Butterfly stroke. 40pf, Breast stroke. 70pf, Water polo.

1962, Aug. 7   Litho.   Perf. 13x13½
Design in Greenish Blue
621	A199	5pf orange	.20	.20
622	A199	10pf grnsh blue	.20	.20
623	A199	25pf ultra	.20	.20
624	A199	40pf brt violet	1.10	1.10
625	A199	70pf red brown	.20	.20
a.		Block of 4, #621-625, B92	2.25	2.25
		Nos. 621-625,B92 (6)	2.10	2.10

10th European Swimming Championships. Leipzig, Aug. 18-25.
Nos. 621-625, B92 each printed in sheets of 50, No. 625a in sheet of 60.

Municipal Store, Leipzig — A200

Engr. & Photo.
1962, Aug. 28   Wmk. 313   Perf. 14

Buildings: 20pf, Mädler Passage. 25pf, Leipzig Air Terminal and plane.
626	A200	10pf black & emerald	.20	.20
627	A200	20pf black & red	.25	.20
628	A200	25pf black & blue	.75	.60
		Nos. 626-628 (3)	1.20	1.00

Leipzig Fall Fair of 1962.

"Transportation and Communication" — A201

1962, Oct. 3   Litho.   Perf. 13½x13
629	A201	5pf light blue & black	.30	.20

10th anniv. of the Friedrich List Transportation College.

Souvenir Sheet

ERSTER GRUPPENFLUG IM KOSMOS

WOSTOK III 11.8.1962. 9.30 Uhr. bis 15.8.1962. 7.55 Uhr (MEZ)
WOSTOK IV 12.8.1962. 9.02 Uhr. bis 15.8.1962. 8.01 Uhr (MEZ)

Pavel R. Popovich, Andrian G. Nikolayev and Space Capsules — A202

1962, Sept. 13   Wmk. 313   Imperf.
630	A202	70pf dk blue, lt grn & yel	2.25	3.50

1st Russian group space flight of Vostoks III and IV, Aug. 11-13, 1962.

DDR Television Signal A203

Young Collectors and World Map — A204

1962, Oct. 25   Perf. 13½x13
631	A203	20pf green & gray	.20	.20
632	A204	40pf brt pink & blk	1.50	1.50

No. 631 for the 10th anniv. of television in the German Democratic Republic; No. 632 is for Stamp Day.

Gerhart Hauptmann A205

1962, Nov. 15　　**Perf. 13x13½**
633 A205 20pf red & black　　.35　.20
Centenary of the birth of Gerhart Hauptmann, playwright.

Souvenir Sheet

Russian Space Flights and Astronauts — A206

1962, Dec. 28　Litho.　Perf. 12½x13
634 A206　Sheet of 8　30.00　30.00
　a.　5pf yellow　1.50　1.50
　b.　10pf emerald　1.50　1.50
　c.　15pf magenta　3.00　3.00
　d.　20pf red　3.00　3.00
　e.　25pf greenish blue　3.00　3.00
　f.　30pf red brown　3.00　3.00
　g.　40pf crimson　1.50　1.50
　h.　50pf ultramarine　1.50　1.50

Issued to show the development of Russian space flights from Sputnik 1 to Vostoks 3 and 4, and to honor the Russian astronauts Gagarin, Titov, Nikolayev and Popovich.

Pierre de Coubertin — A207

Design: 25pf, Stadium and Olympic rings.

1963, Jan. 2　　**Perf. 13½x13**
635 A207 20pf carmine & gray　.20　.20
636 A207 25pf blue & bister　1.50　1.50
Baron Pierre de Coubertin, organizer of the modern Olympic Games, birth cent.

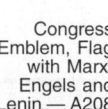

Congress Emblem, Flag with Marx, Engels and Lenin — A208

1963, Jan. 15　　**Perf. 13x13½**
637 A208 10pf yel, org, red & blk　.30　.20
6th congress of Socialist Unity Party of Germany (SED).

World Map and Exterminator — A209

Designs: 25pf, Map, cross and staff of Aesculapius. 50pf, Map, cross, mosquito.

1963, Feb. 6　　**Perf. 13x12½**
638 A209 20pf dp org, dk red
　　　　& blk　.20　.20
639 A209 25pf multicolored　.20　.20
640 A209 50pf multicolored　1.10　1.10
　Nos. 638-640 (3)　1.50　1.50
WHO drive to eradicate malaria.

Silver Fox A210

Design: 25pf, Karakul.

1963, Feb. 14　Photo.　Perf. 14
641 A210 20pf rose & black　.20　.20
642 A210 25pf blue & black　1.40　1.40
Intl. Fur Auctions, Leipzig, 2/14-15, 4/21-24.

Barthels House, Leipzig — A211

Designs: 20pf, New Leipzig City Hall. 25pf, Belltower Building.

Engr. & Photo.
1963, Feb. 26　Wmk. 313　Perf. 14
643 A211 10pf black & citron　.20　.20
644 A211 20pf black & red org　.30　.20
645 A211 25pf black & blue　1.10　1.10
　Nos. 643-645 (3)　1.60　1.50
1963 Leipzig Spring Fair.

Souvenir Sheet
On March 12, 1963, a souvenir sheet publicizing "Chemistry for Peace and Socialism" was issued. It contains two imperforate stamps, 50pf and 70pf, printed on ungummed synthetic tissue. Size: 105x74mm. Value $3.75.

Richard Wagner and "The Flying Dutchman" — A213

Portrait & Scene from Play: 5pf, Johann Gottfried Seume (1763-1810). 10pf, Friedrich Hebbel (1813-63). 20pf, Georg Büchner (1813-37).

1963, Apr. 9　Litho.　Perf. 13x12½
647 A213　5pf brt citron & blk　.20　.20
648 A213 10pf brt green & blk　.20　.20
649 A213 20pf orange & blk　.20　.20
650 A213 25pf dull blue & blk　1.50　1.50
　Nos. 647-650 (4)　2.10　2.10
Anniversaries of German dramatists and the 150th anniv. of the birth of Richard Wagner, composer.

First Aid Station A214

Design: 20pf, Ambulance and hospital.

1963, May 14　　**Wmk. 313**
651 A214 10pf multicolored　1.00　1.00
652 A214 20pf red, blk & gray　.20　.20
Centenary of International Red Cross.

Eugene Pottier, Writer — A215

25pf, Pierre-Chretien Degeyter, composer.

1963, June 18　　**Perf. 13x13½**
653 A215 20pf vermilion & blk　.20　.20
654 A215 25pf vio blue & blk　1.00　1.00
75th anniv. of the communist song "The International."

A216

No. 655, Valentina Tereshkova, Vostok 6. No. 656, Valeri Bykovski, Vostok 5.

1963, July 18　Photo.　Perf. 13½
655　20pf blue, blk & gray bl　.75　.20
656　20pf blue, blk & gray bl　.75　.20
　a. A216　Pair, #655-656　1.50　.40
Space flights of Valeri Bykovski, June 14-19, and Valentina Tereshkova, 1st woman cosmonaut, June 16-19, 1963.

Motorcyclist in "Motocross" at Apolda — A217

Engr. & Photo.
1963, July 30　　**Perf. 14**
20pf, Motorcyclist at Sachsenring, horiz. 25pf, 2 motorcyclists at Sachsenring, horiz.

Size: 23x28mm
657 A217 10pf lt grn & dk grn　3.00　3.00

Size: 48½x21mm
658 A217 20pf rose & dk red　.25　.20
659 A217 25pf lt blue & dk blue　.25　.20
　Nos. 657-659 (3)　3.50　3.40
Motorcycle World Championships.

Monument at Treblinka A218

Perf. 13x13½
1963, Aug. 20　Litho.　Wmk. 313
660 A218 20pf brick red & dk blue　.30　.20
Erection of a memorial at Treblinka (Poland) concentration camp.

Globe, Car and Train — A219

1963, Aug. 27　　**Perf. 13½x13**
Design: No. 662, Globe, plane and bus.
661 A219 10pf multicolored　.65　.20
662 A219 10pf multicolored　.65　.20
　a.　Pair, #661-662　2.00　.40
Issued to publicize the 1963 Leipzig Fall Fair.

Fauna Type of 1962
10pf, Stag beetle. 20pf, Fire salamander. 30pf, Pond turtle. 50pf, Green toad. 70pf, Hedgehogs.

1963, Sept. 10　Photo.　Perf. 14
663 A190 10pf emer, brn & blk　.20　.20
664 A190 20pf crimson, blk & yel　.20　.20
665 A190 30pf multicolored　.20　.20
666 A190 50pf multicolored　3.00　3.00
667 A190 70pf claret brn, brn &
　　　　bis　.50　.50
　Nos. 663-667 (5)　4.10　4.10

Neidhardt von Gneisenau and Gebhard Leberecht von Blücher — A220

Designs: 10pf, Cossacks and home guard, Berlin. 20pf, Ernst Moritz Arndt and Baron Heinrich vom Stein. 25pf, Lützow's volunteers before battle. 40pf, Gerhard von Scharnhorst and Prince Mikhail I. Kutuzov.

1963, Oct. 10　Litho.　Perf. 13½x13
Center in Tan and Black
668 A220　5pf brt yellow　.20　.20
669 A220 10pf emerald　.20　.20
670 A220 20pf dp orange　.20　.20
671 A220 25pf dp ultra　.20　.20
672 A220 40pf dark red　2.00　.75
　Nos. 668-672 (5)　2.80　1.55
150th anniversary of War of Liberation.

Valentina Tereshkova and Space Craft — A221

Burning Synagogue and Star of David in Chains — A222

#674, Tereshkova and map of DDR, vert. #675, Yuri A. Gagarin and map of DDR, vert. 25pf, Tereshkova in space capsule.

1963　　**Perf. 13½x13, 13x13½**
Size: 28x28mm (10pf, 25pf);
28x37mm (20pf)
673 A221 10pf ultra & green　.20　.20
674 A221 20pf red, blk & ocher　.20　.20
675 A221 20pf red, grn & ocher　.20　.20
676 A221 25pf orange & blue　3.50　1.75
　Nos. 673-676 (4)　4.10　2.35
Visit of astronauts Valentina Tereshkova & Yuri A. Gagarin to the German Democratic Republic.

Perf. 13½x13
1963, Nov. 8　　**Wmk. 313**
677 A222 10pf multicolored　.30　.20
25th anniv. of the "Crystal Night," the start of the systematic persecution of the Jews in Germany. Inscribed: "Never again Crystal Night."

Letter Sorting Machine A223

Design: 20pf, Mechanized mail loading.

1963, Nov. 25　　**Perf. 13x12½**
678 A223 10pf multicolored　1.60　1.60
679 A223 20pf multicolored　.20　.20
Issued for Stamp Day.

Ski Jump and Olympic Rings A224

1963, Dec. 16   Litho.   Perf. 13½x13
680 A224 5pf shown   .20   .20
681 A224 10pf Start   .20   .20
682 A224 25pf Landing   2.00   2.00
     Nos. 680-682,B111 (4)   2.60   2.60

9th Winter Olympic Games, Innsbruck, Jan. 29-Feb. 9, 1964.

Admiral — A225

Butterflies: 15pf, Alpine Apollo. 20pf, Swallowtail. 25pf, Postilion. 40pf, Great fox.

Wmk. 313
1964, Jan. 15   Photo.   Perf. 14
Butterflies in Natural Colors
683 A225 10pf citron & blk   .35   .20
684 A225 15pf pale violet & blk   .35   .20
685 A225 20pf lt brick red & blk   .35   .20
686 A225 25pf lt blue & dk brn   .35   .20
687 A225 40pf lt ultra & blk   5.25   1.75
     Nos. 683-687 (5)   6.65   2.55

William Shakespeare — A226

20pf, Quadriga, Brandenburg Gate, Berlin. 25pf, Keystone, History Museum (Zeughaus), Berlin.

1964, Feb. 6   Litho.   Perf. 13x12½
688 A226 20pf rose & dk blue   .25   .20
689 A226 25pf lt blue & mag   .25   .20
690 A226 40pf lt vio & dk bl grn   1.20   .80
     Nos. 688-690 (3)   1.70   1.20

200th anniv. of the birth of the sculptor Johann Gottfried Schadow (20pf); 300th anniv. of the birth of the sculptor Andreas Schlüter (25pf); 400th anniv. of the birth of William Shakespeare, dramatist (40pf).

Electrical Engineering Exhibit — A227

20pf, Bräunigkes Court, exhibition hall, 1700.

Perf. 13x13½
1964, Feb. 26   Wmk. 313
691 A227 10pf brt green & blk   2.25   .25
692 A227 20pf red & black   2.25   .25
a.   Block, 1 each #661-662 + 2 labels   18.00 1.00

Leipzig Spring Fair, Mar. 1-10, 1964.

Khrushchev and Inventors — A228

Youth Training for Leadership A229

40pf, Khrushchev, Tereshkova & Gagarin.

1964, May 15   Perf. 13x13½
693 A228 25pf blue   .25   .20
694 A228 40pf lilac & grnsh blk   2.50   1.50

Issued in honor of Premier Nikita S. Khrushchev of the Soviet Union.

1964, May 13   Litho.

Designs: 20pf, Young athletes. 25pf, Accordion player and girl with flowers.

Center in Black
695 A229 10pf ultra, mag & emer   .20   .20
696 A229 20pf emer, ultra & mag   .20   .20
697 A229 25pf magenta, emer & ultra 1.50   .60
     Nos. 695-697 (3)   1.90   1.00

German Youth Meeting, Berlin.

Television Antenna and Puppets — A230

Children's Day: Various characters from children's television programs.

1964, June 1   Perf. 13x13½
698 A230 5pf multicolored   .20   .20
699 A230 10pf multicolored   .20   .20
700 A230 15pf multicolored   .20   .20
701 A230 20pf multicolored   .20   .20
702 A230 40pf multicolored   1.40   1.40
     Nos. 698-702 (5)   2.20   2.20

Woman as Educator and Portrait of Jenny Marx — A231

Designs: 25pf, Women in industry and transistor diagram. 70pf, Women in agriculture.

Perf. 13½x13
1964, June 26   Litho.   Wmk. 313
703 A231 20pf crimson, gray & yel   .30   .20
704 A231 25pf lt blue, gray & red   .90   .75
705 A231 70pf emerald, gray & yel   .30   .20
     Nos. 703-705 (3)   1.50   1.15

Congress of Women of the German Democratic Republic, June 25-27.

Bicycling A232

Diving — A233

Litho. & Engr.
1964, July 15   Perf. 14
706 A232 5pf shown   .20   .20
707 A232 10pf Volleyball   .20   .20
708 A232 20pf Judo   .20   .20
709 A232 25pf Woman diver   .20   .20
710 A232 70pf Equestrian   1.50   1.50
     Nos. 706-710,B118 (6)   2.60   2.50

Litho.
Perf. 13x13½
711 A233 10pf shown   2.25   2.25
712 A233 10pf Volleyball   2.25   2.25
713 A233 10pf Bicycling   2.25   2.25
714 A233 10pf Judo   2.25   2.25
a.   Block of 6, #711-714   20.00 20.00
      B119-B120

18th Olympic Games, Tokyo, Oct. 10-25, 1964. See Nos. B118-B120. No. 714a printed in 2 horiz. rows: (1st: #711, #B119, #712. 2nd: #713, #B120, #714). The Olympic rings extend over the 6 stamps.

Monument, Leningrad A234

1964, Aug. 8   Litho.   Perf. 13x13½
715 A234 25pf brt blue, blk & yel   .90   .20

Issued to honor the victims of the siege of Leningrad, Sept. 1941-Jan. 1943.

Bertha von Suttner — A235

Medieval Glazier and Goblet — A236

Designs: 20pf, Frederic Joliot Curie. 50pf, Carl von Ossietzky.

1964, Sept. 1   Perf. 14
716 A235 20pf red & black   .20   .20
717 A235 25pf ultra & black   .20   .20
718 A235 50pf lilac & black   1.00   .65
     Nos. 716-718 (3)   1.40   1.05

Issued to promote World Peace.

1964, Sept. 3   Perf. 14

15pf, Jena glass for chemical industry.

719 A236 10pf lt ultra & multi   .50   .20
720 A236 15pf red & multi   .50   .20
a.   Pair, #719-720 + label   2.00   .45

Issued for the Leipzig Fall Fair, 1964.

Handstamp of First Socialist International, 1864 — A237

1964, Sept. 16   Photo.   Wmk. 313
721 A237 20pf orange red & blk   .20   .20
722 A237 25pf dull blue & blk   .60   .50

Centenary of First Socialist International.

Stamp of 1955 (Dürer's Portrait of Young Man) — A238

1964, Sept. 23   Litho.   Perf. 13x13½
723 A238 50pf gray & dk red brn   1.60   1.10
     Nos. 723,B124-B125 (3)   2.15   1.55

Natl. Stamp Exhibition, Berlin, Oct. 3-18.

Coal Transport A239

#724, Navigation. #725, Flag & new Berlin buildings. #727, Chemist. #728, Soldier. #729, Farm woman & cows. #730, Steel worker. #731, Woman scientist & lecture hall. #732, Heavy industry. #733, Optical industry. #734, Consumer goods (woman examining cloth). #735, Foreign trade, Leipzig fair emblem. #736, Buildings industry. #737, Sculptor. #738, Woman skier.

Perf. 13½x13
1964, Oct. 6   Litho.   Wmk. 313
724 A239 10pf blue & multi   .30   .20
725 A239 10pf blue & multi   .30   .20
726 A239 10pf gray & multi   .30   .20
727 A239 10pf red & multi   .30   .20
728 A239 10pf red & multi   .30   .20
729 A239 10pf yel grn & multi   .30   .20
730 A239 10pf red & multi   .30   .20
731 A239 10pf red & multi   .30   .20
732 A239 10pf gray & multi   .30   .20
733 A239 10pf gray & multi   .30   .20
734 A239 10pf blue & multi   .30   .20
735 A239 10pf blue & multi   .30   .20
736 A239 10pf yel grn & multi   .30   .20
737 A239 10pf yel grn & multi   .30   .20
738 A239 10pf blue & multi   .30   .20
     Nos. 724-738 (15)   4.50   3.00

German Democratic Republic, 15th anniv.
A souvenir sheet contains 15 imperf. stamps similar to #724-738. Size: 210x287mm. Value, $45.

For surcharge see No. B134.

Man from Mönchgut, Rügen — A240

1964, Nov. 25   Photo.   Perf. 14

Regional Costumes: No. 740, Woman from Mönchgut, Rügen. No. 741, Man from Spreewald. No. 742, Woman from Spreewald. No. 743, Man from Thuringia. No. 744, Woman from Thuringia.

739 A240 5pf multicolored   7.00   4.25
740 A240 5pf multicolored   7.00   4.25
a.   Pair, #739-740   25.00 10.00
741 A240 10pf multicolored   1.75   .90
742 A240 10pf multicolored   1.75   .90
a.   Pair, #741-742   7.50   3.00
743 A240 20pf multicolored   1.75   .90
744 A240 20pf multicolored   1.75   .90
a.   Pair, #739-740   7.50   3.00
     Nos. 739-744 (6)   21.00 12.10

Printed in checkerboard arrangement.
See Nos. 859-864.

Souvenir Sheets

Exploration of Ionosphere — A241

Designs: 40pf, Exploration of sun activities. 70pf, Exploration of radiation belt.

1964, Dec. 29   Litho.   Perf. 13½x13
745	A241 25pf vio bl & yel	5.50	6.00
746	A241 40pf vio bl, yel & red	2.75	3.00
747	A241 70pf dp grn, vio bl & yel	2.75	3.00
	Nos. 745-747 (3)	11.00	12.00

Intl. Quiet Sun Year, 1964-65.

Albert Schweitzer as Physician A242

August Bebel — A243

Designs (Schweitzer): 20pf, As fighter against war and atom bomb. 25pf, At the organ with score of Organ Prelude by Bach.

Wmk. 313
1965, Jan. 14   Photo.   Perf. 14
748	A242 10pf emerald, blk & bis	.35	.20
749	A242 20pf crimson, blk & bis	.35	.20
750	A242 25pf blue, blk & bis	3.00	1.50
	Nos. 748-750 (3)	3.70	1.90

90th birthday of Dr. Albert Schweitzer, medical missionary.

Ulbricht Type of 1961-63
Currency in "Mark of the Deutsche Notenbank" (MDN)
1965, Feb. 10   Engr.
Size: 24x28½mm
751	A189 1mdn dull green	.45	.35
752	A189 2mdn brown	.50	.40

See note below Nos. 590B-590C.

1965   Photo.   Perf. 14

10pf, Wilhelm Conrad Roentgen. #753A, Adolph von Menzel. 25pf, Wilhelm Külz. 40pf, Erich Weinert. 50pf, Dante Alighieri.
753	A243 10pf dk brn, yel & emer	.35	.20
753A	A243 10pf dk brn, yel & org	.65	.20
754	A243 20pf brn, red & buff	.35	.20
754A	A243 25pf ol brn, yel & bl	.80	.20
754B	A243 40pf ol brn, buff & car rose	.45	.20
755	A243 50pf brn, yel & org	1.60	.20
	Nos. 753-755 (6)	4.20	1.20

Roentgen (1845-1923), physicist, discoverer of X-rays. Sesquicentennial of the birth of Adolph von Menzel, painter and graphic artist.

Bebel, labor leader (1840-1913). 90th anniv. of the birth of Wilhelm Külz, politician. 75th anniv. of the birth of Erich Weinert, poet. Alighieri (1265-1321), Italian poet.
Issued: #753, 3/24; #753A, 12/8; 20pf, 2/22; 25pf, 7/5; 40pf, 7/28; 50pf, 4/15.

A244   A245

Designs: 10pf, Gold Medal, Leipzig Fair. 15pf, Obverse of medal, arms of German Democratic Republic. 25pf, Chemical plant.

1965, Feb. 25   Wmk. 313
756	A244 10pf lilac rose & gold	.20	.20
757	A244 15pf lilac rose & gold	.20	.20
758	A244 25pf brt blue, yel & gold	.50	.20
	Nos. 756-758 (3)	.90	.60

1965 Leipzig Spring Fair; 800th anniv. of the Fair.

1965, Mar. 24

Designs: 10pf, Giraffe. 25pf, Common iguana, horiz. 30pf, White-tailed gnu.
759	A245 10pf green & gray	.20	.20
760	A245 25pf dk vio bl & gray	.25	.20
761	A245 30pf brown & gray	1.75	1.00
	Nos. 759-761 (3)	2.20	1.40

10th anniversary of Berlin Zoo.

Col. Pavel Belyayev and Lt. Col. Alexei Leonov A246

25pf, Lt. Col. Leonov floating in space.

Perf. 13½x13
1965, Apr. 15   Litho.   Wmk. 313
762	A246 10pf red	.30	.20
763	A246 25pf dk ultra	2.00	1.25

Space flight of Voskhod 2 and the first man walking in space, Lt. Col. Alexel Leonov.

Boxing Glove and Laurel Wreath — A247

1965, Apr. 27   Photo.   Perf. 14
764	A247 20pf blk, red & gold	.75	.60

16th European Boxing Championship, Berlin, May, 1965. See No. B126.

Walter Ulbricht and Erich Weinert Distributing "Free Germany" Leaflets on the Eastern Front — A248

50pf, Liberation of concentration camps. 60pf, Russian soldiers raising flag on Reichstag, Berlin. 70pf, Political demonstration.

1965, May 5   Photo.   Perf. 14
Flags in Red, Black & Yellow
765	A248 40pf blue grn & red	.25	.20
766	A248 50pf dull blue & red	.25	.20
767	A248 60pf brown & red	2.50	1.40
768	A248 70pf vio blue & red	.25	.20
	Nos. 765-768,B127-B131 (9)	4.50	3.00

20th anniv. of liberation from fascism.

Radio Tower and Globe A249

ITU Emblem and Frequency Diagram A250

40pf, Workers & broadcasting equipment.

1965, May 12   Litho.   Perf. 12½x13
769	A249 20pf dk car rose & blk	.30	.20
770	A249 40pf vio bl & blk	1.40	.35

20th anniv. of the German Democratic broadcasting system.

1965, May 17

25pf, ITU emblem & telephone diagram.
771	A250 20pf olive, yel & blk	.35	.20
772	A250 25pf vio, pale vio & blk	1.90	.35

Cent. of the ITU.

Emblem of Free German Trade Union — A251

Hemispheres with Crowd of Workers — A252

1965, June 10   Photo.   Perf. 14
773	A251 20pf red & gold	.35	.20
774	A252 25pf gold, blue & blk	1.10	.30

20th anniv. of the Free German Trade Union (FDGB) and of the World Organization of Trade Unions.

Symbols of Industry — A253

Marx and Lenin — A254

Designs: 20pf, Red Tower. 25pf, City Hall.

1965, June 16
775	A253 10pf gold & emerald	.25	.20
776	A253 20pf gold & crimson	.25	.20
777	A253 25pf gold & brt blue	.90	.30
	Nos. 775-777 (3)	1.40	.70

800th anniv. of Chemnitz (Karl Marx City).

1965, June 21   Litho.   Perf. 13½x13
778	A254 20pf red, black & buff	.50	.20

6th Conference of Postal Ministers of Communist Countries, Peking, June 21-July 15.

"Alte Waage" and New Building, Leipzig — A255

25pf, Old City Hall. 40pf, Opera House & General Post Office. 70pf, Hotel "Stadt Leipzig."

Unwmk.
1965, Aug. 25   Photo.   Perf. 14
781	A255 10pf gold, cl brn & ultra	.20	.20
a.	Souv. sheet of 2, #781, 784	3.00	3.00
782	A255 25pf gold, brn, & ocher	.20	.20
a.	Souv. sheet of 2, #782-783	2.50	2.50
783	A255 40pf gold, brn, ocher & yel grn	.25	.20
784	A255 70pf gold & ultra	1.80	.60
	Nos. 781-784 (4)	2.45	1.20

800th anniv. of the City of Leipzig. No. 781a sold for 90pf; No. 782a for 80pf. The souvenir sheets were issued Sept. 4, 1965.

Cameras A256

Equestrian A257

Leipzig Fall Fair: 15pf, Electric guitar and organ. 25pf, Microscope.

1965, Sept. 9   Perf. 14
785	A256 10pf green, blk & gold	.25	.20
786	A256 15pf multicolored	.25	.20
787	A256 25pf multicolored	.70	.20
	Nos. 785-787 (3)	1.20	.60

Perf. 13½x13
1965, Sept. 15   Litho.   Unwmk.
789	A257 10pf shown	.25	.20
790	A257 10pf Swimmer	.25	.20
791	A257 10pf Runner	2.10	2.10
	Nos. 789-791,B135-B136 (5)	3.10	2.90

Intl. Modern Pentathlon Championships, Leipzig.

Alexei Leonov and Brandenburg Gate — A258

Memorial Monument, Putten — A259

Designs: No. 793, Pavel Belyayev and Berlin City Hall. 25pf, Leonov floating in space and space ship.

Wmk. 313
1965, Nov. 1   Litho.   Perf. 14
Size: 23½x28½mm
792	A258 20pf blue, sil & red	.45	.45
793	A258 20pf blue, sil & red	.45	.45

Size: 51x28½mm

794 A258 25pf blue, sil & red .45 .45
   a.   Strip of 3, #792-794   2.90 2.90

Visit of the Russian astronauts to the German Democratic Republic.

1965, Nov. 19   Perf. 13x13½
795 A259 25pf brt bl, pale yel & blk .60 .20

Issued in memory of the victims of a Nazi attack on Putten, Netherlands, Sept. 30, 1944.

Furnace A260

After old woodcuts: 15pf, Ore miners. 20pf, Proustite crystals. 25pf, Sulphur crystals.

Perf. 13x12½
1965, Nov. 11   Litho.   Unwmk.
796 A260 10pf black & multi .25 .20
797 A260 15pf black & multi .55 .55
798 A260 20pf black & multi .25 .20
799 A260 25pf black & multi .25 .20
   Nos. 796-799 (4)   1.30 1.15

Mining Academy in Freiberg, bicent.

Red Kite A261   Otto Grotewohl A262

Birds: 10pf, Lammergeier. 20pf, Buzzard. 25pf, Kestrel. 40pf, Northern goshawk. 70pf, Golden eagle.

1965, Dec. 8   Photo.   Perf. 14
Gold Frame
800 A261 5pf orange & blk .20 .20
801 A261 10pf emer, brn & blk .20 .20
802 A261 20pf car, red brn & blk .25 .20
803 A261 25pf blue, red brn & blk .25 .20
804 A261 40pf lilac, blk & dk red .35 .20
805 A261 70pf brn, blk & yel 3.50 1.75
   Nos. 800-805 (6)   4.75 2.75

1965, Dec. 14   Photo.   Wmk. 313
806 A262 20pf black .70 .20

Issued in memory of Otto Grotewohl (1894-1964), prime minister (1949-1964).

Souvenir Sheet

Spartacus Letter, Karl Liebknecht and Rosa Luxemburg — A263

1966, Jan. 3   Unwmk.
807 A263   Sheet of 2   1.90 4.00
   a.   20pf red & black   .35 .35
   b.   50pf red & black   .35 .35

50th anniv. of the natl. conf. of the Spartacus organization.

Tobogganing, Women's Singles A264

20pf, Men's doubles. 25pf, Men's singles.

Perf. 13½x13
1966, Jan. 25   Litho.   Unwmk.
808 A264 10pf citron & dp grn .20 .20
809 A264 20pf car rose & dk vio bl .20 .20
810 A264 25pf blue & dk blue 1.10 .60
   Nos. 808-810 (3)   1.50 1.00

10th Intl. Tobogganing Championships, Friedrichroda, Feb. 8-13.

Electronic Computer A265

Design: 15pf, Drill and milling machine.

1966, Feb. 24   Perf. 13x12½
811 A265 10pf multicolored .25 .20
812 A265 15pf multicolored .85 .25

Leipzig Spring Fair, 1966.

Jan Arnost Smoler and Linden Leaf — A266

Soldier and National Gallery, Berlin — A267

25pf, House of the Sorbs, Bautzen, Saxony.

1966, Mar. 1   Perf. 13x13½
813 A266 20pf brt bl, blk & brt red .20 .20
814 A266 25pf brt red, blk & brt bl .55 .35

Smoler (1816-84), philologist of the Sorbian language. The Sorbs are a small group of slavic people in Saxony.

Wmk. 313
1966, Mar. 1   Photo.   Perf. 14
Designs (Soldier and): 10pf, Brandenburg Gate. 20pf, Factory. 25pf, Combine.
815 A267 5pf ol gray, blk & yel .20 .20
816 A267 10pf ol gray, blk & yel .20 .20
817 A267 20pf ol gray, blk & yel .20 .20
818 A267 25pf ol gray, blk & yel 1.00 .60
   Nos. 815-818 (4)   1.60 1.20

National People's Army, 10th anniversary.

Luna 9 on Moon — A268

Medal for Scholarship — A269

1966, Mar. 7   Unwmk.
819 A268 20pf multicolored 1.90 .30

1st soft landing on the moon by Luna 9, 2/3/66.

1966, Mar. 7   Litho.   Perf. 13½x13
820 A269 20pf multicolored .55 .20

20th anniv. of the State Youth Organization.

Traffic Signs — A270

Traffic safety: 15pf, Automobile and child with scooter. 25pf, Bicyclist and signaling hand. 50pf, Motorcyclist, ambulance and glass of beer.

1966, Mar. 28   Litho.   Perf. 13
821 A270 10pf dk & lt bl, red & blk .20 .20
822 A270 15pf brt grn, citron & blk .20 .20
823 A270 25pf ol bis, brt bl & blk .20 .20
824 A270 50pf car, yel, gray & blk .90 .60
   Nos. 821-824 (4)   1.50 1.20

Marx, Lenin and Crowd — A271

Designs: 5pf, Party emblem and crowd, vert. 15pf, Marx, Engels and title page of Communist Manifesto, vert. 20pf, Otto Grotewohl and Wilhelm Pieck shaking hands, and Party emblem, vert. 25pf, Chairman Walter Ulbricht receiving flowers.

1966, Mar. 31   Photo.   Perf. 14
825 A271 5pf multicolored .20 .20
826 A271 10pf multicolored .20 .20
827 A271 15pf green & blk .20 .20
828 A271 20pf dk carmine & blk .25 .20
829 A271 25pf multicolored 1.50 .85
   Nos. 825-829 (5)   2.35 1.65

20th anniversary of Socialist Unity Party of Germany (SED).

WHO Headquarters, Geneva — A272

Perf. 13x12½
1966, Apr. 26   Litho.   Unwmk.
830 A272 20pf multicolored .35 .25

Inauguration of WHO Headquarters, Geneva.

Rügen Island, Königsstuhl — A273

National Parks: 10pf, Spree River woodland. 20pf, Saxon Switzerland. 25pf, Dunes at Westdarss. 30pf, Thale in Harz, Devil's Wall. 50pf, Feldberg Lakes, Mecklenburg.

Perf. 13x12½
1966, May 17   Litho.   Unwmk.
831 A273 10pf multicolored .20 .20
832 A273 15pf multicolored .20 .20
833 A273 20pf multicolored .20 .20
834 A273 25pf multicolored .25 .20
835 A273 30pf multicolored 1.60 .75
836 A273 50pf multicolored .25 .20
   Nos. 831-836 (6)   2.70 1.75

Plauen Lace — A274

Various Lace Designs.

1966, May 26   Perf. 13x13½
837 A274 10pf green & lt green .20 .20
838 A274 20pf dk blue & lt blue .20 .20
839 A274 25pf brown red & ver .25 .20
840 A274 50pf dk vio & bluish lil 2.10 .85
   Nos. 837-840 (4)   2.75 1.45

Rhododendron A275

Parachutist Landing on Target — A276

Flowers: 20pf, Lilies of the Valley. 40pf, Dahlias. 50pf, Cyclamen.

Photo. & Engr.
1966   Unwmk.   Perf. 14x13½
841 A275 20pf multicolored .20 .20
842 A275 25pf multicolored .25 .20
843 A275 40pf multicolored .30 .20
844 A275 50pf multicolored 3.50 3.50
   Nos. 841-844 (4)   4.25 4.10

Intl. Flower Show, Erfurt.
Issued: 20pf, Aug. 16; others, June 28.

1966, July 12   Litho.   Perf. 12½x13
15pf, Group parachute jump. 20pf, Free fall.
845 A276 10pf blue, blk & ol .20 .20
846 A276 15pf multicolored .50 .50
847 A276 20pf sky blue, blk & ol .20 .20
   Nos. 845-847 (3)   .90 .90

8th Intl. Parachute Championships, Leipzig.

Hans Kahle, Song of German Fighters and Medal of Spanish Republic — A277

15pf, Hans Beimler and street fighting in Madrid.

1966, July 15   Photo.   Perf. 14
848 A277 5pf multicolored .25 .20
849 A277 15pf multicolored .25 .20
   Nos. 848-849,B137-B140 (6)   2.35 1.90

German fighters in the Spanish Civil War.

Television Set A278

Design: 15pf, Electric typewriter.

Perf. 13x12½
1966, Aug. 29   Litho.   Unwmk.
850 A278 10pf brt grn, blk & gray .60 .20
851 A278 15pf red, blk & gray 1.40 .20

1966 Leipzig Fall Fair.

Women's Doubles Kayak
Race — A279

1966, Aug. 16
852 A279 15pf brt blue & multi   1.00 .75
7th Canoe World Championships, Berlin.
See No. B141.

Oradour sur Glane   Emblem of the
Memorial and   Committee for
French Flag   Health
A280   Education
                    A281

Perf. 13x13½
1966, Sept. 9   **Wmk. 313**
853 A280 25pf ultra, blk & red   .35 .25
Issued in memory of the victims of the Nazi
attack on Oradour, France, June 10, 1944.

1966, Sept. 13   **Perf. 14**
5pf, Symbolic blood donor & recipient, horiz.
854 A281 5pf brt green & red   .25 .20
855 A281 40pf brt blue & red   1.60 .40
    Nos. 854-855,B142 (3)   2.20 .80
Blood donations and health education.

Weight
Lifter — A282

Perf. 13½x13
1966, Sept. 22 Litho. Unwmk.
856 A282 15pf lt brown & blk   1.40 1.10
Intl. and European Weight Lifting Championships, Berlin. See No. B143.

Congress
Hall — A283

Emblem — A284

1966, Oct. 10   **Perf. 13**
857 A283 10pf multicolored   .45 .35
858 A284 20pf dk blue & yellow   .20 .20
6th Cong. of the Intl. Organ. of Journalists,
Berlin.

Costume Type of 1964

Regional Costumes: 5pf, Woman from
Altenburg. No. 860, Man from Altenburg. No.
861, Woman from Mecklenburg. 15pf, Man
from Mecklenburg. 20pf, Woman from Magdeburg area. 30pf, Man from Magdeburg area.

1966, Oct. 25 Photo. Perf. 14
859 A240 5pf multicolored   .35 .20
860 A240 5pf multicolored   .35 .20
  a. Pair, #859-860   1.00 .75
861 A240 10pf lt green & multi   .35 .20
862 A240 15pf lt green & multi   .35 .20
  a. Pair, #861-862   1.00 .75
863 A240 20pf yellow & multi   1.90 1.25
864 A240 30pf yellow & multi   1.90 1.25
  a. Pair, #863-864   4.25 3.00
    Nos. 859-864 (6)   5.20 3.30
Printed in checkerboard arrangement.

Megalamphodus
Megalopterus — A285

Various Tropical Fish in Natural Colors.

1966, Nov. 8 Litho. Perf. 13x12½
865 A285 5pf lt blue & gray   .20 .20
866 A285 10pf blue & indigo   .20 .20
867 A285 15pf citron & blk   2.25 1.50
868 A285 20pf green & blk   .20 .20
869 A285 25pf ultra & blk   .25 .20
870 A285 40pf emerald & blk   .30 .20
    Nos. 865-870 (6)   3.40 2.50

Map of Oil Pipeline and Oil
Field — A286

Design: 25pf, Map of oil pipelines and "Walter Ulbricht" Leuna chemical factory.

1966, Nov. 8   **Perf. 13½x13**
871 A286 20pf red & black   .20 .20
872 A286 25pf blue & black   .75 .30
Chemical industry.

Detail from Ishtar Gate, Babylon, 580
B.C. — A287

Designs from Babylon c. 580 B.C.: 20pf,
Mythological animal from Ishtar Gate. 25pf,
Lion facing right and ornaments, vert. 50pf,
Lion facing left and ornaments, vert.

Perf. 13½x14, 14x13½
1966, Nov. 23   **Photo.**
873 A287 10pf multicolored   .20 .20
874 A287 20pf multicolored   .20 .20
875 A287 25pf multicolored   .20 .20
876 A287 50pf multicolored   .55 .80
    Nos. 873-876 (4)   1.15 1.40
Near East Museum, Berlin.

Wartburg,   Gentian — A289
Thuringia — A288

Design: 25pf, Wartburg, Palace.

1966, Nov. 23 Litho. Perf. 13x13½
877 A288 20pf olive   .20 .20
878 A288 25pf violet brown   .55 .65
    Nos. 877-878,B145 (3)   .95 .65
900th anniv. (in 1967) of the Wartburg (castle) near Eisenach, Thuringia.

1966, Dec. 8 Litho. Perf. 12½x13
Protected Flowers: 20pf, Cephalanthera
rubra (orchid). 25pf, Mountain arnica.

Black Background
879 A289 10pf yel, grn & bl   .20 .20
880 A289 20pf yel, grn & red   .25 .20
881 A289 25pf red, yel & grn   1.25 .70
    Nos. 879-881 (3)   1.70 1.10

Son Leaving
Home — A290

City Hall,
Stralsund — A291

Various Scenes from Fairy Tale "The Table,
the Ass and the Stick."

1966, Dec. 8   **Perf. 13½x13**
882 A290 5pf multicolored   .25 .25
883 A290 10pf multicolored   .25 .25
884 A290 20pf multicolored   .60 .60
885 A290 30pf multicolored   .60 .60
886 A290 30pf multicolored   .25 .25
887 A290 50pf multicolored   .25 .25
  a. Sheet of 6, #882-887   2.75 2.75
See Nos. 968-973, 1063-1068, 1087-1092,
1176-1181, 1339-1344.

Perf. 14x13½, 13½x14
1967, Jan. 24   **Photo.**
Buildings: 5pf, Wörlitz Castle, horiz. 15pf,
Chorin Convent. 20pf, Ribbeck House, Berlin,
horiz. 25pf, Moritzburg, Zeitz. 40pf, Old City
Hall, Potsdam.

888 A291 5pf multicolored   .20 .20
889 A291 10pf multicolored   .20 .20
890 A291 15pf multicolored   .25 .20
891 A291 20pf multicolored   .25 .20
892 A291 25pf multicolored   .25 .20
893 A291 40pf multicolored   1.00 .65
    Nos. 888-893 (6)   2.15 1.65
See Nos. 1018, 1020, 1071-1076.

Rifle Shooting, Prone — A292

Designs: 20pf, Shooting on skis. 25pf, Relay
race with rifles on skis.

1967, Feb. 15 Litho. Perf. 13x12½
894 A292 10pf Prus bl gray & brt
                pink   .20 .20
895 A292 20pf sl grn, brt bl & grn   .20 .20
896 A292 25pf ol grn, ol & grnsh
                bl   .65 .35
    Nos. 894-896 (3)   1.05 .75
World Biathlon Championships (skiing and
shooting), Altenberg, Feb. 15-19.

Circular Knitting
Machine — A293

Mother and
Child — A294

Design: 15pf, Zeiss telescope and galaxy.

1967, Mar. 2   **Perf. 13½x13**
897 A293 10pf dull mag & brt grn   .20 .20
898 A293 15pf ultra & gray   .75 .25
Leipzig Spring Fair of 1967.

1967, Mar. 7   **Perf. 13x13½**
Design: 25pf, Working women.
899 A294 20pf rose brn, red & gray   .25 .20
900 A294 25pf dk bl, brt bl & brn   .60 .50
20th anniv. of the Democratic Women's
Federation of Germany.

Marx, Engels, Lenin and Electronic
Control Center — A295

Designs (Portraits and): 5pf, Farmer driving
combine. No. 903, Students and teacher.
15pf, Family. No. 905, Soldier, sailor and aviator. No. 906, Ulbricht among workers. 25pf,
Soldier, sailor, aviator and factories. 40pf,
Farmers with modern equipment. Nos. 901,
903-905 are vertical.

1967   **Photo.**   **Perf. 14**
901 A295 5pf multicolored   .20 .20
902 A295 10pf multicolored   .20 .20
903 A295 10pf multicolored   .20 .20
904 A295 15pf multicolored   .35 .35
905 A295 20pf multicolored   .20 .20
906 A295 20pf multicolored   .20 .20
907 A295 25pf multicolored   .20 .20
908 A295 40pf multicolored   .40 .45
    Nos. 901-908 (8)   1.95 2.00
7th congress of Socialist Unity Party of Germany (SED), Apr. 17.
Issued: #902, 906-908 3/22; #901, 903-905,
4/6.

Tahitian Women, by Paul
Gauguin — A296

Paintings from Dresden Gallery: 20pf,
Young Woman, by Ferdinand Hodler. 25pf,
Peter in the Zoo, by H. Hakenbeck. 30pf,
Venetian Episode (woman feeding pigeons),
by R. Bergander. 50pf, Grandmother and
Granddaughter, by J. Scholtz. 70pf, Cairn in
the Snow, by Caspar David Friedrich.

1967, Mar. 29
909 A296 20pf multi, vert.   .20 .20
910 A296 25pf multi, vert.   .20 .20
911 A296 30pf multi, vert.   .20 .20
912 A296 40pf multi   .20 .20
913 A296 50pf multi, vert.   1.50 1.10
914 A296 70pf multi   .30 .20
    Nos. 909-914 (6)   2.60 2.10

Barn Owl — A297

Protected Birds: 10pf, Eurasian crane. 20pf, Peregrine falcon. 25pf, Bullfinches. 30pf, European kingfisher. 40pf, European roller.

1967, Apr. 27   Photo.   Perf. 14
Birds in Natural Colors
915	A297	5pf gray blue	.20	.20
916	A297	10pf gray blue	.20	.20
917	A297	20pf gray blue	.20	.20
918	A297	25pf gray blue	.20	.20
919	A297	30pf gray blue	3.50	1.75
920	A297	40pf gray blue	.30	.20
		Nos. 915-920 (6)	4.60	2.75

Arms of Warsaw, Berlin and Prague A298

Design: 25pf, Bicyclists and doves.

Perf. 13x12½
1967, May 10   Litho.   Wmk. 313
921	A298	10pf org, blk & lil	.20	.20
922	A298	25pf lt bl & dk car	.40	.30

20th Intl. Bicycle Peace Race, Berlin-Warsaw-Prague.

Cat A299

Children's Drawings: 10pf, Snow White and the Seven Dwarfs. 15pf, Fire truck. 20pf, Cock. 25pf, Flowers in vase. 30pf, Children playing ball.

1967, June 1   Unwmk.
923	A299	5pf multicolored	.20	.20
924	A299	10pf black & multi	.20	.20
925	A299	15pf dk blue & multi	.20	.20
926	A299	20pf orange & multi	.20	.20
927	A299	25pf multicolored	.20	.20
928	A299	30pf multicolored	1.00	.60
		Nos. 923-928 (6)	2.00	1.60

Issued for International Children's Day.

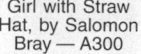

Girl with Straw Hat, by Salomon Bray — A300

Exhibition Emblem and Map of DDR — A301

Paintings: 5pf, Three Horsemen, by Rubens, horiz. 10pf, Girl Gathering Grapes, by Gerard Dou. 20pf, Spring Idyl, by Hans Thoma, horiz. 25pf, Wilhelmine Schroder-Devrient, by Karl Begas. 50pf, The Four Evangelists, by Jacob Jordaens.

1967, June 7   Photo.   Perf. 14
929	A300	5pf lt & dk blue	.20	.20
930	A300	10pf lt red brn & red brn	.20	.20
931	A300	20pf lt & dp yel grn	.20	.20
932	A300	25pf pale rose & rose lil	.20	.20
933	A300	40pf pale grn & ol grn	.20	.20
934	A300	50pf tan & sepia	1.40	.85
		Nos. 929-934 (6)	2.40	1.85

Issued to publicize paintings missing from museums since World War II.

Perf. 12½x13
1967, June 14   Litho.   Unwmk.
935	A301	20pf dk grn, ocher & red	.30	.20

15th Agricultural Exhib., Markkleeberg.

Marie Curie — A302

German Playing Cards — A303

Portraits: 5pf, Georg Herwegh, poet. 20pf, Käthe Kollwitz. 25pf, Johann J. Winckelmann, archaeologist. 40pf, Theodor Storm, writer.

1967   Engr.   Perf. 14
936	A302	5pf brown	.25	.20
937	A302	10pf dark blue	.25	.20
938	A302	20pf dull red	.25	.20
939	A302	25pf gray	.25	.20
940	A302	40pf slate green	.75	.50
		Nos. 936-940 (5)	1.75	1.30

150th anniv. of the birth of Herwegh, Winckelmann and Storm, and the birth centenaries of Curie and Kollwitz.

1967, July 18   Photo.
Designs: Various German playing cards.
941	A303	5pf red & multi	.20	.20
942	A303	10pf green & multi	.20	.20
943	A303	20pf multicolored	.25	.20
944	A303	25pf multicolored	4.75	2.25
		Nos. 941-944 (4)	5.40	2.85

Mare and Foal A304

Horses: 10pf, Stallion. 20pf, Horse race finish. 50pf, Colts, vert.

Perf. 13½x13, 13x13½
1967, Aug. 15   Litho.   Unwmk.
945	A304	5pf multicolored	.20	.20
946	A304	10pf org, blk & dk brn	.20	.20
947	A304	20pf blue & multi	.25	.20
948	A304	50pf multicolored	3.00	1.75
		Nos. 945-948 (4)	3.65	2.35

Thoroughbred Horse Show of Socialist Countries, Hoppegarten, Berlin.

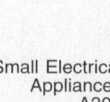

Small Electrical Appliances A305

Leipzig Fall Fair: 15pf, Woman's fur coat and furrier's trademark.

Perf. 14x13½
1967, Aug. 8   Photo.   Unwmk.
949	A305	10pf brt bl, blk & yel	.35	.20
950	A305	15pf yellow, brn & blk	.80	.30

Max Reichpietsch and Warship — A306

15pf, Albin Köbis, warship. 20pf, Sailors marching with red flag, warship.

1967, Sept. 5   Litho.   Perf. 13½x13
Bluish Paper
951	A306	10pf dk blue, gray & red	.20	.20
952	A306	15pf dk blue, gray & red	1.10	.40
953	A306	20pf dk blue, gray & red	.35	.20
		Nos. 951-953 (3)	1.65	.80

50th anniv. of the sailors' uprising at Kiel.

Monument at Kragujevac A307

1967, Sept. 20   Perf. 13x13½
954	A307	25pf dk red, yel & blk	.65	.25

Issued in memory of the victims of the Nazis at Kragujevac, Yugoslavia, Oct. 21, 1941.

Worker and Symbols of Electrification — A308

Communist Emblem and: 5pf, Worker, Communist newspaper masthead. 15pf, Russian War Memorial, Berlin-Treptow. 20pf, Russian and German soldiers, coat of arms. 40pf, Lenin, cruiser Aurora.

1967, Oct. 6   Photo.   Perf. 14x14½
955	A308	5pf multicolored	.20	.20
956	A308	10pf multicolored	.20	.20
957	A308	15pf multicolored	.20	.20
958	A308	20pf multicolored	.30	.20
959	A308	40pf multicolored	2.25	1.40
a.		Souvenir sheet of 2	2.00	2.50
		Nos. 955-959 (5)	3.15	2.20

50th anniv. of the Russian October Revolution. No. 959a contains 2 imperf. stamps similar to Nos. 958-959 with simulated perforations. It commemorates the Red October Jubilee Stamp Exhibition, Karl-Marx-Stadt, Oct. 6-15. Sold for 85pf.

Martin Luther, by Lucas Cranach — A309

Young Inventors and Fair Emblem — A310

Designs: 25pf, Luther's House, Wittenberg, horiz. 40pf, Castle Church, Wittenberg.

Engraved and Photogravure
1967, Oct. 17   Perf. 14
960	A309	20pf black & rose lilac	.20	.20
961	A309	25pf black & blue	.20	.20
962	A309	40pf black & lemon	2.10	.60
		Nos. 960-962 (3)	2.50	1.00

450th anniversary of the Reformation.

1967, Nov. 15   Unwmk.   Perf. 14
Designs: No. 964, Boy's and girl's heads and emblem of the Free German Youth Organization. 25pf, Young workers receiving awards, and medal.

Size: 23x28½mm
963	A310	20pf multicolored	.45	.30
964	A310	20pf multicolored	.45	.30

Size: 51x28½mm
965	A310	25pf multicolored	.45	.30
a.		Strip of 3, #963-965	3.75	3.75

Issued to publicize the 10th Masters of Tomorrow Fair, Leipzig, Nov. 15-26.

Goethe House, Weimar A311

Design: 25pf, Schiller House, Weimar.

1967, Nov. 27   Litho.   Perf. 13x12½
966	A311	20pf gray, blk & brn	.25	.20
967	A311	25pf citron, dk grn & brn	1.40	.40

Honoring German classical humanism.

Fairy Tale Type of 1966
Various Scenes from King Drosselbart.

1967, Nov. 27   Perf. 13½x13
968	A290	5pf multicolored	.20	.20
969	A290	10pf multicolored	.20	.20
970	A290	15pf multicolored	.75	.60
971	A290	20pf multicolored	.75	.60
972	A290	25pf multicolored	.20	.20
973	A290	30pf multicolored	.20	.20
a.		Sheet of 6, #968-973	5.00	5.00

Farmers, Stables and Silos — A312

Perf. 13x12½
1967, Dec. 6   Litho.   Unwmk.
974	A312	10pf multicolored	.30	.20

1st agricultural co-operatives, 15th anniv.

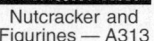

Nutcracker and Figurines — A313

Speed Skating — A314

20pf, Candle holders: angel and miner.

1967, Dec. 6   Photo.   Perf. 13½x14
975	A313	10pf green & multi	.60	.35
976	A313	20pf red & multi	.20	.20

Issued to publicize local handicrafts of the Erzgebirge in Saxony (Ore Mountains).

Perf. 13½x13
1968, Jan. 17   Litho.   Unwmk.
Sport and Olympic Rings: 15pf, Slalom. 20pf, Ice hockey. 25pf, Figure skating, pair. 30pf, Long-distance skiing.
977	A314	5pf blue, dk bl & red	.20	.20
978	A314	15pf multicolored	.20	.20
979	A314	20pf grnsh bl, dk bl & red	.20	.20
980	A314	25pf multicolored	.20	.20

981 A314 30pf grnsh bl, vio bl & red   3.00 1.00
   Nos. 977-981,B146 (6)   4.00 2.00

10th Winter Olympic Games, Grenoble, France, Feb. 6-18.

Actinometer, Sun and Potsdam Meteorological Observatory A315

Designs: 20pf, Antenna, Cloud Formation and Map of Europe. 25pf, Weather influence on farming (fields by day and night, produce).

1968, Jan. 24   *Perf. 13½x13*
   Size: 23x28mm
982 A315 10pf brt mag, org & blk   .35 .25
   Size: 50x28mm
983 A315 20pf multicolored   .35 .25
   Size: 23x28mm
984 A315 25pf olive, blk & yel   .35 .25
   a.   Strip of 3, #982-984   4.00 4.00

75th anniversary of the Meteorological Observatory in Potsdam.

Venus 4 Interplanetary Station — A316

Design: 25pf, Earth satellites Kosmos 186 and 188 orbiting earth.

1968, Jan. 24   **Photo.**   *Perf. 14*
985 A316 20pf multicolored   .20 .20
986 A316 25pf multicolored   1.00 .40

Russian space explorations.

Fighters of The Underground A317

20pf, "The Liberation." 25pf, "The Partisans."

1968, Feb. 21   **Photo.**   *Perf. 14x13½*
987 A317 10pf black & multi   .20 .20
988 A317 20pf black & multi   .20 .20
989 A317 25pf black & multi   .40 .25
   Nos. 987-989 (3)   .80 .65

The designs are from the stained glass window triptych by Walter Womacka in the Sachsenhausen Memorial Museum.

Diesel Locomotive — A318

Design: 15pf, Refrigerator fishing ship.

1968, Feb. 29   *Perf. 14*
990 A318 10pf multicolored   .30 .20
991 A318 15pf multicolored   .85 .30

The 1968 Leipzig Spring Fair.

Woman from Hoyerswerda A319   Maxim Gorky and View of Gorky A320

Sorbian Regional Costumes: 20pf, Woman from Schleife. 40pf, Woman from Crostwitz. 50pf, Woman from Spreewald.

1968, Mar. 14
992 A319 10pf citron & multi   .20 .20
993 A319 20pf fawn & multi   .20 .20
994 A319 40pf blue grn & multi   .25 .20
995 A319 50pf green & multi   2.40 .75
   Nos. 992-995 (4)   3.05 1.35

1968, Mar. 14   **Engr.**
25pf, Stormy petrel and toppling towers.

996 A320 20pf brown & rose car   .20 .20
997 A320 25pf brown & rose car   .45 .25

Maxim Gorky (1868-1936), Russian writer.

Ring-necked Pheasants A321

15pf, Gray partridges. 20pf, Mallards. 25pf, Graylag geese. 30pf, Wood pigeons. 40pf, Hares.

1968, Mar. 26   **Litho.**   *Perf. 13½x13*
998 A321 10pf gray & multi   .20 .20
999 A321 15pf gray & multi   .20 .20
1000 A321 20pf gray & multi   .20 .20
1001 A321 25pf gray & multi   .25 .20
1002 A321 30pf gray & multi   .30 .20
1003 A321 40pf gray & multi   2.75 4.00
   Nos. 998-1003 (6)   3.90 5.00

Karl Marx — A322   Fritz Heckert — A323

Designs: 10pf, Title page of the "Communist Manifesto." 25pf, Title page of "Das Kapital."

1968, Apr. 25   **Photo.**   *Perf. 14*
1004 A322 10pf yel grn & blk   .25 .25
1005 A322 20pf mag, yel & blk   .25 .25
1006 A322 25pf lem, blk & red brn   .25 .25
   a.   Strip of three   1.50 3.00
   b.   Souvenir sheet of 3   1.00 3.00

Karl Marx (1818-83). Nos. 1004-1006 are printed se-tenant. No. 1006a contains 3 imperf. stamps similar to Nos. 1004-1006 with simulated perforations.

1968, Apr. 25
Design: 20pf, Young workers, new apartment buildings and Congress emblem.

1007 A323 10pf multicolored   .20 .20
1008 A323 20pf multicolored   .25 .25

7th Congress of the Free German Trade Unions.

"Right to Work" — A324

Designs: 10pf, "Right to Live," tree and globe. 25pf, "Right for Peace," dove and sun.

1968, May 8   **Litho.**   *Perf. 13½x13*
1009 A324 5pf maroon & pink   .20 .20
1010 A324 10pf brn ol & ol bister   .20 .20
1011 A324 25pf Prus bl & lt bl   .65 .40
   Nos. 1009-1011 (3)   1.05 .80

International Human Rights Year.

Angler A325

Designs: No. 1013, Rowing (woman). No. 1014, High jump (woman).

   Unwmk.
1968, June 6   **Photo.**   *Perf. 14*
1012 A325 20pf ol grn, sl bl & dk red   .75 .65
1013 A325 20pf Prus bl, dk bl & ol   .20 .20
1014 A325 20pf cop red, dp cl & bl   .20 .20
   Nos. 1012-1014 (3)   1.15 1.05

World angling championships, Gustrow (#1012); European women's rowing championships, Berlin (#1013); 2nd European youth athletic competition, Leipzig (#1014).

Brandenburg Gate, Torch — A326   Youth Festival Emblem — A327

Design: 25pf, Stadium and torch.

1968, June 20   **Litho.**   *Perf. 13½x13*
1015 A326 10pf multicolored   .20 .20
1016 A326 25pf multicolored   .85 .40

2nd Children's and Youths' Spartakiad, Berlin.

1968, June 20
1017 A327 25pf multicolored   .70 .35

9th Youth Festival for Peace & Friendship, Sofia.
See No. B148.

    Type of 1967 and

Moritzburg Castle, Dresden — A328

Buildings: 10pf, City Hall, Wernigerode. 25pf, City Hall, Greifswald. 30pf, Sanssouci Palace, Potsdam.

1968, June 25   **Photo.**   *Perf. 13½x14*
1018 A291 10pf multicolored   .20 .20
1019 A328 20pf multicolored   .20 .20
1020 A291 25pf multicolored   .20 .20
1021 A328 30pf multicolored   .60 .60
   Nos. 1018-1021 (4)   1.20 1.20

Walter Ulbricht and Arms of Republic A329

    Photo. & Engr.
1968, June 27   *Perf. 14*
1022 A329 20pf org, dp car & blk   .55 .20

75th birthday of Walter Ulbricht, chairman of the Council of State, Communist party secretary and deputy prime minister.

Old Rostock and Arms A330

Design: 25pf, Historic and modern buildings, 1968, and arms of Rostock.

1968, July 9   **Photo.**
1023 A330 20pf multicolored   .20 .20
1024 A330 25pf multicolored   .50 .40

750th anniv. of Rostock and to publicize the 11th Baltic Sea Week.

Karl Landsteiner, M.D. (1868-1943) A331

Portraits: 15pf, Emanuel Lasker (1868-1941), chess champion and writer. 20pf, Hanns Eisler (1898-1962), composer. 25pf, Ignaz Semmelweis, M.D. (1818-1865). 40pf, Max von Pettenkofer (1818-1901), hygienist.

1968, July 17   **Engr.**   *Perf. 14*
1025 A331 10pf gray green   .20 .20
1026 A331 15pf black   .20 .20
1027 A331 20pf brown   .20 .20
1028 A331 25pf gray blue   .20 .20
1029 A331 40pf rose lake   .70 .70
   Nos. 1025-1029 (5)   1.50 1.50

1968, Aug. 13   **Litho.**   *Perf. 12½x13*
25pf, 2 "Trener" stunt planes in parallel flight.

1030 A332 10pf multicolored   .20 .20
1031 A332 25pf blue & multi   .45 .35

"Trener" Stunt Plane — A332

Peasant Woman, by Wilhelm Leibl — A333

Paintings from Dresden Gallery: 10pf, "On the Beach," by Walter Womacka, horiz. 15pf, Mountain Farmers Mowing, by Albin Egger-Lienz, horiz. 40pf, The Artist's daughter, by Venturelli. 50pf, High School Girl, by Michaelis. 70pf, Girl with Guitar, by Castelli.

    Perf. 14x13½, 13½x14
1968, Aug. 20   **Photo.**
1032 A333 10pf multicolored   .20 .20
1033 A333 15pf multicolored   .20 .20
1034 A333 20pf multicolored   .20 .20
1035 A333 40pf multicolored   .35 .20

1036	A333	50pf multicolored		.35	.20
1037	A333	70pf multicolored		1.90	.95
		Nos. 1032-1037 (6)		3.20	1.95

Model Trains — A334

1968, Aug. 29   *Perf. 14x13½*
1038 A334 10pf lt ultra, red & blk   .30 .25

The 1968 Leipzig Fall Fair.

Spremberg Dam — A335

Designs: 10pf, Pöhl Dam, vert. 15pf, Ohra Dam, vert. 20pf, Rappbode Dam.

     Perf. 13x12½, 12½x13
1968, Sept. 11   Litho.
1039 A335 5pf multicolored   .20 .20
1040 A335 10pf multicolored   .20 .20
1041 A335 15pf multicolored   .35 .35
1042 A335 20pf multicolored   .25 .20
    Nos. 1039-1042 (4)   1.00 .95

Issued to publicize dams built since 1945.

Runner
A336

Designs: 25pf, Woman gymnast, vert. 40pf, Water polo, vert. 70pf, Sculling.

1968, Sept. 18   Photo.   *Perf. 14*
1043 A336 5pf multicolored   .20 .20
1044 A336 25pf multicolored   .20 .20
1045 A336 40pf multicolored   .20 .20
1046 A336 70pf blue & multi   1.25 1.00
  Nos. 1043-1046,B149-B150 (6)   2.25 2.00

19th Olympic Games, Mexico City, 10/12-27.

Monument, Fort Breendonk, Belgium — A337

Tiger Beetle — A338

1968, Oct. 10   Litho.   *Perf. 13x13½*
1047 A337 25pf multicolored   .35 .20

Issued in memory of the victims of the Nazis at the Fort Breendonk Concentration Camp.

1968, Oct. 16   *Perf. 13½x13*

Insects: 15pf, Ground beetle (Cychrus caraboides). 20pf, Ladybug. 25pf, Ground beetle (Carabus arcensis hrbst.). 30pf, Hister beetle. 40pf, Checkered beetle.

1048 A338 10pf yellow & multi   .20 .20
1049 A338 15pf bluish lil & blk   .20 .20
1050 A338 20pf multicolored   .20 .20

1051 A338 25pf lt lilac & blk   1.90 1.50
1052 A338 30pf lt green, blk &   red   .25 .20
1053 A338 40pf pink & black   .25 .20
    Nos. 1048-1053 (6)   3.00 2.50

Lenin and Letter to Spartacists — A339

Designs: 20pf, Workers, soldiers and sailors with masthead and slogans. 25pf, Karl Liebknecht and Rosa Luxemburg.

1968, Oct. 29   Litho.   *Perf. 13x12½*
1054 A339 10pf lemon, red & blk   .20 .20
1055 A339 20pf lemon, red & blk   .20 .20
1056 A339 25pf lemon, red & blk   .45 .35
    Nos. 1054-1056 (3)   .85 .75

November Revolution in Germany, 50th anniv.

Cattleya — A340

Orchids: 10pf, Paphiopedilum albertianum. 15pf, Cattleya fabia. 20pf, Cattleya aclandiae. 40pf, Sobralia macrantha. 50pf, Dendrobium alpha.

1968, Nov. 12   Photo.   *Perf. 13*
Flowers In Natural Colors
1057 A340 5pf bluish lilac   .20 .20
1058 A340 10pf green   .20 .20
1059 A340 15pf bister   .20 .20
1060 A340 20pf green   .20 .20
1061 A340 40pf light brown   .25 .20
1062 A340 50pf gray   1.60 1.10
    Nos. 1057-1062 (6)   2.65 2.10

Fairy Tale Type of 1966

Various Scenes from Puss in Boots.

1968, Nov. 27   Litho.   *Perf. 13½x13*
1063 A290 5pf multicolored   .20 .20
1064 A290 10pf multicolored   .20 .20
1065 A290 15pf multicolored   .90 .75
1066 A290 20pf multicolored   .90 .75
1067 A290 25pf multicolored   .20 .20
1068 A290 30pf multicolored   .20 .20
   a.   Sheet of 6, #1063-1068   5.00 7.50

Young Pioneers
A341

Design: 15pf, Five Young Pioneers.

1968, Dec. 3   *Perf. 13x13½*
1069 A341 10pf blue & multi   .20 .20
1070 A341 15pf multicolored   .60 .25

20th anniv. of the founding of the Ernst Thalmann Young Pioneers' organization.

Buildings Type of 1967

Buildings: 5pf, City Hall, Tangermunde. 10pf, German State Opera, Berlin. 20pf, Wall Pavilion, Dresden. 25pf, Burgher's House, Luckau. 30pf, Rococo Palace, Dornburg. 40pf, "Stockfish" House, Erfurt.

1969, Jan. 1   Photo.   *Perf. 14*
1071 A291 5pf multi   .20 .20
1072 A291 10pf multi, horiz.   .20 .20
1073 A291 20pf multi   .20 .20
1074 A291 25pf multi   .75 .65

1075 A291 30pf multi, horiz.   .20 .20
1076 A291 40pf multi   .25 .20
    Nos. 1071-1076 (6)   1.80 1.65

Martin Andersen Nexö, Danish Writer — A342

Portraits: 20pf, Otto Nagel (1894-1967), painter. 25pf, Alexander von Humboldt (1769-1859), naturalist, traveler, statesman. 40pf, Theodor Fontane (1819-1898), writer.

1969, Feb. 5   Engr.   *Perf. 14*
1077 A342 10pf grnsh black   .20 .20
1078 A342 20pf deep brown   .20 .20
1079 A342 25pf violet blue   .75 .30
1080 A342 40pf brown   .20 .20
    Nos. 1077-1080 (4)   1.35 .90

Issued to honor famous men.

Be Attentive and Considerate! A343

10pf, Watch ahead! (car, truck & traffic signal). 20pf, Watch railroad crossings! (train & car at crossing). 25pf, If in doubt don't pass! (cars & truck).

1969, Feb. 18   Litho.   *Perf. 13x13½*
1081 A343 5pf lt blue & multi   .20 .20
1082 A343 10pf yellow & multi   .20 .20
1083 A343 20pf pink & multi   .20 .20
1084 A343 25pf multicolored   .45 .30
    Nos. 1081-1084 (4)   1.05 .90

Traffic safety campaign.

Combine A344

Leipzig Spring Fair: 15pf, Planeta-Variant offset printing press.

1969, Feb. 26   Photo.   *Perf. 14*
1085 A344 10pf multicolored   .20 .20
1086 A344 15pf crimson, blk & bl   .25 .20

Jorinde and Joringel A345

Various Scenes from Fairy Tale "Jorinde and Joringel."

1969, Mar. 18   Litho.   *Perf. 13½x13*
1087 A345 5pf black & multi   .20 .20
1088 A345 10pf black & multi   .20 .20
1089 A345 15pf black & multi   .45 .45
1090 A345 20pf black & multi   .45 .45
1091 A345 25pf black & multi   .20 .20
1092 A345 30pf black & multi   .20 .20
   a.   Sheet of 6, #1087-1092   2.25 2.25

See Nos. 1176-1181.

Spring Snowflake A346

Red Cross, Crescent, Lion and Sun Emblems A347

Protected Plants: 10pf, Adonis. 15pf, Globeflowers. 20pf, Garden Turk's-cap. 25pf, Button snakeroot. 30pf, Dactylorchis latifolia.

1969, Apr. 4   Photo.   *Perf. 14*
1093 A346 5pf green & multi   .20 .20
1094 A346 10pf green & multi   .20 .20
1095 A346 15pf green & multi   .20 .20
1096 A346 20pf green & multi   .20 .20
1097 A346 25pf green & multi   2.40 1.25
1098 A346 30pf green & multi   .30 .20
    Nos. 1093-1098 (6)   3.50 2.25

1969, Apr. 23   Litho.   *Perf. 12½x13*

Design: 15pf, Large Red Cross, Red Crescent and Lion and Sun Emblems.

1099 A347 10pf gray, red & yel   .25 .20
1100 A347 15pf multicolored   1.10 .35

League of Red Cross Societies, 50th anniv.

Conifer Nursery A348

Erythrite from Schneeberg A349

10pf, Forests as natural resources (timber & resin). 20pf, Forests as regulators of climate. 25pf, Forests as recreation areas (tents along lake).

1969, Apr. 23
1101 A348 5pf multicolored   .25 .20
1102 A348 10pf multicolored   .25 .20
1103 A348 20pf multicolored   .25 .20
1104 A348 25pf multicolored   1.60 .70
    Nos. 1101-1104 (4)   2.35 1.30

Prevention of forest fires.

1969, May 21   Photo.   *Perf. 13½x14*

Minerals: 10pf, Fluorite from Halsbrücke. 15pf, Galena from Neudorf. 20pf, Smoky quartz from Lichtenberg. 25pf, Calcite from Niederrabenstein. 50pf, Silver from Freiberg.

1105 A349 5pf tan & multi   .20 .20
1106 A349 10pf multicolored   .20 .20
1107 A349 15pf gray & multi   .20 .20
1108 A349 20pf lemon & multi   .20 .20
1109 A349 25pf multicolored   .75 .55
1110 A349 50pf lt blue & multi   .25 .20
    Nos. 1105-1110 (6)   1.80 1.55

Women and Symbols of Agriculture, Science and Industry — A350

Design: 25pf, Woman's head and symbols.

1969, May 28   Engr.   *Perf. 14*
1111 A350 20pf dk red & blue   .20 .20
1112 A350 20pf blue & dk red   .85 .30

2nd Women's Congress of the German Democratic Republic.

Ulbricht Type of 1961-67
1969-71   Wmk. 313   Typo.   *Perf. 14*
Size: 17x21mm
1112A	A189	35pf	Prus blue	
			('71)	.30 .30

Unwmk.
Engr.
Size: 24x28½mm
1113	A189	1m	dull green	.35 .35
1114	A189	2m	brown	.45 .45
	Nos. 1112A-1114 (3)			1.10 1.10

See note below Nos. 590B-590C.

Coil Stamp
1970, Jan. 20   Typo.   Wmk. 313
Size: 17x21mm
1114A	A189	1m	olive	.75 3.00

Emblem of DDR Philatelic Society — A351   Worker Protecting Children — A352

1969, June 4   Photo.   Unwmk.
1115	A351	10pf	red, gold & ultra	.30 .20

National Philatelic Exhibition "20 Years DDR," Magdeburg, Oct. 31-Nov. 9.

1969, June 4   Litho.   *Perf. 13*

25pf, Workers of various races. 20pf+5pf, Berlin buildings: Brandenburg Gate, Council of State, Soviet Cenotaph, Town Hall Tower, Television Tower, Teachers' Building & Hall.

Size: 23x28mm
1116	A352	10pf	lemon & multi	.55 .60

Size: 50x28mm
1117	A352	20pf + 5pf multi		.55 .60

Size: 23x28mm
1118	A352	25pf	lemon & multi	.55 .60
	a.	Strip of 3, #1116-1118		2.75 2.75

Intl. Peace Meeting, Berlin. The surtax on No. 1117 was for the Peace Council of the German Democratic Republic.

Opening Ceremony before Battle of Leipzig Monument — A353

15pf, Parading athletes & stadium. 25pf, Running, hurdling, javelin & flag waving. 30pf, Presentation of colors before old Leipzig Town Hall.

Photo. & Engr.
1969, June 18   *Perf. 14*
1119	A353	5pf	multi & black	.20 .20
1120	A353	15pf	multi & black	.20 .20
1121	A353	25pf	multi & black	1.40 .50
1122	A353	30pf	multi & black	.20 .20
	Nos. 1119-1122,B152-B153 (6)			2.40 1.50

5th German Gymnastic and Sports Festival, Leipzig.

Pierre de Coubertin, by Wieland Forster — A354

Knight — A355

Design: 25pf, Coubertin column, Memorial Grove, Olympia.

1969, June 6   *Perf. 14x13½*
1123	A354	10pf	black & lt blue	.20 .20
1124	A354	25pf	black & sal pink	.70 .45

Revival of the Olympic Games, 75th anniv.

1969, July 29   Photo.   *Perf. 14*

#1126, Bicycle wheel. #1127, Volleyball.
1125	A355	20pf	red, gold & dk brn	.25 .20
1126	A355	20pf	green, gold & red	.25 .20
1127	A355	20pf	multicolored	.25 .20
	Nos. 1125-1127 (3)			.75 .60

16th Students' Chess World Championships, Dresden (No. 1125); Indoor Bicycle World Championships, Erfurt (No. 1126); 2nd Volleyball World Cup (No. 1127).

Merchandise A356

1969, Aug. 27   Litho.   *Perf. 12½x13*
1128	A356	10pf	multicolored	.25 .20

Leipzig Fall Fair, Aug. 31-Sept. 7, 1969.

Arms of Republic and View of Rostock A357

1m, DDR Arms, Town Hall, Marienkirche and Television Tower, Berlin, vert.

1969, Sept. 23   Photo.   *Perf. 14*
1129	A357	10pf	Rostock	.20 .20
1130	A357	10pf	Neubrandenburg	.20 .20
1131	A357	10pf	Potsdam	.20 .20
1132	A357	10pf	Eisenhüttenstadt	.20 .20
1133	A357	10pf	Hoyerswerda	.20 .20
1134	A357	10pf	Magdeburg	.20 .20
1135	A357	10pf	Halle-Neustadt	.20 .20
1136	A357	10pf	Suhl	.20 .20
1137	A357	10pf	Dresden	.20 .20
1138	A357	10pf	Leipzig	.20 .20
1139	A357	10pf	Karl-Marx-Stadt	.20 .20
1140	A357	10pf	Berlin	.20 .20
	Nos. 1129-1140 (12)			2.40 2.40

Souvenir Sheet
1141	A357	1m	multicolored	1.60 4.00

#1129-1141, 1142-1145 for 20th anniv. of the German Democratic Republic. No. 1141 contains one 29x52mm stamp.

Television Tower, Berlin — A358

People and Flags — A359

Designs: 20pf, Sphere of Television Tower and TV test picture. No. 1144, Television Tower and TV test picture.

1969, Oct. 6   *Perf. 14*
1142	A358	10pf	multicolored	.20 .20
1143	A358	20pf	multicolored	.25 .20

Souvenir Sheets
1144	A358	1m	dk blue & multi	1.25 3.00

Perf. 13x12½
1145	A359	1m	red & multi	1.20 2.10

No. 1144 contains one 21½x60mm stamp.

Cathedral, Otto von Guericke Monument and Hotel International, Magdeburg — A360

1969, Oct. 28   Litho.   *Perf. 13x12½*
1146	A360	20pf	multicolored	.20 .20

Natl. Postage Stamp Exhibition in honor of the 20th anniv. of the German Democratic Republic, Magdeburg. Oct. 31-Nov. 9. See No. B154.

UFI Emblem — A361

1969, Oct. 28   *Perf. 13x13½*
1147	A361	10pf	multicolored	.20 .20
1148	A361	15pf	multicolored	1.40 .35

36th UFI Congress (Union des Foires Internationales), Leipzig, Oct. 28-30.

Memorial Monument, Copenhagen-Ryvangen — A362

Rostock University Seal and Building — A363

1969, Oct. 28   *Perf. 13*
1149	A362	25pf	multicolored	.60 .20

Issued in memory of the victims of the Nazis in Denmark.

1969, Nov. 12   *Perf. 12½x13*

Design: 15pf, Steam turbine, curve and Rostock University emblem.
1150	A363	10pf	brt blue & multi	.25 .20
1151	A363	15pf	violet & multi	1.10 .25

550th anniversary of Rostock University.

ILO Emblem — A364   Mold for Christmas Cookies — A365

1969, Nov. 12   *Perf. 13½x14*
1152	A364	20pf	dp green & silver	.20 .20
1153	A364	25pf	lil rose & silver	1.40 .30

50th anniv. of the ILO.

1969, Nov. 25   Litho.   *Perf. 13½x13*

50pf, Negro couple, shaped spice cookie.
1154	A365	10pf	dull org, bl & red brn	.90 .75
1155	A365	50pf	lt blue & multi	1.50 1.25
	a.	Pair, #1154-1155		5.50 4.75
	Nos. 1154-1155,B155 (3)			2.70 2.30

Folk art of Lusatia.

Antonov An-24 A366

Planes: 25pf, Ilyushin Il-18. 30pf, Tupolev Tu-134. 50pf, Mi-8 helicopter.

1969, Dec. 2   *Perf. 13x12½*
1156	A366	20pf	blue, red & blk	.20 .20
1157	A366	25pf	vio, red & blk	1.00 .80
1158	A366	30pf	ultra, red & blk	.20 .20
1159	A366	50pf	olive, red & blk	.25 .20
	Nos. 1156-1159 (4)			1.65 1.40

Siberian Teacher, by D. K. Sveshnikov A367

Russian Paintings from Dresden Gallery of Modern Masters: 10pf, Steelworker, by V. A. Serov. 20pf, Still Life, by E. A. Aslamasjan. 25pf, Hot Day (boats on river), by J. D. Romas. 40pf, Spring is Coming (young woman and snow-covered street), by L. V. Kabatchek. 50pf, Man on River Bank, by V. J. Makovskij.

1969, Dec. 10		Photo.	Perf. 13	
1160	A367	5pf gray & multi	.20	.20
1161	A367	10pf gray & multi	.20	.20
1162	A367	20pf gray & multi	.20	.20
1163	A367	25pf gray & multi	.90	.90
1164	A367	40pf gray & multi	.25	.20
1165	A367	50pf gray & multi	.25	.20
		Nos. 1160-1165 (6)	2.00	1.90

Ernst Barlach (1870-1938), Sculptor and Writer — A368

Portraits: 10pf, Johann Gutenberg (1400-68). 15pf, Kurt Tucholsky (1890-1935), writer. 20pf, Ludwig van Beethoven. 25pf, Friedrich Hölderlin (1770-1843), poet. 40pf, Georg Wilhelm Friedrich Hegel (1770-1831), philosopher.

1970, Jan. 20		Engr.	Perf. 14	
1166	A368	5pf blue violet	.25	.20
1167	A368	10pf gray brown	.25	.20
1168	A368	15pf violet blue	.25	.20
1169	A368	20pf rose lilac	.30	.20
1170	A368	25pf blue green	1.90	.50
1171	A368	40pf rose claret	.30	.20
		Nos. 1166-1171 (6)	3.25	1.50

Rabbit — A369

1970, Feb. 5		Photo.	Perf. 13½x14	
1172	A369	10pf shown	.20	.20
1173	A369	20pf Red fox	.20	.20
1174	A369	30pf Mink	2.40	1.60
1175	A369	40pf Hamster	.30	.20
		Nos. 1172-1175 (4)	3.10	2.20

525th International Fur Auctions, Leipzig.

Fairy Tale Type of 1969

Various Scenes from Fairy Tale "Little Brother and Sister."

1970, Feb. 17		Litho.	Perf. 13½x13	
1176	A345	5pf lilac & multi	.20	.20
1177	A345	10pf lilac & multi	.20	.20
1178	A345	15pf lilac & multi	.40	.35
1179	A345	20pf lilac & multi	.40	.35
1180	A345	25pf lilac & multi	.20	.20
1181	A345	30pf lilac & multi	.20	.20
a.		Sheet of 6, #1176-1181	3.00	2.25

Telephone Coordinating Station — A370

15pf, High voltage testing transformer, vert.

1970, Feb. 24		Perf. 13x12½, 12½x13		
1182	A370	10pf multicolored	.20	.20
1183	A370	15pf multicolored	.45	.25

Leipzig Spring Fair, Mar. 1-10, 1970.

Horseman's Tombstone (700 A.D.) — A371

Treasures from the Halle Museum: 20pf, Helmet (500 A.D.). 25pf, Bronze basin (1000 B.C.). 40pf, Clay drum (2500 B.C.).

1970, Mar. 3		Photo.	Perf. 13	
1184	A371	10pf dp grn, gray & dk brn	.20	.20
1185	A371	20pf multicolored	.20	.20
1186	A371	25pf yellow & multi	.60	.80
1187	A371	40pf multicolored	.20	.20
		Nos. 1184-1187 (4)	1.20	1.40

Lenin and Clara Zetkin — A372

Designs: 10pf, Lenin, "ISKRA" (newspaper's name), composing frame and printing press. 25pf, Lenin and title page of German edition of "State and Revolution." 40pf, Lenin statue, Eisleben. 70pf, Lenin monument and Lenin Square, Berlin. 1m, Lenin portrait, vert.

Photogravure and Engraved

1970, Apr. 16			Perf. 14	
1188	A372	10pf multicolored	.20	.20
1189	A372	20pf multicolored	.20	.20
1190	A372	25pf multicolored	1.60	.75
1191	A372	40pf multicolored	.20	.20
1192	A372	70pf multicolored	.30	.20
		Nos. 1188-1192 (5)	2.50	1.55

Souvenir Sheet

1193	A372	1m dk carmine & multi	1.50	6.00

Sea Kale — A373

Red Army Soldier Raising Flag over Berlin Reichstag A374

Protected Plants: 20pf, European pasque-flower. 25pf, Fringed gentian. 30pf, Galeate orchis. 40pf, Marsh tea. 70pf, Round-leaved wintergreen.

1970, Apr. 28			Photo.	
1194	A373	10pf multicolored	.20	.20
1195	A373	20pf violet & multi	.20	.20
1196	A373	25pf multicolored	1.50	1.50
1197	A373	30pf multicolored	.20	.20
1198	A373	40pf multicolored	.25	.20
1199	A373	70pf multicolored	.30	.20
		Nos. 1194-1199 (6)	2.65	2.50

1970, May 5 Litho. Perf. 13x13½

20pf, Spasski Tower, Kremlin; State Council Building, Berlin; coats of arms of USSR and DDR, newspaper clipping about friendship treaty with USSR. 25pf, Mutual Economic Aid Building, Moscow, flags of member countries. 70pf, Memorial monument, Buchenwald.

1200	A374	10pf multi	.25	.20
1201	A374	20pf multi	.25	.20
1202	A374	25pf multi	1.10	.35
		Nos. 1200-1202 (3)	1.60	.75

Souvenir Sheet

1203	A374	70pf multi, horiz.	1.50	4.00

25th anniv. of liberation from Fascism.

Shortwave Antenna, RBI Emblem and Globe — A375

Grain and Globe — A376

15pf, Berlin Radio Station, emblems of Radio Berlin Intl. (RBI), Radio DDR & Radio Germany.

1970, May 13 Litho. Perf. 13½x13
Size: 23x28mm

1204	A375	10pf ap grn, vio bl & bl	.50	.50

Size: 50x28mm

1205	A375	15pf vio bl, dp rose & ap grn	.75	.75
a.		Pair, #1204-1205	3.25	2.00

DDR broadcasting system, 25th anniv.

1970, May 19

25pf, House of Culture, Dresden, and grain.

1206	A376	20pf vio bl, yel & bl	.65	.65
1207	A376	25pf vio bl, yel & bl	.65	.65
a.		Strip of 2, #1206-1207 + label	4.00	4.00

Issued to publicize the 5th World Cereal and Bread Congress, Dresden, May 24-29.

Fritz Heckert Medal A377

Design: 25pf, Globes and "FSM."

1970, June 9			Perf. 13x12½	
1208	A377	20pf red, yel & brn	.20	.20
1209	A377	25pf red, bl & yel	.55	.40

25th anniv. of the Free German Trade Union and of the World Organization of Trade Unions.

Traffic Policeman — A378

Designs: 10pf, Young Pioneers congratulating police woman. 15pf, Volga police car. 20pf, Railroad policeman with radio-telephone. 25pf, River police in Volga wing-type boat.

1970, June 23		Litho.	Perf. 13x12½	
1210	A378	5pf ocher & multi	.25	.20
1211	A378	10pf green & multi	.25	.20
1212	A378	15pf ultra & multi	.25	.20
1213	A378	20pf multicolored	.25	.20
1214	A378	25pf multicolored	1.90	.30
		Nos. 1210-1214 (5)	2.90	1.10

25th anniversary of the People's Police.

Gods Amon, Shu and Tefnut — A379

Designs from Lion Temple in Musawwarat: 15pf, Head of King Arnekhamani. 20pf, Cow from cattle frieze. 25pf, Head of Prince Arka. 30pf, Head of God Arensnuphis, vert. 40pf, Elephants and prisoners of war. 50pf, Lion God Apedemak.

1970, June 23		Perf. 13½x14, 14x13½		
			Photo.	
1215	A379	10pf multicolored	.20	.20
1216	A379	15pf multicolored	.20	.20
1217	A379	20pf multicolored	.20	.20
1218	A379	25pf multicolored	.70	.70
1219	A379	30pf multicolored	.20	.20
1220	A379	40pf multicolored	.20	.20
1221	A379	50pf multicolored	.20	.20
		Nos. 1215-1221 (7)	1.90	1.90

Archaeological work in the Sudan by the Humboldt University, Berlin.

Arms and Flags of DDR and Poland — A380

1970, July 1		Litho.	Perf. 13x12½	
1222	A380	20pf multicolored	.30	.20

20th anniversary of the Görlitz Agreement concerning the Oder-Neisse border.

Culture Association Emblem — A381

Athlete on Pommel Horse — A382

Design: 25pf, Johannes R. Becher medal.

1970, July 1		Photo.	Perf. 14	
1223	A381	10pf ultra, sil & brn	1.60	1.60
1224	A381	25pf ultra, gold & brn	1.60	1.60
a.		Strip of 2, #1223-1224 + label	8.25	8.25

25th anniv. of the German Kulturbund.

1970, July 1			Perf. 14x13½	
1225	A382	10pf blk, yel & brn red	.20	.20

Issued to publicize the 3rd Children's and Youths' Spartakiad. See No. B156.

Meeting of the American, British and Russian Delegations — A383

10pf, Cecilienhof Castle. 20pf, "Potsdam Agreement" in German, English, French & Russian.

1970, July 28		Litho.	Perf. 13	
			Size: 23x28mm	
1226	A383	10pf blk, cit & red	.25	.20
1227	A383	20pf blk, cit & red	.25	.20

Size: 77x28mm
1228 A383 25pf red & blk   .25   .20
a.   Strip of 3, #1226-1228   1.40 2.75
25th anniv. of the Potsdam Agreement among the Allies concerning Germany at the end of WWII.

Men's Pocket and Wrist Watches — A384

1970, Aug. 25 Photo. Perf. 13½x14
1229 A384 10pf ultra, blk & gold   .30   .20
Leipzig Fall Fair, 1970.

Theodor Neubauer and Magnus Poser — A385

"Homeland" from Soviet Cenotaph, Berlin-Treptow A386

1970, Sept. 2 Perf. 13x12½, 12½x13
1230 A385 20pf dk bl, car & pale grn   .20 .20
1231 A386 25pf dp car, pale bl   .25 .20
Issued in memory of fighters against "fascism and imperialistic wars."

Competition Map and Compass — A387

Design: 25pf, Competition map and runner at 3 different stations.

1970, Sept. 15 Litho. Perf. 13x12½
1232 A387 10pf yellow & multi   .20   .20
1233 A387 25pf yellow & multi   1.00 .25
World Orienting Championships.

Mother and Child, by Käthe Kollwitz — A388

Works of Art: 10pf, Forest Worker Scharf's Birthday, by Otto Nagel. 20pf, Portrait of a Girl, by Otto Nagel. 25pf, No More War, (Woman with raised arm) by Käthe Kollwitz. 40pf, Head from Gustrow Memorial, by Ernst Barlach. 50pf, The Flutist, by Ernst Barlach.

Photo.; Litho. (25pf, 30pf)
1970, Sept. 22   Perf. 14x13½
1234 A388 10pf multicolored   .20   .20
1235 A388 20pf multicolored   .20   .20
1236 A388 25pf pink & dk brn   .75   .95
1237 A388 30pf sal & blk   .20   .20
1238 A388 40pf yel & blk   .20   .20
1239 A388 50pf yel & blk   .25   .20
     Nos. 1234-1239 (6)   1.80 1.95
Issued in memory of the artists Otto Nagel, Käthe Kollwitz and Ernst Barlach.

The Little Trumpeter A389

1970, Oct. 1   Photo.
1240 A389 10pf dp ultra, brn & org .20 .20
2nd Natl. Youth Stamp Exhib., Karl-Marx-Stadt, Oct. 4-11. The design shows the memorial in Halle for Fritz Weineck, trumpeter for the Red War Veterans' Organization. See No. B160.

Emblem with Flags of East Block Nations — A390

1970, Oct. 1 Litho. Perf. 13x12½
1241 A390 10pf carmine & multi .20 .20
1242 A390 20pf multicolored   .25 .25
Issued to publicize the Brothers in Arms maneuvers of the East Bloc countries in the territory of the German Democratic Republic.

Musk Ox — A391

Berlin Zoo: 15pf, Shoebill. 20pf, Addax. 25pf, Malayan sun bear.

1970, Oct. 6   Photo.   Perf. 14
1243 A391 10pf blue & multi   .30   .20
1244 A391 15pf green & multi   .30   .20
1245 A391 20pf org & multi   .55   .30
1246 A391 25pf multicolored   5.00 5.00
     Nos. 1243-1246 (4)   6.15 5.70

UN Headquarters and Emblem — A392

1970, Oct. 20   Photo.   Perf. 13
1247 A392 20pf ultra & multi   .55   .25
25th anniversary of the United Nations.

Friedrich Engels   Epiphyllum
A393   A394

20pf, Friedrich Engels and Karl Marx. 25pf, Engels and title page of his polemic against Dühring.

Photogravure and Engraved
1970, Nov. 24   Perf. 14
1248 A393 10pf ver, gray & blk   .25   .20
1249 A393 20pf ver, dk grn & blk   .25   .20
1250 A393 25pf ver, dk car rose
          & blk   1.10 .60
     Nos. 1248-1250 (3)   1.60 1.00
Friedrich Engels (1820-1895), socialist, collaborator with Karl Marx.

1970, Dec. 2   Photo.   Perf. 14
Flowering Cactus Plants: 10pf, Astrophytum myriostigma. 15pf, Echinocereus salm-dyckianus. 20pf, Selenicereus grandiflorus. 25pf, Hamatocactus setispinus. 30pf, Mamillaria boolii.

1251 A394 5pf multicolored   .20   .20
1252 A394 10pf dk blue & multi .20   .20
1253 A394 15pf multicolored   .20   .20
1254 A394 20pf multicolored   .20   .20
1255 A394 25pf dk blue & multi 1.50 1.50
1256 A394 30pf purple & multi   .20   .20
     Nos. 1251-1256 (6)   2.50 2.50

Souvenir Sheet

Ludwig van Beethoven — A395

1970, Dec. 10   Engr.   Perf. 14
1257 A395 1m gray   1.50 3.00
Bicentenary of the birth of Ludwig van Beethoven (1770-1827), composer.

Dancer's Mask, South Seas A396

Works from Ethnological Museum, Leipzig: 20pf, Bronze head, Africa. 25pf, Tea pot, Asia. 40pf, Clay figure (jaguar), Mexico.

1971, Jan. 12   Photo.   Perf. 13
1258 A396 10pf multicolored   .20   .20
1259 A396 20pf multicolored   .20   .20
1260 A396 25pf multicolored   .60   .60
1261 A396 40pf multicolored   .25   .20
     Nos. 1258-1261 (4)   1.25 1.20

Venus 5, Soft-landing on Moon — A397

#1263, Model of space station. #1264, Luna 16 and Luna 10 satellites. #1265, Group flight of Sojuz 6, 7 and 8. #1266, Proton 1, radiation measuring satellite. #1267, Communications

satellite Molniya 1. #1268, Yuri A. Gagarin, first flight of Vostok 1. #1269, Alexei Leonov walking in space, Voskhod 2.

1971, Feb. 11 Litho. Perf. 13x12½
1262 A397 20pf dk blue & multi   .25   .25
1263 A397 20pf dk blue & multi   .25   .25
1264 A397 20pf dk blue & multi   .45   .45
1265 A397 20pf dk blue & multi   .45   .45
1266 A397 20pf dk blue & multi   .45   .45
1267 A397 20pf dk blue & multi   .45   .45
1268 A397 20pf dk blue & multi   .25   .25
1269 A397 20pf dk blue & multi   .25   .25
a.   Sheet of 8, #1262-1269   3.00 3.00
Soviet space research.

Johannes R.   Karl Liebknecht
Becher   A399
A398

Portraits: 10pf, Heinrich Mann. 15pf, John Heartfield. 20pf, Willi Bredel. 25pf, Franz Mehring. 40pf, Rudolf Virchow. 50pf, Johannes Kepler.

1971   Engr.   Perf. 14
1270 A398 5pf brown   .20   .20
1271 A398 10pf vio blue   .20   .20
1272 A398 15pf black   .20   .20
1273 A398 20pf rose lake   .20   .20
1274 A398 25pf green   .45   .50
1274A A398 40pf pale purple .40   .40
1275 A398 50pf dp black   .25   .20
      Nos. 1270-1275 (7)   1.90 1.70
Honoring prominent Germans. See Nos. 1349-1353.

1971, Feb. 23   Photo.
Design: 25pf, Rosa Luxemburg.
1276 A399 20pf gold, mag & blk   .35   .35
1277 A399 25pf gold, mag & blk   .35   .35
a.   Pair, #1276-1277   1.00 1.00
Karl Liebknecht (1871-1919) and Rosa Luxemburg (1871-1919), leaders of Spartacist Movement.

Soldier and Army Emblem — A400

1971, Mar. 1   Perf. 13½x14
1278 A400 20pf gray & multi   .30   .20
15th anniv. of the National People's Army.

Crushing and Conveyor Plant, Magdeburg — A401

Leipzig Spring Fair: 15pf, Dredger for low temperature work.

1971, Mar. 9 Litho. Perf. 13x12½
1279 A401 10pf green & multi   .20   .20
1280 A401 15pf multicolored   .20   .20

Proclamation of the Commune, Town Hall, Paris — A402

Designs: 20pf, Barricade at Place Blanche, defended by women. 25pf, Illustration by Theophile A. Steinlen for the International. 30pf, Title page for "The Civil War in France," by Karl Marx.

1971, Mar. 9   **Perf. 13**
1281 A402 10pf red, bis & blk .25 .20
1282 A402 20pf red, bis & blk .25 .20
1283 A402 25pf red, buff & blk .45 .45
1284 A402 30pf red, gray & blk .25 .20
     Nos. 1281-1284 (4) 1.20 1.05

Centenary of the Paris Commune.

Lunokhod 1 on Moon — A403

1971, Mar. 30   **Photo.**   **Perf. 14**
1285 A403 20pf multicolored .55 .30

Luna 17 unmanned, automated moon mission, Nov. 10-17, and the 24th Communist Party Congress of the Soviet Union.

Discobolus — A404

1971, Apr. 6   **Litho.**   **Perf. 13½x13**
1286 A404 20pf dull bl, lt bl & buff .65 .25

20th anniversary of the Olympic Committee of German Democratic Republic.

Köpenick Castle — A405

Clasped Hands — A406

Berlin Buildings: 10pf, St. Mary's Church, vert. 20pf, Old Library. 25pf, Ermeler House, vert. 50pf, New Guard Memorial. 70pf, Natl. Gallery of Art.

Perf. 13½x14, 14x13½
1971, Apr. 6   **Photo.**
1287 A405 10pf multicolored .20 .20
1288 A405 15pf multicolored .20 .20
1289 A405 20pf multicolored .20 .20
1290 A405 25pf multicolored 2.40 2.25
1291 A405 50pf multicolored .25 .20
1292 A405 70pf multicolored .30 .20
     Nos. 1287-1292 (6) 3.55 3.25

Lithographed and Embossed
1971, Apr. 20   **Perf. 13x13½**
1293 A406 20pf red, blk & gold .30 .20

25th anniversary of Socialist Unity Party of Germany (SED).

Dance Costume, Schleife — A407   Self-Portrait, by Dürer — A408

Sorbian Dance Costumes from: 20pf, Hoyerswerda. 25pf, Cottbus. 40pf, Kamenz.

1971, May 4   **Litho.**   **Perf. 13½x13**
         Size: 33x42mm
1294 A407 10pf multicolored .20 .20
1295 A407 20pf green & multi .20 .20
1296 A407 25pf blue & multi .55 .55
1297 A407 40pf multicolored .25 .20
     Nos. 1294-1297 (4) 1.20 1.15

1971, Nov. 23   **Perf. 13½x13**
         Booklet Stamps
         Size: 23x28mm
1297A A407 10pf multicolored .25 .20
   c.   Booklet pane of 4 1.40 1.10
   d.   Booklet pane, 2 #1297A, 2
         #1297B 3.00 2.50
1297B A407 20pf multicolored .50 .30

1971, May 18   **Perf. 12½x13**

Art Works by Dürer: 40pf, Three Peasants. 70pf, Portrait of Philipp Melanchthon.

1298 A408 10pf multicolored .25 .20
1299 A408 40pf brown & multi .25 .20
1300 A408 70pf gray & multi 1.50 .75
     Nos. 1298-1300 (3) 2.00 1.15

500th anniversary of the birth of Albrecht Dürer (1471-1528), painter and engraver.

Building Industry — A409

Congress Emblem — A410

Designs: 10pf, Science and technology. No. 1303, Farming. 25pf, Civilian defense.

1971, June 9   **Photo.**   **Perf. 14**
1301 A409 5pf cream, red & blk .20 .20
1302 A409 10pf cream, red & blk .20 .20
1303 A409 20pf cream, red, bl &
         blk .20 .20
1304 A410 20pf gold, dp car &
         red .25 .20
1305 A409 25pf cream, red & blk .30 .35
     Nos. 1301-1305 (5) 1.15 1.15

8th Congress of Socialist Unity Party of Germany (SED).

Golden Fleece, 1730 A411

Treasures from the Green Vault, Dresden: 5pf, Cherry stone with 180 heads carved on it, 1590. 15pf, Tankard, Nuremberg, 1530. 20pf, Moor with drums on horseback, 1720. 25pf, Decorated writing box, 1562. 30pf, St. George pendant, 1570.

1971, June 22   **Perf. 13**
1306 A411 5pf dp car & multi .20 .20
1307 A411 10pf green & multi .20 .20
1308 A411 15pf violet & multi .20 .20
1309 A411 20pf multicolored .20 .20
1310 A411 25pf multicolored .55 .75
1311 A411 30pf multicolored .20 .20
     Nos. 1306-1311 (6) 1.55 1.75

Prisoners, by Fritz Cremer A412

Design: 25pf, Brutality in Buchenwald Concentration Camp, by Fritz Cremer.

1971, June 22   **Litho.**   **Perf. 13**
1312 A412 20pf bister & blk .45 .45
1313 A412 25pf lt blue & blk .45 .45
   a.   Pair, #1312-1313 with label between 1.40 1.60

Intl. Federation of Resistance Fighters (FIR), 20th anniv.

Coat of Arms of Mongolia — A413

1971, July 6   **Litho.**   **Perf. 13**
1314 A413 20pf dk red, yel & blk .30 .25

50th anniv. of the Mongolian People's Revolution.

Child's Head, UNICEF Emblem A414

1971, July 13   **Photo.**
1315 A414 20pf multicolored .30 .20

25th anniv. of UNICEF.

Militiaman, Soldier and Brandenburg Gate — A415

Design: 35pf, Brandenburg Gate and new buildings in East Berlin.

1971, Aug. 12
1316 A415 20pf red & multi .60 .25
1317 A415 35pf yel & multi 1.50 .75

10 years of Berlin Wall.

Passenger Ship Iwan Franko — A416

Ships: 15pf, Freighter, type 17. 20pf, Freighter Rostock, type XD. 25pf, Fish processing ship "Junge Welt." 40pf, Container

cargo ship. 50pf, Explorer ship Akademik Kurtschatow.

1971, Aug. 24   **Engr.**
1318 A416 10pf pale purple .20 .20
1319 A416 15pf pale brn & ind .20 .20
1320 A416 20pf gray green .20 .20
1321 A416 25pf slate 1.00 .90
1322 A416 40pf maroon .20 .20
1323 A416 50pf grysh blue .25 .20
     Nos. 1318-1323 (6) 2.05 1.90

Shipbuilding industry.

Butadiene Plant — A417

Leipzig Fall Fair: 25pf, Refinery.

1971, Sept. 2   **Photo.**   **Perf. 13**
1324 A417 10pf olive, vio & mag .20 .20
1325 A417 25pf blue, vio & ol .25 .20

Raised Fists, Photo Montage by John Heartfield, 1937 A418

1971, Sept. 23
1326 A418 35pf grnsh bl, blk & sil .30 .20

Intl. Year Against Racial Discrimination.

Karl Marx Monument A419

1971, Oct. 5   **Photo.**   **Perf. 14x13½**
1327 A419 35pf vio brn, pink & buff .35 .20

Unveiling of Karl Marx memorial at Karl-Marx-Stadt (Chemnitz).

Wiltz Memorial, Flag of Luxembourg A420

1971, Oct. 5
1328 A420 25pf multicolored .25 .20

Memorial for Nazi victims, Wiltz, Luxembourg.

Postal Milestones, Saxony, and Zürner's Surveyor Carriage — A421

Photo. & Engr.

1971, Oct. 5   **Perf. 14**
1329 A421 25pf blue, olive & lilac   .35 .35

Philatelists' Day 1971. See No. B162.

Darbuka, North Africa — A422

Geodetic Apparatus — A423

Musical Instruments: 15pf, Two morin chuur, Mongolia. 20pf, Violin, Germany. 25pf, Mandolin, Italy. 40pf, Bagpipes, Bohemia. 50pf, Kasso, Sudan.

1971, Oct. 26   **Photo.**   **Perf. 14x13½**
1330 A422 10pf multicolored   .20 .20
1331 A422 15pf multicolored   .20 .20
1332 A422 20pf ocher & multi   .20 .20
1333 A422 25pf blue & multi   .20 .20
1334 A422 40pf gray & multi   .20 .20
1335 A422 50pf multicolored   .85 .85
   Nos. 1330-1335 (6)   1.85 1.85

Instruments from the Music Museum in Markneukirchen.

1971, Nov. 9   **Photo.**   **Perf. 13½x14**

20pf, Ergaval microscope. 25pf, Planetarium.

Size: 23½x28½mm
1336 A423 10pf blue, blk & red   .35 .35
1337 A423 20pf blue, blk & red   .35 .35

Size: 50½x28½mm
1338 A423 25pf blue, vio bl & yel   .35 .35
   a.   Strip of 3, #1336-1338   3.00 3.00

Carl Zeiss optical works in Jena, 125th anniv.

Fairy Tale Type of 1966

Designs: Various Scenes from Fairy Tale "The Bremen Town Musicians."

1971, Nov. 23   **Litho.**   **Perf. 13½x13**
1339 A290 5pf multicolored   .20 .20
1340 A290 10pf ocher & multi   .20 .20
1341 A290 15pf gray & multi   .55 .65
1342 A290 20pf ver & multi   .55 .65
1343 A290 25pf violet & multi   .20 .20
1344 A290 30pf yellow & multi   .20 .20
   a.   Sheet of 6, #1339-1344   3.00 7.50

Olympic Rings and Sledding — A424

Olympic Rings and: 20pf, Long-distance skiing. 25pf, Biathlon. 70pf, Ski jump.

1971, Dec. 7   **Photo.**   **Perf. 13½x14**
1345 A424 5pf green, car & blk   .20 .20
1346 A424 20pf car rose, vio & blk   .20 .20
1347 A424 25pf vio, car & blk   1.25 1.00
1348 A424 70pf vio bl, vio & blk   .25 .20
   Nos. 1345-1348,B163-B164 (6)   2.30 2.00

11th Winter Olympic Games, Sapporo, Japan, Feb. 3-13, 1972.

Portrait Type of 1971

Portraits: 10pf, Johannes Tralow (1882-1968), playwright. 20pf, Leonhard Frank (1882-1961), writer. 25pf, K. A. Kocor (1822-1904), composer. 35pf, Heinrich Schliemann (1822-1890), archaeologist. 50pf, F. Caroline Neuber (1697-1760), actress.

1972, Jan. 25   **Engr.**   **Perf. 14**
1349 A398 10pf green   .20 .20
1350 A398 20pf rose claret   .20 .20
1351 A398 25pf dk blue   .20 .20
1352 A398 35pf brown   .20 .20
1353 A398 50pf rose violet   .75 1.00
   Nos. 1349-1353 (5)   1.55 1.80

Honoring famous personalities.

Gypsum, Eisleben A425

Minerals found in East Germany: 10pf, Zinnwaldite, Zinnwald. 20pf, Malachite, Ullersreuth. 25pf, Amethyst, Wiesenbad. 35pf, Halite, Merkers. 50pf, Proustite, Schneeberg.

1972, Feb. 22   **Photo.**   **Perf. 13**
1354 A425 5pf grnsh bl & brn blk   .20 .20
1355 A425 10pf citron, brn & blk   .20 .20
1356 A425 20pf multicolored   .20 .20
1357 A425 25pf multicolored   .20 .20
1358 A425 35pf lt green, ind & blk   .20 .20
1359 A425 50pf gray & multi   .90 1.00
   Nos. 1354-1359 (6)   1.90 2.00

Russian Pavilion and Fair Emblem A426

Design: 25pf, Flags of East Germany and Russia, and Fair emblem.

1972, Mar. 3   **Photo.**   **Perf. 14**
1360 A426 10pf vio blue & multi   .20 .20
1361 A426 25pf claret & multi   .25 .20

50 years of Russian participation in the Leipzig Fair.

Miniature Sheets

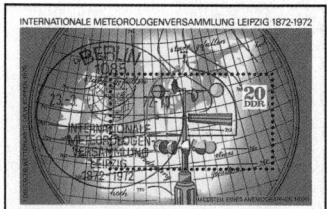

Anemometer, 1896, and Meteorological Chart, 1876 — A427

Designs: 35pf, Dipole and cloud photograph taken by satellite. 70pf, Meteor weather satellite and weather map.

1972, Mar. 23   **Litho.**   **Perf. 13x12½**
1362 A427 20pf multicolored   .70 .80
1363 A427 35pf multicolored   .70 .80
1364 A427 70pf green & multi   .70 .80
   Nos. 1362-1364 (3)   2.10 2.40

Intl. Meteorologists' Cent. Meeting, Leipzig.

World Health Organization Emblem — A428

1972, Apr. 4   **Photo.**   **Perf. 13**
1365 A428 35pf lt bl, vio bl & sil   .30 .20

World Health Day.

Kamov Helicopter A429

Aircraft: 10pf, Agricultural spray plane. 35pf, Ilyushin jet. 1m, Jet and tail with Interflug emblem.

1972, Apr. 25   **Perf. 14**
1366 A429 5pf blue & multi   .20 .20
1367 A429 10pf multicolored   .20 .20
1368 A429 35pf blue grn & multi   .25 .20
1369 A429 1m multicolored   1.00 1.10
   Nos. 1366-1369 (4)   1.65 1.70

Wrestling and Olympic Rings — A430

Sport and Olympic Rings: 20pf, Pole vault. 35pf, Volleyball. 70pf, Women's gymnastics.

1972, May 16   **Photo.**   **Perf. 13½x14**
1370 A430 5pf blue, gold & blk   .20 .20
1371 A430 20pf mag, gold & blk   .20 .20
1372 A430 35pf ol bis, gold & blk   .20 .20
1373 A430 70pf yel grn, gold & blk   2.50 1.50
   Nos. 1370-1373,B166-B167 (6)   3.50 2.50

20th Olympic Games, Munich, 8/26-9/11.

Flags of USSR and German Democratic Republic — A431

20pf, Flags, Leonid Brezhnev & Erich Honecker.

1972, May 24   **Engr. & Photo.**
1374 A431 10pf red, yel & blk   1.00 .60
1375 A431 20pf red, yel & blk   1.00 .60

Soc. for German-Soviet Friendship, 25th anniv.

Workers — A432

Design: 35pf, Students.

1972, May 24   **Litho.**   **Perf. 13**
1376 A432 10pf dull yel, org & mag   .25 .25
1377 A432 35pf dull yel & ultra   .25 .25
   a.   Strip of 2, #1376-1377 + label   1.00 1.00

8th Congress of Free German Trade Unions, Berlin.

Karneol Rose A433

1972, June 13   **Photo.**   **Perf. 13**
Size: 36x36mm
1378 A433 5pf shown   .20 .20
1379 A433 10pf Berger's Erfurt Rose   .20 .20
1380 A433 15pf Charme   1.25 1.25
1381 A433 20pf Izetka Spree-Athens   .20 .20
1382 A433 25pf Kopenick summer   .20 .20
1383 A433 35pf Prof. Knoll   .25 .20
   Nos. 1378-1383 (6)   2.30 2.25

International Rose Exhibition.

Redrawn

1972, Aug. 22   **Perf. 13½x13**
Booklet Stamps
Size: 23x28mm
1383A A433 10pf multicolored   .20 .20
   d.   Booklet pane of 4   1.00 .75
1383B A433 25pf multicolored   1.00 .35
   e.   Booklet pane of 4 (2 #1383B, 2 #1383C)   4.50 3.75
1383C A433 35pf multicolored   1.00 .35
   Nos. 1383A-1383C (3)   2.20 .90

Young Mother and Child, by Cranach A434

Paintings by Lucas Cranach: 5pf, Young man. 35pf, Margarete Luther (Martin's mother). 70pf, Reclining nymph, horiz.

1972, July 4   **Perf. 14x13½, 13½x14**
1384 A434 5pf gold & multi   .20 .20
1385 A434 20pf gold & multi   .20 .20
1386 A434 35pf gold & multi   .25 .25
1387 A434 70pf gold & multi   1.80 2.25
   Nos. 1384-1387 (4)   2.45 2.90

Lucas Cranach (1472-1553), painter.

Compass and Motorcyclist — A435

Designs: 10pf, Parachute and light plane. 20pf, Target and military obstacle race. 25pf, Amateur radio transmitter, Morse key and tape. 35pf, Propeller and sailing ship.

1972, Aug. 8   **Photo.**   **Perf. 14**
1388 A435 5pf multicolored   .20 .20
1389 A435 10pf multicolored   .20 .20
1390 A435 20pf multicolored   .20 .20
1391 A435 25pf multicolored   .55 .65
1392 A435 35pf multicolored   .20 .20
   Nos. 1388-1392 (5)   1.35 1.45

Society for Sport and Technology.

Young Worker Reading, by Jutta Damme — A436

1972, Aug. 22   Photo.   Perf. 13½x14
1393   A436   50pf multicolored   .55   .30
International Book Year 1972.

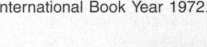

Polylux Writing Projector — A437

George Dimitrov — A438

25pf, Pentacon-audiovision projector, horiz.

Perf. 12½x13, 13x12½
1972, Aug. 29   **Litho.**
1394   A437   10pf crimson & blk   .20   .20
1395   A437   25pf brt green & blk   .25   .20
Leipzig Fall Fair, 1972.

1972, Sept. 19   **Perf. 13x13½**
1396   A438   20pf rose red & blk   .35   .25
George Dimitrov (1882-1949), Bulgarian Communist party leader.

Bird Catchers, Egypt, c. 2400 B.C. — A439

Design: 20pf, Tapestry with animal design, Anatolia, c. 1400 A.D.

1972, Sept. 19   **Photo.**   **Perf. 14**
1397   A439   10pf multicolored   .20   .20
1398   A439   20pf multicolored   .20   .20
Nos. 1397-1398,B168-B169 (4)   1.35   1.35
Interartes Philatelic Exhib., Berlin, Oct. 4-Nov. 11.

Red Cross Trainees and Red Cross — A440

1972, Oct. 3   **Litho.**   **Perf. 13**
Designs: 15pf, Red Cross rescue launch in the Baltic. 35pf, Red Cross with world map, ship, plane and vehicles.

Size: 23x28mm
1399   A440   10pf grnsh bl, dk bl & red   .25   .25

1400   A440   15pf grnsh bl, dk bl & red   .25   .25
Size: 50x28mm
1401   A440   35pf grnsh bl, dk bl & red   .25   .25
a.   Strip of 3, #1399-1401   1.40   1.40
Red Cross at work in the DDR.

Arab Celestial Globe, 1279 — A441

Anti-Fascists Monument — A442

10pf, Globe, by Joachim R. Praetorius, 1568. 15pf, Globe clock, by Reinhold & Roll, 1586. 20pf, Globe clock, by J. Bürgi, c. 1590. 25pf, Armillary sphere, by J. Moeller, 1687. 35pf, Heraldic celestial globe, 1690.

1972, Oct. 17   **Photo.**   **Perf. 14x13½**
1402   A441   5pf gray & multi   .20   .20
1403   A441   10pf gray & multi   .20   .20
1404   A441   15pf gray & multi   1.90   2.00
1405   A441   20pf gray & multi   .20   .20
1406   A441   25pf gray & multi   .20   .20
1407   A441   35pf gray & multi   .25   .20
Nos. 1402-1407 (6)   2.95   3.00
Celestial and terrestrial globes from the National Mathematical and Physics Collection, Dresden.

1972, Oct. 24   **Litho.**   **Perf. 12½x13**
1408   A442   25pf multicolored   .35   .20
Monument for Polish soldiers and German anti-Fascists, unveiled in Berlin, May 14, 1972.

Young Workers Receiving Technical Education — A443

25pf, Workers with modern welding machine.

1972, Nov. 2   **Photo.**   **Perf. 13½x14**
1409   A443   10pf blue & multi   .20   .20
1410   A443   25pf blue & multi   .20   .20
a.   Strip of 2, #1409-1410 + label   .75   .90
15th Central Fair of Masters of Tomorrow.

Mauz and Hoppel A444

Designs: Children's television characters.

1972, Nov. 28   **Litho.**   **Perf. 13½x13**
1411   A444   5pf shown   .20   .20
1412   A444   10pf Fox and magpie   .20   .20
1413   A444   15pf Mr. Owl   .70   .70
1414   A444   20pf Mrs. Hedgehog and Borstel   .70   .70

1415   A444   25pf Schnuffel and Peips   .20   .20
1416   A444   35pf Paul from the Library   .20   .20
a.   Sheet of 6, #1411-1416   2.75   2.75

Grandmother, Children, Magic Mirror — A445

Scenes from Hans Christian Andersen's "Snow Queen": 10pf, Kay and Snow Queen. 15pf, Gerda in magic garden. 20pf, Gerda and crows at palace. 25pf, Gerda and reindeer in Lapland. 35pf, Gerda and Kay at Snow Queen's palace.

1972, Nov. 28   **Perf. 13x13½**
1417   A445   5pf multicolored   .25   .25
1418   A445   10pf multicolored   .55   .75
1419   A445   15pf multicolored   .25   .25
1420   A445   20pf multicolored   .25   .25
1421   A445   25pf multicolored   .55   .75
1422   A445   35pf multicolored   .25   .25
a.   Sheet of 6, #1417-1422   4.00   8.00
See designs A469, A490.

Souvenir Sheet

Heinrich Heine — A446

1972, Dec. 5   **Perf. 12½x13**
1423   A446   1m brn ol, blk & red   1.50   1.50
150th anniversary of the birth of Heinrich Heine (1797-1856), poet.

Coat of Arms of USSR A447

Michelangelo da Caravaggio A448

1972, Dec. 5   **Photo.**   **Perf. 13½x14**
1424   A447   20pf red & multi   .35   .20
50th anniversary of the Soviet Union.

1973   **Litho.**   **Perf. 13½x13**
1425   A448   5pf brown   .60   .70
1426   A448   10pf dull green   .20   .20
1427   A448   20pf rose lilac   .20   .20
1428   A448   25pf blue   .20   .20
1429   A448   35pf brown red   .20   .20
1429A   A448   40pf rose claret   .35   .25
Nos. 1425-1429A (6)   1.75   1.75
Michelangelo da Caravaggio (1565(?)-1609), Italian painter (5pf). Friedrich Wolf (1888-1953), writer (10pf). Max Reger (1873-1916), composer (20pf). Max Reinhardt (1873-1943), Austrian theatrical director (25pf). Johannes Dieckmann (1893-1969), member and president of People's Chamber (35pf). Hermann Matern (1893-1971), vice-president of DDR (40pf).

Lenin Square, Berlin — A449

Coat of Arms of DDR — A449a

Designs: 5pf, Pelican, Berlin Zoo. 10pf, Neptune Fountain, City Hall Street. 15pf, Fisherman's Island, Berlin. 25pf, World clock, Alexander Square, Berlin. 30pf, Workers' Memorial, Halle. 35pf, Marx monument, Karl-Marx-Stadt. 40pf, Brandenburg Gate, Berlin. 50pf, New Guardhouse, Berlin. 60pf, Zwinger, Dresden. 70pf, Old Town Hall, Office Building, Leipzig. 80pf, Old and new buildings, Rostock-Warnemunde. 1m, Soviet War Memorial, Treptow.

1973-74   **Engr.**   **Perf. 14x14**
Size: 29x23½mm
1430   A449   5pf blue green   .20   .20
1431   A449   10pf emerald   .45   .20
1432   A449   15pf rose lilac   .35   .20
1433   A449   20pf rose magenta   .75   .25
1434   A449   25pf grnsh blue   .90   .25
1435   A449   30pf orange   .20   .20
1436   A449   35pf grnsh blue   .75   .25
1437   A449   40pf dull violet   .30   .25
1438   A449   50pf blue, bluish   .35   .25
1439   A449   60pf lilac ('74)   .75   .30
1440   A449   70pf redsh brown   .65   .35
1441   A449   80pf vio blue ('74)   .75   .30
1442   A449   1m olive   1.10   .25
1443   A449a   2m lake   1.80   .20
1443A   A449a   3m rose lilac ('74)   2.25   .50
Nos. 1430-1443A (15)   11.55   3.90
See Nos. 1610-1617, 2071-2085.

Lebachia Speciosa (Oldest Conifer) A450

Fossils from Natural History Museum, Berlin: 15pf, Sphenopteris hollandica (carbon fern). 20pf, Pterodactylus kochi (flying reptile). 25pf, Botryopteris (permian fern). 35pf, Archaeopteryx lithographica (primitive reptile-like bird). 70pf, Odontopieura ovata (trilobite).

1973, Feb. 6   **Photo.**   **Perf. 13**
1444   A450   10pf multicolored   .20   .20
1445   A450   15pf ultra, gray & blk   .20   .20
1446   A450   20pf yellow & multi   .20   .20
1447   A450   25pf emerald, blk & brn   .20   .20
1448   A450   35pf ocher & multi   .20   .20
1449   A450   70pf ind, blk & yel   1.40   1.50
Nos. 1444-1449 (6)   2.40   2.50

Bobsled Track, Oberhof — A451

1973, Feb. 13 Litho. Perf. 12½x13
1450 A451 35pf dk bl, bl & org .35 .30
15th Bobsledding Championships, Oberhof.

Combines A452

Leipzig Spring Fair: 25pf, Computerized threshing and silage producing machine.

1973, Mar. 6 Litho. Perf. 13x12½
1451 A452 10pf olive & multi .20 .20
1452 A452 25pf blue & multi .30 .30

Firecrests A453

Songbirds: 10pf, White-winged crossbill. 15pf, Waxwing. 20pf, White-spotted and red-spotted bluethroats. 25pf, Goldfinch. 35pf, Golden oriole. 40pf, Gray wagtail. 50pf, Wall creeper.

1973, Mar. 20 Photo. Perf. 14x13½
1453 A453 5pf multicolored .20 .20
1454 A453 10pf multicolored .20 .20
1455 A453 15pf multicolored .20 .20
1456 A453 20pf multicolored .20 .20
1457 A453 25pf multicolored .20 .20
1458 A453 35pf multicolored .20 .20
1459 A453 40pf multicolored .25 .20
1460 A453 50pf ocher & multi 2.25 2.25
Nos. 1453-1460 (8) 3.70 3.70

Copernicus and Title Page — A454

1973, Feb. 13 Litho. Perf. 13½x13
1461 A454 70pf multicolored .75 .35
500th anniversary of the birth of Nicolaus Copernicus (1473-1543), astronomer.

Electric Locomotive — A455

Railroad Cars Manufactured in DDR: 10pf, Refrigerator car. 20pf, Long-distance coach. 25pf, Multiple tank car with pneumatic filling device. 35pf, Two-story coach. 85pf, International coaches.

1973, May 22 Litho. Perf. 13x12½
1462 A455 5pf gray & multi .20 .20
1463 A455 10pf brt blue & multi .20 .20
1464 A455 20pf dk blue & multi .20 .20
1465 A455 25pf gray & multi .20 .20
1466 A455 35pf multicolored .20 .20
1467 A455 85pf green & multi 1.90 2.00
Nos. 1462-1467 (6) 2.90 3.00

King Lear, Staged by Wolfgang Langhoff A456

Great Theatrical Productions: 25pf, Midsummer Marriage, staged by Walter Felsenstein. 35pf, Mother Courage, staged by Bertolt Brecht.

1973, May 29 Photo. Perf. 13
1468 A456 10pf maroon, rose & yel .20 .20
1469 A456 25pf vio bl, lt bl & rose .20 .20
1470 A456 35pf dk gray, bis & bl .70 .75
Nos. 1468-1470 (3) 1.10 1.15

Goethe and his Home in Weimar — A457

Fireworks, TV Tower, World Clock — A458

Designs (Portraits and Houses): 15pf, Christoph Martin Wieland. 20pf, Friedrich von Schiller. 25pf, Johann Gottfried Herder. 35pf, Lucas Cranach, the Elder. 50pf, Franz Liszt.

1973, June 26 Litho. Perf. 12½x13
1471 A457 10pf blue & multi .20 .20
1472 A457 15pf multicolored .20 .20
1473 A457 20pf multicolored .20 .20
1474 A457 25pf multicolored .20 .20
1475 A457 35pf green & multi .20 .20
1476 A457 50pf multicolored 1.90 1.10
Nos. 1471-1476 (6) 2.90 2.10
Famous men and their homes in Weimar.

1973

Designs (Festival Emblem and): 15pf, Vietnamese and European men, book and girder. 20pf, Construction workers and valve. 30pf, Negro and European students, dam and retort. 35pf, Emblems of World Federation of Democratic Youth and International Students Union. 50pf, Brandenburg Gate.

1477 A458 5pf vio blue & multi .20 .20
a. Booklet pane of 4 1.50 1.50
1478 A458 15pf olive & multi .20 .20
1479 A458 20pf multicolored .20 .20
a. Booklet pane of 4 1.50 1.50
1480 A458 30pf blue & multi .80 .60
1481 A458 35pf green & multi .20 .20
Nos. 1477-1481 (5) 1.60 1.40

Souvenir Sheet

1482 A458 50pf aqua & multi 1.00 .75
10th Festival of Youths and Students, Berlin, July 1973.
Issued: #1477-1481, July 3; #1482, July 26.

Ulbricht Type of 1961-67
1973, Aug. 8 Engr. Perf. 14
Size: 24x28½mm
1483 A189 20pf black .55 .30
In memory of Walter Ulbricht (1893-1973), chairman of Council of State.

Pylon, Map of Electric Power System — A459

1973, Aug. 14 Photo. Perf. 14
1484 A459 35pf magenta, org & lt bl .35 .30
10th anniversary of the united East European electric power system "Peace."

Sports Equipment — A460

Design: 25pf, Sailboat, guitar, electric drill.

1973, Aug. 28 Photo. Perf. 14
1485 A460 10pf multicolored .20 .20
1486 A460 25pf multicolored .30 .20
Leipzig Fall Fair and EXPOVITA exhibition for leisure time equipment.

Militiaman and Emblem A461

Designs: 20pf, Militia guarding border at Brandenburg Gate. 50pf, Representatives of Red Veterans' League, International Brigade in Spain and Workers' Militia in DDR, vert.

1973, Sept. 11 Litho. Perf. 13x12½
1487 A461 10pf multicolored .20 .20
1488 A461 20pf tan, red & blk .30 .20

Souvenir Sheet
Perf. 12½x13
1489 A461 50pf multicolored .65 .75
20th anniversary of Workers' Militia of the German Democratic Republic.

Globe and Red Flag Emblem A462

1973, Sept. 11 Photo. Perf. 13½x14
1490 A462 20pf gold & red .45 .25
15th anniversary of the review "Problems of Peace and Socialism," published in Prague in 28 languages.

Memorial, Langenstein-Zwieberge — A463

1973, Sept. 18 Perf. 14x13½
1491 A463 25pf multicolored .45 .25
In memory of the workers who perished in the subterranean munitions works at Langenstein-Zwieberge.

UN Headquarters, NY, UN and DDR Emblems — A464

1973, Sept. 21 Perf. 13
1492 A464 35pf multicolored .45 .25
Admission of the DDR to the UN.

Union Emblem A465

Rocket Launching — A466

1973, Oct. 11 Photo. Perf. 14x13½
1493 A465 35pf silver & multi .35 .30
8th Congress of the World Federation of Trade Unions, Varna, Bulgaria.

1973, Oct. 23 Perf. 14
20pf, Emblem with map of Russia & hammer & sickle, horiz. 25pf, Oil refinery, Ryazan.
1494 A466 10pf violet bl & multi .20 .20
1495 A466 20pf vio bl, red & sil .20 .20
1496 A466 25pf multicolored .75 .75
Nos. 1494-1496 (3) 1.15 1.15
Soviet Science & Technology Days in DDR.

Madonna with the Rose, by Parmigianino A467

Paintings: 10pf Child with Doll, by Christian L. Vogel. 20pf, Woman with Plaited Blond Hair, by Rubens. 25pf, Lady in White, by Titian. 35pf, Archimedes, by Domenico Fetti. 70pf, Bouquet with Blue Iris, by Jan D. de Heem.

1973, Nov. 13 Photo. Perf. 14
1497 A467 10pf gold & multi .20 .20
1498 A467 15pf gold & multi .20 .20
1499 A467 20pf gold & multi .20 .20
1500 A467 25pf gold & multi .20 .20
1501 A467 35pf gold & multi .20 .20
1502 A467 70pf gold & multi 2.10 1.40
Nos. 1497-1502 (6) 3.10 2.40

Human Rights Flame A468

1973, Nov. 20   **Perf. 13**
1503 A468 35pf dp rose, dk car &
     sil   .45 .30

25th anniv. of the Universal Declaration of Human Rights.

Boy Holding Pike — A469

Designs: Various scenes from Russian Folktale "At the Bidding of the Pike."

1973, Dec. 4   **Litho.**   **Perf. 13x13½**
1504 A469 5pf multicolored   .25 .25
1505 A469 10pf multicolored   .75 1.00
1506 A469 15pf multicolored   .25 .25
1507 A469 20pf multicolored   .25 .25
1508 A469 25pf multicolored   .75 1.00
1509 A469 35pf multicolored   .25 .25
   a.   Sheet of 6, #1504-1509   2.75 6.50

Edwin
Hoernle — A470

1974   **Litho.**   **Perf. 13½x13**
#1511, Etkar Andre. #1512, Paul Merker. #1513, Hermann Duncker. #1514, Fritz Heckert. #1515, Otto Grotewohl. #1516, Wilhelm Florin. #1517, Georg Handke. #1518, Rudolf Breitschcid. #1519, Kurt Bürgor. #1519A Carl Moltmann.

1510 A470 10pf gray green   .20 .20
1511 A470 10pf rose violet   .20 .20
1512 A470 10pf dark blue   .20 .20
1513 A470 10pf brown   .20 .20
1514 A470 10pf dull green   .20 .20
1515 A470 10pf red brown   .20 .20
1516 A470 10pf vio blue   .20 .20
1517 A470 10pf olive brown   .20 .20
1518 A470 10pf slate green   .20 .20
1519 A470 10pf dull violet   .20 .20
1519A A470 10pf brown   .20 .20
   Nos. 1510-1519A (11)   2.20 2.20

Leaders of German labor movement.
Issued: #1510-1517, Jan. 8; others July 9.

Flags of
Comecon
Members
A471

1974, Jan. 22   **Photo.**   **Perf. 13**
1520 A471 20pf red & multi   .35 .20

25th anniversary of the Council of Mutual Economic Assistance (Comecon).

Pablo
Neruda
and
Chilean
Flag
A472

1974, Jan. 22   **Perf. 14**
1521 A472 20pf multicolored   .35 .25

Pablo Neruda (Neftali Ricardo Reyes, 1904-1973), Chilean poet.

Echinopsis
Multiplex
A473

Fieldball
A474

Various Flowering Cacti: 10pf, Lobivia haageana. 15pf, Parodia sanguiniflora. 20pf, Gymnocal. monvillei. 25pf, Neoporteria rapifera. 35pf, Notocactus concinnus.

1974, Feb. 12   **Photo.**   **Perf. 14**
1522 A473 5pf multicolored   .20 .20
1523 A473 10pf tan & multi   .20 .20
1524 A473 15pf green & multi   1.90 1.90
1525 A473 20pf multicolored   .20 .20
1526 A473 25pf violet & multi   .20 .20
1527 A473 35pf multicolored   .25 .25
   Nos. 1522-1527 (6)   2.95 2.95

1974, Feb. 26   **Litho.**   **Perf. 13**
Design: Various fieldball scenes.

1528 A474 5pf green & multi   .30 .30
1529 A474 10pf green & multi   .30 .30
1530 A474 35pf green & multi   1.10 1.10
   a.   Strip of 3, #1528-1530   1.90 1.90

8th World Fieldball Championships for Men.

Power Testing
Station — A475

Leipzig Spring Fair: 25pf, Robotron EC 2040 data processer, horiz.

1974, Mar. 5   **Photo.**   **Perf. 14**
1531 A475 10pf multicolored   .20 .20
1532 A475 25pf multicolored   .30 .20

Poisonous
European
Mushrooms
A476

1974, Mar. 19   **Litho.**   **Perf. 13x13½**
Designs: 5pf, Rhodophyllus Sinuatus. 10pf, Boletus satanas. 15pf, Amanita pantherina. 20pf, Amanita muscaria. 25pf, Gyromitra esculenta. 30pf, Inocybe patouillardii. 35pf, Amanita phalloides. 40pf, Clitocybe dealbata.

1533 A476 5pf buff & multi   .20 .20
1534 A476 10pf buff & multi   .20 .20
1535 A476 15pf buff & multi   .20 .20
1536 A476 20pf buff & multi   .20 .20
1537 A476 25pf buff & multi   .20 .20
1538 A476 30pf buff & multi   .25 .20
1539 A476 35pf buff & multi   .25 .20
1540 A476 40pf buff & multi   1.25 1.25
   Nos. 1533-1540 (8)   2.75 2.65

Gustav Robert
Kirchhoff — A477

Portraits: 10pf, Immanuel Kant. 20pf, Ehm Welk. 25pf, Johann Gottfried Herder. 35pf, Lion Feuchtwanger.

1974, Mar. 26   **Litho.**   **Perf. 13½x13**
1541 A477 5pf black & gray   .20 .20
1542 A477 10pf vio bl & dull bl   .20 .20
1543 A477 20pf maroon & rose   .20 .20
1544 A477 25pf slate grn & grn   .20 .20
1545 A477 35pf brn & lt brn   .60 .50
   Nos. 1541-1545 (5)   1.40 1.30

"Peace"
A477a

1974, Apr. 16   **Perf. 13**
1548 A477a 35pf silver & multi   .35 .30

1st World Peace Congress, 25th anniv.

Oil Pipeline
Operator
and Arms
of DDR
A477b

1974, Apr. 30   **Photo.**   **Perf. 13**
1549 A477b 10pf shown   .20 .20
1550 A477b 20pf Students   .20 .20
1551 A477b 25pf Woman worker   .20 .20
1552 A477b 35pf Family   .85 .85
   Nos. 1549-1552 (4)   1.45 1.45

25th anniv. of the DDR.

Buk Lighthouse,
1878, and
Map — A478

Lighthouses, Maps and Nautical Charts: 15pf, Warnemünde, 1898. 20pf, Darsser Ort, 1848. 35pf, Arkona, 1827 and 1902. 40pf, Greifswalder Oie, 1855.

1974, May 7   **Litho.**   **Perf. 14**
1553 A478 10pf multicolored   .20 .20
1554 A478 15pf multicolored   .20 .20
1555 A478 20pf multicolored   .20 .20
1556 A478 35pf multicolored   .20 .20
1557 A478 40pf multicolored   1.00 .80
   Nos. 1553-1557 (5)   1.80 1.60

Hydrographic Service of German Democratic Republic. See Nos. 1645-1649.

The Ages of Man, by C. D.
Friedrich — A479

C. D. Friedrich, Self-portrait — A480

Paintings by Friedrich: 10pf, Two Men Observing Moon. 25pf, The Heath near Dresden. 35pf, View of Elbe Valley.

1974, May 21   **Photo.**   **Perf. 13½**
1558 A479 10pf gold & multi   .20 .20
1559 A479 20pf gold & multi   .20 .20
1560 A479 25pf gold & multi   1.50 1.50
1561 A479 35pf gold & multi   .25 .20
   Nos. 1558-1561 (4)   2.15 2.10

Souvenir Sheet
Engr.
Perf. 14x13½
1562 A480 70pf sepia   1.20 1.60

Caspar David Friedrich (1774-1840), German Romantic painter.

Plauen
Lace — A481

Designs: Various Plauen lace patterns.

1974, June 11   **Litho.**   **Perf. 13**
1563 A481 10pf violet, lil & blk   .20 .20
1564 A481 20pf brown ol & blk   .20 .20
1565 A481 25pf bl, lt bl & blk   1.10 1.10
1566 A481 35pf lil rose, rose &
         blk   .20 .20
   Nos. 1563-1566 (4)   1.70 1.70

Trotter — A482

Designs: 10pf, Thoroughbred hurdling, vert. 25pf, Haflinger breed horses. 35pf, British thoroughbred race horse.

Perf. 14x13½, 13½x14
1974, Aug. 13   **Photo.**
1570 A482 10pf olive & multi   .20 .20
1571 A482 20pf multicolored   .20 .20
1572 A482 25pf lt blue & multi   1.25 1.40
1573 A482 35pf ocher & multi   .20 .20
   Nos. 1570-1573 (4)   1.85 2.00

International Horse Breeders' of Socialist Countries Congress, Berlin.

Crane Lifting Diesel
Locomotive — A483

Leipzig Fall Fair: 25pf, Sugar beet harvester, type KS6.

1974, Aug. 27   **Litho.**   **Perf. 13x12½**
1574 A483 10pf multicolored   .20 .20
1575 A483 25pf orange & multi   .30 .25

Miniature China
and Mirror
Exhibits — A484

Designs: Scenes from 18th century Thuringia, Dolls' Village, Arnstadt Castle Museum.

1974, Sept. 10   **Photo.**   **Perf. 14x13½**
1576 A484 5pf shown   .20 .20
1577 A484 10pf Harlequin barker
        at Fair   .20 .20

1578	A484	15pf Wine tasters	.20	.20
1579	A484	20pf Cooper and apprentice	.20	.20
1580	A484	25pf Bagpiper	1.10	1.25
1581	A484	35pf Butcher and beggar, women	.20	.20
		Nos. 1576-1581 (6)	2.10	2.25

Bound Guerrillas, Ardeatine Caves,
Rome — A485

Design: No. 1583, Resistance Fighters,
monument near Chateaubriant, France.

1974, Sept. 24   Perf. 13½x14

1582	A485	35pf green, blk & red	.30	.30
1583	A485	35pf blue, blk & red	.30	.30

International war memorials.

Souvenir Sheet

Family and Flag — A486

1974, Oct. 3   Photo.   Perf. 13

1584	A486	1m multicolored	1.25	1.25

25th anniv. of the DDR.

Freighter and Paddle
Steamer — A487

Cent. of the UPU: 20pf, Old steam locomotive and modern Diesel. 25pf, Bi-plane and jet. 35pf, Mail coach and truck.

1974, Oct. 9   Perf. 14

1585	A487	10pf green & multi	.20	.20
1586	A487	20pf multicolored	.20	.20
1587	A487	25pf blue & multi	.20	.20
1588	A487	35pf multicolored	.90	.75
		Nos. 1585-1588 (4)	1.50	1.35

"In Praise of
Dialectics"
A488

1974, Oct. 24   Litho.   Perf. 13x13½

Designs: 10pf+5pf, "Praise to the Revolutionaries." 25pf, "Praise to the Party." Designs

are from bas-reliefs by Rossdeutscher, Jastram and Wetzel, illustrating poems by Bertholt Brecht.

1589	A488	10pf + 5pf multi	.20	.20
1590	A488	20pf multicolored	.20	.20
1591	A488	25pf multicolored	.20	.20
	a.	Strip of 3, #1589-1591	1.10	1.10

DDR '74 Natl. Stamp Exhib., Karl-Marx-Stadt.

Souvenir Sheet

Drawings by Young Pioneers — A489

1974, Nov. 26   Litho.   Perf. 14

1592	A489	Sheet of 4	1.50	1.50
	a.	20pf Sun shines on everybody	.30	.30
	b.	20pf My Friend Sascha	.30	.30
	c.	20pf Carsten, the Best Swimmer	.30	.30
	d.	20pf Me at the Blackboard	.30	.30

Young Pioneers' drawings (7-10 years old).

Man Cutting Tree,
and Bird — A490

Designs: Various scenes from Russian folktale "Twittering To and Fro."

1974, Dec. 3   Perf. 13x13½

1593	A490	10pf multicolored	.20	.20
1594	A490	15pf multicolored	.85	.85
1595	A490	20pf multicolored	.20	.20
1596	A490	30pf multicolored	.20	.20
1597	A490	35pf multicolored	.85	.85
1598	A490	40pf multicolored	.20	.20
	a.	Sheet of 6, #1593-1598	2.50	3.00

Meditating Girl,
by Wilhelm
Lachnit — A491

1974, Dec. 10   Perf. 13½x14, 14x13½

Paintings: 10pf, Still Life, by Ronald Paris, horiz. 20pf, Fisherman's House, Vitte, by Harald Hakenbeck. 35pf, Girl in Red, by Rudolf Bergander, horiz. 70pf, The Artist's Parents, by Willi Sitte.

1599	A491	10pf multicolored	.20	.20
1600	A491	15pf multicolored	.20	.20
1601	A491	20pf multicolored	.20	.20
1602	A491	35pf multicolored	.25	.20
1603	A491	70pf multicolored	1.50	1.50
		Nos. 1599-1603 (5)	2.35	2.30

Paintings in Berlin Museums.

Banded
Jasper — A492

Minerals from the collection of the Mining Academy in Freiberg: 15pf, Smoky quartz. 20pf, Topaz. 25pf, Amethyst. 35pf, Aquamarine. 70pf, Agate.

1974, Dec. 17   Photo.   Perf. 14

1604	A492	10pf lt yellow & multi	.20	.20
1605	A492	15pf lt yellow & multi	.20	.20
1606	A492	20pf lt yellow & multi	.20	.20
1607	A492	25pf lt yellow & multi	.20	.20
1608	A492	35pf lt yellow & multi	.25	.20
1609	A492	70pf lt yellow & multi	1.50	1.50
		Nos. 1604-1609 (6)	2.55	2.50

Type of 1973
Coil Stamps

1974-75   Photo.   Perf. 14
Size: 21x17½mm

1610	A449	5pf blue grn ('74)	.20	.20
1611	A449	10pf emerald	.35	.35
1612	A449	20pf rose magenta	.35	.35
1613	A449	25pf green ('75)	.35	.25
1615	A449	50pf blue ('74)	.65	.50
1617	A449	1m olive ('74)	.90	.90
		Nos. 1610-1617 (6)	2.80	2.55

Black control number on back of every fifth stamp.

The 20pf was issued in sheets of 100 in 1975.

Martha Arendsee
(1885-1953),
Communist
Politician — A493

1975, Jan. 14   Litho.   Perf. 13½x13

1618	A493	10pf dull red	.30	.20

Souvenir Sheet

Peasants' War, Contemporary
Woodcuts — A494

1975, Feb. 11   Perf. 12½x13

1619	A494	Sheet of 6 + label	3.00	3.00
	a.	5pf Forced labor	.30	.30
	b.	10pf Peasant paying tithe	.30	.30
	c.	20pf Thomas Munzer	.30	.30
	d.	25pf Armed peasants	.55	.55
	e.	35pf Peasant, "Liberty" flag	.55	.55
	f.	50pf Peasant on trial	.30	.30

Peasants' War, 450th anniversary.

Black
Women — A495

Designs: 20pf, Caucasian women. 25pf, Indian woman and child.

1975, Feb. 25   Litho.   Perf. 13

1620	A495	10pf red & multi	.25	.25
1621	A495	20pf red & multi	.25	.25
1622	A495	25pf red & multi	.25	.25
	a.	Strip of 3, Nos. 1620-1622	1.00	.95

International Women's Year 1975.

Microfilm
Pentakta
Camera
A496

Leipzig Spring Fair: 25pf, Sket cement plant.

1975, Mar. 4   Photo.   Perf. 14

1623	A496	10pf ultra & multi	.25	.20
1624	A496	25pf orange & multi	.25	.25

A497

Portraits: 5pf, Hans Otto (1900-33), actor. 10pf, Thomas Mann (1875-1955), writer. 20pf, Albert Schweitzer (1875-1965), medical missionary. 25pf, Michelangelo (1475-1564), painter and sculptor. 35pf, André Marie Ampère (1775-1836), scientist.

1975, Mar. 18   Litho.   Perf. 13½x13

1625	A497	5pf dk blue	.20	.20
1626	A497	10pf dk car rose	.20	.20
1627	A497	20pf dk green	.20	.20
1628	A497	25pf sepia	.20	.20
1629	A497	35pf vio blue	.75	.65
		Nos. 1625-1629 (5)	1.55	1.45

Famous men, birth anniversaries.

A498

German Zoological Gardens: 5pf, Blue and yellow macaws, Magdeburg Zoo. 10pf, Orangutan family, Dresden. 15pf, Siberian chamois, Halle. 20pf, Rhinoceros, Berlin. 25pf, Dwarf hippopotamus, Erfurt. 30pf, Baltic seal and pup, Rostock. 35pf, Siberian tiger, Leipzig. 50pf, Boehm's zebra, Cottbus. 20pf, 25pf, 30pf, 35pf are horiz.

1975, Mar. 25   Perf. 13½x13, 13x13½

1630	A498	5pf multicolored	.20	.20
1631	A498	10pf multicolored	.20	.20
1632	A498	15pf multicolored	.20	.20
1633	A498	20pf multicolored	.20	.20
1634	A498	25pf multicolored	.20	.20
1635	A498	30pf multicolored	.20	.20
1636	A498	35pf multicolored	.20	.20
1637	A498	50pf multicolored	1.40	1.40
		Nos. 1630-1637 (8)	2.80	2.80

Soldiers, Industry and
Agriculture — A499

1975, May 6   Photo.   Perf. 13½x14

1638	A499	20pf multicolored	1.00	.30

20th anniv. of the signing of the Warsaw Treaty (Bulgaria, Czechoslovakia, DDR, Hungary, Poland, Romania, USSR).

Soviet War
Memorial,
Berlin-Treptow
A500

Designs (Arms of German Democratic Rep. and): 20pf, Buchenwald Memorial (detail). 25pf, Woman reconstruction worker. 35pf, Skyscraper and statue at Orenburg (economic integration). 50pf, Soldier raising Red Flag on Reichstag Building, Berlin.

1975, May 6   *Perf. 14x13½*
1639	A500	10pf red & multi	.20 .20
1640	A500	20pf red & multi	.20 .20
1641	A500	25pf red & multi	.20 .20
1642	A500	35pf red & multi	.60 .60
		Nos. 1639-1642 (4)	1.20 1.20

Souvenir Sheet
Imperf
1643	A500	50pf red & multi	.70 .70

30th anniversary of liberation from fascism.

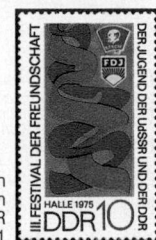

Ribbons, Youth Organization Emblems of DDR and USSR — A501

1975, May 13   *Perf. 14*
1644	A501	10pf multicolored	.35 .20

Third Friendship Festival of Russian and German Youths, Halle, 1975.

Lighthouse Type of 1974

Lighthouses, Maps and Nautical Charts: 5pf, Timmendorf, 1872. 10pf, Gellen, 1905. 20pf, Sassnitz, 1904. 25pf, Dornbush, 1888. 35pf, Peenemünde, 1954.

1975, May 13   *Litho.*   *Perf. 14*
1645	A478	5pf multicolored	.20 .20
1646	A478	10pf multicolored	.20 .20
1647	A478	20pf multicolored	.20 .20
1648	A478	25pf multicolored	.20 .20
1649	A478	35pf multicolored	.75 .75
		Nos. 1645-1649 (5)	1.55 1.55

Hydrographic Service of the DDR.

Wilhelm Liebknecht, August Bebel — A502

20pf, Tivoli House & front page of Protocol of Gotha. 25pf, Karl Marx & Friedrich Engels.

1975, May 21   *Photo.*
1650	A502	10pf buff, brn & red	.20 .20
1651	A502	20pf salmon, brn & red	.20 .20
1652	A502	25pf buff, brn & red	.20 .20
a.		Strip of 3, #1650-1652	1.00 1.00

Centenary of the Congress of Gotha, the beginning of German Socialist Workers' Party.

Construction Workers, Union Emblem — A503

1975, June 10   *Photo.*   *Perf. 14*
1653	A503	20pf red & multi	.30 .20

Free German Association of Trade Unions (FDGB), 30th anniversary.

"Socialist Scientific Cooperation" Mosaic by Walter Womacka A504

1975, June 10   *Litho.*   *Perf. 13*
1654	A504	20pf multicolored	.30 .20

Eisenhüttenstadt, first socialist city of DDR, 25th anniversary.

Automatic Clock by Paulus Schuster, 1585 — A505

Clocks, Dresden Museums: 10pf, Astronomical table clock, Augsburg, c. 1560. 15pf, Automatic clock, Hans Schlottheim, c. 1600. 20pf, Table clock, Johann Heinrich Köhler, c. 1720. 25pf, Table clock, Köhler, c. 1700. 35pf, Astronomical clock, Johannes Klein, 1738.

1975, June 24   *Photo.*   *Perf. 14*
1655	A505	5pf multicolored	.20 .20
1656	A505	10pf ultra & multi	.20 .20
1657	A505	15pf red & multi	1.10 1.10
1658	A505	20pf olive & multi	.20 .20
1659	A505	25pf multicolored	.20 .20
1660	A505	35pf ocher & multi	.20 .20
		Nos. 1655-1660 (6)	2.10 2.10

Dictionary, Compiled by Jacob and Wilhelm Grimm — A506

20pf, Karl-Schwarzschild Observatory, Tautenburg near Jena. 25pf, Electron microscope & chemical plant (scientific & practical cooperation). 35pf, Intercosmos 10 satellite.

1975, July 2   *Litho.*   *Perf. 13½x12½*
1661	A506	10pf plum, ol & blk	.20 .20
1662	A506	20pf vio bl & blk	.20 .20
1663	A506	25pf green, yel & blk	.20 .20
1664	A506	35pf blue & multi	.75 .75
		Nos. 1661-1664 (4)	1.35 1.35

German Academy of Sciences, 275th anniv.

Torch Bearer — A507

1975, July 15   *Perf. 13½x13*
1665	A507	10pf shown	.20 .20
1666	A507	20pf Hurdling	.20 .20
1667	A507	25pf Diving	.20 .20
1668	A507	35pf Gymnast on bar	.75 .75
		Nos. 1665-1668 (4)	1.35 1.35

5th Children and Youths Spartakiad.

Map of Europe A508

1975, July 30   *Photo.*   *Perf. 13*
1669	A508	20pf multicolored	.35 .25

European Security and Cooperation Conference, Helsinki, July 30-Aug. 1.

China Aster — A509

Medimorph Anesthesia Unit — A510

1975, Aug. 19   *Photo.*   *Perf. 13½x14*
1670	A509	5pf shown	.20 .20
1671	A509	10pf Geranium	.20 .20
1672	A509	20pf Transvaal daisies	.20 .20
1673	A509	25pf Carnation	.20 .20
1674	A509	35pf Chrysanthemum	.25 .20
1675	A509	70pf Pansies	2.10 1.90
		Nos. 1670-1675 (6)	3.15 2.90

1975, Aug. 28   *Perf. 14*

Leipzig Fall Fair: 25pf, Motorcycle, type MZ TS 250, horiz.
1676	A510	10pf multicolored	.20 .20
1677	A510	25pf yellow & multi	.35 .25

Children and Child Crossing Guard A511

Designs: 15pf, Traffic policewoman. 20pf, Policeman helping, motorist. 25pf, Motor vehicle inspection. 35pf, Volunteer instructor.

1975, Sept. 9   *Litho.*   *Perf. 13x12½*
1678	A511	10pf multicolored	.20 .20
1679	A511	15pf green & multi	1.20 .75
1680	A511	20pf brown & multi	.20 .20
1681	A511	25pf violet & multi	.20 .20
1682	A511	35pf multicolored	.20 .20
		Nos. 1678-1682 (5)	2.00 1.55

Traffic police serving and instructing the public.

Soyuz Take-off — A512

Designs: 20pf, Soyuz and Apollo in space. 70pf, Spacecraft after link-up, horiz., 79x28mm.

1975, Sept. 15   *Perf. 14x13½, 13½x14*   *Photo.*
1683	A512	10pf multicolored	.20 .20
1684	A512	20pf multicolored	.20 .20
1685	A512	70pf multicolored	1.50 1.50
		Nos. 1683-1685 (3)	1.90 1.90

Apollo Soyuz space test project (Russo-American space cooperation), launching July 15; link-up, July 17.

Weimar, 1630, after Merian — A513

Designs: 20pf, Buchenwald Liberation Monument, vert. 35pf, Composite view of old and new buildings in Weimar.

1975, Sept. 23   *Litho.*   *Perf. 13½x13*
1686	A513	10pf green, gray & blk	.20 .20
1687	A513	20pf red & multi	.20 .20
1688	A513	35pf ultra & multi	.45 .45
		Nos. 1686-1688 (3)	.85 .85

Millennium of Weimar.

Monument, Vienna — A514

1975, Oct. 14   *Photo.*   *Perf. 14x13½*
1689	A514	35pf red & multi	.35 .20

Memorial for the victims of the struggle for a free Austria, 1934-1945.

Louis Braille and Dots — A515

Designs: 35pf, Hands reading Braille. 50pf, Eyeball and protective glasses.

1975, Oct. 14
1690	A515	20pf gray & multi	.20 .20
1691	A515	35pf multicolored	.20 .20
1692	A515	50pf multicolored	1.20 1.20
		Nos. 1690-1692 (3)	1.60 1.60

World Braille Year 1975. Sesquicentennial of the invention of Braille system of writing for the blind, by Louis Braille (1809-1852).

Post Office Bärenfels A516

1975, Oct. 21   *Photo.*   *Perf. 14*
1693	A516	20pf multicolored	.20 .20

Philatelists' Day 1975. See No. B177.

Emperor Ordering Clothes — A517

Designs: Scenes from "The Emperor's New Clothes," by Hans Christian Andersen and Andersen portrait.

1975, Nov. 18   Litho.   Perf. 14x13
1694 A517 20pf ocher & multi   .35   .35
1695 A517 35pf ocher & multi   .60   .60
1696 A517 50pf ocher & multi   .35   .35
  a.   Sheet of 3, #1694-1696   1.90 1.90

Tobogganing and Olympic Rings — A518

Olympic Rings and: 20pf, Speed-skating Rink, Berlin. 35pf, Figure-skating Hall, Karl-Marx Stadt. 70pf, Mass skiing at Schmiedefeld. 1m, Innsbruck & surrounding mountains.

1975, Dec. 2   Photo.   Perf. 14
1697 A518 5pf multicolored   .20   .20
1698 A518 20pf olive & multi   .20   .20
1699 A518 35pf multicolored   .25   .20
1700 A518 70pf multicolored   1.60 1.50
  Nos. 1697-1700,B178-B179 (6)   2.70 2.50

Souvenir Sheet
1701 A518 1m ultra & multi   1.90 1.50
12th Winter Olympic Games, Innsbruck, Austria, Feb. 4-15, 1976.
No. 1701 contains one 32x27mm stamp.

Pres. Wilhelm Pieck (1876-1960) A519

1975, Dec. 30   Litho.   Perf. 13½x13
1702 A519 10pf lt ultra & blk   .25   .20

Ernst Thälmann (1886-1944) A520

Labor Leaders: No. 1704, Georg Schumann (1886-1945). No. 1705, Wilhelm Koenen (1886-1963). No. 1706, John Schehr (1896-1934).

1976, Jan. 13   Perf. 13½x13
1703 A520 10pf rose & blk   .20   .20
1704 A520 10pf emerald & blk   .20   .20
1705 A520 10pf ocher & blk   .20   .20
1706 A520 10pf violet & blk   .20   .20
  Nos. 1703-1706 (4)   .80   .80

See Nos. 1852-1854.

Silbermann Organ, Rötha — A521

Silbermann Organs: 20pf, Freiberg. 35pf, Fraureuth. 50pf, Dresden.

1976, Jan. 27   Photo.   Perf. 14
1707 A521 10pf green & multi   .20   .20
1708 A521 20pf red & multi   .20   .20
1709 A521 35pf multicolored   .20   .20
1710 A521 50pf brown & multi   1.10   .90
  Nos. 1707-1710 (4)   1.70 1.50
Organs built by Gottfried Silbermann (1683-1753).

Souvenir Sheet

Richard Sorge — A522

1976, Feb. 3   Litho.   Imperf.
1711 A522 1m multicolored   1.60 1.60
Dr. Richard Sorge (1895-1944), Soviet intelligence agent. No. 1711 contains one stamp with simulated perforations.

Military Flag, Sailor, Soldier, Aviator — A523

20pf, Military flag, ships, tanks, missile & planes.

1976, Feb. 24   Litho.   Perf. 13½x14
1712 A523 10pf multicolored   .20   .20
1713 A523 20pf multicolored   .30   .25
National People's Army, 20th anniversary.

Telephone A524

Apartment House, Leipzig A525

1976, Mar. 2   Perf. 13
1714 A524 20pf light blue   .30   .20
Centenary of first telephone call by Alexander Graham Bell, March 10, 1876.

1976, Mar. 9   Photo.   Perf. 14
Design: 25pf, Ocean super trawler, horiz.
1715 A525 10pf green & multi   .20   .20
1716 A525 25pf vio blue, blk & grn   .35   .25
Leipzig Spring Fair.

Palace of the Republic — A526

1976, Apr. 22   Photo.   Perf. 14
1717 A526 10pf vio blue & multi   .70   .20
Inauguration of Palace of the Republic, Berlin. See No. 1721.

Post Office Radar Station — A527

1976, Apr. 27   Photo.   Perf. 13½x14
1718 A527 20pf multicolored   .30   .20
Intersputnik 1976.

Marx, Engels, Lenin and Party Flag — A528

20pf, New factories & apartment houses, party flag, horiz. 1m, Palace of the Republic.

1976, May 11   Perf. 14x13½, 13½x14
1719 A528 10pf dp mag, gold & red   .25   .20
1720 A528 20pf multicolored   .25   .20

Souvenir Sheet
Perf. 14
1721 A526 1m multicolored   1.25 1.25
9th Congress of Unity Party (SED).

Peace Bicycle Race and Olympic Rings — A529

Designs: 20pf, Town and sport halls, Suhl. 25pf, Regatta course, Brandenburg. 70pf, 1500-meter race. 1m, Central Stadium, Leipzig.

1976, May 18   Photo.   Perf. 13½x14
1722 A529 5pf green & multi   .20   .20
1723 A529 20pf blue & multi   .20   .20
1724 A529 25pf multicolored   .20   .20
1725 A529 70pf ultra & multi   1.90 1.75
  Nos. 1722-1725,B180-B181 (6)   2.95 2.75

Souvenir Sheet
Perf. 14
1726 A529 1m multicolored   1.40 1.40
21st Olympic Games, Montreal, Canada, July 17-Aug. 1. No. 1726 contains one stamp (32x27mm).

Ribbons and Emblem A530

Design: 20pf, Young man and woman, industrial installations.

1976, May 25   Perf. 14
1727 A530 10pf blue & multi   .20   .20
1728 A530 20pf multicolored   .25   .20
10th Parliamentary Meeting of the Free German Youth Organization.

Himantoglossum Hircinum — A531

Designs: European orchids.

1976, June 15   Litho.   Perf. 12½x13
1729 A531 10pf shown   .20   .20
1730 A531 20pf Dactylorhiza incarnata   .20   .20
1731 A531 25pf Anacamptis pyramidalis   .20   .20
1732 A531 35pf Dactylorhiza sambucina   .25   .20
1733 A531 40pf Orchis coriophora   .25   .20
1734 A531 50pf Cypripedium calceolus   2.10 1.75
  Nos. 1729-1734 (6)   3.20 2.75

Dancer at Rest, by Walter Arnold — A532

Small Sculptures: 10pf, Shetland Pony, by Heinrich Drake, horiz. 25pf, "At the Beach," by Ludwig Engelhardt. 35pf, Hermann Duncker, by Walter Howard. 50pf, "The Conversation," by Gustav Weidanz.

1976, June 22   Photo.   Perf. 14
1735 A532 10pf blk & bl grn   .20   .20
1736 A532 20pf ocher & blk   .20   .20
1737 A532 25pf ocher & blk   .20   .20
1738 A532 35pf yel grn & blk   .20   .20
1739 A532 50pf brick red & blk   1.50 1.50
  Nos. 1735-1739 (5)   2.30 2.30

Marx, Engels, Lenin, Red Flags, Berlin Buildings A533

1976, June 29   Photo.   Perf. 14
1740 A533 20pf blue, red & dk red   .35   .20
European Communist Workers' Congress, Berlin.

Coronation Coach, 1790 — A534

Historic Coaches: 20pf, Open carriage, Russia, 1800. 25pf, Court landau, Saxony, 1840. 35pf, State carriage, Saxony, 1860. 40pf, Mail coach, 1850. 50pf, Town carriage, Saxony, 1889.

1976, July 27
1741 A534 10pf multicolored   .20   .20
1742 A534 20pf multicolored   .20   .20
1743 A534 25pf multicolored   .20   .20
1744 A534 35pf multicolored   .20   .20

1745	A534	40pf multicolored	.25 .20
1746	A534	50pf multicolored	2.25 2.00
		Nos. 1741-1746 (6)	3.30 3.00

View of Gera A535

Design: 10pf+5pf, View of Gera, c. 1652.

1976, Aug. 5   Litho.   Perf. 13
1747	A535	10pf + 5pf multi	.20 .20
1748	A535	20pf multicolored	.20 .20
a.		Pair, #1747-1748 + label	.90 .75

4th German Youth Philatelic Exhib., Gera.

Boxer — A536

Dogs: 10pf, Airedale terrier. 20pf, German shepherd. 25pf, Collie. 35pf, Giant schnauzer. 70pf, Great Dane.

1976, Aug. 17   Perf. 14
1749	A536	5pf multicolored	.20 .20
1750	A536	10pf multicolored	.20 .20
1751	A536	20pf multicolored	.20 .20
1752	A536	25pf multicolored	.20 .20
1753	A536	35pf multicolored	.20 .20
1754	A536	70pf multicolored	2.00 2.10
		Nos. 1749-1754 (6)	3.00 3.10

Oil Distillery A537

Design: 25pf, German Library, Leipzig.

1976, Sept. 1   Perf. 13x12½
1755	A537	10pf multicolored	.20 .20
1756	A537	25pf multicolored	.30 .20

Leipzig Fall Fair.

Templin Lake Bridge — A538

Designs: 15pf, Overpass, Berlin-Adlergestell. 20pf, Elbe River Bridge, Rosslau. 25pf, Göltzschtal Viaduct. 35pf, Elbe River Bridge, Magdeburg. 50pf, Grosser Dreesch Overpass, Schwerin.

1976, Sept. 21   Photo.   Perf. 14
1757	A538	10pf multicolored	.20 .20
1758	A538	15pf multicolored	.20 .20
1759	A538	20pf multicolored	.20 .20
1760	A538	25pf multicolored	.20 .20
1761	A538	35pf multicolored	.20 .20
1762	A538	50pf multicolored	1.50 1.60
		Nos. 1757-1762 (6)	2.50 2.60

Memorial Monument (detail), Budapest — A539

1976, Oct. 5   Photo.   Perf. 14
1763	A539	35pf tan & multi	.35 .30

Memorial to World War II victims.

Brass Jug, c. 1500 — A540

Artistic Handicraft Works: 20pf, Faience vase with lid, c. 1710. 25pf, Porcelain centerpiece (woman carrying bowl), c. 1768. 35pf, Porter, gilded silver, c. 1700. 70pf, Art Nouveau glass vase, c. 1900.

1976, Oct. 19
1764	A540	10pf dk car & multi	.20 .20
1765	A540	20pf ultra & multi	.20 .20
1766	A540	25pf green & multi	.20 .20
1767	A540	35pf vio blue & multi	.20 .20
1768	A540	70pf red brn & multi	1.60 1.60
		Nos. 1764-1768 (5)	2.40 2.40

Guppy A541

Designs: Various guppies.

1976, Nov. 9   Litho.   Perf. 13½x13
1769	A541	10pf multicolored	.20 .20
1770	A541	15pf multicolored	.20 .20
1771	A541	20pf multicolored	.20 .20
1772	A541	25pf multicolored	.20 .20
1773	A541	35pf multicolored	.20 .20
1774	A541	70pf multicolored	1.80 1.80
		Nos. 1769-1774 (6)	2.80 2.80

Vessels, c. 3000 B.C. — A542

20pf, Cult cart, c. 1300 B.C. 25pf, Roman gold coin, 270-273 A.D. 35pf, Gold pendant, 950 A.D. 70pf, Glass cup, 3rd cent. A.D.

1976, Nov. 23   Perf. 13
1775	A542	10pf multicolored	.20 .20
1776	A542	20pf multicolored	.20 .20
1777	A542	25pf multicolored	.20 .20
1778	A542	35pf multicolored	.20 .20
1779	A542	70pf multicolored	1.60 1.60
		Nos. 1775-1779 (5)	2.40 2.40

Archaeological finds in DDR.

"Air," by Rosalba Carriera — A543

Paintings, Dresden Museum: 15pf, Virgin and Child, by Murillo. 20pf, Woman Viola da Gamba Player, by Bernardo Strozzi. 25pf, Ariadne Forsaken, by Angelica Kauffmann. 35pf, Old Man with Black Cap, by Bartolomeo Nazzari. 70pf, Officer Reading a Letter, by Gerard Terborch.

1976, Dec. 14   Photo.   Perf. 13½x14
1780	A543	10pf multicolored	.20 .20
1781	A543	15pf multicolored	.20 .20
1782	A543	20pf multicolored	.20 .20
1783	A543	25pf multicolored	.20 .20
1784	A543	35pf multicolored	.20 .20
1785	A543	70pf multicolored	1.90 1.75
		Nos. 1780-1785 (6)	2.90 2.75

Rumpelstiltskin and King — A544

Scenes from fairy tale "Rumpel-stiltskin."

1976, Dec. 14   Litho.   Perf. 13
1786	A544	5pf multicolored	.20 .20
1787	A544	10pf multicolored	.55 .55
1788	A544	15pf multicolored	.20 .20
1789	A544	20pf multicolored	.20 .20
1790	A544	25pf multicolored	.55 .55
1791	A544	30pf multicolored	.20 .20
a.		Sheet of 6, #1786-1791	2.40 2.40

Arnold Zweig and Quotation A545

Designs: 20pf, Otto von Guericke and Magdeburg hemispheres. 35pf, Albrecht D. Thaer, wheat, plow and sheep. 40pf, Gustav Hertz and diagram of separation of isotopes.

1977, Feb. 8   Litho.   Perf. 13x12½
1792	A545	10pf rose & blk	.20 .20
1793	A545	20pf gray & blk	.20 .20
1794	A545	35pf lt green & blk	.20 .20
1795	A545	40pf blue & blk	.75 .75
		Nos. 1792-1795 (4)	1.35 1.35

Zweig (1887-1968), novelist; von Guericke (1602-86), physicist; Thaer (1752-1828), agronomist & physician; Hertz (1887-1975), physicist.

Spring near Plaue — A546

Natural Monuments: 20pf, Small Organ, Johnsdorf. 25pf, Ivenacker Oaks, Reuterstadt. 35pf, Stone Rose, Saalburg. 50pf, Rauenscher Stein (boulder), Furstenwalde.

1977, Feb. 24   Litho.   Perf. 12½x13
1796	A546	10pf multicolored	.20 .20
1797	A546	20pf multicolored	.20 .20
1798	A546	25pf multicolored	.20 .20
1799	A546	35pf multicolored	.20 .20
1800	A546	50pf multicolored	1.20 1.20
		Nos. 1796-1800 (5)	2.00 2.00

Fair Building, Book Fair A547

Leipzig Spring Fair: 25pf, Wide aluminum roll casting machine, Nachterstedt factory.

1977, Mar. 8   Photo.   Perf. 14
1801	A547	10pf multicolored	.20 .20
1802	A547	25pf multicolored	.25 .20

Costume Senftenberg A548

Start after Wheel Change A549

Sorbian Costumes from: 20pf, Bautzen. 25pf, Klitten. 35pf, Nochten. 70pf, Muskau.

1977, Mar. 22
1803	A548	10pf multicolored	.20 .20
1804	A548	20pf multicolored	.20 .20
1805	A548	25pf multicolored	.20 .20
1806	A548	35pf multicolored	.20 .20
1807	A548	70pf multicolored	2.00 1.75
		Nos. 1803-1807 (5)	2.80 2.55

1977, Apr. 19   Photo.   Perf. 14

Designs: 20pf, Sprint. 35pf, At finish line.
1808	A549	10pf multicolored	.25 .25
1809	A549	20pf multicolored	.25 .25
1810	A549	35pf multicolored	.25 .25
a.		Strip of 3. #1808-1810	1.20 1.20

30th International Peace Bicycling Race.

Carl Friedrich Gauss A550

1977, Apr. 19   Litho.   Perf. 13x12½
1811	A550	20pf lt ultra & blk	.55 .25

Carl Friedrich Gauss (1777-1855), mathematician, 200th birth anniversary.

Flags and Handshake A551

1977, May 3   Photo.   Perf. 13
1812	A551	20pf vio bl & multi	.30 .20

9th German Trade Union Congress, Berlin.

VKM Channel Converter, Filter and ITU Emblem — A552

1977, May 17   Litho.   Perf. 14
1813	A552	20pf multicolored	.30 .20

International Telecommunications Day.

Pistol Shooting A553

Designs: 20pf, Deep-sea diver. 35pf, Radio controlled model boat.

1977, May 17   **Photo.**
1814 A553 10pf lt green & multi   .20   .20
1815 A553 20pf lt blue & multi   .20   .20
1816 A553 35pf salmon & multi   .70   .70
    Nos. 1814-1816 (3)   1.10 1.10

Organization for Physical and Technical Training.

Accordion, c. 1900 — A554

Designs: 20pf, Treble viola da gamba, 1747. 25pf, Oboe, 1785. Clarinet, 1830 and flute, 1817. 35pf, Concert zither, 1891. 70pf, Trumpet, 1860.

1977, June 14
1817 A554 10pf multicolored   .20   .20
1818 A554 20pf multicolored   .20   .20
1819 A554 25pf multicolored   .20   .20
1820 A554 35pf multicolored   .20   .20
1821 A554 70pf multicolored   2.00 2.00
    Nos. 1817-1821 (5)   2.80 2.80

Vogtland musical instruments from Markneukirchen Museum.

Mercury and Argus, by Rubens — A555

Rubens Paintings in Dresden Gallery: 10pf, Bath of Bathsheba, vert. 20pf, The Drunk Hercules, vert. 25pf, Diana Returning from the Hunt. 35pf, Old Woman with Brazier, vert. 50pf, Leda and the Swan.

1977, June 28   **Photo.**   **Perf. 14**
1822 A555 10pf multicolored   .20   .20
1823 A555 15pf multicolored   .20   .20
1824 A555 20pf multicolored   .20   .20
1825 A555 25pf multicolored   .20   .20
1826 A555 35pf multicolored   .25   .20
1827 A555 50pf multicolored   3.00 2.25
    Nos. 1822-1827 (6)   4.05 3.25

Peter Paul Rubens (1577-1640), Flemish painter, 400th birth anniversary.

Souvenir Sheet

Wreath, Flags of USSR and DDR — A556

1977, June 28
1828 A556 50pf multicolored   1.00 1.00

Soc. for German-Soviet Friendship, 30th anniv.

Tractor with Plow — A557

Designs: 20pf, Fertilizer-spreader. 25pf, Potato digger and loader. 35pf, High-pressure harvester. 50pf, Rotating milking machine.

1977, July 12   **Litho.**   **Perf. 13x12½**
1829 A557 10pf multicolored   .20   .20
1830 A557 20pf multicolored   .20   .20
1831 A557 25pf multicolored   .20   .20
1832 A557 35pf multicolored   .20   .20
1833 A557 50pf multicolored   1.60 1.60
    Nos. 1829-1833 (5)   2.40 2.40

Motorized modern agriculture.

High Jump A558

Designs: 20pf, Hurdles, girls. 35pf, Dancing. 40pf, Torch bearer and flags.

1977, July 19
1834 A558 5pf red & multi   .20   .20
1835 A558 20pf lt green & multi   .20   .20
1836 A558 35pf green & multi   .20   .20
1837 A558 40pf blue & multi   1.50 1.50
    Nos. 1834-1837,B183-B184 (4)   2.10 2.10

6th Gymnastics and Sports Festival and 6th Children's and Youth Spartacist Games.

"Bread for all" by Wolfram Schubert A559   Konsument Department Store, Leipzig A560

Design: 25pf, "When Communists Dream," by Walter Womacka (detail) and Sozphilex emblem.

1977, Aug. 16   **Photo.**   **Perf. 14**
1838 A559 10pf multicolored   .25   .20
   a.   Souvenir sheet of 4   1.00   .90
1839 A559 25pf multicolored   .45   .35
   a.   Souvenir sheet of 4   2.00 2.00

SOZPHILEX '77 Philatelic Exhibition, Berlin, Aug. 19-28. See No. B185.

1977, Aug. 30

Design: 25pf, Glasses and wooden plate.
1840 A560 10pf blue & multi   .20   .20
1841 A560 25pf multicolored   .30   .25

Leipzig Fall Fair.

Souvenir Sheet

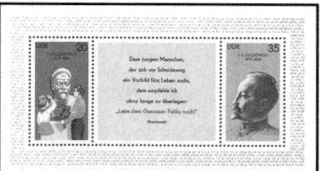

Dzerzhinski and Quotation from Mayakovsky — A561

1977, Sept. 6   **Litho.**   **Perf. 12½x13**
1842 A561 Sheet of 2   1.40 1.40
   a.   20pf multicolored   .30   .30
   b.   35pf multicolored   .45   .45

Feliks E. Dzerzhinski (1877-1926), organizer and head of Russian Secret Police (Cheka), birth centenary.

Muldenthal Locomotive, 1861 — A562

Designs: 10pf, Trolley car, Dresden, 1896. 20pf, First successful German plane, 1909. 25pf, 3-wheel car "Phäno-mobile," 1924. 35pf, Passenger steamship on the Elbe, 1837.

1977, Sept. 13   **Photo.**   **Perf. 14**
1843 A562 5pf green & multi   .25   .20
1844 A562 10pf green & multi   .25   .20
1845 A562 20pf green & multi   .25   .20
1846 A562 25pf green & multi   .25   .20
1847 A562 35pf green & multi   2.25 1.75
    Nos. 1843-1847 (5)   3.25 2.55

Transportation Museum, Dresden.

Cruiser "Aurora" A563

Designs: 25pf, Storming of the Winter Palace. 1m, Lenin, vert.

1977, Sept. 20
1848 A563 10pf multicolored   .25   .20
1849 A563 25pf multicolored   .45   .35

Souvenir Sheet
Perf. 12½x13

1850 A563 1m carmine & blk   2.00 2.00

60th anniversary of the Russian Revolution.

Mother Russia and Obelisk — A564

1977, Sept. 20   **Litho.**   **Perf. 14**
1851 A564 35pf multicolored   .35   .20

Soviet soldiers' memorial, Berlin-Schönholz.

Labor Leaders Type of 1976

Portraits: No. 1852, Ernst Meyer (1887-1930). No. 1853, August Fröhlich (1877-1966). No. 1854, Gerhart Eisler (1897-1968).

1977, Oct. 18   **Litho.**   **Perf. 14**
1852 A520 10pf olive & brown   .20   .20
1853 A520 10pf rose & brown   .20   .20
1854 A520 10pf lt blue & blk brn   .20   .20
    Nos. 1852-1854 (3)   .60   .60

Souvenir Sheet

Heinrich von Kleist, by Peter Friedl, 1801 — A565

1977, Oct. 18
1855 A565 1m multicolored   2.40 2.00

Heinrich von Kleist (1777-1811), poet and playwright, birth bicentenary.

Rocket A566

Design: 20pf, as 10pf, design reversed.

1977, Nov. 8   **Photo.**   **Perf. 14**
1856 A566 10pf red, blk & sil   .20   .20
1857 A566 20pf ultra, blk & gold   .20   .20
   a.   Pair, #1856-1857 + label   .85   .85

20th Central Young Craftsmen's Exhibition (Masters of Tomorrow).

A567   A568

Hunting in East Germany: 10pf, Mouflons. 15pf, Red deer. 20pf, Retriever with pheasant, hunter. 25pf, Red fox, wild duck. 35pf, Tractor driver saving fawn. 70pf, Wild boars.

1977, Nov. 15
1858 A567 10pf multicolored   .20   .20
1859 A567 15pf multicolored   1.90 1.90
1860 A567 20pf multicolored   .20   .20
1861 A567 25pf multicolored   .25   .20
1862 A567 35pf multicolored   .25   .20
1863 A567 70pf multicolored   .30   .20
    Nos. 1858-1863 (6)   3.10 2.90

1977, Nov. 22   **Litho.**   **Perf. 14**

Firemen's Activities: 10pf, Firemen racing with ladders. 20pf, Children Visiting Firehouse. 25pf, Fire engines fighting forest and brush fires. 35pf, Artificial respiration. 50pf, Fireboat alongside freighter.

1864 A568 10pf multi, horiz.   .20   .20
1865 A568 20pf multi   .20   .20
1866 A568 25pf multi, horiz.   .20   .20
1867 A568 35pf multi   .20   .20
1868 A568 50pf multi, horiz.   1.80 1.80
    Nos. 1864-1868 (5)   2.60 2.60

Knight and King — A569

Designs: Various scenes from fairytale: "Six Men Around the World."

1977, Nov. 22   **Perf. 13x13½**
1869 A569 5pf black & multi   .20   .20
1870 A569 10pf black & multi   .70   .70
1871 A569 20pf black & multi   .20   .20
1872 A569 25pf black & multi   .20   .20
1873 A569 35pf black & multi   .70   .70
1874 A569 60pf black & multi   .20   .20
   a.   Sheet of 6, #1869-1874   3.50 3.25

Hips and Dog Rose A570

Medicinal Plants: 15pf, Birch. 20pf, Chamomile. 25pf, Coltsfoot. 35pf, Linden. 50pf, Elder.

1978, Jan. 10   **Photo.**   **Perf. 14**
1875 A570 10pf multicolored   .20   .20
1876 A570 15pf multicolored   .20   .20
1877 A570 20pf multicolored   .20   .20
1878 A570 25pf multicolored   .20   .20
1879 A570 35pf multicolored   .25   .20
1880 A570 50pf multicolored   2.00 2.00
    Nos. 1875-1880 (6)   3.05 3.00

Amilcar
Cabral — A571

1978, Jan. 17   Litho.   *Perf. 14*
1881 A571 20pf multicolored   .35   .30
Amilcar Cabral (1924-1973), freedom movement leader from Guinea-Bissau.

Town Hall, Suhl-
Heinrichs
A572

Half-timbered Buildings, 17th-18th Centuries: 20pf, Farmhouse, Niederoderwitz. 25pf, Farmhouse, Strassen. 35pf, Townhouse, Quedlinburg. 40pf, Townhouse, Eisenach.

1978, Jan. 24   Photo.   *Perf. 14*
1882 A572 10pf multicolored   .20   .20
1883 A572 20pf multicolored   .20   .20
1884 A572 25pf multicolored   .20   .20
1885 A572 35pf multicolored   .20   .20
1886 A572 40pf multicolored   1.80 1.80
        Nos. 1882-1886 (5)   2.60 2.60

Mail Truck, 1921
A573

Past and Present Mail Transport: 20pf, Mail truck, 1978. 25pf, Railroad mail car, 1896. 35pf, Railroad mail car, 1978.

1978, Feb. 9   Litho.   *Perf. 13x12½*
1887 A573 10pf brown & multi   .20   .20
1888 A573 20pf brown & multi   .35   .35
1889 A573 25pf brown & multi   .45   .45
1890 A573 35pf brown & multi   .60   .60
  a. Block of 4, #1887-1890   2.25 2.25

Earring, 11th
Century — A574

Archaeological Artifacts: 20pf, Earring, 10th century. 25pf, Bronze sheath, 10th century. 35pf, Bronze horse, 12th century. 70pf, Arabian coin, 8th century.

1978, Feb. 21   Photo.   *Perf. 14*
1891 A574 10pf multicolored   .20   .20
1892 A574 20pf multicolored   .20   .20
1893 A574 25pf multicolored   .20   .20
1894 A574 35pf multicolored   .25   .24
1895 A574 70pf multicolored   1.50 1.50
        Nos. 1891-1895 (5)   2.35 2.30

Treasures found on Slavic sites.

Royal House,
Leipzig — A575

Leipzig Spring Fair: 25pf, Universal measuring instrument by Carl Zeiss.

1978, Mar. 7
1896 A575 10pf multicolored   .20   .20
1897 A575 25pf multicolored   .35   .30

M-100
Meteorological
Rocket — A576

Designs: 20pf, Intercosmos I satellite. 35pf, Meteor satellite with spectometric complex. 1m, MFK-6 multi-spectral camera over city.

1978, Mar. 21   Photo.   *Perf. 14x13½*
1898 A576 10pf multicolored   .20   .20
1899 A576 20pf multicolored   .20   .20
1900 A576 35pf multicolored   .90   .90
        Nos. 1898-1900 (3)   1.30 1.30

Souvenir Sheet
1901 A576 1m multicolored   2.25 1.75
Achievements in atmospheric and space research.

Samuel
Heinicke,
Leipzig,
c. 1800
A577

25pf, Deaf child learning sign language.

1978, Apr. 4   Litho.   *Perf. 13x12½*
1902 A577 20pf multicolored   .20   .20
1903 A577 25pf multicolored   .60   .60
National Institute for the Education of the Deaf, established by Samuel Heinicke, 200th anniversary.

Radio Tower,
Dequede, TV
Truck — A578

Design: 20pf, TV equipment and tower, vert.

1978, Apr. 25   *Perf. 13½x14, 14x13½*
1904 A578 10pf multicolored   .25   .20
1905 A578 20pf multicolored   .25   .25
World Telecommunications Day.

Saxon Miner, 19th
Century — A579

Dress Uniforms, 19th Century: 20pf, Foundry worker, Freiberg. 25pf, Mining Academy student. 35pf, Chief Inspector of Mines.

1978, May 9   *Perf. 12½x13*
1906 A579 10pf silver & multi   .20   .20
1907 A579 20pf silver & multi   .20   .20
1908 A579 25pf silver & multi   .20   .20
1909 A579 35pf silver & multi   1.10 1.00
        Nos. 1906-1909 (4)   1.70 1.60

Lion
Cub — A580

Young Animals: 20pf, Leopard. 35pf, Tiger. 50pf, Snow leopard.

1978, May 23   Photo.   *Perf. 14*
1910 A580 10pf multicolored   .20   .20
1911 A580 20pf multicolored   .20   .20
1912 A580 35pf multicolored   .20   .20
1913 A580 50pf multicolored   1.10 1.10
        Nos. 1910-1913 (4)   1.70 1.70

Centenary of Leipzig Zoo.

Loading
Container — A581

Designs: 20pf, Loading container on flatbed truck. 35pf, Container trains in terminal. 70pf, Loading container on ship.

1978, June 13   Litho.   *Perf. 12½x13*
1914 A581 10pf multicolored   .20   .20
1915 A581 20pf multicolored   .20   .20
1916 A581 35pf multicolored   .20   .20
1917 A581 70pf multicolored   1.60 1.50
        Nos. 1914-1917 (4)   2.20 2.10

Ceramic
Bull — A582

Designs: 10pf, Woman's head, ceramic. 20pf, Gold armband, horiz. 25pf, Animal head, gold ring. 35pf, Seated family from signet ring. 40pf, Necklace, horiz.

Perf. 14x13½, 13½x14
1978, June 20   Photo.
1918 A582 5pf multicolored   .20   .20
1919 A582 10pf multicolored   .20   .20
1920 A582 20pf multicolored   .20   .20
1921 A582 25pf multicolored   .20   .20
1922 A582 35pf multicolored   .20   .20
1923 A582 40pf multicolored   1.10 1.10
        Nos. 1918-1923 (6)   2.10 2.10

African art from 1st and 2nd centuries in Berlin and Leipzig Egyptian museums.

Old and New Buildings,
Cottbus — A583

Design: 10pf + 5pf, View of Cottbus, 1730.

1978, July 18   Litho.   *Perf. 13x12½*
1924   10pf + 5pf multi   .25   .25
1925 A583 20pf multicolored   .25   .25
  a. A583 Pair, #1924-1925 + label   .60   .60

5th Youth Philatelic Exhibition, Cottbus.

Justus
von
Liebig,
Wheat
and
Retort
A584

Famous Germans: 10pf, Joseph Dietzgen (1828-1888) and title page. 15pf, Alfred Döblin (1878-1957) and title page. 20pf, Hans Loch (1898-1960) and signature, president of Liberal Democratic Party. 25pf, Dr. Theodor Brugsch (1878-1963), and blood circulation. 35pf, Friedrich Ludwig Jahn (1778-1852) and gymnast. 70pf, Dr. Albrecht von Graefe (1828-1870) and ophthalmological instruments.

1978, July 18
1926 A584 5pf yellow & blk   .20   .20
1927 A584 10pf gray & blk   .20   .20
1928 A584 15pf yel grn & blk   .20   .20
1929 A584 20pf ultra & blk   .20   .20
1930 A584 25pf salmon & blk   .20   .20
1931 A584 35pf lt green & blk   .20   .20
1932 A584 70pf ol & blk   1.25 1.25
        Nos. 1926-1932 (7)   2.45 2.45

Festival
Emblem
and New
Buildings,
Havana
A585

35pf, Balloons and new buildings, Berlin.

1978, July 25   Litho.   *Perf. 13x12½*
1933 A585 20pf multicolored   .30   .30
1934 A585 35pf multicolored   .30   .30
  a. Strip of 2, #1933-1934 + label 1.00 1.00

11th World Youth Festival, Havana, 7/28-8/5.

Foot Soldier, by
Hans
Schäufelein — A586

Etchings: 20pf, Woman Reading Letter, by Jean Antoine Watteau. 25pf, Seated Boy, by Gabriel Metsu. 30pf, Seated Young Man, by Cornelis Saftleven. 35pf, St. Anthony, by Matthias Grunewald. 50pf, Seated Man, by Abraham van Diepenbeeck.

1978, July 25   *Perf. 13½x14*
1935 A586 10pf lemon & black   .20   .20
1936 A586 20pf lemon & black   .75   .75
1937 A586 25pf lemon & black   .20   .20
1938 A586 30pf lemon & black   .20   .20
1939 A586 35pf lemon & black   .75   .75
1940 A586 50pf lemon & black   .20   .20
  a. Sheet of 6, #1935-1940   2.75 2.75

Etchings from Berlin Museums.

Fair Building "Three
Kings,"
Leipzig — A587

Leipzig Fall Fair: 10pf, IFA Multicar 25 truck, horiz.

1978, Aug. 29   Photo.   *Perf. 14*
1941 A587 10pf multicolored   .20   .20
1942 A587 25pf multicolored   .35   .30

Mauthausen Memorial — A588

1978, Sept. 5   *Perf. 13½x14*
1943 A588 35pf multicolored   .35   .25

International war memorials.

Soyuz, Intercosmos and German-
Soviet Space Flight Emblems — A589

Soyuz,
Camera and
Space
Complex
A590

Designs: 10pf, Soyuz and Albert Einstein.
20pf, Sigmund Jähn, 1st German cosmonaut,
vert. 35pf, Salyut-Soyuz space station, Otto
Lilienthal and his glider. 1m, Cosmonauts
Bykovsky and Jähn and space ships.

1978, Sept.   Photo.   Perf. 14
1944 A589 20pf multicolored   .35   .25

Litho.
Perf. 13½x13
1945 A590 5pf multicolored   .20   .20
1946 A590 10pf multicolored   .20   .20
1947 A590 20pf multicolored   .20   .20
1948 A590 35pf multicolored   .75   .75
       Nos. 1944-1948 (5)   1.70 1.60

Souvenir Sheet
Perf. 13½x14
1949 A590 1m multicolored   1.80 1.80
1st German cosmonaut on Russian space
mission. #1949 contains 1 54x33mm stamp.
Issued: #1944, Sept. 4; others, Sept. 21.

Marching
Soldiers,
Tractor,
Factory
A591

Design: 35pf, Russian and German
Soldiers, Communist war veteran, 1933.

1978, Sept. 19   Photo.   Perf. 14
1950 A591 20pf multicolored   .30   .30
1951 A591 35pf multicolored   .30   .30
   a.   Strip of 2, #1950-1951 + label 1.20 1.20
Workers' military units, 25th anniv.

Seven-person
Pyramid — A592

10pf, Elephant on tricycle. 20pf, Dressage.
35pf, Polar bear kissing woman trainer.

1978, Sept. 26   Photo.   Perf. 14
1952 A592 5pf black & multi   .30   .50
1953 A592 10pf black & multi   .55   .75
1954 A592 20pf black & multi   .90 1.25
1955 A592 35pf black & multi   1.50 2.50
   a.   Block of 4, #1952-1955   6.00 13.50
Circus in German Democratic Republic.

Construction of Gas Pipe Line,
Drushba Section — A593

1978, Oct. 3   Litho.   Perf. 13x12½
1956 A593 20pf multicolored   .35   .20
German youth helping to build gas pipe line
from Orenburg to Russian border.

African Behind
Barbed
Wire — A594

1978, Oct. 3   Litho.   Perf. 12½x13
1957 A594 20pf multicolored   .35   .20
Anti-Apartheid Year.

Papilio
Hahneli — A595

1978, Oct. 24   Photo.   Perf. 14
20pf, Agama lehmanni (lizards). 25pf, Agate
from Wiederau. 35pf, Paleobatrachus diluvi-
anus. 40pf, Clock, 1720. 50pf, Table telescope, 1750.

1958 A595 10pf multicolored   .20   .20
1959 A595 20pf multicolored   .20   .20
1960 A595 25pf multicolored   .20   .20
1961 A595 35pf multicolored   .20   .20
1962 A595 40pf multicolored   .20   .20
1963 A595 50pf multicolored   1.90 1.90
       Nos. 1958-1963 (6)   2.90 2.90
Dresden Museum of Natural History, 250th
anniversary.

Wheel Lock Gun, 1630 — A596

Hunting Guns: 10pf, Double-barreled gun,
1978. 20pf, Spring-cock gun, 1780. 25pf,
Superimposed double-barreled gun, 1978.
35pf, Percussion gun, 1850. 70pf, Three-bar-
reled gun, 1978.

1978, Nov. 21   Photo.   Perf. 14
1964 A596 5pf silver & multi   .20   .20
1965 A596 10pf silver & multi   .20   .20
1966 A596 20pf silver & multi   .25   .25
1967 A596 25pf silver & multi   .30   .30
1968 A596 35pf silver & multi   .45   .45
   a.   Vert. strip of 3, 5, 20, 35pf 1.40 1.25
1969 A596 70pf silver & multi   .90   .90
   a.   Vert. strip of 3, 10, 25, 70pf 2.40 2.25
       Nos. 1964-1969 (6)   2.30 2.30
Printed in sheets of 9.

Rapunzel's Father
and Witch — A597

Designs: Scenes from fairy tale "Rapunzel."

1978, Nov. 21   Litho.   Perf. 13
1970 A597 10pf multicolored   .20   .20
1971 A597 15pf multicolored   .85   .85
1972 A597 20pf multicolored   .20   .20
1973 A597 25pf multicolored   .20   .20
1974 A597 35pf multicolored   .85   .85
1975 A597 50pf multicolored   .20   .20
   a.   Sheet of 6, #1970-1975   2.90 2.90

Chaffinches
A598

Song Birds: 10pf, Nuthatch. 20pf, Robin.
25pf, Bullfinches. 35pf, Blue tit. 50pf, Red
linnets.

1979, Jan. 9   Photo.   Perf. 13½x14
1976 A598 5pf multicolored   .20   .20
1977 A598 10pf multicolored   .20   .20
1978 A598 20pf multicolored   .20   .20
1979 A598 25pf multicolored   .20   .20
1980 A598 35pf multicolored   .20   .20
1981 A598 50pf multicolored   2.25 1.50
       Nos. 1976-1981 (6)   3.25 2.50

Chabo
Cock — A599

German Cocks: 15pf, Kraienkopp. 20pf,
Porcelain-colored bantam. 25pf, Saxonian.
35pf, Phoenix. 50pf, Striped Italian.

1979, Jan. 23   Perf. 14x13½
1982 A599 10pf multicolored   .20   .20
1983 A599 15pf multicolored   .20   .20
1984 A599 20pf multicolored   .20   .20
1985 A599 25pf multicolored   .20   .20
1986 A599 35pf multicolored   .20   .20
1987 A599 50pf multicolored   1.90 1.90
       Nos. 1982-1987 (6)   2.90 2.90

Telephone Operators, 1900 and
1979 — A600

35pf, Telegraph operators, 1880 and 1979.

1979, Feb. 6   Photo.   Perf. 13½x14
1988 A600 20pf multicolored   .20   .20
1989 A600 35pf multicolored   .65   .65
Development of German postal telephone
and telegraph service.

Souvenir Sheet

$$E = mc^2$$

Albert Einstein (1879-1955),
Theoretical Physicist — A601

1979, Feb. 20   Litho.   Perf. 14
1990 A601 1m multicolored   2.00 1.90

Max Klinger House,
Leipzig — A602

Leipzig Spring Fair: 25pf, Horizontal drilling
and milling machine, horiz.

1979, Mar. 6   Litho.   Perf. 14
1991 A602 10pf multicolored   .20   .20
1992 A602 25pf multicolored   .30   .25

Container Ship, Tug, World Map and
IMCO Emblem — A603

1979, Mar. 20   Photo.
1993 A603 20pf multicolored   .35   .25
World Navigation Day.

Otto
Hahn and
Equation
of
Nuclear
Fission
A604

Famous Germans: 10pf, Max von Laue
(1879-1969) and diagram of sulphide zinc.
20pf, Arthur Scheunert (1879-1957), symbol
of nutrition and health. 25pf, Friedrich August
Kekulé (1829-1896), and benzene ring. 35pf,
George Forster (1754-1794) and Capt. Cook's
ship Resolution. 70pf, Gotthold Ephraim Lessing (1729-1781) and title page for Nathan the
Wise.

1979, Mar. 20   Litho.   Perf. 13x12½
1994 A604 5pf pale salmon &
             blk   .20   .20
1995 A604 10pf blue gray & blk   .20   .20
1996 A604 20pf lemon & blk   .20   .20
1997 A604 25pf lt green & blk   .20   .20
1998 A604 35pf lt blue & blk   .20   .20
1999 A604 70pf pink & blk   1.90 1.50
       Nos. 1994-1999 (6)   2.90 2.50
       See Nos. 2088-2093.

Miniature Sheet

Horch 8,
1911 — A605

Design: 35pf, Trabant 601S de luxe, 1978.

1979, Apr. 3   Litho.   Perf. 14
2000   Sheet of 2 + label   1.50 1.50
   a.   A605 20pf multicolored   .30   .30
   b.   A605 35pf multicolored   .65   .65
Sachsenring automobile plant, Zwickau.

Self-Propelled Car — A606

DDR Railroad Cars: 10pf, Self-unloading
freight car Us-y. 20pf, Diesel locomotive BR
110. 35pf, Laaes automobile carrier.

1979, Apr. 17   Litho.   Perf. 13
2001 A606 5pf multicolored   .20   .20
2002 A606 10pf multicolored   .20   .20
2003 A606 20pf multicolored   .20   .20
2004 A606 35pf multicolored   .75   .75
       Nos. 2001-2004 (4)   1.35 1.35

Durga, 18th Century — A607

Indian Miniatures in Berlin Museums: 35pf, Mahavira, 15th-16th cents. 50pf, Todi Ragini, 17th cent. 70pf, Asavari Ragini, 17th cent.

1979, May 8 Photo. Perf. 14x13½
2005 A607 20pf multicolored   .20 .20
2006 A607 35pf multicolored   .20 .20
2007 A607 50pf multicolored   .25 .20
2008 A607 70pf multicolored   2.10 2.00
      Nos. 2005-2008 (4)   2.75 2.60

Youth Gathering A608

Design: 10pf+5pf, Torchlight parade of German youth, Oct. 7, 1949.

1979, May 22 Photo. Perf. 14
2009 A608 10pf + 5pf multi   .20 .20
2010 A608 20pf multicolored   .25 .25
  a.   Strip of 2, #2009-2010 + label .60 .60

National Youth Festival, Berlin.

Housing Project, Berlin A609

20pf, Berlin-Marzahn building site & surveyors.

1979, May 22 Litho. Perf. 13x12½
2011 A609 10pf multicolored   .20 .20
2012 A609 20pf multicolored   .30 .30

Berlin Project of Free German Youth.

Children Playing and Reading — A610

Exhibition Emblem — A611

20pf, Doctor with black & white children.

1979, May 22 Photo. Perf. 14
2013 A610 10pf multicolored   .20 .20
2014 A610 20pf multicolored   .35 .40

International Year of the Child.

1979, June 5
2015 A611 10pf multicolored   .35 .20

Agra '79 Agricultural Exhib., Markkleeberg.

Ferry Boats A612

1979, June 26 Photo. Perf. 14
2016 A612 20pf Rostock   .30 .30
2017 A612 35pf Rugen   .30 .30
  a.   Strip of 2, #2016-2017 + label 1.10 1.10

Railroad ferry from Sassnitz, DDR, to Trelleborg, Sweden, 70th anniversary.

Hospital Classroom — A613

Design: 35pf, Handicapped workers.

1979, June 26 Litho. Perf. 13x12½
2018 A163 10pf multicolored   .20 .20
2019 A163 35pf multicolored   .45 .35

Rehabilitation in DDR.

Bicyclists A614

Design: 20pf, Roller skating.

1979, July 3
2020 A614 10pf multicolored   .20 .20
2021 A614 10pf multicolored   .45 .35

7th Children's and Youth Spartakiad, Berlin.

Dahlia "Rubens" A615

Dahlias: 20pf, Rosalie. 25pf, Corinna. 35pf, Enzett-Dolli. 50pf, Enzett-Carola. 70pf, Don Lorenzo.

1979, July 17 Photo. Perf. 13
2022 A615 10pf multicolored   .20 .20
2023 A615 20pf multicolored   .20 .20
2024 A615 25pf multicolored   .20 .20
2025 A615 35pf multicolored   .20 .20
2026 A615 50pf multicolored   .25 .20
2027 A615 70pf multicolored   2.25 2.25
      Nos. 2022-2027 (6)   3.30 3.25

Dahlias shown at International Garden Exhibition, Erfurt.

Russian Alphabet Around Congress Emblem A616

1979, Aug. 7 Photo. Perf. 13
2028 A616 20pf multicolored   .30 .20

4th International Congress of Teachers of Russian Language and Literature, Berlin.

Dandelion Fountain, Dresden — A617

Composite of Dresden Buildings — A618

1979, Aug. 7 Perf. 14
2029 A617 20pf multicolored   .20 .20

Souvenir Sheet
Litho. Perf. 13x12½
2030 A618 1m multicolored   1.90 1.75

DDR '79, Natl. Stamp Exhib., Dresden. See No. B187.

Italian Lira da Gamba, 1592 — A619

Musical Instruments, Leipzig Museum: 25pf, French "serpent," 17th-18th centuries. 40pf, French barrel lyre, 18th century. 85pf, German tenor trumpet, 19th century.

1979, Aug. 21 Perf. 14
2031 A619 20pf multicolored   .20 .20
2032 A619 25pf multicolored   .20 .20
2033 A619 40pf multicolored   .25 .20
2034 A619 85pf multicolored   2.10 1.60
      Nos. 2031-2034 (4)   2.75 2.20

Galloping — A620

1979, Aug. 21
2035 A620 10pf shown   .20 .20
2036 A620 25pf Dressage   .75 .65

30th International Horse-breeding Congress of Socialist Countries, Berlin.

Memorial Monument, Nordhausen A621

1979, Aug. 28 Photo. Perf. 14
2037 A621 35pf dull vio & blk   .45 .30

Memorial to World War II victims.

Teddy Bear — A622

Leipzig Autumn Fair: 25pf, Grosser Blumenberg (building), Leipzig, horiz.

1979, Aug. 28
2038 A622 10pf multicolored   .20 .20
2039 A622 25pf multicolored   .25 .20

Philipp Dengel (1888-1948) A623

Working-Class Movement Leaders: No. 2041, Heinrich Rau (1899-1961). No. 2042, Otto Buchwitz (1879-1964). No. 2043, Bernard Koenen (1889-1964).

1979, Sept. 11 Litho.
2040 A623 10pf multicolored   .20 .20
2041 A623 10pf multicolored   .20 .20
2042 A623 10pf multicolored   .20 .20
2043 A623 10pf multicolored   .20 .20
      Nos. 2040-2043 (4)   .80 .80

See Nos. 2166-2169, 2249-2253, 2314-2318, 2390-2392, 2452-2454.

DDR Arms and Flag, Worker A624

DDR Arms, Flag and: 10pf, Young man and woman. 15pf, Soldiers. 20pf, Workers.

1979, Oct. 2 Photo. Perf. 13
2044 A624 5pf multicolored   .20 .20
2045 A624 10pf multicolored   .20 .20
2046 A624 15pf multicolored   .35 .35
2047 A624 20pf multicolored   .20 .20
      Nos. 2044-2047 (4)   .95 .95

Souvenir Sheet
2048 A624 1m multicolored   1.50 1.40

DDR, 30th anniv. No. 2048 contains one stamp (33x55mm).

Altozier Porcelain Coffee Pot — A625

Meissen Porcelain and Hallmark, 18th-20th Centuries: 5pf, Woman applying make-up, 1967. 15pf, "Grosser Ausschnitt" coffee pot, 1974. 20pf, Covered vase. 25pf, Parrot. 35pf, Harlequin drinking. 50pf, Woman selling flowers. 70pf, Sake bottle.

1979, Nov. 6 Photo. Perf. 14
2049 A625 5pf multicolored   .20 .20
2050 A625 10pf multicolored   .20 .20
2051 A625 15pf multicolored   .25 .25
2052 A625 20pf multicolored   .30 .30
  a.   Block of 4, #2049-2052   3.00 2.25

2053	A625	25pf multicolored	.35	.35
2054	A625	35pf multicolored	.60	.60
2055	A625	50pf multicolored	.85	.85
2056	A625	70pf multicolored	1.10	1.10
a.		Block of 4, #2053-2056	6.00	5.50

Rag Doll,
1800 — A626

Historic Dolls: 15pf, Ceramic, 1960. 20pf, Wooden, 1780. 35pf, Straw, 1900. 50pf, Jointed, 1800. 70pf, Tumbler, 1820.

1979, Nov. 20   **Litho.**

2057	A626	10pf multicolored	.20	.20
2058	A626	15pf multicolored	.90	.90
2059	A626	20pf multicolored	.20	.20
2060	A626	35pf multicolored	.20	.20
2061	A626	50pf multicolored	.90	.90
2062	A626	70pf multicolored	.20	.20
a.		Sheet of 6, #2057-2062	3.25	3.25

Bobsledding, by Gunter Rechn,
Olympic Rings — A627

Olympic Rings and: 20pf, Figure Skating, by Johanna Stake, vert. 35pf, Speed Skating, by Axel Wunsch, vert. 1m, Cross-country Skiing, by Lothar Zitzmann.

1980, Jan. 15   **Photo.**   **Perf. 14**

2063	A627	10pf multicolored	.20	.20
2064	A627	20pf multicolored	.20	.20
2065	A627	35pf multicolored	1.10	1.00
		Nos. 2063-2065,B189 (4)	1.70	1.60

Souvenir Sheet

2066	A627	1m multicolored	1.90	1.90

13th Winter Olympic Games, Lake Placid, NY, Feb. 12-24. No. 2066 contains one 29x23½mm stamp. See Nos. 2098-2099, 2119-2121, B190, B192.

"Quiet Music," Grossedlitz — A628

Baroque Gardens: 20pf, Orange grove, Belvedere, Weimar. 50pf, Flower garden, Dornburg Castle. 70pf, Park, Rheinsberg Castle.

1980, Jan. 29

2067	A628	10pf multicolored	.20	.20
2068	A628	20pf multicolored	.20	.20
2069	A628	50pf multicolored	.25	.20
2070	A628	70pf multicolored	1.40	1.40
		Nos. 2067-2070 (4)	2.05	2.00

Type of 1973

Designs as before and: 10pf, Palace of the Republic, Berlin.

1980-81   **Engr.**   **Perf. 14**
Size: 22x17mm

2071	A449	5pf blue green	.20	.20
2072	A449	10pf emerald	.25	.20
2073	A449	15pf rose lilac	.35	.25
2074	A449	20pf rose mag	.45	.25
2075	A449	25pf grnsh bl	.35	.25
2076	A449	30pf org ('81)	.45	.25
2077	A449	35pf blue	.45	.25
2078	A449	40pf dull vio	.90	.50
2079	A449	50pf blue	.55	.25
2080	A449	60pf lilac ('81)	.55	.25
2081	A449	70pf redsh brn ('81)	.70	.50
2082	A449	80pf vio bl ('81)	.85	.50
2083	A449	1m olive	.90	.80
2084	A449a	2m red	1.60	.90
2085	A449a	3m rose lil ('81)	2.60	1.25
		Nos. 2071-2085 (15)	11.15	6.55

Cable-Laying Vehicle, Dish
Antenna — A629

20pf, Radio tower, television screen.

1980, Feb. 5   **Photo.**

2086	A629	10pf multicolored	.20	.20
2087	A629	20pf multicolored	.25	.20

Famous Germans Type of 1979

Designs: 5pf, Johann Wolfgang Dobereiner (1780-1849), chemist. 10pf, Frederic Joliot-Curie (1900-1958), French physicist. 20pf, Johann Friedrich Naumann (1780-1857), ornithologist. 25pf, Alfred Wegener (1880-1930), geophysicist and meteorologist. 35pf, Carl von Clausewitz (1780-1831), Prussian major general. 70pf, Helene Weigel (1900-1971), actress.

1980, Feb. 26   **Litho.**   **Perf. 13x12½**

2088	A604	5pf pale yel & blk	.20	.20
2089	A604	10pf multicolored	.20	.20
2090	A604	20pf lt yel grn & blk	.20	.20
2091	A604	25pf multicolored	.20	.20
2092	A604	35pf lt blue & blk	.20	.20
2093	A604	70pf lt red brn & blk	1.20	1.10
		Nos. 2088-2093 (6)	2.20	2.10

Type ZT-
303
Tractor
A630

1980 Leipzig Spring Fair: 10pf, Karl Marx University, Leipzig, vert.

1980, Mar. 4   **Photo.**   **Perf. 14**

2094	A630	10pf multicolored	.20	.20
2095	A630	25pf multicolored	.30	.25

Werner Eggerath
(1900-1977), Labor
Leader — A631

1980, Mar. 18   **Litho.**

2096	A631	10pf brick red & blk	.45	.30

Souvenir Sheet

Cosmonauts, Salyut 6 and
Soyuz — A632

1980, Apr. 11   **Litho.**   **Perf. 14**

2097	A632	1m multicolored	1.80	1.60

Intercosmos cooperative space program.

Olympic Type of 1980

Designs: 10pf, On the Bars, by Erich Wurzer. 50pf, Scull's Crew, by Wilfried Falkenthal.

1980, Apr. 22   **Photo.**   **Perf. 14**

2098	A627	10pf multicolored	.25	.20
2099	A627	50pf multicolored	1.20	1.00
		Nos. 2098-2099,B190 (3)	1.70	1.40

22nd Summer Olympic Games, Moscow, July 19-Aug. 3. See No. B190.

Flags of
Member
Countries
A633

Bauhaus
Cooperative
Society Building,
1928, Gropius
A634

1980, May 13   **Photo.**

2100	A633	20pf multicolored	.45	.20

Signing of Warsaw Pact (Bulgaria, Czechoslovakia, DDR, Hungary, Poland, Romania, USSR), 25th anniv.

1980, May 27

Bauhaus Architecture: 10pf, Socialists' Memorial, 1926, by Mies van der Rohe, horiz. 15pf, Monument, 1922, by William Gropius. 20pf, Steel building, 1926, by Muche and Paulick, horiz. 50pf, Trade-Union School, 1928, by Meyer. 70pf, Bauhaus Building, 1926, by Gropius, horiz.

2101	A634	5pf multicolored	.25	.20
2102	A634	10pf multicolored	.25	.20
2103	A634	15pf multicolored	.25	.20
2104	A634	20pf multicolored	.25	.20
2105	A634	50pf multicolored	.30	.20
2106	A634	70pf multicolored	1.80	1.60
		Nos. 2101-2106 (6)	3.10	2.60

Rostock
View
A635

1980, June 10   **Photo.**   **Perf. 14**

2107	A635	10pf shown	.20	.20
2108	A635	20pf Dancers	.30	.25

18th Workers' Festival, Rostock, June 27-29.

Dish
Antenna,
Interflug
Airlines
A636

1980, June 10   **Litho.**   **Perf. 13x12½**

2109	A636	20pf shown	.30	.30
2110	A636	25pf Jet	.30	.30
2111	A636	35pf Agricultural plane	.45	.45
2112	A636	70pf Aerial photography	.90	.90
a.		Block of 4, #2109-2112	2.60	2.60

Interflug Airlines. See No. B191.

Okapi — A637

1980, June 24   **Perf. 14**

2113	A637	5pf shown	.20	.20
2114	A637	10pf Wild cats	.20	.20
2115	A637	15pf Prairie wolf	.20	.20
2116	A637	20pf Arabian oryx	.20	.20
2117	A637	25pf White-eared pheasant	.20	.20
2118	A637	35pf Musk oxen	1.60	1.60
		Nos. 2113-2118 (6)	2.60	2.60

Olympic Type of 1980

Designs: 10pf, Judo, by Erhard Schmidt. 50pf, Final Spurt, by Siegfried Schreiber. 1m, Spinnaker Yachts, by Karl Raetsch.

1980, July 8   **Photo.**   **Perf. 14**

2119	A627	10pf multicolored	.20	.20
2120	A627	50pf multicolored	1.25	1.25
		Nos. 2119-2120,B192 (3)	1.65	1.65

Souvenir Sheet

2121	A627	1m multicolored	2.10	1.75

22nd Summer Olympic Games, Moscow, 7/19-8/3. #2121 contains one 29x24mm stamp.

Old and
New
Buildings,
Suhl
A638

Design: 10pf + 5pf, View of Suhl, 1700.

1980, July 22   **Litho.**   **Perf. 13x12½**

2122	A638	10pf + 5pf multi	.30	.30
2123	A638	20pf multicolored	.30	.30
a.		Pair, #2122-2123 + label	1.10	1.10

6th National Youth Philatelic Exhibition, Suhl. Surtax for East German Association of Philatelists.

Huntley Microscope,
London,
1740 — A639

Optical Museum, Karl Zeiss Foundation, Jena: 25pf, Magny microscope, Paris, 1751. 35pf, Amici microscope, Modena, 1845. 70pf, Zeiss microscope, Jena, 1873.

1980, Aug. 12   **Perf. 14**

2124	A639	20pf multicolored	.30	.30
2125	A639	25pf multicolored	.30	.30
2126	A639	35pf multicolored	.55	.55
2127	A639	70pf multicolored	.75	.75
a.		Block of 4, #2124-2127	2.75	2.40

Maidenek Memorial — A640

1980, Aug. 26

2128	A640	35pf multicolored	.45	.30

Leipzig 1980 Autumn Fair, Information
Center — A641

1980, Aug. 26

2129	A641	10pf shown	.20	.20
2130	A641	25pf Carpet loom	.45	.25

67th Interparliamentary Conference,
Berlin — A642

1980, Sept. 9   **Photo.**   **Perf. 14**

2131	A642	20pf Republic Palace, Berlin	.70	.25

Paintings by Frans Hals (1580-1666) A643

1980, Sept. 23
2132	A643	10pf	*Laughing Boy with Flute*	.20 .20
2133	A643	20pf	*Man in Gray Coat*	.20 .20
2134	A643	25pf	*The Mulatto*	.20 .20
2135	A643	35pf	*Man in Black Coat*	.90 .90
		Nos. 2132-2135 (4)		1.50 1.50

Souvenir Sheet
2136	A643	1m	*Self-portrait, horiz.*	1.90 1.50

A644

Edible Mushrooms: 5pf, Leccinum Testaceo Scabrum. 10pf, Boletus erythropus. 15pf, Agaricus campester. 20pf, Xerocomus badius. 35pf, Boletus edulis. 70pf, Cantharellus cibarius.

1980, Oct. 28   Litho.   Perf. 13x13½
2137	A644	5pf multicolored	.20 .20
2138	A644	10pf multicolored	.20 .20
2139	A644	15pf multicolored	.20 .20
2140	A644	20pf multicolored	.20 .20
2141	A644	35pf multicolored	.25 .20
2142	A644	70pf multicolored	1.60 1.60
		Nos. 2137-2142 (6)	2.65 2.60

Exploration of Lignite Deposits (Gravimetry) — A645

Geophysical Exploration: 25pf, Bore-hole measuring (water). 35pf, Seismic geology. (mineral oil, natural gas). 50pf, Seismology.

1980, Nov. 11   Litho.   Perf. 13
2143	A645	20pf multicolored	.30 .20
2144	A645	25pf multicolored	.35 .30
2145	A645	35pf multicolored	.45 .45
2146	A645	50pf multicolored	.75 .75
	a.	Block of 4, #2143-2146	2.25 3.00

Radebeul-Radeburg Railroad Locomotive — A646

1980, Nov. 25   Perf. 13x12½
2147		Strip of 2 + label	1.40 1.00
	a.	A646 20pf shown	.30 .30
	b.	A646 25pf Passenger car	.30 .30
2148		Strip of 2 + label	1.40 1.00
	a.	A646 20pf Bad Doberan-Osteebad Kuhlungsborn Locomotive	.30 .30
	b.	A646 35pf Passenger car	.30 .30

Labels show maps of routes and Moritzburg Castle (No. 2147) and Bad Doberan Street (No. 2148).
See Nos. 2205-2206.

Toy Locomotive, 1850 — A647

1980, Dec. 9   Perf. 14
2149		Sheet of 6	3.00 3.00
	a.	A647 10pf shown	.25 .25
	b.	A647 20pf Airplane, 1914	.90 .90
	c.	A647 25pf Steam roller, 1920	.25 .25
	d.	A647 35pf Ship, 1825	.25 .25
	e.	A647 40pf Car, 1900	.90 .90
	f.	A647 50pf Balloon, 1920	.25 .25

Souvenir Sheet

Wolfgang Amadeus Mozart, 225th Birth Anniv. — A648

1981, Jan. 13   Litho.
2150	A648	1m multicolored	2.25 1.80

St. John's Apple — A649

1981, Jan. 13   Photo.
2151	A649	5pf shown	.20 .20
2152	A649	10pf Snow drop, horiz.	.20 .20
2153	A649	20pf Bladder bush	.20 .20
2154	A649	25pf Paulownia tomentose	.20 .20
2155	A649	35pf German honeysuckle, horiz.	.25 .20
2156	A649	50pf Genuine spice bush	1.90 1.90
		Nos. 2151-2156 (6)	2.95 2.90

Heinrich von Stephan (1831-97), Founder of UPU — A650

1981, Jan. 20   Litho.   Perf. 13x13½
2157	A650	10pf lt lemon & blk	.35 .25

Dedication of National Commemorative Plaza, Sachsenhausen — A651

1981, Jan. 27   Photo.   Perf. 14
2158	A651	10pf shown	.25 .20
2159	A651	20pf Changing of guard	.30 .20

National People's Forces, 25th anniversary.

Socialist Union Party, 10th Congress — A652

1981, Feb. 10
2160	A652	10pf multicolored	.35 .20

Postal and Newspaper Apprentice Training — A653

1981, Feb. 10   Litho.
2161	A653	5pf shown	.20 .20
2162	A653	10pf Telephone and telex service	.20 .20
2163	A653	15pf Radio communications	.20 .20
2164	A653	20pf School of Engineering, Leipzig	.25 .20
2165	A653	25pf Communications Academy, Dresden	1.00 .90
		Nos. 2161-2165 (5)	1.85 1.70

Working-class Leader Type of 1979

Designs: No. 2166, Erich Baron (1881-1933). No. 2167, Conrad Blenkle (1901-1943). No. 2168, Arthur Ewert (1890-1959). No. 2169, Walter Stoecker (1891-1939).

1981, Feb. 24   Litho.   Perf. 14
2166	A623	10pf gray grn & blk	.20 .20
2167	A623	10pf lemon & blk	.20 .20
2168	A623	10pf bl vio & blk	.20 .20
2169	A623	10pf lt red brn & blk	.20 .20
		Nos. 2166-2169 (4)	.80 .80

Merkur Hotel, Leipzig — A654

1981 Leipzig Spring Fair: 25pf, Takraf mining conveyor system, horiz.

1981, Mar. 10   Photo.   Perf. 14
2170	A654	10pf multicolored	.20 .20
2171	A654	25pf multicolored	.35 .25

Ernst Thälmann, by Willi Sitte — A655

10th Communist Party Congress (Paintings): 20pf, Worker, by Bernhard Heising. 25pf, Festivities, by Rudolf Bergander. 35pf, Brotherhood in Arms, by Paul Michaelis. 1m, When Communists Dream, by Walter Womacka.

1981, Mar. 24
2172	A655	10pf multicolored	.20 .20
2173	A655	20pf multicolored	.20 .20
2174	A655	25pf multicolored	.75 .75
2175	A655	35pf multicolored	.20 .20
		Nos. 2172-2175 (4)	1.35 1.35

Souvenir Sheet
2176	A655	1m multicolored	1.50 1.50

Souvenir Sheet

Opening of Sport and Recreation Center, Berlin — A656

1981, Mar. 24   Litho.
2177	A656	1m multicolored	2.10 1.90

Energy Conservation A657

1981, Apr. 21   Litho.   Perf. 12½x13
2178	A657	10pf orange & blk	.25 .20

Heinrich Barkhausen (1881-1956), Physicist — A658

Famous Men: 20pf, Johannes R. Becher (1891-1958), poet. 25pf, Richard Dedekind (1831-1916), mathematician. 35pf, Georg Philipp Telemann (1681-1767), composer. 50pf, Adelbert V. Chamisso (1781-1838), botanist. 70pf, Wilhelm Raabe (1831-1910), writer.

1981, May 5   Perf. 13x12½
2179	A658	10pf dull bl & blk	.20 .20
2180	A658	20pf brick red & blk	.20 .20
2181	A658	25pf dull brn & blk	2.10 1.50
2182	A658	35pf lt vio & blk	.25 .20
2183	A658	50pf yel grn & blk	.30 .20
2184	A658	70pf ol bis & blk	.45 .25
		Nos. 2179-2184 (6)	3.50 2.55

Free German Youth Members A659

1981, May 19
2185	A659	10pf shown	.25 .25
2186	A659	20pf Youths, diff.	.25 .25
	a.	Pair, #2185-2186 + label	.85 .80

Free German Youth, 11th Parliament, Berlin.

View and Map of Worlitz Park — A660

1981, June 9   Litho.   Perf. 12½x13

2187	A660	5pf shown	.20	.20
2188	A660	10pf Tiefurt	.20	.20
2189	A660	15pf Marxwalde	.20	.20
2190	A660	20pf Branitz	.20	.20
2191	A660	25pf Treptow	1.50	1.50
2192	A660	35pf Wiesenburg	.25	.20
		Nos. 2187-2192 (6)	2.55	2.50

Artistic Gymnastics — A661

8th Children's and Youth Spartacist Games: No. 2193, children and youths.

1981, June 23   Photo.   Perf. 14

2193	A661	10pf + 5pf multi	.55	.35
2194	A661	20pf multicolored	.25	.20

Javelin Throwers A662

1981, June 23   Litho.   Perf. 13x12½

2195	A662	5pf shown	.25	.20
2196	A662	15pf Men at museum	.25	.20
a.		Pair, #2195-2196 + label	.60	.55

Intl. Year of the Disabled.

Schinkel's Berlin Playhouse — A663

Karl Friedrich Schinkel, (1781-1841), Architect: 25pf, Old Museum, Berlin.

1981, June 23   Litho. & Engr.

2197	A663	10pf tan & blk	.85	.20
2198	A663	25pf tan & blk	1.90	.85

Sugar Loaf House, Gross Zicker — A664

Frame Houses: 10pf, Zaulsdorf, 19th cent., vert. 25pf, Farmhouse, stable, Weckersdorf, vert. 35pf, Restaurant (former farmhouse), Pillgram. 50pf, Eschenbach, vert. 70pf, Farmhouse, Lüdersdorf.

1981, July 7   Photo.

2199	A664	10pf multicolored	.20	.20
2200	A664	20pf multicolored	.20	.20
2201	A664	25pf multicolored	.25	.20
2202	A664	35pf multicolored	.25	.20
2203	A664	50pf multicolored	.30	.20
2204	A664	70pf multicolored	2.50	2.10
		Nos. 2199-2204 (6)	3.65	3.10

Railroad Type of 1980

1981, July 21   Litho.   Perf. 13x12½

2205		Strip of 2 + label	.75	.60
a.	A646	5pf Locomotive, Freital-Kurort-Kipsdorf line	.20	.20
b.	A646	15pf Luggage car	.20	.20
2206		Strip of 2 + label	.75	.60
a.	A646	5pf Locomotive, Putbus-Gohren line	.20	.20
b.	A646	20pf Passenger car	.20	.20

Labels show maps of train routes.

Ebers Papyrus (Egyptian Medical Text, 1600 B.C.), Leipzig — A665

Literary Treasures in DDR Libraries: 35pf, Maya manuscript, 12th cent., Dresden. 50pf, Petrarch sonnet illustration, 16th century French manuscript, Berlin.

1981, Aug. 18   Photo.   Perf. 14

2207	A665	20pf multicolored	.20	.20
2208	A665	35pf multicolored	.20	.20
2209	A665	50pf multicolored	1.40	1.40
		Nos. 2207-2209 (3)	1.80	1.80

1981, Aug. 18

Leipzig 1981 Autumn Fair: 25pf, Concert Hall, Leipzig, horiz.

Chemical Plant — A666

2210	A666	10pf multicolored	.20	.20
2211	A666	25pf multicolored	.35	.30

Anti-Fascist Resistance Monument, Sassnitz A667

1981, Sept. 8   Photo.   Perf. 14

| 2212 | A667 | 35pf multicolored | .45 | .30 |

Forceps, 18th Cent., Speculum, 17th Cent. — A668

Historic Medical Instruments, Karl Sudhoff Institute, Leipzig: 10pf, Henbana, censer, 16th cent. 20pf, Pelican, dental elevator and extractors, 17th cent. 25pf, Seton forceps, 17th cent. 35pf, Lithotomy knife, 18th cent., hernia scissors, 17th cent. 85pf, Elevators, 17th cent. 10pf, 20pf, 25pf, 35pf horiz.

1981, Sept. 22

2213	A668	10pf multicolored	.20	.20
2214	A668	20pf multicolored	.20	.20
2215	A668	25pf multicolored	.20	.20
2216	A668	35pf multicolored	.25	.20
2217	A668	50pf multicolored	2.75	2.25
2218	A668	85pf multicolored	.45	.30
		Nos. 2213-2218 (6)	4.05	3.35

Philatelists' Day — A669

1981, Oct. 6   Photo.   Perf. 14

2219	A669	10pf + 5pf Letter by Engels, 1840	.75	.50
2220	A669	20pf Postcard by Marx, 1878	.25	.20

River Boat A670

1981, Oct. 20

2221	A670	10pf Tugboat	.20	.20
2222	A670	20pf Tugboat, diff.	.20	.20
2223	A670	25pf Diesel paddle liner	.20	.20
2224	A670	35pf Ice breaker	.25	.20
2225	A670	50pf Motor freighter	.30	.20
2226	A670	85pf Bucket dredger	2.40	2.40
		Nos. 2221-2226 (6)	3.55	3.40

Windmill, Dabel — A671

1981, Nov. 10   Photo.   Perf. 14

2227	A671	10pf shown	.20	.20
2228	A671	20pf Pahrenz	.20	.20
2229	A671	25pf Dresden-Gohlis	.20	.20
2230	A671	70pf Ballstadt	1.50	1.50
		Nos. 2227-2230 (4)	2.10	2.10

Toys — A672

1981, Nov. 24   Litho.   Perf. 13½

2231		Sheet of 6	3.25	3.25
a.	A672	10pf Jointed snake, 1850	.25	.25
b.	A672	20pf Teddy bear, 1910	.25	.25
c.	A672	25pf Fish, 1935	.90	.90
d.	A672	35pf Hobby horse, 1850	.90	.90
e.	A672	40pf Cuckoo, 1800	.25	.25
f.	A672	70pf Frog, 1930	.25	.25

Meissen Porcelain Teapot, 1715 — A673

1982, Jan. 26   Photo.   Perf. 14

2232	A673	10pf shown	.20	.20
2233	A673	20pf Vase, 1715	.30	.30
2234	A673	25pf Oberon figurine, 1969	.45	.45
2235	A673	35pf Day and Night vase, 1979	.60	.60
a.		Block of 4, #2232-2235	2.10	1.80

Souvenir Sheet

2236		Sheet of 2	2.40	1.90
a.	A673	50pf Portrait	.75	.75
b.	A673	50pf Emblem	.75	.75

Johann Friedrich Bottger (1682-1719), inventor of Dresden china. No. 2236 contains two 24x29mm stamps.

Post Offices — A674

1982, Feb. 9

2237	A674	20pf Liebenstein	.20	.20
2238	A674	25pf Berlin	.20	.20
2239	A674	35pf Erfurt	.25	.20
2240	A674	50pf Dresden	1.50	1.50
		Nos. 2237-2240 (4)	2.15	2.10

Intl. Fur Auction, Leipzig A675

1982, Feb. 23   Photo.   Perf. 14

2241	A675	10pf Marmot, vert.	.20	.20
2242	A675	20pf Polecat	.20	.20
2243	A675	25pf Mink	.25	.20
2244	A675	35pf Stone marten	1.10	1.10
		Nos. 2241-2244 (4)	1.75	1.70

Souvenir Sheet

Goethe-Schiller Awards, 1980-1984 — A676

1982, Mar. 9   Litho.

2245	A676	Sheet of 2	2.60	2.10
a.		50pf Goethe	1.00	1.00
b.		50pf Schiller	1.00	1.00

1982 Leipzig Spring Fair A677

1982, Mar. 9   Perf. 13x12½

2246	A677	10pf Entrance	.20	.20
2247	A677	25pf Exhibit	.30	.20

Souvenir Sheet

TB Bacillus Centenary — A678

1982, Mar. 23   Perf. 14

2248	A678	1m multi	2.00	1.60

Working-class Leader Type of 1979

#2249, Max Fechner (1892-1973). #2250, Ottomar Greschke (1882-1957). #2251, Helmut Lehmann (1882-1959). #2252, Herbert Warnke (1902-75). #2253, Otto Winzer (1902-75).

1982, Mar. 23   Engr.

2249	A623	10pf dk red brn	.20	.20
2250	A623	10pf green	.20	.20
2251	A623	10pf violet	.20	.20
2252	A623	10pf dull blue	.20	.20
2253	A623	10pf gray olive	.20	.20
		Nos. 2249-2253 (5)	1.00	1.00

Poisonous Plants — A679

1982, Apr. 6   Litho.   Perf. 14

2254	A679	10pf Meadow saffron	.20	.20
2255	A679	15pf Water arum	.20	.20
2256	A679	20pf Marsh tea	.20	.20
2257	A679	25pf White bryony	.20	.20

2258	A679	35pf Common monks-hood	.25	.20
2259	A679	50pf Henbane	1.20	1.25
		Nos. 2254-2259 (6)	2.25	2.25

Free Federation of German Trade Unions, 10th Congress A680

Paintings: 10pf, Mother and Child, by Walter Womacka. 20pf, Discussion at the Innovator Collective, by Willi Neubert, horiz. 25pf, Young Couple, by Karl-Heinz Jacob.

1982, Apr. 20   **Photo.**

2260	A680	10pf multi	.20	.20
2261	A680	20pf multi	.20	.20
2262	A680	25pf multi	.55	.55
		Nos. 2260-2262 (3)	.95	.95

Intl. Book Art Exhibition, Leipzig — A681

1982, Apr. 20

2263	A681	15pf "I"	.35	.35
2264	A681	35pf Emblem	.35	.35
a.		Pair, #2263-2264 + label	1.25	1.10

A682

Protected species. 10pf, 25pf, 35pf vert.

Perf. 13½x14, 14x13½

1982, May 18   **Photo.**

2265	A682	10pf Fish hawk	.25	.20
2266	A682	20pf Sea eagle	.25	.20
2267	A682	25pf Tawny eagle	.25	.20
2268	A682	35pf Eagle owl	1.25	1.25
		Nos. 2265-2268 (4)	2.00	1.85

19th Workers' Festival, Neubrandenburg — A683

1982, June 8   **Photo.**   **Perf. 14**

2269	A683	10pf View of Neubrandenburg	.20	.20
2270	A683	20pf Traditional costumes	.35	.30

Souvenir Sheet

Dimitrov Memorial Medal — A684

1982, June 8

2271	A684	1m multi	2.25	2.25

George Dimitrov (1882-1947), first prime minister of Bulgaria.

Cargo Ship Frieden — A685

1982, June 22

2272	A685	5pf shown	.20	.20
2273	A685	10pf Fichtelberg	.20	.20
2274	A685	15pf Brocken	.20	.20
2275	A685	20pf Weimar	.20	.20
2276	A685	25pf Vorwarts	.25	.20
2277	A685	35pf Berlin	1.20	1.20
		Nos. 2272-2277 (6)	2.25	2.20

Society for Sport & Technology — A686

1982, June 22   **Litho.**   **Perf. 13x12½**

2278	A686	20pf multi	.35	.20

Bird Wedding — A687

Sorbian Folklore: 20pf, Zampern masqueraders. 25pf, Easter egg game. 35pf, Painting Easter eggs. 40pf, St. John's Day parade. 50pf, Christmas celebration.

1982, July 6   **Litho.**   **Perf. 13x12½**

2279	A687	Block of 6	3.75	3.25
a.		10pf multi	.20	.20
b.		20pf multi	.25	.20
c.		25pf multi	.30	.30
d.		35pf multi	.55	.55
e.		40pf multi	.60	.60
f.		50pf multi	.75	.75

View of Schwerin A688

7th Youth Stamp Exhibition, Schwerin: 10pf + 5pf, View, 1640.

1982, July 6

2280	A688	10pf + 5pf multi	.30	.30
2281	A688	20pf multi	.30	.30
a.		Pair, #2280-2281 + label	1.25	1.00

7th Pioneer Meeting, Dresden A689

1982, July 20   **Photo.**   **Perf. 14x13½**

2282	A689	10pf + 5pf Pioneers, banner	.45	.45
2283	A689	20pf Bugle, pennant	.20	.20

Seascape, by Ludolf Backhuysen (1631-1708) — A690

17th Cent. Paintings in Natl. Museum, Schwerin: 10pf, Music Making at Home, by Frans van Mieris (1635-1681), vert. 20pf, The Gate Guard, by Carel Fabritius (1622-1654), vert. 25pf, Farmers Company, by Adriaen Brouwer (1606-1638). 35pf, Breakfast Table with Ham, by Willem Claesz Heda (1593-1680). 70pf, River Landscape, by Jan van Goyen (1596-1656).

1982, Aug. 10   **Perf. 14**

2284	A690	5pf multi	.20	.20
2285	A690	10pf multi	.20	.20
2286	A690	20pf multi	.20	.20
2287	A690	25pf multi	.25	.20
2288	A690	35pf multi	.25	.20
2289	A690	70pf multi	1.80	1.50
		Nos. 2284-2289 (6)	2.90	2.50

1982 Leipzig Autumn Fair A691

1982, Aug. 24   **Litho.**   **Perf. 13x12½**

2290	A691	10pf Exhibition Hall	.20	.20
2291	A691	25pf Decorative box, ring	.25	.20

Karl-Marx-Stadt Buildings and Monument — A692

1982, Aug. 24   **Photo.**   **Perf. 14**

2292	A692	10pf multi + label	.20	.20

Org. for the Cooperation of Socialist Countries and Posts and Telecommunications Dept., 13th Conference, Karl-Marx-Stadt, Sept. 6-11.

Intl. Federation of Resistance Fighters, 9th Congress, Berlin — A693

1982, Sept. 7   **Litho.**   **Perf. 14**

2293	A693	10pf Emblem	.35	.25

Auschwitz-Birkenau Intl. Memorial A694

1982, Sept. 7   **Photo.**

2294	A694	35pf multi	.35	.30

Autumn Flowers — A695

1982, Sept. 21

2295	A695	5pf Autumn anemones	.20	.20
2296	A695	10pf Student flowers	.20	.20
2297	A695	15pf Hybrid gazanias	.20	.20
2298	A695	20pf Sunflowers	.20	.20
2299	A695	25pf Chrysanthemums	.25	.20
2300	A695	35pf Cosmos bipinnatus	1.80	1.50
		Nos. 2295-2300 (6)	2.85	2.50

Ambulance — A696

1982, Oct. 5   **Litho.**   **Perf. 13x12½**

2301	A696	5pf shown	.20	.20
2302	A696	10pf Street cleaner	.20	.20
2303	A696	20pf Bus	.20	.20
2304	A696	25pf Platform truck	.25	.20
2305	A696	35pf Platform truck, diff.	.25	.20
2306	A696	85pf Milk truck	2.10	1.80
		Nos. 2301-2306 (6)	3.20	2.80

25th Masters of Tomorrow Central Fair — A697

1982, Oct. 19   **Perf. 14**

2307	A697	20pf multicolored	.30	.20

Martin Luther (1483-1546) A698

Designs: 10pf, Seal of Eisleben (town of birth and death). 20pf, Portrait, Eisenach, 1521. 35pf, Wittenberg seal, 1500. 85pf, Portrait, after Cranach, 1528.

1982, Nov. 23   **Photo.**   **Perf. 14x13½**

2308	A698	10pf multi	.25	.20
2309	A698	20pf multi	.25	.20
a.		Miniature sheet of 10	7.50	7.50
2310	A698	35pf multi	.35	.20
2311	A698	85pf multi	3.00	1.90
		Nos. 2308-2311 (4)	3.85	2.50

Toy Carpenter, 1830 — A699

1982, Nov. 23   **Litho.**   **Perf. 14**

2312		Sheet of 6	3.25	3.25
a.	A699	10pf shown	.20	.20
b.	A699	20pf Cobbler	1.00	1.00
c.	A699	25pf Baker	.20	.20
d.	A699	35pf Cooper	.20	.20
e.	A699	40pf Tanner	1.00	1.00
f.	A699	70pf Carter	.20	.20

Souvenir Sheet

Johannes Brahms (1833-1897),
Composer — A700

1983, Jan. 11   Litho.   Perf. 14
2313 A700 1.15m multi   2.60 2.10

Working-class Leader Type of 1979

#2314, Franz Dahlem (1892-1981). #2315,
Karl Maron (1903-75). #2316, Josef Miller
(1883-1964). #2317, Fred Oelssner (1903-77).
#2318, Siegfried Radel (1893-1943).

1983, Jan. 25   Photo.
2314 A623 10pf dark brown   .20 .20
2315 A623 10pf dark green   .20 .20
2316 A623 10pf dark olive grn   .20 .20
2317 A623 10pf deep plum   .20 .20
2318 A623 10pf dark blue   .20 .20
        Nos. 2314-2318 (5)   1.00 1.00

World Communications Year — A701

1983, Feb. 8   Photo.   Perf. 14
2319 A701 5pf Telephone re-
             ceiver, buttons   .20 .20
2320 A701 10pf Rugen radio   .20 .20
2321 A701 20pf Surface and air
             mail   .20 .20
2322 A701 35pf Optical conduc-
             tors   1.10 1.10
        Nos. 2319-2322 (4)   1.70 1.70

Otto Nuschke
(1883-1957),
Statesman
A702

1983, Feb. 8
2323 A702 20pf red brn, bl & blk   .30 .20

Town Hall, Gera,
1576 — A703

1983, Feb. 22   Photo.   Perf. 14
2324 A703 10pf Stolberg, 1482,
             horiz.   .20 .20
2325 A703 20pf shown   .20 .20
2326 A703 25pf Possneck, 1486   .20 .20
2327 A703 35pf Berlin, 1869,
             horiz.   1.20 1.20
        Nos. 2324-2327 (4)   1.80 1.80

1983 Leipzig
Spring
Fair — A704

1983, Mar. 8
2328 A704 10pf Fair building   .20 .20
2329 A704 25pf Robotron
             microcomputer   .30 .25

Paul Robeson (1898-1976),
Singer — A705

1983, Mar. 22   Litho.   Perf. 13x12½
2330 A705 20pf multicolored   .30 .25

Souvenir Sheet

Schulze-Boysen/Harnack Resistance
Org. — A706

Arvid Harnack (1901-42), Harro Schulze-
Boysen (1909-42), John Sieg (1903-42).

1983, Mar. 22
2331 A706 85pf multicolored   1.40 1.40

Karl Marx (1818-1883), and
Newspaper Mastheads — A707

Portraits and: 20pf, Lyons silk weavers'
revolt, 1831, French-German Yearbook. 35pf,
Engels, Communist Manifesto. 50pf, Das
Kapital titlepage. 70pf, Program of German
Workers' Movement text. 85pf, Engels, Lenin,
globe. 1.15m Portrait (24x29mm).

1983, Apr. 11   Photo.   Perf. 13x12½
2332 A707 10pf multicolored   .20 .20
2333 A707 20pf multicolored   .20 .20
2334 A707 35pf multicolored   .25 .20
2335 A707 50pf multicolored   .25 .20
2336 A707 70pf multicolored   .35 .25
2337 A707 85pf multicolored   2.25 2.25
        Nos. 2332-2337 (6)   3.50 3.30

Souvenir Sheet
**   Litho.   Perf. 14**
2338 A707 1.15m multi   2.25 1.80

Works of Art from
Berlin State
Museums — A708

1983, Apr. 19   Photo.   Perf. 14
2339 A708 10pf Athena   .20 .20
2340 A708 20pf Amazon, bronze,
             430 BC   .35 .25

Narrow-Gauge Railroads — A709

1983, May 17   Litho.   Perf. 13x12½
2341   Pair, Wernigerode-Nord-
         hausen line   1.50 1.10
  a. A709 15pf Locomotive   .35 .35
  b. A709 20pf Passenger car   .35 .35
2342   Pair, Zittau-
         Oybin/Johnsdorf line   1.50 1.10
  a. A709 20pf Locomotive   .35 .35
  b. A709 50pf Freight car   .35 .35

Nos. 2341 and 2342 se-tenant with labels
showing maps. See Nos. 2405-2406.

Sand Glasses   Cacti
and Sundials   A711
A710

1983, June 7   Photo.   Perf. 14
2343 A710 5pf Sand glass,
             1674   .20 .20
2344 A710 10pf Sand glass,
             1700   .20 .20
2345 A710 20pf Sundial, 1611   .20 .20
  a.   Sheet of 8   2.25 2.25
2346 A710 30pf Sundial, 1750   .25 .20
2347 A710 50pf Sundial, 1760   .25 .20
2348 A710 85pf Sundial, 1800   2.10 1.90
        Nos. 2343-2348 (6)   3.30 2.90

1983, June 21
2349 A711 5pf Coryphantha ele-
             phantidens   .20 .20
2350 A711 10pf Thelocactus
             schwarzii   .20 .20
2351 A711 20pf Leuchtenbergia
             principis   .20 .20
2352 A711 25pf Submatucana
             madisoniorum   .25 .20
2353 A711 35pf Oroya peruviana   .25 .20
2354 A711 50pf Copiapoa ciner-
             ea   1.50 1.50
        Nos. 2349-2354 (6)   2.60 2.50

Naumberg
Cathedral
Statues,
15th Cent.
A712

1983, July 5   Photo.   Perf. 13
2355 A712 20pf Thimo and Wil-
             helm   .35 .35
2356 A712 25pf Gepa and
             Gerburg   .45 .45
2357 A712 35pf Hermann and
             Reglindis   .55 .55
2358 A712 85pf Eckehard and
             Uta   1.25 1.25
  a.   Block of 4, #2355-2358   3.00 2.90

Technical
Training,
by Harald
Metzkes
(b. 1929)
A713

SOZPHILEX '83 Junior Stamp Exhibition,
Berlin: 10pf+5pf, Glasewaldt and Zinna
Defending the Barricade-18th March, 1848, by
Theodor Hosemann, vert. Surtax was for
exhibition.

1983, July 5   Litho.   Perf. 13x12½
2359 A713 10pf + 5pf multi   .60 .55
2360 A713 20pf multi   .25 .20

Volleyball
A714

1983, July 19   Photo.   Perf. 14
2361 A714 10pf + 5pf Passing
             beach balls   .55 .35
2362 A714 20pf shown   .20 .20

7th Gymnastic and Sports Meeting; 9th Children's and Youth Spartikiade, Leipzig.

Simon Bolivar (1783-1830) — A715

1983, July 19
2363 A715 35pf Bolivar, Alexander
             von Humboldt   .55 .30

A715A   A716

City Arms

1983, Aug. 9
2364 A715A 50pf Berlin   .70 .60
2365 A716 50pf Cottbus   .70 .60
2366 A716 50pf Dresden   .70 .60
2367 A716 50pf Erfurt   .70 .60
2368 A716 50pf Frankfurt   .70 .60
        Nos. 2364-2368 (5)   3.50 3.00

See Nos. 2398-2402, 2464-2468.

1983 Leipzig
Autumn
Fair — A717

1983, Aug. 30
2369 A717 10pf Central Palace   .20 .20
2370 A717 25pf Microelectronic pat-
             tern   .45 .25

Leonhard Euler (1707-1783),
Mathematician — A718

1983, Sept. 6
2371 A718 20pf multi   .45 .25

Souvenir Sheet

30th Anniv. of Working-Class Brigade
Groups — A719

1983, Sept. 6 **Litho.** **Perf. 12½x13**
2372 A719 1m multicolored 2.10 1.50

Governmental Palaces, Potsdam
Gardens — A720

1983, Sept. 20 **Perf. 13x12½**
2373 A720 10pf Sanssouci Palace .20 .20
2374 A720 20pf Chinese tea-
house .25 .20
2375 A720 40pf Charlottenhof
Palace .35 .25
2376 A720 50pf Royal Stables,
Film Museum 2.25 2.25
Nos. 2373-2376 (4) 3.05 2.90

Monument, Mamajew-Kurgan
Hill — A721

1983, Oct. 4 **Perf. 14**
2377 A721 35pf Mother Home .45 .25

Souvenir Sheet

Martin Luther — A722

1983, Oct. 18 **Litho.** **Perf. 14**
2378 A722 1m multi 2.60 2.25
Margin shows title page from Luther Bible,
1541.

Thuringian
Glass — A723

1983, Nov. 8 **Photo.** **Perf. 13½x14**
2379 A723 10pf Cock .25 .20
2380 A723 20pf Cup .25 .20
2381 A723 25pf Vase .25 .20
2382 A723 70pf Ornamental
Glass 1.60 1.50
Nos. 2379-2382 (4) 2.35 2.10

Souvenir Sheet

New Year
1984 — A724

1983, Nov. 22 **Litho.** **Perf. 14**
2383 Sheet of 4 1.60 1.50
a. A724 10pf multi .20 .20
b. A724 20pf multi .25 .20
c. A724 25pf multi .35 .30
d. A724 35pf multi .55 .45

Winter
Olympics
1984,
Sarajevo
A725

1983, Nov. 22 **Photo.** **Perf. 14**
2384 A725 10pf + 5pf 2-man luge .20 .20
2385 A725 20pf + 10pf Ski jump .20 .20
2386 A725 25pf Skiing .20 .20
2387 A725 35pf Biathlon 1.50 1.10
Nos. 2384-2387 (4) 2.10 1.70

Souvenir Sheet
2388 A725 85pf Olympic Center 1.60 1.50

Jena Glass
Centenary — A726

1984, Jan. 10 **Litho.** **Perf. 12½x13**
2389 A726 20pf Otto Schott .35 .25

Working-class Leader Type of 1979
Designs: No. 2390, Friedrich Ebert (1894-
1979). No. 2391, Fritz Grosse (1904-1957).
No. 2392, Albert Norden (1904-1982).

1984, Jan. 24 **Engr.** **Perf. 14**
2390 A623 10pf black .20 .20
2391 A623 10pf dark green .20 .20
2392 A623 10pf dark blue .20 .20
Nos. 2390-2392 (3) .60 .60

Souvenir Sheet

Felix Mendelssohn (1809-1847),
Composer — A727

1984, Jan. 24 **Litho.**
2393 A727 85pf multi 1.00 1.00
Margin shows Song Without Words score.

Postal
Milestones — A728

Designs: 10pf, Muhlau, 1725; Oederan,
1722. 20pf, Johanngeorgenstadt, 1723;
Schonbrunn, 1724. 35pf, Freiberg, 1723. 85pf,
Pegau, 1723.

1984, Feb. 7 **Photo.** **Perf. 14**
2394 A728 10pf multi .20 .20
2395 A728 20pf multi .30 .25
2396 A728 35pf multi .35 .30
2397 A728 85pf multi .75 .75
Nos. 2394-2397 (4) 1.60 1.50

City Arms Type of 1983
1984, Feb. 21
2398 A716 50pf Gera .45 .35
2399 A716 50pf Halle .45 .35
2400 A716 50pf Karl-Marx-Stadt .45 .35
2401 A716 50pf Leipzig .45 .35
2402 A716 50pf Magdeburg .45 .35
Nos. 2398-2402 (5) 2.25 1.75

1984
Leipzig
Spring
Fair
A729

1984, Mar. 6 **Perf. 14**
2403 A729 10pf Old Town Hall .20 .20
2404 A729 25pf Factory .30 .25

Railroad Type of 1983
1984, Mar. 20 **Litho.** **Perf. 13x12½**
2405 Pair, Cranzahl
Oberwiesenthal line 1.40 1.20
a. A709 30pf Locomotive .25 .25
b. A709 80pf Passenger car .60 .60
2406 Pair, Selke Valley line 1.30 1.05
a. A709 40pf Locomotive .30 .30
b. A709 60pf Passenger car .35 .35
Labels show maps of routes.

Stone Door,
Rostock — A730

Council
Building — A731

Intl. Society of Monument Preservation 7th
General Meeting: 10pf, Town Hall, Rostock.
15pf, Albrecht Castle, Meissen. 85pf, Stable
Courtyard, Dresden. 10pf, 15pf, 85pf horiz.

1984, Apr. 24 **Photo.** **Perf. 14**
2407 A730 10pf multi .20 .20
2408 A730 15pf multi .20 .20
2409 A730 40pf multi .45 .35
2410 A730 85pf multi 1.10 1.00
Nos. 2407-2410 (4) 1.95 1.75

1984, May 8
2411 A731 70pf multi .70 .30
Standing Commission of Posts and Telecommunications of Council of Mutual Economic Aid, 25th meeting.

Cast-iron Bowl,
19th Cent.
A732

Marionette
A733

Cast-Iron, Lauchhammer: 85pf, Ascending
Man, by Fritz Cremer, 1967.

1984, May 22
2412 A732 20pf multi .25 .20
2413 A732 85pf multi .85 .85

1984, June 5
2414 A733 50pf shown .55 .55
2415 A733 80pf Puppet .90 .90

Natl.
Youth
Festival
A734

1984, June 5 **Litho.** **Perf. 13x12½**
2416 A734 10pf + 5pt Demon-
stration .20 .20
2417 A734 20pf Construction
workers .25 .25
a. Pair, #2416-2417 + label 1.10 .60

20th
Workers'
Festival
A735

1984, June 19
2418 A735 10pf View of Gera .20 .20
2419 A735 20pf Traditional costumes .25 .25
a. Pair, #2418-2419 + label .85 .55

Natl. Stamp Exhib.,
Halle — A736

1984, July 3 **Perf. 13½x14**
2420 A736 10pf + 5pf Salt carrier .20 .20
2421 A736 20pf Wedding couple .30 .25

Historic Seals,
1442 — A737

1984, Aug. 7 **Litho.** **Perf. 14**
2422 A737 5pf Baker, Berlin .30 .20
2423 A737 10pf Wool weaver,
Berlin .55 .30
2424 A737 20pf Wool weaver,
Cologne 1.00 .35
2425 A737 35pf Shoemaker,
Cologne 1.60 1.50
a. Block of 4, #2422-2425 4.25 2.50

Building
Renovation and
Construction
A738

Ironwork Collective Combine
East — A739

Litho., Photo. (#2427, 2429, 25pf)

1984			Perf. 14x13½	
2426	A738	10pf shown	.20	.20
2427	A739	10pf shown	.20	.20
2428	A738	20pf Surface mining	.30	.30
2429	A739	20pf Armed forces	.25	.25
2430	A739	25pf Petro-chemical Collective Combine, Schwedt	.30	.30
	Nos. 2426-2430 (5)		1.25	1.25

Souvenir Sheets

2431	A738	1m Privy Council Building	1.00	1.00
2432	A739	1m Family	1.00	1.00

DDR, 35th anniv. Issued: A738, 8/21; A739, 9/11.

1984 Leipzig
Autumn Fair — A740

1984, Aug. 28   Photo.   Perf. 14

2433	A740	10pf Frege House, Katharine St.	.20	.20
2434	A740	25pf Crystal bowl, Olbernhau		.30	.25

Members of the Resistance, Sculpture
by Arno Wittig — A741

1984, Sept. 18   Photo.   Perf. 14

2435	A741	35pf multi	.70	.30

View of Magdeburg — A742

1984, Oct. 4   Litho.   Perf. 13x12½

2436	A742	10pf + 5pf shown	.20	.20
2437	A742	20pf Old & modern buildings	.20	.20
a.	Pair, #2436-2437 + label		1.00	.75

8th Youth Stamp Exhibition, Magdeburg.

35th Anniv. of Republic — A743

1984, Oct. 4   Photo.   Perf. 14

2438	A743	10pf Construction	.20	.20
2439	A743	20pf Military	.25	.20
2440	A743	25pf Heavy industry	.30	.30
2441	A743	35pf Agriculture	.35	.35
	Nos. 2438-2441 (4)		1.10	1.05

Souvenir Sheet

2442	A743	1m Arms, dove, vert.	1.00	1.00

Figurines, Green
Vault of
Dresden — A744

1984, Oct. 23

2443	A744	10pf Spring	.20	.20
2444	A744	20pf Summer	.25	.20
a.	Miniature sheet of 8, litho., perf. 12½x13		2.40	2.40
2445	A744	35pf Autumn	.30	.30
2446	A744	70pf Winter	.75	.75
	Nos. 2443-2446 (4)		1.50	1.45

Falkenstein
Castle — A745

1984, Nov. 6   Litho.   Perf. 14

2447	A745	10pf shown	.20	.20
2448	A745	20pf Kriebstein	.25	.25
2449	A745	35pf Ranis	.45	.45
2450	A745	80pf Neuenburg	.75	.75
	Nos. 2447-2450 (4)		1.65	1.65

See Nos. 2504-2507.

Dead Tsar's
Daughter and
the Seven
Warriors
A746

Various scenes from the fairytale.

1984, Nov. 27   Litho.   Perf. 13

2451		Sheet of 6	10.00	4.50
a.	A746	5pf multi	.25	.25
b.	A746	10pf multi	.25	.25
c.	A746	15pf multi	2.60	1.50
d.	A746	20pf multi	2.60	1.50
e.	A746	35pf multi	.25	.25
f.	A746	50pf multi	.25	.25

Working-class Leader Type of 1979

Designs: No. 2452, Anton Ackermann (1905-1973). No. 2453, Alfred Kurella (1895-1975). No. 2454, Otto Schon (1905-1968).

1985, Jan. 8   Engr.   Perf. 14

2452	A623	10pf blk brn	.20	.20
2453	A623	10pf red brn	.20	.20
2454	A623	10pf gray vio	.20	.20
	Nos. 2452-2454 (3)		.60	.60

24th World Luge
Championship — A747

1985, Jan. 22   Photo.

2455	A747	10pf Single seat luge	.30	.20

Antique
Mailboxes — A748

1985, Feb. 5   Litho.   Perf. 14

2456	A748	10pf 1850	.20	.20
2457	A748	20pf 1860	.20	.20
2458	A748	35pf 1900	.30	.30
2459	A748	50pf 1920	.45	.45
a.	Block of 4, Nos. 2456-2459		1.40	1.40

Souvenir Sheet

Dresden Opera House
Reopening — A749

Litho. & Engr.

1985, Feb. 12   Perf. 13

2460	A749	85pf multicolored	1.00	1.00

1985 Leipzig
Spring Fair
A750

Bach, Handel
and Schutz
Tribute
A751

1985, Mar. 5   Photo.   Perf. 14

2461	A750	10pf Statue of Bach, Leipzig	.20	.20
2462	A750	25pf Porcelain pot, Meissen	.30	.25

Souvenir Sheet

1985, Mar. 19   Litho.

2463		Sheet of 3	1.80	1.80
a.	A751	10pf Bach	.25	.25
b.	A751	20pf Handel	.25	.25
c.	A751	85pf Heinrich Schutz (1585-1672)	.75	.75

City Arms Type of 1983

1985, Apr. 9   Photo.   Perf. 14

2464	A716	50pf Neubrandenburg	.45	.35
2465	A716	50pf Potsdam	.45	.35
2466	A716	50pf Rostock	.45	.35
2467	A716	50pf Schwerin	.45	.35
2468	A716	50pf Suhl	.75	.75
	Nos. 2464-2468 (5)		2.55	2.15

Seelow Heights
Memorial — A752

1985, Apr. 16   Photo.   Perf. 14

2469	A752	35pf multi	.45	.30

Egon Erwin Kisch, Journalist (1885-
1948) — A753

1985, Apr. 23   Photo.   Perf. 14

2470	A753	35pf multi	.30	.20

No. 2470 was printed se-tenant with label showing the house where Kisch was born.

Value, single with attached label: unused 45c; used 35c.

Liberation from
Fascism, 40th
Anniv. — A754

Designs: 10pf, German and Soviet astronauts. 20pf, Coal miner Adolf Hennecke, symbols of industry and energy. 25pf, farm workers, symbols of socialist agriculture. 50pf, Technicians manufacturing microchips, science and technology.

1985, May 7   Photo.   Perf. 14x13½

2471	A754	10pf multi	.20	.20
2472	A754	20pf multi	.25	.25
2473	A754	25pf multi	.25	.25
2474	A754	50pf multi	.45	.45
	Nos. 2471-2474 (4)		1.15	1.15

Souvenir Sheet

Perf. 12½x13

2475	A754	1m Berlin-Treptow Soviet Heroes Monument	1.10	1.10

Warsaw Treaty, 30th Anniv. — A755

1985, May 14   Litho.   Perf. 13x12½

2476	A755	20pf Flags of pact nations	.35	.25

Historical
and
Modern
Buildings
A756

12th Youth Parliament, Berlin: 20pf, Ernst Thalmann, flags.

1985, May 21   Litho.

2477	A756	10pf + 5pf multi	.20	.20
2478	A756	20pf multi	.20	.20
a.	Pair, #2477-2478 + label		.60	.60

Intl. Olympic Committee 90th
Meeting — A757

1985, May 28   Litho.   Perf. 14

2479	A757	35pf Flag	.30	.25

No. 2479 was printed setenant with label depicting Olympic Torches. Value of single with attached label: unused 85c; used 60c.

Free German
Trade Unions,
40th
Anniv. — A758

1985, June 11   Photo.

2480	A758	20pf Red flags	.30	.20

Wildlife Preservation A759

1985, June 25   **Photo.**
2481	A759	5pf Harpy eagle, vert.	.20	.20
2482	A759	10pf Red-necked goose	.20	.20
2483	A759	20pf Spectacled bear	.25	.20
2484	A759	50pf Banteng (Javanese) buffalo	.45	.45
2485	A759	85pf Sunda Straits crocodile	.90	.90
		Nos. 2481-2485 (5)	2.00	1.95

19th Century Steam Engines A760

1985, July 9   **Photo.**
2486	A760	10pf Bock engine, vert.	.20	.20
2487	A760	85pf Beam engine	.85	.75

12th World Youth and Student Festival, Moscow A761

1985, July 23   **Litho.**   *Perf. 13x12½*
2488	A761	20pf + 5pf Students reading	.25	.25
2489	A761	50pf Student demonstration	.35	.35
a.		Pair, #2488-2489 + label	1.00	.90

2nd World Orienteering and Deep-sea Diving Championship — A762

1985, Aug. 13   **Photo.**   *Perf. 14*
2490	A762	10pf Diver at turning buoy	.20	.20
2491	A762	70pf Long-distance divers	.75	.75

Bose House Fair Building, St. Thomas Churchyard — A763

1985, Apr. 27   **Photo.**
2492	A763	10pf shown	.20	.20
2493	A763	25pf Bach trumpet	.35	.25

Leipzig Autumn Fair.

A764

SOZPHILEX '85: 19th century coach and team, 1878, bas-relief by Hermann Steinemann, in the court of the former Berlin Post Office.

1985, Sept. 10   **Litho.**   *Perf. 13x12½*
2494	5pf multi	.20	.20
2495	20pf + 5pf multi	.25	.25
a.	Miniature sheet of 4 #2495b	.75	.75
b.	A764 Pair, #2494-2495	.45	.45

No. 2495b has a continuous design.

German Railways 150th Anniv. — A765

Socialist Railway Org.: 20pf, GS II signal box, track diagram. 25pf, 1838 Saxonia, first German locomotive, designer Johann Andreas Schubert (1808-1870), Model 250 electric locomotive. 50pf, Helicopter lifting cable drum, section electrification. 85pf, Leipzig Central Station.

Litho.
Perf. 12½x13
1985, Sept. 24
2496	A765	20pf multi	.25	.20
2497	A765	25pf multi	.30	.25
2498	A765	50pf multi	.60	.55
2499	A765	85pf multi	.90	.90
		Nos. 2496-2499 (4)	2.05	1.90

Bridges in East Berlin A766

Photo.; Litho. (#2501a)
1985, Oct. 8   *Perf. 14*
2500	A766	10pf Gertrauden	.20	.20
2501	A766	20pf Jungfern	.25	.25
a.		Min. sheet of 8, perf. 13x12½	3.00	3.00
2502	A766	35pf Weidendammer	.35	.35
2503	A766	70pf Marx-Engels	.60	.60
		Nos. 2500-2503 (4)	1.40	1.40

Castles Type of 1984
1985, Oct. 15   **Litho.**
2504	A745	10pf Hohnstein	.20	.20
2505	A745	20pf Rochsburg	.20	.20
2506	A745	35pf Schwarzenberg	.30	.30
2507	A745	80pf Stein	.90	.90
		Nos. 2504-2507 (4)	1.60	1.60

Humboldt University, 175th Anniv. — A767

85pf, Charity Hospital, Berlin, 275th anniv.

1985, Oct. 22   *Perf. 14*
2508	A767	20pf Administration bldg.	.25	.20
2509	A767	85pf Buildings, 1897, 1982	.90	.90

Castle Cacilienhof, UN Emblem A768

1985, Oct. 22   **Photo.**   *Perf. 13*
2510	A768	85pf multi	.90	.45

UN, 40th Anniv.

Circus Art — A769

1985, Nov. 12   *Perf. 14*
2511	A769	10pf Elephant training	.25	.25
2512	A769	20pf Trapeze artist	.45	.45
2513	A769	35pf Acrobats on unicycles	.90	.90
2514	A769	50pf Tiger training	1.40	1.40
a.		Block of 4, #2511-2514	5.50	12.50

Souvenir Sheet

Brothers Grimm, Fabulists & Philologists A770

Fairy tales compiled by Wilhelm (1786-1859) and Jacob (1785-1863) Grimm.

1985, Nov. 26   **Litho.**   *Perf. 13½x13*
2515		Sheet of 6	2.75	6.75
a.	A770	5pf multi	.20	.20
b.	A770	10pf Valiant Tailor	.20	.20
c.	A770	20pf Lucky John	.55	1.25
d.	A770	25pf Puss-in-Boots	.55	1.25
e.	A770	35pf Seven Ravens	.20	.20
f.	A770	85pf Sweet Porridge	.20	.20

Monuments to Water Power — A772

Designs: 10pf, Cast iron hand pump, c. 1900. 35pf, Berlin-Altglienicke water tower, c. 1900. 50pf, Berlin-Friedrichshagen waterworks, 1893. 70pf, Rapphoden Hydro-electric Dam, 1959.

Engr., Photo. & Engr. (35pf)
1986, Jan. 21   *Perf. 14*
2516	A772	10pf dk grn & lake	.20	.20
2517	A772	35pf buff, blk & dk grn	.30	.30
2518	A772	50pf dk red brn & lt ol grn	.55	.55
2519	A772	70pf dk bl & brn	.70	.70
		Nos. 2516-2519 (4)	1.75	1.75

Postal Uniforms, c. 1850 — A773

1986, Feb. 4   **Photo.**   *Perf. 14½x14*
2520	A773	10pf Saxon postillion	.20	.20
a.		Litho., perf. 12½x13	.20	.20
2521	A773	20pf Prussian postman	.30	.25
a.		Litho., perf. 12½x13	.30	.25
2522	A773	85pf Prussian P.O. clerk	1.05	1.00
a.		Litho., perf. 12½x13	1.05	1.00
2523	A773	1m Mecklenburg clerk	1.40	1.40
a.		Litho., perf. 12½x13	1.40	1.40

Natl. People's Army, 30th Anniv. A774

1986, Feb. 18   *Perf. 14*
2524	A774	20pf multi	.35	.20

No. 2524 printed se-tenant with gold and red inscribed label. Value of single with attached label: unused 60c; used 45c.

Free German Youth Org., 40th Anniv. — A775

1986, Feb. 18
2525	A775	20pf multi	.35	.30

Leipzig Spring Fair A776

1986, Mar. 11   **Litho.**   *Perf. 13x12½*
2526	A776	35pf Fair grounds entrance, 1946	.30	.25
2527	A776	50pf Trawler Atlantik 488	.45	.35

Manned Space Flight, 25th Anniv. — A777

Designs: 40pf, Yuri Gagarin, Soviet cosmonaut, Vostok rocket, 1961. 50pf, Cosmonauts V. Bykowski, USSR, and S. Jahn, DDR, Vega probe, 1986, Intercosmos emblem. 70pf, Venera probe, Venus, spectrometer. 85pf, MKF-6 multi-spectral reconnaissance camera.

1986, Mar. 25   *Perf. 14*
2528	A777	40pf multi	.30	.30
2529	A777	50pf multi	.35	.35
2530	A777	70pf multi	.55	.55
2531	A777	85pf multi	.70	.70
a.		Block of 4, #2528-2531	3.00	3.25

Socialist Unity 11th Party Day — A778

10pf, Marx, Engels & Lenin. 20pf, Ernst Thalmann. 50pf, Wilhelm Pieck & Otto Grotewohl, Uniting Party Day, 1946. 85pf, Family, motto. 1m, Construction worker, key to economic progress.

1986, Apr. 8   *Perf. 13½x13*
2532	A778	10pf multi	.20	.20
2533	A778	20pf multi	.25	.25
2534	A778	50pf multi	.45	.45
2535	A778	85pf multi	.90	.90
		Nos. 2532-2535 (4)	1.80	1.80

Souvenir Sheet
Perf. 13x14
2536	A778	1m multi	1.05	1.05

Ernst Thalmann Park Opening, Berlin — A779

1986, Apr. 15　Photo.　*Perf. 14*
2537　A779　20pf Memorial statue　.35　.30

Trams and Streetcars — A780

Designs: 10pf, Dresden horse-drawn tram, 1886. 20pf, Leipzig streetcar, 1896. 40pf, Berlin streetcar, 1919. 70pf, Halle streetcar, 1928.

1986, May 20　Photo.　*Perf. 14*
2538　A780　10pf multicolored　.20　.20
2539　A780　20pf multicolored　.25　.25
2540　A780　40pf multicolored　.55　.55
2541　A780　70pf multicolored　.75　.75
　　Nos. 2538-2541 (4)　1.75　1.75

Dresden Zoo, 125th Anniv. — A781

Berlin, 750th Anniv. — A782

1986, May 27　Litho.　*Perf. 14*
2542　A781　10pf Orangutan　.25　.20
2543　A781　20pf Colobus monkey　.35　.30
2544　A781　50pf Mandrill　.75　.75
2545　A781　70pf Lemur　.90　.90
　　Nos. 2542-2545 (4)　2.25　2.15

Litho. & Engr., Engr. (70pf, 1m)
1986, June 3　*Perf. 12½x13, 13x12½*

20pf, 50pf are horiz.

2546　A782　10pf City seal, 1253　.25　.20
2547　A782　20pf Map, 1648　.45　.25
2548　A782　50pf City arms, 1253　.90　.60
2549　A782　70pf Nicholas Church, 1832　1.50　1.00
　　Nos. 2546-2549 (4)　3.10　2.05

Souvenir Sheet

2550　A782　1m Royal Palace, 1986　1.25　1.25

21st Workers' Games, Magdeburg — A783

20pf, Couple in folk dress, house construction. 50pf, Magdeburg Port, River Elbe.

1986, June 17　Litho.　*Perf. 13x12½*
2551　A783　20pf multi　.20　.20
2552　A783　50pf multi　.30　.30
　a.　Pair, #2551-2552 + label　1.00　1.00

9th Youth Stamp Exhibition, Berlin — A784

1986, July 22　Litho.　*Perf. 13x12½*
2553　A784　10pf + 5pf Berlin, c. 1652　.20　.20
2554　A784　20pf Art, architecture, 1986　.20　.20
　a.　Pair, #2553-2554 + label　.45　.60

Castles A785

1986, July 29　*Perf. 13x12½*
2555　A785　10pf Schwerin　.20　.20
　a.　Miniature sheet of 4　.80　.80
2556　A785　20pf Gustrow　.25　.20
　a.　Miniature sheet of 4　1.10　1.10
2557　A785　85pf Rheinsberg　.85　.85
2558　A785　1m Ludwigslust　1.10　1.10
　　Nos. 2555-2558 (4)　2.40　2.35

Intl. Peace Year A786

1986, Aug. 5　Photo.　*Perf. 13*
2559　A786　35pf multi　.55　.35

Berlin Wall, 25th Anniv. — A787

1986, Aug. 5　Litho.　*Perf. 14*
2560　A787　20pf Soldiers, Brandenburg Gate　.60　.35

Souvenir Sheet

Leipzig Autumn Fair — A788

1986, Aug. 19
2561　A788　Sheet of 2　1.20　1.20
　a.　25pf Fair building　.25　.25
　b.　85pf Cloth merchants, 15th cent.　.75　.75

City Coins A789

1986, Sept. 2　Photo.　*Perf. 13*
2562　A789　10pf Rostock, 1637　.20　.20
2563　A789　35pf Nordhausen, 1660　.30　.30
2564　A789　50pf Erfurt, 1633　.45　.35
2565　A789　85pf Magdeburg, 1638　.75　.75
2566　A789　1m Stralsund, 1622　1.10　1.10
　　Nos. 2562-2566 (5)　2.80　2.70

44th World Sports Shooting Championships, Suhl — A790

1986, Sept. 2　*Perf. 14*
2567　A790　20pf Rifle shooting　.25　.20
2568　A790　70pf Woman firing handgun　.75　.70
2569　A790　85pf Skeet-shooting　.90　.85
　　Nos. 2567-2569 (3)　1.90　1.75

11th World Trade Unions Congress, Berlin — A791

1986, Sept. 9
2570　A791　70pf multi+label　.90　.75

Border Guards, 40th Anniv. — A792

1986, Sept. 9
2571　A792　20pf multi　.35　.30

Intl. Brigades in Spain, 50th Anniv. — A793

1986, Sept. 11
2572　A793　20pf Memorial, Friedrichshain　.35　.25

Natl. Memorial for Concentration Camp Victims, Sachsenhausem, 25th Anniv. — A794

1986, Sept. 23
2573　A794　35pf multi　.45　.30

Mukran-Klaipeda Train-Ferry, Inauguration — A795

1986, Sept. 23
2574　A795　50pf Pier, Mukran　.35　.35
2575　A795　50pf Ferry　.35　.35
　a.　Pair, #2574-2575　1.25　1.25

Souvenir Sheet

Carl Maria von Weber (1786-1826), Composer — A796

1986, Nov. 4　Litho.　*Perf. 14*
2576　A796　85pf multi　1.10　1.10

Indira Gandhi (1917-1984), Prime Minister of India — A797

1986, Nov. 18　Photo.
2577　A797　10pf multi　.30　.20

Miniature Sheet

Chandeliers from the Ore Mountains A798

Wrought iron candle-carrying chandeliers presented to Johann Georgenstadt miners annually by the mine blacksmith.

1986, Nov. 18　Photo.　*Perf. 14*
2578　Sheet of 6　2.25　2.25
　a.　A798 10pf 1778　.20　.20
　b.　A798 20pf 1796　.20　.20
　c.　A798 25pf 1810　.55　.55
　d.　A798 35pf 1821　.55　.55
　e.　A798 40pf 1830　.20　.20
　f.　A798 85pf 1925　.20　.20

Statues of Roland, Medieval Hero — A799

1987, Jan. 20　Photo.　*Perf. 14½x14*
2579　A799　10pf Stendal, 1525　.20　.20
2580　A799　20pf Halle, 1719　.25　.20
2581　A799　35pf Brandenburg, 1474　.30　.30
2582　A799　50pf Quedlinburg, 1460　.55　.55
　　Nos. 2579-2582 (4)　1.30　1.25

See Nos. 2782-2785.

Historic Post Offices A800

1987, Feb. 3　Photo.　*Perf. 14x14½*
2583　A800　10pf Freiberg, 1889　.20　.20
2584　A800　20pf Perleberg, 1897　.25　.25
2585　A800　70pf Weimar, 1889　.55　.55
2586　A800　1.20m Kirschau, 1926　1.10　1.10
　a.　Block of 4, #2583-2586　2.25　2.25

Nos. 2583-2586 printed in sheets of fifty and se-tenant in sheets of 40.

Berlin, 750th Anniv. A801

Architecture: 20pf, Reconstructed Palais Ephraim, Nikolai Quarter, demolished 1936, reopened 1987, vert. 35pf, Old Marzahn Village, modern housing. 70pf, Marx-Engels Forum, Central Berlin. 85pf, Reconstructed Friedrichstadt Palace Theater, reopened 1984.

Perf. 12½x13, 13x12½

1987, Feb. 17   **Engr.**
2587	A801	20pf vio brn & bluish grn	.20	.20
2588	A801	35pf sage grn & dk rose brn	.30	.25
2589	A801	70pf org & dk bl	.70	.70
2590	A801	85pf dk ol grn & yel grn	1.00	1.00
		Nos. 2587-2590 (4)	2.20	2.15

See Nos. 2628-2631.

Democratic Women's Federation, 40th Anniv. — A802

1987, Mar. 3   **Litho.**   **Perf. 13½**
2591	A802	10pf sil, dk bl & brt red	.30	.25

Leipzig Spring Fair A803

1987, Mar. 10   **Perf. 13x12½**
2592	A803	35pf New Fair Hall No. 20	.30	.25
2593	A803	50pf Traders at market, c. 1804	.60	.60

Leaders of the German Workers' Movement — A804

#2594, Fritz Gabler (1897-1974). #2595, Robert Siewert (1887-1973). #2596, Walter Vesper (1897-1978). #2597, Clara Zetkin (1857-1933).

1987, Mar. 24   **Engr.**   **Perf. 14**
2594	A804	10pf dark gray	.20	.20
2595	A804	10pf dark green	.20	.20
2596	A804	10pf black	.20	.20
2597	A804	10pf vio black	.20	.20
		Nos. 2594-2597 (4)	.80	.80

See Nos. 2721-2724.

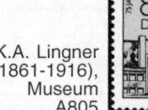

K.A. Lingner (1861-1916), Museum A805

1987, Apr. 7   **Photo.**   **Perf. 14**
2598	A805	85pf multi	.85	.75

German Hygiene Museum, Dresden, 75th anniv.

Free German Trade Unions 11th Congress A806

1987, Apr. 7   **Litho.**   **Perf. 13x12½**
2599	A806	20pf Construction	.20	.20
2600	A806	50pf Computer, ship	.45	.45
a.		Pair, #2599-2600 + label	.90	.90

German Red Cross 10th Congress A807

1987, Apr. 7   **Photo.**   **Perf. 14**
2601	A807	35pf multi	.45	.25

Agricultural Cooperative, 35th Anniv. — A808

1987, Apr. 21   **Litho.**   **Perf. 13x12½**
2602	A808	20pf multi	.35	.30

Famous Men A809

Designs: 10pf, Ludwig Uhland (1787-1862), poet, philologist. 20pf, Arnold Zweig (1887-1968), novelist. 35pf, Gerhart Hauptmann (1862-1946), 1912 Nobel laureate for literature, and scene from The Weavers. 50pf, Gustav Hertz (1887-1975), physicist, and atomic energy transmission diagram.

1987, May 5
2603	A809	10pf multi	.20	.20
2604	A809	20pf multi	.25	.25
2605	A809	35pf multi	.35	.35
2606	A809	50pf multi	.60	.60
		Nos. 2603-2606 (4)	1.40	1.40

Freshwater Fish — A810

1987, May 19   **Litho.**   **Perf. 13x12½**
2607	A810	5pf Abramis brama	.20	.20
2608	A810	10pf Salmo trutta fario	.25	.25
2609	A810	20pf Silurus glanis	.25	.25
2610	A810	35pf Thymallus thymallus	.35	.35
2611	A810	50pf Barbus barbus	.55	.55
2612	A810	70pf Esox lucius	.75	.75
		Nos. 2607-2612 (6)	2.35	2.15

Nos. 2608-2609 exist in sheets of 4.

Fire Engines A811

1987, June 16
2613	A811	10pf Hand-operated, 1756	.20	.20
2614	A811	25pf Steam, 1903	.25	.25
2615	A811	40pf LF 15, 1919	.45	.45
2616	A811	70pf LF 16-TS 8, 1971	.75	.75
a.		Block of 4, Nos. 2613-2616	2.10	1.90

Souvenir Sheet

Esperanto Movement, Cent. — A812

1987, July 7   **Litho.**   **Perf. 14**
2617	A812	85pf L.L. Zamenhof, globe	.90	1.20

World Wildlife Fund A813

1987, July 7   **Photo.**
2618	A813	10pf Two otters	.25	.20
2619	A813	25pf Otter swimming	.60	.20
2620	A813	35pf Otter	1.25	.35
2621	A813	60pf Close-up of head	2.50	1.00
		Nos. 2618-2621 (4)	4.60	1.75

8th Sports Festival and 11th Youth Sports Championships, Leipzig — A814

1987, July 21
2622	A814	5pf Tug-of-war	.20	.20
2623	A814	10pf Handball	.20	.20
2624	A814	20pf + 5pf Girls' long jump	.25	.20
2625	A814	35pf Table tennis	.30	.30
2626	A814	40pf Bowling	.45	.45
2627	A814	70pf Running	.70	.70
		Nos. 2622-2627 (6)	2.10	2.05

Berlin Anniversary Type of 1987

Perf. 12½x13, 13x12½

1987, Feb. 17   **Engr.**
2628	A801	10pf like No. 2587	.25	.25
a.		Miniature sheet of 4	1.00	1.10
2629	A801	10pf like No. 2588	.25	.25
a.		Miniature sheet of 4	1.00	1.10
2630	A801	20pf like No. 2589	.25	.25
a.		Miniature sheet of 4	1.10	1.40
2631	A801	20pf like No. 2590	.25	.25
a.		Miniature sheet of 4	1.00	1.40
		Nos. 2628-2631 (4)	1.00	1.00

Assoc. of Sports and Science, 35th Anniv. A815

1987, Aug. 4   **Litho.**   **Perf. 13x12½**
2632	A815	10pf multi	.30	.20

Stamp Day A816

Designs: 10pf+5pf, Court Post Office, Berlin, 1760. 20pf, Wartenberg Palace, former Prussian General Post Office, 1770.

1987, Aug. 11   **Photo.**   **Perf. 14**
2633	A816	10pf +5pf multi	.20	.20
2634	A816	20pf multi	.20	.20
a.		Pair, #2633-2634 + label	.55	.75

Souvenir Sheet

Leipzig Autumn Fair — A817

1987, Aug. 25   **Litho.**   **Perf. 13½**
2635	A817	Sheet of 2	1.20	1.40
a.		40pf multi	.35	.35
b.		50pf multi	.55	.55

Intl. War Victims' Memorial, Budapest A818

1987, Sept. 8   **Photo.**   **Perf. 14**
2636	A818	35pf Statue by Jozsef Somogyi	.35	.25

Souvenir Sheet

Thalmann Memorial — A819

Litho. & Engr.

1987, Sept. 8   **Perf. 14**
2637	A819	1.35m buff, ver & blk	1.50	1.50

City of Berlin, 750th anniv.

10th Natl. Art Exhibition, Berlin — A820

Designs: 10pf, Weidendamm Bridge, Berlin, 1986, by Arno Mohr. 50pf, They Only Wanted to Learn How to Read and Write, Nicaragua, 1985-86, by Willi Sitte. 70pf, Large Figure of a Man in Mourning, 1983, scupture by Wieland Forster. 1m, Ceramic bowl, 1986, by Gerd Lucke. Nos. 2638-2640, vert.

1987, Sept. 28   **Litho.**
2638	A820	10pf multi	.20	.20
2639	A820	50pf multi	.45	.45
2640	A820	70pf multi	.60	.60
2641	A820	1m multi	.90	.90
		Nos. 2638-2641 (4)	2.15	2.15

Lenin, Flag, Smolny Institute, Cruiser Aurora A821

1987, Oct. 27   Photo.   Perf. 14
2642 A821 10pf shown   .20 .20
2643 A821 20pf Spasski Tower   .25 .20
October Revolution, Russia, 70th anniv.

Robot ZIM 10-S Welding A822

1987, Nov. 3   Litho.   Perf. 13x12½
2644 A822 10pf Personal computer   .20 .20
2645 A822 20pf shown   .25 .20
30th MMM Science Fair and 10th Central Industrial Fair for Students and Youth Scientists, Leipzig.

Miniature Sheet

Christmas Candle Carousels from the Ore Mountains — A823

Designs: 10pf, Annaberg, c. 1810. 20pf, Freiberg, c. 1830. 25pf, Neustadtel, c. 1870. 35pf, Schneeberg, c. 1870. 40pf, Lossnitz, c. 1880. 85pf, Seiffen, c. 1910.

1987, Nov. 3   Litho.   Perf. 12½x13
2646   Sheet of 6   2.25 2.40
  a. A823 10pf multi   .25 .25
  b. A823 20pf multi   .55 .55
  c. A823 25pf multi   .25 .25
  d. A823 35pf multi   .25 .25
  e. A823 40pf multi   .55 .55
  f. A823 85pf multi   .25 .25

1988 Winter Olympics, Calgary — A824

1988, Jan. 19   Photo.   Perf. 14½x14
2647 A824 5pf Ski jumping   .25 .25
2648 A824 10pf Speed skating   .25 .20
2649 A824 20pf +10pf 4-Man bobsled   .35 .30
2650 A824 35pf Biathlon   .45 .35
  Nos. 2647-2650 (4)   1.30 1.05

Souvenir Sheet
Perf. 13x12½
2651 A824 1.20m Single and double luge   1.50 1.30
No. 2649 surtaxed for the Olympic Promotion Society.

Postal Buildings, East Berlin A825

1988, Feb. 2   Perf. 14
2652 A825 15pf Berlin-Buch post office   .25 .20
2653 A825 20pf Natl. Postal Museum   .35 .20

2654 A825 50pf General post office, Berlin-Marzahn   .75 .60
  Nos. 2652-2654 (3)   1.35 1.00

Souvenir Sheet

Bertolt Brecht (1898-1956), Playwright — A826

1988, Feb. 2   Litho.   Perf. 13x12½
2655 A826 70pf multi   1.00 .90

Flowering Plants — A827   Leipzig Spring Fair — A828

1988, Feb. 16   Photo.   Perf. 14
2656 A827 10pf Tillandsia macrochlamys   .20 .20
2657 A827 25pf Tillandsia bulbosa   .25 .25
2658 A827 40pf Tillandsia kalmbacheri   .35 .35
2659 A827 70pf Guzmania blassii   .65 .65
  Nos. 2656-2659 (4)   1.45 1.45

1988, Mar. 8   Litho.   Perf. 12½x13
20pf, Entrance #8. 70pf, Faust & Mephistopheles, bronze statue by Matthieu Molitor.
2660 A828 20pf multi   .20 .20
2661 A828 70pf multi   .75 .60
Madler Passage (arcade), 75th anniv.

A829

Souvenir Sheet
1988, Mar. 8   Perf. 14
2662 A829 70pf multi   1.10 1.10
Joseph von Eichendorff (1788-1857), poet.

Seals — A830

1988, Mar. 22   Photo.   Perf. 14
2663 A830 10pf Muhlhausen saddler, 1565   .20 .20
2664 A830 25pf Dresden butcher, 1564   .25 .25
2665 A830 35pf Nauen smith, 16th cent.   .30 .30
2666 A830 50pf Frankfurt-Oder clothier, 16th cent.   .35 .35
  a. Block of 4, #2663-2666   1.50 1.50

Georg Forster Antarctic Research Station A831

1988, Mar. 22   Litho.   Perf. 13x12½
2667 A831 35pf multi   .45 .25

District Capitals A832

1988, Apr. 5   Photo.   Perf. 14
2668 A832 5pf Wismar   .20 .20
2669 A832 10pf Anklam   .20 .20
2670 A832 25pf Ribnitz-Damgarten   .25 .25
2671 A832 60pf Stralsund   .55 .55
2672 A832 90pf Bergen   .75 .75
2673 A832 1.20m Greifswald   1.00 1.00
  Nos. 2668-2673 (6)   2.95 2.90

Souvenir Sheet

Ulrich von Hutten (1488-1523), Promulgator of the Lutheran Movement — A833

1988, Apr. 5   Litho.   Perf. 12½x13
2674 A833 70pf multi   1.10 .90

USSR-DDR Manned Space Flight, 10th Anniv. — A834

Designs: 5pf, Cosmonauts S. Jahn and Valery Bykowski, Soyuz-29 landing, Sept. 3, 1978. 10pf, MKS-M multi-channel spectrometer. 20pf, MIR space station.

1988, June 21   Litho.   Perf. 14
2675 A834 5pf multi   .20 .20
2676 A834 10pf multi   .20 .20
2677 A834 20pf multi   .25 .25
  Nos. 2675-2677 (3)   .65 .65
See Nos. 2698-2700.

10th Youth Stamp Exhibitions in Erfurt and Karl-Marx-Stadt — A835

Designs: 10pf+5pf, Erfurt. c. 1520. 20+5pf, Chemnitz, c. 1620. 25pf, Historic and modern buildings of Erfurt. 50pf, Historic and modern buildings of Karl-Marx-Stadt.

1988, June 21   Photo.
2678 A835 10pf +5pf multi   .20 .20
2679 A835 20pf +5pf multi   .25 .25
2680 A835 25pf multi   .25 .25
  a. Pair, #2678, 2680 + label   .60 .60
2681 A835 50pf multi   .55 .55
  a. Pair, #2679, 2681 + label   .90 .90
Nos. 2678-2679 surtaxed to benefit the Philatelists' League of the DDR Cultural Union.

22nd Workers' Games, Frankfurt-on-Oder — A836

1988, June 7   Litho.   Perf. 13x12½
2682 20pf multi   .20 .20
2683 A836 50pf multi, diff.   .45 .45
  a. A836 Pair, #2682-2683 + label   .85 .85

Workers' Militia, 35th Anniv. — A837

1988, July 5   Photo.   Perf. 14
2684 A837 5pf Oath   .20 .20
2685 A837 10pf Ernst Thalmann tribute   .20 .20
2686 A837 15pf Roll call   .20 .20
2687 A837 20pf Weapons exchange   .20 .20
  Nos. 2684-2687 (4)   .80 .80

8th Young Pioneers' Congress, Karl-Marx-Stadt — A838

1988, July 19   Litho.   Perf. 13x12½
2688 A838 10pf shown   .20 .20
2689 A838 10pf +5pf Youths playing musical instruments   .20 .20
  a. Pair, #2688-2689 + label   .45 .40
Surtax financed the congress.

1988 Summer Olympics, Seoul A839

1988, Aug. 9   Photo.   Perf. 14
2690 A839 5pf Swimming   .20 .20
2691 A839 10pf Handball   .20 .20
2692 A839 20pf +10pf Hurdles   .35 .35
2693 A839 25pf Rowing   .35 .35
2694 A839 35pf Boxing   .35 .35
2695 A839 50pf +20pf Cycling   .70 .70
  Nos. 2690-2695 (6)   2.15 2.15

Souvenir Sheet
Litho.
Perf. 13x12½
2696 A839 85pf Relay race   1.80 1.60

Souvenir Sheet

Leipzig Autumn Fair — A840

1988, Aug. 30   Litho.   *Perf. 14*
2697 A840 Sheet of 3   1.40 1.20
  a.   5pf Fair, c. 1810   .20   .20
  b.   15pf Battle of Leipzig Memorial .25   .25
  c.   1m Fair, c. 1820   .75   .75

DDR-USSR Manned Space Flight Type

1988, Aug. 30   Litho.   *Perf. 14*
2698 A834 10pf like No. 2675   .25   .25
  a.   Sheet of 4   1.00 1.00
2699 A834 20pf like No. 2676   .25   .25
  a.   Sheet of 4   1.00 1.00
2700 A834 35pf like No. 2677   .45   .45
  a.   Sheet of 4   1.90 1.90
    Nos. 2698-2700 (3)   .95   .95

Fascism Resistance Memorial, Como, Italy — A841

1988, Sept. 13   Photo.
2701 A841 35pf multi   .35   .30

Memorial at Buchenwald, 30th Anniv. — A842

1988, Sept. 13   *Perf. 14*
2702 A842 10pf multi   .25   .20

Mariner's Soc., Stralsund, 500th Anniv. — A843

Paintings: 5pf, *Adolph Friedrich* at Stralsund, by C. Leplow. 10pf, *Die Gartenlaube* (built in 1872) at Stralsund, by J.F. Kruger. 70pf, Brigantine *Auguste Mathilde* (built in 1830) at Stralsund, by I.C. Grunwaldt. 1.20m, Brig *Hoffnung* at Cologne, by G.A. Luther.

1988, Sept. 20   Litho.   *Perf. 13½x13*
2703 A843 5pf multi   .20   .20
2704 A843 10pf multi   .20   .20
2705 A843 70pf multi   .75   .70
2706 A843 1.20m multi   1.10 1.10
    Nos. 2703-2706 (4)   2.25 2.20

Ship Lifts and Bridges A844

1988, Oct. 18   Photo.   *Perf. 14x14½*
2707 A844 5pf Magdeburg   .20   .20
2708 A844 10pf Magdeburg-Rothensee   .20   .20
2709 A844 35pf Niederfinow   .30   .25
2710 A844 70pf Altfriesack   .60   .60
2711 A844 90pf Rugendamm   .75   .75
    Nos. 2707-2711 (5)   2.05 2.00

1st Nazi Pogrom (Kristallnacht), Nov. 9, 1938 — A845

1988, Nov. 8   *Perf. 14*
2712 A845 35pf Menorah   .45   .25

Paintings by Max Lingner (1888-1959) A846

1988, Nov. 8
2713 A846 5pf *In the Boat,* 1931   .20   .20
2714 A846 10pf *Yvonne,* 1939   .20   .20
2715 A846 20pf *Free, Strong and Happy,* 1944   .25   .20
2716 A846 85pf *New Harvest,* 1951   .75   .75
    Nos. 2713-2716 (4)   1.40 1.35

Souvenir Sheet

Friedrich Wolf (1888-1953), Playwright — A847

1988, Nov. 22   Litho.
2717 A847 1.10m multi   1.10 1.10

WHO, 40th Anniv. A848

Bone Lace from Erzgebirge A849

1988, Nov. 22   Photo.
2718 A848 85pf multi   .90   .45

Miniature Sheet

Various lace designs.

1988, Nov. 22   Litho.   *Perf. 12½x13*
2719   Sheet of 6   2.25 2.25
  a.   A849 20pf multi   .25   .25
  b.   A849 25pf multi   .55   .55
  c.   A849 35pf multi   .25   .25
  d.   A849 40pf multi   .25   .25
  e.   A849 50pf multi   .55   .55
  f.   A849 85pf multi   .25   .25

Council for Mutual Economic Aid, 40th Anniv. A850

1989, Jan. 10   Photo.   *Perf. 13*
2720 A850 20pf multi   .30   .25

Labor Leaders Type of 1987

Portraits: No. 2721, Edith Baumann (1909-1973). No. 2722, Otto Meier (1889-1962). No. 2723, Fritz Selbmann (1899-1975). No. 2724, Alfred Oelssner (1879-1962).

1989, Jan. 24   Engr.   *Perf. 14*
2721 A804 10pf dark vio brn   .20   .20
2722 A804 10pf dark grn   .20   .20
2723 A804 10pf dark blue   .20   .20
2724 A804 10pf brn blk   .20   .20
    Nos. 2721-2724 (4)   .80   .80

Telephones A851

Designs: 10pf, Philipp Reis, 1861. 20pf, Siemens & Halske wall model, 1882. 50pf, Wall model OB 03, 1903. 85pf, Table model OB 05, 1905.

1989, Feb. 7   Litho.
2725 A851 10pf shown   .20   .20
2726 A851 20pf multi   .25   .25
2727 A851 50pf multi   .45   .45
2728 A851 85pf multi   .75   .75
  a.   Block of 4, #2725-2728   1.90 1.90

Famous Men A852

1989, Feb. 28   Photo.
2729 A852 10pf Ludwig Renn (1889-1979)   .20   .20
2730 A852 10pf Carl von Ossietzky (1889-1938)   .20   .20
2731 A852 10pf Adam Scharrer (1889-1948)   .20   .20
2732 A852 10pf Rudolf Mauersberger (1889-1971)   .20   .20
2733 A852 10pf Johann Beckmann (1739-1811)   .20   .20
    Nos. 2729-2733 (5)   1.00 1.00

Leipzig Spring Fair — A853

1989, Mar. 7   Litho.
2734 A853 70pf shown   .70   .60
2735 A853 85pf Buildings, 1690   .85   .85

Handelshof, 80th anniv. (70pf).

Souvenir Sheet

Thomas Muntzer (c. 1468-1525), Religious Reformer — A854

1989, Mar. 21   *Perf. 13x12½*
2736 A854 1.10m multi   1.10 1.40

1st Long-distance German Railway, Leipzig-Dresden, Sesquicentennial — A855

15pf, Georg Friedrich List (1789-1846), industrialist, economist. 20pf, Dresden Station in Leipzig, 1839. 50pf, Leipzig Station in Dresden, 1839.

1989, Apr. 4   *Perf. 14*
2737 A855 15pf multi   .30   .25
2738 A855 20pf multi   .30   .20
2739 A855 50pf multi   .55   .55
    Nos. 2737-2739 (3)   1.15 1.00

A856

A857

Designs: Meissen Onion-pattern Porcelain, 250th anniv., and sword emblem.

1989, Apr. 18   Litho.   *Perf. 12½x13*
2740 A856 10pf Tea caddy   .20   .20
2741 A856 20pf Vase   .25   .20
2742 A856 35pf Breadboard   .35   .30
2743 A856 70pf Teapot   .75   .75
    Nos. 2740-2743 (4)   1.55 1.45

Size: 33x56mm
Perf. 14
2744   Block of 4   2.10 2.10
  a.   A856 10pf like No. 2740   .20   .20
  b.   A856 20pf like No. 2741   .25   .25
  c.   A856 35pf like No. 2742   .35   .35
  d.   A856 70pf like No. 2743   .75   .75

1989, May 2   Photo.   *Perf. 14½x14*
2745 A857 20pf "I"   .25   .20
2746 A857 50pf "B"   .45   .35
2747 A857 1.35m "A"   1.25 1.25
    Nos. 2745-2747 (3)   1.95 1.80

Intl. Book Fair (IBA), Leipzig.

Student Government — A858

1989, May 9   Litho.   *Perf. 13½x12½*
2748 A858 20pf 8th World Youth Festival, Pyongyang   .25   .25
2749 A858 20pf +5pf Whitsun meeting of Free German Youth   .25   .25
  a.   Pair, #2748-2749 + label   .55   .55

Princess
Luise — A859

Carl Zeiss
Foundation,
Jena,
Cent. — A860

Sculptures by Johann Gottfried Schadow
(1764-1850), Prussian Court Sculptor.

1989, May 16　Photo.　Perf. 14½x14
2750　A859　50pf shown　.60　.45
2751　A859　85pf Princess Friede-
　　　　rike　1.10　.90

1989, May 16

Modern medical technology: 50pf, Interference microscope Jenaval. 85pf, Bicoordinate
measuring instrument ZKM 01-250C.

2752　A860　50pf multi　.35　.35
2753　A860　85pf multi　.75　.75
　a.　Pair, #2752-2753 + label　1.40　1.40

Label pictures founder Ernst Abbe (1840-
1905).

Jena University
Inaugural Address,
Bicent. — A861

1989, May 23　Photo.　Perf. 14
2754　A861　25pf Frontispiece　.25　.25
2755　A861　85pf Excerpt　.70　.70
　a.　Pair, #2754-2755 + label　1.10　1.10

Label pictures bust of Friedrich Schiller,
author of the address.

Souvenir Sheet

Zoologists — A862

1989, June 13　　　　Litho.
2756　A862　Sheet of 2　1.50　9.00
　a.　50pf Alfred Brehm (1829-1884)　.45　2.25
　b.　85pf Christian Brehm (1787-
　　　1864)　.90　3.50

French
Revolution,
Bicent.
A863

5pf, Storming of the Bastille, July 14, 1789.
20pf, Revolutionaries, flag bearer. 90pf,
Storming Tuileries Palace, Aug. 10, 1792.

1989, July 4　Photo.　Perf. 13
2757　A863　5pf multi　.20　.20
2758　A863　20pf multi　.25　.25
2759　A863　90pf multi　.75　.75
　　　Nos. 2757-2759 (3)　1.20　1.15

Intl. Congress of Horse Breeders from
Socialist States — A864

1989, July 18　Litho.　Perf. 13½
2760　A864　10pf Haflinger　.20　.20
2761　A864　20pf English thor-
　　　　oughbred　.20　.20
2762　A864　70pf Cold blood　.60　.60
2763　A864　110pf Noble warm
　　　　blood　1.00　1.00
　　　Nos. 2760-2763 (4)　2.00　2.00

Natl. Stamp Exhibition,
Magdeburg — A865

1989, Aug. 8　Litho.　Perf. 13x12½
2764　A865　20pf Owlglass Foun-
　　　　tain　.20　.20
2765　A865　70pf +5pf Demons
　　　　Fountain　.75　.70

No. 2765 surtaxed for the philatelic unit of
the Kulturbund.

Souvenir Sheet

Leipzig Autumn Fair — A866

1989, Aug. 22　　　　Perf. 14
2766　A866　Sheet of 2　1.40　1.40
　a.　50pf Fairground　.45　.45
　b.　85pf Fairground, diff.　.75　.75

Thomas
Muntzer (1489-
1525), Religious
Reformer
A867

Various details of the painting *Early Bour-
geois Revolution in Germany in 1525*, by W.
Tübke.

1989, Aug. 22
2767　A867　5pf Globe　.20　.20
2768　A867　10pf Fountain　.20　.20
2769　A867　20pf Battle scene　.25　.20
　a.　Souvenir sheet of 4　1.10　1.00
2770　A867　50pf Ark　.45　.45
2771　A867　85pf Rainbow, battle　1.00　1.00
　　　Nos. 2767-2771 (5)　2.10　2.05

Muttergruppe,
1965, Bronze
Statue in the
Natl. Memorial,
Ravensbruck
A868

1989, Sept. 5　Photo.　Perf. 14
2772　A868　35pf multi　.35　.30
Natl. Memorial, Ravensbruck, 30th anniv.

Flowering
Cacti
(Epiphyllum)
A869

1989, Sept. 19　Litho.　Perf. 13
2773　A869　10m Adriana　.20　.20
2774　A869　35m Feuerzauber　.35　.30
2775　A869　50m Franzisko　.60　.60
　　　Nos. 2773-2775 (3)　1.15　1.10

DDR, 40th Anniv. — A870

1989, Oct. 3　　　　Perf. 14
2776　A870　5pf Education　.20　.20
2777　A870　10pf Agriculture　.20　.20
2778　A870　20pf Construction　.30　.25
2779　A870　25pf Machinist, com-
　　　　puter user　.30　.30
　　　Nos. 2776-2779 (4)　1.00　.95

Souvenir Sheet
2780　A870　135pf Two workers　3.50　1.50

Jawaharlal
Nehru, 1st
Prime Minister
of Independent
India — A871

1989, Nov. 7　Photo.　Perf. 14
2781　A871　35pf multicolored　.35　.30

Statues of Roland Type of 1987
1989, Nov. 7　　　Perf. 14½x14
2782　A799　5pf Zerbst, 1445　.20　.20
2783　A799　10pf Halberstadt,
　　　　1433　.20　.20
2784　A799　20pf Buch-Altmark,
　　　　1611　.25　.25
2785　A799　50pf Perleberg, 1546　.45　.45
　　　Nos. 2782-2785 (4)　1.10　1.10

Miniature Sheet

Chandeliers from
Erzgebirge — A872

Designs: a, Schneeburg, circa 1860. b,
Schwarzenberg, circa 1850. c, Annaberg,
circa 1880. d, Seiffen, circa 1900. e, Seiffen,
circa 1930. f, Annaberg, circa 1925.

Litho. & Engr.
1989, Nov. 28　　　Perf. 14
2786　　Sheet of 6　2.25　2.25
　a.　A872 10pf multicolored　.25　.25
　b.　A872 20pf multicolored　.55　.55
　c.　A872 25pf multicolored　.25　.25
　d.　A872 35pf multicolored　.25　.25
　e.　A872 50pf multicolored　.55　.55
　f.　A872 70pf multicolored　.25　.25

Bees Collecting
Nectar — A873

1990, Jan. 9　　　　Litho.
2787　A873　5pf Apple blossom　.20　.20
2788　A873　10pf Blooming heath-
　　　　er　.20　.20
2789　A873　20pf Rape blossom　.25　.25
2790　A873　50pf Red clover　.60　.60
　　　Nos. 2787-2790 (4)　1.25　1.25

*The Young Post
Rider,* an
Engraving by
Albrecht
Durer — A874

1990, Jan. 12　Litho.　Perf. 13
2791　A874　35pf multi　.45　.35

Postal communications in Europe, 500th
anniv.
　See Austria No. 1486, Belgium No. 1332,
Germany No. 1592 and Berlin No. 9N584.

Labor
Leaders — A875

Portraits: #2792, Bruno Leuschner (1910-
65). #2793, Erich Weinert (1890-1953).

1990, Jan. 16　　　　Perf. 14
2792　A875　10pf gray brown　.25　.25
2793　A875　10pf deep blue　.25　.25

Coats of
Arms — A876

Early postal agency insignia: 10pf,
Schwarzburg-Rudolstadt and Thurn & Taxis.
20pf, Royal Saxon letter collection. 50pf,
Imperial Postal Agency. 1.10pf, Auxiliary post
office.

1990, Feb. 6　Photo.　Perf. 14
2794　A876　10pf multicolored　.20　.20
2795　A876　20pf multicolored　.25　.20
2796　A876　50pf multicolored　.60　.60
2797　A876　110pf multicolored　1.40　1.40
　　　Nos. 2794-2797 (4)　2.45　2.40

Size: 32x42mm
Perf. 13½
Litho.
2798　　Block of 4　2.60　3.00
　a.　A876 10pf like No. 2794　.20　.20
　b.　A876 20pf like No. 2795　.25　.25
　c.　A876 50pf like No. 2796　.60　.60
　d.　A876 110pf like No. 2797　1.40　1.40

Posts & Telecommunications Workers' Day.

August Bebel
(1840-1913),
Co-founder of
the Social
Democratic
Party — A877

1990, Feb. 20   **Photo.**
2799 A877 20pf multicolored   .35 .35

Flying Machine
Designed by
Leonardo da
Vinci — A878

1990, Feb. 20 Litho. Perf. 13½x13
2800 A878 20pf shown   .20 .20
2801 A878 35pf +5pf Melchior
                Bauer   .45 .45
2802 A878 50pf Albrecht
                Berblinger   .60 .55
2803 A878 90pf Otto Lilienthal 1.00 1.00
        Nos. 2800-2803 (4)   2.25 2.20

LILIENTHAL '91 airmail exhibition. No. 2801
surtaxed for philatelic promotion.

Leipzig Spring
Fair
Seals — A879

Dying
Warriors — A880

1990, Mar. 6   **Perf. 12½x13**
2804 A879 70pf Seal, 1268   1.25 .70
2805 A879 85pf Seal, 1497   1.40 .85

City of Leipzig and the Leipzig Spring Fair,
825th annivs.

1990, Mar. 6 Photo. Perf. 13½x14

Sculptures by Andreas Schluter.

2806 A880 40pf shown   .55 .35
2807 A880 70pf multi, diff.   .75 .75

Museum of German History in the
Zeughaus of Berlin.

Famous
Men
A881

Portraits: No. 2808, Friedrich Diesterweg
(1790-1866), educator. No. 2809, Kurt Tucholsky (1890-1935), novelist, journalist.

1990, Mar. 20 Photo. Perf. 14
2808 A881 20pf multicolored   .30 .30
2809 A881 10pf multicolored   .30 .30

Labor Day,
Cent. — A882

1990, Apr. 3
2810 A882 10pf shown   .30 .25
2811 A882 20pf Flower,
                "1890/1990"   .70 .45

Dicraeosaurus — A883

Perf. 13x12½, 12½x13
1990, Apr. 17   **Litho.**
2812 A883 10pf shown   .20 .20
2813 A883 25pf Kentrurosaurus .25 .20
  a.   Miniature sheet of 4   1.40 1.40
2814 A883 35pf Dysalotosaurus .30 .30
2815 A883 50pf Brachiosaurus   .45 .45
2816 A883 85pf Brachiosaurus
                skull   1.00 1.00
        Nos. 2812-2816 (5)   2.20 2.15

Natural History Museum of Berlin, cent.
Nos. 2815-2816 vert.

Penny Black, 150th
Anniv. — A884

1990, May 8   **Perf. 14**
2817 A884 20pf shown   .35 .35
2818 A884 35pf +15pf Saxony
                #1   .70 .70
2819 A884 110pf No. 48   1.80 1.80
        Nos. 2817-2819 (3)   2.85 2.85

A885

Intl. Telecommunications Union, 125th
Anniv.: 10pf, David Edward Hughes (1831-
1900), type-printing telegraph, 1855. 20pf,
Distribution linkage, Berlin-Kopenick post
office. 25pf, TV and microwave tower. 50pf,
Molniya news satellite, globe. 70pf, Philipp
Reis (1834-1874), physicist, designed sound
transmission equipment.

1990, May 15
2820 A885 10pf multicolored   .20 .20
2821 A885 20pf multicolored   .30 .30
2822 A885 25pf multicolored   .30 .30
2823 A885 50pf multicolored   .75 .75
        Nos. 2820-2823 (4)   1.55 1.55

Souvenir Sheet
2824 A885 70pf multicolored   2.00 1.90

Pope John Paul II,
70th
Birthday — A886

1990, May 15
2825 A886 35pf multicolored   .55 .35

11th
Youth
Stamp
Exhibition,
Halle
A887

1990, June 5   **Perf. 13x12½**
2826 A887 10pf +5pf 18th cent.
                Halle   .25 .25
2827 A887 20pf 20th cent. Halle .30 .30
  a.   Pair; #2826-2827 + label .60 .60

Treasures
in the
German
State
Library,
Berlin
A888

Designs: 20pf, Rules of an order, 1264.
25pf, Rudimentum novitiorum, 1475. 50pf,
Chosrou wa Schirin, 18th cent. 110pf, Book-
cover of Amalienbibliothek, 18th cent.

1990, June 19
2828 A888 20pf multicolored   .35 .25
2829 A888 25pf multicolored   .35 .25
2830 A888 50pf multicolored   1.10 .70
2831 A888 110pf multicolored   2.00 1.60
        Nos. 2828-2831 (4)   3.80 2.80

Castle Albrechtsburg
and Cathedral,
Meissen — A889

30pf, Goethe-Schiller Monument, Weimar.
50pf, Brandenburg Gate, Berlin. 60pf, Kyf-
fhauser Monument. 70pf, Semper Opera,
Dresden. 80pf, Castle Sanssouci, Potsdam.
100pf, Wartburg, Eisenach. 200pf, Magdeburg
Cathedral. 500pf, Schwerin Castle.

1990, July 2 Photo. Perf. 14
2832 A889 10pf ultramarine   .20 .20
2833 A889 30pf olive green   .30 .25
2834 A889 50pf bluish green   .45 .35
2835 A889 60pf violet brown   .45 .55
2836 A889 70pf dark brown   .60 .70
2837 A889 80pf red brown   .75 1.00
2838 A889 100pf dark carmine   .75 .60
2839 A889 200pf dark violet   1.50 1.50
2840 A889 500pf green   3.50 3.50
        Nos. 2832-2840 (9)   8.50 8.65

Nos. 2832-2852 have face values based on
the Federal Republic's Deutsche mark and
were valid for postage in both countries.

Postal
System,
500th
Anniv.
A890

30pf, 15th cent. postman. 50pf, 16th cent.
postrider. 70pf, Post carriages c. 1595, 1750.
100pf, Railway mail carriages 1842, 1900.

1990, Aug. 28 Litho. Perf. 13x13½
2841 A890 30pf multicolored   .35 .35
2842 A890 50pf multicolored   .55 .55
2843 A890 70pf multicolored   .70 1.00
2844 A890 100pf multicolored   1.10 1.10
        Nos. 2841-2844 (4)   2.70 3.00

Louis Lewandowski
(1821-94),
Composer — A891

50pf+15pf, New Synagogue, Berlin.

1990, Sept. 18   **Perf. 14**
2845 A891 30pf multicolored   .30 .30
2846 A891 50pf +15pf multi   .60 .60

Heinrich
Schliemann (1822-
1890),
Archaeologist
A892

1990, Oct. 2   **Photo.**

Design: 30pf, shown. 50pf, Schliemann,
double pot c. 2600-1900 B.C., horiz.

2847 A892 30pf multicolored   .30 .30
2848 A892 50pf multicolored   .60 .60

Intl. Astronautics
Federation, 41st
Congress,
Dresden
A893

1990, Oct. 2
2849 A893 30pf Dresden skyline .25 .25
2850 A893 50pf Globe   .45 .45
2851 A893 70pf Moon   .75 1.00
2852 A893 100pf Mars   1.10 1.10
        Nos. 2849-2852 (4)   2.55 2.80

Stamps of the German Democratic Republic
were replaced starting Oct. 3, 1990 by those
of the Federal Republic of Germany. #2832-
2852 remained valid until Dec. 31, 1991.

**FOR USE IN ALL PROVINCES IN
THE RUSSIAN ZONES**

SEMI-POSTALS
Leipzig Fair Issue
Type of German Semi-Postal Stamps

16pf+9pf, 1st New Year's Fair, 1459.
50pf+25pf, Arrival of clothmakers from abroad,
1469.

Wmk. 292
1948, Aug. 29 Litho. Perf. 13½
10NB1 SP252 16 + 9pf dk vio
                brn   .20 .60
10NB2 SP252 50 + 25pf dl vio
                bl   .20 .60
        Set, never hinged   .75

The 1948 Leipzig Autumn Fair.

Emblem of   Goethe — OSP2
Philatelic
Institute — OSP1

1948, Oct. 23   **Perf. 13x13½**
10NB3 OSP1 12 + 3pf red   .20 .55
        Never hinged   .35

Stamp Day, Oct. 24, 1948.

**Type of German Semi-Postal
Stamps of 1947**

30pf+15pf, First fair in newly built Town Hall,
1556. 50pf+25pf, Italians at the Fair, 1536.

1949, Mar. 6 Litho. Perf. 13½
10NB4 SP252 30 + 15pf red   1.10 4.00
10NB5 SP252 50 + 25pf blue   1.50 4.50
        Set, never hinged   6.00

1949 Leipzig Spring Fair.

1949, July 20 Wmk. 292 Perf. 13

Designs: Different Goethe portraits.

10NB6 OSP2 6 + 4pf dl vio   .90 2.60
10NB7 OSP2 12 + 8pf dl brn   .90 2.60
10NB8 OSP2 24 + 16pf red
                brn   .75 2.25
10NB9 OSP2 50 + 25pf dk bl   .75 2.25
10NB10 OSP2 84 + 36pf ol
                gray   1.10 4.50
        Nos. 10NB6-10NB10 (5)   4.40 14.20
        Set, never hinged   10.50

Johann Wolfgang von Goethe, birth bicent.

Souvenir Sheet

Profile of Goethe — OSP3

1949, Aug. 22   Engr.   Perf. 14
10NB11 OSP3 50pf + 4.50m
           blue   110.00 450.00
      Never hinged   175.00

The sheet measures 106x105mm. The sur-tax was for the reconstruction of Weimar.

Type of German Semi-Postal Stamps

12pf+8pf, Russian merchants at the Fair, 1650. 24pf+16pf, Young Goethe at the Fair, 1765.

1949, Aug. 30   Litho.   Perf. 13½
10NB12 SP252 12 + 8pf gray   1.50 6.50
10NB13 SP252 24 + 16pf lake
           brn   1.90 7.75
    Set, never hinged   7.50

1949 Leipzig Autumn Fair.

GERMAN DEMOCRATIC REPUBLIC SEMI-POSTAL STAMPS

> **Catalogue values for unused stamps in this section, from this point to the end of the section, are for Never Hinged items.**

Canceled to Order

Used values are for CTO's from No. B14 to No. B203.

Some se-tenants include a semi-postal stamp. To avoid splitting the se-tenant piece the semi-postal is listed with the regular issue.

Bavaria No. 1 and Magnifier — SP4

Wmk. 292
1949, Oct. 30   Litho.   Perf. 14
B14 SP4   12pf + 3pf gray blk   6.75 6.50

Stamp Day, 1949. See No. B21a.

Leipzig Fair Issue.
German Type of 1947
Inscribed: "Deutsche Demokratische Republik"

Leipzig Spring Fair: 24pf+12pf, First porce-lain at Fair, 1710. 30pf+14pf, First Fair at Municipal Store, 1894.

1950, Mar. 5   Perf. 13
B15 SP252 24 + 12pf red vio   9.00 9.00
B16 SP252 30 + 14pf rose car   10.50 15.00

Shepherd Boy with Double Flute — SP5

"Bach Year": 24pf+6pf, Girl with hand organ. 30pf+8pf, Johann Sebastian Bach. 50pf+16pf, Chorus.

1950, June 14   Perf. 14
B17 SP5 12pf + 4pf bl grn   6.00   5.00
B18 SP5 24pf + 6pf olive   6.00   5.00
B19 SP5 30pf + 8pf dk red   11.50 11.50
B20 SP5 50pf + 16pf blue   18.00 16.50
    Nos. B17-B20 (4)   41.50 38.00

Saxony No. 1, Globe and Dove — SP6

1950, July 1   Photo.   Wmk. 292
B21 SP6 84 + 41pf brn red   45.00 12.00
   a.   Souv. sheet of 2, #B14,
       B21, imperf.   150.00 150.00
       No. B21a hinged   52.50

German Stamp Exhib. (DEBRIA) held at Leipzig for the cent. of Saxony's 1st postage stamp.

Clearing Land — SP7

Reconstruction program: 24pf+6pf, Bricklay-ing. 30pf+10pf, Carpentry. 50pf+10pf, Inspect-ing plans.

1952, May 1   Litho.
B22 SP7 12pf + 3pf brt vio   1.60   .45
B23 SP7 24pf + 6pf henna brn   1.50   .60
B24 SP7 30pf + 8pf dp grn   1.75   .75
B25 SP7 50pf + 10pf vio bl   2.25 1.50
    Nos. B22-B25 (4)   7.10 3.30

Dam — SP8

1954, Aug. 16   Unwmk.
B26 SP8 24pf + 6pf green   .60 .75

The surtax was for flood victims.

Surcharged with New Value and "X"

1955, Feb. 25
B27 SP8 20 +5pf on 24+6pf   .75 .55

The surtax was for flood victims.

Buchenwald Memorial — SP9

Perf. 13½x13
1956, Sept. 8   Wmk. 297
B28 SP9 20pf + 80pf rose red   1.10 3.50

The surtax was for the erection of national memorials at the concentration camps of Buchenwald, Ravensbruck and Sach-senhausen. See No. B43.

Type of 1955 Surcharged "HELFT AGYPTEN +10" (#B29) or "HELFT DEM SOZIALISTISCHEN UNGARN +10" (#B30)

Perf. 13½x13
1956, Dec. 20   Wmk. 313
B29 A75 20pf + 10pf carmine   .45 .35
B30 A75 20pf + 10pf carmine   .45 .35

Monument to Ravensbrück SP10

Memorial Park and Lake — SP11

Perf. 13x13½, 13½x13
1957, Apr. 25   Litho.
B31 SP10 5pf + 5pf grn   .20 .25
B32 SP11 20pf + 10pf rose red   .30 .35

Intl. Day of Liberation. See Nos. B54, B70.

Ernst Thälmann   Bugler, Flag and
SP12   Camp
                  SP13

Portraits: 25pf+15pf, Rudolf Breitscheid. 40pf+20pf, Rev. Paul Schneider.

1957, Dec. 3   Photo.   Perf. 13
Portraits in Gray
B33 SP12 20pf + 10pf dp plum   .20   .20
B34 SP12 25pf + 15pf dk blue   .20   .20
B35 SP12 40pf + 20pf violet   .30   .35
   a.   Souv. sheet of 3, #B33-B35,
       imperf.   57.50 125.00
     Nos. B33-B35 (3)   .70   .75

No. B35a issued Sept. 15, 1958.

1958, July 11   Wmk. 313   Perf. 13
Portraits: 5pf+5pf, Albert Kuntz. 10pf+5pf, Rudi Arndt. 15pf+10pf, Kurt Adams. 20pf+10pf, Rudolf Renner. 25pf+15pf, Walter Stoecker.

Portraits in Gray
B36 SP12   5pf + 5pf brn blk   .20   .75
B37 SP12 10pf + 5pf dk sl grn   .20   .75
B38 SP12 15pf + 10pf dp vio   .20 4.50
B39 SP12 20pf + 10pf dk red
           brn   .20   .75
B40 SP12 25pf + 15pf bl blk   .55 11.50
    Nos. B36-B40 (5)   1.35 18.25

Issued to honor the murdered victims of the Nazis at Buchenwald. The surtax was for the erection of national memorials.
See Nos. B49-B53, B55-B57, B60-B64, B71-B75, B79-B81.

1958, Aug. 7   Litho.   Perf. 12½
Design: 20pf+10pf, Pioneers and flag.
B41 SP13 10pf + 5pf green   .25 .25
B42 SP13 20pf + 10pf red   .35 .25

Pioneer organization, 10th anniversary.

Type of 1956 Overprinted in Black "14. September 1958"

Perf. 13½x13
1958, Sept. 15   Unwmk.
B43 SP9 20pf + 20pf rose red   .50 .50

Dedication of the memorial at Buchenwald concentration camp, Sept. 14, 1958.

Exercises with Hoops — SP14

Designs: 10pf+5pf, High jump. 20pf+10pf Vaulting. 25pf+10pf, Girl gymnasts. 40pf+20pf, Leipzig stadium and fireworks.

Perf. 13x13½
1959, Aug. 10   Litho.   Wmk. 313
B44 SP14   5pf + 5pf org   .20   .20
B45 SP14 10pf + 5pf grn   .20   .20
B46 SP14 20pf + 10pf brt car   .20   .20
B47 SP14 25pf + 10pf brt bl   .20   .20
B48 SP14 40pf + 20pf red vio   2.00   .70
    Nos. B44-B48 (5)   2.80 1.50

3rd German Sports Festival, Leipzig.

Portrait Type of 1957-58

Portraits: 5pf+5pf, Tilde Klose. 10pf+5pf, Kathe Niederkirchner. 15pf+10pf, Charlotte Eisenblatter. 20pf+10pf, Olga Benario-Prestes. 25pf+15pf, Maria Grollmuss.

1959, Sept. 3   Photo.   Perf. 13
Portraits in Gray
B49 SP12   5pf + 5pf sep   .20   .20
B50 SP12 10pf + 5pf dp grn   .20   .20
B51 SP12 15pf + 10pf dp vio   .20   .20
B52 SP12 20pf + 10pf mag   .20   .20
B53 SP12 25pf + 15pf dk bl   .35   .90
    Nos. B49-B53 (5)   1.15 1.70

Issued to honor women murdered by the Nazis at Buchenwald.

Ravensbrück Type of 1957 Dated: "12. September 1959"

Perf. 13½x13
1959, Sept. 11   Litho.   Wmk. 313
B54 SP11 20pf + 10pf dp car &
           blk   .55 .30

Portrait Type of 1957-58

5pf+5pf, Lothar Erdmann. 10pf+5pf, Ernst Schneller. 20pf+10pf, Lambert Horn.

1960, Feb. 25   Photo.   Perf. 13½x13
Portraits in Gray
B55 SP12   5pf + 5pf ol bis   .25   .20
B56 SP12 10pf + 5pf dk grn   .25   .20
B57 SP12 20pf + 10pf dl mag   .25   .20
    Nos. B55-B57 (3)   .75   .60

Issued to honor murdered victims of the Nazis at Sachsenhausen.

Type of Regular Issue, 1960

Designs: 10pf+5pf, Vacation ship under con-struction, Wismar. 20pf+10pf, Ship before Stubbenkammer and sailboat.

Wmk. 313
1960, June 23   Litho.   Perf. 13
B58 A162 10pf + 5pf blk, yel &
          red   .20 .20
B59 A162 20pf + 10pf blk, red &
          bl   .25 .20

Portrait Type of 1957-58

Portraits: 10pf+5pf, Max Lademann. 15pf+5pf, Lorenz Breunig. 20pf+10pf, Mathias Thesen. 25pf+10pf, Gustl Sandtner. 40pf+20pf, Hans Rothbarth.

1960   Wmk. 313   Perf. 13½x13
Portraits in Gray
B60 SP12 10pf + 5pf grn   .20   .20
B61 SP12 15pf + 5pf dp vio   1.00   .70
B62 SP12 20pf + 10pf maroon   .20   .20
B63 SP12 25pf + 10pf dk bl   .25   .25
B64 SP12 40pf + 20pf lt red brn   2.00 1.40
    Nos. B60-B64 (5)   3.65 2.75

Issued to honor the murdered victims of the Nazis at Sachsenhausen.

Bicyclist — SP15

25pf+10pf, Bicyclists and spectators.

1960, Aug. 3   Perf. 13x13½, 13x12½
Size: 28x23mm
B65 SP15 20pf + 10pf multi   .25   .25
Size: 38½x21mm
B66 SP15 25pf + 10pf bl, gray
& brn   1.50   2.50
Bicycling World Championships, Aug. 3-14.

Rook and
Congress
Emblem
SP16

20pf+10pf, Knight. 25pf+10pf, Bishop.

Perf. 14x13½
1960, Sept. 19   Engr.   Wmk. 313
B67 SP16 10pf + 5pf blue green   .20   .20
B68 SP16 20pf + 10pf rose claret   .20   .20
B69 SP16 25pf + 10pf blue   1.10   2.75
Nos. B67-B69 (3)   1.50   3.15
14th Chess Championships, Leipzig.

Type of 1957
Design: Monument and memorial wall of
Sachsenhausen National Memorial.

1960, Sept. 8   Litho.   Perf. 13x13½
B70 SP10 20pf + 10pf dp car   .35   .30
No. B70 was re-issued Apr. 20, 1961, with
gray label adjoining each stamp in sheet, to
commemorate the dedication of Sachsenhausen National Memorial.

Type of 1957
Portraits: 5pf+5pf, Werner Kube. 10pf+5pf,
Hanno Gunther. 15pf+5pf, Elvira
Eisenschneider. 20pf+10pf, Hertha Lindner.
25pf+10pf, Herbert Tschäpe.

1961, Feb. 6   Perf. 13½x13
Portraits in Black
B71 SP12 5pf + 5pf brt brn   .20   .20
B72 SP12 10pf + 5pf bl grn   .20   .20
B73 SP12 15pf + 5pf brt lilac   1.00   2.10
B74 SP12 20pf + 10pf dp rose   .20   .20
B75 SP12 25pf + 10pf brt bl   .20   .20
Nos. B71-B75 (5)   1.80   2.90
Surtax for the erection of natl. memorials.

Pioneers
Playing
Volleyball
SP17

Designs: 20pf+10pf, Folk dancing.
25pf+10pf, Building model airplanes.

1961, May 25   Perf. 13x12½
B76 SP17 10pf + 5pf multi   .20   .20
B77 SP17 20pf + 10pf multi   .20   .20
B78 SP17 25pf + 10pf multi   3.00   2.40
Nos. B76-B78 (3)   3.40   2.80
Young Pioneers' meeting, Erfurt.

Type of 1957 and

Sophie
and
Hans
Scholl
SP18

Portraits: 5pf+5pf, Carlo Schönhaar.
10pf+5pf, Herbert Baum. 20pf+10pf, Liselotte
Herrmann. 40pf+20pf, Hilde and Hans Coppi.

Perf. 13½x13, 13x13½
1961, Sept. 7   Litho.   Wmk. 313
Portraits in Black
B79 SP12 5pf + 5pf green   .20   .20
B80 SP12 10pf + 5pf bl grn   .20   .20
B81 SP12 20pf + 10pf rose car   .20   .20

B82 SP18 25pf + 10pf blue   .20   .20
B83 SP18 40pf + 20pf rose brn   2.10   5.00
Nos. B79-B83 (5)   2.90   5.80
Surtax was the support of natl. memorials at
Buchenwald, Ravensbrück & Sachsenhausen.

Danielle Casanova
of France — SP19

Portraits: 10pf+5pf, Julius Fucik, Czechoslovakia. 20pf+10pf, Johanna Jannetje Schaft,
Netherlands. 25pf+10pf, Pawel Finder,
Poland. 40pf+20pf, Soya Anatolyevna Kos-
modemyanskaya, Russia.

1962, Mar. 22   Engr.   Perf. 13½
B84 SP19 5pf + 5pf gray   .20   .20
B85 SP19 10pf + 5pf green   .20   .20
B86 SP19 20pf + 10pf maroon   .20   .20
B87 SP19 25pf + 10pf deep blue   .25   .20
B88 SP19 40pf + 20pf sepia   1.60   2.25
Nos. B84-B88 (5)   2.45   3.05
Issued in memory of foreign victims of the
Nazis.

Type of Regular Issue, 1962
Design: 20pf+10pf, Three cyclists and Warsaw Palace of Culture and Science.

Perf. 13x12½
1962, Apr. 26   Litho.   Wmk. 313
B89 A192 20pf + 10pf ver, bl, blk &
yel   .20   .20

Folk
Dance — SP20

15pf+5pf, Youths of three nations parading.

1962, July 17   Wmk. 313   Perf. 14
B90 SP20 10pf + 5pf multi   .30   .20
B91 SP20 15pf + 5pf multi   .30   .20
a.   Pair, #B90-B91   1.10   1.00
Issued to publicize the 8th Youth Festival for
Peace and Friendship, Helsinki, July 28-Aug.
6, 1962.
No. B91a forms the festival emblem.

Type of Regular Issue, 1962
Design: 20pf+10pf, Springboard diving.

1962, Aug. 7   Wmk. 313   Perf. 13
B92 A199 20pf + 10pf lil rose &
grnsh bl   .20   .20

René Blieck of
Belgium — SP21

Seven
Cervi
Brothers
of Italy
SP22

Portraits: 10pf+5pf, Dr. Alfred Klahr, Austria.
15pf+5pf, José Diaz, Spain. 20pf+10pf, Julius
Alpari, Hungary.

1962, Oct. 4   Engr.   Perf. 14
B93 SP21 5pf + 5pf dk bl gray   .20   .20
B94 SP21 10pf + 5pf green   .20   .20
B95 SP21 15pf + 5pf brt vio   .20   .20
B96 SP21 20pf + 10pf dl red brn   .20   .20
B97 SP22 70pf + 30pf sepia   1.90   2.50
Nos. B93-B97 (5)   2.70   3.30
Issued to commemorate foreign victims of
the Nazis.

Walter Bohne,
Runner
SP23

Gymnasts
SP24

Portraits: 10pf+5pf, Werner Seelenbinder,
wrestler. 15pf+5pf, Albert Richter, bicyclist.
20pf+10pf, Heinz Steyer, soccer player.
25pf+10pf, Kurt Schlosser, mountaineer.

Engr. & Photo.
1963, May 27   Wmk. 313   Perf. 14
B98 SP23 5pf + 5pf yel & blk   .20   .20
B99 SP23 10pf + 5pf pale yel
grn & blk   .20   .20
B100 SP23 15pf + 5pf rose lil &
blk   .20   .20
B101 SP23 20pf + 10pf pink &
blk   .20   .20
B102 SP23 25pf + 10pf pale bl &
blk   1.90   4.50
Nos. B98-B102 (5)   2.70   5.30
Issued to commemorate sportsmen victims
of the Nazis. Each stamp printed with alternating label showing sporting events connected
with each person honored. The surtax went for
the maintenance of national memorials. See
Nos. B106-B110.

1963, June 13   Litho.   Perf. 12½x13
Designs: 20pf+10pf, Women gymnasts.
25pf+10pf, Relay race.
B103 SP24 10pf + 5pf blk, yel
grn & lem   .20   .20
B104 SP24 20pf + 10pf blk, red
& vio   .25   .20
B105 SP24 25pf + 10pf blk, bl, &
gray   3.00   3.00
Nos. B103-B105 (3)   3.45   3.40
4th German Gymnastic and Sports Festival,
Leipzig. The surtax went to the festival
committee.

Type of 1963
Portraits: 5pf+5pf, Hermann Tops, gymnastics instructor. 10pf+5pf, Käte Tucholla, field
hockey players. 15pf+5pf, Rudolph Seiffert,
long-distance swimmers. 20pf+10pf, Ernst
Grube, sportsmen demonstrating for peace.
40pf+20pf, Kurt Biedermann, kayak in rapids.

Engraved and Photogravure
1963, Sept. 24   Wmk. 313   Perf. 14
B106 SP23 5pf + 5pf yel & blk   .20   .20
B107 SP23 10pf + 5pf grn & blk   .20   .20
B108 SP23 15pf + 5pf lil & blk   .20   .20
B109 SP23 20pf + 10pf pale pink
& blk   .20   .20
B110 SP23 40pf + 20pf lt bl & blk   2.50   2.75
Nos. B106-B110 (5)   3.30   3.55
See note after No. B102.

Type of Regular Issue, 1963
Design: 20pf+10pf, Ski jumper in mid-air.

Perf. 13½x13
1963, Dec. 16   Litho.   Wmk. 313
B111 A224 20pf + 10pf multi   .20   .20
Surtax for the Natl. Olympic Committee.

Anton
Saefkow
SP25

Designs: 10pf+5pf, Franz Jacob. 15pf+5pf,
Bernhard Bästlein. 20pf+5pf, Harro Schulze-
Boysen. 25pf+10pf, Adam Kuckhoff.
40pf+10pf, Mildred and Arvid Harnack. Nos.
B112-B114 show group posting anti-Hitler and
pacifist posters. Nos. B115-B117 show production of anti-fascist pamphlets.

1964, Mar. 24   Wmk. 313   Perf. 13
Size: 41x32mm
B112 SP25 5pf + 5pf   .25   .20
B113 SP25 10pf + 5pf   .25   .20
B114 SP25 15pf + 5pf   .25   .20
B115 SP25 20pf + 5pf   .25   .20
B116 SP25 25pf + 10pf   .35   .25
Size: 48½x28mm
B117 SP25 40pf + 10pf   1.25   1.50
Nos. B112-B117 (6)   2.60   2.55
The surtax was for the support of national
memorials for victims of the Nazis.

Olympic Types of Regular Issues
Designs: 40pf+20pf, Two runners. #B119,
Equestrian. #B120, Three runners.

Lithographed and Engraved
1964, July 15   Wmk. 313   Perf. 14
B118 A232 40pf + 20pf multi   .30   .20
Litho.
Perf. 13
B119 A233 5pf + 5pf multi   2.25   2.75
B120 A233 10pf + 5pf multi   2.25   2.75
Nos. B118-B120 (3)   4.80   5.70
See note after No. 714.

Pioneers Studying — SP26

Designs: 20pf+10pf, Pioneers planting tree.
25pf+10pf, Pioneers playing.

1964, July 29
B121 SP26 10pf + 5pf multi   1.90   .35
B122 SP26 20pf + 10pf multi   1.90   .35
B123 SP26 25pf + 10pf multi   3.50   3.50
Nos. B121-B123 (3)   7.30   4.20
Fifth Young Pioneers Meeting, Karl-Marx-
Stadt.

Stamp Exhibition Type of 1964
Designs: 10pf+5pf, Stamp of 1958 (No.
390). 20pf+10pf, Stamp of 1950 (No. 73).

Perf. 13x13½
1964, Sept. 23   Litho.   Wmk. 313
B124 A238 10pf + 5pf org & emer   .25   .20
B125 A238 20pf + 10pf brt pink &
bl   .30   .25

Boxing Type of Regular Issue
10pf+5pf, Two boxing gloves and laurel.

Perf. 13½x14
1965, Apr. 27   Photo.   Wmk. 313
B126 A247 10pf + 5pf blk, gold,
red & blue   .20   .20
The surtax went to the German Turner and
Sport Organization.

Type of Regular Issue, 1965
5pf+5pf, George Dimitrov at Leipzig trial &
communist newspaper. 10pf+5pf, Anti-fascists
clandestinely distributing leaflets. 15pf+5pf,
Fighting in Spanish Civil War. 20pf+10pf,
Ernst Thalman behind bars & demonstration
for his release. 25pf+10pf, Founding of Natl.
Committee for Free Germany & signatures.

Wmk. 313
1965, May 5   Photo.   Perf. 14
Flags in Red, Black and Yellow
B127 A248 5pf + 5pf blk, org
& red   .25   .20
B128 A248 10pf + 5pf grn & red   .25   .20
B129 A248 15pf + 5pf lil, red &
yel   .25   .20
B130 A248 20pf + 10pf blk &
red   .25   .20
B131 A248 25pf + 10pf ol grn,
yel & blk   .25   .20
Nos. B127-B131 (5)   1.25   1.00
The surtax went for the maintenance of
national memorials.

Doves, Globe and Finnish Flag — SP27

1965, July 5   Litho.   Perf. 13x13½
B132 SP27 10pf + 5pf vio bl & ember   .20 .20
B133 SP27 20pf + 5pf red & vio bl   .45 .30
World Peace Congress, Helsinki, July 10-17. The surtax went to the peace council of the DDR.

No. 725 Surcharged

Perf. 13½x13
1965, Aug. 23   Wmk. 313
B134 A239 10pf + 10pf multi   .35 .20
Surtax was for North Viet Nam.

Sports Type of Regular Issue

Perf. 13½x13
1965, Sept. 15   Litho.   Unwmk.
B135 A257 10pf + 5pf Fencer   .25 .20
B136 A257 10pf + 5pf Pistol shooter   .25 .20
International Modern Pentathlon Championships, Leipzig.

Type of Regular Issue

Designs: 10pf+5pf, Willi Bredel and instruction of International Brigade. 20pf+10pf, Heinrich Rau and parade after battle of Brunete. 25pf+10pf, Hans Marchwitza, international fighters and globe. 40pf+10pf, Artur Becker and battle on the Ebro.

1966, July 15   Photo.   Perf. 14
B137 A277 10pf + 5pf multi   .25 .20
B138 A277 20pf + 10pf multi   .25 .20
B139 A277 25pf + 10pf multi   .25 .20
B140 A277 40pf + 10pf multi   1.10 .90
   Nos. B137-B140 (4)   1.85 1.50
The surtax was for the maintenance of national memorials.

Canoe Type of Regular Issue

Design: 10pf+5pf, Men's single canoe race.

Perf. 13x12½
1966, Aug. 16   Litho.   Unwmk.
B141 A279 10pf + 5pf multi   .25 .20

Red Cross Type of Regular Issue

Design: ICY Red Crescent, Red Cross, and Red Lion and Sun emblems, horiz.

1966, Sept. 13   Wmk. 313   Perf. 14
B142 A281 20pf + 10pf vio & red   .35 .20
International health cooperation. Surtax for German Red Cross.

Sports Type of Regular Issue

Design: 20pf+5pf, Weight lifter.

Perf. 13½x13
1966, Sept. 22   Litho.   Unwmk.
B143 A282 20pf + 5pf ultra & blk   .35 .20

Armed Woman Planting Flower — SP28

1966, Oct. 25   Perf. 13½x13
B144 SP28 20pf + 5pf blk & pink   .35 .25
Surtax was for North Viet Nam.

Wartburg Type of Regular Issue

Design: Wartburg, view from the East.

1966, Nov. 23   Perf. 13x13½
B145 A288 10pf + 5pf slate   .20 .20
See note after No. 878.

Olympic Type of Regular Issue

Design: 10pf+5pf, Tobogganing.

1968, Jan. 17   Litho.   Perf. 13½x13
B146 A314 10pf + 5pf grnsh bl, vio bl & red   .20 .20
The surtax was for the Olympic Committee of the German Democratic Republic.

Armed Mother and Child — SP29   Armed Vietnamese Couple — SP30

1968, May 8   Perf. 13½x13
B147 SP29 10pf + 5pf yel & multi   .25 .20
Surtax was for North Viet Nam.

Festival Type of Regular Issue

1968, June 20   Litho.   Perf. 13½x13
B148 A327 10pf + 5pf multi   .30 .20

Olympic Games Type of Regular Issue, 1968

Designs: 10pf+5pf, Pole vault, vert. 20pf+10pf, Soccer, vert.

1968, Sept. 18   Photo.   Perf. 14
B149 A336 10pf + 5pf multi   .20 .20
B150 A336 20pf + 10pf multi   .20 .20
The surtax was for the Olympic Committee.

1969, June 4
B151 SP30 10pf + 5pf multi   .30 .20
Surtax was for North Viet Nam.

Sports Type of Regular Issue, 1969

Designs: 10pf+5pf, Gymnastics. 20pf+5pf, Art Exhibition with sports motifs.

Photo. & Engr.
1969, June 18   Perf. 14
B152 A353 10pf + 5pf multi   .20 .20
B153 A353 20pf + 5pf multi   .20 .20
The surtax was for the German Gymnastic and Sports League.

Otto von Guericke's Vacuum Test with Magdeburg Hemispheres — SP31

1969, Oct. 28   Litho.   Perf. 13x12½
B154 SP31 40pf + 10pf multi   .95 .45
See note after No. 1146.

Folk Art Type of Regular Issue

Design: 20pf+5pf, Decorative plate.

1969, Nov. 25   Litho.   Perf. 13½x13
B155 A365 20pf + 5pf yel blk & ultra   .30 .30

Sports Type of Regular Issue

Design: 20pf+5pf, Children hurdling.

1970, July 1   Photo.   Perf. 14x13½
B156 A382 20pf + 5pf multi   .35 .20

Pioneer Waving Kerchief, and Pioneer Activities — SP32

Design: 25pf+5pf, Girl Pioneer holding kerchief, and Pioneer activities.

1970, July 28   Litho.   Perf. 13x12½
B157 SP32 10pf + 5pf multi   .25 .25
B158 SP32 25pf + 5pf multi   .25 .25
   a.   Pair, #B157-B158   1.10 2.25
6th Youth Pioneer Meeting, Cottbus. No. B158a has continuous design.

Ho Chi Minh — SP33

1970, Sept. 2   Perf. 13x13½
B159 SP33 20pf + 5pf rose, blk & red   .40 .20
Surtax was for North Viet Nam.

German Democratic Republic No. 460 — SP34

1970, Oct. 1   Photo.   Perf. 14x13½
B160 SP34 15pf + 5pf multi   .20 .30
2nd National Youth Philatelic Exhibition, Karl-Marx-Stadt, Oct. 4-11.

Mother and Child — SP35   Vietnamese Farm Woman — SP36

Photo. & Engr.
1971, Sept. 2   Perf. 14
B161 SP35 10pf + 5pf multi   .30 .20
Surtax was for North Viet Nam.

Type of Regular Issue

10pf+5pf, Loading & unloading mail at airport.

Photo. & Engr.
1971, Oct. 5   Perf. 14
B162 A421 10pf + 5pf multi   .20 .20

Olympic Games Type of Regular Issue

Olympic Rings and: 10pf+5pf, Figure skating, pairs. 15pf+5pf, Speed skating.

1971, Dec. 7   Photo.   Perf. 13½x14
B163 A424 10pf + 5pf bl, car & blk   .20 .20
B164 A424 15pf + 5pf grn, blk & bl   .20 .20

1972, Feb. 22   Litho.   Perf. 13½x13
B165 SP36 10pf + 5pf multi   .30 .20
Surtax was for North Viet Nam.

Olympic Games Type of Regular Issue

Sport and Olympic Rings: 10pf+5pf, Diving. 25pf+10pf, Rowing.

1972, May 16   Photo.   Perf. 13½x14
B166 A430 10pf + 5pf grnsh bl, gold & blk   .20 .20
B167 A430 25pf + 10pf multi   .20 .20

Interartes Type of Regular Issue

Designs: 15pf+5pf, Spear carrier, Persia, 500 B.C. 35pf+5pf, Grape Sellers, by Max Lingner, 1949, horiz.

1972, Sept. 19   Photo.   Perf. 14
B168 A439 15pf + 5pf multi   .75 .75
B169 A439 35pf + 5pf multi   .20 .20

Flags and World Time Clock SP37   Young Couple, by Günter Glombitza SP38

25pf+5pf, Youth group with guitar and dove.

1973, Feb. 13   Litho.   Perf. 12½x13
B170 SP37 10pf + 5pf multi   .20 .20
B171 SP37 25pf + 5pf multi   .30 .25
10th World Youth Festival, Berlin.

1973, Oct. 4   Photo.   Perf. 13½x14
B172 SP38 20pf + 5pf multi   .30 .20
Philatelists' Day and for the 3rd National Youth Philatelic Exhibition, Halle.

Child, Symbols of Reconstruction SP39

Luis Corvalan, Red Flag — SP40

1973, Oct. 11   Perf. 14x13½
B173 SP39 10pf + 5pf multi   .30 .20
Surtax was for North Viet Nam.

1973, Nov. 5   Perf. 13½x14
25pf+5pf, Salvador Allende, Chilean flag.
B174 SP40 10pf + 5pf multi   .20 .20
B175 SP40 25pf + 5pf multi   .50 .50
Solidarity with the people of Chile.

Raised Fist and Star — SP41

1975, Sept. 23   Litho.   Perf. 13x13½
B176 SP41 10pf + 5pf multi   .20 .20
Surtax was for the Solidarity Committee of the German Democratic Republic.

Restored Post Gate, Wurzen, 1734 — SP42

1975, Oct. 21   Photo.   *Perf. 14*
B177 SP42 10pf + 5pf multi   .35 .35
Philatelists' Day 1975.

Olympic Games Type of 1975

Designs: 10pf+5pf, Luge run, Oberhof. 25pf+5pf, Ski jump, Rennsteig at Oberhof.

1975, Dec. 2   Photo.   *Perf. 14*
B178 A518 10pf + 5pf multi   .20 .20
B179 A518 25pf + 5pf multi   .25 .20

Olympic Games Type of 1976

Designs: 10pf+5pf, Swimming pool, High School for Physical Education, Leipzig. 35pf+10pf, Rifle range, Suhl.

1976, May 18   Photo.   *Perf. 13½x14*
B180 A529 10pf + 5pf multi   .20 .20
B181 A529 35pf + 10pf multi   .25 .20

TV Tower, Berlin, and Perforations SP43

1976, Oct. 19   Litho.   *Perf. 13*
B182 SP43 10pf + 5pf org & bl   .30 .20

Surtax was for Sozphilex 77, Philatelic Exhibition of Socialist Countries, in connection with 60th anniversary of October Revolution.

Sports Type of 1977

10pf+5pf, Young milers. 25pf+5pf, Girls artistic gymnastic performance.

1977, July 19   Litho.   *Perf. 13x12½*
B183 A558 10pf + 5pf multi   .20 .20
B184 A558 25pf + 5pf multi   .20 .20

Sozphilex Type of 1977
Souvenir Sheet

Design: 50pf+20pf, World Youth Song, by Lothar Zitzmann, horiz.

1977, Aug. 16   Photo.   *Perf. 13*
B185 A559 50pf + 20pf multi   1.50 1.10

Hand Holding Torch — SP44

1977, Oct. 18   Litho.   *Perf. 14*
B186 SP44 10pf + 5pf multi   .30 .20

Surtax was for East German Solidarity Committee.

Fountain Type of 1979

Design: 10pf+5pf, Goose Boy Fountain.

1979, Aug. 7   Photo.   *Perf. 14*
B187 A617 10pf + 5pf multi   .45 .35

Vietnamese Soldier, Mother and Child — SP45

1979, Nov. 6   Litho.   *Perf. 14*
B188 SP45 10pf + 5pf red org & blk   .35 .25

Surtax was for Vietnam.

Olympic Type of 1980

Ski Jump, sculpture by Gunther Schutz.

1980, Jan. 15   Photo.
B189 A627 25pf + 10pf multi   .20 .20

1980, Apr. 22   Photo.   *Perf. 14*

Design: 20pf+5pf, Runners at the Finish, by Lothar Zitzmann.

B190 A627   20 + 5pf multi   .25 .20

Interflug Type of 1980
Souvenir Sheet

1980, June 10   Litho.   *Perf. 13x12½*
B191 A636 1m + 10pf Jet, globe   2.50 1.90

AEROSOZPHILEX 1980 International Airpost Exhibition, Berlin, Aug. 1-10.

Olympic Type of 1980

Design: Swimmer, by Willi Sitte, vert.

1980, July 8   Photo.   *Perf. 14*
B192 A627 20pf + 10pf multi   .20 .20

22nd Summer Olympic Games, Moscow, July 19-Aug. 3.

International Solidarity
SP46   SP47

1980, Oct. 14   Photo.   *Perf. 14*
B193 SP46 10pf + 5pf multi   .35 .20

1981, Oct. 6   Photo.   *Perf. 14*
B194 SP47 10pf + 5pf multi   .30 .20

Palestinian Solidarity — SP48

Palestinian family, Tree of Life.

1982, Sept. 21   Litho.   *Perf. 14*
B195 SP48 10pf + 5pf multi   .35 .25

Nicaraguan Solidarity SP49

1983, Nov. 8   Litho.   *Perf. 14x13½*

Literacy, home defense.
B196 SP49 10pf + 5pf multi   .30 .20

Solidarity — SP50

1984, Oct. 23   Photo.   *Perf. 14*
B197 SP50 10pf + 5pf Knot   .35 .25

Solidarity SP51

1985, May 28   Photo.
B198 SP51 10pf + 5pf Globe, peace dove   .30 .20

Surtax for the Solidarity Committee.

Technical Assistance to Developing Nations — SP52

1986, Nov. 4   Photo.
B199 SP52 10pf + 5pf multi   .30 .25

Surtax for the Solidarity Committee.

Solidarity with South Africans Opposing Apartheid SP53

1987, June 16   Litho.   *Perf. 14*
B200 SP53 10pf +5pf multi   .30 .25

Solidarity SP54

1988, Oct. 4   Photo.   *Perf. 14*
B201 SP54 10pf +5pf multi   .40 .40

Surtax for the Solidarity Committee. No. B201 printed se-tenant with label containing a Wilhelm Pieck quote.

UNICEF Emblem and Children of Africa — SP55

1989, Sept. 5   Photo.   *Perf. 14½x14*
B202 SP55 10pf +5pf multi   .30 .20

Surtax for the Solidarity Committee.

Leipzig Church, Municipal Arms SP56

1990, Feb. 28   Photo.   *Perf. 13*
B203 SP56 35pf +15pf multi   .75 .50

We are the People.

Intl. Literacy Year — SP57

1990, July 24   Photo.   *Perf. 14*
B204 SP57 30pf+5pf on 10pf+5pf   1.50 1.00

Not issued without surcharge.

AIR POST STAMPS

Catalogue values for unused stamps in this section, from this point to the end of the section, are for Never Hinged items.

Canceled to Order
Used values are for CTO's.

Stylized Plane
AP1   AP2

Perf. 13x12½, 13x13½ (AP2)
1957, Dec. 13   Litho.   Wmk. 313
C1 AP1 5pf gray & blk   3.50 .20
C2 AP1 20pf brt car & blk   .20 .20
C3 AP1 35pf violet & blk   .20 .20
C4 AP1 50pf maroon & blk   .30 .20
C5 AP2 1m olive & yel   1.00 .20
C6 AP2 3m choc & yel   1.60 .45
C7 AP2 5m dk bl & yel   3.75 .70
Nos. C1-C7 (7)   10.55 2.15

Plane and Envelope — AP3

1982-87   Photo.   *Perf. 14*
C8 AP3 5pf lt bl & blk   .20 .20
C9 AP3 15pf brt rose lil & blk   .20 .30
C10 AP3 20pf ocher & blk   .25 .20
C11 AP3 25pf ol bis & blk   .35 .35
C12 AP3 30pf brt grn & blk   .25 .20
C13 AP3 40pf ol grn & blk   .35 .20
C14 AP3 1m blue & blk   1.00 .45
C15 AP3 3m brown & blk   3.00 1.75
C16 AP3 5m dk red & blk   4.50 1.50
Nos. C8-C16 (9)   10.10 5.15

Issued: 30, 40pf, 1m, 10/26; 5, 20pf, 10/4/83; 3m, 4/10/84; 5m, 9/10/85; 15, 25pf, 10/6/87.

OFFICIAL STAMPS

While valid, these Official stamps were not sold to the public unused. After their period of use, some sets were sold abroad by the government stamp sales agency. Used values of Official stamps are for canceled-to-order copies. Reprints of type O1 stamps have printed cancellations.

Catalogue values for unused stamps in this section, from this point to the end of the section, are for Never Hinged items.

Arms of
Republic — O1

Perf. 13x12½

1954	O1		Wmk. 297	Litho.	
O1	O1	5pf emerald		13.50	.20
O2	O1	6pf violet		7.50	.20
O3	O1	8pf org brown		13.50	.20
O4	O1	10pf lt bl grn		13.50	.20
O5	O1	12pf blue		45.00	.20
O6	O1	15pf dark violet		13.50	.20
O7	O1	16pf dark violet		7.50	.20
O8	O1	20pf olive		9.00	.20
O9	O1	24pf brown red		9.00	.20
O10	O1	25pf sage green		9.00	.20
O11	O1	30pf brown red		6.00	.20
O12	O1	40pf red		9.75	.20
O13	O1	48pf rose lilac		5.25	1.10
O14	O1	50pf rose lilac		4.50	.20
O15	O1	60pf bright blue		4.50	.20
O16	O1	70pf brown		4.50	.20
O17	O1	84pf brown		7.50	3.00
	Nos. O1-O17 (17)			183.00	7.10

Type of 1954 Redrawn

Arc of compass projects at right except on
No. O22.

1954-56	O1			Typo.	
O18	O1	5pf emer ('54)		3.75	.25
O19	O1	10pf bl grn		2.25	.25
O20	O1	12pf dk bl ('54)		2.25	.25
O21	O1	15pf dk vio		2.75	.25
O22	O1	20pf ol, arc at left ('55)		52.50	.25
a.		Arc of compass projects at right ('56)		525.00	.25
O23	O1	25pf dark green		2.25	.25
O24	O1	30pf brown red		4.50	.25
O25	O1	40pf red		4.50	.25
O26	O1	50pf rose lilac		2.25	.25
O27	O1	70pf brown		2.25	.25
	Nos. O18-O27 (10)			79.25	2.50

Shaded background of emblem consists of
vertical lines; on Nos. O1-O17 it consists of
dots.

Granite paper was used for a 1956 printing
of the 5pf, 10pf, 15pf, 20pf and 40pf. Value for
set unused $300, used 30 cents.
See Nos. O37-O43.

O2

O3

1956	O2		Wmk. 297	Perf. 13x12½	
O28	O2	5pf black		.25	.20
O29	O2	10pf black		.25	.20
O30	O2	20pf black		.30	.20
O31	O2	40pf black		.40	.20
O32	O2	70pf black		.45	.20
	Nos. O28-O32 (5)			1.65	1.00

1956	O3		Litho.	Wmk. 297	
O33	O3	10pf lilac & black		.90	.75
O34	O3	20pf lilac & black		140.00	1.10
O35	O3	40pf lilac & black		1.50	.75
O36	O3	70pf lilac & black		2.25	2.50
	Nos. O33-O36 (4)			144.65	5.10

Nos. O33-O36 exist also with black or violet
overprint of 4-digit control number.
See Nos. O44-O45.
No. O34 was reprinted with watermark sideways ("DDR" vertical). Value $4.

Redrawn Type of 1954-56
Perf. 13x12½, 14

1957-60	O1		Typo.	Wmk. 313	
			Granite Paper		
O37	O1	5pf emerald		.25	.25
O38	O1	10pf blue green		.25	.25
O39	O1	15pf dark vio		.35	.25
O40	O1	20pf olive		.35	.25
O41	O1	30pf dark red ('58)		.75	.25
O42	O1	40pf red		.55	.25
O42A	O1	50pf rose lilac ('60)		1.60	.35
O43	O1	70pf brown ('58)		1.60	.35
	Nos. O37-O43 (8)			5.70	2.20

Nos. O37-O43 were all issued in perf.
13x12½. Nos. O37-O40 were also issued
perf. 14. Values are the same.

Type of 1956

1957		Litho.	Perf. 13x12½	
O44	O3	10pf lilac & black	.65	.35
O45	O3	20pf lilac & black	.65	.35

Nos. O44-O45 have black or violet overprint
of four-digit control number.
Stamps similar to type O3 were issued later,
with denomination expressed in dashes: one
for 10pf, two for 20pf.

ISSUED UNDER RUSSIAN OCCUPATION

BERLIN-BRANDENBURG

Berlin Bear — OS1

1945		Litho.	Perf. 14	
11N1	OS1	5pf shown	.20	.55
11N2	OS1	6pf Bear holding spade	.20	.35
11N3	OS1	8pf Bear on shield	.20	.35
11N4	OS1	10pf Bear holding brick	.20	.55
11N5	OS1	12pf Bear carrying board	.20	.35
11N6	OS1	20pf Bear on small shield	.20	.35
11N7	OS1	30pf Oak sapling, ruins	.20	.55
	Nos. 11N1-11N7 (7)		1.40	3.05
	Set, never hinged			

Issued: 5pf, 8pf, 6/9; 12pf, 7/5; others, 7/18.

1945, Dec. 6			Serrate Roulette 13½	
11N1a	OS1	5pf	.20	.55
11N2a	OS1	6pf	3.75	90.00
11N3a	OS1	8pf	2.25	90.00
11N4a	OS1	10pf	3.75	90.00
11N5a	OS1	12pf	4.50	125.00
11N6a	OS1	20pf	3.00	97.50
11N7a	OS1	30pf	4.50	125.00
	Nos. 11N1a-11N7a (7)		21.95	618.05
	Set, never hinged		70.00	

No. 11N1a comes with two different roulettes. The roulette that matches Nos. 11N2a-
11N7a is valued at $2. No. 11N5a in the sec-
ond roulette is rare.

MECKLENBURG-VORPOMMERN

OS1

Plowman — OS2

Design: 12pf, Wheat.

1945-46		Typo.	Perf. 10½	
12N1	OS1	6pf black, green	.20	1.90
12N2	OS1	6pf purple	1.10	3.00
12N3	OS1	6pf purple, green	1.10	3.00
12N4	OS2	8pf red, rose	.30	2.25
a.		8pf red lilac, rose	.75	19.00
12N5	OS2	8pf black, rose	1.90	9.75
12N6	OS2	8pf red lilac, green	.55	4.50
12N7	OS2	8pf black, green	3.00	12.00
12N8	OS2	8pf brown	.45	4.50
12N9	OS2	12pf black, rose	.25	1.60
12N10	OS2	12pf brown lilac	.30	1.90
12N11	OS2	12pf red	1.90	12.00
12N12	OS2	12pf red, rose	.30	2.40
	Nos. 12N1-12N12 (12)		11.35	58.80
	Set, never hinged		30.00	

Many shades.
Issued: #12N1, 12N9, 8/28; #12N4, 10/6;
#12N5, 10/19; #12N7, 11/2; #12N6, 11/3;
#12N10, 11/9; #12N2, 11/16; #12N11, 12/20;
#12N8, 1/7/46; #12N3, 1/11/46; #12N12,
1/30/46.

Buildings — OS3

Designs: 4pf, Deer. 5pf, Fishing boats. 6pf,
Harvesting grain. 8pf, Windmill. 10pf, Two-
horse plow. 12pf, Bricklayer on scaffolding.
15pf, Tractor plowing field. 20pf, Ship, warehouse. 30pf, Factory. 40pf, Woman spinning.

1946		Typo.	Imperf.	
12N13	OS3	3pf brown	1.10	35.00
12N14	OS3	4pf blue	13.50	52.50
12N15	OS3	4pf red brown	1.10	45.00
12N16	OS3	5pf green	1.10	35.00
12N17	OS3	8pf orange	1.10	35.00
12N18	OS3	10pf brown	.90	35.00
			Perf. 10½	
12N19	OS3	6pf purple	.75	6.00
12N20	OS3	6pf blue	3.75	18.00
12N21	OS3	12pf red	.60	3.25
12N22	OS3	15pf brown	.60	5.75
12N23	OS3	20pf blue	.90	9.75
12N24	OS3	30pf blue green	.75	7.50
12N25	OS3	40pf red violet	.75	8.25
	Nos. 12N13-12N25 (13)		26.90	296.00
	Set, never hinged		52.50	

Issued: 3pf, #12N14, 5pf, 6pf, 8pf, 1/17;
10pf, 12pf, 40pf, 1/22; 15pf, 1/24; 30pf, 1/26;
20pf, 1/29; #12N15, 2/25.
Nos. 12N13-12N21 exist on both white and
toned paper.

MECKLENBURG-VORPOMMERN SEMI-POSTAL STAMPS

Rudolf
Breitscheid
(1874-1944),
Politician
OSP1

Designs: 8pf+22pf, Dr. Erich Klausener
(1885-1934), theologian. 12pf+28pf, Ernst
Thalmann (1886-1944), politician.

1945, Oct. 21		Typo.	Perf. 10½x11	
12NB1	OSP1	6 +14pf green	10.50	45.00
12NB2	OSP1	8 +22pf purple	10.50	45.00
12NB3	OSP1	12 +28pf red	10.50	45.00
	Nos. 12NB1-12NB3 (3)		31.50	135.00
	Set, never hinged		75.00	

Sower
OSP2

Child Welfare
OSP3

6pf+14pf, Horsedrawn Plow. 12pf+28pf,
Reaper.

1945				
12NB4	OSP2	6 +14pf bl grn	2.25	22.50
12NB5	OSP2	6 +14pf grn	2.25	22.50
12NB6	OSP2	8 +22pf brn	2.25	22.50
12NB7	OSP2	8 +22pf yel brn	2.25	22.50
12NB8	OSP2	12 +28pf red	2.25	22.50
12NB9	OSP2	12 +28pf org	2.25	22.50
	Nos. 12NB4-12NB9 (6)		13.50	135.00
	Set, never hinged		37.50	

Issued: #12NB4, 12NB6, 12NB8, Dec. 8;
others Dec. 31.

1945, Dec. 31			Perf. 11	
12NB10	OSP3	6 +14pf Child in hand	2.75	30.00
12NB11	OSP3	8 +22pf Girl in winter	.95	30.00
12NB12	OSP3	12 +28pf Boy	.95	30.00
	Nos. 12NB10-12NB12 (3)		4.65	90.00
	Set, never hinged		11.00	

SAXONY PROVINCE

Coat of
Arms — OS1

Land
Reform — OS2

Perf. 13x12½

1945-46		Typo.	Wmk. 48	
13N1	OS1	1pf slate	.20	1.90
a.		Imperf.	.20	4.50
		Never hinged	.60	
13N2	OS1	3pf yellow brown	.20	2.25
a.		Imperf.	.20	3.00
		Never hinged	.60	
13N3	OS1	5pf green	.20	2.00
a.		Imperf.	.55	11.00
		Never hinged	1.50	
13N4	OS1	6pf purple	.20	2.25
a.		Imperf.	.35	1.90
		Never hinged	1.00	
13N5	OS1	8pf orange	.20	2.50
a.		Imperf.	.20	3.00
		Never hinged	.60	
13N6	OS1	10pf brown	.20	2.50
a.		Imperf.	2.75	110.00
		Never hinged	6.00	
13N7	OS1	12pf red	.20	1.90
a.		Imperf.	.20	1.90
		Never hinged	.60	
13N8	OS1	15pf red brown	.20	19.00
13N9	OS1	20pf blue	.20	3.00
13N10	OS1	24pf orange brown	.20	3.00
13N11	OS1	30pf olive green	.20	3.00
13N12	OS1	40pf lake	.60	6.75
	Nos. 13N1-13N12 (12)		2.80	50.05
	Set, never hinged			

Issued: #13N1-13N12, 12/1945; #13N1a-
13N5a, 10/10/45; #13N7a, 10/45; #13N6a, 1/1946.

1945-46		Unwmk.	Imperf.	
13N13	OS2	6pf green	.20	1.80
13N14	OS2	12pf red	.20	1.80
		On Thin Transparent Paper		
		Wmk. 397		
		Perf. 13x13½		
13N15	OS2	6pf green	.20	1.80
13N16	OS2	12pf red	.20	1.80
	Nos. 13N13-13N16 (4)		.20	7.20
	Set, never hinged		1.20	

Issued: #13N13-13N14, 12/17/45; others
2/21/46.

SAXONY PROVINCE SEMI-POSTAL STAMPS

Reconstruction
OSP1

Designs: 6+4pf, Housing construction.
12+8pf, Bridge repair. 42+28pf, Locomotives.

1946, Jan. 19		Typo.	Perf. 13	
13NB1	OSP1	6pf +4pf green	.20	1.80
a.		Imperf.	.20	15.00
13NB2	OSP1	12pf +8pf red	.20	1.80
a.		Imperf.	.20	15.00
13NB3	OSP1	42pf +28pf violet	.20	1.80
a.		Imperf.	.20	15.00
	Nos. 13NB1-13NB3 (3)		.70	5.40
	Set, never hinged		.70	
	Set, 13NB1a-13NB3a, never hinged		1.60	

Nos. 13NB1a-13NB3a issued Feb. 21.

WEST SAXONY

OS1

Leipzig
Fair — OS2

1945 Typo. Wmk. 48 *Perf. 13x12½*

14N1	OS1	3pf brown	.20	1.90
14N2	OS1	4pf slate	.20	3.75
14N3	OS1	5pf green	.20	1.90
a.		Imperf.	.20	1.90
		Never hinged	.25	
14N4	OS1	6pf violet	.20	1.90
a.		Imperf.	.20	1.90
		Never hinged	.25	
14N5	OS1	8pf orange	.20	4.50
a.		Imperf.	.20	1.90
		Never hinged	.25	
14N6	OS1	10pf gray	.20	4.00
14N7	OS1	12pf red	.20	1.90
a.		Imperf.	.20	1.90
		Never hinged	.25	
14N8	OS1	15pf red brown	.30	4.25
14N9	OS1	20pf blue	.20	3.75
14N10	OS1	30pf olive green	.30	2.25
14N11	OS1	40pf red lilac	.30	4.50
14N12	OS1	60pf maroon	.30	15.00
		Nos. 14N1-14N12 (12)	2.80	49.60
		Set, never hinged	12.00	

Issued: 3-4, 20-30pf, 11/9; 5-8, 12pf, 11/12; 10, 15, 40-60pf, 11/15; imperfs., 9/28.

1945, Oct. 18

14N13	OS2	6pf green	.25	2.90
14N14	OS2	12pf red	.25	2.90
		Set, never hinged	1.00	

Leipzig Arms — OS3

Designs: 5pf, 6pf, St. Nicholas Church. 8pf, 12pf, Leipzig Town Hall.

1946, Feb. 12

14N15	OS3	3pf brown	.20	6.00
a.		Unwatermarked	.20	9.00
14N16	OS3	4pf slate	.20	6.00
a.		Unwatermarked	.20	9.00
14N17	OS3	5pf green	.20	6.00
a.		Unwatermarked	.20	9.00
14N18	OS3	6pf violet	.20	6.00
a.		Unwatermarked	.20	9.00
14N19	OS3	8pf orange	.20	6.00
a.		Unwatermarked	.20	9.00
14N20	OS3	12pf red	.20	6.00
a.		Unwatermarked	.20	9.00
		Nos. 14N15-14N20 (6)		36.00
		Set, never hinged	1.40	
		Set, 14N15a-14N20a, never hinged	1.50	

Nos. 14N15a-14N20a issued Mar. 15.

WEST SAXONY SEMI-POSTAL STAMPS

OSP1

Market, Old Town Hall — OSP2

1946 Typo. Wmk. 48 *Perf. 13x12½*

14NB1	OSP1	3 +2pf yel brn	.20	2.10
14NB2	OSP1	4 +3pf slate	.20	2.10
14NB3	OSP1	5 +3pf green	.20	2.10
14NB4	OSP1	6 +4pf violet	.20	2.10
14NB5	OSP1	8 +4pf orange	.20	2.10
14NB6	OSP1	10 +5pf gray	.20	2.10
14NB7	OSP1	12 +6pf red	.20	2.10
14NB8	OSP1	15 +10pf red brn	.20	2.10
14NB9	OSP1	20 +10pf blue	.20	2.10
14NB10	OSP1	30 +20pf olive grn	.20	2.10
14NB11	OSP1	40 +30pf red lilac	.20	2.10
14NB12	OSP1	60 +40pf lake	.20	3.00
		Nos. 14NB1-14NB12 (12)	2.40	26.10
		Set, never hinged	4.50	

Issue dates: Nos. 14NB1, 14NB4, 14NB7, 14NB11, Jan. 7; others, Jan. 28.

1946, May 8 *Perf. 13*

14NB13	OSP2	6 +14pf violet	.20	2.50
a.		Imperf.	.35	9.00
b.		Unwatermarked	.35	3.75

14NB14	OSP2	12 +18pf bl gray	.20	4.50
a.		Imperf.	.35	9.00
b.		Unwatermarked	.25	6.00
14NB15	OSP2	24 +26pf org brn	.20	2.50
a.		Imperf.	.35	9.00
b.		Unwatermarked	.25	2.25
14NB16	OSP2	84 +66pf green	.20	6.00
a.		Imperf.	.35	22.50
c.		Sheet of 4, #14NB13a-14NB16a	75.00	240.00
		Nos. 14NB13-14NB16 (4)	.80	15.50
		Set, never hinged	1.50	
		Set, 14NB13a-14NB16a, never hinged	3.50	
		Set, 14NB13b-14NB16b, never hinged	2.10	

Issue date: Imperf., May 20.

EAST SAXONY

OS1

OS2

1945, June 23 Photo. *Imperf.*

15N1	OS1	12pf red	190.00	600.00
		Never hinged	410.00	

Withdrawn on day of issue.

Litho. (3pf, #15N9), Photo.

1945-46

15N2	OS2	3pf sepia	.30	2.25
15N3	OS2	4pf blue gray	.20	1.90
a.		4pf gray	.20	.90
15N4	OS2	5pf brown	.30	2.00
15N5	OS2	6pf green	2.50	6.00
15N6	OS2	6pf violet	.20	.90
15N7	OS2	8pf dark violet	.35	2.00
15N8	OS2	10pf dark brown	.45	4.00
15N9	OS2	10pf gray	.30	2.25
15N10	OS2	12pf red	.30	2.00
15N11	OS2	15pf lemon	.45	2.60
15N12	OS2	20pf blue	.20	1.90
a.		20pf gray blue	.60	2.60
		Never hinged	1.20	
15N13	OS2	25pf blue	.45	2.75
15N14	OS2	30pf yellow	.20	1.90
15N15	OS2	40pf lilac	.45	2.75

Typo.

Perf. 13x12½

15N16	OS2	3pf brown	.20	1.90
15N17	OS2	5pf green	.20	1.90
15N18	OS2	6pf violet	.20	1.90
15N19	OS2	8pf orange	.20	1.90
15N20	OS2	12pf vermilion	.20	1.90
		Nos. 15N2-15N20 (19)	7.65	44.70
		Set, never hinged	17.50	

Issued: 12pf, 6/28; #15N5, 6/30; 8pf, #15N8, 7/3; 25pf, 7/5; 5pf, 6/6; 40pf, 7/7; 15pf, 7/10; #15N12a, 7/26; #15N9, 15N12, 15N17-15N20, 11/3; #15N3, 30pf, 11/5; 3pf, 12/5; #15N15, 12/21; #15N6, 1/22/46.

EAST SAXONY SEMI-POSTAL STAMPS

Zwinger, Dresden — OSP1

Design: 12pf+88pf, Rathaus, Dresden.

1946, Feb. 6 Photo. *Perf. 11*

15NB1	OSP1	6pf +44pf green	.20	4.50
15NB2	OSP1	12pf +88pf red	.20	4.50
		Set, never hinged	.70	

THURINGIA

Fir Trees — OS1

Designs: 6pf, 8pf, Posthorn. 12pf, Schiller. 20pf, 30pf, Goethe.

1945-46 Typo. *Perf. 11*

16N1	OS1	3pf brown	.20	3.00
16N2	OS1	4pf black	.20	3.00
16N3	OS1	5pf green	.20	3.00
a.		Souvenir sheet of 3, #16N1-16N3	150.00	825.00
		Never hinged	300.00	
16N4	OS1	6pf dark green	.20	1.90
16N5	OS1	8pf orange	.20	2.60
16N6	OS1	12pf red	.20	2.50
16N7	OS1	20pf blue	.20	2.25
a.		Imperf.	.20	3.00
		Never hinged	.35	
b.		Souv. sheet of 4, #16N2, 16N4, 16N6-16N7, rouletted x imperf. btwn.	575.00	2,250.
		Never hinged	1,150.	
16N8	OS1	30pf gray	.55	3.00
a.		Imperf.	1.50	15.00
		Never hinged	3.00	
		Nos. 16N1-16N8 (8)	1.95	21.25
		Set, never hinged	3.50	

#16N3a sold for 2m, #16N7b for 10m.
Issued: 6pf, 10/1; 12pf, 10/19; 5pf, 10/20; 8pf, 11/3; 20pf, 11/24; #16N3a, 16N7b, 12/18; 30pf, 12/22; 3pf, 4pf, 1/4/46.

Souvenir Sheet

Rebuilding of German Natl. Theater, Weimar — OS2

a, 6pf, Schiller. b, 10pf, Goethe. c, 12pf, Liszt. d, 16pf, Wieland. e, 40pf, Natl. Theater.

1946, Mar. 27 Wmk. 48 *Imperf.*

16N9	OS2	Sheet of 5, #a.-e.	15.00	60.00
f.		Sheet, unwatermarked, rouletted	26.00	150.00
		Never hinged	52.50	

No. 16N9 was issued without gum. Sold for 7.50 marks.

THURINGIA SEMI-POSTAL STAMPS

Bridge Reconstruction OSP1

Designs: 10pf+60pf, Saalburg Bridge. 12pf+68pf, Camsdorf Bridge, Jena. 16pf+74pf, Goschwitz Bridge. 24pf+76pf, Ilm Bridge, Mellingen.

1946, Mar. 30 Typo. *Imperf.*

16NB1	OSP1	10 +60pf red brn	.20	9.00
16NB2	OSP1	12 +68pf red	.20	9.00
16NB3	OSP1	16 +74pf dark grn	.20	9.00
16NB4	OSP1	24 +76pf brown	.20	9.00
a.		Souv. sheet of 4, #16NB1-16NB4	150.00	1,250.
		Never hinged	300.00	
		Nos. 16NB1-16NB4 (4)		36.00
		Set, never hinged	1.10	

GHANA

ˈgä-nə

LOCATION — West Africa between Benin and Ivory Coast
GOVT. — Republic
AREA — 92,010 sq. mi.
POP. — 18,101,000 (1997 est.)
CAPITAL — Accra

Ghana is the former British colony of Gold Coast, which achieved independence March 6, 1957. It includes the former trusteeship territory of British Togoland.

12 Pence = 1 Shilling
20 Shillings = 1 Pound
100 Pesewas = 1 Cedi (1965, 1972)
100 New Pesewas = 1 New Cedi (1967)

___

Used Values in Italics
In 1961 the government canceled all remainder stocks, using cancellations which closely resemble genuine postmarks. Catalogue values in italics for these stamps (Nos. 1-13, 61-65, 67-77) are for canceled-to-order stamps. Postally used stamps are worth more.

> Catalogue values for all unused stamps in this country are for Never Hinged items.

Watermark

Wmk. 325 — Stars and G Multiple

Kwame Nkrumah, Map and Palm-nut Vulture — A1

Perf. 14x14½
1957, Mar. 6   Wmk. 4   Photo.

1	A1	2p rose red	.25	.20
2	A1	2½p green	.25	.20
3	A1	4p brown	.25	.20
4	A1	1sh3p dark blue	.25	.20
		Nos. 1-4 (4)	1.00	.80

Independence, Mar. 6, 1957.
For overprints see Nos. 28-31.

Stamps of Gold Coast, 1952-54, Overprinted in Black or Red

Perf. 11½x12, 12x11½
1957, Mar. 6   Engr.

5	A14	½p yel brown & car	.60	.20
6	A14	1p deep blue (R)	.60	.20
7	A14	1½p green	.60	.20
8	A14	3p rose	1.00	.20
9	A15	6p org & black (R)	.60	.20
10	A14	1sh red org & black	.60	.20
11	A14	2sh rose car & ol brn	1.50	.20
12	A14	5sh gray & red vio	2.40	.20
13	A15	10sh olive grn & black	2.75	.50
		Nos. 5-13 (9)	10.65	2.15

Nos. 5-6 exist in vertical coils.
See Nos. 25-27.

Viking Ship and Angelfish A2

1sh3p, Medieval galleon and swordfish. 5sh, Modern cargo ship and flyingfish.

Perf. 12x11½
1957, Dec. 27   Engr.   Unwmk.

14	A2	2½p emerald	.20	.20
15	A2	1sh3p dark blue	.35	1.25
16	A2	5sh red lilac	1.25	3.00
		Nos. 14-16 (3)	1.80	4.45

Black Star Line inauguration.

Ambassador Hotel — A3

Coat of Arms — A4

Design: 2½p, Opening of Parliament. 1sh3p, National monument.

Perf. 14x14½, 14½x14
1958, Mar. 6   Photo.   Wmk. 4
Flags in Original Colors

17	A3	½p car rose & black	.20	.40
18	A3	2½p org yel, red & blk	.20	.20
19	A3	1sh3p blue & black	.30	.20
20	A4	2sh multicolored	.45	.50
		Nos. 17-20 (4)	1.15	1.30

First anniversary of Independence.

Map of Africa — A5

Map and Torch — A6

1958, Apr. 15   Perf. 13½x14½

21	A5	2½p multicolored	.20	.20
22	A5	3p multicolored	.20	.20
23	A6	1sh multicolored	.20	.20
24	A6	2sh6p multicolored	.40	.65
		Nos. 21-24 (4)	1.00	1.25

1st conf. of Independent African States, Accra, Apr. 15-22.

Gold Coast Nos. 151-152 and 154 Overprinted Like Nos. 5-13

Perf. 11½x12, 12x11½
1958, May 26   Engr.   Wmk. 4

25	A15	2p chocolate	.75	.35
26	A15	2½p red	2.10	1.40
27	A14	4p deep blue	8.25	8.50
		Nos. 25-27 (3)	11.10	10.25

Nos. 25-27 were prepared in 1957 and some were sold without authorization. The set was officially released in 1958.

Nos. 1-4 Overprinted: "Prime Minister's Visit U. S. A. and Canada"

1958, July 18   Photo.   Perf. 14x14½

28	A1	2p rose red	.20	.40
29	A1	2½p green	.20	.30
30	A1	4p brown	.20	.50
31	A1	1sh3p dark blue	.20	.25
		Nos. 28-31 (4)	.80	1.45

Prime Minister Kwame Nkrumah's visit to the US and Canada, July, 1958.

Palm-nut Vulture over Globe — A7

"Britannia" Plane — A8

Designs: 2sh, Stratocruiser and albatross. 2sh6p, Palm-nut vulture and jet plane, horiz.

1958, July 15   Perf. 14x14½, 14½x14

32	A7	2½p multicolored	.25	.20
33	A8	1sh3p multicolored	.35	.25
34	A8	2sh multicolored	.45	.45
35	A7	2sh6p olive bister & blk	.75	.85
		Nos. 32-35 (4)	1.80	1.75

Inauguration of Ghana Airways.

A9

Perf. 14x14½
1958, Oct. 24   Wmk. 4   Litho.

36	A9	2½p multicolored	.20	.20
37	A9	1sh3p multicolored	.20	.20
38	A9	2sh6p multicolored	.20	.30
		Nos. 36-38 (3)	.60	.70

United Nations Day, Oct. 24.

A10

Perf. 14x14½
1959, Feb. 12   Photo.   Wmk. 325

Lincoln Memorial and Kwame Nkrumah.

39	A10	2½p dp plum & brt pink	.20	.20
40	A10	1sh3p dp blue & lt bl	.20	.20
41	A10	2sh6p ol gray & org yel	.20	.30
a.		Souv. sheet of 3, #39-41, imperf.	.80	1.50
		Nos. 39-41 (3)	.60	.70

Lincoln's birth sesquicentennial.

Kente Cloth with Traditional Symbols A11

Symbol of Greeting — A12

2½p, Talking drums and elephant horn-blower. 2sh, Map of Africa, flag and palm tree.

Perf. 14½x14, 14x14½
1959, Mar. 6   Photo.   Wmk. 325

42	A11	½p multicolored	.20	.20
43	A11	2½p multicolored	.20	.20
44	A12	1sh3p multicolored	.20	.20
45	A11	2sh multicolored	.30	1.00
		Nos. 42-45 (4)	.90	1.60

Independence, 2nd anniversary.

Flags of Independent States of Africa and Globe — A13

1959, Apr. 15   Perf. 14½x14

46	A13	2½p multicolored	.20	.20
47	A13	8½p multicolored	.20	.20

Africa Freedom Day, Apr. 15.

Kente Cloth and "God's Omnipotence" Symbol — A13a

Nkrumah Statue, Accra — A14

Shell Ginger — A15

Cacao A16

"God's Omnipotence" Symbol — A16a

Blackwinged Red Bishop — A17

1½p, Ghana timber. 2p, Volta river. 4p, Diamond and mine. 11p, Golden spider lily. 2sh6p, Great blue turaco. 5sh, Tiger orchid. 10sh, Jewelfish (tropical African cichlid).

Perf. 11½x12, 12x11½, 14x14½, 14½x14

1959, Oct. 5　　Photo.　　Wmk. 325

Size: 30½x21mm, 21x30½mm

| 48 | A13a | ½p | multi (God's Omnipotence) | .45 | .25 |
| 49 | A14 | 1p | multicolored | .45 | .25 |

Size: 26½x37mm, 37x26½mm

50	A15	1½p	multicolored	.45	.25
51	A16	2p	multicolored	.45	.25
52	A16	2½p	multicolored	.45	.25
53	A16a	3p	multi (God's Omnipotence)	.45	.25
54	A16	4p	multicolored	.45	.25
55	A17	6p	multicolored	.45	.25
a.			Booklet pane of 4	2.00	
56	A15	11p	multicolored	.70	.25
57	A15	1sh	multicolored	.50	.25
58	A17	2sh6p	multicolored	1.25	.40
59	A15	5sh	multicolored	2.75	.70

Size: 45x26mm

| 60 | A16 | 10sh | multicolored | 5.00 | 2.25 |
| | | | *Nos. 48-60,C1-C2 (15)* | 15.70 | 6.70 |

Nos. 48 and 53 inscribed "God's Omnipotence." Nos. 95-96 inscribed "Gye Nyame."
For surcharges see Nos. 216-217, 219-225, 277-283.

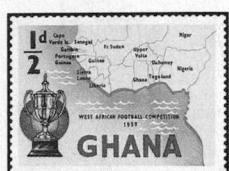

Map and Gold Cup — A18

1p, Soccer players, vert. 3p, Flags and goalkeeper in stadium. 8p, Soccer player at goal. 2sh6p, Kwame Nkrumah Gold Cup, vert.

1959, Oct. 15　　*Perf. 14½x14, 14x14½*

61	A18	½p	multicolored	.20	.20
62	A18	1p	multicolored	.20	.20
63	A18	3p	multicolored	.20	.20
64	A18	8p	multicolored	.30	.20
65	A18	2sh6p	multicolored	.40	.30
			Nos. 61-65 (5)	1.30	1.10

West African Soccer Competitions.

Prince Philip
A19

Perf. 14½x14

1959, Nov. 24　　Photo.　　Wmk. 325

| 66 | A19 | 3p | brt pink & black | .30 | .25 |

Visit of Prince Philip.

Talking Drums
A20

Designs: 6p, 1sh3p, Ghana flag and UN emblem, vert. 2sh6p, Pile of Ceremonial Stools and "UNTC," vert.

1959, Dec. 10　　*Perf. 14½x14, 14x14½*

Flag in Original Colors

67	A20	3p	violet & org yel	.20	.20
68	A20	6p	Prus green & blk	.20	.20
69	A20	1sh3p	grnsh bl, blk & vio	.20	.20
70	A20	2sh6p	dark blue & black	.25	.20
			Nos. 67-70 (4)	.85	.80

United Nations Trusteeship Council.

Three Flying Eagles — A21

Designs: 3p, Three clusters of fireworks. 1sh3p, Ghana flag forming "3" and dove. 2sh, Ghana flag forming triple sail of symbolic ship.

Perf. 13½x14½

1960, Mar. 6　　　　Wmk. 325

71	A21	½p	multicolored	.20	.20
72	A21	3p	multicolored	.20	.20
73	A21	1sh3p	multicolored	.25	.20
74	A21	2sh	multicolored	.30	.20
			Nos. 71-74 (4)	.95	.80

Independence, 3rd anniversary.

Flags Forming "A" and Map
A22

Designs: 6p, Letter "F." 1sh, "D."

1960, Apr. 15　　Photo.　　Wmk. 325

Flags in Original Colors

75	A22	3p	green, red & black	.20	.20
76	A22	6p	rose & black	.20	.20
77	A22	1sh	blue, black & red	.20	.20
			Nos. 75-77 (3)	.60	.60

Africa Freedom Day, Apr. 15.

President Kwame Nkrumah — A23

Olympic Rings and Hand Holding Torch — A24

Designs: 1sh3p, Flag and star. 2sh, Hand holding torch. 10sh, Coat of Arms and flag of Ghana, horiz.

Perf. 14x14½, 14½x14

1960, July 1　　　　Litho.

78	A23	3p	multicolored	.20	.20
79	A23	1sh3p	multicolored	.25	.25
80	A23	2sh	multicolored	.35	.35
81	A23	10sh	multicolored	.75	.75
a.			Souv. sheet of 4, #78-81, imperf.	.50	1.00
			Nos. 78-81 (4)	1.55	1.55

Declaration of the Republic, July 1, 1960.

1960, Aug. 15　　Photo.　　Wmk. 325

Design: 1sh3p, 2sh6p, Runner, Map of Africa and Olympic Rings, horiz.

82	A24	3p	multicolored	.25	.20
83	A24	6p	multicolored	.25	.20
84	A24	1sh3p	multicolored	.25	.20
85	A24	2sh6p	multicolored	.40	.25
			Nos. 82-85 (4)	1.15	.85

17th Olympic Games, Rome, Aug. 25-Sept. 11.

Map and Arch — A25

UN Emblem and Ghana Flag — A26

Designs: 3p, Flag and Kwame Nkrumah, horiz. 6p, Star and Nkrumah.

1960, Sept. 21　　　　Photo.

86	A25	3p	multicolored	.20	.20
87	A25	6p	multicolored	.20	.20
88	A25	1sh3p	multicolored	.20	.30
			Nos. 86-88 (3)	.60	.70

Founder's Day, Sept. 21, birthday of Dr. Kwame Nkrumah.

1960, Dec. 10　　*Perf. 14x14½*

6p, Flame & emblem. 1sh3p, UN Emblem.

89	A26	3p	multicolored	.20	.20
90	A26	6p	multicolored	.20	.20
91	A26	1sh3p	multicolored	.25	.45
			Nos. 89-91 (3)	.65	.85

Human Rights Day, Dec. 10, 1960.

Talking Drums and Map — A27

Designs: 6p, Map of Africa showing 25 independent states. 2sh, Map of Africa and flags of independent nations in 1958, horiz.

Perf. 14x14½, 14½x14

1961, Apr. 15　　　　Wmk. 325

92	A27	3p	multicolored	.20	.20
93	A27	6p	multicolored	.20	.20
94	A27	2sh	multicolored	.40	.35
			Nos. 92-94 (3)	.80	.75

Africa Freedom Day, Apr. 15, 1961.

Types of 1959 Redrawn and

Red-fronted Gazelle — A28

Perf. 11½x12, 14½x14

1961, Apr. 29　　Photo.　　Wmk. 325

95	A13a	½p	"Gye Nyame"	.25	.20
96	A16a	3p	"Gye Nyame"	.25	.20
a.			Booklet pane of 4	1.00	

Perf. 14x14½

| 97 | A28 | £1 | multicolored | 7.00 | 7.00 |
| | | | *Nos. 95-97 (3)* | 7.50 | 7.40 |

Nos. 95-96 are the same sizes as Nos. 48 and 53 which are inscribed "God's Omnipotence."
For surcharges see Nos. 218, 226, 284.

Column, Eagle and Star — A29

Dove with Olive Branch — A30

World Map, Chain and Olive Branch
A31

Designs: 1sh3p, Symbolic flower and star. 2sh, Star and 3 Ghana flags.

1961, July 1　　　　*Perf. 14x14½*

98	A29	3p	multicolored	.20	.20
99	A29	1sh3p	multicolored	.20	.20
100	A29	2sh	multicolored	.25	1.00
			Nos. 98-100 (3)	.65	1.40

First anniversary of the Republic.

1961, Sept. 1　　*Perf. 14x14½, 14½x14*

Design: 5sh, Rostrum and olive branch.

101	A30	3p	green	.20	.20
102	A31	1sh3p	dark blue	.25	.20
103	A31	5sh	rose carmine	.30	.90
			Nos. 101-103 (3)	.75	1.30

Conference of Non-aligned Nations, Belgrade, Sept. 1961.

Kwame Nkrumah and Globe
A32

Designs: 1sh3p, Kente cloth and Nkrumah, vert. 5sh, Kwame Nkrumah, vert.

Perf. 14½x14, 14x14½

1961, Sept. 21　　　　Wmk. 325

104	A32	3p	multicolored	.20	.20
a.			Souvenir sheet of 4, imperf.	1.25	1.75
105	A32	1sh3p	multicolored	.25	.25
a.			Souvenir sheet of 4, imperf.	1.75	2.50
106	A32	5sh	multicolored	.60	2.00
a.			Souvenir sheet of 4, imperf.	4.50	6.00
			Nos. 104-106 (3)	1.05	2.45

Founder's Day.
The souvenir sheets contain four imperf. stamps each with simulated perforations.

Elizabeth II and Map of Africa
A33

1961, Nov. 10　　　　*Perf. 14½x14*

Gold Inscriptions: Design in Black, Red, Yellow & Green

107	A33	3p	claret	.20	.20
108	A33	1sh3p	Prussian blue	.25	.20
109	A33	5sh	violet blue	1.10	.90
a.			Souvenir sheet of 4	4.75	7.00
			Nos. 107-109 (3)	1.55	1.30

Visit of Queen Elizabeth II to Ghana, Nov. 10-22.
No. 109a contains four imperf. copies of No. 109 with simulated perforations.

Map of
Tema
Harbor
and Ships
A34

Perf. 14x13
1962, Feb. 10   Litho.   Unwmk.
110 A34 3p multicolored   .20   .20
    Nos. 110,C3-C4 (3)   1.60 1.60
Opening of Tema Harbor, as part of Volta
River Project.

Dove Flying over
Map of
Africa — A35

1962, Mar. 6   Perf. 13x14
111 A35 3p multicolored   .20   .20
    Nos. 111,C5-C6 (3)   1.25 1.25
Conference of African heads of state at
Casablanca, 1st anniv.

"Freedom"
Illuminating
Africa — A36

"Five Continents
at Peace" — A37

Perf. 14x14½
1962, Apr. 15   Photo.   Wmk. 325
112 A36 3p multicolored   .20   .20
113 A36 6p multicolored   .20   .20
114 A36 1sh3p multicolored   .20   .20
    Nos. 112-114 (3)   .60   .60
Africa Freedom Day, Apr. 15.

1962, June 21   Wmk. 325
Designs: 6p, Atom bomb blast in shape of
skull. 1sh3p, Peace dove and globe.

115 A37 3p deep rose &
          black   .20   .20
116 A37 6p black & dk red   .20   .30
117 A37 1sh3p greenish blue   .40   .50
    Nos. 115-117 (3)   .80 1.00
Accra Assembly of Africans for a "World
Without Bomb," June 21-28.

Patrice
Lumumba
A38

1962, June 30   Perf. 14½x14
118 A38 3p black & orange   .20   .20
119 A38 6p mar, grn & blk   .20   .30
120 A38 1sh3p dk grn, pink & blk .20   .35
    Nos. 118-120 (3)   .60   .85
1st anniv. (on Feb. 12) of the death of
Patrice Lumumba, premier of Congo.

Arch and
Star — A39

Designs: 6p, Torch in flag colors and globe.
1sh3p, Palm-nut vulture trailing flag, horiz.

Perf. 13x13½, 13½x13
1962, July 1   Unwmk.
121 A39 3p multicolored   .20   .20
122 A39 6p multicolored   .20   .20
123 A39 1sh3p multicolored   .35   .35
    Nos. 121-123 (3)   .75   .75
Second anniversary of the republic.

Kwame
Nkrumah — A40

1962, Sept. 21   Litho.   Perf. 13x14
3p, Nkrumah medal. 1sh3p, Nkrumah's
head & stars. 2sh, Hands with trowel & building block.

124 A40 1p multicolored   .20   .20
125 A40 3p multicolored   .20   .20
126 A40 1sh3p ultra & black   .30   .20
127 A40 2sh multicolored   .30 1.00
    Nos. 124-127 (4)   1.00 1.60
Founder's Day, Nkrumah's 53rd birthday.

Malaria
Eradication
Emblem — A41

Wheat Emblem
and Globe — A42

Perf. 14x14½
1962, Dec. 1   Photo.   Wmk. 325
128 A41 1p carmine rose   .20   .20
129 A41 4p yellow green   .20 1.00
130 A41 6p olive bister   .20   .30
131 A41 1sh3p violet   .30   .80
  a. Souvenir sheet of 4, imperf. 1.25 1.50
    Nos. 128-131 (4)   .90 2.30
WHO drive to eradicate malaria.
No. 131a contains one each of Nos. 128-
131, with simulated perforation.

Perf. 14x14½, 14½x14
1963, Mar. 21   Wmk. 325
Designs: 4p, Hands holding Wheat Emblem,
horiz. 1sh3p, Globe, horiz.

132 A42 1p multicolored   .30   .25
133 A42 4p multicolored   .50 1.00
134 A42 1sh3p multicolored   2.00 1.50
    Nos. 132-134 (3)   2.80 2.75
FAO "Freedom from Hunger" campaign.

Map of Africa in
Sun — A43

Cross, Flag and
Centenary
Emblem — A44

Designs: 4p, Symbolic wood carving, horiz.
1sh3p, Map of Africa and ceremonial fire.
2sh6p, Gazelle and flag.

1963, Apr. 15   Photo.
135 A43 1p crimson & gold   .20   .20
136 A43 4p orange, blk & red   .20   .20
137 A43 1sh3p multicolored   .20   .20
138 A43 2sh6p multicolored   .30 1.00
    Nos. 135-138 (4)   .90 1.60
Africa Freedom Day, Apr. 15.

Perf. 14x14½, 14½x14
1963, May 28   Wmk. 325
1½p, Centenary emblem, horiz. 4p, Family
& emblem, horiz. 1sh3p, Emblem & globe.

139 A44 1p multicolored   .50   .20
140 A44 1½p multicolored   .80 1.75
141 A44 4p multicolored   1.25   .20
142 A44 1sh3p multicolored   2.40 2.00
  a. Souvenir sheet of 4, imperf. 5.00 10.00
    Nos. 139-142 (4)   4.95 4.15
Cent. of the founding of the Intl. Red Cross.
No. 142a contains one each of Nos. 139-
142, with simulated perforation.

A45

Designs: 4p, Three flags. 1sh3p, Map of
Africa with Ghana, vert. 2sh6p, Torch, vert.

Perf. 14½x14, 14x14½
1963, July 1   Photo.
143 A45 1p multicolored   .20   .20
144 A45 4p multicolored   .20   .20
145 A45 1sh3p multicolored   .20   .20
146 A45 2sh6p multicolored   .35 1.75
    Nos. 143-146 (4)   .95 2.35
The 3rd anniversary of the republic.

Dancers,
Fireworks
and
Nkrumah
A46

1p, Nkrumah & streamer. 4p, Nkrumah &
flag. 5sh, Wisdom symbol.

Perf. 14x14½, 14½x14
1963, Sept. 21
147 A46 1p multi, vert.   .20   .20
148 A46 4p multi, vert.   .20   .20
149 A46 1sh3p multi   .20   .20
150 A46 5sh multi   .25   .40
    Nos. 147-150 (4)   .85 1.00
Founder's Day, Nkrumah's 54th birthday.

Ramses II at Abu
Simbel — A47

Designs: 1½p, Rock painting, bird and fish,
horiz. 2p, Queen Nefertari, horiz. 4p, Sphinx of
Wadi es-Sebua. 1sh3p, Statues of Ramses II
at Abu Simbel, horiz.

1963, Nov. 1   Unwmk.   Perf. 11½x11
151 A47 1p multicolored   .20   .20
152 A47 1½p multicolored   .20   .50
153 A47 2p multicolored   .20   .20
154 A47 4p multicolored   .50   .20
155 A47 1sh3p multicolored   1.50 1.00
    Nos. 151-155 (5)   2.60 2.10
UNESCO world campaign to save historic
monuments in Nubia.

Steam and
Diesel
Engines
A48

Perf. 14½x14
1963, Nov. 1   Wmk. 325
156 A48 6p multicolored   .20   .20
157 A48 6p multicolored   .75   .20
158 A48 1sh3p multicolored   1.25   .50
159 A48 2sh6p multicolored   1.75 1.75
    Nos. 156-159 (4)   3.95 2.65
The 60th anniversary of Ghana's railroads.

Eleanor Roosevelt
and Flame — A49

IQSY Emblem
and
Satellites — A50

6p, Mrs. Roosevelt & flag. 1sh3p, Mrs.
Roosevelt, flag, flame & Ghanaian symbols,
horiz.

Perf. 11½x11, 11x11½
1963, Dec. 10   Unwmk.
160 A49 1p multicolored   .20   .20
161 A49 4p multicolored   .20   .30
162 A49 6p multicolored   .20   .20
163 A49 1sh3p multicolored   .30   .25
    Nos. 160-163 (4)   .90   .95
Eleanor Roosevelt; 15th anniv. of the Universal Declaration of Human Rights.

Imperforates
Starting in 1964, certain sets of
Ghana exist imperf.

1964, June 1   Photo.   Perf. 14
164 A50 3p multicolored   .20   .20
165 A50 6p multicolored   .20   .20
166 A50 1sh3p multicolored   .35   .25
  a. Souvenir sheet of 4   1.00 2.00
    Nos. 164-166 (3)   .75   .65
Intl. Quiet Sun Year, 1964-65. No. 166a contains 4 imperf. stamps similar to No. 166 with
simulated perforations.
See Nos. 186-188.

Harvest on
State Farm
A51

Designs: 6p, Oil refinery, Tema. 1sh3p,
Communal labor. 5sh, Ghana flag and people.

1964, July 1   *Perf. 13x14*

167	A51	3p multicolored	.20	.20
168	A51	6p multicolored	.20	.20
169	A51	1sh3p multicolored	.20	.20
170	A51	5sh multicolored	.35	.90
a.		Souvenir sheet of 4	.80	*1.50*
		Nos. 167-170 (4)	.95	1.50

4th anniv. of the Republic. No. 170a contains four stamps similar to Nos. 167-170 with simulated perforations.

Dove,
Globe,
Olive
Branch and
Flag — A52

Designs: 6p, Map of Africa and quill pen, vert. 1sh3p, Knotted rope and map of Africa. 5sh, Hands planting symbolic tree, vert.

1964, July 6   *Perf. 14*

171	A52	3p multicolored	.20	.20
172	A52	6p black & red	.20	.20
173	A52	1sh3p blue & multi	.20	.20
174	A52	5sh yel & multi	.35	.60
		Nos. 171-174 (4)	.95	1.20

Signing of the African Unity Charter, 1st anniv.

Nkrumah and
Hibiscus — A53

Boxing — A54

Perf. 14x14½

1964, Sept. 21   **Photo.**   **Wmk. 325**
Design in Brown, Green and Rose Red

175	A53	3p light blue	.20	.20
176	A53	6p yellow	.20	.20
177	A53	1sh3p gray	.20	.20
178	A53	2sh6p emerald	.35	*.90*
a.		Souvenir sheet of 4	1.10	*2.00*
		Nos. 175-178 (4)	.95	1.50

Founder's Day, Nkrumah's 55th birthday. No. 178a contains four of No. 178 with simulated perforation.

1964, Oct. 25   *Perf. 14½x14*

Sport: 1p, Hurdling, horiz. 2½p, Running, horiz. 4p, Broad jump. 6p, Soccer. 1sh3p, Athlete with Olympic torch. 5sh, Banners and Tokyo Olympic emblem, horiz.

179	A54	1p yellow & multi	.20	.20
180	A54	2½p multicolored	.20	1.00
181	A54	3p red & multi	.20	.20
182	A54	4p blue & multi	.20	.20
183	A54	6p multicolored	.20	.20
184	A54	1sh3p blue & multi	.25	.20
185	A54	5sh gray & multi	.40	*2.50*
a.		Souvenir sheet of 3	1.40	*2.25*
		Nos. 179-185 (7)	1.65	4.50

18th Olympic Games, Tokyo, Oct. 10-25. No. 185a contains stamps similar to Nos. 183-185 with simulated perforation.

Quiet Sun Year Type of 1964
Unwmk.

1964, Oct.   **Photo.**   *Perf. 14*

186	A50	3p gray, bl, grn, yel & red	1.25	1.25
187	A50	6p pink, bl, grn, yel & red	2.50	2.50
188	A50	1sh3p tan, bl, grn, yel, & red	4.00	4.00
		Nos. 186-188 (3)	7.75	7.75

Each issued in sheets of 12, with star-strewn blue border inscribed "Ghana International Quiet Sun Year." Stamps arranged in square surrounding vignette of New York World's Fair Unisphere in blue.

G. W.
Carver
and
Sweet
Potato
A55

Design: 1sh3p, Albert Einstein, theory of relativity formula and atom symbol.

1964, Dec. 7   **Wmk. 325**   *Perf. 14½*

189	A55	6p grn & dk blue	.30	.30
190	A55	1sh3p Prus bl & claret	.45	.40
191	A55	5sh org ver & brn blk	1.50	*3.00*
a.		Souvenir sheet of 3	3.00	2.00
		Nos. 189-191 (3)	2.25	3.70

Human Rights Day; Albert Einstein (1878-1955) and George Washington Carver (1864-1943), scientists.
No. 191a commemorates UNESCO Week and contains one each of Nos. 189-191 with simulated perforations.

Secretary
Bird — A56

Designs: 1p, Elephant, vert. 2½p, Purple wreath, vert. 3p, Gray parrot, vert. 4p, Blue-naped mousebird. 6p, African tulip tree flowers. 1sh3p, Amethyst starling. 2sh6p, Hippopotamuses.

Perf. 11½x11, 11x11½

1964, Dec. 14   **Photo.**   **Unwmk.**

192	A56	1p blue & multi	.50	.50
193	A56	1½p org & multi	.80	1.40
194	A56	2½p lt green & multi	.55	.90
a.		Souv. sheet of 3, #192-194, imperf.	3.50	3.50
195	A56	3p lt green & multi	1.40	.50
196	A56	4p multicolored	1.40	.70
197	A56	6p multicolored	.55	.30
198	A56	1sh3p multicolored	1.60	1.00
199	A56	2sh6p multicolored	1.60	3.50
a.		Souv. sheet of 5, #195-199, imperf.	5.75	10.00
		Nos. 192-199 (8)	8.40	8.80

ICY Emblem
A57

1965, Feb. 15   **Litho.**   *Perf. 14x13*
Design in Black, Red and Green

200	A57	1p gray	.40	.60
201	A57	4p bister	1.50	1.50
202	A57	6p tan	1.50	.45
203	A57	1sh3p light green	2.00	2.25
a.		Souvenir sheet of 4	5.50	5.50
		Nos. 200-203 (4)	5.40	4.80

Intl. Cooperation Year. No. 203a contains 4 imperf. stamps similar to No. 203.

ITU Emblem, Old and New
Communication Equipment — A58

1965, Apr. 12   *Perf. 13½*

204	A58	1p multicolored	.20	.20
205	A58	6p multicolored	.20	.20
206	A58	1sh3p multicolored	1.00	.25
207	A58	5sh multicolored	2.50	2.50
a.		Souvenir sheet of 4	12.00	12.00
		Nos. 204-207 (4)	3.90	3.15

Cent. of the ITU. No. 207a contains 4 imperf. stamps similar to Nos. 204-207 with simulated perforations.

Lincoln's
Home,
Springfield,
Ill. — A59

1sh3p, Inaugural Address and Lincoln. 2sh, Lincoln and his signature. 5sh, Adaptation of 1869 US Lincoln stamp (No. 122).

Wmk. 325

1965, Apr.   **Photo.**   *Perf. 12½*

208	A59	6p multicolored	.20	.20
209	A59	1sh3p multicolored	.25	.20
210	A59	2sh multicolored	.30	.35
211	A59	5sh red & black	.65	1.25
a.		Souvenir sheet of 4	1.75	2.50
		Nos. 208-211 (4)	1.40	2.00

Centenary of death of Abraham Lincoln. No. 211a contains one each of Nos. 208-211 with simulated perforation.

5-Pesewa Coin, Nkrumah's
Head — A60

Coins: 10pa, 10 pesewas. 25pa, 25 pesewas. 50pa, 50 pesewas.

Perf. 11x13

1965, July 19   **Unwmk.**   **Litho.**
Coin in Silver and Black
Size: 45x32mm

212	A60	5pa red, grn & lt grn	.20	.20
213	A60	10pa red, grn, & pink	.25	.20

Size: 62x39mm

214	A60	25pa red, grn, & pink	.75	1.00

Size: 71x43½mm

215	A60	50pa red, grn & lt grn	2.00	2.25
		Nos. 212-215 (4)	3.20	3.65

Introduction of decimal currency.

Regular Issue of 1959-61 Surcharged in Red, Blue, Brown, Black or White with New Value and: "Ghana New Currency / 19th July, 1965"

Perf. 12x11½, 14½x14, 14x14½

1965, July 19   **Photo.**   **Wmk. 325**

216	A14	1pa on 1p (R)	.20	.20
217	A16	2pa on 2p (Bl)	.20	.20
218	A16a	3pa on 3p (#96, Br)	1.00	*3.50*
219	A14	4pa on 4p (Bl)	4.00	.50
220	A17	6pa on 6p (Bk)	.50	.20
221	A15	11pa on 11p (W)	.25	.20
222	A15	12pa on 1sh (Bl)	.25	.20
223	A17	30pa on 2sh6p (Bl)	3.00	*6.00*
224	A15	60pa on 5sh (Bl)	4.00	.70
225	A16	1.20c on 10s (Bl)	.75	*1.75*
226	A28	2.40c on £1 (Bl)	1.00	*6.25*
		Nos. 216-226,C7-C8 (13)	19.15	20.75

The two lines of the overprint are diagonal on the 1pa, 11pa, 12pa, 60pa, 1.20c and 2.40c.
The surcharge exists double or inverted on six or more denominations.

Summit Conference, Accra — A61

Map of
Africa and
Flags
A62

Designs: 2pa, "OAU" and three heads (triangle pointing up). 5pa, Symbol of African Unity. 15pa, Sunburst and map of Africa. 24pa, Map of Africa.

Perf. 14, 14½x14   **Photo.**

1965, Oct. 21
Ghana Flag in Red, Black & Green

227	A61	1pa multicolored	.20	.20
228	A61	2pa multicolored	.20	.20
229	A61	5pa multicolored	.20	.20
230	A62	6pa orange & black	.20	.20
231	A62	15pa light blue & blk	.30	.30
232	A62	24pa lt ultra & green	.45	.50
		Nos. 227-232 (6)	1.55	1.60

Summit Conference of the Organization for African Unity, Accra, Oct. 1965.

Soccer Goalkeeper — A63

Designs: 15pa, Soccer player and cup, vert. 24pa, Two soccer players and cup.

Perf. 14x13, 13x14

1965, Nov. 15   **Unwmk.**

233	A63	6pa ocher & multi	.20	.20
234	A63	15pa multicolored	.40	.30
235	A63	24pa lt blue & multi	.45	.60
		Nos. 233-235 (3)	1.05	1.10

African Soccer Cup competition. For overprints see Nos. 244-246.

John F.
Kennedy and
Eternal
Flame — A64

Various Kennedy portraits.

1965, Dec. 15   **Wmk. 325**   *Perf. 12½*

236	A64	6pa blk, yel, gold & grn	.20	.20
237	A64	15pa vio, crim & brt grn	.25	.30
238	A64	24pa dp pur & blk	.30	.50
239	A64	30pa vio brn & blk	.40	.80
a.		Souvenir sheet of 4 ('66)	4.50	5.50
		Nos. 236-239 (4)	1.15	1.80

President John F. Kennedy (1917-1963). No. 239a contains four imperf. stamps similar to Nos. 236-239.

Generators,
Volta River
Project
A65

Designs: 15pa, Dam and Lake Volta. 24pa, "Ghana" forming dam. 30pa, Grain.

Perf. 11x11½

1966, Jan. 22   **Unwmk.**

240	A65	6pa sepia & multi	.20	.20
241	A65	15pa multicolored	.20	.20
242	A65	24pa multicolored	.25	.25
243	A65	30pa brt blue & blk	.40	.50
		Nos. 240-243 (4)	1.05	1.15

Opening of the Volta River dam and electric power station at Akosombo.

Nos. 233-235 Overprinted Diagonally:
"Black Stars Retain Africa Cup / 21st Nov. 1965"

1966, Feb. 7   **Perf. 14x13, 13x14**

244	A63	6pa ocher & multi	.25	.20
245	A63	15pa multicolored	.40	.30
246	A63	24pa lt bl & multi	.65	.65
		Nos. 244-246 (3)	1.30	1.15

Ghana's soccer victory, Nov. 21, 1965.

Inauguration of WHO Headquarters, Geneva — A66

Designs: 24pa, 30pa, WHO Headquarters from the west and WHO emblem.

Perf. 14x14½

1966, July 1   **Photo.**   **Wmk. 325**

247	A66	6pa multicolored	.55	.20
248	A66	15pa multicolored	1.10	.50
249	A66	24pa multicolored	1.40	1.60
250	A66	30pa multicolored	1.60	3.00
a.		Souvenir sheet of 4	30.00	30.00
		Nos. 247-250 (4)	4.65	5.30

No. 250a contains 4 imperf. stamps similar to Nos. 247-250 with simulated perforations.

Herring, Fishermen and Flag A67

Designs: 15pa, Flatfish and canoes. 24pa, Spadefish and schooner. 30pa, Red snapper and fishing trawler "Shama." 60pa, Mackerel and steamer.

1966, Aug. 10   **Unwmk.**   **Perf. 14x13**

251	A67	6pa ocher & multi	.20	.20
252	A67	15pa yel grn & multi	.40	.25
253	A67	24pa ver & multi	.70	.30
254	A67	30pa blue & multi	1.10	1.10
a.		Souvenir sheet of 4	14.00	14.00
255	A67	60pa green & multi	1.50	3.00
		Nos. 251-255 (5)	3.90	4.85

1966 Freedom from Hunger campaign "Young World Against Hunger."
No. 254a contains 4 imperf. stamps similar to No. 254.

Flags of African Unity Charter Signers, Map and Diamond A68

Designs: 6p, Ghana flag and links enclosing map of Africa, vert. 24p, Ship's wheel enclosing map of Africa, and cacao pod.

1966, Sept.   **Unwmk.**   **Perf. 13x13½**

256	A68	6pa brt blue & multi	.20	.20
257	A68	15pa blue & multi	.30	.45
258	A68	24pa dp green & multi	.35	.50
		Nos. 256-258 (3)	.85	1.15

Signing of the African Unity Charter, 3rd anniv.

Soccer Player and Rimet Cup — A69

Various Soccer Scenes.

Perf. 14½x14

1966, Nov. 14   **Photo.**   **Wmk. 325**

259	A69	5pa brown & multi	.25	.20
260	A69	15pa blue & multi	.70	.30
261	A69	24pa green & multi	1.00	.50
262	A69	30pa brt rose & multi	1.25	1.25
263	A69	60pa lilac & multi	1.75	4.00
a.		Souvenir sheet of 4	32.50	32.50
		Nos. 259-263 (5)	4.95	6.25

World Cup Soccer Championship, Wembley, England, July 11-30.
No. 263a contains 4 imperf. stamps similar to No. 263 with simulated perforations.

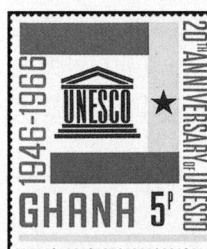

UNESCO Emblem A70

1966, Dec. 23   **Wmk. 325**   **Perf. 14½**

264	A70	5pa multicolored	.25	.25
265	A70	15pa multicolored	.75	.50
266	A70	24pa multicolored	1.00	1.00
267	A70	30pa multicolored	1.50	1.25
268	A70	60pa multicolored	2.25	5.00
a.		Souvenir sheet of 5	32.50	32.50
		Nos. 264-268 (5)	5.75	8.00

UNESCO, 20th anniv. No. 268a contains 5 imperf. stamps similar to Nos. 264-268 with simulated perforations.

Packing Cases and Fair Emblem A71

Fair Emblem and: 15pa, World map and trade routes to Accra. 24pa, Freighters and loading crane, vert. 36pa, Hand holding cargo net.

1967, Feb. 1   **Perf. 14½x14, 14x14½**

269	A71	5pa multicolored	.20	.20
270	A71	15pa multicolored	.20	.20
271	A71	24pa multicolored	.30	.30
272	A71	36pa multicolored	.40	1.50
		Nos. 269-272 (4)	1.10	2.20

International Trade Fair, Accra, Feb. 1-19.

Eagle and Flag — A72

1967, Feb. 24   **Photo.**   **Perf. 14x14½**
Flag in Red, Yellow, Black and Green

273	A72	1np gray bl & dk brn	.20	.75
274	A72	4np ocher & dk brn	.20	.20
275	A72	12½np ol grn & dk brn	.40	.50
276	A72	25np dl cl & dk brn	.85	2.25
a.		Souvenir sheet of 4, #273-276	8.00	8.00
		Nos. 273-276 (4)	1.65	3.70

1st anniv. of the revolution which overthrew the regime of Kwame Nkrumah.
No. 276a has dull claret marginal inscriptions. An imperf. sheet similar to No. 276a has solid margins of dull claret, colorless inscriptions. Value $10.

Nos. 51, 54-58, 60 and 97 Surcharged in Black, Red or White

1967, Feb. 27   **Perf. 14½x14, 14x14½**
Size: 30½x21mm, 21x30½mm

277	A16	1½np on 2p (B)	3.50	7.00
278	A16	3½np on 4p (R)	6.00	3.00
279	A17	5np on 6p (R)	2.00	1.75
280	A15	9np on 11p (W)	.30	.50
281	A15	10np on 1sh (W)	.35	1.00
282	A17	25np on 2sh6p (R)	3.50	7.50

Size: 45x26mm

283	A16	1nc on 10sh (R)	3.00	20.00
284	A28	2nc on £1 (R)	6.00	30.00
		Nos. 277-284,C9-C10 (10)	33.65	77.75

Corn — A73

Forest Kingfisher — A74

African Lungfish A75

Designs: 2np, Ghana Mace (golden staff). 2½np, Commelina flower. 4np, Rufous-crowned roller, vert. 6np, Akosombo Dam, Volta River. 8np, Adomi Bridge, Volta River. 9np, Chameleon. 10np, Quay No. 2, Tema Harbor. 20np, Cape hare. 50np, Black-winged stilt. 1nc, Chief's ceremonial stool. 2nc, Frangipani. 2.50nc, State Chair.

Perf. 11½x12, 12x11½ (A73), 14x14½, 14½x14 (A74-A75)

1967   **Photo.**   **Wmk. 325**

286	A73	1np multicolored	.20	.20
287	A74	1½np multicolored	1.10	2.75
288	A74	2np multicolored	.20	.20
289	A74	2½np multicolored	.40	.20
290	A75	3np multicolored	.25	.45
291	A73	4np multicolored	1.90	.20
292	A75	6np multicolored	.20	1.75
293	A73	8np multicolored	.20	.75
294	A75	9np multicolored	.90	.20
295	A75	10np multicolored	.20	.20
296	A74	20np blue	.25	.20
297	A74	50np multicolored	7.00	2.75
298	A74	1nc multicolored	3.00	1.00
299	A74	2nc multicolored	2.50	4.00
300	A74	2.50nc multicolored	3.75	10.00
		Nos. 286-300 (15)	22.05	24.85

For overprints & surcharges see #356-370, 858, 1091, 1092A-1092C, 1092E-1093, 1095, 1096B.

Kumasi Fort, 1896 A76

Castles on Ghana Coast: 12½np, Christiansborg Castle, 1659, and British galleon. 20np, Elmina Castle, 1482, and Portuguese galleon. 25np, Cape Coast Castle, 1664, and Spanish galleon.

1967, June 12   **Perf. 14½**

301	A76	4np grnsh bl & multi	.20	.20
302	A76	12½np red org & multi	.90	1.00
303	A76	20np brt grn & multi	1.90	2.25
304	A76	25np lt red brn & multi	2.40	3.00
		Nos. 301-304 (4)	5.40	6.45

Orbiter 1 Landing on Moon — A77

Designs: 4np, Luna 10 on the moon, and globe. 12½np, Astronaut walking in space.

1967, Aug. 16   **Unwmk.**   **Perf. 13½**

305	A77	4np multicolored	.20	.20
306	A77	10np multicolored	.20	.30
307	A77	12½np multicolored	.20	.60
a.		Souvenir sheet of 3	2.50	4.00
		Nos. 305-307 (3)	.60	1.10

Achievements in space. Issued in Ghana in sheets of 30. Sheets of 12 with ornamented, inscribed border also exist; these were sold in Ghana in 1968.
No. 307a contains 3 imperf. stamps similar to Nos. 305-307.

Boy Scouts at Campfire A78

Designs: 10np, Hiking Boy Scout. 12½np, Lord Baden-Powell.

1967, Sept. 18   Photo.   Perf. 14x13½

308	A78	4np multicolored	.20	.20
309	A78	10np multicolored	.40	.40
310	A78	12½np multicolored	.50	.70
a.		Souvenir sheet of 3	8.00	10.00
		Nos. 308-310 (3)	1.10	1.30

50th anniv. of the Ghana (Gold Coast) Boy Scouts. Issued in Ghana in sheets of 30. Sheets of 12 with ornamented, inscribed border also exist; these were sold in Ghana in 1968.
No. 310a contains 3 imperf. stamps similar to Nos. 308-310 with simulated perforations.

UN Secretariat Building — A79

Design: 50np, 2.50nc, UN Headquarters.

1967, Oct. 24   Litho.   Perf. 13½x13

311	A79	4np multicolored	.20	.20
312	A79	10np multicolored	.20	.20
313	A79	50np multicolored	.30	.60
314	A79	2.50nc multicolored	1.00	1.00
a.		Souvenir sheet	6.50	9.00
		Nos. 311-314 (4)	1.70	2.00

United Nations Day. No. 314a contains one imperf. stamp similar to No. 314 with simulated perforations.

Leopard — A80

Designs: 12½np, Christmas butterfly. 20np, Nubian carmine bee-eaters. 50np, Waterbuck.

Wmk. 325

1967, Dec. 28   **Photo.**   **Perf. 12½**

315	A80	4np multicolored	1.75	.20
316	A80	12½np multicolored	3.50	1.75
317	A80	20np multicolored	4.25	3.75

318	A80	50np multicolored	7.50	7.50
a.		Souvenir sheet of 3	25.00	25.00
		Nos. 315-318 (4)	17.00	13.20

Intl. Tourist Year. No. 318a contains 3 imperf. stamps similar to Nos. 316-318 with simulated perforations.

Convoy Entering Accra A81

12 ½np, Victory parade. 20np, Waving crowd. 40np, Singing and dancing crowd.

Unwmk.
1968, Feb. 24   Litho.   Perf. 14

319	A81	4np sal & multi	.20	.20
320	A81	12 ½np multicolored	.25	.25
321	A81	20np multicolored	.30	.30
322	A81	40np yel & multi	.60	1.75
		Nos. 319-322 (4)	1.35	2.50

2nd anniversary of Feb. 24th Revolution.

Cacao Beans and Microscope A82

4np, 25np, Cacao tree & beans, microscope.

Perf. 14½x14
1968, Mar. 18   Photo.   Wmk. 325

323	A82	2 ½np grn & multi	.25	1.90
324	A82	4np gray & multi	.25	.25
325	A82	10np scar & multi	.25	.25
326	A82	25np multicolored	.60	1.00
a.		Souvenir sheet of 4	3.50	3.50
		Nos. 323-326 (4)	1.35	3.40

Issued to publicize Ghana's cocoa production. Sheets of 30.
No. 326a contains four imperf. stamps similar to Nos. 323-326 with simulated perforations.
Nos. 323-326 also exist in sheets of 12 believed not to have been on sale in Ghana.

Lt. Gen. E. K. Kotoka A83

Various portraits of Lt. Gen. Kotoka. 40np vert.

1968, Apr. 17   Unwmk.   Perf. 14

327	A83	4np pur & multi	.20	.20
328	A83	12 ½np grn & multi	.25	.25
329	A83	20np multicolored	.45	.60
330	A83	40np gray & multi	.75	1.75
		Nos. 327-330 (4)	1.65	2.80

Lt. Gen. Emmanuel Kwasi Kotoka (1926-1967), leader of the Revolution of 1966 against Nkrumah.

Tobacco — A84

Designs: 5np, Crested porcupine. 12 ½np, Tapped rubber tree. 20np, Cymothoe sangaris butterfly. 40np, Charaxes ameliae butterfly.

1968, Aug.   Photo.   Perf. 14x14½

331	A84	4np multicolored	.20	.20
332	A84	5np multicolored	.20	1.00
333	A84	12 ½np multicolored	.75	.75
334	A84	20np multicolored	2.75	2.75
335	A84	40np multicolored	3.00	5.00
a.		Souvenir sheet of 4	8.00	8.00
		Nos. 331-335 (5)	6.90	9.70

No. 335a contains 4 stamps similar to Nos. 331, 332-335 with simulated perforations.

Surgical Team A85

1968, Nov. 11   Perf. 14x13

336	A85	4np grn & multi	.25	.20
337	A85	12 ½np multicolored	.60	.30
338	A85	20np pur & multi	1.00	1.00
339	A85	40np bl & multi	1.75	2.50
a.		Souvenir sheet of 4	5.25	7.00
		Nos. 336-339 (4)	3.60	4.00

WHO, 20th anniv. No. 339a contains 4 imperf. stamps similar to Nos. 336-339.

Hurdling — A86

12 ½np, Boxing. 20np, Torch bearer, flags & Olympic rings. 40np, Soccer.

1968, Dec.   Unwmk.   Perf. 14x14½

340	A86	4np gray & multi	.20	.20
341	A86	12 ½np gray & multi	.25	.25
342	A86	20np ultra & multi	.50	.70
343	A86	40np gray & multi	.80	2.50
a.		Souvenir sheet of 4	5.25	7.00
		Nos. 340-343 (4)	1.75	3.65

19th Olympic Games, Mexico City, Oct. 12-27, 1968. No. 343a contains 4 imperf. stamps with simulated perforations similar to Nos. 340-343.

UN Headquarters and Flags — A87

UN Day, 1968: 12np, UN emblem and Ghanaian staff and stool. 20np, UN Headquarters, New York, UN emblem and Ghana flag. 40np, UN emblem surrounded by flags.

1969, Feb. 1   Litho.   Perf. 13x13½

344	A87	4np multicolored	.20	.20
345	A87	12 ½np pink & multi	.20	.20
346	A87	20np blk & multi	.25	.35
347	A87	40np lt bl & multi	.50	1.75
a.		Souvenir sheet of 4	1.40	3.25
		Nos. 344-347 (4)	1.15	2.50

No. 347a contains 4 imperf. stamps with simulated perforations similar to #344-347.

Joseph Boakye Danquah A88

12 ½np, 20np, Dr. Martin Luther King, Jr., Human Rights flame & flag of Ghana.

1969, Mar. 7   Photo.   Perf. 14½x14

348	A88	4np gray & multi	.20	.20
349	A88	12 ½np multicolored	.30	.30
350	A88	20np blue & multi	.60	.75

351	A88	40np grn & multi	.75	2.00
a.		Souvenir sheet of 4	2.25	3.50
		Nos. 348-351 (4)	1.75	3.25

Intl. Human Rights Year, Rev. Martin Luther King, Jr. (1929-1968), American civil rights leader, and Joseph Boakye Danquah (1895-1965), lawyer, writer and Ghanaian political leader.
No. 351a contains 4 imperf. stamps with simulated perforations similar to #348-351.

Parliament A89

Design: 12 ½np, 40np, Coat of Arms.

Perf. 14½x14
1969, Sept.   Wmk. 325

352	A89	4np multicolored	.20	.20
353	A89	12 ½p multicolored	.20	.20
354	A89	20np multicolored	.20	.20
355	A89	40np multicolored	.20	.60
a.		Souvenir sheet of 4	1.25	1.20
		Nos. 352-355 (4)	.80	1.20

3rd anniv. of the revolution. No. 355a contains 4 imperf. stamps with simulated perforations similar to Nos. 352-355.

Nos. 286-300 Overprinted in Black, Yellow or Red

Perf. 11½x12, 12x11½ (A73), 14x14½, 14½x14 (A74-A75)
1969, Oct. 1   Photo.   Wmk. 325

356	A73	1np multicolored	.20	2.25
357	A74	1 ½np multicolored	2.00	4.50
358	A73	2np multicolored	.20	3.50
359	A73	2 ½np multicolored	.20	2.25
360	A75	3np multicolored	.80	2.50
361	A73	4np multi (Y)	2.75	.75
362	A75	6np multicolored	.20	2.75
363	A73	8np multicolored	.20	3.00
364	A75	9np multicolored	.20	3.00
365	A75	10np multicolored	.20	3.00
366	A74	20np blue	.75	2.25
367	A74	50np multicolored	6.00	8.50
368	A74	1nc multicolored	2.25	11.00
369	A74	2nc multi (R)	3.00	12.00
370	A74	2.50nc multicolored	3.00	13.00
		Nos. 356-370 (15)	21.95	74.25

Overprint vertical on vertical stamps.
The 4np also exists with overprint in black and in red.

Map of Africa, Two Ghana Flags Rising from Ghana — A90

Designs: 12 ½np, "2" with laurel and star. 20np, Three hands and egg (symbol of rebirth) and Kente cloth. 40np, like 4np.

Unwmk.
1969, Dec. 4   Litho.   Perf. 14

371	A90	4np multicolored	.20	.20
372	A90	12 ½np bl & multi	.35	.35
373	A90	20np multicolored	.50	.50
374	A90	40np bl & multi	1.00	1.00
		Nos. 371-374 (4)	2.05	2.05

Inauguration of the 2nd Republic, Oct. 1969.

Cogwheels and ILO Emblem A91

Perf. 14½x14
1970, Jan. 5   Photo.   Wmk. 325

375	A91	4np rose red & multi	.20	.20
376	A91	12 ½np multicolored	.30	.45
377	A91	20np multicolored	.40	.90
a.		Souvenir sheet of 3	1.75	2.50
		Nos. 375-377 (3)	.90	1.55

ILO, 50th anniv. No. 377a contains 3 imperf. stamps similar to Nos. 375-377 with simulated perforations.
Nos. 375-377 printed in sheets of 12.

Red Cross Helping Wounded A92

4np, Red Cross & globe, vert. 12 ½np, Henri Dunant, Red Cross, Red Crescent, Lion & Sun emblems. 40np, Red Cross and first aid.

1970, Feb. 2   Perf. 14x14½, 14½x14

378	A92	4np gold & multi	.50	.50
379	A92	12 ½np gold & multi	.60	.60
380	A92	20np blue & multi	.70	.85
381	A92	40np multicolored	1.00	2.50
a.		Souvenir sheet of 4	5.00	6.00
		Nos. 378-381 (4)	2.80	4.45

League of Red Cross Societies, 50th anniv. No. 381a contains 4 imperf. stamps similar to Nos. 378-381 with simulated perforations.

Kotoka Airport, Gen. Kotoka and VC10 — A93

12 ½np, Control tower & tail section of VC10. 20np, Bird's eye view of airport and runway. 40np, Flags in front of Kotoka Airport.

Perf. 13x14
1970, Apr.   Unwmk.   Litho.

382	A93	4np multicolored	.20	.20
383	A93	12 ½np multicolored	.30	.20
384	A93	20np multicolored	.50	.50
385	A93	40np multicolored	1.00	1.00
		Nos. 382-385 (4)	2.00	1.90

Inauguration of Kotoka Airport.

Lunar Landing Module and Spacecraft — A94

Designs: 12 ½np, Neil A. Armstrong stepping onto the moon. 20np, Scientific experiments on the moon, horiz. 40np, Neil A. Armstrong, Michael Collins and Edwin E. Aldrin, Jr., after return to earth, horiz.

1970, June 15   Litho.   Perf. 12½

386	A94	4np multicolored	.25	.25
387	A94	12 ½np multicolored	1.10	1.10
388	A94	20np multicolored	1.40	1.40
389	A94	40np multicolored	4.25	4.25
a.		Souvenir sheet of 4	7.50	10.00
		Nos. 386-389 (4)	7.00	7.00

See note after US No. C76. No. 389a contains 4 imperf. stamps similar to Nos. 386-389. Exists with and without simulated perfs.
Nos. 386-389 and 389a were overprinted "PHILYMPIA/LONDON 1970" in black or silver in Sept. 1970. They are believed not to have been regularly issued.

Adult Education A95

Education Year Emblem and. 12½np, Children of various races studying together. 20np, "Ntesie" symbol of wisdom and knowledge. 40np, Nursery school children.

1970, Aug. 10   Litho.   Perf. 13x12½
390	A95	4np blue & multi	.20	.20
391	A95	12½np blue & multi	.30	.30
392	A95	20np blue & multi	.45	.45
393	A95	40np blue & multi	.65	.65
		Nos. 390-393 (4)	1.60	1.60

Issued for International Education Year.

Inauguration of Second Republic
A96

Designs: 12½np, Mace and words of proclamation by K. A. Busia. 20np, Mace and globe with doves. 40np, Opening of Parliament of Second Republic.

1970, Oct. 1   Litho.   Perf. 13
398	A96	4np multicolored	.20	.20
399	A96	12½np multicolored	.35	.35
400	A96	20np multicolored	.55	.55
401	A96	40np lt bl & multi	.65	.65
		Nos. 398-401 (4)	1.75	1.75

First anniversary of the Second Republic.

Amaryllis
A97

Perf. 14½x14
1970   Photo.   Wmk. 325
402	A97	4np shown	3.00	.20
403	A97	12½np Lioness	3.00	1.25
404	A97	20np African orchid	3.25	2.00
405	A97	40np Elephant	9.00	8.50
		Nos. 402-405 (4)	18.25	12.00

Kuduo Brass Casket
A98

Designs: 12½np, Akan traditional house, Danmum. 20np, Larabanga Mosque. 40np, Akan funerary clay head.

1970, Dec. 7   Litho.   Perf. 14½x14
406	A98	4np gray & multi	.20	.20
407	A98	12½np blue & multi	.45	.30
408	A98	20np multicolored	.75	.55
a.		Souvenir sheet of 4	8.00	9.50
409	A98	40np blue & multi	1.60	1.60
		Nos. 406-409 (4)	3.00	2.65

No. 408a contains stamps similar to Nos. 406 and 408, a 12½np (Pompeii Basilica) and a 40np (Pompeii scene). Simulated perforation.

Fair Building and Emblem
A99

Fair Emblem and: 12½np, Drugstore merchandise. 20np, Automotives and tools. 40np, Cranes and trucks. 50np, Cargo, ship and plane, vert.

Perf. 14½x14, 14x14½
1971, Feb. 5   Photo.   Wmk. 325
410	A99	4np multicolored	.20	.20
411	A99	12½np lilac & multi	.45	.45
412	A99	20np blue & multi	.80	.80
413	A99	40np multicolored	1.60	1.60
414	A99	50np multicolored	2.00	2.00
		Nos. 410-414 (5)	5.05	5.05

2nd Ghana International Trade Fair, Accra, Feb. 1-14, 1971.

Crucifixion
A100

Easter: 12½np, Jesus and disciples. 20np, Resurrection.

Perf. 13½
1971, May 19   Litho.   Unwmk.
415	A100	4np multicolored	.20	.20
416	A100	12½np multicolored	.50	.50
417	A100	20np multicolored	.90	.90
		Nos. 415-417 (3)	1.60	1.60

Corn and FAO Emblem — A101

Perf. 14x14½
1971, June   Wmk. 325   Photo.
418	A101	4np lilac & multi	.20	.20
419	A101	12½np lt bl & multi	.45	.45
420	A101	20np multicolored	.75	1.25
		Nos. 418-420 (3)	1.40	1.90

Freedom from Hunger, second development decade, 1970-1980.
The overprint "In Memoriam / Lord Boyd ORR / 1880-1971" was applied to Nos. 418-420 in October, 1971. The 4np was also surcharged "60NP."

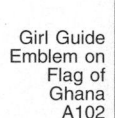

Girl Guide Emblem on Flag of Ghana
A102

12½np, Mrs. Elsie Ofuatey-Kodjoe, national founder. 20np, Girl Guides at play. 40np, Campfire and tent. 50np, Girl Guides signalling.

Unwmk.
1971, July 22   Litho.   Perf. 14
421	A102	4np multicolored	.20	.20
422	A102	12½np yel & multi	.90	.80
423	A102	20np sal & multi	1.75	1.60
424	A102	40np multicolored	3.00	2.50
425	A102	50np lilac & multi	3.25	2.75
a.		Souvenir sheet of 5	15.00	15.00
		Nos. 421-425 (5)	9.10	7.85

50th anniversary of the Girl Guides of Ghana. No. 425a contains 5 imperf. stamps similar to Nos. 421-425.

Child Care Center — A103

YWCA Emblem and: 12½np, World Council Meeting and map of Ghana. 20np, Typing class. 40np, Building fund day.

1971, Aug. 5   Perf. 13
426	A103	4np multicolored	.30	.25
427	A103	12½np ultra & multi	.30	.25
428	A103	20np blue & multi	.30	.25
429	A103	40np yel & multi	.45	.80
a.		Souvenir sheet of 4	1.25	1.25
		Nos. 426-429 (4)	1.35	1.55

World Council Meeting of Young Women's Christian Association, Accra, Aug. 5. No. 429a contains 4 stamps similar to Nos. 426-429 with simulated perforations.

African Nativity Scene
A104

Christmas: 1np, Fireworks, vert. 6np, Flight into Egypt.

Perf. 14x14½, 14½x14
1971, Nov.   Photo.   Wmk. 325
433	A104	1np multicolored	.30	.70
434	A104	3np orange & multi	.30	.30
435	A104	6np blue & multi	.30	.70
		Nos. 433-435 (3)	.90	2.10

UNICEF Emblem, and Child
A105

UNICEF Emblem and: 5np, Infant weighed in net scale, vert. 30np, Student midwife, vert. 50np, Boy in day care center.

Perf. 13½x13, 13x13½
1971, Dec. 20   Litho.   Unwmk.
436	A105	5np grn & multi	.20	.20
437	A105	15np ult & multi	.20	.30
438	A105	30np pink & multi	.45	.70
439	A105	50np blue & multi	.80	1.75
a.		Souvenir sheet of 4	6.00	6.50
		Nos. 436-439 (4)	1.65	2.95

25th anniv. of UNICEF. No. 439a contains 4 stamps with simulated perforations similar to Nos. 436-439.

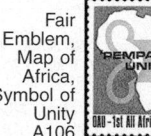

Fair Emblem, Map of Africa, Symbol of Unity
A106

Fair Emblem and: 15np, Horn of Plenty. 30np, Fireworks over Africa. 60np, 1nc, Names of participating nations over map of Africa.

1972, Feb. 23   Litho.   Perf. 14
440	A106	5np lt brn & multi	.20	.20
441	A106	15np lt bl & multi	.20	.30
442	A106	30np green & multi	.30	.60
443	A106	60np yel & multi	.35	1.25
444	A106	1nc lt bl & multi	.60	1.75
		Nos. 440-444 (5)	1.65	4.10

First All-Africa Trade Fair, Nairobi, Kenya, Feb. 23-Mar. 5.
Nos. 440-444 were overprinted "BELGICA 72" in red for release June 24, 1972. The regularity of this issue has been questioned. Value $8.

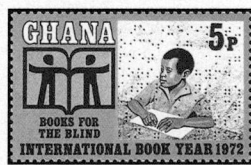

Books for the Blind
A107

Book and Flame of Knowledge
A108

Book Year Emblem and: 15p, Books for Children ("Anansi and Snake the Postman"). 30p, Books for Recreation (Accra Central Library). 50p, Books for Students (2 students).

1972, Apr. 21   Perf. 13½
445	A107	5p blue & multi	.30	.20
446	A107	15p yel & multi	.75	.50
447	A107	30p lilac & multi	1.25	1.00
448	A107	50p green & multi	2.25	2.25
449	A108	1ce blue & multi	3.25	4.25
a.		Souvenir sheet of 5	12.00	12.00
		Nos. 445-449 (5)	7.80	8.20

Intl. Book Year. No. 449a contains one each of Nos. 445-449 with simulated perforations.

Star Grass
A109

1972, July 3   Litho.   Perf. 13½
450	A109	5p shown	.30	.30
451	A109	15p Mona monkey	.90	.90
452	A109	30p Amaryllis	5.50	5.50
453	A109	1ce Side-striped squirrel	6.25	6.25
		Nos. 450-453 (4)	12.95	12.95

Olympic Emblems, Soccer
A110

1972, Sept. 5   Litho.   Perf. 13½x13
454	A110	5p shown	.20	.20
455	A110	15p Running	.30	.20
456	A110	30p Boxing	.55	.55
457	A110	50p Long jump	.90	1.75
458	A110	1ce High jump	2.00	3.00
		Nos. 454-458 (5)	3.95	5.70

Souvenir Sheet
459		Sheet of 2	4.00	6.00
a.	A110	30p like 30p	1.50	2.25
b.	A110	60p like 5p	2.00	3.00

20th Olympic Games, Munich, 8/26-9/11.

Senior and Cub Scouts, Badge
A111

Designs: 15p, Scout in front of tent. 30p, 40p, Sea Scouts in canoe. 50p, Cub Scouts with den mother. 60p, 1ce, Scouts studying.

1972, Oct.   Perf. 14
460	A111	5p blue grn & multi	.20	.20
461	A111	15p ocher & multi	.55	.45
462	A111	30p lilac & multi	1.10	1.10
463	A111	50p multicolored	2.00	2.00
464	A111	1ce blue & multi	4.25	4.25
		Nos. 460-464 (5)	8.10	8.00

Souvenir Sheet
Perf. 13½
465		Sheet of 2	5.00	5.00
a.	A111	40p brown & multi	1.75	1.75
b.	A111	60p green & multi	2.75	2.75

Boy Scout Movement, 65th anniversary. For overprints see Nos. 484-489.

Virgin and Child, by Holbein the Younger — A112

Paintings: 1p, Holy Night, by Correggio. 15p, Virgin and Child, by Andrea Rico. 30p, Melchior. 60p, Virgin and Child with Caspar. 1ce, Balthasar. 30p, 60p, 1ce, are from early 16th century stained glass windows.

1972, Dec. 2   Perf. 14x13½

466	A112	1p black & multi	.20	.20
467	A112	3p black & multi	.20	.20
468	A112	15p black & multi	.40	.35
469	A112	30p black & multi	.80	.80
470	A112	60p black & multi	1.75	1.75
471	A112	1ce black & multi	3.00	3.00
a.		Souvenir sheet of 3	9.50	9.50
		Nos. 466-471 (6)	6.35	6.30

Christmas. No. 471a contains one each of Nos. 469-471 with simulated perforations.

Market A113

Designs: 1p, Unity Declaration at Kumasi Durbar. 5p, Woman with child selling bananas, vert. 15p, Farmer at rest and produce, vert. 30p, Market. 40p, 1ce, Farmer cutting palm nuts with cutlass. 60p, Miners.

Perf. 14x13½, 13½x14

1973, Apr.   Litho.

472	A113	1p multicolored	.20	.20
473	A113	3p multicolored	.20	.20
474	A113	5p multicolored	.20	.20
475	A113	15p multicolored	.30	.25
476	A113	30p multicolored	.30	.40
477	A113	1ce multicolored	.75	1.25
		Nos. 472-477 (6)	1.95	2.50

Souvenir Sheet

478		Sheet of 2	2.75	2.75
a.	A113	40p multicolored	1.00	1.00
b.	A113	60p multicolored	1.50	1.50

Operation "Feed Yourself" and for 1st anniv. of the Oct. 13 Revolution.

Children's Clinic — A114

WHO Emblem and: 15p, Radiology. 30p, Immunization. 50p, Fight against malnutrition (starving child). 1ce, WHO Headquarters, Geneva.

1973, July   Perf. 14x13½

479	A114	5p rose red & multi	.20	.20
480	A114	15p blue & multi	.20	.20
481	A114	30p bister & multi	.40	.40
482	A114	50p green & multi	.65	.75
483	A114	1ce multicolored	1.25	1.75
		Nos. 479-483 (5)	2.70	3.30

WHO, 25th anniversary.

Nos. 460-465 Overprinted: "1st WORLD SCOUTING CONFERENCE IN AFRICA"

1973, July   Litho.   Perf. 14

484	A111	5p green & multi	.20	.20
485	A111	15p ocher & multi	.30	.50
486	A111	30p lilac & multi	.60	1.25
487	A111	50p multicolored	1.00	2.00
488	A111	1ce blue & multi	2.10	3.00
		Nos. 484-488 (5)	4.20	6.95

Souvenir Sheet

Perf. 13½

489		Sheet of 2	4.25	10.00
a.	A111	40p brown & multi	1.50	4.00
b.	A111	60p green & multi	2.25	6.00

24th Boy Scout World Conference (1st in Africa), Nairobi, Kenya, July 16-21.

Poultry Farming A115

FAO/UN Emblem and: 15p, 40p, Tractor. 50p, Cacao harvest. 60p, 1ce, FAO Headquarters, Rome.

1973   Litho.   Perf. 14½x14

490	A115	5p blue & multi	.20	.20
491	A115	15p blue & multi	.20	.20
492	A115	50p blue & multi	.40	.80
493	A115	1ce blue & multi	.60	1.60
		Nos. 490-493 (4)	1.40	2.80

Souvenir Sheet

494		Sheet of 2	1.25	2.25
a.	A115	40p blue & multi	.40	.80
b.	A115	60p blue & multi	.60	1.10

World Food Program, 10th anniversary.

INTERPOL Emblem, Observer A116

INTERPOL Emblem and: 30p, Judge's wig, poison bottle, handcuffs. 50p, photograph and fingerprint. 1ce, Corpse and question mark.

1973   Perf. 13x13½

495	A116	5p emerald & multi	.20	.20
496	A116	30p rose red & multi	.80	.80
497	A116	50p ultra & multi	1.90	1.90
498	A116	1ce gray & multi	3.50	3.50
		Nos. 495-498 (4)	6.40	6.40

50th anniv. the Intl. Criminal Police Org. (INTERPOL).

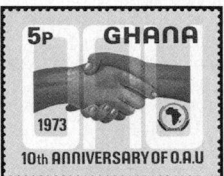

Handclasp and "OAU" A117

"OAU" and: 30p, Africa Hall, Addis Ababa. 50p, OAU emblem (map of Africa). 1ce, "X" in Ghana flag colors.

1973, Oct. 22   Litho.   Perf. 14x14½

499	A117	5p lt bl, blk & brn	.20	.20
500	A117	30p bluish grn, blk & brn	.20	.30
501	A117	50p pink, black & ol	.30	.75
502	A117	1ce multicolored	.45	1.10
		Nos. 499-502 (4)	1.15	2.35

Org. for African Unity, 10th anniv.

Weather Balloon, WMO Emblem A118

WMO Emblem and: 15p, 40p, Tiros weather satellite. 30p, 60p, Computer weather map. 1ce, Radar cloud scanner.

1973, Nov. 16

503	A118	5p multicolored	.20	.20
504	A118	15p multicolored	.20	.20
505	A118	30p multicolored	.40	.60
506	A118	1ce multicolored	.75	1.75
		Nos. 503-506 (4)	1.55	2.75

Souvenir Sheet

507		Sheet of 2	1.75	3.25
a.	A118	40p multicolored	.50	.90
b.	A118	60p multicolored	.90	1.60

Intl. meteorological cooperation, cent. No. 507 exists imperf.

Adoration of the Kings — A119

Christmas: 3p, 40p, Madonna and Child (contemporary). Nos. 510, 511d, Madonna

and Child, by Murillo. No. 511, 60p, Adoration of the Kings, by Tiepolo. No. 511b as 1p.

1973, Dec. 10   Perf. 14

508	A119	1p black & multi	.20	.20
509	A119	3p gray & multi	.20	.20
510	A119	30p multicolored	.55	.55
511	A119	50p multicolored	1.10	1.10
		Nos. 508-511 (4)	2.05	2.05

Souvenir Sheet

Imperf

511A		Sheet of 4	2.50	2.50
b.	A119	30p black & multi	.35	.35
c.	A119	40p gray & multi	.45	.45
d.	A119	50p multicolored	.55	.55
e.	A119	60p multicolored	.65	.65

No. 511A has simulated perforations.

Various Envelopes A120

UPU Emblem and: 9p, 30p, UPU Headquarters, Bern. 40p, 50p, Airmail envelope with Ghana No. 296. 60p, 1ce, Ghana No. 296.

1974, May   Litho.   Perf. 14½

512	A120	5p blue, blk & org	.20	.20
513	A120	9p blue, blk & org	.20	.20
514	A120	50p blue, blk & org	.40	.80
515	A120	1ce blue, blk & org	.65	1.50
		Nos. 512-515 (4)	1.45	2.70

Souvenir Sheet

515A		Sheet of 4	.90	1.40
b.	A120	20p blue, blk & org	.20	.35
c.	A120	30p blue, blk & org	.20	.35
d.	A120	40p blue, blk & org	.20	.35
e.	A120	60p blue, blk & org	.20	.35

Centenary of Universal Postal Union. No. 515A exists imperf. Value $20. For overprints see Nos. 521-524A.

The Betrayal — A121

Designs: 5p, 15p, Jesus Carrying Cross, painting by Thomas de Coloswar, 1427. 20p, 30p, The Betrayal. 25p, 50p, The Deposition. 40p, 1ce, Risen Christ and Mary Magdalene. The designs (except 5p, 15p) are from 15th century English ivory carvings.

1974, Apr.   Litho.   Perf. 14

516	A121	5p black & multi	.20	.20
517	A121	30p sil, ultra & brn	.20	.30
518	A121	50p sil, red & brn	.35	.50
519	A121	1ce silver, ol & brn	.55	.90
		Nos. 516-519 (4)	1.30	1.90

Souvenir Sheet

Imperf

520		Sheet of 4	1.10	1.60
a.	A121	15p black & multi	.20	.40
b.	A121	20p silver, ultra & brn	.20	.40
c.	A121	25p silver, red & brn	.20	.40
d.	A121	40p silver, olive & brn	.20	.40

Easter. No. 520 contains 4 stamps with simulated perforations.

Nos. 512-515A Overprinted "INTERNABA 1974"

1974, June 7   Perf. 14½

521	A120	5p blue, blk & org	.20	.20
522	A120	9p blue, blk & org	.20	.20
523	A120	50p blue, blk & org	.35	.80
524	A120	1ce blue, blk & org	.55	1.25
		Nos. 521-524 (4)	1.30	2.45

Souvenir Sheet

524A		Sheet of 4	2.10	3.50
b.	A120	20p blue, blk & org	.20	.35
c.	A120	30p blue, blk & org	.20	.35
d.	A120	40p blue, blk & org	.30	.50
e.	A120	60p blue, blk & org	.35	.60

INTERNABA 1974 International Philatelic Exhibition, Basel, June 7-16. Overprint is applied to individual stamps of No. 524A.

Soccer and World Cup Emblem A122

Designs: Various soccer scenes and world cup emblem.

1974, June 17   Litho.   Perf. 14½, 13

525	A122	5p multicolored	.20	.20
526	A122	30p multicolored	.20	.50
527	A122	50p multicolored	.30	.75
528	A122	1ce multicolored	.35	1.00
		Nos. 525-528 (4)	1.05	2.45

Souvenir Sheet

Perf. 14½

529		Sheet of 4	2.00	3.00
a.	A122	25p multicolored	.20	.30
b.	A122	40p multicolored	.25	.40
c.	A122	55p multicolored	.30	.45
d.	A122	60p multicolored	.50	.50

World Cup Soccer Championship, June 13-July 7.

Nos. 525-528 were issued in sheets of 30, perf. 14½, and in sheets of 5 plus label, perf. 13.

For overprints, see Nos. 535-539, 549-553.

Traffic Diagram at Traffic Circle A123

Designs: 15p, Traffic sign "Two-way traffic." 30p, "Change to right hand drive," vert. 50p, Warning hands sign, vert. 1ce, 2 hands and car symbolizing traffic change, vert.

1974, July 16   Perf. 13½

Size: 35x28½mm

530	A123	5p yel grn, red & blk	.20	.20
531	A123	15p lilac, red & blk	.20	.30

Size: 28½x41mm

Perf. 14½

532	A123	30p multicolored	.35	.35
533	A123	50p multicolored	.80	.80
534	A123	1ce red, green & blk	1.75	1.75
		Nos. 530-534 (5)	3.30	3.40

Publicity for change to right-hand driving, Aug. 4, 1974.

Nos. 525-529 Overprinted: "WEST GERMANY WINNERS"

1974, Aug. 30   Litho.   Perf. 14½, 13

535	A122	5p multicolored	.20	.20
536	A122	30p multicolored	.45	.45
537	A122	50p multicolored	.65	.65
538	A122	1ce multicolored	1.10	1.10
		Nos. 535-538 (4)	2.40	2.40

Souvenir Sheet

539		Sheet of 4	2.00	2.00
a.	A122	25p multicolored	.25	.25
b.	A122	40p multicolored	.40	.40
c.	A122	55p multicolored	.45	.45
d.	A122	60p multicolored	.50	.50

World Cup Soccer Championship, 1974, victory of German Federal Republic. Overprint is applied to individual stamps of No. 539.

Family and WPY Emblem A124

1974, Sept. 27   Perf. 12½

540	A124	5p shown	.20	.20
541	A124	30p Clinic	.30	.30
542	A124	50p Immunization of children	.35	.50
543	A124	1ce Census	.65	1.25
		Nos. 540-543 (4)	1.50	2.25

World Population Year.

Angel — A125   Nativity — A127

Three Kings, Candles — A126

Design: 60p, 1ce, Annunciation.

Perf. 13½, 14 (7p)

1974, Dec. 19   **Litho.**
544	A125	5p red & multi	.20	.20
545	A126	7p blue & multi	.20	.20
546	A127	9p orange & multl	.20	.20
547	A127	1ce orange & multi	.85	1.25
		Nos. 544-547 (4)	1.45	1.85

Souvenir Sheet
Imperf
548		Sheet of 4	1.25	2.00
a.	A125	15p red & multi	.20	.50
b.	A126	30p blue & multi	.20	.50
c.	A127	45p orange & multi	.20	.50
d.	A127	60p orange & multi	.20	.50

Christmas. No. 548 contains 4 stamps with simulated perforations.

Nos. 525-529 Overprinted "APOLLO / SOYUZ / JULY 15, 1975"

1975, Aug. 15   Litho.   Perf. 14½, 13
549	A122	5p multicolored	.20	.20
550	A122	30p multicolored	.25	.25
551	A122	50p multicolored	.55	.55
552	A122	1ce orange & multi	1.00	1.00
		Nos. 549-552 (4)	2.00	2.00

Souvenir Sheet
Perf. 14½
553		Sheet of 4	2.75	2.75
a.	A122	25p multicolored	.25	.25
b.	A122	40p multicolored	.40	.40
c.	A122	55p multicolored	.60	.60
d.	A122	65p multicolored	.65	.65

Apollo Soyuz space test project (Russo-American cooperation), launching July 15, link-up, July 17.
Overprint is applied to individual stamps of No. 553.
Nos. 549-552 with perf. 13 are from the sheets of 5 plus label.

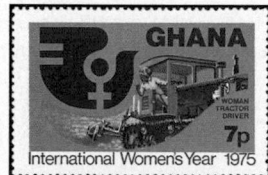

IWY Emblem, Woman Tractor Driver — A128

Intl. Women's Year Emblem and: 15p, like 7p. 30p, 40p, Automobile mechanic. 60p, 65p, Factory workers. 80p, 1ce, Cocoa research.

1975, Sept. 3   **Perf. 14**
554	A128	7p multicolored	.20	.20
555	A128	30p lt violet & multi	.55	.55
556	A128	60p multicolored	1.40	1.40
557	A128	1ce lilac & multi	2.25	2.25
		Nos. 554-557 (4)	4.40	4.40

Souvenir Sheet
Imperf
558		Sheet of 4	4.00	5.00
a.	A128	15p Prus green & multi	.30	.40
b.	A128	40p light violet & multi	.75	.90
c.	A128	65p dull green & multi	1.00	1.25
d.	A128	80p lilac & multi	1.25	1.50

Intl. Women's Year. No. 558 contains 4 stamps with simulated perforations.

Angel over Child in Crib A129

Angel with Harp A130

Designs: 7p, 40p, Angels with lute and bell. 30p, 65p, Angel with viol. 1ce, 80p, Angels with trumpets. 15p, like 5p.

1975, Dec. 31   Litho.   Perf. 14x13½
559	A129	2p org & multi	.20	.20
560	A130	5p yel, brown & grn	.20	.20
561	A130	7p yel, brown & grn	.20	.20
562	A130	30p yel, brown & grn	.35	.20
563	A130	1ce yel, brown & grn	.75	.75
		Nos. 559-563 (5)	1.70	1.55

Souvenir Sheet
Imperf
564		Sheet of 4	2.00	2.50
a.	A130	15p yellow, green & brown	.20	.25
b.	A130	40p yellow, green & brown	.20	.25
c.	A130	65p yellow, green & brown	.50	.65
d.	A130	80p yellow, green & brown	.60	.75

Christmas. No. 564 has simulated perforations.

Boy Scouts Reading Map — A131

30p, 40p, Sailing. 60p, 65p, Hiking. 80p, 1ce, Life saving (swimmers). 15p, like 7p.

1976, Jan. 5   **Perf. 13½x14**
565	A131	7p ocher & multi	.20	.20
566	A131	30p blue & multi	.75	.75
567	A131	60p green & multi	1.75	1.75
568	A131	1ce multicolored	2.75	2.75
		Nos. 565-568 (4)	5.45	5.45

Souvenir Sheet
569		Sheet of 4	5.00	6.00
a.	A131	15p ocher & multi	.40	.50
b.	A131	40p blue & multi	.90	1.10
c.	A131	65p green & multi	1.25	1.50
d.	A131	80p rose claret & multi	1.50	1.75

Nordjamb 75, 14th World Boy Scout Jamboree, Lillehammer, Norway, July 29-Aug. 7.
For overprints, see Nos. 578-582.

1 ¾ Pints Equal 1 Liter A132

Map of Ghana and: 30p, "2 ¼ lbs of jam a little more than a kilogram." 60p, "A meter of cloth will be a little more than 3 foot 3." 1ce, Thermometer, ice and boiling tea kettle.

1976, Jan. 5   Litho.   Perf. 14x13½
570	A132	7p bluish gray & blk	.20	.20
571	A132	30p vio blue & multi	.50	.40
572	A132	60p ocher & multi	.90	.90
573	A132	1ce multicolored	1.60	1.60
		Nos. 570-573 (4)	3.20	3.10

Introduction of metric system, Sept. 1975.

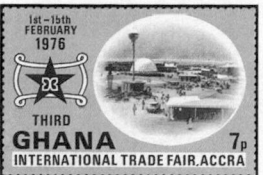

Fair Grounds — A133

Designs: Various exhibition halls.

1976, Apr. 6   **Litho.**   **Perf. 14**
574	A133	7p multicolored	.20	.20
575	A133	30p yellow & multi	.20	.20
576	A133	60p multicolored	.40	.60
577	A133	1ce salmon & multi	.65	1.00
		Nos. 574-577 (4)	1.45	2.00

International Trade Fair, Accra, Feb. 1-15.

Nos. 565-569 Overprinted in Violet Blue

1976, May 29   Litho.   Perf. 13½x14
578	A131	7p ocher & multi	.20	.20
579	A131	30p blue & multi	.55	.50
580	A131	60p green & multi	1.10	.75
581	A131	1ce multicolored	1.60	1.25
		Nos. 578-581 (4)	3.45	2.70

Souvenir Sheet
582		Sheet of 4	2.25	2.25
a.	A131	15p ocher & multi	.20	.20
b.	A131	40p blue & multi	.40	.40
c.	A131	65p green & multi	.50	.50
d.	A131	80p rose claret & multi	.50	.50

Interphil 76 International Philatelic Exhibition, Philadelphia, Pa., May 29-June 6. Overprint applied to individual stamps of No. 582.

Shot Put — A134

Olympic Rings, Map of Ghana and: 15p, like 7p. 30p, 40p, Soccer. 60p, 65p, Women's 1500 meters. 80p, 1ce, Boxing.

1976, Aug. 9   Litho.   Perf. 14x13½
583	A134	7p lt blue & multi	.20	.20
584	A134	30p yellow & multi	.30	.30
585	A134	60p multicolored	.65	.65
586	A134	1ce yellow & multi	1.00	1.00
		Nos. 583-586 (4)	2.15	2.15

Souvenir Sheet
587		Sheet of 4	1.75	1.75
a.	A134	15p light blue & multi	.20	.20
b.	A134	40p yellow & multi	.20	.20
c.	A134	65p emerald & multi	.30	.30
d.	A134	80p yellow & multi	.40	.40

21st Olympic Games, Montreal, Canada, July 17-Aug. 1.
For overprints see Nos. 606-610.

Supreme Court, Accra A135

Designs: Various views of Supreme Court Building, Scales of Justice, law book.

1976, Sept. 7   **Litho.**   **Perf. 14**
588	A135	8p lilac & multi	.20	.20
589	A135	30p blue & multi	.25	.25
590	A135	60p ver & multi	.40	.50
591	A135	1ce multicolored	.85	1.00
		Nos. 588-591 (4)	1.70	1.95

Ghana Supreme Court, centenary.

Examination for River Blindness — A136

Designs: 30p, Ghanaian entomologist with microscope. 60p, Flowers. 1ce, Boatmen checking effectiveness of black fly larvae insecticide.

1976, Oct. 28   Litho.   Perf. 14½x14
592	A136	7p multicolored	.85	.20
593	A136	30p multicolored	2.25	1.75
594	A136	60p multicolored	3.50	3.50
595	A136	1ce multicolored	5.75	5.75
		Nos. 592-595 (4)	12.35	11.20

World Health Day. Prevention of blindness.

Children with Gifts and Christmas Tree — A137

Designs: 6p, 15p, Children with firecrackers. 30p, 65p, Family at Christmas dinner. 40p, 80p, 1ce, like 8p.

1976, Dec. 15   Litho.   Perf. 13½
596	A137	6p multicolored	.20	.20
597	A137	8p multicolored	.20	.20
598	A137	30p multicolored	.65	.65
599	A137	1ce multicolored	1.75	1.75
		Nos. 596-599 (4)	2.80	2.80

Souvenir Sheet
Imperf
600		Sheet of 4	3.25	3.25
a.	A137	15p multicolored	.20	.20
b.	A137	40p multicolored	.55	.55
c.	A137	65p multicolored	.90	.90
d.	A137	80p multicolored	1.10	1.10

Christmas. No. 600 has simulated perfs.

1876 Gallows Frame Telephone and A. G. Bell — A138

A. G. Bell: 15p, like 8p. 30p, 40p, 1895 telephone. 60p, 65p, 1929 telephone. 80p, 1ce, 1976 telephone.

1976, Dec. 17   **Perf. 14½**
601	A138	8p multicolored	.20	.20
602	A138	30p multicolored	.50	.50
603	A138	60p multicolored	1.40	1.40
604	A138	1ce multicolored	2.00	2.00
		Nos. 601-604 (4)	4.10	4.10

Souvenir Sheet
Perf. 13
605		Sheet of 4	3.00	3.00
a.	A138	15p multicolored	.20	.20
b.	A138	40p multicolored	.50	.50
c.	A138	65p multicolored	.85	.85
d.	A138	80p multicolored	1.00	1.00

Centenary of first telephone call by Alexander Graham Bell, Mar. 10, 1876.
For overprints, see Nos. 616-620.

Nos. 583-587 Overprinted:
a. EAST GERMANY / WINNERS
b. U.S.S.R. WINNERS
c. U.S.A. WINNERS

1977, Feb. 22   Litho.   Perf. 14x13½

606	A134(a)	7p multicolored	.20	.20
607	A134(a)	30p multicolored	.35	.20
608	A134(b)	60p multicolored	.75	.75
609	A134(c)	1ce multicolored	1.60	1.60
	Nos. 606-609 (4)		2.90	2.75

Souvenir Sheet

610	Sheet of 4	3.50	2.50
a.	A134(a) 15p multicolored	.30	.30
b.	A134(a) 40p multicolored	.70	.70
c.	A134(c) 65p multicolored	1.00	1.00
d.	A134(c) 80p multicolored	1.10	1.10

1976 Montreal Olympic Games' winners.

Klama Dance, Dipo Tribe — A139

Festival Emblem and: 15p, like 8p. 30p, 40p, African artifacts. 60p, 65p, Acon dance. 80p, 1ce, Mud, straw and wooden huts.

1977, Mar. 24   Litho.   Perf. 14x13½

611	A139	8p multicolored	.20	.20
612	A139	30p multicolored	.50	.60
613	A139	60p multicolored	.80	1.10
614	A139	1ce multicolored	1.25	1.75
	Nos. 611-614 (4)		2.75	3.65

Souvenir Sheet

615	Sheet of 4	3.50	3.50
a.	A139 15p multicolored	.35	.35
b.	A139 40p multicolored	.75	.75
c.	A139 65p multicolored	1.00	1.10
d.	A139 80p multicolored	1.25	1.25

2nd World Black and African Festival of Arts and Culture, Lagos, Nigeria, Jan. 15-Feb. 12.

Nos. 601-605 Overprinted: "PRINCE CHARLES / VISITS GHANA / 17th TO 25th / MARCH, 1977"

1977, June 2   Litho.   Perf. 14½

616	A138	8p multicolored	.75	.75
617	A138	30p multicolored	2.00	2.00
618	A138	60p multicolored	3.00	3.00
619	A138	1ce multicolored	4.00	4.00
	Nos. 616-619 (4)		9.75	9.75

Souvenir Sheet

Perf. 13

620	Sheet of 4	14.00	14.00
a.	A138 15p multicolored	1.50	1.25
b.	A138 40p multicolored	2.75	2.25
c.	A138 65p multicolored	4.00	3.50
d.	A138 80p multicolored	4.50	4.00

Visit of Prince Charles, Mar. 17-25. Overprint applied to individual stamps of No. 620.

Olive Colobus — A140

Wildlife Fund Emblem and: 15p, like 8p. 20p, 40p, Ebien palm squirrel. 30p, 65p, African wild dog. 60p, 80p, West African manatee.

1977, June 22   Litho.   Perf. 13½x14

621	A140	8p multicolored	4.00	1.50
622	A140	20p multicolored	9.00	2.00
623	A140	30p multicolored	12.00	5.00
624	A140	60p multicolored	16.00	7.00
	Nos. 621-624 (4)		41.00	15.50

Souvenir Sheet

625	Sheet of 4	22.50	22.50
a.	A140 15p multicolored	3.00	3.00
b.	A140 40p multicolored	5.00	5.00
c.	A140 65p multicolored	6.00	6.00
d.	A140 80p multicolored	7.00	7.00

Wildlife protection.

Suzanne Fourment in Velvet Hat, by Rubens — A141

Paintings: 15p, like 8p. 30p, 40p, Isabella of Portugal, by Titian. 60p, 65p, Duke and Duchess of Cumberland, by Gainsborough. 80p, 1ce, Rubens and his wife Isabella, by Rubens.

1977, Sept.   Litho.   Perf. 14x13½

626	A141	8p lt blue & multi	.20	.20
627	A141	30p lt blue & multi	.65	.65
628	A141	60p lt blue & multi	1.40	1.40
629	A141	1ce lt blue & multi	2.50	2.50
	Nos. 626-629 (4)		4.75	4.75

Souvenir Sheet

630	Sheet of 4	4.25	4.25
a.	A141 15p light blue & multi	.25	.25
b.	A141 40p light blue & multi	.75	.75
c.	A141 65p light blue & multi	1.25	1.25
d.	A141 80p light blue & multi	1.50	1.50

Painters, birth annivs.: Peter Paul Rubens (1577-1640); Titian (1477-1576); Thomas Gainsborough (1727-1788).

Adoration of the Kings — A142

Guild of the Good Shepherd, Abossey Okai — A143

Designs: 6p, 40p, Methodist Church, Wesley, Accra. 8p, Virgin and Child, and Star. 15p, like 2p. 30p, 65p, Holy Spirit Cathedral, Accra. 80p, 1ce, Ebenezer Presbyterian Church, Osu, Accra. Type A143 designs include score of "Hark the Herald Angels Sing."

Perf. 14x14½, 14

1977, Dec. 30   Litho.

631	A142	1p multicolored	.20	.20
632	A143	2p multicolored	.20	.20
633	A143	6p multicolored	.20	.20
634	A142	8p multicolored	.20	.20
635	A143	30p multicolored	.60	.60
636	A143	1ce multicolored	2.00	2.00
	Nos. 631-636 (6)		3.40	3.40

Souvenir Sheet

Imperf

637	Sheet of 4	4.75	4.75
a.	A143 15p multicolored	.25	.25
b.	A143 40p multicolored	.75	.75
c.	A143 65p multicolored	1.25	1.25
d.	A143 80p multicolored	1.50	1.50

Christmas. No. 637 has simulated perfs.

No. 631-637 Overprinted: "REFERENDUM 1978 VOTE EARLY"

Perf. 14x14½, 14

1978, Mar. 28   Litho.

638	A142	1p multicolored	.20	.20
639	A143	2p multicolored	.20	.20
640	A143	6p multicolored	.20	.20
641	A142	8p multicolored	.20	.20
642	A143	30p multicolored	.70	.70
643	A143	1ce multicolored	2.50	2.50
	Nos. 638-643 (6)		4.00	4.00

Souvenir Sheet

Imperf

644	Sheet of 4	40.00	20.00
a.	A143 15p multicolored	3.00	1.50
b.	A143 40p multicolored	7.50	3.75
c.	A143 65p multicolored	13.00	6.50
d.	A143 80p multicolored	15.00	7.50

Banana Harvest — A144

Designs: 8p, Vegetable garden. 30p, Produce market. 60p, Fishing. 1ce, Tractor.

1978, May 15   Perf. 14

645	A144	2p multicolored	.20	.20
646	A144	8p multicolored	.20	.20
647	A144	30p multicolored	.50	.50
648	A144	60p multicolored	1.10	1.10
649	A144	1ce multicolored	1.90	1.90
	Nos. 645-649 (5)		3.90	3.90

Operation feed yourself.

Wright Biplane and Crowd — A145

Planes and Crowd: 15p, like 8p. 30p, 40p, Heracles, 1st practical airliner. 60p, 65p, D. H. Comet, 1st jet airliner. 80p, 1ce, Concorde, 1st supersonic airliner.

1978, June 6   Litho.   Perf. 14x13½

650	A145	8p multicolored	.30	.20
651	A145	30p multicolored	.70	.55
652	A145	60p multicolored	1.40	1.10
653	A145	1ce multicolored	2.25	1.40
	Nos. 650-653 (4)		4.65	3.25

Souvenir Sheet

654	Sheet of 4	6.50	3.25
a.	A145 15p multicolored	.40	.20
b.	A145 40p multicolored	1.25	.60
c.	A145 65p multicolored	2.00	1.00
d.	A145 80p multicolored	2.25	1.10

75th anniversary of first powered flight. The cheering crowd forms a continuing design on Nos. 650-654.

Nos. 650-653, 654a-654d Overprinted: "CAPEX 78 / JUNE 9-18 1978"

1978, June 9

655	A145	8p multicolored	.30	.20
656	A145	30p multicolored	.45	.25
657	A145	60p multicolored	.75	.50
658	A145	1ce multicolored	2.00	.80
	Nos. 655-658 (4)		3.50	1.75

Souvenir Sheet

659	Sheet of 4	2.50	2.25
a.	A145 15p multicolored	.25	.20
b.	A145 40p multicolored	.45	.40
c.	A145 65p multicolored	.70	.65
d.	A145 80p multicolored	.90	.80

CAPEX, Canadian International Philatelic Exhibition, Toronto, Ont., June 9-18.

Soccer, Africa Cup Emblem and Ghana Flag — A146

15p, like 8p. 30p, 40p, Three soccer players, Africa Cup emblem, Ghana flag. 60p, 65p, Two soccer players. Argentina '78 emblem, Argentina flag. 80p, 1ce, Goalkeeper, Argentina '78 emblem and Argentine flag.

1978, July 1   Litho.   Perf. 13½x14

660	A146	8p multicolored	.20	.20
661	A146	30p multicolored	.35	.35
662	A146	60p multicolored	.85	.85
663	A146	1ce multicolored	1.60	1.60
	Nos. 660-663 (4)		3.00	3.00

Souvenir Sheet

664	Sheet of 4	2.10	2.10
a.	A146 15p multicolored	.20	.20
b.	A146 40p multicolored	.40	.40
c.	A146 65p multicolored	.65	.65
d.	A146 80p multicolored	.80	.80

11th African Cup of Nations, Ghana, Mar. 5-19, and 11th World Cup Soccer Championship, Argentina, June 1-25.

Nos. 660-661, 664a-664b Overprinted: "GHANA WINNERS"

Nos. 662-663, 664c-664d Overprinted: "ARGENTINA WINS"

1978, Aug. 21   Litho.   Perf. 13½x14

665	A146	8p multicolored	.20	.20
666	A146	30p multicolored	.45	.45
667	A146	60p multicolored	.90	.90
668	A146	1ce multicolored	1.60	1.60
	Nos. 665-668 (4)		3.15	3.15

Souvenir Sheet

669	Sheet of 4	1.75	1.75
a.	A146 15p multicolored	.20	.20
b.	A146 40p multicolored	.30	.30
c.	A146 65p multicolored	.45	.45
d.	A146 80p multicolored	.65	.65

Winners, 11th African Cup and 11th World Cup Soccer Championships.
Overprint on 60p and 65p is in two lines.

The Betrayal, by Dürer — A147

Etchings by Albrecht Dürer: 39p, The Crucifixion. 60p, The Deposition. 1ce, The Resurrection.

1978, Sept. 1   Litho.   Perf. 14x13½

670	A147	11p lilac & black	.20	.20
671	A147	39p salmon & black	.35	.35
672	A147	60p orange & black	.55	.55
673	A147	1ce yel green & black	.85	.85
	Nos. 670-673 (4)		1.95	1.95

Easter.

Bauhinia Purpurea A148

Flowers: 39p, Cassia fistula. 60p, Frangipani. 1ce, Jacaranda mimosifolia.

1978, Nov. 20   Litho.   Perf. 14x13½

674	A148	11p multicolored	.20	.20
675	A148	39p multicolored	.25	.25
676	A148	60p multicolored	.55	.55
677	A148	1ce multicolored	.80	.80
	Nos. 674-677 (4)		1.80	1.80

Mail Railroad Car — A149

Ghana railroad, 75th Anniv.: 39p, Pay and bank car. 60p, Locomotive, 1922. 1ce, Diesel locomotive, 1960.

1978, Dec. 4   Litho.   Perf. 13½

678	A149	11p multicolored	.20	.20
679	A149	39p multicolored	.45	.65
680	A149	60p multicolored	.75	1.00
681	A149	1ce multicolored	1.10	1.50
	Nos. 678-681 (4)		2.50	3.35

Orbiter Spacecraft — A150

15p, like 11p. 39p, 40p, Multiprobe spacecraft. 60p, 65p, Orbiter and Multiprobe circling Venus. 2ce, 3ce, Radar chart of Venus.

1979, July 5   Litho.   Perf. 14x13½

682	A150	11p multicolored	.20	.20
683	A150	39p multicolored	.25	.25
684	A150	60p multicolored	.45	.45
685	A150	3ce multicolored	.70	1.10
		Nos. 682-685 (4)	1.60	2.00

Souvenir Sheet
Imperf

686		Sheet of 4	2.25	2.25
a.	A150	15p multicolored	.20	.20
b.	A150	40p multicolored	.25	.25
c.	A150	65p multicolored	.45	.45
d.	A150	2ce multicolored	1.10	1.10

Pioneer Venus Space Project.

O Come All Ye Faithful A152

Christmas Carols: 10p, O Little Town of Bethlehem. 15p, 65p, We Three Kings of Orient Are. 20p, I Saw Three Ships Come Sailing By. 25p, like 8p. No. 696, 1ce, Away in a Manger. 4ce, No. 698d, Ding Dong Merrily on High.

1979, Dec. 20   Perf. 14½

692	A152	8p multicolored	.20	.20
693	A152	10p multicolored	.20	.20
694	A152	15p multicolored	.20	.20
695	A152	20p multicolored	.20	.20
696	A152	2ce multicolored	.35	.60
697	A152	4ce multicolored	.50	1.10
		Nos. 692-697 (6)	1.65	2.50

Souvenir Sheet

698		Sheet of 4	1.25	1.25
a.	A152	25p multicolored	.20	.20
b.	A152	65p multicolored	.20	.20
c.	A152	1ce multicolored	.30	.30
d.	A152	2ce multicolored	.60	.60

Christmas.

J.B. Danquah (1895-1965) A153

National Leaders: 65p, John Mensah Sarbah (1864-1910). 80p, J.E.K. Aggrey (1875-1925). 2ce, Kwame Nkrumah (1909-1972). 4ce, G.E. Grant (1878-1956).

1980, Jan. 21   Litho.   Perf. 13½x14

699	A153	20p multicolored	.20	.20
700	A153	65p multicolored	.20	.20
701	A153	80p multicolored	.20	.20
702	A153	2ce multicolored	.50	.50
703	A153	4ce multicolored	.90	.90
		Nos. 699-703 (5)	2.00	2.00

Man with Clack Bells, Hill A154

Hill and: 25p, Man with clack bells. 50p, 65p, Chief, elephant staff. 1ce, 2ce, Drummer. 4ce, 5ce, Chief, ivory staff.

1980, Mar. 12   Litho.   Perf. 14½

704	A154	20p multicolored	.20	.20
705	A154	65p multicolored	.20	.20
706	A154	2ce multicolored	.55	.55
707	A154	4ce multicolored	1.00	1.00
		Nos. 704-707 (4)	1.95	1.95

Souvenir Sheet

708		Sheet of 4	2.00	2.00
a.	A154	25p multicolored	.20	.20
b.	A154	50p multicolored	.20	.20
c.	A154	1ce multicolored	.40	.40
d.	A154	5ce multicolored	1.00	1.00

Sir Rowland Hill (1795-1879), originator of penny postage.

Nos. 708a-708d also exist perf 13½, issued in small individual sheetlets. Values slightly more than perf 14½.

For overprints see Nos. 714-718.

Students, IYC Emblem — A155

IYC Emblem and: 25p like 20p. 50p, 65p, Boys playing soccer. 1ce, 2ce, Boys in canoe. 3ce, 4ce, Mother and child.

1980, Apr. 2   Litho.   Perf. 15

709	A155	20p multicolored	.20	.20
710	A155	65p multicolored	.20	.30
711	A155	2ce multicolored	.60	.80
712	A155	4ce multicolored	1.25	1.60
		Nos. 709-712 (4)	2.25	2.90

Souvenir Sheet

713		Sheet of 4	2.75	2.75
a.	A155	25p multicolored	.20	.20
b.	A155	50p multicolored	.30	.30
c.	A155	1ce multicolored	.40	.40
d.	A155	3ce multicolored	1.10	1.10

Intl. Year of the Child (in 1979).
For overprints see Nos. 719-723.

Nos. 704-708 Overprinted: "LONDON 1980" / 6th-14th May 1980

1980, May 6   Litho.   Perf. 14½

714	A154	20p multicolored	.20	.20
715	A154	65p multicolored	.35	.35
716	A154	2ce multicolored	.85	.85
717	A154	4ce multicolored	1.40	1.40
		Nos. 714-717 (4)	2.80	2.80

Souvenir Sheet

718		Sheet of 4	3.50	3.50
a.	A154	25p multicolored	.20	.20
b.	A154	50p multicolored	.30	.30
c.	A154	1ce multicolored	.55	.55
d.	A154	5ce multicolored	2.25	2.25

London 1980 Intl. Stamp Exhib., May 6-14. #718a-718d also exist perf 13½, issued in small individual sheetlets. Value, unused or used, $15.

Nos. 709-713 Overprinted: "PAPAL VISIT" / 8th-9th May / 1980

1980, May 8   Perf. 15

719	A155	20p multicolored	.85	.20
720	A155	65p multicolored	1.60	.70
721	A155	2ce multicolored	2.50	1.40
722	A155	4ce multicolored	4.00	2.25
		Nos. 719-722 (4)	8.95	4.55

Souvenir Sheet

723		Sheet of 4	16.00	16.00
a.	A155	25p multicolored	1.10	1.10
b.	A155	50p multicolored	2.25	2.25
c.	A155	1ce multicolored	3.50	3.50
d.	A155	3ce multicolored	8.25	8.25

Visit of Pope John Paul II to Ghana, May 8-9.

Nos. 719-722 exist imperf. Value, set $25.

Parliament House A156

1980, Aug. 4   Litho.   Perf. 14

724	A156	20p shown	.20	.20
725	A156	65p Supreme Court	.20	.20
726	A156	2ce The Castle	.40	.60
		Nos. 724-726 (3)	.80	1.00

Souvenir Sheet

727		Sheet of 3	.75	1.00
a.	A156	25p like #724	.20	.20
b.	A156	1ce like #725	.25	.25
c.	A156	3ce like #726	.30	.30

Third Republic.

Map of West African Member Countries, Flag of Ghana, Jet — A157

1980, Nov. 5   Litho.   Perf. 14½

728	A157	20p shown	.20	.20
729	A157	65p Dish antenna	.20	.20
730	A157	80p Cogwheels	.20	.20
731	A157	2ce Corn	.25	.25
		Nos. 728-731 (4)	.85	.85

5th Anniversary of ECOWAS (Economic Community of West African States).

A158

1980, Nov. 26

732	A158	20p "OAU"	.20	.20
733	A158	65p OAU Banner, Maps	.20	.20
734	A158	80p Waves on map of Africa	.20	.20
735	A158	2ce Flag, banner, map	.25	.25
		Nos. 732-735 (4)	.85	.85

Org. for African Unity summit conference, Lagos, Nigeria, Apr. 28-29.

A159

1980, Dec. 10   Perf. 14

Christmas (Fra Angelico Paintings): 15p, 25p, Adoration of the Magi. 20p, 50p, Virgin and Child Enthroned with Four Angels. 1ce, 2ce, Virgin and Child Enthroned with Eight Angels. 3ce, 4ce, Annunciation.

736	A159	15p multicolored	.20	.20
737	A159	20p multicolored	.20	.20
738	A159	2ce multicolored	.40	.60
739	A159	4ce multicolored	.90	1.25
		Nos. 736-739 (4)	1.70	2.25

Souvenir Sheet

740		Sheet of 4	1.10	1.10
a.	A159	25p multicolored	.20	.20
b.	A159	50p multicolored	.20	.20
c.	A159	1ce multicolored	.25	.25
d.	A159	3ce multicolored	.40	.40

Nurse Weighing Newborn, Rotary Emblem A160

1980, Dec. 18

741	A160	20p shown	.20	.20
742	A160	65p Map of Ghana and world	.20	.20
743	A160	2ce Helping hands, world map	.55	.75
744	A160	4ce Food distribution	1.10	1.40
		Nos. 741-744 (4)	2.05	2.55

Souvenir Sheet

745		Sheet of 4	2.25	2.25
a.	A160	25p like #741	.20	.20
b.	A160	50p like #742	.25	.25
c.	A160	1ce like #743	.30	.30
d.	A160	3ce like #744	1.00	1.00

Rotary International, 75th anniv.

Narina Trogon — A161

1981, Jan. 12   Litho.   Perf. 14

746	A161	20p shown	1.90	.25
747	A161	65p White-crowned robin-chat	3.00	.60
748	A161	2ce Swallow-tailed bee-eater	3.75	1.75
749	A161	4ce Long-tailed parakeet	5.50	3.25
		Nos. 746-749 (4)	14.15	5.85

Souvenir Sheet

750		Sheet of 4	11.50	11.50
a.	A161	25p like #746	.45	.30
b.	A161	50p like #747	1.10	.45
c.	A161	1ce like #748	1.90	.80
d.	A161	3ce like #749	5.50	2.40

Pope John Paul II, Pres. Limann, Archbishop of Canterbury — A162

1981, Mar. 3   Litho.   Perf. 14

751	A162	20p multicolored	.25	.25
752	A162	65p multicolored	.65	.65
753	A162	80p multicolored	.85	.85
754	A162	2ce multicolored	2.50	2.50
		Nos. 751-754 (4)	4.25	4.25

Visit of Pope John Paul II, May 8-10, 1980.

Earth Satellite Station — A163

1981, Sept. 28   Litho.   Perf. 14

755	A163	20p shown	.20	.20
756	A163	65p Satellites orbiting earth	.20	.20
757	A163	80p Satellite	.20	.20
758	A163	4ce Satellite, earth	1.40	1.40
		Nos. 755-758 (4)	2.00	2.00

Souvenir Sheet

758A		Sheet of 4	1.75	1.75
b.	A163	25p like #755	.20	.20
c.	A163	50p like #756	.20	.20
d.	A163	1ce like #757	.20	.20
e.	A163	3ce like #758	.75	.75

Earth Satellite Station commission.

Common Design Types pictured following the introduction.

Royal Wedding Issue
Common Design Type

1981   Litho.   Perf. 14

759	CD331a	20p Couple	.20	.20
759A	CD331a	65p like 20p	.20	.20
760	CD331a	80p Charles	.20	.20
760A	CD331a	1ce like 80p	.20	.20
760B	CD331a	3ce like 4ce	.50	.50
761	CD331a	4ce Royal yacht Britannia	.60	.60
		Nos. 759-761 (6)	1.90	1.90

Souvenir Sheet

762　CD331　7ce St. Paul's Cathedral　1.00 1.00

Nos. 759-761 each printed se-tenant with label showing heraldic design.
Issued: 20p, 80p, 4ce, 7ce, 7/8; 65p, 1ce, 3ce, 9/16.
For surcharges see Nos. 859, 866, 871, 880, 1168-1169, 1195-1197.

1981, Sept. 16　　**Litho.**　　**Perf. 14**
763　CD331　2ce like #4ce　.75　.75
764　CD331　5ce like 20p　1.75　1.75
　a.　Bklt. pane, 2 each #763-764　5.00　5.00

Nos. 763-764 issued only in booklets.

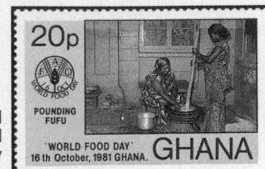

World Food Day A164

1981, Oct. 16　　**Litho.**　　**Perf. 14**
765　A164　20p Women pounding fufu　.20　.20
766　A164　65p Plucking cocoa　.30　.30
767　A164　80p Preparing banku　.45　.45
768　A164　2ce Processing garri　.90　.90
　　Nos. 765-768 (4)　1.85　1.85

Souvenir Sheet

769　　　Sheet of 4　1.75　1.75
　a.　A164　25p like #765　.20　.20
　b.　A164　50p like #766　.20　.20
　c.　A164　1ce like #767　.35　.35
　d.　A164　3ce like #768　1.00　1.00

Angelic Musicians Play for Mary and Child, by Aachener Altares (1480-1520) A165

Christmas (Paintings): 15p, The Betrothal of St. Catherine of Alexandria, by Lucas Cranach (1472-1553). 65p, Child Jesus Embracing His Mother, by Gabriel Metsu (1629-1667). 80p, Virgin and Child, by Fra Filippo Lippi (1406-1469). $2, The Virgin with Infant Jesus, by Barnaba da Modena (1361-1383). $4, The Immaculate Conception, by Bartolome Murillo (1618-1682). $6, Virgin and Child, by Hans Memling (1430-1494).

1981, Nov. 26　　　　　　**Perf. 14**
770　A165　15p multicolored　.20　.20
771　A165　20p multicolored　.20　.20
772　A165　65p multicolored　.20　.20
773　A165　80p multicolored　.20　.20
774　A165　$2 multicolored　.65　.65
775　A165　$4 multicolored　.95　.95
　　Nos. 770-775 (6)　2.40　2.40

Souvenir Sheet

776　A165　$6 multicolored　1.75　1.75

Intl. Year of the Disabled A166

1982, Feb. 8　　**Litho.**　　**Perf. 14**
777　A166　20p Blind man　.20　.20
778　A166　65p Woman, crutch　.35　.35
779　A166　80p Girl reading Braille　.45　.45
780　A166　4ce Couple　1.80　1.80
　　Nos. 777-780 (4)　2.80　2.80

Souvenir Sheet

781　A166　6ce Group　2.50　2.50

Clawless Otter — A167

1982, Feb. 22
782　A167　20p shown　.20　.20
783　A167　65p Bushbuck　.55　.55
784　A167　80p Aardvark　.65　.65
785　A167　1ce Scarlet bell tree　.95　.95
786　A167　2ce Glory lilies　1.75　1.75
787　A167　4ce Blue peas　3.50　3.50
　　Nos. 782-787 (6)　7.60　7.60

Souvenir Sheet

788　A167　5ce Chimpanzees　3.50　3.50

Blue-spot Commodore A168

1982, Apr. 27　　**Litho.**　　**Perf. 14**
789　A168　20p shown　.90　.90
790　A168　65p Emperor swallowtail　1.50　1.50
791　A168　2ce Orange admiral　2.75　2.75
792　A168　4ce Giant charaxes　4.50　4.50
　　Nos. 789-792 (4)　9.65　9.65

Souvenir Sheet

Perf. 14½
793　　　Sheet of 4　10.00　10.00
　a.　A168　25p like #789　.75　.75
　b.　A168　50p like #790　1.25　1.25
　c.　A168　1ce like #791　2.00　2.00
　d.　A168　3ce like #792　5.00　5.00

Scouting Year A169

1982, June 1　　**Litho.**　　**Perf. 15**
794　A169　20p Tree planting　.20　.20
795　A169　65p Camping　.85　.85
796　A169　80p Sailing　1.10　1.10
797　A169　3ce Watching elephant　2.75　2.75
　　Nos. 794-797 (4)　4.90　4.90

Souvenir Sheet

798　A169　5ce Baden-Powell, vert.　5.00　5.00

For surcharges see Nos. 867, 870, 875, 877.

Kpong Hydroelectric Dam Opening — A170

1982, June 28　　**Litho.**　　**Perf. 14**
799　A170　20p Cranes, lifts　.55　.20
800　A170　65p Construction　1.10　.55
801　A170　80p Turbines　1.50　1.50
802　A170　2ce Aerial view　3.25　3.25
　　Nos. 799-802 (4)　6.40　5.50

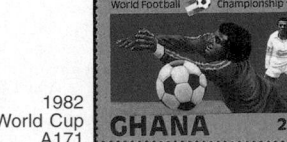

1982 World Cup A171

Perf. 15, 14½x15 (30p, No. 807, 1ce, 3ce)

1982, July 19　　　　　　**Litho.**
803　A171　20p multi　.20　.20
804　A171　30p multi, like 20p　.30　.30
805　A171　65p multi　.90　.90
806　A171　80p multi, like 65p　1.10　1.10
807　A171　80p multi, diff.　.65　.65
808　A171　1ce multi, like #807　.80　.80
809　A171　3ce multi　1.90　1.90
810　A171　4ce multi, like 3ce　2.75　2.75
　　Nos. 803-810 (8)　8.60　8.60

Souvenir Sheet

811　A171　6ce multi　2.25　2.25

Nos. 804, 806, 808-809 in sheets of 5 plus label.
For overprints & surcharges see #826-834, 861-862, 864-865, 868-869, 872-873, 878-879, 912-917.

TB Bacillus Centenary A172

1982, Aug. 9　　　　　　**Perf. 14**
812　A172　20p Child immunization　.55　.55
813　A172　65p Koch, Berlin　1.50　1.50
814　A172　80p Koch, Africa　1.90　1.90
815　A172　1ce Looking through microscope　2.25　2.25
816　A172　2ce Koch, 1905 Nobel medal　3.75　3.75
　　Nos. 812-816 (5)　9.95　9.95

Christmas — A173

1982, Dec.　　**Litho.**　　**Perf. 15**
817　A173　15p Nativity　.20　.20
818　A173　20p Holy Family　.20　.20
819　A173　65p Three Kings　.35　.35
820　A173　4ce Angel with banner　1.25　1.25
　　Nos. 817-820 (4)　2.00　2.00

Souvenir Sheet

821　A173　6ce Nativity, diff.　2.25　2.25

A173a

1983, Mar. 10　　**Litho.**　　**Perf. 15**
822　A173a　20p Flags　.30　.30
823　A173a　55p Aerial view　.55　.55
824　A173a　80p Minerals　1.25　1.25
825　A173a　3ce Eagle　1.90　1.90
　　Nos. 822-825 (4)　4.00　4.00

Commonwealth Day. For surcharges see Nos. 860, 863, 874, 876.

Nos. 803-811 Overprinted in Gold:
"WINNER ITALY / 3-1"

1983, June　　　　　　**Litho.**
826　A171　20p multicolored　.20　.20
827　A171　30p multicolored　.20　.20
828　A171　65p multicolored　.40　.40
829　A171　80p multi, on #806　.40　.40
830　A171　80p multi, on #807　1.25　1.25
831　A171　1ce multicolored　1.40　1.40
832　A171　3ce multicolored　3.00　3.00
833　A171　4ce multicolored　2.75　2.75
　　Nos. 826-833 (8)　9.60　9.60

Souvenir Sheet

834　A171　6ce multicolored　4.00　4.00

Italy's victory in 1982 World Cup.
For surcharges see Nos. 862, 865, 869, 873, 879, 913, 915, 917.

World Communications Year — A173b

1983, Dec. 13　　**Litho.**　　**Perf. 14**
835　A173b　1ce shown　.30　.30
836　A173b　1.40ce Dish antenna　.30　.30
837　A173b　2.30ce Cable ship　.60　.60
838　A173b　3ce Switchboard　.80　.80
839　A173b　5ce Control tower　1.25　1.25
　　Nos. 835-839 (5)　3.25　3.25

Souvenir Sheet

840　A173b　6ce Satellite　.90　.90

For surcharges see Nos. 1107-1111.

Coastal Marine Mammals A173c

1983, Nov. 15　　**Litho.**　　**Perf. 15**
841　A173c　1ce Short fin pilot whale　2.25　2.25
842　A173c　1.40ce Gray dolphin　2.40　2.40
843　A173c　2.30ce False killer whale　2.75　2.75
844　A173c　3ce Spinner dolphin　3.50　3.50
845　A173c　5ce Atlantic humpback dolphin　4.25　4.25
　　Nos. 841-845 (5)　15.15　15.15

Souvenir Sheet

846　A173c　6ce White Alantic humpback dolphin　6.50　6.50

For surcharges see Nos. 918-920.

A174

Christmas A175

1983, Dec. 28　**Perf. 14x13½, 14½x14**
852　A174　70p Children receiving gifts　.20　.20
853　A175　1ce Nativity　.20　.20
854　A175　1.40ce Children playing　.45　.45
855　A175　2.30ce Family praying　.55　.55
856　A174　3ce Bongo drums, festivities　.65　.65
　　Nos. 852-856 (5)　2.05　2.05

Souvenir Sheet

857　A175　6ce like #855　.55　.55

Surcharges

Many inverts, doubles, etc., exist on the surcharged stamps that follow.

Previous Issues Surcharged
1984, Feb. 8
858　A74　1ce on 20np #296　.40　.25
859　CD331　1ce on 20p #759　5.00　4.25
860　A173a　1ce on 20p #822　.40　.25
861　A171　1ce on 20p #803　.60　.40

862	A171	1ce on 20p #826	.40	.25
863	A173a	9ce on 55p #823	.90	.65
864	A171	9ce on 65p #805	1.60	1.00
865	A171	9ce on 65p #828	.90	.65
866	CD331	9ce on 80p #760	6.25	5.50
867	A169	10ce on 20p #794	.90	.65
868	A171	10ce on 80p #806	1.60	1.00
869	A171	10ce on 80p #830	.90	.65
870	A169	20ce on 8p #795	1.75	1.25
871	CD331	20ce on 4ce #761	8.00	8.75
872	A171	20ce on 4ce #810	3.50	2.40
873	A171	20ce on 4ce #833	1.75	1.25
874	A173a	30ce on 80p #824	3.50	2.40
875	A169	30ce on 3ce #797	3.50	2.40
876	A173a	50ce on 3ce #825	6.00	4.00
		Nos. 858-876 (19)	47.85	37.95

Souvenir Sheets

877	A169	60ce on 5ce #798	2.50	4.75
878	A171	60ce on 6ce #811	2.50	3.25
879	A171	60ce on 6ce #834	2.50	4.75
880	CD331	60ce on 7ce #762	2.50	2.50

For surcharges on this issue see #1092A-1092C.

Namibia Day
A176

Scorpion Weight
A177

1984, Jan. 26 — Perf. 14

881	A176	50p Soldiers raising rifles	.20	.20
882	A176	1ce Soldiers, tank	.20	.20
883	A176	1.40ce Machete cutting chains	.20	.20
884	A176	2.30ce Namibian woman	.20	.20
885	A176	3ce Soldiers in combat	.20	.20
		Nos. 881-885 (5)	1.00	1.00

1983, Dec. 12 — Litho. — Perf. 14

886	A177	5p Hemichramis fasciatus, horiz.	.35	.20
887	A177	10p Hemichramis fasciatus, map, horiz.	.60	.20
888	A177	20p Haemanthus rupestris	.70	.20
889	A177	50p Mounted warrior (gold statuette)	.70	.30
890	A177	1ce shown	.80	.20
891	A177	2ce Jet, horiz.	.80	.30
892	A177	3ce Cercocebus torquatus	2.50	.30
893	A177	4ce Galagoides demidovii	.70	.40
894	A177	5ce Kaempheria nigerica	.80	.45
895	A177	10ce Camaroptera brevicaudata	1.00	1.00
		Nos. 886-895 (10)	8.95	3.55

For surcharges see Nos. 1089A-1090, 1092, 1092D, 1093A-1094A, 1096-1096A.

Easter — A178

Local Flowers — A179

1984, Apr. — Litho. — Perf. 14½

906	A178	1ce Cross, crown of thorns	.20	.20
907	A178	1.40ce Jesus praying	.20	.20
908	A178	2.30ce Jesus going to Jerusalem	.20	.20
909	A178	3ce Jesus entering Jerusalem	.20	.20
910	A178	50ce Jesus with Disciples	1.25	2.50
		Nos. 906-910 (5)	2.05	3.30

Souvenir Sheet

911	A178	60ce Cross, crown of thorns	4.00	4.00

Nos. 804, 806, 809, 827, 829, 832 Surcharged

1984, Feb. 8 — Litho.

912	A171	9ce on 3ce #809	.85	.85
913	A171	9ce on 3ce #832	.55	.55
914	A171	10ce on 30p #804	.85	.85
915	A171	10ce on 30p #827	.55	.55
916	A171	20ce on 80p #806	2.00	2.00
917	A171	20ce on 80p #829	1.00	1.00
		Nos. 912-917 (6)	5.80	5.80

Nos. 844-846 Surcharged and Overprinted in Red with UPU Emblem and: "19th U.P.U. CONGRESS-HAMBURG"

1984 — Litho. — Perf. 14½

918	A173c	10ce on 3ce multi	.55	.55
919	A173c	50ce on 5ce multi	2.75	2.75

Souvenir Sheet

920	A173c	60ce on 6ce multi	3.25	3.25

1984, July — Litho. — Perf. 14

921	A179	1ce Amorphophallus johnsonii	.20	.20
922	A179	1.40ce Pancratium trianthum	.20	.20
923	A179	2.30ce Eulophia cucullata	.20	.20
924	A179	3ce Amorphophallus abyssinicus	.20	.20
925	A179	50ce Chlorophytum togoense	3.25	4.00
		Nos. 921-925 (5)	4.05	4.80

Souvenir Sheet

926	A179	60ce like 1ce	3.25	3.25

Endangered Species — A180

1984, Aug. — Perf. 14

927	A180	1ce Bongo	.70	.70
928	A180	2.30ce Males locking horns	1.50	1.50
929	A180	3ce Family	1.75	1.75
930	A180	20ce Herd	5.00	5.00
		Nos. 927-930 (4)	8.95	8.95

Souvenir Sheets

931	A180	70ce Kob	7.00	7.00
932	A180	70ce Bushbuck	7.00	7.00

Nos. 927-930 exist imperf. Value: set, $21.

1984 Summer Olympics — A181

Native Dancers — A182

1984, Aug. — Perf. 15

933	A181	1ce Running	.20	.20
934	A181	1.40ce Boxing	.20	.20
935	A181	2.30ce Field hockey	.20	.20
936	A181	3ce Hurdles	.20	.20
937	A181	50ce Rhythmic gymnastics	3.50	4.00
		Nos. 933-937 (5)	4.30	4.80

Souvenir Sheet

938	A181	70ce Soccer	2.75	2.75

For surcharges see #945-950, 1112-1116.

1984, Sept. — Perf. 14

939	A182	1ce Dipo	.30	.20
940	A182	1.40ce Adowa	.30	.20
941	A182	2.30ce Agbadza	.30	.20
942	A182	3ce Damba	.30	.20
943	A182	50ce Dipo, diff.	2.00	3.00
		Nos. 939-943 (5)	3.20	3.80

Souvenir Sheet

944	A182	70ce Mandolin player	4.00	4.00

Nos. 933-938 Ovptd. in Gold with Winner and Country

1984, Dec. 3 — Perf. 15

945	A181	1ce Valerie Brisco-Hooks, US	.20	.20
946	A181	1.40ce US winners	.20	.20
947	A181	2.30ce Pakistan, (field hockey)	.20	.20
948	A181	3ce Edwin Moses, US	.20	.20
949	A181	50ce Lauri Fung, Canada	2.25	2.25
		Nos. 945-949 (5)	3.05	3.05

Souvenir Sheet

950	A181	70ce France	2.75	2.75

Christmas
A183

Queen Mother, 85th Birthday
A184

1984, Nov. 19 — Perf. 12x12½

951	A183	70p Adoration of the Magi	.20	.20
952	A183	1ce Chorus of angels	.20	.20
953	A183	1.40ce Adoration of the shepherds	.20	.20
954	A183	2.30ce Flight into Egypt	.20	.20
955	A183	3ce King holding Christ	.20	.20
956	A183	50ce Adoration of the angels	2.00	2.00
		Nos. 951-956 (6)	3.00	3.00

Souvenir Sheet

957	A183	70ce like 70p	3.00	3.00

1985 — Perf. 14

Portraits.

958	A184	5ce multicolored	.20	.20
959	A184	8ce like 5ce	.20	.20
960	A184	12ce multicolored	.25	.25
961	A184	20ce like 12ce	.35	.35
962	A184	70ce multicolored	1.10	1.10
963	A184	100ce like 70ce	1.40	1.40
		Nos. 958-963 (6)	3.50	3.50

Souvenir Sheet

964	A184	110ce multicolored	3.50	3.50

Issue dates: 5ce, 12ce, 100ce, 110ce, July 29. 8ce, 20ce, 70ce, Dec.
Nos. 959, 961-962 issued in sheets of 5 + label.
For surcharges see Nos. 1117-1119A, 1198-1200, 1311-1317.

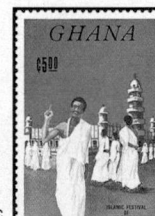

Id-El-Fitr Islamic Festival — A185

1985, Aug. 1

965	A185	5ce Entering mosque	.20	.20
966	A185	8ce Prayer rug	.40	.40
967	A185	12ce Mosque	.65	.65
968	A185	18ce Public Koran reading	1.00	1.00
969	A185	50ce Map, Banda Nkwanta Mosque	2.75	2.75
		Nos. 965-969 (5)	5.00	5.00

Intl. Youth Year — A186

1985, Aug. 9

970	A186	5ce Street clean-up	.20	.20
971	A186	8ce Tree planting	.20	.20
972	A186	12ce Food production	.30	.30
973	A186	100ce Education	1.50	2.50
		Nos. 970-973 (4)	2.20	3.20

Souvenir Sheet

974	A186	110ce like 8ce	2.25	2.25

Motorcycle Centenary — A187

1985, Sept. 9

975	A187	5ce 1984 Honda Interceptor	.60	.30
976	A187	8ce 1938 DKW	.80	.40
977	A187	12ce 1923 BMW R 32	1.25	.85
978	A187	100ce 1900 NSU	7.00	7.00
		Nos. 975-978 (4)	9.65	8.55

Souvenir Sheet

979	A187	110ce 1973 Zundapp	6.00	6.00

Audubon Birth Bicent. — A188

1985, Oct. 16

980	A188	5ce York-tailed flycatcher	1.50	1.50
981	A188	8ce Barred owl	2.50	2.50
982	A188	12ce Black-throated mango	2.50	2.50
983	A188	100ce White-crowned pigeon	6.00	6.00
		Nos. 980-983 (4)	12.50	12.50

Souvenir Sheet

984	A188	110ce Downy woodpecker	8.50	8.50

For surcharges see Nos. 1124-1127.

UN, 40th Anniv.
A189

1985, Oct. 24 — Perf. 14½x14

985	A189	5ce UN building	.20	.20
986	A189	8ce UN building, diff.	.20	.20
987	A189	12ce Dove	.20	.30
988	A189	18ce General Assembly	.30	.40
989	A189	100ce Flags	2.00	2.25
		Nos. 985-989 (5)	2.90	3.35

Souvenir Sheet

990	A189	110ce UN No. 36	2.00	2.00

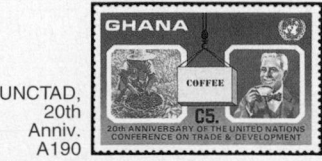

UNCTAD, 20th Anniv.
A190

1985, Nov. 4 — *Perf. 14*
991	A190	5ce	Coffee	.20	.20
992	A190	8ce	Cocoa	.20	.20
993	A190	12ce	Lumber	.30	.30
994	A190	18ce	Bauxite mining	1.25	1.25
995	A190	100ce	Gold mining	7.00	7.00
		Nos. 991-995 (5)		8.95	8.95

Souvenir Sheet
Perf. 15x14
996	A190	110ce	Produce	3.00	3.00

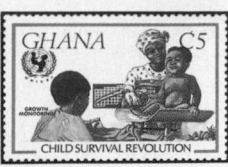

UN Child Survival Campaign A191

1985, Dec. 16 — *Perf. 14*
997	A191	5ce	Weighing	.20	.20
998	A191	8ce	Oral rehydration therapy	.35	.35
999	A191	12ce	Breast-feeding	.60	.60
1000	A191	100ce	Immunization	4.25	4.25
		Nos. 997-1000 (4)		5.40	5.40

Souvenir Sheet
Perf. 15x14
1001	A191	110ce	Emblem, pinwheel	2.25	2.25

AMERIPEX '86 — A192

Perf. 14½x14, 14x14½
1986, Oct. 27 — *Litho.*
1002	A192	5ce	Young collectors	.30	.30
1003	A192	25ce	Earth, jet	.85	.85
1004	A192	100ce	Stewardess, vert.	2.75	2.75
		Nos. 1002-1004 (3)		3.90	3.90

Souvenir Sheet
1005	A192	150ce	Young collectors, diff.	4.00	4.00

INTER-TOURISM '86, Nov. 8-17 — A193

Designs: 5ce, Kejetia Roundabout, Kumasi. 15ce, Fort St. Jago, Elmina. 25ce, Warriors. 100ce, Chief, retinue. 150ce, Elephants.

1986, Nov. 10 — *Perf. 14*
1006	A193	5ce	multi	.25	.25
1007	A193	15ce	multi	.50	.50
1008	A193	25ce	multi	.75	.75
1009	A193	100ce	multi	3.00	3.00
		Nos. 1006-1009 (4)		4.50	4.50

Souvenir Sheet
Perf. 15x14
1010	A193	150ce	multi	5.50	5.50

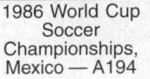

1986 World Cup Soccer Championships, Mexico — A194

Fertility Dolls — A195

Various soccer plays.

1987, Jan. 16 — *Litho.* — *Perf. 14x14½*
1011	A194	5ce	multi	.35	.35
1012	A194	15ce	multi	.45	.45
1013	A194	25ce	multi	.65	.65
1014	A194	100ce	multi	2.25	2.25
		Nos. 1011-1014 (4)		3.70	3.70

Souvenir Sheet
1015	A194	150ce	multi	2.75	2.75

For surcharges see Nos. 1120-1123D.

1987, Jan. 22

Various dolls.
1016	A195	5ce	multi	.30	.30
1017	A195	15ce	multi	.30	.30
1018	A195	25ce	multi	.50	.50
1019	A195	100ce	multi	2.00	2.00
		Nos. 1016-1019 (4)		3.10	3.10

Souvenir Sheet
1020	A195	150ce	like #1016	2.75	2.75

Intl. Peace Year A196

Perf. 14½x14, 14x14½
1987, Mar. 2 — *Litho.*
1021	A196	5ce	Children playing	.30	.30
1022	A196	25ce	Plow	.85	.85
1023	A196	100ce	Earth, doves, vert.	3.25	3.25
		Nos. 1021-1023 (3)		4.40	4.40

Souvenir Sheet
1024	A196	150ce	Dove, plow, vert.	3.00	3.00

GIFEX '87 A197

1987, Mar. 10 — *Perf. 14*
1025	A197	5ce	Lumber, house construction	.20	.20
1026	A197	15ce	Furniture	.20	.20
1027	A197	25ce	Tree stumps	.40	.40
1028	A197	200ce	Logs, art objects	2.50	2.50
		Nos. 1025-1028 (4)		3.30	3.30

Ghana Intl. Forestry Exposition, Accra.

A198

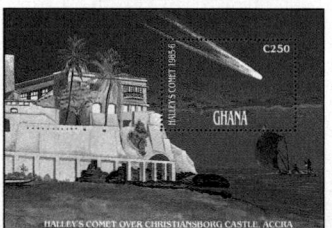

Halley's Comet — A199

Designs: 5ce, Mikhail Vasilyevich Lomonosov (1711-1765), Russian scientist, and the Chamber of Curiosities. 25ce, Landing of the US probe Surveyor on the Moon's surface, 1966. 200ce, Wedgwood memorial to Sir Isaac Newton, the appearance of Halley's Comet in 1790 and US astronauts Armstrong and Aldrin landing Eagle on the Moon in 1969. 250ce, Comet over Fishermen near Christianborg Castle,

---

1987, Apr. 8 — *Perf. 14½x14*
1029	A198	5ce	multi	.30	.20
1030	A198	25ce	multi	.90	.90
1031	A198	200ce	multi	4.75	4.75
		Nos. 1029-1031 (3)		5.95	5.85

Souvenir Sheet
1032	A199	250ce	multi	5.50	5.50

For surcharges see Nos. 1128-1131,

Solidarity with South Africans for Abolition of Apartheid — A200

1987, May 18 — *Perf. 14x14½*
1033	A200	5ce	Liberated prisoner	.20	.20
1034	A200	15ce	Miner, gold ingots	.35	.35
1035	A200	25ce	Zulu warrior	.35	.35
1036	A200	100ce	Nelson Mandela, shackles	1.90	1.90
		Nos. 1033-1036 (4)		2.80	2.80

Souvenir Sheet
1037	A200	150ce	Mandela, map, star	2.75	2.75

Traditional Musical Instruments — A201

1987, July 13 — *Perf. 14½x14*
1038	A201	5ce	Horns	.20	.20
1039	A201	15ce	Xylophone	.30	.30
1040	A201	25ce	String instruments	.55	.55
1041	A201	100ce	Drums	1.40	1.40
		Nos. 1038-1041 (4)		2.45	2.45

Souvenir Sheet
1042	A201	200ce	Percussion instruments	3.25	3.25

Intl. Year of Shelter for the Homeless A202

1987, Sept. 21 — *Litho.* — *Perf. 14*
1043	A202	5ce	Public well	.20	.20
1044	A202	15ce	Home construction	.30	.30
1045	A202	25ce	Village, bridge, car	.45	.45
1046	A202	100ce	Village, electric power lines	1.50	1.50
		Nos. 1043-1046 (4)		2.45	2.45

Festivals — A203

Designs: Preparation of Kpokpoi, Homowo Festival. 15ce, Hunters with catch, Aboakyir Festival. 25ce, Chief dancing, Odwira Festival. 100ce, Chief held aloft in a palanquin, Yam Festival.

1988, Jan. 6 — *Litho.* — *Perf. 15*
1047	A203	5ce	multi	.20	.20
1048	A203	15ce	multi	.25	.25
1049	A203	25ce	multi	.40	.40
1050	A203	100ce	multi	1.40	1.40
		Nos. 1047-1050 (4)		2.25	2.25

December 31, 1981 Revolution — A203a

1988, Jan. 26 — *Litho.* — *Perf. 13*
1050A	A203a	5ce	Ports	1.75	.50
1050B	A203a	15ce	Railways	15.00	3.00
1050C	A203a	25ce	Cocoa industry	3.00	.75
1050D	A203a	100ce	Mining industry	17.50	17.50
		Nos. 1050A-1050D (4)		37.25	21.75

UN Universal Immunization Campaign — A204

Child Survival Campaign emblem and: 5ce, Nurse immunizing woman. 15ce, Child receiving intramuscular vaccine. 25ce, Youth crippled by polio. 100ce, Nurse handing infant to mother.

1988, Feb. 1 — *Perf. 15*
1051	A204	5ce	multi	.20	.20
1052	A204	15ce	multi	.25	.25
1053	A204	25ce	multi	.45	.45
1054	A204	100ce	multi	1.10	1.10
		Nos. 1051-1054 (4)		2.00	2.00

Intl. Fund for Agricultural Development — A204a

1988, Apr. 14 — *Perf. 13*
1054A	A204a	5ce	Fishing	1.60	1.60
1054B	A204a	15ce	Harvesting	2.50	2.50
1054C	A204a	25ce	Cattle	4.25	4.25
1054D	A204a	100ce	Granary	9.50	9.50
		Nos. 1054A-1054D (4)		17.85	17.85

Tribal Costumes — A205

1988, May 9 — *Litho.* — *Perf. 14*
1055	A205	5ce	Akwadjan	.20	.20
1056	A205	25ce	Banaa	.60	.60
1057	A205	250ce	Agwasen	2.75	2.75
		Nos. 1055-1057 (3)		3.55	3.55

1988 Summer Olympics, Seoul A206

1988, Oct. 10
1058	A206	20ce	Boxing	.20	.20
1059	A206	60ce	Running	.65	.65
1060	A206	80ce	Discus	.90	.90

1061	A206	100ce	Javelin	1.10	1.10
1062	A206	350ce	Weight lifting	3.75	3.75
		Nos. 1058-1062 (5)		6.60	6.60

Souvenir Sheet

| 1063 | A206 | 500ce like 80ce | 6.00 | 6.00 |

For overprints see Nos. 1084-1089.

Intl. Red Cross, 125th Anniv. — A207

1988, Dec. 14   Litho.   Perf. 14

1064	A207	20ce	Nutrition	.60	.60
1065	A207	50ce	Voluntary service	1.25	1.25
1066	A207	60ce	Disaster relief (flood)	1.50	1.50
1067	A207	200ce	Medical assistance	4.00	4.00
		Nos. 1064-1067 (4)		7.35	7.35

Christmas Symbolism — A208

1988, Dec. 19   Litho.   Perf. 14

1068	A208	20ce	shown	.20	.20
1069	A208	60ce	Mother and child, vert.	.55	.55
1070	A208	80ce	Mother, child, tree, vert.	.65	.65
1071	A208	100ce	Magi follow star	.85	.85
1072	A208	350ce	Abstract, diff., vert.	3.25	3.25
		Nos. 1068-1072 (5)		5.50	5.50

Souvenir Sheet

| 1073 | A208 | 500ce | Mother and child, diff., vert. | 4.00 | 4.00 |

Organization of African Unity, 25th Anniv. — A209

Titian, 500th Birth Anniv. (in 1988) — A210

1989, Jan. 3

1074	A209	20ce	Solidarity	.20	.20
1075	A209	50ce	OAU, Addis Ababa	.20	.20
1076	A209	60ce	Haile Selassie, Ethiopia	.45	.45
1077	A209	200ce	Kwame Nkrumah, Ghana	.70	.70
		Nos. 1074-1077 (4)		1.55	1.55

"Selassie" is spelled incorrectly on No. 1076. Nos. 1076-1077 horiz.

1989, Jan. 16

1078	A210	20ce	Amor, 1515	.50	.20
1079	A210	60ce	The Appeal	.85	.85
1080	A210	80ce	Bacchus and Ariadne, c. 1523	1.25	1.25
1081	A210	100ce	Portrait of a Musician, c. 1518	1.50	1.50
1082	A210	350ce	Philip II Seated	4.00	4.00
		Nos. 1078-1082 (5)		8.10	7.80

Souvenir Sheet

| 1083 | A210 | 500ce | Portrait of a Gentleman, c. 1550 | 4.00 | 4.00 |

Nos. 1058-1063 Ovptd. with Winners' Names

1989, Jan. 23

1084	A206	20ce	"A. ZUELOW / DDR / 60 KG"	.45	.45
1085	A206	60ce	"G. BORDIN / ITALY / MARATHON"	.55	.55
1086	A206	80ce	"J. SCHULT / DDR"	.65	.65
1087	A206	100ce	"T. KORJUS / FINLAND"	.80	.80
1088	A206	350ce	"B. GUIDIKOV / BULGARIA / 75 KG"	2.00	2.00
		Nos. 1084-1088 (5)		4.45	4.45

Souvenir Sheet

| 1089 | A206 | 500ce multi | 4.25 | 4.25 |

1988 Summer Olympics, Seoul. Margin of No. 1089 ovptd. "GOLD / J. SCHULT DDR / SILVER / R. OUBARTAS USSR / BRONZE / R. DANNEBERG W. GERMANY."

Stamps of 1967-1984 Surcharged

1988-91

1089A	A177	20ce on 50p #889	.35	.30
1090	A177	20ce on 1ce #890	.35	.30
1091	A75	50ce on 10np #295	2.00	2.00
1092	A177	50ce on 10p #887	1.00	2.00
f.		50ce' on 10p Denomination below obliterator	—	—
1092A	A74	50ce on 1ce #858	6.00	5.00
1092B	A74	50ce on 1ce #858	10.00	10.00
1092C	A74	50ce on 1ce #858	10.00	10.00
1092D	A177	50ce on 1ce #890	6.00	.50
1092E	A73	60ce on 1np #286	6.00	.50
1093	A73	60ce on 4np #291	6.00	.50
1093A	A177	60ce on 3ce #892	1.00	.45
1094	A177	80ce on 5p #886	1.00	.45
1094A	A177	80ce on 5ce #894	10.00	10.00
1095	A74	100ce on 20np #296	10.00	10.00
1096	A177	100ce on 20p #888	1.00	1.00
1096A	A177	100ce on 3ce #892	2.00	2.00
1096B	A75	200ce on 6np #292	8.00	8.00

An additional 100ce surcharge exists in this set. The editors would like to examine it.

Surcharge has no decimal on No. 1092A, is vertical on No. 1092B and horizontal on No. 1092C.

No. 1090 also exists with 5mm spacing between block and $20.00.

Surcharge on No. 1093A has decimal point. Unauthorized surcharges exist.

Issued: Nos. 1089A, 1096B, 7/1/88; Nos. 1092A, 1092B, 1092D, 1092E, 1094A, 1096A, 1990; No. 1092C, 1991; others, 1989.

Minamoto-no-Yoritomo, by Fujiwara-no-Takanobu (1142-1205) — A211

Paintings: 50ce, Takami Senseki, by Watanabe Kazan (1793-1841). 60ce, Ikkyu Sojum, by Bokusai, Muromachi period. 75ce, Nakamura Kuranosuke, by Ogata Korin (1658-1716). 125ce, Portrait of a Lady, Kyoto branch of Kano school, Momoyama period. 150ce, Portrait of Zemmui, anonymous, 12th cent. 200ce, Ono no Komachi, the Poetess, by Hokusai. No. 1104, Kobo Daisi as a Child, anonymous, Kamakura period. No. 1105, Portrait of Kodai-no-Kimi, attributed to Fujiwara-no-Nobuzane, 12th cent. No. 1106, Portrait of Emperor Hanazono, by Fujiwara-no-Goshin, 14th cent.

1989, Aug. 21   Litho.   Perf. 13½x14

1097	A211	20ce	shown	.20	.20
1098	A211	50ce	multi	.45	.45
1099	A211	60ce	multi	.50	.50
1100	A211	75ce	multi	.70	.70
1101	A211	125ce	multi	1.10	1.10
1102	A211	150ce	multi	1.50	1.50
1103	A211	200ce	multi	1.90	1.90
1104	A211	500ce	multi	2.75	2.75
		Nos. 1097-1104 (8)		9.10	9.10

Souvenir Sheets

| 1105 | A211 | 500ce multi | 6.50 | 6.50 |
| 1106 | A211 | 500ce multi | 6.50 | 6.50 |

Hirohito (1901-1989) and enthronement of Akihito as emperor of Japan.

Nos. 835-838 and 840 Surcharged

1989, July 3   Litho.   Perf. 14

1107	A173b	60ce on 1ce	1.00	.60
1108	A173b	80ce on 1.40ce	1.25	.75
1109	A173b	200ce on 2.30ce	3.25	3.25
1110	A173b	300ce on 3ce	4.00	4.00
		Nos. 1107-1110 (4)		9.50	8.60

Souvenir Sheet

| 1111 | A173b | 500ce on 6ce | 7.50 | 7.50 |

Nos. 933-936 and 938 Surcharged

1989, July 3   Perf. 15

1112	A181	60ce on 1ce	.45	.45
1113	A181	80ce on 1.40ce	.65	.65
1114	A181	200ce on 2.30ce	1.60	1.60
1115	A181	300ce on 3ce	2.25	2.25
		Nos. 1112-1115 (4)		4.95	4.95

Souvenir Sheet

| 1116 | A181 | 600ce on 70ce | 4.50 | 4.50 |

Nos. 958, 960 and 963-964 Surcharged

1989, Nov. 20   Litho.   Perf. 14

1117	A184	80ce on 5ce #958	.65	.65
1118	A184	250ce on 12ce #960	2.10	2.10
1119	A184	300ce on 100ce #963	2.50	2.50
		Nos. 1117-1119 (3)		5.25	5.25

Souvenir Sheet

| 1119A | A184 | 500ce on 110ce #964 | 5.50 | 5.50 |

Nos. 1011-1013 and 1015 Surcharged

1989   Litho.   Perf. 14x14½

1120	A194	60ce on 5ce #1011	.60	.60
1121	A194	200ce on 15ce #1012	2.00	2.00
1122	A194	300ce on 25ce #1013	2.75	2.75
		Nos. 1120-1122 (3)		5.35	5.35

Souvenir Sheet

| 1123 | A194 | 600ce on 150ce #1015 | 7.50 | 7.50 |

Nos. 1120-1123 Surcharged

1989   Litho.   Perf. 14x14½

1123A	A194	60ce on 5ce	.90	.90
1123B	A194	200ce on 15ce	3.00	3.00
1123C	A194	300ce on 25ce	4.75	4.75
		Nos. 1123A-1123C (3)		8.65	8.65

Souvenir Sheet

| 1123D | A194 | 600ce on 150ce | 10.00 | 10.00 |

Nos. 980-982 and 984 Surcharged

1989, Nov. 20   Litho.   Perf. 14

1124	A188	80ce on 5ce #980	2.00	2.00
1125	A188	100ce on 8ce #981	3.50	3.50
1126	A188	300ce on 12ce #982	4.00	4.00
		Nos. 1124-1126 (3)		9.50	9.50

Souvenir Sheet

| 1127 | A188 | 500ce on 110ce #984 | 10.50 | 10.50 |

Nos. 1029-1032 Surcharged

1989, Nov. 20   Perf. 14½x14

1128	A198	60ce on 5ce #1029	1.00	1.00
a.		With comet logo	1.00	1.00
1129	A198	80ce on 25ce #1030	1.25	1.25
a.		With comet logo	1.25	1.25

1130	A198	500ce on 200ce #1031	4.75	4.75
a.		With comet logo	4.75	4.75
		Nos. 1128-1130 (3)		7.00	7.00
		Nos. 1128a-1130a (3)		7.00	7.00

Souvenir Sheet

| 1131 | A199 | 750ce on 250ce #1032 | 6.50 | 6.50 |
| a. | | With comet logo | 6.50 | 6.50 |

PHILEXFRANCE '89, French Revolution Bicent. — A212

Emblems, French arms and flags: 20ce, Tube-mounted field carriage, flag of 1643 to 1790. 60ce, Infantryman, flag of 1789. 80ce, Handgun, flag of 1789, diff. 350ce, Musket, flag of 1794 to 1814 and 1848 to present. 600ce, Map of Paris.

1989, Sept. 22   Litho.   Perf. 14

1132	A212	20ce	shown	.75	.75
1133	A212	60ce	multi	1.40	1.40
1134	A212	80ce	multi	1.75	1.75
1135	A212	350ce	multi	4.50	4.50
		Nos. 1132-1135 (4)		8.40	8.40

Souvenir Sheet

| 1136 | A212 | 600ce multi | 5.00 | 5.00 |

Mushrooms

A213   A214

1989, Oct. 2   Litho.   Perf. 14

1137	A213	20ce	Collybia	.20	.20
1138	A213	50ce	Lawyer's wig	.40	.40
1139	A214	60ce	Xerocomus subtomentosus	.50	.50
1140	A213	80ce	Wood belwits	.70	.70
1141	A214	150ce	Suillus placidus	1.40	1.40
1142	A214	200ce	Lepista nuda	1.75	1.75
1143	A213	300ce	Fairy rings	2.50	2.50
1144	A213	500ce	Field mushroom	4.25	4.25
		Nos. 1137-1144 (8)		11.70	11.70

Souvenir Sheets

| 1145 | A213 | 600ce | Three Amanita species | 5.00 | 5.00 |
| 1146 | A214 | 600ce | Three Boletus species | 5.00 | 5.00 |

Souvenir Sheet

A Midsummer Night's Dream, by Shakespeare — A215

Designs: a, "The course of true love never did run smooth." b, "Love looks not with the eye but with the mind." c, "Nature here shows art." d, "Things growing are not ripe till their season." e, "He is defiled that draws a sword on thee." f, "It is not enough to speak but to speak true." g, "Thou art wise as thou art beautiful." h, Leopard behind trees. i, Theseus. j, Boy holding flower, trees. k, Oberon and Titania among trees. l, Bottom wearing head of a jackass. m, Bottom's leg, leopard behind trees. n, Hippolyta. o, Leopard, tree trunk. p, Tree trunk, foliage, lower portion of Theseus's robe. q, Wisps of fragrance, clouds, hills, foliage. r, Wisps of fragrance, flowering plants. s, Flowering plants. t, Lion, foliage. u, Lion's mane, foliage.

1989, Oct. 9   Perf. 13½x13
1147	A215	Sheet of 21	18.00	18.00
a.-u.		40ce any single	.80	.80

425th Birth anniv. of William Shakespeare, playwright.

Birds
A216

1989, Oct. 16   Perf. 14
1148	A216	20ce	Spermestes cuculatus	.40	.20
1149	A216	50ce	Motacilla aguimp	.60	.35
1150	A216	60ce	Halcyon malimbicus	1.90	1.90
1151	A216	80ce	Ispidina picta	3.25	3.25
1152	A216	150ce	Striped king-fisher	2.50	2.50
1153	A216	200ce	Shikra	2.25	2.25
1154	A216	300ce	Gray parrot	3.25	3.25
1155	A216	500ce	Black kite	4.50	4.50
		Nos. 1148-1155 (8)		18.65	18.20

Souvenir Sheets
1156	A216	600ce	Four birds	9.00	9.00
1157	A216	600ce	Three birds	9.00	9.00

Nos. 1152-1156 vert.

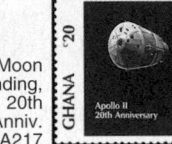

1st Moon Landing, 20th Anniv. A217

Highlights of the Apollo 11 mission.

1989, Nov. 6   Perf. 14
1158	A217	20ce	Columbia	.20	.20
1159	A217	80ce	Footprint	.75	.75
1160	A217	200ce	Aldrin on Moon	1.75	1.75
1161	A217	300ce	Splashdown	2.75	2.75
		Nos. 1158-1161 (4)		5.45	5.45

Souvenir Sheets
1162	A217	500ce	Liftoff, vert.	4.50	4.50
1163	A217	500ce	Earth, vert.	4.50	4.50

World Environment Day — A218

1989, Nov. 20   Litho.   Perf. 14
1164	A218	20ce	Desertifica-tion	.25	.25
1165	A218	60ce	Bush fires	.65	.65
1166	A218	400ce	Industrial pollution	3.75	3.75
1167	A218	500ce	Soil erosion	5.25	5.25
		Nos. 1164-1167 (4)		9.90	9.90

Nos. 760 and 761 Surcharged

1989, Nov. 20   Litho.   Perf. 14
1168	CD331	100ce on 80p	1.00	1.00
1169	CD331	500ce on 4ce	5.00	5.00

French Revolution, Bicent. — A219

Designs: 20ce, Storming of the Bastille, vert. 60ce, Declaration of Human Rights and Citizenship, vert. 80ce, Storming of the Bastille, diff. 200ce, Departure of the Volunteers in 1792, high relief on the Arc de Triomphe, 1833-35, by Francis Rude. 350ce, Planting the Liberty Tree.

Perf. 14x13½, 13½x14
1989, Sept. 22
1170	A219	20ce	multicolored	.55	.55
1171	A219	60ce	multicolored	1.25	1.25
1172	A219	80ce	multicolored	1.50	1.50
1173	A219	200ce	multicolored	2.75	2.75
1174	A219	350ce	multicolored	4.00	4.00
		Nos. 1170-1174 (5)		10.05	10.05

Butterflies
A220

1990, Feb. 15   Litho.   Perf. 14
1175	A220	20ce	Bebearia arcadius	.50	.50
1176	A220	60ce	Charaxes laodice	.65	.65
1177	A220	80ce	Euryphura porphyrion	.85	.85
1178	A220	100ce	Neptis nicomedes	.95	.95
1179	A220	150ce	Citrinophila erastus	1.10	1.10
1180	A220	200ce	Epitola honorius	1.60	1.60
1181	A220	300ce	Precis westermanni	2.10	2.10
1182	A220	500ce	Cymothoe hypatha	2.75	2.75
		Nos. 1175-1182 (8)		10.50	10.50

Souvenir Sheets
1183	A220	600ce	Telipna bimacula	6.00	6.00
1184	A220	600ce	Pentila phidia	6.00	6.00

Seashells — A221

1990, Feb. 20   Perf. 14x14½
1185	A221	20ce	Cymbium glans	.80	.80
1186	A221	60ce	Cardium costatum	1.40	1.40
1187	A221	80ce	Conus genuanus	1.75	1.75
1188	A221	200ce	Ancilla tankervillei	3.25	3.25
1189	A221	350ce	Tectarius coronatus	4.75	4.75
		Nos. 1185-1189 (5)		11.95	11.95

Jawaharlal Nehru, 1st Prime Minister of Independent India — A222

Designs: 20ce, Greeting Pres. Kwame Nkrumah of Ghana. 60ce, Addressing Afro-Asian conference. 80ce, Return from tour of China, vert. 200ce, Releasing dove during a children's celebration in New Delhi, vert. 350ce, Portrait, vert.

Perf. 14½x14, 14x14½
1990, Mar. 27   Litho.
1190	A222	20ce	shown	.75	.75
1191	A222	60ce	multicolored	.90	.90
1192	A222	80ce	multicolored	1.25	1.25
1193	A222	200ce	multicolored	1.75	1.75
1194	A222	350ce	multicolored	2.75	2.75
		Nos. 1190-1194 (5)		7.40	7.40

Nos. 759A and 760A-760B Surcharged

1990   Perf. 14
1195	CD331	80ce on 65p	1.00	1.00
1196	CD331	100ce on 1ce	1.40	1.40
1197	CD331	300ce on 3ce	4.25	4.25
		Nos. 1195-1197 (3)		6.65	6.65

Nos. 961, 959 and 962 Surcharged
1990
1198	A184	80ce on 20ce	.80	.80
1199	A184	200ce on 8ce	2.00	2.00
1200	A184	250ce on 70ce	2.50	2.50
		Nos. 1198-1200 (3)		5.30	5.30

Penny Black, 150th Anniv. A223

Great Britain No. 1 and: 20ce, City Medal containing portrait of Victoria by William Wyon adapted for use on the Penny Black. 60ce, No. 1208, Bath mail coach. 200ce, Heath's engraving, based on the Wyon portrait. 350ce, Penny Black master die. 200ce, Heath's engraving, based on the Wyon portrait. 350ce, Penny Black master die. 400ce, London mail coach. No. 1207, Printers and flat-bed presses of Perkins, Bacon & Petch, 1840.

1990, May 3   Perf. 13½x14
1201	A223	20ce	shown	.35	.35
1202	A223	60ce	multicolored	.65	.65
1203	A223	80ce	multicolored	.90	.90
1204	A223	200ce	multicolored	1.90	1.90
1205	A223	350ce	multicolored	2.50	2.50
1206	A223	400ce	multicolored	2.50	2.50
		Nos. 1201-1206 (6)		8.80	8.80

Souvenir Sheets
1207	A223	600ce	multicolored	5.00	5.00
1208	A223	600ce	multicolored	5.00	5.00

June 4, Revolution, 10th Anniv. (in 1989) — A224

1990, June 5   Litho.   Perf. 14½x14
1209	A224	20ce	shown	.20	.20
1210	A224	60ce	Pineapple, lobsters	.50	.50
1211	A224	80ce	Corn, cacao beans	.65	.65
1212	A224	200ce	Mining	1.75	1.75
1213	A224	350ce	Scales, sword	3.00	3.00
		Nos. 1209-1213 (5)		6.10	6.10

Intelsat, 25th Anniv. A225

Satellites over: 60ce, Pacific Ocean. 80ce, Pacific, diff. 200ce, South Atlantic. 350ce, Pacific, Indian Oceans.

1990, July 12   Perf. 14x14½
1214	A225	20ce	multicolored	.20	.20
1215	A225	60ce	multicolored	.55	.55
1216	A225	80ce	multicolored	.65	.65
1217	A225	200ce	multicolored	1.60	1.60
1218	A225	350ce	multicolored	2.50	2.50
		Nos. 1214-1218 (5)		5.50	5.50

Introduction of Intl. Direct Dialing Service (in 1988) — A226

1990, July 16
1219	A226	20ce	multicolored	.20	.20
1220	A226	60ce	Man using telephone	.55	.55
1221	A226	80ce	Man using pay telephone	.65	.65
1222	A226	200ce	Telephone booths	1.60	1.60
1223	A226	350ce	Satellite dish	2.50	2.50
		Nos. 1219-1223 (5)		5.50	5.50

Miniature Sheet

African Tropical Rain Forest A227

Designs: No. 1224a, Blue fairy flycatcher. b, Boomslang. c, Superb sunbird. d, Bateleur eagle. e, Yellow-casqued hornbill. f, Salamis temora. g, Potto. h, Leopard. i, Bongo. j, Gray parrot. k, Okapi. l, Gorilla. m, Flap-necked chameleon. n, West African dwarf crocodile. o, Python. p, Giant pangolin. q, Pseudacraea boisduvali. r, African crested porcupine. s, Rosy-columned aerangis. t, Cymothoe sangaris.

No. 1225, Leopard, vert.

1990, Oct. 25   Litho.   Perf. 14x14½
1224		Sheet of 20		18.00	18.00
a.-t.	A227	40ce any single		.80	.80

Souvenir Sheet
1225	A227	600ce	multicolored	8.50	8.50

Miniature Sheet

Voyager 2 — A228

Photographs from Voyager 2: No. 1226a, Jupiter. b, Neptune, Triton. c, Ariel, moon of Uranus. d, Saturn, Mimas. e, Saturn. f, Rings of Saturn. g, Neptune. h, Uranus, Miranda. i, Volcano on Io.

1990, Dec. 13   Litho.   Perf. 14
1226	A228	100ce	Sheet of 9, #1226a-1226i	10.00	10.00

Souvenir Sheets
1227	A228	600ce	Voyager 2 liftoff, vert.	4.25	4.25
1228	A228	600ce	Voyager 2, vert.	4.25	4.25

Orchids — A229

Designs: 20ce, Eulophia guineensis. 40ce, Eurychone rothschildiana. 60ce, Bulbophyllum barbigerum. 80ce, Polystachya galeata. 200ce, Diaphananthe kamerunensis. 300ce, Podangis dactyloceras. 400ce, Ancistrochilus rothschildianus. 500ce, Rangaeris muscicola. No. 1237, Bolusiella imbricata. No. 1238, Diaphananthe rutila.

1990, Dec. 17
1229	A229	20ce	multicolored	.20	.20
1230	A229	40ce	multicolored	.30	.30
1231	A229	60ce	multicolored	.55	.55
1232	A229	80ce	multicolored	.70	.70
1233	A229	200ce	multicolored	1.75	1.75
1234	A229	300ce	multicolored	2.75	2.75
1235	A229	400ce	multicolored	3.75	3.75
1236	A229	500ce	multicolored	4.50	4.50
		Nos. 1229-1236 (8)		14.50	14.50

Souvenir Sheets
1237	A229	600ce	multicolored	7.25	7.25
1238	A229	600ce	multicolored	7.25	7.25

Mushrooms — A230

Designs: 20ce, Coprinus atramentarius. 50ce, Marasmius oreades. 60ce, Oudamansiella radicata. 80ce, Cep. 150ce, Hebeloma crustuliniforme. 200ce, Coprinus micaceus. 300ce, Lepiota procera. 500ce, Amanita phalloides.

1990, Dec. 18

1239	A230	20ce multicolored	.85	.55
1240	A230	50ce multicolored	1.10	.85
1241	A230	60ce multicolored	1.40	.85
1242	A230	80ce multicolored	1.75	1.25
1243	A230	150ce multicolored	2.50	1.75
1244	A230	200ce multicolored	3.50	2.50
1245	A230	300ce multicolored	3.50	3.50
a.		Min. sheet of 4, #1240, 1243-1245	7.25	7.25
1246	A230	500ce multicolored	4.50	4.50
a.		Min. sheet of 4, #1239, 1241-1242, 1246	7.25	7.25
		Nos. 1239-1246 (8)	19.10	15.75

World Cup Soccer Championships, Italy — A231

Players from participating countries.

1990, Dec. 18   Litho.   Perf. 14

1247	A231	20ce Italy	.50	.50
1248	A231	50ce Egypt	.65	.65
1249	A231	60ce Cameroun	.70	.70
1250	A231	80ce Romania	.85	.85
1251	A231	100ce Yugoslavia	1.00	1.00
1252	A231	150ce Cameroun, vert.	1.75	1.75
1253	A231	400ce South Korea	2.75	2.75
1254	A231	600ce West Germany	3.25	3.25
		Nos. 1247-1254 (8)	11.45	11.45

Souvenir Sheets

1255	A231	800ce UAE	5.50	5.50
1256	A231	800ce Colombia	5.50	5.50

Peter Paul Rubens (1577-1640), Painter A232

Portraits by Rubens: 20ce, Duke of Mantua. 50ce, Jan Brant. 60ce, Young man. 80ce, Michel Ophovius. 100ce, Caspar Gevaerts. 200ce, Head of a warrior (detail). 300ce, Bearded man. 400ce, Paracelsus. No. 1265. Archduke Ferdinand. No. 1266, Warrior with Two Pages.

1990, Dec. 24   Litho.   Perf. 14

1257	A232	20ce multicolored	.20	.20
1258	A232	50ce multicolored	.40	.40
1259	A232	60ce multicolored	.50	.50
1260	A232	80ce multicolored	.65	.65
1261	A232	100ce multicolored	.80	.80
1262	A232	200ce multicolored	1.90	1.90
1263	A232	300ce multicolored	2.75	2.75
1264	A232	400ce multicolored	3.75	3.75
		Nos. 1257-1264 (8)	10.95	10.95

Souvenir Sheets

1265	A232	600ce multicolored	5.75	5.75
1266	A232	600ce multicolored	5.75	5.75

Minerals — A233

1991, May 2   Litho.   Perf. 14½x14

1267	A233	20ce Manganese ore	.55	.55
1268	A233	60ce Iron ore	.70	.70
1269	A233	80ce Bauxite ore	1.25	1.25
1270	A233	200ce Gold ore	3.00	3.00
1271	A233	350ce Diamond	4.50	4.50
		Nos. 1267-1271 (5)	10.00	10.00

Souvenir Sheet

1272	A233	600ce Diamonds	10.00	10.00

Tribal Drums — A234

1991, May 9

1273	A234	20ce Damba	.45	.20
1274	A234	60ce Atumpan	.85	.55
1275	A234	80ce Kroboto	1.10	.70
1276	A234	200ce Asafo	1.90	1.90
1277	A234	350ce Obonu	3.00	3.00
		Nos. 1273-1277 (5)	7.30	6.35

Souvenir Sheet

1278	A234	600ce Single drum	7.50	7.50

Flowers — A235   A236

1991, May 15

1279	A235	20ce Amorphophallus dracontioides	.75	.35
1280	A235	60ce Anchomanes difformis	1.10	.55
1281	A235	80ce Kaemferia nigerica	1.40	.70
1282	A235	200ce Aframomum sceptrum	2.75	2.75
1283	A235	350ce Amorphophallus flavovirens	3.00	3.00
		Nos. 1279-1283 (5)	9.00	7.35

Souvenir Sheet

1284	A235	600ce White flowers	7.00	7.00

1991, May 17   Litho.   Perf. 14½x14

1285	A235	20ce Urginea indica	.55	.35
1286	A235	60ce Hymenocallis littoralis	1.00	.55
1287	A235	80ce Crinum jagus	1.60	.80
1288	A235	200ce Dipcadi tacazzeanum	2.25	2.25
1289	A235	350ce Haemanthus rupestris	2.75	2.75
		Nos. 1285-1289 (5)	8.15	6.70

Souvenir Sheet

1290	A235	600ce Red flowers	7.50	7.50

1991, June 21   Litho.   Perf. 13½x14

Designs: 20ce, Satellite transmissions, airplane. 60ce, Scientific research, honey bee. 80ce, Literacy instruction. 200ce, Agricultural development. 350ce, Industry.

1291	A236	20ce multicolored	.20	.20
1292	A236	60ce multicolored	1.00	.55
1293	A236	80ce multicolored	1.10	.70
1294	A236	200ce multicolored	1.75	1.75
1295	A236	350ce multicolored	3.00	3.00
		Nos. 1291-1295 (5)	7.05	6.20

UN Development Program, 40th anniv.

Lord Robert Baden-Powell (1857-1941), Founder of Boy Scouts — A237

Designs: 20ce, Sketch by Baden-Powell used in first scouting handbook, vert. 50ce, Portrait, vert. 80ce, Scout handbook illustration by Norman Rockwell. 100ce, Native runner, Cape of Good Hope #178. 200ce, Scouts aiding victims after V-1 attack, London, 1944. 500ce, Scout praying, vert. 600ce, Emblem, Cape of Good Hope No. 178 used. No. 1304, Cover with Cape of Good Hope No. 178 from Mafeking, 1900. No. 1305, Campsites, 17th World Scout Jamboree, Korea, 1991.

1991, July 16   Litho.   Perf. 14

1296	A237	20ce buff & black	.60	.20
1297	A237	50ce multicolored	.75	.40
1298	A237	60ce multicolored	.75	.40
1299	A237	80ce black & buff	1.25	.65
1300	A237	100ce multicolored	1.60	1.00
1301	A237	200ce multicolored	2.00	2.00
1302	A237	500ce multicolored	4.25	4.25
1303	A237	600ce multicolored	5.00	5.00
		Nos. 1296-1303 (8)	16.20	14.00

Souvenir Sheets

1304	A237	800ce multicolored	5.50	5.50
1305	A237	800ce multicolored	5.50	5.50

For overprints see Nos. 1567-1572.

Chorkor Smoker A238

Designs: 20ce, Placing fish on racks. 60ce, Preparing smokers. 80ce, Preparing fish. 200ce, Preparing racks for smoker. 350ce, Placing racks in smoker.

1991, July 22   Litho.   Perf. 14x14½

1306	A238	20ce multicolored	.40	.20
1307	A238	60ce multicolored	.70	.45
1308	A238	80ce multicolored	.80	.65
1309	A238	200ce multicolored	1.90	1.90
1310	A238	350ce multicolored	2.50	2.50
		Nos. 1306-1310 (5)	6.30	5.70

Nos. 958-964 Overprinted "90th Birthday / 4th August 1990" and Surcharged

Perf. 14, 12½x12 (#1312-1313, 1315)

1991, July 22

1311	A184	20ce on 5ce #958	.50	.50
1312	A184	20ce on 8ce #959	.50	.50
1313	A184	40ce on 20ce #961	.80	.80
1314	A184	60ce on 12ce #960	1.50	1.50
1315	A184	80ce on 70ce #962	1.75	1.75
1316	A184	150ce on 100ce #963	3.50	3.50
		Nos. 1311-1316 (6)	8.55	8.55

Souvenir Sheet

1317	A184	200ce on 110ce #964	5.00	5.00

Nos. 1312-1313, 1315 issued in sheets of 5 + label. Overprint is vertical on stamp in No. 1317, horizontal on sheet margin.
The status of this issue is uncertain.

Fish A239

1991, July 29   Litho.   Perf. 14

1318	A239	20ce Cephalopholis taeniops	.20	.20
1319	A239	50ce Synodontis sorex	.40	.40
1320	A239	80ce Balistes forcipatus	.40	.40
1321	A239	100ce Petrocephalus bane	.50	.50
1322	A239	200ce Syngnathus rastellatus	1.00	1.00
1323	A239	300ce Gymnarchus niloticus	2.50	2.50
1324	A239	400ce Hemichromis bimaculatus	3.50	3.50
1325	A239	500ce Sphyrna zygaena	2.75	2.75
		Nos. 1318-1325 (8)	11.25	11.25

Souvenir Sheets

1326	A239	800ce Bagrus bayad	5.25	5.25
1327	A239	800ce Dactyloptena orientalis	3.75	3.75

While Nos. 1320-1322, 1325, 1327 have the same issue date as Nos. 1318-1319, 1323-1324, 1326, the value of Nos. 1320-1322, 1325, 1327 was lower when they were released.
For overprints see Nos. 1573-1578.

Paintings by Vincent Van Gogh A240

Designs: 20ce, Reaper with Sickle. 50ce, The Thresher. 60ce, The Sheaf Binder. 80ce, The Sheep Shearers. 100ce, Peasant Woman Cutting Straw. 200ce, The Sower. 500ce, The Plow and the Harrow, horiz. 600ce, The Woodcutter. No. 1336, Evening: The Watch. No. 1337, Evening: The End of the Day.

Perf. 13x13½, 13½x13

1991, Aug. 12   Litho.

1328	A240	20ce multicolored	.20	.20
1329	A240	50ce multicolored	.40	.40
1330	A240	60ce multicolored	.50	.50
1331	A240	80ce multicolored	.65	.65
1332	A240	100ce multicolored	.80	.80
1333	A240	200ce multicolored	1.60	1.60
1334	A240	500ce multicolored	4.00	4.00
1335	A240	600ce multicolored	4.75	4.75
		Nos. 1328-1335 (8)	12.90	12.90

Size: 106x80mm

Imperf

1336	A240	800ce multicolored	6.50	6.50
1337	A240	800ce multicolored	6.50	6.50

10th Non-aligned Ministers Conference, Accra — A241

Natl. Leaders: 20ce, Nasser, Egypt (1952-1970). 60ce, Tito, Yugoslavia (1945-1980). 80ce, Nehru, India (1947-1964). 200ce, Nkrumah, Ghana (1957-1966). 350ce, Sukarno, Indonesia (1945-1967).

1991, Sept. 2   Perf. 13½x14

1338	A241	20ce multicolored	.50	.35
1339	A241	60ce multicolored	.60	.50
1340	A241	80ce multicolored	4.25	1.50
1341	A241	200ce multicolored	2.25	2.25
1342	A241	350ce multicolored	3.00	3.00
		Nos. 1338-1342 (5)	10.60	7.60

Birds of Ghana — A242

Designs: No. 1343a, Melba finch. b, Orange-cheeked waxbill. c, Paradise flycatcher. d, Blue plantain-eater, e, Red bishop. f, Splendid glossy starling. g, Red-headed lovebird. h, Palm swift. i, Narina trogon. j, Tawny eagle. k, Bateleur eagle. l, Hoopoe. m, Secretary bird. n, White-backed vulture. o, Bare-headed rockfowl. p, Ground hornbill.
No. 1344a, Openbilled stork. b, African spoonbill. c, Pink-backed pelican. d, Little bittern. e, King reed-hen. f, Saddlebill stork. g, Glossy ibis. h, White-faced tree duck. i, Black-headed heron. j, Hammerkop. k, African darter. l, Woolly-necked stork. m, Yellow-billed stork. n, Black-winged stilt. o, Goliath heron. p, Lily trotter.

No. 1345a, Shikra. b, Abyssinian roller (c, g). c, Carmine bee-eater (g). d, Pintailed whydah (h). e, Purple glossy starling. f, Yellow-backed whydah (j). g, Pel's fishing owl. h, Verreaux's touraco (l). i, Red-cheeked cordon-bleu. j, Olive-bellied sunbird. k, Red-billed hornbill. l, Red-billed quelea. m, Crowned crane (i). n, Blue quail. o, Egyptian vulture (p). p, Helmeted guineafowl.

No. 1346, Marabou stork. No. 1347, Saddlebill stork, diff. No. 1348, African river eagle.

1991, Oct. 14   Litho.   Perf. 14½x14
Sheets of 16

1343	A242	80ce	#a.-p.	9.00	9.00
1344	A242	100ce	#a.-p.	13.50	13.50
1345	A242	100ce	#a.-p.	16.00	16.00
	Nos. 1343-1345 (3)			38.50	38.50

Souvenir Sheets

1346	A242	800ce	multicolored	6.00	6.00
1347	A242	800ce	multicolored	6.00	6.00
1348	A242	800ce	multicolored	6.00	6.00

While No. 1344 has the same issue date as No. 1345, the value of No. 1344 was lower when it was released.

Insects
A243

1991, Oct. 25   Perf. 14x13½

1349	A243	20ce	Nularda	.75	.25
1350	A243	50ce	Zonocrus	.90	.40
1351	A243	60ce	Gryllotalpa africana	1.25	.50
1352	A243	80ce	Weevil	1.75	1.25
1353	A243	100ce	Coenagrion	2.25	2.00
1354	A243	150ce	Sahlbergella	2.50	2.25
1355	A243	200ce	Anthia	3.00	3.00
1356	A243	350ce	Megacephala	4.00	3.00
	Nos. 1349-1356 (8)			16.40	12.65

Souvenir Sheet
Perf. 13x12

1357	A243	600ce	Lacetus	13.50	13.50

Landmarks and
Shells — A243a

Designs: 50ce, Boti Falls, vert. 60ce, Larabanga Mosque. 80ce, Fort Sebastian, Shama. 100ce, Cape Coast Castle. 200ce, Leucodon cowrie. 400ce, Achatina achatina.

100ce exists in four types:
Type I, "G" has angled curve, bars in "A"s slope down to left, "c" has straight line, bottom inscription 10mm.
Type II, "G" is rounded, bars in "A"s slope down to right, "c" has slanted line, bottom inscription 13mm.
Type III, "G" is rounded, bars in "A"s slope down to right, "c" has straight line, bottom inscription 10mm.
Type IV, "G" rounded, but cut off at top, bars in "A"s slope to right, "C" with slanted line, bottom inscription 10mm.

200ce, 400ce
Nos. 1357E, 1357Ej, 1357F, Type I: "G" has angled curve, bars in "A"s slope down to left. Nos. 1357Ek, 1357Fl, Type II: "G" is rounded, bars in "A"s slope down to right.

Perf. 13¾x13½, 13½x13¾

1991   Litho.

1357A	A243a	50ce	multi	—	—
1357B	A243a	60ce	multi	—	—
1357C	A243a	80ce	multi	—	—
1357D	A243a	100ce	multi (I)	—	—
g.	Type II			—	—
h.	Type I, perf 14¼x13¾			—	—
i.	Type III, perf 14¼x13¾			—	—
m.	Type IV			—	—
1357E	A243a	200ce	multi (I)	—	—
j.	Type I, perf 14¼x13¾			—	—
k.	Type I, perf 14¼x13¾			—	—
1357F	A243a	400ce	multi (I)	—	—
l.	Type II, perf 14¼x13¾			—	—
n.	Type I, perf 11½			—	—

This set was printed locally. Shades exist. Issue dates: 50ce, Nov. 21; others, Dec. 12. No. 1357Dm, 2004(?).

Adoration of the Magi by Hieronymus Bosch
A244

Details or entire paintings: 50ce, The Annunciation by Robert Campin. 60ce, Virgin and Child by Dirk Bouts. 80ce, Presentation in the Temple by Hans Memling. 100ce, The Virgin and Child Enthroned with an Angel and a Donor by Memling. 200ce, The Virgin and Child with Saints and a Donor by Jan van Eyck. 400ce, St. Luke Painting the Virgin by Rogier van der Weyden. 700ce, Virgin and Child by Bouts, diff. No. 1366, The Annunciation by Memling. No. 1367, The Virgin and Child Standing in a Niche by van der Weyden.

1991, Dec. 23   Perf. 12

1358	A244	20ce	multicolored	.20	.20
1359	A244	50ce	multicolored	.45	.45
1360	A244	60ce	multicolored	.55	.55
1361	A244	80ce	multicolored	.70	.70
1362	A244	100ce	multicolored	.90	.90
1363	A244	200ce	multicolored	1.75	1.75
1364	A244	400ce	multicolored	3.50	3.50
1365	A244	700ce	multicolored	6.00	6.00
	Nos. 1358-1365 (8)			14.05	14.05

Souvenir Sheets
Perf. 14½

1366	A244	800ce	multicolored	5.50	5.50
1367	A244	800ce	multicolored	5.50	5.50

Christmas.

Reunification of Germany — A245

Designs: 20ce, Opening of German border, Nov. 9, 1989. 60ce, Signing of Two Plus Four Treaty, Sept. 12, 1990. 80ce, Opening of Brandenburg Gate, Dec. 22, 1989. 800ce, German leaders, Unity Day, Oct. 3, 1990. 1000ce, Currency union, July 1, 1990.

No. 1371Ab, USSR Pres. Mikhail Gorbachev, vert. c, Chancellor Helmut Kohl, vert. d, Map of West Germany, vert. e, Map of East Germany, vert.

No. 1371g, Doves. h, German Chancellor Helmut Kohl, Foreign Minister Hans-Dietrich Genscher.

1992, Feb. 17   Litho.   Perf. 14

1368	A245	20ce	multi	.30	.20
1369	A245	60ce	multi	.55	.55
1370	A245	80ce	multi	.75	.75
1371	A245	1000ce	multi	9.00	9.00
	Nos. 1368-1371 (4)			10.60	10.50

Souvenir Sheets

1371A	A245	300ce	Sheet of 4, #b.-e.	7.50	7.50
1371F	A245	400ce	Sheet of 2, #g.-h.	2.50	2.50
1372	A245	800ce	multicolored	5.50	5.50

While No. 1371F has the same issue date as No. 1371A, the dollar value of No. 1371F was lower when it was released.

1992 Summer Olympics, Barcelona
A246

Map and: 20ce, Eddie Blay, boxing, Ghana, 1964. 60ce, Mike Ahey, track, Ghana, 1964-1972. 80ce, T. Wilson, ski jumping, US, 1988. 100ce, East German 4-Man bobsled, 1988. 200ce, Greg Louganis, diving, US, 1984. 300ce, L. Visser, speed skating, Netherlands, 1988. 350ce, J. Passler, biathlon, Italy, 1988. 400ce, Mary Lou Retton, gymnastics, US, 1984. 500ce, Jurgen Hingsen, decathlon, Germany, 1984. 600ce, R. Neubert, heptathlon,

West Germany, 1984. No. 1380, Jai alai player, vert. No. 1381, Windmill.

1992, Mar. 3   Litho.   Perf. 14

1373	A246	20ce	multi	.50	.20
1373A	A246	60ce	multi	.60	.45
1374	A246	80ce	multi	.90	.55
1375	A246	100ce	multi	1.25	.90
1376	A246	200ce	multi	2.25	1.60
1377	A246	300ce	multi	2.25	2.10
1378	A246	350ce	multi	2.25	2.10
1378A	A246	400ce	multi	3.00	2.75
1378B	A246	500ce	multi	3.00	2.75
1379	A246	600ce	multi	3.00	2.75
	Nos. 1373-1379 (10)			19.00	16.15

Souvenir Sheets

1380	A246	800ce	multi	7.00	7.00
1381	A246	800ce	multi	7.00	7.00

While Nos. 1373A, 1378A-1378B have the same issue date as rest of the set but the dollar value of Nos. 1373A, 1378A-1378B were lower when they were released.

Phila Nippon '91
A247

1992, Feb. 16   Litho.   Perf. 14

1382	A247	20ce	shown	.20	.20
1383	A247	60ce	Torii of Itsukushima Jingu shrine	.40	.40
1384	A247	80ce	Geisha	.50	.50
1385	A247	100ce	Samurai residence	.65	.65
1386	A247	200ce	Bonsai tree	1.50	1.50
1387	A247	400ce	Olympic sports hall	3.00	3.00
1388	A247	500ce	Great Buddha	3.50	3.50
1389	A247	600ce	Nagoya castle	4.75	4.75
	Nos. 1382-1389 (8)			14.50	14.50

Souvenir Sheets

1390	A247	800ce	Takamatsu castle	6.50	6.50
1391	A247	800ce	Heian shrine	6.50	6.50

Ghana Natl. Railways
A248

Designs: 20c, Engine, 1903, Gold Coast Railway. 50c, Diesel passenger locomotive, Ghana Railways Corp. 60ce, First class coach, 1931 Gold Coast Railway. 80ce, Official inspection coach, Gold Coast Railway. 100ce, Engine No. 401 on turntable. 200c, Twin-bogie cocoa wagon, 1921, Gold Coast Railway. 500ce, Engine No. 223, "Prince of Wales." 600c, Twin-bogie cattle wagon, Gold Coast Railway. No. 1400, German-made locomotive, Gold Coast Railway. No. 1401, Beyer-Garratt #301, 1943, Gold Coast Railway.

1992, Mar. 2

1392	A248	20ce	multicolored	.20	.20
1393	A248	50ce	multicolored	.35	.35
1394	A248	60ce	multicolored	.45	.45
1395	A248	80ce	multicolored	.55	.55
1396	A248	100ce	multicolored	.65	.65
1397	A248	200ce	multicolored	1.40	1.40
1398	A248	500ce	multicolored	3.50	3.50
1399	A248	600ce	multicolored	4.75	4.75
	Nos. 1392-1399 (8)			11.85	11.85

Souvenir Sheets

1400	A248	800ce	multicolored	5.50	5.50
1401	A248	800ce	multicolored	5.50	5.50

Decade of Revolutionary Progress
A249

1992, Feb. 2   Litho.   Perf. 14x13½

1402	A249	20ce	Bore hole water	.30	.30
1403	A249	50ce	Mining industry	.35	.35
1404	A249	60ce	Small scale industry	.45	.45
1405	A249	80ce	Timber industry	.50	.50

1406	A249	200ce	Cocoa rehabilitation	1.00	1.00
1407	A249	350ce	Rural electrification	1.25	1.25
	Nos. 1402-1407 (6)			3.85	3.85

Reptiles
A251

1992, Mar. 30   Litho.   Perf. 14

1414	A251	20ce	Angides lugubris	.20	.20
1415	A251	50ce	Kinixys erosa	.35	.35
1416	A251	60ce	Agama agama	.35	.35
1417	A251	80ce	Chameleo gracilis	.45	.45
1418	A251	100ce	Naja melanleuca	.65	.65
1419	A251	200ce	Crocodylus niloticus	1.10	1.10
1420	A251	400ce	Chelonia mydas	2.25	2.25
1421	A251	500ce	Varanus exanthematicus	2.75	2.75
	Nos. 1414-1421 (8)			8.10	8.10

Souvenir Sheet

1422	A251	600ce	Snake & tortoise	5.25	5.25

Numbers have been reserved for additional values in this set.

Easter
A252

Details from paintings: 20ce, The Four Apostles: Sts. John, Peter, Paul & Mark, by Durer. 50ce, The Last Judgment, by Rubens. 60ce, The Four Apostles: Sts. John, Peter, Paul and Mark, diff. by Durer. 80ce, The Last Judgment, diff. by Rubens. 100ce, Crucifixion, by Rubens. 200ce, The Last Judgment, diff. by Rubens. 500ce, Christum Videre, by Rubens. 600ce, The Last Judgment, diff. by Rubens. No. 1432, Last Communion of St. Francis of Assisi, by Rubens. No. 1432A, Scourging the Money Changers from the Temple, by El Greco, horiz.

1992, Mar. 13   Perf. 13½x14

1424	A252	20ce	multi	.20	.20
1425	A252	50ce	multi	.35	.35
1426	A252	60ce	multi	.45	.45
1427	A252	80ce	multi	.55	.55
1428	A252	100ce	multi	.65	.65
1429	A252	200ce	multi	1.10	1.10
1430	A252	500ce	multi	3.00	3.00
1431	A252	600ce	multi	3.25	3.25
	Nos. 1424-1431 (8)			9.55	9.55

Souvenir Sheets

1432	A252	800ce	multi	5.50	5.50

Perf. 14x13½

1432A	A252	800ce	multi	5.50	5.50

Spanish Art — A253

Paintings by Velazquez: 20ce, Two Men at Table. 60ce, Christ in the House of Mary and Martha (detail). 80ce, The Supper at Emmaus. 100ce, Three Muscians. 200ce, Old Woman Cooking Eggs, vert. 400ce, Old Woman Cooking Eggs (detail), vert. 500ce, The Surrender of Breda (detail) diff., vert. 700ce, The Surrender of Breda (detail), vert.

No. 1441, They Still Say that Fish is Expensive, by Joaquin Sorolla y Bastida. No. 1442, The Waterseller of Seville.

1992, May 4   **Perf. 13½**

1433	A253	20ce multicolored	.20	.20
1434	A253	60ce multicolored	.30	.30
1435	A253	80ce multicolored	.40	.40
1436	A253	100ce multicolored	.60	.60
1437	A253	200ce multicolored	1.25	1.25
1438	A253	400ce multicolored	2.00	2.00
1439	A253	500ce multicolored	2.50	2.50
1440	A253	700ce multicolored	4.25	4.25

Size: 120x95mm
Imperf

1441	A253	900ce multicolored	5.75	5.75
1442	A253	900ce multicolored	5.25	5.25
		Nos. 1433-1442 (10)	22.50	22.50

Granada '92. While Nos. 1434-1435, 1438-1439, 1442 have the same issue date as Nos. 1433, 1436-1437, 1440-1441, the value in relation to the dollar of Nos. 1434-1435, 1438-1439, 1442 was lower when they were released.

Butterflies — A254   Dinosaurs — A255

1992, May 25   **Litho.**   **Perf. 14**

1443	A254	20ce African monarch	.20	.20
1444	A254	60ce Mocker swallowtail	.40	.40
1445	A254	80ce Painted lady	.55	.55
1446	A254	100ce Mountain beauty	.65	.65
1447	A254	200ce Blue temora	1.50	1.50
1448	A254	400ce Foxy charaxes	3.00	3.00
1449	A254	500ce Blue pansy	3.50	3.50
1450	A254	700ce Golden pansy	5.00	5.00
		Nos. 1443-1450 (8)	14.80	14.80

Souvenir Sheets

| 1451 | A254 | 900ce Gaudy commodore | 5.50 | 5.50 |
| 1452 | A254 | 900ce Christmas butterfly | 5.50 | 5.50 |

Genoa '92. For overprints see Nos. 1471-1480.

1992, June 1   **Litho.**   **Perf. 14**

1453	A255	20ce Iguanodon	.45	.35
1454	A255	50ce Anchisaurus	.65	.45
1455	A255	60ce Heterodontosaurus	.70	.45
1456	A255	80ce Ouranosaurus	.75	.55
1457	A255	100ce Anatosaurus	1.00	.65
1458	A255	200ce Elaphrosaurus	1.60	1.60
1459	A255	500ce Coelophysis	3.00	3.00
1460	A255	600ce Rhamphorynchus	3.50	3.50
		Nos. 1453-1460 (8)	11.65	10.55

Souvenir Sheets

| 1461 | A255 | 1500ce like #1459 | 6.75 | 6.75 |
| 1462 | A255 | 1500ce like #1458 | 6.75 | 6.75 |

While Nos. 1453, 1456, 1458-1459 and 1462 have the same issue date as Nos. 1454-1455, 1457, 1460-1461, their value in relation to the dollar was lower when they were released.

Discovery of America, 500th Anniv. — A256

No. 1463: a, Capt. Martin Alonzo Pinzon, Pinta. b, Capt. Vicente Yanez Pinzon, Nina. c, Columbus, Fr. Marchena in La Rabida, 1485. d, Columbus in cabin. e, Land sighted, Oct. 12, 1492. f, Columbus lands on Samana Cay.

g, Shipwreck of Santa Maria. h, Columbus returns to Spanish Court, 1493. No. 1464, Columbus, ship.

1992, July   **Litho.**   **Perf. 14**

| 1463 | A256 | 200ce Sheet of 8, #a.-h. | 10.00 | 10.00 |

Souvenir Sheet

| 1464 | A256 | 500ce multicolored | 4.00 | 4.00 |

World Columbian Stamp Expo '92, Chicago.

Shells — A257

1992, Oct. 5   **Litho.**   **Perf. 14**

1465	A257	20ce Olivancillaria hiatula	.20	.20
1465A	A257	20ce Tympanotonus fuscatus	.20	.20
1466	A257	60ce Donax rugosus	.35	.35
1466A	A257	60ce Murex cornutus	.35	.35
1467	A257	80ce Sigaretus concavus	.45	.45
1467A	A257	80ce Tivola tripla	.45	.45
1468	A257	200ce Pila africana	1.25	1.25
1468A	A257	200ce Cypraea stercoraria	1.25	1.25
1469	A257	350ce Thais hiatula	2.00	2.00
1469A	A257	350ce Cassis tesselata	2.00	2.00
		Nos. 1465-1469A (10)	8.50	8.50

Souvenir Sheet

| 1470 | A257 | 600ce Natica favel | 5.00 | 5.00 |
| 1470A | A257 | 600ce Semifusos morio | 5.00 | 5.00 |

Nos. 1443-1452 Ovptd. "40th / Anniversary / of the / Accession / of / HM Queen / Elizabeth II / 1952-1992" in Silver

1992, Aug. 10   **Litho.**   **Perf. 14**

1471	A254	20ce on #1443	.20	.20
1472	A254	60ce on #1444	.35	.35
1473	A254	80ce on #1445	.50	.50
1474	A254	100ce on #1446	.60	.60
1475	A254	200ce on #1447	1.25	1.25
1476	A254	400ce on #1448	2.25	2.25
1477	A254	500ce on #1449	3.00	3.00
1478	A254	700ce on #1450	4.00	4.00
		Nos. 1471-1478 (8)	12.15	12.15

Souvenir Sheets

| 1479 | A254 | 900ce on #1451 | 6.00 | 6.00 |
| 1480 | A254 | 900ce on #1452 | 6.00 | 6.00 |

Christmas A259

Details or entire paintings: 20ce, Presentation in the Temple, by Master of Brunswick. 50ce, Presentation in the Temple, by Master of St. Severin. 60ce, The Visitation, by Sebastiano del Piombo. 80ce, The Visitation, by Giotto. 100ce, The Circumcision, by Studio of Giovanni Bellini. 200ce, The Circumcision, by Workshop of Benvenuto Garofalo. 500ce, The Visitation, by Workshop of Rogier van der Weyden. 800ce, The Visitation, by Workshop of Rogier Van der Weyden. No. 1491, The Visitation, by Giotto. No. 1492, The Presentation in the Temple, by Bartolo di Fredi.

1992   **Litho.**   **Perf. 13½x14**

1483	A259	20ce multicolored	.20	.20
1484	A259	50ce multicolored	.30	.30
1485	A259	60ce multicolored	.35	.35
1486	A259	80ce multicolored	.40	.40
1487	A259	100ce multicolored	.50	.50
1488	A259	200ce multicolored	1.00	1.00
1489	A259	500ce multicolored	2.75	2.75
1490	A259	800ce multicolored	4.25	4.25
		Nos. 1483-1490 (8)	9.75	9.75

Souvenir Sheet

| 1491 | A259 | 900ce multicolored | 5.50 | 5.50 |
| 1492 | A259 | 900ce multicolored | 5.50 | 5.50 |

No. 1492 exists imperf.

Anniversaries and Events
A260   A261

Designs: 20ce, LZ3, floating hangar at Lake Constance, horiz. 100ce, Lift-off of Ariane 4 rocket, horiz. 200ce, Leopard in tree, horiz. 300ce, Roman Colosseum, fruits and vegetables, horiz. 400ce, Wolfgang Amadeus Mozart. 600ce, Lift-off of H-1 rocket, Japan. 800ce, LZ10, Schwaben, horiz. No. 1501, Scene from "The Marriage of Figaro." No. 1502, Space shuttle, US. No. 1503, Count Ferdinand von Zeppelin. No. 1504, Bongo, horiz.

1992, Dec.   **Litho.**   **Perf. 14**

1493	A260	20ce multicolored	.20	.20
1494	A260	100ce multicolored	.55	.55
1495	A260	200ce multicolored	1.10	1.10
1496	A260	300ce multicolored	1.75	1.75
1497	A261	400ce multicolored	2.50	2.50
1499	A260	600ce multicolored	3.75	3.75
1500	A260	800ce multicolored	5.00	5.00
		Nos. 1493-1500 (7)	14.85	14.85

Souvenir Sheets

1501	A261	900ce multicolored	5.50	5.50
1502	A260	900ce multicolored	5.50	5.50
1503	A260	900ce multicolored	5.50	5.50
1504	A260	900ce multicolored	5.50	5.50

Count Ferdinand von Zeppelin, 75th anniv. of death (#1493, 1500, 1503). Intl. Space Year (#1494, 1499, 1502). UN Earth Summit, Rio de Janeiro (#1495, 1504). WHO, Intl. Conference on Nutrition, Rome (1496). Mozart, bicent. of death (in 1991) (#1497, 1501).

Flowers — A262

Designs: Nos. 1505, 1514d (100ce), Lagerstroemia flos-reginae. No. 1506, Clerodendrum thomsoniae. No. 1507, 1514c (50ce), Spathodea campanulata. No. 1508, Cassia fistula. Nos. 1509, 1514e (150ce), Mellitea ferrugenea. Nos. 1510, 1514j (300ce), Hildegardia barteri. Nos. 1511, 1514i (150ce), Ipomoea asarifolia. No. 1512, Petrea volubilis. Nos. 1513, 1514f (300ce), Ritchiea reflexa. Nos. 1514, 1514h (100ce), Bryphyllum pinnatum.

1993, Mar. 1   **Litho.**   **Perf. 14**

1505	A262	20ce multicolored	.20	.20
1506	A262	20ce multicolored	.20	.20
1507	A262	60ce multicolored	.30	.30
1508	A262	60ce multicolored	.30	.30
1509	A262	80ce multicolored	.40	.40
1510	A262	80ce multicolored	.40	.40
1511	A262	200ce multicolored	1.00	1.00
1512	A262	200ce multicolored	1.00	1.00
1513	A262	350ce multicolored	1.75	1.75
1514	A262	350ce multicolored	1.75	1.75
		Nos. 1505-1514 (10)	7.30	7.30

Souvenir Sheets

| 1514A | A262 | Sheet of 4, #c.-f. | 3.75 | 3.75 |
| 1514B | A262 | Sheet of 4, #g.-j. | 3.75 | 3.75 |

Intl. Conference on Nutrition, Rome — A263

1993, Jan.   **Litho.**   **Perf. 14**

1515	A263	20ce Energy foods	.20	.20
1516	A263	60ce Body-building foods	.30	.30
1517	A263	80ce Protective foods	.40	.40
1518	A263	200ce Disease prevention	1.00	1.00
1519	A263	400ce Food quality control, preservation	2.00	2.00
		Nos. 1515-1519 (5)	3.90	3.90

Crabs A264

Designs: 20ce, Clappa rubroguttata. 60ce, Cardisoma amatum. 80ce, Maia squinado. 400ce, Ocypoda cursor. 800ce, Grapus grapus.

1993, Feb.   **Perf. 14x13½**

1520	A264	20ce multicolored	.20	.20
1521	A264	60ce multicolored	.35	.35
1522	A264	80ce multicolored	.45	.45
1523	A264	400ce multicolored	2.25	2.25
a.		Souv. sheet of 4, #1520-1523	7.50	7.50
1524	A264	800ce multicolored	4.50	4.50
		Nos. 1520-1524 (5)	7.75	7.75

Miniature Sheet of 8

Louvre Museum, Bicent. A265

No. 1525 — Details or entire paintings, by Giovanni Domenico Tiepolo (1727-1804) (a-e) and Giovanni Battista Tiepolo (1696-1770) (f-h): a-c, Carnival Scene, (left, center, right). d-e, Tooth Puller, (left, right). f, Rebecca at the Well. g-h, Presenting Christ to the People, (left, right). 700ce, Chancellor Seguier, by Le Brun, horiz.

1993, Mar. 1   **Litho.**   **Perf. 12**

| 1525 | A265 | 200ce Sheet of 8, #a.-h. + label | 10.00 | 10.00 |

Souvenir Sheet
Perf. 14½

| 1526 | A265 | 700ce multicolored | 4.25 | 4.25 |

No. 1526 contains one 55x88mm stamp.

Oil Palm Fruit — A265a

1993, Apr.   **Litho.**   **Perf. 13½**

| 1526A | A265a | 20ce multi | — | — |

Faberge Eggs — A266

4th Republic — A268

Wild Animals — A267

Easter: 50ce, Resurrection Egg. 80ce, Imperial Red Cross Egg with Resurrection Triptych. 100ce, Imperial Uspensky Cathedral Egg. 150ce, Imperial Red Cross Egg with portraits. 200ce, Orange Tree Egg. 250ce, Rabbit Egg. 400ce, Imperial Coronation Egg. 900ce, Silver-gilt enamel Easter Egg. No. 1535, Spring Flower Egg. No. 1536, Egg charms, horiz.

1993, Apr. 26   **Perf. 14**

1527	A266	50ce multi	.30	.30
1528	A266	80ce multi	.50	.50
1529	A266	100ce multi	.60	.60
1530	A266	150ce multi	.90	.90
1531	A266	200ce multi	1.25	1.25
1532	A266	250ce multi	1.75	1.75
1533	A266	400ce multi	3.50	3.50
1534	A266	900ce multi	7.50	7.50
		Nos. 1527-1534 (8)	16.30	16.30

Souvenir Sheets

1535	A266	1000ce multi	6.50	6.50
1536	A266	1000ce multi	6.50	6.50

1993, May 24   **Litho.**   **Perf. 14**

1537	A267	20ce African buffalo	.20	.20
1538	A267	50ce Giant forest hog	.50	.50
1539	A267	60ce Potto	.60	.60
1540	A267	80ce Bay duiker	.80	.80
1541	A267	100ce Royal antelope	1.00	1.00
1542	A267	200ce Serval	2.00	2.00
1543	A267	500ce Golden cat	5.00	5.00
1544	A267	800ce Megaloglossus woermanni	8.50	8.50
		Nos. 1537-1544 (8)	18.60	18.60

Souvenir Sheets

1545	A267	900ce Dormouse	6.50	6.50
1546	A267	900ce White collared mangabey	6.50	6.50

1993, May   **Litho.**   **Perf. 14**

50ce, Kwame Nkrumah Mausoleum, horiz. 100ce, Kwame Nkrumah Conference Center, horiz. 200ce, Constitution book. 350ce, Independence Square. 400ce, Christiansborg Castle.

1547	A268	50ce multicolored	.30	.30
1548	A268	100ce multicolored	.60	.60
1549	A268	200ce multicolored	1.25	1.25
1550	A268	350ce multicolored	2.25	2.25
1551	A268	400ce multicolored	2.75	2.75
		Nos. 1547-1551 (5)	7.15	7.15

A269

Aviation and Automotive Anniversaries — A270

Designs: 50ce, Graf Zeppelin over Alps, vert. No. 1552, Mercedes Benz 300 SLR in 1955 Mille Miglia. No. 1553, LZ7 Deutschland. No. 1554, Vulcan bomber. No. 1555, Ford Trimotor. No. 1556, 1920 Ford Depot Wagon. No. 1557, Nieuport 27, vert. No. 1558, Graf Zeppelin taking aboard letters, vert. No. 1559, 1970 Ford Mach 1 Mustang.

No. 1560, LZ10 Schwaben. No. 1561, Mercedes wins 1937 Monaco Grand Prix. No. 1562, Graf Zeppelin over Rome. No. 1563, 1955 Mercedes Benz Type 196. No. 1564, Early US air mail flight. No. 1565, S.E.5A, 1918. No. 1566, 1910 Ford Super T, 999.

1993   **Litho.**   **Perf. 14**

1551A	A269	50ce multi	.40	.40
1552	A270	150ce multi	1.00	1.00
1553	A269	150ce multi	1.00	1.00
1554	A269	400ce multi	3.00	3.00
1555	A270	400ce multi	3.00	3.00
1556	A270	400ce multi	3.00	3.00
1557	A269	600ce multi	4.25	4.25
1558	A269	600ce multi	4.25	4.25
1559	A270	600ce multi	4.25	4.25
1560	A269	800ce multi	5.50	5.50
1561	A270	800ce multi	5.50	5.50
		Nos. 1551A-1561 (11)	35.15	35.15

Souvenir Sheets

1562	A269	1000ce multi	5.50	5.50
1563	A270	1000ce multi	5.50	5.50
1564	A269	1000ce multi	5.50	5.50
1565	A269	1000ce multi	5.50	5.50
1566	A270	1000ce multi	5.50	5.50

Capt. Hugo Eckener, 125th birth anniv. (Nos. 1551A, 1553-1554, 1562). Benz's first four-wheeled vehicle, cent. (Nos. 1552, 1561, 1563). Royal Air Force, 75th anniv. (Nos. 1554, 1557, 1564). Henry Ford's first gasoline powered engine, cent. (Nos. 1556, 1559, 1566).

No. 1564 contains one 57x42mm stamp. No. 1563, 1566 contains one 85x28mm stamp.

Issued: Nos. 1555-1556, 1558-1559, 1565-1566, May. Nos. 1551A-1554, 1557, 1560-1564, June.

Nos. 1300-1305 Ovptd.

1993   **Litho.**   **Perf. 14**

1567	A237	100ce multicolored	.75	.75
1568	A237	200ce multicolored	1.75	1.75
1569	A237	500ce multicolored	3.50	3.50
1570	A237	600ce multicolored	5.00	5.00
		Nos. 1567-1570 (4)	11.00	11.00

Souvenir Sheet

1571	A237	800ce on #1304	6.00	6.00
1572	A237	800ce on #1305	6.00	6.00

Nos. 1321, 1323-1327 Ovptd. a. in Black "35 YEARS OF / ROTARY INTERNATIONAL / GHANA 1958" or b. in Red "GHANA / RED CROSS SOCIETY / FOUNDED 1932"

1993

1573	A239(a)	100ce multi	.75	.75
1574	A239(b)	300ce multi	2.00	2.00
1575	A239(b)	400ce multi	3.25	3.25
1576	A239(a)	500ce multi	4.00	4.00
		Nos. 1573-1576 (4)	10.00	10.00

Souvenir Sheets

1577	A239(a)	800ce on #1326	6.50	6.50
1578	A239(b)	800ce on #1327	6.50	6.50

A271

Mushrooms A272

Designs: 20ce, Cantharellus cibarius. 50ce, Russula cyanoxantha. 60ce, Clitocybe rivulosa. No. 1581, Boletus chrysenteron. No. 1582, Cortinarius elatior. No. 1583, Mycena galericulata. No. 1584, Boletus edulis. No. 1585, Tricholoma gambosum. No. 1586, Lepista saeva. 250ce, Gyroporus castaneus. No. 1589, Nolanea sericea. No. 1590, Hygrophorus puiceus. 500ce, Gomphidius glutinosus. No. 1592, Russula olivacea. 1000ce, Russula aurata.

No. 1594a, 100ce, Cantharellus cibarius. b, 150ce, Cortinarius elatior. c, 300ce, Tricholoma gambosum. d, 600ce, Hygrophorus puiceus.

No. 1595: a, 50ce, like #1581. b, 100ce, like #1583. c, 150ce, like #1584. d, 1000ce, like #1589.

1993, July 30   **Litho.**   **Perf. 14**

1579	A271	20ce multi	.20	.20
1580	A271	50ce multi	.25	.25
1581	A271	60ce multi	.30	.30
1582	A271	80ce multi	.40	.40
1583	A271	80ce multi	.40	.40
1584	A271	200ce multi	1.00	1.00
1585	A271	200ce multi	1.00	1.00
1586	A272	200ce multi	1.00	1.00
1587	A272	250ce multi	1.25	1.25
1588	A272	300ce multi	1.50	1.50
1589	A271	350ce multi	2.00	2.00
1590	A271	350ce multi	2.00	2.00
1591	A272	500ce multi	3.00	3.00
1592	A272	800ce multi	3.50	3.50
1593	A272	1000ce multi	6.00	6.00
		Nos. 1579-1593 (15)	23.80	23.80

Souvenir Sheets

1594	A271	Sheet of 4, #a.-d.	8.00	8.00
1595	A271	Sheet of 4, #a.-d.	8.00	8.00

Copernicus (1473-1543) A273

Designs: 20ce, Early astronomical instrument. 200ce, Telescope. No. 1598, Copernicus, long hair. No. 1599, Copernicus, shorter hair.

1993, Oct. 19   **Litho.**   **Perf. 13½x14**

1596	A273	20ce multicolored	.50	.50
1597	A273	200ce multicolored	3.00	3.00

Souvenir Sheets   **Perf. 12x13**

1598	A273	1000ce multicolored	6.00	6.00
1599	A273	1000ce multicolored	6.00	6.00

Picasso (1881-1973) A274

Paintings: 20ce, The Actor, 1905. 80ce, Portrait of Allen Stein, 1906. 800ce, Seated Male Nude, 1908-09.

1993, Oct. 19   **Perf. 14**

1600-1602	A274	Set of 3	5.50	5.50

Souvenir Sheet

1603	A274	900ce Man with a Javelin, 1958	5.50	5.50

Polska '93 — A275

1994 World Cup Soccer, US — A276

Paintings: 200ce, Tattoo, by Sobocki, 1978. 600ce, Prison, by Blonder, 1934. 1000ce, Fable of the Fortunate Man, by Michalak, 1925, horiz.

1993, Oct. 19

1604-1605	A275	Set of 2	5.00	5.00

Souvenir Sheet

1606	A275	1000ce multicolored	5.00	5.00

1993, Dec. 1   **Perf. 13½x14**

Designs: 50ce, Abedi Pele, Ghana. 80ce, Pedro Troglio, Argentina. 100ce, Fernando Alvez, Uruguay. 200ce, Franco Baresi, Italy. 250ce, Gomez, Colombia; Katanec, Yugoslavia. 600ce, Diego Maradona, Argentina. 800ce, Hasek, Czech Republic; Wynalda, US. 1000ce, Lothar Matthaeus, Germany.

No. 1615, Giuseppe Giannini, Italy. No. 1616, Rabie Yassein, Egypt; Ruud Gullit, Holland.

1607	A276	50ce multi	.25	.25
1608	A276	80ce multi	.45	.45
1609	A276	100ce multi	.55	.55
1610	A276	200ce multi	1.10	1.10
1611	A276	250ce multi	1.50	1.50
1612	A276	600ce multi	3.25	3.25
1613	A276	800ce multi	4.25	4.25
1614	A276	1000ce multi	5.00	5.00
		Nos. 1607-1614 (8)	16.35	16.35

Souvenir Sheets   **Perf. 13**

1615	A276	1200ce multi	6.50	6.50
1616	A276	1200ce multi	6.50	6.50

Domestic Animals A277

Designs: 50ce, Meleagris gallopvo. 100ce, Capra hircus. 150ce, Carina moschata. 200ce, Eguus asinus. 250ce, Male gallus gallus. 300ce, Sus vittatus. 400ce, Numida meleagris. 600ce, Canis domesticus. 800ce, Female gallus gallus. 1000ce, Ovis aries.

No. 1627: a, 100ce, Like #1618. b, 250ce, Like #1624. c, 350ce, Like #1622. d, 500ce, Like #1626.

No. 1628: a, 100ce, Like #1623. b, 250ce, Like #1621. c, 350ce, Like #1625. d, 500ce, Like #1617.

1993, Dec. 8   **Perf. 14**

1617-1626	A277	Set of 10	18.50	18.50

Souvenir Sheets

1627	A277	Sheet of 4, #a-d	7.50	7.50
1628	A277	Sheet of 4, #a-d	7.50	7.50

Arts and Crafts — A278

Designs: No. 1629, 50ce, Doll. No. 1630, 50ce, Pot and lid. No. 1631, 200ce, Beads. No. 1632, 200ce, Snake charmers. No. 1633, 250ce, Hoe. No. 1634, 250ce, Scabbard. No. 1635, 600ce, Pipe. No. 1636, 600ce, Deer. No. 1637, 1000ce, Mask. No. 1638, 1000ce, Doll with baby.

No. 1639: a, 100ce, Like #1629. b, 250ce, Like #1631. c, 350ce, Like #1633. d, 500ce, Like #1635.

No. 1640: a, 100ce, Like #1630. b, 250ce, Like #1632. c, 350ce, Like #1634. d, 500ce, Like #1636.

1994, Jan. 24   Litho.   Perf. 14
1629-1638 A278 Set of 10   15.00 15.00

Souvenir Sheets
1639 A278 Sheet of 4, #a-d   4.25 4.25
1640 A278 Sheet of 4, #a-d   4.25 4.25

Christmas
A279

Paintings and Woodcuts: 50ce, Adoration of the Magi. 100ce, The Virgin and Child with Saint John and an Angel, by Botticelli. 150ce, Mary as Queen of Heaven. 200ce, Saint Anne. 250ce, The Madonna of the Magnificat, by Botticelli. 400ce, The Madonna of the Goldfinch, by Tiepolo. 600ce, The Virgin and the Child with the Young St. John the Baptist, by Correggio. 1000ce, Adoration of the Shepherds.
No. 1649, Mystic Nativity (detail), by Botticelli, horiz. No. 1650, Madonna in a Circle, by Durer.
Woodcuts (50ce, 100ce, 200ce, 1000ce) are from Nuremberg Prayer Books, by Durer.

Perf. 13½x14, 14x13½
1993, Dec. 20   Litho.
1641-1648 A279 Set of 8   15.00 15.00

Souvenir Sheets
1649 A279 1000ce multicolored   6.50 6.50
1650 A279 1000ce multicolored   6.50 6.50

A280

Hong Kong '94 — A281

Stamps, tram from Kennedy Town to Shau Kei: No. 1651, Hong Kong #470, back of tram. No. 1652, Front of tram, #1392.
No. 1653 — Imperial Palace clocks: a, Windmill. b, Horse. c, Balloon. d, Zodiac. e, Shar-Pei dog. f, Cat.

1994, Feb. 18   Litho.   Perf. 14
1651 A280 200ce multicolored   1.00 1.00
1652 A280 200ce multicolored   1.00 1.00
a.   Pair, #1651-1652   2.00 2.00

Miniature Sheet
1653 A281 100ce Sheet of 6,
    #a.-f.   6.50 6.50

Nos. 1651-1652 issued in sheets of 5 pairs. No. 1652a is a continuous design.
New Year 1994 (Year of the Dog) (#1653e).

Mickey Mouse, 65th Birthday
A282

Mickey's films: 50ce, Steamboat Willie, 1928. 100ce, The Band Concert, 1937. 150ce, Moose Hunters, 1937. 200ce, Brave Little Taylor, 1938. 250ce, Fantasia, 1940. 400ce, The Nifty Nineties, 1941. 600ce, Canne Caddy,

---

1944. 1000ce, Mickey's Christmas Carol, 1983.
No. 1662, 1200ce, Mickey's Elephant, 1936.
No. 1663, 1200ce, Mickey's Amateurs, 1937.

1994, Mar. 1   Litho.   Perf. 13½x14
1654-1661 A282 Set of 8   12.50 12.50

Souvenir Sheets
1662-1663 A282 Set of 2   11.00 11.00

A283

Hummel Figurines: 50ce, Boy with backpack, walking stick. 100ce, Girl holding basket behind back. 150ce, Boy with rabbits. 200ce, Boy carrying chicks in basket. 250ce, Girl with chicks. 400ce, Girl petting lamb. 600ce, Lamb, girl waving handkerchief. 1000ce, Girl with basket, flowers.
No. 1672: a, 500ce, Like #1665; b, 150ce, Like #1671; c, 1200ce, Like #1667.
No. 1673: a, 300ce, Like #1668; b, 200ce, Like #1669; c, 500ce, Like #1670; d, 1000ce, Like #1666.

1994, Apr. 6   Perf. 14
1664-1671 A283 Set of 8   11.00 11.00

Souvenir Sheets
1672 A283 Sheet of 4, #a.-c.,
    #1664   5.75 5.75
1673 A283 Sheet of 4, #a.-d.   6.00 6.00

World Wildlife Fund — A284

Diana Monkeys: 50ce, Adult, young. 200ce, Sitting in tree. 500ce, Holding food. 800ce, Close-up of face.

1994, May 16   Litho.   Perf. 14
1674-1677 A284 Set of 4   8.50 8.50
1677a   Sheet, 3 each #1674-
    1677   26.00 26.00

For surcharges see Nos. 2530-2533.

Wild Animals
A285

Designs: 100ce, Bushbuck. 150ce, Spotted hyena. 1000ce, Aardvark. No. 1681, 2000ce, Leopard, vert. No. 1682, 2000ce, Waterbuck, vert.

1994, May 16
1678-1680 A285 Set of 3   7.00 7.00

Souvenir Sheets
1681-1682 A285 Set of 2   14.00 14.00

Cats
A286

No. 1683, 200ce: a, Sorrel Abyssinian. b, Silver classic tabby. c, Chocolate-point Siamese. d, Brown tortie Burmese. e, Exotic shorthair. f, Havana brown. g, Devon rex. h, Black manx. i, British blue shorthair. j, Calico American wirehair. k, Spotted oriental Siamese. l, Red classic tabby.
No. 1684, 200ce: a, Norwegian forest cat. b, Blue longhair. c, Red self longhair. d, Black

---

longhair. e, Chinchilla. f, Dilut calico longhair. g, Blue tabby-&-white longhair. h, Ruby somali. i, Blue smoke longhair. j, Calico longhair. k, Brown tabby longhair. l, Balinese.
No. 1685, 2000ce, Brown mackeral tabby Scottish fold. No. 1686, 2000ce, Seal-point colorpoint.

1994, June 6   Litho.   Perf. 14
Sheets of 12, #a-l
1683-1684 A286 Set of 2   16.00 16.00

Souvenir Sheets
1685-1686 A286 Set of 2   11.50 11.50

Birds
A287

No. 1687, 200ce: a, Red-bellied paradise flycatcher (b, e). b, Many-colored bush-shrike. c, Broad-tailed paradise whydah (b, e). d, White-crowned robin-chat. e, Violet plantain-eater. f, Village weaver. g, Fire-crowned bishop. h, Shoveler. i, Spur-winged goose (l). j, African crake. k, King reed-hen. l, Tiger bittern.
No. 1688, 200ce: a, Moho. b, Superb sunbird. c, Blue-breasted kingfisher. d, Blue cuckoo-shrike. e, Blue plantain-eater (d, g). f, Greater flamingo (i). g, Lily-trotter (j). h, Night heron. i, Black-winged stilt (l). j, White-spotted pigmy rail. k, Pigmy goose. k, Angola pitta.
No. 1689, 2000ce, Goliath heron. No. 1690, 2000ce, African spoonbill.

1994, June 13
Sheets of 12, #a-l
1687-1688 A287 Set of 2   21.00 21.00

Souvenir Sheets
1689-1690 A287 Set of 2   14.50 14.50

4th Republic, 1st Anniv.
A288

Designs: 50ce, Rural water projects. 100ce, Honoring farmers. 200ce, Rural electrification. 600ce, Rural bridge construction. 800ce, Natl. Theater. 1000ce, Lighting Perpetual Flame.

1994, July 11   Litho.   Perf. 14
1691-1696 A288 Set of 6   7.50 7.50

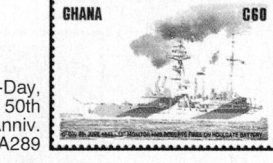

D-Day, 50th Anniv.
A289

Designs: 60ce, 15-inch Monitor HMS Roberts fires on Houlgate Battery. 100ce, HMS Warspite hits Villerville. 200ce, Flagship USS Augusta.
1500ce, USS Nevada bombards Utah Beach.

1994, July 4   Litho.   Perf. 14
1697-1699 A289 Set of 3   4.00 4.00

Souvenir Sheet
1700 A289 1500ce multicolored   7.50 7.50

First Manned Moon Landing, 25th Anniv.
A290

No. 1701 — German, Japanese, scientist-astronauts: a, Sigmund Jahn. b, Ulf Merbold. c, Hans Wilhelm Schlegal. d, Ulrich Walter. e, Reinhard Furrer. f, Ernst Messerschmid. g, Mamoru Mohri. h, Klaus-Dietrich Flade. i, Chaiki Naito-Mukai.
2000ce, "Frau im Mond."

1994, July 4
1701 A290 300ce Sheet of 9,
    #a.-i.   9.50 9.50

Souvenir Sheet
1702 A290 2000ce multicolored   8.75 8.75

Duiker Antelopes
A291

Designs: 50ce, Crowned. 100ce, Red-flanked. 200ce, Yellow-backed. 400ce, Ogilby's. 600ce, Bay. 800ce, Jentink's.
No. 1709, 2000ce, Cephalophus natalensis. No. 1710, 2000ce, Cephalophus niger.

1994, May 16   Litho.   Perf. 14
1703-1708 A291 Set of 6   7.50 7.50

Souvenir Sheets
1709-1710 A291 Set of 2   11.00 11.00

For surcharges see Nos. 2539-2544.

A292

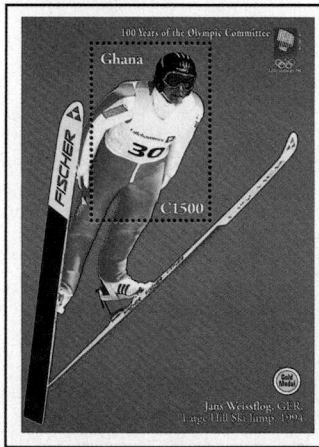

Intl. Olympic Committee, Cent. — A293

Designs: 300ce, Dieter Modenburg, Germany, high jump, 1984. 400ce, Ruth Fuchs, German Democratic Republic, javelin, 1972, 1976.
1500ce, Jans Weissflog, Germany, large hill ski jump, 1994.

1994, July 4   Litho.   Perf. 14
1711 A292 300ce multicolored   1.10 1.10
1712 A292 400ce multicolored   1.40 1.40

Souvenir Sheet
1713 A293 1500ce multicolored   5.50 5.50

A294

PHILAKOREA '94 — A295

Designs: 20ce, Ch'unghak-dong village elder in traditional clothes. 150ce, Stone pagoda, Punhwangsa, Korea. 300ce, Traditional country house, Andong region.

No. 1717 — Letter pictures, eight-panel screen, Choson Dynasty, 20th cent: a, Shown. b, f, Birds. c, Rooster. d, Animal with antennae. e, g, Flowers. h, Fish.

1500ce, Temple judges determine final afterlife judgments, horiz.

1994, July 4   Perf. 14, 13 (#1717)
1714-1716 A294 Set of 3   2.00 2.00
1717 A295 250ce Sheet of 8,
  #a.-h.   7.25 7.25
Souvenir Sheet
1718 A294 1500ce multicolored   6.00 6.00

Miniature Sheet of 6

1994 World Cup Soccer Championships, US — A296

No. 1719: a, Dennis Bergkamp, Netherlands. b, Lothar Matthaus, Germany. c, Giuseppe Signori, Italy. d, Carlos Valderrama, Colombia. e, Jorge Campos, Mexico. f, Tony Meola, US.

No. 1720, 1200ce, Citrus Bowl, Orlando, FL, vert. No. 1721, 1200ce, Giants Stadium, Meadowlands, NJ, vert.

1994, July 25   Perf. 14
1719 A296 200ce Sheet of 6,
  #a.-f.   4.50 4.50
Souvenir Sheets
1720-1721 A296 Set of 2   8.00 .800

Christmas A297

Italian art: 100ce, Madonna of the Annunciation, by Simone Martini. 200ce, Madonna and Child, by Niccolo di Pietro Gerini. 250ce, Virgin and Child on the Throne with Angels and Saints, by Raffaello Botticelli. 300ce, Madonna and Child with Saints, by Antonio Fiorentino. 400ce, Adoration of the Magi, by Bartolo di Fredi. 500ce, The Annunciation, by Cima da Congeliano. 600ce, Virgin and Child with the Young St. John the Baptist, by Workshop of Botticelli. 1000ce, The Holy Family, by Giorgione.

Details from Adoration of the Kings, by Giorgione: No. 1730, 2000ce, Presenting gifts. No. 1731, 20000ce, Madonna & Child.

1994, Dec. 5   Litho.   Perf. 13½x14
1722-1729 A297 Set of 8   10.00 10.00
Souvenir Sheets
1730-1731 A297 Set of 2   12.00 12.00

Intl. Year of the Family — A298

Designs: 50ce, Family. 100ce, Technical training. 200ce, Child care. 400ce, Care for the aged. 600ce, Vocational training. 1000ce, Adult education.

1994, Dec. 20   Perf. 14
1732-1737 A298 Set of 6   6.00 6.00

Ghana Civil Aviation Authority, 50th Anniv. A299

Designs: 100ce, Control tower. 400ce, Insignia, marker light. 1000ce, Airplane leaving runway.

1994, Dec. 20
1738-1740 A299 Set of 3   5.00 5.00

See Nos. 1766-1768. For surcharges see Nos. 2548-2550.

Red Cross & Red Crescent Societies in Ghana, 75th Anniv. A300

Designs: 50ce, Transporting victim. 200ce, Aiding mother, children. 600ce, Erecting tents.

1994, Dec. 20   Litho.   Perf. 14
1741-1743 A300 Set of 3   4.00 4.00
Souvenir Sheet
1744   Sheet of 3, #1741-1742,
           1744a   7.25 7.25
  a. A300 1000ce like #1743   6.00 6.00

For surcharges see Nos. 2545-2547.

Fertility Dolls — A301

Various carvings with background colors of: 50ce, Green. 100ce, Yellow (red frame). 150ce, Blue (black doll). 200ce, Rose. 400ce, Dull orange. 600ce, Yellow green. 800ce, Yellow (green frame). 1000ce, Blue (white doll).

1994, Dec. 20
1745-1752 A301 Set of 8   9.00 9.00
Souvenir Sheet
1753   Sheet of 4, #1745, 1748-
           1749, 1753a   7.25 7.25
  a. A301 250ce like #1752   1.75 1.75

For surcharges see Nos. 2551-2558.

Donald Duck, 60th Birthday (in 1994) — A302

Designs: 40ce, Pluto, Donald, Chip 'n Dale. 50ce, Mickey, pup. 60ce, Daisy. 100ce, Goofy. 150ce, Goofy, diff. 250ce, Donald, Goofy. 400ce, Ludwig Von Drake, Pluto. 500ce, Gramdma Duck, pups. 1000ce, Mickey, Minnie. 1500ce, Pluto.

No. 1764, 2000ce, Daisy, Donald, cake, Mickey, vert. No. 1765, 2000ce, Donald holding fork, spoon, vert.

1995, Feb. 2   Litho.   Perf. 14x13½
1754-1763 A302 Set of 10   11.50 11.50
Souvenir Sheets
Perf. 13½x14
1764-1765 A302 Set of 2   10.00 10.00

Civil Aviation Authority Type of 1994 with ICAO Emblem and New Inscription

Designs: 100ce, Like #1738. 400ce, Like #1739. 1000ce, Like #1740.

1994, Dec. 20   Litho.   Perf. 14
1766-1768 A299 Set of 3   10.00 10.00

Nos. 1766-1768 are inscribed "50th Anniversary of The International Civil Aviation Organization (ICAO)."

For surcharges see Nos. 2559-2561.

Panafest '94 — A303

Designs: 50ce, Northern region dancer. 100ce, Relics with landmark. 200ce, Chief sitting in state. 400ce, Royalist ceremonial dress. 600ce, Cape Coast Castle. 800ce, Clay figurines of West Africa.

1994, Dec. 9   Litho.   Perf. 13½
1769-1774 A303   Set of 6   9.50 9.50

Pan African Historical Theatre Festival, Dec. 1994.

Forts A304

Castles A305

Forts: 50ce, Apolonia, Beyin. 200ce, Patience, Apam. 250ce, Amsterdam, Kormantin. 300ce, St. Jago, Elmina. 400ce, William, Anomabo. 600ce, Kumasi.

Castles: 150ce, Cochem, Germany. 600ce, Hohenzollern, Germany. 800ce, Uwajima, Japan. 100ce, Hohenschwangau, Germany.

Castles: No. 1785a, Windsor, England. b, Osaka, Japan. c, Vaj Dahunyad, Hungary. d, Karlstejn, Czech Republic. e, Kronborg, Denmark. f, Alcazar of Segovia, Spain. g, Chambourd, France. h, Linderhof, Bavaria. i, Red Fort, India.

No. 1786, 800ce, Elmira Castle. No. 1787, 1000ce, Fort St. Antonio, Axim. No. 1788, 2500ce, Himeji Castle, Japan. No. 1789, 2500ce, Neuschwanstein Castle, Germany.

1995, Apr. 3   Perf. 14
1775-1780 A304 Set of 6   6.00 6.00
1781-1784 A305 Set of 4   8.50 8.50
1785 A305 500ce Sheet of 9,
  #a.-i.   12.00 12.00
Souvenir Sheets
1786-1787 A304 Set of 2   5.00 5.00
1788-1789 A305 Set of 2   9.00 9.00

Water Birds A306

Designs: 200ce, Eurasian pochard. 500ce, Maccoa duck. 800ce, Cape shoveler. 1000ce, Red-crested pochard.

No. 1794: a, African pygmy goose. b, Southern pochard. c, Cape teal. d, Ruddy shelduck. e, Fulvous whistling duck. f, White-faced whistling geese. g, Ferruginous white-eye. h, Hottentot teal. i, African black duck. j, Yellow-billed duck. k, White-checked pintail duck. l, Hartlaub's duck.

No. 1795, 2500ce, Roseate tern. No. 1796, 2500ce, Northern shoveler.

1995, Apr. 28
1790-1793 A306 Set of 4   7.00 7.00
1794 A306 400ce Sheet of 12,
  #a.-l.   10.50 10.50
Souvenir Sheets
1795-1796 A306 Set of 2   11.00 11.00

Nos. 1794-1796 have a continuous design. Nos. 1790-1793 have a white border.

1996 Summer Olympics, Atlanta
A307   A308

Athletes: 500ce, Carl Lewis. 800ce, Eric Liddell. 900ce, Runner. 1000ce, Jim Thorpe.

No. 1801: a, Cycling. b, Archery. c, Diving. d, Swimming. e, Gymnastics-Floor Exercise. f, Fencing. g, Boxing. h, Gymnastics-Rings. i, Javelin. j, Tennis. k, Soccer. l, Equestrian.

No. 1802, 1200ce, John Akii Bua. No. 1803, 1200ce, Pierre de Cobertin.

1995, May 2
1797-1800 A307 Set of 4   7.00 7.00
1801 A308 300ce Sheet of 12,
  #a.-l.   8.00 8.00
Souvenir Sheets
1802-1803 A308 Set of 2   5.50 5.50

UN, 50th Anniv. — A309

No. 1804 — Secretaries General: a, 200ce, Trygve Lie, Norway, 1946-52. b, 300ce, Dag Hammarskjold, Sweden, 1953-61. c, 400ce, U Thant, Burma, 1961-71. d, 500ce, Kurt Waldheim, Austria, 1972-81. e, 600ce, Javier Perez de Cuellar, Peru, 1982-91. f, 800ce, Boutros Boutros-Ghali, Egypt, 1992-.

No. 1805, UN flag, horiz.

1995, July 6   Litho.   Perf. 14
1804 A309 Sheet of 6, #a.-f.   6.00 6.00
Souvenir Sheet
1805 A309 1200ce multicolored   3.00 3.00

Miniature Sheets of 6 or 8

A310

End of World War II, 50th Anniv. A311

No. 1806 — Military decorations: a, US Navy Cross, US Purple Heart. b, UK Air Force Cross, UK Distinguished Flying Cross. c, US Navy and Marine Corps Medal, US Distinguished Service Cross. d, UK Distinguished Service Medal, UK Distinguished Conduct Medal. e, UK Military Medal, UK Military Cross. f, UK Distinguished Service Cross, UK Distinguished Service Order.

No. 1807: a, Churchill. b, Eisenhower. c, Air Chief Marshall Sir Arthur Tedder. d, Montgomery. e, Bradley. f, de Gaulle. g, French Resistance Organization. h, Patton.

No. 1808, 1200ce, U.S. Medal of Honor. No. 1809, 1200ce, Fuhrer's promise.

1995, July 6   Litho.   Perf. 14
1806 A310 500ce Sheet of 6, #a.-f. + label   8.00 8.00
1807 A311 400ce Sheet of 8, #a.-h. + label   8.00 8.00

Souvenir Sheets
1808-1809 A310 Set of 2   7.00 7.00

No. 1809 contains one 42x56mm stamp.

FAO, 50th Anniv. A312

Designs: 200ce, Fish preservation. 300ce, Fishing. 400ce, Ox-drawn plow. 600ce, Harvesting. 800ce, Aforestation.
2000ce, Boat, shoreline, oxen, fruit.

1995, July 6   Litho.   Perf. 14
1810-1814 A312 Set of 5   5.00 5.00

Souvenir Sheet
1815 A312 2000ce multicolored   4.50 4.50

For surcharges see Nos. 2534-2538.

Rotary Intl., 90th Anniv. A313

Designs: 600ce, Natl. flag, Rotary emblem. 1200ce, Rotary emblem on banner, vert.

1995, July 6
1816 A313 600ce multicolored   1.75 1.75

Souvenir Sheet
1817 A313 1200ce multicolored   3.00 3.00

1995 Boy Scout Jamboree, Holland — A314

No. 1818: a, 400ce, Two boys. 800ce, Two boys, one wearing glasses. c, 1000ce, Two boys facing left.
1200ce, Boy with bamboo poles.

1995, July 6
1818 A314 Strip of 3, #a.-c.   4.75 4.75

Souvenir Sheet
1819 A314 1200ce multicolored   4.00 4.00

No. 1818 is a continuous design.

Queen Mother, 95th Birthday A315

No. 1820: a, Drawing. b, Bright green blue hat. c, Formal portrait. d, Coral outfit. 2500ce, Pale blue outfit.

1995, July 6   Perf. 13½x14
1820 A315 600ce Strip or block of 4, #a.-d.   5.50 5.50

Souvenir Sheet
1821 A315 2500ce multicolored   4.50 4.50

No. 1820 was issued in sheets of 8 stamps. For surcharges see Nos. 2333-2334.

Singapore '95 — A316

No. 1822, 400ce: a, Seismosaurus (d-f). b, Supersaurus (a, d). c, Ultrasaurus (f). d, Saurolophus (e). e, Lambeosaurus (d, g-h). f, Parasaurolophus (e, i). g, Triceratops (h). h, Styracosaurus (e, g i). i, Pachyrhinosaurus (h).
No. 1823, 400ce: a, Peteinosaurus (b, d-e). b, Quetzalcoatlus (a, c, e). c, Eudimorphodon (b). d, Allosaurus (e-f, h-i). e, Daspletosaurus (f). f, Tarbosaurus (i). g, Velociraptor (h-i). h, Herrerasaurus (i). i, Coelophysis.
No. 1824, 2500ce, Albertosaur. No. 1825, 2500ce, Tyrannosaurus rex.

1995, Aug. 8   Litho.   Perf. 14
Sheets of 9, #a-i
1822-1823 A316 Set of 2   16.00 16.00

Souvenir Sheets
1824-1825 A316 Set of 2   11.00 11.00

Nobel Prize Recipients — A317

No. 1826: a, Nelson Mandela, peace, 1993. b, Albert Schweitzer, peace, 1952. c, Wole Soyinka, literature, 1986. d, Emil Fischer, chemistry, 1902. e, Rudolf Mossbauer, physics, 1961. f, Archbishop Desmond Tutu, peace, 1984. g, Max Born, physics, 1954. h, Max Planck, physics, 1918. i, Hermann Hesse, literature, 1946.
1200ce, Paul Ehrlich, medicine, 1908.

1995, Oct. 2   Litho.   Perf. 14
1826 A317 400ce Sheet of 9, #a.-i.   10.00 10.00

Souvenir Sheet
1827 A317 1200ce multicolored   4.00 4.00

Asantehene, 25th Anniv. — A318

Designs: 50ce, Emblem. 100ce, Silver casket. 200ce, Golden stool. 400ce, Busummuru sword bearer. 600ce, 800ce, Diff. portraits of Otumfuo Opoku Ware II. 1000ce, Mponponsuo sword bearer.

1995   Perf. 13½x13
1828-1834 A318 Set of 7   6.25 6.25

Fauna — A319

Designs: 400ce, Cymothoe beckeri. 500ce, Graphium policene. 1000ce, Urotriorchis macrourus, vert. 2000ce, Xiphias gladius. 3000ce, Monodoctylus sabee. 5000ce, Ardea purpurea, vert.
400ce exists in two types:
Type I — Large flower bud under second "A" in "Ghana," the top of which is above cross line of "A" (shown in illustration).
Type II — Small flower bud under second "A" in "Ghana," the top of which is below cross line of "A."

Perf. 14¼x13¾, 13¾x14¼
1995, June 19   Litho.
1835   A319 400ce multi   .80   .80
1835A A319 400ce multi, type II   —   —
1836   A319 500ce multi   1.00 1.00
1837   A319 1000ce multi   2.00 2.00
  a.   Perf. 11½
1838   A319 2000ce multi   4.25 4.25
1839   A319 3000ce multi   6.25 6.25
1840   A319 5000ce multi   10.50 10.50
       Nos. 1835-1840 (7)   24.80 24.80

No. 1838 has denomination at left. No. 1840 has green frame and "A's" of "Ghana" with cross lines sloping down to right.
An additional stamp exists in this set. The editors would like to examine it.

Christmas A320

Details or entire paintings: 50ce, The Infant Jesus and the Young St. John, by Murillo. 80ce, Rest on Flight to Egypt, by Memling. 300ce, Sacred Family, by Van Dyck. 600ce, The Virgin and the Infant, by Uccello. 800ce, The Virgin and the Infant, by Van Eyck. 1000ce, Head of Christ, by Rembrandt.
No. 1847, 2500ce, Madonna, by Montagna. No. 1848, 2500ce, The Holy Family, by Pulzone.

1995, Dec. 1   Litho.   Perf. 13½x14
1841-1846 A320 Set of 6   6.00 6.00

Souvenir Sheets
1847-1848 A320 Set of 2   18.00 18.00

Motion Pictures, Cent. A321

No. 1849: a, 1903 H. Ernmann camera. b, Charles Chaplin. c, Rudolph Valentino. d, Will Rogers. e, Greta Garbo. f, Jackie Cooper. g, Bette Davis. h, John Barrymore. i, Shirley Temple.
No. 1850, Laurel and Hardy.

1995, Dec. 8
1849 A321 400ce Sheet of 9, #a.-i.   11.00 11.00

Souvenir Sheet
1850 A321 2500ce multi   7.25 7.25

A322

John Lennon (1940-80) A323

No. 1852: a-g, i, Various portraits. h, Like No. 1851.
2000ce, Lennon playing guitar, water in background.

1995, Dec. 8   Perf. 14
1851 A322 400ce shown   3.50 3.50

Miniature Sheet
Perf. 13½x14
1852 A323 400ce Sheet of 9, #a.-i.   12.50 12.50

Souvenir Sheet
1853 A323 2000ce multi   9.00 9.00

No. 1851 was issued in sheets of 16.

Louis Pasteur (1822-95) — A324

No. 1854: a, In laboratory. b, Discovery of rabies virus and vaccine. c, Pneumococcus discovery, 1880. d, Development of first vaccine with birds. e, Perfection of brewer's yeast culture.

1995, Dec. 13   Perf. 14
1854 A324 600ce Sheet of 5, #a.-e.   7.25 7.25

Paintings from the Metropolitan Museum of Art — A325

No. 1855, 400ce: a, Portrait of a Man, by Van Der Goes. b, Paradise, by Giovanni di Paolo. c, Portrait of a Young Man, by Antonello da Messina. d, Tommaso Portinari, by Memling. e, Wife Maria Portinari, by Memling. f, Portrait of a Lady, by Ghirlandaio. g, St. Christopher & Infant Christ, by Ghirlandaio. h, Francesco D'Este, by van der Weyden.

No. 1856, 400ce: a, The Interrupted Sleep, by Boucher. b, Diana and Cupid, by Batoni. c, Boy Blowing Bubbles, by Chardin. d, Ancient Rome, by Pannini. e, Modern Rome, by Pannini. f, The Calmady Children, by Lawrence. g, The Triumph of Marius, by G.B. Tiepolo. h, Garden at Vaucresson, by E. Vuillard.

No. 1857, 2500ce, The Epiphany, by Giotto. No. 1858, 2500ce, The Calling of Matthew, by Hemessen.

1996, Feb. 12   Litho.   Perf. 13½x14
Sheets of 8, #a-h, + Label
1855-1856   A325   Set of 2   15.00 15.00
Souvenir Sheets
Perf. 14
1857-1858   A325   Set of 2   15.00 15.00

Nos. 1857-1858 each contain one 85x57mm stamp.

New Year 1996 (Year of the Rat) — A326

Nos. 1859-1860 — Stylized rats: a, With musical instruments, on horseback. b, Holding banners. c, Carrying rat in palanquin. d, Carrying box, holding fish.
1000ce, Four rats transporting rat in palanquin, horiz.

1996, Jan. 28   Litho.   Perf. 14
Country Name in White
1859   A326   250ce Strip of 4,
              #a.-d.   4.50 4.50
Country Name in Red
1860   A325   250ce Sheet of 4,
              #a.-d.   4.50 4.50
Souvenir Sheet
1861   A325   1000ce red, pink &
              yellow   4.50 4.50

No. 1859 was issued in sheets of 12 stamps.

Fauna of the Rainforest — A327

No. 1862, 400ce: a, Ramphastos toco. b, Choloepus didactylus. c, Pongo pygmaeus. d, Spiaetus cirrhatus. e, Panthera tigris. f, Ibis leucocephallus. g, Ara chloroptera. h, Saimiri sciureus. i, Macaca fascicularis. j, Cithaerias menander, ithomiidae. k, Coryptophanes cristatus, gekkonidae. l, Boa caninus.

No. 1863, 400ce: a, Opisthoccomus hoazin. b, Tarsius bancanus. c, Leontopithecus rosalia. d, Pteropus gouldii. e, Rupicola rupicola. f, Pharomachrus mocino. g, Hyla boans, dendrobates leucomeles. h, Lemur catta. i, Iguana iguana. j, Heliconius burneyi. k, Mellisuga minima. l, Propithecus verreauxi.

No. 1864, 3000ce, Sarcoramphus papa. No. 1865, 3000ce, Pteridophora alberti.

1996, Apr. 15
Sheets of 12, #a-l
1862-1863   A327   Set of 2   20.00 20.00
Souvenir Sheets
1864-1865   A327   Set of 2   15.00 15.00

China '96 — A328

No. 1866: a, Kaiyuan Si Temple, Fujian. b, Kaiyuan Si Temple, Hebei. c, Fogong Si Temple, Shanxi. d, Xiangshan, Beijing.
No. 1867, Baima Si Temple, Henan.

1996, May 13   Litho.   Perf. 14
1866   A328   400ce Strip of 4,
              #a.-d.   7.00 7.00
Souvenir Sheet
1867   A328   1000ce multicolored 5.00 5.00

No. 1866 was issued in sheets of 8 stamps. See No. 1913.

Queen Elizabeth II, 70th Birthday A329

No. 1868: a, Portrait. b, Wearing blue hat, coat. c, Wearing printed dress, wide-brim hat. 2500ce, Riding in horse-drawn carriage, horiz.

1996, June 10   Litho.   Perf. 13½x14
1868   A329   1000ce Strip of 3,
              #a.-c.   7.25 7.25
Souvenir Sheet
Perf. 14x13½
1869   A329   2500ce multicolored 6.50 6.50

No. 1868 was issued in sheets of 9 stamps.

1996 Summer Olympics, Atlanta A330

Designs: 300ce, Two wrestlers, javelin thrower, Bas Relief, 500BC. 500ce, Wilma Rudolph, gold medalist in track and field, Rome, 1960, Olympic torch. 600ce, The Forum, St. Peter's Basilica, Colosseum, Olympic Stadium, Rome, 1960. 800ce, Soviet flag, ladies' kayak pairs gold medal winners, Rome, 1960.

No. 1874, 400ce — Medalists in swimming, diving: a, Aileen Riggin, springboard, 1920. b, Pat McCormick, platform, 1952. c, Dawn Fraser, 100m freestyle, 1956. d, Chris Von Saltza, 400m freestyle, 1960. e, Anita Lonsbrough, 200m breaststroke, 1960. f, Debbie Meyer, 400m freestyle, 1968. g, Shane Gould, 400m freestyle, 1972. h, Petra Thuemer, 800m freestyle, 1976. i, Marjorie Gestring, springboard, 1936.

No. 1875, 400ce, vert. — Soccer players: a, Abedi Pele, Ghana. b, Quico Navarez, Spain. c, Heino Hanson, Denmark. d, Mostafa Ismail, Egypt. e, Anthony Yeboah, Ghana. f, Jurgen Klinsmann, Germany. g, Cobi Jones, US. h, Franco Baresi, Italy. i, Igor Dobrovolski, Russia.

No. 1876, 2000ce, Kornelia Ender, 200m freestyle gold medalist, 1976. No. 1877, 2000ce, Tracy Caulkins, 200m individual medlay gold medalist, 1984.

1996, June 27   Perf. 14
1870-1873   A330   Set of 4   4.50 4.50
Sheets of 9, #a-i
1874-1875   A330   Set of 2   18.00 18.00
Souvenir Sheets
1876-1877   A330   Set of 2   11.00 11.00

Intl. Amateur Boxing Assoc., 50th Anniv. — A331

Boxers: 300ce, Serafim Todorow, Bulgaria. 400ce, Oscar de La Hoya, US. 800ce, Ariel Hernandez, Cuba. 1500ce, Arnaldo Mesa, Cuba.
3000ce, Tadahiro Sasaki, Japan.

1996, July 31
1878-1881   A331   Set of 4   7.00 7.00
Souvenir Sheet
1882   A331   3000ce multicolored 7.00 7.00

UNESCO, 50th Anniv. — A332

Designs: 400ce, The Citadel, Haiti, vert. 800ce, Ait-Ben-Haddou (Fortified Village), Morocco, vert. 1000ce, Spissky Hrad (exterior of castle), Slovakia.
2000ce, Cape Coast, Ghana.

1996, July 31   Litho.   Perf. 14
1883-1885   A332   Set of 3   6.50 6.50
Souvenir Sheet
1886   A332   2000ce multicolored 6.00 6.00

UNICEF, 50th Anniv. — A333

Designs: 400ce, Baby. 500ce, Mother, baby. 600ce, Mother, child drinking from glass. 1000ce, Child, diff.

1996, July 31
1887-1889   A333   Set of 3   3.00 3.00
Souvenir Sheet
1890   A333   1000ce multicolored 2.50 2.50

Jerusalem, 3000th Anniv. — A334

Landmark, flower: 400ce, St. Stephen's (Lion) Gate, Jasminum mesnyi. 600ce, Citadel and Tower of David, nerium oleander. 800ce, Chapel of the Ascension, romulea bulbocodium.
2000ce, Russian Church of St. Mary Magdalene.

1996, July 31   Set of 3   4.00 4.00
1891-1893   A334
Souvenir Sheet
1894   A334   2000ce multicolored 6.00 6.00

For overprints see Nos. 2032-2035.

Musical Instruments A335

No. 1895: a, Fiddles. b, Proverbial drum. c, Double clapless bell & castanet. d, Gourd rattle. e, Horns.

1996, Aug. 5
1895   A335   500ce Sheet of 5,
              #a.-e.   5.25 5.25

Disney's Best Friends — A336

No. 1896, 60ce, Ariel, Flounder, Sebastian. No. 1897, 60ce, Pinocchio, Jiminy Cricket. No. 1898, 60ce, Cogsworth, Lumiere. No. 1899, 60ce, Copper, Tod. No. 1900, 60ce, Pocahontas, Meeko, Flit. No. 1901, 60ce, Bambi, Flower, Thumper.

No. 1902: a, 450ce, Pocahontas, Meeko, Flit. b, 150ce, Pinocchio, Jiminy Cricket. c, 200ce, Copper, Tod. d, 600ce, Aladdin, Abu. e, 700ce, Penny, Rufus. f, 350ce, Cogsworth, Lumiere. g, 800ce, Mowgli, Baloo. h, 200ce, Ariel, Flounder, Sebastian, i, 300ce, Bambi, Flower, Thumper.

No. 1903, Winnie the Pooh, vert. No. 1904, Simba, Pumbaa.

Perf. 14x13½, 13½x14
1996, Aug. 25
1896-1901   A336   Set of 6   2.75 2.75
1902   A336   Sheet of 9, #a.-
              i.   8.50 8.50
Souvenir Sheets
1903   A336   3000ce multicolored 5.00 5.00
1904   A336   3000ce multicolored 5.00 5.00

Stampshow '96 (No. 1902).

E.W. Agyare (1937-72), Ghana Broadcasting Corp. Technician — A337

1996, July 31   Perf. 14
1905   A337   100ce multicolored .45 .45

Radio, Cent. A338

Entertainers: 500ce, Frank Sinatra. No. 1907, 600ce, Judy Garland. No. 1908, 600ce, Bing Crosby. 800ce, Dean Martin, Jerry Lewis. 2000ce, Edgar Bergen, Charlie McCarthy.

1996, July 31   *Perf. 13½x14*
1906-1909   A338   Set of 4   3.50 3.50
Souvenir Sheet
1910   A338   2000ce multicolored   3.50 3.50

Sylvester Stallone in Movie, "Rocky II" — A339

1996, Nov. 21   Litho.   *Perf. 14*
1911   A339   2000ce multi   2.40 2.40
Issued in sheets of 3.

New Year 1997 (Year of the Ox) — A340

Various scenes from Chinese story, "Herd Boy and Girl Weaver."

1997, Jan. 22   Litho.   *Perf. 14*
1912   A340   500ce Sheet of 9, #a.-i.   7.00 7.00

Souvenir Sheet

China '96 — A341

Statue of the Devil.

1996, May 13   Litho.   *Perf. 14*
1913   A341   1000ce multicolored   3.25 3.25
No. 1913 was not available until March 1997.

African Hair Styles — A342

No. 1914, 1000ce: a, Dipo. b, Oduku. c, Dansinkran. d, Mbobom. e, Oduku 2.
No. 1915, 1000ce: a, African corn row. b, Chinese raster. c, Chinese raster 2. d, Corn row. e, Mbakaa.

1997, Mar. 3
Sheets of 5, #a-e
1914-1915   A342   Set of 2   10.00 10.00

GHANA
120th Anniversary of the Birth of Dr Hideyo Noguchi
Tomb of Dr. Noguchi
c1000

Dr. Hideyo Noguchi (1876-1928), Pathologist A343

No. 1916: a, Tomb. b, Portrait. c, Birth place. d, Noguchi Institute, Legon. e, Noguchi Gardens, Accra.
No. 1917, 3000ce, Dr. Noguchi in laboratory. No. 1918, 3000ce, Statue.

1997, Mar. 3
1916   A343   1000ce Sheet of 5, #a.-e.   7.00 7.00
Souvenir Sheets
1917-1918   A343   Set of 2   7.00 7.00

Independence, 40th Anniv. — A344

Designs: 200ce, Emblem. 550ce, Dr. Kwame Nkrumah, first president of Ghana, vert. 800ce, Achievement in education. 1100ce, Akosombo Dam.
2000ce, Declaration of independence, Old Polo Grounds, vert. 3000ce, Kofi Annan, UN Secretary General, vert.

1997, Mar. 6   Litho.   *Perf. 14*
1919-1922   A344   Set of 4   8.00 8.00
Souvenir Sheets
1923   A344   2000ce multicolored   3.00 3.00
1924   A344   3000ce multicolored   5.00 5.00

Deng Xiaoping (1904-97), Chinese Leader — A345

No. 1925: a, 300ce, Smiling. b, 600ce, Wearing glasses. c, 800ce, Like #1925b. d, 1000ce, Like #1925a.
No. 1926: a, 500ce, Lips pursed. b, 600ce, Teeth showing. c, 800ce, Like #1926b. d, 1000ce, Like #1926a.
No. 1927, Reading. No. 1928, Hand in air.

1997, Apr. 28   *Perf. 14x13½*
1925   A345   Sheet of 4, #a.-d.   3.75 3.75
1926   A345   Sheet of 4, #a.-d.   4.00 4.00
Souvenir Sheets
Perf. 13½
1927   A345   3000ce multicolored   3.75 3.75
1928   A345   4000ce multicolored   4.00 4.00
Nos. 1927-1928 each contain one 51x38mm stamp.

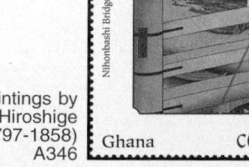

Paintings by Hiroshige (1797-1858) A346

No. 1929: a, Nihonbashi Bridge and Edobashi Bridge. b, View of Nihonbashi Tori 1-chome. c, Open Garden at Fukagawa

---

Hachiman Shrine. d, Inari Bridge and Minato Shrine, Teppozu. e, Bamboo Yards, Kyobashi Bridge. f, Hall of Thirty-Three Bays, Fukagawa.
No. 1930, 3000ce, Teppozu and Tsukiji Honganji Temple. No. 1931, 3000ce, Sumiyoshi Festival, Tsukudajima.

1997, May 29   Litho.   *Perf. 13½x14*
1929   A346   600ce Sheet of 6, #a.-f.   5.00 5.00
Souvenir Sheets
1930-1931   A346   Set of 2   7.00 7.00

Queen Elizabeth II, Prince Philip, 50th Wedding Anniv. A347

No. 1932: a, Queen. b, Royal Arms. c, Queen, Prince waving. d, Queen, Prince. e, Royal carriage. f, Portrait of Prince Philip.
3000ce, Portrait of Queen Elizabeth II.

1997, May 29   *Perf. 14*
1932   A347   800ce Sheet of 6, #a.-f.   5.75 5.75
Souvenir Sheet
1933   A347   3000ce multicolored   2.00 2.00

Heinrich von Stephan (1831-97), Founder of UPU A348

No. 1934 — Portrait of Von Stephan and: a, Automobile used for postal delivery. b, UPU emblem. c, First airmail flight, Pierre Blanchard, 1784.
3000ce, African messenger with cleft stick.

1997, May 29   Litho.   *Perf. 14*
1934   A348   1000ce Sheet of 3, #a.-c.   3.50 3.50
Souvenir Sheet
1935   A348   3000ce multicolored   3.50 3.50
PACIFIC 97.

Paul P. Harris (1868-1947), Founder of Rotary Intl. — A349

Portrait of Harris, Rotary emblem and: 2000ce, PolioPlus oral vaccine administration, Egypt. 3000ce, Emblem for PolioPlus vaccine, "A world free of disease."

1997, May 29
1936   A349   2000ce multicolored   3.50 3.50
Souvenir Sheet
1937   A349   3000ce multicolored   3.50 3.50

Chernobyl, 10th Anniv. A350

Designs: 800ce, UNESCO. 1000ce, Chabad's Children of Chernobyl.

1997, May 29   *Perf. 13½x14*
1938   A350   800ce multicolored   2.25 2.25
1939   A350   1000ce multicolored   2.50 2.50

Cyrestes Camillus — A350a

Designs: 550ce, Ajumpan drums. 1100ce Kente cloth, horiz.

Perf. 13½x14¼, 14¼x13½
1997   Litho.
1939A   A350a   550ce multi   — —
1939B   A350a   800ce multi   — —
1939C   A350a   1100ce multi   — —
Issued: 550ce, 5/30; 800ce, 6/4. 1100ce, 6/7. For surcharges see Nos. 2360, 2360A.

A351

Entertainers — A352

No. 1940: a, Jackie Gleason. b, Danny Kaye. c, John Cleese. d, Lucille Ball. e, Jerry Lewis. f, Sidney James. g, Louis de Fuenes. h, Mae West. i, Bob Hope.
No. 1941: a, Professor Ajax Bukana with fingers making "V." b, Bukana with arms spread.
3000ce, Groucho Marx.

1997, July 1   *Perf. 13½x14*
1940   A351   600ce Sheet of 9, #a.-i.   7.00 7.50
Souvenir Sheets
Perf. 14
1941   A352   2000ce Sheet of 2, #a-b   3.50 3.50
Perf. 13½x14
1942   A351   3000ce multicolored   2.25 2.25

Mushrooms A353

Designs: 200ce, Galerina calyptrata. 300ce, Lepiota ignivolvata. 400ce, Omphalotus olearius. 550ce, Amanita phalloides. 600ce, Entoloma conferendum. 800ce, Entoloma nitidum.
No. 1949: a, Coprinus picaceus. b, Stropharia aurantiaca. c, Cortinarius splendens. d, Gomphidius roseus. e, Russula sardonia. f, Geastrum schmidelia.

No. 1950, 3000ce, Mycena crocata. No. 1951, 3000ce, Craterellus cornucopioides.

1997, July 9   **Perf. 14**
1943-1948 A353 Set of 6   3.50 3.50
1949 A353 800ce Sheet of 6, #a.-f.   5.75 5.75

Souvenir Sheets
1950-1951 A353 Set of 2   7.00 7.00

Fish A354

Seabirds, Marine Life A355

Designs: 400ce, African pygmy angelfish. 600ce, Angelfish. 800ce, Broomtail wrasse. 1000ce, Indian butterfly fish.
No. 1956: a, Violet crested turaco. b, Pied avocet. c, Bottle-nosed dolphin. d, Bottle-nosed dolphin, long-toed lapwing. e, Longfinned spadefish (i). f, Imperial angelfish, manta ray. g, Raccoon butterfly fish, African pompano (h, k). h, Silvertip shark (g, l). i, Longfin banner fish (e, j). j, Longfin banner fish, manta ray (f, i). k, Rusty parrot fish (j). l, Coral trout.
No. 1957, 3000ce, Crown butterfly fish. No. 1958, 3000ce, King angelfish.

1997, July 15
1952-1955 A354 Set of 4   3.50 3.50
1956 A355 500ce Sheet of 12, #a.-l.   7.25 7.25

Souvenir Sheets
1957-1958 A355 Set of 2   8.00 8.00

Flowers A356

Designs: 200ce, Eurychone rothschildiana. 550ce, Bulbophyllum lepidum. No. 1961, 800ce, Ansellia africana. 1100ce, Combretum grandiflorum.
No. 1963, vert: a, Strophanthus preusii. b, Ancistrochilus rothchildianus. c, Mussaenda arcuata. d, Microcoelia guyoniana. e, Gloriosa simplex. f, Brachycorythis kalbreyeri. g, Aframomum sceptrum. h, Thunbergia alata. i, Clerodendrum thomsoniae.
No. 1964, 3000ce, Kigelia africana. No. 1965, 3000ce, Spathodea campanulata.

1997, Aug. 1   **Litho.**   **Perf. 14½**
1959-1962 A356 Set of 4   4.00 4.00
1963 A356 800ce Sheet of 9, #a.-i.   10.00 10.00

Souvenir Sheets
1964-1965 A356 Set of 2   8.00 8.00

1998 World Cup Soccer Championships, France — A357

Stadiums: 200ce, Azteca, Mexico, 1970, 1986. 300ce, Rose Bowl, US, 1994. 400ce, Giuseppe Meazza, Italy, 1990. 500ce, Olympic, Germany, 1974. 1000ce, Maracana, Brazil, 1950. 2000ce, Bernabeu, Spain, 1982.
No. 1972 — Soccer players: a, Patrick Kluivert, Holland. b, Roy Deane, Ireland. c, Abedi Pele Ayew, Ghana. d, Peter Schmeichel, Denmark. e, Roberto di Matteo, Italy. f, Bebeto, Brazil. g, Steve McManaman, England. h, George Appong Weah, Liberia.

No. 1973, 3000ce, Juninho, Brazil. No. 1974, 3000ce, Seaman, England.

1997, July 12   **Perf. 14x13½**
1966-1971 A357 Set of 6   5.00 5.00
1972 A357 600ce Sheet of 8, #a.-h. + label   5.00 5.00

Souvenir Sheets
1973-1974 A357 Set of 2   7.50 7.50
Nos. 1966-1971 were issued in sheets of 10 each.

Birds — A358

Designs: 200ce, Eurasian goldfinch. 300ce, Cape batis. 400ce, Bearded barbet. 500ce, White-necked raven. 600ce, Purple grenadier. 1000ce, Zebra waxbill.
No. 1981: a, Black bustard. b, Northern lapwing. c, Sandgrouse. d, Red-crested turaco. e, White-browed coucal. f, Lilac-breasted roller. g, Golden pipet. h, Crimson-breasted gonolek. i, Blackcap.
No. 1982, 3000ce, Nectarina famosa. No. 1983, 3000ce, Vidua regia.

1997, Oct. 20   **Litho.**   **Perf. 14**
1975-1980 A358 Set of 6   3.50 3.50
1981 A358 800ce Sheet of 9, #a.-i.   8.50 8.50

Souvenir Sheets
1982-1983 A358 Set of 2   8.00 8.00

Cats and Dogs A359

Cats, #1984-1989: 20ce, Havana. 50ce, Singapura. 100ce, Sphinx. 150ce, British white. 300ce, Snowshoe. 600ce, Persian.
Dogs, #1989A-1989F: 80ce, Papillon. 200ce, Bulldog. 400ce, Shetland sheepdog. 500ce, Schnauzer. 800ce, Shih tzu. 2000ce, Chow chow.
No. 1990, 1000ce — Dogs and cats: a, Russian wolfhound. b, Birman. c, Basset hound. d, Silver tabby. e, Afghan. f, Burmilla.
No. 1991, 1000ce: a, Abyssinian. b, Border terrier. c, Scottish fold. d, Boston terrier. e, Oriental. f, Keeshond.
No. 1992, 3000ce, Ragdoll. No. 1992A, 3000ce, Alaskan malamute.

1997, Oct. 20
1984-1989 A359 Set of 6   2.75 2.75
1989A-1989F A359 Set of 6   8.00 8.00

Sheets of 6, #a-f
1990-1991 A359 Set of 2   17.50 17.50

Souvenir Sheets
1992-1992A A359 Set of 2   9.00 9.00

Return of Hong Kong to China — A360

No. 1993: a, Lin Tsi-Hsu (1785-1850). b, Gwan Tian-Pei. Illustration reduced.

1997, Nov. 10
1993 A360 1000ce Sheet of 4, 2 each #a.-b.   6.50 6.50

Huang Binhong (1865-1955) — A361

No. 1994 — Various details of "Color Landscape": a, 200ce. b, 300ce. c, 400ce. d, 500ce. e, 600ce. f, 800ce. g, 1000ce. h, 2000ce.
No. 1995: a, Detail with Chinese inscription. b, Detail without inscription.

1997, Nov. 10
1994 A361 Sheet of 8, #a.-h.   7.00 7.00

Souvenir Sheet
1995 A361 2000ce Sheet of 2, #a.-b.   5.50 5.50
Nos. 1994a-1994h are each 28x90mm.

Christmas A362

Entire paintings or details: 200ce, Cupid by Botticelli. 550ce, Zephyr and Chloris, by Botticelli. 800ce, Trumphant Cupid, by Caravaggio. 1100ce, The Seven Works of Mercy, by Caravaggio. 1500ce, The Toilet of Venus, by Diego Velazquez. 2000ce, Freeing of Saint Peter, by Raphael.
Sculptures: No. 2002, 5000ce, The Cavalcant Annunciation, by Donatello. No. 2003, 5000ce, Isis and Nepthys Protecting the Cartouches of Tutankhamen with their Wings.

1997, Dec. 8   **Litho.**   **Perf. 14**
1996-2001 A362 Set of 6   6.50 6.50

Souvenir Sheets
2002-2003 A362 Set of 2   10.00 10.00

Diana, Princess of Wales (1961-97) — A363

Various portraits, background color of sheet margin: No. 2004, 1200ce, Pink. No. 2005, 1200ce, Blue.
Portraits with (in margin): No. 2006, 3000ce, Elizabeth Taylor. No. 2007, 3000ce, Henry Kissinger.

1997, Dec. 22
Sheets of 6, #a-f
2004-2005 A363 Set of 2   12.00 12.00

Souvenir Sheets
2006-2007 A363 Set of 2   7.00 7.00

Mickey and Friends A364

No. 2008, 1000ce — Characters, month: a, Mortie and Ferdie, Jan. b, Minnie, Feb. c, Goofy, Mar. d, Mickey, Minnie, & Pluto, Apr. e, Minnie, May. f, Daisy, June.
No. 2009, 1000ce: a, Donald, July. b, Donald and Daisy, Aug. c, Morty and Ferdie, Sept. d, Huey, Dewey, & Louie, Oct. e, Mickey, Nov. f, Mickey & Minnie, Dec.
Characters, season: No. 2010, 5000ce, Daisy, nephews, winter, horiz. No. 2011, 5000ce, Goofy, fall. No. 2012, 5000ce, Mickey, spring, horiz. No. 2013, 5000ce, Minnie, summer.

Perf. 13½x14, 14x13½
1998, Jan. 29   **Litho.**
Sheets of 6, #a-f
2008-2009 A364 Set of 2   24.00 24.00
Sheets of 6 With Added Marginal Inscription
2008g-2009g Set of 2   27.50 27.50
Souvenir Sheets
2010-2013 A364 Set of 4   32.50 32.50
Souvenir Sheets With Added Marginal Inscriptions
2012a-2013a Set of 2   57.50 57.50
Nos. 2008g, 2009g, 2012a, 2013a have added inscription in sheet margin showing "Happy Birthday," Mickey Mouse, and "1998" in emblem.
Issued: Nos. 2008g, 2009g, 2012a, 2013a, 8/4/98.

Trains A365

Designs: 300ce, Union Pacific SD60M, US. 500ce, ETR 450, Italy. No. 2018, 800ce, X200 Sweden. 1000ce, TGV Duplex, France. 2000ce, El Class Co-Co, Australia. 3000ce, Eurostar, Britain.
No. 2020, 800ce: a, SPS 4-4-0, Pakistan. b, Class WP 4-6-2, India. c, Class QI 2-10-2, China. d, Class 12 4-4-2, Belgium. e, Class P8 4-6-0, Germany. f, Castle Class 4-6-0, Britain. g, Tank engine 2-6-0, Austria. h, Class P36 4-8-4, Russia. i, William Mason 4-4-0, US.
No. 2021, 800ce: a, AVE, Spain. b, Class 1600, Luxembourg. c, Bullet train, Japan. d, GM F7 Warbonnet, US. e, Class E1500, Morocco. f, Deltic, Great Britain. g, XPT, Australia. h, Le Shuttle, France/Britain. i, Class 201, Ireland.
No. 2022, 5500ce, Duchess Class 4-6-2, Britain. No. 2023, 5500ce, TGV, France.

1998, Feb. 26   **Litho.**   **Perf. 14**
2014-2019 A365 Set of 6   7.75 7.75
Sheets of 9, #a-i
2020-2021 A365 Set of 2   14.50 14.50
Souvenir Sheets
2022-2023 A365 Set of 2   11.00 11.00
Nos. 2022-2023 each contain one 57x42mm stamp.

Lunar New Year — A366

No. 2025 — Signs of Chinese zodiac: a, Horse. b, Monkey. c, Ram. d, Rooster. e, Dog. f, Ox. g, Rabbit. h, Boar. i, Snake. j, Dragon. k, Tiger. l, Rat.

1998   **Litho.**   **Perf. 13½**
2025 A366 400ce Sheet of 12,
    #a.-l.   6.00 6.00

Numbers have been reserved for additional values in this set.

Great Black Writers of the 20th Century — A368

No. 2027: a, Maya Angelou. b, Alex Haley. c, Charles Johnson. d, Richard Wright. e, Toni Cade Bambara. f, Henry Louis Gates, Jr.

1998, Mar. 25   **Litho.**   **Perf. 14**
2027 A368 350ce Sheet of 6,
    #a.-f.   5.00 5.00

Aircraft A369

No. 2028, 800ce: a, Messerschmitt Bf 109 E-7. b, Lockheed PV-2 Harpoon. c, Airspeed Oxford MK1. d, Junkers Ju87D-1. e, Yakovlev Yak-9D. f, North American P-51D Mustang. g, Douglas A-20 Havoc. h, Supermarine Attacker F1. i, Mikoyan-Gurevich MIG-15.
No. 2029, 800ce: a, Breguet 14 B2. b, Curtiss BF2C-1 Goshawk. c, Supermarine Spitfire MK IX. d, Fiat G.50. e, Douglas B-18A. f, Boeing FB-5. g, Bristol F.2B. h, Hawker Fury 1. i, Fiat CR42.
No. 2030, 3000ce, Mitsubishi AGM8 Reisen. No. 2031, 3000ce, Supermarine Spitfire MK XIV, Supermarine Spitfire MK 1.

1998, May 5
    Sheets of 9, #a-i
2028-2029 A369   Set of 2   14.50 14.50
    Souvenir Sheets
2030-2031 A369   Set of 2   6.00 63.00
   #2030-2031 each contain one 57x42mm stamp.

Nos. 1891-1894 Overprinted

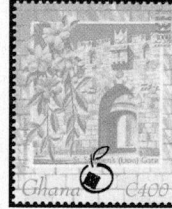

1998, May 13
2032 A334 400ce multi   .90 .90
2033 A334 600ce multi   1.10 1.10
2034 A334 800ce multi   1.50 1.50
    Souvenir Sheet
2035 A334 2000ce multi   4.50 4.50

No. 2035 contains additional inscription in sheet margin: "ISRAEL 98 — WORLD STAMP EXHIBITION / TEL-AVIV 13-21 MAY 1998." No. 2034 exists with an inverted surcharge.

Ships A370

No. 2036, 800ce — Ocean liners: a, Empress of Ireland. b, Transylvania. c, Mauritania. d, Reliance. e, Aquitania. f, Lapland. g, Cap Polonio. h, France. i, Imperator.

No. 2037, 800ce — Warships: a, HMS Rodney. b, USS Alabama. c, HMS Nelson. d, SS Ormonde. e, USS Radford. f, SS Empress of Russia. g, Type XIV, Germany. h, Type A Midget, Japan. i, Brin, Italy.
No. 2038, 5500ce, Titanic. No. 2039, 5500ce, Amistad.

1998, May 5   **Litho.**   **Perf. 14**
    Sheets of 9, #a-i
2036-2037 A370   Set of 2   14.50 14.50
    Souvenir Sheets
2038-2039 A370   Set of 2   11.00 11.00
   #2038-2039 each contain one 42x56mm stamp.

Orchids — A371

No. 2040, 800ce: a, Renanthera imschootiana. b, Arachnis flosaeris. c, Restrepia lansbergi. d, Paphiopedilum tonsum. e, Phalaenopsis ebauche. f, Pleione limprichti.
No. 2041, 800ce: a, Phragmipedium schroderae. b, Zygopetalum clayii. c, Vanda coerulea. d, Odontonia boussole. e, Disa uniflora. f, Dendrobium bigibbum.
No. 2042, 5500ce, Cypripedium calceolus. No. 2043, 5500ce, Sobralia candida.

1998, June 2
    Sheets of 6, #a-f
2040-2041 A371   Set of 2   11.00 11.00
    Souvenir Sheets
2042-2043 A371   Set of 2   12.00 12.00

Elvis Presley (1935-77), Television Comeback Special, 30th Anniv. A372

Various portraits during performance.

1998, June 16   **Litho.**   **Perf. 13½**
2044 A372 800ce Sheet of 6,
    #a.-f.   5.50 5.50

Japanese Flowers — A373

No. 2045, 2000ce — Predominant color of flowers, location of denomination : a, Green (bamboo), UR. b, Red, LR. c, Yellow, LR. d, Pale green & pink, UR.
No. 2046, 2000ce: a, Pale green, yellow & pink, LR. b, Red, UR. c, Pink, LR. d, White, LR.
No. 2047, 5500ce, Small pink & yellow, LR. No. 2048, 5500ce, Pink, UL.

1998, June 2   **Litho.**   **Perf. 14**
    Sheets of 4, #a-d
2045-2046 A373   Set of 2   14.00 14.00
    Souvenir Sheets
2047-2048 A373   Set of 2   11.00 11.00

Ghana Cocoa Board, 50th Anniv. A374

Designs: 200ce, Tetteh Quarshie, pioneer of Ghana Cocoa industry. 550ce, Ripe hybrid cocoa pods. 800ce, Opening of cocoa pods. 1100ce, Fermenting cocoa beans. 1500ce, Shipment of cocoa.

1998, July 8   **Perf. 13x13½**
2049-2053 A374   Set of 5   5.00 5.00

Metropolitan Assembly, Cent. — A375

Designs: 200ce, AMA Centennial emblem. 550ce, King Tackie Tawiah I (1862-1902). 800ce, Achimota School, Accra. 1100ce, Korle Bu Hospital, Accra. 1500ce, Christianborg Castle, Accra.

1998, July 8
2054-2058 A375   Set of 5   5.00 5.00

Intl. Year of the Ocean A376

No. 2059: a, Dolphins. b, Dolphin (f). c, Seagull. d, Least tern, seagulls. e, Emperor angelfish (i). f, Whit ear. g, Blue shark, diver (k). h, Parrotfish. i, Dottyback. j, Blue-spotted stingray (m, n). k, Masked butterfly fish. l, Jack knife fish (h). m, Octopus (i). n, Turkeyfish (lionfish) (j, k, o). o, Seadragon. p, Rock cod.
No. 2060, 3000ce, Devil ray. No. 2061, 3000ce, Great white shark.

1998, Aug. 18   **Perf. 14**
2059 A376 500ce Sheet of
    16, #a.-p.   17.50 17.50
    Souvenir Sheets
2060-2061 A376   Set of 2   14.50 14.50

Inventors and Inventions — A377

No. 2062, 1000ce: a, Edison, light bulb. b, Peephole kinetoscope, Edison. c, Tesla coil, Tesla. d, Nikola Tesla (1856-1943). e, Gottlieb Wilhelm Daimler (1834-1900). f, Motorcycle, Daimler. g, Transmitter circuit for telescope, Marconi. h, Guglielmo Marconi.
#2063, 1000ce: a, Orville & Wright. b, 1st Flyer, Wright Brothers. c, Neon lighting and signs, Claude. d, Georges Claude (1870-1960). e, Alexander Graham Bell. f, The telephone, transmitter, Bell. g, Various uses of lasers, Townes. h, Charles Townes (b. 1915).
No. 2064, 5500ce, Robert Goddard (1882-1945), physicist. No. 2065, 5500ce, Paul Ehrlich (1854-1915), chemist, bacteriologist.

1998, Sept. 1   **Perf. 14**
    Sheets of 8, #a-h
2062-2063 A377   Set of 2   16.00 16.00
    Souenir Sheets
2064-2065 A377   Set of 2   11.00 11.00
   Nos. 2062b-2062c, 2062f-2062g, 2063b-2063c, 2063f-2063g are each 53x38mm.

Christmas — A378

Cats and dogs in Christmas scenes: 500ce, British colorpoint. 600ce, American shorthair-Dilute calico. 800ce, Peke-faced Persian. 1000ce, Small German spitz. 2000ce, British shorthair blue. 3000ce, Persian Dilute calico. No. 2072, 5500ce, English pointer. No. 2073, 5500ce, Rumpy max.

1998, Dec. 1   **Litho.**   **Perf. 14**
2066-2071 A378   Set of 6   10.00 10.00
    Souvenir Sheets
2072-2073 A378   Set of 2   14.00 14.00

Ferrari Automobiles — A378a

No. 2073A: c, : Lampredi. d, 250 GT Cabriolet. e, 121 LM.
3000ce, 365 GTS/4 Spyder.
Illustration reduced.

1998, Dec. 24   **Litho.**   **Perf. 14**
2073A A378a 2000ce Sheet of
    3, #c-e   5.25 5.25
    Souvenir Sheet
    Perf. 13¾x14¼
2073B A378a 3000ce multi   4.00 4.00
No. 2073A contains three 39x25mm stamps.

Diana, Princess of Wales (1961-97) — A379

1998, Dec. 24   **Litho.**   **Perf. 14½**
2074 A379 1000ce multicolored   1.75 1.75
No. 2074 was issued in sheets of 6.

Gandhi — A380

No. 2075: a, After 8 month prison term in Poona, 1931. b, On Salt March, 1930. c, Picking up natural salt at end of Salt March, 1930. d, After graduating from high school in Rajkot, 1887.
5500ce, At age 61, 1931.

1998, Dec. 24
2075 A380 2000ce Sheet of 4,
    #a.-d.   10.00 10.00
    Souvenir Sheet
2076 A380 5500ce multi   9.00 9.00
Nos. 2075b-2075c are each 53x38mm.

Pablo Picasso A381

Designs: No. 2077, 1000ce, Collage, Composition with Butterfly, 1932. No. 2078, 1000ce, Sculpture, Mandolin and Clarinet, 1913, vert. 2000ce, Painting, Ballplayers on the Beach, 1931.
5500ce, Tomato Plant, 1944, vert.

1998, Dec. 24   **Perf. 14x14½**
2077-2079 A381 Set of 3   4.00 4.00
Souenir Sheet
2080 A381 5500ce multicolored   5.50 5.50

19th World Scouting Jamboree, Chile — A382

No. 2081: a, Scout sign. b, Camping. c, Tying a bowline.
5000ce, Robert Baden-Powell.

1998, Dec. 24   **Perf. 14**
2081 A382 2000ce Sheet of 3,
    #a.-c.   6.00 6.00
Souvenir Sheet
2082 A382 5000ce multicolored   5.00 5.00

Royal Air Force, 80th Anniv. A383

No. 2083: a, C130 Hercules. b, Chinook HC2. c, C130 Hercules W2. d, Panavia Tornado F3ADV.
No. 2084, 5500ce, Eurofighter 2000, Chipmunk. No. 2085, 5500ce, Hawk's head, biplane.

1998, Dec. 24
2083 A383 2000ce Sheet of 4,
    #a.-d.   8.00 8.00
Souvenir Sheets
2084-2085 A383 Set of 2   11.00 11.00

New Year 1999 (Year of the Rabbit) A384

No. 2086 — Scenes showing farmer from "Farmer and Rabbit," by Han Fei Tzu: a, Working in field. b, Watching rabbit run into tree. c, Holding rabbit. d, Dreaming of rabbit.

1999, Jan. 4
2086 A384 1400ce Sheet of 4,
    #a.-d.   5.50 5.50

Dinosaurs A385

Designs: 400ce, Corythosaurus. 600ce, Struthiomimus. 1000ce, Lambeosaurus. No. 2089A, 2000ce, Hesperosuchus.
No. 2090, 800ce: a, Ankylosaurus. b, Anatosaurus. c, Diplodocus. d, Monoclonius. e, Tyrannosaurus. f, Camptosaurus. g, Ornitholestes. h, Archaeopteryx. i, Allosaurus.
No. 2091, 800ce: a, Pterodactylus. b, Scelidosaurus. c, Pteranodon. d, Plateosaurus. e, Ornithosuchus. f, Kentrosaurus. g, Hypsognathus. h, Erythrosuchus. i, Stegoceros.
No. 2092, 5000ce, Dimorphodon, vert. No. 2093, 5000ce, Apatosaurus.

1999, Mar. 1   Litho.   Perf. 13½
2087-
2089A A385 Set of 4   4.00 4.00
Sheets of 9, #a-i
2090-2091 A385 800ce Set of
    2   14.50 14.50
Souvenir Sheets
2092-2093 A385 5000ce Set of
    2   10.00 10.00

Australia '99, World Stamp Expo A386

Butterflies: 300ce, California sister. 500ce, Red-splashed sulphur. 600ce, Checked white. 800ce, Blue emperor.
No. 2098, 1000ce, vert: a, Red admiral. b, Buckeye. c, Desert checkered skipper. d, Orange sulphur. e, Tiger swallowtail. f, Orange-bordered blue. g, Agraulis vanillae. h, Monarch.
No. 2099, 1000ce, vert: a, Small tortoiseshell. b, Brimstone. c, Camberwell beauty. d, Marbled white. e, Purple emperor. f, Clouded yellow. g, Ladoga camilla. h, Marsh fritillary.
No. 2100, 5000ce, Papilio homerus, vert. No. 2101, 5000ce, Blue copper.

1999, Apr. 26   Litho.   Perf. 14
2094-2097 A386 Set of 4   3.50 3.50
Sheets of 8, #a-h
2098-2099 A386 Set of 2   16.00 16.00
Souvenir Sheets
2100-2101 A386 Set of 2   10.00 10.00

Shirley Temple as "Curly Top" — A387

No. 2102, vert.: a, Saying prayers. b, Actor John Boles looking at portrait. c, Taking Boles' hand. d, Dressed as old woman.
No. 2103: a, Hugging older sister. b, Dressed as a man. c, Looking at stuffed animals. d, Pulling Boles' tie. e, With family. f, Looking at sister and Boles together.
5000ce, In pink dress, vert.

Perf. 13½x14, 14x13½
1999, Mar. 1   Litho.
2102 A387 1000ce Sheet of 4,
    #a.-d.   3.50 3.50
2103 A387 1000ce Sheet of 6,
    #a.-f.   5.50 5.50
Souvenir Sheet
2104 A387 5000ce multicolored   5.50 5.50

Amorphophallus Flavovirens — A387a

1999, May 6   Litho.   Perf. 14x14¼
2104A A387a 200ce multi   —

Trains A388

Designs: 400ce, ICE 2, Germany, 1966. 500ce, M41, Hungary, 1982. 600ce, DVR, Finland, 1953. 1000ce, AVE 100 class, Spain, 1982.
No. 2109, 1300ce: a, EMD GP7 Illinois Terminal RR, 1949-54. b, EMD SD 38-2, 1972-79. c, EMD SD 60M Soo Line, 1989-96. d, GE U25C, 1963-65. e, EMD GP 28, 1961-63. f, EMD SD 9, 1954-59.
No. 2110, 1300ce: a, Conrail EMD SD80, 1993-99. b, Columbus & Greenville RR EMD SDP35, 1964-66. c, Providence & Worcester RR, MLW M420 Loc. Works, 1973-77. d, Missouri Pacific C36-7, 1978-85. e, Alco C-420 Virginia & Maryland RR, 1963-68. f, Reading RR EMD GP30, 1961-63.
No. 2111, 5000ce, Swiss Federal RR Class RE 6/6 Co-Co, 1972. No. 2112, 5000ce, AGP44, ABB Traction, Inc. 1990-91.

1999, May 10   Perf. 14
2105-2108 A388 Set of 4   2.50 2.50
Sheets of 6, #a-f
2109-2110 A388 Set of 2   14.00 14.00
Souvenir Sheets
2111-2112 A388 Set of 2   10.00 10.00

Paintings by Hokusai (1760-1849) — A389

No. 2113: a, Girl Picking Plum Blossoms. b, Surveying a Region. c, Sumo Wrestlers (rear view). d, Sumo Wrestlers (front view). e, Landscape with Seaside Village. f, Courtiers Crossing a Bridge.
No. 2114: a, Climbing the Mountain. b, Nakahara in Sagami Province. c, Sumo Wrestlers (2 fighting). d, An Oiran and Maid by a Fence. e, Fujiwara Yoshitaka.
No. 2115, 5000ce, Palanquin Bearers on a Steep Hill, vert. No. 2116, 5000ce, Three Ladies by a Well, vert.

1999, Aug. 3   Litho.   Perf. 13¾
2113 A389 1300ce Sheet of 6,
    #a.-f.   7.00 7.00
2114 A389 1300ce Sheet of 6,
    #a.-e., 2113c 7.00 7.00
Souvenir Sheets
2115-2116 A389 Set of 2   9.00 9.00

IBRA '99, World Philatelic Exhibition, Nuremberg — A390

Exhibition emblem, sailing ship Schomberg and: No. 2117, 500ce, Hanover #1. No. 2119, 1000ce, Lubeck #1.
Emblem, Class P8 4-6-0 locomotive and: No. 2118, 800ce, Hamburg #1. No. 2120, 2000ce, Heligoland #1A.
5000ce, Germany #66 tied to airmail label on cover, vert.
Illustration reduced.

1999, Aug. 3   Perf. 14x14½
2117-2120 A390 Set of 4   4.25 4.25
Souvenir Sheet
Perf. 14½x14
2121 A390 5000ce multicolored   4.50 4.50

First Manned Moon Landing, 30th Anniv. — A391

No. 2122: a, Command Module. b, Lunar Module ascension. c, Giant moon rock. d, Lunar module signals home. e, Neil Armstrong. f, One small step.
5000ce, Earth rise, horiz.

1999, Aug. 3   Perf. 14
2122 A391 1300ce Sheet of 6,
    #a.-f.   8.50 8.50
Souvenir Sheet
2123 A391 5000ce multicolored   5.00 5.00

Queen Mother, 100th Birthday (in 2000) — A392

Queen Mother, 100th Birthday (in 2000) — No. 2124: a, Lady Elizabeth Bowles-Lyon with brother David, 1904. b, Queen Elizabeth, 1957. c, Queen Mother, 1970. d, Queen Mother, 1992.
5000ce, Queen Mother, 1970, diff.

1999, Aug. 4
Gold Frames
2124 A392 2000ce Sheet of 4,
    #a.-d. + label   7.75 7.75
Souvenir Sheet
2125 A392 5000ce multicolored   6.50 6.50

No. 2125 contains one 38x50mm stamp. Margins of sheets are embossed.
See Nos. 2273-2274.

Fauna A393

Designs: 200ce, Meles meles. 800ce, Vulpes vulpes.
No. 2128: a, Martes martes. b, Strix aluco. c, Sus scrofa. d, Accipiter gentilis. e, Eliomys quercinus. f, Lucanus cervus.
No. 2129: a, Merops apiaster. b, Upupa epops. c, Cervus elaphus. d, Circaetus gallicus. e, Lacerta ocellata. f, Lynx pardellus.
5000ce, Canis lupus, vert.

1999, Mar. 29   Litho.   Perf. 14
2126-2127 A393 Set of 2   2.00 2.00
2128 A393 1000ce Sheet of 6,
    #a.-f.   5.50 5.50
2129 A393 1000ce Sheet of 6,
    #a.-f.   5.50 5.50
Souvenir Sheet
2130 A393 5000ce multicolored   5.00 5.00

1999

Birds: 400ce, Cyanopica cyana. 600ce, Ciconia ciconia. 2000ce, Aegypius monachus, vert. 3000ce, Garrulus glandarius, vert. 5000ce, Aquila heliaca adalberti.

2131-2134 A393 Set of 4   5.50 5.50
Souvenir Sheet
2135 A393 5000ce multicolored   4.75 4.75

Rights of the Child — A394

No. 2136: a, Child, UN building. b, Dove, earth. c, Mother, child.
5000ce, Child.

1999, Aug. 3   Litho.   **Perf. 14**
2136 A394 3000ce Sheet of 3,
  #a.-c.   8.50 8.50

Souvenir Sheet
2137 A394 5000ce multicolored   5.50 5.50

Souvenir Sheets

PhilexFrance 99 — A395

Locomotives: No. 2138, 5000ce, 232-U1 Four cylinder compound 4-6-4. No. 2139, 5000ce, 0-6-0 Suburban tank engine.

1999, Aug. 3   **Perf. 14x13¾**
2138-2139 A395 Set of 2   15.00 15.00

Johann Wolfgang von Goethe (1749-1832), German Poet — A396

No. 2140: a, Wagner entreats Faust in his study. b, Goethe and Friedrich von Schiller. c, Mephistopheles disguised as the fool.
5000ce, Faust attended by spirits.

1999, Aug. 3   Litho.   **Perf. 14**
2140 A396 2000ce Sheet of 3,
  #a.-c.   6.00 6.00

Souvenir Sheet
2141 A396 5000ce multicolored   5.50 5.50

Return of Macao to People's Republic of China — A397

1999, Aug. 20   Litho.   **Perf. 14x13¾**
2142 A397 1000ce multicolored   3.00 3.00
Issued in sheets of 4.

Save the Ozone Layer — A398

Designs: 200ce, Fish. 550ce, Earth surrounded by ozone layer, man. 800ce, Crying Earth. 1100ce, People holding up shield against sunlight. 1500ce, Objects with ozone-depleting and non-harmful chemicals.

1999   Litho.   **Perf. 13½x13**
2143-2147 A398 Set of 5   8.50 8.50

SOS Children's Villages, 50th Anniv. A399

Designs: 200ce, Grandma Alice. 550ce, Kindergarten. 800ce, SOS Children's Village founder Herrmann Gmeiner (1919-86), Asikawa SOS building. 1100ce, Food preparation.

1999   **Perf. 13x13½**
2148-2151 A399 Set of 4   3.00 3.00

Dr. Ephraim Apu, Musician, Birth Cent. — A400

Designs: 200ce, Apu, clef, note. 800ce, Apu playing Odurugya flute. 1100ce, Apu, indiginous flutes.

1999   **Perf. 13½x13**
2152-2154 A400 Set of 3   2.00 2.00

Millennium — A401

Designs: 300ce, Millennium emblem, vert. 700ce, Emblem, Kwame Nkrumah. 1200ce, Emblem, University of Ghana, vert.

1999, Dec. 28   Litho.   **Perf. 13¼**
2155-2157 A401 Set of 3   6.00 6.00

New Year 2000 — A402

Various scenes from Chinese story, "Daughter of the Dragon King." Stamps from the two sheets are numbered 1-12 in Chinese numeral characters. The numerals are at the bottom of the top group of Chinese characters. See Chinese numerals in Illustrated Identifier.

2000, Feb. 5   **Perf. 14½x14¼**
2158 A402 1600ce Sheet of 6,
  #a.-f.   5.75 5.75
2159 A402 1700ce Sheet of 6,
  #a.-f.   6.25 6.25

Wildlife A403

Designs: 300ce, Black-faced impala. 500ce, Cheetah. 1000ce, Wildebeest. 3000ce, Hippopotamus.

No. 2164, vert.: a, Chimpanzee. b, Boomslang. c, Vulture. d, Leopard. e, Rhinoceros. f, Zebra. g, Crowned crane. h, Lesser kudu.
No. 2165, vert.: a, Purple roller. b, Pelicans. c, Egrets. d, Orange-breasted waxbill. e, Giraffe. f, African buffalo. g, African elephant. h, African lion.
No. 2166, 7000ce, Waterbuck. No. 2167, 7000ce, Ostrich.

2000, Feb. 28   Litho.   **Perf. 14**
2160-2163 A403 Set of 4   3.00 3.00
2164 A403 1100ce Sheet of 8,
  #a.-h.   7.25 7.25
2165 A403 1200ce Sheet of 8,
  #a.-h.   7.50 7.50

Souvenir Sheets
2166-2167 A403   each   9.00 9.00

Tourism A404

No. 2168: a, 300ce, Building, palm trees. b, 300ce, Mud building, natives. c, 300ce, Elephants. d, 1100ce, Natives. e, 1200ce, Natives carrying animal. f, 1800ce, Natives, diff.

2000   Litho.   **Perf. 13x13¼**
2168 A404   Booklet pane of 6,
  #a.-h.   5.00 5.00
  Complete booklet, 4 #2168   20.00

There are 2 types of No. 2168, which differ only by the arrangement of the stamps on the pane. The booklet contains 2 of each type.

Wildlife A405

Designs: 500ce, Zebra duiker. 600ce, Leopard. 2000ce, Bush buck. 3000ce, African wood owl.
No. 2173, 1600ce: a, Blotted genet. b, Tree pangolin. c, Bongo. d, Elephant. e, Flapnecked chameleon. f, West African dwarf crocodile.
No. 2174, 1600ce: a, Lowe's monkey. b, Diana monkey. c, Potto. d, Moustached monkey. e, Thomas's galago. f, Chimpanzee.
No. 2175, 1600ce: a, Gray parrot. b, Hoopoe. c, European roller. d, European beeeater. e, Blue-breasted kingfisher. f, Whitethroated bee-eater.
No. 2176, 6000ce, Hippopotamus, vert. No. 2177, 6000ce, Great blue turaco, vert.

2000, May 1   Litho.   **Perf. 14**
2169-2172 A405 Set of 4   3.50 3.50

Sheets of 6, #a.-f.
2173-2175 A405 Set of 3   14.00 14.00

Souvenir Sheets
2176-2177 A405 Set of 2   8.00 8.00

Mushrooms — A406

No. 2178, horiz.: a, Slippery jack. b, Violet deceiver. c, Fairy stool. d, Honey fungus. e, Shaggy parasol. f, Russula sp.

No. 2179, horiz.: a, Grisette. b, Common puffball. c, Fan. d, Gray chanterelle. e, Fairies' bonnets. f, Russula sp., diff.
5000ce, Great orange elf-cup. 8000ce, Bitter boletus.

2000, May 15
2178 A406 1500ce Sheet of 6,
  #a.-f.   6.50 6.50
2179 A406 2000ce Sheet of 6,
  #a.-f.   8.50 8.50

Souvenir Sheets
2180 A406 5000ce multi   4.00 4.00
2181 A406 8000ce multi   5.00 5.00

The Stamp Show 2000, London.

Eurasian Goldfinch — A406a

2000, June 1   Litho.   **Perf. 13¾x13¼**
2181A A406a 300ce multi   — —

Prince William, 18th Birthday — A407

No. 2182: a, In ski gear. b, With ribbons wrapped around fingers. c, With jacket, no tie. d, Close-up.
8000ce, In sweater.
Illustration reduced.

2000, June 26   Litho.   **Perf. 14**
2182 A407 2000ce Sheet of 4,
  #a-d   6.00 6.00

Souvenir Sheet
Perf. 13¾
2183 A407 8000ce multi   6.00 6.00

No. 2182 contains four 28x42mm stamps.

First Zeppelin Flight, Cent. — A408

No. 2184: a, LZ-129. b, LZ-9. c, LZ-4.
5000ce, LZ-11.
Illustration reduced.

2000, June 26   **Perf. 13¾**
2184 A408 1600ce Sheet of 3,
  #a-c   4.00 4.00

Souvenir Sheet
2185 A408 5000ce multi   4.75 4.75

Berlin Film Festival, 50th
Anniv. — A409

No. 2186: a, Wetherby. b, Die Frau und der
Fremde. c, Hong Gao Liang (Red Sorghum).
d, Skrivánci na Niti. e, Music Box. f, Tema.
6000ce, Justice Est Faite.
Illustration reduced.

2000, June 26   Perf. 14
2186 A409 2000ce Sheet of 6,
#a-f   8.25 8.25
Souvenir Sheet
2187 A409 6000ce multi   5.00 5.00

Apollo-Soyuz Mission, 25th
Anniv. — A410

No. 2188: a, Apollo 18. b, Docked spacecraft. c, Soyuz 19.
8000ce, Soyuz, Earth.
Illustration reduced.

2000, June 26
2188 A410 4000ce Sheet of 3,
#a-c   7.50 7.50
Souvenir Sheet
2189 A410 8000ce multi   5.50 5.50

Souvenir Sheets

2000 Summer Olympics,
Sydney — A411

No. 2190: a, Gymnastics. b, Long jump. c,
Los Angeles Coliseum, and US flag. d,
Ancient Greek chariot racer.
Illustration reduced.

2000, June 26
2190 A411 1300ce Sheet of 4,
#a-d   5.00 5.00

Public Railways, 175th Anniv. — A412

No. 2191: a, Marc Seguin. b, Blenkinsop
locomotive. c, Pumping station, Dawlish.
Illustration reduced.

2000, June 26
2191 A412 4000ce Sheet of 3,
#a-c   7.75 7.75

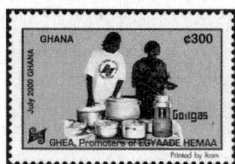

Albert Einstein (1879-1955) — A413

Illustration reduced.

2000, June 26   Perf. 13¾
2192 A413 8000ce multi   10.00 10.00

Ghana Home Economics
Assoc. — A414

Designs: 300ce, Women, cooking pots.
700ce, Woman with home economics text-
book, vert. 1200ce, Emblem, Alberta Ollennu,
Patience A. Adow. 1800ce, Emblems, vert.

2000   Perf. 13x13¼, 13¼x13
2193-2196 A414 Set of 4   4.50 4.50

Space — A415

No. 2197, horiz.: a, Mercury. b, Gemini. c,
Apollo. d, Vostok. e, Voskhod 2. f, Soyuz.
Illustration reduced.

2000, June 26   Litho.   Perf. 14
2197 A415 2000ce Sheet of 6,
#a-f   8.50 8.50
Souvenir Sheet
2198 A415 2000ce Challenger
51-L patch   6.00 6.00
World Stamp Expo 2000, Anaheim.

Cats and
Dogs — A416

Designs: 1100ce, African shorthair.
1200ce, Russian Blue. 1800ce, Basenji.
2000ce, Basset hound.
No. 2203, horiz. a, 1600ce, Weimaraner. b,
1800ce, Keeshond. c, 1800ce, Fox terrier. d,
1800ce, Saluki. e, 1800ce, Dalmatian. f,
1800ce, English setter.
No. 2204, 1800ce, horiz.: a, Silver Persian.
b, Creampoint Himalayan. c, British tortoiseshell shorthair. d, American shorthair tabby. e,
Black Persian. f, Turkish Van.
No. 2205, 8000ce, Cocker spaniels. No.
2206, 8000ce, Lilac Persian.

2000, Aug. 21
2199-2202 A416 Set of 4   3.25 3.25
Sheets of 6, #a-f
2203-2204 A416 Set of 2   12.00 12.00
Souvenir Sheets
2205-2206 A416 Set of 2   9.00 9.00

Scenes from Tale of the White
Snake — A417

No. 2207, 2500ce: a, Xu Xian offers
umbrella to White Lady and maid. b, White
Lady (with basket) helps husband Xu Xian
with business. c, Monk Fa Hai (with necklace)
talks to Xu Xian. d, Xu Xian gives wine to wife.
e, White Lady becomes snake, Xu Xian has
heart attack. f, White Lady (with swords) trying
to get medicinal herbs.
No. 2208, 2500ce: a, White Lady and maid
at Fa Hai's temple. b, Maid threatens to kill Xu
Xian. c, Fa Hai captures White Lady in bowl. d,
Maid, Xu Xian at pagoda. e, Maid with sword
attacks Fa Hai. f, Maid turns Fa Hai into crab.
Illustration reduced.

2001, Jan. 2   Litho.   Perf. 14
Sheets of 6, #a-f
2207-2208 A417 Set of 2   8.75 8.75
New Year 2001 (Year of the snake).

Edward G. Robinson — A418

Color of photograph: a, Gray green. b, Lilac.
c, Red violet (with hat). d, Brown (with cigar).
e, Orange brown (with pipe). f, Blue green.

2001, Apr. 16   Litho.   Perf. 14
2209 A418 4000ce Sheet of 6,
#a-f   6.50 6.50

James Cagney — A419

Color of photograph: a, Olive green. b,
Emerald. c, Blue. d, Brown. e, Red violet. f,
Orange.

2001, Apr. 16
2210 A419 4000ce Sheet of 6,
#a-f   6.50 6.50

Millennium — A420

No. 2211, 2500ce — Architects: a, Walter
Gropius. b, Aldo Rossi. c, Le Corbusier. d,
Antonio Gaudi. e, Paolo Soleri. f, Ludwig Mies
van de Rohe.
No. 2212, 2500ce — Artists: a, Wassily
Kandinsky. b, Henry Moore. c, Marc Chagall.
d, Norman Rockwell. e, Antonio López García.
f, Frida Kahlo.
No. 2213, 14,000ce, Frank Lloyd Wright.
No. 2214, 14,000ce, Pablo Picasso. No. 2215,
14,000ce, Human Genome Project.

2001, Apr. 16
Sheets of 6, #a-f
2211-2212 A420 Set of 2   8.25 8.25
Souvenir Sheets
2213-2215 A420 Set of 3   11.50 11.50

Jazz Musicians — A421

No. 2216, 4000ce: a, Scott Joplin. b, Clar-
ence Williams. c, Sidney Bechet. d, Willie "The
Lion" Smith. e, Ferdinand "Jelly Roll" Morton. f,
Coleman "Bean" Hawkins.
No. 2217, 4000ce: a, Kid Ory. b, Earl
"Fatha" Hines. c, Lil Hardin Armstrong. d, John
Philip Sousa. e, James P. Johnson. f, Johnny
St. Cyr.
No. 2218, 14,000ce, Joe "King" Oliver. No.
2219, 14,000ce, Louis "Satchmo" Armstrong.

2001, Apr. 16
Sheets of 6, #a-f
2216-2217 A421 Set of 2   13.00 13.00
Souvenir Sheets
2218-2219 A421 Set of 2   7.75 7.75

GHANA C500

Oriental Art A422

Designs: 500ce, Cranes, by Kano Eisenin Michinobu. 800ce, Flowers and Trees in Chen Chun's Style, by Tsubaki Chinzan. 1200ce, A Poetry Contest of 42 Matches, by unknown artist. 2000ce, Cranes, by Kano, diff. 5000ce, A Poetry Contest of 42 Matches, diff. 12,000ce, Plum Trees, by Tani Buncho.

No. 2226, vert. — The Tales of Ise, by Sumiyoshi Jokei: a, Chapter 1. b, Chapter 4. c, Chapter 6. d, Chapter 9 (Eastboud Trip, Mt. Utsu). e, Chapter 9, (Eastbound Trip, Mt. Fuji). f, Chapter 9, (Eastbound Trip, Black-headed Gulls). g, Chapter 23, (Crossing Kawachi). h, Chapter 23, (By the Well Wall).

No. 2227, 4000ce, vert. — The Story of Sakyamuni, by unknown artist: a, Siddhartha's Excursion Through the South Gate. b, Siddhartha's Excursion Through the East Gate. c, Siddhartha's Excursion Through the North Gate. d, Siddhartha's Excursion Through the West Gate. e, Sakyamuni Entering Nirvana. f, Untitled.

No. 2228, 14,000ce, Cranes, by Kano (red denomination), diff. No. 2229, 14,000ce, Cranes, by Kano (yellow denomination), diff. No. 2230, 14,000ce, Chapter 1, by Sumiyoshi. No. 2231, Chapter 12, by Sumiyoshi.

2001, Apr. 30
2220-2225	A422	Set of 6	6.00	6.00
2226	A422	3000ce Sheet of 8, #a-h	6.50	6.50
2227	A422	4000ce Sheet of 6, #a-f	6.50	6.50

Souvenir Sheets
| 2228-2231 | A422 | Set of 4 | 15.00 | 15.00 |

Phila Nippon '01, Japan.

Ghana C2000

Automobiles — A423

Designs: 2000ce, 1950 Bentley S Series convertible. 3000ce, 1948 Chrysler Town and Country. 5000ce, 1957 Lotus Elite. 6000ce, 1966 Chevrolet Corvette Sting Ray.

No. 2236, 4000ce: a, 1956-59 BMW 507. b, 1934 Bentley English Tourer. c, 1948 Morris Minor MM. d, 1954 Daimler SP-250 Dart. e, 1950 DeSoto custom convertible. f, 1955-60, Ford Thunderbird.

No. 2237, 4000ce: a,1959-63 Porshe 356B. b, 1962 Rolls-Royce Silver Cloud. c, 1958 Austin Healey Sprite MK-1. d, 1954-57 Mercedes 300SL. e, 1949 Citroen 2CV. f, 1949 Cadillac Series 62.

No. 2238, 14,000ce: a, 1933 Mercedes-Benz. No. 2239, 1953-55 Triumph TR-2.

2001, June 18
| 2232-2235 | A423 | Set of 4 | 4.50 | 4.50 |

Sheets of 6, #a-f
| 2236-2237 | A423 | Set of 2 | 13.00 | 13.00 |

Souvenir Sheets
| 2238-2239 | A423 | Set of 2 | 7.75 | 7.75 |

Belgica 2001 Intl. Stamp Exhibition, Brussels. No. 2238-2239 each contain one 85x28mm stamp.

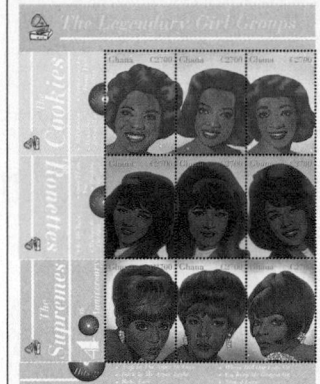

Female Recording Groups of the 1960s — A424

No. 2240 — Various members of: a-c, The Cookies. d-f, The Ronettes. g-i, The Supremes.

2001, Apr. 16   Litho.   Perf. 14
| 2240 | A424 | 2700ce Sheet of 9, #a-i | 6.75 | 6.75 |

Mao Zedong (1893-1976) — A425

No. 2241: a, With arm raised, orange and light orange background. b, Portrait. c, With arm raised, tan gray and blue background. 12,000ce, With flag.

2001, Aug. 27
| 2241 | A425 | 7000ce Sheet of 3, #a-c | 6.00 | 6.00 |

Souvenir Sheet
| 2242 | A425 | 12,000ce multi | 3.50 | 3.50 |

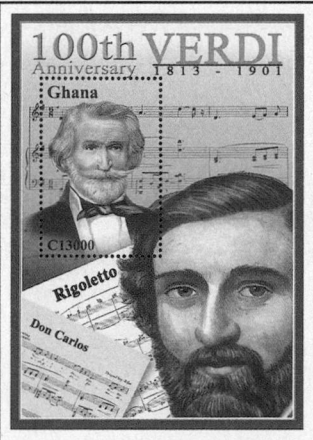

Giuseppe Verdi (1813-1901), Opera Composer — A426

No. 2243: a, Verdi. b, Scores for Aida and Rigoletto. c, Verdi's birthplace. d, Map of Italy. 13,000ce, Verdi and score.

2001, Aug. 27
| 2243 | A426 | 5000ce Sheet of 4, #a-d | 5.75 | 5.75 |

Souvenir Sheet
| 2244 | A426 | 13,000ce multi | 3.75 | 3.75 |

Toulouse-Lautrec Paintings — A427

No. 2245: a, Jane Avril Leaving the Moulin Rouge. b, Jane Avril Dancing. c, Jane Avril Entering the Moulin Rouge.

2001, Aug. 27   Perf. 13¾
| 2245 | A427 | 6700ce Sheet of 3, #a-c | 5.75 | 5.75 |

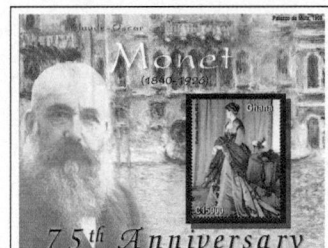

Monet Paintings — A428

No. 2246, horiz.: a, Zaandam. b, On the Seine at Bennecourt. c, The Studio Boat. d, Houses on the Waterfront, Zaandam. 15,000ce, Madame Gaudibert.

2001, Aug. 27
| 2246 | A428 | 5000ce Sheet of 4, #a-d | 5.75 | 5.75 |

Souvenir Sheet
| 2247 | A428 | 15,000ce multi | 4.25 | 4.25 |

Queen Victoria (1819-1901) — A429

No. 2248: a, Victoria. b, Prince Albert. c, Albert and Victoria. d, Victoria and Albert on wedding day. 12,000ce, Victoria with green and white headpiece.

2001, Aug. 27   Perf. 14
| 2248 | A429 | 5000ce Sheet of 4, #a-d | 5.75 | 5.75 |

Souvenir Sheet
| 2249 | A429 | 12,000ce multi | 4.00 | 4.00 |

Queen Elizabeth II, 75th Birthday — A430

No. 2250, vert.: a, Bright pink hat. b, White hat. c, Peach hat. d, Crown. e, Blue and pink hat. f, In uniform. 15,000ce, with Prince Philip.

2001, Aug. 27
| 2250 | A430 | 4000ce Sheet of 6, #a-f | 6.75 | 6.75 |

Souvenir Sheet
| 2251 | A430 | 15,000ce multi | 4.25 | 4.25 |

Whales A431

Designs: 1000ce, Killer whale. 3000ce, Narwhal. 5000ce, Beluga. 6000ce, Bowhead whale.

No. 2256, 4000ce: a, Blue whale. b, Killer whale, diff. c, Northern bottlenose whale. d, Sperm whale. e, Southern right whale. f, Pygmy right whale.

No. 2257, 4000ce: a, Humpback whale. b, Fin whale. c, Bowhead whale, diff. d, Gray whale. e, Narwhal, diff. f, Beluga, diff.

No. 2258, 14,000ce, Sperm whale. No. 2259, 14,000ce, Blue whales.

2001, Oct. 1
| 2252-2255 | A431 | Set of 4 | 7.00 | 7.00 |

Sheets of 6, #a-f
| 2256-2257 | A431 | Set of 2 | 20.00 | 20.00 |

Souvenir Sheets
| 2258-2259 | A431 | Set of 2 | 13.00 | 13.00 |

Rotary Intl. In Ghana, 40th Anniv. (in 1998) A432

Rotary Intl. emblem and: 300ce, Polio victim. 1100ce, Clean water. 1200ce, Founder Paul Harris. 1800ce, Blood donation.

2001 ?   Perf. 13¼
| 2260-2263 | A432 | Set of 4 | 2.25 | 2.25 |

c1100   Ghana

Orchids — A433

Designs: 1100ce, Paphiopedilum hennisianum. 1200ce, Vuylstekeara cambria Plush.

1800ce, Cymbidium ormoulu. 2000ce, Phalaenopsis Barbara Moler.

No. 2268, 4500ce: a, Cattleya capra. b, Odontoglossum rossii. c, Epidendrum pseudepidendrum. d, Encyclia cochleata. e, Cymbidium baldoyle Melbury. f, Phalaenopsis asean.

No. 2269, 4500ce: a, Odontocidium Tigersun. b, Miltonia Emotion. c, Odontonia sappho Excul. d, Cymbidium Bulbarrow. e, Dendrobium nobile. f, Paphiopedilum insigne.

No. 2270, 15,000ce, Calanthe vestita. No. 2271, 15,000ce, Angraecum eburneum.

2001, Oct. 30 **Litho.** **Perf. 14**
2264-2267 A433 Set of 4 3.00 3.00
Sheets of 6, #a-f
2268-2269 A433 Set of 2 17.50 17.50
Souvenir Sheets
2270-2271 A433 Set of 2 10.00 10.00

Musical Instruments — A434

No. 2272: a, Bamboo orchestra. b, Mmensuon. c, Fontomfrom. d, Pati.

2001, Dec. 3 **Perf. 14¼**
2272 A434 4000ce Sheet of 4,
  #a-d 4.50 4.50

Queen Mother Type of 1999 Redrawn

No. 2273: a, Lady Elizabeth Bowles-Lyon with brother David, 1904. b, In Rhodesia, 1957. c, In 1970. d, In 1992.
5000ce, In 1970, diff.

2001, Dec. **Perf. 14**
Yellow Orange Frames
2273 A392 2000ce Sheet of 4,
  #a-d, + label 4.50 4.50
Souvenir Sheet
Perf. 13¾
2274 A392 5000ce multi 3.00 3.00

Queen Mother's 101st birthday. No. 2274 contains one 38x50mm stamp with a darker background than on No. 2125. Sheet margins of Nos. 2273-2274 lack embossing and gold arms and frames found on Nos. 2124-2125.

Kwame Nkrumah University of Science and Technology, Kumasi, 50th Anniv. A435

Designs: 300ce, Emblem. No. 2276, 700ce, No. 2280a, 4000ce, Main gate. No. 2277, 1100ce, No. 2280b, 4000ce, Dairy production. No. 2278, 1200ce, No. 2280c, 4000ce, Pharmacy Department. No. 2279, 1800ce, No. 2280d, 4000ce, Residence hall.

2001 **Perf. 13x13¼**
2275-2279 A435 Set of 5 2.00 2.00
Souvenir Sheet
2280 A435 4000ce Sheet of 4,
  #a-d 4.50 4.50

Nobel Prizes, Cent. (In 2001) — A436

No. 2281, 4000ce — Chemistry laureates: a, George A. Olah, 1994. b, Kary Mullis, 1993. c, Sir Harold W. Kroto, 1996. d, Richard R.

Ernst, 1991. e, Ahmed H. Zewail, 1999. f, Paul Crutzen, 1995.

No. 2282, 4000ce — Chemistry laureates: a, John E. Walker, 1997. b, Jens C. Skou, 1997. c, Alan G. MacDiarmid, 2000. d, Thomas Robert Cech, 1989. e, John Pole, 1998. f, Rudolph A. Marcus, 1992.

No. 2283, 4000ce — Chemistry laureates: a, Walter Kohn, 1998. b, F. Sherwood Rowland, 1995. c, Mario Molina, 1995. d, Hideki Shirakawa, 2000. e, Paul D. Boyer, 1997. f, Richard Smalley, 1996.

No. 2284, 15,000ce, Svante Arrhenius, Chemistry, 1903. No. 2285, 15,000ce, Alfred Werner, Chemistry, 1913. No. 2286, 15,000ce, Peter Debye, Chemistry, 1936. No. 2287, 15,000ce, Wole Soyinka, Literature, 1986. No. 2288, 15,000ce, Nelson Mandela, Peace, 1993.

2002, Jan. 9 **Perf. 14**
Sheets of 6, #a-f
2281-2283 A436 Set of 3 20.00 20.00
Souvenir Sheets
2284-2288 A436 Set of 5 21.00 21.00

Reign of Queen Elizabeth II, 50th Anniv. — A437

No. 2289: a, Wearing pink dress. b, Sitting on horse. c, Looking at horses. d, In carriage with Prince Philip.
15,000ce, Sitting with Prince Philip (black and white photograph).

2002, Feb. 6 **Litho.** **Perf. 14¼**
2289 A437 6500ce Sheet of 4,
  #a-d 7.25 7.25
Souvenir Sheet
2290 A437 15,000ce multi 4.75 4.75

Intl. Copyright Conference, Accra — A438

Designs: 300ce, Conference emblem, vert. 700ce, Person reading. 1100ce, Spider, web, map of Ghana. 1200ce, Map of Ghana, Kente cloth. 1800ce, Drummer.

2002, Feb. 20 **Perf. 14¼x14, 14x14¼**
2291-2295 A438 Set of 5 1.60 1.60

2002 World Cup Soccer Championships, Japan and Korea — A439

World Cup trophy and: 100ce, Jay Jay Okacha, flag of Nigeria. 150ce, South African player and flag. 300ce, Pele, flag of Brazil. 400ce, Roger Milla, flag of Cameroun. 500ce, Bobby Charlton, flag of England. 800ce, Michel Platini, flag of France. 1000ce, Franz Beckenbauer, flag of West Germany. 1500ce,

Ulsan Munsu Stadium, Korea, horiz. 2000ce, German player and flag. 3000ce, Brazilian player and flag. 4000ce, Korean player and flag. 5000ce, Yokohama Intl. Sports Stadium, Japan, horiz. 6000ce, Italian player and flag. 11,000ce, 1950 World Cup poster. 12,000ce, 1934 World Cup poster.

No. 2311, 15,000ce, Geoff Hurst's hat trick for England, 1966. No. 2312, 15,000ce, Gordon Banks making save on Pele, 1970.

2002, Mar. 4 **Perf. 14**
2296-2310 A439 Set of 15 13.00 13.00
Souvenir Sheets
2311-2312 A439 Set of 2 9.00 9.00

Souvenir Sheet

New Year 2002 (Year of the Horse) — A440

No. 2313: a, Brown panel at L, country name at LR. b, Brown panel at R, country name at UR. c, Brown panel at L, country name at LL. d, Brown panel at R, country name at LR.

2002, Mar. 4 **Perf. 13¾**
2313 A440 4000ce Sheet of 4,
  #a-d 5.00 5.00

Visit of Netherlands Prince Willem-Alexander and Princess Máxima to Ghana — A441

Couple: a, With Prince wearing sash. b, Holding hands, Prince wearing hat. c, With windmills and flags. d, At wedding ceremony, with another man. e, In crowd. f, Kissing.

2002 **Perf. 14**
2314 A441 6000ce Sheet of 6,
  #a-f 8.75 8.75
Amphilex 2002 Intl. Stamp Show, Amsterdam.

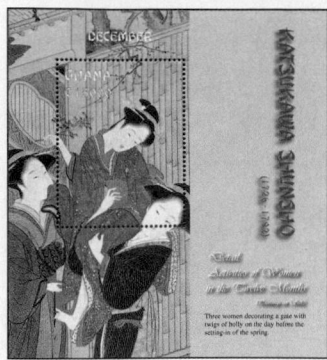

Paintings of Shunsho Katsukawa — A442

No. 2315, 9000ce — Activities of Women in the Twelve Months: a, Trying to retrieve a ball caught in a tree (March). b, Listening to a cuckoo in the bedroom (April). c, Holding a cage filled with fireflies for a woman to read a book (May).

No. 2316, 9000ce — Activities of Women in the Twelve Months: a, Mother and child taking a tub bath while woman holds a revolving lantern (June). b, Strips of paper with wishes and poems are tied on bamboo (July). c, Women enjoying the cool air on a boat (August).

No. 2317, 9000ce — Activities of Women in the Twelve Months: a, Celebrating Feast of the Chrysanthemum (September). b, Looking out for colored leaves (October). c, Mother reading picture book while sitting at a foot warmer (November).

No. 2318, 15,000ce, Three women decorating a gate (woman in blue kimono), from Activities of Women in the Twelve Months. No. 2319, 15,000ce, Part 1 (woman in red kimono) from Snow, Moonlight and Flowers. No. 2320, 15,000ce, Part 2 (woman in black kimono) from Snow, Moonlight and Flowers. No. 2321, 15,000ce, Part 3 (woman in gray kimono) from Snow, Moonlight and Flowers.

2002, July 29 **Litho.** **Perf. 14¼**
Sheets of 3, #a-c
2315-2317 A442 Set of 3 20.00 20.00
Souvenir Sheets
2318-2321 A442 Set of 4 14.50 14.50

United We Stand — A443

2002, Aug. 15 **Perf. 14**
2322 A443 7000ce multi 3.25 3.25
  Printed in sheets of 4.

2002 Winter Olympics, Salt Lake City — A444

Designs: No. 2323, 7000ce, Figure skaters. No. 2324, 7000ce, Freestyle skier.

2002, Aug. 15
2323-2324 A444 Set of 2 3.75 3.75
2324a Souvenir sheet, #2323-2324 4.00 4.00

Intl. Year of Mountains — A445

No. 2325: a, Tateyama, Japan. b, Mt. Shivling, India. c, Wong Leng, Hong Kong. d, Mt. Blanc, France.
15,000ce, Mt. Fuji, Japan.

2002, Aug. 15
2325 A445 6000ce Sheet of 4, #a-d 6.00 6.00
Souvenir Sheet
2326 A445 15,000ce multi 3.75 3.75

20th World Scout Jamboree, Thailand — A446

No. 2327, horiz.: a, Scout with walking stick. b, Scout with backpack. c, Tent and campfire. d, Tent and scout tying knots.
15,000ce, Scout with red neckerchief.

2002, Aug. 15
2327 A446 6500ce Sheet of 4, #a-d 6.25 6.25
Souvenir Sheet
2328 A446 15,000ce multi 5.25 5.25

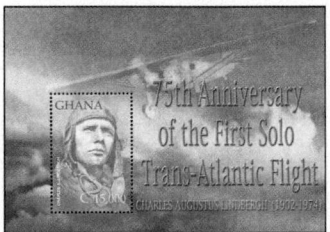

First Solo Transatlantic Flight, 75th Anniv. — A447

No. 2329, 8500ce, horiz.: a, Charles Lindbergh and Spirit of St. Louis. b, Charles and Anne Morrow Lindbergh in airplane.
15,000ce, Lindbergh wearing flying gear.

2002, Aug. 15
2329 A447 8500ce Sheet of 2, #a-b 4.25 4.25
Souvenir Sheet
2330 A447 15,000ce multi 3.75 3.75

Intl. Year of Ecotourism — A448

No. 2331: a, Nectarinia venusta. b, Panthera pardus. c, Kobus kob. d, Syncerus caffer. e, Pan troglodytes. f, Galago.
12,000ce, Loxodonta africana.

2002, Aug. 15
2331 A448 4000ce Sheet of 6, #a-f 9.00 9.00
Souvenir Sheet
2332 A448 12,000ce multi 4.50 4.50

Nos. 1820-1821 Surcharged

2002, Aug. 15 **Perf. 13½x14**
2333 Strip or block of 4 3.00 3.00
  a. A315 3000ce on 600ce #1820a .75 .75
  b. A315 3000ce on 600ce #1820b .75 .75
  c. A315 3000ce on 600ce #1820c .75 .75
  d. A315 3000ce on 600ce #1820d .75 .75
Souvenir Sheet
2334 A315 20,000ce on 2500ce #1821 5.00 5.00

No. 2334 and sheets of No. 2333 are additionally overprinted in margin with black border and inscription "In Memoriam / 1900-2002."

Butterflies, Moths, Insects and Birds — A449

No. 2335, 4500ce — Butterflies: a, Iolaus menas. b, Neptis melicerta. c, Cymothoe lucasi. d, Euphaedra francina. e, Lilac nymph. f, Mocker swallowtail.
No. 2336, 4500ce — Moths: a, Phiala cunina. b, Mazuca strigicincta. c, Steindachner's emperor. d, Amphicallia pactolicus. e, Verdant sphinx. f, Oleander hawkmoth.
No. 2337, 4500ce — Insects: a, Bush hopper. b, Ant lion. c, Digger bee. d, Stag beetle. e, Mantis. f, Longhorn beetle.
No. 2338, 4500ce — Birds: a, Malachite kingfisher. b, Brown harrier eagle. c, Heuglin's masked weaver. d, Egyptian plover. e, Swallow-tailed bee-eater. f, Black-faced fire finch.
No. 2339, 15,000ce, Giant blue swallowtail butterfly. No. 2340, 15,000ce, African moon moth. No. 2341, 15,000ce, Mantis nymph. No. 2342, 15,000ce, Rufous fishing owl.

2002, Aug. 26 **Perf. 14**
Sheets of 6, #a-f
2335-2338 A449 Set of 4 26.00 26.00
Souvenir Sheets
2339-2342 A449 Set of 4 14.50 14.50

Edina Bakatue Festival A450

Designs: No. 2343, 1000ce, No. 2349e, 4000ce, Casting of net. No. 2344, 2000ce, No. 2349b, 4000ce, Chief in palanquin. No. 2345, 2500ce, No. 2349c, 4000ce, Regatta. No. 2346, 3000ce, No. 2349d, 4000ce, Festival boat. No. 2347, 4000ce, Opening ritual. No.

2348, 5000ce, No. 2349a, 4000ce, Priestesses.

2002, Oct. 21 **Perf. 14x13½**
2343-2348 A450 Set of 6 4.25 4.25
2349 A450 Sheet of 6, #2347, 2349a-e 6.00 6.00

Japan Overseas Cooperation Volunteers, 25th Anniv. in Ghana — A451

Designs: No. 2350, 1000ce, Health. No. 2351, 1000ce, Education (Home economics). 2000ce, Education (Science and math). 2500ce, Education (Computer technology). 3000ce, Sports.
No. 2355 (without white inscriptions): a, Like 2000ce. b, Like No. 2350. c, Like 3000ce. d, Like 2500ce. e, Like No. 2351.

2002, Oct. 23 **Perf. 14**
2350-2354 A451 Set of 5 2.40 2.40
2355 A451 4000ce Sheet of 5, #a-e 5.00 5.00

Awarding of Nobel Peace Prize to UN Secretary General Kofi Annan — A452

Designs: 1000ce, With Ghana Pres. J. A. Kufuor at award ceremony. 2000ce, With Nobel medal and citation. 2500ce, Portrait. 3000ce, In academic procession at Kwame Nkrumah University.

2002, Oct. 28
2356-2359 A452 Set of 4 3.50 3.50

Nos. 1939C, 1939B Surcharged

Methods and Perfs As Before
2002, Mar. 7
2360 A350a 1000ce on 1100ce multi #1939C, 10½x6mm obliterator — —
2360A A350a 2500ce on 800ce multi #1939B — —
  b. Obliterator 10½x4mm — —

Obliterator on No. 2360 is 10½x6mm.

Marlene Dietrich (1901-92) — A454

No. 2362 — Background colors: a, Violet black (hair parted in middle, name at left). b, Gray (wearing scarf, name at right). c, Brown (name at left). d, Dark brown (wearing hat). e, Blue gray (name at left). f, Brown black (name at right).
15,000ce, Holding cigarette.

2003, Jan. 14
2362 A454 4500ce Sheet of 6, #a-f 6.50 6.50
Souvenir Sheet
2363 A454 15,000ce multi 3.75 3.75

Popeye in Amsterdam — A455

No. 2364: a, Along the canal. b, Anne Frank House. c, Restaurant Row. d, Downtown. e, Central Station. f, Windmills.

2003, Jan. 14 **Perf. 13¾**
2364 A455 4500ce Sheet of 6, #a-f 6.50 6.50
Souvenir Sheet
2365 A455 15,000ce shown 3.75 3.75

No. 2364 contains six 38x51mm stamps.

New Year 2003 (Year of the Ram) — A456

2003, Feb. 24 **Perf. 14**
2366 A456 5000ce multi 3.00 3.00
  Issued in sheets of 4.

Charlie Chaplin (1889-1977) — A453

No. 2361: a, In suit and tie. b, As "Little Tramp," wearing hat. c, Wearing overalls. d, Holding Academy Award.

2003, Jan. 14 **Litho.** **Perf. 14**
2361 A453 6500ce Sheet of 4, #a-d 6.25 6.25

Famous Women — A457

Designs: 1000ce, Nana Yaa Asantewaa (1822-1923), Asante warrior. 2000ce, Justice Annie Jiagge (1918-96). 2500ce, Dr. Esther Ocloo (1919-2002), industrialist. 3000ce, Dr. Efua T. Sutherland (1924-96), playwright. 5000ce, Rebecca Dedei Aryeetey (1924-60), activist.

2003, Apr. 23   Perf. 13½x14
2367-2371 A457 Set of 5   3.25 3.25

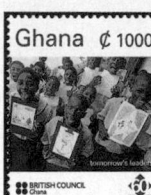

British Council, 60th Anniv. — A458

Designs: 1000ce, Tomorrow's leaders. 2000ce, Women reading Africawoman Newspaper. 2500ce, Partners in culture. 3000ce, Window on the world. 5000ce, Leadership through sport.

2003, June 12
2372-2376 A458 Set of 5   3.25 3.25

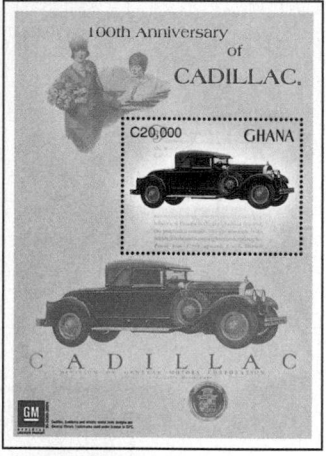

General Motors Automobiles — A459

No. 2377, 7000ce — Cadillacs: a, 1941 Sixty Special. b, 1953 Eldorado. c, 1957 Eldorado Brougham. d, 1959 Eldorado Convertible. No. 2378, 7000ce — Corvettes: a, 1962. b, 1963 Sting Ray. c, 1964 Sting Ray. d, 1968. No. 2379, 20,000ce, Cadillac. No. 2380, 20,000ce, 1966 Corvette Sting Ray.

2003, July 2   Perf. 13¾
Sheets of 4, #a-d
2377-2378 A459 Set of 2   14.50 14.50
Souvenir Sheets
2379-2380 A459 Set of 2   9.50 9.50

Coronation of Queen Elizabeth II, 50th Anniv. — A460

No. 2381: a, Wearing tiara. b, Wearing blue hat. c, Wearing black hat.
20,000ce, Wearing black hat, diff.

2003, July 2   Perf. 14
2381 A460 10,000ce Sheet of 3,
#a-c   7.00 7.00
Souvenir Sheet
2382 A460 20,000ce multi   4.75 4.75

Tour de France Bicycle Race, Cent. — A461

No. 2383: a, Romain Maes, 1935. b, Sylvére Maes, 1936. c, Roger Lapebie, 1937. d, Gino Bartali, 1938.
20,000ce, Henri Pelissier, 1923.

2003, July 2   Perf. 13½x13¼
2383 A461 7000ce Sheet of 4,
#a-d   6.50 6.50
Souvenir Sheet
2384 A461 20,000ce multi   4.75 4.75

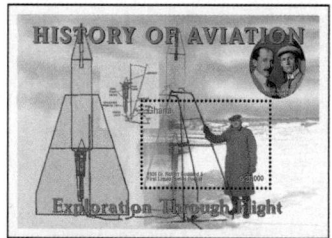

History of Aviation — A462

No. 2385: a, Charles Lindbergh makes first non-stop solo Atlantic crossing, 1927. b, Wiley Post makes first round-the-world solo flight, 1933. c, Heinkel He178, first turbojet powered aircraft, 1939. d, Chuck Yeager flies Bell X-1 to break sound barrier, 1947.
20,000ce, Dr. Robert Goddard and first liquid-fueled rocket, 1926.

2003, July 2   Perf. 14
2385 A462 7000ce Sheet of 4,
#a-d   6.50 6.50
Souvenir Sheet
2386 A462 20,000ce multi   4.75 4.75

Christmas A463

Children's art: 2000ce, Preparation for Christmas, by Kwame Owusu Aduomi. 4000ce, Typical Christmas Present, by Thomas Kyeremateng, vert. 4500ce, Making Merry at Christmas, by Samuel Baffoe Maison. 5000ce, Christmas is Here, by Patrick Annan-Noonoo.

Perf. 14x13¼, 13¼x14
2003, Dec. 1   Litho.
2387-2390 A463 Set of 4   3.75 3.75

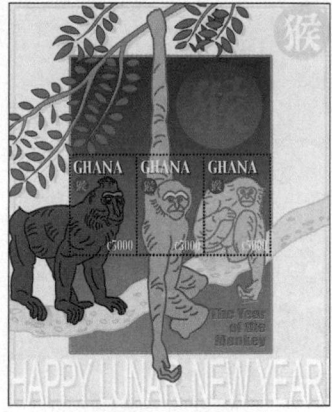

Boletus Edulis — A463a

2003   Litho.   Perf. 14x13½
2390A A463a 1000ce multi   — —

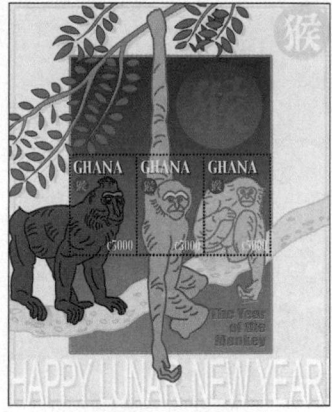

New Year 2004 (Year of the Monkey) — A464

No. 2391: a, Dark gray monkey. b, Light gray monkey. c, Buff monkey.

2004, Jan. 29   Litho.   Perf. 14
2391 A464 5000ce Sheet of 3,
#a-c   5.00 5.00

Chinese Actors — A465

No. 2392, 5000ce — Richie Jen: a, With hair below ears, wearing black shirt. b, With hair above ears, wearing black shirt. c, Wearing helmet. d, With mustache. e, Wearing head covering. f, Wearing red jacket.
No. 2393, 5000ce — Ray Lui: a, Wearing suit and tie. b, With shaved head. c, Wearing black hood. d, Wearing polka dot shirt. e, Wearing costume. f, Wearing costume with red headpiece. g, Wearing costume with wound on forehead.
No. 2394, 5000ce — Jiang Wen: a, Wearing glasses, fingers showing at LR. b, Wearing costume with headpiece. c, Sepia photograph, wearing glasses. d, Wearing suit and tie. e, Sepia photograph, without glasses. f, Wearing striped shirt.

2004, Feb. 1   Perf. 13¾
Sheets of 6, #a-f
2392-2394 A465 Set of 3   21.00 21.00

Kente Cloth Patterns A466

Designs: 2000ce, Edwene Asa. 4000ce, Fatia Fata Nkruma. 4500ce, Asam Takra.

5000ce, Toku Akra Ntoma. 6000ce, Sika Futuro.

2004, Feb. 27   Perf. 14x13¼
2395-2399 A466 Set of 5   5.00 5.00

Hogbetsotso Festival — A467

Designs: 2000ce, Exodus from Notsie. 4000ce, Misego Dance. 4500ce, Royal stools. 5000ce, Pouring libation. 6000ce, King aloft. No. 2405: a, Pouring libation, diff. b, Togbe Adeladza II, Awomefia of Anlo. c, Display of traditional symbols of wealth. d, Exodus from Notsie, diff. e, Procession of the royalty. f, Royalty at Durbar. g, Ewe cultural dance. h, Bountiful harvest. i, Royal stools, diff.

2004, Mar. 1
2400-2404 A467 Set of 5   5.00 5.00
2405 A467 3000ce Sheet of 9,
#a-i   6.25 6.25

Paintings of Scouts by Norman Rockwell (1894-1978) — A468

No. 2406 — Paintings from 1974 Boy Scout Calendar: a, Female scout leader. b, Webelo (plaid neckerchief). c, Boy scout (green cap). d, Cub scout (blue and yellow neckerchief).
20,000ce, Good Friends.

2004, Mar. 18   Perf. 14
2406 A468 7000ce Sheet of 4,
#a-d   6.50 6.50
Souvenir Sheet
2407 A468 20,000ce multi   4.50 4.50

Paintings by Pablo Picasso (1881-1973) — A469

No. 2408: a, Jacqueline in a Black Scarf. b, Portrait of Olga. c, Woman in White (Sara Murphy). d, Portrait of Dora Maar.
16,000ce, Portrait of the Artist's Sister, Lola.

2004, Mar. 18   Perf. 14¼
2408 A469 6500ce Sheet of 4,
#a-d   7.50 7.50
Imperf
2409 A469 16,000ce multi   4.50 4.50
No. 22408 contains four 37x50mm stamps.

Paintings of James Abbott McNeill Whistler (1834-1903) A470

Designs: 2000ce, Head of a Peasant Woman. 4000ce, The Master Smith of Lyme Regis. 5000ce, The Little Rose of Lyme Regis. 6000ce, Arrangement in Gray: Portrait of a Painter (self-portrait).

No. 2414: a, Rose and Siver: La Princesse du Pays de la Porcelaine. b, Variations in Flesh Color and Green: The Balcony. c, Caprice in Purple and Gold: The Golden Screen. d, Purple and Rose: The Lange Lijzen of the Six Marks.

20,000ce, Harmony in Green and Rose: The Music Room, horiz.

2004, Mar. 18   **Perf. 14¼**
2410-2413 A470   Set of 4   4.00 4.00
2414 A470   7500ce Sheet of 4,
     #a-d   6.75 6.75
Souvenir Sheet
2415 A470 20,000ce multi   4.50 4.50

Paintings in the Hermitage, St. Petersburg, Russia A471

Designs: 2000ce, Portrait of Anne of Austria as Minerva, by Simon Vouet. 3000ce, Lasciviousness, by Pompeo Giroloamo Batoni. 10,000ce, Allegory of Faith, by Moretto da Brescia.

No. 2419: a, Allegory of the Arts, by Bernardo Strozzi. b, Vulcan's Forge, by Luca Giordano. c, Daedalus and Icarus, by Charles Lebrun. d, The Infant Hercules Strangling Serpents in His Cradle, by Sir Joshua Reynolds.

No. 2420, Cupid Undoing Venus's Belt, by Reynolds. No. 2421, Perseus Liberating Andromeda, by Peter Paul Rubens, horiz.

2004, Mar. 18   **Perf. 14¼**
2416-2418 A471   Set of 3   3.50 3.50
2419 A471   6500ce Sheet of 4,
     #a-d   6.00 6.00
Imperf
Size: 55x78mm
2420 A471 20,000ce multi   4.50 4.50
Size: 78x55mm
2421 A471 20,000ce multi   4.50 4.50

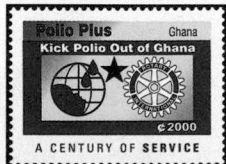

Rotary International, Cent. (in 2005) — A471a

Rotary International emblem and: 2000ce, Polio Plus emblem. 4000ce, Anopheles mosquito, flag of Ghana, vert. 4500ce, Paul P. Harris, flag of Ghana, vert. 5000ce, 2003-04 Rotary International President Jonathan B. Majiyagbe, flag of Ghana, vert. 6000ce, "100 Years," flag of Ghana, vert.

No. 2421F, vert.: g, Women filling water containers. h, Men building shelters. i, Women planting tree.

Perf. 13x13¼, 13¼x13
2004, Sept. 14   **Litho.**
2421A-2421E A471a   Set of 5   4.75 4.75

Souvenir Sheet
2421F A471a 10,000ce Sheet of
    3, #g-i   6.75 6.75
No. 2421F contains three 28x42mm stamps.

Souvenir Sheet

Deng Xiaoping (1904-97), Chinese Leader — A472

2004, Nov. 29   **Litho.**   **Perf. 14**
2422 A472 20,000ce multi   4.50 4.50

Souvenir Sheet

World Peace — A473

No. 2423 — Dr. Martin Luther King, Jr. with: a, Country name at UL. b, Microphone. c, Hands at tie.

2004, Nov. 29
2423 A473 10,000ce Sheet of 3,
     #a-c   9.00 9.00

Miniature Sheet

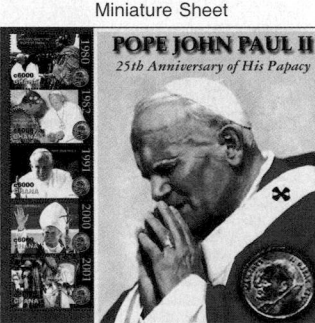

Election of Pope John Paul II, 25th Anniv. (in 2003) — A474

No. 2424 — Photos from: a, 1980. b, 1982. c, 1991. d, 2000. e, 2001.

2004, Nov. 29
2424 A474 6000ce Sheet of 5,
     #a-e   6.75 6.75

2004 Summer Olympics, Athens A475

Designs: 500ce, Intl. Olympic Committee President Jacques Rogge. 800ce, Soccer player Abedi Ayew Pele. 7000ce, Athlete Margaret Simpson. 10,000ce, Art depicting athletes of ancient Greece, horiz.

2004, Nov. 29   **Perf. 14¼**
2425-2428 A475   Set of 4   4.25 4.25

D-Day, 60th Anniv. — A476

No. 2429, vert.: a, Fleet Admiral Ernest J. King. b, Gen. William C. Lee. c, Lt. Commander John D. Bulkeley. d, Admiral Sir Bertram H. Ramsey.
20,000ce, Rear Admiral Alan G. Kirk.

2004, Nov. 29
2429 A476   8000ce Sheet of 4,
     #a-d   7.25 7.25
Souvenir Sheet
2430 A476 20,000ce multi   4.50 4.50

European Soccer Championships, Portugal — A477

No. 2431, vert.: a, Gerd Müller. b, Presentation of European Cup. c, Franz Beckenbauer. d, Heysel Stadium, Brussels.
20,000ce, 1972 German team.

2004, Nov. 29   **Perf. 14**
2431 A477   7500ce Sheet of 4,
     #a-d   6.75 6.75
Souvenir Sheet
Perf. 14¼
2432 A477 20,000ce multi   4.50 4.50
No. 2431 contains four 28x42mm stamps.

Worldwide Fund for Nature (WWF) — A478

No. 2433 — African lions: a, Three cubs. b, Lions in water. c, Male lion. d, Female and cubs.

2004, Dec. 27   **Perf. 14**
2433 A478 5000ce Block or
     strip of 4,
     #a-d   5.00 5.00
e.   Miniature sheet, 2 each
    #2433a-2433d   10.00 10.00

Mushrooms — A479

Designs: 500ce, Boletus badius. 3000ce, Clitocybe nebularis. 5000ce, Amanita muscaria. 8000ce, Russula vesca.

No. 2438, vert.: a, Boletus parasiticus. b, Cortinarius armillatus. c, Gymnopilus spectabilis. d, Cortinarius flexipes.
20,000ce, Chlorosplenium aeruginosum, vert.

2004, Dec. 27
2434-2437 A479   Set of 4   5.00 5.00
2438 A479   7500ce Sheet of 4,
     #a-d   8.00 8.00
Souvenir Sheet
2439 A479 20,000ce multi   5.00 5.00

Orchids A480

Designs: 800ce, Oncidium desertorum. 3500ce, Oncidium variegatum. 4000ce, Anguloa uniflora, vert. 10,000ce, Oncidium gardneri, vert.

No. 2444: a, Vanda rothschildiana. b, Laelia cattleya. c, Laelia anceps. d, Odontioda dalmar.
20,000ce, Renanthera bella, vert.

2004, Dec. 27
2440-2443 A480   Set of 4   6.00 6.00
2444 A480   7500ce Sheet of 4,
     #a-d   7.50 7.50
Souvenir Sheet
2445 A480 20,000ce multi   5.00 5.00

Mammals — A481

Designs: 1000ce, Serval. 1200ce, Sable antelope. 2000ce, Cheetah. 3000ce, Bohor reedbuck.

No. 2450, horiz.: a, White rhinoceros. b, Leopard. c, Burchell's zebra. d, Red river hog.
20,000ce, Hippopotamus, horiz.

2004, Dec. 27
2446-2449 A481   Set of 4   2.50 2.50
2450 A481   7500ce Sheet of 4,
     #a-d   7.50 7.50
Souvenir Sheet
2451 A481 20,000ce multi   5.00 5.00

Sharks — A482

No. 2452: a, Zebra bullhead shark. b, Swellshark. c, Port Jackson shark. d, Leopard shark.
20,000ce, California horn shark.

2004, Dec. 27
2452 A482   7500ce Sheet of 4,
     #a-d   7.50 7.50
Souvenir Sheet
2453 A482 20,000ce multi   5.00 5.00

New Juaben Akwantukese Afahye Festival — A483

Designs: 2000ce, State emblem Yiadom and Hwedie. No. 2455, 4000ce, Migrating to freedom. 4500ce, Crossing Suhyien River.

5000ce, Chief at State Durbar. 6000ce, Sacrificing at the cave.

No. 2459: a, Like 4500ce. b, Palace guards. c, Like 2000ce. d, Like 5000ce. e, Libation pouring. f, Parading the royal treasury.

2005, Mar. 1   **Perf. 13¼x13**
2454-2458 A483   Set of 5   4.75   4.75
2459 A483 4000ce Sheet of 6,
     #a-f   5.50   5.50

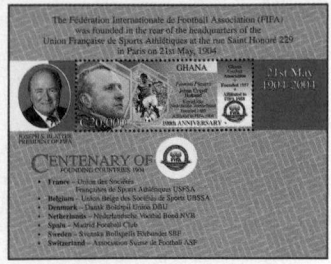

FIFA (Fédération Internationale de Football Association), Cent. — A484

No. 2460: a, Roberto Di Matteo. b, Marcel Desailly. c, Osei Kufuor. d, Eusebio. 20,000ce, Johan Cruyff.

2005, Mar. 14   **Perf. 13¼**
2460 A484   7500ce Sheet of 4,
     #a-d   7.25   7.25
    Souvenir Sheet
2461 A484 20,000ce multi   4.75   4.75

Ipomoea Asarifolia — A485

2005 ?   **Litho.**   **Perf. 13¾x13½**
2462 A485 2000ce multi

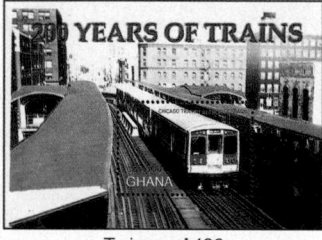

Trains — A486

No. 2463, 5000ce: a, Stanier Class 5-4-6-0. b, Central Pacific Jupiter. c, Robe River RSC3 Class 9401. d, Bangkok BTS train. e, Streamlined tank locomotive. f, ETR450.

No. 2464, 5000ce: a, Talgo train, Spain. b, VIA Turbotrain, Canada. c, Southern Pacific 4-8-4 #4449. d, Union Pacific "City of Portland." e, Shinkansen, Japan (white denomination). f, Deltic Diesel-electric engine, Great Britain.

No. 2465, 5000ce: a, Mogul 2-6-0. b, Milwaukee Railroad 4-6-2. c, Shinkansen (red denomination). d, Former Reading #2101 4-8-4. e, HST Inter-city 125. f, Daylight train.

No. 2466: a, Baldwin 4-6-0 steam train. b, Atchison, Topeka & Santa Fe 4-4-0 "American" steam train. c, Baldwin 4-6-0 Engine #44. d, Baldwin 2-6-0 #3 Three-spot.

No. 2467, 20,000ce, Chicago Transit Authority train. No. 2468, 20,000ce, Santa Fe train. No. 2469, 20,000ce, Empire Builder. No. 2470, 20,000ce, LMS 5305 steam train.

2005, June 1   **Litho.**   **Perf. 12¾**
    Sheets of 6, #a-f
2463-2465 A486   Set of 3   20.00   20.00
2466 A486 8000ce Sheet of 4,
     #a-d   7.25   7.25
    Souvenir Sheets
2467-2470 A486   Set of 4   18.00   18.00

Motor Vehicles A487

Designs: 2000ce, Setra State Transport bus. 4000ce, Album double-decker bus. 4500ce, Bedford Mummy truck and trailer. 5000ce, 1925 Mail carrier. 6000ce, Morris truck.

2005, June 21   **Litho.**   **Perf. 13x13¼**
2471-2475 A487   Set of 5   5.00   5.00

Friedrich von Schiller (1759-1805), Writer — A488

No. 2476: a, Schiller, with hand touching head. b, Schiller and birthplace. c, Brahms with beard.

20,000ce, Portraits of Schiller and Johannes Brahms.

2005   **Litho.**   **Perf. 13¼**
2476 A488   11,000ce Sheet of 3,
     #a-c   7.25   7.25
       Imperf
2477 A488   20,000ce shown   4.75   4.75
No. 2476 contains three 42x28mm stamps.

World Cup Soccer Championships, 75th Anniv. — A489

No. 2478: a, 1938 Italian team. b, Scene from 1938 Italy vs. Hungary match. c, Olympic Stadium. d, Silvio Piola.

20,000ce, Italian team with World Cup.

2005   **Perf. 13¼**
2478 A489   8000ce Sheet of 4,
     #a-d   7.25   7.25
    Souvenir Sheet
2479 A489 20,000ce multi   4.75   4.75

Panafest 05 — A489a

Inscriptions: 2000ce, Biribi wo soro (a symbol of hope). 4000ce, Let's hold hands together, horiz. No. 2479C, 5000ce, Sankofa (back to your roots). No. 2479D, 5000ce, Binnka-bi (bite not one another), horiz.

    Perf. 13½x13¼, 13¼x13½
2005 ?   **Litho.**   —
2479A-2479D A489a   Set of 4   —
The editors would like to examine any examples of any additional stamps that might exist in this set.

Disease Treatment and Prevention — A490

Designs: No. 2480, 2000ce, Emaciated people on rugs. No. 2481, 2000ce, Map of Ghana, symbols of medicine, red ribbon. No. 2482, 2000ce, People holding signs, horiz. 3000ce, Red ribbon, head. 4000ce, Maps of Africa and Ghana, arms, stylized people. No. 2485, 4500ce, Diseases on ladder destroying human body of bricks. No. 2486, 4500ce, Hand holding egg depicting health care workers. No. 2487, 5000ce, Emaciated man carrying bags of diseases. No. 2488, 5000ce, Heart, man lifting stylized globe. 6000ce, Whistle, hands holding cards with slogans.

2006, Jan. 26   **Perf. 13¼x13, 13x13¼**
2480-2489 A490   Set of 10   8.50   8.50

National Basketball Association Players and Team Emblems — A491

No. 2490, 3500ce: a, Carlos Boozer. b, Utah Jazz emblem
No. 2491, 3500ce: a, Carlos Arroyo. b, Detroit Pistons emblem.
No. 2492, 3500ce: a, Corey Magette. b, Los Angeles Clippers emblem.
No. 2493, 3500ce: a, David Wesley. b, Houston Rockets emblem.
No. 2494, 3500ce: a, Manu Ginobili. b, San Antonio Spurs emblem.
No. 2495, 3500ce: a, Al Harrington. b, Atlanta Hawks emblem.

2006, Mar. 15   **Perf. 13¼**
Sheets of 12, 10 each #a, 2 each #b
2490-2495 A491   Set of 6   55.00   55.00

A492

A493

Elvis Presley (1935-77) — A494

No. 2496 — Background color: a, Lilac. b, Green. c, Yellow green. d, Blue.
No. 2497 — Face color: a, Lilac. b, Green. c, Yellow green. d, Blue.
No. 2498: a, Blue background. b, Green background with dark red halo, ghost image at right. c, Yellow background with orange halo. d, Green background with orange red halo, ghost image above head. e, Yellow background, ghost image showing teeth at left. f, Yellow background, gray area at right. g, Green background, blue halo.

2006, Mar. 15   **Perf. 14**
2496 A492 8000ce Sheet of 4,
     #a-d   7.00   7.00
2497 A493 8000ce Sheet of 4,
     #a-d   7.00   7.00
2498 A494 3500ce Sheet of 9,
     #a-f, 3 #g   7.00   7.00

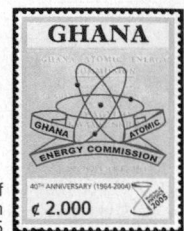

Intl. Year of Physics (in 2005) — A495

Designs: 2000ce, Emblem of Ghana Atomic Energy Commission. 4000ce, Ghana research reactor. 4500ce, Albert Einstein. 5000ce, Prof. Francis K. Allotey, physicist. 6000ce, Electricity experiment in physics laboratory.

2006, Mar. 29   **Perf. 13¼x14**
2499-2503 A495   Set of 5   7.25   7.25

Pope John Paul II (1920-2005) A496

2006, Apr. 7   **Perf. 13¼**
2504 A496 12,000ce multi   2.75   2.75
    Printed in sheets of 4.

Battle of Trafalgar, Bicent. (in 2005) A497

Designs: 2000ce, Sir John Jervis. 3000ce, Chase and Race. 5000ce, Goliath fires at Guerrier, horiz. 10,000ce, Death of Adm. Horatio Nelson, horiz.
20,000ce, Napoleon's flagships, Agamemnon. Vanguard, Elephant and Captain, horiz.

2006, Apr. 7   **Perf. 13x13¼, 13¼x13**
2505-2508 A497   Set of 4   4.50   4.50

Souvenir Sheet
Perf. 12
2509 A497 20,000ce multi 4.50 4.50

Jules Verne (1828-1905),
Writer — A498

No. 2510: a, Verne. b, Original book illustrations of balloons in flight. c, Montgolfier hot air balloon. d, Modern hot air balloon. 20,000ce, The Hindenburg.

2006, Apr. 7 **Perf. 12¾**
2510 A498 8000ce Sheet of 4,
#a-d 7.25 7.25

Souvenir Sheet
2511 A498 20,000ce multi 4.75 4.75

2006 World Cup Soccer
Championships, Germany — A499

Designs: No. 2512, 2000ce, Line of Ghana Black Stars players. No. 2513, 2000ce, Captain Stephen Appiah and opposing player, vert. No. 2514, 4000ce, Exchange of pennants. No. 2515, 4000ce, Joy of success. No. 2516, 4500ce, Michael Essien. No. 2517, 4500ce, Franz Beckenbauer, FIFA World Cup Stadium, Hanover. No. 2518, 5000ce, Scene from Ghana vs. Burkina Faso match. No. 2519, 5000ce, Black Stars team photo. No. 2520, 6000ce, Scene from Ghana vs. South Africa match. No. 2521, 6000ce, Fans celebrating Black Stars victory.
No. 2522, 4000ce: a, Appiah. b, Issah Ahmed. c, John Paintsil. d, Laryea Kingston. e, Essien, diff. f, Sule Ali Muntari. g, Joe Tex Frimpong. h, Coach Ratomir Dujkovic.
No. 2523, 4000ce: a, Asamoah Gyan. b, Sammy Adjei. c, Matthew Amoah. d, John Mensah. e, Emmanuel Pappoe. f, Mark Caniel Edusei. g, Abubakari Yakubu. h, Godwin Attram.

2006, May 18 **Perf. 13½**
2512-2521 A499 Set of 10 9.50 9.50
Sheets of 8, #a-h
Perf. 13¼
2522-2523 A499 Set of 2 14.00 14.00
Nos. 2522-2523 each contain eight 42x28mm stamps.

Tympanotonus
Fuscatus — A500

Synodontis Ocellifer
— A500a

Musa
Sapientum — A501

Gomphidius Glutinosus
— A501a

Bebearia
Arcadius — A502

Polemaetus
Bellicosus —
A502a

Xaphia Gladius
(Denomination
at
Center) — A503

Euphaedra
Francina — A504

Falco Tinnunculus —
A504a

Lagerstroemia Flos-
reginae — A504b

Ardea Purpurea (With
Brown Frame and "A's"
of "Ghana" With
Horizontal Cross Lines
— A504c

Spathodea
Campanulata — A505

2003-2007 **Litho.** **Perf. 13½**
2524	A500	500ce multi	—	—
2524A	A500a	500ce multi	—	—
2525	A501	800ce multi	—	—
2525A	A501a	1000ce multi	—	—
2526	A502	1500ce multi	—	—
2526A	A502a	1500ce multi	—	—
2527	A503	2000ce multi	—	—
2528	A504	2000ce multi	—	—
2528A	A504a	2000ce multi	—	—
2528B	A504b	4000ce multi	—	—
2528C	A504c	5000ce multi	—	—
2529	A505	6000ce multi	—	—

Issued: No. 2524, July 2003; Nos. 2524A, 2528B, Oct. 2005. No. 2525A, 2529, 2006; Nos. 2526A, 2528A, 2528C, 2007; No. 2527, 2005.

Nos. 1674-1677
Surcharged

2006, Aug. 28 **Litho.** **Perf. 14**
2530	A284	2000ce on 50ce #1674	29.00	10.00
2531	A284	2000ce on 200ce #1675	29.00	10.00
2532	A284	2000ce on 500ce #1676	29.00	10.00
2533	A284	2000ce on 800ce #1677	29.00	10.00
		Nos. 2530-2533 (4)	116.00	40.00

Nos. 1810-1814 Surcharged

2006, Aug. 28 **Litho.** **Perf. 14**
2534	A312	2000ce on 200ce #1810	.45	.45
2535	A312	2000ce on 300ce #1811	.45	.45
2536	A312	2000ce on 400ce #1812	.45	.45
2537	A312	2000ce on 600ce #1813	.45	.45
2538	A312	2000ce on 800ce #1814	.45	.45
		Nos. 2534-2538 (5)	2.25	2.25

Nos. 1703-1708 Surcharged

2006, Aug. 28 **Litho.** **Perf. 14**
2539	A291	3000ce on 50ce #1703	.65	.65
2540	A291	3000ce on 100ce #1704	.65	.65
2541	A291	3000ce on 200ce #1705	.65	.65
2542	A291	3000ce on 400ce #1706	.65	.65
2543	A291	3000ce on 600ce #1707	.65	.65
2544	A291	3000ce on 800ce #1708	.65	.65
		Nos. 2539-2544 (6)	3.90	3.90

Nos. 1741-1743 Surcharged

2006, Aug. 28 **Litho.** **Perf. 14**
2545	A300	4000ce on 50ce #1741	.90	.90
2546	A300	4000ce on 200ce #1742	.90	.90
2547	A300	4000ce on 600ce #1743	.90	.90
		Nos. 2545-2547 (3)	2.70	2.70

Nos. 1738-1740 Surcharged

2006, Aug. 28 **Litho.** **Perf. 14**
2548	A299	4500ce on 100ce #1738	1.00	1.00
2549	A299	4500ce on 400ce #1739	1.00	1.00
2550	A299	4500ce on 1000ce #1740	1.00	1.00
		Nos. 2548-2550 (3)	3.00	3.00

Nos. 1745-1752
Surcharged

2006, Aug. 28 **Litho.** **Perf. 14**
2551	A301	5000ce on 50ce #1745	1.10	1.10
2552	A301	5000ce on 100ce #1746	1.10	1.10
2553	A301	5000ce on 150ce #1747	1.10	1.10
2554	A301	5000ce on 200ce #1748	1.10	1.10
2555	A301	5000ce on 400ce #1749	1.10	1.10
2556	A301	5000ce on 600ce #1750	1.10	1.10
2557	A301	5000ce on 800ce #1751	1.10	1.10
2558	A301	5000ce on 1000ce #1752	1.10	1.10
		Nos. 2551-2558 (8)	8.80	8.80

Nos. 1766-1768 Surcharged

2006, Aug. 28 **Litho.** **Perf. 14**
2559	A299	6000ce on 100ce #1766	1.25	1.25
2560	A299	6000ce on 400ce #1767	1.25	1.25
2561	A299	6000ce on 1000ce #1768	1.25	1.25
		Nos. 2559-2561 (3)	3.75	3.75

Miniature Sheets

Ghana Soccer Players — A506

No. 2562, 4000ce: a, Asamoah Gyan. b, Sammy Adjei. c, Matthew Amoah. d, John Mensah. e, Emmanuel Pappoe. f, Mark Daniel Edusei. g, Abubakari Yakubu. h, Godwin Attram.
No. 2563, 4000ce: a, Stephen Appiah. b, Issah Ahmed. c, John Paintsil. d, Laryea Kingston. e, Michael Essien. f, Sule Ali Muntari. g, Joe Tex Frimpong. h, Ghana Team Coach Ratomir Dujkovic.

2007, Jan. 22 **Litho.** **Perf. 13½**
Sheets of 8, #a-h
2562-2563 A506 Set of 2 14.00 14.00

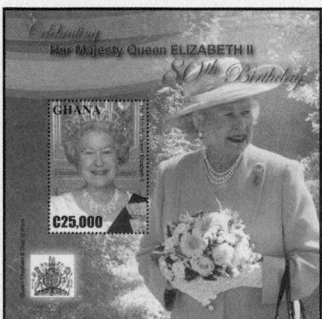

Queen Elizabeth II, 80th
Birthday — A507

No. 2564: a, Holding flowers. b, Wearing
purple hat. c, Wearing light green hat, denomination in purple. d, Wearing light green hat,
denomination in white.
25,000ce, Wearing tiara.

2007, Jan. 22
2564 A507   6000ce Sheet of 4,
                    #a-d   5.25 5.25
Souvenir Sheet
2565 A507   25,000ce multi   5.50 5.50

Marilyn Monroe (1926-62),
Actress — A508

No. 2566: a, Wearing glasses. b, Wearing
bathrobe. c, Looking left. d, Wearing red dress
and earrings.
20,000ce, With eyes closed.

2007, Jan. 22
2566 A508   9000ce Sheet of 4,
                    #a-d   8.00 8.00
Souvenir Sheet
2567 A508   20,000ce multi   4.50 4.50

Space Achievements — A509

No. 2568, horiz. — Luna 9: a, Distant view
of spacecraft and moon, denomination in
black. b, Spacecraft, denomination in white. c,
Close-up view of spacecraft and moon,
denomination in black. d, Spacecraft in frame,
denomination in white.
No. 2569, 6500ce, horiz. — Apollo-Soyuz
Test Project: a, Apollo and Soyuz spacecraft
docked. b, Mission emblem. c, Astronaut Tom
Stafford. d, Cosmonaut Aleksei Leonov. e,
Astronaut Deke Slayton. f, Astronaut Vance
Brand and Cosmonaut Valeri Kubasov.
No. 2570, 6500ce — Giotto Comet Probe: a,
Probe in space, black background. b, Comet,
probe in space, red text at bottom. c, Top of
probe, white background. d, Comet, probe in
space, purple background. e, Probe and sche-
matic diagram. f, Bottom of probe.
No. 2571, 20,000ce, Astronaut Buzz Aldrin.
No. 2572, 20,000ce, Apollo-Soyuz crew mem-
bers shaking hands in space, horiz. No. 2573,
20,000ce, Viking 1, horiz.

2007, Jan. 22
2568 A509   10,000ce Sheet of
                    4, #a-d   8.75 8.75
Sheets of 6, #a-f
2569-2570 A509 Set of 2   17.00 17.00
Souvenir Sheets
2571-2573 A509 Set of 3   13.00 13.00

Scouting, Cent. — A510

No. 2574, vert. — Dove, Scout emblem and
Scout: a, Giving Scout sign. b, Blowing bugle.
c, Carrying injured boy.
20,000ce, Scout emblem, Scout giving
Scout sign.

2007   **Perf. 13¼**
2574 A510   12,000ce Sheet of 3,
                    #a-c   8.00 8.00
Souvenir Sheet
2575 A510   20,000ce multi   4.50 4.50

Independence, 50th Anniv. — A511

2007, Sept. 15   Litho.   Perf. 13¼
2576 A511   4000ce multi   .90   .90

Kente Cloth Designs — A512

Designs: 4000ce, Sika ne Barima. 7300ce,
Edwene Si So. 7500ce, Dakoro Yesere. No.
2580, 9000ce, Agyenegyne Nsu. No. 2581,
9000ce, Nkatoa Sa. 10,000ce, Edwene Asa.

2007, Sept. 15   Perf. 13½x13¼
2577-2582 A512 Set of 6   10.00 10.00

Aburi Botanical Gardens — A513

Designs: 4000ce, Bamboo groves. 7300ce,
School of Horticulture. 7500ce, Silk cotton
tree, vert. 9000ce, Royal Palm Walkway.
10,000ce, Famous ficus tree, vert.
No. 2588: a, Like 9000ce. b, Like 7300ce. c,
Silk cotton tree. d, Famous ficus tree. e, Like
4000ce. f, Sanatorium.

Perf. 13¼x13½, 13½x13¼
2007, Sept. 15
2583-2587 A513 Set of 5   8.25 8.25
2588 A513   6000ce Sheet of 6,
                    #a-f   7.75 7.75

Cocoa — A514

Designs: 4000ce, Cocoa beverages and
spread. 7300ce, Cocoa Pebbles. 7500ce,
Assorted chocolates. 9000ce, Man at cocoa
processing plant. 10,000ce, Finished cocoa
products.
No. 2594: a, Like 10,000ce. b, Cacao pods.
c, Like 7500ce. d, Like 9000ce. e, Like
7300ce. f, Workers packaging cocoa products.

2007, Sept. 15   Perf. 13¼x13½
2589-2593 A514 Set of 5   8.25 8.25
2594 A514   6000ce Sheet of 6,
                    #a-f   7.75 7.75

Cats and
Dogs — A515

Designs: 6000ce, Chartreux cat. 7000ce,
Blue-mitted ragdoll cat. 8000ce, Blue lynx
point Birman cat, horiz. 9000ce, Norwegian
Forest cat.
No. 2599, horiz.: a, American bulldog. b, Old
English sheepdog. c, Shar-pei. d, Boston
terrier.
No. 2600, 20,000ce, Cinnamon point Sia-
mese cat. No. 2601, 20,000ce, Greyhound.

2007, Sept. 15   Perf. 14
2595-2598 A515 Set of 4   6.50 6.50
2599 A515   7500ce Sheet of 4,
                    #a-d   6.50 6.50
Souvenir Sheets
2600-2601 A515 Set of 2   8.75 8.75

Orchids — A516

No. 2602: a, Epipactis atrorubens. b, Galeandra bicarinata. c, Platanthera tipuloides. d,
Platanthera ciliaris.
20,000ce, Spathoglottis plicata.

2007, Sept. 15
2602 A516   7500ce Sheet of 4,
                    #a-d   6.50 6.50
Souvenir Sheet
2603 A516   20,000ce multi   4.50 4.50

Birds — A517

No. 2604, horiz.: a, Red-billed hornbill. b,
Bearded barbet. c, Hoopoe. d, Pygmy
kingfisher.
20,000ce, Gray-crowned crane.

2007, Sept. 15
2604 A517   7500ce Sheet of 4,
                    #a-d   6.50 6.50
Souvenir Sheet
2605 A517   20,000ce multi   4.50 4.50

Traditional
Costumes
A518

Designs: 4000ce, War dress, Northern
Ghana. 7300ce, Woman. 7500ce, Mourning
wear. 9000ce, Smock. 10,000ce, Wulomo
costume.

Perf. 13½x13¼
2007, Sept. 15   Litho.
2606-2610 A518 Set of 5   8.25 8.25

Famous
People — A519

Designs: No. 2611, 4000ce, Sir Arko Kor-
sah, first Chief Justice. No. 2612, 4000ce,
Amon Kotei, designer of national coat of arms.
No. 2613, 4000ce, Philip Gbeho, composer of
national anthem. 4500ce, F. K. Buah, historian. 6000ce, Prof. Albert Adu Boahene, historian and politician. 7300ce, Leticia Obeng,
aquatic biologist. 7500ce, Peter Cardinal
Appiah Turkson, first Ghanaian cardinal.
9000ce, Susanna Alhassan, first femal government minister.

2007, Sept. 15   Perf. 13¼
2611-2618 A519 Set of 8   10.00 10.00

On July 3, 2007, Ghana's currency
was revalued at a rate of 10,000 old
cedis to 1 new cedi. Old cedis continued to be valid until Dec. 31, 2007. Nos.
2576-2618 and 2641-2646 were issued
after July 3, but have denominations
expressed in old cedis.

Antrak Air
A520

Airplane: 40p, On ground. 73p, In flight.

2007, Sept. 15   Perf. 13¼
2619-2620 A520   Set of 2   2.25 2.25

Accra Tourist Attractions — A521

Designs: 20p, Independence Arch. 40p, Independence Square. 73p, Supreme Court. 75p, National Theater. 90p, Intl. Conference Center.

2007, Sept. 15
2621-2625 A521   Set of 5   6.50 6.50

Agricultural Development
Bank — A522

Designs: 40p, Emblem. 75p, Home Link Account, vert. 90p, Young Farmers Program, vert. 1ce, Gold Drive Motor Loan, vert.

2007, Sept. 15
2626-2629 A522   Set of 4   6.75 6.75

Ghana Commercial Bank — A523

Designs: 40p, Emblem. 73p, Eagle, world map. 75p, Ghana Commercial Bank Tower, vert. 90p, Xpress Money Transfer, vert.

2007, Sept. 15
2630-2633 A523   Set of 4   6.00 6.00

State
Insurance
Company
A524

Designs: 40p, Emblem. 73p, Executives. 75p, New office building. 90p, Child pointing. 1ce, Three CIMG Awards, vert.

2007, Sept. 15
2634-2638 A524   Set of 5   8.25 8.25

Ghanaian Heads of State — A525

Dr. Kwame Nkrumah and Pres. J. A.
Kufuor With State Sword — A526

No. 2639: a, Dr. Kwame Nkrumah. b, Lieutenant General J. A. Ankrah. c, General A. A. Afrifa. d, Dr. Kofi Abrefa Busia. e, General I. K. Acheampong. f, Lieutenant General W. A. Akuffo. g, Dr. Hilla Limann. h, Flight Lieutenant J. J. Rawlings. i, Pres. J. A. Kufuor.

2007, Sept. 15   Perf. 13½x13¼
2639 A525 60p Sheet of 9, #a-
     i   11.00 11.00
Souvenir Sheet
2640 A526 1ce multi   1.10 1.10

Pope Benedict
XVI — A527

2007, Nov. 15   Perf. 13¼
2641 A527 4000ce multi   .90 .90
Printed in sheets of 8.

Gold
A528

Designs: 4000ce, Gold ore. 7300ce, Melting gold ore. 7500ce, Woman holding gold bar. 9000ce, Entrance of Obuasi Gold Mines, horiz. 10,000ce, Gold-plated chair.

2007   Perf. 13½x13¼, 13¼x13½
2642-2646 A528   Set of 5   8.25 8.25

24th UPU
Congress,
Nairobi
A529

Designs: 40p, Dancers. 73p, Flags of Ghana and Kenya, warrior with shield, vert. 75p, UPU emblem in opened box. 90p, UPU emblem on map of Africa, vert.

No. 2651: a, Part of UPU emblem, folded map of world, denomination at LL. b, Part of UPU emblem, folded map of world, denomination at UR. c, Folded map of world, map and flag of Kenya.

2007, Dec. 3   Perf. 12½
2647-2650 A529   Set of 4   6.00 6.00
Souvenir Sheet
2651 A529 1ce Sheet of 3, #a-c   6.50 6.50

Miniature Sheet

Wedding of Queen Elizabeth II and
Prince Philip, 60th Anniv. (in
2007) — A530

No. 2652: a, Queen, denomination in green. b, Couple, denomination in green. c, Couple, denomination in orange. d, Queen, denomination in orange. e, Queen, denomination in blue. f, Couple, denomination in blue.

2008, Jan. 31 Litho.   Perf. 13¼x13½
2652 A530 60p Sheet of 6, #a-f   7.75 7.75

Paintings by Qi Baishi (1864-
1957) — A531

No. 2653: a, Top half of Lotus and Mandarin Ducks (lotus). b, Top half of River Landscape with Boats (boats). c, Bottom half of Lotus and Mandarin Ducks (ducks). d, Bottom half of River Landscape with Boats (trees). 3ce, Peony in a Dragon Vase.

2008, Jan. 31   Perf. 12x11½
2653 A531 90p Sheet of 4, #a-d   7.75 7.75
Souvenir Sheet
Perf. 11½
2654 A531 3ce multi   6.50 6.50
No. 2653 contains four 30x40mm stamps.

Miniature Sheet

2008 Summer Olympics,
Beijing — A532

No. 2655: a, Boxing. b, Relay race. c, Long jump. d, Soccer.

2008, May 8   Perf. 12¾
2655 A532 40p Sheet of 4, #a-d   3.25 3.25

Souvenir Sheet

Visit of US Pres. George W. Bush to
Ghana — A533

No. 2656: a, US Pres. George W. Bush. b, Ghana Pres. John Agyekum Kufuor.

2008, Sept. 17   Perf. 13½
2656 A533 1.25ce Sheet of 2,
     #a-b   4.50 4.50

Khilafat Ahmadiyya, Cent. — A533a

Designs: 40p, Flag, minaret, world map. 73p, T. I. Ahmadiyya Senior High School, Kumasi. 90p, Wheat. 1ce, Ahmadiuua Muslim Hospital, Daboase.

2008   Litho.   *Perf. 14½*
2656C-2656F A533a   Set of 4   9.50 9.50

Coat of Arms — A534

Illustration reduced.

2009, Mar. 31   Litho.   *Perf. 14x15*
2657 A534 1ce gray + label   1.40 1.40

Vegetables A535

Designs: 1ce, Tomatoes. 1.20ce, Tomatoes and white eggplants. 1.30ce, White eggplants.

2009, Mar. 31   Litho.   *Perf. 14¾x14*
2658-2660 A535   Set of 3   5.00 5.00

Korle Bu Teaching Hospital A536

Designs: 1ce, Medical block. No. 2662, 1.10ce, Cardiothoracic Center. No. 2663, 1.10ce, New administration block. 1.20ce, Prof. Frimpong Boateng, heart surgeon, vert.

2009, Mar. 31   *Perf. 14¾x14, 14x14¾*
2661-2664 A536   Set of 4   6.25 6.25

Tweneboa Kodua High School A537

Designs: 1ce, Administration block. 1.10ce, Girls domitory. 1.20ce, Students at ICT Center. 1.30ce, Students playing volleyball.

2009, Mar. 31   *Perf. 14¾x14*
2665-2668 A537   Set of 4   6.50 6.50

Soccer Players — A538

Designs: No. 2669, 1ce, Edward Acquah. No. 2670, 1ce, Aggrey Fynn. No. 2671, 1ce,

Nana Gyamfi II. No. 2672, 1ce, Robert Mensah. No. 2673, 1ce, Baba Yara.

2009, Mar. 31   *Perf. 14x14¾*
2669-2673 A538   Set of 5   7.25 7.25

Peony A539

2009, Apr. 10   *Perf. 13¼*
2674 A539 1ce multi   1.40 1.40

Printed in sheets of 8.

Nos. 852, 1055, 1068, 1939B, and 2525 Surcharged

No. 2675

No. 2676

No. 2677

Christmas 1988

No. 2678

No. 2679

Methods and Perfs. As Before

2009 ?
2675	A350a	20p on 800ce #1939B	—	—
2676	A174	1ce on 70p #852	—	—
2677	A205	1ce on 5ce #1055	—	—
2678	A208	1ce on 20ce #1068	—	—
2679	A501	1.20ce on 800ce #2525	—	—

The editors suspect more stamps may have been surcharged and would like to examine any examples.

SEMI-POSTAL STAMPS

Starlets, 1995 Under-17 World Soccer Champions — SP1

200ce+50ce, Holding gold cup won at Ecuador, vert. 550ce+50ce, Starlets '95 team photo. 800ce+50ce, Abu Idorisu, vert. 1100ce+50ce, Emmanuel Bentil, vert. 1500ce+50ce, Bashiru Gambo, vert.

Perf. 13½x13, 13x13½
1997, Aug. 12   Litho.
B1-B5 SP1 Set of 5   6.25 6.25

AIR POST STAMPS

Type of Regular Issue

Designs: 1sh3p, Pennant-winged nightjar. 2sh, Crowned cranes, vert.

Perf. 14½x14, 14x14½
1959, Oct. 5   Photo.   Wmk. 325
C1 A17 1sh3p multicolored   .80 .25
    a.   Booklet pane of 4   4.50
C2 A17 2sh multicolored   1.10 .60

For surcharges see Nos. C7-C10.

Ships, Tema Harbor and Jet — AP1

Perf. 14x13
1962, Feb. 10   Litho.   Unwmk.
C3 AP1 1sh3p multicolored   .40 .40
C4 AP1 2sh6p multicolored   1.00 1.00
   Nos. C3-C4,110 (3)   1.60 1.60

Opening of Tema Harbor, as part of the Volta River Project.

Type of Regular Issue, 1962

1962, Mar. 6   *Perf. 13x14*
C5 A35 1sh3p multicolored   .30 .30
C6 A35 2sh6p multicolored   .75 .75

Nos. C1-C2 Surcharged in White or Green with New Value and: "Ghana New Currency / 19th July, 1965"

Perf. 14½x14, 14x14½
1965, July 19   Photo.   Wmk. 325
C7 A17 15pa on 1sh3p multi (W)   .70
C8 A17 24pa on 2sh multi (G)   2.00 .35

The two lines of the overprint are diagonal on No. C8.

Nos. C1, C8 Surcharged in White or Red

1967, Feb. 27   Photo.   Wmk. 325
C9 A17 12½np on 1sh3p (W)   4.00 3.00
C10 A17 20np on 24pa on 2sh   5.00 4.00

POSTAGE DUE STAMPS

Gold Coast Nos. J2-J6 Overprinted "GHANA" and Bar in Red

Perf. 14
1958, June 25   Wmk. 4   Typo.
J1 D1 1p black   .20 .45
J2 D1 2p black   .20 .45
J3 D1 3p black   .20 .45
J4 D1 6p black   .20 1.00
J5 D1 1sh black   .20 2.00
   Nos. J1-J5 (5)   1.00 4.35

Type of Gold Coast Inscribed "Ghana"

1958, Dec. 1   *Perf. 14*
J6 D1 1p carmine rose   .20 .45
J7 D1 2p green   .20 .45
J8 D1 3p orange   .20 .45

J9 D1 6p ultramarine   .20 1.00
J10 D1 1sh purple   .20 2.00
   Nos. J6-J10 (5)   1.00 4.35

Nos. J6-J10 Surcharged in Black, Blue or Red with New Value and "Ghana New Currency / 19th July, 1965."

1965, July 19
J11 D1 1pa on 1p car rose   .25 .75
J12 D1 2pa on 2p grn (Bl)   .25 1.40
J13 D1 3pa on 3p org (Bl)   .25 1.40
J14 D1 6pa on 6p ultra (R)   .35 2.50
J15 D1 12pa on 1sh pur (Bl)   .60 2.75
   Nos. J11-J15 (5)   1.70 8.80

Surcharge diagonal on Nos. J11 and J15.

No. J12 with additional surcharge, "1½Np" in red, was reported to have been used at one branch post office (Burma Camp) despite official intention. Four similar added surcharges were prepared: 1np on 1pa, 2½np on 3pa, 5np on 6pa, and 10np on 12pa.

D2

1970   Unwmk.   Litho.   *Perf. 14½x14*
J16 D2 1np carmine rose   1.50 5.00
J17 D2 1½np green   1.75 6.00
J18 D2 2½np orange   2.25 8.00
J19 D2 5np ultramarine   2.75 8.50
J20 D2 10np dull purple   4.00 9.50
   Nos. J16-J20 (5)   12.25 37.00

1981   Litho.   *Perf. 14½x14*
J21 D2 2p red orange   1.50 5.25
J22 D2 3p brown   1.50 5.25

GIBRALTAR

jə-ˈbrol-tər

LOCATION — A fortified promontory, including the Rock, extending from Spain's southeast coast at the entrance to the Mediterranean Sea
GOVT. — British Crown Colony
AREA — 2.5 sq. mi.
POP. — 29,165 (1999 est.)
CAPITAL — Gibraltar

12 Pence = 1 Shilling
20 Shillings = 1 Pound
100 Centimos = 1 Peseta (1889-95)
100 Pence = 1 Pound (1971)

> **Catalogue values for unused stamps in this country are for Never Hinged items, beginning with Scott 119 in the regular postage section and Scott J1 in the postage due section.**

Types of Bermuda Overprinted in Black

1886, Jan. 1   Wmk. 2   Perf. 14

1	A6	½p green	18.00	9.00
2	A1	1p rose	75.00	5.50
3	A2	2p violet brown	140.00	92.50
4	A8	2½p ultra	175.00	4.25
5	A7	4p orange brn	175.00	100.00
6	A4	6p violet	300.00	225.00
7	A5	1sh bister brn	500.00	400.00
		Nos. 1-7 (7)	1,383.	836.25

Forged overprints of No. 7 are plentiful.

Victoria
A6   A7

A8   A9

1886-98   Typo.

8	A6	½p dull green ('87)	13.00	4.50
9	A6	½p gray grn ('98)	10.00	2.00
10	A7	1p rose ('87)	50.00	5.00
11	A7	1p car rose ('98)	10.00	.55
12	A8	2p brn violet	35.00	25.00
13	A8	2p brn vio & ultra ('98)	27.50	2.00
14	A9	2½p brt ultra ('98)	36.00	.80
a.		2½p ultramarine	95.00	3.25
16	A8	4p orange brn	90.00	90.00
17	A8	4p org brn & grn ('98)	21.00	7.50
18	A8	6p violet	130.00	130.00
19	A8	6p vio & car rose ('98)	47.50	25.00
20	A8	1sh bister	275.00	225.00
21	A8	1sh bis & car rose ('98)	47.50	18.00
		Nos. 8-14,16-21 (13)	792.50	535.35

Stamps of 1886 Issue Surcharged in Black

1889, July

22	A6	5c on ½p green	8.75	27.50
23	A7	10c on 1p rose	14.50	15.00
24	A8	25c on 2p brn vio	6.00	10.00
a.		Small "I" in "CENTIMOS"	140.00	190.00
b.		Broken "N"	140.00	190.00

25	A9	25c on 2½p ultra	25.00	2.75
a.		Small "I" in "CENTIMOS"	400.00	125.00
b.		Broken "N"	400.00	125.00
26	A8	40c on 4p org brn	62.50	87.50
27	A8	50c on 6p violet	67.50	87.50
28	A8	75c on 1sh bister	67.50	82.50
		Nos. 22-28 (7)	251.75	312.75

There are two varieties of the figure "5" in the 5c, 25c, 50c and 75c.

A11

1889-95

29	A11	5c green	5.50	1.00
30	A11	10c rose	5.50	.60
a.		Value omitted	6,200.	
31	A11	20c ol green ('95)	14.00	82.50
31A	A11	20c ol grn & brn ('95)	50.00	22.50
32	A11	25c ultra	22.50	.90
33	A11	40c orange brn	4.75	3.50
34	A11	50c violet	4.25	2.50
35	A11	75c olive green	42.50	42.50
36	A11	1p bister	92.50	25.00
36A	A11	1p bis & bl ('95)	6.00	7.00
37	A11	2p blk & car rose ('95)	13.00	37.50
38	A11	5p steel blue	52.50	125.00
		Nos. 29-38 (12)	313.00	350.50

A12   A13

King Edward VII

1903, May 1

39	A12	½p grn & bl grn	12.00	11.00
40	A12	1p violet, red	37.50	.70
41	A12	2p grn & car rose	22.50	30.00
42	A12	2½p vio & blk, bl	6.00	.70
43	A12	6p violet & pur	27.50	26.00
44	A12	1sh blk & car rose	32.50	42.50
45	A13	2sh green & ultra	175.00	250.00
46	A13	4sh vio & green	110.00	175.00
47	A13	8sh vio & blk, bl	160.00	175.00
48	A13	£1 vio & blk, red	600.00	700.00
		Nos. 39-48 (10)	1,183.	1,410.

1904-12   Wmk. 3
Ordinary or Chalky Paper

49	A12	½p blue grn		
		grn	9.00	2.00
49A	A12	½p dull grn & br grn	15.00	3.00
50b	A12	1p vio, red ('05)	8.00	1.00
a.		Bisected, used as ½p on card		1,800.
51	A12	1p car ('07)	6.50	.70
52a	A12	2p grn & car rose ('07)	9.50	8.00
53	A12	2p gray ('10)	10.00	13.00
54	A12	2½p vio & blk, bl ('07)	45.00	110.00
55	A12	2½p ultra ('07)	6.25	1.90
56b	A12	6p vio & pur ('08)	35.00	17.50
a.		6p vio & red violet ('12)	160.00	450.00
57	A12	1sh blk & car rose ('05)	62.50	18.00
58	A12	1sh blk, grn ('10)	27.50	25.00
59a	A13	2sh grn & ultra ('07)	97.50	110.00
60	A13	2sh vio & bl, bl ('10)	60.00	57.50
61	A13	4sh vio & grn ('10)	325.00	400.00
62	A13	4sh blk & red ('10)	140.00	175.00
63	A13	8sh vio & grn ('11)	225.00	250.00
64	A12	£1 vio & blk, red	600.00	650.00
		Nos. 49-64 (5)	1,350.	1,532.

Nos. 51, 53, 55 are on ordinary paper. Nos. 54, 58, 60-64 are on chalky paper. Others come on both papers. The least expensive varieties are listed above. For detailed listings, see the *Scott Specialized Catalogue of Stamps and Covers.*
No. 56a, used, must have a 1912 cancellation. Stamps used later sell for about the same as unused.

A14   King George V — A15

1912, July 17   Ordinary Paper

66	A14	½p green	4.00	.80
67	A14	1p carmine	4.00	.90
a.		1p scarlet ('16)	4.25	1.60
68	A14	2p gray	13.00	1.75
69	A14	2½p ultra	9.50	2.50

Chalky Paper

70	A14	6p dl vio & red vio	11.00	19.00
71	A14	1sh black, green	11.00	4.25
a.		1sh black, emerald ('24)	22.50	100.00
b.		1sh blk, bl grn, ol back ('19)	15.00	30.00
c.		1sh blk, emer, ol back ('23)	30.00	82.50
72	A15	2sh vio & ultra, bl	30.00	4.00
73	A15	4sh black & scar	37.50	65.00
74	A15	8sh vio & green	90.00	110.00
75	A15	£1 vio & blk, red	160.00	230.00
		Nos. 66-75 (10)	370.00	438.20

1921-32   Ordinary Paper   Wmk. 4

76	A14	½p green ('26)	1.60	1.90
77	A14	1p rose red	2.25	1.40
78a	A14	1½p pale red brown ('22)	2.25	.40
79	A14	2p gray	1.60	1.60
80	A14	2½p ultra	22.50	47.50
81	A14	3p ultra	2.75	1.75

Chalky Paper

82	A14	6p dl vio & red vio ('26)	1.75	4.00
a.		6p gray lilac & red violet ('23)	7.00	4.50
83	A14	1sh black, emer	12.00	22.00
84	A14	1sh ol grn & blk	17.50	27.50
a.		1sh brn olive & black ('32)	17.50	18.00
85a	A14	2sh red vio & ultra, blue ('25)	8.25	47.50
86	A15	2sh red brn & black	11.00	35.00
87	A15	2sh6p green & blk	11.00	22.50
88	A15	4sh black & scar	75.00	125.00
89	A15	5sh car & black	17.50	65.00
90	A15	8sh vio & green	275.00	450.00
91	A15	10sh ultra & black	37.50	80.00
92	A15	£1 org & black	175.00	275.00
93	A15	£5 dl vio & blk	1,750.	5,000.
		Nos. 76-92 (15)	663.95	1,160.

Years issued: Nos. 83, 85, 4sh, 8sh, 1924. 2sh6p, 5sh, 10sh, £5, 1925. £1, 1927. Nos. 84, 86, 1929.

Type of 1912 Issue
Inscribed: "THREE PENCE"

1930, Apr. 12   Ordinary Paper

94	A14	3p ultramarine	9.50	2.25

Rock of Gibraltar
A16

1931-33   Engr.   Perf. 14

96	A16	1p red	2.25	3.50
		Perf. 13½x14	17.50	6.50
97	A16	1p red brown	2.75	3.25
		Perf. 13½x14	14.50	5.00
98	A16	2p gray ('32)	8.75	2.25
		Perf. 13½x14	18.00	2.75
99	A16	3p dk blue ('33)	7.75	4.25
		Perf. 13½x14	30.00	40.00
		Nos. 96-99 (4)	21.50	13.25
		Set, never hinged	45.00	
		Nos. (4)	80.00	54.25
		Set, never hinged	150.00	

Common Design Types pictured following the introduction.

Silver Jubilee Issue
Common Design Type

1935, May 6   Perf. 11x12

100	CD301	2p black & ultra	1.40	2.50
101	CD301	3p ultra & brown	3.50	4.00
102	CD301	6p indigo & green	12.00	17.50
103	CD301	1sh brown vio & ind	12.00	15.00
		Nos. 100-103 (4)	28.90	39.00
		Set, never hinged	57.50	

Coronation Issue
Common Design Type

1937, May 12   Perf. 11x11½

104	CD302	½p deep green	.20	.45
105	CD302	2p gray black	.85	3.00
106	CD302	3p deep ultra	1.50	3.00
		Nos. 104-106 (3)	2.55	6.45
		Set, never hinged	5.00	

George VI — A17

Rock of Gibraltar
A18

Designs: 2p, Rock from north side. 3p, 5p, Europa Point. 6p, Moorish Castle. 1sh, Southport Gate. 2sh, Eliott Memorial. 5sh, Government House. 10sh, Catalan Bay.

Perf. 13, 13½x14 (½p, No. 118), 14 (1½p)

1938-49   Engr.   Wmk. 4

107	A17	½p gray green	.20	.40
108	A18	1p red brn ('42)	.35	.55
a.		1p chestnut, perf. 14	27.50	2.75
b.		1p chestnut, perf. 13½	27.50	2.50
c.		Perf. 13½, wmk. sideways ('41)	6.75	8.25
109	A18	1½p carmine rose	30.00	.90
b.		Perf. 13½	275.00	45.00
109A	A18	1½p gray vio ('43)	.25	1.60
110	A18	2p dk gray ('42)	.35	1.40
a.		Perf. 14	27.50	.55
c.		Perf. 13½	1.75	.45
d.		Perf. 13½, wmk. sideways ('41)	650.00	52.50
110B	A18	2p car rose ('44)	.30	.55
111	A18	3p blue ('42)	.35	.35
a.		Perf. 14	140.00	6.00
b.		Perf. 13½	22.50	1.10
112	A18	5p red org ('47)	1.00	1.25
113	A18	6p dl vio & car rose	3.75	1.90
a.		Perf. 14	125.00	1.60
b.		Perf. 13½	50.00	4.00
114	A18	1sh grn & blk ('42)	3.00	4.50
a.		Perf. 14	45.00	27.50
b.		Perf. 13½	70.00	8.25
115	A18	2sh org brn & blk ('42)	4.00	6.50
a.		Perf. 14	70.00	30.00
b.		Perf. 13½	140.00	42.50
116	A18	5sh dk car & blk ('44)	12.50	21.00
a.		Perf. 14 ('38)	100.00	175.00
b.		Perf. 13½	40.00	22.50
117	A18	10sh bl & blk ('43)	27.50	27.50
a.		Perf. 14	70.00	150.00
118	A17	£1 orange	37.50	47.50
		Nos. 107-118 (14)	121.05	115.90
		Set, never hinged	190.00	

Nos. 108c and 110d were issued in coils. No. 108 (1p, perf. 13) exists with watermark both normal and sideways. Nos. 110 and 110B (both 2p, perf. 13) have watermark sideways. For overprints see Nos. 127-130.

> **Catalogue values for unused stamps in this section, from this point to the end of the section, are for Never Hinged items.**

Peace Issue
Common Design Type
1946, Dec. 12   **Perf. 13½x14**

119	CD303	½p bright green	.30	.50
120	CD303	3p bright ultra	.40	.50

Silver Wedding Issue
Common Design Types
1948, Dec. 1   **Photo.**   **Perf. 14x14½**

121	CD304	½p dark green	1.00	1.25

Engr.; Name Typo.
Perf. 11½x11

122	CD305	£1 brown orange	70.00	87.50
		Set, hinged	55.00	

UPU Issue
Common Design Types
Engr.; Name Typo. on 3p, 6p
Perf. 13½, 11x11½

1949, Oct. 10   **Wmk. 4**

123	CD306	2p rose carmine	1.00	1.25
124	CD307	3p indigo	2.50	1.50
125	CD308	6p rose violet	2.00	2.50
126	CD309	1sh blue green	1.25	4.25
		Nos. 123-126 (4)	6.75	9.50

Nos. 110B, 111, 113-114 overprinted in Black or Carmine

1950, Aug. 1   **Perf. 13x12½**

127	A18	2p carmine rose	.40	1.25
128	A18	3p blue	1.00	1.25
129	A18	6p dl vio & car rose	1.25	1.75
a.		Double overprint	1,000.	1,250.
130	A18	1sh grn & blk (C)	1.25	1.75
		Nos. 127-130 (4)	3.90	6.00

Adoption of Constitution of 1950.

Coronation Issue
Common Design Type
1953, June 2   **Engr.**   **Perf. 13½x13**

131	CD312	½p olive green & black	.50	.50

Wharves — A26

Moorish Castle — A27

Designs: 1p, South view. 1½p, Tunny fishing industry. 2p, Southport Gate. 2½p, Sailing in the bay. 3p, Ocean liner. 4p, Coaling wharf. 5p, Airport. 6p, Europa Point. 1sh, Strait from Buena Vista. 2sh, Rosia Bay. 5sh, Government House. £1, Arms of Gibraltar.

1953, Oct. 19   **Perf. 12½**

132	A26	½p dk grn & ind	.20	.25
133	A26	1p blue green	1.60	.60
134	A26	1½p dark gray	1.00	1.50
135	A26	2p sepia	1.75	1.25
136	A26	2½p car lake	2.75	1.00
137	A26	3p grnsh blue	4.25	1.25
138	A26	4p ultra	6.00	3.50
139	A26	5p deep plum	1.50	1.00
140	A26	6p blue & black	3.50	1.75
141	A26	1sh red brn & bl	.60	1.25
142	A26	2sh vio & org	29.00	6.00
143	A26	5sh dark brown	37.50	15.00
144	A27	10sh ultra & brn	47.50	40.00
145	A27	£1 yellow & red	57.50	47.50
		Nos. 132-145 (14)	194.65	121.85
		Set, hinged	100.00	

Inscribed: "ROYAL VISIT 1954"
1954, May 10

146	A26	3p greenish blue	.50	.35

Candytuft — A28   Rock and Badge of Gibraltar Regiment — A30

Moorish Castle A29

Designs: 2p, St. George's Hall and cannons. 2½p, The keys. 3p, Rock by moonlight. 4p, Catalan Bay. 6p, Map. 7p, Air terminal. 9p, American war memorial. 1sh, Barbary ape. 2sh, Barbary partridge. 5sh, Blue rock thrush. 10sh, Narcissus.

Wmk. 314
1960, Oct. 29   **Photo.**   **Perf. 12½**

147	A28	½p brt green & lil	.20	.50
148	A29	1p black & yel grn	.20	.20
149	A29	2p org brn & sl	1.00	.20
150	A28	2½p blue & black	1.00	.70
151	A29	3p dk blue & ver	.30	.20
152	A29	4p choc & grnsh bl	3.00	.90
a.		Wmkd. sideways ('66)	.25	1.00
153	A28	6p brown & emer	1.00	.70
154	A28	7p gray & car	2.50	1.75
155	A28	9p grnsh blue & bluish gray	1.00	.95
156	A29	1sh brown & green	1.50	.70
157	A29	2sh dark red brn & ultra	17.50	3.00
158	A29	5sh ol & Prus grn	9.00	7.00
159	A28	10sh blue, yel & grn	22.50	17.50

Perf. 14
Engr.

160	A30	£1 org red & slate	19.00	17.50
		Nos. 147-160 (14)	79.70	51.80

For overprints see Nos. 165-166.

Freedom from Hunger Issue
Common Design Type
1963, June 4   **Perf. 14x14½**

161	CD314	9p sepia	4.00	2.25

Red Cross Centenary Issue
Common Design Type
1963, Sept. 2   **Litho.**   **Perf. 13**

162	CD315	1p black & red	.55	1.40
163	CD315	9p ultra & red	6.50	4.00

Shakespeare Issue
Common Design Type
1964, Apr. 23   **Photo.**   **Perf. 14x14½**

164	CD316	7p brown	.65	.55

Nos. 151 and 153 Overprinted: "NEW / CONSTITUTION / 1964."

1964, Oct. 16   **Perf. 12½**

165	A29	3p dk blue & ver	.20	.20
166	A28	6p brown & emer	.35	.50
a.		No period in overprint	17.00	27.50

ITU Issue
Common Design Type
Perf. 11x11½
1965, May 17   **Litho.**   **Wmk. 314**

167	CD317	4p emerald & yel	2.75	.45
168	CD317	2sh ap grn & dk bl	8.50	5.50

Intl. Cooperation Year Issue
Common Design Type
1965, Oct. 25   **Perf. 14½**

169	CD318	½p lt violet & grn	.20	1.75
170	CD318	4p blue green & cl	1.10	.75

Churchill Memorial Issue
Common Design Type
1966, Jan. 24   **Photo.**   **Perf. 14**
Design in Black, Gold and Carmine Rose

171	CD319	½p bright blue	.20	1.75
172	CD319	1p green	.35	.20
173	CD319	4p brown	1.10	.45
174	CD319	9p violet	2.10	2.50
		Nos. 171-174 (4)	3.75	4.90

World Cup Soccer Issue
Common Design Type
1966, July 1   **Litho.**   **Perf. 14**

175	CD321	2½p multicolored	.75	.75
176	CD321	6p multicolored	1.25	.80

Sea Bream A30a

7p, Orange scorpionfish. 1sh, Stone bass, vert.

Perf. 14x13½, 13½x14
1966, Aug. 27   **Photo.**   **Wmk. 314**

177	A30a	4p ultra, rose red & black	.30	.20
178	A30a	7p ol, rose red & blk	.35	.70
a.		Value omitted	1,500.	
179	A30a	1sh brt grn, brn & blk	.50	.35
		Nos. 177-179 (3)	1.15	1.25

European Sea Angling Championships, Gibraltar, Aug. 28-Sept. 3.

WHO Headquarters Issue
Common Design Type
1966, Sept. 20   **Litho.**   **Perf. 14**

180	CD322	6p multicolored	3.00	1.75
181	CD322	9p multicolored	4.50	2.75

"Our Lady of Europa" A31

Perf. 14x14½
1966, Nov. 15   **Photo.**   **Wmk. 314**

182	A31	2sh ultra & black	.60	1.00

Enthronement of the recovered statue of the Madonna in its new shrine, cent.

UNESCO Anniversary Issue
Common Design Type
1966, Dec. 1   **Litho.**   **Perf. 14**

183	CD323	2p "Education"	.50	.20
184	CD323	7p "Science"	2.00	.20
185	CD323	5sh "Culture"	5.00	3.25
		Nos. 183-185 (3)	7.50	3.65

Cable Ship Mirror — A32

Ships and Arms of Gibraltar: ½p Victory, Nelson's flagship. 1p, S.S. Arab. 2p, H.M.S. Carmania. 2½p, M.V. Mons Calpe. 3p, S.S. Canberra. 4p, H.M.S. Hood. 6p, Xebec, Moorish vessel. 7p, Amerigo Vespucci, Italian training ship (sails). 9p, Raffaello, Italian liner. 1sh, H.M.S. Royal Katherine, 17th century British warship. 2sh, H.M.S. Ark Royal, aircraft carrier. 5sh, H.M.S. Dreadnought, atomic submarine. 10sh, S.S. Neuralia, troopship. £1, Mary Celeste, 19th century mystery ship (sails).

Perf. 14x14½
1967-69   **Photo.**   **Wmk. 314**
Design in Black, Red and Gold; Background as Indicated

186	A32	½p deep rose	.20	.20
187	A32	1p yellow	.20	.20
188	A32	2p ultra	.20	.20

189	A32	2½p orange	.40	.30
190	A32	3p violet	.20	.20
191	A32	4p rose	.35	.20
191A	A32	5p brn & multi ('69)	3.50	.65
192	A32	6p gray	.35	.60
193	A32	7p yellow grn	.35	.50
194	A32	9p green	.35	.95
195	A32	1sh rose brown	.35	.35
196	A32	2sh brt yellow	4.00	2.50
197	A32	5sh brick red	4.00	6.75
198	A32	10sh emerald	14.00	22.50
199	A32	£1 lt ultra	17.00	22.50
		Nos. 186-199 (15)	45.45	58.60

Cable Car and ITY Emblem — A33

ITY emblem and: 9p, Bull shark, horiz. 1sh, Skin diver, horiz.

Perf. 14½x14, 14x14½
1967, June 15   **Photo.**   **Wmk. 314**

200	A33	7p red brn, red & blk	.20	.20
201	A33	9p brt blue, blk & slate	.20	.20
202	A33	1sh emer, blk & org brn	.35	.25
		Nos. 200-202 (3)	.75	.65

International Tourist Year.

Holy Family A34

Christmas: 6p, Church window, vert.

1967, Nov. 1   **Perf. 14½**

203	A34	2p dark red & multi	.20	.20
204	A34	6p dark green & multi	.20	.20

General Eliott and Map of Europe and Great Britain A35

Designs: 9p, Eliott Memorial and tower. 1sh, Gen. Eliott and map of Gibraltar, vert. 2sh, Gen. Eliott directing rescue operations for enemy sailors during Great Siege 1779-83.

Perf. 14½x14, 14x14½
1967, Dec. 11   **Photo.**   **Wmk. 314**
Size: 37x21mm, 21x37mm

205	A35	4p multicolored	.20	.20
206	A35	9p multicolored	.20	.20
207	A35	1sh multicolored	.20	.20

Size: 58x21½mm

208	A35	2sh multicolored	.45	.25
		Nos. 205-208 (4)	1.05	.85

250th anniv. of the birth of General George Augustus Eliott (1717-1790), Governor of Gibraltar during Great Siege.

Lord Baden-Powell — A36

Designs: 7p, Scout flag, Rock of Gibraltar and globe with map of Europe. 9p, Symbolic tents, heads and Scout salute. 1sh, Three Scout badges.

Perf. 14x14½
1968, Mar. 27   **Photo.**   **Wmk. 314**

209	A36	4p dull yellow & pur	.20	.20
210	A36	7p brown org, brn & grn	.20	.20

211 A36 9p ultra, black & org .20 .30
212 A36 1sh yellow & emerald .20 .30
Nos. 209-212 (4) .80 1.00
60th anniv. of the Gibraltar Scout Assoc.

Nurse and WHO Emblem A37

20th anniv. of WHO: 4p, Physician with microscope and WHO emblem.

1968, July 1 Photo. Wmk. 314
213 A37 2p yellow, ultra & blk .20 .20
214 A37 4p pink, black & slate .20 .20

King John Signing Magna Carta — A38

Shepherd, Lamb and Star — A39

Design: 2sh, Rock of Gibraltar, "Freedom" and Human Rights flame.

1968, Aug. 26 Perf. 13½x14½
215 A38 1sh org, gold & dk brn .25 .20
216 A38 2sh brt green & gold .35 .35

International Human Rights Year.

1968, Nov. 1 Perf. 14x13½
Christmas: 9p, Mary, Jesus and lamb.
217 A39 4p lt brown & multi .20 .20
218 A39 9p rose & multi .20 .20

Government House, Gibraltar — A40

9p, Rock of Gibraltar, Commonwealth Parliamentary Association emblem. 2sh, Big Ben, London, arms of Gibraltar.

Perf. 14½x14, 14x14½
1969, May 26 Photo. Wmk. 314
219 A40 4p green & gold .20 .20
220 A40 9p brt violet & gold .20 .20
221 A40 2sh lt ultra, gold & red .35 .20
Nos. 219-221 (3) .75 .60

Meeting of the Executive Committee of the General Council of the Commonwealth Parliamentary Assoc., Gibraltar, May 1969.

Rock of Gibraltar A41

1969, July 30 Perf. 14½x13½
222 A41 ½p orange & gold .20 .20
223 A41 5p emerald & silver .20 .20
224 A41 7p brt rose lil & silver .20 .20
225 A41 5sh ultra & gold 1.40 1.25
Nos. 222-225 (4) 2.00 1.85

Gibraltar's new constitution.
Nos. 222-225 are valued with surrounding selvage.

Royal Artillery Officer, 1758 — A42

Madonna della Seggiola, by Raphael — A43

Uniforms: 6p, Contemporary soldier of the Royal Anglian Regiment. 9p, Soldier, Royal Engineers, 1786. 2sh, Private of Fox's Marines, 1704.

1969, Nov. 6 Photo. Perf. 14
226 A42 1p gold & multi .20 .20
227 A42 6p silver, gold & multi .35 .30
228 A42 9p silver, gold & multi .55 .40
229 A42 2sh gold & multi 1.25 1.00
Nos. 226-229 (4) 2.35 1.90

Descriptions are printed on back on top of gum.
See Nos. 234-237, 276-279, 286-289, 299-302, 310-313, 318-321, 330-333.

1969, Dec. 1 Perf. 13½x Roulette 9
Christmas (Paintings): 7p, Madonna and Child, by Luis Morales. 1sh, Virgin of the Rocks, by Leonardo da Vinci.
230 A43 5p gold & multi .20 .20
231 A43 7p gold & multi .35 .35
232 A43 1sh gold & multi .55 .55
a. Triptych, Nos. 230, 232, 231 1.25 1.25

Europa Issue

Europa Point — A44

1970, June 8 Perf. 13½
233 A44 2sh multicolored .45 .40

Uniform Type of 1969
Uniforms: 2p, Royal Scots officer, 1839. 5p, Private of South Wales Borderers. 7p, Private of Queen's Royal Regiment, 1742. 2sh, Piper of Royal Irish Rangers, 1969.

1970, Aug. 28 Photo. Perf. 14
234 A42 2p gold & multi .40 .20
235 A42 5p gold & multi .60 .45
236 A42 7p gold & multi .60 .55
237 A42 2sh gold & multi 1.50 1.00
Nos. 234-237 (4) 3.10 2.20

Descriptions are printed on back on top of gum.

No. 178a and Rock of Gibraltar A45

Design: 2sh, No. 30a and Moorish Castle.
1970, Sept. 18 Perf. 13
238 A45 1sh red & olive .20 .20
239 A45 2sh ultra & rose .40 .55
Philympia, London Phil. Exhib., Sept. 18-26.

Virgin Mary by Gabriel Loire A46

1970, Dec. 1 Photo. Perf. 13x14
240 A46 2sh multicolored .35 .35

Christmas. The design is after a stained glass window in the Church of Our Lady of Perpetual Succour, Glasgow.

Decimal Currency Issue

Prince George of Cambridge Quarters, and Trinity Church — A47

Designs show for each denomination a 19th century print and a contemporary photograph of the same view: ½p Battery Rosia. 1½p, Wellington Monument, Alameda Gardens. 2p, View from North Bastion. 2½p, Catalan Bay. 3p, Convent, seen from garden. 4p, The Exchange and Spanish Chapel. 5p, Commercial Square, Library and Main Guard. 7p, South Barracks and Rosia Magazine. 8p, Moorish Mosque and Castle. 9p, Europa Pass. 10p, South Barracks, from Rosia Bay. 12½p, Southport Gates. 25p, Guards on Alameda. 50p, Europa Pass Gorge, vert. £1 Prince Edward Gate, vert.

In the listing the 1st number is for the 19th cent. design, the 2nd for the 20th cent. design.

Wmk. 314 Sideways
1971, Feb. 15 Litho. Perf. 14
Multicolored and:
241 ½p brown red .20 .20
242 ½p brown red .20 .20
a. A47 Pair, Nos. 241-242 .35 .40
243 1p light blue .85 .25
244 1p light blue .85 .25
b. A47 Pair, Nos. 243-244 1.75 .60
245 1½p emerald .25 .30
246 1½p emerald .25 .30
a. A47 Pair, Nos. 245-246 .50 .90
247 2p dark brown 1.50 2.50
248 2p dark brown 1.50 2.50
b. A47 Pair, Nos. 247-248 3.00 5.75
249 2½p vermilion .20 .35
250 2½p vermilion .20 .35
a. A47 Pair, Nos. 249-250 .35 .75
251 3p pale green .20 .20
252 3p pale green .20 .20
a. A47 Pair, Nos. 251-252 .35 .40
253 4p gray 2.00 2.50
254 4p gray 2.00 2.50
b. A47 Pair, Nos. 253-254 4.00 6.50
255 5p dark green .35 .35
256 5p dark green .35 .35
a. A47 Pair, Nos. 255-256 .75 .90
257 7p orange .70 .65
258 7p orange .70 .65
a. A47 Pair, Nos. 257-258 1.40 1.50
259 8p dark blue .75 .70
260 8p dark blue .75 .70
a. A47 Pair, Nos. 259-260 1.50 2.00
261 9p brick red .75 .70
262 9p brick red .75 .70
a. A47 Pair, Nos. 261-262 1.50 2.00
263 10p black .85 .80
264 10p black .85 .80
a. A47 Pair, Nos. 263-264 1.75 2.00
265 12½p bister 1.10 1.75
266 12½p bister 1.10 1.75
a. A47 Pair, Nos. 265-266 2.25 5.00
267 25p deep purple 1.10 1.75
268 25p deep purple 1.10 1.75
a. A47 Pair, Nos. 267-268 2.25 5.00
269 50p blue 1.40 2.75
270 50p blue 1.40 2.75
a. A47 Pair, Nos. 269-270 3.25 7.25
271 £1 sepia 2.25 4.25
272 £1 sepia 2.25 4.25
a. A47 Pair, Nos. 271-272 5.00 10.50
Nos. 241-272 (32) 28.90 40.00

Se-tenant both horizontally and vertically.

1973, Sept. 12 Wmk. 314 Upright
247a A47 2p dark brown & multi 1.80 2.75
248a A47 2p dark brown & multi 1.80 2.75
c. Pair, Nos. 247a-248a 4.00 7.00
253a A47 4p gray & multi 2.30 2.50
254a A47 4p gray & multi 2.30 2.50
c. Pair, Nos. 253a-254a 5.00 7.00
Nos. 247a-254a (4) 8.20 10.50

1975, July 9 Wmk. 373
243a A47 1p blue & multi 3.00 3.25
244a A47 1p blue & multi 3.00 3.25
c. Pair, Nos. 243a-244a 6.50 8.00

Elizabeth II — A48

Regimental Coat of Arms — A49

Coil Stamps
Perf. 14½x14
1971, Feb. 15 Photo. Wmk. 314
273 A48 ½p red orange .20 .25
274 A48 1p bright blue .35 .25
275 A48 2p lt yellow green .55 .80
a. Strip of 5 (½p, ½p, 1p, 1p, 2p) 1.60 26.00
Nos. 273-275 (3) 1.10 1.30

Uniform Type of 1969
Uniforms: 1p, Soldier, Black Watch, 1845. 2p, Drum Major with antelope mascot, Royal Fusiliers, 1971. 4p, Soldier, Kings Own Royal Border Regiment, 1704. 10p, Soldier, Devonshire and Dorset Regiment, 1801.

1971, Sept. 6 Litho. Perf. 14
276 A42 1p silver & multi .40 .30
277 A42 2p gold & multi .70 .30
278 A42 4p gold & multi 1.00 .50
279 A42 10p sil, gold & multi 3.25 2.75
Nos. 276-279 (4) 5.35 3.85

Descriptions are printed on back on top of gum.

1971, Sept. 25 Perf. 13x12
280 A49 3p red, bister & black .45 .40

Presentation of colors to Gibraltar Regiment, Sept. 25, 1971.

Nativity — A50

Christmas: 5p, Journey to Bethlehem.

1971, Dec. 1 Photo. Perf. 13x13½
281 A50 3p silver & multi .50 .50
282 A50 5p gold & multi .70 .70

Artificer, 1773 — A51

"Our Lady of Europa" — A52

3p, Tunneler with drill, 1969. 5p, Royal Engineers, 1772 and 1972, and regimental crest, horiz.

1972, Mar. 6 Perf. 14x13½, 13½x14
283 A51 1p dk blue & multi .55 .60
284 A51 3p red & multi .65 .80
285 A51 5p green & multi .75 1.00
Nos. 283-285 (3) 1.95 2.40

Bicent. of the Royal Engineers in Gibraltar.

Uniform Type of 1969

Uniforms: 1p, Soldier, Duke of Cornwall's Light Infantry, 1704. 3p, Officer, King's Royal Rifle Corps, 1830. 7p, Officer, 37th North Hampshire Regiment, 1825. 10p, Sailor, Royal Navy, 1972.

1972, July 19   Litho.   Perf. 14
286	A42	1p silver & multi	.60	.20
287	A42	3p slate & multi	1.40	.40
288	A42	7p silver & multi	2.10	.80
289	A42	10p gold & multi	2.50	1.60
		Nos. 286-289 (4)	6.60	3.00

Design descriptions printed on back on top of gum.

1972, Oct. 1   Perf. 14½x14
| 290 | A52 | 3p brown & multi | .20 | .20 |
| 291 | A52 | 5p green & multi | .20 | .40 |

Christmas. Design description printed on back.

Silver Wedding Issue, 1972
Common Design Type

Design: Queen Elizabeth II, Prince Philip, keys of Gibraltar and white narcissus.

1972, Nov. 20   Photo.   Perf. 14x14½
| 292 | CD324 | 5p car rose & multi | .25 | .20 |
| 293 | CD324 | 7p slate green & multi | .25 | .20 |

Flags of EEC Members and EEC Emblem — A53

Perf. 14½x14
1973, Feb. 22   Litho.   Unwmk.
| 294 | A53 | 5p red & multi | .50 | .40 |
| 295 | A53 | 10p ultra & multi | .80 | .80 |

Entry into European Economic Community.

Gibraltar Skull — A54

Designs: 6p, Head of Neanderthal man. 10p, Neanderthal family.

1973, May 22   Wmk. 314   Perf. 13½
296	A54	4p lilac rose & multi	1.50	.60
297	A54	6p lt ultra & multi	1.60	1.25
298	A54	10p yel green & multi	2.25	2.25
		Nos. 296-298 (3)	5.35	4.10

125th anniv. of the discovery of the Gibraltar skull.

Uniform Type of 1969

Uniforms: 1p, Fifer, King's Own Scottish Borderers, 1770. 4p, Officer, Royal Welsh Fusiliers, 1800. 6p, Soldier, Royal Northumberland Fusiliers, 1736. 10p, Private, Grenadier Guards, 1898.

1973, Aug. 22   Litho.   Perf. 14
299	A42	1p multicolored	.50	.30
300	A42	4p multicolored	1.50	.50
301	A42	6p multicolored	2.25	.95
302	A42	10p multicolored	3.00	2.00
		Nos. 299-302 (4)	7.25	3.80

Descriptions printed on back on top of gum.

Nativity, by Justus Danckerts — A55

1973, Oct. 17   Litho.   Perf. 12½x12
| 303 | A55 | 4p brown org & blue | .40 | .20 |
| 304 | A55 | 6p green & claret | .40 | .80 |

Christmas.

Princess Anne's Wedding Issue
Common Design Type

1973, Nov. 14   Perf. 14
| 305 | CD325 | 6p bl grn & multi | .20 | .20 |
| 306 | CD325 | 14p brt grn & multi | .45 | .45 |

Wedding of Princess Anne and Capt. Mark Phillips, Nov. 14, 1973.

V.R. (Queen Victoria) Pillar Box — A56

Virgin with Green Cushion, Andrea Solario — A57

Pillar Boxes: 6p, G.R. (King George). 14p, E.R. (Queen Elizabeth).

1974, May 2   Litho.   Perf. 14
307	A56	2p yel green & multi	.20	.25
308	A56	6p gray & multi	.35	.35
309	A56	14p dull yel & multi	.65	.65
a.		Souvenir booklet	11.00	
		Nos. 307-309 (3)	1.20	1.25

UPU, cent.
No. 309a contains 2 self-adhesive panes printed on peelable paper backing with multicolored advertising on back. One pane of 6 contains 3 each similar to Nos. 307-308; the other pane of 3 contains one each similar to Nos. 307-309. Stamps are imperf. x roulette.

Uniform Type of 1969

Uniforms: 4p, Officer, East Lancashire Regiment, 1742. 6p, Sergeant, Somerset Light Infantry, 1833. 10p, Company man, Royal Sussex Regiment, 1790. 16p, Officer, Royal Air Force, 1974.

1974, Aug. 21   Perf. 14
310	A42	4p silver & multi	.55	.50
311	A42	6p silver & multi	.95	.85
312	A42	10p silver & multi	1.25	1.40
313	A42	16p silver & multi	2.50	3.75
		Nos. 310-313 (4)	5.25	6.50

Descriptions are printed on back on top of gum.

1974, Nov. 5   Litho.
Christmas (Painting): 6p, Madonna of the Meadow, by Giovanni Bellini.
| 314 | A57 | 4p gold & multi | .40 | .35 |
| 315 | A57 | 6p gold & multi | .70 | 1.00 |

Churchill, Parliament and Big Ben A58

20p, Churchill & George V-class battleship.

1974, Nov. 30   Perf. 14x14½
316	A58	6p violet & multi	.25	.20
317	A58	20p multicolored	.55	.60
a.		Souvenir sheet of 2, #316-317	5.25	6.00

Sir Winston Churchill (1874-1965).

Uniform Type of 1969

Uniforms: 4p, Officer, East Surrey Regiment, 1846. 6p, Private, Highland Light Infantry, 1777. 10p, Officer, Coldstream Guards, 1704. 20p, Sergeant, Gibraltar Regiment, 1974.

1975, Mar. 14   Wmk. 373   Perf. 14
318	A42	4p multicolored	.35	.25
319	A42	6p multicolored	.55	.50
320	A42	10p multicolored	1.00	.90
321	A42	20p multicolored	1.50	2.25
		Nos. 318-321 (4)	3.40	3.90

Descriptions are printed on back on top of gum.

Girl Guides Emblem A59

1975, Oct. 10   Perf. 13½x13
322	A59	5p violet, gold & blue	.35	.45
323	A59	7p red brn, gold & blk	.50	.50
324	A59	15p ocher, silver & blk	.80	1.00
		Nos. 322-324 (3)	1.65	1.95

Girl Guides, 50th anniversary.

Child and Bird — A60

Bruges Madonna, by Michelangelo A61

b, Angel playing lute. c, Singing boy. d, Mother & children. e, Praying child. f, Child & lamb.

1975, Nov. 25   Perf. 14x14½
| 325 | | Block of 6 | 2.75 | 3.25 |
| a.-f. | | A60 6p any single | .45 | .55 |

Christmas. No. 325 printed in sheets of 60 containing 10 blocks of 6 (3x2) stamps with horizontal and vertical gutters between blocks.

1975, Dec. 17   Litho.   Perf. 14x13½
326	A61	6p violet blk & multi	.25	.25
327	A61	9p black brn & multi	.35	.45
328	A61	15p dk purple & multi	.40	.95
a.		Souvenir booklet	5.00	
		Nos. 326-328 (3)	1.00	1.65

500th birth anniv. of Michelangelo Buonarroti (1475-1564), Italian sculptor, painter and architect.
No. 328a contains 2 self-adhesive panes printed on peelable paper backing with stamp dealer's advertisements on back. One pane of 6 contains 2 each similar to Nos. 326-328; the other pane of 3 contains one each similar to Nos. 326-328. Stamps are imperf. x roulette.

American Bicentennial Emblem, Arms of Gibraltar — A62

Holy Family — A63

1976, May 28   Perf. 14x14½
| 329 | A62 | 25p multicolored | .80 | .70 |
| a. | | Souvenir sheet of 4 | 4.50 | 6.50 |

American Bicentennial. No. 329a is rouletted all around.

Uniform Type of 1969

Uniforms: 1p, Suffolk Regiment, 1795. 6p, Northamptonshire Regiment, 1779. 12p, Lancashire Fusiliers, 1793. 25p, Royal Army Ordinance Corps. 1896.

1976, July 21   Perf. 14
330	A42	1p multicolored	.25	.20
331	A42	6p multicolored	.40	.25
332	A42	12p multicolored	.65	.50
333	A42	25p multicolored	.90	1.25
		Nos. 330-333 (4)	2.20	2.20

Descriptions printed on back of top of gum.

1976, Nov. 3   Litho.   Wmk. 373
Stained Glass Windows: 9p, St. Bernard of Clairvaux. 12p, St. John the Evangelist. 20p, Archangel Michael.
334	A63	6p ultra & multi	.25	.20
335	A63	9p brt green & multi	.35	.20
336	A63	12p orange & multi	.50	.60
337	A63	20p dk carmine & multi	.95	1.25
		Nos. 334-337 (4)	2.05	2.25

Christmas.

Elizabeth II and Royal Crest — A64

1977, Feb. 7   Litho.   Perf. 14x13½
338	A64	6p multicolored	.20	.20
339	A64	£1 multicolored	1.50	1.75
a.		Souv. sheet of 2, #338-339, perf. 13	2.00	2.50

25th anniv. of the reign of Queen Elizabeth II. Nos. 338-339 issued in sheets of 9.

Red Mullet A65

Designs: ½p, 3p, 9p, 15p, 25p, Flowers. 1p, 4p, 10p, 50p, Fish. 2p, 5p, 12p, £1, Butterflies. 2½p, 6p, 20p, £2, Birds. ½p, 2½p, 3p, 6p, 9p, 15p, 20p, 25p, £2, £5, vertical.

1977-80   Perf. 14½x14, 14x14½
Inscribed "1977," except as noted
340	A65	½p Toothed orchid	.50	2.00
a.		Chalky paper, inscribed "1982"	5.00	4.00
341	A65	1p shown	.20	.45
342	A65	2p Large blue	.20	1.00
343	A65	2½p Sardinian warbler	1.25	1.50
344	A65	3p Giant squill	.20	.20
345	A65	4p Gray wrasse	.20	.20
346	A65	5p Red admiral	.40	.80
347	A65	6p Black kite	2.00	.45
348	A65	9p Scorpion vetch	.55	.55
a.		Inscribed "1978"	.60	.60
349	A65	10p John Dory	.35	.20
350	A65	12p Clouded yellow	.90	.35
350A	A65	15p Winged asparagus pea (inscr. "1980")	1.50	.45
351	A65	20p Andouin's gull	1.75	2.75
352	A65	25p Barbary nut	1.20	1.75
353	A65	50p Swordfish	1.60	.80
354	A65	£1 Swallowtail	4.00	5.00
355	A65	£2 Hoopoe	8.75	11.00
355A	A65	£5 Coat of Arms (inscr. "1979")	9.00	12.00
		Nos. 340-355A (18)	34.55	41.45

Issued: No. 348a, 2/1/78; £ 5, 5/16/79; 15p, 11/12/80; No. 340a, 2/22/82; others, 4/1/77.

1981, Apr. 21
Chalky Paper, Inscribed "1981"
345a	A65	4p multicolored	.50	.70
349a	A65	10p multicolored	1.00	1.50
350a	A65	12p multicolored	4.00	4.00
352a	A65	25p multicolored	5.00	5.50
353a	A65	50p multicolored	6.50	6.50
		Nos. 345a-353a (5)	17.00	18.20

Gibraltar No. 182 — A66

12p, Gibraltar #233. 25p, Gibraltar #294.

1977, May 27 Litho. Perf. 14
356 A66 6p multi .25 .20
357 A66 12p multi, vert. .30 .45
358 A66 25p multi, vert. .30 .55
Nos. 356-358 (3) .85 1.20

Amphilex 77 Intl. Phil. Exhib., Amsterdam, May 26-June 5. Issued in sheets of 6.

Annunciation, by Rubens — A67

Rubens Paintings: 9p, Nativity. 12p, Adoration of the Kings. 15p, Holy Family under Apple Tree.

Perf. 14x13½, 13½x14
1977, Nov. 2 Litho.
359 A67 3p multi .20 .20
360 A67 9p multi .20 .20
361 A67 12p multi, horiz. .35 .35
362 A67 15p multi .35 .35
a. Souvenir sheet of 4, #359-362 4.00 4.00
Nos. 359-362 (4) 1.10 1.10

Christmas and 400th birth anniv. of Peter Paul Rubens.

Gibraltar from Space A68

Design: 25p, Strait of Gibraltar, aerial view.

1978, May 3 Litho. Perf. 13½
363 A68 12p multicolored .35 .50
Souvenir Sheet
364 A68 25p multicolored .90 .90

No. 363 issued in sheets of 10. No. 364 contains one stamp.

Holyroodhouse — A69

Royal Houses: 9p, St. James Palace. 12p, Sandringham House. 18p, Balmoral.

1978, June 12 Litho. Perf. 13½
365 A69 6p multicolored .20 .20
366 A69 9p multicolored .25 .20
367 A69 12p multicolored .40 .35
368 A69 18p multicolored .50 .50
a. Souvenir booklet 3.00
Nos. 365-368 (4) 1.35 1.25

25th anniv. of coronation of Queen Elizabeth II. No. 368a contains 2 panes printed on peelable paper backing with pictures of castles. One pane contains 6 rouletted stamps, 3 each similar to Nos. 367-368; the other pane contains one 25p (Windsor Castle) rouletted stamp.

Sunderland Seaplane Landing — A70

Gibraltar and: 9p, Two-tiered Caudron taking off, 1918. 12p, Shackleton, 1953-1966. 16p, Hunter warplane, 1954-1966. 18p, Nimrod, 1969-1978.

1978, Sept. 6 Litho. Perf. 14
369 A70 3p multicolored .20 .20
370 A70 9p multicolored .25 .35
371 A70 12p multicolored .40 .45
372 A70 16p multicolored .55 .80
373 A70 18p multicolored .75 1.00
Nos. 369-373 (5) 2.15 2.80

Royal Air Force, 60th anniversary.

Madonna with Goldfinch, by Dürer — A71

Christmas (Paintings by Albrecht Dürer): 5p, Madonna with Animals. 9p, Nativity. 15p, Adoration of the Kings.

1978, Nov. 1 Litho. Perf. 14
374 A71 5p multicolored .20 .20
375 A71 9p multicolored .25 .25
376 A71 12p multicolored .35 .40
377 A71 15p multicolored .40 .75
Nos. 374-377 (4) 1.20 1.60

Rowland Hill and Gibraltar No. 10 — A72

Sir Rowland Hill (1795-1879), originator of penny postage and: 9p, Gibraltar No. 274. 12p, Parchment scroll with early postal regulations. 25p, "Barred G" cancellation used on British stamps in Gibraltar.

1979, Feb. 7 Litho. Perf. 13½
378 A72 3p multicolored .20 .20
379 A72 9p multicolored .20 .20
380 A72 12p yellow grn & black .20 .20
381 A72 25p yellow & black .35 .55
Nos. 378-381 (4) .95 1.15

Satellite Earth Station, Post Horn, Telephone — A73

1979, May 16 Perf. 13½x14
382 A73 3p lt green & green .20 .20
383 A73 9p lt brown & brown .25 .65
384 A73 12p gray & ultra .40 1.10
Nos. 382-384 (3) .85 1.95

European telecommunications system.

Children, IYC Emblem, Nativity — A74

a, African girl. b, Chinese girl. c, Pacific islands girl. d, American Indian girl. e, Shown. f, Scandinavian boy.

Litho.; Silver Embossed
1979, Nov. 14 Perf. 14
385 Block of 6 1.75 1.75
a.-f. A74 12p any single .25 .25

Christmas; IYC No. 385 printed in sheets of 12 containing 2 No. 385 with vertical rouletted gutter between.

Officers, Exchange and Commercial Library, 1830 — A75

Gibraltar Police Force, 150th anniv.: 6p, Early and modern uniforms, Rock of Gibraltar. 12p, Traffic Officer, ambulance. 37p, Policeman and woman, Police Station, Irish Town.

Perf. 14x14½
1980, Feb. 5 Litho. Wmk. 373
386 A75 3p multicolored .20 .20
387 A75 6p multicolored .20 .20
388 A75 12p multicolored .35 .35
389 A75 37p multicolored .55 .95
Nos. 386-389 (4) 1.30 1.70

Archbishop Peter Amigo (1864-1949) A76

Europa: No. 391, Gustavo Charles Bacarisas (1872-1971), artist. No. 392, John Mackintosh (1865-1940), philanthropist.

1980, May 6 Wmk. 373 Perf. 14½
390 A76 12p multicolored .20 .25
391 A76 12p multicolored .20 .25
392 A76 12p multicolored .20 .25
Nos. 390-392 (3) .60 .75

Queen Mother Elizabeth Birthday Issue
Common Design Type
1980, Aug. 4 Litho. Perf. 14
393 CD330 15p multicolored .35 .35

"Victory" and Rock of Gibraltar, by Monamy Swaine A77

Paintings: 3p, Lord Nelson, by John Francis Rigaud, 1781, vert. 15p, Lord Nelson, by William Beechey, vert. 40p, Victory Towed into Gibraltar by Clarkson Stanfield.

1980, Aug. 20 Litho. Perf. 14
394 A77 3p multicolored .20 .20
395 A77 9p multicolored .25 .25
396 A77 15p multicolored .35 .35
a. Souvenir sheet 1.00 1.10
397 A77 40p multicolored .80 .80
Nos. 394-397 (4) 1.60 1.60

Horatio Nelson (1758-1805).

Holy Family A78

1980, Nov. 12
398 A78 15p shown .30 .40
399 A78 15p Three kings .30 .40
a. Pair, #398-399 .80 .80

Christmas. No. 399a has continuous design.

Hercules Separating Africa and Europe — A79

Europa: 15p, Hercules standing on Rock of Gibraltar and Morocco.

Dining Room, The Convent — A80

Perf. 14x13½
1981, Feb. 24 Wmk. 373
400 A79 9p multicolored .20 .20
401 A79 15p multicolored .35 .40

1981, May 22 Litho. Perf. 14½x14
402 A80 4p shown .20 .20
403 A80 14p King's Chapel .25 .20
404 A80 15p Aerial view .40 .20
405 A80 55p Cloister .80 .80
Nos. 402-405 (4) 1.65 1.40

450th anniv. of The Convent (Governor's residence, originally Franciscan monastery).

Prince Charles and Lady Diana A81

1981, July 27 Litho. Perf. 14½
406 A81 £1 multicolored 2.00 2.00

Royal wedding. Se-tenant with decorative label.

Queen Elizabeth II — A82

1981, Sept. 29 Perf. 14½
Booklet Stamps
407 A82 1p black .45 .45
a. Bklt. pane of 10 + 2 labels (2 #407, 2 #408, 6 #409) 2.25
b. Bklt. pane of 5 + label (#407, #408, 3 #409) 1.60
408 A82 4p dark blue .45 .45
409 A82 15p green .45 .45
Nos. 407-409 (3) 1.35 1.35

Airmail Service, 50th Anniv. A83

1981, Sept. 29   *Perf. 14½*
410	A83	14p Paper plane	.35	.35
411	A83	15p Envelopes, aerogram	.35	.35
412	A83	55p Airplane circling globe	1.00	1.00
		Nos. 410-412 (3)	1.70	1.70

Intl. Year of the Disabled A84

1981, Nov. 19   Litho.   Wmk. 373
413	A84	14p multicolored	.35	.35

Christmas A85

1981, Nov. 19   *Perf. 14*
414	A85	15p Children singing carols	.35	.20
415	A85	55p Decorated mailbox, vert.	1.25	.80

Douglas DC-3 — A86

1982, Feb. 10   Litho.   *Perf. 14*
416	A86	1p shown	.20	1.00
417	A86	2p Vickers Viking	.25	1.00
a.		Wmk. 384, dated 1986 ('87)	3.25	
418	A86	3p Airspeed Ambassador	.25	.50
419	A86	4p Vickers Viscount	.40	.20
420	A86	5p Boeing 727	.50	.30
a.		Wmk. 384, dated 1986 ('87)	3.25	
421	A86	10p Vickers Vanguard	.90	.55
422	A86	14p Short Solent	1.00	1.75
423	A86	15p Fokker F-27 Friendship	1.75	2.00
424	A86	17p Boeing 737	.85	.90
425	A86	20p BAC One-eleven	1.00	.65
a.		Inscribed "1985"	1.60	1.60
426	A86	25p Lockheed Constellation	3.75	4.00
427	A86	50p De Havilland Comet 4B	4.00	2.25
428	A86	£1 Saro Windhover	5.50	2.25
429	A86	£2 Hawker Siddeley Trident 2	7.00	7.00
430	A86	£5 DH-89A Dragon Rapide	10.00	15.00
		Nos. 416-430 (15)	37.35	39.35

Royal Navy Ship Crests — A87

1982, Apr. 14   Litho.   *Perf. 14*
431	A87	½p Opossum	.20	.20
432	A87	15½p Norfolk	.50	.50
433	A87	17p Fearless	.65	.65
434	A87	60p Rooke	1.25	2.50
		Nos. 431-434 (4)	2.60	3.85

See Nos. 449-452, 465-468, 474-477, 492-495, 501-504, 528-531, 552-555, 574-577, 587-590.

Europa A88

1982, June 11   Litho.   *Perf. 14*
435	A88	14p Planes preparing for takeoff	.25	.65
436	A88	17p Generals Eisenhower and Giraud	.40	.75

Operation Torch, 1943.

Chamber of Commerce Centenary — A89

Anniversaries: 15½p, British Forces Postal Service centenary. 60p, Scouting year.

1982, Sept. 22
437	A89	½p multicolored	.20	.20
438	A89	15½p multicolored	.45	.45
439	A89	60p multicolored	1.40	1.60
		Nos. 437-439 (3)	2.05	2.25

Intl. Direct Telephone Dialing System Inauguration — A90

1982, Oct. 1   *Perf. 14½*
440	A90	17p Map	.45	.45

Christmas A91

     Perf. 14x14½

1982, Nov. 18   Litho.   Wmk. 373
441	A91	14p Holly	.40	.35
442	A91	17p Mistletoe	.55	.40

A92

1983, Mar. 14   Litho.   *Perf. 14*
443	A92	4p Local street	.20	.20
444	A92	14p Scouts on parade	.35	.35
445	A92	17p Flag, vert.	.45	.45
446	A92	60p Queen Elizabeth II, vert.	1.10	1.40
		Nos. 443-446 (4)	2.10	2.40

Commonwealth Day.

Europa A93

1983, May 21   *Perf. 14x13½*
447	A93	16p St. George's Hall	.35	.35
448	A93	19p Water catchments	.45	.45

Royal Navy Crest Type of 1982

1983, July 1   Litho.   *Perf. 14*
449	A87	4p Faulknor	.20	.20
450	A87	14p Renown	1.10	.40
451	A87	17p Ark Royal	1.25	.50
452	A87	60p Sheffield	1.90	1.75
		Nos. 449-452 (4)	4.45	2.85

Fortresses — A94

1983, Sept. 13   *Perf. 13½x14*
453	A94	4p Landport Gate, 1729	.20	.20
454	A94	17p Koehler gun, 1782	.45	.45
455	A94	77p King's Bastion, 1799	1.50	1.50
a.		Souvenir sheet of 3, #453-455	3.00	3.00
		Nos. 453-455 (3)	2.15	2.15

Christmas A95

Raphael Paintings.

1983, Nov. 17   Litho.   *Perf. 14*
456	A95	4p Adoration of the Magi	.25	.20
457	A95	17p Madonna of Foligno, vert.	.70	.35
458	A95	60p Sistine Madonna, vert.	1.90	1.50
		Nos. 456-458 (3)	2.85	2.05

Europa (1959-1984) A96

Intl. Postal and Telecommunication Links.

1984, Mar. 6   Litho.   *Perf. 14½*
459	A96	17p No. 98	.40	.50
460	A96	23p Communications circuit	.50	.80

Field Hockey A97

1984, May 25   Litho.   *Perf. 14*
461	A97	20p shown	.70	.75
462	A97	21p Basketball	.70	.80
463	A97	26p Rowing	.70	1.00
464	A97	29p Soccer	.80	1.25
		Nos. 461-464 (4)	2.90	3.80

Royal Navy Crest Type of 1982

1984, Sept. 21   Litho.   *Perf. 13½x13*
465	A87	20p Active	1.90	1.60
466	A87	21p Foxhound	1.90	1.90
467	A87	26p Valiant	2.10	1.90
468	A87	29p Hood	2.25	2.25
		Nos. 465-468 (4)	8.15	7.65

Christmas A98

     Perf. 14x14½

1984, Nov. 7   Litho.   Wmk. 373
469	A98	20p Parade float	.55	.55
470	A98	80p Float, diff.	2.25	2.25

Musical Symbols — A99

1985, Feb. 26   Photo.   *Perf. 12½*
Granite Paper
471	A99	20p multi, diff.	.45	.40
472	A99	29p shown	.65	1.60

Save the Children Fund A100

Globe and legend in various positions.

1985, May 3   Litho.   *Perf. 13x13½*
473		Strip of 4	5.00	5.00
a.-d.		A100 26p any single	1.10	1.10

Royal Navy Crests Type of 1982

1985, July 3   Litho.   *Perf. 14*
474	A87	4p Duncan	1.00	.50
475	A87	9p Fury	1.40	1.40
476	A87	21p Firedrake	2.75	2.75
477	A87	80p Malaya	4.50	4.50
		Nos. 474-477 (4)	9.65	9.15

Intl. Youth Year — A101

1985, Sept. 6   *Perf. 14½*
478	A101	4p Emblem	.55	.20
479	A101	20p Hands, diamond	1.90	1.50
480	A101	80p Girl Guides anniv. emblem	4.25	4.00
		Nos. 478-480 (3)	6.70	5.70

St. Joseph's Parish Church, Cent. — A102

Creche, Detail — A103

Perf. 13½xRoulette 7 Between, 13½
1985, Oct. 25   Wmk. 373   Litho.
481 A102 Pair   1.75 1.40
 a. 4p Centenary seal   .85   .60
 b. 4p Church   .85   .60
 c. No. 481a, perf. 13½ on 4 sides .80 .60
482 A103 80p multicolored   5.75 4.75

Christmas. Nos. 481a-481b rouletted between. Printed in sheets of 10 pairs with the bottom row containing 5 No. 481c. Strips of 3, Nos. 481a-481c exist.

Europa
A104

1986, Feb. 10   Litho.   Perf. 13x13½
483 A104 22p Butterfly, house .80   .55
484 A104 29p Seagull, hotel   1.40 2.75

Postage Stamp   Elizabeth II, 60th
Cent. — A105   Birthday — A106

1986, Mar. 25   Perf. 13½x13
485 A105 4p No. 18   .35   .20
486 A105 22p No. 42   1.40 1.25
487 A105 32p No. 67   2.25 2.40
488 A105 36p No. 118   2.25 2.75

Size: 32x48mm
Perf. 14
489 A105 44p No. 131   3.25 3.75
 Nos. 485-489 (5)   9.50 10.35

Souvenir Sheet
490 A105 29p No. 2   4.00 4.00

1986, May 22   Litho.   Perf. 14
491 A106 £1 multicolored   2.50 3.25

Royal Naval Crests Type of 1982
1986, Aug. 28   Litho.   Perf. 14
492 A87 22p Lightning   2.50 1.00
493 A87 29p Hermione   2.75 1.60
494 A87 32p Laforey   3.00 3.00
495 A87 44p Nelson   3.50 3.75
 Nos. 492-495 (4)   11.75 9.35

Christmas, Intl. Peace
Year — A107

1986, Oct. 14   Litho.   Perf. 14½x14
496 A107 18p St. Mary the
           Crowned Cathedral 1.25 .50
497 A107 32p St. Andrew's
           Church   1.75 2.50

Wedding of Prince Andrew and Sarah
Ferguson — A108

1986, Aug. 28   Litho.   Perf. 15
498 A108 44p multicolored   1.50 1.75

Europa — A109

1987, Feb. 17   Wmk. 384   Perf. 15
499 A109 22p Neptune House   1.50   .50
500 A109 29p Ocean Heights   2.00 3.50

Royal Navy Crests Type of 1982
1987, Apr. 2   Perf. 13½x13
501 A87 18p Wishart   1.75   .70
502 A87 22p Charybdis   2.00 1.10
503 A87 32p Antelope   2.75 2.75
504 A87 44p Eagle   3.25 3.50
 Nos. 501-504 (4)   9.75 8.05

Warrant Granted to
the Royal
Engineers, 200th
Anniv. — A110

1987, Apr. 25   Wmk. 373   Perf. 14½
505 A110 18p Victoria Stadium 1.50   .55
506 A110 32p Casket, Freedom
           Scroll   2.25 3.25
507 A110 44p Monogram   3.00 4.00
 Nos. 505-507 (3)   6.75 7.80

Guns and
Artillery
A111

Designs: 1p, 13-inch mortar, 1783. 2p, 6-inch Coast, 1909. 3p, 8-inch Howitzer, 1783. 4p, Bofors L40/70, 1951. 5p, 100-ton RML, 1882. 10p, 5.25 HAA, 1953. 18p, 25-pounder Gun-howitzer, 1943. 19p, 64-pounder RML, 1873. 22p, 12-pounder, 1758. 50p, 10-inch RML, 1870. £1, Russian 24-pounder, 1854. £3, 9.2-inch Coast Mk. 10, 1935. £5, 24-pounder, 1779.

1987, June 1   Wmk. 373   Perf. 12½
508 A111 1p multicolored   .20   .60
509 A111 2p multicolored   .35   .50
510 A111 3p multicolored   .35   .40
511 A111 4p multicolored   .45   .20
512 A111 5p multicolored   .45   .50
513 A111 10p multicolored   .45   .50
514 A111 18p multicolored   .70   .95
515 A111 19p multicolored   .70 1.50
516 A111 22p multicolored   .70   .40
517 A111 50p multicolored 1.40 2.75
518 A111 £1 multicolored   3.00 3.50
519 A111 £3 multicolored   6.00 4.50
520 A111 £5 multicolored 10.00 17.00
 Nos. 508-520 (13)   24.75 33.30

For surcharge see No. 595.

Christmas — A112

1987, Nov. 12   Wmk. 384   Perf. 14½
521 A112 4p Three Wise Men   .20   .20
522 A112 22p Holy Family   1.25   .95
523 A112 44p Shepherds   2.25 3.00
 Nos. 521-523 (3)   3.70 4.15

Europa — A113

Transport and communication: No. 524, Rock of Gibraltar, Cruise Ship. No. 525, Passenger jet, yacht, dish aerial. No. 526, Bus, buggy. No. 527, Rock of Gibraltar, automobile, telephone.

Perf. 14½x14 on 3 Sides; Rouletted Between
1988, Feb. 16   Litho.   Wmk. 373
524   22p multicolored   1.50 1.60
525   22p multicolored   1.50 1.60
 a. A113 Pair, #524-525   3.25 3.25
526   32p multicolored   2.10 2.25
527   32p multicolored   2.10 2.25
 a. A113 Pair, #526-527   4.75 4.75
 Nos. 524-527 (4)   7.20 7.70

Nos. 525a, 527a have continuous design.

Royal Navy Crests Type of 1982
Perf. 13½x13
1988, Apr. 7   Wmk. 384
528 A87 18p Clyde   2.00   .65
529 A87 22p Foresight   2.50 1.25
530 A87 32p Severn   2.75 3.00
531 A87 44p Rodney   3.50 4.75
 Nos. 528-531 (4)   10.75 9.65

Birds
A114

1988, June 15   Wmk. 373   Perf. 14
532 A114 4p Bee eater   .75   .20
533 A114 22p Common puffin 2.25 1.00
534 A114 32p Honey buzzard 3.25 3.25
535 A114 44p Blue rock thrush 4.00 4.25
 Nos. 532-535 (4)   10.25 8.70

Operation
Raleigh,
1984-88
A115

Designs: 19p, Square-rigger. 22p, Sir Walter Raleigh and expedition emblem. 32p, Maps and modern transport ship Sir Walter Raleigh. 44p, Ship Sir Walter Raleigh.

Perf. 13x13½
1988, Sept. 14   Litho.   Wmk. 373
536 A115 19p multicolored   .85   .85
537 A115 22p multicolored 1.00 1.00
538 A115 32p multicolored 1.40 1.40
 Nos. 536-538 (3)   3.25 3.25

Souvenir Sheet
539 Sheet of 2, #537, 539a 5.75 5.75
 a. A115 44p multicolored   2.25 2.25

400th anniv. of Sir Walter Raleigh's voyage to the New World to establish the 1st English-speaking colony, in what is now North Carolina.

Christmas
A116

Children's drawings: 4p, Snowman, by Rebecca Falero. 22p, Nativity, by Dennis Penalver. 44p, Santa Claus, by Gavin Key.

1988, Nov. 2   Wmk. 384   Perf. 14
540 A116 4p multicolored   .20   .20
541 A116 22p multicolored   .60   .75

Size: 25x33mm
542 A116 44p multicolored 1.40 1.90
 Nos. 540-542 (3)   2.20 2.85

Europa
A117

Toys: 32p, Doll, doll house, puppy, ball, boat.

Perf. 13x13½
1989, Feb. 15   Wmk. 384
543 A117 25p shown   1.25   .80
544 A117 32p multicolored 1.75 2.50

Gibraltar Regiment,
50th Anniv. — A118

Perf. 13½x13
1989, Apr. 28   Wmk. 373
545 A118 4p The Port Sergeant   .50   .20
546 A118 22p Regimental colors,
           Queen's colors   1.75   .90
547 A118 32p Drum Major   2.50 2.10
 Nos. 545-547 (3)   4.75 3.20

Souvenir Sheet
548 Sheet of 2, Nos. 546, 548a 5.00 5.00
 a. A118 44p Regimental arms   2.25 2.25

Intl. Red Cross,
125th
Anniv. — A119

Perf. 15x14½
1989, July 7   Wmk. 384
549 A119 25p Mother and child 1.10   .60
550 A119 32p Malnourished chil-
           dren   1.50 1.50
551 A119 44p Accident victims 2.10 2.50
 Nos. 549-551 (3)   4.70 4.60

Royal Navy Crests Type of 1982
1989, Sept. 7   Litho.   Perf. 14
552 A87 22p Blankney   1.75   .70
553 A87 25p Deptford   1.75 1.50
554 A87 32p Exmoor   2.50 2.10
555 A87 44p Stork   3.50 3.50
 Nos. 552-555 (4)   9.50 7.80

Souvenir Sheets

Coins — A120

No. 556: a, 1p Barbary Partridge. b, 2p Lighthouse at Europa Point. c, 10p Tower of Homage. d, 5p Barbary Ape.
No. 557: a, 50p Gibraltar Candytuft. b, £5 Pillars of Hercules. c, £2 Cannon from the Great Siege Period, 1779-1783. d, £1 Natl. coat of arms. e, Common obverse side of coins picturing Maklouf head of Queen Elizabeth II. f, 20p Our Lady of Europa.

	1989, Oct. 10		**Perf. 14½x15**	
556	Sheet of 4		2.25	2.25
a.-d.	A120 4p any single		.55	.55
557	Sheet of 6		7.75	7.75
a.-f.	A120 22p any single		1.25	1.25

Christmas A121

Wmk. 384

	1989, Oct. 11	**Litho.**	**Perf. 14½**	
558	A121	4p Santa's sleigh	.20	.20
559	A121	22p Shepherds see star	1.40	.85
560	A121	32p Holy family	2.10	2.10
561	A121	44p Adoration of the Magi	3.25	3.50
		Nos. 558-561 (4)	6.95	6.65

Europa 1990 — A122

Post offices: No. 562, G.P.O. exterior. No. 563, Carved crown and "VR" from p.o. archway and G.P.O. interior. No. 564, South District P.O. interior. No. 565, South District P.O. exterior.

Perf. 14½, Rouletted 9½ Between

	1990, Mar. 6	**Litho.**	**Unwmk.**	
562	22p multicolored		1.25	1.25
563	22p multicolored		1.25	1.25
a.	A122 Pair, #562-563		3.00	3.00
564	32p multicolored		1.75	1.75
565	32p multicolored		1.75	1.75
a.	A122 Pair, #564-565		4.00	4.00
	Nos. 562-565 (4)		6.00	6.00

Pairs are rouletted between.

Early Fire Truck A123

	1990, Apr. 2		**Perf. 14½x14**	
566	A123	4p Early firemen, hose, vert.	1.50	.20
567	A123	20p shown	3.00	1.00
568	A123	42p Modern truck	3.25	3.00
569	A123	44p Modern fireman, vert.	3.50	3.00
		Nos. 566-569 (4)	11.25	7.20

Fire Service, 125th anniv.

Penny Black, 150th Anniv. — A124

19p, Henry Corbould, Great Britain No. 1. 22p, 1st Royal Mail coach, Bristol-London. 32p, Sir Rowland Hill, Great Britain No. 1. 44p, Great Britain No. 1, Maltese Cross cancel.

	1990, May 3		**Perf. 13½x14**	
570	A124	19p multicolored	1.25	.90
571	A124	22p multicolored	1.50	.95
572	A124	32p multicolored	3.00	3.00
		Nos. 570-572 (3)	5.75	4.85

Souvenir Sheet

573	A124	44p multicolored	6.00	6.00

Royal Navy Crest Type of 1982

	1990, July 10	**Litho.**	**Perf. 14**	
574	A87	22p Calpe	2.00	.80
575	A87	25p Gallant	2.25	1.90
576	A87	32p Wrestler	2.75	3.00
577	A87	44p Greyhound	3.50	4.00
		Nos. 574-577 (4)	10.50	9.70

Europort Model A125

	1990, Oct. 10	**Litho.**	**Perf. 14½**	
578	A125	22p shown	1.10	.95
579	A125	23p Building components	1.10	1.40
580	A125	25p Land reclamation	1.25	1.40
		Nos. 578-580 (3)	3.45	3.75

Christmas — A126

	1990, Oct. 10		**Perf. 13½**	
581	A126	4p shown	.20	.20
582	A126	22p Santa Claus	.90	.55
583	A126	42p Christmas tree	2.25	2.40
584	A126	44p Creche	2.25	2.40
		Nos. 581-584 (4)	5.60	5.55

Europa A127

	1991, Feb. 26	**Litho.**	**Perf. 13½**	
585	A127	25p Spaceplane, satellite	.90	.75
586	A127	32p ERS-1 satellite	1.25	1.75

Royal Navy Crest Type of 1982

	1991, Apr. 9	**Litho.**	**Perf. 13½x13**	
587	A87	4p Hesperus	.50	.20
588	A87	21p Forester	2.00	1.50
589	A87	22p Furious	2.00	1.50
590	A87	62p Scylla	4.75	5.50
		Nos. 587-590 (4)	9.25	8.70

Birds A128

	1991, May 30	**Litho.**	**Perf. 13½**	
591	A128	13p Black stork	1.60	1.25
592	A128	13p Egyptian vulture	1.60	1.25
593	A128	13p Barbary partridge	1.60	1.25
594	A128	13p Shag	1.60	1.25
a.		Block of 4, #591-594	7.00	7.50

World Wildlife Fund.

No. 519 Surcharged

	1991, May 30	**Wmk. 373**		
595	A111	£1.05 on £3 multi	6.50	3.25

Views of Gibraltar A129

Paintings: 22p, North View of Gibraltar, by Gustavo Bacarisas (1873-1971). 26p, Parson's Lodge, by Elena Mifsud (1906-1989). 32p, Governor's Parade, by Jacobo Azabury, OBE (1890-1980). 42p, Waterport Wharf, by Rudesindo Mannia (1899-1982), vert.

	1991, Sept. 10	**Litho.**	**Perf. 15x14**	
596	A129	22p multicolored	1.25	.50
597	A129	26p multicolored	1.40	.90
598	A129	32p multicolored	2.10	2.10

Perf. 14x15

599	A129	42p multicolored	3.00	3.00
		Nos. 596-599 (4)	7.75	6.50

Christmas A130

Christmas carols: 4p, Once in Royal David's City. 24p, Silent Night. 25p, Angels We Have Heard on High. 49p, O Come All Ye Faithful.

	1991, Oct. 15	**Litho.**	**Perf. 14½**	
600	A130	4p multicolored	.25	.20
601	A130	24p multicolored	2.00	.75
602	A130	25p multicolored	2.00	1.50
603	A130	49p multicolored	3.50	3.50
		Nos. 600-603 (4)	7.75	5.95

Souvenir Sheet

Phila Nippon '91 — A131

	1991, Nov. 15			
604	A131	£1.05 Plain tiger	5.25	5.25

Queen Elizabeth II's Accession to the Throne, 40th Anniv.
Common Design Type
Wmk. 373

	1992, Feb. 6	**Litho.**	**Perf. 14**	
605	CD349	4p multicolored	.20	.20
606	CD349	20p multicolored	.80	.80
607	CD349	24p multicolored	1.00	1.10
608	CD349	44p multicolored	2.00	2.10
609	CD349	54p multicolored	2.50	2.75
		Nos. 605-609 (5)	6.50	6.95

Discovery of America, 500th Anniv. — A132

	1992, Feb. 6	**Unwmk.**	**Perf. 14½**	
610	A132	24p Columbus, Santa Maria	2.10	1.75
611	A132	24p Map, Nina	2.10	1.75
a.		Pair, #610-611	4.25	3.50
612	A132	34p Map, Pinta	2.30	1.90
613	A132	34p Map, sailor	2.30	1.90
a.		Pair, #612-613	4.75	3.75
		Nos. 610-613 (4)	8.80	7.30

Europa. Printed in sheets containing 4 pairs.

Around the World Yacht Rally, 1991-92 A133

Compass rose, sail and maps of routes through: 21p, Atlantic Ocean, vert. 24p, Malay Archipelago. 25p, Indian Ocean. 49p, Mediterranean and Red Seas, vert.

	1992, Apr. 15		**Perf. 13½**	
614	A133	21p multicolored	1.10	.90
615	A133	24p multicolored	1.40	1.50
616	A133	25p multicolored	1.40	1.60
		Nos. 614-616 (3)	3.90	4.00

Souvenir Sheet

617	A133	Sheet of 2, #614 & 617a	3.25	3.25
a.		A133 49p multicolored	2.10	2.10

Anglican Diocese of Gibraltar, 150th Anniv. A134

4p, Holy Trinity Cathedral, vert. 24p, Crest and map. 44p, Construction work on Cathedral during 1800's. 54p, Bishop Tomlinson, first Bishop of Diocese (1842-1863), vert.

	1992, Aug. 21	**Litho.**	**Perf. 14**	
618	A134	4p multicolored	.40	.20
619	A134	24p multicolored	1.25	.60
620	A134	44p multicolored	2.25	2.25
621	A134	54p multicolored	2.50	3.00
		Nos. 618-621 (4)	6.40	6.05

Christmas A135

Designs: 4p, Church of the Sacred Heart of Jesus. 24p, Cathedral of St. Mary the Crowned. 34p, St. Andrew's Church. 49p, St. Joseph's Church.

	1992, Nov. 10	**Litho.**	**Perf. 14**	
622	A135	4p multicolored	.20	.20
623	A135	24p multicolored	1.50	.50
624	A135	34p multicolored	2.50	2.25
625	A135	49p multicolored	3.00	4.00
		Nos. 622-625 (4)	7.20	6.95

Contemporary Art — A136

Europa: No. 626, Masks of Comedy and Tragedy, record. No. 627, Painting, dancer, pottery. No. 628, Architecture, sculpture. No. 629, Video camera, 35mm film.

1993, Mar. 2   Litho.   Perf. 14½
626	A136	24p multicolored	1.75	1.50
627	A136	24p multicolored	1.75	1.50
a.		Pair, #626-627	4.25	4.25
628	A136	34p multicolored	2.25	2.25
629	A136	34p multicolored	2.25	2.25
a.		Pair, #628-629	5.25	5.25
		Nos. 626-629 (4)	8.00	7.50

Souvenir Sheet

World War II Warships A137

Designs: a, HMS Hood. b, HMS Ark Royal c, HMAS Waterhen. d, USS Gleaves.

1993, Apr. 27   Litho.   Perf. 14
630 A137 24p Sheet of 4, #a.-d.   12.00 12.00

See Nos. 660, 684, 714, 732.

Architectural Heritage A138

1993-94   Litho.   Perf. 13
631	A138	1p Landport Gate	.20	.75
632	A138	2p St. Mary the Crowned	.30	.75
633	A138	3p Parsons Lodge Battery	.30	.20
634	A138	4p Moorish Castle	.30	.20
635	A138	5p General Post Office	.40	.20
636	A138	10p South Barracks	.40	.25
637	A138	21p American War Memorial	1.00	.85
638	A138	24p Garrison Library	1.10	.95
639	A138	25p Southport Gates	1.10	.95
640	A138	26p Casemates Gate	1.25	1.00
641	A138	50p Central Police Station	2.00	1.75
642	A138	£1 Prince Edward's Gate	3.00	3.00
643	A138	£3 Lighthouse	9.00	10.00
644	A138	£5 Coat of arms, keys to fortress, vert.	15.00	15.00
		Nos. 631-644 (14)	35.35	35.85

Nos. 631, 635, 637, 639, 642-643 are vert.

Portions of the design on No. 644 were applied by a thermographic process producing a shiny, raised effect.
Issued: £5, 6/6/94; others, 6/28/93.
See Nos. 686-693.

Anniversaries — A139

1993, Sept. 21   Litho.   Perf. 13
645	A139	21p Coins	1.25	.75
646	A139	24p Jet, biplane fighters	2.00	1.00
647	A139	34p Garrison Library	2.00	2.25
648	A139	49p Churchill, searchlights	4.00	3.50
		Nos. 645-648 (4)	9.25	7.50

First decimal coins, 25th anniv. Royal Air Force, 75th anniv. Garrison Library, bicent. Churchill's visit to Gibraltar, 50th anniv.

Christmas A140

Mice and: 5p, Christmas tree. 24p, Christmas cracker. 44p, Singing carols. 49p, Snowman.

1993, Nov. 16   Litho.   Perf. 13½
649	A140	5p multicolored	.20	.20
650	A140	24p multicolored	1.25	.70
651	A140	44p multicolored	2.50	2.10
652	A140	49p multicolored	3.25	2.75
		Nos. 649-652 (4)	7.20	5.75

European Discoveries — A141

Europa: No. 653, Atoms exploding, Lord Penney (1909-91). No. 654, Chemistry flasks, polonium, radium, Marie Curie. No. 655, Diesel engine, Rudolf Diesel. No. 656, Telescope, Galileo.

1994, Mar. 1   Litho.   Perf. 13½
653	A141	24p multicolored	1.25	1.25
654	A141	24p multicolored	1.25	1.25
a.		Pair, #653-654	3.00	3.00
655	A141	34p multicolored	1.50	1.50
656	A141	34p multicolored	1.50	1.50
a.		Pair, #655-656	3.75	3.50
		Nos. 653-656 (4)	5.50	5.50

1994 World Cup Soccer Championships, US — A142

26p, FIFA cup, US map, flag. 39p, Players, US map as playing field. 49p, Leg action.

1994, Apr. 19   Litho.   Perf. 13½
657	A142	26p multi	1.25	.65
658	A142	39p multi	1.75	1.75
659	A142	49p multi, vert.	2.25	2.50
		Nos. 657-659 (3)	5.25	4.90

Souvenir Sheet
World War II Warships Type of 1993

Designs: a, 5p, HMS Penelope. b, 25p, HMS Warspite. c, 44p, USS McLanahan. d, 49p, HNLMS Isaac Sweers.

1994, June 6   Litho.   Perf. 13½x13
660 A137 Sheet of 4, #a.-d.   11.50 11.50

Souvenir Sheet

PHILAKOREA '94 — A143

1994, Aug. 16   Litho.   Perf. 13
661 A143 £1.05 multicolored   5.25 5.25

Marine Life — A144

1994, Sept. 27   Litho.   Perf. 14
662	A144	21p Golden star coral	1.00	1.00
663	A144	24p Star fish	1.25	1.25
664	A144	34p Gorgonian sea fan	2.00	2.00
665	A144	49p Turkish wrasse	2.75	2.75
		Nos. 662-665 (4)	7.00	7.00

Intl. Olympic Committee, Cent. — A145

1994, Nov. 22   Litho.   Perf. 14
666	A145	49p Discus	3.00	2.25
667	A145	54p Javelin	3.00	2.50

Christmas Songbirds A146

1994, Nov. 22   Litho.   Perf. 13½
668	A146	5p Great tit, vert.	.50	.20
669	A146	24p Robin	2.50	1.00
670	A146	34p Blue tit	2.75	1.75
671	A146	54p Goldfinch, vert.	3.50	3.25
		Nos. 668-671 (4)	9.25	6.20

New Members in European Union A147

Flags: 24p, Austria. 26p, Finland. 34p, Sweden. 49p, Sweden, Finland, Austria, emblem of European Union.

1995, Jan. 3   Litho.   Perf. 14
672	A147	24p multicolored	.90	.90
673	A147	26p multicolored	1.00	1.00
674	A147	34p multicolored	1.25	1.25
675	A147	49p multicolored	1.90	1.90
		Nos. 672-675 (4)	5.05	5.05

Peace & Freedom — A148

Europa: No. 676, Cross, barbed wire, text. No. 677, Rainbow, dove, hands. No. 678, Shackles, text. No. 679, Doves, hands.

1995, Feb. 28   Litho.   Perf. 13½
676		24p multicolored	1.50	1.25
677		24p multicolored	1.50	1.25
a.		A148 Pair, #676-677	3.25	3.00
678		34p multicolored	1.75	1.75
679		34p multicolored	1.75	1.75
a.		A148 Pair, #678-679	4.25	4.25
		Nos. 676-679 (4)	6.50	6.00

Island Games — A149

1995, May 8   Litho.   Perf. 14x13½
680	A149	24p Sailing	1.00	.90
681	A149	44p Running	2.00	2.00
682	A149	49p Swimming	2.00	2.00
		Nos. 680-682 (3)	5.00	4.90
680a		Booklet pane of 3	3.75	
681a		Booklet pane of 3	6.75	
682a		Booklet pane of 3	8.25	
682b		Bklt. pane, 1 ea. #680-682	6.25	
		Commemorative booklet, 1 each #680a-682b	26.00	

Souvenir Sheet

VE Day, 50th Anniv. — A150

Illustration reduced.

1995, May 8
683 A150 £1.05 multicolored   6.00 6.00

World War II Warships Type of 1993 Souvenir Sheet

Designs: a, 5p, HMS Calpe. b, 24p, HMS Victorious. c, 44p, USS Weehawken. d, 49p, FFS Savorgnan de Brazza.

1995, June 6   Litho.   Perf. 13½x14
684 A137 Sheet of 4, #a.-d.   11.50 11.50

Singapore '95 — A151

Orchids: a, 22p, Bee. b, 23p, Brown bee. c, 24p, Pyramidal. d, 25p, Mirror. e, 26p, Sawfly.

1995, Sept. 1   Litho.   Perf. 14x14½
685 A151 Strip of 5, #a.-e.   9.00 6.25

Architectural Heritage Type of 1993

1995, Sept. 1   Litho.   Perf. 13
686	A138	6p House of Assembly	.75	.40
687	A138	7p Bleak House	.75	.40
688	A138	8p Bust of Gen. Eliott	1.00	.40
689	A138	9p Supreme Court Bldg.	1.25	.65
690	A138	20p Convent	1.50	.70
691	A138	30p St. Bernard's Hospital	1.75	1.50
692	A138	40p City Hall	2.00	2.00
693	A138	£2 Church of Sacred Heart of Jesus	7.50	7.50
		Nos. 686-693 (8)	16.50	13.55

Nos. 686, 688, 691, 693 are vert.

UN, 50th Anniv. A152

1995, Oct. 24   Litho.   Perf. 13½
694	A152	34p shown	1.75	1.75
695	A152	49p Peace dove	2.00	2.00

Miniature Sheets of 4 + 4 Labels

Motion Pictures, Cent. — A153

Designs: No. 696: a, Ingrid Bergman. b, Vittorio De Sica. c, Marlene Dietrich. d, Laurence Olivier.
No. 697: a, 38p, Audrey Hepburn. b, 25p, Romy Schneider. c, 28p, Yves Montand. d, 5p, Marilyn Monroe.

1995, Nov. 13 Litho. Perf. 14½x14
696 A153 24p #a.-d. 4.25 4.25
697 A153 #a.-d. 4.25 4.25

Christmas
A154

Designs: 5p, Santa Claus. 24p, Sack of toys. 34p, Reindeer. 54p, Santa with sleigh, reindeer flying over rooftops.

1995, Nov. 27 Perf. 14
698 A154 5p multicolored .40 .25
699 A154 24p multicolored 1.50 .75
700 A154 34p multicolored 2.00 2.00
701 A154 54p multicolored 3.25 3.25
Nos. 698-701 (4) 7.15 6.25

Miniature Sheet

Puppies
A155

#702: a, 5p, Shih tzu. b, 21p, Dalmatian. c, Cocker spaniel. d, 25p, West Highland white terrier. e, 34p, Labrador. f, 35p, Boxer.

1996, Jan. 24 Litho. Perf. 14
702 A155 Sheet of 6, #a.-f. 7.00 7.00

No. 702 is a continuous design.

Women of the British Royal Family
A156

1996, Feb. 9 Litho. Perf. 13½
703 A156 24p Princess Anne 1.60 1.60
704 A156 24p Princess Diana 1.60 1.60
705 A156 34p Queen Mother 2.00 2.00
706 A156 34p Queen Elizabeth II 2.00 2.00
Nos. 703-706 (4) 7.20 7.20

Europa.

European Soccer — A157

Team members in action scenes: 21p, West Germany, 1980. 24p, France, 1964. 34p, Holland, 1988. £1.20, Denmark, 1992.

1996, Apr. 2 Litho. Perf. 13
707 A157 21p multicolored .70 .70
708 A157 24p multicolored .90 .90
709 A157 34p multicolored 1.40 1.40
710 A157 £1.20 multicolored 3.50 3.50
a. Souvenir sheet, Nos. 707-710 10.00 10.00
Nos. 707-710 (4) 6.50 6.50

Modern Olympic Games, Cent.
A158

1996, May 2 Litho. Perf. 13½
711 A158 34p Ancient athletes 1.25 1.25
712 A158 49p Athletes, 1896 1.75 1.75
713 A158 £1.05 Athletes, 1990s 3.50 3.50
Nos. 711-713 (3) 6.50 6.50

World War II Type of 1993
Souvenir Sheet

a, 5p, HMS Starling. b, 25p, HMS Royalist. c, 49p, USS Philadelphia. d, 54p, HMCS Prescott.

1996, June 8 Litho. Perf. 13½x14
714 A137 Sheet of 4, #a.-d. 8.00 8.00

UNICEF, 50th Anniv.
A159

a, 21p, Girl, boy. b, 24p, Three children. c, 49p, Three children, diff. d, 54p, Girl, boy, diff.

1996, June 8 Perf. 13½x13
715 A159 Strip of 4, #a.-d. 5.75 5.75

World Wildlife Fund
A160

Red kite: a, In flight. b, One adult. c, One on rock, one in flight. d, Adults, young in nest.

1996, July 12 Litho. Perf. 14½
716 A160 34p Block or strip of 4, #a.-d. 9.00 9.00

Christmas Images Formed with "Lego" Blocks — A161

1996, Nov. 27 Litho. Perf. 14
717 A161 5p Pudding .20 .20
718 A161 21p Snowman .85 .85
719 A161 24p Present 1.00 1.00
720 A161 34p Santa Claus 1.25 1.25
721 A161 54p Candle 1.75 1.75
Nos. 717-721 (5) 5.05 5.05

Sailing Ship "Mary Celeste" — A162

Europa: No. 722, "Mary Celeste" in rough seas. No. 723, Men on board ship. No. 724, Boat approaching "Mary Celeste." No. 725, In full sail.

1997, Feb. 12 Litho. Perf. 14
722 A162 28p multicolored 1.10 1.10
723 A162 28p multicolored 1.10 1.10
724 A162 30p multicolored 1.25 1.25
725 A162 30p multicolored 1.25 1.25
Nos. 722-725 (4) 4.70 4.70

Kittens
A163

Designs: a, 5p, Silver tabby American shorthair. b, 24p, "Rumpy" Manx red tabby. c, 26p, Blue point Birmans. d, 28p, Red self longhair. e, 30p, British shorthair, tortoiseshell & white. f, 35p, British bicolor shorthairs.

1997, Feb. 12
726 A163 Sheet of 6, #a.-f. 7.75 7.75
g. Bklt. pane of 3, #726a, 726c, 726e 3.00 3.00
h. Bklt. pane of 3, #726b, 726c, 726d 4.25
i. Bklt. pane of 4, #726a, 726b, 726e, 726f 5.00
j. Bklt. pane of 4, #726c, 726d, 726e, 726f 6.00
k. Booklet pane, #726 8.25
Complete booklet, #726g-726k 26.00

Hong Kong '97. No. 726k is rouletted at left and does not have Hong Kong '97 emblem and inscription in bottom slevage.

Butterflies — A164

Designs: 23p, Anthocharis belia euphenoides. 26p, Charaxes jasius. 30p, Vanessa cardui. £1.20, Iphiclides podalirius.

1997, Apr. 7 Litho. Perf. 14x13½
728 A164 23p multicolored .85 .85
729 A164 26p multicolored .95 .95
730 A164 30p multicolored 1.25 1.25
731 A164 £1.20 multicolored 3.50 3.50
a. Souvenir sheet of 4, #728-731 8.50 8.50
Nos. 728-731 (4) 6.55 6.55

Warships Type of 1993

a, 24p, HMS Enterprise. b, 26p, HMS Cleopatra. c, 38p, USS Iowa. d, 50p, Polish Warship Orkan.

1997, June 9 Litho. Perf. 13½
732 A137 Sheet of 4, #a.-d. 6.25 6.25

Queen Elizabeth II and Prince Philip, 50th Wedding Anniv. — A165

Designs: £1.20, Prince Philip driving a four-in-hand, Queen beside him. £1.40, Queen, Prince Philip at Royal Ascot, Queen "Trooping the Color."

1997, July 10 Litho. Perf. 14x13½
733 A165 £1.20 multicolored 4.75 4.75
734 A165 £1.40 multicolored 5.75 5.75
a. Pair, #733-734 10.50 10.50

1997 Dior Fashion Designs, by John Galliano — A166

30p, Long black dress, hat. 35p, Mini skirt, lace top. 50p, Formal gown. 62p, Suit, hat. £1.20, Formal gown, diff.

1997, Sept. 9 Litho. Perf. 13½x13
735 A166 30p multicolored 1.00 1.00
736 A166 35p multicolored 1.25 1.25
737 A166 50p multicolored 1.40 1.40
a. Pair, #735, 737 3.25 3.25
738 A166 62p multicolored 2.00 2.00
a. Pair, #736, 738 4.25 4.25
Nos. 735-738 (4) 5.65 5.65

Souvenir Sheet

739 A166 £1.20 multicolored 4.50 4.50

Christmas
A167

Stained glass windows: 5p, Our Lady and St. Bernard. 26p, The Epiphany of the Lord. 38p, St. Joseph holding Jesus. 50p, The Holy Family. 62p, The Miraculous Medal Madonna.

1997, Nov. 18 Litho. Perf. 13½
740 A167 5p multicolored .25 .20
741 A167 26p multicolored 1.00 1.00
742 A167 38p multicolored 1.25 1.25
743 A167 50p multicolored 1.75 1.75
744 A167 62p multicolored 2.00 3.00
Nos. 740-744 (5) 6.25 7.20

A168

1997, Dec. 15 Litho. Perf. 13
745 A168 26p multicolored 1.10 1.10

Sir Joshua Hassan (1915-97), government leader.

A169

1998, Jan. 23

Scenes from previous World Cup Championships: 5p, Wales v. Brazil, 1958. 26p, N. Ireland v. France, 1958. 38p, Scotland v. Holland, 1978. £1.20, England v. W. Germany, 1966.

746 A169 5p multicolored .35 .35
747 A169 26p multicolored 1.20 1.20
748 A169 38p multicolored 1.50 1.50
749 A169 £1.20 multicolored 4.00 4.00
a. Souvenir sheet, #746-749 8.00 8.00
Nos. 746-749 (4) 7.05 7.05

1998 World Cup Soccer Championships, France.

Diana, Princess of Wales (1961-97)
Common Design Type

Various portraits: a, 26p, Wearing black & white outfit. b, 26p, Wearing pink & white outfit. c, 38p, In black dress. d, 38p, In blue & gold jacket.

1998, Mar. 31 Litho. Perf. 14½x14
754 CD355 Sheet of 4, #a.-d. 5.50 5.50

The 20p surtax from international sales was donated to the Princess Diana Memorial Fund and the surtax from national sales was donated to a designated local charity.

Royal Air Force, 80th Anniv.
Common Design Type of 1993 Re-inscribed

Designs: 24p, Saro London. 26p, Fairey Fox. 38p, Handley Page Halifax GR.VI. 50p, Hawker Siddeley Buccaneer S.2B.

No. 759: a, 24p, Sopwith 1½ Strutter. b, 26p, Bristol M.1B. c, 38p, Supermarine Spitfire XII. d, 50p, Avro York.

1998, Apr. 1   *Perf. 14*
755	CD350	24p multicolored	1.00	1.00
756	CD350	26p multicolored	1.10	1.10
757	CD350	38p multicolored	1.75	1.75
758	CD350	50p multicolored	2.10	2.10
		Nos. 755-758 (4)	5.95	5.95

Souvenir Sheet of 4
759	CD350	#a.-d.	6.25	6.25

Europa — A170

Costumes worn by Miss Gibraltar for National Day: No. 760, Military style. No. 761, Long skirt, long-sleeved top. No. 762, Short skirt, long cape. No. 763, Black lace scarf, ruffled petticoat.

1998, May 22   **Litho.**   *Perf. 13*
760	A170	26p multicolored	.95	.95
761	A170	26p multicolored	.95	.95
762	A170	38p multicolored	1.40	1.40
763	A170	38p multicolored	1.40	1.40
		Nos. 760-763 (4)	4.70	4.70

UNESCO 1998 Intl. Year of the Ocean A171

Marine life: a, 5p, Striped dolphin. b, 26p, Killer whale, vert. c, £1.20, Blue whale. d, 5p, Common dolphin, vert.

1998, May 22   *Perf. 14*
764	A171	Sheet of 4, #a.-d.	7.50	7.50

Italia '98 and Portugal '98.

Battle of the Nile — A172

1998, Aug. 1   **Litho.**   *Perf. 13½*
765	A172	12p Nileus	.60	.60
766	A172	26p Lord Nelson	1.10	1.10
a.		Booklet pane of 1	1.50	
767	A172	28p Frances Nisbet	1.25	1.25
a.		Bkt. pane, #765-767	3.50	
768	A172	35p HMS Vanguard	1.50	1.50

Size: 45x27mm
769	A172	50p Battle of the Nile	2.25	2.25
a.		Bkt. pane, #768-769, 2 #766	7.00	
b.		Bkt. pane, #766, 768-769	5.75	
c.		Bkt. pane, #765-769	8.00	
		Complete booklet, #766a, 767a, 769a-769c	26.00	
		Nos. 765-769 (5)	6.70	6.70

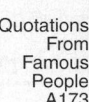

Quotations From Famous People A173

#770, "Love comforts like sunshine after rain," Shakespeare. #771, "The price of greatness is responsibility," Churchill. #772, "Hate the sin, love the sinner," Gandhi. #773, "Imagination is more important than knowledge," Einstein.

1998, Oct. 6   **Litho.**   *Perf. 14½*
770	A173	26p multicolored	1.00	1.00
771	A173	26p multicolored	1.00	1.00
772	A173	38p multicolored	1.75	1.75
773	A173	38p multicolored	1.75	1.75
		Nos. 770-773 (4)	5.50	5.50

Nos. 770-773 were each printed in sheets of 6 with se-tenant labels.

A174   A175

1998, Nov. 10   **Litho.**   *Perf. 13*
774	A174	5p Nativity	.45	.45
775	A174	26p Star over manger	1.10	1.10
776	A174	30p Balthasar	1.25	1.25
777	A174	35p Melchior	1.40	1.40
778	A174	50p Caspar	1.75	1.75
		Nos. 774-778 (5)	5.95	5.95

Christmas.

1999, Mar. 4   **Litho.**   *Perf. 13½*
779	A175	1p claret	.20	.20
780	A175	2p brown	.20	.20
781	A175	4p blue	.20	.20
782	A175	5p green	.20	.20
783	A175	10p brown orange	.40	.40
784	A175	12p red	.45	.45
785	A175	20p blue green	.75	.75
786	A175	28p lilac rose	1.00	1.00
787	A175	30p vermilion	1.10	1.10
788	A175	40p gray olive	1.50	1.50
789	A175	42p slate	1.60	1.60

Size: 22½x28mm
Perf. 14½
790	A175	50p olive bister	1.90	1.90
791	A175	£1 black	4.00	4.00
792	A175	£3 ultramarine	10.00	10.00

Self-Adhesive
Die Cut Perf. 9x9½
793	A175	1st vermilion	1.00	1.00
		Nos. 779-793 (15)	24.50	24.50

No. 793 was valued at 26p on day of issue.

Nature Reserves — A176

1999, Mar. 4   *Perf. 13½x13*
794	A176	30p Barbary macaque	1.75	1.75
795	A176	30p Dartford warbler	1.75	1.75
796	A176	42p Kingfisher	2.25	2.25
797	A176	42p Dusky perch	2.25	2.25
		Nos. 794-797 (4)	8.00	8.00

Europa.

Maritime Heritage — A177

Designs: 5p, Roman Anchorage. 30p, Medieval galley house. 42p, British relief ships. £1.20, HMS Berwick.

1999, Mar. 19   *Perf. 12½*
798	A177	5p multicolored	.25	.25
799	A177	30p multicolored	1.50	1.50
800	A177	42p multicolored	2.25	2.25
801	A177	£1.20 multicolored	5.75	5.75
a.		Souvenir sheet, #798-801	10.00	10.00
		Nos. 798-801 (4)	9.75	9.75

John Lennon (1940-80) A178

Portraits: 20p, With flower over one eye. 30p, Black and white photo. 40p, Wearing glasses.

No. 805, Holding marriage license in front of Rock of Gibraltar. No. 806, Standing in front of airplane.

1999, Mar. 20   *Perf. 13*
802	A178	20p multicolored	.90	.90
803	A178	30p multicolored	1.25	1.25
804	A178	40p multicolored	1.50	1.50
		Nos. 802-804 (3)	3.65	3.65

Souvenir Sheets
805	A178	£1 multicolored	6.00	6.00
806	A178	£1 multicolored	6.00	6.00

UPU, 125th Anniv. — A179

1999, June 7   **Litho.**   *Perf. 12½*
807	A179	5p Postal van	.25	.25
808	A179	30p Space station	1.50	1.50

Fighter Planes and Raptors A180

Designs: No. 809, RAF Eurofighter 2000 Typhoon. No. 810, RAF F3 Tornado. No. 811, RAF GR7 Harrier II. No. 812, Lesser kestrel. No. 813, Peregrine falcon. No. 814, Kestrel.

1999, June 7   *Perf. 13x13¼*
809	A180	30p multicolored	1.10	1.10
810	A180	30p multicolored	1.10	1.10
811	A180	30p multicolored	1.10	1.10
a.		Sheet of 3, #809-811	3.50	3.50
812	A180	42p multicolored	1.25	1.25
a.		Pair, #809, 812	3.25	3.25
813	A180	42p multicolored	1.25	1.25
a.		Pair, #810, 813	3.25	3.25
814	A180	42p multicolored	1.25	1.25
a.		Pair, #811, 814	3.25	3.25
b.		Sheet of 3, #812-814	6.50	6.50

See Nos. 851-853.

Wedding of Prince Edward and Sophie Rhys-Jones A181

1999, June 19   **Litho.**
815	A181	30p shown	1.25	1.25
816	A181	42p Couple, vert.	1.50	1.50

Perf. 13x13¼, 13¼x13

Sports in Gibraltar, Cent. — A182

1999, July 2   *Perf. 13*
817	A182	30p Soccer	1.25	1.25
818	A182	42p Rowing	1.75	1.75
819	A182	£1.20 Cricket	3.75	3.75
		Nos. 817-819 (3)	6.75	6.75

Wedding of Prince Edward to Sophie Rhys-Jones A183

Perf. 13x13¼, 13¼x13

1999, Oct. 11   **Litho.**
820	A183	54p shown	2.00	2.00
821	A183	66p Couple standing, vert.	2.25	2.25

Christmas and New Year's Greetings A184

Designs: No. 822, "Happy Christmas," Santa, sleigh. No. 823, "Season's Greetings." No. 824, "Happy Millennium." No. 825, "Happy Christmas," Santa, reindeer. 42p, "Yo ho ho." 54p, Santa, tree, fireplace.

1999, Nov. 11   **Litho.**   *Perf. 14*
822	A184	5p multicolored	.20	.20
823	A184	5p multicolored	.20	.20
824	A184	30p multicolored	1.00	1.00
825	A184	30p multicolored	1.00	1.00
826	A184	42p multicolored	1.50	1.50
827	A184	54p multicolored	1.75	1.75
		Nos. 822-827 (6)	5.65	5.65

Stampin' the Future Children's Stamp Design Contest Winners A185

Artwork by: 30p, Colin Grech. 42p, Kim Barea. 54p, Stephan Williamson-Fa. 66p, Michael Podesta.

2000, Jan. 28   **Litho.**   *Perf. 14½x14*
828	A185	30p multi	1.50	1.50
829	A185	42p multi	1.50	1.50
830	A185	54p multi	1.50	1.50
831	A185	66p multi	1.50	1.50
a.		Block or strip of 4, #828-831	8.00	8.00

European Soccer — A186

2000, Apr. 17   **Litho.**   *Perf. 12½*
832	A186	30p France	1.00	1.00
833	A186	30p Holland	1.00	1.00
834	A186	42p Denmark	1.25	1.25
835	A186	42p Germany	1.25	1.25
a.		Souvenir sheet, #832-835	5.00	5.00
836	A186	54p England	1.50	1.50
a.		Souvenir sheet of 4	5.50	5.50
		Nos. 832-836 (5)	6.00	6.00

The Stamp Show 2000, London (#836a).

Europa — A187

2000, Apr. 17   *Perf. 13¼x13*
837	A187	30p Fountain	1.25	1.25
838	A187	40p Hands	1.50	1.50
839	A187	42p Airplane	1.50	1.50
840	A187	54p Rainbow	2.00	2.00
		Nos. 837-840 (4)	6.25	6.25

THE HISTORY OF GIBRALTAR

MILLENNIUM STAMPS

Millennium — A188

History of Gibraltar: a, 3000-meter waterfall. b, The sandy plains. c, The Neanderthals. d, The Phoenicians. e, The Romans. f, The Arabs. g, Coat of arms, 1502. h, British Gibraltar. i, The great siege. j, Trafalgar. k, The city. l, Fortifications. m, The evacuation. n, The fortress. o, Queen Elizabeth II. p, European finance center.

Illustration reduced.

2000, May 9			**Perf. 14**	
841	A188	Sheet of 16	14.00	14.00
a.-h.		5p Any single	.30	.30
i.-p.		30p Any single	1.40	1.40
q.		Souvenir booklet	30.00	

No. 841q contains a pane of 2 of each of Nos. 841a-841j and a pane of 3 of each of Nos. 841k-841p.

Prince William, 18th Birthday — A189

Designs: 30p, With Princess Diana. 42p, As child. 54p, With Prince Charles. 66p, In suit.

2000, June 21		Litho.	**Perf. 12½**	
842	A189	30p multi	1.00	1.00
843	A189	42p multi	1.50	1.40
844	A189	54p multi	1.75	1.75
845	A189	66p multi	2.00	2.00
a.		Souvenir sheet, #842-845	8.00	8.00
		Nos. 842-845 (4)	6.25	6.15

Queen Mother, 100th Birthday — A190

Designs: 30p, As young woman. 42p, With King George VI. 54p, With blue hat. 66p, With orange hat.

2000, Aug. 4				
846	A190	30p multi	1.00	1.00
847	A190	42p multi	1.50	1.50
848	A190	54p multi	1.75	1.75
849	A190	66p multi	2.00	2.00
a.		Souvenir sheet, #846-849	7.50	7.50
		Nos. 846-849 (4)	6.25	6.25

Moorish Castle A191

Photo. & Engr.

2000, Sept. 15			**Perf. 11½x11¾**	
850	A191	£5 multi	16.00	16.00

Fighter Planes and Raptors Type

No. 851: a, RAF "Gibraltar" Supermarine Spitfire. b, Male merlin.
No. 852: a, RAF "City of Lincoln" Avro Lancaster B1-3. b, Bonelli's eagle.
No. 853: a, RAF Hawker Hurricane MK IIC. b, Female merlin.

2000, Sept. 15		Litho.	**Perf. 14½x14**	
851		Pair	4.00	4.00
a.	A180	30p multi	1.50	1.50
b.	A180	42p multi	2.00	2.00
852		Pair	4.00	4.00
a.	A180	30p multi	1.50	1.50
b.	A180	42p multi	2.00	2.00
853		Pair	4.00	4.00
a.	A180	30p multi	1.50	1.50
b.	A180	42p multi	2.00	2.00
c.		Souvenir sheet, #851a, 852a, 853a	5.00	5.00
d.		Souvenir sheet, #851b, 852b, 853b	7.50	7.50
		Nos. 851-853 (3)	12.00	12.00

Christmas A192

5p, Baby Jesus. No. 855, 30p, Joseph, Mary, donkey. No. 856, 30p, Mary, Jesus. 40p, Joseph, Mary, innkeeper. 42p, Holy Family, donkey. 54p, Holy Family, Magi.

2000, Nov. 13			**Perf. 14**	
854-859	A192	Set of 6	7.50	7.50

Queen Victoria (1819-1901) A193

Designs: 30p, On wedding day. 42p, Portrait. 54p, In carriage. 66p, Jubilee portrait.

2001, Jan. 22			**Perf. 12¾**	
860-863	A193	Set of 4	8.00	8.00

New Year 2001 (Year of the Snake) — A194

Snakes: No. 864, 5p, Grass. No. 865, 5p, Ladder. No. 866, 5p, Montpelier. No. 867, 30p, Viperine. No. 868, 30p, Southern smooth. No. 869, 30p, False smooth. 66p, Horseshoe whip.

2001, Feb. 1		Litho.	**Perf. 13¾**	
864-870	A194	Set of 7	7.00	7.00
870a		Souvenir sheet, #864-870	10.00	10.00

Size of No. 870: 31x62mm. Hong Kong 2001 Stamp Exhibition (No. 870a).

Europa — A195

Designs: 30p, Long-snouted seahorse. 40p, Snapdragon. 42p, Yellow-legged gull. 54p, Goldfish.

2001, Feb. 1			**Perf. 13¼x13**	
871-874	A195	Set of 4	10.00	10.00

Queen Elizabeth II, 75th Birthday A196

Designs: No. 875, 30p, As child. No. 876, 30p, As young woman. No. 877, 42p, In wedding dress. No. 878, 42p, At coronation. 54p, Wearing hat. £2, In blue dress.

2001, Apr. 21		Litho.	**Perf. 14**	
875-879	A196	Set of 5	8.00	8.00

Souvenir Sheet

Perf. 13¾

880	A196	£2 multi	7.50	7.50

No. 880 contains one 35x48mm stamp.

Gibraltar Chronicle, Bicent. — A197

Designs: 30p, Battle of Trafalgar. 42p, Invention of the telephone. 54p, The end of World War II. 66p, First man on the Moon.

2001, May 21			**Perf. 14x14½**	
881-884	A197	Set of 4	8.00	8.00

Queen Type of 1999

2001, June 1		Litho.	**Perf. 14x14¼**	
			Size: 22x28mm	
885	A175	£1.20 carmine	5.00	5.00
886	A175	£1.40 blue	5.50	5.50

Fighter Planes and Raptors Type of 1999

No. 887: a, 40p, RAF Jaguar GR1B. b, 40p, Hobby.
No. 888: a, 40p, Royal Navy Sea Harrier FA MK 2. b, 40p, Marsh harrier.
No. 889: a, 40p, RAF Hawk T MK 1. b, 40p, Sparrowhawk.

2001, Sept. 3		Litho.	**Perf. 14½x14**	
			Pairs, #a-b	
887-889	A180	Set of 3	10.00	10.00
889c		Souvenir sheet, #887a, 888a, 889a	5.00	5.00
889d		Souvenir sheet, #887b, 888b, 889b	5.00	5.00

Christmas A198

Snoopy, from Peanuts comic strip: 5p, In Santa Claus suit ringing bell, Woodstock. 30p, Charlie Brown, Christmas tree. 40p, Wreath. 42p, In Santa Claus suit carrying cookies, Woodstock. 54p, On dog house.

2001, Nov. 12			**Perf. 14**	
890-894	A198	Set of 5	6.00	6.00
894a		Souvenir sheet, #890-894	7.00	7.00

Souvenir Sheet

Introduction of Euro Coinage to Europe — A199

Coins in denominations of: a, 5p, 1 cent. b, 12p, 2 cents. c, 30p, 5 cents. d, 35p, 10 cents. e, 40p, 20 cents. f, 42p, 50 cents. g, 54p, 1 euro. h, 66p, 2 euro.

2002, Jan. 1		Litho.	**Perf. 13¼x13**	
895	A199	Sheet of 8, #a-h	10.00	10.00

A clear varnish was applied by a thermographic process producing a shiny, raised effect.

Reign Of Queen Elizabeth II, 50th Anniv. Issue
Common Design Type

Designs: No. 896, 30p, Princess Elizabeth in field, 1942. No. 897, 30p, Wearing tiara, 1961. No. 898, 30p, With Princess Margaret, microphones. No. 899, 30p, Wearing hat, 1993. 75p, 1955 portrait by Annigoni (38x50mm).

Perf. 14¼x14½, 13¾ (75p)

2002, Feb. 6		Litho.	**Wmk. 373**	
896-900	CD360	Set of 5	7.00	7.00
a.		Souvenir sheet, #896-900	10.00	10.00

Europa — A200

Famous clowns: 30p, Joseph Grimaldi (1778-1831). 40p, Karl Adrien Wettach (1880-1959). 42p, Nicholai Polakovs (1900-74). 54p, Hubert Jean Charles Cairoli (1910-80).

Perf. 13¼x13

2002, Mar. 4		Litho.	**Unwmk.**	
901-904	A200	Set of 4	6.25	6.25

Bobby Moore, English Soccer Player — A201

Moore in 1966: 30p, Holding up World Cup. 42p, Kissing World Cup. 54p, With Queen Elizabeth II. 66p, In action.

Perf. 13¼x13

2002, May 1		Litho.	**Unwmk.**	
905-908	A201	Set of 4	7.00	7.00
a.		Souvenir sheet, #905-908	7.00	7.00

Wildlife A202

Designs: No. 909, 30p, Red fox. No. 910, 30p, Barbary macaque, vert. 40p, White tooth shrew. £1, Rabbit, vert.

Perf. 14¼x14, 14x14¼

2002, June 6		Litho.	**Unwmk.**	
909-912	A202	Set of 4	7.50	7.50
a.		Souvenir sheet, #909-912	8.00	8.00

Prince Harry, 18th Birthday — A203

Designs: 30p, As child in Princess Diana's arms. 42p, Waving. 54p, Wearing baseball cap. 66p, In suit and tie.

2002, Sept. 15		Litho.	**Perf. 12½**	
913-916	A203	Set of 4	7.25	7.25
a.		Souvenir sheet, #913-916	8.50	8.50

Rock of Gibraltar — A204

View of Rock from: a, North. b, South. c, East (46x38mm). d, West (46x38mm).

2002, Sept. 15   Litho.   Perf. 13¼x13
917   Horiz. strip of 4   10.00 10.00
a.-b.   A204 30p Either single   1.00 1.00
c.-d.   A204 £1 Either single   3.25 3.25

Particles of the Rock of Gibraltar were applied to portions of the designs by a thermographic process.

Christmas — A205

Creche scenes from: 5p, Cathedral of St. Mary the Crowned. 30p, St. Joseph's Parish Church. 40p, St. Theresa's Parish Church. 42p, Our Lady of Sorrows Church, Catalan Bay. 52p, St. Bernard's Church. 54p, Cathedral of the Holy Trinity.

2002, Nov. 13   Perf. 13
918-923 A205   Set of 6   9.00 9.00

Coronation of Queen Elizabeth II, 50th Anniv. — A206

Designs: No. 924, 30p, Queen receiving crown. No. 925, 30p, Queen on throne. 40p, Queen holding orb. £1, Queen in profile.

**   Perf. 12½**
2003, Feb. 20   Litho.   Unwmk.
924-927 A206   Set of 4   7.50 7.50
927a   Souvenir sheet, #924-927 8.00 8.00

Europa — A207

Poster art for: 30p, Drama Festival. 40p, Spring Festival. 42p, Art Festival. 54p, Dance Festival.

2003, Mar. 3   Perf. 14x14½
928-931 A207   Set of 4   6.00 6.00

Powered Flight, Cent. A208

Designs: 30p, Wright Flyer, 1903. No. 933, 40p, Charles Lindbergh and Spirit of St. Louis, 1927. No. 934, 40p, Boeing 314 Yankee Clipper, 1939. 42p, Saunders Roe SARO-21 Windhover Amphibian, 1931 (77x27mm). 44p, Concorde, 1976 (77x27mm). 66p, Space Shuttle Columbia, 1981, vert. (37x57mm).

2003, Mar. 31   Litho.   Perf. 13x13¼
932-937 A208   Set of 6   12.00 12.00
937a   Souvenir sheet, #932-937,
           perf. 12½   13.00 13.00

Martyrdom of St. George, 1700th Anniv. — A209

Designs: 30p, Cross of St. George. 40p, Constantinian Order of St. George. £1.20, Stained glass window depiction of St. George, vert. (31x63mm).

2003, Apr. 23   Perf. 13¾
938-940 A209   Set of 3   7.00 7.00
940a   Souvenir sheet, #938-940 7.50 7.50

Big Ben, Swift and Rock of Gibraltar A210

**   Photo. & Engr.**
2003, June 21   Perf. 11½
941 A210   (£3) multi   11.50 11.50

Prince William, 21st Birthday — A211

Prince William: No. 942, 30p, As a child, with Princess Diana. No. 943, 30p, With hands in pockets. 40p, Close-up, wearing suit. £1, Wearing sweatshirt.

2003, June 21   Litho.   Perf. 12½
942-945 A211   Set of 4   11.50 11.50
945a   Souvenir sheet, #942-945 11.50 11.50

Enlargement of European Union — A212

National flowers of newly-added countries: 30p, Daisy (Latvia), Cornflower (Estonia), Rue (Lithuania). 40p, Rose (Cyprus), Maltese centaury (Malta). 42p, Tulip (Hungary), Carnation (Slovenia), Dog rose (Slovakia). 54p, Corn poppy (Poland), Scented thyme (Czech Republic).

2003, Sept. 15   Litho.   Perf. 13¾
946-949 A212   Set of 4   6.50 6.50

Mushrooms A213

Designs: No. 950, 30p, Lepista nuda. No. 951, 30p, Clitocybe odora. No. 952, 30p, Hypholoma fasciculare. £1.20, Agaricus campestris.

2003, Sept. 15   Perf. 14¼
950-953 A213   Set of 4   9.50 9.50
953a   Souvenir sheet, #950-953 10.00 10.00

A214

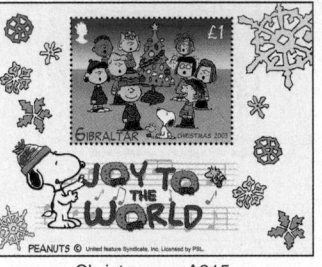

Christmas — A215

Designs: 5p, Baby Jesus crib, Our Lady of Sorrows Church. 30p, Building a traditional creche at home. 40p, Three Kings Cavalcade on January 5. 42p, Children's provisions for Santa and reindeer on Christmas Eve. 54p, Christmas Eve midnight mass at the Cathedral of St. Mary the Crowned.

2003, Nov. 17   Litho.   Perf. 14
954-958 A214   Set of 5   6.00 6.00
**   Souvenir Sheet**
**   Perf. 12¼x12**
959 A215   £1 multi   5.00 5.00

Europa — A216

Designs: No. 960, 40p, Outdoor cafe. No. 961, 40p, St. Michael's Cave. No. 962, 54p, Seaside cafe. No. 963, 54p, Dolphin.

2004, Feb. 20   Litho.   Perf. 14x14½
960-963 A216   Set of 4   7.00 7.00

British Gibraltar, 300th Anniv. A217

Designs: 8p, British flag, Gibraltar coat of arms.
No. 965: a, Ship with large flag. b, Ship, rowboat, cannons. c, Soldiers. d, Military uniform. e, Telephone booth, police hat. f, Mail box. g, Neckties, university documents, graduates in caps and gowns. h, Crowd waving flags. i, British flag.

2004   Litho.   Perf. 13x13¼
964 A217   8p multi   .75 .75
965   Sheet of 9   14.00 14.00
a.-h. A217 30p Any single   1.00 1.00
i.   A217 £1.20 multi   4.00 4.00
j.   Souvenir sheet, #965i   4.75 4.75

Issued: Nos. 964-965i, 4/26. No. 965j, 9/10.
Sir Elton John's Tercentenary Concert (No. 965j).
A perforated "black print" sheet of No. 965 exists with cancels.

Visit of Queen Elizabeth II to Gibraltar, 50th Anniv. — A218

Queen: 38p, Holding flowers. 40p, With arm extended. 47p, In limousine. £1, With children and soldiers. £1.50, Standing in limousine with Prince Philip.

2004, May 4   Perf. 12½
966-969 A218   Set of 4   8.50 8.50
**   Souvenir Sheet**
970 A218   £1.50 multi   6.75 6.75

European Soccer — A219

Designs: 30p, Goalie defending shot. No. 972, 40p, Players near side of goal. No. 973, 40p, Player making scissor kick. £1, Goalie playing ball near goal post. £1.50, Player with arms extended, horiz.

2004, June 6   Set of 4   7.75 7.75
971-974 A219
974a   Souvenir sheet, #971-974 7.75 7.75
**   Souvenir Sheet**
975 A219   £1.50 multi   5.50 5.50

No. 975 contains one 48x37mm stamp.

D-Day, 60th Anniv. A220

Designs: 38p, Soldiers leaving landing craft. 40p, Tank approaching beach. 47p, Airplane. £1, Ships.

2004, June 6   Perf. 13x13¼
976-979 A220   Set of 4   9.25 9.25
979a   Souvenir sheet, #976-979 9.25 9.25

Flowers — A221

Designs: 1p, Mallow-leaved bindweed. 2p, Gibraltar sea lavender. 5p, Gibraltar chickweed. G, Romulea. 10p, Common centaury. G1, Pyramidal orchid. S, Friar's cowl. UK, Corn poppy. E, Giant Tangier fennel. U, Snapdragon. 50p, Common gladiolus. £1, Yellow horned poppy. £3, Gibraltar candytuft.

2004, Sept. 10   Litho.   Perf. 13¼
980 A221   1p multi   .20 .20
a.   Booklet pane of 1   .20
981 A221   2p multi   .20 .20
a.   Booklet pane of 1   .20
982 A221   5p multi   .20 .20
a.   Booklet pane of 1   .20
983 A221   G multi   .25 .25
a.   Booklet pane of 1   .25
984 A221   10p multi   .35 .35
a.   Booklet pane of 1   .35
985 A221   G1 multi   .45 .45
a.   Booklet pane of 1   .45
986 A221   S multi   1.00 1.00
a.   Booklet pane of 1   1.00
987 A221   UK multi   1.40 1.40
a.   Booklet pane of 1   1.40
988 A221   E multi   1.50 1.50
a.   Booklet pane of 1   1.50
989 A221   U multi   1.75 1.75
a.   Booklet pane of 1   1.75
990 A221   50p multi   2.00 2.00
a.   Booklet pane of 1   2.00
991 A221   £1 multi   3.50 3.50
a.   Booklet pane of 1   3.50
992 A221   £3 multi   11.00 11.00
a.   Booklet pane of 1   11.00
       Complete booklet, #980a-
       992a   23.50
       Nos. 980-992 (13)   23.80 23.80

Nos. 983, 985, 986, 987, 988 and 989 sold for 7p, 12p, 28p, 38p, 40p and 47p respectively on day of issue.
See Nos. 1033B-1036.

Ferrari Race Cars
A222

Designs: No. 993, 5p, F2003GA. No. 994, 5p, F2004. No. 995, 30p, F2001. No. 996, 30p, F2002. No. 997, 75p, F399. No. 998, 75p, F1-2000.

2004, Nov. 12   *Perf. 14¾x14¼*
993-998   A222   Set of 6   9.50 9.50
998a   Souvenir sheet, #993-998 9.50 9.50

Christmas
A223

Christmas tree ornaments: 7p, Santa Claus. 28p, Angel. 38p, Red star. 40p, Gold bell. 47p, Red ball. 53p, White star.

2004, Nov. 12   *Perf. 12½*
999-1004 A223   Set of 6   9.50 9.50

Battle of Trafalgar, Bicent. — A224

Designs: 38p, Soldier guarding wine cask containing Admiral Horatio Nelson's body. 40p, HMS Entrepenante. 47p, Admiral Nelson, vert. £1.60, HMS Victory. £2, HMS Vctory being towed to Gibraltar.

2005, Jan. 29   Litho.   *Perf. 13¼*
1005-1008 A224   Set of 4   13.50 13.50
Souvenir Sheet
Perf. 13¾
1009 A224 £2 multi   12.00 12.00

No. 1008 has particles of wood from the HMS Victory embedded in the areas covered by a thermographic process that produces a raised, shiny effect. No. 1009 contains one 44x44mm stamp.
See Nos. 1027-1028.

Europa — A225

Designs: No. 1010, 47p, Sherry trifle. No. 1011, 47p, Spinach pie. No. 1012, 47p, Veal birds. No. 1013, 47p, Grilled sea bass.

Perf. 14¼x14¾
2005, Mar. 31   Litho.
1010-1013 A225   Set of 4   8.50 8.50

V-E Day, 60th Anniv. — A226

Designs: 38p, Winston Churchill. 40p, Woman, children, British flags. 47p, Servicewomen in car waving flags. £1, People at dock.

2005, May 8
1014-1017 A226   Set of 4   9.00 9.00
1017a   Souvenir sheet, #1014-1017   9.00 9.00

Anniversaries — A227

Designs: 38p, Royal Gibraltar Police, 175th anniv. 47p, Gibraltar Museum, 75th anniv. £1, Grant of Charter of Justice, 175th anniv.

2005, June 17   *Perf. 14¾x14¼*
1018-1020 A227   Set of 3   8.25 8.25

Cruise Ships
A228

Designs: 38p, Circassia. 40p, Nevassa. 47p, Black Prince. £1, Arcadia.

2005, June 17   *Perf. 13x13¼*
1021-1024 A228   Set of 4   9.00 9.00
1024a   Souvenir sheet, #1021-1024   9.00 9.00

Pope John Paul II
(1920-2005)
A229

2005, July 15   *Perf. 14¼x14¾*
1025 A229 75p multi   3.50 3.50

Printed in sheets of 6.

Europa Stamps, 50th Anniv. (in 2006) — A230

Litho. With Foil Application
2005, Sept. 30   *Perf. 14¼*
1026 A230 £5 multi   17.50 17.50

Battle of Trafalgar Type of 2005
Souvenir Sheets
Designs: Nos. 1027, 1028a, Admiral Nelson mortally wounded.

2005, Oct. 21   Litho.   *Perf. 13¼*
1027 A224 £1 multi   4.00 4.00
1028   Sheet, #1028a, Isle of Man #1127a   8.00 8.00
  a. A224 £1 multi, 47x30mm   4.00 4.00

No. 1028 has a Gibraltar Post emblem in sheet margin. See Isle of Man No. 1127.

Christmas
A231

Various angels: 7p, 28p, 40p, 47p, 53p.

2005, Oct. 21   *Perf. 13¼x13*
1029-1033 A231   Set of 5   8.00 8.00
1033a   Souvenir sheet, #1029-1033 8.25 8.25

Flowers Type of 2004

Designs: 3p, Gibraltar restharrow. 15p, Paper-white narcissus. 53p, Gibraltar campion. £1.60, Sea daffodil.

2006, Jan. 31   Litho.   *Perf. 13¼*
1033B A221   3p multi   .20   .20
1034   A221   15p multi   .55   .55
1035   A221   53p multi   1.90 1.90
1036   A221   £1.60 multi   5.75 5.75
     Nos. 1033B-1036 (4)   8.40 8.40

Worldwide Fund for Nature (WWF)
A232

Various depictions of Giant devil ray.

2006, Feb. 20   *Perf. 13x13¼*
1037   Strip of 4   10.00 10.00
  a. A232 38p multi   1.50 1.50
  b. A232 40p multi   1.75 1.75
  c. A232 47p multi   2.00 2.00
  d. A232 £1 multi   4.00 4.00

Queen Elizabeth II, 80th Birthday
A233

Various photographs.

2006, Mar. 31   *Perf. 14¾x14*
1038   Block of 4   10.00 10.00
  a. A233 38p multi   1.50 1.50
  b. A233 40p multi   1.75 1.75
  c. A233 47p multi   2.00 2.00
  d. A233 £1 multi   4.00 4.00
  e. Souvenir sheet, #1038b, 1038c   3.25 3.25
  f. Souvenir sheet, #1038a, 1038d   4.75 4.75

Miniature Sheet

2006 World Cup Soccer Championships, Germany — A234

No. 1039 — Children with faces painted as flags of World Cup champions: a, Uruguay. b, Italy. c, Germany. d, Brazil. e, England. f, Argentina. g, France.

2006, May 4   *Perf. 15*
1039 A234   Sheet of 7   11.00 11.00
  a.-g. 38p Any single   1.50 1.50

Europa
A235

Children: No. 1040, 47p, Holding books and notebook paper. No. 1041, 47p, Playing musical instruments. No. 1042, 47p, Building birdhouse. No. 1043, 47p, Playing soccer.

2006, June 30   *Perf. 13x13¼*
1040-1043 A235   Set of 4   7.00 7.00

Gibraltar Packet Agency, Bicent: A236

Ships: 8p, Cornwallis. 40p, Meteor. 42p, Carteret. 68p, Prince Regent.

Perf. 14¾x14¼
2006, Sept. 15   Litho.
1044-1047 A236   Set of 4   7.50 7.50

Airmail Service, 75th Anniv.
A237

Airplanes: 8p, Saro A21 Windhover. 40p, Vickers Vanguard. 49p, Vickers Viscount. £1.60, Boeing 737.

2006, Sept. 15
1048-1051 A237   Set of 4   12.00 12.00

Cruise Ships
A238

Designs: 40p, Coral. 42p, Legend of the Seas. 66p, Saga Ruby. 78p, Costa Concordia.

2006, Sept. 15   *Perf. 13*
1052-1055 A238   Set of 4   10.50 10.50
1055a   Souvenir sheet, #1052-1055   12.50 12.50

See Nos. 1076-1079, 1153-1156.

Christopher Columbus (1451-1506), Explorer — A239

Designs: 40p, Navigational equipment. 42p, Columbus on ship. 66p, Santa Maria. 78p, Columbus and Indian. £1.60, Nina, Pinta and Santa Maria

2006, Nov. 1   Litho.   *Perf. 13x13¼*
1056-1059 A239   Set of 4   10.00 10.00
Souvenir Sheet
Perf. 13¼
1060 A239 £1.60 multi   7.50 7.50

No. 1060 contains one 48x48mm stamp.

Christmas
A240

Various depictions of Santa Claus with panel colors of: 8p, Red brown. 40p, Prussian blue. 42p, Olive bister. 49p, Green. 55p, Gray blue.

2006, Nov. 1   **Perf. 13¼x13**
1061-1065 A240   Set of 5   9.00 9.00
1065a   Souvenir sheet, #1061-1065, perf. 13¼x12½   9.00 9.00

Miniature Sheet

Treaty of Rome, 50th Anniv. — A241

No. 1066 — European Union flag and flag of: a, Belgium. b, Germany. c, France. d, Italy. e, Luxembourg. f, Netherlands.

Perf. 14½x14¼
2007, Feb. 28   **Litho.**
1066 A241 40p Sheet of 6, #a-f   9.75 9.75

Wedding of Queen Elizabeth II and Prince Philip, 60th Anniv. — A242

Designs: 40p, Royal engagement, 1947. 42p, Royal wedding, 1947. 66p, Silver anniversary, 1972. 78p, Ruby anniversary, 1987. £1.60, Wedding party.

2007, Feb. 28   **Perf. 13½**
1067-1070 A242   Set of 4   10.50 10.50
Souvenir Sheet
Perf. 13½x13
1071 A242 £1.60 multi   10.00 10.00
No. 1071 contains one 85x85mm diamond-shaped stamp.

Princess Diana (1961-97)
A243

Various photographs: 8p, 40p, 42p, £1.60.

2007, Mar. 31   **Perf. 13½**
1072-1075 A243   Set of 4   10.00 10.00
1075a   Souvenir sheet, #1072-1075   10.00 10.00

Cruise Ships Type of 2006
Designs: 40p, Oriana. 42p, Oceana. 66p, Queen Elizabeth 2.78p, Queen Mary 2.

2007, May 15   **Litho.**   **Perf. 14¾x14**
1076-1079 A238   Set of 4   9.75 9.75
1079a   Souvenir sheet, #1076-1079   9.75 9.75

Europa — A244

Designs: 8p, Scout from 1908. 40p, Scout from 1950s, 42p, Sea Scout from 1980s. £1, Scout from 2007.

2007, June 30   **Litho.**   **Perf. 13**
1080-1083 A244   Set of 4   7.75 7.75

Gibraltar Postal Anniversaries — A245

Designs: 8p, Last-day-of-validity postcard from Fez, Morocco (cessation of Gibraltar's responsibility for the British postal service in Morocco in 1907). 40p, Stampless cover with last Gibraltar datestamp of the Packet Agency (creation of Gibraltar Post Office in 1857). 42p, Cover franked with stamps of Great Britain (sale of British stamps in Gibraltar in 1857). £1, Cover to London from Morocco via Gibraltar (placement of British postal service in Morocco under control of Gibraltar in 1857).

2007, Sept. 26   **Perf. 14¾x14**
1084-1087 A245   Set of 4   10.00 10.00

Stork Carrying Baby, Baby Bottle, Pacifier, Rubber Duck — A246

Diamond Ring and Heart — A247

Sheep, Lion, Dog at Party — A248

Lamb, Dolphins, Rock of Gibraltar — A249

Shell, Crab and Heart — A250

Illustrations reduced.

2007, Sept. 26   **Perf. 12½x13**
1088	A246	G multi + label	.35	.35
1089	A247	G multi + label	.35	.35
1090	A248	G multi + label	.35	.35
1091	A249	G multi + label	.35	.35
1092	A250	G multi + label	.35	.35
1093	A246	E multi + label	1.75	1.75
1094	A247	E multi + label	1.75	1.75
1095	A248	E multi + label	1.75	1.75
1096	A249	E multi + label	1.75	1.75
1097	A250	E multi + label	1.75	1.75
	Nos. 1088-1097 (10)		10.50	10.50

On day of issue Nos. 1088-1092 each sold for 8p, and Nos. 1093-1097 each sold for 42p. Labels shown with each stamp are the generic labels for that stamp type. Labels could be personalized for an additional fee.

Prehistoric Wildlife of Gibraltar
A251

Designs: 8p, Bears and dolphins. 40p, Eagle owl. 42p, Great auk and eagle. 55p, Red deer and bear. 78p, Wolf and vulture eating horse. £2, Ibex.

2007, Sept. 26   **Perf. 13**
1098-1102 A251   Set of 5   9.25 9.25
1098a   Booklet pane of 1   .35 —
1099a   Booklet pane of 1   1.60 —
1100a   Booklet pane of 1   1.75 —
1101a   Booklet pane of 1   2.25 —
1102a   Booklet pane of 1   3.00 —
   Complete booklet, #1098a-1103a, 1103b   18.00
Souvenir Sheet
1103 A251 £2 multi   8.25 8.25
a.   Booklet pane of 1   8.25
b.   Booklet pane of 6, #1098-1102   9.00 —

No. 1103a has text in margin not found on the margin of No. 1103.

Views of Gibraltar — A252

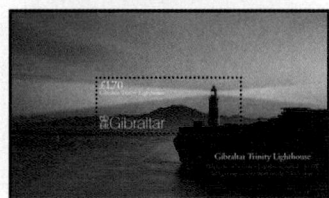

Trinity Lighthouse — A253

Various views: 40p, 42p, 55p, 78p.

2007, Nov. 2   **Litho.**   **Perf. 13¼**
1104-1107 A252   Set of 4   9.00 9.00
Souvenir Sheet
Perf. 13¼x13
1108 A253 £1.70 multi   7.25 7.25

Christmas
A254

Porcelain Nativity figurines: No. 1109, 8p, Joseph. No. 1110, 8p, Baby Jesus. 40p, Mary. 42p, King Melchior. 49p, King Balthasar. 55p, King Gaspar.

2007, Nov. 2   **Perf. 13¼x13**
1109-1114 A254   Set of 6   8.50 8.50
1114a   Miniature sheet, #1109-1114   8.50 8.50
Perf. 12½x13
Size: 32x32mm
1114B A254   8p multi + label   .35 .35
1114C A254   40p multi + label   1.75 1.75

Nos. 1114B and 1114C were available with generic labels. Labels could be personalized for an additional fee.

Birds — A255

Designs: 1p, Woodchat shrike. 2p, Balearic shearwater. 5p, Eagle owl. G, European bee-eater. 10p, Razorbill. S, Egyptian vulture. UK, Blue rock thrush. E, Hoopoe. U, Bonelli's eagle. 50p, Greater flamingo. 55p, Mediterranean shag. £1, Honey buzzard. £5, Lesser kestrel.

2008, Feb. 15   **Litho.**   **Perf. 13x12½**
1115	A255	1p multi	.20	.20
1116	A255	2p multi	.20	.20
1117	A255	5p multi	.20	.20
1118	A255	G multi	.35	.35
1119	A255	10p multi	.40	.40
1120	A255	S multi	1.25	1.25
1121	A255	UK multi	1.60	1.60
1122	A255	E multi	1.75	1.75
1123	A255	U multi	1.90	1.90
1124	A255	50p multi	2.00	2.00
1125	A255	55p multi	2.25	2.25

Size: 32x45mm
Perf. 13x13¼
1126	A255	£1 multi	4.00	4.00
1127	A255	£5 multi	20.00	20.00
	Nos. 1115-1127 (13)		36.10	36.10

On day of issue Nos. 1118, 1120, 1121, 1122 and 1123 sold for 8p, 30p, 40p, 42p and 49p, respectively. See Nos. 1202-1204, 1244-1246.

Admiral Horatio Nelson (1758-1805)
A256

Designs: No. 1128, 40p, HMS Agamemnon. No. 1129, 40p, HMS La Minerve. No. 1130, 42p, HMS Captain. No. 1131, 42p, HMS Vanguard. No. 1132, 49p, HMS Amphion. No. 1133, 49p, HMS Victory.
£2, Nelson's Birthplace, Burnham Thorpe, England, horiz.

Perf. 14¼x14¾
2008, Mar. 15   **Litho.**
1128-1133 A256   Set of 6   10.50 10.50
Souvenir Sheet
Perf. 14¾x14¼
1134 A256 £2 multi   8.00 8.00

Royal Air Force, 90th Anniv. — A257

Rock of Gibraltar and airplanes: No. 1135, 40p, Short 184, Saro London. No. 1136, 40p, Spitfire IV, Hurricane IIc. No. 1137, 42p, Beaufighter II, Lancaster TS III. No. 1138, 42p, Hunter Mk. 6, Shackleton MR2. No. 1139, 49p, Vulcan, Mosquito. No. 1140, 49p, Tornado GR4, Jaguar GR3.
£2, Felixstowe F3.

2008, Mar. 15   Perf. 14¼x14¾
1135-1140 A257   Set of 6   10.50 10.50
Souvenir Sheet
1141 A257   £2 multi   8.00 8.00

Europa — A258

Famous letter writers: 10p, Sir Winston Churchill. 42p, Admiral Horatio Nelson. 44p, Pres. John F. Kennedy. £1, Mohandas K. Gandhi.

2008, June 1   Litho.   Perf. 14x14¾
1142-1145 A258   Set of 4   7.75 7.75

New Seven Wonders of the World — A259

Designs: No. 1146, 8p, Roman Colosseum. No. 1147, 8p, Christ the Redeemer Statue, Rio de Janeiro. No. 1148, 38p, Great Wall of China. No. 1149, 38p, Petra, Jordan. No. 1150, 40p, Chichen Itza Pyramid, Mexico. No. 1151, 40p, Machu Picchu, Peru. 66p, Taj Mahal, India.

2008, June 1
1146-1152   Set of 7   9.50 9.50

Cruise Ships Type of 2006

Designs: 40p, Century. 42p, Grand Princess. 66p, Queen Victoria. 78p, Costa Mediterranea.

2008, Sept. 15   Litho.   Perf. 13x13¼
1153-1156 A238   Set of 4   8.00 8.00
1156a   Souvenir sheet, #1153-
               1156   8.00 8.00

Miniature Sheet

National Aeronautics and Space Administration, 50th Anniv. — A260

No. 1157: a, Liftoff of Apollo 11. b, Earthrise from Moon. c, Lunar Module leaving Moon. d, US flag on Moon.

2008, Sept. 15   Perf. 13¼
1157 A260   Sheet of 4   9.75 9.75
  a.   10p multi   .35   .35
  b.   17p multi   .60   .60
  c.   42p multi   1.50 1.50
  d.   £2 multi   7.25 7.25

Royal Gibraltar Regiment — A261

Designs: No. 1158, 10p, Gibraltar Volunteer Corps in World War I. No. 1159, 10p, Gibraltar Defense Force in World War II. No. 1160, 10p, National Service recruits at Buena Vista Barracks. No. 1161, 42p, Soldiers and large guns, Thomson's Battery of Gibraltar Regiment, 1958-91. No. 1162, 42p, Soldier from Infantry Company of Gibraltar Regiment, 1958-99. No. 1163, 44p, Soldier from Air Defense Troop of Gibraltar Regiment, 1958-91. No. 1164, 44p, Royal Gibraltar Regiment soldier guarding the rock. No. 1165, 51p, Royal Gibraltar Regiment soldier training African Peacekeepers. No. 1166, 51p, Royal Gibraltar Regiment soldier serving in operations in Iraq. £2, Royal Gibraltar Regiment soldier serving in operations in Afghanistan.

2008, Nov. 11   Litho.   Perf. 15x14
1158-1167 A261   Set of 10   15.00 15.00

Christmas A262

Songs: 10p, When Santa Got Stuck in a Chimney. 42p, Rudolph, the Red-nosed Reindeer. 44p, Oh, Christmas Tree. 51p, Away in a Manger. 59p, Jingle Bells.

2008, Nov. 11   Perf. 12½
1168-1172 A262   Set of 5   6.25 6.25

King Henry VIII, 500th Anniv. of Accession to the Throne — A263

Designs: No. 1173, 10p, Catherine of Aragon (first wife). No. 1174, 10p, Anne Boleyn (second wife). No. 1175, 42p, Jane Seymour (third wife). No. 1176, 42p, Anne of Cleves (fourth wife). No. 1177, 44p, Catherine Howard (fifth wife). No. 1178, 44p, Catherine Parr (sixth wife). No. 1179, 51p, Henry VIII. No. 1180, 51p, The Mary Rose.
£2, King Henry VIII at Hampton Court.

2009, Jan. 10   Perf. 12½
1173-1180 A263   Set of 8   8.25 8.25
Souvenir Sheet
1181 A263   £2 multi   5.50 5.50

Gibraltar Shrine to Our Lady of Europe, 700th Anniv. — A264

2009, Feb. 10   Perf. 14x14¾
1182 A264   61p multi   1.75 1.75
Printed in sheets of 4. See Vatican City No. 1402.

Naval Aviation, Cent. — A265

Designs: No. 1183, 42p, Short 184. No. 1184, 42p, Short S27. No. 1185, 42p, SS type non-rigid airship. No. 1186, 42p, Caudron G-III. No. 1187, 42p, Avro 504. No. 1188, 42p, Morane-Saulnier L and Zeppelin LZ-37.
£2, Short 184 and ships.

2009, Mar. 15
1183-1188 A265   Set of 6   7.50 7.50
Souvenir Sheet
1189 A265   £2 multi   6.00 6.00

Grandchildren of Queen Elizabeth II — A266

Designs: No. 1190, 42p, Prince William of Wales. No. 1191, 42p, Prince Henry of Wales. No. 1192, 42p, Princess Beatrice of York. No. 1193, 42p, Princess Eugenie of York. No. 1194, 42p, Viscount Severn. No. 1195, 42p, Lady Louise Windsor. No. 1196, 42p, Peter Phillips. No. 1197, 42p, Zara Phillips.

2009, May 1   Perf. 12½
1190-1197 A266   Set of 8   10.00 10.00

Europa — A267

Designs: 10p, Aristotle (384-322 B.C.), philosopher. 42p, Galileo Galilei (1564-1642), astronomer and physicist. 44p, Nicolaus Copernicus (1473-1543), astronomer. £1.50, Sir Isaac Newton (1642-1727), physicist and mathematician.

2009, June 1   Perf. 13x12½
1198-1201 A267   Set of 4   8.00 8.00
  Intl. Year of Astronomy.

Birds Type of 2008

Designs: 10p, Black stork. £2, Northern gannet. £3, Osprey.

2009, Sept. 16   Litho.   Perf. 13
1202 A255   10p multi   .35   .35
          Size: 32x45mm
             Perf. 13x13¼
1203 A255   £2 multi   6.50 6.50
1204 A255   £3 multi   9.50 9.50
          Nos. 1202-1204 (3)   16.35 16.35

Old Views of Gibraltar — A268

Designs: No. 1205, 10p, Road to the frontier. No. 1206, 42p, Catalan Bay village. No. 1207, 44p, Rock of Gibraltar. 51p, Moorish Castle. 59p, South Barracks.
No. 1210: a, 10p, Garrison Library. b, 42p, Piazza. c, 44p, Piazza Casemates. d, £1, Main Street.

2009, Sept. 16   Perf. 14x14¾
1205-1209 A268   Set of 5   6.75 6.75
Souvenir Sheet
1210 A268   Sheet of 4, #a-d   6.25 6.25

Charles Darwin (1809-82), Naturalist — A269

Darwin and: 10p, HMS Beagle, bird and books. 42p, Books and pages with scientific drawings. 44p, Books and pages with drawings of horse and bone. £2, Book, page with drawing of bird, notebook.
£2.42, Darwin, book and house.

2009, Nov. 12   Perf. 14x14¾
1211-1214 A269   Set of 4   10.00 10.00
Souvenir Sheet
1215 A269   £2.42 multi   8.00 8.00

Christmas A270

Christmas tree ornaments: 10p, Santa Claus. 42p, Angel. 44p, Teddy bear. 51p, Christmas tree. £2, Bells.

2009, Nov. 12   Perf. 13½x13
1216-1220 A270   Set of 5   11.50 11.50

Miniature Sheet

100-Ton Guns of Gibraltar and Malta — A271

No. 1221 — 100-ton gun from: a, Napier of Magdala Battery, Gibraltar, 1880. b, Napier of Magdala Battery, 2010. c, Fort Rinella, Malta, 2010. d, Fort Rinella, 1882.

2010, Feb. 19   Litho.   Perf. 13¾
1221 A271   75p Sheet of 4, #a-d 9.25 9.25
  See Malta No. 1400.

Battle of Britain, 70th Anniv. A272

Airplanes: No. 1222, 50p, Boulton Paul Defiant. No. 1223, 50p, Bristol Blenheim. No. 1224, 50p, Gloster Gladiator. No. 1225, 50p, Hawker Hurricane. No. 1226, 50p, Miles Master. No. 1227, 50p, Supermarine Spitfire. £2, Douglas Bader, British ace pilot, vert.

2010, Feb. 21   Perf. 14
1222-1227 A272   Set of 6   9.25 9.25
Souvenir Sheet
1228 A272   £2 multi   6.25 6.25

Accession to Throne of King George V, Cent. A273

King George V: 10p, As child, with family. 42p, Examining stamp collection. 44p, On horse, reviewing troops. £2, On deck of gunship.

2010, Mar. 26   Perf. 13
1229-1232 A273   Set of 4   9.00 9.00

Europa
A274

Scenes from children's stories by Roald Dahl: 10p, Charlie and the Chocolate Factory. 42p, Matilda. 44p, The Twits. £1.50, The BFG.

2010, May 4   Litho.   Perf. 13
1233-1236 A274   Set of 4   7.50 7.50

Miniature Sheet

Sites in San Marino and Gibraltar — A275

No. 1237: a, Second Tower, San Marino. b, Moorish Castle, Gibraltar. c, Mt. Titano, San Marino. d, Rock of Gibraltar.

2010, June 30   Perf. 14¾x14
1237 A275 75p Sheet of 4, #a-d   9.25 9.25
See San Marino No. 1822.

Souvenir Sheet

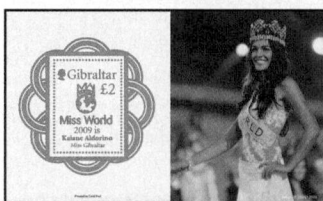

Emblem of Miss World Pageant and Name of 2009 Winner — A276

Litho. With Foil Application
2010, June 30   Perf. 14x14¾
1238 A276 £2 gold & black   6.25 6.25

Aviation Centenaries — A277

Designs: No. 1239, 10p, Airplane of Baroness Raymonde de Laroche, first woman to obtain pilot's license. No. 1240, 42p, LZ-7, first Zeppelin flight with fare-paying customers. No. 1241, 49p, Antoinette VII, airplane of Hubert Latham, setting altitude record of 4,541 feet. No. 1242, £2, Clément-Bayard No. 2, first airship to cross the English Channel.

No. 1243 — Seaplanes: a, 10p, Le Canard, seaplane of Henri Fabre, first seaplane to take off from water. b, 42p, Supermarine S.6B, first aircraft to surpass 400 miles per hour in speed. c, 49p, Short Sunderland of 204th Squadron. d, £2, Saunders-ROE Princess.

2010, Aug. 20   Litho.   Perf. 14¾x14
1239-1242 A277   Set of 4   9.50 9.50
Souvenir Sheet
1243 A277 Sheet of 4, #a-d   9.50 9.50

Birds Type of 2008

Designs: 59p, Barbary partridge. 76p, Ortolan bunting. £2, Pallid swift.

2010, Oct. 20   Litho.   Perf. 13
1244 A255 59p multi   1.90 1.90
1245 A255 76p multi   2.50 2.50
1246 A255 £2 multi   6.50 6.50
   Nos. 1244-1246 (3)   10.90 10.90

Girl Guides, Cent. A278

Uniform of: 10p, Rainbow. 42p, Brownie. 44p, Guide. £2, Senior.

2010, Oct. 20   Perf. 13½
1247-1250 A278   Set of 4   9.75 9.75

Souvenir Sheet

2010 Commonwealth Games, Delhi — A279

2010, Oct. 20   Perf. 14¼x14¾
1251 A279 £2 multi   6.50 6.50

Souvenir Sheet

Dicoese of Gibraltar, Cent. — A280

2010, Nov. 16   Litho.   Perf. 15x14
1252 A280 £2 multi   6.50 6.50

Christmas A281

Designs: 10p, Christmas crackers, gifts, ornaments, stocking, candle, bell and candy cane. 42p, Stockings hung on mantle. 44p, Santa Claus and reindeer in flight. 51p, Three snowmen.

2010, Nov. 26   Perf. 13x13¼
1253-1256 A281   Set of 4   4.75 4.75

Royal British Legion A282

British troops in action in: No. 1257, 50p, World War I. No. 1258, 50p, World War II. No. 1259, 50p, Northern Ireland. No. 1260, 50p, The Falkland Islands. No. 1261, 50p, The Gulf War. No. 1262, 50p, The Balkans. No. 1263, 50p, Afghanistan. No. 1264, 50p, Iraq. £2, Statue, poppies, words from poem, "In Flanders Fields."

2011, Jan. 14   Litho.   Perf. 13
1257-1264 A282   Set of 8   13.00 13.00
Souvenir Sheet
Perf. 13x13½
1265 A282 £2 multi   6.50 6.50
   Nos. 1257-1264 each were printed in sheets of 6.

Souvenir Sheet

Engagement of Prince William and Catherine Middleton — A283

2011, Jan. 14   Perf. 14¾x14¼
1266 A283 £2 multi   6.50 6.50

POSTAGE DUE STAMPS

Catalogue values for unused stamps in this section are for Never Hinged items.

D3

D4

D1   D2

Perf. 14
1956, Dec. 1   Wmk. 4   Typo.
Chalky Paper
J1 D1 1p green   1.75 2.00
J2 D1 2p brown   2.60 3.25
J3 D1 4p ultramarine   3.25 3.75
   Nos. J1-J3 (3)   7.60 9.00

"p" instead of "d"
Perf. 17½x18
1971, Feb. 15   Typo.   Wmk. 314
Chalky Paper
J4 D1 ½p green   .50 .60
J5 D1 1p dark brown   .50 .55
J6 D1 2p dark blue   .60 .60
   Nos. J4-J6 (3)   1.60 1.75

Perf. 14x13½
1976, Oct. 13   Litho.   Wmk. 373
J7   D2 1p orange   .20 .20
J8   D2 3p bright ultra   .20 .20
J9   D2 5p vermilion   .20 .35
J10 D2 7p bright red lilac .25 .40
J11 D2 10p gray   .45 .75
J12 D2 20p green   .80 1.00
   Nos. J7-J12 (6)   2.10 2.90

1984, July 2   Perf. 14½x14
J13 D3 1p black   .20 .20
J14 D3 3p red   .20 .20
J15 D3 5p blue   .20 .20
J16 D3 10p sky blue   .40 .40
J17 D3 25p lilac   1.25 1.25
J18 D3 50p orange   2.25 2.25
J19 D3 £1 green   4.50 4.50
   Nos. J13-J19 (7)   9.00 9.00

1996, Sept. 30   Litho.   Perf. 14½x14
Landmarks: 1p, Water Port Gates. 10p, HM Dockyard. 25p, Military Hospital. 50p, Governor's Cottage. £1, Laguna. £2, Catalan Bay.

J20 D4 1p multicolored   .20 .20
J21 D4 10p multicolored   .35 .35
J22 D4 25p multicolored   .80 .80
J23 D4 50p multicolored 1.60 1.60
J24 D4 £1 multicolored   3.25 3.25
J25 D4 £2 multicolored   7.00 7.00
   Nos. J20-J25 (6)   13.20 13.20

Finches — D5

Designs: 5p, Greenfinch. 10p, Serin. 20p, Siskin. 50p, Linnet. £1, Chaffinch. £2, Goldfinch.

Perf. 13x13¼
2002, June 6   Litho.   Unwmk.
J26-J31 D5 Set of 6   12.50 12.50

WAR TAX STAMP

No. 66 Overprinted

1918, Apr.   Wmk. 3   Perf. 14
MR1 A14 ½p green   1.75 2.40
   a. Double overprint   900.00

GILBERT & ELLICE ISLANDS

'gil-bərt ən,d, 'e-ləs 'i-lənds

LOCATION — Groups of islands in the Pacific Ocean northeast of Australia
GOVT. — British Crown Colony
AREA — 375 sq. mi.
POP. — 57,816 (est. 1973)
CAPITAL — Tarawa

The Gilbert group of which Butaritari, Tarawa and Tamana are the more important, is on the Equator. Ellice Islands, Phoenix Islands, Line Islands (Fanning, Washington and Christmas), and Ocean Island are included in the Colony. The islands were annexed by Great Britain in 1892 and formed into the Gilbert and Ellice Islands Colony in 1915 on request of the native governments.
The colony divided into the Gilbert Islands and Tuvalu, Jan. 1, 1976.

12 Pence = 1 Shilling
20 Shillings = 1 Pound
100 Cents = 1 Dollar (1966)

Catalogue values for unused stamps in this country are for Never Hinged items, beginning with Scott 52.

Stamps and Type of Fiji Overprinted in Black or Red

1911, Jan. 1   Wmk. 3   Perf. 14
Ordinary Paper

1	A22	½p green	7.50	50.00
2	A22	1p carmine	45.00	30.00
a.		Pair, one without overprint		
3	A22	2p gray	14.00	17.50
4	A22	2½p ultramarine	15.00	40.00

Chalky Paper

5	A22	5p violet & ol grn	60.00	90.00
6	A22	6p violet	25.00	50.00
7	A22	1sh black, green	25.00	65.00
		Nos. 1-7 (7)	191.50	342.50

Nos. 1-7 are known with a forged Ocean Island postmark dated "JY 15 11."

Pandanus — A2

1911, Mar.   Engr.
Ordinary Paper

8	A2	½p green	5.00	19.00
9	A2	1p carmine	2.75	8.00
10	A2	2p gray	1.50	7.50
11	A2	2½p ultramarine	5.00	12.50
		Nos. 8-11 (4)	14.25	47.00

King George V — A3

For description of Dies I and II, see front section of the Catalogue.

Die I

1912-24   Typo.

14	A3	½p deep green	.60	6.00
15	A3	1p carmine	2.50	9.00
a.		1p scarlet ('15)	4.25	15.00
16	A3	2p gray ('16)	16.00	25.00
17	A3	2½p ultra ('16)	2.00	6.50

Chalky Paper

18	A3	3p vio, yel ('19)	2.75	8.50
19	A3	4p blk & red, yel	.90	6.50
20	A3	5p vio & ol grn	2.00	6.25
21	A3	6p vio & red vio	1.50	6.75
22	A3	1sh black, green	1.50	5.25
23	A3	2sh vio & ultra, bl	15.00	30.00
24	A3	2sh6p blk & red, bl	18.00	25.00
25	A3	5sh grn & red, yel	37.50	65.00

Die II

26	A3	£1 vio & blk, red ('24)	600.00	1,500.
		Nos. 14-26 (13)	700.25	1,699.

Die II

1921-27   Ordinary Paper   Wmk. 4

27	A3	½p green	3.00	3.00
28	A3	1p deep vio ('27)	5.00	4.50
29	A3	1½p scarlet ('24)	5.00	2.50
30	A3	2p gray	8.00	35.00

Chalky Paper

31	A3	10sh green & red, emer ('24)	160.00	375.00
		Nos. 27-31 (5)	181.00	420.00

Common Design Types pictured following the introduction.

Silver Jubilee Issue
Common Design Type

1935, May 6   Engr.   Perf. 11x12

33	CD301	1p black & ultra	2.25	12.00
34	CD301	1½p car & blue	1.75	4.00
35	CD301	3p ultra & brn	5.50	17.50
36	CD301	1sh brn vio & indigo	30.00	20.00
		Nos. 33-36 (4)	39.50	53.50
		Set, never hinged	65.00	

Coronation Issue
Common Design Type

1937, May 12   Perf. 13½x14

37	CD302	1p dark purple	.20	.65
38	CD302	1½p carmine	.25	.65
39	CD302	3p bright ultra	.45	.70
		Nos. 37-39 (3)	.90	2.00
		Set, never hinged	1.25	

Great Frigate Bird — A4

Pandanus — A5

Designs: 1½p, Canoe crossing reef. 2p, Canoe and boat house. 2½p, Islander's house. 3p, Seascape. 5p, Ellice Islands canoe. 6p, Coconut trees. 1sh, Phosphate loading jetty, Ocean Island. 2sh, Cutter "Nimanoa." 2sh6p, Gilbert Islands canoe. 5sh, Coat of arms of colony.

Perf. 11½x11 (Nos. 40, 43, 50), 12½ (Type A5), 13½ (Nos. 42, 44, 45, 48)

1939, Jan. 14   Engr.   Wmk. 4

40	A4	½p dk grn & sl bl	.40	.90
41	A5	1p dk vio & brt bl	.25	1.25
42	A4	1½p car & black	.25	.90
43	A4	2p black & brn	.40	.95
44	A4	2½p dp olive & blk	.30	.70
45	A4	3p ultra & black	.30	.90
a.		Perf. 12 ('55)	.40	2.25
46	A5	5p dk brn & dp ultra	3.50	1.50
47	A4	6p dl vio & olive	.45	.60
48	A4	1sh gray bl & blk	6.00	3.75
b.		Perf. 12 ('51)	2.00	16.00
49	A5	2sh red org & ultra	7.50	10.00
50	A4	2sh6p brt bl grn & bl	7.50	11.00
51	A5	5sh dp blue & red	9.00	14.00
		Nos. 40-51 (12)	35.85	46.45
		Set, never hinged	80.00	

Catalogue values for unused stamps in this section, from this point to the end of the section, are for Never Hinged items.

Peace Issue
Common Design Type

1946, Dec. 16   Perf. 13½x14

52	CD303	1p deep magenta	.20	.20
53	CD303	3p deep blue	.25	.25

Silver Wedding Issue
Common Design Types

1949, Aug. 29   Photo.   Perf. 14x14½

54	CD304	1p violet	.20	.20

Engraved; Name Typographed   Perf. 11½x11

55	CD305	£1 red	15.00	22.50

UPU Issue
Common Design Types

Engr.; Name Typo. on 2p, 3p

1949, Oct. 1   Perf. 13½, 11x11½

56	CD306	1p rose violet	.75	1.25
57	CD307	2p gray black	2.75	2.75
58	CD308	3p indigo	.80	2.75
59	CD309	1sh blue	.80	2.00
		Nos. 56-59 (4)	5.10	8.75

Coronation Issue
Common Design Type

1953, June 2   Engr.   Perf. 13½x13

60	CD312	2p gray & black	1.00	2.25

Types of 1939-42 with Portrait of Queen Elizabeth II, and

Canoe Crossing Reef — A6

Perf. 11½x11 (Nos. 61, 63, 70), 12½ (Type A5), 12 (Nos. 64-65, 68, 72)

1956, Aug. 1

61	A4	½p brt ultra & blk	.65	1.25
62	A5	1p violet & olive	.60	1.25
63	A4	2p dull pur & brt green	.90	2.50
64	A4	2½p green & black	.50	.60
65	A4	3p dk car & black	.50	.60
66	A5	5p red orange & brt ultra	8.50	2.50
67	A5	6p dk gray & red brown	.85	2.75
68	A4	1sh ol green & blk	3.00	.60
69	A5	2sh dk brown & brt ultra	6.00	4.00
70	A4	2sh6p dp ultra & rose red	9.00	4.50
71	A5	5sh green & blue	10.00	6.00
72	A6	10sh turq blue & blk	27.50	12.00
		Nos. 61-72 (12)	68.00	38.55

See Nos. 84-85.

Loading Phosphate on Freighter A7

2½p, Original lump of phosphate. 1sh, Loading phosphate on truck, Ocean Island.

Wmk. 314

1960, May 1   Photo.   Perf. 12

73	A7	2p rose lilac & green	.80	.85
74	A7	2½p olive & black	.80	.85
75	A7	1sh grnsh blue & blk	.80	.85
		Nos. 73-75 (3)	2.40	2.55

60th anniversary of the discovery of phosphate deposits at Ocean Island.

Freedom from Hunger Issue
Common Design Type

1963, June 4   Perf. 14x14½

76	CD314	10p ultramarine	1.00	.40

Red Cross Centenary Issue
Common Design Type

1963, Sept. 2   Litho.   Perf. 13

77	CD315	2p black & red	.75	.75
78	CD315	10p ultra & red	1.50	2.50

Plane and Fiji-Ellice-Gilbert Route — A8

Designs: 1sh, Eastern reef heron in flight, horiz. 3sh7p, Plane and Tarawa sailboat.

1964, July 20   Perf. 11½x11, 11x11½

79	A8	3p lt blue, bl & blk	.75	.35
80	A8	1sh dk blue, bl & blk	.90	.35
81	A8	3sh7p lt green, grn & blk	1.50	1.50
		Nos. 79-81 (3)	3.15	2.20

Inauguration of air service between Fiji and Gilbert and Ellice Islands.

Queen Types of 1956
Perf. 11½x11, 12½

1964-65   Engr.   Wmk. 314

84	A4	2p dull pur & brt green	1.10	1.60
85	A5	6p dk gray & red brown	1.60	1.60

Issue dates: 2p, Oct. 30. 6p, Apr. 1965.

ITU Issue
Common Design Type

1965, June 4   Litho.   Perf. 11x11½

87	CD317	3p dp org & turq blue	.20	.20
88	CD317	2sh6p grnsh bl & red lilac	.80	.50

Village Elder Blowing Conch and Meeting House (Maneaba) — A9

Designs: 1p, Ellice Islanders torch fishing. 2p, Gilbertese girl weaving frangipani garland. 3p, Gilbertese woman dancing The Ruoia. 4p, Gilbertese man dancing. 5p, Gilbertese woman drawing water. 6p, Ellice kosu dance. 7p, Fatele taua dance, Ellice men. 1sh, Gilbertese woman harvesting taro roots (babai). 1sh6p, Ellice man and woman dancing fatele toka. 2sh, Ellice Islanders pounding taro roots. 3sh7p, Gilbertese sitting dance, ruoia, horiz. 5sh, Gilbertese boys playing stick game, horiz. 10sh, Ellice men beating boxdrum, horiz. £1, Coat of arms, horiz.

Perf. 12x11, 11x12

1965, Aug. 16   Litho.   Wmk. 314

89	A9	½p blue grn & multi	.20	.20
90	A9	1p vio bl & multi	.20	.20
91	A9	2p lt olive & multi	.20	.20
92	A9	3p red & multi	.20	.20
93	A9	4p purple & multi	.20	.20
94	A9	5p car rose & multi	.25	.20
95	A9	6p multicolored	.25	.20
96	A9	7p brown & multi	.40	.20
97	A9	1sh bl vio & multi	.70	.20
98	A9	1sh6p yel & multi	1.40	1.00
99	A9	2sh multicolored	1.40	1.25
100	A9	3sh7p ultra & multi	2.50	.70
101	A9	5sh multicolored	2.50	.90
102	A9	10sh green & multi	3.25	1.40
103	A9	£1 blue & multi	4.00	2.00
		Nos. 89-103 (15)	17.65	9.05

See #135-149. For surcharges see #110-124.

Intl. Cooperation Year Issue
Common Design Type

1965, Oct. 25   Litho.   Perf. 14½

104	CD318	2p blue grn & cl	.20	.20
105	CD318	3sh7p lt violet & grn	.80	.35

Churchill Memorial Issue
Common Design Type

1966, Jan. 24   Photo.   Perf. 14
Design in Black, Gold and Carmine Rose

106	CD319	½p brt blue	.20	.20
107	CD319	3p green	.35	.20
108	CD319	3sh brown	.55	.40
109	CD319	3sh7p violet	.60	.40
		Nos. 106-109 (4)	1.70	1.20

Nos. 89-103 Surcharged with New Value and Three Bars

Perf. 12x11, 11x12

1966, Feb. 14				**Litho.**
110	A9	1c on 1p multi	.20	.20
111	A9	2c on 2p multi	.20	.20
112	A9	3c on 3p multi	.20	.20
113	A9	4c on ½p multi	.20	.20
114	A9	5c on 6p multi	.20	.20
115	A9	6c on 4p multi	.20	.20
116	A9	8c on 5p multi	.20	.20
117	A9	10c on 1sh multi	.20	.20
118	A9	15c on 7p multi	.80	.80
119	A9	20c on 1sh6p multi	.60	.40
120	A9	25c on 2sh multi	.60	.35
121	A9	35c on 3sh7p multi	1.25	.45
122	A9	50c on 5sh multi	.75	.45
123	A9	$1 on 10sh multi	.75	.50
124	A9	$2 on £1 multi	1.75	3.00
		Nos. 110-124 (15)	8.10	7.10

World Cup Soccer Issue
Common Design Type

1966, July 1		**Litho.**		**Perf. 14**
125	CD321	3c multicolored	.20	.20
126	CD321	35c multicolored	.65	.35

WHO Headquarters Issue
Common Design Type

1966, Sept. 20		**Litho.**		**Perf. 14**
127	CD322	3c multicolored	.20	.20
128	CD322	12c multicolored	.55	.45

UNESCO Anniversary Issue
Common Design Type

1966, Dec. 1		**Litho.**		**Perf. 14**
129	CD323	5c "Education"	.50	.50
130	CD323	10c "Science"	.75	.50
131	CD323	20c "Culture"	1.25	.90
		Nos. 129-131 (3)	2.50	1.60

H.M.S. Royalist, 1892, and Union Jack A10

10c, Cutter & canoe at trading post. 35c, Family.

Perf. 14½x14

1967, Sept. 1		**Photo.**		**Wmk. 314**
132	A10	3c green, blue & red	.30	.35
133	A10	10c multicolored	.20	.20
134	A10	35c multicolored	.50	.45
		Nos. 132-134 (3)	1.00	1.00

75th anniv. as a British Protectorate.

Type of 1965

Perf. 12x11, 11x12

1968, Jan. 1		**Litho.**		**Wmk. 314**
135	A9	1c like 1p	.20	.20
136	A9	2c like 2p	.20	.20
137	A9	3c like 3p	.20	.20
138	A9	4c like ½p	.20	.20
139	A9	5c like 6p	.20	.20
140	A9	6c like 4p	.20	.20
141	A9	8c like 5p	.25	.20
142	A9	10c like 1sh	.25	.20
143	A9	15c like 7p	.50	.20
144	A9	20c like 1sh6p	.70	.20
145	A9	25c like 2sh	1.25	.20
146	A9	35c like 3sh7p	1.50	.20
147	A9	50c like 5sh	1.50	2.50
148	A9	$1 like 10sh	1.75	3.50
149	A9	$2 like £1	4.50	3.75
		Nos. 135-149 (15)	13.40	12.15

Map of Tarawa Atoll — A11

Designs: 10c, US Marines wading ashore at Betio. 15c, Battle scene on Betio. 35c, Raising US and British flags on Betio.

1968, Nov. 21		**Photo.**		**Perf. 14**
150	A11	3c multicolored	.20	.20
151	A11	10c multicolored	.20	.20
152	A11	15c multicolored	.35	.35
153	A11	35c multicolored	.45	.45
		Nos. 150-153 (4)	1.20	1.20

Battle of Tarawa against Japan, 25th anniv.

School Boy and Map of Abemama Atoll A12

Designs: 10c, Secondary school boy and girl on map of Tarawa, with rest of Gilbert and Ellice Islands. 35c, Student in cap and grown on main Fiji island (Viti Levu) and map of South Pacific Islands.

1969, June 2		**Litho.**		**Perf. 12½**
154	A12	3c dull org & multi	.20	.20
155	A12	10c black & multi	.20	.20
156	A12	35c dull grn & multi	.25	.35
		Nos. 154-156 (3)	.65	.75

1st anniv. of the University of the South Pacific in Fiji, and to show the progress of education in the area it serves.

Polynesian Madonna A13

1969, Oct. 20				**Perf. 11½**
157	A13	2c multicolored	.20	.20
158	A13	10c multicolored	.20	.20

Christmas.

Canceled to Order
The Philatelic Bureau of Gilbert and Ellice Islands began in 1970 to sell canceled sets of new issues. Values in the second ("used") column are for these canceled-to-order stamps.

Mouth-to-Mouth Resuscitation — A14

1970, Mar. 9		**Litho.**		**Perf. 14½**
159	A14	10c multi	.20	.20
160	A14	15c multi, diff.	.35	.40
161	A14	35c multi, diff.	.60	.85
		Nos. 159-161 (3)	1.15	1.45

Centenary of the British Red Cross.

Mother and Child Care A15

Designs: 10c, Woman physician and laboratory equipment. 15c, Chest X-ray and technician. 35c, Map of Gilbert and Ellice Islands and UN emblem.

Perf. 12½x13

1970, June 26		**Litho.**		**Wmk. 314**
162	A15	5c lilac & multi	.20	.20
163	A15	10c black, gray & red	.20	.20
164	A15	15c yellow & multi	.25	.25
165	A15	35c blue grn, bl & blk	.40	.40
		Nos. 162-165 (4)	1.05	1.05

25th anniv. of the United Nations.

Map of Onotoa, Beru, Tamana and Arorae Islands A16

Designs: 10c, Sailing ship "John Williams III," vert. 25c, Rev. Samuel James Whitmee, vert. 35c, Map of Islands and steamship "John Williams VII."

Perf. 14x14½, 14½x14

1970, Sept. 1		**Litho.**		**Wmk. 314**
166	A16	2c blue & multi	.20	.20
167	A16	10c brt green & black	.35	.20
168	A16	25c lt ultra & red brn	.25	.25
169	A16	35c ver, blk & lt gray	.75	.75
		Nos. 166-169 (4)	1.55	1.40

Centenary of the landing in the Southern Gilbert Islands by the first missionaries of the London Missionary Society.

Island Child with Halo on Pandanus Mat — A17

Christmas: 10c, Sanctuary of New Tarawa Cathedral. 35c, Three Gilbertese sailing canoes within Star of Bethlehem.

1970, Oct. 3				**Perf. 14½**
170	A17	2c ocher & multi	.20	.20
171	A17	10c ocher & multi	.20	.20
172	A17	35c pink & multi	.20	.20
		Nos. 170-172 (3)	.60	.60

Harvesting Copra — A18

Lagoon Fishing A19

3c, Women cleaning pandanus leaves. 4c, Fishermen casting nets. 5c, Gilbertese canoes. 6c, Dehusking coconuts. 8c, Woman weaving pandanus fronds. 10c, Basket weaving. 15c, Tiger shark. 20c, Beating rolled pandanus leaf. 25c, Loading copra. 35c, Night fishing. 50c, Local handicraft. $1, Woman weaving coconut screen. $2, Coat of arms.

Wmk. 314 Upright (A18), Sideways (A19)

1971, May 31		**Litho.**		**Perf. 14**
173	A18	1c multicolored	.20	.20
174	A19	2c multicolored	.20	.20
175	A19	3c multicolored	.20	.20
176	A19	4c multicolored	.35	.20
177	A19	5c multicolored	.70	.25
178	A18	6c multicolored	.45	.35
179	A18	8c multicolored	.55	.35
180	A18	10c multicolored	.60	.45
181	A18	15c multicolored	4.00	.90
182	A18	20c multicolored	2.40	1.75
183	A19	25c multicolored	3.00	1.40
184	A19	35c multicolored	3.50	1.00
185	A18	50c multicolored	1.90	2.40
186	A18	$1 multicolored	2.75	4.75
187	A18	$2 multicolored	7.75	9.25
		Nos. 173-187 (15)	28.55	23.65

Wmk. 314 Upright (A19), Sideways (A18)

1972-73

174a	A19	2c multicolored	12.00	16.50
177a	A19	5c multicolored	4.75	7.75
178a	A18	6c multicolored	12.00	17.50

181a	A18	15c multicolored	5.00	8.00
182a	A19	20c multicolored	5.25	8.50
		Nos. 174a-182a (5)	39.00	58.25

Issue dates: Sept. 7, 1972, June 13, 1973.

Legislative Council, 1971 (former House of Representatives) — A20

New Constitution: 10c, Meeting House.

1971, Aug. 1		**Wmk. 314**		**Perf. 14**
188	A20	3c orange & multi	.20	.20
189	A20	10c green & multi	.30	.30

Nativity Scene — A21

Christmas: 10c, Star of Bethlehem and palm fronds. 35c, Fishermen in outrigger canoe looking at Star.

1971, Oct. 1				
190	A21	3c vio blue, blk & yel	.20	.55
191	A21	10c grnsh bl, blk & gold	.25	.25
192	A21	35c car rose, blk & rose	.35	.35
		Nos. 190-192 (3)	.80	1.15

Children and UNICEF Emblem A22

25th Anniv. of UNICEF: 10c, Seated child. 35c, Child's head.

1971, Dec. 11				
193	A22	3c brt pink & multi	.20	.45
194	A22	10c black & multi	.20	.20
195	A22	35c blue & multi	.65	.80
		Nos. 193-195 (3)	1.05	1.45

Commission Flag, Map of South Pacific — A23

South Pacific Commission, 25th Anniv.: 10c, Island boats. 35c, Flags of 8 member nations plus Tonga, a non-member.

1972, Feb. 21				**Perf. 13½x14**
196	A23	3c gray & multi	.20	.55
197	A23	10c tan, ultra & brown	.25	.25
198	A23	35c ultra & multi	.35	.80
		Nos. 196-198 (3)	.80	1.60

Corals A24

1972, May 26 — Perf. 14x14½

199	A24	3c Alveopora	.20	.35
200	A24	10c Euphyllia	.50	.20
201	A24	15c Melithea	.65	.35
202	A24	35c Spongodes	1.90	1.10
		Nos. 199-202 (4)	3.25	2.00

"Peace" on Star of Bethlehem A25

Christmas: 10c, Holy Family, made of shells. 35c, Christ child sleeping in giant clam and covered with dawn cowrie, horiz.

1972, Sept. 15 — Perf. 13½

203	A25	3c gold & multi	.20	.20
204	A25	10c gold & multi	.20	.20
205	A25	35c gold & multi	.50	.50
		Nos. 203-205 (3)	.90	.90

Silver Wedding Issue, 1972
Common Design Type

Design: Queen Elizabeth II, Prince Philip and kaue floral headdress.

1972, Nov. 20 — Photo. Perf. 14x14½

206	CD324	3c olive & multi	.20	.20
207	CD324	35c rose brown & multi	.20	.20

Funafuti, Land of Bananas A26

Designs: 10c, Butaritari, the smell of the sea. 25c, Tarawa, the center of the world. 35c, Abemama, the land of the moon.

1973, Mar. 5 — Litho. Perf. 14½x14

208	A26	3c yellow & multi	.20	.45
209	A26	10c brt green & multi	.35	.35
210	A26	25c dull blue & multi	.50	.65
211	A26	35c orange & multi	.55	.75
		Nos. 208-211 (4)	1.60	2.20

Legends of island names.

Ellice Dancer — A27

Christmas (Within Outline of Nautilus Shell): 10c, Outrigger canoe in lagoon. 35c, Evening on the lagoon. 50c, Map of Christmas Island, Pacific Ocean.

1973, Sept. 24 — Perf. 14

212	A27	3c vio blue & multi	.20	.20
213	A27	10c multicolored	.20	.20
214	A27	35c multicolored	.25	.25
215	A27	50c vio blue & multi	.35	1.00
		Nos. 212-215 (4)	1.00	1.60

Princess Anne's Wedding Issue
Common Design Type

1973, Nov. 14 — Perf. 14

216	CD325	3c brt green & multi	.20	.20
217	CD325	35c slate & multi	.35	.35

Meteorological Observation — A28

WMO Emblem and: 10c, Island observation station. 35c, Wind finding radar. 50c, Map of Gilbert and Ellice Islands world weather watch stations.

1973, Nov. 26 — Litho. Perf. 14½

218	A28	3c orange & multi	.95	.55
219	A28	10c dp bister & multi	1.00	.40
220	A28	35c gray & multi	1.40	.55
221	A28	50c dk blue & multi	2.25	2.25
		Nos. 218-221 (4)	5.60	3.75

Cent. of intl. meteorological cooperation.

Te-Mataaua Crest and Canoe — A29

Designs: Various family crests and canoes.

1974, Mar. 4 — Litho. Perf. 13½

222	A29	3c tan & multi	.20	.20
223	A29	10c lt blue & multi	.20	.20
224	A29	35c yellow & multi	.35	.20
225	A29	50c pink & multi	.35	.65
a.		Souvenir sheet of 4, #222-225	7.00	8.50
		Nos. 222-225 (4)	1.10	1.25

UPU Emblem, "Te Koroba" and No. 26 — A30

UPU cent.: 10c, Sailing ship "Kiakia" and No. 51. 25c, BAC 111 jet and No. 187. 35c, UPU emblem.

1974, June 10 — Perf. 14

226	A30	4c blue green & multi	.20	.20
227	A30	10c orange & multi	.20	.20
228	A30	25c dp blue & multi	.40	.35
229	A30	35c red orange & black	.55	.45
		Nos. 226-229 (4)	1.35	1.20

Toy Canoe, Star and Boat A31

Star of Bethlehem and: 10c, Pinwheel and boat. 25c, Coconut ball (crate) and boat. 35c, Three boats (Wise Men) and stars.

1974, Sept. 23

230	A31	4c yel green & multi	.20	.25
231	A31	10c red brown & multi	.20	.20
232	A31	25c multicolored	.25	.45
233	A31	35c red brown & multi	.40	.50
		Nos. 230-233 (4)	1.05	1.40

Christmas.

Blenheim Palace, Entrance — A32   Churchill Painting — A33

Design: 35c, Churchill Statue, London.

1974, Nov. 30 — Litho. Perf. 14

234	A32	4c multicolored	.20	.20
235	A33	10c ultra & black	.20	.20
236	A33	35c blue, ocher & blk	.35	.35
		Nos. 234-236 (3)	.75	.75

Sir Winston Churchill (1874-1965).

Carpilius Maculatus — A34

Crabs: 10c, Ranina ranina. 25c, Portunus pelagicus. 35c, Ocypode ceratophthalma.

1975, Jan. 27 — Litho. Perf. 14

237	A34	4c violet & multi	.25	.25
238	A34	10c green & multi	.60	.60
239	A34	25c buff & multi	1.50	1.50
240	A34	35c lt blue & multi	2.00	2.00
		Nos. 237-240 (4)	4.35	4.35

Living Cowries and Empty Shells — A35

1975, May 26 — Wmk. 314 Perf. 14

241	A35	4c Cypraea argus	.60	.60
242	A35	10c Cypraea cribraria	.85	.85
243	A35	25c Cypraea talpa	2.00	2.00
244	A35	35c Cypraea mappa	3.00	3.00
a.		Souvenir sheet of 4, #241-244	17.50	17.50
		Nos. 241-244 (4)	6.45	6.45

Map of Beru (The Bud) A36

Designs: 10c, Map of Onotoa (Six Giants). 25c, Map of Abaiang (Land to the North). 35c, Map of Marakei (Floating fish trap).

Wmk. 314

1975, Aug. 1 — Litho. Perf. 14

245	A36	4c brt green & multi	.20	.20
246	A36	10c brown & multi	.20	.20
247	A36	25c vio blue & multi	.35	.35
248	A36	35c org red & multi	.50	.50
		Nos. 245-248 (4)	1.25	1.25

Legends of island names.

Christ Child Within Coconut — A37

Christmas: 10c, Sadd Memorial Chapel (Protestant), Tarawa. 25c, R.C. Church, Ocean Island. 35c, Fishermen in outrigger canoes seeing star.

1975, Sept. 22 — Perf. 14

249	A37	4c brown & multi	.20	.40
250	A37	10c brt blue & multi	.20	.20
251	A37	25c violet & multi	.45	.55
252	A37	35c green & multi	.55	.80
		Nos. 249-252 (4)	1.40	1.95

POSTAGE DUE STAMPS

D1

1940, Aug. — Typo. Wmk. 4 Perf. 12

J1	D1	1p emerald	5.50	24.00
J2	D1	2p dark red	6.00	24.00
J3	D1	3p chocolate	8.25	25.00
J4	D1	4p deep blue	10.00	35.00
J5	D1	5p deep green	13.00	35.00
J6	D1	6p brt red vio	13.00	40.00
J7	D1	1sh dull violet	22.50	70.00
J8	D1	1sh6p turq green	32.50	100.00
		Nos. J1-J8 (8)	110.75	353.00
		Set, never hinged	165.00	

WAR TAX STAMP

No. 15a Overprinted

1918 — Wmk. 3 Perf. 14

MR1	A3	1p scarlet	.70	6.50

GILBERT ISLANDS

'gil-bərt 'ī-lənds

LOCATION — A group of islands in the Pacific Ocean northeast of Australia.
GOVT. — British Crown Colony
AREA — 270 sq. mi.
POP. — 52,000 (1973)
CAPITAL — Tarawa

The Gilbert Islands Colony consists of the Gilbert Islands, Phoenix, Ocean and Line Islands. They were part of the Gilbert and Ellice Islands colony until 1976. See Tuvalu.

Catalogue values for all unused stamps in this country are for Never Hinged items.

Stamps and Types of Gilbert and Ellice Islands 1971 Overprinted in Red, Black or Gold

Wmk. 373; 314 (2c, 4c)

1976, Jan. 2   Litho.   Perf. 14
253	A18	1c multi (R)	.20	.75
a.		Watermark 314	.25	.30
254	A19	2c multi (R)	.40	.25
a.		Watermark upright	.50	2.25
255	A19	3c multi (R)	.40	1.75
a.		Watermark 314	19.00	15.00
256	A19	4c multi (R)	.30	1.00
257	A19	5c multi (R)	.50	1.00
258	A18	6c multi (R)	.50	1.00
259	A18	8c multi (R)	.50	1.00
260	A18	10c multi (B)	.50	1.00
261	A19	15c multi (B)	2.25	1.25
262	A19	20c multi (B)	1.00	2.00
a.		Watermark 314 sideways	6.00	3.25
b.		Watermark 314 upright		125.00
263	A19	25c multi (B)	1.50	1.25
a.		Watermark 314	30.00	47.50
264	A19	35c multi (G)	2.00	1.75
a.		Watermark 314	950.00	1,000.
265	A18	50c multi (B)	2.00	2.25
a.		Watermark 314	950.00	1,000.
266	A18	$1 multi (R)	5.00	9.00
		Nos. 253-266 (14)	17.05	25.25

Location of overprint varies.

Maps of Tarawa and Funafuti A38

4c, Charts of Gilbert and Tuvalu Islands.

1976, Jan. 2   Wmk. 373
267	A38	4c multicolored	.45	1.00
268	A38	35c multicolored	.80	1.60

Separation of the Gilbert and Ellice Islands.

M.V. Teraaka A39

3c, M.V. Tautunu. 4c, Moorish idol. 5c, Hibiscus. 6c, Reef egret. 7c, Roman Catholic Cathedral, Tarawa. 8c, Frangipani. 10c, Maneaba meeting house. 12c, Betio Harbor. 15c, Sunset. 20c, Marakei Atoll. 35c, Chapel, Tangintebu. 40c, Flamboyant tree. 50c, Hypolimnas bolina elliciana (butterfly). $1, Landing craft, Tabakea. $2, Gilbert Islands flag.

1976, July 1   Litho.   Perf. 14
269	A39	1c multicolored	.45	.60
270	A39	3c multicolored	.65	.70
271	A39	4c multicolored	.35	.60
272	A39	5c multicolored	.40	.75
273	A39	6c multicolored	1.75	.90
274	A39	7c multicolored	.20	.25
275	A39	8c multicolored	.20	.25
276	A39	10c multicolored	.20	.25
277	A39	12c multicolored	.50	.45
278	A39	15c multicolored	.55	.45
279	A39	20c multicolored	.50	.35
280	A39	35c multicolored	.50	.35
281	A39	40c multicolored	.55	.50
282	A39	50c multicolored	1.75	1.75
283	A39	$1 multicolored	1.25	2.50
284	A39	$2 multicolored	1.25	2.50
		Nos. 269-284 (16)	11.05	12.65

Church A40

Children's Drawings: 15c, Feasting (vegetables, fish, pig, chicken), vert. 20c, Communal meeting house, vert. 35c, Children watching dancer.

1976, Sept. 15   Litho.   Perf. 14
285	A40	5c blue & multi	.20	.20
286	A40	15c green & multi	.60	.20
287	A40	20c rose & multi	.60	.60
288	A40	35c salmon & multi	.60	.60
		Nos. 285-288 (4)	2.00	1.60

Christmas.

Porcupine Fish Helmet — A41

Artifacts: 15c, Shark's teeth dagger. 20c, Fighting gauntlet. 35c, Coconut body armor.

1976, Dec. 6   Litho.   Perf. 13½x13
289	A41	5c multicolored	.25	.20
290	A41	15c multicolored	.35	.35
291	A41	20c multicolored	.35	.45
292	A41	35c multicolored	.80	.90
a.		Souvenir sheet of 4, #289-292	9.50	9.50
		Nos. 289-292 (4)	1.75	1.90

Prince Charles, 1970 Visit — A42

1977, Feb. 7   Perf. 14

Designs: 20c, Prince Philip, 1959 visit. 40c, Queen in coronation robes.
293	A42	8c multicolored	.20	.20
294	A42	20c multicolored	.30	.20
295	A42	40c multicolored	.45	.40
		Nos. 293-295 (3)	.95	.80

Reign of Queen Elizabeth II, 25th anniv.

John Byron and Dolphin, 1765 A43

Explorers: 15c, Edmund Fanning, 1798, and "Betsey." 20c, Fabian Gottlieb von Bellingshausen, 1820, and "Vostok." 35c, Charles Wilkes, 1838-42, and "Vincennes."

1977, June 1   Wmk. 373   Perf. 14
296	A43	5c multicolored	.65	1.40
297	A43	15c multicolored	.85	2.75
298	A43	20c multicolored	.85	2.75
299	A43	35c multicolored	1.00	4.25
		Nos. 296-299 (4)	3.35	11.15

Resolution and Discovery off Christmas Island — A44

15c, Capt. Cook's logbook entry, 1777. 20c, Capt. Cook on board ship. 40c, Capt. Cook landing on Christmas Island.

1977, Sept. 12   Litho.   Perf. 14
300	A44	8c multi	.50	.20
301	A44	15c multi, horiz.	.50	.20
302	A44	20c multi	.75	.45
303	A44	40c multi, horiz.	.75	.80
a.		Souvenir sheet of 4, #300-303	9.50	7.50
		Nos. 300-303 (4)	2.50	1.65

Christmas; bicentenary of Capt. Cook's discovery of Christmas Island.

Scout Emblem, Beach Scene — A45

15c, Patrol meeting. 20c, Scout weaving mat. 40c, Canoeing.

1977, Dec. 5   Litho.   Perf. 13
304	A45	8c gold & multi	.40	.20
305	A45	15c gold & multi, horiz.	.45	.25
306	A45	20c gold & multi, horiz.	.50	.45
307	A45	40c gold & multi	1.10	.90
		Nos. 304-307 (4)	2.45	1.80

50th anniversary of Gilbert Islands Scouting.

Taurus with Aldebaran — A46

Night Sky over Gilbert Islands: 20c, Canis Major with Sirius. 25c, Scorpio with Antares. 45c, Orion with Betelgeuse and Rigel.

1978, Feb. 20   Litho.   Perf. 14
308	A46	10c blue & black	.45	.35
309	A46	20c dp rose & black	.50	.25
310	A46	25c olive grn & black	.50	.55
311	A46	45c orange & black	.75	1.00
		Nos. 308-311 (4)	2.20	2.15

Common Design Types pictured following the introduction.

Elizabeth II Coronation Anniversary
Common Design Types
Souvenir Sheet

1978, Apr. 21   Unwmk.
312		Sheet of 6	1.50	1.50
a.		CD326 45c Unicorn of Scotland	.25	.25
b.		CD327 45c Elizabeth II	.25	.25
c.		CD328 45c Great frigate bird	.25	.25

Arrows, Tarawa and Abemama Islands, School Insignia A47

10c, Birds inscribed Bikenibeu, Abemama, Bairiki (school locations). 25c, Children greeting each other from maps of Islands. 45c, Abemama & Tarawa school buildings.

Perf. 14x13½
1978, June 5   Wmk. 373
313	A47	10c multicolored	.20	.20
314	A47	20c multicolored	.25	.25
315	A47	25c multicolored	.25	.25
316	A47	45c multicolored	.35	.35
		Nos. 313-316 (4)	1.05	1.05

King George V School, 25th anniversary of return from Abemama to Tarawa.

Garland A48

Christmas: Various garlands.

1978, Sept. 4   Litho.   Perf. 14
317	A48	10c multicolored	.20	.20
318	A48	20c multicolored	.20	.20
319	A48	25c multicolored	.20	.20
320	A48	45c multicolored	.75	.35
a.		Souvenir sheet of 4, #317-320, perf. 13x13½	2.50	3.50
		Nos. 317-320 (4)	1.35	.95

Endeavour A49

Designs: 20c, Green turtle. 25c, Quadrant. 45c, Capt. Cook after Flaxman/Wedgwood medallion.

1979, Jan. 15   Litho.   Perf. 11
321	A49	10c multicolored	.30	.35
322	A49	20c multicolored	.40	.40
323	A49	25c multicolored	.40	.40

Litho.; Embossed
324	A49	45c multicolored	.40	.80
		Nos. 321-324 (4)	1.50	1.95

Capt. Cook's voyages.
Gilbert Islands stamps were replaced in 1979 by those of Kiribati.

GOLD COAST

'gōld 'kōst

LOCATION — West Africa between Dahomey and Ivory Coast
GOVT. — Former British Crown Colony
AREA — 91,843 sq. mi.
POP. — 3,089,000 (1952)
CAPITAL — Accra

Attached to the colony were Ashanti and Northern Territories (protectorate). Togoland, under British mandate, was also included for administrative purposes.
Gold Coast became the independent state of Ghana in 1957.
See Ghana.

12 Pence = 1 Shilling
20 Shillings = 1 Pound

> Catalogue values for unused stamps in this country are for Never Hinged items, beginning with Scott 128.

Queen Victoria
A1   A3

Perf. 12½

1875, July   Typo.   Wmk. 1

1	A1	1p blue	550.00	95.00
2	A1	4p red violet	525.00	140.00
3	A1	6p orange	825.00	75.00
		Nos. 1-3 (3)	1,900.	310.00

1876-79   Perf. 14

4	A1	½p bister ('79)	90.00	32.50
5	A1	1p blue	30.00	8.00
a.		Half used as ½p on cover		4,500.
6	A1	2p green ('79)	110.00	11.50
a.		Half used as 1p on cover		4,000.
b.		Quarter used as ½p on cover		7,000.
7	A1	4p red violet	250.00	7.25
a.		Quarter used as 1p on cover		10,000.
b.		Half used as 2p on cover		7,750.
8	A1	6p orange	225.00	22.50
a.		One sixth used as 1p on cover		11,500.
				9,250.
		Nos. 4-8 (5)	705.00	81.75

Handstamp Surcharged "1D" in Black

1883, May

9 A1 1p on 4p red violet

Some experts question the status of No. 9. One canceled example is in the British Museum. Another example is supposed to exist (Ferrari).

1883-91   Wmk. 2

10	A1	½p bister ('83)	210.00	75.00
11	A1	½p green ('84)	4.25	1.50
12	A1	1p blue ('83)	1,000.	85.00
13	A1	1p rose ('84)	4.75	.60
a.		Half used as ½p on cover		5,000.
14	A1	2p gray ('84)	25.00	5.00
b.		Half used as 1p on cover		5,000.
15	A1	2½p bl & org ('91)	8.50	.85
16	A1	3p ol green ('89)	17.50	8.00
a.		3p olive bister	17.50	7.50
17	A1	4p dull vio ('84)	16.50	3.00
a.		4p claret	21.00	5.00
b.		Half used as 2p on cover		—
18	A1	6p orange ('89)	17.00	6.00
a.		One sixth used as 1p on cover		—
19	A1	1sh purple ('88)	9.75	1.50
a.		1sh violet	37.50	15.00
20	A1	2sh brown ('84)	60.00	17.50
a.		2sh yellow brown ('88)	95.00	42.50

No. 18 Surcharged in Black

1889, Mar.

21	A1	1p on 6p orange	140.00	60.00
a.		Double surcharge		4,500.

The surcharge exists in two spacings between "PENNY" and bar: 7mm (normal) and 8mm.
No. 21a does not exist unused.

1889

22	A3	5sh lilac & ultra	75.00	20.00
23	A3	10sh lilac & red	95.00	17.50
24	A3	20sh green & red	3,000.	

1894

25	A3	20sh vio & blk, *red*	190.00	40.00

1898-1902

26	A3	½p lilac & green	4.00	1.25
27	A3	1p lil & car rose	5.00	.60
28	A3	2p lil & red ('02)	60.00	175.00
29	A3	2½p lilac & ultra	7.25	7.25
30	A3	3p lilac & yel	8.00	3.00
31	A3	6p lilac & purple	8.50	2.75
32	A3	1sh gray grn & blk	13.00	25.00
33	A3	2sh gray grn & car rose	22.50	27.50
34	A3	5sh grn & lil ('00)	72.50	42.50
35	A3	10sh grn & brn ('00)	175.00	65.00
		Nos. 26-35 (10)	375.75	349.85

Numerals of 2p, 3p and 6p of type A3 are in color on colorless tablet.

Nos. 29 and 31 Surcharged in Black

1901, Oct. 6

36	A3	1p on 2½p lil & ultra	5.50	5.00
a.		"ONE" omitted	1,200.	
37	A3	1p on 6p lilac & pur	5.50	4.25
a.		"ONE" omitted	325.00	650.00

Beware of copies offered as No. 37a that have part of "ONE" showing.

King Edward VII
A5   A6

1902   Wmk. 2

38	A5	½p violet & green	1.75	.50
39	A5	1p vio & car rose	1.75	.25
40	A5	2p vio & red org	27.50	8.50
41	A5	2½p vio & ultra	5.50	11.00
42	A5	3p vio & orange	3.50	1.75
43	A5	6p violet & pur	4.50	1.75
44	A5	1sh green & blk	17.00	4.00
45	A5	2sh grn & car rose	17.50	25.00
46	A5	5sh green & violet	57.50	110.00
47	A5	10sh green & brn	72.50	150.00
48	A5	20sh vio & blk, *red*	160.00	210.00
		Nos. 38-48 (11)	369.00	522.75

Numerals of 2p, 3p, 6p and 2sh6p of type A5 are in color on colorless tablet.

1904-07   Wmk. 3

Ordinary Paper

49	A5	½p vio & grn ('07)	3.00	*8.50*
50	A5	1p vio & car rose	11.00	.40
51	A5	2p vio & red org	6.50	.60
52	A5	2½p vio & ultra ('06)	57.50	57.50
53a	A5	3p vio & org ('06)	20.00	.70
54	A5	6p vio & pur ('06)	80.00	4.00
55	A5	2sh6p grn & yel ('06)	32.50	130.00
		Nos. 49-55 (7)	210.50	201.70

Nos. 49 and 52 are on ordinary paper. Nos. 50, 51, 53 and 54 are on both ordinary and chalky paper. No. 55 is on chalky paper. For detailed listings, see the *Scott Classic Specialized Catalogue of Stamps and Covers*.

1907-13   Ordinary Paper

56	A5	½p green	8.00	.40
57	A5	1p carmine	14.50	.50
58	A5	2p gray ('09)	2.75	.55
59	A5	2½p ultramarine	14.00	3.50

Chalky Paper

60	A5	3p violet, *yel* ('09)	9.50	.65
61	A5	6p dull violet ('08)	25.00	.65
a.		6p dull violet & red violet	4.50	4.25

62	A5	1sh blk, *grn* ('09)	17.50	.65
63	A5	2sh violet & bl, *bl* ('10)	9.50	19.00
64	A5	2sh6p blk & red, *blue* ('11)	37.50	105.00
65	A5	5sh grn & red, *yel* ('13)	65.00	225.00
		Nos. 56-65 (10)	203.25	355.90

No. 63 is on both ordinary and chalky paper.

1908, Nov.   Ordinary Paper

66	A6	1p carmine	6.00	.20

King George V
A7   A8

For description of Dies I and II, see front section of the Catalogue.

Die I

1913-21   Ordinary Paper

69	A7	½p green	3.00	1.50
70	A8	1p carmine	1.50	.20
a.		1p scarlet	2.25	.60
71	A7	2p gray	7.00	3.00
72	A7	2½p ultramarine	10.00	1.25

Chalky Paper

73	A7	3p vio, *yel* ('15)	2.50	1.00
a.		Die II ('19)	57.50	6.00
74	A7	6p dull vio & red vio	6.25	2.75
75	A7	1sh black, *green*	4.50	1.50
a.		1sh black, *emerald*	2.50	2.50
b.		1sh black, *bl grn,* ol back	10.00	.95
c.		Die II ('21)	1.75	.60
76	A7	2sh vio & bl, *bl*	10.50	3.75
a.		Die II ('21)	190.00	77.50
77	A7	2sh6p blk & red, *bl*	9.50	16.00
a.		Die II ('21)	27.50	50.00
78	A7	5sh grn & red, *yel*	22.50	65.00
a.		Die II ('21)	35.00	160.00
79	A7	10sh grn & red, *grn* ('16)	60.00	110.00
a.		10sh grn & red, *emer*	37.50	175.00
b.		10sh grn & red, *bl grn,* ol back	26.00	85.00
80	A7	20sh vio & blk, *red* ('16)	150.00	100.00

Surface-colored Paper

81	A7	3p violet, *yel*	2.10	1.00
82	A7	5sh grn & red, *yel*	20.00	72.50
		Nos. 69-82 (14)	309.35	379.45

Numerals of 2p, 3p, 6p and 2sh6p of type A7 are in color on plain tablet.

Die II

1921-25   Ordinary Paper   Wmk. 4

83	A7	½p green ('22)	1.00	.60
84	A8	1p brown ('22)	.90	.20
85	A7	1½p carmine ('22)	2.10	.20
86	A7	2p gray	2.10	.40
87	A7	2½p orange ('23)	1.50	11.00
88	A7	3p ultra ('22)	2.10	.70

Chalky Paper

89	A7	6p dl vio & red vio ('22)	2.75	3.50
90	A7	1sh blk, *emer* ('25)	4.75	4.00
91	A7	2sh vio & bl, *bl* ('24)	4.00	4.00
92	A7	2sh6p blk & red, *bl* ('25)	8.50	32.50
93	A7	5sh grn & red, *yel* ('25)	18.00	77.50

Die I

94	A7	15sh dl vio & grn ('21)	175.00	475.00
a.		Die II ('25)	140.00	475.00
95	A7	£2 grn & org	500.00	1,300.
		Nos. 83-95 (13)	722.70	1,909.

Christiansborg Castle — A9

1928, Aug. 1 Photo. Perf. 13½x14½

98	A9	½p green	1.20	.50
99	A9	1p red brown	1.00	.50
100	A9	1½p scarlet	2.50	1.75
101	A9	2p slate	2.50	.20
102	A9	2½p yellow	3.00	4.25
103	A9	3p ultramarine	2.50	.50
104	A9	6p dull vio & blk	3.00	.50
105	A9	1sh red org & blk	4.25	.95
106	A9	2sh purple & black	30.00	6.00
107	A9	5sh ol green & car	72.50	52.50
		Nos. 98-107 (10)	122.45	67.35

Common Design Types pictured following the introduction.

Silver Jubilee Issue
Common Design Type

1935, May 6   Engr.   Perf. 11x12

108	CD301	1p black & ultra	1.00	.60
109	CD301	3p ultra & brown	3.25	7.25
110	CD301	6p indigo & green	16.00	22.50
111	CD301	1sh brn vio & indigo	5.50	27.50
		Nos. 108-111 (4)	25.75	57.85
		Set, never hinged	38.00	

Coronation Issue
Common Design Type

1937, May 12   Perf. 11x11½

112	CD302	1p brown	.85	2.50
113	CD302	2p dark gray	.95	4.50
114	CD302	3p deep ultra	1.25	2.75
		Nos. 112-114 (3)	3.05	9.75
		Set, never hinged	6.00	

A10

George VI and Christiansborg Castle — A11

1938-41   Wmk. 4   Perf. 12

115	A10	½p green	.35	.50
116	A10	1p red brown	.35	.20
117	A10	1½p rose red	.35	.50
118	A10	2p gray black	.35	.20
119	A10	3p ultramarine	.35	.35
120	A10	4p rose lilac	.70	1.10
121	A10	6p rose violet	.70	.55
122	A10	9p red orange	1.10	.55
123	A11	1sh gray grn & blk	1.40	.55
124	A11	1sh3p turq grn & red brown	1.75	.45
125	A11	2sh dk vio & dp bl	4.75	14.00
126	A11	5sh rose car & ol green	9.25	17.50
127	A11	10sh purple & black	6.50	26.00
		Nos. 115-127 (13)	27.90	62.10
		Set, never hinged	40.00	

Issued: 10sh, July, 1940; 1sh3p, Apr. 12, 1941; others, Apr. 1.

> Catalogue values for unused stamps in this section, from this point to the end of the section, are for Never Hinged items.

Peace Issue
Common Design Type

1946, Oct. 14   Perf. 13½

128	CD303	2p purple	.25	.20
a.		Perf. 13½x14	18.00	3.00
129	CD303	4p deep red violet	1.60	3.50
a.		Perf. 13½x14	3.00	3.75

A12

A13

½p, Mounted Constable. 1p, Christiansborg Castle. 1½p, Emblem of Joint Provincial Council. 2p, Talking Drums. 2½p, Map. 3p, Manganese mine. 4p, Lake Bosumtwi. 6p, Cacao

farmer. 1sh, Breaking cacao pods. 2sh, Trooping the colors. 5sh, Surfboats. 10sh, Forest.

1948, July 1   Engr.   Perf. 12

130	A12	½p emerald	.20	.40
131	A13	1p deep blue	.20	.20
132	A13	1½p red	1.50	.90
133	A13	2p chocolate	.65	.20
134	A13	2½p lt brown & red	2.50	4.25
135	A13	3p blue	5.00	.60
136	A13	4p dk car rose	4.25	3.25
137	A12	6p org & black	.40	.40
138	A13	1sh red org & blk	2.00	.40
139	A13	2sh rose car & ol brn	4.00	2.50
140	A13	5sh gray & red vio	30.00	9.50
141	A12	10sh ol grn & black	14.00	10.00
		Nos. 130-141 (12)	64.70	32.60

Silver Wedding Issue
Common Design Types

1948, Dec. 20 Photo. Perf. 14x14½

142	CD304	1½p scarlet	.20	.20

Engraved; Name Typographed
Perf. 11½x11

143	CD305	10sh dk brn olive	29.00	29.00

UPU Issue
Common Design Types
Engr.; Name Typo. on 2½p and 3p

1949, Oct. 10   Perf. 13½, 11x11½

144	CD306	2p red brown	.25	.25
145	CD307	2½p deep orange	1.90	4.50
146	CD308	3p indigo	.45	1.75
147	CD309	1sh blue green	.45	.45
		Nos. 144-147 (4)	3.05	6.95

Map of West
Africa — A14

Mounted
Constable — A15

Designs: 1p, Christiansborg Castle. 1½p,
Emblem of Joint Provincial Council. 2p, Talk-
ing drums. 3p, Manganese mine. 4p, Lake
Bosumtwi. 6p, Cacao farmer. 1sh, Breaking
cacao pods. 2sh, Trooping the colors. 5sh,
Surfboats. 10sh, Forest.

Perf. 11½x12, 12x11½
1952-54   Engr.

148	A14	½p yel brn & car	.20	.20
149	A14	1p deep blue	.40	.20
150	A14	1½p green	.40	1.50
151	A15	2p chocolate	.40	.20
152	A15	2½p red	.45	.75
153	A14	3p rose	.95	.20
154	A14	4p deep blue	.45	.45
155	A15	6p orange & black	.50	.20
156	A14	1sh red org & black	1.50	.20
157	A14	2sh rose car & ol brn	13.00	1.00
158	A14	5sh gray & red vio	22.50	6.00
159	A15	10sh olive grn & blk	20.00	15.00
		Nos. 148-159 (12)	60.75	25.90

Nos. 148-149 exist in vertical coils.
Issued: 2½p, 12/19/52; ½p, 1½p, 3p, 4p,
4/1/53; 1p, 2p, 6p, 1sh-10sh, 3/1/54.
For overprints see Ghana #5-13, 25-27.

Coronation Issue
Common Design Type

1953, June 2   Perf. 13½x13

160	CD312	2p dk brown & black	.95	.20

POSTAGE DUE STAMPS

D1

1923   Typo.   Wmk. 4   Perf. 14
Yellowish Toned Paper

J1	D1	½p black	19.00	125.00
J2	D1	1p black	.95	1.50
J3	D1	2p black	13.00	3.50
J4	D1	3p black	22.50	2.00
		Nos. J1-J4 (4)	55.45	133.00

1951-52   Typo.   Wmk. 4   Perf. 14
Chalk-Surfaced Paper

J5	D1	2p black	3.75	22.50
a.		Wmk. 4a (error)	550.00	
b.		Wmk. 4, crown missing (error)	1,100.	
J6	D1	3p black	3.00	21.00
a.		Wmk. 4a (error)	500.00	
b.		Wmk. 4, crown missing (error)	1,000.	
J7	D1	6p black ('52)	2.10	10.00
a.		Wmk. 4a (error)	950.00	
b.		Wmk. 4, crown missing (error)	1,500.	
J8	D1	1sh black ('52)	2.10	80.00
a.		Wmk. 4a (error)	1,200.	
		Nos. J5-J8 (4)	10.95	133.50

Issued: #J7-J8, 10/1.

WAR TAX STAMP

Regular Issue of 1913
Surcharged

1918, June   Wmk. 3   Perf. 14

MR1	A8	1p on 1p scarlet	3.00	1.00

GRAND COMORO

ˈgrand ˈkä-mə-ˌrō

LOCATION — One of the Comoro
Islands in the Mozambique Channel
between Madagascar and
Mozambique.
GOVT. — French Colony
AREA — 385 sq. mi. (approx.)
POP. — 50,000 (approx.)
CAPITAL — Moroni

100 Centimes = 1 Franc

See Comoro Islands.

Navigation and
Commerce — A1

Perf. 14x13½
1897-1907   Typo.   Unwmk.
Name of Colony in Blue or Carmine

1	A1	1c blk, *lil bl*	1.25	1.25
2	A1	2c brn, *buff*	2.00	2.00
3	A1	4c claret, *lav*	2.50	2.50
4	A1	5c grn, *grnsh*	4.50	4.50
5	A1	10c blk, *lavender*	10.00	6.50
6	A1	10c red ('00)	11.00	11.00
7	A1	15c blue, quadrille paper	20.00	14.50
8	A1	15c gray, *lt gray* ('00)	11.00	11.00
9	A1	20c red, *grn*	12.50	12.50
10	A1	25c blk, *rose*	18.50	17.00
11	A1	25c blue ('00)	21.50	21.50
12	A1	30c brn, *bister*	22.50	20.00
13	A1	35c blk, *yel* ('06)	21.00	20.00
14	A1	40c red, *straw*	22.50	20.00
15	A1	45c blk, *gray grn* ('07)	80.00	67.50
16	A1	50c car, *rose*	45.00	24.00
17	A1	50c brn, *bluish* ('00)	47.50	45.00
18	A1	75c dp vio, *org*	60.00	40.00
19	A1	1fr brnz grn, *straw*	42.50	36.00
		Nos. 1-19 (19)	455.75	376.75

Perf. 13½x14 stamps are counterfeits.

Issues of 1897-1907 Surcharged in
Black or Carmine

1912

20	A1	5c on 2c brn, *buff*	1.50	1.50
a.		Inverted surcharge	240.00	
21	A1	5c on 4c cl, *lav* (C)	1.60	1.60
22	A1	5c on 15c blue (C)	1.50	1.50
23	A1	5c on 20c red, *grn*	1.75	1.75
24	A1	5c on 25c blk, *rose* (C)	1.60	1.60
25	A1	5c on 30c brn, *bis* (C)	1.75	1.75
26	A1	10c on 40c red, *straw*	1.75	1.75
27	A1	10c on 45c blk, *gray grn* (C)	2.50	2.50
28	A1	10c on 50c car, *rose*	2.25	2.25
29	A1	10c on 75c dp vio, *org*	2.75	2.75
		Nos. 20-29 (10)	18.95	18.95

Two spacings between the surcharged
numerals are found on Nos. 20-29. For
detailed listings, see the *Scott Classic Specialized Catalogue of Stamps and Covers.*
Nos. 20-29 were available for use in Madagascar and the entire Comoro archipelago.
Stamps of Grand Comoro were superseded
by those of Madagascar, and in 1950 by those
of Comoro Islands.

Two spacings between the surcharged
numerals are found on Nos. 20-29. For
detailed listings, see the *Scott Classic Specialized Catalogue of Stamps and Covers.*
Nos. 20-29 were available for use in Madagascar and the entire Comoro archipelago.
Stamps of Grand Comoro were superseded
by those of Madagascar, and in 1950 by those
of Comoro Islands.

GREAT BRITAIN

'grāt 'bri-tən

(United Kingdom)

LOCATION — Northwest of the continent of Europe and separated from it by the English Channel
GOVT. — Constitutional monarchy
AREA — 94,511 sq. mi.
POP. — 59,128,000 (1998 est.)
CAPITAL — London

12 Pence = 1 Shilling
20 Shillings = 1 Pound
100 Pence = 1 Pound (1970)

> **Catalogue values for unused stamps in this country are for Never Hinged items, beginning with Scott 264 in the regular postage section, Scott B1 in the semi-postal section, Scott J34 in the postage due section, and Scott 93, Scott 246 and Scott 521 in British Offices in Morocco. All of the listings in British Offices — Middle East Forces, for Use in Eritrea, for Use in Somalia and for Use in Tripolitania are valued as never-hinged.**

The letters in the corners of the early postage issues indicate position in the horizontal and vertical rows in which that particular specimen was placed.

In the case of illustration A1, this stamp came from the 15th horizontal row (O) and was the second stamp (B) from the left in that row. The left corner refers to the horizontal row and the right corner to the vertical row. Thus no two stamps on the plate bore the same combination of letters.

When four corner letters are used (starting in 1858), the lower ones indicate the stamp's position in the sheet and the top ones are the same letters reversed.

Watermarks

Wmk. 18 — Small Crown

Wmk. 20 — Large Crown

Wmk. 19 — V R

Wmk. 21 — Small Garter

Wmk. 22 — Medium Garter

Wmk. 23 — Large Garter

Wmk. 24 — Heraldic Emblems

Wmk. 25 — Spray of Rose

Wmk. 26 — Maltese Cross

Wmk. 27 — "Half Penny" in Script

Wmk. 28 — Anchor

Wmk. 29 — Orb

Wmk. 30 — Imperial Crown

Wmk. 31 — Anchor

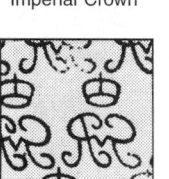

Wmk. 32 — Crown and GvR Multiple

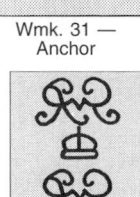

Wmk. 33 — Crown and GvR

Wmk. 33 — In the normal watermark (sometimes termed the "repeated" watermark) the letters "GvR" are extended. The royal cyphers are placed one above the other and usually two appear on each stamp. In the multiple watermark the letters "GvR" are condensed, the cyphers are smaller and are so placed that those in each succeeding row are below the spaces between the cyphers in the row above.

Wmk. 34 — Large Crown and GvR

Wmk. 35 — Crown and Block GvR Multiple

Wmk. 219 — Large Crown and GvR

Wmk. 250 — Crown and E8R Multiple

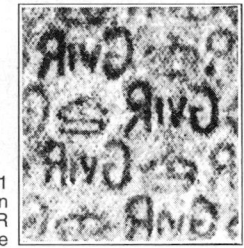

Wmk. 251 — Crown and GviR Multiple

Wmk. 259 — Crown and Large G VI R

Wmk. 298 — Tudor Crown and E 2 R Multiple

Wmk. 308 — St. Edward's Crown and E 2 R Multiple

Wmk. 322 — St. Edward's Crown Multiple

Wmk. 401

Values for unused stamps are for examples with original gum as defined in the catalogue introduction. Very fine stamps will be sound and have fresh color, but expect Nos. 8-56, 58-73, 78-89, 94-95, and the Official overprints on these designs, to have perforations touching the design on at least one side due to the narrow spacing of the stamps on the plates. Stamps with perfs clear of the design on all four sides range from scarce to very rare and command substantially higher prices.

Cancellations on stamps from the 1847 issue to the 1884 issues, and in many cases beyond, are usually heavy. Values quoted are for stamps with better than average cancellations. Stamps with circular date stamps (especially those with a steel cds) range from scarce to very rare and command much higher prices.

Queen Victoria — A1

1840, May   Wmk. 18   Engr.   _Imperf._
White Paper

1	A1	1p black	9,000.	350.00
2	A1	2p blue	30,000.	800.00

Full margins = ½mm.

No. 1 was printed from 11 plates; No. 2 from 2 plates. The 1p plates 1, 2, 5, 6, 8 and 9 can be found in two or more states. Stamp values are for the most common plates.
Issue dates: 1p, May 6; 2p, May 7.
See Nos. 3, 8-9, 11-12, 14, 16, 18, 20, O1.
Compare designs A1-A2 with A8, A10.

A1a   A2

1841   **Bluish Paper**

3	A1a 1p red brown	550.00	24.00
c.	Rouletted 12	17,000.	
d.	"A" missing in lower right corner (position BA, P77)	—	22,500.
4	A2 2p blue	4,000.	85.00
c.	2p violet blue	20,000.	1,400.

Full margins = ½mm.

No. 3 exists on silk thread paper, but was not regularly issued.
No. 4 was printed from two plates.
See Nos. 10, 13, 15, 17, 19, 21.
For shades, see the *Scott Classic Specialized Catalogue of Stamps and Covers.*

During the reigns of Victoria and Edward VII, many color trials were produced on perfed, gummed and watermarked papers.

A3   A3a

A4

With Vertical Silk Threads

1847   **Embossed**   **Unwmk.**

5	A3 1sh pale green	16,000.	850.00
a.	1sh green	16,000.	900.00
	Cut to shape		25.00

Die numbers (on base of bust): 1 and 2.

Nos. 5-7 were printed one stamp at a time on the sheet. Space between the stamps usually is very small. Impressions that touch, or even overlap, are numerous.

Stamps with margins ½mm beyond the outer frame are considered as having full margins.

Values for Nos. 5-6 are for examples with complete frames and clear white margins on all four sides. Values for No. 7 are for examples with complete design but not necessarily clear margins around the design.

1848

6	A3a 10p red brown	7,750.	1,200.
	Cut to shape	500.00	35.00

Die numbers (on base of bust): 1, 2, 3, 4; also without die number.

1854   **Wmk. 19**

7	A4 6p red violet	12,500.	875.00
a.	6p dull violet	12,500.	875.00
b.	6p deep violet	20,000.	3,250.
	Cut to shape		20.00

1854-55   **Wmk. 18**   **Engr.**   **Perf. 16**
Bluish Paper

8	A1 1p red brown	325.00	29.00
a.	1p yellow brown	375.00	52.50
9	A1 1p red brown, re-engraved ('55)	450.00	70.00
a.	Imperf.		—
10	A2 2p blue	4,000.	100.00
a.	2p pale blue	4,500.	115.00

In the re-engraved 1p stamps, the lines of the features are deeper and stronger, the fillet behind the ear more distinct, the shading about the eye heavier, the line of the nostril is turned downward at right and an indentation of color appears between lower lip and chin.

Perf. 14

11	A1 1p red brown ('55)	625.00	90.00
a.	Imperf.		—
12	A1 1p red brown, re-engraved ('55)	575.00	67.50
a.	1p org brn, re-engraved	1,700.	175.00
13	A2 2p blue ('55)	8,500.	225.00
a.	Imperf. (P5)		—

Wmk. 20 exists in two types. The first includes two vertical prongs, rising from the top of the crown's headband and extending into each of the two balancing midsections. The second type (illustrated), introduced in 1861, omits these prongs.

1855   **Wmk. 20**   **Perf. 16**
Bluish Paper

14	A1 1p red brown, re-engraved	1,050.	125.00
15	A2 2p blue	11,000.	425.00
a.	Imperf. (P5)		7,500.

1855   **Bluish Paper**   **Perf. 14**

16	A1 1p red brown, re-engraved	225.00	21.00
a.	1p orange brn, re-engraved	650.00	62.50
b.	1p brown rose, re-engraved	340.00	57.50
c.	Imperf.	4,250.	3,500.
17	A2 2p blue	2,250.	67.50

1856-58   **White Paper**   **Perf. 16**

18	A1 1p rose red, re-engraved ('57)	2,400.	72.50
19	A2 2p blue, thin lines ('58)	11,000.	375.00

Perf. 14

20	A1 1p rose red, re-engraved ('57)	52.50	11.50
a.	Imperf.	4,500.	3,250.
b.	1p red brown, re-engraved	1,100.	340.00
21	A2 2p blue, thin lines ('57)	2,850.	67.50
a.	Imperf.		8,000.
b.	Vertical pair, imperf horiz.		—

Queen Victoria — A5

1855   **Typo.**   **Wmk. 21**

22	A5 4p rose, *bluish*	7,000.	400.00
23	A5 4p rose, *white*		850.00

Compare design A5 with A11, A16, A31.

1856   **Wmk. 22**

24	A5 4p rose, *bluish*	8,500.	450.
25	A5 4p rose, *white*	7,000.	375.

1857   **Wmk. 23**

26	A5 4p rose, *white*	1,300.	110.00

A6   A7

1856   **Wmk. 24**

27	A6 6p lilac	1,100.	100.00
a.	6p deep lilac	1,300.	130.00
b.	Wmk. 3 roses and shamrock		
28	A7 1sh green	2,500.	275.00
a.	1sh pale green	2,500.	275.00
b.	1sh deep green	4,250.	450.00
e.	Imperf		—

Compare design A6 with A13, A18, A22.
Compare A7 with A15, A21, A29.

A8   A9

1858-69   **Engr.**   **Wmk. 20**   **Perf. 14**

29	A8 2p deep blue (P9)	325.00	12.50
	Plate 7	1,400.	52.50
	Plate 8	1,300.	37.50
	Plate 12	2,100.	125.00
b.	Imperf. (P9)		6,000.

Plate numbers are contained in the scroll work at the sides of the stamp.

Lines Above and Below Head Thinner

30	A8 2p blue ('69) (P13)	350.00	32.50
	Plate 14	450.00	32.50
	Plate 15	425.00	32.50
a.	Imperf. (P13)		8,000.

1860-70

31	A9 1½p lilac rose, *bluish* ('60)	6,500.	
32	A9 1½p dull rose ('70) (P3)	425.00	52.50
a.	1½p lake red	425.00	52.50
	Plate 1	600.00	75.00
c.	Imperf (P1, 3)		5,500.

The 1½p stamps from Plate 1 carry no plate number. The Plate 3 number is in the border at each side above the lower corner letters.
No. 31 was prepared but not issued.
The "OP-PC" variety is a broken letter.

Queen Victoria — A10

1864

33	A10 1p rose red	19.00	2.50
a.	1p brick red	19.00	2.50
b.	1p lake red	19.00	2.50
c.	Imperf. (P116, see footnote)	1,800.	1,000.

Plate numbers are contained in the scroll work at the sides of the stamp.
Thirty-nine plate numbers besides Plate 116 (No. 33c) are also known imperforate and used. Values for used copies start at $450.
Stamps from plate 177 have been altered and offered as plate 77.

Plate Numbers

Plate 71	42.50	3.75
Plate 72	47.50	4.75
Plate 73	47.50	3.75
Plate 74	47.50	2.50
Plate 76	42.50	2.50
Plate 77	—	175,000.
Plate 78	110.00	2.50
Plate 79	37.50	2.50
Plate 80	52.50	2.50
Plate 81	52.50	3.00
Plate 82	110.00	4.75
Plate 83	140.00	8.50
Plate 84	70.00	3.00
Plate 85	47.50	4.00
Plate 86	60.00	4.75
Plate 87	37.50	2.50
Plate 88	170.00	9.00
Plate 89	50.00	2.50
Plate 90	50.00	2.50
Plate 91	65.00	7.00
Plate 92	42.50	2.50
Plate 93	60.00	2.50
Plate 94	52.50	6.00
Plate 95	47.50	2.50
Plate 96	52.50	2.50
Plate 97	47.50	4.25
Plate 98	60.00	7.00
Plate 99	65.00	6.00
Plate 100	70.00	3.00
Plate 101	70.00	10.50
Plate 102	52.50	2.50
Plate 103	60.00	4.25

Plate 104	85.00	6.00
Plate 105	105.00	8.50
Plate 106	65.00	2.50
Plate 107	70.00	8.50
Plate 108	90.00	3.00
Plate 109	95.00	4.25
Plate 110	70.00	10.75
Plate 111	60.00	3.00
Plate 112	80.00	3.00
Plate 113	60.00	15.00
Plate 114	300.00	15.00
Plate 115	110.00	3.00
Plate 116	85.00	10.75
Plate 117	52.50	2.50
Plate 118	60.00	2.50
Plate 119	52.50	2.50
Plate 120	29.00	2.50
Plate 121	47.50	10.75
Plate 122	19.00	2.50
Plate 123	47.50	2.50
Plate 124	35.00	2.50
Plate 125	47.50	3.00
Plate 127	65.00	3.00
Plate 129	47.50	9.50
Plate 130	65.00	3.00
Plate 131	75.00	20.00
Plate 132	160.00	27.50
Plate 133	135.00	10.75
Plate 134	19.00	2.25
Plate 135	105.00	30.00
Plate 136	105.00	24.00
Plate 137	35.00	3.00
Plate 138	24.00	2.50
Plate 139	70.00	20.00
Plate 140	24.00	2.50
Plate 141	135.00	10.75
Plate 142	80.00	30.00
Plate 143	70.00	17.00
Plate 144	105.00	24.00
Plate 145	37.50	2.50
Plate 146	47.50	7.00
Plate 147	60.00	3.75
Plate 148	47.50	3.75
Plate 149	47.50	7.00
Plate 150	19.00	2.50
Plate 151	70.00	10.75
Plate 152	70.00	6.50
Plate 153	115.00	10.75
Plate 154	60.00	2.50
Plate 155	60.00	2.50
Plate 156	52.50	2.50
Plate 157	60.00	2.60
Plate 158	37.50	2.50
Plate 159	37.50	2.50
Plate 160	37.50	2.50
Plate 161	70.00	8.50
Plate 162	60.00	8.50
Plate 163	60.00	3.75
Plate 164	60.00	3.75
Plate 165	52.50	2.50
Plate 166	52.50	7.00
Plate 167	52.50	2.50
Plate 168	60.00	9.50
Plate 169	70.00	8.50
Plate 170	42.50	2.50
Plate 171	19.00	2.50
Plate 172	37.50	2.50
Plate 173	80.00	10.75
Plate 174	37.50	2.50
Plate 175	70.00	4.25
Plate 176	70.00	3.00
Plate 177	47.50	2.50
Plate 178	70.00	4.25
Plate 179	60.00	2.50
Plate 180	70.00	6.00
Plate 181	52.50	2.50
Plate 182	105.00	6.00
Plate 183	65.00	3.75
Plate 184	37.50	2.50
Plate 185	60.00	3.75
Plate 186	75.00	3.00
Plate 187	60.00	2.50
Plate 188	80.00	12.00
Plate 189	80.00	8.00
Plate 190	60.00	7.00
Plate 191	37.50	8.50
Plate 192	60.00	2.50
Plate 193	37.50	2.50
Plates 194-195	60.00	9.50
Plate 196	60.00	6.00
Plate 197	65.00	10.75
Plate 198	47.50	7.00
Plate 199	65.00	7.00
Plate 200	70.00	2.50
Plate 201	37.50	6.00
Plate 202	70.00	9.50
Plate 203	37.50	20.00
Plate 204	65.00	2.50
Plate 205	65.00	3.75
Plate 206	65.00	8.25

Plate 207	70.00	10.75
Plate 208	65.00	20.00
Plate 209	60.00	10.75
Plate 210	75.00	14.00
Plate 211	80.00	24.00
Plate 212	70.00	13.00
Plate 213	70.00	13.00
Plate 214	75.00	21.50
Plate 215	75.00	21.50
Plate 216	80.00	21.50
Plate 217	80.00	8.50
Plate 218	75.00	9.50
Plate 219	105.00	80.00
Plate 220	47.50	8.50
Plate 221	80.00	20.00
Plate 222	90.00	47.50
Plate 223	120.00	70.00
Plate 224	150.00	60.00
Plate 225	3,000.	750.00

Plate numbers are contained in the scroll work at the sides of the stamp.

Thirty-nine plate numbers besides Plate 116 (No. 33c) are also known imperforate. Values for used copies start at $450.

A11

1862   **Typo.**   **Wmk. 23**
34	A11	4p vermilion	1,500.	95.00
b.		Hair lines (P4)	1,800.	120.00
d.		Imperf. (P4)	3,500.	

Hair lines on No. 34a are fine colorless lines drawn diagonally across the corners of the stamp.

A12   A13

A14   A15

1862   **Wmk. 24**
37	A12	3p pale rose	2,000.	260.00
a.		3p deep rose	4,000.	450.00
b.		With white dots under side ornaments	37,500.	11,000.
39	A13	6p lilac	1,700.	95.00
c.		6p lilac, wmk. 3 roses & thistle	—	8,000.
d.		6p lilac, hair lines (P4) ('64)	2,400.	190.00
h.		6p deep lilac (P3)	2,000.	115.00
40	A14	9p straw	3,500.	375.00
c.		9p straw, wmk. 3 roses & thistle	—	—
d.		9p bister (P2)	4,500.	425.00
e.		9p bister, hair lines (P3)	27,500.	10,000.
42	A15	1sh green	2,500.	210.00
a.		1sh deep green (P1)	3,500.	375.00
b.		As "c," imperf.	5,500.	
c.		1sh deep green, with hair lines (P2)	32,000.	

Hair lines on Nos. 39b, 39c, 39e, 40c and 42d are fine colorless lines drawn diagonally across the corners of the stamp.
Compare design A14 with A19.

A16

1865   **Wmk. 23**
43	A16	4p vermilion (P12)	475.00	60.00
		Plate 9	525.00	65.00
		Plate 10	700.00	140.00
		Plate 11	525.00	65.00
		Plate 13	550.00	60.00
		Plate 14	600.00	90.00
a.		4p dull vermilion (P8)	550.00	90.00
		Plate 7	600.00	100.00
		Plates 9, 13	525.00	65.00
b.		Imperf. (P11,12)	4,000.	

A17   (Hyphen after SIX) — A18

A19   A20

A21

1865   **Wmk. 24**
44	A17	3p rose (P4)	1,800.	190.00
a.		Wmk. 3 roses & shamrock	4,250.	950.00
45	A18	6p lilac (P5)	875.00	85.00
a.		6p deep lilac	1,500.	135.00
		Plate 6	2,700.	160.00
b.		Double impression		13,000.
c.		Wmk. 3 roses & shamrock (P5)		1,400.
		As "c," Plate 6		1,600.
46	A19	9p straw (P4)	4,250.	525.00
		Plate 5	20,000.	
a.		Wmk. 3 roses & shamrock (P4)	—	2,250.
47	A20	10p red brn (P1)		40,000.
48	A21	1sh green (P4)	2,250.	210.00
b.		Wmk. 3 roses & shamrock		1,400.
c.		Vert. pair, imperf. btwn.		15,000.

No. 46, plate 5 is from a proof sheet.
See Nos.49-50, 52-54. Compare design A17 with A27.

(No hyphen after SIX) — A22   A23

1867-80   **Wmk. 25**
49	A17	3p rose (P5)	475.00	60.00
a.		3p deep rose	850.00	90.00
		Plate 4	1,500.	250.00
		Plate 6	475.00	60.00
		Plate 7	600.00	65.00
		Plate 8	575.00	60.00
		Plate 9	575.00	65.00
		Plate 10	775.00	120.00
b.		Imperf. (P5,6,8,9)	5,000.	
50	A18	6p dull violet (P6)	1,500.	85.00
a.		6p bright violet (P6)	1,400.	95.00
b.		Imperf. (P6)		5,000.
51	A22	6p red violet ('69) (P9)	575.00	85.00
		6p violet (P9)	700.00	85.00
		Plate 8	600.00	115.00
		Plate 10		30,000.
b.		Imperf. (P8, 9)	7,500.	4,000.
52	A19	9p bister (P4) ('67)	2,000.	300.00
a.		Imperf. (P4)	10,000.	
53	A20	10p red brown (P1)	2,750.	325.00
		Plate 2	45,000.	14,000.
a.		10p deep red brown	4,000.	525.00
b.		Imperf. (P1)	10,000.	
54	A21	1sh green (P4)	1,200.	60.00
		Plate 5	700.00	37.50
		Plate 6	1,100.	37.50
		Plate 7	1,200.	70.00
a.		1sh deep green	775.00	42.50
b.		Imperf. (P4)	8,000.	5,000.
55	A23	2sh blue (P1)	3,000.	180.00
a.		2sh pale blue	3,500.	210.00
		Plate 3		12,000.
b.		Imperf. (P1)	15,000.	
56	A23	2sh pale brn (P1) ('80)	20,000.	3,500.
a.		Imperf.	24,000.	

No. 51, plate 10 and No. 53, plate 2, are from proof sheets.

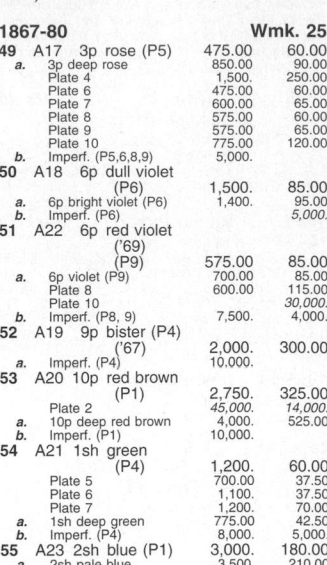

A24

1867   **Wmk. 26**   **Perf. 15½x15**
57	A24	5sh rose (P1)	8,000.	650.00
		Plate 2	12,000.	1,100.
a.		5sh pale rose	8,000.	650.00
		Plate 2	11,000.	1,100.
b.		Imperf. (P1)	15,000.	

See No. 90. Compare design A24 with A51.

A25

1870   **Engr.**   **Wmk. 27**   **Perf. 14**
58	A25	½p rose (P5)	95.00	19.00
		Plate 1	275.00	80.00
		Plate 3	200.00	42.50
		Plate 4	140.00	32.50
		Plate 6	105.00	19.00
		Plate 8	500.00	100.00
		Plate 9	5,500.	750.00
		Plate 10	115.00	19.00
		Plate 11-14	105.00	19.00
		Plate 15	160.00	42.50
		Plate 19	180.00	60.00
		Plate 20	275.00	80.00
a.		Imperf (see footnote)	—	—

Plates 1, 4-6, 8, and 14 are known imperf. Values: from $3,750 unused, $2,500 used.

A26   A27

A28   A29

Type A28 has a lined background.

1872-73   **Wmk. 25**   **Typo.**
59	A26	6p brown (P11)	725.00	52.50
		Plate 12		3,500.
a.		6p deep brown (P11)	1,100.	110.00
		Plate 12		3,250.
b.		6p pale buff (P11)	725.00	90.00
		Plate 12	3,000.	265.00
60	A26	6p gray (P12) ('73)	1,600.	240.00
a.		Imperf.	10,000.	

1873-80
61	A27	3p rose (shades) (P11)	350.00	47.50
		Plates 12	400.00	47.50
		Plate 14	450.00	47.50
		Plates 15-16	350.00	45.00
		Plates 17-18	400.00	47.50
		Plate 19	350.00	45.00
		Plate 20	650.00	100.00
62	A28	6p gray (P13-16)	425.00	65.00
		Plate 17	750.00	150.00
63	A28	6p buff (P13)		21,000.
64	A29	1sh pale green (P12, 13)	525.00	105.00
		Plate 10	625.00	150.00
		Plate 11	625.00	130.00
		Plate 14		16,500.
a.		1sh deep green (P8, 9)	625.00	130.00
65	A29	1sh sal (P13) ('80)	4,000.	625.00

No. 64, plate 14, is from a proof sheet.
See Nos. 83, 86-87. For surcharges see Nos. 94-95. For overprints see Nos. O6, O30.

A30

1875   **Wmk. 28**
66	A30	2½p claret (P1, 2)	550.00	85.00
		Plate 3	850.00	130.00
a.		Bluish paper (P1)	800.00	130.00
		Plate 2	7,500.	1,450.
		Plate 3		5,000.
b.		Lettered "LH-FL"	20,000.	2,250.

1876-80   **Wmk. 29**
67	A30	2½p claret (P4-9, 11-16)	450.00	52.50
		Plate 3	1,100.	115.00
		Plate 10	500.00	70.00
		Plate 17	1,400.	275.00
68	A30	2½p ultra ('80) (P19, 20)	500.00	42.50
		Plate 17	500.00	60.00
		Plate 18	475.00	40.00

A31   A32

1876-80   **Wmk. 23**
69	A31	4p vermilion (P15)	2,400.	450.00
		Plate 16		30,000.
70	A31	4p pale ol grn ('77) (P16)	1,000.	275.00
		Plate 15	1,100.	300.00
		Plate 17		17,500.
a.		Imperf (P15)	1,300.	
71	A31	4p gray brn (P17) ('80)	2,400.	475.00
72	A32	8p brn lilac (P1) ('76)	11,750.	
73	A32	8p org (P1) ('76)	1,500.	325.00

No. 72 was never placed in use.
No. 69, plate 16, is from proof sheets.

A33   A34

1878   **Wmk. 26**   **Perf. 15½x15**
74	A33	10sh slate (P1)	50,000.	2,900.
75	A34	£1 brn lilac (P1)	80,000.	4,000.

See Nos. 91-92. Compare design A34 with A52.

A35   A36

A37   A38

A39   A40

1880-81   **Wmk. 30**   **Perf. 14**
78	A35	½p deep green	47.50	13.00
a.		Imperf.	3,000.	
b.		No watermark	7,500.	
79	A36	1p red brown	24.00	13.00
a.		Wmk. 29, error	3,750.	
80	A37	1½p red brown	200.00	47.50
81	A38	2p lilac rose	275.00	95.00
82	A30	2½p ultra ('81) (P23)	375.00	30.00
		Plate 21	400.00	37.50
		Plate 22	375.00	37.50
a.		Imperf. (P23)	600.00	
83	A27	3p rose ('81) (P21)	425.00	85.00
		Plate 20	750.00	150.00
84	A31	4p gray brown (P17, 18)	375.00	65.00
85	A39	5p dp indigo ('81)	675.00	115.00
a.		Imperf.	6,000.	4,000.
86	A28	6p gray (P18)	375.00	65.00
		Plate 17	400.00	65.00
87	A29	1sh salmon (P14) ('81)	525.00	150.00
		Plate 13	675.00	150.00
		Nos. 78-87 (10)	3,296.	678.50

The 1sh in purple was not issued. Value, unused, $8,750.
See No. 98. For overprints see Nos. O2-O3, O37, O45, O55.
Compare design A35 with A54.

1881
88	A40	1p lilac (14 dots in each angle)	220.	32.50
89	A40	1p lilac (16 dots in each angle)	2.75	2.00
a.		Printed on both sides	800.	
b.		Imperf., pair	7,000.	
c.		Unwmkd.	7,000.	
d.		Bluish paper	4,500.	
e.		Printed on the gummed side	800.	

For overprint see No. O4.

1882-83   **Wmk. 31**
90	A24	5sh rose, *bluish* (P4)	32,000.	4,250.
a.		White paper	27,000.	3,250.
91	A33	10sh slate, *bluish* (P1)	120,000.	5,250.
a.		White paper	130,000.	4,000.
92	A34	£1 brown lilac, *bluish* (P1)	135,000.	9,250.
		White paper	160,000.	7,750.

A41

1882   **Wmk. Two Anchors (31)**
93	A41	£5 brt orange (P1)	12,750.	5,000.
a.		£5 pale dull orange, *bluish*	57,000.	13,000.
b.		£5 bright orange, *bluish*	60,000.	13,000.

The paper of No. 93b is less bluish than that of No. 93a, and it is a later printing.

Types of 1873-80
Surcharged in Carmine

1883   **Wmk. 30**
94	A27	3p on 3p violet	500.00	140.00
95	A28	6p on 6p violet	550.00	140.00
a.		Double surcharge		10,000.

A44

1883   **Wmk. 31**
96	A44	2sh6p lilac	500.00	150.00
a.		Bluish paper	8,000.	3,500.

See British Offices Abroad for overprints on types A44-A133. These overprints include "M.E.F.," "B.A.," "B.M.A.," "E.A.F.," "CHINA," "Morocco Agencies," "TANGIER," "LEVANT," "PARAS," and "PIASTRE(S)."

A45   A46

A47   A48

A49   A50

1883-84   **Wmk. 30**
98	A35	½p slate blue ('84)	27.50	8.50
99	A45	1½p lilac ('84)	110.00	40.00
100	A46	2p lilac ('84)	185.00	75.00
101	A47	2½p lilac ('84)	80.00	16.00
102	A48	3p lilac ('84)	225.00	95.00
103	A49	4p green ('84)	450.00	200.00
104	A45	5p green ('84)	450.00	200.00
105	A46	6p green ('84)	475.00	225.00
106	A50	9p green	950.00	425.00
107	A48	1sh green ('84)	1,100.	250.00
		Nos. 98-107 (10)	4,052.	1,534.

Nos. 99-107 were printed by De La Rue in a newly invented doubly fugitive ink that was only available in lilac and green. The stamps were unpopular with the public and postal clerks because they were unattractive and the different denominations were difficult to distinguish from one another.

Values are for stamps of good color. Faded stamps sell for much less. Soaking stamps will cause the color to run.
No. 104 with line instead of period under "d" was not regularly issued. Value, $27,500.
Nos. 98-105 and 107 exist imperf. Values from $2,150 to $3,000 each for Nos. 98-105, $4,500 for No. 107.
For overprints see Nos. O5, O7, O27-O29.

A51   A52

1884   **Wmk. 31**
108	A51	5sh carmine rose	950.00	220.00
a.		Bluish paper	15,000.	3,750.
109	A52	10sh ultra	2,000.	500.00
a.		10sh cobalt	35,000.	7,500.
b.		Bluish paper	37,500.	8,000.
c.		As "a," bluish paper	60,000.	14,000.

For overprints see Nos. O8-O9.

A53

1884   **Wmk. 30**
110	A53	£1 brown violet	30,000.	3,250.

See Nos. 123-124. For overprints see Nos. O10, O13, O15.

Queen Victoria Jubilee Issue

A54   A55

A56   A57

A58   A59

A60   A61

A62   A63

A64   A65

Two types of 5p:
I — Squarish dots beside "d."
II — Tiny vertical dashes beside "d."

1887-92   **Wmk. 30**
111	A54	½p vermilion	1.60	1.00
a.		Printed on both sides		
b.		Double impression	20,000.	
112	A55	1½p violet & grn	16.00	7.50
113	A56	2p grn & car rose	30.00	13.00
a.		2p green & vermilion	375.00	240.00
114	A57	2½p violet, *blue*	24.00	3.25
115	A58	3p violet, *yellow*	24.00	3.50
a.		3p violet, *orange*	725.00	175.00
116	A59	4p brown & grn	32.50	14.00
117	A60	4½p car rose & grn ('92)	10.50	42.50
118	A61	5p lilac & bl, II	37.50	11.50
a.		Type I	600.00	100.00
119	A62	6p violet, *rose*	32.50	10.50
120	A63	9p blue & lilac	65.00	42.50
121	A64	10p car rose & lilac ('90)	82.50	50.00
122	A65	1sh green	220.00	65.00
		Nos. 111-122 (12)	576.10	264.25

The unpopular green and lilac issue (Nos. 98-107) were replaced by these stamps in colored inks and papers that made it easier to distinguish the different denominations.
See Nos. 125-126. For overprints see Nos. O11-O12, O14, O16-O18, O31-O36, O38, O44, O46-O48, O54, O56-O58, O65-O66.

1888   **Wmk. Three Orbs (29)**
123 A53 £1 brown violet   65,000.   4,250.

1891   **Wmk. 30**
124 A53 £1 green   3,750.   750.00

1900   **Wmk. 30**
125 A54 ½p blue green   1.90   2.10
  a.   Imperf   6,250.
126 A65 1sh car rose &
    green   52.50   135.00

No. 125 in bright blue is a color changeling.

King Edward VII
A66   A67

A68   A69

A70   A71

A72   A73

A74   A75

A76   A77

A78

1902-11   **Wmk. 30**   *Perf. 14*
ORDINARY PAPER
127 A66 ½p gray green   2.25   1.75
128 A66 1p scarlet   2.20   1.60
  c.   1p aniline rose ('11)   225.00   160.00
  e.   Booklet pane of 6   50.00
  f.   No watermark ('11)   45.00   45.00
  g.   Imperf., pair   27,500.
129 A67 1½p vio & green   45.00   22.50
130 A68 2p yel grn & car   52.50   22.50
  a.   2p deep grn & red ('11)   30.00   22.50
131 A66 2½p ultra   22.50   11.50
132 A69 3p dull pur, *org*
    yel   45.00   19.00
133 A70 4p gray brn & grn   57.50   35.00
134 A71 5p dull pur & ultra   67.50   22.50
135 A66 6p pale dull vio   45.00   22.50
  a.   6p slate purple   45.00   22.50
  b.   6p reddish violet   45.00   30.00
  c.   6p dark violet   45.00   40.00

136 A72 9p ultra & dull vio   100.00   70.00
137 A73 10p car & dull pur   100.00   70.00
    10p scarlet & dull pur   92.50   85.00
138 A74 1sh car & dull grn   92.50   40.00
    1sh scar & dark green ('11)   115.00   70.00

Wmk. 31
139 A75 2sh6p lilac   260.00   150.00
  a.   2sh6p dark violet ('11)   260.00   175.00
140 A76 5sh car rose   400.00   225.00
  b.   5sh carmine   400.00   225.00
141 A77 10sh ultra   775.00   525.00

Wmk. Three Imperial Crowns (30)
142 A78 £1 blue green   2,000.   750.00
   Nos. 127-138 (12)   631.95   338.85

Nos. 129, 130 and 132 to 139 inclusive exist on both ordinary and chalky paper.

See Nos. 143, 144, 146-150. For overprints see Nos. O19-O26, O39-O43, O49-O53, O59-O64, O67-O83.

See British Offices Abroad for overprints on types A44-A133.
These overprints include "M.E.F.," "B.A.," "B.M.A.," "E.A.F.," "CHINA," "Morocco Agencies," "TANGIER," "LEVANT," "PARAS," and "PIASTRE(S)."

1904   **Wmk. 30**
143 A66 ½p pale yel grn   2.25   1.75
  b.   Booklet pane of 5 + label   450.00
  c.   Booklet pane of 6   37.50
  d.   Double impression   29,000.
  e.   Imperf., pair   27,500.

Edward VII — A79

1909-10
144 A70 4p pale orange
    ('10)   22.50   17.50
145 A79 7p gray ('10)   13.50   22.50

1911   *Perf. 15x14*
146 A66 ½p dull yel
    green   45.00   50.00
147 A66 1p carmine
    rose   17.50   17.50
148 A66 2½p brt ultra   25.00   17.50
149 A69 3p violet, *yel-low*   52.50   17.50
  a.   3p gray, *lemon*   3,000.
150 A70 4p orange   35.00   17.50
   Nos. 146-150 (5)   175.00   120.00

King George V
A80   A81

Perf. 15x14

1911, June 22   **Wmk. 30**
151 A80 ½p yellow green   5.75   4.50
  a.   Booklet pane of 6   62.50
  b.   Perf. 14 (error)   17,500.   900.00
152 A81 1p carmine   5.25   3.00
  a.   Booklet pane of 6   62.50
  b.   Perf. 14 (error)   —   3.50
  c.   1p pale carmine   16.00   3.50
  d.   As "c," booklet pane of 6   125.00

1912, Jan. 1   **Re-engraved**
153 A80 ½p yellow green   10.00   4.50
154 A81 1p scarlet   7.50   3.50
  b.   1p aniline scarlet   225.00   125.00

In the re-engraved stamps the lines of the hair and beard are clearer; the re-engraved ½p has 3 lines of shading instead of 4 between the point of neck and frame; in the 1p the body of the lion is nearly covered by lines of shading.

1912, Aug.   **Wmk. 33**   *Perf. 15x14*
Die I (Before Re-engraving)
155 A80 ½p yellow green   45.00   45.00
  a.   Booklet pane of 6   270.00
156 A81 1p scarlet   35.00   35.00
  a.   Booklet pane of 6   210.00

Die II (Re-engraved)
157 A80 ½p yellow green   8.00   3.50
158 A81 1p scarlet   9.25   3.50

1912-21   **Wmk. 32**
158A A80 ½p yellow green   14.00   9.25
  e.   Imperf., pair   300.00
158B A81 1p scarlet   20.00   11.50
  g.   Imperf., pair   300.00

A82   A83

A84   A85

A86   A87

A88   A89

King George V — A90

"Britannia Rule the Waves"
A91

TWO PENCE:
Die I — Four horizontal lines above the head. Heavy colored lines above and below the bottom tablet. The inner frame line is closer to the central design than it is to the outer frame line.
Die II — Three lines above the head. Thinner lines above and below the bottom tablet. The inner frame line is midway between the central design and the outer frame line.

1912-13   **Wmk. 33**   *Perf. 15x14*
159 A82 ½p green ('13)   1.10   1.10
  a.   Double impression   22,500.
  b.   Booklet pane of 6   15.00
160 A83 1p scarlet   1.10   1.10
  a.   Booklet pane of 6   15.00
  b.   Tete beche pair   67,500.
161 A84 1½p red brown   4.50   1.75
  a.   "PENCF"   220.00   175.00
  d.   1½p orange brown   24.00   19.00
  e.   1½p chocolate brown   10.50   2.25
  f.   As "e," Unwmkd.   200.00   140.00
  g.   Booklet pane of 6   30.00
  h.   Booklet pane of 4 + 2 labels   525.00
162 A85 2p deep org (I)   5.00   3.50
  a.   2p deep orange (II) ('21)   5.75   4.25
  b.   Booklet pane of 6 (I)   67.50
  c.   Booklet pane of 6 (II)   110.00
163 A86 2½p ultramarine   14.00   4.50
164 A87 3p bluish violet
    ('13)   8.00   2.25
165 A88 4p slate green   17.50   2.25
166 A89 5p yellow brown   17.50   5.75
  a.   Unwmkd.   950.00
167 A89 6p rose lilac   17.50   8.00
  a.   6p dull violet ('13)   30.00   11.50
  b.   Perf. 14   105.00   125.00
168 A89 7p ol grn ('13)   22.50   11.50
169 A89 8p black, *yellow*
    ('13)   37.50   12.50
170 A90 9p black brown
    ('13)   22.50   6.75
171 A90 10p light blue
    ('13)   25.00   22.50
172 A90 1sh bister ('13)   24.00   4.50
   Nos. 159-172 (14)   217.70   87.95

No. 167 is on chalky paper.
Nos. 159-172 were printed in a variety of shades.

See #177-178, 183, 187-200, 210, 212-220. Compare design A82 with A97.

See British Offices Abroad for overprints on types A44-A133.
These overprints include "M.E.F.," "B.A.," "B.M.A.," "E.A.F.," "CHINA," "Morocco Agencies," "TANGIER," "LEVANT," "PARAS," and "PIASTRE(S)."

Waterlow Brothers & Layton Printing (1913)

Measure 22mm vertically. Perforation holes are larger and evenly spaced.

1913   **Engr.**   **Wmk. 34**   *Perf. 11x12*
173 A91 2sh6p dark
    brown   275.00   190.00
174 A91 5sh rose car   500.00   375.00
175 A91 10sh indigo blue   950.00   475.00
176 A91 £1 green   2,900.   1,550.
   Nos. 173-176 (4)   4,625.   2,590.

De La Rue & Co. Printing (1915)

Measure 22mm vertically. Gum tends to be yellowish and patchy. The top right and top left perf teeth are wider than the others. Perforation holes are smaller.

1915   **Engr.**   **Wmk. 34**   *Perf. 11x12*
173a A91 2sh6p lt brn
    (worn
    plate)   290.00   220.00
174a A91 5sh br carmine   475.00   375.00
175a A91 10sh light blue   2,500.   800.00

See Nos. 179-181, 222-224.

1913   **Wmk. 32**   **Typo.**   *Perf. 15x14*
Coil Stamps
177 A82 ½p green   175.00   210.00
178 A83 1p scarlet   260.00   260.00

Bradbury, Wilkinson & Co. Printing (1918-19)
Seahorses Types of 1913-15 Retouched

1919   **Engr.**   **Wmk. 34**   *Perf. 11x12*
179 A91 2sh6p olive brown   115.00   75.00
180 A91 5sh car rose   290.00   125.00
181 A91 10sh blue   425.00   180.00
   Nos. 179-181 (3)   830.00   380.00

The retouched stamps usually have a dot above the middle of the top frame. They are 22¾mm high, whereas Nos. 173-176 are 22mm high.

Type of 1912-13

1922   **Typo.**   **Wmk. 33**   *Perf. 15x14*
183 A90 9p olive green   120.00   35.00

British Empire Exhibition Issue

British Lion and George V
A92

Wmk. 35
1924, Apr. 23   **Engr.**   *Perf. 14*
185 A92 1p vermilion   11.50   12.50
    Never hinged   17.50
186 A92 1½p dark brown   17.50   17.50
    Never hinged   26.00

See Nos. 203-204.

Types of 1912-13 Issue

1924   **Typo.**   *Perf. 15x14*
187 A82 ½p green   1.10   1.10
    Never hinged   1.50
  a.   Wmk. sideways   10.00   3.75
    Never hinged   18.00
  b.   Booklet pane of 6   12.00
    Never hinged   18.00
  c.   Double impression   9,250.
188 A83 1p scarlet   1.10   1.10
    Never hinged   1.40
  a.   Wmk. sideways   22.50   17.50
    Never hinged   45.00
  b.   Booklet pane of 6   12.50
    Never hinged   18.50
189 A84 1½p red brown   1.10   1.10
    Never hinged   1.40
  a.   Tête bêche pair   550.00   875.00
    Never hinged   775.00
  b.   Wmk. sideways   20.00   4.00
    Never hinged   40.00
  c.   Booklet pane of 6   12.50
    Never hinged   18.50
  d.   Bklt. pane of 4 + 2 labels   160.00

	Never hinged	260.00	
e.	Double impression	16,500.	
190 A85	2p dp orange (II)	2.90	2.90
	Never hinged	3.75	
a.	Wmk. sideways	110.00	110.00
	Never hinged	200.00	
b.	Unwatermarked	925.00	
	Never hinged	1,400.	
191 A86	2½p ultra	5.75	3.50
	Never hinged	10.00	
	Unwatermarked	1,750.	
	Never hinged	2,250.	
192 A87	3p violet	11.50	2.75
	Never hinged	19.00	
193 A88	4p slate green	14.00	2.75
	Never hinged	29.00	
194 A89	5p yel brown	22.50	3.50
	Never hinged	45.00	
195 A89	6p dull violet	3.50	1.75
	Never hinged	5.00	
198 A90	9p olive green	13.50	4.00
	Never hinged	21.50	
199 A90	10p dull blue	45.00	45.00
	Never hinged	110.00	
200 A90	1sh bister	25.00	3.50
	Never hinged	50.00	
	Nos. 187-200 (12)	146.95	72.95

Nos. 187a, 188a, 189b, 190a issued in coils. Inverted watermarks on the three lowest values are usually from booklet panes.

Nos. 188-189 were issued also on experimental paper with variety of Wmk. 35: closer spacing; letters shorter, rounder.

British Empire Exhibition Issue
Type of 1924, Dated "1925"

			Engr.	**Perf. 14**
1925, May 9				
203 A92	1p vermilion		17.00	35.00
	Never hinged		25.00	
204 A92	1½p brown		45.00	80.00
	Never hinged		67.50	

A93

A94

A95

St. George Slaying the Dragon
A96

		Typo.	**Perf. 15x14**
1929, May 10			
205 A93	½p green	2.50	2.50
	Never hinged	3.75	
a.	Wmk. sideways	45.00	45.00
	Never hinged	120.00	
b.	Booklet pane of 6	27.50	
206 A94	1p scarlet	2.50	2.50
	Never hinged	3.75	
a.	Wmk. sideways	82.50	82.50
	Never hinged	120.00	
b.	Booklet pane of 6	27.50	
207 A94	1½p dark brown	2.60	2.00
	Never hinged	4.00	
a.	Wmk. sideways	45.00	45.00
	Never hinged	90.00	
b.	Booklet pane of 6	20.00	
c.	Booklet pane of 4 + 2 labels	250.00	
208 A95	2½p deep blue	11.50	11.50
	Never hinged	24.00	
	Nos. 205-208 (4)	19.10	18.50

Nos. 205a, 206a and 207a were issued in coils.

Wmk. 219

		Engr.	**Perf. 12**
209 A96	£1 black	875.00	625.00
	Never hinged	1,400.	

Universal Postal Union, 9th Congress.

A97

Type A97 designs are re-engraved versions of the types of the 1912-13 issue, with the most obvious difference being the solid appearance of the central field. The backgrounds appear to be solid, although the photoengraving screen can be seen under magnification.

		Photo.	**Wmk. 35**
1934-36		**Perf. 14½x14**	
210 A97	½p dark green	.60	.60
	Never hinged	1.10	
a.	Wmk. sideways	10.00	4.00
	Never hinged	19.00	
b.	Booklet pane of 6	11.00	
211 A97	1p carmine	.60	.60
	Never hinged	1.00	
a.	Wmk. sideways	22.50	9.00
	Never hinged	45.00	
b.	Booklet pane of 6	11.00	
c.	Imperf., pair	4,000.	
d.	Pair, imperf. btwn.	5,000.	
212 A97	1½p red brown	.60	.60
	Never hinged	1.00	
a.	Imperf., pair	1,000.	
b.	Wmk. sideways	9.00	4.50
	Never hinged	13.00	
c.	Booklet pane of 6	5.50	
d.	Booklet pane of 4 + 2 labels	110.00	
213 A97	2p red org ('35)	.85	.85
	Never hinged	1.25	
a.	Imperf., pair	4,750.	
b.	Wmk. sideways	140.00	100.00
	Never hinged	250.00	
214 A97	2½p ultra ('35)	1.75	1.40
	Never hinged	2.50	
215 A97	3p dk violet ('35)	1.75	1.40
	Never hinged	2.50	
216 A97	4p dk sl grn ('35)	2.25	1.40
	Never hinged	3.50	
217 A97	5p yel brown ('36)	7.00	3.00
	Never hinged	11.00	
218 A97	9p dk ol grn ('35)	14.00	2.75
	Never hinged	20.00	
219 A97	10p Prus blue ('36)	17.50	11.50
	Never hinged	30.00	
220 A97	1sh bister brn ('36)	17.50	1.40
	Never hinged	35.00	
	Nos. 210-220 (11)	64.40	25.50

The designs in this set are slightly smaller than the 1912-13 issue.

Nos. 210a, 211a, 212b and 213b were issued in coils.

Britannia Type of 1913-19 Reengraved

		Engr.	**Wmk. 34**	**Perf. 11x12**
1934				
222 A91	2sh6p brown		90.00	45.00
	Never hinged		150.00	
223 A91	5sh carmine		190.00	100.00
	Never hinged		340.00	
224 A91	10sh dark blue		400.00	92.50
	Never hinged		650.00	
	Nos. 222-224 (3)		680.00	237.50

Printed by Waterlow & Sons. Can be distinguished by the crossed lines in background of portrait. Previous issues have horizontal lines only.

Silver Jubilee Issue

A98

		Photo.	**Wmk. 35**
1935, May 7		**Perf. 14½x14**	
226 A98	½p dark green	1.10	.60
	Never hinged	1.55	
a.	Booklet pane of 4	18.50	
227 A98	1p carmine	1.60	1.90
	Never hinged	2.30	
a.	Booklet pane of 4	18.50	
228 A98	1½p red brown	1.10	.60
	Never hinged	1.55	
a.	Booklet pane of 4	9.50	
229 A98	2½p ultra	5.50	6.25
	Never hinged	7.75	
a.	2½p Prussian blue	9,500.	11,000.
	Never hinged	11,000.	
	Nos. 226-229 (4)	9.30	9.35

25th anniv. of the reign of George V. Device at right differs on 1½p and 2½p.

Edward VIII — A99

			Wmk. 250
1936			
230 A99	½p dark green	.20	.20
	Never hinged	.40	
a.	Booklet pane of 6	2.00	
	Never hinged	2.75	
231 A99	1p crimson	.50	.50
	Never hinged	.70	
a.	Booklet pane of 6	3.00	
	Never hinged	4.50	

---

232 A99	1½p red brown	.20	.35
	Never hinged	.40	
a.	Booklet pane of 6	2.00	
	Never hinged	2.75	
b.	Booklet pane of 4 + 2 labels	62.50	
	Never hinged	85.00	
c.	Booklet pane of 2	6.00	
	Never hinged	10.00	
233 A99	2½p bright ultra	.20	1.00
	Never hinged	.40	
	Nos. 230-233 (4)	1.10	2.05

King George VI and Queen Elizabeth
A100

			Wmk. 251
1937, May 13		**Perf. 14½x14**	
234 A100	1½p purple brown	.25	.25
	Never hinged	.35	

Coronation of George VI and Elizabeth.

See British Offices Abroad for overprints on types A44-A133. These overprints include "M.E.F.," "B.A.," "B.M.A.," "E.A.F.," "CHINA," "Morocco Agencies," "TANGIER," "LEVANT," "PARAS," and "PIASTRE(S)."

A101

A102

King George VI — A103

Nos. 235-240 show face and neck highlighted, background solid.

1937-39			
235 A101	½p deep green	.20	.25
	Never hinged	.25	
a.	Wmk. sideways	.40	.45
	Never hinged	.55	
b.	Booklet pane of 6	5.50	
	Never hinged	7.50	
c.	Booklet pane of 4	25.00	32.50
	Never hinged	50.00	
d.	Booklet pane of 2	8.50	
	Never hinged	12.50	
236 A101	1p scarlet	.20	.20
	Never hinged	.25	
a.	Wmk. sideways	8.50	9.50
	Never hinged	22.50	
b.	Booklet pane of 6	8.50	
	Never hinged	12.50	
c.	Booklet pane of 4	55.00	55.00
	Never hinged	110.00	
d.	Booklet pane of 2	8.50	
	Never hinged	12.50	
237 A101	1½p red brown	.20	.20
	Never hinged	.25	
a.	Wmk. sideways	.80	1.25
	Never hinged	1.10	
b.	Booklet pane of 6	8.50	
	Never hinged	12.50	
c.	Booklet pane of 4 + 2 labels	57.50	
	Never hinged	80.00	
d.	Booklet pane of 2	6.25	
	Never hinged	9.00	
238 A101	2p orange ('38)	.60	.50
	Never hinged	1.00	
a.	Wmk. sideways	50.00	45.00
	Never hinged	85.00	
b.	Booklet pane of 6	25.00	
	Never hinged	37.50	
239 A101	2½p bright ultra	.20	.20
	Never hinged	.35	
a.	Wmk. sideways	45.00	25.00
	Never hinged	80.00	
b.	Booklet pane of 6	25.00	
	Never hinged	37.50	
c.	Tête bêche pair	2,400.	
240 A101	3p dk purple ('38)	3.00	1.10
	Never hinged	5.25	
241 A102	4p gray green ('38)	.45	.80
	Never hinged	.70	
a.	Imperf., pair	4,750.	
	Never hinged	6,000.	
b.	Horiz. pair, imperf. on 3 sides	4,500.	
	Never hinged	6,000.	
242 A102	5p lt brown ('38)	1.70	.90
	Never hinged	3.00	
a.	Imperf., pair	5,500.	
	Never hinged	7,000.	
b.	Horiz. pair, imperf. on 3 sides	4,500.	
	Never hinged	6,000.	
243 A102	6p rose lilac ('39)	1.10	.65
	Never hinged	1.50	

---

244 A103	7p emerald ('39)	2.75	.65
	Never hinged	5.50	
a.	Horiz. pair, imperf. on 3 sides	4,400.	
	Never hinged	5,750.	
245 A103	8p brt rose ('39)	3.75	.90
	Never hinged	6.00	
246 A103	9p dp ol green ('39)	3.50	.90
	Never hinged	6.50	
247 A103	10p royal bl ('39)	4.00	.85
	Never hinged	7.50	
a.	Imperf., pair	5,700.	
	Never hinged	7,000.	
248 A103	1sh brown ('39)	4.75	1.00
	Never hinged	7.50	
	Nos. 235-248 (14)	26.40	9.10
	Set, never hinged	47.00	

Nos. 235a, 236a, 237a, 238a and 239a were issued in coils.

Nos. 235c and 236c are watermarked sideways.

The 1½p, 1p, 1½p, 2p and 2½p with watermark inverted are from booklet panes.

No. 238 bisects were used in Guernsey from 12/27/40 to 2/24/41. Value, on cover $32.50.

See Nos. 258-263, 266, 280-285.

Oman Surcharges
Various definitive and commemorative stamps between Nos. 243 and 372 were surcharged in annas (a), new paisa (np) and rupees (r) for use in Oman. The surcharges do not indicate where the stamps were used.

King George VI and Royal Arms — A104

King George VI — A105

		Engr.	**Wmk. 259**	**Perf. 14**
1939-42				
249 A104	2sh6p chestnut		30.00	8.50
	Never hinged		77.50	
249A A104	2sh6p yel green ('42)		6.00	1.75
	Never hinged		16.00	
250 A104	5sh dull red		8.50	2.25
	Never hinged		25.00	
251 A105	10sh indigo		150.00	24.00
	Never hinged		325.00	
251A A105	10sh ultra ('42)		17.50	5.75
	Never hinged		40.00	
	Nos. 249-251A (5)		212.00	42.25

See No. 275.

Victoria and George VI
A106

		Photo.	**Wmk. 251**
1940, May 6		**Perf. 14½x14**	
252 A106	½p deep green	.20	.25
	Never hinged	.30	
253 A106	1p scarlet	.55	.40
	Never hinged	1.10	
254 A106	1½p red brown	.25	.85
	Never hinged	.55	
255 A106	2p orange	.60	.85
	Never hinged	1.10	
256 A106	2½p brt ultra	1.25	.55
	Never hinged	2.50	
257 A106	3p dark purple	1.90	4.50
	Never hinged	3.50	
	Nos. 252-257 (6)	4.75	7.40

Centenary of the postage stamp.

No. 255 bisects were used in Guernsey from 12/27/40 to 2/24/41. Value, on cover, $40.

Type of 1937-39, with Background Lightened

1941-42			
258 A101	½p green	.20	.20
	Never hinged	.25	
a.	Booklet pane of 6	3.00	

	Never hinged	4.25	
b.	Booklet pane of 2	1.20	
	Never hinged	1.50	
c.	Imperf., pair	5,000.	
	Never hinged	7,000.	
d.	Tete beche pair	8,000.	
	Never hinged	17,500.	
e.	Booklet pane of 4		
259	A101 1p vermilion	.20	.25
	Never hinged	.25	
a.	Wmk. sideways ('42)	3.00	5.75
	Never hinged	5.00	
b.	Booklet pane of 2	1.25	
	Never hinged	1.60	
c.	Imperf., pair	5,000.	
	Never hinged	7,000.	
d.	Booklet pane of 4		
e.	Horiz. pair, imperf on 3 sides	5,000.	
	Never hinged	7,000.	
260	A101 1½p lt red brn ('42)	.30	.85
	Never hinged	.60	
a.	Booklet pane of 2	2.75	
	Never hinged	4.00	
b.	Booklet pane of 4		
261	A101 2p light orange	.25	.50
	Never hinged	.50	
a.	Wmk. sideways ('42)	16.50	21.00
	Never hinged	32.50	
b.	Booklet pane of 6	6.75	
	Never hinged	10.00	
c.	Imperf., pair	4,350.	
	Never hinged	6,000.	
d.	Tete beche pair	11,500.	
	Never hinged	17,500.	
262	A101 2½p ultra	.25	.40
	Never hinged	.35	
a.	Wmk. sideways ('42)	9.00	11.00
	Never hinged	17.50	
b.	Booklet pane of 6	3.75	
	Never hinged	5.00	
c.	Imperf., pair	3,350.	
	Never hinged	4,750.	
d.	Tete beche pair	11,500.	
	Never hinged	17,500.	
263	A101 3p violet	1.40	1.10
	Nos. 258-263 (6)	2.60	3.30

Nos. 259a, 261a and 262a were issued in coils.

Nos. 258b, 258e, 259b, 259d, 260a-260b are made from sheets.

> **Catalogue values for unused stamps in this section, from this point to the end of the section, are for Never Hinged items.**

Peace Issue

A107

King George VI and Symbols of Peace and Industry A108

Perf. 14½x14

1946, June 11   Photo.   Wmk. 251

264	A107 2½p bright ultra	.20	.20
265	A108 3p violet	.20	.45

Return to peace at the close of WW II.

George VI Type of 1939

1947, Dec. 29

266	A103 11p violet brown	3.50	4.00

A109

King George VI and Queen Elizabeth A110

1948, Apr. 26   Perf. 14½x14, 14x14½

267	A109 2½p brt ultra	.40	.20
268	A110 £1 dp chalky blue	50.00	50.00

25th anniv. of the marriage of King George VI and Queen Elizabeth.

A111

Vraicking (Gathering Seaweed) A112

1948, May 10   Perf. 14½x14

269	A111 1p red	.20	.20
270	A112 2½p bright ultra	.20	.20

3rd anniversary of the liberation of the Channel Islands from German occupation.
Sold at post offices in the Channel Islands and at major philatelic windows in the United Kingdom, and valid for postage throughout Great Britain.

A113

A114

A115

A116

1948, July 29

271	A113 2½p bright ultra	.40	.20
272	A114 3p deep violet	.65	.65
273	A115 6p red violet	2.75	.75
274	A116 1sh dark brown	4.25	2.00
	Nos. 271-274 (4)	8.05	3.60

1948 Olympic Games held at Wembley during July and August.

George VI Type of 1939
Wmk. 259

1948, Oct. 1   Engr.   Perf. 14

275	A105 £1 red brown	25.00	27.50

A117

A118

A119

A120

Perf. 14½x14

1949, Oct. 10   Photo.   Wmk. 251

276	A117 2½p bright ultra	.20	.20
277	A118 3p brt violet	.20	.55
278	A119 6p red violet	.50	.55
279	A120 1sh brown	1.10	1.40
	Nos. 276-279 (4)	2.00	2.70

UPU, 75th anniversary.

Types of 1937

1950-51   Wmk. 251   Perf. 14½x14

280	A101 ½p light orange	.20	.20
a.	Booklet pane of 2	1.20	
b.	Booklet pane of 4	2.00	
c.	Booklet pane of 6	3.00	
d.	Imperf., pair	5,000.	
e.	Tete beche pair	17,500.	
281	A101 1p ultramarine	.20	.20
a.	Wmk. sideways	1.25	1.40
b.	Booklet pane of 2	1.40	
c.	Booklet pane of 4	2.10	
d.	Booklet pane of 6	3.00	
e.	Booklet pane of 3 + 3 labels	20.00	
f.	Imperf., pair	5,000.	
g.	Horiz. pair, imperf on 3 sides	6,000.	
282	A101 1½p green	.75	.70
a.	Wmk. sideways	3.75	5.75
b.	Booklet pane of 2	2.00	
c.	Booklet pane of 4	3.75	
d.	Booklet pane of 6	5.50	
283	A101 2p lt red brown	.85	.45
a.	Wmk. sideways	2.00	2.25
b.	Booklet pane of 6	9.00	
c.	Tete beche pair	17,500.	
d.	Horiz. pair, imperf on 3 sides	6,000.	
284	A101 2½p vermilion	.70	.45
a.	Wmk. sideways	2.00	2.00
b.	Booklet pane of 6	4.75	
c.	Tete beche pair		
285	A102 4p ultra ('50)	2.25	2.00
a.	Double impression	8,250.	
	Nos. 280-285 (6)	4.95	4.00

Nos. 281a, 282a, 283a and 284a were issued in coils.

H.M.S. Victory A121

St. George Slaying the Dragon A122

Royal Arms A123

Design: 5sh, White Cliffs, Dover.

Perf. 11x12

1951, May 3   Engr.   Wmk. 259

286	A121 2sh6p green	6.50	1.10
287	A121 5sh dull red	45.00	1.75
288	A122 10sh ultra	16.00	9.75
289	A123 £1 lt red brown	55.00	22.50
	Nos. 286-289 (4)	122.50	35.10

Britannia, Symbols of Commerce and Prosperity, King George VI — A124

Festival Symbol A125

Perf. 14½x14

1951, May 3   Photo.   Wmk. 251

290	A124 2½p scarlet	.25	.25
291	A125 4p bright ultra	.35	.75

Festival of Britain, 1951.

Queen Elizabeth
A126   A127

A128   A129

A130   A131

A132

The 2½d exists in two types: Type I, in the front cross of the diadem, the top line extends half the width of the cross; Type II, the top line extends across the full width of the top of the cross.

Perf. 14½x14

1952-54   Photo.   Wmk. 298

292	A126 ½p red orange ('53)	.20	.20
a.	Booklet pane of 2	.70	
b.	Booklet pane of 4	1.25	
c.	Booklet pane of 6	1.50	
293	A126 1p ultra ('53)	.20	.20
a.	Booklet pane of 2	.90	
b.	Booklet pane of 4	1.75	
c.	Booklet pane of 6	2.25	
d.	Booklet pane 3 + 3 labels	32.50	
294	A126 1½p green ('52)	.20	.20
a.	Booklet pane of 2	.70	
b.	Booklet pane of 4	1.25	
c.	Booklet pane of 6 ('53)	1.50	
d.	Wmk. sideways	.55	.80
e.	As "c," imperf. (error)	750.00	
295	A126 2p red brn ('53)	.20	.20
a.	Booklet pane of 6	25.00	
b.	Wmk. sideways	1.10	2.25
296	A127 2½p scarlet, Type I ('52)	.20	.20
a.	Booklet pane of 6, Type II ('53)	7.00	
b.	Wmk. sideways, Type I ('54)	8.00	9.25
c.	Type II	1.40	1.40
297	A127 3p dk purple	.85	.65
298	A128 4p ultra ('53)	3.75	1.40
299	A129 5p lt brn ('53)	.85	4.00
300	A129 6p lilac rose	4.50	1.10
301	A129 7p emerald	11.00	6.25
302	A130 8p brt rose ('53)	.80	1.00
303	A130 9p dp ol grn	26.00	5.50
304	A130 10p royal blue	21.00	5.50
305	A130 11p vio brown	35.00	17.50
306	A131 1sh brown ('53)	.90	.55
307	A132 1sh3p dk grn ('53)	5.25	3.75
308	A131 1sh6p dk bl ('53)	16.00	4.25
	Nos. 292-308 (17)	126.90	52.45

Nos. 294d, 295b, 296b issued in coils.

Nos. 292-296 with watermark inverted are from booklets.

Type II stamps of No. 296 come only from booklet panes.

See Nos. 317-333, 353-369, 1801-1803, 2022-2023, 2086, 2125.

Compare design A128 with A139.

See regional issues, Guernsey, Jersey and Isle of Man for other stamps showing this portrait of the Queen, which have different frames or devices added to the design.

See British Offices Abroad for overprints on types A44-A133.

These overprints include "M.E.F.," "B.A.," "B.M.A.," "E.A.F.," "CHINA," "Morocco Agencies," "TANGIER," "LEVANT," "PARAS," and "PIASTRE(S)."

Windsor,
England
A133

Castles: 2sh6p, Carrickfergus, Ireland. 5sh, Caernarfon Castle, Wales. 10sh, Edinburgh, Scotland.

1955 Engr. Wmk. 308 Perf. 11x12

309	A133	2sh6p dark brown	12.50	2.25
310	A133	5sh crimson	40.00	4.50
311	A133	10sh brt ultra	100.00	16.00
312	A133	£1 intense blk	150.00	40.00
		Nos. 309-312 (4)	302.50	62.75

See Nos. 371-374, 525-528, 2278.

A134

A135

A136

A137

Perf. 14½x14

1953, June 3 Photo. Wmk. 298

313	A134	2½p scarlet	.30	.25
314	A135	4p ultra	1.40	2.25
315	A135	1sh3p dark green	5.50	3.50
316	A137	1sh6p dark blue	11.00	5.50
		Nos. 313-316 (4)	18.20	11.50

See Nos. 1942, 2126.

Types of 1952-54

1955-57 Wmk. 308 Perf. 14½x14

317	A126	½p red orange ('56)	.20	.20
a.		Booklet pane of 6	1.75	
b.		Booklet pane of 4	1.50	
c.		Booklet pane of 2	.70	
318	A126	1p ultra ('56)	.20	.20
a.		Bklt. pane of 3 + 3 labels	19.00	
b.		Booklet pane of 6	2.00	
c.		Booklet pane of 4	1.50	
e.		Tete Beche pair	—	
f.		Booklet pane of 2	.80	
319	A126	1½p green ('56)	.25	.25
a.		Booklet pane of 6	8.50	
b.		Booklet pane of 4	6.50	
c.		Wmk. sideways ('56)	.40	.80
e.		Tete beche pair	3,000.	
f.		Booklet pane of 2	1.50	
320	A126	2p red brown ('56)	.20	.25
a.		Wmk. sideways ('56)	7.50	6.00
b.		Booklet pane of 6	3.00	

d.		Tete beche pair	2,000.	
e.		Vert. pair, imperf. between	3,000.	
f.		As "a," horiz. pair, imperf. between	3,000.	
h.		Imperf., pair	350.00	
321	A127	2½p scar, Type I ('56)	.20	.25
a.		Booklet pane of 6, Type II	4.50	
b.		Wmk. sideways, Type I ('56)	1.75	2.00
d.		Type II	.50	.50
e.		Tete beche pair	2,100.	
f.		Imperf., pair		
322	A127	3p dk purple ('56)	.20	.25
a.		Booklet pane of 6	4.50	
b.		Booklet pane of 4	6.00	
c.		Wmk. sideways	22.50	20.00
e.		Tete beche pair	2,100.	
323	A128	4p ultra	1.40	.50
324	A129	5p lt brn ('56)	6.75	6.75
325	A129	6p lilac rose ('56)	5.00	1.40
326	A129	7p emerald	60.00	12.50
327	A130	8p brt rose ('56)	8.00	1.40
328	A130	9p dp ol grn ('56)	22.50	3.25
329	A130	10p royal bl ('56)	22.50	3.25
330	A130	11p vio brown	.55	1.40
331	A131	1sh brown	25.00	.75
332	A132	1sh3p dk grn ('56)	35.00	1.90
333	A131	1sh6p dark blue	26.00	1.90
		Nos. 317-333 (17)	213.95	36.40

Nos. 319c, 320a, 321b, 322c issued in coils.

Nos. 317-322 with watermark inverted are from booklets. See Nos. 353-369.

Black Graphite Lines on Back

1957-59 Wmk. 308

317c	A126	½p red orange	.25	.25
p.		Phosphor. ('59)	4.50	4.50
318d	A126	1p ultra	.25	.25
p.		Phosphor. ('59)	12.50	12.50
319d	A126	1½p green	1.30	1.60
p.		Phosphor. ('59)	4.50	4.50
320c	A126	2p red brown	1.75	2.50
p.		Phosphor. ('59)	210.00	175.00
321c	A127	2½p scarlet (II)	10.00	8.25
322d	A127	3p dark purple	.95	.60
		Nos. 317c-322d (6)	14.50	13.40

The vertical black graphite lines were applied to facilitate mail sorting by an electronic machine. The 2p has one line (at right, seen from back), the others two.

Phosphorescent bands were overprinted vertically in Nov. 1959 on the face of the preceding ½p, 1p, 1½p and 2p graphite-lined stamps, plus the 2p, 2½p, 3p, 4p and 4½p graphite-lined stamps with Wmk. 322, in a letter-sorting experiment. These faint bands can be seen best with an ultraviolet lamp; without it they can be seen best on unused stamps.

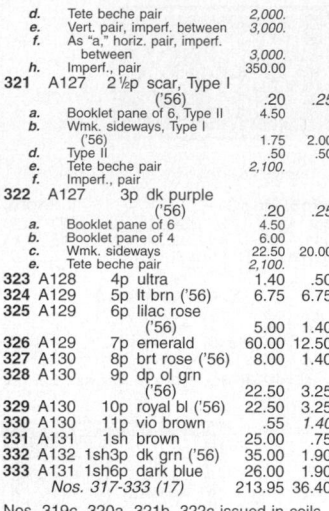

Scout
Emblem
and Rolling
Hitch Knot
A138

4p, Swallows. 1sh3p, Globe encircled by compass.

Perf. 14½x14

1957, Aug. 1 Wmk. 308

334	A138	2½p scarlet	.25	.20
335	A138	4p ultra	.60	1.00
336	A138	1sh3p dk green	5.50	4.00
		Nos. 334-336 (3)	6.35	5.20

50th anniv. of the Boy Scout movement and the World Scout Jubilee Jamboree, Sutton Coldfield, Aug. 1-12.

A139

1957, Sept. 12 Photo.

337	A139	4p ultra	1.10	1.10

46th Conf. of the Inter-Parliamentary Union, London, Sept. 12-19.

Welsh
Dragon
A140

Designs: 6p, Flag with British Empire and Commonwealth Games Emblem. 1sh3p, Welsh dragon holding laurel.

1958, July 18 Perf. 14½x14

338	A140	3p dk purple	.20	.20
339	A140	6p red lilac	.45	.50
340	A140	1sh3p green	2.50	2.75
		Nos. 338-340 (3)	3.15	3.45

6th British Empire and Commonwealth Games, Cardiff, July 18-26.

Regional Issues of Great Britain for Guernsey, Jersey, Isle of Man, Northern Ireland, Scotland and Wales-Monmouthshire are listed in separate sections following Great Britain Envelopes.

Types of 1952-55

Perf. 14½x14

1958-65 Photo. Wmk. 322

353	A126	½p red orange	.20	.20
a.		Booklet pane of 6	.70	
b.		Booklet pane of 4	4.00	
e.		Booklet pane of 4 (3 No. 353 + No. 357) ('63)	10.50	10.50
f.		Tete beche pair	850.00	
g.		Booklet pane of 4 (2 Nos. 353 + 2 No. 357) ('64)	2.50	2.50
354	A126	1p ultra ('59)	.20	.20
a.		Booklet pane of 6 ('59)	1.00	
b.		Booklet pane of 4	5.25	
e.		Imperf., pair		
f.		Bklt. pane, #2 #354, 2 #358 ('65)	11.50	11.50
355	A126	1½p green	.20	.20
a.		Booklet pane of 6	1.00	
b.		Booklet pane of 4	40.00	
356	A126	2p red brown	.20	.20
a.		Wmk. sideways	.55	1.10
b.		Booklet pane of 6	6.00	
357	A127	2½p scarlt, type II	.20	.20
a.		Type I ('61)	.80	.80
b.		Wmk. sideways, type I	.30	.50
c.		Booklet pane of 6, Type II ('59)	1.00	
f.		Tete beche pair, type II	5,000.	
g.		Booklet pane of 4, type II ('64)	2.50	
h.		Imperf., pair		
358	A127	3p dark purple	.20	.20
a.		Booklet pane of 6	1.75	
b.		Booklet pane of 4	3.75	
e.		Imperf., pair	250.00	
g.		Wmk. sideways	.30	.40
359	A128	4p ultra	.50	.40
b.		Booklet pane of 6 ('65)	6.00	
c.		Booklet pane of 4 ('65)	3.75	
d.		Wmk. sideways	.80	.65
360	A128	4½p henna brn	.20	.20
361	A129	5p light brown	.30	.40
362	A129	6p lil rose ('59)	.35	.25
363	A129	7p emerald	.60	.50
364	A130	8p brt rose ('60)	.70	.40
365	A130	9p dp ol grn ('59)	.70	.45
366	A130	10p royal blue	1.00	.55
367	A131	1sh brown	.50	.35
368	A132	1sh3p dk grn ('59)	.50	.35
369	A131	1sh6p dark blue	4.50	.70
		Nos. 353-369 (17)	11.05	5.80

Nos. 356a and 357b were issued in coils. The 3p and 4p watermarked sideways may be from a coil or booklet pane of 4.

Booklet panes of this issue have watermarks normal, inverted or sideways.

Part perf. booklet panes exist of No. 353a and No. 354a.

Black Graphite Lines on Back

1958-59 Wmk. 322

353c	A126	½p red orange ('59)	10.50	10.50
d.		Booklet pane of 6	27.50	
354c	A126	1p ultra ('59)	1.50	1.75
d.		Booklet pane of 6	17.50	
355c	A126	1½p green ('59)	100.00	92.50
d.		Booklet pane of 6	600.00	
356c	A126	2p red brown	8.75	4.00
cp.		Phosphor. ('59)	5.50	5.00
357d	A127	2½p scarlet (II) ('59)	10.50	11.50
dp.		Phosphor. ('59)	25.00	20.00
e.		Booklet pane of 6	100.00	
358c	A127	3p dark purple	.75	.75
cp.		Phosphor. ('59)	10.00	8.00
d.		Booklet pane of 6	5.50	
359a	A128	4p ultra ('59)	5.25	5.75
ap.		Phosphor. ('59)	22.50	20.00
360a	A128	4½p henna brn ('59)	7.50	5.75
ap.		Phosphor. ('59)	35.00	25.00
		Nos. 353c-360a (8)	144.75	132.50

The vertical black graphite lines were applied to facilitate mail sorting by an electronic machine. The 2p has one line; the others two. Missing or misplaced lines occur on 1p, 3p and 4p.

Nos. 353c and 354c were issued only in booklets or coils; No. 355c only in booklets.

Phosphorescent Stamps of 1958-65

1960-67 Wmk. 322

353p	A126	½p red orange	.20	.20
ap.		Booklet pane of 6	4.00	
bp.		Booklet pane of 4	50.00	
354p	A126	1p ultra	.20	.20
ap.		Booklet pane of 6	5.00	
bp.		Booklet pane of 4	12.00	

fp.		Booklet pane of 2 each #354p, 358p	40.00	
355p	A126	1½p green	.20	.20
ap.		Booklet pane of 6	5.00	
bp.		Booklet pane of 4	50.00	
356p	A126	2p red brown	.20	.20
ap.		Watermark sideways	.20	.40
357p	A127	2½p scarlet (II)	.20	.40
ap.		Type I ('61)	47.50	37.50
cp.		Booklet pane of 6	60.00	
358p	A127	3p dark purple	.70	.65
ap.		Booklet pane of 6	7.50	
bp.		Booklet pane of 12	12.50	
gp.		Watermark sideways	1.25	.50
359p	A128	4p ultramarine	.25	.25
ap.		Booklet pane of 6	6.25	
cp.		Booklet pane of 4		
dp.		Watermark sideways	.40	.60
360p	A128	4½p henna brown ('61)	.25	.25
361p	A129	5p lt brown ('67)	.25	.25
362p	A129	6p lilac rose	.40	.35
363p	A129	7p emerald ('67)	.65	.60
364p	A130	8p brt rose ('67)	.45	.50
365p	A130	9p dp ol grn ('67)	.65	.65
366p	A130	10p royal blue ('67)	.80	.70
367p	A131	1sh brown ('67)	.40	.40
368p	A132	1sh3p dark green	2.25	2.75
369p	A131	1sh6p dark blue ('66)	2.40	1.75
		Nos. 353p-369p (17)	10.45	10.30

The 2p, 2½p (II) and 3p were issued with both one and two phosphorescent bands. The less expensive is valued here.

Watermarked sideways, the 2p is from a coil; the 3p and 4p from booklet pane or coil; the ½p, 1p and 1½p from booklet panes (hence unlisted in this state).

Booklet panes of 4 with phosphorescent bands; ½p, 1p, 1½p, 3p (2 bands), 4p, and 1p se-tenant with 3p (1 or 2 bands). Booklet panes of 6 with phosphorescent bands: ½p, 1p, 1½p, 2½p (II) (1 or 2 bands), 3p (1 or 2 bands), 4p.

1959 Engr. Wmk. 322 Perf. 11x12

371	A133	2sh6p dark brown	.40	.45
372	A133	5sh crimson	1.00	.60
373	A133	10sh bright ultra	4.50	5.25
374	A133	£1 intense blk	12.50	8.00
		Nos. 371-374 (4)	18.40	14.30

Postboy on
Horseback
A147

Queen Elizabeth II,
Oak Leaves and
1660 Post
Horn — A148

Perf. 14½x14, 14x14½

1960, July 7 Photo. Wmk. 322

375	A147	3p bright violet	.50	.50
376	A148	1sh3p dark green	3.50	4.25

Tercentenary of the act establishing the General Letter Office (General Post Office).

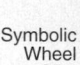

Symbolic
Wheel
CD3

Perf. 14½x14

1960, Sept. 19 Wmk. 322

377	CD3	6p red lilac & grn	1.75	.60
378	CD3	1sh3p dk bl & red brn	13.50	6.25

1st anniv. of the establishment of CEPT.

Symbolic Thrift
Plant — A150

Nut Tree, Nest, Squirrel, Owl A151

Thrift Plant A152

Perf. 14x14½, 14½x14

1961, Aug. 28		**Photo.**	**Wmk. 322**	
379	A150	2½p scar & blk	.20	.20
a.		Black omitted	18,500.	
380	A151	3p pur & org	.20	.20
a.		Orange omitted	190.00	90.00
381	A152	1sh6p dk bl & ver	2.50	2.50
		Nos. 379-381 (3)	2.90	2.90

Centenary of Post Office Savings Bank.

CEPT Emblem A153

Nineteen Doves Flying as One CD4

Design: 10p, Queen at right.

1961, Sept. 18			**Perf. 14½x14**	
382	A153	2p red brn, yel & rose	.20	.20
383	CD4	4p ultra, pink & buff	.20	.20
384	CD4	10p dk bl, yel grn & Prus blue	.20	.90
a.		Yellow green omitted	13,500.	
b.		Dark blue omitted	4,500.	
		Nos. 382-384 (3)	.60	1.30

Hammer Beam Roof of Westminster Hall — A155

Parliament — A156

Perf. 14½x14, 14x14½

1961, Sept. 25			**Wmk. 322**	
385	A155	6p red lil & gold	.30	.20
a.		Gold omitted	1,600.	
386	A156	1sh3p green & slate	3.00	3.25
a.		Slate (Queen's head) omitted	16,500.	

7th Commonwealth Parliamentary Conf.

National Productivity Symbol — A157

Designs: 3p, Two arrows and map of the British Isles. 1sh3p, Five arrows pointing up.

Perf. 14½x14

1962, Nov. 14		**Photo.**	**Wmk. 322**	
387	A157	2½p car rose & dk grn	.20	.20
388	A157	3p violet & blue	.30	.20
a.		Queen's head omitted	2,250.	
389	A157	1sh3p dk grn, car rose & bl	2.00	2.00
a.		Queen's head omitted	10,000.	
		Nos. 387-389 (3)	2.50	2.40

Phosphorescent

387p	A157	2½p car rose & dk grn	.70	.60
388p	A157	3p violet & blue	1.75	.95
389p	A157	1sh3p dk grn, car rose & bl	40.00	25.00
		Nos. 387p-389p (3)	42.45	26.55

National Productivity Year. The watermark on Nos. 387-388 is inverted.

Phosphorescent Commemorative stamps between Nos. 387-493 were issued both with and without phosphorescence on the front unless otherwise noted with the issue.
Starting with No. 514, commemorative stamps were issued only with phosphorescence on the front unless otherwise noted.
Phosphorescent Regulars: Starting in 1967, all small stamps (lower values) of the regular series were issued only with phosphorescence.

Wheat Emblem and People A158

1sh3p, Children of different races.

1963, Mar. 21			**Wmk. 322**	
390	A158	2½p pink & dp car	.25	.20
p.		Phosphor.	3.50	1.40
391	A158	1sh3p yellow & brn	2.25	2.25
p.		Phosphor.	35.00	26.00

FAO "Freedom from Hunger" campaign.

Paris Postal Conference A159

1963, May 7			**Wmk. 322**	
392	A159	6p purple & green	.35	.45
a.		Green omitted	4,000.	
p.		Phosphor.	7.25	7.25

Cent. of the 1st Intl. Postal Conf., Paris, 1863, and Paris Postal Conf., May 7-9, 1963.

Buttercups, Daisies and Bee A160

Design: 4½p, Badger, Fawn, woodpecker, lark, titmouse, butterfly, mouse and wild plants.

1963, May 16			**Perf. 14½x14**	
393	A160	3p multicolored	.20	.20
p.		Phosphor.	.70	.70
394	A160	4½p multicolored	.20	.40
p.		Phosphor.	3.50	3.50

Natl. Nature Week, May 18-25, and the importance of wildlife conservation.

Helicopter Lifting Man from Lifeboat A161

Lifeboat Men A162

Design: 4p, 19th cent. lifeboat under sail.

1963, May 31		**Photo.**		
395	A161	2½p multicolored	.20	.20
396	A161	4p multicolored	.45	.45
397	A162	1sh6p multicolored	2.75	3.00
		Nos. 395-397 (3)	3.40	3.65

Phosphorescent

395p	A161	2½p multicolored	.60	.70
396p	A161	4p multicolored	.60	.70
397p	A162	1sh6p multicolored	55.00	32.50
		Nos. 395p-397p (3)	56.20	33.90

9th Intl. Life-Boat Conf., Edinburgh, 6/3-5.

Red Cross and Elizabeth II — A163

1sh3p, Cross at UL. 1sh6p, Cross in center.

1963, Aug. 15			**Wmk. 322**	
		Cross in Red		
398	A163	3p purple	.20	.20
a.		Red cross omitted	5,750.	
399	A163	1sh3p gray & blue	2.75	2.75
400	A163	1sh6p dl bl & ol bister	2.75	2.75
		Nos. 398-400 (3)	5.70	5.70

Phosphorescent

398p	A163	3p purple	1.25	1.00
399p	A163	1sh3p gray & blue	42.50	35.00
400p	A163	1sh6p dull blue & ol bister	40.00	32.50
		Nos. 398p-400p (3)	83.75	68.50

Red Cross Cent. Cong., Geneva, Sept. 2.

Cable Around World and Under Sea A164

1963, Dec. 3			**Perf. 14½x14**	
401	A164	1sh6p blue & blk	3.25	2.75
a.		Black omitted	4,000.	
p.		Phosphor.	19.00	18.00

Opening of the Commonwealth Pacific (telephone) cable service, COMPAC.

Puck and Bottom from "A Midsummer Night's Dream," Shakespeare — A165

Hamlet Holding Yorick's Skull A166

First Folio Portrait of Shakespeare and: 6p, Feste the Clown, from "Twelfth Night." 1sh3p, Romeo and Juliet. 1sh6p, Henry V praying at Agincourt.

		Perf. 14½x14		
1964, Apr. 23		**Photo.**	**Wmk. 322**	
402	A165	3p multicolored	.20	.20
403	A165	6p multicolored	.45	.35
404	A165	1sh3p multicolored	1.00	1.00
405	A165	1sh6p multicolored	1.60	1.25
		Perf. 11x12		
		Engr.		
406	A166	2sh6p dark gray	2.00	1.50
		Nos. 402-406 (5)	5.25	4.30

Phosphorescent

402p	A165	3p multicolored	.30	.35
403p	A165	6p multicolored	.90	1.10
404p	A165	1sh3p multicolored	4.75	7.50
405p	A165	1sh6p multicolored	9.25	5.25
		Nos. 402p-405p (4)	15.20	14.20

400th anniv. of the birth of William Shakespeare. No. 406 was not issued with phosphorescence.

Apartment Buildings, London A170

Designs: 4p, Shipyards, Belfast. 8p, Beddgelert Forest Park, Snowdonia. 1sh6p, Dounreay nuclear reactor and sheaves of wheat.

1964, July 1		**Photo.**	**Perf. 14½x14**	
410	A170	2½p multicolored	.20	.20
411	A170	4p multicolored	.40	.35
a.		Violet ("4d") omitted	225.00	
b.		Ocher omitted	475.00	
c.		Violet & ocher omitted	475.00	
412	A170	8p multicolored	.85	.85
a.		Green omitted	13,500.	
413	A170	1sh6p multicolored	3.75	3.50
		Nos. 410-413 (4)	5.20	4.90

Phosphorescent

410p	A170	2½p multicolored	.45	.60
411p	A170	4p multicolored	1.40	1.40
412p	A170	8p multicolored	3.00	3.25
413p	A170	1sh6p multicolored	32.50	25.00
		Nos. 410p-413p (4)	37.35	30.25

20th Intl. Geographical Cong., London, July 20-28.

Spring Gentian A171

1964, Aug. 5			**Wmk. 322**	
414	A171	3p shown	.20	.20
a.		Blue omitted	8,000.	
b.		Sage green omitted	13,500.	
415	A171	6p Dog rose	.35	.40
416	A171	9p Honeysuckle	2.00	2.50
a.		Light green omitted	13,500.	
417	A171	1sh3p Fringed water lily	2.75	2.75
		Nos. 414-417 (4)	5.30	5.85

Phosphorescent

414p	A171	3p shown	.45	.45
415p	A171	6p Dog rose	2.75	3.25
416p	A171	9p Honeysuckle	5.25	4.50
417p	A171	1sh3p Fringed water lily	27.50	22.50
		Nos. 414p-417p (4)	35.95	30.70

10th Intl. Botanical Cong., Edinburgh, Aug. 3-12.

Forth Road Bridge A172

Design: 6p, Bridge and railroad bridge.

1964, Sept. 4			**Perf. 14½x14**	
418	A172	3p blk, lil & blue	.20	.20
p.		Phosphor.	.75	.75
419	A172	6p vio blk, grnsh bl & car lake	.45	.45
a.		Greenish blue omitted	4,250.	1,500.
p.		Phosphor.	5.50	5.25

Opening of Forth Road Bridge, Scotland.

Winston Churchill A173

Design: 1sh3p, Large portrait.

1965, July 8		**Photo.**	**Wmk. 322**	
420	A173	4p dk brown & blk	.20	.20
p.		Phosphor.	.30	.30
421	A173	1sh3p gray & black	.35	.45
p.		Phosphor.	3.00	3.50

Sir Winston Spencer Churchill (1874-1965), statesman and WWII leader.

Seal of Simon de Montfort A174

700th ANNIVERSARY OF PARLIAMENT 2/6

St. Stephen's Hall, Westminster Hall and Abbey, Engraving by Wenceslaus Hollar, 1647 — A175

1965, July 19   *Perf. 14½x14*
422 A174   6p dark olive   .20   .20
   p.   Phosphor.   .70   .85
423 A175 2sh6p brown black   .90   1.10

700th anniv. of Parliament. No. 423 was not issued with phosphorescence; size: 58x21mm.

Salvation Army Band and "Blood and Fire" Flag A176

1sh6p, Salvation Army officers and flag.

1965, Aug. 9
424 A176   3p dk bl, yel & brt car   .25   .25
   p.   Phosphor.   .35   .45
425 A176 1sh6p red, yel & brt bl   1.00   *1.50*
   p.   Phosphor.   3.00   3.50

Centenary of the Salvation Army.

Lister's Carbolic Spray A177

1sh, Joseph Lister & carbolic acid formula.

1965, Sept. 1
426 A177   4p gray, bluish blk & red brn   .20   .20
   a.   Red brown (tubing) omitted   425.00
   b.   Bluish black omitted   5,750.
   p.   Phosphor.   .25   .25
427 A177 1sh blk, blue & pur   .80   *1.25*
   p.   Phosphor.   2.25   2.60

Introduction of antiseptic surgery by Joseph Lister, cent.

Trinidad Folk Dancers, Shrove Monday Carnival A178

Design: 1sh6p, French Canadian folk dancers, Les Feux Follets.

     Perf. 14½x14
1965, Sept. 1   Photo.   Wmk. 322
428 A178   6p orange & blk   .20   .20
   p.   Phosphor.   .35   .45
429 A178 1sh6p brt vio & blk   .90   *1.25*
   p.   Phosphor.   3.00   3.50

1st Commonwealth Arts Festival, 9/16-10/2.

Supermarine Spitfire Fighters — A179

Anti-Aircraft Gun Battery in Action A180

Designs: No. 431, Pilot in cockpit of Hawker Hurricane fighter. No. 432, Wing tips of Messerschmitt ME-109 and Spitfire. No. 433, Two Spitfires attacking Heinkel HE-111 bomber. No. 434, Spitfire attacking Junkers JU-187B Stuka dive bomber. No. 435, Hurricanes returning over wreckage of Dornier DO-17 Z bomber. 1sh3p, Vapor trails over St. Paul's Cathedral, London.

     Perf. 14½x14
1965, Sept. 13   Photo.   Wmk. 322
430 A179   4p slate & dk ol   .60   .80
431 A179   4p slate & dk ol   .60   .80
432 A179   4p sl, dk ol, brt bl & red   .60   .80
433 A179   4p slate & dk ol   .60   .80
434 A179   4p slate & dk ol   .60   .80
435 A179   4p sl, dk ol & brt blue   .60   .80
   a.   Bright blue omitted   5,500.
   b.   Block of 6, #430-435   5.00   5.00
436 A180   9p vio bl, org & vio black   2.25   1.75
437 A180 1sh3p brt bl, sl & grnsh gray   2.25   1.75
   Nos. 430-437 (8)   8.10   8.30

Phosphorescent
430p A179   4p slate & dark ol   1.10   1.10
431p A179   4p slate & dark ol   1.10   1.10
432p A179   4p sl, dk ol, brt bl & red   1.10   1.10
433p A179   4p slate & dark ol   1.10   1.10
434p A179   4p slate & dark ol   1.10   1.10
435p A179   4p sl, dk ol & brt bl   1.10   1.10
   a.   Block of 6, #430p-435p   11.00   11.00
436p A180   9p vio bl, org & vio black   2.50   2.50
437p A180 1sh3p brt bl, slate & grnsh gray   2.50   2.50
   Nos. 430p-437p (8)   11.60   11.60

25th anniv. of the Battle of Britain. Nos. 430-435 printed in blocks of 6 (3x2) in sheets of 120.

Post Office Tower and Georgian Buildings — A181

Design: 1sh3p, Post Office Tower and Nash Terrace, Regents Park, horiz.

1965, Oct. 8   *Perf. 14x14½, 14½x14*
438 A181   3p brt bl, lem & ol green   .20   .20
   p.   Phosphor.   .20   .20
439 A181 1sh3p grn, ol grn & bl   .35   .50
   p.   Phosphor.   .35   .60

Opening of the Post Office Tower, London.

UN Emblem A182

ICY Emblem A183

1965, Oct. 25   *Perf. 14½x14*
440 A182   3p multicolored   .20   .20
   p.   Phosphor.   .35   .35
441 A183 1sh6p multicolored   .85   .85
   p.   Phosphor.   3.25   3.50

20th anniv. of the UN and Intl. Cooperation Year, 1965.

INTERNATIONAL TELECOMMUNICATION UNION 1865 1965 9d

"World Telecommunication Stations" — A184

ITU Cent.: 1sh6p, "Radio waves & switchboard."

1965, Nov. 15   Photo.   Wmk. 322
442 A184   9p multicolored   .35   .45
   p.   Phosphor.   1.00   .85
443 A184 1sh6p bl, red, blk, ind & pink   1.10   1.40
   a.   Pink omitted   3,000.
   p.   Phosphor.   5.50   6.00

Robert Burns and Saltier Cross of St. Andrew A185

Design: 1sh3p, Alexander Nasmyth portrait of Burns, his signature and symbols of his life. Portrait of Burns on 4p stamp is adaptation of Archibald Skirvings', chalk drawing, 1798.

1966, Jan. 25   *Perf. 14½x14*
444 A185   4p blue, blk & dk sl   .20   .20
   p.   Phosphor.   .25   .45
445 A185 1sh3p org, blk & Prus blue   .45   .80
   p.   Phosphor.   2.50   2.50

Robert Burns (1759-1796), Scottish national poet.

Westminster Abbey — A186

Fan Vaulting, Chapel of Henry VII A187

1966, Feb. 28   Photo.   *Perf. 14½x14*
452 A186   3p blue, blk, & red brn   .20   .20
   p.   Phosphor.   .20   .20

     Perf. 11x12
     Engr.
453 A187 2sh6p black   .65   *.90*

900th anniv. of Westminster Abbey. No. 453 issued only without phosphor.

Landscape near Hassock, Sussex A188

Views: 6p, Antrim, Northern Ireland. 1sh3p, Harlech Castle, Wales. 1sh6p, The Cairngorms (mountains), Scotland.

     Perf. 14½x14
1966, May 2   Photo.   Wmk. 322
454 A188   4p multicolored   .20   .20
455 A188   6p multicolored   .20   .20
456 A188 1sh3p multicolored   .25   .40
457 A188 1sh6p multicolored   .45   .40
   Nos. 454-457 (4)   1.10   1.20

Phosphorescent
454p A188   4p multicolored   .20   .20
455p A188   6p multicolored   .20   .20
456p A188 1sh3p multicolored   .25   .40
457p A188 1sh6p multicolored   .45   .45
   Nos. 454p-457p (4)   1.10   1.25

Soccer Players — A189

Players and Crowd A190

1sh3p, Goalkeeper and two players.

     Perf. 14x14½, 14½x14
1966, June 1   Photo.   Wmk. 322
458 A189   4p multicolored   .20   .20
459 A190   6p multicolored   .20   .20
   a.   Black omitted   175.00
   b.   Yellow green omitted   4,500.
   c.   Red omitted   7,250.
460 A190 1sh3p multicolored   .60   .80
   a.   Blue omitted   300.00
   Nos. 458-460 (3)   1.00   1.20

Phosphorescent
458p A189   4p multicolored   .20   .20
459p A190   6p multicolored   .20   .20
   d.   Black omitted   1,900.
460p A190 1sh3p multicolored   .50   .75
   Nos. 458p-460p (3)   .90   1.15

Final games of the 1965-66 World Soccer Championship for the Jules Rimet Cup, Wembley, July 11-30.
See No. 465.

BLACK-HEADED GULL 4d

Blackheaded Gull — A191

     Perf. 14½x14
1966, Aug. 8   Photo.   Wmk. 322
     Birds in Natural Colors
461 A191   4p shown   .20   .20
   p.   Phosphor.   .20   .20
462 A191   4p Blue tit   .20   .20
   p.   Phosphor.   .20   .20
463 A191   4p European robin   .20   .20
   p.   Phosphor.   .20   .20
464 A191   4p European blackbird   .20   .20
   p.   Phosphor.   .20   .20
   a.   Block of 4, #461-464   .90   .60
   b.   Block of 4, #461p-464p   .90   .80

Seven colors have been found omitted (singly or in combinations) on Nos. 461-464; green, red, ultramarine, brown, red brown, yellow and black.

No. 458 Inscribed: "ENGLAND WINNERS"

1966, Aug. 18   *Perf. 14x14½*
465 A189   4p multicolored   .25   .25

England's victory in the World Soccer Cup Championship.

Jodrell Bank Radio Telescope A192

Designs: 6p, Automobiles (Jaguar and 3 Mini-Minors). 1sh3p, SR N6 Hovercraft. 1sh6p, Windscale atomic reactor.

1966, Sept. 19   *Perf. 14½x14*
466 A192   4p yellow & blk   .20   .20
467 A192   6p org, red & dk bl   .20   .20
   a.   Red (Mini-Minors) omitted   11,500.
   b.   Dark blue (Jaguar & imprint) omitted   8,000.
468 A192 1sh3p sl, blk, org & bl   .30   .45
469 A192 1sh6p multicolored   .40   .45
   Nos. 466-469 (4)   1.10   1.30

Phosphorescent

466p	A192	4p yellow & black	.20	.20
467p	A192	6p org, red & dk bl	.20	.20
468p	A192	1sh3p slate, blk, org & bl	.40	.45
469p	A192	1sh6p multicolored	.60	.70
		Nos. 466p-469p (4)	1.40	1.55

British technology.

Battle of Hastings A193

Battle of Hastings from Bayeux Tapestry: No. 471, Two knights on horseback, one killed, one attacking. No. 472, Slain Harold on horseback and knight with shield. No. 473, Knight with shield and axe fighting horseman. No. 474, Knight on foot killing man, and horseman attacking with lance. No. 475, Four knights and two horses in battle scene. 6p, Norman ship. 1sh3p, King Harold's housecarls (body guard) battling Normans.

Photo.; Gold Impressed on 6p, 1sh3p
Perf. 14½x14

		1966, Oct. 14	Wmk. 322

Size: 38½x22mm

470	A193	4p multicolored	.20	.20
471	A193	4p multicolored	.20	.20
472	A193	4p multicolored	.20	.20
473	A193	4p multicolored	.20	.20
474	A193	4p multicolored	.20	.20
475	A193	4p multicolored	.20	.20
a.		Strip of 6, #470-475	2.25	
476	A193	6p multi & gold	.30	.30

Size: 58x22mm

477	A193	1sh3p multi & gold	.75	.65
		Nos. 470-477 (8)	2.25	2.15

Phosphorescent

470p	A193	4p multicolored	.20	.20
471p	A193	4p multicolored	.20	.20
472p	A193	4p multicolored	.20	.20
473p	A193	4p multicolored	.20	.20
474p	A193	4p multicolored	.20	.20
475p	A193	4p multicolored	.20	.20
b.		Strip of 6, #470p-475p	2.25	
476p	A193	6p multi & gold	.30	.30
477p	A193	1sh3p multi & gold	.85	.85
		Nos. 470p-477p (8)	2.35	2.35

900th anniv. of the Battle of Hastings.

Eight colors have been found omitted (singly or in pair) on Nos. 470-475 and 470p-477p: gray, orange, blue, dark blue, bright green, olive green, brown and magenta. Also violet on 1sh3p.

Gold Omitted

The variety "Gold (Queen's head) omitted" can be counterfeited by chemically removing the gold.

Christmas — A194

Photo.; Gold Impressed

		1966, Dec. 1	Perf. 14x14½

478	A194	3p King	.20	.20
b.		Green omitted		
p.		Phosphor.	.20	.20
479	A194	1sh6p Snowman	.35	.35
b.		Pink omitted	2,500.	
p.		Phosphor.	.35	.40

EFTA

Loading Ship at Dock and Train A195

Design: 1sh6p, Loading plane from trucks and flags of EFTA members.

Perf. 14½x14

		1967, Feb. 20	Photo.	Wmk. 322

480	A195	9p blue & multi	.20	.20
p.		Phosphor.	.20	.20

481	A195	1sh6p violet & multi	.35	.50
p.		Phosphor.	.30	.45

European Free Trade Assoc. Tariffs were abolished Dec. 31, 1966, among EFTA members (Austria, Denmark, Finland, Great Britain, Norway, Portugal, Sweden, Switzerland).

Colors omitted include: 9p — yellow, brown, light blue, light violet and green singly; black, brown, light blue and yellow simultaneously. 1sh6p — dark blue, bister, yellow, red, ultramarine and gray. 9p, value range for one-color omissions, $75 to $200. 1sh6p, value for red omitted $5,000 (used), dark blue omitted $500, value for other color-omitted errors $75 to $125 each.

Hawthorn and Wild Blackberry A196

Flowers: No. 489, Morning-glory and viper's bugloss. No. 490, Ox-eye daisy, coltsfoot and buttercup. No. 491, Bluebell, red campion and wood anemone. 9p, Dog violet. 1sh9p, Primrose.

Perf. 14½x14

		1967, Apr. 24	Photo.	Wmk. 322

488	A196	4p multicolored	.20	.20
489	A196	4p multicolored	.20	.20
490	A196	4p multicolored	.20	.20
491	A196	4p multicolored	.20	.20
492	A196	9p multicolored	.30	.40
493	A196	1sh9p multicolored	.40	.35
		Nos. 488-493 (6)	1.50	1.55

Phosphorescent

488p	A196	4p multicolored	.20	.20
489p	A196	4p multicolored	.20	.20
490p	A196	4p multicolored	.20	.20
491p	A196	4p multicolored	.20	.20
492p	A196	9p multicolored	.25	.40
493p	A196	1sh9p multicolored	.35	.35
		Nos. 488p-493p (6)	1.40	1.55

Four colors have been found omitted on Nos. 488-491 and three on 488p-491p: dark brown, red, violet and dull purple.

> For QEII Machin definitives, see listings following Regional Issues and preceding Booklets.

Master Lambton, by Thomas Lawrence — A198

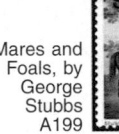

Mares and Foals, by George Stubbs A199

Design: 1sh6p, Children Coming out of School, by Laurence Stephen Lowry.

Photo.; Gold Impressed on 4p, 1sh6p
Perf. 14x14½, 14½x14

		1967, July 10	Unwmk.

514	A198	4p multi	.20	.20
a.		Gold (Queen's head & value) omitted	325.00	
515	A199	9p multi	.20	.20
a.		Black (Queen's head & value) omitted	750.00	
b.		Black (Queen's head only) omitted	1,750.	
516	A199	1sh6p multi	.20	.20
a.		Blue omitted	250.00	
b.		Gray omitted	150.00	
c.		Gold (Queen's head) omitted	13,500.	
		Nos. 514-516 (3)	.60	.60

See Nos. 568-571.

Gipsy Moth IV — A200

		1967, July 24	Photo.	Perf. 14½x14

517	A200	1sh9p multicolored	.20	.20

Sir Francis Chichester's one-man voyage around the world, Aug. 27, 1966-May 28, 1967.

Radar Screen A201

British Discoveries: 1sh, Penicillin mold. 1sh6p, Vickers 10 twin jet engines. 1sh9p, Television camera, vert.

Perf. 14½x14, 14x14½

		1967, Sept. 19	Photo.	Wmk. 322

518	A201	4p multicolored	.20	.20
519	A201	1sh multicolored	.20	.20
520	A201	1sh6p multicolored	.20	.20
521	A201	1sh9p multicolored	.20	.20
a.		Gray omitted	4,500.	
		Nos. 518-521 (4)	.80	.80

Adoration of the Shepherds, Ascribed to School of Seville — A202

Adoration of the Shepherds, by Le Nain A203

Christmas 1967: 4p, Madonna and Child, by Murillo.

Photo.; Gold Impressed
Perf. 14x14½, 14½x14

		1967		Unwmk.

522	A202	3p multi	.20	.20
a.		Gold (Queen's head & value) omitted	100.00	
b.		Pink omitted	3,250.	
523	A202	4p multi	.20	.20
a.		Gold (Queen's head & value) omitted	90.00	
b.		Gold ("4d" only) omitted	2,750.	
c.		Yellow omitted	7,000.	
d.		Greenish yellow & gold omitted	11,500.	
524	A203	1sh6p multi	.20	.20
a.		Gold (Queen's head & value) omitted	7,000.	
b.		Blue omitted	500.00	
c.		Yellow omitted	13,500.	
d.		Gold (Queen's head only) omitted	2,250.	
		Nos. 522-524 (3)	.60	.60

Issue dates: 4p, Oct. 18; 3p, 1sh6p, Nov. 27.

Castle Type of 1955
Perf. 11x12

		1967-68	Engr.	Unwmk.

525	A133	2sh6p dk brown ('68)	.35	.50
526	A133	5sh crimson ('68)	.80	.85
527	A133	10sh brt ultra ('68)	5.50	7.25
528	A133	£1 intense black	5.25	7.00
		Nos. 525-528 (4)	11.90	15.60

Aberfeldy Bridge, Perthshire A204

Designs: 4p, Prehistoric Tarr Steps, Exmoor. 1sh6p, Menai Bridge, North Wales, 1826. 1sh9p, Viaduct, Highway M4.

Perf. 14½x14

		1968, Apr. 29	Photo.	Unwmk.

560	A204	4p gold & multi	.20	.20
561	A204	9p gold & multi	.20	.20
a.		Blue omitted	6,500.	
b.		Gold (Queen's head) omitted	190.00	
562	A204	1sh6p gold & multi	.20	.30
a.		Gold (Queen's head) omitted	250.00	
b.		Red omitted	350.00	
563	A204	1sh9p gold & multi	.20	.35
a.		Gold (Queen's head) omitted	250.00	
		Nos. 560-563 (4)	.80	1.05

Emmeline Pankhurst Statue A205

Designs: 4p, Letters "TUC" and faces. 1sh, Sopwith Camel 1914-1918 fighter plane and formation of Lightning jets. 1sh9p, Capt. Cook's "Endeavour" and signature.

		1968, May 29		

564	A205	4p brt grn, blk, ol & bl	.20	.20
565	A205	9p gray, violet & blk	.20	.20
566	A205	1sh gray, ol, red, bl & blk	.20	.20
567	A205	1sh9p blk & bister	.40	.45
		Nos. 564-567 (4)	1.00	1.05

Cent. of Trades Union Congress (4p); 50th anniv. of women's suffrage (9p); 50th anniv. of the Royal Air Force (1sh); bicent. of Captain Cook's first discovery voyage (1sh9p).

Paintings Types of 1967

Paintings: 4p, Elizabeth I, c. 1575, artist unknown. 1sh, Pinkie (Miss Sarah Moulton-Barrett) by Sir Thomas Lawrence. 1sh6p, St. Mary le Port, by John Piper. 1sh9p, The Hay Wain (landscape), by John Constable.

Photo.; Gold Impressed
Perf. 14x14½, 14½x14

		1968, Aug. 12		

568	A198	4p multi	.20	.20
a.		Gold (Queen's head & value) omitted	250.00	
b.		Vermilion omitted	525.00	
569	A198	1sh multi	.20	.25
a.		Gold (Queen's head & value) omitted	5,750.	
570	A198	1sh6p multi	.20	.30
a.		Gold (Queen's head & value) omitted	200.00	
571	A199	1sh9p multi	.25	.45
a.		Gold (Queen's head & value) omitted	825.00	
b.		Red omitted	13,500.	
		Nos. 568-571 (4)	.85	1.20

Sizes: 4p, 27x37½mm; 1sh, 25½x37½mm; 1sh6p, 31x37½mm; 1sh9p, 38x28mm.

Boy and Girl with Rocking Horse A206

Girl Playing with Dolls and Dollhouse — A207

Christmas: 1sh6p, Boy with toy train and building blocks.

Perf. 14½x14, 14x14½

		1968, Nov. 25		Photo.

572	A206	4p gold & multi	.20	.20
a.		Gold omitted	8,000.	
b.		Vermilion omitted	500.00	
c.		Ultramarine omitted	375.00	
573	A207	9p gold & multi	.20	.20
a.		Yellow omitted	100.00	
574	A207	1sh6p gold & multi	.20	.35
		Nos. 572-574 (3)	.60	.75

British Ships — A208

Designs: 5p, R.M.S. Queen Elizabeth 2. No. 576, Elizabethan Galleon. No. 577, East Indiaman. No. 578, Cutty Sark. No. 579, S.S. Great Britain. No. 580, R.M.S. Mauretania.

1969, Jan. 15   *Perf. 14½x14*

Size: 58x22mm

575	A208	5p multicolored	.20	.20
a.		Black omitted	1,600.	
b.		Gray omitted	200.00	
c.		Red omitted	110.00	

Size: 38½x22mm

576	A208	9p multicolored	.20	.20
a.		Red & blue omitted	2,400.	
b.		Blue omitted	2,750.	
577	A208	9p multicolored	.20	.30
578	A208	9p multicolored	.20	.30
a.		Strip of 3, #576-578	.60	

Size: 58x22mm

579	A208	1sh multicolored	.45	.40
a.		Greenish yellow omitted	3,500.	
580	A208	1sh multicolored	.45	.40
a.		Pair, #579-580	1.40	
b.		Carmine (hull overlay) omitted	20,000.	
c.		Red (funnels) omitted	18,000.	
d.		Carmine and red omitted	18,000.	
		Nos. 575-580 (6)	1.70	1.80

British seamen and shipbuilders.

Concorde over Great Britain and France
A209

Designs: 9p, Concorde seen from above and from side, flags of France and Great Britain. 1sh6p, Outlines of plane's nose and tail superimposed.

1969, Mar. 3 **Photo.** *Perf. 14½x14*

581	A209	4p multicolored	.30	.30
a.		Violet omitted	500.00	
b.		Orange omitted	500.00	
582	A209	9p multicolored	.65	.90
583	A209	1sh6p multicolored	1.00	1.25
a.		Silver omitted	500.00	
		Nos. 581-583 (3)	1.95	2.45

First flight of the prototype Concorde plane at Toulouse, France, Mar. 1, 1969.

Alcock, Brown, Daily Mail and Vickers Vimy Plane
A210

"EUROPA" and "CEPT"
CD12

Hand Holding Wrench
A212

Flags of NATO Nations Forming one Flag
A213

Vickers-Vimy Plane and Globe — A214

1969, Apr. 2

584	A210	5p multicolored	.25	.20
585	CD12	9p multicolored	.25	.25
586	A212	1sh multicolored	.25	.25
587	A213	1sh multicolored	.25	.30
a.		Black omitted	110.00	
b.		Green omitted	90.00	
c.		Yellow omitted	4,000.	
588	A214	1sh9p multicolored	.25	.40
		Nos. 584-588 (5)	1.25	1.40

50th anniv. of the 1st non-stop Atlantic flight from Newfoundland to Ireland of Capt. John Alcock and Lt. Arthur Whitten Brown; 10th anniv. of the Conference of European Postal and Telecommunications Administrations; 50th anniv. of the ILO (1sh); 20th anniv. of NATO; 50th anniv. of the first England to Australia flight (1sh9p).

Durham Cathedral
A215

British Cathedrals: No. 590, York Minster. No. 591, St. Giles', Edinburgh. No. 592, Canterbury. 9p, St. Paul's. 1sh6p, Liverpool Metropolitan.

Perf. 14½x14

1969, May 28   **Photo.**   **Unwmk.**

589	A215	5p multicolored	.20	.20
a.		Bluish violet omitted	6,500.	
590	A215	5p multicolored	.20	.20
a.		Bluish violet omitted	6,500.	
591	A215	5p multicolored	.20	.20
a.		Green omitted	90.00	
592	A215	5p multicolored	.20	.20
593	A215	9p multicolored	.25	.30
a.		Black (denomination) omitted	160.00	
594	A215	1sh6p multicolored	.40	.40
a.		Black (denomination) omitted	4,500.	
		Nos. 589-594 (6)	1.45	1.50

King's Gate, Caernarvon Castle, Wales — A216

Celtic Cross, Margam Abbey, Glamorgan
A217

Prince of Wales — A218

Designs: No. 596, Eagle Tower, Caernarvon Castle (2 flags). No. 597, Queen Eleanor's Gate, Caernarvon Castle.

Perf. 14x14½

1969, July 1   **Photo.**   **Unwmk.**

595	A216	5p silver & multi	.20	.20
596	A216	5p silver & multi	.20	.20
597	A216	5p silver & multi	.20	.20
a.		Strip of 3, #595-597	.25	.25
598	A217	9p gold, gray & black	.20	.20
599	A218	1sh black & gold	.20	.20
		Nos. 595-599 (5)	1.00	1.00

Investiture of Prince Charles as Prince of Wales, July 1.

Mahatma Gandhi and Flag of India
A219

1969, Aug. 13   *Perf. 14½x14*

600	A219	1sh6p orange, blk & grn	.20	.20

Mohandas K. Gandhi (1869-1948), leader in India's fight for independence.

Emblem of Post Office Bank
A220

International Subscriber Dialing — A221

Automatic Letter Sorting
A222

Design: 1sh, Telecommunications (pulse code modulation graph).

Perf. 13½x14

1969, Oct. 1   **Litho.**   **Unwmk.**

601	A220	5p blue & multi	.20	.20
602	A221	9p ultra & multi	.20	.20
603	A221	1sh green & multi	.20	.20
604	A222	1sh6p multicolored	.20	.40
		Nos. 601-604 (4)	.80	1.00

Technological advancements of the British Post Office, transfer of responsibility from the government to the Post Office Corporation.

Angel
A223

Christmas: 5p, Three shepherds. 1sh6p, The Three Kings.

Photo.; Gold Embossed

1969, Nov. 26   *Perf. 14x15*

605	A223	4p multicolored	.20	.20
606	A223	5p multicolored	.20	.20
607	A223	1sh6p multicolored	.20	.20
		Nos. 605-607 (3)	.60	.60

Fife Harling House, Scotland
A224

British Rural Architecture: 9p, Cotswold limestone house, Gloucestershire, England. 1sh, Aberaeron town house, Wales. 1sh6p, Irish cottage with Ulster thatching.

Perf. 14x15

1970, Feb. 11   **Photo.**   **Unwmk.**

Size: 38½x22mm

608	A224	5p multicolored	.20	.20
609	A224	9p multicolored	.20	.20

Size: 38½x27mm

610	A224	1sh multicolored	.20	.20
611	A224	1sh6p multicolored	.25	.25
		Nos. 608-611 (4)	.85	.85

Mayflower Leaving Plymouth, England
A225

Designs: 5p, Signing of the Declaration of Arbroath. 9p, Florence Nightingale and soldiers in Scutari Hospital. 1sh, Earl Grey, Great Britain; Charles Robert, France; Victor Bohmert, Germany; De Keussler, Russia, and document in 4 languages. 1sh9p, Sir William Herschel, Francis Bailey, Sir John Herschel and telescope.

Photo.; Gold Embossed

1970, Apr. 1   *Perf. 14x15*

612	A225	5p red & multi	.20	.20
613	A225	9p blue & multi	.20	.20
614	A225	1sh lt blue & multi	.25	.25
615	A225	1sh6p olive & multi	.30	.35
616	A225	1sh9p brt pink & multi	.30	.35
		Nos. 612-616 (5)	1.25	1.35

650th anniv. of the Declaration of Arbroath (5p); Florence Nightingale (1820-1910), nurse and hospital reformer (9p); Intl.Cooperative Alliance, 75th anniv. (1sh); 350th anniv. of Mayflower sailing (1sh6p); sesquicentennial of the Royal Astronomical Soc. (1sh9p).

Missing colors or embossing occur on each denomination.

"The Pickwick Papers," by Dickens
A226

Wordsworth's Grasmere, Lake District
A227

Designs: No. 618, Mr. and Mrs. Micawber ("David Copperfield"). No. 619, David Copperfield and Betsy Trotwood ("David Copperfield"). No. 620, "Oliver Twist."

Perf. 14x14½

1970, June 3   **Photo.**   **Unwmk.**

617	A226	5p orange & multi	.20	.20
618	A226	5p lil rose & multi	.20	.20
619	A226	5p grnsh blue & multi	.20	.20
620	A226	5p lemon & multi	.20	.20
621	A227	1sh9p citron & multi	.30	.40
		Nos. 617-621 (5)	1.10	1.20

Charles Dickens (1812-70), novelist. William Wordsworth (1770-1850), poet, No. 621.

Athletics
A228

1970, July 15   **Litho.**   *Perf. 14x14½*

639	A228	5p shown	.20	.20
640	A228	1sh6p Swimming	.30	.40
641	A228	1sh9p Bicycling	.35	.40
		Nos. 639-641 (3)	.85	1.00

9th British Commonwealth Games, Edinburgh, July 16-25.

Philympia, London Phil. Exhib., Sept. 18-26 — A229

5p, Penny black. 9p, 1847 1-shilling stamp, #5. 1sh6p, 1855 4-pence stamp, #22.

1970, Sept. 18   Photo.   Perf. 14x14½

642	A229	5p multicolored	.20	.20
643	A229	9p multicolored	.20	.35
644	A229	1sh6p multicolored	.20	.50
		Nos. 642-644 (3)	.60	1.05

Christmas (Illuminations from 14th Century de Lisle Psalter) — A230

Designs: 4p, Angel and Shepherds. 5p, Nativity. 1sh6p, Adoration of the Kings.

1970, Nov. 25   Photo.   Perf. 14x14½

645	A230	4p red & multi	.20	.20
646	A230	5p violet & multi	.20	.20
a.		Imperf., pair	400.00	
647	A230	1sh6p olive & multi	.25	.35
		Nos. 645-647 (3)	.65	.75

Decimal Currency Issue
"P" instead of "D"

Mountain Road, by T.P. Flanagan A231

Paintings from Northern Ireland: 7½p, Deer's Meadow, by Thomas Carr. 9p, Tollymore Forest Park, by Colin Middleton.

1971, June 16   Photo.   Perf. 14½x14

648	A231	3p multicolored	.20	.20
649	A231	7½p multicolored	.35	.35
650	A231	9p multicolored	.45	.45
		Nos. 648-650 (3)	1.00	1.00

Ulster '71 Festival, Belfast, May-Oct.

John Keats (1795-1821) — A232

Writers and their signatures: 5p, Thomas Gray (1716-71). 7½p, Sir Walter Scott (1771-1832).

1971, July 28   Photo.   Perf. 14½x14

651	A232	3p dull bl, blk & gold	.20	.20
652	A232	5p olive, blk & gold	.35	.35
653	A232	7½p yel brn, blk & gold	.45	.45
		Nos. 651-653 (3)	1.00	1.00

Soldier, Sailor, Airman, Nurse, 1921, and Poppy A233

Designs: 7½p, Roman centurion on horseback, York Castle and coat of arms. 9p, Rugby players 100 years ago, and rose.

1971, Aug. 25

654	A233	3p ultra & multi	.20	.20
655	A233	7½p ocher & multi	.40	.40
656	A233	9p olive & multi	.40	.40
		Nos. 654-656 (3)	1.00	1.00

50th anniv. of the British Legion (3p); 1900th anniv. of the founding of York (7½p); cent. of the Rugby Football Union (9p).

Physical Sciences Building, University College of Wales, Aberystwyth — A234

Modern University Buildings: 5p, Faraday Building, Engineering Faculty, University of Southampton. 7½p, Engineering Building, University of Leicester. 9p, Hexagon Restaurant, University of Essex.

1971, Sept. 22   Photo.   Perf. 14½x14

657	A234	3p citron & multi	.20	.20
658	A234	5p rose vio & multi	.20	.20
659	A234	7½p dp brn & multi	.45	.45
660	A234	9p dk blue & multi	.75	.75
		Nos. 657-660 (4)	1.60	1.60

No. 658 exists with large "p" in "5p." These are from plate combination 1A1B1C1D and were not officially issued.

Dream of the Kings A235

Christmas (from Stained Glass Windows, Canterbury Cathedral): 3p, Adoration of the Kings. 7½p, Journey of the Kings.

1971, Oct. 13

661	A235	2½p scarlet & multi	.20	.20
662	A235	3p ultra & multi	.20	.20
663	A235	7½p green & multi	.75	.75
		Nos. 661-663 (3)	1.15	1.15

James Clark Ross (1800-1862) and Map of South Polar Sea — A236

British Polar Explorers: 5p, Martin Frobisher (1535-1594), and Desceliers map, 1550. 7½p, Henry Hudson (c. 1560-1611) and Petrus Plancius map, 1592. 9p, Robert Falcon Scott (1868-1912) and map of Antarctica.

1972, Feb. 16   Perf. 14x14½

664	A236	3p dp bister & multi	.20	.20
665	A236	5p brick red & multi	.20	.20
666	A236	7½p violet & multi	.40	.40
667	A236	9p blue & multi	.60	.60
		Nos. 664-667 (4)	1.40	1.40

See Nos. 689-693.

Head of Tutankhamen as Fisherman — A237

Coast Guard A238

Ralph Vaughan Williams and "Sea Symphony" A239

1972, Apr. 26   Photo.   Perf. 14½x14

668	A237	3p gold & multi	.20	.20

Photo.; Queen's Head Gold Embossed

669	A238	7½p blue & multi	.35	.35
670	A239	9p multicolored	.70	.70
		Nos. 668-670 (3)	1.25	1.25

50th anniv. of the discovery of the tomb of Tutankhamen by Howard Carter and Lord Carnarvon; sesquicentennial of the British Coast guard; Ralph Vaughan Williams (1872-1958), composer.

St. Andrew's, Greensted-Juxta-Ongar — A240

Old Village Churches: 4p, All Saints, Earls Barton. 5p, St. Andrew's, Letheringsett. 7½p, St. Andrew's, Helpringham. 9p, St. Mary the Virgin, Huish Episcopi.

Photo.; Queen's Head Gold Embossed

1972, June 21   Perf. 14x14½

671	A240	3p dull blue & multi	.20	.20
672	A240	4p olive & multi	.20	.20
673	A240	5p dp grn & multi	.20	.20
674	A240	7½p red & multi	.70	.70
675	A240	9p blue & multi	.70	.70
		Nos. 671-675 (5)	2.00	2.00

Various BBC Microphones — A241

Designs: 5p, Wooden horn loudspeaker 1925. 7½p, Color TV camera, 1972. 9p, Marconi's oscillator and spark transmitter, 1897.

1972, Sept. 13   Photo.   Perf. 14½x14

676	A241	3p black, brn & yel	.20	.20
677	A241	5p henna brn & blk	.20	.20
678	A241	7½p black & magenta	.45	.45
679	A241	9p black & yel	.50	.50
		Nos. 676-679 (4)	1.35	1.35

Daily broadcasting in the United Kingdom, 50th anniv. (British Broadcasting Corp., #676-678), Marconi-Kemp experiments resulting in the 1st radio transmission across water, 75th anniv. (#679).

Angel with Trumpet — A242

Photo.; Gold Embossed

1972, Oct. 18   Perf. 14x14½

680	A242	2½p shown	.20	.20
681	A242	3p Angel with lute	.20	.20
682	A242	7½p Angel with harp	.30	.30
		Nos. 680-682 (3)	.70	.70

Christmas.

Queen Elizabeth II, Prince Philip — A243

1972, Nov. 20   Photo.   Perf. 14x14½

683	A243	3p dk bl, sep & sil	.25	.25
684	A243	20p dk pur, sepia & sil	.75	.75

25th anniv. of the marriage of Queen Elizabeth II and Prince Philip. No. 684 is without phosphor.

Britain as Part of European Community A244

1973, Jan. 3

685	A244	3p brown org & multi	.20	.20
686	A244	5p blue & multi	.45	.45
687	A244	5p emerald & multi	.45	.45
a.		Pair, #686-687	.90	1.50
		Nos. 685-687 (3)	1.10	1.10

Britain's entry into the European Community.

Oak A245

1973, Feb. 28   Photo.   Perf. 14½x14

688	A245	9p multicolored	.40	.40

Tree Planting Year.

Explorer Type of 1972

British Explorers: No. 689, David Livingstone and map of Africa. No. 690, Henry Stanley and map of Africa. 5p, Sir Francis Drake and world map. 7½p, Sir Walter Raleigh and world map. 9p, Charles Sturt and map of Australia.

1973, Apr. 8   Photo.   Perf. 14x14½

689	A236	3p multicolored	.20	.20
690	A236	3p multicolored	.20	.20
a.		Pair, #689-690	.75	1.00
691	A236	5p multicolored	.30	.30
692	A236	7½p multicolored	.35	.35
693	A236	9p multicolored	1.00	.90
		Nos. 689-693 (5)	2.05	1.95

William Gilbert Grace — A246

Designs: Caricatures of William Gilbert Grace, the Great Cricketer, by Harry Furniss.

1973, May 16   Photo.   Perf. 14x14½

694	A246	3p brown & black	.20	.20
695	A246	7½p green & black	.60	.60
696	A246	9p blue & black	.80	.80
		Nos. 694-696 (3)	1.60	1.60

Centenary of British County Cricket.

Sir Joshua Reynolds, Self-portrait A247

1973, July 4   Photo.   Perf. 14x14½

Paintings: 5p, Sir Henry Raeburn (1756-1823), self-portrait. 7½p, Nelly O'Brien, by Reynolds (1723-92). 9p, Rev. R. Walker (The Skater), by Raeburn.

697	A247	3p multicolored	.20	.20
698	A247	5p multicolored	.20	.20
699	A247	7½p multicolored	.40	.40
700	A247	9p gray & multi	.45	.45
		Nos. 697-700 (4)	1.25	1.25

Tuscan Portico, St. Paul's Church, Covent Garden A248

Designs: No. 701, Costumes for Oberon and Titania. No. 703, Prince's Lodging, Newmarket. No. 704, Stage scenery for Oberon.

Litho. and Typo.

1973, Aug. 15   Perf. 14½x14

701	A248	3p black, pur & gold	.20	.20
702	A248	3p gold, brn & blk	.20	.20
a.		Pair, #701-702	.45	.30
703	A248	5p black, blue & gold	.50	.50
704	A248	5p gold, olive & blk	.50	.50
a.		Pair, #703-704	1.25	1.25
		Nos. 701-704 (4)	1.40	1.40

400th birth anniv. of Inigo Jones (1573-1652), architect and designer.

Parliament, from Millbank A249

Design: 8p, Parliament, from Whitehall.

1973, Sept. 12   Engr. and Typo.

705	A249	8p buff, gray & blk	.35	.35
706	A249	10p black & gold	.45	.45

Opening by the Queen of the 19th Commonwealth Parliamentary Assoc. Conf., Westminster Hall.

Princess Anne and Mark Phillips A250

1973, Nov. 14   Photo.   Perf. 14½x14

707	A250	3½p violet & silver	.20	.20
708	A250	20p brown & silver	.75	.75

Wedding of Princess Anne and Captain Mark Phillips, Nov. 14, 1973.

Good King Wenceslas A251

Christmas: Illustrations for Christmas carol "Good King Wenceslas" showing king and page.

1973, Nov. 28

709	A251	3p shown	.40	.35
710	A251	3p Page looking out of window	.40	.35
711	A251	3p Page leaving castle	.40	.35
712	A251	3p Page in storm	.40	.35
713	A251	3p Page bringing gifts	.40	.35
a.		Strip of 5, #709-713	2.50	2.50
714	A251	3½p Page and peasant	.40	.35
		Nos. 709-714 (6)	2.40	2.10

Horse Chestnut A252

1974, Feb. 27   Photo.   Perf. 14½x14

715	A252	10p green & multi	.40	.40

Fire Engine, 1766 A253

Designs: 3½p, First motorized fire engine, 1904. 5½p, Prize winning Sutherland fire engine, 1863. 8p, First steam engine, 1830.

1974, Apr. 24

716	A253	3½p multicolored	.20	.20
717	A253	5½p multicolored	.30	.30
718	A253	8p multicolored	.35	.35
719	A253	10p multicolored	.45	.45
		Nos. 716-719 (4)	1.30	1.30

Fire Prevention (Metropolis) Act, bicent.

Packet "Peninsular," 1888, and "Southampton Packet Letter" Postmark — A254

Development of Overseas Mail Transport: 5½p, Farnham Biplane and "Aerial Post" postmark. 8p, Truck and pillar box for airmail and "London F.S. Air Mail" postmark. 10p, Imperial Airways flying boat and "Southampton Airport" postmark.

1974, June 12   Perf. 14½x14

720	A254	3½p multicolored	.20	.20
721	A254	5½p multicolored	.20	.20
722	A254	8p multicolored	.30	.30
723	A254	10p multicolored	.40	.40
		Nos. 720-723 (4)	1.10	1.10

UPU, Cent.

Robert the Bruce A255

"Great Britons" on caparisoned chargers.

1974, July 10   Perf. 14½x14

724	A255	4½p shown	.20	.20
725	A255	5½p Owain Glyndwr	.20	.20
726	A255	8p King Henry V	.35	.35
727	A255	10p Black Prince	.45	.45
		Nos. 724-727 (4)	1.20	1.20

Churchill, Lord Warden of the Cinque Ports, 1942 — A256

Designs (Churchill): 5½p, with bowler and cigar, 1940. 8p, with top hat, as Secretary of War and Air, 1919. 10p, in uniform of South African Light Horse Regiment, 1899.

1974, Oct. 9   Photo.   Perf. 14x14½

728	A256	4½p silver & multi	.20	.20
729	A256	5½p silver & multi	.30	.30
730	A256	8p silver & multi	.40	.40
731	A256	10p silver & multi	.55	.55
		Nos. 728-731 (4)	1.45	1.45

Sir Winston Spencer Churchill (1874-1965).

Adoration of the Kings, York Minster, c. 1355 A257

Christmas (Roof Bosses): 4½p, Nativity, St. Helen's, Norwich, c. 1480. 8p, Virgin and Child, Church of Ottery St. Mary, Devonshire, c. 1350. 10p, Virgin and Child, Lady Chapel, Worcester Cathedral, c. 1224.

1974, Nov. 27   Perf. 14½x14

732	A257	3½p gold & multi	.20	.20
733	A257	4½p gold & multi	.20	.20
734	A257	8p gold & multi	.30	.30
735	A257	10p gold & multi	.40	.40
		Nos. 732-735 (4)	1.10	1.10

"Peace-Burial at Sea," by Turner — A258

Paintings: 5½p, "Snowstorm-Steamer off a Harbour's Mouth." 8p, "Arsenal, Venice." 10p, "View of St. Laurent."

1975, Feb. 19   Photo.   Perf. 14½x14

736	A258	4½p multicolored	.20	.20
737	A258	5½p multicolored	.20	.20
738	A258	8p multicolored	.30	.30
739	A258	10p multicolored	.40	.40
		Nos. 736-739 (4)	1.10	1.10

Birth bicent. of Joseph Mallord William Turner (1775-1851), painter.

Charlotte Square, Edinburgh A259

National Theater, London A260

Designs: No. 740, The Rows, Chester (double-storied medieval shopping streets). 8p, Sir Christopher Wren's Flamsteed House, Royal Observatory, Greenwich. 10p, St. George's Chapel, Windsor.

1975, Apr. 23   Perf. 14½x14

740	A259	7p multicolored	.25	.25
741	A259	7p multicolored	.25	.25
a.		Pair, #740-741	.50	.50

742	A259	8p multicolored	.30	.30
743	A259	10p multicolored	.40	.40
744	A260	12p multicolored	.45	.45
		Nos. 740-744 (5)	1.65	1.65

European Architectural Heritage Year 1975. Nos. 740-741 printed se-tenant in sheets of 100. 300th anniv. of Royal Observatory, (No. 742) and 500th anniv. of St. George's Chapel (No. 743).

Dinghies A261

1975, June 11   Photo. & Engr.

745	A261	7p shown	.25	.25
746	A261	8p Racing keelboats	.30	.30
747	A261	10p Cruising yachts	.40	.40
748	A261	12p Multihulls	.50	.50
		Nos. 745-748 (4)	1.45	1.45

Royal Thames Yacht Club bicent. and other sailing club anniversaries.

Stephenson's Locomotion, 1825 — A262

Locomotives: 8p, Abbotsford, Waverley Class, 1876. 10p, Caerphilly Castle, 1923. 12p, High-speed train, 1975.

1975, Aug. 13   Photo.   Perf. 14½x14

749	A262	7p multicolored	.25	.20
750	A262	8p multicolored	.30	.30
751	A262	10p multicolored	.40	.40
752	A262	12p multicolored	.50	.50
		Nos. 749-752 (4)	1.45	1.40

Sesquicentennial of public railroads in Great Britain.

Parliament A263

1975, Sept. 3

753	A263	12p multicolored	.50	.50

62nd Inter-Parliamentary Conference, London, Sept. 1975.

Emma and Mr. Woodhouse from "Emma" — A264

Designs (Illustrations by Barbara Brown of Characters from Jane Austen's Novels): 10p, Catherine Morland from "Northanger Abbey." 11p, Mr. Darcy from "Pride and Prejudice." 13p, Mary and Henry Crawford from "Mansfield Park."

1975, Oct. 22   Photo.   Perf. 14x14½

754	A264	8½p multicolored	.30	.30
755	A264	10p multicolored	.40	.40
756	A264	11p multicolored	.45	.45
757	A264	13p multicolored	.50	.50
		Nos. 754-757 (4)	1.65	1.65

Jane Austen (1775-1817), novelist.

Angels with Lute and Harp A265

Christmas: 8½p, Angel with mandolin. 11p, Angel with horn. 13p, Angel with trumpet.

1975, Nov. 26   Photo.   Perf. 14½x14
758	A265	6½p violet & multi	.25	.25
759	A265	8½p multicolored	.30	.30
760	A265	11p multicolored	.45	.45
761	A265	13p ocher & multi	.50	.50
		Nos. 758-761 (4)	1.50	1.50

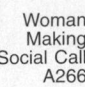

Woman Making Social Call A266

Designs: 10p, Policeman making emergency call. 11p, District nurse making social welfare call. 13p, Refinery worker making field call.

1976, Mar. 10   Photo.   Perf. 14½x14
777	A266	8½p multicolored	.30	.30
778	A266	10p multicolored	.40	.40
779	A266	11p multicolored	.45	.45
780	A266	13p multicolored	.50	.50
		Nos. 777-780 (4)	1.65	1.65

1st telephone call by Alexander Graham Bell, Mar. 10, 1876.

Coal Miner's Hands (Thomas Hepburn) A267

Designs: 10p, Child's hands, textile mill (Robert Owen). 11p, Boy's hand sweeping chimney (Lord Shaftesbury). 13p, Woman's hands holding prison bars (Elizabeth Frey).

1976, Apr. 28   Photo.   Perf. 14½x14
781	A267	8½p gray & black	.30	.30
782	A267	10p multicolored	.40	.40
783	A267	11p multicolored	.45	.45
784	A267	13p multicolored	.50	.50
		Nos. 781-784 (4)	1.65	1.65

19th cent. industrial & social reformers: Hepburn formed 1st miners' union in 1831; Owen, improved working conditions in his mill and established schools; Lord Shaftesbury, philanthropist and sponsor of reform work laws; Frey, pioneer of women's prison reforms.

Benjamin Franklin, by Jean-Jacques Caffieri — A268

1976, June 2   Perf. 14x14½
785	A268	11p multicolored	.45	.45

American Bicentennial.

Royal National Rose Society, Centenary A269

Roses Painted by Kristin Rosenberg.

1976, June 30   Photo.   Perf. 14x14½
786	A269	8½p Elizabeth of Glamis Rose	.30	.30
787	A269	10p Grandpa Dickson	.40	.40
788	A269	11p Rosa Mundi	.45	.45
789	A269	13p Sweet Briar	.50	.50
		Nos. 786-789 (4)	1.65	1.65

Archdruid, Eisteddfod A270

Morris Dancing — A271

British Cultural Traditions: 11p, Piper and dancers, Highland gathering. 13p, Woman playing Welsh harp (telyn), Eisteddfod.

1976, Aug. 4   Photo.   Perf. 14x14½
790	A270	8½p multicolored	.30	.30
791	A271	10p multicolored	.40	.40
792	A271	11p multicolored	.45	.45
793	A270	13p multicolored	.50	.50
		Nos. 790-793 (4)	1.65	1.65

Squire, from Canterbury Tales — A272

Designs: 10p, Page from Tretyse of Love, c. 1493, set in Caxton typeface. 11p, Philosopher, from The Game and Playe of Chesse, c. 1483. 13p, Printing press and printers, early 16th century woodcut.

Photo.; Queen's Head Gold Embossed
1976, Sept. 29   Perf. 14x14½
794	A272	8½p blue & indigo	.30	.30
795	A272	10p olive & dk grn	.40	.40
796	A272	11p gray & black	.40	.40
797	A272	13p ocher & red brn	.50	.50
		Nos. 794-797 (4)	1.60	1.60

500 years of British printing, introduced by William Caxton (1422-1491).

Virgin and Child, Clare Chasuble A273

Christmas (English medieval embroideries): 8½p, Angel with crown. 11p, Angel appearing to the shepherds. 13p, Three Kings bringing gifts, Butler-Bowden cope.

1976, Nov. 24   Photo.   Perf. 14½x14
798	A273	6½p multicolored	.30	.30
799	A273	8½p multicolored	.35	.35
800	A273	11p multicolored	.45	.45
801	A273	13p multicolored	.50	.50
		Nos. 798-801 (4)	1.60	1.60

Racket Sports A274

1977, Jan. 12   Photo.   Perf. 14½x14
802	A274	8½p Tennis	.30	.30
803	A274	10p Table tennis	.40	.40
804	A274	11p Squash	.45	.45
805	A274	13p Badminton	.50	.50
		Nos. 802-805 (4)	1.65	1.65

Wimbledon Tennis Championships, cent. and 1977 World Table Tennis Championships, Birmingham.

Steroids Conformational Analysis — A275

Designs: 10p, Vitamin C synthesis (formula and orange). 11p, Starch chromatography. 13p, Salt crystallography.

1977, Mar. 2   Photo.   Perf. 14½x14
806	A275	8½p multicolored	.30	.30
807	A275	10p multicolored	.40	.40
808	A275	11p multicolored	.45	.45
809	A275	13p multicolored	.50	.50
		Nos. 806-809 (4)	1.65	1.65

British chemists who won Nobel prize. Derek Barton, 1969 (8½p); Walter Norman Haworth, 1937 (10p); Archer J. P. Martin and Richard L. M. Synge, 1952 (11p); William and Lawrence Bragg, 1915 (13p).

Queen Elizabeth II — A276

1977   Photo.   Perf. 14½x14
810	A276	8½p silver & multi	.30	.30
811	A276	9p silver & multi	.35	.35
812	A276	10p silver & multi	.40	.40
813	A276	11p silver & multi	.45	.45
814	A276	13p silver & multi	.50	.50
		Nos. 810-814 (5)	2.00	2.00

25th anniv. of the reign of Elizabeth II. Issue dates: 9p, June 15; others, May 11.

Pentagons, Symbolic of Continents and Nations — A277

1977, June 8   Photo.   Perf. 14x14½
815	A277	13p multicolored	.50	.50

Summit Conference of Commonwealth Heads of Government, London, June 1977.

Wildlife Protection — A278

1977, Oct. 5   Photo.   Perf. 14x14½
816	A278	9p Hedgehog	.35	.25
817	A278	9p Brown hare	.35	.25
818	A278	9p Red squirrel	.35	.25
819	A278	9p Otter	.35	.25
820	A278	9p Badger	.35	.25
a.		Strip of 5, #816-820	2.00	

"Two Turtle Doves, Three French Hens. . ." — A279

The Twelve Days of Christmas: No. 822, 4 colly birds, 5 gold rings, 6 geese a-laying. No. 823, 7 swans a-swimming, 8 maids a-milking. No. 824, 9 drummers drumming, 10 pipers piping. No. 825, 11 ladies dancing, 12 lords a-leaping. 9p, A partridge in a pear tree.

1977, Nov. 23   Photo.   Perf. 14½x14
821	A279	7p multicolored	.25	.20
822	A279	7p multicolored	.25	.20
823	A279	7p multicolored	.25	.20
824	A279	7p multicolored	.25	.20
825	A279	7p multicolored	.25	.20
a.		Strip of 5, #821-825	1.00	
826	A279	9p multicolored	.35	.20
		Nos. 821-826 (6)	1.60	1.20

Oil Production Platform, North Sea — A280

Designs: 10½p, Coal, pithead. 11p, Natural gas, flame. 13p, Electricity-producing nuclear power plant and uranium atom diagram.

1978, Jan. 25   Photo.   Perf. 14x14½
827	A280	9p multicolored	.35	.20
828	A280	10½p multicolored	.35	.20
829	A280	11p multicolored	.45	.20
830	A280	13p multicolored	.50	.25
		Nos. 827-830 (4)	1.65	.85

Great Britain's wealth of energy resources.

Tower of London A281

British Architecture: 10½p, Abbey and Palace, Holyrood House, Edinburgh. 11p, Caernarvon Castle, Wales. 13p, Hampton Court Palace, London.

1978, Mar. 1   Photo.   Perf. 14½x14
831	A281	9p multicolored	.35	.20
832	A281	10½p multicolored	.40	.25
833	A281	11p multicolored	.40	.25
834	A281	13p multicolored	.50	.25
a.		Souv. sheet of 4, #831-834	1.75	1.75
		Nos. 831-834 (4)	1.65	.95

No. 834a issued to publicize London 1980 Intl. Stamp Exhib. and sold for 53½p. The surtax went to exhibition fund.

Gold State Coach — A282

Designs: 10½p, St. Edward's crown. 11p, Orb. 13p, Imperial State crown.

1978, May 31 Photo. *Perf. 14x14½*
835	A282	9p vio blue & gold	.35	.25
836	A282	10½p car lake & gold	.40	.25
837	A282	11p dp green & gold	.45	.30
838	A282	13p purple & gold	.50	.35
		Nos. 835-838 (4)	1.70	1.15

25th anniv. of coronation of Elizabeth II.

Shire Horse A283

British Horses: 10½p, Shetland pony. 11p, Merlyn Cymreig Welsh pony. 13p, Thoroughbred.

1978, July 5 Photo. *Perf. 14½x14*
839	A283	9p multicolored	.35	.25
840	A283	10½p multicolored	.40	.25
841	A283	11p multicolored	.45	.25
842	A283	13p multicolored	.50	.35
		Nos. 839-842 (4)	1.70	1.10

"Penny-farthing," 19th Century — A284

British bicycles: 10½p, 1920 touring bicycles. 11p, Modern small-wheel bicycles. 13p, Road racers.

1978, Aug. 2 Photo. *Perf. 14½x14*
843	A284	9p multicolored	.35	.25
844	A284	10½p multicolored	.40	.25
845	A284	11p multicolored	.45	.25
846	A284	13p multicolored	.50	.35
		Nos. 843-846 (4)	1.70	1.10

Cent. of 1st natl. cycling organizations: British Cycling Fed. and Cyclists Touring Club.

Carolers Around Christmas Tree A285

Christmas: 9p, Christmas waits (watchmen). 11p, 18th century carolers. 13p, Boar's head carol.

1978, Nov. 22 Photo. *Perf. 14½x14*
847	A285	7p multicolored	.25	.25
848	A285	9p multicolored	.35	.25
849	A285	11p multicolored	.45	.25
850	A285	13p multicolored	.50	.35
		Nos. 847-850 (4)	1.55	1.10

Old English Sheepdog A286

British dogs: 10½p, Welsh springer spaniel. 11p, West Highland white terrier. 13p, Irish setter.

1979, Feb. 7 Photo. *Perf. 14½x14*
851	A286	9p multicolored	.35	.25
852	A286	10½p multicolored	.40	.25
853	A286	11p multicolored	.45	.25
854	A286	13p multicolored	.50	.35
		Nos. 851-854 (4)	1.70	1.10

British Wild Flowers — A287

1979, Mar. 21 Photo. *Perf. 14x14½*
855	A287	9p Primroses	.35	.25
856	A287	10½p Daffodils	.40	.25
857	A287	11p Bluebells	.45	.25
858	A287	13p Snowdrops	.50	.35
		Nos. 855-858 (4)	1.70	1.10

Flags of Member Nations as Ballots A288

Flags of European Community Members: United Kingdom, Italy, Denmark, Belgium, Fed. Rep. of Germany, France, Netherlands, Ireland, Luxembourg. Positions of hands and flags different on each denomination.

1979, May 9 Photo. *Perf. 14½x14*
859	A288	9p multicolored	.35	.25
860	A288	10½p multicolored	.40	.25
861	A288	11p multicolored	.45	.25
862	A288	13p multicolored	.50	.35
		Nos. 859-862 (4)	1.70	1.10

European Parliament, 1st direct elections, 6/7-10.

Saddling of Mahmoud, 1936 Derby, by Alfred Munnings A289

200th Anniv. of the Derby: 10½p, Liverpool Great National Steeple Chase, 1839, aquatint by F. C. Turner. 11p, First Spring Meeting, Newmarket, 1793, by J. N. Sartorius. 13p, Charles II watching racing at Dorsett Ferry, Windsor, 1684, by Francis Barlow.

1979, June 6 Photo. *Perf. 14½x14*
863	A289	9p multicolored	.35	.25
864	A289	10½p multicolored	.40	.25
865	A289	11p multicolored	.45	.25
866	A289	13p multicolored	.50	.35
		Nos. 863-866 (4)	1.70	1.10

Peter Rabbit — A290

Children's books: 10½p, The Wind in the Willows. 11p, Winnie the Pooh. 13p, Alice's Adventures in Wonderland.

1979, July 11 Photo. *Perf. 14x14½*
867	A290	9p multicolored	.40	.20
868	A290	10½p multicolored	.45	.20
869	A290	11p multicolored	.45	.25
870	A290	13p multicolored	.55	.25
		Nos. 867-870 (4)	1.85	.90

International Year of the Child.

Rowland Hill — A291

Designs: 11½p, Bellman, early 19th cent. 13p, London post office and mailman, early 19th cent. 15p, Victorian woman and child mailing letter.

1979, Aug. 22 Photo. *Perf. 14x14½*
871	A291	10p multicolored	.40	.25
872	A291	11½p multicolored	.45	.25
873	A291	13p multicolored	.50	.25
874	A291	15p multicolored	.60	.30
a.		Souvenir sheet of 4, #871-874	2.00	1.75
		Nos. 871-874 (4)	1.95	1.05

Sir Rowland Hill (1795-1879), originator of penny postage.
No. 874a issued 10/24/79 to publicize London 1980 Intl. Stamp Exhib. and sold for 59½p. The surtax went to exhibition fund.

Police Constable and Children A292

Designs: 11½p, Police constable directing traffic. 13p, Police woman on horseback. 15p, River patrol boat.

1979, Sept. 26 Photo. *Perf. 14½x14*
875	A292	10p multicolored	.40	.25
876	A292	11½p multicolored	.45	.25
877	A292	13p multicolored	.50	.25
878	A292	15p multicolored	.60	.35
		Nos. 875-878 (4)	1.95	1.10

London Metropolitan Police, 150th anniv.

Three Kings Following Star A293

Christmas: 10p, Angel appearing before the shepherds. 11½p, Nativity. 13p, Joseph and Mary traveling to Bethlehem. 15p, Annunciation.

1979, Nov. 21 Photo. *Perf. 14½x14*
879	A293	8p multicolored	.30	.25
880	A293	10p multicolored	.40	.25
881	A293	11½p multicolored	.45	.30
882	A293	13p multicolored	.50	.35
883	A293	15p multicolored	.60	.35
		Nos. 879-883 (5)	2.25	1.50

Kingfisher — A294

1980, Jan. 16 Photo. *Perf. 14x14½*
884	A294	10p shown	.40	.25
885	A294	11½p Dipper	.45	.25
886	A294	13p Moorhen	.50	.25
887	A294	15p Yellow wagtail	.60	.35
		Nos. 884-887 (4)	1.95	1.10

"Rocket" Locomotive A295

1980, Mar. 12 Photo. *Perf. 14½x14*
904	A295	12p shown	.50	.30
905	A295	12p 1st, 2nd class cars	.50	.30
906	A295	12p 3rd class and sheep cars	.50	.30
907	A295	12p Flat cars	.50	.30
908	A295	12p Flat car, mail coach	.50	.30
a.		Strip of 5, #904-908	2.50	2.50

Liverpool-Manchester Railroad, 150th anniv. No. 908a has a continuous design.

London View A296

1980, Apr. 9 Engr. *Perf. 14½*
909	A296	50p multicolored	2.00	1.25
a.		Souvenir sheet	2.00	2.00

London 1980, Intl. Stamp Exhib., May 6-14. No. 909a, issued May 7, sold for 75p.

Buckingham Palace — A297

1980, May 7 Photo. *Perf. 14x14½*
910	A297	10½p shown	.40	.25
911	A297	12p Albert Memorial	.50	.25
912	A297	13½p Royal Opera House	.50	.25
913	A297	15p Hampton Court	.60	.25
914	A297	17½p Kensington Palace	.70	.35
		Nos. 910-914 (5)	2.70	1.35

Emily Bronte and "Wuthering Heights" A298

Victorian novelists and scenes from their novels: 12p, Charlotte Bronte, "Jane Eyre." 13½p, George Eliot, "The Mill on the Floss." 17½p, Mrs. Gaskell, "North and South." 12p and 13½p show CEPT (Europa) emblem.

1980, July 9 Photo. *Perf. 15x14*
915	A298	12p multicolored	.50	.30
916	A298	13½p multicolored	.55	.35
917	A298	15p multicolored	.60	.40
918	A298	17½p multicolored	.70	.55
		Nos. 915-918 (4)	2.35	1.60

Queen Mother
Elizabeth, 80th
Birthday — A299

1980, Aug. 4   Photo.   Perf. 14x14½
919 A299 12p multicolored   .45   .20

English
Conductors
A300

Designs: 12p, Henry Wood, (1869-1944)
Conductor. 13½p, Thomas Beecham (1879-
1961). 15p, Malcolm Sargent (1895-1967).
17½p, John Barbirolli (1899-1970).

1980, Sept. 10
920 A300 12p multicolored   .50   .30
921 A300 13½p multicolored   .55   .30
922 A300 15p multicolored   .60   .40
923 A300 17½p multicolored   .70   .45
  Nos. 920-923 (4)   2.35 1.45

Running — A301

1980, Oct. 10   Litho.   Perf. 14x14½
924 A301 12p shown   .50   .30
925 A301 13½p Rugby   .55   .30
926 A301 15p Boxing   .60   .40
927 A301 17½p Cricket   .70   .45
  Nos. 924-927 (4)   2.35 1.45

Centenaries: Amateur Athletics Assoc.;
Welsh Rugby Union; Amateur Boxing Assoc.;
1st cricket test match against Australia.

Christmas
Tree with
Candles
A302

Christmas (Traditional Decorations): 12p,
Candles, ivy, ribbons. 13½p, Mistletoe,
apples. 15p, Paper chain and bell. 17½p, Holly
wreath.

1980, Nov. 19   Photo.   Perf. 14½x14
928 A302 10p multicolored   .40   .25
929 A302 12p multicolored   .50   .30
930 A302 13½p multicolored   .55   .35
931 A302 15p multicolored   .60   .40
932 A302 17½p multicolored   .70   .50
  Nos. 928-932 (5)   2.75 1.80

Lovebirds,
Angels and
Heart
(Valentine's
Day)
A303

Folklore: 18p, Morris Dancers, 16th century
window, Shropshire. 22p, Wheat, fruit, farm
couple dancing (Lammastide). 25p, Medieval
mummers, 14th century manuscript illustration. 14p and 18p show CEPT (Europa)
emblem.

1981, Feb. 6   Photo.   Perf. 14½x14
933 A303 14p multicolored   .50   .30
934 A303 18p multicolored   .65   .65
935 A303 22p multicolored   .90   .75
936 A303 25p multicolored   1.00 .85
  Nos. 933-936 (4)   3.05 2.55

Guide Dog
Leading
Blind Man
A304

1981, Mar. 25   Photo.
937 A304 14p shown   .50   .30
938 A304 18p Sign language   .70   .45
939 A304 22p Man in wheelchair   .90   .65
940 A304 25p Foot painting   1.00 .75
  Nos. 937-940 (4)   3.10 2.15

International Year of the Disabled.

Small
Tortoiseshell
A305

1981, May 13   Perf. 14x14½
941 A305 14p shown   .55   .30
942 A305 18p Large blue   .70   .45
943 A305 22p Peacock   .90   .70
944 A305 25p Checkered skipper   1.00 .80
  Nos. 941-944 (4)   3.15 2.25

Glenfinnan,
Highlands,
Scotland
A306

50th anniv. of National Trust for Scotland:
18p, Derwentwater, Lake District, England.
20p, Stackpole Head, Dyfed, Wales. 22p,
Giant's Causeway, County Antrim, Northern
Ireland. 25p, St. Kilda, Scotland.

1981, June 24   Photo.   Perf. 14½x14
945 A306 14p multicolored   .55   .25
946 A306 18p multicolored   .70   .35
947 A306 20p multicolored   .80   .45
948 A306 22p multicolored   .90   .65
949 A306 25p multicolored   1.00 .75
  Nos. 945-949 (5)   3.95 2.45

Prince Charles
and Lady
Diana — A307

1981, July 22   Photo.   Perf. 14x14½
950 A307 14p multicolored   .90   .40
951 A307 25p multicolored   1.60 .75

Wedding of Charles, Prince of Wales, and
Lady Diana Spencer, St. Paul's Cathedral,
July 29.

Hikers
Reading
Map
A308

1981, Aug. 12   Litho.   Perf. 14
952 A308 14p shown   .55   .25
953 A308 18p Girl at potter's
         wheel   .70   .50
954 A308 22p Woman adminis-
         tering artificial
         respiration   .90   .65
955 A308 25p Hurdler   1.00 .75
  Nos. 952-955 (4)   3.15 2.15

The Duke of Edinburgh's Awards (expeditions, skills, service, recreation), 25th anniv.

Cockle
Dredging
A309

1981, Sept. 23   Photo.   Perf. 14½x14
956 A309 14p shown   .55   .25
957 A309 18p Hauling trawl net   .70   .50
958 A309 22p Lobster potting   .90   .65
959 A309 25p Hauling seine net   1.00 .75
  Nos. 956-959 (4)   3.15 2.15

Fishermen's Year and Royal Natl. Mission to
Deep Sea Fishermen centenary.

Joseph
and Mary
Arriving at
Bethlehem
A310

Christmas: Children's Drawings.

1981, Nov. 18   Photo.
960 A310 11½p Santa Claus   .45   .25
961 A310 14p Jesus   .55   .30
962 A310 18p Angel   .70   .40
963 A310 22p shown   .90   .50
964 A310 25p Three Kings   1.00 .60
  Nos. 960-964 (5)   3.60 2.05

Death Centenary of Charles Darwin
(1809-1882) — A311

1982, Feb. 10   Photo.
965 A311 15½p Giant tortoises   .60   .35
966 A311 19½p Iguanas   .80   .50
967 A311 26p Darwin's finches   1.05 .80
968 A311 29p Skulls   1.15 .95
  Nos. 965-968 (4)   3.60 2.60

Youth
Organizations
A312

1982, Mar. 24   Photo.   Perf. 14x14½
983 A312 15½p Boy's Brigade   .60   .35
984 A312 19½p Girl's Brigade   .80   .50
985 A312 26p Boy Scouts   1.05 .80
986 A312 29p Girl Guides   1.15 .95
  Nos. 983-986 (4)   3.60 2.60

75th anniv. of scouting and 125th birth
anniv. of founder Robert Baden-Powell (26p).

Performing
Arts — A313

1982, Apr. 28   Photo.   Perf. 14x14½
987 A313 15½p Ballet   .65   .25
988 A313 19½p Pantomime   .85   .50
989 A313 26p Shakespearean
         drama   1.15 .90
990 A313 29p Opera   1.25 1.00
  Nos. 987-990 (4)   3.90 2.65

Nos. 987-990 show CEPT (Europa) emblem.

King Henry
VIII and the
Mary Rose
A314

1982, June 16   Perf. 14½x14
991 A314 15½p shown   .60   .25
992 A314 19½p Admiral Blake,
         Triumph   .75   .50
993 A314 24p Lord Nelson,
         Victory   .90   .65
994 A314 26p Lord Fisher,
         Dreadnought   1.05 .75
995 A314 29p Viscount Cun-
         ningham, War-
         spite   1.15 .90
  Nos. 991-995 (5)   4.45 3.05

Textile
Designs — A315

1982, July 23   Photo.   Perf. 14x14½
996 A315 15½p Strawberry Thief,
         1883   .60   .20
997 A315 19½p Tulips, 1906   .80   .50
998 A315 26p Cherry Orchard,
         1930   1.05 .75
999 A315 29p Chevron, 1973   1.15 .85
  Nos. 996-999 (4)   3.60 2.30

Information Technology — A316

15½p, Hieroglyphics, library, word proces-
sor. 26p, Viewdata set, satellite, laser pen.

1982, Sept. 8   Photo.
1000 A316 15½p multicolored   .60   .25
1001 A316 26p multicolored   1.05 .70

Austin's
Seven
(1922) and
Metro
A317

Cars: 19½p, Ford Model T (1913) and
Escort. 26p, Jaguar SS (1931) and XJ6
(1967). 29p, Rolls-Royce Silver Ghost (1907)
and Silver Spirit (1982).

1982, Oct. 13   Litho.   Perf. 14½x14
1002 A317 15½p multicolored   .60   .45
1003 A317 19½p multicolored   .80   .60
1004 A317 26p multicolored   1.05 .75
1005 A317 29p multicolored   1.15 .85
  Nos. 1002-1005 (4)   3.60 2.65

Christmas 1982 A318

Designs: Christmas carols.

1982, Nov. 17   **Photo.**
1006	A318	12½p	While Shepherds Watched	.50 .20
1007	A318	15½p	The Holly and the Ivy	.60 .35
1008	A318	19½p	I Saw Three Ships	.80 .60
1009	A318	26p	We Three Kings	1.05 .70
1010	A318	29p	Good King Wenceslas	1.15 .80
			Nos. 1006-1010 (5)	4.10 2.65

River Fish A319

1983, Jan. 26   **Photo.**   **Perf. 15x14**
1011	A319	15½p	Salmon	.60 .25
1012	A319	19½p	Pike	.80 .55
1013	A319	26p	Trout	1.05 .65
1014	A319	29p	Perch	1.15 .75
			Nos. 1011-1014 (4)	3.60 2.20

Commonwealth Day — A320

Landscapes by Donald Hamilton Fraser.

1983, Mar. 9   **Photo.**   **Perf. 14x14½**
1015	A320	15½p	Tropical island	.60 .35
1016	A320	19½p	Desert	.80 .55
1017	A320	26p	Farmland	1.05 .65
1018	A320	29p	Mountains	1.15 .75
			Nos. 1015-1018 (4)	3.60 2.30

Engineering Achievements (Europa) — A321

1983, May 25   **Photo.**   **Perf. 15x14**
1019	A321	16p	Humber Bridge	.60 .20
1020	A321	20½p	Thames Flood Barrier	1.25 1.10
1021	A321	28p	Emergency oil rig support vessel Iolair	1.75 1.40
			Nos. 1019-1021 (3)	3.60 2.70

A322

Designs: 16p, The Royal Scots (Royal Regiment). 20½p, Royal Welsh Fusiliers. 26p, Royal Green Jackets. 28p, Irish Guards. 31p, Parachute Regiment.

1983, July 6   **Perf. 14x14½**
1022	A322	16p	multicolored	.65 .35
1023	A322	20½p	multicolored	.80 .55
1024	A322	26p	multicolored	1.05 .65
1025	A322	28p	multicolored	1.10 .70
1026	A322	31p	multicolored	1.20 .75
			Nos. 1022-1026 (5)	4.80 3.00

A323

Designs: 16p, 20th cent. garden, Sissinghurst. 20½p, Biddulph Grange, 19th cent. 28p, Blenheim, 18th cent. 31p, Pitmeeden, 17th cent.

1983, Aug. 24   **Litho.**   **Perf. 14**
1027	A323	16p	multicolored	.65 .35
1028	A323	20½p	multicolored	.80 .55
1029	A323	28p	multicolored	1.10 .70
1030	A323	31p	multicolored	1.20 .75
			Nos. 1027-1030 (4)	3.75 2.35

British Fairs A324

1983, Oct. 5   **Photo.**   **Perf. 14½x14**
1031	A324	16p	Merry-go-round	.65 .40
1032	A324	20½p	Animals, rides	.80 .50
1033	A324	28p	Games	1.10 .75
1034	A324	31p	Ancient market fair	1.20 .75
			Nos. 1031-1034 (4)	3.75 2.40

850th anniv. of St. Bartholomew's Fair.

Christmas A325

1983, Nov. 16   **Photo.**
1035	A325	12½p	Birds mailing cards	.50 .30
1036	A325	16p	Three Kings chimney pots	.65 .40
1037	A325	20½p	Birds under umbrella	.80 .55
1038	A325	28p	Birds under street lamp	1.10 .70
1039	A325	31p	Topiary dove	1.20 .80
			Nos. 1035-1039 (5)	4.25 2.80

Heraldry A326

Designs: 16p, Arms of The College of Arms. 20½p, Arms of Richard III, founder. 28p, Arms of The Earl Marshal. 31p, Arms of The City of London.

1984, Jan. 17   **Photo.**   **Perf. 14½**
1040	A326	16p	multicolored	.65 .40
1041	A326	20½p	multicolored	.80 .50
1042	A326	28p	multicolored	1.10 .75
1043	A326	31p	multicolored	1.20 .80
			Nos. 1040-1043 (4)	3.75 2.45

National Cattle Breeders' Association A327

1984, Mar. 6   **Litho.**   **Perf. 15x14½**
1044	A327	16p	Highland Cow	.65 .40
1045	A327	20½p	Chillingham Wild Bull	.80 .55
1046	A327	26p	Hereford Bull	1.05 .65
1047	A327	28p	Welsh Black Bull	1.10 .70
1048	A327	31p	Irish Moiled Cow	1.20 .75
			Nos. 1044-1048 (5)	4.80 3.05

Royal Institute of British Architects Sesquicentennial — A328

Urban renewal projects and plans.

1984, Apr. 3   **Photo.**
1049	A328	16p	Liverpool	.65 .40
1050	A328	20½p	Durham	.80 .55
1051	A328	28p	Bristol	1.10 .70
1052	A328	31p	Perth	1.20 .75
			Nos. 1049-1052 (4)	3.75 2.40

Europa (1959-1984) — A329

1984, May 9   **Photo.**   **Perf. 14½x14**
1053	A329	16p	Bridge	.75 .25
1054	A329	16p	Abduction of Europa	.75 .25
a,			Pair, #1053-1054	1.50 .75
1055	A329	20½p	like No. 1053	1.75 1.25
1056	A329	20½p	like No. 1054	1.75 1.25
a,			Pair, #1055-1056	3.50 3.00
			Nos. 1053-1056 (4)	5.00 3.00

Nos. 1054, 1056 also for 2nd Election of the European Parliament.

London Economic Summit, June 7-9 — A330

1984, June 5   **Photo.**   **Perf. 14x15**
1057	A330	31p	Lancaster House	1.20 .80

Greenwich Meridian, Cent. — A331

1984, June 26   **Litho.**   **Perf. 14x14½**
1058	A331	16p	View from Apollo 11	.65 .40
1059	A331	20½p	English Channel map	.80 .55
1060	A331	28p	Greenwich Observatory	1.10 .70

1061   A331   31p   Airy's transit telescope, 1850   1.20 .75
Nos. 1058-1061 (4)   3.75 2.35

Bath-Bristol-London Mail Coach Bicentenary — A332

18th century drawings by James Pollard.

1984, July 31   **Photo. & Engr.**   **Perf. 14½x14**
1062	A332	16p	Bath, 1784	.65 .40
1063	A332	16p	Exeter, 1816	.65 .40
1064	A332	16p	Norwich, 1827	.65 .40
1065	A332	16p	Holyhead & Liverpool	.65 .40
1066	A332	16p	Edinburgh, 1831	.65 .40
a.			Strip of 5, #1062-1066	3.25 2.75

50th Anniv. of British Council A333

1984, Sept. 25   **Photo.**
1067	A333	17p	Education for development	.65 .35
1068	A333	22p	Promoting the arts	.85 .45
1069	A333	31p	Technical training	1.20 .65
1070	A333	34p	Language & libraries	1.35 .80
			Nos. 1067-1070 (4)	4.05 2.25

Christmas 1984 A334

Crayon Sketches by Yvonne Gilbert.

1984, Nov. 20   **Photo.**   **Perf. 15x14**
1088	A334	13p	Holy Family	.50 .30
a.			Booklet pane of 20 (BK770)	10.50
1089	A334	17p	Arrival in Bethlehem	.70 .35
1090	A334	22p	Shephard and Lamb	.90 .50
1091	A334	31p	Virgin and child	1.20 .75
1092	A334	34p	Offering Frankincense	1.35 .90
			Nos. 1088-1092 (5)	4.65 2.80

Bklt. of 20 13p sold at 30p discount. Stamps have blue stars printed on the back.

Great Western Railway Sesquicentennial — A335

1985, Jan. 22   **Photo.**   **Perf. 15x14**
1093	A335	17p	Flying Scotsman	.65 .45
1094	A335	22p	Golden Arrow	.85 .60
1095	A335	29p	Cheltenham Flyer	1.20 .85
1096	A335	31p	Royal Scot	1.25 1.00
1097	A335	34p	Cornish Riviera	1.25 1.05
			Nos. 1093-1097 (5)	5.20 3.95

Insects — A336

1985, Mar. 12　Photo.　Perf. 15x14½

1098	A336	17p Buff tailed bumble bee	.70	.40
1099	A336	22p Seven spotted ladybird	.90	.60
1100	A336	29p Wart-biter bushcricket	1.20	.80
1101	A336	31p Stag beetle	1.25	.85
1102	A336	34p Emperor dragonfly	1.35	.90
		Nos. 1098-1102 (5)	5.40	3.55

Music Year (Europa) A337

British Composers: 17p, Water Music, by George Frideric Handel. 22p, The Planets Suite, by Gustav Holst. 31p, The First Cockoo, by Frederick Delius. 34p, Sea Pictures, by Edward Elgar.

1985, May 14　　　　　　Perf. 14½

1103	A337	17p Reflections in pool	.75	.20
1104	A337	22p View of planets	1.10	1.25
1105	A337	31p Roosting cuckoo	1.75	1.50
1106	A337	34p Waves, wing	2.00	1.75
		Nos. 1103-1106 (4)	5.60	4.70

Safety at Sea A338

1985, June 18　Litho.　Perf. 14

1107	A338	17p Lifeboat	.70	.40
1108	A338	22p Beachy Head Lighthouse, chart	.90	.55
1109	A338	31p Marecs-A satellite	1.25	.80
1110	A338	34p Signal buoy, yacht	1.35	.85
		Nos. 1107-1110 (4)	4.20	2.60

Royal Mail Service, 350th Anniv. — A339

Designs: 17p, Royal Mail Datapost motorcyclist and plane. 22p, Postbus on country road. 31p, Parcel service delivery. 34p, Postman delivering mail.

1985, July 30　Photo.　Perf. 14x14½

1111	A339	17p multicolored	.70	.45
1112	A339	22p multicolored	.90	.55
1113	A339	31p multicolored	1.25	.80
1114	A339	34p multicolored	1.35	.85
		Nos. 1111-1114 (4)	4.20	2.65

Arthurian Legends A340

Designs: 17p, Arthur consulting with Merlin. 22p, The Lady of the Lake with the sword "Excalibur." 31p, Guinevere and Lancelot fleeing from Camelot. 34p, Sir Galahad praying during his quest for the Holy Grail.

1985, Sept. 3　Photo.　Perf. 15x14

1115	A340	17p multicolored	.70	.45
1116	A340	22p multicolored	.90	.55
1117	A340	31p multicolored	1.25	.80
1118	A340	34p multicolored	1.35	.85
		Nos. 1115-1118 (4)	4.20	2.65

500th anniv. of William Caxton's edition of Le Morte D'Arthur, by Sir Thomas Mallory.

20th Cent. Stars and Directors of Film — A341

Photographs: 17p, Peter Sellers (1925-80). 22p, David Niven (1910-83). 29p, Charlie Chaplin (1889-1977). 31p, Vivien Leigh (1913-67). 34p, Sir Alfred Hitchcock (1899-1980), director.

1985, Oct. 8　Photo.　Perf. 14½

1119	A341	17p multicolored	.70	.45
1120	A341	22p multicolored	.90	.60
1121	A341	29p multicolored	1.15	.80
1122	A341	31p multicolored	1.25	.90
1123	A341	34p multicolored	1.35	1.00
		Nos. 1119-1123 (5)	5.35	3.75

Christmas Pantomime A342

1985, Nov. 19　Photo.　Perf. 15x14½

1124	A342	12p Principal boy	.50	.30
a.		Booklet pane of 20 (BK 780)	10.00	
1125	A342	17p Genie	.70	.50
1126	A342	22p Grande dame	.90	.60
1127	A342	31p Good fairy	1.25	.75
1128	A342	34p Cat	1.35	.85
		Nos. 1124-1128 (5)	4.70	3.00

No. 1124a has random star design printed on back.

Industry Year A343

1986, Jan. 14　Litho.　Perf. 15x14

1129	A343	17p North Sea oil rig, light bulb	.70	.40
1130	A343	22p Medical research lab, thermometer	.90	.60
1131	A343	31p Steel mill, garden hoe	1.25	.75
1132	A343	34p Cornfield, bread	1.35	.85
		Nos. 1129-1132 (4)	4.20	2.60

Halley's Comet A344

Designs: 17p, Caricature, Edmond Halley (1656-1742), astronomer. 22p, European Space Agency Giotto spacecraft pursuing comet. 31p, Comet and legend, Maybe Twice in a Lifetime. 34p, Comet orbiting sun.

1986, Feb. 18　　　　　　Photo.

1133	A344	17p multicolored	.70	.40
1134	A344	22p multicolored	.90	.60
1135	A344	31p multicolored	1.25	.75
1136	A344	34p multicolored	1.35	.85
		Nos. 1133-1136 (4)	4.20	2.60

A345

Queen Elizabeth II, 60th Birthday A346

1986, Apr. 21　　　　　　Photo.

1137	A345	17p multicolored	.75	.50
1138	A346	17p multicolored	.75	.50
a.		Pair, #1137-1138	1.50	1.25
1139	A345	34p multicolored	1.40	.90
1140	A346	34p multicolored	1.40	.90
a.		Pair, #1139-1140	2.80	2.50

Europa A347

1986, May 20　Photo.　Perf. 14½

1141	A347	17p Barn owl	.70	.55
1142	A347	22p Pine marten	.90	.85
1143	A347	31p Wild cat	1.25	1.00
1144	A347	34p Natterjack toad	1.40	1.25
		Nos. 1141-1144 (4)	4.25	3.65

Domesday Book, 900th Anniv. A348

1986, June 17　　　　　　Photo.

1145	A348	17p Peasant	.70	.50
1146	A348	22p Freeman	.90	.60
1147	A348	31p Knight	1.25	.80
1148	A348	34p Lord	1.40	.90
		Nos. 1145-1148 (4)	4.25	2.80

Domesday Book, first nationwide survey in British history.

Sports A349

1986, July 15　Photo.　Perf. 15x14

1149	A349	17p Track and field	.70	.45
1150	A349	22p Rowing	.90	.65
1151	A349	29p Weight lifting	1.20	.80
1152	A349	31p Shooting	1.25	.85
1153	A349	34p Field hockey	1.35	.90
		Nos. 1149-1153 (5)	5.40	3.65

1986 Commonwealth Games, Edinburgh. World Hockey Cup, London.

Wedding of Prince Andrew and Sarah Ferguson — A350

1986, July 22　　　　　Perf. 14x15

1154	A350	12p multicolored	.60	.40
1155	A350	17p multicolored	.80	.50

Commonwealth Parliamentary Assoc. Conf., London — A351

1986, Aug. 19　Litho.　Perf. 14x14½

1156	A351	34p multicolored	1.35	.85

Royal Air Force Commanders and Aircraft A352

Designs: 17p, Lord Dowding (1882-1970), Hurricane. 22p, Lord Tedder (1890-1967), Hawker Typhoon. 29p, Lord Trenchard (1873-1956), De Havilland 9A World War I bomber. 31p, Sir Arthur Harris (1892-1984), Avro Lancaster. 34p, Lord Portal (1893-1971), De Havilland Mosquito.

1986, Sept. 16　Photo.　Perf. 14½

1157	A352	17p multicolored	.70	.45
1158	A352	22p multicolored	.90	.65
1159	A352	29p multicolored	1.15	.75
1160	A352	31p multicolored	1.25	.80
1161	A352	34p multicolored	1.35	.90
		Nos. 1157-1161 (5)	5.35	3.55

Christmas A353

Customs: 12p, 13p, Glastonbury Thorn. 18p, Tanad Valley Plygain. 22p, Hebrides Tribute. 31p, Dewsbury Church Knell. 34p, Hereford Boy Bishop.

1986, Nov. 18　Photo.　Perf. 15x14½

1162	A353	12p multicolored	.50	.30
1163	A353	13p multicolored	.50	.35
a.		Pane of 36	18.00	
1164	A353	18p multicolored	.70	.45
1165	A353	22p multicolored	.90	.70
1166	A353	31p multicolored	1.25	.80
1167	A353	34p multicolored	1.35	.90
		Nos. 1162-1167 (6)	5.20	3.50

No. 1163a printed in two panes of 18 with gutter between, stars on back; folded and sold in discount booklet for £4.30.

Flora — A354

Photographs by Alfred Lammer.

1987, Jan. 20　Photo.　Perf. 14½

1168	A354	18p Gaillardia	.70	.40
1169	A354	22p Echinops	.90	.65
1170	A354	31p Echeveria	1.25	.80
1171	A354	34p Colchicum	1.35	.90
		Nos. 1168-1171 (4)	4.20	2.75

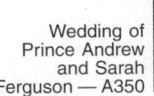

Sir Isaac Newton (1642-1727), Physicist, Mathematician A355

Manuscripts and principles. 18p, Philosophiae Naturalis Principia Mathematica, 1687. 22p, Motion of bodies in ellipses. 31p, Opticks Treatise of the Refraction, Reflections and Colors of Light. 34p, The System of the World.

1987, Mar. 24		Photo.	Perf. 14	
1172	A355	18p multicolored	.70	.40
1173	A355	22p multicolored	.90	.65
1174	A355	31p multicolored	1.25	.80
1175	A355	34p multicolored	1.35	.90
	Nos. 1172-1175 (4)		4.20	2.75

Europa
A356

Modern architecture: 18p, Willis Faber & Dumas Building, Ipswich, designed by Norman Foster. 22p, Pompidou Centre, Paris, designed by Richard Rogers and Renzo Piano. 31p, Staatsgalerie, Stuttgart, designed by James Stirling and Michael Wilford. 34p, European Investment Bank, Luxembourg, designed by Sir Denys Lasdun.

1987, May 12		Photo.	Perf. 15x14	
1176	A356	18p multicolored	.70	.30
1177	A356	22p multicolored	1.00	.80
1178	A356	31p multicolored	1.40	1.25
1179	A356	34p multicolored	1.75	1.25
	Nos. 1176-1179 (4)		4.85	3.60

St. John Ambulance, Cent. — A357

First aid.

1987, June 16		Litho.	Perf. 14x14½	
1180	A357	18p Ambulance, 1887	.70	.50
1181	A357	22p War victims, 1940	.90	.60
1182	A357	31p Public event, 1965	1.25	.80
1183	A357	34p Transplant organ flight, 1987	1.35	.90
	Nos. 1180-1183 (4)		4.20	2.80

Order of the Thistle, Scotland, 300th Anniv. of Revival A358

Coats of arms: 18p, Lord Lyon, King of Arms, 1687. 22p, Duke of Rothesay, bestowed on Prince Charles in 1974. 31p, Royal Scottish Academy of Painting, Sculpture & Architecture, 1826. 34p, The Royal Society of Edinburgh, 1783.

1987, July 21		Photo.	Perf. 14½	
1184	A358	18p multicolored	.70	.50
1185	A358	22p multicolored	.90	.60
1186	A358	31p multicolored	1.25	.80
1187	A358	34p multicolored	1.35	.90
	Nos. 1184-1187 (4)		4.20	2.80

Accession of Queen Victoria, 150th Anniv. A359

Portraits of Victoria and: 18p, Great Exhibition (1851) at the Crystal Palace, Grace Darling's rescue (1838) of the Forfarshire's survivors, and Monarch of the Glen, by Sir Edwin Henry Landseer. 22p, Launching of Brunel's ship Great Eastern, portrait of Prince Consort Albert, Mrs. Beeton's Book of Household Management (1889). 31p, The Albert Memorial,

---

Prime Minister Disraeli and 1st ballot box. 34p, The Boer War, Guglielmo Marconi's wireless telegraph communications linking Paris and London (1898), and diamond jubilee emblem.

Photo. & Engr.

1987, Sept. 8			Perf. 15x14	
1188	A359	18p multicolored	.70	.45
1189	A359	22p multicolored	.90	.60
1190	A359	31p multicolored	1.25	.80
1191	A359	34p multicolored	1.35	.90
	Nos. 1188-1191 (4)		4.20	2.75

Studio Pottery
A360

1987, Oct. 13		Photo.	Perf. 14½	
1192	A360	18p Bernard Leach	.70	.45
1193	A360	26p Elizabeth Fritsch	1.05	.60
1194	A360	31p Lucie Rie	1.25	.80
1195	A360	34p Hans Coper	1.35	.90
	Nos. 1192-1195 (4)		4.35	2.75

Christmas
A361

Childhood memories: 13p, Decorating tree. 18p, Looking out window, Christmas eve. 26p, Sweet dreams. 31p, Reading new book to toys, Christmas morning. 34p, Playing horn, snowman.

1987, Nov. 17		Photo.	Perf. 15x14	
1196	A361	13p multicolored	.50	.30
a.		Pane of 36	18.00	
1197	A361	18p multicolored	.70	.45
1198	A361	26p multicolored	1.05	.60
1199	A361	31p multicolored	1.25	.80
1200	A361	34p multicolored	1.35	.90
	Nos. 1196-1200 (5)		4.85	3.05

No. 1196a printed in two panes of 18 with gutter between, stars on back; folded and sold in discount booklets for £4.30.

Linnean Society of London, 200th Anniv. A362

1988, Jan. 19			Perf. 15x14½	
1201	A362	18p Bull-rout fish	.70	.45
1202	A362	26p Yellow waterlily	1.05	.60
1203	A362	31p Bewick's swan	1.25	.80
1204	A362	34p Morel	1.35	.90
	Nos. 1201-1204 (4)		4.35	2.75

Linnaeus (Carl von Linne, 1707-78), inventor of system of taxonomic nomenclature.

Welsh Bible, 400th Anniv. — A363

1988, Mar. 1		Photo.	Perf. 14½	
1205	A363	18p William Morgan	.70	.50
1206	A363	26p William Salesbury	1.05	.70
1207	A363	31p Richard Davies	1.25	.80
1208	A363	34p Richard Parry	1.35	.90
	Nos. 1205-1208 (4)		4.35	2.90

Sports — A364

1988, Mar. 22		Photo.	Perf. 14½	
1209	A364	18p Balance beam	.70	.50
1210	A364	26p Downhill skiing	1.05	.70
1211	A364	31p Tennis	1.25	.80
1212	A364	34p Soccer	1.35	.90
	Nos. 1209-1212 (4)		4.35	2.90

Ski Club of Great Britain and centenaries of the British Amateur Gymnastics Assoc., Lawn Tennis Assoc. and the Soccer League.

Europa
1988
A365

Transportation and communication, 1938.

1988, May 10			Perf. 15x14	
1213	A365	18p Mallard locomotive	.75	.50
1214	A365	26p Queen Elizabeth ocean liner	1.10	.70
1215	A365	31p Tram No. 1173, Glasgow	1.25	.85
1216	A365	34p Handley Page aircraft, Croydon Airport	1.40	1.00
	Nos. 1213-1216 (4)		4.50	3.05

Defeat of the Spanish Armada by the Royal Navy, 400th Anniv. A366

Designs: No. 1217, Armada approaching The Lizard, July 19, 1588. No. 1218, Royal Navy vessels sailing from Plymouth to engage Spaniards in battle, July 21. No. 1219, Battle scene off the Isle of Wight, July 25. No. 1220, Battle scene off Calais, France, July 28-29. No. 1221, Spanish ships foundering in the North Sea storms, July 30-Aug. 2. Printed in a continuous design.

1988, July 19				
1217	A366	18p multicolored	.70	.45
1218	A366	18p multicolored	.70	.45
1219	A366	18p multicolored	.70	.45
1220	A366	18p multicolored	.70	.45
1221	A366	18p multicolored	.70	.45
a.		Strip of 5, Nos. 1217-1221	3.50	2.50

Australia Bicentennial A367

Designs: No. 1222, Colonist, First Fleet vessel. No. 1223, British and Australian parliaments, Queen Elizabeth II. No. 1224, Cricketer W.G. Grace. No. 1225, John Lennon (1940-1980), William Shakespeare (1564-1616) and Sydney Opera House. Flag of Australia appears on #1223a, 1225a.

1988, June 21		Litho.	Perf. 14½	
1222	A367	18p multicolored	.70	.50
1223	A367	18p multicolored	.70	.50
a.		Pair, #1222-1223	1.40	1.00
1224	A367	34p multicolored	1.35	.90
1225	A367	34p multicolored	1.35	.90
a.		Pair, #1224-1225	2.70	1.80
	Nos. 1222-1225 (4)		4.10	2.80

See Australia Nos. 1082-1085.

Nonsensical Drawings by Edward Lear (1812-1888) — A368

Illustrations and text: 19p, The Owl and the Pussycat, 1867. 27p, Self-portrait as a bird, pen-and-ink sketch from a letter. 32p, "C" is for Cat, alphabet book character. 35p, Girl, birds and part of a limerick.

1988, Sept. 6		Photo.	Perf. 15x14	
1226	A368	19p multicolored	.75	.45
1227	A368	27p multicolored	1.10	.70
1228	A368	32p multicolored	1.30	.90
1229	A368	35p multicolored	1.30	.90
a.		Souv. sheet of 4, #1226-1229	10.00	10.00
	Nos. 1226-1229 (4)		4.45	2.95

No. 1229a sold for £1.35. The surtax benefited Stamp World London '90.

Photographs of Castles by Prince Andrew — A369

1988, Oct 18			Engr.	
1230	A369	£1 Carrickfergus	4.00	1.00
1231	A369	£1.50 Caernarfon	6.00	1.75
1232	A369	£2 Edinburgh	8.00	2.00
1233	A369	£5 Windsor	20.00	7.00
	Nos. 1230-1233 (4)		38.00	11.75

See Nos. 1445-1448.

Christmas Cards A370

1988, Nov. 15		Photo.	Perf. 15x14½	
1234	A370	14p Journey to Bethlehem	.55	.25
1235	A370	19p Shepherds see star	.75	.45
1236	A370	27p Magi follow star	1.10	.70
1237	A370	32p Nativity	1.30	.80
1238	A370	35p The Annunciation	1.40	.90
	Nos. 1234-1238 (5)		5.10	3.10

Birds — A371

1989, Jan. 17			Perf. 14x15	
1239	A371	19p Puffin	.75	.55
1240	A371	27p Avocet	1.10	.70
1241	A371	32p Oystercatcher	1.30	.80
1242	A371	35p Gannet	1.40	.90
	Nos. 1239-1242 (4)		4.55	2.95

Special Occasions A372

1989, Jan. 31   Photo.   *Perf. 15x14*
Booklet Stamps
1243	A372	19p Rose	6.50	4.50
1244	A372	19p Cupid	6.50	4.50
1245	A372	19p Ships	6.50	4.50
1246	A372	19p Fruit bowl	6.50	4.50
1247	A372	19p Teddy Bear	6.50	4.50
a.		Bklt. pane of 10 (2 each #1243-1247) +12 labels (BK733)	65.00	
		Nos. 1243-1247 (5)	32.50	22.50

Labels inscribed "CONGRATULATIONS," "BEST WISHES," "HAPPY BIRTHDAY," "HAPPY ANNIVERSARY," "WITH LOVE," or "THANK YOU."
No. 1247a is valued with perfs guillotined. Full perfs sell for more.

Food and Farming Year — A373

Foods and tile mosaics in agricultural motifs.

1989, Mar. 7   Photo.   *Perf. 14½*
1248	A373	19p Fruit and vegetables	.75	.50
1249	A373	27p Meat, fish, fruit	1.10	.75
1250	A373	32p Dairy products	1.30	.90
1251	A373	35p Breads, cake, cereal	1.40	1.00
		Nos. 1248-1251 (4)	4.55	3.15

Fireworks — A374

1989, Apr. 11   Photo.   *Perf. 14x14½*
1252	A374	19p Mortarboard	1.00	.75
1253	A374	19p "X" on ballot	1.00	.75
a.		Pair, #1252-1253	2.00	2.00
1254	A374	35p Posthorn	1.75	1.50
1255	A374	35p Globe	1.75	1.50
a.		Pair, #1254-1255	3.50	3.50
		Nos. 1252-1255 (4)	5.50	4.50

Public education in England and Wales, 150th anniv. (#1252); European Parliament 3rd elections (#1253); 26th world congress of Postal Telegraph and Telephone Intl., Brighton, Sept. 18-23 (#1254); Interparliamentary Union Cent. Conf., 82nd session, Sept. 4-9 (#1255).

Europa 1989 — A375

1989, May 16   *Perf. 14x15*

Children's toys.
1256	A375	19p Airplane, locomotive	.90	.50
1257	A375	27p Building-block tower	1.25	.80
1258	A375	32p Checkerboard, die, ladder, chips	1.40	.90
1259	A375	35p Doll house, boat, robot	1.50	1.00
		Nos. 1256-1259 (4)	5.05	3.20

Industrial Archaeology
A376

1989, July 4   Photo.   *Perf. 14x15*
1280	A376	19p Ironbridge	.75	.50
1281	A376	27p Tin Mine	1.10	.70
1282	A376	32p Mills	1.30	.80
1283	A376	35p Pontcysyllte Aqueduct	1.40	.90
		Nos. 1280-1283 (4)	4.55	2.90

1989, July 25   Souvenir Sheet
1284		Sheet of 4	7.50	7.50
a.	A376	19p like #1280, horiz.	.85	.85
b.	A376	27p like #1281, horiz.	1.25	1.25
c.	A376	32p like #1282, horiz.	1.50	1.50
d.	A376	35p like #1283, horiz.	1.75	1.75

No. 1284 sold for £1.40.

Microscopy A377

Specimens under magnification: 19p, Snowflake, the soc. emblem. 27p, Blue fly. 32p, Blood cells. 35p, Microchip.

1989, Sept. 5   Litho.   *Perf. 14½x14*
1285	A377	19p multicolored	.75	.55
1286	A377	27p multicolored	1.10	.70
1287	A377	32p multicolored	1.30	.80
1288	A377	35p multicolored	1.40	.90
		Nos. 1285-1288 (4)	4.55	2.95

Royal Microscopical Soc., 150th anniv.

The Lord Mayor's Show,
London — A378

Procession of the Lord Mayor's coach from Guildhall to the Law Courts in the Strand: No. 1289, Royal mail coach and The Guildhall. No. 1290, Drummer, cavalrymen and Mansion House. No. 1291, Gold coach, 1757, and The Royal Exchange. No. 1292, Coachman and St. Paul's Cathedral. No. 1293, Drummer, cavalryman and the Law Courts.

1989, Oct. 17   Litho.   *Perf. 14x15*
1289	A378	20p multicolored	.80	.55
a.		Perf. 14x14¼	.70	.35
b.		Booklet pane of 4 #1289a (BK189)	2.80	—
1290	A378	20p multicolored	.80	.55
1291	A378	20p multicolored	.80	.55
1292	A378	20p multicolored	.80	.55
1293	A378	20p multicolored	.80	.55
a.		Strip of 5, #1289-1293	4.00	3.75

Issued. Nos. 1289a, 1289b, 8/19/09.

Ely Cathedral, Cambridgeshire, 800th
Anniv. — A379

1989, Nov. 14   Photo.   *Perf. 15x14*
1294	A379	15p Gothic arches, 4 peasants	.60	.30
		Nos. 1294,B2-B5 (5)	4.85	3.05

Christmas.

Royal Soc. for the Prevention of Cruelty to Animals, 150th Anniv. — A381

1990, Jan. 23   Litho.   *Perf. 14x15*
1300	A381	20p Kitten	.80	.55
1301	A381	29p Rabbit	1.15	.85
1302	A381	34p Duckling	1.35	1.00
1303	A381	37p Puppy	1.50	1.10
		Nos. 1300-1303 (4)	4.80	3.50

Miniature Sheet

Famous Smiles
A382

1990, Feb. 6   Photo.   *Perf. 15x14*
1304	A382	20p Teddy bear	3.25	2.50
1305	A382	20p Dennis the Menace	3.25	2.50
1306	A382	20p Mr. Punch	3.25	2.50
1307	A382	20p Cheshire Cat	3.25	2.50
1308	A382	20p Man in the Moon	3.25	2.50
1309	A382	20p The Laughing Policeman	3.25	2.50
1310	A382	20p Clown	3.25	2.50
1311	A382	20p Mona Lisa	3.25	2.50
1312	A382	20p Queen of Hearts	3.25	2.50
1313	A382	20p Stan Laurel	3.25	2.50
a.		Pane of 10, #1304-1313	37.50	37.50
		Nos. 1304-1313 (10)	32.50	25.00

No. 1313a sold folded and unattached in booklet cover.
See Nos. 1364-1373.

A383

Europa 1990: No. 1314, Alexandra Palace. No. 1315, School of Art, Glasgow. 29p, British Philatelic Bureau, Edinburgh. 37p, Templeton Carpet Factory, Glasgow.

1990, Mar. 6   Photo.   *Perf. 14x15*
1314	A383	20p multicolored	.80	.45
a.		Bklt. pane of 4 + printed margin	5.00	
1315	A383	20p multicolored	.80	.45
1316	A383	29p multicolored	1.15	.65
1317	A383	37p multicolored	1.50	.85
		Nos. 1314-1317 (4)	4.25	2.40

Stamp World '90, London (No. 1314); Glasgow, European City of Culture (Nos. 1315, 1317).
For Prestige booklet containing pane #1314a, see listings in the Booklets section.

Kew Gardens, 150th Anniv. — A385

1990, June 5   Photo.
1322	A385	20p Cycad	.80	.50
1323	A385	29p Stone pine	1.15	.70
1324	A385	34p Willow tree	1.35	.80
1325	A385	37p Cedar	1.50	.90
		Nos. 1322-1325 (4)	4.80	2.90

Thomas Hardy (1840-1928), Writer and Clyffe Clump, Dorset — A386

1990, July 10   Photo.   *Perf. 14x15*
1326	A386	20p multicolored	.80	.50

Queen Mother, 90th Birthday — A387

Designs: Portraits of Queen Elizabeth, The Queen Mother.

1990, Aug. 2   *Perf. 14x15, 14½*
1327	A387	20p Recent portrait	.80	.35
1328	A387	29p As Queen Consort, 1937	1.25	1.25
1329	A387	34p As Duchess of York	1.70	1.70
1330	A387	37p As Lady Elizabeth Bowes-Lyon	1.80	1.80
		Nos. 1327-1330 (4)	5.55	5.10

Gallantry Awards — A388

Designs: No. 1331, Victoria Cross. No. 1332, George Cross. No. 1333, Military Cross, Military Medal. No. 1334, Distinguished Flying Cross, Distinguished Flying Medal. No. 1335, Distinguished Service Cross, Distinguished Service Medal. Nos. 1333-1335 horiz.

1990, Sept. 11   *Perf. 14x15, 15x14*
1331	A388	20p multicolored	.80	.55
a.		Litho., perf. 14x14¼, black denomination ('06)	.80	.35
b.		Booklet pane of 4 #1331a (BK180)	3.25	—
1332	A388	20p multicolored	.80	.55
1333	A388	20p multicolored	.80	.55
1334	A388	20p multicolored	.80	.55
1335	A388	20p multicolored	.80	.55
		Nos. 1331-1335 (5)	4.00	2.75

Denomination on No. 1331 is gray.
Nos. 1331a, 1331b issued 9/21/2006.

Queen's Awards for Export and Technological Achievement, 25th Anniv. — A384

1990, Apr. 10   Litho.
1318	A384	20p Export	.80	.45
1319	A384	20p Technology	.80	.45
a.		Pair, #1318-1319	1.60	1.50
1320	A384	37p like No. 1318	1.50	1.00
1321	A384	37p like No. 1319	1.50	1.00
a.		Pair, #1320-1321	3.00	2.80
		Nos. 1318-1321 (4)	4.60	2.90

Se-tenant pairs have continuous designs.

Astronomy
A389

Designs: 22p, Armagh Observatory, Jodrell Bank and La Palma telescopes. 26p, Early telescope, celestial diagram. 31p, Greenwich Old Observatory, sextant, chronometer. 37p, Stonehenge, celestial navigation.

1990, Oct. 16   **Perf. 14**
1336	A389	22p multicolored	.90	.60
1337	A389	26p multicolored	1.05	.70
1338	A389	31p multicolored	1.25	.80
1339	A389	37p multicolored	1.50	.90
		Nos. 1336-1339 (4)	4.70	3.00

Christmas
A390

1990, Nov. 13   **Litho.**   **Perf. 15x14**
1340	A390	17p Building snow-man	.70	.25
	a.	Booklet pane of 20	15.00	
1341	A390	22p Carrying Christmas tree	.90	.30
1342	A390	26p Caroling	1.05	.70
1343	A390	31p Sledding	1.25	.80
1344	A390	37p Ice skating	1.50	.90
		Nos. 1340-1344 (5)	5.40	2.95

Dogs — A391

Paintings by George Stubbs: 22p, King Charles Spaniel. 26p, A Pointer. 31p, Two Hounds in a Landscape. 33p, A Rough Dog. 37p, Fino and Tiny.

1991, Jan. 8   **Photo.**   **Perf. 14x14½**
1345	A391	22p multicolored	.90	.55
1346	A391	26p multicolored	1.05	.70
1347	A391	31p multicolored	1.25	.80
1348	A391	33p multicolored	1.30	.90
1349	A391	37p multicolored	1.50	1.00
		Nos. 1345-1349 (5)	6.00	3.95

Royal Veterinary College bicentennial, National Canine Defense League and Cruft's Dog Show, centennial.

Symbols of Good Luck
A392

1991, Feb. 5   **Photo.**   **Perf. 15x14**
Booklet Stamps
1350	A392	1st shown	1.50	1.00
1351	A392	1st Shooting star, rainbow	1.50	1.00
1352	A392	1st Bird, charm bracelet	1.50	1.00
1353	A392	1st Black cat	1.50	1.00
1354	A392	1st Bluebird, key	1.50	1.00
1355	A392	1st Duck, frog	1.50	1.00
1356	A392	1st Black boot, shamrocks	1.50	1.00
1357	A392	1st Rainbow, pot of gold	1.50	1.00
1358	A392	1st Peacock moths	1.50	1.00
1359	A392	1st Wishing well, sixpence	1.50	1.00
	a.	Bklt. pane of 10, #1350-1359 (BK1160)	16.00	

No. 1359a printed se-tenant with 12 greetings labels. No. 1359a sold for £2.20 at date of issue.

Scientists & Their Technology
A393

Designs: No. 1360, Michael Faraday, electricity. No. 1361, Charles Babbage, computers. 31p, Radar, developed by Robert Watson-Watt. 37p, Jet engine developed by Frank Whittle.

1991, Mar. 5   **Perf. 14x15**
1360	A393	22p multicolored	.90	.60
1361	A393	22p multicolored	.90	.60
1362	A393	31p multicolored	1.25	.80
1363	A393	37p multicolored	1.50	.90
		Nos. 1360-1363 (4)	4.55	2.90

Famous Smiles Type of 1990
1991, Mar. 26   **Photo.**   **Perf. 15x14**
Booklet Stamps
1364	A382	1st Teddy bear	1.10	1.10
	a.	Sheet of 20 + 20 labels, litho., perf. 14¼x14	37.50	—
1365	A382	1st Dennis the Menace	1.10	1.10
	a.	Sheet, 10 each #1364-1365 + 20 labels	32.50	
	b.	Sheet of 20 + 20 labels, litho., perf. 14¼x14	37.50	—
1366	A382	1st Mr. Punch	1.10	1.10
1367	A382	1st Cheshire Cat	1.10	1.10
1368	A382	1st Man in the Moon	1.10	1.10
1369	A382	1st The Laughing Policeman	1.10	1.10
1370	A382	1st Clown	1.10	1.10
1371	A382	1st Mona Lisa	1.10	1.10
1372	A382	1st Queen of Hearts	1.10	1.10
1373	A382	1st Stan Laurel	1.10	1.10
	a.	Booklet pane of 10	12.00	
	b.	Sheet, #1364-1373 + 10 labels	22.00	

No. 1373a sold for £2.20 at date of issue. No. 1373a was affixed to booklet cover and was printed se-tenant with 12 greetings labels.
No. 1373b issued 5/22/00. Labels depict ribbons and are inscribed "The Stamp Show / 2000". The sheet with ribbon labels sold for £2.95, while the sheet with personalized labels sold for £5.95.
A sheet similar to No. 1373b with labels inscribed "Collect British Stamps" was specially produced for stamp dealers. Value, $225.
No. 1365a issued 2002. It sold for £5.95 and had labels that could be personalized.
Nos. 1364a, 1365b issued 2002. Each sold for £14.95 and has labels that can be personalized.

A394

Europa — A395

1991, Apr. 23   **Photo.**   **Perf. 14x15**
1374	A394	22p Planets	.90	.55
1375	A394	22p Stars	.90	.55
	a.	Pair, #1374-1375	1.80	1.10
1376	A395	37p shown	2.00	1.40
1377	A395	37p Crescent eye	2.00	1.40
	a.	Pair, #1376-1377	4.50	3.25
		Nos. 1374-1377 (4)	5.80	3.90

Sports — A396

1991, June 11   **Photo.**   **Perf. 14½x14**
1378	A396	22p Fencing	.80	.60
1379	A396	26p Hurdling	1.05	.70
1380	A396	31p Diving	1.25	.80
1381	A396	37p Rugby	1.50	.90
		Nos. 1378-1381 (4)	4.60	3.00

World Student Games, Nos. 1378-1380. Rugby World Cup, No. 1381.

Roses — A397

1991, July 16   **Litho.**   **Perf. 14½x14**
1382	A397	22p Silver Jubilee	.90	.50
1383	A397	26p Mme. Alfred Carriere	1.05	.60
1384	A397	31p Rosa moyesii	1.25	.70
1385	A397	33p Harvest Fayre	1.30	.80
1386	A397	37p Mutabilis	1.50	.90
		Nos. 1382-1386 (5)	6.00	3.50

Dinosaurs
A398

1991, Aug. 20   **Photo.**   **Perf. 14½x14**
1387	A398	22p Iguanodon	.90	.65
1388	A398	26p Stegosaurus	1.05	.70
1389	A398	31p Tyrannosaurus	1.25	.75
1390	A398	33p Protoceratops	1.30	.80
1391	A398	37p Triceratops	1.50	.90
		Nos. 1387-1391 (5)	6.00	3.80

First use of word "dinosaur" by Sir Richard Owen, 150th anniv.

Ordnance Survey Maps, Bicent. — A399

Maps of village of Hamstreet, Kent.

1991, Sept. 17   **Litho. & Engr.**
1392	A399	24p 1816	.90	.50

Litho.
1393	A399	28p 1906	1.10	.70
1394	A399	33p 1959	1.30	.80
1395	A399	39p 1991	1.55	.90
		Nos. 1392-1395 (4)	4.85	2.90

Christmas
A400

Illuminated leters from Venetian manuscript "Acts of Mary and Jesus": 18p, "P," Adoration of the Magi. 24p, "M," Mary placing Jesus in manger. 28p, "A," Angel warning Joseph. 33p, "Q," The Annunciation. 39p, "N," Flight into Egypt.

Animals in Winter
A401

1992, Jan. 14   **Photo.**   **Perf. 15x14**
1421	A401	18p Fallow deer	.70	.45
1422	A401	24p Brown hare	.95	.60
1423	A401	28p Fox	1.10	.75
1424	A401	33p Redwing	1.25	.90
1425	A401	39p Welsh mountain sheep	1.55	1.00
	a.	Booklet pane of 4	6.00	
		Nos. 1421-1425 (5)	5.55	3.70

For Prestige booklet containing pane #1425a, see BK156.
Issue date: No. 1425a, Mar. 1.

1991, Nov. 12   **Photo.**   **Perf. 15x14**
1416	A400	18p multicolored	.70	.25
	a.	Booklet pane of 20	14.00	
1417	A400	24p multicolored	.95	.30
1418	A400	28p multicolored	1.10	.80
1419	A400	33p multicolored	1.25	.85
1420	A400	39p multicolored	1.55	1.10
		Nos. 1416-1420 (5)	5.55	3.30

Memories
A402

1992, Jan. 28   **Litho.**   **Perf. 15x14**
Booklet Stamps
1426	A402	1st Flowers	1.30	1.00
1427	A402	1st Locket	1.30	1.00
1428	A402	1st Key	1.30	1.00
1429	A402	1st Model car	1.30	1.00
1430	A402	1st Compass, 4-leaf clover	1.30	1.00
1431	A402	1st Pocket watch	1.30	1.00
1432	A402	1st Envelope, fountain pen	1.30	1.00
1433	A402	1st Buttons, pearls	1.30	1.00
1434	A402	1st Marbles	1.30	1.00
1435	A402	1st Starfish, shovel and bucket	1.30	1.00
	a.	Bklt. pane of 10, #1426-1435 (BK1171)	13.00	

No. 1435a printed se-tenant with 12 greeting labels and sold for £2.40 at date of issue.

Queen Elizabeth II's Accession to the Throne, 40th Anniv. A403

Queen Elizabeth II: No. 1436, In coronation regalia. No. 1437, Facing right, wearing garter robes as head of Church of England. No. 1438, Holding infant Prince Andrew. No. 1439, Wearing military uniform at Trooping of the Color. No. 1440, Wearing purple hat.

1992, Feb. 6   **Litho.**   **Perf. 14½x14**
1436	A403	24p multicolored	1.20	.90
1437	A403	24p multicolored	1.20	.90
1438	A403	24p multicolored	1.20	.90
1439	A403	24p multicolored	1.20	.90
1440	A403	24p multicolored	1.20	.90
	a.	Strip of 5, #1436-1440	6.00	6.00

Alfred, Lord Tennyson, Death Cent. — A404

Portraits and illustrations for poems: 24p, The Beguiling of Merlin by Sir Edward Burne-Jones. 28p, April Love by Arthur Hughes. 33p, The Lady of Shalott by John William Waterhouse. 39p, Mariana by Dante Gabriel Rossetti.

1992, Mar. 10   **Photo.**
1441	A404	24p multicolored	.95 .65
1442	A404	28p multicolored	1.10 .80
1443	A404	33p multicolored	1.25 .90
1444	A404	39p multicolored	1.55 1.00
	Nos. 1441-1444 (4)		4.85 3.35

CARRICKFERGUS CASTLE

Castle Type of 1988

Nos. 1445-1448 have been re-engraved to show greater detail than on Nos. 1230-1233. The silhouette of the Queen's head on Nos. 1445-1448 is printed in a special ink that changes color from green to gold.

Perf. 15x14 Syncopated
1992-95   **Engr.**
1445	A369	£1 like #1230	4.00 1.00
1446	A369	£1.50 like #1231	6.00 1.10
1447	A369	£2 like #1232	8.00 1.10
1447A	A369	£3 like #1230	17.50 3.00
1448	A369	£5 like #1233	20.00 4.00
	Nos. 1445-1448 (5)		55.50 10.20

Nos. 1445-1447, 1448 were re-issued 12/6/94 with lines strengthened. Castles appear darker than on original issue.
Issued: £3, 8/22/95; others, 3/24/92.

Castle Type Re-engraved

1997, July 29
1446a	A369	£1.50 Caernarfon	10.00 3.00
1447b	A369	£2 Edinburgh	12.00 1.50
1447Ac	A369	£3 Carrickfergus	30.00 2.50
1448a	A369	£5 Windsor	35.00 6.00

Queen's head is silkscreened and feels smooth on Nos. 1446a, 1447b, 1447Ac, 1448a. Letters "C" and "S" in Castle do not have serifs. Letters in castle names also differ from the 1992 and 1995 printings. The elliptical perforation begins one perf hole higher than on the earlier printings.

Discovery of America, 500th Anniv. A405

LANDFALL IN THE AMERICAS 1492 CHRISTOPHER COLUMBUS

Design: 39p, Sailing ship, Operation Raleigh Grand Regatta.

Litho. & Engr.
1992, Apr. 7   **Perf. 14½**
1449	A405	24p multicolored	*1.50 .40*
1450	A405	39p multicolored	*2.25 .90*

Europa.

Events A406

OLYMPICS '92 BARCELONA

Designs: No. 1451, British Olympic Assoc. flag. No. 1452, Flying torch flag of British Paralympic Assoc. No. 1453, British pavilion.

1992, Apr. 7   **Litho.**
1451	A406	24p multicolored	.95 .60
1452	A406	24p multicolored	.95 .60
a.	Pair, #1451-1452		1.80 1.50
1453	A406	39p multicolored	1.75 1.00
	Nos. 1451-1453 (3)		3.65 2.20

1992 Summer Olympics (No. 1451) and Paralympics (No. 1452), Barcelona. Expo '92, Seville (No. 1453).

THE CIVIL WAR 1642-51 fought between the forces of KING & PARLIAMENT: *Pikeman*

English Civil War, 350th Anniv. — A407

1992, June 16   **Photo.**   **Perf. 14½**
1454	A407	24p Pikeman	.95 .65
1455	A407	28p Drummer	1.10 .80
1456	A407	33p Musketeer	1.25 .90
1457	A407	39p Standard bearer	1.55 1.00
	Nos. 1454-1457 (4)		4.85 3.35

GILBERT & SULLIVAN
The Yeomen of the Guard

Yeoman of the Guard, by Gilbert & Sullivan A408

Scenes from comic operas: 24p, The Gondoliers. 28p, The Mikado. 33p, The Pirates of Penzance. 39p, Iolanthe.

1992, July 21   **Photo.**   **Perf. 14½x14**
1458	A408	18p multicolored	.70 .50
1459	A408	24p multicolored	.95 .65
1460	A408	28p multicolored	1.10 .80
1461	A408	33p multicolored	1.25 .90
1462	A408	39p multicolored	1.55 1.00
	Nos. 1458-1462 (5)		5.55 3.85

Sir Arthur Sullivan, 150th anniv. of birth.

ACID RAIN KILLS

Protect the Environment A409

Children's drawings: 24p, Acid rain kills. 28p, Ozone layer. 33p, Greenhouse effect. 39p, Bird of hope.

1992, Sept. 15   **Photo.**   **Perf. 14½**
1463	A409	24p multicolored	.95 .60
1464	A409	28p multicolored	1.10 .80
1465	A409	33p multicolored	1.25 .90
1466	A409	39p multicolored	1.55 1.00
	Nos. 1463-1466 (4)		4.85 3.30

Single European Market A410

1992, Oct. 13   **Photo.**   **Perf. 15x14**
1467	A410	24p multicolored	.95 .80

Christmas A411

Stained glass windows: 18p, Angel Gabriel. 24p, Madonna and Child. 28p, King offering gold crown. 33p, Shepherds. 39p, Kings offering frankincense and myrrh.

1992, Nov. 10   **Photo.**   **Perf. 15x14**
1468	A411	18p multicolored	.70 .25
a.	Booklet pane of 20		14.00
1469	A411	24p multicolored	.95 .25
1470	A411	28p multicolored	1.10 .80
1471	A411	33p multicolored	1.25 .90
1472	A411	39p multicolored	1.55 1.00
	Nos. 1468-1472 (5)		5.55 3.20

Mute Swans — A412

Designs: 18p, Male, St. Catherine's Chapel, Abbotsbury. 24p, Cygnet, reed bed, Abbotsbury Swannery. 28p, Pair, cygnet. 33p, Eggs in nest, Tithe Barn. 39p, Head of young swan.

1993, Jan. 19   **Photo.**   **Perf. 14x15**
1473	A412	18p multicolored	1.10 .40
1474	A412	24p multicolored	1.10 .50
1475	A412	28p multicolored	1.40 1.00
1476	A412	33p multicolored	1.80 1.75
1477	A412	39p multicolored	2.00 1.75
	Nos. 1473-1477 (5)		7.40 5.40

Abbotsbury Swannery, 600th anniv.

Britannia — A413

Litho., Typo. and Embossed
Perf. 14x14½ Syncopated
1993, Mar. 2
Granite Paper
1478	A413	£10 multicolored	37.50 12.50
a.	Silver (Queen's head, security crosses) omitted		*1,750.*

Soaking may damage these stamps.

Greetings Stamps A414

Children's Characters: No. 1479, Long John Silver, parrot. No. 1480, Tweedledum, Tweedledee. No. 1481, Just William, Violet Elizabeth. No. 1482, Toad, Mole. No. 1483, Bash Street Kids, teacher. No. 1484, Peter Rabbit, Mrs. Rabbit. No. 1485, Father Christmas, Snowman. No. 1486, Big Friendly Giant, Sophie. No. 1487, Rupert Bear, Bill Badger. No. 1488, Aladdin, Genie.

Perf. 15x14 Syncopated
1993, Feb. 2   **Litho.**
1479	A414	(1st) multicolored	1.30 1.00
1480	A414	(1st) multicolored	1.30 1.00
1481	A414	(1st) multicolored	1.30 1.00
1482	A414	(1st) multicolored	1.30 1.00
1483	A414	(1st) multicolored	1.30 1.00
1484	A414	(1st) multicolored	1.30 1.00
a.	Booklet pane of 4 (BK1172)		5.00
1485	A414	(1st) multicolored	1.30 1.00
1486	A414	(1st) multicolored	1.30 1.00
1487	A414	(1st) multicolored	1.30 1.00
1488	A414	(1st) multicolored	1.30 1.00
a.	Bklt. pane of 10, #1479-1488		12.50

No. 1479-1488 sold for 24p on day of issue. No. 1488a printed se-tenant with 20 greetings labels. See note above No. 1445.
Issue date: No. 1484a, Aug. 10.
For booklets containing panes of #1484a and #1488a, see BK158 and BK1172, respectively.

Marine Chronometer No. 4 — A415

MARINE TIMEKEEPER NO. 4

Designs: 24p, Face. 28p, Escapement, remontoire and fusee. 33p, Balance spring, temperature compensator. 39p, Back of movement.

1993, Feb. 16   **Litho.**   **Perf. 14½**
1489	A415	24p multicolored	.95 .45
1490	A415	28p multicolored	1.10 .70
1491	A415	33p multicolored	1.25 .65
1492	A415	39p multicolored	1.55 .90
	Nos. 1489-1492 (4)		4.85 2.70

John Harrison (1693-1776), inventor of marine chronometer.

Orchids A416

14th World Orchid Conf., Glasgow: 18p, Dendrobium hellwigianum. 24p, Paphiopedilum Maudiae "Magnificum." 28p, Cymbidium Iowianum. 33p, Vanda Rothschildiana. 39p, Dendrobium vexillarius.

1993, Mar. 16   **Litho.**   **Perf. 15x14**
1493	A416	18p multicolored	.70 .40
1494	A416	24p multicolored	.95 .55
1495	A416	28p multicolored	1.10 .70
1496	A416	33p multicolored	1.25 .80
1497	A416	39p multicolored	1.55 .90
	Nos. 1493-1497 (5)		5.55 3.35

Contemporary Art — A417

Europa: 24p, Sculpture, Family Group, by Henry Moore. 28p, Print, Kew Gardens, by Edward Bawden. 33p, Painting, St. Francis and the Birds, by Stanley Spencer. 39p, Painting, Still Life, Odyssey 1, by Ben Nicholson.

1993, May 11   **Photo.**   **Perf. 14x14½**
1498	A417	24p multicolored	.95 .20
1499	A417	28p multicolored	1.10 .85
1500	A417	33p multicolored	1.25 .90
1501	A417	39p multicolored	1.55 .90
	Nos. 1498-1501 (4)		4.85 2.85

Roman Artifacts A418

24p, Gold aureus of Claudius. 28p, Bronze bust of Hadrian. 33p, Gemstone carved with head of Roma. 39p, Mosaic of Christ.

1993, June 15   **Photo.**   **Perf. 14½x14**
1502	A418	24p multicolored	.95 .60
1503	A418	28p multicolored	1.10 .90
1504	A418	33p multicolored	1.25 .90
1505	A418	39p multicolored	1.55 1.00
	Nos. 1502-1505 (4)		4.85 3.40

British Canals, Bicent. A419

Designs: 24p, Grand Junction Canal boats. 28p, Stainforth and Keadby Canal. 33p, Brecknock and Abergavenny Canal boats, horse. 39p, Crinan Canal, steamers and fishing boats.

1993, July 20   **Litho.**   **Perf. 14½x14**
1506	A419	24p multicolored	.95 .60
1507	A419	28p multicolored	1.10 .90
1508	A419	33p multicolored	1.25 .90
1509	A419	39p multicolored	1.55 1.00
	Nos. 1506-1509 (4)		4.85 3.40

Autumn
Fruits
A420

1993, Sept. 14   Photo.   *Perf. 15x14*
1510 A420 18p Horse chestnut   .70   .35
1511 A420 24p Blackberries   .95   .55
1512 A420 28p Filbert   1.10   .90
1513 A420 33p Rowanberries   1.25   .90
1514 A420 39p Pears   1.55   1.00
    Nos. 1510-1514 (5)   5.55   3.70

Sherlock
Holmes — A421

Holmes and: No. 1515, Dr. Watson, The Reigate Square. No. 1516, Sir Henry, The Hound of the Baskervilles. No. 1517, Lestrade, The Six Napoleons. No. 1518, Mycroft, The Greek Interpreter. No. 1519, Moriarty, The Final Problem.

1993, Oct. 12   Litho.   *Perf. 14x14½*
1515 A421 24p multicolored   1.00   .75
1516 A421 24p multicolored   1.00   .75
1517 A421 24p multicolored   1.00   .75
1518 A421 24p multicolored   1.00   .75
1519 A421 24p multicolored   1.00   .75
    a. Strip of 5, #1515-1519 5.00   4.50

"A
Christmas
Carol," by
Charles
Dickens,
150th
Anniv.
A423

Designs: 19p, Tiny Tim, Bob Cratchit. 25p, Mr. & Mrs. Fezziwig. 30p, Scrooge. 35p, Prize Turkey. 41p, Mr. Scrooge's Nephew.

1993, Nov. 9   Photo.   *Perf. 15x14*
1528 A423 19p multicolored   .75   .25
    a. Booklet pane of 20   15.00
1529 A423 25p multicolored   1.00   .25
1530 A423 30p multicolored   1.20   .90
1531 A423 35p multicolored   1.40   .90
1532 A423 41p multicolored   1.65   1.00
    Nos. 1528-1532 (5)   6.00   3.30

For booklet containing #1528a, see BK857.

Age of
Steam — A424

Designs: 19p, Tandem locomotives, West Highland Line, North British Railway. 25p, Locomotive #60149, Kings Cross Station, London. 30p, Locomotive #43000 on turntable, Blyth North engine shed. 35p, Locomotive entering station. 41p, Locomotive on bridge over Worcester & Birmingham Canal.

1994, Jan. 18   Photo.   *Perf. 14½*
1533 A424 19p black & green   .75   .35
1534 A424 25p black & purple 1.00   .55
1535 A424 30p black & red brn 1.20   .90
1536 A424 35p black & red violet 1.40   .90
1537 A424 41p black & dark blue 1.65 1.00
    Nos. 1533-1537 (5)   6.00   3.70

Dan Dare
A425

The Three
Bears
A426

Rupert the
Bear
A427

Alice in Wonderland — A428

Noggin the
Nog
A429

Peter
Rabbit
A430

Little Red
Riding
Hood
A431

Orlando,
the
Marmalade
Cat
A432

Biggles
A433

Paddington
A434

1994, Feb. 1   Photo.
Booklet Stamps
1538 A425 (1st) multicolored 1.35   1.00
1539 A426 (1st) multicolored 1.35   1.00
1540 A427 (1st) multicolored 1.35   1.00
1541 A428 (1st) multicolored 1.35   1.00
1542 A429 (1st) multicolored 1.35   1.00
1543 A430 (1st) multicolored 1.35   1.00
1544 A431 (1st) multicolored 1.35   1.00
1545 A432 (1st) multicolored 1.35   1.00
1546 A433 (1st) multicolored 1.35   1.00
1547 A434 (1st) multicolored 1.35   1.00
    a. Bklt. pane of 10, #1538-1547 13.50

Nos. 1538-1547 sold for 25p on day of issue. No. 1547a was printed se-tenant with 20 greetings labels.
For booklet containing #1547a, see BK1182.

Investiture
of Prince
of Wales,
25th Anniv.
A435

Watercolor landscapes, by Prince Charles: 19p, Chirk Castle, Clwyd, Wales. 25p, Ben Arkle, Sutherland, Scotland. 30p, Mourne Mountains, County Down, Northern Ireland. 35p, Dersingham, Norfolk, England. 41p, Dolwyddelan, Gwynedd, Wales.

1994, Mar. 1   Photo.   *Perf. 15x14*
1548 A435 19p multicolored   .75   .35
1549 A435 25p multicolored   1.00   .55
1550 A435 30p multicolored   1.20   .90
    a. Booklet pane of 4   4.80
1551 A435 35p multicolored   1.40   .90
1552 A435 41p multicolored   1.65   1.00
    Nos. 1548-1552 (5)   6.00   3.70

For booklet containing pane #1550a, see No. BK159.

British Picture
Postcards,
Cent. — A436

Seaside characters: 19p, "Bather at Blackpool." 25p, "Where's my Little Lad." 30p, "Wish You Were Here." 35p, "Punch and Judy Show." 41p, "The Tower Crane."

1994, Apr. 12   Litho.   *Perf. 14x14½*
1553 A436 19p multicolored   .75   .35
1554 A436 25p multicolored   1.00   .55
1555 A436 30p multicolored   1.20   .90
1556 A436 35p multicolored   1.40   .90
1557 A436 41p multicolored   1.65   1.00
    Nos. 1553-1557 (5)   6.00   3.70

Blackpool Tower, cent. (#1553). Tower Bridge, cent. (#1557).

Opening of Channel Tunnel — A437

Nos. 1558, 1560, British lion, French rooster, meeting over Channel. Nos. 1559, 1561, Joined hands above speeding train.

1994, May 3   Photo.   *Perf. 14x14½*
1558 A437 25p dk blue & multi 1.00   .60
1559 A437 25p dk blue & multi 1.00   .60
    a. Pair, #1558-1559   2.00   1.25
1560 A437 41p lt blue & multi 1.65   1.00
1561 A437 41p multicolored   1.65   1.00
    a. Pair, #1560-1561   3.30   2.75
    Nos. 1558-1561 (4)   5.30   3.20

See France Nos. 2421-2424.

D-Day, 50th
Anniv. — A438

Photographs from Imperial War Museum's archives: No. 1562, Ground crew reloading FAF Bostons. No. 1563, Coastal bombardment by HMS Warspite. No. 1564, Commandos landing on Gold Beach. No. 1565, Infantry regrouping on Sword Beach. No. 1566, Advancing inland from Ouistreham.

1994, June 6   Litho.   *Perf. 14*
1562 A438 25p multicolored   1.00   .65
1563 A438 25p multicolored   1.00   .65
1564 A438 25p multicolored   1.00   .65
1565 A438 25p multicolored   1.00   .65
1566 A438 25p multicolored   1.00   .65
    a. Strip of 5, #1562-1566 5.00   3.50

Honorable
Company of
Edinburgh
Golfers, 250th
Anniv. — A439

Golf courses: 19p, St. Andrews, old course. 25p, Muirfield, 18th hole. 30p, Carnoustie, 15th hole. 35p, Royal Troon, "postage stamp" 8th hole. 41p, Turnberry, 9th hole.

1994, July 5   Photo.   *Perf. 14*
1567 A439 19p multicolored   .75   .35
1568 A439 25p multicolored   1.00   .55
1569 A439 30p multicolored   1.20   .90
1570 A439 35p multicolored   1.40   .90
1571 A439 41p multicolored   1.65   1.00
    Nos. 1567-1571 (5)   6.00   3.70

Summertime Events — A440

Designs: 19p, Royal Welsh Agricultural Show, Llanelwedd. 25p, Wimbledon. 30p, Yachts on Solent during Cowes Week. 35p, Cricket at Lord's. 41p, Scottish Highland Games, Braemar.

1994, Aug. 2   *Perf. 14½x14*
1572 A440 19p multicolored   .75   .35
1573 A440 25p multicolored   1.00   .55
1574 A440 30p multicolored   1.20   .90
1575 A440 35p multicolored   1.40   .90
1576 A440 41p multicolored   1.65   1.00
    Nos. 1572-1576 (5)   6.00   3.70

Medical Discoveries — A441

Europa: 25p, Ultrasonic imaging. 30p, Scanning electron microscopy. 35p, Magnetic resonance imaging. 41p, Computed tomography.

1994, Sept. 27   Photo.   *Perf. 14x14½*
1577 A441 25p multicolored   1.00   .20
1578 A441 30p multicolored   1.20   .80
1579 A441 35p multicolored   1.40   .90
1580 A441 41p multicolored   1.65   1.00
    Nos. 1577-1580 (4)   5.25   2.90

Christmas
A442

School children portraying: 19p, Mary, Joseph, with infant Jesus. 25p, Magi. 30p, Mary holding Jesus. 35p, Shepherds. 41p, Angels.

1994, Nov. 1   Photo.   Perf. 15x14

1581	A442	19p multicolored	.75	.25
a.		Booklet pane of 20	15.00	
1582	A442	25p multicolored	1.00	.25
1583	A442	30p multicolored	1.20	.90
1584	A442	35p multicolored	1.40	.90
1585	A442	41p multicolored	1.65	1.00
		Nos. 1581-1585 (5)	6.00	3.30

For booklet containing #1581a, see #BK858.

Cats
A443

Designs: 19p, Black cat. 25p, Siamese, tabby cats. 30p, Yellow cat. 35p, Calico, Abyssinian cats. 41p, Black & white cat.

1995, Jan. 17   Litho.   Perf. 15x14

1586	A443	19p multicolored	.75	.35
1587	A443	25p multicolored	1.00	.55
1588	A443	30p multicolored	1.20	.90
1589	A443	35p multicolored	1.40	.90
1590	A443	41p multicolored	1.65	1.00
		Nos. 1586-1590 (5)	6.00	3.70

Springtime
A444

Sculptures from natural materials, by Andy Goldsworthy: 19p, Dandelions. 25p, Chestnut leaves. 30p, Garlic leaves. 35p, Hazel leaves. 41p, Spring grass.

1995, Mar. 14   Photo.   Perf. 15x14

1591	A444	19p multicolored	.75	.35
1592	A444	25p multicolored	1.00	.55
1593	A444	30p multicolored	1.20	.90
1594	A444	35p multicolored	1.40	.90
1595	A444	41p multicolored	1.65	1.00
		Nos. 1591-1595 (5)	6.00	3.70

La Danse a la Campagne, by Renoir A445

Troilus and Criseyde, by Peter Brookes A446

The Kiss, by Rodin A447

Girls on the Town, by Beryl Cook A448

Jazz, by Andrew Mockett A449

Girls Performing aKathal Dance (Aurangzeb Period) A450

Alice Keppel with her Daughter, by Alice Hughes A451

Children Playing, by L.S. Lowry A452

Circus Clowns, by Emily Firmin and Justin Mitchell A453

Decoration from All the Love Poems of Shakespeare, by Eric Gill — A454

Perf. 14 Syncopated

1995, Mar. 21   Litho.

1596	A445	1st multicolored	1.35	1.00
1597	A446	1st multicolored	1.35	1.00
1598	A447	1st multicolored	1.35	1.00
1599	A448	1st multicolored	1.35	1.00
1600	A449	1st multicolored	1.35	1.00
1601	A450	1st multicolored	1.35	1.00
1602	A451	1st multicolored	1.35	1.00
1603	A452	1st multicolored	1.35	1.00
1604	A453	1st multicolored	1.35	1.00
1605	A454	1st multicolored	1.35	1.00
a.		Bklt. pane of 10, #1596-1605	13.50	

Complete booklet sold for $2.50 on day of issue.
For booklet containing #1605a, see #BK1183.

National Trust, Cent. — A455

Designs: 19p, Celebrating 100 years. 25p, Protecting land. 30p, Conserving art. 35p, Saving coast. 41p, Repairing buildings.

1995, Apr. 11   Photo.   Perf. 14x15

1606	A455	19p multicolored	.75	.35
1607	A455	25p multicolored	1.00	.55
a.		Booklet pane of 6	6.00	
1608	A455	30p multicolored	1.20	.90
1609	A455	35p multicolored	1.40	.90
1610	A455	41p multicolored	1.65	1.00
		Nos. 1606-1610 (5)	6.00	3.70

For booklet containing panes #1607a, see #BK160.
Issued: #1607a, 4/25/95.

Peace & Freedom A456

Designs: No. 1611, Hands, British Red Cross 1870-1995. No. 1612, British troops, people celebrating liberation of Paris. No. 1613, Dove, outstretched hand, UN, 1945-95. No. 1614, St. Paul's Cathedral, floodlights forming Victory V. 30p, Hands above earth, UN 1945-95.

1995, May 2   Photo.   Perf. 14½x14

1611	A456	19p multicolored	.75	.40
1612	A456	19p multicolored	.75	.40
1613	A456	25p multicolored	1.00	.55
1614	A456	25p multicolored	1.00	.55
1615	A456	30p multicolored	1.20	.80
		Nos. 1611-1615 (5)	4.70	2.70

End of World War II, 50th anniv. (#1612, 1614), Europa (#1613, 1615).
See No. 2294a.

H. G. Wells (1866-1946), Science Fiction Writer — A457

Novels: 25p, The Time Machine. 30p, The First Men on the Moon. 35p, The War of the Worlds. 41p, The Shape of Things to Come.

1995, June 6   Litho.   Perf. 14½x14

1616	A457	25p multicolored	1.00	.55
1617	A457	30p multicolored	1.20	.90
1618	A457	35p multicolored	1.40	.90
1619	A457	41p multicolored	1.65	1.00
		Nos. 1616-1619 (4)	5.25	3.35

Opening of Shakespeare's New Globe Theatre A458

Bankside theatres: No. 1620, Swan, 1595. No. 1621, The Rose, 1595. No. 1622, The Globe, 1599. No. 1623, The Hope, 1613. No. 1624, The Globe, 1614.

1995, Aug. 8   Litho.   Perf. 14½x14

1620	A458	25p multicolored	1.00	.60
1621	A458	25p multicolored	1.00	.60
1622	A458	25p multicolored	1.00	.60
1623	A458	25p multicolored	1.00	.60
1624	A458	25p multicolored	1.00	.60
a.		Strip of 5, #1620-1624	5.00	4.50

Pioneers of Communication — A459

Designs: 19p, Sir Rowland Hill, introduction of uniform penny postage. 25p, Hill as older man, design A1. 41p, Guglielmo Marconi, early wireless equipment. 60p, Marconi as older man using radiophone, sinking *Titanic*.

Litho. & Engr.

1995, Sept. 5   Perf. 14½

1625	A459	19p multicolored	.75	.35
1626	A459	25p multicolored	1.00	.50
1627	A459	41p multicolored	1.65	1.00
1628	A459	60p multicolored	2.40	1.25
		Nos. 1625-1628 (4)	5.80	3.10

Rugby League, Cent. — A460

1995, Oct. 3   Photo.   Perf. 14x14½

1629	A460	19p Harold Wagstaff	.75	.35
1630	A460	25p Gus Risman	1.00	.55
1631	A460	30p Jim Sullivan	1.20	.90
1632	A460	35p Billy Batten	1.40	.90
1633	A460	41p Brian Bevan	1.65	1.00
		Nos. 1629-1633 (5)	6.00	3.70

Christmas — A461

Designs showing robin in winter scene: 19p, In pillar box. 25p, On fence rail, holly bush. 30p, Standing on snow covered milk bottle. 41p, Sitting on snow covered road sign, blue fence. 60p, Sitting on door knob, Chistmas decoration on door.

1995, Oct. 30   Photo.   Perf. 14¾x14

1634	A461	19p multicolored	.75	.25
a.		Booklet pane of 20	15.00	
b.		Sheet of 20 + 20 labels	*210.00*	
1635	A461	25p multicolored	1.00	.25
1636	A461	30p multicolored	1.20	.90
1637	A461	41p multicolored	1.65	1.00
1638	A461	60p multicolored	2.40	1.40
a.		Booklet pane of 4	9.75	
		Nos. 1634-1638 (5)	7.00	3.80

No. 1634b was issued 10/3/00. It sold for £3.99 and has labels that read "Seasons Greetings" and "Glad Tidings." Sheets with personalized labels were made available only to select Royal Post customers via mail order purchases, and sold for more.
For booklets containing Nos. 1634a and 1638a, see Nos. BK859 and BK792, respectively.

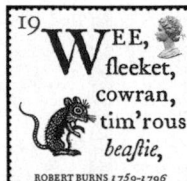

Robert Burns (1759-1796), Poet — A462

Lines from poems: 19p, "Wee sleeket, cowran, tim'rous beastie." 25p, "O my luve's like a red, red rose." 41p, "Scots, wha hae wi Wallace bled." 60p, "Should auld acquaintance be forgot."

1996, Jan. 25 Litho. Perf. 14½

1639	A462 19p multicolored	.75	.35
1640	A462 25p multicolored	1.00	.55
1641	A462 41p multicolored	1.65	1.00
1642	A462 60p multicolored	2.40	1.40
	Nos. 1639-1642 (4)	5.80	3.30

Greetings Cartoons A463

#1643, More Love. #1644, Sincerely. #1645, Human condition. #1646, Mental Floss. #1647, Don't ring. #1648, Dear lottery prize winner. #1649, I'm writing to you... #1650, Fetch this... #1651, My day starts... #1652, The check in the post.

Perf. 14½ Syncopated

1996-2001			Litho.
1643	A463 1st black & lilac	1.35	.85
1644	A463 1st black & green	1.35	.85
1645	A463 1st black & blue	1.35	.85
1646	A463 1st black & purple	1.35	.85
1647	A463 1st black & red	1.35	.85
1648	A463 1st black & blue	1.35	.85
1649	A463 1st black & red	1.35	.85
1650	A463 1st black & purple	1.35	.85
1651	A463 1st black & blue	1.35	.85
1652	A463 1st black & lilac	1.35	.85
a.	Booklet pane, #1643-1652+20 labels	13.50	
b.	Sheet of 10, #1643-1652, 10 labels, perf. 14½x14	60.00	—
c.	Sheet of 20, 2 each #1643-1652, + 20 labels, perf. 14¼	—	—

Issued: No. 1652b, 12/18/01. 1652a, 2/26/96. 1652c, 7/29/03.
No. 1652b lacks perforation syncopation. Labels could be personalized for an additional amount.
Nos. 1643-1652 sold for 25p on day of issue.
No. 1652c sold for £6.15.
For booklet containing #1652a, see #BK1184.

Wildfowl and Wetlands Trust, 50th Anniv. A464

Paintings by Charles Tunnicliffe RA (1901-79): 19p, Muscovy duck. 25p, Lapwing. 30p, White-fronted goose. 35p, Bittern. 41p, Whooper swan.

1996, Mar. 12 Photo. Perf. 14x14½

1653	A464 19p multicolored	.75	.35
1654	A464 25p multicolored	1.00	.55
1655	A464 30p multicolored	1.20	.90
1656	A464 35p multicolored	1.40	.90
1657	A464 41p multicolored	1.65	1.00
	Nos. 1653-1657 (5)	6.00	3.70

Motion Pictures, Cent. — A465

Designs: 19p, Exterior of Odeon at Harrogate, 1930s theater. 25p, Laurance Olivier, Vivien Leigh in scene from "That Hamilton Woman." 30p, Cinema ticket from "The Picture House." 35p, Rooster emblem of Pathe News, motion picture newsreels. 41p, Theater marquee.

1996, Apr. 16 Photo. Perf. 14x14½

1658	A465 19p multicolored	.75	.35
1659	A465 25p multicolored	1.00	.55
1660	A465 30p multicolored	1.20	.90
1661	A465 35p multicolored	1.40	.90
1662	A465 41p multicolored	1.65	1.00
	Nos. 1658-1662 (5)	6.00	3.70

1996 European Soccer Championships — A466

Lengendary players: 19p, Dixie Dean (1907-80). 25p, Bobby Moore (1941-93). 35p, Duncan Edwards (1936-58). 41p, Billy Wright (1924-94). 60p, Danny Blanchflower (1926-93).

1996, May 14 Litho. Perf. 15x14

1663	A466 19p gray, red & blk	.75	.35
a.	Bklt. pane of 4 + printed margin (BK161)	3.00	
1664	A466 25p gray, grn & blk	1.00	.55
a.	Bklt. pane of 4 + printed margin (BK161)	4.00	
1665	A466 35p gray, yel & blk	1.40	.90
1666	A466 41p blk, blue & gray	1.65	1.00
1667	A466 60p gray, org & blk	2.40	1.40
a.	Bklt. pane, 2 ea #1665-1667 (BK161)	9.75	
	Nos. 1663-1667 (5)	7.20	4.20

1996 Summer Olympic, Paralympic Games, Atlanta A467

1996, July 9 Litho. Perf. 15x14

1688	A467 26p Sprinting	1.05	.60
1689	A467 26p Javelin	1.05	.60
1690	A467 26p Basketball	1.05	.60
1691	A467 26p Swimming	1.05	.60
1692	A467 26p Victorious athlete	1.05	.60
a.	Strip of 5, #1688-1692	5.25	4.00

Compare with Type A588.

20th Century Women of Achievement A468

Designs: 20p, Dorothy Hodgkin (1910-94), chemist. 26p, Margot Fonteyn (1919-91), ballerina. 31p, Elisabeth Frink (1930-93), sculptor. 37p, Daphne du Maurier (1907-89), novelist. 43p, Marea Hartman (1920-94), sports administrator.

1996, Aug. 6 Photo. Perf. 14½

1693	A468 20p multicolored	.80	.35
1694	A468 26p multicolored	1.05	.55
1695	A468 31p multicolored	1.25	.90
1696	A468 37p multicolored	1.50	.90
1697	A468 43p multicolored	1.70	1.10
	Nos. 1693-1697 (5)	6.30	3.80

Europa, Nos. 1694-1695.

British Television Programs for Children, 50th Anniv. A469

Designs: 20p, Annette Mills, "Muffin the Mule." 26p, Sooty. 31p, String puppets Troy Tempest and Lord Titan. 37p, The Clangers. 43p, Dangermouse.

1996, Sept. 3 Perf. 14½x14

1698	A469 20p multicolored	.80	.30
a.	Pane of 4 +#1698b + printed margin	8.00	
b.	Perf. 15x14	2.00	1.50
1699	A469 26p multicolored	1.05	.40
1700	A469 31p multicolored	1.25	1.00
1701	A469 37p multicolored	1.50	1.10
1702	A469 43p multicolored	1.70	1.50
	Nos. 1698-1702 (5)	6.30	4.30

For Prestige booklet containing pane #1698a, see BK162.
Issued: #1698a, 9/23/97.

Classic British Sports Cars — A470

Designs: 20p, 1955 Triumph TR3. 26p, MG TD. 37p, Austin-Healy 100. 43p, 1948 Jaguar XK 120. 63p, Morgan Plus Four.

1996, Oct. 1 Photo. Perf. 14½

1703	A470 20p multicolored	.80	.35
1704	A470 26p multicolored	1.05	.55
1705	A470 37p multicolored	1.50	1.10
1706	A470 43p multicolored	1.70	1.25
1707	A470 63p multicolored	2.50	1.60
	Nos. 1703-1707 (5)	7.55	4.85

Christmas A471

Designs: 2nd, Three kings, star. 1st, The Annunciation. 31p, Mary, Joseph on journey to Bethlehem. 43p, Madonna and Child. 63p, Angel telling shepherds of Christ's birth.

1996, Oct. 28 Photo. Perf. 14½x14

1708	A471 2nd multicolored	.95	.25
a.	Booklet pane of 20	19.00	
1709	A471 1st multicolored	1.35	.25
1710	A471 31p multicolored	1.25	1.10
1711	A471 43p multicolored	1.70	1.25
1712	A471 63p multicolored	2.50	1.50
	Nos. 1708-1712 (5)	7.75	4.35

Nos. 1708-1709 sold for 20p and 26p respectively on day of issue.
For booklet containing #1708a, see #BK1220.

Gentiana Acaulis A472

Magnolia Altissima A473

Camellia Japonica A474

Tulip A475

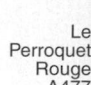

Fuchsia "Princess of Wales" A476

Le Perroquet Rouge A477

Gazania Splendens A478

Iris Latifolia A479

Amaryllis Bresiliensis A480

Granadilla A481

Perf. 14½x14 Syncopated

1997, Jan. 6			Litho.
Booklet Stamps			
1713	A472 1st multicolored	1.35	.85
a.	Perf 15x14	3.25	3.25
1714	A473 1st multicolored	1.35	.85
1715	A474 1st multicolored	1.35	.85
1716	A475 1st multicolored	1.35	.85
a.	Perf 15x14	2.00	2.00
1717	A476 1st multicolored	1.35	.85
1718	A477 1st multicolored	1.35	.85
1719	A478 1st multicolored	1.35	.85
1720	A479 1st multicolored	1.35	.85
a.	Perf 15x14	3.25	3.25
b.	Booklet pane, #1713a, 1720a, 2 #1716a (BK176)	8.50	—
1721	A480 1st multicolored	1.35	.85
1722	A481 1st multicolored	1.35	.85
a.	Bklt. pane of 10, #1713-1722	13.50	
b.	Sheet, 2 each #1713-1722, + 20 labels, perf. 14¼	45.00	

Nos. 1713-1722, 1722a issued 1/9/97. 1722a sold for £2.50 on day of issue, but stamps each had 26p of franking value.
No. 1722b issued 2003. It sold for £14.95 and had labels that could be personalized.
No. 1720a issued 5/25/04. 1720a sold for £1.12 on day of issue.
For booklet containing #1722a, see #BK1195.
See Nos. 2671-2672.

King Henry VIII and His Six Wives A482

1997, Jan. 21 Photo. Perf. 15

1723	A482 26p shown	1.05	.60

Size: 27x38mm
Perf. 14x15

1724	A482 26p Catherine of Aragon	1.05	.65
1725	A482 26p Anne Boleyn	1.05	.65
1726	A482 26p Jane Seymour	1.05	.65
1727	A482 26p Anne of Cleves	1.05	.65
1728	A482 26p Catherine Howard	1.05	.65

1729 A482 26p Catherine Parr   1.05   .65
    a.   Strip of 6, #1724-1729   6.25   5.25
     Nos. 1723-1729 (7)   7.35   4.50

St. Augustine
of Canterbury
& St. Columba
of
Iona — A483

Designs: 26p, St. Columba's journey across Irish Sea to Iona. 37p, St. Columba at work, Ionian Sea. 43p, St. Augustine baptizing King Ethelbert. 63p, St. Augustine outside Cathedral at Canterbury, Kent coastline.

1997, Mar. 11   Photo.   Perf. 14½x14
1730 A483 26p multicolored   1.05   .50
1731 A483 37p multicolored   1.50   1.10
1732 A483 43p multicolored   1.70   1.25
1733 A483 63p multicolored   2.50   1.60
     Nos. 1730-1733 (4)   6.75   4.45

Stories and
Legends — A484

Europa: 26p, Dracula. 31p, Frankenstein. 37p, Dr. Jekyll and Mr. Hyde. 43p, The Hound of the Baskervilles.

1997, May 13   Photo.   Perf. 14x15
1754 A484 26p multicolored   *1.05*   *.45*
1755 A484 31p multicolored   *1.25*   *1.10*
1756 A484 37p multicolored   *1.50*   *1.25*
1757 A484 43p multicolored   *1.70*   *1.40*
     Nos. 1754-1757 (4)   *5.50*   *4.20*

Aircraft,
Designers
A485

20p, Supermarine Spitfire, R.J. Mitchell. 26p, Avro Lancaster, Roy Chadwick. 37p, DeHavilland Mosquito, R.E. Bishop. 43p, Gloster Meteor, George Carter. 63p, Hawker Hunter, Sidney Camm.

1997, June 10   Photo.   Perf. 15x14
1758 A485 20p multicolored   .80   .45
    a.   Litho., perf. 14¼x14 (#2587b)
      ('08)   .75   .35
1759 A485 26p multicolored   1.05   .80
1760 A485 37p multicolored   1.50   1.10
1761 A485 43p multicolored   1.70   1.25
1762 A485 63p multicolored   2.50   1.60
     Nos. 1758-1762 (5)   7.55   5.20

Issued: No. 1758a, 9/18/08.

All the
Queen's
Horses
A486

20p, 43p, Carriage horses from Royal Mews. 26p, 63p, Mount horses from Household Cavalry.

1997, July 9   Litho.   Perf. 14x14½
1763 A486 20p multicolored   .80   .35
1764 A486 26p multicolored   1.05   .80
1765 A486 43p multicolored   1.70   1.40
1766 A486 63p multicolored   2.50   1.75
     Nos. 1763-1766 (4)   6.05   4.30

British Horse Society, 50th anniv.

Post Offices
A487

Designs: 20p, Haroldswick, Shetland Islands, Scotland. 26p, Painswick, Gloucestershire, England. 43p, Beddgelert, Gwynedd, Wales. 63p, Ballyroney, County Down, Northern Ireland.

1997, Aug. 12   Litho.   Perf. 14½x14
1767 A487 20p multicolored   .80   .35
1768 A487 26p multicolored   1.05   .80
1769 A487 43p multicolored   1.70   1.40
1770 A487 63p multicolored   2.50   1.75
     Nos. 1767-1770 (4)   6.05   4.30

Enid Blyton,
Author of
Children's
Stories, Birth
Cent. — A488

Characters from books: 20p, "Noddy." 26p, "Famous Five." 37p, "Secret Seven." 43p, "Faraway Tree." 63p, "Malory Towers."

1997, Sept. 9   Litho.   Perf. 14x14½
1771 A488 20p multicolored   .80   .25
1772 A488 26p multicolored   1.05   .25
1773 A488 37p multicolored   1.50   .85
1774 A488 43p multicolored   1.70   1.40
1775 A488 63p multicolored   2.50   1.75
     Nos. 1771-1775 (5)   7.55   4.50

Christmas
Crackers
A489

Designs: 2nd, Santa as Man in Moon sharing cracker with two children. 1st, Santa bursting through wrapping paper with cracker. 31p, Santa riding across sky on giant cracker. 43p, Santa on giant snowball holding cracker. 63p, Santa climbing into chimney with sack full of crackers.

1997, Oct. 27   Photo.   Perf. 15x14
1776 A489 2nd multicolored   .95   .30
    a.   Booklet pane of 20   19.00
1777 A489 1st multicolored   1.35   .35
    b.   Sheet of 10 + 10 labels   17.50
    c.   Sheet of 20 + 20 labels,
      litho., perf 14½x14   37.50
1778 A489 31p multicolored   1.35   .80
1779 A489 43p multicolored   1.70   1.25
1780 A489 63p multicolored   2.50   1.60
     Nos. 1776-1780 (5)   7.85   4.30

Nos. 1776-1777 were sold for 20p and 26p, respectively, on day of issue.
No. 1777b issued 10/3/00. It sold for £2.95 and has labels that read "Seasons Greetings" and "Ho Ho Ho." Sheets with personalized labels were made available only to select Royal Post customers via mail order purchases, and sold for more.
No. 1777c issued 2003. It sold for £5.95 and had labels that could be personalized.
For booklet containing #1776a, see #BK1221.

Queen
Elizabeth
II, Prince
Philip, 50th
Wedding
Anniv.
A490

Designs: 20p, 43p, Wedding portrait, 1947. 26p, 63p, Anniversary portrait, 1997.

1997, Nov. 13   Photo.   Perf. 15
1781 A490 20p multicolored   .80   .30
1782 A490 26p multicolored   1.05   .55
1783 A490 43p multicolored   1.70   1.25
1784 A490 63p multicolored   2.50   1.60
     Nos. 1781-1784 (4)   6.05   3.70

Endangered
Species — A491

Designs: 20p, Common dormouse. 26p, Lady's slipper orchid. 31p, Song thrush. 37p, Shining ram's horn snail. 43p, Mole cricket. 63p, Devil's bolete.

1998, Jan. 20   Litho.   Perf. 14x14½
1785 A491 20p multicolored   .80   .35
1786 A491 26p multicolored   1.05   .45
1787 A491 31p multicolored   1.35   .80
1788 A491 37p multicolored   1.50   1.10
1789 A491 43p multicolored   1.70   1.40
1790 A491 63p multicolored   2.50   1.75
     Nos. 1785-1790 (6)   8.90   5.85

Diana, Princess of
Wales (1961-
97) — A492

Portraits of Diana wearing: No. 1791, Choker. No. 1792, Blue dress. No. 1793, Tiara. No. 1794, Checked dress. No. 1795, Black dress.

1998, Feb. 3   Photo.   Perf. 14x15
1791 A492 26p multicolored   1.25   .65
1792 A492 26p multicolored   1.25   .65
1793 A492 26p multicolored   1.25   .65
1794 A492 26p multicolored   1.25   .65
1795 A492 26p multicolored   1.25   .65
    a.   Strip of 5, #1791-1795   6.25   6.00
    b.   As "a," imperf.   —

Order of
the Garter,
650th
Anniv.
A493

Queen's Beasts (supporters of Royal Arms created for Queen Elizabeth II's coronation in 1953): No. 1796, Lion of England, Griffin of Edward III. No. 1797, Falcon of Plantagenet, Bull of Clarence. No. 1798, Lion of Mortimer, Yale of Beaufort. No. 1799, Greyhound of Richmond, Dragon of Wales. No. 1800, Unicorn of Scotland, Horse of Hanover.

Litho. & Engr.
1998, Feb. 24   Perf. 15x14
1796 A493 26p multicolored   1.05   .65
1797 A493 26p multicolored   1.05   .65
1798 A493 26p multicolored   1.05   .65
1799 A493 26p multicolored   1.05   .65
1800 A493 26p multicolored   1.05   .65
    a.   Strip of 5, #1796-1800   5.25   4.75

**Queen Type of 1952 with Face
Values in Decimal Currency
Perf. 14 Syncopated**
1998, Mar. 10   Litho.
1801 A129 20p dk grn & lt grn   .80   .50
    a.   Booklet pane of 6 + printed
      margin (BK163)   4.75
1802 A129 26p dk brn & lt brn   1.05   .80
    a.   Booklet pane of 9 + printed
      margin (BK163)   10.50
1803 A129 37p dk red lil & lt lil   2.50   2.00
    a.   Booklet pane 3 each #1802-
      1803 + printed margin
      (BK163)   11.00
    b.   Booklet pane, 4 #1801, 2 ea
      #1802-1803 + printed mar-
      gin (BK163)   11.00

Lighthouses
A494

1998, Mar. 24   Perf. 14x14½
1804 A494 20p St. John's Point   .80   .30
1805 A494 26p The Smalls   1.05   .55
1806 A494 37p Needles Rocks   1.50   1.10
1807 A494 43p Bell Rock   1.70   1.40
1808 A494 63p Eddystone   2.50   1.75
     Nos. 1804-1808 (5)   7.55   5.10

Comedians
A495

20p, Tommy Cooper (1922-84). 26p, Eric Morecambe (1926-84). 37p, Joyce Grenfell (1910-79). 43p, Les Dawson (1933-93). 63p, Peter Cook (1937-95).

1998, Apr. 23   Litho.   Perf. 14½x14
1809 A495 20p multicolored   .80   .35
1810 A495 26p multicolored   1.05   .60
1811 A495 37p multicolored   1.50   .80
1812 A495 43p multicolored   1.70   1.20
1813 A495 63p multicolored   2.50   1.60
     Nos. 1809-1813 (5)   7.55   4.55

National Health
Service, 50th
Anniv. — A496

Designs: 20p, Hands forming heart, "10,000 donors give blood every day." 26p, Adult hand clasping child's, "1,700,000 prescriptions dispensed every day." 43p, Hands forming cradle, "2,000 babies delivered every day." 63p, Taking pulse, "130,000 hospital outpatients seen every day."

1998, June 23   Litho.   Perf. 14x14½
1814 A496 20p multicolored   .80   .35
1815 A496 26p multicolored   1.05   .60
1816 A496 43p multicolored   1.70   1.40
1817 A496 63p multicolored   2.50   1.75
     Nos. 1814-1817 (4)   6.05   4.10

Magical
World of
Children's
Literature
A496a

Stories depicted: 20p, "The Hobbit," by J.R.R. Tolkien. 26p, "The Lion, The Witch and the Wardrobe," by C.S. Lewis. 37p, "The Phoenix and the Carpet," by E. Nesbit. 43p, "The Borrowers," by Mary Norton. 63p, "Through the Looking Glass," by Lewis Carroll.

1998, July 21   Photo.   Perf. 15x14
1820 A496a 20p multicolored   .80   .35
1821 A496a 26p multicolored   1.05   .55
1822 A496a 37p multicolored   1.50   .80
1823 A496a 43p multicolored   1.70   1.40
1824 A496a 63p multicolored   2.50   1.75
     Nos. 1820-1824 (5)   7.55   4.85

Notting Hill
Carnival
A497

Expressionist photographic images of dancers, color of costumes: 20p, Yellow. 26p, Blue. 43p, Gold and white. 63p, Green.

1998, Aug. 25   *Perf. 14x14½*
1825	A497	20p multicolored	.80	.35
1826	A497	26p multicolored	1.05	.50
1827	A497	43p multicolored	1.70	1.20
1828	A497	63p multicolored	2.50	1.60
	Nos. 1825-1828 (4)		6.05	3.65

Europa (#1825-1826).

Land
Speed
Records
A498

Car, driver, year, record speed: 20p, Bluebird, Sir Malcolm Campbell, 1925, 151 mph. 26p, Red Sunbeam, Sir Henry Segrave, 1926, 152 mph. 30p, Babs, John G. Parry Thomas, 1926, 171 mph. 43p, Railton Mobil Special, John R. Cobb, 1947, 394 mph. 63p, Bluebird CN7, Donald Campbell, 1964, 403 mph.

1998, Sept. 29   Photo.   *Perf. 15x14*
1829	A498	20p multicolored	.80	.35
a.		Perf. 14½x13½	2.25	1.25
b.		As "a," booklet pane of 4 + printed margin (BK164)	9.00	
1830	A498	26p multicolored	1.05	.55
1831	A498	30p multicolored	1.20	.80
1832	A498	43p multicolored	1.70	1.40
1833	A498	63p multicolored	2.50	1.75
	Nos. 1829-1833 (5)		7.25	4.85

Christmas
Angels
A499

1998, Nov. 2   Photo.   *Perf. 15x14*
1834	A499	20p shown	.80	.25
a.		Booklet pane of 20	16.00	
1835	A499	26p Praying	1.05	.25
1836	A499	30p Playing flute	1.20	.80
1837	A499	43p Playing lute	1.70	1.40
1838	A499	63p Praying, diff.	2.50	1.75
	Nos. 1834-1838 (5)		7.25	4.45

British
Achievements
During Past
1000
Years — A500

Inventions: 20p, Timekeeping, John Harrison's chronometer. 26p, Development of steam power. 43p, William Henry Fox Talbot's use of negatives to create photographs. 63p, Development of computers.

Transportation: 20p, Jet travel. 26p, Development of bicycle. 43p, Isambard Kingdom Brunel's Clifton Suspension Bridge, Great Western Railway. 63p, Capt. Cook's expeditions.

Health care: 20p, First smallpox vaccination, by Edward Jenner. 26p, Development of nursing care. 43p, Discovery of penicillin, by Alexander Fleming. 63p, First "test tube" baby (invitro fertilization), pioneered by Patrick Steptoe and Robert Edwards.

Emigration: 20p, Migration to Scotland. 26p, Pilgrim fathers. 43p, Destination Australia. 63p, Migration to UK.

Workers: 19p, Weavers. 26p, Mill towns. 44p, Ship building. 64p, City finance.

Entertainment and sports: 19p, Freddie Mercury, lead singer of Queen. 26p, Bobby Moore, 1966 World Cup Soccer Champions. 44p, Dalek from "Dr. Who" television series. 64p, Charlie Chaplin.

Citizens' Rights: 19p, Equal rights. 26p, Right to health. 44p, Right to learn. 64p, First rights.

Scientists: 19p, Decoding DNA. 26p, Darwin's theory. 44p, Faraday's electricity. 64p, Newton, Hubble Telescope.

Farmers: 19p, Strip farming (Europa). 26p, Mechanical farming. 44p, Food from afar. 64p, Satellite agriculture.

Soldiers: 19p, Battle of Bannockburn. 26p, Civil War. 44p, World Wars, cemetery. 64p, Peace keeping.

Christians: 19p, John Wesley (1703-91), founder of Methodism, and "Hark, The Herald Angels Sing," hymn by brother Charles (1707-88). 26p, King James Bible. 44p, St. Andrews Pilgrimage. 64p, First Christmas.

Artists: 19p, World of the stage. 26p, World of music. 44p, World of literature. 64p, New worlds.

1999   Photo.   *Perf. 14¼x14½*

Inventions
1839	A500	20p multi (48)	.80	.40
1840	A500	26p multi (47)	1.05	.80
1841	A500	43p multi (46)	1.70	1.40
1842	A500	63p multi (45)	2.50	1.75
a.		Perf. 13¾	4.25	
b.		Booklet pane, 4 #1842a (BK165)	17.00	

Transportation
1843	A500	20p multi (44)	.80	.40
1844	A500	26p multi (43)	1.05	.80
1845	A500	43p multi (42)	1.70	1.40
1846	A500	63p multi (41)	2.50	1.75

Health Care
Perf. 13¾x14
1847	A500	20p multi (40)	.80	.40
a.		Booklet pane of 4 (BK165)	3.25	
1848	A500	26p multi (39)	1.05	.80
1849	A500	43p multi (38)	1.70	1.40
1850	A500	63p multi (37)	2.25	1.75

Emigration
Perf. 14¼x14½
1851	A500	20p multi (36)	.80	.40
1852	A500	26p multi (35)	1.05	.80
1853	A500	43p multi (34)	1.70	1.40
1854	A500	63p multi (33)	2.50	1.75

Workers
Perf. 14¼x14½
1855	A500	19p multi (32)	.75	.40
1856	A500	26p multi (31)	1.05	.80
a.		Booklet pane #1852, 1856 (BK1141)	2.10	
1857	A500	44p multi (30)	1.75	1.40
1858	A500	64p multi (29)	2.60	1.75

Entertainment & Sports
Perf. 14¼x14½
1859	A500	19p multi (28)	.75	.40
1860	A500	26p multi (27)	1.05	.80
1861	A500	44p multi (26)	1.75	1.40
1862	A500	64p multi (25)	2.60	1.75

Citizen's Rights
Perf. 14¼x14½
1863	A500	19p multi (24)	.80	.40
1864	A500	26p multi (23)	1.05	.80
1865	A500	44p multi (22)	1.75	1.40
1866	A500	64p multi (21)	2.60	1.75

Scientists
Perf. 14¼ (#1868-1869), 13¾ (#1867, 1870)
1867	A500	19p multi (20)	.75	.40
1868	A500	26p multi (19)	1.05	.80
a.		Perf. 14¼x14	3.00	3.00
b.		Booklet pane, 4 #1868a (BK165)	12.00	
1869	A500	44p multi (18)	1.75	1.40
a.		Perf. 14¼x14	4.00	4.00
b.		Booklet pane, 4 #1869a (BK165)	12.00	
1870	A500	64p multi (17)	2.60	1.75
a.		Perf. 14¼	6.50	6.50
b.		Souvenir sheet, 4 #1870a	30.00	25.00

Farmers
Perf. 14¼x14½
1871	A500	19p multi (16)	.75	.40
1872	A500	26p multi (15)	1.05	.80
a.		Booklet pane of 2 (BK1142)	2.10	
1873	A500	44p multi (14)	1.75	1.40
1874	A500	64p multi (13)	2.60	1.75

Europa, No. 1871.

Soldiers
Perf. 14¼x14½
1875	A500	19p multi (12)	.75	.40
1876	A500	26p multi (11)	1.05	.80
1877	A500	44p multi (10)	1.75	1.40
1878	A500	64p multi (9)	2.60	1.75

Christians
1879	A500	19p multi (8)	.75	.40
a.		Booklet pane of 20	15.00	
1880	A500	26p multi (7)	1.05	.80
1881	A500	44p multi (6)	1.75	1.40
1882	A500	64p multi (5)	2.60	1.75

Artists
Perf. 14¼x14½
1883	A500	19p multi (4)	.75	.40
1884	A500	26p multi (3)	1.05	.80
1885	A500	44p multi (2)	1.75	1.40
1886	A500	64p multi (1)	2.60	1.75
	Nos. 1839-1886 (48)		73.20	52.20

Issued: #1839-1842, 1/12; #1843-1846, 2/2; #1847-1850, 3/2; #1851-1854, 4/6; #1855-1858, 5/4; #1859-1862, 6/1; #1863-1866, 7/6; #1867-1870, 8/3; #1871-1874, 9/7; #1870b, 8/11; #1875-1878, 10/5; #1879-1882, 11/2; #1883-1886, 12/7.

See #1889, 1890-1929, 1938, 1942-1943.

Marriage of Prince Edward and Sophie
Rhys-Jones — A501

1999, June 15   Photo.   *Perf. 15x14*
1887	A501	26p shown	1.05	.80
1888	A501	64p Profile portrait	2.60	1.75

Souvenir Sheet

Millennium
A502

Clock and globe showing: a, North America. b, Southeast Asia. c, Middle East. d, Europe.

Perf. 14¼x14½
1999, Dec. 14   Photo.
1889		Sheet of 4	32.50	27.50
a.-d.		A502 64p any single	8.00	4.00

No. 1889 exists overprinted "EARLS COURT, LONDON...STAMP SHOW 2000." It was sold at a substantial premium as part of a premium entrance fee.

Millennium
Projects
A503

Above and Beyond: 19p, Barn owl's head, 3rd Millennium conservation projects, Muncaster. 26p, Night sky, National Space Center, Leicester. 44p, Buildings and waterfall, Torrs Walkway project, Derbyshire. 64p, Sea birds, Scottish Sea Bird Center.

Fire & Light: 19p, Beacon, Beacon Millennium project. 26p, Rheilffordd Eryri / Snowdonia, Welsh Highland Railway rebuilding project. 44p, Lightning bolt, Dynamic Earth project. 64p, Lights, Croydon Skyline project.

Water & Coast: 19p, Stones, Durham Coast restoration project. 26p, Frog, flowers, National Pondlife Center, conservation project. 44p, Parc Arfordirol project. 64p, Portsmouth Harbor project.

Life & Earth: 2nd, Wetlands, ECOS/Ballymena Project. 1st, Ants, Web of Life Exhibition at London Zoo. 44p, Solar cells, Earth Center, Doncaster. 64p, Plant leaves in water, Project SUZY, Teeside.

Art & Craft: 2nd, Ceramica project, Stoke-on-Trent. 1st, Tate Gallery of Modern Art, London. 45p, Cycle Network Artworks Project. 65p, The Lowry Arts Complex, Balford.

People & Place: 2nd, Millennium Greens project. 1st, Gateshead Millennium Bridge, Newcastle. 45p, Mile End Park, London. 65p, On the Line project.

Stone & Soil: 2nd, Raising of Strangford Stone, Killyleagh, Northern Ireland. 1st, Trans Pennine Trail project. 45p, Kingdom of Fife Cycle Ways project, Scotland. 65p, Changing Places project of Groundwork Foundation.

Tree & Leaf: 2nd, Yews for the Millennium project. 1st, Eden Project, St. Austell. 45p, Millennium Seed Bank project, Ardingly. 65p, Forest for Scotland project.

Mind & Matter: 2nd, Ant's head, Wildscreen at Bristol Project. 1st, People in rowboat, Norfolk and Norwich Project, Newport. 45p, X-ray image of hand and computer mouse, Millennium Point Project, Birmingham. 65p, Plaid globe, Scottish Cultural Resources Access Network.

Body & Bone: 2nd, Dancers, Millennium Dome project, Greenwich. 1st, Soccer players, Hampden Park project, Glasgow. 45p, Bath Spa project. 65p, Center for Life, Newcastle.

Spirit & Faith: 2nd, Stained glass window, St. Edmundsbury Cathedral project. 1st, Church floodlighting project. 45p, St. Patrick Center project, Downpatrick. 65p, York mystery plays.

Sound & Vision: 2nd, Bells, Ringing in the Millennium project. 1st, Eye, Year of the Artist. 45p, Harp, Carnofym Millennium Center, Cardiff. 65p, TS2K Talent and Skills project.

Photo., Litho. (#1892, 1900, 1911, 1913)

2000

Above & Beyond
Perf. 13¾x14, 14¼x14½ (#1892)
1890	A503	19p multi (1)	.75	.40
1891	A503	26p multi (2)	1.05	.80
1892	A503	44p multi (3)	1.75	1.40
1893	A503	64p multi (4)	2.60	1.75

Perf. 14¼x14½
Fire & Light
1894	A503	19p multi (5)	.75	.40
1895	A503	26p multi (6)	1.05	.80
1896	A503	44p multi (7)	1.75	1.40
1897	A503	64p multi (8)	2.60	1.75

Water & Coast
1898	A503	19p multi (9)	.75	.40
1899	A503	26p multi (10)	1.05	.80
1900	A503	44p multi (11)	1.75	1.40
1901	A503	64p multi (12)	2.60	1.75

Life & Earth
1902	A503	2nd multi (13)	.95	.40
1903	A503	1st multi (14)	1.35	.80
1904	A503	44p multi (15)	1.75	1.40
1905	A503	64p multi (16)	2.60	1.75

Art & Craft
1906	A503	2nd multi (17)	.95	.40
1907	A503	1st multi (18)	1.35	.80
1908	A503	45p multi (19)	1.80	1.40
1909	A503	65p multi (20)	2.60	1.75

People & Place
1910	A503	2nd multi (21)	.95	.40
1911	A503	1st multi (22)	1.35	.80
1912	A503	45p multi (23)	1.80	1.40
1913	A503	65p multi (24)	2.60	1.75

Stone & Soil
1914	A503	2nd multi (25)	.95	.40
1915	A503	1st multi (26)	1.35	.80
1916	A503	45p multi (27)	1.80	1.40
1917	A503	65p multi (28)	2.60	1.75
a.		Booklet pane of 2 (BK169)	5.25	

Tree & Leaf
1918	A503	2nd multi (29)	.95	.40
a.		Bklt. pane of 4 (BK169)	3.75	
1919	A503	1st multi (30)	1.35	.80
a.		Bklt. pane, #1915, 1919 (BK1202)	2.70	
1920	A503	45p multi (31)	1.80	1.40
a.		Bklt. pane of 4 (BK169)	8.00	
1921	A503	65p multi (32)	2.60	1.75
a.		Bklt. pane of 2 (BK169)	5.25	

Mind & Matter
Litho.
1922	A503	2nd multi (33)	.95	.40
1923	A503	1st multi (34)	1.35	.80
1924	A503	45p multi (35)	1.80	1.40
1925	A503	65p multi (36)	2.60	1.75

Body & Bone
1926	A503	2nd multi (37)	.95	.40

Photo.
Perf. 13¾
1927	A503	1st multi (38)	1.35	.80
1928	A503	45p multi (39)	1.80	1.40
1929	A503	65p multi (40)	2.60	1.75

Perf. 14¼
Spirit & Faith
1930	A503	2nd multi (41)	.95	.40
a.		Bklt. pane of 20 (BK1211)	19.00	
1931	A503	1st multi (42)	1.35	.80
1932	A503	45p multi (43)	1.80	1.40
1933	A503	65p multi (44)	2.60	1.75

Sound & Vision
1934	A503	2nd multi (45)	.95	.40
1935	A503	1st multi (46)	1.35	.80
1936	A503	45p multi (47)	1.80	1.40
1937	A503	65p multi (48)	2.60	1.75
	Nos. 1890-1937 (48)		78.70	52.20

#1902, 1906, 1910, 1914, 1918, 1922, 1926, 1930, 1934 sold for 19p; #1903, sold for 26p; #1907, 1911, 1915, 1919, 1923, 1927, 1931, 1935 sold for 27p on day of issue.

Issued: #1890-1893, 1/18; #1894-1897, 2/1; #1898-1901, 3/7; #1902-1905, 4/4; #1906-1909, 5/2; #1910-1913, 6/6; #1914-1917, 7/4; #1918-1921, 8/1; #1917a-1921a, 9/18; #1922-1925, 9/5; #1926-1929, 10/3; #1930-1933, 11/7; #1934-1937, 12/5.

2000-02   Photo.   *Perf. 14¼x14½*
1938	A503	1st multi Like #1891	7.50	5.00
a.		Booklet pane, #1903, 1938 (BK1201)	9.00	
b.		Booklet pane of 4 (BK172)	30.00	

Issued: No. 1938, 5/26. No. 1938b, 9/24/02. Nos. 1938 sold for 27p on day of issue, and was issued only in booklets.

Types of 1953 and 2000

Stamp Show 2000, London — A503a

Souvenir Sheet

2000, May 23 Photo. *Perf. 14¾x14*
1942   Sheet, #1942a, 4
       #MH335   25.00   25.00
   a.   A136 £1 dark green   20.00   17.50

Souvenir Sheet

Queen Mother's 100th
Birthday — A504

Designs: a, Queen Elizabeth II. b, Prince William. c, Queen Mother. d, Prince Charles. Illustration reduced.

2000, Aug. 4   Photo.   *Perf. 14½*
1943   A504   Sheet of 4   11.00   11.00
   a.-d.   27p Any single   1.10   .50
   e.   Booklet pane, #1943 with
       silver border (BK168)   11.00   11.00
   f.   Booklet pane, 4 #1943c
       (BK168)   5.00

Millennium
2001
A505

Painted faces of children: 2nd, Flower. 1st, Tiger. 45p, Owl. 65p, Butterfly.

Perf. 14¼x14½

2001, Jan. 16   Photo.
1944   A505   2nd multi   .95   .50
1945   A505   1st multi   1.35   .90
1946   A505   45p multi   1.80   1.40
1947   A505   65p multi   2.60   1.75
     Nos. 1944-1947 (4)   6.70   4.55

Stamps inscribed "2nd" and "1st" sold for 19p and 27p respectively on day of issue.

Greetings
A506

2001, Feb. 6   Photo.   *Perf. 14¼*
1948   A506   1st shown   1.35   .70
1949   A506   1st Cheers   1.35   .70
1950   A506   1st Love   1.35   .70
1951   A506   1st Thanks   1.35   .70
1952   A506   1st Welcome   1.35   .70
   a.   Sheet, 4 vert. strips
      #1948-1952 + 20 labels,
      litho.   130.00   25.00
     Nos. 1948-1952 (5)   6.75   3.50

Nos. 1948-1952 each sold for 27p on day of issue.
No. 1952a issued 6/5/01. No. 1952a sold for £5.95.
A sheet containing 7 #1949 and 3 #1951 + 10 labels depicting Spiderman was specially produced for stamp dealers.

Dogs and
Cats
A507

Designs: No. 1953, Dog and man on park bench. No. 1954, Dog in bathtub. No. 1955, Dog looking over carrel. No. 1956, Cat in handbag. No. 1957, Cat on fence. No. 1958, Dog in automobile. No. 1959, Cat in curtained window. No. 1960, Dog looking over fence. No. 1961, Cat looking at bird through window. No. 1962, Cat in sink.

2001, Feb. 13   *Die Cut Perf. 14½x14*
Self-Adhesive
Booklet Stamps

1953   A507   1st blk & sil   1.50   1.00
1954   A507   1st blk & sil   1.50   1.00
1955   A507   1st blk & sil   1.50   1.00
1956   A507   1st blk & sil   1.50   1.00
1957   A507   1st blk & sil   1.50   1.00
1958   A507   1st blk & sil   1.50   1.00
1959   A507   1st blk & sil   1.50   1.00
1960   A507   1st blk & sil   1.50   1.00
1961   A507   1st blk & sil   1.50   1.00
1962   A507   1st blk & sil   1.50   1.00
   a.   Booklet, #1953-1962   15.00
   b.   Booklet, #1953-1962, 2
      #MH297   32.50
     Nos. 1953-1962 (10)   15.00   10.00

Nos. 1953-1962 each sold for 27p on day of issue.

The Weather
A508

Designs: 19p, Rain. 27p, Fair. 45p, Much rain, storms. 65p, Very dry, set fair.

Perf. 14¼x14½

2001, Mar. 13   Photo.
1963   A508   19p multi   .75   .40
1964   A508   27p multi   1.10   .80
1965   A508   45p multi   1.80   1.40
1966   A508   65p multi   2.60   1.75
   a.   Souvenir sheet, #1963-1966   20.00   14.00
     Nos. 1963-1966 (4)   6.25   4.35

Purple cloud at bottom of No. 1964 is printed with thermochromic ink and changes color to blue when warmed.

Submarines — A509

Designs: 2nd, Vanguard Class, 1992. 1st, Swiftsure Class, 1973. 45p, Unity Class, 1939. 65p, Holland Class, 1901.

2001   Photo.   *Perf. 14¾x14*
1967   A509   2nd multi   .95   .40
   a.   Perf. 15¼x14¾   5.00   5.00
1968   A509   1st multi   1.35   .80
   a.   Perf. 15¼x14¾   5.00   4.00
1969   A509   45p multi   1.80   1.25
   a.   Perf. 15¼x14¾   5.00   4.00
   b.   Booklet pane, 2 each
      #1967a, 1969a (BK170)   12.00
1970   A509   65p multi   2.60   1.60
   a.   Perf. 15¼x14¾   5.00   4.00
   b.   Booklet pane, 2 each
      #1968a, 1970a (BK170)   20.00
     Nos. 1967-1970 (4)   6.70   4.05

Self-Adhesive
Die Cut Perf. 15½x14¼

2001   A509   1st multi   60.00   30.00
1971
   a.   Booklet, #1971, 4
      #MH298   125.00

Issued: Nos. 1967-1970, 4/10; No. 1971, 4/17; Nos. 1967a, 1968a, 1969a, 1970a, 10/22/01.
On day of issue No. 1967 sold for 19p and Nos. 1968 and 1971 sold for 27p.

Buses
A510

Designs: No. 1972, Blue and red Leyland X-type (half), London General (#11), yellow green and orange Leyland Titan, dark green and yellow AEC Regent I (half). No. 1973, AEC Regent I (half), Daimler COG5 (#8), Guy Arab Mk II (#51), green and yellow AEC Regent (half). No. 1974, AEC Regent (half), Bristol KSW 5G (#68), AEC Routemaster (#21), red and yellow Bristol Lodekka (half). No. 1975, Bristol Lodekka (half), Leyland Titan (#12B), Leyland Atlantean (#53X), red and yellow Daimler Fleetline (half). No. 1976, Daimler Fleetline (half), MCW Metrobus (#770), Leyland Olympian (#12), red and blue Dennis Trident (half).

2001, May 15   Photo.   *Perf. 14¼x14*
1972   A510   1st multi   1.35   .90
1973   A510   1st multi   1.35   .90
1974   A510   1st multi   1.35   .90
1975   A510   1st multi   1.35   .90
1976   A510   1st multi   1.35   .90
   a.   Horiz. strip, #1972-1976   6.75   5.75
   b.   Souvenir sheet, #1972-1976   12.50   10.00

Nos. 1972-1976 each sold for 27p on day of issue.

Women's
Hats — A511

Hats designed by: 1st, Pip Hackett. E, Dai Rees. 45p, Stephen Jones. 65p, Philip Treacy.

Perf. 14½x14¼

2001, June 19   Litho.
1977   A511   1st multi   1.35   .60
1978   A511   E multi   1.90   1.20
1979   A511   45p multi   1.80   1.40
1980   A511   65p multi   2.60   1.75
     Nos. 1977-1980 (4)   7.65   4.95

Nos. 1977 and 1978 sold for 27p and 36p respectively on day of issue.

Europa
A512

2001, July 10   Photo.   *Perf. 14¾x14*
1981   A512   1st Frog   1.35   .60
1982   A512   E Great diving
      beetle   1.90   1.20
1983   A512   45p Stickleback   1.80   1.40
1984   A512   65p Dragonfly   2.60   1.75
     Nos. 1981-1984 (4)   7.65   4.95

Nos. 1981 and 1982 sold for 27p and 36p respectively on day of issue.

Puppets — A513

2001, Sept. 4   Photo.   *Perf. 14x15*
1985   A513   1st Policeman   1.35   .80
1986   A513   1st Clown   1.35   .80
1987   A513   1st Punch   1.35   .80
1988   A513   1st Judy   1.35   .80
1989   A513   1st Beadle   1.35   .80

1990   A513   1st Crocodile   1.35   .80
   a.   Horiz. strip of 6, #1985-
      1990   8.00   6.00
     Nos. 1985-1990 (6)   8.10   4.80

Booklet Stamps
Self-Adhesive
Die Cut Perf. 14x15½

1991   A513   1st Punch   12.50   10.00
1992   A513   1st Judy   12.50   10.00
   a.   Booklet, Nos. 1991-1992, 4
      #MH298   30.00

Nos. 1985-1992 sold for 27p on day of issue.

Nobel Prizes,
Cent. — A514

Items symbolic of prize categories: 2nd, Carbon 60 molecule (Chemistry). 1st, Globe (Economics). E, Dove (Peace). 40p, Crosses (Physiology or Medicine). 45p, The Addressing of Cats, by T.S. Eliot (Literature). 65p, Boron atom (Physics).

2001, Oct. 2   Photo.   *Perf. 14½x14¼*
1993   A514   2nd multi   .95   .50
Photo. & Engr.
1994   A514   1st multi   1.35   .65
Photo. & Embossed
1995   A514   E multi   1.90   .90
Photo.
1996   A514   40p multi   1.60   .65
1997   A514   45p multi   1.60   .65
Photo. With Hologram Affixed
1998   A514   65p multi   2.60   1.75
     Nos. 1993-1998 (6)   10.20   5.85

Nos. 1993-1995 each sold for 19p, 27p and 37p respectively on day of issue. Molecule on No. 1993 is covered with a thermochromic film that changes color when warmed. No. 1996 has a scrach and sniff coating with a eucalyptus odor. Soaking in water may affect holographic images.

Flags — A515

Designs: Nos. 1999a, 2001, White ensign. No. 1999b, Union flag. Nos. 1999c, 2000, Jolly Roger. No. 1999d, Flag of the Chief of the Defense Staff.

2001, Oct. 22   Photo.   *Perf. 14¾*
Miniature Sheet

1999   A515   Sheet of 4   12.00   10.00
   a.-d.   1st Any single   3.00   1.50
   e.   Booklet pane, #1999 +
      selvage at L (BK170)   12.00
   f.   Sheet of 20 #1999b + 20
      labels, litho.   60.00   —
   g.   Sheet of 20 #1999a + 20
      labels, litho.   30.00   —
   h.   Booklet pane of 3 #1999a,
      litho. (BK178)   4.75
   i.   Booklet pane of 4, 2 each
      #1999a, 1999b, litho.
      (BK184)   5.50
   j.   Booklet pane of 4, 2 each
      #1999a, 1999b, litho.
      (BK190)   5.00

Booklet Stamps
Self-Adhesive
Die Cut Perf. 14¾

2000   A515   1st multi   12.50   9.00
2001   A515   1st multi   12.50   9.00
   a.   Booklet, #2000-2001, 4
      #MH298   32.50

Nos. 1999a-1999d, 2000-2001 each sold for 27p on day of issue. The left edge of No. 1999 is straight while rouletting separates the selvage from the sheet on No. 1999e.

No. 1999f issued 2004. It sold for £14.95 and has labels that can be personalized.

No. 1999h issued 10/18/2005. No. 1999i issued 1/8/2008. No. 1999j issued 9/17/2009.

Christmas
A516

Robins and: 2nd, Snowman. 1st, Birdhouse. E, Birdbath. 45p, Suet ball. 65b, Nest.

Die Cut Perf. 14¼x14½

				Photo.
2001, Nov. 6				
Self-Adhesive				
2002	A516	2nd multi	.95	.25
a.	Booklet of 24		23.00	
b.	Sheet of 20 + 20 labels, litho.		35.00	
2003	A516	1st multi	1.35	.25
a.	Booklet of 12		16.50	
b.	Sheet of 20 + 20 labels, litho.		27.50	
c.	Sheet, 10 each #2002-2003 +20 labels, litho.		27.50	—
2004	A516	E multi	1.90	1.00
2005	A516	45p multi	1.80	1.40
2006	A516	65p multi	2.60	1.75
	Nos. 2002-2006 (5)		8.60	4.65

Nos. 2002-2004 each sold for 19p, 27p, and 37p respectively on day of issue.

Issued: No. 2003b, 9/30/03. No. 2003b sold for £6.15 and had labels that could be personalized.

Issued: No. 2202b, 2203c, 2005. No. 2002b sold for £9.95 and had labels that could be personalized. No. 2003c sold for £5.60.

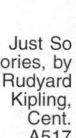

Just So Stories, by Rudyard Kipling, Cent.
A517

Designs: No. 2007, How the Whale Got His Throat (whale in bed). No. 2008, How the Camel Got His Hump (genie, camel). No. 2009, How the Rhinoceros Got His Skin (man in palm tree, rhinoceros). No. 2010, How the Leopard Got His Spots (man putting spots on leopard). No. 2011, The Elephant's Child (crocodile, elephant, snake). No. 2012, The Sing-song of Old Man Kangaroo (dog chasing kangaroo). No. 2013, The Beginning of the Armadilloes (jaguar, armadillo). No. 2014, The Crab That Played With the Sea (people in boat, giant crab). No. 2015, The Cat That Walked by Himself (people, dog, cat and shadow in cave). No. 2016, The Butterfly That Stamped (castle, giant butterfly).

Serpentine Die Cut 14½x14

				Photo.
2002, Jan. 15				
Booklet Stamps				
Self-Adhesive				
2007	A517	1st multi	1.35	.85
2008	A517	1st multi	1.35	.85
2009	A517	1st multi	1.35	.85
2010	A517	1st multi	1.35	.85
2011	A517	1st multi	1.35	.85
2012	A517	1st multi	1.35	.85
2013	A517	1st multi	1.35	.85
2014	A517	1st multi	1.35	.85
2015	A517	1st multi	1.35	.85
2016	A517	1st multi	1.35	.85
a.	Booklet, #2007-2016		13.50	

Nos. 2007-2016 each sold for 27p on day of issue. Titles of stories are not on stamps, but in margin.

Reign of Queen Elizabeth II, 50th Anniv. — A518

Photographs of Queen by: 2nd, Dorothy Wilding, 1952. 1st, Cecil Beaton, 1968. E, Lord Snowdon, 1978, 45p, Yousef Karsh, 1984. 65p, Tim Graham, 1996.

Perf. 14½x14¼

			Wmk. 401
2002, Feb. 6	**Photo.**		
2017	A518	2nd blk & sil	.95	.50
2018	A518	1st blk & sil	1.35	.85
2019	A518	E blk & sil	1.90	.90
2020	A518	45p blk & sil	1.80	1.40
a.	Booklet pane, #2017-2020 (BK171)	6.00	
2021	A518	65p blk & sil	2.60	1.75
a.	Booklet pane, #2018-2021 (BK171)	7.75	
	Nos. 2017-2021 (5)	8.60	5.40

Nos. 2017-2019 sold for 19p, 27p, and 37p respectively on day of issue.

Queen Types of 1952
Tan Surface-colored Paper
Perf. 14¾x14 Syncopated

			Wmk. 401
2002, Feb. 6	**Photo.**		
2022	A127	2nd red	1.50	1.00
2023	A126	1st green	1.75	1.50
a.	Booklet pane, 5 #2022, 4 #2023, + label (BK171)	14.50	—

Nos. 2022 and 2023 sold for 19p and 27p respectively on day of issue.

A New Baby
A519

Hello
A520

Moving
A521

Best Wishes
A522

Love
A523

Perf. 14¾x14

				Unwmk.
2002-3		**Litho.**		
2024	A519	1st multi	1.35	.60
a.	Perf. 14¼ + label		2.50	2.50
2025	A520	1st multi	1.35	.60
a.	Perf. 14¼ + label		2.50	2.50
2026	A521	1st multi	1.35	.60
a.	Perf. 14¼ + label		2.50	2.50
2027	A522	1st multi	1.35	.60
a.	Perf. 14¼ + label		2.50	2.50
2028	A523	1st multi	1.35	.65
a.	Perf. 14¼ + label		2.50	2.50
c.	Sheet of 20, 4 each #2024-2028, + 20 labels, perf. 14¼	—	—
	Nos. 2024-2028 (5)		6.75	3.05

Self-Adhesive
Booklet Stamp
Die Cut Perf. 14¾x14

2028A	A520	1st multi	6.00	.65
b.	Booklet pane, 2 #2028A, 4 #MH300	15.00	

Nos. 2024-2028A each sold for 27p on day of issue.

Nos. 2024a-2028a sold for £14.95 and have labels that can be personalized. No. 2028c sold for £5.95.

Sheets of No. 2025a with a Washington 2006 World Philatelic Exhibition margin and labels sold for £6.95. Value $27.50. Sheets with other margins exist.

Aerial Photographs of Coastline
A524

Issued, Nos. 2024-2028, 3/5/02; No. 2028c, 4/23/02; Nos. 2024a-2028a, 2002; No. 2028A, 3/4/03.

Perf. 14¼x14½

2002, Mar. 19				
2029	A524	27p Studland Bay	1.10	.80
2030	A524	27p Luskentyre	1.10	.80
2031	A524	27p Dover	1.10	.80
2032	A524	27p Padstow	1.10	.80
2033	A524	27p Broadstairs	1.10	.80
2034	A524	27p St. Abb's Head	1.10	.80
2035	A524	27p Dunster Beach	1.10	.80
2036	A524	27p Newquay	1.10	.80
2037	A524	27p Portrush	1.10	.80
2038	A524	27p Conwy	1.10	.80
a.	Block of 10, #2029-2038	11.00	10.00

Circus — A525

Designs: 2nd, High wire performer. 1st, Lion tamer. E, Trick tricyclists. 45p, Krazy kar. 65p, Equestrienne.

Perf. 14¼x14½

2002, Apr. 9	**Photo.**			
2039	A525	2nd multi	.95	.50
2040	A525	1st multi	1.35	.80
2041	A525	E multi	1.90	1.00
2042	A525	45p multi	1.80	1.40
2043	A525	65p multi	2.60	1.75
	Nos. 2039-2043 (5)		8.60	5.45

Europa (Nos. 2040-2041). Nos. 2039-2041 sold for 19p, 27p and 37p respectively on day of issue.

First day covers of Nos. 2039-2043 bear an April 9, 2001, date, but the issue of the stamps was delayed until April 10 due to the funeral of the Queen Mother.

Queen Mother (1900-2002)
A526

Perf. 14x14¾

2002, Apr. 25				
2044	A526	1st 1990 photo	1.35	.80
2045	A526	E 1948 photo	1.90	1.00
2046	A526	45p 1930 photo	1.80	1.40
2047	A526	65p 1907 photo	2.60	1.75
	Nos. 2044-2047 (4)		7.65	4.95

Nos. 2044-2045 sold for 27p and 37p respectively on day of issue. Compare with Type A387.

Jet Aircraft — A527

Designs: 2nd, Airbus A340-600, 2002. 1st, Concorde, 1976. E, Trident, 1964. 45p, VC10, 1964. 65p, Comet, 1952.

Perf. 14½

2002, May 2				
2048	A527	2nd multi	.95	.50
2049	A527	1st multi	1.35	.80
a.	Litho. (#2619a) ('09)	1.10	.55
2050	A527	E multi	1.90	1.00
2051	A527	45p multi	1.80	1.40
2052	A527	65p multi	2.60	1.75
a.	Souvenir sheet, #2048-2052	13.00	9.50
	Nos. 2048-2052 (5)		8.60	5.45

Booklet Stamp
Self-Adhesive
Die Cut Perf. 14½

2053	A527	1st multi	6.00	5.00
a.	Booklet, 2 #2053, 4 #MH297	16.00	

Nos. 2048-2052 sold for 19p, 27p and 37p respectively on day of issue.

No. 2049a issued 1/13/09. No. 2049a sold for 36p on day of issue.

A528

2002 World Cup Soccer Championships, Japan and Korea — A529

Soccer ball and: Nos. 2056a, 2057, Upper left portion of English flag. Nos. 2056b, 2058, Upper right portion of English flag. No. 2056c, Lower left portion of English flag. Nos. 2055, 2056d, Lower right portion of English flag.

Photo., Litho. (#2055)

			Perf. 14¼
2002, May 21			
2054	A528	1st multi	1.80	1.50
2055	A529	1st dull blue & multi	1.80	1.50

Souvenir Sheet

2056	Sheet, #2054, #2056a-2056d	9.00	9.00
a.-d.	A529 1st deep blue & multi, perf. 14¾x14, any single	1.80	1.50

Booklet Stamps
Die Cut Perf. 14¾x14
Self-Adhesive

2057	A529	1st deep blue & multi	7.00	3.50
2058	A529	1st deep blue & multi	7.00	3.50
a.	Booklet, #2057, 2058, 4 #MH298	17.50	

Nos. 2054, 2056a-2056d, 2057-2058 sold for 27p on day of sale. No. 2055 was issued only in sheets of 20 stamps + 16 labels that sold for £5.95, and which could have the labels personalized for an additional fee.

17th Commonwealth Games, Manchester — A530

Designs: 2nd, Swimming. 1st, Running. E, Cycling. 47p, Long jump. 68p, Wheelchair racing.

Perf. 14¾x14¼

				Photo.
2002, July 16				
2059	A530	2nd multi	.95	.35
2060	A530	1st multi	1.35	.55
2061	A530	E multi	1.90	1.00
2062	A530	47p multi	1.90	1.00
2063	A530	68p multi	2.70	1.40
	Nos. 2059-2063 (5)		8.80	4.30

Nos. 2059-2061 each sold for 19p, 27p and 37p respectively on day of issue.

Peter Pan, by J. M. Barrie, 150th Anniv.
A531

Designs: 2nd, Tinkerbell. 1st, Darling children. E, Crocodile and clock. 47p, Captain Hook. 68p, Peter Pan.

Perf. 14¾x14¼

2002, Aug. 20				**Photo.**	
2064	A531	2nd multi		.95	.35
2065	A531	1st multi		1.35	.55
2066	A531	E multi		1.90	1.00
2067	A531	47p multi		1.90	1.00
2068	A531	68p multi		2.70	1.40
	Nos. 2064-2068 (5)			8.80	4.30

Nos. 2064-2066 each sold for 19p, 27p and 37p respectively on day of issue.

Thames River Bridges in London
A532

2002, Sept. 10		**Litho.**	**Perf. 14¾x14**		
2069	A532	2nd Millennium		1.25	.35
2070	A532	1st Tower		1.50	.55
2071	A532	E Westminster		2.25	1.00
2072	A532	47p Blackfriars		2.25	1.00
2073	A532	68p London		3.00	1.40
	Nos. 2069-2073 (5)			10.25	4.30

Booklet Stamp
Serpentine Die Cut 14¾x14

2074	A532	1st Tower		7.50	6.00
a.		Booklet, 2 #2074, 4 #MH300		19.00	

Nos. 2070 and 2074 sold for 27p; Nos. 2069, 2071 sold for 19p and 37p respectively on day of sale.

Souvenir Sheet

Astronomy — A533

No. 2075: a, Planetary nebula in Aquila. b, Seyfert 2 galaxy in Pegasus. c, Planetary nebula in Norma. d, Seyfert 2 galaxy in Circinus.

Perf. 14¾x14¼

2002, Sept. 24				**Photo.**	
2075	A533	Sheet of 4		6.00	5.00
a.-d.		(1st) Any single		1.50	.75
e.		Booklet pane, #2075, rouletted at left (BK172)		5.50	

Nos. 2075a-2075d each sold for 27p on day of issue.

Pillar Boxes, 150th Anniv. — A534

Designs: 2nd, Decorative box, 1857. 1st, Mainland box, 1874. E, Airmail box, 1934. 47p, Oval dual-aperture box, 1939. 68p, Modern box, 1980.

2002, Oct. 8		**Litho. & Engr.**	**Perf. 14x14¼**		
2076	A534	2nd multi		.95	.35
2077	A534	1st multi		1.35	.55
2078	A534	E multi		1.90	1.00
2079	A534	47p multi		1.90	1.00
2080	A534	68p multi		2.70	1.40
	Nos. 2076-2080 (5)			8.80	4.30

Nos. 2076-2078 each sold for 19p, 27p and 37p on day of issue.

Christmas
A535

Die Cut Perf. 14½x14

2002, Nov. 5				**Photo.**	
		Self-Adhesive			
2081	A535	2nd Spruce branches		.95	.25
a.		Booklet pane of 24		23.00	
2082	A535	1st Holly		1.35	.25
a.		Booklet pane of 12		16.50	
2083	A535	E Ivy		1.90	.80
2084	A535	47p Mistletoe		1.90	.95
2085	A535	68p Pine cone		2.70	1.40
	Nos. 2081-2085 (5)			8.80	3.65

Nos. 2081-2085 each sold for 19p, 27p and 37p on day of issue.

Types of 1952-54
Souvenir Sheet
Tan Surface-colored Paper

Perf. 14¾x14 Syncopated

2002, Dec. 5		**Photo.**		**Wmk.**	**401**
2086		Sheet of 9, #2022-2023, 2086a-2086g + label		12.50	8.50
a.	A126	1p red orange		.30	.25
b.	A126	2p ultramarine		.30	.25
c.	A126	5p brown		.30	.25
d	A129	33p light brown		2.00	.90
e.	A130	37p bright rose		2.50	1.00
f.	A131	47p brown		3.00	1.10
g.	A132	50p dark green		3.50	1.25

Barn Owl in Flight — A536

Barn Owl in Flight — A537

Barn Owl in Flight — A538

Barn Owl in Flight — A539

Barn Owl in Flight — A540

Kestrel in Flight — A541

Kestrel in Flight — A542

Kestrel in Flight — A543

Kestrel in Flight — A544

Kestrel in Flight — A545

2003, Jan. 14		**Litho.**	**Perf. 14¼x14½**		
2087	A536	1st multi		1.35	.80
2088	A537	1st multi		1.35	.80
2089	A538	1st multi		1.35	.80
2090	A539	1st multi		1.35	.80
2091	A540	1st multi		1.35	.80
2092	A541	1st multi		1.35	.80
2093	A542	1st multi		1.35	.80
2094	A543	1st multi		1.35	.80
2095	A544	1st multi		1.35	.80
2096	A545	1st multi		1.35	.80
a.		Block of 10, #2087-2096		13.50	11.50

Nos. 2087-2096 each sold for 27p on day of issue.

Check-off Slogans
A546

Designs: No. 2097, Gold star, See me, Playtime. No. 2098, I love you, XXXX, S.W.A.L.K. No. 2099, Angel, Poppet, Little terror. No. 2100, Yes, No, Maybe. No. 2101, Oops!, Sorry, Will try harder. No. 2102, I did it!, You did it!, We did it!

2003, Feb. 4		**Litho.**	**Perf. 14¼x14**		
2097	A546	1st multi		1.35	.80
2098	A546	1st multi		1.35	.80
2099	A546	1st multi		1.35	.80
2100	A546	1st multi		1.35	.80
2101	A546	1st multi		1.35	.80
2102	A546	1st multi		1.35	.80
a.		Block of 6, #2097-2102		8.25	6.25
b.		Sheet, 3 each #2097, 2099, 2101-2102, 4 each #2098, 2100 + 20 labels		35.00	

No. 2102b sold for $5.95 and had labels that could be personalized.

Genetics
A548

Designs: 2nd, Scientists with jigsaw puzzle. 1st, Chimpanzee and scientist. E, Scientist, DNA double helix, snake. 47p, Scientists with animals. 68p, Scientist with doctor's satchel, crystal ball.

Perf. 14¼x14½

2003, Feb. 25				**Litho.**	
2103	A548	2nd multi		.95	.35
2104	A548	1st multi		1.35	.45
a.		Booklet pane, 2 each #2103-2104 (BK173)		4.50	
2105	A548	E multi		1.90	.90
a.		Booklet pane of 4 (BK173)		7.50	
2106	A548	47p multi		1.90	.90
2107	A548	68p multi		2.70	1.40
	Nos. 2103-2107 (5)			8.80	4.00

Nos. 2103-2105 sold for 19p, 27p and 37p respectively on day of issue.

Fruit and Vegetables
A549

Die Cut Perf. 14¼x14

2003, Mar. 25				**Photo.**	
		Self-Adhesive			
		Booklet Stamps			
2108	A549	1st Strawberry		1.35	.75
2109	A549	1st Potato		1.35	.75
2110	A549	1st Apple		1.35	.75
2111	A549	1st Pepper		1.35	.75
2112	A549	1st Pear		1.35	.75
2113	A549	1st Orange		1.35	.75
2114	A549	1st Tomato		1.35	.75
2115	A549	1st Lemon		1.35	.75
2116	A549	1st Brussels sprout		1.35	.75
2117	A549	1st Eggplant		1.35	.75
a.		Pane, #2108-2117 + 76 stickers		13.50	
b.		Sheet, 2 each #2108-2117, litho., + 20 labels +93 stickers ('06)		35.00	

Nos. 2108-2117 each sold for 27p on day of issue.

No. 2117b issued 3/7/06. No. 2117b sold for £6.55.

Adventurers — A550

Designs: 2nd, Amy Johnson (1903-41), first woman to fly to Australia. 1st, British Mount Everest expedition of 1953. E, Freya Stark (1893-1993), Middle East traveler and writer. 42p, Ernest Shackleton (1874-1922), Antarctic explorer. 47p, Francis Chichester (1901-72), sailor. 68p, Robert Falcon Scott (1868-1912), Antarctic explorer.

Perf. 14¾x14¼

2003, Apr. 29		**Photo.**		**Unwmk.**	
2118	A550	2nd multi		.95	.35
2119	A550	1st multi		1.35	.50
2120	A550	E multi		1.90	.85
2121	A550	42p multi		1.70	.85
2122	A550	47p multi		1.90	1.00
2123	A550	68p multi		2.70	1.40
	Nos. 2118-2123 (6)			10.50	4.95

Booklet Stamp
Self-Adhesive
Die Cut Perf. 14¾x14¼

2124	A550	1st multi		6.00	1.25
a.		Booklet pane, 2 #2124, 4 #MH300		14.00	

Nos. 2118-2120 each sold for 19p, 27p and 38p respectively on day of issue.

Types of 1952-54

A550a

Perf. 14¾x14 Syncopated
2003, May 20   Photo.   Wmk. 401
Tan Surface-colored Paper
Souvenir Sheet

2125		Sheet of 9 + label	13.00 13.00
a.	A127	4p purple	.20 .20
b.	A128	8p ultramarine	.30 .20
c.	A129	10p lilac rose	.40 .20
d.	A129	20p emerald	.80 .40
e.	A130	28p deep olive green	1.10 .50
f.	A130	34p violet brown	1.35 .65
g.	A128	E henna brown	1.90 .80
h.	A130	42p royal blue	1.75 .75
i.	A131	68p dark blue	3.00 1.25

Booklet Stamp
Perf. 14¾x14

2126	A136	£1 dark green	65.00 55.00
a.		Booklet pane, #2126, 2 each #2086f, 2125i (BK174)	72.50

No. 2125g sold for 38p on day of issue.

Coronation of Queen Elizabeth II, 50th Anniv. — A551

Designs: No. 2127, Aerial view of parade entering circle. No. 2128, Children reading coronation party sign. No. 2129, Queen at coronation. No. 2130, Children at wall of pictures. No. 2131, Queen holding orb and scepter. No. 2132, Children running in street. No. 2133, Royal carriage under arch. No. 2134, Children standing in front of house. No. 2135, Royal carriage. No. 2136, Children at party.

Perf. 14½x14¼
2003, June 2   Photo.   Wmk. 401

2127	A551	1st multi	1.35 .80
2128	A551	1st multi	1.35 .80
2129	A551	1st multi	1.35 .80
2130	A551	1st multi	1.35 .80
2131	A551	1st multi	1.35 .80
2132	A551	1st multi	1.35 .80
2133	A551	1st multi	1.35 .80
2134	A551	1st multi	1.35 .80
a.		Booklet pane, #2127, 2129, 2132, 2134 (BK174)	5.50
2135	A551	1st multi	1.35 .80
2136	A551	1st multi	1.35 .80
a.		Block of 10, #2127-2136	13.50 12.00
b.		Booklet pane, #2128, 2131, 2133, 2136 (BK174)	5.50

Nos. 2127-2136 each sold for 28p on day of issue.

Prince William, 21st Birthday A552

Various portraits.

2003, June 17   Photo.   Perf. 14¼
Background Color

2137	A552	28p silver	1.10 .50
2138	A552	E brown	2.25 1.00
2139	A552	47p green	2.50 1.50
2140	A552	68p olive green	3.75 1.50
		Nos. 2137-2140 (4)	9.60 5.50

No. 2138 sold for 38p on day of issue. Background colors are printed with Iriodin ink, giving the stamp a three dimensional appearance.

Scottish Scenery A553

Designs: 2nd: Loch Assynt, Sutherland. 1st, Ben More, Isle of Mull. E, Rothiemurchus, Cairngorms. 42p, Dalveen Pass, Lowther Hills. 47p, Glenfinnan Viaduct, Lochaber. 68p, Papa Little, Shetland Islands.

2003, July 15   Photo.   Perf. 14½

2141	A553	2nd multi	.95 .35
2142	A553	1st multi	1.35 .50
2143	A553	E multi	1.90 .75
2144	A553	42p multi	1.70 .90
2145	A553	47p multi	1.90 1.00
2146	A553	68p multi	2.70 1.40
		Nos. 2141-2146 (6)	10.50 4.90

Booklet Stamp
Self-Adhesive
Die Cut Perf. 14½

2147	A553	1st multi	6.00 1.00
a.		Booklet pane, 2 #2147, 4 #MH300	16.00

Nos. 2141 and 2143 each sold for 20p and 38p respectively on day of issue, while Nos. 2142 and 2147 sold for 28p on day of issue.

Pub Signs — A554

Designs: 1st, The Station, Thurnscoe. E, Black Swan, Lincoln. 42p, The Cross Keys, London. 47p, The Mayflower, Southsea. 68p, The Barley Sheaf, Bodmin.

2003, Aug. 12   Photo.   Perf. 14x14¼

2148	A554	1st multi	1.35 .50
a.		Booklet pane of 4 (BK175)	5.50 —
2149	A554	E multi	1.90 .75
2150	A554	42p multi	1.70 .90
2151	A554	47p multi	1.90 1.00
2152	A554	68p multi	2.70 1.40
		Nos. 2148-2152 (5)	9.55 4.55

Europa (#2148-2149).
Nos. 2148 and 2149 each sold for 28p and 38p, respectively, on day of issue.

Toys A555

Designs: 1st, Meccano Constructor Biplane, c. 1931. E, Wells-Brimtoy Clockwork Double-decker Omnibus, c. 1938. 42p, Hornby M1 Clockwork Locomotive and Tender, c. 1948. 47p, Dinky Toys Ford Zephyr, c. 1956. 68p, Mettoy Friction drive Space Ship Eagle c. 1960.

2003, Sept. 18   Photo.   Perf. 14¼x14¼

2153	A555	1st multi	1.35 .50
2154	A555	E multi	1.90 .75
2155	A555	42p multi	1.70 .90
2156	A555	47p multi	1.90 1.00
2157	A555	68p multi	2.70 1.40
a.		Souvenir sheet, #2153-2157	10.00 10.00
		Nos. 2153-2157 (5)	9.55 4.55

Booklet Stamp
Self-Adhesive
Die Cut Perf. 14¼x14

2158	A555	1st multi	6.00 1.00
a.		Booklet, 2 #2158, 4 #MH300	16.00

Nos. 2153 and 2158 each sold for 28p on day of issue. No. 2154 sold for 38p on day of issue.

British Museum, 250th Anniv. — A556

Museum Exhibits: 2nd, Coffin of Denytenamun, c. 900 B.C. 1st, Bust of Alexander the Great, c. 200 B.C. E, Sutton Hoo Helmet, c. 600. 42p, Sculpture of Indian Goddess Parvati, c. 1500. 47p, Mask of Xiuhtecuhtli, c. 1500. 68p, Hoa Hakananai'a Easter Island moai, c. 1000.

2003, Oct. 7   Perf. 14x14¼

2159	A556	2nd multi	.95 .40
2160	A556	1st multi	1.35 .50
2161	A556	E multi	1.90 .75
2162	A556	42p multi	1.70 .90
2163	A556	47p multi	1.90 1.00
2164	A556	68p multi	2.70 1.40
		Nos. 2159-2164 (6)	10.50 4.95

Nos. 2159-2161 each sold for 20p, 28p and 38p respectively on day of issue.

Christmas A557

Ice and snow sculptures by Andy Goldsworthy: 2nd, Ice Spiral. 1st, Icicle Star. E, Wall of Frozen Snow. 53p, Ice Ball. 68p, Ice Hole. £1.12, Snow Pyramids.

Die Cut Perf. 14¼x14
2003, Nov. 4   Photo.
Self-Adhesive

2165	A557	2nd multi	.95 .25
a.		Booklet pane of 24	23.00
b.		Sheet of 20 + 20 labels, litho.	25.00
2166	A557	1st multi	1.35 .25
a.		Booklet pane of 12	16.00
b.		Sheet of 20 + 20 labels, litho.	37.50
2167	A557	E multi	1.90 .85
2168	A557	53p multi	2.10 1.00
2169	A557	68p multi	2.70 1.40
2170	A557	£1.12 multi	4.50 2.00
		Nos. 2165-2170 (6)	13.50 5.75

Nos. 2165-2167 sold for 20p, 28p and 38p respectively on day of issue.
Nos. 2165b and 2166b sold for £4.20 and £6.15 respectively and had labels that could be personalized.

Souvenir Sheet

England, Winners of 2003 Rugby World Cup Championships — A558

No. 2171: a, English flags. b, Players with red shirts in huddle. c, World Cup. d, Players in white jerseys, celebrating.

2003, Dec. 19   Litho.   Perf. 13¾x14

2171	A558	Sheet of 4	19.50 19.50
a.-b.		1st Either single	2.00 .75
c.-d.		68p Either single	4.00 1.75

Nos. 2171a-2171b sold for 28p on day of issue.

Locomotives — A559

Designs: 20p, Dolgoch 0-4-0T. 28p, CR 439 0-4-4T. E, GCR 8K 2-8-0. 42p, GWR Manor 4-6-0. 47p, SR West Country 4-6-2. 68p, BR Standard 4 2-6-4T.

2004, Jan. 13   Litho.   Perf. 14¾x14¼

2172	A559	20p multi	.80 .35
2173	A559	28p multi	1.10 .55
2174	A559	E multi	1.90 .80
2175	A559	42p multi	1.70 .90
a.		Booklet pane, #2173-2175 (BK175)	4.50
2176	A559	47p multi	1.90 1.00
2177	A559	68p multi	2.70 1.40
a.		Souvenir sheet, #2172-2177	45.00 45.00
		Nos. 2172-2177 (6)	10.10 5.00

First steam locomotive, bicent. No. 2174 sold for 38p on day of issue.

Special Occasions A560

2004, Feb. 3   Litho.   Perf. 14¼x14

2178	A560	1st Postman	1.35 .55
2179	A560	1st Face	1.35 .55
2180	A560	1st Duck	1.35 .55
2181	A560	1st Baby	1.35 .55
2182	A560	1st Airplane	1.35 .55
a.		Horiz. strip of 5, #2178-2182	6.75 3.25
c.		Sheet, 4 each #2178-2182, + 20 labels	27.50 —

Nos. 2178-2182 each sold for 28p on day of issue. No. 2182c sold for £6.15 and had labels that could not be personalized.

Map — A561

Forest of Lothlórien A562

The Fellowship of the Ring — A563

Rivendell A564

Hall at Bag-End A565

Orthanc
A566

Doors of
Durin — A567

Barad-Dur
A568

Minas
Tirith — A569

Fangorn
Forest
A570

2004, Feb. 26   Perf. 14½x14¼

2183	A561	1st multi	1.35	.55
2184	A562	1st multi	1.35	.55
2185	A563	1st multi	1.35	.55
2186	A564	1st multi	1.35	.55
2187	A565	1st multi	1.35	.55
2188	A566	1st multi	1.35	.55
2189	A567	1st multi	1.35	.55
2190	A568	1st multi	1.35	.55
2191	A569	1st multi	1.35	.55
2192	A570	1st multi	1.35	.55
a.		Block of 10, #2183-2192	13.50	5.50

Publication of *The Lord of the Rings*, by
J.R.R. Tolkein, 50th anniv. Nos. 2183-2192
each sold for 28p on day of issue.

Northern
Ireland
Scenery
A571

Designs: 2nd, Ely, Island, Lower Lough
Erne. 1st, Giant's Causeway, Antrim Coast. E,
Slemish, Antrim Mountains. 42p, Banns Road,
Mourne Mountain. 47p, Glenelly Valley, Sper-
rins. 68p, Islandmore, Strangford Lough.

2004, Mar. 16   Photo.   Perf. 14½

2193	A571	2nd multi	.95	.35
2194	A571	1st multi	1.35	.50
2195	A571	E multi	1.90	.70
2196	A571	42p multi	1.70	.75
2197	A571	47p multi	1.90	.85
2198	A571	68p multi	2.70	1.25
		Nos. 2193-2198 (6)	10.50	4.40

Booklet Stamp
Self-Adhesive
Die Cut Perf. 14½

2199	A571	1st multi	5.75	.90
a.		Booklet, 2 #2199, 4 #MH300	15.00	

Nos. 2193-2195 each sold for 20p, 28p and
38p respectively on day of issue.

Entente Cordiale,
Cent. — A572

Designs: 28p, Lace 1 (trial proof) 1968, by
Sir Terry Frost. 57p, Coccinelle, by Sonia
Delaunay.

2004, Apr. 6   Photo.   Perf. 14x14¼

2200	A572	28p multi	1.10	.50
2201	A572	57p multi	2.25	1.10

See France Nos. 3009-3010.

Ocean
Liners
A573

Designs: 1st, RMS Queen Mary 2, 2004. E,
SS Canberra, 1961. 42p, RMS Queen Mary,
1936. 47p, RMS Mauretania, 1907. 57p, SS
City of New York, 1888. 68p, PS Great Western, 1838.

2004, Apr. 13   Perf. 14¼x14

2202	A573	1st multi	1.35	.50
2203	A573	E multi	1.90	.80
2204	A573	42p multi	1.70	.85
2205	A573	47p multi	1.90	.90
2206	A573	57p multi	2.30	1.40
2207	A573	68p multi	2.70	1.40
a.		Souvenir sheet, #2202-2207	22.50	12.50
b.		Litho. (from #2356a)	2.70	1.40
		Nos. 2202-2207 (6)	11.85	5.85

Booklet Stamp
Self-Adhesive
Serpentine Die Cut 14¼x14

2208	A573	1st multi	6.00	1.00
a.		Booklet pane, 2 #2208, 4 #MH300	16.00	

Nos. 2202 and 2203 sold for 28p and 40p
respectively on day of issue.
No. 2207b is contained in the booklet pane
No. 2356a, issued 2/23/06.

Royal
Horticultural
Society,
Bicent.
A574

Designs: 2nd, Dianthus Allwoodii Group.
1st, Dahlia "Garden Princess." E, Clematis
"Arabella." 42p, Miltonia "French Lake." 47p,
Lilium "Lemon Pixie." 68p, Delphinium "Clifford
Sky."

2004, May 25   Photo.   Perf. 14½

2209	A574	2nd multi	.95	.35
2210	A574	1st multi	1.35	.50
a.		Perf. 14¼ + label, litho.	1.40	1.10
2211	A574	E multi	1.90	.85
2212	A574	42p multi	1.70	.85
2213	A574	47p multi	1.90	1.00
a.		Booklet pane, 2 each #2210, 2213 (BK176)	6.50	—
2214	A574	68p multi	2.70	1.40
a.		Souvenir sheet, #2209-2214 (BK176)	15.00	9.00
b.		Booklet pane, #2209, 2211, 2212, 2214 (BK176)	7.25	—
		Nos. 2209-2214 (6)	10.50	4.95

Nos. 2209-2211 each sold for 21p, 28p and
40p respectively on day of issue.
No. 2210a was printed in sheets of 20
stamps + 20 labels that sold for £6.15.

Wales Scenery
A575

Designs: 2nd, Barmouth Bridge. 1st,
Hyddgen, Plynlimon. 40p, Brecon Beacons
National Park. 43p, Pen-pych, Rhondda Val-
ley. 47p, Rhewl, Dee Valley. 68p, Marloes
Sands.

2004, June 15   Photo.   Perf. 14½

2215	A575	2nd multi	.95	.40
2216	A575	1st multi	1.35	.50
2217	A575	40p multi	1.60	.80
2218	A575	43p multi	1.70	.90
2219	A575	47p multi	1.90	1.00
2220	A575	68p multi	2.70	1.40
		Nos. 2215-2220 (6)	10.20	5.00

Booklet Stamp
Self-Adhesive
Die Cut Perf. 14½

2221	A575	1st multi	7.50	.90
a.		Booklet pane, 2 #2221, 4 #MH300	19.00	

Europa (#2216, 2217, 2221). Nos. 2215-
2216 each sold for 21p and 28p respectively
on day of issue.

Royal
Society of
Arts, 250th
Anniv.
A576

Designs: 1st, Great Britain #1. 40p, William
Shipley, Society founder. 43p, Stylized typewriter keys, shorthand. 47p, Apparatus for
sweeping chimneys invented by George
Smart. 57p, Typeface designed by Eric Gill.
68p, Zero waste.

Perf. 13¾x14¼

2004, Aug. 10   Litho.

2222	A576	1st multi	1.35	.50
2223	A576	40p multi	1.60	.80
2224	A576	43p multi	1.70	.90
2225	A576	47p multi	1.90	1.00
2226	A576	57p multi	2.30	1.25
2227	A576	68p multi	2.70	1.40
		Nos. 2222-2227 (6)	11.55	5.85

No. 2222 sold for 28p on day of issue.

Mammals
A577

Perf. 14½x14¼

2004, Sept. 16   Photo.

2228	A577	1st	Pine marten	1.35	.50
2229	A577	1st	Roe deer	1.35	.50
2230	A577	1st	Badger	1.35	.50
2231	A577	1st	Yellow-necked mouse	1.35	.50
2232	A577	1st	Wild cat	1.35	.50
2233	A577	1st	Red squirrel	1.35	.50
2234	A577	1st	Stoat	1.35	.50
2235	A577	1st	Natterer's bat	1.35	.50
2236	A577	1st	Mole	1.35	.50
2237	A577	1st	Fox	1.35	.50
a.			Block of 10, #2228-2237	13.50	7.50

Nos. 2228-2237 each sold for 28p on day of
issue.

Crimean War,
150th
Anniv. — A578

Photographs of Crimean War heroes: 2nd,
Private Michael MacNamara. 1st, Piper David
Muir. 40p, Sergeant Major Edward Edwards.
57p, Sergeant William Powell. 68p, Sergeant
Major John Poole. £1.12, Sergeant Robert
Glasgow.

2004, Oct. 12   Litho.   Perf. 14x13¾

2238	A578	2nd multi	.95	.40
2239	A578	1st multi	1.35	.50
2240	A578	40p multi	1.60	.85
2241	A578	57p multi	2.30	1.25
2242	A578	68p multi	2.70	1.40
2243	A578	£1.12 multi	4.50	2.00
		Nos. 2238-2243 (6)	13.40	6.40

Nos. 2238-2239 each sold for 21p and 28p
respectively on day of issue.

Christmas
A579

Santa Claus: Nos. 2244a, 2245, Walking
toward chimney in snow. Nos. 2244b, 2246,
Looking at rising sun. Nos. 2244c, 2247, In
wind. Nos. 2244d, 2248, With umbrella in rain
storm. Nos. 2244e, 2249, With flashlight in
fog. Nos. 2244f, 2250, Taking protection from
hail storm.

2004, Nov. 2   Photo.   Perf. 14½x14

2244		Sheet of 6	13.50	7.00
a.	A579	(2nd) multi	.95	.40
b.	A579	(1st) multi	1.35	.55
c.	A579	40p multi	1.60	.85
d.	A579	57p multi	2.30	1.25
e.	A579	68p multi	2.70	1.40
f.	A579	£1.12 multi	4.50	2.10

Self-Adhesive
Die Cut Perf. 14½x14

2245	A579	(2nd) multi	.95	.25
a.		Booklet pane of 24	23.00	
b.		Sheet of 20 + 20 personal-ized labels, litho.	40.00	
2246	A579	(1st) multi	1.35	.55
a.		Booklet pane of 12	16.00	.25
b.		Sheet, 10 each #2245-2246, + 20 labels, litho.	27.50	
c.		Sheet of 20 + 20 personal-ized labels, litho.	57.50	
2247	A579	40p multi	1.60	.85
2248	A579	57p multi	2.30	1.25
2249	A579	68p multi	2.70	1.40
2250	A579	£1.12 multi	4.50	2.10
		Nos. 2245-2250 (6)	13.40	6.40

Nos. 2244a and 2245 each sold for 21p and
Nos. 2244b and 2246 each sold for 28p on day
of issue.
No. 2245b sold for £9.95; No. 2246b sold for
£5.40; No. 2246c sold for £14.95.

Farm Animals
A580

Designs: No. 2251, British Saddleback pigs.
No. 2252, Two Khaki Campbell ducks. No.
2253, Clydesdale horses. No. 2254, Shorthorn
cattle. No. 2255, Border collie. No. 2256,
Chicks. No. 2257, Suffolk sheep. No. 2258,
Bagot goat. No. 2259, Norfolk Black turkeys.
No. 2260, Three Embden geese.

2005, Jan. 11   Photo.   Perf. 14½

2251	A580	1st multi	1.35	.55
2252	A580	1st multi	1.35	.55
2253	A580	1st multi	1.35	.55
2254	A580	1st multi	1.35	.55
2255	A580	1st multi	1.35	.55
2256	A580	1st multi	1.35	.55
2257	A580	1st multi	1.35	.55
2258	A580	1st multi	1.35	.55
2259	A580	1st multi	1.35	.55

2260 A580 1st multi 1.35 .55
   a.   Block of 10, #2251-2260 13.50 5.50
   b.   Sheet, 2 each #2251-2260 +
      20 labels, litho. 34.00 —

Nos. 2251-2260 each sold for 28p on day of issue. No. 2260b sold for £6.15.

Southwestern
England
Scenery
A581

Designs: 2nd, Old Harry Rocks, Studland Bay. 1st, Wheal Coates mine, St. Agnes. 40p, Start Point and Start Bay. 43p, Norton Down, Wiltshire. 57p, Chiselcombe, Exmoor. 68p, St. James Stone, Lundy.

2005, Feb. 8   **Photo.**   ***Perf. 14½***
2261 A581 2nd multi .95 .40
2262 A581 1st multi 1.35 .50
2263 A581 40p multi 1.60 .80
2264 A581 43p multi 1.70 .90
2265 A581 57p multi 2.30 1.25
2266 A581 68p multi 2.70 1.40
    Nos. 2261-2266 (6) 10.60 5.25

Nos. 2261 and 2262 sold for 21p and 28p respectively on day of issue.

Jane Eyre, by
Charlotte Bronte
(1816-55) — A582

Various characters.

2005, Feb. 24   **Litho.**   ***Perf. 14¼***
2267 A582 2nd multi .95 .40
2268 A582 1st multi 1.35 .50
   a.   Booklet pane, 2 each #2267-
      2268 (BK177) 5.50 —
2269 A582 40p multi 1.60 .85
2270 A582 57p multi 2.30 1.25
2271 A582 68p multi 2.70 1.40
2272 A582 £1.12 multi 4.50 2.10
   a.   Souvenir sheet, #2267-2272 14.00 7.00
   b.   Booklet pane, #2269-2272
      (BK177) 11.00 —
    Nos. 2267-2272 (6) 13.40 6.50

Nos. 2267 and 2268 sold for 21p and 28p respectively on day of issue.

Magic
Tricks
A583

Designs: 1st, Magician, "heads or tails" coin. 40p, Rabbit and hat. 47p, Popper. 68p, Ace of Hearts. £1.12, Pyramids and fezzes.

2005, Mar. 15   **Photo.**   ***Perf. 14¼x14***
2273 A583 1st multi, un-
      scratched
      coin 1.35 .55
   a.   Scratched coin, heads 1.35 .55
   b.   Scratched coin, tails 1.35 .55
   c.   Vert. pair, unscratched 2.70 1.10
   d.   Sheet of 20 + 20 labels, un-
      scratched, litho. 27.00 —
2274 A583 40p multi 1.60 .80
2275 A583 47p multi 1.90 .95
2276 A583 68p multi 2.70 1.40
2277 A583 £1.12 multi 4.50 2.10
    Nos. 2273-2277 (5) 12.05 5.80

No. 2273 sold for 28p on day of issue. No. 2273 has a chalky covering over the coin that can be scratched away with a coin or other metal object to reveal a "heads" picture, showing a face composed of a planet, star and a crescent, or a "tails" picture, showing a shooting star. The chalky covering may, like earlier British chalky paper stamps, dissolve in any fluid.

No. 2273c will have both versions of the stamp. Vertical or horizontal pairs from No. 2273d will have both versions of the stamp. No. 2273d sold for £6.15.

Portions of the designs of Nos. 2275 and 2277 are printed with a thermochromic ink that changes color when warmed.

Castles Type of 1955
Miniature Sheet
Litho. & Engr.
2005, Mar. 22   ***Perf. 11x11¾***
On Cream-Colored Paper
2278   Sheet of 4 12.00 12.00
   a.   A133 50p Carrickfergus
      (brown) 2.00 1.00
   b.   A133 50p Windsor (black) 2.00 1.00
   c.   A133 £1 Caernarfon (red) 4.00 2.00
   d.   A133 £1 Edinburgh (blue) 4.00 2.00

Miniature Sheet

Wedding of Prince Charles and
Camilla Parker Bowles — A584

No. 2279 — Couple: a, 30p, Prince wearing blue, red and green tie. b, 68p, Prince wearing vest.

2005, Apr. 8   **Litho.**   ***Perf. 13½x14***
2279 A584   Sheet, 2 each #a-b 8.50 8.50
   a.   30p multi 1.75 .60
   b.   68p multi 2.75 1.40

The marginal inscription states that the wedding took place on Apr. 8, but it was delayed until Apr. 9, due to Prince Charles's attendance at the Apr. 8 funeral of Pope John Paul II. Post offices were requested not to sell the stamps until Apr. 9, but first day covers have Apr. 8 cancels.

UNESCO
World Heritage
Sites in Great
Britain and
Australia
A585

Designs: No. 2280, Hadrian's Wall, England. No. 2281, Ayers Rock, Uluru-Kata Tjuta National Park, Australia. No. 2282, Stonehenge, England No. 2283, Wet Tropics of Queensland, Australia. No. 2284, Blenheim Palace, England. No. 2285, Greater Blue Mountains Area, Australia. No. 2286, Heart of Neolithic Orkney, Scotland. No. 2287, Purnululu National Park, Australia.

2005, Apr. 21   ***Perf. 14½***
2280 A585 2nd multi .95 .40
2281 A585 2nd multi .95 .40
   a.   Horiz. pair, #2280-2281 1.80 1.00
2282 A585 1st multi 1.35 .55
2283 A585 1st multi 1.35 .55
   a.   Horiz. pair, #2282-2283 2.70 1.50
2284 A585 47p multi 1.90 1.00
2285 A585 47p multi 1.90 1.00
   a.   Horiz. pair, #2284-2285 3.75 2.25
2286 A585 68p multi 2.70 1.40
2287 A585 68p multi 2.70 1.40
   a.   Horiz. pair, #2286-2287 5.50 3.00
    Nos. 2280-2287 (8) 13.80 6.70

Nos. 2280 and 2281 each sold for 21p and Nos. 2282 and 2283 each sold for 30p on day of issue.

See Australia Nos. 2369-2376.

Trooping the
Color
Ceremony
A586

Designs: 2nd, Soldier holding regimental flag. 1st, Queen Elizabeth II saluting. 42p, Bugler on horseback. 60p, Soldier holding scabbard. 68p, Queen on horseback. £1.12, Queen and soldier in phaeton.

2005, June 7   **Litho.**   ***Perf. 14½***
2288 A586 2nd multi .95 .40
2289 A586 1st multi 1.35 .55
2290 A586 42p multi 1.70 .85
2291 A586 60p multi 2.40 1.25
2292 A586 68p multi 2.70 1.25
2293 A586 £1.12 multi 4.50 2.00
   a.   Souvenir sheet, #2288-2293 14.00 14.00
    Nos. 2288-2293 (6) 13.60 6.30

Nos. 2288 and 2289 sold for 21p and 30p respectively on day of issue.

St. Paul's Cathedral Type of 1995
Souvenir Sheet
2005, July 5   **Photo.**   ***Perf. 14½***
2294   Sheet of 6, #2294a, 5
      #MH287 8.50 7.50
   a.   A456 (1st) deep blue & silver 1.35 .50

No. 2294a issued 6/21/2005 and sold for 30p on day of issue. End of World War II, 60th anniv.

Motorcycles — A587

Designs: 1st, 1991 Norton F.1. 40p, 1969 BSA Rocket 3. 42p, 1949 Vincent Black Shadow. 47p, 1938 Triumph Speed Twin. 60p, 1930 Brough Superior. 68p, 1914 Royal Enfield.

2005, July 19   **Litho.**   ***Perf. 13¾x14***
2295 A587 1st multi 1.35 .55
2296 A587 40p multi 1.60 .80
2297 A587 42p multi 1.70 .85
2298 A587 47p multi 1.90 1.00
2299 A587 60p multi 2.40 1.25
2300 A587 68p multi 2.70 1.40
    Nos. 2295-2300 (6) 11.65 5.85

No. 2295 sold for 30p on day of issue.

Miniature Sheet

Selection of London as Host of 2012
Summer Olympics — A588

No. 2301: a, Javelin. b, Swimming. c, Sprinting. d, Basketball. e, Victorious athlete.

2005, Aug. 5   ***Perf. 14¼***
2301 A588   Sheet of 6, #a-d, 2
      #e 8.50 7.50
   a.-e.   1st Any single 1.35 .55

Nos. 2301a-2301e each sold for 30p on day of issue. Compare with Type A467.

Changing
Tastes in
Britain — A589

Designs: 2nd, Woman with rice bowl and chopsticks. 1st, Woman with mug of tea. 42p, Man eating sushi. 47p, Woman with pasta bowl and wine glass. 60p, Woman with bag of French fries. 68p, Man with bowl of fruit.

2005, Aug. 23   **Photo.**   ***Perf. 14½***
2302 A589 2nd multi .95 .40
2303 A589 1st multi 1.35 .55
2304 A589 42p multi 1.70 .90
2305 A589 47p multi 1.90 1.00
2306 A589 60p multi 2.40 1.25
2307 A589 68p multi 2.70 1.40
    Nos. 2302-2307 (6) 11.00 5.50

Europa (#2303, 2304). Nos. 2302 and 2303 sold for 21p and 30p respectively on day of issue.

Television
Shows
A590

Designs: 2nd, Inspector Morse. 1st, Emmerdale. 42p, Rising Damp. 47p, The Avengers. 60p, The South Bank Show. 68p, Who Wants To Be a Millionaire?

2005, Sept. 15   **Litho.**   ***Perf. 14¼x14***
2308 A590 2nd multi .95 .40
2309 A590 1st multi 1.35 .55
   a.   Sheet of 20 + 20 labels 27.00 —
2310 A590 42p multi 1.70 .85
2311 A590 47p multi 1.90 1.00
2312 A590 60p multi 2.40 1.25
2313 A590 68p multi 2.70 1.40
    Nos. 2308-2313 (6) 11.00 5.45

Independent Television, 50th anniv. Nos. 2308 and 2309 sold for 21p and 30p respectively on day of issue. No. 2309a sold for £6.65.

Labels on No. 2309a could be personalized for a fee.

 Flower A591

 Hello A592

 Love — A593

 Flag — A594

 Teddy Bear — A595

 Bird — A596

Serpentine Die Cut 14¾x14
2005, Oct. 4   **Photo.**
Self-Adhesive
Booklet Stamps
2314 A591 1st multi 2.00 .75
   a.   Sheet of 20 + 20 labels, litho. 52.50 —
2315 A592 1st multi 2.00 .75
   a.   Sheet of 20 + 20 labels, litho. 52.50 —
2316 A593 1st multi 2.00 .75
   a.   Sheet of 20 + 20 labels, litho. 52.50 —
2317 A594 1st multi 2.00 .75
   a.   Sheet of 20 + 20 labels, litho. 52.50 —
2318 A595 1st multi 2.00 .75
   a.   Sheet of 20 + 20 labels, litho. 52.50 —
2319 A596 1st multi 2.00 .75
   a.   Booklet pane, #2314-2319 13.00 —
   b.   Sheet of 20 + 20 labels, litho. 52.50 —
   c.   Sheet, 4 each #2315-2316, 3
      each #2314, 2317-2319, +
      20 labels, litho. ('06) 42.50 —

Each stamp sold for 30p on day of issue. Nos. 2314a-2318a, 2319b each sold for £14.95 and had labels that could be personalized.

No. 2319 issued 7/4/06. No. 2319c sold for £6.95.

See Nos. 2427, 2537-2538a, 2545, 2793.

Souvenir Sheet

THE ASHES ENGLAND WINNERS 2005

Great Britain's Victory Over Australia in Ashes Cricket Test Match Series — A597

No. 2320: a, Players celebrating with trophy. b, Players celebrating. c, Batsman. d, Players in action.

2005, Oct. 6	**Litho.**	**Perf. 14¼x14**		
2320	A597	Sheet of 4	8.50	8.50
a.-b.		1st Either single	1.35	.55
c.-d.		68p Either single	2.70	1.40

Nos. 2320a and 2320b each sold for 30p on day of issue.

Battle of Trafalgar, Bicent. — A598

Designs: No. 2321, Ships in battle. No. 2322, Wounded Admiral Horatio Nelson on deck of HMS Victory. No. 2323, Ship on fire. No. 2324, Ships in battle, diff. No. 2325, Columns of British ships. No. 2326, French and Spanish ships.

2005, Oct. 18	**Litho.**	**Perf. 14¾x14¼**		
2321	A598	1st multi	1.35	.55
2322	A598	1st multi	1.35	.55
a.		Horiz. pair, #2321-2322	2.70	1.40
2323	A598	42p multi	1.70	.85
2324	A598	42p multi	1.70	.85
a.		Horiz. pair, #2323-2324	3.50	2.00
2325	A598	68p multi	2.70	1.40
a.		Booklet pane, #2321, 2323, 2325 (BK178)	5.25	—
2326	A598	68p multi	2.70	1.40
a.		Horiz. pair, #2325-2326	5.50	3.50
b.		Booklet pane, #2322, 2324, 2326 (BK178)	5.75	—
c.		Souvenir sheet, #2321-2326	12.00	12.00

Nos. 2321-2322 each sold for 30p on day of issue.

Christmas A599

2ND

Madonna and Child in artistic style of: 2nd, Haiti. 1st, Europe. 42p, Europe. 60p, Native Americans. 68p, India. £1.12, Australian Aborigines.

2005, Nov. 1	**Photo.**	**Perf. 14½x14**		
2327		Sheet of 6	14.00	14.00
a.	A599	2nd multi	.95	.40
b.	A599	1st multi	1.35	.55
c.	A599	42p multi	1.70	.90
d.	A599	60p multi	2.40	1.25
e.	A599	68p multi	2.70	1.40
f.	A599	£1.12 multi	4.50	2.00

Self-Adhesive

Die Cut Perf. 14½x14

2328	A599	2nd multi	.95	.25
a.		Booklet pane of 24	23.00	
2329	A599	1st multi	1.35	.25
a.		Booklet pane of 12	16.50	
2330	A599	42p multi	1.70	.90
2331	A599	60p multi	2.40	1.25
2332	A599	68p multi	2.70	1.40
2333	A599	£1.12 multi	4.50	2.00
		Nos. 2328-2333 (6)	13.60	6.05

Nos. 2327a and 2328 each sold for 21p and Nos. 2327b and 2329 each sold for 30p on day of issue.

Animals From Children's Books — A600

Designs: No. 2334, Jeremy Fisher, from *The Tale of Mr. Jeremy Fisher*, by Beatrix Potter. No. 2335, Kipper, from *Kipper*, by Mick Inkpen. No. 2336, The Enormous Crocodile, from *The Enormous Crocodile*, by Roald Dahl. No. 2337, Paddington Bear, from *More About Paddington*, by Michael Bond. No. 2338, Boots, from *The Comic Adventures of Boots*, by Satoshi Kitamura. No. 2339, White Rabbit, from *Alice's Adventures in Wonderland*, by Lewis Carroll. No. 2340, The Very Hungry Caterpillar, from *The Very Hungry Caterpillar*, by Eric Carle. No. 2341, Maisy, from *Maisy's ABC*, by Lucy Cousins. No. 2342, Like #2337.

2006, Jan. 10	**Litho.**	**Perf. 14½**		
2334	A600	2nd multi	.95	.40
2335	A600	2nd multi	.95	.40
a.		Horiz. pair, #2334-2335	1.90	.95
2336	A600	1st multi	1.35	.55
2337	A600	1st multi	1.35	.55
a.		Horiz. pair, #2336-2337	2.70	1.40
2338	A600	42p multi	1.70	.75
2339	A600	42p multi	1.70	.75
a.		Horiz. pair, #2338-2339	3.50	1.75
2340	A600	68p multi	2.70	1.40
2341	A600	68p multi	2.70	1.40
a.		Horiz. pair, #2340-2341	5.50	3.00
		Nos. 2334-2341 (8)	13.40	6.20

Self-Adhesive

Serpentine Die Cut 14½

2342	A600	1st multi + label	2.25	.75

Nos. 2334-2335 each sold for 21p, and Nos. 2336-2337 each sold for 30p on day of issue. No. 2340 has two die cut holes repesenting holes eaten by the caterpillar.

See United States Nos. 3987, 3990.

No. 2342 had a franking value of 30p on the day of issue, and was issued in sheets of 20 stamps + 20 different labels that sold for £6.55.

English Scenery A601

Designs: No. 2343, Carding Mill Valley, Shropshire. No. 2344, Beachy Head, Sussex coast. No. 2345, St. Paul's Cathedral, London. No. 2346, Brancastle, Norfolk coast. No. 2347, Derwent Edge, Peak District. No. 2348, Robin Hood's Bay, Yorkshire coast. No. 2349, Buttermere, Lake District. No. 2350, Chipping Campden, Cotswolds. No. 2351, St. Boniface Down, Isle of Wight. No. 2352, Chamberlain Square, Birmingham.

2006, Feb. 7	**Photo.**	**Perf. 14½**		
2343	A601	1st multi	1.35	.55
2344	A601	1st multi	1.35	.55
2345	A601	1st multi	1.35	.55
2346	A601	1st multi	1.35	.55
2347	A601	1st multi	1.35	.55
2348	A601	1st multi	1.35	.55
2349	A601	1st multi	1.35	.55
2350	A601	1st multi	1.35	.55
2351	A601	1st multi	1.35	.55
2352	A601	1st multi	1.35	.55
a.		Block of 10, #2343-2352	13.50	7.50

Nos. 2343-2352 each sold for 30p on day of issue.

Isambard Kingdom Brunel (1806-1859), Engineer — A602

Engineering projects of Brunel: 1st, Royal Albert Bridge. 40p, Box Tunnel. 42p, Paddington Station. 47p, PSS Great Eastern. 60p, Clifton Suspension Bridge design. 68p, Maidenhead Bridge.

2006, Feb. 23	**Litho.**	**Perf. 14x13¼**		
2353	A602	1st multi	1.35	.55
2354	A602	40p multi	1.60	.80
2355	A602	42p multi	1.70	.90
2356	A602	47p multi	1.90	1.00
a.		Booklet pane, #2356, 2 #2207b (BK179)	7.25	—
2357	A602	60p multi	2.40	1.25
a.		Booklet pane, #2354, 2356, 2357 (BK179)	6.00	—
2358	A602	68p multi	2.70	1.40
a.		Souvenir sheet, #2353-2358	12.00	7.50
b.		Booklet pane, #2353, 2355, 2358 (BK179)	5.75	—
		Nos. 2353-2358 (6)	11.65	5.90

No. 2353 sold for 30p on day of issue.

Ice Age Animals A603

Designs: 1st, Saber-tooth cat. 42p, Giant deer. 47p, Woolly rhinoceros. 68p, Woolly mammoth. £1.12, Cave bear.

	Perf. 14¼x14½			
2006, Mar. 21			**Litho.**	
2359	A603	1st gray & blk	1.35	.55
2360	A603	42p gray & blk	1.70	.90
2361	A603	47p gray & blk	1.90	1.00
2362	A603	68p gray & blk	2.70	1.40
2363	A603	£1.12 gray & blk	4.50	2.00
		Nos. 2359-2363 (5)	12.15	5.85

No. 2359 sold for 30p on day of issue.

Queen Elizabeth II, 80th Birthday A604

Queen: No. 2364, Wearing sunglasses, 1972. No. 2365, With horse, 1985. No. 2366, Wearing hat, 2001. No. 2367, As child, with mother, 1931. No. 2368, Wearing tiara, 1951. No. 2369, Wearing hat, 1960. No. 2370, As teenager, 1940. No. 2371, With Prince Philip, 1950.

2006, Apr. 18	**Photo.**	**Perf. 14¼x14**		
2364	A604	2nd gray & blk	.95	.40
2365	A604	2nd gray & blk	.95	.40
a.		Horiz. pair, #2364-2365	1.90	1.00
2366	A604	1st gray & blk	1.35	.55
2367	A604	1st gray & blk	1.35	.55
a.		Horiz. pair, #2366-2367	2.70	1.50
2368	A604	44p gray & blk	1.75	.90
2369	A604	44p gray & blk	1.75	.90
a.		Horiz. pair, #2368-2369	3.50	2.25
2370	A604	72p gray & blk	2.90	1.40
2371	A604	72p gray & blk	2.90	1.40
a.		Horiz. pair, #2370-2371	5.75	3.00
		Nos. 2364-2371 (8)	13.90	6.50

On day of issue, Nos. 2364-2365 each sold of 23p; Nos. 2366-2367 each sold for 32p.

2006 World Cup Soccer Championships, Germany — A605

Globe, soccer player and flag from: 1st, England. 42p, Italy. 44p, Argentina. 50p, Germany. 64p, France. 72p, Brazil.

2006, June 6	**Litho.**	**Perf. 14½**		
2372	A605	1st multi	1.35	.60
a.		Sheet of 20 + 20 labels	27.00	
2373	A605	42p multi	1.70	.85
2374	A605	44p multi	1.75	.90
2375	A605	50p multi	2.00	1.00
2376	A605	64p multi	2.50	1.25
2377	A605	72p multi	2.90	1.40
		Nos. 2372-2377 (6)	12.20	6.00

No. 2372 sold for 32p on day of issue. No.2372a sold for £6.95.

Modern Architecture A606

Designs: 1st, 30 St. Mary Axe, London, designed by Sir Norman Foster. 42p, Maggie's Center, Dundee, designed by Frank Gehry. 44p, Selfridges, Birmingham, designed by Future Systems. 50p, Downland Gridshell, Chichester, by Edward Cullinan. 64p, An Turas, Isle of Tiree, by Sutherland Hussey Architects. 72p, The Deep Hull, by Terry Farrell and Partners.

2006, June 20			**Photo.**	
2378	A606	1st multi	1.35	.60
2379	A606	42p multi	1.70	.85
2380	A606	44p multi	1.75	.90
2381	A606	50p multi	2.00	1.00
2382	A606	64p multi	2.50	1.40
2383	A606	72p multi	2.90	1.50
		Nos. 2378-2383 (6)	12.20	6.25

No. 2378 sold for 32p on day of issue.

National Portrait Gallery, 150th Anniv. — A607

Famous Britons in art from National Portrait Gallery: No. 2384, Sir Winston Churchill, by Walter Sickert. No. 2385, Self-portrait of Sir Joshua Reynolds. No. 2386, T. S. Eliot, by Patrick Heron. No. 2387, Emmeline Pankhurst, by Georgina Brakenbury. No. 2388, Virginia Woolf, photograph by George Beresford. No. 2389, Sir Walter Scott, bust by Sir Francis Chantry. No. 2390, Mary Seacole, by Albert Challen. No. 2391, William Shakespeare, by John Taylor. No. 2392, Dame Cicely Saunders, by Catherine Goodman. No. 2393, Charles Darwin, by John Collier.

2006, July 18			**Perf. 14¼**	
2384	A607	1st multi	1.35	.60
2385	A607	1st multi	1.35	.60
2386	A607	1st multi	1.35	.60
2387	A607	1st multi	1.35	.60
2388	A607	1st multi	1.35	.60
2389	A607	1st multi	1.35	.60
2390	A607	1st multi	1.35	.60
2391	A607	1st multi	1.35	.60
2392	A607	1st multi	1.35	.60
2393	A607	1st multi	1.35	.60
a.		Block of 10, #2384-2393	13.50	7.50
		Nos. 2384-2393 (10)	13.50	6.00

Nos. 2384-2393 each sold for 32p on day of issue.

Recipients of Victoria Cross A608

Designs: No. 2394, Corporal Agansing Rai. No. 2395, Boy Seaman First Class Jack Cornwell. No. 2396, Midshipman Charles Lucas. No. 2397, Captain Noel Chavasse. No. 2398, Captain Albert Ball. No. 2399, Captain Charles Upham.

2006, Sept. 21	**Litho.**	**Perf. 14¼x14**		
2394	A608	1st multi	1.35	.60
2395	A608	1st multi	1.35	.60
a.		Horiz. pair, #2394-2395	2.70	1.50
2396	A608	64p multi	2.50	1.40
2397	A608	64p multi	2.50	1.40
a.		Horiz. pair, #2396-2397	5.00	3.25
2398	A608	72p multi	2.90	1.00
a.		Booklet pane, #2394, 2396, 2398 (BK180)	6.75	—
2399	A608	72p multi	2.90	1.50
a.		Horiz. pair, #2398-2399	5.75	3.75
b.		Booklet pane #2395, 2397, 2399 (BK180)	6.75	—
c.		Souvenir sheet, #1331a, 2394-2399	14.00	8.00
		Nos. 2394-2399 (6)	13.50	6.50

Nos. 2394-2395 each sold for 32p on day of issue.

Musicians
and Dancers
A609

Designs: 1st, Sitar player and dancer. 42p, Guitarist and drummer. 50p, Violinist and harpist. 72p, Saxophone player and guitarist. £1.19, Maracas player and dancers.

2006, Oct. 3		Perf. 14¼x14½	
2400	A609	1st multi	1.35	.60
2401	A609	42p multi	1.70	.90
2402	A609	50p multi	2.00	1.05
2403	A609	72p multi	2.90	1.50
2404	A609	£1.19 multi	4.75	2.25
	Nos. 2400-2404 (5)		12.70	6.30

Europa (#2402).

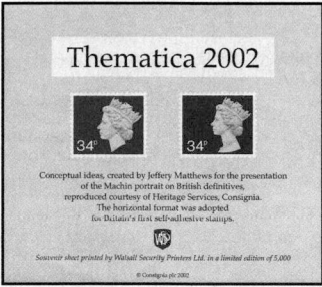

The gummed souvenir sheets shown above, created for the 2002 and 2006 Thematica stamp shows, contain invalid imperforate stamps with simulated perforations that were never issued by Royal Mail. The stamps on these sheets have no obliterators.

The gummed 2005 Thematica sheet reproduces reduced versions of Nos. 440, 441, 683, 1040 and 1796. These reproduced images lack obliterators, and are also invalid for postage.

Gummed Thematica sheets for other years exist, each showing reproductions of other stamps with obliterations to invalidate the images.

"New Baby"
A610

"Best Wishes"
A611

"Thank You"
A612

Balloons
A613

Fireworks
A614

Flowers,
Butterflies
and
Champagne
Bottle
A615

Die Cut Perf. 14¾x14¼

2006, Oct. 17			Photo.	
Self-Adhesive				
2405	A610	1st multi	1.50	.80
2406	A611	1st multi	1.50	.80
2407	A612	1st multi	1.50	.80
2408	A613	1st multi	1.50	.80
2409	A614	1st multi	1.50	.80
2410	A615	1st multi	1.50	.80
a.	Booklet pane, #2405-2410		10.00	
b.	Sheet, 3 each #2406-2409, 4 each #2405, 2410 + 20 labels, litho.		32.50	
	Nos. 2405-2410 (6)		9.00	4.80

Nos. 2405-2410 each sold for 32p on day of issue. No. 2410b sold for £6.95.
See Nos. 2546-2548, 2794.

Christmas
A616   A617

Designs: Nos. 2411a, 2411c, 2412, 2414, Snowman. Nos. 2411b, 2411d, 2413, 2415, Santa Claus. Nos. 2411e, 2416, Reindeer. Nos. 2411f, 2417, Christmas tree.

2006, Nov. 7		Photo.	Perf. 14¾x14	
2411		Sheet of 6	13.00	6.50
a.	A616	2nd multi	.95	.45
b.	A616	1st multi	1.35	.60
c.	A617	2nd Large multi	1.50	.80
d.	A617	1st Large multi	1.75	.90
e.	A616	72p multi	2.90	1.50
f.	A616	£1.19 multi	4.75	2.40

Self-Adhesive
Die Cut Perf. 14¾x14

2412	A616	2nd multi	.95	.25
a.	Booklet pane of 12		11.50	
2413	A616	1st multi	1.35	.25
a.	Booklet pane of 12		16.00	
b.	Sheet, 10 each #2412-2413, + 20 labels, litho.		24.00	—
2414	A617	2nd Large multi	1.50	.90
2415	A617	1st Large multi	1.75	.90
2416	A616	72p multi	2.90	1.50
2417	A616	£1.19 multi	4.75	2.40
	Nos. 2412-2417 (6)		13.20	6.10

On day of issue, Nos. 2411a and 2412 each sold for 23p, Nos. 2411b and 2413 each sold for 32p, Nos. 2411c and 2414 each sold for 37p, and Nos. 2411d and 2415 each sold for 44p. No. 2413b sold for £6.

Souvenir Sheet

Battle of the Somme, 90th
Anniv. — A618

Perf. 14½x14¼ (#2418a), 14¾x14 Syncopated

2006, Nov. 9			Photo.	
2418	A618	Sheet of 5	13.00	6.50
a.		1st Poppies	1.35	.60
b.		Sheet of 20 #2418a + 20 labels, litho.	27.50	
c.		Single stamp, litho. (#2614b) ('08)	1.10	.55

No. 2418 contains #2418a, England #13, Northern Ireland #24, Scotland #27 and Wales & Monmouthshire #27. No. 2418a sold for 32p on day of issue. No. 2418b sold for £6.95.
No. 2418c issued 11/6/08. It sold for 36p on day of issue.

Souvenir Sheet

Heritage of Scotland — A619

No. 2419: a, National flag (Scotland type A5). b, St. Andrew (58x22mm). c, Edinburgh Castle (58x22mm).

Perf. 14¾x14 Syncopated, 14¾x14 (#2419b, 2419c)

2006, Nov. 30			Photo.	
2419	A619	Sheet of 4, #2419a-2419c, Scotland #21	9.50	6.50
a.		1st multi	1.50	.75
b.-c.		72p Either single	3.25	1.75

No. 2419a sold for 32p on day of issue.

Beatles Memorabilia — A620

Beatles Album
Covers
A621

No. 2420: a, Toy guitar, button. b, Lunch box, buttons. c, 45RPM record of "Love Me Do." d, Tray picturing the Beatles, buttons.
No. 2421, "With The Beatles." No. 2422, "Sgt. Pepper's Lonely Hearts Club Band." No. 2423, "Help!" No. 2424, "Abbey Road." No. 2425, "Let It Be." No. 2426, "Revolver."

2007, Jan. 9		Litho.	Perf. 14	
2420	A620	Sheet of 4	5.50	3.00
a.-d.		1st Any single	1.35	.60

Self-Adhesive
Photo.
Die Cut Perf. 13x13¾

2421	A621	1st multi	1.35	.60
2422	A621	1st multi	1.35	.60
2423	A621	64p multi	2.50	1.25
2424	A621	64p multi	2.50	1.25
2425	A621	72p multi	3.00	1.50
2426	A621	72p multi	3.00	1.50
	Nos. 2421-2426 (6)		13.70	6.70

Nos. 2420a-2420d, 2421-2422 each sold for 32p on day of issue.

Love Type of 2005
Serpentine Die Cut 14¾x14 Syncopated

2007-08			Photo.	
Self-Adhesive				
Booklet Stamp				
2427	A593	1st multi	10.00	.65
a.	Booklet pane, #2427, 5 #MH380		15.00	
b.	Booklet pane, 2 #2427, 4 #MH300 + 3 labels		8.25	
c.	As #2427, litho. (from 2538a)		1.50	1.50

No. 2427 sold for 32p on day of issue. Compare with No. 2316 which is not syncopated.
Issued: Nos. 2427, 2427a, 1/16/07. Nos. 2427b, 2427c, 1/15/08.
No. 2427c had a franking value of 34p on day of issue.

Marine
Life — A622

Designs: No. 2428, Moon jellyfish. No. 2429, Common starfish. No. 2430, Beadlet anemone. No. 2431, Bass. No. 2432, Thornback ray. No. 2433, Lesser octopus. No. 2434, Common mussels. No. 2435, Gray seal. No. 2436, Shore crab. No. 2437, Common sun star.

2007, Feb. 1		Litho.	Perf. 14½	
2428	A622	1st multi	1.35	.65
2429	A622	1st multi	1.35	.65
2430	A622	1st multi	1.35	.65
2431	A622	1st multi	1.35	.65
2432	A622	1st multi	1.35	.65
2433	A622	1st multi	1.35	.65
2434	A622	1st multi	1.35	.65
2435	A622	1st multi	1.35	.65
2436	A622	1st multi	1.35	.65
2437	A622	1st multi	1.35	.65
a.	Block of 10, #2428-2437		13.50	6.50

Nos. 2428-2437 each sold for 32p on day of issue.

Astronomical
Objects — A623

Designs: No. 2438, Saturen Nebula (C55). No. 2439, Eskimo Nebula (C39). No. 2440, Cat's Eye Nebula (C6). No. 2441, Helix Nebula (C63). No. 2442, Flaming Star Nebula (C31). No. 2443, Spindle Galaxy (C53).

Serpentine Die Cut 14¼x14

2007, Feb. 13			Photo.	
2438	A623	1st multi	1.35	.65
2439	A623	1st multi	1.35	.65
2440	A623	50p multi	2.00	1.00
2441	A623	50p multi	2.00	1.00
2442	A623	72p multi	3.00	1.50
2443	A623	72p multi	3.00	1.50
	Nos. 2438-2443 (6)		12.70	6.30

Nos. 2438-2439 each sold for 32p on day of issue.

World of
Invention
A624

Designs: Nos. 2444, 2450, Man thinking about bridge. Nos. 2445, 2451, Locomotive and tracks. Nos. 2446, 2452, People using telephones, maps of Great Britain, Ireland and Australia. Nos. 2447, 2453, Television camera, man with microphone, man watching television. Nos. 2448, 2454, Man at computer with cord in large ball. Nos. 2449, 2455, Man and woman travelers on cratered planet.

2007, Mar. 1		Photo.	Perf. 14½x14	
2444	A624	1st multi	1.75	.65
2445	A624	1st multi	1.75	.65
2446	A624	64p multi	3.00	1.40
2447	A624	64p multi	3.00	1.40
a.	Booklet pane, #2444-2447 (BK181)		9.75	—
2448	A624	72p multi	5.00	2.00
2449	A624	72p multi	5.00	2.00
a.	Souvenir sheet, #2444-2449		19.50	10.00
b.	Booklet pane, #2444-2445, 2448-2449		11.00	—
	Nos. 2444-2449 (6)		19.50	8.10

Self-Adhesive
Die Cut Perf. 14½x14

2450	A624	1st multi	1.35	.60
2451	A624	1st multi	1.35	.60
2452	A624	64p multi	2.50	1.25
2453	A624	64p multi	2.50	1.25
2454	A624	72p multi	3.00	1.50
2455	A624	72p multi	3.00	1.50
	Nos. 2450-2455 (6)		13.70	6.70

Nos. 2444-2445, 2450-2451 each sold for 32p on day of issue.

Abolition of the
Slave Trade,
Bicent. — A625

Designs: No. 2456, William Wilberforce (1759-1833), abolitionist leader in Parliament, and poster. No. 2457, Olaudah Equiano (c. 1750-97), freed slave and abolitionist writer, and map. No. 2458, Granville Sharp (1735-1813), abolitionist, and ship. No. 2459, Thomas Clarkson (1760-1846), abolitionist and diagram of slaves in slave ship. No. 2460, Hannah More (1745-1833), religious writer, and illustration from Cheap Repository Tracts. No. 2461, Ignatius Sancho (c. 1729-80), abolitionist and actor, poster for performance by Sancho.

2007, Mar. 22   **Litho.**   **Perf. 14¼**

2456	A625	1st multi	1.25	.60
2457	A625	1st multi	1.25	.60
a.		Horiz. pair, #2456-2457	2.50	1.20
2458	A625	50p multi	2.00	1.00
2459	A625	50p multi	2.00	1.00
a.		Horiz. pair, #2458-2459	4.00	2.00
2460	A625	72p multi	3.00	1.50
2461	A625	72p multi	3.00	1.50
a.		Horiz. pair, #2460-2461	6.00	3.00
		Nos. 2456-2461 (6)	12.50	6.20

Nos. 2456-2457 each sold for 32p on day of issue.

Souvenir Sheet

Heritage of England — A626

No. 2462: a, English flag (18x22mm). b, St. George slaying dragon (59x22mm). c, Parliament (59x22mm).

**Perf. 14 Syncopated, 14¾x14
(#2462b, 2642c)**

2007, Apr. 23   **Photo.**

2462	A626	Sheet of 4, #2462a-2462c, England #7	9.00	4.50
a.		1st multi	1.40	.70
b.-c.		78p Either single	3.00	1.50

On day of issue, No. 2462a and England #7 sold for 34p.

Seaside
Resort
Scenes
A627

Designs: 1st, Giant ice cream cone. 46p, Sand castle. 48p, Carousel horses. 54p, Beach cabins. 69p, Beach chairs. 78p, Hitched donkeys.

2007, May 15   **Photo.**   **Perf. 14½**

2463	A627	1st multi	1.40	.70
2464	A627	46p multi	1.90	.95
2465	A627	48p multi	2.00	1.00
2466	A627	54p multi	2.10	1.10
2467	A627	69p multi	2.75	1.40
2468	A627	78p multi	3.25	1.60
		Nos. 2463-2468 (6)	13.40	6.75

No. 2463 sold for 34p on day of issue.
See No. 2573.

Crowned Lion of England — A628

2007, May 17   **Litho.**   **Perf. 14½x14¼**

2469	A628	1st gray bl & dk red + label	2.25	2.25

Souvenir Sheet
Photo.

2470		Sheet, #2470a, 2 each England #6, 15 + label	9.50	9.50
a.		A628 1st bl grn & brt red	1.40	.70

No. 2469 was issued in sheets of 20 stamps + 20 labels that sold for £7.35. No. 2470 sold for £2.38 on day of issue. Nos. 2469 and 2470 each had a franking value of 34p on day of issue.

Souvenir Sheet

Definitive Stamps Designed by Arnold
Machin, 40th Anniv. — A629

Design: No. 2472, Arnold Machin.

**Perf. 14½x14¼ (#2471a-2471b, 2472)
Photo. & Embossed (#2471a-2471b)
2007, June 5**

2471	A629	Sheet, #2471a, 2471b, MH237, MH373	11.50	11.50
a.		1st Arnold Machin	1.40	.70
b.		1st #MH6	1.40	.70
c.		Booklet pane, 2 each #2471a, 2471b (BK182)	5.75	—

Photo.

2472	A629	1st multi + label	1.50	.75

Nos. 2471a and 2471b each sold for 34p on day of issue and were only issued in the souvenir sheet and the booklet pane.

No. 2472, having a franking value of 34p on day of issue, was issued only in sheets of 20 stamps + 20 labels. The sheets sold for £7.35.

Grand
Prix
Race Cars
and
Drivers
A630

Designs: No. 2473, 1957 Vanwall 2.5-liter, Stirling Moss. No. 2474, 1962 BRM P57, Graham Hill. No. 2475, 1963 Lotus 25 Climax, Jim Clark. No. 2476, 1973 Tyrrell 006/2, Jackie Stewart. No. 2477, 1976 McLaren M23, James Hunt. No. 2478, 1986 Williams FW11, Nigel Mansell.

2007, July 3   **Litho.**   **Perf. 14¼x14**

2473	A630	1st multi	1.40	.70
2474	A630	1st multi	1.40	.70
2475	A630	54p multi	2.25	1.10
2476	A630	54p multi	2.25	1.10
2477	A630	78p multi	3.25	1.60
2478	A630	78p multi	3.25	1.60
		Nos. 2473-2478 (6)	13.80	6.80

Nos. 2473 and 2474 each sold for 34p on day of issue.

Publication of
Last Harry Potter
Novel by J. K.
Rowling
A631

Coats of
Arms From
Harry Potter
Novels
A632

Novels: No. 2479, Harry Potter and the Philosopher's Stone. No. 2480, Harry Potter and the Chamber of Secrets. No. 2481, Harry Potter and the Prisoner of Azkaban. No. 2482, Harry Potter and the Goblet of Fire. No. 2483, Harry Potter and the Order of the Phoenix. No. 2484, Harry Potter and the Half-Blood Prince. No. 2485, Harry Potter and the Deathly Hallows.

Arms of: Nos. 2486a, 2487, Gryffindor. Nos. 2486b, 2488, Hufflepuff. Nos. 2486c, 2489, Hogwarts. Nos. 2486d, 2490, Ravenclaw. Nos. 2486e, 2491, Slytherin.

2007, July 17   **Perf. 14x14¼**

2479	A631	1st multi	1.40	.70
2480	A631	1st multi	1.40	.70
2481	A631	1st multi	1.40	.70
2482	A631	1st multi	1.40	.70
2483	A631	1st multi	1.40	.70
2484	A631	1st multi	1.40	.70
2485	A631	1st multi	1.40	.70
a.		Horiz. strip of 7, #2479-2485	9.80	4.90

Souvenir Sheet
Perf. 14¾x14

2486		Sheet of 5	7.00	7.00
a.-e.		A632 1st Any single	1.40	.70

Self-Adhesive
Die Cut Perf. 14¾x14

2487	A632	1st multi + label	2.00	2.00
2488	A632	1st multi + label	2.00	2.00
2489	A632	1st multi + label	2.00	2.00
2490	A632	1st multi + label	2.00	2.00
2491	A632	1st multi + label	2.00	2.00
a.		Vert. strip of 5, #2487-2491, + 5 labels	11.00	
		Nos. 2487-2491 (5)	10.00	10.00

Nos. 2479-2485, 2486a-2486e, each sold for 34p on day of issue. Nos. 2487-2491, having a franking value of 34p on day of issue, were issued in a sheet of 20 stamps + 20 labels that sold for £7.35. Labels could be personalized for an extra fee.

Scouting,
Cent.
A633

Designs: 1st, Scouts around campfire, Scout looking at sky. 46p, Scouts climbing rocks. 48p, Scout planting tree. 54p, Scout learning archery from volunteer. 69p, Scouts and glider. 78p, Nine Scouts.

2007, July 26   **Perf. 14¼x14**

2492	A633	1st multi	1.40	.70
2493	A633	46p multi	1.90	.95
2494	A633	48p multi	2.00	1.00
2495	A633	54p multi	2.25	1.10
2496	A633	69p multi	2.75	1.40
2497	A633	78p multi	3.25	1.60
		Nos. 2492-2497 (6)	13.55	6.75

Europa (#2492, 2494). No. 2492 sold for 34p on day of issue.

Endangered
Birds — A634

2007, Sept. 4   **Litho.**   **Perf. 14½**

2498	A634	1st White-tailed eagle	1.40	.70
2499	A634	1st Bearded tit	1.40	.70
2500	A634	1st Red kite	1.40	.70
2501	A634	1st Cirl bunting	1.40	.70

2502	A634	1st Marsh harrier	1.40	.70
2503	A634	1st Avocet	1.40	.70
2504	A634	1st Bittern	1.40	.70
2505	A634	1st Dartford warbler	1.40	.70
2506	A634	1st Corncrake	1.40	.70
2507	A634	1st Peregrine falcon	1.40	.70
a.		Block of 10, #2498-2507	14.00	7.00

Nos. 2498-2507 each sold for 34p on day of issue.

British Army
Uniforms — A635

Designs: No. 2508, Non-commissioned officer, Royal Military Police, 1999. No. 2509, Tank commander, 5th Royal Tank Regiment, 1944. No. 2510, Observer, Royal Field Artillery, 1917. No. 2511, Rifleman, 95th Rifles, 1813. No. 2512, Grenadier, Royal Regiment of Foot of Ireland, 1704. No. 2513, Trooper, Earl of Oxford's Horse, 1661.

2007, Sept. 20   **Litho.**   **Perf. 14¼**

2508	A635	1st multi	1.40	.70
2509	A635	1st multi	1.40	.70
2510	A635	1st multi	1.40	.70
a.		Horiz. strip of 3, #2508-2510	4.20	2.10
b.		Booklet pane of 3, #2508-2510 (BK183)	4.20	
2511	A635	78p multi	3.25	1.60
2512	A635	78p multi	3.25	1.60
2513	A635	78p multi	3.25	1.60
a.		Horiz. strip of 3, #2511-2513	9.75	4.80
b.		Booklet pane of 3, #2511-2513 (BK183)	9.75	—
		Nos. 2508-2513 (6)	13.95	6.90

Nos. 2508-2510 each sold for 34p on day of sale.

Wedding
of Queen
Elizabeth II
and Prince
Philip, 60th
Anniv.
A636

Royal Family — A637

Various photographs of couple from: No. 2514, 2006. No. 2515, 1997. No. 2516, 1980. No. 2517, 1969. No. 2518, 1961. No. 2519, 1947.

No. 2520: a, Royal family, log and flowers (35x35mm). b, Queen Elizabeth II and Prince Philip (40x30mm). c, Royal family, baby carriage (41x30mm). d, Queen Elizabeth II, Prince Philip, Princess Anne and Prince Charles (27x38mm).

2007, Oct. 26   **Litho.**   **Perf. 14¼x14**

2514	A636	1st black	1.40	.70
2515	A636	1st black	1.40	.70
a.		Horiz. pair, #2514-2515	2.80	1.40
2516	A636	54p black	2.25	1.10
2517	A636	54p black	2.25	1.10
a.		Horiz. pair, #2516-2517	4.50	2.10
2518	A636	78p black	3.25	1.60
2519	A636	78p black	3.25	1.60
a.		Horiz. pair, #2518-2519	6.50	3.20
		Nos. 2514-2519 (6)	13.80	6.80

Souvenir Sheet
Self-Adhesive

2520	A637	Sheet of 4	9.00	
a.		1st multi, die cut perf. 14½	1.40	.70
b.		1st multi, die cut perf. 14½x14¼	1.40	.70
c.		69p multi, die cut perf. 14¼x14	2.75	1.40
d.		78p multi, die cut perf. 14¼	3.25	1.60

Nos. 2514-2515, 2520a and 2520b each sold for 34p on day of sale.

Madonna and Child, by William Dyce
A638

Madonna of Humility, by Lippo di Dalmasio
A639

Die Cut Perf. 14¾x14 Syncopated
2007, Nov. 6   Photo.
Self-Adhesive
| 2521 | A638 | 2nd multi | 1.00 | .50 |
| 2522 | A639 | 1st multi | 1.50 | .75 |

On day of issue, No. 2521 sold for 24p; No. 2522 for 34p.

Christmas
A640   A641

Angels with banners inscribed: Nos. 2523a, 2523c, 2524, 2526, Peace. Nos. 2523b, 2523d, 2525, 2527, Goodwill. Nos. 2523e, 2528, Joy. Nos. 2523f, 2529, Glory.

2007, Nov. 6   Photo.   Perf. 14¾x14
2523		Sheet of 6	15.00	15.00
a.		A640 2nd multi	1.00	.50
b.		A640 1st multi	1.50	.75
c.		A641 2nd Large multi	1.75	.85
d.		A641 1st Large multi	2.00	1.00
e.		A640 78p multi	3.25	1.60
f.		A640 £1.24 multi	5.25	2.60

Self-Adhesive
Die Cut Perf. 14¾x14
2524	A640	2nd multi	1.00	.50
a.		Booklet pane of 12	12.00	
b.		Sheet of 20 + 20 labels, litho.	35.00	
2525	A640	1st multi	1.50	.75
a.		Booklet pane of 12	18.00	
b.		Sheet of 20 + 20 labels, litho.	57.50	
2526	A641	2nd Large multi	1.75	.85
2527	A641	1st Large multi	2.00	1.00
2528	A640	78p multi	3.25	1.60
a.		Sheet, 8 each #2524-2525, 4 #2528, + 20 labels, litho.	35.00	
b.		Sheet of 10 + 10 labels, litho.	57.50	
2529	A640	£1.24 multi	5.25	2.60
		Nos. 2524-2529 (6)	14.75	7.30

On day of issue, Nos. 2523a and 2524 sold for 24p, Nos. 2523b and 2425 sold for 34p, Nos. 2523c and 2426 sold for 40p, and Nos. 2523d and 2427 sold for 48p. No. 2528a sold for 18.30, No. 2524b sold for 18.50, Nos. 2525b and 2528b each sold for £13.50. Labels on Nos. 2524b, 2525b, and 2528b were personalizable.

Poppy and Soldiers
A642

2007, Nov. 8   Litho.   Perf. 14½x14¼
| 2530 | A642 | 1st multi | 2.25 | .90 |
| a. | | Souvenir sheet of 5 | 14.50 | 14.50 |

Battle of Passchendaele, 90th anniv. No. 2530a contains #2530, England #15, Northern Ireland #26, Scotland #29, and Wales & Monmouthshire #30. No. 2530 was also printed in a sheet of 20 + 5 labels that sold for £7.35, and a limited-quantity privately-contracted sheet of 10 + 10 labels, that sold for £28.50.

Book Covers of James Bond Novels by Ian Fleming — A643

Designs: No. 2531, Casino Royale. No. 2532, Doctor No. No. 2533, Goldfinger. No. 2534, Diamonds Are Forever. No. 2535, For Your Eyes Only. No. 2536, From Russia, with Love.
Illustration reduced.

2008, Jan. 8   Litho.   Perf. 14¾x14¼
2531	A643	1st multi	1.40	.70
2532	A643	1st multi	1.40	.70
2533	A643	54p multi	2.10	1.10
2534	A643	54p multi	2.10	1.10
2535	A643	78p multi	3.25	1.60
a.		Booklet pane of 3, #2531, 2533, 2535 (BK184)	6.75	
2536	A643	78p multi	3.25	1.60
a.		Miniature sheet of 6, #2531-2536	13.50	13.50
b.		Booklet pane of 3, #2532, 2534, 2536 (BK184)	6.75	—
		Nos. 2531-2536 (6)	13.50	6.80

On day of issue, Nos. 2531-2532 each sold for 34p.

Hello and Flag Types of 2005
Die Cut Perf 14¾x14 Syncopated
2008, Jan. 15   Litho.
Self-Adhesive
| 2537 | A592 | 1st Hello | 1.50 | 1.50 |
| a. | | Sheet of 20 + 20 labels | 25.00 | |

Issued: No. 2537a, 5/8/10. 2537a sold for £8.50. Labels could not be personalized.

| 2538 | A594 | 1st Flag | 1.50 | 1.50 |
| a. | | Sheet, 8 #2427c, 6 each #2537-2538, + 20 labels | 30.00 | |

No. 2538a sold for £7.35. Nos. 2537-2538 each had a franking value of 34p on day of issue.

Working Dogs — A644

Designs: 1st, Assistance dog. 46p, Mountain rescue dog. 48p, Police dog. 54p, Customs dog. 69p, Sheepdog. 78p, Guide dog.

2008, Feb. 5   Litho.   Perf. 14¼x14½
2539	A644	1st multi	1.40	.70
2540	A644	46p multi	1.75	.90
2541	A644	48p multi	1.90	.95
2542	A644	54p multi	2.10	1.10
2543	A644	69p multi	2.75	1.40
2544	A644	78p multi	3.25	1.60
		Nos. 2539-2544 (6)	13.15	6.65

No. 2539 sold for 34p on day of issue. Europa (#2539).

Types of 2005-06
Die Cut Perf. 14¾x14 Syncopated
2008, Feb. 28   Litho.
Booklet Stamps
Self-Adhesive
2545	A591	1st multi	1.40	.70
2546	A613	1st multi	1.40	.70
2547	A614	1st multi	1.40	.70
2548	A615	1st multi	1.40	.70
a.		Booklet pane of 6, #2537-2538, 2545-2548	8.50	

On day of issue, Nos. 2545-2548 each sold for 34p.

British Royalty and History — A645

Designs: No. 2549, King Henry IV. No. 2550, King Henry V. No. 2551, King Henry VI. No. 2552, King Edward IV. No. 2553, King Edward V. No. 2554, King Richard III.
No. 2555: a, Owen Glendower (Owain Glyn Dwr), Welsh rebel. b, Battle of Agincourt. c, Battle of Tewkesbury. d, William Caxton, first English printer.

2008, Feb. 28   Litho.   Perf. 14¼
2549	A645	1st multi	1.40	.70
2550	A645	1st multi	1.40	.70
2551	A645	54p multi	2.25	1.10
2552	A645	54p multi	2.25	1.10
2553	A645	69p multi	2.75	1.40
2554	A645	69p multi	2.75	1.40
		Nos. 2549-2554 (6)	12.80	6.40

Souvenir Sheet
2555		Sheet of 4	9.50	9.50
a.-b.		A645 1st Either single	1.40	.70
c.-d.		A645 78p Either single	3.25	1.60

On day of issue, Nos. 2549, 2550, 2555a and 2555b each sold for 34p.
See Nos. 2653-2659, 2767-2774, 2807-2814.

Souvenir Sheet

Heritage of Northern Ireland — A646

No. 2556: a, Carrickfergus Castle (18x21mm). b, Giant's Causeway, ocean and sky (18x21mm). c, St. Patrick (57x21mm). d, Queen's Bridge and Friendship Beacon, Belfast (57x21mm).

Perf. 14¾x14¼ Syncopated, 14¾x14¼ (78p)
2008, Mar. 11   Litho.
2556	A646	Sheet of 4	9.50	9.50
a.-b.		1st Either single	1.40	.70
c.-d.		78p Either single	3.25	1.60

On day of issue Nos. 2556a-2556b each sold for 34p.

Rescue at Sea
A647

Sea rescuers in action near: 1st, Barra. 46p, Appledore. 48p, Portland. 54p, St. Ives. 69p, Lee-on-Solent. 78p, Tenby.

Perf. 14¼x14 Syncopated
2008, Mar. 13
2557	A647	1st multi	1.40	.70
2558	A647	46p multi	1.90	.95
2559	A647	48p multi	2.00	1.00
2560	A647	54p multi	2.25	1.10
2561	A647	69p multi	2.75	1.40
2562	A647	78p multi	3.25	1.60
		Nos. 2557-2562 (6)	13.55	6.75

No. 2557 sold for 34p on day of issue.

Endangered Insects
A648

Designs: No. 2563, Adonis blue butterfly. No. 2564, Southern damselfly. No. 2565, Red-barbed ant. No. 2566, Barberry carpet moth. No. 2567, Stag beetle. No. 2568, Hazel pot beetle. No. 2569, Field cricket. No. 2570, Silver-spotted skipper. No. 2571, Purbeck mason wasp. No. 2572, Noble chafer.

2008, Apr. 15   Litho.   Perf. 14½
2563	A648	1st multi	1.50	.75
2564	A648	1st multi	1.50	.75
2565	A648	1st multi	1.50	.75
2566	A648	1st multi	1.50	.75
2567	A648	1st multi	1.50	.75
2568	A648	1st multi	1.50	.75
2569	A648	1st multi	1.50	.75
2570	A648	1st multi	1.50	.75
2571	A648	1st multi	1.50	.75
2572	A648	1st multi	1.50	.75
a.		Block of 10, #2563-2572	15.00	7.50

Nos. 2563-2572 each sold for 36p on day of issue.

Seaside Resorts Type of 2007
Die Cut Perf. 14½
2008, May 13   Photo.
Booklet Stamp
Self-Adhesive
| 2573 | A627 | 1st Like #2463 | 3.50 | 1.00 |
| a. | | Booklet pane, 2 #2573, 4 #MH300 | 12.00 | |

No. 2573 sold for 36p on day of issue.

A649

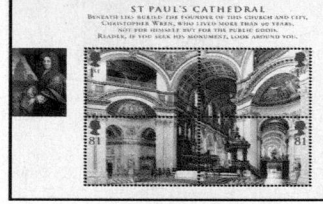
Cathedrals — A650

Designs: No. 2574, Lichfield Cathedral. 48p, Belfast Cathedral. 50p, Gloucester Cathedral. 56p, St. David's Cathedral, Wales. 72p, Westminster Cathedral. 81p, St. Magnus Cathedral, Orkney.
No. 2580 — St. Paul's Cathedral: a, Ceiling, denomination at UL. b, Ceiling, denomination at UR. c, Floor, denomination at UL. d, Floor, denomination at UR.

2008, May 13   Litho.   Perf. 14¼
2574	A649	1st black	1.40	.70
2575	A649	48p black	1.90	.95
2576	A649	50p black	2.00	1.00
2577	A649	56p black	2.25	1.10
2578	A649	72p black	3.00	1.50
2579	A649	81p black	3.25	1.60
		Nos. 2574-2579 (6)	13.80	6.85

Souvenir Sheet
2580	A650	Sheet of 4	9.50	9.50
a.-b.		1st Either single	1.40	.70
c.-d.		81p Either single	3.25	1.60

Nos. 2574, 2580a-2580b each sold for 36p on day of issue.

Posters of British Comedy and Horror Films
A651

Poster for: 1st, Carry On Sergeant. 48p, Dracula. 50p, Carry On Cleo. 56p, The Curse of Frankenstein. 72p, Carry On Screaming. 81p, The Mummy.

2008, June 10   Litho.   Perf. 13¾x14
2581	A651	1st multi	1.40	.70
2582	A651	48p multi	1.90	.95
2583	A651	50p multi	2.00	1.00
2584	A651	56p multi	2.25	1.10
2585	A651	72p multi	3.00	1.50
2586	A651	81p multi	3.25	1.60
		Nos. 2581-2586 (6)	13.80	6.85

No. 2581 sold for 36p on day of issue.

First Powered Flight in Great Britain, Cent.
A652

Air displays: 1st, Red Arrow aerobatic team. 48p, Royal Air Force Falcons parachuting squad. 50p, Boy watching airplanes in formation. 56p, Avro Vulcans and Avro 707s in flight. 72p, Parachutist Robert Wyndham on wing of Avro 504 biplane. 81p, Blériot airplane and air race tower.

2008, July 17　Photo.　*Perf. 14¼x14*

2587	A652	1st multi	1.50	.75
a.		Sheet of 20 + 17 labels, litho.	31.00	—
b.		Litho.	1.25	.65
c.		Booklet pane of 4, 2 each		
		#1758a, 2587b (BK185)	4.00	—
2588	A652	48p multi	1.90	.95
2589	A652	50p multi	2.00	1.00
2590	A652	56p multi	2.25	1.10
2591	A652	72p multi	3.00	1.50
2592	A652	81p multi	3.25	1.60
		Nos. 2587-2592 (6)	13.90	6.90

No. 2587 sold for 36p on day of issue. No. 2587a sold for £7.75. Labels could not be personalized.
No. 2587c issued 9/18.

Souvenir Sheet

2008 Olympic Games, Beijing and 2012 Olympic Games, London — A653

No. 2593: a, National Stadium, Beijing. b, London Eye. c, Tower of London. d, Corner Tower, Forbidden City, Beijing.

Litho. & Silk Screened

2008, Aug. 22　*Perf. 14½*

2593	A653	Sheet of 4	5.75	5.75
a.-d.		1st Any single	1.40	.70

On day of issue Nos. 2593a-2593d each sold for 36p.

Royal Air Force Uniforms — A654

Designs: No. 2594, Drum major, Royal Air Force Central Band, 2007. No. 2595, Helicopter rescue winchman, 1984. No. 2596, Hawker Hunter pilot, 1951. No. 2597, Lancaster air gunner, 1944. No. 2598, Plotter, Women's Army Air Force, 1940. No. 2599, Pilot, 1918.

2008, Sept. 18　Litho.　*Perf. 14¼*

2594	A654	1st multi	1.25	.65
2595	A654	1st multi	1.25	.65
2596	A654	1st multi	1.25	.65
a.		Horiz. strip of 3, #2594-2596	3.75	2.00
b.		Booklet pane of 3, #2594-2596 (BK185)	3.75	—
2597	A654	81p multi	3.00	1.50
2598	A654	81p multi	3.00	1.50
2599	A654	81p multi	3.00	1.50
a.		Horiz. strip of 3, #2597-2599	9.00	4.50
b.		Booklet pane of 3, #2597-2599 (BK185)	9.00	—
		Nos. 2594-2599 (6)	12.75	6.45

Nos. 2594-2596 each sold for 36p on day of issue.

Miniature Sheet

Country Definitive Stamps, 50th Anniv. — A655

Perf. 14¾x14 Syncopated

2008, Sept. 29　Photo.

Buff Paper

2600	A655	Sheet of 9 + label	11.50	6.00
a.		1st Wales & Monmouthshire Type A1	1.25	.65
b.		1st Scotland Type A1	1.25	.65
c.		1st Wales & Monmouthshire Type A3	1.25	.65
d.		1st Scotland Type A3	1.25	.65
e.		1st Northern Ireland Type A1	1.25	.65
f.		1st Wales & Monmouthshire Type A2	1.25	.65
g.		1st Scotland Type A2	1.25	.65

h.		1st Northern Ireland Type A2	1.25	.65
i.		1st Northern Ireland Type A3	1.25	.65
j.		As #2600e, litho., white paper	1.25	.65
k.		As #2600i, litho., white paper	1.25	.65
l.		As #2600h, litho., white paper	1.25	.65
m.		As #2600a, litho., white paper	1.25	.65
n.		As #2600c, litho., white paper	1.25	.65
o.		As #2600f, litho., white paper	1.25	.65
p.		As #2600b, litho., white paper	1.25	.65
q.		As #2600d, litho., white paper	1.25	.65
r.		As #2600g, litho., white paper	1.25	.65
s.		Booklet pane of 9, #2600j-2600r (BK186)	11.50	—
t.		Booklet pane of 6, #2600p-2600r, 3 Scotland #21a (BK186)		7.50
u.		Booklet pane of 6, #2600j-2600l, 3 Northern Ireland #18a (BK186)		7.50
v.		Booklet pane of 6, #2600m-2600o, 3 Wales & Monmouthshire #21b (BK186)		7.50

Nos. 2600a-2600r each sold for 36p on day of issue.

Famous Women A656

Designs: 1st, Millicent Garrett Fawcett (1847-1929), suffragist. 48p, Elizabeth Garrett Anderson (1836-1917), first female physician in Britain. 50p, Marie Stopes (1880-1958), birth control advocate. 56p, Eleanor Rathbone (1872-1946), politician and advocate for family allowance. 72p, Claudia Jones (1915-64), civil rights activist. 81p, Barbara Castle (1910-2002), politician and advocate for equal pay for women.

Perf. 14¼x14½

2008, Oct. 14　　　　Photo.

2601	A656	1st multi	1.25	.60
2602	A656	48p multi	1.60	.80
2603	A656	50p multi	1.60	.80
2604	A656	56p multi	1.90	.95
2605	A656	72p multi	2.40	1.25
2606	A656	81p multi	2.60	1.40
		Nos. 2601-2606 (6)	11.35	5.80

On day of issue, No. 2601 sold for 36p.

Christmas

A657　　　　　　　A658

Pantomime actors: Nos. 2607a, 2607c, 2608, 2610, Ugly sisters from Cinderella. Nos. 2607b, 2607e, 2609, 2612, Genie from Aladdin. 50p, Captain Hook from Peter Pan. 81p, Wicked queen from Snow White.

2008, Nov. 4　Photo.　*Perf. 14¾x14*

2607		Sheet of 6	9.25	9.25
a.		A657 2nd multi	.85	.40
b.		A657 1st multi	1.10	.55
c.		A658 2nd Large multi	1.40	.70
d.		A657 50p multi	1.60	.80
e.		A658 1st Large multi	1.60	.80
f.		A657 81p multi	2.60	1.40

Self-Adhesive

Die Cut Perf. 14¾x14 Syncopated

2608	A657	2nd multi	.85	.40
a.		Booklet pane of 12	10.50	—
b.		Litho. + label	.90	.90
2609	A657	1st multi	1.10	.55
a.		Booklet pane of 12	13.50	—
b.		Litho. + label	1.25	1.25
2610	A658	2nd Large multi	1.40	.70
2611	A657	50p multi	1.60	.80
2612	A658	1st Large multi	1.60	.80
2613	A657	81p multi	2.60	1.40
a.		Litho. + label	2.75	2.75
b.		Sheet of 20, 8 each #2608b, 2609b, 4 #2613a + 20 labels	32.50	—
		Nos. 2608-2613 (6)	9.15	4.65

On day of issue, the franking value of Nos. 2607a, 2608, and 2608b was 27p, and that of Nos. 2607b, 2609 and 2609b was 36p. On day of issue, Nos. 2607c and 2610 sold for 42p, and Nos. 2607e and 2612 sold for 52p. No. 2613b sold for £8.85. Labels could not be personalized.

No. 2608 was also printed in sheets of 20 stamps + 20 labels that could be personalized. No. 2609b was also printed in sheets of 10 stamps + 10 labels and 20 stamps + 20 labels that could be personalized. No. 2613a was also available in a sheet of 10 stamps + 10 labels that could be personalized.

Poppy With Soldier's Face — A659

2008, Nov. 6　Litho.　*Perf. 14½x14¼*

2614	A659	1st multi	2.25	.75
a.		Souvenir sheet of 5	11.50	11.50
b.		Horiz. strip, #2418c, 2530, 2614	3.75	2.50

End of World War I, 90th anniv. On day of issue, No. 2614 sold for 36p. No. 2614a contains 2614, England #18, Northern Ireland #29, Scotland #32, and Wales & Monmouthshire #32. No. 2614 also was printed in a sheet of 20 + 5 labels that sold for £7.75, and in a series of limited-quantity privately contracted sheets of 10 + 10 labels that sold for various prices.

British Design A660

Designs: No. 2615, Supermarine Spitfire, designed by R. J. Mitchell. No. 2616, Miniskirt, designed by Mary Quant. No. 2617, Mini Cooper, designed by Sir Alec Issigonis. No. 2618, Anglepoise lamp, designed by George Carwardine. No. 2619, Concorde, designed by Aérospatiale-BAC. No. 2620, K2 telephone kiosk, designed by Sir Giles Gilbert Scott. No. 2621, Polypropylene chair, designed by Robin Day. No. 2622, Penguin books, designed by Edward Young. No. 2623, London Underground map, designed by Harry Beck. No. 2624, Routemaster Bus, designed by AAM Durrant.

2009, Jan. 13　Litho.　*Perf. 14½*

2615	A660	1st multi	1.10	.55
a.		Sheet of 20 + 20 labels	26.00	—
2616	A660	1st multi	1.10	.55
2617	A660	1st multi	1.10	.55
a.		Sheet of 20 + 20 labels	24.00	—
2618	A660	1st multi	1.10	.55
2619	A660	1st multi	1.10	.55
a.		Booklet pane of 4, 2 each #2049a, 2619 (BK187)	4.50	—
b.		Sheet of 20 + 20 labels	25.00	—
2620	A660	1st multi	1.10	.55
2621	A660	1st multi	1.10	.55
2622	A660	1st multi	1.10	.55
2623	A660	1st multi	1.10	.55
a.		Booklet pane of 6, #2616, 2618, 2620-2623 (BK187)	6.75	—
2624	A660	1st multi	1.10	.55
a.		Block of 10, #2615-2624	11.00	5.50
b.		Booklet pane of 4, #2615, 2617, 2 #2624 (BK187)	4.50	—

On day of issue, Nos. 2615-2624 each sold for 36p. Nos. 2617a, 2619b sold for £7.74. Labels on No. 2617a, No. 2619b could not be personalized.
Issued: No. 2619b, 3/2.
See Nos. 2640-2644, 2833.
Issued: No. 2615a, 9/15/10. No. 2615a sold for £8.50 and labels could not be personalized.

Miniature Sheet

Robert Burns (1759-96), Poet — A661

No. 2625: a, Man with plow, text, "A Man's a Man for a' that". b, Portrait of Burns by Alexander Naysmith.

Perf. 14½ (#2625a, 2625b), 14¾x14 Syncopated

2009, Jan. 22　　　　Photo.

2625	A661	Sheet of 6, #2625a, 2625b, Scotland #20, 21, 31, 32	9.00	5.00
a.-b.		1st Either single	1.25	.60

On day of issue, Nos. 2625a and 2625b each sold for 36p.

Miniature Sheet

Wildlife and HMS Beagle Map of Galapagos Islands — A662

No. 2626: a, Flightless cormorant. b, Giant tortoise, cactus finch. c, Marine iguana. d, Floreana mockingbird.

2009, Feb. 12　　　　*Perf. 14¼*

2626	A662	Sheet of 4	7.00	3.50
a.-b.		1st Either single	1.10	.55
c.-d.		81p Either single	2.40	1.25
e.		Booklet pane, #2626, litho. (BK188)	7.00	—

On day of issue, Nos. 2626a and 2626b each sold for 36p. No. 2626e has a rouletted label to the left of the sheet.

Charles Darwin (1809-82), Naturalist A663

Designs: Nos. 2627, 2633, Photograph of Darwin. Nos. 2628, 2634, Head of marine iguana (zoology). Nos. 2629, 2635, Heads of finches (ornithology). Nos. 2630, 2636, Island (geology). Nos. 2631, 2637, Bee orchid (botany). Nos. 2632, 2638, Orangutan (anthropology).

2009, Feb. 12　*Perf. 14 Syncopated*

Booklet Stamps (#2627-2632)

2627	A663	1st multi (2632a)	1.25	.75
2628	A663	48p multi (2630a)	1.50	.90
2629	A663	50p multi (2630a)	2.75	1.00
2630	A663	56p multi (2630a)	3.25	1.25
a.		Booklet pane of 3, #2628-2630 (BK188)	9.00	—
2631	A663	72p multi (2632a)	3.50	2.00
2632	A663	81p multi (2632a)	4.25	2.50
a.		Booklet pane of 3, #2627, 2631, 2632 (BK188)	9.50	—
		Nos. 2627-2632 (6)	16.50	8.40

Self-Adhesive

Die Cut Perf. 14 Syncopated

2633	A663	1st multi	1.10	.55
2634	A663	48p multi	1.40	.70
2635	A663	50p multi	1.50	.75
2636	A663	56p multi	1.60	.80
2637	A663	72p multi	2.10	1.10
2638	A663	81p multi	2.40	1.25
		Nos. 2633-2638 (6)	10.10	5.15

On day of issue, Nos. 2627 and 2633 each sold for 36p.

Miniature Sheet

Heritage of Wales — A664

No. 2639: a, Flag of Wales (18x22mm). b, Red dragon (18x21mm). c, St. David (58x22mm). d, Welsh Assembly, Cardiff (58x22mm).

Perf. 14¾x14 Syncopated (#2639a), 14¾x14 (#2639b, 2639c)

2009, Feb. 26　　　　Litho.

2639	A664	Sheet of 4	8.75	5.00
a.-b.		1st Either single	1.25	.60
c.-d.		81p Either single	2.50	1.40

On day of issue, Nos. 2639a and 2639b each sold for 36p.

British Design Types of 2009

Designs: No. 2640, K2 telephone kiosk. No. 2641, Routemaster Bus. No. 2642, Mini Cooper automobile. No. 2643, Concorde. No. 2644, Miniskirt.

2009 Photo. *Die Cut Perf. 14½*
Booklet Stamps
Self-Adhesive

2640	A660	1st multi	2.50	1.00
2641	A660	1st multi	2.50	1.00
a.	Booklet pane, #2640-2641, 4 #MH384a		9.50	
2642	A660	1st multi	2.75	1.25
a.	Booklet pane, 2 #2642, 4 #MH384a		11.00	
2643	A660	1st multi	2.75	1.25
a.	Booklet pane of 6, 2 #2643, 4 #MH384a		11.00	
2644	A660	1st multi	2.75	1.25
a.	Booklet pane of 6, 2 #2644, 4 #MH384a		11.00	

Issued: Nos. 2640, 2641, 2641a, 3/10; Nos. 2642, 2642a, 4/21; Nos. 2643, 2643a, 8/18; Nos. 2644, 2644a, 9/17. On day of issue, Nos. 2640-2641 each sold for 36p; Nos. 2642, 2643, 2644 sold for 39p.

Pioneers of the Industrial Revolution
A665

Designs: No. 2645, Matthew Boulton (1728-1809), steam engine manufacturer. No. 2646, James Watt (1736-1819), steam engine pioneer and inventor. No. 2647, Richard Arkwright (1732-92), inventor of textile machines. No. 2648, Josiah Wedgwood (1730-95), manufacturer of decorative ceramics. No. 2649, George Stephenson (1781-1848), steam locomotive inventor. No. 2650, Henry Maudslay (1771-1831), engineer and machine tool inventor. No. 2651, James Brindley (1716-72), canal engineer. No. 2652, John McAdam (1756-1836), engineer, road builder.

Perf. 14¼x14½

2009, Mar. 10 Litho.

2645	A665	1st multi	1.10	.55
2646	A665	1st multi	1.10	.55
a.	Horiz. pair, #2645-2646		2.25	1.10
2647	A665	50p multi	1.50	.75
2648	A665	50p multi	1.50	.75
a.	Horiz. pair, #2647-2648		3.00	1.50
2649	A665	56p multi	1.75	.85
2650	A665	56p multi	1.75	.85
a.	Horiz. pair, #2649-2650		3.50	1.75
2651	A665	72p multi	2.25	1.10
2652	A665	72p multi	2.25	1.10
a.	Horiz. pair, #2651-2652		4.50	2.25
	Nos. 2645-2652 (8)		13.20	6.50

On day of issue, Nos. 2645-2646 each sold for 36p.

British Royalty and History Type of 2008

Designs: No. 2653, King Henry VII. No. 2654, King Henry VIII. No. 2655, King Edward VI. No. 2656, Lady Jane Grey. No. 2657, Queen Mary I. No. 2658, Queen Elizabeth I. No. 2659: a, Warship Mary Rose. b, Field of Cloth of Gold Royal Conference. c, Royal Exchange. d, Sir Francis Drake, first English circumnavigator.

2009, Apr. 21 *Perf. 14¼*

2653	A645	1st multi	1.25	.60
2654	A645	1st multi	1.25	.60
2655	A645	62p multi	1.90	.95
2656	A645	62p multi	1.90	.95
2657	A645	81p multi	2.40	1.25
2658	A645	81p multi	2.40	1.25
	Nos. 2653-2658 (6)		11.10	5.60

Souvenir Sheet

2659		Sheet of 4	7.75	4.00
a.-b.	A645 1st Either single		1.25	.60
c.-d.	A645 90p Either single		2.60	1.25

On day of issue, Nos. 2653, 2654, 2659a and 2659b sold for 39p.

Endangered Plants
A666

Designs: No. 2660, Round-headed leek. No. 2661, Floating water plantain. No. 2662, Lady's slipper orchid. No. 2663, Dwarf milkwort. No. 2664, Marsh saxifrage. No. 2665, Downy woundwort. No. 2666, Upright spurge. No. 2667, Plymouth pear. No. 2668, Sea knotgrass. No. 2669, Deptford pink.

2009, May 19 *Perf. 14½*

2660	A666	1st multi	1.25	.60
2661	A666	1st multi	1.25	.60
2662	A666	1st multi	1.25	.60
2663	A666	1st multi	1.25	.60
2664	A666	1st multi	1.25	.60
2665	A666	1st multi	1.25	.60
2666	A666	1st multi	1.25	.60
2667	A666	1st multi	1.25	.60
2668	A666	1st multi	1.25	.60
2669	A666	1st multi	1.25	.60
a.	Block of 10, #2660-2669		12.50	6.00

On day of issue, Nos. 2660-2669 each sold for 39p.

Miniature Sheet

Royal Botanic Gardens, Kew — A667

No. 2670: a, Palm House. b, Millennium Seed Bank, Wakehurst Place. c, Pagoda. d, Sackler Crossing.

2009, May 19 *Perf. 14¼x14½*

2670	A667	Sheet of 4	8.00	4.00
a.-b.	1st Either single		1.25	.60
c.-d.	90p Either single		2.75	1.40

On day of issue, Nos. 2670a and 2670b each sold for 39p.

Flowers Type of 1997

Die Cut Perf. 14½x14 Syncopated

2009, May 21 Photo.
Booklet Stamps
Self-Adhesive

2671	A475	1st multi	3.00	.85
2672	A479	1st multi	3.00	.85
a.	Booklet pane, #2671-2672, 4 #MH384a		11.00	

On day of issue Nos. 2671-2672 each sold for 39p.

Mythical Creatures
A668

2009, June 16 Photo. *Perf. 14½*

2673	A668	1st Dragon	1.40	.70
2674	A668	1st Unicorn	1.40	.70
2675	A668	62p Giant	2.10	1.10
2676	A668	62p Pixie	2.10	1.10
2677	A668	90p Mermaid	3.00	1.50
2678	A668	90p Fairy	3.00	1.50
	Nos. 2673-2678 (6)		13.00	6.60

On day of issue, Nos. 2673-2674 each sold for 39p.

Miniature Sheet

Post Boxes — A669

No. 2679: a, George V type B wall box. b, Edward VII Ludlow box. c, Victorian lamp box. d, Elizabeth II type A wall box.

2009, Aug. 18 Litho. *Perf. 14¼*

2679	A669	Sheet of 4	9.00	9.00
a.	1st multi		1.25	.65
b.	56p multi		1.90	.95
c.	81p multi		2.75	1.40
d.	90p multi		3.00	1.50
e.	Booklet pane of 4, #2679a-2679d (BK189)		9.00	—
f.	Sheet of 20 #2679a + 20 labels		27.50	

No. 2679 sold for 39p on day of issue. No. 2679f sold for £8.35 on day of issue and its labels could not be personalized.

Fire and Rescue Service
A670

Designs: 1st, Firefighting. 54p, Chemical fire. 56p, Emergency rescue. 62p, Flood rescue. 81p, Search and rescue. 90p, Fire safety.

Perf. 14¼x14½

2009, Sept. 1 Photo.

2680	A670	1st multi	1.25	.65
2681	A670	54p multi	1.75	.90
2682	A670	56p multi	1.90	.95
2683	A670	62p multi	2.10	1.10
2684	A670	81p multi	2.75	1.40
2685	A670	90p multi	3.00	1.50
	Nos. 2680-2685 (6)		12.75	6.50

No. 2680 sold for 39p on day of issue.

Royal Navy Uniforms — A671

Designs: No. 2686, Flight deck officer, 2009. No. 2687, Captain, 1941. No. 2688, Second officer WRNS, 1918. No. 2689, Able seaman, 1880. No. 2690, Royal Marine, 1805. No. 2691, Admiral, 1795.

2009, Sept. 17 Litho. *Perf. 14¼*

2686	A671	1st multi	1.25	.60
2687	A671	1st multi	1.25	.60
2688	A671	1st multi	1.25	.60
a.	Horiz. strip of 3, #2686-2688		3.75	1.90
b.	Booklet pane of 3, #2686-2688 (BK190)		3.75	—
2689	A671	90p multi	3.00	1.50
2690	A671	90p multi	3.00	1.50
2691	A671	90p multi	3.00	1.50
a.	Horiz. strip of 3, #2689-2691		9.00	4.50
b.	Booklet pane of 3, #2689-2691 (BK190)		9.00	—
	Nos. 2686-2691 (6)		12.75	6.30

Nos. 2686-2688 each sold for 39p on day of issue.

Famous People
A672

Designs: No. 2692, Fred Perry (1909-95), tennis player. No. 2693, Henry Purcell (1659-95), composer and musician. No. 2694, Sir Matt Busby (1909-94), soccer player and manager. No. 2695, William Gladstone (1809-98), prime minister. No. 2696, Mary Wollstonecraft (1759-97), writer on feminist themes. No. 2697, Sir Arthur Conan Doyle (1859-1930), writer and creator of Sherlock Holmes stories. No. 2698, Donald Campbell (1921-67), breaker of land and water speed records. No. 2699, Judy Fryd (1909-2000), founder of Royal Society for Mentally Handicapped Children. No. 2700, Samuel Johnson (1709-84), lexicographer, critic and poet. No. 2701, Sir Martin Ryle (1918-84), radio astronomer.

2009, Oct. 8 Litho. *Perf. 14½*

2692	A672	1st multi	1.25	.60
2693	A672	1st multi	1.25	.60
2694	A672	1st multi	1.25	.60
2695	A672	1st multi	1.25	.60

2696	A672	1st multi	1.25	.60
a.	Horiz. strip of 5, #2692-2696		6.25	3.00
2697	A672	1st multi	1.25	.60
2698	A672	1st multi	1.25	.60
2699	A672	1st multi	1.25	.60
2700	A672	1st multi	1.25	.60
2701	A672	1st multi	1.25	.60
a.	Horiz. strip of 5, #2697-2701		6.25	3.00
	Nos. 2692-2701 (10)		12.50	6.00

On day of issue, Nos. 2692-2701 each sold for 39p. Europa (#2701).

Sports of the 2012 Summer Olympics and Paralympics, London
A673

Olympics or Paralympics emblem and: No. 2702, Canoe slalom. Nos. 2703, 2713, Archery (Paralympics). Nos. 2704, 2714, Track. No. 2705, Aquatics. No. 2706, Boccie (Paralympics). Nos. 2707, 2712, Judo. No. 2708, Equestrian (Paralympics). No. 2709, Badminton. No. 2710, Weight lifting. Nos. 2711, 2715, Basketball.

2009-10 Litho. *Perf. 14½*

2702	A673	1st multi	1.40	.70
2703	A673	1st multi	1.40	.70
2704	A673	1st multi	1.40	.70
2705	A673	1st multi	1.40	.70
2706	A673	1st multi	1.40	.70
a.	Horiz. strip of 5, #2702-2706		7.00	3.50
2707	A673	1st multi	1.40	.70
2708	A673	1st multi	1.40	.70
2709	A673	1st multi	1.40	.70
2710	A673	1st multi	1.40	.70
2711	A673	1st multi	1.40	.70
a.	Horiz. strip of 5, #2707-2711		7.00	3.50
	Nos. 2702-2711 (10)		14.00	7.00

Booklet Stamps
Self-Adhesive
Photo.
Die Cut Perf. 14½

2712	A673	1st multi (2713a)	2.75	.90
2713	A673	1st multi (2713a)	2.75	.90
a.	Booklet pane of 6, #2712, 2713, 4 #MH384a		11.50	
2714	A673	1st multi	2.75	.85
2715	A673	1st multi	2.75	.85
a.	Booklet pane of 6, #2714-2715, 4 #MH384a		11.50	

On day of issue, Nos. 2702-2715 each sold for 39p. Issued: Nos. 2702-2711, 10/22; Nos. 2712-2713, 1/7/10; Nos. 2714-2715, 2/25/10. See Nos. 2815-2826.

Christmas
A674   A675

Stained-glass windows: Nos. 2716a, 2716c, 2717, 2719, Angel, Church of St. James, Staveley. Nos. 2716b, 2716e, 2718, 2721, Madonna and Child, Church of Ormesby St. Michael, Great Yarmouth. 56p, Joseph, Church of St. Michael, Minehead. 90p, Wise Man, Church of St. Mary the Virgin, Rye. £1.35, Shepherd, Church of St. Mary's, Upavon.

Perf. 14¾x14 Syncopated

2009, Nov. 3 Photo.

2716		Sheet of 7	15.50	7.75
a.	A674 2nd multi		1.00	.50
b.	A674 1st multi		1.40	.70
c.	A675 2nd Large multi		1.50	.75
d.	A674 56p multi		1.90	.95
e.	A675 1st Large multi		2.00	1.00
f.	A674 90p multi		3.00	1.50
g.	A674 £1.35 multi		4.50	2.25

Self-Adhesive
Die Cut Perf. 14¾x14 Syncopated

2717	A674	2nd multi	1.00	.50
a.	Booklet pane of 12		12.00	
b.	Litho., serpentine die cut 14¾x14 + label		1.10	1.10
2718	A674	1st multi	1.40	.70
a.	Booklet pane of 12		17.00	
b.	Litho., serpentine die cut 14¾x14 + label		1.50	1.50
2719	A675	2nd Large multi	1.50	.75
2720	A674	56p multi	1.90	.95
a.	Litho., serpentine die cut 14¾x14 + label		2.00	2.00
2721	A675	1st Large multi	2.00	1.00
2722	A674	90p multi	3.00	1.50
a.	Litho., serpentine die cut 14¾x14 + label		3.25	3.25

b. Sheet of 20, 8 each #2717b, 2718b, 2 each #2720a, 2722a, + 20 labels — 32.00
2723 A674 £1.35 multi — 4.50 2.25
Nos. 2717-2723 (7) — 15.30 7.65

On day of issue, Nos. 2716a and 2717 each sold for 30p; Nos. 2716b and 2718, 39p; Nos. 2716c and 2719, 47p; Nos. 2716e and 2721, 61p. No. 2722b sold for £9, and contains 20 labels that could not be personalized. No. 2717b was additionally sold in a sheet of 20 + 20 labels that could be personalized that sold for £9.50. No. 2718b was additionally sold in a sheet of 20 + 20 labels that could be personalized that sold for £13.50. No. 2720a was additionally sold in a sheet of 10 + 10 labels that could be personalized that sold for £9.50. No. 2722b was additionally sold in a sheet of 10 + 10 labels that could be personalized that sold for £13.50.

Let It Bleed, by The Rolling Stones A676

Led Zeppelin IV, by Led Zeppelin A677

The Rise and Fall of Ziggy Stardust and the Spiders from Mars, by David Bowie A678

Power, Corruption and Lies, by New Order — A679

Screamadelica, by Primal Scream — A680

The Division Bell, by Pink Floyd — A681

Tubular Bells, by Mike Oldfield A682

London Calling, by The Clash — A683

Parklife, by Blur — A684

A Rush of Blood to the Head, by Coldplay A685

Perf. 14¾ Syncopated
2010, Jan. 7 — Litho.
2724	A676	1st multi	1.40	.70
2725	A677	1st multi	1.40	.70
2726	A678	1st multi	1.40	.70
2727	A679	1st multi	1.40	.70
2728	A680	1st multi	1.40	.70
2729	A681	1st multi	1.40	.70
a.		Booklet pane of 6, #2724-2729 (BK191)	8.50	—
2730	A682	1st multi	1.40	.70
2731	A683	1st multi	1.40	.70
2732	A684	1st multi	1.40	.70
2733	A685	1st multi	1.40	.70
a.		Booklet pane of 4, #2730-2733 (BK191)	5.75	—
b.		Souvenir sheet, #2724-2733	14.00	14.00

No. 2733b has simulated creases and toning at the sides and corners of the album cover sheet margin.

Self-Adhesive
Photo.
Die Cut Perf. 14¾
2734	A681	1st multi	1.40	.70
2735	A685	1st multi	1.40	.70
2736	A684	1st multi	1.40	.70
2737	A679	1st multi	1.40	.70
2738	A676	1st multi	1.40	.70
a.		Horiz. strip of 5, #2734-2738	7.00	
2739	A683	1st multi	1.40	.70
2740	A682	1st multi	1.40	.70
2741	A677	1st multi	1.40	.70
2742	A680	1st multi	1.40	.70
2743	A678	1st multi	1.40	.70
a.		Horiz. strip of 5, #2739-2743	7.00	

On day of issue, Nos. 2724-2743 each sold for 39p.

Miniature Sheet

A686

Nos. 2744 and 2745: a, Airplane with propellers. b, Automobile. c, Sealing wax with crown impression. d, Birthday cake. e, Steam locomotive. f, Ocean liner. g, Poppies. h, Gift box. i, Bird carrying airmail letter. j, "Hello" in airplane's contrail.

Perf. 14¾x14 Syncopated
2010, Jan. 26 — Litho.
2744	A686	Sheet of 10	15.00	15.00
a.-h.		1st Any single	1.25	.60
i.		(56p) multi	1.90	.95
j.		(90p) multi	3.00	1.50

Self-Adhesive
Die Cut Perf. 14¾x14 Syncopated
2745	A686	Sheet of 20, 2 each #a-j, + 20 labels	33.00	
a.-h.		1st Any single + label	1.40	1.40
i.		(56p) multi + label	2.00	2.00
j.		(90p) multi + label	3.25	3.25
k.		Sheet of 20 #2745d + 20 labels	44.00	
l.		Sheet of 20 #2745g + 20 labels	44.00	

m.		Sheet of 10 #2745h + 10 labels	31.00	
n.		Sheet of 10 #2745i + 10 labels	44.00	

On day of issue, Nos. 2744a-2744h sold for 39p. No. 2745 sold for £9.70, and Nos. 2745a-2745h had a franking value of 39p. Labels could not be personalized.
Nos. 2745k and 2745l each sold for £13.63; No. 2745m for £9.58; and No. 2745n for £13.60. Labels could be personalized on Nos. 2745k-2745n.

Miniature Sheet

Girl Guides, Cent. — A687

No. 2746 — Girl Guides and: a, Kite, handprint, drawing of flower. b, Cupcake, magnifying glass, leaves, colored pencils. c, Archery target, climber's rope. d, Photographs, swimming goggles, map of Manchester.

2010, Feb. 2 — **Perf. 14¼x14½**
2746	A687	Sheet of 4	8.75	8.75
a.		1st multi	1.25	.60
b.		56p multi	1.75	.85
c.		81p multi	2.60	1.25
d.		90p multi	3.00	1.50

No. 2746a sold for 39p on day of issue.

Royal Society, 350th Anniv. A688

Scientists: No. 2747, Robert Boyle (1627-91), air pump. No. 2748, Sir Isaac Newton (1642-1727), color spectrum and optics diagram. No. 2749, Benjamin Franklin (1706-90), lightning. No. 2750, Edward Jenner (1749-1823), smallpox virus. No. 2751, Charles Babbage (1792-1871), gear diagram. No. 2752, Alfred Russel Wallace (1823-1913), oak tree. No. 2753, Sir Joseph Lister (1827-1912), spray. No. 2754, Ernest Rutherford (1871-1937), atom. No. 2755, Dorothy Hodgkin (1910-94), crystal diagram. No. 2756, Sir Nicholas Shackleton (1937-2006), microfossils.

2010, Feb. 25 — Litho. — **Perf. 14½**
2747	A688	1st multi	1.25	.60
2748	A688	1st multi	1.25	.60
2749	A688	1st multi	1.25	.60
2750	A688	1st multi	1.25	.60
2751	A688	1st multi	1.25	.60
2752	A688	1st multi	1.25	.60
2753	A688	1st multi	1.25	.60
2754	A688	1st multi	1.25	.60
a.		Booklet pane of 4, #2748, 2749, 2 #2754 (BK192)	5.00	—
2755	A688	1st multi	1.25	.60
a.		Booklet pane of 4, #2753, 2755, 2 #2750 (BK192)	5.00	—
2756	A688	1st multi	1.25	.60
a.		Block of 10, #2747-2756	12.50	6.00
b.		Booklet pane of 4, #2747, 2751, 2752, 2756 (BK192)	5.00	—
		Nos. 2747-2756 (10)	12.50	6.00

On day of issue, Nos. 2747-2756 each sold for 39p.

Battersea Dogs and Cats Home, 150th Anniv. A689

Designs: No. 2757, Pixie (dog). No. 2758, Button (cat). No. 2759, Herbie (dog). No. 2760, Mr. Tumnus (cat). No. 2761, Tafka (dog). No. 2762, Boris (dog). No. 2763, Casey (dog). No. 2764, Tigger (cat). No. 2765, Leonard (dog). No. 2766, Tia (dog).

2010, Mar. 11 — **Perf. 14½**
2757	A689	1st multi	1.25	.60
2758	A689	1st multi	1.25	.60
2759	A689	1st multi	1.25	.60
2760	A689	1st multi	1.25	.60
2761	A689	1st multi	1.25	.60
2762	A689	1st multi	1.25	.60
2763	A689	1st multi	1.25	.60
2764	A689	1st multi	1.25	.60
2765	A689	1st multi	1.25	.60
2766	A689	1st multi	1.25	.60
a.		Block of 10, #2757-2766	12.50	6.00
		Nos. 2757-2766 (10)	12.50	6.00

On day of issue, Nos. 2757-2766 each sold for 39p.

British Royalty and History Type of 2008

Designs: No. 2767, King James I of Scotland (1406-37). No. 2768, King James II of Scotland (1437-60). No. 2769, King James III. No. 2770, King James IV. No. 2771, King James V. No. 2772, Mary, Queen of Scots. No. 2773, King James VI.
No. 2774: a, Founding of St. Andrew's University, 1413. b, College of Surgeons, Edinburgh, 1505. c, Court of Session, 1532. d, John Knox, religious reformer.

2010, Mar. 23 — **Perf. 14¼**
2767	A645	1st multi	1.25	.60
2768	A645	1st multi	1.25	.60
2769	A645	1st multi	1.25	.60
2770	A645	62p multi	1.90	.95
2771	A645	62p multi	1.90	.95
2772	A645	81p multi	2.50	1.25
2773	A645	81p multi	2.50	1.25
		Nos. 2767-2773 (7)	12.55	6.20

Souvenir Sheet
2774		Sheet of 4	7.50	7.50
a.-b.	A645	1st Either single	1.25	.60
c.-d.	A645	81p Either single	2.50	1.25

On day of issue, Nos. 2767-2769, 2774a-2774b each sold for 39p.

Land and Sea Mammals A690

Designs: No. 2775, Humpback whale. No. 2776, Wildcat. No. 2777, Brown long-eared bat. No. 2778, Polecat. No. 2779, Sperm whale. No. 2780, Water vole. No. 2781, Greater horseshoe bat. Nos. 2782, 2785, Otter. No. 2783, Dormouse. Nos. 2784, 2786, Hedgehog.

2010 — **Perf. 14½**
2775	A690	1st multi	1.25	.65
2776	A690	1st multi	1.25	.65
2777	A690	1st multi	1.25	.65
2778	A690	1st multi	1.25	.65
2779	A690	1st multi	1.25	.65
2780	A690	1st multi	1.25	.65
2781	A690	1st multi	1.25	.65
2782	A690	1st multi	1.25	.65
2783	A690	1st multi	1.25	.65
2784	A690	1st multi	1.25	.65
a.		Block of 10, #2775-2784	12.50	6.50
		Nos. 2775-2784 (10)	12.50	6.50

Photo.
Booklet Stamps
Self-Adhesive
Die Cut Perf. 14½
2785	A690	1st multi	1.25	.65
2786	A690	1st multi	1.25	.65
a.		Booklet pane of 6, #2785-2786, 4 #MH384a	7.50	

Issued: Nos. 2775-2784, 4/13; Nos. 2785-2786, 6/15. On day of issue, Nos. 2775-2786 each sold for 41p.

King George V and Queen Elizabeth II — A691

British Empire Exhibition Stamps of 1924 — A692

"Britannia Rules the Waves" Stamps of 1913 — A693

Heads of King George V and Lion From Types A81 and A82 — A694

Designs: No. 2788, Great Britain #185. No. 2789, Great Britain #186. No. 2790, Great Britain #176. No. 2791, Great Britain #175.

Perf. 14½x14 (#2787, 2792), 14¾x14¼

Litho. (#2787, 2792), Litho. & Engr.

2010
2787	A691	1st red	1.25	.60
2788	A692	1st multi	1.25	.60
2789	A692	1st multi	1.25	.60
a.		Booklet pane of 4, 2 each #2788-2789 (BK193)	5.00	—
2790	A693	£1 multi	3.00	1.50
2791	A693	£1 multi	3.00	1.50
a.		Souvenir sheet of 4, #2788-2791	8.50	4.25
b.		Booklet pane of 2, #2790-2791 (BK193)	6.00	—
2792	A694	£1 brown & silver	3.00	1.50
a.		Souvenir sheet of 2, #2787, 2792	4.25	2.10
b.		Booklet pane of 6, 3 each #2787, 2792 (BK193)	13.00	—
		Nos. 2787-2792 (6)	12.75	6.30

Issued: No. 2787, 5/6; others, 5/8. London 2010 Festival of Stamps. Nos. 2787-2789 each sold for 41p on day of issue.

Bird and Thank You Types of 2005-06

Die Cut Perf. 14¾x14 Syncopated
2010, May 8 Litho.
Self-Adhesive
2793	A596	1st multi + label (2794a)	5.00	5.00
2794	A612	1st multi + label (2794a)	5.00	5.00
a.		Sheet of 20, #2427, 2546, 2547, 2793, 2794, 2 each #2745i, 2745j, 3 #2538, 4 each #2745d, 2745g + 20 labels	40.00	

No. 2794a sold for £10. Labels could not be personalized. Nos. 2793 and 2794 each had a franking value of 41p on day of issue.

Britain in World War II — A695

Designs: No. 2795, Prime Minister Winston Churchill reviewing troops. No. 2796, Girl on tractor. No. 2797, Home Guard. No. 2798, Evacuees. No. 2799, Air raid warden. No. 2800, Woman in factory. No. 2801, Firemen at fire. No. 2802, Royal broadcast.
No. 2803, Soldiers in water. No. 2804, Flotilla of small boats. No. 2805, Soldiers in boat. No. 2806, Soldiers on two boats.

2010, May 13 *Perf. 14½*
2795	A695	1st multi	1.25	.60
2796	A695	1st multi	1.25	.60
2797	A695	60p multi	1.75	.85
2798	A695	60p multi	1.75	.85
2799	A695	67p multi	2.00	1.00
2800	A695	67p multi	2.00	1.00
2801	A695	97p multi	3.00	1.50
a.		Booklet pane of 4, #2797-2799, 2801 (BK194)	8.50	—
2802	A695	97p multi	3.00	1.50
a.		Booklet pane of 4, #2795-2796, 2800, 2802 (BK194)	7.50	—

Inscribed "Dunkirk"
2803	A695	1st multi	1.25	.60
2804	A695	60p multi	1.75	.85
2805	A695	88p multi	2.60	1.25

2806	A695	97p multi	3.00	1.50
a.		Souvenir sheet of 4, #2803-2806	8.75	8.75
b.		Booklet pane of 4, #2803-2806 (BK194)	8.75	—
		Nos. 2795-2806 (12)	24.60	12.10

Nos. 2795, 2796 and 2803 each sold for 41p on day of issue.

British Royalty and History Type of 2008

Designs: No. 2807, King James I of Great Britain (1603-25). No. 2808, King Charles I. No. 2809, King Charles II. No. 2810, King James II of Great Britain (1685-88). No. 2811, King William III. No. 2812, Queen Mary II. No. 2813, Queen Anne.
No. 2814: a, William Harvey, discoverer of blood circulation, 1628. b, Civil War Battle of Naseby, 1645. c, John Milton, author of Paradise Lost, 1667. d, Castle Howard, designed by John Vanbrugh.

2010, June 15 *Perf. 14¼*
2807	A645	1st multi	1.25	.60
2808	A645	1st multi	1.25	.60
2809	A645	60p multi	1.90	.95
2810	A645	60p multi	1.90	.95
2811	A645	67p multi	2.10	1.10
2812	A645	67p multi	2.10	1.10
2813	A645	88p multi	2.75	1.40
		Nos. 2807-2813 (7)	13.25	6.70

Souvenir Sheet
2814		Sheet of 4	9.00	9.00
a.		A645 1st multi	1.25	.60
b.		A645 60p multi	1.90	.95
c.		A645 88p multi	2.75	1.40
d.		A645 97p multi	3.00	1.50

On day of issue, Nos. 2807, 2808 and 2814a each sold for 41p.

Sports of the 2012 Olympics and Paralympics Type of 2009-10

Olympics or Paralympics emblem and: Nos. 2815, 2825, Rowing (Paralympics). No. 2816, Shooting. Nos. 2817, Modern pentathlon. No. 2818, Taekwondo. No. 2819, Cycling. Nos. 2820, 2826, Table tennis (Paralympics). No. 2821, Field hockey. No. 2822, Soccer. No. 2823, Goalball (Paralympics). No. 2824, Boxing.

2010, July 27 Litho. *Perf. 14½*
2815	A673	1st multi	1.40	.70
2816	A673	1st multi	1.40	.70
2817	A673	1st multi	1.40	.70
2818	A673	1st multi	1.40	.70
2819	A673	1st multi	1.40	.70
a.		Horiz. strip of 5, #2815-2819	7.00	3.50
2820	A673	1st multi	1.40	.70
2821	A673	1st multi	1.40	.70
2822	A673	1st multi	1.40	.70
2823	A673	1st multi	1.40	.70
2824	A673	1st multi	1.40	.70
a.		Horiz. strip of 5, #2820-2824	7.00	3.50
		Nos. 2815-2824 (10)	14.00	7.00

Booklet Stamps
Self-Adhesive
Photo.
Die Cut Perf. 14½
2825	A673	1st multi (2826a)	1.40	.70
2826	A673	1st multi (2826a)	1.40	.70
a.		Booklet pane of 6, #2825, 2826, 4 #MH384a	8.50	

Nos. 2815-2826 each sold for 41p on day of issue. See Nos. 2840-2841.

Locomotives — A696

Designs: No. 2827, London Midland and Scottish Railway Coronation Class. No. 2828, British Rail Class 9F. No. 2829, Great Western Railway King Class. No. 2830, London North Eastern Railway Class A1. No. 2831, London Midland and Scottish Railway Northern Counties Committee Class WT. No. 2832, Southern Railway King Arthur Class.

2010, Aug. 19 Photo. *Perf. 14¼x14*
2827	A696	1st multi	1.40	.70
2828	A696	1st multi	1.40	.70
2829	A696	60p multi	2.10	1.10
2830	A696	67p multi	2.10	1.10
2831	A696	88p multi	3.25	1.60
2832	A696	97p multi	3.25	1.60
		Nos. 2827-2832 (6)	13.50	6.80

Nos. 2827-2828 each sold for 41p on day of issue.

British Design Type of 2009
Design: Supermarine Spitfire.
Die Cut Perf. 14½
2010, Sept. 15 Photo.
Booklet Stamp
Self-Adhesive
2833	A660	1st multi	1.25	.65
a.		Booklet pane of 6, 2 #2833, 4 #MH384a	7.50	

No. 2833 sold for 41p on day of issue.

Medical Breakthroughs — A697

Designs: 1st, Heart-regulating beta blockers synthesized by Sir James Black, 1962. 58p, Antibiotic properties of penicillin discovered by Sir Alexander Fleming, 1928. 60p, Total hip replacement operation pioneered by Sir John Charnley, 1962. 67p, Artificial lens implant surgery pioneered by Sir Harold Ridley, 1949. 88p, Malaria parasite transmitted by mosquitoes proved by Sir Ronald Ross, 1897. 97p, Computed tomography scanner invented by Sir Godfrey Hounsfield, 1971.

Perf. 14¼x14½
2010, Sept. 16 Litho.
2834	A697	1st multi	1.25	.65
2835	A697	58p multi	1.75	.90
2836	A697	60p multi	1.90	.95
2837	A697	67p multi	2.10	1.10
2838	A697	88p multi	2.75	1.40
2839	A697	97p multi	3.00	1.50
		Nos. 2834-2839 (6)	12.75	6.50

No. 2834 sold for 41p on day of issue.

Sports of the 2012 Olympics and Paralympics Type of 2009-10
Designs: No. 2840, Soccer. No. 2841, Cycling.
Die Cut Perf. 14½
2010, Oct. 12 Photo.
Booklet Stamps
Self-Adhesive
2840	A673	1st multi (2841a)	1.40	.70
2841	A673	1st multi (2841a)	1.40	.70
a.		Booklet pane of 6, #2840, 2841, 4 #MH384a	8.50	

Nos. 2840-2841 each sold for 41p on day of issue.

Characters From Winnie-the-Pooh Stories by A. A. Milne — A698

Winnie-the-Pooh and: No. 2842, Christopher Robin. 58p, Piglet. No. 2844, Rabbit. 67p, Eeyore. No. 2846, Friends. No. 2847, Tigger.
No. 2848 — Winnie-the-Pooh and Christopher Robin with inscriptions: a, Wherever I am, there's always Pooh. b, There's always Pooh and Me, Whatever I do, he wants to do. c, "Where are you going to-day?" says Pooh: "Well, that's very odd 'cos I was too. d, "Let's go together," says Pooh, says he. "Let's go together," says Pooh.

2010, Oct. 12 Litho. *Perf. 14¼x14½*
2842	A698	1st multi	1.40	.70
2843	A698	58p multi	1.90	.95
2844	A698	60p multi	1.90	.95
2845	A698	67p multi	2.10	1.10
2846	A698	88p multi	2.75	1.40
2847	A698	97p multi	3.25	1.60
		Nos. 2842-2847 (6)	13.30	6.70

Souvenir Sheet
Perf. 14½
2848		Sheet of 4	9.50	9.50
a.		A698 1st multi	1.40	.70
b.		A698 60p multi	1.90	.95
c.		A698 88p multi	2.75	1.40
d.		A698 97p multi	3.25	1.60

Europa (Nos. 2842, 2848a). Nos. 2842 and 2848a each sold for 41p on day of issue.

Christmas
A699   A700

Designs: 2nd, Wallace and Gromit singing Christmas carols. 1st, Gromit mailing Christmas cards. 2nd Large, Wallace and Gromit singing Christmas carols, Christmas tree at left. 60p, Wallace and Gromit decorating Christmas tree. 1st Large, Gromit mailing Christmas cards, Feathers McGraw at left. 97p, Gromit carrying Christmas pudding. £1.46, Gromit wearing large sweater.

Perf. 14¾x14 Syncopated
2010, Nov. 2 Photo.
2849		Sheet of 7	16.50	8.25
a.		A699 2nd multi	1.10	.55
b.		A699 1st multi	1.40	.70
c.		A700 2nd Large multi	1.75	.85
d.		A699 60p multi	2.00	1.00
e.		A700 1st Large multi	2.10	1.10
f.		A699 97p multi	3.25	1.60
g.		A699 £1.46 multi	4.75	2.40

Self-Adhesive
Die Cut Perf. 14¾x14 Syncopated
2850	A699	2nd multi	1.10	.55
a.		Booklet pane of 12	13.50	
b.		Litho., serpentine die cut 14¾x14 syncopated, + label (2855b)	1.10	1.10
c.		Sheet of 20 #2850b	32.50	
2851	A699	1st multi	1.40	.70
a.		Booklet pane of 12	17.00	
b.		Litho., serpentine die cut 14¾x14 syncopated, + label (2855b)	1.40	1.40
c.		Sheet of 20 #2851b	45.00	
2852	A700	2nd Large multi	1.75	.85
2853	A699	60p multi	2.00	1.00
a.		Litho., serpentine die cut 14¾x14 syncopated, + label (2855b)	2.00	2.00
b.		Sheet of 10 #2853a	32.50	
2854	A700	1st Large multi	2.10	1.10
2855	A699	97p multi	3.25	1.60
a.		Litho., serpentine die cut 14¾x14 syncopated, + label (2855b)	3.25	3.25
b.		Sheet of 20, 8 each #2850b, 2851b, 2 each #2853a, 2855a, + 20 labels	31.00	
c.		Sheet of 10 #2855a	47.50	
2856	A699	£1.46 multi	4.75	2.40
		Nos. 2850-2856 (7)	16.35	8.20

On day of issue, Nos. 2849a and 2850 each sold for 32p, Nos. 2849b and 2851 each sold for 41p, Nos. 2849c and 2852 each sold for 51p, and Nos. 2849e and 2854 each sold for 66p. No. 2855b sold for £9.30 and contained 20 labels that could not be personalized.
Nos. 2850c, 2851c, 2853b and 2855c had labels that could be personalized. Nos. 2850a and 2853b each sold for £9.95; No. 2851c sold for £13.95; No. 2855c sold for £14.50. Sheets of 10 No. 2850b were also sold but these were halves of No. 2850c torn along the sheet's central row of rouletting. Nos. 2853b and 2855c have rouletting along the left or right side of the sheet, but these stamps were not sold in sheets of 20.

Television Shows Created By Gerry Anderson A701

Designs: No. 2857, Joe 90. No. 2858, Captain Scarlet. Nos. 2859, 2864, Thunderbirds. No. 2860, Stingray. No. 2861, Fireball XL5. No. 2862, Supercar.
No. 2863 — Opening sequence of Thunderbirds depicting rocket and: a, "4." b, "3." c, "2." d, "1."

2011, Jan. 11 Litho. *Perf. 14¼*
2857	A701	1st multi	1.40	.70
2858	A701	1st multi	1.40	.70
2859	A701	1st multi	1.40	.70
a.		Horiz. strip of 3, #2857-2859	4.20	2.10
2860	A701	97p multi	3.25	1.60
2861	A701	97p multi	3.25	1.60

2862	A701	97p multi	3.25	1.60
a.		Horiz. strip of 3, #2860-2862	9.75	4.80
		Nos. 2857-2862 (6)	13.95	6.90

Souvenir Sheet
Litho. With Three-Dimensional Plastic Affixed

2863		Sheet of 4	9.50	9.50
a.	A701	41p multi	1.40	1.40
b.	A701	60p multi	1.90	1.90
c.	A701	88p multi	2.75	2.75
d.	A701	97p multi	3.25	3.25

Booklet Stamp
Self-Adhesive
Die Cut Perf. 14¼x14

2864	A701	1st multi	1.40	.70
a.		Booklet pane of 6, 2 #2864, 4 #MH384a	8.00	

On day of issue, Nos. 2857-2859, 2864 each sold for 41p.

Miniature Sheet

Locomotives — A702

No. 2865: a, British Railways Dean Goods No. 2532. b, Peckett R2 Thor. c, Lancashire & Yorkshire Railway 1093 No. 1100. d, British Railways No. 90662.

			Perf. 14¼	
2011, Feb. 1		**Litho.**	**Perf. 14¼**	
2865	A702	Sheet of 4	9.75	9.75
a.		1st multi	1.40	.70
b.		60p multi	2.00	1.00
c.		88p multi	3.00	1.50
d.		97p multi	3.25	1.60

No. 2865a sold for 41p on day of issue.

SEMI-POSTAL STAMPS

Catalogue values for unused stamps in this section are for Never Hinged items.

Handicapped Person — SP1

			Photo.	Unwmk.
1975, Jan. 22			**Photo.**	**Unwmk.**
B1	SP1	4½p +1½p blue & lt blue	.25	.25

For the benefit of health and handicap charities. No. B1 is phosphorescent.

Christmas Type of 1989

Ely Cathedral, Cambridgeshire: No. B2, Romanesque arches, west front. No. B3, Central tower. No. B4, Interlocking arches, Romanesque arcades, west transept. No. B5, Peasant, stained-glass window in triple arch, west front.

			Photo.	Perf. 15x14
1989, Nov. 14			**Photo.**	**Perf. 15x14**
B2	A379	15p +1p multicolored	.60	.40
B3	A379	20p +1p multicolored	.80	.55
B4	A379	34p +1p multicolored	1.35	.85
B5	A379	37p +1p multicolored	1.50	.95
		Nos. B2-B5 (4)	4.25	2.75

AIR POST STAMPS

Queen Elizabeth II
AP1   AP2

Serpentine Die Cut 14¾x14 Syncopated

			Photo.	
2003, Mar. 27			**Photo.**	
Self-Adhesive			**Booklet Stamps**	
C1	AP1	(52p) blue & red	2.75	.85
a.		Booklet pane of 4	11.00	

C2	AP2	(£1.12) red & blue	5.00	1.90
a.		Booklet pane of 4	20.00	

Queen Elizabeth
II — AP3

Die Cut Perf. 14¾x14 Syncopated

			Photo.	
2004, Apr. 1	**Self-Adhesive**		**Photo.**	
C3	AP3	(43p) blk, red & blue	2.00	.80
a.		Booklet of 4 + 4 etiquettes	8.00	

Nos. C1-C3 were sold for 52p, £1.12 and 43p, respectively, when issued.

Queen Elizabeth II
AP4   AP5

Die Cut Perf. 14¾x14 Syncopated

			Photo.	
2010, Mar. 30			**Photo.**	
Self-Adhesive			**Booklet Stamps**	
C4	AP4	(60p) grn, red & blue	1.90	.95
a.		Booklet pane of 4	7.75	
C5	AP5	(97p) pur, red & blue	3.00	1.50
a.		Booklet pane of 4	12.00	

SPECIAL DELIVERY STAMPS

Queen Elizabeth II
SD1   SD2

Die Cut Perf. 14¾x14 Syncopated

			Photo.	
2010, Oct. 26	**Self-Adhesive**		**Photo.**	
E1	SD1	(£5.05) dk bl & gray	16.50	8.25
E2	SD2	(£5.50) gray & dk bl	18.00	9.00

POSTAGE DUE STAMPS

D1   D2

			Perf. 14x14½	
1914-24		**Typo.**	**Wmk. 33**	
J1	D1	½p emerald	.60	.30
		Never hinged	1.25	
J2	D1	1p rose	.60	.30
		Never hinged	1.75	
J3	D1	1½p red brown ('22)	55.00	22.50
		Never hinged	160.00	
J4	D1	2p brown black	.60	.30
		Never hinged	1.75	
J5	D1	3p violet ('18)	5.75	.85
		Never hinged	27.50	
J6	D1	4p gray green ('21)	40.00	5.75
		Never hinged	140.00	
J7	D1	5p org brown	7.00	4.00
		Never hinged	16.00	
J8	D1	1sh blue ('15)	45.00	5.50
		Never hinged	150.00	
		Nos. J1-J8 (8)	154.55	39.50

1924-30			**Wmk. 35**	
J9	D1	½p emerald	1.10	.85
		Never hinged	3.00	
J10	D1	1p car rose	.65	.30
		Never hinged	3.00	
J11	D1	1½p red brown	52.50	20.00
		Never hinged	150.00	
J12	D1	2p black brown	1.40	.30
		Never hinged	10.50	
J13	D1	3p violet	1.75	.30
		Never hinged	11.50	
a.		Experimental wmk.	45.00	40.00
		Never hinged	92.50	
b.		Printed on the gummed side	87.50	
		Never hinged	140.00	
J14	D1	4p deep green	17.50	3.50
		Never hinged	57.50	
J15	D1	5p org brown ('30)	65.00	45.00
		Never hinged	125.00	
J16	D1	1sh blue	11.50	1.10
		Never hinged	35.00	
J17	D2	2sh6p brown, yellow	85.00	2.25
		Never hinged	250.00	
		Nos. J9-J17 (9)	236.40	73.60

The experimental watermark of No. J13a resembles Wmk. 35 but is spaced more closely, with letters short and rounded, crown with flat arch and sides high, lines thicker.

			Wmk. 250	
1936-37			**Wmk. 250**	
J18	D1	½p emerald ('37)	5.00	10.00
		Never hinged	12.00	
J19	D1	1p car rose ('37)	1.25	2.25
		Never hinged	2.50	
J20	D1	2p blk brown ('37)	5.25	12.50
		Never hinged	12.00	
J21	D1	3p violet ('37)	1.50	2.50
		Never hinged	2.75	
J22	D1	4p slate green	20.00	40.00
		Never hinged	50.00	
J23	D1	5p bister ('37)	9.00	26.00
		Never hinged	18.00	
a.		5p orange brown	35.00	30.00
		Never hinged	75.00	
J24	D1	1sh blue ('36)	7.50	10.50
		Never hinged	16.00	
J25	D2	2sh6p brn, yel ('37)	190.00	12.50
		Never hinged	350.00	
		Nos. J18-J25 (8)	239.50	116.25

			Wmk. 251	
1938-39			**Wmk. 251**	
J26	D1	½p emerald	5.25	5.75
		Never hinged	13.00	
J27	D1	1p carmine rose	1.75	.85
		Never hinged	3.50	
J28	D1	2p black brown	1.50	.85
		Never hinged	3.00	
J29	D1	3p violet	7.00	1.10
		Never hinged	14.00	
J30	D1	4p slate green	40.00	15.00
		Never hinged	110.00	
J31	D1	5p bister ('39)	6.00	.85
		Never hinged	16.00	
J32	D1	1sh blue	35.00	2.25
		Never hinged	80.00	
J33	D2	2sh6p brown, yel ('39)	40.00	3.00
		Never hinged	85.00	
		Nos. J26-J33 (8)	136.50	29.65

Catalogue values for unused stamps in this section, from this point to the end of the section, are for Never Hinged items.

1951-52				
J34	D1	½p orange	1.10	3.50
J35	D1	1p violet blue	1.50	1.75
J36	D1	1½p green ('52)	2.00	3.50
J37	D1	4p bright blue	50.00	24.00
J38	D1	1sh olive bister	32.50	10.00
		Nos. J34-J38 (5)	87.10	42.75

1954-55			**Wmk. 298**	
J39	D1	½p orange ('55)	7.00	9.25
J40	D1	2p brn black ('55)	25.00	20.00
J41	D1	3p purple ('55)	70.00	60.00
J42	D1	4p brt blue ('55)	25.00	32.50
a.		Imperf., pair	300.00	
J43	D1	5p bister brn ('55)	22.50	19.00
J44	D2	2sh6p dk pur brn, yel	150.00	9.00
		Nos. J39-J44 (6)	299.50	149.75

1955-57		**Wmk. 308**	**Perf. 14x14½**	
J45	D1	½p orange ('56)	2.25	4.50
J46	D1	1p ultra ('56)	6.25	2.00
J47	D1	1½p green ('56)	8.00	7.00
J48	D1	2p brown blk ('56)	52.50	4.50
J49	D1	3p purple ('56)	8.00	2.25
J50	D1	4p brt blue ('56)	25.00	6.00
J51	D1	5p bister brn ('56)	27.50	17.50
J52	D1	1sh dp olive bister	65.00	2.75
J53	D2	2sh6p dk red brn, yel ('57)	200.00	12.50
J54	D2	5sh red, yellow	140.00	32.50
		Nos. J45-J54 (10)	534.50	91.50

1959-63		**Wmk. 322**	**Perf. 14x14½**	
J55	D1	½p orange ('61)	.20	1.40
J56	D1	1p ultra ('60)	.20	.60
J57	D1	1½p green ('60)	2.00	4.00
J58	D1	2p brown black	1.25	.60
J59	D1	3p purple	.40	.35
J60	D1	4p brt blue ('60)	.40	.35
J61	D1	5p bister brn ('62)	.50	.70
J62	D1	6p dp mag ('62)	.60	.35
J63	D1	1sh dp ol bis ('60)	1.00	.35
J64	D2	2sh6p dark red brown, yellow ('61)	5.50	.85
J65	D2	5sh red, yellow ('61)	8.25	1.10
J66	D2	10sh ultra, yel ('63)	11.50	6.25
J67	D2	£1 blk, yellow ('63)	47.50	8.75
		Nos. J55-J67 (13)	79.30	25.65

Nos. J1-J67 are watermarked sideways.

			Perf. 14x14½	
1968-69		**Unwmk.**	**Typo.**	
J68	D1	2p greenish black	.50	1.00
J69	D1	3p purple	1.00	.85
J70	D1	4p bright blue	1.00	.35
J71	D1	5p brown org ('69)	8.00	11.50
J72	D1	6p deep magenta	2.00	1.50
J73	D1	1sh bister ('69)	4.00	2.00
		Nos. J68-J73 (6)	16.50	17.60

1968-69			**Photo.**	
J74	D1	4p bright blue ('69)	7.00	6.00
J75	D1	8p bright red	1.25	1.00

D3   D4

			Perf. 14x14½	
1970-75		**Photo.**	**Unwmk.**	
J79	D3	½p grnsh blue ('71)	.20	.60
J80	D3	1p magenta ('71)	.20	.60
J81	D3	2p green ('71)	.20	.20
J82	D3	3p ultra ('71)	.20	.20
J83	D3	4p olive bister ('71)	.25	.25
J84	D3	5p bluish lilac ('71)	.25	.20
J85	D3	7p brown red ('74)	.40	.90
J86	D4	10p carmine rose	.40	.25
J87	D4	11p slate ('75)	.60	1.10
J88	D4	20p olive	.75	.50
J89	D4	50p ultramarine	2.00	1.00
J90	D4	£1 black	4.00	2.25
J91	D4	£5 org & black ('73)	40.00	3.50
		Nos. J79-J91 (13)	49.45	11.10

D5   D6

1982, June 9		**Photo.**	**Perf. 14x14½**	
J92	D5	1p rose carmine	.20	.35
J93	D5	2p ultramarine	.35	.35
J94	D5	3p deep rose lilac	.20	.35
J95	D5	4p dark blue	.20	.30
J96	D5	5p sepia	.20	.30
J97	D5	10p brown	.35	.45
J98	D5	20p dark ol green	.60	.70
J99	D5	25p slate blue	.90	1.00
J100	D5	50p black	1.75	1.25
J101	D5	£1 vermilion	3.50	1.40
J102	D5	£2 greenish blue	7.00	2.75
J103	D5	£5 yellow bister	16.00	2.25
		Nos. J92-J103 (12)	31.25	11.45

Perf. 15x14 Syncopated, Type C (2 Sides)

1994, Feb. 15		**Photo. & Embossed**		
J104	D6	1p vermilion & org	.20	.60
J105	D6	2p red lilac & red	.20	.60
J106	D6	5p yel & brn	.20	.40
J107	D6	10p yel & grn	.50	.50
J108	D6	20p green & blue	1.00	.80
J109	D6	25p red	1.50	.85
J110	D6	£1 vio & red lilac	7.50	3.00
J111	D6	£1.20 blue & green	10.00	4.00
J112	D6	£5 green & black	27.50	20.00
		Nos. J104-J112 (9)	48.60	30.75

OFFICIAL STAMPS

O1

Type of Regular Issue of 1840
"V R" in Upper Corners

			Imperf.	
1840		**Wmk. 18**	**Imperf.**	
O1	O1	1p black	25,000.	27,500.

No. O1 was never placed in use but examples are known used and on covers that passed through the mails by oversight.
Postage stamps perforated with a crown and initials "H.M.O.W.," "O.W.," "B.T." or "S.O.," or with only the initials "H.M.S.O." or "D.S.I.R.," were used for official purposes.

Counterfeits exist of Nos. O2-O83.

Inland Revenue
Regular Issues Overprinted in Black:

a

b

Type "a" is overprinted on the stamps of ½ penny to 1 shilling inclusive, type "b" on the higher values.

1882-85   Wmk. 30   Perf. 14
O2	A35	½p green	110.00	37.50
O3	A35	½p slate bl		
		('85)	75.00	26.00
O4	A40	1p lilac	4.75	2.50
a.		"OFFICIAL" omitted		8,250.
b.		Ovpt. lines transposed		
O5	A47	2½p lilac ('85)	350.00	120.00
O6	A28	6p gray	475.00	150.00
O7	A48	1sh green ('85)	4,750.	1,400.

Wmk. 31
O8	A51	5sh car rose		
		('85)	4,000.	1,400.
a.		Bluish paper ('85)	8,750.	3,250.
O9	A52	10sh ultra	6,000.	2,150.
a.		10sh cobalt	18,500.	5,500.
b.		Bluish paper	14,000.	4,250.

Wmk. Three Imperial Crowns (30)
O10	A53	£1 brown vio	42,500.	22,500.

1888-89   Wmk. 30
O11	A54	½p vermilion	9.50	3.50
a.		"I.R." omitted	4,250.	
O12	A65	1sh green ('89)	650.00	220.00

1890   Wmk. Three Orbs (29)
O13	A53	£1 brown vio	65,000.	30,000.

1891   Wmk. 30
O14	A57	2½p violet, blue	130.00	16.00

Wmk. Three Imperial Crowns (30)
1892
O15	A53	£1 green	8,750.	2,250.
a.		No period after "R"	—	3,000.

1901   Wmk. 30
O16	A54	½p blue green	16.00	11.00
O17	A62	6p violet, rose	350.00	100.00
O18	A65	1sh car rose &		
		green	3,000.	1,000.

1902-04
O19	A66	½p gray		
		green	26.00	2.75
O20	A66	1p carmine	19.00	1.90
O21	A66	2½p ultra	825.00	100.00
O22	A66	6p dull vio		
		('04)	165,000.	75,000.
O23	A74	1sh car rose		
		& green	2,750.	140.00

Wmk. 31
O24	A76	5sh car rose	12,000.	7,000.
O25	A77	10sh ultra	65,000.	30,000.

Wmk. Three Imperial Crowns (30)
O26	A78	£1 green	58,000.	22,500.

Nos. O4, O8, O9 and O15 also exist with overprint in blue black.

Government Parcels

Overprinted

1883-86   Wmk. 30
O27	A45	1½p lilac ('86)	350.00	70.00
O28	A46	6p green ('86)	2,100.	875.00
O29	A50	9p green	1,750.	700.00
O30	A29	1sh salmon		
		(P13)	1,050.	250.00
		Plate 14	2,500.	350.00
		Nos. O27-O30 (4)	5,250.	1,895.

1887-92
O31	A55	1½p violet &		
		green	100.00	8.50
O32	A56	2p green & car		
		rose ('91)	175.00	24.00
O33	A60	4½p car rose &		
		grn ('92)	300.00	220.00
O34	A62	6p violet, rose		
		('88)	175.00	37.50
O35	A63	9p blue & lil	275.00	55.00
O36	A65	1sh green	500.00	200.00
		Nos. O31-O36 (6)	1,525.	545.00

1897
O37	A40	1p lilac	82.50	17.50
a.		Inverted overprint	4,500.	2,100.

1900
O38	A65	1sh car rose &		
		grn	525.00	200.00
a.		Inverted overprint		11,000.

1902
O39	A66	1p carmine	35.00	14.00
O40	A68	2p green & car	160.00	40.00
O41	A66	6p dull violet	275.00	40.00
O42	A72	9p ultra & violet	550.00	175.00
O43	A74	1sh car rose &		
		grn	1,000.	275.00
		Nos. O39-O43 (5)	2,020.	544.00

Office of Works

Overprinted

1896
O44	A54	½p vermilion	250.00	120.00
O45	A40	1p lilac	400.00	120.00

1901-02
O46	A54	½p blue green	350.00	175.00
O47	A61	5p lilac & ultra	2,500.	1,000.
O48	A64	10p car rose &		
		lil	4,500.	1,400.

1902
O49	A66	½p gray		
		green	600.00	175.00
O50	A66	1p carmine	600.00	175.00
O51	A68	2p green &		
		car	1,750.	425.00
O52	A66	2½p ul-		
		tramarine	2,400.	650.00
O53	A73	10p car rose &		
		vio	30,000.	6,000.

Army
Overprinted:

a   b

1896
O54	A54(a)	½p vermilion	5.25	2.75
a.		"OFFICIA"	240.00	110.00
O55	A40(a)	1p lilac	4.25	3.00
a.		"OFFICIA"	175.00	105.00
O56	A57(b)	2½p violet, blue	35.00	24.00
		Nos. O54-O56 (3)	44.50	29.75

1900
O57	A54(a)	½p blue green	5.00	8.25

1901
O58	A62(b)	6p violet, rose	87.50	47.50

1902
O59	A66(a)	½p gray green	6.00	2.40
O60	A66(a)	1p carmine	6.00	2.40
a.		"ARMY" omitted		
O61	A66(a)	6p dull violet	175.00	80.00
		Nos. O59-O61 (3)	187.00	84.80

Overprinted

1903
O62	A66	6p dull violet	3,000.	1,200.

Royal Household

Overprinted

1902
O63	A66	½p gray green	400.00	220.00
O64	A66	1p carmine	350.00	190.00

Board of Education

Overprinted

1902
O65	A61	5p lilac & ultra	3,500.	800.00
O66	A65	1sh car rose &		
		grn	8,500.	4,500.

1902-04
O67	A66	½p gray green	175.00	40.00
O68	A66	1p carmine	175.00	40.00
O69	A66	2½p ultramarine	4,250.	350.00
O70	A71	5p lilac & ultra		
		('04)	25,000.	8,000.
O71	A74	1sh car rose &		
		grn	125,000.	—

Admiralty

Overprinted

1903
O72	A66	½p gray green	30.00	14.00
O73	A66	1p carmine	17.50	7.00
O74	A67	1½p vio & green	300.00	140.00
O75	A68	2p green & car	325.00	150.00
O76	A66	2½p ultra	450.00	140.00
O77	A69	3p violet, yel	375.00	150.00
		Nos. O72-O77 (6)	1,497.	601.00

Overprinted

1903
O78	A66	½p gray green	60.00	24.00
O79	A66	1p carmine	60.00	24.00
O80	A67	1½p vio &		
		green	1,000.	600.00
O81	A68	2p green &		
		car	2,000.	650.00
O82	A66	2½p ultramarine	2,400.	850.00
O83	A69	3p violet, yel	2,000.	350.00

The two types of the "Admiralty Official" overprint differ principally in the shape of the letter "M."

ENVELOPES

Britannia Sending Letters to World
(William Mulready, Designer) — E1

1840
U1	E1	1p black	375.00	500.00
U2	E1	2p blue	450.00	2,000.

LETTER SHEETS
U3	E1	1p black	375.00	500.00
U4	E1	2p blue	425.00	2,000.

REGIONAL ISSUES

Sold only at post offices within the respective regions, but valid for postage throughout Great Britain. Issues for Guernsey, Jersey and Isle of Man are listed with the Bailiwick issues that follow.

Starting in 1967, all Regional stamps were issued only with phosphorescence.

> Catalogue values for unused stamps in this section are for Never Hinged items.

ENGLAND

Three Lions — A1

Perf. 15x14 Syncopated
			Photo.	
2001-02				
1	A1	2nd shown	.95	.40
2	A1	1st Crowned Lion	1.35	.55
3	A1	E Oak tree	1.90	1.00
4	A1	65p Tudor rose	2.60	2.00
5	A1	68p Tudor rose	2.90	1.50
		Nos. 1-5 (5)	9.70	5.45

Issued: Nos. 1-4, 4/23/01. No. 5, 7/4/02.

Nos. 1-3 sold for 19p, 27p and 36p respectively on day of issue.

Type of 2001 With White Frames
Perf. 14¾x14 Syncopated
			Photo.	
2003, Oct. 14				
6	A1	2nd Three lions	.95	.40
7	A1	1st Crowned lion	1.35	.60
a.		Litho. (Wales #21a)	1.35	.60
8	A1	E Oak tree	1.90	1.00
9	A1	68p Tudor rose	2.90	1.50
		Nos. 6-9 (4)	7.10	3.50

Nos. 6-8 each sold for 20p, 28p and 38p respectively on day of issue.

Type of 2001 With White Frames
Perf. 14¾x14 Syncopated
			Photo.	
2004, May 11				
10	A1	40p Oak tree	1.60	.80
a.		Booklet pane, 2 each #6, 10 + label		
		(BK177)	5.00	—

No. 10a issued 2/24/05.

Type of 2001 With White Frames
Perf. 14¾x14 Syncopated
			Photo.	
2005, Apr. 5				
11	A1	42p Oak tree	1.70	.85

Type of 2001 With White Frames
Perf. 14¾x14 Syncopated
			Photo.	
2006, Mar. 28				
12	A1	44p Oak tree	1.75	.90
13	A1	72p Tudor rose	2.90	1.50

Type of 2001 With White Frames
Perf. 14¾x14 Syncopated
			Photo.	
2007				
14	A1	48p Oak tree	1.90	.95
15	A1	78p Tudor rose	3.25	1.60

Litho.
Self-Adhesive
Die Cut Perf. 14¾x14
Stamp + Label
16	A1	1st Crowned lion	1.50	1.50

Issued: Nos. 14, 15, 3/27; No. 16, 4/23. No. 16 was issued in sheets of 20 stamps + 20 labels that sold for £7.35 and had a franking value of 34p on day of issue.

Types of 2001 With White Frames

Perf. 14¾x14 Syncopated

			Photo.	
2008, Apr. 1			**Photo.**	
17	A1	50p Oak tree	2.00	1.00
18	A1	81p Tudor rose	3.25	1.60

Types of 2001 With White Frames

Perf. 14¾x14 Syncopated

2009, Mar. 31				
19	A1	56p Oak tree	1.75	.85
20	A1	90p Tudor rose	2.75	1.40

Heritage of England Type of 2007

Design: English flag (like #2462a).

Die Cut Perf. 14¾x14

2009, Apr. 21			Litho.	
		Self-Adhesive		
21	A626	1st multi + label	1.25	1.25

No. 21 was issued in a sheet of 20 stamps + 20 labels that sold for £8.35, and had a franking value of 39p on day of issue.

Types of 2001 With White Frames

Perf. 14¾x14 Syncopated

2010, Mar. 30			**Photo.**	
22	A1	60p Oak tree	1.90	.95
23	A1	97p Tudor rose	3.00	1.50

NORTHERN IRELAND

A1   A2

Flax and Red Hand of Ulster — A3

Perf. 15x14

1958-67			**Photo.**	**Wmk. 322**
1	A1	3p dark purple	.20	.20
p.		Phosphor. ('67)	.20	.20
2	A1	4p ultra ('66)	.20	.20
p.		Phosphor. ('67)	.20	.20
3	A2	6p rose lilac	.30	.20
4	A2	9p dk green ('67)	.35	.80
5	A3	1sh3p dark green	.35	.80
6	A3	1sh6p dark blue ('67)	.35	.80
		Nos. 1-6 (6)	1.75	3.00

Nos. 4, 6 and following are phosphorescent. For stamps with denomination of "1st" see No. 2600.

1968-69				**Unwmk.**

Design: 1sh6p, Flax plant, Red Right Hand of Ulster and Ulster field gate.

7	A1	4p ultramarine	.20	.20
8	A1	4p olive brown	.20	.20
9	A1	4p bright red ('69)	.30	.20
10	A1	5p dark blue	.20	.20
11	A3	1sh6p dark blue ('69)	3.00	3.00
		Nos. 7-11 (5)	3.90	3.80

Giants Causeway — A4

Perf. 14¾x14 Syncopated

2001-02			**Litho.**	
12	A4	2nd shown	.95	.25
13	A4	1st Farm fields	1.35	.60
a.		Booklet pane, 5 #12, 4 #13 (BK173)	10.00	
14	A4	E Linen	1.90	.90
15	A4	65p Parian China	2.60	1.35
16	A4	68p Parian China	2.70	1.40
		Nos. 12-16 (5)	9.50	4.50

Issued: Nos. 12-15, 3/6/01; No. 16, 7/4/02; No. 13a, 2/25/03.
Nos. 12-14 sold for 19p, 27p and 36p respectively on day of issue.

Type of 2001 With White Frames

Perf. 14¾x14 Syncopated

2003, Oct. 14			**Litho.**	
17	A4	2nd Giant's Causeway	.95	.40
a.		Photo.	.95	.40
18	A4	1st Farm fields	1.35	.50
a.		Photo. ('07)	1.25	.65
19	A4	E Linen	1.90	.90
20	A4	68p Parian China	2.70	1.40
		Nos. 17-20 (4)	6.90	3.20

Nos. 17-19 each sold for 20p, 28p and 38p respectively on day of issue.
No. 21a issued 9/28/08.

Type of 2001 With White Frames

Perf. 14¾x14 Syncopated

2004, May 11			**Litho.**	
21	A4	40p Linen	1.60	.80

Type of 2001 With White Frames

Perf. 14¾x14 Syncopated

2005, Apr. 5			**Litho.**	
22	A4	42p Linen	1.70	.90

Type of 2001 With White Frames

Perf. 14¾x14 Syncopated

2006, Mar. 28			**Litho.**	
23	A4	44p Linen	1.75	.90
24	A4	72p Parian China	2.90	1.50

Type of 2001 With White Frames

Perf. 14¾x14 Syncopated

2007, Mar. 27			**Photo.**	
25	A4	48p Parian China	1.90	.95
26	A4	78p Parian China	3.25	1.60

Type of 2001 With White Frames

Die Cut Perf. 14¾x14

2008, Mar. 11			**Litho.**	
		Self-Adhesive		
		Stamp + Label		
27	A4	1st Farm fields	1.50	1.50

No. 27 was issued in sheets of 20 stamps + 20 labels that sold for £7.35, and had a franking value of 34p on day of issue.

Types of 2001 With White Frames

Perf. 14¾x14 Syncopated

2008, Apr. 1			**Photo.**	
28	A4	50p Linen	2.00	1.00
29	A4	81p Parian China	3.25	1.60

Types of 2001 With White Frames

2009

2009				
30	A4	56p Linen	1.75	.85
31	A4	90p Parian China	2.75	1.40

Litho.
Self-Adhesive
Stamp + Label
Die Cut Perf. 14¾x14 Syncopated

32	A4	1st Farm fields	1.25	1.25
		Nos. 30-32 (3)	5.75	3.50

Issued: Nos. 30-31, 3/31; No. 32, 4/21. No. 32 was issued in a sheet of 20 stamps + 20 labels that sold for £8.35, and had a franking value of 39p on day of issue.

Types of 2001 With White Frames

Perf. 14¾x14 Syncopated

2010, Mar. 30			**Photo.**	
33	A4	60p Linen	1.90	.95
34	A4	97p Parian China	3.00	1.50

SCOTLAND

St. Andrew's Cross and Thistle — A1   A2

A3

Perf. 15x14

1958-67			**Photo.**	**Wmk. 322**
1	A1	3p dark purple	.20	.20
p.		Phosphor.	.20	.20
2	A1	4p ultra ('66)	.20	.20
p.		Phosphor. ('67)	.20	.20
3	A2	6p rose lilac	.25	.20
4	A2	9p dark green ('67)	.40	.45
5	A3	1sh3p dark green	.45	.45
p.		Phosphor. ('63)	.45	.45
6	A3	1sh6p dark blue ('67)	.50	.55
		Nos. 1-6 (6)	2.00	2.05

The 3p with two phosphorescent bands was issued in 1963; with one side band in 1965, and one center band in 1967. The value of No. 1p is for one center band. Nos. 4, 6 and following are phosphorescent. For stamps with denomination of "1st" see No. 2600.

1967-70				**Unwmk.**
7	A1	3p purple ('68)	.20	.20
8	A1	4p ultramarine	.20	.20
9	A1	4p olive brown ('68)	.20	.20
10	A1	4p brt red ('69)	.20	.20
11	A1	5p dark blue ('68)	.25	.20
12	A2	9p dark green ('70)	6.50	5.75
13	A3	1sh6p dark blue ('68)	1.60	1.60
		Nos. 7-13 (7)	9.15	8.35

Natl. Flag (St. Andrew's Cross) — A4

Perf. 14¾x14 Syncopated

1999-2002			**Photo.**	
14	A4	(2nd) shown	.95	.30
15	A4	(1st) Lion Rampant	1.35	.45
a.		Booklet pane, #15, 4 England #1, 4 England #2 (BK172)	10.50	
16	A4	(E) Thistle	1.10	.50
a.		Booklet pane, 4 each #15-16, + label (BK170)	8.25	
17	A4	64p Tartan	10.00	2.50
18	A4	65p As #17	2.40	1.25
a.		Booklet pane, 6 #14, 2 #18 + label (BK168)	9.00	
19	A4	68p Tartan	2.50	1.40
		Nos. 14-19 (6)	18.30	6.40

#14-16 sold for 19p, 26p, & 30p, respectively, on day of issue.
Issued: #14-17, 6/8; #18, 4/25/00; #18a, 8/4/00; #16a, 10/22/01. #19, 7/4/02. #15a, 9/24/02.

Type of 1999 With White Frames

Perf. 14¾x14 Syncopated

2003, Oct. 14			**Photo.**	
20	A4	2nd National flag	.95	.40
a.		Booklet pane, 3 each England #9, Scotland #20 (BK175)	11.50	—
21	A4	1st Lion rampant	1.35	.50
21a		Litho. (Wales #21a, GB 2600t)	1.25	.65
22	A4	E Thistle	1.90	.90
23	A4	68p Tartan	2.70	1.30
		Nos. 20-23 (5)	8.15	3.75

Nos. 20-22 each sold for 20p, 28p and 38p respectively on day of issue.
No. 20a issued 3/16/04. No. 21a issued 9/28/08.
See Great Britain No. 2419a for National Flag stamp inscribed "1st."

Type of 1999 With White Frames

Perf. 14¾x14 Syncopated

2004, May 11			**Photo.**	
24	A4	40p Thistle	1.60	.80
a.		Souvenir sheet, #20, 2 each #21, 24	6.75	4.50

No. 24a issued 10/5/04.

Type of 1999 With White Frames

Perf. 14¾x14 Syncopated

2005, Apr. 5			**Photo.**	
25	A4	42p Thistle	1.70	.85

Type of 1999 With White Frames

Perf. 14¾x14 Syncopated

2006, Mar. 28			**Photo.**	
26	A4	44p Thistle	1.75	.90
27	A4	72p Tartan	2.90	1.50

Type of 1999 With White Frames

Perf. 14¾x14 Syncopated

2007, Mar. 27			**Photo.**	
28	A4	48p Thistle	1.90	.95
29	A4	78p Tartan	3.25	1.60

Type of 1999 With White Frames

Die Cut Perf. 14¾x14

2007, Nov. 30			**Litho.**	
		Self-Adhesive		
		Stamp + Label		
30	A4	1st Lion rampant	1.75	1.75

No. 30 was issued in sheets of 20 stamps + 20 labels that sold for £8.50, and had a franking value of 34p on day of issue.

Types of 1999 With White Frames

Perf. 14¾x14 Syncopated

2008, Apr. 1			**Photo.**	
31	A4	50p Thistle	2.00	1.00
32	A4	81p Tartan	3.25	1.60

Types of 1999 With White Frames

2009, Mar. 31

2009, Mar. 31				
33	A4	56p Thistle	1.75	.85
34	A4	90p Tartan	2.75	1.40

Flag of Scotland — A5

35	A5	1st multi + label	1.40	1.40

No. 35 was printed in a sheet of 20 + 20 labels that could not be personalizd that sold for £8.35. See No. 2419a for similar stamp with water-activated gum.

Types of 1999 With White Frames

2010, Mar. 30

2010, Mar. 30				
36	A4	60p Thistle	1.90	.95
37	A4	97p Tartan	3.00	1.50

WALES & MONMOUTHSHIRE

A1   A2

Welsh Dragon — A3

Designs: 6p, 9p, Dragon in rectangular panel at bottom. 1sh3p, 1sh6p, Dragon and leek.

Perf. 15x14

1958-67			**Photo.**	**Wmk. 322**
1	A1	3p dark purple	.20	.20
p.		Phosphor. band ('67)	.20	.20
2	A1	4p ultra ('66)	.20	.20
p.		Phosphor. bands ('67)	.20	.20
3	A2	6p rose lilac	.40	.35
4	A2	9p dark green ('67)	.45	.40
5	A3	1sh3p dark green	.45	.45
6	A3	1sh6p dark blue ('67)	.45	.45
		Nos. 1-6 (6)	2.15	2.05

Nos. 4, 6 and following are phosphorescent. For stamps with denomination of "1st" see No. 2600.

1967-69				**Unwmk.**
7	A1	3p dark purple	.20	.20
8	A1	4p ultra ('68)	.20	.20
9	A1	4p olive brown ('68)	.20	.20
10	A1	4p brt red ('69)	.20	.20
11	A1	5p dark blue ('68)	.20	.20
12	A3	1sh6p dark blue ('69)	4.00	4.00
		Nos. 7-12 (6)	5.00	5.00

Leek — A4

Perf. 15x14 Syncopated

			Photo.	
1999-2002			**Photo.**	
13	A4	2nd shown	.95	.30
14	A4	1st Dragon	1.35	.45
15	A4	E Daffodil	1.90	.75
16	A4	64p Prince of Wales feathers	10.00	3.50
17	A4	65p Prince of Wales feathers	2.60	1.30
		Nos. 13-17 (5)	16.80	6.30
18	A2	2nd Leek, perf 13¾x14¼	5.50	.30
a.		Booklet pane, 4 each #18, MH336 + label (BK169)	27.50	
19	A4	68p Prince of Wales Feathers	3.00	1.50

#13, 18 sold for 19p; #14, 26p; & #15, 30p, on day of issue.
Issued: #13-16, 6/8; #17, 4/25/00. #19, 7/4/02.
No. 18 is a booklet stamp.

Type of 1999 With White Frames
Perf. 14¾x14 Syncopated

2003, Oct. 14			**Photo.**	
20	A4	2nd Leek	.95	.40
21	A4	1st Dragon	1.35	.50
a.		Booklet pane, litho., England #7a, Northern Ireland #18, Scotland, #21a, Wales & Monmouthshire #21b, + 5 labels (BK183) ('07)	5.75	
b.		Litho. (#21a, GB #2600v) ('07)	1.25	.65
22	A4	E Daffodil	1.90	.70
23	A4	68p Prince of Wales feathers	2.70	1.40
a.		Souvenir sheet, #20, 2 each #21, 23 ('06)	9.00	5.00
		Nos. 20-23 (4)	6.90	3.00

Nos. 20-22 each sold for 20p, 28p and 38p respectively on day of issue.
No. 23a issued 3/1/06. No. 21b issued 9/28/08.

Type of 1999 With White Frames
Perf. 14¾x14 Syncopated

2004, May 11			**Photo.**	
24	A4	40p Daffodil	1.60	.80

Type of 1999 With White Frames
Perf. 14¾x14 Syncopated

2005, Apr. 5			**Photo.**	
25	A4	42p Daffodil	1.70	.85

Type of 1999 With White Frames
Perf. 14¾x14 Syncopated

2006-07			**Photo.**	
26	A4	44p Daffodil	1.75	.90
a.		Booklet pane, 3 each Scotland #20, Wales & Monmouthshire #26 (BK181) ('07)	8.00	—
27	A4	72p Prince of Wales feathers	2.90	1.50

Self-Adhesive
Litho.
Stamp + Label
Die Cut Perf. 14¾x14

28	A4	1st Dragon	1.40	1.40
a.		Sheet, 5 each #28, England #16, Northern Ireland #27, Scotland #30, + 20 labels ('08)	27.50	

No. 28 was issued in a sheet of 20 stamps + 20 different se-tenant labels that sold for £6.95. The franking value of No. 28 was 32p on day of issue.
No. 28a issued 9/29/08. No. 28a sold for £7.74. Labels could not be personalized.
Issued: Nos. 26, 27, 3/28; Nos. 26a, 28 issued 3/1/07.

Type of 1999 With White Frames
Perf. 14¾x14 Syncopated

2007, Mar. 27			**Photo.**	
29	A4	48p Daffodil	1.90	.95
30	A4	78p Prince of Wales feathers	3.25	1.60

Types of 1999 With White Frames
Perf. 14¾x14 Syncopated

2008, Apr. 1			**Photo.**	
31	A4	50p Daffodil	2.00	1.00
32	A4	81p Prince of Wales feathers	3.25	1.60

Types of 1999 With White Frames
Perf. 14¾x14 Syncopated

2009, Mar. 31			**Photo.**	
33	A4	56p Daffodil	1.75	.85
34	A4	90p Prince of Wales feathers	2.75	1.40

Flag of Wales — A5

Die Cut Perf. 14¾x14 Syncopated
Self-Adhesive

2010, Mar. 1			**Litho.**	
35	A5	1st multi + label	1.25	1.25

No. 35 was printed in a sheet of 20 + 20 labels that could not be personalized that sold for £8.35. See No. 2639a for similar stamp with water-activated gum.

Types of 1999 With White Frames
Perf. 14¾x14 Syncopated

2010, Mar. 30			**Photo.**	
36	A4	60p Daffodil	1.90	.95
37	A4	97p Prince of Wales feathers	3.00	1.50

MACHINS

MACHIN DEFINITIVE STAMPS

Sterling Currency Issue

MA1

Type I   Type II

Two types of 2p.
Type I — Head off-center to right. Foot of "2" 1mm from left margin.
Type II — Head centered. Foot of "2" ½mm from left margin.

MH21   MH168

Two types of "£" symbol:
No. MH21 has a loop at the bottom and the numeral is a figure "1."
No. MH168 has no loop and numeral is like a capital "I."

Perf. 15x14

1967-69			**Photo.**	**Unwmk.**
		Size: 17½x21½mm		
MH1		½ brown orange	.20	.20
MH2		1p olive	.20	.20
a.		Booklet pane of 6 (BK101-BK104, BK121)	1.00	
MH3		2p maroon (I)	.25	.20
MH4		2p maroon (II)	.35	.20
MH5		3p dark violet	.20	.20
a.		Booklet pane of 6 (BK121)	12.00	
b.		Booklet pane, 2 ea #MH2, MH5 (BK83)	3.50	
c.		imperf. pair	800.00	
MH6		4p brown black	.20	.20
a.		Bklt. pane of 2 + 2 labels (BK84)	1.10	
b.		Bklt. pane of 4 (BK83-BK84)	1.10	
c.		Booklet pane of 6 (BK101-BK102, BK114-BK115, BK121-BK122)	1.50	
d.		Booklet pane, 4 #MH2, 2 #MH6 (BK122)	4.50	
MH7		4p bright red	.20	.20
a.		Bklt. pane of 2 + 2 labels (BK85)	1.10	
b.		Booklet pane of 4 (BK85)	1.10	
c.		Booklet pane of 6 (BK103-BK104, BK116-BK117, BK123-BK124)	1.10	
d.		Booklet pane of 15 + recipe (BK125-BK126)	5.00	
e.		Booklet pane, 4 #MH2, 2 #MH7 (BK123-BK124)	4.00	
f.		Coil strip of 5, #MH2, #MH5, MH7, 2 #MH4	3.00	
MH8		5p dark blue	.20	.20
a.		Booklet pane of 6 (BK110-BK112, BK122-BK124)	1.50	

---

b.		Booklet pane, 6 each #MH2, #MH7, 3 #MH8 + recipe (BK125-BK126)	16.00	
c.		Booklet pane of 15 + recipe (BK125-BK126)	6.00	
MH9		6p magenta	.30	.30
MH10		7p bright green	.45	.40
MH11		8p scarlet	.20	.50
MH12		8p lt greenish blue	.60	.70
MH13		9p dark green	.45	.30
MH14		10p gray	.65	.65
MH15		1sh light violet	.50	.30
MH16		1sh6p indigo & greenish bl	.60	.60
a.		Greenish blue omitted	110.00	
MH17		1sh9p black & orange	.60	.50

Perf. 12
Engr.
Size: 27x31mm

MH18		2sh6p brown	.90	.20
MH19		5sh dark carmine	2.25	.70
MH20		10sh ultramarine	7.00	7.00
MH21		£1 bluish black	4.00	1.75
		Nos. MH1-MH21 (21)	20.30	15.50

Nos. MH10-MH13 have denomination at right. Many of Nos. MH1-MH17 exist with phosphor bands omitted in error.
Issued: ½p, 1p, #MH3, 6p, 2/5/68; #MH4, 8/27/69; 3p, 4/6/68; #MH6, 1sh, 1sh9p, 6/5/67; #MH7, #MH12, 1/6/69; 5p, 7p, #MH11, 10p, 7/1/68; 9p, 1sh6p, 8/8/67; #MH18-MH21, 3/5/69.

Decimal Currency Issues
(P Instead of D)

MA2

Nos. MH22-MH189, MH199-MH243 are Type MA2. Specialized illustrations are shown for identification purposes.
Two types of 1p: Type I: Thick numeral and "p," which are 2½mm from bottom of design. Type II: Thinner numeral and "p," which are 3mm from bottom of design.

Perf. 15x14

1970-95			**Photo.**	**Unwmk.**
		Size: 17½x21½mm		
MH22		½p greenish blue	.20	.20
a.		Booklet pane of 5 + label (BK129-BK130, BK132, BK138, BK143)	4.50	
MH23		1p magenta, Type I	.20	.20
MH23A		1p magenta, Type II	.60	.60
MH24		1½p black	.20	.20
a.		Booklet pane, 2 each #MH23-MH24 (BK127-BK128)	2.00	

Issued: ½p, #MH23, 1½p, 2/15/71. #MH23A, 8/4/80.

a   b   c

Three types of 2p:
a, Wide "2," thick at bottom of curve.
b, Wide "2," thin at bottom of curve.
c, Narrow "2."

MH25		2p light green (a)	.20	.20
a.		Coil strip, 2 ea #MH22-MH23, 1 #MH25	.60	
MH26		2p light green (b)	.55	.20
a.		Booklet pane, 2 each #MH22, MH26 (BK127-BK128)	4.00	
b.		Booklet pane of 6 + printed margin (BK145)	.60	
MH27		2p dark green (c)	.35	.20
MH28		2p light green (c)	5.75	3.00

Litho.

MH29		2p dk grn, perf 14 (a)	.40	.20
MH30		2p dark green (a)	.55	.20
MH31		2p dark green (c)	1.00	.80
MH31A		2p dk grn, perf 14 (c)	2.00	2.00

Nos. MH24a, MH26a exist with with stamps se-tenant vertically or horizontally.
Issued: #MH25, 12/12/79; #MH26, 2/15/71; #MH27, 9/5/88; #MH28, 7/26/88; #MH29, 5/21/80; #MH30, 7/10/84; #MH31, 2/23/88; MH31A, 2/9/93.
No. MH31A comes from #MH128a (BK420) only.

---

a   b   c

Three types of 2½p:
a, Thick numerals & "P," end of curve of small "2" is thick.
b, Thinner numerals & "P," end of curve of small "2" is thin.
c, Very thin numerals & "P," end of curve of small "2" is pointy.

MH32		2½p pink (a)	.20	.20
a.		Booklet pane of 4 + 2 labels (BK129-BK130, BK132)	5.75	
b.		Booklet pane of 5 + label (BK129-BK130, BK132, BK138, BK143)	5.50	
MH33		2½p pink (b)	.30	.60
MH34		2½p pink (c)	2.00	3.00
a.		Booklet pane, 5 #MH22, 9 #MH34 + printed margin (BK144)	25.00	
b.		Booklet pane, 4 #MH22, 2 #MH34 + printed margin (BK144)	75.00	

#MH34a, MH34b valued in F-VF condition.

MH35		2½p vermilion (b)	.45	.70

Issued: #MH32 2/15/71; MH33, 5/21/75; #MH34, 5/24/72; MH35, 1/14/81.
#MH34 issued only in booklets.

a   b

Two types of 3p:
a, Thick numeral with top serif.
b, Thin numeral without serif.

MH36		3p ultramarine (a)	.20	.20
a.		Booklet pane, 2 #MH32, 4 #MH36 (BK138, BK143)	8.00	
b.		Booklet pane, 5 + label (BK131, BK133-BK136, BK139)	5.00	
c.		Bklt. pane of 6 (BK138, BK143)	5.00	
d.		Booklet pane of 12, 6 each #MH34, #MH36 + printed margin (BK144)	18.00	
e.		Booklet pane of 12 + printed margin (BK144)	10.00	
MH37		3p deep lilac rose (a)	.20	.20
a.		Coil strip, #MH35, 3 #MH37	.75	.35
MH38		3p deep lilac rose (b)	1.75	.75

Issued: #MH36, 9/10/73; #MH37, 10/22/80; #MH38, 1/21/92.

a   b

Two types of 3½p:
a, Numerals in fraction aligned diagonally.
b, Numerals in fraction aligned vertically.

MH39		3½p gray green (a)	.40	.40
a.		Booklet pane of 5 + label (BK137, BK139-BK141)	6.00	
MH40		3½p violet brown (b)	1.25	1.40

Issued: #MH39, 6/24/74; #MH40, 3/30/83.

a   b   c

Three types of 4p:
a, Wide "4" with large serif and thick crossbar.
b, Wide "4" with small serif and thin crossbar.
c, Narrow "4."

MH41		4p olive bister (a)	.30	.20
a.		Imperf., pair		
MH42		4p greenish blue (a)	.75	.75
a.		Coil strip, #MH22, 3 #MH42	1.75	2.50
MH43		4p brt greenish bl (a)	.20	.20
a.		Coil strip, #MH23, 3 #MH43	3.25	
b.		Coil strip, #MH28, 3 #MH43	4.25	
MH44		4p greenish blue (b)	2.25	2.25
MH45		4p brt greenish bl (c)	1.90	2.25
MH46		4p bright blue (c)	1.25	.20
a.		Coil strip, #MH38, 3 #MH46	5.25	
MH47		4p Prussian blue litho., perf 13½x14 (b)	.40	.40
MH48		4p Prus blue, litho. (c)	1.10	.85
MH49		4½p grayish blue	.50	.20
a.		Booklet pane of 5 + label (BK140, BK142)	6.00	

Issued: #MH41, 2/15/71; #MH42-MH42a, 12/30/81; #MH43-MH43a, 8/14/84; #MH43b, 9/5/88. #MH44, 8/26/81; #MH45, 9/3/84;

#MH46, 7/26/88; #MH46a, 9/19/89. #MH47, 1/30/80; #MH48, 5/13/86; 4 1/2p, 10/24/73. #MH43 issued only in strips.

a   b

Two types of 5p:
a, 5p is 3.25mm wide.
b, 5p is 2.75mm wide.

MH50	5p bluish lilac (a)	.30	.20
MH51	5p lilac, litho., perf 13½x14 (a)	.45	.45
MH52	5p red brown, litho., perf 13½x14 (a)	.75	.60
MH53	5p red brown, litho. (a)	.90	.20
MH54	5p red brown (b)	2.50	1.25
MH55	5p brown (b)	.45	.35
	a. Coil strip, #MH55, 3 #MH46	4.00	
	b. Coil strip, 2 ea #MH46, MH55	2.75	
	c. Coil strip, #MH46, 3 MH55	1.75	
MH56	5½p dark violet	.35	.35

Issued: #MH50, 2/15/71; #MH51, 5/21/80; #MH52, 1/27/82; #MH53, 2/21/84; #MH54, 10/20/86; #MH55, 7/26/88; #MH55a, 11/27/90; #MH55b, 10/1/91. #MH55c, 1/31/95. 5 1/2p, 10/24/73.

a   b   c

Three types of 6p:
a, Thick numeral and "P."
b, Thinner numeral and "P," numeral is pointed at top and very thin where loop joins.
c, Narrow numeral.

MH57	6p light emerald (a)	.35	.20
MH58	6p light emerald (b)	.85	.20
	a. Booklet pane, #MH58, 2 MH22, 3 MH23 (BK225)	1.50	
	b. Coil strip, #MH23, MH26, MH58, 2 #MH22	1.10	
MH59	6p brt olive green (c)	.40	.20
MH60	6½p Prussian blue	.35	.40

Issued: #MH57, 2/15/71; #MH58, 6/9/76; #MH58b, 12/3/75. #MH59, 9/10/91; 6 1/2p, 9/4/74. #MH58 issued only in booklets and strips.

a   b

Two types of 7p:
a, Wide numeral.
b, Narrow numeral.

MH61	7p dark red brown (a)	.35	.40
	a. Coil strip, #MH61, 2 ea MH22-MH23	.60	
	b. Booklet pane, #MH61, 2 ea MH22-MH23 + label (BK226)	.75	
MH62	7p henna brown (b)	1.25	*1.50*
MH63	7½p lt red brown	.40	.40
MH64	8p red	.35	.20
	a. Coil strip, #MH64, 2 MH23 + 2 labels	.60	
	b. Booklet pane, #MH64, 2 MH23 + label (BK227)	.75	
MH65	8½p yellow green	.35	.20
	a. Bklt. pane, 2 ea #MH22-MH23, MH60, 4 MH65 (BK228)	5.25	

No. MH65a exists with the four 8 1/2p stamps se-tenant on either the left or right side of the pane.

MH66	9p black & ocher	.65	.25
MH67	9p violet blue	.45	.20
	a. Booklet pane, 2 #MH23, 3 ea MH61, MH67 (BK229-BK230)	3.50	
	b. Booklet pane, 10 ea #MH61, MH67 (BK672)	6.50	

No. MH67a exists with the three 9p stamps se-tenant on either the left or right side of the pane.

MH68	9½p bright lilac	.40	.50

Issued: #MH61, 1/15/75; #MH61a, 12/14/77. #MH62, 10/29/85; 7 1/2p, 2/15/71; 8p, 10/24/73; #MH64a, 1/16/80. 8 1/2p, 9/24/75; #MH66, 2/15/71; #MH67, 9 1/2p, 2/25/76.

a   b   c

Three types of 10p:
a, Round "0."

b, Thin part of "0" at upper left, lower right.
c, Thin part of "0" at top, bottom.

MH69	10p org brn & lt org (a)	.65	.35
MH70	10p light org brn (b)	.45	.30
	a. Bklt. pane of 9 + printed margin (BK145)	2.50	
	b. Booklet pane, 2 ea #MH26, MH64, 3 #MH70 + label (BK231-BK232)	2.50	
	c. Booklet pane, 10 ea #MH64, MH70 (BK709)	6.25	
MH70D	10p light org brn (c)	35.00	20.00

No. MH70b exists with the three 10p stamps se-tenant on either the left or right side of the pane.

MH71	10p brn orange (c)	.60	.50
MH72	10½p yellow	.50	.50
MH73	10½p steel blue	.80	.60
MH74	11p pink	.50	.20

Issued: #MH69, 8/11/71; #MH70, MH72, 11p, 2/25/76; #MH71, 9/4/90; #MH73, 4/26/78; #MH70D, 9/4/84.

a   b

Two types of 11 ½p:
a, Thin numerals in fraction.
b, Thick numerals in fraction.

MH75	11 ½p olive bister (a)	.65	.65
MH76	11 ½p gray brown (a)	.55	.40
	a. Booklet pane, 2 #MH42, 3 each MH35, MH76 (BK236)	4.50	
MH77	11 ½p gray brown (b)	1.00	.20

#MH77 comes from #MH86c (BK826), only.
Issued: #MH75, 8/15/79; #MH76, 1/14/81; #MH77, 11/11/81;

a   b

Two types of 12p:
a, Wide numerals.
b, Narrow, thin numerals.

MH78	12p yellow green (a)	.55	.50
	a. Booklet pane of 9 + printed margin (BK145)	3.00	
	b. Booklet pane of 9 (#MH26, 4 each #MH70, MH78) + printed margin (BK145)	13.50	
	c. Booklet pane of 10 each #MH70, MH78 (BK759)	9.00	
	d. Booklet pane, 3 #MH26, 2 each MH70, MH78 + label (BK233)	2.25	
MH79	12p bright green (b)	.60	.35
	a. Booklet pane of 9 + printed margin (BK140)	6.00	
	b. Booklet pane, 2 #MH23, 4 MH79 (BK245)	8.00	

Issued: #MH78, 1/30/80; #MH79, 10/29/85.

a   b

Two types of 12 ½p:
a, Thin, narrow numerals.
b, Thick, wider numerals.

MH80	12 ½p light emerald (a)	.50	.25
	a. Booklet pane of 6 + printed margin (BK146-BK147)	5.00	
	b. Booklet pane of 9, #MH25, MH37, 7 MH80 + printed margin (BK146)	6.00	
	c. Booklet pane, #MH22, 4 MH37, 3 MH80 (BK237-BK238)	3.00	
	d. Booklet pane, 2 #MH23, 3 each MH40, MH80 (BK239)	7.50	
	e. Booklet pane of 20 (BK760)	8.00	

No. MH80c exists with the three 12½p stamps se-tenant on either the left or right side of the pane. Booklets with 20 #MH80 were sold at a discount. Stamps in these booklets had 5-point double-lined stars printed on the reverse.

MH81	12 ½p green (b)	.80	.25

No. MH81 comes from #MH93d (BK572).
Issued: #MH80, 1/27/82; #MH81, 2/1/82.

a   b

Two types of 13p:
a, "3" with serif.

b, "3" without serif.

MH82	13p gray green (a)	.60	.55
MH83	13p lt red brown (b)	.50	.20
	a. Booklet pane of 6 + printed margin (BK148, BK151)	3.50	
	b. Booklet pane of 9 + printed margin (BK149, BK151)	5.00	
	c. Booklet pane, 2 each MH45, 3 each MH23, MH83 (BK240)	4.75	
	d. Booklet pane, #MH23, 2 MH54, 3 MH83 (BK244, BK248)	5.00	
	e. Booklet pane of 4, margins all around (BK285)	3.00	
	f. Booklet pane of 10, margins all around (BK534)	6.00	
	g. As "d," imperf edges (BK248A, BK250-BK251)	6.00	

Panes of #MH83 with stars printed on the reverse were sold at a discount.

MH84	13p lt red brn, litho. (b)	1.00	.85
	a. Booklet pane of 6 + printed margin (BK152)	6.00	

Issued: #MH82, 8/15/79; #MH83, 8/28/84; #MH84, 2/9/88; 13 1/2p, 1/30/80.

a   b

Two types of 14p:
a, Wide "4."
b, Narrow "4."

MH86	14p gray blue (a)	.70	.60
	a. Bklt. pane, #MH22-MH23, MH86, 3 MH76 (BK234-BK235)	2.25	
	b. Booklet pane, 4 #MH76, 6 MH86 (BK524)	5.25	
	c. Booklet pane, 10 each MH77, MH86 (BK826)	12.50	
MH87	14p dark blue (b)	.60	.40
	a. Booklet pane of 4, margins all around (BK295)	5.00	
	b. Booklet pane of 4, imperf on T, B (BK296)	5.00	
	c. Booklet pane of 4, imperf on T, B, R (BK297)	19.00	
	d. Booklet pane of 10, margins all around (BK558)	5.50	
	e. Booklet pane of 10, imperf on T, B (BK560)	8.00	
MH88	14p dark blue, litho. (b)	2.50	2.00
MH89	14p dark blue, litho., perf 14 (b)	6.25	1.00

No. MH89 comes from #MH108a (BK412), only.

MH90	15p deep ultramarine	.70	.70
MH91	15p bright blue	.75	.25

Issued: #MH86, 1/14/81; #MH87, 9/5/88; #MH88, 10/11/88; #MH89, 4/25/89; #MH90, 8/15/79; #MH91, 9/26/89.

a   b

Two types of 15 ½p:
a, Thin numerals in fraction, top bar of "5" thin.
b, Thick numerals in fraction, top bar of "5" thick.

MH92	15 ½p light violet (a)	.70	.60
	a. Booklet pane of 6 + printed margin (BK146)	4.25	
	b. Booklet pane of 9 + printed margin (BK146)	6.50	
MH93	15 ½p light violet (b)	.80	.35
	c. Booklet pane, 4 #MH80, 6 MH93 (BK573-BK574)	6.75	
	d. Booklet pane, 4 #MH81, 6 MH93 (BK572)	8.25	
	e. Booklet pane, 10 each #MH80, MH93 (BK802)	11.00	

No. MH93e was printed with 10-point single-line blue stars on the reverse over the gum.

MH94	16p brownish gray	.65	.65
	a. Booklet pane, #MH37, 2 MH40, 6 MH94 + printed margin (BK147)	4.50	
	b. Booklet pane of 9 + printed margin (BK147)	5.50	
	c. Booklet pane, 4 #MH80, 6 MH94 (BK594)	12.00	

Panes of #MH94 with double-line D printed on reverse were sold at a discount in BK584.

MH95	16 ½p fawn	1.00	.85

Issued: #MH92, 1/14/81; #MH93, 2/1/82; 16p, 3/30/83; 16 1/2p, 1/27/82. #MH93 issued only in booklets.

a   b

Two types of 17p:
a, Wide "7."
b, Narrow "7."

MH96	17p light green (a)	.85	.70
MH97	17p blue gray (b)	.70	.70
	a. Booklet pane of 3 + label (star printed on reverse-BK241-BK242)	2.50	
	b. Booklet pane of 9 + printed margin (BK149-BK150)	7.00	
	c. Booklet pane of 6 + printed margin (BK148-BK150)	20.00	
	d. Booklet pane, #MH70D, MH83, 7 MH97 + printed margin (BK148)	45.00	
	e. Booklet pane, 4 #MH79, 6 MH97 (BK616-BK618)	7.00	
	f. Booklet pane, 4 #MH83, 6 MH97 (BK641)	6.00	
	g. Booklet pane of 10 (double-lined "D" printed on reverse-BK652)	6.00	
MH98	17p dark blue (b)	1.25	.35
	a. Bklt. pane of 3 + label (BK256)	3.00	
MH99	17p dk bl, litho. (b)	1.20	.35
	a. Booklet pane of 6 + printed margin (BK155)	7.50	
MH100	17 ½p lt red brown	.90	.85
MH101	18p violet blue	.80	.70
MH102	18p olive green	.85	.70
	a. Booklet pane of 9 + printed margin (BK151)	7.00	
	b. Booklet pane, #MH23, MH83, 2 MH102 (BK246-BK247, BK249)	3.00	
	c. Booklet pane of 4, margins all around (BK328)	4.00	
	d. Booklet pane, #MH83, 5 MH102 (BK406-BK407)	6.00	
	e. Booklet pane of 10, margins all around (BK714)	8.75	
	f. As "d," imperf edges (BK408-BK410)	6.00	
MH103	18p ol grn, litho.	1.00	1.10
	a. Booklet pane of 6 + printed margin (BK152)	5.75	
	b. Booklet pane of 9 + printed margin (BK152)	7.75	
MH104	18p brt yel grn	.90	.40
MH105	18p brt yel grn, litho.	1.40	1.60
	a. Booklet pane of 6 + printed margin (BK157)	7.75	
MH106	19p brt orange	1.25	.35
	a. Bklt. pane, #MH87, 2 #MH106 + label (BK252-BK253)	3.75	
	b. Booklet pane, 2 #MH87, 4 MH106 (BK411, BK413)	8.00	
	c. Booklet pane of 4, margins all around (BK348)	8.00	
	d. Booklet pane of 4, imperf on T, B (BK349)	9.75	
	e. Booklet pane of 4, imperf on T, B, R (BK350)	19.00	
	f. Booklet pane of 10, margins all around (BK729)	14.00	
	g. Booklet pane of 10, imperf on T, B (BK730)	10.00	
MH107	19p red org, litho.	2.25	2.25
MH108	19p red org, litho., perf 14	3.50	1.25
	a. Booklet pane of 2 #MH89, 4 #MH108 (BK412)	22.50	
MH110	19 ½p olive gray	2.25	1.50

Issued: #MH96, 1/30/80; #MH97, 3/30/80; #MH98, 9/4/90; #MH99, 3/19/91; 17 1/2p, 1/30/80; #MH101, 1/14/81; #MH102, 8/28/84; #MH103, 2/9/88; #MH104, 9/10/91; #MH105, 10/27/92; #MH106, 8/3/88; #MH107, 10/11/88; #MH108, 4/25/89; 19 1/2p, 1/27/82. #MH99, MH103, MH105, MH108 issued only in booklets.

a   b

Two types of 20p:
a, Thin part of "0" at upper left, lower right.
b, Thin part of "0" at top, bottom.

MH111	20p dp pur brn (a)	1.25	.20
MH112	20p dp pur brn, litho., perf 13¾x14 (a)	1.75	1.10
MH113	20p dp pur brn, litho., perf 15x14 (b)	2.00	1.25
MH114	20p greenish bl (b)	1.00	.80
MH115	20p brown black (b)	1.10	1.10
	a. Booklet pane, 2 #MH91, MH115 + label (BK254)	5.00	
	b. Booklet pane of 5 + label (BK414)	8.00	
MH116	20½p ultramarine	1.50	1.10
MH117	22p dark blue	1.00	.85
MH118	22p yellow green	1.00	.90
MH119	22p yel grn, litho. (MH150a)	14.00	3.00
MH120	22p orange red	1.20	.90
	a. Booklet pane, 2 #MH98, 3 MH120 + 3 labels (BK417)	4.00	
MH121	22p org red, litho.	1.40	1.00
	a. Booklet pane of 9 + printed margin (BK155)	10.00	
MH122	23p rose pink	1.50	.50
MH123	23p brt yel grn	1.40	1.00
MH124	24p violet	1.75	1.75
MH125	24p brown red	2.25	1.90

MH126	24p brown	1.00	.90
	a. Booklet pane, 2 each #MH23, MH126 (BK257-BK259)	1.75	
	b. Booklet pane, 2 #MH27, 4 MH126 + 2 labels (BK418-BK419)	3.50	
MH127	24p brown, litho.	1.25	1.25
	a. Booklet pane of 6 + printed margin (BK157)	8.00	
MH128	24p brn, litho. perf 14	1.50	.35
	a. Booklet pane, 2 #MH31A, 4 MH128 + 2 labels (BK420)	9.50	
MH129	25p lilac	1.00	1.10
MH129A	25p salmon	15.00	14.00

Issued: #MH111, 2/25/76; #MH112, 5/21/80; #MH113, 5/13/86; #MH114, 8/23/88; #MH115, 9/26/89; 20 ½p, 3/30/83; #MH117, 10/22/80; #MH118, 8/28/84; #MH119, 2/9/88; #MH120, 9/4/90; #MH121, 3/19/91; #MH122, 3/30/83; #MH123, 8/3/88; #MH124, 8/28/84; MH125, 9/26/89; #MH126, 9/10/91; #MH127, 10/27/92; #MH128, 2/9/93; 25p, 1/14/81.

#MH119, MH121, MH127 issued only in booklets.

No. MH129A was issued 2/6/96 only in coils.

a   b

Two types of 26p:
a, Wide numerals.
b, Narrow numerals.

MH130	26p red (a)	1.25	.70
	a. Booklet pane, #MH23, MH130, 2 MH83, 5 MH102 + printed margin (BK151)	20.00	
MH131	26p red (b)	6.00	6.00
	a. Booklet pane of 4, margins all around (BK446)	24.00	
MH132	26p olive gray (b)	1.75	1.40
MH133	27p brown	1.50	1.50
	a. Booklet pane of 4, margins all around (BK456)	14.50	
	b. Booklet pane of 4, horiz. edges imperf (BK457)	35.00	
MH134	27p violet	1.75	1.40
MH135	28p deep violet blue	1.40	1.40
MH136	28p dk olive bister	1.60	1.40
MH137	28p dull blue green	1.60	1.40

Issued: #MH130, 1/27/82; #MH131, 8/4/87; #MH132, 9/4/90; #MH133, 8/3/88; #MH134, 9/4/90; #MH135, 3/30/83; #MH136, 8/23/88; #MH137, 9/10/91.

#MH131 issued only in booklets.

a   b

Two types of 29p:
a, Wide numerals.
b, Narrow numerals.

MH138	29p brown olive (a)	2.25	2.00
MH139	29p dp rose lilac (b)	2.50	2.00
MH140	29p dp rose lilac, litho., perf 14 (b)	4.75	3.00
	a. Booklet pane of 4, imperf edges (BK478)	20.00	
MH141	30p dk olive green	1.75	1.40
MH142	31p brt rose lilac	1.40	1.40
	a. Bklt. pane, 6 #MH121, 2 MH79, 2 MH97 + printed margin (BK150)	17.00	
MH143	31p ultramarine	1.90	1.75
MH144	31p ultra, litho., perf 14	2.75	1.60
	a. Booklet pane of 4, imperf on T, B (BK503)	11.00	
MH145	32p Prussian blue	2.25	2.00
MH146	33p emerald	2.00	1.90
MH147	33p emerald, litho.	3.00	3.00
	a. Bklt. pane, 6 #MH121, 2 MH147 + label, printed margin (BK155)	15.00	
MH148	33p emer, litho. perf 14	2.75	.45
	a. Booklet pane of 4, margins all around (BK544)	11.00	
MH149	34p dark brown	2.00	2.00
	a. Bklt. pane, 2 #MN149, 2 MH45, 4 MH83, 2 MH97 + printed margin (BK149)	17.00	
MH150	34p dark brn, litho.	11.00	2.00
	a. Bklt. pane, 6 #MH84, 1 ea MH103, MH119, MH150 + printed margin (BK152)	27.50	
MH151	34p dull blue green	2.25	2.10
MH152	34p brt rose lilac	2.00	2.00
MH153	35p dark brown	2.25	1.90
MH154	35p orange yellow	2.00	1.90
MH155	37p scarlet	2.25	2.00
MH156	39p brt rose lilac	2.25	1.75
MH157	39p brt rose lil, litho. perf 14	3.00	.80
	a. Booklet pane of 4, imperf on T, B (BK662)	12.00	

MH158	39p brt rose lil, litho. (MH178a, MH187b)	2.50	.80

Issued: #MH138, 1/27/82; #MH139, 9/26/89; #MH140, 10/2/89; #MH141, 9/26/89; #MH142, 3/30/83; #MH143, 9/4/90; #MH144, 9/17/90; #MH145, 8/23/88; #MH146, 9/4/90; #MH147, 3/19/91; #MN148, 9/16/91; #MH149, 8/28/84; #MH150, 2/9/88; #MH151, 9/26/89; #MH152, 9/10/91; #MH153, 8/23/88; #MH154, 9/10/91; #MH155, 9/26/89; #MH156, 9/10/91; #MH157, 9/16/91; #MH158, 10/27/92.

#MH144, MH147-MH148, MH150 issued only in booklets.

a   b

Two types of 50p:
a, Wide numerals.
b, Narrow numerals.

MH159	50p bister brown (a)	2.75	.35
MH160	50p ocher (b)	2.50	.80

Issued: #MH159, 2/2/77; #MH160, 5/21/80.

a   b

Two types of 75p:
a, Wide numerals.
b, Narrow numerals.

MH161	75p black, litho., perf 13 ½x14 (a)	4.00	1.50
MH162	75p black, litho. (a)	4.00	1.50
MH163	75p black, litho. (b)	12.00	9.75
MH164	75p black (b)	4.00	2.00

Issued: #MH161, 3/1/80; #MH162, 2/21/84; #MH163, 2/23/88; #MH164, 7/26/88.

Engr.
Perf. 12
Size: 27x31mm

MH165	10p carmine rose	.90	*1.00*
MH166	20p olive	1.00	.20
MH167	50p ultramarine	2.00	.60
	p. Phosphor	2.50	.60
MH168	£1 bluish black	4.75	1.25

For illustration of £1, see above #MH1.
No. MH168, imperf, are from printers' waste.
Issued: #MH165-MH167, 6/17/70; £1, 12/6/72.

Photo.
Perf. 14x15
Size: 27x38mm

MH169	£1 olive grn & yel	4.00	.60
MH170	£1.30 slate bl & buff	6.25	*7.00*
MH171	£1.33 black & pale rose lilac	8.75	8.00
MH172	£1.41 indigo & buff	11.00	9.75
MH173	£1.50 blk & lt pink	7.50	5.75
MH174	£1.60 indigo & buff	7.50	8.00
MH175	£2 mar & lt grn	14.00	1.50
MH176	£5 dk bl & pink	32.50	4.00

Issued: £1, 2/2/77; £1.30, 8/3/83; £1.33, 8/28/84; £1.41, 9/17/85; £1.50, 9/2/86; £1.60, 9/15/87; £2, £5, 2/2/77.

2nd or 1st Class (Non-Denominated)

2nd and 1st class stamps sell for the current rates and remain valid indefinitely for the indicated service

Perf. 15x14

MH177	2nd bright blue	1.50	1.10
	a. Booklet pane of 4, imperf on T, B, R (BK961)	25.00	
	b. Booklet pane of 10, imperf on T, B (BK1028, BK1078)	15.00	
MH178	2nd bright blue, litho.	1.25	1.00
	a. Booklet pane, 2 each #MH105, MH147, MH158, MH178 + label, printed margin (BK158)	15.00	
MH179	2nd bright blue, litho., perf 14	1.25	1.10
	a. Booklet pane of 4, imperf on T, B, R (BK960)	5.00	
	b. Booklet pane of 10, imperf on T, B (BK963-BK964)	5.00	
	c. Booklet pane of 10, imperf on T, B (BK1034-BK1035)	12.50	

Nos. MH177-MH179 each sold for 14p on day of issue.

MH180	2nd dark blue	1.75	.30
	a. Booklet pane of 10, imperf on T, B (BK1030)	17.50	

MH181	2nd dark blue, litho.	2.50	.30
MH182	2nd dark blue, litho., perf 14	.95	.30
	a. Booklet pane of 4, imperf on T, B (BK962)	3.75	
	b. Booklet pane of 10, imperf on T, B (BK1032)	9.50	

Nos. MH180-MH182 each sold for 15p on day of issue.

MH183	1st brown black	2.00	.65
	a. Booklet pane of 4, imperf on T, B, R (BK995)	25.00	
	b. Booklet pane of 10, imperf on T, B (BK1041)	20.00	
MH184	1st brown black, litho., perf 14	3.00	.75
	a. Booklet pane of 4, imperf on T, B, R (BK994)	12.00	
MH185	1st brown black, litho.	2.50	.65

Nos. MH183-MH185 each sold for 19p on day of issue.

MH186	1st orange red	1.35	.40
	a. Booklet pane of 10, imperf on T, B (BK1068, BK1091)	13.50	
MH187	1st orange red, litho.	1.35	.40
	a. Booklet pane, 3 each #MH178, MH187 + printed margin (BK158)	7.75	
	b. Booklet pane, #MH178, MH187, 2 ea MH105, MH127, MH158 + label, printed margin (BK157)	15.00	
	c. Booklet pane of 8+ label, printed margin (BK156)	10.50	
	d. Booklet pane of 10, imperf on T, B (BK1092-BK1093)	13.50	

No. MH187c contains #MH178, MH187, 2 each MH147, WMMH34, WMMH45.

MH188	1st orange red, litho., perf 14	1.35	.40
	a. Booklet pane of 4, imperf on T, B (BK996-BK997)	5.50	
	b. Booklet pane of 10, imperf on T, B (BK1070)	13.50	
MH189	1st orange red, litho., perf 13x13 ½	4.25	1.50

Nos. MH186-MH189 each sold for 20p on day of issue.
Distance of denomination to the margin and bust may vary on different printings of the same stamp.
Issued: #MH177, 8/22/89; #MH178, 9/18/89; #MH179, 8/22/89; #MH180-MH182, 8/7/90; #MH183-MH184, 8/22/89; #MH185, 9/19/89; #MH186-MH188, 8/7/90; #MH189, 10/90.

#MH177-MH189 issued only in booklets.

Victoria and Elizabeth II — MA3

1990-2000	**Photo.**	**Perf. 15x14**	
MH190	15p bright blue	.90	.90
	a. Booklet pane of 10, imperf on T, B (BK619)	11.50	
MH191	15p brt bl, litho., perf 14	1.75	2.00
	a. Booklet pane of 4 with imperf on T, B, R (BK307)	8.00	
	b. Booklet pane of 10 with imperf on T, B (BK620)	14.00	
MH192	15p bright blue, litho.	2.50	2.50
	a. Booklet pane of 10 (BK621)	22.50	
MH193	20p black & brown black	.90	.90
	a. Booklet pane, #MH193, 2 MH190 + label (BK255)	3.00	
	b. Booklet pane of 4 with imperf on T, B, R (BK371)	6.00	
	c. Bklt. pane of 5 + label (BK415)	4.00	
	d. Booklet pane of 6 + printed margin (BK154)	4.00	
	e. Booklet pane of 10 with imperf on T, B (BK743)	12.00	
	f. Souvenir sheet of 1	7.00	7.00
MH194	20p black & brn blk, litho., perf 14	2.25	2.00
	a. Booklet pane of 4 with imperf on T, B (BK372)	11.50	
	b. Bklt. pane of 5 + label (BK416)	12.00	
	c. Booklet pane of 10 with imperf on T, B (BK744)	22.50	
MH195	20p black & brn blk, litho.	2.75	2.75
	a. Booklet pane of 10 (BK745)	27.50	
MH196	29p deep rose lilac	2.00	2.00
	a. Booklet pane, #MH91, MH115, MH160, MH177, MH183, MH190, MH193, MH196 + label, printed margin (BK154)	22.50	
MH197	34p dull blue green	2.25	2.25
MH198	37p scarlet	2.50	2.50

Perf. 13¾x14¼ Syncopated

MH198A	1st blk & yel	2.50	1.60
	a. Booklet pane of 6 (BK167)	15.00	

Nos. MH191-MH192, MH194-MH195, MH198A were issued only in booklets.
No. MH198A sold for 26p on day of issue.
Issued: #MH190, MH193, MH196-MH198, 1/10; #MH191, MH194, 1/30; #MH192, MH195, 4/17; #MH198A, 2/15/00.

1P

Syncopated Perf. 15x14

1993-97		**Type MA2**	
MH199	1p magenta	.20	.20
MH200	1p mag, litho. (MH216b)	.90	.45
MH201	2p dark green	.25	.20
MH202	4p Prussian blue	.45	.20
MH203	5p rose brown	.35	.20
MH204	6p bright olive green	.55	.35
MH205	6p bright olive green, litho. (MH214a)	15.00	15.00
MH206	10p brown orange	.50	.35
MH207	10p brown orange, litho. (MH231a)	7.25	5.50
MH208	19p olive green	.75	.70
MH209	19p ol grn, litho. (MH214a, MH231a)	2.25	2.00
	a. Booklet pane of 6 + printed margin (BK160)	13.50	
MH210	20p greenish blue	1.20	1.00
MH211	20p bright yel grn	1.40	.80
MH212	20p brt yel grn, litho. (MH216a-MH216b)	3.75	2.50
MH213	25p salmon	1.00	.40
	a. Booklet pane of 2 + 2 labels (BK260-BK262)	2.00	
	b. 25p sal, litho.		
MH214	25p sal, litho. (MH231a)	1.25	1.25
	a. Bklt. pane, #MH205, MH209, 4 MH214 + printed margin (BK159)	22.50	
	b. Booklet pane of 8 + label, printed margin (see footnote) (BK161)	11.00	

No. MH214b contains 2 each #MH214, NIMH59, SMH65, WMMH60.

MH215	26p brown	1.75	1.25
MH216	26p brown, litho.	1.10	1.10
	a. Bklt. pane, #MH212, 7 MH216 (BK749)	10.00	
	b. Bklt. pane, #MH212, 2 MH200, 3 MH216 + 2 labels (BK426)	4.00	
MH218	29p gray	1.50	1.40
MH219	30p olive green	1.50	1.25
MH220	30p olive green, litho. (MH231a)	8.00	4.75
MH221	31p deep rose lilac	1.75	1.25
MH222	35p orange yellow	1.75	1.75
MH223	35p org yel, litho.	2.00	2.00
	a. Booklet pane of 4 (BK562-BK563)	10.00	
MH224	36p blue	1.75	1.75
MH225	37p bright rose lilac	2.10	2.10
MH226	37p brt rose lilac, litho.	4.25	3.00
	a. Booklet pane of 4 (BK605)	18.00	
MH227	38p red	2.00	2.00
MH228	39p bright pink	2.10	2.10
MH230	41p drab	2.50	1.60
MH231	41p drab, litho.	3.50	2.00
	a. Booklet pane, #MH207, MH220, MH223, MH231, 2 each MH209, MH214 + label, printed margin (BK160)	17.50	
	b. Booklet pane of 4 (BK685-BK686)	15.00	
MH232	43p dark brown	2.75	2.75
MH233	50p ocher	2.75	1.10
MH234	60p slate blue, litho.	2.75	2.75
	a. Booklet pane of 4 (BK790-BK791)	11.00	
MH235	63p bright green	3.25	2.25
MH236	63p brt grn, litho.	5.00	3.50
	a. Bklt. pane of 4 (BK815)	18.00	
MH237	£1 violet	4.50	3.25

No. MH237 is printed with Iriodin ink, giving stamp design a three dimensional appearance.

MH238	2nd bright blue	1.00	1.00
MH239	2nd bright blue, litho.	1.00	1.00
MH240	1st orange red	1.75	1.40
MH241	1st orange red, litho.	1.35	1.00
	a. Miniature sheet of 1	6.50	6.50
	b. Booklet pane of 4 + label (BK1000, BK1002, BK1004)	6.50	
	c. Booklet pane of 9 + printed margin (BK165)	12.00	

No. MH241a was sold for £1 on day of issue in pre-packaged greeting cards at Boots pharmacy. Unfolded examples were later sold by British Philatelic Bureau. Value indicated is for unfolded example.

Size: 21½x17½mm
Self-Adhesive

MH243

MH309

Die Cut 14x15 Syncopated
Litho.

MH243	1st orange red	1.60	1.25
a.	Booklet pane of 20	32.50	

#MH238-MH239 each sold for 18p on day of issue; #MH240-MH241, MH243 each for 24p.

Issued: #MH201, 4/11/95; #MH204, 4/27/93; #MH219, 7/27/93; #MH222, 8/17/93; #MH234, 8/9/94; #MH237, 8/22/95; #MH238, 9/7/93; #MH241, 9/6/93. #MH241c, 2/16/99.

Nos. MH239, MH240, 4/6/93.

Nos. MH199, MH203, MH212, MH206, 6/8/93.

Nos. MH243, 10/19/93.

Nos. MH208, MH213, MH218, MH224, MH227, MH230, 10/26/93.

Nos. MH214, MH223, MH222, 11/1/93. Nos. MH202, MH210, MH233, 12/14/93. Nos. MH205, MH209, 7/26/94. Nos. MH207, MH220, 4/25/95. Nos. MH215, MH221, MH225, MH228, MH232, MH235, 6/25/96.

Nos. MH200, MH205, MH216, MH226, MH236, 7/8/96.

Nos. MH200, MH203, MH207, MH209, MH212, MH216, MH219, MH226, MH231, MH236 issued only in booklets.

No. MH243a is a complete booklet.

Queen Type of 1970 with Redrawn Portrait

Type MA2: Upper lip not defined by sharp line, nostril is incomplete, hairlines not sharply defined, upper corners of cross formeé are widely separated.

Redrawn portrait: Upper lip sharply outlined, nostril is complete and defined by two lines, hairlines are sharply defined, upper corners of cross formeé are close together so they nearly complete a square.

5p Type c — The top line of the 5 has a curved top edge.

Perf. 15x14 Syncopated, 13¾x14¼ Syncopated (#MH251, MH254A, MH264B, MH269, MH285, MH289)

1997-2004			Photo.
MH245	1p magenta	.20	.20
a.	Litho. (MH372c)	3.50	1.75
MH246	2p dark green	.20	.20
a.	Litho. (MH401b)	.20	.20
MH247	4p Prussian blue	.70	.30
MH248	5p rose brown (b)	.20	.20
a.	Litho. (b) (MH363c)	1.25	.30
MH248B	5p red brown, litho. (c) (MH350Ad)	5.25	.30
MH249	6p bright olive green	1.00	.30
MH249A	7p gray	5.00	1.00
MH249B	8p dk olive bister	.90	.90
MH250	10p brown orange	.40	.20
a.	Litho. (MH363c)	1.75	.35
MH251	10p brn org, perf 13¾x14¼	4.00	.30
MH254	19p bister	1.75	.40
MH254A	19p bister (MH264c), perf 13¾x14¼	2.25	2.25
MH255	20p bright yellow green	1.60	1.60
a.	Litho. (MH368c)	.65	.30
MH256	26p gold	1.75	1.10
MH257	26p brown	1.50	.40
a.	Booklet pane, 3 each #MH255, MH257 + printed margin (BK162)	9.50	
b.	Bklt. pane, #MH255, 2 MH245, 3 MH257 + 2 labels (BK427)	16.50	
c.	Booklet pane, #MH255, 7 MH257 (BK751)	22.00	
d.	Booklet pane, #MH245-MH246, MH254, 3 #MH257 + 2 labels (BK428)	9.00	
e.	Booklet pane, #MH254, 7 #MH257 (BK752)	13.00	
f.	Booklet pane, 4 #MH245, 3 #MH254, 1 #MH257 + label	4.50	
MH259	30p olive green	2.00	.50
MH260	31p deep rose lil	2.00	.55
MH261	33p dk blue green	1.75	1.25
MH261A	34p olive green	7.50	1.40
MH262	37p brt rose lilac	2.50	1.75
MH263	37p black	1.90	1.25
MH264	38p dark blue	2.25	1.75
MH264B	38p dk blue, perf 13¾x14¼	7.50	1.00
c.	Booklet pane, 4 #MH254A, 2 #MH264B (BK167)	20.00	
MH265	39p brt pink	2.50	.30
MH266	40p chalky blue	2.00	1.40
a.	Booklet pane of 4 (BK676)	8.00	
MH267	41p carmine rose	2.00	1.40
MH267A	42p olive	2.00	1.40
MH268	43p dark brown	3.00	.70
MH269	43p dk brn, perf 13¾x14¼	2.25	2.25
a.	Booklet pane, #NIMH70, SMH76, WMMH71, 3 MH269 + printed margin (BK164)	12.00	
MH270	44p brown	6.75	2.50
MH270A	45p brt rose lilac	2.10	1.50
MH270B	47p blue green	2.25	1.75
MH271	50p ocher	2.00	1.10
MH275	63p bright green	4.00	1.25
MH276	64p greenish blue	3.50	2.50
MH277	65p Prussian blue	3.50	2.10
a.	Booklet pane of 4 (BK830)	14.00	
MH278	68p drab	3.25	2.10
MH279	£1 violet	4.50	3.00
a.	Souv. sheet, see footnote	32.50	12.00

No. MH279 is printed with Iriodin ink, giving stamp design a three dimensional appearance.

No. MH279a contains #MH247-MH249, MH250, MH260, MH265, MH276, MH279 + 2 labels.

Issued: No. MH246a, 5/8/10.

MH280	£1.50 red, engr.	6.00	2.25
MH281	£2 slate blue, engr.	8.00	3.25
MH282	£3 purple, engr.	12.00	4.75
MH283	£5 brown, engr.	20.00	8.00
MH284	2nd bright blue	.95	.30
a.	Litho. (#MH287h) ('08)	4.00	.75
MH285	2nd bright blue, perf 13¾x14¼	1.75	.30
a.	Booklet pane, #NIMH74, SMH80, WMMH75, 3 MH285 + printed margin (BK164)	11.00	
b.	Booklet pane, 2 #MH251, 3 each MH269, MH285 + label, printed margin (BK164)	16.50	
MH287	1st gold	1.35	.30
a.	Bklt. pane, 4 ea #MH256, MH287 + label, printed margin (BK162)	10.50	
b.	Booklet pane, 4 each #MH284, MH287 + label (BK174)	9.25	
c.	Booklet pane, 4 each #MH263, MH287 + label	11.50	—
d.	Booklet pane, 2 each #MH267A, MH270B, 4 #MH287, + label (BK176)	11.00	
e.	Booklet pane, 2 each #MH271, MH278, 4 #MH287 + label (BK178)	15.00	—
f.	Booklet pane of 8 + central label , litho. (#MH284, 4 #MH287 + label)	11.00	—
g.	Litho. (#MH287f) ('08)	2.00	.75
h.	Booklet pane of 8, 4 each #MH284a, MH287g + label (BK185) ('08)	9.00	—
MH288	1st orange red (BK1005, BK1140)	1.35	.30
a.	Booklet pane of 8, label + printed margin (BK165)	11.00	
b.	Booklet pane of 8 (BK1141-BK1142)	11.00	
c.	Booklet pane of 4 + label (BK1006)	5.50	
d.	Booklet pane, #MH284, 3 #MH288 + 4 labels (BK429)	6.25	
e.	Bklt. pane, 2 #MH284, 4 #MH288 (BK753)	7.25	
MH289	1st org red, perf 13¾x14¼	3.25	.50
a.	Booklet pane of 10 (BK1139A)	20.00	
MH290	E dark blue	2.10	.50
a.	Booklet pane of 4 (BK1010)	8.50	
b.	Booklet pane, 4 each #MH284, MH290, + label (BK171)	13.00	—
c.	Booklet pane, 4 #MH287, 4 #MH290 + label (BK172, BK173)	14.50	

#MH284-MH285 sold for 20p on day of issue; #MH287-MH289 for 26p; #MH290 for 30p. #MH284 MH285 were later sold for 19p. Selling prices for booklets containing these stamps will be considered to have 20p stamps.

Queen Type of 1970 with Redrawn Portrait

MH292

MH294

MH297

MH299

MH300   MH301

On Nos. MH292 and MH297, the numeral and letters are thinner, and perf tips are flat with distinct corners, while on MH294 and MH299, numeral and letters are thicker and bolder, and perf tips have a slight arc and are rounded at the corners.

On No. MH300 the numeral and letters are thick and bold and perf tips have a slight arc and are rounded at the corners, while on No. MH301, the numeral and letters are thin and perf tips are distinctly serpentine with little flatness on the peaks or valleys.

Die Cut Perf. 14¾x14 Sync., Die Cut Perf. 15x14¼ Sync. (MH 293, MH298)
Self-Adhesive Stamps
Booklet Stamps (MH293, MH298)

MH292	2nd bright blue	1.75	.35
a.	Booklet pane of 6	10.50	
b.	Booklet pane of 12	20.00	
MH293	2nd bright blue	1.50	.30
a.	Booklet pane of 10	15.00	
b.	Booklet pane of 12	18.00	
MH294	2nd bright blue	1.75	.30
a.	Booklet of 12	21.00	
MH297	1st vermilion	1.75	.45
a.	Booklet pane of 6	10.50	
b.	Booklet pane of 12	21.00	
MH298	1st vermilion	1.75	.40
a.	Booklet pane of 10	17.50	
b.	Booklet pane of 12	21.00	
MH299	1st vermilion	2.50	.40
a.	Booklet of 6	15.00	
MH300	1st gold	1.35	.40
a.	Booklet of 6	8.00	
MH301	1st gold	1.35	.40
a.	Booklet of 6	8.00	
b.	Booklet of 12	16.00	
MH302	E dark blue	3.75	.75
a.	Booklet of 6	22.00	

MH304	42p olive	7.00	1.25
a.	Booklet of 6	42.50	
MH306	68p drab	7.00	1.25
a.	Booklet of 6	42.50	

Nos. MH292, MH297 and MH301 were also issued as coils, which have no selvage surrounding stamps.

Nos. MH293 & single stamps from No. MH292a sold for 19p on day of issue; #MH292, 20p; #MH297, 26p; #MH298 & single stamps from #MH297a, MH297b, 27p.

Nos. MH292a, MH293a, MH293b, MH297a, MH297b, MH298a, and MH298b are complete booklets.

No. MH297a exists with self-adhesive label depicting Queen Victoria.

Die Cut Perf. 14x15 Syncopated
Self-Adhesive Coil Stamps
Size: 21x17mm

MH308	2nd bright blue	7.00	3.00
MH309	1st orange red	3.50	3.50

Size: 30x40mm
Perf. 14x14½

MH310	1st black, engr.	4.00	3.00
a.	Booklet pane of 4 + printed margin (BK165)	16.00	
MH311	1st black, typo.	3.50	2.50
a.	Booklet pane of 4 + printed margin (BK165)	14.00	

Self-Adhesive
Die Cut Perf. 14x14½

MH312	1st gray, litho. & embossed	3.75	.50
a.	Booklet pane of 4 + printed margin (BK165)	15.00	

#MH312 is valued in used condition on piece. Soaking and pressing #MH312 removes the embossed image of the Queen.

No. MH300 sold for 20p on day of issue. Nos. MH305, MH310-MH312 sold for 26p on day of issue.

Issued: #MH245, MH249, MH268, MH271, MH279, 4/1/97; #MH256, MH287, 4/21/97. #MH255, MH284, MH308, MH309, 4/29/97; #MH246-MH248, MH250, MH265, 5/27/97; #MH260, MH262, MH275, MH288, 8/26/97; #MH257, 11/18/97; #MH292, MH297, 4/6/98; #MH251, MH269, MH285, 10/13/98; #MH289, 12/1/98; #MH290, 1/12/99; #MH288c, 5/12/99; #MH280-MH283, 3/9/99; #MH310-MH312, 2/16/99; #MH289, 3/16/99; #MH249A, MH254, MH264, MH270, MH276, 4/20/99; #MH254A, MH264B, 2/15/00; 8p, 33p, 40p, 41p, 45p, 65p, #MH288d, MH288e, 4/25/00; #MH279a, 5/22/00; #MH292a, MH293, MH293a, MH297a, MH297b, MH298, 1/29/01.

Nos. MH293c, MH298c issued 1/29/01.

Nos. MH251, MH254A, MH264B, MH269, MH285 (BK164), MH289 (BK1139A), MH290 (BK1010) issued only in booklets.

No. MH290b issued 2/6/02. E stamps from MH 290b sold for 37p on day of issue.

No. MH290c issued 9/24/02.

Nos. MH263, MH267A, MH278, MH270B, MH294, MH299, MH302, MH304, MH306, 7/4/02; Nos. MH300-MH301, 6/5/02. No. MH294 sold for 19p, Nos. MH299, MH300 and MH301 sold for 27p, and No. MH302 sold for 37p on day of issue.

No. MH261A, 5/6/03; No. MH287b, 6/2/03. Nos. MH284a, MH287h, 9/18/08; No. MH287g, 1/8/08.

Nos. MH248a, MH250a, 2/12/09. Nos. MH249B, MH255a, 1/7/10.

This is an expanding set. Nos. MH245-MH312 may change.

Queen Type of 1970 With Redrawn Portraits
Perf. 14¾x14 Syncopated

2003, July 1			Photo.
	Printed in Iriodin Ink		
MH321	£1.50 rose	6.00	5.00
MH322	£2 greenish blue	8.00	7.00
a.	Pound symbol missing in denomination	200.00	—
MH323	£3 violet	12.00	11.00
a.	Souvenir sheet of 1 ('06)	12.00	11.00
MH324	£5 light blue	20.00	17.50
	Nos. MH321-MH324 (4)	46.00	40.50

Issued: £1.50, £2, £3, £5, 7/1. No. MH323a, 8/31/06.

No. MH323a has margin depicting invalid imperforate examples of Nos. 211, 231, and 236.

Queen Elizabeth II (No Frame, Perforations Touch Vignette) — MA4

Perf. 14¾x14 Syncopated

2000	Photo.	Design MA4	
MH335	1st olive green	1.35	.45
a.	Bklt. pane of 8 (BK1201)	11.00	
b.	Bkt. pane of 9 (BK168)	12.25	
c.	Bkt. pane of 4 + label (BK1007)	5.50	

Perf. 13¾x14¼ Syncopated

MH336	1st olive green	1.75	.50
a.	Booklet pane of 10 (BK1144)	17.50	
b.	Booklet pane of 8 + label (BK167)	14.00	

Issued: #MH335, MH336, 1/6; #MH336b, 2/15; #MH335a, 5/26; #MH335b, 8/4.

No. MH335c comes in two versions (as does No. BK1007): with Postman Pat on label and with Botanical Garden of Wales on label.

No. MH336 issued only in booklets. Perforations are Syncopated.

No. MH335 and MH336 sold for 26p on day of issue.

Queen Type of 1970 With Redrawn Portraits

54p Type a — "5" has thick straight top line, "4" has thick cross line.

Type b — "5" has thinner, slightly curved top line, "4" has thin cross line.

Perf. 14¾x14 Syncopated

2004-10		Photo.	
Type MA2			
MH344	7p bright pink	.75	.20
MH346	9p brt orange	.35	.20
a.	Litho. (MH401b)	.25	.20
MH347	12p blue green	.75	.25
MH348	14p vermilion	.70	.25
MH348A	15p brt pink	.75	.30
MH349	16p lilac rose	.75	.30
a.	Litho. (MH365b) ('09)	2.00	.35
MH350	17p olive green	.55	.25
b.	Litho. (MH368b)	1.00	.30
MH350A	22p brown	.65	.30
c.	Litho. (MH368b)	3.50	.40
d.	Booklet pane of 9, 5 #MH250a, 2 each #MH248A, MH350Ac (BK191)	14.00	—
MH351	35p brown	1.75	.65
MH352	35p olive green	1.75	.75
MH353	37p olive green	1.75	.75
MH354	39p gray	2.00	.75
a.	Booklet pane, 4 #MH284, 2 each #MH267A, MH354 + label (BK177)	11.00	—
MH355	40p Prussian blue	2.00	.75
a.	Booklet pane, 4 #MH287, 2 each #MH352, MH355 + central label (BK179)	12.50	—
MH358	43p emerald	2.50	.80
MH359	44p bright blue	2.00	.80
MH361	46p dk ol bister	2.00	.85
MH363	48p brt rose lil	2.00	.95
a.	Booklet pane, 4 #MH246, 2 each #MH361, MH363, + label (BK182)	7.75	—
b.	Litho. (MH363c)	4.25	.80
c.	Booklet pane, 2 each #MH248a, MH250a, MH287g, MH363b + label (BK188)	9.50	—
MH364	49p brown	2.25	.85
MH365	50p gray	2.25	1.00
a.	Litho. (MH365b) ('09)	3.75	.75
b.	Booklet pane, 4 each #MH349a, MH365a, + central label (BK187) ('09)	10.50	—
MH366	54p brown (a)	2.25	1.10
a.	Booklet pane, 2 each #MH245, MH366, 4 #MH361, + label (BK183)	12.50	
MH366B	54p brown, litho. (b) (MH368c)	4.75	.85
c.	Booklet pane of 8, 4#MH350Ac, 4 #MH366B, + label (BK192)	11.00	—
MH367	56p lt olive grn	2.25	1.10
MH368	62p carmine	1.90	.95
a.	Litho. (MH368b)	4.00	1.25
b.	Booklet pane of 8, 4 #MH350b, 2 each #MH350c, MH368a + central label (BK189)	10.00	—
c.	Booklet pane of 8, 4 #MH255a, 2 each #MH366B, MH368a + label (BK191)	12.50	—
MH370	72p carmine rose	3.00	1.25
MH371	78p emerald	3.25	1.60
MH372	81p greenish blue	3.25	1.60
MH372A	90p dark blue	2.75	1.40
b.	Litho. (MH372c)	6.25	1.75
c.	Booklet pane of 8, 4 #MH350b, 2 each #MH345a, MH372Ab + central label (BK190)	8.75	—
MH373	£1 cerise	4.25	2.00
a.	Booklet pane of 2 + label (BK182)	8.50	—
Nos. MH344-MH373 (28)		55.15	22.80

Issued: 7p, 35p, 39p, 40p, 43p, 4/1; MH354a, 2/24/05. 9p, No. MH352, 46p, 4/5/05. No. MH355a, 2/23/06. 37p, 44p, 49p, 72p, 3/28/06. 12p, 14p, 8/1/06. 16p, 48p, 50p, 54p, 78p, 3/27/07. Nos. MH363a, MH373, 6/5/07. MH366a, 9/20/07. 15p, 56p, 81p, 4/1/08. Nos. MH349a, MH365a, MH365b, 1/13/09. Nos. MH363b, MH363c, 2/17/09. Nos. MH350, MH350A, MH368, MH372A, 3/31/09. Nos. MH350b, MH350c, MH368a,

MH368b, 8/18/09. Nos. MH350Ad, MH366Bb, MH368c, 1/7/10. No. MH366Bc, 2/25/10. MH356a, 5/8/10.

This is an expanding set, numbers may change.

Queen Elizabeth II

MA5   MA6

Perf. 14¾x14 Syncopated

2006		Photo.	
MH375	MA5 2nd bright blue	1.25	.45
MH376	MA5 1st gold	1.60	.60
a.	Booklet pane, 4 each #MH271, MH376 + central label (BK180)	19.50	—
b.	Booklet pane, 4 each #MH248, MH376, + central label (BK181)	8.50	—
Inscribed "Large"			
MH377	MA6 2nd bright blue	1.60	.70
MH378	MA6 1st gold	2.00	.85
a.	Booklet pane, #MH375, MH376, 2 each #MH377-MH378, + label (BK182)	11.00	—
Nos. MH375-MH378 (4)		6.45	2.60

Booklet Stamps
Self-Adhesive
Serpentine Die Cut 14¾x14 Syncopated

MH379	MA5 2nd bright blue	1.50	.45
a.	Booklet pane of 12	18.00	
MH380	MA5 1st gold	1.60	.60
a.	Booklet pane of 6	9.75	
b.	Booklet pane of 12	19.50	
Inscribed "Large"			
MH381	MA6 2nd bright blue	2.25	.70
a.	Booklet pane of 4	9.00	
MH382	MA6 1st gold	2.50	.85
a.	Booklet pane of 4	10.00	
Nos. MH379-MH382 (4)		7.85	2.60

Issued: Nos. MH375-MH378, 8/1; Nos. MH379-MH380, 9/12; Nos. MH381-MH382, 8/15. No. MH376a, 9/21. No. MH376b, 3/1/07. No. MH378a, 6/5/07.

On day of issue, Nos. MH375 and MH379 each sold for 23p, Nos. MH376 and MH380 each sold for 32p, Nos. MH377 and MH381 each sold for 37p, and Nos. MH378 and MH382 each sold for 44p.

Queen Type of 1970 With Redrawn Portraits and Type of 2006 With Two Die Cut Slits on Stamp and Iridescent Overprint of "Royal Mail" in Wavy Lines

Slit Types:
Type I: Oval slits have breaks at sides only.
Type II: Oval slits have breaks at top, bottom and sides (booklet stamps only).

Die Cut Perf. 14¾x14 Syncopated

2009		Photo.	
Type MA2			
Self-Adhesive			
MH383	2nd bright blue, type I	.80	.40
a.	Type II	1.10	.40
b.	Booklet pane of 12 #MH383a	9.75	
MH384	1st gold, type I	1.10	.55
a.	Type II	1.40	.55
b.	Booklet pane of 6 #MH384a	6.75	
c.	Booklet pane of 12 #MH384a	13.50	
MH385	50p gray	1.50	.75
a.	Booklet pane of 8, 4 #MH384, 2 each #MH383, MH385, + central label (BK193)	9.00	
MH386	£1 cerise	3.00	1.50
MH387	£1.50 brown red	4.25	2.10
MH388	£2 greenish blue	5.75	2.75
MH389	£3 violet	8.75	4.25
MH390	£5 light blue	14.50	7.25
Type MA6			
MH391	2nd Large bright blue, type I	1.25	.60
a.	Type II	1.60	.60
b.	Booklet pane of 4 #MH391a	5.00	
MH392	1st Large gold, type I	1.50	.75
a.	Type II	2.10	.75
b.	Booklet pane of 4 #MH392a	6.00	
Nos. MH383-MH392 (10)		42.40	20.90

Issued: Nos. MH383-MH392, 2/17; Nos. MH383a, MH383b, MH384a, MH384b, MH384c, MH391a, MH391b, MH392a, MH392b, 3/31. MH385a, 5/8/10. On day of issue, No. MH383 sold for 27p; No. MH384, 36p; No. MH391, 42p; No. MH392, 52p.

Victoria and Elizabeth II Type of 1990
Perf. 14¾x14 Syncopated

2009		Litho.	
Booklet Stamps			
Type MA3			
MH393	20p black (MH394a)	2.00	.35
MH394	1st black (MH394a)	2.75	.45
a.	Booklet pane of 8, 4 each #MH393-MH394 + central label (BK189)	19.00	—

No. MH394 sold for 39p on day of issue.

MA7

MA8

Die Cut Perf. 14¾x14 Syncopated

2009, Nov. 17		Photo.	
Self-Adhesive			
Type II Slits			
MH395	MA7 1st yel & org	3.75	1.90
Die Cut Perf. 14½x14			
MH396	MA8 1st Large yel & org	4.50	2.25

On day of issue, No. MH395 sold for £1.14; No. MH396, £1.36.

Queen Type of 1970 With Redrawn Portraits
Perf. 14¾x14 Syncopated

2010, Mar. 30		Photo.	
Type MA2			
MH397	60p emerald	1.90	.95
a.	Litho. (MH397b)	1.75	.85
b.	Booklet pane of 8, 4 #MH248a, 2 each #MH250a, MH397a, + central label (BK194)	5.00	—
MH398	67p red violet	2.10	1.10
a.	Litho. (MH401b)	2.00	1.00
MH399	88p cerise	2.75	1.40
a.	Litho. (MH401b)	2.60	1.40
MH400	97p violet	3.00	1.50
a.	Litho. (MH401b)	3.00	1.50
MH401	£1.46 Prussian blue	4.50	2.25
a.	Litho. (MH401b)	4.25	2.10
b.	Sheet of 11 + label (see contents below)	16.00	16.00
Nos. MH397-MH401 (5)		14.25	7.20

Issued: Nos. MH397a, MH397b, 5/13/10. London 2010 Festival of Stamps (No. MH401b). Issued: Nos. MH398a, MH399a, MH400a, MH401a, MH401b, 5/8/10. No. MH401b contains Nos. MH245a, MH246a, MH248a, MH250a, MH255a, MH346a, MH397a, MH398a, MH399a, MH400a, MH401a + label.

MACHINS REGIONAL ISSUES

NORTHERN IRELAND

All stamps are Design MA2 unless noted.

Type I   Type II

Two types of crown:
Type I: All pearls individually drawn, screened background.

Type II: Large pearls with strong white line below them.

First three pearls at left joined together. Solid background.

1971-93		Photo.	*Perf. 15x14*	
NIMH1	2½p bright pink		.75	.50
NIMH2	3p ultramarine		.40	.30
NIMH3	3½p slate		.30	.30
NIMH4	4½p dark blue		.30	.30
NIMH5	5p bright violet		1.40	1.40
NIMH6	5½p dark violet		.30	.20
NIMH7	6½p Prussian blue		.30	.20
NIMH8	7p dark red brn		.40	.30
NIMH9	7½p chestnut		2.25	2.00
NIMH10	8p red		.40	.40
NIMH11	8½p yellow green		.40	.45
NIMH12	9p violet blue		.45	.45
NIMH13	10p orange brown		.45	.55
NIMH14	10½p steel blue		.55	.55
NIMH15	11p red		.55	.55
NIMH16	11½p gray brn, litho., perf 13½x14		1.00	1.00
NIMH17	12p yellow green		.70	.60
NIMH18	12p brt grn, litho.		.95	.90
NIMH19	12½p lt emer, litho., perf 13½x14		.70	.70
NIMH20	12½p lt emer, litho.		6.00	4.50
NIMH21	13p lt red brown, litho., type II		2.00	.55
a.	Type I		1.25	.50
NIMH22	13½p brown purple		.80	.70
NIMH23	14p gray bl, litho., perf 13½x14		.90	.85
NIMH24	14p dark bl, litho.		1.00	.70
NIMH25	15p deep ultra		.90	.70
Litho.				
NIMH26	15p bright blue		1.00	.70
NIMH27	15½p light violet, perf 13½x14		.90	.90
NIMH28	16p brownish gray, perf 13½x14		1.10	1.25
NIMH29	16p brownish gray		9.50	6.00
NIMH30	17p blue gray, type I		.95	1.10
a.	Type II		210.00	
NIMH31	17p dark blue		1.10	.90
NIMH32	18p violet blue, perf 13½x14		1.10	1.10
NIMH33	18p olive green		1.10	1.00
NIMH34	18p bright yel grn		1.10	1.00
NIMH35	18p bright yel grn, perf 13½x14		7.00	1.90
NIMH36	19p red orange		1.10	1.10
NIMH37	19½p olive gray, perf 13½x14		2.25	2.50
NIMH38	20p brown black		1.10	.90
NIMH39	20½p ultramarine, perf 13½x14		4.75	4.00
NIMH40	22p dark blue, perf 13½x14		1.25	1.25
NIMH41	22p yellow green		1.25	1.25
NIMH42	22p red orange		1.40	1.00
NIMH43	23p bright yel grn		1.40	1.25
NIMH44	24p brown red		1.75	1.10
NIMH45	24p brown		1.25	1.00
a.	Bklt. pane, see footnote (BK158)		4.25	

#NIMH45a contains NIMH34, NIMH45, SMH35, SMH47, WMMH34, WMMH45.

NIMH46	26p red, perf 13½x14, type I		1.40	1.40
NIMH47	26p red, type II		4.50	4.00
NIMH48	26p olive gray		1.75	1.50
NIMH49	28p deep viol bl, perf 13½x14, type I		1.60	1.40
NIMH50	28p deep viol bl, type II		2.25	1.40
NIMH51	28p dull blue green		1.90	1.60
NIMH52	31p brt rose lil, type I		1.75	1.40
a.	Type II		3.75	1.90
NIMH53	32p Prussian blue		2.00	2.00
NIMH54	34p dull blue green		2.25	2.25
NIMH55	37p scarlet		2.50	2.50
NIMH56	39p brt rose lilac		2.50	2.50

Issued: #NIMH1, 3p, 5p, NIMH9, 7/7/71; #NIMH3, NIMH6, 8p, 1/23/74; #NIMH4, 11/6/74;

#NIMH7, NIMH11, 1/14/76; 10p, 11p, 10/20/76; 7p, 9p, NIMH14, 1/18/78.

#NIMH17, NIMH22, #NIMH25, 7/23/80; #NIMH16, #NIMH23, NIMH32, NIMH40, 4/8/81; #NIMH19, 1/24/82; #NIMH27, #NIMH28, NIMH37, NIMH46, 2/24/82; NIMH39, #NIMH49, 4/27/83;

#NIMH20, #NIMH29, 2/28/84; 13p, #NIMH30, NIMH41, 31p, 10/23/84; #NIMH18, 1/7/86; #NIMH33, 1/6/87; #NIMH50, 1/27/87; #NIMH24, 19p, 23p, 32p, 11/8/88; #NIMH26, 30p, NIMH44, 34p, 11/28/89; #NIMH31, NIMH42, NIMH48, 37p, 12/4/90; #NIMH35, NIMH45, NIMH51, 39p, 12/3/91; #NIMH35, #NIMH45a, 8/10/93; #NIMH47, 12/7/93.

Perf. 15x14 Syncopated

1993-96		Litho.	
NIMH57	19p olive green	1.00	1.00
NIMH58	20p brt yel green	1.75	1.40
NIMH59	25p salmon	1.00	.90
a.	Bklt. pane, see footnote (BK160)	5.00	

No. NIMH59a contains #NIMH57, NIMH59, SMH63, SMH65, WMMH58, WMMH60 + label, printed margin.

NIMH60	26p brown	2.25	1.60
NIMH61	30p olive green	1.75	1.60

Column 1 (Northern Ireland continued)

NIMH62	37p bright rose lilac	3.25	2.50
NIMH63	41p drab	2.00	1.75

a. Bklt. pane, #NIMH61, NIMH63, 2 #NIMH57, 4 #NIMH59 + label, printed margin (BK159) — 6.25

b. Bklt. pane, #NIMH57, NIMH59, NIMH61, NIMH63 + printed margin (BK159) — 3.50

NIMH64	63p bright green	5.50	4.00

Issued: 19p, 25p, 30p, 41p, 12/7/93; #NIMH59a, 4/25/95; 20p, 26, 37p, 63p, 7/23/96.

Queen Design of 1970 with Redrawn Portrait
Perf. 15x14 Syncopated

1997-2000			Photo.
NIMH68	19p olive green	4.50	4.50
NIMH69	20p brt yel grn	1.75	.80
NIMH70	20p brt yel grn, perf 14	5.50	2.10
NIMH73	26p brown	2.50	1.10
NIMH74	26p brown, perf 14	5.50	2.00
NIMH81	37p bright rose lilac	3.25	1.40

a. Bklt. pane, see footnote (BK162) — 7.50

No. NIMH81a contains #NIMH73, NIMH81, SMH79, SMH87, WMMH74, WMMH82 + printed margin.

NIMH82	38p dark blue	10.00	7.50
NIMH83	40p chalky blue	5.00	2.50
NIMH91	63p bright green	6.50	5.00
NIMH92	64p greenish blue	11.00	8.00
NIMH93	65p Prussian blue	4.00	3.00

Issued: #NIMH69, NIMH73, 37p, 63p, 7/1/97; #NIMH81a, 9/24/97; #NIMH70, NIMH74, 10/13/98; #NIMH68, NIMH82, NIMH92, 6/8/99; 40p, 65p, 4/25/00.
Nos. NIMH70, NIMH74 issued only in booklets (BK164).

Perf. 13¾x14¼ Syncopated

2000			Photo.
NIMH96	1st orange red (WM-MH96a)	3.50	2.75

Perf. 15x14 Syncopated

NIMH99	1st org red	11.00	7.50

#NIMH96, NIMH99 sold for 26p on day of issue. #NIMH96 issued only in booklets.
Issued: #NIMH96, 2/15/00; #NIMH99, 4/25/00.

SCOTLAND

All stamps are Design MA2 unless noted.

Type I   Type II

Two types of lion:
Type I: Thin tongue, no line across bridge of nose, three "feathers" on left of tail are widely separated.
Type II: Thick tongue where it enters mouth, eye connected to background by solid line, three "feathers" on left of tail are close together.

1971-93		Photo.	Perf. 15x14
SMH1	2½p bright pink	.30	.20
SMH2	3p ultramarine	.40	.20
SMH3	3½p slate	.30	.20
SMH4	4½p dark blue	.35	.30
SMH5	5p brt violet	1.50	1.25
SMH6	5½p dark violet	.30	.20
SMH7	6½p Prussian blue	.30	.20
SMH8	7p dark red brn	.35	.35
SMH9	7½p chestnut	1.50	1.50
SMH10	8p red	.50	.40
SMH11	8½p yellow green	.50	.45
SMH12	9p violet blue	.50	.45
SMH13	10p orange brown	.50	.60
SMH14	10½p steel blue	.55	.55
SMH15	11p red	.55	.55
SMH16	11½p gray brn, litho., perf 13½x14	1.00	.90
SMH17	12p yellow green	.55	.55

Column 2 (Scotland continued)

SMH18	12p brt green, litho., perf 13½x14	2.25	1.90
SMH19	12p green, litho.	2.10	2.10
SMH20	12½p lt emer, litho., perf 13½x14	.70	.80
SMH21	13p lt red brown, litho., perf 13½x14, type I	1.10	1.10
a.	Type II	11.00	5.00
SMH22	13p lt red brn, litho.	1.25	.85
SMH23	13½p brown purple	.80	.90
SMH24	14p gray blue, litho., perf 13½x14	.85	.85
SMH25	14p dk bl, litho.	.75	.35
a.	Booklet pane of 6 + printed margin (BK153)	3.50	
SMH26	15p deep ultra	.70	.80

Litho.

SMH27	15p bright blue	.80	.80

Perf. 13½x14

SMH28	15½p light violet	.90	.90
SMH29	16p brownish gray	.90	.95
SMH30	17p blue gray, type II	2.50	1.10
a.	Type I	4.50	2.50

Perf. 15x14

SMH31	17p blue gray	4.50	4.50
SMH32	17p dark blue	1.10	1.25
SMH33	18p violet blue, perf 13½x14	1.00	.75
SMH34	18p olive green	1.25	1.00
SMH35	18p bright yel grn	1.00	.30
SMH36	18p brt yel grn, perf 13½x14	2.50	1.00
SMH37	19p red orange	.80	.80
a.	Booklet pane of 6 + printed margin (BK153)	5.25	
b.	Booklet pane of 9 + printed margin (BK153)	6.50	
SMH38	19½p olive gray, perf 13½x14	2.00	2.00
SMH39	20p brown black	1.10	1.10

Perf. 13½x14

SMH40	20½p ultra	4.75	.75
SMH41	22p dk blue	1.25	1.00
SMH42	22p yel grn, type I	4.50	2.00
a.	Type II	50.00	40.00

Perf. 15x14

SMH43	22p yellow green	2.00	1.75
SMH44	22p red orange	1.40	1.00
SMH45	23p bright yel grn	1.50	1.25
a.	Booklet pane #SMH45, 2 #SMH37, 5 #SMH25 + printed margin (BK153)	5.25	
SMH46	24p brown red	1.75	1.10
SMH47	24p brown	1.60	1.40
SMH48	24p chestnut, perf 13½x14	9.25	3.25
SMH49	26p red, perf 13½x14, type I	4.50	.90
SMH50	26p red	3.75	3.50
SMH51	26p olive gray	1.40	1.40
SMH52	28p dp vio bl, perf 13½x14	1.40	1.40
SMH53	28p deep violet blue	1.75	.90
SMH54	28p dull bl grn	1.75	1.60
SMH55	28p dull bl grn, perf 13½x14	10.00	4.00
SMH56	31p brt rose lilac, perf 13½x14	3.00	2.10
a.	Type II	190.00	90.00
SMH57	31p brt rose lilac	2.50	.90
SMH58	32p Prussian blue	2.00	1.75
SMH59	34p dull bl grn	2.25	2.25
SMH60	37p scarlet	2.25	2.25
SMH61	39p brt rose lilac	2.25	2.25
SMH62	39p brt rose lilac, perf 13½x14	16.00	2.75

Issued: #SMH1, 3p, 5p, #SMH9, 7/7/71; #SMH3, SMH6, 8p, 1/23/74; #SMH4, 11/6/74; #SMH7, SMH11, 1/14/76; 10p, 11p, 10/20/76; 7p, 9p, #SMH14, 1/18/78; #SMH17, SMH23, #SMH26, 7/23/80.
#SMH16, #SMH24, SMH33, SMH41, 4/8/81; #SMH20, SMH28, SMH49, 2/24/82;
16p, #SMH40, #SMH52, 4/27/83; #SMH21, SMH30, SMH42, SMH56, 10/23/84; #SMH18, 1/7/86; #SMH19, 1/24/86; #SMH31, SMH57, 4/29/86; #SMH22, 11/4/86; #SMH34, 1/6/87.
#SMH43, SMH50, SMH53, 1/27/87; #SMH25, 19p, 23p, 32p, 11/8/88; #SMH27, 20p, SMH46, 34p, 1/28/89; #SMH32, SMH44, SMH51, 37p, 12/4/90;
#SMH35, SMH47, SMH54, SMH61, 12/3/91; #SMH36, 9/26/92; #SMH48, 10/92; #SMH62, 11/92; #SMH55, 2/18/93.

Perf. 15x14 Syncopated

1993-96			Litho.
SMH63	19p olive green	1.00	.80
SMH64	20p brt yel green	1.75	1.10
SMH65	25p salmon	1.25	1.10
SMH66	26p brown	2.25	1.75
SMH67	30p olive green	2.00	1.40
SMH68	37p bright rose lilac	3.25	2.50
SMH69	41p drab	2.25	2.25
SMH70	63p bright green	4.75	3.75

Issued: 19p, 20p, 30p, 41p, 12/7/93; 20p, 26p, 37p, 63p, 7/23/96.

Queen Design of 1970 with Redrawn Portrait
Perf. 15x14 Syncopated

1997-98			Photo.
SMH75	20p brt yel green	1.50	.70
SMH76	20p brt yel grn, perf 14	5.75	2.50
SMH79	26p brown	2.25	1.25
SMH80	26p brown, perf 14	5.75	3.00
SMH87	37p bright rose lilac	3.50	1.50
SMH97	63p bright green	6.00	3.75

Issued: #SMH75, SMH79, 37p, 63p, 7/1/97; #SMH76, SMH80, 10/13/98.
Nos. SMH76, SMH80 issued only in booklets (BK164).
This is an expanding set, numbers may change.

Perf. 13¾x14¼ Syncopated

2000			Photo.
SMH101	1st org red (WM-MH96a)	3.50	3.00

Issued: No. SMH96, 2/15/00. No. SMH96 sold for 26p on day of issue and was issued only in booklets.

WALES & MONMOUTHSHIRE

All stamps are Design MA2 unless noted.

Type I   Type II

Two types of dragon:
Type I: Eye is complete with white dot in center. Wing tips, tail and tongue are thin.
Type II: Eye is joined to nose by solid line. Wing tips, tail and tongue are thick.

1971-93		Photo.	Perf. 15x14
WMMH1	2½p bright pink	.30	.20
WMMH2	3p ultra	.30	.20
WMMH3	3½p slate	.30	.35
WMMH4	4½p dark blue	.35	.35
WMMH5	5p brt violet	1.25	1.25
WMMH6	5½p dark violet	.30	.35
WMMH7	6½p Prussian blue	.30	.20
WMMH8	7p dark red brn	.30	.20
WMMH9	7½p chestnut	1.75	2.00
WMMH10	8p red	.40	.40
WMMH11	8½p yel grn	.40	.40
WMMH12	9p violet blue	.45	.45
WMMH13	10p orange brn	.45	.45
WMMH14	10½p steel blue	.55	.50
WMMH15	11p red	.55	.50
WMMH16	11½p gray brn, litho., perf 13½x14	1.00	.90
WMMH17	12p yel grn	.60	.55

Litho.

WMMH18	12p brt grn	1.75	1.40
WMMH19	12½p lt emer, perf 13½x14	.80	.80
WMMH20	12½p lt emer	6.00	5.75
WMMH21	13p lt red brn, type I	.70	.70
a.	Type II	3.50	

Photo.

WMMH22	13½p brown pur	.85	.75
WMMH23	14p gray blue, litho., perf 13½x14	.85	.85
WMMH24	14p dark blue	.85	.85
WMMH25	15p deep ultra	.70	.80

Litho.

WMMH26	15p bright blue	.90	.85
WMMH27	15½p light violet	1.10	.85
WMMH28	16p brownish gray, perf 13½x14	1.75	1.90
WMMH29	16p brownish gray	2.00	2.25
WMMH30	17p blue gray, type I	.95	.90
a.	Type II	72.50	25.00
WMMH31	17p dark blue	1.00	.90
WMMH32	18p vio bl, perf 13½x14	1.10	1.10
WMMH33	18p olive blue	1.10	1.00

WMMH34	18p brt yel grn	.85	.85
a.	Booklet pane of 6 + printed margin (BK156)	3.90	
WMMH35	18p brt yel grn, perf 13½x14	13.00	4.00
WMMH36	19p red orange	1.10	.90
WMMH37	19½p ol gray, perf 13½x14	2.00	2.00
WMMH38	20p brown black	1.00	1.00
WMMH39	20½p blue ultra	3.75	3.75
WMMH40	22p dk bl, perf 13½x14	1.25	1.25
WMMH41	22p yel grn	1.10	1.25
WMMH42	22p orange red	1.10	1.25
WMMH43	23p brt yel grn	1.40	1.25
WMMH44	24p brown red	1.50	1.25
WMMH45	24p brown	.95	.85
a.	Booklet pane of 6 + printed margin (BK156)	5.75	
WMMH46	24p brown, perf 13½x14	12.50	3.25
WMMH47	26p red, type I, perf 13½x14	1.25	1.25
WMMH48	26p red, type II	6.25	5.75
WMMH49	26p olive gray	1.60	1.60
WMMH50	28p dp vio bl, type I, perf 13½x14	1.40	1.40
WMMH51	28p dp vio bl, type II	2.00	2.00
WMMH52	28p dull bl grn	1.75	1.60
WMMH53	31p brt rose lil	1.60	1.60
WMMH54	32p Prus blue	1.75	1.75
WMMH55	34p dull bl grn	1.75	1.75
WMMH56	37p scarlet	2.25	2.25
WMMH57	39p brt rose lil	2.50	2.50

Issued: #WMMH1, 3p, 5p, WMMH9, 7/7/71; #WMMH3, WMMH6, 8p, 1/23/74; #WMMH4, 11/6/74; #WMMH7, WMMH11, 1/14/76; 10p, 11p, 10/20/76.
7p, 9p, WMMH14, 1/18/78; #WMMH17, WMMH22, WMMH25, 7/23/80; #WMMH16, #WMMH23, WMMH32, WMMH40, 4/8/81;
#WMMH19, WMMH27, WMMH37, WMMH47, 2/24/82; #WMMH28, WMMH39, WMMH50, 4/27/83; #WMMH20, WMMH29, 1/10/84.
#WMMH30, WMMH41, 31p, 10/23/84; #WMMH18, 1/7/86; #WMMH33, 1/6/87; #WMMH48, WMMH51, 1/27/87; #WMMH24, 19p, 23p, 32p, 8/11/88; #WMMH26, 20p, WMMH44, 34p, 11/28/89.
#WMMH31, WMMH42, WMMH49, 37p, 12/4/90; #WMMH34, WMMH45, WMMH52, 39p, 12/3/91; #WMMH46, 9/14/92; #WMMH35, 1/12/93.

Perf. 15x14 Syncopated

1993-96			Litho.
WMMH58	19p olive green	1.10	1.00
WMMH59	20p brt yel grn	2.00	1.75
WMMH60	25p salmon	1.40	1.10
WMMH61	26p brown	2.25	2.00
WMMH62	30p olive green	2.00	1.50
WMMH63	37p bright rose lilac	3.25	2.75
WMMH64	41p drab	2.25	2.25
WMMH65	63p bright green	5.00	4.50

Issued: 19p, 25p, 30p, 41p, 12/7/93. 20p, 26p, 37p, 63p, 7/23/96.

Queen Design of 1970 with Redrawn Portrait
"P" Removed
Perf. 15x14 Syncopated

1997-98			Photo.
WMMH70	20p brt yel grn	1.75	.90
WMMH71	20p brt yel grn, perf 14	5.50	2.25
WMMH74	26p brown	2.00	1.10
WMMH75	26p brown, perf 14	5.50	2.25
WMMH82	37p bright rose lilac	6.00	2.50
WMMH92	63p bright green	5.00	4.00

Issued: #WMMH70, WMMH74, 37p, 63p, 7/1/97; #WMMH71, WMMH75, 10/13/98.
Nos. WMMH71, WMMH75 issued only in booklets (BK164).
This is an expanding set, numbers may change.

Perf. 13¾x14¼ Syncopated

2000			Photo.
WMMH96	1st orange red	3.50	2.50
a.	Bklt. pane, 3 ea #NIMH96, SMH101, WMMH96 (BK167)	30.00	

Issued: No. WMMH96, 2/15/00. No. WMMH96 sold for 26p on day of issue and was issued only in booklets.

See Isle of Man #8-11 for additional Machin Head definitives.

BOOKLETS

Booklets are listed in denomination sequence by reign. Numbers in parenthesis following each listing reflect the number of cover varieties or edition numbers that apply to each cover style.

Values shown for complete booklets are for examples containing most panes having full perforations on two edges of the pane only. Booklets containing most or all panes with very fine, full perforations on all sides are scarce and will sell for more. Also, in booklets where most of the value is contained in only one pane of several, it is assumed that this pane has full perforations on two sides only. If this pane is very fine, the booklet will be worth a considerable premium over the value given.

This section does not contain complete booklets consisting solely of self-adhesive stamps. These are catalogued as minors under stamp listings.

Sterling Currency

BC1

1904
BK1 BC1 2sh ½p red, 4 #128e   350.00

1906-11
BK2 BC1 2sh red, 2 #128e, 3
          #143c, #143b   950.00
BK3 BC1 2sh red, 3 #128e, 1
          each #143b-
          143c (4)   1,150.

Cover inscription on Nos. BK2-BK3 revised to reflect changed contents.

1911
BK4 BC1 2sh red, 2#151a, 3
          #152a   750.00

BC2

1912-13
BK5 BC2 2sh red, 2 #151a, 3
          #152a   1,050.
BK6 BC2 2sh red, 2 #155a, 3
          #156a (4)   1,000.

Cover inscription on Nos. BK5-BK6 shows only Inland Postage Rates.

1913
BK7 BC2 2sh red, 2 #159b, 3
          #160a (35)   500.00
BK8 BC2 2sh org, 2 #159b,3
          #160a (20)   525.00

BC3

1917
BK9 BC3 2sh org, 2 #159b, 3
          #160a (17)   500.00

BC4

1924-34
BK10 BC4 2sh blue, #159b,
           160a, 161d-
           161e (2)   1,250.
BK11 BC4 2sh blue, #187b,
           188b, 189c-
           189d (277)   475.00

BC5

1929
BK12 BC5 2sh blue, buff,
           #205b-207b,
           207c   550.00

1935
BK13 BC4 2sh blue, #210b-
           211b, 212c-
           212d (58)   550.00

BC6

1935
BK14 BC6 2sh blue, buff,
           #226a-227a,
           3 #228a   100.00

1918-19
BK15 BC4 3sh org, 2 each
           #159b, 160a,
           161d (11)   650.00
BK16 BC4 3sh org, #159b,
           160a, 3
           #161d (15)   650.00

Cover used for Nos. BK15-BK16 does not have inscription above top line.

1921
BK17 BC4 3sh blue, 3 #162b
           (3)   850.00
BK18 BC4 3sh blue, 3 #162c
           (3)   900.00

1922
BK19 BC4 3sh scar, #159b,
           160a, 3 #161d
           (33)   850.00
BK20 BC4 3sh blue, 4 #161d
           (2)   900.00

1924-34
BK21 BC4 3sh scar, #187b-
           188b, 3
           #189c (237)   375.00

1929
BK22 BC5 3sh blue, buff,
           #205b-206b,
           3 #207b (5)   450.00

1935
BK23 BC4 3sh scar, #210b-
           211b, 3
           #212c (27)   375.00
BK24 BC6 3sh red, buff,
           #226a-227a,
           5 #228a (4)   100.00

1920
BK25 BC4 3sh6p org, #160a, 3
           #162b (6)   850.00

Cover used for No. BK25 does not have inscription above top line.

1921
BK26 BC4 3sh6p org red,
           #159b,
           160a, 161d,
           2 #162b (7)   900.00
BK27 BC4 3sh6p org red,
           #159b,
           160a, 161d,
           2 #162c
           (13)   900.00

1931-35
BK28 BC4 5sh grn, #187b-
           188b, 189d,
           5 #189c   4,000.
BK29 BC4 5sh buff, #187b-
           188b, 189d,
           5 #189c (7)   1,250.
BK30 BC4 5sh buff, #210b-
           211b, 212d,
           5 #212c (7)   450.00

BC7

1936
BK31 BC7 6p buff, 2 #232c   70.00

BC8

BK32 BC8 2sh blue, #230a-
           231a, #232a-
           232b (31)   140.00
BK33 BC8 3sh scar, #230a-
           231a, 3 #232a
           (12)   110.00
BK34 BC8 5sh buff, #230a-
           231a, 6 #232a
           (2)   250.00

1938-40
BK35 BC7 6p buff, 2 #237d   70.00
BK36 BC7 6p pink, #235d-
           237d   325.00
BK37 BC7 6p pale grn, #235c-
           236c   150.00

No. BK37 is 53x41mm.

1947-51
BK38 BC7 1sh buff, 2 each
           #258b-259b,
           260a   27.50
BK39 BC7 1sh buff, 2 each
           #280b, 281b-
           282b   27.50

BK40 BC7 1sh buff, #258e,
           259d, 260b   6,000.
BK41 BC7 1sh buff, #280b-
           282b   32.50

Nos. BK40-BK41 are 53x41mm.

Round GPO Emblem — BC9

1952-53
BK42 BC9 1sh buff, #280b, 281c-
           282c   22.50
  a. Inland postage rate corrected
      in ink on inside booklet cover 25.00

Oval GPO Emblem — BC10

1954
BK43 BC10 1sh buff, #280b,
            281c-282c   32.50

1937
BK44 BC8 2sh blue, #235b-
           236b, #237c (26)   450.00

BC11

1938
BK45 BC11 2sh blue, #235b-
            236b, #237b-
            237c (95)   450.00

1940-42
                2sh6p Booklets
BK46 BC11 scar, #235b,
            #238b-239b (7)   1,050.
BK47 BC11 blue, #235b,
            #238b-239b (6)   1,050.

Denomination part of cover of Nos. BK46-BK47 is printed in white on black background.

BK48 BC11 grn, #235b,
            #238b-239b (80)   550.00
BK49 BC11 grn, #258b,
            #261b-262b
            (120)   550.00

BC12

1943
BK50 BC12 *grn,* #258a, #261b-
262b (90)   65.00

With booklets issued in August and September 1943, commercial advertising on British booklets was discontinued. Covers and interleaving were used for Post Office slogans. Booklets were no longer numbered, but carried the month and year of issue.

1951-52
BK51 BC12 *grn,* #280c, #283b-
284b (10)   42.50
BK52 BC12 *grn,* #280c, 281e,
#282d, 284b (15)   40.00

1937-38
3sh Booklets
BK53 BC8 *scar,* #235a-236a,
3 #237b (10)   850.00
BK54 BC11 *scar,* #235a-236a,
3 #237b (34)   850.00

1937-43
5sh Booklets
BK55 BC8 *buff,* #235b-236b,
237c, 5 #237b (3)   1,000.
BK56 BC11 *buff,* #235b-236b,
237c, 5 #237b (9)   950.00
BK57 BC11 *buff,* #235b, 238b,
3 #239b (16)   975.00
BK58 BC11 *buff,* #258a, 261b,
3 #262b (20)   950.00

1943-53
BK59 BC12 *tan,* #258a, 261b,
3 #262b (49)   110.00
BK60 BC12 *tan,* #258a, 261b,
3 #262b (20)   1,250.

Cover on No. BK60 has thick horizontal lines separating the GPO emblem and the various inscriptions.

BK61 BC12 *tan,* #280a, 283b,
3 #284b (5)   62.50
BK62 BC12 *tan,* #280c, 281e,
282d, 3 #284b (5)   62.50
BK63 BC12 *tan,* #280c, 281d-
282d, 283b, 2
#284b (2)   62.50

BC13

1953-54
2sh6p Booklets
BK64 BC12 *grn,* #280c, 281e,
294c, #296a (6)   29.00
BK65 BC13 *grn,* #280c, 281e,
294c, 296a (7)   32.50
BK66 BC13 *grn,* #281e, 292c,
294c, 296a   500.00

5sh Booklets
BK67 BC12 *brn,* #280c, 281d,
283b, 294c, 2
#296a (3)   40.00
BK68 BC13 *brn,* #280c, 281d,
283b, 294c, 2
#296a (2)   45.00
BK69 BC13 *brn,* #281d, 283b,
292c, 294c, 2
#296a   300.00
BK70 BC13 *brn,* #283b, 292c-
294c, 2 #296a   160.00

1953-57
1sh Booklets
BK71 BC7 *buff,* 2 each
#292a-294a   8.50
BK72 BC7 *buff,* 2 each #317d,
318f, 319f   25.00

1954-59
BK73 BC10 *buff,* #292b-294b (2)   8.00
BK74 BC10 *buff,* #317b, 318c,
319b (3)   8.00
BK75 BC10 *buff,* #353b-355b (2)   10.00

1959
2sh Booklets
BK76 BC10 *salmon,* #317b,
318c, 319b, 322b   6.50

BC14

1960-65
2sh Booklets
BK77 BC14 *sal,* #353b-355b,
358b   40.00
BK77A BC14 *pale yel,* 353b-
355b, 358b   40.00
BK78 BC14 *red, pale yel,*
#353e, 2 #357g   4.00
  a.   White stiching   4.00
BK79 BC14 *pale yel,* #353b-
355b, 358b (17)   40.00
  a.   #353bp-355bp, 358bp (13)   100.00
BK80 BC14 *red, pale yel,* 4
#353g   5.00
BK81 BC14 *org yel,* #354f,
359c (7)   3.50
  a.   #354fp, 359cp (12)   17.50
BK82 BC14 *red, org yel,* 2
#358b   8.00

1968-69
BK83 BC14 *org yel,* #MH5b,
MH6b (3)   1.40
BK84 BC14 *gray,* #MH6a-MH6b
(5)   1.00
BK85 BC14 *gray,* #MH7a-MH7b
(12)   1.25

1954, Mar.
2sh6p Booklets
BK86 BC13 *grn,* #292c, 293d,
294c, 296a (19)   37.50

No. BK86 inscribed Apr. 1954 through Aug. 1955 are valued. Booklet inscribed Mar. 1954 is valued at $325.

No. BK86 inscribed Aug. 1955 through Nov. 1955, may contain one or more panes watermarked 308 substituted for those listed. Value $50.

1955, Dec.
BK87 BC13 *grn,* #317a, 318b,
319a, 321a (16)   40.00

No. BK87 inscribed Dec. 1955 through June 1956 may contain one or more panes watermarked 298 substituted for those listed. Value $15.

1957
BK88 BC13 *grn,* #317a, 320b, 321a
(9)   40.00

3sh Booklets
1958, Jan.
BK89 BC13 *red,* #317a, 318b,
319a, 322a (9)   25.00

No. BK89 inscribed Nov. 1958, may contain one or more panes watermarked 322 substituted for those listed. Value $13.

1958, Dec.-59
BK90 BC13 *red,* #353a-355a,
358a (5)   29.00
  a.   #353d, 354d, 355d, 358d (2)   300.00

No. BK90 dated Dec. 1958, may contain one or more panes watermarked 308 substituted for those listed. Value $14.

BK91 BC13 *brick red,* #353a-355a,
358a (14)   32.50
  a.   #353d, 354d, 355d, 358d (4)   325.00
  b.   #353ap, 354ap, 355ap, 358ap (2)   65.00

BC15

1960
BK92 BC15 *brick red,* #353a-355a,
358a (46)   32.50
  a.   #353ap-355ap, 358ap (35)   75.00

3sh9p Booklets
1953, Nov.
BK93 BC15 *red,* 3 #296a (10)   35.00

No. BK93 inscribed Oct. or Dec. 1955 may contain one or more panes watermarked 308 substituted for those listed. Value $16.

1956, Feb.
BK94 BC13 *red,* 3 #321a (10)   25.00

1957, Oct.-Dec. 1960
4sh6p Booklets
BK95 BC13 *dull mauve,* 3 #322a
(7)   25.00
BK96 BC13 *dull mauve,* 3 #358a
(4)   90.00
BK97 BC14 *dull mauve,* 3 #358a
(4)   26.00
  a.   3 #358d   37.50
BK98 BC14 *pale reddish lil,* 3
#358a (9)   37.50
  a.   3 #358d (4)   25.00
  b.   3 #358ap   30.00
BK99 BC15 *pale reddish lil,* 3
#358a (36)   45.00
  a.   3 #358ap (31)   35.00

1965
BK100 BC15 *slate bl,* #354a, 2
#359b (7)   25.00
  a.   #354ap, 2 #359bp (13)   32.50

1968
BK101 BC15 *slate bl,* #MH2a, 2
#MH6c   7.50

Ship with GPO Emblem — BC16

1968-70
4sh6p Booklets
BK102 BC16 *blue,* #MH2a, 2
#MH6c (3)   2.00
BK103 BC16 *blue,* #MH2a, 2
#MH7c (9)   3.75

Ship Type with St. Edward's Crown instead of GPO emblem
BK104 BC16 *blue,* #MH2a, 2
#MH7c (2)   4.50

5sh Booklets
1954, Mar.
BK105 BC13 *brn,* #292c-294c,
295a-296a (10)   45.00

No. BK105 inscribed Sept. 1955 may contain one or more panes watermarked 308 substituted for those listed. Value $16.

1955, Nov.
BK106 BC13 *brn,* #317a, 318b,
319a, 320b, 321a
(14)   40.00

No. BK106 inscribed Nov. 1955, Jan. 1956 or May 1956 may contain one or more panes watermarked 298 substituted for those listed. Value $17.

1958
BK107 BC13 *brn,* #317a, 318b,
321a, 2 #322a (5)   40.00

No. BK107 inscribed July or Nov. 1958 may contain one or more panes watermarked 322 substituted for those listed. Value $15.

1959, Jan.
BK108 BC14 *bl,* #353a-354a,
357c, 2 #358a (11)   32.50
  a.   #353d-354d, 357e, 2 #358d (3)   150.00
  b.   #353ap-354ap, 357cp, 2
#358ap   125.00

No. BK108 inscribed Jan. 1959 may contain one or more panes watermarked 308 substituted for those listed. Value $15.

1961, Jan.
BK109 BC15 *bl,* #353a-354a, 357c,
2 #358a (27)   50.00
  a.   #353ap-354ap, 357cp, 2 #358ap
(24)   150.00

House with GPO Emblem — BC17

1968-70
BK110 BC17 *org brn,* 2 #MH8a
(5)   3.00

House Type with St. Edward's Crown instead of GPO Emblem
BK111 BC17 5sh *org brn,* 2 #MH8a
(7)   3.25

BC18

1970
BK112 BC18 *org brn,* 2 #MH8a   3.50

6sh Booklets
1965
BK113 BC15 *claret,* 3 #359b (23)   30.00
  a.   3 #359bp (27)   37.50

1967
BK114 BC15 *claret,* 3 #MH6c (10)   50.00

Bird with GPO Emblem — BC19

1968-70
BK115 BC19 *org,* 3 #MH6c (8)   2.25
BK116 BC19 *org,* 3 #MH7c (5)   2.25

Bird Type with St. Edward's Crown instead of GPO Emblem
BK117 BC19 *org,* 3 #MH7c (5)   4.25

1961-67
10sh Booklets
BK118 BC15 *grn,* #353a-355a,
356b, 5 #358a (2)   140.00
BK119 BC15 *gray grn,* #354a-
355a, 357c, 5
#358a (7)   115.00
BK120 BC15 *tan,* #354a, 358a, 4
#359b (5)   30.00
  a.   #354ap, 358ap, 4 #359bp (3)   9.25

Explorers with GPO Emblem — BC20

1968-70
BK121 BC20 *pur,* #MH2a, MH5a, 4 #MH6c (2) 6.75

Explorer Type with clear GPO Emblem
BK122 BC20 *yel grn,* #MH6d, 2 ea #MH6c, #MH8a 6.75
BK123 BC20 *yel grn,* #MH7c, MH7e, MH8a (4) 4.00

Explorer Type with St. Edward's Crown instead of GPO Emblem
BK124 BC20 *yel grn,* #MH7e, 2 ea #MH7c, MH8a (2) 8.00

BC21

£1 Booklets
1969
BK125 BC21 multi, 2 #MH7d, MH8b-MH8c 17.50
BK126 BC21 2 #MH7d, MH8b-MH8c, stapled 400.00

Decimal Currency Booklets (Stitched)

BC22

1971-74
BK127 BC22 10p *org yel,* #MH24a, MH26a (21) 2.50

BC23

1974-76
BK128 BC23 10p *org yel,* #MH24a, MH26a (9) 2.75

BC24

1971-73
BK129 BC24 25p *dull purple* (12) 5.00
Contents: #MH22a, MH32a-MH32b.

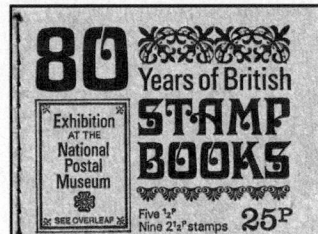

BC25

1971
BK130 BC25 25p *dull purple* 8.25
Contents: #MH22a, MH32a-MH32b.
BK131 BC25 30p *bright pur,* #MH36b 5.75

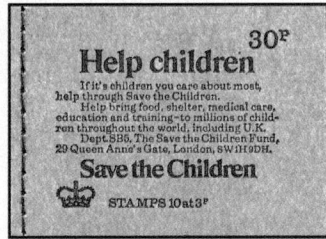

BC26

1973-74
BK132 BC26 25p *dull mauve* 10.50
Contents: #MH22a, MH32a-MH32b.
BK133 BC26 30p *vermilion,* 2 #MH36b 6.50

Bird Type with St. Edward's Crown instead of GPO Emblem
1971-73
BK134 BC19 30p *pur,* 2 #MH36b (16) 5.50
BK135 BC19 30p *buff,* 2 #MH36b 8.25

BC27

1973-74
BK136 BC27 30p *red,* 2 #MH36b 6.00
BK137 BC27 35p *blue,* 2 #MH39a 4.00
BK138 BC27 50p *pale bluish grn* 12.00
Contents: #MH22a, MH32b, MH36a, MH36c (4).
BK139 BC27 50p *pale grn,* MH36b, 2 #MH39a (2) 10.50
BK140 BC27 85p *purple,* #MH39a, 3 #MH49a 10.50

BC28

1973-74
BK141 BC28 35p *bl,* 2 #MH39a (3) 4.25
BK142 BC28 45p *yel brn,* 2 #MH49a (3) 7.00

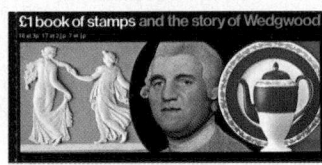

BC29

1971-72
BK143 BC29 50p *pale bluish green* 11.50
Contents: #MH22a, MH32b, MH36a, MH36c (8).

Prestige Booklets

BC30

1972, May 24
BK144 BC30 £1 *Wedgwood* 150.00
Contents: #MH34a-MH34b, #MH36d-MH36e. Valued with a F-VF 1/2p stamp.

BC31

1980, Apr. 16
BK145 BC31 £3 *Wedgwood* 20.00
Contents: #MH26b, MH70a, MH78a-MH78b.

1982, May 19
BK146 £4 *Stanley Gibbons* 20.00
Contents: #MH80a-MH80b, MH92a-MH92b.

1983, Sept. 14
BK147 £4 *Royal Mint* 19.00
Contents: #MH94a-MH94b, 2 #MH80a.

1984, Sept. 4
BK148 £4 *Christian Heritage* 55.00
Contents: #MH97c-MH97d, 2 #MH83a.

1985, Jan. 8
BK149 £5 *The Times* 50.00
Contents: #MH83b, MH97b-MH97c, MH149a.

1986, Mar. 18
BK150 £5 *British Rail* 50.00
Contents: #MH79a, MH97b-MH97c, MH142a.

1987, Mar. 3
BK151 £5 *P & O* 32.50
Contents: #MH83a-MH83b, MH102a, MH130a.

1988, Feb. 9
BK152 £5 *The Financial Times* 47.50
Contents: #MH84a, MH103a-MH103b, MH150a.

1989, Mar. 21
BK153 £5 *Scots Connection* 30.00
Contents: #SMH25a,SMH37a-SMH37b, SMH45a.

1990, Mar. 20
BK154 £5 *London Life* 37.50
Contents: #1314a, MH196a, 2 #MH193d.

1991, Mar. 19
BK155 £6 *Agatha Christie* 37.50
Contents: #MH121a, MH147a, 2 #MH99a.

1992, Feb. 25
BK156 £6 *Cymru-Wales* 30.00
Contents: #1425a, MH187c, WMMH34a, WMMH45a.

1992, Oct. 27
BK157 £6 *J.R.R. Tolkien* 32.50
Contents: #MH105a, MH187b, 2 #MH127a.

1993, Aug. 10
BK158 £5.64 *Beatrix Potter* 30.00
Although inscribed £6 on the cover, No. BK158 was sold for £5.64, the face value of its contents, which were #1484a, MH178a, MH187a, NIMH45a.

1994, July 26
BK159 £6.04 *N. Ireland* 45.00
Contents: #1550a, MH214a, NIMH63a-NIMH63b, 2 postal cards.

1995, Apr. 25
BK160 £6 *National Trust* 40.00
Contents: #1607a, MH209a, MH231a, NIMH59a.

1996, May 14
BK161　£6.48　*European Soccer Championships*　25.00
Contents: #1663a, 1664a, 1667a, MH214b.

1997, Sept. 23
BK162　£6.15　*75th Anniv. of BBC*　30.00
Contents: #1698a, MH287a, MH257a, NIMH81a.

1998, Mar. 10
BK163　£7.49　*Definitive Portrait*　35.00
Contents: #1801a, 1802a, 1803a-1803b.

1998, Oct. 13
BK164　£6.16　*Breaking Barriers*　45.00
Contents: #1829b, MH269a, MH285a-MH285b.

1999, Feb. 16
BK165　(£7.54)　*Profile on Print*　50.00
Contents: #MH241c, MH288a, MH310a-MH312a.

1999, Sept. 21
BK166　(£6.99)　*World Changers*　50.00
Contents: #1842b, 1847a, 1868b, 1869b, MH257f.

2000, Feb. 15
BK167　£7.50　*Special by Design*　60.00
Contents: #MH198Ab, MH264Bc, MH336b, WMMH96a.

2000, Aug. 4
BK168　(£7.03)　*The Life of the Century*　35.00
Contents: #1943e, 1943f, Scotland 18a, MH335b.

2000, Sept. 18
BK169　(£7)　*A Treasury of Trees*　40.00
Contents: #1917a, 1918a, 1920a, 1921a, Wales and Monmouthshire 18a.

2001, Oct. 22
BK170　(£6.76)　*Unseen and Unheard*　45.00
Contents: #1969b, 1970b, 1999e, Scotland 16a.

2002, Feb. 6
BK171　(£7.23)　*A Gracious Accession*　35.00
Contents: #2020a, 2021a, 2023a, MH290b.

2002, Sept. 24
BK172　(£6.83)　*Across the Universe*　45.00
Contents: 1938b, 2075e, Scotland 15a, MH290c.

2003, Feb. 25
BK173　(£6.99)　*Microcosmos*　30.00
Contents: #2104a, 2105a, Northern Ireland 13a, MH290c.

2003, June 2
BK174　(£7.46)　*A Perfect Coronation*　90.00
Contents: #2126a, 2134a, 2136b, MH287b.

2004, Mar. 16
BK175　(£7.44)　*Letters by Night*　27.00
Contents: #2148a, 2175a, Scotland 20a, MH287c.

2004, May 25
BK176　(£7.23)　*The Glory of the Garden*　32.50
Contents: #1720b, 2213a, 2214b, MH287d.

2005, Feb. 24
BK177　(£7.43)　*The Bronte Sisters*　30.00
Contents: #2268a, 2272b, England 10a, MH354a.

2005, Oct. 18
BK178　(£7.26)　*Battle of Trafalgar*　30.00
Contents: #1999h, 2325a, 2326b, MH287e.

2006, Feb. 23
BK179　(£7.40)　*Isambard Kingdom Brunel*　30.00
Contents: #2356a, 2357a, 2358b, MH355a.

2006, Sept. 21
BK180　(£7.44)　*Victoria Cross*　30.00
Contents: #1331b, 2398a, 2399b, MH376a.

2007, Mar. 1
BK181　(£7.49)　*World of Invention*　37.50
Contents: #2447a, 2449b, Wales & Monmouthshire 26a, MH376b.

2007, June 5
BK182　(£7.66)　*The Machin*　31.00
Contents: #2471c, MH363a, MH373a, MH378a.

2007, Sept. 20
BK183　(£7.66)　*British Army Uniforms*　32.00
Contents: #2510b, 2513b, MH366a, Wales & Monmouthshire #21a.

2008, Jan. 8
BK184　(£7.40)　*Ian Fleming's James Bond*　30.00
Contents: #1999i, 2535a, 2536b, MH287f.

2008, Sept. 18
BK185　(£7.15)　*RAF Uniforms*　26.00
Contents: #2587c, 2596b, 2599b, MH287h.

2008, Sept. 29
BK186　(£9.72)　*The Regional Definitives: Heraldry and Symbol*　34.00
Contents: #2600s, 2600t, 2600u, 2600v.

2009, Jan. 13
BK187　(£7.68)　*British Design Classics*　24.00
Contents: #2619a, 2623a, 2624b, MH365b.

2009, Feb. 12
BK188　(£7.75)　*Charles Darwin*　30.00
Contents: #2626e, 2630a, 2632a, MH363c.

2009, Aug. 18
BK189　(£8.18)　*Treasures of the Archive*　28.00
Contents: #1289b, 2679e, MH368b, MH394a.

2009, Sept. 17
BK190　(£7.93)　*Royal Navy Uniforms*　26.50
Contents: #1999j, 2688b, 2691b, MH372Ac.

2010, Jan. 7
BK191　(£8.06)　*Classic Album Covers*　40.00
Contents: #2729a, 2733a, MH350Ad, MH368c.

2010, Feb. 25
BK192　(£7.72)　*The Royal Society*　25.00
Contents: #2754a, 2755b, 2756b, MH366Bc.

2010, May 8
BK193　(£11.15)　*King George V*　33.00
Contents: #2792b, 2791b, 2789a, MH385a.

2010, May 13
BK194　(£9.76)　*Britain Alone*　30.00
Contents: #MH397b, 2802a, 2801a, 2806b.

Numbers have been reserved for future prestige booklets.

Decimal Currency Booklets (Folded)

Booklets are listed in denomination sequence in chronological order in this section.

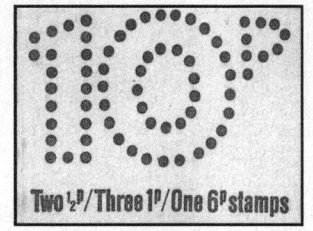

BC32

1976-77
BK225　BC32　10p red, *gray*, #MH58a (3)　1.25

BC33

1978
BK226　BC33　10p brn, *bl*, #MH61b (6)　1.25

1979-80
BK227　BC33　10p *London '80*, #MH64b (2)　.75

BC34

1977
BK228　BC34　50p #MH65a　5.25
BK229　BC34　50p #MH67a　3.50

Nos. BK228-BK229, BK230-BK231, BK237-BK238 exist with either version of #MH65a, MH67a, MH70b, MH80c. See the notes following the listings for these panes.

Commercial Vehicles — BC35

1978-95
50p Booklets, Cover BC35

BK230	Commercial Vehicles, #MH67a (6)	5.75
BK231	Commercial Vehicles, #MH70b	3.75
BK232	Veteran Cars, #MH70b	3.00
BK233	Veteran Cars, #MH78d (3)	3.00
BK234	Veteran Cars, #MH86a (2)	3.00
BK235	Follies, #MH86a	3.00
BK236	Follies, #MH76a (2)	8.25
BK237	Follies, #MH80c (4)	3.50
BK238	Rare Farm Animals, #MH80c	3.75
BK239	Rare Farm Animals, #MH80d (4)	7.50
BK240	Orchids, #MH83c (4)	4.75
BK241	Pillar Box, #MH97a	5.50
BK242	Pond Life, #MH97a (2)	3.50

Nos. BK241-BK242 sold for a 1p discount. Some panes have stars on reverse.

BK244	Pond Life, #MH83d (2)	5.00
BK245	Roman Britain, #MH79b	11.50
BK246	Roman Britain, #MH102b (2)	5.25
BK247	Marylebone Cricket Club, #MH102b (4)	3.50
BK248	Botanical Gardens, #MH83d (2)	6.00
BK248A	Botanical Gardens, #MH83g (2)	5.75
BK249	London Zoo, #MH102b (2)	4.00
BK250	London Zoo, #MH83g	5.00
BK251	Marine Life, #MH83g	5.00
BK252	Marine Life, #MH106a (2)	4.00
BK253	Gilbert & Sullivan Operas, #MH106a (3)	6.00
BK254	Aircraft, #MH115a	14.00
BK255	Aircraft, #MH193a	10.50
BK256	Aircraft, #MH98a (2)	6.25
BK257	Archaeology, #MH126a (4)	3.50
BK258	Sheriff's Millennium, #MH126a	2.50
BK259	Postal History, #MH126a (3)	3.00
BK260	Postal History, #MH213a	3.00
BK261	Coaching Inns, #MH213a (4)	3.00
BK262	Sea Charts, #MH213a (4)	3.00

With Window — BC36

Without Window — BC37

1987
BK285　BC36　52p #MH83e　4.50

1988-89
BK295	BC36	56p #MH87a (2)	7.00
BK296	BC37	56p #MH87b	11.00
BK297	BC37	56p #MH87c	45.00

1990
BK307	BC37	60p #MH191a	7.50

1976-77
BK317	BC34	65p 10 #MH60	10.50
BK325	BC34	70p 10 #MH61	7.00

Nos. BK317, BK325-BK327, BK370, BK394, BK404-BK405, BK467-BK468, BK488-BK492, BK513-BK514, BK524-BK533, BK554-BK557, BK573-BK574, BK584, BK594, BK616-BK618, BK631, BK641, BK651-BK652, BK673-BK675, BK696-BK699, BK709-BK713, BK715-BK718, BK728, BK732-BK733 exist with stamps affixed to cover by selvage at either right or left edges of block or pane of stamps.

BC38

1978-79

70p Booklets
BK326	BC38	Country Crafts, 10 #MH61 (6)	5.75
BK327	BC38	Derby Mechanized Letter Office, 10 #MH61	10.50

1987
BK338	BC36	72p red, yel & blk, #MH102c	4.50

1988-89
BK348	BC36	76p #MH106c (2)	9.00
BK349	BC37	76p #MH106d	9.00
BK350	BC37	76p #MH106e	45.00

BC39

1992
BK360	BC39	78p 2 #MH157	4.00

Cover of #BK360 does not show the numeral four. Contents of #BK360 is 1/2 of #MH157a, the right hand vertical pair of stamps being removed.

1979
BK370	BC38	80p Military Aircraft, 10 #MH64	3.00

1990
BK371	BC37	80p red, yel & blk, #MH193b	10.00
BK372	BC37	80p red, yel & blk, #MH194a	7.50

1976-79
BK382	BC34	85p gray & ol grn, 10 #MH65	10.50
BK392	BC34	90p lt & dk bl, 10 #MH67	7.00
BK393	BC38	90p British Canals, 10 #MH67 (6)	8.00
BK394	BC38	90p Derby Letter Office, 10 #MH67	12.50

1979-95

£1 Booklets
BK403	BC38	Industrial Archaeology, 10 #MH70	5.25
BK404	BC38	Military Aircraft, 10 #MH70 (3)	5.25
BK405	BC35	Violin, 6 #MH97	5.75
BK406	BC35	Musical Instruments, #MH102d (2)	6.00
BK407	BC35	Sherlock Holmes, #MH102d (2)	6.00
BK408	BC35	Sherlock Holmes, #MH102f (2)	6.00
BK409	BC35	London Zoo, #MH102f	6.00
BK410	BC35	Oliver Twist, #MH102f	8.00
BK411	BC35	Nicholas Nickleby, #MH106b (2)	8.00
BK412	BC35	Great Expectations, #MH108a	15.00
BK413	BC35	Marine Life, #MH106b	8.00
BK414	BC35	Wicken Fen, #MH115b	11.00
BK415	BC35	Click Mill, #MH193c	8.50
BK416	BC35	Wicken Fen, #MH194b	8.00
BK417	BC35	Jack & Jill Mills, #MH120a (2)	5.00
BK418	BC35	Punch Magazine, #MH126b (4)	4.00
BK419	BC35	Sheriff's Millennium, #MH126b	4.25
BK420	BC35	Educational Institutions, #MH128a (3)	8.25
BK421	BC35	Educational Institutions, 4 #MH214	8.25
BK422	BC35	Prime Ministers, 4 #MH214	3.75
BK423	BC35	Prime Ministers, 4 #MH213 (3)	4.00
BK424	BC35	End of World War II, 4 #MH213 (4)	4.00

BC40

1996-2000
BK425	BC40	£1 multi, 4 #MH214	8.00
BK426	BC40	£1 multi, #MH216b	8.00
BK427	BC40	£1 multi, #MH257b	12.50
BK428	BC40	£1 multi, #MH257d	7.00
BK429	BC40	£1 #MH288d	6.00

1987-88

£1.04 Booklet
BK446	BC36	#MH131a	24.00

£1.08 Booklets
BK456	BC36	#MH133a	16.00
BK457	BC37	#MH133b	40.00

1981

£1.15 Booklets
BK467	BC38	Military Aircraft, 10 #MH76 (2)	5.75
BK468	BC38	Museums, 10 #MH76 (2)	5.75

1989

£1.16 Booklet
BK478	BC37	multi, #MH140a	25.00

1980-86

£1.20 Booklets
BK488	BC38	Industrial Archaeology, 10 #MH78 (3)	5.75
BK489	BC38	Pillar Box, 10 #MH79	8.00
BK490	BC38	National Gallery, 10 #MH79	7.50
BK491	BC38	Handwriting, 10 #MH79	7.50
BK492	BC38	Christmas, 10 #MH83	10.00

No. BK492 was sold at a discount. Each stamp has a blue double-line star printed on reverse.

BC41

1998

£1.20 Booklet
BK493	BC41	multi, 4 #MH259	4.75

1990

£1.24 Booklet
BK503	BC39	multi, #MH144a	8.00

1982-83

£1.25 Booklets
BK513	BC38	Museums, 10 #MH81 (4)	6.25
BK514	BC38	Railway Engines, 10 #MH81 (5)	8.00

1981-88

£1.30 Booklets
BK524	BC38	Postal History, #MH86b (2)	8.00
BK525	BC38	Trams, 10 #MH83 (4)	6.25
BK526	BC38	Books for Children, 10 #MH83	6.25
BK527	BC38	Keep in Touch, 10 #MH83	6.25
BK528	BC38	Ideas for your Garden, 10 #MH83	6.25
BK529	BC38	Brighter Writer, 10 #MH83	6.25
BK530	BC38	Jolly Postman, 10 #MH83	6.50
BK531	BC38	Linnean Society, 10 #MH83	7.75
BK532	BC38	Recipe Cards, 10 #MH83	6.25
BK533	BC38	Party Pack, 10 #MH83	6.25
BK534	BC36	red, yel & blk, #MH83f	7.00

1991

£1.32 Booklet
BK544	BC39	multi, #MH148a	8.50

1981-89

£1.40 Booklets
BK554	BC38	Industrial Archaeology, 10 #MH86 (2)	6.25
BK555	BC38	Women's Costumes, 10 #MH86 (2)	6.25
BK556	BC38	Pocket Planner, 10 #MH87	6.25
BK557	BC38	William Henry Fox Talbot, 10 #MH87	6.50

1988-95

£1.40 Booklets
BK558	BC36	#MH87d	9.50
BK559	BC36	10 #MH88	20.00
BK560	BC37	#MH87e	11.50
BK561	BC37	10 #MH88	20.00
BK562	BC39	4 #MH223	8.00
BK563	BC41	4 #MH223 (2)	8.00

1982

£1.43 Booklets
BK572	BC38	James Chalmers, #MH93d	7.00
BK573	BC38	Postal History, #MH93c (4)	7.00
BK574	BC38	Holiday Postcard Stamp Book, #MH93c	7.00

1983

£1.45 Booklet
BK584	BC38	Britain's Countryside, 10 #MH94	5.50

Stamps in #BK584 have double-lined D printed on reverse.

1983

£1.46 Booklet
BK594	BC38	Postal History, #MH94c (4)	12.50

BC42

1996-97

£1.48 Booklets
BK605	BC41	#MH226a (2)	11.50
BK606	BC42	4 #MH264	11.50

1986-90

£1.50 Booklets
BK616	BC38	Pillar Box, #MH97e	8.00
BK617	BC38	National Gallery, #MH97e	8.00
BK618	BC38	Handwriting, #MH97e	8.00
BK619	BC37	#MH190a	7.50
BK620	BC37	#MH191b	12.00
BK621	BC37	#MH192a	11.00

1999

£1.52 Booklet
BK630	BC41	4 #MH264	8.00

1985

£1.53 Booklet
BK631	BC38	Royal Mail, 350th Anniv., 10 #1111	7.00

1984

£1.54 Booklet
BK641	BC38	Postal History, #MH97f (4)	7.00

1982-85

£1.55 Booklets
BK651	BC38	Women's Costumes, 10 #MH93 (4)	6.50
BK652	BC38	Social Letter Writing, 10 #MH97	6.50

No. BK652 sold for a 15p discount. Panes have double-lined "D" printed on reverse.

1991

£1.56 Booklet
BK662	BC39	#MH157a	12.50

1978-2000

£1.60 Booklets
BK672	BC38	Christmas, #MH67b	8.00
BK673	BC38	Birthday Box, 10 #MH97 (2)	8.00
BK674	BC38	Britain's Countryside, 10 #MH94	7.00
BK675	BC38	Write It, 10 #MH97	8.00
BK676	BC41	#MH266a	8.75

1993-96

£1.64 Booklets
BK685	BC39	#MH231b	10.00
BK686	BC41	#MH231b (2)	10.00

1984-86

£1.70 Booklets
BK696	BC38	Love Letters, 10 #MH97 (2)	8.00
BK697	BC38	Pillar Box, 10 #MH97 (2)	8.00
BK698	BC38	National Gallery, 10 #MH97	8.00
BK699	BC38	Handwriting, 10 #MH97	8.00

1979-88

£1.80 Booklets
BK709	BC38	Christmas, #MH70c	10.50
BK710	BC38	Books for Children, 10 #MH102	8.00
BK711	BC38	Keep in Touch, 10 #MH102	8.00
BK712	BC38	Ideas for your Garden, 10 #MH102	8.00
BK713	BC38	Brighter Writer, 10 #MH102	8.00
BK714	BC36	red, yel & blk, #MH102e	10.50

BK715	BC38	*Jolly Postman*, 10 #MH102	8.00
BK716	BC38	*Linnean Society*, 10 #MH102	8.00
BK717	BC38	*Recipe Cards*, 10 #MH102	8.00
BK718	BC38	*Party Pack*, 10 #MH102	8.00

1988-89
£1.90 Booklets

BK728	BC38	*Pocket Planner*, 10 #MH106	10.00
BK729	BC36	red, yel & blk, #MH106f	14.00
BK730	BC37	#MH106g	14.00
BK731	BC37	10 #MH107	27.50
BK732	BC38	*William Henry Fox Talbot*, 10 #MH106	10.00

BC43

1989
£1.90 Booklet

BK733	BC43	*Greetings*, #1247a	65.00

Artwork for #BC43 spanned six booklet covers. Only portions of the design appear on each cover.

Value is for pane with perfs guillotined. Value for booklet with pane having full perfs is approximately 60% more.

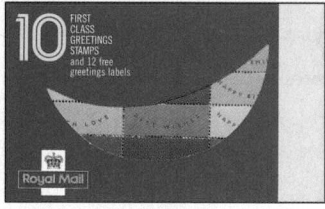

BC44

1990
£2 Booklets

BK742	BC44	#1313a	40.00
BK743	BC37	#MH193e	12.00
BK744	BC37	#MH194c	12.00
BK745	BC37	#MH195a	20.00
BK746	BC35	*Postal Vehicles*, 8 #MH213 (3)	8.50
BK747	BC35	*Rowland Hill*, 8 #MH213 (4)	8.50
BK748	BC40	8 #MH214	8.00
BK749	BC40	#MH216a	9.00

1998-2000

BK751	BC40	#MH257c	15.00
BK752	BC40	#MH257e	8.50
BK753	BC40	#MH288e	8.00

1980-93
£2.20 Booklets

BK759	BC38	*Christmas*, #MH78c	9.00
BK760	BC38	*Christmas*, 20 #MH80	8.00

£2.30 Booklet

BK770	BC38	*Christmas*, 20 #1088	11.00

£2.40 Booklet

BK780	BC38	*Christmas*, 20 #1124	10.50

Stamps in #BK760, BK770, BK780 have double-line star printed on reverse over gum.

BC45

1994-95
£2.40 Booklets

BK790	BC39	#MH234a (2)	9.25
BK791	BC41	#MH234a (2)	9.25
BK792	BC45	#1638a	9.50

1981-94
£2.50 Booklets

BK802	BC38	*Christmas*, #MH93e	10.50

No. BK802 was sold for a 30p discount. Stamps in #BK802 have a 10-point single-line blue star printed on reverse over gum.

BK803	BC45	*Santa, Reindeer*, 10 #1529	11.50
BK804	BC45	*Christmas Play Props*, 10 #1582	9.00
BK805	BC45	*Christmas Robin*, 10 #1635	9.00

1996-97
£2.52 Booklet

BK815	BC41	#MH236a (3)	15.00

1981
£2.55 Booklet

BK826	BC38	*Christmas*, #MH86c	11.00

1999
£2.56 Booklet

BK827	BC41	4 #MH276	10.50

2000
£2.60 Booklet

BK830	BC41	#MH277a	11.50

1990-95
£3.40 Booklet

BK836	BC45	*Snowman*, #1340a	14.00

£3.60 Booklets

BK846	BC45	*Holly*, #1416a	14.00
BK847	BC45	*Santa, Reindeer*, #1468a	14.00

£3.80 Booklets

BK857	BC45	*Santa, Reindeer*, #1528a	15.00
BK858	BC45	*Christmas Play Props*, #1581a	15.00
BK859	BC45	*Christmas Robin*, #1634a	15.00

No-Value Indicated Booklets

BC46

1989-2000

BK960	BC37	(56p)	#MH179a	10.00
BK961	BC37	(60p)	#MH177a	30.00
BK962	BC39	(60p)	#MH182a	4.50
BK963	BC39	(68p)	#MH179b	5.00
BK964	BC46	(72p)	#MH179b	8.00
BK965	BC39	(72p)	4 #MH238	4.50
BK966	BC39	(72p)	4 #MH239	4.50
BK967	BC41	(76p)	4 #MH238	4.50
BK968	BC41	(76p)	4 #MH239 (2)	4.50
BK969	BC41	(80p)	4 #MH284 (2)	5.00
BK994	BC37	(76p)	#MH184a	10.00
BK995	BC37	(80p)	#MH183a	40.00
BK996	BC39	(80p)	#MH188a (2)	4.50
BK997	BC46	(96p)	#MH188a	4.00
BK998	BC39	(96p)	4 #MH240	4.50

BK999	BC39	(96p)	4 #MH241	5.00
BK1000	BC39	(£1)	#MH241b	11.00
BK1001	BC41	(£1)	#MH241 (4)	5.00
BK1002	BC41	(£1)	#MH241b (4)	7.00

(£1.04) Booklets

BK1003	BC41	4 #MH288	5.75
BK1004	BC41	#MH241b	7.00
BK1005	BC41	4 #MH288	8.50
BK1006	BC41	4 #MH288+label	9.75

(£1.20) Booklet

BK1007	BC41	#MH335c	5.50
BK1010	BC41	#MH290a	6.50

(£1.40) Booklets

BK1028	BC37	#MH177b	15.00
BK1029	BC37	10 #MH178	12.50

(£1.50) Booklets

BK1030	BC39	#MH180a	8.50
BK1031	BC39	10 #MH181	20.00
BK1032	BC39	#MH182b	9.50

(£1.70) Booklets

BK1033	BC39	10 #MH178	12.50
BK1034	BC39	#MH179c	12.50

(£1.80) Booklets

BK1035	BC46	#MH179c	12.50
BK1036	BC46	10 #MH178	12.50
BK1037	BC39	#MH177b	15.00
BK1038	BC39	10 #MH239 (3)	10.00

(£1.90) Booklets

BK1039	BC41	10 #MH239 (5)	10.00
BK1040	BC41	10 #MH238 (4)	10.00
BK1041	BC37	#MH183b	20.00

(£2) Booklets

BK1068	BC39	#MH186a (2)	13.50
BK1069	BC39	10 #MH187 (3)	13.50
BK1070	BC39	#MH188b (3)	13.50
BK1071	BC41	10 #MH284	9.50
BK1072	BC41	10 #MH285	9.50

(£2.40) Booklets

BK1091	BC46	#MH186a	13.50
BK1092	BC46	#MH187d	13.50
BK1093	BC39	#MH187d	13.50
BK1094	BC39	10 #MH240	14.00
BK1095	BC39	10 #MH241 (11)	14.00

(£2.50) Booklets

BK1116	BC41	10 #MH240 (11)	12.50
BK1117	BC41	10 #MH241 (12)	11.00

(£2.60) Booklets

BK1137	BC41	10 #MH287	12.50
BK1139	BC41	10 #MH288	12.50
BK1139A	BC41	#MH289a	20.00
BK1140	BC41	10 #MH288	12.50
BK1141	BC41	#1856a, MH288b	11.00
BK1142	BC41	#1872a, MH288b	11.00
BK1143	BC41	10 #MH335	12.50
BK1144	BC41	#MH336a	12.50

BC47

1991-2000
(£2.20) Booklets

BK1160	BC47	#1359a	16.00
BK1161	BC47	*Laughing Pillar Box*, #1373a	12.00

(£2.40) Booklets

BK1171	BC47	*Memories*, #1435a	11.00
BK1172	BC47	*Rupert Bear*, #1488a (3)	12.00

(£2.50) Booklets

BK1182	BC47	*Rupert Bear, Paddington Bear*, #1547a	13.50
BK1183	BC47	*Clown*, #1605a	13.50
BK1184	BC47	*More Love*, #1652a	13.50

(£2.60) Booklets

BK1194	BC47	*Christmas*, 10 #1709	15.00
BK1195	BC47	*Flower*, #1722a (4)	12.50
BK1196	BC47	*Chocolates*, #1722a	14.00

BK1197	BC47	*Memorable Post*, #1722a	14.00
BK1198	BC47	*Santa Claus*, 10 #1777	11.50
BK1199	BC47	*Christmas*, 10 #1835	10.50
BK1200	BC47	10 #1880	10.50

(£2.70) Booklets

BK1201	BC41	#1938a, MH335a	11.00
BK1202	BC47	#1919a, MH335a	11.00
BK1203	BC47	10 #1931	13.50

(£3.80) Booklet

BK1210	BC47	#1879a	15.00
BK1211	BC47	#1930a	19.00

(£4) Booklets

BK1220	BC47	*Magi*, #1708a	19.00
BK1221	BC47	*Santa Claus, Children*, #1776a	19.00
BK1222	BC47	*Christmas*, #1834a	16.00

BRITISH OFFICES ABROAD

OFFICES IN AFRICA

> Catalogue values for unused stamps in this section are for Never Hinged stamps.

MIDDLE EAST FORCES

For use in Ethiopia, Cyrenaica, Eritrea, the Dodecanese and Somalia
Stamps of Great Britain, 1937-42
Overprinted in Black or Blue Black

London Printing — ovpt. 14mm long, square dots

1942-43		**Wmk. 251**	**Perf. 14½x14**	
1	A101	1p scarlet	2.00	3.00
2	A101	2p orange	1.50	4.00
3	A101	2½p bright ultra	1.10	1.40
4	A101	3p dark purple	.90	.35
a.		Double overprint		4,000.
5	A102	5p lt brn (Blk)	.80	.35
a.		Blue black overprint ('43)	4.25	.20
6	A102	6p rose lilac ('43)	.45	.20
7	A103	9p dp olive grn ('43)	1.00	.20
8	A103	1sh brown ('43)	.55	.20
		Wmk. 259		
		Perf. 14		
9	A104	2sh6p yel green ('43)	8.00	1.10
		Nos. 1-9 (9)	16.30	10.80

Same Overprint in Blue Black on Nos. 259, 261, 262 and 263

1943, Jan. 1			**Wmk. 251**	
10	A101	1p vermilion	1.75	.20
11	A101	2p light orange	1.75	1.40
12	A101	2½p ultramarine	.55	.20
13	A101	3p violet	1.75	.20
		Nos. 10-13 (4)	5.80	2.00

There were two printings of Nos. 1-5, both issued Mar. 2, 1942, and both black. Nos. 5a and 6-13 compose a third printing, also made in London. On these stamps, issued Jan. 1, 1943, the overprint is 13½mm wide. The 2sh6p overprint is black, the others blue black.

Same Ovpt. in Black on #250, 251A

1947		**Wmk. 259**	**Perf. 14**	
14	A104	5sh dull red	15.00	20.00
15	A105	10sh ultramarine	17.50	11.50

In 1950 Nos. 1-15 were declared valid for use in Great Britain. Used values are for stamps postmarked in territory of issue. Others sell for about 25 percent less.

POSTAGE DUE STAMPS

> Catalogue values for unused stamps in this section are for Never Hinged items.

Postage Due Stamps of Great Britain Overprinted in Blue

1942		**Wmk. 251**	**Perf. 14x14½**	
J1	D1	½p emerald	.35	14.00
J2	D1	1p carmine rose	.35	4.00
J3	D1	2p black brown	1.40	1.40
J4	D1	3p violet	.55	4.75
J5	D1	1sh blue	4.25	14.00
		Nos. J1-J5 (5)	6.90	36.15

No. J1-J5 were used in Eritrea.

FOR USE IN ERITREA

> Catalogue values for unused stamps in this section are for Never Hinged items.

100 Cents = 1 Shilling
Stamps of Great Britain 1937-42 Surcharged

a

		Perf. 14½x14		
1948, June -49			**Wmk. 251**	
1	A101	5c on ½p green (II)	1.60	.75
2	A101	10c on 1p vermilion (II)	1.60	2.75
3	A101	20c on 2p light org (II)	1.10	2.50
4	A101	25c on 2½p ultra (II)	1.40	.70
5	A101	30c on 3p violet (II)	1.60	5.00
6	A101	40c on 5p light brown	1.10	4.75
7	A101	50c on 6p rose lilac	.70	1.10
8	A103	75c on 9p deep ol grn	1.40	.85
9	A103	1sh on 1sh brown	1.40	.55

Great Britain Nos. 249A, 250 and 251A Surcharged

		Wmk. 259		
		Perf. 14		
10	A104	2sh50c on 2sh6p yel grn	9.25	11.50
11	A104	5sh on 5sh dl red	9.25	18.00
12	A105	10sh on 10sh ultra	25.00	25.00

Great Britain No. 245 Surcharged Type "a"

		Wmk. 251		
		Perf. 14½x14		
13	A103	65c on 8p brt rose ('49)	8.00	2.25
		Nos. 1-13 (13)	63.40	75.70

"B. M. A." stands for British Military Administration.

Stamps of Great Britain 1937-42 Surcharged

c

1950, Feb. 6				
14	A101	5c on ½p green (II)	1.60	9.25
15	A101	10c on 1p ver (II)	.45	3.50
16	A101	20c on 2p lt orange (II)	.55	.90
17	A101	25c on 2½p ultra (II)	.55	.70
18	A101	30c on 3p violet (II)	.45	2.50
19	A102	40c on 5p light brown	.80	2.00
20	A102	50c on 6p rose lilac	.45	.25
21	A103	65c on 8p bright rose	3.25	1.75
22	A103	75c on 9p dp ol grn	.65	.30
23	A103	1sh on 1sh brown	.45	.20

Great Britain Nos. 249A, 250, 251A Surcharged

		Wmk. 259	**Perf. 14**	
24	A104	2sh50c on 2sh6p yel grn	8.00	5.50
25	A104	5sh on 5sh dl red	8.00	14.00
26	A105	10sh on 10sh ultra	70.00	62.50
		Nos. 14-26 (13)	95.20	103.35

Great Britain Nos. 280, 281, 283 and 284 Surcharged Type "c"

		Perf. 14½x14		
1951, May 3			**Wmk. 251**	
27	A101	5c on ½p lt orange	.55	.95
28	A101	10c on 1p ultra	.55	.85
29	A101	20c on 2p lt red brown	.55	.35
30	A101	25c on 2½p vermilion	.55	.35

Great Britain Nos. 286-288 Surcharged

		Perf. 11x12		
1951, May 31			**Wmk. 259**	
31	A121	2sh50c on 2sh6p grn	11.50	26.00
32	A121	5sh on 5sh dl red	24.00	26.00
33	A122	10sh on 10sh ultra	25.00	26.00
		Nos. 27-33 (7)	62.70	80.50

Surcharge arranged to fit the design on #33.

POSTAGE DUE STAMPS

> Catalogue values for unused stamps in this section are for Never Hinged items.

Great Britain Nos. J26-J29, J32 Surcharged

1948		**Wmk. 251**	**Perf. 14x14½**	
J1	D1	5c on ½p emer	11.00	25.00
J2	D1	10c on 1p car rose	11.00	27.50
J3	D1	20c on 2p blk brn	12.00	18.00
J4	D1	30c on 3p violet	11.00	18.00
J5	D1	1sh on 1sh blue	20.00	35.00
		Nos. J1-J5 (5)	65.00	123.50

Great Britain Nos. J26 to J29 and J32 Surcharged

1950, Feb. 6				
J6	D1	5c on ½p emer	13.00	55.00
J7	D1	10c on 1p car rose	13.00	18.50
a.		"C" of CENTS omitted	2,750.	
		Lightly hinged	1,850.	
J8	D1	20c on 2p blk brn	13.00	20.00
J9	D1	30c on 3p violet	17.50	28.00
J10	D1	1sh on 1sh blue	17.50	28.00
		Nos. J6-J10 (5)	74.00	149.50

EAST AFRICAN FORCES

FOR USE IN SOMALIA (ITALIAN SOMALILAND)

> Catalogue values for unused stamps in this section are for Never Hinged items.

12 Pence = 1 Shilling
100 Cents = 1 Shilling

Stamps of Great Britain 1938-42 Overprinted in Blue

		Perf. 14½x14		
1943, Jan. 15			**Wmk. 251**	
1	A101	1p vermilion	.80	.65
2	A101	2p light orange	1.75	1.40
3	A101	2½p ultramarine	.80	3.75
4	A101	3p violet	1.10	.20
5	A101	5p light brown	1.90	.45

6	A101	6p rose lilac	1.10	1.40
7	A103	9p dp olive green	1.60	2.40
8	A103	1sh brown	3.00	.20

On Great Britain No. 249A

1946		**Wmk. 259**	**Perf. 14**	
9	A104	2sh6p yellow green	16.00	8.00
		Nos. 1-9 (9)	28.05	18.45

Stamps of Great Britain, 1937-42 Surcharged

		Perf. 14½x14		
1948, May 27			**Wmk. 251**	
10	A101	5c on ½p grn (II)	1.40	2.10
11	A101	15c on 1½p lt red brn (II)	2.00	17.50
12	A101	20c on 2p lt org (II)	3.50	5.00
13	A101	25c on 2½p ultra (II)	2.50	5.00
14	A101	30c on 3p vio (II)	2.50	10.50
15	A102	40c on 5p lt brown	1.40	.20
16	A102	50c on 6p rose lilac	.55	2.25
17	A103	75c on 9p dp ol grn	2.25	21.00
18	A103	1sh on 1sh brown	1.40	.20

Great Britain Nos. 249A and 250 Surcharged

		Wmk. 259	**Perf. 14**	
19	A104	2sh50c on 2sh6p yel grn	5.00	29.00
20	A104	5sh on 5sh dl red	11.00	45.00
		Nos. 10-20 (11)	33.50	137.75

Stamps of Great Britain 1937-42 Surcharged

		Perf. 14½x14		
1950, Jan. 2			**Wmk. 251**	
21	A101	5c on ½p grn (II)	.20	3.50
22	A101	15c on 1½p lt red brn (II)	.85	19.00
23	A101	20c on 2p lt org (II)	.85	8.50
24	A101	25c on 2½p ultra (II)	.55	8.50
25	A101	30c on 3p violet (II)	1.40	5.00
26	A102	40c on 5p light brn	.65	1.10
27	A102	50c on 6p rose lilac	.55	1.10
28	A103	75c on 9p deep ol grn	2.25	8.00
29	A103	1sh on 1sh brown	.70	1.75

Great Britain Nos. 249A and 250 Surcharged

		Wmk. 259	**Perf. 14**	
30	A104	2sh50c on 2sh 6p yel grn	4.50	27.50
31	A104	5sh on 5sh dull red	12.50	35.00
		Nos. 21-31 (11)	25.00	118.95

FOR USE IN TRIPOLITANIA

> Catalogue values for unused stamps in this section are for Never Hinged items.

Stamps of Great Britain,
1937-42, Surcharged

M.A.L.=Military Authority Lire

Perf. 14½x14

1948, July 1   **Wmk. 251**

1	A101	1 l on ½p green (II)	1.00	1.75
2	A101	2 l on 1p ver (II)	.35	.20
3	A101	3 l on 1½p lt red brn (II)	.35	.55
4	A101	4 l on 2p lt org (II)	.35	.80
5	A101	5 l on 2½p ultra (II)	.35	.20
6	A101	6 l on 3p violet (II)	.35	.45
7	A102	10 l on 5p lt brown	.35	.20
8	A102	12 l on 6p rose lilac	.35	.20
9	A103	18 l on 9p dp ol grn	.90	.75
10	A103	24 l on 1sh brown	.80	1.75

Great Britain Nos.
249A, 250 and
251A Surcharged

Wmk. 259   **Perf. 14**

11	A104	60 l on 2sh6p yel grn	4.00	9.75
12	A104	120 l on 5sh dl red	17.50	21.00
13	A105	240 l on 10sh ultra	25.00	110.00
		Nos. 1-13 (13)	51.65	147.60

Stamps of Great Britain
1937-42 Surcharged

Perf. 14½x14

1950, Feb. 6   **Wmk. 251**

14	A101	1 l on ½p green (II)	3.00	14.00
15	A101	2 l on 1p ver (II)	2.75	.45
16	A101	3 l on 1½p lt red brn (II)	1.10	14.00
17	A101	4 l on 2p lt org (II)	1.10	5.00
18	A101	5 l on 2½p ultra (II)	.80	.80
19	A101	6 l on 3p violet (II)	2.00	3.75
20	A102	10 l on 5p lt brown	.55	4.50
21	A102	12 l on 6p rose lilac	2.25	.55
22	A103	18 l on 9p dp ol grn	2.50	2.75
23	A103	24 l on 1sh brown	2.75	4.25

Great Britain Nos.
249A, 250 and
251A Surcharged

Wmk. 259   **Perf. 14**

24	A104	60 l on 2sh6p yel grn	7.50	14.00
25	A104	120 l on 5sh dl red	22.50	25.00
26	A105	240 l on 10sh ultra	42.50	57.50
		Nos. 14-26 (13)	91.30	146.55

Great Britain Nos. 280-284
Surcharged like Nos. 14-23

Perf. 14½x14

1951, May 3   **Wmk. 251**

27	A101	1 l on ½p lt org	.20	7.00
28	A101	2 l on 1p ultra	.20	1.10
29	A101	3 l on 1½p green	.35	6.25
30	A101	4 l on 2p lt red brown	.20	1.40
31	A101	5 l on 2½p ver	.30	8.50

Great Britain Nos. 286-288
Surcharged

1951, May 3   **Wmk. 259**   **Perf. 11x12**

32	A121	60 l on 2sh6p grn	6.25	25.00
33	A121	120 l on 5sh dl red	10.00	30.00
34	A122	240 l on 10sh ultra	42.50	57.50
		Nos. 27-34 (8)	60.00	139.75

Surcharge arranged to fit the design on #34.

POSTAGE DUE STAMPS

Catalogue values for unused stamps in this section are for Never Hinged items.

Great Britain Nos.
J26-J29, J32
Surcharged

1948   **Wmk. 251**   **Perf. 14x14½**

J1	D1	1 l on ½p emer	6.25	57.50
J2	D1	2 l on 1p car rose	2.75	30.00
J3	D1	4 l on 2p blk brn	8.50	37.50
J4	D1	6 l on 3p violet	8.50	24.00
J5	D1	24 l on 1sh blue	32.50	110.00
		Nos. J1-J5 (5)	58.50	259.00

Great Britain Nos.
J26-J29, J32
Surcharged

1950, Feb. 6

J6	D1	1 l on ½p emer	14.00	92.50
J7	D1	2 l on 1p car rose	3.00	30.00
J8	D1	4 l on 2p blk brn	4.50	40.00
J9	D1	6 l on 3p violet	21.00	70.00
J10	D1	24 l on 1sh blue	55.00	160.00
		Nos. J6-J10 (5)	97.50	392.50

CHINA

100 Cents = 1 Dollar

Stamps of Hong Kong,
1912-14, Overprinted

1917   **Wmk. 3**   **Perf. 14**

Ordinary Paper

1	A11	1c brown	4.50	3.00
2	A11	2c deep green	8.00	.35
3	A12	4c scarlet	6.25	.35
4	A13	6c orange	6.25	.70
5	A12	8c gray	14.00	1.40
6	A11	10c ultramarine	14.00	.35

Chalky Paper

7	A14	12c violet, yel	12.50	5.00
8	A14	20c olive grn & vio	14.00	.70
9	A15	25c red vio & dl vio (on #117)	9.25	17.50
10	A13	30c orange & violet	40.00	6.25
11	A14	50c black, emerald	40.00	6.50
a.		50c blk, blue green, ol back	75.00	1.75
b.		50c blk, emerald, ol back	50.00	9.75
12	A11	$1 blue & vio, bl	80.00	2.90
13	A14	$2 black & red	260.00	62.50
14	A14	$3 violet & grn	625.00	210.00
15	A14	$5 red & grn, bl grn, ol back	400.00	290.00
16	A13	$10 blk & vio, red	1,000.	550.00
		Nos. 1-16 (16)	2,533.	1,157.

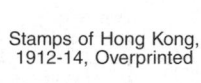

Stamps of Hong Kong,
1921-26, Overprinted

1922-27   **Wmk. 4**

Ordinary Paper

17	A11	1c brown	2.60	4.25
18	A11	2c green	4.00	2.60
19	A12	4c scarlet	7.00	2.60
20	A13	6c orange	5.00	4.75
21	A12	8c gray	9.25	17.50
22	A11	10c ultramarine	10.00	4.00

Chalky Paper

23	A14	20c olive grn & vio	16.00	5.75
24	A15	25c red violet & dull vio	26.00	80.00
25	A14	50c blk, emerald ('27)	70.00	210.00
26	A11	$1 ultra & vio, bl	85.00	70.00
27	A14	$2 black & red	225.00	290.00
		Nos. 17-27 (11)	459.85	691.45

MOROCCO

100 Centimos = 1 Peseta
12 Pence = 1 Shilling
20 Shillings = 1 Pound
100 Centimes = 1 Franc

These stamps were issued for various purposes:

a — For general use at the British Post Offices throughout Morocco.

b — For use in the Spanish Zone of Northern Morocco.

c — For use in the French Zone of Southern Morocco.

d — For use in the International Zone of Tangier.

For convenience these stamps are listed in four groups according to the coinage expressed or surcharged on the stamps, namely:

#1-100: Value expressed in Spanish currency.

#201-280: Value in British currency.

#401-440: Value in French currency.

#501-611: Stamps overprinted "Tangier."

Spanish Currency

Gibraltar Stamps of
1889-95 Overprinted

1898   **Wmk. 2**   **Perf. 14**

Black Overprint

1	A11	5c green	3.00	3.00
2	A11	10c carmine rose	5.00	.85
b.		Double overprint	625.00	
3	A11	20c olive green	11.00	6.25
4	A11	25c ultramarine	4.50	.70
5	A11	40c orange brown	7.00	3.75
6	A11	50c violet	20.00	26.00
7	A11	1pe bister & blue	20.00	30.00
8	A11	2pe blk & car rose	25.00	30.00
		Nos. 1-8 (8)	95.50	100.55

Dark Blue Overprint

9	A11	40c orange brown	50.00	35.00
10	A11	50c violet	14.00	14.00
11	A11	1pe bister & blue	175.00	210.00

Inverted "V" for "A"

1a	A11	5c	40.00	50.00
2a	A11	10c	260.00	310.00
3a	A11	20c	85.00	95.00
4a	A11	25c	140.00	150.00
5a	A11	40c	190.00	210.00
6a	A11	50c	290.00	375.00
7a	A11	1pe	275.00	400.00
8a	A11	2pe	350.00	400.00

Overprinted in Black

(Narrower "M," ear of "g" horiz.)

1899

12	A11	5c green	.55	1.10
13	A11	10c carmine rose	2.90	.35
14	A11	20c olive green	8.00	.80
15	A11	25c ultramarine	12.50	1.00
16	A11	40c orange brown	47.50	35.00
17	A11	50c violet	11.00	4.00
18	A11	1pe bister & blue	32.50	50.00
19	A11	2pe blk & car rose	62.50	55.00
		Nos. 12-19 (8)	177.45	147.25

"M" with long serif

12a	A11	5c	10.00	15.00
13a	A11	10c	11.50	13.50
14a	A11	20c	40.00	42.50
15a	A11	25c	50.00	55.00
16a	A11	40c	260.00	290.00
17a	A11	50c	125.00	140.00
18a	A11	1pe	175.00	290.00
19a	A11	2pe	375.00	400.00

Type of Gibraltar, 1903, with Value in
Spanish Currency, Overprinted

1903-05

20	A12	5c gray grn & bl	11.00	4.00
21	A12	10c violet, red	9.75	.45
22	A12	20c gray grn & car rose ('04)	20.00	52.50
23	A12	25c vio & blk, bl	9.25	.35
24	A12	50c violet	100.00	190.00
25	A12	1pe blk & car rose	47.50	175.00
26	A12	2pe black & ultra	57.50	140.00
		Nos. 20-26 (7)	255.00	562.30

"M" with long serif

20a	A12	5c	57.50	62.50
21a	A12	10c	50.00	45.00
22a	A12	20c	110.00	210.00
23a	A12	25c	57.50	50.00
24a	A12	50c	400.00	700.00
25a	A12	1pe	260.00	575.00
26a	A12	2pe	300.00	550.00

1905-06   **Wmk. 3**   **Chalky Paper**

27	A12	5c gray grn & bl grn	11.00	3.50
28	A12	10c violet, red	12.50	2.25
29	A12	20c gray grn & car rose ('06)	6.25	35.00
30	A12	25c violet & blk, bl ('06)	45.00	9.75
31	A12	50c violet	8.50	50.00
32	A12	1pe blk & car rose	32.50	92.50
33	A12	2pe black & ultra	18.00	40.00
		Nos. 27-33 (7)	133.75	233.00

No. 29 is on ordinary paper. Nos. 27 and 28 are on both ordinary and chalky paper.

"M" with long serif

27a	A12	5c	62.50	50.00
28a	A12	10c	62.50	42.50
29a	A12	20c	57.50	175.00
30a	A12	25c	350.00	175.00
31a	A12	50c	175.00	290.00
32a	A12	1pe	225.00	375.00
33a	A12	2pe	210.00	290.00

Numerous other minor overprint varieties exist of Nos. 1-33.

British Stamps of 1902-10 Surcharged
in Spanish Currency:

#34-42, 46-48   #43-45

1907-10   **Wmk. 30**

34	A66	5c on ½p pale grn	9.25	.20
35	A66	10c on 1p car	13.50	.20
36	A67	15c on 1½p vio & grn	3.50	.25
a.		"1" of "15" omitted	5,400.	
37	A68	20c on 2p grn & car	3.00	.25
38	A66	25c on 2½p ultra	2.00	.25
39	A70	40c on 4p brn & grn	1.40	3.50
40	A70	40c on 4p org ('10)	1.10	.70
41	A71	50c on 5p lil & ultra	2.25	3.75
42	A73	1pe on 10p car rose & blk	25.00	14.00

Wmk. 31

43	A75	3pe on 2sh6p vio	24.00	29.00
44	A76	6pe on 5sh car rose	40.00	52.50
45	A77	12pe on 10sh ultra	85.00	85.00
		Nos. 34-45 (12)	210.00	189.60

Nos. 36-37, 39-43 are on chalky paper.

Great Britain Nos. 153, 154 and 148
Surcharged

1912   **Wmk. 30**   **Perf. 15x14**

46	A80	5c on ½p yel grn	3.50	.20
47	A81	10c on 1p scarlet	1.10	.20
48	A66	25c on 2½p ultra	42.50	10.00
		Nos. 46-48 (3)	47.10	30.40

British Stamps of 1912-18 Surcharged
in Black or Carmine:

c   d

e

1914-18   Wmk. 33
49	A82(a)	5c on ½p grn	.85	.20
50	A83(d)	10c on 1p scar	1.75	.20
51	A84(c)	15c on 1½p red brn('15)	1.10	.25
52	A85(d)	20c on 2p org (I)	1.10	.25
53	A86(d)	25c on 2½p ultra	2.00	.25
54	A90(d)	1pe on 10p lt bl	4.00	8.00

Wmk. 34
Perf. 11x12
55	A91(e)	3pe on 2sh6p lt brn	35.00	160.00
a.		3pe on 2sh6p dark brown	45.00	125.00
56	A91(e)	6pe on 5sh car	32.50	55.00
a.		6pe on 5sh light carmine	150.00	210.00
57	A91(e)	12pe on 10sh dk bl(C)	110.00	190.00
a.		12pe on 10sh blue	100.00	190.00
		Nos. 49-57 (9)	188.30	414.15

Great Britain Nos. 159, 165 Surcharged in Spanish Currency

f   g

1917-23   Wmk. 33   Perf. 15x14
58	A82(f)	3c on ½p green	1.40	5.00
59	A88(g)	40c on 4p sl green	3.50	4.50

Great Britain Nos. 189, 191, 179 Surcharged in Spanish Currency

1926   Wmk. 35
60	A84(c)	15c on 1½p red brn	8.50	26.00
61	A86(d)	25c on 2½p ultra	2.90	2.90

Wmk. 34
Perf. 11x12
62	A91(e)	3pe on 2sh6p brn	26.00	85.00
		Nos. 60-62 (3)	37.40	113.90

British Stamps of 1924 Surcharged in Spanish Currency

1929-31   Wmk. 35   Perf. 15x14
63	A82(a)	5c on ½p grn('31)	3.00	17.50
64	A83(d)	10c on 1p scar	21.00	30.00
65	A85(d)	20c on 2p org (II) ('31)	3.50	10.00
66	A88(g)	40c on 4p sl grn ('30)	2.90	2.90
		Nos. 63-66 (4)	30.40	60.40

Silver Jubilee Issue
Great Britain Nos. 226-229 Surcharged in Blue or Red

1935, May 8   Perf. 14½x14
67	A98	5c on ½p dk grn	1.10	1.10
68	A98	10c on 1p car	3.00	2.50
a.		Pair, one reading "CEN-TIMES"	1,600.	1,800.
69	A98	15c on 1½p red brn	6.25	20.00
70	A98	25c on 2½p ultra (R)	4.00	2.50
		Nos. 67-70 (4)	14.35	26.10

25th anniv. of the reign of King George V.

> **Catalogue values for unused stamps in this section, from this point to the end of the section, are for Never Hinged items.**

Great Britain Nos. 210-214, 216, 219 Surcharged in Spanish Currency

1935-37   Photo.
71	A97(a)	5c on ½p dk grn('36)	1.25	21.00
72	A97(d)	10c on 1p car	3.25	11.00
73	A97(c)	15c on 1½p red brn	7.00	3.75

74	A97(d)	20c on 2p red org ('36)	.75	.30
75	A97(d)	25c on 2½p ul-tra('36)	1.75	5.00
76	A97(d)	40c on 4p dk sl grn ('37)	.75	3.50
77	A97(d)	1pe on 10p Prus bl ('37)	7.00	.35
		Nos. 71-77 (7)	21.75	44.90

Great Britain Nos. 230-233 Surcharged

"MOROCCO" 14mm
1936   Wmk. 250
78	A99	5c on ½p dk green	.20	.20
79	A99	10c on 1p crimson	.55	2.25
a.		"Morocco" 15mm long	4.00	16.00
80	A99	15c on 1½p red brown	.20	.20
81	A99	25c on 2½p brt ultra	.20	.20
		Nos. 78-81 (4)	1.15	2.85

Great Britain #234 Surcharged in Blue

Perf. 14½x14
1937, May 13   Wmk. 251
82	A100	15c on 1½p purple brn	.80	.80

Coronation of George VI and Elizabeth.

Great Britain Nos. 235-237, 239, 241, 244 Surcharged in Blue or Black

h

1937-40
83	A101	5c on ½p dp grn (Bl)	1.40	.35
84	A101	10c on 1p scarlet	1.10	.20
85	A101	15c on 1½p red brown (Bl)	1.40	.30
86	A101	25c on 2½p brt ultra	2.25	1.40
87	A102	40c on 4p gray green ('40)	35.00	15.00
88	A103	70c on 7p emer ('40)	2.00	16.00
		Nos. 83-88 (6)	43.15	33.25

Great Britain Nos. 252-254, 256 Surcharged in Blue or Black

1940, May 6
89	A106	5c on ½p deep grn (Bl)	.35	3.00
90	A106	10c on 1p scarlet	4.25	2.90
91	A106	15c on 1½p red brn (Bl)	.80	2.90
92	A106	25c on 2½p brt ultra	.90	1.10
		Nos. 89-92 (4)	6.30	9.90

Centenary of the postage stamp.

Great Britain Nos. 267 and 268 Surcharged in Black:

i

---

j

Perf. 14½x14, 14x14½
1948, Apr. 26   Wmk. 251
93	A109(i)	25c on 2½p	1.10	.35
94	A110(j)	45pe on £1	19.00	25.00

25th anniv. of the marriage of King George VI and Queen Elizabeth.

Great Britain Nos. 271-274 Surcharged "MOROCCO AGENCIES" and New Value
1948, July 29   Perf. 14½x14
95	A113	25c on 2½p brt ultra	.55	1.40
96	A114	30c on 3p dp vio	.55	1.40
97	A115	60c on 6p red vio	.55	1.40
98	A116	1.20pe on 1sh dk brn	.70	1.40
a.		Double surcharge	925.00	
		Nos. 95-98 (4)	2.35	5.60

1948 Olympic Games, Wembley, July-Aug. A square of dots obliterates the original denomination on No. 98.

Great Britain Nos. 280-282, 284-285, 247 Surcharged Type "h"
1951-52   Wmk. 251   Perf. 14½x14
99	A101	5c on ½p lt or-ange	2.25	5.00
100	A101	10c on 1p ultra	3.75	8.50
101	A101	15c on 1½p green	2.00	19.00
102	A101	25c on 2½p ver	2.00	11.00
103	A102	40c on 4p ultra ('52)	.70	11.50
104	A103	1pe on 10p ryl bl ('52)	2.50	4.00
		Nos. 99-104 (6)	13.20	59.00

Great Britain Nos. 292-293 Surcharged Type "h"
1954-55   Wmk. 298
105	A126	5c on ½c red org	.25	2.00
106	A126	10c on 1p ultra ('55)	.50	3.00

Great Britain Nos. 317 and 323 Wurcharged type "h"
1956   Wmk. 308   Perf. 14x14½
107	A126	5c on ½p red org	.25	2.00
108	A128	40c on 4p ultra	1.10	3.00

BRITISH CURRENCY

Stamps of Morocco Agencies were accepted for postage in Great Britain, starting in mid-1950. Examples with contemporary Morocco cancellations sell for more.

British Stamps of 1902-11 Overprinted

a   b

Overprint "a" 14½mm long
1907-12   Wmk. 30   Perf. 14
Ordinary Paper
201	A66	½p pale yel grn	2.50	9.75
202	A66	1p carmine	11.00	6.25

Chalky Paper
203	A68	2p green & car	11.50	6.25
204	A70	4p brown & grn	4.25	4.50
205	A70	4p orange ('12)	11.50	12.50
a.		Perf. 15x14	25.00	27.50
206	A66	6p dull vio	17.00	21.00
207	A74	1sh car rose & grn	30.00	19.00

Overprinted Type "b"
Wmk. 31
208	A75	2sh6p violet	92.50	140.00
		Nos. 201-208 (8)	180.25	219.25

British Stamps of 1912-18 Overprinted Type "a"
Perf. 14½x14, 15x14
1914-21   Wmk. 33
209	A82	½p green ('18)	4.00	.55
210	A83	1p scarlet ('17)	1.00	.20
211	A84	1½p red brn ('21)	3.75	14.00
212	A85	2p orange ('18)	4.50	.70
213	A87	3p violet ('21)	1.40	.40
214	A88	4p slate grn ('21)	3.75	1.40
215	A89	6p dull vio ('21)	5.50	17.50
216	A90	1sh bister ('17)	6.25	1.40

c

217	A91	2sh6p lt brown	42.50	57.50
a.		2sh6p brown	55.00	35.00
b.		2sh6p black brown	52.50	62.50
c.		Double overprint	1,900.	1,350.
		Nos. 209-217 (9)	72.65	93.65

Same Overprint on Great Britain Nos. 179-180
1925-31
218	A91	2sh6p gray brown	42.50	29.00
219	A91	5sh car rose ('31)	62.50	100.00

British Stamps of 1924 Overprinted Type "a" (14½mm long)
1925-31   Wmk. 35   Perf. 15x14
220	A82	½p green	2.25	.55
221	A84	1½p red brn ('31)	13.50	15.00
222	A85	2p dp org (Die II)	2.50	1.10
223	A86	2½p ultra	2.50	5.75
224	A89	6p red vio ('31)	2.25	9.50
225	A90	1sh bister	19.00	5.75
		Nos. 220-225 (6)	42.00	37.65

Silver Jubilee Issue
Great Britain Nos. 226-229 Overprinted in Blue or Red

1935, May 8   Perf. 14½x14
226	A98	½p dark green (Bl)	1.40	7.50
227	A98	1p carmine (Bl)	1.40	7.50
228	A98	1½p red brown (Bl)	2.50	11.00
229	A98	2½p ultramarine (R)	2.90	2.90
		Nos. 226-229 (4)	8.20	28.90

25th anniversary of the reign of King George V.

British Stamps of 1924 Overprinted Type "a" (15½mm long)
1935-36
230	A82	½p green	9.50	45.00
231	A86	2½p ultra	110.00	35.00
232	A88	4p slate green	8.00	40.00
233	A89	6p red violet	1.10	.70
234	A90	1sh bister	62.50	57.50
		Nos. 230-234 (5)	191.10	178.20

British Stamps of 1934-36 Overprinted "MOROCCO AGENCIES"
1935-36
235	A97	1p carmine	3.50	16.00
236	A84	1½p red brn ('36)	3.50	19.00
237	A85	2p red org ('36)	1.40	9.00
238	A97	2½p ultra ('36)	2.00	4.75
239	A87	3p dk violet ('36)	.55	.35
240	A88	4p dk slate grn ('36)	.55	.35
241	A90	1sh bis brn ('36)	.90	4.00

Great Britain #234 Surcharged in Blue

Overprinted Type "c"
Wmk. 34
Perf. 11x12

242	A91	2sh6p brown	45.00	70.00
243	A91	5sh carmine ('37)	27.50	110.00
		Nos. 235-243 (9)	84.90	233.45

Catalogue values for unused stamps in this section, from this point to the end of the section, are for Never Hinged items.

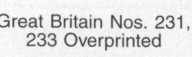

Great Britain Nos. 231, 233 Overprinted

"MOROCCO" 14mm

1936   **Wmk. 250**   **Perf. 14½x14**

244	A99	1p crimson	.20	.20
a.		"Morocco" 15mm long	7.00	19.00
245	A99	2½p bright ultra	.20	.20
a.		"Morocco" 15mm long	1.10	4.75

Great Britain Nos. 258-263, 241-248, 266, 249A-250 Overprinted "MOROCCO AGENCIES" (14½mm long)

1949, Aug. 16   **Wmk. 251**

246	A101	½p green	2.00	8.00
247	A101	1p vermilion	3.00	10.00
248	A101	1½p lt red brown	3.00	9.50
249	A101	2p lt orange	3.50	10.00
250	A101	2½p ultra	3.75	11.50
251	A101	3p violet	1.75	2.00
252	A102	4p gray green	.55	1.40
253	A102	5p lt brown	3.50	17.00
254	A102	6p rose lilac	1.75	1.75
255	A103	7p emerald	.55	18.00
256	A103	8p brt rose	3.50	7.50
257	A103	9p dp olive grn	.55	12.50
258	A103	10p royal blue	.55	7.50
259	A103	11p scarlet brn	.80	8.50
260	A103	1sh brown	3.00	7.00

"MOROCCO AGENCIES"
17½mm long
Wmk. 259
Perf. 14

261	A104	2sh6p yellow grn	18.00	40.00
262	A104	5sh dull red	32.50	70.00
		Nos. 246-262 (17)	82.25	242.15

Great Britain Nos. 280-284, 286-287 Overprinted "MOROCCO AGENCIES" (14½mm long)
Perf. 14½x14

1951, May 3   **Wmk. 251**

263	A101	½p lt orange	2.25	1.10
264	A101	1p ultra	2.25	1.60
265	A101	1½p green	2.25	3.00
266	A101	2p lt red brown	2.50	4.50
267	A101	2½p vermilion	2.25	4.75

"MOROCCO AGENCIES"
17½mm long
Wmk. 259
Perf. 11x12

268	A121	2sh6p green	15.00	24.00
269	A121	5sh dull red	15.00	26.00
		Nos. 263-269 (7)	41.50	64.95

Great Britain Nos. 292-296, 298-300, 302 and 306 Overprinted "MOROCCO AGENCIES" (14½mm long)

1952-55   **Wmk. 298**   **Perf. 14½x14**

270	A126	½p green	.20	.20
271	A126	1p ultramarine	.20	2.00
272	A126	1½p green ('52)	.20	.20
273	A126	2p red brown	.30	2.25
274	A127	2½p carmine ('52)	.20	1.40
275	A128	4p ultra ('55)	1.75	4.00
276	A129	5p light brown	.75	.70
277	A129	6p lilac rose ('55)	1.00	4.00
278	A130	8p bright rose	.80	.80
279	A131	1sh brown	.80	.70
		Nos. 270-279 (10)	6.20	16.25

Same Ovpt. on Great Britain No. 321
1956   **Wmk. 308**

280	A127	2½p scarlet	1.00	3.75

French Currency
British Stamps of 1912-22 Surcharged in French Currency in Red or Black:

h   i

Perf. 14½x14, 15x14

1917-24   **Wmk. 33**

401	A82(h)	3c on ½p green (R)	1.10	2.90
402	A82(h)	5c on ½p green	.45	1.75
403	A83(h)	10c on 1p scarlet	3.75	.45
404	A84(h)	15c on 1½p red brn	2.90	.20
405	A86(h)	25c on 2½p ultra	2.25	.20
406	A88(h)	40c on 4p slate grn	2.90	1.75
407	A89(h)	50c on 5p yel brn ('23)	.90	3.00
408	A90(h)	75c on 9p ol grn ('24)	1.10	.85
409	A90(i)	1fr on 10p lt blue	8.00	3.50
		Nos. 401-409 (9)	23.35	14.60

Great Britain No. 179 Surcharged:

k

1924   **Wmk. 34**   **Perf. 11x12**

410	A91(k)	3fr on 2sh6p brn	8.50	1.75

British Stamps of 1924 Surcharged in French Currency as in 1917-24

1925-26   **Wmk. 35**   **Perf. 15x14**

411	A82(h)	5c on ½p green	.35	7.50
412	A83(h)	10c on 1p scarlet	.35	2.25
413	A84(h)	15c on 1½p red brn	1.10	2.00
414	A86(h)	25c on 2½p ultra	1.75	.55
415	A88(h)	40c on 4p sl green	.70	.90
416	A89(h)	50c on 5p yel brown	1.75	.20
417	A90(h)	75c on 9p ol green	4.00	.20
418	A90(i)	1fr on 10p dl blue	1.40	.20
		Nos. 411-418 (8)	11.40	13.80

Great Britain Nos. 180, 198 and 200 Surcharged type "k"

1932   **Wmk. 34**   **Perf. 11x12**

419	A91	6fr on 5sh car rose	42.50	47.50

1934   **Wmk. 35**   **Perf. 14½x14**

420	A90	90c on 9p ol green	18.00	8.50
421	A90	1.50fr on 1sh bister	11.50	2.50

Silver Jubilee Issue
Great Britain Nos. 226-229 Surcharged in Blue or Red

1935, May 8   **Perf. 14½x14**

422	A98	5c on ½p dk green	.20	.20
423	A98	10c on 1p carmine	3.00	.85
424	A98	15c on 1½p red brn	.40	.55
425	A98	25c on 2½p ultra (R)	.25	.35
		Nos. 422-425 (4)	3.85	1.95

25th anniv. of the reign of King George V.

British Stamps of 1934-36 Surcharged Types "h" or "k"
Perf. 14½x14

1935-37   **Photo.**   **Wmk. 35**

426	A82(h)	5c on ½p dk grn	.55	5.75
427	A97(h)	10c on 1p car ('36)	.40	.35
428	A84(h)	15c on 1½p red brn	5.50	6.25
429	A97(h)	25c on 2½p ultra	.35	.20
430	A88(h)	40c on 4p dk sl grn	.35	.20
431	A89(h)	50c on 5p yel brn	.35	.20
432	A90(h)	90c on 9p dk ol grn	.40	2.00
433	A90(k)	1fr on 10p Prus bl	.35	.35
434	A90(h)	1.50fr on 1sh bister brn ('37)	.85	3.75

Waterlow Printing
Wmk. 34   **Perf. 11x12**

435	A91(k)	3fr on 2sh6p brn	5.50	14.00
436	A91(k)	6fr on 5sh car ('36)	7.00	24.00
		Nos. 426-436 (11)	21.60	57.05

Great Britain Nos. 230, 232 Surcharged

1936   **Wmk. 250**   **Perf. 14½x14**

437	A99	5c on ½p dark green	.20	.20
438	A99	15c on 1½p red brown	.20	.20

Great Britain No. 234 Surcharged in Blue

1937, May 13   **Wmk. 251**

439	A100	15c on 1½p purple brn	.35	.20

Coronation of George VI and Elizabeth.

Great Britain No. 235 Surcharged in Blue

1937

440	A101	5c on ½p deep green	2.50	2.90

For Use in the International Zone of Tangier
Great Britain Nos. 187-190 Overprinted in Black

a

1927   **Wmk. 35**   **Perf. 15x14**

501	A82	½p green	3.50	.20
502	A83	1p scarlet	3.50	.30
503	A84	1½p red brown	7.00	4.25
504	A85	2p orange (II)	3.75	.20
		Nos. 501-504 (4)	17.75	4.95

Same Overprint on Great Britain Nos. 210-212

1934-35   **Photo.**   **Perf. 14½x14**

505	A97	½p dark green	1.40	1.75
506	A83	1p carmine	4.75	2.75
507	A97	1½p red brown	.55	.20
		Nos. 505-507 (3)	6.70	4.70

Silver Jubilee Issue
Great Britain Nos. 226-228 Overprinted in Blue

b

1935, May 8

508	A98	½p dark green	1.40	5.75
509	A98	1p carmine	16.00	17.00
510	A98	1½p red brown	1.40	1.10
		Nos. 508-510 (3)	18.80	23.85

25th anniv. of the reign of King George V.

Great Britain Nos. 230-232 Overprinted Type "a"

1936   **Wmk. 250**

511	A99	½p dark green	.20	.20
512	A99	1p crimson	.20	.20
513	A99	1½p red brown	.20	.20
		Nos. 511-513 (3)	.60	.60

Great Britain No. 234 Overprinted Type "b" in Blue

1937, May 13   **Wmk. 251**

514	A100	1½p purple brown	.55	.55

Coronation of George VI and Elizabeth.

Great Britain Nos. 235-237 Overprinted in Blue or Black

c

1937   **Perf. 14½x14**

515	A101	½p deep green (Bl)	2.75	1.75
516	A101	1p scarlet (Bk)	8.00	1.75
517	A101	1½p red brown (Bl)	2.75	.30
		Nos. 515-517 (3)	13.50	3.80

Great Britain Nos. 252-254 Ovptd. Type "a" in Blue or Black

1940, May 6

518	A106	½p deep green (Bl)	.35	5.50
519	A106	1p scarlet (Bk)	.50	.60
520	A106	1½p red brown (Bl)	2.25	5.75
		Nos. 518-520 (3)	3.10	11.85

Centenary of the postage stamp.

Great Britain Nos. 258 and 259 Overprinted Type "c" in Blue or Black

1944-45

521	A101	½p green (Bl)	12.50	5.00
522	A101	1p ver (Bk) ('45)	12.50	3.50

Catalogue values for unused stamps in this section, from this point to the end of the section, are for Never Hinged items.

Great Britain Nos. 264-265 Overprinted:

d

e

1946, June 11

523	A107(d)	2½p bright ultra	.75	.75
524	A108(e)	3p violet	.75	2.25

Return to peace at close of World War II.

Great Britain Nos. 267 and 268 Overprinted Type "a"

1948, Apr. 26   **Perf. 14½x14, 14x14½**

525	A109	2½p bright ultra	.60	.20
a.		Pair, one without overprint	5,400.	
526	A110	£1 dp chalky bl	22.50	29.00

25th anniv. of the marriage of King George VI and Queen Elizabeth.

Great Britain Nos. 271 to 274 Overprinted Type "a"

1948, July 29   **Perf. 14½x14**

527	A113	2½p bright ultra	1.10	2.25
528	A114	3p deep violet	1.10	2.25
529	A115	6p red violet	1.10	2.25
530	A116	1sh dark brown	1.10	1.40
		Nos. 527-530 (4)	4.40	8.15

1948 Olympic Games, Wembley, July-Aug.

Stamps of Great Britain, 1937-47, and Nos. 249A, 250 and 251A Overprinted Type "c"

1949, Jan. 1

531	A101	2p lt org (II)	5.75	7.00
532	A101	2½p ultra (II)	2.00	7.00
533	A101	3p violet (II)	.80	1.40
534	A102	4p gray green	12.50	11.50
535	A102	5p light brown	4.25	22.50
536	A102	6p rose lilac	.80	.35
537	A103	7p emerald	1.40	15.00
538	A103	8p bright rose	4.25	12.50

539	A103	9p deep ol grn	1.40	13.50
540	A103	10p royal blue	1.40	15.00
541	A103	11p violet brn	1.75	12.50
542	A103	1sh brown	1.40	3.00

Wmk. 259

Perf. 14

543	A104	2sh6p yellow grn	5.00	13.50
544	A104	5sh dull red	15.00	42.50
545	A105	10sh ultra	50.00	110.00
		Nos. 531-545 (15)	107.70	287.25

Great Britain Nos. 276 to 279
Overprinted Type "a"

Perf. 14½x14

1949, Oct. 10 — **Wmk. 251**

546	A117	2½p bright ultra	.80	3.00
547	A118	3p bright violet	.80	2.00
548	A119	6p red violet	.80	1.40
549	A120	1sh brown	.80	3.75
		Nos. 546-549 (4)	3.20	10.15

Great Britain Nos. 280-288
Overprinted Type "c" or "a" (Shilling Values)

1950-51

550	A101	½p lt orange	1.00	1.75
551	A101	1p ultra	1.10	3.50
552	A101	1½p green	1.10	16.00
553	A101	2p lt red brn	1.10	2.90
554	A101	2½p vermilion	1.10	5.75
555	A102	4p ultra ('50)	3.50	3.50

Wmk. 259

Perf. 11x12

556	A121	2sh6p green	11.00	5.75
557	A121	5sh dull red	17.50	19.00
558	A122	10sh ultra	22.50	19.00
		Nos. 550-558 (9)	59.90	77.15

Great Britain Nos. 292-308
Overprinted Type c

1952-54 — **Wmk. 298** — **Perf. 14½x14**

559	A126	½p red org ('53)	.20	.35
560	A126	1p ultra ('53)	.20	.45
561	A126	1½p green ('52)	.20	.35
562	A126	2p red brn ('53)	.20	.90
563	A127	2½p scarlet ('52)	.20	1.10
564	A127	3p dk pur (Dk Bl)	.25	1.40
565	A128	4p ultra ('53)	.70	2.25
566	A129	5p lt brown ('53)	.70	2.25
567	A129	6p lilac rose	.50	.20
568	A129	7p emerald	.90	3.00
569	A130	8p brt rose ('53)	.70	1.75
570	A130	9p dp olive grn	1.60	.85
571	A130	10p royal blue	1.60	3.00
572	A130	11p violet brn	1.60	3.75
573	A131	1sh brown ('53)	.55	.80
574	A132	1sh3p dk grn ('53)	.75	4.75
575	A131	1sh6p dk blue ('53)	1.10	2.00
		Nos. 559-575 (17)	11.95	29.15

Stamp and Type of Great Britain
1955 Overprinted Type a

Perf. 11x12

1955, Sept. 23 — **Engr.** — **Wmk. 308**

576	A133	2sh6p dark brown	4.00	10.00
577	A133	5sh crimson	5.00	18.00
578	A133	10sh brt ultra	18.00	24.00
		Nos. 576-578 (3)	27.00	52.00

Coronation Issue
Great Britain Nos. 313-316
Overprinted Type a

1953, June 3 — **Photo.** — **Wmk. 298**

579	A134	2½p scarlet	.50	.40
580	A135	4p brt ultra	.90	.65
581	A136	1sh3p dark green	2.75	1.90
582	A137	1sh6p dark blue	3.25	2.25
		Nos. 579-582 (4)	7.40	5.20

Great Britain Nos. 317-323, 325 and 332 Overprinted Type c

1956 — **Wmk. 308** — **Perf. 14½x14**

583	A126	½p red orange	.20	.55
584	A126	1p ultramarine	.35	.55
585	A126	1½p green	.65	1.40
586	A126	2p red brown	1.10	.55
587	A127	2½p scarlet	.75	.55
588	A127	3p dark purple	.85	1.00
589	A128	4p ultra	1.75	4.00
590	A129	6p lilac rose	1.10	1.00
591	A132	1sh3p dark green	1.25	15.00
		Nos. 583-591 (9)	8.00	24.60

Great Britain Nos. 317-333 and 309-311 Overprinted 1857-1957
TANGIER

1957, Apr. 1 — **Photo.** — **Wmk. 308**

592	A126	½p red orange	.20	.20
593	A126	1p ultramarine	.20	.20
594	A126	1½p green	.20	.20
595	A126	2p red brown	.20	.20
596	A127	2½p scarlet	.20	1.40
597	A127	3p dark purple	.20	.45
598	A128	4p ultramarine	.35	.20
599	A129	5p lt brown	.35	.40
600	A129	6p lilac rose	.35	.40
601	A129	7p emerald	.35	.40

602	A130	8p brt rose	.35	1.10
603	A130	9p dp olive grn	.35	.35
a.		"TANGIER" omitted	5,500.	
604	A130	10p royal blue	.35	.35
605	A130	11p violet brown	.35	.35
606	A131	1sh brown	.35	.35
607	A132	1sh3p dark green	.50	5.50
608	A131	1sh6p dark blue	.55	1.75

Engr.

Perf. 11x12

609	A133	2sh6p dark brown	2.25	4.25
610	A133	5sh crimson	3.00	7.00
611	A133	10sh ultramarine	4.25	8.50
		Nos. 592-611 (20)	14.90	33.55

Centenary of British P.O. in Tangier.
Nos. 609-611 are found with hyphen omitted (one stamp in sheet of 40).
British stamps overprinted "Tangier" were discontinued Apr. 30, 1957.

TURKISH EMPIRE

40 Paras = 1 Piaster
12 Pence = 1 Shilling (1905)

a   b

c   d

Surcharged on Great Britain Nos. 101, 104, 96

1885, Apr. 1 — **Wmk. 30** — **Perf. 14**

1	A47(a)	40pa on 2½p lil	110.00	1.50
2	A45(b)	80pa on 5p grn	210.00	12.50

Wmk. 31

3	A44(c)	12pi on 2sh6p lilac	52.50	27.50
a.		Bluish paper	400.00	260.00
		Nos. 1-3 (3)	372.50	41.50

Great Britain Nos. 114, 118
Surcharged

1887 — **Wmk. 30**

4	A57(a)	40pa on 2½p vio, bl	4.75	.20
a.		Double surcharge	2,250.	2,900.
5	A61(b)	80pa on 5p lil & bl	17.50	.35
a.		Small "0" in "80"	225.00	100.00

Great Britain No. 111 Handstamp Surcharged

1893, Feb. 25

6	A54(d)	40pa on ½p ver	500.00	125.00

No. 6 was a provisional, made and used at Constantinople for five days. Excellent forgeries are known.

Great Britain No. 121 Surcharged

e

1896

7	A64(e)	4pi on 10p car rose & lil	47.50	9.25

British Stamps of 1902 Surcharged

1902-05 — **Wmk. 30**

8	A66(a)	40pa on 2½p ultra	17.50	.20
9	A71(b)	80pa on 5p lil & bl	9.00	2.90
a.		Small "0" in "80"	250.00	210.00
10	A73(e)	4pi on 10p car rose & vio	13.50	4.50

Wmk. 31

11	A75(c)	12pi on 2sh6p vio ('03)	40.00	40.00
12	A76(c)	24pi on 5sh car rose ('05)	35.00	47.50
		Nos. 8-12 (5)	115.00	95.10

Great Britain Nos. 131, 134
Surcharged

f

1906 — **Wmk. 30**

13	A66(f)	1pi on 2½p ultra	17.50	.20
14	A71(f)	2pi on 5p lil & ultra	32.50	2.75

Nos. 10, 11, 14 are on both ordinary and chalky paper.

Great Britain Nos. 127-135, 138
Overprinted

g

1905

15	A66	½p pale green	10.00	.20
16	A66	1p carmine	9.50	.20
17	A67	1½p violet & grn	6.25	2.00
18	A68	2p green & car	3.50	8.00
19	A66	2½p ultra	10.00	22.50
20	A69	3p violet, yel	7.25	13.50
21	A70	4p brown & grn	10.00	50.00
22	A71	5p lilac & ultra	19.00	32.50
23	A66	6p dull violet	15.00	29.00
24	A74	1sh car rose & grn	42.50	57.50
		Nos. 15-24 (10)	133.00	215.40

Nos. 17, 18 and 24 are on both ordinary and chalky paper.

No. 18 Surcharged

1906, July 2

25	A68	1pi on 2p grn & car	1,500.	700.00

British Stamps of 1902-09 Surcharged:

j   k

1909

26	A67	30pa on 1½p vio & grn	11.50	1.40
27	A69	1pi10pa on 3p vio, yel	13.50	40.00
28	A70	1pi30pa on 4p brn & grn	5.75	19.00
29	A70	1pi30pa on 4p org	20.00	70.00
30	A66	2pi20pa on 6p dl violet	22.50	70.00
31	A74	5pi on 1sh car rose & grn	5.00	11.00
		Nos. 26-31 (6)	78.25	211.40

No. 29 is on ordinary paper, the others are on chalky paper.

Great Britain Nos. 132, 144, 135
Surcharged:

m   n

1910

32	A69(m)	1¼pi on 3p vio, yel	.60	1.25
33	A70(m)	1¾pi on 4p orange	.60	.75
34	A66(n)	2½pi on 6p dl vio	1.60	.80
		Nos. 32-34 (3)	2.80	2.80

There are three different varieties of "4" in the fraction of the 1¾ piastre.

Great Britain Nos. 151-154
Overprinted Type g

1911-12 — **Perf. 15x14**

35	A80	½p yellow green	2.25	1.75
36	A81	1p carmine	.55	7.00

Re-engraved

37	A80	½p yel grn ('12)	.90	.20
38	A81	1p scarlet ('12)	.90	1.75

Great Britain No. 148 Surcharged

o

39	A66(o)	1pi on 2½p ultra	15.00	3.00
		Nos. 35-39 (5)	19.60	13.70

The surcharge on No. 39 exists in two types with the letters 2½ and 3mm high respectively. The stamp also differs from No. 13 in the perforation.

British Stamps of 1912-13 Surcharged with New Values

1913-14 — **Wmk. 33**

40	A84(j)	30pa on 1½p red brown	4.00	16.00
41	A86(o)	1pi on 2½p ultra	8.50	2.00
42	A87(m)	1¼pi on 3p vio	5.50	4.75
43	A88(m)	1¾pi on 4p sl grn	3.50	7.00
44	A90(o)	4pi on 10p lt bl	9.00	22.50
45	A90(o)	5pi on 1sh bis	45.00	70.00
		Nos. 40-45 (6)	75.50	120.45

British Stamps of 1912-19 Overprinted Type "g"

1913-21

46	A82	½p green	.45	1.40
47	A83	1p scarlet	.35	5.75
48	A85	2p orange ('21)	1.40	32.50
49	A87	3p violet ('21)	8.50	11.50
50	A88	4p sl grn ('21)	5.75	16.00
51	A89	5p yel brn ('21)	13.50	32.50
52	A89	6p dl vio ('21)	30.00	10.00
53	A90	1sh bister ('21)	15.00	10.00

Wmk. 34

Perf. 11x12

54	A91	2sh6p brn ('21)	42.50	100.00
		Nos. 46-54 (9)	117.45	219.65

British Stamps of 1912-19 Surcharged as in 1909-10 and

p

q

1921 — **Wmk. 33** — **Perf. 14½x14**

55	A82(j)	30pa on ½p grn	.90	13.50
a.		Inverted surcharge	100.00	
56	A83(p)	1½pi on 1p scar	1.75	1.40
57	A86(p)	3¾pi on 2½p ultra	1.50	.35
58	A87(p)	4½pi on 3p vio	2.25	4.25
59	A89(p)	7½pi on 5p yel brn	.60	.20
60	A90(p)	15pi on 10p lt bl	.85	.20
61	A90(p)	18¾pi on 1sh bis	5.00	5.00

Wmk. 34

Perf. 11x12

62	A91(q)	45pi on 2sh6p brown	22.50	52.50
63	A91(q)	90pi on 5sh car rose	30.00	35.00
64	A91(q)	180pi on 10sh blue	52.50	45.00
		Nos. 55-64 (10)	117.85	157.40

GUERNSEY

'gərn-zē

LOCATION — A group of islands in the English Channel
GOVT. — Dependent territory (bailiwick) of the British Crown
AREA — 30 sq. mi.
POP. — 58,681 (1996)
CAPITAL — St. Peter Port

The bailiwick includes the islands of Guernsey, Alderney, Sark, Herm, Jethou and Lithou.

Following the establishment of the British General Post Office as a public corporation on October 1, 1969, the post office of the Bailiwick of Guernsey became a separate entity and British postage stamps ceased to be valid.

> Catalogue values for unused stamps in this country are for Never Hinged items.

Watermark

Wmk. 396 — Link Fence

British Regional Issue

Guernsey Lily and Crown of William the Conqueror
A1   A2

Perf. 15x14

1958-69   Photo.   Wmk. 322
1	A1	2½p rose red ('64)	.35 .35
2	A2	3p light purple	.30 .20
p.		Phosphor. ('67)	.20 .20
3	A2	4p ultra ('66)	.30 .20
p.		Phosphor. ('67)	.20 .20

Unwmk.
4	A2	4p ultra ('68)	.20 .20
5	A2	4p olive brown ('68)	.20 .20
6	A2	4p bright red ('69)	.20 .20
7	A2	5p dark blue ('68)	.20 .20
		Nos. 1-7 (7)	1.75 1.55

Nos. 4-7 are phosphorescent.
Sold to the general public only at post offices within Guernsey, but valid for postage throughout Great Britain.
See also Great Britain Nos. 269-270, which were sold only in the Channel Islands and at a few philatelic windows in Great Britain, and may be considered to be precursors to the regional issues.

Bailiwick Issues

William the Conqueror, Queen Elizabeth II and Map of Bailiwick — A3

Creux Harbor, Sark — A4

Designs (Queen Elizabeth II and): ½p, Castle Cornet and Edward the Confessor. 1½p, Martello Tower and Henry II. 2p, Arms of Sark and King John. 3p, Arms of Alderney and Edward III. 4p, Guernsey lily and Henry V. 5p, Arms of Guernsey and Queen Elizabeth I. 6p, Arms of Alderney and Charles II. 9p, Arms of Sark and George III. 1sh, Arms of Guernsey and Queen Victoria. 1sh6p, Map of Bailiwick and William I. 1sh9p, Guernsey lily and Queen Elizabeth I. 2sh6p, Martello Tower and King John. 10sh, Braye Harbor, Alderney. £1, St. Peter Port, Guernsey.

Perf. 14½x14

1969-70   Photo.   Unwmk.
8	A3	½p magenta & blk	.25 .20
9	A3	1p ultra & black	.25 .20
10	A3	1½p bister & blk	.25 .20
11	A3	2p dk brown & blk	.25 .20
12	A3	3p deep org & multi	.30 .20
13	A3	4p yel green & multi	.40 .40
a.		Booklet pane of 1	1.00 1.00
14	A3	5p vio blue & multi	.35 .20
a.		Booklet pane of 1	1.50 1.50
15	A3	6p ol green & multi	.40 .50
16	A3	9p plum & multi	.50 .60
17	A3	1sh dk olive & multi	.40 .50
18	A3	1sh6p blue grn & blk	.40 .50
19	A3	1sh9p magenta & multi	1.50 1.40
20	A3	2sh6p purple & blk	7.00 6.00

Perf. 12½
21	A4	5sh multicolored	4.00 3.00
22	A4	10sh multicolored	27.50 25.00
a.		Perf. 13½x13	57.50 50.00

Perf. 13½x13
23	A4	£1 multicolored	3.75 3.50
a.		Perf. 12½	4.50 4.50
		Nos. 8-23 (16)	47.50 42.60

Issued: #22a, 23, 3/4/70; others, 10/1/69.
Nos. 9 and 18 are inscribed "40o 30' N."
See Nos. 28-29, 41-55, 749.

Col. Isaac Brock — A5

Designs: 5p, Sir Isaac Brock as major general. 1sh9p, as ensign, flags of 1789 and 1969. 2sh6p, Regimental coat of arms and flags, horiz.

Perf. 14x13½, 13½x14

1969, Dec. 1   Litho.   Unwmk.
24	A5	4p multicolored	.25 .20
25	A5	5p black & multi	.25 .20
26	A5	1sh9p dp blue & multi	1.25 1.10
27	A5	2sh6p purple & multi	1.25 1.10
		Nos. 24-27 (4)	3.00 2.60

Sir Isaac Brock (1769-1812), born on Guernsey, commander of Quebec garrison.

Map Type of 1969 Redrawn

1969-70   Photo.   Perf. 14½x14
28	A3	1p "49o 30'N"	.25 .25
a.		Booklet pane of 1	.45 .45
29	A3	1sh6p "49o 30'N"	.25 .25

No. 28a was issued Dec. 12, 1969, in booklets containing Nos. 13a, 14a, 28a. Nos. 28-29 issued 2/4/70.
Nos. 9 and 18 are inscribed "40o 30' N."

Destroyer "Bulldog" near Castle Cornet — A6

Designs: 5p, Liberation fleet in roadsteads between Guernsey, Herm and Jethou. 1sh6p, Brigadier A. E. Snow reading proclamation of King George VI on steps of Elizabeth College in Guernsey, vert.

1970, May 9   Photo.   Perf. 11½
30	A6	4p vio blue & lt blue	.25 .20
31	A6	5p dp plum & gray	.25 .20
32	A6	1sh6p dk brown & bis	1.75 1.75
		Nos. 30-32 (3)	2.25 2.15

25th anniv. of Guernsey's liberation from the Germans.

Guernsey Cow — A7

1970, Aug. 12   Photo.   Perf. 11½
33	A7	4p Tomatoes	1.10 .45
34	A7	5p shown	1.10 .45
35	A7	9p Guernsey bull	5.50 2.25
36	A7	1sh6p Freesias	6.00 4.50
		Nos. 33-36 (4)	13.70 7.65

For similar design see No. 68.

St. Anne, Alderney A8

Christmas (Churches): 5p, St. Peter, Town Church, Guernsey. 9p, St. Peter, Sark, vert. 1sh6p, St. Tugual Chapel, Herm, vert.

1970, Nov. 11   Photo.   Perf. 11½
37	A8	4p blue, gold & brn	.30 .20
38	A8	5p brt grn, gold & brn	.40 .20
39	A8	9p rose red, gold & brown	1.10 1.00
40	A8	1sh6p brt purple, gold & brown	2.10 1.60
		Nos. 37-40 (4)	3.90 3.00

Decimal Currency Issue
Types of 1969
"p" instead of "d"

Designs: ½p, Castle Cornet and Edward the Confessor. 1p, 5p, Map of Bailiwick and William the Conqueror. 1½p, Martello Tower and Henry II. 2p, Guernsey lily and Henry V. 2½p, Arms of Guernsey and Elizabeth I. 3p, Arms of Alderney and Edward III. 3½p, Guernsey lily and Elizabeth I. 4p, Arms of Sark and King John. 6p, Arms of Alderney and Charles II. 7½p, Arms of Guernsey and Queen Victoria. 9p, Arms of Sark and George III. 10p, Martello Tower and King John. 20p, Creux Harbor. 50p, Braye Harbor.

1971   Photo.   Perf. 14½x14
41	A3	½p magenta & blk	.20 .20
a.		Booklet pane of 1	.20
42	A3	1p ultra & black	.20 .20
43	A3	1½p bister & blk	.25 .25
44	A3	2p yel green & multi	.25 .25
a.		Booklet pane of 1	.35
45	A3	2½p vio blue & multi	.25 .25
a.		Booklet pane of 1	.35
46	A3	3p dp orange & multi	.30 .30
47	A3	3½p magenta & multi	.30 .30
48	A3	4p dk blue & multi	.30 .30
49	A3	5p brt green & multi	.30 .30
50	A3	6p dk green & multi	.30 .30
51	A3	7½p brn olive & multi	.40 .40
52	A3	9p plum & multi	.80 .80
53	A3	10p purple & black	1.60 1.60

Perf. 13
54	A4	20p dk red & multi	1.00 1.00
55	A4	50p multicolored	2.40 2.40
		Nos. 41-55 (15)	8.85 8.85

Issue dates: #53-55, Jan. 6; others Feb. 15.

Thomas de la Rue, Hong Kong No. 1 — A9

Thomas de la Rue and: 2½p, GB No. 22. 4p, Italy No. 26. 7½p, US Confederate States No. 6.

Ebenezer Methodist Church — A10

Historic Churches of Guernsey: 2½p, St. Pierre du Bois. 5p, St. Joseph's, vert. 7½p, St. Philippe de Torteval, vert.

1971, June 2   Engr.   Perf. 14x13½
56	A9	2p brown	.60 .20
57	A9	2½p carmine	.60 .20
58	A9	4p dark green	1.90 1.60
59	A9	7½p violet blue	2.25 1.60
		Nos. 56-59 (4)	5.35 3.60

Thomas de la Rue (1793-1866), founder of Thomas de la Rue & Co., Ltd., security printers.

1971, Oct. 27   Photo.   Perf. 11½
60	A10	2p green, sil & blk	.35 .35
61	A10	2½p blue, sil & blk	.40 .35
62	A10	5p pur, silver & blk	1.75 1.40
63	A10	7½p red, silver & blk	2.50 2.25
		Nos. 60-63 (4)	5.00 4.35

Christmas 1971.

Mail Boat, Earl of Chesterfield, 1794 — A11

1972, Feb. 10   Photo.   Perf. 11½
64	A11	2p shown	.20 .20
65	A11	2½p Dasher, 1827	.20 .20
66	A11	7½p Ibex, 1891	.35 .35
67	A11	9p Alberta, 1900	.55 .55
		Nos. 64-67 (4)	1.30 1.30

See Nos. 77-80.

Guernsey Bull — A12

1972, May 22   Photo.   Perf. 11½
68	A12	5p brown & multi	.65 .55

Guernsey Breeders, 2nd World Conf. For similar designs see Nos. 33-36.

Wild Flowers A13

1972, May 24
69	A13	2p Sorrel	.20 .20
70	A13	2½p Orchis maculata, vert.	.20 .20
71	A13	7½p Carpobrotus edulis	.40 .40
72	A13	9p Pimpernel, vert.	.50 .50
		Nos. 69-72 (4)	1.30 1.30

Angels, St. Martin's Church — A14

Stained Glass Windows from Guernsey Churches: 2½p, Virgin and Child, St. André's.

7½p, Virgin Mary, St. Sampson's. 9p, Christ Victorious, St. Pierre's.

1972, Nov. 20 Photo. Perf. 11½
73	A14	2p brick red & multi	.20	.20
74	A14	2½p lt violet & multi	.20	.20
75	A14	7½p yellow & multi	.30	.30
76	A14	9p lt green & multi	.30	.30
		Nos. 73-76 (4)	1.00	1.00

Christmas 1972 and for the 25th anniv. of the marriage of Queen Elizabeth II and Prince Philip.

Mail Boat Type of 1972

1973, Mar. 9 Photo. Perf. 11½
77	A11	2p St. Julien, 1925	.20	.20
78	A11	3p Isle of Sark, 1932	.25	.25
79	A11	7½p St. Patrick, 1947	.40	.40
80	A11	9p Sarnia, 1961	.40	.40
		Nos. 77-80 (4)	1.25	1.25

No. 78 is incorrectly inscribed "Isle of Guernsey 1930."

Supermarine Sea Eagle — A15

Airplanes: 3p, Westland Wessex. 5p, De Havilland Rapide. 7½p, Douglas Dakota. 9p, Vickers Viscount.

1973, July 4 Photo. Perf. 11½
81	A15	2½p multicolored	.20	.20
82	A15	3p multicolored	.20	.20
83	A15	5p multicolored	.20	.20
84	A15	7½p multicolored	.40	.40
85	A15	9p multicolored	.50	.50
		Nos. 81-85 (5)	1.50	1.50

50th anniversary of air service to Guernsey.

The Good Shepherd, St. Michel du Valle — A16

Stained-glass Windows from Guernsey Churches: 3p, Jesus preaching, St. Marie du Castel. 7½p, St. Dominic, Notre Dame du Rosaire. 20p, Virgin and Child, St. Sauveur.

1973, Oct. 24 Photo. Perf. 11½
86	A16	2½p salmon & multi	.20	.20
87	A16	3p blue & multi	.20	.20
88	A16	7½p yellow & multi	.20	.20
89	A16	20p multicolored	.50	.50
		Nos. 86-89 (4)	1.10	1.10

Christmas 1973.

Princess Anne and Mark Phillips — A17

1973, Nov. 14
90	A17	25p blue & multi	.70	.70

Wedding of Princess Anne and Capt. Mark Phillips, Nov. 14, 1973.

"John Lockett," 1875 — A18

Guernsey Lifeboats: 3p, "Arthur Lionel," 1875. 8p, "Euphrosyne Kendal," 1954. 10p, "Arun," 1972.

1974, Jan. 15 Photo. Perf. 11½
Granite Paper
91	A18	2½p multicolored	.20	.20
92	A18	3p multicolored	.20	.20
93	A18	8p multicolored	.20	.20
94	A18	10p multicolored	.20	.20
		Nos. 91-94 (4)	.80	.80

Sesqui. of Royal Natl. Lifeboat Institution.

A19

Militia — A20

1974-78 Photo. Perf. 11½
Granite Paper (Nos. 95-107)
95	A19	½p 1815	.20	.20
96	A19	1p 1825	.20	.20
97	A19	1½p 1787	.20	.20
98	A19	2p 1815	.20	.20
99	A19	2½p Royal, 1868	.20	.20
		Complete booklet, pane of 8 (5 #95, 3 #99)		.35
100	A19	3p Royal, 1895	.20	.20
		Complete booklet, pane of 16 (4 #95, 6 #99 and 6 #100)		1.10
101	A19	3½p Royal, 1867	.20	.20
102	A19	4p 1822	.20	.20
102A	A19	5p Royal, 1895	.25	.25
		Complete booklet, pane of 8 (4 #96, #100, 2 #102, #102A) ('77)		.85
		Complete booklet, pane of 4 (#96, 2 #98, #102A) ('78)		.55
103	A19	5½p Royal, 1833	.20	.20
104	A19	6p Royal, 1832	.20	.20
104A	A19	7p 1822	.35	.35
105	A19	8p Royal, 1868	.20	.20
106	A19	9p 1785	.20	.20
107	A19	10p 1824	.20	.20

Perf. 13x13½, 13½x13
108	A20	20p Royal, 1848, vert.	.70	.50
109	A20	50p Royal, 1868, vert.	1.50	1.40
110	A20	£1 1814	3.00	2.50
		Nos. 95-110 (18)	8.40	7.60

Issued: #95-107, 4/2/74; #108-110, 4/1/75; #102A, 104A, 5/2976; #96a, 2/8/77; #96b, 2/7/78.

Stamps in booklet panes are from special sheets of 80 (two 8x5 panes) which were sold separately.

Bailiwick Seal and UPU Emblem — A21

UPU Cent.: 3p, Map of Guernsey. 8p, UPU Headquarters, Bern, flag of Guernsey. 10p, Legislative Chamber, Parliament.

1974, June 11 Photo. Perf. 11½
Granite Paper
111	A21	2½p multicolored	.20	.20
112	A21	3p ultra & multi	.20	.20
113	A21	8p multicolored	.20	.20
114	A21	10p multicolored	.20	.20
		Nos. 111-114 (4)	.80	.80

Cradle Rock, by Renoir A22

Paintings by Renoir: 5½p, Moulin-Huet Bay. 8p, Woman at the Shore, vert. 10p, Self-portrait, vert.

1974, Sept. 21 Photo. Perf. 13¼
115	A22	3p multicolored	.20	.20
116	A22	5½p multicolored	.20	.20
117	A22	8p multicolored	.20	.20
118	A22	10p multicolored	.20	.20
		Nos. 115-118 (4)	.80	.80

Pierre Auguste Renoir (1841-1919), who painted pictures shown on Nos. 115-117 while visiting Guernsey.

Guernsey Spleenwort — A23

Designs: Guernsey ferns.

1975, Jan. 7 Photo. Perf. 11½
119	A23	3½p shown	.20	.20
120	A23	4p Sand quillwort	.20	.20
121	A23	8p Guernsey fern	.20	.20
122	A23	10p Least adder's tongue	.20	.20
		Nos. 119-122 (4)	.80	.80

Hauteville, Hugo's House A24

Victor Hugo Statue, Candie Gardens — A25

Designs: 8p, United Europe Oak, Hauteville (planted by Hugo). 10p, Departure for the Hunt, Aubusson tapestry, Hauteville.

1975, June 6 Photo. Perf. 11½
Granite Paper
123	A24	3½p dull yel & multi	.20	.20
124	A25	4p lt blue & multi	.20	.20
125	A25	8p yel green & multi	.20	.20
126	A24	10p multicolored	.20	.20
a.		Souvenir sheet of 4, #123-126	.80	.80
		Nos. 123-126 (4)	.80	.80

Victor Hugo (1802-85), French writer, political exile in Guernsey (1855-70).

Arms and Map of Guernsey — A26

Designs (Globe with Map of Bailiwick): 6p, Flag of Guernsey. 10p, Flag of Guernsey and arms of Alderney, horiz. 12p, Flag of Guernsey and arms of Sark, horiz.

1975, Oct. 7 Photo. Perf. 13½
127	A26	4p olive green & multi	.20	.20
128	A26	6p rose lilac & multi	.20	.20
129	A26	10p brt green & multi	.20	.20
130	A26	12p orange & multi	.20	.20
		Nos. 127-130 (4)	.80	.80

Christmas 1975.

Lighthouses — A27

1976, Feb. 10 Photo. Perf. 11½
131	A27	4p Les Hanois	.20	.20
132	A27	6p Les Casquets	.20	.20
133	A27	11p Quesnard, Alderney	.20	.20
134	A27	13p Point Robert, Sark	.30	.30
		Nos. 131-134 (4)	.90	.90

Guernsey Milk Can — A28

Europa: 25p, Silver christening cup.

1976, May 29 Photo. Perf. 11½
Granite Paper
135	A28	10p multicolored	.35	.30
136	A28	25p multicolored	.70	.50

Sheets of 9.

Pine Forest, Guernsey — A29

Guernsey Views: 7p, Herm Harbor and Jethou. 11p, Grande Grave Bay, Sark Cliffs, vert. 13p, Trois Vaux Bay, Alderney Cliffs, vert.

1976, Aug. 3 Photo. Perf. 11½
Granite Paper
137	A29	5p multicolored	.20	.20
138	A29	7p multicolored	.20	.20
139	A29	11p multicolored	.25	.25
140	A29	13p multicolored	.25	.25
		Nos. 137-140 (4)	.90	.90

Royal Court House, Guernsey — A30

Christmas (Buildings in the Bailiwick): 7p, Elizabeth College, Guernsey. 11p, La Seigneurie, Sark. 13p, Island Hall, Alderney.

1976, Oct. 14 Photo. Perf. 11½
Granite Paper
141	A30	5p multicolored	.20	.20
142	A30	7p multicolored	.20	.20
143	A30	11p multicolored	.25	.25
144	A30	13p multicolored	.25	.25
		Nos. 141-144 (4)	.90	.90

Elizabeth II with Order of the Garter — A31

Design: 7p, Queen Elizabeth II.

1977, Feb. 8   Photo.   Perf. 12x11½
145 A31 7p blue & multi   .20   .20
146 A31 35p purple & multi   .70   .70
25th anniv. of the reign of Elizabeth II.

Talbots Valley — A32

Europa: 25p, Fields and hedges, Talbots Valley.

1977, May 17   Photo.   Perf. 11½
Granite Paper
147 A32 7p multicolored   .20   .20
148 A32 25p multicolored   .70   .70

Megalithic Tomb, Le Catioroc — A33

Prehistoric monuments: 5p, Menhir (statue), Castel, vert. 11p, Cist (tomb), Alderney. 13p, Menhir, St. Martin, vert.

1977, Aug. 2   Photo.   Perf. 11½
149 A33 5p multicolored   .20   .20
150 A33 7p multicolored   .20   .20
151 A33 11p multicolored   .30   .30
152 A33 13p multicolored   .30   .30
       Nos. 149-152 (4)   1.00 1.00

Mobile First Aid Unit A34

7p, Mobile radar & rescue coordination unit, for ships in distress. 11p, Marine ambulance "Flying Christine II," vert. 13p, Cliff rescue, vert.

1977, Oct. 25   Photo.   Perf. 11½
153 A34 5p multicolored   .20   .20
154 A34 7p multicolored   .20   .20
155 A34 11p multicolored   .30   .30
156 A34 13p multicolored   .30   .30
       Nos. 153-156 (4)   1.00 1.00
St. John Ambulance Assoc. cent. (in GB).

View from Clifton, c. 1830 A35

19th Century Prints, Guernsey: 7p, Market Square, c. 1838. 11p, Petit-Bo Bay, c. 1839. 13p, The Quay, c. 1830.

1978, Feb. 7   Litho.   Perf. 14x13½
157 A35 5p pale green & black   .20   .20
158 A35 7p buff & black   .20   .20
159 A35 11p pink & black   .30   .30
160 A35 13p lt violet & black   .30   .30
       Nos. 157-160 (4)   1.00 1.00
       See Nos. 236-239.

Memorial to Seamen of Ship Prosperity; Sank 1974 — A36

Europa: 7p, Victoria monument, vert.

1978, May 2   Litho.   Perf. 14½
161 A36 5p multicolored   .20   .20
162 A36 7p multicolored   .25   .25

Elizabeth II — A37

1978, May 2   Photo.   Perf. 11½
163 A37 20p ultra & black   .70   .70
25th anniv. of coronation of Elizabeth II.

Inscribed: "VISIT OF/H.M. THE QUEEN AND/H.R.H. THE DUKE OF EDINBURGH/JUNE 28-29, 1978"
1978, June 28
164 A37 7p emerald & black   .30   .30

Gannet A38

Birds: 7p, Firecrest. 11p, Dartford warbler. 13p, Spotted redshank.

1978, Aug. 29   Photo.   Perf. 11½
165 A38 5p multicolored   .20   .20
166 A38 7p multicolored   .20   .20
167 A38 11p multicolored   .30   .30
168 A38 13p multicolored   .40   .40
       Nos. 165-168 (4)   1.10 1.10

Solanum — A39

Christmas: 7p, Christmas rose. 11p, Holly, vert. 13p, Mistletoe, vert.

1978, Oct. 31   Photo.   Perf. 11½
169 A39 5p multicolored   .20   .20
170 A39 7p multicolored   .20   .20
171 A39 11p multicolored   .30   .30
172 A39 13p multicolored   .30   .30
       Nos. 169-172 (4)   1.00 1.00

1 Double, 1930 — A40

1979, Feb. 13
Granite Paper
173 A40 ½p 1 double, 1930   .20   .20
174 A40 1p 2 doubles, 1899   .20   .20
175 A40 2p 4 doubles, 1902   .20   .20
176 A40 4p 8 doubles, 1959   .20   .20
177 A40 5p 3 pence, 1956   .20   .20
178 A40 6p 5 new pence, 1968   .20   .20
  a.   Horiz. strip of 4, #175, 178, 2
       #174   1.00
179 A40 7p 50 new pence,
          1969   .20   .20
180 A40 8p 10 new pence,
          1970   .20   .20
  a.   Horiz. strip of 5, #175, 2 each
       #178, 180   1.25
       Complete booklet of 10, 5 each
       #176, 180   2.25
181 A40 9p ½ new penny, 1971   .20   .20
182 A40 10p 1 new penny, 1971   .30   .20
183 A40 11p 2 new penny, 1971   .30   .20
184 A40 12p 1 penny, 1977   .30   .20
       Complete booklet of 15, 5 each
       #176, 180, 184   3.50
185 A40 13p 2 pence, 1977   .30   .20
       Complete booklet of 10, 2 #176,
       3 #181, 5 #185   2.25
       Complete booklet of 15, 5 each
       #176, 181, 185   3.50
186 A40 14p 5 pence, 1977   .35   .20
187 A40 15p 10 pence, 1977   .35   .20
188 A40 20p 25 pence, 1977   .45   .20
       Nos. 173-188 (16)   4.15 3.20

No. 177 is dark brown, No. 182, green & bronze. See Nos. 198B-203A.

Booklets were produced from sheets of 40, 30 and 20. These sheets were sold both as complete sheets and as strips, folded and affixed by the sheet salvage or inserted unattached into booklet covers.

Oldest Pillar Box, 1853 Cancel, Truck — A41

Europa: 8p, Telephone, 1897, telex machine.

1979, May 8   Photo.   Perf. 11½
189 A41 6p multicolored   .20   .20
190 A41 8p multicolored   .20   .20

Steam Tram, 1879 A42

Public Transportation: 8p, Electric tram, 1896. 11p, Autobus, 1911. 13p, Autobus, 1979.

1979, Aug. 7   Photo.   Perf. 11½
191 A42 6p multicolored   .20   .20
192 A42 8p multicolored   .20   .20
193 A42 11p multicolored   .30   .30
194 A42 13p multicolored   .30   .30
       Nos. 191-194 (4)   1.00 1.00
Centenary of public transportation.

Postal Bureau and Headquarters — A43

Designs: 8p, Mail and telegram delivery-men. 13p, Parcel trucks. 15p, Post Office philatelic room.

1979, Oct. 1   Photo.   Perf. 11½
195 A43 6p multicolored   .20   .20
196 A43 8p multicolored   .20   .20
197 A43 13p multicolored   .30   .30
198 A43 15p multicolored   .40   .40
  a.   Souvenir sheet of 4, Nos. 195-
       198   1.25 1.25
       Nos. 195-198 (4)   1.10 1.10
Guernsey PO, 10th anniv.; Christmas 1979.

Coin Type of 1979

Designs: 10p, like No. 182. 11½p, ½ pence, 1979. 50p, Battle of Hastings coin, 1966. £1, Queen Elizabeth II 25th anniv., 1977, horiz. £2, Queen Elizabeth II 25th wedding anniv., 1972, horiz. £5, Official seal.

1980-81   Photo.   Perf. 11½
198B A40 5p orange brown
           & multi   .45   .45
       Complete booklet of 15, 5
       each #180, 185, 198B   2.00
       Complete booklet of 10,
       #185, 4 #180, 5 #198B   3.50
199   A40 10p orange &
           bronze   .25   .20
       Complete booklet of 10,
       #177, 179, 199, 2 each
       #173, 175, 3 each #174   2.00
       Complete booklet of 10,
       #174, 2 each #173, 175,
       179, 3 #199   2.50
200   A40 11½p red & bronze   .30   .20

Size: 26x45, 45x26mm
201   A40 50p red org & sil   1.60 1.25
202   A40 £1 green & sil   3.25 2.25
203   A40 £2 blue & silver   6.50 3.50
203A A40 £5 multi ('81)   16.00 12.00
       Nos. 198B-203A (7)   28.35 19.85

No. 177 is dark brown.
For booklets, see note following No. 188.
Issue dates: £5, May 22, others, Feb. 5.

Policewoman Helping Child — A44

Guernsey Police Force, 60th Anniv.: 15p, Policeman on motorcycle. 17½p, Police dog and officer.

1980, May 6   Litho.   Perf. 14
204   A44 7p multicolored   .20   .20
205   A44 15p multicolored   .40   .40
206   A44 17½p multicolored   .45   .45
       Nos. 204-206 (3)   1.05 1.05

Major Gen. John Gaspard Le Marchant — A45

Europa: 13½p, Admiral James Lord de Saumarez (1757-1836).

1980, May 6   Photo.   Perf. 11½
Granite Paper
207   A45 10p multicolored   .25   .25
208   A45 13½p multicolored   .40   .40

Guernsey Golden Goat — A46

Designs: Various Guernsey golden goats.

1980, Aug. 5   Photo.   Perf. 13
209   A46 7p multicolored   .20   .20
210   A46 10p multicolored   .20   .20
211   A46 15p multicolored   .40   .40
212   A46 17½p multicolored   .50   .50
       Nos. 209-212 (4)   1.30 1.30

Sark Cottage, by Peter Le Lievre, 1847 — A47

Christmas 1980 (Le Lievre Paintings): 10p, Moulin Huet, 1850. 13½p, Boats at Sea, 1850. 15p, Cow Lane, 1852, vert. 17½p, Portrait, by Le Lievre's sister, vert.

1980, Nov. 15   Photo.   Perf. 12
Granite Paper
213	A47	7p multicolored	.20	.20
214	A47	10p multicolored	.25	.25
215	A47	13½p multicolored	.40	.40
216	A47	15p multicolored	.45	.45
217	A47	17½p multicolored	.50	.50
		Nos. 213-217 (5)	1.80	1.80

Common Blue — A48

1981, Feb. 24   Photo.   Perf. 14½
218	A48	8p shown	.20	.20
219	A48	12p Red Admiral	.20	.20
220	A48	22p Small Tortoiseshell	.60	.60
221	A48	25p Wall Brown	.70	.70
		Nos. 218-221 (4)	1.70	1.70

Le Petit Bonhomme Andriou (Head-shaped Rock) — A49

1981, May 22   Litho.   Perf. 14½
222	A49	12p shown	.35	.35
223	A49	18p Guernsey lily	.55	.55

Europa.

Prince Charles and Lady Diana — A50

Royal Wedding: a, Charles. c, Diana.

1981, July 29   Litho.   Perf. 14½x15
224		Strip of 3	.90	.90
a.-c.		A50 8p any single	.30	.30
225		Strip of 3	1.25	1.25
a.-c.		A50 12p any single	.40	.40

Size: 49x32mm
226	A50	25p Royal family	.90	.90
a.		Souv. sheet, #224-226, perf. 14x14½	3.25	3.25
		Nos. 224-226 (3)	3.05	3.05

Sark Launch — A51

Designs: Interisland transportation.

1981, Aug. 25   Photo.   Perf. 11½
Granite Paper
227	A51	8p shown	.20	.20
228	A51	12p Trislander plane	.35	.35
229	A51	18p Hydrofoil	.55	.55

230	A51	22p Herm catamaran	.75	.75
231	A51	25p Alderney coaster	.80	.80
		Nos. 227-231 (5)	2.65	2.65

Rifle-shooting Competition A52

1981, Nov. 17   Litho.   Perf. 14¾
232	A52	8p shown	.20	.20
233	A52	12p Riding	.35	.35
234	A52	22p Swimming	.70	.70
235	A52	25p Electronics workers	.80	.80
		Nos. 232-235 (4)	2.05	2.05

Intl. Year of the Disabled.

Print Type of 1978
1982, Feb. 2   Litho. & Engr.
236	A35	8p Jethou	.20	.20
237	A35	12p Fermain Bay	.35	.35
238	A35	22p The Terres	.70	.70
239	A35	25p St. Pierre Port	.80	.80
		Nos. 236-239 (4)	2.05	2.05

La Societe Guernesiaise Centenary A53

Society Emblem and Activities: 8p, Sir Edgar MacCulloch, founding president. 13p, William the Conqueror's fleet, Battle at Hastings (history). 20p, Sir James Saumarez's Crescent rescued from French fleet (history). 24p, Dragonfly (entomology). 26p, Vale Parish Church bird sanctuary (ornithology). 29p, Samian bowl, King's Road excavation (archaeology). 13p and 20p show CEPT (Europa) emblem.

1982, Apr. 28   Photo.   Perf. 11½
Granite Paper
240	A53	8p multicolored	.30	.30
241	A53	13p multicolored	.40	.40
242	A53	20p multicolored	.65	.65
243	A53	24p multicolored	.80	.80
244	A53	26p multicolored	.80	.80
245	A53	29p multicolored	.85	.85
		Nos. 240-245 (6)	3.80	3.80

Scouting Year — A54

1982, July 13   Litho.   Perf. 14½
246	A54	8p Sea scouts, Castle Cornet, St. Peter Port	.25	.25
247	A54	13p Boy scouts building bridge	.35	.35
248	A54	26p Cub scouts parading	.80	.80
249	A54	29p Air scouts reading chart	.85	.85
		Nos. 246-249 (4)	2.25	2.25

Christmas 1982 — A55

1982, Oct. 12   Photo.   Perf. 14½
250	A55	8p Midnight mass, St. Peter Port Church	.20	.20
251	A55	13p Exchanging presents	.35	.35
252	A55	24p Dinner	.70	.70
253	A55	26p Exchanging cards	.75	.75
254	A55	29p Watching Queen's TV greeting	.90	.90
		Nos. 250-254 (5)	2.90	2.90

Centenary of Boys' Brigade — A56

Designs: Various brigade activities.

1983, Jan. 18   Perf. 14
255	A56	8p multicolored	.25	.25
256	A56	13p multicolored	.40	.40
257	A56	24p multicolored	.75	.75
258	A56	26p multicolored	.90	.90
259	A56	29p multicolored	1.10	1.10
		Nos. 255-259 (5)	3.40	3.40

Europa 1983 — A57

Views of the development of St. Peter Port Harbor.

1983, Mar. 14   Photo.   Perf. 11½
Granite Paper
260	A57	13p multicolored	.40	.40
261	A57	13p multicolored	.40	.40
a.		Pair, #260-261	.90	.90
262	A57	20p multicolored	.65	.65
263	A57	20p multicolored	.65	.65
a.		Pair, #262-263	1.40	1.40

View at Guernsey, by Renoir — A58

Centenary of Renoir's Visit: 13p, Children at the Seashore (26x39mm). 26p, Marine Guernsey. 28p, Moulin Huet Bay through the Trees. 31p, Fog in Guernsey.

Perf. 12, 11½x12 (13p)
1983, Sept. 6   Photo.
Granite Paper
264	A58	9p multicolored	.30	.30
265	A58	13p multicolored	.40	.40
266	A58	26p multicolored	.85	.85
267	A58	28p multicolored	.90	.90
268	A58	31p multicolored	1.00	1.00
		Nos. 264-268 (5)	3.45	3.45

Star of the West, 1869 Merchant Ship, Capt. J.G. Lenfestey — A59

1983, Nov. 15   Photo.   Perf. 14½
269	A59	9p Launching	.30	.30
270	A59	13p Leaving St. Peter Port	.40	.40
271	A59	26p Rio Grande Bar	.85	.85
272	A59	28p St. Lucia	.90	.90
273	A59	31p Voyage Map	1.00	1.00
		Nos. 269-273 (5)	3.45	3.45

Dame of Sark (Sibyl Hathaway, 1884-1974) — A60

Biographical Scenes: 9p, Portrait, La Seigneurie (residence). 13p, German occupation, 1940-45. 26p, Royal visit, 1957. 28p, Chief Pleas (parliament). 31p, Dame of Sark rose.

1984, Feb. 7   Litho.   Perf. 14½
274	A60	9p multicolored	.30	.30
275	A60	13p multicolored	.40	.40
276	A60	26p multicolored	.85	.85
277	A60	28p multicolored	1.00	1.00
278	A60	31p multicolored	1.10	1.10
		Nos. 274-278 (5)	3.65	3.65

Links with the Commonwealth — A61

Designs: 9p, Flag of Guernsey, Royal Court. 31p, Union Jack, Castle Cornet.

1984, Apr. 10   Litho.   Perf. 14½
279	A61	9p multicolored	.30	.30
280	A61	31p multicolored	1.25	1.25

Europa (1959-84) — A62

1984, Apr. 10   Perf. 15
281	A62	13p multicolored	.50	.50
282	A62	20½p multicolored	.75	.75

Petit Port — A63

Perf. 15x14½, 14½x15
1984-85   Litho.
283	A63	1p Little Chapel, vert. ('85)	.20	.20
284	A63	2p Ft. Grey ('85)	.20	.20
285	A63	3p St. Apolline Chapel, vert.	.20	.20
286	A63	4p shown	.20	.20
287	A63	5p Little Russel ('85)	.20	.20
288	A63	6p The Harbour, Herm ('85)	.20	.20
289	A63	7p Saints ('85)	.20	.20
290	A63	8p St. Saviour, vert. ('85)	.20	.20
291	A63	9p Cambridge Berth	.20	.20
292	A63	10p Belvoir, Herm	.35	.20
a.		Min. sheet, 2 2p, 4 4p, 2 5p, 2 10p	2.50	
293	A63	11p La Seigneurie, Sark ('85)	.20	.20
294	A63	13p St. Saviour's Reservoir	.35	.35
a.		Min. sheet, 2 4p, 3 9p, 5 13p	3.00	
b.		Min. sheet, 5 each 4p, 9p, 13p	5.00	
295	A63	14p St. Peter Port, vert.	.20	.20
a.		Min. sheet, 4 9p, 6 14p	4.50	
b.		Min. sheet, 2 9p, 8 14p	4.75	
c.		Min. sheet, 5 10p, 5 14p	4.50	
296	A63	15p Havelet, vert. ('85)	.35	.20
a.		Min. sheet, 3p, 2 4p, 4 11p, 3 15p	3.75	
b.		Min. sheet, 5 each 11p, 15p	4.50	
297	A63	20p La Coupee, Sark	.60	.20
a.		Booklet pane, 6 4p, 4 14p, 2 20p	3.00	
b.		Booklet pane, 5 14p, 5 20p	3.50	
298	A63	30p Grandes Rocques ('85)	1.00	1.00
299	A63	40p St. Torteval Church, vert.	1.25	1.25
300	A63	50p Bordeaux	1.60	1.60
301	A63	£1 Albecq	3.50	3.50
302	A63	£2 L'Ancresse ('85)	7.00	7.00
		Nos. 283-302 (20)	18.20	17.50

Issued: 1p, 2p, 5p, 6p, 7p, 8p, 11p, 15p, 30p, £2, 7/23/84; 3p, 4p, 9p, 10p, 13p, 14p, 20p, 40p, 50p, £1, 9/18/84; #292a, 12/2/85; #294a-294b, 9/18/84; #295a-295b, 3/19/85; #295c, 4/1/86; #296a-296b, 3/30/87; #297a-297b, 12/27/89.

Miniature sheets have surrounding selvage and were sold folded and unattached in booklet covers. Nos. 297a, 297b with straight edges around stamps and attached to booklet covers by tabs.

See Nos. 372-378, 453-454.

Lieutenant-General John Doyle (1756-1834) — A64

Designs: 13p, Portrait by James Ramsey, 1817. 29p, American War of Independence battle. 31p, Land fill, Grand Havre Bay. 34p, Ship approaching Casquets Reef, 1811. 29p, 31p, 34p horiz.

1984, Nov. 20   **Photo.**   *Perf. 11½*
303 A64 13p multicolored   .40   .40
304 A64 29p multicolored   .95   .95
305 A64 31p multicolored   1.00 1.00
306 A64 34p multicolored   1.10 1.00
   Nos. 303-306 (4)   3.45 3.35

Christmas 1984 — A65

Twelve Days of Christmas: a, Partridge in a Pear Tree. b, 2 Turtle Doves. c, 3 French Hens. d, 4 Colly Birds. e, 5 Golden Rings. f, 6 Geese-a-Laying. g, 7 Swans a-Swimming. h, 8 Maids a-Milking. i, 9 Drummers Drumming. j, 10 Pipers Piping. k, 11 Ladies Dancing. l, 12 Lords a-Leaping. Illustration reduced.

1984, Nov. 20   **Litho.**   *Perf. 14½*
307 A65   Sheet of 12   2.50 2.50
  a.-l.   5p any single   .20   .20

Indigenous Fish — A66

1985, Jan. 22   **Photo.**   *Perf. 12*
308 A66   9p Cockoo Wrasse   .40   .40
309 A66 13p Red Gurnard   .65   .65
310 A66 29p Red Mullet   1.25 1.25
311 A66 31p Mackerel   1.60 1.60
312 A66 34p Sunfish   1.75 1.75
   Nos. 308-312 (5)   5.65 5.65

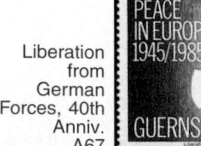

Liberation from German Forces, 40th Anniv. A67

1985, May 9   **Litho.**   *Perf. 14x14½*
313 A67 22p Peace dove   1.00 1.00

Celebrating the end of the war in Europe (VE-Day).

Europa 1985 — A68

Designs: 14p, Musical staff, flags of Great Britain, Netherlands, Germany, Italy, Cross of St. George. 22p, Music, cello, French horn.

1985, May 14   **Litho.**   *Perf. 14½*
314 A68 14p multicolored   .55   .55
315 A68 22p multicolored   .90   .90

Intl. Youth Year — A69

1985, May 14   **Litho.**   *Perf. 14*
316 A69   9p IYY emblem, circle of children   .35   .35
317 A69 31p Girl Guides in camp   1.25 1.25

Children's drawings.

Girl Guides, 75th Anniv. — A70

1985, May 14   **Litho.**   *Perf. 14*
318 A70 34p Leader, guide and brownie   1.40 1.40

Child's drawing.

Christmas 1985 — A71

Religious and folk figures: a, Santa Claus. b, Lussibruden. c, Balthasar. d, St. Nicholas. e, La Befana. f, Julenisse. g, Christkind. h, King Wenceslas. i, Shepherd of Les Baux. j, Caspar. k, Baboushka. l, Melchior.

1985, Nov. 19   **Litho.**   *Perf. 12½*
   Granite Paper
319   A71   Sheet of 12   5.00 5.00
  a.-l.   5p any single   .40   .40

Watercolors by Paul Jacob Naftel — A72

1985, Nov. 19   **Litho.**   *Perf. 15x14½*
320 A72   9p Vraicing   .35   .35
321 A72 14p Castle Cornet   .55   .55
322 A72 22p Rocquaine Bay   .90   .90
323 A72 31p Little Russel   1.25 1.25
324 A72 34p Seaweed Gatherers   1.40 1.40
   Nos. 320-324 (5)   4.45 4.45

Adm. Lord De Saumarez, 150th Death Anniv. — A73

Designs: 9p, Squadron off Nargue Is., 1809. 14p, Battle of the Nile, 1798. 29p, Battle of St. Vincent, 1797. 31p, HMS Crescent off Cherbourg, 1793. 34p, Battle of the Saints, 1782.

1986, Feb. 4   **Litho.**   *Perf. 12x11½*
   Granite Paper
325 A73   9p multicolored   .35   .35
326 A73 14p multicolored   .55   .55
327 A73 29p multicolored   1.10 1.10
328 A73 31p multicolored   1.40 1.40
329 A73 34p multicolored   1.50 1.50
   Nos. 325-329 (5)   4.90 4.90

Queen Elizabeth II, 60th Birthday — A74

1986, Apr. 21   *Perf. 14*
330 A74 60p multicolored   2.50 2.50

Europa 1986 — A75

1986, May 22   *Perf. 11½*
   Granite Paper
331 A75 10p Operation Gannet   .40   .40
332 A75 14p Whitsun orchid   .55   .55
333 A75 22p Guernsey elm   .90   .90
   Nos. 331-333 (3)   1.85 1.85

Wedding of Prince Andrew and Sarah Ferguson — A76

1986, July 23   **Litho.**   *Perf. 14*
334 A76 14p Couple   .60   .60
   Size: 48x32mm
335 A76 34p Couple, diff.   1.50 1.50

Sports A77

1986, July 24   *Perf. 14½*
336 A77 10p Lawn bowling, vert.   .40   .40
337 A77 14p Cricket, vert.   .55   .55
338 A77 22p Badminton, vert.   .90   .90
339 A77 29p Field hockey, vert.   1.10 1.10
340 A77 31p Swimming   1.25 1.25
341 A77 34p Rifle shooting   1.40 1.40
   Nos. 336-341 (6)   5.60 5.60

Museums A78

1986, Nov. 18   **Litho.**   *Perf. 14½*
342 A78 14p Guernsey Museum and Art Gallery   .55   .55
343 A78 29p Ft. Grey Maritime Museum   1.10 1.10
344 A78 31p Castle Cornet   1.25 1.25
345 A78 34p Natl. Trust of Guernsey Folk Museum   1.40 1.40
   Nos. 342-345 (4)   4.30 4.30

     Miniature Sheet

Christmas — A79

Carols: a, "While Shepherds Watched Their Flocks by Night." b, "In the Bleak Mid-Winter." c, "O Little Town of Bethlehem." d, "The Holly and the Ivy." e, "O Little Christmas Tree." f, "Away in a Manger." g, "Good King Wenceslas." h, "We Three Kings of Orient Are." i, "Hark the Herald Angels Sing." j, "I Saw Three Ships." k, "Little Donkey." l, "Jingle Bells."

1986, Nov. 18   *Perf. 12½*
346 A79   Sheet of 12   2.75 2.75
  a.-l.   6p any single   .20   .20

     Souvenir Sheet

Duke of Richmond, 18th Century Map Detail — A80

1987, Feb. 10   **Litho.**   *Perf. 14½*
347   Sheet of 4   4.50 4.50
  a. A80 14p shown   .55   .55
  b. A80 29p North   1.10 1.10
  c. A80 31p Southwest   1.25 1.25
  d. A80 34p Southeast   1.40 1.40

Duke of Richmond's survey of Guernsey, bicent.

Europa 1987 — A81

Modern architecture.

1987, May 5   **Litho.**   *Perf. 13x13½*
348 A81 15p Postal headquarters   .60   .60
349 A81 15p Headquarters, schematic view   .60   .60
  a.   Pair, #348-349   1.25 1.25
350 A81 22p Grammar school entrance   .90   .90
351 A81 22p School, schematic view   .90   .90
  a.   Pair, #350-351   1.90 1.90

Andros and La Plaiderie Court House, Guernsey A82

Andros and: 29p, Governor's Palace, Virginia. 31p, "Governor Andros and the Boston People," print from Harper's New Monthly Magazine. 34p, Map of New Amsterdam (New York City).

1987, July 7 — Perf. 12
Granite Paper

352	A82 15p multicolored	.60	.60
353	A82 29p multicolored	1.10	1.10
354	A82 31p multicolored	1.25	1.25
355	A82 34p multicolored	1.40	1.40
	Nos. 352-355 (4)	4.35	4.35

Sir Edmund Andros (1637-1714), lieutenant-governor of Guernsey (1704-1706) and statesman of Colonial America (1672-1710).

William the Conqueror (c. 1028-1087), King of England (1066-1087) — A83

11p, Jester warning young William of a plot to murder him. #357, Battle of Hastings. #358, King William, his banner at the Battle of Hastings. #359, William the Conqueror. #360, Abbey at Caen & Queen Matilda of Flanders (d. 1083). 34p, Halley's Comet & regalia of William I.

1987, Sept. 9 — Perf. 13½x14

356	A83 11p multicolored	.45	.50
357	A83 15p multicolored	.60	.65
358	A83 15p multicolored	.60	.65
a.	Pair, #357-350	1.25	1.40
359	A83 22p multicolored	.90	.95
360	A83 22p multicolored	.90	.95
a.	Pair, #359-360	1.90	2.00
361	A83 34p multicolored	1.40	1.50
	Nos. 356-361 (6)	4.85	5.20

Visit of John Wesley (1703-1791), Religious Reformer, Bicent. — A84

Designs: 7p, Preaching at the quay, Alderney. 15p, Preaching at Mon Plaisir. 29p, Preaching at Assembly Rooms, St. Peter Port. 31p, Wesley and La Ville Baudu, an early Methodist meeting place, Vale Parish. 34p, Wesley and Ebenezer Methodist Church, first Methodist chapel, Union Street, 1816.

1987, Nov. 17 — Litho. — Perf. 14½

362	A84 7p multicolored	.30	.30
363	A84 15p multicolored	.60	.60
364	A84 29p multicolored	1.10	1.10
365	A84 31p multicolored	1.25	1.25
366	A84 34p multicolored	1.40	1.40
	Nos. 362-366 (5)	4.65	4.65

Voyage of the Golden Spur, Apr. 12, 1872-Jan. 4, 1874 — A85

Designs: 11p, Off St. Sampson's Harbor. 15p, Entering Hong Kong Harbor. 29p, Anchored off Macao. 31p, In China Tea Race. 34p, Golden Spur, map of voyage.

1988, Feb. 9 — Litho. — Perf. 13½x14

367	A85 11p multicolored	.45	.45
368	A85 15p multicolored	.60	.60
369	A85 29p multicolored	1.10	1.10
370	A85 31p multicolored	1.25	1.25
371	A85 34p multicolored	1.40	1.40
	Nos. 367-371 (5)	4.80	4.80

Guernsey's Golden Age of Shipping: largest vessel built on Guernsey, the Golden Spur, launched Oct. 15, 1864, wrecked at Haiphong on Feb. 27, 1879.

Landscape Type of 1984
Perf. 14½x15, 15x14½
1988-89 — Litho.

372	A63 12p Petit Bot beach, vert.	.50	.50
373	A63 16p St. John's Hostel for the Aged	.65	.65
a.	Min. sheet, 5 each 12p, 16p	6.50	
b.	Min. sheet, 4 4p, 3 12p, 3 16p	5.00	
374	A63 18p Le Variouf, vert.	.70	.70
a.	Booklet pane, 4p, 6p, 3 12p, 3 18p	4.00	
b.	Booklet pane, 4 12p, 4 18p	3.50	
	Nos. 372-374 (3)	1.85	1.85

Nos. 373a-373b have surrounding selvage and were sold unattached in booklet covers. Nos. 374a, 374b with straight edges around stamps and attached to booklet covers by tabs.
Issued: Nos. 372-373b, 3/28/88; Nos. 374-374b, 2/28/89.

Coil Stamps
Sizes: 21½x17½mm, 17½x21½mm
Perf. 14x14½, 14½x14

375	A63 11p La Seigneurie, Sark	.45	.45
376	A63 12p Petit Bot beach	.50	.50
377	A63 15p Havelet, vert.	.60	.60
378	A63 16p St. John's Hostel for the Aged	.65	.65
	Nos. 375-378 (4)	2.20	2.20

Issued: 11p, 15p, 5/15/87; 12p, 16p, 3/28/88.

Waves, Map — A85a

Perf. 14½x14
1989, Apr. 3 — Photo. — Coil Stamp

380	A85a (18p) green	1.00	1.00

Inscribed "MINIMUM FIRST CLASS POSTAGE TO UK PAID." See No. 431.

Europa 1988 A86

Communication and transportation: No. 381, Bedford Rascal postal van, Lihou Is. rowboat. No. 382, Rowboat, Viscount plane. No. 383, Horse and buggy, front wheel of bicycle. No. 384, Back wheel of bicycle, No. 4 coach.

1988, May 10 — Litho. — Perf. 14½

381	A86 16p multicolored	.65	.65
382	A86 16p multicolored	.65	.65
a.	Pair, #381-382	1.40	1.40
383	A86 22p multicolored	.90	.90
384	A86 22p multicolored	.90	.90
a.	Pair, #383-384	1.90	1.90
	Nos. 381-384 (4)	3.10	3.10

#382a, 384a have continuous designs.

Frederick Corbin Lukis (1788-1871), Archaeologist A87

Designs: 12p, Entrance to Lukis House, St. Peter Port, and portrait. 16p, Bound manuscript containing illustrations painted by Lukis's daughter Mary Anne (born 1822). 29p, Lukis supervising excavation of Le Creux es Faies dolmen at L'Eree, Guernsey. 31p, Rear of Lukis House and garden. 34p, Artifacts recovered by Lukis and preserved as part of the museum collection.

1988, July 12 — Photo. — Perf. 12½
Granite Paper

385	A87 12p multicolored	.50	.50
386	A87 16p multicolored	.65	.65
387	A87 29p multicolored	1.10	1.10
388	A87 31p multicolored	1.25	1.25
389	A87 34p multicolored	1.40	1.40
	Nos. 385-389 (5)	4.90	4.90

1988 World Offshore Powerboat Championships — A88

Designs: 16p, Racing boats, Royal Navy helicopter. 30p, Boats racing through Gouliot Passage (separating Sark from Brecqhou). 32p, Boats, helicopter, St. John's Ambulance rescue ship, vert. 35p, Race course marked in red on Admiralty Chart, vert.

1988, Sept. 6 — Perf. 12
Granite Paper

390	A88 16p multicolored	.65	.65
391	A88 30p multicolored	1.25	1.25
392	A88 32p multicolored	1.25	1.25
393	A88 35p multicolored	1.40	1.40
	Nos. 390-393 (4)	4.55	4.55

Publication of *Flora Sarniensis*, Bicent. — A89

Designs: 12p, Joshua Gosselin (1739-1813), botanist, and herbarium made by Rollo Sherwill in 1976. No. 395, *Lagurus ovatus*, diff. No. 397, *Silene gallica quinquevulnera* (pressed specimen). No. 398, *Silene gallica quinquevulnera*, diff. 35p, *Limonium binervosum sarniense serquense*.

1988, Nov. 15 — Litho. — Perf. 14

394	A89 12p shown	.50	.50
395	A89 16p multicolored	.65	.65
396	A89 16p multicolored	.65	.65
a.	Pair, #395-396	1.40	1.40
397	A89 23p multicolored	.90	.90
398	A89 23p multicolored	.90	.90
a.	Pair, #397-398	1.90	1.90
399	A89 35p multicolored	1.40	1.40
	Nos. 394-399 (6)	5.00	5.00

Miniature Sheet

Ecclesiastical Links to France and Great Britain — A90

Church interiors, exteriors and artifacts: a, Coutances Cathedral, France. b, Notre Dame du Rosaire Church interior, Guernsey. c, Stained-glass window, St. Sampson's Church, Guernsey. d, Dol-de-Bretagne Cathedral, France. e, Bishop's Throne, Town Church, Guernsey. f, Winchester Cathedral, England. g, St. John's Cathedral, Portsmouth, England. h, High Altar, St. Joseph's Church, Guernsey. i, Mont Saint-Michel, France. j, Chancel, Vale Church, Guernsey. k, The Lychgate, Forest Church, Guernsey. l, Marmoutier Abbey, France.

1988, Nov. 15 — Perf. 14½x15

400	A90 Sheet of 12	4.00	4.00
a.-l.	8p any single	.30	.30

Christmas 1988.

Europa 1989 — A91

Traditional children's toys and games.

1989, Feb. 28 — Litho. — Perf. 13½

401	A91 12p Tip cat (Le Cat)	.50	.50
402	A91 16p Girl, Cobo Alice doll	.65	.65
403	A91 23p Hopscotch (Le Colimachaon)	.90	.90
	Nos. 401-403 (3)	2.05	2.05

Aircraft A92

1989, May 5

404	A92 12p DH86 Express	.50	.50
a.	Booklet pane of 6	3.25	
405	A92 12p Southampton	.50	.50
406	A92 18p DH89 Rapide	.70	.70
a.	Booklet pane of 6	4.75	
407	A92 18p Sunderland	.70	.70
408	A92 35p BAe 146	1.40	1.40
a.	Booklet pane of 6	9.50	
	Complete booklet, #404a, 406a, 408a	17.50	
409	A92 35p Shackleton	1.40	1.40
	Nos. 404-409 (6)	5.20	5.20

Guernsey Airport, 50th anniv. (Nos. 404, 406, 408); others, 201st Squadron Affiliation, 50th anniv.

Visit of Queen Elizabeth II, May 23-24 — A93

1989, May 23 — Perf. 15x14

410	A93 30p Portrait by June Mendoza	1.25	1.25

Great Western Railway Steamer Service Between Weymouth and the Channel Isls., Cent. — A94

1989, Sept. 5 — Litho. — Perf. 13½

411	A94 12p S.S. *Ibex*, 1891	.50	.50
412	A94 18p P.S. *Great Western*, 1872	.70	.70
413	A94 29p S.S. *St. Julien*, 1925	1.10	1.10
414	A94 34p S.S. *Roebuck*, 1925	1.40	1.40
415	A94 37p S.S. *Antelope*, 1889	1.50	1.50
a.	Souvenir sheet of 5, #411-415	5.50	5.50
	Nos. 411-415 (5)	5.20	5.20

Zoological Trust of Guernsey — A95

1989, Nov. 17   Litho.   *Perf. 14x13½*

416	A95	18p Two-toed sloth	.70	.70
417	A95	29p Capuchin monkey	1.10	1.10
418	A95	32p White-lipped tamarin	1.25	1.25
419	A95	34p Squirrel monkey	1.40	1.40
420	A95	37p Lar gibbon	1.50	1.50
a.		Strip of 5, #416-420	6.00	6.00

Animals of the rainforest.

Miniature Sheet

Christmas — A96

Ornaments on tree: a, Star. b, Angel. c, Candles. d, Robin red breast. e, Presents on sled. f, Caroler. g, Santa Claus pictured on Christmas cracker. h, Herald and stars pictured on glass ball. i, Presents in stocking. j, Bell. k, Reindeer. l, Chapel.

1989, Nov. 17   *Perf. 13*

421	A96	Sheet of 12	5.00	5.00
a.-l.		10p any single	.40	.40

Europa 1990 — A97

Post offices.

1990, Feb. 27   Litho.   *Perf. 13½x14*

422	A97	20p Sark, c. 1890	.80	.80
423	A97	20p Sark, 1990	.80	.80
424	A97	24p Arcade, c. 1840	.95	.95
425	A97	24p Arcade, 1990	.95	.95
		Nos. 422-425 (4)	3.50	3.50

Penny Black, 150th Anniv. A98

Designs: 14p, Great Britain No. 1, Maltese Cross cancellation in red, mail steamer in St. Peter Port Harbor. 20p, Great Britain No. 3, Maltese Cross cancellation in black, pedestrians, mailbox at Elm Grove and Union Street in 1852. 32p, Great Britain No. 255 bisected, 1940, and military band. 34p, Guernsey No. 2, crown of William the Conqueror, Guernsey lily. 37p, Guernsey No. 10, crowd in line outside Guernsey P.O.

1990, May 3   *Perf. 14*

426	A98	14p multicolored	.55	.55
427	A98	20p multicolored	.80	.80
428	A98	32p multicolored	1.25	1.25
429	A98	34p multicolored	1.40	1.40
430	A98	37p multicolored	1.50	1.50
a.		Souvenir sheet, #426-430	6.00	6.00
b.		No. 430a ovptd. "NZ 1990" emblem, "FROM LONDON 90 TO NEW ZEALAND 90"	16.00	16.00
		Nos. 426-430 (5)	5.50	5.50

Map and Waves Type of 1989

1989, Dec. 27   Photo.   *Perf. 14½x14*
Coil Stamp

431	A85a	(14p) ultra & lt ultra	.85	.85

Inscribed "MINIMUM BAILIWICK POSTAGE PAID."

Lord Anson's Circumnavigation of the World, 250th Anniv. — A99

Designs: 14p, Philip Saumarez writing ship's log. 20p, *Centurion, Gloucester, Severn, Pearle, Wager* and *Tryal* departing from Portsmouth. 29p, Landfall at St. Catherine's Is. off Brazil, 1740. 34p, *Tryal* rounding Cape Horn, 1741. 37p, Camp at Juan Fernandez, 1741.

1990, July 24   Litho.   *Perf. 13½x14*

436	A99	14p multicolored	.55	.55
437	A99	20p multicolored	.80	.80
438	A99	29p multicolored	1.10	1.10
439	A99	34p multicolored	1.40	1.40
440	A99	37p multicolored	1.50	1.50
		Nos. 436-440 (5)	5.35	5.35

Gray Seal A100

1990, Oct. 16   Litho.   *Perf. 14½*

441	A100	20p shown	1.25	.75
442	A100	26p Bottlenose dolphin	2.25	1.10
443	A100	31p Basking shark	2.50	1.40
444	A100	37p Harbor porpoise	2.75	1.60
		Nos. 441-444 (4)	8.75	4.85

World Wildlife Fund.

Miniature Sheet

Christmas — A101

Winter birds: a, Blue and Great Tits. b, Snow Bunting. c, Kestrel. d, Starling. e, Greenfinch. f, Robin. g, Wren. h, Barn owl. i, Mistle Thrush. j, Heron. k, Chaffinch. l, Kingfisher.

1990, Oct. 16   *Perf. 13½*

445	A101	Sheet of 12	5.00	5.00
a.-l.		10p any single	.40	.40

Occupation Stamp No. N1, 50th Anniv. — A102

1991, Feb. 18   Litho.   *Perf. 13½*

446	A102	37p shown	1.50	1.50
447	A102	53p No. N2	2.10	2.10
448	A102	57p No. N3	2.25	2.25
a.		Booklet pane of 3, #446-448	6.00	
		Complete booklet, 3 #448a	18.00	

No. 448a printed in three formats with Nos. 446-448 in different order.

Europa — A103

Designs: No. 449, Royal Visit to Guernsey, discovery of Neptune, 1846. No. 450, Royal Visit to Sark, launch of Sputnik, 1957. No. 451, Maiden voyage of ferry Sarnia, first manned space flight, 1961. No. 452, Independence of Guernsey Post Office, first man on moon, 1969.

1991, Apr. 1   Litho.   *Perf. 13½x14*

449	A103	21p multicolored	.85	.85
450	A103	21p multicolored	.85	.85
451	A103	26p multicolored	1.00	1.00
452	A103	26p multicolored	1.00	1.00
		Nos. 449-452 (4)	3.70	3.70

Landscape Type of 1984

1991   Litho.   *Perf. 15x14½, 14½x15*

453	A63	21p King's Mills, St. Saviours	.85	.85
a.		Booklet pane, 3 each #453, #296, 2 each #287, #288)	3.50	
b.		Booklet pane, 5 each #453, #296)	6.00	
454	A63	26p Town Church, St. Peter Port, vert.	1.00	1.00

Issued: 21p, 26p, 4/1; #453a, 453b, 4/2. #453a, 453b with straight edges around stamps and attached to booklet covers by tabs.

Guernsey Yacht Club, Cent. — A104

1991, July 2   Litho.   *Perf. 14*

459	A104	15p Guernsey Sailing Trust	.60	.60
460	A104	21p Guernsey Regatta	.80	.80
461	A104	26p Channel Islands Challenge	1.00	1.00
462	A104	31p Rolex Swan Regatta	1.25	1.25
463	A104	37p Old Gaffers Assoc.	1.50	1.50
a.		Souvenir sheet of 5, #459-463	5.50	5.50
		Nos. 459-463 (5)	5.15	5.15

"Guernsey" and denomination in white on sheet stamps, yellow on souvenir sheet stamps.

Miniature Sheet

Christmas — A105

Children's Paintings: a, Reindeer by Melanie Sharpe. b, Christmas pudding by James Quinn. c, Snowman by Lisa Marie Guille. d, Snowman by Jessica Ede-Golightly. e, Birds by Sharon Le Page. f, Shepherds, sheep, angels by Anna Coquelin. g, Manger scene by Claudine Lihou. h, Three kings by Jonathan Le Noury. i, Children, angels, Star of Bethlehem by Marcia Mahy. j, Christmas tree, presents by Laurel Garfield. k, Santa Claus by Rebecca Driscoll. l, Snowman by Ian Lowe.

1991, Oct. 15   Litho.   *Perf. 13*

464	A105	Sheet of 12	5.75	5.75
a.-l.		12p any single	.45	.45

Nature Conservation A106

Birds and plants: No. 465: a, Two oyster catchers. b, Three turnstones. c, Two turnstones. d, Curlew, two turnstones. e, Ringed plover, chicks.
No. 466: a, Violet and white flowers. b, Yellow flowers. c, Small yellow flowers. d, Violet, yellow and white flowers. e, Long-stemmed yellow flowers.

1991, Oct. 15   *Perf. 14½*

465		Strip of 5	3.00	3.00
a.-e.	A106	15p any single	.60	.60
466		Strip of 5	4.25	4.25
a.-e.	A106	21p any single	.85	.85

Discovery of America, 500th Anniv. — A107

1992, Feb. 6   Litho.   *Perf. 13½x14*

467	A107	23p Columbus	.90	.90
468	A107	23p Columbus' signatures	.90	.90
469	A107	28p Map of 1st voyage	1.10	1.10
470	A107	28p Santa Maria	1.10	1.10
a.		Souvenir sheet, #467-470	7.00	7.00
b.		No. 470a overprinted in brown in sheet margin	8.00	8.00
		Nos. 467-470 (4)	4.00	4.00

Europa. No. 470b overprint shows emblem of World Columbian Stamp Expo '92. Issue date: No. 470b, May 22.

Queen Elizabeth II's Accession to Throne, 40th Anniv. — A108

Various portraits of Queen Elizabeth II from 1952, 1977, 1986 and 1992.

1992, Feb. 6   Litho.   *Perf. 14*

471	A108	23p multicolored	.90	.90
472	A108	28p multicolored	1.10	1.10
473	A108	33p multicolored	1.25	1.25
474	A108	39p multicolored	1.60	1.60
		Nos. 471-474 (4)	4.85	4.85

Souvenir Sheet

Guernsey Cows — A109

1992, May 22   Litho.   *Perf. 14*

475	A109	75p multicolored	3.00	3.00

Royal Guernsey Agricultural and Horticultural Society, 150th anniv.

Flowers — A110

1992-96   **Perf. 13**

476	A110	1p Stephanotis floribunda	.20	.20
477	A110	2p Potted hydrangea	.20	.20
478	A110	3p Stock	.20	.20
479	A110	4p Anemones	.20	.20
480	A110	5p Gladiolus	.20	.20
481	A110	6p Gypsophila paniculata, asparagus plumosus	.25	.25
482	A110	7p Guernsey lily	.25	.25
483	A110	8p Enchantment lily	.30	.30
484	A110	9p Clematis freckles	.35	.35
485	A110	10p Alstroemeria	.40	.40
486	A110	16p Standard carnation, horiz.	.65	.55
a.		Perf. 14 on 3 sides, inscribed "1993"	.65	.55
b.		Booklet pane of 8 #486a	5.00	
		Complete booklet, 1 #486b	5.00	
c.		Inscribed "1992"	.65	.55
487	A110	20p Spray rose	.80	.75
488	A110	23p Mixed freesia, horiz.	.90	.85
a.		Perf. 14 on 3 sides	.90	.85
b.		Bklt. pane of 5 #486c, 3 #488a	6.50	6.50
		Complete booklet, 1 #488b	6.50	
c.		Booklet pane of 8, #488a	8.00	8.00
		Complete booklet, 1 #488c	8.00	
489	A110	24p Standard rose, horiz.	.95	.80
a.		Perf. 14 on 3 sides	1.00	.80
b.		Booklet pane of 8 #489a	8.00	
		Complete booklet, 1 #489b	8.00	
490	A110	25p Iris ideal	1.00	.80
a.		Perf. 14½ on 3 sides	1.10	.80
b.		As "a," booklet pane of 4	4.50	
		Complete booklet, 1 #490b	4.50	
491	A110	28p Lisianthus, horiz.	1.10	.75
a.		Perf. 14 on 3 sides	1.25	.80
b.		Booklet pane of 4 #491a	5.00	
		Complete booklet, 1 #491b	5.00	
492	A110	30p Spray chrysanthemum, horiz.	1.25	1.10
493	A110	40p Spray carnation	1.60	1.25
494	A110	50p Single freesia, horiz.	2.00	1.50

Size: 39x30mm
Perf. 13¾

495	A110	£1 Bouquet, horiz., inscribed "1992"	4.00	3.00
a.		Souv. sheet of 1 + label, perf. 13, inscribed "1994"	4.50	4.50
b.		Souv. sheet of 1 + label, perf. 13, inscribed "1995"	4.50	4.50
496	A110	£2 Chelsea flower show, horiz.	8.00	8.00

Size: 39x31mm
Perf. 13¼

497	A110	£3 Floral fantasia, horiz.	12.00	10.00
		Nos. 476-497 (22)	36.80	31.90

PHILAKOREA '94 (#495a). Singapore '95 (#495b).

Issued: 3p, 4p, 5p, 10p, 16p, 20p, 23p, 40p, 50p, £1, 5/22/92; 1p, 2p, 6p, 7p, 8p, 9p, 24p, 28p, 30p, £2, #486a, 3/2/93; #486b, 489b, 491b, 3/3/93; #488a, 488b, 5/22/92; 25p, 2/18/94; #490b, 2/18/94; #495a, 8/94; #495b, 9/1/95; £3, 1/24/96.

Perf 14 or 14½ stamps issued only in booklets.

See Nos. 584-585.

Operation Asterix A111

1992, Sept. 18   **Litho.**   **Perf. 13**

498	A111	16p Ship construction	.65	.65
499	A111	23p Loading cargo	.90	.90
500	A111	28p Ship at sea	1.10	1.10
501	A111	33p Ship on fire	1.25	1.25
502	A111	39p Ship sinking	1.50	1.50
a.		Bklt. pane of #498-502 + label	5.50	
		Complete booklet, 4 #502a	22.50	
		Nos. 498-502 (5)	5.40	5.40

No. 502a exists with four different labels: Great Britain, France, Italy, Germany. Booklet contains one of each type.

Historic Trams A112

Designs: 16p, Tram No. 10 decorated for Battle of Flowers. 23p, No. 10 passing Hougue a la Perre. 28p, Tram No. 1 at St. Sampsons. 33p, First steam tram, St. Peter Port, 1879. 39p, Last electric tram, 1934.

1992, Nov. 17   **Litho.**   **Perf. 13½x14**

503	A112	16p multicolored	.65	.65
504	A112	23p multicolored	.90	.90
505	A112	28p multicolored	1.10	1.10
506	A112	33p multicolored	1.25	1.25
507	A112	39p multicolored	1.50	1.50
		Nos. 503-507 (5)	5.40	5.40

Christmas — A113

a, Father dressed as Santa. b, Girl pulling end of cracker. c, Mother. d, Champagne, mince pies. e, Turkey. f, Plum pudding. g, Cake. h, Cookies. i, Wine, blue cheese. j, Nuts. k, Ham. l, Cake roll.

1992, Nov. 17   **Perf. 13½**

508	A113	Sheet of 12	6.25	6.25
a.-l.		13p any single	.50	.50

A114

Rupert Bear and friends, created by Mary Tourtel: No. 509: Rupert Bear, Bingo, and dog. No. 510a, 24p, Bill Badger, Willie Mouse, Reggie Rabbit, and Podgy Pig with snowman. No. 510b, 16p, Airplane above castle tower. No. 510c, 24p, Balloonist leaping away from Gregory on sled. No. 510d, 16p, Professor's servant and Autumn Elf. No. 510e, 16p, Algy Pug. No. 510f, 16p, Baby Badger on sled. No. 510g, 24p, Tiger Lily and Edward Trunk.

1993, Feb. 2   **Litho.**   **Perf. 13½x13**

509	A114	24p multicolored	.95	.95
510	A114	Sheet of 8, #a.-g. & #509	7.00	7.00

No. 510 printed in continuous design. Nos. 510b, 510d-510f are 25x26mm.

Contemporary Art — A115

Europa: No. 511, Tapestry, by Kelly Fletcher. No. 512, The Fish Market, by Sally Reed. No. 513, Dress Shop, King's Road, by

Damon Bell. No. 514, Red Abstract, by Molly Harris.

1993, May 7   **Litho.**   **Perf. 13½x14**
Size: 45x30mm (#512, 513)

511	A115	24p multicolored	.95	.95
512	A115	24p multicolored	.95	.95
513	A115	28p multicolored	1.10	1.10
514	A115	28p multicolored	1.10	1.10
		Nos. 511-514 (4)	4.10	4.10

Siege of Castle Cornet, 1643-51 — A116

16p, Shipboard arrest of Parliamentarian officials. 24p, Parliamentarian warships firing on castle. 28p, Captured officials fleeing from castle. 33p, Cannon firing from castle into St. Peter Port. 39p, Surrender of castle.

1993, May 7   **Perf. 15x14**

515	A116	16p multicolored	.65	.65
516	A116	24p multicolored	.95	.95
517	A116	28p multicolored	1.10	1.10
518	A116	33p multicolored	1.25	1.25
519	A116	39p multicolored	1.50	1.50
a.		Souvenir sheet of 5, #515-519	5.50	5.50
		Nos. 515-519 (5)	5.45	5.45

Thomas de la Rue, Printer, Birth Bicent. — A117

Designs: 16p, Playing card king, queen and jack. 24p, Swift reservoir fountain pens. 28p, Envelope folding machine. 33p, Great Britain type A5. 39p, £1 Mauritius bank note, portrait of de la Rue.

1993, July 27   **Litho.**   **Perf. 13½**

520	A117	16p multicolored	.65	.65
521	A117	24p multicolored	.95	.95
522	A117	28p multicolored	1.10	1.10

Engr.

523	A117	33p rose carmine	1.25	1.25
524	A117	39p green	1.50	1.50
		Nos. 520-524 (5)	5.45	5.45

520a		Booklet pane of 4	3.00
521a		Booklet pane of 4	4.25
522a		Booklet pane of 4	4.75
523a		Booklet pane of 4	5.50
524a		Booklet pane of 4	6.50
		Complete booklet, #520a-524a	24.00

Miniature Sheet

Christmas — A118

Stained glass windows, Chapel of Christ the Healer: a, Sunburst. b, Light from sun. c, Hand of God. d, Doves descending left. e, Christ raising hand. f, Doves descending right. g, Christ Child sitting in temple. h, Christ raising daughter of Jairus from dead. i, "Suffer little children to come unto me." j, Scene from Pilgrim's Progress. k, The Light of the World. l, Archangel of Healing.

1993, Nov. 2   **Litho.**   **Perf. 13x13½**

525	A118	Sheet of 12	6.25	6.25
a.-l.		13p any single	.50	.45

Archaeological Discoveries — A119

Europa: No. 526, Warrior on horseback. No. 527, Burial site, Les Fouaillages. No. 528, Sword, scabbard, spear. No. 529, Cerny-style pots, arrowheads, axe.

1994, Feb. 18   **Litho.**   **Perf. 13½**

526	A119	24p multicolored	.95	.95
a.		Sheet of 10 with added inscription	12.00	12.00
527	A119	24p multicolored	.95	.95
528	A119	30p multicolored	1.25	1.25
529	A119	30p multicolored	1.25	1.25
		Nos. 526-529 (4)	4.40	4.40

No. 526a inscribed in sheet margin with Hong Kong '94 emblem and "PHILATELIC EXHIBITION / 18-21 FEBRUARY 1994" in English and Chinese.

Souvenir Sheet

D-Day, 50th Anniv. — A120

£2, Canadian Wing Spitfires flying over Normandy coastline.

1994, June 6   **Litho.**   **Perf. 14**

530	A120	£2 multicolored	8.00	5.00

Classic Cars A121

Designs: 16p, 1894 Peugeot Type 3. 24p, 1903 Mercedes Simplex. 35p, 1906 Humber 14.4hp. 41p, 1936 Bentley 4¼ L. 60p, 1948 MG TC.

1994, July 19   **Litho.**   **Perf. 15x14**

531	A121	16p multicolored	.65	.65
532	A121	24p multicolored	.95	.95
533	A121	35p multicolored	1.40	1.40
534	A121	41p multicolored	1.60	1.60
535	A121	60p multicolored	2.40	2.40
		Nos. 531-535 (5)	7.00	7.00

531a		Booklet pane of 4	3.00
532a		Booklet pane of 4	4.25
533a		Booklet pane of 4	6.00
534a		Booklet pane of 4	6.50
535a		Booklet pane or 4	9.75
		Complete booklet, #531a-535a	29.50

Guernsey Post Office, 25th Anniv. A122

Designs: 16p, Trident ferry. 24p, Handley Page Super Dart Herald of Channel Express. 35p, Aurigny Air Services' JOEY. 41p, Bon Marin de Serk ferry. 60p, Map of Guernsey, Herm, Alderney, Sark.

1994, Oct. 1   **Litho.**   **Perf. 14**

536	A122	16p multicolored	.65	.65
537	A122	24p multicolored	.95	.95
538	A122	35p multicolored	1.40	1.40
539	A122	41p multicolored	1.60	1.60

540	A122 60p multicolored	2.40	2.40
a.	Souvenir sheet, #536-540	7.50	7.50
	Nos. 536-540 (5)	7.00	7.00

See Jersey Nos. 685-689a.

Miniature Sheets

Christmas — A123

Antique toys — #541: a, Doll house. b, Doll. c, Small teddy bear in carriage. d, Cards, post boxes with candy. e, Top. f, Picture puzzle blocks.
#542: a, Rocking horse. b, Large teddy bear. c, Tricycle. d, Wooden pull duck. e, Tin plate locomotive. f, Ludo game.

1994, Oct. 1		**Perf. 13**	
541	A123 Sheet of 6	3.25	3.25
a.-f.	13p any single	.50	.50
542	A123 Sheet of 6	5.75	5.75
a.-f.	24p any single	.90	.90

Greetings — A124

Faces formed by: No. 543, Shrimp, oyster, lobster, fish. No. 544, Sand buckets, shovel, sand. No. 545, Flowers. No. 546, Lettuce, tomatoes, mushroom, squash. No. 547, Seaweed, shells. No. 548, Anchor, life preservers. No. 549, Wine, cork, knife, fork. No. 550, Butterflies, caterpillars.

1995, Feb. 2	**Litho.**	**Perf. 14**	
543	A124 24p multicolored	.95	.95
544	A124 24p multicolored	.95	.95
545	A124 24p multicolored	.95	.95
546	A124 24p multicolored	.95	.95
547	A124 24p multicolored	.95	.95
548	A124 24p multicolored	.95	.95
549	A124 24p multicolored	.95	.95
550	A124 24p multicolored	.95	.95
a.	Miniature sheet of 8, #543-550	8.00	7.25
	Complete booklet, #550a	8.00	
	Nos. 543-550 (8)	7.60	7.60

Doves — A125

Europa: 25p, Doves standing. 30p, Doves in flight. Illustration reduced.

1995, May 9	**Litho.**	**Perf. 14**	
551	A125 25p green	1.00	1.00
552	A125 30p blue	1.25	1.25

Nos. 551-552 contain a three-dimensional image hidden in the patterns composed of doves.

Liberation of Guernsey, 50th Anniv. — A126

Designs: 16p, Churchill making broadcast, crowd. 24p, St. Peter Port harbor. 35p, Military band. 41p, Red Cross ship Vega. 60p, Soldier kissing civilian woman.

1995, May 9		**Perf. 13½x14**	
553	A126 16p multicolored	.65	.65
554	A126 24p multicolored	.95	.95
555	A126 35p multicolored	1.40	1.40
556	A126 41p multicolored	1.60	1.60
557	A126 60p multicolored	2.40	2.40
a.	Souvenir sheet of 5, #553-557	7.50	7.50
	Nos. 553-557 (5)	7.00	7.00

Visit by Prince of Wales A127

1995, May 9		**Perf. 14**	
558	A127 £1.50 multicolored	6.00	6.00

UN, 50th Anniv. — A128

Portion of UN emblem, denomination: a, UL. b, UR. c, LL. d, LR.

Litho. & Embossed

1995, Oct. 24		**Perf. 14x13½**	
559	A128 Block of 4	8.00	8.00
a.-d.	50p any single	2.00	2.00

Christmas — A129

Designs, with denomination at:
Shops in the city, children playing in snow — No. 560: a, LL. b, LR.
Homes in winter, children playing in snow — #561: a, LL. b, LR.
Children playing instruments, singing — #562: a, LL. b, LR.
Children of many nations — #563: a, LL. b, LR.

1995, Nov. 16	**Litho.**	**Perf. 13½x13**	
560	A129 Pair	1.00	1.00
a.-b.	13p any single	.50	.50
561	A129 Pair	1.00	1.00
a.-b.	13p +1p, any single	.50	.50
562	A129 Pair	1.90	1.90
a.-b.	24p any single	.95	.95
563	A129 Pair	1.90	1.90
a.-b.	24p +2p, any single	.95	.95
	Nos. 560-563 (4)	5.80	5.80

Nos. 560-563 are each continuous designs. UNICEF, 50th anniv.

Women of Achievement — A130

Europa: 25p, Princess Anne, children of different nations. 30p, Queen Elizabeth II, people of different nations.

1996, Apr. 21	**Litho.**	**Perf. 14**	
564	A130 25p multicolored	1.00	1.00
565	A130 30p multicolored	1.25	1.25

Queen Elizabeth II, 70th birthday (#565).
See Isle of Man Nos. 679-680.

1996 European Soccer Championships — A131

Various flags from participating countries and: No. 566a, USSR player kicking ball. No. 566b, English players in white shirts, 1968. No. 567a, Italian player in blue shirt with ball. No. 567b, Belgium player in red, Italian players, 1972. No. 568a, Irish player in green kicking. No. 568b, Dutch player in blue, 1988. No. 569a, German player in white with ball. No. 569b, Danish player in red, 1992.

1996, Apr. 25		**Perf. 14x13½**	
566	A131 Pair	1.25	1.25
a.-b.	16p any single	.60	.60
567	A131 Pair	1.90	1.90
a.-b.	24p any single	.95	.95
568	A131 Pair	3.00	3.00
a.-b.	35p any single	1.40	1.40
569	A131 Pair	3.25	3.25
a.-b.	41p any single	1.60	1.60
	Nos. 566-569 (4)	9.40	9.40

Souvenir Sheet

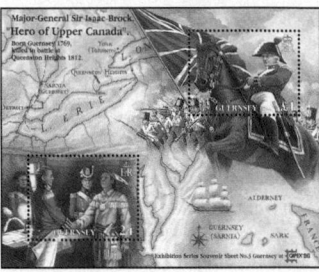

Sir Isaac Brock (1769-1812), British Commander in Upper Canada — A132

Designs: a, 24p, Brock shaking hands with Tecumseh. b, £1, Brock on horse.

1996, June 8	**Litho.**	**Perf. 14x13½**	
570	A132 Sheet of 2, #a.-b.	5.00	5.00

CAPEX '96.

Modern Olympic Games, Cent. — A133

The original pentathlon.

1996, July 19	**Litho.**	**Perf. 14**	
571	A133 16p Running	.65	.65
572	A133 24p Javelin	.95	.95
573	A133 41p Discus	1.60	1.60
574	A133 55p Wrestling	2.25	2.25
575	A133 60p Jumping	2.40	2.40
a.	Souvenir sheet, #571-575	8.00	8.00
	Nos. 571-575 (5)	7.85	7.85

No. 574 is 53x31mm. Olymphilex'96 (#574).

Motion Pictures, Cent. A134

Classic Movie Detectives: 16p, Humphrey Bogart as Philip Marlowe. 24p, Peter Sellers as Inspector Clouseau. 35p, Basil Rathbone as Sherlock Holmes. 41p, Margaret Rutherford as Miss Marple. 60p, Warner Oland as Charlie Chan.

1996, Nov. 6	**Litho.**	**Perf. 15x14**	
576	A134 16p multicolored	.65	.65
577	A134 24p multicolored	.95	.95
578	A134 35p multicolored	1.40	1.40

579	A134 41p multicolored	1.60	1.60
580	A134 60p multicolored	2.40	2.40
	Nos. 576-580 (5)	7.00	7.00

576a	Booklet pane of 3	2.00	
577a	Booklet pane of 3	3.00	
578a	Booklet pane of 3	4.25	
579a	Booklet pane of 3	5.00	
580a	Booklet pane of 3	7.25	
580b	Bklt. pane of 5, #576-580	7.50	
	Complete booklet, #576a-580b	30.00	

Christmas A135

Scenes depicting the Christmas story: 24p, Madonna and Child. 25p, Nativity.
No. 583, vert: a, Annunciation by Angel Gabriel. b, Mary, Joseph on way to Bethlehem. c, Inn keeper turning them away. d, Angel appearing before shepherds. e, Holy Family in stable. f, Adoration of the shepherds. g, Magi following star. h, Magi presenting gifts. i, Prophet's warning to Mary, Joseph. j, Madonna and Child. k, Angel appearing in Joseph's dream. l, Flight into Egypt.

1996, Nov. 6		**Perf. 13**	
581	A135 24p multicolored	.95	.95
582	A135 25p multicolored	1.00	1.00

Miniature Sheet

583	Sheet of 12	6.25	6.25
a.-l.	A135 13p Any single	.50	.50

Flower Type of 1992

1997	**Litho.**	**Perf. 13**	
584	A110 18p Standard rose	.70	.60
a.	Perf. 14 on 3 Sides	.75	.65
b.	As "a," booklet pane of 8	7.50	
	Complete booklet, #584b	7.50	
585	A110 26p Freesia pink glow, horiz.	1.00	.80
a.	Perf. 14 on 3 Sides	1.10	.80
b.	As "a," booklet pane of 4	5.25	
	Complete booklet, #585b	5.25	

Butterflies and Moths A136

Designs: 18p, Holly blue. 25p, Hummingbird hawk-moth. 26p, Emperor moth. 37p, Brimstone. £1, Painted lady.

1997, Feb. 12	**Litho.**	**Perf. 14**	
586	A136 18p multicolored	1.10	1.10
587	A136 25p multicolored	1.40	1.40
588	A136 26p multicolored	1.60	1.60
589	A136 37p multicolored	2.25	2.25
	Nos. 586-589 (4)	6.35	6.35

Souvenir Sheet

Perf. 13½

590	A136 £1 multicolored	4.00	4.00

World Wildlife Fund (#586-589), Hong Kong '97 (#590).

Stories and Legends — A137

The Toilers of the Sea, by Victor Hugo: 26p, Man fighting sea monster, face in sea, ship. 31p, Ship, man seated on rock visualizing woman.

1997, Apr. 24	**Litho.**	**Perf. 13½**	
591	A137 26p multicolored	1.00	1.00
592	A137 31p multicolored	1.25	1.25

Nos. 591-592 each issued in sheets of 10. Europa.

Island
Scenes — A138

18p, Shell Beach, Herm. 25p, La Seigneurie, Sark, vert. 26p, Castle Comet, Guernsey.

Die Cut Perf. 9½x9, 9x9½
1997, Apr. 24
Self-Adhesive

593	A138	18p multicolored	.70	.70
a.		Booklet pane of 8	6.50	
		Complete booklet, #593a	6.50	
594	A138	25p multicolored	1.00	1.00
a.		Booklet pane of 8	9.00	
		Complete booklet, #594a	9.00	
595	A138	26p multicolored	1.00	1.00
a.		Booklet pane of 4	4.50	
		Complete booklet, #595a	4.50	
		Nos. 593-595 (3)	2.70	2.70

See Nos. 625-628.

Souvenir Sheet

PACIFIC 97 — A139

a, 30p, St. Peter Port, 1868. b, £1, Sailing ships.

1997, May 29   Litho.   Perf. 14
596	A139	Sheet of 2, #a.-b.	5.25	5.25

Communications — A140

1997, Aug. 21   Litho.   Perf. 13½x13
597	A140	18p Radio	.70	.70
598	A140	25p Television	1.00	1.00
599	A140	26p Telephone	1.00	1.00
600	A140	37p Newspaper	1.50	1.50
601	A140	43p Post system	1.60	1.60
602	A140	63p Computer network	2.50	2.50
		Nos. 597-602 (6)	8.30	8.30

Queen Elizabeth II and Prince Philip, 50th Wedding Anniv. — A141

Designs: 18p, At St. George's Hall, Guernsey, 1957. 25p, Queen being saluted by guardsman, 1953. 26p, Queen, family on horseback, 1957. 37p, Prince, Queen in casual attire, 1972. 43p, Queen saluting, at Trooping of the Color, 1987. 63p, Portrait, 1997.

1997, Nov. 20   Litho.   Perf. 14
603	A141	18p multicolored	.70	.70
604	A141	25p multicolored	1.00	1.00
a.		Bklt. pane, 3 each #603-604	5.75	
605	A141	26p multicolored	1.00	1.00
606	A141	37p multicolored	1.50	1.50
a.		Bklt. pane, 3 each #605-606	8.50	
607	A141	43p multicolored	1.60	1.60
608	A141	63p multicolored	2.50	2.50
a.		Bklt. pane, 3 each #607-608	13.50	
b.		Booklet pane #603-608	9.00	
		Complete booklet, #604a, 606a, 608a, 608b	37.50	
		Nos. 603-608 (6)	8.30	8.30

A142

Teddy Bears celebrating Christmas: 15p, Baking in kitchen. 25p, Beside Christmas tree. 26p, Seated in chair reading story. 37p, As Santa Claus. 43p, With presents. 63p, Seated at Christmas dinner.

1997, Nov. 6
609	A142	15p multicolored	.60	.60
610	A142	25p multicolored	1.00	1.00
611	A142	26p multicolored	1.00	1.00
612	A142	37p multicolored	1.50	1.50
613	A142	43p multicolored	1.60	1.60
614	A142	63p multicolored	2.50	2.50
a.		Souvenir sheet #609-614	8.25	7.50
		Nos. 609-614 (6)	8.20	8.20

A143

1998, Feb. 10   Litho.   Perf. 14½

Millennium Tapestries: Embroidered panels showing images of Guernsey during last ten centuries, Guernsey-French inscriptions.

615	A143	25p 11th century	1.00	1.00
616	A143	25p 12th century	1.00	1.00
617	A143	25p 13th century	1.00	1.00
618	A143	25p 14th century	1.00	1.00
a.		Bklt. pane, 2 each #615-616, 1 each #617-618	6.50	
619	A143	25p 15th century	1.00	1.00
620	A143	25p 16th century	1.00	1.00
a.		Bklt. pane, 2 each #617-618, 1 each #619-620	6.50	
621	A143	25p 17th century	1.00	1.00
622	A143	25p 18th century	1.00	1.00
a.		Bklt. pane, 2 each #619-620, 1 each #621-622	6.50	
623	A143	25p 19th century	1.00	1.00
624	A143	25p 20th century	1.00	1.00
a.		Bklt. pane, 2 each #621-622, 1 each #623-624	6.50	
b.		Bklt. pane, 2 each #623-624, 1 each #615-616	6.50	
		Complete booklet, #618a, 620a, 622a, 624a-624b	35.00	
c.		Strip of 10, #615-624	10.00	10.00

Island Scenes Type of 1997
Die Cut Perf. 9½x9
1998, Mar. 25   Litho.
Self-Adhesive

625	A138	(20p) Fort Grey	.80	.80
626	A138	(20p) Grand Havre	.80	.80
a.		Booklet pane, 4 each #625-626	7.50	
		Complete booklet, #626a	7.50	
627	A138	(25p) Little Chapel	1.00	1.00
628	A138	(25p) Guernsey cow	1.00	1.00
a.		Booklet pane, 4 each #627-628	8.75	
		Complete booklet, #628a	8.75	
		Nos. 625-628 (4)	3.60	3.60

Nos. 625-626 are inscribed "Bailwick Minimum Postage Paid" and were valued at 20p on day of issue. Nos. 627-628 are inscribed "UK Minimum Postage Paid" and were valued at 25p on day of issue.

Aircraft
A144

Designs: 20p, Fairey IIIC, Balloon, Sopwith Camel, Avro 504. 25p, Fairey Swordfish, Tiger Moth, Supermarine Walrus, Gloster Gladiator. 30p, Hawker Hurricane, Supermarine Spitfire, Vickers Wellington, Short Sunderland, Westland Lysander, Bristol Blenheim. 37p, De Havilland Mosquito, Avro Lancaster, Auster III, Gloster Meteor, Horsa glider. 43p, Canberra, Hawker Sea Fury, Bristol Sycamore, Hawker Hunter, Handley Page Victor, BAe Lightning. 63p, Pavania Tornado GRI, BAe Hawk, BAe Sea Harrier, Westland Lynx, Hawker Siddeley Nimrod.

1998, May 7   Perf. 13½x13
629	A144	20p multicolored	.80	.80
630	A144	25p multicolored	1.00	1.00
631	A144	30p multicolored	1.25	1.25
632	A144	37p multicolored	1.50	1.50
633	A144	43p multicolored	1.60	1.60
634	A144	63p multicolored	2.50	2.50
		Nos. 629-634 (6)	8.65	8.65

Royal Air Force, 80th anniv.

Souvenir Sheet

Cambridge Rules for Soccer, 150th Anniv. — A145

a, 30p, Jules Rimet, first president of FIFA. b, £1.75, Bobby Moore, Queen Elizabeth II.

1998, May 7   Perf. 13½x14
635	A145	Sheet of 2, #a.-b.	8.25	8.25

Natl. Holidays and Festivals — A146

Europa: 20p, People in traditional costumes watching animals, West Show. 25p, Band in parade, Battle of Flowers, North Show. 30p, Prince Charles, Liberation Monument under Guernsey flag, tank, Liberation Day. 37p, Goat, equestrian event, flowers, South Show.

1998, Aug. 11   Litho.   Perf. 13½
636	A146	20p multicolored	.80	.80
637	A146	25p multicolored	1.00	1.00
638	A146	30p multicolored	1.25	1.25
639	A146	37p multicolored	1.50	1.50
		Nos. 636-639 (4)	4.55	4.55

A147

Royal Yacht Britannia — A148

Designs: 1p, Small fishing boat. 2p, St. John Ambulance Inshore Rescue inflatable dinghy. 3p, Pilot boat. 4p, St. John Ambulance boat, Flying Christine III. 5p, Crab boat. 6p, Ferry. 7p, Workboat, Sarnia. 8p, Fisheries Protecton vessel, Leopardess. 9p, Large fishing boat. 10p, Powerboat. 20p, Dart 18 racing catamaran. 30p, Bermudan rigged sloop. 40p, Motor cruiser. 50p, Ocean-going yacht. 75p, Motor cruiser anchored. £1, Cruise ship, Queen Elizabeth II. £3, Cruise ship Oriana

1998-2000   Litho.   Perf. 14
640	A147	1p multicolored	.20	.20
641	A147	2p multicolored	.20	.20
642	A147	3p multicolored	.20	.20
643	A147	4p multicolored	.20	.20
644	A147	5p multicolored	.20	.20
645	A147	6p multicolored	.25	.25
646	A147	7p multicolored	.25	.25
647	A147	8p multicolored	.30	.30
648	A147	9p multicolored	.35	.35

Size: 27x27mm
Perf. 14½x14¼
649	A147	10p multicolored	.40	.40
650	A147	20p multicolored	.80	.80
651	A147	30p multicolored	1.25	1.25
652	A147	40p multicolored	1.60	1.60
654	A147	50p multicolored	2.00	2.00
656	A147	75p multicolored	3.00	3.00

Size: 34x26mm
Litho. & Embossed
Perf. 14¼x14½
658	A148	£1 multicolored	4.00	4.00
660	A148	£3 multicolored	12.00	12.00

Size: 48x36mm
Perf. 14¾x14½
663	A148	£5 gold & multi	20.00	20.00
		Nos. 640-663 (18)	47.20	47.20

Issued: £5, 8/11; 1p, 2p, 3p, 4p, 5p, 6p, 7p, 8p, 10p, 40p, 50p, 75p, £1, 7/27/99; 20p, 30p, £3, 8/4/00.
See also No. 867.

Introduction of Christmas Tree to Britain, 150th Anniv. — A149

Christmas tree and toys from past 150 years: 17p, Teletubby "Po," video game machine, 1998. 25p, Doll, double decker bus, c. 1968. 30p, Stuffed panda, toy army tank, c. 1938. 37p, Model of Bluebird race car, doll, c. 1928. 43p, Teddy bear, train pull toy, c. 1908. 63p, Spinning top, wooden doll, c. 1850.

1998, Nov. 10   Litho.   Perf. 13½
664	A149	17p multicolored	.65	.65
665	A149	25p multicolored	1.00	1.00
666	A149	30p multicolored	1.25	1.25
667	A149	37p multicolored	1.50	1.50
668	A149	43p multicolored	1.60	1.60
669	A149	63p multicolored	2.50	2.50
a.		Souvenir sheet #664-669	8.50	8.50
		Nos. 664-669 (6)	8.50	8.50

Queen Elizabeth, the Queen Mother — A150

Three strings of pearls and photographs: No. 670, As a child, 1907. No. 671, At wedding, 1923. No. 672, Holding newly-born Princess Elizabeth, 1926. No. 673, Wearing crown at coronation of King George VI, 1937. No. 674, In green hat, 1940. No. 675, Holding fishing pole, 1966. No. 676, Wearing tiara, 1963. No. 677, Holding flowers, 1992. No. 678, Presenting trophy, 1989. No. 679, In blue hat, 1990.

1999, Feb. 4   Litho.   Perf. 13
Color of LL Corner
670	A150	25p pink	1.00	1.00
671	A150	25p blue	1.00	1.00
672	A150	25p red brown	1.00	1.00
673	A150	25p purple	1.00	1.00
a.		Bklt. pane, 2 each #670-671, 1 each #672-673	6.50	
674	A150	25p green	1.00	1.00
675	A150	25p green	1.00	1.00
a.		Bklt. pane, 2 each #672-673, 1 each #673-674	6.50	
676	A150	25p purple	1.00	1.00
677	A150	25p red brown	1.00	1.00
678	A150	25p blue	1.00	1.00
a.		Bklt. pane, 2 each #674-675, 1 each #676-677	6.50	
679	A150	25p pink	1.00	1.00
a.		Bklt. pane, 2 each #676-677, 1 each #678-679	6.50	
b.		Bklt. pane, 2 each #678-679, 1 each #670-671	6.50	
		Complete booklet, #673a, 675a, 678a, 679a, 679b	35.00	
c.		Strip of 10, #670-679	10.00	10.00

Herm Island — A151

Local Carriage Labels and: 20p, Burnet roses, Shell Beach. 25p, Puffins, Belvoir Bay. 30p, Small Heath butterfly. 38p, Various shells, Shell Beach.

1999, Apr. 27		**Litho.**	***Perf. 13½x13***	
680	A151	20p multicolored	.80	.80
681	A151	25p multicolored	1.00	1.00
682	A151	30p multicolored	1.25	1.25
683	A151	38p multicolored	1.50	1.50
		Nos. 680-683 (4)	4.55	4.55

Europa.

Royal Lifeboat Assoc., 175th Anniv. A152

20p, Spirit of Guernsey, 1995. 25p, Sir William Arnold, 1973. 30p, Euphrosyne Kendal, 1954. 38p, Queen Victoria, 1929. 44p, Arthur Lionel, 1912. 64p, Vincent Kirk Ella, 1888.

1999, Apr. 27				
684	A152	20p multicolored	.80	.80
685	A152	25p multicolored	1.00	1.00
686	A152	30p multicolored	1.25	1.25
687	A152	38p multicolored	1.50	1.50
688	A152	44p multicolored	1.75	1.75
689	A152	64p multicolored	2.50	2.50
		Nos. 684-689 (6)	8.80	8.80

Souvenir Sheet

Wedding of Prince Edward and Sophie Rhys-Jones — A153

Illustration reduced.

1999, June 19		**Litho.**	***Perf. 13½***	
690	A153	£1 multicolored	4.00	4.00

Royal Military Academy, Sandhurst, Bicent. — A154

20p, Major General Le Marchant, founder, 1799. 25p, Duke of York, sponsor, 1802. 30p, Field Marshal Earl Haig, 1884-85. 38p, Field Marshal Montgomery, 1907-08. 44p, Major David Niven, actor, 1928-30. 64p, Sir Winston Churchill, 1893-95.

1999, July 27		**Litho.**	***Perf. 14***	
691	A154	20p multicolored	.80	.80
692	A154	25p multicolored	1.00	1.00
693	A154	30p multicolored	1.25	1.25
694	A154	38p multicolored	1.50	1.50
695	A154	44p multicolored	1.75	1.75
696	A154	64p multicolored	2.50	2.50
		Nos. 691-696 (6)	8.80	8.80

Christmas A155

Creche figures around manger: 17p, Magus, shepherd, Mary, Joseph, donkey. 25p, Mary. 30p, Joseph, Mary. 38p, Donkey, Mary, cow. 44p, Mary, two shepherds. 64p, Three Magi.

1999, Oct. 19		**Litho.**	***Perf. 13¾x14¼***	
697	A155	17p multicolored	.65	.65
698	A155	25p multicolored	1.00	1.00
699	A155	30p multicolored	1.25	1.25
700	A155	38p multicolored	1.50	1.50
701	A155	44p multicolored	1.75	1.75
702	A155	64p multicolored	2.50	2.50
a.		Souvenir sheet, #697-702	11.00	11.00
		Nos. 697-702 (6)	8.65	8.65

Millennium A156

Children's drawings by: 20p, Fallon Ephgrave. 25p, Abigail Downing. 30p, Laura Martin. 38p, Sarah Haddow. 44p, Sophie Medland. 64p, Danielle McIver.

2000, Jan. 1		**Litho.**	***Perf. 14¼x14½***	
703	A156	20p multi	.80	.80
704	A156	25p multi	1.00	1.00
705	A156	30p multi	1.25	1.25
706	A156	38p multi	1.50	1.50
707	A156	44p multi	1.75	1.75
708	A156	64p multi	2.50	2.50
		Nos. 703-708 (6)	8.80	8.80

Nos. 703-708 depict the winning designs in the Future Children's Stamp Design Contest.

Europa, 2000
Common Design Type and

A157

Designs: 21p, Kite. 26p, Yacht sails. 65p, Rainbow and doves.

2000, May 9		**Litho.**	***Perf. 13¼***	
709	A157	21p multi	.85	.85
710	A157	26p multi	1.00	1.00
711	CD17	36p multi	1.40	1.40
712	A157	65p multi	2.50	2.50
		Nos. 709-712 (4)	5.75	5.75

Battle of Britain, 60th Anniv. A158

Designs: 21p, Bristol Blenheim. 26p, Hawker Hurricane. 36p, Boulton Paul Defiant II. 40p, Gloster Gladiator. 45p, Bristol Beaufighter IF. 65p, Supermarine Spitfire IIc.

2000, April 28		**Litho.**	***Perf. 13¼x13***	
713	A158	21p multi	.85	.85
714	A158	26p multi	1.00	1.00
715	A158	36p multi	1.40	1.40
716	A158	40p multi	1.60	1.60
717	A158	45p multi	1.75	1.75
a.		Booklet pane, #713-715, 717	5.75	
b.		Booklet pane, #713, 715-717	6.25	
c.		Booklet pane, #714-717	6.25	
718	A158	65p multi	2.50	2.50
a.		Booklet pane of 2	5.75	
b.		Bklt. pane, #713-714, 716, 718	6.50	
		Complete booklet, #717a-717c, 718a-718b	32.50	
		Nos. 713-718 (6)	9.10	9.10

The Stamp Show 2000, London (Nos. 717a-717c, 718a-718b).

Flowers in Candie Gardens — A159

No. 719: a, Long styled iris. b, Watsonia. c, Arum lily. d, Hoop petticoat daffodil. e, Triteleia laxa. f, Peacock flower. g, African blue lily. h, Corn lily. i, Sea lily. j, Guernsey lily.

2000, Aug. 4		**Litho.**	***Perf. 13½x13***	
719		Horiz. strip of 10	10.50	10.50
a.-j.		A159 26p Any single	1.00	1.00

Christmas A160

Snow-covered churches: 18p, Town Church, St. Peter's Port. 26p, St. Sampson's Church. 36p, Vale Church. 40p, St. Pierre du Bois Church. 45p, St. Martin's Church. 65p, St. John's Church, St. Peter's Port.

2000, Oct. 19		**Litho.**	***Perf. 14¼x13¾***	
720	A160	18p multi	.70	.70
721	A160	26p multi	1.00	1.00
722	A160	36p multi	1.40	1.40
723	A160	40p multi	1.60	1.60
724	A160	45p multi	1.75	1.75
725	A160	65p multi	2.50	2.50
a.		Souvenir sheet, #720-725	9.25	9.25
		Nos. 720-725 (6)	8.95	8.95

Queen Victoria (1819-1901) — A161

Various portraits and: 21p, Statue of Victoria. 26p, Document. 36p, Statues of Victoria and Prince Albert. 40p, Commemoration stone, St. Peter's Port. 45p, Statue of Prince Albert. 65p, Victoria Tower.

2001, Jan. 22			***Perf. 14¾***	
726	A161	21p multi	.85	.85
727	A161	26p multi	1.00	1.00
728	A161	36p multi	1.40	1.40
729	A161	40p multi	1.60	1.60
730	A161	45p multi	1.75	1.75
731	A161	65p multi	2.50	2.50
a.		Souvenir sheet, #726-731	9.25	9.25
		Nos. 726-731 (6)	9.10	9.10

Hong Kong 2001 Stamp Exhibition (No. 731a).

Birds A162

2001, Feb. 1		**Litho.**	***Perf. 14x14¾***	
732	A162	21p Kingfisher	.85	.85
733	A162	26p Garganey	1.00	1.00
734	A162	36p Little egret	1.40	1.40
735	A162	65p Little ringed plover	2.50	2.50
		Nos. 732-735 (4)	5.75	5.75

Europa (26p, 36p).

Guernsey Dog Club, Cent. — A163

Designs: 22p, Cavalier King Charles spaniel. 27p, Miniature schnauzer. 36p, German shepherd. 40p, Cocker spaniel. 45p, West Highland terrier. 65p, Dachshund.

2001, Apr. 26		**Litho.**	***Perf. 13x13¼***	
736	A163	22p multi	.85	.85
737	A163	27p multi	1.00	1.00
738	A163	36p multi	1.40	1.40
739	A163	40p multi	1.60	1.60
740	A163	45p multi	1.75	1.75
741	A163	65p multi	2.50	2.50
		Nos. 736-741 (6)	9.10	9.10

Island Views — A164

Serpentine Die Cut 14¼x14

2001, Apr. 26   **Litho.**

No. 742: a, La Corbière sunset. b, Rue des Hougues. c, St. Saviour's Reservoir. d, Shell Beach, Herm. e, Telegraph Bay, Alderney. f, Alderney Railway. g, Vazon Bay. h, La Coupée, Sark. i, Les Hanois. j, Albecq.

Self-Adhesive

742	Sheet of 10	9.50	
a.-e.	A164 GY Any single	.85	.85
f.-j.	A164 UK Any single	1.00	1.00
k.	Booklet, 2 each #742a-742e	9.50	
l.	Booklet, 2 each #742f-742j	11.00	
m.-q.	As "a-e," photo., any single	.85	.85
r.	Strip, #742m-742q	4.25	
s.-w.	As "f-j," photo., any single	1.00	1.00
x.	Strip, #742s-742w	5.00	

The photogravure stamps have a fuzzier appearance overall than the lithographed stamps. This is most noticeable in the crown where under magnification the bumps on the crown's outline are clearly distinct and well-defined as semicircles on the lithographed stamps, while ragged and ill-defined with a pointy appearance, on the photogravure stamps.

Nos. 742a-742e each sold for 22p, and Nos. 742f-742j each sold for 27p on day of issue.

No. 742 itself was available only from the Philatelic Bureau.

Type of 1969 and

Change of Guernsey Post Office to Guernsey Post Ltd., Oct. 1, 2001 — A165

Designs: 22p, Vision (water droplet on leaf). 27p, Understanding (hummingbird and flower). 36p, Individuality (butterfly's wing). 40p, Strength (nautilus shell cross-section). 45p, Community (honeycomb). 65p, Maturity (Dandelion gone to seed). £1, Like No. 23.

2001, Aug. 1		**Litho.**	***Perf. 13¼x13***	
743	A165	22p multi	.85	.85
a.		Booklet pane of 3	3.00	
744	A165	27p multi	1.00	1.00
a.		Booklet pane of 3	3.25	
745	A165	36p multi	1.40	1.40
a.		Booklet pane of 3	4.50	
746	A165	40p multi	1.60	1.60
a.		Booklet pane of 3	5.50	
747	A165	45p multi	1.75	1.75
a.		Booklet pane of 3	6.00	
748	A165	65p multi	2.50	2.50
a.		Booklet pane of 3	8.25	
		Perf. 14x14¼		
749	A4	£1 Booklet pane of 1	8.50	8.50
		Booklet, #743a, 744a, 745a, 746a, 747a, 748a, 749	40.00	
		Nos. 743-749 (7)	17.60	17.60

Panels on the top and bottom of No. 749 are dark blue and clouds in silver margin are distinct. Never-bound examples of No. 749 with Prussian blue panels and less distinct clouds in the silver margin were given to standing order subscribers at no charge.

Christmas
A166

Decorations: 19p, Tree of Joy, St. Peter Port. 27p, Cross, Les Cotils Christian Center. 36p, Les Ruettes Cottage, St. Saviour's. 40p, 17th cent. farmhouse. 45p, Sark Post Office. 65p, High Street, St. Peter Port.

2001, Oct. 16   Perf. 14¼x14½

750	A166 19p multi	.75	.75
751	A166 27p multi	1.00	1.00
752	A166 36p multi	1.40	1.40
753	A166 40p multi	1.60	1.60
754	A166 45p multi	1.75	1.75
755	A166 65p multi	2.50	2.50
a.	Souvenir sheet, #750-755	9.00	9.00
	Nos. 750-755 (6)	9.00	9.00

Hafnia 01 Philatelic Exhibition, Copenhagen (#755a).

Circus — A167

Designs: 22p, Juggler. 27p, Clowns. 36p, Trapeze artists. 40p, Knife thrower. 45p, Acrobat. 65p, High-wire cyclist.

2002, Feb. 6   Litho.   Perf. 14¾x14½

756	A167 22p multi	.85	.85
757	A167 27p multi	1.00	1.00
758	A167 36p multi	1.40	1.40
759	A167 40p multi	1.60	1.60
760	A167 45p multi	1.75	1.75
761	A167 65p multi	2.50	2.50
	Nos. 756-761 (6)	9.10	9.10

Europa (27p, 36p).

Victor Hugo (1802-85), Writer — A168

Designs: 22p, Hugo and St. Peter Port. 27p, Cosette from Les Misérables. 36p, Valjean from Les Misérables. 40p, Javert from Les Misérables. 45p, Cosette and Marius from Les Misérables. 65p, Les Misérables, score from play based on book.

2002, Feb. 6   Perf. 13¼x13

762	A168 22p multi	.85	.85
763	A168 27p multi	1.00	1.00
764	A168 36p multi	1.40	1.40
765	A168 40p multi	1.60	1.60
766	A168 45p multi	1.75	1.75
767	A168 65p multi	2.50	2.50
a.	Souvenir sheet of 6, #762-767	9.25	9.25
	Nos. 762-767 (6)	9.10	9.10

Souvenir Sheet

Pillar Boxes, 150th Anniv. — A169

2002, Apr. 30   Perf. 14½x14¼

768	A169 £1.75 multi	5.25	5.25

Reign of Queen Elizabeth II, 50th Anniv. — A170

Various views of Queen.

2002, Apr. 30   Perf. 13½

769	A170 22p multi	.85	.85
770	A170 27p multi	1.00	1.00
771	A170 36p multi	1.40	1.40
772	A170 40p multi	1.60	1.60
773	A170 45p multi	1.75	1.75
a.	Booklet pane, #770-773	6.00	
774	A170 65p multi	2.50	2.50
a.	Booklet pane, #769, 772-774	6.50	
b.	Booklet pane, #769-771, 774	5.75	
c.	Booklet pane, #769-774	9.00	
	Nos. 769-774 (6)	9.10	9.10

For complete booklet, see Alderney No. 184a.

Vacations in Sark — A171

No. 775: a, Family on dock, boat near dock. b, Family disembarking tractor-pulled transport. c, Family at campground. d, Family with bicycles at La Coupée. e, Swimming at Venus Pool. f, Family at La Seigneurie Gardens. g, Family at village pillar box. h, Family in horse-drawn cart. i, Family dining outdoors. j, Family at beach.

2002, July 30   Perf. 13¼

775	Block of 10	10.00	10.00
a.-j.	A171 27p Any single	1.00	1.00

Awarding of Victoria Cross to Major Herbert Wallace Le Patourel, 60th Anniv.
A172

Designs: 22p, Parade of Elizabeth College Combined Cadet Corps, 1934. 27p, In battle, Tunisia, 1942. 36p, As repatriated prisoner of war, 1943. 40p, Presentation of Victoria Cross ribbon, 1943. 45p, Return to Guernsey, 1948. 65p, Carrying King's Colors, 1968.

2002, July 30   Perf. 13¼x13

777	A172 22p multi	.85	.85
778	A172 27p multi	1.00	1.00
779	A172 36p multi	1.40	1.40
780	A172 40p multi	1.60	1.60
781	A172 45p multi	1.75	1.75
782	A172 65p multi	2.50	2.50
	Nos. 777-782 (6)	9.10	9.10

Souvenir Sheet

Queen Mother Elizabeth (1900-2002) — A173

Litho. With Foil Application

2002, Aug. 4   Perf. 13¼

783	A173 £2 multi	8.00	8.00

Christmas
A174

Designs: 22p, Madonna and Child. 27p, Holy Family. 36p, Angel announcing birth to shepherds. 40p, Adoration of the shepherds. 45p, Three Kings. 65p, Star of Bethlehem.

2002, Oct. 17   Litho.   Perf. 13¼x13

784	A174 22p multi	.85	.85
785	A174 27p multi	1.00	1.00
786	A174 36p multi	1.40	1.40
787	A174 40p multi	1.60	1.60
788	A174 45p multi	1.75	1.75
789	A174 65p multi	2.50	2.50
a.	Souvenir sheet, #784-789	9.25	9.25
	Nos. 784-789 (6)	9.10	9.10

World War II — A175

Designs: 22p, Pilots and airplanes. 27p, Airplanes over shoreline. 36p, Airplanes and searchlights. 40p, Airplanes dropping bombs. £1.50, HMS Charybdis and HMS Limbourne.

2003, Jan. 30   Perf. 14

790	A175 22p multi	.85	.85
791	A175 27p multi	1.00	1.00
792	A175 36p multi	1.40	1.40
793	A175 40p multi	1.60	1.60

Size: 40x31mm
Perf. 14¼x14½

794	A175 £1.50 multi	6.00	6.00
	Nos. 790-794 (5)	10.85	10.85

Dambusters Raid (#790-793), Operation Tunnel (#794), 60th anniv. See Nos. 827-831, 855-859.

Island Games — A176

Designs: 22c, Hurdles. 27p, Cycling. 36p, Gymnastics. 40p, Windsurfing. 45p, Golf. 65p, Triathlon.

2003, Jan. 30   Perf. 12½

795	A176 22p multi	.85	.85
796	A176 27p multi	1.00	1.00
797	A176 36p multi	1.40	1.40
798	A176 40p multi	1.60	1.60
799	A176 45p multi	1.75	1.75

800	A176 65p multi	2.50	2.50
a.	Souvenir sheet, #795-800	9.25	9.25
	Nos. 795-800 (6)	9.10	9.10

Poster Art — A177

Poster art from: 22p, 2003. 27p, 1995. 36p, 1988. 40p, 1978. 45p, 1968. 65p, 1956.

2003, Apr. 10   Perf. 14¾x14½

801	A177 22p multi	.85	.85
802	A177 27p multi	1.00	1.00
803	A177 36p multi	1.40	1.40
804	A177 40p multi	1.60	1.60
805	A177 45p multi	1.75	1.75
806	A177 65p multi	2.50	2.50
	Nos. 801-806 (6)	9.10	9.10

Europa (#802, 803).

Souvenir Sheet

Decommissioning of HMS Guernsey — A178

2003, Apr. 10   Perf. 13¾x14¼

807	A178 £1.50 multi	6.00	6.00

Prince William, 21st Birthday — A179

No. 808: a, With Princess Diana, 1983. b, With Princes Charles and Harry, 1985. c, At play in military uniform, 1986. d, In school uniform, with Prince Harry, 1989. e, Holding hand of Prince Charles, 1990. f, In ski jacket, with Princess Diana, 1991. g, In suit, 1995. h, With Princes Charles and Harry, 1997. i, Wearing helmet, 2000. j, Playing polo, 2002.

2003, June 21   Perf. 13½x13

808	Horiz. strip of 10	10.00	10.00
a.-j.	A179 27p Any single	1.00	1.00
k.	As #808a, perf. 13½x14	1.00	1.00
l.	As #808b, perf. 13½x14	1.00	1.00
m.	As #808c, perf. 13½x14	1.00	1.00
n.	As #808d, perf. 13½x14	1.00	1.00
o.	As #808e, perf. 13½x14	1.00	1.00
p.	As #808f, perf. 13½x14	1.00	1.00
q.	As #808g, perf. 13½x14	1.00	1.00
r.	As #808h, perf. 13½x14	1.00	1.00
s.	As #808i, perf. 13½x14	1.00	1.00
t.	As #808j, perf. 13½x14	1.00	1.00
u.	Booklet pane, #808k, 808m, 808q, 808s, 808t	6.00	—
v.	Booklet pane, #808l, 808m, 808np, 808o, 808r, 808s	6.00	—
w.	Booklet pane, #808k, 808n, 808p, 808q, 808r, 808t	6.00	—
x.	Booklet pane, #808k, 808l, 808m, 808o, 808r, 808t	6.00	—
y.	Booklet pane, #808l, 808n, 808o, 808p, 808q, 808s	6.00	—
	Complete booklet, #808u-808y	30.00	

Nos. 808k-808t come only from Nos. 808u-808y.

Letters
A180

Litho. With Foil Application

2003, July 3   *Perf. 13¼*
809 A180 £5 multi   20.00 20.00

No. 809 is printed with thermochromatic ink that changes color when warmed.

Christmas
A181

Scenes from *'Twas the Night Before Christmas:* 10p, Boy in bed, Christmas tree. 27p, Arrival of St. Nicholas. 36p, St. Nicholas near chimney. 40p, St. Nicholas carrying gifts. 45p, St. Nicholas placing gifts near tree. 65p, Departure of St. Nicholas.

2003, Oct. 16   Litho.   *Perf. 14¼*
810 A181 10p multi   .40   .40
811 A181 27p multi   1.00 1.00
812 A181 36p multi   1.40 1.40
813 A181 40p multi   1.60 1.60
814 A181 45p multi   1.75 1.75
815 A181 65p multi   2.50 2.50
  a.   Souvenir sheet, #810-815   8.75 8.75
       Nos. 810-815 (6)   8.65 8.65

Souvenir Sheet

Golden Snub-nosed Monkey — A182

2004, Jan. 29 Litho. *Perf. 13¾x14¼*
816 A182 £2 multi   8.25 8.25

Clematis Flower
Varieties — A183

Serpentine Die Cut 12½

2004, Jan. 29   Litho.

Self-Adhesive
Inscribed "GY"

817 A183 (22p) Rosemoor   .85   .85
818 A183 (22p) Arctic Queen   .85   .85
819 A183 (22p) Harlow Carr   .85   .85
820 A183 (22p) Guernsey
              Cream   .85   .85
821 A183 (22p) Josephine   .85   .85
  a.   Booklet pane, 2 each #817-
       821   8.50
       Complete booklet, No. 821a   8.50
  b.   Booklet pane, 2 each #817-
       821 (see note)   8.50
       Complete booklet, 10 No.
       821b   85.00

Inscribed "UK"

822 A183 (27p) Blue Moon   1.10 1.10
823 A183 (27p) Wisley   1.10 1.10
824 A183 (27p) Liberation   1.10 1.10
825 A183 (27p) Royal Velvet   1.10 1.10
826 A183 (27p) Hyde Hall   1.10 1.10
  a.   Sheetlet, #817-826   10.00
  b.   Booklet pane, 2 each #822-
       826   11.00
       Complete booklet, #826b   11.00
  c.   Booklet pane, 2 each #822-
       826 (see note)   11.00
       Complete booklet, 10 #826c   110.00
       Nos. 817-826 (10)   9.75 9.75

Booklet panes Nos. 821a and 826b have blocks of 6 and 4 separated by a space with text. Nos. 821b and 826c do not have a space between stamps.

World War II Type of 2003

Scenes of D-Day: 26p, Royal Air Force Spitfire. 32p, Arrival of landing craft. 36p, Soldiers approaching Gold Beach, open door of landing craft. 40p, Soldiers seeking shelter behind obstacles. £1.50, SS Vega.

2004, May 12   *Perf. 14¼*
827 A175 26p multi   1.00 1.00
828 A175 32p multi   1.25 1.25
829 A175 36p multi   1.40 1.40
830 A175 40p multi   1.60 1.60

                     Perf. 14¾x14¼
                     Size: 40x30mm
831 A175 £1.50 multi   6.00 6.00
       Nos. 827-831 (5)   11.25 11.25

Vacations — A184

Inscriptions: 26p, Sand, Beaches, Sunshine. 32p, Views, Walking, Cliff top trails. 36p, Marina, Yachts, Cruisers. 40p, Dining, Seafood, A la carte. 45p, Churches, History, Monuments. 65p, Fauna, Flora, Colors.

2004, May 12   *Perf. 13½*
832 A184 26p multi   1.00 1.00
833 A184 32p multi   1.25 1.25
834 A184 36p multi   1.40 1.40
835 A184 40p multi   1.60 1.60
836 A184 45p multi   1.75 1.75
837 A184 65p multi   2.50 2.50
       Nos. 832-837 (6)   9.50 9.50

Europa (32p, 36p).

Loyalty to the
British Crown,
800th
Anniv. — A185

2004, June 24   *Perf. 13¼x14*
838 A185 26p Loyalty   1.00 1.00
839 A185 32p Trade   1.25 1.25
840 A185 36p Unity   1.40 1.40
841 A185 40p Protection   1.60 1.60
842 A185 45p Justice   1.75 1.75
843 A185 65p Industry   2.50 2.50
  a.   Souvenir sheet, #838-843,
       perf. 14x13¼   10.00 10.00
       Nos. 838-843 (6)   9.50 9.50

2004 Summer
Olympics,
Athens — A186

2004, July 29   *Perf. 13½*
844 A186 32p Discus   1.25 1.25
845 A186 36p Javelin   1.40 1.40
846 A186 45p Runners   1.75 1.75
  a.   Booklet pane, #845, 846, 2
       #844   5.75
847 A186 65p Wrestlers   2.50 2.50
  a.   Booklet pane, #846, 847, 2
       #845   7.25   —
  b.   Booklet pane, #844, 847, 2
       #846   7.25   —
  c.   Booklet pane, #844, 845, 2
       #847   7.75   —
  d.   Booklet pane, #844-847   7.00   —
       Nos. 844-847 (4)   6.90 6.90

Nos. 846a, 847a-847d are perf 14¾x14.

Souvenir Sheet
Perf. 14¾x14

848 A186 £1 Athletes, horiz.   4.00 4.00
  a.   Booklet pane, #848   4.00
       Complete booklet, Nos. 846a,
       847a-847d, 848   40.00

No. 848 contains one 40x30mm stamp. No. 848a has binding stub at left.

Christmas
A187

Designs: No. 849a, Little Donkey. No. 849b, While Shepherds Watched. No. 849c, Away in a Manger. No. 849d, Unto Us a Child is Born. No. 849e, We Three Kings.

32p, Angel wings. 36p, Christmas tree ornament. 40p, Holly leaf and berries. 45p, Snowman's scarf and buttons. 65p, Christmas tree star.

2004, Oct. 28   Litho.   *Perf. 13*
849   Horiz. strip of 5   4.00 4.00
  a.-e. A187 20p Any single   .80   .80
850 A187 32p multi   1.25 1.25
851 A187 36p multi   1.40 1.40
852 A187 40p multi   1.60 1.60
853 A187 45p multi   1.75 1.75
854 A187 65p multi   2.50 2.50
       Nos. 849-854 (6)   12.50 12.50

World War II Type of 2003

Designs: 26p, Soldiers greet Guernsey residents on Army Landrover. 32p, Woman celebrating liberation from German rule. 36p, Parents reunite with children. 40p, Soldiers return home. £1.50, Winston Churchill.

2005, Feb. 3   Litho.   *Perf. 14¼*
855 A175 26p multi   1.00 1.00
856 A175 32p multi   1.25 1.25
857 A175 36p multi   1.40 1.40
858 A175 40p multi   1.60 1.60

                     Size: 40x30mm
                     Perf. 14¾x14¼
859 A175 £1.50 multi   6.00 6.00
       Nos. 855-859 (5)   11.25 11.25

Paintings of Flowers
by William John
Caparne — A188

Designs: 26p, Iris "Dorothea" and "Royal." 32p, Nerine fothergilli "Major." 36p, Iris "Garnet." 40p, Narcissus "Sir Watkin." 45p, Narcissus "Rip Van Winkle." 65p, Narcissus "Sulphur Phoenix."

2005, Feb. 3   *Perf. 13¼*
860 A188 26p multi   1.00 1.00
861 A188 32p multi   1.25 1.25
862 A188 36p multi   1.40 1.40
863 A188 40p multi   1.60 1.60
864 A188 45p multi   1.75 1.75
865 A188 65p multi   2.50 2.50
  a.   Souvenir sheet, #860-865   10.00 10.00
       Nos. 860-865 (6)   9.50 9.50

Liberation
of
Guernsey,
60th Anniv.
A189

No. 866: a, King George VI. b, Queen Elizabeth II.

Litho. With Foil Application

2005, May 9   *Perf. 14¾x14*
866   Horiz. pair   8.50 8.50
  a.-b. A189 £1 Either single   4.00 4.00

Queen Mary 2 Ocean Liner — A190

Litho. & Embossed With Foil Application

2005, May 9   *Perf. 13¼*
867 A190 £4 multi   16.00 16.00

Gastronomy
A191

Dishes: 26p, Spider crab. 32p, Red mullet and crab cake. 36p, Lobster salad. 40p, Brill on spinach with mussels. 45p, Prawn salad. 65p, Salmon wrapped in spinach with mussels.

2005, May 9   Litho.   *Perf. 14x13¼*
868 A191 26p multi   1.00 1.00
869 A191 32p multi   1.25 1.25
870 A191 36p multi   1.40 1.40
871 A191 40p multi   1.60 1.60
872 A191 45p multi   1.75 1.75
873 A191 65p multi   2.50 2.50
       Nos. 868-873 (6)   9.50 9.50

Europa (32p, 36p).

Souvenir Sheet

Basking Shark — A192

2005, July 21   *Perf. 13¼*
874 A192 £2 multi   8.50 8.50

SeaGuernsey 2005 — A193

Designs: 26p, Fishing boat and gulls. 32p, Sailboat. 36p, Windsurfer. 40p, Fisherman. 65p, Horse and rider on beach.

2005, July 21   *Perf. 13¼x13¾*
875 A193 26p multi   1.00 1.00
876 A193 32p multi   1.25 1.25
  a.   Booklet pane, 2 each #875-876   4.75
877 A193 36p multi   1.40 1.40
  a.   Booklet pane, 2 each #876-877   5.50   —
878 A193 40p multi   1.60 1.60
  a.   Booklet pane, 2 each #877-878   6.25   —
879 A193 65p multi   2.50 2.50
  a.   Booklet pane, 2 each #878-879   8.50   —
  b.   Booklet pane, 2 each #875,
       879   7.50   —
  c.   Booklet pane, #876-879   7.00   —
       Complete booklet, #876a,
       877a, 878a, 879a, 879b,
       879c   40.00
       Nos. 875-879 (5)   7.75 7.75

Christmas — A194

No. 880 — Stained glass windows from: a, St. Pierre du Bois Church. b, St. Saviour's Church. c, St. Martin's Church. d, Torteval Church. e, St. Sampson's Church.

32p, Vale Church. 36p, Castel Church. 40p, St. Anne's Church, Alderney. 45p, St. Andrew's Church. 65p, Forest Church.

2005, Oct. 27   *Perf. 14x14¼*
880   Horiz. strip of 5   4.00 4.00
  a.-e. A194 20p Any single   .80   .80
881 A194 32p multi   1.25 1.25
882 A194 36p multi   1.40 1.40
883 A194 40p multi   1.60 1.60
884 A194 45p multi   1.75 1.75
885 A194 65p multi   2.50 2.50
       Nos. 880-885 (6)   12.50 12.50

Victoria
Cross,
150th
Anniv.
A195

Battle scenes and medals from: 29p, Iraq Conflict, 2004. 34p, Falklands Conflict, 1982. 38p, Battle of El Alamein, World War II, 1942. 42p, Battle of Gallipoli, World War I, 1915. 47p, Battle of Rorke's Drift, Zulu War, 1879. 68p, Charge of the Light Brigade, Crimean War, 1854.

Perf. 13¾x13½

2006, Feb. 16		Litho.	
886	A195 29p multi	1.10	1.10
887	A195 34p multi	1.40	1.40
888	A195 38p multi	1.50	1.50
889	A195 42p multi	1.60	1.60
890	A195 47p multi	1.90	1.90
891	A195 68p multi	2.75	2.75
	Nos. 886-891 (6)	10.25	10.25

Souvenir Sheet

Endangered Species of the Florida Everglades — A196

No. 892: a, £1, Leatherback turtle. b, £1.50, Wood stork.

2006, Feb. 16		Perf. 14x14¾	
892	A196 Sheet of 2, #a-b	10.00	10.00

International Tourist Attractions — A197

Designs: 29p, Eiffel Tower, Paris. 34p, Sphinx, Egypt. 42p, Great Wall of China. 45p, Uluru (Ayers Rock), Australia. 47p, Statue of Liberty, New York. 68p, Taj Mahal, India.

2006, May 20		Perf. 13¼x13½	
893	A197 29p multi	1.10	1.10
894	A197 34p multi	1.40	1.40
895	A197 42p multi	1.60	1.60
896	A197 45p multi	1.75	1.75
897	A197 47p multi	1.90	1.90
898	A197 68p multi	2.75	2.75
	Nos. 893-898 (6)	10.50	10.50

Europa (34p, 42p).

Isambard Kingdom Brunel (1806-59) — A198

Designs: 29p, Brunel, mailbags for Guernsey at Paddington Station, London. 34p, Mail train leaving Paddington Station. 42p, Train on Wharncliffe Viaduct. 45p, Mail train and ship at harbor, Weymouth. 47p, Mailboat Ibex in English Channel. 68p, Ibex at St. Peter Port.

2006, May 20		Perf. 13¼x13	
899	A198 29p multi	1.10	1.10
900	A198 34p multi	1.40	1.40
901	A198 42p multi	1.60	1.60
902	A198 45p multi	1.75	1.75
a.	Booklet pane, #899-902	6.00	—
903	A198 47p multi	1.90	1.90
a.	Booklet pane, #900-903	6.75	—
904	A198 68p multi	2.75	2.75
a.	Booklet pane, #901-904	8.00	—
b.	Booklet pane, #899, 902-904	7.50	—
c.	Booklet pane, #899-900, 903-904	7.00	—
d.	Booklet pane, #899-901, 904	7.00	—
	Complete booklet, #902a, 903a, 904a-904d	42.50	
	Nos. 899-904 (6)	10.50	10.50

Andy Priaulx, Race Car Driver A199

Priaulx, car and events: 29p, British Speed Hill Climb Championship, 1995. 34p, Renault Spider Cup, 1999. 42p, British Formula 3, 2001. 45p, FIA European Touring Car Championship, 2004. 47p, Nürburgring, Germany, 2005. 68p, FIA World Touring Car Championship, 2005.

2006, May 20		Perf. 13½	
905	A199 29p multi	1.10	1.10
906	A199 34p multi	1.40	1.40
907	A199 42p multi	1.60	1.60
908	A199 45p multi	1.75	1.75
909	A199 47p multi	1.90	1.90
910	A199 68p multi	2.75	2.75
a.	Souvenir sheet, #905-910	11.00	11.00
	Nos. 905-910 (6)	10.50	10.50

Queen Elizabeth II, 80th Birthday A200

Litho. & Embossed with Foil Application

2006, June 17		Perf. 14¾x14¼	
911	A200 £10 multi	40.00	40.00

L'Erée Wetlands A201

Designs: 29p, Gray seal. 34p, Ormer. 42p, Common blenny. 45p, Le Creux ès Faies. 47p, Yellow-horned poppy. 68p, Oyster catchers.

2006, July 27	Litho.	Perf. 14x13¼	
912	A201 29p multi	1.10	1.10
913	A201 34p multi	1.40	1.40
914	A201 42p multi	1.60	1.60
915	A201 45p multi	1.75	1.75
916	A201 47p multi	1.90	1.90
917	A201 68p multi	2.75	2.75
a.	Souvenir sheet, #912-917	11.00	11.00
	Nos. 912-917 (6)	10.50	10.50

Addition of L'Erée Wetlands to Ramsar Convention Protected Wetlands List. See Nos. 972-977.

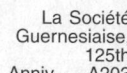

The Twelve Days of Christmas — A202

No. 918: a, A partridge in a pear tree. b, Two turtle doves. c, Three French hens. d, Four calling birds. e, Five gold rings. f, Six geese a-laying.

29p, Seven swans a-swimming. 34p, Eight maids a-milking. 42p, Nine ladies dancing. 45p, Ten lords a-leaping. 47p, Eleven pipers piping. 68p, Twelve drummers drumming.

2006, Nov. 2	Litho.	Perf. 14¾x15	
918	Horiz. strip of 6	5.00	5.00
a.-f.	A202 22p Any single	.80	.80
919	A202 29p multi	1.10	1.10
920	A202 34p multi	1.40	1.40
921	A202 42p multi	1.60	1.60
922	A202 45p multi	1.75	1.75
923	A202 47p multi	1.90	1.90
924	A202 68p multi	2.60	2.60
	Nos. 918-924 (7)	15.35	15.35

La Société Guernesiaise, 125th Anniv. — A203

No. 925: a, Rocks, Albecq. b, Ivy bee. c, Vale Church. d, Common frog. e, Parasol mushroom. f, Southern marsh orchid. g, Shore crab. h, Alderney blonde hedgehog. i, Barn owl. j, Le Trépied dolmen.

Serpentine Die Cut 12½

2007, Mar. 8			
Self-Adhesive			
925	Sheet of 10	13.50	
a.-e.	A203 (32p) Any single	1.25	1.25
f.-j.	A203 (37p) Any single	1.40	1.40
k.	Booklet pane of 10, 2 each #925a-925e	12.50	
	Complete booklet, 1 #925k	12.50	
l.	Booklet pane of 10, 2 each #925j	14.00	
	Complete booklet, 1 #925l	14.00	
m.	Booklet pane of 10, 2 each #925a-925c (see note)	12.50	
	Complete booklet, 10 #925m	125.00	
n.	Booklet pane of 10, 2 each #925f-925j (see note)	14.00	
	Complete booklet, 10 #925n	140.00	

Nos. 925a-925e are inscribed "GY"; Nos. 925f-925j, "UK."

Booklet panes Nos. 925k and 925l have blocks of 6 and 4 separated by a space between stamps. Booklet panes Nos. 925m and 925n do not have a space between stamps.

See No. 997.

Falkland Islands War, 25th Anniv. A204

Designs: 32p, Troops leaving for war. 37p, Landing at San Carlos Bay. 45p, Harriers flying over SS Canberra. 48p, Lieutenant Colonel H. Jones firing gun. 50p, Helicopter evacuating men from ship. 71p, Troops marching toward Port Stanley.

2007, Mar. 8		Perf. 13½	
926	A204 32p multi	1.25	1.25
927	A204 37p multi	1.40	1.40
928	A204 45p multi	1.75	1.75
929	A204 48p multi	1.90	1.90
930	A204 50p multi	1.90	1.90
931	A204 71p multi	2.75	2.75
a.	Souvenir sheet, #926-931	11.00	11.00

Scouting, Cent. — A205

Designs: 32p, 1907 Scout camping. 37p, 1924 Scout sailing. 45p, 1947 Scouts fishing. 48p, 1968 Scouts making model airplanes. 50p, 1990 Scouts exploring cave. 71p, 2007 Scouts on rollerblades.

2007, May 24	Litho.	Perf. 13¼x13	
932	A205 32p multi	1.25	1.25
933	A205 37p multi	1.50	1.50
934	A205 45p multi	1.75	1.75
935	A205 48p multi	1.90	1.90
936	A205 50p multi	2.00	2.00
937	A205 71p multi	3.00	3.00
	Nos. 932-937 (6)	11.40	11.40

Europa (37p, 45p).

British Formula 1 World Championship Cars and Drivers — A206

Driver and championship year: No. 938, Mike Hawthorn, 1958. No. 939, Jackie Stewart, 1971. No. 940, Graham Hill, 1962. No. 941, James Hunt, 1976. 45p, Jim Clark, 1963. 48p, Nigel Mansell, 1992. 50p, John Surtees, 1964. 71p, Damon Hill, 1996.

2007, May 24		Perf. 14x13¾	
938	A206 32p multi	1.25	1.25
939	A206 32p multi	1.25	1.25
940	A206 37p multi	1.50	1.50
941	A206 37p multi	1.50	1.50
942	A206 45p multi	1.75	1.75
943	A206 48p multi	1.90	1.90
944	A206 50p multi	2.00	2.00
945	A206 71p multi	3.00	3.00
	Nos. 938-945 (8)	14.15	14.15

Wedding of Queen Elizabeth II and Prince Philip, 60th Anniv. — A207

Designs: 32p, Princess Elizabeth and Prince Philip, c. 1967. 37p, With baby Princess Anne. 45p, Off duty, wearing casual clothes. 48p, On tour, Queen in jacket and hat. 50p, With grandchildren Princes William and Henry. 71p, Recent photo.

2007, Aug. 2		Perf. 13¼x13¾	
Background Color			
946	A207 32p red brown	1.40	1.40
947	A207 37p tan	1.50	1.50
a.	Booklet pane, 2 each #946-947	6.00	—
948	A207 45p light blue	1.90	1.90
a.	Booklet pane, 2 each #947-948	7.00	—
949	A207 48p light green	2.00	2.00
a.	Booklet pane, 2 each #948-949	8.00	—
950	A207 50p orange	2.10	2.10
a.	Booklet pane, 2 each #949-950	8.25	—
951	A207 71p lilac	3.00	3.00
a.	Booklet pane, 2 each #950-951	10.50	—
b.	Booklet pane, 2 each #946, 951	9.00	—
	Complete booklet, #947a, 948a, 949a, 950a, 951a, 951b	49.00	
	Nos. 946-951 (6)	11.90	11.90

Souvenir Sheet

Mountain Gorilla — A208

2007, Aug. 2		Perf. 14	
952	A208 £2.50 multi	10.50	10.50

Seaside Views A209

Designs: 32p, St. Peter Port Harbor. 37p, Fort Grey, Rocquaine. 45p, Point Robert Lighthouse, Sark. 48p, Brecqhou Island as seen from Sark. 50p, Vazon Bay. 71p, Fontenelle Bay.

2007, Oct. 1	Litho.	Perf. 13¾x13½	
953	A209 32p multi	1.40	1.40
954	A209 37p multi	1.50	1.50
955	A209 45p multi	1.90	1.90
956	A209 48p multi	2.00	2.00
957	A209 50p multi	2.10	2.10
958	A209 71p multi	3.00	3.00
	Nos. 953-958 (6)	11.90	11.90

See Nos. 1057-1062, 1098.

Christmas — A210

Decorations: No. 959, Crystal snowflake in snow. No. 960, Crystal snowflake pendant. No. 961, Angel candle accent. No. 962, Crystal angel pendant. No. 963, Pine cone in snow. No. 964, Spherical ornament with leaf pattern. 32p, Spherical ornament with spiral pattern. 37p, Candles. 45p, Bell. 48p, Ribbon bow. 50p, Christmas tree star. 71p, Porcelain angel.

2007, Oct. 25   *Perf. 14½x15*

959	A210 27p multi		1.10	1.10
960	A210 27p multi		1.10	1.10
961	A210 27p multi		1.10	1.10
962	A210 27p multi		1.10	1.10
963	A210 27p multi		1.10	1.10
964	A210 27p multi		1.10	1.10
965	A210 32p multi		1.40	1.40
966	A210 37p multi		1.50	1.50
967	A210 45p multi		1.90	1.90
968	A210 48p multi		2.00	2.00
969	A210 50p multi		2.10	2.10
970	A210 71p multi		3.00	3.00
	Nos. 959-970 (12)		18.50	18.50

Souvenir Sheet

Race Cars Used by World Touring Car Champion Andy Priaulx — A211

Race cars used by Priaulx in: a, 2005 (40x30mm). b, 2006 (40x30mm). c, 2007 (60x48mm).

2008, Jan. 18   **Litho.**   *Perf. 13¾x14¼*

971	A211	Sheet of 3	12.00	12.00
a.-c.		£1 Any single	4.00	4.00

Wetlands Type of 2006

Designs: 34p, Beadlet anemones. 40p, Sand crocus. 48p, Fulmars. 51p, Sheep's bit. 53p, Thick-lipped gray mullets. 74p, Light bulb sea squirts.

2008, Feb. 28   *Perf. 13x13¼*

972	A201 34p multi		1.40	1.40
973	A201 40p multi		1.60	1.60
974	A201 48p multi		1.90	1.90
975	A201 51p multi		2.00	2.00
976	A201 53p multi		2.10	2.10
977	A201 74p multi		3.00	3.00
a.	Miniature sheet, #972-977		12.00	12.00
	Nos. 972-977 (6)		12.00	12.00

Addition of Sark to Ramsar Convention Protected Wetlands List.

Flowers — A212

Designs: 10p, Red campion. 20p, Great bindweed. 30p, Spear thistle. 40p, Greater bird's foot trefoil. 50p, Sheep's bit. £1, Marguerite, vert. £2, Sea campion, vert.

2008, Feb. 28   **Litho.**   *Perf. 14*

978	A212 10p multi		.40	.40
979	A212 20p multi		.80	.80
980	A212 30p multi		1.25	1.25
981	A212 40p multi		1.60	1.60
982	A212 50p multi		2.00	2.00

Litho. & Embossed

983	A212 £1 multi		4.00	4.00
984	A212 £2 multi		8.00	8.00
	Nos. 978-984 (7)		18.05	18.05

See Nos. 1029-1038.

Mr. Men and Little Miss Children's Book Characters A213

Designs: 34p, Mr. Happy. 40p, Mr. Bump. 48p, Little Miss Naughty. 51p, Mr. Greedy. 53p, Mr. Strong. 74p, Mr. Tickle.

2008, May 15   **Litho.**   *Perf. 14x13½*

985	A213 34p multi		1.40	1.40
986	A213 40p multi		1.60	1.60
987	A213 48p multi		1.90	1.90
988	A213 51p multi		2.00	2.00
989	A213 53p multi		2.10	2.10
990	A213 74p multi		3.00	3.00
	Nos. 985-990 (6)		12.00	12.00

Guernesiais Phrases — A214

Guernesias phrases for: 34p, Till the next time. 40p, Hello. 48p, Oh! There you are. 51p, Good gracious. 53p, Cor blimey. 74p, How are things?

2008, May 15   *Perf. 13¼x13*

991	A214 34p multi		1.40	1.40
992	A214 40p multi		1.60	1.60
993	A214 48p multi		1.90	1.90
994	A214 51p multi		2.00	2.00
995	A214 53p multi		2.10	2.10
996	A214 74p multi		3.00	3.00
	Nos. 991-996 (6)		12.00	12.00

Europa (40p, 48p).

La Société Guernsiaise Type of 2007

No. 997 — Photographs of Guernsey: a, Pleimont Point. b, Saint's Harbor. c, Rocks at Albecq. d, Groins at Vazon Bay. e, La Bette Bay. f, Bordeaux Harbor. g, St. Saviour's Reservoir. h, Vazon Bay. i, St. Peter Port Lighthouse. j, Petit Port.

Serpentine Die Cut 12½

2008, June 9   **Litho.**

Self-Adhesive

997		Sheet of 10	15.00	
a.-e.	A203 (34p) Any single		1.40	1.40
f.-j.	A203 (40p) Any single		1.60	1.60
k.	Booklet pane of 10, 2 each #997a-997e		14.00	
l.	Booklet pane of 10, 2 each #997f-997j		16.00	

Nos. 997a-997e are inscribed "GY"; Nos. 997f-997j, "UK."

Ford Model T, Cent. A215

Model T: 34p, And house. 40p, Converted to truck. 48p, Converted to pickup truck. 51p, On tree-lined street. 53p, Converted to World War I army ambulance. 74p, Red 1912 Roadster.

2008, July 31   *Perf. 13¼*

998	A215 34p multi		1.40	1.40
999	A215 40p multi		1.60	1.60
1000	A215 48p multi		1.90	1.90
1001	A215 51p multi		2.00	2.00
a.	Booklet pane of 4, #998-1001		7.00	
1002	A215 53p multi		2.10	2.10
a.	Booklet pane of 4, #998-999, 1001-1002		7.25	
1003	A215 74p multi		3.00	3.00
a.	Booklet pane of 4, #1000-1003		9.00	
b.	Booklet pane of 4, #998-999, 1002-1003		8.25	
c.	Booklet pane of 4, #999-1000, 1002-1003		8.75	
d.	Booklet pane of 4, #998, 1000-1001, 1003		8.50	

Complete booklet, #1001a, 1002a, 1003a, 1003b, 1003c, 1003d	49.00	
Nos. 998-1003 (6)	12.00	12.00

St. Paul's Cathedral, London, 300th Anniv. — A216

Blocks of granite from Guernsey and various depictions of cathedral.

2008, Oct. 30   *Perf. 13¼*

1004	A216 34p multi		1.10	1.10
1005	A216 40p multi		1.40	1.40
1006	A216 48p multi		1.60	1.60
1007	A216 51p multi		1.75	1.75
1008	A216 53p multi		1.75	1.75
1009	A216 74p multi		2.40	2.40
	Nos. 1004-1009 (6)		10.00	10.00

Particles of granite were applied to parts of the designs by a thermographic process.

Christmas — A217

2008, Oct. 30   *Perf. 13¾x13¼*

1010	A217 29p Spruce		.95	.95
1011	A217 29p Butchers broom		.95	.95
1012	A217 29p Mistletoe		.95	.95
1013	A217 29p Ivy		.95	.95
1014	A217 29p Christmas cactus		.95	.95
1015	A217 29p Cyclamen		.95	.95
1016	A217 34p Holly		1.10	1.10
1017	A217 40p Poinsettia		1.40	1.40
1018	A217 48p Bracken		1.60	1.60
1019	A217 51p Hawthorn		1.75	1.75
1020	A217 53p Clematis peppermint		1.75	1.75
1021	A217 74p Pyracantha		2.40	2.40
	Nos. 1010-1021 (12)		15.70	15.70

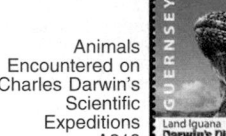

Animals Encountered on Charles Darwin's Scientific Expeditions A218

Designs: 36p, Land iguana. 43p, Wallaby. 51p, Giant tortoise. 54p, Marine iguana. 56p, Guanaco. 77p, Komodo dragon.

2009, Feb. 26   **Litho.**   *Perf. 14*

1022	A218 36p multi		1.10	1.10
1023	A218 43p multi		1.25	1.25
1024	A218 51p multi		1.50	1.50
1025	A218 54p multi		1.60	1.60
1026	A218 56p multi		1.60	1.60
1027	A218 77p multi		2.25	2.25
a.	Miniature sheet of 6, #1022-1027		9.50	9.50
	Nos. 1022-1027 (6)		9.30	9.30

Souvenir Sheet

Amur Leopard — A219

2009, Feb. 26   *Perf. 13¼x14*

1028	A219 £3 multi		8.75	8.75

Flowers Type of 2008

Designs: 1p, Stinking onion. 2p, Common mallow. 3p, Primrose. 4p, Loose-flowered orchid. 5p, Common centaury. 6p, Yellow horned poppy. 7p, Sea kale. 8p, Bluebell. 9p, Sea bindweed. £3, Common poppy, vert.

2009, May 28   **Litho.**   *Perf. 13¼*

1029	A212 1p multi		.20	.20
1030	A212 2p multi		.20	.20
1031	A212 3p multi		.20	.20
1032	A212 4p multi		.20	.20
1033	A212 5p multi		.20	.20
1034	A212 6p multi		.20	.20
1035	A212 7p multi		.25	.25
1036	A212 8p multi		.25	.25
1037	A212 9p multi		.30	.30

Litho. & Embossed

1038	A212 £3 multi		9.75	9.75
	Nos. 1029-1038 (10)		11.75	11.75

Invention of Telescope, 400th Anniv. A220

Designs: 36p, Quasar. 43p, Asteroid. 51p, Sun and Earth. 54p, Sun and Jupiter. 56p, Total solar eclipse. 77p, Solar eruption.

2009, May 28   **Litho.**   *Perf. 13¼*

1039	A220 36p multi		1.25	1.25
1040	A220 43p multi		1.40	1.40
1041	A220 51p multi		1.60	1.60
1042	A220 54p multi		1.75	1.75
1043	A220 56p multi		1.90	1.90
1044	A220 77p multi		2.50	2.50
	Nos. 1039-1044 (6)		10.40	10.40

Europa (43p, 51p).

Coronation of King Henry VIII, 500th Anniv. A221

King Henry VIII: 36p, With hawk. 43p, On throne beside Catherine of Aragon. 51p, Meeting Francis I of France. 54p, With Cardinal Wolsey. 56p, With Anne Boleyn. 77p, And ships.

2009, July 30   **Litho.**   *Perf. 13½*

1045	A221 36p multi		1.25	1.25
a.	Booklet pane of 4		5.00	
1046	A221 43p multi		1.50	1.50
a.	Booklet pane of 4		6.00	
1047	A221 51p multi		1.75	1.75
a.	Booklet pane of 4		7.00	
1048	A221 54p multi		2.00	2.00
a.	Booklet pane of 4		8.00	
1049	A221 56p multi		2.00	2.00
a.	Booklet pane of 4		8.00	
1050	A221 77p multi		2.60	2.60
a.	Booklet pane of 4		10.50	10.50
	Complete booklet, #1045a-1050a		44.50	
	Nos. 1045-1050 (6)		11.10	11.10

Postal Independence, 40th Anniv. — A222

"1969" and "2009" with inscription: 36p, The Psychedelic 60's. 43p, God Save the 70's. 51p, The POPular 80's. 54p, The Urban 90's. 56p, The Seductive 00's. 77p, Looking to the Future.

2009, July 30   Litho.   Perf. 14x13¾
1051	A222	36p multi	1.25	1.25
1052	A222	43p multi	1.50	1.50
1053	A222	51p multi	1.75	1.75
1054	A222	54p multi	1.90	1.90
1055	A222	56p multi	1.90	1.90
1056	A222	77p multi	2.60	2.60
		Nos. 1051-1056 (6)	10.90	10.90

Seaside Views Type of 2007

Designs: 36p, Jerbourg Point. 43p, Vazon Bay. 51p, Saints Bay Moorings. 54p, Le Jaonnet Bay. 56p, Rocquaine Bay. 77p, Bordeaux Harbor.

2009, Sept. 16   Litho.   Perf. 13½
1057	A209	36p multi	1.25	1.25
1058	A209	43p multi	1.40	1.40
1059	A209	51p multi	1.60	1.60
1060	A209	54p multi	1.75	1.75
1061	A209	56p multi	1.75	1.75
1062	A209	77p multi	2.50	2.50
		Nos. 1057-1062 (6)	10.25	10.25

Christmas — A223

Designs: No. 1063, St. Martin's Church. No. 1064, Castel Church. No. 1065, Torteval Church. No. 1066, St. John's Church. No. 1067, St. Peter Port Church. No. 1068, St. Sampson's Church. 36p, St. Matthew's Church. 43p, St. Saviour's Church. 51p, Forest Church. 54p, St. Andrew's Church. 56p, Vale Church. 77p, St. Peter's Church.

2009, Oct. 29
1063	A223	31p multi	1.10	1.10
1064	A223	31p multi	1.10	1.10
1065	A223	31p multi	1.10	1.10
1066	A223	31p multi	1.10	1.10
1067	A223	31p multi	1.10	1.10
1068	A223	31p multi	1.10	1.10
1069	A223	36p multi	1.25	1.25
1070	A223	43p multi	1.40	1.40
1071	A223	51p multi	1.75	1.75
1072	A223	54p multi	1.75	1.75
1073	A223	56p multi	1.90	1.90
1074	A223	77p multi	2.60	2.60
		Nos. 1063-1074 (12)	17.25	17.25

Souvenir Sheet

Asian Elephant — A224

2010, Feb. 25   Litho.   Perf. 14
1075	A224	£3.07 multi	9.50	9.50

Views of Guernsey A225

Designs: Nos. 1076, 1082a, Port à la Jument, Sark. Nos. 1077, 1082b, Dog and Lion Rocks. Nos. 1078, 1082c, Fort Grey. Nos. 1079, 1082d, West coast of Guernsey. Nos. 1080, 1082e, Slipway, Havelet Bay. Nos. 1081, 1082f, Castle Cornet.

2010, Mar. 18   Perf. 13¼
1076	A225	(48p) multi	1.50	1.50
1077	A225	(48p) multi	1.50	1.50
a.		Vert. pair, #1076-1077	3.00	3.00
1078	A225	(50p) multi	1.60	1.60
1079	A225	(58p) multi	1.75	1.75
1080	A225	(58p) multi	1.75	1.75
a.		Vert. pair, #1079-1080	3.50	3.50
1081	A225	(80p) multi	2.50	2.50
		Nos. 1076-1081 (6)	10.60	10.60

Self-Adhesive
Serpentine Die Cut 12½
1082		Sheet of 6	11.00	
a.-b.		A225 (48p) Either single	1.50	1.50
c.		A225 (50p) multi	1.60	1.60
d.-e.		A225 (58p) Either single	1.75	1.75
f.		A225 (80p) multi	2.50	2.50
g.		Booklet pane of 4, 2 each #1082a-1082b	6.00	
h.		Booklet pane of 4, 2 each #1082d-1082e	7.00	

Nos. 1076-1077, 1082a-1082b are inscribed "GY LARGE"; Nos. 1078, 1082c, "EUR"; Nos. 1079-1080, 1082d-1082e, "UK LARGE"; Nos. 1081, 1082f, "ROW."

The Adventures of Penny the Postie A226

Children on treasure chest with sail and: 45p, Volcano. 50p, Map. £2, Pirate and ship.

2010, May 4   Litho.   Perf. 13¼
1083	A226	45p multi	1.40	1.40

Size: 38x51mm
Perf. 14¼
1084	A226	50p multi	1.50	1.50
1085	A226	£2 multi	6.00	6.00
a.		Souvenir sheet, #1083-1085	9.00	9.00
		Nos. 1083-1085 (3)	8.90	8.90

Europa (Nos. 1083-1084).

Girl Guides, Cent. — A227

Designs: 36p, Outdoor activities. 45p, Help during World Wars I and II. 48p, Crystal Palace Maze. 50p, Agnes Baden-Powell. 58p, Mount Everest. 80p, Queen's Guide award.

2010, May 27   Litho.   Perf. 13¼
1086	A227	36p multi	1.10	1.10
1087	A227	45p multi	1.40	1.40
1088	A227	48p multi	1.40	1.40
1089	A227	50p multi	1.50	1.50
1090	A227	58p multi	1.75	1.75
1091	A227	80p multi	2.40	2.40
		Nos. 1086-1091 (6)	9.55	9.55

National Trust of Guernsey, 50th Anniv. — A228

Designs: 36p, Victorian Shop, 26 Cornet Street, St. Peter Port. 45p, Field, Jerbourg. 48p, Martello Tower, Fermain Bay. 50p, Ivy Gates. 58p, Pleinmont Headland. 80p, Moulin de Quanteraine.

2010, July 5   Litho.   Perf. 13½
1092	A228	36p multi	1.10	1.10
1093	A228	45p multi	1.40	1.40
1094	A228	48p multi	1.50	1.50
1095	A228	50p multi	1.50	1.50
1096	A228	58p multi	1.75	1.75
1097	A228	80p multi	2.40	2.40
		Nos. 1092-1097 (6)	9.65	9.65

Seaside Views Type of 2007

Design: Point Robert Lighthouse, Sark.

2010, July 29   Perf. 13¾x13½
1098	A209	55p multi	1.75	1.75

Evacuation of Guernsey, 70th Anniv. A229

Designs: 36p, Gas masks being loaded onto a truck, 1939. 45p, Guernsey children waiting to leave, 1940. 48p, German soldiers leaving Guernsey, 1945. 50p, Evacuees arriving back in Guernsey, 1945. 58p, Royal visit to Guernsey, June 1945. 80p, Liberation Day, 1946.

2010, July 29   Perf. 13¾
1099	A229	36p multi	1.10	1.10
1100	A229	45p multi	1.40	1.40
1101	A229	48p multi	1.50	1.50
1102	A229	50p multi	1.60	1.60
1103	A229	58p multi	1.90	1.90
1104	A229	80p multi	2.50	2.50
		Nos. 1099-1104 (6)	10.00	10.00

2010 Commonwealth Games, Delhi — A230

Designs: 36p, Tennis. 45p, Lawn bowling. 48p, Shooting. 50p, Swimming. 58p, Track. 80p, Cycling.

2010, Sept. 23   Perf. 13½
1105	A230	36p multi	1.25	1.25
a.		Booklet pane of 4	5.00	
1106	A230	45p multi	1.50	1.50
a.		Booklet pane of 4	6.00	
1107	A230	48p multi	1.60	1.60
a.		Booklet pane of 4	6.50	
1108	A230	50p multi	1.60	1.60
a.		Booklet pane of 4	6.50	
1109	A230	58p multi	1.90	1.90
a.		Booklet pane of 4	7.75	
1110	A230	80p multi	2.60	2.60
a.		Booklet pane of 4	10.50	
		Complete booklet, #1005a, 1106a, 1107a, 1108a, 1109a, 1110a	42.50	
		Nos. 1105-1110 (6)	10.45	10.45

Christmas Carols A231

Designs: 31p, The Holly and the Ivy. 36p, Little Donkey. 45p, Silent Night. 48p, I Saw Three Ships. 50p, Joy to the World. 58p, Ding Dong Merrily on High. 80p, We Three Kings.

2010, Nov. 4   Litho.   Perf. 13¼x14
1111	A231	31p multi	1.00	1.00
1112	A231	36p multi	1.25	1.25
1113	A231	45p multi	1.50	1.50
1114	A231	48p multi	1.60	1.60
1115	A231	50p multi	1.60	1.60
1116	A231	58p multi	1.90	1.90
1117	A231	80p multi	2.60	2.60
		Nos. 1111-1117 (7)	11.45	11.45

POSTAGE DUE STAMPS

Castle Cornet and St. Peter Port — D1

Perf. 12½x12
1969, Oct. 1   Photo.   Unwmk.
Black Numeral
J1	D1	1p deep magenta	1.75	1.00
J2	D1	2p yellow green	2.25	1.75
J3	D1	3p red	3.00	3.00
J4	D1	4p ultra	4.00	4.00
J5	D1	5p yellow bister	7.00	4.00
J6	D1	6p greenish blue	8.00	4.50
J7	D1	1sh red brown	21.00	13.00
		Nos. J1-J7 (7)	47.00	31.25

Type of 1969
"p" instead of "d"
1971-76
Black Numeral
J8	D1	½p deep magenta	.20	.20
J9	D1	1p yellow green	.20	.20
J10	D1	2p red	.20	.20
J11	D1	3p ultra	.20	.20
J12	D1	4p yellow bister	.20	.20
J13	D1	5p greenish blue	.25	.25
J14	D1	6p purple	.25	.25
J15	D1	8p orange ('75)	.25	.25
J16	D1	10p red brown	.50	.50
J17	D1	15p gray ('76)	.50	.50
		Nos. J8-J17 (10)	2.75	2.75

Town Church, St. Peter Port — D2

1977-80   Photo.   Perf. 13½x13
Arms and Denomination in Black
J18	D2	½p red brown	.20	.20
J19	D2	1p lilac rose	.20	.20
J20	D2	2p orange	.20	.20
J21	D2	3p red	.20	.20
J22	D2	4p greenish blue	.20	.20
J23	D2	5p olive green	.20	.20
J24	D2	6p greenish blue	.20	.20
J25	D2	8p rose	.25	.25
J26	D2	10p dark blue	.30	.30
J27	D2	14p green ('80)	.40	.40
J28	D2	15p purple	.40	.40
J29	D2	16p salmon rose ('80)	.50	.50
		Nos. J18-J29 (12)	3.25	3.25

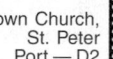

Woman Milking Cow — D3

1982, July 13   Litho.   Perf. 14½
J30	D3	1p shown	.20	.20
J31	D3	2p Vale Mill	.20	.20
J32	D3	3p Sark cottage	.20	.20
J33	D3	4p St. Peter Port	.20	.20
J34	D3	5p Well, Moulin Huet	.20	.20
J35	D3	16p Seaweed gathering	.40	.40
J36	D3	18p Upper Walk, White Rock	.45	.45
J37	D3	20p Cobo Bay	.50	.50
J38	D3	25p Saints' Bay	.55	.55
J39	D3	30p La Coupee, Sark	.75	.75
J40	D3	50p Old Harbor, St. Peter Port	1.10	1.10
J41	D3	£1 Greenhouses, Victoria Tower	2.50	2.50
		Nos. J30-J41 (12)	7.25	7.25

OCCUPATION STAMPS

Issued Under German Occupation

Bisects of Great Britain Nos. 238 and 255 were used in Guernsey from 12/27/40 to 2./24/41. Values, on cover or postcard: No. 238, $45; No. 255, $40.

OS1

Rouletted 14x7

		Typo.		
1941-44				**Unwmk.**
N1	OS1	½p light green	5.50	3.25
N2	OS1	1p red	3.00	2.00
N3	OS1	2½p ultramarine	12.00	11.00
		Nos. N1-N3 (3)	20.50	16.25

Issued: #N1b, 4/7/41; #N1c, 6/41; #N1d, 11/41; #N1e, 2/42; #N1a, 9/42; #N1f, 2/43; #N1, from 7/43; #N2, 2/18/41; #N2a, 7/43; #N2b, 1943; #N3, 4/12/44; #N3a, 7/44.

Additional shades and papers exist. The rouletting is very crude and may not be measurable. This is not a defect.

Wmk. 396 Chain Link Fence

1942   Rouletted 14x7
Bluish French Bank Note Paper

N4	OS1	½p green	27.50	27.50
N5	OS1	1p red	14.50	21.00

Issue dates: ½p, Mar. 11; 1p, Apr. 9.

Nos. N1-N5 remained valid until 4/13/46.

ALDERNEY

'ol-dər-nē

LOCATION — Northernmost of the Channel Islands in the Guernsey Bailiwick
GOVT. — Dependent territory under Bailiwick of Guernsey.
AREA — 3 sq. mi.
POP. — 2,373 (1994 est.)
CAPITAL — St. Anne's

Part of the Bailiwick of Guernsey, this island began issuing its own stamps.

> **Catalogue values for unused stamps in this section are for Never Hinged items.**

Map of Alderney, Arms — A1

1983, June 14		**Litho.**	**Perf. 12**	
1	A1	1p shown	.40	.40
2	A1	4p Hanging Rock	.40	.40
3	A1	9p States Building	.45	.45
4	A1	10p St. Anne's Church	.45	.45
5	A1	11p Yachts, Braye Bay	.50	.50
6	A1	12p Victoria St., St. Anne	.50	.50
7	A1	13p Map, arms	.50	.50
8	A1	14p Ft. Clonque	.55	.55
9	A1	15p Corblets Bay Port	.55	.55
10	A1	16p Old Tower, St. Anne	.65	.65
11	A1	17p Essex Castle Golf Course	.70	.70
12	A1	18p Ships in Old Harbor	.70	.70
		Nos. 1-12 (12)	6.35	6.35

See Nos. 42-46, which is considered to be the higher-denomination continuation of this definitive set.

Oystercatcher, Telegraph Bay — A2

1984, June 12			**Perf. 14½**	
13	A2	9p shown	1.50	1.10
14	A2	13p Turnstone, Corblets Bay	1.50	1.00

15	A2	26p Ringed plover, Corblets Bay	4.00	3.00
16	A2	28p Dunlin, Arch Bay	4.00	3.25
17	A2	31p Curlew, Old Harbor	4.00	3.25
		Nos. 13-17 (5)	15.00	11.60

Alderney Airport, 50th Anniv. — A3

Aircraft: 9p, Wessex helicopter of the Queen's Flight, 1984. 13p, Aurigny Air Joey Britten-Norman Trislander, 1981. 29p, Morton Air Services DeHavilland Heron, 1946. 31p, DeHavilland Dragon Rapide, c. 1930. 34p, Saunders-Roe Saro Windhover, 1935.

1985, Mar. 19			**Perf. 12x11½**	
18	A3	9p multicolored	1.75	1.50
19	A3	13p multicolored	2.50	1.50
20	A3	29p multicolored	4.25	3.50
21	A3	31p multicolored	5.25	3.75
22	A3	34p multicolored	5.25	3.75
		Nos. 18-22 (5)	19.00	14.00

Regimental Uniforms, Alderney Garrison — A4

1985, Sept. 24			**Perf. 14½**	
23	A4	9p Royal Engineers, 1890	.30	.30
24	A4	14p Duke of Albany's Own Highlanders, 1856	1.10	.55
25	A4	29p Royal Artillery, 1855	1.10	1.10
26	A4	31p South Hampshire Regiment, 1810	1.50	1.25
27	A4	34p Royal Irish Regiment, 1782	1.75	1.40
		Nos. 23-27 (5)	5.75	4.60

Forts — A5

1986, Sept. 23		**Litho.**	**Perf. 13x13½**	
28	A5	10p Grosnez	1.25	1.25
29	A5	14p Tourgis	1.50	1.50
30	A5	31p Clonque	3.50	3.50
31	A5	34p Albert	3.75	3.75
		Nos. 28-31 (4)	10.00	10.00

Shipwrecks — A6

1987, May 5		**Litho.**	**Perf. 14½**	
32	A6	11p Liverpool, 1902	2.00	.80
33	A6	15p Petit Raymond, 1906	2.50	.80
34	A6	29p Maina, 1910	5.00	5.00
35	A6	31p Burton, 1911	5.25	5.00
36	A6	34p Point Law, 1975	5.25	5.25
		Nos. 32-36 (5)	20.00	16.85

18th-20th Cent. Maps — A7

Designs: 12p, Herman Moll map, 1724. 18p, Survey by J.H. Bastide, 1739. 27p, Land survey by M.P. Goodwin, 1830. 32p, Wartime occupation map, 1943. 35p, Ordnance survey, 1988.

1989, July 7		**Litho.**	**Perf. 13½x14**	
37	A7	12p multicolored	.50	.50
38	A7	18p multicolored	.75	.75
39	A7	27p multicolored	1.10	1.10
40	A7	32p multicolored	1.25	1.25
41	A7	35p multicolored	1.40	1.40
		Nos. 37-41 (5)	5.00	5.00

Quesnard Lighthouse A8

Designs: 21p, Inner Harbor, Braye. 23p, The Island Hall, Alderney. 24p, Alderney Railway locomotive, J. T. Daly. 28p, Lifeboat, Louis Marchesi of Round Table.

1989-93		**Litho.**	**Perf. 15x14**	
42	A8	20p multicolored	1.25	1.00
43	A8	21p multicolored	1.25	1.00
44	A8	23p multicolored	.85	.75
45	A8	24p multicolored	2.25	2.00
46	A8	28p multicolored	2.40	2.00
		Nos. 42-46 (5)	8.00	6.75

Issued: 20p, 12/27; 21p, 4/2/91; 23p, 2/6/92; 24p, 28p, 3/3/93.

Ships Called HMS Alderney A9

1990, May 3		**Litho.**	**Perf. 13½**	
55	A9	14p Bomb ketch, 1738	.55	.55
56	A9	20p Sixth-rate, 1742	.70	.70
57	A9	29p Sloop, 1755	1.00	1.00
58	A9	34p A-Class submarine, 1945	1.25	1.25
59	A9	37p Fishery protection vessel, 1979	1.50	1.50
		Nos. 55-59 (5)	5.00	5.00

Automation of Casquets Lighthouse — A10

1991, Apr. 20		**Litho.**	**Perf. 14x13½**	
60	A10	21p Wreck of HMS Victory, 1744	1.90	1.90
61	A10	26p Returning by rowboat	2.10	2.10
62	A10	31p Helicopter relief	2.50	2.50
63	A10	37p Lighthouse, birds	3.00	3.00
64	A10	50p MV Patricia	4.00	4.00
		Nos. 60-64 (5)	13.50	13.50

Battle of La Hogue, 300th Anniv. — A11

23p, 28p, and 33p, Various details from painting by unknown artist. 50p, Entire painting.

1992, Sept. 18		**Litho.**	**Perf. 13½**	
65	A11	23p multicolored	2.00	2.00
66	A11	28p multicolored	2.50	2.50
67	A11	33p multicolored	3.00	3.00

Size: 45x30mm				
		Perf. 14x14½		
68	A11	50p multicolored	3.75	3.75
		Nos. 65-68 (4)	11.25	11.25

Marine Life — A12

Designs: a, 24p, Palinurus elephas. b, 28p, Metridium senile. c, 33p, Luidia ciliaris. d, 39p, Psammechinus miliaris.

1993, Nov. 2		**Litho.**	**Perf. 15x14½**	
69	A12	Strip of 4, #a.-d.	9.50	9.50

Flora and Fauna — A13

Designs: 1p, Ischnura elegans, ranunculus trichophyllus, sparganium erectum. 2p, Crocidura russula, hypericum linarifolium. 3p, Fulmarus glacialis, carpobrotus edulis. 4p, Colias croceus, trifolium pratense. 5p, Bombus lucorum, orobanche rapum-genistae, cytisus scoparius. 6p, Sylvia undata, cuscuta epithymum, ulex europaeus. 7p, Inachis io, cirsium acaule. 8p, Talpa europaea, endymion non-scripta. 9p, Tettigonia viridissima, ulex europaeus. 10p, Zygaena filipendulae, echium vulgare. 16p, Polyommatus icarus, anacamptis pyramidalis. 20p, Oryctolagus cuniculus, rannunculus repens, pteridium aquilinum. 24p, Larus marinus, romulea columnae. 30p, Fratercula arctica, sedum anglicum. 40p, Saturnia pavonia, rubus fruticosus. 50p, Erinaceus europaeus, oxalis articulata. £1, Sterna hirundo, cynodon dactylon, horiz. £2, Morus bassanus, fucus vesiculosus.

1994-95		**Litho.**	**Perf. 14**	
70	A13	1p multicolored	.20	.20
71	A13	2p multicolored	.20	.20
72	A13	3p multicolored	.20	.20
73	A13	4p multicolored	.20	.20
74	A13	5p multicolored	.20	.20
75	A13	6p multicolored	.25	.25
76	A13	7p multicolored	.25	.25
77	A13	8p multicolored	.30	.30
78	A13	9p multicolored	.35	.35
79	A13	10p multicolored	.40	.40
80	A13	16p multicolored	.60	.60
a.		Perf. 14x15 on three sides	.65	.65
b.		As "a," booklet pane of 8	5.75	
		Complete booklet, #80b	5.75	
81	A13	20p multicolored	.80	.80
a.		Perf. 14x15 on three sides	.85	.85
b.		As "a," booklet pane of 8	7.25	
		Complete booklet, #81b	7.25	
82	A13	24p multicolored	.95	.95
a.		Perf. 14x15 on three sides	1.00	1.00
b.		As "a," booklet pane of 8	9.00	
		Complete booklet, #82b	9.00	
83	A13	30p multicolored	1.10	1.10
84	A13	40p multicolored	1.60	1.60
85	A13	50p multicolored	2.00	2.00
86	A13	£1 multicolored	4.00	4.00

		Perf. 14x15		
87	A13	£2 multicolored	8.00	8.00
		Nos. 70-87 (18)	21.60	21.60

No. 81 is dated "1994." Nos. 81a-81b are dated "1998."
Issued: £2, 2/28/95; others, 5/5/94.
See Nos. 98-100.

Career of Flt. Lt. Tommy Rose DFC
(1895-1968) — A14

No. 88: a, 1917-18 Royal Flying Corps. b, 1939-45 Chief Test Pilot. c, Phillips & Powis (Miles) Aircraft.
No. 89: a, Winner, 1935 King's Cup Air Race. b, Winner, 1947 Manx Air Derby. c, UK-Cape-UK Speed Record, 1936.

1995, Sept. 1   Litho.   Perf. 14x15
88   A14   35p Strip of 3, #a.-c.   4.25   4.25
89   A14   41p Strip of 3, #a.-c.   5.00   5.00

Nos. 88-89 printed in sheets of 12 stamps + 3 labels.

Souvenir Sheet

Return of Islanders, 50th
Anniv. — A15

Illustration reduced.

1995, Nov. 16   Litho.   Perf. 13½
90   A15   £1.65 multicolored   6.50   6.50

30th Signal Regiment Activities in
Alderney, 25th Anniv.
A16

a, 24p, Training. b, 41p, Natl. contingencies overseas. c, 60p, Strategic communications. d, 75p, UN operations.

1996, Jan. 24   Litho.   Perf. 14
91   A16   Strip of 4, #a.-d.   8.00   8.00

Domestic
Cats — A17

16p, Butterfly, brown & white cat. 24p, Gray cat on table. 25p, Two cats on chair. 35p, Cat pulling on table cloth. 41p, Calico cat in toy cart, white cat. 60p, Siamese cat with yarn.

1996, July 19   Litho.   Perf. 13½
92   A17   16p multicolored   .60   .60
93   A17   24p multicolored   .95   .95
94   A17   25p multicolored   1.00   1.00
95   A17   35p multicolored   1.40   1.40
96   A17   41p multicolored   1.60   1.60
97   A17   60p multicolored   2.40   2.40
a.   Souvenir sheet, #92-97   8.00   8.00
      Nos. 92-97 (6)   7.95   7.95

No. 97a is a continuous design.

Fauna and Flora Type of 1994

Designs: 18p, Aglais urticae, Buddleja davidii. 25p, Anthus petrosus, matthiola incana. 26p, Ammophila sabulosa, calystegia soldanella, horiz.

1997, Jan. 2   Litho.   Perf. 14½
98   A13   18p multicolored   .70   .70
a.   Perf. 14x15 on 3 sides   1.00
b.   As "a," booklet pane of 8   8.75
      Complete booklet, #98b   8.75
99   A13   25p multicolored   1.00   1.00
a.   Perf. 14x15 on 3 sides   1.00
b.   As "a," booklet pane of 8   8.75
      Complete booklet, #99b   8.75
100 A13   26p multicolored   1.00   1.00
      Nos. 98-100 (3)   2.70   2.70

Alderney Cricket
Club, 150th
Anniv. — A18

1997, Aug. 21   Litho.   Perf. 13½
101 A18   18p Harold Larwood   .70   .70
102 A18   25p John Arlott   1.00   1.00
103 A18   37p Pelham J. Warner   1.40   1.40
104 A18   43p W.G. Grace   1.60   1.60
105 A18   63p John Wisden   2.50   2.50
a.   Souvenir sheet, #101-105 + label   8.00   8.00
      Nos. 101-105 (5)   7.20   7.20

Garrison
Island — A19

#106, Founding of the harbor. #107, Ariadne at anchor. #108, Quarrying at Mannez. #109, Earliest train ferrying stone. #110, Queen Victoria arrives ashore. #111, Royal yacht at anchor. #112, Railway and quarry workers greet the Queen. #113, Queen Victoria tours the island.

1997, Nov. 20   Litho.   Perf. 14½x14
106 A19   18p multicolored   .70   .70
107 A19   18p multicolored   .70   .70
a.   Pair, #106-107   1.40   1.40
108 A19   25p multicolored   1.00   1.00
109 A19   25p multicolored   1.00   1.00
a.   Pair, #108-109   2.00   2.00
b.   Booklet pane, #107a, 109a ('98)   3.75
110 A19   26p multicolored   1.00   1.00
111 A19   26p multicolored   1.00   1.00
a.   Pair, #110-111   2.00   2.00
b.   Booklet pane, #107a, 111a ('98)   3.75
112 A19   31p multicolored   1.25   1.25
113 A19   31p multicolored   1.25   1.25
a.   Pair, #112-113   2.50   2.50
b.   Booklet pane, #111a, 113a ('98)   4.75
c.   Booklet pane, #109a, 113a ('98)   4.75
      Nos. 106-113 (8)   7.90   7.90

Nos. 109b, 111b, 113b, 113c issued 11/10/98.
See Nos. 119-126, 134-141, 155-162, 176-183.

Alderney Diving
Club, 21st
Anniv. — A20

20p, Modern superlite helmet. 30p, Cousteau-Gagnan demand valve, 1943. 37p, Heinke closed helmet, 1845. 43p, Siebe closed helmet, 1840. 63p, Deane open helmet, 1829.

1998, Feb. 10   Litho.   Perf. 13
114 A20   20p multicolored   .80   .80
115 A20   30p multicolored   1.10   1.10
116 A20   37p multicolored   1.40   1.40
117 A20   43p multicolored   1.60   1.60
118 A20   63p multicolored   2.50   2.50
a.   Souvenir sheet, #114-118 + label   7.50   7.50
      Nos. 114-118 (5)   7.40   7.40

Garrison Island Type of 1997

#119, Alderney Post Office. #120, Traders in Victoria Street. #121, Court House. #122, Police Station and Fire Service. #123, St. Anne's Church. #124, Wedding Party at The Albert Gate. #125, SS Courier unloading. #126, Fishermen at quay.

1998, Nov. 10   Litho.   Perf. 14½x14
119 A19   20p multicolored   .80   .80
120 A19   20p multicolored   .80   .80
a.   Pair, #119-120   1.60   1.60
121 A19   25p multicolored   1.00   1.00
122 A19   25p multicolored   1.00   1.00
a.   Pair, #121-122   2.00   2.00
b.   Booklet pane, #120a, 122a   3.75
123 A19   30p multicolored   1.25   1.25
124 A19   30p multicolored   1.25   1.25
a.   Pair, #123-124   2.50   2.50
b.   Booklet pane, #120a, 124a   4.25
125 A19   37p multicolored   1.60   1.60
126 A19   37p multicolored   1.60   1.60
a.   Pair, #125-126   3.25   3.25
b.   Booklet pane, #124a, 126a   6.00
c.   Booklet pane, #122a, 126a   5.75
      Complete booklet, #109b, 111b, 113b, 113c, 122b, 124b, 126b, 126c   37.50
      Nos. 119-126 (8)   9.30   9.30

Souvenir Sheet

The Wreck of the SS Stella,
Cent. — A21

a, 25p, Stained glass window, Anglican Cathedral, Liverpool, dedicated to Mary Rogers, chief stewardess. b, £1.75, Ship leaving Southampton.

1999, Feb. 4   Litho.   Perf. 14
127 A21   Sheet of 2, #a.-b.   8.00   8.00

Total Solar
Eclipse — A22

Stages of eclipse on 8/11/99: 20p, 10:15. 25p, 10:51. 30p, 11:14. 38p, 11:16. 44p, 11:17. 64p, 11:36.

1999, Apr. 27   Litho.   Perf. 13½x13
128 A22   20p multicolored   .80   .80
129 A22   25p multicolored   1.00   1.00
130 A22   30p multicolored   1.25   1.25
131 A22   38p multicolored   1.50   1.50
132 A22   44p multicolored   1.75   1.75
133 A22   64p multicolored   2.50   2.50
a.   Souvenir sheet, #128-133 + label   8.75   8.75
      Nos. 128-133 (6)   8.80   8.80

Garrison Island Type of 1997

Designs: No. 134, Fort Grosnez, c. 1855. No. 135, Ninth Battalion, Royal Garrison Artillery. No. 136, Arsenal, Fort Albert. No. 137, Royal Engineer Unit. No. 138, Fort Tourgis, c. 1865. No. 139, Second Battalion, Royal Scots Regiment. No. 140, Fort Houmet Herbé, c. 1870. No. 141, Royal Alderney Artillery Militia.

1999, Oct. 19   Litho.   Perf. 14¼x13¾
134 A19   20p multicolored   .80   .80
135 A19   20p multicolored   .80   .80
a.   Pair, #134-135   1.60   1.60
136 A19   25p multicolored   1.00   1.00
137 A19   25p multicolored   1.00   1.00
a.   Pair, #136-137   2.00   2.00
b.   Booklet pane, #135a, 137a   3.75
138 A19   30p multicolored   1.25   1.25
139 A19   30p multicolored   1.25   1.25
a.   Pair, #138-139   2.50   2.50
b.   Booklet pane, #135a, 139a   4.50
c.   Booklet pane, #137a, 139a   4.75
140 A19   38p multicolored   1.50   1.50
141 A19   38p multicolored   1.50   1.50
a.   Pair, #140-141   3.25   3.25
b.   Booklet pane, #135a, 141a   5.25
c.   Booklet pane, #137a, 141a   5.50
d.   Booklet pane, #139a, 141a   6.25
      Complete booklet, #137b, 139b, 139c, 141b, 141c, 141d   32.50
      Nos. 134-141 (8)   9.10   9.10

Peregrine
Falcon — A23

Falcons: 21p, Attacking turnstone near lighthouse. 26p, With prey. 34p, With eggs. 38p, With chicks. 44p, With young near Fort Clonque. 64p, Preparing to fly.

2000, Feb. 4   Litho.   Perf. 14½x14
142 A23   21p multi   1.10   1.10
a.   Booklet pane of 10   11.00
      Complete booklet   11.00
143 A23   26p multi   1.25   1.25
a.   Booklet pane of 10   12.00
      Complete booklet   12.00
144 A23   34p multi   1.50   1.50
145 A23   38p multi   1.60   1.60
146 A23   44p multi   2.00   2.00
147 A23   64p multi   2.75   2.75
      Nos. 142-147 (6)   10.20   10.20

Worldwide Fund for Nature, Nos. 144-147.

The Wombles
on Vacation
A24

Wombles: 21p, With map. 26p, On beach. 36p, At lighthouse. 40p, Picnicking. 45p, On golf course. 65p, At airport.

2000, Apr. 28   Litho.   Perf. 14¼x13¾
148 A24   21p multi   .85   .85
149 A24   26p multi   1.00   1.00
150 A24   36p multi   1.40   1.40
151 A24   40p multi   1.60   1.60
152 A24   45p multi   1.75   1.75
153 A24   65p multi   2.50   2.50
a.   Souvenir sheet, #148-153   9.25   9.25
      Nos. 148-153 (6)   9.10   9.10

The Stamp Show 2000, London (No. 153a).

Souvenir Sheet

Queen Mother, 100th Birthday — A25

Illustration reduced.

Litho. with Foil Application
2000, Aug. 4   Perf. 13¼
154 A25   £1.50 multi   6.00   6.00

Garrison Island Type of 1997

#155, Regimental boxing tournament. #156, Sports Day of Alderney Gala Week, 1924. #157, Regimenal Band of 15th entertains. #158, Garrison Ball, 1873, Fort Albert mess room. #159, Garrison assembly for Queen's birthday celebrations, 1859. #160, Demonstration of field guns on the Butes. #161, Inspection of honor guard, 1863. #162, Arrival of Lt. Gov. Major Gen. Marcus Slade.

2000, Oct. 19   Litho.   Perf. 13¼x13
155 A19   21p multi   .85   .85
156 A19   21p multi   .85   .85
a.   Pair, #155-156   1.75   1.75
157 A19   26p multi   1.00   1.00
158 A19   26p multi   1.00   1.00
a.   Pair, #157-158   2.00   2.00
b.   Booklet pane, #156a, 158a   4.00
159 A19   36p multi   1.40   1.40
160 A19   36p multi   1.40   1.40
a.   Pair, #159-160   3.00   3.00
b.   Booklet pane, #158a, 160a   5.50
161 A19   40p multi   1.60   1.60
162 A19   40p multi   1.60   1.60
a.   Pair, #161-162   3.25   3.25
b.   Booklet pane, #156a, 162a   5.00
c.   Booklet pane, #160a, 162a   6.25
      Booklet, #158b, 162c, 2 each #160b, 162b   30.00
      Nos. 155-162 (8)   9.70   9.70

Each of the two panes of Nos. 160b and 162b in the booklet have different selvages.

Souvenir Sheet

Queen Elizabeth, 75th Birthday — A26

2001, Feb. 1   Litho.   Perf. 14¼
163 A26 £1.75 multi   7.00 7.00

Community Health Services A27

Health care workers and: 22p, Hospital x-ray department. 27p, Mignot Memorial Hospital in 1980s. 36p, Princess Anne visiting hospital, 1972. 40p, Nurse with infant, 1960s. 45p, Queen Elizabeth II laying hospital cornerstone, 1957. 65p, Opening of original hospital, 1920s.

2001-02   Litho.   Perf. 14¼x14½
164 A27 22p multi   .85   .85
  a.   Perf. 13¼x13   .90   .90
165 A27 27p multi   1.00 1.00
  a.   Perf. 13¼x13   1.40 1.40
166 A27 36p multi   1.40 1.40
  a.   Perf. 13¼x13   1.40 1.40
167 A27 40p multi   1.60 1.60
  a.   Perf. 13¼x13   1.60 1.60
  b.   Booklet pane, #164a, 165a,
        166a, 167a   5.50   —
168 A27 45p multi   1.75 1.75
  a.   Perf. 13¼x13   1.75 1.75
169 A27 65p multi   2.50 2.50
  a.   Perf. 13¼x13   2.40 2.40
  b.   Booklet pane, #166a, 167a,
        168a, 169a   7.25   —
  c.   Booklet pane, #164a, 165a,
        168a, 169a   6.50   —
      Nos. 164-169 (6)   9.10 9.10

Issued: Nos. 164-169, 4/26/01; Nos. 164a-169a, 10/17/02.

Alderney Golf Club — A28

Designs: 22p, Golf ball with core of feathers, 1901. 27p, Golfing fashions, 1920s. 36p, Player and ball on Alderney Golf Club green, 1970s. 40p, Modern putter. 45p, Golf accessories. 65p, Modern lofted wood.

2001, Aug. 1   Litho.   Perf. 14¾
170 A28 22p multi   .85   .85
171 A28 27p multi   1.00 1.00
172 A28 36p multi   1.40 1.40
173 A28 40p multi   1.60 1.60
174 A28 45p multi   1.75 1.75
175 A28 65p multi   2.50 2.50
  a.   Souvenir sheet, #170-175 9.25 9.25
      Nos. 170-175 (6)   9.10 9.10

Phila Nippon '01 (#175a).

Garrison Island Type of 1997

Designs: No. 176, Work continues at the breakwater. No. 177, Officials observe work in progress. No. 178, Steam frigate Emerald grounded. No. 179, Soldiers disembarking Emerald. No. 180, Torpedo boats moored at breakwater. No. 181, Railway provides mobile artillery. No. 182, HMS Majestic at anchor, 1901. No. 183, Torpedo boats maneuver at speed.

2001, Oct. 16   Litho.   Perf. 13¼x13
176 A19 22p multi   .85   .85
177 A19 22p multi   .85   .85
  a.   Pair, #176-177   1.75 1.75
178 A19 27p multi   1.00 1.00
179 A19 27p multi   1.00 1.00
  a.   Pair, #178-179   2.00 2.00
  b.   Booklet pane, #177a, 179a 4.00
180 A19 36p multi   1.40 1.40
181 A19 36p multi   1.40 1.40
  a.   Pair, #180-181   3.00 3.00
  b.   Booklet pane, #179a, 181a 5.25   —
182 A19 40p multi   1.60 1.60
183 A19 40p multi   1.60 1.60
  a.   Pair, #182-183   3.25 3.25
  b.   Booklet pane, #177a, 183a 4.75   —
  c.   Booklet pane, #179a, 183a 5.25   —
  d.   Booklet pane, #181a, 183a 5.25   —
      Booklet, #179b, 181b, 183c,
        183d, 2 #183b   32.50
      Nos. 176-183 (8)   9.70 9.70

Booklet sold for £7.50. Each of the two panes of No. 183b in the booklet have different selvages.

Souvenir Sheet

Reign of Queen Elizabeth II, 50th Anniv. — A29

2002, Feb. 6   Litho.   Perf. 13¾x13½
184 A29 £2 multi   8.00 8.00
  a.   Booklet pane of 1   8.00
      Complete booklet, #184a,
        Guernsey #773a, 774a, 774b,
        774c   37.50

No. 184a is sewn into booklets, but is otherwise identical to No. 184.

Issued: #184: 2/6; #184a, 4/30.

Birds — A30

2002, Apr. 30   Perf. 13¾
185 A30 22p Hobby   .85   .85
186 A30 27p Black kite   1.00 1.00
187 A30 36p Merlin   1.40 1.40
188 A30 40p Honey buzzard   1.60 1.60
189 A30 45p Osprey   1.75 1.75
190 A30 65p Marsh harrier   2.50 2.50
  a.   Souvenir sheet, #185-190 9.25 9.25
      Nos. 185-190 (6)   9.10 9.10

See Nos. 209-214, 233-238, 256-261.

Lighting at Les Casquets Lighthouse — A31

Designs: 22p, Coal fire, 1725. 27p, Oil lantern, 1779. 36p, Argand lamp, 1790. 45p, Revolving apparatus, 1818. 65p, Electrification, 1952.

2002, July 30   Perf. 12¾x13¼
191 A31 22p multi   .85   .85
192 A31 27p multi   1.00 1.00
193 A31 36p multi   1.40 1.40
194 A31 45p multi   1.75 1.75
195 A31 65p multi   2.50 2.50
      Nos. 191-195 (5)   7.50 7.50

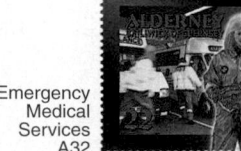

Emergency Medical Services A32

Designs: 22p, Ambulance technician, crew running to ambulance. 27p, Emergency medical technician on radio, ambulance on road.

36p, Doctor, transfer of patient to airplane. 40p, Pilot, Aurigny Trislander airplane. 45p, Emergency dispatch operator, transfer of patient to lifeboat. 65p, Lifeboat crewman, speeding lifeboat.

2002, Oct. 17   Litho.   Perf. 14x14½
196 A32 22p multi   .85   .85
  a.   Perf. 13¼x13   .85   .85
197 A32 27p multi   1.00 1.00
  a.   Perf. 13¼x13   1.00 1.00
198 A32 36p multi   1.40 1.40
  a.   Perf. 13¼x13   1.40 1.40
199 A32 40p multi   1.60 1.60
  a.   Perf. 13¼x13   1.60 1.60
  b.   Booklet pane, #196a, 197a,
        198a, 199a   5.00   —
200 A32 45p multi   1.75 1.75
  a.   Perf. 13¼x13   1.75 1.75
201 A32 65p multi   2.50 2.50
  a.   Perf. 13¼x13   2.50 2.50
  b.   Booklet pane, #198a, 199a,
        200a, 201a   6.25   —
  c.   Booklet pane, #196a, 197a,
        200a, 201a   6.25   —
      Complete booklet, #167b, 169b,
        169c, 199b, 201b, 201c   35.00
      Nos. 196-201 (6)   9.10 9.10

Souvenir Sheet

Coronation of Queen Elizabeth II, 50th Anniv. — A33

Litho. & Embossed

2003, Jan. 30   Perf. 13½
202 A33 £2 multi   8.00 8.00

Powered Flight, Cent. A34

Designs: 22p, Wright Flyer, 1903. 27p, Vickers Vimy, 1919. 36p, Douglas DC-3, 1936. 40p, Comet, 1946. 45p, Concorde, 1969. 65p, Airbus A380.

2003, Apr. 10   Litho.
203 A34 22p multi   .85   .85
204 A34 27p multi   1.00 1.00
205 A34 36p multi   1.40 1.40
206 A34 40p multi   1.60 1.60
207 A34 45p multi   1.75 1.75
208 A34 65p multi   2.50 2.50
      Nos. 203-208 (6)   9.10 9.10

Bird Type of 2002

2003, July 3   Perf. 13¾
209 A30 22p Arctic tern   .85   .85
210 A30 27p Great skua   1.00 1.00
211 A30 36p Sandwich tern   1.40 1.40
212 A30 40p Sooty shearwater 1.60 1.60
213 A30 45p Arctic skua   1.75 1.75
214 A30 65p Manx shearwater   2.50 2.50
  a.   Souvenir sheet, #209-214 9.25 9.25
      Nos. 209-214 (6)   9.10 9.10

Island Police — A35

Police officer and: 22p, Policemen patrolling streets. 27p, Police vehicle. 36p, Member of forensics team. 40p, Policeman assisting child on bicycle. 45p, Police at car accident. 65p, Policeman working with customs officer.

2003, Oct. 16   Litho.   Perf. 13¼x13
215 A35 22p multi   .85   .85
216 A35 27p multi   1.00 1.00
217 A35 36p multi   1.40 1.40
218 A35 40p multi   1.60 1.60
  a.   Booklet pane, #215-218   5.00
219 A35 45p multi   1.75 1.75
  a.   Booklet pane, #215-217, 219 5.75 —
220 A35 65p multi   2.50 2.50
  a.   Booklet pane, #215-216, 219-
        220   6.25   —
  b.   Booklet pane, #217-220   7.25   —

  c.   Booklet pane, #215-216, 218,
        220   6.00   —
      Complete booklet, #218a, 219a,
        220a, 220c, 2 #220b   37.50
      Nos. 215-220 (6)   9.10 9.10

The two examples of No. 220b in the booklet have different margins.

Fungi — A36

Designs: 22p, Sulphur tuft. 27p, Orange peel fungus. 36p, Shining ink-cap. 40p, Giant puffball. 45p, Parasol. 65p, Candle snuff fungus.

2004, Jan. 29   Litho.   Perf. 13¼
221 A36 22p multi   .85   .85
222 A36 27p multi   1.00 1.00
223 A36 36p multi   1.40 1.40
224 A36 40p multi   1.60 1.60
225 A36 45p multi   1.75 1.75
226 A36 65p multi   2.50 2.50
      Nos. 221-226 (6)   9.10 9.10

FIFA (Fédération Internationale de Football Association), Cent. — A37

Designs: 26p, Challenge on Tourgis Close. 32p, Soccer on the beach. 36p, Playground school soccer. 40p, Friendly kickabout. 45p, Turning the defender. 65p, Tackling Dad at Arch Bay.

2004, May 12   Litho.   Perf. 13¼
227 A37 26p multi   1.00 1.00
228 A37 32p multi   1.25 1.25
229 A37 36p multi   1.40 1.40
230 A37 40p multi   1.60 1.60
231 A37 45p multi   1.75 1.75
232 A37 65p multi   2.50 2.50
      Nos. 227-232 (6)   9.50 9.50

Values are for stamps with surrounding selvage.

Birds Type of 2002

2004, July 29   Litho.   Perf. 13¼
233 A30 26p Wheatear   1.00 1.00
234 A30 32p Redstart   1.25 1.25
235 A30 36p Yellow wagtail   1.40 1.40
236 A30 40p Hoopoe   1.60 1.60
237 A30 45p Ring ouzel   1.75 1.75
238 A30 65p Sand martin   2.50 2.50
  a.   Souvenir sheet, #233-238 9.50 9.50
      Nos. 233-238 (6)   9.50 9.50

Fire Services A38

Designs: 26p, Fireman and fire truck. 32p, Firemen and fire truck. 36p, Fireman and airport fire truck. 40p, Fire chief, fire truck at station. 45p, Training grounds at airport. 65p, Road accicent training exercise.

2004, Oct. 28   Litho.   Perf. 13¼x13
239 A38 26p multi   1.00 1.00
240 A38 32p multi   1.25 1.25
241 A38 36p multi   1.40 1.40
242 A38 40p multi   1.60 1.60
  a.   Booklet pane, #239-242   5.00
243 A38 45p multi   1.75 1.75
  a.   Booklet pane, #239-241, 243 5.75 —
244 A38 65p multi   2.50 2.50
  a.   Booklet pane, #239-240, 243-
        244   6.75   —
  b.   Booklet pane, #241-244   7.50   —
  c.   Booklet pane, #239-240, 242,
        244   6.50   —
      Complete booklet, #242a,
        243a, 244a, 244c, 2 #244b 42.50
      Nos. 239-244 (6)   9.50 9.50

The two examples of No. 244b in the complete booklet have different margins.

Hans Christian Andersen (1805-75),
Author — A39

Scenes from "The Little Mermaid": 26p,
Mermaid, fish, castle. 32p, Mermaid rescues
prince. 36p, Mermaid and sea witch. 40p, Mermaid and prince on land. 65p, Dead mermaid
and angels.

2005, Feb. 3   Litho.   Perf. 13½
245 A39 26p multi   1.00   1.00
246 A39 32p multi   1.25   1.25
247 A39 36p multi   1.40   1.40
248 A39 40p multi   1.60   1.60
249 A39 65p multi   2.50   2.50
        Nos. 245-249 (5)   7.75   7.75

Battle of
Trafalgar,
Bicent. — A40

Designs: 26p, Admiral Horatio Nelson. 32p,
HMS Victory. 36p, Enemy in sight. 40p, Fall of
Nelson. 45p, Breaking the line. 65p, Admiral
James de Saumarez.

2005, May 9   Litho.   Perf. 14x13¼
250 A40 26p multi   1.00   1.00
251 A40 32p multi   1.25   1.25
252 A40 36p multi   1.40   1.40
253 A40 40p multi   1.60   1.60
  a.   Booklet pane, #250-253   5.50
254 A40 45p multi   1.75   1.75
255 A40 65p multi   2.50   2.50
  a.   Booklet pane, #250-251, 254-255   6.50
  b.   Booklet pane, #252-255   7.25
  c.   Booklet pane, #251-252, 254-255 7.00
  d.   Booklet pane, #250, 253-255   6.75
       Complete booklet, #255a, 255b, 255c, 255d, 2 #253a 42.50
       Nos. 250-255 (6)   9.50   9.50

The two examples of No. 253a in the complete booklet have different pane margins.

Bird Type of 2002
2005, July 21   Perf. 13¼
256 A30 26p Little stint   1.00   1.00
257 A30 32p Greenshank   1.25   1.25
258 A30 36p Golden plover   1.40   1.40
259 A30 40p Bar-tailed god-
                wit   1.60   1.60
260 A30 45p Green sandpi-
                per   1.75   1.75
261 A30 65p Sanderling   2.50   2.50
  a.   Souvenir sheet, #256-261   11.00 11.00
        Nos. 256-261 (6)   9.50   9.50

Souvenir Sheet

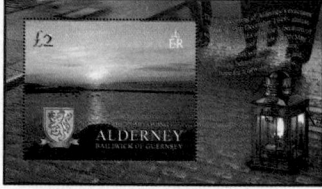

Homecoming of World War II
Evacuees, 60th Anniv. — A41

2005, Oct. 27   Perf. 13¾
262 A41 £2 multi   8.00   8.00

T.H. White, Author
of The Once and
Future King, Birth
Centenary — A42

Authorian legends: 29p, King Arthur. 34p,
Merlyn. 38p, Morgause. 42p, Queen
Guenever. 47p, Lancelot. 68p, Mordred.

2006, Feb. 16 Litho. Perf. 13½x14
263 A42 29p multi   1.10   1.10
264 A42 34p multi   1.40   1.40
265 A42 38p multi   1.50   1.50
266 A42 42p multi   1.60   1.60
267 A42 47p multi   1.90   1.90
268 A42 68p multi   2.75   2.75
  a.   Souvenir sheet, #263-268   10.50 10.50
        Nos. 263-268 (6)   10.25 10.25

Queen Elizabeth II, 80th
Birthday — A43

Various photographs of Queen with predom-
inant background colors of:
No. 269: a, Blue violet. b, Red violet.
No. 270: a, Green. b, Orange brown.
No. 271: a, Yellow brown. b, Bright red.
No. 272: a, Red. b, Violet.
Illustration reduced.

2006, Apr. 21   Perf. 13¾
269 A43 Horiz. pair   2.25   2.25
  a.-b. 29p Either single   1.10   1.10
270 A43 Horiz. pair   3.00   3.00
  a.-b. 34p Either single   1.50   1.50
271 A43 Horiz. pair   3.25   3.25
  a.-b. 42p Either single   1.60   1.60
272 A43 Horiz. pair   3.50   3.50
  a.-b. 45p Either single   1.75   1.75
        Nos. 269-272 (4)   12.00 12.00

Birds — A44

Designs: 29p, Fulmar. 34p, Gannet. 42p,
Lesser black-backed gull. 45p, Storm petrel.
47p, Kittiwake. 68p, Puffin.

2006, July 27   Litho.   Perf. 13¾
273 A44 29p multi   1.10   1.10
  a.   Booklet pane of 4   4.50
274 A44 34p multi   1.50   1.50
  a.   Booklet pane of 4   6.00
275 A44 42p multi   1.60   1.60
  a.   Booklet pane of 4   6.50
276 A44 45p multi   1.75   1.75
  a.   Booklet pane of 4   7.00
277 A44 47p multi   2.00   2.00
  a.   Booklet pane of 4   8.00
278 A44 68p multi   2.75   2.75
  a.   Booklet pane of 4   11.00
       Complete booklet, #273a, 274a, 275a, 276a, 277a, 278a   45.00
       Nos. 273-278 (6)   10.70 10.70

See Nos. 297-302, 319-324, 344-349.

Corals and
Anemones — A45

Designs: 1p, Burrowing anemone. 2p, Colonial anemone. 3p, Jewel anemone. 4p, Sagar-
tia elegans. 5p, Plumose anemone. 6p, Plumose
anemone. 7p, Fan coral. 8p, Jewel anemone,
diff. 9p, Actinothoe sphyrodeta. 10p,
Snakelocks anemone. £1, Beadlet anemone.
£2, Sunset cup coral.

2006, Nov. 2   Litho.   Perf. 13x13½
279 A45 1p multi   .20   .20
280 A45 2p multi   .20   .20
281 A45 3p multi   .20   .20
282 A45 4p multi   .20   .20
283 A45 5p multi   .20   .20
284 A45 6p multi   .20   .20
285 A45 7p multi   .25   .25
286 A45 8p multi   .30   .30
287 A45 9p multi   .35   .35
288 A45 10p multi   .40   .40

Litho. & Embossed
Size: 22x27mm
Perf. 12¾x13¼
289 A45 £1 multi   3.75   3.75
290 A45 £2 multi   7.75   7.75
        Nos. 279-290 (12)   14.00 14.00
        See Nos. 303-306.

Alderney
Wetlands
A46

Designs: 32p, Cushion starfish. 37p, Gannet. 45p, Squat lobster. 48p, Gray seal. 50p,
Golden samphire. 71p, Little egret.

2007, Mar. 8   Litho.   Perf. 13¼
291 A46 32p multi   1.25   1.25
292 A46 37p multi   1.50   1.50
293 A46 45p multi   1.75   1.75
294 A46 48p multi   1.90   1.90
295 A46 50p multi   2.00   2.00
296 A46 71p multi   2.75   2.75
  a.   Souvenir sheet, #291-296   11.50 11.50
        Nos. 291-296 (6)   11.15 11.15

Addition of Alderney Wetlands and Burhou
Islands to Ramsar Convention Protected Wetlands List.

Birds Type of 2006
Designs: 32p, Blackbird. 37p, Dartford warbler. 45p, Blue tit. 48p, Wren. 50p, House
sparrow. 71p, Jackdaw.

2007, May 24   Litho.   Perf. 13¾
297 A44 32p multi   1.25   1.25
  a.   Booklet pane of 4   5.00
298 A44 37p multi   1.50   1.50
  a.   Booklet pane of 4   6.00
299 A44 45p multi   1.75   1.75
  a.   Booklet pane of 4   7.00
300 A44 48p multi   1.90   1.90
  a.   Booklet pane of 4   7.75
301 A44 50p multi   2.00   2.00
  a.   Booklet pane of 4   8.00
302 A44 71p multi   3.00   3.00
  a.   Booklet pane of 4   12.00
       Complete booklet, #297a-302a   46.00
       Nos. 297-302 (6)   11.40 11.40

Corals and Anemones Type of 2006
Designs: 20p, Devonshire cup coral. 40p,
Fried egg anemone. 50p, Parasitic anemone.
£4, Strawberry anemone.

2007, Aug. 2   Litho.   Perf. 14
Size: 27x23mm
303 A45 20p multi   .80   .80
304 A45 40p multi   1.60   1.60
305 A45 50p multi   2.10   2.10

Litho. & Embossed
Size: 27x28mm
306 A45 £4 multi   16.00 16.00
        Nos. 303-306 (4)   20.50 20.50

Just So Stories, by
Rudyard
Kipling — A47

Designs: 32p, How the Camel Got His
Hump. 37p, How the Whale Got His Throat.
45p, The Elephant's Child. 48p, How the
Leopard Got His Spots. 50p, The Cat That
Walked by Himself. 71p, How the Rhinoceros
Got His Skin.

2007, Oct. 25   Litho.   Perf. 13x13¼
307 A47 32p multi   1.40   1.40
308 A47 37p multi   1.50   1.50
309 A47 45p multi   1.90   1.90
310 A47 48p multi   2.00   2.00
311 A47 50p multi   2.10   2.10
312 A47 71p multi   3.00   3.00
  a.   Miniature sheet, #307-312   12.00 12.00
        Nos. 307-312 (6)   11.90 11.90

Butterflies
A48

Butterflies: 34p, Painted lady. 40p, Grayling.
48p, Green hairstreak. 51p, Speckled wood.
53c, Common blue. 74p, Glanville fritillary.

2008, Feb. 28   Litho.   Perf. 13¾
313 A48 34p multi   1.40   1.40
314 A48 40p multi   1.60   1.60
315 A48 48p multi   1.90   1.90
316 A48 51p multi   2.00   2.00
317 A48 53p multi   2.10   2.10
318 A48 74p multi   3.00   3.00
  a.   Miniature sheet, #313-318   12.00 12.00
        Nos. 313-318 (6)   12.00 12.00

Birds Type of 2006
Designs: 34p, Common buzzard. 40p, Pere-
grine falcon. 48p, Kestrel. 51p, Barn owl. 53p,
Long-eared owl. 74p, Sparrowhawk.

2008, May 15   Litho.   Perf. 13¾
319 A44 34p multi   1.40   1.40
  a.   Booklet pane of 4   5.75
320 A44 40p multi   1.60   1.60
  a.   Booklet pane of 4   6.50
321 A44 48p multi   1.90   1.90
  a.   Booklet pane of 4   7.75
322 A44 51p multi   2.00   2.00
  a.   Booklet pane of 4   8.00
323 A44 53p multi   2.10   2.10
  a.   Booklet pane of 4   8.50
324 A44 74p multi   3.00   3.00
  a.   Booklet pane of 4   12.00
       Complete booklet, #319a-324a   49.00
       Nos. 319-324 (6)   12.00 12.00

Alderney Postage Stamps, 25th
Anniv. — A49

Flag and tourist sites: 34p, Old Harbor. 40p,
Breakwater. 48p, Fort Clonque Causeway.
51p, Golf course. 53p, Hanging Rock. 74p,
Fort Clonque.

2008, June 14   Litho.   Perf. 14x13¾
325 A49 34p multi   1.40   1.40
326 A49 40p multi   1.60   1.60
327 A49 48p multi   1.90   1.90
328 A49 51p multi   2.00   2.00
329 A49 53p multi   2.10   2.10
330 A49 74p multi   3.00   3.00
        Nos. 325-330 (6)   12.00 12.00
        See No. 376.

Heraldic
Lion — A50

Litho. & Embossed With Foil
Application
2008, June 14   Perf. 14¼x13½
331 A50 £5 multi   20.00 20.00

Aurigny Air Services, 40th
Anniv. — A51

Airplanes: 34p, Britten-Norman Islander.
40p, Britten-Norman Trislander. 48p, DHC-6
Twin Otter. 51p, Short 360. 53p, Saab 340.
74p, ATR 72.

2008, Oct. 30　　Litho.　　Perf. 13½

332	A51	34p multi	1.10	1.10
333	A51	40p multi	1.25	1.25
334	A51	48p multi	1.60	1.60
335	A51	51p multi	1.75	1.75
336	A51	53p multi	1.75	1.75
337	A51	74p multi	2.40	2.40
a.		Souvenir sheet, #332-337	10.00	10.00
		Nos. 332-337 (6)	9.85	9.85

Bees — A52

Flowers and: 36p, Tawny mining bee. 43p, Early bumblebee. 51p, Bug mining bee. 54p, Cuckoo bee. 56p, Solitary bee. 77p, Honey bee.

2009, Feb. 26　　Litho.　　Perf. 13¾

338	A52	36p multi	1.10	1.10
339	A52	43p multi	1.25	1.25
340	A52	51p multi	1.50	1.50
341	A52	54p multi	1.60	1.60
342	A52	56p multi	1.60	1.60
343	A52	77p multi	2.25	2.25
a.		Miniature sheet of 6, #338-343	9.50	9.50
		Nos. 338-343 (6)	9.30	9.30

Birds Type of 2006

Designs: 36p, Turnstone. 43p, Curlew. 51p, Oystercatcher. 54p, Snipe. 56p, Dunlin. 77p, Ringed plover.

2009, May 28　　Litho.　　Perf. 13¾

344	A44	36p multi	1.25	1.25
a.		Booklet pane of 4	5.00	—
345	A44	43p multi	1.40	1.40
a.		Booklet pane of 4	5.75	—
346	A44	51p multi	1.60	1.60
a.		Booklet pane of 4	6.50	—
347	A44	54p multi	1.75	1.75
a.		Booklet pane of 4	7.00	—
348	A44	56p multi	1.90	1.90
a.		Booklet pane of 4	7.75	—
349	A44	77p multi	2.50	2.50
a.		Booklet pane of 4	10.00	—
		Complete booklet, #344a-349a	42.00	
		Nos. 344-349 (6)	10.40	10.40

Naval Aviation, Cent. — A53

Designs: 36p, Flying Boat over Castle Cornet. 43p, Swordfish attacking U-boat. 51p, Skuas divebombing Scharnhorst. 54p, Sea Fury over Alderney. 56p, Sea Hawk and Sea Fury. 77p, Merlin helicopter landing on HMS Daring.

2009, July 30　　Perf. 14¼x13¾

350	A53	36p multi	1.25	1.25
351	A53	43p multi	1.50	1.50
352	A53	51p multi	1.75	1.75
353	A53	54p multi	1.90	1.90
354	A53	56p multi	1.90	1.90
355	A53	77p multi	2.60	2.60
		Nos. 350-355 (6)	10.90	10.90

Scenes From Sherlock Holmes and the Curious Case of the Alderney Bull, by Sir Arthur Conan Doyle (1859-1930) — A54

Designs: 36p, Alice West reporting theft to Holmes. 43p, Holmes and policeman studying message, arrest of suspect. 51p, Holmes looking for clues with magnifying glass. 54p, Holmes with two men outside building. 56p, Holmes pointing to partially-built lighthouse. 77p, Holmes pointing to thief.

2009, Oct. 29　　Litho.　　Perf. 13¼x13

356	A54	36p multi	1.25	1.25
357	A54	43p multi	1.50	1.50
358	A54	51p multi	1.75	1.75
359	A54	54p multi	1.90	1.90
360	A54	56p multi	1.90	1.90
361	A54	77p multi	2.60	2.60
		Nos. 356-361 (6)	10.90	10.90

A miniature sheet of six containing one of each stamp was sold together with a DVD for £9.99. The sheet was not available separately.

Dragonflies A55

Designs: 36p, Common darter. 45p, Emperor dragonfly. 56p, Blue-tailed damselfly. 66p, Brown hawker. 75p, Black-tailed skimmer. 83p, Red-veined darter.

2010, Feb. 25　　Litho.　　Perf. 13¾

362	A55	36p multi	1.10	1.10
363	A55	45p multi	1.40	1.40
364	A55	56p multi	1.75	1.75
365	A55	66p multi	2.00	2.00
366	A55	75p multi	2.40	2.40
367	A55	83p multi	2.60	2.60
a.		Souvenir sheet, #362-367	11.50	11.50
		Nos. 362-367 (6)	11.25	11.25

Battle of Britain, 70th Anniv. A56

Designs: 36p, Pilot Keith Gilman. 45p, Hawker Hurricanes in flight. 48p, Pilots scrambling to planes. 50p, Spitfire sortie. 58p, Air raid warden. 80p, Evacuees. £2, Sir Douglas Bader, vert.

2010, May 4　　　Perf. 14

369	A56	36p blk & gray	1.10	1.10
370	A56	45p blk & gray	1.40	1.40
371	A56	48p blk & gray	1.50	1.50
372	A56	50p blk & gray	1.50	1.50
373	A56	58p blk & gray	1.75	1.75
374	A56	80p blk & gray	2.40	2.40
		Nos. 369-374 (6)	9.65	9.65

Souvenir Sheet

375	A56	£2 blk & gray	6.00	6.00

Alderney Postage Stamps, 25th Anniv. Type of 2008

Design: Hanging Rock.

2010, July 29　　Perf. 14x13¾

376	A49	55p multi	1.75	1.75

Florence Nightingale (1820-1910), Nurse — A57

Various quotes of Nightingale and: 36p, Hand carrying lantern. 45p, Hand reaching out. 48p, Hand holding bucket. 50p, Hands unwrapping gauze bandage. 58p, Hand writing. 80p, Hands in prayer.

2010, July 29　　Perf. 14½x14

377	A57	36p multi	1.10	1.10
378	A57	45p multi	1.40	1.40
379	A57	48p multi	1.50	1.50
380	A57	50p multi	1.60	1.60
381	A57	58p multi	1.90	1.90
382	A57	80p multi	2.50	2.50
		Nos. 377-382 (6)	10.00	10.00

Peter Pan, by Sir James M. Barrie (1860-1937) — A58

Designs: 36p, Children flying above London. 45p, Captain Hook and crocodile. 48p, Peter Pan visits Captain Hook's ship. 50p, Peter Pan waving a rainbow. 58p, Children on Neverpeak. 80p, Bonfire. £3, Peter Pan, vert.

2010, Nov. 4　　Litho.　　Perf. 13¼x13½

383	A58	36p multi	1.25	1.25
384	A58	45p multi	1.50	1.50
385	A58	48p multi	1.60	1.60
386	A58	50p multi	1.60	1.60
387	A58	58p multi	1.90	1.90
388	A58	80p multi	2.60	2.60
		Nos. 383-388 (6)	10.45	10.45

Souvenir Sheet
Perf. 13½x13¼

389	A58	£3 multi	10.00	10.00

Christmas Carols A59

Designs: 31p, O Christmas Tree. 36p, Away in a Manger. 45p, While Shepherds Watched Their Flocks By Night. 48p, Hark the Herald Angels Sing. 50p, O Holy Night. 58p, O Little Town of Bethlehem. 80p, Good King Wenceslas.

2010, Nov. 4　　Litho.　　Perf. 13¼x14

390	A59	31p multi	1.00	1.00
391	A59	36p multi	1.25	1.25
392	A59	45p multi	1.50	1.50
393	A59	48p multi	1.60	1.60
394	A59	50p multi	1.60	1.60
395	A59	58p multi	1.90	1.90
396	A59	80p multi	2.60	2.60
		Nos. 390-396 (7)	11.45	11.45

JERSEY

jər-zē

LOCATION — Island in the English Channel
GOVT. — Dependent territory (bailiwick) of the British Crown
AREA — 45 sq. mi.
POP. — 89,721 (1999 est.)
CAPITAL — St. Helier

Following the establishment of the British General Post Office as a public corporation on October 1, 1969, the post office of the Bailiwick of Jersey became a separate entity and British postage stamps ceased to be valid.

Catalogue values for unused stamps in this country are for Never Hinged items.

British Regional Issue

A1

Royal Mace and Arms of Jersey — A2

Perf. 15x14

1958-69　　Photo.　　Wmk. 322

1	A1	2½p rose red ('64)	.35	.25
2	A2	3p light purple	.35	.20
p.		Phosphor. ('67)	.20	.20
3	A2	4p ultra ('66)	.35	.20
p.		Phosphor. ('67)	.20	.20
		Unwmk.		
4	A2	4p olive brown ('68)	.20	.20
5	A2	4p brt red ('69)	.20	.20
6	A2	5p dark blue ('68)	.20	.20
		Nos. 1-6 (6)	1.65	1.25

Nos. 4-6 are phosphorescent.
Sold to the general public only at post offices within Jersey, but valid for postage throughout Great Britain.
See also Great Britain Nos. 269-270, which were sold only in the Channel Islands and at a few philatelic windows in Great Britain, and may be considered to be precursors to the regional issues.

Bailiwick Issues

Elizabeth Castle and Queen Elizabeth II — A3

Queen Elizabeth II — A4

Designs (Queen Elizabeth II and): 1p, La Hougue Bie (prehistoric tomb). 2p, Portelet Bay. 3p, La Corbière Lighthouse. 4p, Mont Orgueil by night. 5p, Arms of Jersey and Royal Mace. 6p, Jersey cow. 9p, 1sh6p, Map of English Channel with Jersey. 1sh, Mont Orgueil. 2sh6p, Airport. 5sh, Legislative Chamber. 10sh, Royal Court. £1, Queen Elizabeth II, photograph by Cecil Beaton.

Perf. 14½

1969, Oct. 1　　Photo.　　Unwmk.

7	A3	½p ocher & multi	.20	.20
8	A3	1p brown & multi	.20	.20
a.		Booklet pane of 1	.35	
b.		Booklet pane of 2	.90	
9	A3	2p multicolored	.20	.20
10	A3	3p dp blue & multi	.20	.20
11	A3	4p multicolored	.20	.20
a.		Booklet pane of 4	.60	
b.		Booklet pane of 2	1.10	
12	A3	5p multicolored	.20	.20
a.		Booklet pane of 2	1.75	
13	A3	6p multicolored	.40	.20
14	A3	9p multicolored	.60	.30
15	A3	1sh lilac & multi	.80	.70
16	A3	1sh6p green & multi	1.40	1.40
17	A4	1sh9p multicolored	2.00	2.00
		Perf. 12		
18	A3	2sh6p multicolored	3.50	2.75
19	A3	5sh multicolored	12.00	10.00
20	A3	10sh gray & multi	27.50	20.00
a.		10sh green & multi (error)	4,000.	
21	A4	£1 tan & multi	4.00	3.50
		Nos. 7-21 (15)	53.40	42.05

A second post-1971 printing of No. 21 shows the background drapery less purple and more blue. Value, $3.
See Nos. 34-48, 107-109.

Jersey Post Office First Day Cover A5

Inauguration of the Jersey Post Office, 1969

1969, Oct. 1　　Perf. 14½

22	A5	4p multicolored	.35	.20
23	A5	5p blue & multi	.40	.20
24	A5	1sh6p brown & multi	1.10	1.25
25	A5	1sh9p emerald & multi	1.75	2.10
		Nos. 22-25 (4)	3.60	3.75

Inauguration of independent postal service.

Jersey Woman Reaching for Royal Mace, Flags of USSR, US and Great Britain — A6

4p, Lord Coutanche, Bailiff of Jersey, by James Gunn, vert. 5p, Sir Winston Churchill, by D. Van Praag, vert. 1sh9p, Swedish Red Cross ship "Vega."

1970, May 9   Photo.   Perf. 11½

26	A6	4p gold & multi	.50	.20
27	A6	5p gold & multi	.50	.20
28	A6	1sh6p gold & multi	2.00	2.00
29	A6	1sh9p gold & multi	2.00	2.00
		Nos. 26-29 (4)	5.00	4.40

25th anniv. of Jersey's liberation from the Germans.

"Rags to Riches" Cinderella — A7

Designs (Parade Floats Made of Flowers): 4p, "A Tribute to Enid Blyton," author of children's books. 1sh6p, "Gourmet's Delight." 1sh9p, "We're the Greatest" (ostriches and trees).

1970, July 28   Photo.   Perf. 11½

30	A7	4p gold & multi	.60	.20
31	A7	5p gold & multi	.60	.60
32	A7	1sh6p gold & multi	8.00	5.00
33	A7	1sh9p gold & multi	8.00	6.50
		Nos. 30-33 (4)	17.20	12.30

"Battle of Flowers" annual parade.

**Decimal Currency Issue
Types of 1969
"p" instead of "d"**

Designs: ½p, Elizabeth Castle. 1p, La Corbiere Lighthouse. 1½p, Jersey cow. 2p, Mont Orgueil by night. 2½p, Arms of Jersey and Royal Mace. 3p, La Hougue Bie. 3½p, Portelet Bay. 4p, 7½p, Map of English Channel and Jersey. 5p, Mont Orgueil by day. 6p, Martello Tower at Archirondel. 9p, Queen Elizabeth II, by Cecil Beaton. 10p, Airport. 20p, Legislative Chamber. 50p, Royal Court.

1970-75   Photo.   Perf. 14½

34	A3	½p ocher & multi ('71)	.20	.20
a.		Booklet pane of 1		.20
35	A3	1p multicolored ('71)	.20	.20
a.		Booklet pane of 2 ('75)		.20
b.		Booklet pane of 4 ('75)		.35
36	A3	1½p multicolored ('71)	.20	.20
37	A3	2p multicolored ('71)	.20	.20
a.		Booklet pane of 1		.20
b.		Booklet pane of 2		.35
38	A3	2½p multicolored ('71)	.20	.20
a.		Booklet pane of 1		.35
b.		Booklet pane of 2		.45
39	A3	3p brn & multicolored ('71)	.20	.20
a.		Booklet pane of 1 ('72)		.35
b.		Booklet pane of 2 ('72)		.45
40	A3	3½p multicolored ('71)	.20	.20
a.		Booklet pane of 1 ('74)		.35
b.		Booklet pane of 2 ('74)		.50
41	A3	4p multicolored ('71)	.20	.20
a.		Booklet pane of 2 ('75)		.50
b.		Booklet pane of 4 ('75)		.75
42	A3	5p lilac & multi ('71)	.20	.20
a.		Booklet pane of 2 ('75)		.55
b.		Booklet pane of 4 ('75)		.95
43	A3	6p green & multi ('71)	.20	.20
44	A3	7½p multicolored ('71)	.25	.25
45	A4	9p multicolored ('71)	.35	.35

Perf. 12

46	A3	10p multicolored	.40	.40
47	A3	20p multicolored	.75	.75
48	A3	50p multicolored	1.90	1.90
		Nos. 34-48 (15)	5.65	5.65

See also Nos. 107-109.

White-eared Pheasant — A8

2½p, Thick-billed parrots, vert. 7½p, Ursine colobus monkeys, vert. 9p, Ring-tailed lemurs.

1971, Mar. 9   Photo.   Perf. 11½

49	A8	2p deep plum & multi	.70	.20
50	A8	2½p dark gray & multi	.80	.20
51	A8	7½p olive & multi	6.00	5.00
52	A8	9p vio blue & multi	8.00	8.00
		Nos. 49-52 (4)	15.50	13.40

Jersey Wildlife Preservation Trust.
See Nos. 65-68.

British Legion Emblem A9

2½p, Poppy field & poppy emblem. 7½p, Jack Counter (1899-1970) & Victoria Cross. 9p, Flags of France & Great Britain.

1971, June 15   Litho.   Perf. 14½

53	A9	2p multicolored	.35	.20
54	A9	2½p multicolored	.35	.20
55	A9	7½p multicolored	2.25	2.00
56	A9	9p multicolored	2.25	2.25
		Nos. 53-56 (4)	5.20	4.65

50th anniversary of the British Legion.

English Fleet in Channel, by Peter Monamy A10

Paintings by Jersey Artists: 2p, Tante Elizabeth (women in farm kitchen), by Edmund Blampied, vert. 7½p, Boyhood of Raleigh (man and boys at seashore), by Sir John Millais. 9p, The Blind Beggar (old man and girl), by W. W. Ouless, vert.

1971, Oct. 5   Photo.   Perf. 11½

57	A10	2p gold & multi	.30	.20
58	A10	2½p gold & multi	.40	.20
59	A10	7½p gold & multi	3.00	2.50
60	A10	9p gold & multi	3.00	2.50
		Nos. 57-60 (4)	6.70	5.40

Jersey Fern — A11   Jersey Royal Artillery Shako — A12

Jersey Wild Flowers: 5p, Thrift. 7½p, Orchid (laxiflora). 9p, Viper's bugloss.

**1972, Jan. 18
Flowers in Natural Colors**

61	A11	3p brown & blk	.35	.20
62	A11	5p lt blue & blk	.75	.35
63	A11	7½p lilac & blk	2.25	1.90
64	A11	9p green & blk	2.25	2.00
		Nos. 61-64 (4)	5.60	4.45

Wildlife Type of 1971

2½p, Cheetahs. 3p, Rothschild's mynahs, vert. 7½p, Spectacled bear. 9p, Tuatara reptiles.

**1972, Mar. 17   Photo.   Perf. 11½
Queen's Head in Gold**

65	A8	2½p Prus blue & multi	.85	.20
66	A8	3p dk pur & multi	.60	.20
67	A8	7½p yel bis & multi	1.25	1.25
68	A8	9p multicolored	1.75	1.75
		Nos. 65-68 (4)	4.45	3.40

Jersey Wildlife Preservation Trust.

1972, June 27

69	A12	2½p shown	.25	.20
70	A12	3p 2nd North Regiment	.25	.20
71	A12	7½p South West Regiment	.60	.30
72	A12	9p 3rd (South) Light Infantry	.85	.65
		Nos. 69-72 (4)	1.95	1.35

Royal Jersey Militia shakos of 19th century.

Princess Anne — A13

Designs: 3p, Queen Elizabeth II and Prince Philip, horiz. 7½p, Prince Charles. 20p, Queen Elizabeth II and family, horiz.

1972, Nov. 1   Photo.   Perf. 11½

73	A13	2½p citron & multi	.20	.20
74	A13	3p rose & multi	.20	.20
75	A13	7½p blue & multi	.25	.20
76	A13	20p gray & multi	.75	.50
		Nos. 73-76 (4)	1.40	1.10

25th anniversary of the marriage of Queen Elizabeth II and Prince Philip.

Silver Wine and Christening Cups, 18th Century A14

Designs: 3p, Gold torque, Bronze Age, vert. 7½p, Seal of Charles II, 1659, vert. 9p, Armorican (Brittany) coins, c. 55 B.C.

1973, Jan. 23   Photo.   Perf. 11½

77	A14	2½p ultra & multi	.20	.20
78	A14	3p dp car & multi	.20	.20
79	A14	7½p org & multi	.25	.25
80	A14	9p blue & multi	.35	.25
		Nos. 77-80 (4)	1.00	.90

Cent. of the Jersey Soc. Designs are from exhibits in the Soc. museum in St. Helier.

Balloon, Letter to Jersey from Siege of Paris, 1870 — A15

5p, Astra seaplane, 1912. 7½p, Supermarine Sea Eagle, 1923. 9p, De Havilland DH86, 1933.

1973, May 16   Photo.   Perf. 11½

81	A15	3p brt blue & multi	.20	.20
82	A15	5p blue grn & multi	.20	.20
83	A15	7½p ultra & multi	.35	.35
84	A15	9p vio blue & multi	.45	.45
		Nos. 81-84 (4)	1.20	1.20

Aviation history connected with Jersey before 1939.

19th Century Locomotives A16

1973, Aug. 6   Photo.   Perf. 11½

85	A16	2½p North Western	.20	.20
86	A16	3p Calvados	.20	.20
87	A16	7½p Carteret	.35	.30
88	A16	9p Caesarea	.45	.35
		Nos. 85-88 (4)	1.20	1.05

Centenary of Jersey Eastern Railroad.

Princess Anne and Mark Phillips A17

1973, Nov. 14   Photo.   Perf. 11½

89	A17	3p lt blue & multi	.20	.20
90	A17	20p pink & multi	.60	.80

Wedding of Princess Anne and Capt. Mark Phillips, Nov. 14, 1973.

Spider Crab A18

1973, Nov. 15   Photo.   Perf. 11½

91	A18	2½p shown	.20	.20
92	A18	3p Conger eel	.20	.20
93	A18	7½p Lobster	.30	.25
94	A18	20p Ormer	.60	.30
		Nos. 91-94 (4)	1.30	.95

Jersey Spring Flowers — A19

1974, Feb. 13   Photo.   Perf. 12x11½

95	A19	3p Freesias	.20	.20
96	A19	5½p Anemones	.20	.20
97	A19	8p Carnations & gladioli	.25	.25
98	A19	10p Daffodils & iris	.35	.35
		Nos. 95-98 (4)	1.00	1.00

First Letter Box, Letter with 1852 Cancel A20

UPU Cent.: 3p, Postmen, 1862 and 1969. 5½p, Contemporary pillar box and first day cover of No. 101. 20p, BAC 111 and paddle steamer "Aquila," 1874.

1974, June 7   Photo.   Perf. 11½

99	A20	2½p multicolored	.20	.20
100	A20	3p ultra & multi	.20	.20
101	A20	5½p olive & multi	.20	.20
102	A20	20p gray & multi	.75	.40
		Nos. 99-102 (4)	1.35	1.00

John Wesley — A21

Lithographed and Engraved

1974, July 31		**Perf. 13½x14**		
103	A21	3p shown	.20	.20
104	A21	3½p Hillary	.20	.20
105	A21	8p Wace	.25	.25
106	A21	20p Churchill	.75	.50
		Nos. 103-106 (4)	1.40	1.15

Anniversaries: Methodism in Jersey, bicen.; John Wesley, theologian, founder of Methodism. Sesquicentennial of Royal Natl. Lifeboat Institution, Lt. Col. Sir William Hillary, founder. 800th death anniv. of Canon Wace, poet and chronicler. Sir Winston Churchill, birth centenary.

Type of 1969

4½p, Arms of Jersey and Royal Mace. 5½p, Jersey cow. 8p, Mont Orgueil by night.

1974, Oct. 31		**Photo.**	**Perf. 14½**	
107	A3	4½p olive & multi	.20	.20
108	A3	5½p magenta & multi	.20	.20
109	A3	8p yellow & multi	.30	.30
		Nos. 107-109 (3)	.70	.70

English Yacht, 1660, by Peter Monamy A22

Marine paintings by Peter Monamy (d. 1749): 5½p, French ship. 8p, Dutch ship, horiz. 25p, Naval battle, 1662.

1974, Nov. 22		**Photo.**	**Perf. 11½**	
		Size: 31x38, 38x31mm		
116	A22	3½p gold & multi	.20	.20
117	A22	5½p gold & multi	.20	.20
118	A22	8p gold & multi	.25	.25
		Size: 54x25mm		
119	A22	25p gold & multi	.65	.65
		Nos. 116-119 (4)	1.30	1.30

Potato Digger — A23

19th cent. farming tools: 3½p, Cider apple crusher. 8p, Six-horse plow. 10p, Hay cart.

1975, Feb. 25		**Photo.**	**Perf. 11½**	
120	A23	3p multicolored	.20	.20
121	A23	3½p multicolored	.20	.20
122	A23	8p multicolored	.40	.30
123	A23	10p multicolored	.70	.35
		Nos. 120-123 (4)	1.50	1.05

Shell Design as Letter "J" — A24

Posters: 8p, Beach umbrella. 10p, Beach chair. 12p, Sand castle with Union Jacks & Jersey flag.

1975, June 8		**Photo.**	**Perf. 11½**	
124	A24	5p multicolored	.20	.20
125	A24	8p multicolored	.20	.20
126	A24	10p multicolored	.30	.30
127	A24	12p multicolored	.40	.40
a.		Souvenir sheet of 4	1.25	1.25
		Nos. 124-127 (4)	1.10	1.10

Tourist publicity. No. 127a contains Nos. 124-127 in continuous design extending into margin.

Queen Mother Elizabeth A25

1975, May 30		**Photo.**	**Perf. 11½**	
128	A25	20p multicolored	.75	.50

Visit of Queen Mother Elizabeth to Jersey.

Common Tern — A26

1975, July 28		**Photo.**	**Perf. 11½**	
129	A26	4p shown	.20	.20
130	A26	5p Storm petrel	.20	.20
131	A26	8p Brent geese	.40	.20
132	A26	25p Shag	.80	.35
		Nos. 129-132 (4)	1.60	.95

Siskin 3A, 1925 — A27

R.A.F. Planes: 5p, Southampton 1, 1925. 10p, Spitfire 1, 1931. 25p, Gnat T.1, 1962.

1975, Oct. 30		**Photo.**	**Perf. 11½**	
133	A27	4p blue & multi	.20	.20
134	A27	5p lt green & multi	.20	.20
135	A27	10p yellow & multi	.40	.35
136	A27	25p ultra & multi	.70	.70
		Nos. 133-136 (4)	1.50	1.45

Royal Air Force Assoc., Jersey Branch, 50th anniv.

Map of Jersey with 12 Parishes A28

Arms of Trinity and Zoo — A29

1976-77		**Litho.**	**Perf. 14½**	
		Size: 33x23mm		
137	A28	½p lt blue & multi	.20	.20
138	A29	1p bister & multi	.20	.20
a.		Bklt. pane of 2 + 2 labels	.80	
b.		Booklet pane of 4	.80	
139	A29	5p rose & multi	.20	.20
a.		Booklet pane of 4	.80	
140	A29	6p vio blue & multi	.25	.25
a.		Booklet pane of 4 ('78)	1.00	
141	A29	7p fawn & multi	.25	.25
a.		Booklet pane of 4 ('78)	1.10	
142	A29	8p yel grn & multi	.25	.25
a.		Booklet pane of 4 ('78)	1.10	
143	A29	9p lil rose & multi	.25	.25
a.		Booklet pane of 4 ('80)	1.25	
144	A29	10p ol bis & multi	.30	.30
145	A29	11p bl grn & multi	.35	.35
146	A29	12p org & multi	.35	.35
147	A29	13p blue & multi	.35	.35
148	A29	14p yel org & multi	.50	.50
149	A29	15p vio & multi	.50	.50

		Photo.		
		Perf. 12		
		Size: 41x26mm, 26x41mm		
150	A29	20p gold & multi	.55	.55
151	A28	30p gold & multi	.70	.70
152	A29	40p gold & multi	1.00	1.00
153	A29	50p gold & multi	1.25	1.25
154	A29	£1 gold & multi	3.50	3.50
155	A30	£2 multicolored ('77)	5.00	5.00
		Nos. 137-155 (19)	15.95	15.95

Issue dates: Nos. 137-149, Jan. 29; Nos. 150-154, Aug. 20. No. 155, Nov. 16.

Sir Walter Raleigh and Old Map of Virginia — A31

US Bicentennial: 7p, Sir George Carteret and old map of New Jersey. 11p, Philippe Dauvergne and ships landing on Long Island. 13p, John Singleton Copley and his "Death of Major Pierson."

1976, May 29		**Photo.**	**Perf. 11½**	
160	A31	5p multicolored	.20	.20
161	A31	7p multicolored	.25	.25
162	A31	11p multicolored	.35	.35
163	A31	13p multicolored	.45	.45
		Nos. 160-163 (4)	1.25	1.25

Dr. Grandin, Central and Southern China Map A32

7p, Yangtze River journey. 11p, On horseback to Chaotung. 13p, Dr. Grandin holding infant.

1976, Nov. 25		**Photo.**	**Perf. 11½**	
164	A32	5p multicolored	.20	.20
165	A32	7p multicolored	.25	.25
166	A32	11p multicolored	.35	.35
167	A32	13p multicolored	.45	.45
		Nos. 164-167 (4)	1.25	1.25

Lilian Mary Grandin (1876-1924), Jersey-born missionary doctor in China.

Queen Wearing St. Edward's Crown — A33

7p, Queen with Jersey Bailiff Sir Alexander Coutanche, 1957. 25p, Portrait, 1976.

Queen Elizabeth II — A30

Arms and scene: 5p, Church of St. Mary. 6p, Grouville, Seymour Tower. 7p, St. Brelade, La Corbière Lighthouse. 8p, Church of St. Saviour. 9p, St. Helier, Elizabeth Castle. 10p, St. Martin, Gorey Harbor. 11p, St. Peter, Jersey Airport. 12p, St. Ouen, Grosnez Castle. 13p, St. John, Bonne Nuit Harbor. 14p, St. Clement and Le Hocq Tower. 15p, St. Lawrence, Morel Farm. 20p, 12 Parishes, view of harbor. 30p, Jersey flag, map of Island. 40p, Postal Administration emblem, PO Headquarters. 50p, Jersey, Parliament and Royal Court. £1, Flag of Lt.-Governor, Government House.

1977, Feb. 7		**Photo.**	**Perf. 11½**	
168	A33	5p multicolored	.20	.20
169	A33	7p multicolored	.30	.30
170	A33	25p multicolored	.70	.70
		Nos. 168-170 (3)	1.20	1.20

25th anniv. of the reign of Elizabeth II.

1/13th sh, 1871 and 1/12th sh, 1877 A34

Coins: 7p, 1/12th sh, 1949. 11p, Silver crown, 1966. 13p, Silver £2, 1972.

1977, Mar. 25		**Litho.**	**Perf. 14**	
171	A34	5p multicolored	.20	.20
172	A34	7p multicolored	.25	.25
173	A34	11p multicolored	.40	.40
174	A34	13p multicolored	.45	.45
		Nos. 171-174 (4)	1.30	1.30

Centenary of Jersey's currency reform.

Sir William Weston and Santa Anna, 1530 A35

Designs: 7p, Sir William Drogo and horse-drawn ambulance, 1877. 11p, Duke of Connaught and Jersey ambulance, 1917. 13p, Richard, Duke of Gloucester and ambulance team, 1977.

1977, June 24		**Litho.**	**Perf. 14x13½**	
175	A35	5p multicolored	.20	.20
176	A35	7p multicolored	.25	.25
177	A35	11p multicolored	.35	.35
178	A35	13p multicolored	.45	.45
		Nos. 175-178 (4)	1.25	1.25

St. John Ambulance Assoc. cent. (in GB).

Victoria and Albert Arriving in Jersey, 1846 A36

Designs: 10½p, Victoria College, 1852. 11p, Statue of Sir Galahad near college gate, vert. 13p, College Hall, interior, vert.

1977, Sept. 29		**Litho.**	**Perf. 14½**	
179	A36	7p multicolored	.20	.20
180	A36	10½p multicolored	.25	.25
181	A36	11p multicolored	.35	.35
182	A36	13p multicolored	.45	.45
		Nos. 179-182 (4)	1.25	1.25

Jersey Victoria College, 125th anniv.

Harry Vardon Statuette, Layout of Golf Course A37

Designs: 8p, Golf grip and swing perfected by Vardon. 11p, Vardon's putting grip and stance. 13p, Vardon's British and US Open Golf trophies, his book "The Complete Golfer" and biography.

1978, Feb. 28		**Litho.**	**Perf. 14**	
183	A37	6p multicolored	.20	.20
184	A37	8p multicolored	.30	.30
185	A37	11p multicolored	.35	.35
186	A37	13p multicolored	.40	.40
		Nos. 183-186 (4)	1.25	1.25

Cent. of Royal Jersey Golf Club and to honor Vardon (1870-1937), Jersey-born golfer.

Europa: 8p, St. Aubin's Fort. 10½p, Elizabeth Castle.

Mont Orgueil — A38

1978, May 1   Photo.   Perf. 11½
187	A38	6p multicolored	.20	.20
188	A38	8p multicolored	.25	.25
189	A38	10½p multicolored	.35	.35
		Nos. 187-189 (3)	.80	.80

Gaspe Basin, by P. J. Ouless — A39

8p, Early map of Gaspe Peninsula, after Capt. Cook. 10½p, Sailing ship Century. 11p, Early map of Jersey. 13p, St. Aubin's Bay Town & Harbor.

1978, June 9   Litho.   Perf. 14x15
190	A39	6p multicolored	.20	.20
191	A39	8p multicolored	.25	.25
192	A39	10½p multicolored	.30	.25
193	A39	11p multicolored	.35	.25
194	A39	13p multicolored	.45	.30
		Nos. 190-194 (5)	1.55	1.25

Jersey's links with Canada and for CAPEX, Canadian Intl. Phil. Exhib., Toronto, Ont., June 9-18.

Elizabeth II, Portraits 1953 and 1977 — A40

Design: 8p, Elizabeth II and Prince Philip.

1978, June 27   Photo.   Perf. 11½
195	A40	8p car, sil & black	.25	.25
196	A40	25p blue, sil & black	.75	.70

25th anniv. of coronation of Queen Elizabeth II and for Royal visit, June 27.

Mail Cutter — A41

Packets: 8p, Flamer, paddle vessel. 10½p, Diana, screw steamer. 11p, Ibex, steamer. 13p, Caesarea, mini-liner.

1978, Oct. 18   Litho.   Perf. 14½x14
197	A41	6p multicolored	.20	.20
198	A41	8p multicolored	.25	.25
199	A41	10½p multicolored	.30	.25
200	A41	11p multicolored	.35	.25
201	A41	13p multicolored	.45	.30
		Nos. 197-201 (5)	1.55	1.25

First Government packet between Britain and Jersey, bicentenary.

Jersey Pillar Box, 1860 — A42

Europa: No. 203, Mailman emptying 1979 mailbox. No. 204, Telephone switchboard, c. 1900. No. 205, Technician working on contemporary telecommunications system.

Perf. 14, 14½x15
1979, Mar. 1   Litho.
202	A42	8p yellow & blk	.25	.25
203	A42	8p carmine & blk	.25	.25
a.		Pair, #202-203	.50	.50
204	A42	10½p violet & blk	.45	.45
205	A42	10½p blue & blk	.45	.45
a.		Pair, #204-205	.90	.90
		Nos. 202-205 (4)	1.40	1.40

Nos. 203a, 205a have continuous design. Both exist perf. 14 and 14½x15.

Soft-colored Jersey Heifer — A43

25p, Milk-laden Jersey cow with 1st Prize ribbon.

Perf. 14 (#206), 13¾ (#207)
1979, Mar. 1
206	A43	6p multicolored	.30	.30

Size: 48x31mm
207	A43	25p multicolored	.95	.95

30th anniv. of 1st Intl. Conf. of Jersey Breed Societies and 9th Conf. of the World Jersey Cattle Bureau.

Percival Mew Gull — A44

Planes: 8p, De Havilland Chipmunk. 10½p, Druine D-31 Turbulent. 11p, De Havilland Tiger Moth. 13p, North American Harvard Mk. 4.

1979, Apr. 24   Photo.   Perf. 11½
208	A44	6p multicolored	.20	.20
209	A44	8p multicolored	.25	.25
210	A44	10½p multicolored	.25	.25
211	A44	11p multicolored	.40	.40
212	A44	13p multicolored	.50	.50
		Nos. 208-212 (5)	1.60	1.60

25th International Air Rally.

My First Sermon, by Millais — A45

Paintings by Millais: 10½p, Orphan. 11p, The Princes in the Tower. 25p, Jesus in the Home of His Parents, horiz.

1979, Aug. 13   Photo.   Perf. 11½
Size: 25x35mm
213	A45	8p multicolored	.30	.30
214	A45	10½p multicolored	.35	.35
215	A45	11p multicolored	.35	.35

Size: 49x30mm
Perf. 12x12½
216	A45	25p multicolored	.75	.75
		Nos. 213-216 (4)	1.75	1.75

IYC and for John Everett Millais (1829-96).

Waldrapp Ibis — A46

1979, Nov. 8   Photo.   Perf. 11½
217	A46	6p Pink pigeons	.20	.20
218	A46	8p Orangutans	.25	.25
219	A46	11½p shown	.25	.25
220	A46	13p Lowland gorillas	.40	.40

221	A46	15p Rodrigues fruit bats	.60	.60
		Nos. 217-221 (5)	1.70	1.70

Nos. 217-218, 220-221 vertical.

Mont Orgueil Fortress A47

Fortresses, 300th Anniversary: 11½p, St. Aubin Tower. 13p, Elizabeth. 25p, Map of Jersey showing fortress locations.

1980, Feb. 5   Litho.   Perf. 14½x13½
222	A47	8p multicolored	.25	.25
223	A47	11p multicolored	.30	.30
224	A47	13p multicolored	.35	.35

Perf. 13½x14
Size: 37½x26mm
225	A47	25p multicolored	.70	.70
		Nos. 222-225 (4)	1.60	1.60

Potato Harvest — A48

Royal Jersey Potato Cent.: 7p, Planting potatoes. 17½p, Loading dock, Weighbridge.

1980, May 6   Litho.   Perf. 14
226	A48	7p multicolored	.25	.25
227	A48	15p multicolored	.40	.40
228	A48	17½p multicolored	.55	.55
		Nos. 226-228 (3)	1.20	1.20

A49

Europa (Wax Figures from Mont Orgueil and Elizabeth Castles): No. 229a, Sir Walter Raleigh; 229b, Paul Ivy. No. 230a, Charles II and Sir George Carteret; 230b, Lady Carteret. Pairs in continuous design.

1980, May 6
229	A49	Pair	.60	.60
a.-b.		9p any single	.30	.30
230	A49	Pair	.70	.70
a.-b.		13½p any single	.35	.35

Three-lap Motorcycle Race — A51

1980, July 24   Litho.   Perf. 12
Granite Paper
231	A51	7p shown	.25	.25
232	A51	9p Intl. road race	.25	.25
233	A51	13½p Motorcycle scrambling	.45	.45
234	A51	15p Sand racing, saloon cars	.50	.50
235	A51	17½p Natl. Hill climb	.55	.55
		Nos. 231-235 (5)	2.00	2.00

Jersey Motorcycle and Light Car Club, 60th anniv.

"Eye of the Wind" Leaving St. Helier — A52

Designs: 9p, Medical research, Cuna Indians, Panama. 13½p, Exploration, Papua New Guinea. 14p, Capt. Scott's ship, Antarctica. 15p, Conservation, Sulawesi. 17½p, Marine studies.

1980, Oct. 1   Litho.   Perf. 14½
236	A52	7p multicolored	.25	.25
237	A52	9p multicolored	.25	.25
238	A52	13½p multicolored	.30	.30
239	A52	14p multicolored	.30	.30
240	A52	15p multicolored	.45	.45
241	A52	17½p multicolored	.55	.55
		Nos. 236-241 (6)	2.10	2.10

Operation Drake, a two-year, round-the-world scientific expedition in tribute to Royal Geographic Society sesquicentennial.

Armed Soldiers and Wounded Drummer A53

Designs: Details from The Death of Major Peirson, by John Singleton Copley.

1981, Jan. 6   Photo.   Perf. 12½
Granite Paper
242	A53	7p multicolored	.25	.25
243	A53	10p multicolored	.30	.30
244	A53	15p multicolored	.45	.45
245	A53	17½p multicolored	.60	.60
a.		Souvenir sheet of 4, #242-245	2.00	2.00
		Nos. 242-245 (4)	1.60	1.60

Battle of Jersey bicentenary. No. 245a has continuous design.

De Bagot Family Arms — A54

Jersey, Channel Map A54a

Queen Elizabeth II, by Norman Hepple — A54b

1981-83   Litho.   Perf. 14
246	A54	½p shown	.20	.20
247	A54	1p De Carteret	.20	.20
a.		Booklet pane of 6	.35	
248	A54	2p La Cloche	.20	.20
a.		Booklet pane of 6	.55	
249	A54	3p Dumaresq	.20	.20
a.		Booklet pane of 6	.65	
250	A54	4p Payn	.20	.20
251	A54	5p Janvrin	.20	.20
252	A54	6p Poingdestre	.20	.20

253	A54	7p Pipon	.30	.25
a.		Booklet pane of 6	1.90	
254	A54	8p Marett	.35	.30
		Booklet pane of 6 ('83)	2.40	
255	A54	9p Le Breton	.35	.25
256	A54	10p Le Maistre	.40	.25
a.		Booklet pane of 6	2.75	
257	A54	11p Bisson	.45	.25
b.		Booklet pane of 6 ('83)	3.25	
258	A54	12p Robin	.45	.30
259	A54	13p Herault	.50	.30
260	A54	14p Messervy	.55	.30
261	A54	15p Fiott	.60	.35
262	A54	20p Badier	.80	.35
263	A54	25p L'Arbalestier	1.00	.35
264	A54	30p Journeaulx	1.25	.45
265	A54	40p Lempriere	1.40	.60
266	A54	50p D'Auvergne	1.60	.75
267	A54a	£1 shown	3.00	1.50

Photo.
Perf. 12½x12

268	A54b	£5 multi	15.00	10.00
	Nos. 246-268 (23)		29.40	17.95

Issued: #246-256, 2/24; #248a, 12/1; #257-262, 7/28; #263-267, 2/23/82; #254a, 257a, 4/19/83; £5, 11/17/83.

1984-88   **Perf. 15x14**

247b	A54	1p ('88)	.35	.25
248b	A54	2p Bklt. pane of 6 ('86)	.65	
248c	A54	2p ('84)	.25	.20
249b	A54	3p Bklt. pane of 6 ('84)	.75	
249c	A54	3p ('84)	.30	.20
250a	A54	4p Bklt. pane of 6 ('87)	1.25	
250b	A54	4p ('86)	.30	.25
251a	A54	5p ('86)	.35	.30
252a	A54	6p ('86)	.30	.30
255a	A54	9p Bklt. pane of 6 ('84)	1.75	
255b	A54	9p ('84)	.60	.50
256b	A54	10p Bklt. pane of 6 ('86)	2.50	
256c	A54	10p ('86)	.50	.35
257a	A54	11p Bklt. pane of 6 ('87)	3.00	
257c	A54	11p ('87)	.55	.45
258a	A54	12p Bklt. pane of 6 ('84)	3.00	
258b	A54	12p ('84)	.80	.60
259a	A54	13p ('84)	.50	.25
260a	A54	14p Bklt. pane of 6 ('86)	3.25	
260b	A54	14p ('86)	.45	.35
261a	A54	15p ('87)	.60	.45
261b	A54	15p Bklt. pane of 6 ('87)	3.50	
262a	A54	20p ('86)	.85	.60
264a	A54	30p ('86)	1.50	1.25
265a	A54	40p ('87)	2.00	1.50
266a	A54	50p ('87)	2.75	2.25

Issued: #251a, 252a, 262a, 264a, Mar. 4.
No. 247a dated "February 1981," "December 1981" or "April 1983"; No. 248a dated "December 1981" or "April 1983"; Nos. 253a, 256a dated "February 1981" or "December 1981;" No. 250a dated "April 1987" or "May 1988." No. 258a dated "April 1984" or "May 1988."

See Nos. 381-388.

Knight of Hamby Killing the Dragon A55

Europa (Legends): 10p, La Hougue Bie. 18p, Easter Voyage of St. Brelade. No. 272, Servant killing Knight of Hamby. No. 273, Shipwreck of St. Brelade. No. 274, Fish, ships' departure.

1981, Apr. 7   **Perf. 14½**

271	A55	10p multicolored	.35	.35
272	A55	10p multicolored	.35	.35
a.		Pair, #271-272	.70	.70
273	A55	18p multicolored	.55	.55
274	A55	18p multicolored	.55	.55
a.		Pair, #273-274	1.10	1.10
	Nos. 271-274 (4)		1.80	1.80

Royal Square by Gaslight A56

1981, May 22   **Photo.**
Granite Paper   **Perf. 12**

275	A56	7p The Harbor	.25	.25
276	A56	10p The Quay	.30	.30
277	A56	18p shown	.45	.45
278	A56	22p Halkett Place	.55	.55
279	A56	25p Central Market	.65	.65
	Nos. 275-279 (5)		2.20	2.20

Gas light sesquicentennial.

Prince Charles and Lady Diana A57

1981, July 28   **Photo.**
Granite Paper   **Perf. 12**

280	A57	10p multicolored	.30	.30
281	A57	25p multicolored	1.40	1.40

Royal Wedding.

Christmas Tree, Royal Square, St. Helier — A58

1981, Sept. 29   **Litho.**   **Perf. 14½**

282	A58	7p shown	.25	.25
283	A58	10p East window, St. Helier's Church, choir	.35	.35
284	A58	18p Boxing Day, Jersey Drag Hunt	.60	.60
	Nos. 282-284 (3)		1.20	1.20

Christmas 1981.

Europa 1982 — A59

Designs: Maps showing formation of Channel Islands resulting from rise in sea level.

1982, Apr. 20   **Litho.**   **Perf. 14½**

285	A59	11p 16,000 BC	.35	.35
286	A59	11p 10,000 BC, vert.	.35	.35
287	A59	19½p 7,000 BC, vert.	.55	.55
288	A59	19½p 4,000 BC	.55	.55
	Nos. 285-288 (4)		1.80	1.80

Rollon Duke of Normandy, William the Conqueror, Clameur de Haro (Plea of Injunction) — A60

Links with France: No. 290, Kings John and Philippe Auguste, Siege of Rouen. No. 291, Jean Martxell (1694-1753), brandy merchant. No. 292, Victor Hugo. No. 293, Pierre Teilhard de Chardin (1881-1955), theologian. No. 294, Charles Rey (1897-1981), meteorologist.

1982, June 11   **Litho.**   **Perf. 14**

289	A60	8p multicolored	.25	.25
290	A60	8p multicolored	.25	.25
a.		Bklt. pane of 4+label, 2 each #289-290	1.00	1.00
b.		Pair, #289-290	.50	.50
291	A60	11p multicolored	.35	.35
292	A60	11p multicolored	.35	.35
a.		Bklt. pane of 4+label, 2 each #291-292	1.50	1.50
b.		Pair, #291-292	.70	.70
293	A60	19½p multicolored	.60	.60
294	A60	19½p multicolored	.60	.60
a.		Bklt. pane of 4+label, 2 each #293-294	2.75	2.75
b.		Pair, #293-294	1.25	1.25
		Complete booklet, 2 each #290a, 292a, 294a	11.00	
	Nos. 289-294 (6)		2.40	2.40

Issue date: Nos. 290a-294a, Sept. 7. Two versions of Nos. 290a, 292a and 294a exist: the label is inscribed in English or French.

Scouting Year A61

Designs: 8p, Sir William Smith (Boys Brigade founder). 11p, Liberation parade, 1945, vert. 24p, Boys Brigade annual display, 1903. 26p, The Baden-Powells, 1924, vert. 29p, Scouts.

1982, Nov. 18   **Photo.**
Granite Paper   **Perf. 12**

295	A61	8p multicolored	.30	.30
296	A61	11p multicolored	.40	.40
297	A61	24p multicolored	.75	.75
298	A61	26p multicolored	.80	.80
299	A61	29p multicolored	.95	.85
	Nos. 295-299 (5)		3.20	3.10

Port Egmont A62

250th Birth Anniv. of Capt. Philippe de Carteret (1733-97): 18th cent. engravings.

1983, Feb. 15   **Litho.**   **Perf. 14¼**

300	A62	8p shown	.30	.30
301	A62	11p Dolphin, Swallow	.40	.40
302	A62	19½p Discovering Pitcairn Is.	.65	.65
303	A62	24p English Cove, New Ireland	.80	.80
304	A62	26p Sinking pirate ship	.85	.85
305	A62	29p Endymion	1.00	1.00
	Nos. 300-305 (6)		4.00	4.00

No. 19 A63

Royal Mace — A64

1983, Apr. 19   **Litho.**

306	A63	11p shown	.45	.45
307	A64	11p shown	.45	.45
a.		Pair, #306-307	.90	.90
308	A63	19½p No. 20a	.65	.65
309	A64	19½p Bailiff's seal	.65	.65
a.		Pair, #308-309	1.40	1.40
	Nos. 306-309 (4)		2.20	2.20

Europa.

World Communications Year — A65

1st Postmaster Charles William LeGeyt (1733-1827): 8p, Commanding Grenadier Co., 25th Foot, Battle of Minden, 1759. 11p, London-Weymouth mail coach. 24p, PO Mail Packet attacked by French privateer. 26p, Hue St. PO. 29p, St. Helier Harbor.

1983, June 21   **Litho.**   **Perf. 14**

310	A65	8p multicolored	.35	.35
311	A65	11p multicolored	.45	.45
312	A65	24p multicolored	.85	.85
313	A65	26p multicolored	.90	.90
314	A65	29p multicolored	1.10	1.10
	Nos. 310-314 (5)		3.65	3.65

Intl. Assoc. of French-Speaking Parliamentarians 1983 General Assembly — A66

1983, June 21   **Perf. 15**

315	A66	19½p multicolored	.80	.80

Cardinal Newman, by Walter William Ouless (1848-1933) A67

1983, Sept. 20   **Photo.**   **Perf. 11½**

316	A67	8p shown	.35	.35
317	A67	11p M. De Cazotte and his Daughter	.55	.55
318	A67	20½p Thomas Hardy	.85	.85

Size: 41x34mm

319	A67	31p David with the Head of Goliath	1.25	1.25
	Nos. 316-319 (4)		3.00	3.00

Jersey Wildlife Preservation Trust — A68

1984, Jan. 17   **Litho.**   **Perf. 14**

320	A68	9p Golden Lion Tamarin	.40	.40
321	A68	12p Snow Leopard	.45	.45
322	A68	20½p Jamaican Boa	.75	.75
323	A68	26p Round Island Gecko	1.00	1.00
324	A68	28p Coscoroba Swan	1.00	1.00
325	A68	31p St. Lucia Parrot	1.10	1.10
	Nos. 320-325 (6)		4.70	4.70

Europa 1984 (25th Anniv.) — A69

1984, Mar. 12   **Perf. 14½x15**

326	A69	9p multicolored	.35	.35
327	A69	12p multicolored	.40	.40
328	A69	20½p multicolored	.70	.70
	Nos. 326-328 (3)		1.45	1.45

Souvenir Sheet

Jersey Links with the Commonwealth — A70

1984, Mar. 12   **Perf. 15x14½**

329	A70	75p multicolored	3.00	3.00

Commonwealth Postal Administrations Conf.

JERSEY

407

Royal Natl. Lifeboat Institution Centenary A71

Rescue Scenes (Lifeboats and Ships).

1984, June 1   Litho.   Perf. 14½
330 A71 9p Sarah Brooshoft, Demie de Pas Light .35 .35
331 A71 9p Hearts of Oak, Maurice Georges .35 .35
332 A71 12p Elizabeth Rippon, Hanna .45 .45
333 A71 12p Elizabeth Rippon, Santa Maria .45 .45
334 A71 20½p Elizabeth Rippon, Bacchus .75 .75
335 A71 20½p Thomas James King, Cythara .75 .75
Nos. 330-335 (6) 3.10 3.10

40th Anniv. of Intl. Civil Aviation Org. A72

1984, July 24   Litho.   Perf. 14
Granite Paper
336 A72 9p Bristol Type 170 .35 .35
337 A72 12p Airspeed AS-57 Ambassador 2 .50 .50
338 A72 26p De Havilland Heron 1B .90 .90
339 A72 31p DH-89A Dragon Rapide 1.25 1.25
Nos. 336-339 (4) 3.00 3.00

Robinson Crusoe, by John Alexander Gilfillan (1793-1864) — A73

"Links with Australia" paintings by J.A. Gilfillan.

1984, Sept. 21   Photo.   Perf. 11½
340 A73 9p shown .35 .35
341 A73 12p Edinburgh Castle .45 .45
342 A73 20½p Maori Village .70 .70
343 A73 26p Australian Landscape .95 .95
344 A73 28p Waterhouse's Corner, Adelaide 1.00 1.00
345 A73 31p Capt. Cook at Botany Bay 1.10 1.10
Nos. 340-345 (6) 4.55 4.55

Christmas 1984 — A74

1984, Nov. 15   Photo.   Perf. 12x11½
346 A74 9p St. Helier orchid .60 .60
347 A74 12p Mt. Bingham orchid .80 .80

Ship Paintings by Philip John Ouless (1817-85) — A75

1985, Feb. 26   Photo.   Perf. 14x14½
348 A75 9p Hebe, 1874 .30 .30
349 A75 12p Gaspe .35 .35
350 A75 22p London, 1856 .75 .75
351 A75 31p Rambler 1.25 1.25
352 A75 34p Elizabeth Castle 1.40 1.40
Nos. 348-352 (5) 4.05 4.05

Europa 1985 A76

Performing Arts: 10p, John Ireland, composer (1879-1962). 13p, Ivy St. Helier, actress (1886-1971). 22p, Claude Debussy, composer.

1985, Apr. 23   Litho.   Perf. 14
353 A76 10p multicolored .35 .35
354 A76 13p multicolored .45 .45
355 A76 22p multicolored .80 .80
Nos. 353-355 (3) 1.60 1.60

Intl. Youth Year — A77

1985, May 30   Litho.   Perf. 14½
356 A77 10p Girls' Brigade .35 .35
357 A77 13p Girl Guides .45 .45
358 A77 29p Jersey Youth Service .95 .95
359 A77 31p Sea Cadet Corps 1.00 1.00
360 A77 34p Air Training Corps 1.25 1.25
Nos. 356-360 (5) 4.00 4.00

Railway History A78

1985, July 16   Photo.   Perf. 12x11½
361 A78 10p Duke of Normandy, Cheapside .45 .45
362 A78 13p Saddletank, First Tower .50 .50
363 A78 22p La Moye, Millbrook .90 .90
364 A78 29p St. Helier's, St. Aubin 1.10 1.10
365 A78 34p St. Aubyns, Corbiere 1.40 1.40
Nos. 361-365 (5) 4.35 4.35

Centenary of Jersey's first train from St. Helier to Corbiere.

Huguenot Heritage A79

300th anniv. of revocation of the Edict of Nantes (religious tolerance) by King Louis XIV of France: No. 366, James Hemery (1814-1849), Dean of Jersey, Rector of St. Helier. No. 367, Francis Henry Jeune, Baron St. Helier, law lord and junior counsel in the Tichbourne case. No. 368, Francois Voisin, merchant. No. 369, Pierre Amiraux, silversmith. No. 370, George Henry Ingouville, Victoria Cross recipient. No. 371, Robert Brohier, co-founder of Schweppes soft-drink company.

1985, Sept. 10   Litho.   Perf. 14
366 A79 10p Memorial window, St. Helier Town Church .40 .40
  a. Booklet pane of 4 1.60
367 A79 10p Houses of Parliament, Westminster .40 .40
  a. Booklet pane of 4 1.60
368 A79 13p Great Fair, Nijni-Novgorod, Russia .45 .45
  a. Booklet pane of 4 1.90

369 A79 13p Silver coffee pot, pitcher .45 .45
  a. Booklet pane of 4 1.90
370 A79 22p Naval Battle of Viborg .70 .70
  a. Booklet pane of 4 3.25
371 A79 22p Glass bottles, carbonated water commercial patent .70 .70
  a. Booklet pane of 4 3.25
  Complete booklet, #366a-371a 14.00
Nos. 366-371 (6) 3.10 3.10

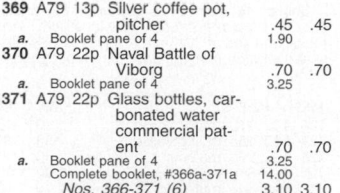

Thomas Benjamin Frederick Davis (1867-1942), Shipping Magnate, Philanthropist — A80

Portrait and endowments: 10p, Howard Davis Hall, Victoria College. 13p, Yacht, racing schooner Westward. 31p, Howard Davis Park, St. Helier. 34p, Howard Davis Agricultural Development Farm, Trinity.

1985, Oct. 25   Perf. 13½
372 A80 10p multicolored .40 .40
373 A80 13p multicolored .45 .45
374 A80 31p multicolored 1.10 1.10
375 A80 34p multicolored 1.25 1.25
Nos. 372-375 (4) 3.20 3.20

50th anniv. of Howard Davis Hall, Victoria College, donated by Davis in memory of his son.

Arms Type of 1981-82 and

Elizabeth II, 60th Birthday — A80a

1985-91   Litho.   Perf. 15x14
381 A54 16p Malet .55 .35
  a. Booklet pane of 6 ('88) 3.50
382 A54 17p Mabon .55 .45
383 A54 18p De St. Martin ('88) .80 .75
384 A54 19p Hamptonne ('88) .95 .80
386 A54 26p De Bagot ('88) .80 .65
388 A54 75p Remon ('87) 2.40 1.75

Perf. 11½x12
389 A80a £1 multicolored 3.50 3.25

Photo.
Granite Paper
390 A80a £2 multicolored 6.50 4.00
Nos. 381-390 (8) 16.05 12.00

Issued: 16, 17p, 10/25; £1, 4/21/86; 75p, 4/23/87; 18, 19, 26p, 4/26/88; £2, 3/19/91. No. 381a inscribed "May 1988."

Jersey Lily — A81

Lillie Langtry, by Sir John Millais — A82

1986, Jan. 28   Litho.   Perf. 15x14½
391 A81 13p multicolored .60 .60
392 A82 34p multicolored 1.40 1.40
  a. Souvenir sheet of 5 (4 13p, 34p) 4.25 4.25

Intl. Flower Gala, June 10-14.

Halley's Comet Sightings A83

Comet and coinciding historic events: 10p, Conquest of England, Bayeux Tapestry, A.D. 912 and 1066 sightings. 22p, Lady Carteret signing New Jersey over to William Penn, Edmond Halley observing comet, comets of 1301 & 1682. 31p, Giotto spacecraft and technology developed in 1910, 1986. Caesarea maiden voyage.

1986, Mar. 4   Perf. 13½x13
393 A83 10p multicolored .35 .35
394 A83 22p multicolored .90 .90
395 A83 31p multicolored 1.25 1.25
Nos. 393-395 (3) 2.50 2.50

Europa 1986 — A84

1986, Apr. 21   Perf. 14½
396 A84 10p Viola kitaibeliana .35 .35
397 A84 14p Matthiola sinuata .60 .60
398 A84 22p Romulea columnae .95 .95
Nos. 396-398 (3) 1.90 1.90

Environmental conservation.

Jersey Natl. Trust, 50th Anniv. A85

1986, June 17   Litho.   Perf. 13½x13
399 A85 10p Le Rat cottage .40 .40
400 A85 14p The Elms, headquarters .45 .45
401 A85 22p Morel Farm entrance .70 .70
402 A85 29p Quetivel Mill 1.10 1.10
403 A85 31p La Vallette 1.25 1.25
Nos. 399-403 (5) 3.90 3.90

Wedding of Prince Andrew and Sarah Ferguson — A86

1986, July 23   Perf. 13½
404 A86 14p multicolored .55 .55
405 A86 40p multicolored 1.90 1.90

Paintings by Edmund Blampied (1886-1966), Artist — A87

1986, Aug. 28   **Litho.**   **Perf. 14**
406	A87	10p Gathering Vraic	.40	.40
407	A87	14p Driving Home in the Rain	.55	.55
408	A87	29p The Miller	1.10	1.10
409	A87	31p The Joy Ride	1.25	1.25
410	A87	34p Tante Elizabeth	1.40	1.40
		Nos. 406-410 (5)	4.70	4.70

Christmas, Intl.
Peace
Year — A88

1986, Nov. 4   **Perf. 14½**
411	A88	10p Dove, map, flower	.40	.40
412	A88	14p Lovebirds	.55	.55
413	A88	34p Dove, noise-maker	1.40	1.40
		Nos. 411-413 (3)	2.35	2.35

Racing
Schooner
Westward
A89

1987, Jan. 15   **Litho.**   **Perf. 13½**
414	A89	10p Under full sail	.40	.40
415	A89	14p T.B. Davis, owner	.55	.55
416	A89	31p Overhauling Britannia	1.25	1.25
417	A89	34p Dry dock, St. Helier	1.50	1.50
		Nos. 414-417 (4)	3.70	3.70

Jersey
Airport,
50th
Anniv.
A90

1987, Mar. 3   **Litho.**   **Perf. 14**
418	A90	10p DH86 Belcroute Bay	.40	.40
419	A90	14p Boeing 757, Douglas DC-9	.55	.55
420	A90	22p Britten Norman Trislander, Islander	.85	.85
421	A90	29p Short SD330, Vickers Viscount	1.10	1.10
422	A90	31p BAC1-11, HPR.7 Dart Herald	1.25	1.25
		Nos. 418-422 (5)	4.15	4.15

Europa
1987
A91

Modern architecture.

1987, Apr. 23   **Perf. 15x14**
423	A91	11p St. Mary and St. Peter's Church	.45	.45
424	A91	15p Villa Devereux	.60	.60

Size: 61x31mm
425	A91	22p Fort Regent, St. Helier	.85	.85
		Nos. 423-425 (3)	1.90	1.90

Adm. Philippe D'Auvergne (1754-1816) — A92

Ships: 11p, Racehorse trapped in the Arctic. 15p, Alarm burned off Rhode Island. 29p, Arethusa wrecked off Ushant, France. 31p, Rattlesnake stranded on Trinidad. 34p, Mont Orgueil Castle.

1987, July 9   **Perf. 14**
426	A92	11p multicolored	.40	.40
427	A92	15p multicolored	.50	.50
428	A92	29p multicolored	1.00	1.00
429	A92	31p multicolored	1.00	1.00
430	A92	34p multicolored	1.10	1.10
		Nos. 426-430 (5)	4.00	4.00

William the Conqueror (c. 1028-87), King of England (1066-87) — A93

Designs in the style of the Bayeux Tapestry: 11p, King Charles negotiating peace with the Vikings, 911, and cession of Jersey to Rollo's son William, 933. 15p, Duke Robert I and King Edward ashore Jersey after storm, 1030; Edward's succession to the throne of England, 1042. 22p, William the Conqueror's coronation, 1066, and succession of William II, 1087. 29p, Death of King William Rufus, and Henry defeating Duke Robert to unite England and Normandy, 1106. 31p, Death of Henry, battle for the throne and succession of King Stephen, 1135. 34p, Successions of Henry II, 1154, and John Lackland, 1189.

1987   **Perf. 13½**
431	A93	11p multicolored	.45	.45
a.		Booklet pane of 4 + label	2.00	
432	A93	15p multicolored	.60	.60
a.		Booklet pane of 4 + label	2.50	
433	A93	22p multicolored	.85	.85
a.		Booklet pane of 4 + label	3.75	
434	A93	29p multicolored	1.10	1.10
a.		Booklet pane of 4 + label	4.75	4.75
435	A93	31p multicolored	1.25	1.25
a.		Booklet pane of 4 + label	5.50	
436	A93	34p multicolored	1.40	1.40
a.		Booklet pane of 4 + label	6.50	
		Complete booklet, #431a-436a	26.00	
		Nos. 431-436 (6)	5.65	5.65

Paintings by John Le Capelain (1812-1848) — A94

1987, Nov. 3   **Photo.**   **Perf. 12x11½**
437	A94	11p Grosnez Castle	.45	.45
438	A94	15p St. Aubin's Bay	.60	.60
439	A94	22p Mt. Orgueil Castle	.85	.85
440	A94	31p Town Fort and Harbor, St. Helier	1.25	1.25
441	A94	34p The Hermitage	1.40	1.40
		Nos. 437-441 (5)	4.55	4.55

Christmas.

Hybrids, Eric Young Orchid Foundation, Trinity — A95

Nos. 443, 445 are vertical.

1988, Jan. 12   **Litho.**   **Perf. 14**
442	A95	11p Cymbidium pontac	.45	.45
443	A95	15p Odontioda Eric Young	.60	.60
444	A95	29p Lycaste auburn Seaford and Ditchling	1.10	1.10
445	A95	31p Odontoglossum St. Brelade	1.25	1.25
446	A95	34p Cymbidium mavourneen Jester	1.40	1.40
		Nos. 442-446 (5)	4.80	4.80

Jersey
Dog Club,
Cent.
A96

1988, Mar. 2
447	A96	11p Labrador retriever	.45	.45
448	A96	15p Wire-haired dachshund	.60	.60
449	A96	22p Pekingese	.85	.85
450	A96	31p Cavalier King Charles spaniel	1.25	1.25
451	A96	34p Dalmatian	1.40	1.40
		Nos. 447-451 (5)	4.55	4.55

Europa
1988
A97

Nos. 453 and 455 vert.

Perf. 14x13½, 13½x14
1988, Apr. 26   **Litho.**
452	A97	16p Air transport	.65	.65
453	A97	16p Air communication	.65	.65
454	A97	22p Sea transport	.85	.85
455	A97	22p Sea communication	.85	.85
		Nos. 452-455 (4)	3.00	3.00

Wildlife Preservation Trust, 25th Anniv. — A98

1988, July 6   **Litho.**
456	A98	12p Rodrigues fody, vert.	.45	.45
457	A98	16p Volcano rabbit	.65	.65
458	A98	29p White-faced marmoset, vert.	1.10	1.10
459	A98	31p Ploughshare tortoise	1.25	1.25
460	A98	34p Mauritius kestrel, vert.	1.40	1.40
		Nos. 456-460 (5)	4.85	4.85

Operation
Raleigh
A99

Activities: 12p, Rain Forest Leaf Frog, Costa Rica. 16p, Archaeological Survey, Peru. 22p, Glacier Climbing, Chile. 29p, Medical Assistance, Solomon Isls. 31p, Underwater Exploration, Australia. 34p, Zebu returns to St. Helier, Jersey.

1988, Sept. 27   **Photo.**   **Perf. 12**
461	A99	12p multicolored	.45	.45
462	A99	16p multicolored	.65	.65
463	A99	22p multicolored	.85	.85
464	A99	29p multicolored	1.10	1.10
465	A99	31p multicolored	1.25	1.25
466	A99	34p multicolored	1.40	1.40
		Nos. 461-466 (6)	5.70	5.70

Operation Raleigh: voyage of the Zebu, on which youths were trained with the aim of remotivating them and helping them to earn new self-respect.
WHO 40th anniv. (29p).

Parish
Churches
A100

1988, Nov. 15   **Litho.**   **Perf. 14**
467	A100	12p St. Clement	.45	.45
468	A100	16p St. Ouen	.55	.55
469	A100	31p St. Brelade	1.10	1.10
470	A100	34p St. Lawrence	1.25	1.25
		Nos. 467-470 (4)	3.35	3.35

Christmas. See Nos. 549-552, 610-613.

Classic
Cars
A101

Designs: 12p, 1912 Talbot Tourer, seaweed harvest at Le Hocq. 16p, 1920 De Dion Bouton, Grosnez Castle ruins. 23p, 1926 Austin Chummy, brick kiln at Mont a l'Abbe. 30p, 1926 Ford Model T, harvest of the Jersey royal potato crop. 32p, 1930 Bentley 8-Litre, Guard House and Gate at Government House. 35p, 1931 Cadillac V16 Fleetwood Sports Phaeton, St. Ouen's Manor.

1989, Jan. 31
471	A101	12p multicolored	.45	.45
472	A101	16p multicolored	.60	.60
473	A101	23p multicolored	.80	.80
474	A101	30p multicolored	1.00	1.00
475	A101	32p multicolored	1.10	1.10
476	A101	35p multicolored	1.25	1.25
		Nos. 471-476 (6)	5.20	5.20

See Nos. 604-609, 903-908.

Scenic
Views — A102

Coronation of Queen Elizabeth II, 40th Anniv. — A102a

Royal
Arms
A102b

1989-95   **Litho.**   **Perf. 13½**
477	A102	1p Belcroute Bay	.20	.20
478	A102	2p High St., St. Aubin	.20	.20
480	A102	4p Royal Jersey Golf Course	.20	.20
a.		Booklet pane of 6	.80	.80
481	A102	5p Portelet Bay	.20	.20
a.		Booklet pane of 6	1.40	1.40
485	A102	10p Les Charrieres D'Anneport	.30	.30
486	A102	13p St. Helier Marina	.45	.45
487	A102	14p St. Ouen's Bay	.45	.45
a.		Booklet pane of 6	3.00	3.00
b.		Booklet pane of 8	4.25	4.25
		Complete booklet, #487b ('92)	4.25	
488	A102	15p Rozel Harbor	.50	.50
a.		Booklet pane of 6	3.25	3.25
489	A102	16p St. Aubin's Harbor	.55	.55
a.		Booklet pane of 6	5.00	5.00
		Complete booklet, #489a ('92)	5.00	
490	A102	17p Jersey Airport	.55	.55
491	A102	18p Corbiere Lighthouse	.60	.60
a.		Booklet pane of 6	4.25	4.25
		Complete booklet, 2 each #480a, 487a, 491a ('90)	17.50	
492	A102	19p Val de la Mare	.60	.60
493	A102	20p Elizabeth Castle	.50	.50
a.		Booklet pane of 8	3.25	3.25
494	A102	21p Greve de Lecq	.55	.55
495	A102	22p Samares Manor	.50	.50
a.		Booklet pane of 8	4.50	4.50
		Complete booklet, #495a ('92)	4.50	

	Complete booklet, 2 each #481a, 493a, 495a ('91)	20.00		
496	A102	23p Bonne Nuit Harbor	.85	.85
497	A102	24p Grosnez Castle	.70	.70
498	A102	25p Augres Manor	.80	.80
499	A102	26p Central Market	.90	.90
500	A102	27p St. Brelade's Bay	1.00	1.00
501	A102	30p St. Ouen's Manor	1.10	1.10
502	A102	40p La Hougue Bie	1.40	1.40
503	A102	50p Mont Orgueil Castle	1.60	1.60
504	A102	75p Royal Square	2.50	2.50

Perf. 14½

505	A102a	£1 multicolored	3.50	3.50

Perf. 15x14

506	A102b	£4 multicolored	13.00	13.00
	Nos. 477-506 (26)		33.70	33.70

Pane Nos. 480a, 487a and 491a issued for Stamp World London '90 and are inscribed "May 1990."

Issued: 1p-20p, 3/21/89; 21p-27p, 1/16/90; 30p-75p, 3/13/90; #481a, 488a, 493a, 2/12/91; £1, 6/2/93; £4, 1/2/95. Nos. 487b, 489a, 495a were released on May 22, but were not readily available until September 1992. Other booklet panes, 1990.

World Wildlife Fund — A103

1989, Apr. 25   Litho.   Perf. 13x13¼

507	A103	13p Large checkered skipper	2.50	2.50

Perf. 13¼x13

508	A103	13p Agile frog, horiz.	2.50	2.50
509	A103	17p Green lizard, horiz.	2.50	2.50

Perf. 13½x13¾

510	A103	17p Barn owl	2.50	2.50
	Nos 507-510 (4)		10.00	10.00

Europa 1989 — A104

Children's games.

1989, Apr. 25   Perf. 14

511	A104	17p Playpen	.65	.65
512	A104	17p Playground	.65	.65
513	A104	23p Magician, games	.90	.90
514	A104	23p Cricket, rugby, tennis	.90	.90
	Nos. 511-514 (4)		3.10	3.10

Visit of Queen Elizabeth II — A105

1989, May 24   Litho.   Perf. 14½

515	A105	£1 Ferry Terminal, St. Helier	4.00	4.00

French Revolution, Bicent. A106

Designs: 13p, D'Auvergne meets Louis XVI, 1786. 17p, Storming the Bastille, 1789. 23p,

Marie de Bouillon at the Chateau de Navarre, 1790. 30p, Mission from Mont Orgueil, 1795. 32p, Support for the Chouans, 1796. 35p, The last Chouannerie, 1799.

1989, July 7   Perf. 13½

516	A106	13p multicolored	.45	.45
517	A106	17p multicolored	.55	.55
518	A106	23p multicolored	.75	.75
519	A106	30p multicolored	1.00	1.00
520	A106	32p multicolored	1.10	1.10
521	A106	35p multicolored	1.25	1.25
	Nos. 516-521 (6)		5.10	5.10

516a	Booklet pane of 4	1.90
517a	Booklet pane of 4	2.50
518a	Booklet pane of 4	3.50
519a	Booklet pane of 4	4.25
520a	Booklet pane of 4	5.50
521a	Booklet pane of 4	5.00
	Complete booklet, #516a-521a	23.00

Great Western Railway Steamer Service Between Weymouth and the Channel Isls., Cent. — A107

1989, Sept. 5   Litho.   Perf. 13½x14

522	A107	13p St. Helier, 1925	.45	.45
523	A107	17p Caesarea II, 1910	.55	.55
524	A107	27p Reindeer, 1897	.95	.95
525	A107	32p Ibex and Frederica, 1891	1.25	1.10
526	A107	35p Lynx, 1889	1.40	1.40
	Nos. 522-526 (5)		4.60	4.45

Paintings by Sarah Louisa Kilpack (1839-1909) — A108

1989, Oct. 24   Litho.   Perf. 13x12½

527	A108	13p Gorey Harbour	.50	.50
528	A108	17p La Corbiere	.65	.65
529	A108	23p Greve de Lecq	.90	.90
530	A108	32p Bouley Bay	1.25	1.25
531	A108	35p Mont Orgueil	1.40	1.40
	Nos. 527-531 (5)		4.70	4.70

Europa 1990 A109

Post offices.

Perf. 13½x14, 14x13½

1990, Mar. 13   Litho.

532	A109	18p Broad Street, 1969	.70	.70
533	A109	18p Mont Millais, 1990	.70	.70
534	A109	24p Hue Street, 1815	.95	.95
535	A109	24p Halkett Place, 1890	.95	.95
	Nos. 532-535 (4)		3.30	3.30

Nos. 532-533 vert.

Festival of Tourism — A110

1990, May 3   Litho.   Perf. 14x13½

536	A110	18p Battle of Flowers	.80	.80
537	A110	24p Recreation	1.00	1.00
538	A110	29p History	1.10	1.10
539	A110	32p Salon Culinaire	1.25	1.25
a.	Souvenir sheet of 4, #536-539	4.50	4.50
	Nos. 536-539 (4)		4.15	4.15

News Media A111

1990, June 26   Litho.   Perf. 13½

540	A111	14p Print (newspapers), 1784-1889	.55	.55
541	A111	18p The Evening Post, 1890	.70	.70
542	A111	34p BBC Radio Jersey, 1982	1.50	1.50
543	A111	37p Channel Television, 1962	1.60	1.60
	Nos. 540-543 (4)		4.35	4.35

UNESCO World Literacy Year.

Battle of Britain, 50th Anniv. A112

1990, Sept. 4   Perf. 14

544	A112	14p Hawk	.65	.65
545	A112	18p Spitfire	.75	.75
546	A112	24p Hurricane	1.00	1.00
547	A112	34p Wellington	1.50	1.50
548	A112	37p Lancaster	1.60	1.60
	Nos. 544-548 (5)		5.50	5.50

Parish Churches Type of 1988

1990, Nov. 13   Litho.   Perf. 13½x14

549	A100	14p St. Helier	.55	.55
550	A100	18p Grouville	.70	.70
551	A100	34p St. Saviour	1.50	1.50
552	A100	37p St. John	1.60	1.60
	Nos. 549-552 (4)		4.35	4.35

Christmas.

Prince's Tower, La Hougue Bie, 1801 A113

Philippe d'Auvergne: 20p, Arrested in Paris, 1802. 26p, Plotting against Napoleon, 1803. 31p, Execution of Cadoudal, 1804. 37p, H.M. Cutter Surly, 1809. 44p, Prince de Bouillon, 1816.

1991, Jan. 22   Litho.   Perf. 13½

553	A113	15p multicolored	.60	.60
554	A113	20p multicolored	.80	.80
555	A113	26p multicolored	1.00	1.00
556	A113	31p multicolored	1.25	1.25
557	A113	37p multicolored	1.50	1.50
558	A113	44p multicolored	1.75	1.75
	Nos. 553-558 (6)		6.90	6.90

A114

Europa (Satellites and their functions): No. 559, ERS-1, oceanography. No. 560, Landsat, Earth resources. No. 561, Meteosat, meteorology. No. 562, Olympus, communications.

1991, Mar. 19   Litho.   Perf. 14½x13

559	A114	20p multicolored	.80	.80
560	A114	20p multicolored	.80	.80
561	A114	26p multicolored	1.00	1.00
562	A114	26p multicolored	1.00	1.00
	Nos. 559-562 (4)		3.60	3.60

A115

15p, German Occupation Stamps for Jersey, 50th anniv. 20p, Eastern Railway extension to Gorey Pier, 100th anniv. 26p, Jersey Herd Book, 125th anniv. 31p, Victoria Harbor, 150th anniv. 53p, Hospital bequest of Marie Bartlett, 250th anniv.

1991, May 16   Litho.   Perf. 13½

563	A115	15p multicolored	.60	.60
564	A115	20p multicolored	.80	.80
565	A115	26p multicolored	1.00	1.00
566	A115	31p multicolored	1.25	1.25
567	A115	53p multicolored	2.10	2.10
	Nos. 563-567 (5)		5.75	5.75

Butterflies & Moths A116

1991, July 9   Litho.   Perf. 13x12½

568	A116	15p Glanville fritillary	.60	.60
569	A116	20p Jersey tiger	.80	.80
570	A116	37p Small elephant hawk-moth	1.90	1.90
571	A116	57p Peacock	2.40	2.40
	Nos. 568-571 (4)		5.70	5.70

See Nos. 727-731.

Overseas Aid — A117

Designs: 15p, Water drilling rig, Ethiopia. 20p, Construction work, Rwanda. 26p, Technical school, Kenya. 31p, Leprosy and eye care, Tanzania. 37p, Agriculture and cultivation aid, Zambia. 44p, Health care and immunization, Lesotho.

1991, Sept. 3   Litho.   Perf. 13½

572	A117	15p multicolored	.60	.60
573	A117	20p multicolored	.80	.80
574	A117	26p multicolored	1.00	1.00
575	A117	31p multicolored	1.25	1.25
576	A117	37p multicolored	1.50	1.50
577	A117	44p multicolored	1.75	1.75
	Nos. 572-577 (6)		6.90	6.90

Christmas — A118

Illustrations by Edmund Blampied from Peter Pan: 15p, This is the place for me. 20p, The Island Come True. 37p, The Never Bird. 53p, The Great White Father.

1991, Nov. 5   Litho.   Perf. 14

578	A118	15p multicolored	.60	.60
579	A118	20p multicolored	.80	.80
580	A118	37p multicolored	1.50	1.50
581	A118	53p multicolored	2.10	2.10
	Nos. 578-581 (4)		5.00	5.00

Winter Birds — A119

1992, Jan. 7   Litho.   Perf. 13½x14
582	A119	16p Pied wagtail	.55	.55
583	A119	22p Firecrest	.75	.75
584	A119	28p Snipe	1.00	1.00
585	A119	39p Lapwing	1.50	1.50
586	A119	57p Fieldfare	2.10	2.10
		Nos. 582-586 (5)	5.90	5.90

Shanghai Harbor, 1860 A120

William Mesny, 150th birth anniv: No. 588, Running the Taiping blockade, 1862. No. 589, General Mesny, River Gate, 1874. No. 590, Mesny accompanying Gill to Burma, 1877. No. 591, Mesny advises Governor Chang, 1882. No. 592, Mesny, Mandarin First Class, 1886.

1992, Feb. 25   Litho.   Perf. 13½
587	A120	16p multicolored	.60	.60
588	A120	16p multicolored	.60	.60
589	A120	22p multicolored	.90	.90
590	A120	22p multicolored	.90	.90
591	A120	33p multicolored	1.25	1.25
592	A120	33p multicolored	1.25	1.25
		Nos. 587-592 (6)	5.50	5.50

587a	Booklet pane of 4	2.40	2.40
588a	Booklet pane of 4	2.40	2.40
589a	Booklet pane of 4	3.75	3.75
590a	Booklet pane of 4	3.75	3.75
591a	Booklet pane of 4	5.25	5.25
592a	Booklet pane of 4	5.25	5.25
	Complete booklet, #587a-592a	23.00	

Discovery of America, 500th Anniv. A121

Columbus, ship and: 22p, John Bertram (1796-1882). 28p, Sir George Carteret (1610-1680). 39p, Sir Walter Raleigh (1554-1618).

1992, Apr. 14   Litho.   Perf. 14½
593	A121	22p multicolored	.85	.85
594	A121	28p multicolored	1.10	1.10
595	A121	39p multicolored	1.60	1.60
		Nos. 593-595 (3)	3.55	3.55

Europa.

Jersey-Built Sailing Ships — A122

1992, Apr. 14   Litho.   Perf. 14
596	A122	16p Tickler	.55	.55
597	A122	22p Hebe	.75	.75
598	A122	50p Gemini	1.75	1.75
599	A122	57p Percy Douglas	1.90	1.90
a.	Souvenir sheet of 4, #596-599	5.25	5.25
		Nos. 596-599 (4)	4.95	4.95

Batik — A123

16p, Snow leopards. 22p, Three elements. 39p, Three men in a tub. 57p, Cockatoos.

1992, June 23   Litho.   Perf. 14½
600	A123	16p multicolored	.65	.65
601	A123	22p multicolored	.90	.90
602	A123	39p multicolored	1.50	1.50
603	A123	57p multicolored	2.10	2.10
		Nos. 600-603 (4)	5.15	5.15

Classic Car Type of 1989

Designs: 16p, 1925 Morris Cowley "Bull-nose." 22p, 1932 Rolls Royce 20/25. 28p, 1924 Chenard & Walcker T5. 33p, 1932 Packard 900 Series Light Eight. 39p, 1927 Lanchester 21. 50p, 1913 Buick 30 Roadster.

1992, Sept. 8   Litho.   Perf. 13x12½
604	A101	16p multicolored	.50	.50
605	A101	22p multicolored	.70	.70
606	A101	28p multicolored	.90	.90
607	A101	33p multicolored	1.10	1.10
608	A101	39p multicolored	1.25	1.25
609	A101	50p multicolored	1.60	1.60
		Nos. 604-609 (6)	6.05	6.05

Parish Church Type of 1988

1992, Nov. 3   Litho.   Perf. 13½x14
610	A100	16p Trinity	.50	.50
611	A100	22p St. Mary	.70	.65
612	A100	33p St. Martin	1.25	1.25
613	A100	57p St. Peter	1.75	1.75
		Nos. 610-613 (4)	4.20	4.15

Christmas.

Non-Value Indicator Stamps — A124

Scenic views: No. 614, Building with arches. No. 615, Cemetery, Trinity Church. No. 616, Daffodils, cattle. No. 617, Cattle in pasture.
Beach scenes: No. 618, People lying on beach with umbrella. No. 619, Man with windsurfer. No. 620, Crab facing right. No. 621, Crab, facing left.
Parade floats: No. 622, Smiling face, rainbow. No. 623, Dragon head, Oriental theme. No. 624, Umbrellas, Asian theme. No. 625, Elephant's tusks, African theme.

1993, Jan. 26   Litho.   Perf. 13½
614	A124	(17p) Bailiwick	.55	.55
615	A124	(17p) Bailiwick	.55	.55
616	A124	(17p) Bailiwick	.55	.55
617	A124	(17p) Bailiwick	.55	.55
a.	Block of 4, #614-617		2.25	2.25
b.	Booklet pane of 8, 2 each #614-617		4.50	
618	A124	(23p) UK	.70	.70
619	A124	(23p) UK	.70	.70
620	A124	(23p) UK	.70	.70
621	A124	(23p) UK	.70	.70
a.	Block of 4, #618-621		3.00	3.00
b.	Booklet pane of 8, 2 each #618-621		6.00	
622	A124	(28p) European	.85	.85
623	A124	(28p) European	.85	.85
624	A124	(28p) European	.85	.85
625	A124	(28p) European	.85	.85
a.	Block of 4, #622-625		3.25	3.25
b.	Booklet pane of 8, 2 each #622-625		7.00	7.00
		Nos. 614-625 (12)	8.40	8.40

The minimum postage rate is represented for each area where mail is delivered.

Orchids — A125

17p, Phragmipedium Eric Young "Jersey." 23p, Odontoglossum Augres "Trinity." 28p, Miltonia Saint Helier "Colomberie." 39p, Phragmipedium pearcei. 57p, Calanthe Grouville "Gorey."

1993, Jan. 26   Litho.   Perf. 14½x13
626	A125	17p multicolored	.60	.60
627	A125	23p multicolored	.90	.90
628	A125	28p multicolored	1.10	1.10
629	A125	39p multicolored	1.50	1.50
630	A125	57p multicolored	2.00	2.00
		Nos. 626-630 (5)	6.10	6.10

Europa — A126

Contemporary Art: 23p, Jersey Opera House, by Ian Rolls. 28p, The Ham and Tomato Bap, by Jonathan Hubbard. 39p, Vase of Flowers, by Neil MacKenzie.

1993, Apr. 1   Litho.   Perf. 13½x14
631	A126	23p multicolored	.90	.90
632	A126	28p multicolored	1.10	1.10
633	A126	39p multicolored	1.50	1.50
		Nos. 631-633 (3)	3.50	3.50

Royal Air Force, 75th Anniv. A127

Designs: 17p, Douglas Dakota. 23p, Wight Seaplane. 28p, Avro Shakleton AEW2. 33p, Gloster Meteor, DeHavilland Vampire. 39p, BAe Harrier GR1A. 57p, Panavia Tornado F3.

1993, Apr. 1   Perf. 14
634	A127	17p multicolored	.65	.65
635	A127	23p multicolored	.90	.90
636	A127	28p multicolored	1.10	1.10
637	A127	33p multicolored	1.25	1.25
638	A127	39p multicolored	1.50	1.50
639	A127	57p multicolored	2.25	2.25
a.	Souvenir sheet of 2, #635, 639		7.75	7.75
		Nos. 634-639 (6)	7.65	7.65

Stamps from No. 639a do not have white border.

German Occupation Stamps by Edmund Blampied, 50th Anniv. A128

1993, June 2   Litho.   Perf. 13½
640	A128	17p No. N3	.65	.65
641	A128	23p No. N4	.90	.90
642	A128	28p No. N5	1.10	1.10
643	A128	33p No. N6	1.25	1.25
644	A128	39p No. N7	1.50	1.50
645	A128	50p No. N8	2.00	2.00
		Nos. 640-645 (6)	7.40	7.40

Birds — A129

1993, Sept. 7   Litho.   Perf. 13½x14
646	A129	17p Short-toed treecreeper	.65	.65
647	A129	23p Dartford warbler	.90	.90
648	A129	28p Wheatear	1.10	1.10
649	A129	39p Cirl bunting	1.50	1.50
650	A129	57p Jay	2.25	2.25
		Nos. 646-650 (5)	6.40	6.40

Christmas — A130

Stained glass windows by Henry Bosdet, from St. Aubin on the Hill.

1993, Nov. 2   Litho.   Perf. 14½x13
651	A130	17p multicolored	.65	.65
652	A130	23p multicolored	.90	.90
653	A130	39p multicolored	1.50	1.50
654	A130	57p multicolored	2.25	2.25
		Nos. 651-654 (4)	5.30	5.30

Mushrooms A131

1994, Jan. 11   Litho.   Perf. 14½
655	A131	18p Shaggy ink cap	.70	.70
656	A131	23p Fly agaric	.90	.90
657	A131	30p Chanterelle	1.25	1.25
658	A131	41p Parasol mushroom	1.60	1.60
659	A131	60p Latticed stinkhorn	2.40	2.40
		Nos. 655-659 (5)	6.85	6.85

Souvenir Sheet

New Year 1994 (Year of the Dog) — A132

1994, Feb. 18   Litho.   Perf. 15x14½
660	A132	£1 multicolored	4.00	4.00

Hong Kong '94.

Cats — A133

1994, Apr. 5   Litho.   Perf. 13½
661	A133	18p Maine coon, vert.	.70	.70
662	A133	23p British shorthair	.90	.90
663	A133	35p Persian, vert.	1.40	1.40
664	A133	41p Siamese	1.60	1.60
665	A133	60p Non-pedigree, vert.	2.40	2.40
		Nos. 661-665 (5)	7.00	7.00

Jersey Cat Club, 21st anniv., and 4th Championship Show.

Europa — A134

Designs: No. 666, Mammoths on cliff, c. 250,000 B.C. No. 667, Paleolithic hunters dragging mammoth by tusks. No. 668, Neolithic dolmen, "La Hougue Bie," c. 4,000 B.C. No. 669, Exterior of "La Hougue Bie," during construction.

1994, Apr. 5   Litho.   Perf. 13½x14

666	A134	23p multicolored	.90	.90
667	A134	23p multicolored	.90	.90
a.		Pair, #666-667	1.90	1.90
668	A134	30p multicolored	1.25	1.25
669	A134	30p multicolored	1.25	1.25
a.		Pair, #668-669	2.50	2.50
		Nos. 666-669 (4)	4.30	4.30

D-Day, 50th Anniv. A135

#670, Airborne Forces enroute to drop zones. #671, Allied Fleet of Normandy Coast. #672, Coming ashore, Gold Beach. #673, Coming ashore, Sword Beach. #674, Spitfires on beachead patrol. #675, Normandy invasion map.

1994, June 6   Litho.   Perf. 13½

670	A135	18p multicolored	.70	.70
671	A135	18p multicolored	.70	.70
a.		Bklt. pane, 3 each #670-671	4.50	
672	A135	23p multicolored	.90	.90
673	A135	23p multicolored	.90	.90
a.		Bklt. pane, 3 each #672-673	6.00	
674	A135	30p multicolored	1.25	1.25
675	A135	30p multicolored	1.25	1.25
a.		Bklt. pane, 3 each #674-675	8.00	
b.		Bklt. pane of 6, #670-675	6.50	
		Complete booklet, #671a, 673a, 675a, 675b	25.00	
		Nos. 670-675 (6)	5.70	5.70

No. 675b also sold by the Philatelic Bureau separate from the booklet, without stitching, as a souvenir sheet.

Intl. Olympic Committee, Cent. — A136

1994, June 6   Perf. 14

676	A136	18p Sailing	.70	.70
677	A136	23p Rifle shooting	.90	.90
678	A136	30p Hurdles	1.25	1.25
679	A136	41p Swimming	1.60	1.60
680	A136	60p Field hockey	2.40	2.40
		Nos. 676-680 (5)	6.85	6.85

Marine Life A137

Designs: 18p, Strawberry anemone. 23p, Hermit crab, parasitic anemone. 41p, Velvet swimming crab. 60p, Common jellyfish.

1994, Aug. 2   Litho.   Perf. 13½x13

681	A137	18p multicolored	.70	.70
682	A137	23p multicolored	.90	.90
683	A137	41p multicolored	1.60	1.60
684	A137	60p multicolored	2.40	2.40
		Nos. 681-684 (4)	5.60	5.60

Postal Independence, 25th Anniv. — A138

Designs: 18p, Condor 10 Wavepiercer. 23p, Map of Jersey, postbox. 35p, BEA "Vanguard" aircraft. 41p, Aurigny "Short 360" aircraft. 60p, Sealink vessel "Caesarea."

1994, Oct. 1   Litho.   Perf. 14

685	A138	18p multicolored	.70	.70
686	A138	23p multicolored	.90	.90
687	A138	35p multicolored	1.40	1.40
688	A138	41p multicolored	1.60	1.60

689	A138	60p multicolored	2.40	2.40
a.		Souvenir sheet, #685-689 + label	7.25	7.25
		Nos. 685-689 (5)	7.00	7.00

See Guernsey Nos. 536-540a.

Christmas A139

Christmas carols: 18p, "Away in the manger..." 23p, "Hark! the herald angels sing..." 41p, "While shepherds watched..." 60p, "We three kings of Orient are..."

1994, Nov. 8

690	A139	18p multicolored	.70	.70
691	A139	23p multicolored	.90	.90
692	A139	41p multicolored	1.60	1.60
693	A139	60p multicolored	2.40	2.40
		Nos. 690-693 (4)	5.60	5.60

Greetings Stamps — A140

Designs: No. 694, Dog, "Good Luck." No. 695, Rose, "With Love." No. 696, Chick, "Congratulations." No. 697, Bouquet of flowers, "Thank You."
No. 698, Dove, "With love." No. 699, Cat, "Good Luck." No. 700, Carnations, "Thank You." No. 701, Parrot, "Congratulations." 60p, Boar, "Happy New Year."

1995, Jan. 24   Litho.   Perf. 13½x13

694	A140	18p multicolored	.70	.70
695	A140	18p multicolored	.70	.70
696	A140	18p multicolored	.70	.70
697	A140	18p multicolored	.70	.70
a.		Strip of 4, #694-697	3.00	3.00
698	A140	23p multicolored	.90	.90
699	A140	23p multicolored	.90	.90
700	A140	23p multicolored	.90	.90
701	A140	23p multicolored	.90	.90
a.		Strip of 4, #698-701	3.75	3.75

Size: 25x64mm

702	A140	60p multicolored	2.40	2.40
a.		Booklet pane, #697a, 701a, #702	10.00	
		Complete booklet, #702a	10.00	
		Nos. 694-702 (9)	8.80	8.80

New Year 1995 (Year of the Boar) (#702).

Camellias A141

1995, Mar. 21   Litho.   Perf. 14

703	A141	18p Captain Rawes	.70	.70
704	A141	23p Brigadoon	.90	.90
705	A141	30p Elsie Jury	1.25	1.25
706	A141	35p Augusto L'Gouveia Pinto	1.40	1.40
707	A141	41p Bella Romana	1.60	1.60
		Nos. 703-707 (5)	5.85	5.85

International Camellia Society conference, Jersey, Mar. 30-Apr. 4, 1995.

Liberation, by Philip Jackson A142

1995, May 9   Litho.   Perf. 13½

708	A142	23p gray & black	.90	.90
709	A142	30p pink & black	1.25	1.25

Europa.

Liberation, 50th Anniv. A143

#710, Bailiff, Crown Officers taken to HMS Beagle. #711, Red Cross ship SS Vega. #712, Germans surrender on board HMS Beagle. #713, First troops of task force 135, Ordinance Yard, St. Helier. #714, Royal visitors, June 1945. #715, Supplies come ashore from LSTs, Operation Nestegg.
£1, Princess Elizabeth, Queen Elizabeth, Winston Churchill, King George VI, Princess Margaret at Buckingham Palace, VE Day.

1995, May 9   Litho.   Perf. 14½x14

710	A143	18p multicolored	.70	.70
711	A143	18p multicolored	.70	.70
a.		Bklt. pane, 3 each #710-711	4.75	
712	A143	23p multicolored	.90	.90
713	A143	23p multicolored	.90	.90
a.		Bklt. pane, 3 each #712-713	6.25	
714	A143	60p multicolored	2.40	2.40
715	A143	60p multicolored	2.40	2.40
a.		Bklt. pane, 3 each #714-715	16.00	
		Nos. 710-715 (6)	8.00	8.00

Souvenir Sheet

716	A143	£1 multicolored	4.00	4.00
a.		Booklet pane, #716	4.50	
		Complete booklet, #711a, #713a, #715a, #716a	32.50	

No. 716 contains one 81x29mm stamp.

Wild Flowers — A144

1995, July 4   Litho.   Perf. 13½

717	A144	19p Bell heather	.75	.75
718	A144	19p Sea campion	.75	.75
719	A144	19p Spotted rock-rose	.75	.75
720	A144	19p Thrift	.75	.75
721	A144	19p Sheep's-bit scabious	.75	.75
a.		Strip of 5, #717-721	3.75	3.75
722	A144	23p Field bind-weed	.90	.90
723	A144	23p Common bird's-foot trefoil	.90	.90
724	A144	23p Sea holly	.90	.90
725	A144	23p Common centaury	.90	.90
726	A144	23p Dwarf pansy	.90	.90
a.		Strip of 5, #722-726	4.75	4.75
		Nos. 717-726 (10)	8.25	8.25

Butterfly & Moth Type of 1991

1995, Sept. 1   Litho.   Perf. 14

727	A116	19p Peacock pansy	.75	.75
728	A116	23p Green-barred swallowtail	.90	.90
729	A116	30p Orange emigrant	1.25	1.25
730	A116	41p Scarlet mormon	1.60	1.60
731	A116	60p Common birdwing	2.40	2.40
a.		Souvenir sheet of 2, #730-731	4.00	4.00
		Nos. 727-731 (5)	6.90	6.90

Singapore '95 (#731a).
Stamps from No. 731a do not have border around the designs or inscriptions at bottom.

Christmas Pantomimes — A145

Childrens' stories: 19p, Puss in Boots. 23p, Cinderella. 41p, Sleeping Beauty. 60p, Aladdin.

1995, Oct. 24   Litho.   Perf. 13½

732	A145	19p multicolored	.75	.75
733	A145	23p multicolored	.90	.90
734	A145	41p multicolored	1.60	1.60
735	A145	60p multicolored	2.40	2.40
		Nos. 732-735 (4)	5.65	5.65

UN, 50th Anniv. A146

1995, Oct. 24   Litho.   Perf. 13x14

736	A146	19p Doves, emblem	.75	.75
737	A146	23p Wheat ear, emblem	.90	.90
738	A146	41p As 23p	1.60	1.60
739	A146	60p As 19p	2.40	2.40
		Nos. 736-739 (4)	5.65	5.65

UNICEF, 50th Anniv. A147

Children, map areas of UNICEF activities: 19p, Africa. 23p, Globe. 30p, Europe, Balkans. 35p, South America, Caribbean. 41p, South Asia. 60p, Australasia, South Pacific.

1996, Feb. 19   Litho.   Perf. 14½

740	A147	19p multicolored	.75	.75
741	A147	23p multicolored	.90	.90
742	A147	30p multicolored	1.25	1.25
743	A147	35p multicolored	1.40	1.40
744	A147	41p multicolored	1.60	1.60
745	A147	60p multicolored	2.40	2.40
		Nos. 740-745 (6)	8.30	8.30

Souvenir Sheet

New Year 1996 (Year of the Rat) — A148

1996, Feb. 19   Perf. 14

746	A148	£1 multicolored	4.00	4.00

Queen Elizabeth II, 70th Birthday — A149

1996, Apr. 21   Litho.   Perf. 14x15

747	A149	£5 multicolored	20.00	20.00

Women of Achievement A150

Europa: 23p, Elizabeth Garrett, first British woman physician. 30p, Emmeline Pankhurst (1858-1928), suffragist.

1996, Apr. 25   Perf. 14

748	A150	23p multicolored	.90	.90
749	A150	30p multicolored	1.25	1.25

1996 European Soccer Chamionships — A151

Various soccer plays.

1996, Apr. 25
750	A151	19p multicolored	.75	.75
751	A151	23p multicolored	.90	.90
752	A151	35p multicolored	1.40	1.40
753	A151	41p multicolored	1.60	1.60
754	A151	60p multicolored	2.40	2.40
		Nos. 750-754 (5)	7.05	7.05

Modern Olympic Games, Cent. A152

1996, June 8   Litho.   Perf. 14
755	A152	19p Rowing	.75	.75
756	A152	23p Judo	.90	.90
757	A152	35p Fencing	1.40	1.40
758	A152	41p Boxing	1.60	1.60
759	A152	60p Basketball	2.40	2.40
		Nos. 755-759 (5)	7.05	7.05

Souvenir Sheet
760	A152	£1 Olympic torch, flame	4.00	4.00

Intl. Amateur Boxing Assoc., 50th anniv. (#758). CAPEX '96 (#760). No. 760 contains one 50x38mm stamp.

Tourism A153

1996, June 8   Litho.   Perf. 14
761	A153	19p North Coast	.75	.75
762	A153	23p Portelet Bay	.90	.90
a.		Bklt. pane, 3 each #761-762	5.75	
763	A153	30p Greve de Lecq Bay	1.25	1.25
764	A153	35p Beauport Beach	1.25	1.25
a.		Bklt. pane, 3 each #763-764	8.50	
765	A153	41p Plemont Bay	1.60	1.60
766	A153	60p St. Brelade's Bay	2.40	2.40
a.		Bklt. pane, 1 each #761-766	8.75	
b.		Bklt. pane, 1 each #765-766	13.00	
		Complete booklet, #762a, 764a, 766a, 766b	37.50	
		Nos. 761-766 (6)	8.15	8.15

Horses A154

1996, Sept. 13   Litho.   Perf. 13½x14
767	A154	19p Drag hunt	.75	.75
768	A154	23p Horse driving	.90	.90
769	A154	30p Race training	1.25	1.25
770	A154	35p Show jumping	1.40	1.40
771	A154	41p Pony club	1.60	1.60
772	A154	60p Shire horses	2.40	2.40
		Nos. 767-772 (6)	8.30	8.30

Christmas A155

19p, Journey to Bethlehem. 23p, Archangel Gabriel visits shepherds. 30p, Nativity. 60p, Magi.

1996, Nov. 12   Perf. 13x13½
773	A155	19p multicolored	.75	.75
774	A155	23p multicolored	.90	.90
775	A155	30p multicolored	1.25	1.25
776	A155	60p multicolored	2.40	2.40
		Nos. 773-776 (4)	5.30	5.30

Souvenir Sheet

New Year 1997 (Year of the Ox) — A156

Illustration reduced.

1997, Feb. 7   Litho.   Perf. 13½
777	A156	£1 multicolored	4.00	4.00
a.		With added inscription in sheet margin	4.00	4.00

No. 777a inscribed in sheet margin with "JERSEY AT HONG KONG '97" in red and Hong Kong '97 emblem in black.

Birds — A157

1997, Feb. 12   Perf. 14½
Inscribed "1997"
778	A157	1p Red-breasted merganser	.20	.20
779	A157	10p Common tern	.40	.40
780	A157	15p Black-headed gull	.60	.60
781	A157	20p Dunlin	.80	.80
782	A157	24p Puffin	.95	.95
783	A157	37p Oystercatcher	1.50	1.50
784	A157	75p Redshank	3.00	3.00
785	A157	£2 Shag	8.00	8.00
a.		Souv. sheet of 8, #778-785	16.00	16.00
b.		As "a," with added inscription in sheet margin	16.00	16.00

No. 785b contains PACIFIC '97 World Philatelic Exhibition emblem in sheet margin. Issued: 5/29.

See Nos. 825-832, 864-871, 909-916.

1998, Jan. 28
Inscribed "1998"
778a	A157	1p Red-breasted merganser	—	—
779a	A157	10p Common tern	—	—
780a	A157	15p Black-headed gull	—	—
781a	A157	20p Dunlin	—	—
782a	A157	24p Puffin	—	—
783a	A157	37p Oystercatcher	—	—
784a	A157	75p Redshank	—	—
785a	A157	£2 Shag	—	—

1999, Aug. 21
Inscribed "1999"
778b	A157	1p Red-breasted merganser	—	—
779b	A157	10p Common tern	—	—
780b	A157	15p Black-headed gull	—	—
781b	A157	20p Dunlin	—	—
782b	A157	24p Puffin	—	—
783b	A157	37p Oystercatcher	—	—
784b	A157	75p Redshank	—	—
785b	A157	£2 Shag	—	—

Lillie the Cow — A158

Designs: No. 786, Building sand castle. No. 787, Taking photographs. No. 788, Lying on beach. No. 789, In restaurant.

1997, Feb. 12   Die Cut Perf 9½x9
Self-Adhesive
Inscribed "1997"
786	A158	(23p) multicolored	.90	.90
a.		With copyright symbol after date	5.00	5.00
787	A158	(23p) multicolored	.90	.90
a.		With copyright symbol after date	5.00	5.00

788	A158	(23p) multicolored	.90	.90
a.		With copyright symbol after date	5.00	5.00
789	A158	(23p) multicolored	.90	.90
a.		With copyright symbol after date	5.00	5.00
b.		Strip of 4, #786-789	3.75	
c.		Strip of 4, #786a-789a	20.00	20.00

Peelable backing is rouletted 9 between stamps.

1999, Apr. 16
Inscribed "1999"
786d		(23p) multi	7.00	7.00
787d		(23p) multi	7.00	7.00
788d		(23p) multi	7.00	7.00
789d		(23p) multi	7.00	7.00
789e		Strip of 4, #786d-789d	28.00	

2000, Dec. 9
Coil Stamps
Inscribed "2000"
786f		Die cut perf. 8¾x9	6.00	6.00
787f		Die cut perf. 8¾x9	6.00	6.00
788f		Die cut perf. 8¾x9	6.00	6.00
789f		Die cut perf. 8¾x9	6.00	6.00
789g		Strip of 4, #786f-789f	25.00	

Nos. 786-789 are inscribed "U.K. MINIMUM POSTAGE PAID."

Jersey Airport, 60th Anniv. A159

1997, Mar. 10   Litho.   Perf. 13½x14
790	A159	20p DH95 Flamingo	.80	.80
791	A159	24p HPR1 Marathon	.95	.95
792	A159	31p DH114 Heron	1.25	1.25
793	A159	37p Boeing 737-236	1.40	1.40
794	A159	43p BN Trislander	1.75	1.75
795	A159	63p BAe 146-200	2.50	2.50
		Nos. 790-795 (6)	8.65	8.65

Stories and Legends A160

Europa: 20p, Bull of St. Clement. 24p, Black Horse of St. Ouen. 31p, Black Dog of Bouley Bay. 63p, Les Fontaines des Mittes.

1997, Apr. 15   Litho.   Perf. 14½x14
796	A160	20p multicolored	.75	.75
797	A160	24p multicolored	.85	.85
798	A160	31p multicolored	1.10	1.10
799	A160	63p multicolored	2.10	2.10
		Nos. 796-799 (4)	4.80	4.80

1997 Jersey Island Games A161

1997, June 28   Litho.   Perf. 13½x14
800	A161	20p Cycling	.75	.75
801	A161	24p Archery	.85	.85
a.		Booklet pane, 3 each #800-801	4.75	
802	A161	31p Windsurfing	1.10	1.10
803	A161	37p Gymnastics	1.40	1.40
a.		Booklet pane, 3 each #802-803	7.50	
804	A161	43p Volleyball	1.60	1.60
805	A161	63p Running	2.50	2.50
a.		Booklet pane, 3 each #804-805	12.00	
b.		Booklet pane, #800-805	8.25	
		Complete booklet, #801a, 803a, 805a-805b	32.50	
		Nos. 800-805 (6)	8.20	8.20

Jesey Wildlife Preservation Trust A162

Endangered species: 20p, Mallorcan midwife toad. 24p, Aye-aye. 31p, Echo parakeet. 37p, Pigmy hog. 43p, St. Lucia whip-tail. 63p, Madagascar teal.

1997, Sept. 2   Litho.   Perf. 13
806	A162	20p multicolored	.80	.80
807	A162	24p multicolored	.95	.95
808	A162	31p multicolored	1.25	1.25
809	A162	37p multicolored	1.50	1.50
810	A162	43p multicolored	1.75	1.75
811	A162	63p multicolored	2.50	2.50
		Nos. 806-811 (6)	8.75	8.75

Trees — A163

1997, Sept. 2   Perf. 14½
812	A163	20p Ash	.80	.80
813	A163	24p Elder	.95	.95
814	A163	31p Beech	1.25	1.25
815	A163	37p Sweet chestnut	1.50	1.50
816	A163	43p Hawthorn	1.75	1.75
817	A163	63p Common oak	2.50	2.50
		Nos. 812-817 (6)	8.75	8.75

Christmas A164

Santa Claus at various Jersey landmarks: 20p, Jersey Airport. 24p, St. Aubin's Harbor. 31p, Mont Orgueil Castle. 63p, Royal Square, St. Helier.

1997, Nov. 11   Litho.   Perf. 14
818	A164	20p multicolored	.80	.80
819	A164	24p multicolored	.95	.95
820	A164	31p multicolored	1.25	1.25
821	A164	63p multicolored	2.50	2.50
		Nos. 818-821 (4)	5.50	5.50

Queen Elizabeth II and Prince Philip, 50th Wedding Anniv. A165

Designs: No. 822, Wedding portrait. No. 823, Anniversary portrait.
£1.50, Full length wedding portrait, vert.

1997, Nov. 20   Litho.   Perf. 14½
822	A165	50p multicolored	2.00	2.00
823	A165	50p multicolored	2.00	2.00
a.		Pair, #822-823	4.00	4.00

Souvenir Sheet
Perf. 13½x14
824	A165	£1.50 multicolored	4.75	4.75

No. 824 contains one 38x51mm stamp.

Bird Type of 1997

1998, Jan. 28   Litho.   Perf. 14½
825	A157	2p Sanderling	.20	.20
826	A157	5p Great crested grebe	.20	.20
827	A157	21p Sandwich tern	.80	.80
828	A157	25p Brent goose	1.00	1.00
829	A157	30p Fulmar	1.25	1.25
830	A157	40p Turnstone	1.60	1.60
831	A157	60p Avocet	2.50	2.50
832	A157	£1 Razorbill	4.00	4.00
a.		Souvenir sheet of 8, #825-832	12.00	12.00
		Nos. 825-832 (8)	11.55	11.55

Souvenir Sheet

New Year 1998 (Year of the Tiger) — A166

1998, Jan. 28   *Perf. 14*
833 A166 £1 multicolored   4.00 4.00

Buses A167

Designs: 20p, JMT Bristol 4 Tonner, 1923. 24p, SCS Regent Double Decker, 1934. 31p, Slade's Dennis Lancet, 1936. 37p, Tantivy Leyland PLSC Lion, 1947. 43p, JBS Morris Bus, 1958. 63p, JMT Leyland Titan TD4 Double Decker, 1961.

1998, Apr. 2   **Litho.**   *Perf. 14*
834	A167	20p multicolored	.80	.80
835	A167	24p multicolored	.95	.95
a.		Bklt. pane, 3 each #834-835	5.75	
836	A167	31p multicolored	1.25	1.25
837	A167	37p multicolored	1.50	1.50
a.		Bklt. pane, 3 each #836-837	8.50	
838	A167	43p multicolored	1.75	1.75
839	A167	63p multicolored	2.50	2.50
a.		Bklt. pane, 3 each #838-839	13.50	
b.		Bklt. pane, 1 each, #834-839	9.00	
		Complete booklet, #835a, 837a, 839a, 839b	37.50	
		Nos. 834-839 (6)	8.75	8.75

National Festivals — A168

Europa: 20p, Creative Arts Festival. 24p, Jazz Festival. 31p, Good Food Festival. 63p, Floral Festival.

1998, Apr. 2   *Perf. 14x13½*
840	A168	20p multicolored	.80	.80
841	A168	24p multicolored	.95	.95
842	A168	31p multicolored	1.25	1.25
843	A168	63p multicolored	2.50	2.50
		Nos. 840-843 (4)	5.50	5.50

Yachting — A169

Nos. 844-848: Various Hobie Cats sailing in St. Aubin's Bay.
Nos. 849-853: Various yachts racing in annual "Lombard Challenge."

1998, May 18   **Litho.**   *Perf. 13*
844	A169	20p multicolored	.80	.80
845	A169	20p multicolored	.80	.80
846	A169	20p multicolored	.80	.80
847	A169	20p multicolored	.80	.80
848	A169	20p multicolored	.80	.80
a.		Strip of 5, #844-848	4.25	4.25
849	A169	24p multicolored	.95	.95
850	A169	24p multicolored	.95	.95
851	A169	24p multicolored	.95	.95
852	A169	24p multicolored	.95	.95
853	A169	24p multicolored	.95	.95
a.		Strip of 5, #849-853	5.00	5.00

"Days Gone By" — A170

Jersey lily and: No. 854, Cider making. No. 855, Potato barrels transported by horse and cart. No. 856, Gathering seaweed for fertilizer. No. 857, Milking Jersey cows by hand.

Serpentine Die Cut Perf. 11¼
1998, Aug. 11   **Litho.**
Self-Adhesive
854	A170	(20p) multicolored	1.10	1.10
855	A170	(20p) multicolored	1.10	1.10
856	A170	(20p) multicolored	1.10	1.10
857	A170	(20p) multicolored	1.10	1.10
a.		Strip of 4, #854-857	4.50	

Nos. 854-857 are inscribed "Bailiwick / Minimum Postage Paid." They were sold for 22p. Stamps from the first printing are dated "1998." Stamps from subsequent printings are dated "1999," "2000," "2001" and "2003."

Marine Life A171

1998, Aug. 11   **Litho.**   *Perf. 15x14½*
858	A171	20p Bass	.80	.80
859	A171	24p Red gurnard	.95	.95
860	A171	31p Skate	1.25	1.25
861	A171	37p Mackerel	1.50	1.50
862	A171	43p Tope	1.75	1.75
863	A171	63p Cuckoo wrasse	2.50	2.50
		Nos. 858-863 (6)	8.75	8.75

Intl. Year of the Ocean.

Bird Type of 1997

1998, Aug. 11   *Perf. 14½*
864	A157	4p Gannet	.20	.20
865	A157	22p Ringed plover	.85	.85
866	A157	26p Grey plover	1.00	1.00
867	A157	31p Golden plover	1.25	1.25
868	A157	32p Greenshank	1.25	1.25
869	A157	35p Curlew	1.40	1.40
870	A157	44p Herring gull	1.75	1.75
871	A157	50p Great black-backed gull	2.00	2.00
a.		Souvenir sheet of 8, #864-871	9.75	9.75
		Nos. 864-871 (8)	9.70	9.70

Jersey Autumn Flowers A172

1998, Oct. 23   **Litho.**   *Perf. 14½*
872	A172	20p Iris	.80	.80
873	A172	24p Carnations	.95	.95
874	A172	31p Chrysanthemums	1.25	1.25
875	A172	37p Pinks	1.50	1.50
876	A172	43p Roses	1.75	1.75
877	A172	63p Lilies	2.50	2.50
		Nos. 872-877 (6)	8.75	8.75

Souvenir Sheet
Perf. 14
878 A172 £1.50 Lilium star gazer   6.00 6.00

No. 878 contains one 50x38mm stamp. Italia '98 (#878).

Christmas A173

Island manger (crib), service club sponsor: 20p, Central Market, Jersey Round Table. 24p, St. Thomas' Church, Soroptimist Intl. of

Jersey. 31p, Trinity Parish Church, Rotary Club of Jersey. 63p, Royal Square, Lions Club of Jersey.

1998, Nov. 10   *Perf. 13x13½*
879	A173	20p multicolored	.80	.80
880	A173	24p multicolored	.95	.95
881	A173	31p multicolored	1.25	1.25
882	A173	63p multicolored	2.50	2.50
		Nos. 879-882 (4)	5.50	5.50

Souvenir Sheet

New Year 1999 (Year of the Rabbit) — A174

1999, Feb. 16   **Litho.**   *Perf. 13½*
883 A174 £1 multicolored   4.00 4.00

UPU, 125th Anniv. A175

Jersey mail transport: 20p, Eastern Railway train. 24p, Mail steamer, "Brighton." 43p, DH 86A, first airmail arrival. 63p, Morris Minor P.O. van.

1999, Feb. 16   *Perf. 14*
884	A175	20p multicolored	.80	.80
885	A175	24p multicolored	.95	.95
886	A175	43p multicolored	1.75	1.75
887	A175	63p multicolored	2.50	2.50
		Nos. 884-887 (4)	6.00	6.00

Royal Natl. Lifeboat Institution, 175th Anniv. A176

1999, Feb. 16   *Perf. 14½*
888	A176	75p Jessica Eliza, St. Catherine	3.00	3.00
889	A176	£1 Alexander Coutanche, St. Helier	4.00	4.00
a.		Pair, #888-889	7.00	7.00

Orchids — A177

Designs: 21p, Cymbidium Maufant "Jersey." 25p, Miltonia Millbrook "Jersey." 31p, Paphiopedilum Transvaal. 37p, Paphiopedilum Elizabeth Castle. 43p, Calanthe Five Oaks. 63p, Cymbidium Icho Tower "Trinity." £1.50, Miltonia Portelet.

Perf. 14¼x13¼
1999, Mar. 19   **Litho.**
890	A177	21p multicolored	.80	.80
891	A177	25p multicolored	1.00	1.00
892	A177	31p multicolored	1.25	1.25
893	A177	37p multicolored	1.50	1.50
894	A177	43p multicolored	1.75	1.75
895	A177	63p multicolored	2.50	2.50
		Nos. 890-895 (6)	8.80	8.80

Souvenir Sheet
Perf. 13½
896 A177 £1.50 multicolored   6.00 6.00

Australia '99 World Stamp Expo (#896).

IBRA'99 Intl. Philatelic Exhibition, Nuremberg A178

National Parks: 21p, Howard Davis Park. 25p, Sir Winston Churchill Memorial Park. 31p, Coronation Park. 63p, La Collette Gardens.

1999, Apr. 27   *Perf. 13x13½*
897	A178	21p multicolored	.80	.80
898	A178	25p multicolored	1.00	1.00
899	A178	31p multicolored	1.25	1.25
900	A178	63p multicolored	2.25	2.25
		Nos. 897-900 (4)	5.30	5.30

Europa (#898-899).

Wedding of Prince Edward and Sophie Rhys-Jones — A179

1999, June 19   **Litho.**   *Perf. 14½*
901	A179	35p yellow & multi	1.40	1.40
902	A179	35p blue & multi	1.40	1.40
a.		Pair, #901-902	3.00	3.00

Classic Car Type of 1989

Designs: 21p, 1899 Jersey-built Benz. 25p, 1910 Star Tourer. 31p, 1938 Citroen "Traction Avant." 37p, 1937 Talbot BG110 Tourer. 43p, 1934 Morris Cowley Six Special Coupé. 63p, 1946 Ford Anglia E04A Saloon.

1999, July 2   **Litho.**   *Perf. 14*
903	A101	21p multicolored	.80	.80
904	A101	25p multicolored	1.00	1.00
a.		Bklt. pane, 3 each #903-904	5.75	
905	A101	31p multicolored	1.25	1.25
906	A101	37p multicolored	1.50	1.50
a.		Bklt. pane, 3 each #905-906	8.75	
907	A101	43p multicolored	1.75	1.75
908	A101	63p multicolored	2.50	2.50
a.		Bklt. pane, 3 each #907-908	13.50	
b.		Booklet pane, #903-908	9.25	
		Complete booklet, #904a, 906a, 908a, 908b	40.00	
		Nos. 903-908 (6)	8.80	8.80

PhilexFrance '99 (#904a, 906a, 908a-908b).

Bird Type of 1997

1999, Aug. 21   *Perf. 14¾*
909	A157	23p Bar-tailed godwit	.90	.90
910	A157	27p Common scoter	1.10	1.10
911	A157	28p Lesser black-backed gull	1.10	1.10
912	A157	29p Little egret	1.10	1.10
913	A157	33p Little grebe	1.25	1.25
914	A157	34p Cormorant	1.25	1.25
915	A157	45p Rock pipit	1.75	1.75
916	A157	65p Gray heron	2.50	2.50
a.		Souvenir sheet of 8, #909-916	11.00	11.00
		Nos. 909-916 (8)	10.95	10.95

Small Mammals A180

Designs: 21p, Hedgehog. 25p, Red squirrel. 31p, Nathusius pipestrelle. 37p, Jersey bank vole. 43p, Lesser white-toothed shrew. 63p, Common mole.

1999, Aug. 21   **Litho.**   *Perf. 13¼x13*
917	A180	21p multicolored	.80	.80
918	A180	25p multicolored	1.00	1.00
919	A180	31p multicolored	1.25	1.25
920	A180	37p multicolored	1.50	1.50
921	A180	43p multicolored	1.75	1.75
922	A180	63p multicolored	2.50	2.50
		Nos. 917-922 (6)	8.80	8.80

Lighthouses
A181

1999, Oct. 5   Litho.   Perf. 14
923 A181 21p Gorey Pierhead   .80   .80
924 A181 25p La Corbiere   1.00   1.00
925 A181 34p Noirmont Point   1.40   1.40
926 A181 38p Demie de Pas   1.50   1.50
927 A181 44p Greve d'Azette   1.75   1.75
928 A181 64p Sorel Point   2.50   2.50
     Nos. 923-928 (6)   8.95   8.95

Christmas
A182

Poinsettias and: 21p, Mistletoe. 25p, Holly.
34p, Ivy. 64p, Christmas rose.

1999, Nov. 9   Litho.   Perf. 13¾
929 A182 21p multi   .80   .80
930 A182 25p multi   1.00   1.00
931 A182 34p multi   1.40   1.40
932 A182 64p multi   2.50   2.50
     Nos. 929-932 (4)   5.70   5.70

Coat of
Arms
A183

**Litho. & Embossed with Foil
Application**
2000, Jan. 1   Perf. 13¼
933 A183 £10 gold & multi   40.00 40.00
     Millennium.

Souvenir Sheet

New Year 2000 (Year of the
Dragon) — A184

2000, Feb. 5   Litho.   Perf. 13¾
934 A184 £1 multi   4.00   4.00

Europa, 2000
Common Design Type and

A185

2000, May 9   Perf. 13¼x13
935 A185 26p multi   1.00   1.00
936 CD17 34p multi   1.40   1.40

Stampin' the Future — A186

Children's Stamp Design Contest Winners:
No. 937, Ocean Adventure, by Gemma Carré.
No. 938, Solar Power, by Chantal Varley-Best.
No. 939, Floating City and Space Cars, by
Nicola Singleton. No. 940, Conservation, by
Carly Logan.

2000, May 9   Litho.   Perf. 14
937 A186 22p multi   .85   .85
938 A186 22p multi   .85   .85
939 A186 22p multi   .85   .85
940 A186 22p multi   .85   .85
 a.   Souvenir sheet, #937-940   3.50   3.50
     Nos. 937-940 (4)   3.40   3.40

Ships — A187

#941, Roman merchant ship. #942, Viking
long boat. #943, Warship, 13th cent. #944,
Merchant ship, 14th-15th cent. #945, Tudor
warship, 16th cent.
    #946, Warship, 17th cent. #947, Navy cut-
ter, 18th cent. #948, Barque, 19th cent. #949,
Oyster cutter, 19th cent. #950, Ketch, 20th
cent.

2000, May 22   Perf. 13¾
941 A187 22p multi   .85   .85
942 A187 22p multi   .85   .85
943 A187 22p multi   .85   .85
944 A187 22p multi   .85   .85
945 A187 22p multi   .85   .85
 a.   Strip of 5, #941-945   4.25   4.25
946 A187 26p multi   1.00   1.00
947 A187 26p multi   1.00   1.00
948 A187 26p multi   1.00   1.00
949 A187 26p multi   1.00   1.00
 a.   Booklet pane, #941-944, 946-
        949   7.50   7.50
950 A187 26p multi   1.00   1.00
 a.   Strip of 5, #946-950   5.00   5.00
 b.   Souvenir sheet, #941-950   9.25   9.25
 c.   Booklet pane, #941-942, 944-
        946, 948-950   7.50
 d.   Booklet pane, #941, 943-947,
        949-950   7.50
 e.   Booklet pane, #941-943, 945-
        948, 950   7.50
 f.   Bklt. pane, #942-945, 947-950   7.50
        Booklet, #949a, 950c-950f   37.50
 g.   As "b," with Stamp Show 2000
        emblem added in sheet mar-
        gin   9.25   9.25

Marine
Mammals
A188

Designs: 22p, Bottle-nosed dolphin. 26p,
Long-finned pilot whale. 34p, Harbor porpoise.
38p, Atlantic gray seal. 44p, Risso's dolphin.
64p, White-beaked dolphin.
£1.50, Common dolphin.

2000, June 5   Perf. 14¾x14
951 A188 22p multi   .85   .85
952 A188 26p multi   1.00   1.00
953 A188 34p multi   1.25   1.25
954 A188 38p multi   1.50   1.50
955 A188 44p multi   1.75   1.75
956 A188 64p multi   2.50   2.50
     Nos. 951-956 (6)   8.85   8.85

Souvenir Sheet
957 A188 £1.50 multi   6.00   6.00
 a.   As #957, with World Stamp Ex-
        po 2000 emblem in margin   6.00   6.00

No. 957 contains one 81x29mm stamp.
Issued: No. 957a, 7/7/00.

Prince
William,
18th
Birthday
A189

William &: #958, Mountain. #959, Polo
player. #960, Fireworks. #961, Beaumarais
Castle.

2000, June 21   Perf. 14¼x14½
958 A189 75p multi   3.00   3.00
959 A189 75p multi   3.00   3.00
960 A189 75p multi   3.00   3.00
961 A189 75p multi   3.00   3.00
     Nos. 958-961 (4)   12.00 12.00

Queen Mother,
100th Birthday
A190

Litho. with Foil Application
2000, Aug. 4   Perf. 14½x14¼
962 A190 50p Purple hat   2.00   2.00
963 A190 50p Pink hat   2.00   2.00
 a.   Souvenir sheet, #962-963   4.00   4.00

Battle of
Britain,
60th
Anniv.
A191

Designs: 22p, Supermarine Spitfire Mk. Ia.
26p, Hawker Hurricane Mk. I. 36p, Bristol
Blenheim Mk. IV. 40p, Vickers Wellington Mk.
Ic. 45p, Boulton Paul Defiant Mk. I. 65p, Short
Sunderland Mk. I.

2000, Sept. 15 Litho.   Perf. 14¼x14
964 A191 22p multi   .85   .85
965 A191 26p multi   1.00   1.00
966 A191 36p multi   1.40   1.40
967 A191 40p multi   1.60   1.60
968 A191 45p multi   1.75   1.75
969 A191 65p multi   2.50   2.50
     Nos. 964-969 (6)   9.10   9.10

Christmas
A192

2000, Nov. 7   Perf. 13
970 A192 22p Virgin Mary   .85   .85
971 A192 26p Shepherd   1.00   1.00
972 A192 36p Angel   1.40   1.40
973 A192 65p Magus   2.50   2.50
     Nos. 970-973 (4)   5.75   5.75

Souvenir Sheet

New Year 2001 (Year of the
Snake) — A193

2001, Jan. 24   Litho.   Perf. 13¾
974 A193 £1 multi   4.25   4.25

Steamships on Jersey-France
Route — A194

2001, Jan. 24   Perf. 13x13¼
975 A194 22p Rose   .85   .85
976 A194 26p Comete   1.00   1.00
977 A194 36p Cygne   1.40   1.40
978 A194 40p Victoria   1.60   1.60
979 A194 45p Attala   1.75   1.75
980 A194 65p Brittany   2.50   2.50
     Nos. 975-980 (6)   9.10   9.10

Agricultural
Products — A195

No. 981: a, Jersey cows. b, Royal potatoes.
c, Tomatoes. d, Cauliflower and purple broc-
coli. e, Zucchini and peppers.

Serpentine Die Cut 11¼
2001, Apr. 3
**Self-Adhesive
Inscribed "2001"**
981   Strip of 5   14.00
 a.-e. A195 (26p) Any single   2.75   2.75
 f.   As No. 981, inscribed "2002"   14.00
 g.   As No. 981, inscribed "2003"   14.00
 h.   As No. 981, inscribed "2005"   14.00

Navy
Ships
Named
Jersey
A196

Ships in service from: 23p, 1654-91. 26p,
1694-98. 37p, 1698-1731. 41p, 1736-83. 46p,
1860-73. 66p, 1938-41.

2001, Apr. 3   Perf. 14
982 A196 23p multi   .90   .90
983 A196 26p multi   1.00   1.00
984 A196 37p multi   1.50   1.50
985 A196 41p multi   1.60   1.60
986 A196 46p multi   1.75   1.75
987 A196 66p multi   2.50   2.50
     Nos. 982-987 (6)   9.25   9.25

Queen Elizabeth II, 75th
Birthday — A197

2001, Apr. 21　　　　**Perf. 14x14¾**
988　A197　£3 multi　　　12.00 12.00

Pond Life
A198

Designs: 23p, Agile frog. 26p, Trout. 37p,
White water lily. 41p, Common blue damselfly.
46p, Palmate newt. 66p, Tufted duck.

2001, May 22　　　　**Perf. 14¾x14**
989　A198　23p multi　　　.90　.90
990　A198　26p multi　　　1.00　1.00
991　A198　37p multi　　　1.40　1.40
992　A198　41p multi　　　1.50　1.50
993　A198　46p multi　　　1.00　1.60
994　A198　66p multi　　　2.40　2.40
　　　Nos. 989-994 (6)　　　8.80　8.80

Souvenir Sheet
Perf. 14¼
995　A198　£1.50 Kingfisher　6.00　6.00
　a.　As #995, with Belgica 2001
　　　emblem in margin　　　6.50　6.50

Europa (#990-991). No. 995 contains one
38x50mm stamp.
Issued: No. 995a, 6/9/01.

Birds of
Prey — A199

Designs: 23p, Long-eared owl. 26p, Peregrine falcon. 37p, Short-eared owl. 41p, Marsh
harrier. 46p, Sparrowhawk. 66p, Tawny owl.
£1.50, Barn owl.

2001, July 3　**Litho.**　**Perf. 13½**
996　A199　23p multi　　　.90　.90
997　A199　26p multi　　　1.00　1.00
998　A199　37p multi　　　1.50　1.50
999　A199　41p multi　　　1.60　1.60
1000　A199　46p multi　　　1.75　1.75
　a.　Booklet pane, #997, 998, 2
　　　each #996, 1000　　　8.00　—
1001　A199　66p multi　　　2.50　2.50
　a.　Booklet pane, #996-1001　9.25　—
　b.　Booklet pane, 2 each #996,
　　　998, 1001　　　9.75　—
　c.　Booklet pane, #996-998,
　　　1001, 2 #999　　　8.75　—
　　　Nos. 996-1001 (6)　9.25　9.25
1002　A199　£1.50 Booklet pane
　　　of 1　　　17.50 12.50
　　　Booklet, #1000a, 1001a,
　　　1001b, 1001c, 1002　55.00

Souvenir Sheet
1003　A199　£1.50 multi　　6.00　6.00
　a.　Like #1003, with Hafnia 01
　　　emblem　　　6.00　6.00

Issued: No. 1003a, 10/16/01.
On No. 1002, "Tyto" is 4mm from the owl's
head (owl is in center of stamp), while on No.
1003, it is 9mm from the head (owl is at right of
stamp). The size of No. 1002 is 154x100mm,
while the size of No. 1003 is 110x75.

Souvenir Sheet

Racing Yacht Jersey Clipper — A200

2001, Sept. 17　　　**Perf. 13¾**
1004　A200　£1.50 multi　　6.00　6.00

Fire
Engines
A201

Designs: 23p, Tilley 26 manual, c. 1845.
26p, Albion Merryweather, c. 1935. 37p, Dennis Ace, c. 1940. 41p, Dennis F8 pump
escape, c. 1952. 46p, Land Rover Merryweather, c. 1968. 66p, Dennis Carmichael,
c. 1989.

2001, Sept. 25　　　**Perf. 13x13¼**
1005　A201　23p multi　　　1.00　1.00
1006　A201　26p multi　　　1.25　1.25
1007　A201　37p multi　　　1.50　1.50
1008　A201　41p multi　　　1.75　1.75
1009　A201　46p multi　　　1.90　1.90
1010　A201　66p multi　　　2.50　2.50
　　　Nos. 1005-1010 (6)　9.90　9.90

Christmas
A202

No. 1011: a, Nativity. b, Street decorations.
c, Carolers. d, Santa Claus. c, Bells and other
ornaments on Christmas tree.
No. 1012: a, Adoration of the Shepherds. b,
Carolers, Santa Claus, reindeer. c, Bell ornament, Christmas tree with candles. d, Church
bells. e, Cracker with bells on wrapper.

Serpentine Die Cut 11x11¼
2001, Nov. 6
Coil Stamps
Self-Adhesive
Inscribed "2001"

1011　Horiz. strip of 5　　4.75
　a.-e.　A202 (23p) green & multi, any
　　　single　　　.90　.90
1012　Horiz. strip of 5　　5.75　—
　a.-e.　A202 (29p) red & multi, any
　　　single　　　1.10　1.10
　f.　Booklet pane of 16, 2 each
　　　#1011a, 1011c-1011e,
　　　1012a-1012b, 1012d-1012e　16.00

On Nos. 1011-1012, the matrix was stripped
from around the stamps; on the booklets, the
matrix remains surrounding the stamps.

2002, Nov. 23
Inscribed "2002"
1011f　Horiz. strip of 5　　4.75
　g.-k.　A202 (23p) any single　.90　.90
1012g　Horiz. strip of 5　　5.75
　h.-l.　A202 (29p) any single　1.10　1.10

2003, Nov. 10
Inscribed "2003"
1011l　Horiz. strip of 5　　4.75
　m.-q.　A202 (23p) any single　.90　.90
1012m　Horiz. strip of 5　　5.75
　n.-r.　A202 (29p) any single　1.10　1.10

Jersey State
Vessels
A203

Designs: 23p, Launch "Duchess of Normandy." 29p, Tugboat "Duke of Normandy."
38p, Customs patrol boat "Challenger." 47p,

Pilot boat "Le Fret." 68p, Sea fisheries protection boat "Norman Le Brocq."

2002, Jan. 22　**Litho.**　**Perf. 13x13¼**
1013　A203　23p multi　　　.90　.90
1014　A203　29p multi　　　1.10　1.10
1015　A203　38p multi　　　1.50　1.50
1016　A203　47p multi　　　1.75　1.75
1017　A203　68p multi　　　2.75　2.75
　　　Nos. 1013-1017 (5)　8.00　8.00

Reign of
Queen
Elizabeth II,
50th
Anniv. — A204

Litho. & Embossed With Foil
Application
2002, Feb. 6　　　**Perf. 13¼**
1018　A204　£3 multi　　　12.00 12.00

Souvenir Sheet

New Year 2002 (Year of the
Horse) — A205

2002, Feb. 12　**Litho.**　**Perf. 13¾**
1019　A205　£1 multi　　　4.75　4.75

Battle of Flowers
Depictions of
Circus
Figures — A206

2002, Mar. 12　**Litho.**　**Perf. 13¾**
1020　A206　23p Elephant, cats　.90　.90
1021　A206　29p Clown　　　1.10　1.10
1022　A206　38p Clown, diff.　1.50　1.50
1023　A206　68p Seal　　　2.75　2.75
　　　Nos. 1020-1023 (4)　6.25　6.25

Europa (#1021-1022).

La Moye
Golf Club,
Cent.
A207

Designs: 23p, Aubrey Boomer. 29p, Harry
Vardon. 38p, Sir Henry Cotton. 47p, Golfer's
swing. 68p, Golfer addressing ball.

2002, Apr. 16　　　**Perf. 14**
1024　A207　23p multi　　　1.00　1.00
1025　A207　29p multi　　　1.25　1.25
1026　A207　38p multi　　　1.50　1.50
1027　A207　47p multi　　　2.00　2.00
1028　A207　68p multi　　　3.00　3.00
　　　Nos. 1024-1028 (5)　8.75　8.75

Police
Vehicles
A208

Designs: 23p, Vauxhall 12, c. 1952. 29p,
1959-60 Jaguar 2.4 MkII. 38p, 1972-73 Austin
1800. 40p, Ford Cortina MkIV, c. 1978. 47p,
1995-2000 Honda motorcycle. 68p, 1998-
2000 Vauxhall Vectra.

2002, May 24　**Litho.**　**Perf. 13x13¼**
1029　A208　23p multi　　　.90　.90
1030　A208　29p multi　　　1.10　1.10
1031　A208　38p multi　　　1.50　1.50
1032　A208　40p multi　　　1.60　1.60
1033　A208　47p multi　　　1.75　1.75
1034　A208　68p multi　　　2.75　2.75
　　　Nos. 1029-1034 (6)　9.60　9.60

Insects
A209

Designs: 23p, Honeybee. 29p, Seven-spot
ladybug. 38p, Great green bush cricket. 40p,
Greater horntail. 47p, Emperor dragonfly. 68p,
Hawthorn shield bug.

2002, June 18　　　**Perf. 14¾x14**
1035　A209　23p multi　　　.90　.90
1036　A209　29p multi　　　1.10　1.10
1037　A209　38p multi　　　1.50　1.50
1038　A209　40p multi　　　1.60　1.60
1039　A209　47p multi　　　1.75　1.75
1040　A209　68p multi　　　2.75　2.75
　　　Nos. 1035-1040 (6)　9.60　9.60

Queen Mother Elizabeth (1900-
2002) — A210

Litho. with Foil Application
2002, Aug. 4　　　**Perf. 14x14¾**
1041　A210　£2 multi　　　8.00　8.00

Battle of
Flowers,
Cent.
A211

Designs: 23p, Hydrangeas. 29p, Chrysanthemums. 38p, Hare's tails, pampas grass.
40p, Asters. 47p, Carnations. 68p, Gladioli.
£2, Float "Zanzibar."

2002, Aug. 8　**Litho.**　**Perf. 13x13¼**
1042　A211　23p multi　　　.90　.90
1043　A211　29p multi　　　1.10　1.10
1044　A211　38p multi　　　1.50　1.50
1045　A211　40p multi　　　1.60　1.60
1046　A211　47p multi　　　1.75　1.75
1047　A211　68p multi　　　2.75　2.75
　a.　Booklet pane, #1042-1047　9.75
　　　Nos. 1042-1047 (6)　9.60　9.60

Souvenir Sheet
Perf. 13
1048　A211　£2 multi　　　8.00　8.00
　a.　Booklet pane of 1　　8.00
　　　Booklet, #1048a, 3 #1047a　37.50

No. 1047a has three different layouts of
stamps on pane. No. 1048 contains one
76x39mm stamp. No. 1048a is larger than No.
1048, having extra selvage at left, with rouletting separating the selvage from the rest of the
sheet.

Cats
A212

Designs: 23p, British dilute tortoiseshell.
29p, Cream Persian. 38p, Blue exotic

shorthair. 40p, Black smoke Devon Rex. 47p, British silver tabby. 68p, Usual Abyssinian. £2, British cream and white bi-color, vert.

2002, Oct. 12		Perf. 14¾x14¼	
1049	A212 23p multi	.90	.90
1050	A212 29p multi	1.10	1.10
1051	A212 38p multi	1.50	1.50
1052	A212 40p multi	1.60	1.60
1053	A212 47p multi	1.75	1.75
1054	A212 68p multi	2.75	2.75
	Nos. 1049-1054 (6)	9.60	9.60

Souvenir Sheet
Perf. 14¼

1055	A212 £2 multi	8.00	8.00

No. 1055 contains one 38x50mm stamp.

Letter Boxes, 150th Anniv. — A213

Designs: 23p, Pillar box, Central Market. 29p, Wall box, Colomberie. 38p, Wall box, St. Clement's Inner Road. 40p, Ship box. 47p, Pillar box, Parade, 1952. 68p, Pillar box, La Collette, 2000.
£2, First letter box, David Place, 1852.

2002, Nov. 23		Perf. 14½x14¼	
1056	A213 23p multi	.90	.90
1057	A213 29p multi	1.10	1.10
1058	A213 38p multi	1.50	1.50
1059	A213 40p multi	1.60	1.60
1060	A213 47p multi	1.75	1.75
1061	A213 68p multi	2.75	2.75
	Nos. 1056-1061 (6)	9.60	9.60

Souvenir Sheet
Perf. 14¾

1062	A213 £2 multi	8.50	8.50

No. 1062 contains one 39x76mm stamp.

Airplanes A214

Designs: 23p, Sanchez-Besa Hydroplane. 29p, Supermarine S.6B. 38p, De Havilland DH84 Dragon. 40p, De Havilland DH89a Rapide. 47p, Vickers 701 Viscount. 68p, BAC One-Eleven.
£2, 1906 Biplane of Jacob Christian Hansen Ellehammer.

2003, Jan. 21	Litho.	Perf. 13x13¼	
1063	A214 23p multi	.90	.90
1064	A214 29p multi	1.10	1.10
1065	A214 38p multi	1.50	1.50
1066	A214 40p multi	1.60	1.60
1067	A214 47p multi	1.75	1.75
1068	A214 68p multi	2.75	2.75
a.	Booklet pane, #1063-1068	9.75	
	Nos. 1063-1068 (6)	9.60	9.60

Souvenir Sheet
Perf. 13¼x13

1069	A214 £2 multi	8.00	8.00
a.	Booklet pane, #1069	8.00	
	Complete booklet, #1069a, 3 #1068a	37.50	

No. 1069 contains one 60x40mm stamp. The booklet contains three examples of No. 1068a, each with different margins. No. 1069a has a larger margin than No. 1069, which contains additional text and illustrations. The £2 stamp from the booklet pane No. 1069a has the date under the second "e" of "Ellehammer," while the date on the stamp from the souvenir sheet No. 1069 has the date under the first "m" of "Ellehammer."

Souvenir Sheet

New Year 2003 (Year of the Ram) — A215

2003, Feb. 1		Perf. 13¾	
1070	A215 £1 multi	4.50	4.50

Poster Art A216

Designs: 23p, Portelet, c. 1935. 29p, Southern British Railways, c. 1952, vert. 38p, Chemins de Fer de l'Ouest, c. 1910, vert. 68p, Jersey, the Sunny Channel Island, c. 1947.

2003, Mar. 11		Perf. 13½	
1071	A216 23p multi	.90	.90
1072	A216 29p multi	1.10	1.10
1073	A216 38p multi	1.50	1.50
1074	A216 68p multi	2.75	2.75
	Nos. 1071-1074 (4)	6.25	6.25

Europa (29p, 38p).

Lighthouses and Buoys — A217

No. 1075: a, St. Catherine's Breakwater Light. b, Violet Channel Buoy.
No. 1076: a, Mont Ubé Lighthouse. b, Frouquie Aubert Buoy.
No. 1077: a, Gronez Point Lighthouse. b, Banc des Ormes Buoy.

2003, Apr. 15		Perf. 13¾	
1075	A217 Horiz. pair	2.25	2.25
a.-b.	29p Either single	1.10	1.10
1076	A217 Horiz. pair	2.50	2.50
a.-b.	30p Either single	1.25	1.25
1077	A217 Horiz. pair	4.00	4.00
a.-b.	48p Either single	1.90	1.90
	Nos. 1075-1077 (3)	8.75	8.75

Wild Orchids — A218

Designs: 29p, Southern-marsh orchid. 30p, Loose-flowered orchid. 39p, Spotted orchid. 50p, Autumn Ladies Tresses. 53p, Green-winged orchid. 69p, Pyramidal orchid.

2003, May 13		Perf. 13¼x13	
1078	A218 29p multi	1.10	1.10
1079	A218 30p multi	1.25	1.25
1080	A218 39p multi	1.60	1.60
1081	A218 50p multi	2.00	2.00
1082	A218 53p multi	2.25	2.25
1083	A218 69p multi	2.75	2.75
	Nos. 1078-1083 (6)	10.95	10.95

Souvenir Sheet

1084	A218 £2 multi	8.00	8.00
a.	As #1084, with added marginal inscription	8.25	8.25

No. 1084a has Bangkok 2003 Philatelic Exhibition emblem and text, "Jersey at Bangkok 2003," added in margin. Issued, 10/4.

Coronation of Queen Elizabeth II, 50th Anniv. A219

Designs: 29p, Sovereign's orb. 30p, St. Edward's Crown. 39p, Scepter with Cross. 50p, Ampulla and Spoon. 53p, Sovereign's Ring. 69p, Armills.

Litho. With Foil Application

2003, June 2		Perf. 14¾x14	
1085	A219 29p multi	1.10	1.10
1086	A219 30p multi	1.25	1.25
1087	A219 39p multi	1.60	1.60
1088	A219 50p multi	2.00	2.00
1089	A219 53p multi	2.10	2.10
1090	A219 69p multi	2.75	2.75
a.	Souvenir sheet, #1085-1090	11.00	11.00
	Nos. 1085-1090 (6)	10.80	10.80

Souvenir Sheet

Prince William, Prince Charles and Queen Elizabeth II — A220

2003, June 21	Litho.	Perf. 13¾	
1091	A220 £2 multi	8.00	8.00

Prince William, 21st birthday.

Offshore Reefs and Flowers — A221

No. 1092: a, Les Ecrehous Reef, tree mallow. b, Les Minquiers Reef, smooth sow-thistle. c, Les Minquiers Reef, thrift. d, Paternosters Reef, rock samphire. e, Les Ecrehous Reef, bluebells.
No. 1092g, Like No. 1092a. No. 1092h, Like No. 1092b. No. 1092i, Like No. 1092c. No. 1092j, Like No. 1092d. No. 1092k, Like No. 1092e.

Serpentine Die Cut 11

2003, Aug. 5		Photo.	
	Coil Stamps		
	Self-Adhesive		
1092	Horiz. strip of 5	5.50	5.50
a.-e.	A221 (29p) Any single	1.10	1.10
f.	Like #1092, serp. die cut 11¼, inscribed "2004"	7.00	
g.-k.	A221 (32p) Any single, serp. die cut 11¼	1.40	1.40
l.	Like #1092, serp. die cut 11¼, inscribed "2006"	7.00	
m.-q.	A221 (32p) Any single, serp. die cut 11¼, inscribed "2006"	1.40	1.40

Nos. 1092f-1092k issued 11/3/04. Nos. 1092l-1092q issued 11/16/06.

Pets — A222

Designs: 29p, Albino Rex rabbit. 30p, Labrador retriever. 38p, Canary and budgerigar. 53p, Hamster. 69p, Guinea pig.
£2, Border collie.

2003, Sept. 9	Litho.	Perf. 13¾	
1093	A222 29p multi	1.10	1.10
1094	A222 30p multi	1.25	1.25
1095	A222 38p multi	1.50	1.50
1096	A222 53p multi	2.10	2.10
1097	A222 69p multi	2.75	2.75
	Nos. 1093-1097 (5)	8.70	8.70

Souvenir Sheet
Perf. 13¼

1098	A222 £2 multi	8.00	8.00

No. 1098 contains one 39x51mm stamp.

Winter Flowers A223

Designs: 29p, Japanese quince. 30p, Winter jasmine. 39p, Snowdrop. 48p, Winter heath. 53p, Chinese witch hazel. 69p, Winter daphne.

2003, Nov. 10		Perf. 14¼	
1099	A223 29p multi	1.10	1.10
1100	A223 30p multi	1.25	1.25
1101	A223 39p multi	1.60	1.60
1102	A223 48p multi	1.90	1.90
1103	A223 53p multi	2.10	2.10
1104	A223 69p multi	2.75	2.75
	Nos. 1099-1104 (6)	10.70	10.70

Souvenir Sheet

New Year 2004 (Year of the Monkey) — A224

2004, Jan. 22	Litho.	Perf. 13¾	
1105	A224 £1 multi	4.75	4.75

British Chess Federation, Cent. — A225

2004, Jan. 22			
1106	A225 29p Rook	1.10	1.10
1107	A225 30p Knight	1.25	1.25
1108	A225 39p Bishop	1.75	1.75
1109	A225 48p Pawn	2.00	2.00
1110	A225 53p Queen	2.25	2.25
1111	A225 69p King	2.75	2.75
	Nos. 1106-1111 (6)	11.10	11.10

Tourist Attractions A226

Designs: 29p, St. Aubin's Harbor. 30p, Mont Orgueil Castle. 39p, Corbiere Lighthouse. 69p, Rozel Harbor.

2004, Mar. 9		Perf. 13x13¼	
1112	A226 29p multi	1.10	1.10
1113	A226 30p multi	1.25	1.25
1114	A226 39p multi	1.60	1.60
1115	A226 69p multi	2.75	2.75
	Nos. 1112-1115 (4)	6.70	6.70

Europa (#1113, 1114).

Waterfowl A227

Designs: 32p, Eurasian teal. 33p, Mute swan. 40p, Northern shoveler. 49p, Common pochard. 62p, Black swan. 70p, Eurasian wigeon. £2, Mallard, vert.

2004, Apr. 6   *Perf. 14¾x14*

1116	A227	32p multi	1.25	1.25
1117	A227	33p multi	1.25	1.25
1118	A227	40p multi	1.60	1.60
1119	A227	49p multi	2.00	2.00
1120	A227	62p multi	2.50	2.50
1121	A227	70p multi	2.75	2.75
		Nos. 1116-1121 (6)	11.35	11.35

Souvenir Sheet
Perf. 14¼

1122	A227	£2 multi	8.00	8.00

No. 1122 contains one 38x50mm stamp.

Orchids
A228

Designs: 32p, Cymbidium lowianum "Concolor." 33p, Phragmipedium besseae var. flavum. 40p, Peristeria elata. 54p, Cymbidium tracyanum. 62p, Paphiopedilum "Victoria Village Isle of Jersey." 70p, Paphiopedilum hirsutissimum. £2, Phragmipedium "Jason Fischer."

2004, May 25   *Perf. 13x13¼*

1123	A228	32p multi	1.25	1.25
1124	A228	33p multi	1.25	1.25
1125	A228	40p multi	1.60	1.60
1126	A228	54p multi	2.10	2.10
1127	A228	62p multi	2.50	2.50
1128	A228	70p multi	2.75	2.75
a.		Booklet pane, #1123-1128	11.50	
		Nos. 1123-1128 (6)	11.45	11.45

Souvenir Sheet

1129	A228	£2 multi	8.00	8.00
a.		Booklet pane #1129	8.00	
		Complete booklet, #1129a, 3 #1128a	42.50	
b.		Like #1129, with added marginal inscription	8.25	8.25

The booklet contains three examples of No. 1128a each with different arrangements of the stamps. No. 1129a has a larger margin than No. 1129.

No. 1129b issued 6/26. It is inscribed "Jersey at / Le Salon du Timbre 2004" in margin.

Souvenir Sheet

D-Day, 60th Anniv. — A229

2004, June 4   *Perf. 13*

1130	A229	£2 multi	8.00	8.00

Mont Orgueil Castle and Monarchs — A230

No. 1131: a, Castle in 13th century (49x32mm). b, King John, vert. (29x32mm). No. 1132: a, Castle in 17th century (49x32mm). b, King Charles II, vert. (29x32mm). No. 1133: a, Castle in 21st century (49x32mm). b, Queen Elizabeth II, vert. (29x32mm).

Illustration reduced.

2004, June 25   *Perf. 14¾*

1131	A230	Horiz. pair	2.50	2.50
a.-b.		32p Either single	1.25	1.25
1132	A230	Horiz. pair	2.50	2.50
a.-b.		33p Either single	1.25	1.25

1133	A230	Horiz. pair	3.25	3.25
a.-b.		40p Either single	1.60	1.60
		Nos. 1131-1133 (3)	8.25	8.25

Worldwide Fund for Nature (WWF)
A231

Designs: 32p, Wall lizard. 33p, Ant lion. 49p, Field cricket. 70p, Dartford warbler.

2004, July 27   *Perf. 14¾x14*

1134	A231	32p multi	1.25	1.25
1135	A231	33p multi	1.25	1.25
1136	A231	49p multi	2.00	2.00
1137	A231	70p multi	2.75	2.75
a.		Miniature sheet, 2 each #1134-1137	14.50	14.50
		Nos. 1134-1137 (4)	7.25	7.25

Corals
A232

Designs: 32p, Dead man's fingers. 33p, Devonshire cup. 40p, White sea fan. 54p, Pink sea fan. 62p, Sunset cup. 70p, Red fingers.

2004, Sept. 28   Litho.   *Perf. 13x13¼*

1138	A232	32p multi	1.25	1.25
1139	A232	33p multi	1.25	1.25
1140	A232	40p multi	1.60	1.60
1141	A232	54p multi	2.10	2.10
1142	A232	62p multi	2.50	2.50
1143	A232	70p multi	2.75	2.75
a.		Souvenir sheet, #1141-1143	7.50	7.50
		Nos. 1138-1143 (6)	11.45	11.45

Christmas
A233

No. 1144: a, Nativity. b, Street with Christmas decorations. c, Santa Claus, children, Christmas tree. d, Church interior. e, Candles and holly. Each inscribed "Jersey Minimum Postage Paid."

No. 1145: a, Madonna and Child, lilies. b, Christmas stocking on mantle. c, Candles and flowers. d, Angel and candle. e, Candles in window. Each inscribed "U.K. Minimum Postage Paid."

Serpentine Die Cut 11¼x11½

2004, Nov. 2   Litho.

Self-Adhesive
Coil Stamps

1144		Horiz. strip of 5	6.00	
a.-e.		A233 (32p) Any single	1.25	1.25
1145		Horiz. strip of 5	6.25	
a.-e.		A233 (33p) Any single	1.25	1.25

Nos. 1144 and 1145 exist dated "2005" and "2006." Values the same.

Rescue Craft
A234

Designs: 32p, Channel Islands Air Search airplane. 33p, Burby helicopter. 40p, Beach Lifeguard Service Surf Rescue boat. 49p, Fire Rescue inflatable boat. 70p, Royal Air Force Sea King helicopter.

2005, Jan. 18   Litho.   *Perf. 13x13¼*

1146	A234	32p multi	1.25	1.25
1147	A234	33p multi	1.25	1.25
1148	A234	40p multi	1.60	1.60
1149	A234	49p multi	2.00	2.00
1150	A234	70p multi	2.75	2.75
		Nos. 1146-1150 (5)	8.85	8.85

Souvenir Sheet

New Year 2005 (Year of the Rooster) — A235

2005, Feb. 9   *Perf. 14¼*

1151	A235	£1 multi	5.00	5.00

Gastronomy
A236

Designs: 32p, Conger eel soup. 33p, Oysters. 40p, Bean crock. 70p, Bourdélots with black butter.

2005, Mar. 8   Litho.   *Perf. 13¾*

1152	A236	32p multi	1.25	1.25
1153	A236	33p multi	1.50	1.50
1154	A236	40p multi	1.75	1.75
1155	A236	70p multi	2.75	2.75
		Nos. 1152-1155 (4)	7.25	7.25

Europa (33p, 40p).

Fairy Tales
A237

Designs: 33p, Little Red Riding Hood. 34p, The Little Mermaid. 41p, Beauty and the Beast. 50p, Rumpelstiltskin. 73p, The Goose That Laid the Golden Egg. £2, The Ugly Duckling.

2005, Apr. 2   *Perf. 13x13¼*

1156	A237	33p multi	1.25	1.25
1157	A237	34p multi	1.40	1.40
1158	A237	41p multi	1.60	1.60
1159	A237	50p multi	2.00	2.00
1160	A237	73p multi	3.00	3.00
		Nos. 1156-1160 (5)	9.25	9.25

Souvenir Sheet
Perf. 13¼

1161	A237	£2 multi	8.00	8.00
a.		As No. 1161, with Nordia 2005 emblem in sheet margin	7.75	7.75

No. 1161 contains one 49x35mm stamp, and has a hologram applied in the sheet margin.
No. 1161a issued 5/26.

Souvenir Sheet

Jersey Soccer Association and Muratti Vase Soccer Competition, Cent. — A238

2005, Apr. 27   *Perf.*

1162	A238	£2 multi	8.00	8.00

Souvenir Sheet

End of World War II, 60th Anniv. — A239

2005, May 9   Litho.   *Perf. 14¼*

1163	A239	£2 multi	8.00	8.00

Jersey Motor Festival
A240

Automobiles: 33p, MGB GT. 34p, Mini Cooper. 41p, Citroen DS. 50p, Jaguar E Type. 56p, Volkswagen Beetle. 73p, Aston Martin DB5.

2005, June 6   *Perf. 13x13¼*

1164	A240	33p multi	1.25	1.25
1165	A240	34p multi	1.40	1.40
1166	A240	41p multi	1.60	1.60
1167	A240	50p multi	2.00	2.00
1168	A240	56p multi	2.25	2.25
1169	A240	73p multi	3.00	3.00
a.		Booklet pane, #1164-1169	11.50	
		Complete booklet, 3 #1169a	35.00	
		Nos. 1164-1169 (6)	11.50	11.50

Complete booklet contains three examples of No. 1169a, each with a different margin and layout of the stamps.

Flowers — A241

Designs: 2p, Scarlet pimpernel. 4p, Common knapweed. 20p, Greater stitchwort. 30p, Common mallow. 40p, White campion. 50p, Common dog-violet. 65p, Herb Robert. £1, Three-cornered garlic.

2005, July 19   *Perf. 13¼*

1170	A241	2p multi	.20	.20
1171	A241	4p multi	.20	.20
1172	A241	20p multi	.80	.80
1173	A241	30p multi	1.25	1.25
1174	A241	40p multi	1.60	1.60
1175	A241	50p multi	2.00	2.00
1176	A241	65p multi	2.50	2.50
1177	A241	£1 multi	4.00	4.00
a.		Souvenir sheet, #1170-1177	12.50	12.50
		Nos. 1170-1177 (8)	12.55	12.55

See Nos. 1228-1235a, 1267-1274a.

Martello Towers — A242

2005, Aug. 9   *Perf. 13¾*

1178	A242	33p Le Hocq	1.25	1.25
1179	A242	34p Seymour	1.40	1.40
1180	A242	41p Archirondel	1.60	1.60
1181	A242	56p Kempt	2.25	2.25
1182	A242	73p Le Rocco	3.00	3.00
		Nos. 1178-1182 (5)	9.50	9.50

Designs: 33p, Pink waxcap. 34p, Boletus erythropus. 41p, Inocybe godeyi. 50p, Pepperpot earthstar. 56p, White elfin saddle. 73p, Red waxy cap.
£2, Fairy ring mushrooms, horiz.

Mushrooms
A243

2005, Sept. 13   *Perf. 13¾*
1183	A243	33p multi	1.25	1.25
1184	A243	34p multi	1.40	1.40
1185	A243	41p multi	1.60	1.60
1186	A243	50p multi	2.00	2.00
1187	A243	56p multi	2.25	2.25
1188	A243	73p multi	3.00	3.00
	Nos. 1183-1188 (6)		11.50	11.50

Souvenir Sheet
Perf. 14¼
| 1189 | A243 | £2 multi | 8.00 | 8.00 |

No. 1189 contains one 50x38mm stamp.

Battle of Trafalgar, Bicent. A244

Designs: 33p, HMS Belleisle. 34p, HMS Royal Sovereign. 41p, HMS Neptune. 50p, HMS Euryalus. 73p, HMS Mars.
£2, HMS Victory.

2005, Oct. 21   *Perf. 14*
1190	A244	33p multi	1.25	1.25
1191	A244	34p multi	1.40	1.40
1192	A244	41p multi	1.60	1.60
1193	A244	50p multi	2.00	2.00
1194	A244	73p multi	3.00	3.00
	Nos. 1190-1194 (5)		9.25	9.25

Souvenir Sheet
Perf. 14¼
| 1195 | A244 | £2 multi | 8.00 | 8.00 |

No. 1195 contains one 50x38mm stamp.

Royal Jersey Militia Uniforms and Badges A245

Uniforms and badges from: 33p, Royal Jersey Regiment, ca. 1830. 34p, Royal Jersey Regiment, ca. 1844. 41p, Royal Jersey Artillery, ca. 1881. 50p, Royal Jersey Light Infantry ca. 1890. 73p, Royal Engineers, present day.

2006, Jan. 6   **Litho.**   *Perf. 13¼*
1196	A245	33p multi	1.25	1.25
1197	A245	34p multi	1.40	1.40
1198	A245	41p multi	1.60	1.60
1199	A245	50p multi	2.00	2.00
1200	A245	73p multi	3.00	3.00
	Nos. 1196-1200 (5)		9.25	9.25

Souvenir Sheet

New Year 2006 (Year of the Dog) — A246

2006, Jan. 29   **Litho.**   *Perf. 14¼*
| 1201 | A246 | £1 multi | 5.00 | 5.00 |

Souvenir Sheet

Victoria Cross, 150th Anniv. — A247

2006, Jan. 29   *Perf. 13¼x14*
| 1202 | A247 | £2 multi | 9.00 | 9.00 |

Multiculturalism — A248

Designs: 33p, Chinese costumes. 34p, Portuguese Fado Music Festival. 41p, Polish Pisanki Easter egg tradition. 73p, Indian costumes.

2006, Mar. 7   *Perf. 14*
1203	A248	33p multi	1.25	1.25
1204	A248	34p multi	1.40	1.40
1205	A248	41p multi	1.60	1.60
1206	A248	73p multi	3.00	3.00
	Nos. 1203-1206 (4)		7.25	7.25

Europa (34p, 41p).

Shells A249

Designs: 34p, Flat periwinkle. 37p, Painted top shell. 42p, Dog cockle. 51p, Variegated scallop. 57p, Blue-rayed limpet. 74p, European cowrie.
£2, Ormer shell.

2006, Apr. 4   **Litho.**   *Perf. 13x13¼*
1207	A249	34p multi	1.40	1.40
1208	A249	37p multi	1.50	1.50
1209	A249	42p multi	1.60	1.60
1210	A249	51p multi	2.00	2.00
1211	A249	57p multi	2.25	2.25
1212	A249	74p multi	3.00	3.00
	Nos. 1207-1212 (6)		11.75	11.75

Souvenir Sheet
Litho. & Embossed With Hologram Affixed
Perf.
| 1213 | A249 | £2 multi | 8.00 | 8.00 |
| *a.* | Like #1213, with Belgica '06 emblem added in sheet margin | | 9.00 | 9.00 |

Portions of the designs of Nos. 1207-1212 were applied by a thermographic process producing a shiny, raised effect. No. 1213 contains one 46x30 oval stamp.
Issued: No. 1213a, 11/16.

Souvenir Sheet

Wedding of Prince Charles and Camilla Parker-Bowles, 1st Anniv. — A250

2006, Apr. 9   **Litho.**   *Perf. 13¼*
| 1214 | A250 | £2 multi | 8.00 | 8.00 |

Queen Elizabeth II, 80th Birthday A251

Litho. & Embossed With Foil Application

2006, Apr. 21   *Perf. 13½*
1215	A251	£5 dk bl & multi	20.00	20.00
a.	Prussian blue & multi	20.00	20.00
b.	Souvenir sheet, #1215a, New Zealand #2068a	27.50	27.50

See New Zealand No. 2068. No. 1215b sold for £7.

Souvenir Sheet

2006 World Cup Soccer Championships, Germany — A252

2006, June 9   **Litho.**   *Perf. 14¼*
| 1216 | A252 | £2 multi | 9.00 | 9.00 |

Island Views — A253

Serpentine Die Cut 11¼
2006, July 11
Self-Adhesive
Coil Stamps
Inscribed "2006"
1217	A253	(37p) Greve de Lecq	1.75	1.75
a.	Inscribed "2009"	1.75	1.75
1218	A253	(37p) La Rocque	1.75	1.75
a.	Inscribed "2009"	1.75	1.75
1219	A253	(37p) Portelet	1.75	1.75
a.	Inscribed "2009"	1.75	1.75
1220	A253	(37p) St. Brelade's Bay	1.75	1.75
a.	Inscribed "2009"	1.75	1.75
b.	Horiz. strip of 4, #1217-1220	7.50	
c.	Horiz. strip of 4, #1217a-1220a	7.50	

Butterflies & Moths A254

Designs: 34p, Red underwing moth. 37p, Comma butterfly. 42p, Black arches moth. 51p, Small copper butterfly. 57p, Holly blue butterfly. 74p, Orange-tip butterfly.

2006, Aug. 1   *Perf. 14¾x14*
Stamps With White Margin
1221	A254	34p multi	1.50	1.50
1222	A254	37p multi	1.60	1.60
1223	A254	42p multi	1.75	1.75
1224	A254	51p multi	2.25	2.25
1225	A254	57p multi	2.50	2.50
1226	A254	74p multi	3.25	3.25
	Nos. 1221-1226 (6)		12.85	12.85

Souvenir Sheet
Stamps Without White Margin
1227		Sheet of 3	8.50	8.50
a.	A254 51p multi	2.25	2.25
b.	A254 57p multi	2.50	2.50
c.	A254 74p multi	3.25	3.00

Flowers Type of 2005

Designs: 1p, Yellow bartsia. 3p, Wild angelica. 5p, Marsh St. John's wort. 15p, Bog pimpernel. 70p, Ragged robin. 75p, Brooklime. 85p, Cuckoo flower. 90p, Yellow iris.

2006, Sept. 26   **Litho.**   *Perf. 13¼*
1228	A241	1p multi	.20	.20
1229	A241	3p multi	.20	.20
1230	A241	5p multi	.20	.20
1231	A241	15p multi	.75	.75
1232	A241	70p multi	3.00	3.00
1233	A241	75p multi	3.25	3.25
1234	A241	85p multi	3.75	3.75
1235	A241	90p multi	4.00	4.00
a.	Souvenir sheet, #1228-1235	15.00	15.00
	Nos. 1228-1235 (8)		15.35	15.35

Jersey Post Vehicles A255

Designs: 34p, 2004 LDV Luton Van. 37p, 1999-2004 Renault Kangaroo. 42p, 1994-2004 LDV Pilot. 51p, 1988-96 Ford Transit Luton Body. 57p, Morris Marina 440/575, c. 1978. 74p, Morris Minor, c. 1969.

2006, Oct. 31   *Perf. 13x13¼*
1236	A255	34p multi	1.40	1.40
1237	A255	37p multi	1.50	1.50
1238	A255	42p multi	1.60	1.60
1239	A255	51p multi	2.00	2.00
1240	A255	57p multi	2.25	2.25
1241	A255	74p multi	3.00	3.00
a.	Booklet pane, #1236-1241	12.00	
b.	Booklet pane, #1239-1241 + binding stub	7.50	—
	Complete booklet, #1241b, 3 #1241a	45.00	
c.	Souvenir sheet, #1239-1241	7.50	7.50

No. 1241a has three different layouts of stamps on pane and three different margins. No. 1241c has a straight edge at left, while No. 1241b is separated from binding stub by a row of rouletting.

Minerals A256

Designs: 34p, Molybdenite. 37p, Muscovite in pegmatite vein, feldspar and quartz. 42p, Orthoclase and plagioclase. 51p, Quartz coated with manganese oxide. 74p, Smoky quartz.

2007, Jan. 23   **Litho.**   *Perf. 13x13¼*
1242	A256	34p multi	1.50	1.50
1243	A256	37p multi	1.75	1.75
1244	A256	42p multi	1.75	1.75
1245	A256	51p multi	2.25	2.25
1246	A256	74p multi	3.25	3.25
	Nos. 1242-1246 (5)		10.50	10.50

Souvenir Sheet

New Year 2007 (Year of the Pig) — A257

2007, Feb. 18   *Perf. 14¼*
| 1247 | A257 | £1 multi | 5.00 | 5.00 |

Scouting, Cent. A258

Lord Robert Baden-Powell and Scouts: 34p, With kayak, sailboard and kite-propelled vehicle. 37p, With musical instruments and flags. 42p, In go-carts and wagons, scouts climbing. 74p, With uniform patches.

2007, Mar. 6   *Perf. 14*
1248	A258	34p multi	1.40	1.40
1249	A258	37p multi	1.50	1.50
1250	A258	42p multi	1.60	1.60
1251	A258	74p multi	3.00	3.00
	Nos. 1248-1251 (4)		7.50	7.50

Europa (37p, 42p).

Mammals
A259

Designs: 34p, Long-tailed field mouse. 37p, Rabbits. 42p, Polecat. 51p, Common shrew. 57p, Stoat. 74p, Brown rat.

2007, Apr. 10   *Perf. 14¾x14*
Stamps With White Frames
1252	A259	34p multi	1.50	1.50
1253	A259	37p multi	1.75	1.75
1254	A259	42p multi	2.00	2.00
1255	A259	51p multi	2.25	2.25
1256	A259	57p multi	2.50	2.50
1257	A259	74p multi	3.25	3.25
	Nos. 1252-1257 (6)		13.25	13.25

Souvenir Sheet
Stamps Without White Frames
1258		Sheet of 3	8.00	8.00
a.	A259 51p multi		2.25	2.25
b.	A259 57p multi		2.50	2.50
c.	A259 74p multi		3.25	3.25

Birds
A260

Designs: 34p, House sparrow. 37p, Chaffinch. 42p, Blue tit. 51p, Blackbird. 57p, Magpie. 74p, Great tit.

2007, June 19   Litho.   *Perf. 13x13½*
Stamps With White Frames
1259	A260	34p multi	1.50	1.50
1260	A260	37p multi	1.75	1.75
1261	A260	42p multi	2.00	2.00
1262	A260	51p multi	2.25	2.25
1263	A260	57p multi	2.50	2.50
1264	A260	74p multi	3.25	3.25
a.	Miniature sheet, #1259-1264		13.00	13.00
	Nos. 1259-1264 (6)		13.25	13.25

Souvenir Sheet
Stamps Without White Frames
1265		Sheet of 3	8.00	8.00
a.	A260 51p multi		2.25	2.25
b.	A260 57p multi		2.50	2.50
c.	A260 74p multi		3.25	3.25

See Nos. 1342-1348, 1389-1395.

Souvenir Sheet

Gorey Regatta — A261

2007, June 22   *Perf. 12¾x13½*
1266	A261	£2 multi	8.50	8.50

Flowers Type of 2005

Designs: 10p, Black bryony. 25p, Horseshoe vetch. 35p, English stonecrop. 45p, Tutsan. 55p, Ox-eye daisy. 60p, Rock sea-spurrey. 80p, Mouse-ear hawkweed. £1.50, Devil's-bit scabious.

2007, July 25   *Perf. 13¼*
1267	A241	10p multi	.40	.40
1268	A241	25p multi	1.00	1.00
1269	A241	35p multi	1.40	1.40
1270	A241	45p multi	1.90	1.90
1271	A241	55p multi	2.25	2.25
1272	A241	60p multi	2.50	2.50
1273	A241	80p multi	3.25	3.25
1274	A241	£1.50 multi	6.25	6.25
a.	Miniature sheet, #1267-1274		19.00	19.00
	Nos. 1267-1274 (8)		18.95	18.95

Summer Flowers
A262

Designs: 34p, Clematis. 37p, Roses. 42p, Honeysuckles. 51p, Fuchsias. 57p, Sweet peas. 74p, Lilacs.

2007, July 25   *Perf. 13½*
1275	A262	34p multi	1.50	1.50
1276	A262	37p multi	1.75	1.75
1277	A262	42p multi	2.00	2.00
1278	A262	51p multi	2.25	2.25
1279	A262	57p multi	2.50	2.50
1280	A262	74p multi	3.25	3.25
	Nos. 1275-1280 (6)		13.25	13.25

Airplanes
A263

Designs: 34p, Dornier Do 24 ATT. 37p, Avro Vulcan B-2. 42p, Junkers Ju-52. 51p, Sukhoi Su-27 Flanker. 57p, Boeing B-52 Stratofortress. 74p, Concorde.
£2.50, Red Arrows in formation.

2007, Sept. 13   *Perf. 13x13¼*
1281	A263	34p multi	1.40	1.40
1282	A263	37p multi	1.50	1.50
1283	A263	42p multi	1.75	1.75
1284	A263	51p multi	2.10	2.10
1285	A263	57p multi	2.40	2.40
1286	A263	74p multi	3.00	3.00
a.	Booklet pane, #1281-1286		12.50	—
	Complete booklet, #1287a, 3 #1286a		48.00	
	Nos. 1281-1286 (6)		12.15	12.15

Souvenir Sheet
Perf. 13¼x13
1287	A263	£2.50 multi	10.50	10.50
a.	Booklet pane, #1287		10.50	

No. 1287 contains one 60x40mm stamp. Size of No. 1287a: 150x100mm. The complete booklet contains three examples of No. 1286a, each of which has a different arrangement of the stamps.

Jersey Attractions — A264

Designs: 34p, Queen's Valley Reservoir. 37p, Mont Orgueil Castle. 42p, Bonne Nuit Harbor. 51p, La Hogue Bie. 57p, Bouley Bay. 74p, Le Corbiere Lighthouse.

2007, Oct. 1   *Perf. 14x13½*
1288	A264	34p multi	1.50	1.50
1289	A264	37p multi	1.75	1.75
1290	A264	42p multi	2.00	2.00
1291	A264	51p multi	2.25	2.25
1292	A264	57p multi	2.50	2.50
1293	A264	74p multi	3.25	3.25
	Nos. 1288-1293 (6)		13.25	13.25

See Nos. 1396-1401.

Christmas Songs
A265

No. 1294: a, Minuit Chrétiens. b, While Shepherds Watched. c, O Come, All Ye Faithful. d, O Christmas Tree. e, Jingle Bells.
No. 1295: a, Hark! The Herald Angels Sing. b, We Three Kings. c, Ding Dong! Merrily On High. d, Holly and the Ivy. e, Good King Wenceslas.

Serpentine Die Cut 11¼
2007, Nov. 7   Litho.
Self-Adhesive
Coil Stamps
Inscribed "2007"
1294		Horiz. strip of 5	7.50	
a.-e.	A265 (35p) Any single		1.40	1.40
g.	As #1294, inscribed "2008"		5.50	
h.-l.	A265 (35p) As #1294a-1294e,			
	any single, inscribed "2008"		1.10	1.10
m.	As #1294, inscribed "2009"		7.00	
n.-r.	A265 (35p) As #1294a-1294e,			
	any single, inscribed "2009"		1.40	1.40
1295		Horiz. strip of 5	8.50	
a.-e.	A265 (39p) Any single		1.60	1.60
g.	As #1295, inscribed "2008"		6.25	
h.-l.	A265 (39p) As #1295a-1295e,			
	any single, inscribed "2008"		1.25	1.25
m.	As #1295, inscribed "2009"		7.00	
n.-r.	A265 (42p) As #1295a-1295e,			
	any single, inscribed "2009"		1.40	1.40

Issued: Nos. 1294g, 1295g, 11/14/08; Nos. 1294m, 1295m, 11/10/09.

Wedding of Queen Elizabeth II and Prince Philip, 60th Anniv. — A266

2007, Nov. 20   *Perf. 13¼*
1296	A266	£3 multi	12.50	12.50

Jersey Signal Station, 300th Anniv.
A267

Designs: 35p, Sun, sunshine recorder, clouds. 39p, Clouds, weather symbols for wind speed, weather vane. 43p, Clouds, raindrops, weather symbols and barometer. 58p, Sun, thermometer and weather station. 76p, Tide measuring device, French flag, Moon.

2008, Jan. 15   Litho.   *Perf. 14*
1297	A267	35p multi	1.40	1.40
1298	A267	39p multi	1.60	1.60
1299	A267	43p multi	1.75	1.75
1300	A267	58p multi	2.40	2.40
1301	A267	76p multi	3.00	3.00
	Nos. 1297-1301 (5)		10.15	10.15

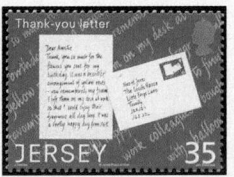

Letters
A268

Designs: 35p, Thank-you letter. 39p, Love letter. 43p, Letter to Santa Claus. 76p, Family letter.

2008, Feb. 14   *Perf. 13½x14*
1302	A268	35p multi	1.40	1.40
1303	A268	39p multi	1.60	1.60
1304	A268	43p multi	1.75	1.75
1305	A268	76p multi	3.00	3.00
	Nos. 1302-1305 (4)		7.75	7.75

Europa (39p, 43p).

Jersey Eisteddfod, Cent.
A269

Designs: 35p, Arts and crafts. 39p, Dance and drama. 43p, Speech. 58p, Films and photography. 76p, Music.

2008, Mar. 3   *Perf. 14*
1306	A269	35p multi	1.40	1.40
1307	A269	39p multi	1.60	1.60
1308	A269	43p multi	1.75	1.75
1309	A269	58p multi	2.40	2.40
1310	A269	76p multi	3.25	3.25
	Nos. 1306-1310 (5)		10.40	10.40

Buses
A270

Designs: 35p, Grey Bus Services Daimler CB bus. 39p, Safety Coach Service Ex LGOC K single decker bus. 43p, Jersey Motor Transport horse-drawn town bus. 52p, Jersey Motor Transport Leyland Lion Charcoal Burner bus. 58p, Jersey Bus Service Bedford WLB bus. 76p, Jersey Motor Transport Commer Commando bus.
£2.50, Jersey Motor Transport Ford Willowbrook bus.

2008, Apr. 8   *Perf. 14¼x14*
1311	A270	35p multi	1.40	1.40
1312	A270	39p multi	1.60	1.60
1313	A270	43p multi	1.75	1.75
1314	A270	52p multi	2.10	2.10
1315	A270	58p multi	2.40	2.40
1316	A270	76p multi	3.00	3.00
	Nos. 1311-1316 (6)		12.25	12.25

Souvenir Sheet
Perf. 13½x13¾
1317	A270	£2.50 multi	10.00	10.00
a.	As #1317, with WIPA 08 emblem in sheet margin		9.00	9.00

No. 1317 contains one 75x30mm stamp. No. 1317a issued 9/18.

Souvenir Sheet

World Jersey Cattle Bureau Conference — A271

2008, May 18   *Perf. 13*
1318	A271	£2 multi	8.00	8.00

Orchids
A272

Designs: 35p, Cymbidium Avranches "Victoria Village." 39p, Miltonia "Tesson Mill." 43p, Anguloa Victoire "Trinity." 52p, Phragmipedium La Hougette. 58p, Phragmipedium Havre des Pas "Jersey." 76p, Paphiopedilum Rolfei "Trinity."
£2.50, Paphiopedilum Rocco Tower.

2008, May 20   *Perf. 13x13¼*
1319	A272	35p multi	1.40	1.40
1320	A272	39p multi	1.60	1.60
1321	A272	43p multi	1.75	1.75
1322	A272	52p multi	2.10	2.10

1323	A272	58p multi	2.40	2.40
1324	A272	76p multi	3.00	3.00
	Nos. 1319-1324 (6)		12.25	12.25

Souvenir Sheet

1325	A272	£2.50 multi	10.00	10.00

Souvenir Sheet

2008 World Cricket League Division 5
Tournament, Jersey — A273

2008, May 23 Litho. Perf. 12¾x13¼

1326	A273	£2 multi	8.00	8.00

Royal
Navy
Vessels
A274

Designs: 35p, HMS Roebuck. 39p, HMS
Monmouth. 43p, HMS Edinburgh. 52p, HMS
Express. 58p, HMS Severn. 76p, HMS
Cottesmore.
£2.50, HMY Britannia.

2008, June 24 Litho. Perf. 13x13¼

1327	A274	35p multi	1.40	1.40
1328	A274	39p multi	1.60	1.60
1329	A274	43p multi	1.75	1.75
1330	A274	52p multi	2.10	2.10
1331	A274	58p multi	2.40	2.40
1332	A274	76p multi	3.00	3.00
a.		Booklet pane, #1327-1332	12.50	12.50
	Nos. 1327-1332 (6)		12.25	12.25

Souvenir Sheet
Perf. 13¼x13

1333	A274	£2.50 multi	10.00	10.00
a.		Booklet pane of 1 #1333	10.00	10.00
		Complete booklet, #1333a, 3 #1332a		47.50

No. 1333 contains one 60x40mm stamp.
No. 1333a has a binding stub at left. Complete booklet contains 3 examples of No.
1332a, each with a different margin and different arrangement of the stamps.

Souvenir Sheet

Jersey Festival of Speed — A275

2008, Aug. 23 Litho. Perf. 13x13¼

1334	A275	£2.50 multi	9.25	9.25

Farm Animals
and Their
Young — A276

No. 1335: a, Rooster, hen and chicks. b,
Sheep and lambs. c, Sow and piglets. d,
Ducks and ducklings. e, Cows and calf.

Serpentine Die Cut 11¼
2008, Aug. 26
Coil Stamps
Self-Adhesive

1335		Horiz. strip of 5	6.50	
a.-e.	A276	(35p) Any single	1.25	1.25

Insects
A277

Designs: 35p, Carpenter bee. 39p, Buff-
tailed bumblebee. 43p, Clown-faced bug. 52p,
Large migrant hoverfly. 58p, Ruby-tailed wasp.
76p, 22-spot ladybug.

2008, Sept. 8 **Perf. 13x13¼**

1336	A277	35p multi	1.25	1.25
1337	A277	39p multi	1.40	1.40
1338	A277	43p multi	1.60	1.60
1339	A277	52p multi	1.90	1.90
1340	A277	58p multi	2.10	2.10
1341	A277	76p multi	2.75	2.75
	Nos. 1336-1341 (6)		11.00	11.00

Birds Type of 2007

Designs: 35p, Northern wheatear. 39p,
Whinchat. 43p, Pied flycatcher. 52p, Yellow
wagtail. 58p, Ring ouzel. 76p, Common
redstart.

2008, Oct. 21 **Litho.**
Stamps With White Frames

1342	A260	35p multi	1.10	1.10
1343	A260	39p multi	1.25	1.25
1344	A260	43p multi	1.40	1.40
1345	A260	52p multi	1.75	1.75
1346	A260	58p multi	1.90	1.90
1347	A260	76p multi	2.50	2.50
a.		Souvenir sheet, #1342-1347	10.00	10.00
	Nos. 1342-1347 (6)		9.90	9.90

Souvenir Sheet
Stamps Without White Frames

1348		Sheet of 3	6.25	6.25
a.	A260	52p multi	1.75	1.75
b.	A260	58p multi	1.90	1.90
c.	A260	76p multi	2.50	2.50

Prince
Charles,
60th
Birthday
A278

2008, Nov. 14 **Perf. 13¼**

1349	A278	£4 multi	12.00	12.00
a.		Souvenir sheet of 1	12.00	12.00

Airplanes
A279

Designs: 35p, Douglas C-47 Dakota 3 Pion-
air. 39p, Vickers Viscount 833. 43p, Handley
Page HPR7 Dart-Herald. 52p, Bristol Super-
freighter 32. 58p, Fokker F-27 Friendship. 76p,
Bombardier Q400 Dash 8.
£3, De Havilland D.H. 84 Dragon 2.

2009, Jan. 13 **Litho.** **Perf. 14**

1350	A279	35p multi	1.00	1.00
1351	A279	39p multi	1.10	1.10
1352	A279	43p multi	1.25	1.25
1353	A279	52p multi	1.50	1.50
1354	A279	58p multi	1.60	1.60
1355	A279	76p multi	2.10	2.10
	Nos. 1350-1355 (6)		8.55	8.55

Souvenir Sheet

1356	A279	£3 multi	8.25	8.25

First flight from Jersey to Southampton, 75th
anniv. (#1356).

Intl. Year
of
Astronomy
A280

Galileo Galilei, one quarter of Jupiter and:
35p, Jupiter's moon Io, Ursa Major and Cassi-
opeia constellations. 39p, Jupiter's moon
Europa, Boötes and Corona Borealis constellations. 43p, Jupiter's moon Ganymede,
Cygnus and Pegasus constellations. 76p,
Jupiter's moon Callisto, Perseus and Orion
constellations.

Litho. & Embossed With Foil Application
2009, Feb. 10 **Perf. 13x13¼**

1357	A280	35p multi	1.00	1.00
1358	A280	39p multi	1.10	1.10
1359	A280	43p multi	1.25	1.25
1360	A280	76p multi	2.25	2.25
	Nos. 1357-1360 (4)		5.60	5.60

Europa (39p, 43p).

Endangered Species — A281

Designs: 35p, Blue iguana. 39p, Madagascar giant jumping rat. 43p, Mountain chicken
frog. 52p, Livingstone's fruit bat. 58p, Andean
bear. 76p, Western lowland gorilla.

2009, Mar. 10 Litho. Perf. 14¾x14

1361	A281	35p multi	1.10	1.10
1362	A281	39p multi	1.25	1.25
1363	A281	43p multi	1.25	1.25
1364	A281	52p multi	1.60	1.60
1365	A281	58p multi	1.75	1.75
1366	A281	76p multi	2.25	2.25
	Nos. 1361-1366 (6)		9.20	9.20

Durrell Wildlife Conservation Trust, 50th
anniv.

Spring
Flowers
A282

Designs: 35p, Crocus and grape hyacinth.
39p, Daffodils. 43p, Anemones de Caen. 52p,
Tulips. 58p, Hyacinths. 76p, Polyanthus and
primulas.

2009, Apr. 1 **Perf. 13¼**

1367	A282	35p multi	1.10	1.10
1368	A282	39p multi	1.25	1.25
1369	A282	43p multi	1.25	1.25
1370	A282	52p multi	1.60	1.60
1371	A282	58p multi	1.75	1.75
1372	A282	76p multi	2.25	2.25
	Nos. 1367-1372 (6)		9.20	9.20

Locomotives and Rail Cars — A283

Designs: 37p, 0-4-2T Mont Orgueil locomotive. 42p, 2-4-0T Corbière locomotive. 45p, 0-
4-2T Carteret locomotive. 55p, Pioneer rail
car. 61p, 2-4-0T La Moye locomotive. 80p, 2-
4-0T St. Brelades locomotive.
£3, 2-4-0T Corbière locomotive, diff.

2009, May 6 **Perf. 13x13¼**

1373	A283	37p multi	1.25	1.25
1374	A283	42p multi	1.40	1.40
1375	A283	45p multi	1.50	1.50
1376	A283	55p multi	1.75	1.75
1377	A283	61p multi	2.00	2.00
1378	A283	80p multi	2.60	2.60
a.		Booklet pane of 6, #1373-1378	10.50	10.50
	Nos. 1373-1378 (6)		10.50	10.50

Souvenir Sheet
Perf. 13¼x13

1379	A283	£3 multi	9.75	9.75
a.		Booklet pane of 1 #1379	9.75	9.75
		Complete booklet, #1379a, 3 #1378a		42.00
b.		As #1379, with IBRA emblem in sheet margin	9.75	9.75

No. 1379 contains one 60x40mm stamp.
No. 1379a has a binding stub at left.
Complete booklet contains three examples
of No. 1378a, each with a different margin and
different arrangement of the stamps.

Souvenir Sheet

Surfing — A284

2009, June 2 **Perf. 13¼**

1380	A284	£3 multi	9.75	9.75

Jersey Surfboard Club, 50th anniv.

Souvenir Sheet

St. Helier Broad Street Post Office,
Cent. — A285

2009, June 21 **Perf. 14**

1381	A285	£3 multi	9.75	9.75

Souvenir Sheet

Investiture of Prince Charles as Prince
of Wales, 40th Anniv. — A286

2009, July 1 **Perf. 13¼**

1382	A286	£3 multi	9.75	9.75

Seaweeds
A287

Designs: 37p, Egg wrack. 42p, Gutweed.
45p, Red rags. 55p, Sea lettuce. 61p, Lamina-
ria hyperborea. 80p, Velvet horn.

2009, July 7 **Perf. 13x13¼**

1383	A287	37p multi	1.25	1.25
1384	A287	42p multi	1.40	1.40
1385	A287	45p multi	1.50	1.50
1386	A287	55p multi	1.90	1.90
1387	A287	61p multi	2.00	2.00
1388	A287	80p multi	2.60	2.60
	Nos. 1383-1388 (6)		10.65	10.65

Birds Type of 2007

Designs: 37p, Dunnock. 42p, Song thrush. 45p, Wren. 55p, Blackcap. 61p, Mistle thrush. 80p, Robin.

2009, Aug. 4   Litho.   Perf. 13x13¼

Stamps With White Frames

1389	A260	37p multi	1.25	1.25
1390	A260	42p multi	1.40	1.40
1391	A260	45p multi	1.50	1.50
1392	A260	55p multi	1.90	1.90
1393	A260	61p multi	2.10	2.10
1394	A260	80p multi	2.75	2.75
a.		Souvenir sheet, #1389-1394	11.00	11.00
		Nos. 1389-1394 (6)	10.90	10.90

Souvenir Sheet
Stamps Without White Frames

1395		Sheet of 3	6.75	6.75
a.	A260	55p multi	1.90	1.90
b.	A260	61p multi	2.10	2.10
c.	A260	80p multi	2.75	2.75

Jersey Attractions Type of 2007

Designs: 37p, Green Island. 42p, Gorey Castle. 45p, St. Aubin's Harbor. 55p, St. Peter's Valley. 61p, La Rocque Harbor. 80p, Greve de Lecq.

2009, Sept. 16   Litho.   Perf. 14x13½

1396	A264	37p multi	1.25	1.25
1397	A264	42p multi	1.40	1.40
1398	A264	45p multi	1.50	1.50
1399	A264	55p multi	1.75	1.75
1400	A264	61p multi	2.00	2.00
1401	A264	80p multi	2.60	2.60
		Nos. 1396-1401 (6)	10.50	10.50

Mushrooms
A288

Designs: 37p, Parrot wax-cap. 42p, Russula sardonia. 45p, Velvet foot. 55p, Honey fungus. 61p, Orange peel fungus. 80p, Jewelled deathcap.

2009, Oct. 15   Litho.   Perf. 13¼x13

1402	A288	37p multi	1.25	1.25
1403	A288	42p multi	1.40	1.40
1404	A288	45p multi	1.50	1.50
1405	A288	55p multi	1.90	1.90
1406	A288	61p multi	2.10	2.10
1407	A288	80p multi	2.75	2.75
		Nos. 1402-1407 (6)	10.90	10.90

Ships on Which Sir George Carteret Sailed
A289

Designs: 37p, HMS Garland. 42p, HMS Eighth Lion's Whelp. 45p, HMS Unicorn. 55p, HMS Mary Rose. 61p, HMS Antelope. 80p, HMS Rainbow.

2009, Oct. 15   Litho.   Perf. 13¼x13

1408	A289	37p multi	1.25	1.25
1409	A289	42p multi	1.40	1.40
1410	A289	45p multi	1.50	1.50
1411	A289	55p multi	1.90	1.90
1412	A289	61p multi	2.10	2.10
1413	A289	80p multi	2.75	2.75
		Nos. 1408-1413 (6)	10.90	10.90

Girl Guides, Cent.
A290

Inscriptions: 37p, Healthy lifestyles. 42p, Global awareness. 45p, Skills & relationships. 61p, Celebrating diversity. 80p, Discovery.

2010, Jan. 12   Litho.   Perf. 14

1414	A290	37p multi	1.25	1.25
1415	A290	42p multi	1.40	1.40
1416	A290	45p multi	1.50	1.50
1417	A290	61p multi	2.00	2.00
1418	A290	80p multi	2.60	2.60
		Nos. 1414-1418 (5)	8.75	8.75

Maps of Jersey — A291

No. 1419 — Map: a, Circa 1685. b, Circa 1844. c, Circa 1980s. d, Circa 2000. e, Satellite view.

Serpentine Die Cut 11¼

2010, Feb. 9

Coil Stamps
Self-Adhesive

1419		Horiz. strip of 5	6.50	
a.-e.	A291	(42p) Any single	1.25	1.25

Children's Book Characters
A292

Designs: 37p, Pushmi-pullyu from *Dr. Doolittle*, by Hugh Lofting. 42p, Elephant from *How the Elephant Got His Trunk*, by Rudyard Kipling. 45p, Mad Hatter from *Alice in Wonderland*, by Lewis Carroll. 80p, *The Dong with a Luminous Nose*, by Edward Lear.

2010, Feb. 9   Perf. 13x13¼

1420	A292	37p multi	1.10	1.10
1421	A292	42p multi	1.25	1.25
1422	A292	45p multi	1.40	1.40
1423	A292	80p multi	2.50	2.50
		Nos. 1420-1423 (4)	6.25	6.25

Europa (42p, 45p).

Rocks
A293

Designs: 37p, Brecciated pegmatite, orthoclase feldspar crystals re-cemented with chalcedony. 42p, Diorite with incipient orbicular structure. 45p, Granite. 61p, Jasper in andesite. 80p, Pebbles of granite, andesite and shale in Rozel conglomerate.

2010, Mar. 9   Perf. 13x13¼

1424	A293	37p multi	1.10	1.10
1425	A293	42p multi	1.25	1.25
1426	A293	45p multi	1.40	1.40
1427	A293	61p multi	1.90	1.90
1428	A293	80p multi	2.50	2.50
		Nos. 1424-1428 (5)	8.15	8.15

Birds Type of 2007

Designs: 37p, Jay. 42p, Great spotted woodpecker. 45p, Short-toed treecreeper. 55p, Chiffchaff. 61p, Long-tailed tit. 80p, Turtle dove.

2010, Apr. 1

Stamps With White Frames

1429	A260	37p multi	1.10	1.10
1430	A260	42p multi	1.25	1.25
1431	A260	45p multi	1.40	1.40
1432	A260	55p multi	1.75	1.75
1433	A260	61p multi	1.90	1.90
1434	A260	80p multi	2.50	2.50
a.		Souvenir sheet, #1429-1434	10.00	10.00
		Nos. 1429-1434 (6)	9.90	9.90

Souvenir Sheet
Stamps Without White Frames

1435		Sheet of 3	6.25	6.25
a.	A260	55p multi	1.75	1.75
b.	A260	61p multi	1.90	1.90
c.	A260	80p multi	2.50	2.50

British Regional Stamps of 1958-69
A294

Designs: 36p, Jersey #2. 39p, Jersey #1. 45p, Jersey #3. 55p, Jersey #4. 60p, Jersey #6. 72p, Jersey #5.

2010, May 8   Perf. 13x13¼

1436	A294	36p multi	1.10	1.10
1437	A294	39p multi	1.10	1.10
1438	A294	45p multi	1.40	1.40
1439	A294	55p multi	1.60	1.60
1440	A294	60p multi	1.75	1.75
1441	A294	72p multi	2.10	2.10
a.		Souvenir sheet, #1436-1441	9.25	9.25
		Nos. 1436-1441 (6)	9.05	9.05

Mail Ships
A295

Designs: 39p, Royal Charlotte. 45p, Dispatch. 55p, Diana. 60p, Reindeer. 72p, Caesarea (II). 80p, St. Patrick (III). £3, Watersprite.

2010, May 8   Perf. 13x13¼

1442	A295	39p multi	1.10	1.10
1443	A295	45p multi	1.40	1.40
1444	A295	55p multi	1.60	1.60
1445	A295	60p multi	1.75	1.75
1446	A295	72p multi	2.10	2.10
1447	A295	80p multi	2.40	2.40
a.		Booklet pane, #1442-1447	10.50	—
b.		Souvenir sheet, #1442-1447	10.50	10.50
		Nos. 1442-1447 (6)	10.35	10.35

Souvenir Sheet
Perf. 13¼x13

1448	A295	£3 multi	8.75	8.75
a.		Booklet pane of 1 + binding stub	8.75	—
		Complete booklet, #1448a, 3 #1447a	41.00	

No. 1448 contains one 60x40mm stamp. Complete booklet contains three examples of No. 1447a, each with a different margin and different arrangement of the stamps.

Roses
A296

Rose varieties: 36p, Nostalgia. 39p, Mountbatten. 45p, Royal William. 55p, Elina. 60p, New Dawn. 72p, Lovers Meeting. £3, Pride of England.

2010, June 8   Perf. 13x13¼

1449	A296	36p multi	1.10	1.10
1450	A296	39p multi	1.10	1.10
1451	A296	45p multi	1.40	1.40
1452	A296	55p multi	1.60	1.60
1453	A296	60p multi	1.75	1.75
1454	A296	72p multi	2.10	2.10
		Nos. 1449-1454 (6)	9.05	9.05

Souvenir Sheet

1455	A296	£3 multi	8.75	8.75
a.		As #1455, with Salon du Timbre emblem in sheet margin	9.25	9.25

Issued: No. 1455a, 6/12.

Sea Anemones
A297

Designs: 36p, Strawberry anemone. 39p, Snakelock anemone. 45p, Jewel anemone. 55p, Parasitic anemone. 60p, Tube anemone. 72p, Beadlet anemone. £3, Dahlia anemone.

2010, July 6   Litho.

1456	A297	36p multi	1.10	1.10
1457	A297	39p multi	1.25	1.25
1458	A297	45p multi	1.40	1.40
1459	A297	55p multi	1.75	1.75
1460	A297	60p multi	1.90	1.90
1461	A297	72p multi	2.25	2.25
		Nos. 1456-1461 (6)	9.65	9.65

Souvenir Sheet

1462	A297	£3 multi	9.00	9.00

Automobiles — A298

Designs: 39p, 1912 Rolls Royce Silver Ghost. 45p, 1926 Bugatti Type 37. 55p, 1933 Austin Seven. 60p, 1938 Citroen Light 15. 72p, 1946 Morris 10. 80p, 1949 Rover 75 Sports Saloon.

2010, Aug. 3   Perf. 14¼x14

1463	A298	39p multi	1.25	1.25
1464	A298	45p multi	1.50	1.50
1465	A298	55p multi	1.75	1.75
1466	A298	60p multi	1.90	1.90
1467	A298	72p multi	2.40	2.40
1468	A298	80p multi	2.60	2.60
		Nos. 1463-1468 (6)	11.40	11.40

Fish
A299

Designs: 36p, Perch. 39p, Tench. 45p, Roach. 55p, Rudd. 60p, Mirror carp. 72p, Common bream. £3, Brown trout.

2010, Sept. 7   Litho.   Perf. 14¾x14

1469	A299	36p multi	1.10	1.10
1470	A299	39p multi	1.25	1.25
1471	A299	45p multi	1.40	1.40
1472	A299	55p multl	1.75	1.75
1473	A299	60p multi	1.90	1.90
1474	A299	72p multi	2.25	2.25
		Nos. 1469-1474 (6)	9.65	9.65

Souvenir Sheet

1475	A299	£3 multi	9.25	9.25

La Cotte de St. Brelade Archaeological Site — A300

Designs: 39p, Human teeth, models of head of Neanderthal man. 45p, Skull of Woolly rhinoceros. 55p, Tooth and tusks of Woolly mammoth. 60p, Flint tools and timeline. 80p, Antler of Giant deer.

2010, Oct. 12   Perf. 14

1476	A300	39p multi	1.25	1.25
1477	A300	45p multi	1.50	1.50
1478	A300	55p multi	1.90	1.90
1479	A300	60p multi	2.00	2.00
1480	A300	80p multi	2.60	2.60
		Nos. 1476-1480 (5)	9.25	9.25

Map of Jersey and Heraldic Lions — A301

Inscriptions: (36p), Standard Letter. (39p), Priority Letter. (45p), UK Letter.

Serpentine Die Cut 11½x11¼

2010, Nov. 1
Coil Stamps
Self-Adhesive
Background Color

1481	A301	(36p) dark red	1.25	1.25
1482	A301	(39p) blue	1.25	1.25
1483	A301	(45p) green	1.50	1.50
		Nos. 1481-1483 (3)	4.00	4.00

Buses
A302

Designs: 36p, Paragon C10 AEC B, c. 1926. 45p, Ramblers Tours Chevrolet, c. 1935. 55p, JMT Leyland Lioness, c. 1938. 60p, JMT Leyland PLSC1 Lion, c. 1939. 72p, Mascot Motors Morris C/F 13/5, c. 1948. 80p, Mascot Motors AEC Regal 4, c. 1961.

2011, Jan. 11   Litho.   Perf. 14

1484	A302	36p multi	1.25	1.25
1485	A302	45p multi	1.50	1.50
1486	A302	55p multi	1.75	1.75
1487	A302	60p multi	1.90	1.90
1488	A302	72p multi	2.40	2.40
1489	A302	80p multi	2.60	2.60
		Nos. 1484-1489 (6)	11.40	11.40

POSTAGE DUE STAMPS

Numeral — D1   Map of
                    Jersey — D2

Unwmk.

1969, Oct. 1   Litho.   Perf. 14

J1	D1	1p violet blue	2.75	2.50
J2	D1	2p sepia	4.00	3.75
J3	D1	3p brt carmine	5.50	5.25
J4	D2	1sh emerald	15.00	14.50
J5	D2	2sh6p gray green	25.00	27.50
J6	D2	5sh red orange	42.50	42.50
		Nos. J1-J6 (6)	94.75	96.00

Type of 1969
Decimal Currency

1971-75   Litho.   Perf. 14

J7	D2	½p black	.20	.20
J8	D2	1p pale violet	.20	.20
J9	D2	2p brown	.20	.20
J10	D2	3p bright pink	.20	.20
J11	D2	4p orange	.20	.20
J12	D2	5p emerald	.20	.20
J13	D2	6p orange ('74)	.20	.20
J14	D2	7p brt yellow ('74)	.25	.25
J15	D2	8p grnsh blue ('75)	.30	.30
J16	D2	10p gray	.35	.35
J17	D2	11p bister ('75)	.40	.40
J18	D2	14p lilac	.50	.50
J19	D2	25p dull green ('74)	.90	.90
J20	D2	50p plum ('75)	1.90	1.90
		Nos. J7-J20 (14)	6.00	6.00

St. Clement Arms,
Dovecote,
Samares — D3

Arms and Scenes from Jersey Parishes: 2p, St. Lawrence and Handois Reservoir. 3p, St. John and Sorel Point. 4p, St. Ouen and Pinnacle Rock. 5p, St. Peter and Quetivel Mill. 10p, St. Martin and St. Catherine's Breakwater. 12p, St. Helier and St. Helier Harbor. 14p, St. Saviour and Highlands College. 15p, St. Brelade and Beauport Bay. 20p, Grouville and La Hougue Bie. 50p, St. Mary and Perry Farm. £1, Trinity and Bouley Bay.

1978, Jan. 17   Litho.   Perf. 14

J21	D3	1p brt green & blk	.20	.20
J22	D3	2p orange & blk	.20	.20
J23	D3	3p maroon & blk	.20	.20
J24	D3	4p vermilion & blk	.20	.20
J25	D3	5p dp ultra & blk	.20	.20
J26	D3	10p olive & blk	.25	.25
J27	D3	12p blue & blk	.30	.30
J28	D3	14p red org & blk	.35	.35

J29	D3	15p lilac rose & blk	.40	.40
J30	D3	20p yel green & blk	.45	.45
J31	D3	50p brown & blk	1.10	1.10
J32	D3	£1 violet & blk	2.40	2.40
		Nos. J21-J32 (12)	6.25	6.25

St. Brelade — D4

1982, Sept. 4   Litho.   Perf. 13½x14

J33	D4	1p shown	.20	.20
J34	D4	2p St. Aubin	.20	.20
J35	D4	3p Rozel	.20	.20
J36	D4	4p Greve de Lecq	.20	.20
J37	D4	5p Bouley Bay	.20	.20
J38	D4	6p St. Catherine	.25	.25
J39	D4	7p Gorey	.25	.25
J40	D4	8p Bonne Nuit	.25	.25
J41	D4	9p La Rocque	.30	.30
J42	D4	10p St. Helier	.35	.35
J43	D4	20p Ronez	.60	.60
J44	D4	30p La Collette	1.00	1.00
J45	D4	40p Elizabeth Castle	1.25	1.25
J46	D4	£1 Upper Harbor Marina	2.75	2.75
		Nos. J33-J46 (14)	8.00	8.00

OCCUPATION STAMPS

Issued Under German Occupation

OS1

1941-42   Typo.   Unwmk.   Perf. 11

N1	OS1	½p bright green	7.25	5.00
N2	OS1	1p vermilion	7.25	5.00

Issue dates: #N1, 1/29/42; #N1d, 1/43; #N2, 4/1/41; #N2e, 1/43.

Jersey Views — OS2

Designs: ½p, Old Jersey farm; 1p, Portelet Bay; 1½p, Corbiere Lighthouse; 2p, Elizabeth Castle; 2½, Mont Orgueil Castle; 3p, Gathering seaweed.

1943-44   Perf. 13½

N3	OS2	½p dark green	11.00	11.00
a.		On rough, gray paper	13.50	12.50
N4	OS2	1p scarlet	2.75	.80
a.		On newsprint	3.00	1.50
N5	OS2	1½p brown	7.25	5.25
N6	OS2	2p orange	6.75	3.25
N7	OS2	2½p blue	2.75	1.40
a.		On newsprint	.90	1.50
N8	OS2	3p red violet	2.75	3.25
		Nos. N3-N8 (6)	33.25	24.95

Issued: ½p, 1p, 6/1/43; 1½p, 2p, 6/8/43; 2½p, 3p, 6/29/43; #N4a, 2/28/44; #N7a, 2/25/44.

Nos. N1-N8 remained valid until 4/13/46.

ISLE OF MAN

ˈaɪ.əl əv ˈman

LOCATION — In the Irish Sea, off Northwest coast of England
GOVT. — Semi-autonomous within the British Commonwealth
AREA — 221 sq. mi.
POP. — 75,686 (1999 est.)

CAPITAL — Douglas

Catalogue values for unused stamps in this section are for **Never Hinged** items, beginning with Scott 1 in the regular postage section and Scott J1 in the postage due section.

British Regional Issues

A1   A2

Manx Emblem — A3

Perf. 15x14

1958-69   Photo.   Wmk. 322

1	A1	2½p rose red ('64)	.60	.50
2	A2	3p purple	.20	.20
p.		Phosphor. ('68)	.20	.20
3	A2	4p ultra ('66)	1.50	.20
p.		Phosphor. ('67)	.20	.20

Unwmk.

4	A2	4p ultra ('68)	.20	.20
5	A2	4p olive brown ('68)	.20	.20
6	A2	4p bright red ('69)	.65	.30
7	A2	5p dark blue ('68)	.65	.30
		Nos. 1-7 (7)	4.00	1.90

Nos. 4-7 are phosphorescent.
A 1963 printing of No. 2 is on chalky paper.

1971, July 7   Photo.   Unwmk.

8	A3	2½p bright pink	.35	.20
9	A3	3p ultramarine	.35	.20
10	A3	5p bluish lilac	.65	.60
11	A3	7½p light red brown	.65	.70
		Nos. 8-11 (4)	2.00	1.70

Sold to the general public only at post offices within the Isle of Man, but valid for postage throughout Great Britain.

Bailiwick Issues

Castletown
and Manx
Emblem
A4

Manx Cat — A5

Perf. 11½

1973, July 5   Photo.   Unwmk.

12	A4	½p shown	.20	.20
a.		Booklet pane of 2	2.75	
b.		Booklet pane of 4 ('74)	.90	
13	A4	1p Port Erin	.20	.20
14	A4	1½p Mt. Snaefell	.20	.20
15	A4	2p Laxey Village	.20	.20
a.		Booklet pane of 2	2.75	
16	A4	2½p Tynwald Hill	.20	.20
a.		Booklet pane of 2	.75	
17	A4	3p Douglas Promenade	.20	.20
a.		Booklet pane of 2	.70	
b.		Booklet pane of 4 ('74)	.90	
18	A4	3½p Port St. Mary	.20	.20
a.		Booklet pane of 4 ('74)	1.40	
19	A4	4p Fairy Bridge	.20	.20
20	A4	5p Peel, Castle and shore	.20	.20
21	A4	6p Cregneish Village	.35	.35
22	A4	7½p Ramsey Bay	.35	.35
23	A4	9p Douglas Bay	.35	.35
24	A5	10p shown	.45	.45
25	A5	20p Manx ram	.75	.75
26	A5	50p Manx shearwaters	2.00	2.00
27	A5	£1 Viking longship	4.00	4.00
		Nos. 12-27 (16)	10.05	10.05

See Nos. 52-59.

Vikings
Landing on
Man, 938 — A6

1973, July 5   Perf. 14

28	A6	15p multicolored	.60	.60

Inauguration of postal independence. Compare with No. 251. Inscription under "Isle of Man" reads "Post Office Decennium" on No. 251.

 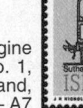

Engine
No. 1,
Sutherland,
1873 — A7

1973, Aug. 4   Perf. 14½x14

29	A7	2½p shown	.20	.20
30	A7	3p Caledonia, 1885	.20	.20
31	A7	7½p Kissack, 1910	.50	.50
32	A7	9p Pender, 1873	.60	.60
		Nos. 29-32 (4)	1.50	1.50

Centenary of Manx steam railroad.

Leslie
Randles,
1923
Winner
A8

3½p, Alan Holmes, 1957 double winner.

1973, Sept. 4   Litho.   Perf. 14

33	A8	3p multicolored	.20	.20
34	A8	3½p multicolored	.20	.20

Manx Grand Prix Motorcycle Race, 50th anniversary.

Princess Anne and Mark Phillips — A9

Litho. & Engr.

1973 Nov. 14   Perf. 14x13½

35	A9	25p lt blue & multi	.95	.95

Wedding of Princess Anne and Capt. Mark Phillips, Nov. 14, 1973.

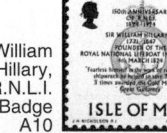

William
Hillary,
R.N.L.I.
Badge
A10

Wreck of
"St.
George"
A11

Designs: 8p, Tower of Refuge and lifeboat "Manchester & Salford." 10p, "Osman Gabriel" at Port Erin. 3½p and 8p are from paintings.

1974, Mar. 4   Photo.   Perf. 11½

36	A10	3p black & multl	.20	.20
37	A11	3½p black & multi	.20	.20
38	A11	8p black & multi	.45	.45
39	A11	10p black & multi	.55	.55
		Nos. 36-39 (4)	1.40	1.40

Sesqui. of the founding of the Royal Natl. Lifeboat Institution by Sir William Hillary.

Stanley Woods on Moto Guzzi Motorcycle — A12

Designs: 3½p, Freddie Frith on Norton. 8p, Max Deubel on BMW with sidecar. 10p, Mike Hailwood on Honda.

1974, May 29   Litho.   Perf. 13

40	A12	3p yellow grn & multi	.20	.20
41	A12	3½p crimson & multi	.20	.20
42	A12	8p yellow & multi	.30	.25
43	A12	10p ultra & multi	.40	.35
		Nos. 40-43 (4)	1.10	1.00

Tourist Trophy Motorcycle Races on the Isle of Man.

Arms and Ruins of Rushen Abbey A13

Designs: 4½p, King Edgar of England visiting Chester in boat rowed by 8 kings including King Magnus Haraldson. 8p, Fleet under King Magnus' command and arms he gave to Isle of Man. 10p, Bridge at Avignon, Bishop's mitre and Three Legs of Man.

1974, Sept. 18   Litho.   Perf. 14

44	A13	3½p multicolored	.20	.20
45	A13	4½p multicolored	.20	.20
46	A13	8p multicolored	.30	.30
47	A13	10p multicolored	.40	.40
		Nos. 44-47 (4)	1.10	1.10

1,000th death anniv. of Magnus Haraldson, King of Many Islands (Nos. 45-46), and 600th death anniv. of William Russell, Bishop of Sodor and Mann (Nos. 44, 47).

Churchill and "Bugler Dunne at Colenso, 1899" — A14

Sir Winston Churchill: 4½p, Government Buildings, Douglas, and Warrant of Appointment. 8p, Manx A.A. Regiment in action. 20p, Freedom of Douglas Scroll, and casket.

1974, Nov. 22   Photo.   Perf. 11½

48	A14	3½p multicolored	.20	.20
49	A14	4½p multicolored	.20	.20
50	A14	8p multicolored	.25	.25
51	A14	20p multicolored	.65	.65
a.		Souvenir sheet of 4, #48-51	1.40	1.40
		Nos. 48-51 (4)	1.30	1.30

Type of 1973

1975   Unwmk.   Perf. 11½

52	A4	4½p Tynwald Hill	.20	.20
53	A4	5½p Douglas Promenade	.20	.20
54	A4	7p Laxey Village	.40	.40
55	A4	8p Ramsey Bay	.40	.40
58	A4	11p Monk's Bridge	.45	.45
59	A4	13p Derbyhaven	.60	.60
		Nos. 52-59 (6)	2.25	2.25

Issued: #52, 55, 1/8; #53-54, 5/28; #58-59, 10/29.

Log Cabin School, Cleveland Medal, Names of Settlers A15

Designs: 5½p, Terminal Tower Building, Cleveland, John Gill and Robert Carran. 8p, Clague House Museum, Margaret and Robert Clague. 10p, Thomas Quayle and S. S. William T. Graves.

1975, Mar. 14   Photo.   Perf. 11½

62	A15	4½p multicolored	.20	.20
63	A15	5½p multicolored	.20	.20
64	A15	8p multicolored	.30	.30
65	A15	10p multicolored	.35	.35
		Nos. 62-65 (4)	1.05	1.05

Sesquicentennial of arrival of Manx settlers in Cleveland, Ohio area.

Tom Sheard and "Douglas" — A16

Designs: 7p, Walter L. Handley and "Rex-Acme." 10p, Geoffrey Duke and "Gilera." 12p, Peter Williams and "Norton."

1975, May 28   Litho.   Perf. 13½

66	A16	5½p bister & multi	.20	.20
67	A16	7p salmon & multi	.25	.25
68	A16	10p lt green & multi	.35	.35
69	A16	12p ultra & multi	.40	.40
		Nos. 66-69 (4)	1.20	1.20

Tourist Trophy Motorcycle races on Isle of Man.

Sir George Goldie and his Birthplace A17

Designs (Sir George Goldie and): 7p, Map of Africa with Niger River basin, vert. 10p, Goldie as president of Royal Geographical Society and Society emblem, vert. 12p, River boats: trading hulk, native canoe, sternwheeler.

1975, Sept. 9   Photo.   Perf. 11½

70	A17	5½p multicolored	.20	.20
71	A17	7p multicolored	.25	.25
72	A17	10p multicolored	.35	.35
73	A17	12p multicolored	.40	.40
		Nos. 70-73 (4)	1.20	1.20

Sir George Dashwood Goldie-Taubman (1846-1925), founder of Royal Niger Company.

Manx Bible — A18

Bicentenary of Manx Bible and Christmas 1975: 7p, Rev. Philip Moore and Old Ballaugh Church. 11p, Bishop Mark Hildesley and Bishops Court. 13p, Shipwreck off Cumberland Coast with John Kelly holding manuscript above water.

1975, Oct. 29   Litho.   Perf. 14

74	A18	5½p multicolored	.20	.20
75	A18	7p multicolored	.25	.25
76	A18	11p multicolored	.35	.35
77	A18	13p multicolored	.40	.40
		Nos. 74-77 (4)	1.20	1.20

William Christian Listening to Patrick Henry — A19

Designs: 7p, Christian carrying Fincastle Resolutions to Williamsburg. 13p, Col. Patrick Henry and Lt. Col. William Christian of 1st Virginia Regiment. 20p, Christian as frontiersman and Indians.

1976, Mar. 12   Litho.   Perf. 13½

78	A19	5½p multicolored	.20	.20
79	A19	7p multicolored	.25	.25
80	A19	13p multicolored	.40	.40
81	A19	20p multicolored	.45	.45
a.		Souv. sheet of 4, #78-81, perf. 14	1.75	1.75
		Nos. 78-81 (4)	1.30	1.30

American Bicentennial. William Christian (1743-1786), patriot, son of a Manx-man and Patrick Henry's brother-in-law.

First Double-decker Tram Car — A20

Designs: 7p, Toast-rack tram, 1890. 11p, Horse bus, 1895. 13p, Decorated tram with Queen Elizabeth II and Prince Philip.

1976, May 26   Photo.   Perf. 11½

82	A20	5½p multicolored	.20	.20
83	A20	7p multicolored	.25	.25
84	A20	11p multicolored	.40	.40
85	A20	13p multicolored	.40	.40
		Nos. 82-85 (4)	1.25	1.25

Douglas horse trams, centenary.

Barroose Beaker, Bronze Age — A21

Virgin and Child, on Sodor and Man Banner — A22

Europa (Manx Ceramic Art): No. 87, Souvenir teapot (3-legged man), 19th cent. No. 88, Laxey jug, 1854. No. 89, Cronk Aust food vessel, early Bronze Age. No. 90, Sansbury bowl, 1851. No. 91, Knox urn, 20th cent. Nos. 89-91, horiz.

1976, July 28   Photo.   Perf. 11½

86	A21	5p multicolored	.25	.25
87	A21	5p multicolored	.25	.25
88	A21	5p multicolored	.25	.25
a.		Strip of 3, #86-88	.80	.80
89	A21	10p multicolored	.25	.25
90	A21	10p multicolored	.25	.25
91	A21	10p multicolored	.25	.25
a.		Strip of 3, #89-91	.80	.80
		Nos. 86-91 (6)	1.50	1.50

Printed in sheets of 9 (3x3).

1976, Oct. 14   Litho.   Perf. 14¾x14½

Virgin and Child on Embroidered Church Banners: 7p, St. Peter's, Onchan, Mothers' Union. 11p, Castletown. 13p, St. Olav's, Ramsey.

92	A22	6p multicolored	.25	.25
93	A22	7p multicolored	.25	.25
94	A22	11p multicolored	.35	.35
95	A22	13p multicolored	.45	.45
		Nos. 92-95 (4)	1.30	1.30

Christmas 1976 & cent. of Mothers' Union.

Elizabeth II and Arms of Man A23

Designs: 7p, Queen Elizabeth II and Prince Philip, vert. 25p, Queen, 1976 portrait.

Perf. 13½x14, 14x13½

1977, Mar. 1   Litho. & Engr.

96	A23	6p multicolored	.25	.25
97	A23	7p multicolored	.25	.25
98	A23	25p multicolored	.75	.75
		Nos. 96-98 (3)	1.25	1.25

25th anniv. of the reign of Elizabeth II.

Carrick Bay from Tom-the-Dipper's — A24

Europa: 10p, Looking south from Mooragh Park, Ramsey.

1977, May 25   Litho.   Perf. 14

99	A24	6p multicolored	.25	.25
100	A24	10p multicolored	.35	.35

"Pa" Applebee at Ballig Bridge, 1912 — A25

Designs: 7p, Hairpin curve at Governor's Bridge and ambulance attendants. 11p, Boy Scouts tending scoreboards. 13p, John Williams at Windy Corner on Snaefell Mountain, winner of 1976 Open Classic Race.

1977, May 25   Perf. 13½

101	A25	6p multicolored	.20	.20
102	A25	7p multicolored	.30	.30
103	A25	11p multicolored	.40	.40
104	A25	13p multicolored	.45	.45
		Nos. 101-104 (4)	1.35	1.35

Tourist Trophy Motorcycle Races, and Boy Scouts, 70th anniv.; St. John Ambulance Assoc. cent. (in GB).

Meeting House, Mt. Morrison — A26

Designs: 7p, John Wesley preaching at Castletown, 1777. 11p, Wesley preaching outside Braddan Church. 13p, Methodist Church on Douglas Promenade, 1976.

1977, Oct. 19   Photo.   Perf. 11½
Size: 30x24mm

105	A26	6p multicolored	.20	.20

Size: 37½x24mm

106	A26	7p multicolored	.30	.30
107	A26	11p multicolored	.40	.40

Size: 30x24mm

108	A26	13p multicolored	.45	.45
		Nos. 105-108 (4)	1.35	1.35

Bicentenary of John Wesley's first visit to the Isle of Man.

Seaplane and Carrier Ben My Chree — A27

Royal Air Force, 60th Anniv.: 7p, Bristol Scout and carrier Vindex, 1915. 11p, Boulton Paul Defiant over Douglas Bay, 1941. 13p, RAF Jaguar over Ramsey, 1977.

1978, Feb. 28   Litho.   Perf. 13½x14
109	A27	6p multicolored	.20	.20
110	A27	7p multicolored	.30	.30
111	A27	11p multicolored	.40	.40
112	A27	13p multicolored	.45	.45
		Nos. 109-112 (4)	1.35	1.35

Watch Tower, Langness — A28

Jurby Church — A29

Fuchsia — A30

Landmarks: 6p, Government buildings. 7p, Tynwald Hill. 8p, Milner's Tower. 9p, Laxey Wheel. 10p, Castle Rushen. 11p, St. Ninian's Church. 12p, Tower of Refuge. 13p, St. German's Cathedral. 14p, Point of Ayre Lighthouse. 15p, Corrin's Tower. 16p, Douglas Head Lighthouse. 25p, Manx cat. 50p, Chough (crows). £1, Viking warrior.

1978   Litho.   Perf. 14
113	A28	½p multicolored	.20	.20
114	A29	1p multicolored	.20	.20
115	A28	6p multicolored	.20	.20
116	A29	7p multicolored	.20	.20
117	A28	8p multicolored	.25	.25
118	A28	9p multicolored	.30	.30
119	A29	10p multicolored	.45	.45
120	A28	11p multicolored	.45	.45
121	A29	12p multicolored	.50	.50
122	A29	13p multicolored	.70	.70
123	A29	14p multicolored	.70	.70
124	A29	15p multicolored	.85	.85
125	A29	16p multicolored	.60	.60

Photo.
Perf. 11½
126	A30	20p multicolored	.60	.60
127	A30	25p multicolored	.90	.90
128	A30	50p multicolored	1.60	1.60
129	A30	£1 multicolored	3.50	3.50
		Nos. 113-129 (17)	12.20	12.20

Issued: #113-125, 2/28; #126-129, 10/18.

Perf. 14½
113a	A28	½p multicolored	.25	.20
114a	A29	1p multicolored	.25	.20
116a	A29	7p multicolored	9.00	7.00
117a	A28	8p multicolored	.40	.40
118a	A28	9p multicolored	.30	.30
119a	A29	10p multicolored	.40	.40
120a	A28	11p multicolored	.45	.45
121a	A29	12p multicolored	.60	.60
122a	A29	13p multicolored	.35	.35
123a	A29	14p multicolored	.35	.35
124a	A29	15p multicolored	.35	.35
125a	A29	16p multicolored	30.00	25.00
		Nos. 113a-125a (12)	42.70	35.60

Elizabeth II — A31

1978, May 24   Litho.   Perf. 14½x14¼
130	A31	25p blue & multi	.80	.80

25th anniv. of coronation of Elizabeth II.

Keeil Chiggyrt Stone — A32

Europa (Carved Gravestones): No. 132, Wheel-headed cross slab. No. 133, Celtic Wheel cross. No. 134, Thor cross. No. 135, Olaf Liotulfson cross. No. 136, Odd's and Thorleif's crosses.

1978, May 24   Perf. 11½
131	A32	6p multicolored	.20	.20
132	A32	6p multicolored	.20	.20
133	A32	6p multicolored	.20	.20
a.		Strip of 3, #131-133	.50	.50
134	A32	11p multicolored	.35	.35
135	A32	11p multicolored	.35	.35
136	A32	11p multicolored	.35	.35
a.		Strip of 3, #134-136	1.10	1.10
		Nos. 131-136 (6)	1.65	1.65

Printed se-tenant in sheets of 9 (3x3).

J. K. Ward, Ward Library, Peel — A33

13p, Lumber camp at Three Rivers & J. K. Ward.

1978, June 10   Litho.   Perf. 13½
137	A33	6p multicolored	.20	.20
138	A33	13p multicolored	.35	.35

James K. Ward (1819-1910), Manx pioneer in Canada.

Athletes, Games' Emblem and Manx Arms A34

Eagle, Manx Arms, Maple Leaf A35

1978, June 10
139	A34	7p multicolored	.25	.25
140	A35	11p multicolored	.35	.35

11th Commonwealth Games, Edmonton, Aug. 3-12 (7p); North American Manx Soc., 50th anniv. (11p).

"Hunt the Wren" — A36

1978, Oct. 18   Litho.   Perf. 13
141	A36	5p multicolored	.35	.25

Christmas 1978.

Philip M. C. Kermode and Nassa Kermodei A37

7p, Peregrine falcons. 11p, Fulmars. 13p, Asilid fly.

1979, Feb. 27   Litho.   Perf. 14
142	A37	6p multicolored	.20	.20
143	A37	7p multicolored	.30	.30
144	A37	11p multicolored	.35	.35
145	A37	13p multicolored	.45	.45
		Nos. 142-145 (4)	1.30	1.30

Isle of Man Natural History and Antiquarian Society.

Viking Ship — A38

A39

Viking Raid at Garwick A40

Designs (Tynwald Emblem and): 7p, 10th century meeting at Tynwald. 11p, Tynwald Hill and St. John's Church. 13p, Contemporary Tynwald Day parade.

Perf. 14½x14 (#146-147), 13¼ (#148-151)

1979, May 16   Litho.
146	A38	3p Insularem	.20	.20
a.		Bklt. pane, 4 #146b, 2 #147a	.60	
b.		Insularum (inscribed "1980")	.20	.20
c.		Bklt. pane, 4 #146b, 2 #147	1.25	
147	A39	4p multicolored	.20	.20
a.		Inscribed "1980"	.20	.20
148	A40	6p multicolored	.20	.20
149	A40	7p multicolored	.25	.25
150	A40	11p multicolored	.30	.30
151	A40	13p multicolored	.35	.35
		Nos. 146-151 (6)	1.50	1.50

Millennium of Tynwald, Legislative Council. #146-147 printed se-tenant in sheets of 80. No. 146a comes in two arrangements. The Nos. 147 in Nos. 146c and 190a are dated "1980."

19th Century Mailman — A41

Europa: 11p, Contemporary mailman.

1979, May 16   Perf. 14½
152	A41	6p multicolored	.20	.20
153	A41	11p multicolored	.40	.40

Ceremony on Tynwald Hill — A42

Design: 13p, Procession from St. John's Church to Tynwald Hill.

1979, July 5   Litho.   Perf. 14½
154	A42	7p multicolored	.25	.25
155	A42	13p multicolored	.45	.45

Visit of Queen Elizabeth II for the celebration of millennium of Tynwald.

Girl Holding Teddy Bear — A43

Christmas and IYC: 7p, Children with Santa.

1979, Oct. 19   Litho.   Perf. 13¼x13½
156	A43	5p multicolored	.20	.20
157	A43	7p multicolored	.30	.30

Capt. John Quilliam and Spencer A44

Capt. Quilliam: 6p, Seized by press gang. 8p, Battle of Trafalgar. 15p, Castle Rushen.

1979, Oct. 19   Perf. 14
158	A44	6p multicolored	.25	.25
159	A44	8p multicolored	.25	.25
160	A44	13p multicolored	.35	.35
161	A44	15p multicolored	.45	.45
		Nos. 158-161 (4)	1.30	1.30

Capt. John Quilliam (1771-1829), British naval hero and member of House of Keys.

"Odin's Raven" A45

1979, Oct. 19   Perf. 14x14½
162	A45	15p multicolored	.65	.65

Voyage of replica Viking longboat across North Sea (Trondheim to Peel), May 27-July 4. See No. 176a.

Conglomerate Arch, Langness, and Emblem — A46

Royal Geographical Society Emblem and: 8p, Braaid Circle. 12p, Cashtal yn Ard (Neolithic burial ground). 13p, Volcanic rocks, Scarlett. 15p, Sugar-loaf Rock.

1980, Feb. 5   Litho.   Perf. 14½
163	A46	7p multicolored	.25	.25
164	A46	8p multicolored	.30	.30
165	A46	12p multicolored	.40	.40
166	A46	13p multicolored	.40	.40
167	A46	15p multicolored	.40	.40
		Nos. 163-167 (5)	1.75	1.75

Royal Geographical Society, 150th anniv.

"Mona's Isle I" A47

1980, May 6   Photo.   Perf. 11½
Granite Paper

168	A47	7p *shown*	.25	.25
169	A47	8p Douglas I	.25	.25
170	A47	11½p Mona's Queen II, sinking U-boat	.30	.30
171	A47	12p King Orry III	.35	.35
172	A47	13p Ben-My-Chree IV	.40	.40
173	A47	15p Lady of Mann II	.50	.50
a.		Souvenir sheet of 6, #168-173	2.25	2.25
		Nos. 168-173 (6)	2.05	2.05

Isle of Man Steam Packet Co. sesqui.; London 80 Intl. Stamp Exhib., May 6-14.

Thomas Edward Brown and Characters from his Poems — A48

Europa (Brown (1830-1897), Poet and Scholar): 13½p, Cricket game, Clifton College Bristol.

1980, May 6

174	A48	7p multicolored	.30	.30
175	A48	13½p multicolored	.40	.40

Visit of King Olav V of Norway A49

1980, June 13   Litho.   Perf. 14½

176	A49	12p multicolored	.75	.75
a.		Souv. sheet of 2, #162, 176	1.25	1.25

Visit of King Olav V of Norway, Aug. 2-7, 1979, and NORWEX 80 stamp exhibition, Oslo, June 13-22.

William Kermode and "Robert Quayle" A50

Kermode Family (First Manx Pioneers in Tasmania): 9p, First homestead, Mona Vale, Merino sheep, 1834. 13½p, Ross Bridge, W. Kermode. 15p, Calendar House, 1868. 17½p, Parliament Buildings, Hobart, Robert Quayle Kermode.

1980, Sept. 29   Litho.

177	A50	7p multicolored	.25	.25
178	A50	9p multicolored	.30	.30
179	A50	13½p multicolored	.45	.45
180	A50	15p multicolored	.50	.50
181	A50	17½p multicolored	.55	.55
		Nos. 177-181 (5)	2.05	2.05

Wren A51

1980, Sept. 29   Litho.   Perf. 13½x14

182	A51	6p shown	.20	.20
183	A51	8p Robin	.20	.20

Wildlife conservation and Christmas 1980.

Luggers, Red Pier, Douglas A52

1981, Feb. 24   Litho.   Perf. 14

184	A52	8p *shown*	.25	.25
185	A52	9p Wanderer saving Lusitania Survivors	.25	.25
186	A52	18p Nickey, Port St. Mary	.50	.50
187	A52	20p Nobby, Ramsey Harbor	.60	.60
188	A52	22p Sunbeam and Zebra, Port Erin	.65	.65
		Nos. 184-188 (5)	2.25	2.25

Royal National Mission to Deep Sea Fishermen centenary.

Peregrine Falcon — A53

1980, Sept. 29   Litho.   Perf. 14½x14
Booklet Stamps

189	A53	1p shown	.35	.35
190	A53	5p Loaghtyn ram	.35	.35
a.		Bklt. pane, 2 each #147, 189, 190	1.25	

Crosh Cuirn (Cross of Mountain Ash Twigs, Harvest Charm) — A54

Europa: 18p, Bollan fish cross-bone (fishermen's charm).

1981, May 22   Litho.   Perf. 14½

191	A54	8p multicolored	.25	.25
192	A54	18p multicolored	.65	.65

Col. Mark Wilks, Peel Castle A55

1981, May 22   Perf. 14

193	A55	8p shown	.30	.30
194	A55	20p Wilks, Fort. St. George, Madras	.50	.50
195	A55	22p Wilks, Napoleon	.65	.65
196	A55	25p Wilks at Kirby estate	.75	.75
		Nos. 193-196 (4)	2.20	2.20

Wilks (d. 1831), governor of St. Helena.

Suffragettes Emmeline Goulden Pankhurst and Sophia Jane Goulden — A56

1981, May 22   Perf. 14

197	A56	9p multicolored	.40	.40

Centenary of women's suffrage and of House of Keys Election Act (granting widows and unmarried women voting rights).

Prince Charles and Lady Diana A57

1981, July 29   Litho.   Perf. 14

198	A57	9p multicolored	.25	.25
199	A57	25p multicolored	1.00	1.00
a.		Souv. sheet, 2 each #198-199	2.75	2.75

Royal Wedding.

Queen Elizabeth II — A58

1981, Sept. 29   Photo.   Perf. 11½
Granite paper

200	A58	£2 multicolored	6.00	6.00

Douglas War Memorial, Poppies, Quote from Laurence Binyon's For the Fallen — A59

1981, Sept. 29
Granite Paper

201	A59	8p shown	.25	.25
202	A59	10p Maj. R.H. Cain, Battle of Arnhem, 1944	.30	.30
203	A59	18p Festival of Remembrance	.60	.60
204	A59	20p Tynwald and Spitfire, Dunkirk, 1940	.70	.70
		Nos. 201-204 (4)	1.85	1.85

Royal British Legion, 60th anniv.

Nativity Stained-glass Window, 1865, St. George's Church, Douglas — A60

9p: Christmas pageant, Glencrutchery Special School, Douglas.

1981, Sept. 29   Litho.   Perf. 14½x14

205	A60	7p multicolored	.25	.25

Size: 47x28mm

206	A60	9p multicolored	.35	.35

Christmas and St. George's Church bicen. (7p), IYD (9p).

Scouting Year — A61

Designs: 9p, Cunningham House (Man Scout Headquarters). 10p, Baden-Powell's

---

visit, 1911. 19½p, Portrait (32x41mm., Perf. 14½). 24p, Baden-Powell with scouts, message. 29p, Sign, handshake, globe, emblem.

1982, Feb. 23   Perf. 13½x14

207	A61	9p multicolored	.25	.25
208	A61	10p multicolored	.25	.25
209	A61	19½p multicolored	.65	.65
210	A61	24p multicolored	.80	.80
211	A61	29p multicolored	1.00	1.00
		Nos. 207-211 (5)	2.95	2.95

Europa 1982 — A62

Designs: 9p, Bishop Thomas Wilson (1663-1755) and his "The Principles and Duties of Christianity," first book printed in Manx, 1707. 19½p, Visit of Thomas, 2nd Earl of Derby, 1507.

1982, June 1   Photo.   Perf. 12½
Granite Paper

212	A62	9p multicolored	.30	.30
213	A62	19½p multicolored	.60	.60

75th Anniv. of Tourist Trophy Motorcycle Races — A63

Designs: Winners on their bikes.

1982, June 1   Litho.   Perf. 14

214	A63	9p Charlie Collier, 431 Matchless, 1907	.25	.25
215	A63	10p Freddie Dixon, Douglas, 1923	.25	.25
216	A63	24p Jimmie Simpson, Norton, 1932	.90	.90
217	A63	26p Mike Hailwood, Norton, 1961	.90	.90
218	A63	29p Jock Taylor, 700 Fowler Yamaha, '80	.90	.90
		Nos. 214-218 (5)	3.20	3.20

Isle of Man Steam Packet Co. Mail Contract Sesquicentennial — A64

1982, Oct. 5   Litho.   Perf. 13½x14

219	A64	12p Mona I	.55	.55
220	A64	19½p Manx Maid II	.80	.80

Christmas 1982 A65

Perf. 13¼x13½, 13½x13¼
1982, Oct. 5

221	A65	8p Three Kings	.30	.30
222	A65	11p Robin, Christmas tree, vert.	.55	.55

Souvenir Sheet

Princess Diana and Prince
William — A66

1982, Oct. 12   *Perf. 14½x14¼*
223 A66 50p multicolored   2.75 2.75
Birth of Prince William of Wales (June 21)
and 21st birthday of Princess Diana (July 1).

Marine
Birds
A67

1983, Feb. 15   Litho.   *Perf. 14½*
224 A67 1p Puffins, Cranstal   .20   .20
225 A67 2p Gannets, Point of
           Ayre   .20   .20
226 A67 5p Lesser black-backed
           gulls, Santon   .20   .20
227 A67 8p Cormorants,
           Maughold Head   .35   .35
228 A67 10p Kittiwakes, White
           Strand   .45   .45
229 A67 11p Shags, Calf of Man   .50   .50
230 A67 12p Herons, Douglas
           Foreshore   .55   .55
231 A67 13p Herring gulls, Peel   .60   .60
232 A67 14p Razorbills, Calf of
           Man   .60   .60
233 A67 15p Great black-backed
           gulls, Calf of Man   .70   .70
234 A67 16p Shelducks, Poyll
           Vaaish   .75   .75
235 A67 18p Oystercatchers,
           Langness   .80   .80

1983, Sept. 14   Perf. 14
Size: 39x25mm
236 A67 20p Arctic terns, Blue
           Point   .90   .90
237 A67 25p Guillemots, Calf
           of Man   1.10 1.10
238 A67 50p Redshanks,
           Langness   2.00 2.00
239 A67 £1 Mute swans, Port
           St. Mary Bay   4.00 4.00
    Nos. 224-239 (16)   13.90 13.90

Centenary of Salvation Army in Isle of
Man — A68

Designs: 10p, Citadel opening ceremony,
1932, T.H. Cannell. 12p, Founder William
Booth, early meeting place (former Unitarian
Church, Douglas). 19½p, Band, Bandmaster
Gordon Cowley, 1981. 26p, Lt.-Col. Thomas
Bridson, treating lepers in Dutch East Indies.

1983, Feb. 15   Photo.   *Perf. 11½*
Granite Paper
240 A68 10p multicolored   .35   .35
241 A68 12p multicolored   .45   .45
242 A68 19½p multicolored   .75   .75
243 A68 26p multicolored   .95   .95
    Nos. 240-243 (4)   2.50 2.50

Europa 1983 — A69

1983, May 18   *Perf. 14*
244 A69 10p Laxey Wheel   .45   .45
245 A69 20½p Designer Robert
            Casement   .80   .80

King William's College
Sesquicentennial — A70

Graduates: 10p, Nick Keig, Yachtsman. 12p,
College, arms. 28p, William Bragg, 1915
Nobel Prize winner in physics, ionization spec-
trometer. 31p, Gen. George Stuart White,
Defense of Ladysmith, Boer War.

1983, May 18   Photo.   *Perf. 11½*
Granite Paper
246 A70 10p multicolored   .30   .30
247 A70 12p multicolored   .40   .40
248 A70 28p multicolored   1.10 1.10
249 A70 31p multicolored   1.25 1.25
    Nos. 246-249 (4)   3.05 3.05

World Communications Year and 10th
Anniv. of Post Office — A71

1983, July 5   Litho.   *Perf. 15*
250 A71 10p New P.O. Head-
           quarters   .45   .45
251 A6 15p Viking landing, 938   .75   .75
    Compare No. 251 with No. 28.

Christmas
1983
A72

1983, Sept. 14   Litho.   *Perf. 13x13½*
252 A72 9p Shepherds   .40   .40
253 A72 12p Three Kings   .50   .50

Karran
Fleet
A73

Links with Falkland Islands — A74

1984, Feb. 14   Litho.   *Perf. 14*
254 A73 10p Manx King, 1884   .30   .30
255 A73 13p Hope, 1858   .45   .45
256 A73 20½p Rio Grande, 1868   .65   .65
257 A73 28p Lady Elizabeth,
           1879   1.10 1.10
258 A73 31p Sumatra, 1858   1.25 1.25
    Nos. 254-258 (5)   3.75 3.75

1984, Feb. 14
259   Sheet of 2, #257, 259a   3.50 3.50
 a. A74 31p multicolored   1.50 1.50

Europa
(1959-1984)
A75

1984, Apr. 27   Photo.   *Perf. 11½*
260 A75 10p dk yel org, dk brn
           & buff   .40   .40
261 A75 20½p blue, dk bl & lt bl   .75   .75

DH-48, Ronaldsway Airport — A76

1984, Apr. 27   Litho.   *Perf. 14*
262 A76 11p shown   .50   .50
263 A76 13p DH-86, Calf of Man   .55   .55
264 A76 26p DC-3, Ronaldsway
           Airport   1.00 1.00
265 A76 28p Vickers Viscount,
           Douglas   1.00 1.00
266 A76 31p Islander, Ronald-
           sway Airport   1.00 1.00
    Nos. 262-266 (5)   4.05 4.05
50th Anniv. of official airmail service and
40th anniv. of Intl. Civil Aviation Org.

William Cain as Mayor of Melbourne,
1886-87 — A77

1984, Sept. 21   Litho.   *Perf. 14½*
267 A77 11p Ballasalla (birth-
           place)   .45   .45
268 A77 22p Voyage to Australia   .80   .80
269 A77 28p Railway, Victoria   1.00 1.00
270 A77 30p shown   1.10 1.10
271 A77 33p Royal Exhibition
           Buildings, Mel-
           bourne   1.10 1.10
    Nos. 267-271 (5)   4.45 4.45
William Cain (1831-1914), building contractor and public servant in Australia.

Queen
Elizabeth
II, CPA
Emblem
A78

1984, Sept. 21   Perf. 14
272 A78 11p shown   .50   .50
273 A78 33p Arms, Elizabeth II   1.25 1.25
30th Conference of Commonwealth Parliamentary Assoc., Sept. 28-Oct. 5.

Christmas — A79

Stained-glass windows.

1984, Sept. 21
274 A79 10p Birds, Glencrutch-
           ery House   .50   .50
275 A79 13p Arms, Lonan Old
           Church   .60   .60

75th Anniv. of Girl Guides — A80

Designs: 11p, Cunningham House (headquarters), Mrs. W. and J. Cunningham (early
Island Commissioners). 14p, Princess Margaret (president), color guard. 29p, Lady
Olave Baden-Powell, headquarters opening.
31p, Uniforms, 1910-85. 34p, Sign, handclasp,
trefoil.

1985, Jan. 31   Photo.   *Perf. 12*
276 A80 11p multicolored   .50   .50
277 A80 14p multicolored   .65   .65
278 A80 29p multicolored   1.10 1.10
279 A80 31p multicolored   1.25 1.25
280 A80 34p multicolored   1.50 1.50
    Nos. 276-280 (5)   5.00 5.00

Elizabeth II
A81

1985, Jan. 31   Litho.   *Perf. 14*
281 A81 £5 multicolored   15.00 15.00

Europa 1985 — A82

Manx composers and excerpts from their
works: No. 282a, "O'Land of our Birth." No.
282b, William H. Gill (1839-1922). No. 283a,
Hymn "Crofton;" No. 283b, Dr. John Clague
(1842-1908).

1985, Apr. 24   Photo.   *Perf. 12*
282 A82 Pair   1.25 1.25
 a.-b.   12p any single   .65   .65
283 A82 Pair   1.50 1.50
 a.-b.   22p any single   .75   .75

Motoring — A83

Motor races and winning vehicles: No. 284a,
1906 Tourist Trophy Race. No. 284b, 1922
Tourist Trophy Race. No. 285a, 1950 British
Empire Trophy Race. No. 285b, 1934 Manin
Moar Race. No. 286a, 1984 Tourist Trophy
Motorcycle Race (official car). No. 286b, 1981
Rothmans Manx Intl. Rally.

1985, May 25   Litho.   *Perf. 14*
284 A83 Pair   1.00 1.00
 a.-b.   12p any single   .45   .45
285 A83 Pair   1.25 1.25
 a.-b.   14p any single   .60   .60
286 A83 Pair   2.50 2.50
 a.-b.   31p any single   1.25 1.25
    Nos. 284-286 (3)   4.75 4.75

H.R.H. Alexandra (1885-1925),
Princess of Wales — A84

SSA presidents: 15p, Queen Mary (1925-
1953). 29p, Earl Mountbatten of Burma (1953-
1979). 34p, Prince Michael of Kent (1982-).

1985, Sept. 4   Litho.   Perf. 14
287 A84 12p multicolored   .45   .45
288 A84 15p multicolored   .60   .60
289 A84 29p multicolored   1.10 1.10
290 A84 34p multicolored   1.40 1.40
    Nos. 287-290 (4)   3.55 3.55

Soldier's, Sailors' & Airmen's Families
Assoc., cent.

Lt.-Gen. Sir Mark Cubbon, K.C.B.
(1785-1861), Commissioner of
Mysore — A85

1985, Oct. 2   Litho.   Perf. 14
291 A85 12p Kirk Maughold Par-
        ish Church, 14th
        century   .50   .50
292 A85 22p Portrait, vert.   .90   .90
293 A85 45p Equestrian monu-
        ment, 1866 Ban-
        galore, India, vert. 1.75 1.75
    Nos. 291-293 (3)   3.15 3.15

Christmas
1985
A86

1985, Oct. 2   Litho.   Perf. 13½
294 A86 11p Onchan Parish
        Church, 1833   .40   .40
295 A86 14p St. John's Church .65   .65
296 A86 31p Bride Parish
        Church, 1876   1.50 1.50
    Nos. 294-296 (3)   2.55 2.55

1986 Commonwealth Games,
Edinburgh — A87

1986, Feb. 5   Litho.   Perf. 14
297 A87 12p Women's swimming .50   .50
298 A87 15p Walking   .65   .65
299 A87 31p Rifle shooting   1.10 1.10
300 A87 34p Bicycling   1.50 1.50
    Nos. 297-300 (4)   3.75 3.75

Viking
Necklace,
Peel
Castle
A88

Artifacts, architecture: 15p, Meayll Circle
burial ground, Rushen. 22p, Prehistoric
Cervus giganteus skeleton, Glose-y-Garey,
vert. 26p, Norwegian viking longship, vert.
29p, Open-air Museum, Cregneash.

1986, Feb. 5   Perf. 14½x14, 14x14½
301 A88 12p multicolored   .50   .50
302 A88 15p multicolored   .60   .60
303 A88 22p multicolored   .90   .90

304 A88 26p multicolored   1.00 1.00
305 A88 29p multicolored   1.25 1.25
    Nos. 301-305 (5)   4.25 4.25
Centenaries of Manx Museum and Ancient
Monuments Act.

Europa 1986, Manx National
Trust — A89

Designs: No. 306a, Bride hills and the
Ayres. No. 306b, Calf of Man. No. 307a, Eary
Cushlin. No. 307b, St. Michael's Isle.

1986, Apr. 10   Litho.   Perf. 12
306 A89 Pair   1.00 1.00
  a.-b. 12p any single   .50   .50
307 A89 Pair   2.00 2.00
  a.-b. 22p any single   1.00 1.00

Settling of
Plymouth — A90

Designs: 12p, Ellanbane, Isle of Man, Myles
Standish's home. 15p, The Mayflower. 31p,
Pilgrims landing, 1620. 34p, Capt. Myles
Standish (c. 1584-1656).

1986, May 22   Perf. 13½
308 A90 12p multicolored   .50   .50
309 A90 15p multicolored   .60   .60
310 A90 31p multicolored   1.25 1.25
311 A90 34p multicolored   1.50 1.50
  a. Souvenir sheet of 2, #310-311,
      perf. 13x12½   3.00 3.00
    Nos. 308-311 (4)   3.85 3.85
AMERIPEX '86, Chicago, May 22-June 1.

Heritage Year — A91

1986, Apr. 10   Litho.   Perf. 15x14
312 A91 2p Viking longship bow .20   .20
  a. Bklt. pane of 6, 2 #312, 4 #313 4.50
313 A91 10p Celtic cross   .90   .90
  a. Bklt. pane of 3 + 3 labels   2.75
    Issued in booklets only.

Wedding of
Prince
Andrew
and Sarah
Ferguson
A92

1986, July 23
314 A92 15p Wedding date   .80   .80
315 A92 40p Engagement date 1.75 1.75

Royal Birthdays — A93

No. 316: a, Prince Philip, 65. #b, Elizabeth
II, 60. No. 317 is the same size as No. 316.

1986, Aug. 28   Perf. 11½
316 A93 Pair   1.40 1.40
  a.-b. 15p any single   .70   .70
317 A93 34p Royal couple   1.40 1.40
STOCKHOLMIA '86, Swedish Post Office
350th anniv. Stamps issued in sheets of 6.

Intl. Peace
Year — A94

1986, Sept. 25   Litho.   Perf. 14
318 A94 11p Robins, globe,
        Braille   .45   .45
319 A94 14p Hands, dove   .55   .55
320 A94 31p Hand-holding, sign
        language   1.25 1.25
    Nos. 318-320 (3)   2.25 2.25

Accession of
Queen
Victoria to
the British
Throne,
150th Anniv.
A95

Photographs of Victorian Douglas, by John
Miller Nicholson.

1987, Jan. 21   Litho.   Perf. 14½
321 A95 2p North Quay   .20   .20
322 A95 3p The Old Fish Mar-
        ket   .20   .20
323 A95 10p Breakwater   .40   .40
  a. Bklt. pane of 8 (2 2p, 2 3p, 4
      10p) ('87)   2.10
      Complete booklet, #323a 2.10
324 A95 15p Jubilee Clock   .60   .60
  a. Bklt. pane of 8 (2 2p, 2 3p, 2
      10p, 2 15p) ('87)   2.40
      Complete booklet, #323a, #324a 4.50
325 A95 31p Loch Promenade 1.40 1.40
326 A95 34p Beach   1.50 1.50
    Nos. 321-326 (6)   4.30 4.30

No. 323a comes in two arrangements.

19th Century Paintings by John Miller
Nicholson (1840-1913) — A96

Harbor scenes: 12p, The Old Fish Market
and Harbor, Douglas. 26p, Red Sails at Douglas. 29p, The Double Corner. 34p, Peel
Harbor.

1987, Feb. 18   Perf. 13½
327 A96 12p multicolored   .50   .50
328 A96 26p multicolored   1.00 1.00
329 A96 29p multicolored   1.10 1.10
330 A96 34p multicolored   1.40 1.40
    Nos. 327-330 (4)   4.00 4.00

Promenade, Douglas — A97

1987, Apr. 29   Litho.   Perf. 13½
331 A97 12p Sea Terminal, 1965 .65 .65
332 A97 12p Tower of Refuge,
        1832   .65   .65
  a. Pair, #331-332   1.25 1.25
333 A97 22p Gaiety Theater, c.
        1900   1.00 1.00
334 A97 22p Villa Marina   1.00 1.00
  a. Pair, #333-334   2.00 2.00
    Nos. 331-334 (4)   3.30 3.30
Europa 1987.

Tourist Trophy Motorcycle Races, 80th
Anniv. — A98

1987, May 27   Perf. 13½x13
335 A98 12p 1939 Supercharged
        BMW 500CC   .45   .45
336 A98 15p 1953 Manx "Kneel-
        er" Norton 350CC   .60   .60
337 A98 29p 1956 MV Agusta
        500CC 4   1.10 1.10
338 A98 31p 1957 Guzzi 500CC
        V8   1.25 1.25
339 A98 34p 1967 Honda 250CC
        6   1.40 1.40
  a. Souv. sheet of 5, #335-339 + 7
      labels, perf 14x13½   5.00 5.00
    Nos. 335-339 (5)   4.80 4.80

Wildflowers — A99

1987, Sept. 9 Litho. Perf. 14½x13½
340 A99 16p Fuchsia, wild roses .60 .60
341 A99 29p Field scabius, rag-
        wort   1.10 1.10
342 A99 31p Wood anemone,
        celandine   1.25 1.25
343 A99 34p Violets, primroses 1.40 1.40
    Nos. 340-343 (4)   4.35 4.35

Christmas — A100

Victorian family scenes based on drawings
by Alfred Hunt for The Illustrated London
News, c. 1870-1890.

1987, Oct. 16   Perf. 14
344 A100 12p Stirring the pud-
        ding   .50   .50
345 A100 15p Christmas tree se-
        lection   .60   .60
346 A100 31p Decorating tree 1.40 1.40
    Nos. 344-346 (3)   2.50 2.50

Railways &
Tramways
A101

Designs: 1p, Horse-drawn "Toast Rack"
tram, Douglas Bay, 1884. 2p, No. 5 electric
tram, Snaefell Mountain Railway, 1895. 3p,
No. 3 open-top double-deck electric tram,
Marine Drive-Port Soderick line, Douglas
Southern Electric Tramway, 1896. 5p, Tower of
Refuge and open tram, Douglas Head Incline
Railway. 10p, Electric tram at Maughold Head,
1893, Douglas and Laxey Coast Electric Tram-
way. 13p, Douglas Cable Car No. 72, 1896.
14p, Manx Northern Railway No. 4 Caledonia,
a Dubs 0-6-0T, 1885, at Gob-y-Deigan. 15p,
Great Laxey Mine Railway Lewin steam
engine Ant pulling coal cars. 16p, Henry B.
Loch, first locomotive on the island, Port Erin
Breakwater Railway, 1864. 17p, Locomotive
No. 1, Ramsey Harbor Tramway. 18p, Engine
No. 7 Tynwald, 1880, Foxdale Railway. 19p,
Douglas Corp. engine, Baldwin Reservoir
Railway. 20p, "Kissack" leaving St. John's for
Peel. 25p, "Hutchinson" leaving Douglas Sta-
tion. 50p, "Polar Bear" of Groudle Glen Rail-
way. £1, The Royal Train.

1988 Litho. Perf. 13½
Inscribed 1988

347	A101	1p multicolored	.20	.20
348	A101	2p multicolored	.20	.20
349	A101	3p multicolored	.20	.20
a.		Inscribed "1989"	.20	.20
350	A101	5p multicolored	.20	.20
351	A101	10p multicolored	.40	.40
352	A101	13p multicolored	.50	.50
a.		Inscribed "1989"	.20	.20
353	A101	14p multicolored	.55	.55
a.		Inscribed "1989"	.55	.55
354	A101	15p multicolored	.60	.60
a.		Inscribed "1990"	.60	.60
355	A101	16p multicolored	.65	.65
a.		Inscribed "1989"	.65	.65
b.		Bklt. pane, 2 #349a, 2 #352a, 2 #355a	2.25	
c.		Bklt. pane, 4 #352a, 6 #355a	6.00	
356	A101	17p multicolored	.70	.70
a.		Bklt. pane, 2 #349a, 2 #353a, 2 #356c	2.25	
b.		Booklet pane, 4 #353a, 6 #356c	6.50	
c.		Inscribed "1989"	.70	.70
d.		Inscribed "1991"	.70	.70
357	A101	18p multicolored	.70	.70
358	A101	19p multicolored	.75	.75
e.		Inscribed "1990"	.75	.75
f.		Bklt. pane, 4 #354a, 6 #358e	7.00	
g.		Bklt. pane, 1 #354a, 2 #358e	2.10	

Perf. 15

358A	A101	20p multicolored	.80	.80
358B	A101	25p multicolored	1.00	1.00
358C	A101	50p multicolored	2.00	2.00
a.		Inscribed "1992"	4.00	4.00
358D	A101	£1 multicolored	4.00	4.00
a.		Inscribed "1992"	8.50	8.50
		Nos. 347-358D (16)	13.45	13.45

Nos. 356a and 356b also exist in special booklet sheets of 50 stamps containing either 10 #356a or 5 #356b.

Issued: 1p-19p, 2/10; #355b-355c, 3/16; 20p-£1, 9/21; #356a, 356b, 10/16/89; #358f, 2/14/90.

See Nos. 448-459.

Car Racing — A102

Winning automobiles, drivers: 13p, Vauxhall Opel, Russell Brookes, 1985. 26p, Ford Escort, Ari Vatanen of Finland, 1976. 31p, Repco March 761, Terry Smith, 1980. 34p, Williams/Honda Nigel Mansell, 1986-87.

1988, Feb. 10 Perf. 13½x14½

359	A102	13p multicolored	.60	.60
360	A102	26p multicolored	1.25	1.25
361	A102	31p multicolored	1.40	1.40
362	A102	34p multicolored	1.50	1.50
		Nos. 359-362 (4)	4.75	4.75

Europa 1988 A103

Telecommunications: No. 363, IOM-UK optical fiber cable-laying plow. No. 364, Cable-laying ship. No. 365, 1st IOM Earth station, Braddan, established by Manx Telecom. No. 366, Intelsat V satellite.

1988, Apr. 14 Litho. Perf. 14x13½

363	A103	13p multicolored	.60	.60
364	A103	13p multicolored	.60	.60
a.		Pair, #363-364	1.25	1.25
365	A103	22p multicolored	1.00	1.00
366	A103	22p multicolored	1.00	1.00
a.		Pair, #365-366	2.00	2.00
		Nos. 363-366 (4)	3.20	3.20

Submarine cable linking the Isle of Man and Silecroft in Cumbria, 1987 (13p). Nos. 364a, 366a have continuous designs.

Historic Ships Built on the Isle A104

Isle of Man flag, Australia bicen. emblem or US flag and: 16p, Euterpe, 1863, built in Ramsey. 29p, Vixen leaving Peel for Australia, 1853. 31p, Ramsey, an immigrant ship in Brisbane, 1870. 34p, Star of India (renamed in

1906, was the Euterpe), restored 1960-1976, Maritime Museum at San Diego.

1988, May 11 Litho. Perf. 14

367	A104	16p multicolored	.60	.60
368	A104	29p multicolored	1.10	1.10
369	A104	31p multicolored	1.10	1.10
370	A104	34p multicolored	1.25	1.25
a.		Souvenir sheet of 2 (16p, 34p)	2.75	2.75
		Nos. 367-370 (4)	4.05	4.05

Fuchsia Blossoms — A105

1988, Sept. 21 Litho. Perf. 13½x14

371	A105	13p Magellanica	.45	.45
372	A105	16p Pink cloud	.55	.55
373	A105	22p Leonora	.80	.80
374	A105	29p Satellite	1.10	1.10
375	A105	31p Preston Guild	1.25	1.25
376	A105	34p Thalia	1.40	1.40
		Nos. 371-376 (6)	5.55	5.55

British Fuchsia Society, 50th anniv.

Christmas A106

1988, Oct. 12 Perf. 14

377	A106	12p Long-eared owl	.75	.75
378	A106	15p Robin	.90	.90
379	A106	31p Partridge	1.75	1.75
		Nos. 377-379 (3)	3.40	3.40

Manx Cats A107

Designs: 16p, Ginger. 27p, Black and white. 30p, Tortoiseshell and white. 40p, Tortoiseshell.

1989, Feb. 8

380	A107	16p multicolored	.65	.65
381	A107	27p multicolored	1.10	1.10
382	A107	30p multicolored	1.40	1.40
383	A107	40p multicolored	1.60	1.60
		Nos. 380-383 (4)	4.75	4.75

Celtic Works of Art by Archibald Knox (1864-1933) — A108

Designs: 13p, Tudric pewter and enamel clock, 1903, vert. 16p, Cross, a watercolor, vert. 23p, Silver tankard, 1902, vert. 32p, Liberty silver and Cymric gold brooches. 35p, Silver jewel box with inlaid turquoise, mother-of-pearl and enamel, 1900.

1989, Feb. 8 Litho. Perf. 13

384	A108	13p multicolored	.50	.50
385	A108	16p multicolored	.60	.60
386	A108	23p multicolored	.85	.85
387	A108	32p multicolored	1.10	1.10
388	A108	35p multicolored	1.40	1.40
		Nos. 384-388 (5)	4.45	4.45

Mutiny on the Bounty A109

Designs: 13p, William Bligh, Old Onchan Church. 16p, Bligh and crewmen cast adrift. 30p, Peter Heywood on Tahiti, 1770. 32p, Bounty off Pitcairn. 35p, Fletcher Christian on Pitcairn.

1989, Apr. 28 Litho. Perf. 14

389	A109	13p multicolored	.45	.45
390	A109	16p multicolored	.60	.60
391	A109	30p multicolored	1.00	1.00
392	A109	32p multicolored	1.10	1.10
393	A109	35p multicolored	1.25	1.25
		Nos. 389-393 (5)	4.40	4.40

Souvenir Sheet

394		Sheet of 3 + label	4.50	4.50
a.		A109 23p Pitcairn Isls. No. 321d	.80	.80
b.		A109 27p Norfolk Is. No. 453	.95	.95
c.		Booklet pane, #394	4.50	
d.		Booklet pane, 1 each #389-393, 394a	5.50	
e.		Bklt. pane of 6, #389-393, #394b	5.50	
f.		Booklet pane, 3 each #394a, #394b	5.25	
		Complete booklet, #394c, 394d, 394e, 394f	22.00	

See Norfolk Is. Nos. 452-456 and Pitcairn Isls. Nos. 320-322.

No. 394 contains Nos. 393, 394a-394b.

No. 394c is 145x101mm and is rouletted at left.

Europa 1989 A110

Children's games: No. 395, Jumping rope, hopscotch, London Bridge is falling down. No. 396, Running, wheelbarrow race, leap frog, piggyback ride. No. 397, Boy building fort, girl blowing soap bubbles, puzzle. No. 398, Doll house, blocks, girl playing with rag doll and puzzle.

1989, May 17 Perf. 13½

395	A110	13p multicolored	.50	.50
396	A110	13p multicolored	.50	.50
a.		Pair, #395-396	1.00	1.00
397	A110	23p multicolored	1.00	1.00
398	A110	23p multicolored	1.00	1.00
a.		Pair, #397-398	2.00	2.00
		Nos. 395-398 (4)	3.00	3.00

Nos. 396a, 398a have continuous designs.

World Wildlife Fund — A111

1989, Sept. 20 Litho. Perf. 14

399	A111	13p Puffin	1.50	1.50
400	A111	13p Black guillemot	1.50	1.50
401	A111	13p Cormorant	1.50	1.50
402	A111	13p Kittiwake	1.50	1.50
a.		Block or strip of 4, #399-402	7.50	7.50
		Nos. 399-402 (4)	6.00	6.00

Exists as sheetlet of 16 with "World Stamp Expo '89" printed in selvage.

Intl. Red Cross, 125th Anniv. A112

1989, Oct. 16 Litho. Perf. 14

403	A112	14p Training youths	.55	.55
404	A112	17p Emblems	.65	.65
405	A112	23p Signing 1st Geneva convention, 1864	.90	.90
406	A112	30p Ambulance services	1.25	1.25
407	A112	35p Henri Dunant, founder	1.40	1.40
		Nos. 403-407 (5)	4.75	4.75

Noble's Hospital, Douglas, cent.

Christmas — A113

1989, Oct. 16 Perf. 14½x15

408	A113	13p Maternity home	.45	.45
409	A113	16p Mother and child	.55	.55
410	A113	34p Madonna and child, scripture	1.25	1.25
411	A113	37p Church, baptismal ceremony	1.40	1.40
		Nos. 408-411 (4)	3.65	3.65

Jane Crookall Maternity Home 50th anniv. (13p) and 75th anniv. of the consecration of St. Ninian's Church (37p).

Queen Elizabeth II, Lord of Man, Trooping the Colors — A114

1990, Feb. 14 Litho. Perf. 14½

412	A114	£2 multicolored	6.50	6.50

Humorous Edwardian Postcards — A115

15p, The Isle of Man Express Going Up a Gradient. 19p, A Way We Have in the Isle of Man. 32p, Douglas — Waiting for the Male Boat. 34p, The Last Toast Rack Home Douglas Parade. 37p, The Last Isle of Man Boat.

1990, Feb. 14 Perf. 14

413	A115	15p multicolored	.55	.55
414	A115	19p multicolored	.75	.75
415	A115	32p multicolored	1.25	1.25
416	A115	34p multicolored	1.50	1.50
417	A115	37p multicolored	1.75	1.75
		Nos. 413-417 (5)	5.80	5.80

Europa 1990 — A116

Mailmen and post offices.

1990, Apr. 18 Litho. Perf. 13½
Size of Nos. 419, 421: 42x28mm

418	A116	15p Mailman, 1990	.75	.75
419	A116	15p Ramsey P.O., 1990	.75	.75
a.		Pair, #418-419	1.50	1.50
420	A116	24p Mailman, c. 1890	1.25	1.25
421	A116	24p Douglas P.O., c. 1890	1.25	1.25
a.		Pair, #420-421	2.50	2.50
		Nos. 418-421 (4)	4.00	4.00

Great Britain No. 1 — A117

Designs: 19p, Wyon Medal. 32p, William Wyon's essay. 34p, Perkins Bacon engine-turned essay of 1839. 37p, Great Britain No. 2.

No. 423 (various Penny Blacks and text): a.-e. Positions AA-AE. f.-j. Positions BA-BE. k.-n. Positions CA-CE. p.-t. Positions DA-DE. u.-y. Positions EA-EE.

Note that A-A top of square on No. 423a, centered on No. 422a.

1990, May 3   Litho.   Perf. 14x13½

422		Pane of 5	5.25	5.25
a.	A117	1p shown	.20	.20
b.	A117	19p multicolored	.75	.75
c.	A117	32p multicolored	1.25	1.25
d.	A117	34p multicolored	1.40	1.40
e.	A117	37p multicolored	1.50	1.50
g.		Bkt. pane, 2 each #422b-422e	10.00	
h.		No. 422 ovptd. "From STAMP WORLD LONDON '90 / To NEW ZEALAND '90"	16.00	16.00

Miniature Sheet

423		Sheet of 25	2.50	2.50
a.-y.	A117	1p like #422a, any single	.20	.20
z.		Pane of 8, #a.-d., f.-i.	.55	

Souvenir Sheet
Litho. & Engr.

424	A117	£1 4 Great Britain #1	4.50	4.50
a.		Booklet pane of 1	4.50	4.50
		Complete booklet, #422g, 423z, 424a	15.00	

Left margin of #422g, 423z and 424a rouletted.

Queen Mother, 90th Birthday — A118

1990, Aug. 4   Litho.   Perf. 13x13½

425	A118	90p multicolored	3.75	3.75

Sheets of 10 alternating with 10 labels.

Battle of Britain, 50th Anniv. A119

1990, Sept. 5   Litho.   Perf. 14

426	A119	15p Home defense	.70	.70
427	A119	15p Air sea rescue	.70	.70
a.		Pair, #426-427	1.40	1.40
428	A119	24p Rearming fighters	1.00	1.00
429	A119	24p Height of battle	1.00	1.00
a.		Pair, #428-429	2.00	2.00
430	A119	29p Civil defense	1.25	1.25
431	A119	29p Anti-aircraft defense	1.25	1.25
a.		Pair, #430-431	2.50	2.50
		Nos. 426-431 (6)	5.90	5.90

Sir Winston Churchill (1874-1965) — A120

1990, Sept. 5   Perf. 13½

432	A120	19p multicolored	.75	.75
433	A120	32p multicolored	1.25	1.25
434	A120	34p multicolored	1.40	1.40
435	A120	37p multicolored	1.50	1.50
		Nos. 432-435 (4)	4.90	4.90

Christmas — A121

1990, Oct. 10   Perf. 13x13½

436	A121	14p Mailing letters	.55	.55
437	A121	18p Sledding, skating	.70	.70
438	A121	34p Snowman	1.25	1.25

439	A121	37p Throwing snowball	1.40	1.40
a.		Souvenir sheet of 4, #436-439	4.25	4.25
		Nos. 436-439 (4)	3.90	3.90

Denominations on stamps in No. 439a are black.

Manx Photographers A122

Designs: 17p, Henry Bloom Noble, by Marshall Wane. 21p, Douglas, by Frederic Frith & Co. 26p, Studio Portrait, by Hilda Newby. 31p, Cashtal yn Ard, by Christopher Killip. 40p, Peel, by Colleen Corlett.

1991, Jan. 6   Litho.   Perf. 14x14½

440	A122	17p multicolored	.60	.60
441	A122	21p multicolored	.70	.70
442	A122	26p multicolored	.90	.90
443	A122	31p multicolored	1.25	1.25
444	A122	40p multicolored	1.60	1.60
		Nos. 440-444 (5)	5.05	5.05

Railways and Tramways Type of 1988 with Queen's Head in White (#448, 458-459)

Designs: 18p, TPO Special leaving Douglas Station, 1991. 23p, Double decker horse tram.

1991-92   Litho.   Perf. 13½

448	A101	4p like No. 352	.20	.20
456	A101	18p multicolored	.70	.70
458	A101	21p like No. 353	.85	.85
a.		Souv. sheet, 2 each #448, #458	2.75	2.75
b.		Bklt. pane, #450, 3 #440, 4 #356	3.75	
c.		Bklt. pane, 3 #448, 1 each #356, #458	1.90	
459	A101	23p multicolored	.90	.90
a.		Bklt. pane, 6 #456, 4 #459	8.00	
b.		Bklt. pane, 3 #456, 2 #459	4.00	
		Nos. 448-459 (4)	2.65	2.65

No. 458a for Ninth Conf. of Commonwealth Postal Administrations, Douglas, Isle of Man. Issued: 4p, 21p, #458b, 458c, 1/9; #458a, 7/1; 18p, 23p, #459a, 1/8/92.
No. 458b exists in special booklet sheets containing 5 #458b and 5 each #448, #458. No. 458b dated 1991.

Manx Lifeboats A123

1991, Feb. 13   Perf. 14

463	A123	17p Sir William Hillary	.65	.65
464	A123	21p Osman Gabriel	.85	.85
465	A123	26p James & Ann Ritchie	1.00	1.00
466	A123	31p The Gough Ritchie	1.25	1.25
467	A123	37p John Batstone	1.40	1.40
		Nos. 463-467 (5)	5.15	5.15

Europa — A124

1991, Apr. 24   Litho.   Perf. 14

468	A124	17p Satellites	.80	.80
469	A124	17p Boats, Ariane rocket	.80	.80
a.		Vert. pair, #468-469	1.60	1.60
470	A124	26p Satellites, diff.	1.25	1.25
471	A124	26p Space shuttle, jet	1.25	1.25
a.		Vert. pair, #470-471	2.50	2.50
		Nos. 468-471 (4)	4.10	4.10

Tourist Trophy Mountain Course, 80th Anniv. A125

Designs: 17p, Oliver Godfrey, Indian 500cc, Bray Hill, 1911. 21p, Freddie Dixon, Douglas banking sidecar, Ballacraine, 1923. 26p, Bill Ivy, Yamaha 125cc, Waterworks, 1968. 31p, Giacomo Agostini, MV Agusta 500cc, Cregny-Baa, 1972. 37p, Joey Dunlop, RVF Honda 750cc, Ballaugh Bridge, 1985.

1991, May 30   Litho.   Perf. 14½x13

472	A125	17p multicolored	.70	.70
473	A125	21p multicolored	.85	.85
474	A125	26p multicolored	1.00	1.00
475	A125	31p multicolored	1.25	1.25
476	A125	37p multicolored	1.50	1.50
a.		Souv. sheet of 5, #472-476 + 7 labels	5.50	5.50
b.		As "a," ovptd. in black & red in sheet margin	15.00	15.00
		Nos. 472-476 (5)	5.30	5.30

No. 476b overprint includes show emblem and "PHILA / NIPPON '91."
Issue date: No. 476b, Nov. 16.

Fire Engines A126

Designs: 17p, Laxey hand cart. 21p, Douglas horse drawn steamer. 30p, Merryweather Hatfield pump. 33p, Dennis F8 pumping appliance. 37p, Volvo turntable ladder.

1991, Sept. 18   Litho.   Perf. 14½

477	A126	17p multicolored	.00	.00
478	A126	21p multicolored	.80	.80
479	A126	30p multicolored	1.10	1.10
480	A126	33p multicolored	1.25	1.25
481	A126	37p multicolored	1.40	1.40
		Nos. 477-481 (5)	5.15	5.15

Swans A127

Designs: No. 482, Mute swans, Douglas Harbor. No. 483, Black swans, Curraghs Wildlife Park. No. 484, Whooper swans, Bishops Dub, Ballaugh. No. 485, Bewick's swans, Eairy Dam, Foxdale. No. 486, Coscaroba swans, Curraghs Wildlife Park. No. 487, Trumpeter swans, Corraghs Wildlife Park.

1991, Sept. 18   Perf. 13

482	A127	17p multicolored	.75	.75
483	A127	17p multicolored	.75	.75
a.		Pair, #482-483	1.50	1.50
484	A127	26p multicolored	1.25	1.25
485	A127	26p multicolored	1.25	1.25
a.		Pair, #484-485	2.75	2.75
486	A127	37p multicolored	1.60	1.60
487	A127	37p multicolored	1.60	1.60
a.		Pair, #486-487	3.50	3.50
		Nos. 482-487 (6)	7.20	7.20

Pairs have continuous designs.

Christmas — A128

1991, Oct. 14   Perf. 14x14½

488	A128	16p Three kings	.55	.55
489	A128	20p Jesus in manger, Mary	.70	.70
490	A128	26p Shepherds	.90	.90
491	A128	37p Angels	1.25	1.25
		Nos. 488-491 (4)	3.40	3.40

Litho.
Die Cut
Self-Adhesive Booklet Stamps

492	A128	16p like #488	1.00	1.00
493	A128	20p like #489	1.25	1.25
a.		Bklt. pane, 8 #492, 4 #493	13.50	13.50
		Complete booklet, 2 #493a	27.00	

Queen Elizabeth II's Accession to the Throne, 40th Anniv. — A129

Various portraits of Queen Elizabeth II.

1992, Feb. 6   Litho.   Perf. 14

494	A129	18p multicolored	.60	.60
495	A129	23p multicolored	.80	.80
496	A129	28p multicolored	1.00	1.00
497	A129	33p multicolored	1.10	1.10
498	A129	39p multicolored	1.50	1.50
		Nos. 494-498 (5)	5.00	5.00

Parachute Regiment, 50th Anniv. A130

Designs: No. 499, North Africa & Italy, 1942-43. No. 500, Operation Overlord, Normandy, 1944. No. 501, Operation Market Garden, Arnhem, 1944. No. 502, Operation Varsity, Rhine, 1945. No. 503, Near, Middle and Far East, 1945-68. No. 504, Operation Corporate, Falkland Islands, 1982, and Utrinque Paratus, 1992.

1992, Feb. 6   Perf. 14

499	A130	23p multicolored	.80	.80
500	A130	23p multicolored	.80	.80
a.		Pair, #499-500	1.60	1.60
501	A130	28p multicolored	1.00	1.00
502	A130	28p multicolored	1.00	1.00
a.		Pair, #501-502	2.00	2.00
503	A130	39p multicolored	1.50	1.50
504	A130	39p multicolored	1.50	1.50
a.		Pair, #503-504	3.00	3.00
		Nos. 499-504 (6)	6.60	6.60

Printed in sheets of 8.

Pilgrims' Voyage to America, 1620 — A131

Europa: No. 505, Pilgrims in longboats. No. 506, Speedwell, Delfshaven, Holland. No. 507, Mayflower. No. 508, Speedwell, Dartmouth, England.

1992, Apr. 16   Litho.   Perf. 14x13½

505	A131	18p multicolored	.80	.80
506	A131	18p multicolored	.80	.80
a.		Pair, #505-506	1.60	1.60
507	A131	28p multicolored	1.75	1.75
508	A131	28p multicolored	1.75	1.75
a.		Pair, #507-508	3.50	3.50
		Nos. 505-508 (4)	5.10	5.10

Nos. 506a, 508a have continuous design.

Port Erin Marine Laboratory, Cent. A132

1992, Apr. 16   Perf. 14½

509	A132	18p Brittle stars	.65	.65
510	A132	23p Phytoplankton	.85	.85
511	A132	28p Herring	1.00	1.00
512	A132	33p Great scallop	1.10	1.10
513	A132	39p Dahlia anemone, delesseria	1.40	1.40
		Nos. 509-513 (5)	5.00	5.00

Union Pacific, First Transcontinental Railroad — A133

#514, "Jupiter," 1869. #515, "#119," 1869. #516, "#844," 1992. #517, "#3985," 1992. £1.50, Golden Spike Ceremony, Union Pacific and Central Pacific Railroads, 1869.

1992, May 22   Litho.   Perf. 13½x14

514	A133	33p multicolored	1.10	1.10
515	A133	33p multicolored	1.10	1.10
a.		Pair, #514-515 + label	2.25	2.25
516	A133	39p multicolored	1.40	1.40
517	A133	39p multicolored	1.40	1.40
a.		Pair, #516-517 + label	3.00	3.00
b.		Bklt. pane, 1 ea #515a, 517a	5.25	

Souvenir Sheet

518	A133	£1.50 multicolored	6.00	6.00
a.		Booklet pane, #518	6.00	
b.		Bklt. pane, #518a, 2 #517b	17.00	
		Complete booklet, #518b	17.00	

World Columbian Stamp Expo '92. No. 518 contains one 60x50mm stamp. Nos. 514-515 and 516-517 issued in sheets of 10. Nos. 515a, 517a have 3 different labels. No. 517b exists with two different pairs of labels. No. 518a has a rouletted white border at left and right.

Manx Harbors — A134

#519, King Orry V, Douglas Harbor. 23p, Castletown Harbor. 37p, Port St. Mary Harbor. 40p, Ramsey Harbor. a, King Orry V. b, St. Eloi. Illustration reduced.

1992, Sept. 18   Litho.   Perf. 14½x14

519	A134	18p multicolored	.60	.60
520	A134	23p multicolored	.75	.75
521	A134	37p multicolored	1.40	1.40
522	A134	40p multicolored	1.75	1.75
		Nos. 519-522 (4)	4.50	4.50

Souvenir Sheet

523		Sheet of 2	4.75	4.75
a.		A134 18p multicolored	.75	.75
b.		A134 £1 multicolored	4.00	4.00

Genoa '92. #523 contains 30x24mm stamps.

Christmas — A135

Designs: 17p, Nativity window, St. German's Cathedral, Peel. 22p, Adoration of the Magi panel, St. Matthew's Church, Douglas. 28p, Nativity window, St. George's Church, Douglas. 37p, Reredos of The Annunciation, St. Mary of the Isle, Douglas. 40p, Good Shepherd window, Trinity Methodist Church, Douglas.

1992, Oct. 13   Litho.   Perf. 14½

524	A135	17p multicolored	.55	.55
525	A135	22p multicolored	.75	.75
526	A135	28p multicolored	1.00	1.00
527	A135	37p multicolored	1.25	1.25
528	A135	40p multicolored	1.40	1.40
		Nos. 524-528 (5)	4.95	4.95

Nigel Mansell, Formula I World Champion, 1992 — A136

Williams Renault FW 14B at: 20p, British Grand Prix, 1992. 24p, French Grand Prix, 1992.

1992, Nov. 8   Perf. 13½

529	A136	20p multicolored	.85	.85
530	A136	24p multicolored	1.00	1.00

Ships A137

Royal Ensign of the Isle of Man — A137a

Queen Elizabeth II — A137b

1993-96   Litho.   Perf. 13½

531	A137	1p HMS Amazon	.20	.20
532	A137	2p Fingal	.20	.20
533	A137	4p Sir Winston Churchill	.20	.20
a.		Inscribed "1997"	.20	.20
534	A137	5p Dar Mlodziezy	.20	.20
543	A137	20p Tynwald I	.45	.45
a.		Inscribed "1995"	.45	.45
544	A137	21p Ben Veg	.55	.55
a.		Inscribed "1997"	.55	.55
545	A137	22p Waverley	.55	.55
546	A137	23p HMY Britannia	.60	.60
a.		Souv. sheet of 1, Perf. 13	1.00	1.00
547	A137	24p Francis Drake	.55	.55
a.		Bklt. pane, 4 #543, 6 #547	5.50	
		Complete booklet, #547a	5.50	
b.		Bklt. pane, 2 #543, 3 #547	2.75	
		Complete booklet, #547b	2.75	
c.		Inscribed "1995"	.55	.55
548	A137	25p Royal Viking Sky	.65	.65
a.		Booklet pane, 2 #533, 2 #544, 2 #548	4.25	
		Complete booklet, #548a	4.25	
b.		Inscribed "1997"	.65	.65
549	A137	26p Lord Nelson	.70	.70
550	A137	27p Europa	.70	.70
551	A137	30p Snaefell V	.80	.80
551A	A137	35p Sea Cat	.95	.95
552	A137	40p Lady of Mann I	1.10	1.10
553	A137	50p Mona's Queen II	1.40	1.40
553A	A137	£1 QE2, Mona's Queen V	3.50	3.50
a.		Inscribed "1997"	3.50	3.50

Perf. 14½

553B	A137a	£2 multicolored	6.00	6.00
553C	A137b	£5 multicolored	17.00	17.00
		Nos. 531-553C (19)	36.30	36.30

#546a, for return of Hong Kong to China, is wmk. 373.
No. 553C has a holographic image. Soaking in water may affect the hologram.
Issued: 1p-5p, 20p-27p, 1/4/93; 30p, 40p-£1, 9/15/93; £2, 1/24/94; £5, 7/5/94; 35p, 1/11/96; #546a, 7/1/97; #548a, 1997. Nos. 533, 544, 546a, 548, 548a, 553A dated "1997."
See Nos. 683-697.

Manx Electric Railway, Cent. — A138

20p, #13 trailer, #1 motor car. 24p, #19 trailer, #9 tunnel car. 28p, #59 Royal trailer special saloon car, #19 motor car. 39p, #33 motor car, #45 trailer, #13 small van. Illustration reduced.

1993, Feb. 3   Perf. 14

554	A138	20p multicolored	.75	.75
555	A138	24p multicolored	.85	.85
556	A138	28p multicolored	1.10	1.10
557	A138	39p multicolored	1.25	1.25
a.		Booklet pane of #554-557	4.25	4.25
		Complete booklet, 4 #557a	17.00	
		Nos. 554-557 (4)	3.95	3.95

No. 557a exists with four different marginal inscriptions and in four different arrangements.

Contemporary Art by Bryan Kneale — A139

Europa: No. 558, Statue of Sir Hall Caine. No. 559, Painting, The Brass Bedstead. No. 560, Abstract bronze. No. 561, Drawing of polar bear skeleton.

1993, Apr. 14   Litho.   Perf. 14

558	A139	20p multicolored	.80	.80
559	A139	20p multicolored	.80	.80
a.		Pair, #558-559	1.60	1.60
560	A139	28p multicolored	1.00	1.00
561	A139	28p multicolored	1.00	1.00
a.		Pair, #560-561	2.00	2.00
		Nos. 558-561 (4)	3.60	3.60

Motorcycling Events — A140

Riders and events: 20p, Gold Medalists Graham Oates, Bill Marshall, Intl. Six-Day Trial, 1933, Ariel Square Four. 24p, Geoff Duke, Team Sergeant, Royal Signals Display Team, 1947, Triumph Twin. 28p, Denis Parkinson, winner of Senior Manx Grand Prix, 1953, Manx Norton. 33p, Richard Swallow, winner of Junior Classic Manx Grand Prix, 1991, Aermacchi. 39p, Steve Colley, winner of Scottish Six-Day Trial, 1992, Beta Zero.

1993, June 3   Litho.   Perf. 13½x14

562	A140	20p multicolored	.80	.80
563	A140	24p multicolored	.85	.85
564	A140	28p multicolored	1.00	1.00
565	A140	33p multicolored	1.25	1.25
566	A140	39p multicolored	1.40	1.40
a.		Souv. sheet of 5, #562-566 + 4 labels	5.50	5.50
		Nos. 562-566 (5)	5.30	5.30

Butterflies A141

1993, Sept. 15   Litho.   Perf. 14½

567	A141	24p Dark green fritillary	.85	.85
568	A141	24p Painted lady	.85	.85
569	A141	24p Holly blue	.85	.85
570	A141	24p Red admiral	.85	.85
571	A141	24p Peacock	.85	.85
a.		Strip of 5, #567-571	4.50	4.50

Christmas — A142

Designs: 19p, Children decorating Christmas tree. 23p, Snowman, girl. 28p, Boy unwrapping presents. 39p, Girl with holly basket, boy on sled.

Tourism A143

No. 577, Gaiety Theatre, Douglas. No. 578, Field hockey, golf, soccer (#577). No. 579, Yacht racing, artist's hand painting picture of castle (#580). No. 580, TT Motorcycle Races, Red Arrows demonstration squadron. (#581). No. 581, Musical instruments. No. 582, Laxey Wheel, Manx cat. No. 583, Tower of Refuge, beach, sand bucket (#584). No. 584, Cyclist. No. 585, Tynwald Day, classic racing car (#579, 580, 584, 586). No. 586, Santa Claus riding Mince Pie Train, Groudle Glen.

1994, Feb, 18   Litho.   Perf. 13½
Booklet Stamps

577	A143	24p multicolored	.80	.80
578	A143	24p multicolored	.80	.80
579	A143	24p multicolored	.80	.80
580	A143	24p multicolored	.80	.80
581	A143	24p multicolored	.80	.80
582	A143	24p multicolored	.80	.80
583	A143	24p multicolored	.80	.80
584	A143	24p multicolored	.80	.80
585	A143	24p multicolored	.80	.80
586	A143	24p multicolored	.80	.80
a.		Booklet pane of 10, #577-586	8.25	
		Complete booklet, #586a	8.25	

Birds A144

Magpie, Calf of Man Bird Observatory — A145

1994, Feb. 18   Perf. 14

587	A144	20p White-throated robin	.80	.80
588	A144	20p Black-eared wheatear	.80	.80
a.		Pair, #587-588	1.60	1.60
589	A144	24p Goldcrest	.95	.95
590	A144	24p Northern oriole	.95	.95
a.		Pair, #589-590	1.90	1.90
591	A144	30p Kingfisher	1.25	1.25
592	A144	30p Hoopoe	1.25	1.25
a.		Pair, #591-592	2.50	2.50
		Nos. 587-592 (6)	6.00	6.00

Souvenir Sheet
Perf. 13½x13

593	A145	£1 shown	4.00	4.00

Hong Kong '94 (#593).

Europa A146

Designs, Forbes and Discoveries: No. 594, Eubranchus tricolor. No. 595, Loligo forbesii. No. 596, Edward Forbes (1815-54), naturalist. No. 597, Solaster moretonis. No. 598, Adamsia carciniopados on hermit crab. No. 599, Solaster endeca.

1994, May 5   Litho.   Perf. 13¼x14½

594	A146	20p multicolored	.80	.80
595	A146	20p multicolored	.80	.80
596	A146	20p multicolored	.80	.80
a.		Strip of 3, #594-596	2.40	2.40
597	A146	30p multicolored	1.25	1.25
598	A146	30p multicolored	1.25	1.25
599	A146	30p multicolored	1.25	1.25
a.		Strip of 3, #597-599	3.75	3.75

D-Day, 50th Anniv. A147

Designs: No. 600, Transport Ben-My-Chree IV, landing ships, US Maj. Gen. Walter Bedell Smith. No. 601, Transports Victoria, Lady of Mann I, Adm. Sir Bertram Ramsay, RN, Naval Commander. No. 602, Infantry, tanks on Gold, Juno, Sword Beaches, Gen. Montgomery, Commander, 21st Army Group. No. 603, Tanks, landing craft on Gold, Juno, Sword Beaches, Lt. Gen. Sir Miles C. Dempsey, Commander, British 2nd Army. No. 604, US 8th, 9th Air Forces, Air Chief Marshal Sir Trafford Leigh-Mallory, RAF, Air Force Commander. No. 605, Air Chief Marshall Sir Arthur Tedder, RAF, Deputy Supreme Allied Commander, RAF 2nd Tactical Air Force & Bomber Command. No. 606, Landing craft, Omaha, Utah Beaches, Lt. Gen. Omar N. Bradley, Commander, US 1st Army. No. 607, Infantry, tanks on Omaha, Utah Beaches, Gen. Eisenhower, Supreme Allied Commander.

1994, June 6   Litho.   Perf. 14

600	A147	4p multicolored	.20	.20
601	A147	4p multicolored	.20	.20
a.		Pair, #600-601	.25	.25
602	A147	20p multicolored	.75	.75
603	A147	20p multicolored	.75	.75
a.		Pair, #602-603	1.50	1.50
604	A147	30p multicolored	1.10	1.10
605	A147	30p multicolored	1.10	1.10
a.		Pair, #604-605	2.25	2.25
606	A147	41p multicolored	1.60	1.60
607	A147	41p multicolored	1.60	1.60
a.		Pair, #606-607	3.25	3.25
		Nos. 600-607 (8)	7.30	7.30

Nos. 601a, 603a, 605a, 607a are continuous designs.

Postman Pat A148

Postman Pat at: 1p, Sea Terminal, Douglas. 20p, Laxey Wheel. 24p, Cregneash. 30p, Manx Electric Railway. 36p, Peel Harbor. 41p, Tourist office, Douglas Promenade. £1, Postman Pat.

1994, Sept. 14   Litho.   Perf. 14½x14

608	A148	1p multicolored	.20	.20
a.		Booklet pane of 2	.20	
609	A148	20p multicolored	.65	.65
a.		Booklet pane of 2	1.40	
610	A148	24p multicolored	.80	.80
a.		Booklet pane of 2	1.60	
611	A148	30p multicolored	1.00	1.00
a.		Booklet pane of 2	2.10	
612	A148	36p multicolored	1.25	1.25
a.		Booklet pane of 2	2.50	
613	A148	41p multicolored	1.40	1.40
a.		Booklet pane of 2	3.00	
		Nos. 608-613 (6)	5.30	5.30

Souvenir Sheet

614	A148	£1 multicolored	4.00	4.00
a.		Booklet pane of 1	4.00	4.00
		Complete booklet, #608a-614a	16.00	

No. 614a is rouletted 9 at left.

Intl. Olympic Committee, Cent. — A149

1994, Oct. 11   Perf. 14

615	A149	10p Cycling	.40	.40
616	A149	20p Alpine skiing	.75	.75
617	A149	24p Swimming	.90	.90

618	A149	35p Steeplechase	1.40	1.40
619	A149	48p Emblem	1.60	1.60
		Nos. 615-619 (5)	5.05	5.05

A150

1994, Oct. 11

Christmas: 19p, Santa, Mrs. Claus greeting children on Santa Train to Santon, horiz. 23p, Santa Claus on tractor, Postman Pat. 60p, Santa Claus arriving by boat, Port St. Mary, horiz.

620	A150	19p multicolored	.75	.75
621	A150	23p multicolored	1.00	1.00
622	A150	60p multicolored	2.00	2.00
		Nos. 620-622 (3)	3.75	3.75

Snaefell Mountain Electric Railway, Cent. — A151

Designs: 20p, Opening day, Car No. 2. 24p, Car 3 ascending Laxey Valley, Car 4 in green livery. 35p, Car 5, Car 6. 42p, Caledonia on construction duty, Goods Car 7. £1, Bungalow Hotel & Station, Snaefell. Illustration reduced.

1995, Feb. 8   Litho.   Perf. 14

623	A151	20p multicolored	.75	.75
624	A151	24p multicolored	.95	.95
625	A151	35p multicolored	1.40	1.40
626	A151	42p multicolored	1.60	1.60
a.		Bklt. pane, #623-626	4.75	
		Nos. 623-626 (4)	4.70	4.70

Souvenir Sheet
Perf. 14x13½

627	A151	£1 multicolored	4.00	4.00
a.		Sheet from souvenir booklet	4.00	4.00
		Complete booklet, 3 #626a, #627a	18.50	

No. 627 contains one 61x38mm stamp.
No. 626a comes with three different arrangements of the stamps. Value the same for each.
No. 627a is rouletted in margin at left with additional vertical sheet margin inscriptions. At left is a description of the design. At right is "1895-Centenary Snaefell Mountain Railway-1995."

Steam-Powered Vehicles — A152

Designs: 20p, Foden Wagon, 5 ton. 24p, Clayton & Shuttleworth, 7hp, Fowler, 6hp. 30p, Wallis & Steevens, 6hp. 35p, Marshall, 6hp. 41p, Marshall Convertible, 5hp.

1995, Feb. 8   Perf. 13½

628	A152	20p multicolored	.70	.70
629	A152	24p multicolored	.90	.90
630	A152	30p multicolored	1.10	1.10
631	A152	35p multicolored	1.40	1.40
632	A152	41p multicolored	1.50	1.50
		Nos. 628-632 (5)	5.60	5.60

Peace & Freedom — A153

Europa: 20p, Flight of doves forming tidal wave, Tower of Refuge, Douglas Bay. 30p, Dove with olive branch breaking barbed wire.

1995, Apr. 28   Litho.   Perf. 13½

633	A153	20p multicolored	.80	.80
634	A153	30p multicolored	1.25	1.25

VE Day, 50th Anniv. A154

Designs: No. 635, Spitfire, tank, 1939-45 Star, African Star. No. 636, France and Germany Star, Italy Star, Hawker Typhoon, artillery. No. 637, Lancaster bomber, aircraft carrier, Air Crew Europe Star, Atlantic Star. No. 638, Pacific Star, Burma Star, Avenger torpedo bomber, soldiers. No. 639, Parliament, Manx flag. No. 640, British flag, crowd celebrating. No. 641, Children celebrating at street party, Manx flag. No. 642, British flag, visit of Queen Elizabeth, King George VI, 1945.

1995, May 8   Perf. 14

635	A154	10p multicolored	.40	.40
636	A154	10p multicolored	.40	.40
a.		Pair, #635-636	.80	.80
637	A154	24p multicolored	.75	.75
638	A154	24p multicolored	.75	.75
a.		Pair, #637-638	1.50	1.50
639	A154	24p multicolored	.85	.85
640	A154	24p multicolored	.85	.85
a.		Pair, #639-640	1.75	1.75
641	A154	40p multicolored	1.50	1.50
642	A154	40p multicolored	1.50	1.50
a.		Pair, #641-642	3.25	3.25
		Nos. 635-642 (8)	7.00	7.00

British Motor Car Racing, 90th Anniv. A155

Tourist Trophy Race drivers, cars: 20p, R. Parnell, 1951 Maserati 4 CLT. 24p, S. Moss, 1951 Frazer Nash. 30p, R.J.B. Seaman, 1936 Delage. 36p, Prince Bira, 1937 ERA R2B Romulus. 41p, K. Lee Guinness, 1914 Sunbeam 1. 42p, F. Dixon, 1934 Riley. £1, John S. Napier, 1905 Arrol Johnston.

1995, May 8

643	A155	20p multicolored	.75	.75
644	A155	24p multicolored	.90	.90
645	A155	30p multicolored	1.10	1.10
646	A155	36p multicolored	1.40	1.40
647	A155	41p multicolored	1.50	1.50
648	A155	42p multicolored	1.60	1.60
		Nos. 643-648 (6)	7.25	7.25

Souvenir Sheet

649	A155	£1 multicolored	4.00	4.00

No. 649 contains one 47x58mm stamp.

Mushrooms A156

Designs: 20p, Amanita muscaria. 24p, Boletus edulis. 30p, Coprinus disseminatus. 35p, Pleurotus ostreatus. 45p, Geastrum triplex. £1, Shaggy ink cap, bee orchid.

1995, Sept. 1   Litho.   Perf. 13½x14

650	A156	20p multicolored	.80	.80
651	A156	24p multicolored	.95	.95
652	A156	30p multicolored	1.25	1.25

653	A156	35p multicolored	1.40	1.40
654	A156	45p multicolored	1.75	1.75
		Nos. 650-654 (5)	6.15	6.15

Souvenir Sheet
Perf. 14x13½

655	A156	£1 multicolored	4.00	4.00

No. 655 contains one 51x60mm stamp. Singapore '95 (#655).

Thomas the Tank Engine A157

Designs: 20p, Bertie arrives on the quayside. 24p, Mail train and Thomas. 30p, Bertie and trains at Ballasalla. 36p, Viking and Thomas at Port Erin. 41p, The mail gets through. 45p, Race at Laxey Wheel.

1995, Sept. 1   Perf. 14

656	A157	20p multicolored	.75	.75
657	A157	24p multicolored	.85	.85
a.		Booklet pane of 2, #656-657	1.60	
658	A157	30p multicolored	1.10	1.10
a.		Booklet pane of 2, #657-658	2.00	
659	A157	36p multicolored	1.40	1.40
a.		Booklet pane of 2, #658-659	2.50	
660	A157	41p multicolored	1.50	1.50
a.		Booklet pane of 2, #659-660	3.00	
661	A157	45p multicolored	1.60	1.60
a.		Booklet pane of 2, #656, 661	2.50	
b.		Booklet pane of 2, #660-661	3.25	
		Complete booklet, #657a, 658a, 659a, 660a, 661a-661b	16.00	
		Nos. 656-661 (6)	7.20	7.20

Christmas A158

Designs: 19p, Church, holly. 23p, Bird on holly branch. 42p, Snow crocuses, church. 50p, Antique farming equipment in snow.

1995, Oct. 10   Litho.   Perf. 14x14½

662	A158	19p multicolored	.70	.70
663	A158	23p multicolored	.80	.80
664	A158	42p multicolored	1.50	1.50
665	A158	50p multicolored	1.75	1.75
		Nos. 662-665 (4)	4.75	4.75

Lighthouses — A159

Location, year opened: 20p, Langness, 1880, vert. 24p, Point of Ayre, 1818. 30p, Chicken Rock, 1873, vert. 36p, Calf of Man, 1818. 41p, Douglas Head, 1832. vert. 42p, Maughold Head, 1914.

1996, Feb. 27   Litho.   Perf. 14

666	A159	20p multicolored	.70	.70
a.		Booklet pane of 4 + 4 labels	3.00	
667	A159	24p multicolored	.80	.80
a.		Booklet pane of 4	3.25	
668	A159	30p multicolored	1.10	1.10
669	A159	36p multicolored	1.25	1.25
670	A159	41p multicolored	1.50	1.50
a.		Booklet pane, 2 each #668, 670 + 4 labels	5.25	
671	A159	42p multicolored	1.50	1.50
a.		Bklt. pane, 2 ea #669, 671	5.50	
		Complete booklet, #666a, 667a, 670a, 671a	17.50	
		Nos. 666-671 (6)	6.85	6.85

Manx Cats A160

Various cats and: 20p, Arms of Man. 24p, British Union Flag as of ball yarn. 36p, Brandenburg Gate. 42p, US flag, Statue of Liberty. 48p, Australian flag, map.
£1.50, Gray adult cat, gray and yellow kittens.

1996, Mar. 14
672	A160	20p multicolored	.70	.70
673	A160	24p multicolored	.80	.80
674	A160	36p multicolored	1.25	1.25
675	A160	42p multicolored	1.50	1.50
676	A160	48p multicolored	1.75	1.75
		Nos. 672-676 (5)	6.00	6.00

Souvenir Sheet
677	A160	£1.50 multicolored	6.00	6.00
a.		With additional inscription	12.00	12.00

No. 677 contains one 51x60mm stamp. No. 677a contains CAPEX '96 exhibition emblem in sheet margin. Issued 6/8/96.

Douglas Borough, Cent. — A161

Die Cut Perf. 9x9½
1996, Mar. 14   **Litho.**
Self-Adhesive
678	A161	(40p) multicolored	1.50	1.50

The backing of No. 678 is rouletted 13.

Women of Achievement — A162

Europa: 24p, Princess Anne, children of different nations. 30p, Queen Elizabeth II, people of different nations.

1996   **Perf. 14**
679	A162	24p multicolored	.90	.90
680	A162	30p multicolored	1.25	1.25

Queen Elizabeth II, 70th birthday (#680). See Guernsey Nos. 564-565.

Ship Type of 1993
1996   **Litho.**   **Perf. 14**
Size: 21x19mm
683	A137	4p like #533	.20	.20
693	A137	20p like #543	.80	.80
697	A137	24p like #547	.90	.90
		Nos. 683-697 (3)	1.90	1.90
a.		Bklt. pane, 2 ea 4p, 20p, 24p	4.00	
		Complete booklet, No. 697a	4.00	

Irish Winners of Tourist Trophy Motorcycle Races — A163

20p, Alec Bennett. 24p, Stanley Woods. 45p, Artie Bell. 60p, Robert & Joey Dunlop.
£1, Demonstration squadron Hawks flying over motorcycles, vert.

1996, May 30   **Litho.**   **Perf. 14**
701	A163	20p multicolored	.75	.75
702	A163	24p multicolored	.85	.85
703	A163	45p multicolored	1.60	1.60
704	A163	60p multicolored	2.10	2.10
		Nos. 701-704 (4)	5.30	5.30

Souvenir Sheet
705	A163	£1 multicolored	3.75	3.75

See Ireland Nos. 1010-1014.

Royal British Legion, 75th Anniv. — A164

Poppies and: 20p, National poppy appeal trophy. 24p, Manx war memorial. 42p, Poppy appeal. 75p, Crest.

1996, June 8
706	A164	20p multicolored	.75	.75
707	A164	24p multicolored	.85	.85
708	A164	42p multicolored	1.60	1.60
709	A164	75p multicolored	2.75	2.75
		Nos. 706-709 (4)	5.95	5.95

UNICEF, 50th Anniv. A165

Children receiving aid, map of country: #710, Mexico. #711, Sri Lanka. #712, Colombia. #713, Zambia. #714, Afghanistan. #715, Viet Nam.

1996, Sept. 18   Litho.   Perf. 13½x14
710	A165	24p multicolored	.85	.85
711	A165	24p multicolored	.85	.85
a.		Pair, #710-711	1.75	1.75
712	A165	30p multicolored	1.10	1.10
713	A165	30p multicolored	1.10	1.10
a.		Pair, #712-713	2.25	2.25
714	A165	42p multicolored	1.60	1.60
715	A165	42p multicolored	1.60	1.60
a.		Pair, #714-715	3.25	3.25
		Nos. 710-715 (6)	7.10	7.10

Dogs — A166

1996, Sept. 18   **Perf. 14½**
716	A166	20p Labrador	.75	.75
a.		Booklet pane of 4	3.00	
717	A166	24p Border collie	.80	.80
a.		Booklet pane of 4	3.25	
718	A166	31p Dalmatian	1.10	1.10
719	A166	38p Mongrel	1.40	1.40
720	A166	43p English setter	1.60	1.60
721	A166	63p Alsatian	2.40	2.40
a.		Booklet pane, 1 each #718-721	6.50	
		Nos. 716-721 (6)	8.05	8.05

Souvenir Sheet
Perf. 13½x14
722	A166	£1.20 Border collie, labrador	4.75	4.75
a.		Booklet pane of 1	4.75	
		Complete booklet, #716a, 717a, 721a, 722a	19.00	

Nos. 716-721 are each printed with se-tenant label. No. 722 contains one 38x50mm stamp. No. 722a is rouletted around margin of sheet.

Christmas A167

Children's drawings: 19p, Snowman. 23p, Santa, "Happy Christmas" in Manx. 50p, Family, Christmas tree, presents. 75p, Santa in sleigh flying over rooftops.

1996, Nov. 2   Litho.   Perf. 14x14½
723	A167	19p multicolored	.70	.70
724	A167	23p multicolored	.80	.80
725	A167	50p multicolored	1.60	1.60
726	A167	75p multicolored	2.75	2.75
		Nos. 723-726 (4)	5.85	5.85

Owls — A168

1997, Feb. 12   Litho.   Perf. 14
727	A168	20p Barn owl	.75	.75
a.		Booklet pane of 4	3.00	
728	A168	24p Short-eared owl	.85	.85
a.		Booklet pane of 4	3.50	
729	A168	31p Long-eared owl	1.10	1.10
730	A168	36p Little owl	1.25	1.25
731	A168	43p Snowy owl	1.60	1.60
732	A168	56p Tawny owl	2.00	2.00
a.		Booklet pane of 4, #729-732	6.00	
		Nos. 727-732 (6)	7.55	7.55

Souvenir Sheet
Perf. 13
733	A168	£1.20 Long-eared owl	4.00	4.00
a.		Booklet pane of 1	4.00	
		Complete booklet, #727a, 728a, 732a, 733a	16.50	

No. 733, 733a each contain one 56x60mm stamp. No. 733a is rouletted at left. Hong Kong '97 (#733, 733a).

Springtime A169

1997, Feb. 12   **Perf. 14**
734	A169	20p Spring flowers	.70	.70
735	A169	24p Sheep	.80	.80
736	A169	43p Waterfowl	1.60	1.60
737	A169	63p Frog, ducks	2.40	2.40
		Nos. 734-737 (4)	5.50	5.50

Stories and Legends A170

21p, Moddey Dhoo. 25p, The Trammen Tree. 31p, Fairy Bridge. 36p, Fin Macooil. 37p, The Buggane of St. Trinian's. 43p, Fynoderee.

1997, Apr. 24   Litho.   Perf. 13½x14
738	A170	21p multicolored	.70	.70
739	A170	25p multicolored	.85	.85
740	A170	31p multicolored	1.10	1.10
741	A170	36p multicolored	1.25	1.25
742	A170	37p multicolored	1.25	1.25
743	A170	43p multicolored	1.60	1.60
		Nos. 738-743 (6)	6.75	6.75

Europa (#739-740).

Aircraft A171

Designs: No. 744, Sopwith Tabloid. No. 745, Grumman Tiger. No. 746, Manx Airlines BAe ATP. No. 747, Manx Airlines BAe 146-200. No. 748 Boeing 757-200. No. 749, Farman biplane. No. 750, Spitfire. No. 751, Hurricane.

1997, Apr. 24   **Perf. 14**
744	A171	21p multicolored	.70	.70
745	A171	21p multicolored	.70	.70
a.		Pair, #744-745	1.40	1.40
746	A171	25p multicolored	.85	.85
747	A171	25p multicolored	.85	.85
a.		Pair, #746-747	1.75	1.75
748	A171	31p multicolored	1.10	1.10
749	A171	31p multicolored	1.10	1.10
a.		Pair, #748-749	2.25	2.25
750	A171	36p multicolored	1.25	1.25
751	A171	36p multicolored	1.25	1.25
a.		Pair, #750-751	2.50	2.50
		Nos. 744-751 (8)	7.80	7.80

Golf Courses A172

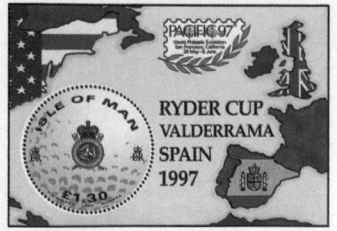

1997 Ryder Cup, Valderrama, Spain — A173

21p, 14th Hole, Ramsey Golf Club. 25p, 15th Hole, King Edward Bay Golf and Country Club. 43p, 17th Hole, Rowany Golf Club. 50p, 8th Hole, Castletown Golf Links.

1997, May 29   **Perf. 14**
752	A172	21p multicolored	.70	.70
a.		Booklet pane of 3	2.10	
753	A172	25p multicolored	.90	.90
a.		Booklet pane of 3	2.75	
754	A172	43p multicolored	1.60	1.60
755	A172	50p multicolored	1.75	1.75
a.		Bklt. pane, 2 ea #754-755	6.75	
		Nos. 752-755 (4)	4.95	4.95

Souvenir Sheet
756	A173	£1.30 multicolored	5.25	5.25
a.		Booklet pane of 1	5.25	
		Complete booklet, #752a, 753a, 753a, 756a	17.00	

PACIFIC 97 (#756). No. 756 contains one 40mm diameter stamp.
No. 756a has a large white border, is 155x96mm and is sewn into booklet.

Trial of Nations Motorcycle Competition — A174

Various motorcyclists: 21p, Steve Colley. 25p, Steve Saunders. 37p, Sammy Miller. 44p, Don Smith.

1997, Sept. 29   Litho.   Perf. 13½
757	A174	21p multicolored	.70	.70
758	A174	25p multi, vert.	.85	.85
759	A174	37p multi, vert.	1.40	1.40
760	A174	44p multicolored	1.60	1.60
		Nos. 757-760 (4)	4.55	4.55

Queen Elizabeth II and Prince Philip, 50th Wedding Anniv. — A175

Designs: a, Early drawing of couple. b, Wedding portrait. c, Drawing of Queen waving, Prince in top hat. d, Portrait, 1997.
£1, Queen, Prince touring Isle of Man, 1989.

1997, Nov. 3   Litho.   Perf. 14x14½
761	A175	50p Strip of 4, #a.-d.	7.00	7.00

Souvenir Sheet
Perf. 14
762	A175	£1 multicolored	3.75	3.75

No. 761 was issued in sheets of 16 stamps. No. 762 contains one 48x58mm stamp.

Christmas — A176

1997, Nov. 3   *Perf. 14*
763 A176 20p Angel, shepherd   .75   .75
764 A176 24p Wise man, angel   .85   .85

Size: 54x39mm
765 A176 63p Angel and one of
             the Three Kings   2.40 2.40
       Nos. 763-765 (3)   4.00 4.00

Flowers — A177

1998, Feb. 12 Litho. Perf. 13x13½
766 A177   4p Shamrocks   .20   .20
767 A177 21p Cushag   .80   .80
768 A177 25p Princess of
             Wales Rose   1.00 1.00
       Complete booklet, 2 each #766-
             768   4.00
769 A177 50p Daffodil   2.00 2.00
770 A177 £1 Spear thistle   4.00 4.00
       Nos. 766-770 (5)   8.00 8.00

Nos. 766-768 also exist in special booklet sheets containing 10 of each denomination. Booklet panes made from these sheets contain 2 each #766-768.
No. 766 exists dated "1999."
See Nos. 794-801.

A178

Viking Longships: 21p, Dragon's head figurehead. 25p, Ship under full sail. 31p, Ship with sail furled. 75p Ship's stern.
£1, Man on ship pointing, fortress.

1998, Feb. 14   *Perf. 14*
771 A178 21p multicolored   .80   .80
772 A178 25p multicolored   1.00 1.00
773 A178 31p multicolored   1.25 1.25
774 A178 75p multicolored   3.00 3.00
       Nos. 771-774 (4)   6.05 6.05
       Souvenir Sheet
775 A178 £1 multicolored   4.00 4.00

Marine
Life
A179

Designs: 10p, Bottle-nosed dolphin. 21p, Basking shark swimming right. 25p, Basking shark swimming forward. 31p, Minke whale. 63p, Killer whale.

1998, Mar. 14 Litho. Perf. 14
776 A179 10p multicolored   .40   .40
777 A179 21p multicolored   .80   .80
  a.   Booklet pane of 6, 3 each
         #776-777 + 3 labels   3.75
778 A179 25p multicolored   1.00 1.00
779 A179 31p multicolored   1.25 1.25
780 A179 63p multicolored   2.40 2.40
  a.   Bklt. pane of 8, #776-777, 2 ea
         #778-780 + label   11.00
       Souvenir booklet, #777a, 780a 15.00
       Nos. 776-780 (5)   5.85 5.85

Trains
A180

Designs: 21p, Hutchinson 2-4-0. 25p, G.H. Wood 2-4-0. 31p, Maitland 2-4-0. 63p, Loch 2-4-0.

1998, May 2 Litho. Perf. 14½x14
781 A180 21p multicolored   .80   .80
782 A180 25p multicolored   1.00 1.00
783 A180 31p multicolored   1.25 1.25
784 A180 63p multicolored   2.40 2.40
  a.   Bklt. pane of 4, #781-784   5.50 5.50
       Nos. 781-784 (4)   5.45 5.45
       Souvenir Sheet
785 A180   Sheet of 2   5.50 5.50
  a.   £1 Engine   4.50 4.50
  b.   25p Passenger cars   1.00 1.00
  c.   Booklet pane of 1   5.50 5.50
       Complete bklt., #785c, 2 #784a 17.00
  d.   As #785, inscribed in sheet
         margin   5.50 5.50

No. 784a exists with two different backgrounds and stamps in different order. Complete booklets contain one of each pane.
No. 785d is inscribed in sheet margin with PhilexFrance '99, World Philatelic Exhibition emblem and was issued 7/2/99.

Europa
A181

National Days celebration: 25p, People under tent, seated in stand, watching ceremony. 30p, Women dancing in traditional costumes.

1998, July 2   *Perf. 13x13½*
786 A181 25p multicolored   1.00 1.00
787 A181 30p multicolored   1.25 1.25

1998 Tourist Trophy Motorcycle
Races — A182

Designs: 21p, Eight-man pyramid. 25p, Joey Dunlop rounding curve. 31p, Dave Molyneux with side car. 43p, Naomi Taniguchi racing. 63p, Mike Hailwood racing.

1998, June 1 Litho. Perf. 14
788 A182 21p multicolored   .80   .80
789 A182 25p multicolored   1.00 1.00
790 A182 31p multicolored   1.25 1.25
791 A182 43p multicolored   1.60 1.60
792 A182 63p multicolored   2.50 2.50
       Nos. 788-792 (5)   7.15 7.15

A183

Diana, Princess of Wales (1961-97): a, In black evening dress. b, Accepting flowers. c, Holding hand to face. d, In protective clothing.

1998, June 19   *Perf. 13*
793 A183 25p Strip of 4, #a.-d.   4.00 4.00

Flower Type
Perf. 13, 13x13½ (5p, 22p, 26p)
1998-99   Litho.

Flowers: 1p, Bearded iris. 2p, Daisy. 5p, Silver jubilee rose. 10p, Oriental poppy. 20p,

Heath spotted orchid. 22p, Gorse. 26p, Dog rose. 30p, Fuchsia - lady thumb.

794 A177   1p multicolored   .20   .20
795 A177   2p multicolored   .20   .20
796 A177   5p multicolored   .20   .20
797 A177 10p multicolored   .40   .40
798 A177 20p multicolored   .80   .80
799 A177 22p multicolored   .85   .85
800 A177 26p multicolored   1.00 1.00
  a.   Bklt. pane, #800, 2 #766, 3 #799 4.00
       Complete booklet, #800a   4.00
801 A177 30p multicolored   1.25 1.25
       Nos. 794-801 (8)   4.90 4.90

Issued: 5p, 22p, 26p, 4/26/99; others, 7/2/98.

Queen
Mother and
Queen
Elizabeth II
A185

1998, July 2 Litho. Perf. 13
802 A185 £2.50 multicolored   10.00 10.00

Christmas
A186

Santa Claus: 20p, Loading sleigh at North Pole. 24p, With list, reindeer standing in clouds, Isle of Man below. 30p, Going over Spring Valley Sorting Office. 43p, Passing through Baldrine. 63p, Leaving presents, children inside house.

1998, Sept. 25 Litho. Perf. 14½x14
803 A186 20p multicolored   .70   .70
804 A186 24p multicolored   .85   .85
805 A186 30p multicolored   1.25 1.25
806 A186 43p multicolored   1.60 1.60
807 A186 63p multicolored   2.50 2.50
       Nos. 803-807 (5)   6.90 6.90

Manx Nature
Reserve and Parks
(Europa) — A187

Designs: 25p, Cottage, Ballaglass Glen. 30p, Glen Maye Waterfall.

1999, Mar. 4 Litho. Perf. 14
808 A187 25p multicolored   1.00 1.00
809 A187 30p multicolored   1.25 1.25

Post
Boxes — A188

10p, Oval box, Kirk Onchan Post Office. 20p, Wall box, Ballaterson, Ballaugh. 21p, Cylindrical box, Laxey Station. 25p, Wall box, Spaldrick, Port Erin. 44p, Oval box, Derby Road, Douglas. 63p, Wall box, Baldrine Station.

1999, Mar. 4
810 A188 10p multicolored   .40   .40
811 A188 20p multicolored   .80   .80
812 A188 21p multicolored   .80   .80
813 A188 25p multicolored   .95   .95
814 A188 44p multicolored   1.60 1.60
815 A188 63p multicolored   2.40 2.40
       Nos. 810-815 (6)   6.95 6.95

Royal Natl. Lifeboat Institution, 175th
Anniv. — A189

1999, Mar. 4
816 A189 21p Ramsey lifeboat   .80   .80
817 A189 25p Douglas lifeboat   1.00 1.00
818 A189 37p Peel lifeboat   1.50 1.50
819 A189 43p Port Erin lifeboat   1.60 1.60
820 A189 56p Port St. Mary life-
             boat   2.25 2.25
  a.   Bklt. pane, #816-820 + 4 labels 7.25
       Nos. 816-820 (5)   7.15 7.15
       Booklet Stamps
821 A189 43p #38   1.60 1.60
822 A189 56p #464   2.25 2.25
  a.   Booklet pane, #816-818, #821-
         822 + 4 labels   7.25
       Souvenir Sheet
823 A189 £1 William Hillary
             (1771-1847)   4.00 4.00
  a.   Booklet pane of 1   4.00
       Complete booklet, #820a,
         #822a, #823a   19.00

IBRA '99 (#822a), Australia '99, World Stamp Expo. (#823). No. 823 contains one 38x50mm stamp.

Celtic Jewelry
Depicting
Seasons — A190

1999, May 14   *Perf. 14½x14*
824 A190 22p Winter   .85   .85
825 A190 26p Spring   1.00 1.00
826 A190 50p Summer   1.90 1.90
827 A190 63p Autumn   2.50 2.50
       Nos. 824-827 (4)   6.25 6.25

20th
Century
British
Monarchs
A191

Monarch: a, Victoria. b, Edward VII. c, George V. d, Edward VIII. e, George VI. f, Elizabeth II.

1999, June 2 Litho. Perf. 14
828 A191 26p Sheet of 6, #a.-f.   6.00 6.00

Manx
Buses
A192

22p, 1922 Tilling Stevens 46 double-decker. 26p, 1928 Thornycroft BC 28-seat. 28p, 1927 ADC 416 28-seat. 37p, 1914 Staker Squire 25-seat. 38p, 1927 Thornycroft A2 20-seat. 40p, 1938 Leyland Lion LT9 34-seat.

1999, June 18
829 A192 22p multicolored   .85   .85
830 A192 26p multicolored   1.00 1.00
831 A192 28p multicolored   1.10 1.10
832 A192 37p multicolored   1.50 1.50
833 A192 38p multicolored   1.50 1.50
834 A192 40p multicolored   1.60 1.60
       Nos. 829-834 (6)   7.55 7.55

831a   Bklt. pane, #829-830, 2 #831   4.25
832a   Bklt. pane, #829-830, 2 #832   5.00
833a   Bklt. pane, #829-830, 2 #833   5.00
834a   Bklt. pane, #829-830, 2 #834   5.25
       Complete booklet, #831a-834a 19.50

Wedding of Prince Edward and Sophie
Rhys-Jones — A193

1999, June 19
835 A193 22p Sophie, vert. .85 .85
836 A193 39p Prince Edward,
vert. 1.40 1.40
837 A193 44p Couple 1.60 1.60
Nos. 835-837 (3) 3.85 3.85

Royal Wedding
Photos — A193a

Designs: 26p, Couple standing, vert. 53p,
Couple seated in carriage.

1999, Sept. 1 Litho. Perf. 14¼
837A A193a 26p multi 1.00 1.00
837B A193a 53p multi 2.00 2.00

Churches — A194

Illustration reduced.

Perf. 13¼x13½
1999, Sept. 22 **Litho.**
838 A194 21p St. Luke, Baldwin .80 .80
839 A194 25p St. Mark's, Malew .95 .95
840 A194 30p St. Germain Parish
Church and Cathedral, Peel 1.10 1.10
841 A194 64p Kirk Christ Church,
Rushan 2.50 2.50
Nos. 838-841 (4) 5.35 5.35

Bee Gees
Songs
A195

Designs: 22p, "Massachusetts." 26p,
"Words." 29p, "I've Gotta Get a Message to
You." 37p, "Ellan Vannin." 38p, "You Win
Again." 66p, "Night Fever."
60p, "Immortality." 90p, "Stayin' Alive."

1999, Oct. 12 Litho. Perf. 13¼x13½
842 A195 22p multicolored .85 .85
843 A195 26p multicolored 1.00 1.00
844 A195 29p multicolored 1.10 1.10
845 A195 37p multicolored 1.40 1.40
846 A195 38p multicolored 1.40 1.40
847 A195 66p multicolored 2.50 2.50
Nos. 842-847 (6) 8.25 8.25

Souvenir Sheets
848 A195 60p multicolored 4.00 4.00
849 A195 90p multicolored 6.00 6.00

Nos. 848-849 each contain one 40mm
diameter stamp. Nos. 842-847 each issued in
sheets of 9 stamps and 3 labels.

Souvenir Sheet

Millennium
A196

Objects in the night sky: a, 50p, Mars, stars
Deneb, Altair, Vega. b, £2, Constellations
Lynx, Draco, Ursa Minor, Ursa Major. c, 50p,
Mercury, Venus, Deneb, Vega, Altair, orbit of
International Space Station (ISS).

Perf. 14¼x14½
1999, Dec. 31 **Litho.**
850 A196 Sheet of 3, #a.-c. 13.00 13.00

History of
Time — A197

Clock escapements of: 22p, 1735 by John
Harrison. 26p, 2000 by George Daniels. 29p,
1767 by Harrison. 34p, 1769 by Thomas
Mudge. 38p, 1779 by John Arnold. 44p, 1780
by Thomas Earnshaw.

2000, Jan. 24 Litho. Perf. 13x13½
851 A197 22p multi 1.00 1.00
852 A197 26p multi 1.10 1.10
853 A197 29p multi 1.25 1.25
854 A197 34p multi 1.50 1.50
855 A197 38p multi 1.75 1.75
856 A197 44p multi 2.00 2.00
Nos. 851-856 (6) 8.60 8.60

Queen Mother (b. 1900) — A198

Pictures of Queen Mother from — No. 857:
a, 1923. b, 1940. c, 1944.
No. 858: a, 1954. b, 1985. c, 1988.
No. 859, 1984.
£1, Queen Mother on Isle of Man.
Illustration reduced.

2000, Feb. 29 Litho. Perf. 14
857 Strip of 3 3.00 3.00
a. A198 22p multi .80 .80
b. A198 26p multi 1.00 1.00
c. A198 30p multi 1.10 1.10
858 Strip of 3 6.00 6.00
a. A198 44p multi 1.60 1.60
b. A198 52p multi 1.90 1.90
c. A198 64p multi 2.40 2.40

Souvenir Sheet
Perf. 14¼
859 A198 £1 multi 3.75 3.75
a. With emblem of The Stamp
Show 2000 in margin 7.00 7.00

Size of Nos. 857a-857c, 858a-858c,
42x28mm.
Issued: No. 859a, 5/22/00.

Song
Birds — A199

2000, May 5 Perf. 14½x14¼
860 Strip of 4 8.50 8.50
a. A199 22p Swallow 1.00 1.00
b. A199 26p Spotted flycatcher 1.10 1.10
c. A199 64p Skylark 2.75 2.75
d. A199 77p Yellowhammer 3.25 3.25

World Wildlife Fund.

Military
Leaders
and Isle of
Man
Military
Personnel
A200

Battle of Britain, 60th Anniv. — A201

#861: a, John Quilliam (1771-1829), Admiral
Lord Nelson (1758-1805). b, Caesar Bacon
(1791-1876), Duke of Wellington (1769-1852).
#862: a, Thomas Leigh Goldie (1807-54),
Earl of Cardigan (1797-1868). b, John Dunne
(1884-1950), Sir Robert Baden-Powell (1857-
1941).
#863: a, George Kneale (1896-1917), Viscount Kitchener (1850-1916). b, Alan Watterson (1910-42), Sir Winston Churchill (1874-
1965).
#864: a, Planes in air. b, Plane on ground.
Illustration A201 reduced.

2000, May 22 Litho. Perf. 13¼
861 Pair, #a-b, + central label 1.90 1.90
a. A200 22p multi .80 .80
b. A200 26p multi 1.00 1.00
862 Pair, #a-b, + central label 3.25 3.25
a. A200 36p multi 1.40 1.40
b. A200 48p multi 1.75 1.75
863 Pair, #a-b, + central label 4.75 4.75
a. A200 50p multi 1.90 1.90
b. A200 77p multi 2.75 2.75
c. Booklet pane, #861a, 861b,
862a, 862b, 863a 7.00
d. Booklet pane, #861a, 862a,
863a, 863b 6.75
Nos. 861-863 (3) 9.90 9.90

Souvenir Sheet
Perf. 14¾x14¼
864 A201 60p Sheet of 2, #a-b 5.25 5.25
c. Booklet pane, #864 5.25
Booklet, #863c, 863d, 864c 21.00

No. 864c has stitched margin at left.

Souvenir Sheet

Prince William,
18th
Birthday — A202

2000, June 21 Litho. Perf. 14
865 Sheet of 5 6.50 6.50
a. A202 22p As toddler .80 .80
b. A202 26p With Queen Mother 1.00 1.00
c. A202 45p In checked shirt 1.75 1.75
d. A202 52p With Princes Charles,
Harry 1.90 1.90
e. A202 56p In ski gear 2.00 2.00

Gaiety
Theater,
Cent.
A203

2000, July 16
866 A203 22p Ballet .80 .80
867 A203 26p Comedy 1.00 1.00
868 A203 36p Drama 1.40 1.40
869 A203 45p Pantomime 1.75 1.75
870 A203 52p Opera 1.90 1.90
871 A203 65p Musicals 2.40 2.40
Nos. 866-871 (6) 9.25 9.25

Global Challenge Yacht Race — A204

Sail from yacht "Isle of Man," and ports of
call: 22p, Southampton. 26p, Sydney. 36p,
Wellington. 40p, Buenos Aires. 44p, Boston.
65p, Cape Town.

Perf. 13¼x13¾
2000, Sept. 10 **Litho.**
872 A204 22p multi .80 .80
873 A204 26p multi 1.00 1.00
874 A204 36p multi 1.40 1.40
875 A204 40p multi 1.50 1.50
876 A204 44p multi 1.60 1.60
877 A204 65p multi 2.40 2.40
Nos. 872-877 (6) 8.70 8.70

Travel Poster Art
of Isle of Man
Steam Packet
Co. — A205

Designs: 22p, Three legs of Man, ship. 26p,
Cliffs and sailboats. 36p, Woman and Isle of
Man. 45p, Woman, ship, flag. 65p, Ship.

2000, Oct. 16 Perf. 13½x13¼
878 A205 22p multi .80 .80
879 A205 26p multi 1.00 1.00
880 A205 36p multi 1.40 1.40
881 A205 45p multi 1.75 1.75
882 A205 65p multi 2.40 2.40
Nos. 878-882 (5) 7.35 7.35

Europa, 2000
Common Design Type

2000, Nov. 7 Perf. 14
883 CD17 36p multi 1.50 1.50

Christmas
A206

2000, Nov. 7
884 A206 21p Peace .80 .80
885 A206 25p Hope .90 .90
886 A206 45p Love 1.75 1.75
887 A206 65p Faith 2.40 2.40
Nos. 884-887 (4) 5.85 5.85

Souvenir Sheet

New Year 2001 (Year of the
Snake) — A207

Litho. with Foil Application

2001, Jan. 22   **Perf. 13¾**
888 A207 £1 St. Patrick   4.50 4.50

Hong Kong 2001 Stamp Exhibition.

Queen Victoria (1819-1901) — A208

Designs: 22p, Wyon medal, Queen Victoria, Great Britain Type A1. 26p, Great Exhibition medal, Albert Tower. 34p, Coin, Steamship Great Britain. 39p, Coin, scene from Oliver Twist, St. Thomas' Church, Douglas. 40p, Coin, first train to arrive in Vancouver, Canada and Jubilee streetlamp standard. 52p, Coin, Foxdale Clock Tower, family of diamond magnate Joe Mylchreest.

2001, Jan. 22   **Litho.**   **Perf. 13½**
889 A208 22p multi   .85 .85
890 A208 26p multi   1.00 1.00
891 A208 34p multi   1.40 1.40
892 A208 39p multi   1.50 1.50
893 A208 40p multi   1.60 1.60
894 A208 52p multi   2.00 2.00
   Nos. 889-894 (6)   8.35 8.35

Insects A209

Designs: 22p, White-tailed bumblebee. 26p, Seven-spot ladybug. 29p, Lesser mottled grasshopper. 58p, Manx robber fly. 66p, Elephant hawkmoth.

2001, Feb. 1   **Perf. 14½**
895 A209 22p multi   .85 .85
896 A209 26p multi   1.00 1.00
897 A209 29p multi   1.10 1.10
898 A209 58p multi   2.25 2.25
899 A209 66p multi   2.50 2.50
   Nos. 895-899 (5)   7.70 7.70

Souvenir Sheet

Queen Elizabeth II, 75th Birthday — A210

Stamps: 29p, Great Britain #MH1. 34p, Great Britain #300. 37p, Isle of Man #8. 50p, Isle of Man #3.

2001, Apr. 18   **Litho.**   **Perf. 14**
900 A210 Sheet of 4, #a-d   6.00 6.00
  e. As #900, with Hafnia 01 emblem added in sheet margin   7.50 7.50

No. 900e issued 10/29.

Manx Postmen and Cancels — A211

2001, Apr. 18
901 A211 22p 1805   .85 .85
902 A211 26p 1859   1.00 1.00
903 A211 36p 1910   1.40 1.40
904 A211 39p 1933   1.50 1.50
905 A211 40p 1983   1.60 1.60
906 A211 66p 2001   2.50 2.50
   Nos. 901-906 (6)   8.85 8.85

William Joseph Dunlop (1952-2000), Motorcycle Racer — A212

Various photographs.

2001, May 17
907 A212 22p multi   .85 .85
908 A212 26p multi   1.00 1.00
909 A212 36p multi   1.40 1.40
910 A212 45p multi   1.75 1.75
911 A212 65p multi   2.50 2.50
912 A212 77p multi   2.75 2.75
   Nos. 907-912 (6)   10.25 10.25

Horse Racing A213

Designs: 22p, Manx Derby. 26p, Post Haste. 36p, Red Rum. 52p, Hyperion. 63p, Isle of Man.

2001, May 18   **Perf. 13¼x13½**
913 A213 22p multi   .85 .85
914 A213 26p multi   1.00 1.00
915 A213 36p multi   1.40 1.40
916 A213 52p multi   1.90 1.90
917 A213 63p multi   2.40 2.40
   Nos. 913-917 (5)   7.55 7.55

Gourmet Food — A214

2001, Aug. 10   **Litho.**   **Perf. 14¼**
918 A214 22p Beef   .80 .80
919 A214 26p Queenies   .90 .90
  a. Sheet of 10   9.00
920 A214 36p Seafood   1.25 1.25
  a. Sheet of 10   12.50
921 A214 45p Lamb   1.60 1.60
922 A214 50p Kippers   1.90 1.90
923 A214 66p Lemon tart   2.40 2.40
   Nos. 918-923 (6)   8.85 8.85

Europa (#919, 920).

Architecture of Mackay Hugh Baillie Scott — A215

Designs: 22p, Castletown Police Station, 1901. 26p, Leafield/Braeside, 1897. 37p, Red House, 1893. 40p, Ivydene, 1893. 80p, Onchan Village Hall, 1898.

2001, Sept. 3   **Perf. 13¼x13½**
924 A215 22p multi   .85 .85
925 A215 26p multi   1.00 1.00
926 A215 37p multi   1.40 1.40
927 A215 40p multi   1.60 1.60
928 A215 80p multi   3.00 3.00
   Nos. 924-928 (5)   7.85 7.85

Reign of Queen Elizabeth II, 50th Anniv. (in 2002) — A216

Drawings of Queen: 22p, At dining table. 26p, With crowd, holding flower bouquet. 39p, With dogs. 40p, With men wearing hats. 45p, With correspondence. 65p, Alone, holding flower bouquet.

Litho. With Foil Application

2001-02   **Perf. 14¼**
929 A216 22p multi   .85 .85
930 A216 26p multi   1.00 1.00
931 A216 39p multi   1.60 1.60
  a. Booklet pane of 3, #929-931   3.50
932 A216 40p multi   1.60 1.60
933 A216 45p multi   1.75 1.75
934 A216 65p multi   2.50 2.50
  a. Booklet pane of 3, #932-934   6.00
   Nos. 929-934 (6)   9.30 9.30

Issued: Nos. 929-934, 10/29/01. Nos. 931a, 934a, 2/6/02.

Christmas A217

Floral arrangements: 21p, Holly on Christmas tree-shaped frame. 25p, Wreath. 37p, Table decoration with candles. 45p, Topiary tree. 65p, Wreath, diff.

2001, Nov. 5   **Litho.**   **Perf. 14x14½**
Stamp + Label
Background Color
935 A217 21p green   .80 .80
936 A217 25p red   1.00 1.00
937 A217 37p gold   1.40 1.40
938 A217 45p silver   1.75 1.75
939 A217 65p violet   2.40 2.40
   Nos. 935-939 (5)   7.35 7.35

Reign of Queen Elizabeth II, 50th Anniv. — A218

No. 940 — Paintings: a, The Coronation, by Terence Cuneo. b, Her Majesty the Queen as Colonel in Chief, Grenadier Guards on Imperial, by Cuneo (Queen on horse). c, Her Majesty in Evening Dress, by June Mendoza. d, Her Majesty the Queen, by Chen Yan Ning. e, The Royal Family, by John Wonnacott.
£1, Her Majesty Queen Elizabeth II Lord of Mann, sculpture by David Cregeen.

Litho. with Foil Application

2002, Feb. 6   **Perf. 14**
940   Vert. strip of 5   10.00 10.00
  a.-e. A218 50p Any single   2.00 2.00
  f. Booklet pane of 3, #940a-940c   6.25 —
  g. Booklet pane of 2, #940d-940e   4.25 —

Souvenir Sheet
Perf. 14½x14
941 A218 £1 multi   4.00 4.00
  a. Booklet pane of 1 with larger margin   4.00 —
  Booklet, #931a, 934a, 940f, 940g, 941a   24.00

No. 941 contains one 60x40mm stamp.

No. 941 exists with purple inscription in sheet margin, "The Isle of Man Celebrates The Jubilee / 4th June 2002."

17th Commonwealth Games, Manchester, England — A219

Designs: 22p, Cycling. 26p, Running. 29p, Javelin, women's high jump. 34p, Swimming. 40p, Hurdles, pole vault. 45p, Wheelchair racing.

2002, Mar. 11   **Litho.**   **Perf. 14**
942 A219 22p multi   .80 .80
943 A219 26p multi   .90 .90
944 A219 29p multi   1.10 1.10
945 A219 34p multi   1.25 1.25
946 A219 40p multi   1.50 1.50
947 A219 45p multi   1.60 1.60
   Nos. 942-947 (6)   7.15 7.15

Queen Mother Elizabeth (1900-2002) A220

2002, Apr. 23   **Perf. 13x13¼**
948 A220 £3 multi   12.00 12.00

Paintings by Toni Onley A221

Designs: 22p, Monks' Bridge, Ballasalla. 26p, Laxey. 37p, Langness Lighthouse. 45p, King William's College. 65p, The Mull Circle & Bradda Head.

2002, May 1   **Perf. 13¼x13½**
949 A221 22p multi   .85 .85
950 A221 26p multi   1.00 1.00
951 A221 37p multi   1.50 1.50
952 A221 45p multi   1.75 1.75
953 A221 65p multi   2.50 2.50
   Nos. 949-953 (5)   7.60 7.60

2002 World Cup Soccer Championships, Japan and Korea — A222

Various players.

2002, May 1   **Perf. 13½**
954 A222 22p multi   .85 .85
955 A222 26p multi   1.00 1.00
956 A222 39p multi   1.60 1.60
957 A222 40p multi   1.60 1.60
958 A222 66p multi   2.50 2.50
959 A222 68p multi   2.75 2.75
   Nos. 954-959 (6)   10.30 10.30

Flower Sketches by Sir Paul McCartney A223

Various sketches.

2002, July 1   Litho.   Perf. 13¼x12¾
960	A223	22p multi	.85	.85
961	A223	26p multi	1.00	1.00
962	A223	29p multi	1.10	1.10
963	A223	52p multi	2.00	2.00
964	A223	63p multi	2.50	2.50
965	A223	77p multi	3.00	3.00
	Nos. 960-965 (6)		10.45	10.45

Photographs of Local Scenes — A224

Nos. 966-967: a, Laxey Wheel, by Kathy Brown. b, Sheep at Druidale, by John Hall. c, Carousel at Silverdale, by Colin Edwards. d, Grandma, by Stephanie Corkill. e, Manx Rock, by Ruth Nicholls. f, TT Riders at Signpost, by Neil Brew. g, Groudle Railway, by Albert Lowe. h, Royal Cascade, by Brian Speedie. i, St. Johns, by John Hall. j, Niarbyl Cottages with Poppies, by Cathy Galbraith.

2002   Litho.   Perf. 14
966		Block of 10	11.00	11.00
a.-j.	A224	27p Any single	1.10	1.10

Self-Adhesive
Serpentine Die Cut 6¼
967		Booklet of 10	11.00	
a.-j.	A224	27p Any single	1.10	1.10

Designs: a, Manx Milestone, by Mrs. B. J. Trimble. b, Plow Horses, by Miss D. Flint. c, Manx Emblem, by Ruth Nicholls. d, Loaghtan Sheep, by Diana Buford. e, Fishing Fleet at Port St. Mary, by Phil Thomas. f, Peel, by Michael Thompson. g, Daffodils, by Michael Thompson. h, Millennium Sword, by Mr. F. K. Smith. i, Peel Castle, by Kathy Brown. j, Snaefell Railway, by Joan Burgess.

Litho.
Perf. 14
968		Block of 10	9.00	9.00
a.-j.	A224	23p Any single	.90	.90

Self-Adhesive
Serpentine Die Cut 6¼
969		Booklet of 10	9.00	
a.-j.	A224	23p Any single	.90	.90

Issued: Nos. 966-967, 8/30; Nos. 968-969, 10/1.

Christmas and Europa — A225

Designs: 22p, Santa Claus. 26p, Madonna and Child. 37p, Clown. 47p, Cymbal player. 68p, Fairy. £1.30, "Christmas."

2002, Nov. 5   Perf. 14x14½
970	A225	22p multi	.80	.80
971	A225	26p multi	.95	.95
972	A225	37p multi	1.50	1.50
a.		Sheet of 10 + 10 labels	15.00	15.00
973	A225	47p multi	1.75	1.75
974	A225	68p multi	2.75	2.75
	Nos. 970-974 (5)		7.75	7.75

Miniature Sheet
Perf. 14¾
975	A225	£1.30 multi	5.25	5.25

Europa (#972). No. 975 contains one 99x38mm stamp.

Post Office Vehicles A226

Designs: 23p, Handcart. 27p, Morris Z van. 37p, Morris LD van. 42p, DI BSA Bantam motorcycle. 89p, Ford Escort 55 delivery van.

2003, Feb. 14   Perf. 14¼
976	A226	23p multi	1.00	1.00
977	A226	27p multi	1.25	1.25
978	A226	37p multi	1.50	1.50
979	A226	42p multi	1.75	1.75
980	A226	89p multi	3.50	3.50
	Nos. 976-980 (5)		9.00	9.00

Space Exploration — A227

No. 981: a, Tromode Teleport. b, Satellite earth station.
No. 982: a, Pioneering the space frontier (denomination at left). b, Pioneering the space frontier (denomination at right).
No. 983: a, Sea Launch Odyssey launch platform. b, Sea Launch Commander.
No. 984: a, Loral Skynet Telstar 1. b, Loral Skynet Telstar 8.
No. 985: a, Space station, Phobos. b, Astronauts, Mars.
Illustration reduced.

2003, Feb. 14   Perf. 13¼x13½
981	A227	Horiz. pair	1.90	1.90
a.-b.		23p Either single	.90	.90
982	A227	Horiz. pair	2.25	2.25
a.-b.		27p Either single	1.10	1.10
983	A227	Horiz. pair	3.00	3.00
a.-b.		37p Either single	1.50	1.50
984	A227	Horiz. pair	3.25	3.25
a.-b.		42p Either single	1.60	1.60
	Nos. 981-984 (4)		10.40	10.40

Souvenir Sheet
Perf. 13¼x13
985	A227	Horiz. pair	6.00	6.00
a.-b.		75p Either single	3.00	3.00

No. 985 contains two 29x38mm stamps.

Coronation of Queen Elizabeth II, 50th Anniv. — A228

No. 986: a, Queen wearing St. Edward's Crown (brown background, 29x59mm). b, Queen wearing Sovereign's ring and armills (29x29mm). c, Sovereign's orb (29x29mm). d, Scepter with Cross, Rod with Dove (29x29mm). e, Queen wearing Imperial State Crown (blue green background, 29x59mm) f, Queen in State Coach (89x29mm).
Illustration reduced.

Litho. With Foil Application
2003, Apr. 12   Perf. 13¼
986	A228	Block of 6	12.00	12.00
a.-f.		50p Any single	2.00	2.00

Powered Flight, Cent. — A229

No. 987: a, DH 83 Fox Moth, Saro Cloud. b, DH 61 Giant Moth, DH Puss Moth. c, Avro Anson, B-17 Flying Fortress.
No. 988: a, Eurofighter Typhoon, Avro Vulcan. b, Handley Page Herald, Bristol Wayfarer. c, Concorde, A380 Airbus.

2003, May 9   Litho.   Perf. 13¼
987		Strip of 3	3.50	3.50
a.	A229	23p multi	.90	.90
b.	A229	27p multi	1.10	1.10
c.	A229	37p multi	1.50	1.50
988		Strip of 3	8.00	8.00
a.	A229	40p multi	1.60	1.60
b.	A229	67p multi	2.75	2.75
c.	A229	89p multi	3.50	3.50

Souvenir Sheet

Dambuster's Raid, 60th Anniv. — A230

2003
989	A230	£2 multi	8.00	8.00
a.		With "Ticino 2003" emblem in margin	8.50	8.50

Issued: No. 989, 5/9; No. 989a, 6/18.

Prince William, 21st Birthday A231

Various photographs.

2003, June 9   Perf. 13¼x13½
990	A231	42p black	1.60	1.60
991	A231	47p black	1.90	1.90
992	A231	52p black	2.00	2.00
993	A231	68p black	2.50	2.50
	Nos. 990-993 (4)		8.00	8.00

Literature With Manx Connections — A232

Designs: 23p, Manx Gold, by Agatha Christie. 27p, Quartermass and the Pit, by Nigel Kneale. 30p, Flashman at the Charge, by George MacDonald Fraser. 38p, The Eternal City, by Hall Caine. 40p, Islanders, by Mona Douglas. 53p, Emma's Secret, by Barbara Taylor Bradford.

2003, July 9   Perf. 13¼
Stamp + Label
994	A232	23p multi	.90	.90
995	A232	27p multi	1.10	1.10
996	A232	30p multi	1.25	1.25
997	A232	38p multi	1.50	1.50
a.		Sheet of 10 + 10 labels	15.00	15.00
998	A232	40p multi	1.60	1.60
999	A232	53p multi	2.00	2.00
	Nos. 994-999 (6)		8.35	8.35

Europa (#997).

End of Tudor Reign, 400th Anniv. A233

Designs: 23p, Crowning of King Henry VII at Bosworth. 27p, King Henry VIII, Dissolution of the Monasteries. 38p, Queen Elizabeth I, Sir Francis Drake circumnavigates the globe. 40p, King Henry VIII, Hampton Court. 47p, Queen Mary I, Tudor rose. 67p, Queen Elizabeth I, Spanish Armada.

2003, Sept. 15   Perf. 14
1000	A233	23p multi	.90	.90
1001	A233	27p multi	1.10	1.10
1002	A233	38p multi	1.50	1.50
1003	A233	40p multi	1.60	1.60
1004	A233	47p multi	1.90	1.90
1005	A233	67p multi	2.50	2.50
	Nos. 1000-1005 (6)		9.50	9.50

Henry Bloom Noble Trust, Cent. — A234

No. 1006: a, Boys' Orphanage. b, Ramsey Cottage Hospital. c, Children's Home. d, Noble's Baths. e, Scout Headquarters.
No. 1007: a, Noble's Hospital. b, Villa Marina. c, Noble's Park. d, St. Ninian's Church. e, Noble's Library.

2003, Oct. 1
1006		Horiz. strip of 5	4.50	4.50
a.-e.	A234	23p Any single	.90	.90
1007		Horiz. strip of 5	5.50	5.50
a.-e.	A234	23p Any single	1.10	1.10

Booklet Stamps
Self-Adhesive
Serpentine Die Cut 6¼
1007F	A234	23p Like #1006a	.90	.90
1007G	A234	23p Like #1006b	.90	.90
1007H	A234	23p Like #1006c	.90	.90
1007I	A234	23p Like #1006d	.90	.90
1007J	A234	23p Like #1006e	.90	.90
p.		Booklet pane, 2 each #1007F-1007J	9.00	
1007K	A234	27p Like #1007a	1.10	1.10
1007L	A234	27p Like #1007b	1.10	1.10
1007M	A234	27p Like #1007c	1.10	1.10
1007N	A234	27p Like #1007d	1.10	1.10
1007O	A234	27p Like #1007e	1.10	1.10
q.		Booklet pane, 2 each #1007K-1007O	11.00	
	Nos. 1007F-1007O (10)		10.00	10.00

Nos. 1007Jp and 1007Oq are complete booklets, the backing serving as the booklet covers.

Christmas A235

Various snowmen, based on Raymond Briggs' children's story *The Snowman*.

Litho. With Foil Application
2003, Nov. 5   Perf. 14¼
Background Color
1008	A235	22p red	.90	.90
1009	A235	26p deep blue	1.00	1.00
1010	A235	38p blue green	1.50	1.50
1011	A235	47p orange	1.90	1.90
1012	A235	68p yellow	2.50	2.50
	Nos. 1008-1012 (5)		7.80	7.80

Debut of Movie *The Lord of the Rings: The Return of the King* — A236

Designs: 23p, Aragorn. 27p, Gimli. 30p, Gandalf the White. 38p, Legolas on horseback. 42p, Gollum. 47p, Frodo Baggins and Samwise Gamgee. 68p, Legolas with bow and arrow. 85p, Aragorn on horseback. £2, Ring.

2003, Dec. 17   Litho.   Perf. 13¼
1013	A236	23p multi	.90	.90
1014	A236	27p multi	1.10	1.10
1015	A236	30p multi	1.25	1.25
1016	A236	38p multi	1.50	1.50
1017	A236	42p multi	1.60	1.60
1018	A236	47p multi	1.90	1.90
1019	A236	68p multi	2.75	2.75
1020	A236	85p multi	3.50	3.50
	Nos. 1013-1020 (8)		14.50	14.50

Souvenir Sheet
Perf. 13½
1021	A236	£2 multi	8.50	8.50

No. 1021 contains one 44x39mm stamp. Nos. 1013-1020 were each printed in sheets of six.

Steam Locomotives — A237

Designs: 23p, Maitland. 27p, Evening Star. 40p, Penydarren Tramroad locomotive. 57p, Duchess of Hamilton. 61p, City of Truro. 90p, Mallard.

2004, Feb. 21   Litho.   Perf. 13x13½
1022	A237	23p multi	1.00	1.00
1023	A237	27p multi	1.25	1.25
1024	A237	40p multi	1.75	1.75
1025	A237	57p multi	2.25	2.25
1026	A237	61p multi	2.50	2.50
1027	A237	90p multi	3.50	3.50
	Nos. 1022-1027 (6)		12.25	12.25

D-Day, 60th Anniv. — A238

No. 1028: a, Two soldiers near walkways, tanks on beach. b, Soldiers in water, tanks on beach.
No. 1029: a, Soldiers in water between two boats. b, Soldiers in water, landing craft with gangway open.
No. 1030: a, Lady of Mann, two blimps. b, Ben-my-Chree, three landing craft, five blimps.
No. 1031: a, Two US B-24 Liberators, RAF Horsa glider. b, Three RAF Horsa gliders.
No. 1032: a, Sir Winston Churchill. b, Soldiers near airplane propeller. c, Military vehicles on street in residential area. d, Soldiers reading book.
Illustration reduced.

2004, Apr. 6   Perf. 14
1028	A238	Horiz. pair	1.90	1.90
a.-b.		23p Either single	.90	.90
1029	A238	Horiz. pair	2.25	2.25
a.-b.		27p Either single	1.10	1.10
1030	A238	Horiz. pair	4.00	4.00
a.-b.		47p Either single	1.90	1.90
1031	A238	Horiz. pair	5.50	5.50
a.-b.		68p Either single	2.75	2.75
	Nos. 1028-1031 (4)		13.65	13.65

Souvenir Sheet
Perf. 13¼x13¾
1032	A238	Sheet of 4	8.00	8.00
a.-d.		50p Any single	2.00	2.00

Flowers
A239

Designs: 25p, Lesser celandine. 28p, Red campion. 37p, Devil's bit scabious. 40p, Northern harebell. 68p, Wood anemone. 85p, Common spotted orchid.

2004, May 3   Perf. 13½
1033	A239	25p multi	1.00	1.00
1034	A239	28p multi	1.10	1.10
1035	A239	37p multi	1.50	1.50
1036	A239	40p multi	1.60	1.60
1037	A239	68p multi	2.75	2.75
1038	A239	85p multi	3.50	3.50
	Nos. 1033-1038 (6)		11.45	11.45

George Formby (1904-61), Movie Actor — A240

Various scenes from film *No Limit* and text: 25p, No Limit. 28p, George. 40p, Speed Demon. 43p, Florence. 50p, Shuttleworth. 74p, Formby.

2004, May 26   Perf. 13¼
1039	A240	25p multi	1.00	1.00
1040	A240	28p multi	1.10	1.10
1041	A240	40p multi	1.60	1.60

1042	A240	43p multi	1.75	1.75
1043	A240	50p multi	2.00	2.00
1044	A240	74p multi	3.00	3.00
	Nos. 1039-1044 (6)		10.45	10.45

2004 Summer Olympics, Athens — A241

Designs: 25p, Johnny Weismuller, Paris Olympics, 1924. 28p, Jesse Owens, runners, Berlin Olympics, 1936. 43p, John Mark, torch bearer, London Olympics, 1948. 55p, Fanny Blankers-Koen, runners, London Olympics, 1948. 91p, Sir Steve Redgrave, rowers, Sydney Olympics, 2000.

2004, July 1   Litho.   Perf. 14
1045	A241	25p multi	1.00	1.00
1046	A241	28p multi	1.25	1.25
1047	A241	43p multi	1.75	1.75
1048	A241	55p multi	2.25	2.25
1049	A241	91p multi	3.75	3.75
	Nos. 1045-1049 (5)		10.00	10.00

Manx History — A242

Designs: Nos. 1050a, 1052, Celtic islander and Viking invaders. Nos. 1050b, 1053, Ships and the sea. Nos. 1050c, 1054, Laxey miners. Nos. 1050d, 1055, Kings and Lords of Mann. Nos. 1050e, 1056, Farmers and crofters. Nos. 1051a, 1057, Calf of Man. Nos. 1051b, 1058, Peel Castle. Nos. 1051c, 1059, Laxey Wheel. Nos. 1051d, 1060, Castle Rushen. Nos. 1051e, 1061, Cregneash.

2004, Aug. 3   Perf. 14¼
1050		Horiz. strip of 5	5.00	5.00
a.-e.	A242 (25p) any single		1.00	1.00
1051		Horiz. strip of 5	5.50	5.50
a.-e.	A242 (28p) any single		1.10	1.10

Booklet Stamps
Self-Adhesive
Serpentine Die Cut 12½
1052	A242	(25p) multi	1.00	1.00
1053	A242	(25p) multi	1.00	1.00
1054	A242	(25p) multi	1.00	1.00
1055	A242	(25p) multi	1.00	1.00
1056	A242	(25p) multi	1.00	1.00
a.		Booklet pane, 2 each #1052-1056	10.00	
1057	A242	(28p) multi	1.10	1.10
1058	A242	(28p) multi	1.10	1.10
1059	A242	(28p) multi	1.10	1.10
1060	A242	(28p) multi	1.10	1.10
1061	A242	(28p) multi	1.10	1.10
a.		Booklet pane, 2 each #1057-1061	11.00	
	Nos. 1050-1061 (12)		21.00	21.00

Nos. 1056a and 1061a are complete booklets, the backing serving as the booklet covers.

Souvenir Sheet

Laxey Wheel, 150th Anniv. — A243

2004, Aug. 3   Perf. 14¼
1062	A243	£2 multi	8.00	8.00
a.		With Sindelfingen 2004 emblem added in sheet margin	10.00	10.00

No. 1062a issued 10/29.

Watercolors by Alfred Heaton Cooper (1864-1929) A244

Designs: 25p, Maughold Church. 28p, Port St. Mary. 40p, Ballaugh Old Church. 41p, Douglas Bay (A Midsummer's Night). 43p, Point of Ayre. 74p, Peel Harbor and Castle.

2004, Oct. 21   Litho.   Perf. 13¼x12¾
1063	A244	25p multi	1.00	1.00
1064	A244	28p multi	1.10	1.10
a.		Sheet of 10 + 10 labels	11.00	11.00
1065	A244	40p multi	1.60	1.60
a.		Sheet of 10 + 10 labels	16.00	16.00
1066	A244	41p multi	1.60	1.60
1067	A244	43p multi	1.75	1.75
1068	A244	74p multi	3.00	3.00
	Nos. 1063-1068 (6)		10.05	10.05

Europa (#1064-1065).

Robins A245

Robin on: 25p, Flowerpot. 28p, Rock. 40p, Branch. 47p, Window sill. 68p, Log.

2004, Nov. 9   Perf. 12½x13
1069	A245	25p multi	1.00	1.00
1070	A245	28p multi	1.25	1.25
1071	A245	40p multi	1.75	1.75
1072	A245	47p multi	2.00	2.00
1073	A245	68p multi	2.75	2.75
a.		Miniature sheet, 2 each #1069-1073	22.50	22.50
	Nos. 1069-1073 (5)		8.75	8.75

Scenes from *Harry Potter and the Prisoner of Azkaban* A246

Designs: 25p, Harry Potter, Ron Weasley and Hermione Granger. 28p, Owl Post. 39p, Harry and Petronus. 40p, Hogwarts Express. 49p, Hagrid. 55p, Knight Bus. 57p, Harry and Dementor. 68p, Harry and Buckbeak.

2004, Dec. 7   Perf. 13¼
1074	A246	25p multi	1.00	1.00
1075	A246	28p multi	1.25	1.25
1076	A246	39p multi	1.75	1.75
1077	A246	40p multi	1.90	1.90
1078	A246	49p multi	2.00	2.00
1079	A246	55p multi	2.25	2.25
1080	A246	57p multi	2.50	2.50
1081	A246	68p multi	2.75	2.75
	Nos. 1074-1081 (8)		15.40	15.40

Each printed in sheets of 5.

Battle of Trafalgar, Bicent. — A247

No. 1082: a, Nile Campaign. b, Battle of Copenhagen.
No. 1083: a, Emma Horatia Nelson. b, Band of brothers.
No. 1084: a, Prepare for battle. b, Victory in sight.
No. 1085: a, Fall of Nelson. b, Death of Nelson.
No. 1086: a, #861a. b, #159.
Illustration reduced.

2005   Perf. 12½x13
1082	A247	Horiz. pair	2.00	2.00
a.-b.		25p Either single	1.00	1.00
1083	A247	Horiz. pair	2.25	2.25
a.-b.		28p Either single	1.10	1.10
1084	A247	Horiz. pair	4.00	4.00
a.-b.		50p Either single		

1085	A247	Horiz. pair	5.00	5.00
a.-b.		65p Either single	2.50	2.50
	Nos. 1082-1085 (4)		13.25	13.25

Souvenir Sheet
1086	A247	Sheet of 2	8.00	8.00
a.-b.		£1 Either single	4.00	4.00

Issued: Nos. 1082-1085, 1/9; No. 1086, 2/1.

Victory in World War II, 60th Anniv. — A248

No. 1087: a, Women and sailors. b, Soldiers and women marching together.
No. 1088: a, Soldier trying on hat. b, Servicewomen.
No. 1089: a, Winston Churchill and Royal family waving. b, Royal family in carriage.
No. 1090: a, Servicemen without shirts. b, Cemetery.
No. 1091: a, Manx Regiment. b, Royal visit, 1945.
Illustration reduced.

2005, Apr. 15   Litho.   Perf. 13¼x13¾
1087	A248	Horiz. pair	2.25	2.25
a.-b.		26p Either single	1.10	1.10
1088	A248	Horiz. pair	2.50	2.50
a.-b.		29p Either single	1.25	1.25
1089	A248	Horiz. pair	5.00	5.00
a.-b.		60p Either single	2.50	2.50
1090	A248	Horiz. pair	5.50	5.50
a.-b.		65p Either single	2.75	2.75
	Nos. 1087-1090 (4)		15.25	15.25

Souvenir Sheet
1091	A248	Sheet of 2	9.00	9.00
a.-b.		£1 Either single	4.50	4.50

Paintings of Isle of Man Steam Packet Company Ships — A249

No. 1092: a, Mona's Isle, by Samuel Walters. b, Viking, by Norman Wilkinson.
No. 1093: a, King Orry, by Robert Lloyd. b, Mona's Queen, by Arthur Burgess.
No. 1094: a, Ben-my-Chree, by John Nicholson. b, King Orry, by Robert Lloyd, diff.
No. 1095: a, Ben-my-Chree, by Robert Lloyd. b, Lady of Mann, by Robert Lloyd.
Illustration reduced.

2005, May 6   Perf. 14
1092	A249	Horiz. pair	2.25	2.25
a.-b.		26p Either single	1.10	1.10
1093	A249	Horiz. pair	2.50	2.50
a.-b.		29p Either single	1.25	1.25
c.		Booklet pane, #1092, 1093	4.75	
1094	A249	Horiz. pair	3.50	3.50
a.-b.		40p Either single	1.75	1.75
c.		Booklet pane, #1092, 1094	5.75	
1095	A249	Horiz. pair	5.50	5.50
a.-b.		66p Either single	2.75	2.75
c.		Booklet pane, #1093, 1095	8.00	
d.		Booklet pane, #1094, 1095	9.00	—
e.		Booklet pane, #1095	5.50	—
		Complete booklet, #1093c, 1094c, 1095c, 1095d, 1095e	35.00	
	Nos. 1092-1095 (4)		13.75	13.75

Complete booklet sold for £7.80.

Motorcycle Racers — A250

Designs: 26p, Bill Ivy, Phil Read. 29p, Joey Dunlop, Ray McCullough. 40p, Steve Hislop. 42p, Carl Fogarty. 68p, David Jefferies. 78p, John McGuinness.

2005, May 17
1096	A250	26p multi	1.00	1.00
1097	A250	29p multi	1.10	1.10
1098	A250	40p multi	1.60	1.60
1099	A250	42p multi	1.75	1.75
1100	A250	68p multi	2.75	2.75
1101	A250	78p multi	3.00	3.00
a.		Miniature sheet, 2 each #1096-1101	22.50	22.50
	Nos. 1096-1101 (6)		11.20	11.20

Yamaha motorcycles, 50th anniv.

Rotary International, Cent. — A251

Rotary International emblem, various photos and inscription: 26p, Paul Harris, The Man Behind The Movement. 29p, Rotary's Dreams For The Future. 40p, Polioplus: Rotary's Finest Hour. 42p, Youth Programme: Junior Masterchef. 64p, A Day In The Life of Rotary International. 68p, Serving The World Community.

Perf. 13¼x13½

2005, June 15		**Litho.**	
1102 A251	26p multi	1.00	1.00
1103 A251	29p multi	1.10	1.10
1104 A251	40p multi	1.60	1.60
1105 A251	42p multi	1.75	1.75
a.	Sheet of 10 + 10 labels	17.50	17.50
1106 A251	64p multi	2.50	2.50
1107 A251	68p multi	2.75	2.75
	Nos. 1102-1107 (6)	10.70	10.70

No. 1105 is inscribed "Europa 2005."

Photographs of Everyday Life — A252

Inscriptions: Nos. 1108a, 1110, Guttin' Herrin'. Nos. 1108b, 1111, Pickin' Spuds. Nos. 1108c, 1112, Master Butcher. Nos. 1108d, 1113, Winckles: Foxdale. Nos. 1108e, 1114, Palace Ballroom. Nos. 1109a, 1115, Land Army. Nos. 1109b, 1116, Farmyard Glen Maye. Nos. 1109c, 1117, Summer Season Stars. Nos. 1109d, 1118, Donkey Rides. Nos. 1109e, 1119, Give us a go Mister!

2005, Aug. 12		**Perf. 12½x13**	
1108	Horiz. strip of 5	5.00	5.00
a.-e.	A252 26p Any single	1.00	1.00
1109	Horiz. strip of 5	5.50	5.50
a.-e.	A252 29p Any single	1.10	1.10

Booklet Stamps
Self-Adhesive
Serpentine Die Cut 10½x10¼

1110 A252	26p multi	1.00	1.00
a.	Die cut perf 12½x13	1.00	1.00
1111 A252	26p multi	1.00	1.00
a.	Die cut perf 12½x13	1.00	1.00
1112 A252	26p multi	1.00	1.00
a.	Die cut perf 12½x13	1.00	1.00
1113 A252	26p multi	1.00	1.00
a.	Die cut perf 12½x13	1.00	1.00
1114 A252	26p multi	1.00	1.00
a.	Booklet pane, 2 each #1110-1114	10.00	
	Complete booklet, #1114a	10.00	
b.	Die cut perf 12½x13	1.00	1.00
c.	Strip 5, #1110a-1113a, 1114b	5.00	
1115 A252	29p multi	1.10	1.10
a.	Die cut perf 12½x13	1.10	1.10
1116 A252	29p multi	1.10	1.10
a.	Die cut perf 12½x13	1.10	1.10
1117 A252	29p multi	1.10	1.10
a.	Die cut perf 12½x13	1.10	1.10
1118 A252	29p multi	1.10	1.10
a.	Die cut perf 12½x13	1.10	1.10
1119 A252	29p multi	1.10	1.10
a.	Booklet pane, 2 each #1115-1119	11.00	
	Complete booklet, #1119a	11.00	
b.	Die cut perf 12½x13	1.10	1.10
c.	Strip 5, #1115a-1118a, 1119b	5.50	
	Nos. 1110-1119 (10)	10.50	10.50

Nos. 1114a and 1119a are complete booklets, the backing serving as booklet covers. The die-cut 12½x13 stamps are from sheets of 50.

Souvenir Sheet

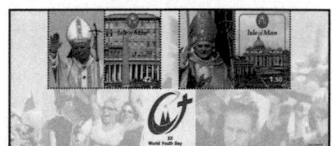

20th World Youth Day, Cologne, Germany — A253

Perf. 14x14¾ on 3 Sides

2005, Aug. 15			
1120 A253	Sheet of 2 + 2 labels	8.00	8.00
a.	42p Apostolic Palace	1.75	1.75
b.	£1.50 St. Peter's Basilica	6.00	6.00

Scenes From *Harry Potter and the Goblet of Fire* — A254

Designs: 26p, Harry Potter. 29p, Harry, Ron Weasley, Hermione Granger, Goblet of Fire. 33p, Triwizard Cup. 64p, Hungarian Horntail. 68p, Hogwarts coat of arms. 75p, Murcus.

2005, Oct. 21		**Perf. 13¼**	
1121 A254	26p multi	1.00	1.00
1122 A254	29p multi	1.10	1.10
1123 A254	33p multi	1.40	1.40
1124 A254	64p multi	2.50	2.50
1125 A254	68p multi	2.75	2.75
1126 A254	75p multi	3.00	3.00
	Nos. 1121-1126 (6)	11.75	11.75

Souvenir Sheet

Battle of Trafalgar, Bicent. — A255

2005, Oct. 21	**Litho.**	**Perf. 13¼**	
1127 A255	Sheet, #1127a, Gibraltar #1028a	8.00	8.00
a.	£1 Funeral of Admiral Nelson	4.00	4.00

See Gibraltar No. 1028. No. 1127 has an Isle of Man Post emblem in the margin.

Christmas — A256

Stained glass windows: 26p, Madonna and Child, St. German's Cathedral, Peel. 29p, Angel with Crown of Glory, St. German's Cathedral. 42p, Adoration of the Shepherds, St. German's Cathedral. 60p, Nativity, Kirk Church, Rushen. 68p, Adoration of the Magi, Kirk Church.

2005, Nov. 7	**Litho.**	**Perf. 13½x13**	
1128 A256	26p multi	1.00	1.00
1129 A256	29p multi	1.10	1.10
1130 A256	42p multi	1.75	1.75
1131 A256	60p multi	2.40	2.40
1132 A256	68p multi	2.75	2.75
	Nos. 1128-1132 (5)	9.00	9.00

Queen Elizabeth II, 80th Birthday — A257

No. 1133: a, At age 5 with family, 1931. b, In uniform, 1944. c, Wearing tiara, 1952. d, With husband and children, 1972.
No. 1134: a, With Prince Philip, 1972. b, Seated in Throne Room, 2001. c, With Prince William. d, With crowd, 2002.

2006, Jan. 16		**Perf. 13¾**	
1133	Horiz. strip of 4	3.25	3.25
a.-d.	A257 20p Any single	.80	.80
1134	Horiz. strip of 4	13.00	13.00
a.-d.	A257 80p Any single	3.25	3.25

Isle of Man Natural History and Antiquarian Society — A258

Designs: 26p, Jurby Church, chalice. 29p, Peel Castle, Viking pinhead. 64p, Meayll Hill, Neolithic potsherd. 68p, Cronk Sumark, Manx stoat. 78p, South Barrule Hill, hen harrier. 97p, Scarlett Point, ammonite fossil.

2006, Feb. 15	**Litho.**	**Perf. 14**	
1135 A258	26p multi	1.00	1.00
1136 A258	29p multi	1.10	1.10
1137 A258	64p multi	2.50	2.50
1138 A258	68p multi	2.75	2.75
1139 A258	78p multi	3.00	3.00
1140 A258	97p multi	3.75	3.75
	Nos. 1135-1140 (6)	14.10	14.10

Birds — A259

No. 1141: a, Peregrine falcon. b, Puffin. c, Manx shearwater. d, Chough. e, Guillemot.
No. 1142: a, Whinchat. b, Hen harrier. c, Goldcrest. d, Gray wagtail. e, Wren.
No. 1142G: i, Peregrine falcon. j, Puffin. k, Manx shearwater. l, Chough. m, Guillemot.
No. 1142H: n, Whinchat. o, Hen harrier. p, Goldcrest. q, Gray wagtail. r, Wren.

2006, Apr. 17		**Perf. 12½**	
1141	Horiz. strip of 5	5.50	5.50
a.-e.	A259 28p multi	1.10	1.10
1142	Horiz. strip of 5	6.25	6.25
a.-e.	A259 31p multi	1.25	1.25
f.	Miniature sheet, #1141a-1141e, 1142a-1142e	12.00	12.00

Self-Adhesive

1142G	Horiz. strip of 5	5.25	5.25
i.-m.	A259 28p Any single	1.00	1.00
1142H	Horiz. strip of 5	5.75	5.75
n.-r.	A259 31p Any single	1.10	1.10

No. 1142f issued 10/11, for Belgica '06 Intl. Philatelic Exhibition.

Souvenir Sheet

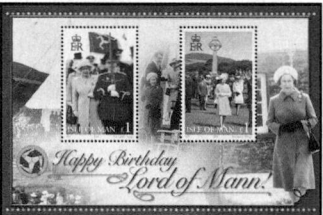

Queen Elizabeth II, 80th Birthday — A260

No. 1143: a, Queen, swordbearer, Manx flag, 2003. b, Queen, crowd, cross, 1972.

2006, Apr. 21		**Perf. 14**	
1143 A260	Sheet of 2	8.00	8.00
a.-b.	£1 Either single	4.00	4.00

Souvenir Sheet

Europa Stamps, 50th Anniv. — A261

No. 1144: a, #100. b, #419a.

2006, May 2		**Perf. 13¼x13¾**	
1144 A261	Sheet of 2	5.25	5.25
a.	42p multi	1.75	1.75
b.	83p multi	3.50	3.50

2006 World Cup Soccer Championships, Germany — A262

Various photographs of English team's 1966 World Cup championship match and celebrations.

2006, May 2		**Perf. 12½**	
1145 A262	28p multi	1.10	1.10
1146 A262	31p multi	1.25	1.25
1147 A262	44p multi	1.75	1.75
1148 A262	72p multi	2.75	2.75
1149 A262	83p multi	3.25	3.25
1150 A262	94p multi	3.75	3.75
	Nos. 1145-1150 (6)	13.85	13.85

Manx Ties to Washington, D.C. A263

Designs: 28p, Letitia Tyler, wife of Pres. John Tyler, White House. 31p, Speaker of the House Joseph G. Cannon, Cannon House Office Building. 45p, Matthew Quay, Medal of Honor recipient, battle scene. 50p, Mary Clemmer, journalist, inkwell and U.S. Constitution. 76p, Ewan Clague, economist, Castletown. 83p, Henry "Marse" Watterson, newspaper publisher, Pres. Theodore Roosevelt.

2006, May 23		**Perf. 13¾**	
1151 A263	28p multi	1.10	1.10
1152 A263	31p multi	1.25	1.25
1153 A263	45p multi	1.75	1.75
1154 A263	50p multi	2.00	2.00
1155 A263	76p multi	3.00	3.00
1156 A263	83p multi	3.25	3.25
	Nos. 1151-1156 (6)	12.35	12.35

Peel Cars — A264

Designs: 28p, Peel P50. 31p, Trident. 38p, Viking Sport. 41p, BMC GRP Mini. 54p, Manxcar. 94p, P1000.

2006, July 23		**Perf. 13¼**	
1157 A264	28p multi	1.10	1.10
1158 A264	31p multi	1.25	1.25
1159 A264	38p multi	1.50	1.50
1160 A264	41p multi	1.60	1.60
1161 A264	54p multi	2.10	2.10
1162 A264	94p multi	3.75	3.75
	Nos. 1157-1162 (6)	11.30	11.30

National Portrait Gallery, London, 150th Anniv. — A265

Portraits: 28p, Ewan Christian, by unknown artist. 31p, Dame Agatha Christie, by John Gay. 38p, Sir Hall Caine, by Harry Furniss. 41p, William Bligh, by John Condé. 44p, Lady Maria Callcott, by Sir Thomas Lawrence. 54p, John Martin, by Henry Warren. 64p, Sir John Betjeman, by Stephen Hyde. 96p, Sir Edward Elgar, by Herbert Lambert.

2006, Aug. 25   **Litho.**   **Perf. 13½**

1163	A265	28p multi	1.10	1.10
1164	A265	31p multi	1.25	1.25
1165	A265	38p multi	1.50	1.50
1166	A265	41p multi	1.60	1.60
1167	A265	42p multi	1.75	1.75
1168	A265	54p multi	2.10	2.10
1169	A265	64p multi	2.50	2.50
1170	A265	96p multi	3.75	3.75
	Nos. 1163-1170 (8)		15.55	15.55

Souvenir Sheet

Tales of Beatrix Potter — A266

No. 1171: a, Benjamin Bunny. b, Jemima Puddle-duck, horiz. c, Peter Rabbit, horiz. d, Jeremy Fisher.

2006, Oct. 11   **Perf. 13**

1171	A266	Sheet of 4	9.00	9.00
a.		28p multi	1.10	1.10
b.		50p multi	2.00	2.00
c.		72p multi	2.75	2.75
d.		75p multi	3.00	3.00

Christmas — A267

Various Christmas trees with panel colors of: 28p, Red. 31p, Dark violet. 41p, Green. 44p, Light blue. 72p, Purple. 94p, Orange.

Litho. with Foil Application

2006, Oct. 11   **Perf. 14¼**

1172	A267	28p multi	1.10	1.10
1173	A267	31p multi	1.25	1.25
a.		Sheet of 10	12.50	
1174	A267	41p multi	1.60	1.60
1175	A267	44p multi	1.75	1.75
a.		Sheet of 10	17.50	
1176	A267	72p multi	2.75	2.75
1177	A267	94p multi	3.75	3.75
	Nos. 1172-1177 (6)		12.20	12.20

Self-Adhesive
Booklet Stamps
Die Cut Perf. 9x9½

1178	A267	28p multi	1.10	1.10
a.		Booklet pane of 10	11.00	
1179	A267	31p multi	1.25	1.25
a.		Booklet pane of 10	12.50	

Europa (31p, 44p).
Nos. 1178a and 1179a are complete booklets, the backing serving as the booklet covers.

TT Motorcycle Races, Cent. — A268

No. 1180 — Various racers with panel color of: a, Pink. b, Light blue. c, Purple. d, Indigo. e, Orange.
No. 1181: a, Red violet. b, Green. c, Gray blue. d, Red. e, Red brown.

2007, Jan. 1   **Litho.**   **Perf. 14¼**

1180		Horiz. strip of 5	6.25	6.25
a.-e.		A268 UK Any single	1.25	1.25
1181		Horiz. strip of 5	8.75	8.75
a.-e.		A268 E Any single	1.75	1.75
f.		Sheet of 10, #1180a-1180e, 1181a-1181e, + 10 labels	15.00	15.00

On day of issue Nos. 1180a-1180e each sold for 31p, Nos. 1181a-1181e each sold for 44p.
Issued: No. 1181f, 7/9.

A269

Scouting, Cent. — A270

Designs: 28p, Hiking expedition near South Barrule. 31p, Scout investiture on Douglas Beach. 44p, Backpacking below Cronk-ny-Arrey-Laa. 72p, Manx Scouts on parade at St. Johns. 83p, Sea kayaking off Laxey Beach. £1, Manx Scouts operating the TT scoreboard.
No. 1188: a, Scouts and table (43x29mm). b, Scouts, tent and campfire (43x57mm).

2007, Feb. 22   **Litho.**   **Perf. 14**

1182	A269	28p multi	1.10	1.10
1183	A269	31p multi	1.25	1.25
a.		Sheet of 10	12.50	
1104	A209	44p multi	1.75	1.75
a.		Booklet pane, #1182-1184	4.25	
a.		Sheet of 10	17.50	
1185	A269	72p multi	2.75	2.75
1186	A269	83p multi	3.25	3.25
a.		Booklet pane, #1182, 1184, 1186	6.25	—
1187	A269	£1 multi	4.00	4.00
a.		Booklet pane, #1185-1187	10.00	—
b.		Booklet pane, #1183, 1185, 1187	8.00	—
	Nos. 1182-1187 (6)		14.10	14.10

Souvenir Sheet

1188	A270	Sheet of 2	7.75	7.75
a.		50p multi	2.00	2.00
b.		£1.50 multi	5.75	5.75
c.		Booklet pane, #1188 (154x96mm)	7.75	—
		Complete booklet, #1184a, 1186a, 1187a, 1187b, 1188c	36.50	
d.		As No. 1188, with 2007 Intl. Scout Jamboree emblem in margin	8.25	8.25

Europa (31p, 44p).
No. 1188d issued 7/26.

Wedding of Queen Elizabeth II and Prince Philip, 60th Anniv. — A271

Various photos of Queen and Prince with denomination colors of: a, Dark blue. b, Lilac. c, Rose pink. d, Light blue. e, Dark green. f, Yellow bister.

2007, Feb. 22   **Perf. 14**

1189		Horiz. strip of 6	14.00	14.00
a.-f.		A271 60p Any single	2.25	2.25

Paintings by Norman Sayle A272

Designs: Nos. 1190, 1198, Headland, Cornaa. Nos. 1191, 1199, Headland, Sound. Nos. 1192, 1200, St. Mark's Church. Nos. 1193, 1201, Castletown Harbour Moonlight. 42p, Bridge House, Castletown. 65p, In Ancient Times. 75p, Bracken Mountain.

2007, Apr. 12   **Perf. 12½x13**

1190	A272	28p multi	1.10	1.10
1191	A272	28p multi	1.10	1.10
1192	A272	31p multi	1.25	1.25
1193	A272	31p multi	1.25	1.25
1194	A272	42p multi	1.75	1.75
1195	A272	44p multi	1.75	1.75
1196	A272	65p multi	2.60	2.60
1197	A272	75p multi	3.00	3.00
	Nos. 1190-1197 (8)		13.80	13.80

Booklet Stamps
Self-Adhesive
Serpentine Die Cut 10x9½

1198	A272	28p multi	1.10	1.10
1199	A272	28p multi	1.10	1.10
a.		Booklet pane, 5 each #1198-1199	11.00	
1200	A272	31p multi	1.25	1.25
1201	A272	31p multi	1.25	1.25
a.		Booklet pane, 5 each #1200-1201	12.50	
	Nos. 1198-1201 (4)		4.70	4.70

Nos. 1199a and 1201a are complete booklets, the backing serving as the booklet covers.

Settlement of Jamestown, Virginia, 400th Anniv. — A273

Designs: 28p, Map. 31p, Capt. John Smith and ships. 44p, Aerial view of settlement. 78p, Indians and colonists. 90p, Settlement buildings. 90p, Indian village.

2007, Apr. 26   **Perf. 13½**

1202	A273	28p multi	1.10	1.10
1203	A273	31p multi	1.25	1.25
1204	A273	44p multi	1.75	1.75
1205	A273	54p multi	2.25	2.25
1206	A273	78p multi	3.25	3.25
1207	A273	90p multi	3.75	3.75
	Nos. 1202-1207 (6)		13.35	13.35

Royal Charter of Liverpool, 800th Anniv. A274

Designs: 31p, King John and Royal Charter. 48p, The spiritual heart of Liverpool. 54p, Liverpool war heroes. 74p, Liverpool heritage. 80p, Port of Liverpool. £1, Wall of Fame.
No. 1214: a, James Brown, Manx election pioneer. b, Joseph Cunningham, philanthropist. c, William Gill, ship captain. d, Dalrymple Maitland, industrialist.

2007, Apr. 26   **Perf. 14**

1208	A274	31p multi	1.25	1.25
1209	A274	48p multi	1.90	1.90
1210	A274	54p multi	2.25	2.25
1211	A274	74p multi	3.00	3.00
1212	A274	80p multi	3.25	3.25
1213	A274	£1 multi	4.00	4.00
	Nos. 1208-1213 (6)		15.65	15.65

Souvenir Sheet

2007, May 10

1214		Sheet of 4	9.00	9.00
a.		A274 25p multi	1.00	1.00
b.		A274 40p multi	1.50	1.50
c.-d.		A274 80p Either single	3.25	3.25

Historical Maps of Isle of Man A275

Designs: 28p, Map by John Speed, 1605. 31p, Map by Capt. Greenville Collins, 1693. 44p, Map by John Drinkwater, 1826. 48p, Ordnance Survey County map, 1870. 75p, Six-inch Series map, 1975. 88p, 1:100,000 map by Isle of Man Government Mapping Office, 2006.

2007, Aug. 1   **Litho.**   **Perf. 12½x13**

1215	A275	28p multi	1.10	1.10
1216	A275	31p multi	1.25	1.25
1217	A275	44p multi	1.75	1.75

1218	A275	48p multi	2.00	2.00
1219	A275	75p multi	3.00	3.00
1220	A275	88p multi	3.75	3.75
	Nos. 1215-1220 (6)		12.85	12.85

Intl. Polar Year A276

Designs: 28p, Capt. John Ross, ship Victory trapped in ice. 31p, Flares shot from Victory. 55p, Victory crewmen hunting with Inuit. 75p, Musk ox hunted by Victory crewmen. 90p, Victory crewmen pulling sled after abandoning ship. 117p, Whaler Isabella rescuing Victory crewmen.

2007, Aug. 20

1221	A276	28p multi	1.10	1.10
1222	A276	31p multi	1.25	1.25
1223	A276	55p multi	2.25	2.25
1224	A276	75p multi	3.00	3.00
1225	A276	90p multi	3.75	3.75
1226	A276	117p multi	4.75	4.75
	Nos. 1221-1226 (6)		16.10	16.10

Souvenir Sheet

Manx Connections With Northern Canada — A277

No. 1227: a, Ben-My-Chree Cabin, British Columbia. b, Graham "Jimmy" Oates, first man to reach Hudson Bay on rubber-tired vehicle, vert. c, Kermode bear, vert. d, Hudson Bay Post Office and dog team.

2007, Aug. 20   **Perf. 13**

1227	A277	Sheet of 4	10.00	10.00
a.-b.		50p Either single	2.00	2.00
c.-d.		75p Either single	3.00	3.00

Intl. Polar Year.

Europen Vintage Plowing Championships — A278

Designs: 28p, Manx-style plowing. 31p, Vintage plowing. 48p, Horse and digger plow. 71p, Swing plow. 90p, World-style plowing. £1.27, Jean Burns, first woman to compete in Manx plowing contest, on tractor.

2007, Sept. 1   **Perf. 13¼**

1228	A278	28p multi	1.10	1.10
1229	A278	31p multi	1.25	1.25
1230	A278	48p multi	2.00	2.00
1231	A278	71p multi	3.00	3.00
1232	A278	90p multi	3.75	3.75
1233	A278	£1.27 multi	5.25	5.25
	Nos. 1228-1233 (6)		16.35	16.35

Christmas — A279

Various angels with panel color of: 28p, Blue. 31p, Pink. 69p, Orange. 78p, Green. £1.24, Dark blue.

Serpentine Die Cut 13x13¼
2007, Oct. 19
Self-Adhesive

1234	A279	28p multi	1.25	1.25
1235	A279	31p multi	1.40	1.40
1236	A279	69p multi	3.00	3.00
1237	A279	78p multi	3.25	3.25
1238	A279	£1.24 multi	5.25	5.25
	Nos. 1234-1238 (5)		14.15	14.15

Souvenir Sheet

Cunard Ocean Liners — A280

No. 1239: a, Queen Elizabeth 2. b, Queen Mary 2. c, Queen Victoria.

2008, Jan. 13   Litho.   Perf. 14x13¼

1239	A280	Sheet of 3	12.00	12.00
a.-c.		£1 Any single	4.00	4.00
d.		Sheet of 10 #1239a + 10 labels	40.00	—
e.		Sheet of 10 #1239b + 10 labels	40.00	—
f.		Sheet of 10 #1239c + 10 labels	40.00	—

Royal Air Force, 90th Anniv. A281

Aircraft: No. 1240, H.P. 0/400, Bristol F2B fighter. No. 1241, Avro 504N, Westland Wapiti. No. 1242, Hawker Hurricane, Short Sunderland. No. 1243, Gloster Meteor, Westland Whirlwind. No. 1244, Hawker Hunter, E.E. Canberra. No. 1245, BAE Harrier, Lockheed Hercules.

2008, Jan. 15   Perf. 13¼

1240	A281	31p multi	1.25	1.25
1241	A281	31p multi	1.25	1.25
1242	A281	31p multi	1.25	1.25
a.		Horiz. strip, #1240-1242	3.75	3.75
1243	A281	90p multi	3.75	3.75
a.		Booklet pane, #1240-1243	7.50	
1244	A281	90p multi	3.75	3.75
a.		Booklet pane, #1240-1241, 1243-1244	10.00	
1245	A281	90p multi	3.75	3.75
a.		Horiz. strip, #1243-1245	11.25	11.25
b.		Booklet pane, #1242-1245	12.50	
c.		Booklet pane, #1240-1241, 1244-1245	10.00	
		Complete booklet, #1243a, 1244a, 1245b, 1245c	40.00	
	Nos. 1240-1245 (6)		15.00	15.00

Vikings on Isle of Man — A282

Designs: 28p, Pagan Lady of Peel. 31p, Ship burial. 44p, Godred Crovan (King Orry). 54p, Gautr Bjornsson the Sculptor. 69p, Sigurd the Dragon Slayer. £1.24, Coming of Christianity.

2008, Feb. 18   Litho.   Perf. 13¼

1246	A282	28p multi	1.10	1.10
1247	A282	31p multi	1.25	1.25
1248	A282	44p multi	1.75	1.75
1249	A282	54p multi	2.25	2.25
1250	A282	69p multi	2.75	2.750
1251	A282	£1.24 multi	5.00	5.00
	Nos. 1246-1251 (6)		14.10	14.10

Manx Bank Notes A283

Designs: 30p, 1956 Isle of Man one-pound note. 31p, 1972 Isle of Man Government ten-pound note. 44p, 1882 Manx Bank one-pound note. 56p, 1969 Isle of Man Government fifty-pence note. 85p, 1983 Isle of Man Government fifty-pound note. 114p, 1918 Parr's Bank one-pound note.

2008, Apr. 7   Perf. 14

1252	A283	30p multi	1.25	1.25
1253	A283	31p multi	1.25	1.25
1254	A283	44p multi	1.75	1.75
1255	A283	56p multi	2.25	2.25
1256	A283	85p multi	3.50	3.50
1257	A283	114p multi	4.50	4.50
	Nos. 1252-1257 (6)		14.50	14.50

Booklet Stamp
Self-Adhesive
Die Cut Perf. 12x12¼

1258	A283	30p multi	1.25	1.25
a.		Booklet pane of 10	10.00	
		Complete booklet, #1258a	12.50	

Miniature Sheet

2008 Summer Olympics, Beijing — A284

2008, Apr. 21   Perf. 13¼

1259	A284	Sheet of 4	4.00	4.00
a.		1p Archery	.20	.20
b.		2p Equestrian	.20	.20
c.		3p Cycling	.20	.20
d.		94p Olympic torch	3.75	3.75
e.		As No. 1259, with Olympex inscription in sheet margin	4.00	4.00
f.		Souvenir sheet, #1259c, #1259d	4.00	4.00

Issued: No. 1259e, 8/8; No. 1259f, 8/9.

Interceltic Music Festival, Lorient, France A285

Flags of regions with Celtic language heritage: 20p, Cornwall. 30p, Isle of Man. 31p, Scotland. 48p, Brittany. 50p, Ireland. 56p, Asturias. 72p, Wales. £1.13, Galicia.

2008, May 12   Perf. 13¼

1260	A285	20p multi	.80	.80
1261	A285	30p multi	1.25	1.25
1262	A285	31p multi	1.25	1.25
a.		Sheet of 10	12.50	12.50
1263	A285	48p multi	1.90	1.90
1264	A285	50p multi	2.00	2.00
a.		Sheet of 10	20.00	20.00
1265	A285	56p multi	2.25	2.25
1266	A285	72p multi	3.00	3.00
1267	A285	£1.13 multi	4.50	4.50
a.		Sheet of 8, #1260-1267 (Aug. 1)	17.00	—
	Nos. 1260-1267 (8)		16.95	16.95

Europa (31p, 50p).

Famous Race Drivers and Their Cars A286

Designs: 20p, Reg Parnell. 30p, Mike Hawthorn. 70p, Tony Brooks. 81p, Roy Salvadori. 94p, Stirling Moss. £1.22, Jim Clark.

2008, July 10   Litho.   Perf. 14

1268	A286	20p multi	.80	.80
1269	A286	30p multi	1.25	1.25
1270	A286	70p multi	2.75	2.75
1271	A286	81p multi	3.25	3.25
1272	A286	94p multi	3.75	3.75
1273	A286	£1.22 multi	5.00	5.00
	Nos. 1268-1273 (6)		16.80	16.80

Miniature Sheet

Race Cars — A287

No. 1274: a, 1961 Aston Martin DB4 GT Zagato. b, 1965 Ferrari 250 LM. c, 1962 Ferrari 250 GTO. d, 1965 Ford GT40. e, 1955 Mercedes-Benz 300 SLR. f, 1964 Shelby Cobra.

2008, July 10   Perf. 14⅜x14

1274	A287	Sheet of 6	12.00	12.00
a.-f.		50p Any single	2.00	2.00

Famous People — A288

No. 1275: a, Mary Louisa Wood (1839-1925), founder of Isle of Man Fine Arts and Industrial Guild. b, Harry Kelly (1852-1935), last native Manx speaker. c, Sir Frank Gill (1866-1950), telephone and communications engineer. d, Ramsey Gelling Johnson (1889-1972), judge, president of Royal Manx Agricultural Society. e, John Nicholson (1911-88), stamp designer.

No. 1276: a, Dr. Dorothy Pantin (1896-1985), first female doctor. b, Richard Costain (1839-1902), construction business entrepreneur. c, Sir William Percy Cowley (1886-1958), judge. d, Rev. Fred Cubbon (1902-80), philanthropist. e, William Henry Gill (1839-1922), author, musician.

2008, Aug. 1   Perf. 13¼

1275		Horiz. strip of 5	6.25	6.25
a.-e.		A288 31p Any single	1.25	1.25
1276		Horiz. strip of 5	10.00	10.00
a.-e.		A288 50p Any single	2.00	2.00

End of World War I, 90th Anniv. — A289

Poppy and letter from soldier: 30p, Second Lieutenant Roy F. Corlett. 31p, Second Lieutenant John W. Lewis. 44p, Private Joseph Killey. 56p, Lieutenant Colonel W. A. W. Crellin. 81p, Lance Corporal Tom Quilliam. 94p, Private Robert Oates. £2, National War Memorial, St. John's.

2008, Oct. 1   Litho.   Perf. 14

1277	A289	30p multi	1.10	1.10
1278	A289	31p multi	1.10	1.10
1279	A289	44p multi	1.60	1.60
1280	A289	56p multi	2.00	2.00
1281	A289	81p multi	3.00	3.00
1282	A289	94p multi	3.50	3.50
	Nos. 1277-1282 (6)		12.30	12.30

Souvenir Sheet

1283	A289	£2 multi	7.25	7.25

Flora and Fauna of Ballaugh Curragh A290

Designs: 30p, Orange-tip butterfly. 31p, Curlew. 50p, Birch bracket fungus. 70p, Large red damselfly. 82p, Marsh cinquefoil. £1.38, Royal fern.

2008, Oct. 1   Perf. 13¼

1284	A290	30p multi	1.10	1.10
1285	A290	31p multi	1.10	1.10
1286	A290	50p multi	1.75	1.75
1287	A290	70p multi	2.50	2.50
1288	A290	82p multi	3.00	3.00
1289	A290	£1.38 multi	5.00	5.00
	Nos. 1284-1289 (6)		14.45	14.45

Christmas A291

Postman from *The Jolly Christmas Postman*, by Janet and Allen Ahlberg: 28p, On bicycle, letters. 31p, And mouse in cracker box. 48p, And bear family. 50p, And Toy Town. 56p, On bicycle, with truck and horsecart on winding road. £1.56, At home.

2008, Oct. 20   Perf. 14x14¼

1290	A291	28p multi	.90	.90
1291	A291	31p multi	1.00	1.00
1292	A291	48p multi	1.60	1.60
1293	A291	50p multi	1.60	1.60
1294	A291	56p multi	1.90	1.90
1295	A291	£1.56 multi	5.00	5.00
	Nos. 1290-1295 (6)		12.00	12.00

Lewis Hamilton, Formula 1 Race Car Driver A292

No. 1296: a, Hamilton driving race car. b, Hamilton celebrating victory with champagne spray.

No. 1297: a, Hamilton driving past finish line. b, Hamilton in race car cockpit.

No. 1298: a, Hamilton driving race car, diff. b, Hamilton in helmet with arms extended.

2009, Jan. 15   Litho.   Perf. 14

1296		Horiz. pair	1.75	1.75
a.		A292 30p multi	.85	.85
b.		A292 31p multi	.90	.90
1297		Horiz. pair	4.00	4.00
a.		A292 56p multi	1.60	1.60
b.		A292 85p multi	2.40	2.40
1298		Horiz. pair	6.75	6.75
a.		A292 98p multi	2.75	2.75
b.		A292 £1.42 multi	4.00	4.00
	Nos. 1296-1298 (3)		12.50	12.50

Naval Aviation, Cent. A293

No. 1299: a, Fairey Barracuda II. b, Blackburn Buccaneer S.2. c, Fairey Flycatcher.

No. 1300: a, EH101 Merlin helicopter. b, BAe Sea Harrier FRS.1. c, Sea Scout SS.24 airship.

2009, Jan. 15

1299		Horiz. strip of 3	3.75	3.75
a.		A293 30p multi	.85	.85
b.		A293 31p multi	.90	.90
c.		A293 72p multi	2.00	2.00
d.		Booklet pane of 4, 2 each #1299a, 1299b	3.50	—
1300		Horiz. strip of 3	9.00	9.00
a.		A293 85p multi	2.40	2.40
b.		A293 98p multi	2.75	2.75
c.		A293 £1.36 multi	3.75	3.75
d.		Booklet pane of 4, #1299a, 1299b, 1299c, 1300a	6.25	—
e.		Booklet pane of 4, #1299a, 1299b, 1300b, 1300c	8.25	—
f.		Booklet pane of 4, #1299c, 1300a, 1300b, 1300c	11.00	—
		Complete booklet, #1299d, 1300d, 1300e, 1300f	29.00	

Accession to the Throne of Henry VIII, 500th Anniv. A294

No. 1301: a, King Henry VIII. b, Catherine of Aragon (first wife). c, Anne Boleyn (second wife). d, Jane Seymour (third wife).

No. 1302: a, Anne of Cleves (fourth wife). b, Catherine Howard (fifth wife). c, Catherine Parr (sixth wife). d, Hampton Court.

2009, Feb. 18   **Perf. 13¼**

1301	Horiz. strip of 4	5.75	5.75
a.-d.	A294 50p Any single	1.40	1.40
1302	Horiz. strip of 4	5.75	5.75
a.-d.	A294 50p Any single	1.40	1.40

Photographs of Mills and Millers by Chris Killip — A295

No. 1303: a, Ballakilley Farm. b, Grenaby Farm.

No. 1304: a, Mr. Cubbon. b, Glenmoar Mill.

No. 1305: a, Golden Meadow Mill. b, Bernie Mylcraine.

No. 1306: a, Golden Meadow Mill, diff. b, Loughtan Farm.

No. 1307, Like #1303a. No. 1308, Like #1303b. No. 1309, Like #1304b. No. 1310, Like #1304a.

2009, Apr. 1   **Perf. 13¼**

1303	Pair	1.90	1.90
a.-b.	A295 32p Either single	.95	.95
1304	Pair	2.00	2.00
a.-b.	A295 33p Either single	1.00	1.00
1305	Pair	3.00	3.00
a.-b.	A295 50p Either single	1.50	1.50
1306	Pair	4.75	4.75
a.-b.	A295 78p Either single	2.25	2.25
	Nos. 1303-1306 (4)	11.65	11.65

Booklet Stamps
Self-Adhesive
Serpentine Die Cut 12½

1307	A295 32p black	.95	.95
1308	A295 32p black	.95	.95
a.	Booklet pane of 10, 5 each #1307-1308	9.00	
	Complete booklet, #1308a	9.00	
1309	A295 33p black	1.00	1.00
1310	A295 33p black	1.00	1.00
a.	Booklet pane of 10, 5 each #1309-1310	9.50	
	Complete booklet, #1310a	10.00	
	Nos. 1307-1310 (4)	3.90	3.90

Miniature Sheet

Peonies — A296

No. 1311 — Denomination color: a, Yellow. b, Light green. c, Pink. d, Blue. e, Violet. f, Red. g, Blue green. h, Olive green.

2009, Apr. 10   **Perf. 13¼**

1311	A296 Sheet of 8	2.40	2.40
a.-h.	10p Any single	.30	.30

First Man on the Moon, 40th Anniv. A297

Paintings by Astronaut Alan Bean: 33p, First Boot Print, Sunrise Over Antares. 50p, Clan MacBean Arrives on the Moon, Documenting the Sample. 56p, Pete and Me. 81p, Headed for the Last Parking Lot. 105p, The Eagle is Headed Home, In the Beginning. 135p, Ceremony on the Plain at Hadley, The Hoer. £2.50, On the Rim, vert.

2009, Apr. 12   **Perf. 12½**

1312	A297 33p multi	1.00	1.00
a.	Sheet of 10	10.00	10.00
1313	A297 50p multi	1.50	1.50
1314	A297 56p multi	1.75	1.75
a.	Sheet of 10	17.50	17.50
1315	A297 81p multi	2.40	2.40
1316	A297 105p multi	3.25	3.25
1317	A297 135p multi	4.00	4.00
	Nos. 1312-1317 (6)	13.90	13.90

Souvenir Sheet

1318	A297 £2.50 multi	7.50	7.50
1318a		As #1318, with 40th anniversary emblem in sheet margin, perf. 12	8.50	8.50

Europa (33p, 56p).
Issued: No. 1318a, 7/20.

Honda Racing Motorcycles — A298

Motorcycle from the: 32p, 1950s. 33p, 1960s. 56p, 1970s. 62p, 1980s. 90p, 1990s. £1.77, 2000s.

2009, May 11   **Perf. 14**

1319	A298 32p multi	1.00	1.00
1320	A298 33p multi	1.10	1.10
1321	A298 56p multi	1.75	1.75
1322	A298 62p multi	2.00	2.00
1323	A298 90p multi	3.00	3.00
1324	A298 £1.77 multi	5.75	5.75
	Nos. 1319-1324 (6)	14.60	14.60

Souvenir Sheet

2009 England Vs. Australia The Ashes Cricket Test Match — A299

No. 1325: a, W. G. Grace at Lord's Cricket Ground (42x28mm). b, Marylebone Cricket Club Ashes trophy and urn (30x40mm). c, England vs. Australia, Lord's Cricket Ground, 2005 (42x28mm).

Perf. 14 (#1325a, 1325c), 14x14¾

2009, June 20

1325	A299 Sheet of 3	9.75	9.75
a.-c.	£1 Any single	3.25	3.25

The Bee Gees, 50th Anniv. — A300

No. 1326: a, Barry, Robin and Maurice Gibb as children. b, "Children of the World" album cover. c, "Spirits Having Flown" album cover. d, "Still Waters" album cover.

No. 1327: a, "One Night Only" album cover. b, "This Is Where I Came In" album cover. c, "Number Ones" album cover. d, "The Studio Albums 1967-1968" album cover.

2009, July 1   **Perf. 13x12½**

1326	Horiz. strip of 4 + central label	5.50	5.50
a.	A300 32p multi	1.00	1.00
b.	A300 33p multi	1.10	1.10
c.	A300 50p multi	1.60	1.60
d.	A300 54p multi	1.75	1.75
1327	Horiz. strip of 4 + central label	11.00	11.00
a.	A300 56p multi	1.90	1.90
b.	A300 62p multi	2.10	2.10
c.	A300 78p multi	2.60	2.60
d.	A300 £1.28 multi	4.25	4.25

Paintings of Wildlife by Jeremy Paul A301

Paintings: 32p, Brown Hare. 33p, Hedgehogs. 54p, Pheasants. 90p, Barn Owl. 92p, Cockerel. £1.58, On the Hill.

2009, Sept. 1   **Litho.**   **Perf. 12½**

1328	A301 32p multi	1.10	1.10
1329	A301 33p multi	1.10	1.10
1330	A301 54p multi	1.75	1.75
1331	A301 90p multi	3.00	3.00
1332	A301 92p multi	3.00	3.00
1333	A301 £1.58 multi	5.25	5.25
a.	Sheet of 6, #1328-1333	15.50	15.50
	Nos. 1328-1333 (6)	15.20	15.20

Watercolors by Archibald Knox A302

Watercolors: 32p, Bridge Possibly at Laxey. 33p, Willows and Blue Mountain Possibly Greeba. 56p, Kew. 62p, Eairy Beg Glen Helen. 81p, Leaning Trees. 182p, Old Laxey.

2009, Sept. 16   **Perf. 12½**

1334	A302 32p multi	1.00	1.00
1335	A302 33p multi	1.10	1.10
1336	A302 56p multi	1.75	1.75
1337	A302 62p multi	2.00	2.00
1338	A302 81p multi	2.60	2.60
1339	A302 182p multi	5.75	5.75
	Nos. 1334-1339 (6)	14.20	14.20

Souvenir Sheet

Sinking of the Ellan Vannin, Cent. — A303

No. 1340: a, Captain James Teare and Ellan Vannan at sea. b, Ellan Vannan in harbor.

2009, Oct. 1   **Perf. 14**

1340	A303 Sheet of 2	9.50	9.50
a.-b.	£1.50 Either single	4.75	4.75

Christmas — A304

Santa Claus: 30p, Filling stocking. 33p, Making a list. 56p, Holding bag of toys. 62p, Near chimney, holding gift. 81p, Holding staff and bag. 90p, Holding chalice.

2009, Oct. 20   **Perf. 14**

1341	A304 30p multi	1.00	1.00
1342	A304 33p multi	1.10	1.10
1343	A304 56p multi	1.90	1.90
1344	A304 62p multi	2.10	2.10
1345	A304 81p multi	2.75	2.75
1346	A304 90p multi	3.00	3.00
	Nos. 1341-1346 (6)	11.85	11.85

Christmas Type of 2009

Designs as before.

Die Cut Perf. 13x13½

2009, Oct. 20   **Litho.**

Size: 23x34mm

Self-Adhesive

1347	A304 30p multi	1.00	1.00
1348	A304 33p multi	1.10	1.10

A305

A306

A307

A308

A309

A310

A311

A312

A313

Island Life — A314

2010, Jan. 12 — Perf. 12½

1349		Horiz. strip of 4	4.25	4.25
a.	A305	(32p) multi	1.00	1.00
b.	A306	(32p) multi	1.00	1.00
c.	A307	(32p) multi	1.00	1.00
d.	A308	(32p) multi	1.00	1.00
1350		Horiz. strip of 4	4.50	4.50
a.	A309	(33p) multi	1.10	1.10
b.	A310	(33p) multi	1.10	1.10
c.	A311	(33p) multi	1.10	1.10
d.	A312	(33p) multi	1.10	1.10
1351	A313	56p multi	1.75	1.75
1352	A314	90p multi	3.00	3.00
		Nos. 1349-1352 (4)	13.50	13.50

Booklet Stamps
Self-Adhesive
Serpentine Die Cut 13¾x13

1353	A305	(32p) multi	1.00	1.00
1354	A306	(32p) multi	1.00	1.00
1355	A307	(32p) multi	1.00	1.00
1356	A308	(32p) multi	1.00	1.00
a.		Booklet pane of 12, 3 each		
		#1353-1356	12.00	
1357	A309	(33p) multi	1.10	1.10
1358	A310	(33p) multi	1.10	1.10
1359	A311	(33p) multi	1.10	1.10
1360	A312	(33p) multi	1.10	1.10
a.		Booklet pane of 12, 3 each		
		#1357-1360	13.50	
		Nos. 1353-1360 (8)	8.40	8.40

Girl Guides, Cent. — A315

No. 1361 — Rainbows with denomination in: a, Red. b, Blue.
No. 1362 — Brownies with denomination in: a, Red. b, Blue.
No. 1363 — Girl Guides with denomination in: a, Red. b, Blue.
No. 1364 — Senior Section members with denomination in: a, Red. b, Blue.
No. 1365 — Adult volunteers with denomination in: a, Red. b, Blue.

2010 — Perf. 14

1361	A315	Horiz. pair	2.00	2.00
a.-b.		32p Either single	1.00	1.00
1362	A315	Horiz. pair	2.00	2.00
a.-b.		33p Either single	1.00	1.00
1363	A315	Horiz. pair	3.50	3.50
a.-b.		56p Either single	1.75	1.75
1364	A315	Horiz. pair	6.00	6.00
a.-b.		£1 Either single	3.00	3.00
		Nos. 1361-1364 (4)	13.50	13.50

Souvenir Sheet

1365	A315	Sheet of 2	9.00	9.00
a.-b.		£1.50 Either single	4.50	4.50
c.		As #1365, with Centenary Camp emblem added in sheet margin	9.75	9.75

Issued: Nos. 1361-1365, 2/18; No. 1365c, 7/31. Europa (Nos. 1362a, 1363a).

A316

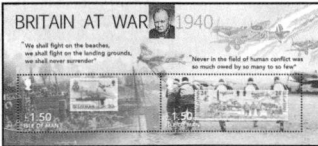

Battle of Britain, 70th Anniv. — A317

No. 1366: a, Messerschmitt BF110 and Hurricane. b, Blenheim I and Junkers 88. c, Heinkel HE 111 and Spitfire.
No. 1367: a, Messerschmitt BF109 and Defiant. b, Spitfire and Messerschmitt BF109. c, Junkers JU-87 and Hurricane.
No. 1368: a, Ben My Chree arriving at Folkstone with troops evacuated from Dunkirk, Isle of Man #204. b, Airmen running to planes, Isle of Man #429a.

2010, Apr. 20 — Perf. 13¼

1366		Horiz. strip of 3	6.50	6.50
a.-c.	A316	70p Any single	2.10	2.10
1367		Horiz. strip of 3	6.50	6.50
a.-c.	A316	70p Any single	2.10	2.10

Souvenir Sheet
Perf. 13¾

1368	A317	Sheet of 2	9.25	9.25
a.-b.		£1.50 Either single	4.50	4.50

Accession to Throne of King George V, Cent. — A318

Photographs of 1920 royal visit to Isle of Man and items from Royal Philatelic Collection: 55p, Royal party at Bishops Court, Ballaugh, cast of proposed 1913 stamp depicting King George V. 60p, King George V and Queen Mary on Tynwald Hill, two used pairs of Cape of Good Hope 1p triangle stamps. 67p, Queen's Pier, Ramsey, unissued 2p plum stamp of Great Britain. 96p, Visit to war disabled at Ramsey Cottage Hospital, Niger Coast Protectorates #35. 97p, Tree planting at Bishops Court, Great Britain #151. £1.10, Royal party at Castletown, Mauritius #2.

2010, May 6 — Perf. 14

1369	A318	55p multi	1.60	1.60
1370	A318	60p multi	1.75	1.75
1371	A318	67p multi	2.00	2.00
1372	A318	96p multi	3.00	3.00
1373	A318	97p multi	3.00	3.00
1374	A318	£1.10 multi	3.25	3.25
		Nos. 1369-1374 (6)	14.60	14.60

Model T Fords — A319

Designs: 35p, 1915 Speedster. 36p, 1926 Coupe. 60p, 1923 Van. 74p, 1912 Town Car. 97p, 1922 Charabanc. 172p, 1912 Tourer.

2010, May 7 — Perf. 13¼

1375	A319	35p multi	1.10	1.10
1376	A319	36p multi	1.10	1.10
1377	A319	60p multi	1.75	1.75
1378	A319	74p multi	2.25	2.25
1379	A319	97p multi	3.00	3.00
1380	A319	172p multi	5.25	5.25
		Nos. 1375-1380 (6)	14.45	14.45

Railways A320

Designs: 35p, Caledonia at summit of Snaefell Mountain. 36p, Isle of Man Railways steam locomotive No. 1 and Manx Electric Railway car 1 at Laxey. 55p, Caledonia at Bulgham. 88p, Isle of Man Railways Loch locomotive at Skinscoe Curve. £1.32, Manx Electric Railway car No. 33 approaching Keristal. £1.46, Loch and Maitland locomotives near White Hoe.

2010, June 24 — Perf. 14

1381	A320	35p multi	1.10	1.10
1382	A320	36p multi	1.10	1.10
1383	A320	55p multi	1.75	1.75
1384	A320	88p multi	2.75	2.75
1385	A320	£1.32 multi	4.00	4.00
1386	A320	£1.46 multi	4.50	4.50
		Nos. 1381-1386 (6)	15.20	15.20

History of Manx Coinage A321

Designs: 35p, 1709 Lord Derby halfpenny, Castle Rushen. 36p, 1798 Cartwheel penny, Soho Mint, Birmingham. 55p, 1839 Queen Victoria Farthing, Douglas. 60p, 1965 gold coin, Castle Rushen. 67p, 1971 Decimal currency 5p coin, Tower of Refuge. £1.87, 2010 £5 Laxey Wheel coin, Laxey Wheel.

2010, June 24 — Perf. 12¾

1387	A321	35p multi	1.10	1.10
1388	A321	36p multi	1.10	1.10
1389	A321	55p multi	1.75	1.75
1390	A321	60p multi	1.90	1.90
1391	A321	67p multi	2.10	2.10
1392	A321	£1.87 multi	5.75	5.75
		Nos. 1387-1392 (6)	13.70	13.70

Souvenir Sheet

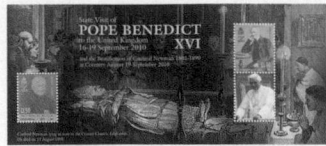

Beatification of Cardinal John Henry Newman (1801-90) — A322

No. 1393: a, Newman, table and book. b, Newman.

2010, Aug. 11 — Perf. 13¼

1393	A322	Sheet of 2 + label	9.50	9.50
a.-b.		£1.50 Either single	4.75	4.75

State visit of Pope Benedict XVI.

Artwork by Internees in Isle of Man World War II Internment Camps A323

Designs: 35p, Three-legged Postman, by Bertram. 36p, Peveril Camp, Peel, by Herbert Kaden. 55p, Life at Palace Camp, Douglas, by Imre Goth. 67p, Douglas, Isle of Man, by Hermann Fechenbach. 132p, Violinist at Onchan Camp, by Ernst Eisenmayer. 172p, Portrait of Klaus E. Hinrichsen, by Kurt Schwitters.

2010, Sept. 24 — Litho.

1394	A323	35p multi	1.10	1.10
1395	A323	36p multi	1.10	1.10
1396	A323	55p multi	1.75	1.75
1397	A323	67p multi	2.10	2.10
1398	A323	132p multi	4.00	4.00
1399	A323	172p multi	5.25	5.25
		Nos. 1394-1399 (6)	15.30	15.30

Souvenir Sheet

The Christmas Story — A324

No. 1400 — Characters from Friends and Heroes animated TV show depicting the Nativity: a, Jesus is born. b, Shepherds hear first. c, The Magi see a star.

2010, Oct. 1 — Litho. — Perf. 13¼x13¾

1400	A324	Sheet of 3	9.75	9.75
a.-c.		£1 Any single	3.25	3.25

Photographs of Snowfall of 2009-10 Winter — A325

Photographs of: 35p, Old Braddan Church, by Bill Dale. 36p, The Braaid, by Seamus Whelan. 60p, Dhoon Glen, by Simon Park. 88p, Dhoon Beach, by Park. 97p, Cronk ny Aree Laa, by Dale. £1.46, St. Patrick's Isle in Snow, by Victoria Harrop.

2010, Oct. 20 — Perf. 13x13¼

1401	A325	35p multi	1.25	1.25
1402	A325	36p multi	1.25	1.25
1403	A325	60p multi	2.00	2.00
1404	A325	88p multi	3.00	3.00
1405	A325	97p multi	3.25	3.25
1406	A325	£1.46 multi	4.75	4.75
		Nos. 1401-1406 (6)	15.50	15.50

Souvenir Sheet

Engagement of Prince William of Wales and Catherine Middleton — A326

No. 1407 — Prince William: a, Close-up, no shirt visible. b, Shirt visible.

2010, Nov. 26 — Litho. — Perf. 14¾x14

1407	A326	Sheet of 2	9.50	9.50
a.-b.		£1.50 Either single	4.75	4.75

Queen Elizabeth II, 60th Anniv. of Reign (in 2012) — A327

Designs: 35p, Queen Elizabeth II, 1953 coronation photograph. 36p, Queen and Prince Philip, 2007. 55p, Queen and Prince Philip as newlyweds, 1971. 60p, Queen and Prince Philip in uniforms, 1971. £1.14, Queen and Prince Philip, 2002. £1.46, Prince Philip at 1953 coronation.
£3, Queen and Prince Philip, 1970s.

2011, Feb. 6 — Perf. 13¼

1408	A327	35p multi	1.10	1.10
1409	A327	36p multi	1.25	1.25
1410	A327	55p multi	1.75	1.75
1411	A327	60p multi	1.90	1.90
1412	A327	£1.14 multi	3.75	3.75
1413	A327	£1.46 multi	4.75	4.75
		Nos. 1408-1413 (6)	14.50	14.50

Souvenir Sheet

1414	A327	£3 multi	9.75	9.75

Genealogy A328

Inscription in frame at UL: No. 1415, Baptisms. No. 1416, School Days. No. 1417, Working Life. No. 1418, Weddings. No. 1419, Family Album. No. 1420, Emigration. No. 1421, Memorials. No. 1422, Family Tree.

2011, Feb. 18 — Litho. — Perf. 13½
Frame Color

1415	A328	35p org brown	1.10	1.10
1416	A328	35p deep claret	1.10	1.10
1417	A328	36p car rose	1.25	1.25
1418	A328	36p Prus blue	1.25	1.25
1419	A328	67p slate grn	2.25	2.25
1420	A328	67p emerald	2.25	2.25
1421	A328	£1.10 ol green	3.50	3.50
1422	A328	£1.10 brown	3.50	3.50
		Nos. 1415-1422 (8)	16.20	16.20

POSTAGE DUE STAMPS

Catalogue values for unused stamps in this section are for Never Hinged items.

D1 D2

Imprint: "1973 Questa"
Perf. 13½

1973, July 5   Litho.   Unwmk.
Inscriptions and Coat of Arms in
Black and Red

J1	D1	½p yellow	.20	.20
J2	D1	1p buff	.30	.30
J3	D1	2p lt yellow grn	1.10	1.10
J4	D1	3p gray	2.00	2.00
J5	D1	4p dull rose	3.00	3.00
J6	D1	5p light blue	3.25	3.25
J7	D1	10p light violet	7.50	7.50
J8	D1	20p lt grnsh blue	18.00	18.00
		Nos. J1-J8 (8)	35.35	35.35

Inscribed: "1973 A Questa"

1973, Sept.

J1a	D1	½p	1.75	1.50
J2a	D1	1p	.90	.45
J3a	D1	2p	.25	.20
J4a	D1	3p	.20	.20
J5a	D1	4p	.25	.20
J6a	D1	5p	.25	.20
J7a	D1	10p	.45	.40
J8a	D1	20p	.90	.65
		Nos. J1a-J8a (8)	4.95	3.80

1975, Jan. 8   Litho.   Perf. 14
Inscriptions and Coat of Arms in
Black and Red

J9	D2	½p yellow	.20	.20
J10	D2	1p buff	.20	.20
J11	D2	4p lilac rose	.20	.20
J12	D2	7p blue	.30	.30
J13	D2	9p sepia	.35	.35
J14	D2	10p lilac	.40	.40
J15	D2	50p orange	1.25	1.25
J16	D2	£1 bright green	2.50	2.50
		Nos. J9-J16 (8)	5.40	5.40

D3 D4

1982-92   Litho.   Perf. 15x14

J17	D3	1p light green	.20	.20
J18	D3	2p bright pink	.20	.20
J19	D3	5p grnsh blue	.20	.20
J20	D3	10p bright lilac	.40	.40
J21	D3	20p gray	.75	.75
J22	D3	50p dull yellow	2.00	2.00
J23	D3	£1 brick red	3.00	3.00
J24	D3	£2 blue	6.00	6.00

Litho.
Perf. 13x13½

J25	D4	£5 multicolored	15.00	15.00
		Nos. J17-J25 (9)	27.75	27.75

Issued: £5, 9/16/92; others, 10/5/82.

GREECE

'grēs

(Hellas)

LOCATION — Southern part of the Balkan Peninsula in southeastern Europe, bordering on the Ionian, Aegean and Mediterranean Seas
GOVT. — Republic
AREA — 50,949 sq. mi.
POP. — 10,511,000 (1997 est.)
CAPITAL — Athens

In 1923 the reigning king was forced to abdicate and the following year Greece was declared a republic. In 1935, the king was recalled by a "plebiscite" of the people. Greece became a republic in June 1973. The country today includes the Aegean Islands of Chios, Mytilene (Lesbos), Samos, Icaria (Nicaria) and Lemnos, the Ionian Islands (Corfu, etc.) Crete, Macedonia, Western Thrace and part of Eastern Thrace, the Mount Athos District, Epirus and the Dodecanese Islands.

100 Lepta = 1 Drachma
100 Cents = 1 Euro (2002)

> Catalogue values for unused stamps in this country are for Never Hinged items, beginning with Scott 472 in the regular postage section, Scott B1 in the semi-postal section, Scott C48 in the airpost section, Scott CB1 in the airpost semi-postal section, Scott RA69 in the postal tax section, and Scott N239 in the occupation and annexation section.

Values for unused stamps are for examples with original gum as defined in the catalogue introduction. Any exceptions will be noted.

Values for Large Hermes Head stamps with double control numbers on the back, Nos. 20e, 21c, 27a, et al, are for examples with two distinct and separate impressions, not for blurred or "slide doubles" caused by paper slippage on the press.

Watermarks

Wmk. 129 — Crown and ET

Wmk. 252 — Crowns

Paris Print

Paris Print, Fine Impression

The enlarged illustrations show the head in various states of the plates. The differences are best seen in the shading lines on the cheek and neck.

1861   Unwmk.   Typo.   Imperf.
Without Figures on Back

1	A1	1 l choc, *brnish*	600.00	550.00
a.		1 l red brown, *brnish*	725.00	600.00
b.		1 l brown	575.00	475.00
2	A1	2 l ol bis, *straw*	67.50	87.50
a.		2 l brown buff, *buff*	55.00	75.00
b.		2 l yellowish bister	55.00	75.00
3	A1	5 l yel grn, *grnsh*	700.00	150.00
a.		5 l emerald green	875.00	175.00
4	A1	20 l bl, *bluish*	1,150.	95.00
a.		20 l deep blue, *bluish*	1,100.	340.00
b.		On pelure paper	1,350.	275.00
5	A1	40 l vio, *bl*	325.00	130.00
6	A1	80 l rose, *pink*	250.00	120.00
a.		80 l carmine, *pink*	250.00	120.00

Large Figures, 8mm high, on Back

7	A1	10 l red org, *bl*	1,040.	500.00
a.		"10" on back inverted	—	
c.		"0" of "10" invtd. on back	—	1,850.
d.		"1" of "10" invtd. on back	—	2,750.

No. 7 without "10" on back is a proof.
Trial impressions of Paris prints exist in many shades, some being close to those of the issued stamps. The gum used was thin and smooth instead of thick, brownish and crackly as on the issued stamps.
See #8-58. For surcharges see #130, 132-133, 137-139, 141-143, 147-149, 153-154, 157-158.

Faint quadrille, horizontal or vertical lines are visible in the background of some Athens print large Hermes head stamps.
Nos. 16, 16a, 16b are the only 1 l stamps that have these lines.

Athens Prints

Athens Print, Typical Clear Impression

Hermes (Mercury) — A1

Athens Print, Typical Coarse Impression

Figures on Back
5 l:

#11

#18-45

Fine Printing (F)
Fine Printing (F, '62) see footnote
Coarse Printing (C)

1861-62
Without Figures on Back

8	A1	1 l choc, *brnish* (F, '62)	490.00	490.00
		No gum	350.00	
a.		1 l dk chocolate, *brnish* (F)	1,300.	1,325.
		No gum	700.00	
b.		1 l chocolate, *brnish* (F)	590.00	590.00
		No gum	460.00	
9	A1	2 l bis brn, *bister* (F)	75.00	110.00
		No gum	40.00	
a.		2 l dark brown, *straw,* (C)	6,750.	—
b.		2 l bister brown, *bister* (C)	90.00	135.00
c.		2 l bister brown, *bister* (F, '62)	90.00	135.00
10	A1	20 l dk bl, *bluish* (C)		15,000.

With Figures on Back

11	A1	5 l grn, *grnsh* (F)	300.00	135.00
		No gum	175.00	
a.		5 l green, *greenish* (C)	375.00	190.00
b.		As "a," double "5" on back (F, C)		2,850.
c.		5 l green, *greenish,* bl grn figures on back (F, '62)	350.00	135.00
12	A1	10 l org, *grnsh* (F, '62)	600.00	90.00
		No gum	325.00	
a.		10 l orange, *greenish* (C)	1,950.	300.00
c.		10 l orange, *greenish* (F)	600.00	135.00
13	A1	20 l blue, *bluish* (F, '62)	475.00	57.50
a.		20 l dull blue, *bluish* (C)	6,750.	245.00
b.		20 l dark blue, *bluish* (F)	3,500.	110.00
14	A1	40 l red vio, *pale bl* (F, '62)	5,250.	475.00
a.		40 l red violet, *blue* (C)	10,000.	600.00
b.		40 l red violet, *blue,* (F)	5,250.	475.00
15	A1	80 l carmine, *pink* (F, '62)	1,200.	165.00
a.		80 l carmine, *pink* (F)	1,200.	165.00
b.		80 l dl rose, *pink* (F)	1,200.	165.00

Nos. 8-15 are known as the "Athens Provisionals." The first printings were not very successful, producing the "coarse printings." Later printings used an altered printing method that gave better results (the "fine printings"). All these were issued in the normal manner by the Post Office.

Nos. 8, 9c, 11c, 12, 13, 14, 15 have uninterrupted and even shading lines that do not taper off at the ends. They were produced in May 1862 (F, '62). Other fine printing stamps were produced in Feb.-Apr. 1862 (F).
The numerals on the back are strongly shaded in the right lines with the corresponding left lines being quite thin. The colors of the numerals are generally strong and often show clumps of ink.
Nos. 15a and 15b have vermilion figures on the back, while those of all later printings are carmine.

1862-67
With Figures on Back
Except 1 l, 2 l

16	A1	1 l brn, *brnish* (poor print)	60.00	60.00
a.		1 l red brn, *brnish* (poor print)	150.00	150.00
b.		1 l choc, *brnish*	67.50	67.50
17	A1	2 l bister, *bister*	55.00	60.00
a.		2 l brnsh bis, *bister*	13.00	24.00
18	A1	5 l grn, *grnsh*	250.00	24.00
a.		5 l yellowish green, *grnsh*	250.00	12.00
19	A1	10 l org, *blue* ('64)	400.00	47.50
a.		10 l yel org, *bluish*	650.00	60.00
b.		As "b," "10" inverted on front of stamp		23,500.
c.		10 l red org, *bl* (Dec. '65)	650.00	27.50
d.		"01" on back	9,000.	175.00
20	A1	20 l bl, *bluish*	250.00	24.00
a.		20 l lt bl, *bluish* (fine print)	375.00	24.00
b.		20 l dark blue, *bluish*	2,000.	67.50
c.		20 l blue, *greenish*	1,700.	37.50
d.		"80" on back		2,450.
e.		Double "20" on back		1,500.
f.		Without "20" on back		5,500.
21	A1	40 l lilac, *bl*	550.00	37.50
a.		40 l grayish lilac, *blue*	1,750.	37.50
b.		40 l lilac brown, *lil gray*	1,500.	47.50
c.		Double "40" on back		1,600.
22	A1	80 l car, *pale rose*	80.00	24.00
a.		80 l rose, *pale rose*	80.00	24.00
b.		"8" on back inverted		550.00
c.		"80" on back inverted		
d.		"8" only on back		700.00
e.		"0" only on back		700.00

Nos. 16-22 represent a series of printings for each value, from 1862 through 1867, until a major cleaning of the plates was done in 1868. Impressions range from very fine and clear to coarse and blotchy.
Some printings of Nos. 16, 16a, 16b show faint vertical, horizontal or quadrilled lines in the background. Later 1 l stamps do not show these lines.
Many stamps of this and succeeding issues which are normally imperforate are known privately rouletted, pin-perforated, percé en scie, etc.

1868
From Cleaned Plates
With Figures on Back,
Except 1 l, 2 l

23	A1	1 l gray brn, *brnish*	67.50	75.00
24	A1	2 l gray bis, *bister*	32.50	47.50
25	A1	5 l grn, *grnsh*	6,500.	150.00
a.		5 l yellow green, *grnsh*	6,500.	50.00
26	A1	10 l pale org, *bluish*	1,650.	40.00
a.		"01" on back		—
27	A1	20 l pale bl, *bluish*	1,500.	24.00
a.		Double "20" on back	—	1,450.
28	A1	40 l rose vio, *bl*	325.00	37.50
a.		"20" on back, corrected to "40"	—	2,750.
29	A1	80 l rose car, *pale rose*	190.00	250.00

The "0" on the back of No. 29 is printed more heavily than the "8."

1870
With Figures on Back, Except 1 l

30	A1	1 l deep reddish brn, *brnish*	175.00	200.00
a.		1 l redsh brn, *brnish*	200.00	240.00
31	A1	20 l lt bl, *bluish*	1,900.	24.00
a.		20 l blue, *bluish*	2,000.	35.00
b.		"02" on back		1,225.
c.		"20" on back inverted		675.00

Nos. 30 and 30a have short lines of shading on cheek. The spandrels of No. 31 are very pale with the lines often broken or missing.

This was an Athens Printing made under supervision of German workmen.

1870
Medium to Thin Paper
Without Mesh
With Figures on Back, Except 1 l, 2 l

32	A1	1 l brn, *brnish*	325.00	325.00
a.		1 l purple brown, *brnish*	325.00	325.00
33	A1	2 l sal bis, *bister*	19.00	45.00
34	A1	5 l grn, *grnsh*	6,000.	120.00
35	A1	10 l lt red org, *grnsh*	—	240.00
a.		"01" on back	—	—
b.		"10" on back inverted	—	—
36	A1	20 l bl, *bluish*	1,400.	24.00
a.		"02" on back	—	600.00
b.		Double "20" on back		1,375.
37	A1	40 l sal, *grnsh*	825.00	82.50
a.		40 l lilac, *greenish*		75,000.

The stamps of this issue have rather coarse figures on back.

No. 37a is printed in the exact shade of the numerals on the back of No. 37.

1872
Thin Transparent Paper
Showing Mesh
With Figures on Back, Except 1 l

38	A1	1 l grayish brown, *straw*	55.00	75.00
a.		1 l red brn, *yelsh*	82.50	115.00
39	A1	5 l grn, *greenish*	675.00	30.00
a.		5 l dark green, *grnsh*	725.00	40.00
b.		Double "5" on back		225.00
40	A1	10 l red org, *grnsh*	1,050.	37.50
a.		10 l red orange, *pale lilac*	7,750.	150.00
b.		As #40, "10" on back inverted	—	90.00
c.		Double "10" on back	—	1,125.
d.		"0" on back	—	525.00
e.		"01" on back	—	2,100.
41	A1	20 l dp bl, *bluish*	1,375.	30.00
a.		20 l blue, *bluish*	1,375	32.50
b.		20 l dark blue, *blue*	2,500.	55.00
42	A1	40 l brn, *bl*	45.00	67.50
a.		40 l olive brown, *blue*	45.00	70.00
b.		40 l red violet, *blue*	1,000.	95.00
c.		40 l gray violet, *blue*	825.00	75.00
d.		Figures on back bister (#42b, 42c)	1,100.	95.00

The mesh is not apparent on Nos. 38, 38a.

1875
On Cream Paper Unless Otherwise Stated
With Figures on Back, Except 1 l, 2 l

43	A1	1 l gray brn	15.00	12.00
a.		1 l Deep red brown	35.00	20.00
b.		1 l black brown, *yellowish*	175.00	160.00
c.		1 l red brown	45.00	60.00
d.		1 l dark red brown	75.00	87.50
e.		1 l purple brown	75.00	87.50
44	A1	2 l bister	30.00	32.50
45	A1	5 l pale yellow green	200.00	30.00
a.		5 l dk yel grn	275.00	40.00
46	A1	10 l orange	425.00	45.00
a.		10 l orange, *yellow*	240.00	25.00
b.		"00" on back	925.00	200.00
c.		"1" on back	—	260.00
d.		"0" on back	—	225.00
e.		"01" on back	—	535.00
f.		Double "10" on back	—	800.00
47	A1	20 l ultra	160.00	24.00
a.		20 l blue	290.00	24.00
b.		20 l deep Prussian blue	1,600.	60.00
c.		"02" on back	—	475.00
d.		"20" on back inverted	—	11,000.
e.		"2" instead of "20," inverted	—	3,000.
f.		Double "20" on back	—	1,350.
g.		"20" inverted, on front of stamp	210,000.	
48	A1	40 l salmon	30.00	90.00

The back figures are found in many varieties, including "1" and "0" inverted in "10."

Value for No. 47e is for example with "2" of "02" broken (deformed). Also known with unbroken "2"; value used about $600.

1876
Without Figures on Back
Paris Print, Clear Impression

49	A1	30 l ol brn, *yelsh*	290.00	60.00
a.		30 l brown, *yellowish*	500.00	135.00
50	A1	60 l grn, *grnsh*	40.00	115.00

Athens Print, Coarse Impression, Yellowish Paper

51	A1	30 l dark brown	75.00	13.50
a.		30 l black brown	75.00	13.50
52	A1	60 l green	625.00	67.50

1880-82 — Cream Paper
Without Figures on Back

53	A1	5 l green	30.00	9.50
54	A1	10 l orange	27.50	9.50
a.		10 l yellow	27.50	9.50
b.		10 l red orange	8,250.	75.00
55	A1	20 l ultra	450.00	190.00
56	A1	20 l pale rose (aniline ink) ('82)	8.25	8.25
a.		20 l rose (aniline ink) ('82)	8.25	8.25
b.		20 l deep carmine	275.00	17.50
57	A1	30 l ultra ('82)	225.00	17.50
a.		30 l slate blue	230.00	17.50
58	A1	40 l lilac	67.50	15.00
a.		40 l violet	67.50	24.00

Stamps of type A1 were not regularly issued with perf. 11½ but were freely used on mail.

Hermes — A2

Lepta denominations have white numeral tablets.

Belgian Print, Clear Impression

1886-88				*Imperf.*
64	A2	1 l brown ('88)	4.00	4.00
65	A2	2 l bister ('88)	9.50	225.00
66	A2	5 l yel grn ('88)	12.00	2.75
67	A2	10 l yellow ('88)	16.00	2.40
68	A2	20 l car rose ('88)	45.00	4.00
69	A2	25 l blue	160.00	2.75
70	A2	40 l violet ('88)	105.00	30.00
71	A2	50 l gray grn	8.25	2.75
72	A2	1d gray	120.00	4.00
		Nos. 64-72 (9)	479.75	277.65

See Nos. 81-116. For surcharges see Nos. 129, 134, 140, 144, 150, 151-152, 155-156.

1891				*Perf. 11½*
81	A2	1 l brown	8.25	3.50
82	A2	2 l bister	13.50	
83	A2	5 l yel grn	27.50	13.00
84	A2	10 l yellow	40.00	13.00
85	A2	20 l car rose	55.00	18.00
86	A2	25 l blue	275.00	25.00
87	A2	40 l violet	190.00	190.00
88	A2	50 l gray grn	22.50	6.50
89	A2	1d gray	200.00	8.25
		Nos. 81-89 (9)	831.75	277.25

The Belgian Printings perf. 13½ and most of the values perf. 11½ (Nos. 82-86) were perforated on request of philatelists at the main post office in Athens. While not regularly issued they were freely used for postage.

Athens Print, Poor Impression
Wmk. Greek Words in Some Sheets

1889-95				*Imperf.*
90	A2	1 l black brn	6.75	2.75
a.		1 l brown	6.75	4.00
91	A2	2 l pale bister	1.75	1.60
a.		2 l buff	2.75	2.75
92	A2	5 l green	11.00	1.60
a.		Double impression	200.00	
b.		5 l deep green	40.00	9.50
93	A2	10 l yellow	125.00	5.50
a.		10 l orange	47.50	4.00
b.		10 l dull yellow	125.00	5.50
94	A2	20 l carmine	11.00	8.25
a.		20 l rose	75.00	40.00
95	A2	25 l dull blue	125.00	9.50
a.		25 l indigo	150.00	6.75
b.		25 l ultra	125.00	6.75
c.		25 l brt blue	135.00	9.50
96	A2	25 l lilac	13.50	2.75
a.		25 l red vio ('93)	20.00	4.00
97	A2	40 l red vio ('91)	125.00	27.50
98	A2	40 l blue ('93)	9.50	2.75
99	A2	1d gray ('95)	475.00	8.25

				Perf. 13½
100	A2	1 l brown	80.00	—
101	A2	2 l buff	2.00	1.60
104	A2	20 l carmine	67.50	5.25
a.		20 l rose	80.00	6.25
105	A2	40 l red violet	130.00	47.50

Other denominations of type A2 were not officially issued with perf. 13½.

				Perf. 11½
107	A2	1 l brown	3.00	1.60
a.		1 l black brown	7.25	5.75
108	A2	2 l pale bister	2.50	2.00
a.		2 l buff	2.75	2.75
109	A2	5 l pale green	13.50	2.00
a.		5 l deep green	55.00	3.00
110	A2	10 l yellow	95.00	1.25
a.		10 l dull yellow	165.00	2.50
b.		10 l orange	300.00	5.75

111	A2	20 l carmine	55.00	.75
a.		20 l rose	160.00	1.60
112	A2	25 l dull blue	110.00	3.75
a.		25 l indigo	300.00	21.00
b.		25 l ultra	110.00	52.50
c.		25 l bright blue	160.00	9.00
113	A2	25 l lilac	6.75	1.60
a.		25 l red violet	20.00	2.75
114	A2	40 l red violet	160.00	37.50
115	A2	40 l blue	16.50	5.00
116	A2	1d gray	600.00	10.00

Partly-perforated varieties sell for about twice as much as normal stamps.

The watermark on Nos. 90-116 consists of three Greek words meaning Paper for Public Service. It is in double-lined capitals, measures 270x35mm, and extends across three panes.

Boxers — A3

Discobolus by Myron — A4

Vase Depicting Pallas Athene (Minerva) — A5

Chariot Driving A6

Stadium and Acropolis A7

Statue of Hermes by Praxiteles — A8

Statue of Victory by Paeonius — A9

Acropolis and Parthenon A10

Perf. 14x13½, 13½x14

1896				Unwmk.
117	A3	1 l ocher	4.00	3.00
118	A3	2 l rose	3.00	3.00
a.		Without engraver's name	30.00	21.00
119	A4	5 l lilac	12.50	5.25
120	A4	10 l slate gray	12.50	7.25
121	A5	20 l red brn	25.00	8.25
122	A6	25 l red	30.00	10.50
123	A5	40 l violet	14.50	9.50
124	A6	60 l black	42.50	21.00
125	A7	1d blue	115.00	26.00
126	A8	2d bister	325.00	105.00
a.		Horiz. pair, imperf. btwn.	—	—
127	A9	5d green	575.00	500.00
128	A10	10d brown	625.00	550.00
		Nos. 117-128 (12)	1,784.	1,248.

1st intl. Olympic Games of the modern era, held at Athens. Counterfeits of Nos. 123-124 and 126-128 exist.

For surcharges see Nos. 159-164.

Preceding Issues Surcharged

1900				*Imperf.*
129	A2	20 l on 25 l dl bl, #95c	3.00	1.60
a.		20 l on 25 l indigo, #95a	67.50	47.50
b.		20 l on 25 l ultra, #95b	70.00	55.00
c.		Double surcharge	57.50	57.50
d.		Triple surcharge	85.00	85.00
e.		Inverted surcharge	60.00	57.50
f.		"20" above word	110.00	105.00
g.		Pair, one without surcharge	250.00	250.00
h.		"20" without word	165.00	165.00
130	A1	30 l on 40 l vio, *cr*, #58a	6.50	6.25
a.		30 l on 40 l lilac, #58	15.50	15.50
b.		Broad "0" in "30"	10.50	8.25
c.		First letter of word is "A"	135.00	135.00
d.		Double surcharge	625.00	625.00
132	A1	40 l on 2 l bis, *cr*, #44	8.50	8.25
a.		Broad "0" in "40"	12.50	12.50
b.		First letter of word is "A"	165.00	165.00
133	A1	50 l on 40 l sal, *cr*, #48	6.25	6.25
a.		Broad "0" in "50"	10.00	8.25
b.		First letter of word is "A"	135.00	135.00
c.		"50" without word	200.00	175.00
d.		"50" above word	200.00	175.00
134	A2	1d on 40 l red vio (No. 97)	15.50	6.25
137	A1	3d on 10 l org, *cr*, #54	52.50	52.50
a.		3d on 10 l yellow, #54a	52.50	52.50
138	A1	5d on 40 l red vio, *bl*, #21	150.00	150.00
a.		5d on 40 l red vio, *bl*, #28	190.00	190.00
b.		"20" on back corrected to "40"	1,400.	
139	A1	5d on 40 l red vio, *bl*, #42b	575.00	

				Perf. 11½
140	A2	20 l on 25 l dl bl, #112	3.25	3.25
a.		20 l on 25 l indigo, #112a	100.00	90.00
b.		20 l on 25 l ultra, #112b	80.00	77.50
c.		Double surcharge	67.50	70.00
d.		Triple surcharge	95.00	95.00
e.		Inverted surcharge	67.50	67.50
f.		"20" above word	150.00	150.00
141	A1	30 l on 40 l vio, *cr*, #58a	10.50	10.50
a.		30 l on 40 l lilac, #58	17.50	17.50
b.		Broad "0" in "30"	12.50	12.50
c.		First letter of word "A"	150.00	150.00
d.		Double surcharge		
142	A1	40 l on 2 l bis, *cr*, #44	15.50	15.50
a.		Broad "0" in "40"	15.50	15.50
b.		First letter of word is "A"	165.00	165.00
143	A1	50 l on 40 l sal, *cr*, #48	10.50	10.50
a.		Broad "0" in "50"	12.50	12.50
b.		First letter of word "A"	135.00	135.00
c.		"50" without word	200.00	175.00
144	A2	1d on 40 l red vio, #114	145.00	160.00
147	A1	3d on 10 l yel, *cream*, #54a	57.50	57.50
a.		3d on 10 l org, *cr*, #54	60.00	65.00
148	A1	5d on 40 l red vio, *bl*, #21	150.00	175.00
a.		5d on 40 l red vio, *bl*, #28	175.00	225.00
149	A1	5d on 40 l red vio, *bl*, #42b	625.00	

				Perf. 13½
150	A2	2d on 40 l red vio, #105	12.00	12.50

The 1d on 40 l perf. 13½ and the 2d on 40 l, both imperf. and perf. 13½, were not officially issued.

Surcharge Including "A M"

"A M" = "Axia Metalliki" or "Value in Metal (gold)."

1900				*Imperf.*
151	A2	25 l on 40 l vio, #70	6.00	10.50
152	A2	50 l on 25 l bl, #69	26.50	24.00
153	A1	1d on 40 l brn, *bl*, #42b	125.00	150.00
154	A1	2d on 5 l grn, *cr*, #53	16.00	21.00

				Perf. 11½
155	A2	25 l on 40 l vio, #87	12.00	15.50
156	A2	50 l on 25 l bl, #86	52.50	62.50
157	A1	1d on 40 l brn, *bl*, #42b	160.00	160.00
158	A1	2d on 5 l grn, *cr*, #53	20.00	26.00
		Nos. 151-158 (8)	418.00	469.50

Partly-perforated varieties of Nos. 129-158 sell for about two to three times as much as normal stamps.

Surcharge in Red

1900-01   **Perf. 14x13½**

159	A7	5 l on 1d blue		15.00	9.50
a.		Wrong font "M" with serifs		75.00	80.00
b.		Double surcharge		225.00	200.00
160	A5	25 l on 40 l vio		70.00	67.50
a.		Double surcharge		900.00	
161	A8	50 l on 2d bister		80.00	62.50
a.		Broad "0" in "50"		80.00	62.50
162	A9	1d on 5d grn ('01)		250.00	200.00
a.		Greek "D" instead of "A" as 3rd letter		650.00	700.00
163	A10	2d on 10d brn ('01)		70.00	100.00
a.		Greek "D" instead of "A" as 3rd letter		275.00	250.00
		Nos. 159-163 (5)		485.00	439.50

Black Surcharge on No. 160

164	A5	50 l on 25 l on 40 l vio (R + Bk)	500.00	475.00
a.		Broad "0" in "50"	475.00	575.00

Nos. 151-164 and 179-183, gold currency stamps, were generally used for parcel post and foreign money orders. They were also available for use on letters, but cost about 10 per cent more than the regular stamps of the same denomination.

Counterfeit surcharges exist of #159-164.

Giovanni da Bologna's Hermes
A11   A12

A13

FIVE LEPTA.
Type I — Letters of "ELLAS" not outlined at top and left. Only a few faint horizontal lines between the outer vertical lines at sides.
Type II — Letters of "ELLAS" fully outlined. Heavy horizontal lines between the vertical frame lines.

Perf. 11½, 12½, 13½

1901		**Engr.**		**Wmk. 129**
165	A11	1 l yellow brn	.40	.20
166	A11	2 l gray	.60	.20
167	A11	3 l orange	.65	.30
168	A12	5 l grn, type I	.80	.20
a.		5 l yellow green, type I	.60	.20
b.		5 l yellow green, type II	.60	.20
169	A12	10 l rose	3.25	.20
170	A11	20 l red lilac	6.50	.20
171	A12	25 l ultra	6.50	.20
172	A11	30 l dl vio	12.00	2.00
173	A11	40 l dk brn	25.00	3.00
174	A11	50 l brn lake	10.00	1.50

Perf. 12½, 14 and Compound

175	A13	1d black	47.50	3.00
a.		Horiz. pair, imperf. btwn.	325.00	
c.		Horiz. pair, imperf. vert.	300.00	
d.		Vert. pair, imperf. horiz.	300.00	

Litho.
Perf. 12½

176	A13	2d bronze		11.00	8.00
177	A13	3d silver		11.00	12.00
178	A13	5d gold		13.00	15.00
		Nos. 165-178 (14)		158.20	46.00
		Set, never hinged		325.00	

All values 1 l through 1d issued on both thick and thin paper. Nos. 173-174 are values for thin paper — values for thick paper are higher. For overprints and surcharges see Nos. RA3-RA13, N16, N109.

Imperf., Pairs

165a	A11	1 l		12.00
166a	A11	2 l		15.00
167a	A11	3 l		15.00
168c	A12	5 l		12.00
169a	A12	10 l		19.00
170a	A11	20 l		15.00
171a	A12	25 l		15.00
172a	A11	30 l		250.00
173a	A11	40 l		300.00
174a	A11	50 l		70.00
175b	A13	1d		250.00

Nos. 165a-175a were issued on both thick and thin paper. Values are for the less expensive thin paper.

Hermes — A14

1902, Jan. 1   **Engr.**   **Perf. 13½**

179	A14	5 l deep orange	2.00	1.10
a.		Imperf., pair	82.50	
180	A14	25 l emerald	30.00	3.00
181	A14	50 l ultra	30.00	3.75
a.		Imperf., pair	550.00	
182	A14	1d rose red	30.00	8.25
183	A14	2d orange brn	52.50	50.00
		Nos. 179-183 (5)	144.50	66.10
		Set, never hinged	375.00	

See note after No. 164. In 1913 remainders of Nos. 179-183 were used as postage dues.

Apollo Throwing Discus A15   Jumper, with Jumping Weights A16

Victory — A17

Atlas and Hercules A18

Struggle of Hercules and Antaeus A19

Wrestlers A20   Daemon of the Games A21

Foot Race A22

Nike, Priest and Athletes in Pre-Games Offering to Zeus A23

Wmk. Crown and ET (129)

1906, Mar.   **Engr.**   **Perf. 13½, 14**

184	A15	1 l brown	.55	.40
a.		Imperf., pair	300.00	
185	A15	2 l gray	.55	.40
a.		Imperf., pair	300.00	
186	A16	3 l orange	.55	.40
a.		Imperf., pair	300.00	
187	A16	5 l green	1.25	.40
a.		Imperf., pair	110.00	
188	A17	10 l rose red	3.00	.60
a.		Imperf., pair	300.00	
189	A18	20 l magenta	5.00	.60
a.		Imperf., pair	575.00	
190	A19	25 l ultra	6.00	.85
a.		Imperf., pair	575.00	
191	A20	30 l dl pur	5.00	2.75
a.		Double impression	1,100.	
192	A21	40 l dk brown	5.00	2.75
193	A18	50 l brn lake	10.00	3.25
194	A22	1d gray blk	65.00	13.00
a.		Imperf., pair	1,100.	
195	A22	2d rose	100.00	35.00
196	A22	3d olive yel	155.00	125.00
197	A23	5d dull blue	160.00	140.00
		Nos. 184-197 (14)	516.90	325.40
		Set, never hinged	1,500.	

Greek Special Olympic Games of 1906 at Athens, celebrating the 10th anniv. of the modern Olympic Games.
Surcharged stamps of this issue are revenues.

A24

Iris Holding Caduceus A25   Hermes Donning Sandals A26

Hermes Carrying Infant Arcas — A27   Hermes, from Old Cretan Coin — A28

Designs A24 to A28 are from Cretan and Arcadian coins of the 4th Century, B.C.

Serrate Roulette 13½

1911-21		**Engr.**	**Unwmk.**	
198	A24	1 l green	.65	.30
199	A25	2 l car rose	.65	.30
200	A24	3 l vermilion	.95	.30
201	A26	5 l green	2.00	.30
202	A24	10 l car rose	9.50	.30
203	A25	20 l gray lilac	3.00	.80
204	A25	25 l ultra	15.00	.80
a.		Rouletted in black	190.00	140.00
205	A26	30 l car rose	4.50	1.60
206	A25	40 l deep blue	10.00	4.00
207	A26	50 l dl vio	15.00	3.00
208	A27	1d ultra	20.00	.80
209	A27	2d vermilion	27.50	.95
210	A27	3d car rose	27.50	1.40
a.		Size 20 ¼x25 ½mm ('21)	100.00	50.00
211	A27	5d ultra	35.00	4.00
a.		Size 20 ¼x25 ½mm ('21)	200.00	25.00

212	A27	10d dp bl ('21)	140.00	70.00
a.		Size 20x26 ½mm ('11)	300.00	125.00
213	A28	25d deep blue	87.50	55.00
		Nos. 198-213 (16)	398.75	143.85
		Set, never hinged	750.00	

The 1921 reissues of the 3d, 5d and 10d measure 20¼x25½mm instead of 20x26½mm. See Nos. 214-231. For overprints see Nos. 233-248B, N1, N10-N15, N17-N52A, N110-N148, Thrace 22-30, N26-N75.

Imperf., Pairs

198a	A24	1 l	90.00	90.00
200a	A24	3 l	240.00	240.00
201a	A26	5 l	30.00	30.00
202a	A24	10 l	52.50	52.50
203a	A25	20 l	225.00	225.00
204b	A25	25 l	300.00	300.00
206a	A25	40 l	350.00	
207a	A26	50 l	350.00	
208a	A27	1d	350.00	
209a	A27	2d	350.00	
210b	A27	3d	350.00	
211b	A27	5d	350.00	
212b	A27	10d As "a"	1,600.	
213a	A28	25d	2,250.	

Serrate Roulette 10½x13½, 13½

1913-23			**Litho.**	
214	A24	1 l green	.20	.20
a.		Without period after "El-las"	77.50	—
215	A25	2 l rose	.20	.20
216	A24	3 l vermilion	.20	.20
217	A26	5 l green	.20	.20
218	A24	10 l carmine	.20	.20
219	A25	15 l dl bl ('18)	.35	.20
220	A25	20 l slate	.35	.20
221	A25	25 l ultra	4.00	.50
a.		25 l blue	.20	
c.		Double impression		
222	A26	30 l rose ('14)	.95	.40
223	A25	40 l indigo ('14)	2.10	.70
224	A26	50 l vio brn ('14)	4.25	.35
225	A26	80 l vio brn ('23)	5.25	1.40
226	A27	1d ultra ('19)	7.00	.70
227	A27	2d ver ('19)	6.50	.70
228	A27	3d car rose ('20)	8.50	.80
229	A27	5d ultra ('22)	12.00	1.00
230	A27	10d dp bl ('22)	12.00	1.25
231	A28	25d indigo ('22)	16.00	4.75
		Nos. 214-231 (18)	80.25	13.95
		Set, never hinged	225.00	

Nos. 221, 223 and 226 were re-issued in 1926, printed in Vienna from new plates. There are slight differences in minor details.
The 10 lepta brown, on thick paper, type A28, is not a postage stamp. It was issued in 1922 to replace coins of this denomination during a shortage of copper.

Imperf., Pairs

214b	A24	1 l	65.00	
215a	A25	2 l	110.00	
216a	A24	3 l	175.00	
217a	A26	5 l	65.00	
218a	A24	10 l	82.50	
220a	A25	20 l	82.50	
221b	A25	25 l	175.00	
222a	A26	30 l	175.00	
223a	A25	40 l	175.00	
224a	A26	50 l	300.00	
225b	A26	80 l	92.50	
226a	A27	1d		250.00
227a	A27	2d	100.00	
228b	A27	3d	300.00	
229a	A27	5d	360.00	

Raising Greek Flag at Suda Bay, Crete A29

1913, Dec. 1   **Engr.**   **Perf. 14½**

232	A29	25 l blue & black	8.00	5.00
		Never hinged	16.00	
a.		Imperf., pair	1,400.	

Union of Crete with Greece. Used only in Crete.

Stamps of 1911-14 Overprinted in Red or Black

Serrate Roulette 13½

1916, Nov. 1			**Litho.**	
233	A24	1 l green (R)	.20	.20
234	A25	2 l rose	.20	.20
235	A24	3 l vermilion	.20	.20
236	A26	5 l green (R)	.50	.40
237	A24	10 l carmine	.75	.40
238	A25	20 l slate (R)	1.50	.40
239	A25	25 l blue (R)	1.50	.40
a.		25 l ultra	140.00	26.00
240	A26	30 l rose	1.50	.90
a.		Pair, one without ovpt.		

241	A25	40 l indigo (R)	11.00	3.00
242	A26	50 l vio brn (R)	37.50	2.50

Engr.

243	A24	3 l vermilion	.50	.50
244	A26	2 l car rose	1.25	1.25
245	A27	1d ultra (R)	40.00	.80
a.		Rouletted in black	325.00	225.00
246	A27	2d vermilion	24.00	3.50
247	A27	3d car rose	14.00	3.50
248	A27	5d ultra (R)	95.00	15.00
248B	A27	10d dp bl (R)	24.00	22.50
		Nos. 233-248B (17)	253.60	55.65
		Set, never hinged	500.00	

Most of Nos. 233-248B exist with overprint double, inverted, etc. Minimum value of errors $18. Excellent counterfeits of the overprint varieties exist.

Issued by the Venizelist Provisional Government

Iris — A32

1917, Feb. 5   Litho.   Perf. 14

249	A32	1 l dp green	.40	.20
250	A32	5 l yel grn	.40	.20
251	A32	10 l rose	.80	.35
252	A32	25 l lt blue	1.10	.35
253	A32	50 l gray vio	9.00	2.50
254	A32	1d ultra	2.25	.75
255	A32	2d lt red	4.50	1.50
256	A32	3d claret	25.00	7.75
257	A32	5d gray bl	5.75	3.00
258	A32	10d dk blue	70.00	20.00
259	A32	25d slate	125.00	160.00
		Nos. 249-259 (11)	244.20	196.60
		Set, never hinged	400.00	

The 4d was used only as a revenue stamp.

Imperf., Pairs

249a	A32	1 l	9.50
250a	A32	5 l	9.50
251a	A32	10 l	9.50
252a	A32	25 l	17.50
253a	A32	50 l	25.00
254a	A32	1d	22.50
255a	A32	2d	30.00
256a	A32	3d	65.00
257a	A32	5d	65.00
258a	A32	10d	110.00
259a	A32	25d	125.00

Stamps of 1917 Surcharged

1923

260	A32	5 l on 10 l rose	.25	.25
a.		Inverted surcharge	24.00	35.00
261	A32	50 l on 50 l gray vio	.25	.25
262	A32	10 l on 1d ultra	.25	.25
a.		1d on 1d gray	.25	.25
263	A32	2d on 2d lt red	.55	.55
264	A32	3d on 3d claret	1.60	1.60
265	A32	5d on 5d dk bl	2.00	2.00
266	A32	25d on 25d slate	27.50	27.50
		Nos. 260-266 (7)	32.40	32.40
		Set, never hinged	125.00	

Same Surcharge on Occupation of Turkey Stamps, 1913
Perf. 13½

267	O2	5 l on 3 l org	.25	.25
a.		Inverted surcharge	19.00	
268	O1	10 l on 20 l vio	1.50	1.50
a.		Inverted surcharge	82.50	
269	O2	10 l on 25 l pale bl	.25	.25
a.		Inverted surcharge	60.00	35.00
270	O1	10 l on 30 l gray grn	.25	.25
271	O2	10 l on 40 l ind	1.25	1.25
272	O1	50 l on 50 l dk bl	.25	.25
a.		Inverted surcharge	72.50	37.50
273	O1	2d on 2d gray brn	60.00	60.00
274	O2	3d on 3d dl bl	4.50	6.00
a.		Imperf., pair	500.00	
275	O1	5d on 5d gray	4.00	7.00
276	O2	10d on 1d vio brn	15.00	22.50
276A		10d on 10d car	800.00	
		Nos. 267-276 (10)	87.25	99.25
		Set, never hinged	150.00	

Dangerous counterfeits of No. 276A exist.

Same Surcharge on Stamps of Crete
Perf. 14

On Crete #50, 52, 59

276B	A6	5 l on 1 l red brn	27.50	27.50
277	A8	10 l on 10 l red	.25	.25
277B	A8	10 l on 25 l bl	110.00	110.00

On Crete #66-69, 71

278	A8	10 l on 25 l blue	.25	.25
279	A8	50 l on 50 l lilac	.45	.70
279A	A6	50 l on 50 l ultra	8.50	14.00
280	A9	50 l on 1d gray vio	3.00	4.00
280A	A11	50 l on 5d grn & blk	27.50	27.50

On Crete #77-82

281	A15	10 l on 20 l bl grn	125.00	125.00
282	A16	10 l on 25 l ultra	.45	.45
a.		Double surcharge	50.00	50.00
283	A17	50 l on 50 l yel brn	.25	.35
284	A18	50 l on 1d rose car & brn	2.00	1.75
a.		Imperf., pair	425.00	
285	A19	3d on 3d org & blk	14.00	14.00
286	A20	5d on 5d ol grn & blk	9.00	9.00

On Crete #83-84

287	A21	10 l on 25 l bl & blk	3.25	1.75
a.		Imperf., pair		
287B	A22	50 l on 1d grn & blk	8.00	4.50

On Crete #96

288	A23	10 l on 10 l red	.25	.25
a.		Inverted surcharge	45.00	40.00

On Crete #91

288B	A17	50 l on 50 l yel brn		800.00

Dangerous counterfeits of the overprint on No. 288B are plentiful.

On Crete #109

289	A19	3d on 3d org & blk	17.50	17.50

On Crete #111, 113-120

290	A6	5 l on 1 l vio brn	.25	.25
a.		Inverted surcharge	25.00	
291	A13	5 l on 5 l grn	.25	.25
a.		Inverted surcharge	47.50	
292	A23	10 l on 10 l red	.25	.25
a.		Inverted surcharge	47.50	
293	A15	10 l on 20 l bl grn	.30	.30
a.		Inverted surcharge	47.50	
294	A16	10 l on 25 l ultra	.35	.35
a.		Inverted surcharge	47.50	
295	A17	50 l on 50 l yel brn	.40	.40
296	A18	50 l on 1d rose car & brn	5.25	5.25
a.		Inverted surcharge		
b.		Double surcharge	225.00	
c.		Double surch., one invtd.		
d.		Imperf., pair		
297	A19	3d on 3d org & blk	16.00	16.00
298	A20	5d on 5d ol grn & blk	200.00	200.00

Dangerous counterfeits of No. 298 exist.

Crete #J2-J9

299	D1	5 l on 5 l red	.25	.25
a.		Inverted surcharge	45.00	6.75
300	D1	5 l on 10 l red	.30	.30
301	D1	10 l on 20 l red	12.00	12.00
a.		Inverted surcharge		
302	D1	10 l on 40 l red	.30	.30
303	D1	50 l on 50 l red	.30	.55
304	D1	50 l on 1d red	.30	.50
a.		Double surcharge		
305	D1	50 l on 1d on 1d red	9.50	9.50
306	D1	2d on 2d red	1.25	1.25

On Crete #J11-J13

307	D1	5 l on 5 l red	6.00	6.00
308	D1	5 l on 10 l red	1.50	1.50
a.		"Ellas" inverted	6.50	
309	D1	50 l on 1d red	55.00	55.00

On Crete #J20-J22, J24-J26

310	D1	5 l on 5 l red	.25	.25
311	D1	5 l on 10 l red	.25	.25
a.		Inverted surcharge	12.00	
312	D1	10 l on 20 l red	.25	.25
313	D1	50 l on 50 l red	.55	.55
314	D1	50 l on 1d red	4.00	4.00
315	D1	2d on 2d red	7.00	7.00

These surcharged Postage Due stamps were intended for the payment of ordinary postage.

Nos. 260 to 315 were surcharged in commemoration of the revolution of 1922.

Nos. 59, 91, 109, 111, 113-120, J11-J13, J20-J22, J24-J26 are on stamps previously overprinted by Crete.

Issues of the Republic

Lord Byron — A33

Byron at Missolonghi — A34

1924, Apr. 16   Engr.   Perf. 12

316	A33	80 l dark blue	.55	.20
317	A34	2d dk vio & blk	1.25	.65
		Set, never hinged	3.25	

Death of Lord Byron (1788-1824) at Missolonghi.

Tomb of Markos Botsaris — A35

Serrate Roulette 13½

1926, Apr. 24   Litho.

318	A35	25 l lilac	.85	.50
		Never hinged	1.75	

Centenary of the defense of Missolonghi against the Turks.

Corinth Canal A36

Dodecanese Costume A37

Macedonian Costume A38

Monastery of Simon Peter on Mt. Athos A39

White Tower of Salonika A40

Temple of Hephaestus A41

The Acropolis — A42

Cruiser "Georgios Averoff" — A43

Academy of Sciences, Athens — A44

Temple of Hephaestus A45

Acropolis A46

Perf. 12½x13, 13, 13x12½, 13½, 13½x13

1927, Apr. 1   Engr.

321	A36	5 l dark green	.20	.20
a.		Vert. pair, imperf. horiz.	140.00	92.50
322	A37	10 l orange red	.30	.20
a.		Horiz. pair, imperf. between	140.00	92.50
c.		Double impression	77.50	
323	A38	20 l violet	.30	.20
324	A39	25 l slate blue	.50	.20
a.		Imperf., pair	140.00	140.00
b.		Vert. pair, imperf. between	150.00	110.00
325	A40	40 l slate blue	.50	.20
326	A36	50 l violet	1.10	.20
327	A36	80 l dk bl & blk	.95	.20
a.		Imperf., pair	825.00	
328	A41	1d dk bl & bis brn (I)	1.10	.20
a.		Imperf., pair	150.00	125.00
b.		Center inverted		6,500.
c.		Double impression of center	325.00	225.00
d.		Double impression of frame	325.00	225.00
329	A42	2d dk green & blk	6.50	.30
a.		Imperf., pair	600.00	800.00
330	A43	3d dp violet & blk	6.00	.30
a.		Double impression of center	225.00	275.00
b.		Center inverted		8,000.
331	A44	5d yellow & blk	15.00	2.00
a.		Imperf., pair	925.00	925.00
b.		Center inverted	10,000.	4,500.
c.		5d yellow & green	110.00	37.50
332	A45	10d brn car & blk	45.00	11.00
333	A44	15d brt yel grn & blk	57.50	16.00
334	A46	25d green & blk	110.00	18.00
a.		Double impression of center		
		Nos. 321-334 (14)	244.95	49.20
		Set, never hinged	700.00	

See Nos. 364-371 and notes preceding No. 364. For overprints see Nos. RA55, RA57, RA60, RA66, RA70-RA71.

This series as prepared, included a 1 lepton dark brown, type A37, but that value was never issued. Most stamps were burned. Value $300.

Gen. Charles N. Fabvier and Acropolis A47

1927, Aug. 1   Perf. 12

335	A47	1d red	.30	.20
336	A47	3d dark blue	2.00	.60
337	A47	6d green	12.00	9.00
		Nos. 335-337 (3)	14.30	9.80
		Set, never hinged	42.50	

Cent. of the liberation of Athens from the Turks in 1826.

For surcharges see Nos. 376-377.

Bay of Navarino and Pylos A48

Battle of Navarino A49

"Edward" omitted — A50 | "Edward" added — A51

Admiral de Rigny — A52 | Admiral van der Heyden — A53

Designs: #340-341, Sir Edward Codrington.

Perf. 13½x12½, 12½x13½, 13x12½, 12½x13

			1927-28		Litho.
338	A48	1.50d gray green		1.60	.35
a.		Imperf., pair		275.00	
b.		Horiz. pair, imperf. btwn.		875.00	
c.		Horiz. pair, imperf. vert.		250.00	
339	A49	4d dk gray bl ('28)		7.00	1.50
340	A50	5d dk brn & gray		5.50	4.75
a.		5d blk brn & blk ('28)		13.00	6.50
341	A51	5d dk brn & blk ('28)		35.00	12.00
342	A52	5d vio bl & blk ('28)		35.00	12.00
343	A53	5d lake & blk ('28)		20.00	9.50
		Nos. 338-343 (6)		104.10	40.10
		Set, never hinged		275.00	

Centenary of the naval battle of Navarino. For surcharges see Nos. 372-375.

Admiral Lascarina Bouboulina A54 | Athanasios Diakos A55

Map of Greece in 1830 and 1930 — A56

Sortie from Missolonghi A58

Patriots Declaring Independence — A57

Portraits: 10 l, Constantine Rhigas Ferreos. 20 l, Gregorios V. 40 l, Prince Alexandros Ypsilantis. No. 345, Bouboulina. No. 355, Diakos. No. 346, Theodoros Kolokotronis. No. 356, Konstantinos Kanaris. No.347, Georgios Karaiskakis. No. 357, Markos Botsaris. 2d, Andreas Miaoulis. 3d, Lazaros Koundouriotis. 5d, Count John Capo d'Istria (Capodistria), statesman and doctor. 10d, Petros Mavromichalis. 15d, Dionysios Solomos. 20d, Adamantios Korais.

Various Frames

1930, Apr. 1   Engr.   Perf. 13½, 14
Imprint of Perkins, Bacon & Co.

344	A55	10 l	brown	.20	.20
345	A54	50 l	red	.20	.20
346	A54	1d	car rose	.30	.30
347	A55	1.50d	lt blue	.40	.40
348	A55	2d	orange	.45	.45
349	A55	5d	purple	1.50	1.50
350	A54	10d	gray blk	6.50	6.50
351	A54	15d	yellow grn	12.00	12.00
352	A55	20d	blue blk	17.50	17.50

Imprint of Bradbury, Wilkinson & Co.
Perf. 12

353	A55	20 l	black	.20	.20
354	A55	40 l	blue grn	.20	.20
355	A55	50 l	brt blue	.20	.20
356	A55	1d	brown org	.30	.30
357	A55	1.50d	dk red	.40	.40
358	A55	3d	dk brown	.65	.65
359	A56	4d	dk blue	3.00	3.00
360	A57	25d	black	17.50	17.50
361	A58	50d	red brn	45.00	45.00
		Nos. 344-361 (18)		106.50	106.50
		Set, never hinged		275.00	

Greek independence, cent. Some exist imperf.

Arcadi Monastery and Abbot Gabriel (Mt. Ida in Background) A60

1930, Nov. 8   Perf. 12

363	A60	8d deep violet	13.00	1.10
		Never hinged	55.00	

Issue of 1927 Re-engraved

50 l, Design is clearer, especially "50" and the 10 letters.

Type I

Type II

1d. Type I — Greek letters "L," "A," "D" have sharp pointed tops; numerals "1" are 1 ½mm wide at the foot, and have a straight slanting serif at top.

1d. Type II — Greek letters "L," "A," "D" have flat tops; numerals "1" are 2mm wide at foot and the serif at top is slightly curved. Perf. 14.

There are many minor differences in the lines of the two designs.

1d. Type III — The "1" in lower left corner has no serif at left of foot. Lines of temple have been deepened, so details stand out more clearly.

2d. On 1927 stamp the Parthenon is indistinct and blurred. On 1933 stamp it is strongly outlined and clear. Between the two pillars at lower right are four blocks of marble. These blocks are clear and distinct on the 1933 stamp but run together on the 1927 issue.

3d. Design is clearer, especially vertical lines of shading in smoke stacks and reflections in the water. Two or more sides perf. 11 ½.

10d. Background and shading of entire stamp have been lightened. Detail of frame is clearer and more distinct.

15d. Many more lines of shading in sky and foreground. Engraving is sharp and clear, particularly in frame. Two or more sides perf. 11 ½.

25d. Background has been lightened and foreground reduced until base of larger upright column is removed and fallen column appears nearly submerged.

Sizes in millimeters:

50 l, 1927, 18x24¾. 1933, 18 ½x24 ½.

1d, 1927, 24¾x17¾. 1931, 24¾x17¼. 1933, 24 ½x18 ¼.

2d, 1927, 24 ½x17¾. 1933, 24 ½x18 ½.

Perf. 11½, 11½x12½, 12½x10, 13, 13x12½, 14
1931-35

364	A36	50 l	dk vio ('33)	4.00	1.00
365	A41	1d	dk bl & org brn, type II	10.00	1.00
366	A41	1d	dk bl & org brn, type III ('33)	5.75	.20
367	A42	2d	dk grn & blk ('33)	2.75	.50
368	A43	3d	red vio & blk ('34)	3.25	.25
a.		Imperf., pair			
369	A45	10d	brn car & blk ('35)	47.50	1.50
370	A44	15d	pale yel grn & blk ('34)	82.50	17.50
a.		Imperf., pair		1,100.	
371	A46	25d	dk grn & blk ('35)	25.00	17.00
		Nos. 364-371 (8)		180.75	38.95
		Set, never hinged		600.00	

Nos. 336-337, 340-343 Surcharged in Red

1932   Perf. 12½x13½, 12½x13

372	A52	1.50d on 5d	2.00	.20
373	A53	1.50d on 5d	2.00	.20
a.		Double surcharge	110.00	
374	A50	2d on 5d	5.00	.20
375	A51	2d on 5d	9.00	.20

Perf. 12

376	A47	2d on 3d	2.25	.20
a.		Double surcharge	125.00	
377	A47	4d on 6d	2.50	1.10
		Nos. 372-377 (6)	22.75	2.10
		Set, never hinged	50.00	

Adm. Pavlos Koundouriotis and Cruiser "Averoff" — A61

Pallas Athene — A62 | Youth of Marathon — A63

1933   Perf. 13½x13, 13x13½

378	A61	50d black & ind	50.00	1.60
a.		Imperf., pair	2,250.	
379	A62	75d blk & vio brn	110.00	175.00
a.		Imperf., pair	825.00	
		Never hinged	1,700.	
380	A63	100d brn & dull grn	625.00	29.00
a.		Imperf., pair	2,750.	
		Nos. 378-380 (3)	785.00	205.60
		Set, never hinged	1,800.	

The imperf pairs are without gum. For surcharges see Nos. 386-387.

Approach to Athens Stadium A64

Perf. 11½, 11½x10, 13½x11½
1934, Dec. 10

381	A64	8d blue	65.00	2.25
		Never hinged	200.00	

Perforations on No. 381 range from 10 ½ to 13, including compounds.

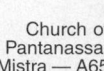

Church of Pantanassa, Mistra — A65

1935, Nov. 1   Perf. 13x12½

382	A65	4d brown	17.00	1.60
		Never hinged	47.50	
a.		Horiz. pair, imperf. between	725.00	
b.		Imperf., pair	725.00	

Issues of the Monarchy

J71, J76, J82, 380, 379 Surcharged in Red or Blue

Nos. 383-385 | Nos. 386-387

Serrate Roulette 13½
1935, Nov. 24   Litho.

383	D3	50 l on 40 l indigo (R)	.20	.20
a.		Double surcharge		27.50
384	D3	3d on 3d car (Bl)	.55	.40

Perf. 13

385	D3	3d on 3d rose red (Bl)	2.75	2.00

Perf. 13x13½

386	A63	5d on 100d (R)	2.25	2.00
387	A62	15d on 75d (Bl)	6.50	6.00
		Nos. 383-387 (5)	12.25	10.60
		Set, never hinged	30.00	

King Constantine — A66

Center Engr., Frame Litho.
Perf. 12x13½
1936, Nov. 18   Wmk. 252

389	A66	3d black & brown	.55	.40
a.		Pair, printer's name in Greek	22.50	
b.		Pair, printer's name in English	22.50	
390	A66	8d black & blue	1.10	.90
a.		Pair, printer's name in Greek	22.50	
b.		Pair, printer's name in English	22.50	
		Set, never hinged	3.25	

Re-burial of the remains of King Constantine and Queen Sophia.

Two printings exist, the first containing varieties "a" and "b" with gray border; second with black border.

King George II — A67 | Pallas Athene — A68

1937, Jan. 24   Engr.   Perf. 12½x12

391	A67	1d green	.20	.20
392	A67	3d red brown	.25	.20
393	A67	8d dp blue	.90	.40
394	A67	100d carmine lake	12.00	12.00
		Nos. 391-394 (4)	13.35	12.80
		Set, never hinged	30.00	

For surcharges see Nos. 484-487, 498-500, RA86-RA87, N241-N242.

1937, Apr. 17   Unwmk.   Perf. 11½

395	A68	3d yellow brown	.55	.25
		Never hinged	1.10	

Centenary of the University of Athens.

Contest with Bull — A69

Lady of Tiryns — A70

Zeus of Dodona — A71

Coin of Amphictyonic League A72

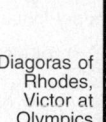

Diagoras of Rhodes, Victor at Olympics A73

Venus of Melos — A74

Battle of Salamis A75

Chariot of Panathenaic Festival A76

Alexander the Great at Battle of Issos — A77

St. Paul Preaching to Athenians A78

St. Demetrius' Church at Salonika A79

Leo III Victory over Arabs — A80

Allegorical Figure of Glory — A81

Perf. 13½x12, 12x13½

1937, Nov. 1   Litho.   Wmk. 252

396	A69	5 l brn red & bl	.20	.20
a.		Double impression of frame	60.00	
397	A70	10 l bl & brn red	.20	.20
a.		Double impression of frame	60.00	
398	A71	20 l black & grn	.20	.20
399	A72	40 l green & blk	.20	.20
a.		Green impression doubled	60.00	
400	A73	50 l brown & blk	.20	.20
401	A74	80 l ind & yel brn	.20	.20

Engr.

402	A75	2d ultra	.20	.20
403	A76	5d red	.20	.20
a.		Printer's name omitted	5.50	
404	A77	6d olive brn	.20	.20
405	A78	7d dk brown	.55	.50
406	A79	10d red brown	.20	.20
407	A80	15d green	.20	.20
408	A81	25d dk blue	.20	.20
		Nos. 396-408 (13)	2.95	2.90
		Set, never hinged	4.00	

See Nos. 413, 459-466. For overprints and surcharges see Nos. 455-458, 476-477, RA75-RA78, RA83-RA85, N202-N217, N246-N247.

Cerigo, Paxos, Lefkas

Greek stamps with Italian overprints for the islands of Cerigo (Kithyra), Paxos and Lefkas (Santa Maura) are fraudulent.

Royal Wedding Issue

Princess Frederika-Louise and Crown Prince Paul — A82

1938   Wmk. 252   Perf. 13½x12

409	A82	1d green	.20	.20
410	A82	3d orange brn	.30	.20
411	A82	8d dark blue	.55	.65
		Nos. 409-411 (3)	1.05	1.05
		Set, never hinged	2.75	

Arms of Greece, Romania, Yugoslavia and Turkey A83

Statue of King Constantine A84

Perf. 12x12½

1938, Feb. 8   Litho.   Unwmk.

412	A83	6d blue	5.50	1.75
		Never hinged	14.00	

Balkan Entente.

Tiryns Lady Type of 1937
Corrected Inscription

1938   Wmk. 252   Perf. 12x13½

413	A70	10 l blue & brn red	.50	.70
			.85	

The first four letters of the third word of the inscription read "TIPY" instead of "TYPI."

Perf. 12x13½

1938, Oct. 8   Engr.   Unwmk.

414	A84	1.50d green	.45	.20
415	A84	30d orange brn	2.25	3.25
		Set, never hinged	5.50	

For overprint see No. N218.

Coats of Arms of Ionian Islands — A85

Fort at Corfu — A86

King George I of Greece and Queen Victoria of England A87

Perf. 12½x12, 13½x12

1939, May 21   Engr.   Unwmk.

416	A85	1d dk blue	.85	.25
417	A86	4d green	2.90	1.00
418	A87	20d yellow org	17.00	17.00
419	A87	20d dull blue	17.00	17.00
420	A87	20d car lake	17.00	17.00
		Nos. 416-420 (5)	54.75	52.25
		Set, never hinged	125.00	

75th anniv. of the union of the Ionian Islands with Greece.

Runner with Shield — A88

10th Pan-Balkan Games: 3d, Javelin thrower. 6d, Discus thrower. 8d, Jumper.

Perf. 12x13½

1939, Oct. 1   Litho.   Unwmk.

421	A88	50 l slate grn & grn	.25	.20
422	A88	3d henna brn & dl rose	1.25	.55
423	A88	6d cop brn & dl org	3.00	2.25
424	A88	8d ultra & gray	3.00	2.50
		Nos. 421-424 (4)	7.50	5.50
		Set, never hinged	18.00	

Arms of Greece, Romania, Turkey and Yugoslavia — A92

Perf. 13x12½

1940, May 27   Wmk. 252

425	A92	6d blue	10.00	2.25
426	A92	8d blue gray	7.00	2.25
		Set, never hinged	45.00	

Balkan Entente.

Emblem of Youth Organization A93

Boy Member — A94

Designs: 3d, 100d, Emblem of Greek Youth Organization. 10d, Girl member. 15d, Javelin Thrower. 20d, Column of members. 25d, Flag bearers and buglers. 30d, Three youths. 50d, Line formation. 75d, Coat of arms.

Perf. 12½, 13½x12½

1940, Aug. 3   Litho.   Wmk. 252

427	A93	3d sil, dp ultra & red	.85	1.25
428	A94	5d dk bl & blk	6.50	7.50
429	A94	10d red org & blk	7.50	10.00
430	A94	15d dk grn & blk	30.00	32.50
431	A94	20d lake & blk	25.00	25.00
432	A94	25d dk bl & blk	25.00	25.00
433	A94	30d rose vio & blk	25.00	25.00
434	A94	50d lake & blk	30.00	30.00
435	A94	75d dk bl, brn & gold	30.00	32.50
436	A93	100d sil, dp ultra & red	50.00	37.50
		Nos. 427-436,C38-C47 (20)	555.70	529.00
		Set, never hinged	1,000.	

4th anniv. of the founding of the Greek Youth Organization. The stamps were good for postal duty Aug. 3-5, 1940, only. They remained on sale until Feb. 3, 1941.
For overprints see Nos. N219-N238.

Windmills on Mykonos A103

Bourtzi Fort — A104

Aspropotamos River — A105

Candia Harbor, Crete — A106

Houses at Hydra — A107

Meteora Monasteries A108

Edessa A109

Pantokratoros Monastery and Port — A110

Bridge at Konitsa A111

Ekatontapiliani Church, Paros — A112

Ponticonissi, Corfu (Mouse Island) A113

Perf. 12½, 13½x12½

1942-44		Litho.	Wmk. 252	
437	A103	2d red brown	.20	.20
438	A104	5d lt bl grn	.20	.20
a.		"NAYO . . ."	8.25	8.25
439	A105	10d lt blue	.20	.20
440	A106	15d red vio	.20	.20
441	A107	25d org red	.20	.20
442	A108	50d sapphire	.20	.20
443	A109	75d dp rose	.20	.20
444	A110	100d black	.20	.20
445	A110	200d ultra	.20	.20
a.		Imprint omitted	3.90	3.90
446	A111	500d dk olive	.20	.20
447	A112	1000d org brn	.20	.20
448	A113	2000d dp blue	.20	.20
449	A111	5000d rose red	.20	.20
450	A112	15,000d rose lil	.20	.20
451	A113	25,000d green	.20	.20
452	A105	500,000d blue	.20	.25
453	A103	2,000,000d turq grn	.20	.25
454	A104	5,000,000d rose brn	.20	.30
		Nos. 437-454 (18)	3.60	3.80
		Set, never hinged	4.50	

Double impressions exist of 10d, 25d, 50d, 100d, 200d, 1,000d and 2,000d. Value, each $30.

Issued: #439-442, 9/1; 200d, 12/1; #446-448, 3/15/44; #449-451, 7/1/44; #452-454, 9/15/44.

For surcharges and overprint see Nos. 472C, 473B-475, 478-481, 501-505, B1-B5, B11-B15, RA72-RA74, N239-N240, N243-N245, N248.

Imperf., Pairs

439a	A105	10d	57.50
440a	A106	15d	57.50
441a	A107	25d	45.00
442a	A108	50d	45.00
446a	A111	500d	45.00
447a	A112	1000d	45.00
448a	A113	2000d	45.00
449a	A111	5000d	45.00
450a	A112	15,000d	45.00
451a	A113	25,000d	45.00
452a	A105	500,000d	45.00
454a	A104	5,000,000d	45.00

Nos. 400, 402-404 Surcharged in Blue Black

1944-45			Perf. 13½x12	
455	A73	50 l brn & blk	.20	.20
a.		Double surcharge	40.00	40.00
456	A75	2d ultra	.20	.20
457	A76	5d red	.20	.20
a.		Inverted surcharge	47.50	
b.		Double surcharge	47.50	
c.		Printer's name omitted (403a)	12.00	12.00
d.		Pair, one without surcharge	20.00	
458	A77	6d olive brn ('45)	.20	.25
		Nos. 455-458 (4)		.85
		Set, never hinged	.90	

Glory Type of 1937
Perf. 12½x13½

1945		Litho.	Wmk. 252	
459	A81	1d dull rose vio	.40	.20
460	A81	3d rose brown	.40	.20
a.		Imperf., pair	160.00	
461	A81	5d ultra	.40	.20
a.		Imperf., pair	160.00	
462	A81	10d dull brown	.40	.20
463	A81	20d dull violet	.40	.20
464	A81	50d olive black	.40	.20
465	A81	100d pale blue	6.00	6.00
a.		Imperf., pair	190.00	
466	A81	200d slate	5.25	4.75
		Nos. 459-466 (8)	13.65	12.00
		Set, never hinged	27.50	

Doric Column and Greek Flag A114

Franklin D. Roosevelt A115

1945, Oct. 28			Unwmk.	
467	A114	20d orange brown	.25	.20
468	A114	40d blue	.25	.20
a.		Double impression	30.00	
		Set, never hinged	.75	

Vote of Oct. 28, 1940, refusing Italy's ultimatum. "OXI" means "No."
Exist imperf.

1945, Dec. 21			Unwmk.	
469	A115	30d blk & red brn	.30	.20
a.		Center double	27.00	
c.		Inverted frame	72.50	
d.		Imperf., pair	45.00	
470	A115	60d blk & sl gray	.30	.20
a.		Center double	27.50	
b.		60d black & blue gray	11.00	11.00
c.		Imperf., pair	27.50	
d.		Inverted frame	65.00	
471	A115	200d blk & vio brn	.30	.20
a.		Center double	27.50	77.50
b.		Imperf., pair	45.00	
		Nos. 469-471 (3)	.90	.60
		Set, never hinged	1.50	

Death of Pres. Franklin D. Roosevelt.

> **Catalogue values for unused stamps in this section, from this point to the end of the section, are for Never Hinged items.**

Nos. C61, C63, 447-451, 453, 398, 401, 454 and 452 Surcharged in Black or Carmine

Perf. 12½, 12x13½, 13½x12½

1946			Wmk. 252	
472	AP35	10d on 10d	.40	.20
a.		Inverted surcharge	100.00	—
b.		Double surcharge	22.50	
472C	A113	10d on 2000d (C)	.40	.20
473	AP35	20d on 50d (C)	.40	.20
a.		Inverted surcharge	125.00	
473B	A112	20d on 1000d	.40	.20
474	A113	50d on 25,000d (C)	.55	.20
475	A103	100d on 2,000,000d (C)	.95	.30
476	A71	130d on 20 l (C)	1.00	.20
b.		Double surcharge	27.50	
476A	A71	250d on 20 l (C)	1.25	.20
c.		Double surcharge	92.50	
477	A74	300d on 80 l (C)	1.00	.20
a.		Purple brown surcharge	17.00	17.00
b.		Double surcharge	90.00	
478	A104	500d on 5,000,000d	4.00	.80
a.		Inverted surcharge	85.00	
b.		Double surcharge	85.00	
479	A105	1000d on 500,000d (C)	14.00	2.25
a.		Double surcharge	45.00	
480	A111	2000d on 5000d	52.50	4.50
481	A112	5000d on 15,000d	160.00	35.00
a.		Blue surcharge	160.00	140.00
		Nos. 472-481 (13)	236.85	44.45

The surcharge exists in various shades on most denominations. A 150d on 20 l is fraudulent.

Eleutherios K. Venizelos A116

Panaghiotis Tsaldaris A117

Perf. 12x13½

1946, Mar. 25		Litho.	Wmk. 252	
482	A116	130d brn ol & buff	.40	.20
a.		Double impression of brn olive	7.25	
483	A116	300d brn & pale brn	.40	.20
a.		Double impression of red brown	14.00	

Venizelos (1864-1936), statesman.

Nos. 391 to 394 Surcharged in Blue Black

1946, Sept. 28			Perf. 12½x12	
484	A67	50d on 1d	.70	.20
485	A67	250d on 3d	1.60	.20
a.		Date omitted	32.50	
b.		Inverted surcharge	32.50	—
486	A67	600d on 8d	11.00	1.25
a.		Additional surcharge on back, inverted	72.50	
b.		Carmine surcharge	150.00	
487	A67	3000d on 100d	27.50	2.00
		Nos. 484-487 (4)	40.80	3.65

Plebiscite of Sept. 1, 1946, which resulted in the return of King George II to Greece.

Perf. 12½x13½

1946, Nov. 15		Litho.	Unwmk.	
488	A117	250d red brn & buff	4.00	1.25
489	A117	600d dp bl & pale bl	4.00	1.25
a.		Double impression	22.50	

Naval Convoy A118

Torpedoing of Cruiser Helle — A119

Women Carrying Ammunition in Pindus Mountains A120

Troops in Albania A121

Campaign of Greek Troops in Italy — A122

Allegory of Flight — A123

Greek Torpedo Boat Towing Captive Submarine A124

Design: 5000d, Memorial Tomb, El Alamein.

1946-47		Unwmk.	Engr.	Perf. 13	
490	A118	50d dk bl grn		.25	.20
491	A119	100d dp ultra		.65	.20
492	A120	250d yel grn ('46)		.65	.20
493	A121	500d yel brn		1.05	.20
494	A122	600d dk brown		1.40	.85
495	A123	1000d dull lil		7.25	.40
496	A124	2000d dp ultra		30.00	2.50
497	A119	5000d dk car		40.00	2.50
a.		Imperf., pair		1,500.	
		Nos. 490-497 (8)		81.25	7.05

1947 stamps issued May 1.

King George II Memorial Issue

Nos. 391-393 Surcharged in Black

Perf. 12½x12

1947, Apr. 15			Wmk. 252	
498	A67	50d on 1d grn	.60	.20
a.		Double surcharge	72.50	
499	A67	250d on 3d red brn	1.25	.20
a.		Double surcharge	72.50	
b.		Pair, one without surcharge	72.50	
500	A67	600d on 8d dp bl	10.00	.55
a.		Double surcharge	72.50	
		Nos. 498-500 (3)	11.85	.95

Nos. 446, 438, 442, 439 and 443 Surcharged in Carmine or Black

1947			Perf. 12½	
501	A111	20d on 500d	.30	.20
a.		Double surcharge	27.50	
502	A104	30d on 5d	.95	.40
503	A108	50d on 50d	.45	.20
504	A105	100d on 10d	1.60	.20
505	A109	450d on 75d (Bk)	2.50	.25
		Nos. 501-505 (5)	5.80	1.25

Castellorizo Castle A126

Dodecanese Vase A127

Dodecanese Costume A128

Monastery where St. John Preached, Patmos A129

Emanuel
Xanthos — A130

Sailing Vessel of
1824 — A131

Revolutionary Stamp
of 1912 — A132

Statue of
Hippocrates
A133

Colossus of
Rhodes
A134

Perf. 12½x13½, 13½x12½

1947-48		Litho.	Wmk. 252
506	A126	20d ultra	.30	.20
507	A127	30d blk brn & buff	.30	.20
508	A128	50d chlky bl	.50	.20
509	A129	100d blk grn & pale grn	.50	.20
510	A130	250d gray grn & pale grn	1.00	.20
511	A132	450d dp bl ('48)	2.25	.20
512	A131	450d dp bl & pale bl ('48)	1.75	.20
a.		Imperf., pair	275.00	
513	A132	500d red	1.40	.20
514	A133	600d vio brn & pale pink	1.40	.20
515	A134	1000d brn & cream	2.00	.20
a.		Imperf., pair	250.00	
		Nos. 506-515 (10)	11.40	2.00

Return of the Dodecanese to Greece. See Nos. 520-522, 525-534.

Battle of
Crete — A135

1948, Sept. 15   Engr.   Perf. 13x13½

516	A135	1000d dark green	6.50	.50

Battle of Crete, 7th anniversary.

Abduction of
Children
A136

Concentration
Camp — A137

Protective
Mother — A138

Perf. 13½x12½, 12½x13½

1949, Feb. 1		Litho.	Wmk. 252
517	A136	450d dk & lt violet	3.75	.65
518	A137	1000d dk & lt brown	13.50	4.00
519	A138	1800d dk red & cream	17.50	.40
		Nos. 517-519 (3)	34.75	5.05

Types of 1947

1950, Apr. 5			Perf. 12½x13½
520	A127	2000d org brn & sal	50.00	.55
a.		Imperf., pair	140.00	
521	A133	5000d rose vio	55.00	.55
522	A134	10,000d ultra	95.00	1.25
		Nos. 520-522 (3)	200.00	2.35

Map of
Crete and
Flags
A139

Perf. 13½x13

1950, Apr. 28		Engr.	Wmk. 252
523	A139	1000d deep blue	17.50	.40
a.		Imperf., pair	1,500.	

Battle of Crete, 9th anniversary.

Youth of
Marathon — A140

Engraved and Lithographed

1950, May 21   Perf. 13x13½

524	A140	1000d cream & dp grn	2.00	.60
a.		Without dates	450.00	
b.		"1949" only	450.00	
c.		Dates inverted	450.00	
d.		Dates doubled	450.00	

75th anniv. (in 1949) of the UPU.
Exists imperf., used only.

Types of 1947-48
Perf. 12½x13½, 13½x12½

1950		Litho.	Wmk. 252
525	A130	200d orange	.70	.20
526	A128	300d orange	.95	.20
527	A129	400d blue	1.75	.20
528	A133	700d lilac rose	2.25	.20
529	A133	700d blue green	27.50	.25
a.		Imperf., pair	290.00	
530	A131	800d pur & pale grn	2.75	.20
531	A132	1300d carmine	12.00	.20
532	A126	1500d brn org	82.50	1.10
533	A127	1600d ultra & bl gray	8.50	.25
534	A134	2600d emer & pale grn	11.50	.85
		Nos. 525-534 (10)	150.40	3.65

Altar and
Sword
A141

St. Paul — A142

St. Paul by El
Greco — A143

Preaching to
Athenians — A144

Perf. 13½x12, 12x13½

1951, June 15		Engr.	Unwmk.
535	A141	700d red vio	3.50	1.00
536	A142	1600d lt blue	14.50	8.75
537	A143	2600d dk ol bis	25.00	9.00
538	A144	10,000d red brn	175.00	80.00
		Nos. 535-538 (4)	218.00	98.75

1900th anniv. of St. Paul's visit to Athens.

Industrialization
A145

Designs: 800d, Fishing. 1300d, Rebuilding. 1600d, Farming. 2600d, Home Industries. 5000d, Electrification and map of Greece.

Perf. 12½x13½

1951, Sept. 20			Wmk. 252
539	A145	700d red org	5.00	.30
540	A145	800d aqua	7.25	.30
541	A145	1300d grnsh bl	10.00	.30
542	A145	1600d olive grn	30.00	.50
543	A145	2600d vio gray	75.00	2.25
544	A145	5000d dp plum	100.00	.50
		Nos. 539-544 (6)	227.25	4.15

Issued to publicize Greek recovery under the Marshall Plan.

King Paul
I — A146

Allegorical
Figure and
Medal — A147

1952, Dec. 14   Engr.   Perf. 12½x12

545	A146	200d deep green	2.00	.20
546	A146	1000d red	6.00	.35
547	A147	1400d blue	20.00	2.25
548	A147	10,000d dk red lil	60.00	14.00
		Nos. 545-548 (4)	88.00	16.80

50th birthday of King Paul I.

Oranges
A148

Tobacco — A149

National Products: 1000d, Olive oil, Pallas Athene. 1300d, Wine. 2000d, Figs. 2600d, Grapes and bread. 5000d, Bacchus holding grapes.

1953, July 1		Perf. 13½x13, 13x13½
549	A148	500d dp car & org	1.90	.20
550	A149	700d dk brn & org yel	1.90	.20
551	A148	1000d bl & lt ol grn	4.00	.20
a.		Imperf., pair	450.00	
552	A149	1300d dp plum & org brn	5.50	.20
553	A149	2000d dk brn & lt grn	13.50	.40
554	A149	2600d vio & ol bis	37.50	1.75
555	A149	5000d dk brn & yel grn	37.50	.90
		Nos. 549-555 (7)	101.80	3.85

Pericles
A150

Homer
A151

Hunting Wild
Boar — A152

Shepherd
Carrying
Calf — A152a

Designs: 200d, Mycenaean oxhead vase. 500d, Zeus of Istiaea. 600d, Head of a youth. 1000d, Alexander the Great. 1200d, Charioteer of Delphi. 2000d, Vase of Dipylon. 4000d, Voyage of Dionysus. 20,000d, Pitcher bearers.

Perf. 13½x13, 12½x12, 13x13½

1954, Jan. 15			Litho.
556	A150	100d red brn	.50	.20
557	A150	200d black	.50	.20
558	A151	300d blue vio	1.25	.20
559	A151	500d green	2.00	.20
560	A151	600d rose pink	2.00	.20
561	A151	1000d dl bl & blk	2.50	.20
562	A150	1200d ol grn	2.50	.20
563	A150	2000d red brn	11.00	.20
564	A152	2400d grnsh bl	11.00	.40
a.		Double impression	150.00	
565	A152a	2500d dk bl grn	11.00	.20
566	A151	4000d dk car	27.50	.40
567	A150	20,000d rose lilac	225.00	1.25
		Nos. 556-567 (12)	296.75	3.90

See Nos. 574-581, 632-638, and 689.

British
Parliamentary
Debate and Ink
Blot — A153

1954, Sept.   Perf. 12½
Center in Black

568	A153	1.20d cream	4.00	.45
569	A153	2d orange	20.00	3.75
570	A153	2d lt bl	20.00	9.25
571	A153	2.40d lilac	20.00	2.50
572	A153	2.50d pink	20.00	2.50
573	A153	4d citron	60.00	3.75
		Nos. 568-573 (6)	144.00	22.20

Document in English on Nos. 569, 572, 573; in French on Nos. 570, 571 and in Greek on No. 568.

Issued to promote the proposed union between Cyprus and Greece.

Types of 1954
Perf. 13½x13, 12½x12, 13x13½

1955		Litho.	Wmk. 252

Designs: 20 l, Mycenaean oxhead vase. 30 l, Pericles. 50 l, Zeus of Istiaea. 1d, Head of a youth. 2d, Alexander the Great. 3d, Hunting wild boar. 3.50d, Homer. 4d, Voyage of Dionysus.

574	A150	20 l	dk green	.40	.20
575	A150	30 l	yellow brn	.60	.20
576	A151	50 l	car lake	.90	.20
577	A151	1d	blue grn	2.25	.20
578	A151	2d	brown & blk	7.25	.20
579	A152	3d	red org	11.00	.20

580	A151	3.50d rose crim	11.00	.70
581	A151	4d violet bl	82.50	.45
		Nos. 574-581 (8)	115.90	2.35

Samos Coin Picturing Pythagoras A154

Pythagorean Theorem A155

Samos Mapped in Antique Style — A156

1955, Aug. 20   Perf. 12x13½

582	A154	2d green	3.75	.40
583	A155	3.50d intense blk	13.50	3.00
584	A154	5d plum	45.00	2.00
585	A156	6d blue	57.50	32.50
		Nos. 582-585 (4)	119.75	37.90

2500th anniv. of the founding of the 1st School of Philosophy by Pythagoras on Samos.

Globe and Rotary Emblem — A157

1956, May 15   Litho.   Wmk. 252

586	A157	2d ultra	17.50	.40

50th anniv. of Rotary Intl. (in 1955).

King Alexander A158

Crown Prince Constantine — A159

Portraits: 30 l, George I. 50 l, Queen Olga. 70 l, King Otto. 1d, Queen Amalia. 1.50d, King Constantine. 2d, 7.50d, King Paul. 3d, George II. 3.50d, Queen Sophia. 4d, Queen Frederica. 5d, King Paul and Queen Frederica. 10d, King, Queen and Crown Prince.

Perf. 13½x12, 12x13½

1956, May 21   Engr.

587	A158	10 l blue vio	.20	.20
588	A159	20 l dull pur	.20	.20
589	A159	30 l sepia	.20	.20
590	A159	50 l red brn	.30	.20
591	A159	70 l lt ultra	.50	.20
592	A159	1d grnsh bl	.50	.20
593	A159	1.50d gray bl	3.50	.20
594	A159	2d black	4.75	.20
595	A159	3d brown	3.50	.20
596	A159	3.50d copper brn	11.50	.25
597	A159	4d gray green	11.50	.20
598	A159	5d rose car	11.50	.20
599	A159	7.50d ultra	11.50	2.00
600	A158	10d dk blue	60.00	1.10
		Nos. 587-600 (14)	119.65	5.55

See Nos. 604-617.

Dionysios Solomos and Nicolaos Mantzaros A160

Dionysios Solomos — A161

5d, View on Zante and bust of Solomos.

Perf. 13½x12, 12x13½

1957, Mar. 26   Litho.   Wmk. 252

601	A160	2d red brn & ocher	4.25	.50
602	A161	3.50d bl & gray	6.75	3.25
603	A160	5d dk grn & ol bis	9.00	4.75
		Nos. 601-603 (3)	20.00	8.50

Centenary of the death of Dionysios Solomos (1798-1857), nationalist poet best known for the poem *Hymn to Liberty,* the first two stanzas of which were adopted as the lyrics of the Greek national anthem.

Types of 1956

Designs as before.

Perf. 13½x12

1957		**Wmk. 252**	**Engr.**	
604	A158	10 l rose lake	.50	.20
605	A159	20 l orange	.50	.20
606	A159	30 l gray blk	.50	.20
607	A159	50 l grnsh blk	.50	.20
608	A159	70 l rose lil	1.50	.65
609	A159	1d rose red	1.00	.20
610	A159	1.50d lt ol grn	1.75	.20
611	A159	2d carmine	3.25	.20
612	A159	3d dk blue	4.00	.20
613	A159	3.50d blk vio	10.00	.20
a.		Imperf., pair		
614	A159	4d red brn	10.00	.20
615	A159	5d gray blue	10.00	.20
616	A159	7.50d yel org	3.00	1.25
617	A158	10d green	75.00	.80
		Nos. 604-617 (14)	121.50	4.90

Oil Tanker A162

Ships: 1d, Ocean liner. 1.50d, Sailing ship, 1820. 2d, Byzantine vessel. 3.50d, Ship from 6th century B. C. 5d, "Argo."

1958, Jan. 30   Litho.   Perf. 13½x12

618	A162	50 l multi	.50	.20
619	A162	1d ultra, blk & bis	.50	.20
620	A162	1.50d blk & car	1.50	.95
a.		Double impression of blk	160.00	
621	A162	2d vio bl, blk & red brn	.50	.30
622	A162	3.50d lt bl, blk & red	2.00	1.25
a.		Double impression of blk	160.00	125.00
623	A162	5d bl grn, blk & car	13.50	10.00
		Nos. 618-623 (6)	18.50	12.90

Issued to honor the Greek merchant marine.

Narcissus — A163

Designs: 30 l, Daphne (laurel) and Apollo. 50 l, Adonis (hibiscus) and Aphrodite. 70 l, Pitys (pine) and Pan. 1d, Crocus. 2d, Iris. 3.50d, Tulips. 5d, Cyclamen.

1958, Sept. 15   Wmk. 252   Perf. 13

Size: 22½x38mm

624	A163	20 l multi	.20	.20
625	A163	30 l multi	.20	.20
626	A163	50 l multi	.20	.20
627	A163	70 l multi	.20	.20

Perf. 12½x12

Size: 21½x26mm

628	A163	1d multi	.45	.40

Perf. 12x13½

Size: 22x32mm

629	A163	2d multi	.20	.20
630	A163	3.50d multi	1.75	1.75
a.		Imperf., pair	325.00	
631	A163	5d multi	5.00	5.00
		Nos. 624-631 (8)	8.20	8.15

International Congress for the Protection of Nature, held in Athens.

Types of 1954

Designs: 10 l, Pericles. 20 l, Mycenaean oxhead vase. 50 l, Zeus of Istiaea. 70 l, Charioteer of Delphi. 1d, Head of a youth. 1.50d, Pitcher bearers. 2.50d, Alexander the Great. Two types of 2.50d:
I — 9 dots in upper half of right border.
II — 10 dots.

Perf. 13½x13, 12½x12

1959		**Litho.**	**Wmk. 252**	
632	A150	10 l emerald	.50	.20
633	A150	20 l magenta	.80	.20
634	A150	50 l lt bl grn	1.75	.20
635	A150	70 l red org	.50	.20
636	A151	1d reddish brn	4.50	.20
637	A150	1.50d brt bl	25.00	.20
638	A151	2.50d mag & blk (II)	17.50	.30
a.		Type I	60.00	.55
		Nos. 632-638 (7)	50.55	1.50

Zeus-Eagle Coin — A164

Helios-Rose Coin — A165

Ancient Greek Coins: 20 l, Athena & Owl. 50 l, Nymph Arethusa & Chariot. 70 l, Hercules & Zeus. 1.50d, Griffin & Square. 2.50d, Apollo & Lyre. 4.50d, Apollo & Labyrinth. 6d, Aphrodite & Apollo. 8.50d, Ram's Head & Incuse Squares.

1959, Mar. 24   Wmk. 252   Perf. 14

Coins in Various Shades of Gray

639	A164	10 l red brn & blk	.45	.20
640	A164	20 l dp bl & blk	.45	.20
641	A164	50 l plum & blk	.60	.20
642	A164	70 l ultra & blk	1.10	.30
643	A165	1d dk car rose & blk	1.50	.20
644	A164	1.50d ocher & blk	1.75	.20
645	A164	2.50d dp mag & blk	2.50	.20
646	A165	4.50d Prus grn & blk	5.50	.40
647	A165	6d ol grn & blk	25.00	1.75
648	A165	8.50d dp car & blk	10.00	1.75
		Nos. 639-648 (10)	48.85	3.85

See Nos. 750-758.

Audience, Vase 580 B. C. — A166

Theater, Delphi A167

Designs: 50 l, Clay tragedy mask, 3rd cent. B.C. 1d, Flute, drum and lyre. 2.50d, Clay statue of an actor, 3rd cent. B.C. 4.50d, Andromeda, vase, 4th cent. B.C. 6d, Actors, bowl 410 B.C.

Perf. 13x13½, 13½x13

1959, June 20   Litho.   Wmk. 252

649	A166	20 l blk, fawn & gray	.30	.20
650	A166	50 l dk red brn & ol bis	.30	.25
651	A166	1d grn, brn & ocher	.30	.25
652	A166	2.50d brn & bl	.80	.65
653	A167	3.50d red brn, grn & sep	15.00	10.50
654	A167	4.50d blk & fawn	1.50	1.25
655	A166	6d blk, fawn & gray	1.75	1.50
		Nos. 649-655 (7)	19.95	14.60

Ancient Greek theater.

"Victory" and Soldiers — A168

Perf. 13x13½

1959, Aug. 29   Wmk. 252

656	A168	2.50d red brn, ultra & blk	5.00	.50

10th anniversary of civil war.

St. Basil — A169

The Good Samaritan A170

Designs: 20 l, Plane tree of Hippocrates. 50 l, Aesculapius. 2.50d, Achilles and Patroclus. 3d, Globe and Red Cross over people receiving help. 4.50d, Henri Dunant.

Perf. 13½x12, 12x13½

1959, Sept. 21   Litho.

657	A170	20 l multi	.20	.20
658	A169	50 l multi	.20	.20
659	A169	70 l multi	.20	.20
660	A169	2.50d multi	.60	.50
661	A169	3d multi	10.00	10.00
662	A169	4.50d multi	1.60	1.60
663	A170	6d multi	1.50	1.50
		Nos. 657-663 (7)	14.30	14.20

Cent. of the Red Cross idea. Sizes: Nos. 658-660, 662 24½x32mm, No. 661 32x47mm.

Imre
Nagy — A171

Costis
Palamas — A172

Perf. 13x13½

1959, Dec. 8
664 A171 4.50d org brn & dk brn 1.75 1.75
665 A171 6d brt bl, bl & blk 1.75 1.75

3rd anniv. of the crushing of the 1956 Hungarian Revolution, and to honor Premier Imre Nagy, its leader.

1960, Jan. 25 **Perf. 12x13½**
666 A172 2.50d multi 7.00 .75

Centenary of the birth of Costis Palamas (1859-1943), poet.

Ship
Battling
Storm
A173

4.50d, Ship in calm sea and rainbow.

Perf. 13½x13

1960, Apr. 7 **Wmk. 252**
667 A173 2.50d multi .50 .40
668 A173 4.50d multi 2.00 1.40

Issued to publicize World Refugee Year, July 1, 1959-June 30, 1960.

Boy Scout on
Horseback, St.
George and
Dragon — A174

Scouts
Planting
Tree
A175

30 l, Scout taking oath & boy of ancient Athens. 40 l, Scouts helping in disaster. 70 l, Scouts reading map & tent. 1d, Boy Scout, Sea Scout & Air Scout. 2.50d, Crown Prince Constantine. 6d, Scout flag of Greece & Military Merit medal.

Perf. 13x13½, 13½x13

1960, Apr. 23 **Litho.**
669 A174 20 l multi .20 .20
670 A174 30 l multi .20 .20
671 A174 40 l multi .20 .20
672 A175 50 l multi .20 .20
673 A175 70 l multi .20 .20
674 A174 1d multi .80 .40
675 A174 2.50d multi 2.00 1.25
676 A175 6d multi 2.50 1.50
Nos. 669-676 (8) 6.30 4.15

Greek Boy Scout Organization, 50th anniv.

Greek Holding
Sacred Disk
Proclaiming
Armistice During
Games — A176

Lighting
Olympic
Flame
A177

Designs: 70 l, Youth taking oath. 80 l, Boy cutting olive branches for Olympic prizes. 1d, Judges entering stadium. 1.50d, Long jump. 2.50d, Discus thrower. 4.50d, Sprinters. 5d, Javelin thrower. 6d, Crowning the victors. 12.50d, Victor in chariot entering home town.

Perf. 13x13½, 13½x13

1960, Aug. 12 **Wmk. 252**
677 A176 20 l multi .25 .20
678 A177 50 l multi .25 .20
679 A177 70 l multi .25 .20
680 A177 80 l multi .25 .20
a. Imperf., pair 450.00
681 A177 1d multi .40 .30
682 A177 1.50d multi .40 .30
683 A177 2.50d multi .80 .50
684 A177 4.50d multi .95 .70
a. Dbl. impression of black 350.00 200.00
685 A177 5d multi 2.75 1.60
686 A177 6d multi 2.75 1.60
687 A177 12.50d multi 15.00 10.00
Nos. 677-687 (11) 24.05 15.80

17th Olympic Games, Rome, 8/25-9/11.

Common Design Types
pictured following the introduction.

Europa Issue, 1960
Common Design Type
Perf. 13½x12
1960, Sept. 19 **Litho.** **Wmk. 252**
Size: 33x23mm
688 CD3 4.50d ultra 5.00 2.00
a. Double impression 190.00

Shepherd Type of 1954
1960, Sept. 1 **Wmk. 252** **Perf. 13**
689 A152a 3d ultra 2.25 .40

Crown Prince Constantine and
Yacht — A178

1961, Jan. 18 **Perf. 13½x13**
690 A178 2.50d multi 1.00 .25

Victory of Crown Prince Constantine and his crew at the 17th Olympic Games, Rome (Gold medal, Yachting, Dragon class).

Castoria
A179

Delphi — A180

Landscapes and Ancient Monuments: 20 l, Meteora. 50 l, Hydra harbor. 70 l, Acropolis, Athens. 80 l, Mykonos. 1d, St. Catherine's Church, Salonika. 1.50d, Olympia. 2.50d, Knossos. 3.50d, Rhodes. 4d, Epidauros amphitheater. 4.50d, Temple of Poseidon, Sounion. 5d, Temple of Zeus, Athens. 7.50d, Aslan's mosque, Ioannina. 8d, Mount Athos. 8.50d, Santorini. 12.50d, Marble lions, Delos.

Perf. 13½x12½, 12½x13½

1961, Feb. 15 **Engr.** **Wmk. 252**
691 A179 10 l dk gray bl .20 .20
692 A179 20 l dk purple .20 .20
693 A179 50 l blue .20 .20
694 A179 70 l dk purple .20 .20

695 A179 80 l brt ultra .40 .20
696 A179 1d red brn .70 .20
697 A179 1.50d brt grn 1.00 .25
698 A179 2.50d carmine 3.50 .20
699 A179 3.50d purple 1.40 .20
700 A179 4d sl grn 11.00 .20
701 A179 4.50d dk blue 1.25 .20
702 A179 5d claret 11.00 .25
703 A180 6d slate grn 2.50 .20
704 A179 7.50d black .70 .25
705 A180 8d dk vio bl 4.50 .25
706 A179 8.50d org ver 7.00 .65
707 A179 12.50d dk brn 2.75 1.50
Nos. 691-707 (17) 48.50 5.35

Issued for tourist publicity.

Lily Vase — A181

Partridge
and Fig
Pecker
A182

Minoan Art: 1d, Fruit dish. 1.50d, Rhyton bearer. 2.50d, Ladies of Knossos Palace. 4.50d, Sarcophagus of Hagia Trias. 6d, Dancer. 10d, Two vessels with spouts.

Perf. 13x13½, 13½x13

1961, June 30 **Litho.**
708 A181 20 l multi .50 .20
709 A182 50 l multi .50 .20
710 A182 1d multi .50 .20
711 A181 1.50d multi 1.00 .25
712 A182 2.50d multi 7.00 .20
713 A181 4.50d multi 3.00 2.00
714 A182 6d multi 13.50 1.60
715 A182 10d multi 15.00 8.00
Nos. 708-715 (8) 41.00 12.65

Democritus Nuclear Research
Center — A183

Democritus — A184

1961, July 31 **Perf. 13½x13**
716 A183 2.50d dp lil rose & rose lil .50 .20
717 A184 4.50d vio bl & pale vio bl 1.00 .60

Inauguration of the Democritus Nuclear Research Center at Aghia Paraskevi.

Europa Issue, 1961
Common Design Type
1961, Sept. 18 **Perf. 13½x12**
Size: 32½x22mm
718 CD4 2.50d ver & pink .40 .20
a. Pink omitted (inscriptions white) 20.00 18.00
719 CD4 4.50d ultra & lt ultra .40 .20

Nicephoros
Phocas — A185

1961, Sept. 22 **Wmk. 252**
720 A185 2.50d multi 1.00 .60

1000th anniv. of the liberation of Crete from the Saracens by the Byzantine general (later emperor) Phocas.

Hermes Head of
1861 — A186

1961, Dec. 20 **Litho.** **Perf. 13x13½**

Each denomination shows a different stamp of 1861 issue.

721 A186 20 l brn, red brn & cream .20 .20
722 A186 50 l brn, bis & straw .20 .20
723 A186 1.50d emer & gray .20 .25
724 A186 2.50d red org & ol bis .20 .20
725 A186 4.50d dk bl, bl & gray .45 .30
726 A186 6d rose lil, pale rose & bl .75 .50
727 A186 10d car, rose & cr 1.50 1.50
Nos. 721-727 (7) 3.50 3.15

Centenary of Greek postage stamps.

Tauropos Dam and
Lake — A187

Ptolemais
Power
Station
A188

Designs: 50 l, Ladhon river hydroelectric plant. 1.50d, Louros river dam. 2.50d, Aliverion power plant. 4.50d, Salonika hydroelectric sub-station. 6d, Agra river hydroelectric station, interior.

Perf. 13x13½, 13½x13

1962, Apr. 14 **Wmk. 252**
728 A187 20 l multi .20 .20
729 A187 50 l multi .20 .20
730 A188 1d multi .20 .20
731 A188 1.50d multi .20 .20
732 A188 2.50d multi 1.25 .20
733 A188 4.50d multi .95 .70
734 A188 6d multi 4.00 4.00
Nos. 728-734 (7) 7.00 5.70

National electrification project.

Youth with Shield
and Helmet from
Ancient
Vase — A189

Designs: 2.50d, Zappion hall, horiz. 4.50d,
Kneeling soldier from Temple of Aphaea,
Aegina. 6d, Standing soldier from stele of
Ariston.

Perf. 13¼x14, 12x13½
1962, May 3   Litho.   Wmk. 252
Sizes: 22x33mm, 33x22mm
735	A189	2.50d grn, bl, red & brn	.25	.20
736	A189	3d brn, buff & red		
		brn	.25	.20
737	A189	4.50d bl & gray	.40	.40

Size: 21x37mm
738	A189	6d brn red & blk	.40	.30
		Nos. 735-738 (4)	1.30	1.10

Ministerial congress of NATO countries, Athens, May 3-5.

Europa Issue, 1962
Common Design Type
1962, Sept. 17   Perf. 13½x12
Size: 33x23mm
739	CD5	ver & blk	.75	.40
740	CD5	4.50d ultra & blk	1.50	.75

Hands and   Demeter — A191
Grain — A190

1962, Oct. 30   Perf. 13x13½
741	A190	1.50d dp car, blk & brn	.50	.20
742	A190	2.50d brt grn, blk & brn	.75	.25

Agricultural Insurance Program.

Perf. 12x13½
1963, Apr. 25   Wmk. 252

Design: 4.50d, Wheat and globe.
743	A191	2.50d brn car, gray &		
		blk	.40	.20
744	A191	4.50d multicolored	.85	.35

FAO "Freedom from Hunger" campaign.

George I, Constantine XII, Alexander I,
George II and Paul I — A192

Perf. 13½x12½
1963, June 29   Engr.
745	A192	50 l rose car	.20	.20
746	A192	1.50d green	.45	.20
747	A192	2.50d redsh brn	1.00	.20
748	A192	4.50d dk blue	1.60	1.25
749	A192	6d violet	3.50	.60
		Nos. 745-749 (5)	6.75	2.45

Centenary of the Greek dynasty.

Coin Types of 1959

Ancient Greek Coins: 50 l, Nymph Arethusa
& Chariot. 80 l, Hercules & Zeus. 1d, Helios &
Rose. 1.50d, Griffin & Square. 3d, Zeus &
Eagle. 3.50d, Athena & Owl. 4.50d, Apollo &
Labyrinth. 6d, Aphrodite & Apollo. 8.50d,
Ram's head & Incuse Squares.

Perf. 13½x13, 13x13½
1963, July 5   Litho.   Wmk. 252
Coins in Various Shades of Gray
750	A164	50 l violet bl	.20	.20
751	A164	80 l dp magenta	.20	.20
752	A165	1d emerald	.20	.20
753	A164	1.50d lilac rose	.85	.20
754	A164	3d olive	.60	.20
755	A164	3.50d vermilion	.70	.20
756	A165	4.50d redsh brn	.85	.50
757	A165	6d blue grn	1.10	.20
758	A165	8.50d brt blue	2.00	.85
		Nos. 750-758 (9)	6.70	2.75

"Acropolis at Dawn" by Lord Baden-
Powell — A193

Jamboree Badge   Athenian
(Boeotian   Treasury,
Shield) — A194   Delphi — A195

Designs: 2.50d, Crown Prince Constantine,
Chief Scout. 3d, Athanassios Lefkadites
(founder of Greek Scouts) and Lord Baden-
Powell. 4.50d, Scout bugling with conch shell.

1963, Aug. 1
759	A193	1d bl, sal & ol	.20	.20
760	A194	1.50d dk bl, org brn &		
		brn	.20	.20
761	A194	2.50d multi	1.25	.20
762	A193	3d multi	.50	.55
763	A194	4.50d multi	1.25	.55
		Nos. 759-763 (5)	3.40	1.70

11th Boy Scout Jamboree, Marathon, July
29-Aug. 16, 1963.

1963, Sept. 16   Perf. 12x13½

2d, Centenary emblem. 2.50d, Queen Olga,
founder of Greek Red Cross. 4.50d, Henri
Dunant.
764	A195	1d multi	.50	.25
765	A195	2d multi	.20	.20
766	A195	2.50d multi	.30	.20
767	A195	4.50d multi	.75	.50
		Nos. 764-767 (4)	1.75	1.15

International Red Cross Centenary.

Europa Issue, 1963
Common Design Type
1963, Sept. 16   Perf. 13½x12
Size: 33x23mm
768	CD6	2.50d green	2.25	.40
769	CD6	4.50d brt magenta	3.00	1.50

Vatopethion   King Paul I
Monastery   (1901-1964)
A196   A197

Designs: 80 l, St. Denys' Monastery. 1d,
"Protaton" (Founder's) Church, horiz. 2d,
Stavronikita Monastery. 2.50d, Jeweled cover
of Nicephoros Phocas Gospel. 3.50d, Fresco
of St. Athanassios, founder of community.
4.50d, Presentation of Christ, 11th century
manuscript. 6d, Great Lavra Church, horiz.

Perf. 13x13½, 13½x13
1963, Dec. 5   Litho.   Wmk. 252
770	A196	30 l multi	.20	.20
771	A196	80 l multi	.20	.20
772	A196	1d multi	.20	.20
773	A196	2d multi	1.00	.20
774	A196	2.50d multi	3.00	.20
775	A196	3.50d multi	1.00	.85
776	A196	4.50d multi	1.00	.55
777	A196	6d multi	1.10	.55
		Nos. 770-777 (8)	7.70	2.95

Millennium of the founding of the monastic
community on Mt. Athos.

1964, May 6   Perf. 12x13½
778	A197	30 l brown	.20	.20
779	A197	50 l purple	.20	.20
780	A197	1d green	.75	.20
781	A197	1.50d orange	.40	.20
782	A197	2d blue	.75	.20
783	A197	2.50d chocolate	.75	.20
784	A197	3.50d red brn	.75	.20
785	A197	4d ultra	2.00	.20
786	A197	4.50d bluish blk	2.00	.80
787	A197	6d rose pink	3.00	1.00
		Nos. 778-787 (10)	10.80	3.40

Archangel
Michael — A198

Designs: 1d, Bulgaroctonus coin of Emperor
Basil II. 1.50d, Two armed saints from ivory
triptych by Harbaville, Louvre. 2.50d, Lady,
fresco by Panselinos, Protaton Church, Mt.
Athos. 4.50d, Angel, mosaic, Daphni Church,
Athens.

1964, June 10   Perf. 12x13½
788	A198	1d multi	.20	.20
789	A198	1.50d multi	.20	.20
790	A198	2d multi	.20	.20
791	A198	2.50d multi	.20	.20
792	A198	4.50d multi	.80	.50
		Nos. 788-792 (5)	1.60	1.30

Byzantine Art and for the Byzantine Art
Exhibition, Athens, Apr.-June, 1964.
Exist imperf.

Birth of
Aphrodite,
Emblem of
Kythera
A199

Designs (emblems of islands): 20 l, Trident,
Paxos. 1d, Head of Ulysses, Ithaca. 2d, St.
George slaying dragon, Lefkas. 2.50d,
Zakyntnos, Zante. 4.50d, Cephalus, dog and
spear, Cephalonia. 6d, Trireme, Corfu.

Perf. 13½x12
1964, July 20   Litho.   Wmk. 252
793	A199	20 l multi	.20	.20
794	A199	30 l multi	.20	.20
795	A199	1d multi	.20	.20
796	A199	2d multi	.20	.20
797	A199	2.50d sl grn & dl grn	.50	.20
798	A199	4.50d multi	1.00	.75
799	A199	6d multi	1.00	.40
		Nos. 793-799 (7)	3.30	2.15

Centenary of the union of the Ionian Islands
with Greece.

Child and
Sun — A200

1964, Sept. 10   Wmk. 252
800	A200	2.50d multi	.80	.20

50th anniv. of the Natl. Institute of Social
Welfare for the Protection of Children and
Mothers (P.I.K.P.A.).

Europa Issue, 1964
Common Design Type
1964, Sept. 14   Litho.   Perf. 13x13½
Size: 23x39mm
801	CD7	2.50d lt grn & dk red	2.25	.40
802	CD7	4.50d gray & brn	2.75	1.50

King Constantine   Peleus and
II and Queen   Atalante
Anne-Marie   Fighting, 6th
A201   Cent. B.C. Vase
                         A202

1964, Sept. 18   Engr.   Perf. 13½x14
803	A201	1.50d green	.20	.20
804	A201	2.50d rose car	.20	.20
805	A201	4.50d brt ultra	.50	.25
		Nos. 803-805 (3)	.90	.65

Wedding of King Constantine II and Princess Anne-Marie of Denmark, Sept. 18, 1964.

Perf. 12x13½, 13½x12
1964, Oct. 24   Litho.   Wmk. 252

Designs: 1d, Runners on amphora, horiz.
2d, Athlete on vase, horiz. 2.50d, Discus
thrower and judge, pitcher. 4.50d, Charioteer,
sculpture, horiz. 6d, Boxers, vase, horiz. 10d,
Apollo, frieze from Zeus Temple at Olympia.
806	A202	10 l multi	.20	.20
807	A202	1d multi	.20	.20
808	A202	2d multi	.20	.20
809	A202	2.50d multi	.20	.20
810	A202	4.50d multi	.40	.30
811	A202	6d multi	.20	.20
812	A202	10d multi	.30	.20
		Nos. 806-812 (7)	1.70	1.50

18th Olympic Games, Tokyo, Oct. 10-25.

Detail from   Aesculapius
"Christ Stripped   Theatre,
of His   Epidauros
Garments" by El   A204
Greco
A203

Paintings by El Greco: 1d, Concert of the
Angels. 1.50d, El Greco's painted signature,
horiz. 2.50d, Self-portrait. 4.50d, Storm-lashed
Toledo.

Perf. 12x13½, 13½x12
1965, Mar. 6   Litho.   Wmk. 252
813	A203	50 l sepia &		
		multi	.20	.20
814	A203	1d gray & multi	.20	.20
a.		Double impression of black	100.00	
815	A203	1.50d multi	.20	.20
816	A203	2.50d slate & mul-		
		ti	.20	.20
817	A203	4.50d multi	.30	.25
		Nos. 813-817 (5)	1.10	1.05

350th anniv. of the death of Domenico Theotocopoulos, El Greco (1541-1614).

1965, Apr. 30   Litho.   Perf. 12x13½

Design: 4.50d, Herod Atticus Theatre, and
Acropolis, Athens.
818	A204	1.50d multi	.25	.20
819	A204	4.50d multi	.30	.30

Epidauros and Athens theatrical festivals.

ITU Emblem, Old and New
Telecommunication Equipment — A205

1965, Apr. 30   *Perf. 13½x12*
820 A205 2.50d multi   .40   .20
Cent. of the ITU.

Swearing-in
Ceremony
A206

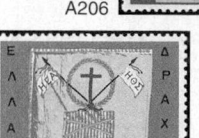

Flag of Philiki
Hetaeria, the
Friends'
Society
A207

Perf. 13½x12
1965, May 31   Litho.   Wmk. 252
821 A206 1.50d multi   .20   .20
822 A207 4.50d gray & multi   .20   .20
150th anniv. of the Friends' Society, a
secret organization for the liberation of Greece
from Turkey.

Emblem of
A.H.E.P.A.
A208

1965, June 30
823 A208 6d lt bl, blk & ol   .50   .20
Congress of the American Hellenic Educational Progressive Association, Athens.

Eleutherios
Venizelos,
Therissos,
1905 — A209

Designs: 2d, Venizelos signing Treaty of
Sevres, 1920. 2.50d, Venizelos portrait.

1965, June 30 Engr.   Perf. 12½x13
824 A209 1.50d green   .20   .20
825 A209 2d dark blue   .40   .30
826 A209 2.50d brown   .20   .20
    Nos. 824-826 (3)   .80   .70
Cent. of the birth of Eleutherios Venizelos
(1864-1936), statesman and prime minister.

Symbols of   Astronaut in
Planets — A210   Space — A211

Design: 6d, Two space ships over globe.

Perf. 12½x13½
1965, Sept. 11   Litho.   Wmk. 252
827 A210 50 l multi   .20   .20
828 A211 2.50d multi   .20   .20
829 A211   6d multi   .20   .20
    Nos. 827-829 (3)   .60   .60
16th Astronautical Cong., Athens, 9/12-18.

Victory
Medal — A212

Stadium,
Phaleron
A213

Design: 1d, Games' emblem and "JBA."

Perf. 13½x13, 13x13½
1965, Sept. 11
830 A213 1d multicolored   .20   .20
831 A212 2d multicolored   .20   .20
832 A213 6d multicolored   .20   .20
    Nos. 830-832 (3)   .60   .60
24th Balkan Games, Sept. 1-10.

Europa Issue, 1965
Common Design Type
1965, Oct. 21   *Perf. 13½x12*
Size: 33x23mm
833 CD8 2.50d bl gray, blk & dk
bl   .75   .40
834 CD8 4.50d olive, blk & grn   1.50   .75

Hipparchus
and Astrolabe
A214

1965, Oct. 21   Litho.   Wmk. 252
835 A214 2.50d bl grn, blk & dk
red   .40   .20
Opening of the Evghenides Planetarium,
Athens.

St. Andrew's   St.
Church,   Andrew — A216
Patras — A215

1965, Nov. 30   *Perf. 12x13½*
836 A215 1d multicolored   .20   .20
837 A216 5d multicolored   .25   .20
Return of the head of St. Andrew from St.
Peter's, Rome to St. Andrew's, Patras. The
design of the 5d is from an 11th cent. mosaic
at St. Luke's Monastery, Boeotia.

Ants and
Anthill — A217

Savings Bank
and
Book — A218

1965, Nov. 30   Litho.   Wmk. 252
838 A217 10 l grn, blk & bis   .20   .20
839 A218 2.50d multi   .30   .20
50th anniv. of the Post Office Savings Bank.

Theodore   Jean Gabriel
Brysakes   Eynard
A219   A220

Banknote of 1867 — A221

Greek Painters: 1d, Nikeforus Lytras. 2.50d,
Constantin Volonakis. 4d, Nicolas Gyses. 5d,
George Jacobides.

Perf. 13x13½
1966, Feb. 28   Litho.   Wmk. 252
840 A219 80 l multi   .20   .20
841 A219   1d multi   .20   .20
842 A219 2.50d multi   .20   .20
843 A219   4d multi   .20   .20
844 A219   5d multi   .20   .20
    Nos. 840-844 (5)   1.00 1.00

Perf. 12x13½
1966, Mar. 30   Engr.   Wmk. 252
2.50d, Georgios Stavros. 4d, Bank's 1st
headquarters, etching by Yannis Kefallinos.
845 A220 1.50d gray grn   .20   .20
846 A220 2.50d brown   .20   .20
847 A221   4d ultra   .20   .20
848 A221   6d black   .20   .20
    Nos. 845-848 (4)   .80   .80
National Bank of Greece, 125th anniv.

Symbolic Water   UNESCO
Cycle — A222   Emblem — A223

WHO Headquarters, Geneva — A224

Perf. 12x13½, 13½x12
1966, Apr. 18   Litho.
849 A222 1d multicolored   .20   .20
850 A223 3d multicolored   .20   .20
851 A224 5d multicolored   .60   .60
    Nos. 849-851 (3)   .60   .60
Hydrological Decade (UNESCO), 1965-74,
(1d); 20th anniv. of UNESCO (3d); inauguration of the WHO Headquarters, Geneva (5d).

Geannares Michael
(Hatzes) — A225

Explosion at
Arkadi
Monastery
A226

Map of
Crete — A227

1966, Apr. 18
852 A225   2d multi   .20   .20
853 A226 2.50d multi   .20   .20
854 A227 4.50d multi   .25   .20
    Nos. 852-854 (3)   .65   .60
Cent. of the Cretan revolt against the Turks.
Geannares Michael (Hatzes), the leader of the
revolt, was a member of Cretan government
and a writer.

Copper Mask, 4th
Century,
B.C. — A228

Dionysus on
a Thespian
Ship-Chariot
A229

Designs: 2.50d, Old Theater of Dionysus,
Athens, 6th Century B.C. 4.50d, Dancing Dionysus, from vase by Kleophrades, c. 500 B.C.

Perf. 12x13½, 13½x12
1966, May 26   Litho.   Wmk. 252
855 A228   1d multi   .20   .20
856 A229 1.50d multi   .20   .20
857 A229 2.50d multi   .20   .20
858 A228 4.50d multi   .20   .20
    Nos. 855-858 (4)   .80   .80
2500th anniversary of Greek theater.

Boeing 707-320 over New York
Buildings and Greek Column
A230

1966, May 26   *Perf. 13x12½*
859 A230 6d blue & dark blue   .40   .20
Inauguration of transatlantic flights of
Olympic Airways.

Tobacco Worker — A231

Design: 5d, Woman sorting tobacco leaves.

Perf. 12½x13½

1966, Sept. 19   Litho.   Wmk. 252
860 A231 1d multicolored   .25   .20
861 A231 5d multicolored   .45   .20

Greek tobacco industry, and 4th Intl. Scientific Tobacco Congress, Athens, Sept. 19-26.

Europa Issue, 1966
Common Design Type
1966, Sept. 19   Litho.   Wmk. 252
Size: 23x33mm
862 CD9 1.50d olive   .75   .35
863 CD9 4.50d lt red brown   1.50   .70

Carved Cases for Knitting Needles — A232

Bridegroom, Embroidery from Epirus A233

Designs (Popular Art): 50 l, Lyre, Crete. 1d, Massa (stringed instrument). 1.50d, Bas-relief (cross and angels). 2d, Icon (Sts. Constantine and Helena). 2.50d, Virgin (wood carving, Church of St. Nicholas, Galaxeidon). 3d, Embroidery (sailing ship from Skyros). 4d, Embroidery (wedding parade). 4.50d, Carved wooden distaff (Sts. George and Barbara). 5d, Silver and agate necklace and earrings. 20d, Handwoven cloth, Cyprus.

Perf. 12x13½, 13½x12

1966, Nov. 21   Litho.   Wmk. 252
864 A232 10 l multi   .20   .20
865 A232 30 l multi   .20   .20
866 A232 50 l multi   .20   .20
867 A232   1d multi   .20   .20
868 A232 1.50d multi   .20   .20
869 A232   2d multi   1.60   .20
870 A232 2.50d multi   .20   .20
871 A233   3d multi   .20   .20
872 A233   4d multi   .65   .20
873 A232 4.50d multi   .30   .30
874 A232   5d multi   .70   .20
875 A233 20d multi   1.50 1.50
      Nos. 864-875 (12)   6.15 2.80

King Constantine II, Queen Anne-Marie and Princess Alexia — A234

Designs: 2d, Princess Alexia. 3.50d, Queen Anne-Marie and Princess Alexia.

Perf. 13½x14

1966, Dec. 19   Engr.   Wmk. 252
876 A234   2d green   .30   .20
877 A234 2.50d brown   .30   .20
878 A234 3.50d ultra   .40   .20
      Nos. 876-878 (3)   1.00   .60

Princess Alexia, successor to the throne of Greece.

"Night" by John Cossos (1830-73) — A235

Sculptures: 50 l, Penelope by Leonides Drosses (1836-1882). 80 l, Shepherd by George Fytales. 2d, Woman's torso by Constantine Demetriades (1881-1943). 2.50d, "Colocotrones" (equestrian statue) by Lazarus Sochos (1862-1911). 3d, Sleeping Young Lady by John Halepas (1851-1938), horiz. 10d, Woodcutter by George Filippotes (1839-1919), horiz.

Perf. 12x13½, 13½x12

1967, Feb. 28   Litho.   Wmk. 252
879 A235 20 l Prus bl, gray &
                 blk   .20   .20
880 A235 50 l brn, gray & blk   .20   .20
881 A235 80 l brn red, gray &
                 blk   .20   .20
882 A235   2d vio bl, gray & blk .20   .20
883 A235 2.50d ultra, blk & grn .20   .20
884 A235   3d bl, lt bl, gray &
                 blk   .40   .25
885 A235 10d bl & multi   .30   .25
      Nos. 879-885 (7)   1.70 1.50

Issued to honor modern Greek sculptors.

World Map and Olympic Rings A236

Discus Thrower by C. Demetriades A237

Designs: 1.50d, Runners on ancient clay vessel. 2.50d, Hurdler and map of Europe and Near East. 6d, Rising sun over Altis ruins at Olympia.

Perf. 13½x12, 12x13½

1967, Apr. 6   Litho.   Wmk. 252
886 A236   1d multi   .20   .20
887 A236 1.50d multi   .20   .20
888 A236 2.50d multi   .20   .20
889 A237   5d multi   .40   .30
890 A236   6d multi   .45   .25
      Nos. 886-890 (5)   1.45 1.15

Olympic Games Day, Apr. 6 (1d); Classic Marathon Race, Apr. 6 (1.5d); athletic qualifying rounds for the Cup of Europe, June 24-25 (2.50d); 9th contest for the European Athletic Championships, 1969 (5d); founding of the Intl. Academy at Olympia and the 7th meeting of the Academy, July 29-Aug. 14, 1967 (6d).

Europa Issue, 1967
Common Design Type
Perf. 12x13½
1967, May 2   Litho.   Wmk. 252
Size: 23x33½mm
891 CD10 2.50d buff, lt & dk brn 1.00   .25
892 CD10 4.50d grn, lt & dk grn 2.75   .75

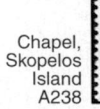

Chapel, Skopelos Island A238

Plaka District, Athens — A239

Intl. Tourist Year: 4.50d, Doric Temple of Epicurean Apollo, by Itkinus, c. 430 B.C.

Perf. 13½x12, 12x13½

1967, June 26   Litho.   Wmk. 252
893 A238 2.50d multi   .20   .20
894 A238 4.50d multi   .50   .30
  a.   Double impression of black
895 A239   6d multi   .50   .20
      Nos. 893-895 (3)   1.20   .70

Destroyer and Sailor A240

Training Ship, Merchant Marine Academy — A241

Maritime Week: 2.50d, Merchant Marine Academy, Aspropyrgos, Attica, and rowing crew. 3d, Cruiser Georgios Averoff and Naval School, Poros. 6d, Merchant ship and bearded figurehead.

1967, June 26
896 A240 20 l multi   .20   .20
897 A241   1d multi   .20   .20
898 A240 2.50d multi   .20   .20
899 A240   3d multi   .30   .25
900 A240   6d multi   .40   .25
      Nos. 896-900 (5)   1.30 1.10

Soldier and Rising Phoenix A242

Blast Furnaces A243

Perf. 12x13½

1967, Aug. 30   Litho.   Wmk. 252
901 A242 2.50d blue & multi   .20   .20
902 A242   3d orange & multi   .20   .20
903 A242 4.50d multi   .20   .20
      Nos. 901-903 (3)   .60   .60

Revolution of Apr. 21, 1967.

1967, Nov. 29   Perf. 13x14
904 A243 4.50d brt bl & dk vio bl .40   .40

1st meeting of the UN Industrial Development Organization, Athens, Nov. 29-Dec. 20.

Sailboats A244

Children's Drawings: 1.50d, Steamship and island. 3.50d, Farmhouse. 6d, Church on hill.

1967, Dec. 20   Perf. 13½x12½
905 A244 20 l multi   .20   .20
906 A244 1.50d dk bl & blk   .20   .20
907 A244 3.50d multi   .40   .40
908 A244   6d multi   .40   .40
      Nos. 905-908 (4)   1.20 1.20

Javelin A245

Apollo, Olympic Academy Seal A246

Discus Thrower by Demetriades A247

Designs: 1d, Jumping. 2.50d, Attic vase showing lighting of Olympic torch. 4d, Olympic rings and world map, horiz. 6d, Long-distance runners, vert.

Wmk. 252

1968, Feb. 28   Litho.   Perf. 12½
909 A245 50 l ultra & bis   .20   .20
910 A245   1d grn, yel, blk &
                 gray   .20   .20
911 A246 1.50d blk, bl & buff   .20   .20
912 A246 2.50d ol grn, blk & org
                 brn   .20   .20
913 A246   4d gray & multi   .35   .20
914 A247 4.50d bl, grn, yel & blk 1.25   .35
915 A245   6d brn, red & bl   .30   .20
      Nos. 909-915 (7)   2.70 1.55

50 l, 1d, 6d, 27th Balkan Games, Athens, Aug. 29-Sept. 1; 1.50d, Meeting of the Intl. Olympic Academy; 2.50d, Lighting of the Olympic torch for 19th Olympic Games, Mexico City; 4d, Olympic Day, Apr. 6; 4.50d, 9th European Athletic Championships, 1969.

Europa Issue, 1968
Common Design Type
Perf. 13½x12
1968, Mar. 29   Litho.   Wmk. 252
Size: 33x23mm
916 CD11 2.50d cop red, bis &
                 blk   1.25   .40
917 CD11 4.50d vio, bister & blk 2.50 1.25

Emblems of Greek and International Automobile Clubs — A248

1968, Mar. 29   Perf. 13x14
918 A248 5d ultra & org brn   1.00   .40

General Assembly of the International Automobile Federation, Athens, Apr. 8-14.

Athena Defeating Alkyoneus, from Pergamos Altar, 180 B.C. — A249

Athena, 2nd Century, B.C. — A250

Winged Victory of Samothrace, c. 190 B.C. — A251

Designs: 50 l, Alexander the Great on horseback, from sarcophagus, c. 310 B.C. 1.50d, Emperors Constantine and Justinian bringing offerings to Virgin Mary, Byzantine mosaic. 2.50d, Emperor Constantine Paleologos, lithograph by D. Tsokos, 1859. 3d, Greece in Missolonghi, by Delacroix. 4.50d, Greek Soldier (evzone), by G. B. Scott.

Perf. 13½x13, 13x13½, 13½x14
(A249)
1968, Apr. 27

919	A249	10 l	gray & multi	.20	.20
920	A250	20 l	grn & multi	.20	.20
921	A250	50 l	pur & multi	.20	.20
922	A249	1.50d	gray & multi	.20	.20
923	A250	2.50d	multicolored	.20	.20
924	A251	3d	multi	.20	.20
925	A251	4.50d	multi	.25	.20
926	A251	6d	multi	.35	.30
		Nos. 919-926 (8)		1.80	1.70

"The Hellenic Fight for Civilization" exhibition

Monument to the Unknown Priest and Teacher, Rhodes A252

Map & Flag of Greece — A253

Cross and Globe — A254

Perf. 14x13½, 13½x14
1968, July 11   Litho.   Wmk. 252

927	A252	2d multicolored	.40	.25
928	A253	5d multicolored	.80	.80

20th anniv. of the union of the Dodecanese Islands with Greece.

1968, July 11   Perf. 13½x14
929 A254 6d multicolored   .55 .40

19th Biennial Congress of the Greek Orthodox Archdiocese of North and South America.

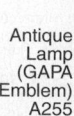

Antique Lamp (GAPA Emblem) A255

1968, July 11   Perf. 14x13½
930 A255 6d multicolored   .50 .30

Regional Congress of the Greek-American Progressive Association, G.A.P.A.

Fragment of Bas-relief, Temple of Aesculapius, Athens — A256

Perf. 13½x14
1968, Sept. 8   Litho.   Wmk. 252
931 A256 4.50d multicolored   1.50 .90

Issued to publicize the 5th European Cardiology Congress, Athens, Sept. 8-14.

View of Olympia, Site of Ancient Games A257

Pindar and Olympic Ode — A258

Hygeia and WHO Emblem — A259

Design: 2.50d, Panathenaic Stadium, site of 1896 Olympic Games.

Perf. 14x13½, 13x13½
1968, Sept. 25   Litho.   Wmk. 252

932	A257	2.50d multicolored	.30	.20
933	A257	5d green & multi	.60	.20
934	A258	10d bl, yel & brn	1.50	.80
		Nos. 932-934 (3)	2.40	1.20

19th Olympic Games, Mexico City, 10/12-27. On 10d, hyphen is omitted at end of 5th line of ode on 5 of 50 stamps in each sheet.

1968, Nov. 8   Perf. 13½x14
935 A259 5d gray & multi   .70 .40

20th anniv. of WHO.

Mediterranean, Breguet 19 and Flight Route, 1928 — A260

Farman, 1912, Plane and F-104G Jet — A261

St. Zeno, The Letter Bearer — A262

Design: 2.50d, Greek air force pilot ramming enemy plane over Langada.

1968, Nov. 8   Perf. 14x13½, 13½x14

936	A260	2.50d ultra, blk & yel	.20	.20
937	A260	3.50d multicolored	.20	.20
938	A261	8d multicolored	1.25	.90
		Nos. 936-938 (3)	1.65	1.30

Exploits of Royal Hellenic Air Force.

Perf. 13½x14
1969, Feb. 10   Litho.   Wmk. 252
939 A262 2.50d multicolored   .50 .20

Establishment of the feast day of St. Zeno as the day of Greek p.o. personnel.

Hephaestus and Cyclops, Bas-relief A263

Parade of Harvesters, Minoan Vase — A264

1969, Feb. 10   Perf. 13½x12½

940	A263	1.50d multicolored	.35	.20
941	A264	10d multicolored	.90	.65

50th anniv. of the ILO.

Yachts in Vouliagmeni Harbor — A265

Athens Festival, Chorus of Elders — A266

View of Astypalaia — A267

Perf. 13½x12½, 12½x13½
1969, Mar. 3

942	A265	1d multicolored	.20	.20
943	A266	5d multicolored	.80	.70
944	A267	6d multicolored	.40	.20
		Nos. 942-944 (3)	1.40	1.10

Issued for tourist publicity.

Attic Shield and Helmet on Greek Coin, 461-450 B.C. — A268

Hoplites and Flutist, from Proto-Corinthian Pitcher, 640-630 B.C. — A269

Perf. 12½x13½, 13½x12½
1969, Apr. 4   Litho.   Wmk. 252

945	A268	2.50d rose red, blk & sl	.35	.20
946	A269	4.50d multi	1.00	.65

20th anniv. of NATO.

Europa Issue, 1969
Common Design Type
1969, May 5   Perf. 13½x12½
Size: 33x23mm

947	CD12	2.50d multi	1.75	.25
948	CD12	4.50d multi	3.25	1.25

Victory Medal A270

Pole Vault and Pentathlon (from Panathenaic Amphora) A271

5d, Relay race and runners from amphora, 525 B.C., horiz. 8d, Modern and ancient (Panathenaic amphora, c. 480 B.C.) discus throwers.

Perf. 12½x13½, 13½x12½
1969, May 5

949	A270	20 l	red & multi	.20	.20
950	A271	3d	gray & multi	.20	.20
951	A271	5d	multicolored	.20	.20
952	A271	8d	multicolored	1.40	.75
		Nos. 949-952 (4)		2.00	1.35

Issued to publicize the 9th European Athletic Championships, Athens, Sept. 16-21.

Greece and the Sea Issue

Oil Tanker A272

Merchant Vessels and Warships, 1821 — A273

Designs: 80 l, Brig and steamship, painting by Ioannis Poulakas, vert. 4.50d, Warships on maneuvers. 6d, Battle of Salamis, 480 B.C., painting by Constantine Volonakis.

Perf. 12½x13½, 13½x12½, 13½x13
1969, June 28   Litho.   Wmk. 252

953	A272	80 l	multicolored	.20	.20
954	A272	2d	blk, bl & gray	.20	.20
955	A272	2.50d	dk bl & multi	.20	.20
956	A272	4.50d	brn, gray & bl	1.00	.35
957	A273	6d	multicolored	1.50	.45
		Nos. 953-957 (5)		3.10	1.40

Raising Greek Flag — A274

1969, Aug. 31 *Perf. 13x13½*
958 A274 2.50d blue & multi .70 .20
20th anniv. of the Grammos-Vitsi victory.

Athena Promachos and Map of Greece A275

"National Resistance" A276

Greek Participation in World War II — A277

Perf. 13x13½, 13½x14
1969, Oct. 12 Litho. Wmk. 252
959 A275 4d multicolored .20 .20
960 A276 5d multicolored 1.50 .70
961 A277 6d multicolored .65 .20
Nos. 959-961 (3) 2.35 1.10

25th anniv. of the liberation of Greece in WW II.
No. 960 exists imperf.

Demetrius Tsames Karatasios, by G. Demetriades A278

Pavlos Melas, by P. Mathiopoulos A279

2.50d, Emmanuel Pappas, statue by Nicholas Perantinos. 4.50d, Capetan Kotas.

Perf. 12x13½
1969, Nov. 12 Litho. Wmk. 252
962 A278 1.50d multicolored .20 .20
963 A278 2.50d blue & multi .20 .20
964 A279 3.50d gray & multi .20 .20
965 A279 4.50d multicolored .95 .55
Nos. 962-965 (4) 1.55 1.15

Issued to honor Greek heroes in Macedonia's struggle for liberation.

Angel of the Annunciation, Daphni Church, 11th Century — A280

Dolphins, Delos, 110 B.C. A281

Christ's Descent into Hell, Nea Moni Church, 11th Cent. A282

Greek Mosaics: 1.50d, The Holy Ghost (dove), Hosios Loukas Monastery, 11th cent. 2d, The Hunter, Pella, 4th cent. B.C. 5d, Bird, St. George's Church, Salonica, 5th cent.

Perf. 12x13½, 13½x12 (1d), 13x13½ (6d)
1970, Jan. 16 Litho. Wmk. 252
966 A280 20 l multicolored .20 .20
967 A281 1d multicolored .20 .20
968 A280 1.50d blue & multi .20 .20
969 A280 2d gray & multi .45 .20
970 A280 5d bister & multi .55 .35
971 A282 6d multicolored .75 .75
Nos. 966-971 (6) 2.35 1.90

Hercules and the Cretan Bull — A283

Hercules and the Erymanthian Boar — A284

Labors of Hercules: 30 l, Capture of Cerberus. 1d, Capture of the golden apples of the Hesperides. 1.50d, Lernean Hydra. 2d, Slaying of Geryon. 3d, Centaur Nessus. 4.50d, Fight with the river god Achelos. 5d, Nemean lion. 6d, Stymphalian birds. 20d, Giant Antaeus. Designs of 20 l and 1d are from Temple of Zeus, Olympia; others from various vessels; all from 7th-5th cent. B.C.

Perf. 13½x12, 12x13½
1970, Mar. 16 Litho. Wmk. 252
972 A283 20 l gray, blk & yel .20 .20
973 A283 30 l ocher & multi .20 .20
974 A284 1d bl gray, blk & bl .20 .20
975 A283 1.50d dk brn, bis & sl grn .30 .20
976 A283 2d ocher & multi 2.25 .20
977 A284 2.50d ocher, dk brn & dl red .30 .20
978 A284 3d multicolored 2.25 .20
979 A283 4.50d dk bl & multi .50 .20
980 A283 5d multicolored .50 .20
981 A283 6d multicolored .50 .20
982 A283 20d black & multi 1.75 .85
Nos. 972-982 (11) 8.95 2.85

Satellite, Earth Station and Hemispheres A285

1970, Apr. 21 *Perf. 13½x12*
983 A285 2.50d bl, gray & yel .50 .30
984 A285 4.50d brn, ol & bl 1.25 1.10

Opening of the Earth Satellite Telecommunications Station "Thermopylae," Apr. 21, 1970.

Europa Issue, 1970
Common Design Type and

Owl (Post Horns and CEPT) — A287

1970, Apr. 21 Perf. 13½x12, 12x13½
985 CD13 2.50d rose red & org 2.00 .75
986 A287 3d brt bl, gray & vio bl 2.00 1.00
987 CD13 4.50d ultra & org 5.75 1.25
Nos. 985-987 (3) 9.75 2.75

St. Demetrius with Cyril and Methodius as Children A288

Emperor Michael III with Sts. Cyril and Methodius A290

A289

Perf. 13½x14 (50 l); 12x13½ (2d, 10d); 13x13½ (5d)
1970, Apr. 17 Litho. Wmk. 252
988 A288 50 l multi .20 .20
989 2d St. Cyril .60 .45
990 A290 5d multi .50 .20
991 10d St. Methodius .70 .50
a. A289 Pair, #989, 991 1.25 1.25
Nos. 988-991 (4) 2.00 1.35

Sts. Cyril and Methodius who translated the Bible into Slavonic.

Greek Fir A292

Jankaea Heldreichii A293

6d, Rock partridge, horiz. 8d, Wild goat.

Perf. 13x14, 14x13, 12x13½ (2.50d)
1970, June 16 Litho. Wmk. 252
992 A292 80 l multi .35 .35
993 A293 2.50d multi 1.25 .20
994 A292 6d multi 2.40 .55
995 A292 8d multi 2.75 2.40
Nos. 992-995 (4) 6.75 3.50

European Nature Conservation Year, 1970.

Map Showing Link Between AHEPA Members and Greece A294

1970, Aug. 1 *Perf. 13½x13*
996 A294 6d blue & multi 1.00 .40

48th annual AHEPA (American Hellenic Educational Progressive Assoc.) Cong., Athens, Aug. 1970.

UPU Headquarters, Bern — A295

Education Year Emblem — A296

Mahatma Gandhi — A297

United Nations Emblem — A298

Ludwig van Beethoven — A299

Perf. 13½x12, 13x14, 12x13½
1970, Oct. 7 Litho. Wmk. 252
997 A295 50 l bis & multi .20 .20
998 A296 2.50d bl & multi .40 .20
999 A297 3.50d multi .25 .20
1000 A298 4d bl & multi .75 .20
1001 A299 4.50d blk & multi 1.50 1.10
Nos. 997-1001 (5) 3.10 1.90

Inauguration of the UPU Headquarters, Bern (50 l); Intl. Education Year (2.50d); cent. of the birth of Mohandas K. Gandhi (1869-1948), leader in India's struggle for independence (3.50d); 25th anniv. of the UN (4d); Ludwig van Beethoven (1770-1827), composer (4.50d).

The Shepherds (Mosaic) — A300

Christmas (from Mosaic in the Monastery of Hosios Loukas, Boetia, 11th cent.): 4.50d, The Three Kings and Angel. 6d, Nativity, horiz.

1970, Dec. 5 *Perf. 13x14, 14x13*
1002 A300 2d bister & multi .20 .20
1003 A300 4.50d bister & multi .40 .30
1004 A300 6d bister & multi .80 .80
Nos. 1002-1004 (3) 1.40 1.30

"Leonidas"
A301

Priest Sworn in as
Fighter, from
Commemorative
Medal — A302

Eugenius
Voùlgaris (1716-
1806)
A303

Battle of Corinth
A304

Kaltetsi Monastery, Seal of
Peloponnesian Senate — A305

Death of Bishop Isaias, Battle of
Alamana — A306

Designs: No. 1009, *Pericles.* No. 1010, Sacrifice of Kapsalis. 1.50d, *Terpsichore.* No. 1012, Patriarch Grigorius IV. No. 1013, Suliot women in battle, horiz. No. 1015, *Karteria.* No. 1016, Adamantios Korais, M.D. No. 1017, Memorial column, provincial administrative seal of Epidaurus. 3d, Naval battle, Samos, horiz. 5d, Battle of Athens. 6d, Naval battle, Yeronda. 6.50d, Battle of Maniaki. 9d, Battle of Karpenisi, death of Marcos Botsaris. 10d, Bishop Germanos blessing flag. 15d, *Secret School.* 20d, John Capodistrias' signature and seal.

1971		Litho.	Wmk. 252	
1005	A301	20 l multi	.20	.20
1006	A302	50 l multi	.20	.20
1007	A303	50 l multi	.20	.20
1008	A304	50 l multi	.20	.20
1009	A301	1d multi	.20	.20
1010	A304	1d multi	.20	.20
1011	A301	1.50d multi	.20	.20
1012	A302	2d multi	.20	.20
1013	A304	2d multi	.20	.20
1014	A305	2d multi	.20	.20
1015	A301	2.50d multi	.20	.20
1016	A303	2.50d multi	.25	.20
1017	A305	2.50d multi	.25	.20
1018	A304	3d multi	.65	.40
1019	A306	4d multi	.20	.20
1020	A304	5d multi	.40	.20
1021	A301	6d multi	1.25	.90
1022	A301	6.50d multi	.40	.25
1023	A301	9d multi	1.00	.90
1024	A306	10d multi	1.10	.90
1025	A306	15d multi	1.25	1.10
1026	A306	20d multi	2.25	1.40
		Nos. 1005-1026 (22)	11.20	8.85

Sesquicentennial of Greece's uprising against the Turks. Emphasize role of Navy (#1005, 1009, 1011, 1015, 1018, 1021), issued 3/15; Church (#1006, 1012, 1019,

1024), 2/8; Instructors (#1007, 1016, 1025), 6/21; Land Forces (#1008, 1010, 1013, 1020, 1022-1023), 9/21; Provincial Administrations (#1014, 1017, 1026), 10/19.
Sizes: 37x24mm: #1005, 1009, 1011, 1015; 40x27½mm, #1021; 48x33mm, #1022, 1023.
Perfs.: 14x13, #1005, 1009, 1011, 1013, 1015, 1018; 13½x14, #1006, 1012; 12x13½, #1007, 1016, 1019, 1022-1025; 13x14, #1008, 1010, 1020; 13½x13, #1014, 1017, 1021, 1026.

Spyridon Louis, Winner of 1896
Marathon Race, Arriving at Stadium
A307

Pierre de Coubertin
and Memorial
Column — A308

Perf. 13½x13, 13x13½

1971, Apr. 10		Litho.	Wmk. 252	
1027	A307	3d multi	.50	.20
1028	A308	8d multi	1.25	.90

Olympic Games revival, 75th anniv.

Europa Issue, 1971
Common Design Type

1971, May 18		*Perf. 13½x12*		
		Size: 33x22½mm		
1029	CD14	2.50d grn, yel & blk	1.00	.30
1030	CD14	5d org, yel & blk	3.00	1.50

Hosios
Lukas
Monastery
A309

Monasteries and Churches: 1d, Daphni Church. 2d, St. John the Divine, Patmos. 2.50d, Koumbelidiki Church, Kastoria. 4.50d, Chalkeon Church, Thessalonica. 6.50d, Paregoritissa Church, Arta. 8.50d, St. Paul's Monastery, Mt. Athos.

1972, Jan. 17		*Perf. 14x13*		
1031	A309	50 l multi	.20	.20
1032	A309	1d multi	.20	.20
1033	A309	2d multi	.20	.20
1034	A309	2.50d multi	.20	.20
1035	A309	4.50d multi	.25	.20
1036	A309	6.50d multi	.25	.20
1037	A309	8.50d multi	1.00	1.00
		Nos. 1031-1037 (7)	2.30	2.20

Cretan
Costume — A310

Designs: Greek regional costumes.

1972, Mar. 1		*Perf. 12½x13½*		
1038	A310	50 l shown	.20	.20
1039	A310	1d Woman, Pindus	.20	.20
1040	A310	2d Man, Missolonghi	.20	.20
1041	A310	2.50d Woman, Sarakatsan, Attica	.20	.20
a.		"1972" omitted	10.00	10.00
1042	A310	3d Woman, Island of Nisyros	.20	.20
1043	A310	4.50d Woman, Megara	.20	.20

1044	A310	6.50d Woman, Trikeri	.30	.25
1045	A310	10d Woman, Pylaia, Macedonia	3.00	1.00
		Nos. 1038-1045 (8)	4.50	2.45

See Nos. 1073-1089, 1121-1135.

Memorial
Medal,
Science
and
Industry
A311

Flag and Map of
Greece — A312

Honeycomb,
Transportation
and
Industry — A313

Perf. 13½x13, 13x13½

1972, Apr. 21			Wmk. 252	
1046	A311	2.50d blue & multi	.20	.20
1047	A312	4.50d ocher & multi	.25	.25
1048	A313	5d multi	.40	.40
		Nos. 1046-1048 (3)	.85	.85

5th anniversary of the revolution.

Europa Issue 1972
Common Design Type

1972, May 2		*Perf. 12x13½*		
		Size: 23x33mm		
1049	CD15	3d multi	.50	.30
1050	CD15	4.50d blue & multi	1.50	1.25

Acropolis and
Car — A314

Route of
Automobile
Rally — A315

1972, May 26		*Perf. 13½x12*		
1051	A314	4.50d multi	.60	.60
1052	A315	5d bl & multi	.60	.60

20th Acropolis Automobile Rally, May 26-29.

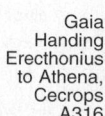

Gaia
Handing
Erecthonius
to Athena,
Cecrops
A316

Designs: 2d, Uranus, from altar of Zeus at Pergamum. 2.50d, Gods defeating the Giants, Treasury of Siphnos. 5d, Zeus of Dodona.

1972, June 26		Litho.	*Perf. 14x13½*	
1053	A316	1.50d yel grn & blk	.20	.20
1054	A316	2d dk bl & blk	.20	.20
1055	A316	2.50d org brn & blk	.20	.20
1056	A316	5d dk brn & blk	.50	.40
a.		Strip of 4, #1053-1056	2.00	2.00

Greek mythology. No. 1056 issued only setenant with Nos. 1053-1055 in sheets of 40 (4x10). Nos. 1053-1055 issued also in sheets of 50 each.

Olympic
Rings,
Wrestlers
A317

50 l, Young athlete, crowning himself, c. 480 B.C., vert. 3.50d, Spartan woman running, Archaic period, vert. 4.50d, Episkyros ball game, 6th century B.C. 10d, Running youths, from Panathenaic amphora.

Perf. 13½x14, 14x13½

1972, July 28		Litho.	Wmk. 252	
1057	A317	50 l mar, blk & gray	.25	.20
1058	A317	1.50d brn, gray & blk	.25	.20
1059	A317	3.50d ocher & multi	.50	.20
1060	A317	4.50d grn, buff & blk	.25	.20
1061	A317	10d blk & fawn	1.00	.55
		Nos. 1057-1061 (5)	2.25	1.35

20th Olympic Games, Munich, 8/26-9/11.

Young Stamp
Collector — A318

Three Kings and
Angels — A319

1972, Nov. 15		*Perf. 13x14*		
1062	A318	2.50d multi	.25	.20

Stamp Day.

1972, Nov. 15				
1063	A319	2.50d shown	.20	.20
1064	A319	4.50d Nativity	.20	.20
a.		Pair, #1063-1064	.40	.40

Christmas 1972.

Technical University, 1885, by Luigi
Lanza — A320

1973, Mar. 30		*Perf. 13½x13*		
1065	A320	2.50d multi	.40	.20

Centenary of the Metsovion National Technical University.

"Spring,"
Fresco — A321

Breast-form Jug — A322

"Wooing and Twittering Swallows" Fresco — A323

Designs: 30 l, "Blue Apes" fresco. 1.50d, Jug decorated with birds. 5d, "Wild Goats" fresco. 6.50d, Wrestlers, fresco.

1973, Mar. 30   Perf. 13x13½, 13½x13
1066	A321	10 l multi	.20	.20
1067	A322	20 l multi	.20	.20
1068	A323	30 l multi	.20	.20
1069	A322	1.50d grn & multi	.20	.20
1070	A323	2.50d multi	.20	.20
1071	A323	5d multi	.20	.20
1072	A323	6.50d multi	.80	.80
		Nos. 1066-1072 (7)	2.00	2.00

Archaeological treasures from Santorini Island (Thera).

Costume Type of 1972

Women's costumes except 10 l, 20 l, 50 l, 5d, 15d.

1973, Apr. 18   Perf. 12½x13½
1073	A310	10 l Peloponnesus	.20	.20
1074	A310	20 l Central Greece	.20	.20
1075	A310	30 l Locris	.20	.20
1076	A310	50 l Skyros	.20	.20
1077	A310	1d Spetsai	.20	.20
1078	A310	1.50d Almyros	.20	.20
1079	A310	2.50d Macedonia	.20	.20
1080	A310	3.50d Salamis	.20	.20
1081	A310	4.50d Epirus	.20	.20
1082	A310	5d Lefkas	.20	.20
1083	A310	6.50d Skyros	.20	.20
1084	A310	8.50d Corinth	.40	.25
1085	A310	10d Corfu	.40	.25
1086	A310	15d Epirus	.40	.25
1087	A310	20d Thessaly	1.25	.25
1088	A310	30d Macedonia	1.60	.35
1089	A310	50d Thrace	3.25	1.60
		Nos. 1073-1089 (17)	9.50	5.05

Europa Issue 1973
Common Design Type

1973, May 2   Perf. 13½x12½
Size: 35x22mm
1090	CD16	2.50d dp bl & lt bl	.30	.25
1091	CD16	3d dp car & dp org	.30	.30
1092	CD16	4.50d ol grn & yel	1.50	.85
		Nos. 1090-1092 (3)	2.10	1.40

Zeus Battling Typhoeus, from Amphora A324

1d, Mount Olympus, after photograph. 2.50d, Zeus battling Giants, from Pergamum Altar. 4.50d, Punishment of Atlas and Prometheus, from vase.

Perf. 14x13½
1973, June 25   Wmk. 252
1093	A324	1d gray & blk	.25	.20
1094	A324	2d multi	.25	.20
1095	A324	2.50d gray, blk & buff	.25	.20
1096	A324	4.50d ocher & multi	.45	.45
a.		Strip of 4, #1093-1096	1.75	1.75

Greek mythology.

Dr. George Papanicolaou A325

Icon, The Annunciation A326

Perf. 13x13½
1973, Aug. 10   Litho.   Wmk. 252
1097	A325	2.50d multi	.20	.20
1098	A325	6.50d multi	.25	.25

Dr. George Papanicolaou (1883-1962), cytologist and cancer researcher.

1973, Aug. 10
1099	A326	2.50d multi	.40	.25

Miraculous icon of Our Lady of the Annunciation found on Tinos, 1823.

A327

A328

Triptolemus holding wheat on chariot.

Perf. 13x14
1973, Oct. 22   Litho.   Wmk. 252
1100	A327	4.50d buff, dk brn & red	.30	.25

5th Symposium of the European Conf. of Transport Ministers, Athens, Oct. 22-25.

1973, Nov. 15   Engr.

National Benefactors: 1d, Georgios Averoff. 2d, Apostolos Arsakis. 2.50d, Constantine Zappas. 4d, Andrea Sygros. 6.50d, John Varvakis.
1101	A328	1.50d dk red brn	.20	.20
1102	A328	2d car rose	.20	.20
1103	A328	2.50d slate green	.20	.20
1104	A328	4d purple	.20	.20
1105	A328	6.50d black	.25	.25
		Nos. 1101-1105 (5)	1.05	1.05

Child Examining Stamp — A329

1973, Nov. 15   Litho.   Perf. 14x13
1106	A329	2.50d multi	.25	.20

Stamp Day.

Lord Byron in Souliot Costume — A330

Byron Taking Oath at Grave of Botsaris — A331

Perf. 13x14
1974, Apr. 4   Wmk. 252   Litho.
1107	A330	2.50d multi	.20	.20
1108	A331	4.50d multi	.20	.20

George Gordon, Lord Byron (1788-1824), English poet involved in Greek struggle for independence.

Harpist of Keros, c. 2800-2200 B.C. — A332

Europa: 4.50d, Statue of Young Women, c. 510 B.C. 6.50d, Charioteer of Delphi, c. 480-450 B.C.

1974, May 10   Perf. 13x14
1109	A332	3d dp bl & multi	.45	.25
1110	A332	4.50d dl red & multi	.65	.30
1111	A332	6.50d yel & multi	1.75	.80
		Nos. 1109-1111 (3)	2.85	1.35

Zeus and Hera Enthroned, and Iris — A333

Design from Mycenean Vase and UPU Emblem — A334

Greek mythology (from Vases, 5th Cent. B.C.): 2d, Birth of Athena, horiz. 2.50d, Artemis, Apollo, Leto, horiz. 10d, Hermes, the messenger.

1974, June 24   Perf. 13x14, 14x13
1112	A333	1.50d ocher, blk & brn	.20	.20
1113	A333	2d blk, ocher & brn	.20	.20
1114	A333	2.50d blk, ocher & brn	.20	.20
1115	A333	10d blk, ocher & brn	.25	.25
		Nos. 1112-1115 (4)	.85	.85

1974, Sept. 14   Perf. 12½x13½

UPU cent.: 4.50d, Hermes on the Move, horiz. 6.50d, Woman reading letter.
1116	A334	2d vio & blk	.20	.20
1117	A334	4.50d vio & blk	.20	.20
1118	A334	6.50d vio & blk	.25	.30
		Nos. 1116-1118 (3)	.65	.70

Crete No. 80 A335

1974, Nov. 15   Litho.   Perf. 13½x13
1119	A335	2.50d multi	.25	.20

Stamp Day.

Flight into Egypt — A336

1974, Nov. 15   Perf. 13½x14
1120	A336	Strip of 3	.80	.80
a.		2d ocher & multi	.20	.20
b.		4.50d ocher & multi	.20	.20
c.		8.50d ocher & multi	.20	.20

Christmas 1974. Design is from 11th cent. Codex of Dionysos Monastery on Mount Athos.

Costume Type of 1972

Designs: Women's costumes, except 1.50d.

1974, Dec. 5   Perf. 12½x13½
1121	A310	20 l Megara	.20	.20
1122	A310	30 l Salamis	.20	.20
1123	A310	50 l Edipsos	.20	.20
1124	A310	1d Kyme	.20	.20
1125	A310	1.50d Sterea Hellas	.20	.20
1126	A310	2d Desfina	.20	.20
1127	A310	3d Epirus	.20	.20
1128	A310	3.50d Naousa	.20	.20
1129	A310	4d Hasia	.20	.20
1130	A310	4.50d Thasos	.20	.20
1131	A310	5d Skopelos	.20	.20
1132	A310	6.50d Epirus	.20	.20
1133	A310	10d Pelion	.30	.20
1134	A310	25d Kerkyra	.70	.20
1135	A310	30d Boeotia	2.25	.60
		Nos. 1121-1135 (15)	5.65	3.40

Secret Vostitsa Assembly, 1821 — A337

Grigorios Dikeos-Papaflessas A338

Aghioi Apostoli Church, Kalamata A339

Perf. 13½x12½, 12½x13½

1975, Mar. 24

1136	A337	4d multi	.20	.20
1137	A338	7d multi	.20	.20
1138	A339	11d multi	.25	.25
	Nos. 1136-1138 (3)		.65	.65

Grigorios Dikeos-Papaflessas (1788-1825), priest and leader in Greece's uprising against the Turks, sesquicentennial of death.

Vase with Flowers — A340

Erotokritos and Aretussa — A341

Europa: 11d, Girl with Hat. All designs are after paintings by Theophilos Hatzimichael (d. 1934).

Perf. 12½x13½

1975, May 10   Litho.   Wmk. 252

1139	A340	4d multi	.50	.45
1140	A341	7d multi	.70	.65
1141	A340	11d multi	2.00	1.25
	Nos. 1139-1141 (3)		3.20	2.35

House, Kastoria A342

Greek Houses, 18th Cent.: 40 l, Arnea, Halkidiki. 4d, Veria. 6d, Siatista. 11d, Ambelakia, Thessaly.

1975, June 26   Perf. 13½x12½

1142	A342	10 l brt bl & blk	.20	.20
1143	A342	40 l red org & blk	.20	.20
1144	A342	4d bister & blk	.25	.20
1145	A342	6d ultra & multi	.20	.20
1146	A342	11d org & blk	.25	.25
	Nos. 1142-1146 (5)		1.10	1.05

IWY Emblem, Neolithic Goddess — A343

"Looking to the Future" — A344

8.50d, Confrontation between Antigone & Creon.

Perf. 12½x13½

1975, Sept. 29   Litho.   Wmk. 252

1147	A343	1.50d lilac & dk brn	.20	.20
1148	A343	8.50d bis, blk & brn	.20	.20
1149	A344	11d bl & blk	.25	.25
	Nos. 1147-1149 (3)		.65	.65

International Women's Year 1975.

Papanastasiou and University Buildings — A345

First University Building A346

University City Plan A347

1975, Sept. 29   Perf. 14x13½

1150	A345	1.50d tan & sepia	.20	.20
1151	A346	4d multi	.20	.20
1152	A347	11d multi	.25	.25
	Nos. 1150-1152 (3)		.65	.65

Thessaloniki University, 50th anniversary. Alexandros Papanastasiou (1876-1936), founded University while Prime Minister.

Evangelos Zappas and Zappeion Building — A348

National Benefactors: 4d, Georgios Rizaris and Rizarios Ecclesiastical School. 6d, Michael Tositsas and Metsovion Technical University. 11d, Nicolaos Zosimas and Zosimea Academy.

Perf. 14x13

1975, Nov. 15   Litho.   Wmk. 252

1153	A348	1d blk & grn	.20	.20
1154	A348	4d blk & brn	.20	.20
1155	A348	6d blk & org	.20	.20
1156	A348	11d blk & brick red	.20	.20
	Nos. 1153-1156 (4)		.80	.80

Greece No. 380 — A349

1975, Nov. 15   Perf. 13x14

1157	A349	11d dull grn & brn	.40	.35

Stamp Day 1975.

Pontos Lyre — A350

Musicians, Byzantine Mural — A351

Designs: 1d, Cretan lyre. 1.50d, Tambourine. 4d, Guitarist, from amphora, horiz. 6d, Bagpipes. 7d, Lute. 10d, Barrel organ. 11d, Pipes and zournadas. 20d, Musicians and singers praising God, Byzantine mural, horiz. 25d, Drums. 30d, Kanonaki, horiz.

Perf. 12½x13½, 13½x12½

1975, Dec. 15   Litho.   Wmk. 252

1158	A350	10 l multi	.20	.20
1159	A351	20 l multi	.20	.20
1160	A350	1d ultra & multi	.20	.20
1161	A350	1.50d multi	.20	.20
1162	A351	4d multi	.20	.20
1163	A350	6d multi	.20	.20
1164	A350	7d multi	.20	.20
1165	A350	10d multi	.20	.20
1166	A350	11d red & multi	.20	.20
1167	A351	20d multi	.25	.20
1168	A350	25d multi	.45	.20
1169	A350	30d multi	1.00	1.00
	Nos. 1158-1169 (12)		3.50	3.20

Popular musical instruments.

Early Telephone, Globe, Waves A352

11d, Globe, waves, telephone 1976.

Perf. 13½x12½

1976, Mar. 23   Litho.   Wmk. 252

1170	A352	7d blk & multi	.20	.20
1171	A352	11d blk & multi	.20	.20
a.	Pair, Nos. 1170-1171		.50	.50

1st telephone call by Alexander Graham Bell, Mar. 10, 1876.

Sortie of Missolonghi — A353

1976, Mar. 23   Perf. 13½x13

1172	A353	4d multi	.25	.25

Sortie of the garrison of Missolonghi, sesquicentennial.

Florina Jugn — A354

Avramidis Plate — A355

Europa: 11d, Egina pitcher with Greek flags.

Perf. 13x14, 12½x12 (A355)

1976, May 10   Litho.   Wmk. 252

1173	A354	7d buff & multi	.40	.30
1174	A355	8.50d blk & multi	.50	.30
1175	A354	11d gray & multi	1.50	.90
	Nos. 1173-1175 (3)		2.40	1.50

Lion Attacking Bull — A356

Head of Silenus — A357

Designs: 4.50d, Flying aquatic birds. 7d, Wounded bull. 11d, Cow feeding calf, horiz. Designs from Creto-Mycenaean engraved seals, c. 1400 B.C.

Perf. 13x12½, 13½x14, 14x13½

1976, May 10

1176	A356	2d bis & multi	.20	.20
1177	A356	4.50d multi	.20	.20
1178	A356	7d multi	.20	.20
1179	A357	8.50d pur & multi	.20	.20
1180	A357	11d brn & multi	.20	.20
	Nos. 1176-1180 (5)		1.00	1.00

Long Jump A358

Montreal and Athens Stadiums — A359

Designs (Classical and Modern Events): 2d, Basketball. 3.50d, Wrestling. 4d, Swimming. 25d, Lighting Olympic flame and Montreal Olympic Games torch.

Perf. 14x13½, 12½x13½ (A359)

1976, June 25   Litho.   Wmk. 252

1181	A358	50 l org & multi	.20	.20
1182	A358	2d org & multi	.20	.20
1183	A358	3.50d org & multi	.20	.20
1184	A358	4d bl & multi	.20	.20
1185	A359	11d multi	.20	.20
1186	A358	25d org & multi	.75	.75
	Nos. 1181-1186 (6)		1.75	1.75

21st Olympic Games, Montreal, Canada, July 17-Aug. 1.

Lesbos, View and Map A360

Perf. 13½x14, 14x13½

1976, July 26   Litho.   Wmk. 252

1187	A360	30d Lemnos, vert.	.45	.20
1188	A360	50d shown	.75	.20
1189	A360	75d Chios	.90	.25
1190	A360	100d Samos	2.10	1.75
	Nos. 1187-1190 (4)		4.20	2.40

Greek Aegean Islands.

GREECE

462

Three Kings
Speaking to the
Jews — A361

Christmas: 7d, Nativity. Designs from manuscripts in Esfigmenou Monastery, Mount Athos.

1976, Dec. 8   *Perf. 13½x14*
1191 A361 4d yellow & multi   .20 .20
1192 A361 7d yellow & multi   .20 .20

Greek
Grammar
of 1478
A362

1976, Dec. 8   *Perf. 14x13*
1193 A362 4d multi   .25 .20

500th anniversary of printing of first Greek book by Constantin Lascaris, Milan.

Heinrich
Schliemann
A363

Brooch with
Figure of
Goddess — A364

Designs: 4d, Gold bracelet, horiz. 7d, Gold diadem, horiz. 11d, Gold mask (Agamemnon). Treasures from Mycenaean tombs.

1976, Dec. 8   *Perf. 13x14, 14x13*
1194 A363 2d multi   .20 .20
1195 A364 4d multi   .20 .20
1196 A364 5d grn & multi   .20 .20
1197 A364 7d multi   .20 .20
1198 A364 11d multi   .50 .50
   Nos. 1194-1198 (5)   1.30 1.30

Cent. of the discovery of the Mycenaean royal shaft graves by Heinrich Schliemann.

Aesculapius with   Patient in
Patients — A365   Clinic — A366

Designs: 1.50d, Aesculapius curing young man. 2d, Young Hercules with old nurse. 20d, Old man with votive offering of large leg.

Perf. 12½x13½ (A365); 13x12 (A366)
1977, Mar. 15   Litho.   Wmk. 252
1199 A365 50 l multi   .20 .20
1200 A366 1d multi   .20 .20
1201 A366 1.50d multi   .20 .20
1202 A366 2d multi   .20 .20
1203 A365 20d multi   .20 .20
   Nos. 1199-1203 (5)   1.00 1.00

International Rheumatism Year.

Winged Wheel, Modern
Transportation — A367

1977, May 16   Litho.   *Perf. 14x13½*
1204 A367 7d multi   .25 .20

European Conference of Ministers of Transport (E.C.M.T.), Athens, June 1-3.

Mani
Castle,
Vathia
A368

Europa: 7d, Santorini, vert. 15d, Windmills on Lasithi plateau.

Perf. 14x13½, 13½x14
1977, May 16   Litho.   Wmk. 252
1205 A368 5d multicolored   .45 .25
1206 A368 7d multicolored   .45 .35
1207 A368 15d multicolored   1.50 .50
   Nos. 1205-1207 (3)   2.40 1.10

Alexandria Lighthouse, from Roman
Coin — A369

Designs: 1d, Alexander places Homer's works into Achilles' tomb, fresco by Raphael. 1.50d, Alexander descends to the bottom of the sea, Flemish miniature. 3d, Alexander searching for water of life, Hindu plate. 7d, Alexander on horseback, Coptic carpet. 11d, Alexander hearing oracle that his days are numbered, Byzantine manuscript. 30d, Death of Alexander, Persian miniature. All designs include gold coin of Lysimachus with Alexander's head.

1977, July 23   *Perf. 14x13*
1208 A369 50 l silver & multi .20 .20
1209 A369 1d silver & multi   .20 .20
1210 A369 1.50d silver & multi .20 .20
1211 A369 3d silver & multi   .20 .20
1212 A369 7d silver & multi   .20 .20
1213 A369 11d silver & multi   .25 .25
1214 A369 30d silver & multi   .35 .35
   Nos. 1208-1214 (7)   1.60 1.60

Cultural influence of Alexander the Great (356-323 B.C.), King of Macedonia.

"Greece
Rising Again"
A370

People in Front of   Greek Flags,
University   Laurel,
A371   University
                         A372

Perf. 13½x12½, 12x12½, 12½x12
1977, July 23   Unwmk.
1215 A370 4d multi   .20 .20
1216 A371 7d multi   .20 .20
1217 A372 20d multi   .25 .25
   Nos. 1215-1217 (3)   .65 .65

Restoration of Democracy in Greece.

Archbishop Makarios, Map of
Cyprus — A373

Design: 4d, Archbishop Makarios, vert.

Perf. 13x13½, 13½x13
1977, Sept. 10   Litho.   Unwmk.
1218 A373 4d sepia & blk   .20 .20
1219 A373 7d buff, brn & blk   .20 .20

Archbishop Makarios (1913-1977), President of Cyprus.

Old
Athens
Post
Office
A374

Neo-Hellenic architecture: 1d, Institution for the Blind, Salonika. 1.50d, Townhall, Syros. 2d, National Bank of Greece, Piraeus. 5d, Byzantine Museum, Athens. 50d, Municipal Theater, Patras.

1977, Sept. 22   *Perf. 13½x13*
1220 A374 50 l multi   .20 .20
1221 A374 1d multi   .20 .20
1222 A374 1.50d multi   .20 .20
1223 A374 2d multi   .20 .20
1224 A374 5d multi   .20 .20
1225 A374 50d multi   .35 .35
   Nos. 1220-1225 (6)   1.35 1.35

Battle of Navarino, Lithograph — A375

Adm. Van Heyden, Sir Edward
Codrington, Count de Rigny — A376

1977, Oct. 20   *Perf. 13½x13*
1226 A375 4d brn, buff & blk   .20 .20
1227 A376 7d multi   .20 .20

150th anniversary of Battle of Navarino.

Parthenon and   Caryatid and
Refinery — A377   Factories — A379

Fish and
Birds
Suffering
from
Pollution
A378

Design: 7d, Birds and trees in polluted air.

1977, Oct. 20   *Perf. 13½x14, 14x13½*
1228 A377 3d org & blk   .20 .20
1229 A378 4d multi   .20 .20
1230 A378 7d multi   .20 .20
1231 A379 30d blk, gray & slate .40 .40
   Nos. 1228-1231 (4)   1.00 1.00

Protection of the environment.

Map of
Greece and
Ships — A380

Globe and
Swallows
A381

Letter with
Flags,
Swallow
A382

5d, Globe with Greek flag. 13d, World map showing dispersion of Greeks abroad.

1977, Dec. 15   *Perf. 13½x12½*
1232 A380 4d multi   .20 .20
1233 A380 5d multi   .20 .20
1234 A381 7d multi   .20 .20
1235 A382 11d multi   .20 .20
1236 A380 13d multi   .25 .25
   Nos. 1232-1236 (5)   1.05 1.05

Greeks living abroad.

Kalamata Harbor, by Constantine
Parthenis — A383

Greek Paintings: 2.50d, Boats, Arsanas, by Spyros Papaloucas, vert. 4d, Santorini, by Constantine Maleas. 7d, The Engagement, by Nicolaus Gyzis. 11d, Woman with Straw Hat, by Nicolaus Lytras, vert. 15d, "Spring" (nude), by Georgio Iacovidis.

1977, Dec. 15   *Perf. 13½x13, 13x13½*
1237 A383 1.50d yel & multi   .20 .20
1238 A383 2.50d yel & multi   .20 .20
1239 A383 4d yel & multi   .20 .20
1240 A383 7d yel & multi   .20 .20
1241 A383 11d yel & multi   .20 .20
1242 A383 15d yel & multi   .25 .25
   Nos. 1237-1242 (6)   1.25 1.25

Ebenus
Cretica — A384

Greek Flora: 2.50d, Dwarf lily. 3d, Campanula oreadum. 4d, Tiger lily. 7d, Viola delphinantha. 25d, Paeonia rhodia.

1978, Mar. 30   Litho.   Perf. 13x13½

1243	A384	1.50d multi	.20	.20
1244	A384	2.50d multi	.20	.20
1245	A384	3d multi	.20	.20
1246	A384	4d multi	.20	.20
1247	A384	7d multi	.25	.20
1248	A384	25d multi	.30	.25
		Nos. 1243-1248 (6)	1.35	1.25

Postrider, Cancellation A385

5d, S.S. Maximilianos & Hermes Head. 7d, 19th cent. mail train & #122. 30d, Mailmen on motorcycles & #1062.

1978, May 15   Perf. 13½x12½

1249	A385	4d buff & multi	.20	.20
1250	A385	5d buff & multi	.20	.20
1251	A385	7d buff & multi	.20	.20
1252	A385	30d buff & multi	.25	.20
a.		Souvenir sheet of 4	1.00	1.00
		Nos. 1249-1252 (4)	.85	.80

150th anniv. of Greek postal service. No. 1252a issued Sept. 25, contains Nos. 1249-1252 in slightly changed colors. Sold for 60d.

Lighting Olympic Flame, Olympia — A386

Start of 100-meter Race — A387

1978, May 15   Perf. 13x14

1253	A386	7d multi	.40	.20
1254	A387	13d multi	.85	.40

80th session of International Olympic Committee, Athens, May 10-21.

Europa Issue 1978

St. Sophia, Salonica A388

Lysicrates Monument, Athens — A389

1978, May 15   Perf. 13x14, 14x13

1255	A388	4d multi	.75	.30
1256	A389	7d multi	1.50	.70

Aristotle, Roman Bust — A390

School of Athens, by Raphael — A391

Map of Chalcidice, Base of Statue from Attalus Arcade A392

Aristotle the Wise, Byzantine Fresco, St. George's Church, Ioannina A393

Perf. 13x13½, 13½x14 (20d)
1978, July 10   Litho.

1257	A390	2d multi	.20	.20
1258	A391	4d multi	.20	.20
1259	A392	7d multi	.20	.20
1260	A393	20d multi	.25	.25
		Nos. 1257-1260 (4)	.85	.85

Aristotle (384-322 B.C.), systematic philosopher.

Rotary Emblem A394

Surgeons Operating — A395

Ugo Foscolo, View of Zante — A396

Hellenistic Bronze Head — A397

Charioteer's Hand, Delphi — A398

Wright Brothers' Plane, Daedalus and Icarus — A399

1978, Sept. 21   Litho.   Perf. 12½

1261	A394	1d multi	.20	.20
1262	A395	1.50d multi	.20	.20
1263	A396	2.50d multi	.20	.20
1264	A397	5d multi	.40	.30
1265	A398	7d multi	.40	.30
1266	A399	13d multi	.40	.40
		Nos. 1261-1266 (6)	1.60	1.50

Rotary in Greece, 50th anniv. (1d); 11th Greek Surgery Cong., Salonica (1.50d); Ugo Foscolo (1778-1827), Italian writer (2.50d); European Convention on Human Rights, 25th anniv. (5d); 2nd Conf. of Ministers of Culture of the Council of Europe member countries, Athens, Oct. 23-27 (7d); 75th anniv. of 1st powered flight (13d).

Poor Woman and her 5 Children A400

Scenes from Fairy Tale "The 12 Months": 3d, The poor woman and the 12 months. 4d, The poor woman and the gold coins. 20d, Punishment of the greedy woman.

1978, Nov. 6   Litho.   Perf. 13½x13

1267	A400	2d multi	.20	.20
1268	A400	3d multi	.20	.20
1269	A400	4d multi	.20	.20
1270	A400	20d multi	.25	.25
		Nos. 1267-1270 (4)	.85	.85

"Transplants" A401

The Miracle of St. Anarghiri A402

1978, Nov. 6   Perf. 12½x13½

1271	A401	4d multi	.20	.20
1272	A402	10d multi	.20	.20

Advancements in organ transplants.

Cruiser A403

New and Old Greek Naval Ships: 1d, Torpedo boats. 2.50d, Submarine Papanicolis. 4d, Battleship Psara. 5d, Sailing ship "Madonna of Hydra." 7d, Byzantine corvette. 50d, Archaic trireme.

1978, Dec. 15   Litho.   Perf. 13½x12

1273	A403	50 l multi	.20	.20
1274	A403	1d multi	.20	.20
1275	A403	2.50d multi	.20	.20
1276	A403	4d multi	.20	.20
1277	A403	5d multi	.20	.20
1278	A403	7d multi	.20	.20
1279	A403	50d multi	.45	.45
		Nos. 1273-1279 (7)	1.65	1.65

Cadet Officer, Military School, Nauplia A404

Cadet Officers' School Emblem — A405

Design: 10d, Cadet Officers Military School, Athens, Cadet's uniform, 1978.

1978, Dec. 15   Perf. 13½x12, 12x13½

1280	A404	1.50d multi	.20	.20
1281	A405	2d multi	.20	.20
1282	A404	10d multi	.25	.25
		Nos. 1280-1282 (3)	.65	.65

Cadet Officers Military School, 150th anniv.

Virgin and Child — A406

Baptism of Christ — A407

Designs from 16th century icon stands in Stavronikita Monastery.

1978, Dec. 15   Perf. 13x13½

1283	A406	4d multi	.20	.20
1284	A407	7d multi	.20	.20

Christmas 1978.

Map of Greece A408

1978, Dec. 28   Perf. 14x13

1285	A408	7d multi	.20	.20
1286	A408	11d multi	.20	.20
1287	A408	13d multi	.25	.25
		Nos. 1285-1287 (3)	.65	.65

Kitsos Tzavellas — A409

Souli Castle A410

10d, Fighting Souliots. 20d, Fight of Zalongo.

Perf. 12½x13½, 13½x12½
1979, Mar. 12   Litho.

1288	A409	1.50d buff, blk & brn	.20	.20
1289	A410	3d multi	.20	.20
1290	A410	10d multi	.20	.20
1291	A409	20d buff, blk & brn	.25	.25
		Nos. 1288-1291 (4)	.85	.85

Struggle of the Souliots, 18th century fighters for freedom from Turkey.

Cycladic Figure from Amorgos — A411

Mailmen from Crete — A412

1979, Apr. 26 Litho. Perf. 12x13½
1292 A411 20d multi .35 .35
Aegean art.

1979, May 11 Perf. 13½x14
Europa: 7d, Rural mailman on horseback, Crete.
1293 A412 4d multi 1.00 .25
1294 A412 7d multi 1.00 .55
a. Pair, #1293-1294 2.25 2.25

Nicolas Scoufas A413

Basketball A415

Locomotives — A414

Mene Psarianosi Symeonidis Fossil A416

Temple of Hephaestus and Byzantine Church A417

Victory of Paeonius Statue, Flags of Balkan Countries A418

1979, May 12 Perf. 13x14, 14x13
1295 A413 1.50d multi .20 .20
1296 A414 2d multi .20 .20
1297 A415 3d multi .20 .20
1298 A416 4d multi .20 .20
1299 A417 10d multi .20 .20
1300 A418 20d multi .35 .35
Nos. 1295-1300 (6) 1.35 1.35

Nicolas Scoufas (1779-1818), founder of (patriotic) Friendly Society; Piraeus-Athens-to-the-frontier railroad, 75th anniv.; European Basketball Championship; 7th Intl. Cong. for the Study of the Neocene Period in the Mediterranean; Balkan Tourist Year 1979; 50 years of track and field competitions in Balkan countries.

Wheat with Members' Flags, Greek Coins — A419

European Parliament, Strasbourg — A420

Perf. 13x14, 14x13
1979, May 28 Litho.
1301 A419 7d multi .20 .20
1302 A420 30d multi .35 .35
Greece's entry into European Economic Community and Parliament.

Statue of a Girl, IYC Emblem — A421

Intl. Year of the Child: 8d, Girl & pigeons. 20d, Mother & Children, painting by Iacovides.

1979, June 27 Litho. Perf. 13x14
1303 A421 5d multi .20 .20
1304 A421 8d multi .20 .20
1305 A421 20d multi .20 .20
Nos. 1303-1305 (3) .60 .60

Philip II, Bust — A422

Purple Heron — A423

Designs: 8d, Golden wreath. 10d, Copper vessel. 14d, Golden casket, horiz. 18d, Silver ewer. 20d, Golden quiver (detail). 30d, Gold and iron cuirass.

Perf. 13½x14, 14x13½
1979, Sept. 15 Litho.
1306 A422 6d multi .20 .20
1307 A422 8d multi .20 .20
1308 A422 10d multi .20 .20
1309 A422 14d multi .20 .20
1310 A422 18d multi .20 .20
1311 A422 20d multi .25 .25
1312 A422 30d multi .40 .40
Nos. 1306-1312 (7) 1.65 1.65

Archaeological finds from Vergina, Macedonia.

1979, Oct. 15
Protected Birds: 8d, Gull. 10d, Falcon, horiz. 14d, Kingfisher, horiz. 20d, Pelican. 25d, White-tailed sea eagle.
1313 A423 6d multi .20 .20
1314 A423 8d multi .20 .20
1315 A423 10d multi .20 .20
1316 A423 14d multi .20 .20
1317 A423 20d multi .20 .20
1318 A423 25d multi .75 .60
Nos. 1313-1318 (6) 1.75 1.60

Council of Europe wildlife and natural habitat protection campaign.

Agricultural Bank A424

St. Cosmas — A425

Basil the Great — A426

Balkan Countries, Magnifier — A427

Aristotelis Valaoritis — A428

Golfer A429

Hippocrates A430

Parliament in Session A431

Perf. 14x13½, 13½x14
1979, Nov. 24 Litho.
1319 A424 3d multi .20 .20
1320 A425 4d multi .20 .20
1321 A426 6d multi .20 .20
1322 A427 8d multi .20 .20
1323 A427 10d multi, horiz. .20 .20
1324 A428 12d multi .20 .20
1325 A429 14d multi .20 .20
1326 A430 18d multi .30 .30
1327 A431 25d multi .40 .40
Nos. 1319-1327 (9) 2.10 2.10

Agricultural Bank of Greece, 50th anniv.; Cosmas the Aetolian (1714-79), Greek missionary and martyr; Basil the Great (330-379), Archbishop of Caesarea; Balkanfila, Balkan Stamp Exhibition, Athens, Nov. 24-Dec. 2; Aristotelis Valaoritis (1824-1879), Greek poet; 27th World Golf Championship, Nov. 8-11; Intl. Hippocratic Foundation of Cos; Greek Parliament, 104th anniv.

Parnassus — A432

Tempe Valley A433

Perf. 12½x13½, 13½x12½
1979, Dec. 15 Litho.
1328 A432 50 l shown .20 .20
1329 A433 1d shown .20 .20
1330 A432 2d Melos .20 .20
1331 A432 4d Vikos Gorge .20 .20
1332 A433 5d Missolonghi Salt Lake .20 .20
1333 A432 6d Louros Aqueduct .20 .20
1334 A432 7d Samothrace .20 .20
1335 A433 8d Sithonia-Halkidiki .20 .20
1336 A433 10d Samarias Gorge, vert. .20 .20
1337 A432 12d Siphnos .20 .20
1338 A433 14d Kyme .20 .20
1339 A432 18d Ios .20 .20
1340 A432 20d Thasos .20 .20
1341 A433 30d Paros .30 .30
1342 A432 50d Cephalonia .50 .40
Nos. 1328-1342 (15) 3.40 3.20

Byzantine Castle of Thessalonica A434

4d, Aegosthena Castle, vert. 8d, Cave of Perama Ioannina, vert. 10d, Cave of Dyros, Mani, vert. 14d, Arta Bridge. 20d, Kalogiros Bridge, Epirus.

Perf. 12½x14, 14x12½
1980, Mar. 15 Litho.
1343 A434 4d multi .20 .20
1344 A434 6d multi .20 .20
1345 A434 8d multi .20 .20
1346 A434 10d multi .20 .20
1347 A434 14d multi .20 .20
1348 A434 20d multi .20 .20
Nos. 1343-1348 (6) 1.20 1.20

Gate of Galerius A435

1980, Mar. 15
1349 A435 8d multi .25 .20
1st Hellenic Congress of Nephrology, Thessalonica, Mar. 20-22.

Solar System A436

Design: 10d, Temple of Hera, Aristarchus' theory and diagram.

1980, May 5 Litho. Perf. 13½x12½
1350 A436 10d multi .20 .20
1351 A436 20d multi .40 .35

Aristarchus of Samos, first astronomer to discover heliocentric theory of universe, 2300th birth anniv.; Intl. Scientific Congress on Aristarchus, Samos, June 17-19.

Maria Callas (1923-1977), Opera Singer A437

Europa: 8d, Georges Seferis (1900-1971), writer and diplomat.

1980, May 5
1352 A437 8d multi .40 .40
1353 A437 14d multi 1.60 1.20

Energy Conservation Manual A438

Perf. 13½x12½, 12½x13½

1980, May 5
1354 A438 8d shown .20 .20
1355 A438 20d Candle in bulb, vert. .30 .30

Firemen
A439

St. Demetrius, Angel, Fresco — A440

Soldiers Marching through Crete — A441

Ancient Vase, Olives A442

Federation Emblem, Newspaper A443

Constantinos Ikonomos — A444

1980, July 14   Litho.   Perf. 12½
1356 A439 4d multi .20 .20
1357 A440 6d multi .20 .20
1358 A441 8d multi .20 .20
1359 A442 10d multi .20 .20
1360 A443 14d multi .20 .20
1361 A444 20d multi .40 .40
Nos. 1356-1361 (6) 1.40 1.40

Fire Brigade, 50th anniv.; St. Demetrius, 1700th birth anniv.; Therissos Revolution, 75th anniv.; 2nd Intl. Olive Oil Year; Intl. Federation of Journalists, 15th Cong., Athens, May 12-16; Constantinos Ikonomos (1780-1857), writer and revolutionary.

Olympic Stadium, Temple Coin, Olympia A445

Olympic Rings and: 14d, Stadium and coin of Delphi 18d, Epidaurus theater, coin of Olympia 20d, Rhodes Stadium, Cos coin. 50d, Panathenean Stadium; 1st Olympic Games medal.

1980, Aug. 11   Litho.   Perf. 13½x13
1362 A445 8d multi .20 .20
1363 A445 14d multi .35 .30
1364 A445 18d multi .25 .20
1365 A445 20d multi .30 .20
1366 A445 50d multi .65 .55
Nos. 1362-1366 (5) 1.75 1.45

22nd Summer Olympic Games, Moscow, July 19-Aug. 3.

Asbestos A446

Perf. 13½x12½

1980, Sept. 22   Litho.
1367 A446 6d shown .20 .20
1368 A446 8d Gypsum, vert. .20 .20
1369 A446 10d Copper ore .20 .20
1370 A446 14d Barite, vert. .35 .35
1371 A446 18d Chromite .25 .20
1372 A446 20d Mixed sulphides, vert. .25 .20
1373 A446 30d Bauxite, vert. .35 .35
Nos. 1367-1373 (7) 1.80 1.70

Tow Truck — A447

Air Force Jet — A448

Airplane and Hangar A449

Ships in Port A450

Students' Association Headquarters A451

1980, Oct. 31   Litho.   Perf. 12½
1374 A447 6d multi .20 .20
1375 A448 8d multi .20 .20
1376 A449 12d multi .20 .20
1377 A450 20d multi .35 .30
1378 A451 25d multi .40 .40
Nos. 1374-1378 (5) 1.35 1.30

Road Assistance Service of Automobile and Touring Club of Greece, 20th anniv.; Air Force, 50th anniv.; Flyers' Club of Thessaloniki, 50th anniv.; Piraeus Port Organization, 50th anniv.; Association for Macedonian Studies, 40th anniv.

Madonna and Child, by Theodore Poulakis — A452

Christmas 1980: He is Happy Thanks to You, by Theodore Poulakis. No. 1381a has continuous design.

1980, Dec. 10   Perf. 13½
1379 6d multi .20 .20
1380 14d multi .20 .20
1381 20d multi .30 .30
a. A452 Strip of 3, #1379-1381 .75 .75

Vegetables for Export — A453

1981, Mar. 16   Litho.   Perf. 12½
1382 A453 9d shown .20 .20
1383 A453 17d Fruits .25 .25
1384 A453 20d Cotton .25 .25
1385 A453 25d Marble .40 .40
Nos. 1382-1385 (4) 1.10 1.10

Europa Issue 1981

Kira Maria Folk Dance, Alexandria — A454

1981, May 4   Litho.   Perf. 14x13
1386 A454 12d shown .50 .20
1387 A454 17d Cretan Sousta (dance) 1.00 .75

Runner, Olympic Stadium, Kalogreza A455

1981, May 4
1388 A455 12d shown .25 .20
1389 A455 17d Runners, Europe .40 .40

13th European Athletic Championship, Athens, 1982.

Torso Showing Kidneys A456

Sky Diver and Airplanes A457

Views of Thessaly and Epirus — A458

Oil Rig and Map of Thassos Island — A460

Vase with Painted Eyes A459

Globes and Ancient Coin A461

Heart and Vessels — A462

Perf. 13½x14, 14x13½

1981, May 22   Litho.
1390 A456 2d multi .20 .20
1391 A457 3d multi .20 .20
1392 A458 6d multi .20 .20
1393 A459 9d multi .20 .20
1394 A460 12d multi .20 .20
1395 A461 21d multi .50 .45
1396 A462 40d multi .75 .75
Nos. 1390-1396 (7) 2.25 2.20

8th Intl. Nephrology Conf., Athens, June 7-12; Greek National Air Club, 50th anniv.; Intl. Historical Symposium, Volos, Sept. 27-30; Greek Ophthalmological Society, 50th anniv.; inauguration of oil production at Thassos Island; World Assoc. for Intl. Relations, Athens, 2nd anniv.; 15th Intl. Cardiovascular Surgery Conference, Athens, Sept. 6-10.

Cockles A463

1981, June 30   Litho.   Perf. 14x13½
1397 A463 4d shown .20 .20
1398 A463 5d Parrot fish .20 .20
1399 A463 12d Painted comber .25 .20
1400 A463 15d Common dentex .25 .25
1401 A463 17d Parnassius apollo .50 .30
1402 A463 50d Colias hyale 1.10 .90
Nos. 1397-1402 (6) 2.50 2.05

Bell Tower, Epirus — A464

Altar Gate, St. Paraskevi's Church — A465

Bell Towers and Wood Altar Gates (Iconostases): 9d, Pelion, horiz. 12d, Church of Sts. Constantine and Helen, Epirus. 17d, St. Nicolas Church, Velvendos, horiz. 30d, St. Jacob icon, Church Museum, Alexandroupolis. 40d, St. Nicholas Church, Makrinitsa.

1981, Sept. 30   Litho.
1403 A464 4d multi .20 .20
1404 A465 6d multi .20 .20
1405 A465 9d multi .20 .20
1406 A464 12d multi .20 .20
1407 A465 17d multi .25 .25
1408 A465 30d multi .35 .35
1409 A465 40d multi .60 .60
Nos. 1403-1409 (7) 2.00 2.00

European Urban Renaissance Year — A466

St. Simeon, Archbishop of Thessalonica A467

Promotion of Breastfeeding A468

Gina Bachauer, Pianist, 5th Death Anniv. A469

Constantine Broumidis, Artist, Death Centenary A470

Sesquicentennial of Greek Banknotes — A471

Perf. 14x13½, 13½x14

1981, Nov. 20 Litho.

1410	A466	3d multi		.20	.20
1411	A467	9d multi		.20	.20
1412	A468	12d multi		.25	.20
1413	A469	17d multi		.40	.25
1414	A470	21d multi		.45	.25
1415	A471	50d multi		.75	.60
		Nos. 1410-1415 (6)		2.25	1.70

Old Parliament Building, Athens A472

Angelos Sikelianos (1884-1951), Poet A473

Harilaos Tricoupis, Politician, Birth Sesquicentennial A474

Aegean Islands Exhib., Rhodes, Athens — A475

Petralona Cave and Skull — A477

Europa 1982 — A478

Olympic Airlines, 25th Anniv. A476

Perf. 13½x12½, 12½x13½

1982, Mar. 15 Litho.

1416	A472	2d multi		.20	.20
1417	A473	9d multi		.20	.20
1418	A474	15d multi		.20	.20
1419	A475	21d multi		.40	.40
1420	A476	30d multi		.65	.55
1421	A477	50d multi		1.10	1.00
		Nos. 1416-1421 (6)		2.75	2.55

Historical and Ethnological Society centennial (2d); 3rd European Anthropology Congress, Halkidiki, Sept. (50d).

1982, May 10 Litho. **Perf. 13½x14**

1422	A478	21d Battle of Marathon, 490 BC		*2.00*	1.00
1423	A478	30d 1826 Revolution		*4.00*	2.00

13th European Athletic Championships, Athens — A479

1982, May 10 **Perf. 14x13½, 13½x14**

1424	A479	21d Pole vaulting, horiz.		.30	.25
1425	A479	25d Running		.40	.25
1426	A479	40d Sports, horiz.		.80	.65
		Nos. 1424-1426 (3)		1.50	1.15

Byzantine Book Illustrations A480

Perf. 13½x12½, 12½x13½

1982, June 26 Litho.

1427	A480	4d Gospel book heading		.25	.20
1428	A480	6d Illuminated "E," vert.		.25	.20
1429	A480	12d Illuminated "T," vert.		.25	.20
1430	A480	15d Gospel reading canon table, vert.		.25	.20
1431	A480	80d Zoology book heading		1.50	1.25
		Nos. 1427-1431 (5)		2.50	2.05

Georgios Karaiskakis (1782-1827), Liberation Hero — A481

Amnesty Intl. — A482

Designs: 12d, Camp in Piraeus, by von Krazeisen. 50d, Meditating.

1982, Sept. 20 Litho. **Perf. 13x13½**

1432	A481	12d multi		.40	.20
1433	A481	50d multi		.80	.50

1982, Sept. 20 **Perf. 13x14**

1434	A482	15d Vigil		.45	.20
1435	A482	75d Prisoners		1.25	1.00

Natl. Resistance Movement, 1941-44 A483

Designs: 1d, Demonstration of Mar. 24, 1942. 2d, Sacrifice of Inhabitants of Kalavrita, by S. Vasiliou. 5d, Resistance Fighters in Thrace, by A. Tassos. 9d, The Start of Resistance in Crete, by P. Gravalos. 12d, Partisan Men and Women, by P. Gravalos. 21d, Blowing Up a Bridge, by A. Tassos. 30d, Fighters at a Barricade, by G. Sikeliotis. 50d, The Fight in Northern Greece, by B. Katraki, 5d, 9d, 12d, 21d vert.

1982, Nov. 8 Litho. **Perf. 12½**

1436	A483	1d multi		.20	.20
1437	A483	2d multi		.20	.20
1438	A483	5d multi		.20	.20
1439	A483	9d multi		.20	.20
1440	A483	12d multi		.20	.20
1441	A483	21d multi		.20	.20
a.		Souv. sheet, 5d, 9d, 12d, 21d		1.75	1.75
1442	A483	30d multi		.50	.35
1443	A483	50d multi		1.25	.55
a.		Souv. sheet, 1d, 2d, 30d, 50d		2.00	2.00
		Nos. 1436-1443 (8)		2.95	2.10

Christmas 1982 — A484

Designs: Various Byzantine Nativity bas-reliefs, Byzantine Museum.

1982, Dec. 6 Litho. **Perf. 13½x12½**

1444	A484	9d multi		.20	.20
1445	A484	21d multi		.30	.25
a.		Pair, #1444-1445		.65	.65

25th Anniv. of Intl. Maritime Org. A485

Ship Figureheads. 15d, 18d, 25d, 40d vert.

1983, Mar. 14 **Perf. 14x13½, 13½x14**

1446	A485	11d Ares, Tsamados		.20	.30
1447	A485	15d Ares, Miaoulis		.20	.20
1448	A485	18d Female figure		.25	.20
1449	A485	25d Spetses, Bouboulina		.40	.25
1450	A485	40d Epameinondas, K. Babas		.60	.35
1451	A485	50d Carteria		1.25	1.00
		Nos. 1446-1451 (6)		2.90	2.30

Postal Code Inauguration A486

1983, Mar. 14 Litho. **Perf. 12½**

1452	A486	15d Cover, map		.20	.20
1453	A486	25d Hermes, post horn, vert.		.45	.40

Rowing A487

1983, Apr. 28 **Perf. 14x13, 13x14**

1454	A487	15d shown		.25	.20
1455	A487	18d Water skiing, vert.		.35	.20
1456	A487	27d Wind surfing, vert.		.65	.60
1457	A487	50d Skiiers on chairlift, vert.		.65	.60
1458	A487	80d Skiing		2.00	1.75
		Nos. 1454-1458 (5)		3.90	3.35

Europa Issue 1983

Acropolis — A488

Archimedes and His Hydrostatic Principle — A489

Perf. 12½x13½, 13x13½

1983, Apr. 28 Litho.

1459	A488	25d multi		*2.00*	1.00
1460	A489	80d multi		*4.00*	3.00

Marinos Antypas (1873-1907), Farmers' Movement Leader — A490

Designs: 9d, Nicholas Plastiras (1883-1953), prime minister. 15d, George Papandreou (1888-1968), statesman. 20d, Constantine Cavafy (1863-1933), poet. 27d, Nikos Kazantzakis (1883-1957), writer. 32d, Manolis Calomiris (1883-1962), composer. 40d, George Papanicolaou (1883-1962), medical researcher. 50d, Despina Achladioti (1890-1982), nationalist.

1983, July 11 Litho. **Perf. 13½x14**

1461	A490	6d multi		.20	.20
1462	A490	9d multi		.20	.20
1463	A490	15d multi		.20	.20
1464	A490	20d multi		.30	.20
1465	A490	27d multi		.35	.20
1466	A490	32d multi		.60	.30
1467	A490	40d multi		.70	.30
1468	A490	50d multi		.85	.60
		Nos. 1461-1468 (8)		3.40	2.20

A491

1983, Sept. 26 Litho. **Perf. 13½x13**

1469	A491	50d Portrait bust		1.00	.50

1st Intl. Conf. on the Works of Democritus (Philosopher, 460-370 BC), Xanthe, Oct.

A492

1983, Nov. 17   Litho.   Perf. 13
1470 A492 15d Poster .25 .25
1471 A492 30d Flight from school .45 .35

Polytechnic School Uprising, 1st anniv.

The Deification of Homer — A493

Homer Inspired Artworks: 3d, The Abduction of Helen by Paris, horiz. 4d, The Wooden Horse, horiz. 5d, Achilles Throwing Dice with Ajax, horiz. 6d, Achilles. 10d, Hector Receiving His Arms from His Parents. 14d, Single-handed Battle Between Ajax and Hector, horiz. 15d, Priam Requesting the Body of Hector, horiz. 20d, The Blinding of Polyphemus. 27d, Ulysses Escaping from Polyphemus' Cave, horiz. 30d, Ulysses Meeting with Nausica. 32d, Ulysses on the Island of the Sirens, horiz. 50d, Ulysses Slaying the Suitors, horiz. 75d, The Heroes of the Iliad, horiz. 100d, Homer.

1983, Dec. 19   Litho.   Perf. 13
1472 A493 2d multi .20 .20
1473 A493 3d multi .20 .20
1474 A493 4d multi .20 .20
1475 A493 5d multi .20 .20
1476 A493 6d multi .20 .20
1477 A493 10d multi .20 .20
1478 A493 14d multi .20 .20
1479 A493 15d multi .20 .20
1480 A493 20d multi .20 .20
1481 A493 27d multi .30 .20
1482 A493 30d multi .40 .20
1483 A493 32d multi .50 .20
1484 A493 50d multi .60 .20
1485 A493 75d multi 1.25 .60
1486 A493 100d multi 1.90 .80
   Nos. 1472-1486 (15) 6.75 4.00

Horse's Head from Chariot of Seline A494

Horsemen and Heroes A495

Nos. 1492a-1492b, Equestrian scene. Nos. 1492c-1492d, Athenian Elders.

1984, Mar. 15   Litho.   Perf. 14½x14
1487 A494 14d shown .20 .20
1488 A494 15d Dionysus .35 .20
1489 A494 20d Hestia, Dione, Aphrodite .65 .30
1490 A494 27d Ilissus .85 .30
1491 A494 32d Lapith, centaur 1.50 .75
   Nos. 1487-1491 (5) 3.55 1.75

Souvenir Sheet
Perf. 13x13½
1492   Sheet of 4 4.50 4.50
   a.   A495 15d multi .75 .75
   b.   A495 21d multi .90 .90
   c.   A495 27d multi 1.00 1.00
   d.   A495 32d multi 1.25 1.25

Marble from the Parthenon. No. 1492 sold for 107d.
Nos. 1492a-1492b and 1492c-1492d have continuous designs.

Europa (1959-84) A496

1984, Apr. 30   Litho.   Perf. 14x13½
1493 A496 15d multi .75 .40
1494 A496 27d multi 1.75 1.00
   a.   Pair, #1493-1494 3.25 3.25

1984 Summer Olympics — A497

Designs: 14d, Ancient Olympic stadium crypt. 15d, Athletes training. 20d, Broad jump, discus thrower. 32d, Athletes, diff. 80d, Stadium, Demetrius Bikelos, poet, organizer of 1896 Athens games.

1984, Apr. 30   Perf. 13½x14
1495 A497 14d multi .30 .25
1496 A497 15d multi .40 .35
1497 A497 20d multi .50 .45
1498 A497 32d multi .75 .65
1499 A497 80d multi 1.75 1.40
   a.   Strip of 5, #1495-1499 4.50 4.50

Also issued in booklets.

Turkish Invasion of Cyprus, 10th Anniv. — A498

1984, July 10   Litho.   Perf. 13
1500 A498 20d Tank, map, vert. .40 .20
1501 A498 32d Map, barbed wire .60 .50

Also issued in booklets.

Greek Railway Centenary A499

Perf. 13x13½, 13½x13
1984, July 20   Litho.
1502 A499 15d Pelion .65 .35
1503 A499 20d Papadia Bridge, vert. 2.00 1.40
1504 A499 30d Piraeus-Peloponnese .65 .35
1505 A499 50d Cogwheel Calavryta, vert. 2.00 1.40
   Nos. 1502-1505 (4) 5.30 3.50

Sesquicentenary of Athens as Capital City — A500

15d, 4d silver coin, 5th cent. BC, city plan, vert. 100d, Views of ancient & modern Athens.

Perf. 13½x13, 13x13½
1984, Oct. 12   Litho.
1506 A500 15d multi .40 .25
1507 A500 100d multi 1.60 1.00

10th Anniv. of Democratic Govt. — A501

1984, Oct. 12   Litho.   Perf. 13x13½
1508 A501 95d "10" on flag 1.75 .75

Christmas 1984 — A502

Scenes from 18th cent. icon by Athanasios Tountas.

1984, Dec. 6   Litho.   Perf. 13½x13
1509 A502 14d Annunciation .50 .30
1510 A502 20d Nativity .50 .30
1511 A502 25d Presentation in the Temple .50 .40
1512 A502 32d Baptism of Christ .50 .50

Also issued in booklets.

Runner A503

Palais des Sports A504

Perf. 13, 13x13½ (#1515)
1985, Mar. 1   Litho.
1513 A503 12d shown .20 .20
1514 A503 15d Shot put .35 .20
1515 A504 20d shown .35 .25
1516 A503 25d Hurdles .70 .25
1517 A503 80d Women's high jump 1.40 .80
   Nos. 1513-1517 (5) 3.00 1.70

European Indoor Athletics Championships, Palais des Sports, New Phaleron.

Europa 1985 — A505

CEPT emblem and: 27d, Musical contest between Marsyas and Apollo. 80d, Dimitris Mitropoulos (1896-1960) and Nikos Skalkottas (1904-1949), composers.

1985, Apr. 29   Perf. 14x14½
1518 A505 27d multi .80 .50
1519 A505 80d multi 1.50 1.00

Exist se-tenant as strip of 3, 27d+80d+27d in booklets.

Melos Catacombs, A.D. 2nd Cent., Trypete A506

1985, Apr. 29   Perf. 14½x14
1520 A506 15d Niche .20 .20
1521 A506 20d Altar, Central Gallery .50 .20
1522 A506 100d Catacombs 1.60 1.10
   Nos. 1520-1522 (3) 2.30 1.50

Republic of Cyprus, 25th Anniv. — A507

1985, June 24   Perf. 13x13½
1523 A507 32d Map of Cyprus, urn 1.00 .50

Coin of King Cassander (315 B.C.), Personification of Salonika, Galerius Era Bas-relief — A508

Sts. Demetrius and Methodius, Mosaics — A509

Designs: 15d, Emperor sacrificing at Altar, Arch of Galerius, Roman era. 20d, Eastern walls of Salonika, Byzantine era. 32d, Houses in the Upper City. 50d, Liberation of Salonika by the Greek Army, 1912. 80d, German occupation, 1941-44, the Old Mosque. 95d, View of city, Trade Fair grounds, Aristotelian University tower.

Perf. 14½x14 (A508), 14x14½ (A509)
1985, June 24
1524 A508 1d multi .20 .20
1525 A509 5d multi .35 .20
1526 A508 15d multi .40 .20
1527 A508 20d multi .40 .20
1528 A508 32d multi .45 .20
1529 A508 50d multi .60 .20
1530 A508 80d multi 1.25 .50
1531 A509 95d multi 1.75 1.50
   Nos. 1524-1531 (8) 5.40 3.20

Salonika City, 2300th anniv. Aristotelian University, Trade Fair, 60th annivs.

Athenian Cultural Heritage A510

Ancient art and architecture: 15d, Democracy Crowning the City, bas-relief from a column, Ancient Agora of Athens, vert. 20d, Mosaic pavement of tritons, nereids, dolphins, etc., Roman baths at Hieratus, Isthmia, A.D. 2nd cent. 32d, Angel, fresco, Grotto of Pentheli, A.D. 13th cent., vert. 80d, Capodistrian University, Athens.

1985, Oct. 7   Perf. 13½x13, 13x13½
1532 A510 15d multi .25 .20
1533 A510 20d multi .25 .20
1534 A510 32d multi .65 .30
1535 A510 80d multi 1.40 1.10
   Nos. 1532-1535 (4) 2.55 1.80

Intl. Youth
Year — A511

UN 40th
Anniv. — A512

#1540, Girl crowned with flowers, Stadium of Peace and Friendship, Athens.

1985, Oct. 7　　Perf. 14x14½
1536 A511 15d Children, olive
　　　　　　wreath　　　.25　.20
1537 A511 25d Children, doves　.45　.20
1538 A512 27d UN General As-
　　　　　　sembly, dove　.55　.20
1539 A512 100d UN building,
　　　　　　emblem　1.60　1.50
　　　Nos. 1536-1539 (4)　2.85　2.10

Souvenir Sheet
1985, Nov. 22　　Perf. 14x13
1540 A511 100d multi　　2.00　2.00

No. 1540 contains one 43x47mm stamp.

Pontic Hellenism Cultural Reformation A513

Perf. 14x12½, 12½x14
1985, Dec. 9　　　　Litho.
1541 A513 12d Folk dance　.20　.20
1542 A513 15d Our Lady Soume-
　　　　　　la Monastery　.20　.20
1543 A513 27d Folk costumes,
　　　　　　vert.　　　.45　.30
1544 A513 32d Trapezus High
　　　　　　School　.45　.30
1545 A513 80d Sinope Castle　1.10　1.00
　　　Nos. 1541-1545 (5)　2.40　2.00

Greek
Gods — A514

1986, Feb. 17　Litho.　Perf. 13
1546 A514　5d Hestia　.20　.20
1547 A514 18d Hermes　.20　.20
1548 A514 27d Aphrodite　.30　.20
1549 A514 32d Ares　.45　.35
1550 A514 35d Athena　.60　.35
1551 A514 40d Hephaestus　.70　.20
1552 A514 50d Artemis　.95　.35
1553 A514 110d Apollo　1.10　.35
1554 A514 150d Demeter　1.75　.35
1555 A514 200d Poseidon　2.50　.45
1556 A514 300d Hera　4.25　.95
1557 A514 500d Zeus　9.50　4.50
　　　Nos. 1546-1557 (12)　22.50　8.45

Each denomination also sold in booklets containing 20 panes of 5 stamps, perf 13 horizontally only. Value for set of unused booklet stamps $25; used booklet stamps sell for approximately half the values shown for used sheet stamps.

Youth of
Antikythera
A515

Soccer Players
A517

Diadoumenos,
by Polycleitus
A516

Wrestlers,
Hellenic Era
Statue — A518

Cyclists — A520

Volleyball
Players
A519

Commemorative Design for 1st
Modern Olympic Games — A521

1986, Mar. 3　　　Perf. 12
1558 A515 18d multi　.40　.20
1559 A516 27d multi　1.40　.40
1560 A517 32d multi　2.75　.90
1561 A518 35d multi　1.40　1.25
1562 A519 40d multi　1.40　.45
1563 A520 50d multi　1.40　.45
1564 A521 110d multi　4.50　1.60
　　　Nos. 1558-1564 (7)　13.25　5.25

First World Junior Athletic Championships. Pan-European Junior Soccer Championships. Pan-European Free-style and Greco-Roman Wrestling Championships. Men's World Volleyball Championships. Sixth International Round-Europe Cycling Meet. Modern Olympic Games, 90th anniv.

European Traffic
Safety Year — A522

1986, Mar. 3　　　Perf. 12½x14
1565 A522 18d Seat belts　.25　.20
1566 A522 27d Motorcycle　.95　.95
1567 A522 110d Speed limits　1.50　.50
　　　Nos. 1565-1567 (3)　2.70　1.65

Prevention
of Forest
Fires
A523

1986, Apr. 23　Litho.　Perf. 14x13½
1568 A523 35d shown　3.00　2.00
1569 A523 110d Prespa Lakes
　　　　　　wetlands　5.00　4.00
　　a.　Pair, 35d, 110d　9.00　9.00
　　b.　Bklt. pane, 2 each 35d,
　　　　110d　25.00
　　c.　As "b," pair, 35d, 110d　12.50　12.50

Europa.
No. 1569a is imperf horizontally.

New Postal
Services — A524

May Day Strike,
Chicago,
Cent. — A525

1986, Apr. 23　Perf. 13½x14, 14x13½
1570 A524 18d Intelpost　.40　.20
1571 A524 110d Express mail,
　　　　　　horiz.　1.60　.80

1986, Apr. 23　　　Perf. 12½
1572 A525 40d Strikers, monu-
　　　　　　ment　.65　.50

Eleutherios K.
Venizelos
(1864-1936),
Premier
A526

18d, Venizelos, Ministers taking oath of office, 1917. 110d, Old Hania Harbor, Crete.

1986, June 30　Litho.　Perf. 14x12½
1573 A526 18d multi　.25　.20
1574 A526 110d multi　1.75　.70

6th Intl. Cretological Conference, Crete.

Intl. Peace
Year — A527

1986, Oct. 6　Litho.　Perf. 12½
1575 A527 18d Dove, sun, vert.　.25　.20
1576 A527 35d Flags, dove,
　　　　　　vert.　.60　.40
1577 A527 110d World cage,
　　　　　　dove　1.50　.70
　　　Nos. 1575-1577 (3)　2.35　1.30

Christmas
A528

Aesop's Fables
A529

Religious art in the Benaki Museum: 22d, Madonna and Child Enthroned, triptych center panel, 15th cent. 46d, Adoration of the Magi, 15th cent. 130d, Christ Enthroned with St. John the Evangelist, triptych panel.

1986, Dec. 1　Litho.　Perf. 13½x14
1578 A528 22d multi　.30　.20
1579 A528 46d multi　.65　.50
1580 A528 130d multi　1.75　.40
　　　Nos. 1578-1580 (3)　2.70　1.10

Size of No. 1579: 27x35mm.

1987, Mar. 5　Litho.　Perf. 12½
1581 A529　2d Fox and the
　　　　　　Grapes　.25　.20
1582 A529　5d North Wind
　　　　　　and the Sun　.25　.20
1583 A529 10d Stag and the
　　　　　　Lion　.30　.30
1584 A529 22d Zeus and the
　　　　　　Snake　.60　.20
1585 A529 32d Crow and the
　　　　　　Fox　1.10　.30
1586 A529 40d Woodcutter
　　　　　　and Hermes　1.25　.40
1587 A529 46d Ass in a Lion's
　　　　　　Skin　2.10　.65

1588 A529 130d Tortoise and
　　　　　　the Hare　4.50　1.60
　　　Nos. 1581-1588 (8)　10.35　3.85

Each denomination also sold in booklets containing 20 panes of 5 stamps, perf 13½ horizontally only. Value for set of unused booklet stamps $32.50; used booklet stamps sell for approximately half the values shown for used sheet stamps.

Europa
1987 — A530

Modern art: 40d, Composition, by Achilleas Apergis. 130d, Delphic Light, by Gerassimos Sklavos.

1987, May 4　Litho.　Perf. 12½
1589 A530 40d multi　3.00　2.00
1590 A530 130d multi　4.00　3.00
　　a.　Pair, #1589-1590　7.50　7.50
　　b.　Bklt. pane, 2 each #1589-
　　　　1590　21.00
　　c.　As "b," pair, #1589-1590　10.00　10.00

Nos. 1590b and 1590c are imperf horizontally.

25th European
Basketball
Championships,
Stadium of Peace
and
Friendship — A531

A532

1987, May 4　Perf. 13½x14, 12½
1591 A531 22d Jump shot, sta-
　　　　　　dium, vert.　.60　.60
1592 A532 25d Emblem, spec-
　　　　　　tators　.40　.20
1593 A531 130d Two players,
　　　　　　vert.　1.90　1.10
　　　Nos. 1591-1593 (3)　2.90　1.90

Higher Education
Sesquicentenary — A533

Perf. 14x13½, 13½x14
1987, May 4　　　　Litho.
1594 A533　3d Students, tapes-
　　　　　　try　.20　.20
1595 A533 23d Owl, medallion　.40　.20
1596 A533 40d Institute, symbols
　　　　　　of science　.70　.40
1597 A533 60d Institute, students 1.00　.75
　　　Nos. 1594-1597 (4)　2.30　1.55

Capodistrias University of Athens (Nos. 1594-1595); The Natl. Metsovio Polytechnic Institute (Nos. 1596-1597). #1596-1597 vert.

Souvenir Sheet

25th European
Men's Basketball
Championships
A534

1987, June 3 Litho. Perf. 13x14
1598	Sheet of 3	6.00	6.00
a.	A534 40d Jump ball	.90	.90
b.	A534 60d Layup	1.25	1.25
c.	A534 100d Dunk shot	2.25	2.25

Architecture
A535

Designs: 2d, Ionic and Corinthian capitals, Archaic Era. 26d, Doric capital, the Parthenon (detail). 40d, Ionic capital and the Erechteum. 60d, Corinthian capital and the Tholos in Epidaurus.

1987, July 1 Litho. Perf. 13½x12½
1599	A535	2d multi	.20	.20
1600	A535	26d multi	.35	.20
1601	A535	40d multi	.55	.35
1602	A535	60d multi	1.10	1.00
	Nos. 1599-1602 (4)		2.20	1.75

Engraving by Yiannis Kephalinos — A536

Panteios School
A537

Perf. 12½x14, 14x12½
1987, Oct. 1 Litho.
1603	A536	26d multi	.35	.20
1604	A537	60d multi	.85	.75

School of Fine Arts, 150th anniv. (26d), and Panteios School of Political Science, 60th anniv. (60d).

Greek Natl. Team, Winner, 25th European Men's Basketball Championship
A538

1987, Oct. 1 Perf. 13x14
1605	A538	40d multi	.90	.90

Traditional and Modern Greek Theater
A539

Designs: 2d, Eleni Papadaki in Hecuba, by Euripides, and outdoor theater, Philippi. 4d, Christopher Nezer in The Wasps, by Aristophane, and outdoor theater, Dodona. 7d, Emilios Veakis in Oedipus Rex and theater, Delphi. 26d, Marika Cotopouli in The Shepherdess's Love, by Dimitris Koromilas. 40d, Katina Paxinou in Abraham's Sacrifice, by Vitzentzos Cornaros. 50d, Kyveli in Countess Valeraina's Secret, by Gregory Xenopoulos. 60d, Director Carolos Koun, stage setting. 100d, Dimitris Rontiris teaching ancient dance, Greek National Theater.

1987, Dec. 2 Litho. Perf. 14x13½
1606	A539	2d multi	.20	.20
1607	A539	4d multi	.20	.20
1608	A539	7d multi	.20	.20
1609	A539	26d multi	.35	.20
1610	A539	40d multi	.55	.20
1611	A539	50d multi	.65	.20
1612	A539	60d multi	.90	.90
1613	A539	100d multi	1.75	.35
	Nos. 1606-1613 (8)		4.80	2.50

Christmas — A540

1987, Dec. 2 Perf. 13x12½
1614	26d Angel facing right		.50	.20
1615	26d Angel facing left		.50	.20
a.	Bklt. pane, 5 each #1614-1615		5.00	
b.	A540 Pair, #1614-1615		1.00	1.00

Marine Life — A541

1988, Mar. 2 Perf. 14x12½
1616	A541	30d Codonellina	.80	.40
1617	A541	40d Diaperoecia major	1.25	.60
1618	A541	50d Artemia	1.75	.90
1619	A541	60d Posidonia oceanica	4.00	2.00
1620	A541	100d Padina pavonica	4.00	2.00
	Nos. 1616-1620 (5)		11.80	5.90

Each denomination sold in booklets containing 20 panes of 5 stamps, perf 12½ vertically only. Value for set of unused booklet stamps $27.50; used booklet stamps sell for somewhat less than the values shown for sheet stamps.

Europa 1988 — A542

Communication and transport: 60d, Telecommunications satellite, telephone and facsimile machine. 150d, Passenger trains.

1988, May 6 Litho. Perf. 12½
1621	60d multi		5.00	3.00
1622	150d multi		5.50	4.00
a.	A542 Pair, 60d, 150d		11.50	11.50
b.	Bklt. pane of 4, 2 each #1621-1622, perf. 14 vert.		26.00	—
c.	A542 As "b," pair, 60d, 150d		12.00	12.00

Nos. 1622b and 1622c perf 14 vertically and imperf horizontally.

1988 Olympics
A543

Designs: 4d, Ancient Olympia and Temple of Zeus. 20d, Javelin thrower and ancient Olympians in open-air gymnasium. 30d, Centenary emblem of the modern Games (cent. in 1996). 60d, Wrestlers, runners and other ancient athletes in training. 170d, Modern torch-bearer.

1988, May 6 Perf. 14x12
1623	A543	4d multi	.50	.35
1624	A543	20d multi	1.10	.60
1625	A543	30d multi	2.00	.90
1626	A543	60d multi	3.75	2.75
1627	A543	170d multi	5.25	3.25
a.	Strip of 5, #1623-1627		14.00	14.00
b.	Bklt. pane of 5, #1623-1627, perf. 12½ vert.		19.00	19.00

Each denomination also sold in bklts. containing 20 panes of 5 stamps, perf. 12½ vert. Value for set of unused booklet stamps $20; used booklet stamps sell for somewhat less than the values shown for used sheet stamps.
See Korea No. B53.

A544   A545

Waterfalls: 10d, Catarractis village falls at the foot of the Tzoumerca Mountain Range. 60d, Edessa Waterfalls. 100d, Edessaios River cascades.

1988, July 4 Litho. Perf. 12½x14
1628	A544	10d multi	2.00	.40
1629	A544	60d multi	7.00	2.25
1630	A544	100d multi	10.00	2.25
	Nos. 1628-1630 (3)		19.00	4.90

Each denomination also sold in booklets containing 20 panes of 5 stamps, perf. 14 vertically. Value for set of unused booklet stamps $35; used booklet stamps sell for about half the values shown for used sheet stamps.

1988, July 4 Perf. 13x12½
1631	A545	60d multi	8.00	2.50

20th Pan-European Postal Trade Unions Congress. No. 1631 also sold in booklets containing 20 panes of 5 stamps, perf. 14 vertically. Value of unused booklet stamp $12; the used booklet stamp sells for about half the value shown for the used sheet stamp.

A546

A547

Designs: 30d, Premier Eleutherios Venizelos (1864-1936), natl. flag and map. 70d, Lady liberty, flag and map.

1988, Oct. 7 Litho. Perf. 12½x13
1632	A546	30d shown	.85	.30
1633	A546	70d multi	1.40	.75

Union of Crete with Greece and liberation of Epirus and Macedonia from Turkish rule, 75th anniv.
Each denomination also sold in booklets containing 20 panes of 5 stamps, perf. 14 horizontally. Value for set of unused booklet stamps $6; used booklet stamps sell for somewhat less than the values shown for used sheet stamps.

1988, Oct. 7 Perf. 13
Departmental Seats: 2d, Mytilene-Lesbos Harbor, painting by Theophilos. 3d, Alexandroupolis lighthouse. 4d, St. Nicholas bell tower, Kozane. 5d, Labor Center, Hermoupolis. 7d, Sparta Town Hall. 8d, Pegasus of Leukas. 10d, Castle of the Knights, Rhodes. 20d, The Acropolis, Athens. 25d, Kavalla aqueduct. 30d, Statue of Athanasios Diakos and castle, Lamia. 50d, Preveza cathedral bell tower and Venetian clock. 60d, Corfu promenade. 70d, Harbor view of Hagios Nicolaos. 100d, Poligiros public fountains. 200d, Church of the Apostle Paul, Corinth.

1634	A547	2d multi	.20	.20
1635	A547	3d multi	.20	.20
1636	A547	4d multi	.20	.20
1637	A547	5d multi	.20	.20
1638	A547	7d multi	.20	.20
1639	A547	8d multi	.25	.20
1640	A547	10d multi	.25	.20
1641	A547	20d multi	.30	.20
a.	Bklt. pane, 4 each 3d, 5d, 10d, 20d		4.25	—
1642	A547	25d multi	.35	.20
1643	A547	30d multi	.40	.20
1644	A547	50d multi	.60	.20
1645	A547	60d multi	1.25	.60
1646	A547	70d multi	1.25	.60
1647	A547	100d multi	2.00	.40
1648	A547	200d multi	4.00	2.00
	Nos. 1634-1648 (15)		11.65	4.50

Each denomination was also sold in booklets containing 20 panes of 5 stamps, perf 13 vertically or horizontally. Value for set of unused booklet stamps $12; used booklet stamps sell for slightly less than the values shown for used sheet stamps.

Council of Europe, Rhodes, Dec. 2-3
A548

Christmas
A549

Designs: 60d, Map and Castle of the Knights, Rhodes. 100d, Head of Helios, Rhodian 2nd-3rd cent. B.C. coin, and flags.

1988, Dec. 2 Litho. Perf. 12½
1649	A548	60d multi	2.00	1.75
1650	A548	100d multi	3.00	1.25

Nos. 1649-1650 were also issued in booklets containing 20 panes of 5, perf. 14 horizontally. Value for set of unused booklet stamps $6.50; used booklet stamps sell for somewhat less than the values shown for used sheet stamps.

1988, Dec. 2 Perf. 12½
Paintings: 30d, Adoration of the Magi, by El Greco. 70d, The Annunciation, by Costas Parthenis, horiz.

1651	A549	30d multi	.80	.40
a.	Bklt. pane of 10		24.00	—

Perf. 14
1652	A549	70d multi	1.75	.85

No. 1651 was issued in booklets of 10 stamps perf 12½ on three sides. No. 1652 was also issued in booklets containing 20 panes of 5 stamps, perf. 14 vertically. Value for booklet stamp of No. 1651 $2.50; value for booklet stamp of No. 1652 $5; used values for booklet stamps are the same as for sheet stamps.

A550   A551

Athens '96 emblem and: 30d, High jumper and ancient Olympia. 60d, Wrestlers and view of Delphi. 70d, Swimmers and The Acropolis, Athens. 170d, Sports complex.

Perf. 13¼x13½ Vert.
1989, Mar. 17 Litho.
1653	A550	30d multi	.50	.30
1654	A550	60d multi	1.00	.90
1655	A550	70d multi	1.50	1.40
1656	A550	170d multi	3.00	2.00
a.	Strip of 4, Nos. 1653-1656		7.00	7.00
b.	Bklt. pane of 4, #1653-1656, perf 13¼ vert.		10.00	—

1989, May 22 Litho. Perf. 12½x14
Europa: Children's toys.

1657	A551	60d Whistling bird	4.50	2.50
1658	A551	170d Butterfly	5.00	2.50
a.	Pair, #1657-1658		10.00	10.00
b.	Bklt. pane, 2 each #1657-1658, perf 13¼ vert.		22.00	22.00
c.	As "b," pair, #1657-1658		11.00	11.00

Printed se-tenant in sheets of 16. Nos. 1657-1658 were also issued separately in booklets containing 20 panes of 5 stamps, perf. 13¼ vertically.

Anniversaries — A552

1989, May 22   **Perf. 14x13½**

1659	A552	30d Flags	.75	.40
1660	A552	50d Flag, La Liberte	.75	.40
1661	A552	60d Flag, ballot box	1.75	1.10
1662	A552	70d Coin, emblem	1.75	1.10
1663	A552	200d Flag, "40"	4.00	1.50
		Nos. 1659-1663 (5)	9.00	4.50

Six-nation Initiative for Peace and Disarmament, 5th anniv. (30d); French revolution, bicent. (50d); European Parliament Elections in Greece, 10th anniv. (60d); Interparliamentary Union, cent. (70d); and Council of Europe, 40th anniv. (200d).

Nos. 1659-1663 also issued in booklets containing 20 panes of 5 stamps, perf. 13¼ horizontally. Values for unused booklet stamps: 1659 $1; 1660 $2.75; 1661 $7.25; 1662 $7.25; 1663 $9. Used booklet stamps sell for up to 5 times the values shown for used sheet stamps.

A553

BALKANFILA XII, Sept. 30-Oct. 8, Salonica — A554

1989, Sept. 25   **Litho.**   **Perf. 14x12½**

1664	A553	60d shown	.85	.50
1665	A553	70d Eye, magnifying glass	.85	.75

Souvenir Sheet
Perf. 14x13

1666	A554	200d shown	3.50	3.50

Wildflowers
A555

1989, Dec. 8   **Litho.**   **Perf. 14x12½**

1667	A555	8d Wild rose	.20	.20
1668	A555	10d Common myrtle	.20	.20
1669	A555	20d Field poppy	.25	.20
1670	A555	30d Anemone	.40	.25
1671	A555	60d Dandelion, chicory	.80	.40
1672	A555	70d Mallow	.90	.50
1673	A555	200d Thistle	2.50	1.90
		Nos. 1667-1673 (7)	5.25	3.65

Ursus arctos
A556

Rare and endangered species.

1990, Mar. 16   **Litho.**   **Perf. 14x12½**

1674	A556	40d shown	.55	.20
1675	A556	70d *Caretta caretta*	1.90	.45
1676	A556	90d *Monachus monachus*	2.40	.50
1677	A556	100d *Lynx lynx*	2.50	1.10
		Nos. 1674-1677 (4)	7.35	2.25

Europa
1990 — A557

Post offices: 70d, Old Central P.O. interior. 210d, Contemporary p.o. exterior.

1990, May 11   **Litho.**   **Perf. 13½x12½**

1678	A557	70d multicolored	3.25	2.75
1679	A557	210d multicolored	5.75	4.75
a.		Pair, #1678-1679	9.50	9.50
b.		Bklt. pane, 2 each #1678-1679, perf 12½	20.00	
c.		As "b," pair, #1678-1679	10.00	10.00

Nos. 1678-1679 were printed setenant in sheets of 16 and separately in booklets. Nos. 1679b and 1679c are perf 12½ vertically and imperf horizontally.

Natl. Reconciliation   Political Reformers
A558   A559

1990, May 11   **Perf. 12½x13½**

1680	A558	40d Flag, handshake	.50	.20
1681	A558	70d Dove, ribbon	.85	.35
1682	A558	100d Map, gift of flowers	1.25	1.25
		Nos. 1680-1682 (3)	2.60	1.80

1990, May 11

1683	A559	40d Gregoris Lambrakis (1912-63)	.65	.40
1684	A559	40d Pavlos Bakoyiannis (1935-89)	.65	.40

A560   A561

Department Seats: 2d, Karditsa, the commercial-animal fair. 5d, Trikkala fort and clock tower. 8d, Veroia, street with traditional architecture. 10d, Mesolongion, Central Monument of Fallen Heroes in the Exodus. 15d, Chios, view. 20d, Tripolis, street with neoclassical architecture. 25d, Volos, view with town hall, woodcut by A. Tassou. 40d, Kalamata, neoclassical town hall. 50d, Pyrgos, central marketplace. 70d, Ioannina, view of lake and island. 80d, Rethymnon, sculpture at the port. 90d, Argostolion, view before earthquake. 100d, Nauplia, Bourtzi with Palamidi in the background. 200d, Patras, central lighthouse. 250d, Florina, street with neoclassical architecture. Nos. 1685, 1687, 1695, 1698 vert.

1990, June 20   **Litho.**   **Perf. 12½**

1685	A560	2d multicolored	.20	.20
1686	A560	5d multicolored	.20	.20
1687	A560	8d multicolored	.20	.20
1688	A560	10d multicolored	.20	.20
1689	A560	15d multicolored	.20	.20
1690	A560	20d multicolored	.20	.20
1691	A560	25d multicolored	.40	.20
1692	A560	40d multicolored	.60	.20
1693	A560	50d multicolored	.75	.20
1694	A560	70d multicolored	1.00	.40
1695	A560	80d multicolored	1.10	.45
1696	A560	90d multicolored	1.40	.50
1697	A560	100d multicolored	2.25	.60
1698	A560	200d multicolored	4.50	1.10
1699	A560	250d multicolored	6.00	1.50
		Nos. 1685-1699 (15)	19.20	6.35

Each denomination was also sold in booklets containing 20 panes of 5 stamps, perf 13½ vertically or horizontally. Value for set of unused booklet stamps $10; used booklet stamps sell for about half of the value of used sheet stamps.

See Nos. 1749-1760, 1792-1801.

1990, July 13   **Perf. 12½x13½**

1700	A561	20d Sailing	.25	.20
1701	A561	50d Wrestling	.60	.25
1702	A561	80d Sprinting	.90	.90
1703	A561	100d Basketball	1.25	.90
1704	A561	250d Soccer	3.00	1.50
a.		Strip of 5, #1700-1704	7.00	7.00

1996 Summer Olympics. Athens, proposed site for centennial Summer Olympic Games. Exists perf. 13½ vert.

Heinrich Schliemann (1822-1890), Archaeologist — A562

1990, Oct. 11   **Litho.**   **Perf. 14x13½**

1705	A562	80d multicolored	5.00	3.00

See Germany No. 1615.

Greco-Italian War, 50th Anniv. — A563

1990, Oct. 11   **Perf. 12½**

1706	A563	50d Woman knitting	.60	.20
1707	A563	80d Virgin Mary, soldier	1.00	.80
1708	A563	100d Women volunteers	1.40	.80
		Nos. 1706-1708 (3)	3.00	1.80

Souvenir Sheet

Stamp Day — A564

1990, Dec. 14   **Litho.**   **Perf. 14x13**

1709	A564	300d multicolored	10.00	10.00

The Muses — A565

Designs: 50d, Calliope, Euterpe, Erato. 80d, Terpsichore, Polyhymnia, Melpomene. 250d, Thalia, Clio, Urania.

1991, Mar. 11   **Litho.**   **Perf. 12½**

1710	A565	50d multicolored	.60	.20
1711	A565	80d multicolored	.95	.40
1712	A565	250d multicolored	2.75	1.25
		Nos. 1710-1712 (3)	4.30	1.85

Battle of Crete by Ioannis Anousakis — A566

300d, Map, flags of participating allied armies.

1991, May 20   **Litho.**   **Perf. 12½x13½**

1713	A566	60d multicolored	1.60	.40

Size: 32x24mm
Perf. 12½

1714	A566	300d multicolored	3.25	1.50

Battle of Crete, 50th anniv.

Europa
A567

Designs: 80d, Icarus pushing modern satellite. 300d, Chariot of the Sun.

1991, May 20   **Perf. 12½**

1715	A567	80d multicolored	4.00	3.00
1716	A567	300d multicolored	5.50	4.50
a.		Pair, #1715-1716	10.00	10.00
b.		Bklt. pane, 2 ea. #1715-1716	22.00	22.00
c.		As "b," pair, 80d, 300d	11.00	11.00

No. 1716a printed in continuous design in sheets of 16. Nos. 1715-1716 were also issued separately in booklets (#1716b), perf 12½ vertically and imperf horizontally.

A568   A569

1991, June 25   **Litho.**   **Perf. 13½x14**

1717	A568	10d Swimming	.20	.20
1718	A568	60d Basketball	.50	.25
1719	A568	90d Gymnastics	.90	.30
1720	A568	130d Weight lifting	1.25	.50
1721	A568	300d Hammer throw	3.50	2.00
		Nos. 1717-1721 (5)	6.35	3.25

1991 Mediterranean Games, Athens.

1991, Sept. 20   **Litho.**   **Perf. 13½x14**

1722	A569	100d multicolored	1.10	.60

Athenian Democracy, 2500th anniv.

Europa Souvenir Sheet

Greek Presidency of CEPT — A570

Europe with Zeus metmorphosed into a bull, from Attic vase, c. 500 B.C.

1991, Sept. 20   **Perf. 14x13**

1723	A570	300d multicolored	20.00	20.00

A571   A572

Greek Membership in EEC, 10th anniv.: 50d, Pres. Konstantin Karamanlis signing Treaty of Greek entrance into EEC. 80d, Map showing EEC members, Pres. Karamanlis.

1991, Dec. 9   **Litho.**   **Perf. 13x14**

1724	A571	50d multicolored	.55	.25
1725	A571	80d multicolored	.90	.50

1991, Dec. 9   **Perf. 12½x13½**

1726	A572	80d Speed skaters	.90	.80
1727	A572	300d Slalom skier	3.25	1.10
a.		Pair, #1726-1727	4.25	4.25

16th Winter Olympics, Albertville.

A573

1992 Summer Olympics, Barcelona A574

Perf. 12½, 14x13½ (90d, 340d)

1992, Apr. 3			Litho.	
1728	A573	10d Javelin	.25	.20
1729	A573	60d Equestrian	.90	.30
1730	A574	90d Runner	1.40	.75
1731	A573	120d Gymnastics	2.75	.80
1732	A574	340d Runners	4.50	2.25
		Nos. 1728-1732 (5)	9.80	4.30

Health — A575

Designs: 60d, Protection against AIDS. 80d, Diseases of digestive system. 90d, Dying flower symbolizing cancer. 120d, Hephaestus at his forge, 6th century BC. 280d, Alexandros S. Onassis Cardiosurgical Center.

1992, May 22			Litho.	Perf. 12½	
1733	A575	60d multicolored	.60	.30
1734	A575	80d multicolored	.85	.40
1735	A575	90d multicolored	.90	.45
1736	A575	120d multicolored	1.50	.65
1737	A575	280d multicolored	3.25	1.75
		Nos. 1733-1737 (5)	7.10	3.55

No. 1734, 1st United European Gastroenterology Week. No. 1736, European Year of Social Security, Hygiene and Health in the Workplace.

Discovery of America, 500th Anniv. A576

Europa: 340d, Map of 15th century Chios, Columbus.

1992, May 22			Perf. 13½x12¼	
1738	A576	90d shown	2.75	2.00
a.		Perf. 12½ vert.	3.00	2.25
1739	A576	340d multicolored	6.50	4.75
a.		Pair, #1738-1739	10.00	10.00
b.		Perf. 12½ vert.	6.75	5.50
c.		Bklt. pane, 2 each #1738a, 1739b	20.00	20.00
d.		Pair, #1738a, 1739b	10.00	10.00

No. 1739a was printed in continuous design in sheets of 16. Nos. 1738-1739 were also issued separately in booklets (#1739c), perf 12¼ vertically and imperf horizontally.

Souvenir Sheet

European Conference on Transportation — A577

1992, June 8			Perf. 14x13	
1740	A577	300d multicolored	8.50	8.50

Macedonian Treasures — A578

Designs: 10d, Head of Hercules wearing lion skin, Vergina treasures. 20d, Bust of Aristotle, map of Macedonia. 60d, Alexander the Great at Battle of Issus, horiz. 80d, Archaeologist Manolis Andronikos, tomb of King Philip II. 90d, Deer hunt mosaic, Pella. 120d, Macedonian tetradrachm. 340d, St. Paul, 4th century church near Philippi.

1992, July 17			Litho.	Perf. 12½	
1741	A578	10d multicolored	.50	.20
1742	A578	20d multicolored	.50	.20
1743	A578	60d multicolored	.60	.20
1744	A578	80d multicolored	1.60	.25
1745	A578	90d multicolored	1.90	.25
1746	A578	120d multicolored	2.40	1.00
1747	A578	340d multicolored	8.50	2.50
		Nos. 1741-1747 (7)	16.00	4.60

European Unification — A579

1992, Oct. 12			Litho.	Perf. 14x13	
1748	A579	90d multicolored	1.00	1.00

Departmental Seat Type of 1990

Designs: 10d, Piraeus, the old clock. 20d, Amphissa, view of city with citadel. 30d, Samos (Vathy), the Heraion. 40d, Canea, city in 1800s. 50d, Zakinthos (Zante), view in 1800s. 60d, Karpenision, Velouchi and city. 70d, Kilkis, the cave, vert. 80d, Xanthe, door of Town Hall, vert. 90d, Salonika, Macedonian Struggle Museum. 120d, Komotine, Tsanakleous School. 340d, Drama, spring. 400d, Larissa, Pinios bridge.

1992, Oct. 12			Perf. 12¾	
1749	A560	10d multicolored	.20	.20
1750	A560	20d multicolored	.20	.20
1751	A560	30d multicolored	.20	.20
1752	A560	40d multicolored	.35	.20
1753	A560	50d multicolored	.40	.20
1754	A560	60d multicolored	.45	.30
1755	A560	70d multicolored	.60	.35
1756	A560	80d multicolored	.60	.35
1757	A560	90d multicolored	1.25	.40
1758	A560	120d multicolored	2.50	.65
1759	A560	340d multicolored	4.00	1.60
1760	A560	400d multicolored	5.50	2.25
		Nos. 1749-1760 (12)	16.25	6.90

Each denomination was also sold in booklets containing 20 panes of 5 stamps, perf 10½ vertically or horizontally. Value for set of unused booklet stamps $14.50; used booklet stamps sell for about half the listed values for used sheet stamps.

City of Rhodes, 2400th Anniv. — A580

Designs: 60d, Headstone, 4th cent. B.C. 90d, Bathing Aphrodite, 1st cent. B.C. 120d, St. Irene, Church of St. Catherine, 14th cent. 250d, St. Paul's Gate, 15th cent.

1993, Feb. 26			Litho.	Perf. 13x14	
1761	A580	60d multicolored	.65	.35
1762	A580	90d multicolored	1.10	.80
1763	A580	120d multicolored	1.25	.70
1764	A580	250d multicolored	4.00	1.75
		Nos. 1761-1764 (4)	7.00	3.60

Remembrances of Greek Wars — A581

Designs: 10d, Death of Georgakis Olympios, 1821. 30d, Theodore Kolokotronis in battle, 1821. 60d, Pavlos Melas. 90d, Glory lays wreath over graves of dead from Balkan Wars. 120d, Greek soldiers at Battle of El Alamein, 1942, horiz. 150d, Greek troops in Aegean Islands, 1943-45, horiz. 200d, Kalavryta Massacre Memorial.

Perf. 13x14, 14x13

1993, May 25			Litho.	
1765	A581	10d multicolored	.25	.20
1766	A581	30d multicolored	.40	.20
1767	A581	60d multicolored	.55	.30
1768	A581	90d multicolored	1.00	.40
1769	A581	120d multicolored	2.40	1.00
1770	A581	150d multicolored	2.40	1.60
1771	A581	200d multicolored	4.75	2.25
		Nos. 1765-1771 (7)	11.75	5.95

The Benefits of Transportation, by K. Parthenis — A582

Europa: 90d, Tree, three people, ships. 350d, Woman and children, town.

1993, May 25			Perf. 13x14	
1772		90d multicolored	1.50	1.25
a.		Perf. 13½ vert.	1.50	1.25
1773		350d multicolored	6.75	5.50
a.		A582 Pair, #1772-1773	9.00	9.00
b.		Perf. 13½ vert.	6.75	5.50
c.		Bklt. pane, 2 each #1772a, 1773b	18.00	18.00
d.		Pair, #1772a, 1773b	9.00	9.00

No. 1773a was printed in continuous design in sheets of 16. Nos. 1772-1773 were also issued separately in booklets (#1773c), perf 13½ vertically and imperf horizontally.

Buildings in Athens A583

Designs: 30d, Concert Hall. 60d, Numismatic Museum (Iliou Melathron). 90d, Natl. Library of Greece. 200d, Opthalmology Hospital.

1993, Oct. 4			Litho.	Perf. 14	
1774	A583	30d multicolored	.85	.20
1775	A583	60d multicolored	.85	.30
1776	A583	90d multicolored	1.00	.80
1777	A583	200d multicolored	5.00	2.00
		Nos. 1774-1777 (4)	7.70	3.30

Souvenir Sheet

Greek Presidency of the European Community Council of Ministers — A584

1993, Dec. 20			Litho.	Perf. 14	
1778	A584	400d multicolored	5.00	5.00

Chariot of Selene Driven by Hermes A585

1994, Mar. 7			Litho.	Perf. 13x13½	
1779	A585	200d multicolored	2.25	1.50

2nd Pan-European Transportation Conference.

Passion of Christ A586

Designs: 30d, Last Supper, 16th cent. icon, St. Catherine's Church, Crete, vert. 60d, Crucifixion, detail from 1552 wall drawing, Great Meteoron, vert. 90d, Burial, 1620-45 icon, Church of the Presentation of the Lord, Patmos. 150d, Resurrection, illustrated manuscript of Mt. Athos, 11th cent.

1994, Apr. 8			Litho.	Perf. 14	
1780	A586	30d multicolored	.40	.25
1781	A586	60d multicolored	.50	.25
1782	A586	90d multicolored	.75	.40
1783	A586	150d multicolored	1.60	.90
		Nos. 1780-1783 (4)	3.25	1.80

European Inventors, Discoverers A587

Europa: 90d, Thales of Miletus (625?-547? B.C.), philosopher, mathematician. 350d, Konstantinos Karatheodoris (1873-1950).

1994, May 9			Litho.	Perf. 14x13½	
1784	A587	90d multicolored	1.75	1.50
a.		Perf. 13¾ vert.	2.00	1.75
1785	A587	350d multicolored	3.75	3.25
a.		Pair, #1784-1785	6.00	6.00
b.		Perf. 13¾ vert.	4.00	3.50
c.		Bklt. pane, 2 each #1784a-1785b	13.00	13.00
d.		Pair, #1784a, 1785b	6.50	6.50

Nos. 1784-1785 was issued in sheets of 16 and in booklets (#1785c), perf 13¾ vertically and imperf horizontally.

Athletic Events, Anniversaries A588

Designs: 60d, Demetrios Vikelas (1835-1908), first president Intl. Olympic Committee, vert. 90, Modern, ancient soccer players. 120d, Volleyball, net, vert. 400d, Statue of Liberty, modern, ancient soccer players.

1994, June 6　　Litho.　　Perf. 14
1786	A588	60d multicolored	.70	.30
1787	A588	90d multicolored	.85	.60
1788	A588	120d multicolored	1.75	.90
		Nos. 1786-1788 (3)	3.30	1.80

Souvenir Sheet
Perf. 14x13½
1789	A588	400d multicolored	4.50	4.50

Intl. Olympic Committee, cent. (#1786). 1994 World Cup Soccer Championships, US (#1787, #1789). World Volleyball Championships, Piraeus & Salonika (#1788).
No. 1789 contains one 42x52mm stamp.

Greek Presidency of European Community Council of Ministers
A589

Designs: 90d, Winged chariot driven by Greece. 120d, Doric columns, European Community flag.

1994, June 21　　　　　Perf. 13
1790	A589	90d multicolored	1.00	.90
1791	A589	120d multicolored	1.25	.90

Departmental Seat Type of 1990

Designs: 10d, Katerine, Tsalopoulou mansion house, vert. 20d, Arta, Byzantine Church Parigoritissas. 30d, Lebadea, medieval bridge, tower of catalanian castle, Krias springs vert. 40d, Kastoria, Church of Panagia Koumbelidkis. 50d, Grevena, outdoor theatre. 60d, Edessa, waterfall. 80d, Chalcis, red house. 90d, Serrai, government house, Merarchias road, Acropolis of Koulas. 120d, Candia (Herakleion), town hall. 150d, Egoumenitsa, Church of Evangelistria, vert.

1994, Oct. 5　　Litho.　　Perf. 12¾
1792	A560	10d multicolored	.20	.20
1793	A560	20d multicolored	.20	.20
1794	A560	30d multicolored	.30	.20
1795	A560	40d multicolored	.40	.25
1796	A560	50d multicolored	.50	.25
1797	A560	60d multicolored	.65	.25
1798	A560	80d multicolored	.75	.30
1799	A560	90d multicolored	.80	.30
1800	A560	120d multicolored	1.00	.40
1801	A560	150d multicolored	1.25	.50
		Nos. 1792-1801 (10)	6.05	2.85

Each denomination was also sold in booklets containing 20 panes of 5 stamps, perf 10½ vertically or horizontally. Unused booklet stamps sell for the same price as the sheet stamp values listed; used booklet stamps sell for about half the listed values for the used sheet stamps.

Constitution, 150th Anniv. — A590

Designs: 60d, People, army demonstrating, by Carl Howpt, vert. 150d, Portraits of Ioannis Makriyannis, Andreas Metaxas, Demetrios Kallergis. 200d, Painting of night of Sept. 3, 1843. 340d, Article 107, seal of Greek Parliament, signature of President.

1994, Nov. 21　　Litho.　　Perf. 14x13
1802	A590	60d multicolored	.65	.40
1803	A590	150d multicolored	1.10	.65
1804	A590	200d multicolored	2.25	1.00
1805	A590	340d multicolored	4.25	2.00
		Nos. 1802-1805 (4)	8.25	4.05

Melina Mercouri (1925-94), Actress, Politician — A591

1995, Mar. 7　　Litho.　　Perf. 14x13
1806	A591	60d shown	.65	.25
1807	A591	90d Portrait, Parthenon	.80	.40

1808	A591	100d Portraits as actress	3.00	1.00
1809	A591	340d Portrait, vert.	6.75	2.25
		Nos. 1806-1809 (4)	11.20	3.90

Liberation of Concentration Camps, 50th Anniv.
A592

Europa: 90d, Prisoners. 340d, Peace doves, broken barbed wire fence.

1995, May 3　　Litho.　　Perf. 14
1810	A592	90d multicolored	2.00	2.00
a.		Perf. 13½ vert.	2.00	2.00
1811	A592	340d multicolored	4.00	4.00
a.		Perf. 13½ vert.	4.00	4.00
b.		Pair, #1810-1811	6.50	6.50
c.		Bklt. pane, 2 each #1810a, 1811b	13.00	13.00
		Complete booklet, #1811c	13.00	
d.		Pair, #1810a, 1811b	6.50	6.50

Anniversaries & Events — A593

Designs: 10d, Stylized emblem, basketball, vert. 70d, University building. 90d, Architectural ruins, vert. 100d, Flag, soldier, vert. 120d, Statue of Peace, by Kifissodotos, vert. 150d, Dolphins. 200d, Early telephone, push buttons, vert. 300d, Owl, basketball, vert.

Perf. 13½x13, 13x13½
1995, June 21　　　　　　Litho.
1812	A593	10d multicolored	.20	.20
1813	A593	70d multicolored	1.00	.30
1814	A593	90d multicolored	1.25	.40
1815	A593	100d multicolored	1.40	.45
1816	A593	120d multicolored	1.75	.55
1817	A593	150d multicolored	2.00	.65
1818	A593	200d multicolored	2.75	.90
1819	A593	300d multicolored	4.50	1.25
		Nos. 1812-1819 (8)	14.85	4.70

5th World Junior Basketball Championships (#1812). Agricultural University of Athens, 75th anniv. (#1813). UN, 50th anniv. (#1814, #1816). End of World War II, 50th anniv. (#1815). European Nature Conservation Year (#1817). Telephone in Greece, cent. (#1818). 29th European Basketball Championships (#1819).

Book of Revelation, 1900th Anniv. — A594

Visions of the Apocalypse: 80d, First vision, Angels of the Seven Churches of Asia Minor, icon by Thomas Bathas, vert. 110d, Apostle John at Cave of the Apocalypse dictating to Prochoros, miniature from manuscript of Four Gospels, vert. 300d, First Angel with trumpet from silver gilded Gospel cover.

1995, Sept. 18　　Litho.　　Perf. 14
1820	A594	80d multicolored	2.00	.35
1821	A594	110d multicolored	2.75	.90
1822	A594	300d multicolored	3.75	2.00
		Nos. 1820-1822 (3)	8.50	3.25

Jason & the Argonauts
A595

Designs: 80d, Argonauts, the Argus, goddess Athena setting out for Colchis. 120d, Phineas, Hermes, one of the Voreadae, Harpy. 150d, Jason taming the bull, Medea and Nike. 200d, Jason takes Golden Fleece,

kills serpent with Medea's help. 300d, Medea watches, Jason, crowned by Nike, giving Golden Fleece to Pelias.

1995, Nov. 6　　Litho.　　Perf. 13x13½
1823	A595	80d multicolored	.90	.40
1824	A595	120d multicolored	.90	.75
1825	A595	150d multicolored	1.10	.65
1826	A595	200d multicolored	1.60	.75
1827	A595	300d multicolored	4.50	1.60
		Nos. 1823-1827 (5)	9.00	4.15

Lighthouses — A596

1995, Dec. 18　　Litho.　　Perf. 14
1828	A596	80d Psyttaleia	1.00	.40
1829	A596	120d Sapienza	1.50	.60
1830	A596	150d Kastri (Othonoi)	2.00	1.10
1831	A596	500d Zourva (Hydra)	7.25	2.40
		Nos. 1828-1831 (4)	11.75	4.50

Souvenir Sheets

Modern Olympic Games, Cent.
A597

Perf. 13½x13, 13x13½
1996, Mar. 25　　　　　　Litho.
1832		Sheet of 4	15.00	15.00
a.	A597	80d like #117, vert.	3.00	3.00
b.	A597	120d like #118, vert.	3.00	3.00
c.	A597	150d like #119, vert.	3.00	3.00
d.	A597	650d like #120, vert.	3.00	3.00
1833		Sheet of 4	15.00	15.00
a.	A597	80d like #122	3.00	3.00
b.	A597	120d like #124	3.00	3.00
c.	A597	150d like #125	3.00	3.00
d.	A597	650d like #128	3.00	3.00
1834		Sheet of 4	15.00	15.00
a.	A597	80d like #121, vert.	3.00	3.00
b.	A597	120d like #123, vert.	3.00	3.00
c.	A597	150d like #126, vert.	3.00	3.00
d.	A597	650d like #127, vert.	3.00	3.00

Famous Women — A598

Europa: 120d, Sappho (c.610-580BC), lyric poet. 430d, Amalia Fleming.

1996, Apr. 22　　Litho.　　Perf. 14x14½
1835		120d multicolored	1.50	1.50
a.		Perf. 14½ vert.	1.50	1.50
1836		430d multicolored	4.50	4.50
a.	A598	Pair, #1835-1836	6.25	6.25
b.		Perf. 14½ vert.	4.50	4.50
c.		Booklet pane, 2 each #1835a, 1836b	12.50	12.50
		Complete booklet, #1836c	12.50	
d.		Pair, #1835a, 1836b	6.25	6.25

Modern Olympic Games, Cent.
A599

Stylized designs: 10d, Greek runners, vert. 80d, Discus thrower, vert. 120d, Weight lifter, vert. 200d, Wrestlers.

Perf. 13½x14, 14x13½
1996, June 4　　　　　　Litho.
1837	A599	10d multicolored	.45	.20
1838	A599	80d multicolored	1.60	.45
1839	A599	120d multicolored	3.00	.75
1840	A599	200d multicolored	4.75	2.00
		Nos. 1837-1840 (4)	9.80	3.40

First Intl. Medical Olympiad — A600

1996, July 8　　Litho.　　Perf. 13½
1841	A600	80d Hippocrates	2.00	.80
1842	A600	120d Galen	2.50	1.25

Castles
A601

1996, Oct. 7　　Litho.　　Perf. 13x13½
1843	A601	10d Mytilene	.20	.20
1844	A601	20d Lindos	.20	.20
1845	A601	30d Rethymnon	.30	.25
1846	A601	70d Assos Cephalonia	.65	.35
1847	A601	80d Serbs	.80	.60
1848	A601	120d Monemvasia	1.00	.65
1849	A601	200d Didimotihon	1.75	1.00
1850	A601	430d Vonitsas	4.25	3.00
1851	A601	1000d Nikopolis	10.00	6.50
		Nos. 1843-1851 (9)	19.15	12.75

Each denomination was also sold in booklets containing 20 panes of 5 stamps, perf. 13 vertically. Unused booklet stamps sell for the same price as the listed sheet stamps; used booklet stamps sell for about half the values shown for used sheet stamps.

Figures from Shadow Theatre — A602

100d, Four characters, diff. 120d, Three characters. 200d, Two characters, dragon.

1996, Nov. 15　　　　　　Perf. 14
1852	A602	80d multicolored	1.00	.45
1853	A602	100d multicolored	1.00	.55
1854	A602	120d multicolored	2.00	.70
1855	A602	200d multicolored	3.00	1.10
		Nos. 1852-1855 (4)	7.00	2.80

Hellenic Language
A603

Designs: 80d, Oldest Hellenic inscription, wine pitcher, 720BC. 120d, Verse IX, 436-445 from Homer's Iliad, 1st-2nd cent. AD. 150d, Psalm of the Holy Apostles, 6th cent. AD. 350d, Reference to Hellenic language, Dionysios Solomos, 1824.

1996, Dec. 18　　Litho.　　Perf. 13x13½
1856	A603	80d multicolored	.85	.55
1857	A603	120d multicolored	1.10	.85
1858	A603	150d multicolored	1.75	1.40
1859	A603	350d multicolored	4.25	2.10
		Nos. 1856-1859 (4)	7.95	4.90

Andreas G. Papandreou (1919-96), Prime Minister — A604

Papandreou at various ages and: 80d, Graduation cap, books, diploma. 120d, Leaving airplane. 150d, Building. 500d, Greek flag, dove.

1997, Feb. 12   Litho.   Perf. 13
1860	A604	80d multicolored	1.10	.30
1861	A604	120d multicolored	1.10	.45
1862	A604	150d multicolored	1.75	.85
1863	A604	500d multicolored	4.00	.95
		Nos. 1860-1863 (4)	7.95	2.55

Thessaloniki, European Cultural Capital A605

Designs: 80d, Fresco of St. Dimitrios, patron saint of Thessaloniki, Church of Aghios Nikolaos Orphanos, vert. 100d, Hippocratic Hospital. 120d, Marble pedestal with inscription, medallion with woman's head. 150d, Detail of mosaic from Rotunda cupola, vert. 300d, "Iaspis" chalice, 14th cent., Mt. Athos.

1997, Mar. 26   Perf. 13½
1864	A605	80d multicolored	.90	.50
1865	A605	100d multicolored	1.40	.65
1866	A605	120d multicolored	1.50	.75
1867	A605	150d multicolored	1.75	1.00
1868	A605	300d multicolored	4.50	2.00
		Nos. 1864-1868 (5)	10.05	4.90

Bridges of Macedonia A606

1997, Apr. 24   Litho.   Perf. 14
1869	A606	80d Village of Trikomo	.70	.45
1870	A606	120d Portitsa	1.10	.65
1871	A606	150d Village of Ziakas	2.00	.85
1872	A606	350d Village of Kastro	5.25	1.90
		Nos. 1869-1872 (4)	9.05	3.85

Stories and Legends A607

Europa: 120d, Prometheus, the giver of fire. 430d, Digenis Akritas, Greek swordsmen on horseback.

1997, May 19   Litho.   Perf. 14
1873	A607	120d multicolored	1.75	1.50
a.		Perf. 13½vert.	1.75	1.50
1874	A607	430d multicolored	4.00	3.50
a.		Perf. 13½vert.	4.00	3.50
b.		Pair, #1873-1874	5.75	5.75
c.		Booklet pane, 2 each #1873a, 1874b	11.50	11.50
		Complete booklet, #1874c	11.50	
d.		Pair, #1873a, 1874b	5.75	5.75

6th IAAF World Track & Field Championships, Athens — A608

Official IAAF emblem, Greek flag and: 20d, Runners. 100d, Nike. 140d, High jump. 170d, Hurdles. 500d, Olympic Stadium, Athens.

1997, July 11   Litho.   Perf. 13x13½
1875	A608	20d multicolored	.20	.20
1876	A608	100d multicolored	.85	.40
1877	A608	140d multicolored	1.25	.80
1878	A608	170d multicolored	1.60	1.00
1879	A608	500d multicolored	5.25	2.50
		Nos. 1875-1879 (5)	9.15	4.90

Famous People A609

Designs: 20d, Alexandros Panagoulis (1939-76), resistance leader, vert. 30d, Grigorios Xenopoulos (1867-1951), novelist, vert. 40d, Odysseus Elytis (1911-96), poet. 50d, Panayiotis Kanellopoulos (1902-86), prime minister, vert. 100d, Harilaos Trikoupis (1832-96), politician. 170d, Maria Callas (1923-77), opera singer. 200d, Rigas Vélestinlis-Feraios (1757-98), revolutionary, vert.

Perf. 13½x13, 13x13½
1997, Oct. 31   Litho.
1880	A609	20d multicolored	.20	.20
1881	A609	30d multicolored	.50	.20
1882	A609	40d multicolored	.60	.20
1883	A609	50d multicolored	.90	.20
1884	A609	100d multicolored	1.50	.75
1885	A609	170d multicolored	3.00	1.40
1886	A609	200d multicolored	3.50	1.60
		Nos. 1880-1886 (7)	10.20	4.55

Film Comedians A610

Designs: 20d, Vassilis Avlonitis. 30d, Vassilis Argyropoulos. 50d, Georgia Vassileiadou. 70d, Lambros Constantaras. 100d, Vassilis Logothetidis. 140d, Dionysis Papagiannopoulos. 170d, Nikos Stavrides. 200d, Mimis Fotopoulos.

1997, Dec. 17   Litho.   Perf. 13x13½
1887	A610	20d multicolored	.20	.20
1888	A610	30d multicolored	.40	.20
1889	A610	50d multicolored	.60	.45
1890	A610	70d multicolored	.85	.70
1891	A610	100d multicolored	1.10	.85
1892	A610	140d multicolored	1.60	1.60
1893	A610	170d multicolored	2.40	1.60
1894	A610	200d multicolored	5.00	1.60
		Nos. 1887-1894 (8)	12.15	7.20

Incorporation of the Dodecanese Islands into Greece, 50th Anniv. — A611

100d, German commander signing treaty turning islands over to English and Greek military, Symi (Simi), May 8, 1945. 140d, Greece and Colossus of Rhodes, Greek flag. 170d, English general turns islands over to Greek military command, Rhodes, 3/31/47. 500d, Greek flag raised over Dodencanese, Kasos (Caso), 3/7/47.

1998, Feb. 27   Litho.   Perf. 13½x13
1895	A611	100d multicolored	1.00	.65
1896	A611	140d multicolored	1.40	1.40
1897	A611	170d multicolored	2.00	1.75
1898	A611	500d multicolored	5.50	1.25
		Nos. 1895-1898 (4)	9.90	5.05

Hagia Sophia General Children's Hospital, Cent. — A612

Holy Monastery of Xenon, 1000th Anniv. A613

4th World Congress of Thracians, Nea Orestiada A614

16th World Congress of Cardiology Research, Athens — A615

European Movement, 50th Anniv. — A616

Perf. 13x13½, 13½x13
1998, Apr. 30   Litho.
1899	A612	20d multicolored	.20	.20
1900	A613	100d multicolored	.90	.50
1901	A614	140d multicolored	1.25	1.25
1902	A615	150d Building, heart, horiz.	1.25	1.25
1903	A615	170d multicolored	2.00	1.60
1904	A616	500d multicolored	6.50	1.90
		Nos. 1899-1904 (6)	12.10	6.70

Souvenir Sheet

1998 FIBA World Basketball Championships, Greece — A617

Illustration reduced.

1998, June 15   Litho.   Perf. 14
1905	A617	300d multicolored	3.50	3.50

Natl. Festivals A618

Europa: 140d, Culture Festival, Grecian Theatre, Epidaurus. 500d, Culture Festival, Herod Atticus Theatre, Athens.

1998, May 29   Litho.   Perf. 14x13½
1906	A618	140d multicolored	1.50	1.50
a.		Perf. 13 vert.	1.75	1.75
1907	A618	500d multicolored	4.25	4.25
a.		Pair, #1906-1907	6.25	6.25
b.		Perf. 13 vert.	5.00	5.00
c.		Bklt. pane, 2 ea. #1906a, 1907b	14.50	14.50
		Complete booklet, #1907c	14.50	
d.		Pair, #1906a, 1907b	7.25	7.25

Castle Ruins in Greece A619

1998, July 15   Litho.   Perf. 13½
1908	A619	30d Hierapetra	.25	.20
1909	A619	50d Korfu	.40	.20
1910	A619	70d Limnos	.55	.30
1911	A619	100d Argolis	.75	.40
1912	A619	150d Iraklion	.75	.65
1913	A619	170d Navpaktos, vert.	1.25	.90
1914	A619	200d Ioannina, vert.	2.00	1.00
1915	A619	400d Plataea	4.50	1.50
1916	A619	550d Karitainas, vert.	6.25	2.25
1917	A619	600d Fragkokastello, Crete	6.50	2.75
		Nos. 1908-1917 (10)	23.20	10.15

Each denomination was also sold in booklets containing 20 panes of stamps, perf. 13⅓ horizontally or vertically. Unused booklet stamps sell for the same price as the listed sheet stamps; used booklet stamps sell for somewhat less than the values shown for used sheet stamps.

Greek Orthodox Community of Venice, 500th Anniv. — A620

Designs: 30d, Cathedral. 40d, Icon, vert. 140d, Illuminated manuscript, vert. 230d, Icon of Madonna and Child surrounded by saints.

1998, Oct. 26   Litho.   Perf. 14
1918	A620	30d multicolored	.30	.25
1919	A620	40d multicolored	.55	.35
1920	A620	140d multicolored	1.50	.85
1921	A620	230d multicolored	3.50	2.00
		Nos. 1918-1921 (4)	5.85	3.45

Greek Writers of Antiquity — A621

1998   Litho.   Perf. 13½x13
1922	A621	20d Homer	.20	.20
1923	A621	100d Sophocles	1.60	1.60
1924	A621	140d Thucydides	1.90	1.90
1925	A621	200d Plato	2.40	2.40
1926	A621	250d Demosthenes	3.75	3.75
		Nos. 1922-1926 (5)	9.85	9.85

Intl. Year of the Ocean A622

Designs: 40d, Ancient ship, map of Mediterranean Sea. 100d, Sailing ship, Neptune. 200d, Modern ship. 500d, Silver tetradrachm of Antigonos Doson, 229-221 B.C.

1999, Feb. 19   Litho.   Perf. 13x13½
1927	A622	40d multicolored	.30	.25
1928	A622	100d multicolored	.90	.40
1929	A622	200d multicolored	1.60	1.00
1930	A622	500d multicolored	3.25	1.50
		Nos. 1927-1930 (4)	6.05	3.15

Pres. Konstantin Karamanlis (1907-98) — A623

Various portraits of Karamanlis and: 100d, Representations of economic development, 1955-63. 170d, People celebrating. 200d, Emblem of European Union. 500d, National flag, vert.

1999, Apr. 19   Litho.   Perf. 14
1931	A623	100d multicolored	.70	.35
1932	A623	170d multicolored	1.25	.75
1933	A623	200d multicolored	1.50	.85
1934	A623	500d multicolored	3.00	2.00
		Nos. 1931-1934 (4)	6.45	3.95

Europa A624

Various views Mytikas peak (Mt. Olympus) and wildflowers.

1999, May 24	Litho.	Perf. 14	
1935 A624 170d multicolored		1.75	1.75
a.	Perf. 13¼ vert.	2.00	1.75
1936 A624 550d multicolored		4.50	4.00
a.	Pair, #1935-1936	6.75	6.75
b.	Perf. 13¼ vert.	4.75	4.00
c.	Booklet pane, 2 each #1935a, 1936b	14.00	14.00
	Complete booklet, #1936c	14.00	
d.	Pair, #1935a, 1936b	7.00	7.00

Greece-Japan Diplomatic Relations, Cent. — A625

1999, June 28	Litho.	Perf. 13¾x14	
1937 A625 120d multicolored		.90	.75

4000 Years of Hellenism — A626

Designs: a, Sanctuary of Apollo Hylates, Kourion. b, Mycenaean "Krater of the Warriors," Athens. c, Mycenaean amphoral krater, Cyprus Museum. d, Sanctuary of Apollo Epikourios, Delphi.

1999, June 28	Litho.	Perf. 13½x13	
1938 A626 120d Block of 4, #a.-d.		3.50	3.50

See Cyprus No. 936.

Community Support Framework, 5th Anniv. A627

Designs: 20d, Modernization of Greek Railway Organization. 120d, Rio-Antirrio Bridge. 140d, Modernization of Greek Post Office. 250d, Athens Metro train. 500d, Eleftherios Venizelos Airport, Athens.

1999, Nov. 8	Litho.	Perf. 13x13¼	
1939 A627 20d multi		.20	.20
1940 A627 120d multi		.75	.75
1941 A627 140d multi		.85	.85
1942 A627 250d multi		1.50	1.50
1943 A627 500d multi		3.00	3.00
Nos. 1939-1943 (5)		6.30	6.30

Armed Forces A628

20d, Exercise with helicopters, rafts. 30d, Patrol boat. 40d, F-16s in flight. 50d, CL-215 dousing forest fire. 70d, Destroyers. 120d, Distribution of goods in Bosnia. 170d, Mirage 2000 in flight. 250d, Exercise with helicopters, tanks. 600d, Submarine Okeanos.

		Perf. 13¾x13½	
1999, Dec. 13			Litho.
1944 A628 20d multi		.20	.20
1945 A628 30d multi		.20	.20
1946 A628 40d multi		.25	.25
1947 A628 50d multi		.30	.30
1948 A628 70d multi		.40	.40
1949 A628 120d multi		.70	.50
1950 A628 170d multi		1.25	1.10
1951 A628 250d multi		1.75	1.50
1952 A628 600d multi		3.75	3.50
Nos. 1944-1952 (9)		8.80	7.95

Christianity, 2000th Anniv. A629

Designs: 20d, Birth of Christ, vert. 50d, Inter-religious dialogue, vert. 120d, Angels with instruments, vert. 170d, Dove. 200d, Communion. 500d, Providence, vert.

2000, Jan. 1		Perf. 14¼x14	
1953 A629 20d multi		.20	.20
1954 A629 50d multi		.30	.30
1955 A629 120d multi		.70	.70
		Perf. 14x14¼	
1956 A629 170d multi		1.00	1.00
		Size: 35x35mm	
		Perf. 13¾	
1957 A629 200d multi		1.25	1.25
		Size: 27x57mm	
		Perf. 13½x14	
1958 A629 500d multi		3.00	3.00
Nos. 1953-1958 (6)		6.45	6.45

Europa, 2000
Common Design Type

2000, May 9	Litho.	Perf. 13¼x13	
1959 CD17 170d multi		3.00	3.00
a.	Perf. 13 vert.	3.50	3.50
b.	Booklet pane, 4 #1959a	14.00	14.00
	Complete booklet, #1959b	14.00	

Ships — A630

Designs: 10d, Steamship Ilissos. 120d, Destroyer Adrias. 170d, Steamship Ia II. 400d, Destroyer Vas. Olga.

		Perf. 14¼x13¾	
2000, June 26			Litho.
1960 A630 10d multi		.30	.25
1961 A630 120d multi		1.00	.65
1962 A630 170d multi		1.90	1.10
1963 A630 400d multi		4.75	3.00
Nos. 1960-1963 (4)		7.95	5.00

Stampin' the Future Children's Stamp Design Contest Winners A631

Art by: 130d, Spyros Dalakos (rainbow). 180d, Ornella Moshovaki-Chaiger (robots). 200d, Zisis Zariotis (building, tree, vehicles). 620d, Athina Limoudi (rocket).

2000, June 26			
1964 A631 130d multi		.70	.70
1965 A631 180d multi		1.10	1.10
1966 A631 200d multi		1.75	1.75
1967 A631 620d multi		4.25	4.25
Nos. 1964-1967 (4)		7.80	7.80

Sydney and Athens — A632

Olympic torch, flag and: 200d, Parthenon. 650d, Sydney Opera House.

		Perf. 13¼x13¾	
2000, Sept. 15			Litho.
1968-1969 A632 Set of 2		5.00	5.00

See Australia Nos. 1873-1874.

Emblem of 2004 Athens Olympic Games — A633

Various backgrounds. Denominations: 10d, 50d, 130d, 180d, 200d, 650d.

2000, Nov. 7		Perf. 14x14¼	
1970-1975 A633 Set of 6		8.00	8.00

Souvenir Sheet

Stamps of the Cretan Government, Cent. — A634

No. 1976: a, 200d, Crete #69. b, 650d, Crete #71.
Illustration reduced.

2000, Dec. 18	Litho.	Perf. 14x14¼	
1976 A634 Sheet of 2, #a-b		15.00	15.00

Christianity, 2000th Anniv. A635

Designs: 20d, Sculpture of Christ as Orpheus, vert. 30d, Sculpture of The Good Shepherd, vert. 40d, Mosaic of Christ, vert. 100d, Mural of Christ. 130d, Icon of Christ (green frame), vert. 150d, Icon of Christ with open Bible, vert. 180d, Icon of Christ with closed Bible (dark blue frame), vert. 1000d, Byzantine coin depicting Christ.

2000, Dec. 18	Perf. 14x14¼, 14¼x14		
1977-1984 A635 Set of 8		10.00	10.00

Post Office Savings Bank, Cent. A636

Designs: 20d, Mother and child, vert. 130d, Emblem and 2-euro coin.

	Perf. 13¼x13¾, 13¾x13¼		
2001, May 15			Litho.
1985-1986 A636 Set of 2		1.10	1.10

UN High Commissioner for Refugees, 50th Anniv. — A637

2001, May 15		Perf. 13¾x13¼	
1987 A637 140d multi		1.25	1.25

Thessaloniki Intl. Trade Fair, 75th Anniv. — A638

2001, May 15		Perf. 13¼x13¾	
1988 A638 180d multi		1.25	1.25

Aristotle University, Thessaloniki, 75th Anniv. — A639

2001, May 15		Perf. 13¾x13¼	
1989 A639 200d multi		1.50	1.50

Academy of Athens, 75th Anniv. A640

2001, May 15			
1990 A640 500d multi		3.75	3.75

Ioannis Zigdis (1913-97), Politician — A641

2001, May 15		Perf. 13¼x13¾	
1991 A641 700d multi		5.00	5.00

Europa — A642

Designs: Nos. 1992a, 1992c, Dry leaf, parched earth. Nos. 1992b, 1992d, Water, fresh leaves.

2001, May 15		Perf. 14¼x13¾	
1992 A642 Horiz. pair		8.50	8.50
a.	180d multi	2.00	2.00
b.	650d multi	6.50	6.50
c.	Horiz. pair, perf. 13¼ vert.	8.50	8.50
d.	As "a," perf. 13¼ vert.	2.00	2.00
e.	As "b," perf. 13¼ vert.	6.50	6.50
f.	Booklet pane, 2 # 1992c	17.00	
	Booklet, #1992f	17.00	

Birds and Flowers A643

Designs: 20d, Little egret. 50d, White stork. 100d, Bearded vulture. 140d, Orchid, vert. 150d, Dalmatian pelican, vert. 200d, Lily, Plastira Lake. 700d, Egyptian vulture. 850d, Black vulture.

Perf. 13¾x13¼, 13¼x13¾
2001, June 27
1993-2000 A643 Set of 8   17.00 17.00

Symbol of Hellenic Post — A644

Illustration reduced.

2001, Sept. 8   Litho.   Perf. 13x12¾
2001   Pair + 2 labels   2.50 2.50
   a.   A644 140d blue & yellow   1.00 1.00
   b.   A644 200d blue   1.50 1.50

Wording on label varies. No. 2001 could be personalized by adding photos to the labels.

Souvenir Sheet

Christianity in Armenia, 1700th Anniv. — A645

2001, Dec. 5   Perf. 13
2002 A645 850d multi   9.50 9.50

Souvenir Sheet

2004 Summer Olympics, Athens — A646

2001, Dec. 5   Perf. 13¾
2003 A646 1200d multi   9.50 9.50

100 Cents = 1 Euro (€)

Dances A647

Designs: 2c, Kamakaki. 3c, Bride's dowry. 5c, Zagorissios, vert. 10c, Balos. 15c, Synkathistos. 20c, Tsakonikos, vert. 30c, Pyrrichios. 35c, Fourles, vert. 40c, Apokriatikos. 45c, Kotsari. 50c, Pentozalis, vert. 55c, Karagouna. 60c, Hassapiko. 65c, Zalistos. 85c, Pogonissios. €1, Kalamatianos. €2, Maleviziotis. €2.15, Tsamikos. €2.60, Zeibekikos, vert. €3, Nyfiatikos. €4, Paschaliatikos.

Perf. 13x13¼, 13¼x13
2002, Jan. 2   Litho.

2004	A647	2c multi	.20 .20
2005	A647	3c multi	.20 .20
2006	A647	5c multi	.20 .20
2007	A647	10c multi	.30 .30
2008	A647	15c multi	.45 .45
2009	A647	20c multi	.60 .60
2010	A647	30c multi	.90 .90
2011	A647	35c multi	1.00 1.00
2012	A647	40c multi	1.25 1.25
2013	A647	45c multi	1.40 1.40
2014	A647	50c multi	1.50 1.50
2015	A647	55c multi	1.60 1.60
2016	A647	60c multi	1.75 1.75
2017	A647	65c multi	1.90 1.90
2018	A647	85c multi	2.50 2.50
2019	A647	€1 multi	3.00 3.00
2020	A647	€2 multi	6.00 6.00
2021	A647	€2.15 multi	6.50 6.50
2022	A647	€2.60 multi	7.75 7.75
2023	A647	€3 multi	9.00 9.00
2024	A647	€4 multi	12.00 12.00

Nos. 2004-2024 (21)   60.00 60.00

Each denomination also sold in booklets containing 20 panes of stamps, perf 13¼ vertically or horizontally. Unused booklet stamps sell for the same prices as the sheet stamps listed; most used booklet stamps sell for significantly less than the values shown for used sheet stamps.

2004 Summer Olympics, Athens A648

Ancient Olympics: 41c, Runners. 59c, Sculpture of charioteer, vert. 80c, Javelin thrower. €2.05, Doryphoros of Polycleitos, vert. €2.35, Weight lifter. €5, Stadium archway.

Perf. 13¾x13¼, 13¼x13¾
2002, Mar. 15   Litho.
2025-2029 A648 Set of 5   19.00 19.00

Souvenir Sheet
Perf. 12¾
2030 A648 €5 multi   15.00 15.00

No. 2030 contains one 49x28mm stamp.

Europa — A649

2002, May 9   Perf. 13¼x13¾
2031 A649   Horiz. pair, #a-b   8.50 8.50
  a.   60c Elephant   1.75 1.75
  b.   €2.60 Equestrian act   6.75 6.75
  c.   Horiz. pair, perf. 13¼ vert.   8.50 8.50
  d.   As "a," perf. 13¼ vert.   1.75 1.75
  e.   As "b," perf. 13¼ vert.   6.75 6.75
  f.   Booklet pane, 2, #2031c   17.00 —
    Booklet, #2031f   17.00

Scouting A650

Designs: 45c, Navy Scout, sailboats. 60c, Scout, emblem of World Conference. 70c, Scouts planting tree. €2.15, Scouts, map and mountain.

2002, June 26   Litho.   Perf. 13x13½
2032-2035 A650 Set of 4   11.50 11.50
2035a   Miniature sheet, 2 each
    #2032-2035 + 4 labels   25.00 25.00

Greek Language A651

Designs: 45c, Hieros Nomos, Athens Acropolis, 5th cent. B.C. 60c, Linear B script, 13th cent. B.C., vert. 90c, The Memoirs of General Makriyiannis. €2.15, Byzantine script, 11th cent., vert.

Perf. 13¾x13¼, 13¼x13¾
2002, Sept. 23
2036-2039 A651 Set of 4   10.00 10.00

Ancient Olympic Winners With Laurel Wreaths — A652

Head color: 45c, Green. 60c, Dark blue. €2.15, Pink. €2.60, Light blue.

2002, Oct. 30   Litho.   Perf. 13¼x13¾
2040-2043 A652   Set of 4   17.50 17.50
2043a   Miniature sheet, 2 each
    #2040-2043   35.00 35.00

Souvenir Sheet

Stadia of First Olympics — A653

2002, Oct. 30   Perf. 12¾
2044 A653 €6 multi   18.00 18.00

Archbishops of Athens A654

Archbishop and years of reign: 10c, Chrystostomos I (1923-38). 45c, Chrysanthos (1938-41). €2.15, Damaskinos (1941-49). €2.60, Serapheim (1974-98).

2002, Dec. 10   Perf. 13x13½
2045-2048 A654   Set of 4   16.00 16.00

Olympic Sports Equipment — A655

Designs: 2c, Discus. 5c, Hammer. 47c, Javelin. 65c, Pole vault pole and bar. €2.17, Hurdles. €2.85, Weights.

2003, Feb. 11   Perf. 13¾x14¼
2049-2054 A655   Set of 6   19.00 19.00
2054a   Sheet, #2049-2054   16.00 16.00

2004 Summer Olympics, Athens.

Souvenir Sheet

Mascots for 2004 Summer Olympics, Athens — A656

No. 2055: a, €2.50, Mascot with red shirt. b, €2.85, Mascot with blue shirt.

2003, Feb. 11   Perf. 13¼
2055 A656   Sheet of 2, #a-b   16.00 16.00

Greetings — A657

No. 2056: a, Globe. b, Athens 2004 Olympic Games emblem and Olympic rings. c, Ancient Greek athlete with laurel wreath. d, Roses and wedding headband. e, Spheres and grid. f, Child's drawing of train. g, Man and woman holding flowers. h, Stone carving of face. i, Acropolis.

2003, Mar. 18   Litho.   Perf. 14x13¾
2056   A657   Sheet of 9   13.50 13.50
  a.-g.   47c Any single   1.40 1.40
  h.-i.   65c Either single   2.00 2.00
  q.   No. 2056h + label   3.75 3.75
  r.   #2056a + label   2.00 2.00
  s.   #2056b + label   2.00 2.00
  t.   #2056c + label   2.00 2.00
  u.   #2056d + label   2.00 2.00
  v.   #2056e + label   2.00 2.00
  w.   #2056f + label   2.00 2.00

No. 2056q was issued in sheets of 15 stamps and 15 labels that sold for €19.50. Labels could be personalized. No. 2056q exists dated "2004." Stamps dated "2004" were issued in sheets of 5 stamps + 5 preprinted labels that sold for €4 per sheet. Additional stamps in this set were available with personalized labels. The editors would like to examine any examples.

Nos. 2056r-2056w were printed in sheets of 15 + 15 labels that sold for €14.10. Labels could be personalized. Two additional personalized stamps exist in this set. The editors would like to examine any examples.

Dove and Stars — A658

White Tower of Thessaloniki in Letters — A659

Fresco of Birds — A660

Jigsaw Puzzle Pieces — A661

2003, Apr. 16   **Perf. 14x13¾**
2057	A658	47c multi	1.40	1.40
2058	A659	65c multi	2.00	2.00
2059	A660	€2.17 multi	6.50	6.50
2060	A661	€2.85 multi	8.50	8.50
2060a		Sheet, 2 each #2057-2060	37.50	37.50
		Nos. 2057-2060 (4)	18.40	18.40

Greek Presidency of European Union.

Europa — A662

Poster art: a, 65c, Abstract. b, €2.85, Tourist poster.

2003, May 9   **Litho.**   **Perf. 13¼x13¾**
2061	A662	Horiz. pair	10.50	10.50
a.		65c multi	2.00	2.00
b.		€2.85 multi	8.50	8.50
c.		Horiz. pair, perf. 13¼ vert.	10.50	10.50
d.		As "a," perf. 13¼ vert.	2.00	2.00
e.		As "b," perf. 13¼ vert.	8.50	8.50
f.		Booklet pane, 2 #2061c	21.00	—
		Complete booklet, #2061f	21.00	

A663

No. 2062: a, Water polo. b, Diving. c, Swimming.

No. 2063, vert.: a, Table tennis. b, Basketball. c, Soccer. d, Handball.

No. 2064: a, Kayak slalom. b, Windsurfing.

No. 2065, vert.: a, Rhythmic gymnastics. b, Judo. c, Archery. d, Trampoline.

No. 2066: a, Kayak (flatwater). b, Rowing (coxswain). c, Rowing (rower).

No. 2067, vert.: a, Badminton. b, Fencing. c, Tennis. d, Taekwondo.

No. 2068: a, Cycling. b, Triathlon.

No. 2069, vert.: a, Baseball. b, Beach volleyball. c, Field hockey. d, Boxing.

No. 2070, vert.: a, Weight lifting (figure in red) b, Weight lifting (figure in blue).

2003, May 9   **Litho.**   **Perf. 13¼**
2062	A663	Booklet pane of 3 + label	4.75	—
a.-c.		47c Any single	1.50	1.40
2063	A663	Booklet pane of 4	6.00	—
a.-d.		47c Any single	1.50	1.40
2064	A663	Booklet pane of 2	3.50	—
a.-b.		47c Either single	1.75	1.40
2065	A663	Booklet pane of 4	6.00	—
a.		30c multi	1.25	1.00
b.-d.		47c Any single	1.50	1.40
2066	A663	Booklet pane of 3 + label	4.75	—
a.-c.		47c Any single	1.50	1.40
2067	A663	Booklet pane of 4	6.00	—
a.		30c multi	1.25	1.00
b.-d.		47c Any single	1.50	1.40
2068	A663	Booklet pane of 2	3.50	—
a.-b.		47c Either single	1.75	1.40
2069	A663	Booklet pane of 4	6.00	—
a.		35c multi	1.25	1.10
b.-d.		47c Any single	1.50	1.40
2070	A663	Booklet pane of 2	3.50	—
a.-b.		47c Either single	1.75	1.40
		Complete booklet, #2062-2070	50.00	

Booklet containing Nos. 2062-2070 sold for €14.99.

Environmental Protection — A664

Designs: 15c, Apple falling from tree. 47c, Apple in water. 65c, Laurel wreath over seacoast. €2.85, Moon over tree.

2003, June 5   **Perf. 13¼x13¾**
2071-2074	A664	Set of 4	12.50 12.50

Olympic Sports A665

Designs: 5c, High jump. 47c, Wrestling. 65c, Running. 80c, Cycling, vert. €4, Windsurfing, vert.

Perf. 13¾x13¼, 13¼x13¾
2003, Sept. 9
2075-2079	A665	Set of 5	18.00	18.00
2079a		Miniature sheet, #2075-2079	18.00	18.00

Souvenir Sheet

Mascots for 2004 Summer Olympics, Athens — A666

No. 2080: a, Figure in red. b, Figure in blue.

2003, Sept. 9   **Perf. 13¼**
2080	A666	Sheet of 2	16.00	16.00
a.		€2.50 multi	7.50	7.50
b.		€2.85 multi	8.50	8.50

Trades of the Past — A667

Designs: 3c, Stair carving. 10c, Shoemaking. 50c, Blacksmithing. €1, Typesetting by hand. €1.40, Sponge fishing. €4, Weaving.

2003, Oct. 17   **Perf. 13¾x13¼**
2081-2086	A667	Set of 6	21.00	21.00
2086a		Miniature sheet, #2081-2086	21.00	21.00

Olympic Athletes — A668

Various athletes: 20c, 30c, 40c, 47c, €2, €2.85.

Perf. 13¼x13¾
2003, Nov. 28   **Litho.**
2087-2092	A668	Set of 6	19.00	19.00
2092a		Miniature sheet, #2087-2092	19.00	19.00

Greek Olympians A669

Athletes: 3c, Spyridon Louis, marathon, 1896 gold medalist. 10c, Aristides Konstantinides, cycling road race, 1896 gold medalist. €2, Ioannis Fokianos, gymnastics coach. €2.17, Ioannis Mitropoulos, rings, 1896 gold medalist. €3.60, Konstantinos Tsiklitiras, standing long jump, 1912 gold medalist.

Litho. with Foil Application
2004, Jan. 15   **Perf. 13x13½**
2093-2097	A669	Set of 5	24.00 24.00

Cities Hosting Events at 2004 Olympics A670

Designs: 1c, Volos. 2c, Patra. 5c, Iraklion. 47c, Athens. €1.40, Thessaloniki. €4, Athens, diff.

2004, Jan. 15   **Litho.**
2098-2103	A670	Set of 6	18.00 18.00

Olympic Sports A671

Designs: 5c, Swimmer. 10c, Gymnast chalking hands. 20c, Kayak. 47c, Relay race. €2, Rhythmic gymnastics, vert. €5, Men's rings, vert.

2004, Mar. 24   **Litho.**   **Perf. 13¼**
2104-2109	A671	Set of 6	24.00	24.00
2109a		Miniature sheet, #2104-2109	24.00	24.00

Europa — A672

2004, May 4   **Perf. 13¼x13¾**
2110	A672	Horiz. pair	10.50	10.50
a.		65c Sailboat	2.00	2.00
b.		€2.85 Balloon	8.50	8.50
c.		Horiz. pair, perf. 13¼ vert.	10.50	10.50
d.		As "a," perf. 13¼ vert.	2.00	2.00
e.		As "b," perf. 13¼ vert.	8.50	8.50
f.		Booklet pane, 2 #2110c	21.00	—
		Complete booklet, #2110f	21.00	

Souvenir Sheets

Olympic Flame — A673

Olympic Dove — A674

2004, May 4   **Perf. 13¾x14**
2111	A673	Sheet of 2	9.00	9.00
a.		47c Torch bearer	1.40	1.40
b.		€2.50 Torch bearer, city	7.50	7.50
c.		#2111a + label, perf. 14x13¾	2.40	2.40

Perf. 13¼
2112	A674	Sheet of 2	9.00	9.00
a.		47c Dove, Olympic rings	1.40	1.40
b.		€2.50 Dove, people	7.50	7.50

No. 2111c was printed in sheets of 15 + 15 labels that sold for €15. Labels could be personalized.

Olympic Coins — A675

Obverse and reverse of: 47c, Silver three-drachma of Cos, 480-450 BC. 65c, Gold stater of Philip II of Macedonia. €2, Silver two-drachma of Elis, 460 BC. €2.17, Silver four-drachma of Philip II of Macedonia.

2004, June 15   **Perf. 13¼**
2113-2116	A675	Set of 4	16.00	16.00
2116a		Miniature sheet, #2113-2116	16.00	16.00

Souvenir Sheets

Modern Art and the Olympics — A676

2004, July 23   **Perf. 13x13¼**
2117	A676	Sheet of 2	9.00	9.00
a.		50c Wavy lines	1.50	1.50
b.		€2.50 Stripes of color	7.50	7.50

Perf. 13¼x13
2118	A676	Sheet of 2	9.00	9.00
a.		€1 Paint brush, vert.	3.00	3.00
b.		€2 Paint roller, vert.	6.00	6.00
c.		Miniature sheet, #2117a-2117b, 2118a-2118b	18.00	18.00

Greece, 2004 European Soccer Champions A677

Designs: 47c, Greek flag, trophy. 65c, Greek players celebrating. €1, Greek players holding trophy. €2.88, Greek players, trophy.

2004, July 16   **Litho.**   **Perf. 13x13¼**
2119-2122	A677	Set of 4	15.00	15.00
a.		Souvenir sheet, #2119-2122	15.00	15.00

Greek Flag and Trophy — A678

2004, July   Litho.   Perf. 14x13¾

2123	A678	47c multi + label	1.60	1.60
a.		Sheet of 5 + 5 labels	8.25	—
b.		Sheet of 10 + 10 labels	16.50	—

No. 2123 was printed in sheets of 15 + 15 labels that could be personalized. The sheet sold for €15. Nos. 2123a and 2123b have labels that depict soccer players or emblems, which cannot be personalized. Nos. 2123a and 2123b exist with two different sets of labels, and the set of 4 sheets sold for €20.

2004 Summer
Olympics,
Athens — A679

Designs: 50c, Hall of Good Harvest, Temple of Heaven, Beijing. 65c, Parthenon, Athens.

2004, Aug. 9   Litho.   Perf. 14

2124-2125	A679	Set of 2	4.00	4.00
a.		Souvenir sheet, #2124-2125	4.00	4.00

See People's Republic of China Nos. 3376-3377.

Souvenir Sheet

Olymphilex 2004 Philatelic
Exhibition — A680

2004, Aug. 13   Perf. 13½x13¼

2126	A680	€6 multi	18.00	18.00

Nikos Syranidis and Thomas Bimis, Synchronized Diving Gold Medalists A681

Leonidas Sampanis, Disqualified Bronze Medalist in 62 Kilogram Weight Lifting — A682

Ilias Iliadis, Judo Gold Medalist A683

Sofia Bekatorou and Emilia Tsoulfa, Women's 470 Sailing Gold Medalists A684

Pyrros Dimas, 85 Kilogram Weight Lifting Bronze Medalist A685

Dimosthenis Tampakos, Rings Gold Medalist A686

Anastasia Kelesidou, Women's Discus Silver Medalist A687

Vasilis Polymeros and Nikos Skiathitis, Lightweight Double Sculls Bronze Medalists A688

Athanasia Tzoumeleka, Women's 20 Kilometer Walk Gold Medalist A689

Chrysopigi Devezi, Women's Triple Jump Silver Medalist A690

Fani Chalkia, Women's 400-Meter Hurdles Gold Medalist A691

Nikos Kaklamanakis, Men's Mistral Sailing Silver Medalist A692

Artiom Kiouregian, 55 Kilogram Greco-Roman Wrestling Bronze Medalist A693

Women's Water Polo Team, Silver Medalist A694

Mirela Maniani, Women's Javelin Bronze Medalist A695

Elisavet Mystakidou, Women's 67 Kilogram Taekwondo Silver Medalist A696

Alexandros Nikolaidis, Men's 80 Kilogram Taekwondo Silver Medalist A697

Digitally Printed

2004, Aug.   Perf. 13¼

2127	A681	65c multi	1.90	1.90
2128	A682	65c multi	19.00	19.00
2129	A683	65c multi	1.90	1.90
2130	A684	65c multi	1.90	1.90
2131	A685	65c multi	1.90	1.90
2132	A686	65c multi	1.90	1.90
2133	A687	65c multi	1.90	1.90
2134	A688	65c multi	1.90	1.90
2135	A689	65c multi	1.90	1.90
2136	A690	65c multi	1.90	1.90
2137	A691	65c multi	1.90	1.90
2138	A692	65c multi	1.90	1.90
2139	A693	65c multi	1.90	1.90
2140	A694	65c multi	1.90	1.90
2141	A695	65c multi	1.90	1.90
2142	A696	65c multi	1.90	1.90
2143	A697	65c multi	1.90	1.90
		Nos. 2127-2143 (17)	49.40	49.40

Litho.

2144	A681	65c multi	1.90	1.90
2145	A682	65c multi	15.00	15.00
2146	A683	65c multi	1.90	1.90
2147	A684	65c multi	1.90	1.90
2148	A685	65c multi	1.90	1.90
2149	A686	65c multi	1.90	1.90
2150	A687	65c multi	1.90	1.90
2151	A688	65c multi	1.90	1.90
2152	A689	65c multi	1.90	1.90
2153	A690	65c multi	1.90	1.90
2154	A691	65c multi	1.90	1.90
2155	A692	65c multi	1.90	1.90
2156	A693	65c multi	1.90	1.90
2157	A694	65c multi	1.90	1.90
2158	A695	65c multi	1.90	1.90
2159	A696	65c multi	1.90	1.90
2160	A697	65c multi	1.90	1.90
a.		Souvenir sheet, #2144, 2146-2160	30.00	30.00
		Nos. 2144-2160 (17)	45.40	45.40

Issued: Nos. 2127-2128, 8/17; No. 2129, 8/18; Nos. 2130-2131, 8/22; Nos. 2132-2134, 8/23; Nos. 2135-2136, 8/24; Nos. 2137-2139, 8/26; No. 2140, 8/27; No. 2141, 8/28; No. 2142, 8/29; No. 2143, 8/30. Nos. 2144-2160 were to have been issued within days of the digitally printed stamp with the same design. The digitally printed stamps have almost illegible lettering above the Olympic rings at upper right, and fuzzy, indistinct details in the emblem above this lettering. These details are clearer and more readable on the lithographed stamps.

Nos. 2128 and 2145 were withdrawn from circulation after the athlete shown was stripped of his medal after failing a drug test.

2004
Paralympics,
Athens — A698

Designs: 20c, Horses and riders. 49c, Handicapped runner. €2, Wheelchair basketball. €2.24, Archer in wheelchair.

2004, Sept. 22   Litho.

2161-2164	A698	Set of 4	12.50	12.50

Island Views — A699

2004, Dec. 27   Perf. 14x13¾

2165	A699	2c Santorini	.20	.20
a.		Perf. 13¼ horiz.	.20	.20
2166	A699	3c Karpathos	.20	.20
a.		Perf. 13¼ horiz.	.20	.20
2167	A699	5c Crete-Vai	.20	.20
a.		Perf. 13¼ horiz.	.20	.20
2168	A699	10c Mykonos	.30	.30
a.		Perf. 13¼ horiz.	.30	.30
2169	A699	49c Canea	1.50	1.50
a.		Perf. 13¼ horiz.	1.50	1.50
2170	A699	50c Castellorizo	1.50	1.50
a.		Perf. 13¼ horiz.	1.50	1.50
2171	A699	€1 Astipalaia	3.00	3.00
a.		Perf. 13¼ horiz.	3.00	3.00
2172	A699	€2 Serifos	6.00	6.00
a.		Perf. 13¼ horiz.	6.00	6.00
2173	A699	€2.24 Melos	6.75	6.75
a.		Perf. 13¼ horiz.	6.75	6.75
2174	A699	€4 Skiathos	12.00	12.00
a.		Perf. 13¼ horiz.	12.00	12.00
		Nos. 2165-2174 (10)	31.65	31.65

Jewelry
A700

Designs: 1c, Necklace, 730 B.C. 15c, Snake-shaped bracelet, 2nd-3rd cent. B.C., vert. 30c, Necklace, 5th cent. 49c, Crown, 2nd cent. €4, Earring, 8th cent. B.C., vert.

Perf. 13¾x13¼, 13¼x13¾

2005, Feb. 25

2175-2179	A700	Set of 5	15.00	15.00

State Laboratory, 75th Anniv. — A701   European Diabetes Association, 41st Meeting — A702

European Society for Cardiovascular Surgery, 54th Congress — A703

I. Kondilakis, First President of Athens Journalists Union — A704

Year of Economic Competitiveness — A705

Greek Mastological Society, 25th Anniv. — A706

Angel, by Alekos Kontopoulos — A707

2005, Apr. 5   *Perf. 13¼x13, 13x13¼*

2180	A701	1c multi	.20	.20
2181	A702	4c multi	.20	.20
2182	A703	5c multi	.20	.20
2183	A704	40c multi	1.25	1.25
2184	A705	49c multi	1.50	1.50
2185	A706	€1.40 multi	4.25	4.25
2186	A707	€3.50 multi	10.50	10.50
	Nos. 2180-2186 (7)		18.10	18.10

Flowers — A708

Designs: 20c, Gladiolus illyricus. 40c, Crocus sieberi. 49c, Narcissus tazetta. €1.40, Rhododendron luteum. €3, Tulipa boeotica.

2005, Apr. 5   *Perf. 13¼x13¾*

2187-2191	A708	Set of 5	16.00	16.00

Europa — A709

2005, May 19   *Perf. 14¼x13¾*

2192	A709	Horiz. pair	9.00	9.00
a.		65c Finished dish	2.00	2.00
b.		€2.35 Ingredients	7.00	7.00
c.		Horiz. pair, perf. 13¼ vert.	9.00	9.00
d.		As "a," perf. 13¼ vert.	2.00	2.00
e.		As "b," perf. 13¼ vert.	7.00	7.00
f.		Booklet pane, 2 #2192c	18.00	—
		Complete booklet, #2192f	18.00	

Wine Grapes A710

Designs: 20c, Agiorgitiko grapes and grape pickers, Peloponnisos. 49c, Assyrtiko grapes, Santorini. 65c, Xinomavro grapes and coin, Macedonia. €2.24, Robolla grapes, Cephalonia. €2.40, Moschofilero, Peloponnisos.

2005, May 19   *Perf. 13¾x14*

2193-2197	A710	Set of 5	18.00	18.00

Blackboard A711

Girl Reading — A712

Envelope A713

Stylized People — A714

Grid — A715

Globe and Stylized Stamp — A716

Flowers — A717

Church — A718

2005, July 15   *Perf. 14x13¾*

2198	A711	49c multi	1.50	1.50
a.		#2198 + label	2.50	2.50
2199	A712	49c multi	1.50	1.50
a.		#2199 + label	2.50	2.50
2200	A713	49c multi	1.50	1.50
2201	A714	49c multi	1.50	1.50
a.		#2201 + label	2.50	2.50
2202	A715	49c multi	1.50	1.50
a.		#2202 + label	2.50	2.50
2203	A716	49c multi	1.50	1.50
2204	A717	49c multi	1.50	1.50
a.		#2204 + label	2.50	2.50
2205	A718	65c multi	1.90	1.90
a.		#2205 + label	3.25	3.25
	Nos. 2198-2205 (8)		12.40	12.40

Nos. 2198a and 2199a were printed in sheets of 10 + 10 labels that sold for €10. Nos. 2201a, 2202a and 2204a were printed in sheets of 15 + 15 labels that sold for €15. No. 2205a was printed in sheets of 10 + 10 labels that sold for €13. Labels could be personalized. Two additional personalized stamps exist in this set. The editors would like to examine any examples.

Drawing by Fokion Dimitriadis A719

Drawing by Archelaos A720

Drawing by Themos Anninos — A721

Drawing by Dimitris Galanis — A722

Drawing by Kostas Mitropoulos A723

Unattributed Odyssey Scene — A724

2005, Sept. 16   *Perf. 13¼x13¾*

2206	A719	15c multi	.45	.45
2207	A720	20c multi	.60	.60
2208	A721	30c multi	.90	.90
2209	A722	50c multi	1.50	1.50

2210	A723	65c multi	1.90	1.90
2211	A724	€4 multi	12.00	12.00
	Nos. 2206-2211 (6)		17.35	17.35

Booklet Panes of 1
Self-Adhesive

2212	A719	15c multi	.45	.45
2213	A720	20c multi	.60	.60
2214	A721	30c multi	.90	.90
2215	A722	50c multi	1.50	1.50
2216	A723	65c multi	1.90	1.90
2217	A724	€4 multi	12.00	12.00
	Complete booklet, #2212-2217		17.50	
	Nos. 2212-2217 (6)		17.35	17.35

Greece, 2005 European Basketball Champions — A725

Basketball, net and: 30c, Players in game. 50c, Championship bowl. 65c, Fans. €3.55, Players celebrating.

2005, Oct. 7   Litho.   *Perf. 13x13¼*

2218-2221	A725	Set of 4	15.00	15.00
2221a		Souvenir sheet, #2218-2221	15.00	15.00

Automobiles — A726

Designs: 1c, Mini Cooper. 30c, Fiat 500. 50c, Citroen 2CV. €2.25, Volkswagen Beetle. €2.85, Ford Model T.

2005, Nov. 4   *Perf. 13x13¼*

2222-2226	A726	Set of 5	17.50	17.50
2226a		As #2226, without inscription "Ford Model T"	10.00	10.00
2226b		Booklet pane, #2222-2225, 2226a	20.00	—
		Complete booklet, #2226b	20.00	

Panathinaikos Soccer Team Emblem — A727

Panionios Soccer Team Emblem — A728

Iraklis Soccer Team Emblem — A729

PAOK Soccer Team Emblem — A730

Panellinios Sports Club Emblem — A731

Designs: 30c, Ethnikos Sports Club emblem. €4, Omilos Ereton emblem.

2005, Nov. 30 Litho.   Perf. 14x13¾

2227	A727	30c multi	.90	.90
2228	A727	50c multi	1.50	1.50
a.		#2228 + label	2.40	2.40
2229	A728	50c multi	1.50	1.50
a.		#2229 + label	2.40	2.40
2230	A729	50c multi	1.50	1.50
a.		#2230 + label	2.40	2.40
2231	A730	65c multi	1.90	1.90
a.		#2231 + label	3.25	3.25
2232	A731	65c multi	1.90	1.90
a.		#2232 + label	3.25	3.25
2233	A727	€4 multi	12.00	12.00
		Nos. 2227-2233 (7)	21.20	21.20

Nos. 2228a, 2229a and 2230a were printed in sheets of 10 + 10 labels that sold for €10. Nos. 2231a and 2232a were printed in sheets of 10 + 10 labels that sold for €13. Labels could be personalized.

Christmas
A732

Icons: 1c, Hodeghetria Virgin. 20c, Kardiotissa Virgin. 70c, Glykophiloussa Virgin. €3.20, Virgin with Symbols of the Passion.

Litho. With Foil Application

2005, Dec. 20   Perf. 13¾

2234-2237	A732	Set of 4	12.50	12.50

Souvenir Sheet

Europa Stamps, 50th Anniv. — A733

2006, Jan. 10 Litho.   Perf. 13x13¼

2238	A733	Sheet of 2	12.00	12.00
a.		€1.50 Greece #1255	4.50	4.50
b.		€2.50 Greece #1459	7.50	7.50

Patras, 2006 European Cultural Capital
A734

Designs: 1c, Drama masks. 15c, Buildings, sailboat, lighthouse. 20c, Child. 50c, Carnival dragon and clown. 65c, Emblem, vert. €2.25, Jars, containers and boxes. €2.30, Icon, vert.

2006, Feb. 28   Perf. 13x13¼, 13¼x13

2239-2245	A734	Set of 7	18.00	18.00

Carnival Dragon and Clown — A734a

Emblem — A734b

2006, Feb. 28 Litho.   Perf. 14x13¾

2245A	A734a	50c multi + label	2.40	2.40
2245B	A734b	65c multi + label	3.25	3.25

Patras, 2006 European Cultural Capital. Nos. 2245A and 2245B were issued in sheets of 10 stamps and 10 labels that could be personalized. Sheets of No. 2245A sold for €10; No. 2245B for €13.

Items in Greek Museums
A735

Designs: 5c, Kouros of Anavissos, sculpture, 530 B.C., Natl. Archaeological Museum. 20c, Seated figure, 2800-2300 B.C., Museum of Cycladic Art. 50c, Spiral (28x28mm). 65c, Pediment from Parthenon, Acropolis Museum, horiz. €1.40, Greco-Roman portrait of an Egyptian, 4th cent. €2.25, Concert of the Angels, by El Greco, Natl. Art Gallery, horiz.

Litho with Foil Application, Litho. (50c)

2006, Apr. 7   Perf. 14x13¾, 13¾x14

2246-2251	A735	Set of 6	15.00	15.00
2248a		#2248 + label	2.50	2.50

No. 2248a was printed in sheets of 10 + 10 labels that sold for €10. Labels could be personalized.

Pediment From Parthenon — A735a

2006, Apr. 7 Litho.   Perf. 14x13¾

2251A	A735a	65c multi + label	3.25	3.25

No. 2251A was printed in sheets of 10 + 10 labels that sold for €13. Labels could be personalized.

Souvenir Sheets

Stamps Issued for 1906 Interim Olympic Games — A736

No. 2252: a, 20c, #187. b, 30c, #191. c, 50c, #188. d, €2, #192.
No. 2253: a, 50c, #189. b, 65c, #194. c, 85c, #197. d, €1, #190.

2006, Apr. 7 Litho.   Perf. 13x13¼
Sheets of 4, #a-d

2252-2253	A736	Set of 2	18.00	18.00

Europa — A737

2006, May 15   Perf. 13¾x14¼

2254	A737	Horiz. pair	11.00	11.00
a.		65c Rope and moon	1.90	1.90
b.		€3 Rope and sun	9.00	9.00
c.		Horiz. pair, perf. 13¼ vert.	11.00	11.00
d.		As "a," perf. 13¼ vert.	1.90	1.90
e.		As "b," perf. 13¼ vert.	9.00	9.00
f.		Booklet pane, 2 #2254c	22.50	
		Complete booklet, #2254f	22.50	

State General Archives — A738

Admission to European Union, 25th Anniv. — A739

2006 Eurovision Song Contest, Athens — A740

Olive and Olive Oil Year — A741

Tinia, Etruscan Sky God — A742

Greek Participation in 2005-06 UN Security Council — A743

2006, May 15   Perf. 14x13¾

2255	A738	15c multi	.45	.45
2256	A739	20c multi	.60	.60
2257	A740	50c multi	1.50	1.50
a.		#2257 + label	2.60	2.60
2258	A741	65c multi	1.90	1.90
a.		#2258 + label	3.50	3.50
2259	A742	€1.40 multi	4.25	4.25
2260	A743	€3 multi	9.00	9.00
		Nos. 2255-2260 (6)	17.70	17.70

No. 2257a was printed in sheets of 10 + 10 labels that sold for €10. No. 2258a was printed in sheets of 10 + 10 labels that sold for €13. Labels could be personalized.

Island Views
A744

2006, June 16 Litho.   Perf. 14¼x14

2261	A744	1c Lesbos	.20	.20
a.		Perf. 13¼ vert.	.20	.20
2262	A744	3c Hydra	.20	.20
a.		Perf. 13¼ vert.	.20	.20
2263	A744	10c Sifnos	.30	.30
a.		Perf. 13¼ vert.	.30	.30
2264	A744	20c Levkas	.60	.60
a.		Perf. 13¼ vert.	.60	.60
2265	A744	40c Samothrace	1.25	1.25
a.		Perf. 13¼ vert.	1.25	1.25
2266	A744	50c Syros	1.50	1.50
a.		Perf. 13¼ vert.	1.50	1.50
2267	A744	65c Rhodes	1.90	1.90
a.		Perf. 13¼ vert.	1.90	1.90
2268	A744	85c Cephalonia	2.50	2.50
a.		Perf. 13¼ vert.	2.50	2.50
2269	A744	€2.25 Corfu	6.75	6.75
a.		Perf. 13¼ vert.	6.75	6.75
2270	A744	€5 Naxos	15.00	15.00
a.		Perf. 13¼ vert.	15.00	15.00
		Nos. 2261-2270 (10)	30.20	30.20

Syros — A744a

2006, June 16 Litho.   Perf. 14x13¾

2270B	A744a	50c multi + label	2.60	2.60

No. 2270B was printed in sheets of 10 + 10 labels that could be personalized. An additional personalized stamp was issued in this set. The editors would like to examine any example.

Ancient Greek Technology
A745

Designs: 3c, Trireme "Olympias." 5c, Odometer, by Hero of Alexandria. 50c, Piston water pump, vert. 65c, Antikythera Mechanism, vert. €3.80, Automatic temple gates, by Hero of Alexandria, vert.

Litho. With Foil Application
Perf. 13¾x13¼, 13¼x13¾

2006, Sept. 14

2271-2275	A745	Set of 5	15.00	15.00

Souvenir Sheet

Second Place Finish of Greek Team at 2006 World Basketball Championships — A746

Litho. With Foil Application

2006, Oct. 16   Perf. 13¼

2276	A746	Sheet of 3	17.00	17.00
a.		50c Silver medal	1.50	1.50
b.		€2 Team	6.00	6.00
c.		€3 Team, medal ribbon	9.00	9.00

Soccer Team Emblems A747

Designs: 2c, Apollon Kalamaria. 3c, Atromitos Athinon. 52c, Aris Thessaloniki. €2.27, Ethnikos Piraeus. €3.20, Apollon Smyrnis.

2006, Nov. 29   Litho.   Perf. 14x13¾
2277-2281 A747   Set of 5   18.00 18.00
2279a   #2279 + label   2.75 2.75

No. 2279a was printed in sheets of 10 + 10 labels that sold for €10. Labels could be personalized.

Items in Toys, Games and Childhood Section of Benaki Museum A748

Designs: 5c, Doll, chest and clothing from France, c. 1905. 15c, Wooden airplanes, c. 1940. 30c, Dolls made by Skonouchi Karopoulos, c. 1925. 40c, Horses on wheels made by Anestis Romeopoulos, c. 1920. 52c, Dominos, toy cat, duck on wheels. 72c, Parachutist, c. 1950, vert. €2.27, Airplane carousel, 1950s, vert. €4, Puppet theater of the Resistance, 1941-45, vert.

Perf. 13¾x13¼, 13¼x13¾
2006, Dec. 22
2282-2289 A748   Set of 8   25.00 25.00

Faces — A749

Globe — A750

Crescents A751

Artemis — A752

Ring Around Earth — A753

Parthenon A754

Phrasikleia Kore — A755

2007, Mar. 12   Litho.   Perf. 14x13¾
2290 A749 52c multi   1.40 1.40
a.   #2290 + label   2.75 2.75
2291 A750 52c multi   1.40 1.40
a.   #2291 + label   2.75 2.75
2292 A751 52c multi   1.40 1.40
a.   #2292 + label   2.75 2.75
2293 A752 52c multi   1.40 1.40
a.   #2293 + label   2.75 2.75
2294 A753 52c multi   1.40 1.40
a.   #2294 + label   2.75 2.75
2295 A754 65c multi   1.75 1.75
a.   #2295 + label   3.50 3.50
2296 A755 65c multi   1.75 1.75
a.   Miniature sheet, #2290-2296   10.50 10.50
b.   #2296 + label   3.50 3.50
Nos. 2290-2296 (7)   10.50 10.50

Nos. 2290a, 2292a amd 2293a were printed in sheets of 10 + 10 labels that sold for €10. Nos. 2291a and 2294a were printed in sheets of 15 + 15 labels that sold for €15. Nos. 2295a and 2296a were printed in sheets of 10 + 10 labels that sold for € 13. Labels could be personalized.

Kostis Palamas (1859-1943), Poet — A756

Greek Cultural Year in China A757

Symposium of Seven Cardiovascular Surgeons, Athens and Delphi — A758

2nd Union Network International World Postal Conference A759

Treaty of Rome, 50th Anniv. — A760

Georgios Kotzias (1918-77) A761

Rigas Velestinlis (1757-98), Poet — A762

Year of Innovation A763

State Legal Council, 125th Anniv. A764

Perf. 13¼x13¾, 13¾x13¼
2007, Apr. 25
2297 A756   2c multi   .20 .20
2298 A757   10c multi   .30 .30
2299 A758   20c multi   .55 .55
2300 A759   52c multi   1.40 1.40
2301 A760   65c multi   1.75 1.75
2302 A761   85c multi   2.40 2.40
2303 A762   €1 multi   2.75 2.75
2304 A763 €2.27 multi   6.25 6.25
2305 A764   €3 multi   8.25 8.25
Nos. 2297-2305 (9)   23.85 23.85

Europa — A765

No. 2306: a, Scouting fleur-de-lis, dove's tail. b, Scouts, dove's head.

2007, May 25   Perf. 14¼x14
2306 A765 Horiz. pair   10.50 10.50
a.   65c multi   1.75 1.75
b.   €3.15 multi   8.75 8.75
c.   Horiz. pair, perf. 13¾ vert.   10.50 10.50
d.   As "a," perf. 13¾ vert.   1.75 1.75
e.   As "b," perf. 13¾ vert.   8.75 8.75
f.   Booklet pane, 2 #2306c   21.00 —
    Complete booklet, #2306f   21.00

Scouting, cent.

Signs of the Zodiac A766

Litho. With Foil Application
Perf. 13¾x13¼, 13¼x13¾
2007, May 25
2307 A766   2c Scorpio   .20 .20
2308 A766   3c Cancer   .20 .20
2309 A766   5c Capricorn   .20 .20
2310 A766   10c Taurus   .30 .30
2311 A766   20c Sagittarius, vert.   .55 .55
2312 A766   40c Leo, vert.   1.10 1.10
2313 A766   52c Virgo, vert.   1.40 1.40
2314 A766   65c Aries   1.75 1.75
2315 A766   85c Aquarius   2.40 2.40
2316 A766   €1 Libra   2.75 2.75
2317 A766 €2.27 Pisces   6.25 6.25
2318 A766 €2.80 Gemini   7.50 7.50
Nos. 2307-2318 (12)   24.60 24.60

Souvenir Sheet

Statues of Asclepius, Greek God of Medicine — A767

No. 2319: a, Statue from Museum of Ampurias, Spain. b, Statue from National Archaeological Museum, Athens.

2007, June 28   Litho.   Perf. 13¾
2319 A767   Sheet of 2   13.50 13.50
a.-b. €2.50 Either single   6.75 6.75
See Spain No. 3521.

Discovery of the Tomb of St. Cyril, 150th Anniv. A768

University of Macedonia, 50th Anniv. — A769

Konstantinos Tsatsos (1899-1987), Politician — A770

Litho. With Foil Application
2007, Sept. 28   Perf. 13¾x14
2320 A768   2c multi   .20 .20
Litho.
2321 A769   3c multi   .20 .20
Perf. 14x13¾
2322 A770   €4 multi   11.50 11.50
Nos. 2320-2322 (3)   11.90 11.90

Sports Team Emblems A771

Designs: 2c, Ergotelis Sports Club. 4c, OFI. 54c, Olympiacos C.F.P. €2.29, Doxa Dramas Sports Club. €5, Nautical Club of Mytilini.

2007, Nov. 2   Litho.   Perf. 14x13¾
2323-2327 A771   Set of 5   23.00 23.00
2325a   #2325 + label   3.00 3.00

No. 2325a was printed in sheets of 10 + 10 labels that sold for €10. Labels could be personalized.

Busts of Goddesses — A772

Designs: 54c, Bust of Aphrodite. €2.40, Bust of Goddess Anahit, Armenia.

2007, Dec. 14   **Perf. 14x14¼**
2328-2329   A772   Set of 2   8.75   8.75
   See Armenia Nos. 774-775.

Islands A773

2008, Feb. 27   **Litho.**   **Perf. 14¼x14**
2330	A773	2c Chios	.20	.20
a.		Perf. 13¼ vert.	.20	.20
2331	A773	5c Amorgos	.20	.20
a.		Perf. 13¼ vert.	.20	.20
2332	A773	10c Nísiros	.30	.30
a.		Perf. 13¼ vert.	.30	.30
2333	A773	20c Paxos	.60	.60
a.		Perf. 13¼ vert.	.60	.60
2334	A773	40c Leros	1.25	1.25
a.		Perf. 13¼ vert.	1.25	1.25
2335	A773	54c Kalymnos	1.75	1.75
a.		Perf. 13¼ vert.	1.75	1.75
2336	A773	67c Kos	2.10	2.10
a.		Perf. 13¼ vert.	2.10	2.10
2337	A773	€1 Simi	3.00	3.00
a.		Perf. 13¼ vert.	3.00	3.00
2338	A773	€2.29 Zákinthos	7.00	7.00
a.		Perf. 13¼ vert.	7.00	7.00
2339	A773	€4 Inousses	12.50	12.50
a.		Perf. 13¼ vert.	12.50	12.50
		Nos. 2330-2339 (10)	28.90	28.90

2008 Summer Olympics, Beijing — A774

Designs: 3c, Discus thrower. 35c, Lighting of Olympic flame. No. 2342, 67c, Torch bearer. No. 2343, 67c, Three cyclists, horiz.

2008, Mar. 14   **Perf. 13½x13, 13x13½**
2340-2343   A774   Set of 4   5.50   5.50

Letter — A775

Numbers — A776

Heart — A777

Kites — A778

Pillar — A779

Greek Flag — A780

2008, Apr. 21   **Litho.**   **Perf. 14x13¾**
2344	A775	54c multi	1.75	1.75
2345	A776	54c multi	1.75	1.75
2346	A777	54c multi	1.75	1.75
2347	A778	54c multi	1.75	1.75
2348	A779	67c multi	2.10	2.10
2349	A780	67c multi	2.10	2.10
a.		Miniature sheet, #2044-2049	11.50	11.50
		Nos. 2344-2349 (6)	11.20	11.20

Europa — A781

No. 2350: a, Inkwell, pen and papers. b, Fountain pen and papers.
Illustration reduced.

2008, May 26   **Perf. 14¼x14**
2350	A781	Horiz. pair	12.50	12.50
a.		67c multi	2.25	2.25
b.		€3.17 multi	10.00	10.00
c.		Horiz. pair, perf. 13¾ vert.	12.50	12.50
d.		As "a," perf. 13¾ vert.	2.25	2.25
e.		As "b," perf. 13¾ vert.	10.00	10.00
f.		Booklet pane, 2 #2350c	25.00	—
		Complete booklet, #2350f	25.00	

Anniversaries A782

Curved lines and: 3c, Emblem of Hellenic Post. 5c, Posthorn, Greek men. 10c, Ioannis Kapodistrias (1776-1831), provisional president of Greece. 57c, M. Karagatsis (1908-60), writer. 70c, Fish. €1.85, Emblem of National Hellenic Research Foundation. €3, Emblem of National Council of Women.

2008, June 20   **Perf. 13¼x13¾**
2351-2357   A782   Set of 7   20.00   20.00
   Hellenic Post, 180th anniv. (#2351-2352); Inauguration of Kapodistrias, 180th anniv. (#2353); Intl. Year of Planet Earth (#2355); National Hellenic Research Foundation, 50th anniv. (#2356), National Council of Women, cent. (#2357).

Greek Products — A783

Designs: 3c, Feta cheese and tomatoes. 5c, Mastic. 20c, Olive, bottle of olive oil, horiz. 57c, Bottle of ouzo, marine life and boat. €1, Pistachio nuts. €4, Bees, rose, jar of honey.

    Perf. 13¼x13¾, 13¾x13¼
2008, Sept. 19
2358-2363   A783   Set of 6   16.50   16.50

Sports Team Emblems A784

Designs: 40c, Diagoras Rhodos Sports Club. 57c, A.E.K. soccer team. 70c, Asteras Tripolis soccer team. €2, Panserraoikos soccer team. €3, Kerkiraikos Sports Club.

2008, Oct. 20   **Perf. 14x13¾**
2364-2368   A784   Set of 5   17.00   17.00

Fairy Tales, Fables and Children's Literature A785

Designs: 10c, The Mermaid and Alexander the Great. 57c, Little Red Riding Hood. €1, The Fairies. €1.85, The Little Match Girl. €3, Arion and the Lyre.

2008, Dec. 16   **Perf. 13¾x14**
2369-2373   A785   Set of 5   18.00   18.00

Actors and Actresses A786

Designs: 1c, Manos Katrakis (1908-84). 20c, Dinos Iliopoulos (1915-2001). 35c, Elli Lambeti (1926-83). 40c, Alekos Alexandrakis (1928-2005). 50c, Aliki Vougioklaki (1934-96). 57c, Jenny Karezi (1932-92). €1, Dimitris Horn (1921-98). €2.42, Nikos Kourkoulos (1934-2007). €3.50, Thanos Kotsopoulos (1911-94).

2009, Feb. 9   **Litho.**   **Perf. 13¾x13¼**
2374-2382	A786	Set of 9	23.00	23.00
2382a		Miniature sheet of 9, #2374-2382	23.00	23.00

Souvenir Sheet

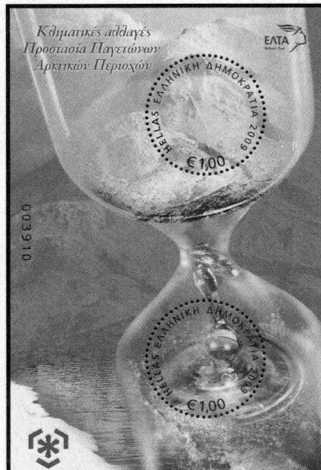

Preservation of Polar Regions and Glaciers — A787

No. 2383: a, Snow-covered mountain. b, Droplet of water.

2009, Mar. 3   **Perf.**
2383   A787   €1 Sheet of 2, #a-b   5.75   5.75
   No. 2383 contains two 30mm diameter stamps.

Sivitanidios School, 80th Anniv. A788

University of Piraeus, 70th Anniv. — A789

Natl. Archaeological Museum, 180th Anniv. — A790

Greek Presidency of UPU Postal Operations Council A791

Eye, Braille Script, Hands Touching Braille Book A792

Introduction of Euro, 10th Anniv. A793

Lord Byron (1788-1824), Poet — A794

Natl. Real Estate Registry A795

Litho., Litho. With Foil Application (10c, 50c), Litho. & Embossed (57c)
    Perf. 13¾x13¼, 13¼x13¾
2009, Mar. 30
2384	A788	5c multi	.20	.20
2385	A789	10c multi	.30	.30
2386	A790	20c multi	.60	.60
2387	A791	50c multi	1.50	1.50
2388	A792	57c multi	1.75	1.75

2389	A793	70c multi	2.10 2.10
2390	A794	€2.42 multi	7.25 7.25
2391	A795	€3 multi	9.00 9.00
		Nos. 2384-2391 (8)	22.70 22.70

Louis Braille (1809-52), educator of the blind (#2388), Hellenophile and Intl. Solidarity Day (#2390).

Europa — A796

No. 2392: a, Pulsar diagram. b, Aristarchos Telescope.
Illustration reduced.

2009, May 11   Litho.   *Perf. 14¾x14*
2392	A796	Horiz. pair	11.00 11.00
a.		70c multi	2.00 2.00
b.		€3.20 multi	9.00 9.00
c.		Horiz. pair, perf. 13¾ vert.	11.00 11.00
d.		As "a," perf. 13¾ vert.	2.00 2.00
e.		As "b," perf. 13¾ vert.	9.00 9.00
f.		Booklet pane, 2 #2392c	22.00 —
		Complete booklet, #2392f	22.00

Intl. Year of Astronomy.

UNESCO World Heritage Sites A797

Designs: No. 2393, 57c, Acropolis (denomination at LL). No. 2394, 57c, Meteora (denomination at UR). No. 2395, 70c, Delphi (denomination at UR). No. 2396, 70c, Mycenae (denomination at LL). €2, Mystras. €3, Delos.

Litho. With Foil Application
2009, June 20   *Perf. 13¾x14*
2393-2398	A797	Set of 6	21.00 21.00
2398a		Miniature sheet of 6, #2393-2398	21.00 21.00

Lighthouses A798

Designs: 1c, Didimi Islet Lighthouse. 57c, Tourlitis Lighthouse. 70c, Chania Lighthouse. €1, Korakas Paros Lighthouse, horiz. €4.20, Strongyli Lighthouse, horiz.

Litho. With Foil Application
**   *Perf. 13¼x13¾, 13¾x13¼***
2009, Aug. 21
2399-2403	A798	Set of 5	19.00 19.00
2403a		Souvenir sheet, #2399-2403	19.00 19.00

Greek Mythology A799

Designs: 1c, Theseus against the Minotaur. 5c, Heracles and Triton. 57c, Odysseus and the Sirens, vert. 70c, Talos and the Dioskuroi. €5, Vellerofontis riding Pegasus, vert.

**   *Perf. 13¾x14, 14x13¾***
2009, Oct. 20   Litho.
2404-2408	A799	Set of 5	19.00 19.00

Convention on Rights of the Child, 20th Anniv. — A800

Designs: 20c, Hands of adult and child. 58c, Child standing against wall, horiz. 72c, Clasped hands of children, horiz. €1, Child looking through barred window. €4, Child in darkness.

**   *Perf. 13¼x13, 13x13¼***
2009, Dec. 7   Litho.
2409-2413	A800	Set of 5	19.00 19.00

Souvenir Sheets

Medals For Greek National Basketball Teams — A801

Designs: No. 2414, €2, Gold medal for men's under-20 team at 2009 European Basketball Championships. No. 2415, €2, Silver medal for men's under-19 team at 2009 World Basketball Championships. No. 2416, €2, Bronze medal for men's team at 2009 European Basketball Championships.

Litho. & Embossed With Foil Application
2009, Dec. 15   *Perf. 13x13¼*
2414-2416	A801	Set of 3	17.50 17.50

20th Century Paintings by Greeks — A802

Designs: 1c, Stuffed Head, by Giannis Gaitis. 5c, Orpheus, Hermes and Eurydice, by Nikos Engonopoulos. 50c, Erotic, by Yannis Moralis. 58c, Sailor Sitting at the Table, Pink Background, by Yannis Tsarouchis. €2.43, Wattle Fences, by Nikos Hadjikyriakos-Ghika. €3, The Drawing, by Diamantis Diamantopoulos.

2010, Feb. 11   Litho.   *Perf. 14x13¾*
2417-2422	A802	Set of 6	18.00 18.00
2422a		Sheet of 6, #2417-2422	18.00 18.00

Renewable Energy Development A803

Designs: 1c, Solar energy. 40c, Water energy. 58c, Wind energy, horiz. 72c, Self-contained man. €2.43, Wave energy. €2.50, Bioenergy.

**   *Perf. 13¼x13¾, 13¾x13¼***
2010, Apr. 26
2423-2428	A803	Set of 6	18.00 18.00

Europa — A804

No. 2429: a, Boy in balloon, Puss in Boots. b, Girl on books.

2008, May 26   Litho.   *Perf. 14¼x14*
2429	A804	Horiz. pair	9.50 9.50
a.		72c multi	1.75 1.75
b.		€3.22 multi	7.75 7.75
c.		Horiz. pair, perf. 13¾ vert.	9.50 9.50
d.		As "a," perf. 13¾ vert.	1.75 1.75
e.		As "b," perf. 13¾ vert.	7.75 7.75
f.		Booklet pane, 2 #2429c	19.00 —
		Complete booklet, #2429f	19.00

New Acropolis Museum — A805

Designs: 5c, Peplos kore. 58c, Parthenon gallery, horiz. 72c, Fragment of Parthenon frieze, horiz. €1, Entrance to new museum, horiz. €4, Marble sculpture of dog, horiz.

**   *Perf. 13¼x13¾, 13¾x13¼***
2010, June 21   Litho.
2430-2434	A805	Set of 5	16.00 16.00
2434a		Souvenir sheet, #2430-2434	16.00 16.00

Battle of Marathon, 2500th Anniv. A806

Designs: 50c, Athenian and Persian fighting. 58c, Phalanx marching into battle. 72c, Battle scene. €3, Bronze Corinthian helmet.

Litho. With Foil Application
2010, June 23   *Perf. 13¾x14*
2437-2440	A806	Set of 4	12.50 12.50

Popular Musicians A807

Designs: 10c, Vasilis Tsitsanis (1915-84). 20c, Giorgos Zampetas (1925-92). 58c, Stelios Kazantzidis (1931-2001). 72c, Grigoris Bithikotsis (1922-2005). €1, Vicky Moscholiou (1945-2005). €4.80, Sotiria Bellou (1921-97).

**   *Perf. 13¾x13¼***
2010, Sept. 16   Litho.
2441-2446	A807	Set of 6	21.00 21.00
2446a		Souvenir sheet, #2441-2446	21.00 21.00

Paper Boat — A808

Spiral Staircase — A809

2010, Oct. 14   *Perf. 14x13¾*
2447	A808	(58c) multi	1.75 1.75
a.		Perf. 12¾ vert.	1.75 1.75
2448	A809	(72c) multi	2.10 2.10
a.		Perf. 12¾ vert.	2.10 2.10

Islands A810

2010, Oct. 14   *Perf. 14¼x14*
2449	A810	2c Limnos	.20 .20
a.		Perf. 12¾ vert.	.20 .20
2450	A810	5c Paros	.20 .20
a.		Perf. 12¾ vert.	.20 .20
2451	A810	20c Ithaki	.60 .60
a.		Perf. 12¾ vert.	.60 .60
2452	A810	40c Tinos	1.25 1.25
a.		Perf. 12¾ vert.	1.25 1.25
2453	A810	50c Skyros	1.40 1.40
a.		Perf. 12¾ vert.	1.40 1.40
2454	A810	€1 Evia-Chalkida	3.00 3.00
a.		Perf. 12¾ vert.	3.00 3.00
2455	A810	€2 Samos	5.75 5.75
a.		Perf. 12¾ vert.	5.75 5.75
2456	A810	€4 Kassos	11.50 11.50
a.		Perf. 12¾ vert.	11.50 11.50
		Nos. 2449-2456 (8)	23.90 23.90

Buildings A811

Designs: 20c, Municipal Theater of Piraeus. 58c, Benaki Museum. €2.43, National Theater. €2.50, National Gallery of Nafplio.

Litho. With Foil Application
2010, Nov. 16   *Perf. 13¾x14*
2457-2460	A811	Set of 4	15.50 15.50

Christmas — A812

Designs: 50c, Doves, holly leaves, stars. 58c, Angel with horn. €1, Ship with Christmas decorations. €3.50, Christmas tree, birds, holly leaves.

2010, Dec. 10   Litho.   *Perf. 13¾x14*
2461-2464	A812	Set of 4	15.00 15.00

SEMI-POSTAL STAMPS

Nos. 440-444 Surcharged in Blue

1944   Wmk. 252   *Perf. 12½*
B1	A106	100,000d on 15d	.40 .90
B2	A107	100,000d on 25d	.40 .90
B3	A108	100,000d on 50d	.40 .90

B4	A109	100,000d on 75d	.40	.90
B5	A110	100,000d on 100d	.40	.90

Nos. B1-B5,CB1-CB5 (10)   4.00   8.75
Set, never hinged   6.50

The proceeds aided victims of the Piraeus bombing, Jan. 11, 1944. The exceptionally high face value discouraged the use of these stamps.

Nos. 437-441 Surcharged in Blue

1944, July 20
50,000d + 450,000d

B11	A103	on 2d	.30	.65
B12	A104	on 5d	.30	.65
B13	A105	on 10d	.30	.65
B14	A106	on 15d	.30	.65
a.	Pair, one without surcharge		65.00	
B15	A107	on 25d	.30	.65

Nos. B11-B15,CB6-CB10 (10)   3.50   6.50
Set, never hinged   5.50

The surtax aided children's camps.

AIR POST STAMPS

Italy-Greece-Turkey-Rhodes Service

Flying Boat off Phaleron Bay — AP1

Flying Boat over Acropolis — AP2

Flying Boat over Map of Southern Europe — AP3

Flying Boat Seen through Colonnade — AP4

Perf. 11½

1926, Oct. 20   **Unwmk.**   **Litho.**

C1	AP1	2d multicolored	1.60	1.25
a.	Horiz. pair, imperf. vert.		725.00	
C2	AP2	3d multicolored	12.00	11.00
C3	AP3	5d multicolored	1.60	1.25
C4	AP4	10d multicolored	12.00	12.00

Nos. C1-C4 (4)   27.20   25.50
Set, never hinged   80.00

Graf Zeppelin Issue

Zeppelin over Acropolis AP5

1933, May 2   **Perf. 13½x12½**

C5	AP5	30d rose red	13.00	13.00
C6	AP5	100d deep blue	52.50	52.50
C7	AP5	120d dark brown	52.50	52.50

Nos. C5-C7 (3)   118.00   118.00
Set, never hinged   325.00

Propeller and Pilot's Head AP6

Temple of Apollo, Corinth AP7

Plane over Hermoupolis, Syros — AP8

Allegory of Flight
AP9   AP12

Map of Italy-Greece-Turkey-Rhodes Airmail Route — AP10

Head of Hermes and Airplane — AP11

1933, Oct. 10   **Engr.**   **Perf. 12**

C8	AP6	50 l green & org	.20	.20
C9	AP7	1d bl & brn org	.30	.25
C10	AP8	3d dk vio & org brn	.50	.50
C11	AP9	5d brn org & dk bl	7.25	4.50
C12	AP10	10d dp red & blk	1.50	1.40
C13	AP11	20d black & grn	7.25	4.00
C14	AP12	50d dp brn & dp bl	50.00	55.00

Nos. C8-C14 (7)   67.00   65.85
Set, never hinged   200.00

By error the 1d stamp is inscribed in the plural "Draxmai" instead of the singular "Draxmh." This stamp exists bisected, used as a 50 lepta denomination.

All values of this set exist imperforate but were not regularly issued.

For General Air Post Service

Airplane over Map of Greece — AP13

Airplane over Map of Icarian Sea — AP14

Airplane over Acropolis AP15

Perf. 13x13½, 13x12½, 13½x13, 12½x13

1933, Nov. 2

C15	AP13	50 l green	.20	.25
C16	AP13	1d red brown	.30	.55
C17	AP14	2d lt violet	.60	.85
C18	AP15	5d ultra	3.50	3.50
a.	Imperf., pair		650.00	550.00
b.	Horiz. pair, imperf. vert.		650.00	
C19	AP14	10d car rose	6.50	7.75
C20	AP13	25d dark blue	30.00	20.00
C21	AP15	50d dark brown	30.00	42.50
a.	Imperf., pair		775.00	650.00

Nos. C15-C21 (7)   71.10   75.40
Set, never hinged   225.00

Helios Driving the Sun Chariot AP16

Iris — AP17

Daedalus Preparing Icarus for Flying — AP18

Pallas Athene Holding Pegasus — AP19

Hermes AP20   Zeus Carrying off Ganymede AP21

Triptolemos, King of Eleusis AP22

Bellerophon and Pegasus — AP23

Phrixos and Helle on the Ram Flying over the Hellespont AP24

Perf. 13x12½, 12½x13

1935, Nov. 10   **Engr.**
Grayish Paper
Size: 34x23½mm, 23½x34mm

C22	AP16	1d deep red	1.50	1.50
C23	AP17	2d dull blue	1.50	1.50
C24	AP18	5d dk violet	17.50	4.00
C25	AP19	7d blue violet	25.00	7.25
C26	AP20	10d bister brown	5.00	5.00
C27	AP21	25d rose	6.00	5.75
C28	AP22	30d dark green	2.00	2.00
C29	AP23	50d violet	8.00	6.00
C30	AP24	100d brown	2.50	2.25

Nos. C22-C30 (9)   69.00   35.25
Set, never hinged   150.00

Re-engraved
1937-39
White Paper
Size: 34¼x24mm, 24x34¼mm

C31	AP16	1d red	.30	.25
C32	AP17	2d gray blue	.30	.25
C33	AP18	5d violet	.30	.25
C34	AP19	7d dp ultra	.30	.25
C35	AP20	10d brn org	2.40	3.50

Nos. C31-C35 (5)   3.60   4.50
Set, never hinged   7.00

Issued: #C35, 3/1/39; others 8/3/37.

Postage Due Stamp, 1913, Overprinted in Red

Serrate Roulette 13½
1938, Aug. 8   **Litho.**   **Unwmk.**

C36	D3	50 l violet brown	.20	.20
	Never hinged		.25	
a.	"O" for "P" in word at foot		30.00	30.00

Same Overprint on No. J79 in Red
1939, June 26   **Perf. 13½x12½**

C37	D3	50 l dark brown	.20	.20
	Never hinged		.25	

Meteora Monasteries, near Trikkala — AP25

Designs: 4d, Simon Peter Monastery. 6d, View of Santorin. 8d, Church of Pantanassa. 16d, Santorin view. 32d, Ponticonissi, Corfu. 45d, Acropolis, Athens. 55d, Erechtheum. 65d, Temple Nea Apteros. 100d, Temple of the Olympian Zeus, Athens.

Wmk. Crowns (252)
1940, Aug. 3   **Litho.**   **Perf. 12½**

C38	AP25	2d red org & blk	.85	1.25
C39	AP25	4d dk grn & blk	4.00	3.50
C40	AP25	6d lake & blk	7.25	6.50
C41	AP25	8d dk bl & blk	18.75	16.50
C42	AP25	16d rose vio & blk	30.00	25.00
C43	AP25	32d red org & blk	40.00	47.50
C44	AP25	45d dk grn & blk	52.50	47.50
C45	AP25	55d lake & blk	52.50	47.50
C46	AP25	65d dk bl & blk	52.50	47.50

C47 AP25 100d rose vio & blk 67.50 60.00
Nos. C38-C47 (10) 325.85 302.75
Set, never hinged 800.00

4th anniv. of the founding of the Greek Youth Organization. The stamps were good for postal duty on Aug. 3-5, 1940, only. They remained on sale until Feb. 3, 1941.
For overprints see Nos. N229-N238.

> **Catalogue values for unused stamps in this section, from this point to the end of the section, are for Never Hinged items.**

Postage Due Stamps Nos. J81 and J75 Surcharged in Red

1941-42　Unwmk.　Perf. 13x12½
C48 D3 1d on 2d lt red .20 .20
　a. Inverted surcharge 45.00

Serrate Roulette 13½
C49 D3 1d on 2d ver ('42) .20 .20
　a. Inverted surcharge 32.50
　b. Double surcharge 22.50

Nos. J83, J84, J86, J87 Overprinted in Red

1941-42　Perf. 13, 12½x13
C50 D3 5d gray bl ('42) .20 .20
　a. Inverted overprint 45.00
　b. Double overprint 32.50
　c. Pair, one without ovpt. 22.50
　d. Surcharge on back 22.50
　e. On No. J78 ('42) 140.00 160.00
C51 D3 10d gray grn .30 .30
　a. Inverted overprint 16.00
　b. Vert. pair, imperf. btwn. 325.00
C52 D3 25d lt red .85 .85
　a. Inverted overprint 110.00
C53 D3 50d orange 1.50 1.50
　Nos. C50-C53 (4) 2.85 2.85

Boreas, North Wind — AP35

Winds: 5d, Notus, South. 10d, Apeliotes, East. 20d, Lips, Southwest. 25d, Zephyrus, West. 50d, Kaikias, Northeast.

Wmk. 252
1942, Aug. 15　Litho.　Perf. 12½
C55 AP35 2d emerald .20 .20
C56 AP35 5d red org .20 .20
　a. Imperf., pair 325.00
　b. Double impression 55.00
C57 AP35 10d red brown .45 .45
C58 AP35 20d brt blue .50 .50
C59 AP35 25d dk red org .50 .50
C60 AP35 50d gray blk 2.00 2.00
　a. Double impression 110.00
　Nos. C55-C60 (6) 3.85 3.85

1943, Sept. 15
Winds: 10d, Apeliotes, East. 25d, Zephyrus, West. 50d, Kaikias, Northeast. 100d, Boreas, North. 200d, Eurus, Southeast. 400d, Skiron, Northwest.

C61 AP35 10d rose red .20 .20
C62 AP35 25d Prus green .20 .20
C63 AP35 50d violet blue .20 .20
C64 AP35 100d slate black .20 .20
C65 AP35 200d dull claret .20 .20
C66 AP35 400d steel blue .20 .20
　Nos. C61-C66 (6) 1.20 1.20

Double impressions exist of 10d and 400d. Value, each $30.
For surcharges see #472, 473, CB1-CB10.

Imperf., Pairs
C61a AP35 10d 110.00
C62a AP35 25d 110.00
C63a AP35 50d 110.00
C64a AP35 100d 110.00
C65a AP35 200d 110.00
C66a AP35 400d 110.00

Priest Blessing Troops on Summit of Mt. Grammos AP36

Torchbearer AP37

Designs: 1700d, Victory above Mt. Vitsi. 2700d, Battle Scene. 7000d, Victory leading infantry.

1952, Aug. 29　Engr.　Perf. 12x13½
C67 AP36 1000d deep blue 1.50 .30
C68 AP36 1700d dp blue grn 5.00 2.00
C69 AP36 2700d brown 15.00 6.00
C70 AP36 7000d olive green 45.00 15.00
　Nos. C67-C70 (4) 66.50 23.30

Greek army's struggle against communism.

1954, May 15　　　Perf. 13
Designs: 2400dr, Coin of Amphictyonic League. 4000dr, Pallas Athene.

C71 AP37 1200d dp orange 7.50 .35
C72 AP37 2400d dk green 37.50 2.50
C73 AP37 4000d dp ultra 65.00 3.50
　Nos. C71-C73 (3) 110.00 6.35

5th anniv. of the signing of the North Atlantic Treaty.

Piraeus AP38

Harbors: 15d, Salonika. 20d, Patras. 25d, Hermoupolis (Syra). 30d, Volos. 50d, Cavalla. 100d, Herakleion (Candia).

Perf. 13½x13
1958, July 1　Wmk. 252　Litho.
C74 AP38 10d multicolored 12.50 .25
C75 AP38 15d multicolored 1.75 .40
C76 AP38 20d multicolored 12.50 .25
C77 AP38 25d multicolored 2.00 .80
C78 AP38 30d multicolored 2.25 .80
C79 AP38 50d multicolored 8.00 .80
C80 AP38 100d multicolored 40.00 4.00
　Nos. C74-C80 (7) 79.00 7.30

AIR POST SEMI-POSTAL STAMPS

#C61-C65 Surcharged in Blue like #B1-B5

1944, June　Wmk. 252　Perf. 12½
CB1 AP35 100,000d on 10d .40 .85
CB2 AP35 100,000d on 25d .40 .85
CB3 AP35 100,000d on 50d .40 .85
　a. Inverted overprint 32.50
CB4 AP35 100,000d on 100d .40 .85
CB5 AP35 100,000d on 200d .40 .85
　Nos. CB1-CB5 (5) 2.00 4.25
　Set, never hinged 7.00

The exceptionally high face value discouraged the use of these stamps.
The proceeds aided victims of the Piraeus bombing, January 11, 1944.

#C61-C65 Surcharged in Blue like #B11-B15

1944, July
50,000d + 450,000d
CB6 AP35 on 10d .40 .65
CB7 AP35 on 25d .40 .65
CB8 AP35 on 50d .40 .65
CB9 AP35 on 100d .40 .65
CB10 AP35 on 200d .40 .65
　Nos. CB6-CB10 (5) 2.00 3.25
　Set, never hinged 8.00

The surtax aided children's camps. Surcharge exists inverted or double. Value, each $55.

POSTAGE DUE STAMPS

D1　　　　　　　D2

Perf. 9, 9½, and 10, 10½ and Compound
1875　　Litho.　　Unwmk.
J1 D1 1 l green & black 1.50 1.50
J2 D1 2 l green & black 1.50 1.50
J3 D1 5 l green & black 1.75 1.25
J4 D1 10 l green & black 1.75 1.25
J5 D1 20 l green & black 42.50 30.00
J6 D1 40 l green & black 8.25 5.50
J7 D1 60 l green & black 42.50 30.00
J8 D1 70 l green & black 8.25 5.50
J9 D1 80 l green & black 17.50 14.50
J10 D1 90 l green & black 11.00 11.00
J11 D1 1d green & black 12.00 11.00
J12 D1 2d green & black 13.00 11.00
　Nos. J1-J12 (12) 161.50 124.00

Imperforate and part perforated, double and inverted center varieties of Nos. J1-J12 are believed to be printers' waste.

Perf. 12, 13 and 10½x13
J13 D1 1 l green & black 1.60 1.60
J14 D1 2 l green & black 22.50 22.50
J15 D1 5 l green & black 2.75 2.75
J16 D1 10 l green & black 3.25 3.25
J17 D1 20 l green & black 40.00 27.50
J18 D1 40 l green & black 10.00 7.75
J19 D1 60 l green & black 42.50 27.50
J20 D1 70 l green & black 7.75 7.75
J21 D1 80 l green & black 12.00 12.00
J22 D1 90 l green & black 17.50 12.00
J23 D1 1d green & black 27.50 17.50
J24 D1 2d green & black 22.50 17.50
　Nos. J13-J24 (12) 209.85 159.60

Redrawn
"Lepton" or "Lepta" in Larger Greek Letters
1876　Perf. 9, 9½, and 10, 10½
J25 D2 1 l green & black 4.50 4.50
J26 D2 2 l dk grn & blk 6.00 5.75
J27 D2 5 l dk grn & blk 360.00 275.00
J28 D2 10 l green & black 3.00 2.10
J29 D2 20 l green & black 4.00 3.00
J30 D2 40 l green & black 32.50 25.00
J31 D2 60 l green & black 27.50 15.00
J32 D2 70 l green & black 22.50 25.00
J33 D2 80 l green & black 17.50 15.00
J34 D2 90 l green & black 17.50 16.00
J35 D2 100 l green & black 22.50 15.00
J36 D2 200 l green & black 22.50 15.00
　Nos. J25-J36 (12) 540.00 416.35

Perf. 11½ to 13
J37 D2 1 l yel grn & blk 1.75 .95
J38 D2 2 l yel grn & blk 1.75 .95
J39 D2 5 l yel grn & blk 4.75 1.25
J40 D2 10 l yel grn & blk 2.75 2.00
　a. Perf. 10-10½x11½-13 4.00
J41 D2 20 l yel grn & blk 2.75 2.00
J42 D2 40 l yel grn & blk 15.00 11.00
J43 D2 60 l yel grn & blk 9.50 9.50
J47 D2 100 l yel grn & blk 12.00 12.00
J48 D2 200 l yel grn & blk 13.50 11.00
　Nos. J37-J48 (9) 63.75 50.65

Footnote below #J12 applies also to #J25-J48.

D3

1902　Engr.　Wmk. 129　Perf. 13½
J49 D3 1 l chocolate .30 .25
J50 D3 2 l gray .30 .25
J51 D3 3 l orange .30 .25
J52 D3 5 l yel grn .30 .25
J53 D3 10 l scarlet .30 .25
J54 D3 20 l lilac .45 .25
J55 D3 25 l ultra 8.00 4.00
J56 D3 30 l dp vio .50 .30
J57 D3 40 l dk brn .60 .25
J58 D3 50 l red brn .60 .40
J59 D3 1d black 1.50 .90

Litho.
J60 D3 2d bronze 2.00 1.25
J61 D3 3d silver 3.00 3.00
J62 D3 5d gold 6.50 9.00
　Nos. J49-J62 (14) 24.65 20.85

See Nos. J63-J88, J90-J93. For overprints and surcharges see Nos. 383-385, J89, RA56, RA58-RA59, NJ1-NJ31.

Imperf., Pairs
J50a D3 2 l 90.00
J51a D3 3 l 90.00
J52a D3 5 l 90.00
J55a D3 25 l 150.00
J56a D3 30 l 150.00
J58a D3 50 l 150.00
J59a D3 1d 150.00

Serrate Roulette 13½
1913-26　　　　　　Unwmk.
J63 D3 1 l green .20 .20
J64 D3 2 l carmine .20 .20
J65 D3 3 l vermilion .20 .20
J66 D3 5 l green .20 .20
　a. Imperf., pair 150.00
　b. Double impression 60.00
　c. "o" for "p" in lowest word 5.00 5.00
J67 D3 10 l carmine .20 .20
J68 D3 20 l slate .20 .20
J69 D3 25 l ultra .20 .20
J70 D3 30 l carmine .20 .20
J71 D3 40 l indigo .20 .20
J72 D3 50 l vio brn .30 .25
　a. "o" for "p" in lowest word 25.00 20.00
J73 D3 80 l lil brn ('24) .40 .20
J74 D3 1d blue 8.00 1.25
　a. 1d ultramarine 12.00 5.00
J75 D3 2d vermilion 8.00 1.50
J76 D3 3d carmine 8.00 1.50
J77 D3 5d ultra 30.00 12.00
J78 D3 5d gray bl ('26) 8.00 4.00
　Nos. J63-J78 (16) 64.50 22.50

In 1922-23 and 1941-42 some postage due stamps were used for ordinary postage.
In 1916 Nos. J52, and J63 to J75 were surcharged for the Mount Athos District (see note after No. N166) but were never issued there. By error some of them were put in use as ordinary postage due stamps in Dec., 1924. In 1932 the balance of them was burned.

Type of 1902 Issue
Perf. 13, 13½x12½, 13½x13
1930　　　　　　　　Litho.
J79 D3 50 l dk brown .30 .30
J80 D3 1d lt blue .30 .30
J81 D3 2d lt red .30 .30
J82 D3 3d rose red 27.50 25.00
J83 D3 5d gray blue .30 .30
J84 D3 10d gray green .30 .30
J85 D3 15d red brown .30 .30
J86 D3 25d light red .70 .65
　Nos. J79-J86 (8) 30.00 27.45

Type of 1902 Issue
1935　Engr.　Perf. 12½x13
J87 D3 50d orange .30 .30
J88 D3 100d slate green .30 .30

No. J70 Surcharged with New Value in Black
1942
J89 D3 50 (l) on 30 l carmine 1.50 1.50

Type of 1902
1943　Wmk. 252　Litho.　Perf. 12½
J90 D3 10d red orange .20 .20
J91 D3 25d ultramarine .20 .20
J92 D3 100d black brown .20 .20
J93 D3 200d violet .20 .20
　Nos. J90-J93 (4) .80 .80

POSTAL TAX STAMPS

"The Tragedy of War" — PT1

Red Cross, Nurses, Wounded and Bearers PT1a

Serrate Roulette 13½

1914		**Litho.**		**Unwmk.**
RA1	PT1	2 l red ('18)	.30	.25
a.		2 l carmine	.35	.25
b.		Imperf., pair	200.00	
RA2	PT1	5 l blue	.50	.75
a.		Imperf., pair	250.00	

1915		**Serrate Roulette 13**	
RA2B	PT1a (5 l) dk bl & red	10.00	2.00

The tax was for the Red Cross.

Women's Patriotic League
Badge — PT1b

1915, Nov.			**Perf. 11½**
RA2C	PT1b (5 l) dk bl & car	1.25	1.00
d.	Horiz. pair, imperf. btwn.	55.00	

The tax was for the Greek Women's Patriotic League.

Nos. 165, 167, 170, 172-175
Surcharged in Black or Brown:

a   b

In type "b" the letters, especially those in the first line, are thinner than in type "a," making them appear taller.

Perf. 11½, 12½, 13½ and Compound

1917		**Engr.**		**Wmk. 129**
RA3	A11(a)	1 l on 1 l	1.50	1.50
a.		Double surcharge	7.00	
RA4	A11(a)	1 l on 1 l (Br)	22.50	22.50
RA5	A11(a)	1 l on 3 l	.30	.30
RA6	A11(b)	1 l on 3 l	.30	.30
a.		Triple surcharge	5.00	
b.		Dbl. surch., one invtd.	5.00	
c.		"K.M." for "K.II."	20.00	
RA7	A11(a)	1 l on 1 l	2.00	2.00
a.		Double surcharge	10.00	
b.		Dbl. surch., one invtd.	10.00	
c.		Inverted surcharge	12.00	
RA8	A11(a)	5 l on 20 l	.65	.65
a.		Double surcharge	12.00	
b.		Dbl. surch., one invtd.	12.00	
RA9	A11(b)	5 l on 40 l	.65	.65
a.		Imperf.		
RA10	A11(b)	5 l on 50 l	.65	.65
a.		Double surcharge	25.00	
b.		Dbl. surch., one invtd.	25.00	
RA11	A13(b)	5 l on 1d	2.25	2.25
a.		Imperf.		
b.		Inverted surcharge	50.00	
RA12	A11(a)	10 l on 30 l	.80	.80
a.		Imperf.		
b.		Double surcharge	20.00	
RA13	A11(a)	30 l on 30 l	.90	.90
a.		Double surcharge	20.00	
		Nos. RA3-RA13 (11)	32.50	32.50

Same Surcharge On Occupation
Stamps of 1912

Serrate Roulette 13½

1917		**Litho.**		**Unwmk.**
RA14	O2 (b)	5 l on 25 l pale bl	.55	.55
a.		Triple surch., one invtd.	15.00	
b.		Double surcharge	8.00	
RA15	O2 (b)	5 l on 40 l indigo	.55	.55
a.		Double surch., one invtd.	8.00	
b.		Double surcharge	8.00	
RA16	O1 (b)	5 l on 50 l dk bl	.55	.55
a.		Double surcharge	10.00	
b.		Inverted surcharge	10.00	
		Nos. RA14-RA16 (3)	1.65	1.65

There are many wrong font, omitted and misplaced letters and punctuation marks and similar varieties in the surcharges on Nos. RA3 to RA16.

Revenue Stamps Surcharged in Brown

"Victory"

1917				
RA17	R1	1 l on 10 l blue	.70	.70
RA18	R1	1 l on 80 l blue	.70	.70
RA19	R1	5 l on 10 l blue	15.00	20.00
RA20	R1	5 l on 60 l blue	4.00	4.00
a.		Perf. vert. through middle	6.00	10.00
RA21	R1	5 l on 10 l blue	3.00	3.00
a.		Perf. vert. through middle	8.00	6.00
b.		Inverted surcharge		
RA22	R1	10 l on 70 l blue	16.00	12.00
a.		Perf. vert. through middle	6.00	8.00
RA23	R1	10 l on 90 l blue	12.00	8.00
a.		Perf. vert. through middle	20.00	25.00
RA24	R1	20 l on 20 l blue	725.00	525.00
RA25	R1	20 l on 30 l blue	4.00	4.00
RA26	R1	20 l on 40 l blue	12.00	10.00
RA27	R1	20 l on 50 l blue	8.00	6.00
RA28	R1	20 l on 60 l blue	400.00	250.00
RA29	R1	20 l on 80 l blue	40.00	32.50
RA30	R1	20 l on 90 l blue	4.00	6.00
a.		Inverted surcharge	70.00	
		Nos. RA17-RA30 (14)	1,244.	881.90

No. RA19 is known only with vertical perforation through the middle.
Counterfeits exist of Nos. RA17-RA43, used.

Surcharged in
Brown or Black

RA31	R1	1 l on 50 l vio (Bk)	.80	1.25
RA32	R1	5 l on 10 l bl (Br)	.80	1.25
a.		Inverted surcharge	80.00	
b.		Left "5" invert.	80.00	
RA33	R1	5 l on 10 l vio (Br)	.80	1.25
RA34	R1	10 l on 50 l vio (Br)	5.50	10.00
RA35	R1	10 l on 50 l vio (Bk)	22.50	20.00
RA36	R1	20 l on 2d bl (Bk)	8.00	8.00
a.		Surcharged "20 lept. 30"	65.00	65.00
b.		Horiz. pair, imperf. btwn.		
		Nos. RA31-RA36 (6)	38.40	41.75

The "t," fourth Greek letter of the denomination in the surcharge ("Lept."), is normally omitted on Nos. RA31, RA34-RA36.

Corfu Issue

Surcharged in
Black

1917				
RA37	R1	1 l on 10 l blue	2.00	2.00
RA38	R1	5 l on 50 l blue	55.00	75.00
RA39	R1	10 l on 50 l blue	675.00	575.00
RA40	R1	20 l on 50 l blue	2,850.	1,075.

Surcharged in
Black

RA41	R1	10 l on 50 l blue	12.00	9.00
RA42	R1	20 l on 50 l blue	26.00	17.50
RA43	R1	30 l on 50 l blue	17.50	12.00

Surcharged in
Black

RA44	R1	5 l on 10 l vio & red	8.00	12.00
a.		"K" with serifs	12.00	20.00

Counterfeits exist of Nos. RA17-RA44. Similar stamps with denominations higher than 30 lepta were for revenue use.

Wounded
Soldier — PT2

1918		**Serrate Roulette 13½, 11½**		
RA45	PT2	5 l bl, yel & red	8.00	2.00

Overprinted

RA46	PT2	5 l blue, yel & red	9.50	2.00

The letters are the initials of Greek words equivalent to "Patriotic Relief Institution." The proceeds were given to the Patriotic League, for the aid of disabled soldiers.
Counterfeits exist of Nos. RA45-RA46.

PT3

Surcharge in Red

1922		**Litho.**		**Perf. 11½**
		Dark Blue & Red		
RA46A	PT3	5 l on 10 l	300.00	14.00
RA46B	PT3	5 l on 20 l	95.00	50.00
RA46C	PT3	5 l on 50 l	275.00	240.00
RA46D	PT3	5 l on 1d	9.50	60.00

Counterfeit surcharges exist. Examples of Nos. RA46A-RA46C without surcharge, each 50 cents.

Red Cross Help
to Soldier and
Family
PT3a

St. Demetrius
PT4

1924		**Perf. 11½, 13½ x 12½**		
RA47	PT3a	10 l blue, buff & red	.70	.25
a.		Imperf., pair	40.00	
b.		Horiz. pair, imperf. btwn.	40.00	

Proceeds were given to the Red Cross.

1934				**Perf. 11½**
RA48	PT4	20 l brown	.40	.20
a.		Horizontal pair, imperf. between		
b.		Vertical pair, imperf. between	10.00	
c.		Imperf., pair	15.00	
			20.00	

No. RA48 was obligatory as a tax on all interior mail, including air post, mailed from Salonica.

For surcharge see No. RA69.

"Health"

PT5   PT6

1934, Dec. 28		**Perf. 13, 13x13½**		
RA49	PT5	10 l bl grn, org & buff	.25	.20
a.		Vert. pair, imperf. horiz.		
RA50	PT5	20 l ultra, org & buff	.55	.20
RA51	PT5	50 l grn, org & buff	2.00	.50
		Nos. RA49-RA51 (3)	2.80	.90

For surcharge see No. RA67.

1935				
RA52	PT6	10 l yel grn, org & buff	.40	.20
RA53	PT6	20 l ultra, org & buff	.40	.20
RA54	PT6	50 l grn, org & buff	1.25	.65
		Nos. RA52-RA54 (3)	2.05	1.05

The use of #RA49-RA54 was obligatory on all mail during 4 weeks each year including Christmas, the New Year and Easter, and on parcel post packages at all times. For the benefit of the tubercular clerks and officials of the Post, Telephone and Telegraph Service. See No. RA64. For surcharge see No. RA68.

No. 364 Overprinted in
Red

1937, Jan. 20		**Engr.**		**Perf. 13x12½**
RA55	A36	50 l violet	1.40	.25
a.		Inverted overprint	.75	.20

No. RA55a first appeared as an error, then was issued deliberately in quantity to avoid speculation.

Same Overprint in Blue on No. J67
Litho.

Serrate Roulette 13½

RA56	D3	10 l carmine	.80	.25
a.		Inverted overprint	50.00	

No. RA56 with blue overprint double exists only with additional black overprint of Ionian Islands No. NRA1a.

Same Overprint in Green on No. 364

1937		**Engr.**		**Perf. 13x12½**
RA57	A36	50 l violet	.75	.20

Same Overprint, with Surcharge of
New Value, on Nos. J66, J68 and 323
in Blue or Black

Serrate Roulette 13½

1938		**Litho.**		**Unwmk.**
RA58	D3	50 l on 5 l grn	2.40	.80
a.		"o" for "p" in lowest word	25.00	25.00
b.		Vert. pair, imperf. horiz.	55.00	
RA59	D3	50 l on 20 l slate	2.40	.80
		Engr.		**Perf. 13x12½**
RA60	A38	50 l on 20 l vio (Bk)	.75	.20
		Nos. RA58-RA60 (3)	5.55	1.80

Surcharge on No. RA60 is 14½x16½mm.

Queens Olga
and Sophia
PT7

1939, Feb. 1		**Litho.**		**Perf. 13½x12**
RA61	PT7	10 l brt rose, pale rose	.20	.20
RA62	PT7	50 l gray grn, pale grn	.20	.20
RA63	PT7	1d dk bl, lt bl	.20	.20
		Nos. RA61-RA63 (3)	.60	.60

For overprints and surcharges see Nos. RA65, RA79-RA81A, NRA1-NRA3.

"Health" Type of 1935

			Perf. 12½
1939			
RA64	PT6	50 l brn & buff	.55 .30

No. RA62 Overprinted in Red

			Perf. 13½x12
1940			
RA65	PT7	50 l gray grn, pale grn	.25 .25
a.		Inverted overprint	35.00
b.		Pair, one without surcharge	20.00

Proceeds of #RA64-RA65 were used for the benefit of tubercular clerks and officials of the Post, Telephone and Telegraph Service. #RA65 was used in Albania during the Greek occupation, 1940-41 without additional overprint.

No. 321 Surcharged in Carmine

			Perf. 13½x13
1941	**Unwmk.**	**Engr.**	
RA66	A36	50 l on 5 l dk grn	.20 .20
a.		Inverted surcharge	15.00

No. RA49 and Type of 1935 Surcharged with New Value in Black

Perf. 12½x13, 13x13½
Litho.

RA67	PT5	50 l on 10 l	2.00 2.00
RA68	PT6	50 l on 10 l dp bl grn, dl org & buff	.20 .20
a.		Inverted surcharge	40.00
b.		Double surcharge	40.00

> Catalogue values for unused stamps in this section, from this point to the end of the section, are for Never Hinged items.

No. RA48 Surcharged in Green

			Perf. 11½
1942			
RA69	PT4	1d on 20 l brn	.40 .20
a.		Pair, one without surcharge	25.00
b.		Imperf., pair	32.50
c.		Double surcharge	15.00

Nos. 321, 324 Surcharged In Red or Carmine

			Perf. 13½x13
1942-43	**Engr.**		
RA70	A36	10d on 5 l ('43)	.25 .20
a.		Double surcharge	25.00
RA71	A39	10d on 25 l (C)	.25 .20
a.		Inverted surcharge	25.00

No. 444 Overprinted in Red

1944	**Wmk. 252**	**Litho.**	**Perf. 12½**
RA72	A110	100d black	.20 .20
a.		Double overprint	12.00
b.		Inverted overprint	9.00

No. 443 Surcharged in Blue

RA73	A109	5000d on 75d	.20 .20
a.		Double surcharge	25.00

No. 437 Surcharged in Blue

RA74	A103	25000d on 2d	.20 .20
a.		Double surcharge	25.00
b.		Additional surcharge on back	17.50

No. 399 Surcharged in Blue or Carmine

			Perf. 13½x12
1945			
RA75	A72	1d on 40 l	.20 .20
a.		Double surcharge	17.50
RA76	A72	2d on 40 l (C)	.20 .20
a.		Vert. pair, one without surch.	20.00
b.		Surcharged on back	15.00
c.		Inverted surcharge	22.50

Tax on Nos. RA67, RA68-RA70 to RA76 aided the postal clerks' tuberculosis fund.

Nos. 396 and 399 Surcharged in Carmine

1946			
RA77	A72	20d on 40 l	.50 .25
a.		Pair, one without surcharge	25.00
RA78	A69	20d on 5 l	1.25 .60

Same Surcharge in Carmine on Nos. RA62 and RA63

1946-47	**Unwmk.**		**Perf. 13½x12**
RA79	PT7	50d on 50 l ('47)	.50 .25
a.		Inverted surcharge	27.50
RA80	PT7	50d on 1d	.40 .25
a.		Violet black surcharge	4.75 3.00

The tax on Nos. RA77 to RA80 was for the Postal Clerks' Welfare Fund.

Nos. RA65 and RA62 Surcharged in Carmine

1947			
RA81		50d on 50 l (RA65)	2.00 .25
RA81A		50d on 50 l (RA62)	40.00 40.00

Tax for the postal clerks' tuberculosis fund.

St. Demetrius — PT8

1948	**Litho.**		**Perf. 12x13½**
RA82	PT8	50d yellow brown	.25 .25

Obligatory on all domestic mail. The tax was for restoration of historical monuments and churches destroyed during World War II.

Nos. 397 and 413 Surcharged in Blue

1950			**Wmk. 252**
RA83	A70	50d on 10 l (#397)	1.25 .30
a.		Stamp with double frame	125.00
b.		Surcharge reading down	22.50 22.50
RA84	A70	50d on 10 l (#413)	1.00 .20
a.		Surcharge reading down	22.50 22.50

Tax for the Postal Clerks' Welfare Fund.

No. 396 Surcharged in Carmine

1951			**Perf. 13½x12**
RA85	A69	50d on 5 l	2.00 .20

Tax for the Postal Employees' Welfare Fund.

No. 392 Surcharged in Black

1951	**Wmk. 252**		**Perf. 12½x12**
RA86	A67	50d on 3d red brn	2.00 .20
a.		Pair, one without surcharge	30.00
b.		"50" omitted	18.00

Tax for the postal clerks' tuberculosis fund.

No. 393 Surcharged in Carmine

1952			
RA87	A67	100d on 8d deep blue	1.00 .20

The tax was for the State Welfare Fund.

Ruins of Church of Phaneromeni, Zante — PT9

Zeus on Macedonian Coin of Philip II — PT10

500d, Map & scene of destruction, Argostoli.

1953	**Wmk. 252**	**Litho.**	**Perf. 12½**
RA88	PT9	300d indigo & pale grn	1.25
RA89	PT9	500d dk brn & buff	4.50 .70

The tax was for the reconstruction of Cephalonia, Ithaca, and Zante, Ionian Islands destroyed by earthquake.

1956			**Perf. 13½**

Design: 1d, Aristotle.

RA90	PT10	50 l dk car rose	1.25 .20
a.		Imperf., pair	125.00
RA91	PT10	1d brt blue	4.50 1.25

Tax for archaeological research in Macedonia. The coin on No. RA90 portrays Zeus despite inscription of Philip's name.

POSTAL TAX SEMI-POSTAL STAMPS

Child — PTSP1

Mother and Child — PTSP2

Virgin and Christ Child — PTSP3

		Perf. 12x13½	
1943	**Wmk. 252**		**Litho.**
RAB1	PTSP1	25d + 25d bl grn	.20 .20
RAB2	PTSP2	100d + 50d rose vio	.20 .20
RAB3	PTSP3	200d + 100d red brn	.20 .20
		Nos. RAB1-RAB3 (3)	.60 .60

Surtax aided needy children. These stamps were compulsory on domestic mail in Oct. 1943.

OCCUPATION AND ANNEXATION STAMPS

During the Balkan wars, 1912-13, Greece occupied certain of the Aegean Islands and part of Western Turkey. She subsequently acquired these territories and they were known as the New Greece.

Most of the special issues for the Aegean Islands were made by order of the military commanders.

For Use in the Aegean Islands Occupied by Greece

CHIOS

Greece No. 221 Overprinted in Red

		Serrate Roulette 13½	
1913	**Litho.**		**Unwmk.**
N1	A25	25 l ultramarine	60.00 75.00
a.		Inverted overprint	225.00 175.00
b.		Greek "L" instead of "D"	225.00 175.00

ICARIA (NICARIA)

Penelope — I1

1912	**Unwmk.**	**Litho.**	**Perf. 11½**
N2	I1	2 l orange	1.25	2.40
N3	I1	5 l blue green	1.25	2.40
N4	I1	10 l rose	1.25	2.40
N5	I1	25 l ultra	1.25	2.40
N6	I1	50 l gray lilac	1.50	3.25
N7	I1	1d dark brown	2.40	9.00
N8	I1	2d claret	3.25	15.00
N9	I1	5d slate	4.75	22.50
		Nos. N2-N9 (8)	16.90	59.35

Counterfeits of Nos. N1-N15 are plentiful.

Stamps of Greece, 1911-23, Overprinted Reading Up

1913   **Engr.**

On Issue of 1911-21

N10	A25	2 l car rose	40.00	30.00
N11	A24	3 l vermilion	40.00	30.00

Litho.

On Issue of 1912-23

N12	A24	1 l green	40.00	30.00
N13	A24	3 l vermilion	40.00	30.00
N14	A26	5 l green	40.00	30.00
N15	A24	10 l carmine	40.00	30.00
		Nos. N10-N15 (6)	240.00	180.00

LEMNOS

Regular Issues of Greece Overprinted in Black

On Issue of 1901

1912	**Wmk. 129**	**Engr.**	**Perf. 13½**
N16	A11	20 l red lilac	7.00	5.00

On Issue of 1911-21

Unwmk.

Serrate Roulette 13½

N17	A24	1 l green	1.00	1.00
N18	A25	2 l carmine rose	1.00	1.00
N19	A24	3 l vermilion	1.00	1.00
N20	A26	5 l green	1.00	1.00
N21	A24	10 l car rose	1.00	1.00
N22	A26	20 l gray lilac	1.00	1.00
N23	A25	25 l ultra	2.00	2.00
N24	A25	30 l car rose	2.00	2.00
N25	A25	40 l deep blue	4.00	4.00
N26	A26	50 l dl violet	4.00	4.00
N27	A27	1d ultra	6.00	6.00
N28	A27	2d vermilion	20.00	20.00
N29	A27	3d car rose	22.50	22.50
N30	A27	5d ultra	27.50	27.50
N31	A27	10d deep blue	92.50	92.50
N32	A28	25d deep blue	150.00	150.00

On Issue of 1912-23

Litho.

N33	A24	1 l green	.40	.40
a.		Without period after "Ellas"	150.00	150.00
N34	A26	5 l green	.40	.40
N35	A24	10 l carmine	.40	.40
N36	A25	25 l ultra	1.75	1.75
		Nos. N16-N36 (21)	346.45	344.45

Red Overprint

On Issue of 1911-21

Engr.

N37	A25	2 l car rose	.80	.80
N38	A24	3 l vermilion	.80	.80
N39	A26	20 l gray lilac	6.00	6.00
N40	A26	30 l car rose	4.25	4.25
N41	A24	40 l deep blue	4.25	4.25
N42	A26	50 l dull violet	4.25	4.25
N43	A27	1d ultra	4.25	4.25
N44	A27	2d vermilion	42.50	42.50
N45	A27	3d car rose	25.00	25.00

N46	A27	5d ultra	47.50	47.50
N47	A27	10d deep blue	110.00	110.00
N48	A28	25d deep blue	150.00	150.00

On Issue of 1912-23

Litho.

N49	A24	1 l green	.80	.80
a.		Without period after "Ellas"	150.00	150.00
N50	A26	5 l green	.40	.40
N51	A24	10 l carmine	2.00	2.00
N52	A25	25 l ultra	2.50	2.50
		Nos. N37-N52 (16)	405.30	405.30

The overprint is found inverted or double on many of Nos. N16-N52. There are several varieties in the overprint: Greek "D" for "L," large Greek "S" or "O," and small "O."

No. N49 with Added "Greek Administration" Overprint, as on Nos. N109-N148, in Black

1913

N52A	A24	1 l green	29.00	29.00

Counterfeits of #N16-N52A are plentiful.

MYTILENE (LESBOS)

Turkey Nos. 162, 158 Overprinted in Blue

Perf. 12, 13½ and Compound

1912		**Typo.**	**Unwmk.**
N53	A21	20pa rose	22.50	22.50
N54	A21	10pi dull red	110.00	110.00

On Turkey Nos. P68, 151-155, 137, 157-158 in Black

N55	A21	2pa olive green	2.00	2.00
N56	A21	5pa ocher	2.00	2.00
N57	A21	10pa blue green	2.00	2.00
N58	A21	20pa rose	2.00	2.00
N59	A21	1pi ultra	4.00	4.00
N60	A21	2pi blue black	22.50	22.50
N61	A19	2½pi dk brown	11.00	11.00
N62	A21	5pi dk violet	22.50	22.50
N63	A21	10pi dull red	110.00	110.00
		Nos. N55-N63 (9)	178.00	178.00

On Turkey Nos. 161-163, 145 in Black

N64	A21	10pa blue green	5.50	5.50
a.		Double overprint	40.00	40.00
N65	A21	20pa rose	5.50	5.50
N66	A21	1pi ultra	5.50	5.50
N67	A19	2pi blue black	52.50	52.50

Nos. N55, N58, N65, N59 Surcharged in Blue or Black

N68	A21	25 l on 2pa	8.00	8.00
a.		New value inverted	40.00	
N69	A21	50 l on 20pa	10.00	10.00
b.		New value inverted	45.00	
N70	A21	1d on 20pa		
		(N65) (Bk)	30.00	30.00
a.		New value inverted	60.00	60.00
N71	A21	2d on 1pi (Bk)	22.50	22.50
a.		New value inverted		

Same Overprint on Turkey No. J49

N72	A19	1pi blk, dp rose	50.00	50.00

The overprint is found on all values reading up or down with inverted "i" in the first word and inverted "e" in the third word.
No. N72 was only used for postage.
Counterfeits of Nos. N53-N72 are plentiful.

SAMOS

Issues of the Provisional Government

Map of Samos OS1

1912	**Unwmk.**	**Typo.**	**Imperf.**
N73	OS1	5 l gray green	20.00	7.00
N74	OS1	10 l red	20.00	7.00
N75	OS1	25 l blue	40.00	20.00
a.		25 l green (error)	500.00	600.00
		Nos. N73-N75 (3)	80.00	34.00

Nos. N73-N75 exist in tête bêche pairs.
Value per set, $2,000 unused, $1,200 used.

Counterfeits exist of Nos. N73 to N75.

Hermes — OS2

1912		**Litho.**	**Perf. 11½**
	Without Overprint		
N76	OS2	1 l gray	3.00	1.50
N77	OS2	5 l lt green	3.75	1.50
N78	OS2	10 l rose	4.00	1.50
b.		Half used as 5 l on cover		200.00
N79	OS2	25 l lt blue	7.00	1.50
N80	OS2	50 l violet brn	12.50	10.00

With Overprint

N81	OS2	1 l gray	1.00	1.10
N82	OS2	5 l blue grn	1.00	1.10
N83	OS2	10 l rose	1.75	1.50
b.		Half used as 5 l on cover		200.00
N84	OS2	25 l blue	2.00	2.00
N85	OS2	50 l violet brn	11.00	6.50
N86	OS2	1d orange	10.00	10.00
		Nos. N76-N86 (11)	57.00	38.20

For overprints and surcharge see Nos. N92-N103.

Imperf., Pairs
Without Overprint

N76a	OS2	1 l	40.00
N77a	OS2	5 l	40.00
N78a	OS2	10 l	40.00
N79a	OS2	25 l	40.00
N80a	OS2	50 l	40.00

With Overprint

N81a	OS2	1 l	100.00
N82a	OS2	5 l	100.00
N83a	OS2	10 l	100.00
N85a	OS2	50 l	100.00	100.00

Church in Savior's Name and Fort Ruins OS3

Manuscript Initials in Red or Black

1913

N87	OS3	1d brown (R)	16.00	14.00
N88	OS3	2d deep blue (R)	16.00	14.00
N89	OS3	5d gray grn (R)	30.00	25.00
N90	OS3	10d yellow grn (R)	90.00	80.00
N91	OS3	25d red (Bk)	80.00	67.50
		Nos. N87-N91 (5)	232.00	200.50

Victory of the Greek fleet in 1824 and the union with Greece of Samos in 1912. The manuscript initials are those of Pres. Themistokles Sofulis.
Values the same for stamps without initials. Exist imperf. Counterfeits of Nos. N87-N91 are plentiful.
For overprints see Nos. N104-N108.

Nos. N76 to N80 Overprinted

1914

N92	OS2	1 l gray	4.00	4.00
N93	OS2	5 l lt green	4.00	4.00
N94	OS2	10 l rose	4.25	4.00
a.		Double overprint	60.00	
N95	OS2	25 l lt blue	12.00	12.00
N96	OS2	50 l violet brn	8.00	8.00
a.		Double overprint	100.00	
		Nos. N92-N96 (5)	32.25	32.00

Charity Issues of Greek Administration

Nos. N81 to N86 Overprinted in Red or Black

1915

N97	OS2	1 l gray (R)	20.00	20.00
a.		Black overprint	125.00	
N98	OS2	5 l blue grn (Bk)	.80	.80
a.		Red overprint	125.00	
b.		Double overprint	125.00	
N99	OS2	10 l rose (Bk)	.90	.90
a.		Red overprint	125.00	
b.		Inverted overprint	125.00	
N100	OS2	25 l blue (Bk)	.80	.80
a.		Red overprint	125.00	
N101	OS2	50 l violet brn (Bk)	1.00	1.00
a.		Red overprint	125.00	
N102	OS2	1d orange (R)	2.00	2.00
a.		Inverted overprint	125.00	
b.		Black overprint	100.00	
c.		Double black overprint	150.00	

No. N102 With Additional Surcharge in Black

N103	OS2	1 l on 1d orange	15.00	15.00
a.		Black surcharge double	160.00	
b.		Black surcharge inverted	160.00	
		Nos. N97-N103 (7)	40.50	40.50

Issue of 1913 Overprinted in Red or Black

Manuscript Initials in Red or Black

1915

N104	OS3	1d brown (R)	20.00	20.00
N105	OS3	2d dp blue (R)	24.00	24.00
a.		Double overprint		
N106	OS3	5d gray grn (R)	40.00	40.00
N107	OS3	10d yellow grn (Bk)	60.00	60.00
a.		Inverted overprint		
N108	OS3	25d red (Bk)	750.00	750.00
		Nos. N104-N108 (5)	894.00	894.00

Nos. N97 to N108 inclusive have an embossed control mark, consisting of a cross encircled by a Greek inscription.
Most examples of Nos. N104-N108 lack the initials.
Counterfeits of Nos. N104-N108 are plentiful.

FOR USE IN PARTS OF TURKEY OCCUPIED BY GREECE (NEW GREECE)

Regular Issues of Greece Overprinted

Black Overprint Meaning "Greek Administration" On Issue of 1901

1912	**Wmk. 129**	**Engr.**	**Perf. 13½**
N109	A11	20 l red lilac	3.25	2.40

On Issue of 1911-21

Unwmk.

Serrate Roulette 13½

N110	A24	1 l green	.80	.60
N111	A25	2 l car rose	.80	.60
N112	A24	3 l vermilion	.80	.60
N113	A26	5 l green	1.40	1.25
N114	A24	10 l car rose	2.00	1.90

N115	A25	20 l	gray lilac	3.50	2.50
N116	A25	25 l	ultra	3.50	3.50
N117	A26	30 l	car rose	4.25	3.75
N118	A25	40 l	deep blue	6.75	5.50
N119	A26	50 l	dl violet	7.00	5.50
N120	A27	1d	ultra	17.00	3.50
N121	A27	2d	vermilion	67.50	42.50
N122	A27	3d	car rose	90.00	90.00
N123	A27	5d	ultra	60.00	35.00
N124	A27	10d	deep blue	225.00	225.00
N125	A28	25d	dp bl, ovpt. horiz.	225.00	225.00

On Issue of 1913-23

Litho.

N126	A24	1 l	green	.80	.80
b.		Without period after "El-las"		100.00	100.00
N127	A26	5 l	green	.80	.80
N128	A24	10 l	carmine	3.25	2.40
N129	A25	25 l	blue	9.50	7.25
	Nos. N109-N129 (21)			732.90	660.35

Red Overprint

On Issue of 1911-21

Engr.

N130	A24	1 l	green	1.25	1.25
N131	A25	2 l	car rose	9.00	9.00
N132	A24	3 l	vermilion	8.00	8.00
N133	A26	5 l	green	.90	.70
N134	A25	20 l	gray lilac	12.00	1.50
N135	A25	25 l	ultra	55.00	55.00
N136	A26	30 l	car rose	60.00	60.00
N137	A25	40 l	deep blue	3.00	3.00
N138	A26	50 l	dl violet	3.00	3.00
N139	A27	1d	ultra	12.00	12.00
N140	A27	2d	vermilion	60.00	60.00
N141	A27	3d	car rose	24.00	24.00
N142	A27	5d	ultra	250.00	225.00
N143	A27	10d	deep blue	35.00	30.00
N144	A28	25d	dp bl, ovpt. horiz.	55.00	55.00
a.		Vertical overprint		400.00	400.00

On Issue of 1913-23

Litho.

N145	A24	1 l	green	7.00	7.00
a.		Without period after "El-las"		175.00	
N146	A26	5 l	green	.85	.85
N147	A24	10 l	carmine	60.00	55.00
N148	A25	25 l	blue	2.25	1.75
	Nos. N130-N148 (19)			658.25	612.05

The normal overprint is vertical, reading upward on N109-N124, N126-N143, N145-N148. It is often double or reading downward. There are numerous broken, missing and wrong font letters with a Greek "L" instead of "D" as the first letter of the second word.
Counterfeits exist of Nos. N109-N148.

Cross of Constantine
O1

Eagle of Zeus
O2

1912   **Litho.**

N150	O1	1 l	brown	.25	.25
N151	O2	2 l	red	.25	.25
a.		2 l rose		.80	.60
N153	O2	3 l	orange	.30	.25
N154	O1	5 l	green	1.25	.25
N155	O1	10 l	rose red	10.00	.25
N156	O1	20 l	violet	21.00	4.50
N157	O2	25 l	pale blue	4.75	1.25
N158	O1	30 l	gray grn	75.00	3.25
N159	O2	40 l	indigo	15.00	8.75
N160	O1	50 l	dark blue	8.00	4.50
N161	O2	1d	violet brn	8.75	4.50
N162	O1	2d	gray brn	60.00	12.00
N163	O2	3d	dull blue	175.00	27.50
N164	O1	5d	gray	175.00	32.50
N165	O2	10d	carmine	250.00	350.00
N166	O1	25d	gray blk	250.00	350.00
	Nos. N150-N166 (16)			1,054.	800.00

Occupation of Macedonia, Epirus and some of the Aegean Islands.
Sold only in New Greece.
Dangerous forgeries of #N165-N166 exist.
In 1916 some stamps of this issue were overprinted in Greek: "l (era) Koinotis Ag (iou) Orous" for the Mount Athos Monastery District. They were never placed in use and most of them were destroyed.
For surcharges and overprints see Nos. 267-276A, RA14-RA16, Thrace 31-33.

Imperf., Pairs

Without Overprint

N150a	O1	1 l		500.00
N151b	O2	2 l		500.00
N153a	O2	3 l		500.00
N154a	O1	5 l		200.00
N155a	O1	10 l		200.00
N156a	O1	20 l		1,750.

N157a	O2	25 l		1,750.
N158a	O1	30 l		1,750.
N159a	O2	40 l		1,750.
N163a	O2	3d		2,500.

CAVALLA

Bulgaria Nos. 89-97 Surcharged in Red

1913   **Unwmk.**   **Engr.**   *Perf. 12*

N167	A20	5 l	on 1s	22.50	22.50
N169	A25	10 l	on 15s	65.00	65.00
N170	A26	10 l	on 2s	32.50	32.50
N171	A21	15 l	on 25s	65.00	65.00
N172	A22	20 l	on 3s	65.00	65.00
N173	A23	25 l	on 5s	20.00	12.00
N174	A24	50 l	on 10s	35.00	22.50
N175	A25	1d	on 15s	225.00	200.00
N176	A27	1d	on 30s	95.00	95.00
N177	A28	1d	on 50s	140.00	140.00

Blue Surcharge

N178	A24	50 l	on 10s	20.00	20.00
	Nos. N167-N178 (11)			785.00	739.50

The counterfeits and reprints of Nos. N167-N178 are difficult to distinguish from originals. Many overprint varieties exist.
Some specialists question the status of Nos. N167-N178.

DEDEAGATCH

(Alexandroupolis)

D1-(10 lepta)

1913   **Unwmk.**   **Typeset**   *Perf. 11½*

Control Mark in Red

N179	D1	5 l	black	40.00	30.00
N180	D1	10 l	black	5.50	4.00
N181	D1	25 l	black	6.50	4.50
a.		Sheet of 8		125.00	125.00
	Nos. N179-N181 (3)			52.00	38.50

Nos. N179-N181 issued without gum in sheets of 8, consisting of one 5 l, three 10 l normal, one 10 l inverted, three 25 l and one blank. The sheet yields se-tenant pairs of 5 l & 10 l, 10 l & 25 l; tete beche pairs of 5 l & 10 l, 10 l & 25 l and 10 l & 10 l.
Also issued imperf., value $200 unused, $150 canceled.
The 5 l reads "PENTE LEPTA" in Greek letters; the 10 l is illustrated; the 25 l carries the numeral "25."

Bulgaria Nos. 89-90, 92-93, 95 Surcharged

Red Surcharge

1913   *Perf. 12*

N182	A20	5 l	on 1s	65.00	42.50
N183	A26	1d	on 25s	80.00	52.50

Blue Surcharge

N184	A24	10 l	on 10s	30.00	25.00
N185	A23	25 l	on 5s	35.00	25.00
N187	A21	50 l	on 2s	65.00	42.50
	Nos. N182-N185, N187 (5)			275.00	187.50

The surcharges on Nos. N182 to N187 are printed from a setting of eight, which was used for all, with the necessary changes of value. No. 6 in the setting has a Greek "L" instead of "D" for the third letter of the third word of the surcharge.
The 25 l surcharge also exists on 8 examples of the 25s, Bulgaria No. 95.

D2

D3

1913, Sept. 15   **Typeset**   *Perf. 11½*

Control Mark in Blue

N188	D2	1 l	blue	200.00	65.00
N189	D2	2 l	blue	200.00	65.00
N190	D2	3 l	blue	200.00	65.00
N191	D2	5 l	blue	200.00	65.00
N192	D2	10 l	blue	200.00	65.00
N193	D2	25 l	blue	200.00	65.00
N194	D2	40 l	blue	200.00	65.00
N195	D2	50 l	blue	200.00	65.00
	Nos. N188-N195 (8)			1,600.	

Issued without gum in sheets of 8 containing all values.

1913, Sept. 25   **Typeset**

Control Mark in Blue

N196	D3	1 l	blue, *gray blue*	160.00	50.00
N197	D3	5 l	blue, *gray blue*	160.00	50.00
N198	D3	10 l	blue, *gray blue*	160.00	50.00
N199	D3	25 l	blue, *gray blue*	160.00	50.00
N200	D3	30 l	blue, *gray blue*	160.00	50.00
N201	D3	50 l	blue, *gray blue*	160.00	50.00
	Nos. N196-N201 (6)			960.00	

Nos. N196 to N201 were issued without gum in sheets of six containing all values.
Counterfeits of Nos. N182-N201 are plentiful.

FOR USE IN NORTH EPIRUS (ALBANIA)

Greek Stamps of 1937-38 Overprinted in Black

Perf. 13½x12, 12x13½

1940   **Litho.**   **Wmk. 252**

N202	A69	1 l	brn red & bl	.25	.25
a.		Inverted overprint		55.00	
N203	A70	10 l	bl & brn red (No. 413)	.25	.25
a.		Double impression of frame		160.00	
N204	A71	20 l	blk & grn	.25	.25
a.		Inverted overprint		55.00	
N205	A72	40 l	grn & blk	.25	.25
a.		Inverted overprint		55.00	
N206	A73	50 l	brn & blk	.25	.25
N207	A74	80 l	ind & yel brn	.40	.40
N208	A67	1d	green	.40	.40
a.		Inverted overprint		100.00	
N209	A75	2d	ultra	.40	.40
N210	A67	3d	red brn	.80	.80
N211	A76	5d	red	.80	.80
N212	A77	6d	ol brn	.80	.80
N213	A78	7d	dk brn	.80	.80
N214	A67	8d	deep blue	.80	.80
N215	A79	10d	red brn	2.00	2.00
N216	A80	15d	green	2.00	2.00
N217	A81	25d	dark blue	2.75	4.00
a.		Inverted overprint		90.00	

Engr.

Unwmk.

N218	A84	30d	org brn	5.00	*8.00*
	Nos. N202-N218 (17)			18.20	22.45

Same Overprinted in Carmine on National Youth Issue

1941   **Litho.**   *Perf. 12½, 13½x12½*

N219	A93	3d	sil, dp ultra & red	1.00	1.00
N220	A94	5d	dk bl & blk	3.75	3.75
N221	A94	10d	red org & blk	6.00	6.00
N222	A94	15d	dk grn & blk	26.00	26.00
N223	A94	20d	lake & blk	15.00	12.00
N224	A94	25d	dk bl & blk	15.00	12.00

N225	A94	30d	rose vio & blk	15.00	12.00
N226	A94	50d	lake & blk	15.00	12.00
N227	A94	75d	dk bl, brn & gold	20.00	12.00
N228	A93	100d	sil, dp ultra & red	20.00	15.00
a.		Inverted overprint		350.00	
	Nos. N219-N228 (10)			136.75	111.75

Same Overprint in Carmine on National Youth Air Post Stamps

N229	AP25	2d	red org & blk	1.10	1.10
a.		Inverted overprint		150.00	
N230	AP25	4d	dk grn & blk	4.50	4.50
a.		Inverted overprint		150.00	
N231	AP25	6d	lake & blk	6.50	6.50
a.		Inverted overprint		150.00	
N232	AP25	8d	dk bl & blk	6.50	6.50
N233	AP25	16d	rose vio & blk	11.00	6.50
N234	AP25	32d	red org & blk	15.00	12.00
N235	AP25	45d	dk grn & blk	15.00	12.00
N236	AP25	55d	lake & blk	15.00	12.00
N237	AP25	65d	dk bl & blk	15.00	12.00
N238	AP25	100d	rose vio & blk	20.00	15.00
	Nos. N229-N238 (10)			109.60	88.10

Some specialists have questioned the status of Nos. N230a and N231a.
For other stamps issued by Greece for use in occupied parts of Epirus and Thrace, see the catalogue listings of those countries.

> **Catalogue values for unused stamps in this section, from this point to the end of the section, are for Never Hinged items.**

FOR USE IN THE DODECANESE ISLANDS

Greece, No. 472C, with Additional Overprint in Carmine or Silver

1947   **Wmk. 252**   **Litho.**   *Perf. 12½*

N239	A113	10d	on 2,000d (C)	2.40	2.40
N240	A113	10d	on 2,000d (S)	2.40	2.40

These stamps sold for 5 lire (100 drachmas) and paid postage for that amount.

King George II Memorial Issue

Greece, Nos. 484 and 485, With Additional Overprint in Black

1947   **Engr.**   *Perf. 12½x12*

N241	A67	50d	on 1d green	1.60	1.60
N242	A67	250d	on 3d red brown	1.60	1.60

The letters are initials of the Greek words for "Military Administration of the Dodecanese."

Greece, Nos. 501 and 502 Overprinted in Carmine

1947   **Wmk. 252**   **Litho.**   *Perf. 12½*

N243	A111	20d	on 500d dk ol	2.40	2.40
N244	A104	30d	on 5d lt bl grn	2.40	2.40

Greece, Nos. 437, 406, 407 and 445, Surcharged in Black or Carmine

1947   *Perf. 12½, 13½x12*

N245	A103	50d	on 2d	2.40	2.40

Engr.

N246	A79	250d on 10d	7.25	7.25
N247	A80	400d on 15d (C)	8.75	8.75
a.		Inverted surcharge	150.00	

Litho.

N248	A110	1000d on 200 (C)	5.50	5.50
a.		Imprint omitted	40.00	
		Nos. N245-N248 (4)	23.90	23.90

POSTAGE DUE STAMPS

FOR USE IN PARTS OF TURKEY OCCUPIED BY GREECE (NEW GREECE)

Postage Due Stamps of Greece, 1902, Overprinted

1912   Wmk. 129   Engr.   Perf. 13½

Black Overprint

NJ1	D3	1 l chocolate	.50	.50
NJ2	D3	2 l gray	.50	.50
NJ3	D3	3 l orange	.50	.50
NJ4	D3	5 l yel grn	.50	.50
NJ5	D3	10 l scarlet	1.00	1.00
NJ6	D3	20 l lilac	1.00	1.00
NJ7	D3	30 l dp vio	3.00	3.00
NJ8	D3	40 l dk brn	6.00	6.00
NJ9	D3	50 l red brn	8.75	8.75
NJ10	D3	1d black	27.50	27.50
NJ11	D3	2d bronze	25.00	25.00
NJ12	D3	3d silver	60.00	60.00
NJ13	D3	5d gold	100.00	100.00
		Nos. NJ1-NJ13 (13)	234.25	234.25

Red Overprint

NJ14	D3	1 l chocolate	.60	.60
NJ15	D3	2 l gray	.60	.60
NJ16	D3	3 l orange	.60	.60
NJ17	D3	5 l yel grn	.60	.60
NJ18	D3	10 l scar, down	6.00	6.00
NJ19	D3	20 l lilac	.60	.60
NJ20	D3	30 l dp vio	4.50	4.50
NJ21	D3	40 l dk brn	1.40	1.40
NJ22	D3	50 l red brn	1.40	1.40
NJ23	D3	1d black	8.00	8.00
NJ24	D3	2d bronze	13.50	13.50
NJ25	D3	3d silver	20.00	20.00
NJ26	D3	5d gold	50.00	50.00
		Nos. NJ14-NJ26 (13)	107.80	107.80

The normal position of the overprint is reading upward but it is often reversed. Some of the varieties of lettering which occur on the postage stamps are also found on the postage due stamps. Double overprints exist on some denominations.

FOR USE IN NORTH EPIRUS (ALBANIA)

Postage Due Stamps of Greece, 1930, Surcharged or Overprinted in Black:

a   b

Perf. 13, 13x12½

1940		Litho.	Unwmk.	
NJ27	D3(a)	50 l on 25d lt red	.80	.80
NJ28	D3(b)	2d light red	1.25	1.40
a.		Inverted overprint	52.50	
NJ29	D3(b)	5d blue gray	.80	1.25
NJ30	D3(b)	10d green	1.25	1.40
NJ31	D3(b)	15d red brown	1.25	1.60
		Nos. NJ27-NJ31 (5)	5.35	6.45

POSTAL TAX STAMPS

FOR USE IN NORTH EPIRUS (ALBANIA)

Postal Tax Stamps of Greece, Nos. RA61-RA63, Overprinted Type "b" in Black

1940   Unwmk.   Litho.   Perf. 13½x12

NRA1	PT7	10 l	.25	.30
NRA2	PT7	50 l	.40	.65
a.		Inverted overprint	55.00	
NRA3	PT7	1d	.95	1.40
		Nos. NRA1-NRA3 (3)	1.60	2.35

MOUNT ATHOS

> Catalogue values for unused stamps in this section are for **Never Hinged items.**

All stamps also are available for postage in Greece.

Nikiforos Fokas A1

Ioannis Tsimiskis A2

Map of Mount Athos A3

Church of the Protaton A4

Staff of Protepistates — A5

Litho. With Foil Application
Perf. 13¼x13

2008, May 16			Unwmk.	
1	A1	40c multi + label	1.25	1.25
2	A2	60c multi + label	1.90	1.90
3	A3	70c multi + label	2.25	2.25
4	A4	€2 multi + label	6.50	6.50
5	A5	€4 multi + label	13.00	13.00
		Nos. 1-5 (5)	24.90	24.90

Vatopedis Monastery A7

Koutloumousiou Monastery — A8

Iveron Monastery A9

Chilandari Monastery A10

2008, June 13

6	A6	57c multi + label	1.75	1.75
7	A7	70c multi + label	2.25	2.25
8	A8	€1 multi + label	3.25	3.25
9	A9	€1.85 multi + label	5.75	5.75
10	A10	€3 multi + label	9.25	9.25
		Nos. 6-10 (5)	22.25	22.25

Pantokrator Monastery — A11

Xeropotamou Monastery — A12

Karakallou Monastery A13

Zographou Monastery A14

Docheiariou Monastery — A15

2008, July 4

11	A11	57c multi + label	1.90	1.90
12	A12	70c multi + label	2.25	2.25
13	A13	80c multi + label	2.50	2.50
14	A14	€1.50 multi + label	4.75	4.75
15	A15	€3.50 multi + label	11.00	11.00
		Nos. 11-15 (5)	22.40	22.40

Agiou Pavlou Monastery A16

Dionysiou Monastery A17

Stavronikita Monastery — A18

Simonos Petras Monastery A19

Philotheou Monastery A20

2008, Aug. 22

16	A16	57c multi + label	1.75	1.75
17	A17	70c multi + label	2.10	2.10
18	A18	€1.20 multi + label	3.50	3.50
19	A19	€1.80 multi + label	5.25	5.25
20	A20	€3 multi + label	9.00	9.00
		Nos. 16-20 (5)	21.60	21.60

Xenophontos Monastery — A21

Gregoriou Monastery A22

Esphigmenou Monastery — A23

Konstamonitou Monastery — A24

Panteleimonos-Rossikou Monastery — A25

2008, Nov. 7

21	A21	57c multi + label	1.50	1.50
22	A22	70c multi + label	1.90	1.90
23	A23	85c multi + label	2.25	2.25
24	A24	€2.42 multi + label	6.25	6.25
25	A25	€3 multi + label	7.75	7.75
		Nos. 21-25 (5)	19.65	19.65

Monk Ringing Talanton A26

Monk in Library A27

Protepistate Konstantinos Prigoumenos Vatopaidinos — A28

Monk Sculpting Wood A29

Monk Packing Mule A30

2009, May 11

26	A26	57c multi + label	1.60	1.60
27	A27	70c multi + label	2.00	2.00
28	A28	85c multi + label	2.40	2.40
29	A29	€2.42 multi + label	6.75	6.75
30	A30	€3 multi + label	8.50	8.50
		Nos. 26-30 (5)	21.25	21.25

Monk Sewing Clothes A31

Monk Binding Book A32

Monk Cooking A33

Monk Watering Flowers A34

Monk Hiking A35

2009, June 12

31	A31	57c multi + label	1.60	1.60
32	A32	70c multi + label	2.00	2.00
33	A33	€1 multi + label	2.75	2.75
34	A34	€1.85 multi + label	5.25	5.25
35	A35	€3.30 multi + label	9.25	9.25
		Nos. 31-35 (5)	20.85	20.85

Olive Collecting, by Polykleitos Rengos A36

Old Apostolos with His Lines, by Fotis Kontoglou A37

Shipwright, by Kontoglou A38

Icon Painter on Mount Athos, by Theodoros Rallis A39

Monk at Study, by Dimitris Gioldasis A40

2009, Sept. 18

36	A36	57c multi + label	1.75	1.75
37	A37	70c multi + label	2.10	2.10
38	A38	80c multi + label	2.40	2.40
39	A39	€1 multi + label	3.00	3.00
40	A40	€4.50 multi + label	13.50	13.50
		Nos. 36-40 (5)	22.75	22.75

Holy Epistiasia of the Holy Community of Mount Athos, 1938 — A41

Athonias School, 1936 — A42

Archimandrite Gabriel Celebrating Feast of the Holy Monastery of Xenophon, 1967 — A43

Holy Community of Mount Athos, 1951 — A44

Archimandrite Vyssarion, 1998 — A45

2009, Nov. 17 **Perf. 13½**

41	A41	58c multi + label	1.75	1.75
42	A42	70c multi + label	2.10	2.10
43	A43	€1.20 multi + label	3.75	3.75
44	A44	€1.85 multi + label	5.50	5.50
45	A45	€3 multi + label	9.00	9.00
		Nos. 41-45 (5)	22.10	22.10

Flora and Fauna A46

Designs: No. 46, 58c, Pansy. No. 47, 72c, Judas tree. No. 48, €1, Arbutus. No. 49, €2.43, European tree frog. No. 50, €3, Heath.

Litho. With Foil Application
2010, May 11 **Perf. 13½x13**
Stamps + Label

46-50	A46	Set of 5	18.50	18.50

2010, June 21

Designs: No. 51, 50c, Silene orphanidis. No. 52, 58c, Nightingale. No. 53, 72c, European roe deer. No. 54, €2, Laurel. No. 55, €3.50, European green lizard.

Stamps + Label

51-55	A46	Set of 5	18.50	18.50

Flora and Fauna Type of 2010

Designs: No. 56, 58c, Two-tailed pasha butterfly. No. 57, 72c, Golden eagle. No. 58, €1, Mountain tea (white flowers and mountain).

No. 59, €2.43, Amaranth (plant). No. 60, €3, Mediterranean monk seal.

Litho. With Foil Application
2010, Sept. 16   **Perf. 13½x13**
Stamps + Label

56-60 A46 Set of 5   21.50 21.50

2010, Nov. 16

Designs: No. 61, 50c, Chestnut. No. 62, 58c, Fir tree. No. 63, 72c, Sage. No. 64, €2, Wild boar. No. 65, €3.50, Spiny puffball mushroom.

Stamps + Label

61-65 A46 Set of 5   19.50 19.50

GREENLAND

ˈgrēn-lənd

LOCATION — North Atlantic Ocean
GOVT. — Danish
AREA — 840,000 sq. mi.
POP. — 56,076 (1998)
CAPITAL — Nuuk (Godthaab)

In 1953 the colony of Greenland became an integral part of Denmark.

100 Ore = 1 Krone

> Catalogue values for unused stamps in this country are for Never Hinged items, beginning with Scott 28 in the regular postage section, Scott B1 in the semi-postal section.

Christian X — A1

Polar Bear — A2

Perf. 13x12½

			Unwmk.	Engr.
1938-46				
1	A1	1o olive black	.30	.30
2	A1	5o rose lake	2.00	1.40
3	A1	7o yellow green	2.75	3.25
4	A1	10o dk violet	.85	.65
5	A1	15o red	.85	.65
6	A1	20o red ('46)	1.25	1.40
7	A2	30o blue	5.00	7.00
8	A2	40o blue ('46)	24.00	11.50
9	A2	1k light brown	5.75	10.00
		Nos. 1-9 (9)	42.75	36.15
		Set, never hinged	110.00	

Issued: Nov. 1, 1938; Aug. 1, 1946.
For surcharges see Nos. 39-40.

Harp Seal — A3

Christian X — A4

Dog Team — A5

Designs: 1k, Polar bear. 2k, Eskimo in kayak. 5k, Eider duck.

				Perf. 12
1945, Feb. 1				
10	A3	1o ol blk & vio	25.00	42.50
11	A3	5o rose lake & ol bister	25.00	42.50
12	A3	7o green & blk	25.00	42.50
13	A4	10o purple & olive	25.00	42.50
14	A4	15o red & brt ultra	25.00	42.50
15	A5	30o dk blue & red brn	25.00	42.50
16	A5	1k brown & gray blk	25.00	42.50

17	A5	2k sepia & dp grn	25.00	42.50
18	A5	5k dk pur & dl brn	25.00	42.50
		Nos. 10-18 (9)	225.00	382.50
		Set, never hinged	450.00	

Nos. 10-18 Overprinted in Carmine or Blue

1945				
19	A3	1o (C)	67.50	85.00
20	A3	5o (Bl)	67.50	85.00
21	A3	7o (C)	67.50	85.00
22	A4	10o (Bl)	125.00	150.00
a.		Overprint in carmine	400.00	700.00
23	A4	15o (C)	125.00	150.00
a.		Overprint in blue	200.00	240.00
24	A5	30o (Bl)	125.00	150.00
a.		Overprint in carmine	200.00	240.00
25	A5	1k (C)	125.00	150.00
a.		Overprint in blue	225.00	240.00
26	A5	2k (C)	125.00	150.00
a.		Overprint in blue	200.00	240.00
27	A5	5k (Bl)	125.00	150.00
a.		Overprint in carmine	200.00	240.00
		Nos. 19-27 (9)	952.50	1,155.
		Set, never hinged	1,450.	
		Nos. 22a-27a (6)	1,425.	1,900.
		Set, never hinged	3,000.	

Liberation of Denmark from the Germans. Overprint illustrated as on Nos. 19-21. Larger type and different settings used for Types A4 and A5. Overprint often smudged. Nos. 19-27 exist with overprint inverted. Values: 1k and 30o, each $1,200; others, each $1,000.

> Catalogue values for unused stamps in this section, from this point to the end of the section, are for Never Hinged items.

Frederik IX — A6

Polar Ship "Gustav Holm" — A7

1950-60		**Unwmk.**	**Engr.**	**Perf. 13**
28	A6	1o dark olive green	.30	.30
29	A6	5o deep carmine	.30	.30
30	A6	10o green	.35	.35
31	A6	15o purple	.60	.40
a.		15o dull purple	4.50	1.60
32	A6	25o vermilion	2.75	1.00
33	A6	30o dark blue	45.00	2.25
34	A6	30o vermilion	.50	.35
35	A7	50o deep blue	52.50	15.00
36	A7	1k brown	17.00	3.25
37	A7	2k dull red	9.25	3.25
38	A7	5k gray	3.00	2.00
		Nos. 28-38 (11)	131.55	28.45

Issued: #28-30, 31a, 32, 35-37, 8/15/50; #33, 12/1/53; #38, 8/14/58; #34, 10/29/59; #31, 10/60.
For surcharges see Nos. B1-B2.

Nos. 8 and 9 Surcharged

1956, Mar. 8				
39	A2	60o on 40o blue	9.00	1.75
40	A2	60o on 1k lt brown	67.50	8.00

Drum Dancer — A8

Designs: 50o, The Boy and the Fox. 60o, The Mother of the Sea. 80o, The Girl and the Eagle. 90o, The Great Northern Diver and the Raven.

1957-69		**Engr.**		**Perf. 13**
41	A8	35o gray olive	1.40	1.00
42	A8	50o brown red	1.25	1.40
43	A8	60o blue	4.00	1.40
44	A8	80o light brown	1.40	1.40
45	A8	90o dark blue	4.50	4.00
		Nos. 41-45 (5)	12.55	9.20

Issued: 35o, 3/16/61; 50o, 9/22/66; 60o, 5/2/57; 80o, 9/18/69; 90o, 11/23/67.

Hans Egede A9

Knud Rasmussen A10

1958, Nov. 5

46 A9 30o henna brown   10.00 1.75

200th anniv. of death of Hans Egede, missionary to Eskimos in Greenland.

1960, Nov. 24   **Perf. 13**

47 A10 30o dull red   1.60 1.10

50th anniv. of establishment by Rasmussen of the mission and trading station at Thule (Dundas).

Northern Lights and Crossed Anchors — A11

Frederick IX — A12

Polar Bear — A13

1963-68			**Engr.**	
48	A11	1o gray	.30	.35
49	A11	5o rose claret	.30	.35
50	A11	10o green	.40	.50
51	A11	12o yellow grn	.40	.40
52	A11	15o rose vio	1.00	1.25
53	A12	20o ultra	4.50	3.50
54	A12	25o lt brown	.75	.75
55	A12	30o green	.30	.50
56	A12	35o dull red	.30	.30
57	A12	40o gray	.35	.55
58	A12	50o grnsh blue	10.00	10.00
59	A12	50o dark red	.35	.45
60	A12	60o rose claret	.40	.45
61	A12	80o orange	.80	.85
62	A13	1k brown	.65	.35
63	A13	2k dull red	3.50	1.10

64	A13	5k dark blue	3.00	2.25
65	A13	10k dull slate grn	5.00	1.10
		Nos. 48-65 (18)	32.30	25.00

Issued: #48-52, 3/7/63; #53, 61, 7/25/63; #62-65, 9/17/63; #54, 56-58, 3/11/64; #59, 9/9/65; #60, 2/29/68; #55, 11/21/68.

Niels Bohr (1885-1962) and Atom Diagram — A14

1963, Nov. 21   **Unwmk.**

66 A14 35o red brown   .40 .55
67 A14 60o dark blue   4.75 4.75

50th anniv. of atom theory of Prof. Bohr.

A15   A16

1964, Nov. 26

68 A15 35o brown red   .65 .65

Samuel Kleinschmidt (1814-1886), philologist.

1967, June 10

69 A16 50o red   3.50 3.50

Wedding of Crown Princess Margrethe and Prince Henri de Monpezat.

Frederik IX and Map of Greenland A17

1969, Mar. 11 **Engr.** **Perf. 13**

70 A17 60o dull red   1.40 1.40

70th birthday of King Frederik IX.

Musk Ox — A18

Liberation Celebration at Jakobshaven A19

Designs: 1k, Right whale diving off Disko Island. 2k, Narwhal. 5k, Polar bear. 10k, Walruses.

1969-76   Engr.   Perf. 13

71	A18	1k dark blue	.40	.40
72	A18	2k gray green	.90	.60
73	A18	5k blue	2.00	.75
74	A18	10k sepia	4.00	1.90
75	A18	25k greenish gray	11.00	4.00
		Nos. 71-75 (5)	18.30	7.65

Issued: 1k, 3/5/70; 2k, 2/20/75; 5k, 2/19/76; 10k, 2/15/73; 25k, 11/27/69.

1970, May 4
76   A19   60o red brown   2.25 2.25

Hans Egede and Gertrude Rask on the Haabet — A20

1971, May 6   Engr.   Perf. 13
77   A20   60o brown red   1.75 1.75

250th anniv. of arrival of Hans Egede in Greenland and the beginning of its colonization.

Mail-carrying Kayaks — A21

Designs: 70o, Umiak (women's rowboat). 80o, Catalina seaplane dropping mail by parachute. 90o, Dog sled. 1k, Coaster Kununguak and pilot boat. 1.30k, Schooner Sokongen. 1.50k, Longboat off Greenland coast. 2k, Helicopter over mountains.

1971-77   Engr.   Perf. 13

78	A21	50o green	.30	.25
79	A21	70o dull red ('72)	.35	.25
80	A21	80o black ('76)	.40	.40
81	A21	90o blue ('72)	.35	.20
82	A21	1k red ('76)	.40	.40
83	A21	1.30k dull bl ('75)	.85	.65
84	A21	1.50k gray grn ('74)	.80	.55
85	A21	2k blue ('77)	1.00	.85
		Nos. 78-85 (8)	4.45	3.55

Issued: #78, 11/4; #81, 2/29; #79, 9/21; #84, 2/21; #83, 4/17; #80, 10/11; #85, 2/24.

Queen Margrethe — A22

1973-79   Engr.   Perf. 13

86	A22	5o car rose ('78)	.30	.25
87	A22	10o gray green	.30	.25
a.		10o emerald ('89)	6.50	6.50
88	A22	60o sepia	.60	.60
89	A22	80o sepia ('79)	.40	.30
90	A22	90o red brown ('74)	.70	.70
91	A22	1k dark red ('77)	.40	.30
a.		Bklt. pane, 4 #87a, 6 #91b	37.50	
b.		1k carmine ('89)	5.00	5.00
92	A22	1.20k dk blue ('74)	.70	1.00
93	A22	1.20k maroon ('78)	.75	.50
94	A22	1.30k dk blue ('77)	.60	.60
95	A22	1.30k red ('79)	.60	.50
96	A22	1.60k blue ('79)	.70	.70
97	A22	1.80k dl green ('78)	.85	.70
		Nos. 86-97 (12)	6.90	6.40

#86, 89, 93, 95-97 inscribed "Kalaallit Nunaat."

The background lines on Nos. 87, 91 are sharp and complete. On No. 87a, 91b they are irregular and broken.

Issue dates: Nos. 87-88, Apr. 16. Nos. 90, 92, Oct. 24. Nos. 91, 94, May 26. Nos. 86, 93, 97, Apr. 17. Nos. 89, 95-96, Mar. 29.

Trawler and Kayaks — A23

Falcon and Radar — A24

2k, Old Trade Buildings, Copenhagen, vert.

1974, May 16   Engr.   Perf. 13

98	A23	1k lt red brown	.60	.90
99	A23	2k sepia	.70	.60

Royal Greenland Trade Dept. Bicentennial.

1975, Sept. 4   Engr.   Perf. 13
100 A24 90o red   .60 .60

50th anniversary of Greenland's telecommunications system.

Sirius Sled Patrol A25

1975, Oct. 16   Engr.   Perf. 13
101 A25 1.20k sepia   .40 .40

Sirius sled patrol in northeast Greenland, 25th anniversary.

Inuit Cult Mask — A26

Jorgen Bronlund, Jakobshavn, Disko Bay — A27

Designs: 6k, Tupilac, a magical creature, carved whalebone. 7k, Soapstone sculpture. 8k, Eskimo with Family, driftwood sculpture, by Johannes Kreutzmann (1862-1940).

1977-80

102	A26	6k deep rose lilac	2.50	1.90
103	A26	7k gray olive	2.75	2.40
104	A26	8k dark blue	3.25	2.50
105	A26	9k black	3.50	3.25
		Nos. 102-105 (4)	12.00	10.05

Issue dates: 6k, Oct. 5, 1978. 7k, Sept. 6, 1979. 8k, Feb. 29, 1980. 9k, Sept. 6, 1977. The 6k, 7k, 8k are inscribed "Kalaallit Nunaat."

1977, Oct. 20
106 A27 1k red brown   .40 .25

Jorgen Bronlund, arctic explorer, birth centenary.

Meteorite — A28

1978, Jan. 20   Engr.   Perf. 13
107 A28 1.20k dull red   .55 .50

Scientific Research Commission, centenary.

Sun Rising over Mountains — A29

1978, June 5   Engr.   Perf. 13
108 A29 1.50k dark blue   .55 .55

25th anniversary of Constitution.

Hans Egede, Settlers, Troops and Drummer — A30

1978, Aug. 29   Engr.   Perf. 13
109 A30 2.50k red brown   .95 .70

Founding of Godthaab, 250th anniversary.

A31   A32

1979, May 1   Engr.
110 A31 1.10k Navigator   .40 .40

Establishment of home rule, May 1, 1979.

1979, Oct. 18   Engr.   Perf. 13

Eskimo Boy, aurora borealis, IYC emblem.

111 A32 2k olive green   .80 .80

International Year of the Child.

The Legend of the Reindeer and the Larva, by Jens Kreutzmann, 1860 — A33

Designs: 2.70k, Harpooning a Walrus, Jakob Danielsen. No. 114, Life in Thule, c. 1900, by Aninaaq. No. 115, Landscape, Ammassalik Fjord, Eastern Greenland, Peter Rosing (1892-1965). 3k, Footrace, woodcut by Aron from Kagec (1822-1869). 3.70k, Polar Bear Killing Seal Hunter, K. Andreassen (1890-1934). 9k, Hares Hunting, Gerhard Kleist (1855-1931).

1980-87   Engr.   Perf. 13

112	A33	1.60k red	.65	.65
113	A33	2.70k deep violet	1.10	1.00
114	A33	2.80k lake	1.10	.95
115	A33	2.80k lake	1.40	1.00
116	A33	3k black	1.25	1.10
117	A33	3.70k blue black	1.75	1.50
118	A33	9k dark green	4.00	2.75
		Nos. 112-118 (7)	11.25	8.95

Issued: 1.60k, 3/26/81; 2.70k, 6/24/82; #114, 9/4/86; #115, 4/9/87; 3k, 9/4/80; 3.70k, 2/9/84; 9k, 9/5/85.

Queen Margrethe, Map of Greenland A34

1980-89   Engr.   Perf. 13

120	A34	50o purple ('81)	.30	.30
a.		50o dull purple ('89)	7.50	7.50
121	A34	80o sepia	.40	.40
122	A34	1.30k red	.60	.60
123	A34	1.50k royal blue ('82)	.70	.70
124	A34	1.60k ultra	1.00	1.00
125	A34	1.80k dull red ('82)	1.00	.70
126	A34	2.30k dk grn ('81)	1.00	.75
127	A34	2.50k red ('83)	1.25	.75
128	A34	2.80k copper red ('85)	2.00	.80
129	A34	3k fawn ('88)	2.25	2.00
130	A34	3.20k rose ('89)	2.25	2.00
a.		Bklt. pane of 10 (4 #120a, 6 #130)	42.50	

131	A34	3.80k slate blue ('85)	2.00	2.00
132	A34	4.10k brt blue ('88)	2.25	2.25
133	A34	4.40k ultra ('89)	4.50	2.75
		Nos. 120-133 (14)	21.50	17.00

Issued: #121-122, 124, 4/16; #120, 126, 1/29; #123, 125, 5/13; #127, 3/30; #128, 131, 2/7; #129, 132, 2/4; #130, 133, 1/30.

Rasmus Berthelsen (Teacher, Hymnist), in Training College Library, 1830 — A35

1980, May 29   Engr.   Perf. 13
134 A35 2k brown, cream   .80 .75

Greenland Public Library Service, 150th anniv.

Ejnar Mikkelsen on board Gustav Holm, 1934 — A36

1980, Oct. 16   Engr.   Perf. 13
135 A36 4k slate green   1.40 1.25

Ejnar Mikkelsen, inspector of East Greenland, birth centenary.

Pandalus Borealis — A37

Designs: No. 137, Anarhicas minor. No. 138, Reinhardtius Hippoglossoides. No. 139, Mallotus villosus. 25k, Codfish. 50k, Salmo salar.

1981-86   Engr.   Perf. 13

136	A37	10k multicolored	4.00	2.00
137	A37	10k dk bl & blk	6.00	4.00
138	A37	10k multicolored	4.50	4.00
139	A37	10k grnsh blk & blk	4.75	4.75
140	A37	25k multicolored	9.75	4.25
141	A37	50k multicolored	20.00	10.00
		Nos. 136-141 (6)	49.00	29.00

Issued: 25k, 5/21; #136, 4/1/82; 50k, 1/27/83; #137, 10/11/84; #138, 10/10/85; #139, 10/16/86.

Saqqaq Eskimo in Kayak, Reindeer — A38

5k, Tunit-Dorset hunters hauling seal.

1981, Oct. 15   Engr.   Perf. 12½
146 A38 3.50k dark blue   1.50 1.50
147 A38 5k brown   2.10 2.10

Thule District Eskimos Catching Whale, 1000AD — A39

Greenland history: No. 149, Bishop Joen Smyrill's house and staff, 12th cent. No. 150, Wooden dolls, 13th cent. No. 151, Eskimo mummy, sacrificial stones, 14th cent. No. 152, Hans Pothorst, explorer, 15th cent. No. 153, Glass pearls, 16th cent. No. 154, Apostle spoons, 17th cent. No. 155, Key, trading station, 18th cent. No. 156, Trade Ship Hvalfisken, masthead, 19th cent. No. 157, Communications satellite, Earth, 20th cent.

1982, Sept. 30
148 A39 2k brown red   .90 .90
149 A39 2.70k dark blue   1.25 1.25

1983, Sept. 15
150 A39 2.50k red   1.00 1.00
151 A39 3.50k brown   1.50 1.50
152 A39 4.50k blue   1.75 1.75

1984, Mar. 29
153	A39	2.70k red brown	1.75	1.75
154	A39	3.70k dark blue	1.75	1.75
155	A39	5.50k brown	2.25	2.25

1985, Mar. 21
156	A39	2.80k violet	1.75	1.75
157	A39	6k blue black	2.75	2.75
		Nos. 148-157,B10 (11)	17.90	17.90

250th Anniv. of Settlement of New Herrnhut — A40

1983, Nov. 2   Engr.
158	A40	2.50k brown	1.00	1.00

Henrik Lund, Natl. Anthem Score, Lichtenau Fjord — A41

1984, Sept. 6   Engr.
159	A41	5k dark green	3.25	3.25

Henrik Lund (1875-1948), natl. anthem composer, artist, only Greenlander to win Ingenio et Arti medal.

A42   A43

1984, June 6   Engr.   Perf. 13
160	A42	2.70k dull red	2.25	2.25

Prince Henrik, 50th birthday.

1984, July 25   Engr.   Perf. 13
161	A43	3.70k Danish grenadier, 1734	1.75	1.75

Town of Christianshab, 250th anniv.

Ingrid, Queen Mother of Denmark, Chrysanthemums — A44

1985, May 21   Litho. & Engr.
162	A44	2.80k multi	1.40	1.40

Arrival in Denmark of Princess Ingrid, 50th anniv. See Denmark No. 775.

Intl. Youth Year — A45

1985, June 27   Litho.
163	A45	3.80k Emblem, birds nesting, fiord	1.40	1.40

Greenland Port Post Office, Flags — A46

1986, Mar. 6   Engr.   Perf. 13
164	A46	2.80k dark red	1.40	1.40

Transfer of postal control under Greenland Home Rule, Jan. 1, 1986.

Artifacts — A47

1986-88   Engr.   Perf. 13
165	A47	2.80k Sewing needles, case	1.40	.95
165A	A47	3k Buckets, bowl, scoop	1.25	.90
166	A47	3.80k Ulos	1.50	1.50
167	A47	3.80k Masks	1.75	1.75
168	A47	5k Harpoon points	2.00	1.50
169	A47	6.50k Lard lamps	2.75	2.75
172	A47	10k Carved faces	4.50	3.25
		Nos. 165-172 (7)	15.15	12.60

Issued: #166, 6.50k, May 22. 2.80k, 3.80k, June 11, 1987. 3k, 5k, 10k, Oct. 27, 1988.

Souvenir Sheet

HAFNIA '87 — A48

1987, Jan. 23   Litho.   Perf. 13
175	A48	Sheet of 3	11.00	11.00
a.		2.80k Gull in flight	3.00	3.00
b.		3.80k Mountain	3.75	3.75
c.		6.50k Gulls in water	3.75	3.75

No. 175 sold for 19.50k. See No. 199.

Year of the Fishing, Sealing and Whaling Industries — A49

1987, Apr. 9   Litho.   Perf. 13
176	A49	3.80k multi	1.75	1.50

Lagopus Mutus — A50   Birds of Prey — A51

1987-90   Litho.   Perf. 13
177	A51	3k Falco rusticolus	1.75	1.75
178	A51	3.20k Clangula hyemalis	2.40	1.40
179	A51	4k Anser caerulescens	1.75	1.40
180	A51	4.10k Corvus corax	2.25	2.25
181	A51	4.40k Plectrophenax nivalis	2.50	2.50
182	A50	5k shown	3.00	1.90
183	A51	5.50k Haliaeetus albicilla	3.75	2.50
184	A51	5.50k Cepphus grylle	3.00	3.25
185	A51	6.50k Uria lomvia	4.00	2.25
186	A51	7k Gavia immer	3.75	2.75
187	A51	7.50k Stercorarius longicaudus	3.25	3.75
188	A50	10k Nyctea scandiaca	4.50	3.50
		Nos. 177-188 (12)	35.90	29.20

Issued: 5k, 10k, 9/3; 3k, 4.10k, #183, 7k, 4/14/88; 3.20k, 4.40k, #184, 6.50k, 3/16/89; 4k, 7.50k, 1/15/90.

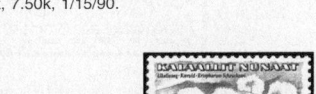

Plants — A52

1989-92   Litho.   Perf. 13
189	A52	4k Campanula gieseckiana	1.75	1.50
190	A52	4k Pedicularis hirsuta	2.25	1.50
191	A52	5k Eriophorum scheuchzeri	2.75	2.10
192	A52	5.50k Ledum groenlandicum	2.50	2.25
193	A52	6.50k Cassiope tetragona	3.25	3.00
194	A52	7.25k Saxifraga oppositifolia	3.75	3.25
196	A52	10k Papaver radicatum, vert.	5.25	4.00
		Nos. 189-196 (7)	21.50	17.60

Issued: 5k, 10k, 10/12/89; #189, 5.50k, 6.50k, 6/7/90; #190, 7.25k, 3/26/92. #189-190 vert.

HAFNIA type of 1987
Souvenir Sheet
Uummannaq Mountain in winter, horiz.

1987, Oct. 16   Litho.   Perf. 13x12½
199	A48	2.80k slate blue & lake	3.25	3.75

No. 199 sold for 4k.

Greenland Home Rule, 10th Anniv.

A53   A54

1989, May 1   Litho.   Perf. 13
200	A53	3.20k Flag, landscape	1.50	1.40
201	A54	4.40k Coat of arms	2.50	1.75

Queen Margrethe — A55

and Nos. 214, 217 Surcharged in Red or Blue

1990-96   Engr.   Perf. 13
214	A55	25o green	.30	.30
217	A55	1k brown	.55	.45
a.		Bklt. pane, 4 #214, 6 #217	32.50	
b.		Bklt. pane, 4 each #214, 217	16.00	
224	A55	4k carmine rose	1.75	1.75
		Complete booklet, 217a, 10 #224	47.50	
225	A55	4.25k red	2.40	2.40
226	A55	4.25k on 25o #214 (R)	5.00	5.00
a.		Inverted surcharge	1,100.	
227	A55	4.50k on 1k #217 (Bl)	5.00	5.00
228	A55	6.50k blue	2.75	2.75
229	A55	7k violet	3.50	3.50
		Nos. 214-229 (8)	21.25	21.15

Issued: #217a, 5/3/90; #217b, 9/9/93; 7k, 2/10/94; #225, 1996; #226-227, 12/31/95; others, 4/5/90.

Frederik Lynge (1889-1957), Politician — A56

25k, Augo Lynge (1899-1959), politician

1990, Oct. 18   Engr.   Perf. 13x12½
231	A56	10k rose brn & dk bl	4.25	4.25
232	A56	25k vio & dk bl	10.00	10.00

See Nos. 242-243, 249.

Walrus and Seals.

Phoca Hispida — A57

1991, Mar. 14   Litho. & Engr.   Perf. 13
233	A57	4k shown	1.75	1.75
234	A57	4k Pagophilus groenlandicus	1.75	1.75
235	A57	7.25k Cystophora cristata	3.00	3.00
236	A57	7.25k Odobenus rosmarus	3.00	3.00
237	A57	8.50k Erignatus barbatus	3.25	3.25
238	A57	8.50k Phoca vitulina	3.25	3.25
a.		Miniature sheet of 6, #233-238	18.00	18.00
		Nos. 233-238 (6)	16.00	16.00

Village of Ilulissat, 250th Anniv. — A58

1991, May 15   Litho.   Perf. 13
239	A58	4k multicolored	1.75	1.75

Tourism — A59

1991, May 15   Perf. 12½x13
240	A59	4k Iceberg	1.50	1.50
241	A59	8.50k Skiers, sled dogs	3.50	3.50

See Nos. 259-260, 289-290.

Famous Men Type of 1990

10k, Jonathan Petersen (1881-1961), musician. 50k, Hans Lynge (1906-88), artist & writer. 100k, Lars Moller (1842-1926), newspaper editor.

1991-92   Engr.   Perf. 13x12½
242	A56	10k black & dk blue	4.75	3.50
243	A56	50k red brn & blue	20.00	17.00
249	A56	100k claret & slate	35.00	30.00
		Nos. 242-249 (3)	59.75	50.50

Issued: 10k, 50k, 9/5; 100k, 9/15/92.

Settlement of Paamiut, 250th Anniv. A60

1992, May 14   Engr.   Perf. 13
252	A60	7.25k dk bl & ol brn	3.50	3.00

Denmark's Queen Margrethe and
Prince Henrik, Silver Wedding
Anniv. — A61

1992, June 10　Litho.　Perf. 12½x13
253　A61　4k multicolored　　　2.40　2.40
See Denmark No. 946.

A62

1992, Nov. 12　Litho.　Perf. 13
254　A62　4k Christmas　　　2.75　2.10

1993, Feb. 4　Litho.　Perf. 13
255　A63　4k multicolored　　　2.25　2.00
Intl. Year of Indigenous Peoples.

A63

Crabs — A64

4k, Neolithodes grimaldii. 7.25k, Chionoecetes oiliqo. 8.50k, Hyas coarctatus, Hyas araneus.

Litho. & Engr.
1993, Mar. 25　　Perf. 13
256　A64　4k multicolored　　1.50　1.50
257　A64　7.25k multicolored　4.00　4.00
　a.　Chionoecetes opilio　　10.50　13.00
　b.　Booklet pane, 4 each #256,
　　　257a　　　　　　　50.00
258　A64　8.50k multicolored　5.00　5.00
　　　Nos. 256-258 (3)　　10.50　10.50
Issue date: No. 257b, Sept. 9.

Tourism Type of 1991
1993, May 6　Litho.　Perf. 12½x13
259　A57　4k Village in winter　2.00　2.00
260　A57　8.50k Ruins, coastline　4.00　4.00

AIDS
Research
A66

1993, Sept. 9　Litho.　Perf. 13
261　A66　4k multicolored　　　2.00　2.00

Native
Animals — A67

Litho. & Engr.
1993, Oct. 14　　Perf. 13
262　A67　5k Canis lupus　　2.50　2.50
263　A67　8.50k Alopex lagopus　4.00　4.00
264　A67　10k Rangifer
　　　tarandus　　　　4.50　4.50
　　　Nos. 262-264 (3)　　11.00　11.00
See Nos. 270-272, 296-298.

Christmas
A68

1993, Nov. 11　Litho.　Perf. 13
265　A68　4k multicolored　　　2.25　2.25

Buksefjord Electrical Project — A69

Litho. & Engr.
1994, Mar. 24　　Perf. 13
266　A69　4k multicolored　　　1.50　1.50

Ammassalik,
Cent. — A70

1994, Mar. 24
267　A70　7.25k multicolored　　3.00　3.00

Expedition
to North
East
Greenland,
1906-08
A71

Europa: 4k, Icebound Danmark. 7.25k, Danmark, expedition car, dogs.

1994, May 5　Litho.　Perf. 13
268　A71　4k multicolored　　2.00　2.00
269　A71　7.25k multicolored　3.50　3.25

Native Animal Type of 1993
Designs: 5.50k, Mustela erminea. 7.25k, Dicrostonyx torquatus. 9k, Lepus arcticus.

Litho. & Engr.
1994, Sept. 8　　Perf. 13
270　A67　5.50k multicolored　2.50　2.50
271　A67　7.25k multicolored　4.00　4.00
272　A67　9k multicolored　　4.50　4.50
　　　Nos. 270-272 (3)　　11.00　11.00

Ship's Figureheads — A72

Litho. & Engr.
1994, Oct. 13　　Perf. 13
273　A72　4k Ceres　　　1.50　1.50
274　A72　8.50k Nordlyset　4.00　4.00
See Nos. 299-300, 309-310.

Christmas Paintings, by Julia
Pars — A73

1994, Nov. 10　Litho.　Perf. 12½x13
275　A73　4k shown　　　2.00　2.00
276　A73　5k Santa, dogs, igloo　3.25　3.25

Orchids — A74

Litho. & Engr.
1995-96　　　Perf. 13x12½
279　A74　4k Listera cordata　2.00　2.00
280　A74　4.25k Corallorhiza
　　　trifida　　　　1.75　1.75
281　A74　4.50k Amerorchis
　　　rotundifolia　　1.90　1.90
282　A74　7.25k Leucorchis al-
　　　bida　　　　3.00　3.00
283　A74　7.50k Plantanthera
　　　hyperborea　　3.25　3.25
　a.　Booklet pane, #281, 283, 2 ea
　　　#225, 280 + 4 labels　12.50
　　　Complete booklet, 2 #283a　25.00
　　　Nos. 279-283 (5)　11.90　11.90
No. 283a exists with different labels and
stamps in different order. Complete booklet
contains one of each type of No. 283a.
Issued: 4k, 7.25k, 2/9/95.

Ilinniarfissuaq Seminarium, Nuuk (The
Greenland Training College), 150th
Anniv. — A75

Litho. & Engr.
1995, Mar. 23　　Perf. 13
287　A75　4k multicolored　　　2.00　2.00

United Nations,
50th Anniv. — A76

1995, Mar. 23
288　A76　7.25k multicolored　　3.50　3.50

Tourism Type of 1991
1995, Apr. 20　Litho.　Perf. 12½x13
289　A59　4k Iceberg, inlet　2.25　2.25
290　A59　8.50k Mountains　4.50　4.50

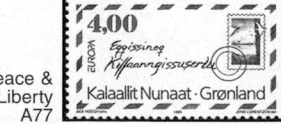

Peace &
Liberty
A77

Europa: 4k, Envelope, simulated stamp.
8.50k, Doves flying over Greenland.

1995, May 5　　　Perf. 12½x13
291　A77　4k multicolored　　1.75　1.75
292　A77　8.50k multicolored　4.00　4.00

America Series — A78

Designs: No. 295a, Dog team. b, Polar bear.
c, Eskimo in kayak. d, Eider duck.
Illustration reduced.

1995, May 5　　Litho.　Perf. 13
293　A78　Sheet of 2 + 4 labels　6.50　6.50
　a.　5k on 10o pur & ol (Type A4)　3.00　3.00
　b.　5k on 15o red & vio (Type A4)　3.00　3.00
294　A78　Sheet of 3　　7.75　7.75
　a.　1k on 1o dk ol & vio bl (Type
　　　A3)　　　　　　.60　.60
　b.　5k on 5o rose lake & brn
　　　(Type A3)　　　3.00　3.00
　c.　7k on 7o dk grn & blk (Type
　　　A3)　　　　　4.25　4.25
295　A78　Sheet of 4　10.00　10.00
　a.　4k on 30o dk bl & red brn
　　　(Type A5)　　　2.40　2.40
　b.　4k on 1k brn & gray blk (Type
　　　A5)　　　　　2.40　2.40
　c.　4k on 2k sep & dp grn (Type
　　　A5)　　　　　2.40　2.40
　d.　4k on 5k dp pur & dl brn (Type
　　　A5)　　　　　2.40　2.40

Native Animal Type of 1993
Litho. & Engr.
1995, Sept. 7　　Perf. 13
296　A67　4k Ursus maritimus　2.00　2.00
297　A67　7.25k Gulo gulo　3.25　3.25
298　A67　7.50k Ovibus moschatus　3.25　3.25
　　　Nos. 296-298 (3)　8.50　8.50

Ship's Figureheads Type of 1994
Litho. & Engr.
1995, Oct. 12　　Perf. 13
299　A72　4k Hvalfisken, vert.　1.60　1.60
300　A72　8.50k Tjalfe　3.75　3.75

Christmas
A79

1995, Nov. 9　Litho.　Perf. 13
301　A79　4k Boy running in snow　1.60　1.60
302　A79　5k Girl running in snow　2.10　2.10

Whales
A80

Designs: 25o, Orcinus orca. 50o, Megaptera
novaeangliae. 1k, Delphinapterus leucas.
4.50k, Physeter catodon. 6.50k, Balaena mysticetus. 9.50k, Balaenoptera acutorostrata.

1996, Apr. 25　Litho.　Perf. 13
303　A80　25o blue, black &
　　　red　　　　.20　.20
304　A80　50o blue, black &
　　　red　　　　.20　.20
305　A80　1k blue, black &
　　　red　　　　.65　.65
306　A80　4.50k blue, black &
　　　red　　　　2.00　2.00
　a.　Bklt. pane, #304, 2 ea #303,
　　　306　　　　　6.00
　　　Complete booklet, 2 #306a　13.00
307　A80　6.50k blue, black &
　　　red　　　　3.25　3.25
308　A80　9.50k blue, black &
　　　red　　　　4.50　4.50
　a.　Souvenir sheet, Nos. 303-308　12.00　12.00
　　　Nos. 303-308 (6)　10.80　10.80
No. 306a exists with stamps in different
order. Issued: No. 306a, 1/1/97.
See Nos. 319-322, 329-334.

Ship's Figureheads Type of 1994
Litho. & Engr.
1996, Sept. 5　　Perf. 13
309　A72　15k Blaahejren, vert.　6.50　6.50
310　A72　20k Gertrud Rask　8.50　8.50

Arnarulunnguaq (1896-1933), Member of Thule Expedition — A81

1996, Sept. 5   Engr.
311 A81 4.50k dark blue   1.75 1.75

Europa.

Christmas A82

Designs: 4.25k, Girl looking through frozen window pane, angels scratched in ice. 4.50k, Paper star, children singing.

1996, Nov. 7   Litho.   Perf. 13
312 A82 4.25k multicolored   2.00 2.00
313 A82 4.50k multicolored   2.50 2.50
  a.   Booklet pane, 3 each #312-313   13.00
       Complete booklet, 2 #313a   26.00

No. 313a was issued in two formats, one with No. 312 at the UL, the other with No. 313 at the UL. The complete booklet contains one of each format.

A83

A84

Litho. & Engr.
1997, Jan. 14   Perf. 13
314 A83 4.50k multicolored   2.50 2.50

Coronation of Queen Margrethe II, 25th anniv.

1997, Jan. 14

Butterflies: 2k, Clossiana chariclea. 3k, Colias hecla. 4.75k, Plebejus franklinii. 8k, Lycaena phlaeas.

315 A84   2k multicolored   1.10 1.10
316 A84   3k multicolored   1.75 1.75
317 A84   4.75k multicolored   1.75 1.75
318 A84   8k multicolored   3.50 3.50
  a.   Booklet pane of 6, 2 #314, 1 ea
       #315-318 + 2 labels   13.00
       Complete booklet, 2 #318a   26.00
       Nos. 315-318 (4)   8.10 8.10

Issued: No. 318a, 5/5.

No. 318a exists with stamps in two different orders and with two different backgrounds, one of green plants, the other of red flowers. The complete booklet contains one of each type of pane.

Whale Type of 1996

Designs: 5k, Balaenoptera musculus. 5.75k, Balaenoptera physalus. 6k, Balaenoptera borealis. 8k, Monodon monoceros.

1997, May 5   Litho.   Perf. 13
319 A80 5k blue, black &
         red   1.90 1.90
320 A80 5.75k blue, black &
         red   2.25 2.25
321 A80 6k blue, black &
         red   2.25 2.25
322 A80 8k blue, black &
         red   3.25 3.25
  a.   Souvenir sheet of 4, #319-322   9.75 9.75
       Nos. 319-322 (4)   9.65 9.65

Story of the "Bear of the Sea" — A85

1997, May 5   Litho. & Engr.   Perf. 13
323 A85 4.75k black & blue black 2.00 2.00

Europa.

Town of Nanortalik, Bicent. A86

Litho. & Engr.
1997, Aug. 15   Perf. 13
324 A86 4.50k multicolored   2.00 2.00

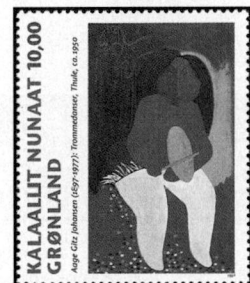

Paintings by Aage Gitz-Johansen (1897-1977) — A87

Designs: 10k, Native dancer, Thule. 16k, Nude woman, Ammassalik.

1997, Aug. 15   Litho.   Perf. 13x12½
325 A87 10k multicolored   4.00 4.00
326 A87 16k multicolored   6.00 6.00

Christmas A88

Designs: 4.50k, Child with dogs in snow. 4.75k, Family in sled with Christmas presents, tree, father preparing harness.

1997, Nov. 6   Litho.   Perf. 13x12½
327 A88 4.50k multicolored   2.00 2.00
328 A88 4.75k multicolored   2.00 2.00
  a.   Booklet pane, 3 each #327-328   14.00
       Complete booklet, 2 #328a   28.00

No. 328a comes in two configurations. One has #327 at UL, the second has #328 at UL. Complete booklet has one of each pane.

Whale Type of 1996

Designs: 2k, Phocoena phocoena. 3k, Lagenorhynchus albirostris. No. 331, Globicephala melaena. No. 332, Hyperoodon ampullatus. No. 333, Lagenorhynchus acutus. No. 334, Eubalaena glacialis.

1998, Feb. 5   Litho.   Perf. 13
329 A80   2k multicolored   .75 .75
330 A80   3k multicolored   1.50 1.50
331 A80   4.50k multicolored   2.40 2.40
332 A80   4.50k multicolored   2.40 2.40
333 A80   4.75k multicolored   2.40 2.40
334 A80   4.75k multicolored   2.40 2.40
  a.   Souvenir sheet of 6, #329-334   12.00 12.00
       Nos. 329-334 (6)   11.85 11.85

Intl. Year of the Ocean.

New Order of 1950 — A89

Design: Augo Lynge, Frederik Lynge, first Greenland politicians in Danish Parliament.

1998, Feb. 5   Engr.   Perf. 13
335 A89 4.50k multicolored   2.00 2.00

Europa — A90

Children's drawings of "Children's Day in Greenland:" 4.75k, Happy faces beside lake. 10k, People celebrating across Greenland.

1998, May 29   Litho.   Perf. 13
336 A90 4.75k multicolored   1.75 1.75
337 A90 10k multicolored   4.00 4.00

Ships — A91

Litho. & Engr.
1998, Aug. 20   Perf. 13
338 A91 4.50k Gertrud Rask   2.00 2.00
  a.   Booklet pane of 6   12.00
339 A91 4.75k Hans Egede   2.00 2.00
  a.   Booklet pane of 6   12.00
       Complete booklet, #338a, 339a   24.00

Paintings by Hans Lynge (1906-88) — A92

Designs: 11k, "Brother Gets Breast-fed." 25k, "Refuelling" (men in boat).

1998, Aug. 20   Litho.   Perf. 13
340 A92 11k multicolored   4.50 4.50
341 A92 25k multicolored   9.50 9.50

Christmas A93

1998, Nov. 5   Litho.   Perf. 13
342 A93 4.50k Dickey, kamikker   2.00 2.00
  a.   Booklet pane of 6   15.00
343 A93 4.75k Kamikker, hat   2.50 2.50
  a.   Booklet pane of 6   15.00
       Complete booklet, #342a, 343a   30.00

World Wildlife Fund — A94

Nyctea scandiaca (snowy owl): 1k, Nesting with young. 4.75k, In flight. 5.50k, Two adults. 5.75k, Perched on rock.

Litho. & Engr.
1999, Feb. 8   Perf. 13
344 A94   1k multicolored   .60 .60
345 A94 4.75k multicolored   2.00 2.00
  a.   Booklet pane, 3 each #344-345   8.50
346 A94 5.50k multicolored   2.25 2.25
347 A94 5.75k multicolored   2.50 2.50
  a.   Booklet pane, 3 each #346-347   14.50
       Complete booklet, #345a, 347a   25.00
       Nos. 344-347 (4)   7.35 7.35

Europa A95

1999, May 7   Litho. & Engr.   Perf. 13
348 A95 6k Polar bear   2.25 2.25

Paintings, by Peter Rosing (1892-1965) — A96

Designs: 7k, The Man from Aluk, 1944. 20k, Homecoming, 1956.

1999, May 7   Litho.   Perf. 12½x13
349 A96 7k multicolored   2.50 2.50
350 A96 20k multicolored   7.50 7.50

Arctic Vikings A97

1999, Aug. 13   Engr.   Perf. 13x13¼
351 A97 4.50k Viking ship   2.00 2.00
352 A97 4.75k Man on drift-
         wood   2.00 2.00
353 A97 5.75k Arrowhead,
         coins   2.50 2.50
354 A97 8k Tjodhilde's
         church   3.25 3.25
  a.   Souvenir sheet, #351-354   9.00 9.00
       Nos. 351-354 (4)   9.75 9.75

See Nos. 358-361, 380-383.

Christmas A98

1999, Nov. 11   Litho.   Perf. 13x13¼
355 A98 4.50k Writing letter   1.60 1.60
  a.   Booklet pane of 6   9.75
356 A98 4.75k Handshake   1.75 1.75
  a.   Booklet pane of 6   10.50
       Complete booklet, #355a, 356a   21.00

Millennium A99

1999, Nov. 11   Litho.   Perf. 13x13¼
357 A99 5.75k multicolored   2.10 2.10

Arctic Vikings Type of 1999

Designs: 25o, Hunter, four walruses. 3k, Storyteller. 5.50k, Dog chasing reindeer. 21k, Man, gyrfalcon, polar bear, narwhal tusk, items made from animals.

2000, Feb. 21   Engr.   Perf. 13x13¼
358 A97 25o bl gray & brn   .20 .20
359 A97 3k bl gray & brn   1.40 1.40
360 A97 5.75k bl gray & brn   2.25 2.25
361 A97 21k bl gray   9.00 9.00
  a.   Souvenir sheet, #358-361   13.00 13.00
       Nos. 358-361 (4)   12.85 12.85

Navy Dog Sled Patrol
A100

Litho. & Engr.

2000, Feb. 21   Perf. 12¾
362 A100 10k multi   3.25 3.25

Europa, 2000
Common Design Type

2000, May 9   Litho.   Perf. 13¼x13
363 CD17 4.75k multi   1.90 1.90

Queen Margrethe
A101

2000-01   Engr.   Perf. 13x13¼
364 A101 25o blk & bl gray   .30 .20
365 A101 50o red brn & bl gray   .25 .20
367 A101 4.50k red & bl gray   1.75 1.75
368 A101 4.75k bl & bl gray   1.90 1.90
   Complete booklet, 4 each
   #364, #368   8.50
372 A101 8k yel grn & bl gray   3.25 3.25
374 A101 10k grn & bl gray   4.00 4.00
375 A101 12k pur & bl gray   4.75 4.75
   Nos. 364-375 (7)   16.20 16.05

Issued: 4.50k, 4.75k, 8k, 10k, 5/9/00. 25o, 12k, 5/9/01. 50o, 10/21/02.
This is an expanding set.

Cultural Heritage — A102

2000, Aug. 18   Litho.   Perf. 13¼x13
376 A102 4.50k Wooden map   1.75 1.75
   a.   Booklet pane of 6 + 2 labels   10.50
377 A102 4.75k Sealskin   1.90 1.90
   a.   Booklet pane of 6 + 2 labels   11.50
   Booklet, #376a, 377a   22.50

See Nos. 384-385, 392-393, 414-415

Christmas
A103

2000, Nov. 9   Litho.   Perf. 13x13¼
378 A103 4.50k Stars, candles   1.75 1.75
   a.   Booklet pane of 6   10.50
379 A103 4.75k Star   1.90 1.90
   a.   Booklet pane of 6   11.50
   Booklet, #378a, 379a   22.50

Arctic Vikings Type of 1999

Designs: 1k, Hunter, dead seals. 4.50k, Mice eating food. 5k, Man and pack animals leaving. 10k, Birds on ruins.

2001, Feb. 5   Perf. 13x13¼
380 A97 1k indigo & red   1.50 1.50
381 A97 4.50k indigo & blue   1.75 1.75
382 A97 5k indigo & blue   3.25 3.25
383 A97 10k indigo & red   6.50 6.50
   a.   Souvenir sheet, #380-383   8.25 8.25
   Nos. 380-383 (4)   13.00 13.00

Cultural Heritage Type of 2000

Designs: 4.50k, Smoked fish. 4.75k, Fishing spear.

2001, May 9   Litho.   Perf. 13¼x13
384 A102 4.50k multi   1.50 1.50
   a.   Booklet pane of 6 + 2 labels   10.00
385 A102 4.75k multi   2.00 2.00
   a.   Booklet pane of 6 + 2 labels   10.00
   Complete booklet, #384a, 385a   20.00

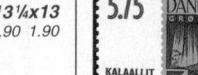

Europa
A104

2001, May 9   Litho. & Engr.   Perf. 13
386 A104 15k Krill   6.00 6.00

Unissued Stamps from the 1930s — A105

Designs: 5.75k, 5o Northern lights. 8k, 10o Seal. 21k, 15o Polar bear.

Litho. & Engr.

2001, Oct. 16   Perf. 12¾
387 A105 5.75k blk & brn   2.25 2.25
388 A105 8k blk & brn   3.25 3.25
389 A105 21k blk & brn   8.25 8.25
   a.   Souvenir sheet, #387-389 + 3 labels   14.00 14.00

Christmas
A106

Grouse and: 4.50k, Berries. 4.75k, Mountain.

2001, Oct. 16   Litho.   Perf. 13x13¼
390 A106 4.50k multi   1.75 1.75
   a.   Booklet pane of 6   10.50
391 A106 4.75k multi   1.90 1.90
   a.   Booklet pane of 6   11.50
   Complete booklet, #390a, 391a   22.50

Cultural Heritage Type of 2000

Designs: 4.50k, Thule drum. 4.75k, Mask.

2002, Mar. 5   Litho.   Perf. 13x13¼
392 A102 4.50k multi   1.75 1.75
   a.   Miniature sheet of 8 + label   14.00
393 A102 4.75k multi   1.90 1.90
   a.   Miniature sheet of 8 + label   15.00

Sculptures
A107

Designs: 1k, Stone and Man, by various sculptors. 31k, Nuuk Snow Festival snow sculpture.

2002, Mar. 5   Perf. 12¾
394 A107 1k multi   .40 .40
395 A107 31k multi   12.00 12.00

Europa — A108

2002, June 24   Litho.   Perf. 12¾
396 A108 11k multi   4.00 4.00

Ships
A109

2002, June 24   Engr.   Perf. 13x13¼
397 A109 2k Nordlyset   .80 .80
398 A109 4k Hvidbjornen   1.60 1.60
399 A109 6k Staerkodder   2.40 2.40
   a.   Booklet pane of 4, 2 each #398-399   8.00

400 A109 16k Haabet   6.25 6.25
   a.   Booklet pane of 4, 2 each #397, 400   14.00 —
   Complete booklet, #399a, 400a   22.50
   Nos. 397-400 (4)   11.05 11.05

See Nos. 416-419, 434-437, 452-455.

Intl. Council for Exploration of the Seas, Cent. — A110

Designs: 7k, Somniosus microcephalus and iceberg. 19k, Sebastes mentella and exploration ship Paamiut.

Litho. & Engr.

2002, Oct. 21   Perf. 13¼x13
401 A110 7k multi   2.75 2.75
402 A110 19k multi   7.50 7.50
   a.   Souvenir sheet, #401-402   10.50 10.50

See Denmark Nos. 1237-1238, Faroe Islands No. 426.

Christmas — A111

Designs: 4.50k, Man with gifts, children on sled with tree. 4.75k, Family with gifts near fire.
Illustration reduced.

2002, Oct. 21   Litho.   Perf. 12¾
403 A111 4.50k multi   1.90 1.90
404 A111 4.75k multi   2.00 2.00

Booklet Stamps
Self-Adhesive
Serpentine Die Cut 14

405 A111 4.50k multi   1.90 1.90
406 A111 4.75k multi   2.00 2.00
   a.   Horiz. pair, #405-406   4.00
   b.   Booklet, 6 each #405-406   25.00

Danish Literary Greenland Expedition, Cent. — A112

Designs: 15k, Campsite. 21k, Knud Rasmussen.
Illustration reduced.

2003, Mar. 12   Engr.   Perf. 12¾
407 A112 15k multi   6.00 6.00

Size: 28x21mm
408 A112 21k blue gray   8.25 8.25
   a.   Souvenir sheet, #407-408 + label   14.50 14.50

Sled Dogs
A113

Designs: 4.50k, Puppies playing. 4.75k, Close-up of dog. 6k, Dog in harness.

2003, Mar. 12   Perf. 13x13¼
409 A113 4.50k blue gray   1.75 1.75
   a.   Sheet of 8 + central label   14.00 14.00
410 A113 4.75k blue gray   1.90 1.90
   a.   Sheet of 8 + central label   15.00 15.00
411 A113 6k blue gray   2.40 2.40
   a.   Booklet pane, 2 each #409-411, with #411 at UL   12.00
   b.   Booklet pane, 2 each #409-411, with #409 at UL   12.00
   Complete booklet, #411a, 411b   24.00

Europa — A114

2003, June 16   Litho.   Perf. 13¼x13
412 A114 5.50k multi   2.25 2.25

Town of Qaanaaq, 50th Anniv. — A115

2003, June 16   Perf. 12¾
413 A115 15k multi   6.00 6.00

Cultural Heritage Type of 2000

Designs: 25o, Comb. 1k, Ice bucket.

2003, June 16   Perf. 13¼x13
414 A102 25o multi   .25 .25
415 A102 1k multi   .45 .45

Ship Type of 2002
Litho. & Engr.

2003, Oct. 20   Perf. 13x13¼
416 A109 6.75k Emma   2.75 2.75
417 A109 7.75k Gamle Fox   3.00 3.00
418 A109 8.75k Godthaab   3.50 3.50
419 A109 26k Sonja   10.00 10.00
   Nos. 416-419 (4)   19.25 19.25

Christmas
A116

Designs: Nos. 420, 422, Christmas tree. Nos. 421, 423, Church.

2003, Oct. 20   Litho.   Perf. 12¾
420 A116 5k multi   2.00 2.00
421 A116 5.50k multi   2.25 2.25

Booklet Stamps
Self-Adhesive
Serpentine Die Cut 12¼x12¾

422 A116 5k multi   2.00 2.00
423 A116 5.50k multi   2.25 2.25
   a.   Horiz. pair, #422-423   4.25
   b.   Booklet pane, 6 each #423a   26.00
   Nos. 420-423 (4)   8.50 8.50

Polar Air Route, 50th Anniv. — A117

2004, Mar. 26   Litho.   Perf. 13¼x13
424 A117 8.75k multi   3.50 3.50

Home Rule, 25th Anniv. — A118

2004, Mar. 26   Perf. 12¾x12½
425 A118 11k multi   4.25 4.25

Landing Boat From Expedition of Arctic Explorer Otto Sverdrup (1854-1930) — A119

Litho. & Engr.
2004, Mar. 26　　　**Perf. 13¼x13**
426　A119　17.50k multi　　7.00　7.00
　a.　Souvenir sheet of 1 + 2 labels　7.00　7.00

See Canada Nos. 2026-2027, Norway Nos. 1398-1399.

Norse Mythology A120

Designs: 5.50k, Moon Man. 6.50k, Northern Lights.

2004, Mar. 26　Litho.　**Perf. 12¾**
427　A120　5.50k multi　　2.50　2.50
428　A120　6.50k multi　　2.75　2.75
　a.　Souvenir sheet, #427-428　5.25　5.25

Wedding of Crown Prince Frederik and Mary Donaldson A121

Designs: 5k, Couple facing right. 5.50k, Couple facing left.

2004, May 14　　　**Perf. 13¼**
429　A121　5k multi　　　2.00　2.00
430　A121　5.50k multi　　2.25　2.25
　a.　Souvenir sheet, #429-430 +
　　　central label　　　　4.25　4.25
　b.　Booklet pane, 3 each #429-
　　　430, with #429 at top　13.00　—
　c.　As "b," with #430 at top　13.00　—
　　　Complete booklet, #430b-430c　26.00

Edible Plants A122

Designs: 5k, Angelica archangelica. 5.50k, Thymus praecox. 17k, Empetrum hermaphroditum.

2004, May 14　　　**Perf. 13x13¼**
431　A122　5k multi　　　2.00　2.00
　a.　Sheet of 8 + central label　16.00　16.00
432　A122　5.50k multi　　2.25　2.25
　a.　Sheet of 8 + central label　18.00　18.00
433　A122　17k multi　　　6.75　6.75
　　　Nos. 431-433 (3)　　11.00　11.00

See Nos. 459-461

Ships Type of 2002
Litho. & Engr.
2004, Oct. 18　　　**Perf. 13x13¼**
434　A109　6.50k Constance　2.50　2.50
435　A109　8.75k Disko　　　3.50　3.50
436　A109　14k Julius Thom-
　　　　　　sen　　　　　　5.50　5.50
437　A109　21.75k Misigssut　8.75　8.75
　　　Nos. 434-437 (4)　　20.25　20.25

Europa — A123

2004, Oct. 18　Litho.　**Perf. 13¼x13**
438　A123　6.50k multi　　2.50　2.50

Christmas A124

Designs: 5k, Family, Christmas tree. 5.50k, Carolers with lanterns.

2004, Oct. 18　　　**Perf. 12¾**
439　A124　5k multi　　　2.00　2.00
440　A124　5.50k multi　　2.25　2.25

Booklet Stamps
Self-Adhesive
Serpentine Die Cut 12¼x12¾
441　A124　5k multi　　　2.00　2.00
442　A124　5.50k multi　　2.25　2.25
　a.　Horiz. pair, #441-442　4.25
　b.　Complete booklet, 6 #442a　26.00
　　　Nos. 439-442 (4)　　8.50　8.50

Ilulissat Ice Fjord, UNESCO World Heritage Site — A125

2005, Jan. 17　Litho.　**Perf. 12¾**
443　A125　6k multi　　　2.40　2.40

Church and School Systems Law, Cent. — A126

2005, Jan. 17　　　**Perf. 12¾**
444　A126　9.25k multi　　3.75　3.75

Europa — A127

2005, Jan. 17　　　**Perf. 13¼x13**
445　A127　11.75k multi　　4.75　4.75

Mushrooms — A128

Designs: 5.25k, Leccinum sp. 6k, Russula subrubens. 7k, Amanita groenlandica.

2005, Jan. 17　　　**Perf. 13x13¼**
446　A128　5.25k multi　　2.10　2.10
　a.　Sheet of 8 + central label　17.00
447　A128　6k multi　　　2.40　2.40
　a.　Sheet of 8 + central label　19.00
448　A128　7k multi　　　2.75　2.75
　　　Nos. 446-448 (3)　　7.25　7.25

Booklet Stamps
Self-Adhesive
Serpentine Die Cut 9¾x10¼
449　A128　5.25k multi　　2.10　2.10
450　A128　6k multi　　　2.40　2.40
451　A128　7k multi　　　2.75　2.75
　a.　Booklet pane, 2 each #449-451　14.50
　　　Complete booklet, 2 #451a　29.00
　　　Nos. 449-451 (3)　　7.25　7.25

No. 451a has two different marginal designs.

See Nos. 476-480.

Ships Type of 2002
Litho. & Engr.
2005, June 20　　　**Perf. 13x13¼**
452　A109　5.25k Dannebrog　2.10　2.10
453　A109　6k Kista Arctica　2.40　2.40
454　A109　18.50k Sarpik Ittuk　7.25　7.25
455　A109　23k Triton　　　9.25　9.25
　　　Nos. 452-455 (4)　　21.00　21.00

Science In Greenland — A129

Designs: 7.25k, Geological map. 9.25k, Diver at limestone columns in Ikka Fjord, horiz. 10k, Limnognathia maerski, horiz.

Perf. 13¼x13, 13x13¼
2005, June 20
456　A129　7.25k multi　　3.00　3.00
457　A129　9.25k multi　　3.75　3.75
458　A129　10k multi　　　4.00　4.00
　　　Nos. 456-458 (3)　　10.75　10.75

Edible Plants Type of 2004
Designs: 75o, Ligusticum scoticum. 6.50k, Rhodiola rosea. 8.25k, Oxyria digyna.

2005, Oct. 31　Litho.　**Perf. 13x13¼**
459　A122　75o multi　　　.30　.30
460　A122　6.50k multi　　2.50　2.50
461　A122　8.25k multi　　3.25　3.25
　　　Nos. 459-461 (3)　　6.05　6.05

Admiral Robert E. Peary (1856-1920), Explorer — A130

Litho. & Engr.
2005, Oct. 31　　　**Perf. 13**
462　A130　27.50k multi　　11.00　11.00
　a.　Souvenir sheet of 1　11.00　11.00

Parcel Post Stamps, Cent. — A131

2005-07　Litho.　**Perf. 14x13½**
463　A131　25k #Q3　　　10.00　10.00
　　　　　Perf. 12¾x13
464　A131　50k #Q4　　　20.00　20.00
　a.　Perf. 14x13½, dated "2007"　18.00　18.00

Issued: 25k, 1/16/06; No. 464, 10/3; No. 464a, 2007.
No. 464a is found only in No. 497a, along with an example of No. 463 dated "2007."
Issued: No. 464a, 5/21/07.
See No. 497.

Christmas A132

Designs: 5.25k, Boy at left. 6k, Girl at right.

2005, Oct. 31　　　**Perf. 12¾**
465　A132　5.25k multi　　2.10　2.10
466　A132　6k multi　　　2.40　2.40

Booklet Stamps
Self-Adhesive
Serpentine Die Cut 12¾x13
467　A132　5.25k multi　　2.10　2.10
468　A132　6k multi　　　2.40　2.40
　a.　Pair, #467-468　　　4.50　4.50
　b.　Booklet pane, 6 each #467-468　27.50

Whale Jaw Gate and Blue Church, Sisimiut — A138

2006, Jan. 16　　　**Perf. 13¾x13¼**
469　A138　9.75k multi　　4.00　4.00

Sisimiut, 250th anniv.

Nordic Union "Norden" Stamps, 50th Anniv. — A139

2006, Jan. 16
470　A139　19.50k multi　　7.75　7.75

European Philatelic Cooperation, 50th Anniv. — A140

2006, Jan. 16　　　**Perf. 14x13¼**
471　A140　26.50k #438 and
　　　　　　stars　　　　10.50　10.50

Europa stamps, 50th anniv.

Norse Mythology A141

Designs: 7.50k, The Mother of the Sea. 13.50k, Asiaq, Mistress of the Weather.

Perf. 13¾x13½
2006, Mar. 29　　　**Litho.**
472　A141　7.50k multi　　3.00　3.00
473　A141　13.50k multi　　5.25　5.25
　a.　Souvenir sheet, #472-473　8.25　8.25

Sheep Farming in Greenland, Cent. A142

2006, May 22
474　A142　7.50k multi　　3.00　3.00

Alfred Wegener (1880-1930), Geophysicist A143

2006, May 22　Engr.　**Perf. 13x13¼**
475　A143　20.75k red & blue　8.25　8.25
　a.　Souvenir sheet of 1　8.25　8.25

Mushrooms Type of 2005
Designs: 5.50k, Rozites caperatus. 7k, Lactarius dryadophilus. 10k, Calvatia cretacea.

2006, May 22 Litho. Perf. 14x13¼
476	A128	5.50k multi	2.25	2.25
a.		Sheet of 8 + central label	18.00	18.00
477	A128	7k multi	2.75	2.75
a.		Sheet of 8 + central label	22.00	22.00
478	A128	10k multi	4.00	4.00
		Nos. 476-478 (3)	9.00	9.00

Self-Adhesive
Booklet Stamps
Serpentine Die Cut 12¼x12
479	A128	5.50k multi	2.25	2.25
480	A128	7k multi	2.75	2.75
a.		Booklet pane, 3 each #479-480	15.00	
		Complete booklet, 2 #480a	30.00	

No. 480a has two different marginal designs.

Galathea 3
Research
Expedition — A144

2006, Sept. 9 Litho. Perf. 13½x14
481	A144	9.75k multi	4.00	4.00

Science — A145

Designs: 50o, Larch tree preserved in Kap Kobenhavn Formation. 8k, Geologist obtaining rock sample from mountains at Isua. 15.50k, Qeqertarsuaq Arctic Station, cent.

Litho. & Engr.
2006, Nov. 6 Perf. 13¼x13
482	A145	50o multi	.20	.20
483	A145	8k multi	3.25	3.25
484	A145	15.50k multi	6.25	6.25
		Nos. 482-484 (3)	9.70	9.70

See Nos. 502-504, 524-526.

Christmas
A146

Music for hymn and: 5.50k, Angel. 7k, Candle.

2006, Nov. 6 Litho. Perf. 13¾x13½
485	A146	5.50k multi	2.25	2.25
486	A146	7k multi	2.75	2.75

Booklet Stamps
Self-Adhesive
Serpentine Die Cut 12¼x12
487	A146	5.50k multi	2.00	2.00
488	A146	7k multi	2.50	2.50
a.		Booklet pane, 3 each #487-488	13.50	
		Complete booklet, 2 #488a	27.00	

Hydroelectric
Power — A147

2007, Jan. 15 Litho. Perf. 13¾x13½
489	A147	5k multi	1.75	1.75

West Nordic Council, 10th anniv.

Crown Prince
Frederik, Crown
Princess Mary and
Prince
Christian — A148

2007, Jan. 15 Perf. 13¼x14
490	A148	14.25k multi	5.00	5.00

Intl. Polar
Year
A149

Designs: 7.50k, Scientists drilling ice cores. 8k, Urbanization.

Litho. & Engr.
2007, Jan. 15 Perf. 13x13¼
491	A149	7.50k multi	2.60	2.60
492	A149	8k multi	2.75	2.75
a.		Souvenir sheet, #491-492	5.50	5.50

Europa — A150

Scouts: 5.75k, And rock pile. 7.50k, At campsite.

2007, Jan. 15 Litho. Perf. 13¾x13¼
493	A150	5.75k multi	2.00	2.00
a.		Sheet of 8 + central label	16.00	16.00
494	A150	7.50k multi	2.60	2.60
a.		Sheet of 8 + central label	21.00	21.00

Booklet Stamps
Self-Adhesive
Serpentine Die Cut 12¼x12
495	A150	5.75k multi	2.00	2.00
496	A150	7.50k multi	2.60	2.60
a.		Booklet pane, 3 each #495-496	14.00	—
		Complete booklet, 2 #496a	28.00	

Parcel Post Stamp Centenary Type
of 2005-06
2007, May 21 Litho. Perf. 14x13½
497	A131	100k #Q6	37.50	37.50
a.		Souvenir sheet, #463, 464a, 497	65.00	65.00

Examples of Nos. 463 and 464a in No. 497a are dated "2007."

A151

Contemporary Art — A152

Unnamed paintings by: 3k, Jens Rosing. 8.50k, Anne-Birthe Hove. 10.50k, Linda Riber Sorensen.
Illustration A151 reduced.

2007, May 21
498	A151	3k multi	1.10	1.10
499	A152	8.50k multi	3.25	3.25
500	A152	10.50k multi	3.75	3.75
		Nos. 498-500 (3)	8.10	8.10

Greenlandic Landscape — A153

2007, Oct. 1
501	A153	6.50k multi	2.50	2.50

Science Type of 2006

Designs: 75o, Planting of Greenlandic flag on Tubbiap Queqertaa. 2k, Soapstone bowl and quarry. 10.25k, Cyanobacteria.

Litho. & Engr.
2007, Oct. 1 Perf. 13¼x13
502	A145	75o multi	.30	.30
503	A145	2k multi	.75	.75
504	A145	10.25k multi	4.00	4.00
		Nos. 502-504 (3)	5.05	5.05

Ship Pourquois-Pas? — A154

Paul-Emile Victor
(1907-95), Arctic
Explorer — A155

2007, Nov. 8 Engr. Perf. 13½
505	A154	5.75k multi	2.25	2.25
506	A155	7.50k multi	3.00	3.00
a.		Souvenir sheet, #505-506, + label	5.25	5.25

See France No. 3369.

Christmas — A156

Snowflakes and: 5.75k, Angel. 7.50k, Star.

2007, Nov. 8 Litho. Perf. 13½x13¾
507	A156	5.75k multi	2.25	2.25
508	A156	7.50k multi	3.00	3.00

Self-Adhesive
Booklet Stamps
Serpentine Die Cut 12x12¼
509	A156	5.75k multi	2.25	2.25
510	A156	7.50k multi	3.00	3.00
a.		Pair, #509-510	5.25	
b.		Booklet pane of 12, 6 each #509-510	31.50	

Europa — A157

Envelope half and: 5.75k, Man. 7.50k, Woman.

2008, Jan. 31 Litho. Perf. 13¾x13½
511	A157	5.75k multi	2.40	2.40
a.		Sheet of 8 + central label	19.50	19.50
512	A157	7.50k multi	3.00	3.00
a.		Sheet of 8 + central label	24.00	24.00

Booklet Stamps
Self-Adhesive
Serpentine Die Cut 12¼x12
513	A157	5.75k multi	2.40	2.40
514	A157	7.50k multi	3.00	3.00
a.		Booklet pane, 6 each #513-514	32.50	

Contemporary Art — A158

Unnamed paintings by: 5.50k, Ina Rosing. 14.25k, Buuti Pedersen. 30.50k, Aka Hoegh.

2008, Jan. 31 Perf. 14x13½
515	A158	5.50k multi	2.25	2.25
516	A158	14.25k multi	5.75	5.75
517	A158	30.50k multi	12.50	12.50
		Nos. 515-517 (3)	20.50	20.50

Mythical
Places — A159

Myths of: 7k, Kayaker and river rocks. 8k, Bear of the Lake.

Perf. 13¾x13½
2008, Mar. 27 Litho.
518	A159	7k multi	3.00	3.00
519	A159	8k multi	3.50	3.50
a.		Souvenir sheet, #518-519	6.50	6.50

Wedding of Prince
Joachim and
Marie
Cavallier — A160

2008, May 24 Litho. Perf. 13½x14
520	A160	10.25k multi	4.50	4.50

Fossils
A161

Designs: 1k, Halkieria evangelista. 20.50k, Ichthyostega stensioei. 25k, Eudimorphodon cromptonellus.

Litho. & Engr.
2008, May 24 Perf. 13x13¼
521	A161	1k multi	.45	.45
522	A161	20.50k multi	8.75	8.75
523	A161	25k multi	10.50	10.50
		Nos. 521-523 (3)	19.70	19.70

Science Type of 2006

Designs: 6.50k, Scientist, equipment hauler, satellite above Greenland. 10.50k, French station at Scoresbysund. 28k, Danish Arctic station at Nuuk.

Litho. & Engr.

2008, Oct. 20			Perf. 13¼x13	
524	A145	6.50k multi	2.25	2.25
525	A145	10.50k multi	3.75	3.75
526	A145	28k multi	9.75	9.75
a.		Souvenir sheet, #524-526	16.00	16.00
		Nos. 524-526 (3)	15.75	15.75

International Geophysical Year, 50th anniv. (#524); French station at Scoresbysund, 75th anniv. (#525); Danish Arctic station at Nuuk, 125th anniv. (#526).

Expedition Ship Sofia — A162

Adolf Erik Nordenskiöld (1832-1901), Arctic Explorer — A163

2008, Oct. 20			Perf. 13¼x13	
527	A162	8.50k multi	3.00	3.00
528	A163	16.25k multi	5.75	5.75
a.		Souvenir sheet, #527-528, + label	8.75	8.75

See Finland No. 1321.

Christmas A164

Designs: 5.75k, Reindeer and house. 7.50k, Christmas tree and houses.

2008, Oct. 20 Litho.			Perf. 13¾x13¼	
529	A164	5.75k multi	2.00	2.00
530	A164	7.50k multi	2.60	2.60

Booklet Stamps
Self-Adhesive
Serpentine Die Cut 12¼x12

531	A164	5.75k multi	2.00	2.00
532	A164	7.50k multi	2.60	2.60
a.		Pair, #531-532		4.60
b.		Booklet pane of 12, 6 each #531-532		28.00

Fossils Type of 2008

Designs: 2k, Schizoneura carcinoides. 11.50k, Scaphites rosenkrantzi. 22k, Mallotus villosus.

Litho. & Engr.

2009, Jan. 19			Perf. 13x13¼	
533	A161	2k multi	.70	.70
534	A161	11.50k multi	4.00	4.00
535	A161	22k multi	7.75	7.75
		Nos. 533-535 (3)	12.45	12.45

Preservation of Polar Regions and Glaciers — A165

2009, Jan. 19 Litho.			Perf. 14x13¼	
536	A165	5k multi	1.75	1.75

Europa — A166

Designs: 6.25k, Ursa Major constellation. 8k, Ursa Major constellation and outline of bear.

2009, Jan. 19			Perf. 13¼x13¾	
537	A166	6.25k multi	2.25	2.25
a.		Sheet of 8 + central label	18.00	18.00
538	A166	8k multi	2.75	2.75
a.		Sheet of 8 + central label	22.00	22.00

Booklet Stamps
Self-Adhesive
Serpentine Die Cut 12x12¼

539	A166	6.25k multi	2.25	2.25
540	A166	8k multi	2.75	2.75
a.		Booklet pane of 12, 6 each #539-540		30.00

Intl. Year of Astronomy.

Prince Henri, 75th Birthday — A167

2009, June 11 Litho.			Perf. 13¼x14	
541	A167	8k multi	3.00	3.00

Self-Governance — A168

2009, June 21			Perf. 14x13¼	
542	A168	6.25k multi	2.40	2.40

Matthew Henson (1866-1955), Polar Explorer — A169

2009, June 21			Perf. 13¼x13¾	
543	A169	9k multi	3.50	3.50

First Steps, Comic Strip by Nuka K. Godtfredsen — A170

2009, June 21			Perf. 14x13¼	
544	A170	15.50k multi	6.00	6.00
a.		Souvenir sheet of 1	6.00	6.00

Contemporary Art — A171

Designs: 6k, Two Polar Bears From Above, by Ivalo Abelsen. 18k, Window to the World, by Camilla Nielsen. 33k, Gletscher, by Naja Abelsen.

2009, June 21				
545	A171	6k multi	2.25	2.25
546	A171	18k multi	6.75	6.75
547	A171	33k multi	12.50	12.50
		Nos. 545-547 (3)	21.50	21.50

Greenlandic Landscape — A172

2009, Sept. 16 Litho.			Perf. 14x13¼	
548	A172	7k multi	2.75	2.75

North Star Mission Station, Thule, Cent. — A173

2009, Oct. 19 Engr.			Perf. 13¼x13	
549	A173	15.25k black	6.25	6.25

Otto Nordenskjold (1869-1928), Arctic Explorer — A174

Litho. & Engr.
2009, Oct. 19   Perf. 13¼x13
Sans-Serif Inscriptions

550	A174	30k multi	12.00	12.00

Souvenir Sheet
Serifed Inscriptions

551	A174	30k multi + label	12.00	12.00

Science Type of 2006

Designs: 1k, Cryolite mine, Ivittuut. 15.50k, Himantolophus groenlandicus. 23.50k, Gold mine, Nalunaq.

2009, Oct. 19			Perf. 13¼x14	
552	A145	1k multi	.40	.40
553	A145	15.50k multi	6.25	6.25
554	A145	23.50k multi	9.50	9.50
a.		Souvenir sheet, #552-554	16.50	16.50
		Nos. 552-554 (3)	16.15	16.15

Christmas A175

Star and: 6.25k, Family. 8k, Baby.

2009, Oct. 19 Litho.			Perf. 13¾x13¼	
555	A175	6.25k multi	2.50	2.50
556	A175	8k multi	3.25	3.25

Booklet Stamps
Self-Adhesive
Serpentine Die Cut 12¼x12

557	A175	6.25k multi	2.50	2.50
558	A175	8k multi	3.25	3.25
a.		Pair, #557-558		5.75
b.		Booklet pane, 6 each #557-558		35.00

Air Greenland, 50th Anniv. — A176

2010, Jan. 18 Litho.			Perf. 12½x12¾	
559	A176	16.50k multi	6.25	6.25

Contemporary Art — A177

Designs: 6.50k, Polar Bear, by Maria Panínguak' Kjærulff. 7.50k, Sun, by Miki Jacobsen. 50k, Greenland Razorbills, by Bolatta Silis-Hoegh.

2010, Jan. 18			Perf. 14x13¼, 13¼x14	
560	A177	6.50k multi	2.50	2.50
561	A177	7.50k multi	2.75	2.75
562	A177	50k multi	19.00	19.00
		Nos. 560-562 (3)	24.25	24.25

Europa — A178

Designs: 8.50k, Boy reading book. 9.50k, Children reading book.

2010, Jan. 18			Perf. 13¾x13¼	
563	A178	8.50k multi	3.25	3.25
a.		Sheet of 8 + central label	26.00	26.00
564	A178	9.50k multi	3.50	3.50
a.		Sheet of 8 + central label	28.00	28.00

Booklet Stamps
Self-Adhesive
Serpentine Die Cut 12¼x12

565	A178	8.50k multi	3.25	3.25
566	A178	9.50k multi	3.50	3.50
a.		Booklet pane of 12, 6 each #565-566		41.00

Intl. Women's Day, Cent. — A179

2010, Mar. 8 Litho.			Perf. 13¼x14	
567	A179	12.50k multi	4.50	4.50

Life by the Sea — A180

Designs: 7k, Sea ice. 8.50k, Port and sea ice.

2010, Mar. 24   *Perf. 13¾x13¼*
568 A180   7k multi   2.50 2.50
569 A180 8.50k multi   3.25 3.25
  a.   Souvenir sheet, #568-569   5.75 5.75

Queen Margrethe II, 70th
Birthday — A181

2010, Apr. 16   *Perf. 13¼x14*
570 A181 35k multi   12.50 12.50

Flag of Greenland,
25th
Anniv. — A182

2010, May 1
571 A182   7k multi   2.40 2.40

Buuarsikkut, Comic Strip by Robert
Holmene — A183

2010, May 1   *Perf. 14x13¼*
572 A183 23.50k multi   8.00 8.00
  a.   Souvenir sheet of 1   8.00 8.00

Thule Trading
Station,
Cent. — A184

2010, Oct. 18 Engr. *Perf. 12¼x12½*
573 A184 25k black   9.50 9.50

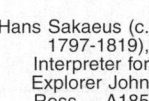

Hans Sakaeus (c.
1797-1819),
Interpreter for
Explorer John
Ross — A185

Ross Expedition Ships Isabella and
Alexander — A186

2010, Oct. 18   *Perf. 12½x12*
574 A185 25o pur & bl blk   .20   .20
575 A186 32k pur & bl blk   12.00 12.00
  a.   Souvenir sheet, #574-575, +
       label   12.50 12.50

Mining in
Greenland
A187

Designs: 50o, King Frederik VII's copper
mine. 26.50k, Ivituut cryolite mine.

Die Cut Perf. 13x13¼
2010, Oct. 18   Litho.
Self-Adhesive
576 A187   50o multi   .20   .20
577 A187 26.50k multi   10.00 10.00

Christmas
A188

Santa Claus and: 7k, Two children. 8.50k,
One child.

2010, Oct. 18   *Perf. 13¾x13¼*
578 A188   7k multi   2.75 2.75
579 A188 8.50k multi   3.25 3.25

Booklet Stamps
Self-Adhesive
Serpentine Die Cut 12¼x12
580 A188   7k multi   2.75 2.75
581 A188 8.50k multi   3.25 3.25
  a.   Pair, #580-581   6.00
  b.   Booklet pane of 12, 6 each
       #580-581   36.00

SEMI-POSTAL STAMPS

Catalogue values for unused
stamps in this section are for
Never Hinged items.

No. 35
Surcharged in
Red

1958, May 22 Engr.   *Perf. 13*
B1   A7   30o + 10o on 50o   6.00 1.90
  The surtax was for the campaign against
tuberculosis in Greenland.

No. 32 Surcharged: "Gronlandsfonden
30+10" and Bars
1959, Feb. 23   Unwmk.
B2   A6   30o + 10o on 25o   5.25 5.25
  The surtax was for the benefit of the Greenland Fund.

Two Greenland
Boys in Round
Tower — SP1

1968, Sept. 12 Engr.   *Perf. 13*
B3   SP1 60o + 10o dark red   1.25 1.25
  Surtax for child welfare work in Greenland.

Hans Egede
Explaining Bible
to Natives — SP2

1971, July 3   Engr.   *Perf. 13*
B4   SP2 60o + 10o red brown   2.75 2.75
  See footnote after No. 77.

Frederik IX,
"Dannebrog" off
Umanak — SP3

1972, Apr. 20
B5   SP3 60o + 10o dull red   1.75 1.75
  King Frederik IX (1899-1972). The surtax
was for humanitarian and charitable purposes.

Heimaey Town
and
Volcano — SP4

1973, Oct. 18 Engr.   *Perf. 13*
B6   SP4 70o + 20o gray & red   1.75 1.75
  The surtax was for the victims of the erup-
tion of Heimaey Volcano.

Arm Pulling, by
Hans
Egede — SP5

1976, Apr. 8   Engr.   *Perf. 12½*
B7   SP5 100o + 20o multi   .70   .70
  Surtax for the Greenland Athletic Union.

Rasmussen and
Eskimos — SP6

1979, June 7   Engr.   *Perf. 13*
B8   SP6 1.30k + 20o brown red   .95   .95
  Knud Rasmussen (1879-1933), arctic
explorer and ethnologist.

Stone Tent Ring,
Polar Wolf, King
Eider
Ducks — SP7

1981, Sept. 3   Engr.   *Perf. 13*
B9   SP7 1.60k + 20o lt red brn   .90   .90
  Surtax was for Peary Land Expeditions.

History Type of 1982
Design: Eric the Red sailing for Greenland.

1982, Aug. 2   Engr.   *Perf. 12½*
B10 A39 2k + 40o dk red brn   1.25 1.25
  Surtax was for Cultural House, Julianehab.

Blind Man — SP8

1983, May 19   Engr.
B11 SP8 2.50k + 40o multi   1.40 1.40
  Surtax was for the handicapped.

Greenland
Sports
Union — SP9

1986, Apr. 17   Litho.
B12 SP9 2.80k + 50o Water
            game   2.00 2.00
  Surtax for the Sports Union.

Greenland PO, 50th Anniv. — SP10

1988, Sept. 16 Litho.   *Perf. 12½x13*
B13 SP10 300o +50o multi   3.00 3.00
  Surtax for the purchase of postal artifacts.

Sled Dog,
Common
Eider — SP11

Litho. & Engr.
1990, Sept. 6   *Perf. 13*
B14 SP11 400o + 50o multi   3.75 3.75
  Surtax for the Greenland Environmental
Foundation.

SP12   SP13

1991, Sept. 5   Litho.   *Perf. 13*
B15 SP12 4k +50o multi   15.00 15.00
  Blue Cross of Greenland, 75th Anniv. Sur-
tax benefits Blue Cross of Greenland.

1992, Oct. 8   Litho.   *Perf. 13*
B16 SP13 4k +50o multi   4.25 4.25
  Cancer research in Greenland.

Red
Cross — SP14

Boy Scouts
in
Greenland,
50th Anniv.
SP15

1993, June 17 Litho.   *Perf. 13*
B17 SP14 4k +50o red & blue   2.50 2.50
B18 SP15 4k +50o multi   2.50 2.50
  a.   Souv. sheet, 2 ea #B17-B18   20.00 20.00

1994 Winter Olympics, Lillehammer SP16

1994, Feb. 10   Litho.   Perf. 13
B19 SP16 4k +50o Skiers   3.00 3.00
a.   Souvenir sheet of 4   12.00 12.00

Surtax to support Greenlandic athletes.

Natl. Flag, 10th Anniv. — SP17

1995, June 21   Litho.   Perf. 13
B20 SP17 4k +50o multi   3.00 3.00
a.   Souvenir sheet of 4   12.00 12.00

Surtax for benefit of Greenland Flag Society.

Handicapped and Disabled in Greenland — SP18

1996, Sept. 5   Litho.   Perf. 13
B21 SP18 4.25k +50o multi   2.50 2.50
a.   Souvenir sheet of 4   10.00 10.00

Katuaq Cultural Center, Nuuk SP19

Litho. & Engr.
1997, Jan. 14   Perf. 13
B22 SP19 4.50k +50o multi   2.50 2.50
a.   Souvenir sheet of 4   10.00 10.00

SP20   SP21

Women's Society of Greenland: Kathrine Chemnitz (1894-1978), first Gen. Secretary.

1998, May 29   Litho.   Perf. 13
B23 SP20 4.50k +50o multi   2.50 2.50
a.   Souvenir sheet of 4   10.00 10.00

1999, May 7   Engr.   Perf. 13
B24 SP21 4.50k +50o Pincush-
         ion, Natl. Mu-
         seum   1.60 1.60
a.   Souvenir sheet of 4   7.00 7.00

Surtax for the benefit of Greenland National Museum & Archives.

Drum Dance — SP22

Litho. & Engr.
2000, Aug. 18   Perf. 13¼x13
B25 SP22 4.50k + 1k multi   1.75 1.75
a.   Souvenir sheet of 4   7.00 7.00

Surtax to benefit the Hafnia 01 Philatelic Exhibition, Copenhagen.

2002 Arctic Winter Games — SP23

2001, Feb. 5   Litho.   Perf. 13¼x13
B26 SP23 4.50k +50o multi   1.75 1.75
a.   Souvenir sheet of 4   7.00 7.00

SP24

2002, Mar. 5   Perf. 12¾
B27 SP24 4.50k +50o multi   1.75 1.75
a.   Souvenir sheet of 4   7.00 7.00

Surtax for "Children Are People, Too" Project of Paarisa.

Ornament With Santa Claus, Map of Greenland, House — SP25

2003, Oct. 20   Perf. 13¼
B28 SP25 5k +50o multi   2.00 2.00
a.   Souvenir sheet of 4   8.00 8.00

Society of Greenlandic Children, 80th Anniv. — SP26

2004, May 14   Perf. 13x13¼
B29 SP26 5k +50o multi   2.00 2.00
a.   Souvenir sheet of 4   8.00 8.00

Surtax for Society of Greenlandic Children.

Child — SP27

2005, Jan. 17   Perf. 12¾
B30 SP27 5.25k +50o multi   2.10 2.10
a.   Souvenir sheet of 4   8.50 8.50

Surtax for Save the Children Fund.

Crown Prince Frederik and Crown Princess Mary — SP28

2006, Mar. 29   Perf. 13¼x13¾
B31 SP28 5.50k +50o multi   2.10 2.10
a.   Souvenir sheet of 4   8.50 8.50

Surtax for children's charities.

Amnesty Greenland SP29

2007, Jan. 15   Perf. 13¾x13¼
B32 SP29 575o +50o multi   2.25 2.25
a.   Souvenir sheet of 4   9.00 9.00

Fight Against Tuberculosis SP30

2008, May 24   Perf. 13¾x13½
B33 SP30 575o +50o multi   2.75 2.75
a.   Souvenir sheet of 4   11.00 11.00

Fight Against Cancer SP31

2009, Jan. 19   Perf. 13¼x14
B34 SP31 6.25k +50o blk & red 2.40 2.40
a.   Souvenir sheet of 4   9.75 9.75

Surtax for Greenlandic Cancer Society.

Performer SP32

2010, Jan. 18   Perf. 14x13¼
B35 SP32 7k +50o multi   2.75 2.75
a.   Souvenir sheet of 4   11.00 11.00

Surtax for Silamiut Theater Group.

PARCEL POST STAMPS

Arms of Greenland PP1

Perf. 10¾, 11½

1905-37   Unwmk.   Typo.
Q1 PP1 1o ol grn ('16-
         '26)   57.50 60.00
a.   Perf. 12½ ('05)   775.00 775.00
Q2 PP1 2o yellow ('16-
         '24)   350.00 125.00
Q3 PP1 5o brown ('18-
         '28)   125.00 125.00
a.   Perf. 12½ ('05)   750.00 775.00
Q4 PP1 10o blue ('37)   40.00 72.50
a.   Perf. 12½ ('05)   950.00 625.00
b.   Perf. 11½ ('16)   60.00 65.00
Q5 PP1 15o violet ('15-'28) 275.00 275.00
Q6 PP1 20o red ('15-'33)   17.00 13.00
a.   Perf. 11 ('37)   40.00 60.00

Q7 PP1 70o violet ('37)   40.00 125.00
a.   Perf. 11½ ('30)   275.00 275.00
Q8 PP1 1k yellow ('37)   40.00 140.00
a.   Perf. 11½ ('30)   52.50 65.00
Q9 PP1 3k brown ('30)   140.00 175.00
         Nos. Q1-Q9 (9)   1,009. 1,035.

1937   Litho.   Perf. 11
Q10 PP1 70o pale violet   42.50 150.00
Q11 PP1 1k yellow   50.00 77.50
         Nos. Q10-Q11, never
         hinged   150.00

On lithographed stamps, PAKKE-PORTO is slightly larger, hyphen has rounded ends and lines in shield are fine, straight and evenly spaced.

On typographed stamps, hyphen has squared ends and shield lines are coarse, uneven and inclined to be slightly wavy.

Used values are for stamps postally used from Denmark. Numeral cancels indicate use as postal savings stamps and are worth less. Greenland village cancels are worth more.

Sheets of 25. Certain printings of Nos. Q1-Q2, Q3a, Q4a and Q5-Q6 were issued without sheet margins. Stamps from the outer rows are straight edged. Some of these sheets were reperfed later.

GRENADA

grə-'nä-də

LOCATION — Windward Islands, West Indies
GOVT. — Independent nation in the British Commonwealth
AREA — 133 sq. mi.
POP. — 98,600 (1998 est.)
CAPITAL — St. George's

Grenada consists of Grenada Island and the southern Grenadines, including Carriacou. This colony was granted associated statehood with Great Britain in 1967 and became an independent state Feb. 7, 1974.

12 Pence = 1 Shilling
100 Cents = 1 Dollar (1949)

Catalogue values for unused stamps in this country are for Never Hinged items, beginning with Scott 143 in the regular postage section, Scott B1 in the semipostal section, Scott C1 in the air post section, Scott J15 in the postage due section, and Scott O1 in the official section.

Watermarks

Wmk. 5 — Small Star

Wmk. 6 — Large Star

Wmk. 7 — Large Star with Broad Points

Values for unused stamps are for examples with original gum as defined in the catalogue introduction. Very fine examples of Nos. 1-19, 27-29, and 31-38 will have perforations touching the design on at least one side due to the narrow spacing of the stamps on the plates. Stamps with perfs clear of the design on all four sides are scarce and will command higher prices.

Queen Victoria — A1

Rough Perf. 14 to 16

1861　　Engr.　　Unwmk.

1	A1 1p green		57.50	50.00
a.	1p blue green		5,250.	350.00
b.	As No. 1, horiz. pair, imperf. btwn.			
2	A1 6p rose		1,050.	110.00
b.	6p lake red, perf. 11-12½		1,000.	

No. 2b was not issued. No. 2 imperf is a proof.

1863-71　　　　　　Wmk. 5

3	A1 1p green ('64)	100.00	15.00
a.	1p yellow green	125.00	30.00

4	A1 6p rose	775.00	20.00
5	A1 6p vermilion ('71)	875.00	20.00
a.	6p dull red	4,000.	275.00
g.	Double impression		2,350.
i.	6p orange red ('66)	750.00	14.00

No. 5a always has sideways watermark. Other colors sometimes have sideways watermark.

1873-78　　Clean-Cut Perf. about 15

5B	A1 1p deep green	120.00	47.50
j.	Pair, imperf between		11,000.
c.	1p blue green ('78)	275.00	45.00
h.	Half used as ½p on cover		11,000.
5D	A1 6p vermilion ('75)	925.00	40.00
e.	6p dull red	950.00	40.00
f.	Double impression		2,350.

1873　　　　　　　　Wmk. 6

6	A1 1p blue green	105.00	22.50
a.	Diagonal half used as ½p on cover		11,000.
7	A1 6p vermilion	775.00	35.00

1875　　　　　　　　Perf. 14

7A	A1 1p yellow green	90.00	9.00
b.	Half used as ½p on cover		16,000.
c.	Perf. 15	10,000.	2,600.

A2　　　　　　　　　A2a

Revenue Designs Surcharged in Black
Perf. 14, 14½

1875-81

8	A2 ½p purple ('81)	15.50	7.50
a.	"OSTAGE"	225.00	150.00
b.	Imperf., pair	350.00	
c.	"ALF"	4,000.	
d.	"PEN"		
e.	No hyphen between "HALF" and "PENNY"	225.00	150.00
f.	Double surcharge	350.00	350.00
9	A2a 2½p lake ('81)	70.00	10.00
a.	Imperf., pair	650.00	
b.	Imperf. vertically, pair	4,500.	
c.	"PENCF"	525.00	225.00
d.	No period after "PENNY"	290.00	90.00
e.	"PENOE"	175.00	
10	A2 4p blue ('81)	120.00	10.00

Revenue Designs Surcharged in Dark Blue

11	A2 1sh purple	775.00	20.00
a.	"SHLLIING"	6,500.	800.00
b.	"NE SHILLING"		3,250.
c.	"OSTAGE"	7,250.	3,000.
d.	Invtd. "S" in "POSTAGE"	4,500.	750.00

See Nos. 27-35.

1881　　　　　　　　Wmk. 7

12	A2 2½p lake	200.00	57.50
a.	2½p claret	500.00	140.00
b.	As No. 12, "PENCF"	875.00	325.00
c.	As No. 12, No period after "PENNY"	650.00	230.00
d.	As "a," "PENCF"	1,850.	825.00
e.	As "a," no period after "PENNY"	1,275.	575.00
13	A2 4p blue	325.00	210.00

Revenue Stamp Overprinted "POSTAGE" in Black

A3　　　　　　　　　A4

A5

Revenue Stamp Handstamped "POSTAGE" in Manuscript

A6

1883　　　　　　　　Wmk. 5
Denomination & Crown in 2nd Color

14	A3 ½p orange & grn	900.00	275.00
a.	Unsevered pair	5,000.	1,500.
b.	"POSTAGE" omitted		1,500.
15	A4 ½p orange & grn	325.00	150.00
a.	Unsevered pair	2,000.	525.00
16	A5 1p orange & grn	400.00	65.00
a.	Inverted overprint	3,500.	2,600.
b.	Double overprint	1,625.	1,275.
c.	Inverted "S" in "Postage"	1,150.	700.00
d.	Diagonal half used as ½p on cover		3,500.

"Postage" in Manuscript, Red or Black

18	A6 1p orange & grn (R)		21,000.
19	A6 1p orange & green	—	15,000.

On Nos. 14-19 the words "ONE PENNY" measure from 10-11¼mm in length.
On No. 15, the lower "POSTAGE" is always inverted.
It has been claimed that although Nos. 18 and 19 were used, they were not officially authorized by Grenada's postmaster.

A8　　　　　　　　　A10

1883　　Wmk. 2　　Perf. 14

20	A8 ½p green	1.50	1.25
a.	Tete beche pair	5.00	18.50
21	A8 1p rose	80.00	4.00
a.	Tete beche pair	260.00	290.00
22	A8 2½p ultra	8.00	1.25
a.	Tete beche pair	30.00	57.50
23	A8 4p slate	8.00	2.25
a.	Tete beche pair	22.50	65.00
24	A8 6p red lilac	5.00	6.50
a.	Tete beche pair	21.00	65.00
25	A8 8p bister	10.50	14.00
a.	Tete beche pair	37.50	87.50
26	A8 1sh vin violet	140.00	65.00
a.	Tete beche pair	1,650.	2,250.
	Nos. 20-26 (7)	253.50	94.25

Stamps of types A8, A10 and D2 are printed with alternate horizontal rows inverted. For surcharges see Nos. 36-38, J4-J7.

Revenue Stamps Surcharged

1886　　1p on 1½ org & grn　　Wmk. 6

27	A2 1p on 1½ org & grn	50.00	35.00
a.	Inverted surcharge	350.00	
b.	Diagonal half used as ½ on cover		2,250.
c.	Double surcharge	600.00	350.00
d.	"HALH" instead of "HALF"	300.00	275.00
e.	"F" for first "E" in "THREE"	300.00	225.00
f.	"PFNCE" for "PENCE"	300.00	225.00
28	A2 1p on 1sh org & grn	47.50	37.50
a.	"SHILLNG" instead of "SHILLING"	525.00	450.00
b.	No period after "POSTAGE"	475.00	
c.	Half used as ½p on cover		2,350.

Wmk. 5

29	A2 1p on 4p org & grn	190.00	110.00

1887　　　　　　　　Wmk. 2

30	A10 1p rose	3.50	1.75
a.	Tete beche pair	10.00	24.00

Revenue Stamps Surcharged:

h　　　　　　　　　i

j　　　　　　　　　k

I

1888-91　　Wmk. 5　　Perf. 14½

31	A2 (h) ½p on 2sh & grn ('89)	14.00	26.00
a.	Double surcharge	350.00	375.00
b.	First "S" in "SHILLINGS" inverted	325.00	350.00
32	A2 (i) 4p on 2sh org & grn	45.00	22.50
a.	"4d" and "POSTAGE" 5mm apart	80.00	35.00
b.	"S" inverted, as in #31b	550.00	400.00
c.	As "a," inverted "S," as in #31b	750.00	650.00

"d" Vertical instead of Slanting

33	A2 (j) 4p on 2sh org & grn	875.00	475.00
34	A2 (k) 1p on 2sh org & grn ('90)	92.50	87.50
a.	Inverted surcharge	875.00	—
b.	"S" inverted	825.00	750.00
35	A2 (l) 1p on 2sh org & grn ('91)	70.00	65.00
a.	Inverted surcharge		
b.	No period after "d"	450.00	—
c.	"S" inverted	575.00	575.00

No. 25 Surcharged in Black:

Wmk. 2

36	A8 1p on 8p bister	12.00	16.00
a.	Tete beche pair	50.00	70.00
b.	Inverted surcharge	375.00	325.00
c.	No period after "d"	300.00	300.00

"2" of "½" Upright

37	A8 2½p on 8p bister	11.00	14.00
a.	Tete beche pair	50.00	70.00
b.	Inverted surcharge		
c.	Double surcharge	1,000.	925.00
d.	Triple surcharge		1,100.
e.	Double surcharge, one inverted	650.00	575.00

"2" of "½" Italic

38	A8 2½p on 8p bister	14.00	13.00
	Ovptd. "SPECIMEN"	75.00	
a.	Tete beche pair	50.00	70.00
b.	Tete beche pair, #37, 38	125.00	
c.	Inverted surcharge		
d.	Double surcharge	875.00	925.00
e.	Triple surcharge		1,050.
f.	Triple surch., two inverted		1,000.
g.	Double surcharge, one inverted	625.00	575.00

Queen Victoria — A17

1895-99　　Wmk. 2　Typo.　Perf. 14

39	A17 ½p lilac & green	3.00	2.00
40	A17 1p lilac & car rose	5.25	.90
41	A17 2p lilac & brown	47.50	37.50
42	A17 2½p lilac & ultra	7.50	1.75
43	A17 3p lilac & orange	8.00	18.00
44	A17 6p lilac & green	18.00	50.00
45	A17 8p lilac & black	15.00	52.50
46	A17 1sh green & org	22.50	57.50
	Nos. 39-46 (8)	126.75	220.15

Numerals of ½p, 3p, 8p and 1sh of type A17 are in color on colorless tablet.
Issue dates: 1p, May, 1896; ½p, 2p, Sept. 1899; others, Sept. 5, 1895.

Columbus'
Flagship, La
Concepcion
A18

King Edward
VII
A19

1898, Aug. 15   Engr.   Wmk. 1
47 A18 2½p ultra   17.50 8.00
 a.   Bluish paper   37.50 47.50
Discovery of the island by Columbus, Aug.
15th, 1498.

1902   Wmk. 2   Typo.
48 A19 ½p violet & grn   3.75 1.50
49 A19 1p vio & car
          rose   5.25   .35
50 A19 2p vio & brown   3.50 11.50
51 A19 2½p vio & ultra   4.00 3.25
52 A19 3p vio & org   4.50 10.50
53 A19 6p vio & green   3.00 20.00
54 A19 1sh green & org   5.50 32.50
55 A19 2sh grn & ultra   29.00 65.00
56 A19 5sh grn & car
          rose   47.50 75.00
57 A19 10sh green & vio 140.00 300.00
     Nos. 48-57 (10)   246.00 519.60
Numerals of ½p, 3p, 1sh, 2sh and 10sh of
type A19 are in color on colorless tablet.

1904-06   Wmk. 3   Perf. 14
58 A19 ½p vio & green   20.00 35.00
59 A19 1p vio & car
          rose   15.00 3.00
60 A19 2p vio & brown   65.00 125.00
61 A19 2½p vio & ultra   65.00 75.00
62 A19 3p vio & org   3.25 8.00
63 A19 6p vio & green   9.00 22.50
64 A19 1sh green & org   7.00 32.50
65 A19 2sh grn & ultra   57.50 80.00
66 A19 5sh grn & car
          rose   75.00 110.00
67 A19 10sh green & vio 175.00 300.00
     Nos. 58-67 (10)   491.75 791.00
Nos. 62, 63 and 65 are on both ordinary and
chalky paper.
Issued: #58, 60-62, 64, 1905; #63, 65-67,
1906.

Seal of
Colony
A20

King George
V
A21

1906-11   Engr.
68 A20 ½p green   5.25   .35
69 A20 1p carmine   7.50   .20
70 A20 2p yellow   3.50 3.50
71 A20 2½p blue   7.00 2.00
 a.   2½p ultramarine   9.50 3.75

Typo.
Chalky Paper
Numerals white on dark ground
72 A20 3p vio, yel ('08) 5.50 1.90
73 A20 6p violet ('08)   22.50 25.00
74 A20 1sh blk, grn ('11) 8.00 5.00
75 A20 2sh vio & blue,
          blue ('08)   22.50 14.00
76 A20 5sh red & green,
          yel ('08)   67.50 80.00
     Nos. 68-76 (9)   149.25 131.95

1908   Wmk. 2
77 A20 1sh black, green   37.50 70.00
78 A20 10sh red & grn, grn 120.00 250.00

1913   Ordinary Paper   Wmk. 3
79 A21 ½p green   1.10 1.25
80 A21 1p carmine   2.50   .35
 a.   1p scarlet ('16)   5.00 1.10
81 A21 2p orange   1.90   .35
82 A21 2½p ultra   2.00 4.00

Chalky Paper
83 A21 3p violet, yel   .75 1.00
84 A21 6p dull vio &
          red vio   1.75 10.00
85 A21 1sh black, green   1.10 11.50
 a.   1sh black, emerald   1.75 16.00
 b.   1sh blk, bl grn, olive back 52.50 90.00
 c.   As "a," olive back   1.75 15.00

---

86 A21 2sh vio & ultra,
          bl   7.25 14.00
87 A21 5sh grn & red,
          yel   20.00 67.50
88 A21 10sh grn & red,
          grn   62.50 100.00
 a.   10sh grn & red, emer 60.00 175.00
     Nos. 79-88 (10)   100.85 209.95

1914   Surface-colored Paper
89 A21 3p violet, yel   .70 1.60
90 A21 1sh black, green   1.40 8.50

1921-29   Ordinary Paper   Wmk. 4
91 A21 ½p green   1.40   .35
92 A21 1p rose red   .90   .85
93 A21 1p brown ('23)   1.75   .35
94 A21 1½p rose red
          ('22)   1.75 1.75
95 A21 2p orange   1.40   .35
96 A21 2p gray ('26)   2.75 3.00
97 A21 2½p ultramarine   5.25 10.00
98 A21 2½p gray ('22)   1.10 10.00
99 A21 3p ultra ('22)   1.75 12.50

Chalky Paper
100 A21 3p vio, yel ('26) 3.50 5.75
101 A21 4p blk & red,
          yel ('26)   1.10 4.25
102 A21 5p gray vio & ol
          grn ('22)   1.75 4.75
103 A21 6p dl vio & red
          vio   1.50 22.50
104 A21 6p blk & red
          ('26)   2.50 2.75
105 A21 9p gray vio &
          blk ('22)   2.50 11.00
106 A21 1sh blk, emer
          ('23)   3.00 55.00
107 A21 1sh org brn ('26) 4.50 11.00
108 A21 2sh vio & ultra,
          bl ('22)   7.00 19.00
109 A21 2sh6p blk & red, bl
          ('29)   8.00 22.50
110 A21 3sh grn & vio
          ('22)   6.75 30.00
111 A21 5sh green & red,
          yel ('23)   14.00 40.00
112 A21 10sh green & red,
          emer ('23)   57.50 150.00
     Nos. 91-112 (22)   131.65 417.65

Grand Anse
Beach — A22

Seal of the
Colony — A23

View of Grand
Etang — A24

View of St.
George's — A25

1934, Oct. 23   Engr.   Perf. 12½
114 A22 ½p black brn & blk .20 1.25
 a.   Perf. 12½x13 ('36)   5.00 50.00

Perf. 13½x12½
115 A23 1p blk brn & blk   .65   .35
 a.   Perf 12½   1.10 3.50

Perf. 12½x13½
116 A24 1½p car & black   .90   .45
 a.   Perf 12½ ('36)   5.25 3.75

Perf. 12½
117 A23 2p org & black   1.10   .80
118 A25 2½p deep blue   .55   .55
119 A23 3p ol grn & blk   1.10 3.25
120 A23 6p claret & blk   2.25 2.00
121 A23 1sh brown & blk   2.25 4.50
122 A23 2sh6p ultra & blk 9.00 30.00
123 A23 5sh vio & black   45.00 55.00
     Nos. 114-123 (10)   63.00 98.15
Set, never hinged   125.00

Common Design Types
pictured following the introduction.

Silver Jubilee Issue
Common Design Type
1935, May 6   Perf. 11x12
124 CD301 ½p green & blk   1.10 1.50
125 CD301 1p black & ultra 1.25 2.25
126 CD301 1½p car & blue   1.25 3.25
127 CD301 1sh brn vio & ind 13.00 32.50
     Nos. 124-127 (4)   16.60 39.50
Set, never hinged   27.50

Coronation Issue
Common Design Type
1937, May 12   Wmk. 4   Perf. 11x11½
128 CD302 1p dark purple   .25   .25
129 CD302 1½p dark carmine .25   .20
130 CD302 2½p deep ultra   .50   .35
     Nos. 128-130 (3)   1.00   .80
Set, never hinged   1.60

George
VI — A26

Seal of the
Colony — A28

Grand Anse
Beach — A27

View of Grand
Etang — A29

View of St.
George's — A30

Seal of the
Colony — A31

1937, July 12   Photo.   Perf. 14½x14
131 A26 ¼p chestnut   .50   .75
1938, Mar. 16   Engr.   Perf. 12½
132 A27 ½p green   .80 1.40
133 A28 1p blk brn & blk   .55   .55
134 A29 1½p scarlet & blk   .25   .95
135 A28 2p orange & blk   .20   .55
136 A30 2½p ultramarine   .20   .35
137 A28 3p olive grn &
          blk   .20 2.10
138 A28 6p red vio & blk   1.25   .45
139 A28 1sh org brn & blk 2.50   .45
140 A28 2sh ultra & black 15.00 2.00
141 A28 5sh purple & blk   2.25 2.75

Perf. 14
142 A31 10sh rose car &
          gray blue   20.00 13.00
 a.   10sh deep car & gray blue,
          perf. 12 ('43) 700.00 1,750.
 b.   Perf. 12x13   42.50 12.00
     Nos. 131-142 (12)   43.70 25.30
Set, never hinged   62.50

1938-42   Perf. 12½x13½, 13½x12½
132a A27 ½p   3.50   .90
133a A28 1p   .30   .20
134a A29 1½p car & blk   1.25   .40
135a A28 2p   1.40   .75
136a A30 2½p   7,500. 240.00
137a A28 3p   2.50 1.00
138a A28 6p ('42)   1.25   .35
139a A28 1sh ('42)   2.50 1.50
140a A28 2sh ('41)   17.50 2.00
141a A28 5sh ('47)   2.00 4.50

┌─────────────────────────────┐
│ Catalogue values for unused │
│ stamps in this section, from this │
│ point to the end of the section, are │
│ for Never Hinged items.   │
└─────────────────────────────┘

Peace Issue
Common Design Type
1946, Sept. 25   Perf. 13½x14
143 CD303 1½p carmine   .20   .20
144 CD303 3½p deep blue .20   .70

Silver Wedding Issue
Common Design Types
1948, Oct. 27   Photo.   Perf. 14x14½
145 CD304 1½p scarlet   .20   .20

Engr.; Name Typo.
Perf. 11½x11
146 CD305 10sh gray green 20.00 20.00

UPU Issue
Common Design Types
Engr.; Name Typo. on 6c, 12c
Perf. 13½, 11x11½
1949, Oct. 10   Wmk. 4
147 CD306 5c ultra   .25   .25
148 CD307 6c deep olive 1.50 2.25
149 CD308 12c red lilac .30   .50
150 CD309 24c red brown .25   .55
     Nos. 147-150 (4)   2.30 3.55

A32

A33

A34

1951, Jan. 8   Engr.   Perf. 11½
Center in Black
151 A32 ½c chestnut   .20 1.50
152 A32 1c blue green   .20   .60
153 A32 2c dark brown   .20   .20
154 A32 3c carmine   .25   .20
155 A32 4c deep orange   .40   .25
156 A32 5c purple   .50   .30
157 A32 6c olive   .50   .65
158 A32 7c blue   2.00   .30
159 A32 12c red violet 2.25   .75

Perf. 11½x12½
160 A33 25c dark brown 2.50 1.00
161 A33 50c ultra   6.50   .60
162 A33 $1.50 orange   8.25 8.00

Perf. 11½x13
Center in Gray Blue
163 A34 $2.50 deep carmine 9.50 6.50
     Nos. 151-163 (13)   33.25 20.85
See #180-183, 202. For overprints see
#166-169.

University Issue
Common Design Types
1951, Feb. 16   Perf. 14x14½
164 CD310 3c dp car & gray blk .55 1.00
165 CD311 6c olive & black .65   .60

Nos. 154-156 and 159
Overprinted in Black or
Carmine

1951, Sept. 21   Perf. 11½
166 A32 3c carmine & black .25   .40
167 A32 4c dp orange & black .25 .40
168 A32 5c purple & black (C) .30 .65
169 A32 12c red violet & black .30 .90
     Nos. 166-169 (4)   1.10 2.35
Adoption of a new constitution for the Windward Islands.

Coronation Issue
Common Design Type
1953, June 3   Perf. 13½x13
170 CD312 3c carmine & black .25 .20

Types of 1951 Inscribed "E II R" and

Queen
Elizabeth II — A35

1953-59 Engr. Perf. 11½
Center in Black

171	A35	½c chestnut ('54)	.20	.20
172	A35	1c blue green	.20	.20
173	A35	2c dark brown	.30	.20
174	A35	3c carmine ('54)	.20	.20
175	A35	4c dp orange ('54)	.20	.20
176	A35	5c purple ('54)	.20	.20
177	A35	6c olive	2.00	1.50
178	A35	7c blue ('55)	2.50	.20
179	A35	12c red violet	.30	.20

Perf. 11½x12½
180	A33	25c dark brown ('55)	1.40	.35
181	A33	50c ultra ('55)	6.00	1.00
182	A33	$1.50 orange ('55)	12.50	14.00

Perf. 11½x13
Center in Gray Blue
183	A34	$2.50 deep car ('59)	27.50	11.00
		Nos. 171-183 (13)	53.50	29.45

See Nos. 195-202.

No. 182 was locally surcharged "2" and two black horizontal lines and issued Dec. 23, 1965, for revenue use. It was used postally, though not authorized for postal use. The "2" is found in two type faces.

West Indies Federation
Common Design Type
1958, Apr. 22 Perf. 11½x11 Wmk. 314
184	CD313	3c green	.35	.20
185	CD313	6c blue	.55	.70
186	CD313	12c carmine rose	.60	.20
		Nos. 184-186 (3)	1.50	1.10

Victoria and Elizabeth II and Mail Truck — A36

Queens and: 8c, "La Concepcion" and Dakota plane. 25c, Steam Packet "Solent" and B.O.A.C. plane.

1961, June 1 Photo. Perf. 14½x14
187	A36	3c gray & deep car	.30	.20
188	A36	8c orange & ultra	.60	.25
189	A36	25c blue & maroon	.65	.25
		Nos. 187-189 (3)	1.55	.70

Centenary of first Grenada postage stamps.

Freedom from Hunger Issue
Common Design Type
1963, June 4 Perf. 14x14½
190	CD314	8c green	.30	.20

Red Cross Centenary Issue
Common Design Type
1963, Sept. 2 Litho. Perf. 13
191	CD315	3c black & red	.25	.20
192	CD315	25c ultra & red	.55	.20

Types of 1953-55
Wmk. 314
1963-64 Engr. Perf. 11½
Center in Black
195	A35	2c dark brown	.20	.20
196	A35	3c carmine	.20	.20
197	A35	4c dp orange	.20	.80
198	A35	5c purple	.20	.20
199	A35	6c olive	200.00	95.00
201	A35	12c red violet	.30	.20

Perf. 11½x12½
202	A33	25c dark brown	2.75	1.00
		Nos. 195-198,201-202 (6)	3.85	2.60

Issued: 6c, 1963; others, May 12, 1964.

ITU Issue
Common Design Type
1965, May 17 Litho. Perf. 11x11½
205	CD317	2c vermilion & olive	.20	.20
206	CD317	50c yellow & ver	.25	.20

Intl. Cooperation Year Issue
Common Design Type
1965, Oct. 25 Litho. Perf. 14½
207	CD318	1c blue grn & claret	.20	.20
208	CD318	25c lt violet & green	.20	.20

Churchill Memorial Issue
Common Design Type
1966, Jan. 24 Photo. Perf. 14
Design in Black, Gold and Carmine Rose
209	CD319	1c bright blue	.20	.20
210	CD319	3c green	.20	.20
211	CD319	25c brown	.25	.25
212	CD319	35c violet	.35	.35
		Nos. 209-212 (4)	1.00	1.00

Royal Visit Issue
Common Design Type
1966, Feb. 4 Litho. Perf. 11x12
213	CD320	3c violet blue	.20	.20
214	CD320	35c dark car rose	1.00	.20

Careenage, St. George's A37

Queen Elizabeth II — A38

Designs: 1c, Hillsborough, Carriacou. 2c, Bougainvillea. 3c, Flamboyant plant. 5c, Levera Beach. 8c, Annandale Falls. 10c, Cacao pods. 12c, Inner Harbor. 15c, Nutmeg. 25c, St. George's. 35c, Grand Anse Beach. 50c, Bananas. $1, Seal of Colony. $3, Map of Grenada.

Perf. 14½x13½, 14½ (A38)
1966, Apr. 1 Photo. Wmk. 314
215	A37	1c blue, grn & yel	.20	.80
216	A37	2c dk grn & dp car rose	.20	.20
217	A37	3c multicolored	1.00	.90
218	A37	5c multicolored	1.25	.20
219	A37	6c ultra, grn & car rose	.95	.20
220	A37	8c dp grn, ind & yel	.95	.20
221	A37	10c yel grn, brn & dk car	.50	.20
222	A37	12c multicolored	.30	.90
223	A37	15c multicolored	.30	.20
224	A37	25c dk bl, grn & car rose	.30	.20
225	A37	35c multicolored	.40	.20
226	A37	50c violet & green	1.25	2.00
227	A38	$1 brn, ultra & dull grn	7.00	3.50
228	A38	$2 multicolored	5.00	9.00
229	A38	$3 brt grnsh bl, dk bl & dl yel	4.50	15.00
		Nos. 215-229 (15)	24.10	34.40

For overprints and surcharges see Nos. 237-261.

World Cup Soccer Issue
Common Design Type
1966, July 1 Litho. Perf. 14
230	CD321	5c multicolored	.20	.20
231	CD321	50c multicolored	.45	.70

WHO Headquarters Issue
Common Design Type
1966, Sept. 20 Litho. Perf. 14
232	CD322	8c multicolored	.25	.20
233	CD322	50c multicolored	.55	.25

UNESCO Anniversary Issue
Common Design Type
1966, Dec. 1 Litho. Perf. 14
234	CD323	2c "Education"	.20	.20
235	CD323	15c "Science"	.20	.20
236	CD323	50c "Culture"	.60	.70
		Nos. 234-236 (3)	1.00	1.10

Nos. 216-217, 220 and 224 Overprinted "ASSOCIATED STATEHOOD 1967" in Silver

Perf. 14½x13½
1967, Mar. 3 Photo. Wmk. 314
237	A37	2c dk grn & dp car rose	.20	.20
238	A37	3c multicolored	.20	.20
239	A37	8c dp grn, ind & yel	.20	.20
240	A37	25c dk bl, grn & car rose	.20	.20
		Nos. 237-240 (4)	.80	.80

Nos. 216, 221, 223 and 227-228 Surcharged

Perf. 14½x13½, 14½ (A38)
1967, July 1 Photo. Wmk. 314
241	A37	1c on 15c multi	.20	.20
242	A37	2c dk grn & dp car rose	.20	.20
243	A37	3c on 10c multi	.20	.20
244	A38	$1 multicolored	.30	.25
245	A38	$2 multicolored	.40	.40
		Nos. 241-245 (5)	1.30	1.25

EXPO '67 Intl. Exhib., Montreal, Apr. 28-Oct. 27.

Nos. 215-229 Overprinted in Black: "ASSOCIATED STATEHOOD"

1967-68 Photo. Wmk. 314
246	A37	1c multicolored	.20	.20
247	A37	2c multicolored	.20	.20
248	A37	3c multicolored	.20	.20
249	A37	5c multicolored	.20	.20
250	A37	6c multicolored	.20	.20
251	A37	8c multicolored	.20	.20
252	A37	10c multicolored	.20	.20
253	A37	12c multicolored	.20	.20
254	A37	15c multicolored	.20	.20
255	A37	25c multicolored	.20	.20
256	A37	35c multicolored	.60	.20
257	A37	50c multicolored	1.00	.30
258	A38	$1 multicolored	1.40	.75
259	A38	$2 multicolored	1.25	3.00
260	A38	$3 multicolored	2.50	5.00

Overprinted and Surcharged
261	A38	$5 on $2 multi	1.75	4.50
		Nos. 246-261 (16)	10.50	15.75

Issued: $5, 5/18/68; others, 10/19/67.
For surcharges, see Nos. B1A-B1D.

Pres. John F. Kennedy — A39

Pres. Kennedy and: 25c, 50c, Bird-of-paradise flower. 35c, $1, Roses.

Perf. 14½x14
1968, Jan. 13 Unwmk.
262	A39	1c lt blue & multi	.20	.20
263	A39	15c orange & multi	.20	.20
264	A39	25c violet & multi	.20	.20
265	A39	35c multicolored	.20	.20
266	A39	50c blue & multi	.35	.25
267	A39	$1 multicolored	.50	.70
		Nos. 262-267 (6)	1.65	1.75

50th anniv. of the birth of Pres. John F. Kennedy (1917-1963).

Bugler and Jamboree Emblem — A40

Jamboree Emblem and: 2c, 50c, Boy Scouts sitting in tent. 3c, $1, Lord Baden-Powell.

1968, Feb. 1 Photo. Perf. 13x14
268	A40	1c orange & multi	.20	.20
269	A40	2c emer & multi	.20	.20
270	A40	3c yellow & multi	.20	.20
271	A40	35c multicolored	.30	.20
272	A40	50c blue & multi	.50	.40
273	A40	$1 multicolored	.70	.70
		Nos. 268-273 (6)	2.10	1.90

12th Boy Scout Jamboree, Farragut State Park, Idaho, Aug. 1-9, 1967.

Seascape, by Winston Churchill — A41

Paintings: 12c, Pine at the shore. 15c, 35c, Houses at the shore. 50c, Churchill painting a seascape.

Perf. 14x14½
1968, Mar. 23 Unwmk.
274	A41	10c multicolored	.20	.20
275	A41	12c multicolored	.20	.20
276	A41	15c multicolored	.20	.20
277	A41	25c multicolored	.30	.20
278	A41	35c multicolored	.30	.20
279	A41	50c multicolored	.45	.25
		Nos. 274-279 (6)	1.55	1.25

Winston Churchill as a painter.

Edith McGuire, US, 200m. Dash, 1964 A42

Gold Medal Winners: 2c, 50c, Arthur Wint, Jamaica, 400m run, 1948. 3c, 60c, Adhemar Ferreira da Silva, Brazil, hop, step and jump, 1952 & 1956. 10c, Like 1c.

1968, Sept. 24 Photo. Perf. 12½
280	A42	1c ultra & multi	.20	.30
281	A42	2c lilac & multi	.20	.30
282	A42	3c green & multi	.20	.30
283	A42	10c red org & multi	.20	.30
284	A42	50c Prus blue & multi	.60	.75
285	A42	60c orange & multi	.70	.85
		Nos. 280-285 (6)	2.10	2.80

19th Olympic Games, Mexico City, Oct. 12-27. Nos. 280-282 and 283-285 are printed in sheets of 9 (3 of each denomination).
For surcharges see Nos. 310-315.

Transplant Operations — A43

Perf. 13x13½
1968, Nov. 25 Photo. Unwmk.
286	A43	5c Kidney	.20	.20
287	A43	25c Heart	.35	.20
288	A43	35c Lung	.45	.20
289	A43	50c Cornea	.55	.60
		Nos. 286-289 (4)	1.55	1.20

20th anniv. of WHO.

Adoration of the Magi, by Veronese A44

Paintings: 15c, Madonna and Child with St. John and St. Catherine, by Titian. 35c, Adoration of the Magi, by Botticelli. $1, "A Knight Adoring the Infant Christ" by Vincenzo di Biagio Catena.

GRENADA   505

1968, Dec. 3   *Perf. 12½*

290	A44	5c vio blue & multi	.20	.20
291	A44	15c crimson & multi	.20	.20
292	A44	35c dk green & multi	.20	.20
293	A44	$1 dk blue & multi	.25	.25
		Nos. 290-293 (4)	.85	.85

Christmas. For overprints see Nos. 341-344.

Hibiscus and "La Concepcion" — A45

Yacht in St. George's Harbour — A45a

Designs: 2c, Bird-of-paradise flower. 3c, Bougainvillea. 5c, Rock hind (fish; horiz.). 6c, Sailfish. 8c, Red snapper, horiz. 10c, Giant toad, horiz. 12c, Yellowfoot tortoise. No. 302, Tree boa, horiz. No. 302A, Thunbergia. 25c, Mouse opossum. 35c Armadillo, horiz. 50c, Mona monkey. $1, Bananaquit (bird). $2, Brown pelican. $3, Magnificent frigate bird. $5, Bare-eyed thrush.

Perf. 14x14½, 14½x14; 14x13½ (#302A); 13½x14 (#305A)
Photo.; Litho. (#302A, 305A)

1968-71   Unwmk.

294	A45	1c dl yel & multi	.20	.20
295	A45	2c brt pink & multi	.20	.20
296	A45	3c blue & multi	.20	.20
297	A45	5c violet & multi	.20	.20
298	A45	6c emer & multi	.20	.20
299	A45	8c multicolored	.20	.25
300	A45	10c multicolored	.20	.20
301	A45	12c ver & multi	.20	.20
302	A45	15c emer & multi	.90	.85
302A	A45	15c gray & multi	5.00	3.25
303	A45	25c multicolored	.30	.20
304	A45	35c multicolored	.35	.20
305	A45	50c ultra & multi	.45	.25
305A	A45a	75c blue & multi	10.00	8.00
306	A45	$1 multicolored	3.00	2.40
307	A45	$2 multicolored	4.25	10.00
308	A45	$3 yel & multi	4.25	5.00
309	A45	$5 multicolored	6.00	19.00
		Nos. 294-309 (18)	36.10	50.80

Nos. 294-309 vary in size from 25x44mm to 29x46mm.
The overprint "VOTE/FEB. 28 1972" was applied to the 2c, 3c, 6c and 25c in Feb., 1972.
Issued: 5c, 10c, 25c, $2, 2/4/69; 3c, 8c, 35c, $5, 7/1/69; #302A, 1970; 75c, 10/9/71; others, 10/68.
For surcharges see Nos. 462-464. For overprints see Nos. 528-541, C3-C19.

Nos. 280-285 Surcharged in Carmine

1969, Feb.   *Perf. 12½*

310	A42	5c on 1c multi	.20	.20
311	A42	8c on 2c multi	.20	.20
312	A42	25c on 3c multi	.20	.20
313	A42	35c on 10c multi	.20	.20
314	A42	$1 on 50c multi	.25	.25
315	A42	$2 on 60c multi	.50	.60
		Nos. 310-315 (6)	1.55	1.65

Gov. Hilda Bynoe and View of St. George's A46

Designs: 15c, Premier Eric M. Gairy, fruits and St. George's. 60c, Emblems of Brussels, New York and Montreal World's Fairs.

1969, May 1   Litho.   *Perf. 13x13½*

316	A46	5c multicolored	.20	.20
317	A46	15c multicolored	.20	.20
318	A46	50c multicolored	.20	.20
319	A46	60c multicolored	.20	.30
		Nos. 316-319 (4)	.80	.90

Nos. 310-319 issued to publicize CARIFTA (Caribbean Free Trade Area) Exposition, St. George's, Apr. 5-30.

Gov. Hilda Bynoe — A47

Designs: 25c, Dr. Martin Luther King, Jr. $1, Belshazzar's Feast, by Rembrandt, horiz.

Perf. 13x12½, 12½x13
1969, June 8   Photo.   Unwmk.

320	A47	5c multicolored	.20	.20
321	A47	25c multicolored	.20	.20
322	A47	35c multicolored	.20	.20
323	A47	$1 multicolored	.30	.40
		Nos. 320-323 (4)	.90	1.00

International Human Rights Year.

Batsman Playing Off-drive — A48

Cricket: 10c, Batsman playing defensive stroke. 25c, Batsman sweeping ball. 35c, Batsman playing on-drive.

1969, Aug. 1   *Perf. 14x14½*

324	A48	3c dk blue & multi	.25	.95
325	A48	10c fawn & multi	.30	.40
326	A48	25c dp green & multi	.55	.80
327	A48	35c brt purple & multi	.70	.85
		Nos. 324-327 (4)	1.80	3.00

Astronaut Collecting Moon Rocks, Landing Module and Earth — A49

Designs: ½c, like $1. 1c, Apollo 11, moon and earth. 2c, Landing module "Eagle." 3c, Memorial tablet left on moon. 8c, Separation of rocket and spaceship. 25c, Take off from Cape Kennedy, vert. 35c, Apollo 11 circling the moon, vert. 50c, Splashdown, vert. ½c, 2c, 25c, 50c, $1 inscribed: "We came in peace for all mankind." 1c, 3c, 8c, 35c inscribed: "Like the moon it shall be established forever" Psalms 89:37.

Perf. 13x13½ (½c), 12½
1969, Sept. 24   Litho.   Unwmk.
Size: 56x35mm

| 328 | A49 | ½c multicolored | .20 | .20 |

Size: 44½x28mm, 28x44½mm

329	A49	1c multicolored	.20	.20
330	A49	2c multicolored	.20	.20
331	A49	3c multicolored	.20	.20
332	A49	8c multicolored	.20	.20
333	A49	25c multicolored	.20	.20
334	A49	35c multicolored	.20	.20
335	A49	50c multicolored	.20	.20
336	A49	$1 multicolored	.40	.60
a.		Souvenir sheet of 2	2.25	2.25
		Nos. 328-336 (9)	2.00	2.20

Man's first moonlanding (Apollo 11), July 20, 1969.
No. 336a contains stamps similar to Nos. 331 and 336 with simulated perforations.
For surcharge and overprints see #349, 379-382.

Mahatma Gandhi — A50

Gandhi in various positions. 15c, 25c are vert.

1969, Oct. 8   *Perf. 11½x12, 12x11½*
Queen's Head in Gold

337	A50	6c multicolored	.20	.20
338	A50	15c multicolored	.20	.20
339	A50	25c multicolored	.60	.20
340	A50	$1 multicolored	1.00	1.10
a.		Souvenir sheet of 4	4.50	4.50
		Nos. 337-340 (4)	2.00	1.70

Mohandas K. Gandhi (1869-1948), leader in India's fight for independence.
No. 340a contains stamps similar to Nos. 337-340 with simulated perforation.

Nos. 290-293 Overprinted in Black or Silver with Bars and "1969"

1969, Dec. 23   Photo.   *Perf. 12½*

341	A44	2c on 15c multi	.20	.75
342	A44	5c multi (S)	.20	.20
343	A44	35c multi (S)	.20	.20
344	A44	$1 multi (S)	.85	1.75
		Nos. 341-344 (4)	1.45	2.90

Christmas.

Edward Teach (Blackbeard) A51

Pirates: 25c, Anne Bonney and sailboats. 50c, Jean Lafitte and sailboats. $1, Mary Read, ships and fighting pirates.

1970, Feb. 1   Engr.   *Perf. 13x13½*

345	A51	15c black	.50	.20
346	A51	25c emerald	.80	.20
347	A51	50c purple	1.50	.20
348	A51	$1 carmine	2.40	.95
		Nos. 345-348 (4)	5.20	1.55

No. 328 Surcharged

Type I

Type II

1970, Mar. 18   Litho.   *Perf. 13x13½*

| 349 | A49 | 5c on ½c multi (I) | .40 | .40 |
| a. | | Type II | 1.25 | 1.50 |

Christ, from "The Last Supper," by Andrea del Sarto — A52

Paintings: No. 351 (5c), St. John, from Last Supper by Andrea del Sarto. Nos. 352-353 (15c), Christ Crowned with Thorns, by Anthony Van Dyck. Nos. 354-355 (25c), Passion of Christ, by Hans Memling. Nos. 356-357 (60c), Christ in the Tomb, by Peter Paul Rubens. Nos. 350, 352, 354 and 356 have denomination in lower right corner; others in lower left corner. The stamps of the same denomination are printed se-tenant without separating margin, reproducing continuous picture.

1970, Apr. 13   Litho.   *Perf. 11½x11*

350	A52	5c rose car & multi	.20	.20
351	A52	5c rose car & multi	.20	.20
a.		A52 Pair, #350-351	.40	.40
352	A52	15c ultra & multi	.20	.25
353	A52	15c ultra & multi	.20	.25
a.		A52 Pair, #352-353	.40	.50
354	A52	25c brt vio & multi	.20	.25
355	A52	25c brt vio & multi	.20	.25
a.		A52 Pair, #354-355	.40	.50
356	A52	60c dull org & multi	.40	.55
357	A52	60c dull org & multi	.40	.55
a.		A52 Pair, #354-355	.85	1.10
b.		Souvenir sheet of 4, #354-357	1.40	1.40
		Nos. 350-357 (8)	2.00	2.50

Easter.

Girl Pushing Carriage with Kittens — A53

Designs: 15c, Girl playing with puppy and kitten. 30c, Boy fishing and cat. 60c, Children with pets.

1970, May 27   Litho.   *Perf. 11*

358	A53	5c multicolored	.20	.20
359	A53	15c multicolored	.20	.20
360	A53	30c multicolored	.35	.35
a.		Souvenir sheet of 2	2.25	2.25
361	A53	60c multicolored	.75	1.00
a.		Souvenir sheet of 2	2.25	2.25
		Nos. 358-361 (4)	1.50	1.75

William Wordsworth (1770-1850). English poet. No. 360a contains stamps similar to Nos. 358 and 360; No. 361a contains stamps similar to Nos. 359 and 361. Sheets have simulated perforations.

Indian Parliament — A54

Commonwealth Parliamentary Association Emblem and: 25c, British Parliament. 50c, Canadian Parliament. 60c, Grenadian Parliament.

1970, June 15   **Perf. 14½x14**
362 A54 5c multicolored .20 .20
363 A54 25c multicolored .20 .20
364 A54 50c multicolored .20 .20
365 A54 60c multicolored .20 .20
   a. Souvenir sheet of 4, #362-365 1.25 1.25
   Nos. 362-365 (4) .80 .80

7th Caribbean Regional Conf. of the Commonwealth Parliamentary Assoc., St. George's. June 13-20.

Sun Tower and EXPO Emblem
A55

EXPO Emblem and: 2c, Livelihood Industry pavilion, horiz. 3c, Ikenobo, Japanese floral art, vert. 10c, Adam and Eve, by Tintoretto and Italian pavilion, horiz. 25c, UN pavilion and flags reflected in pool, 50c, Peace statue of St. Francis, San Francisco pavilion, cable car and Golden Gate Bridge, $1, Toshiba-Ihi pavilion, horiz.

1970, Aug. 8   **Litho.**   **Perf. 13½**
366 A55 1c brt blue & multi .20 .20
367 A55 2c multicolored .20 .20
368 A55 3c buff & multi .20 .20
369 A55 10c multicolored .20 .20
370 A55 25c gray & multi .20 .20
371 A55 50c gray & multi .25 1.00
   Nos. 366-371 (6) 1.25 2.00

Souvenir Sheet
372 A55 $1 gold & multi 1.25 1.75

EXPO '70 Intl. Exhib., Osaka, Japan, Mar. 15-Sept. 13.

Pres. Roosevelt and Flag-Raising on Iwo Jima — A56

Designs: 5c, Marshal Georgi K. Zhukov and fall of Berlin. 15c, Winston Churchill and evacuation of Dunkirk. 25c, Charles de Gaulle and liberation of Paris. 50c, General Dwight D. Eisenhower and D-Day landing. 60c, Field Marshal Bernard Montgomery and Battle of Alamein.

1970, Sept. 3   **Perf. 11**
373 A56 ½c multicolored .20 .60
374 A56 5c multicolored 1.00 .35
375 A56 15c multicolored 1.50 .55
376 A56 25c multicolored 1.75 .55
377 A56 50c multicolored 2.00 1.60
378 A56 60c multicolored 2.25 3.00
   a. Souv. sheet of 4 #373, 375, 377-378 6.75 6.75
   Nos. 373-378 (6) 8.70 6.65

End of World War II, 25th anniversary.

Nos. 333-336 Overprinted in Black or Silver: "PHILYMPIA / LONDON 1970"
1970, Sept. 18   **Perf. 12½**
379 A49 25c multicolored .20 .20
380 A49 35c multicolored .20 .20
381 A49 50c multicolored .25 .25
382 A49 $1 multi (S) .50 .50
   Nos. 379-382 (4) 1.15 1.15

Philympia 1970, London philatelic exhibition, Sept. 18-26. The overprint on No. 382 is vertical, reading up.
This overprint was applied in silver to No. 336a. Value $45.

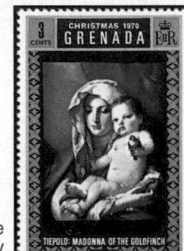

UPU Headquarters, Emblem and Old Transportation — A57

UPU Headquarters, emblem and: 25c, Jet plane, ship and diesel train. 50c, Rowland Hill, vert. $1, Abraham Lincoln, vert.

1970, Oct. 17   **Litho.**   **Perf. 14½**
383 A57 15c orange & multi .65 .25
384 A57 25c blue & multi .65 .25
385 A57 50c multicolored .40 .40
386 A57 $1 rose & multi .60 2.00
   a. Souvenir sheet of 2 2.10 3.00
   Nos. 383-386 (4) 2.30 2.85

Opening of the new UPU Headquarters in Bern. No. 386a contains stamps similar to Nos. 385-386.

Madonna of the Goldfinch, by Tiepolo — A58

Christmas (Paintings): No. 388, 35c, Virgin and Child with Sts. Peter and Paul, by Dirk Bouts. No. 389, $1, Virgin and Child, by Bellini. 3c, Like No. 387. 2c, 50c, Madonna of the Basket, by Correggio.

1970, Dec. 5   **Perf. 14x13½**
387 A58 ½c yel grn & multi .20 .20
388 A58 ½c pink & multi .20 .20
389 A58 ½c yellow & multi .20 .20
390 A58 2c lt blue & multi .20 .20
391 A58 3c dp rose & multi .20 .20
392 A58 35c dk green & multi .30 .40
393 A58 50c brown & multi .45 .50
394 A58 $1 purple & multi .70 1.10
   a. Souvenir sheet of 2, #393-394 2.75 3.00
   Nos. 387-394 (8) 2.45 3.00

Nursing in 19th Century A59

Designs: 15c, Horse-drawn ambulance, Northern France, 1918. 25c, First aid station, 1941. 60c, Red Cross truck loaded on plane, 1970 emergency aid.

1970, Dec. 12   **Litho.**   **Perf. 14½x14**
395 A59 5c red & multi .20 .20
396 A59 15c red & multi .30 .20
397 A59 25c red & multi .50 .35
398 A59 60c red & multi 1.00 1.25
   a. Souvenir sheet of 4, #395-398 2.25 2.00
   Nos. 395-398 (4) 2.00 2.00

Centenary of the British Red Cross Society.

John Dewey, Children Learning to Paint — A60

Designs: 10c, Jean-Jacques Rousseau and students. 50c, Moses Maimonides and biology student. $1, Bertrand Russell and boys.

1971, May 8   **Litho.**   **Perf. 13½**
399 A60 5c multicolored .20 .20
400 A60 10c multicolored .20 .20
401 A60 50c multicolored .50 .50

402 A60 $1 multicolored 1.10 .75
   a. Souvenir sheet of 2, #401-402 2.00 2.25
   Nos. 399-402 (4) 2.00 1.65

International Education Year.

Jennifer Hosten and Map of Grenada A61

1971, June 1   **Litho.**   **Perf. 13½**
403 A61 5c vio blue & multi .20 .20
404 A61 10c red lilac & multi .20 .20
405 A61 15c brt rose & multi .25 .20
406 A61 25c violet & multi .30 .25
407 A61 35c blue & multi .35 .45
408 A61 50c red & multi .75 .75
   a. Souvenir sheet of 1 1.90 1.90
   Nos. 403-408 (6) 2.05 2.05

Honoring Miss Jennifer Hosten of Grenada, Miss World, 1971. No. 408a, printed on silk, contains imperf. stamp similar to No. 408.
Nos. 403-408 and 408a were overprinted "INTERPEX/1972" in Mar. 1972. Value $9.50.
For surcharge and overprints #465, C23-C26.

Canadian and French Boy Scouts — A62

Boy Scouts from: 35c, West Germany and US. 50c, Australia and Japan. 75c, Grenada and Great Britain.

1971, Aug.   **Litho.**   **Perf. 11**
409 A62 5c multicolored .20 .20
410 A62 35c multicolored .40 .40
411 A62 50c multicolored .50 .60
412 A62 75c multicolored .65 .90
   a. Souvenir sheet of 2, #411-412 2.40 2.75
   Nos. 409-412 (4) 1.75 2.10

13th Boy Scout World Jamboree, Asagiri Plain, Japan, Aug. 2-10.

Grenada No. 1 — A64

15c, Grenada #2 & Queen Elizabeth II. 35c, Grenada #1, 2. 50c, Grenada #1 & scroll.

1971, Nov. 6   **Litho.**   **Perf. 11**
417 A64 5c dk red & multi .25 .20
418 A64 15c multicolored .35 .20
419 A64 35c dull org & multi .55 .25
420 A64 50c dk green & multi .75 1.75
   a. Souvenir sheet of 2, #419-420 1.75 1.75
   Nos. 417-420 (4) 1.90 2.40

110th anniversary of postal service.

Splashdown, Apollo 13 — A65

Designs: 2c, Capsule and rafts in ocean, Apollo 13. 3c, Separation of landing module from rocket, Apollo 14. 10c, Astronauts collecting moon rocks, Apollo 14. 25c, Astronauts in moon rover, Apollo 15. 50c, $1, Rocket blast-off, Apollo 15, vert.

1971, Nov.
421 A65 1c multicolored .20 .30
422 A65 2c multicolored .20 .30
423 A65 3c black & multi .20 .30
424 A65 10c black & multi .40 .20
425 A65 25c multicolored 1.25 .35
426 A65 $1 multicolored 2.75 3.50
   Nos. 421-426 (6) 5.00 4.95

Souvenir Sheet
427 A65 50c multicolored 2.75 2.75

US moon missions of Apollo 13, 14 and 15.

67th Regiment of Foot, 1787 — A66

Designs: 1c, 45th Regiment of Foot, 1792. 2c, 29th Regiment of Foot, 1794. 10c, 9th Regiment of Foot, 1801. 25c, 2nd Regiment of Foot, 1815. $1, 70th Regiment of Foot, 1764.

1971, Dec.   **Perf. 13½x14**
428 A66 ½c red & multi .20 .20
429 A66 1c red & multi .20 .20
430 A66 2c red & multi .20 .20
431 A66 10c red & multi .55 .20
432 A66 25c red & multi 1.00 .30
433 A66 $1 red & multi 3.00 2.75
   a. Souv. sheet of 2, #432-433, perf. 15 4.25 4.25
   Nos. 428-433 (6) 5.15 3.85

Uniforms of British units stationed in Grenada.
For surcharges see Nos. 439, C1-C2.

Napoleon, by Edouard Détaille A63

Paintings of Napoleon: 15c, Outside Madrid, by Carle Vernet. 35c, Crossing the Alps, by Jacques Louis David. $2, Portrait, by David.

1971, Sept.   **Perf. 13x13½**
413 A63 5c multicolored .20 .20
414 A63 15c multicolored .20 .20
415 A63 35c multicolored .35 .35
   a. Souvenir sheet of 1 2.75 3.00
416 A63 $2 multicolored 1.25 1.50
   Nos. 413-416 (4) 2.00 2.25

Sesquicentennial of the death of Napoleon Bonaparte (1769-1821).
No. 415a contains stamp similar to No. 415 with simulated perforations.

Adoration of the Kings, by Memling — A67

Christmas: 25c, Madonna and Child, sculpture by Michelangelo. 35c, Madonna and Child, by Murillo. 50c, Madonna with the Apple, by Memling. $1, Adoration of the Kings, by Jan Mostaert.

1971, Dec.   *Perf. 14x13½*
434	A67	15c gold & multi	.20	.20
435	A67	25c gold & multi	.30	.20
436	A67	35c gold & multi	.35	.20
437	A67	50c gold & multi	.50	.75
		Nos. 434-437 (4)	1.35	1.35

Souvenir Sheet
| 438 | A67 | $1 gold & multi | 1.10 | 1.10 |

No. 430 Surcharged with New Value, Olympic Rings and: "WINTER OLYMPICS / FEB. 3-13, 1972 / SAPPORO, JAPAN"

1972, Feb. 3   *Perf. 13½x14*
| 439 | A66 | $2 on 2c red & multi | 1.50 | 1.50 |
| a. | | Souvenir sheet of 2 | 2.25 | 2.25 |

11th Winter Olympic Games, Sapporo, Japan, Feb. 3-13. See Nos. C1-C2.
No. 439a is overprinted in red on No. 433a (no surcharge); margin inscribed in red: "SAPPORO 1972."

King Arthur, UNICEF Emblem A68

UNICEF Emblem and: 1c, 50c, Robin Hood. 2c, 75c, Robinson Crusoe, vert. 25c, like ½c. $1, Mary and her Little Lamb, vert.

1972, Mar. 4   *Perf. 14½x14, 14x14½*
450	A68	½c dp blue & multi	.20	.20
451	A68	1c yellow & multi	.20	.20
452	A68	2c dp yel & multi	.20	.20
453	A68	25c salmon & multi	.20	.20
454	A68	50c multicolored	.25	.35
455	A68	75c blue & multi	.35	.60
456	A68	$1 multicolored	.45	.85
a.		Souvenir sheet of 1	1.10	1.10
		Nos. 450-456 (7)	1.85	2.60

25th anniv. (in 1971) of UNICEF.

Yachting A69

1c, 50c, Equestrian. 2c, 35c, Running, vert.

1972, Sept. 8   *Litho.*   *Perf. 14*
457	A69	½c multicolored	.20	.20
458	A69	1c lt blue & multi	.20	.20
459	A69	2c orange & multi	.20	.20
460	A69	35c yellow & multi	.50	.80
461	A69	50c yel grn & multi	.70	1.10
		Nos. 457-461,C20-C21 (7)	3.20	3.55

20th Olympic Games, Munich, Aug. 26-Sept. 11. See No. C22.

Nos. 294-296, 403 Surcharged with New Value and Two Bars

Perf. 14x14½, 13½
1972, Oct.   *Photo.*
462	A45	12c on 1c multi	.50	.55
463	A45	12c on 2c multi	.50	.55
464	A45	12c on 3c multi	.50	.55
465	A61	12c on 5c multi	.50	.55
		Nos. 462-465 (4)	2.00	2.20

Silver Wedding Issue, 1972
Common Design Type

Design: Queen Elizabeth II, Prince Philip, seal of Grenada and myristica fragrans.

Perf. 14x14½
1972, Nov. 20   *Wmk. 314*
| 466 | CD324 | 8c olive & multi | .20 | .20 |
| 467 | CD324 | $1 multicolored | .45 | .45 |

Boy Scout Saluting A70

Designs: 1c, Two Scouts knotting ropes. 2c, 70c, 75c, Scouts from different nations. 3c, 60c, $1, Lord Baden-Powell.

Unwmk.
1972, Dec. 2   *Litho.*   *Perf. 14*
468	A70	½c yellow & multi	.20	.20
469	A70	1c red & multi	.20	.20
470	A70	2c yellow & multi	.20	.20
471	A70	3c brt lilac & multi	.20	.20
472	A70	75c lt blue & multi	1.00	1.00
473	A70	$1 multicolored	1.50	1.50
		Nos. 468-473,C27-C28 (8)	4.30	4.20

Souvenir Sheet
474		Sheet of 2	3.00	3.00
a.		A70 60c ocher & multi	1.40	1.40
b.		A70 70c pale lilac & multi	1.60	1.60

Boy Scouts, 65th anniversary.

Virgin and Child, Crosier — A71

Christmas: 3c, 35c, 70c, The Three Kings. 5c, $1, Holy Family. 25c, 60c, Like 1c.

1972, Dec. 9   *Litho.*   *Perf. 14x13½*
475	A71	1c blue & multi	.20	.20
476	A71	3c gray & multi	.20	.20
477	A71	5c multicolored	.20	.20
478	A71	25c multicolored	.20	.20
479	A71	35c lt blue & multi	.25	.25
480	A71	$1 ocher & multi	.80	.80
		Nos. 475-480 (6)	1.85	1.85

Souvenir Sheet
Perf. 15
481		Sheet of 2	1.25	1.25
a.		A71 60c blue & multi	.50	.50
b.		A71 70c bright pink & multi	.70	.70

Flamingos — A72

1973, Jan. 5   *Litho.*   *Perf. 14*
482	A72	25c shown	.90	.25
483	A72	35c Tapir	.70	.25
484	A72	60c Macaws	1.50	1.75
485	A72	70c Ocelot	1.40	2.25
		Nos. 482-485 (4)	4.50	4.50

National Zoo of Grenada.

Class II Ocean Racing Yacht — A73

1973, Jan. 26   *Litho.*   *Perf. 13½x14*
486	A73	25c shown	.40	.35
487	A73	35c Boats in St. George's Harbour	.55	.50
488	A73	60c Yacht "Bloodhound"	.90	.85
489	A73	70c St. George's Harbour	.95	1.10
		Nos. 486-489 (4)	2.80	2.80

Yachting off Grenada.

Sun God Helios, Equinoxes and Solstices — A74

WMO Emblem and: 1c, Poseidon and Nomad automatic storm detector. 2c, Zeus and radarscope. 3c, Goddess Iris, rainbow, weather balloon. 35c, Hermes, ATS 3 satellite. 50c, Zephyr and circulation of atmosphere. 75c, Demeter, space photograph of storm. $1, Selene, globe showing world rainfall. $2, Computer weather map (42x31mm).

1973, July 6   *Litho.*   *Perf. 13½*
490	A74	½c multicolored	.20	.20
491	A74	1c multicolored	.20	.20
492	A74	2c multicolored	.20	.20
493	A74	3c multicolored	.20	.20
494	A74	35c multicolored	.30	.20
495	A74	50c multicolored	.45	.25
496	A74	75c multicolored	.55	.45
497	A74	$1 multicolored	.55	.55
		Nos. 490-497 (8)	2.65	2.25

Souvenir Sheet
| 498 | A74 | $2 multicolored | 1.75 | 1.75 |

Intl. meteorological cooperation, cent.

Racing Class Yachts — A75

1973, Aug. 3   *Litho.*   *Perf. 13½*
499	A75	½c shown	.20	.20
500	A75	1c Cruising class	.20	.20
501	A75	2c Open-decked sloops	.20	.20
502	A75	35c Sloop Mermaid	.35	.20
503	A75	50c St. George's Harbour	.45	.25
504	A75	75c Map of Carriacou	.65	.65
505	A75	$1 Boat building	.80	.80
		Nos. 499-505 (7)	2.85	2.50

Souvenir Sheet
| 506 | A75 | $2 End of race | 1.50 | 1.75 |

Carriacou Regatta, August 1973.

Ignaz Philipp Semmelweiss A76

Designs: Physicians and scientists.

1973, Sept. 17   *Litho.*   *Perf. 14½*
507	A76	½c shown	.25	.20
508	A76	1c Louis Pasteur	.25	.20
509	A76	2c Edward Jenner	.25	.20
510	A76	3c Sigmund Freud	.25	.20
511	A76	25c Emil von Behring	.45	.45
512	A76	35c Carl Jung	.60	.60
513	A76	50c Charles Calmette	.90	.90
514	A76	$1 William Harvey	1.75	1.75
		Nos. 507-514 (8)	4.70	4.50

Souvenir Sheet
| 515 | A76 | $2 Marie Curie | 2.50 | 2.50 |

WHO, 25th anniv.

Princess Anne and Mark Phillips — A77

1973, Nov. 14   *Wmk. 314*   *Perf. 13½*
516	A77	25c dp orange & multi	.30	.80
517	A77	$2 green & multi	.30	.80
a.		Souv. sheet of 2 (75c, $1)	.75	.75

Wedding of Princess Anne and Capt. Mark Phillips.
Nos. 516-517 were issued only in sheets of 5 plus label. Colors of 75c and $1 are as those of 25c and $2.

Virgin and Child, by Carlo Maratti — A78

Christmas (Paintings): 1c, Virgin and Child, by Carlo Crivelli. 2c, Virgin and Child, by Verrocchio. 3c, Adoration of the Shepherds, by Roberti. 25c, Holy Family, by Federigo Baroccio. 35c, Holy Family, by Bronzino. 75c, Mystic Nativity, by Botticelli. $1, Adoration of the Kings, by Geertgen tot Sint Jans. $2, Adoration of the Kings, by Jan Mostaert (30x45mm).

1973, Nov.   *Unwmk.*   *Perf. 14½*
519	A78	½c lt brown & multi	.20	.20
520	A78	1c citron & multi	.20	.20
521	A78	2c blue & multi	.20	.20
522	A78	3c green & multi	.20	.20
523	A78	25c multicolored	.25	.25
524	A78	35c multicolored	.25	.25
525	A78	75c vio blue & multi	.30	.80
526	A78	$1 multicolored	.35	1.00
		Nos. 519-526 (8)	1.95	3.10

Souvenir Sheet
Perf. 13½x14
| 527 | A78 | $2 red & multi | 2.10 | 2.10 |

Nos. 294-297, 299-301, 303-304, 305A-309 Overprinted

Perf. 14x14½, 14½x14
1974, Feb. 7   *Photo.*
528	A45	1c multicolored	.20	.20
529	A45	2c multicolored	.20	.20
530	A45	3c multicolored	.20	.20
531	A45	5c multicolored	.20	.20
532	A45	8c multicolored	.20	.20
533	A45	10c multicolored	.20	.20
534	A45	12c multicolored	.20	.20
535	A45	25c multicolored	.50	.35
536	A45	35c multicolored	.75	.50

Litho.
Perf. 13½x14
| 537 | A45a | 75c multicolored | 2.75 | 1.25 |

Photo.
Perf. 14x14½
538	A45	$1 multicolored	4.75	1.50
539	A45	$2 multicolored	7.25	6.00
540	A45	$3 multicolored	9.25	7.50
541	A45	$5 multicolored	14.50	17.00
		Nos. 528-541 (14)	41.15	35.50

Grenada's independence, Feb. 7, 1974. Size of overprint on vertical stamps 16x5mm; on horizontal stamps 20x6mm.

Creative Arts Theater, Jamaica Campus — A79

Designs: 25c, Marryshow House, University Center. 50c, Chapel, vert. $1, $2, University coat of arms, vert.

1974, Apr. 10		**Litho.**	**Perf. 13½**	
542	A79	10c multicolored	.20	.20
543	A79	25c multicolored	.20	.20
544	A79	50c multicolored	.25	.25
545	A79	$1 multicolored	.30	.30
		Nos. 542-545 (4)	.95	.95
		Souvenir Sheet		
546	A79	$2 multicolored	.90	.90

25th anniv. of the University of the West Indies.

Prime Minister Eric M. Gairy — A80

1974, Aug. 19		**Litho.**	**Perf. 13½**	
547	A80	3c Nutmeg and mace	.20	.20
548	A80	8c Map of Grenada	.20	.20
549	A80	25c shown	.30	.30
550	A80	35c Anse Beach and Flag	.45	.30
551	A80	$1 Coat of arms	1.10	1.10
		Nos. 547-551 (5)	2.25	2.10
		Souvenir Sheet		
552	A80	$2 Coat of arms	1.25	1.25

Grenada's independence.

Soccer, Flags of West Germany and Chile — A81

1974, Sept. 3 **Litho.** **Perf. 14½**

Soccer Games and Flags: 1c, East Germany and Australia. 2c, Yugoslavia and Brazil. 10c, Scotland and Zaire. 25c, Netherlands and Uruguay. 50c, Sweden and Bulgaria. 75c, Italy and Haiti. $1, Poland and Argentina. $2, Flags of participating nations, horiz.

553	A81	½c multicolored	.20	.20
554	A81	1c multicolored	.20	.20
555	A81	2c multicolored	.20	.20
556	A81	10c multicolored	.20	.20
557	A81	25c multicolored	.20	.20
558	A81	50c multicolored	.20	.20
559	A81	75c multicolored	.40	.40
560	A81	$1 multicolored	.60	.60
		Nos. 553-560 (8)	2.20	2.20
		Souvenir Sheet		
		Perf. 13		
561	A81	$2 multicolored	1.75	1.75

World Cup Soccer Championship, Munich, June 13-July 7.

19th Century US Mail Train, Concorde and UPU Emblem — A82

UPU Emblem and: 1c, Sailing ship "Caesar," 1839, and helicopter. 2c, Zeppelin, jet and early planes. 8c, Pigeon post, 1480, telephone dial. 15c, Bellman, 18th cent. and radar. 25c, German Imperial messenger, 1450, satellite. 35c, French pillar box and ocean liner. $1, German mailman, 18th cent., and futuristic mail train. $2, St. Gotthard mail coach, 1735, vert.

1974, Oct. 8		**Litho.**	**Perf. 14½**	
562	A82	½c rose & multi	.20	.20
563	A82	1c gray & multi	.20	.20
564	A82	2c dull pink & multi	.20	.20
565	A82	8c yellow & multi	.20	.20
566	A82	15c yel grn & multi	.45	.20
567	A82	25c dull yel & multi	.50	.20
568	A82	35c lilac & multi	.75	.20
569	A82	$1 lt blue & multi	2.00	1.60
		Nos. 562-569 (8)	4.50	3.00
		Souvenir Sheet		
		Perf. 13		
570	A82	$2 multicolored	1.75	2.25
		UPU, cent.		

Sir Winston Churchill — A83

Design: $2, Churchill, different portrait.

1974, Oct. 28		**Litho.**	**Perf. 13½**	
571	A83	35c multicolored	.25	.25
572	A83	$2 multicolored	.75	.75
		Souvenir Sheet		
573		Sheet of 2	1.10	1.10
a.		A83 75c like 35c	.45	.45
b.		A83 $1 like $2	.65	.65

Winston Churchill (1874-1965).

Virgin and Child, by Botticelli — A84

Christmas: Paintings of the Virgin and Child.

1974, Nov. 18			**Perf. 14½**	
574	A84	½ shown	.20	.20
575	A84	1c Niccolo di Pietro	.20	.20
576	A84	2c Van der Weyden	.20	.20
577	A84	3c Bastiani	.20	.20
578	A84	10c Giovanni	.20	.20
579	A84	25c Van der Weyden	.20	.20
580	A84	50c Botticelli	.25	.25
581	A84	$1 Mantegna	.40	.40
		Nos. 574-581 (8)	1.85	1.85
		Souvenir Sheet		
		Perf. 13½		
582	A84	$2 Niccolo di Pietro	1.40	1.40

Yachts and Point Saline A85

1c, Grenada Yacht Club race, St. George's. 2c, Careenage taxi (boat). 3c, Large working boats. 5c, Deep Water Dock, St. George's. 6c, Cacao beans in drying trays. 8c, Nutmeg

branch. 10c, River Antoine Estate rum distillery, c. 1785. 12c, Cacao branch. 15c, Fishermen landing catch at Fontenoy. 20c, Parliament Building, St. George's. 25c, Fort George cannons. 35c, Pearls Airport. 50c, General Post Office. 75c, Carib Leap, Sauteurs Bay. $1, Careenage, St. George's. $2, St. George's harbor at night. $3, Grand Anse Beach. $5, Canoe Bay and Black Bay from Point Saline Lighthouse. $10, Sugar-loaf Island from Levera Beach.

1975		**Litho.**	**Perf. 14½**	
		Size: 38x25mm		
583	A85	½c multicolored	.20	.55
584	A85	1c multicolored	.20	.20
585	A85	2c multicolored	.20	.20
586	A85	3c multicolored	.20	.20
587	A85	5c multicolored	.25	.20
588	A85	6c multicolored	.20	.20
589	A85	8c multicolored	1.25	.20
590	A85	10c multicolored	.20	.20
591	A85	12c multicolored	.35	.20
592	A85	15c multicolored	.20	.20
593	A85	20c multicolored	.20	.20
594	A85	25c multicolored	.25	.20
595	A85	35c multicolored	.25	.20
596	A85	50c multicolored	.20	.25
		Perf. 13½x14		
		Size: 45x28mm		
597	A85	75c multicolored	.55	.40
598	A85	$1 multicolored	.60	.60
599	A85	$2 multicolored	.60	1.25
600	A85	$3 multicolored	.65	1.75
601	A85	$5 multicolored	.80	2.50
602	A85	$10 multicolored	2.40	5.50
		Nos. 583-602 (20)	9.75	15.20

Issue dates: Nos. 583-596, Jan. 13; Nos. 597-601, Jan. 22; No. 602, Mar. 26.
For overprints, see Nos. 965-979.

1978			**Perf. 13**	
584a	A85	1c	.20	.20
585a	A85	2c	.20	.20
586a	A85	3c	.20	.20
587a	A85	5c	.20	.20
588a	A85	6c	.20	.25
590a	A85	10c	.20	.30
592a	A85	15c	.20	.35
593a	A85	20c	.20	.40
594a	A85	25c	.20	.50
596a	A85	50c	.40	.55
		Nos. 584a-596a (10)	2.20	3.00

Sailfish A86

Designs: Big game fish.

1975, Feb. 3			**Perf. 14½**	
603	A86	½c shown	.20	.20
604	A86	1c Blue marlin	.20	.20
605	A86	2c White marlin	.20	.20
606	A86	10c Yellowfin tuna	.20	.20
607	A86	25c Wahoo	.35	.30
608	A86	50c Dolphin	.60	.40
609	A86	70c Grouper	.85	.40
610	A86	$1 Great barracuda	1.10	.50
		Nos. 603-610 (8)	3.70	2.40
		Souvenir Sheet		
		Perf. 13		
611	A86	$2 Mako shark	2.40	2.40

Passiflora Quadrangularis — A87

Designs: Flowers of Grenada.

1975, Feb. 26		**Litho.**	**Perf. 14½**	
612	A87	½c shown	.20	.20
613	A87	1c Bleeding heart	.20	.20
614	A87	2c Poinsettia	.20	.20
615	A87	3c Obroma cacao	.20	.20
616	A87	10c Gladioli	.25	.20
617	A87	25c Red head-yellow head	.45	.20
618	A87	50c Plumbago	.65	.25
619	A87	$1 Orange blossoms	.95	.45
		Nos. 612-619 (8)	3.10	1.90
		Souvenir Sheet		
		Perf. 13½		
620	A87	$2 Barbados gooseberry	1.90	1.90

Grenada Flag and UN Emblem — A88

Designs: 1c, UN and Grenada flags. 2c, $1, UN emblem and Grenada coat of arms. 35c, UN emblem over map of Grenada. 50c, Grenada flag in front of UN Headquarters. 75c, like ½c. $2, UN emblem and scroll.

1975, Mar. 19			**Perf. 14½**	
621	A88	½c multicolored	.20	.20
622	A88	1c multicolored	.20	.20
623	A88	2c multicolored	.20	.20
624	A88	35c multicolored	.25	.25
625	A88	50c multicolored	.25	.25
626	A88	$2 multicolored	.60	.60
		Nos. 621-626 (6)	1.70	1.70
		Souvenir Sheet		
		Perf. 13½		
627		Sheet of 2	1.40	1.40
a.		A88 75c multicolored	.55	.55
b.		A88 $1 multicolored	.90	.90

Grenada's admission to the United Nations, Sept. 17, 1974.

Remainders of Grenada stamps between Scott Nos. 630 and 872, except Nos. 747-748 and 802-804, were later canceled to order and sold at a fraction of their face value. Our used values for these stamps are for c-t-o examples. Postally used stamps are worth the same as unused, never hinged examples.

Midnight Ride of Paul Revere — A89

1c, Crispus Attucks at Boston Massacre. 2c, Patrick Henry. 3c, Franklin visiting Washington at the front. 5c, Lexington-Concord. 10c, John Paul Jones. #634, Arms of Grenada & US. #635, Flags of Grenada & US.

1975, May 6		**Litho.**	**Perf. 14½, 13**
628	A89	½c Prus blue & multi	.20	.20
629	A89	1c buff & multi	.20	.20
630	A89	2c dp org & multi	.20	.20
631	A89	3c orange & multi	.20	.20
632	A89	5c Prus blue & multi	.20	.20
633	A89	10c ultra & multi	.20	.20
		Nos. 628-633,C29-C32 (10)	3.10	2.05
		Souvenir Sheets		
		Perf. 13½		
634	A89	$2 tan & multi	1.00	.45
635	A89	$2 gray & multi	1.00	.45

American Revolution Bicentennial. Size of stamps on Nos. 634-635: 47x34mm.
Nos. 628-633 issued in sheets of 40. Each denomination was also printed in sheets of 5 plus label, perf. 13.

Angel Collecting Jesus' Blood in Grail, by Bellini — A90

Easter (Paintings): 1c, Pieta, by Bellini. 2c, The Deposition, by Rogier van der Weyden. 3c, Pieta, by Bellini. 35c, Descent from the Cross, by Bellini. 75c, Jesus Rising from the Tomb, by Bellini. $1, Descent from the Cross, by Procaccini. $2, Pieta, by Botticelli.

1975, May 21

636	A90	½c multicolored	.20	.20
637	A90	1c multicolored	.20	.20
638	A90	2c multicolored	.20	.20
639	A90	3c multicolored	.20	.20
640	A90	35c multicolored	.30	.20
641	A90	75c multicolored	.35	.20
642	A90	$1 multicolored	.45	.20
		Nos. 636-642 (7)	1.90	1.40

Souvenir Sheet
Perf. 13½

643	A90	$2 multicolored	1.60	.65

Scouts Studying Wildlife, Nordjamb 75 Emblem — A91

Nordjamb 75 Emblem and: 1c, Seamanship; Scouts in sailboat. 2c, Survival; Scouts reading map. 35c, First aid. 40c, Physical fitness; gymnastics. 75c, Mountaineering. $1, Emergency boat building. $2, Scouts singing.

1975, July 2   Litho.   Perf. 14

644	A91	½c blue & multi	.20	.20
645	A91	1c blue & multi	.20	.20
646	A91	2c blue & multi	.20	.20
647	A91	35c blue & multi	.55	.20
648	A91	40c blue & multi	.60	.20
649	A91	75c blue & multi	.70	.20
650	A91	$2 blue & multi	1.60	.35
		Nos. 644-650 (7)	4.05	1.55

Souvenir Sheet

651	A91	$1 blue & multi	1.60	.35

Nordjamb 75, 14th Boy Scout World Jamboree, Lillehammer, Norway, July 29-Aug. 7.

Leafy Jewel Box — A92

Designs: Sea shells.

1975, Aug. 1   Litho.   Perf. 14

652	A92	½c shown	.20	.20
653	A92	1c Emerald nerite	.20	.20
654	A92	2c Yellow cockle	.20	.20
655	A92	25c Purple sea snail	1.00	.20
656	A92	50c Turkey wing	2.00	.40
657	A92	75c West Indian fighting conch	2.75	.50
658	A92	$1 Noble wentletrap	2.75	.50
		Nos. 652-658 (7)	9.10	2.20

Souvenir Sheet

659	A92	$2 Music volute	4.50	.90

Butterflies — A93

1975, Sept. 22   Litho.   Perf. 14

660	A93	½c Large tiger	.20	.20
661	A93	1c Five continents	.20	.20
662	A93	2c Large striped blue	.20	.20
663	A93	35c Gonatryx	.85	.25
664	A93	45c Spear-winged cattle heart	1.00	.30
665	A93	75c Risty nymula	1.50	.40
666	A93	$2 Blue night	3.75	.75
		Nos. 660-666 (7)	7.70	2.30

Souvenir Sheet

667	A93	$1 Lycrophon	2.40	1.00

Crew Race — A94

Young Man, by Michelangelo — A95

1975, Oct. 13   Litho.   Perf. 14

668	A94	½c shown	.20	.20
669	A94	1c Women's swimming	.20	.20
670	A94	2c Steeplechase	.20	.20
671	A94	35c Gymnastics	.25	.20
672	A94	45c Soccer	.25	.20
673	A94	75c Boxing	.30	.25
674	A94	$2 Bicycling	1.75	.40
		Nos. 668-674 (7)	3.15	1.65

Souvenir Sheet

675	A94	$1 Sailing	2.00	.45

7th Pan-American Games, Mexico City, Oct. 13-26.

1975, Nov. 3

Works by Michelangelo (except 50c): ½c, David. 2c, Moses. 40c, Zachariah. 50c, St. John the Baptist (sculpture). 75c, Judith and Holofernes (detail). $1, Madonna (head from Pietà). $2, Doni Madonna (detail from Holy Family).

676	A95	½c black & multi	.20	.20
677	A95	1c black & multi	.20	.20
678	A95	2c black & multi	.20	.20
679	A95	40c black & multi	.40	.20
680	A95	50c black & multi	.50	.20
681	A95	75c black & multi	.75	.25
682	A95	$2 black & multi	2.00	.45
		Nos. 676-682 (7)	4.25	1.70

Souvenir Sheet

683	A95	$1 black & multi	2.40	.40

Michelangelo Buonarroti (1475-1564), Italian painter, sculptor and architect.

Virgin and Child Paintings — A96

Bananaquit — A97

1975, Dec. 8

684	A96	½c Filippino Lippi	.20	.20
685	A96	1c Mantegna	.20	.20
686	A96	2c Luis de Morales	.20	.20
687	A96	35c G. M. Morandi	.25	.20
688	A96	50c Antonello da Messina	.25	.20
689	A96	75c Durer	.30	.20
690	A96	$1 Velazquez	.35	.20
		Nos. 684-690 (7)	1.75	1.40

Souvenir Sheet

691	A96	$2 Bellini	1.75	.45

Christmas.

1976, Jan. 20   Litho.   Perf. 14

Designs: 1c, Orange-rumped agouti. 2c, Hawksbill turtle, horiz. 5c, Dwarf poinciana. 35c, Albacores, horiz. 40c, Cardinal's guard flower. $1, Belted kingfisher. $2, Antillean armadillo, horiz.

692	A97	½c multicolored	.20	.20
693	A97	1c multicolored	.20	.20
694	A97	2c multicolored	.20	.20
695	A97	5c multicolored	.20	.20
696	A97	35c multicolored	1.10	.20
697	A97	40c multicolored	1.25	.20
698	A97	$2 multicolored	3.00	.75
		Nos. 692-698 (7)	6.15	1.95

Souvenir Sheet

699	A97	$1 multicolored	8.00	1.00

Carnival Dancers — A98

Designs: 1c, Scuba diving. 2c, Cruise ship in St. George's Harbor. 35c, Game fishing. 50c, St. George's Golf Course. 75c, Tennis. $1, Mount Rich rock carvings. $2, Sailboats.

1976, Feb. 25   Litho.   Perf. 14

700	A98	½c multicolored	.20	.20
701	A98	1c multicolored	.20	.20
702	A98	2c multicolored	.20	.20
703	A98	35c multicolored	.90	.20
704	A98	50c multicolored	3.00	.20
705	A98	75c multicolored	3.25	.35
706	A98	$1 multicolored	3.50	.35
		Nos. 700-706 (7)	11.25	1.75

Souvenir Sheet

707	A98	$2 multicolored	3.00	.75

Tourist publicity.

Descent from the Cross, by Master of Okolicsno — A99

Easter (Paintings): 1c, Pieta, by Correggio. 2c, Crucifixion, by van der Weyden. 3c, Burial of Christ, by Dürer. 35c, God the Father Holding Crucified Christ, by unknown master (Florence). 75c, Ascension, by Raphael. $1, Burial of Christ, by Raphael. $2, Pieta, by Crespi.

1976, Mar. 29

708	A99	½c multicolored	.20	.20
709	A99	1c multicolored	.20	.20
710	A99	2c multicolored	.20	.20
711	A99	3c multicolored	.20	.20
712	A99	35c multicolored	.20	.20
713	A99	75c multicolored	.35	.20
714	A99	$1 multicolored	.50	.25
		Nos. 708-714 (7)	1.85	1.45

Souvenir Sheet

715	A99	$2 multicolored	1.25	1.25

Sharpshooters, 1780 — A100

First Stars and Stripes and: 1c, Defense of Liberty Pole. 2c, Men loading muskets. 35c, 75c, Fight for Liberty. 50c, $2, Peace Treaty, 1783. $1, Drumming march on Breed's Hill. $3, Gunboat, c. 1776.

1976, Apr. 15   Litho.   Perf. 14

716	A100	½c multicolored	.20	.20
717	A100	1c multicolored	.20	.20
718	A100	2c multicolored	.20	.20
719	A100	35c multicolored	.45	.20
720	A100	50c multicolored	.55	.20
721	A100	$1 multicolored	1.00	.20
722	A100	$3 multicolored	2.40	.25
		Nos. 716-722 (7)	5.00	1.45

Souvenir Sheet

723		Sheet of 2	2.00	1.40
a.		A100 75c multicolored	.65	.55
b.		A100 $2 multicolored	1.40	.75

American Bicentennial.

Girl Guide Emblems, Nature Study — A101

Volleyball — A102

Various Girl Guide Emblems and: 1c, Cooking. 2c, $2, First aid, diff. 50c, Tenting. 75c, Home economics. $1, Drawing.

1976, June 1   Litho.   Perf. 14

724	A101	½c multicolored	.20	.20
725	A101	1c multicolored	.20	.20
726	A101	2c multicolored	.20	.20
727	A101	50c multicolored	.55	.20
728	A101	75c multicolored	.85	.25
729	A101	$2 multicolored	2.10	.45
		Nos. 724-729 (6)	4.10	1.50

Souvenir Sheet

730	A101	$1 multicolored	1.75	.80

Girl Guides of Grenada, 50th anniv.

1976, June 21   Litho.   Perf. 14

Olympic Rings and: 1c, Bicycling. 2c, Rowing. 35c, Judo. 45c, Hockey. 75c, Women's gymnastics. $1, High jump. $3, Equestrian.

731	A102	½c multicolored	.20	.20
732	A102	1c multicolored	.20	.20
733	A102	2c multicolored	.20	.20
734	A102	35c multicolored	.35	.20
735	A102	45c multicolored	.65	.20
736	A102	75c multicolored	.70	.40
737	A102	$1 multicolored	.80	.40
		Nos. 731-737 (7)	3.10	1.80

Souvenir Sheet

738	A102	$3 multicolored	2.00	1.25

21st Olympic Games, Montreal, Canada, July 17-Aug. 1.

Moulin Rouge, by Toulouse-Lautrec — A103

Paintings by Toulouse-Lautrec: 1c, Start of the Quadrille. 2c, Woman's Head. 3c, Hall at the Moulin Rouge. 40c, Man Delivering Laundry. 50c, Dancing the Bolero. $1, Lady with Boa. $2, Signor Boileau at the Cafe.

1976, July 20   Litho.   Perf. 14

739	A103	½c multicolored	.20	.20
740	A103	1c multicolored	.20	.20
741	A103	2c multicolored	.20	.20
742	A103	3c multicolored	.20	.20
743	A103	40c multicolored	.75	.20
744	A103	50c multicolored	.95	.20
745	A103	$2 multicolored	2.50	.50
		Nos. 739-745 (7)	5.00	1.70

Souvenir Sheet

746	A103	$1 multicolored	4.00	1.25

Henri de Toulouse-Lautrec (1864-1901), painter, 75th death anniv.

Map of West Indies, Bats, Wicket and Ball — A103a

Prudential
Cup — A103b

1976, July 26
747 A103a 35c lt blue & multi .60 .60
748 A103b $1 lilac rose & blk 1.75 1.75
World Cricket Cup, won by West Indies
Team, 1975.

Piper
Apache
A104

Airplanes: 1c, Beech Twin Bonanza. 2c,
D.H. Twin Otter. 40c, Britten Norman Islander.
50c, D.H. Heron. $2, Hawker Siddeley Avro
748. $3, B.A.C. One-Eleven.

1976, Aug. 18
749 A104 ½c multicolored .20 .20
750 A104 1c multicolored .20 .20
751 A104 2c multicolored .20 .20
752 A104 40c multicolored .75 .20
753 A104 50c multicolored .80 .20
754 A104 $2 multicolored 2.75 .75
　　　Nos. 749-754 (6) 4.90 1.75

Souvenir Sheet
755 A104 $3 multicolored 3.25 1.10

Helios Mission,
Assembly — A105

Designs: 1c, Helios spacecraft in space 2c,
Helios assembled. 15c, Helios, system test
and checkout. 45c, Viking nearing Mars, horiz.
75c, Viking on Mars. $2, Viking spacecraft
assembled. $3, Helios orbiter and Viking
lander.

1976, Sept. 1　Litho.　Perf. 14
756 A105 ½c multicolored .20 .20
757 A105 1c multicolored .20 .20
758 A105 2c multicolored .20 .20
759 A105 15c multicolored .20 .20
760 A105 45c multicolored .25 .20
761 A105 75c multicolored .40 .25
762 A105 $2 multicolored .80 .35
　　　Nos. 756-762 (7) 2.25 1.60

Souvenir Sheet
763 A105 $3 multicolored 1.75 1.00
Helios (solar probe) mission and Viking
Mars missions.

S.S. Geestland, Geest Line
Flag — A106

Ships: 1c, M.V. Federal Palm, West Indies
Shipping Service. 2c, H.M.S. Blake and ship's
crest. 25c, M.V. Vlstafjord and Norwegian-
American Line flag. 75c, S.S. Canberra and P.
& O. Line flag. $1, S.S. Regina and Chandris
Line flag. $2, Santa Maria and Spanish flag,
1492. $5, S.S. Arandora and Blue Star Line
flag.

1976, Nov. 3　Litho.　Perf. 14½
764 A106 ½c blue & multi .20 .20
765 A106 1c blue & multi .20 .20
766 A106 2c blue & multi .20 .20
767 A106 25c blue & multi .55 .20
768 A106 75c blue & multi 1.10 .25
769 A106 $1 blue & multi 1.40 .40
770 A106 $5 blue & multi 2.75 .65
　　　Nos. 764-770 (7) 6.40 2.00

Souvenir Sheet
771 A106 $2 multicolored 2.50 2.50
Ships connected with Grenada's
development.

Altarpiece
of San
Barnaba,
by
Botticelli
A107

Christmas (Paintings): 1c, Annunciation, by
Botticelli. 2c, Madonna with Chancellor Rolin,
by Jan van Eyck. 35c, Annunciation, by Fra
Filippo Lippi. 50c, Madonna of the Magnificat,
by Botticelli. 75c, Madonna of the Pomegran-
ate, by Botticelli. $2, Gipsy Madonna, by
Titian. $3, Madonna with St. Cosmas and
Saints, by Botticelli.

1976, Dec. 8　Litho.　Perf. 14
772 A107 ½c multicolored .20 .20
773 A107 1c multicolored .20 .20
774 A107 2c multicolored .20 .20
775 A107 35c multicolored .35 .20
776 A107 50c multicolored .30 .20
777 A107 75c multicolored .40 .25
778 A107 $3 multicolored 1.00 .40
　　　Nos. 772-778 (7) 2.50 1.65

Souvenir Sheet
779 A107 $3 multicolored 1.60 .75

Globe
and
Telephone
Users
A108

Designs: ½c, A. G. Bell, 1876 and modern
telephones. 2c, Satellites around globe, world
map. 18c, Videophone. 40c, Satellite and
ground stations. $1, Satellite and telephone
communication with ships. $2, British
"Triphone" and radar station. $5, Flags of the
world surrounding globe, and telephone.

1976, Dec. 17　Litho.　Perf. 14
780 A108 ½c multicolored .20 .20
781 A108 1c multicolored .20 .20
782 A108 2c multicolored .20 .20
783 A108 18c multicolored .25 .20
784 A108 40c multicolored .35 .20
785 A108 $1 multicolored .50 .25
786 A108 $2 multicolored .80 .45
　　　Nos. 780-786 (7) 2.50 1.70

Souvenir Sheet
787 A108 $5 multicolored 2.50 .90
Centenary of first telephone conversation by
Alexander Graham Bell, Mar. 10, 1876.

Coronation of
Elizabeth
II — A109

Designs: ½c, Coronation. 1c, $1, Orb and
scepter. 35c, $3, Trooping of the Guards. 50c,
$2, Spoon and ampulla. 35c, (bklt.), $2.50,
Elizabeth II and Prince Philip. $5, Royal visit
to Grenada.

1977, Feb. 8　Litho.　Perf. 14, 12
788 A109 ½c multicolored .20 .20
789 A109 1c multicolored .20 .20
790 A109 35c multicolored .20 .20
791 A109 $2 multicolored .35 .30

792 A109 $2.50 multicolored .40 .30
a. Booklet pane of 6 (35c) .95
b. Booklet pane of 3 (50c, $1, $3) 3.25
　　　Nos. 788-792 (5) 1.35 1.20

Souvenir Sheet
793 A109 $5 multicolored 1.10 1.10
Reign of Queen Elizabeth II, 25th anniv.
Nos. 792a-792b are self-adhesive, roulette
x imperf. Marginal inscriptions.
Nos. 788-792 were printed in sheets of 40
(10x4), perf. 14, and sheets of 5 plus label,
perf. 12, in changed colors.
For overprints see Nos. 821-826.

Water
Skiing,
One-ski
Slalom
A110

Designs: 1c, Speedboat racing around
Grand Anse. 2c, Crew racing, St. George's.
22c, Swimming, Grand Anse. 35c, Local work
boat races. 75c, Water polo, careenage, St.
George's. $2, Game fishing. $3, South Coast
yacht race.

1977, Apr. 13　Litho.　Perf. 14
794 A110 ½c multicolored .20 .20
795 A110 1c multicolored .20 .20
796 A110 2c multicolored .20 .20
797 A110 22c multicolored .20 .20
798 A110 35c multicolored .35 .20
799 A110 75c multicolored .55 .20
800 A110 $2 multicolored 1.10 .35
　　　Nos. 794-800 (7) 2.80 1.55

Souvenir Sheet
801 A110 $2 multicolored 1.75 1.25
1977 Easter Water Parade.

Tent, OAS
Emblem
A111

1977, June 14　Litho.　Perf. 14
802 A111 35c multicolored .20 .20
803 A111 $1 multicolored .45 .45
804 A111 $2 multicolored .75 .75
　　　Nos. 802-804 (3) 1.40 1.40
7th Regular Session, General Assembly of
Organization of American States.

Scouts on
Raft
A112

Designs: 1c, Tug-of-war. 2c, Boy Scout
regatta. 18c, Scouts around camp fire. 40c,
Field kitchen. $1, Boy Scouts and Sea Scouts.
$2, Hiking and map reading. $3, Semaphore.

1977, Sept. 6　Litho.　Perf. 14
805 A112 ½c multicolored .20 .20
806 A112 1c multicolored .20 .20
807 A112 2c multicolored .20 .20
808 A112 18c multicolored .30 .20
809 A112 40c multicolored .45 .20
810 A112 $1 multicolored 1.10 .35
811 A112 $2 multicolored 2.00 .55
　　　Nos. 805-811 (7) 4.45 1.90

Souvenir Sheet
812 A112 $3 multicolored 3.00 1.25
6th Caribbean Jamboree, Kingston,
Jamaica, Aug. 5-14.

Annunciation to the
Shepherds — A113

Ceiling Paintings, St. Martin's Church, Zillis,
Switzerland, 12th Century: 1c, Joseph on his
way. 2c, Virgin and Child, Flight into Egypt.
22c, Angel leading the way. 35c, King on way
to Herod. 75c, Three horses. $2, Virgin and
Child. $3, Adoration of the Kings.

1977, Nov. 3　Litho.　Perf. 14
813 A113 ½c multicolored .20 .20
814 A113 1c multicolored .20 .20
815 A113 2c multicolored .20 .20
816 A113 22c multicolored .20 .20
817 A113 35c multicolored .20 .20
818 A113 75c multicolored .20 .20
819 A113 $2 multicolored .35 .25
　　　Nos. 813-819 (7) 1.55 1.45

Souvenir Sheet
820 A113 $3 multicolored 1.25 1.00
Christmas.

Nos. 788-793 Overprinted "Royal Visit
W.I. 1977"

1977, Nov. 10　Perf. 12, 14
821 A109 ½c multicolored .20 .20
822 A109 1c multicolored .20 .20
823 A109 35c multicolored .20 .20
824 A109 $2 multicolored .25 .35
825 A109 $2.50 multicolored .25 .45
　　　Nos. 821-825 (5) 1.10 1.40

Souvenir Sheet
Perf. 14
826 A109 $5 multicolored .90 1.40
Caribbean visit of Queen Elizabeth II. Nos.
821-822 are perf. 12, others perf. 12 and 14.

Christjaan
Eijkman — A114

Portraits: 1c, Winston Churchill, Literature,
1953. 2c, Woodrow Wilson, Peace, 1919. 35c,
Frederic Passy, Peace 1901. $1, Albert Ein-
stein, Physics, 1921. $2, Alfred Nobel,
founder. $3, Carl Bosch, Chemistry, 1931.

1978, Jan. 25　Litho.　Perf. 14
827 A114 ½c multicolored .20 .20
828 A114 1c multicolored .20 .20
829 A114 2c multicolored .20 .20
830 A114 35c multicolored .30 .20
831 A114 $1 multicolored .85 .30
832 A114 $3 multicolored 2.25 .55
　　　Nos. 827-832 (6) 4.00 1.65

Souvenir Sheet
833 A114 $2 multicolored 2.00 1.00
Nobel Prize winners.

Early
Zeppelin
and Count
Zeppelin
A115

Designs: 1c, Lindbergh and Spirit of St.
Louis. 2c, "Deutschland" airship. 22c,
Lindbergh landing in Paris. 35c, Lindbergh in
cockpit. 75c, Lindbergh and Spirit of St. Louis
in flight. $1, Zeppelin over Alps. $2, Count
Zeppelin and early airship. $3, Zeppelin over
Capitol.

1978, Feb. 13　Litho.　Perf. 14
834 A115 ½c multicolored .20 .20
835 A115 1c multicolored .20 .20
836 A115 2c multicolored .20 .20
837 A115 22c multicolored .40 .20
838 A115 75c multicolored .75 .20
839 A115 $1 multicolored .90 .25
840 A115 $3 multicolored 2.00 .50
　　　Nos. 834-840 (7) 4.65 1.75

Souvenir Sheet
041 Sheet of 2 3.25 1.00
a. A115 35c multicolored .75
b. A115 $2 multicolored 2.50

Aviation history.

Launching of Space Shuttle — A116

Black- headed Gulls — A117

Space Shuttle: 1c, Booster separation. 2c, External tank separation. 18c, In orbit. 75c, Satellite placement. $2, Landing approach. $3, On landing pad.

1978, Feb. 28

842	A116	½c multicolored	.20	.20
843	A116	1c multicolored	.20	.20
844	A116	2c multicolored	.20	.20
845	A116	18c multicolored	.40	.20
846	A116	75c multicolored	.90	.20
847	A116	$2 multicolored	1.75	.40
		Nos. 842-847 (6)	3.65	1.40

Souvenir Sheet

848	A116	$3 multicolored	2.10	1.00

US space shuttle.

1978, Mar. 8   Litho.   Perf. 14

Wild Birds of Grenada and Wildlife Fund Emblem: 1c, Wilson's petrels. 2c, Killdeers. 50c, White-necked jacobin and hibiscus. 75c, Blue-faced booby. $1, Broad-winged hawk. $2, Scaley-necked pigeon. $3, Scarlet ibis.

849	A117	½c multicolored	.30	.25
850	A117	1c multicolored	.30	.25
851	A117	2c multicolored	.30	.25
852	A117	50c multicolored	3.00	.40
853	A117	75c multicolored	3.50	.60
854	A117	$1 multicolored	5.00	.80
855	A117	$2 multicolored	7.50	1.50
		Nos. 849-855 (7)	19.90	4.05

Souvenir Sheet

856	A117	$3 multicolored	13.50	2.00

Marquise de Spinola, by Rubens A118

Ludwig van Beethoven A119

Paintings by Peter Paul Rubens (1577-1640): 5c, Reception of Marie de Medicis. 15c, Rubens and Helena Fourment. 25c, Ludovicus Nonnius. 45c, Helena Fourment with her Children. 75c, Child's head. $3, Suzanne Fourment in Velvet Hat.

1978, Mar. 30   Litho.   Perf. 13½x14

857	A118	5c lt blue & multi	.30	.20
858	A118	15c lt blue & multi	.30	.20
859	A118	18c lt blue & multi	.30	.20
860	A118	25c lt blue & multi	.30	.20
861	A118	45c lt blue & multi	.55	.20
862	A118	75c lt blue & multi	.80	.20
863	A118	$3 lt blue & multi	1.75	.55
		Nos. 857-863 (7)	4.30	1.75

Souvenir Sheet

864	A118	$5 lt blue & multi	3.75	1.00

1978, Apr. 24   Perf. 14

Designs: 15c, Woman violinist playing concerto. 18c, Various musical instruments. 22c, Piano. 50c, Two violins. 75c, Beethoven's piano and score. $2, Beethoven and score. $3, Beethoven and his house. 15c, 18c, 22c, 75c, $2, $3, horiz.

865	A119	5c multicolored	.20	.20
866	A119	15c multicolored	.20	.20
867	A119	18c multicolored	.45	.20
868	A119	22c multicolored	.45	.20
869	A119	50c multicolored	.90	.35

870	A119	75c multicolored	1.60	.50
871	A119	$3 multicolored	3.00	.65
		Nos. 865-871 (7)	6.80	2.30

Souvenir Sheet

872	A119	$2 multicolored	3.25	1.25

Ludwig van Beethoven (1770-1827), composer, death sesquicentennial.

Elizabeth II with Crown, Scepter and Orb — A120

Trooping of the Colors — A121

Designs: 35c, Coronation. $2.50, St. Edward's crown. $5, Elizabeth II and Prince Philip.

1978, June 2   Litho.   Perf. 14

873	A120	35c multicolored	.20	.20
874	A120	$2 multicolored	.50	.50
875	A120	$2.50 multicolored	.50	.50
		Nos. 873-875 (3)	1.20	1.20

Souvenir Sheet

876	A120	$5 multicolored	.95	.95

Imperf

Self-adhesive

35c, Elizabeth II at Maundy Money distribution ceremony. $5, Elizabeth II and Prince Philip.

877		Souvenir booklet	3.25
a.	A121	Bklt. pane, 3 each 25c, 35c	1.00
b.	A121	Booklet pane of 1, $5	2.50

Coronation of Queen Elizabeth II, 25th anniv. Nos. 873-875 were printed in sheets of 40 (10x4), perf. 14, and sheets of 3 plus label, perf. 12, in changed colors. Labels show royal insignia.

No. 877 contains 2 booklet panes printed on peelable paper backing showing coins.

Goalkeeper Reaching for Ball — A122

Designs: Goalkeeper reaching for ball, various stages of motion.

1978, Aug. 1   Litho.   Perf. 15

878	A122	40c multicolored	.20	.20
879	A122	60c multicolored	.25	.25
880	A122	90c multicolored	.35	.35
881	A122	$2 multicolored	.85	.85
		Nos. 878-881 (4)	1.65	1.65

Souvenir Sheet

882	A122	$2.50 multicolored	1.75	1.75

11th World Cup Soccer Championship, Argentina, June 1-25.

Flying Objects, 16th Century Drawing and Flying Saucer, 1962 A123

Designs: 35c, Radar probing skies, and Mars surface. $2, Prime Minister Eric Gairy and UN General Assembly Building. $3, Flying saucer with downwards beam, and UFO photograph.

1978, Aug. 17

883	A123	5c multicolored	.25	.20
884	A123	35c multicolored	.50	.35
885	A123	$3 multicolored	3.25	3.00
		Nos. 883-885 (3)	4.00	3.55

Souvenir Sheet

886	A123	$2 multicolored	3.25	3.25

Proposal by Prime Minister Eric Gairy of Grenada to the UN General Assembly to study unidentified flying objects, Oct. 7, 1977.

Wright Glider and Allegory of Flight A124

15c, Flyer I, 1903, & eagle. 18c, Flyer III & allegory of flight. 22c, Flyer III & eagle. 50c, Orville Wright, Flyer & allegory of flight. 75c, Flyer, 1908, & eagle. $2, Flyer & allegory of flight. $3, Wilbur Wright, Flyer & allegory of flight.

1978, Aug. 24   Perf. 14

887	A124	5c multicolored	.20	.20
888	A124	15c multicolored	.20	.20
889	A124	18c multicolored	.25	.20
890	A124	22c multicolored	.25	.20
891	A124	50c multicolored	.40	.30
892	A124	75c multicolored	.50	.40
893	A124	$3 multicolored	1.25	1.25
		Nos. 887-893 (7)	3.05	2.75

Souvenir Sheet

894	A124	$2 multicolored	2.75	2.75

75th anniversary of first powered flight by Wright brothers, Dec. 17, 1903.

Hawaiian Feast in Capt. Cook's Honor A125

Capt. Cook and: 35c, Hawaiian warriors' dance. 75c, Honolulu harbor. $3, "Resolution." $4, Death scene.

1978, Dec. 5   Litho.   Perf. 14

895	A125	18c multicolored	.90	.50
896	A125	35c multicolored	1.10	.60
897	A125	75c multicolored	2.00	1.90
898	A125	$3 multicolored	2.75	4.50
		Nos. 895-898 (4)	6.75	7.50

Souvenir Sheet

899	A125	$4 multicolored	5.00	5.00

Bicentenary of Capt. Cook's arrival in Hawaii and 250th anniversary of his birth.

Christmas 1978 GRENADA Dürer 40c

Detail from Paumgartner Altar, by Dürer — A126

Convention and Cultural Center — A127

Dürer Paintings: 60c, The Three Kings. 90c, Virgin and Child. $2, Head of the Virgin. $4, Virgin and Child.

1978, Dec. 20   Litho.   Perf. 14

900	A126	40c multicolored	.25	.25
901	A126	60c multicolored	.35	.35
902	A126	90c multicolored	.40	.40
903	A126	$2 multicolored	.75	.75
		Nos. 900-903 (4)	1.75	1.75

Souvenir Sheet

904	A126	$4 multicolored	2.00	2.00

Christmas and 450th death anniv. of Albrecht Dürer (1471-1528), German painter.

1979, Feb. 8   Litho.   Perf. 14

18c, Geodesic Dome. 22c, Rowboat race, Easter parade, St. George's. 35c, Prime Minister Eric M. Gairy. $3, Cross at Fort Frederick at night.

905	A127	5c multicolored	.20	.20
906	A127	18c multicolored	.20	.20
907	A127	22c multicolored	.20	.20
908	A127	35c multicolored	.20	.20
909	A127	$3 multicolored	.50	.50
		Nos. 905-909 (5)	1.30	1.30

5th anniversary of independence.

Chenille Plant — A128

Birds in Flight — A129

Native Flowers: 50c, Red hibiscus. $1, Skyflower. $2, Pink pride of India. $3, Rosebay.

1979, Feb. 26

910	A128	18c multicolored	.20	.20
911	A128	50c multicolored	.30	.25
912	A128	$1 multicolored	.50	.45
913	A128	$3 multicolored	1.25	1.10
		Nos. 910-913 (4)	2.25	2.00

Souvenir Sheet

914	A128	$4 multicolored	1.60	1.60

1979, Mar. 15

$2, Bird in flight & Human Rights emblem.

915	A129	15c multicolored	.20	.20
916	A129	$2 multicolored	.75	.75

Universal Declaration of Human Rights, 30th anniversary.

Children Playing Cricket — A130

IYC Emblem and: 22c, Boys playing baseball. $4, Children with model spaceship. $5, Three children.

1979, Apr. 23   Litho.   Perf. 14

917	A130	18c multicolored	1.00	.50
918	A130	22c multicolored	.50	.30
919	A130	$5 multicolored	4.50	6.00
		Nos. 917-919 (3)	6.00	6.80

Souvenir Sheet

920	A130	$4 multicolored	2.50	2.50

Intl. Year of the Child.

Balloon and Space Shuttle A131

Designs: 35c, Octopus holding sailors, nuclear submarine. 75c, Rocket and moon. $3, Imaginary plane and space ship. $4, Multi-propelled ship and US space shuttle.

1979, May 4

921	A131	18c multicolored	.40	.20
922	A131	35c multicolored	.70	.25
923	A131	75c multicolored	.90	.65
924	A131	$3 multicolored	2.40	3.00
		Nos. 921-924 (4)	4.40	4.10

Souvenir Sheet

925	A131	$4 multicolored	2.50	2.50

Jules Verne (1828-1905), science fiction writer.

African Mail Runner A132

Sir Rowland Hill (1795-1879), originator of penny postage, and: 40c, American Pony Express. $1, Oriental pigeon post. $3, European mail coach. $5, Tete-beche stamps with revenue surcharge, 1883.

1979, July 23　　Litho.　　Perf. 14

926	A132	20c multicolored	.20	.20
927	A132	40c multicolored	.20	.20
928	A132	$1 multicolored	.20	.20
929	A132	$3 multicolored	.60	.60
		Nos. 926-929 (4)	1.20	1.20

Souvenir Sheet

930	A132	$5 multicolored	1.10	1.10

Nos. 926-929 were printed in sheets of 40, perf. 14, and in sheets of 5 plus label, perf. 12, in changed colors.
For overprints see Nos. 989A-989D.

Boys, Map of Grenada, Vaccination Gun — A133

1979, Aug. 2　　Litho.　　Perf. 14

931	A133	5c multicolored	.20	.20
932	A133	$1 multicolored	.90	.90

Intl. Year of the Child, immunization of children.

Reef Shark A134

Designs: 45c, Spotted eagle ray. 50c, Many-tooth conger. 60c, Golden olive shells. 70c, West Indian murex. 75c, Giant tuns. 90c, Brown boobies. $1, Magnificent frigate bird. $2.50, Sooty tern.

1979, Aug. 22　　Litho.　　Perf. 14

933	A134	40c multicolored	.40	.35
934	A134	45c multicolored	.40	.40
935	A134	50c multicolored	.45	.40
936	A134	60c multicolored	.75	.60
937	A134	70c multicolored	.90	.70
938	A134	75c multicolored	1.10	1.10
939	A134	90c multicolored	1.90	2.25
940	A134	$1 multicolored	1.90	2.25
		Nos. 933-940 (8)	7.80	8.00

Souvenir Sheet

941	A134	$2.50 multicolored	3.50	3.50

Flight into Egypt, Tapestry A135

Tapestries: 25c, Virgin and Child. 30c, Angel, vert. 40c, Infant Jesus, by Doge Marino Grimani, vert. 90c, Shepherds, vert. $1, Flight into Egypt, vert. $2, Virgin in Glory, vert. $4, Virgin and Child, by Grimani, vert.

1979, Oct. 16　　Litho.　　Perf. 14

942	A135	6c multicolored	.20	.20
943	A135	25c multicolored	.20	.20
944	A135	30c multicolored	.20	.20
945	A135	40c multicolored	.20	.20
946	A135	90c multicolored	.20	.20
947	A135	$1 multicolored	.20	.20
948	A135	$2 multicolored	.40	.40
		Nos. 942-948 (7)	1.60	1.60

Souvenir Sheet

949	A135	$4 multicolored	1.40	1.40

Christmas.

Disney Characters and IYC Emblem A135a

Designs: Sport scenes.

1979, Nov. 2　　Litho.　　Perf. 11

950	A135a	½c Mickey Mouse, baseball	.20	.20
951	A135a	1c Donald, high jump	.20	.20
952	A135a	2c Goofy, basketball	.20	.20
953	A135a	3c Goofy, hurdles	.20	.20
954	A135a	4c Donald Duck, golf	.20	.20
955	A135a	5c Mickey, cricket	.20	.20
956	A135a	10c Mickey, soccer	.20	.20
957	A135a	$2 Mickey, tennis	3.00	3.50
958	A135a	$2.50 Minnie, equestrian	3.00	3.50
		Nos. 950-958 (9)	7.40	8.40

Souvenir Sheet

Perf. 13½

959	CD329	$3 Goofy in riding habit	2.75	2.75

See Nos. 1031-1032.

Hands, Paul P. Harris, Rotary Emblem — A136

Rotary Emblem and Hands Holding: 30c, Caduceus. 90c, Wheat. $2, Family. $4, Emblem.

1980, Feb. 25　　Litho.　　Perf. 14

960	A136	6c multicolored	.20	.20
961	A136	30c multicolored	.20	.20
962	A136	90c multicolored	.25	.25
963	A136	$2 multicolored	.70	.70
		Nos. 960-963 (4)	1.35	1.35

Souvenir Sheet

964	A136	$4 multicolored	1.60	1.60

Rotary International, 75th anniversary.

Nos. 585-586, 588-591, 593-594, 596-602 Overprinted in Black: PEOPLE'S REVOLUTION / 13 MARCH 1979

1980　　　　　　　Perf. 15, 13½

965	A85	2c multicolored	.20	.20
966	A85	3c multicolored	.20	.20
967	A85	6c multicolored	.20	.20
968	A85	8c multicolored	.20	.20
969	A85	10c multicolored	.20	.20
970	A85	12c multicolored	.20	.20
971	A85	20c multicolored	.20	.20
972	A85	25c multicolored	.40	.60
973	A85	50c multicolored	.40	.60
974	A85	75c multicolored	.65	.95
975	A85	$1 multicolored	1.00	1.25
976	A85	$2 multicolored	1.75	2.40
977	A85	$3 multicolored	2.25	3.25
978	A85	$5 multicolored	3.00	5.50
979	A85	$10 multicolored	4.25	8.00
		Nos. 965-979 (15)	15.10	23.95

Issue dates: 25c, Apr. 7; others, Feb. 28.

Boxing, Kremlin, Olympic Rings A137

1980, Mar. 24　　　　　Perf. 14

980	A137	25c shown	.20	.20
981	A137	40c Bicycling	.20	.20
982	A137	90c Equestrian	.25	.25
983	A137	$2 Running	.60	.60
		Nos. 980-983 (4)	1.25	1.25

Souvenir Sheet

984	A137	$4 Yachting	1.10	1.10

22nd Summer Olympic Games, Moscow, July 19-Aug. 3.

Tropical Kingbirds — A138

1980, Apr. 8

985	A138	20c shown	1.00	.80
986	A138	40c Rufous-breasted hermits	1.40	1.10
987	A138	$1 Troupials	1.90	1.60
988	A138	$2 Ruddy quail doves	2.25	4.00
		Nos. 985-988 (4)	6.55	7.50

Souvenir Sheet

989	A138	$3 Prairie warblers	5.25	5.25

Nos. 926-929 Overprinted: "LONDON 1980"

1980, May 6　　Litho.　　Perf. 12

989A	A132	20c multicolored	.20	.20
989B	A132	40c multicolored	.30	.30
989C	A132	$1 multicolored	.50	.50
989D	A132	$3 multicolored	1.75	1.75
		Nos. 989A-989D (4)	2.75	2.75

London '80 Intl. Stamp Exhib., May 6-14.

Free School Hot Lunches A139

1980, May 19　　Litho.　　Perf. 14

990	A139	10c shown	.20	.20
991	A139	40c Food canning	.25	.25
992	A139	$1 Health care	.50	.50
993	A139	$2 Housing projects	.75	.75
		Nos. 990-993 (4)	1.70	1.70

Souvenir Sheet

994	A139	$5 Prime Minister Bishop, vert.	1.50	1.50

People's Revolution, 1st anniv.

Jamb Statues, West Portal, Chartres Cathedral — A140

Masterpieces: 10c, Les Desmoiselles d'Avignon, by Picasso. 40c, Winged Victory of Samothrace. 50c, The Night Watch, by Rembrandt. $1, Edward VI as a Child, by Holbein, the Younger. $3, Queen Nefertiti. $4, Weier Haws, by Dürer, vert.

1980, June　　　　Litho.　　　Perf. 14

995	A140	8c multicolored	.20	.20
996	A140	10c multicolored	.20	.20
997	A140	40c multicolored	.25	.25
998	A140	50c multicolored	.25	.25
999	A140	$1 multicolored	.40	.40
1000	A140	$3 multicolored	1.10	1.10
		Nos. 995-1000 (6)	2.40	2.40

Souvenir Sheet

1001	A140	$4 multicolored	1.50	1.50

Carib Canoes A141

Designs: 1c, Boat building. 2c, Small workboat. 4c, "Santa Maria." 5c, West India man barque, 1840. 6c, "Orinoco," 1851. 10c, Schooner. 12c, Trimaran. 15c, "Petite Amie," Spice Island cruising yacht. 20c, Fishing pirogue. 25c, Harbor police launch. 30c, Grand Anse speedboat. 40c, "Seimstrand." 50c, "Ariadne," 3-masted schooner. 90c, "Geestide," banana boat. $1, "Cunard Countess," cruise ship. $3, Rumrunner. $5, "Statendam." $10, Coast Guard patrol boat.

1980, Sept. 9　　Litho.　　Perf. 14

1002	A141	½c multicolored	.20	.20
1003	A141	1c multicolored	.20	.20
1004	A141	2c multicolored	.20	.20
1005	A141	4c multicolored	.40	.55
1006	A141	5c multicolored	.40	.55
1007	A141	6c multicolored	.40	.55
1008	A141	10c multicolored	.45	.20
1009	A141	12c multicolored	1.00	.70
1010	A141	15c multicolored	.50	.20
1011	A141	20c multicolored	1.00	.70
1012	A141	25c multicolored	2.00	.45
1013	A141	30c multicolored	1.50	.45
1014	A141	40c multicolored	2.25	.55
1015	A141	50c multicolored	.60	.70
1016	A141	90c multicolored	2.00	.70
1017	A141	$1 multicolored	3.50	1.10
1018	A141	$3 multicolored	3.00	4.00
1019	A141	$5 multicolored	4.25	6.50
1020	A141	$10 multicolored	5.00	8.50
		Nos. 1002-1020 (19)	28.85	26.50

#1017 reprinted inscribed 1982, #1015, 1984.
For overprints see #O1-O10, O12-O13, O15, O17.

1982-84　　　　　Perf. 12½x12

1002a	A141	½c	.20	.20
1006a	A141	5c	.60	.60
1008a	A141	10c	.65	.65
1011a	A141	20c	1.00	1.00
1012a	A141	25c	2.00	2.00
1013a	A141	30c	1.50	1.50
1014a	A141	40c	2.00	2.00
1015a	A141	50c ('84)	.80	.80
1018a	A141	$3	3.00	3.00
1019a	A141	$5	4.25	4.25
1020a	A141	$10 ('84)	9.50	9.50
		Nos. 1002a-1020a (11)	25.50	25.50

Snow White at Well — A142

Christmas: Various scenes from Walt Disney's Snow White and the Seven Dwarfs.

1980, Sept. 25　　Litho.　　Perf. 11

1021	A142	½c multicolored	.20	.20
1022	A142	1c multicolored	.20	.20
1023	A142	2c multicolored	.20	.20
1024	A142	3c multicolored	.20	.20
1025	A142	4c multicolored	.20	.20
1026	A142	5c multicolored	.20	.20
1027	A142	10c multicolored	.20	.20
1028	A142	$2.50 multicolored	3.25	2.75
1029	A142	$3 multicolored	3.75	3.25
		Nos. 1021-1029 (9)	8.40	7.40

Souvenir Sheet

1030	A142	$4 multicolored	5.75	5.75

No. 1030 contains a vertical stamp.

Disney Type of 1980
50th anniversary of Pluto character: $2, Pluto and birthday cake. $4, Pluto.

1981, Jan. 19   Litho.   Perf. 14
1031 A135a $2 multicolored   2.00 2.00

Souvenir Sheet
1032 A135a $4 multicolored   2.50 2.50
No. 1031 issued in sheets of 8.

Adult Education — A143

1981, Mar. 13   Litho.   Perf. 12½
1033 A143 5c Flags of the
        Revolution and
        Grenada   .20 .20
1034 A143 10c shown   .20 .20
1035 A143 15c Food processing
        plant   .20 .20
1036 A143 25c Agriculture   .20 .20
1037 A143 40c Fishing boat,
        crawfish   .25 .25
1038 A143 90c Ships   .65 .65
1039 A143 $1 Palm trees   .70 .70
1040 A143 $3 Map   2.10 2.10
    Nos. 1033-1040 (8)   4.50 4.50
2nd Festival of the Revolution.

Mickey Mouse and Goofy with Easter Basket A144

Easter: Various Disney characters with Easter baskets.

1981, Apr. 7   Perf. 11
1041 A144 35c multi   .25 .25
1042 A144 40c multi   .30 .30
1043 A144 $2 multi   1.50 1.50
1044 A144 $2.50 multi   2.00 2.00
    Nos. 1041-1044 (4)   4.05 4.05

Souvenir Sheet
1045 A144 $4 multi   3.00 3.00

Large Heads, by Picasso — A145

Paintings by Pablo Picasso (1881-1973): 25c, Woman-Flower. 30c, Portrait of Madame. 90c, Cavalier with Pipe. $5, Woman on the Bank of the Seine.

1981, Apr. 28   Perf. 14
1046 A145 25c multicolored   .20 .20
1047 A145 30c multicolored   .20 .20
1048 A145 90c multicolored   .50 .50
1049 A145 $4 multicolored   2.25 2.25
    Nos. 1046-1049 (4)   3.15 3.15

Souvenir Sheet
1050 A145 $5 multicolored   5.00 5.00

Royal Wedding Issue
Common Design Type

1981, June 16   Litho.   Perf. 15
1051 CD331 50c Couple   .20 .20
1052 CD331 $2 Holyrood
        House   .30 .30
1053 CD331a $4 Charles   .50 .50
    Nos. 1051-1053 (3)   1.00 1.00

Souvenir Sheet
1054 CD331 $5 Glass coach   1.00 1.00

Souvenir Booklet
1055 CD331   9.00
a.   Pane of 6 (3x$1, Lady Di-
        ana, 3x$2, Charles)   6.00
b.   Pane of 1, $5, Couple   3.00
No. 1055 contains imperf., self-adhesive stamps.
    Sheets of 5 plus label contain 30c, 40c or $4 in changed colors, perf. 14x14½.
    For overprints see Nos. O11, O14, O16,

The Bath, by Mary Cassatt (1845-1926) A146

Decade for Women (Paintings by Women): 40c, Mademoiselle Charlotte du Val d'Ognes, by Constance Marie Charpentier. 60c, Self-portrait, by Mary Beale. $3, Woman in White Stockings, by Suzanne Valadon. $5, The Artist Hesitating between the Arts of Music and Painting, horiz.

1981, Oct. 13   Litho.   Perf. 14
1058 A146 15c multicolored   .20 .20
1059 A146 40c multicolored   .30 .30
1060 A146 60c multicolored   .45 .45
1061 A146 $3 multicolored   2.00 2.00
    Nos. 1058-1061 (4)   2.95 2.95

Souvenir Sheet
1062 A146 $5 multicolored   3.00 3.00

Cinderella and Prince Charming Dancing at the Ball — A147

Christmas: Scenes from Walt Disney's Cinderella.

1981, Nov. 2   Litho.   Perf. 14x13½
1063 A147 ½c multi   .20 .20
1064 A147 1c multi   .20 .20
1065 A147 2c multi   .20 .20
1066 A147 3c multi   .20 .20
1067 A147 4c multi   .20 .20
1068 A147 5c multi   .25 .25
1069 A147 10c multi   .25 .25
1070 A147 $2.50 multi   3.75 3.00
1071 A147 $3 multi   4.00 3.50
    Nos. 1063-1071 (9)   9.25 8.00

Souvenir Sheet
1072 A147 $5 multi   7.00 7.00

Columbia Space Shuttle — A148

Views of the Columbia space shuttle.

1981, Nov. 12
1073 A148 30c multicolored   .20 .20
1074 A148 60c multicolored   .40 .40
1075 A148 70c multicolored   .50 .50
1076 A148 $3 multicolored   2.25 2.00
    Nos. 1073-1076 (4)   3.35 3.10

Souvenir Sheet
1077 A148 $5 multicolored   3.50 3.50

UPU Membership Centenary — A149

1981, Dec. 10   Litho.   Perf. 15
1078 A149 25c St. George's P.O.   .20 .20
1079 A149 30c No. 1   .20 .20
1080 A149 90c No. 384   .60 .60
1081 A149 $4 No. 189   2.50 2.50
    Nos. 1078-1081 (4)   3.50 3.50

Souvenir Sheet
1082 A149 $5 No. 562   4.00 4.00

Intl. Year of the Disabled (1981) — A150

1982, Feb. 4   Perf. 14
1083 A150 30c Artist   .20 .20
1084 A150 40c Computer opera-
        tor   .30 .30
1085 A150 70c Teaching Braille   .50 .50
1086 A150 $3 Drummer   2.00 2.00
    Nos. 1083-1086 (4)   3.00 3.00

Souvenir Sheet
1087 A150 $4 Auto mechanic   3.75 3.75

Scouting Year A151

1982, Feb. 19   Perf. 15
1088 A151 70c Gardening   .60 .60
1089 A151 90c Map reading   .75 .75
1090 A151 $1 Bee keeping   .85 .80
1091 A151 $4 Hospital reading   2.75 2.75
    Nos. 1088-1091 (4)   4.95 4.90

Souvenir Sheet
1092 A151 $5 Trophy presenta-
        tion   3.50 3.50

Flambeaux A152

1982, Mar. 24   Litho.   Perf. 14
1093 A152 10c shown   .65 .20
1094 A152 60c Large orange
        sulphurs   2.25 1.25
1095 A152 $1 Red anartias   2.75 2.10
1096 A152 $3 Polydamas
        swallowtails   7.25 7.25
    Nos. 1093-1096 (4)   12.90 10.80

Souvenir Sheet
1097 A152 $5 Caribbean
        buckeyes   8.25 8.25

Norman Rockwell A153

1982, Apr. 12   Litho.   Perf. 14x13½
1098 A153 15c shown   .40 .20
1099 A153 30c Card Tricks   .65 .25
1100 A153 60c Pharmacist   1.10 1.00
1101 A153 70c Pals   1.40 1.25
    Nos. 1098-1101 (4)   3.55 2.70

Princess Diana Issue
Common Design Type

1982, July 1   Litho.   Perf. 14½x14
1101A CD332 50c Kensington
        Palace   .55 .75
1102 CD332 60c like 50c   .60 .50
1102A CD332 $1 Couple in
        field   1.00 .80
1103 CD332 $2 like $1   2.50 1.75
1103A CD332 $3 Diana in
        green
        dress   2.75 2.75
1104 CD332 $4 like $3   3.50 3.50
    Nos. 1101A-1104 (6)   10.90 10.05

Souvenir Sheet
1105 CD332 $5 Diana, diff.   6.75 6.75
For overprints see Nos. 1115A-1119.

Franklin Roosevelt Birth Centenary A154

Designs: 10c, Mary McLeod Bethune, director of Negro Affairs, 1942. 60c, Leadbelly (Huddie Ledbetter, Works Progress Administration). $1.10, Signing Fair Employment Act, 1941. $3, Farm Security Administration.

1982, July 27   Litho.   Perf. 14
1106 A154 10c multi   .20 .20
1107 A154 60c multi   .30 .30
1108 A154 $1.10 multi   .60 .60
1109 A154 $3 multi   1.60 1.60
    Nos. 1106-1109 (4)   2.70 2.70

Souvenir Sheet
1110 A154 $5 multi   2.75 2.75

Easter A155

Details from Raphael's "On the Way to Calvary." 70c, $1.10, $4, $5, vert.

1982, Sept. 2   Perf. 14½
1111 A155 40c multi   .25 .25
1112 A155 70c multi   .30 .30
1113 A155 $1.10 multi   .55 .55
1114 A155 $4 multi   2.25 2.25
    Nos. 1111-1114 (4)   3.35 3.35

Souvenir Sheet
1115 A155 $5 multi   3.75 3.75

Nos. 1101A-1105 Overprinted:
"ROYAL BABY / 21.6.82"

1982, Sept. 27   Litho.   Perf. 14½x14
1115A CD332 50c multi   .35 .35
1116 CD332 60c multi   .40 .40
1116A CD332 $1 multi   .65 .65
1117 CD332 $2 multi   1.40 1.40
1117A CD332 $3 multi   2.25 2.00
1118 CD332 $4 multi   2.75 2.75
    Nos. 1115A-1118 (6)   7.80 7.55

Souvenir Sheet
1119 CD332 $5 multi   5.00 5.00
Birth of Prince William of Wales, June 21.

Orient Express A156

1982, Oct. 4
1120 A156 30c shown   .35 .40
1121 A156 60c Trans-Siberian
        Express   .65 .65
1122 A156 70c Fleche D'or   .75 .75
1123 A156 90c Flying Scotsman   .95 .95
1124 A156 $1 German Federal
        Railways   1.25 1.25

1125	A156	$3 German Natl. Railways	3.00	4.00
		Nos. 1120-1125 (6)	6.95	8.00

Souvenir Sheet

1126	A156	$5 20th Century Limited, US	4.00	4.00

Christmas — A157

Scenes from Walt Disney's Robin Hood.

1982, Dec. 7   Litho.   *Perf. 14*

1127	A157	½c multi	.20	.20
1128	A157	1c multi	.20	.20
1129	A157	2c multi	.20	.20
1130	A157	3c multi	.20	.20
1131	A157	4c multi	.20	.20
1132	A157	5c multi	.20	.20
1133	A157	10c multi	.20	.20
1134	A157	$2.50 multi	3.00	3.00
1135	A157	$3 multi	3.25	3.25
		Nos. 1127-1135 (9)	7.65	7.65

Souvenir Sheet

1136	A157	$5 multi	7.50	7.50

Italy's Victory in 1982 World Cup A158

1982, Dec. 2   *Perf. 14x13½*

1137	A158	60c Stolen ball	.50	.50
1138	A158	$4 Captain holding trophy	3.25	3.25

Souvenir Sheet

1139	A158	$5 Flags	3.75	3.75

Killer Whale — A159

1982, Dec. 15   *Perf. 14*

1140	A159	15c shown	1.00	.50
1141	A159	40c Sperm whale	2.00	.75
1142	A159	70c Blue whale	2.75	2.75
1143	A159	$3 Common dolphins	5.00	6.00
		Nos. 1140-1143 (4)	10.75	10.00

Souvenir Sheet

1144	A159	$5 Humpback whale	8.75	8.75

500th Birth Anniv. of Raphael — A160

1983, Feb. 15   Litho.   *Perf. 14*

1145	A160	25c Construction of the Ark	.20	.20
1146	A160	30c Jacob's Vision	.25	.25
1147	A160	90c Joseph Interprets the Dreams	.55	.55
1148	A160	$4 Joseph Interprets Pharaoh's Dream	2.00	2.00
		Nos. 1145-1148 (4)	3.00	3.00

Souvenir Sheet

1149	A160	$5 Creation of the Animals	2.75	2.75

A161

1983, Mar. 14

1150	A161	10c Dental care	.20	.20
1151	A161	70c Airport runway construction	.40	.40
1152	A161	$1.10 Beach	.65	.65
1153	A161	$3 Boat building	1.25	1.75
		Nos. 1150-1153 (4)	2.50	3.00

Commonwealth Day.

World Communication Year — A162

1983, Apr. 18

1154	A162	30c Ship-satellite communication	.20	.20
1155	A162	40c Rural telephone installation	.25	.25
1156	A162	$2.50 Weather map	1.40	1.40
1157	A162	$3 Airport control tower	1.75	1.75
		Nos. 1154-1157 (4)	3.60	3.60

Souvenir Sheet

1158	A162	$5 Satellite	3.00	3.00

For overprints see Nos. 1248-1250.

Franklin Sport Sedan, 1928 A163

1983, May 4   Litho.   *Perf. 15*

1159	A163	6c shown	.20	.20
1160	A163	10c Delage D8, 1933	.20	.20
1161	A163	40c Alvis, 1938	.25	.25
1162	A163	60c Invicta S-type Tourer, 1931	.40	.40
1163	A163	70c Alfa-Romeo 1750 Gran Sport, 1930	.45	.45
1164	A163	90c Isotta Fraschini, 1930	.65	.60
1165	A163	$1 Bugatti Royal Type 41, 1941	.70	.70
1166	A163	$2 BMV 328, 1938	1.40	1.40
1167	A163	$3 Marmon V-16, 1931	2.00	2.00
1168	A163	$4 Lincoln KB Saloon, 1932	2.75	2.75
		Nos. 1159-1168 (10)	9.00	8.95

Souvenir Sheet

1169	A163	$5 Cougar XR-7, 1972	3.50	3.50

Manned Flight Bicentenary — A164

1983, July 18   Litho.   *Perf. 14*

1170	A164	30c Norge blimp	.60	.60
1171	A164	60c Gloster-VI sea plane	1.00	1.00
1172	A164	$1.10 Curtiss NC-4	1.75	1.75
1173	A164	$3 Dornier Do-18	4.25	4.25
		Nos. 1170-1173 (4)	7.60	7.60

Souvenir Sheet

1174	A164	$5 Hot air ballooning, vert.	4.50	4.50

Christmas A165

Designs: Walt Disney's It's Beginning to look a lot like Christmas.

1983, Nov.   *Perf. 11*

1175	A165	½c Morty and Patches	.20	.20
1176	A165	1c Ludwig von Drake	.20	.20
1177	A165	2c Gyro Gearloose	.20	.20
1178	A165	3c Pluto and Figaro	.20	.20
1179	A165	4c Morty and Ferdy	.20	.20
1180	A165	5c Mickey Mouse and Goofy	.30	.25
1181	A165	10c Chip'n'Dale	.30	.25
1182	A165	$2.50 Mickey and Minnie	3.25	3.25
1183	A165	$3 Donald and Grandma Duck	3.25	3.25
		Nos. 1175-1183 (9)	8.10	8.00

Souvenir Sheet

1184	A165	$5 Goofy	8.25	8.25

1984 Olympics — A166

Designs: Various Disney characters.

1983, Dec. 19   Litho.   *Perf. 13½*

1185	A166	½c Pommel Horse	.20	.20
1186	A166	1c Boxing	.20	.20
1187	A166	2c Archery	.20	.20
1188	A166	3c Uneven bars	.20	.20
1189	A166	4c Hurdles	.20	.20
1190	A166	5c Weightlifting	.25	.25
1191	A166	$1 Kayak	2.00	2.00
1192	A166	$2 Marathon	2.75	2.75
1193	A166	$3 Pole Vault	3.25	3.75
		Nos. 1185-1193 (9)	9.25	9.75

Souvenir Sheet

1194	A166	$5 Medley Relay, vert.	8.25	8.25

Inscribed with Olympic Rings Emblem

1984   *Perf. 12½x12*

1185a	A166	½c	.20	.20
1186a	A166	1c	.20	.20
1187a	A166	2c	.20	.20
1188a	A166	3c	.20	.20
1189a	A166	4c	.20	.20
1190a	A166	5c	.25	.25
1191a	A166	$1	2.00	2.00
1192a	A166	$2	2.75	2.75
1193a	A166	$3	3.25	3.75
		Nos. 1185a-1193a (9)	9.25	9.75

Souvenir Sheet

1194a	A166	$5 Olympic rings emblem inscribed	8.25	8.25

Nos. 1185a-1193a printed in sheets of 5.

Banana Boat A167

1984, July 16   Litho.   *Perf. 15*

1195	A167	40c shown	1.00	.60
1196	A167	70c Queen Elizabeth J	1.50	1.00
1197	A167	90c Working sailboats	1.60	2.00
1198	A167	$4 Amerikanis	6.00	8.00
		Nos. 1195-1198 (4)	10.10	11.60

Souvenir Sheet

1199	A167	$5 Spanish galleon, flotilla	7.00	7.00

King William I, 1066-87 — A168

British Kings or Queens and Years of their reigns: No. 1200b, William II, 1087-1100. b, Henry I, 1100-35. d, Stephen, 1135-54. e, Henry II, 1154-89. f, Richard I, 1189-99. g, John, 1199-1216.

No. 1201a, Henry III, 1216-72. b, Edward I, 1272-1307. c, Edward II, 1307-27. d, Edward III, 1327-77. e, Richard II, 1377-99. f, Henry IV, 1399-1413. g, Henry V, 1413-22.

No. 1202a, Henry VI, 1422-61. b, Edward IV, 1461-83. c, Edward V, 1483. d, Richard III, 1483-85. e, Henry VII, 1485-1509. f, Henry VIII, 1509-47. g, Edward VI, 1547-53.

No. 1203a, Jane Grey, 1553. b, Mary I, 1553-58. c, Elizabeth I, 1558-1603. d, James I, 1603-25. e, Charles I, 1625-49. f, Charles II, 1660-85. g, James II, 1685-88.

No. 1204a, William III, 1688-1702. b, Mary II, 1688-94. c, Anne, 1702-14. d, George I, 1714-27. e, George II, 1727-60. f, George III, 1760-1820. g, George IV, 1820-30.

No. 1205a, William IV, 1830-37. b, Victoria, 1837-1901. c, Edward VII, 1901-10. d, George V, 1910-36. e, Edward VIII, 1936. f, George VI, 1936-52. g, Elizabeth II, since 1952. Size: 141x128mm.

1984, Jan. 25   Litho.   *Perf. 14*

1200		Sheet of 7 + label	21.00	21.00
a.-g.	A168	$4, any single	3.00	3.00
1201		Sheet of 7 + label	21.00	21.00
a.-g.	A168	$4, any single	3.00	3.00
1202		Sheet of 7 + label	21.00	21.00
a.-g.	A168	$4, any single	3.00	3.00
1203		Sheet of 7 + label	21.00	21.00
a.-g.	A168	$4, any single	3.00	3.00
1204		Sheet of 7 + label	21.00	21.00
a.-g.	A168	$4, any single	3.00	3.00
1205		Sheet of 7 + label	21.00	21.00
a.-g.	A168	$4, any single	3.00	3.00

Local Flowers A169

1984, May   *Perf. 15*

1206	A169	25c Lantana	.25	.20
1207	A169	30c Plumbago	.30	.20
1208	A169	90c Spider lily	.70	.60
1209	A169	$4 Giant alocasia	2.75	2.75
		Nos. 1206-1209 (4)	4.00	3.75

Souvenir Sheet

1210	A169	$5 Orange trumpet vine	3.50	3.50

For overprints see Nos. 1216-1218.

Coral Reef Fish, World Wildlife Fund Emblem A170

1984, May   Litho.   *Perf. 14*

1211	A170	10c Blue parrot fish	3.25	.95
1212	A170	30c Flame-back cherub fish	5.25	1.60
1213	A170	70c Painted wrasse	9.00	4.00
1214	A170	90c Straight-tailed razorfish	12.00	5.25
		Nos. 1211-1214 (4)	29.50	11.80

Souvenir Sheet

1215	A170	$5 Spanish hogfish	11.00	11.00

Nos. 1208-1210 Overprinted: "19th U.P.U CONGRESS — HAMBURG"

1984   Litho.   *Perf. 15*

1216	A169	90c multi	.70	.70

1217	A169	$4 multi	3.00	3.00

Souvenir Sheet

1218	A169	$5 multi	3.75	3.75

AUSIPEX '84 — A171   Correggio & Degas — A171a

1984, Sept. 21 *Perf. 14*

1219	A171	$1.10 Puffing Billy	1.25	1.25
1220	A171	$4 Australia II	5.50	5.50

Souvenir Sheet

1221	A171	$5 Melbourne tram	7.00	7.00

1984, Aug. **Litho.** **Perf. 14**

Paintings by Correggio: 10c, The Night (detail). 30c, Virgin Adoring the Child. 90c, Mystical Marriage of St. Catherine with St. Sebastian. $4, Madonna and the Fruit Basket. No. 1230, Madonna at the Spring.

Paintings by Degas: 25c, L'Absinthe. 70c, Pouting, horiz. $1.10, The Millinery Shop. $3, The Bellelli Family. No. 1231, The Cotton Market.

1222	A171a	10c multi	.45	.20
1223	A171a	25c multi	.60	.30
1224	A171a	30c multi	.80	.40
1225	A171a	70c multi	1.25	1.00
1226	A171a	90c multi	1.50	1.00
1227	A171a	$1.10 multi	1.75	1.75
1228	A171a	$3 multi	3.00	4.00
1229	A171a	$4 multi	4.00	5.00
		Nos. 1222-1229 (8)	13.35	13.65

Souvenir Sheets

1230	A171a	$5 multi	6.25	6.25
1231	A171a	$5 multi	6.25	6.25

19th Cent. Locomotives — A172

1984, Oct. *Perf. 14½*

1232	A172	30c Locomotion, 1825	.80	.35
1233	A172	40c Novelty, 1829	.90	.45
1234	A172	60c Washington Farmer, 1836	1.00	.70
1235	A172	70c French Crampton, 1859	1.00	1.00
1236	A172	90c Dutch State, 1873	1.25	1.00
1237	A172	$1.10 Champion, 1882	1.50	2.00
1238	A172	$2 Webb Compound, 1893	2.40	3.00
1239	A172	$4 Berlin 74, 1900	4.75	5.00
		Nos. 1232-1239 (8)	13.60	13.50

Souvenir Sheets

1240	A172	$5 Crampton Phoenix, 1863	4.50	4.50
1241	A172	$5 2-8-2 Mikado, 1897	4.50	4.50

Christmas and 50th Anniv. of Donald Duck A173

Scenes from various Donald Duck movies.

Perf. 13½x14, 12 ($2)

1984, Nov. **Litho.**

1242	A173	45c multicolored	1.00	.65
1243	A173	60c multicolored	1.25	.95
1244	A173	90c multicolored	2.00	1.50
1245	A173	$2 multicolored	3.50	3.50
1246	A173	$4 multicolored	6.75	6.75
		Nos. 1242-1246 (5)	14.50	13.35

Souvenir Sheet

1247	A173	$5 multicolored	8.75	8.75

Nos. 1155. 1157, and 1158
Overprinted: "OPENING OF / POINT SALINE / INT'L AIRPORT"

1984, Oct. 28 **Litho.** *Perf. 14½x14*

1248	A162	40c on #1155	.50	.50
1249	A162	$3 on #1157	3.00	3.00

Souvenir Sheet

Same Overprint in Margin in 2 Lines

1250	A162	$5 on #1158	4.50	4.50

Audubon Birth Bicentenary A174

1985, Feb. **Litho.** *Perf. 14*

1251	A174	50c Clapper Rail	2.00	.75
1252	A174	70c Hooded Warbler	2.50	1.50
1253	A174	90c Flicker	3.25	1.75
1254	A174	$4 Bohemian Waxwing	6.75	7.50
		Nos. 1251-1254 (4)	14.50	11.50

Souvenir Sheet

1255	A174	$5 Pigeon Hawk, horiz.	12.00	12.00

See Nos. 1352-1356.

Motorcycle Centenary — A175

1985, Mar. 11 **Litho.** *Perf. 14*

1256	A175	25c Honda XL500R	1.50	.75
1257	A175	50c Suzuki GS1100ES	1.75	1.50
1258	A175	90c Kawasaki KZ700	2.75	1.60
1259	A175	$4 BMW K100	6.00	7.50
		Nos. 1256-1259 (4)	12.00	11.35

Souvenir Sheet

1260	A175	$5 Yamaha 500CC	9.25	9.25

Girl Guides, 75th Anniv. A176

1985, Apr. 15

1261	A176	25c Nature hike	.65	.40
1262	A176	60c Cookout	1.00	.90
1263	A176	90c Singing around campfire	1.50	1.25
1264	A176	$3 Public service	4.50	4.50
		Nos. 1261-1264 (4)	7.65	7.05

Souvenir Sheet

1265	A176	$5 Flags	5.00	5.00

Opening of Point Saline Intl. Airport, Oct. 28, 1984 A177

Inaugural flights.

1985, Apr. 30

1266	A177	70c From Barbados	2.75	1.40
1267	A177	$1 From New York	3.75	2.00
1268	A177	$4 To Miami	7.75	8.50
		Nos. 1266-1268 (3)	14.25	11.90

Souvenir Sheet

1269	A177	$5 Point Saline Intl. Airport	8.00	8.00

Intl. Civil Aviation Org., 40th Anniv. A178

1985, May 15

1270	A178	10c McDonnell Douglas DC-8	.40	.20
1271	A178	50c Super Constellation	1.00	.65
1272	A178	60c Vickers Vanguard	1.50	.80
1273	A178	$4 DeHavilland Twin Otter	5.00	6.50
		Nos. 1270-1273 (4)	7.90	8.15

Souvenir Sheet

1274	A178	$5 Avro 748 Turboprop	5.25	5.25

Water Sports A179

1985, June 15 *Perf. 15*

1275	A179	10c Model boat racing	.20	.20
1276	A179	50c Snorkeling, Sandy Island carriacou	.40	.40
1277	A179	$1.10 Sailing, Grand Anse Beach	.90	.90
1278	A179	$4 Windsurfing	3.00	3.00
		Nos. 1275-1278 (4)	4.50	4.50

Miniature Sheet

1279	A179	$5 Snorkelers, surfers, sailboats	5.00	5.00

Island Flowers — A180

½c, Strelitzia reginae. 1c, Passiflora coccinea. 2c, Nerium oleander. 4c, Ananas comosus. 5c, Anthurium andraeanum. 6c, Bougainvillea glabra. 10c, Hibiscus rosasinensis. 15c, Alpinia purpurata. 25c, Euphorbia pulcherrima. 30c, Antigonon leptopus. 40c, Datura candida. 50c, Hippeastrum punicum. 60c, Opuntia megacantha. 70c, Acalypha hispida. 75c, Cordia sebestina. $1, Catharan-thus roseus. $1.10, Ixora macrothyrsa. $3, Justicia brandegeeana. $5, Plumbago capensis. $10, Lantana camara. $20, Jatropha integerrima.

1985-88 *Perf. 14*

1280	A180	½c multi	.20	.20
1281	A180	1c multi	.20	.20
1282	A180	2c multi	.20	.20
1283	A180	4c multi	.20	.20
1284	A180	5c multi	.20	.20
1285	A180	6c multi	.20	.20
1286	A180	10c multi	.20	.20
1287	A180	15c multi	.20	.20
1288	A180	25c multi	.20	.20
1289	A180	30c multi	.20	.20
1290	A180	40c multi	.45	.45
1291	A180	50c multi	.50	.50
1292	A180	60c multi	.60	.60
1293	A180	70c multi	.65	.65
1293B	A180	75c multi	.85	.85
1294	A180	$1 multi	1.00	1.00
1295	A180	$1.10 multi	1.10	1.10
1296	A180	$3 multi	2.75	2.75
1297	A180	$5 multi	4.50	4.50

1297A	A180	$10 multi	9.25	9.25
1297B	A180	$20 multi	18.00	18.00
		Nos. 1280-1297B (21)	41.65	41.65

Issued: #1280-1293, 1294-1297, 7/1; $10, 11/11; $20, 8/1/86; 75c, 1/12/88.
For overprints see #1357-1358, 1558-1560.

1986 *Perf. 12x12½*

No date inscription

1280a	A180	½c	.20	.20
1281a	A180	1c	.20	.20
1282a	A180	2c	.20	.20
1283a	A180	4c	.20	.20
1284a	A180	5c	.20	.20
1285a	A180	6c	.20	.20
1286a	A180	10c	.20	.20
b.		Inscribed "1988"	3.00	3.00
1287a	A180	15c	.20	.20
1288a	A180	25c	.20	.20
1289a	A180	30c	.20	.20
1290a	A180	40c	.30	.30
1291a	A180	50c	.35	.35
1292a	A180	60c	.40	.40
1293a	A180	70c	.45	.45
1294a	A180	$1	.70	.70
1295a	A180	$1.10	.75	.75
1296a	A180	$3	2.00	2.00
1297c	A180	$5	3.25	3.25
1297d	A180	$10	6.50	6.50
		Nos. 1280a-1297d (19)	16.70	16.70

Issued: #1280a-1285a, 1287a-1292a, 1294a-1296a, Mar.; 10c, 70c, $5, July; $10, Dec.

1987

Inscribed "1987"

1289b	A180	30c	.30	.65
1291b	A180	50c	.40	.80
1292b	A180	60c	.50	1.25
1294b	A180	$1	.70	1.25
		Nos. 1289b-1294b (4)	1.90	3.95

Queen Mother, 85th Birthday A181

Photographs: $1, At the Royal Opera, vert. $1.50, Playing pool, London Press Club. $2.50, At Epsom for the Oaks Day races, vert. $5, In open carriage with Prince Charles, Thanksgiving Day, 1980, vert.

1985, July 5

1298	A181	$1 multicolored	.70	.70
1299	A181	$1.50 multicolored	1.10	1.10
1300	A181	$2.50 multicolored	1.75	1.75
		Nos. 1298-1300 (3)	3.55	3.55

Souvenir Sheet

1301	A181	$5 multicolored	4.00	4.00

1986, Jan. 20 **Litho.** *Perf. 12x12½*

1301A	A181	90c like #1298	.65	.65
1301B	A181	$1 like #1299	.75	.75
1301C	A181	$3 like #1300	2.25	2.25
		Nos. 1301A-1301C (3)	3.65	3.65

#1301A-1301C issued in sheets of 5 + label.

Intl. Youth Year — A182

1985, Aug. 21 *Perf. 15*

1302	A182	25c Gardening	.40	.25
1303	A182	50c At the beach	.50	.40
1304	A182	$1.10 Education	1.00	1.00
1305	A182	$3 Health care	2.40	2.40
		Nos. 1302-1305 (4)	4.30	4.05

Souvenir Sheet

1306	A182	$5 Harmonizing	4.50	4.50

4th Caribbean Cuboree, Aug. 17-23 A183

1985, Sept. 5 — Perf. 14

1307	A183	10c Pitching tents	.40	.20
1308	A183	50c Swimming	.80	.65
1309	A183	$1 Stamp collecting	1.90	1.40
1310	A183	$4 Bird watching	5.25	5.25
		Nos. 1307-1310 (4)	8.35	7.50

Souvenir Sheet

1311	A183	$5 Grand Circle ritual	6.00	6.00

Johann Sebastian Bach — A184

Portrait, signature, music from Ciaccona and: 25c, Crumhorn. 70c, Oboe d'amore. $1, Violin. $3, Harpsichord. $5, Portrait.

1985, Sept. 19

1312	A184	25c multicolored	.80	.20
1313	A184	70c multicolored	1.50	.85
1314	A184	$1 multicolored	2.00	1.25
1315	A184	$3 multicolored	3.75	3.75
		Nos. 1312-1315 (4)	8.05	6.05

Souvenir Sheet

1316	A184	$5 multicolored	6.25	6.25

The Prince & the Pauper — A185

Walt Disney characters.

1985, Oct. 30

1317	A185	25c Prince & Pauper meet	1.25	.40
1318	A185	50c Exchange clothes	1.50	.80
1319	A185	$1.10 Prince as the Pauper	2.00	1.75
1320	A185	$1.50 Prince rescued	2.75	2.50
1321	A185	$2 Pauper as the Prince	4.50	4.50
		Nos. 1317-1321 (5)	12.00	9.95

Souvenir Sheet

1322	A185	$5 Prince & Pauper celebrate	9.75	9.75

IYY, Mark Twain (1835-1910), author.

Elizabeth II, Royal Visit to Spice Island — A186

1985, Oct. 31 — Perf. 14½

1323	A186	50c Flags of Grenada, U.K.	1.00	.50
1324	A186	$1 Elizabeth II, vert.	1.00	1.00
1325	A186	$4 HMS Britannia	3.50	3.50
		Nos. 1323-1325 (3)	5.50	5.25

Souvenir Sheet

1326	A186	$5 Map	4.25	4.25

The Brothers Grimm — A187

Disney characters in The Fisherman and His Wife.

1985, Nov. 4 — Litho. — Perf. 14

1327	A187	30c multicolored	1.00	.50
1328	A187	60c multicolored	1.50	1.00
1329	A187	70c multicolored	2.00	1.10
1330	A187	$1 multicolored	3.00	1.60
1331	A187	$3 multicolored	5.25	5.25
		Nos. 1327-1331 (5)	12.75	9.45

Souvenir Sheet

1332	A187	$5 multicolored	9.75	9.75

Indigenous Fish and Coral — A188

1985, Nov. 15

1333	A188	25c Red-spotted hawkfish	1.75	.80
1334	A188	50c Spotfin butterflyfish	2.75	1.25
1335	A188	$1.10 Fire coral, orange sponge	5.00	3.25
1336	A188	$3 Pillar coral	8.75	8.75
		Nos. 1333-1336 (4)	18.25	14.05

Souvenir Sheet

1337	A188	$5 Bigeye	7.00	7.00

UN, 40th Anniv. A189

UN stamps and famous people: 50c, No. 258, Mary McLeod Bethune (1875-1955), American educator. $2, No. 156, Maimonides (1135-1204), Judaic scholar. $2.50, No. 41, Alexander Graham Bell (1847-1922), inventor of the telephone. $5, Dag Hammarskjold (1905-1961), 2nd UN secretary general.

1985, Nov. 22 — Perf. 14½

1338	A189	50c multicolored	.75	.65
1339	A189	$2 multicolored	3.50	3.50
1340	A189	$2.50 multicolored	3.50	4.00
		Nos. 1338-1340 (3)	7.75	8.15

Souvenir Sheet

1341	A189	$5 multicolored	4.75	4.75

Christmas A190

Religious paintings: 25c, Adoration of the Shepherds, by Andre Mantegna (1431-1506). 60c, Journey of the Magi, by Sassetta (d. 1450). 90c, Madonna and Child Enthroned with Saints, by Raphael (1483-1520). $4, Nativity, by Monaco. $5, Madonna and Child Enthroned with Saints, by Agnolo Gaddi (c. 1350-1396).

1985, Dec. 23 — Perf. 15

1342	A190	25c multicolored	.20	.20
1343	A190	60c multicolored	.35	.35
1344	A190	90c multicolored	.55	.55
1345	A190	$4 multicolored	2.50	2.50
		Nos. 1342-1345 (4)	3.60	3.60

Souvenir Sheet

1346	A190	$5 multicolored	3.25	3.25

Statue of Liberty, Cent. A191

Views of New York City.

1986, Jan. 6

1347	A191	5c Columbus Circle, 1893	.50	.20
1348	A191	25c Circle, 1986	1.00	.45
1349	A191	40c Central Park Mounted Police, 1895	1.75	1.25
1350	A191	$4 Mounted Police, 1986	6.50	8.00
		Nos. 1347-1350 (4)	9.75	9.90

Souvenir Sheet

1351	A191	$5 Statue of Liberty	4.50	4.50

Nos. 1347-1348, 1351 vert.

Audubon Type of 1985

1986, Jan. 20 — Perf. 12x12½

1352	A174	50c Snowy egret	2.00	1.00
1353	A174	90c Red flamingo	2.75	1.60
1354	A174	$1.10 Barnacle goose	3.00	2.50
1355	A174	$3 Smew	5.50	5.50
		Nos. 1352-1355 (4)	13.25	10.60

Souvenir Sheet
Perf. 14

1356	A174	$5 Brant Goose, horiz.	16.00	16.00

Nos. 1291 and 1297 Overprinted "VISIT OF PRES. REAGAN 20 FEB. 1986"

1986, Feb. 20 — Perf. 14

1357	A180	50c multicolored	.45	.45
1358	A180	$5 multicolored	4.50	4.50

St. George Methodist Church, Bicent. A192

1986, Feb. 24 — Perf. 15

1359	A192	60c multicolored	.90	.90

Souvenir Sheet

1360	A192	$5 multicolored	3.50	3.50

Heritage Year.

1986 World Cup Soccer Championships, Mexico — A193

Various soccer plays.

1986, Mar. 6 — Perf. 14

1361	A193	50c multicolored	.80	.70
1362	A193	70c multicolored	1.00	1.00
1363	A193	90c multicolored	1.50	1.50
1364	A193	$4 multicolored	5.25	5.25
		Nos. 1361-1364 (4)	8.55	8.45

Souvenir Sheet

1365	A193	$5 multicolored	6.25	6.25

For overprints see Nos. 1399-1403.

Halley's Comet A194

5c, Clyde Tombaugh, discovered Pluto, 1930, & Dudley Observatory. 20c, US X-24B

space shuttle prototype, 1973. 40c, Medallic art, Catholic Church, 1618. $4, Lot & his daughters fleeing Sodom & Gomorrah, 1949 B.C. $5, Comet over Grand Anse Beach.

1986, Mar. 20

1366	A194	5c multicolored	.50	.50
1367	A194	20c multicolored	.75	.25
1368	A194	40c multicolored	1.00	.40
1369	A194	$4 multicolored	4.25	4.25
		Nos. 1366-1369 (4)	6.50	5.40

Souvenir Sheet

1370	A194	$5 multicolored	8.00	8.00

For overprints see Nos. 1416-1420.

Queen Elizabeth II, 60th Birthday
Common Design Type

2c, Signing the log, 1951. $1.50, Presenting polo trophy, Windsor, 1965. $4, Derby Day, 1977. $5, Royal family portrait, 1939.

1986, Apr. 21 — Perf. 14

1371	CD339	2c yel & blk	.20	.20
1372	CD339	$1.50 pale grn & multi	.90	.90
1373	CD339	$4 dl lil & multi	2.40	2.40
		Nos. 1371-1373 (3)	3.50	3.50

Souvenir Sheet

1374	CD339	$5 tan & blk	3.25	3.25

AMERIPEX '86 — A195

Walt Disney characters playing baseball.

1986, May 22 — Litho. — Perf. 11

1375	A195	1c Pitcher	.20	.20
1376	A195	2c Catcher	.20	.20
1377	A195	3c Strike	.20	.20
1378	A195	4c Force out	.20	.20
1379	A195	5c Fly ball	.20	.20
1380	A195	6c Third base	.25	.25
1381	A195	$2 Manager	2.25	1.90
1382	A195	$3 Error	3.25	3.25
		Nos. 1375-1382 (8)	6.75	6.40

Souvenir Sheets
Perf. 14

1383	A195	$5 Batter	7.00	7.00
1384	A195	$5 Grand slam	7.00	7.00

Royal Wedding Issue, 1986
Common Design Type

Designs: 2c, Prince Andrew and Sarah Ferguson. $1.10, Andrew. $4, Andrew in flight suit, helicopter. $5, Couple, diff.

1986, July 23 — Perf. 14

1385	CD340	2c multicolored	.20	.20
1386	CD340	$1.10 multicolored	.80	.80
1387	CD340	$4 multicolored	3.00	3.00
		Nos. 1385-1387 (3)	4.00	4.00

Souvenir Sheet

1388	CD340	$5 multicolored	4.25	4.25

Seashells A196

Designs: 25c, Gmelin brown-lined latirus. 60c, Lamarck lamellose wentletrap. 70c, Swainson turkey wing. $4, Linne rooster-tail conch. $5, Linne angular triton.

1986, July 15 — Litho. — Perf. 15

1389	A196	25c multicolored	.50	.20
1390	A196	60c multicolored	.75	.55
1391	A196	70c multicolored	.90	.90
1392	A196	$4 multicolored	3.75	3.75
		Nos. 1389-1392 (4)	5.90	5.40

Souvenir Sheet

1393	A196	$5 multicolored	3.75	3.75

Mushrooms
A197

1986, Aug. 1   *Perf. 15*
1394	A197	10c Lepiota rose-lamellata	.65	.40
1395	A197	60c Lentinus bertieri	1.25	1.00
1396	A197	$1 Lentinus re-tinervis	2.75	2.00
1397	A197	$4 Eccilia cysti-ophorus	6.50	6.50
		Nos. 1394-1397 (4)	11.15	9.90

Souvenir Sheet
1398	A197	$5 Cystolepiota eriophora	14.00	14.00

Nos. 1361-1365 Ovptd. "WINNERS Argentina 3 / W. Germany 2" in Gold

1986, Sept. 15   Litho.   *Perf. 14*
1399	A193	50c multicolored	.95	.95
1400	A193	70c multicolored	1.25	1.25
1401	A193	90c multicolored	1.50	1.50
1402	A193	$4 multicolored	6.00	6.00
		Nos. 1399-1402 (4)	9.70	9.70

Souvenir Sheet
1403	A193	$5 multicolored	5.75	5.75

Disarmament Week and Intl. Peace Year — A198

60c, Mahatma Gandhi, rifles, dove. $4, Martin Luther King, Jr., hands, olive branch.

1986, Sept. 15   *Perf. 15*
1404	A198	60c multi, vert.	.40	.40
1405	A198	$4 multi	3.00	3.00

Christmas — A199

Disney characters. Nos. 1406-1407, 1411-1412 vert.

1986, Nov. 3   *Perf. 11*
1406	A199	30c Mickey, hearth	.50	.30
1407	A199	45c Mickey, Santa	.75	.45
1408	A199	60c Donald, Mickey Mouse phone	.90	.60
1409	A199	70c Goofy, toy band	1.10	.70
1410	A199	$1.10 Daisy, dolls	1.25	1.10
1411	A199	$2 Goofy as Santa	2.00	2.00
1412	A199	$2.50 Goofy playing piano	2.40	2.40
1413	A199	$3 Train ride	3.00	3.00
		Nos. 1406-1413 (8)	11.90	10.55

Souvenir Sheets
1414	A199	$5 Donald, Goofy, Mickey	7.00	7.00
1415	A199	$5 Dewey	7.00	7.00

Nos. 1366-1370 Ovptd. with Halley's Comet Emblem

1986, Oct. 15   Litho.   *Perf. 14*
1416	A194	5c multicolored	.60	.60
1417	A194	20c multicolored	.85	.60
1418	A194	40c multicolored	1.25	.70
1419	A194	$4 multicolored	7.25	7.25
		Nos. 1416-1419 (4)	9.95	9.15

Souvenir Sheet
1420	A194	$5 multicolored	5.50	5.50

Fauna and Flora
A200

1986, Nov. 17   *Perf. 14*
1421	A200	10c Chicken, rooster	.25	.20
1422	A200	30c Fish-eating bat	.40	.25
1423	A200	60c Goat	.85	.75
1424	A200	70c Cow	1.00	.90
1425	A200	$1 Anthurium	1.50	1.10
1426	A200	$1.10 Royal poinci-ana	1.50	1.25
1427	A200	$2 Frangipani	2.50	2.50
1428	A200	$4 Orchid	5.00	6.50
		Nos. 1421-1428 (8)	13.00	13.45

Souvenir Sheets
1429	A200	$5 Horse	4.75	4.75
1430	A200	$5 Trees	4.75	4.75

Automobile, Cent. — A202

1886 Daimler and modern automobiles.

1986, Nov. 20   *Perf. 15*
1431	A202	10c 1984 Maserati Biturbo	.25	.25
1432	A202	30c 1960 AC Cobra	.35	.35
1433	A202	60c 1963 Corvette	.55	.55
1434	A202	70c 1932 Duesen-berg SJ7	.65	.65
1435	A202	90c 1957 Porsche	.75	.75
1436	A202	$1.10 1930 Stoewer	1.00	1.00
1437	A202	$2 1957 VW Beetle	1.60	1.60
1438	A202	$3 1963 Mercedes 600 Limo	2.40	2.75
		Nos. 1431-1438 (8)	7.55	7.90

Souvenir Sheets
1439	A202	$5 1914 Stutz	4.00	4.00
1440	A202	$5 1941 Packard	4.00	4.00

Song of Songs, by Marc Chagall (1887-1984) — A203

Paintings: No. 1441, The Rooster. No. 1442, Lovers in the Moonlight. No. 1443, Woman and Haystack. No. 1444, Snow-Covered Church. No. 1445, Peasant Life. No. 1446, Moses Receiving the Tablets. No. 1447, Vitebsk: From Mt. Zadunuv. No. 1449, Song of Songs, diff. No. 1450, The Creation of Man. No. 1451, Spring. No. 1452, Jacob's Struggle with the Angel. No. 1453, Song of Songs (wedding detail). No. 1454, The Painter to the Moon, 1917. No. 1455, Moses Striking the

Rock. No. 1456, To My Betrothed, 1911. No. 1457, Sacrifice of Isaac. No. 1458, Monkey Acting as Judge Over Dispute Between Wolf and Fox, 1925. No. 1459, Song of Songs (bride riding Pegasus). No. 1460, Lovers in the Lilac, 1930. No. 1461, Song of Songs (sun, spirits). No. 1462, Jacob's Dream. No. 1463, Purim, 1916. No. 1464, Fantastic Horsecart. No. 1465, Listening to the Cock, 1944. No. 1466, Self-portrait, 1914. No. 1467, The Juggler, 1943. No. 1468, Noah and the Rainbow. No. 1469, Moses Before the Burning Bush. No. 1470, Around Her, 1945. No. 1471, The Trough, 1925. No. 1472, The Poet of Half-Past-Three. No. 1473, The Tree of Life, 1948. No. 1474, Woman with the Blue Face, 1932. No. 1475, Chrysanthemums, 1926. No. 1476, Spoonful of Milk, 1912. No. 1477, The Soldier Drinks, 1911. No. 1478, Noah's Ark. No. 1479, Flowers and Fruit. No. 1480, Adam and Eve Expelled fron Paradise. No. 1481. Return from Synagogue. No. 1482, Aleko: A Fantasy of St. Petersburg. No. 1483, The Orchard. No. 1484, Solitude. No. 1485, Paris Through the Window, 1913. No. 1486, The Wedding, 1910. No. 1487, Paradise. No. 1488, The Dream, 1939. No. 1489, Abraham and the Three Angels. No. 1490, Water Carrier Under the Moon, 1914.

1986-87
1441-1480	A203	$1 each	1.00	1.00

Size: 110x95mm

Imperf
1481-1490	A203	$5 each	4.00	4.00

Nos. 1441-1446, 1450-1452 1455-1458, 1464-1467 and 1470-1479 vert.
Issued: #1441-1452, 1481-1483, 1986; #1453-1480, 1484-1490, 1987.

A204

America's Cup — A205

1987, Feb. 5   Litho.   *Perf. 15*
1491	A204	10c Columbia, 1958	.20	.20
1492	A204	60c Resolute, 1920	.50	.50
1493	A204	$1.10 Endeavor, 1934	.90	.90
1494	A204	$4 Rainbow, 1934	3.25	3.25
		Nos. 1491-1494 (4)	4.85	4.85

Souvenir Sheet
1495	A205	$5 Weatherly, 1962	4.00	4.00

Virgin Mary — A206

Map of Voyage, Columbus' Signature — A207

1987, Apr. 27   *Perf. 15*
1496	A206	10c shown	.30	.20
1497	A206	30c Nina, Pinta, Santa Maria	.55	.25
1498	A206	50c Columbus, map	.65	.40
1499	A206	60c Columbus	.75	.45
1500	A206	90c Isabella, Ferdi-nand	.85	.70
1501	A206	$1.10 Discovering the Antilles	.90	.80
1502	A206	$2 Carib Indians	1.50	1.50
a.		Souv. sheet of 3, 30c, 90c, $2	2.40	2.40
1503	A206	$3 American Indi-ans, 1493	2.25	2.25
a.		Souv. sheet of 5 + label, 10c, 50c, 60c, $1.10, $3	4.00	4.00
		Nos. 1496-1503 (8)	7.75	6.55

Souvenir Sheets
1504	A207	$5 shown	3.75	3.75
1505	A207	$5 Columbus, Christ child	3.75	3.75

Discovery of America 500th anniv. (in 1992). Nos. 1497, 1500 and 1502 horiz.

CAPEX '87
A208

Fish. Nos. 1506, 1508 vert.

1987, June 15
1506	A208	10c Black group-er	.40	.20
1507	A208	30c Blue marlin	.60	.25
1508	A208	60c White marlin	.75	.50
1509	A208	70c Big-eye thresher shark	.85	.60
1510	A208	$1 Bonefish	1.25	1.00
1511	A208	$1.10 Wahoo	1.50	1.25
1512	A208	$2 Sailfish	2.25	2.00
1513	A208	$4 Albacore	3.50	3.50
		Nos. 1506-1513 (8)	11.10	9.30

Souvenir Sheets
1514	A208	$5 Barracuda	4.50	4.50
1515	A208	$5 Yellowfin tu-na, vert.	4.50	4.50

Transportation Innovations — A209

1987, May 18   *Perf. 14*
1516	A209	10c Cornu's Heli-copter, 1907	.80	.60
1517	A209	15c The Monitor and Merri-mack, 1862	.80	.60
1518	A209	30c LZ1 Zeppelin, c. 1900	1.00	.80
1519	A209	50c S.S. Sirius, 1838	1.10	.85
1520	A209	60c Trans-Siberi-an Railway	1.25	1.00
1521	A209	70c USS Enter-prise, 1960	1.40	1.10
1522	A209	90c Blanchard's Balloon, 1785	1.50	1.40
1523	A209	$1.50 USS Holland 1, 1900	2.25	2.25
1524	A209	$2 S.S. Ocean-ic, 1871	3.00	3.00
1525	A209	$3 1984 Lamborghini Countach	4.50	4.50
		Nos. 1516-1525 (10)	17.60	16.10

For overprints see Nos. 1599-1602.

Statue of Liberty, Cent. A210

1987, Aug. 5
1526	A210	10c Computer structural di-agrams	.20	.20

1527	A210	25c	Fireworks around statue	.20	.20
1528	A210	50c	Fireworks in front of statue	.50	.50
1529	A210	60c	Statue, boats	.65	.60
1530	A210	70c	Structural diagram, close-up	1.00	.65
1531	A210	$1	Rear of statue, close-up	1.10	.95
1532	A210	$1.10	Liberty and Manhattan Isls.	1.25	1.25
1533	A210	$2	Statue, boats, diff.	2.25	2.25
1534	A210	$4	Ocean liner, New York Harbor	3.75	4.50
			Nos. 1526-1534 (9)	10.90	11.10

Nos. 1529, 1531-1534 vert.

Inventors and Innovators
A211

Designs: 50c, Sir Isaac Newton (1642-1727), law of gravity. $1.10, Jons Jakob Berzelius (1779-1848), symbols of chemical elements. $2, Robert Boyle (1627-1691), and Boyle's Law of pressure and volume. $3, James Watt (1736-1819), and diagram of steam engine. $5, Wright Flyer, Voyager.

1987, Sept. 9

1535	A211	50c	multicolored	.90	.90
1536	A211	$1.10	multicolored	2.00	2.00
1537	A211	$2	multicolored	2.75	2.75
1538	A211	$3	multicolored	5.00	5.00
			Nos. 1535-1538 (4)	10.65	10.65

Souvenir Sheet

1539	A211	$5	multicolored	5.25	5.25

No. 1536 inscribed with incorrect spelling of inventors name, "John Jacob Berzelius." No. 1538 inscribed with incorrect caption; James Watt and Watt engine are pictured, not Rudolf Diesel and the Diesel engine.

Miniature Sheets

Fairy Tales — A212

Snow White (50th Anniv.): No. 1540a, Snow White scrubs stairs. b, Wicked Queen, looking glass. c, Snow White fleeing. d, Dwarfs, mine. e, Snow White at cottage. f, Snow White, dwarfs. g, Snow White dancing with dwarfs. h, Eating poison apple. i, Prince kissing Snow White.
Sleeping Beauty: No. 1541a, Royal family. b, Maleficent cursing infant (Aurora). c, Merryweather altering curse. d, Three good fairies. e, Briar Rose (Aurora), forest animals. f, Aurora, spinning wheel. g, Sleeping Beauty (Aurora). h, Prince Phillip battling dragon (Maleficent). i, Sleeping Beauty awakes.
Cinderella: No. 1542a, Ella (Cinderella) and father. b, Cinderella sweeping. c, Cinderella, animals in barn. d, Cinderella, stepmother, stepsisters. e, Mice. f, Fairy Godmother. g, Cinderella transformed, coach. h, i, Duke puts glass slipper on Cinderella's foot.
Pinocchio: No. 1543a, Geppetto and puppet. b, Jiminy Cricket. c, Pinocchio, J. Worthington Foulfellow and Gideon. d, Pinocchio, Master Stromboli. e, Blue Fairy rescues Pinocchio. f, Pinocchio, donkeys. g, Pinocchio riding fish. h, Pinocchio and Geppetto at sea. i, Pinocchio transformed into a boy.
Alice in Wonderland: No. 1544a, Alice, rabbit hole. b, Alice in bottle. c, Walrus and Carpenter. d, White Rabbit in pink house. e, Alice, pink butterfly. f, March Hare, Mad Hatter. g, Alice in garden. h, Queen of Hearts. i, Alice on trial.
Peter Pan: No. 1545a, Nana. b, Peter Pan. c, Peter Pan, Tinker Bell, Wendy, John and Michael Darling flying. d, In NeverNever Land. e, Peter Pan and Tiger Lily. f, Captain Hook and First Mate Smee. g, Peter Pan dueling with Captain Hook. h, Tinker Bell, pirate ship. i, Captain Hook, crocodile.

No. 1546, Snow White and Prince riding off into sunset. No. 1547, Aurora and Prince Phillip dancing. No. 1548, Cinderella and Prince Charming marry. No. 1549, Pinocchio, Jiminy Cricket and Gepetto. No. 1550, Alice, cat, mother. No. 1551, Darling children waving goodbye to Peter Pan.

1987, Sept. 9   Perf. 14x13½

1540		Sheet of 9	4.25	4.25
a.-i.	A212	30c any single	.45	.45
1541		Sheet of 9	4.25	4.25
a.-i.	A212	30c any single	.45	.45
1542		Sheet of 9	4.25	4.25
a.-i.	A212	30c any single	.45	.45
1543		Sheet of 9	4.25	4.25
a.-i.	A212	30c any single	.45	.45
1544		Sheet of 9	4.25	4.25
a.-i.	A212	30c any single	.45	.45
1545		Sheet of 9	4.25	4.25
a.-i.	A212	30c any single	.45	.45
		Nos. 1540-1545 (6)	25.50	25.50

Souvenir Sheets

1546-1551	A212	$5 each	6.75	6.75

Souvenir Sheet

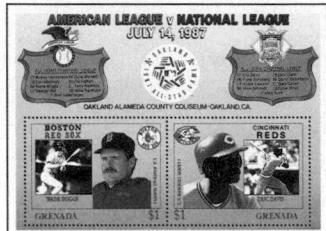

Baseball All-Star Game, Oakland, July 14 — A213

Athletes, team emblems: a, Wade Boggs, Boston Red Sox. b, Eric Davis, Cincinnati Reds.

1987, Nov. 2   Litho.   Perf. 14

1552	A213	Sheet of 2	1.45	1.45
a.-b.		$1 any single	.70	.70

Massachusetts State Crest — A214

Designs: 15c, Independence Hall, Philadelphia. 50c, Benjamin Franklin. $4, Robert Morris (1734-1806), financier of American Revolution. $5, Pres. James Madison.

1987, Nov. 2

1553	A214	15c	multi, vert.	.20	.20
1554	A214	50c	multi, vert.	.30	.30
1555	A214	60c	shown	.40	.40
1556	A214	$4	multi, vert.	2.50	2.50
			Nos. 1553-1556 (4)	3.40	3.40

Souvenir Sheet

1557	A214	$5	multi, vert.	3.25	3.25

US Constitution bicent.

Nos. 1286, 1291 and 1296 Overprinted

1987, Nov. 2

1558	A180	10c	multicolored	.20	.20
1559	A180	50c	multicolored	.35	.35
1560	A180	$3	multicolored	2.00	2.00
			Nos. 1558-1560 (3)	2.55	2.55

HAFNIA '87 — A215

Disney animated characters in adaptation of fairy tales by Hans Christian Andersen.

1987, Nov. 16   Litho.   Perf. 14

1561	A215	25c	The Shadow	.50	.30
1562	A215	30c	The Storks	.50	.35
1563	A215	50c	The Emperor's New Clothes	.75	.60
1564	A215	60c	The Tinderbox	1.00	.65
1565	A215	70c	The Shepherdess and the Chimney Sweep	1.25	.80
1566	A215	$1.50	The Little Mermaid	2.25	1.75
1567	A215	$3	The Princess and the Pea	3.25	3.25
1568	A215	$4	The Marsh King's Daughter	4.25	4.25
			Nos. 1561-1568 (8)	13.75	11.95

Souvenir Sheets

1569	A215	$5	The Flying Trunk, horiz.	8.00	8.00
1570	A215	$5	The Sandman, horiz.	8.00	8.00

Christmas — A216

Religious paintings: 15c, The Annunciation, by Fra Angelico. 30c, The Annunciation, attributed to Hubert van Eyck (c. 1370-1426). 60c, Adoration of the Magi, by Januarius Zick (1730-1797). $4, The Flight Into Egypt, by David. $5, The Circumcision, produced by artists of the Giovanni Bellini Studio, 14th cent.

1987, Dec. 15

1571	A216	15c	multicolored	.55	.45
1572	A216	30c	multicolored	1.00	.50
1573	A216	60c	multicolored	1.75	1.40
1574	A216	$4	multicolored	6.75	6.75
			Nos. 1571-1574 (4)	10.05	9.10

Souvenir Sheet

1575	A216	$5	multicolored	8.50	8.50

T. Albert Marryshow (b. 1887) — A217

1988, Jan. 22   Litho.   Perf. 14

1576	A217	25c scarlet, red brn & brn blk	.30	.30

40th Wedding Anniv. of Queen Elizabeth II and Prince Philip — A218

1988, Feb. 15

1577	A218	15c	Wedding portrait, 1947	.30	.20
1578	A218	50c	Elizabeth, Charles, Anne	.60	.45
1579	A218	$1	Elizabeth, Anne	1.00	1.00
1580	A218	$4	Elizabeth, c. 1980	3.25	3.25
			Nos. 1577-1580 (4)	5.15	4.90

Souvenir Sheet

1581	A218	$5	Elizabeth, 1947	3.75	3.75

Disney Animated Characters and 1988 Summer Olympics, Seoul
A219

1988, Apr. 13   Litho.   Perf. 13½x14

1582	A219	1c	Lighting torch, Olympia	.20	.20
1583	A219	2c	Torch bearers	.20	.20
1584	A219	3c	Flag bearers	.20	.20
1585	A219	4c	Releasing doves	.20	.20
1586	A219	5c	Opening ceremony	.20	.20
1587	A219	10c	Olympic motto	.20	.20
1588	A219	$6	Tiger character trademark	6.00	5.50
1589	A219	$7	Oldest Korean p.o.	6.50	5.50
			Nos. 1582-1589 (8)	13.70	12.20

Souvenir Sheets

1590	A219	$5	Sportsmanship oath	5.75	5.75
1591	A219	$5	Closing ceremony	5.75	5.75

Boy Scouts
A220

1988, May 3   Litho.   Perf. 14

1592	A220	20c	Fishing, vert.	.40	.20
1593	A220	70c	Hiking	1.25	1.00
1594	A220	90c	First-aid	1.75	1.40
1595	A220	$3	Canoeing, vert.	4.00	4.00
			Nos. 1592-1595 (4)	7.40	6.60

Souvenir Sheet

1596	A220	$5	Scout holding koala, vert.	3.75	3.75

Rotary Conference, District 405, St. George, May 5-7 — A221

Rotary Intl. emblem and: $2, Map of District 405 island nations (Grenada, Guyana, Surinam and French Guiana), 15th cent. Spanish galleon Santa Maria, vert. $10, Motto "Service Above Self."

1988, May 5   Perf. 13½x14

1597	A221	$2	multicolored	1.50	1.50

Souvenir Sheet

Perf. 14x13½

1598	A221	$10	shown	7.50	7.50

Nos. 1522-1525 Overprinted for Philatelic Exhibitions

a

b

c

d

1988, Apr. 19	Litho.		Perf. 14	
1599	A209 (a)	90c multi	1.25	.85
1600	A209 (b)	$1.50 multi	1.75	1.50
1601	A209 (c)	$2 multi	2.25	2.25
1602	A209 (d)	$3 multi	2.75	2.75
	Nos. 1599-1602 (4)		8.00	7.35

Birds — A222

1988, May 31				
1603	A222	10c Roseate tern	.80	.30
1604	A222	25c Laughing gull	1.00	.30
1605	A222	50c Osprey	1.25	.60
1606	A222	60c Rose-breasted grosbeak	1.25	.60
1607	A222	90c Purple gallinule	1.25	.95
1608	A222	$1.10 White-tailed tropicbird	1.25	1.10
1609	A222	$3 Blue-faced booby	3.00	3.00
1610	A222	$4 Northern shoveler	4.25	4.25
	Nos. 1603-1610 (8)		14.05	11.10

Souvenir Sheet

1611	A222	$5 Belted kingfisher	5.00	5.00
1612	A222	$5 Rusty-tailed flycatcher	5.00	5.00

Miniature Sheets

Classic Automobiles
A223

Cars (U.S. unless otherwise stated): No. 1613a, 1934 Tatra Type 77, Czechoslovakia. b, 1938 Rolls-Royce Phantom III, Britain. c, 1947 Studebaker Champion Starlight. d, 1948 Porsche Gmund, Germany. e, 1948 Tucker. f, 1931 Peerless V-16. g, 1931 Minerva AL, Belgium. h, 1933 REO Royale. i, 1933 Pierce-Arrow Silver Arrow. j, 1934 Hupmobile Aerodynamic.
No. 1614a, 1925 Vauxhall Type OE30/98, Britain. b, 1926 Wills Sainte Claire. c, 1928 Bucciali, France. d, 1929 Irving Napier Golden Arrow, Britain. e, 1930 Studebaker President. f, 1907 Thomas Flyer. g, 1908 Isotta-Fraschini Tipo J, Italy. h, 1910 Fiat 10/14HP, Italy. i, 1911 Mercer Type 35 Raceabout. j, 1917 Marmon Model 34 Cloverleaf.
No. 1615a, 1965 Peugeot 404, France. b, 1969 Ford Capri, Britain. c, 1975 Ferrari 312T, Italy. d, 1978 Lotus T-79, Britain. e, 1979 Williams-Cosworth FW07, Britain. f, 1948 H.R.G. 1500 Sports, Britain. g, 1949 Crosley Hotshot. h, 1955 Volvo PV444, Sweden. i, 1960 Maserati Tipo 61, Italy. j, 1963 Saab 96, Sweden.

1988, June 1			Perf. 13x13½	
1613		Sheet of 10	14.50	14.50
a.-j.	A223 $2 any single		1.40	1.40
1614		Sheet of 10	14.50	14.50
a.-j.	A223 $2 any single		1.40	1.40
1615		Sheet of 10	14.50	14.50
a.-j.	A223 $2 any single		1.40	1.40

Paintings by Titian (c. 1488-1576)
A224

Paintings by Titian: 10c, Lavinia Vecellio, c. 1546. 20c, Portrait of a Man, c. 1510. 25c, Andrea De Franceschi, 1532. 90c, Head of a Soldier, 1511. $1, Man With a Flute. $2, Lucrezia and Tarquinius, c. 1515. $3, Duke of Mantua with Dog, 1525. $4, La Bella Di Tiziano, 1536. No. 1624, Allegory of Alfonso D'Avalos. No. 1625, Fall of Man, 1570, horiz.

1988, June 15			Perf. 13½x14	
1616	A224	10c multicolored	.20	.20
1617	A224	20c multicolored	.20	.20
1618	A224	25c multicolored	.20	.20
1619	A224	90c multicolored	.60	.60
1620	A224	$1 multicolored	.65	.65
1621	A224	$2 multicolored	1.40	1.40
1622	A224	$3 multicolored	2.10	2.10
1623	A224	$4 multicolored	2.75	2.75
	Nos. 1616-1623 (8)		8.10	8.10

Souvenir Sheets

1624	A224	$5 multicolored	3.75	3.75

			Perf. 14x13½	
1625	A224	$5 multicolored	3.75	3.75

Zeppelins
A225

Designs: 10c, Graf Zeppelin over the Federal Building, Chicago, 1933 World's Fair, vert. 15c, LZ-1 over Lake Constance, 1900. 25c, Washington aerial balloon lifting off the aircraft carrier USS George Washington Parke Custis off Port Royal, South Carolina, 1862, vert. 45c, Hindenburg over a Maybach Zeppelin automobile, Friedrichshaven, 1936. 50c, Goodyear Blimp over the Statue of Liberty, 1986, vert. 60c, Hindenburg passing over the Statue of Liberty during its final flight, 1937. 90c, Experimental docking of aircraft (piloted by Ernst Udet) with the Hindenburg, 1936. $2, Hindenburg over the Olympic stadium, Berlin, 1936, vert. $3, Hindenburg over Christ the Redeemer statue, Rio de Janeiro, 1937, vert. $4, Hindenburg over mail plane catapult ship Bremen, 1936. No. 1636, Zepplin over DLH base, Bathurst, Gambia, 1935. No. 1637, Graf Zeppelin over St. Basil's Cathedral, Moscow, 1930.

1988, July 1			Perf. 14	
1626	A225	10c multicolored	.50	.20
1627	A225	15c multicolored	.60	.25
1628	A225	25c multicolored	.70	.35
1629	A225	45c multicolored	.75	.40
1630	A225	50c multicolored	.80	.45
1631	A225	60c multicolored	.85	.50
1632	A225	90c multicolored	1.00	.80
1633	A225	$2 multicolored	1.75	1.75
1634	A225	$3 multicolored	2.50	2.50
1635	A225	$4 multicolored	3.50	3.50
	Nos. 1626-1635 (10)		12.95	10.70

Souvenir Sheets

1636	A225	$5 multicolored	3.75	3.75
1637	A225	$5 multicolored	3.75	3.75

The ship name on No. 1628 is incorrect.

SYDPEX '88, Sydney, Australia — A226

Walt Disney characters in Australian settings: 1c, Camping in the Outback, a howling Tasmanian wolf. 2c, Offering peanuts to wallabies. 3c, With a kangaroo and joey against Ayers Rock. 4c, Riding emus, emu-wrens. 5c, Camp and wombat. 10c, Duck-billed platypuses. No. 1644, Photographing a kookaburra. $6, Koala and Mickey waving flags of Grenada, Australia and the United States, map. No. 1646, Flags and candles atop Cake in the shape of Australia. No. 1647, Mickey, Minnie Pluto and Goofy taking a break during a walkabout.

1988, Aug. 1	Litho.		Perf. 14x13½	
1638	A226	1c multicolored	.20	.20
1639	A226	2c multicolored	.20	.20
1640	A226	3c multicolored	.20	.20
1641	A226	4c multicolored	.20	.20
1642	A226	5c multicolored	.20	.20
1643	A226	10c multicolored	.20	.20
1644	A226	$5 multicolored	5.75	5.75
1645	A226	$6 multicolored	6.75	6.75
	Nos. 1638-1645 (8)		13.70	13.70

Souvenir Sheet

1646	A226	$5 multicolored	6.75	6.75
1647	A226	$5 multicolored	6.75	6.75

Mickey Mouse, 60th anniversary.

Intl. Fund for Agricultural Development, 10th Anniv. — A227

1988, Aug. 11	Litho.		Perf. 14	
1648	A227	25c Pineapple, vert.	.40	.40
1649	A227	75c Banana, vert.	.80	.80
1650	A227	$3 Mace, nutmeg	2.75	2.25
	Nos. 1648-1650 (3)		3.95	3.45

Flowering Trees and Shrubs of the Caribbean
A228

1988, Sept. 30			Litho.	
1651	A228	15c Lignum vitae	.20	.20
1652	A228	25c Saman	.20	.20
1653	A228	35c Red frangipani	.25	.25
1654	A228	45c Flowering maple	.30	.30
1655	A228	60c Yellow poui	.40	.40
1656	A228	$1 Wild chestnut	.70	.70
1657	A228	$2 Mountain immortelle	2.10	2.10
1658	A228	$4 Queen of flowers	2.75	2.75
	Nos. 1651-1658 (8)		6.90	6.90

Souvenir Sheets

1659	A228	$5 Flamboyant	3.50	3.50
1660	A228	$5 Orchid tree	3.50	3.50

Miniature Sheet

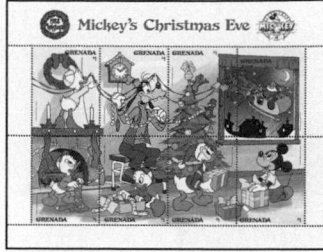

Christmas, Mickey Mouse 60th Anniv. — A229

Designs: a, Huey draping garland. b, Goofy stringing popcorn. c, Chip'n'Dale decorating tree. d, Santa Claus in his sleigh. e, Dewey hanging stockings. f, Louie unpacking decorations. g, Donald Duck. h, Mickey Mouse. No. 1662, Morty and Ferdie leaving milk and cookies for Santa, horiz. No. 1663, Morty and Ferdie dreaming of presents, horiz.
Illustration reduced.

		Perf. 13½x14, 14x13½		
1988, Dec. 1	A229	Sheet of 8	Litho.	
1661	A229	Sheet of 8	7.50	7.50
a.-h.	$1 any single		.90	.90

Souvenir Sheets

1662	A229	$5 multicolored	5.50	5.50
1663	A229	$5 multicolored	5.50	5.50

Miniature Sheets

Major League Baseball Players — A230

No. 1664: a, Mickey Mantle. b, Roger Clemens. c, Rod Carew. d, Ryne Sandberg. e, Mike Scott. f, Tim Raines. g, Willie Mays. h, Bret Saberhagen. i, Honus Wagner.
No. 1665: a, Roberto Clemente. b, Cal Ripken, Jr. c, Bob Feller. d, George Bell. e, Mark McGwire. f, Alvin Davis. g, Pete Rose. h, Dan Quisenberry. i, Babe Ruth.
No. 1666: a, Jackie Robinson. b, Dwight Gooden. c, Brooks Robinson, Jr. d, Nolan Ryan. e, Mike Schmidt. f, Gary Gaetti. g, Nellie Fox. h, Tony Gwynn. i, Dizzy Dean.
No. 1667: a, Ernie Banks. b, National League emblem. c, Julio Franco. d, Jack Morris. e, Fernando Valenzuela. f, Lefty Grove. g, Ted Williams. h, Darryl Strawberry. i, Dale Murphy.
No. 1668: a, Johnny Bench. b, Dave Stieb. c, Reggie Jackson. d, Harold Baines. e, Wade Boggs. f, Pete O'Brien. g, Stan Musial. h, Wally Joyner. i, Grover Cleveland Alexander.
No. 1669: a, Jose Cruz. b, American League emblem. c, Al Kaline. d, Chuck Klein. e, Don Mattingly. f, Mike Witt. g, Mark Langston. h, Hubie Brooks. i, Harmon Killebrew.
No. 1670: a, George Brett. b, Joe Carter. c, Frank Robinson. d, Mel Ott. e, Benito Santiago. f, Teddy Higuera. g, Lloyd Moseby. h, Bobby Bonilla. i, Warren Spahn.
No. 1671: a, Gary Carter. b, Hank Aaron. c, Gaylord Perry. d, Ty Cobb. e, Andre Dawson. f, Charlie Hough. g, Kirby Puckett. h, Robin Yount. i, Don Drysdale.
No. 1672: a, Luis Aparicio. b, Paul Molitor. c, Lou Gehrig. d, Jeffrey Leonard. e, Eric Davis. f, Pete Incaviglia. g, Steve Rogers. h, Ozzie Smith. i, Randy Jones.

1988, Nov. 28			Litho.	Perf. 14	
1664		Sheet of 9		1.90	1.90
a.-i.	A230 30c any single			.20	.20
1665		Sheet of 9		1.90	1.90
a.-i.	A230 30c any single			.20	.20
1666		Sheet of 9		1.90	1.90
a.-i.	A230 30c any single			.20	.20
1667		Sheet of 9		1.90	1.90
a.-i.	A230 30c any single			.20	.20
1668		Sheet of 9		1.90	1.90
a.-i.	A230 30c any single			.20	.20
1669		Sheet of 9		1.90	1.90
a.-i.	A230 30c any single			.20	.20
1670		Sheet of 9		1.90	1.90
a.-i.	A230 30c any single			.20	.20
1671		Sheet of 9		1.90	1.90
a.-i.	A230 30c any single			.20	.20

1672		Sheet of 9	1.90	1.90
a.-i.	A230	30c any single	.20	.20
		Nos. 1664-1672 (9)	17.10	17.10

No. 1665 was reprinted with No. 1665g replaced by a label inscribed "U.S. Baseball Series."

Singers — A231

1988, Dec. 5   Litho.   Perf. 14

1673	A231	10c Tina Turner	.30	.20
1674	A231	25c Lionel Ritchie	.30	.20
1675	A231	45c Whitney Houston	.45	.40
1676	A231	60c Joan Armatrading	.60	.50
1677	A231	75c Madonna	1.00	.65
1678	A231	$1 Elton John	1.25	.85
1679	A231	$3 Bruce Springsteen	2.50	2.50
1680	A231	$4 Bob Marley	3.25	3.25
		Nos. 1673-1680 (8)	9.65	8.55

Souvenir Sheet

1681		Sheet of 4 (2 55c,2 $1)	3.50	3.50
a.	A231	55c Yoko Minamino	.75	.75
b.	A231	$1 Yoko Minamino, diff.	2.50	2.50

Armatrading is misspelled "Ammertrading."

Car Type of 1988
Miniature Sheets

Locomotives.
No. 1682: a, 1889 Canada Atlantic Railway No. 2 0-6-0, Canada. b, 1875 Virginia & Truckee Railroad J.W. Bowker 2-4-0, US. c, 1872 Philadelphia & Reading Railway Ariel 2-2-2, US. d, 1867 Chicago & Rock Is. Railroad America 4-4-0, US. e, 1866 Lehigh Valley Railroad Consolidation No. 63 2-8-0, US. f, 1860 Great Western Railway Scotia 0-6-0, Canada. g, 1854 Grand Trunk Railway Birkenhead Class 4-4-0, Canada. h, 1837 Camden & Amboy Railroad Monster 0-8-0, US. i, 1834 B&O Railroad Grasshopper Class 0-4-0, US. j, 1829 B&O Railroad Tom Thumb 0-2-2, US.

No. 1683: a, 1925 United Railways of Yucatan Yucatan 4-4-0, Mexico. b, 1924 Canadian Natl. Railways Class T2 2-10-2, Canada. c, 1919 St. Louis-San Francisco Railroad USRA Light Mikado 2-8-2, US. d, 1919 Atlantic Coast Line Railroad USRA Light Pacific 4-6-2, US. e, 1913 Edaville Railroad (Bridgton & Saco River Railroad) No. 7 2-4-4-T, US. f, 1903 Denver & Rio Grande Western Railroad Mudhens Class K27 2-8-2, US. g, 1902 PRR Class E-2 No. 7002 4-4-2, US. h, 1899 PRR Class H6 2-8-0, US. i, 1893 Mohawk & Hudson Railroad De Witt Clinton 0-4-0, US. j, 1891 St. Clair Tunnel Company No. 598 0-10-0, Canada.

No. 1684: a, 1947 Chesapeake & Ohio Railroad M-1 Class No. 500 steam turbine electric, US. b, 1946 Rutland Railroad No. 93 4-8-2, US. c, 1942 PRR Class T1 4-4-4-4, US. d, 1942 Chesapeake & Ohio Railroad Class H-8 2-6-6-6, US. e, 1941 Atchison, Topeka & Santa Fe Railway EMD Model FT Bo-Bo, US. f, 1940 Gulf, Mobile & Ohio Railroad ALCO Models S-1 & S-2 Bo-Bo, US. g, 1937 New York, New Haven & Hartford Railroad Class 15 4-6-4, US. h, 1936 Seaboard Air Line Railroad Class R 2-6-6-4, US. i, 1930 Newfoundland Railway Class R-2 2-8-2, Canada. j, 1928 Canadian Natl. Railway No. 9000 2-Do-1 + 1-Do-2, Canada.

1989, Jan. 23   Litho.   Perf. 13x13½

1682		Sheet of 10	14.50	14.50
a.-j.	A223	$2 any single	1.40	1.40
1683		Sheet of 10	14.50	14.50
a.-j.	A223	$2 any single	1.40	1.40
1684		Sheet of 10	14.50	14.50
a.-j.	A223	$2 any single	1.40	1.40

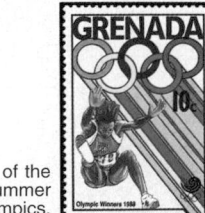

Medalists of the
1988 Summer
Olympics,
Seoul — A232

Designs: 10c, Jackie Joyner-Kersee, US, long jump. 25c, Steffi Graf, Federal Republic of Germany, women's singles tennis. 45c, Peter Rono, Kenya, 1500m run. 75c, Greg

Barton, US, kayak singles. $1, Italy, women's team foil. $2, Kristin Otto, German Democratic Republic, women's 100m freestyle swimming. $3, Holger Behrendt, German Democratic Republic, still rings. $4, Japan, duet synchronized swimming. No. 1693, Yukio Iketani, Japan, men's floor exercise. No. 1694, West Germany, 400m relay, and (Olympic) flame over track.

1989, Apr. 6   Litho.   Perf. 14

1685	A232	10c multicolored	.30	.30
1686	A232	25c multicolored	.70	.35
1687	A232	45c multicolored	.80	.40
1688	A232	75c multicolored	.90	.60
1689	A232	$1 multicolored	1.00	.75
1690	A232	$2 multicolored	1.50	1.50
1691	A232	$3 multicolored	2.25	2.25
1692	A232	$4 multicolored	3.00	3.00
		Nos. 1685-1692 (8)	10.45	9.15

Souvenir Sheets

1693	A232	$6 multicolored	5.00	5.00
1694	A232	$6 multicolored	5.00	5.00

"The Fifty-three Stations on the
Tokaido" — A233

Prints by Hiroshige (1797-1858): 10c, Shinagawa on Edo Bay. 25c, Pine Trees on the Road to Totsuka. 60c, Kanagawa on Edo Bay. 75c, Crossing Banyu River to Hiratsuka. $1, Windy Shore at Odawara. $2, Snow-covered Post Station of Mishima. $3, Full Moon at Fuchu. $4, Crossing the Stream at Okitsu. No. 1703, Mt. Uzu at Okabe. No. 1704, Mountain Pass at Nissaka.

1989, May 15   Litho.   Perf. 14x13½

1695	A233	10c multicolored	.20	.20
1696	A233	25c multicolored	.20	.20
1697	A233	60c multicolored	.45	.45
1698	A233	75c multicolored	.65	.65
1699	A233	$1 multicolored	1.00	.75
1700	A233	$2 multicolored	1.50	1.50
1701	A233	$3 multicolored	2.25	2.25
1702	A233	$4 multicolored	3.00	3.00
		Nos. 1695-1702 (8)	9.25	9.00

Souvenir Sheets

1703	A233	$5 multicolored	3.75	3.75
1704	A233	$5 multicolored	3.75	3.75

Hirohito (1901-1989) and enthronement of Akihito as emperor of Japan.

Indigenous Birds — A234

1989, June 6   Litho.   Perf. 14

1705	A234	5c Great blue heron	.75	*1.00*
1706	A234	10c Green heron	.75	.60
1707	A234	15c Ruddy turnstone	.80	.60
1708	A234	25c Blue-winged teal	.90	.30
1709	A234	35c Ring-necked plover	1.10	.30
1710	A234	45c Emerald-throated hummingbird	1.10	.40
1711	A234	50c Hairy hermit	1.25	.45
1712	A234	60c Lesser Antillean bullfinch	1.40	.55
1713	A234	75c Brown pelican	1.50	.60
1714	A234	$1 Black-crowned night heron	1.60	1.00
1715	A234	$3 Sparrow hawk	2.40	2.40
1716	A234	$5 Barn swallow	4.00	4.00
1717	A234	$10 Red-billed tropicbird	8.00	8.00
1718	A234	$20 Barn owl	21.50	21.50
		Nos. 1705-1718 (14)	47.05	41.75

Nos. 1709-1718 vert.

1990-93   Litho.   Perf. 11½x13

1705a	A234	5c	.70	.70
1706a	A234	10c	.70	.60
1707a	A234	15c	.75	.70
1708a	A234	25c	.85	.30

Perf. 13x11½

1709a	A234	35c	1.00	.30
1710a	A234	45c	1.00	.35
1711a	A234	50c	1.10	.45
1712a	A234	60c	1.25	.50
1713a	A234	75c	1.40	.55
1714a	A234	$1	1.50	.90
1715a	A234	$3	2.40	2.40
1716a	A234	$5	4.00	4.00
1717a	A234	$10	8.00	8.00
1718a	A234	$20	21.50	21.50
		Nos. 1705a-1718a (14)	46.15	41.15

Issued: #1718a, 1/22/90.

1990 World Cup
Soccer
Championships,
Italy — A235

1989, June 12   Perf. 14

1719	A235	10c Scotland	.50	.30
1720	A235	25c England vs. Brazil	.60	.50
1721	A235	60c Paolo Rossi, Italy	.80	.70
1722	A235	75c Jairzinho of Brazil	1.00	.80
1723	A235	$1 Swedish Striker	1.25	1.00
1724	A235	$2 Pele, Brazil	2.50	2.00
1725	A235	$3 Mario Kempes, Argentina	3.00	3.00
1726	A235	$4 Pat Jennings	4.00	4.00
		Nos. 1719-1726 (8)	13.65	12.30

Souvenir Sheets

1727	A235	$6 Argentina vs. Holland	5.75	5.75
a.		$6 1990 score ovptd. in margin	5.75	5.75
1728	A235	$6 Goalie	5.75	5.75

Issue date: No. 1727a, Nov. 30, 1990.

PHILEXFRANCE '89 — A236

19th Cent. ships and cargo: 25c, Chebeck, sugarcane. 75c, Lugger, cotton. $1, Merchantman, cocoa. $4, Ketch, coffee. $6, Vue du Fort et Ville de St. George dans l'Isle de la Grenade et du Morne, 1779.

1989, July 7   Perf. 14

1729	A236	25c multicolored	1.00	.30
1730	A236	75c multicolored	1.25	.85
1731	A236	$1 multicolored	1.60	1.10
1732	A236	$4 multicolored	5.50	5.50

Size: 114x71mm
Imperf

1733	A236	$6 multicolored	6.50	6.50
		Nos. 1729-1733 (5)	15.85	14.25

First
Moon
Landing,
20th
Anniv.
A237

Space achievements: 15c, Alan Shepard, 1st American in space, 1961. 35c, Friendship 7, piloted by John Glenn, 1st manned orbit of the Earth, 1962. 45c, Apollo 8 mission, 1st manned orbit of the Moon, 1968. 70c, Lunar rover on Moon, 1972. $1, Apollo 11 mission emblem and Eagle lunar module on the Moon, 1969. $2, Gemini 8-Agena, 1st space docking, 1969. $3, Edward White, 1st American to walk in space, 1965. $4, Apollo 7 mission emblem. No. 1742, Simple flight plan for the Apollo 11 mission. No. 1743, Raising of the American flag on the Moon.

1989, July 20   Perf. 14

1734	A237	15c multicolored	.50	.40
1735	A237	35c multicolored	.60	.45
1736	A237	45c multicolored	.80	.60
1737	A237	70c multicolored	1.00	.70
1738	A237	$1 multicolored	1.50	1.10
1739	A237	$2 multicolored	2.50	2.10
1740	A237	$3 multicolored	3.25	3.25
1741	A237	$4 multicolored	4.25	4.25
		Nos. 1734-1741 (8)	14.40	12.85

Souvenir Sheets

1742	A237	$5 multicolored	5.50	5.50
1743	A237	$5 multicolored	5.50	5.50

Mushrooms
A238

YWCA, Cent.
A239

15c, Hygrocybe occidentalis scarletina. 40c, Marasmius haemato- cephalus. 50c, Hygrocybe hypohaemacta. 70c, Lepiota pseudoignicolor. 90c, Cookeina tricholoma. $1.10, Leucopaxillus gracillimus. $2.25, Hygrocybe nigrescens. $4, Clathrus crispus.
#1752, Mycena holoporphyra. #1753, Xeromphalina tenuipes.

1989, Aug. 17   Litho.   Perf. 14

1744-1751	A238	Set of 8	16.00	16.00

Souvenir Sheets

1752-1753	A238	$6 Set of 2	16.00	16.00

1989, Sept. 11   Perf. 14

1754	A239	50c shown	.70	.70
1755	A239	75c Emblem, horiz.	.90	.90

Butterflies
A240

1989, Oct. 2   Perf. 14

1756	A240	6c Orion	.35	.35
1757	A240	30c Southern daggertail	.50	.50
1758	A240	40c Soldier	.65	.65
1759	A240	60c Silver spot	1.00	1.00
1760	A240	$1.10 Gulf fritillary	1.60	1.60
1761	A240	$1.25 Monarch	1.90	1.90
1762	A240	$4 Polydamas swallowtail	4.00	4.00
1763	A240	$5 Flambeau	4.75	4.75
		Nos. 1756-1763 (8)	14.75	14.75

Souvenir Sheets

1764	A240	$6 St. Christopher hairstreak	6.25	6.25
1765	A240	$6 White peacock	6.25	6.25

Discovery of
America, 500th
Anniv. (in
1992) — A241

Anniv. and UPAE emblems and various pre-Columbian petroglyphs.

1989, Oct. 16   Litho.   Perf. 14

1766	A241	45c multicolored	.90	.90
1767	A241	60c multi, diff.	1.10	1.10
1768	A241	$1 multi, diff.	1.25	1.25
1769	A241	$4 multi, diff.	4.75	4.75
		Nos. 1766-1769 (4)	8.00	8.00

Souvenir Sheet

1770	A241	$6 multi, diff.	5.50	5.50

World Stamp Expo '89, Scenes from
Ben and Me — A242

Walt Disney characters, story of the American Revolution: 1c, Amos leaves home. 2c, Amos meets young Benjamin Franklin. 3c, Invention of the Franklin stove. 4c, Invention of bifocals. 5c, *Pennsylvania Gazette.* 6c, Franklin at printing press. 10c, Experimenting with electricity. $5, As an American diplomat in England. No. 1779, Amos's "Document of Agreement." No. 1780, Franklin presiding over meeting of the Ben Franklin Stamp Club. No. 1781, 2nd Continental Congress, Philadelphia, 1775.

Perf. 14x13½, 13½x14

1989, Nov. 17			Litho.	
1771	A242	1c multi	.20	.20
1772	A242	2c multi	.20	.20
1773	A242	3c multi	.20	.20
1774	A242	4c multi	.20	.20
1775	A242	5c multi	.20	.20
1776	A242	6c multi	.20	.20
1777	A242	10c multi	.20	.20
1778	A242	$5 multi	6.00	6.00
1779	A242	$6 multi	6.50	6.75
		Nos. 1771-1779 (9)	13.90	14.15

Souvenir Sheets

1780	A242	$6 multi, vert.	5.75	5.75
1781	A242	$6 multi	5.75	5.75

Christmas — A243

Paintings by Rubens: 20c, *Christ in the House of Mary and Martha.* 35c, *The Circumcision.* 60c, *Trinity Adored by Duke of Mantua and Family.* $2, *Holy Family with St. Francis.* $3, *The Ildefonso Altarpiece.* $4, *Madonna and Child with Garland and Putti,* by Rubens and Jan Brueghel. No. 1788, *Adoration of the Magi.* No. 1789, *Virgin and Child Adored by Angels.*

1990, Jan. 4			Litho.	Perf. 14
1782	A243	20c multicolored	.50	.25
1783	A243	35c multicolored	.65	.45
1784	A243	60c multicolored	1.00	.65
1785	A243	$2 multicolored	2.00	2.00
1786	A243	$3 multicolored	2.50	2.50
1787	A243	$4 multicolored	3.50	3.50
		Nos. 1782-1787 (6)	10.15	9.35

Souvenir Sheets

1788	A243	$5 multicolored	5.00	5.00
1789	A243	$5 multicolored	5.00	5.00

Anniversaries and Events (in 1989) — A244

Designs: 10c, Alexander Graham Bell, early telephone, telephone lines. 25c, George Washington, the Capitol Building. 35c, William Shakespeare, birthplace, Stratford-on-Avon. 75c, Jawaharlal Nehru, Mahatma Gandhi. $1, Hugo Eckener, Ferdinand von Zeppelin, zeppelin *Delag.* $2, Charlie Chaplin. $3, Ship in port. $4, Pres. Friedrich Ebert, Heidelberg Gate. No. 1798, Concorde jet. No. 1799, Ship, 13th century, vert.

1990, Feb. 12			Litho.	Perf. 14
1790	A244	10c multicolored	.35	.20
1791	A244	25c multicolored	.35	.20
1792	A244	35c multicolored	1.10	.55
1793	A244	75c multicolored	2.25	1.60
1794	A244	$1 multicolored	1.60	1.40
1795	A244	$2 multicolored	3.25	2.75
1796	A244	$3 multicolored	3.50	3.50
1797	A244	$4 multicolored	4.75	4.75
		Nos. 1790-1797 (8)	17.15	14.95

Souvenir Sheets

1798	A244	$6 multicolored	6.25	6.25
1799	A244	$6 multicolored	6.25	6.25

Invention of the telephone, 1876 (10c); American presidency, 200th anniv. (25c); 425th birth anniv. of Shakespeare (35c); birth cent. of Nehru (75c); 1st passenger zeppelin, 80th anniv. ($1); birth cent. of Charlie Chaplin ($2); Hamburg, 800th anniv. ($3, No. 1799); Federal Republic of Germany, 40th anniv. ($4); and test flight of the Concorde supersonic jet, 20th anniv. (No. 1798).

Orchids — A245

1990, Mar. 6			Litho.	Perf. 14
1800	A245	1c *Odontoglossum triumphans*	.20	.20
1801	A245	25c *Oncidium splendidum*	.30	.30
1802	A245	60c *Laelia anceps*	.65	.65
1803	A245	75c *Cattleya trianaei*	.80	.80
1804	A245	$1 *Odontoglossum rossii*	1.25	1.25
1805	A245	$2 *Brassia gireoudiana*	1.75	1.75
1806	A245	$3 *Cattleya dowiana*	2.50	2.50
1807	A245	$4 *Sobralia macrantha*	3.25	3.25
		Nos. 1800-1807 (8)	10.70	10.70

Souvenir Sheets

1808	A245	$6 *Laelia rubescens*	5.50	5.50
1809	A245	$6 *Oncidium lanceanum*	5.50	5.50

EXPO '90 Intl. Garden and Greenery Exposition, Japan.

America Issue — A246

Butterflies, UPAE and discovery of America 500th anniv. emblems: 15c, Southern dagger tail. 25c, Caribbean buckeye. 75c, Malachite. 90c, Orion. $1, St. Lucia mestra. $2, Red rim. $3, Flambeau. $4, Red anartia. No. 1818, Giant hairstreak. No. 1819, Orange-barred sulphur.

1990, Mar. 16			Litho.	Perf. 14
1810	A246	15c multicolored	.65	.20
1811	A246	25c multicolored	.80	.25
1812	A246	75c multicolored	1.25	.80
1813	A246	90c multicolored	1.40	.95
1814	A246	$1 multicolored	1.50	1.00
1815	A246	$2 multicolored	2.00	2.00
1816	A246	$3 multicolored	3.00	3.00
1817	A246	$4 multicolored	4.00	4.00
		Nos. 1810-1817 (8)	14.60	12.20

Souvenir Sheets

1818	A246	$6 multicolored	7.00	7.00
1819	A246	$6 multicolored	7.00	7.00

Wildlife — A247

1990, Apr. 3			Litho.	Perf. 14
1820	A247	10c Caribbean monk seal	.50	.30
1821	A247	15c Little brown bat	.55	.30
1822	A247	45c Norway rat	.65	.50
1823	A247	60c Old-world rabbit	.75	.60
1824	A247	$1 Water opossum	1.00	.90
1825	A247	$2 White-nosed ichneumon	1.60	1.60
1826	A247	$3 Little big-eared bat	2.40	2.40
1827	A247	$4 Mouse opossums	3.25	3.25
		Nos. 1820-1827 (8)	10.70	9.85

Souvenir Sheets

1828	A247	$6 Old-world rabbit, diff.	5.50	5.50
1829	A247	$6 Water opossum	5.50	5.50

No. 1826 is vert. Nos. 1828-1829 have multicolored decorative margins contininuing the designs and picturing little brown bat, prehensile-tailed porcupine and mouse opossum (No. 1828) or four-eyed opossum, West Indies manatee and Norway rat (No. 1829).

World War II A248

Designs: 25c, Operation Battleaxe, June 15, 1941. 35c, Allied landing in southern France, Aug. 15, 1944. 45c, US invasion of Guadalcanal, Aug. 7, 1942. 50c, Allied defeat of Japanese army in New Guinea, Jan. 22, 1943. 60c, US forces secure Leyte, Dec. 11, 1944. 75c, US forces enter Cologne, Mar. 5, 1945. $1, Allied offensive to break out of Anzio, May 23, 1944. $2, Battle of the Bismarck Sea, Mar. 3, 1943. $3, US fleet under Adm. Nimitz, Dec. 17, 1941. $4, Allied landing at Salerno, Sept. 9, 1943. $6, German U-boat.

1990, Apr. 30			Litho.	Perf. 14x13½
1830	A248	25c multicolored	.40	.40
1831	A248	35c multicolored	.50	.50
1832	A248	45c multicolored	.60	.60
1833	A248	50c multicolored	.70	.70
1834	A248	60c multicolored	.80	.80
1835	A248	75c multicolored	1.00	1.00
1836	A248	$1 multicolored	1.50	1.50
1837	A248	$2 multicolored	1.75	1.75
1838	A248	$3 multicolored	2.50	2.50
1839	A248	$4 multicolored	3.50	3.50
		Nos. 1830-1839 (10)	13.25	13.25

Souvenir Sheet

1840	A248	$6 multicolored	7.00	7.00

Souvenir Sheet

Penny Black, 150th Anniv. — A249

1990, May 3			Litho.	Perf. 14
1841	A249	$6 violet	5.75	5.75

Stamp World London '90.

Stamp World London '90 — A250

Walt Disney characters and British trains.

1990, June 21				Perf. 14
1844	A250	5c 1925 King Arthur Class	.45	.20
1845	A250	10c 1813 Puffing Billy	.45	.20
1846	A250	20c 1765 Colliery Tram-wagon	.60	.20
1847	A250	45c 1935 No. 2509 Silver Link	1.00	.55
1848	A250	$1 1948 No. 60149 Amadis	1.50	1.10
1849	A250	$2 1830 Liverpool	2.25	2.10
1850	A250	$4 1870 Flying Scotsman	4.25	4.25
1851	A250	$5 1972 Advanced Passenger Train	5.25	4.50
		Nos. 1844-1851 (8)	15.75	13.10

Souvenir Sheets

1852	A250	$6 Stockton & Darlington Railway Opening, 1825, vert.	6.75	6.75
1853	A250	$6 1809 *Catch-Me-Who-Can*	6.75	6.75

Queen Mother, 90th Birthday — A251

1990, July 5			Litho.	Perf. 14
1854	A251	$2 Wearing black hat	2.25	2.25
1855	A251	$2 shown	2.25	2.25
1856	A251	$2 Wearing crown	2.25	2.25
		Nos. 1854-1856 (3)	6.75	6.75

Souvenir Sheet

1857	A251	$6 Like No. 1855	5.25	5.25

1992 Summer Olympics, Barcelona — A252

Character trademark and: 10c, Men's steeplechase. 15c, Men's 200 meter butterfly. 45c, Men's 200 meter butterfly. 50c, Field hockey. 65c, Balance beam. 75c, Flying Dutchman Class yachting. $2, Freestyle wrestling. $3, Men's diving. $4, Women's cycling. $5, Men's basketball. No. 1863, Three-day equestrian event. No. 1863A, Men's 10,000 M race.

1990, July 9				
1858	A252	10c multicolored	.35	.30
1858A	A252	15c multicolored	.45	.35
1859	A252	45c multicolored	.55	.40
1859A	A252	50c multicolored	.80	.60
1860	A252	65c multicolored	.80	.60
1860A	A252	75c multicolored	1.00	.80
1861	A252	$2 multicolored	1.75	1.75
1861A	A252	$3 multicolored	2.50	2.50
1862	A252	$4 multicolored	3.75	3.75
1862A	A252	$5 multicolored	4.00	4.00
		Nos. 1858-1862A (10)	15.95	15.05

Souvenir Sheet

1863	A252	$8 multicolored	6.25	6.25
1863A	A252	$8 multicolored	6.25	6.25

Nos. 1858A, 1859A, 1860A, 1861A, 1862A, 1863A were not available until 1991.

US Airborne, 50th Anniv. A253

1990, July 3				
1864	A253	75c Mass jump	2.00	2.00

Souvenir Sheets

1865	A253	$2.50 Paratrooper landing	2.50	2.50
1866	A253	$6 Paratroopers 1940, 1990	5.75	5.75

Yellow Goatfish
A254

1990, Aug. 8
1867	A254	10c shown	.40	.40
1868	A254	25c Black margate	.60	.60
1869	A254	65c Bluehead wrasse	1.00	1.00
1870	A254	75c Puddingwife	1.25	1.25
1871	A254	$1 Foureye butterflyfish	1.50	1.50
1872	A254	$2 Honey damselfish	1.90	1.90
1873	A254	$3 Queen angelfish	2.75	2.75
1874	A254	$5 Cherubfish	4.75	4.75
		Nos. 1867-1874 (8)	14.15	14.15

Souvenir Sheets
1875	A254	$6 Smooth trunkfish	6.75	6.75
1876	A254	$6 Sergeant major	6.75	6.75

Birds
A255

1990, Sept. 10   Litho.   Perf. 14
1877	A255	15c Tropical mockingbird	.45	.45
1878	A255	25c Gray kingbird	.50	.50
1879	A255	65c Bare-eyed thrush	.80	.80
1880	A255	75c Antillean crested hummingbird	1.00	1.00
1881	A255	$1 House wren	1.50	1.50
1882	A255	$2 Purple martin	1.90	1.90
1883	A255	$4 Hooded tanager	3.75	3.75
1884	A255	$5 Common ground dove	4.50	4.50
		Nos. 1877-1884 (8)	14.40	14.40

Souvenir Sheets
1885	A255	$6 Fork-tailed flycatcher	8.00	8.00
1886	A255	$6 Smooth-billed ani	8.00	8.00

Crustaceans — A256

1990, Sept. 17
1887	A256	5c Coral crab	.20	.20
1888	A256	10c Smoothtail spiny lobster	.20	.20
1889	A256	15c Flamestreaked box crab	.20	.20
1890	A256	25c Spotted swimming crab	.20	.20
1891	A256	75c Sally lightfoot rock crab	.60	.60
1892	A256	$1 Spotted spiny lobster	.80	.80
1893	A256	$3 Longarm spiny lobster	2.40	2.40
1894	A256	$20 Caribbean spiny lobster	16.00	16.00
		Nos. 1887-1894 (8)	20.60	20.60

Souvenir Sheets
1895	A256	$6 Spanish lobster	6.25	6.25
1896	A256	$6 Copper lobster	6.25	6.25

World Cup Soccer Championships, Italy — A257

Players from participating countries.

1990, Sept. 24
1897	A257	10c Cameroun	.20	.20
1898	A257	25c Spain	.20	.20
1899	A257	$1 West Germany	.80	.80
1900	A257	$5 Scotland	4.00	4.00
		Nos. 1897-1900 (4)	5.20	5.20

Souvenir Sheets
1901	A257	$6 Uruguay	6.00	6.00
1902	A257	$6 Italy	6.00	6.00

Christmas
A258

Paintings by Raphael: 10c, The Ansidei Madonna. 15c, The Sistine Madonna. $1, Madonna of the Baldacchino. $2, The Large Holy Family. $5, Madonna in the Meadow. No. 1908, Madonna of the Veil. No. 1909, Madonna of the Diadem.

1990, Dec. 31   Litho.   Perf. 14
1903	A258	10c multicolored	.30	.20
1904	A258	15c multicolored	.30	.20
1905	A258	$1 multicolored	1.50	1.00
1906	A258	$2 multicolored	2.50	2.50
1907	A258	$5 multicolored	5.25	5.25
		Nos. 1903-1907 (5)	9.85	9.15

Souvenir Sheets
1908	A258	$6 multicolored	6.75	6.75
1909	A258	$6 multicolored	6.75	6.75

Peter Paul Rubens (1577-1640), Painter — A259

Entire paintings or different details from: 5c, $1, $4, The Brazen Serpent. 10c, Garden of Love. 25c, Head of Cyrus. 75c, Tournament in Front of a Castle. $2, Judgement of Paris. $5, The Kermesse. No. 1918, The Prodigal Son. No. 1919, Anger of Neptune.

1991, Jan. 31   Litho.   Perf. 14
1910	A259	5c multicolored	.35	.20
1911	A259	10c multicolored	.35	.20
1912	A259	25c multicolored	.60	.20
1913	A259	75c multicolored	.80	.60
1914	A259	$1 multicolored	1.00	.80
1915	A259	$2 multicolored	1.60	1.60
1916	A259	$4 multicolored	3.25	3.25
1917	A259	$5 multicolored	4.00	4.00
		Nos. 1910-1917 (8)	11.95	10.85

Souvenir Sheets
1918	A259	$6 multicolored	6.75	6.75
1919	A259	$6 multicolored	6.75	6.75

Disney Film *Fantasia*, 50th Anniv. — A260

5c, Mickey as Sorcerer's apprentice, walking broom. 10c, Mushroom Dance Ensemble from The Nutcracker Suite. 20c, Pterodactyls from The Rite of Spring. 45c, Centaurs from The Pastoral Symphony. $1, Bacchus & Jacchus from The Pastoral Symphony. $2, Ostrich ballerina in Dance of the Hours. $4, Elephant dance from Dance of the Hours. $5, Diana, Goddess of the Moon from Dance of the Hours. #1928, Mickey as Sorcerer's apprentice. #1929, Mickey, Leopold Stokowski. $12, Mickey as Sorcerer's Apprentice, vert.

1991, Feb. 4   Litho.   Perf. 14
1920	A260	5c multicolored	.75	.20
1921	A260	10c multicolored	.75	.20
1922	A260	20c multicolored	1.10	.20
1923	A260	45c multicolored	1.25	.55
1924	A260	$1 multicolored	1.75	1.75
1925	A260	$2 multicolored	2.75	2.75
1926	A260	$4 multicolored	5.00	5.00
1927	A260	$5 multicolored	6.50	6.50
		Nos. 1920-1927 (8)	19.85	17.15

Souvenir Sheets
1928	A260	$6 multicolored	8.50	8.50
1929	A260	$6 multicolored	8.50	8.50
1930	A260	$12 multicolored	16.50	16.50

Butterflies
A261

5c, Adelphia iphicla. 10c, Nymphalidae claudina. 15c, Brassolidae polyxena. 20c, Zebra longwing. 25c, Marpesia corinna. 30c, Morpho hecuba. 45c, Morpho rhetenor. 50c, Dismorphia spio. 60c, Prepona omphale. 70c, Morpho anaxibia. 75c, Marpesia iole. $1, Metalmark. $2, Morpho cisseis. $3, Danaidae plexippus. $4, Morpho achilleana. $5, Calliona argenissa. #1947, Anteos clorinde. #1948, Haetera piera. #1949, Papilio cresphontes. #1950, Prepona pheridames.

1991, Apr. 8   Litho.   Perf. 14
1931	A261	5c multicolored	.45	.40
1932	A261	10c multicolored	.50	.40
1933	A261	15c multicolored	.55	.40
1934	A261	20c multicolored	.60	.30
1935	A261	25c multicolored	.65	.30
1936	A261	30c multicolored	.70	.30
1937	A261	45c multicolored	.80	.50
1938	A261	50c multicolored	.85	.55
1939	A261	60c multicolored	1.00	.65
1940	A261	70c multicolored	1.10	.80
1941	A261	75c multicolored	1.25	1.25
1942	A261	$1 multicolored	1.40	1.40
1943	A261	$2 multicolored	1.90	1.90
1944	A261	$3 multicolored	2.75	2.75
1945	A261	$4 multicolored	3.75	3.75
1946	A261	$5 multicolored	4.75	4.75
		Nos. 1931-1946 (16)	23.00	20.40

Souvenir Sheets
1947	A261	$6 multicolored	6.50	6.50
1948	A261	$6 multicolored	6.50	6.50
1949	A261	$6 multicolored	6.50	6.50
1950	A261	$6 multicolored	6.50	6.50

Voyages of Discovery
A262

Explorer's ships: 5c, Vitus Bering, 1728-1729. 10c, Louis de Bougainville, 1766-1769. 25c, Polynesians. 50c, Álvaro de Mendana, 1567-1569. 75c, Charles Darwin, 1831-1835. $2, Capt. James Cook, 1768-1771. $4, Capt. Willem Schouten, 1615-1617. $5, Abel Tasman, 1642-1644. No. 1959, Columbus' ship Santa Maria. No. 1960, Loss of Santa Maria.

1991, Apr. 29
1951	A262	5c multicolored	.50	.40
1952	A262	10c multicolored	.50	.40
1953	A262	25c multicolored	.50	.30
1954	A262	50c multicolored	.90	.50
1955	A262	$1 multicolored	1.50	1.25
1956	A262	$2 multicolored	2.75	2.50
1957	A262	$4 multicolored	3.75	3.75
1958	A262	$5 multicolored	4.75	4.75
		Nos. 1951-1958 (8)	15.15	13.85

Souvenir Sheets
1959	A262	$6 multicolored	6.75	6.75
1960	A262	$6 multicolored	6.75	6.75

Discovery of America, 500th anniv. (in 1992).

PHILANIPPON '91 — A263

Walt Disney characters celebrating festivals of Japan: 5c, Daisy Duck and Minnie Mouse, Peach Fete, Festival of the Dolls. 10c, Morty and Ferdie, Tango Festival, Boys' Day Festival. 20c, Mickey, Minnie Mouse, Hoshi-Matsuri, Star Festival. 45c, Minnie, Daisy folk dancing at Bon-Odori Summer Festival. $1, Huey, Dewey and Louie wearing Eboshi headdresses at Yari-Matsuri, Spear Festival of Ohji. $2, Mickey, Goofy pulling Daisy, Minnie in Yamaboko, Gion Festival of Kyoto. $4, Minnie, Daisy preparing rice broth for Nanakusa, Festival of the Seven Plants. $5, Huey, Dewey floating straw boat at O-Bon, Festival of Lanterns. No. 1969, Goofy, Tori-No-Hichi or Rake Festival, vert. No. 1970, Minnie Mouse, Japanese New Year, vert. No. 1971, Mickey, Snow Festival, vert.

1991, May 6   Litho.   Perf. 13½x14
1961	A263	5c multicolored	.45	.20
1962	A263	10c multicolored	.45	.20
1963	A263	20c multicolored	.95	.20
1964	A263	45c multicolored	1.25	.80
1965	A263	$1 multicolored	2.25	1.25
1966	A263	$2 multicolored	3.00	3.00
1967	A263	$4 multicolored	4.25	4.25
1968	A263	$5 multicolored	5.00	5.00
		Nos. 1961-1968 (8)	17.60	14.90

Souvenir Sheets
1969	A263	$6 multicolored	6.00	6.00
1970	A263	$6 multicolored	6.00	6.00
1971	A263	$6 multicolored	6.00	6.00

Paintings by Vincent Van Gogh — A264

Designs: 20c, Blossoming Almond Branch in a Glass, vert. 25c, La Mousme, Sitting, vert. 30c, Still Life with Red Cabbages and Onions. 40c, Japonaiserie: Flowering Plum Tree, vert. 45c, Japonaiserie: Bridge in Rain, vert. 60c, Still Life with Basket of Apples. 75c, Italian Woman (Agostina Segatori), vert. $1, The Painter on His Way to Work, vert. $2, Portrait of Pere Tanguy, vert. $3, Still Life with Plaster Statuette, a Rose and Two Novels, vert. $4, Still Life: Bottle, Lemons and Oranges. $5, Orchard with Blossoming Apricot Trees. No. 1984, Farmhouse in a Wheatfield. No. 1985, The "Roubine du Roi" Canal with Washerwoman, vert. No. 1986, Japonaiserie: Oiran, vert. No. 1987, The Gleize Bridge over the Viguerat Canal. No. 1988, Rocks with Oak Tree.

1991, May 13   Litho.   Perf. 13½
1972	A264	20c multicolored	.50	.25
1973	A264	25c multicolored	.50	.25
1974	A264	30c multicolored	.55	.30
1975	A264	40c multicolored	.75	.40
1976	A264	45c multicolored	.75	.50
1977	A264	60c multicolored	1.00	.70
1978	A264	75c multicolored	1.10	1.00
1979	A264	$1 multicolored	1.25	1.25
1980	A264	$2 multicolored	1.60	1.60
1981	A264	$3 multicolored	2.40	2.40
1982	A264	$4 multicolored	3.25	3.25
1983	A264	$5 multicolored	4.00	4.00
		Nos. 1972-1983 (12)	17.65	15.90

Size: 100x75mm, 75x100mm

Imperf
1984-1988	A264	$6 each	4.75	4.75

Mushrooms
A265

Designs: 15c, Psilocybe cubensis. 25c, Leptonia caeruleocapitata. 65c, Cystolepiota eriophora. 75c, Chlorophyllum molybdites. $1, Xerocomus hypoxanthus. $2, Volvariella cubensis. $4, Xerocomus coccolobae. $5, Pluteus chrysophlebius. No. 1997, Hygrocybe miniata. No. 1998, Psathyrella tuberculata.

1991, June 1   **Perf. 14**

1989	A265	15c multicolored	.70	.30
1990	A265	25c multicolored	.85	.30
1991	A265	65c multicolored	1.25	.75
1992	A265	75c multicolored	1.50	1.00
1993	A265	$1 multicolored	1.75	1.00
1994	A265	$2 multicolored	2.00	2.00
1995	A265	$4 multicolored	4.50	4.50
1996	A265	$5 multicolored	5.00	5.00
		Nos. 1989-1996 (8)	17.55	14.85

Souvenir Sheet

1997	A265	$6 multicolored	8.50	8.50
1998	A265	$6 multicolored	8.50	8.50

Miniature Sheets

Exploration of Mars — A266

Designs (all different): No. 1999: a, Johannes Kepler, 1571-1630. b, Galileo Galilei, 1564-1642. c, Martian canals drawn by Giovanni Schiaparelli, 1886. d, Sir William Herschel, 1738-1882. e, Mars, planets. f, Percival Lowell at telescope. g, Mariner 4. h, Mars 2. i, Mars 3.

No. 2000: a, e, Profiles of Mars. b, Olympus Mons. c, Dusty face of Mars. d, Martian moon Phobos. f, Martian moon Deimos. g, Nix Olympica. h, Terrain feature resembling human face. i, South Polar Cap.

No. 2001: a, Mars from Phobus. b, Martian dusk. c, "Voyager descent." d, Viking 2 lander on Mars. e, f, Martian landscape. g, h, i, Panorama view from Viking 2 lander.

No. 2002: a, b, Mariner 9. c, Mars. d, Polar cycle. e, Plain of Sinai. f, South pole. g, Nix Olympica. h, Martian surface. i, Outflow channel.

No. 2003, Phobos spacecraft over Mars. No. 2004, Future spacecraft. No. 2005, Future spacecraft, Mars.

1991, June 21   **Perf. 14x13½**
Sheets of 9

1999	A266	75c #a.-i.	5.50	5.50
2000	A266	$1.25 #a.-i.	9.00	9.00
2001	A266	$2 #a.-i.	14.50	14.50
2002	A266	$7 #a.-i.	50.00	50.00

Souvenir Sheets

2003	A266	$6 multicolored	5.75	5.75
2004	A266	$6 multicolored	5.75	5.75
2005	A266	$6 multicolored	5.75	5.75

Royal Family Birthday, Anniversary
Common Design Type

1991, July 5   **Litho.**   **Perf. 14**

2006	CD347	10c multicolored	.50	.20
2007	CD347	15c multicolored	.50	.20
2008	CD347	40c multicolored	.95	.35
2009	CD347	50c multicolored	1.50	1.50
2010	CD347	$1 multicolored	1.75	1.50
2011	CD347	$2 multicolored	2.75	1.75
2012	CD347	$4 multicolored	3.25	3.25
2013	CD347	$5 multicolored	4.00	4.00
		Nos. 2006-2013 (8)	15.20	11.75

Souvenir Sheet

2014	CD347	$5 Philip, Elizabeth	5.75	5.75
2015	CD347	$5 Diana, sons, Charles	5.25	5.25

10c, 50c, $1, Nos. 2013, 2015, Charles and Diana, 10th Wedding anniversary. Others, Queen Elizabeth II, 65th birthday.

University of West Indies, 40th Anniv. — A266a

Designs: 45c, Marryshow House, Grenada. 50c, Administrative Building, Barbados.

1991, July 19

2016	A266a	45c multicolored	.85	.50
2017	A266a	50c multicolored	.90	.90

Anglican High School, 75th Anniv. A267

1991, July 29

2018	A267	10c Existing school	.35	.25
2019	A267	25c New school design	.60	.25

Railways of the World — A269

Railways of Great Britain: No. 2020a, Stephenson's first engine, 1814. b, George Stephenson (1781-1848). c, Stephenson's Killingworth engine, 1816. d, Locomotion No. 1, 1825. e, Locomotion in Darlington, 1825. f, Opening of Stockton & Darlington Railway, 1825. g, Royal George No. 5, 1827. h, Northumbrian Rocket, 1829. i, Planet Class engine, 1830.

No. 2021a, Old Ironsides, US, 1832. b, Wilberforce, Stockton & Darlington Railway, Great Britain, 1832. c, Stephenson's Der Adler, Germany, 1835. d, Stephenson's North Star, Great Britain, 1837. e, London & Birmingham No. 1, Great Britain, 1838. f, Stephenson's 1st Austrian locomotive, 1838. g, Mud Digger, US, 1840. h, Standard Norris, US, 1840. i, Fire Fly Class, Great Britain, 1840.

No. 2022a, Lion, Liverpool and Manchester, Great Britain, 1841. b, Beuth 2-2-2, Berlin-Anhalt Railway, Germany, 1843. c, Derwent No. 25, Stockton & Darlington Railway, Great Britain, 1845. d, MKpV, WCB, Vienna, 1846. e, First railway in Hungary, Budapest to Vac, 1846. f, Stockton & Darlington, 1846. g, Stephenson's long boiler type, Paris, 1847. h, Baldwin 4-4-0, US, 1850. i, 2-4-0, Germany, 1850. No. 2023, Boiler of Locomotion No. 1. No. 2024, Liverpool & Manchester Railway, Great Britain, 1833.

1991-92   **Litho.**   **Perf. 14**
Sheets of 9

2020	A269	75c #a.-i.	6.75	6.75
2021	A269	$1 #a.-i.	9.00	9.00
2022	A269	$2 #a.-i.	18.00	18.00

Souvenir Sheet

2023	A269	$6 multicolored	8.00	8.00
2024	A269	$6 multicolored	8.00	8.00

Issued: 75c, #2023, Dec. 2; others, May 7, 1992.

Miniature Sheet

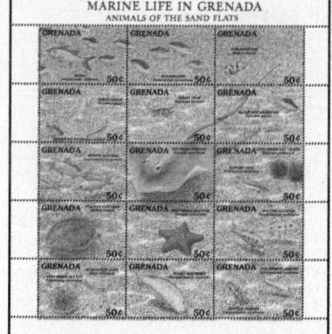

Marine Life in the Sand Flats — A270

Designs: No. 2025a, Barbu. b, Beaugregory. c, Porcupinefish. d, Conchfish, queen conch. e, Hermit crab. f, Bluestripe lizardfish. g, Spotfin mojarra. h, Southern stingray. i, Slippery dick, long-spined sea urchin. j, Peacock flounder. k, West Indian sea star. l, Spotted goatfish. m, West Indian sea egg, reticulated olive. n, Pearly razorfish. o, Mottled and yellowhead jawfish. $6, Shortnose batfish.

1991, Dec. 5   **Litho.**   **Perf. 14**

2025	A270	50c Sheet of 15, #a.-o.	12.50	12.50

Souvenir Sheet

2026	A270	$6 multicolored	11.50	11.50

Christmas
A271

Details from paintings by Albrecht Durer: 10c, Adoration of the Magi. 35c, The Madonna with the Siskin. 50c, The Feast of the Rose Garlands. 75c, Madonna and Child (Virgin with the Pear). $1, The Virgin in Half-Length. $2, Madonna and Child. $4, Virgin and Child with St. Anne. $5, Virgin and Child, diff. No. 2035, Virgin with a Multitude of Animals. No. 2036, The Nativity.

1991, Dec. 9   **Perf. 12**

2027	A271	10c multicolored	.40	.20
2028	A271	35c multicolored	.60	.35
2029	A271	50c multicolored	.65	.45
2030	A271	75c multicolored	1.00	.70
2031	A271	$1 multicolored	1.10	.90
2032	A271	$2 multicolored	1.75	1.75
2033	A271	$4 multicolored	4.00	4.00
2034	A271	$5 multicolored	4.50	4.50
		Nos. 2027-2034 (8)	14.00	12.85

Souvenir Sheets
Perf. 14½

2035	A271	$6 multicolored	7.50	7.50
2036	A271	$6 multicolored	7.50	7.50

Thrill Sports — A272

Walt Disney characters enjoying thrill sports.

1992, Feb. 11   **Litho.**   **Perf. 14x13½**

2037	A272	5c Windsurfing	.45	.35
2038	A272	10c Skateboarding	.55	.35
2039	A272	20c Gliding	.80	.35
2040	A272	45c Stunt kite flying	1.25	.35
2041	A272	$1 Mountain biking	1.50	1.00

2042	A272	$2 Parachuting	2.25	2.25
2043	A272	$4 Go-carting	4.75	4.75
2044	A272	$5 Water skiing	5.50	5.50
		Nos. 2037-2044 (8)	17.05	14.90

Souvenir Sheets

2045	A272	$6 Rollor blade hockey	6.00	6.00
2046	A272	$6 Bungee jumping	6.00	6.00
2046A	A272	$6 Hang gliding	6.00	6.00
2046B	A272	$6 River rafting	6.00	6.00

Queen Elizabeth II's Accession to the Throne, 40th Anniv.
Common Design Type

1992, Feb. 6   **Perf. 14**

2047	CD348	10c multicolored	.20	.20
2048	CD348	50c multicolored	.40	.40
2049	CD348	$1 multicolored	.80	.80
2050	CD348	$5 multicolored	4.00	4.00
		Nos. 2047-2050 (4)	5.40	5.40

Souvenir Sheets

2051	CD348	$6 Queen at left	5.75	5.75
2052	CD348	$6 Queen at right	5.75	5.75

Spanish Art — A273

Paintings: 10c, The Corpus Christi Procession in Seville, by Manuel Cabral y Aguado, horiz. 35c, The Mancorbo Channel, by Carlos de Haes. 50c, Countess of Vilches, by Federico de Madrazo y Kuntz. 75c, Countess of Santovenia, by Eduardo Rosales Gallina. $1, Queen Maria Isabel de Braganza, by Bernardo Lopez Piquer. $2, $4, The Presentation of Don John of Austria to Charles V (different details), by Gallina. $5, The Testament of Isabella the Catholic, by Eduardo Rosales Gallina, horiz. No. 2061, Meeting of Poets in Antonio Maria Esquivel's Studio, by Antonio Maria Esquivel y Suarez de Urbina. No. 2062, The Horse Corral in the Old Madrid Bullring, by Manuel Castellano, horiz.

1992, Apr. 30   **Litho.**   **Perf. 13**

2053	A273	10c multicolored	.35	.20
2054	A273	35c multicolored	.45	.35
2055	A273	50c multicolored	.55	.45
2056	A273	75c multicolored	.80	.65
2057	A273	$1 multicolored	1.25	.85
2058	A273	$2 multicolored	1.75	1.75
2059	A273	$4 multicolored	3.50	3.50
2060	A273	$5 multicolored	4.25	4.25

Size: 120x95mm
Imperf

2061	A273	$6 multicolored	5.75	5.75
2062	A273	$6 multicolored	5.75	5.75
		Nos. 2053-2062 (10)	24.40	23.50

Granada '92.

A274

Discovery of America, 500th Anniv. — A275

1992, May 7   **Litho.**   **Perf. 14**

2063	A274	10c Green-winged parrot	.50	.25
2064	A274	25c Santa Maria	.50	.25
2065	A274	35c Columbus	.50	.45

2066	A274	50c Hourglass	.70	.60
2067	A274	75c Queen Isabella	1.25	1.00
2068	A274	$4 Cantino map, 1502	4.50	4.50
		Nos. 2063-2068 (6)	7.95	7.05

Souvenir Sheets

2069	A274	$6 Map, ship, fish	6.25	6.25
2070	A274	$6 Map, arms, Genoa	6.25	6.25

World Columbian Stamp Expo '92, Chicago.

1992 — **Perf. 14½**

2071	A275	$1 Coming ashore	1.10	1.10
2072	A275	$2 Native, ships	2.00	2.00

Organization of East Caribbean States.

Hummingbirds
A276

1992, May 28

2073	A276	10c Ruby-throated	.75	.30
2074	A276	25c Vervain	.90	.30
2075	A276	35c Blue-headed	.95	.35
2076	A276	50c Cuban Emerald	1.25	.50
2077	A276	75c Antillean Mango	1.50	.75
2078	A276	$2 Purple-throated carib	1.60	1.60
2079	A276	$4 Puerto Rican emerald	3.25	3.25
2080	A276	$5 Green-throated carib	4.00	4.00
		Nos. 2073-2080 (8)	14.20	11.05

Souvenir Sheets

2081	A276	$6 Rufous-breasted hermit	7.50	7.50
2082	A276	$6 Antillean crested	7.50	7.50

Genoa '92.

USO, 50th Anniv. — A277　　1992 Summer Olympics, Barcelona — A278

1992, June 1 — **Perf. 14**

2083	A277	15c Gracie Fields	.35	.25
2084	A277	25c Jack Benny	.45	.25
2085	A277	35c Jinx Falkenburg	.50	.40
2086	A277	50c Frances Langford	.65	.50
2087	A277	75c Joe E. Brown	1.00	1.00
2088	A277	$1 Phil Silvers	1.25	1.25
2089	A277	$2 Danny Kaye	2.50	2.50
2090	A277	$2 Frank Sinatra	6.00	6.00
		Nos. 2083-2090 (8)	12.70	12.15

Souvenir Sheets

2091	A277	$6 Anna May Wong	6.75	6.75
2092	A277	$6 Bob Hope	6.75	6.75

1992

2093	A278	10c Badminton	.50	.30
2094	A278	25c Women's long jump	.50	.20
2095	A278	35c Women's 100-meter dash	.50	.30
2096	A278	50c Cycling	1.00	.50
2097	A278	75c Decathlon (pole vault), horiz.	1.00	.70
2098	A278	$2 Judo, horiz.	1.60	1.60
2099	A278	$4 Women's gymnastics	3.25	3.25
2100	A278	$5 Javelin	4.00	4.00
		Nos. 2093-2100 (8)	12.35	10.85

Souvenir Sheets

2101	A278	$6 Men's floor exercise	5.75	5.75
2102	A278	$6 Men's vault	5.75	5.75

Model Trains
A279

Designs: 10c, The Blue Comet, standard gauge, US, 1933. 35c, Switching locomotive, 2-inch gauge, 1906. 40c, B & O Tunnel locomotive, 2-inch gauge, 1905. 75c, Grand Canyon, standard gauge, US, 1931. $1, Lithographed tin streamliner, O gauge, 1930's. $2, Switching locomotive #237, No. 1 gauge, US, 1911. $4, Parlor car, standard gauge, US, 1928. $5, Locomotive #4687 of Improved President's Special, standard gauge, 1927. No. 2111, Engine #3239, No. 1 gauge, US, 1912. No. 2112, Ives engine #1132, 1921.

1992, Oct. 22 — **Litho.** — **Perf. 14**

2103	A279	10c multicolored	.45	.25
2104	A279	35c multicolored	.50	.30
2105	A279	40c multicolored	.50	.35
2106	A279	75c multicolored	.90	.50
2107	A279	$1 multicolored	1.25	1.00
2108	A279	$2 multicolored	1.50	1.50
2109	A279	$4 multicolored	3.00	3.00
2110	A279	$5 multicolored	3.75	3.75
		Nos. 2103-2110 (8)	11.85	10.65

Souvenir Sheet
Perf. 13

2111	A279	$6 multicolored	6.25	6.25
2112	A279	$6 multicolored	6.25	6.25

Nos. 2111-2112 contains one 51x40mm stamp.

Souvenir Sheet

Guggenheim Museum, NYC — A280

1992, Oct. 28 — **Perf. 14**

2113	A280	$6 multicolored	5.25	5.25

Postage Stamp Mega Event '92, NYC.

Christmas
A281

Details or entire paintings: 10c, The Adoration of the Magi, by Fra Filippo Lippi. 15c, Madonna Adoring Child in a Wood, by Fra Filippo Lippi. 25c, Adoration of the Magi, by Botticelli. 35c, The Epiphany-Adoration of the Magi, by Hieronymus Bosch. 50c, Adoration of the Magi, by Giovanni de Paolo. 75c, The Adoration of the Magi, by Gentile da Fabriano. 90c, Adoration of the Magi, by Juan Batista Maino. $1, The Adoration of the Child, by Master of Liesborn. $2, The Adoration of the Kings, by Master of Liesborn. $3, The Adoration of the Three Wise Men, by Pedro Berruguete. $4, The Adoration of the Child, by Filippo Lippi. $5, Adoration of the Child, by Correggio. No. 2126, Adoration of the Magi, by Andrea Mantegna. No. 2127, Adoration of the Magi, by Hans Memling. No. 2128, Adoration of the Shepherds, by De La Tour.

1992, Nov. 16 — **Litho.** — **Perf. 13½x14**

2114	A281	10c multicolored	.45	.20
2115	A281	15c multicolored	.50	.20
2116	A281	25c multicolored	.55	.20
2117	A281	35c multicolored	.75	.40
2118	A281	50c multicolored	.90	.50
2119	A281	75c multicolored	1.10	.80
2120	A281	90c multicolored	1.25	.90
2121	A281	$1 multicolored	1.50	1.00
2122	A281	$2 multicolored	2.00	2.00
2123	A281	$3 multicolored	3.00	3.00

2124	A281	$4 multicolored	4.00	4.00
2125	A281	$5 multicolored	5.00	5.00
		Nos. 2114-2125 (12)	21.00	18.20

Souvenir Sheet

2126	A281	$6 multicolored	6.25	6.25
2127	A281	$6 multicolored	6.25	6.25
2128	A281	$6 multicolored	6.25	6.25

Regattas of the World — A282

Yachts, races: 15c, Matador, Newport News Regatta. 25c, Awesome, Antigua Regatta. 35c, Mistress Quickly, Bermuda Regatta. 50c, Emeraude, St. Tropez Regatta. $1, Diva G, German Admirals Cup. $2, Lady Be, French Admirals Cup. $4, Midnight Sun, Admirals Cup Regatta. $5, Carat, Sardinia Cup Regatta. No. 2137, 1979 Fastnet Race, horiz. No. 2138, Grenada Regatta, horiz.

1992, Oct. — **Litho.** — **Perf. 14**

2129	A282	15c multicolored	.20	.20
2130	A282	25c multicolored	.20	.20
2131	A282	35c multicolored	.30	.30
2132	A282	50c multicolored	.75	.40
2133	A282	$1 multicolored	1.00	.75
2134	A282	$2 multicolored	1.40	1.40
2135	A282	$4 multicolored	3.00	3.00
2136	A282	$5 multicolored	3.75	3.75
		Nos. 2129-2136 (8)	10.60	10.00

Souvenir Sheets

2137	A282	$6 multicolored	7.00	7.00
2138	A282	$6 multicolored	7.00	7.00

A283

Anniversaries and Events — A284

Designs: 25c, LZ1 on maiden flight, 1900. 50c, Endosat, proposed robot plane. 75c, Konrad Adenauer, factory. $1.50, Golden lion tamarin. No. 2143 Mountain gorilla. No. 2144, WHO emblem and "Heartbeat-the Rhythm of Health." $3, Wolfgang Amadeus Mozart. No. 2146, German flag, map, Adenauer. No. 2147, Voyager 2, Neptune. $5, Count Zeppelin, Graf Zeppelin. $6, Lion's Club emblem, Admiral Richard E. Byrd. No. 2150, Scene from "The Magic Flute." No. 2151, Konrad Adenauer. No. 2152, Earth Summit emblem, northern spotted owl. No. 2153, Count Zeppelin. No. 2154, Satellite rescue, vert.

1992 — **Litho.** — **Perf. 14**

2139	A283	25c multicolored	1.50	1.50
2140	A283	50c multicolored	1.50	1.50
2141	A283	75c multicolored	1.50	1.50
2142	A283	$1.50 multicolored	3.50	3.50
2143	A283	$2 multicolored	4.00	4.00
2144	A283	$2 multicolored	4.75	4.75
2145	A283	$3 multicolored	5.75	5.75
2146	A283	$4 multicolored	4.00	4.00
2147	A283	$4 multicolored	5.50	5.50
2148	A283	$5 multicolored	8.00	8.00
2149	A283	$6 multicolored	5.50	5.50
		Nos. 2139-2149 (11)	45.50	45.50

Souvenir Sheets

2150	A284	$6 multicolored	6.50	6.50
2151	A283	$6 multicolored	6.50	6.50
2152	A283	$6 multicolored	5.75	5.75
2153	A283	$6 multicolored	6.00	6.00
2154	A283	$6 multicolored	5.75	5.75

Count Ferdinand von Zeppelin, 75th anniv. of death (#2139, 2148, 2153). Intl. Space Year (#2140, 2147, 2154). Konrad Adenauer, 25th anniv. of death (#2141, 2146, 2151). Earth Summit, Rio de Janeiro (#2142-2143, 2152).

Mozart, bicent. of death (in 1991) (#2145, 2150). Lions Intl., 75th anniv. (#2149).

Issue dates: Nos. 2145, 2150, Oct. Nos. 2140-2141, 2144, 2146-2147, 2149, 2151, 2154, Nov. Nos. 2139, 2142-2143, 2148, 2152-2153, Dec.

Grenada Dove — A285

1992

2155	A285	10c multicolored	.85	.85

Entertainers — A286

Gold record award winners: No. 2156a, Cher. b, Michael Jackson. c, Elvis Presley. d, Dolly Parton. e, Johnny Mathis. f, Madonna. g, Nat King Cole. h, Janis Joplin.
No. 2157a, Frank Sinatra. b, Perry Como.
No. 2158a, Chuck Berry. b, James Brown.

1992, Nov. 19 — **Litho.** — **Perf. 14**

Miniature Sheet

2156	A286	90c Sheet of 8, #a.-h.	11.50	11.50

Souvenir Sheets

2157	A286	$3 Sheet of 2, #a.-b.	8.00	8.00
2158	A286	$3 Sheet of 2, #a.-b.	8.00	8.00

Care Bears Promote Conservation — A287

75c, Bear on uncontaminated beachfront. $2, Bear with parasol, butterfly on flower, vert.

1992, Dec. 15 — **Litho.** — **Perf. 14**

2159	A287	75c multicolored	1.00	1.00

Souvenir Sheet

2160	A287	$2 multicolored	3.00	3.00

Dogs
A288

Designs: 10c, Samoyed, St. Basil's Cathedral, Moscow. 15c, Chow chow, Ling Yin Monastery, China. 25c, Boxer, Traitor's Gate, United Kingdom. 90c, Basenji, Yamma Mosque, Niger. $1, Golden Labrador Retriever, Parliament, Ottawa, Canada. $3, Saint Bernard, Parsenn, Switzerland. $4, Rhodesian ridgeback, Melrose House, South Africa. $5, Afghan, Mazar-i-Sharif, Afghanistan. No. 2169, Alaskan malamute, Alaska. No. 2170, Australian cattle dog, Australia.

1993, Jan. 20 — **Litho.** — **Perf. 14**

2161	A288	10c multicolored	.70	.40
2162	A288	15c multicolored	.85	.40
2163	A288	25c multicolored	.90	.40
2164	A288	90c multicolored	1.25	.75
2165	A288	$1 multicolored	1.50	1.00

2166	A288	$3 multicolored	2.25	2.25
2167	A288	$4 multicolored	3.00	3.00
2168	A288	$5 multicolored	3.75	3.75
		Nos. 2161-2168 (8)	14.20	11.95

Souvenir Sheet

2169	A288	$6 multicolored	5.75	5.75
2170	A288	$6 multicolored	5.75	5.75

Miniature Sheet

PAINTINGS FROM THE LOUVRE
BICENTENNIAL 1793-1993

Louvre Museum, Bicent. — A289

Paintings by Jean-Antoine Watteau (1684-1721): a, The Faux-Pas. b, A Gentleman. c, Young Lady with Archlute. d, Young Man Dancing. e, Autumn. f, The Judgement of Paris. g-h, Pierrot (diff. details).
No. 2172, The Embarkation for Cythera, horiz.

1993, Mar. 8   Litho.   Perf. 12

2171	A289	$1 Sheet of 8, #a.-h. + label	10.00	10.00

Souvenir Sheet
Perf. 14½

2172	A289	$6 multicolored	7.50	7.50

No. 2172 contains one 88x55mm stamp.

Moths
A290

1993, Apr. 13   Litho.   Perf. 14

2173	A290	10c Magnificant	.35	.25
2174	A290	35c Metzl's io	.50	.35
2175	A290	45c Owl	.60	.40
2176	A290	75c Pink-spotted hawk	1.00	.60
2177	A290	$1 Faithful beauty	1.25	.75
2178	A290	$2 Green geometrid	2.50	1.50
2179	A290	$4 Gaudy sphinx	3.00	3.00
2180	A290	$5 Black witch	3.75	3.75
		Nos. 2173-2180 (8)	12.95	10.60

Souvenir Sheets

2181	A290	$6 Titan hawk, vert.	5.50	5.50
2182	A290	$6 Avocado, vert.	5.50	5.50

Flowers — A291

1993, May 17   Litho.   Perf. 14

2183	A291	10c Heliconia	.35	.25
2184	A291	35c Pansy	.50	.35
2185	A291	45c Water lily	.60	.40
2186	A291	75c Bougainvillea	.85	.60
2187	A291	$1 Calla lily	1.00	.75
2188	A291	$2 California poppy	1.50	1.50
2189	A291	$4 Red ginger	3.00	3.00
2190	A291	$5 Anthurium	3.75	3.75
		Nos. 2183-2190 (8)	11.55	10.60

Souvenir Sheet

2191	A291	$6 Christmas rose, horiz.	5.25	5.25
2192	A291	$6 Moth orchids, horiz.	5.25	5.25

Baha'i Shrine, Haifa, Israel — A292

1993, May   Litho.   Perf. 13½x14

2193	A292	75c multicolored	1.60	1.60

Baha'i faith in Grenada, cent.

Miniature Sheet

The 40th Anniversary of the Coronation of HM Queen Elizabeth II

Coronation of Queen Elizabeth II, 40th Anniv. — A293

Designs: a, 35c, Official coronation photograph. b, 70c, Queen Consort's Ivory Rod, Queen Consort's Scepter. c, $1, Elizabeth accepting scepter during ceremony. $5, Queen, family, 1960s.
$6, Portrait, by Peter George Greenham, 1965.

1993, June 2   Perf. 13½x14

2194	A293	Sheet, 2 each #a.-d.	12.00	12.00

Souvenir Sheet
Perf. 14

2195	A293	$6 multicolored	6.50	6.50

No. 2195 contains one 28x42mm stamp.

A294

Anniversaries and Events — A295

Designs: 35c, Telescope. 50c, Willy Brandt, Sen. Edward Kennedy, Mrs. Robert Kennedy, 1973. $4, Astronaut standing on moon. No. 2199, Willy Brandt, Kurt Waldheim. No. 2200, Copernicus. $6, Newspaper headline announcing Brandt's resignation.

1993, July 1   Litho.   Perf. 14

2196	A294	35c multicolored	.50	.50
2197	A295	50c black & brown	.75	.75
2198	A294	$4 multicolored	4.50	4.50
2199	A295	$5 black & brown	4.25	4.25
		Nos. 2196-2199 (4)	10.00	10.00

Souvenir Sheets

2200	A294	$5 multicolored	5.50	5.50
2201	A295	$6 brown & black	5.75	5.75

Nicolaus Copernicus, 450th anniv. of death (#2196, 2198, 2200). Willy Brandt, 1st anniv. of death (#2197, 2199, 2201).

Grenada Carnival, 1992
A296

1993, July 1

2202	A296	35c Public Library, vert.	.50	.50
2203	A296	75c Dancers	.95	.95

Public Library, cent. (in 1992) (#2202).

Miniature Sheet

Songbirds
A297

Designs: No. 2204a, 15c, Red-eyed vireo. b, 25c, Scissor-tailed flycatcher (g). c, 35c, Palmchat. d, 35c, Chaffinch. e, 45c, Yellow wagtail. f, 45c Painted bunting. g, 50c, Short-tailed pygmy flycatcher. h, 65c, Rainbow bunting. i, 75c, Red crossbill. j, 75c, Kauai akialoa. k, $1, Yellow-throated wagtail. l, $4, Barn swallow.
No. 2205, Song thrush. No. 2206, White-crested laughing thrush.

1993, July 13

2204	A297	Sheet of 12, #a.-l.	13.00	13.00

Souvenir Sheets

2205	A297	$6 multicolored	5.00	5.00
2206	A297	$6 multicolored	5.00	5.00

Miniature Sheet

Seashells of Grenada

Seashells — A298

Designs: No. 2207a, 15c, Atlantic gray cowrie, Atlantic yellow cowrie. b, 15c, Candy stick tellin, sunrise tellin. c, 25c, Common Atlantic vase. d, 35c, Lightning venus, royal comb venus. e, 45c, Crown cone. f, 45c, Reticulated cowrie-helmet. g, 50c, Barbados miter, variegated turret shell. h, 50c, Common egg cockle, Atlantic strawberry cockle. i, 75c, Measled cowrie. j, 75c, Rooster tail conch. k, $1, Lion's paw, Antillean scallop. l, $4, Dog-head triton.
No. 2208, Dyson's keyhole limpet. No. 2209, Virgin nerite, emerald nerite.

1993, July 19   Litho.   Perf. 14

2207	A298	Sheet of 12, #a.-l.	13.00	13.00

Souvenir Sheets

2208	A298	$6 multicolored	7.00	7.00
2209	A298	$6 multicolored	7.00	7.00

A299

Picasso (1881-1973): 25c, Woman with Loaves, 1906. 90c, Weeping Woman, 1937. $4, Woman Seated in Armchair, 1947. $6, Three Women at the Spring, 1921.

1993, July 1   Litho.   Perf. 14

2210	A299	25c multicolored	.35	.35
2211	A299	90c multicolored	1.25	1.00
2212	A299	$4 multicolored	4.00	4.00
		Nos. 2210-2212 (3)	5.60	5.35

Souvenir Sheet

2213	A299	$6 multicolored	4.75	4.75

A300

1993, July 1

1994 Winter Olympics, Lillehammer, Norway: 35c, Gaeten Boucher, speedskating gold medalist, 1984. $5, Norbert Schramm, figure skater. $6, Michela Figini, Sigrid Wolf, Karen Percy, Super G medalists, 1988, horiz.

2214	A300	35c multicolored	.50	.30
2215	A300	$5 multicolored	4.50	4.50

Souvenir Sheet

2216	A300	$6 multicolored	5.75	5.75

Polska '93 — A301

Paintings: $1, Portrait of Marii Prohaska, by Tytus Czyzewski, 1923. $3, Marysia et Burek a Geylan, by S.I. Wirkiewicz, 1920-21. $6, Parting, by Witold Wojtkiewicz, 1908.

1993, July 1   Litho.   Perf. 14

2217	A301	$1 multicolored	1.25	1.25
2218	A301	$3 multicolored	3.75	3.75

Souvenir Sheet

2219	A301	$6 multicolored	6.25	6.25

Taipei '93 — A302

Designs: 35c, Fire-breathing dragon, New Year's Fair, Chongqing. 45c, Stone elephant, Spirit Way to Ming Tomb, Nanjing. $2, Marble peifang, Ming Tombs, Beijing. $4, Stone pillar, Nanjing.
Paintings by Han Meilin: No. 2224a, Ornamental cock. b, Tiger cub. c, Owl. d, Cat. e, Gorillas. f, Leopard.
No. 2225, Orangutan.

1993, Aug. 13   Litho.   Perf. 14

2220	A302	35c multicolored	.25	.25
2221	A302	45c multicolored	.75	.75
2222	A302	$2 multicolored	3.25	3.25
2223	A302	$6 multicolored	6.25	6.25
		Nos. 2220-2223 (4)	10.50	10.50

Miniature Sheet

2224	A302	$1.50 Sheet of 6, #a.-f.	6.75	6.75

Souvenir Sheet

2225	A302	$6 multicolored	5.50	5.50

With Bangkok '93 Emblem

Designs: 35c, Nora Nair, Prasad Phra Thepidon, Wat Phra Kaew. 45c, Stucco deities, Library, Wat Phra Singh. $2, Naga snake, Chiang Mai's Temple. $4, Stucco elephants, Wat Chang Lom.

Thai sculpture: No. 2230a, Horses. b, Wheel of the Law, 7th-8th cent. c, Lanna bronze elephant, 1575. d, Kendi in form of elephant. e, Bronze duck, 14th-15th cent. f, Horseman, 14th-15th cent.
No. 2231, Elephants, horiz.

1993, Aug. 13
2226	A302	35c multicolored	.25	.25
2227	A302	45c multicolored	.35	.35
2228	A302	$2 multicolored	1.50	1.50
2229	A302	$4 multicolored	3.00	3.00
	Nos. 2226-2229 (4)		5.10	5.10

Miniature
2230	A302	$1.50 Sheet of 6, #a.-f.	6.75	6.75

Souvenir Sheet
2231	A302	$6 multicolored	4.50	4.50

With Indopex '93 Emblem

35c, Megalithic carving, Sumba Island, Indonesia. 45c, Entrance to Gao Gaja (Elephant Cave), Bali. $2, Loving Mother Bridge, Taroko Gorge Natl. Park. $4, Kala head gateway to Balinese Temple, Northern Bali.
Indonesian sculpture - #2236: a, Kris holder and Kris, 19th cent. b, Hanuman protecting Sita, I. Dojotan of Mas. c, Sendi of Visnu mounted on Garuda, 19th cent. d, Wahana (mini vehicle for votive fig.), 20th cent. e, Mercurial monkey warrior Hanuman, Rodja of Mas. f, Singa (polychrome lion).
No. 2237, Loris.

1993, Aug. 13 — Perf. 13½x14
2232	A302	35c multicolored	.25	.25
2233	A302	45c multicolored	.35	.35
2234	A302	$2 multicolored	1.50	1.50
2235	A302	$4 multicolored	3.00	3.00
	Nos. 2232-2235 (4)		5.10	5.10

Miniature
2236	A302	$1.50 Sheet of 6, #a.-f.	11.00	11.00

Souvenir Sheet
2237	A302	$6 multicolored	5.50	5.50

Miniature Sheets of 6

Italian Soccer Assoc. and Genoa Soccer Club, Cent. — A303

Players for Genoa Soccer Club, each $3: No. 2238a, Vittorio Sardelli. b, Juan Carlos Verdeal. c, Fosco Becattini. d, Julio Cesar Abadie. e, Luigi Meroni. f, Roberto Pruzzo.
No. 2239a, each $3: James K. Spensley. b, Renzo de Vecchi. c, Giovanni de Pra. d, Luigi Burlando. e, Felice Levratto. f, Guglielmo Stabile.
Each $15: No. 2240, 1991 Genoa team photo, horiz. No. 2241, Genoa team emblem.

1993, Sept. 7 Litho. Perf. 14
Sheets of 6, #a-f
2238-2239	A303	Set of 2	40.00	40.00

Souvenir Sheets
2240-2241	A303	Set of 2	37.00	37.00

No. 2240 contains one 48x35mm stamp. No. 2241 contains one 29x45mm stamp.

1994 World Cup Soccer Championships, US — A304

Designs: 10c, Nikolai Larionov, Russia. 25c, Andrea Carnevale, Italy. 35c, Enzo Scifo,

---

Belgium, Soon-Ho Choi, South Korea. 45c, Gary Lineker, England. $1, Diego Maradona, Argentina. $2, Lothar Matthaeus, Germany. $4, Jan Karas, Poland, Julio Cesar Silva, Brazil. $5, Claudio Caniggia, Argentina.
Each $6: No. 2250, Wlodzimierz, Poland. No. 2251, Jose Basualdo, Argentina.

1993, Sept. 7 Litho. Perf. 14
2242-2249	A304	Set of 8	12.00	12.00

Souvenir Sheets
2250-2251	A304	Set of 2	11.00	11.00

Mickey Mouse, 65th Birthday — A305

Movie clips: 25c, The Band Concert, 1935. 35c, Mickey's Circus, 1936. 50c, Magician Mickey, 1937. 75c, Moose Hunters, 1937. $1, Mickey's Amateurs, 1937. $2, Tugboat Mickey, 1940. $4, Orphan's Benefit, 1941. $5, Mickey's Christmas, 1983.
Each $6: No. 2260, Mickey's Birthday Party, 1942. No. 2261, Mickey's Trailer, 1938.

1993, Nov. 11 Litho. Perf. 14x13½
2252-2259	A305	Set of 8	13.00	13.00

Souvenir Sheets
2260-2261	A305	Set of 2	13.50	13.50

Christmas A306

Woodcuts by Durer: 10c, The Nativity. 25c, "The Annunciation." $1, "Adoration of the Magi." $5, "The Virgin Mary in the Sun."
Paintings by Leonardo Da Vinci: 35c, The Litta Madonna. 60c, Madonna and Child with St. Anne and the Infant St. John. 90c, Madonna with the Carnation. $4, The Benois Madonna.
Each $6: No. 2270, The Holy Family with Three Hares, by Durer. No. 2271, Adoration of the Magi, by Da Vinci.
The 25c actually shows the Adoration of the Magi. The $1 actually shows The Virgin Mary in the Sun. The $5 actually shows The Annunciation.

1993, Nov. 22 Litho. Perf. 13½x14
2262-2269	A306	Set of 8	10.50	10.50

Souvenir Sheets
2270-2271	A306	Set of 2	10.50	10.50

Hugo Eckener (1868-1954) — A307

Graf Zeppelin over: 35c, Vienna. 75c, Pyramids at Giza. $5, Rio de Janeiro. #2275, Flensburg.

1993, Dec. 21 Perf. 14
2272-2274	A307	Set of 3	5.50	5.50

Souvenir Sheet
2275	A307	$6 multicolored	5.50	5.50

Royal Air Force, 75th Anniv. A308

1993, Dec. 21
2276	A308	50c Lysander	1.00	1.00
2277	A308	$3 Hawker Typhoon	4.25	4.25

Souvenir Sheet
2278	A308	$6 Hawker Hurricane	5.25	5.25

Automotive Anniversaries — A309

35c, 1932 Mercedes Benz 370 S Cabriolet. 45c, 1966 Ford Mustang. $3, 1930 Model A Ford Phaeton. $4, Mercedes Benz 300 SL Gullwing.
Each $6: No. 2283, 1903 Ford Model A. No. 2284, 1934 Mercedes Benz 290.

1993, Dec. 21 Litho. Perf. 14
2279-2282	A309	Set of 4	10.00	10.00

Souvenir Sheets
2283-2284	A309	Set of 2	10.50	10.50

1st Benz 4-wheel car, cent. 1st Ford engine, cent.

First Gas Balloon Flight in America, Bicent. A310

Designs: 45c, Lift-off from Philadelphia. $2, Balloon in flight, vert. $6, Blanchard's balloon in flight, diff., vert.

1993, Dec. 21 Litho. Perf. 14
2285-2286	A310	Set of 2	3.00	3.00

Souvenir Sheet
2287	A310	$6 multicolored	6.50	6.50

Fine Art — A311

Self-portraits, by Matisse: 15c, 1900. 45c, 1918. $2, 1906. $4, 1900, diff.
Self-portraits, by Rembrandt: 35c, 1629. 50c, 1640. 75c, 1652. $5, 1625-31.
No. 2296, The Painter in His Studio, by Matisse. No. 2297, The Sampling Officials of the Draper's Guild, by Rembrandt, horiz.

1993, Dec. 31 Litho. Perf. 13½x14
2288	A311	15c multicolored	.40	.20
2289	A311	35c multicolored	.50	.25
2290	A311	45c multicolored	.55	.40
2291	A311	50c multicolored	.65	.45
2292	A311	75c multicolored	1.00	.60
2293	A311	$2 multicolored	1.75	1.60
2294	A311	$4 multicolored	3.25	3.25
2295	A311	$5 multicolored	4.00	4.00
	Nos. 2288-2295 (8)		12.10	10.75

Souvenir Sheets
2296	A311	$6 multicolored	5.25	5.25

Perf. 14x13½
2297	A311	$6 multicolored	5.25	5.25

Spice Islands Billfish Tournament, 25th Anniv. — A312

15c, Blue marlin. 25c, Sailfish with angler. 35c, Yellowfin tuna with angler. 50c, White marlin with angler. 75c, Catching a sailfish.

1993, Dec. Litho. Perf. 14
2302-2306	A312	Set of 5	4.25	4.25

A313

Hong Kong '94 — A314

Stamps, painting, Hong Kong Post Office-1846, by M. Bruce: No. 2307, Hong Kong #263, left detail. No. 2308, Right detail, #1597.
Porcelain ware, Qing Dynasty: No. 2309a, Vase with dragon decor. b, Hat stand. c, Gourd-shaped vase. d, Rotating vase with openwork. e, Candlestick with dogs. f, Hat stand, diff.

1994, Feb. 18 Litho. Perf. 14
2307	A313	40c multicolored	.65	.65
2308	A313	40c multicolored	.65	.65
a.	A313	Pair, #2307-2308	1.40	1.40

Miniature Sheet
2309	A314	45c Sheet of 6, #a.-f.	3.75	3.75

Nos. 2307-2308 issued in sheets of 5 pairs. No. 2308a is a continuous design.
New Year 1994 (Year of the Dog) (#2309e).

Independence, 20th Anniv. — A315

1994, Feb. 8 Litho. Perf. 14
2310	A315	35c Natl. flag, boat	.85	.85

Souvenir Sheet
2311	A315	$6 Map of Grenada	6.50	6.50

Miniature Sheets

Dinosaurs A316

Jurassic: No. 2312a, Germanodactylus. b, Dimorphodon. c, Ramphorhynchus. d, Apatosaurus (h). e, Pterodactylus. f, Stegosaurus. g, Brachiosaurus. h, Allosaurus (l). i,

Plesiosaurus. j, Ceratosaurus. k, Compsognathus. l, Elaphosaurus.

Cretaceous: No. 2313a, Quetzalcoatlus. b, Pteranodon ingens (c). c, Tropeognathus. d, Phobetor. e, Alamosaurus (i). f, Triceratops (e). g, Tyrannosaurus rex (h). h, Tyrannosaurus rex (up close) (l). i, Lambeosaurus. j, Spinosaurus. k, Parasaurolophus (l). l, Hadrosaurus.

No. 2314, Plateosaurus, vert. No. 2315, Pteranodon ingens.

1994, Apr. 13
Sheets of 12
2312	A316	75c #a.-l.	7.75	7.75
2313	A316	75c #a.-l.	7.75	7.75

Souvenir Sheets
2314	A316	$6 multicolored	5.50	5.50
2315	A316	$6 multicolored	5.50	5.50

Mushrooms
A317

Designs: 35c, Hygrocybe acutoconica. 45c, Leucopaxillus gracillimus. 50c, Leptonia caeruleocapitata. 75c, Leucoprinus birnbaumii. $1, Marasmius atrorubens. $2, Boletellus cubensis. $4, Chlorophyllum molybdites. $5, Psilocybe cubensis.

No. 2324, Mycena pura. No. 2325, Pyrrhoglossum lilaceipes.

1994, Apr. 6
2316	A317	35c multicolored	.50	.25
2317	A317	45c multicolored	.60	.35
2318	A317	50c multicolored	.70	.40
2319	A317	75c multicolored	.90	.50
2320	A317	$1 multicolored	1.25	.75
2321	A317	$2 multicolored	1.60	1.25
2322	A317	$4 multicolored	3.25	3.25
2323	A317	$5 multicolored	4.00	4.00
		Nos. 2316-2323 (8)	12.80	10.75

Souvenir Sheets
2324	A317	$6 multicolored	6.25	6.25
2325	A317	$6 multicolored	6.25	6.25

D-Day,
50th
Anniv.
A318

Designs: 40c, Sherman Dual-Drive swimming tanks. $2, Churchill "Ark" in operation. $3, Churchill "Bobbin" lays path over soft ground.
$6, Churchill "Avre."

1994, Aug. 4   Litho.   Perf. 14
2326-2328	A318	Set of 3	6.50	6.50

Souvenir Sheet
2329	A318	$6 multicolored	6.25	6.25

Miniature Sheet of 6

First Manned Moon Landing, 25th
Anniv. — A319

Tribute to crew of space shuttle Challenger: No. 2330a, Flame erupting before explosion. b, Judith A. Resnick. c, Aircraft flyover in "Missing Man" formation. d, Dick Scobee. e, Challenger 51-L patch. f, Michael J. Smith.
$6, Crew of mission 51-L.

1994, Aug. 4
2330	A319	$2 #a.-f.	8.50	8.50

Souvenir Sheet
2331	A319	$6 multicolored	5.25	5.25

A320

Paintings by Sin Yunbok, Late Chosŏn Dynasty

PHILAKOREA '94 — A321

Designs: 40c, Wonson Park & Garden. $1, Port of Pusan. $4, National Theatre, Seoul.
Paintings by Sin Yunbok, Late Choson Dynasty: No. 2335a-2335b, Lady in a Hooded Cloak. c-d, Kiaseng House. e-f, Amorous Youth on a Picnic. g-h, Chasing a Cat.
$6, Roof Tiling, by Kim Hongdo, vert.

1994, Aug. 4   Perf. 14, 13½ (#2335)
2332-2334	A320	Set of 3	4.00	4.00

Miniature Sheet
2335	A321	$1 Sheet of 8, #a.-h.	6.00	6.00

Souvenir Sheet
2336	A320	$6 multicolored	4.50	4.50

A322

Orchids: 15c, Brassavola cuculatta. 25c, Comparettia falcata. 45c, Epidendrum ciliare. 75c, Epidendrum cochleatum. $1, Ionopsis utriculariodes. $2, Oncidium ceboletta. $4, Oncidium luridium. $5, Rodriquezia secunda.
Each $6: No. 2345, Ionopis utriculariodes, diff. No. 2346, Onicium luridum, diff.

1994, Aug. 7   Perf. 14
2337-2344	A322	Set of 8	10.50	10.50

Souvenir Sheets
2345-2346	A322	Set of 2	11.00	11.00

A323

1994 World Cup Soccer Championships, US: No. 2347a, Tony Meola, US. b, Steve Mark, Grenada. c, Gianluigi Lentini, Italy. d, Belloumi, Algeria. e, Nunoz, Spain. f, Lothar Matthaus, Germany.
Each $6: #2348, Steve Mark, diff. #2349, Poster from 1st World Cup Championships, Uruguay, 1930.

1994, Aug. 11   Perf. 14
Miniature Sheet
2347	A323	75c Sheet of 6, #a.-f.	5.50	5.50

Souvenir Sheet
2348-2349	A323	Set of 2	10.00	10.00

Fish
A324

Designs: 15c, Yellowtail snapper. 20c, Blue tang. 25c, Porkfish. 45c, Foureye butterflyfish. $1, Longsnout seahorse, vert. $2, Spotted moray eel, vert. $4, Fairy basslet. $5, Queen triggerfish, vert.
Each $6: #2358, Queen angelfish. #2359, Squirrelfish.

1994, Sept. 1
2350-2357	A324	Set of 8	10.00	10.00

Souvenir Sheets
2358-2359	A324	Set of 2	10.50	10.50

A325

Intl. Olympic Committee,
Cent. — A326

Designs: 50c, Heike Dreschler, Germany, long jump, 1992. $1.50, Nadia Comaneci, Romania, Gymnastics, 1976, 1980.
$6, Dan Jansen, US, 1000-meters long track speed skating, 1994.

1994, Aug. 4
2360	A325	50c multicolored	1.00	1.00
2361	A325	$1.50 multicolored	2.25	2.25

Souvenir Sheet
2362	A326	$6 multicolored	5.00	5.00

1994, Year of the Dog — A327

Scenes from Disney's Society Dog Show: 2c, Mickey bathing Pluto. 3c, Using atomizer. 4c, Having tail "set." 5c, Putting on mascara. 10c, Having nails done. 15c, Mickey using flea powder on Pluto. 20c, On judge's stand. $4, Judge looking at Pluto. $5, Pluto in chair with first prize.
No. 2372, Pluto wearing "13," first prize ribbon. No. 2373, Little dog beside judge. No. 2374, Pluto with first prize ribbon.

1994, Sept. 22   Litho.   Perf. 14x13½
2363-2371	A327	Set of 9	10.50	10.50

Souvenir Sheets
2372-2374	A327	$6 each	5.25	5.25

Butterflies — A328

1994, Sept. 28   Perf. 14
2375	A328	10c	Red anartia	.35	.20
2376	A328	15c	Ruddy daggerwing	.35	.20
2377	A328	25c	Fiery skipper	.40	.20
a.			Inscribed "1996"	.40	.20
2378	A328	35c	Caribbean buckeye	.45	.40
a.			Inscribed "1996"	.45	.25
2379	A328	45c	Giant hairstreak	.50	.40
2380	A328	50c	Zebra longwing	.60	.50
2381	A328	75c	Diadem	.70	.70
2382	A328	$1	Blue night	1.00	1.00
2383	A328	$2	Orion	2.00	2.00
2384	A328	$3	Orange-barred sulphur	3.00	3.00
2385	A328	$4	Long-tail skipper	4.00	4.00
2386	A328	$5	Polydamas swallowtail	4.75	4.75
2386A	A328	$10	Bamboo page	9.50	9.50
2386B	A328	$20	Queen cracker	15.25	15.25
			Nos. 2375-2386B (14)	42.85	42.10

See Nos. 2585-2586.

Intl. Year
of the
Family
A329

1994, Aug. 4
2387	A329	$1 multicolored	.95	.95

Order of the Caribbean
Community — A330

First award recipients: 15c, Sir Shridath Ramphal, statesman, Guyana. 65c, William Demas, economist, Trinidad & Tobago. $2, Derek Walcott, writer, St. Lucia.

1994, Sept. 1
2388-2390	A330	Set of 3	3.00	3.00

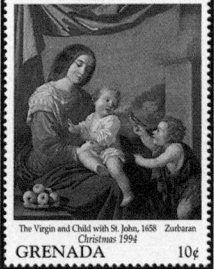

Christmas
A331

Paintings, by Zurbaran: 10c, The Virgin and Child with St. John. 15c, The Circumcision. 25c, Adoration of St. Joseph. 35c, Adoration of the Magi. 75c, The Portiuncula. $1, The Virgin and Child with St. John, 1662. $2, The Virgin and Child with St. John, 1658-64. $4, The Flight into Egypt.
Each $6: No. 2399, Adoration of the Shepherds, horiz. No. 2400, Our Lady of Ransom and Two Mercedarians.

1994, Dec. 5   Litho.   Perf. 13½x14
2391-2398 A331 Set of 8   7.50 7.50
Souvenir Sheets
2399-2400 A331 Set of 2   10.50 10.50

A332

A333

Birds: 25c, Grenada dove, horiz. 35c, Grenada doves, horiz. 45c, Cuban tody. No. 2404, 75c, Grenada dove, diff. No. 2405, 75c, Painted bunting, horiz. No. 2406, $1, Grenada dove, in flight. No. 2407, $1, Red-legged honeycreeper, horiz. $5, Green jay, horiz.
Each $6: No. 2409, Chestnut-sided shrike-vireo, horiz. No. 2410, Chaffinch, horiz.

1995, Jan. 10   Litho.   Perf. 14
2401-2408 A332 Set of 8   15.00 15.00
Souvenir Sheet
2409-2410 A332 Set of 2   13.00 13.00
World Wildlife Fund (#2401-2402, 2404, 2406).

1995, Jan. 12
Designs: 25c, Junior Murray, Grenada/W. Indies. 35c, R.B. Richardson, Leeward Isl./W. Indies. $2, A.J. Steward, England, horiz.
No. 2414, West Indies team, horiz.
2411-2413 A333 Set of 3   3.00 3.00
Souvenir Sheet
2414 A333 $3 multicolored   4.00 4.00
English Touring Cricket, cent.

Water Birds A334

25c, Hooded merganser. 35c, Teal. $1, Harlequin duck. $3, European wigeon.
No. 2419a, King eider. b, Shoveler. c, Long-tailed duck. d, Chiloe wigeon. e, Red-breasted merganser. f, Falcated teal. g, Vericolor teal. h, Smew. i, Red-crested pochard. j, Northern pintail. k, Barrow's goldeneye. l, Stellar's eider.
No. 2420, European wigeon, diff. No. 2421, Egyptian goose.

1995, Mar. 27   Litho.   Perf. 14
2415-2418 A334 Set of 4   5.00 5.00
Miniature Sheet
2419 A334 75c Sheet of 12, #a.-l. 9.50 9.50
Souvenir Sheets
2420 A334 $5 multicolored   4.00 4.00
2421 A334 $6 multicolored   4.75 4.75

New Year 1995 (Year of the Boar) — A335

a, 50c, Pig priest, China. b, 75c, Porcelain pig, Scotland. c, $1, Porcelain pig, Italy. $2, Jade pig, China.

1995, Apr. 21   Litho.   Perf. 14
2422 A335 Strip of 3, #a.-c.   2.50 2.50
Souvenir Sheet
2423 A335 $2 multicolored   2.75 2.75
No. 2422 was issued in miniature sheets containing 3 #2422.

Miniature Sheets of 6 and 8

End of World War II, 50th Anniv. A336

No. 2423A: b, Great Marianas Turkey Shoot. c, Battle of Midway. d, Battle of the Bismarck Sea. e, Musashi sinks at Leyte Gulf. f, Henderson Field. g, Battle of Guadalcanal.
Fighter planes: No. 2424a, Lavochkin LA7, Soviet Air Force. b, Hawker Hurricane, Royal Air Force (RAF). c, North American P-51D, US Army Air Force (USAAF). d, Messerschmitt ME 109F, Luftwaffe. e, Bristol Beaufighter, RAF. f, Messerschmitt ME 262, Luftwaffe. g, Republic P-47D, USAAF. h, Hawker Tempest V, RAF.
No. 2425, Nose of P-47D. No. 2425A, B-29 bomber.

1995, May 8
2423A A336 $2 #b.-g. + label   12.00 12.00
2424 A336 $2 #a.-h. + label   15.00 15.00
Souvenir Sheets
2425 A336 $6 multicolored   7.00 7.00
2425A A336 $6 multicolored   6.50 6.50

18th World Scout Jamboree, Holland — A337

Designs: a, 75c, Palm trees, scout. b, $1, Mountain climbing. c, $2, Scout salute, flag. $6, Canoeing.

1995, May 8
2426 A337 Strip of 3, #a.-c.   3.25 3.25
Souvenir Sheet
2427 A337 $6 multicolored   5.25 5.25
No. 2426 issued in sheets of 9 stamps.

UN, 50th Anniv. — A338

Designs: a, 75c, Man bending sword into plowshare. b, $1, Earth, dove. c, $2, UN Headquarters.
$6, Emblem.

1995, May 8
2428 A338 Strip of 3, #a.-c.   3.25 3.25
Souvenir Sheet
2429 A338 $6 multicolored   5.00 5.00
No. 2428 is a continuous design and was issued in sheets of 9 stamps.

Grenada-Republic of China Friendship — A339

Designs: 75c, Flags of Grenada, Republic of China. $1, Prime Minister Nicholas Brathwaite, Grenada, Pres. Lee Teng-hui, Republic of China.

1995, Apr. 27   Litho.   Perf. 14
2430 A339 75c multicolored   1.25 1.25
2431 A339 $1 multicolored   1.50 1.50
  a.   Souvenir sheet, #2430-2431   2.75 2.75

Domesticated Animals — A340

Designs: 10c, Cocker spaniel. 15c, Pinto. 25c, Rottweiler. 35c, German shepherd. 45c, Persian. 50c, Snowshoe. 75c, Percheron. $1, Scottish fold. $2, Arabian. $3, Andalusian. $4, C.P. shorthair. $5, Chihuahua.
No. 2444, $5, Manx. No. 2445, $5, Donkey. No. 2446, $6, Shar pei.

1995, May 3
2432-2443 A340 Set of 12   16.00 16.00
Souvenir Sheets
2444-2445 A340 Set of 2   8.00 8.00
2446 A340 multi   5.25 5.25

Miniature Sheets of 9

Sierra Club, Cent. A341

No. 2447, vert., each $1: a, Margay, mouth open. b, Margay seated. c, Margay up close. d, Condor facing left. e, Condor facing right. f, Condor looking back. g, White-faced saki on tree limb. h, White-faced saki, face in light. i, Patagonia Region, South America.
No. 2448, each $1: a, Darwin's rhea, two facing right. b, Darwin's rhea, two facing left. c, One Darwin's rhea. d, Snow covered mountains, Patagonia Region. e, Mountain peaks, Patagonia Region. f, White-faced saki. g, Crested caracara facing right. h, Two crested caracara. i, Crested caracara facing left.

1995, May 5
2447-2448 A341 Set of 2   17.00 17.00

FAO, 50th Anniv. — A342

Rotary Intl., 90th Anniv. — A343

No. 2449: a, 75c, Woman with baskets. b, $1, Boy with basket. c, $2, Men working in field.
$6, FAO emblem.

1995, May 8
2449 A342 Strip of 3, #a.-c.   3.25 3.25
Souvenir Sheet
2450 A342 $6 multicolored   5.00 5.00
No. 2449 was issued in sheets of 9 stamps.

1995, May 8
2451 A343 $5 shown   4.25 4.25
Souvenir Sheet
2452 A343 $6 Paul Harris, emblem   5.00 5.00

Queen Mother, 95th Birthday — A344

No. 2453: a, Drawing. b, Holding flower. c, Formal portrait. d, Blue hat, white coat.
$6, As younger woman.

1995, May 8   Perf. 13½x14
2453 A344 $1.50 Strip or block of 4, #a.-d.   7.00 7.00
Souvenir Sheet
2454 A344 $6 multicolored   6.25 6.25
No. 2453 was issued in sheets of 8 stamps.
Sheets of Nos. 2453 and 2454 exist with black border and text "In Memoriam 1900-2002" overprinted in sheet margins.

1996 Summer Olympics, Atlanta — A345

No. 2455: a, Tian Bingyi, China, badminton. b, Waldemar Leigien, Poland, Frank Wieneke, Germany, judo. c, Nelli Kim, USSR, women's gymnastics. d, Allessandro Andri, Italy, shot put.
No. 2456: a, Jackie Joyner, US, heptathlon. b, Mitsuo Tsukahara, Japan, gymnastics. c, Flo Hyman, US, Zhang Rung Fang, China, volleyball. d, Steffi Graf, Germany, tennis.
Each $6: No. 2457, Sailing. No. 2458, Wilma Rudolph, US, track.

1995, June 23
2455 A345 75c Strip of 4, #a.-d.   3.00 3.00
2456 A345 $2 Strip of 4, #a.-d.   7.75 7.75
Souvenir Sheets
2457-2458 A345 Set of 2   10.00 10.00

Anniversaries & Events — A346

25c, Junior Murray, cricket player. 75c, Spices. #2461, $1, Sendall Tunnel, cent. #2462, $1, Caribbean Development Bank, 25th anniv.

1995, Aug. 18   Litho.   Perf. 14
2459-2462 A346 Set of 4   3.50 3.50

Miniature Sheets of 9

Trains of the World A347

No. 2463: a, ETR 450, Italy. b, Isparta to Bozanonu, Turkey. c, TGV, France. d, ICE Inter-City Express, Germany. e, Nishi Nippon Rail, Japan. f, Bullet Train, Japan. g, Standard 4-4-0, Central Pacific RR, US. h, Amtrak 900 Bo-Bo Electric, US. i, Sir Nigel Gresley LNER, Great Britain.
No. 2464: a, Bi Level Vista Dome, Kinki Nippon Rail, Japan. b, Rolios Rail, South Africa. c, Class 460 Bo-Bo, Switzerland. d, The Central, Peru. e, X2000 Tilt Body Train, Sweden. f, Toronto-Vancouver, Canada. g, Talisman 125 Class 31, Great Britain. h, Flying Scotsman, Great Britain. i, Indian Pacific, Australia.
$5, Diesel Hydraulic, Korea. $6, Trans-Mongolian Beijing to Ulan Bator.

1995, Sept. 5
2463-2464 A347 $1 #a.-i., each   8.75 8.75
Souvenir Sheets
2465 A347 $5 multicolored   4.25 4.25
2466 A347 $6 multicolored   5.00 5.00
Singapore '95 (#2463).

Miniature Sheet of 9

Elvis Presley (1935-77) A348

Various portraits.

1995, Sept. 5   **Perf. 13½x14**
2467 A348 $1 #a.-i.   7.50 7.50

A349

Motion Picture, Cent. A350

No. 2470: a, Film reel, Oscar statuette. b, "HOLLYWOOD" sign. c, Charlie Chaplin. d, Shirley Temple. e, Spencer Tracy, Katherine Hepburn. f, Marilyn Monroe. g, John Wayne. h, Marlon Brando. i, Tom Cruise.
$5, Orson Welles as Citizen Kane, horiz.

1995, Sept. 5   **Perf. 14**
2468 A349 75c Marilyn Monroe   1.00 1.00
2469 A349 75c Elvis Presley   1.00 1.00
Miniature Sheet
Perf. 13½x14
2470 A350 $1 Sheet of 9, #a.-i.   8.00 8.00
Souvenir Sheet
Perf. 14x13½
2471 A350 $5 multicolored   8.75 8.75
Nos. 2468-2469 were each issued in miniature sheets of 16. No. 2470 is a continuous design.

Local Entertainers A351

Designs: No. 2472, 35c, Ajamu, white outfit. No. 2473, 35c, Mighty Sparrow, blue suit. 50c, Mighty Sparrow, black tuxedo. 75c, Ajamu, checkered shirt, sailor hat.

1995, Sept. 5   **Litho.**   **Perf. 14**
2472-2475 A351 Set of 4   2.75 2.75

Miniature Sheets

Marine Life A352

No. 2476: a, Yellowtail damselfish. b, Bluehead wrasse. c, Balloonfish. d, Shy hamlet. e, Orange tube coral. f, Rock beauty.
No. 2477: a, Creole wrasse. b, Queen angelfish. c, Trumpetfish (e, f). d, Barred hamlet. e, Tube sponge (b, f, h, i). f, Porcupine fish. g, Fire coral (d, e, h). h, Fairy basslet. i, Anemone.
Each $6: No. 2478, Elkhorn coral. No. 2479, Common seahorse, gulfweed.

1995, Apr. 24
2476 A352 $1 Sheet of 6, #a.-f.   5.25 5.25
2477 A352 $1 Sheet of 9, #a.-i.   7.25 7.25
Souvenir Sheets
2478-2479 A352 Set of 2   9.00 9.00
Issued: No. 2477, 2478, 4/24/95; Nos. 2476, 2479, 9/19/95.

Mickey's High Sea Adventure A353

Designs: 15c, Mickey sword fighting with pirate. 25c, Mickey with treasure chest. 35c, Minnie trying on jewelry from chest. 75c, Pluto with telescope, Mickey over barrel. $3, Pirate. $5, Mickey holding scarf with Minnie's name.
Each $6: No. 2486, Pirate fox fighting on ratlines. No. 2487, Minnie lowered from pirate ship to Mickey.

1995, Oct. 2   **Perf. 13½x14**
2480-2485 A353 Set of 6   8.75 8.75
Souvenir Sheets
2486-2487 A353 Set of 2   10.50 10.50

Miniature Sheets

Nobel Prize Fund Established, Cent. — A354

Recipients: No. 2488a, Albert A. Michelson, physics, 1907. b, Ralph Bunche, peace, 1950. c, Edwin Neher, physiology or medicine, 1991. d, Klaus von Klitzing, physics, 1985. e, Johann Deisenhofer, chemistry, 1988. f, Max Delbrück, physiology or medicine, 1969. g, J. Georg Bednorz, physics, 1987. h, Feodor Lynen, physiology or medicine, 1964. i, Walther Bothe, physics, 1954.
No. 2489: a, Hans G. Dehmelt, physics, 1989. b, Heinrich Böll, literature, 1972. c, Georges Köhler, physiology or medicine, 1984. d, Wolfgang Pauli, physics, 1945. e, Sir Bernard Katz, physiology or medicine, 1970. f, Ernest Ruska, physics, 1986. g, William Golding, literature, 1983. h, Hartmut Michel, chemistry, 1988. i, Hans A. Bethe, physics, 1967.
No. 2490: a, James Franck, physics, 1925. b, Gustav Hertz, physics, 1925. c, Friedrich Bergius, chemistry, 1931. d, Otto Loewi, physiology or medicine, 1936. e, Fritz Lipmann, physiology or medicine, 1953. f, Otto Meyerhof, physiology or medicine, 1922. g, Paul Heyse, literature, 1910. h, Jane Addams, peace, 1931. i, Carl F. Braun, physics, 1909.
Each $6: No. 2491, Winston Churchill, literature, 1953. No. 2492, Woodrow Wilson, peace, 1919. No. 2493, Theodore Roosevelt, peace, 1906.

1995, Oct. 18   **Litho.**   **Perf. 14**
2488-2490 A354 $1 Sheets of 9, #a.-i., each   8.25 8.25
Souvenir Sheets
2491-2493 A354 Set of 3   14.50 14.50

Teresa Teng, Chinese Entertainer A355

Nos. 2495-2496: Various portraits.

1995, Sept. 29
2494 A355 75c shown   1.00 1.00
Miniature Sheets
2495 A355 35c Sheet of 16, #a.-p.   5.50 5.50
2496 A355 75c Sheet of 9, #a.-i.   7.00 7.00
Nos. 2495a-2495p are 24x38mm.

Christmas A356

Details or entire paintings: 15c, The Madonna, by Montagna. 25c, Sacred Conversation Piece, by dei Pitati. 35c, Nativity, by Van Loo. 75c, The Virgin of the Fountain, Van Eyck. $2, Apparition of the Virgin, by Tiepolo. $5, The Holy Family, by Ribera.
Each $6: No. 1503, Madonna with the Christ Child, by Van Dyck. No. 1504, Vision of St. Anthony, by Van Dyck.

1995, Nov. 28   **Litho.**   **Perf. 13½x14**
2497-2502 A356 Set of 6   6.50 6.50
Souvenir Sheets
2503-2504 A356 Set of 2   10.50 10.50

Liberation of Grenada, 12th Anniv. A357

US Pres. Ronald Reagan and: No. 2505: a, Fort George. b, US, Grenada flags. c, St. George. No. 2506, Island scene, map. No. 2507, Waterfall.

1995, Dec. 8   **Perf. 14**
2505 A357 75c Strip of 3, #a.-c.   2.50 2.50
Souvenir Sheets
2506 A357 $5 multicolored   5.25 5.25
2507 A357 $6 multicolored   6.00 6.00
No. 2505 was issued in sheets of 9 stamps.

Pope John Paul II, 1995 Visit to New York City — A358

A358a

Pope John Paul II and: No. 2508, Statue of Liberty. No. 2509, St. Patrick's Cathedral. No. 2510, New York skyline.
Illustration A358a reduced.

1995, Dec. 13
2508 A358 $1 multicolored   1.00 1.00
2509 A358 $1 multicolored   1.00 1.00
Souvenir Sheet
2510 A358 $6 multicolored   5.25 5.25
Litho. & Embossed
Perf. 9
2510A A358a $30 gold & multi   30.00
Nos. 2508-2509 were each issued in sheets of 9.

New Year 1996 (Year of the Rat) — A359

Stylized rats: a, green & multi. b, red & multi. c, orange brown & multi.
$1, Two rats, horiz.

1996, Jan. 2   **Litho.**   **Perf. 14**
2511 A359 75c Strip of 3, #a.-c.   2.10 2.10
Miniature Sheet
2512 A359 75c Sheet of 1 #2511   2.10 2.10
Souvenir Sheet
2513 A359 $1 multicolored   1.25 1.25
No. 2511 was issued in sheets of 9 stamps.

Woodcuts by Dürer and Paintings by Rubens A360

Details or entire works: 15c, Young Woman, by Dürer. 25c, Four Horsemen from Apocalypse, by Dürer. 35c, Assumption and Coronation of Virgin, by Dürer. 75c, Mulay Ahmed, by Rubens. $1, Anthony Van Dyck Aged 15, by Rubens. $2, Head of a Young Monk, by Rubens. $3, A Scholar Inspired by Nature, by Rubens. $5, Hanns Dürer, by Dürer.
$5, Martyrdom of St. Ursula, by Rubens. $6, The Death and Life of a Virgin, by Dürer.

1996. Jan. 29   **Litho.**   **Perf. 13½x14**
2514-2521 A360 Set of 8   10.50 10.50
Souvenir Sheets
2522 A360 $5 multicolored   5.00 5.00
2523 A360 $6 multicolored   5.50 5.50

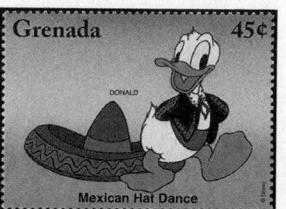

Disney Dancers — A361

Character, dance: 35c, Goofy, tap dance, vert. 45c, Donald, Mexican hat dance. 75c, Daisy, hula. vert. 90c, Mickey, Minnie, tango. $1, Daisy, Donald, jitterbug. vert. $2, Mickey, Minnie, Ukrainian folk dance. $3, Goofy, Pluto, ballet. $4, Minnie, Mickey, line dancing. $5, Minnie, the can-can. $6, Scrooge McDuck, Scottish sword dance.

Perf. 13½x14, 14x 13½

1996, Feb. 26				Litho.
2524-2531	A361	Set of 8	12.00	12.00

Souvenir Sheets

2532	A361	$5 multicolored	5.50	5.50
2533	A361	$6 multicolored	6.50	6.50

Queen Elizabeth II, 70th Birthday A362

Designs: No. 2534a, 35c, In blue dress. b, 75c, In white hat. c, $4, In black hat. $6, Younger picture with Prince Phillip.

1996, May 8	Litho.		Perf. 13½x14
2534	A362	Strip of 3, #a.-c.	4.50 4.50

Souvenir Sheet

2535	A362	$6 multicolored	5.25	5.25

No. 2534 was issued in sheets of 9 stamps.

Ferrari Race Cars — A363

Designs: a, 125-F1. b, Tipo 625. c, P4. d, 312P. e, 312, Formula 1. f, 312B. $6, F333 SP.

1996, May 8			Perf. 14
2536	A363	$1.50 Sheet of 6, #a.-f.	8.00 8.00

Souvenir Sheet

2537	A363	$6 multicolored	5.00	5.00

China '96, 9th Asian Intl. Philatelic Exhibition (#2536). No. 2537 contains one 85x28mm stamp.

Modern Olympic Games, Cent. A364

Designs: 35c, 1896 Olympic Gold Medal, vert. 75c, Olympic Stadium, Athens, 1896. $2, Ancient Greek Olympic runners. $3, Spiridon Louis, 1896 marathon winner.

1996, May 8		Litho.	Perf. 14
2538-2541	A364	Set of 4	5.00 5.00

See Nos. 2599-2602.

Jerusalem, 3000th Anniv. — A365

Various city gates: 75c, $2, $3. $5, Buildings inside city, horiz.

1996, June 26			
2542-2544	A365	Set of 3	4.50 4.50

Souvenir Sheet

2545	A365	$5 multicolored	4.25	4.25

UNICEF, 50th Anniv. A366

Designs: 35c, Child writing in book. $2, Child planting seedling. $3, Faces of boy, girl. $5, Boy, vert.

1996, June 26			
2546-2548	A366	Set of 3	4.25 4.25

Souvenir Sheet

2549	A366	$5 multicolored	4.00	4.00

Radio, Cent. A367

Entertainers: 35c, Jack Benny. 75c, Gertrude Berg. $1, Eddie Cantor. $2, Groucho Marx. $6, George Burns, Gracie Allen, horiz.

Perf. 13½x14, 14x13½

1996, June 26			
2550-2553	A367	Set of 4	4.25 4.25

Souvenir Sheet

2554	A367	$6 multicolored	5.25	5.25

Ships A369

War ships, No. 2559, each $1: a, Bounty, Britain, 1788. b, Bismark, Germany, 1941. c, Chuii Apoo, China, 1849. d, F224 Lubeck, Germany, 1970. e, Barbary Corsair, France, 1655. f, Augsburg, Germany, 1970. g, Henri Grace A Dieu, 1514. France. h, Prince of Wales, Britain, 1941. i, Santa Anna, Spain, 1512.

Sailing ships, each $1: No. 2560a, Gorch Fock, Germany, 1916. b, Henry B. Hyde, US, 1886. c, Resolution, Britain, 1652. d, USS Constitution, 1797. e, Nippon Maru, Japan, 1930. f, Preussen, Germany, 1902. g, Taeping, Britain, 1852. h, Chariot of Fame, US, 1853. i, Star of India, US, 1861.

$5, Victory, Britain, 1805. $6, Cutty Sark, Britain, 1869.

1996, Aug. 14			

Sheets of 9, #a-i

2559-2560	A368	Set of 2	16.00 16.00

Souvenir Sheets

2561	A369	$5 multicolored	4.50	4.50
2562	A369	$6 multicolored	5.25	5.25

Trains A370

Designs: 35c, C51 Imperial Train, Japan. 75c, Reingold, Germany. $2, Pioneer, US. $3, LA France, France.

Trains of the Orient, each $1: No. 2567: a, C62 4-6-4, Japanese Natl. Railways. b, 4-6-0, Shantung Railways, China. c, C57 Light 4-6-2, Japanese Natl. Railways. d, Diesel Express, Japanese Natl. Railways. e, 4-6-2, Shanghai-Nanking Railway, China. f, 051 2-8-2, Japanese Natl. Railways.

Trains of the world, each $1: No. 2568a, Atlantic Coast Line, US. b, #1619, Pioneer Smith Compound, England. c, 4-8-4 Trans-Siberian Railway. d, "Atlantic type," Palatinate Railway, Germany. e, 4-6-0 Paris, Lyons and Mediterranean Railway, France. f, 0341 Diesel Electric, Italian State Railways.

$5, Baden State Railways, Germany. $6, C11 2-6-4, Japanese National Railways.

1996, Aug. 28			
2563-2566	A370	Set of 4	4.50 4.50

Sheets of 6, #a-f

2567-2568	A370	Set of 2	9.00 9.00

Souvenir Sheets

2569	A370	$5 multicolored	4.25	4.25
2570	A370	$6 multicolored	5.00	5.00

Flowers A371

No. 2571, each $1: a, Winter jasmine. b, Chrysanthemum. c, Lilac. d, Japanese iris. e, Hibiscus. f, Sacred lotus. g, Apple blossom. h, Gladiolus. i, Japanese quince.

No. 2572, vert. each $1: a, Canterbury bell. b, Rose. c, Nasturtium. d, Daffodil. e, Tulip. f, Snapdragon. g, Zinnia. h, Sweetpea. i, Pansy. $5, Aster. $6, Peony, vert.

1996, Sept. 9		Litho.	Perf. 14

Sheets of 9, #a-i

2571-2572	A371	Set of 2	16.00 16.00

Souvenir Sheets

2573	A371	$5 multicolored	5.00	5.00
2574	A371	$6 multicolored	5.75	5.75

Zeppelins A372

No. 2575: a, 30c, L31, Germany. b, 30c, L35, Germany. c, 50c, L30, Germany. d, 75c, LZ10, Germany. e, $3, L3, Germany. f, $3, Beardmore No. 24, British.

No. 2576: a, Zeppelin L21, Germany. b, Zodiac Type 13 Spiess, France. c, NI "Norge." d, D-LZ 127 "Graf Zeppelin," Germany. e, D-LZ 129 "Hindenburg," Germany. f, Zeppelin NT, Germany, 1996.

Each $6: No. 2577, L13, Germany. No. 2578, Zeppelin ZT, Germany.

1996, Sept. 9			

Sheets of 6

2575	A372	#a.-f.	7.50	7.50
2576	A372	$1.50 #a.-f.	8.25	8.25

Souvenir Sheets

2577-2578	A372	Set of 2	10.50 10.50

Birds A373

No. 2579: a, Horned guan. b, St. Lucia parrot. c, Black penelopina. d, Grenada dove. e, St. Vincent parrot. f, White-breasted thrasher. $5, Barbados yellow warbler. $6, Semper's warbler.

1996			
2579	A373	$1.50 Sheet of 6, #a.-f.	8.75 8.75

Souvenir Sheets

2580	A373	$5 multicolored	4.50	4.50
2581	A373	$6 multicolored	5.25	5.25

Endangered Species — A374

Designs: a, Blue whale. b, Humpback whale. c, Right whale. d, Hawksbill turtle. e, Leatherback turtle. f, Green turtle.

1996, Sept. 18		Litho.	Perf. 14
2582	A374	$1.50 Sheet of 6, #a.-f.	8.75 8.75

Jacqueline Kennedy Onassis (1929-94) — A375

Various portraits.

1996, Aug. 26			
2583	A375	$1 Sheet of 9, #a.-i.	8.75 8.75

Souvenir Sheet

2584	A375	$6 multicolored	5.25	5.25

Butterfly Type of 1994

90c, Tropical chequered skipper. $1.50, Godman's hairstreak.

1996, Nov. 7		Litho.	Perf. 12
2585	A328	90c multicolored	.80 .80
2586	A328	$1.50 multicolored	1.25 1.25

A376

1996, Nov. 7 — Perf. 14

Sea Creatures: No. 2587, each $1: a, Killer whale. b, Dolphin. c, Dolphins. d, Sea lion, royal angelfish. e, Dolphins, hawksbill turtle. f, Hawksbill turtles (e). g, Royal angelfish. h, Pennant butterflyfish. i, Sea lion, squirrel fish.

No. 2588, each $1: a, Brown pelican. b, Killer whale. c, Whale (c). d, Dolphins, sea lion. e, Shortfin pilot whale, blue ringed octopus, sea lion (d, f, h). f, Hammerhead sharks, sea lion. g, Blue striped grunts. h, Stingray, Van Gogh fusiliers (i). i, Van Gogh fusiliers, golden coney, ribbon moray eel (h).

Each $6: No. 2589, Sea lions, horiz. No. 2590, Dolphins, horiz.

Sheets of 9, #a-i

2587-2588	A376	Set of 2	16.00 16.00

Souvenir Sheets

2589-2590	A376	Set of 2	10.50 10.50

Christmas A377

Details or entire paintings: 25c, The Visitation, by Tintoretto. 35c, Virgin with the Child, by Palma Vecchio. 50c, The Adoration of the Magi, by Botticeli. 75c, The Annunciation, by Titian. $1, The Flight into Egypt, by Tintoretto. $3, The Holy Family with the Infant Saint John, by Andrea Del Sarto.

Each $6: #2597, Adoration of the Magi, by Paolo Schiavo. #2598, Madonna and Child with Saints, by Vincenzo Foppa.

1996, Nov. 18 — Perf. 13½x14

2591-2596	A377	Set of 6	5.50 5.50

Souvenir Sheets

2597-2598	A377	Set of 2	10.50 10.50

Modern Olympic Games Type of 1996

Marathon medalists: No. 2599: a, Boughera El Quafi, 1928. b, Gustav Jansson, 1952. c, Spiridon Louis, 1896. d, Basil Heatley, 1964. e, Emil Zatopek, 1952. f, Frank Shorter, 1972. g, Alain Mimoun, 1956. h, Kokichi Tsuburaya, 1964. i, Delfo Cabrera, 1948.

Weight lifting medalists: No. 2600: a, Harald Sakata, 1948. b, Tom Kono, 1952. c, Naim Suleymanoglu, 1988. d, Lee Hyung Kun, 1988. e, Vassily Alexeyev, 1972. f, Chen Weiqiang, 1984. g, Ye Huanming, 1988. h, Manfred Nerlinger, 1984. i, Joseph Depietro, 1948.

$5, Manfred Nerlinger, vert. $6, Thomas Hicks, 1904, vert.

1996, July 8 — Litho. — Perf. 14

Sheets of 9

2599-2600	A364	$1 #a.-i., each	7.25 7.25

Souvenir Sheets

2601	A364	$5 multicolored	4.25 4.25
2602	A364	$6 multicolored	5.00 5.00

US Pres. Ronald Reagan A378

Various portraits.

1996, Aug. 26 — Perf. 13½

2603	A378	$1 Sheet of 9, #a.-i.	7.00 7.00

Sylvester Stallone in Movie, "Rocky" — A379

1996, Nov. 21 — Litho. — Perf. 14

2604	A379	$2 Sheet of 3	5.25 5.25

New Year 1997 (Year of the Ox) — A380

Oxen: Nos. 2605a, 2606a, Horns pointed down. Nos. 2605b, 2606b, Horns pointed up. Nos. 2605c, 2606c, Shown.
Illustration reduced.

Serpentine Die Cut 11

1997, Jan. 2 — Litho.

Self-Adhesive

Sheets of 3

2605	A380	$2 #a.-c., gold & multi	4.50 4.50
2606	A380	$2 #a.-c., sil & multi	4.50 4.50

Mickey Visits Hong Kong — A381

No. 2607: a, Pet birds. b, Kung-fu tea. c, Chinese Wet Market. d, Handmade grasshopper. e, Mid-Autumn Festival. f, Tai-chi.

No. 2608: a, 35c, Tram. b, 50c, Victoria Harbor. c, 75c, Buddha. d, 90c, Bank of China. e, $2, Bottle gas. f, $3, Seafood restaurant.

No. 2609, Mickey at The Peak, vert. $4, Minnie, Mickey, Hong Kong mail, vert. $5, Mickey pulling rickshaw, vert. $6, Mickey at Peking Noodle Show, vert.

1997, Feb. 12 — Litho. — Perf. 14x13½

2607	A381	$1 Sheet of 6, #a.-f.	7.00 7.00
2608	A381	Sheet of 6, #a.-f.	8.75 8.75

Souvenir Sheets

Perf. 13½x14

2609	A381	$3 multicolored	3.50 3.50
2610	A381	$4 multicolored	4.25 4.25
2611	A381	$5 multicolored	5.50 5.50
2612	A381	$6 multicolored	6.25 6.25

Hong Kong '97.

UNESCO, 50th Anniv. — A382

Designs: 35c, Kyoto, Japan. 75c, Quedlinburg, Germany. 90c, Dubrovnik, Croatia. $1, Ruins, Delphi, Greece. $2, Tomar, Portugal. $3, Palace of Chaillot, Paris, France.

No. 2619, Chinese sites, vert, each $1: a, Entrance to caves, Desert of Taklamakan. b, House, Taklamakan. c, Monument, Taklamakan. d, Palace of Cielos Purpuras, Wudang. e, House, Wudang. f, Stone Guard, Great Wall. g, Ming Dynasty, Wudang. h, Section, Great Wall.

No. 2620, vert, each $1: a, Bryggen Wharf, Bergen, Norway. b, Old City of Bern, Switzerland. c, Warsaw, Poland. d, Fortress Walls, Luxembourg. e, Palace of Drottningholm, Sweden. f, Petäj ävesi Old Church, Finland. g, Vilnius, Lithuania. h, Church of Jelling, Denmark.

No. 2621: a, Cathedral, Segovia, Spain. b, Würzburg, Germany. c, Lakes of Plitvice, Croatia. d, Monastery of Batalha, Portugal. e, River Seine, Paris, France.

Each $6: No. 2622, Monastery of Popocatepetl, Mexico. No. 2623, Shirakami-Sanchi, Japan. No. 2624, Monastery of the Hieronymites and Tower of Belem, Portugal.

1997, Apr. 3 — Litho. — Perf. 14

2613-2618	A382	Set of 6	7.50 7.50

Sheets of 8 or 5 + Label

2619-2620	A382	Set of 2	15.00 15.00
2621	A382	$1.50 #a.-e.	7.00 7.00

Souvenir Sheets

2622-2624	A382	Set of 2	11.00 11.00

Cats — A383   Dogs — A384

Cats: 35c, Devon rex. 90c, Japanese bobtail. $2, Cornish rex.

No. 2628: a, Turkish van. b, Ragdoll. c, Siberian. d, Egyptian mau. e, American shorthair. f, Bengal. g, Asian longhair. h, Somali. i, Turkish angora.

1997, Apr. 10

2625-2627	A383	Set of 3	3.50 3.50

Sheet of 9

2628	A383	$1 #a.-i.	8.50 8.50

Souvenir Sheet

2629	A383	$6 Singapura	5.75 5.75

1997, Apr. 10

Dogs: 75c, Cavalier King Charles spaniel. $1, Afghan hound. $3, Pekingese.

No. 2633: a, Lhasa apso. b, Rough collie. c, Norwich terrier. d, America cocker spaniel. e, Chinese crested dog. f, Old English sheepdog. g, Standard poodle. h, German shepherd. i, German shorthaired pointer.

No. 2634, Bernese mountain dog.

2630-2632	A384	Set of 3	4.00 4.00

Sheet of 9

2633	A384	$1 #a.-i.	8.50 8.50

Souvenir Sheet

2634	A384	$6 multicolored	5.75 5.75

Prehistoric Animals — A385

Designs: 35c, Dunkleosteus. 75c, Tyrannosaurus rex. $2, Askeptosaurus, vert. $3, Triceratops, vert.

No. 2639: a, Sordes. b, Dimorphodon. c, Diplodocus. d, Allosaurus. e, Pentaceratops. f, Protoceratops.

Each $6: No. 2640, Maiasaura, vert. No. 2641, Tristychius, Cladoselache, vert.

1997, Apr. 15

2635-2638	A385	Set of 4	6.50 6.50
2639	A385	$1.50 Sheet of 6, #a.-f.	8.25 8.25

Souvenir Sheets

2640-2641	A385	Set of 2	12.50 12.50

Marine Life A386

Designs: 45c, Porcelain crab. 75c, Humpback whale. 90c, Hermit crab. $1, Great white shark. $3, Green sea turtle. $4, Whale shark.

No. 2648, vert: a, Octopus. b, Lei triggerfish. c, Lionfish. d, Harlequin wrasse. e, Clown fish. f, Moray eel.

Each $6: No. 2649, Pacific barracudas. No. 2650, Scalloped hammerhead shark.

1997, May 2

2642-2647	A386	Set of 6	9.00 9.00
2648	A386	$1.50 Sheet of 6, #a.-f.	8.50 8.50

Souvenir Sheets

2649-2650	A386	Set of 2	11.50 11.50

Queen Elizabeth II, Prince Philip, 50th Wedding Anniv. A386a

No. 2651: a, Queen, Prince waving. b, Royal Arms. c, Formal portrait in royal attire. d, Formal portrait in street clothes. e, Windsor Castle. f, Prince Philip.

$6, Formal portrait in royal attire, diff.

1997, May 28 — Litho. — Perf. 14

2651	A386a	$1 Sheet of 6, #a.-f.	5.75 5.75

Souvenir Sheet

2652	A386a	$6 multicolored	5.75 5.75

Paintings by Hiroshige (1797-1858) A387

No. 2653: a, Nihon Embankment, Yoshiwara. b, Asakusa Ricefields and Torinomachi Festival. c, Senju Great Bridge. d, Dawn Inside the Yoshiwara. e, Tile Kilns and Hasiba Ferry, Sumida River. f, View from Massaki of Suijin Shrine, Uchigawa Inlet and Sekiya.

Each $6: No. 2654, Kinryuzan Temple, Asakusa. No. 2655, Night View of Saruwakamachi.

1997, May 28 — Perf. 13½x14

2653	A387	$1.50 Sheet of 6, #a.-f.	9.50 9.50

Souvenir Sheets

2654-2655	A387	Set of 2	11.50 11.50

Heinrich von Stephan (1831-97), Founder of UPU A388

No. 2656: a, Postal delivery on motorcycle. b, UPU emblem. c, Postal delivery on skis and snowshoes, Rockies, 1900. $6, Chinese long distance carrier.

1997, May 28 — Litho. — Perf. 14

2656	A388	$2 Sheet of 3, #a.-c.	6.00 6.00

Souvenir Sheet

2657	A388	$6 multicolored	6.00 6.00

PACIFIC 97.

Paul P. Harris (1868-1947), Founder of Rotary, Intl. — A389

Designs: $3, Rotary emblem, vocational training service program, The Philippines, portrait of Harris.

$6, Doves, hands holding globe inscribed "Act with Integrity, Serve with love, Work for Peace".

1997, May 28
2658 A389 $3 multicolored   2.75 2.75

Souvenir Sheet

2659 A389 $6 multicolored   5.25 5.25

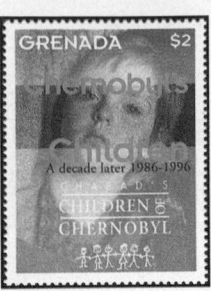

Chernobyl Disaster, 10th Anniv. A390

Designs: No. 2660, Chabad's Children of Chernobyl. No. 2661, UNESCO.

1997, May 28   **Perf. 13½x14**
2660 A390 $2 multicolored   2.00 2.00
2661 A390 $2 multicolored   2.00 2.00

Grimm's Fairy Tales A391

Mother Goose — A392

Scenes from "Snow White and the Seven Dwarfs:" No. 2662: a, Witch as woman looking into mirror. b, Dwarfs looking at Snow White as she sleeps. c, Snow White awakening, Prince. $6, Witch holding out apple for Snow White.

$5, "Little Johnny" walking in rain with umbrella.

1997, May 28   **Perf. 13½x14**
2662 A391 $2 Sheet of 3, #a.-c.   6.25 6.25

Souvenir Sheets
Perf. 14, 13½x14
2663 A392 $5 multicolored   4.00 4.00
2664 A391 $6 multicolored   5.00 5.00

1998 Winter Olympics Games, Nagano A393

Designs: 45c, Luge. 75c, Speed skater in red. $2, Male figure skater. $3, Slalom skier.

No. 2669: a, Luge, diff. b, Ski jumper. c, Downhill skier. d, Speed skater in blue. e, Two-man bobsled. f, Female figure skater. g, Biathlon. h, Hockey. i, Freestyle skier upside down.

Each $6: No. 2670, Downhill skier in air, vert. No. 2671, 4-Man bobsled.

1997, June 26   **Perf. 14**
2665-2668 A393 Set of 4   6.50 6.50
2669 A393 $1 Sheet of 9, #a.-
     i.   9.00 9.00

Souvenir Sheets
2670-2671 A393 Set of 2   11.50 11.50

Return of Hong Kong to China — A394

Views of city, Chinese flag as Chinese inscription: 90c, Bank of China, night scene. $1, Skyscrapers. $1.75, "Hong Kong," city in lights, horiz. $2, Deng Xiaoping (1904-97), Hong Kong, horiz.

1997, July 1
2672-2675 A394 Set of 4   7.00 7.00

Nos. 2672-2673 were issued in sheets of 4. Nos. 2674-2675 are 59x28mm and were issued in sheets of 3.

Disney's Hercules A395

No. 2676: a, Hercules. b, Pegasus. c, Megara. d, Philoctetes. e, Nessus. f, Hydra. g, Pain and Panic. h, Hades.

Each $6: No. 2677, Young Hercules. No. 2678, Calliope surrounded by Terpsichore, Melpomene, Clio, Thalia.

1997, Aug. 7   **Litho.**   **Perf. 13½x14**
2676 A395 $1 Sheet of 8, #a.-
     h.   10.00 10.00

Souvenir Sheets
2677-2678 A396 Set of 2   13.50 13.50

Butterflies A396

Designs: 45c, Peacock. 75c, Orange flambeau. 90c, Eastern tailed blue. $2, Black and red. $3, Large white. $4, Oriental swallowtail.

No. 2685: a, Brimstone. b, Mocker swallowtail. c, American painted lady. d, Tiger swallowtail. e, Long wing. f, Sunset moth. g, Australian blue mountain swallowtail. h, Bird wing.

Each $5: No. 2686, Monarch. No. 2687, Blue morpho.

1997, Aug. 12   **Perf. 14**
2679-2684 A396 Set of 6   10.00 10.00
2685 A396 $1 Sheet of 8, #a.-
     h.   7.50 7.50

Souvenir Sheets
2686-2687 A396 Set of 2   10.50 10.50

1998 World Cup Soccer Championships, France — A397

Various actions scenes from Italy v. West Germany, 1982. 15c, 75c, 90c, $2, $3, $4, vert.

Winning teams: No. 2694, each $1: a, Uruguay. b, Brazil, 1958. c, Germany. d, Argentina. e, Italy. f, West Germany. g, Italy. h, Brazil, 1970.

Soccer players: No. 2695, each $1: a, Seaman, England. b, Klinsmann, Germany. c, Berger, Czech Rep. d, McCoist, Scotland. e, Gascoigne, England. f, Djorkaeff, France. g, Sammer, Germany. h, Futre, Portugal.

Each $6: No. 2696, Beckenbauer, Germany, vert. No. 2697, Moore, England.

1997   **Perf. 13½x14**
2688-2693 A397 Set of 6   10.00 10.00

Sheets of 8, #a-h
Perf. 14x13½
2694-2695 A397 Set of 2   14.50 14.50

Souvenir Sheets
2696-2697 A397 Set of 2   12.00 12.00

Minnie Mouse in Hawaiian Holiday — A398

Stamps in flip book sequence showing Minnie doing Hula dance: No. 2698: a, 1. b, 2. c, 3. d, 4. e, 5. f, 6. g, 7. h, 8.
No. 2699: a, 9. b, 10. c, 11. d, 12. e, 13. f, 14. g, 15. h, 16. i, 17.
$6, 18.

1997, Aug. 7   **Litho.**   **Perf. 14x13½**
Sheets of 8 or 9
2698 A398 50c #a.-h. + label   6.00 6.00
2699 A398 50c #a.-i.   6.50 6.50

Souvenir Sheet
2700 A398 $6 multicolored   8.50 8.50

PACIFIC 97.

Mushrooms — A399

Designs: 35c, Boletus erythropus. 75c, Armillariella mellea. 90c, Amanita flavorubens. $1, Indigo milky. $2, Tylopilus balloui. $4, Boletus parasiticus.

No. 2707, each $1.50: a, Boletus parasiticus, diff. b, Frostis bolete. c, Amanita myscara flavilolvata. d, Volvariella volvacea. e, Stuntz's blue legs. f, Orange-latex milky.

No. 2708, each $1.50: a, Agaricus solidipes. b, Salmon waxy cap. c, Fused marasmius. d, Shellfish-scented russula. e, Red-capped scaber stalk. f, Calocybe tricholoma gambosum.

Each $6: No. 2709, Omphalotus illudens. No. 2710, Agaricus argenteus.

1997, Sept. 4   **Perf. 14**
2701-2706 A399 Set of 6   8.75 8.75

Sheets of 6, #a-f
2707-2708 A399 Set of 2   16.50 16.50

Souvenir Sheets
2709-2710 A399 Set of 2   11.50 11.50

Orchids A400

Designs: 20c, Paphiopedilum urbanianum. 35c, Trichoceros parviflorus. 45c, Euanthe sanderiana, vert. 75c, Oncidium macranthum, vert. 90c, Psychopsis kramerianum, vert. $1, Oncidium hastatum, vert. $3, Masdevallia saltatrix, vert. $4, Cattleya luteola.

No. 2719, vert, each $2: a, Odontoglossum crispum. b, Cattleya brabantiae. c, Cattleya bicolor. d, Trichopilia suavia. e, Encyclia mariae. f, Angraecum leonis.

No. 2720, vert, each $2: a, Broughtonia sanguinea. b, Anguloa virginalis. c, Dendrobium Bigibbum. d, T. forcia, L. lucasiana. e, Cymbidium. f, Cymbidium, diff.

Each $6: No. 2721, Oncidium onustum. No. 2722, Laelia milleri.

1997, Sept. 4
2711-2718 A400 Set of 8   11.00 11.00

Sheets of 6, #a-f
2719-2720 A400 Set of 2   22.00 22.00

Souvenir Sheets
2721-2722 A400 Set of 2   11.50 11.50

Diana, Princess of Wales (1961-97) — A401

Various portraits.

1997, Oct. 15   **Litho.**   **Perf. 14½**
2723 A401 $1.50 Sheet of 6, #a.-
     f.   8.75 8.75

Souvenir Sheet
2724 A401 $5 multicolored   5.00 5.00

Christmas — A402

Works of art, entire paintings, or details: 35c, Angel, by Matthias Grunewald. 50c, Saint Demetrius (icon). 75c, Reliquary in the Form of a Triptych. $1, Angel of the Annunciation, by Jan van Eyck. $3, The Annunciation, by Simone Martini. $4, Saint Michael (mosaic).

Each $6: No. 2731, The Annunciation, by Titian, horiz. No. 2732, The Coronation of the Virgin, by Fra Angelico.

1997, Dec. 5   **Litho.**   **Perf. 14**
2725-2730 A402 Set of 6   8.75 8.75

Souvenir Sheets
2731-2732 A402 Set of 2   12.50 12.50

New Year 1998 (Year of the Tiger) — A403

Designs: a, shown. b, With mouth open. c, With ears rolled back. Illustration reduced.

1998, Jan. 5 Litho. *Die Cut Perf. 9*
Self-Adhesive
Sheets of 3, #a.-c.

2733	A403	$1.50 gold & multi		
2734	A403	$1.50 sil & multi		

Nos. 2733b, 2734b have point of triangle down.

Fish
A404

65c, Black-tailed humbug. 90c, Yellow sweetlips. $1, Common squrrelfish. $2, Powder blue surgeon.

No. 2739, each $1.50: a, Blue tang. b, Porkfish. c, Banded butterflyfish. d, Threadfin butterflyfish. e, Red-headed. f, Emperor angelfish.

No. 2740, each $1.50: a, Scribbled angelfish. b, Lemonpeel angelfish. c, Bandit angelfish. d, Bicolor cherub. e, Regal tang. f, Yellow tang.

Each $6: No. 2741, Two-banded anemonefish. No. 2742, Long-nosed butterflyfish.

1998, Feb. 10 Litho. *Perf. 14*

2735-2738	A404	Set of 4	5.50	5.50

Sheets of 6, #a.-f.

2739-2740	A404	Set of 2	17.00	17.00

Souvenir Sheets

2741-2742	A404	Set of 2	13.50	13.50

Orchids
A405

No. 2743, each $1.50: a, Arachnis clarkei. b, Cymbidium eburneum. c, Dendrobium chrysotoxum. d, Paphiopedilum insigne. e, Paphiopedilum venustum. f, Renanthera imschootiana.

No. 2744, each $1.50: a, Sophronitis grandiflora. b, Phalaenopsis amboinensis. c, Zygopetalum intermedium. d, Paphiopedilum purpuratum. e, Miltonia regnellii. f, Dendrobium parishii.

Each $6: No. 2745, Lycaste aromatica. No. 2746, Pleione maculata.

1998, Apr. 21 Litho. *Perf. 14*
Sheets of 6, #a.-f.

2743-2744	A405	Set of 2	19.00	19.00

Souvenir Sheets

2745-2746	A405	Set of 2	12.50	12.50

Ships
A406

No. 2747, each $1: a, Brig. b, Clipper. c, Caique. d, Mississippi Riverboat. e, Luxury liner. f, The Mayflower. g, Frigate. h, Janggolan. i, Junk.

No. 2748, each $1: a, Dhow. b, Galleon. c, Felucca. d, Schooner. e, Aircraft carrier. f, Knau. g, Destroyer. h, Longship. i, Queen Elizabeth 2.

Each $6: #2749, The Lusitania. #2750, Submarine.

1998, Apr. 26 Litho. *Perf. 14*
Sheets of 9, #a-i

2747-2748	A406	Set of 2	19.00	19.00

Souvenir Sheets

2749-2750	A406	Set of 2	12.50	12.50

No. 2749 contains one 85x28mm stamp; No. 2750 one 56x42mm stamp.

Disney's Hercules
A407

Hercules grows up — #2751: a, Hercules, Zeus. b, Hercules and Pegasus walking past creature. c, Phil, Hercules. d, Hercules swinging through air. e, Centaur carrying captured Meg. f, Hercules attacking centaur. g, Hercules fighting lion. h, Hercules, Pegasus looking at prints.

Birth and childhood of Hercules — #2752: each $1: a, Zeus and Hera with newborn Hercules. b, Hades finds baby. c, Hades in the night. d, Baby sleeping. e, Baby swept away by Pain and Panic. f, Old couple with Baby Hercules. g, Hercules pulling cart. h, Hercules looking into mirror.

Hercules triumphant — #2753, each $1: a, Hercules carrying Meg. b, Meg, Hades. c, Hercules being trained by Phil. d, Hercules meeting Hades. e, Monster coming through city. f, Zeus. g, Hercules lifting column off Meg. h, Hercules diving into water.

Each $6: #2754, Hercules with sword, fighting Hydra. #2755, Hades on fire. #2756, Hercules, Meg on Pegasus, horiz. #2757, Zeus, Hercules, horiz. #2758, Hades. #2759, Zeus with baby Pegasus.

1998, June 16 Litho. *Perf. 13½x14*
Sheets of 8

2751	A407	10c #a.-h.	3.75	3.75
2752-2753	A407	Set of 2	18.00	18.00

Souvenir Sheets

2754-2759	A407	Set of 6	40.00	40.00

Sea Birds — A408

Designs: 90c, Arctic skua. $1.10, Humboldt penguin. $2, Herring gull. $3, Red knot.

No. 2764, horiz.: a, Northern fulmar. b, Black-legged kittiwake. c, Cape petrel. d, Mediterranean gull. e, Brandt's cormorant (h). f, Greater shearwater. g, Black-footed albatross. h, Red-necked phalarope. i, Black skimmer (f).

Each $5: No. 2765, Black-browed albatross. No. 2766, King penguin.

1998, June 30 Litho. *Perf. 14*

2760-2763	A408	Set of 4	6.25	6.25
2764	A408	$1 Sheet of 9, #a.-i.	9.25	9.25

Souvenir Sheets

2765-2766	A408	Set of 2	10.50	10.50

Diana, Princess of Wales (1961-97) — A409

Portrait of Diana with rose: No. 2767, Wearing hat. No. 2768, Without hat. Illustration reduced.

Litho. & Embossed

1998, July 14 *Die Cut 7½*

2767	A409	$20 gold & multi		
2768	A409	$20 gold & multi		

Supermarine Spitfires — A410

No. 2769, each $1.50: a, MK IX. b, MK XIV. c, MK XII. d, MK XI. e, H.F. MK VIII. f, MK VB. No. 2770, each $1.50: a, MK I. b, MK VIII. c, MK III. d, MK XVI. e, MK V. f, MK XIX. Each $6: No. 2771, MK IX. No. 2772, MK IA.

1998, July 20 Litho. *Perf. 14*
Sheets of 6, #a.-f.

2769-2770	A410	Set of 2	15.50	15.50

Souvenir Sheets

2771-2772	A410	Set of 2	12.50	12.50

Nos. 2771-2772 each contain one 57x43mm stamp.

Intl. Year of the Ocean
A411

No. 2773: a, Walrus. b, African black footed penguins. c, African black-footed penguin. d, California sea lion. e, Green turtle. f, Redfin anthias. g, Sperm whale. h, French angelfish. Australian sea lion. i, Jellyfish. j, Sawfish. k, Male and female cuckoo wrasse. l, Garibaldi. m, Spinecheek anemonefish. n, Leafy seadragon. o, Blue-spotted goatfish. p, Two-spot gobies.

No. 2774, Atlantic spotted dolphins. No. 2775, Octopus.

1998, Aug. 19

2773	A411	75c Sheet of 16, #a.-p.	12.50	12.50

Souvenir Sheets

2774	A411	$5 multicolored	5.00	5.00
2775	A411	$6 multicolored	6.25	6.25

CARICOM, 25th Anniv. — A412

1998, Sept. 15 Litho. *Perf. 13½*

2776	A412	$1 multicolored	1.10	1.10

Mahatma Gandhi (1869-1948)
A413

Design: $6, Portrait, head down.

1998, Sept. 13 *Perf. 14*

2777	A413	$1 multicolored	1.50	1.50

Souvenir Sheet

2778	A413	$6 multicolored	6.25	6.25

No. 2777 was issued in sheets of 4.

Paintings by Pablo Picasso (1881-1973) — A414

45c, The Bathers, 1918, vert. $2, Luncheon on the Grass, 1960. $3, The Swimmer, 1929. $5, Woman Reading, 1944, vert.

Perf. 14½x14, 14x14½
1998, Sept. 15

2779-2781	A414	Set of 3	5.25	5.25

Souvenir Sheet

2782	A414	$5 multicolored	5.25	5.25

Paintings by Eugéne Delacroix (1798-1863) — A415

No. 2783: a, Horsemen Fighting in the Plain. b, The Assassination of the Bishop of Liege. c, Still-life with Lobsters. d, The Battle of Nancy. e, The Shipwreck of Don Juan. f, The Death of Ophelia. g, Attila and the Barbarians. h, Entertaining the Arabians.

$5, Entry of the Crusaders into Constantinople.

1998, Sept. 15 *Perf. 14*

2783	A415	$1 #a.-h.	7.75	7.75

Souvenir Sheet

2784	A415	$5 multicolored	5.25	5.25

Organization of American States, 50th Anniv.
A416

1998, Sept. 15 Litho. *Perf. 14*

2785	A416	$1 multicolored	1.10	1.10

Diana, Princess of Wales (1961-97)
A417

1998 *Perf. 14½*

2786	A417	$1 multicolored	1.10	1.10

Self-Adhesive
Serpentine Die Cut Perf. 11½
Sheet of 1
Size: 52x65mm

2786A	A417	$6 Diana, buildings	6.00	

No. 2786 was issued in sheets of 6. Soaking in water may affect the multi-layer image of No. 2786A.
Issued: $1, 9/15; $6, 11/5/98.

Enzo Ferrari (1898-1988), Automobile Manufacturer — A418

No. 2787: a, 250 GT Berlinetta Lusso. b, 250 GTO. c, 250 GT Boano/Ellena cabriolet. $5, Dino 246 GTS.

1998, Sept. 15 — Perf. 14
2787 A418 $2 Sheet of 3, #a.-c.   5.25 5.25
Souvenir Sheet
2788 A418 $5 multicolored   5.25 5.25

No. 2786 was issued in sheets of 6. No. 2788 contains one 91x35mm stamp.

1998 World Scouting Jamboree, Chile — A419

Designs: $2, Scout salute. $3, World Scout flag. $4, Scout first aid. $6, World Scout flag.

1998, Sept. 15
2789-2791 A419 Set of 3   8.75 8.75
Souvenir Sheet
2792 A419 $6 multi, horiz.   7.00 7.00

Royal Air Force, 80th Anniv. A420

No. 2793, each $2: a, Vickers Supermarine Spitfire Mk2a. b, Vickers Supermarine Spitfire HF Mk1XB flying right. c, Vickers Supermarine Spitfire HF Mk1Xb flying left. d, Hawker Hurricane 11C.

No. 2794, each $2: a, EF-2000 Eurofighter prototype. b, Nimrod MR2P. c, Eurofighter 2000, diff. d, C-47 Dakota.

Each $6: No. 2795, Eurofighter 2000, VC10. No. 2796, Biplane, hawk's head. No. 2797, Biplane, hawk. No. 2798, Eurofighter 2000, Jet Provost.

1998, Sept. 15
Sheets of 4, #a-d
2793-2794 A420 Set of 2   16.00 16.00
Souvenir Sheets
2795-2798 A420 Set of 4   25.00 25.00

Tennis Stars A421

45c, Arthur Ashe. 75c, Martina Hingis. 90c, Chris Evert. $1, Steffi Graf. $1.50, Arantxa Sanchez Vicario. $3, Martina Navratilova. $2, Monica Seles. $6, Martina Hingis, diff.

1998, Oct. 28
2799-2805 A421 Set of 7   8.75 8.75
Souvenir Sheet
2806 A421 $6 multicolored   7.00 7.00

Peacekeepers, Beirut, Lebanon, 1982-84 — A422

1998, Nov. 30 — Litho. — Perf. 14
2807 A422 $1 multicolored   1.25 1.25

Christmas A423

Birds: 45c, Blue-hooded Euphonia. 75c, Black-bellied whistling duck. 90c, Purple martin. $1, Imperial parrot. $2, Adelaide's warbler. $3, Roseate flamingo.

$5, Green-throated carib. $6, Purple-throated carib, Canada #85.

1998, Dec. 1
2808-2813 A423 Set of 6   7.75 7.75
Souvenir Sheet
2814 A423 $5 multicolored   5.25 5.25
2815 A423 $6 multicolored   8.00 8.00

No. 2815 contains one 38x61mm stamp.

Christmas — A424

Works of art: 35c, Painting, The Angel's Parting from Tobias, by Jean Bilevelt. 45c, Painting, Allegory of Faith, by Moretto da Brescia. 90c, Painting, Cross, with Depiction of the Crucifixion, by Ugolino di Tedice. $1, The Triumphal Entry into Jerusalem, Master of the Thuison Altarpiece.

1998, Dec. 1
2816-2819 A424 Set of 4   2.75 2.75

New Year 1999 (Year of the Rabbit) — A425

Various rabbits, color of country name: a, green. b, orange. c, red. Illustration reduced.

1999, Jan. 4 — Litho. — Die Cut Perf. 9
Self-Adhesive
Sheet of 3
2820 A425 $1 sil & multi, #a.-c.   3.50 3.50

No. 2820b has point of triangle down.

A426

Famous People: No. 2821: a, Martin Luther King, Jr. (1929-68). b, Socrates (470-399BC). c, Thomas Moore (1478-1535). d, Chaim Weizmann (1874-1952). e, Alexander Solzhenitsyn (b. 1918). f, Galileo Galilei (1564-1642). g, Michael Servetus (1511-53). h, Salman Rushdie (b. 1947).

$6, Mother Teresa (1910-97).

1999, Mar. 1 — Litho. — Perf. 14
2821 A426 $1 Sheet of 8, #a.-h.   10.00 10.00
Souvenir Sheet
2822 A426 $6 multicolored   7.00 7.00

Nos. 2821b-2821c, 2821e-2821f are 53x38mm.

GRENADA $1.50   A427

Space Exploration — #2823, each $1.50: a, Robert H. Goddard. b, Werner von Braun. c, Yuri Gagarin. d, Freedom 7 rocket. e, Aleksei Leonov. f, Apollo 11 astronauts on moon.

No. 2824, each $1.50: a, Mariner 9. b, Voyager 1. c, Bruce McCandless. d, Giotto probe. e, Space Shuttle. f, Magellan probe.

Each $6: No. 2825, John H. Glenn, Jr. No. 2826, Neil A. Armstrong.

1999, Mar. 5
Sheets of 6, #a-f
2823-2824 A427 Set of 2   16.00 16.00
Souvenir Sheets
2825-2826 A427 Set of 2   12.00 12.00

Mickey's Dream Wedding A428

No. 2827: a, Goofy. b, Mickey. c, Minnie. d, Daisy Duck. e, Donald Duck. f, Pluto. g, Huey, Dewey & Louie. h, Dog.

Each $6: No. 2828, Mickey eating cake. No. 2829, Mickey, Minnie in back of carriage, horiz.

1999, Mar. 12 — Perf. 13½x14, 14x13½
2827 A428 $1 Sheet of 8, #a.-h.   8.00 8.00
Souvenir Sheets
2828-2829 A428 Set of 2   13.50 13.50

Mickey Mouse, 70th anniv.

Trains A429

Designs: 25c, Grand Trunk Western. 35c, Louisville & Nashville. 45c, Gulf, Mobile & Ohio. 75c, Missouri Pacific. 90c, RTG, French Natl. Railway. $1, Florida East Coast. $3, Kansas City Southern. $4, New Haven.

No. 2838, each $1.50: a, Western Pacific. b, Union Pacific. c, Chesapeake & Ohio. d, Southern Pacific. e, Baltimore & Ohio. f, Wabash.

No. 2839, each $1.50: a, Burlington Route. b, Texas Special, Missouri, Kansas & Texas. c, City of Los Angeles. d, Northwestern. e, Canadian National. f, Rock Island.

No. 2840, each $1.50: a, Rio Grande. b, Erie Lackawanna. c, New York Central. d, Pennsylvania. e, Milwaukee Road. f, Illinois Central.

No. 2841, each $1.50: a, TGV, French National Railways. b, HST, British Railways. c, TEE, Trans Europe Express. d, Ancona Express Itay. e, XPT, Australia. f, APT-P, British Railways.

Each $6: No. 2842, Bullet Train, Japan. No. 2843, Inter City Express, Germany. No. 2844, Santa Fe. No. 2845, ELD 4, Netherlands.

1999, Mar. 15 — Perf. 14
2830-2837 A429 Set of 8   9.75 9.75
Sheets of 6, #a-f
2838-2841 A429 Set of 4   36.00 36.00
Souvenir Sheets
2842-2845 A429 Set of 4   25.00 25.00

Australia '99, World Stamp Expo A430

Flora and fauna: $1, Orangutan. $2, Dourocouli. $3. Black caiman. $4, Black leopard, vert.

No. 2850, vert, each 75c: a, African binturong. b, Two elephants. c, One elephant. d, Garkulax mitratus. e, Vanda hookeriana (a, f). f, Heron. g, Fur seal (f). h, Pied shag (g). i, Round batfish (e). j, Loggerhead turtle (f, k). k, Three harlequin sweet lips (l). l, Two harlequin sweet lips (k).

No. 2851, each 75c: a, Papilio blumei (d). b, Egret (e). c, Kumarahou (b, f). d, Javan rhinoceros (g). e, Silver eye. f, Kiore (i). g, Cyclorana novaehollandiae. h, Caterpillar. i, Grey duck (h). j, Honey blue-eye. k, Krefft's tortoise. l, Archer fish.

Each $6: No. 2852, Impalas. No. 2853, Ring-tailed lemurs.

1999, Apr. 12 — Litho. — Perf. 14
2846-2849 A430 Set of 4   9.50 9.50
Sheets of 12, #a-l
2850-2851 A430 Set of 2   17.50 17.50
Souvenir Sheets
2852-2853 A430 Set of 2   12.50 12.50

Paintings by Hokusai (1760-1849) A431

Entire paintings or details — #2854, each $1.50: a, The Actor Ichikawa Danjuro as Tomoe Gozen. b, E-Tehon drawings (washing clothes). c, The Prostitute of Eguchi. d, Sudden Shower from a Fine Sky. e, E-tehon drawings (hanging clothes up to dry). f, Shimada.

No. 2855, each $1.50: a, Head of Old Man. b, Horse Drawings (with head down). c, Girl Making Cord for Binding Hats. d, Li Po Admiring the Waterfall of Lo-Shan. e, Horse drawings (with head up). f, Potted Dwarf Pine with Basin.

Each $6: No. 2856, Women on the Beach at Enoshima. No. 2857, The Guardian God Fudo Myoo and His Two Young Attendants.

1999, May 24 — Litho. — Perf. 13½x14
Sheets of 6, #a-f
2854-2855 A431 Set of 2   17.00 17.00
Souvenir Sheets
2856-2857 A431 Set of 2   12.50 12.50

Johann Wolfgang von Goethe (1749-1832), Poet — A432

No. 2858: a, Faust contempates the moon in his story. b, Portrait of Goethe and Freidrich von Schiller (1759-1805). c, Faust converses with Wagner outside the town gate. d, No. 2860, Margaret Muses in "Faust."

1999, May 24 — Perf. 14
2858 A432 $3 Sheet of 3, #a.-c.   8.75 8.75
Souvenir Sheet
2860 A432 $6 multi   6.75 6.75

IBRA '99, World Philatelic Exhibition, Nuremberg — A433

IBRA'99 emblem, 1893 4-4-0 locomotive and: No. 2862, 75c, Prussia #2. No. 2864, $1, Saxony #1.
Emblem, Humboldt sailing ship and: No. 2863, 90c, Mecklenburg-Schwerin #1. No. 2865, $2, Mecklenburg-Strelitz #1.
$6, Saxony #1. Illustration reduced.

1999, May 24		Litho.		Perf. 14
2862-2865	A433	Set of 4		5.25 5.25

Souvenir Sheet

2866	A433	$6 multicolored		7.75 7.75

Apollo 11 Moon Landing, 30th Anniv. A434

#2867, each $1.50: a, Footprint on moon. b, V2 Rocket. c, Command module, Columbia. d, Lunar rover. e, Lunar lander, Eagle. f, Command module during re-entry.
#2868, each $1.50: a, Moon. b, Edward H. White during first spacewalk. c, Edwin "Buzz" Aldrin. d, Earth. e, Michael Collins. f, Neal A. Armstrong, first man to walk on moon.
Each $6: a, #2869, Launch of Apollo 11, vert. #2870, US flag, Armstrong on Moon.

1999, May 24

Sheets of 6, #a-f

2867-2868	A434	Set of 2	19.00 19.00

Souvenir Sheets

2869-2870	A434	Set of 2	12.50 12.50

Souvenir Sheets

PhilexFrance '99, World Philatelic Exhibition — A435

Designs, each $6: No. 2871, 2-8-0 Heavy freight locomotive, French State Railways. No. 2872, 4 Cylinder Compound Pacific, Paris-Lyons and Mediterranean Railway.
Illustration reduced.

1999, May 24			Perf. 13¾
2871-2872	A435	Set of 2	12.50 12.50

A436

Wedding of Prince Edward and Sophie Rhys-Jones — #2873: a, Edward. b, Sophie and Edward. c, Sophie.
$6, Couple, horiz.

1999, June 18		Litho.	Perf. 13½
2873	A436	$3 Sheet of 3, #a.-c.	8.75 8.75

Souvenir Sheet

2874	A436	$6 multicolored	7.00 7.00

A437

Children: a, Two with fur hats. b, One with pink hat. c, Boy without shirt, girl with shawl.
$6, Wearing white shirt.

1999, May 24		Litho.		Perf. 14
2875	A437	$3 Sheet of 3, #a.-c.		8.75 8.75

Souvenir Sheet

2876	A437	$6 multicolored		7.00 7.00

UN Rights of the Child, 10th anniv.

British Comedy "Carry On" — A438

a, Dick. b, Doctor. c, England. d, Matron. e, Round the Bend. f, Up the Jungle. g, Loving. h, Up the Khyber.
$6, Various characters.

1999, May 24			Perf. 13½x14
2877	A438	$1 Sheet of 8, #a.-h.	8.75 8.75

			Perf. 13¾
2877I	A438	$6 multicolored	6.75 6.75

Variety Club of Great Britain, 50th anniv.

UPU, 125th Anniv. A439

Mail from space: a, Cosmonaut with letter from home. b, Supply and mail ship, "Progress." c, Postmark of space station Mir. d, Buran shuttle, Mir in space.
$6, Space station Mir.

1999, May 24			Perf. 14
2878	A439	$2 Sheet of 4, #a.-d.	8.75 8.75

Souvenir Sheet

2879	A439	$6 multicolored	7.00 7.00

Queen Mother, 100th Birthday (in 2000) — A440

A440a

Gold Frames

No. 2880: a, Queen Mother, Prince Charles, 1948. b, Queen Mother, 1970. c, Queen Mother in Australia, 1958. d, Queen Mother.
$6, Queen Mother, 1953.

1999, Aug. 16

Sheet of 4

2880	A440	$2 #a.-d. + label	8.75 8.75

Souvenir Sheet

2881	A440	$6 multicolored	7.00 7.00

Litho. & Embossed
Die Cut Perf. 8¾
Without Gum

2881A	A440a	$20 gold & multi	20.00

No. 2881 contains one 38x50mm stamp. Margins of sheet are embossed.
See Nos. 3212-3213.

Birth of the Silver Screen A441

Musicians — #2882, each $1: a, George Gershwin, 1929. b, Florence Mills, 1928. c, Sam Beckett, 1925. d, Bessie Smith, 1923. e, Billie Holiday, 1933. f, Bert Williams, 1914. g, Cole Porter, 1934. h, Sophie Tucker, 1915.
Actors — #2883, each $1: a, Lon Chaney, 1930. b, Buster Keaton, 1930. c, Norma Shearer, 1934. d, James Cagney, 1930. e, Hedda Hopper, 1933. f, Jean Harlow, 1931. g, Marlene Dietrich, 1930. h, Ramon Novarro, 1928.
Each $6: No. 2884, Louis Armstrong. No. 2885, Clark Gable, 1932,

1999, Aug. 18

Sheets of 8, #a-h

2882-2883	A441	Set of 2	16.00 16.00

Souvenir Sheets

2884-2885	A441	Set of 2	14.00 14.00

Star Trek A442

Various starships.

1999, July 20		Litho.	Perf. 13¼
2886	A442	$1.50 Sheet of 9, #a.-i.	14.50 14.50

Dinosaurs A443

35c, Ouranosaurus. 45c, Struthiomimus, vert. 75c, Parasaurolophus, vert. $2, Triceratops. $3, Stegoceras. $4, Stegosaurus.
No. 2893, each $1: a, Agathaumus. b, Camarosaurus. c, Quetzalcoatlus. d, Alioramus. e, Camptosaurus. f, Albertosaurus. g, Anatosaurus. h, Spinosaurus. i, Centrosaurus.
No. 2894, each $1: a, Archaeopteryx. b, Brachiosaurus. c, Dilophosaurus. d, Dimetrodon. e, Psittacosaurus. f, Acrocanthosaurus. g, Stenonychosaurus. h, Dryosaurus. i, Compsognathus.
Each $6: No. 2895, Velociraptor, vert. No. 2896, Tyrannosaurus, vert.

1999, Sept. 1		Litho.		Perf. 14
2887-2892	A443	Set of 6		10.00 10.00

Sheets of 9, #a-i

2893-2894	A443	Set of 2	18.00 18.00

Souvenir Sheets

2895-2896	A443	Set of 2	12.50 12.50

Christmas — A444

Candle and: 20c, Rose. 75c, Tulip. 90c, Pear. $1, Hibiscus. $4, Lily.
$6, The Nativity, by Sandro Botticelli.

1999, Dec. 7		Litho.		Perf. 14
2897-2901	A444	Set of 5		6.75 6.75

Souvenir Sheet

2902	A444	$6 multi		7.00 7.00

Flowers A445

Various flowers making up a photomosaic of Princess Diana.

1999, Dec. 31		Litho.	Perf. 13¾
2903	A445	$1 Sheet of 8, #a.-h.	8.00 8.00

See No. 3055.

New Year 2000 (Year of the Dragon) — A446

Inscription color: a, Blue green. b, Red. c, Violet.

2000, Feb. 5			Perf. 12½x12¾
2904	A446	$2 Sheet of 3, #a.-c.	6.75 6.75

No. 2904b has point of triangle down.

Birds
A447

Designs: 75c, Roseate spoonbill. 90c, Scarlet ibis. $1.50, Sparkling violet-ear. $2, Northern jacana.

No. 2909, each $1: a, Blue-headed euphonia. b, Troupial. c, Caribbean parakeet. d, Forest thrush. e, Hooded tanager. f, Stripe-headed tanager. g, Ringed kingfisher. h, Zenaida dove.

No. 2910, each $1: a, Adelaide's warbler. b, Hispaniolan trogon. c, Sun parakeet. d, Black-necked stilt. e, Sora rail. f, Fulvous tree duck. g, Blue-headed parrot. h, Tropical mockingbird.

Each $6: No. 2911, Antillean siskin. No. 2912, Cedar waxwing, vert.

2000, Mar. 1   Litho.   Perf. 14
2905-2908 A447 Set of 4   5.00 5.00
Sheets of 8, #a-h
2909-2910 A447 Set of 2   14.00 14.00
Souvenir Sheets
2911-2912 A447 Set of 2   10.00 10.00

No. 2911 contains one 50x37mm stamp.
No. 2912 contains one 37x50mm stamp.

Mushrooms
A448

Designs: 35c, Clitocybe geotropa. 45c, Psalliota augusta. $1, Amanita rubescens. $4, Boletus satanas.

No. 2917, each $1.50: a, Ungulina marginata. b, Pleurotus ostreatus. c, Flammula penetrans. d, Morchella crassipes. e, Lepiota procera. f, Tricholoma aurantium.

No. 2918, each $1.50: a, Pholiota spectabilis. b, Mycena polygramma. c, Collybia iocephala. d, Corinus cornatus. e, Amanita muscaria. f, Boletus aereus.

Each $6: No. 2919, Lepiota acutes-quamosa. No. 2920, Daedala quercina.

2000, May 1   Perf. 14
2913-2916 A448 Set of 4   6.25 6.25
Sheets of 6, #a-f
2917-2918 A448 Set of 2   17.00 17.00
Souvenir Sheets
2919-2920 A448 Set of 2   12.00 12.00

Paintings of Anthony Van Dyck
A449

No. 2921, each $1: a, Young Woman Resting Her Head on Her Hand. b, Self-portrait. c, Woman Looking Upwards. d, Head of an Old Man, c. 1621. e, Head of a Boy. f, Head of an Old Man, 1616-18.

No. 2922, each $1: a, Charles I on Horseback with Seigneur de St. Antoine. b, St. Martin Dividing His Cloak. c, Giovanni Paolo Balbi on Horseback. d, Marchese Anton Giulio Brignole-Sale on Horseback. e, Study of a Horse. f, An Oriental on Horseback.

No. 2923, each $1.50: a, Portrait of a Man. b, Portrait of a Man Aged Seventy. c, Portrait of a Woman. d, An Elderly Man. e, Portrait of a Young Man. f, Man with a Glove.

No. 2924, each $1.50: a, St. John the Baptist. b, St. Anthony of Padua and the Ass of Rimini. c, The Stoning of St. Stephen. d, The Martyrdom of St. Sebastian. e, St. Sebastian Bound for Martyrdom. f, St. Jerome.

No. 2925, each $1.50: a, Inscribed "Portrait of Anthony Van Dyck," actually a self-portrait of Rubens. b, Inscribed "Self-portrait (after Peter Paul Rubens)." c, Isabella Brant, Wife of Peter Paul Rubens. d, The Penitent Apostle Peter. e, Head of a Robber. f, The Heads of the Apostles, by Rubens.

Each $5: No. 2926, Prince Thomas-Francis of Savoy-Carignan on Horseback. No. 2927, Charles I on Horseback. No. 2928, The Emperor Theodosius Refused Entry in Milan Cathedral, horiz.

Each $6: No. 2929, St. Jerome (in the Wilderness). No. 2930, St. Martin Dividing His Cloak, horiz. No. 2931, Portrait of a Man and His Wife.

2000, May 1   Perf. 13¾
Sheets of 6, #a-f.
2921-2922 A449 Set of 2   10.50 10.50
2923-2925 A449 Set of 3   22.50 22.50
Souvenir Sheets
2926-2928 A449 Set of 3   13.00 13.00
2929-2931 A449 Set of 3   14.50 14.50

Millennium
A450

Highlights of 1650-1700: a, Painter Jan Vermeer dies. b, Birth of microbiology. c, Salem Witch Trials. d, Sir Isaac Newton builds first reflecting telescope. e, Voltaire born. f, Ivan V and Peter become joint rulers of Russia. g, First Qing Dynasty Emperor, Shun Zhi, dies. h, Christiaan Huygens discovers rings of Saturn. i, Robert Hooke identifies cells. j, Wang Shih-min paints "Verdant Peaks." k, René Descartes dies. l, Canal du Midi completed. m, Glorious Revolution. n, King William's War ends. o, Gian Domenico Cassini observes polar caps on Mars. p, Newton formulates law of gravitation (60x40mm). q, Ole Roemer discovers that light moves at a finite speed.

2000, May 1   Perf. 12½
2932 A450 50c Sheet of 17, #a.-
          q., + label   8.75 8.75

Orchids — A451

Designs: 75c, Brassolaeliocattleya. 90c, Maxilbera. $1, Isochilius. $2, Oncidium.

No. 2937, each $1.50: a, Laeliocattleya. b, Sophrocattleya (red). c, Epidendrum. d, Cattleya. e, Ionopsis. f, Brassoepidendrum.

No. 2938, each $1.50: a, Lycaste. b, Cochleanthes. c, Brassocattleya. d, Brassolaeliacattleya, diff. e, Iwanagaara. f, Sophrocattleya (orange).

Each $6: No. 2939, Vanilla. No. 2940, Brassocattleya, diff.

2000, May 15   Litho.   Perf. 14
2933-2936 A451 Set of 4   4.25 4.25
Sheets of 6, #a.-f.
2937-2938 A451 Set of 2   17.00 17.00
Souvenir Sheets
2939-2940 A451 Set of 2   11.00 11.00

100th Test Match at Lord's Ground — A452

90c, Junior Murray. $5, Rawl Lewis.

$6, Lord's Ground, horiz.

2000, May 15   Litho.   Perf. 14
2941-2942 A452 Set of 2   4.75 4.75
Souvenir Sheet
2943 A452 $6 multi   5.25 5.25

Prince William, 18th Birthday — A453

No. 2944: a, In suit. b, In suit, with person in tan suit. c, In suit, waving. d, In ski jacket. $6, In suit, diff.
Illustration reduced.

2000, May 15   Perf. 14
2944 A453 $1.50 Sheet of 4,
          #a-d   4.50 4.50
Souvenir Sheet   Perf. 13¾
2945 A453 $6 multi   4.50 4.50

No. 2944 contains four 28x42mm stamps.

First Zeppelin Flight, Cent. — A454

No. 2946 — Ferdinand von Zeppelin and: a, LZ-130. b, LZ-2. c, LZ-127.
$6, LZ-129.
Illustration reduced.

2000, May 15   Perf. 14
2946 A454 $3 Sheet of 3, #a-c   8.00 8.00
Souvenir Sheet
2947 A454 $6 multi   5.25 5.25

No. 2946 contains three 42x28mm stamps.

Berlin Film Festival, 50th Anniv. — A455

No. 2948: a, Alphaville. b, Rod Steiger. c, Os Fuzis. d, Jean-Pierre Leaud. e, Cul-de-sac. f, Ikiru.
$6, Hsi Yen.
Illustration reduced.

2000, May 15
2948 A455 $1.50 Sheet of 6, #a-f 6.75 6.75
Souvenir Sheet
2949 A455 $6 multi   4.50 4.50

Apollo-Soyuz Mission, 25th Anniv. — A456

No. 2950, vert.: a, Soyuz launch vehicle. b, Soyuz 19. c, Apollo 18 and Soyuz 19 docked. $6, Valeri Kubasov and Thomas Stafford.
Illustration reduced.

2000, May 15
2950 A456 $3 Sheet of 3, #a-c   7.75 7.75
Souvenir Sheet
2951 A456 $6 multi   5.75 5.75

Souvenir Sheets

2000 Summer Olympics, Sydney — A457

No. 2952: a, Archibald Hahn. b, Show jumping. c, Sports Palace, Rome, and Italian flag. d, Ancient Greek chariot racing.
Illustration reduced.

2000, May 15
2952 A457 $2 Sheet of 4, #a-d   7.00 7.00

Public Railways, 175th Anniv. — A458

No. 2953: a, Locomotion No. 1, George Stephenson. b, John Bull.
Illustration reduced.

2000, May 15
2953 A458 $3 Sheet of 2, #a-b   5.75 5.75

Johann Sebastian Bach (1685-1750) — A459

Illustration reduced.

2000, May 15
2954 A459 $6 multi   4.50 4.50

Souvenir Sheet

Albert Einstein (1879-1955) — A460

Illustration reduced.

2000, May 15   Litho.   Perf. 14¼
2955 A460 $6 multi   4.50 4.50

Space — A461

No. 2956: a, Luna 4. b, Clementine. c, Luna 12. d, Luna 16. e, Apollo 11 Lunar module. f, Ranger 7.
$6, Apollo command and service modules.
Illustration reduced.

2000, May 15   Litho.   Perf. 14
2956 A461 $1.50 Sheet of 6, #a-f 7.75 7.75

Souvenir Sheet
2957 A461 $6 multi   5.25 5.25

World Stamp Expo 2000, Anaheim

Marine Life A462

Designs: 45c, Porkfish. 75c, Short bigeye. 90c, Red snapper. $1, Creole wrasse. $2, Indigo hamlet. $3, Blue tang.
No. 2964: a, Juvenile French angelfish. b, Beaugregory. c, Queen angelfish. d, Sergeant major. e, Bank butterflyfish. f, Spanish hogfish. g, Porkfish. h, Banded butterflyfish. i, Longsnout seahorse.
No. 2965: a, Hawksbill turtle. b, Foureye butterflyfish. c, Porcupinefish. d, Yellowtail damselfish. e, Adult French angelfish. f, Yellow goatfish. g, Blue-striped grunt. h, Spanish grunt. i, Queen triggerfish.
No. 2966, Queen angelfish. No. 2967, Blue tang.

2000, Aug. 8
2958-2963 A462   Set of 5   7.00 7.00
Sheets of 9, #a-i
2964-2965 A462 $1 Set of 2   14.50 14.50
Souvenir Sheets
2966-2967 A462 $6 Set of 2   9.00 9.00

Grenada National Stadium A463

Designs: $2, Aerial view.
No. 2969: a, Cricket team photo. b, Cricketers playing.

2000, Aug. 8
2968 A463 $2 multi   1.50 1.50
Souvenir Sheet
2969 A463 $1 Sheet of 2, #a-b 1.50 1.50

European Soccer Championships — A464

No. 2970, horiz. — Belgium: a, Vanderhaege. b, Belgian team. c, Ronny Gaspercic. d, Lorenzo Staelens. e, Stadium Koning Boudewijn. f, Strupar and Mpenza.
No. 2971, horiz. — Spain: a, Sergi Barjuan. b, Spanish team. c, Luis Enrique. d, Hierro. e, De Kuip Stadium. f, Raul Gonzales.
No. 2972, horiz. — Yugoslavia: a, Dejan Savicevic. b, Yugoslavian team. c, Predrag Migatovic. d, Savo Milosevic. e, Jan Breydel Stadium. f, Darko Kovacevic.
No. 2973, Belgian coach Robert Waseige. No. 2974, Spanish coach José Antonio Camacho. No. 2975, Yugoslavian coach Vujadin Boskov.
Illustration reduced.

2000, Aug. 8   Perf. 13¾
Sheets of 6, #a-f
2970-2972 A464 $1.50 Set of 3   20.00 20.00
Souvenir Sheets
2973-2975 A464 $6 Set of 3   13.50 13.50

Ferrari Automobiles — A465

20c, 1953 500 Mondial. 45c, 1948 166 Inter. 75c, 1953 340 MM. 90c, 1964 500 Superfast. $1, 1948 166 MM. $1.50, 1952 250 S. $2, 1957 250 California. $3, 1966 365 California.

2000, Sept. 5   Perf. 14
2976-2983 A465   Set of 8   8.00 8.00

Antique Automobiles A466

45c, 1921 Marmon Model 34. 75c, 1917 Buick D44. 90c, 1918 Hudson Runabout Landau. $1, 1915 Chevrolet Royal Mail. $2, 1925 Kissel Speedster. $3, 1915 Ford Model T.
No. 2990: a, 1925 Cadillac V63. b, 1939 Plymouth. c, 1934 Franklin Club Sedan. d, 1933 Fiat Ardita. e, 1929 Essex Speedabout. f, 1932 Stutz Bearcat.
No. 2991: a, 1929 Rolls Royce. b, 1932 Graham Convertible. c, 1937 Mercedes-Benz 540K. d, 1948 Jaguar MkV. e, 1939 Lagonda Drophead Coupe. f, 1930 Alfa Romeo Gran Sport.
No. 2992, 1915 Dodge Tourer. No. 2993, 1924 Chrysler.

2000, Sept. 5
2984-2989 A466   Set of 6   6.00 6.00
Sheets of 6, #a-f
2990-2991 A466 $1.50 Set of 2   13.50 13.50
Souvenir Sheets
2992-2993 A466 $6 Set of 2   9.00 9.00

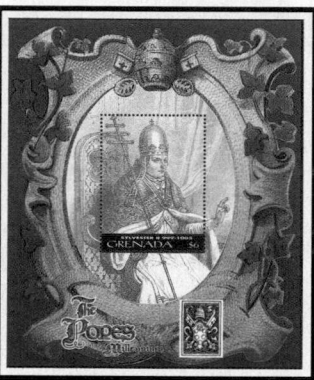

Popes — A467

No. 2994: a, Stephen VIII, 939-42. b, Theodore I, 642-49. c, Theodore II, 897. d, Valentine, 827. e, Vitalian, 657-72. f, Zacharias, 741-52.
$6, Sylvester II, 999-1003.

2000, Sept. 5   Perf. 13¾
2994 A467 $1.50 Sheet of 6, #a-f 6.75 6.75
Souvenir Sheet
2995 A467 $6 multi   4.50 4.50

Monarchs — A468

No. 2996: a, George III of Great Britain, 1760-1820. b, George IV of Great Britain, 1820-30. c, Duchess Charlotte of Luxembourg, 1964-present. d, Grand Duke Jean of Luxembourg, 1964-present.
$6, Charles VIII of France, 1483-98.

2000, Sept. 5   Perf. 13¾
2996 A468 $1.50 Sheet of 4, #a-d 4.50 4.50
Souvenir Sheet
2997 A468 $6 multi   4.50 4.50

Shirley Temple in "Heidi" — A469

No. 2998, horiz.: a, With woman holding candle. b, With girl in green dress c, On stairs. d, With Christmas gift.
No. 2999, horiz.: a, Walking with woman. b, Touching bearded man. c, Holding goat. d, With doves. e, With bearded man. f, Seated with woman.
Illustration reduced.

2000, Oct. 6   Litho.   Perf. 13¾
2998 A469 $1.50 Sheet of 4, #a-d 4.50 4.50
2999 A469 $1.50 Sheet of 6, #a-f 6.75 6.75
Souvenir Sheet
3000 A469 $6 Seated near tree   4.50 4.50

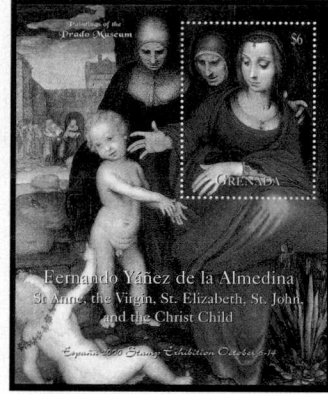

Paintings from the Prado — A470

#3001: a, Monk and king from The Virgin of the Catholic Monarchs, by an Anonymous Castilian. b, Madonna and child from The Virgin of the Catholic Monarchs. c, Monk and queen from The Virgin of the Catholic Monarchs. d, The Flagellation, by Alexo Fernandez. e, The Virgin and Souls in Purgatory, by Pedro Machuca. f, The Holy Trinity, by El Greco.
#3002: a, Playing at Giants, by El Greco. b, The Holy Family Under the Oak Tree, by Raphael. c, Don Gaspar Melchior de Jovellanos, by Francisco de Goya. d, Man with arm on hip from Joseph in the Pharaoh's Palace, by Jacopo Amiconi. e, Man and woman from Joseph in the Pharaoh's Palace. f, Man on bended knee from Joseph in the Pharaoh's Palace.
#3003: a, The Savior Blessing, by Francisco de Zurbarán. b, St. John the Baptist, by Francisco Solimena. c, Noli Me Tangere, by Correggio. d, St. Casilda, by Zurbarán. e, Nicolás Omazur by Bartolomé Esteban Murillo. f, Juan Martínez Montañés, by Diego Velázquez.
#3004, St. Anne, the Virgin, St. Elizabeth, St. John and the Christ child, by Fernando Yáñez de la Almedina. #3005, The Virgin of the Catholic Monarchs. #3006, Joseph in the Pharaoh's Palace, horiz.
Illustration reduced.

2000, Oct. 19   Perf. 12x12¼, 12¼x12
Sheets of 6, #a-f
3001-3003 A470 $1.50 Set of 3   20.00 20.00
Souvenir Sheets
3004-3006 A470 $6 Set of 3   13.50 13.50

Espana 2000 Intl. Philatelic Exhibition.

Battle of Britain, 60th Anniv. — A471

No. 3007: a, Messerschmitt BF 109E and bomb blast. b, Supermarine Spitfire MK XI. c, V1 flying bomb. d, U-boat. e, Ack-ack gun unit. f, Bedford field ambulance.
No. 3008: a, Messerschmitt BF 109E. b, German paratrooper. c, Hawker Hurricane HK 1. d, RAF airfield. e, Heinkel HE 111 H. f, Nose of Supermarine Spitfire MK XI.
No. 3009, Line of Hawker Hurricanes. No. 3010, Supermarine Spitfire MK XI.
Illustration reduced.

2000, Oct. 30   *Perf. 14*
Sheets of 6, #a-f
3007-3008 A471 $1.50 Set of 2   16.00 16.00
Souvenir Sheets
3009-3010 A471 $6 Set of 2   12.00 12.00

A472   A473

Birds: 25c, Purple gallinule. 40c, Limpkin. 50c, Black-necked stilt. 60c, Painted bunting. 75c, Yellow-breasted warbler. $1, Blackburnian warbler. $1.25, Blue grosbeak. $1.50, Black-and-white warbler. $1.60, Blue whistling thrush. $3, Common yellowthroat. $4, Indigo bunting. $5, Gray catbird. $10, Bananaquit. $20, Blue-gray gnatcatcher.

2000, Oct. 30   *Perf. 14¾x14*
3011-3024 A472 Set of 14   37.50 37.50

2000, June 23   Litho.   *Perf. 14*

Dogs: $2, Shetland sheepdog. $3, Central Asian sheepdog.
No. 3027, horiz.: a, Labrador retriever. b, Standard poodle. c, Boxer. d, Rough-coated Jack Russell terrier. e, Tibetan terrier. f, Welsh corgi.
$6, Irish red and white setter, horiz.
3025-3026 A473 Set of 2   3.75 3.75
3027 A473 $1.50 Sheet of 6, #a-f   6.75 6.75
Souvenir Sheet
3028 A473 $6 multi   4.50 4.50

Butterflies A474

45c, Marpesia eleuchea bahamaensis. 75c, Pterourus palamedes. 90c, Dryas julia framptoni. $1, Hypna clytemnestra iphegenia.
No. 3033, $1.50: a, Danaus plexippus. b, Anartia amathea. c, Colobura dirce. d, Parides gundiachianus. e, Spiroeta stelenes. f, Hammadryas feronia.
No. 3034, $1.50: a, Merchantis isthmia. b, Colias eurytheme. c, Papilio troilus d, Junonia coenia. e, Doxocopa laure. f, Pierella hyalinus.
No. 3035, $6, Agraulis vanilae insularis. No. 3036, $6, Danaus gilippus.

2000, June 26
3029-3032 A474 Set of 4   3.00 3.00
Sheets of 6, #a-f
3033-3034 A474 Set of 2   17.00 17.00
Souvenir Sheets
3035-3036 A474 Set of 2   10.00 10.00

Trains — A476

No. 3037, $1.50: a, Diesel-electric locomotive, Royal State Railway of Thailand. b, Diesel-electric locomotive, Danish Railways. c, French-built Turbo train. d, Diesel, Spanish Railways. e, Virgen del Rosario, Spanish Railways. f, 22 Class Co-Co Diesel-electric locomotive, Malayan Railways.
No. 3038, $1.50: a, Class 87 electric locomotive, British Railways. b, Electric-Diesel locomotive, Iraqi Railway. c, Electric locomotive, Austrian Railway. d, 1.4 meter gauge locomotive, South Australia Railways. e, Automated electric locomotive, Black Mesa & Lake Powell Railroad. f, Diesel-electric, Yugoslav Railways.
No. 3039, $1.50: a, Class 10 4-6-2, German Federal Railway. b, Class E.10 Bo-Bo Electric locomotive, German Federal Railways. c, Class 23 2-6-2, German Federal Railway. d, 2-8-4 locomotive, German Federal Railway. e, Rebuilt 01 Class Pacific, East German State Railway. f, High speed Diesel railcar, Deutschen Reichsbahn.
No. 3040, $1.50: a, Borsig Standard 2-2-2. b, Austerity 2-10-0 Series 52, German Federal Railway. c, Adler, facing right, Nuremburg-Furth Railway. d, Bardenia, Baden State Railways. e, Drache. f, Adler, facing left.
No. 3041, $6, Diesel T.E.E. Parsifal. No. 3042, $6, High speed electric, Netherlands Railway. No. 3043, $6, Electric train, Swiss Railways. No. 3044, $6, Silver Fern, New Zealand Railways. No. 3045, $6, Borsig locomotive, Berlin and Anhalt Railway. No. 3046, $6, Krauss-Maffei V.200 Diesel-hydraulic locomotive, German Federal Railway.
Illustrations reduced.

2000, Sept. 5
Sheets of 6, #a-f
3037-3038 A475 Set of 2   15.00 15.00
3039-3040 A476 Set of 2   15.00 15.00
Souvenir Sheets
3041-3044 A475 Set of 4   21.00 21.00
3045-3046 A476 Set of 2   11.00 11.00

Descriptions of trains are in margins on Nos. 3039-3940, 3045-3046.

Nursery Rhymes — A477

No. 3047, Little Bo Peep, $1.50, vert.: a, Crook, tree, dove. b, Little Bo Peep. c, Sheep. d, Geese. e, Goose, Little Bo Peep's leg. f, Dog.
No. 3048, The Old Woman Who Lived in a Shoe, $1.50, vert.: a, Child, roof. b, Child with hat, rainbow. c, Cow, sun, rainbow. d, Child at door. e, Old woman, child. f, Child on shoe.
No. 3049, Little Boy Blue, $1.50, vert.: a, Sheep, house. b, Sun. c, Cow. d, Geese, path. e, Dog, Little Boy Blue's leg. f, Little Boy Blue.
No. 3050, The Cat and the Fiddle, $1.50, vert. a, Bird, house. b, Cow jumping over moon. c, Spoon. d, Dog, house. e, Cat and fiddle. f, Dish.
No. 3051, $6, Little Bo Peep. No. 3052, $6, The Old Woman Who Lived in a Shoe. No. 3053, $6, Little Boy Blue. No. 3054, Cow jumping over the moon.
Illustration reduced.

2000, Sept. 9   *Perf. 13¾x13¼*
Sheets of 6, #a-f
3047-3050 A477 Set of 4   27.50 27.50
Souvenir Sheets
Perf. 13¼x13¾
3051-3054 A477 Set of 4   18.00 18.00

Flower Photomosaic Type of 1999
Queen Mother

Various flowers making up photomosaic.

2000, Nov. 20   *Perf. 13¾*
3055 A445 $1 Sheet of 8, #a-h   6.00 6.00

Cats — A478

75c, Maine Coon cat. 90c, Selkirk Rex.
No. 3058, horiz.: a, Spotted tabby British shorthair. b, Burmilla. c, British blue shorthair. d, Siamese. e, Japanese bobtail. f, Oriental shorthair.

2000, June 23   Litho.   *Perf. 14*
3056-3057 A478 Set of 2   1.75 1.75
3058 A478 $1.50 Sheet of 6, #a-f   8.00 8.00
Souvenir Sheet
3059 A478 $6 Scottish Fold   5.75 5.75

Queen Mother, 100th Birthday — A479

2000, Nov. 20
3060 A479 $1.50 multi   1.10 1.10
Printed in sheets of 6.

Christmas — A480

Designs: 15c, 50c, No. 3065b, Angel looking left. 25c, $5, No. 3065a, Angel looking right.

2000, Dec. 4
3061-3064 A480 Set of 4   4.50 4.50
3065 A480 $2 Sheet, 2 ea #a-b   6.00 6.00
Souvenir Sheet
3066 A480 $6 Baby Jesus   4.50 4.50

Souvenir Sheets

Betty Boop — A481

Designs: No. 3067, $6, Wearing lei. No. 3068, $6, Holding fishing pole and fish. No. 3069, $6, Wearing polka dot hat. No. 3070, $6, Holding castanets. No. 3071, $6, At Japanese tea ceremony. No. 3072, $6, Wearing pink hat. No. 3073, $6, In mountains, wearing flowered hat. No. 3074, $6, Wearing beret. No. 3075, $6, As Statue of Liberty. No. 3076, $6, In Hollywood. No. 3077, $6, On horse. No. 3078, $6, On camel's back.
Illustration reduced.

2000, Oct. 11   Litho.   *Perf. 13¾*
3067-3078 A481 Set of 12   60.00 60.00

Souvenir Sheet

New Year 2001 (Year of the Snake) — A482

No. 3079: a, Blue green denomination. b, Red denomination. c, Purple denomination.
Illustration reduced.

2001, Jan. 2   *Perf. 12½x13*
3079 A482 $2 Sheet of 3, #a-c   4.50 4.50

Rijksmuseum, Amsterdam, Bicent. — A483

No. 3080, $1.50: a, William I, Prince of Orange, by Adriaen Thomasz Key. b, Rutger Jan Schimmelpennick and Family, by Pierre Paul Prud'hon. c, Johan Rudolf Thorbecke, by Johan Heinrich Neuman. d, St. Sebastian, by Joachim Wtewael. e, St. Sebastian, by Hendrick ter Brugghen. f, Portrait of a Man With a Ring, by Werner Van Den Valckert.
No. 3081, $1.50: a, The Syndics of the Amsterdam Goldsmith's Guild, by Thomas de Keyser. b, Portrait of a Gentleman, by de Keyser. c, Portrait of Eva Wtewael, by Wtewael. d, The Cattle Ferry, by Esaias van de Velde. e, Landscape With the Parable of the Tares Among the Wheat, by Abraham Bloemaert. f, Princess Henrietta Marie Stuart, by Bartholomeus van der Helst.
No. 3082, $1.50: a, The Merry Fiddler, by Gerard van Honthorst. b, The Merry Drinker, by Frans Hals. c, Granida and Daifilo, by van Honthorst. d, Vertumnus and Pomona, by Paulus Moreelse. e, Flutist from The Concert, by ter Brugghen. f, A Young Student at His Desk: Melancholy, by Pieter Codde.
No. 3083, $1.50: a, The Haarlem Painter Abraham Casteleyn and His Wife Margarieta van Bancken, by Jan de Bray. b, Two figures from The Concert. c, The Procuress, by Dirck van Baburen. d, Woman Seated at a Virginal, by Johannes Vermeer. e, Dignified Couples Courting, by Willem Buytewech. f, The Young Flute Player, by Judith Leyster.
No. 3084, $6, Interior of the Portuguese Synagogue in Amsterdam, by Emanuel de Witte. No. 3085, $6, The Denial of St. Peter, by Rembrandt, horiz. No. 3086, $6, Winter Landscape With Skaters, by Hendrick Avercamp, horiz. No. 3087, $6, The Raampoortje, by Wouter Johannes van Troostwijk, horiz.
Illustration reduced.

2001, Jan. 15   *Perf. 13¾*
Sheets of 6, #a-f
3080-3083 A483 Set of 4   27.50 27.50
Souvenir Sheets
3084-3087 A483 Set of 4   18.00 18.00

Pokémon — A484

No. 3088: a, Rattata. b, Sandshrew. c, Wartortle. d, Primeape. e, Golduck. f, Persian. Illustration reduced.

2001, Feb. 1
3088 A484 $1.50 Sheet of 6, #a-f 6.75 6.75
Souvenir Sheet
3089 A484 $6 Jolteon 4.50 4.50

Waterfowl — A485

No. 3090, $1.25: a, African pygmy goose. b, Silver teal. c, Marbled teal. d, Garganey. e, Wandering whistling duck. f, Northern shoveler.
No. 3091, $1.25: a, Female flightless steamer duck. b, Radjah. c, Cape teal. d, Hartlaub's duck. e, Ruddy shelduck. f, White-cheeked pintail.
No. 3092, $1.25, vert.: a, Fulvous whistling duck. b, African black duck. c, Madagascar white-eye. d, Female pygmy goose. e, Female wood duck. f, Male wood duck.
No. 3093, $6, Flightless steamer duck. No. 3094, $6, Female pygmy goose. No. 3095, $6, Australian shelduck, vert.

Perf. 13¼x13¾, 13¾x13¼
2001, Mar. 5 **Litho.**
Sheets of 6, #a-f
3090-3092 A485 Set of 3 17.00 17.00
Souvenir Sheets
3093-3095 A485 Set of 3 13.50 13.50
Hong Kong 2001 Stamp Exhibition.

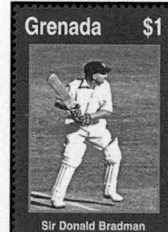

Cricket
Players — A486

No. 3096: Various photos of Sir Donald Bradman swinging bat.
No. 3097, Various photos of Shane Warne bowling.
No. 3098, Various photos of Sir Jack Hobbs.
No. 3099, Various photos of Sir Vivian Richards.
No. 3100, Various photos of Sir Garfield Sobers.
No. 3101, oval vignettes: a, Bradman. b, Sobers. c, Hobbs. d, Warne. e, Richards.

2001, May 15 **Perf. 14**
3096 Sheet of 8, #a-h 6.00 6.00
a.-h. A486 $1 Any single .75 .75
3097 Sheet of 8, #a-h 6.00 6.00
a.-h. A486 $1 Any single .75 .75
3098 Sheet of 4, #a-d 6.00 6.00
a.-d. A486 $2 Any single 1.50 1.50
3099 Sheet of 4, #a-d 6.00 6.00
a.-d. A486 $2 Any single 1.50 1.50
3100 Sheet of 4, #a-d 6.00 6.00
a.-d. A486 $2 Any single 1.50 1.50
3101 Sheet of 5, #a-e 7.50 7.50
a.-e. A486 $2 Any single 1.50 1.50
Nos. 3096-3101 (6) 37.50 37.50

A487

Phila Nippon '01, Japan — A488

Art: 75c, Scenes of Daily Life in Edo, by Miyagawa Choshun. 90c, Twelve Famous Places in Japan, by Kano Isenin Naganobu. $1, After the Rain, by Kawai Gyokudo. $1.25, Ryogoku Bridge Crowded With People, by Kano Kyuei. No. 3106, $2, A Courtesan of Fukagawa, by Katsukawa Shunei. $3, Rite of Bear Killing, by unknown artist.
No. 3108 — Details from the Lotus Sutra, $2, vert.: a, Figure in white at left. b, Figure with flag at lower right. c, Water in center. d, White pagoda at top right.
No. 3109 — Details from the Tale of Genji, $2 (size: 84x28mm): a, Yugao Chapter. b, Suetsumuhana Chapter. c, Wakamurasaki Chapter. d, Momiji-no-ga Chapter.
No. 3110, $6, Pomegranates and a Small Bird, by Onishi Keisai. No. 3111, $6, Bodhisattva from the Lotus Sutra, vert.

2001, May 1 **Litho.** **Perf. 14**
3102-3107 A487 Set of 6 6.75 6.75
Sheets of 4, #a-d
3108-3109 A488 Set of 2 12.00 12.00
Souvenir Sheets
3110-3111 A488 Set of 2 9.00 9.00

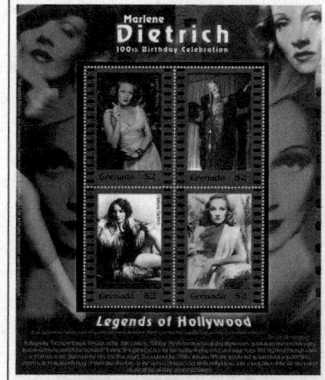

Marlene Dietrich — A489

No. 3112: a, With cigarette. b, Behind microphone. c, Seated, showing legs. d, Seated.

2001, May 15 **Perf. 13¾**
3112 A489 $2 Sheet of 4, #a-d 6.00 6.00

Queen Victoria (1819-1901) — A490

No. 3113: a, In white, as young girl. b, Wearing crown as young woman. c, Wearing crown as old woman.
$6, On throne.

2001, May 15 **Perf. 14**
3113 A490 $3 Sheet of 3, #a-c 6.75 6.75
Souvenir Sheet
3114 A490 $6 multi 4.50 4.50

Queen Elizabeth II, 75th
Birthday — A491

No. 3115: a, Straw hat. b, Red hat. c, Flowered hat. d, Blue hat.
$6, Blue hat with brim.

2001, May 15 **Perf. 14**
3115 A491 $2 Sheet of 4, #a-d 6.00 6.00
Souvenir Sheet
Perf. 13¾
3116 A491 $6 multi 4.50 4.50
No. 3116 contains one 38x51mm stamp.

UN Women's
Human Rights
Campaign — A492

Designs: 90c, Woman, bird, torch. $1, Woman.

2001, May 15 **Litho.** **Perf. 14**
3117-3118 A492 Set of 2 1.40 1.40

Mao Zedong (1893-1976) — A493

No. 3119 — background colors: a, Deep purple. b, Pinkish gray. c, Mottled red violet. $6, Mao with cap.

2001, May 15 **Perf. 13¾**
3119 A493 $2 Sheet of 3, #a-c 4.50 4.50
Souvenir Sheet
3120 A493 $3 multi 2.25 2.25

Giuseppe Verdi (1813-1910), Opera
Composer — A494

No. 3121: a, Actor with crown. b, Score from Ernani. c, Verdi. d, La Scala Theater, Milan. $6, Verdi with hat.

2001, May 15 **Perf. 14**
3121 A494 $2 Sheet of 4, #a-d 6.00 6.00
Souvenir Sheet
3122 A494 $6 multi 4.50 4.50

Toulouse-Lautrec Paintings — A495

No. 3123: a, Alone. b, Two Half-naked Women. c, The Toilette. d, Justine Dieuhl. $6, Mademoiselle Dihau at the Piano.

2001, May 15 **Perf. 13¾**
3123 A495 $2 Sheet of 4, #a-d 6.00 6.00
Souvenir Sheet
3124 A495 $6 multi 4.50 4.50

A496

Ships — A497

Designs: 45c, Phoenician trading ship. 75c, Portuguese caravel. 90c, Marblehead schooner. No. 3128, Mala pansi. $1.50, US corvette. $2, Racing schooner.

No. 3131, $1: a, English carrack. b, Mediterranean carrack. c, Spanish galleon. d, Elizabeth Grumster. e, British East Indiaman. f, Clipper ship. g, British gunship. h, British flagship. i, English hoy.

No. 3132, $1: a, English cog. b, Roman merchantman. c, Greek war galley. d, Greek merchantman. e, Norse Oseberg ship. f, Egyptian sailboat. g, Egyptian oared ship. h, 16th cent. galleass. i, Norman sailing ship.

No. 3133, $1: a, Gloucester fishing schooner. b, Racing sloop. c, Chinese junk. d, Sambuk. e, Baltimore clipper schooner. f, Schooner yacht. g, US Clipper ship. h, US frigate. i Steam naval packet.

No. 3134, $6, Gulf Streamer. No. 3135, $6, Suhaili.

Illustration A497 reduced.

2001, June 18   **Perf. 14**
3125-3130	A496	Set of 6	5.00	5.00

Sheets of 9, #a-i
3131-3133	A496	Set of 3	21.00	21.00

Miniature Sheets
3134-3135	A497	Set of 2	9.00	9.00

Belgica 2001 Intl. Stamp Exhibition, Brussels (Nos. 3131-3133).

A498

Flowers
A499

Designs: 25c, Brassavola nodosa. No. 3137, $1, Allamanda cathartica. No. 3138, $2, Aspasia epidendroides. $3, Oncidium splendidum.

35c, Flor de San Miguel. 75c, Red frangipani. No. 3142, $1, Paper flower. No. 3143, $2, Flor de muerto.

No. 3144, $1.50: a, Candlebush. b, Flamingo flower. c, Bush morning glory. d, Laelia anceps. e, Galeandra baueri. f, Chinese hibiscus.

No. 3145, $1.50: a, Red ginger. b, Bird of paradise. c, Psychlis atropurpurea. d, Cattleya velutina. e, Caularthron bicornutum. f, Cattleya warneri.

No. 3146, $1.50, vert.: a, Mandeville. b, Tithonia rotundifolia. c, June rose. d, Columnea argentea. e, Chameleon plant. f, Protlandia albiflora.

No. 3147, $1.50, vert.: a, Wild chestnut. b, Jatropha integerrima. c, Fern tree. d, Geiger tree. e, Golden trumpet. f, Saman.

No. 3148, $6, Ipomoea learii, horiz. No. 3149, $6, Anthurium scherzerianum, horiz.

No. 3150, $6, Ladies eardrops. No. 3151, $6, Heliconia psittacorum, vert.

2001
3136-3139	A498	Set of 4	6.25	6.25
3140-3143	A499	Set of 4	4.75	4.75

Sheets of 6, #a-f
3144-3145	A498	Set of 2	15.00	15.00
3146-3147	A499	Set of 2	15.00	15.00

Souvenir Sheets
3148-3149	A498	Set of 2	11.00	11.00
3150-3151	A499	Set of 2	11.00	11.00

Kane — A500

No. 3152 — Kane: a, In air, above ring ropes. b, On one knee. c, In air. d, With red background. e, With gradiated gray and yellow background. f, Holding up opponent with both hands. g, With spotlight background. h, Holding up shirtless opponent. i, Holding up opponent with one hand.

No. 3153, $5, With red background, diff. No. 3154, $5, With opponent.

2001   **Perf. 13¾**
3152	A500	$1 Sheet of 9, #a-i	6.75	6.75

Souvenir Sheets
3153-3154	A500	Set of 2	7.50	7.50

The Three Stooges — A501

No. 3155, $1: a, Larry, Moe, two cowboys. b, Moe and Shemp with hats, Larry. c, Shemp and Larry in drag, Moe with mustache. d, Moe with gun, Larry, Shemp, woman. e, Larry, Moe, Shemp with certificate. f, Shemp, Moe. g, Larry, picture. h, Moe, picture. i, Shemp.

No. 3156, $1: a, Larry, Curly, Moe with tool. b, Joe DeRita eating hay, horse, Larry, Moe. c, Shemp, Larry with flowers, Moe. d, Moe, Shemp, Larry, reading paper. e, Larry, Moe, Shemp with pots. f, Moe, Shemp, Larry with money. g, Shemp with knight. h, Joe DeRita, horse, Moe, Larry. i, Larry with knight.

No. 3157, $5, Larry, Moe, Shemp, woman from movie poster. No. 3158, $5, Shemp pulling Moe's arm. No. 3159, $5, Joe DeRita and Larry. No. 3160, $5, Larry and Joe DeRita, jet engine. No. 3161, $5, Moe, Larry holding woman's hand. No. 3162, $5, Larry, Moe listening to jet engine, horiz. No. 3163, $5, Larry, Moe, Shemp and cowboy, horiz. No. 3164, $5, Shemp behind bar, cowboys fighting Larry and Moe, horiz. No. 3165, $5, Curly, Moe, Larry

and propeller, horiz. No. 3166, $5, Moe, Larry, woman with drink, horiz. No. 3167, $6, Moe, Larry with knight, horiz. No. 3168, $6, Curly in wringer, Moe, horiz.

2001

Sheets of 9, #a-i
3155-3156	A501	Set of 2	13.50	13.50

Souvenir Sheets
3157-3168	A501	Set of 12	47.50	47.50

Lighthouses
A502

Designs: 25c, Montauk Point, NY. 50c, Alcatraz, CA. $1, Barnegat, NJ. $2, St. Augustine, FL.

No. 3173, $1.50: a, Admiralty Head, WA. b, Hooper's Strait, MD. c, Hunting Island, SC. d, Key West Lighthouse Museum, FL. e, Old Point Loma, CA. f, Old Mackinac Moint, MI.

No. 3174, $1.50: a, Point Amour, Canada. b, Inubo-Saki, Japan. c, Belle-Ile. France. d, Faerder, Norway. e, Cape Agulhas, South Africa. f, Minicoy, India.

No. 3175, $1.50: a, Keri, Estonia. b, Anholt, Denmark. c, Porer, Croatia. d, Laotieshan, China. e, Sapientza Methoni, Greece. f, Arkona, Germany.

No. 3176, $6, Boston, MA. No. 3177, $6, Pellworm, Germany. No. 3178, $6, Kvitsoy, Norway. No. 3179, Mahota Pagoda, China.

2001, Aug. 27   **Litho.**   **Perf. 14**
3169-3172	A502	Set of 4	2.75	2.75

Sheets of 6, #a-f
3173-3175	A502	Set of 3	20.00	20.00

Souvenir Sheets
3176-3179	A502	Set of 4	18.00	18.00

Marine
Mammals
A503

Designs: 25c, Commerson's dolphin. 50c, Pacific white-sided dolphin. $2, Northern bottlenosed whale. $3, Baird's beaked whale.

No. 3184, $1.50: a, Risso's dolphin. b, Fraser's dolphin. c, Dall's porpoise. d, Right whale. e, Gray whale. f, Minke whale.

No. 3185, $1.50: a, Common dolphin. b, Antillean beaked whale. c, Killer whale. d, Bryde's whale. e, Cuvier's beaked whale. f, Sei whale.

No. 3186, $1.50: a, Harbor porpoise. b, Beluga. c, White-beaked dolphin. d, Narwhal. e, Bowhead whale. f, Fin whale.

No. 3187, $6, Sperm whale. No. 3188, $6, Blue whale. No. 3189, $6, Southern right whale. No. 3190, $6, Humpback whale.

2001, Sept. 10
3180-3183	A503	Set of 4	4.25	4.25

Sheets of 6, #a-f
3184-3186	A503	Set of 3	20.00	20.00

Souvenir Sheets
3187-3190	A503	Set of 4	18.00	18.00

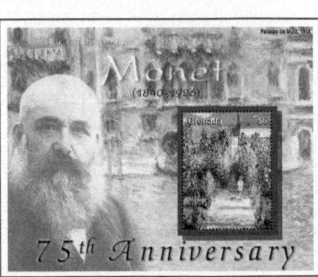

Monet Paintings — A504

No. 3191, horiz.: a, Boats in Winter Quarters, Etretat. b, Regatta at Sainte Adresse. c, The Bridge at Bougival. d, The Beach at Sainte Adresse.

$6, Monet's Garden at Vétheuil.

2002 World Cup Soccer Championships, Japan and Korea — A505

No. 3193, $1.50: a, Poster, 1950. b, West German championship team, 1954. c, Just Fontaine, 1958. d, Garrincha, Brazil, 1962. e, Bobby Moore, England, 1966. f, Pelé, Brazil, 1970.

No. 3194, $1.50: a, Osvaldo Ardiles, Argentina, 1978. b, Lakhdar Belloumi, Algeria, 1982. c, Diego Maradona, Argentina, 1986. d, Matthaüs and Völler, West Germany, 1990. e, Seo Jung Won, South Korea, 1994. f, Ronaldo, Brazil, 1998.

No. 3195, $6, Face from Jules Rimet trophy. No. 3196, $6, Face and globe from World Cup trophy.

2001, May 15   **Litho.**   **Perf. 13¾**
3191	A504	$2 Sheet of 4, #a-d	6.00	6.00

Souvenir Sheet
3192	A504	$6 multi	4.50	4.50

2001, Nov. 29   **Perf. 13¾x14¼**

Sheets of 6, #a-f
3193-3194	A505	Set of 2	13.50	13.50

Souvenir Sheet
3195-3196	A505	Set of 2	9.00	9.00

Christmas
A506

Santa Claus and: 15c, House, Christmas tree. 50c, Trees, snowman. $1, Tree, ice skates. $4, Children.

$6, Santa eating cookie.

2001, Dec. 3   **Perf. 14**
3197-3200	A506	Set of 4	4.25	4.25

Souvneir Sheet
3201	A506	$6 multi	4.50	4.50

A507

Nobel Prizes, Cent. — A508

1901 Laureates: 75c, Emil A. von Behring, Medicine. 90c, Wilhelm C. Röntgen, Physics. $1, Jacobus H. van't Hoff, Chemistry. No. 3205, $1.50, Frederic Passy, Peace. $2, Jean-Henri Dunant, Peace. $3, René Sully-Prudhomme, Literature.

No. 3208, horiz. — Albert Einstein, 1921 Physics laureate, with: a, Dark hair, black suit. b, Pipe. c, Gray suit. d, Pink sweater. e, Gray hair, black suit. f, Blue sweater.

$6, Einstein wearing hat.

2001, Dec. 13
3202-3207	A507	Set of 6	7.00	7.00
3208	A508	$1.50 Sheet of 6, #a-f	6.75	6.75

Souvenir Sheet
3209	A508	$6 multi	4.50	4.50

Princess Diana (1961-97) — A509

No. 3210: a, Blue gown. b. White gown. c, Red gown.
$6, With pink curtain.

2001, Dec. 13
3210	A509	$1.50 Sheet, 2 each #a-c	6.75	6.75

Souvenir Sheet
3211	A509	$6 multi	4.50	4.50

Queen Mother Type of 1999

No. 3212: a, Queen Mother, Prince Charles, 1948. b, Queen Mother, 1970. c, Queen Mother in Australia, 1958. d, Queen Mother.
$6, Queen Mother, 1953.

2001, Dec. 13   *Perf. 14*
Yellow Orange Frames
3212	A440	$2 Sheet of 4, #a-d, + label	6.00	6.00

Souvenir Sheet   *Perf. 13¾*
3213	A440	$6 multi	4.50	4.50

Queen Mother's 101st birthday. No. 3213 contains one 38x50mm stamp with a redder backdrop than that found on No. 2881. Sheet margins of Nos. 3212-3213 lack embossing and gold arms found on Nos. 2880-2881.

New Year 2002 (Year of the Horse) — A510

Ceramic horses of T'ang dynasty — No. 3214: a, Brown horse with long, tan mane. b, Blue horse with pink hooves. c, Black horse with gray mane. d, Tan horse with round ornaments.
$4, Brown horse with gray and green saddle.

2001, Dec. 17   *Perf. 13¾*
3214	A510	$1.50 Sheet of 4, #a-d	4.50	4.50

Souvenir Sheet
3215	A510	$4 multi	3.00	3.00

A511

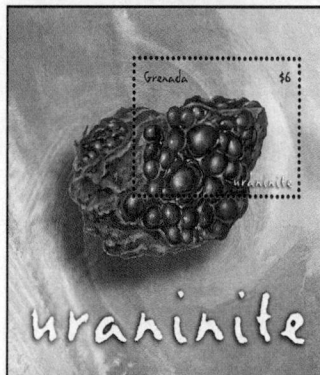

Gemstones and Minerals — A512

Monthly gemstones — No. 3216, $1.50: a, Garnet (January). b, Amethyst (February). c, Aquamarine (March). d, Diamond (April). e, Emerald (May). f, Pearl (June).

No. 3217, $1.50: a, Ruby (July). b, Sardonyx (August). c, Sapphire (September). d, Opal (October). e, Topaz (November). f, Turquoise (December).

Gemstones in mineral form — No. 3218: a, Ruby. b, Diamond. c, Sapphire. d, Opal. e, Turquoise. f, Jade.

No. 3219, $6, Uraninite. No. 3220, $6, Calcite. No. 3221, $6, Quartz, vert.

2001, Dec. 31   *Perf. 14*
Sheets of 6, #a-f
3216-3217	A511	Set of 2	14.50	14.50
3218	A512	$1.50 Sheet of 6, #a-f	7.50	7.50

Souvenir Sheets
3219-3221	A512	Set of 3	14.50	14.50

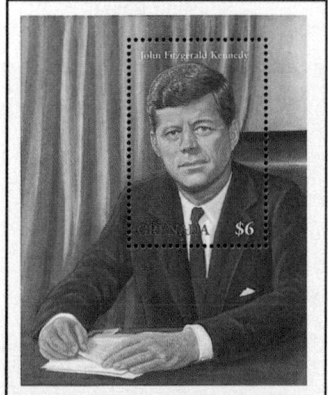

US Presidents — A513

No. 3222, $1.50 — John F. Kennedy and: a, Field. b, Flag, building, microphone. c, Airplane.

No. 3223, $1.50 — Ronald Reagan: a, In uniform with binoculars. b, With red tie. c, With flag.

No. 3224, $6, Kennedy. No. 3225, $6, Reagan.

2001, Dec. 31
Sheets, 2 each #a-c
3222-3223	A513	Set of 2	13.50	13.50

Souvenir Sheets
3224-3225	A513	Set of 2	9.00	9.00

I Love Lucy — A514

Designs: No. 3226, $6, Ethel watching Lucy and Desi dance. No. 3227, $6, Desi, Lucy, Fred and Ethel near door. No. 3228, $6, Desi holding Lucy. No. 3229, $6, Lucy in plaid shirt.

2001   *Perf. 13¾*
3226-3229	A514	Set of 4	18.00	18.00

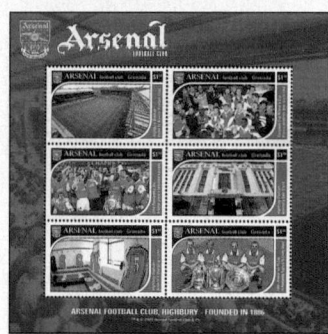

English Soccer Teams — A515

No. 3230, $1.50 — Arsenal: a, Inside of Highbury Stadium. b, Players celebrate 1994 European Cup and Winner's Cup. c, Players celebrate 1998 premiership. d, East stands, Highbury Stadium. e, Locker rooms. f, Four players with trophies, 1998.

No. 3231, $1.50 — Aston Villa: a, Sign on Villa Park. b, Fans watching night game. c, Empty stadium, field at right. d, Empty stadium, field at left. e, Holte End of stadium. f, Fans in stands.

No. 3232, $1.50 — Bolton Wanderers: a, Empty Reebok Stadium. b, Players celebrating 2001 Division 1 playoff win. c, Promotion to Premier League. d, Fans celebrate. e, Players, coaches with trophy. f, Game played in Reebok Stadium.

No. 3233, $1.50 — Everton: a, 2001-02 team. b, Re-signing of Duncan Ferguson. c, Statue of William Ralph "Dixie" Dean. d, Fans. e, Goodison Park. f, 1969-70 league championship team.

No. 3234, $1.50 — Ipswich Town: a, Players holding banner and trophy after 2000 Division 1 playoff final. b, 2001-02 team. c, Manager George Burley and Chairman David Sheepshanks. d, Pablo Counago fights for ball. e, Captain Matt Holland. f, George Burley receives Manager of the Year award.

No. 3235, $1.50 — Liverpool: a, Anfield. b, 2000-01 Worthington Cup winners. c, 2000-01 FA Cup winners. d, Fans. e, 2000-01 UEFA Cup winners. f, Treble Cup parade.

No. 3236, $1.50 — Manchester United: a, Legends Meredith, Law and Charlton. b, Three 1998-99 trophies. c, Views of Old Trafford, 1948, 1956. d, Recent views of Old Trafford. e, Third premiership in three years, 2000-01. f, Heroes, Best, Robson and Beckham.

No. 3237, $1.50 — Rangers: a, View of Ibrox Stadium from street. b, 1972 European Cup and Winner's Cup team. c, Scottish FA Cup, Scottish Premier League Trophy. d, Aerial view of Ibrox Stadium. e, Fans in stadium. f, Nine consecutive Scottish League wins.

2001, Sept. 12   *Litho.*   *Perf. 13¼*
Sheets of 6, #a-f
3230-3237	A515	Set of 8	55.00	55.00

Reign of Queen Elizabeth II, 50th Anniv. — A516

No. 3238: a, With Prince Philip. b, Wearing flowered hat. c, Wearing tiara. d, Wearing gray coat with white collar.
$6, Wearing uniform.

2002, Feb. 6   *Perf. 14½*
3238	A516	$2 Sheet of 4, #a-d	6.00	6.00

Souvenir Sheet
3239	A516	$6 multi	4.50	4.50

United We Stand — A517

2002, Feb.   *Perf. 13¾x13½*
3240	A517	$2 multi	1.50	1.50

Issued in sheets of 4.

Dale Earnhardt, Race Car Driver — A518

Years of Winston Cup Championships: No. 3241, $2, 1980. No. 3242, $2, 1986. No. 3243, $2, 1987. No. 3244, $2, 1990. No. 3245, $2, 1991. No. 3246, $2, 1993. No. 3247, $2, 1994.

2002, Mar. 4   *Litho.*   *Perf. 14x13¾*
3241-3247	A518	Set of 7	12.00	12.00

Mickey Mouse A519

No. 3249 — Scenes from: a, The Nifty Nineties, 1941. b, Magician Mickey, 1937. c, Steamboat Willie, 1928. d, Fantasia, 1940. e, Mickey Mouse Club, 1955. f, Cactus Kid, 1930. g, The Prince and the Pauper, 1990. h, Brave Little Tailor, 1938. i, Canine Caddy, 1941.

2002, Apr. 24   **Perf. 13¾**
3248 A519 $1 shown   .90   .90
3249 A519 $1 Sheet of 9, #a-i   8.75   8.75

No. 3248 was printed in sheets of nine.

American Civil War Naval
History — A520

No. 3250, $1: a, CSS Teaser. b, US gun-boats on the James River. c, USS Tyler. d, USS Maratanza. e, USS Metacomet. f, USS Rattler.
No. 3251, $1.25: a, CSS Tennessee. b, USS Hartford. c, USS Chickasaw. d, USS Ossipee. e, Battle of Mobile Bay. f, USS Chickasaw at Mobile Bay.
No. 3252, $1.50: a, USS H.L. Hunley. b, USS Cumberland. c, CSS Old Dominion. d, USS Housatonic. e, USS Hartford. f, USS Essex.
No. 3253, $1.50: a, CSS Alabama. b, USS Kearsarge and CSS Alabama. c, USS Hatteras. d, CSS Alabama and decoy. e, CSS Sumter. f, USS Kearsarge.
No. 3254, $6, USS Monitor. No. 3255, $6, CSS Florida. No. 3256, $6, CSS Tennessee. No. 3257, $6, Capt. Raphael Semmes aboard CSS Alabama.

2002, Apr. 8   **Litho.**   **Perf. 13¼x13½**
Sheets of 6, #a-f
3250-3253 A520   Set of 4   28.00   28.00
Souvenir Sheets
3254-3257 A520   Set of 4   22.00   22.00

Chiune Sugihara, Japanese Diplomat Who Saved Jews in World War II — A521

2002, July 1   **Perf. 13½x13¾**
3258 A521 $2 multi   1.50   1.50

Printed in sheets of 4.

2002 Winter Olympics, Salt Lake City A522

Skier with: No. 3259, $2, Red skis. No. 3260, $2, Yellow skis.

2002, July 1   **Perf. 13¼x13½**
3259-3260 A522   Set of 2   3.00   3.00
   a. Souvenir sheet, #3259-3260   3.00   3.00

Intl. Year of Mountains — A523

No. 3261: a, Mt. Mawensi, Kenya. b, Mt. Stanley, Uganda. c, Mt. Taweche, Nepal. d, Mt. San Exupery, Argentina.
$6, Mt. Aso, Japan.

2002, July 1
3261 A523 $2 Sheet of 4, #a-d   6.00   6.00
Souvenir Sheet
3262 A523 $6 multi   4.50   4.50

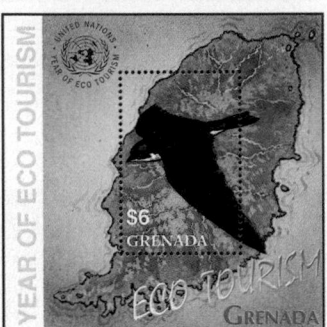

Intl. Year of Ecotourism — A524

No. 3263, horiz.: a, Tower and pennants. b, Bird. c, Flower, vacationer on chair. d, Diver, fish. e, Fish. f, Sailboats.
$6, Map of Grenada, bird.

2002, July 1   **Perf. 13¼x13½**
3263 A524 $1 Sheet of 6, #a-f   4.50   4.50
Souvenir Sheet
Perf. 13½x13¼
3264 A524 $6 multi   4.50   4.50

No. 3263 was overprinted in sheet margin "Hurricane Relief 2004" in 2005.

20th World Scout Jamboree, Thailand — A525

No. 3265, horiz.: a, Scout in canoe with oar out of water. b, Scout in canoe with oar in water. c, Bugler. d, Scout making Scout sign.
$6, Scout saluting.

2002, July 1   **Perf. 13¼x13½**
3265 A525 $2 Sheet of 4, #a-d   7.50   7.50
Souvenir Sheet
Perf. 13½x13¼
3266 A525 $6 multi   5.00   5.00

Model Heidi Klum — A526

No. 3267: a, Arms up. b, Arms down. c, No arms shown.
Illustration reduced.

2002, Aug. 16   **Perf. 14**
3267 A526 $1.50 Horiz. strip of
          3, #a-c   3.50   3.50

Printed in sheets containing two strips.

Elvis Presley (1935-77) A527

2002, Aug. 26   **Perf. 13½x13¾**
3268 A527 $1 multi   .75   .75

Printed in sheets of 9.

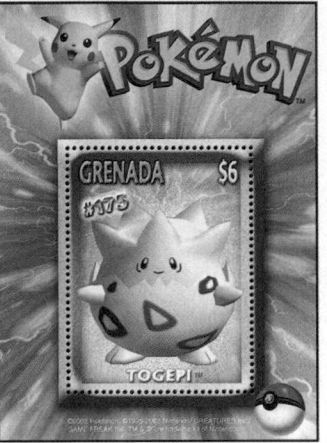

Pokémon — A528

No. 3269: a, Mareep. b, Sunkern. c, Teddiursa. d, Swinub. e, Murkrow. f, Snubbull.
$6, Togepi.

2002, Aug. 26   **Perf. 13¾**
3269 A528 $1.50 Sheet of 6, #a-f   6.75   6.75
Souvenir Sheet
3270 A528 $6 multi   4.50   4.50

A529

A530

Teddy Bears, Cent. — A531

No. 3271: a, 25c, Bear with red hat, lace collar, cheese wheels. b, $1.25, Bear with black cap. c, $3, Bear with wooden shoes. d, $5, Bear with red hat and ribbon.
No. 3272: a, Army bear. b, Navy bear. c, Air Force bear. d, Marines bear.
No. 3273: a, Basketball bear. b, Martial arts bear. c, Golf bear. d, Baseball bear.

2002, Aug. 26   **Perf. 14**
3271 A529   Sheet of 4, #a-d   7.25   7.25
Perf. 14¼
3272 A530 $2 Sheet of 4, #a-d   6.00   6.00
3273 A531 $2 Sheet of 4, #a-d   6.00   6.00

Dutch Nobel Prize Winners — A532

Dutch Lighthouses — A533

Traditional Dutch Women's
Costumes — A534

No. 3274: a, Jacobus H. van't Hoff, Chemistry, 1901. b, Nobel Peace medal. c, Pieter Zeeman, Physics, 1902. d, Johannes D. van der Waals, Physics, 1910. e, Tobias M. C. Asser, Peace, 1911. f, Heike Kammerlingh-Onnes, Physics, 1913.

No. 3275: a, Schiermonnikoog. b, Texel. c, Egmond. d, Scheveningen. e, Schouwen. f, Hellevoetsluis.

No. 3276: a, Zeeland (woman with red necklace, patterned dress). b, Noord-Brabant (woman with black shawl). c, Noord-Holland (woman with flowered neckpiece).

2002, Aug. 29		**Perf. 13½x13¼**	
3274	A532	$1.50 Sheet of 6, #a-f	6.75 6.75
3275	A533	$1.50 Sheet of 6, #a-f	6.75 6.75
		Perf. 13¼	
3276	A534	$3 Sheet of 3, #a-c	6.75 6.75

Amphilex 2002 Intl. Stamp Exhibition, Amsterdam.

Shirley Temple — A535

Scenes from "Our Little Girl" — No. 3277, horiz.: a, With man. b, With man and woman. c, With dog and man. d, With woman and two men. e, On seesaw with dog. f, With dog.

No. 3278: a, With woman. b, With man and clown. c, Kneeling beside chair. d, With man and woman.

$6, In pink dress.

2002, Sept. 3		**Perf. 14¼**	
3277	A535	$1.50 Sheet of 6, #a-f	6.75 6.75
3278	A535	$2 Sheet of 4, #a-d	6.00 6.00
		Souvenir Sheet	
3279	A535	$6 multi	4.50 4.50

Souvenir Sheet

Terrorist Attack on World Trade
Center, 1st Anniv. — A536

2002, Sept. 11		**Perf. 13¾**	
3280	A536	$6 multi	4.50 4.50

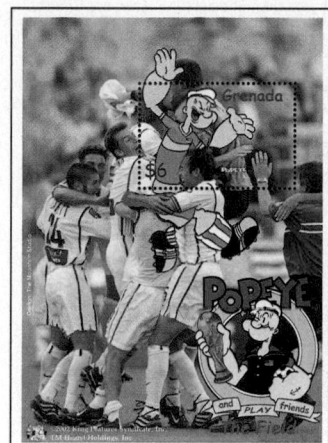

Popeye — A537

No. 3281, vert.: a, Popeye in Florence, Italy. b, Popeye and Brutus in Paris, France. c, Popeye in Athens, Greece. d, Popeye and Olive Oyl in Venice, Italy. e, Popeye in London, England. f, Popeye in Norway.

No. 3282, vert. — At soccer match: a, Swee'Pea. b, Jeep. c, Popeye. d, Brutus.

No. 3283, $6, Popeye playing soccer. No. 3284, $6, Brutus playing soccer. No. 3285, $6, Popeye at Leaning Tower of Pisa, vert.

		Perf. 14¼ (#3281, 3285), 14	
2002, Sept. 23			
3281	A537	$1.50 Sheet of 6, #a-f	6.75 6.75
3282	A537	$2 Sheet of 4, #a-d	6.00 6.00
		Souvenir Sheets	
3283-3285	A537	Set of 3	13.50 13.50

No. 3218 contains six 38x50mm stamps; No. 3285 contains one 50x75mm stamp.

English Soccer Teams Type of 2001

No. 3286, $1.50 — Tottenham Hotspur: a, Fans watching match in White Hart Lane Stadium. b, Sheringham and Anderton in action against Fulham. c, Poyet scoring against Liverpool. d, Tottenham Hotspur wins UEFA Cup, 1972. e, Celebrations after win against Chelsea. f, Fans in stadium, team insignia.

No. 3287, $1.50 — Manchester City: a, Maine Road Stadium from stands. b, Fans celebrate becoming Division One champions. c, Manager Kevin Keegan and trophy. d, Team with trophy. e, Players wearing medals, with trophy. f, Field level view of Maine Road Stadium.

No. 3288, $1.50 — Norwich City: a, Match at the Nest. b, Promotion to the Top Flight, 1971-72. c, Milk Cup win, 1985. d, Carrow Road Stadium. e, Win against Bayern Munich, 1993. f, Action from 1958-59 Cup run.

No. 3289, $1.50 — Arsenal, Double Winners: a, Tony Adams and Patrick Vieira hold FA Cup. b, Team wearing tan shirts, holding championship banners. c, Team without banners, at Premiership trophy presentation. d, Photo of 2001-02 Premiership team, standing and wearing red shirts. e, Four players celebrate winning goal against Chelsea. f, Manager Arsene Wenger and Tony Adams at Double Winners Parade.

No. 3290, $1.50 — Arsenal, Premiership Winners: a, Inside of Highbury Stadium, team emblem and name in red panels. b, Celebrations after Gilberto scores winning goal. c, Team with FA Community Shield sign. d, Team photo, empty stands. e, Gilberto with FA Community Shield. f, Highbury Stadium with fans, team emblem.

No. 3291, $1.50 — Manchester United: a, David Beckham after free kick. b, Team photo,

empty stands. c, Aerial view of Old Trafford Stadium. d, Celebration after Ole Gunnar Solskjaer's 100th goal for Manchester United. e, Fans at Old Trafford Stadium. f, North stand of Old Trafford Stadium.

No. 3292, $1.50 — Liverpool: a, Anfield's Centenary stand, as seen from Main stand. b, 2002-03 team photo. c, Gerard Houllier and Phil Thompson. d, Milan Baros celebrates goal. e, Vladimir Smicer congratulating Danny Murphy. f, The Kop, as seen from Anfield Road end.

No. 3293, $1.50 — Celtic: a, Interior of Celtic Park. b, Martin O'Neill with SPL Trophy. c, Henrik Larsson celebrating goal. d, 2002-03 team photo. e, Players celebrating a goal. f, Exterior of Celtic Park.

No. 3294, $1.50 — Chelsea: a, Night match at Stamford Bridge Stadium. b, Team with 1998 Cup Winners' Cup Final trophy. c, Fans in stadium. d, Sign for the Shed End. e, Field level view of Stamford Bridge Stadium. f, Players celebrating 2000 FA Cup victory.

2002		**Perf. 14x13¾**	
		Sheets of 6, #a-f	
3286-3294	A515	Set of 9	60.00 60.00

Issued: Nos. 3286-3289, 9/23; Nos. 3290-3294, 11/14.

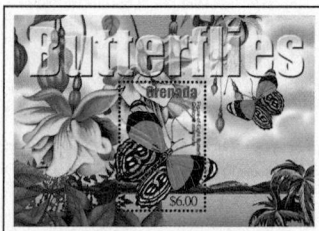

Butterflies, Insects, Mushrooms and
Whales — A538

No. 3295, $1.50 — Butterflies: a, Common morpho. b, Blue night. c, Small flambeau. d, Grecian shoemaker. e, Orange-barred sulphur. f, Cramer's mesene.

No. 3296, $1.50 — Insects: a, Honeybees. b, Dragonfly. c, Milkweed bug. d, Bumblebee. e, Migratory grasshopper. f, Monarch caterpillar.

No. 3297, $1.50 — Mushrooms: a, Boletus crocipodius. b, King bolete. c, Velvet shank. d, Death cap. e, Golden cavalier. f, Fly agaric.

No. 3298, $1.50 — Whales: a, Blue. b, Pygmy sperm. c, Humpback. d, Killer. e, Bowhead. f, Gray.

No. 3299, $6, Figure-of-eight butterfly. No. 3300, $6, Hercules beetle. No. 3301, $6, Sharp-scaled parasol mushroom. No. 3302, $6, Blue whale, horiz.

2002, Oct. 21		**Perf. 14**	
		Sheets of 6, #a-f	
3295-3298	A538	Set of 4	27.50 27.50
		Souvenir Sheets	
3299-3302	A538	Set of 4	18.00 18.00

Sir Norman
Wisdom, British
Comedian
A539

2002, Nov. 3		**Perf. 13¾**	
3303	A539	$1.50 multi	1.10 1.10

Printed in sheets of 6.

Amerigo Vespucci (1454-1512),
Explorer — A540

No. 3304, $3: a, Map of South America, ship. b, Compass rose, ship. c, Map of Europe and Africa.

No. 3305, $3, horiz.: a, Sextant, map of northern South America. b, Vespucci, map of central South America. c, Ship, map of southern South America.

No. 3306, $6, Compass rose. No. 3307, $6, Globe.

2002, Nov. 4		**Perf. 13¾**	
		Sheets of 3, #a-c	
3304-3305	A540	Set of 2	13.50 13.50
		Souvenir Sheets	
		Perf. 14	
3306-3307	A540	Set of 2	9.00 9.00

No. 3304 contains three 38x50mm stamps; No. 3305 contains three 50x38mm stamps.

Christmas
A541

Cimabue paintings: 15c, Madonna and Child, Four Angels and St. Francis, entire. 25c, Madonna and Child and Two Angels, vert. 50c, Madonna Enthroned, detail, vert. $1, Madonna Enthroned, entire, vert. $4, Madonna and Child, Four Angels and St. Francis, detail, vert. $6, Nativity by Perugino, vert.

2002, Nov. 4		**Perf. 14**	
3308-3312	A541	Set of 5	4.50 4.50
		Souvenir Sheet	
3313	A541	$6 multi	4.50 4.50

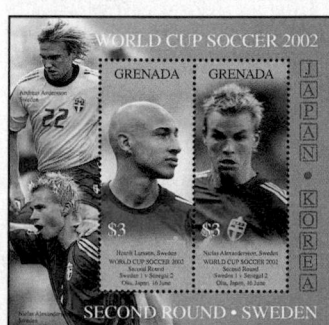

Second Round Matches of 2002 World
Cup Soccer Championships, Japan
and Korea — A542

No. 3314, $1.50 — Sweden vs. Senegal: a, Johan Mjalby. b, Magnus Hedman. c, Fredrik Ljungberg. d, Khalilou Fadiga. e, El Hadji Diouf. f, Papa Bouba Diop.

No. 3315, $1.50 — Brazil vs. Belgium: a, Roberto Carlos. b, Juninho Paulista. c, Ronaldinho. d, Johan Walem. e, Marc Wilmots. f, Bart Goor.

No. 3316, $3 — Swedish players: a, Henrik Larsson. b, Niclas Alexandersson.

No. 3317, $3 — Senegal players: a, Fadiga. b, Coach Bruno Metsu.

No. 3318, $3 — Brazil players: a, Coach Luiz Felipe Scolari. b, Ronaldo.

No. 3319, $3 — Belgium players: a, Wesley Sonck. b, Coach Robert Waseige.

2002, Nov. 18   **Perf. 13¼**
Sheets of 6, #a-f
3314-3315 A542   Set of 2   13.50 13.50
Souvenir Sheets of 2, #a-b
3316-3319 A542   Set of 4   18.00 18.00

Souvenir Sheet

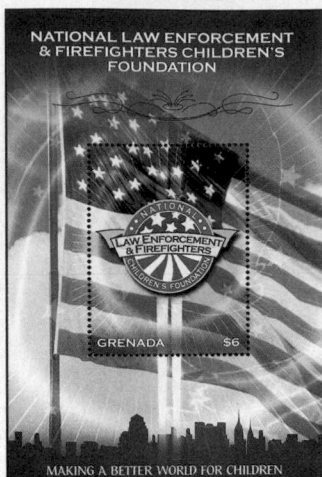

United States Natl. Law Enforcement
and Firefighters Children's
Foundation — A543

2002, Nov. 28   **Perf. 14¼**
3320 A543 $6 multi   4.50 4.50

Pres. John F. Kennedy (1917-
63) — A544

No. 3321, horiz.: a, Meeting with Cabinet. b,
Signing bill into law. c, Meeting civil rights
leaders. d, With Astronaut John Glenn. e, On
campaign trail. f, Arrival in Dallas, Nov. 22,
1963.
$6, At microphone.

2002, Dec. 4   **Perf. 14**
3321 A544 $1.50 Sheet of 6, #a-f 6.75 6.75
Souvenir Sheet
3322 A544 $6 multi   4.50 4.50

Intl. Federation of Stamp Dealers
Associations, 50th Anniv. — A545

2002, Dec. 16   **Litho.**
3323 A545 $2 multi   1.50 1.50

Princess Diana (1961-97) — A546

No. 3324: a, Wearing bow tie. b, Wearing
blue dress. c, Wearing red and white hat. d,
Holding flowers.
$6, Wearing earphones and microphone.

2002   **Perf. 14**
3324 A546 $2 Sheet of 4, #a-d   6.00 6.00
Souvenir Sheet
3325 A546 $6 multi   4.50 4.50

I Love Lucy Type of 2001
Souvenir Sheets

No. 3326, $6, Lucy standing near fireplace.
No. 3327, $6, Lucy and Ethel at desk. No.
3328, $6, Fred and Desi standing. No. 3329,
$6, Fred and Desi at desk, horiz.

2002   **Perf. 13¾**
3326-3329 A514   Set of 4   18.00 18.00

New Year
2003 (Year
of the Ram)
A547

2003, Jan. 27   **Perf. 13¾**
3330 A547 $1.25 multi   .95 .95
Printed in sheets of 4.

M-Gears — A548

No. 3331: a, Airplane. b, Vehicle. c, Monster. d, Race car.

2003, Feb. 16   **Litho.**   **Perf. 14¼**
3331 A548 $2 Sheet of 4, #a-d   6.00 6.00

Astronauts Killed in Space Shuttle
Columbia Accident — A549

No. 3332: a, Mission Specialist 1 David M.
Brown. b, Commander Rick D. Husband. c,
Mission Specialist 4 Laurel Blair Salton Clark.
d, Mission Specialist 4 Kalpana Chawla. e,
Payload Commander Michael P. Anderson. f,
Pilot William C. McCool. g, Payload Specialist
4 Ilan Ramon.

2003, Apr. 7   **Perf. 13¼**
3332 A549 $1 Sheet of 7, #a-g   6.00 6.00

Paintings of
Gustav Klimt
(1862-1918)
A550

Designs: 15c, Jardin aux Tournesols. 25c,
L'Allée aux Poulets. 75c, Allée dans le Parc du
Schloss Kammer. $1, Portrait of Johanna
Staude. $1.25, Portrait of Friederike Maria
Beer. $3, Portrait of Mäda Primavesi.
No. 3339: a, La Jeune Fille. b, Les Amies. c,
Le Berceau. d, La Vie et la Mort.
$6, Portrait of Margaret Stonborough-
Wittgenstein.

2003, Apr. 28   **Perf. 14¼**
3333-3338 A550   Set of 6   5.00 5.00
3339 A550 $2 Sheet of 4, #a-d   6.00 6.00
Size: 82x103mm
Imperf
3340 A550 $6 multi   4.50 4.50

Art of
Yoshitoshi
Taiso (1839-
92)
A551

Designs: 75c, A Harlot in Repose. $1, A
"Shakuni," or Geisha, Who Serves Wine or
Sake. $1.25, A "Joro," or Low Ranking Prosti-
tute, Having a Snack. $3, A Geisha Known as
a "Geiko," or Entertainer Relaxing.
No. 3345: a, Enjoying a Cool Evening
Breeze in a Pleasure Boat. b, A Fukagawa
Waitress Carrying a Wooden Table Laden
With Food. c, A Spoiled Unmarried Woman
Pretending to Be Displeased With an Admirer.
d, A Coy Young Girl, Biting Her Sleeve Pre-
tending to Be Embarrassed.
$6, A Geisha About to Board a Party Boat.

2003, Apr. 28   **Perf. 14¼**
3341-3344 A551   Set of 4   4.50 4.50
3345 A551 $2 Sheet of 4, #a-d   6.00 6.00
Souvenir Sheet
3346 A551 $6 multi   4.50 4.50

Paintings by Lucas Cranach the Elder
(1472-1553) — A552

Details from St. Catherine Altarpiece: 50c,
Sts. Dorothy, Agnes and Cunigonde. 75c, St.
Margaret, vert. $1.25, St. Barbara, vert. $3,
Detail from left wing, vert.
No. 3351 — Painting details: a, Lot and His
Daughters. b, David and Bathsheba. c, The
Agony in the Garden. d, The Adoration of the
Magi.
$6, Detail of Samson and Delilah, vert.

2003, Apr. 28
3347-3350 A552   Set of 4   4.25 4.25
3351 A552 $2 Sheet of 4, #a-d   6.00 6.00
Souvenir Sheet
3352 A552 $6 multi   4.50 4.50

Teddy
Bear
A553

2003, Apr. 29   Embroidered   Imperf.
Self-Adhesive
3353 A553 $15 multi   11.50 11.50
Issued in sheets of 4.

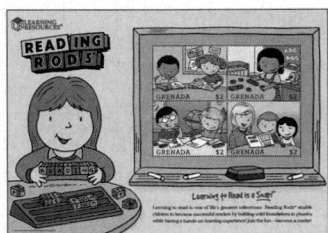

Reading Rods — A554

No. 3354 — Children and: a, Bulletin board.
b, Blackboard. c, Globe. d, Teacher.

2003, May 5   Litho.   Perf. 13¾
3354 A554 $2 Sheet of 4, #a-d   6.00 6.00

Tour de France Bicycle Race,
Cent. — A555

No. 3355, $2: a, Sylvère Maes, 1939. b,
Jean Lazaridés, 1946. c, Jean Robic, 1947. d,
Gino Bartali, 1948.
No. 3356, $2: a, Fausto Coppl, 1949. b, Fer-
dinand Kubler, 1950. c, Hugo Koblet, 1951. d,
Coppi, 1952.
No. 3357, $2: a, Roger Walkowiak, 1956. b,
Jacques Anquetil, 1957. c, Charly Gaul, 1958.
d, Federico Bahamontes, 1959.

No. 3358, $6, Coppi, 1949, diff. No. 3359, $6, Kubler, 1950, diff. No. 3360, $6, Anquetil, 1964.

2003, June 17 **Perf. 13¼**
Sheets of 4, #a-d
3355-3357 A555 Set of 3 18.00 18.00
Souvenir Sheets
3358-3360 A555 Set of 3 13.50 13.50

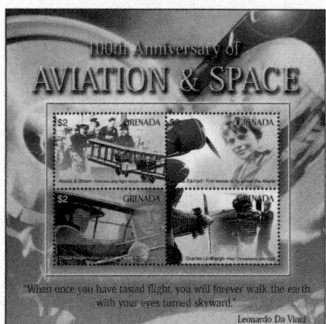

Powered Flight, Cent. — A556

No. 3361, $2: a: First non-stop transatlantic flight by Alcock & Brown. b, Amelia Earhart, first woman to fly across Atlantic. c, Chuck Yeager, first man to break sound barrier. d, Charles Lindbergh, first solo transatlantic flight.
No. 3362, $2: a, Louis Bleriot, first flight across English Channel. b, Johnnie Johnson, ace pilot in World War II. c, Wright Brothers, first powered flight. d, Jacqueline Cochran, first woman to break sound barrier.

2003, June 24 **Perf. 13¼x13½**
Sheets of 4, #a-d
3361-3362 A556 Set of 2 12.00 12.00

Coronation of Queen Elizabeth II, 50th Anniv. — A557

Designs: No. 3363, $2, Enthroning of the Queen. No. 3364, $2, Duke pays homage to the Queen. No. 3365, $2, Celebration of Holy Communion. No. 3366, $2, Floodlit mall. No. 3367, $2, Queen on balcony. No. 3368, $2, St. Edward's Chair. No. 3369, $2, Official coronation portrait. No. 3370, $2, Queen leaves Abbey.
$6, Queen in coach.

2003, June 30 **Perf. 13½x14**
3363-3370 A557 Set of 8 12.00 12.00
Souvenir Sheet
3371 A557 $6 multi 4.50 4.50
No. 3371 contains one 38x51mm stamp.

CARICOM, 30th Anniv. — A558

2003, July 4 **Perf. 14**
3372 A558 $1 multi .75 .75

Intl. Year of Fresh Water — A559

No. 3373: a, Levera Pond. b, Concord Falls. c, Lake Antoine.
$6, Lake Grand Etang.

2003, July 4 **Perf. 13½x13¼**
3373 A559 $2 Sheet of 3, #a-c 4.50 4.50
Souvenir Sheet
3374 A559 $6 multi 4.50 4.50

Circus Performers — A560

No. 3375, $2: a, Clive Andrews. b, Bell Bozo. c, Bumpsy. d, Annie Frattellini.
No. 3376, $2: a, Stag. b, Olga and Regina Kolpensky. c, Brad Byers. d, Tiger.

2003, July 14 **Perf. 14**
Sheets of 4, #a-d
3375-3376 A560 Set of 2 12.00 12.00

St. George's University School of Medicine A561

Designs: 75c, Aerial view of campus. $1, Campus buildings.

2003, July 23
3377-3378 A561 Set of 2 1.40 1.40

Prince William, 21st Birthday — A562

No. 3379, vert.: a, With bouquet of flowers. b, Wearing blue shirt. c, Wearing blue shirt, close-up.
$6, Wearing plaid shirt.

2003, Aug. 25
3379 A562 $3 Sheet of 3, #a-c 6.75 6.75
Souvenir Sheet
3380 A562 $6 multi 4.50 4.50

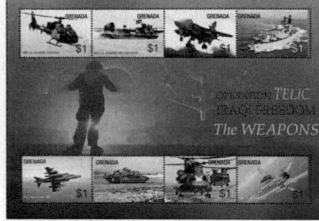

Operation Iraqi Freedom — A563

No. 3381, $1: a, Gazelle helicopter. b, Hovercraft. c, Jaguar. d, HMS Liverpool. e, Harrier GR7. f, Challenger 2 tank. g, Chinook helicopters. h, Tornado F3.
No. 3382, $1: a, Gen. Sir Mike Jackson. b, Air Vice-marshal Glenn Torpy. c, Air Marshal Brian Burridge. d, Maj. Gen. Tony Milton. e, Maj. Gen. Peter Wall. f, Maj. Gen. Barney White-Spunner. g, Adm. Sir Alan West. h, Air Chief Marshal Sir Peter Squire.

2003, Aug. 29
Sheets of 8, #a-h
3381-3382 A563 Set of 2 12.00 12.00

Pres. Ronald Reagan — A564

No. 3383: a, On Korean demilitarized zone, 1983. b, With British Prime Minister Margaret Thatcher. c, Speaking at the Berlin Wall, 1987. d, Signing IMF treaty with Soviet Secretary General Mikhail Gorbachev. e, With Egyptian President Anwar Sadat, 1981. f, At home with his horse.
$6, Addressing the nation.

2003
3383 A564 $1.50 Sheet of 6, #a-f 6.75 6.75
Souvenir Sheet
3384 A564 $6 multi 4.50 4.50

Souvenir Sheet

Anatoly Karpov, Chess Champion — A565

2003 **Perf. 13¼**
3385 A565 $20 multi 15.00 15.00

Prehistoric Animals — A566

No. 3386, $2, horiz.: a, Spinosaurus. b, Herrerasaurus. c, Protarchaeopteryx. d, Sinosauropteryx.
No. 3387, $2, horiz.: a, Allosaurus. b, Crylophosaurus. c, Eoraptor. d, Caudipteryx.
No. 3388, $6, Archaeopteryx. No. 3389, $6, Triceratops.

2003, Oct. 23 Litho. Perf. 13¼x13½
Sheets of 4, #a-d
3386-3387 A566 Set of 2 14.00 14.00
Souvenir Sheets
Perf. 13½x13¼
3388-3389 A566 Set of 2 10.00 10.00

Flowers A567

Designs: 25c, Yellow allamanda. 50c, Queen of the night. 75c, Anthurium. $3, Oleander.
No. 3394: a, Blue passion flower. b, Chinese hibiscus. c, Poinsettia. d, Bird of paradise.
$6, Shrimp flower.

2003, Oct. 23 **Perf. 14**
3390-3393 A567 Set of 4 3.50 3.50
3394 A567 $2 Sheet of 4, #a-d 6.00 6.00
Souvenir Sheet
3395 A567 $6 multi 4.50 4.50

Fish A568

Designs: No. 3396, $1, Gold coney. No. 3397, $1, Spotfin butterflyfish. No. 3398, $1, Smallmouth grunt. $3, Night sergeant.
No. 3400: a, Cuban hogfish. b, Bluehead wrasse. c, Black cap gramma. d, Cherubfish.
$6, Banded butterflyfish.

2003, Oct. 23
3396-3399 A568 Set of 4 4.50 4.50
3400 A568 $2 Sheet of 4, #a-d 6.00 6.00
Souvenir Sheet
3401 A568 $6 multi 4.50 4.50

Birds A569

Designs: No. 3402, $1.25, Osprey. No. 3403, $1.25, Northern oriole. No. 3404, $1.25, Red-eyed vireo. $3, Bahama pintail.
No. 3406: a, Slaty-capped shrike vireor. b, Northern flicker. c, Blackburnian warbler. d, Common tody-flycatcher.
$6, Blue grosbeak, vert.

2003, Oct. 23
3402-3405 A569 Set of 4 5.00 5.00
3406 A569 $2 Sheet of 4, #a-d 6.00 6.00
Souvenir Sheet
3407 A569 $6 multi 4.50 4.50

Christmas
A570

Paintings by Giotto: 35c, Madonna and Child, from the Church of the Ognissanti. 75c, Ognissanti Madonna. $1, Madonna of the Angels. $4, Madonna and Child, from the Florentine Church of San Giorgio alla Costa.
$6, Holy Family with John the Baptist and St. Elizabeth, horiz.

2003, Nov. 17   *Perf. 14¼*
3408-3411 A570   Set of 4   4.75   4.75
     Souvenir Sheet
3412 A570 $6 multi   4.50   4.50
St. Petersburg, Russia, 300th anniv. (#3412).

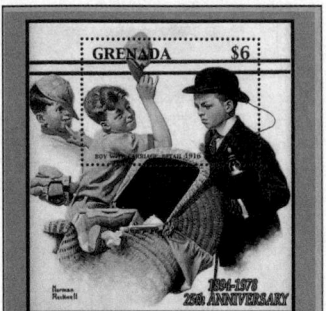

Paintings by Norman Rockwell (1894-1978) — A571

No. 3413, vert.: a, The Spring Tonic. b, The Facts of Life. c, The Proper Gratuity. d, The Runaway.
$6, Boy with Carriage.

2003, Dec. 8   *Perf. 13¼*
3413 A571 $2 Sheet of 4, #a-d   6.00   6.00
     Souvenir Sheet
3414 A571 $6 multi   4.50   4.50

Paintings in the Hermitage, St. Petersburg, Russia — A572

Designs: 45c, At the Palmist's, by Jean-Baptiste Le Prince, vert. $1, A Visit to Grandmother, by Louis Le Nain. $1.50, Musicale, by Dirck Hals. $3, A Young Woman in the Morning, by Frans van Mieris the Elder, vert.
No. 3419, vert.: a, Louis, Grand Dauphin de France, by Louis Tocqué. b, Count P. A. Stroganov as a Child, by Jean-Baptiste Greuze. c, A Boy with a Book, by Jean-Baptiste Perronneau. d, A Girl with a Doll, by Greuze.
No. 3420, The Lute Player, by Caravaggio.
No. 3421, The Spoiled Child, by Greuze, vert.

2003, Dec. 8   *Perf. 13¼*
3415-3418 A572   Set of 4   4.50   4.50
3419 A572 $2 Sheet of 4, #a-d   6.00   6.00
     Imperf
     Size: 78x65mm
3420 A572 $6 multi   4.50   4.50
     Size: 67x78mm
3421 A572 $6 multi   4.50   4.50

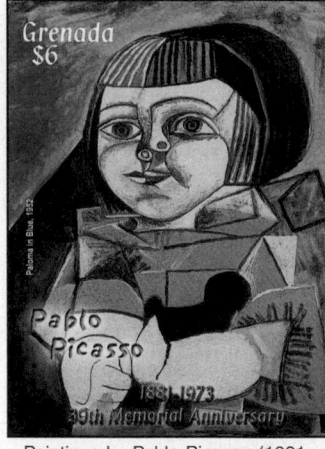

Paintings by Pablo Picasso (1881-1973) — A573

No. 3422: a, Claude Drawing. b, Claude and Paloma at Play. c, Paloma at Three Years Old. d, Paloma with an Orange.
$6, Paloma in Blue.

2003, Dec. 8   Litho.   *Perf. 13¼*
3422 A573 $2 Sheet of 4, #a-d   6.00   6.00
     Imperf
3423 A573 $6 multi   4.50   4.50
No. 3422 contains four 37x50mm stamps.

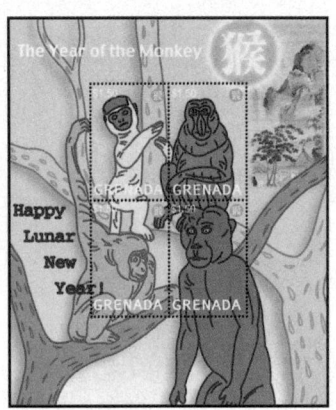

New Year 2004 (Year of the Monkey) — A574

No. 3424: a, Buff monkey with brown features. b, Brown monkey. c, Tan monkey. d, Gray monkey.

2004, Jan. 4   *Perf. 14*
3424 A574 $1.50 Sheet of 4, #a-d   4.50   4.50

     Souvenir Sheet

Training Ship "Lissy" — A575

2004, Jan. 16   Litho.   *Perf. 14¼*
3425 A575 $6 multi   4.50   4.50
Opening of Weser Tunnel, Dedesdorf, Germany.

Paintings by Pu Hsin-yu (1896-1963) — A576

No. 3426: a, Woman. b, Monkeys in tree. c, Landscape. d, Bird in tree. e, Man seated. f, Man standing.
No. 3427: a, Branch. b, Man.

2004, Jan. 29   *Perf. 13½x13¼*
3426 A576 $1.50 Sheet of 6, #a-f   6.75   6.75
3427 A576 $3 Sheet of 2, #a-b   4.50   4.50

2004 Hong Kong Stamp Expo.

Arthur and Friends — A577

No. 3428, $1.50: a, Arthur. b, D. W. with Valentine's Day card. c, Binky. d, Muffy. e, D. W. as Cupid. f, Francine.
No. 3429, $1.50: a, Muffy giving speech about butterflies. b, Francine giving presentation about butterflies. c, Brain with plants. d, D. W. in space. e, Sue Ellen with insects. f, Arthur with model of solar system.
No. 3430, $2: a, Robinson Crusoe. b, Treasure Island. c, Tom Sawyer. d, Jungle Book.
No. 3431, $2: a, Robin Hood. b, Rumplestiltskin. c, How Arthur Drew Forth His Sword. d, King Arthur.

2004, Jan. 29   *Perf. 13¼*
     Sheets of 6, #a-f
3428-3429 A577   Set of 2   13.50   13.50
     Sheets of 4, #a-d
3430-3431 A577   Set of 2   12.00   12.00

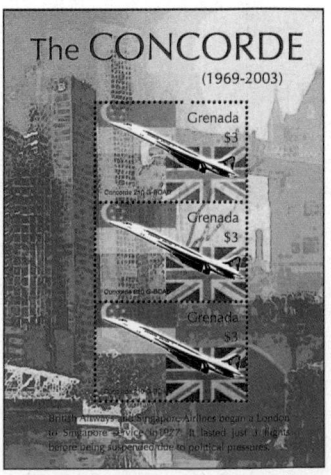

Cessation of Conorde Flights (in 2003) — A578

No. 3432, $3 — Concorde 210 G-BOAD, British and Singapore flags and: a, Roof line of buildings at UR. b, Curved and jagged lines at UR. c, Dark gray background at UR.
No. 3433, $3 — Concorde 001 F-WTSS, French flag and: a, Concorde above runway. b, Spectators near airport fence. c, Cockpit control panel.
No. 3434, $3 — Concorde 203 F-BVFA and: a, Top of US Capitol. b, Middle part of Capitol dome, head of statue. c, Base of Capitol and statue.

2004, Feb. 16   *Perf. 13¼x13½*
     Sheets of 3, #a-c
3432-3434 A578   Set of 3   21.00   21.00

2004 Summer Olympics, Athens
A579

Designs: 75c, Lord Killanin, Intl. Olympic Committee President, 1972-80. $1, 10,000 meter run, 1928 Olympics, horiz. $1.25, Commemorative plaque from 1900 Paris Olympics. $3, Presentation of olive wreath.

2004, Apr. 8   *Perf. 13¼*
3435-3438 A579   Set of 4   4.50   4.50

American Indian Chiefs — A580

Paintings of American Indians — A581

No. 3439: a, American Horse. b, Blue Bird. c, Crow King. d, Crow Man. e, Gall. f, Good Horse. g, Goose. h, John Grass. i, Rain-in-the-Face. j, Red Cloud. k, Sitting Bull. l, Wild Horse.
No. 3440: a, Return of the Blackfoot War Party, by Frederic Remington. b, Ridden Down, by Remington. c, Smoke Signal, by Remington. d, Buffalo Hunt, by Charles Russell. e, Scouts, by Russell. f, Piegans, by Russell.

2004, Apr. 19   *Perf. 13¾*
3439 A580   75c Sheet of 12, #a-l   6.75   6.75
3440 A581 $1.25 Sheet of 6, #a-f   5.75   5.75

Souvenir Sheet

Deng Xiaoping (1904-97), Chinese Communist Party Leader — A582

2004, May 3   **Perf. 13½x13¼**
3441 A582 $6 multi   4.50 4.50

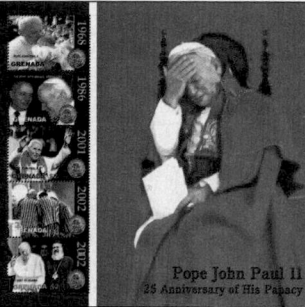

Election of Pope John Paul II, 25th Anniv. — A583

No. 3442: a, Kissing baby. b, With Mikhail Gorbachev. c, Waving to crowd. d, Meeting with Polish deportees. e, Visit to Russia.

2004, May 3   **Perf. 13¼x13½**
3442 A583 $2 Sheet of 5, #a-e   7.50 7.50

Marilyn Monroe (1926-62) — A584

No. 3444: a, Wearing red dress with strap over shoulder, mouth wide open. b, Wearing orange red dress, mouth closed. c, Wearing white dress. d, Wearing red dress, mouth partially open.

2004, May 3   **Perf. 14**
3443 A584 50c shown   .60 .60
         Perf. 13½x13¼
3444 A584 $2 Sheet of 4, #a-d   7.50 7.50
No. 3443 printed in sheets of 16.

European Soccer Championships, Portugal — A585

No. 3445, vert.: a, Jan Svehlik. b, Franz Beckenbauer. c, Karol Dobias. d, Crvena Zvezda Stadium, Belgrade.
$6, 1976 Czechoslovakian team.

2004, May 3   **Perf. 13½x13¼**
3445 A585 $2 Sheet of 4, #a-d   6.00 6.00

Souvenir Sheet
Perf. 13¼
3446 A585 $6 multi   4.50 4.50
No. 3445 contains four 28x42mm stamps.

D-Day, 60th Anniv. A586

Designs: 45c, Don Sheppard, Royal Engineers. $1, Air Chief Marshall Sir Arthur Tedder. $1.50, Douglas Kay, 13th/18th Royal Hussars. $3, Gen. Bernard Montgomery.
No. 3451, $2: a, Germans detect Allied invasion. b, Germans prepare to engage Allied invasion fleet. c, Soldier, Merville Battery. d, Paratroopers capture Merville Battery.
No. 3452, $2: a, HMS Belfast fires on German shore batteries. b, Allies pound German coastal defenses. c, Air strikes over Utah Beach. d, Allied troops head towards Omaha Beach.
No. 3453, $6, Fake landing craft. No. 3454, $6, Pipeline under the ocean.

2004, May 3   **Perf. 14**
Stamps + Labels (#3447-3450)
3447-3450 A586 Set of 4   4.50 4.50
Sheets of 4, #a-d
3451-3452 A586 Set of 2   12.00 12.00
Souvenir Sheets
3453-3454 A586 Set of 2   9.00 9.00

Locomotives and Famous Men — A587

No. 3455, $1: a, Sir Lord Nelson 4-6-0. b, South African 16CR Class Pacific. c, Florisdorf 0-6-0 Fireless, Austria. d, GWR 57XX Class 0-6-0. e, GWR Castle Class 4-6-0. f, GWR Saint Class 4-6-0. g, GWR Star Class 4-6-0. h, GWR 28XX Class 2-8-0. i, GWR 51XX Class 2-6-2T.
No. 3456, $1, vert.: a, GN Stirling Single 4-2-2. b, Beyer Peacock Mogul 2-6-0. c, Prussian G8 0-8-0. d, George Stephenson. e, James Nasmyth. f, Nasmyth's steam hammer. g, Raven Z Class 4-4-2. h, Sir Vincent Raven. i, Thomas Cook.
No. 3457, $1, vert.: a, SR Schools Class 4-4-0. b, Indian Railways SGS Class 0-6-0. c, Borsig 0-4-0 Tram, Paraguay. d, Richard Trevithick. e, Herbert Garratt. f, Isambard Kingdom Brunel. g, Replica of Trevithick's Coalbrookdale Engine. h, Rhodesian 20th Class Garratt. i, Train on Brunel's Royal Saltash Bridge.
No. 3458, $6, California Zephyr. No. 3459, $6, Indian Pacific. No. 3460, $6, Cumbres and Toltec.

2004, July 19   **Litho.**
Sheets of 9, #a-i
3455-3457 A587 Set of 3   21.00 21.00
Souvenir Sheets
3458-3460 A587 Set of 3   13.50 13.50

Elvis Presley (1935-77) — A588

No. 3461: a, Holding guitar (brown). b, Playing guitar (green). c, Playing guitar, diff. (red violet). d, Portrait (brown). e, Like #3461b, (blue).

2004, Aug. 3   **Perf. 14**
3461 A588 $1.50 Sheet, #a-d,   2 #e   7.25 7.25

Operation Iraqi Freedom — A589

No. 3462: a, Pres. George W. Bush. b, Paul Bremer. c, Col. James Hickey, US Special Forces. d, A friendly welcome.

2004, Aug. 25   **Perf. 13¼x13½**
3462 A589 $2 Sheet of 4, #a-d   6.00 6.00

Queen Juliana of the Netherlands (1909-2004) — A590

2004, Aug. 25   **Litho.**   **Perf. 13¼**
3463 A590 $2 multi   1.50 1.50
Printed in sheets of 6.

Miniature Sheet

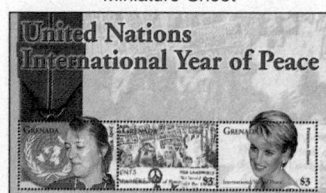

Intl. Year of Peace — A591

No. 3464: a, Jody Williams, 1997 Nobel Peace laureate. b, Protesters against landmines. c, Princess Diana.

2004, Sept. 7   **Perf. 14**
3464 A591 $3 Sheet of 3, #a-c   6.75 6.75

Miniature Sheet

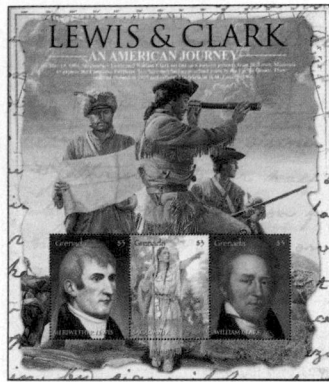

Lewis and Clark Expedition, Bicent. — A592

No. 3465: a, Meriwether Lewis. b, Sacajawea. c, William Clark.

2004, Sept. 7   **Perf. 14¼**
3465 A592 $3 Sheet of 3, #a-c   6.75 6.75

Miniature Sheet

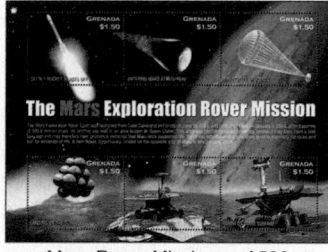

Mars Rover Mission — A593

No. 3466: a, Delta II rocket blasts off. b, Entering Mars atmosphere. c, Parachute descent. d, Landing on the surface. e, Rover leaving lander. f, Rover on Mars surface.

2004, Sept. 7
3466 A593 $1.50 Sheet of 6, #a-f 6.75 6.75

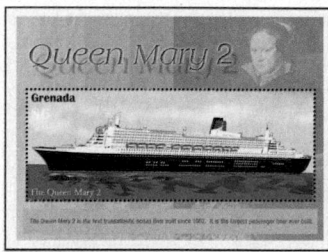

Ocean Liners — A594

No. 3467, $2: a, RMS Titanic. b, TSS Normandie. c, Mauritania. d, Lusitania.
No. 3468, $2: a, Queen Mary 2. b, Queen Elizabeth II. c, Queen Mary. d, Queen Elizabeth.
$6, Queen Mary 2, diff.

2004, Sept. 7   **Perf. 13¼x13**
Sheets of 4, #a-d
3467-3468 A594 Set of 2   12.00 12.00
Souvenir Sheet
3469 A594 $6 multi   4.50 4.50

FIFA (Fédération Internationale de Football Association), Cent. — A595

No. 3470: a, Gabriel Batistuta. b, Cafu. c,
Michel Platini. d, Gianluca Vialli.
$6, Oliver Kahn.

2004, Nov. 1   *Perf. 12¾x12½*
3470 A595 $2 Sheet of 4, #a-d   6.00 6.00
Souvenir Sheet
3471 A595 $6 multi   4.50 4.50

National
Basketball
Association
Players — A596

Designs: No. 3472, 75c, Pau Gasol, Mem-
phis Grizzlies. No. 3473, 75c, Allen Iverson,
Philadelphia 76ers. No. 3474, 75c, Stephon
Marbury, New York Knicks.

2004   *Perf. 14*
3472-3474 A596   Set of 3   1.75 1.75

Issued: No. 3472, 11/3; No. 3473, 11/5; No.
3474, 11/6. Each printed in sheets of 12.

Miniature Sheet

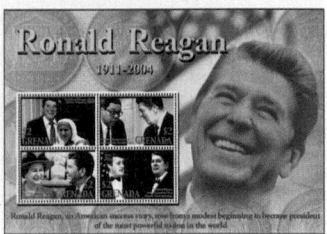

Pres. Ronald Reagan (1911-
2004) — A597

No. 3475: a, With Mother Teresa. b, With
Colin Powell. c, With Queen Elizabeth II. d,
With Brian Mulroney.

2004   *Perf. 13½*
3475 A597 $2 Sheet of 4, #a-d   6.00 6.00

A598

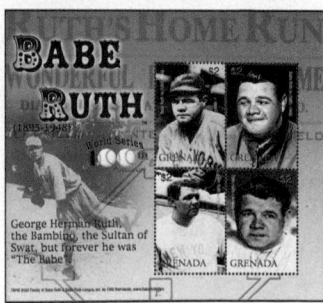

George Herman "Babe" Ruth (1895-
1948), Baseball Player — A599

Various portraits.

2004   *Perf. 14*
3476 A598 $2 Sheet of 4, #a-d   6.00 6.00
            Perf. 13¾x13¼
3477 A599 $2 Sheet of 4, #a-d   6.00 6.00

Christmas
A600

Paintings by Norman Rockwell: 35c, Merry
Christmas. 75c, Yuletide Merriment. $1,
Dressing Up. $4, Christmas.
$6, The London Coach.

2004, Dec. 9   *Perf. 12*
3478-3481 A600 Set of 4   4.75 4.75
Souvenir Sheet
3482 A600 $6 multi   4.50 4.50

New Year 2005
(Year of the
Rooster) — A601

Paintings by Qi Baishi: $1, Chrysanthe-
mums, Cocks and Hens. $4, Taro Leaves and
Double Hens.

2005, Jan. 17 Litho. *Perf. 11¾x12¼*
3483 A601 $1 multi   .75 .75
Souvenir Sheet
            Perf. 12¾x13
3484 A601 $4 multi   3.00 3.00

No. 3483 printed in sheets of 4. No. 3484
contains one 22x76mm stamp.

Basketball Players Type of 2004

Designs: No. 3485, 75c, Zydrunas Ilgaus-
kas, Cleveland Cavaliers. No. 3486, 75c,
Dwayne Wade, Miami Heat. $3, Tracy
McGrady, Orlando Magic.

2005, Feb. 10   *Perf. 14*
3485-3487 A596   Set of 3   3.50 3.50

Souvenir Sheet

Intl. Year of Rice — A602

No. 3488: a, Detail from Deities Overseeing
the Transplanting of Rice, by unknown artist.
b, Detail from the Taoist God Overseeing the
Rice Planting, by unknown artist. c, Women
Transplanting Rice in Late Spring Rain, by
Hiroshige.

2005, Feb. 10
3488 A602 $3 Sheet of 3, #a-c   6.75 6.75

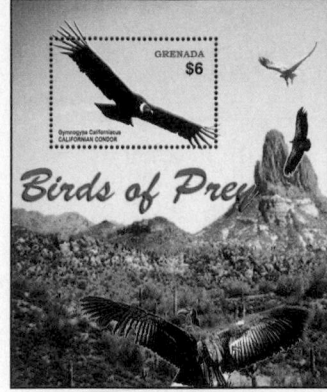

Birds, Wild Cats and
Butterflies — A603

No. 3489, $1.50, vert. — Birds: a, Turkey
vulture. b, Bald eagle. c, Peregrine falcon. d,
Prairie falcon. e, Northern goshawk. f,
Cooper's hawk.
No. 3490, $1.50, vert. — Wild cats: a, Chee-
tah. b, Lion. c, White tiger. d, Leopard. e, Bob-
cat. f, Bengal tiger.
No. 3491, $1.50 — Butterflies: a, Machao-
nides's swallowtail. b, Viceroy. c, Glasswing
satyr. d, Birdwing. e, Ornithoptera goliath
procus. f, Ornithoptera priamus alberio.
No. 3492, $6, California condor. No. 3493,
$6, Jaguar, vert. No. 3494, $6, Lime butterfly.

2005, Feb. 10   *Litho.*
Sheets of 6, #a-f
3489-3491 A603   Set of 3   21.00 21.00
Souvenir Sheets
3492-3494 A603   Set of 3   13.50 13.50

A604

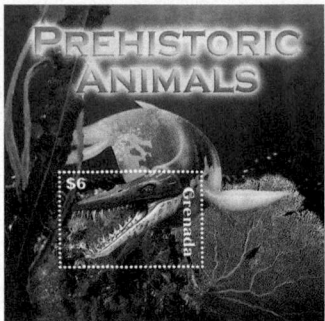

Prehistoric Animals — A605

No. 3495: a, Majungatholus. b, Diplodocus.
c, Willo. d, Velociraptor.
No. 3496, $2: a, Archelon. b, Ammonite. c,
Plesiosaur. d, Xiphactinus.
No. 3497, $2: a, Pteranodon. b,
Dimorphodon. c, Pterodactylus. d,
Rhamphorhynchus.
No. 3498, Spinosaurus.
No. 3499, $6, Pliosaur. No. 3500, $6,
Tapejara imperator.

2005, Feb. 10
3495 A604 $2 Sheet of 4, #a-d   6.00 6.00
Sheets of 4, #a-d
3496-3497 A605   Set of 2   12.00 12.00
Souvenir Sheets
3498 A604 $6 multi   4.50 4.50
3499-3500 A605   Set of 2   9.00 9.00

Souvenir Sheet

Buildings Damaged in Hurricane
Ivan — A606

No. 3501: a, Cathedral of Immaculate Conception. b, Anglican Church. c, York House. d,
Springs Sub-office.

2005, Mar. 8   *Perf. 12¾*
3501 A606 $2 Sheet of 4, #a-d   6.00 6.00

Elvis Presley (1935-77) — A607

No. 3502, $1.50: a, Singing, 1955. b, Hold-
ing microphone, 1957. c, Playing guitar, 1959.
d, Singing, 1961. e, Singing, 1968. f, With guitar, 1970.
No. 3503, $1.50: a, Dancing, 1957. b, Play-
ing guitar, 1964. c, On saddle, 1965. d, Playing guitar, 1968. e, Playing piano, 1969. f,
Singing, 1970.

2005, Apr. 4   *Perf. 13¾*
Sheets of 6, #a-f
3502-3503 A607   Set of 2   13.50 13.50

Yasujiro Ozu (1903-63), Film
Director — A608

No. 3504: a, Tenement Gentleman, 1947. b,
Tokyo Story, 1953. c, A Hen in the Wind, 1948.
d, Floating Weeds, 1959.

2005, Apr. 8   *Perf. 14¼*
3504 A608 $2 Sheet of 4, #a-d   6.00 6.00

Dutch Royalty — A609

No. 3505: a, King William I. b, King William II. c, King William III. d, Queen Wilhelmina. e, Queen Juliana. f, Queen Beatrix. g, Prince Willem-Alexander. h, Princess Catharina-Amalia.

2005, Apr. 14   Litho.   Perf. 12
3505 A609 $2 Sheet of 8, #a-h 12.00 12.00

End of World War II, 60th Anniv. — A610

No. 3506, $2 — Burma Campaign: a, "21 Curves" Road. b, British advance through the jungle of Burma. c, Troops at Magwe airstrip. d, Allied troops escorting prisoners.
No. 3507, $2 — Operation Market Garden: a, Allied troops landing behind enemy lines. b, Allied troops fire on German defenders. c, German troops move up to counterattack. d, Bridges still remain in German hands.
No. 3508, $6, Troops discuss next move.
No. 3509, $6, Allied troops meet stiff resistance.

2005, May 10   Perf. 13¼
Sheets of 4, #a-d
3506-3507 A610 Set of 2 12.00 12.00
Souvenir Sheets
3508-3509 A610 Set of 2   9.00 9.00

V-E Day, 60th Anniv. — A611

No. 3510: a, D-Day. b, Allied troops break through enemy lines. c, German troops begin to surrender. d, The war in Europe is over.
$6, Berlin falls to the armies of the Soviet Union.

2005, May 10   Perf. 14
3510 A611 $2 Sheet of 4, #a-d 6.00 6.00
Souvenir Sheet
3511 A611 $6 multi 4.50 4.50

V-J Day, 60th Anniv. — A612

No. 3512: a, Airplanes over islands of the Pacific. b, Allied forces storm the beaches of Japanese-held islands. c, Gen. Douglas MacArthur returns to the Philippines. d, The Japanese armies surrender.
$6, Allies enjoy victory celebration.

2005, May 10
3512 A612 $2 Sheet of 4, #a-d 6.00 6.00
Souvenir Sheet
3513 A612 $6 multi 4.50 4.50

Rotary International, Cent. — A613

No. 3514: a, Child receiving polio vaccination. b, District 7030 Governor David Edwards and wife, Donna. c, Paul P. Harris, Rotary International founder.
$6, 2001-02 Rotary President Richard D. King, children.

2005, May 10   Perf. 14
3514 A613 $3 Sheet of 3, #a-c 6.75 6.75
Souvenir Sheet
3515 A613 $6 multi 4.50 4.50

Miniature Sheet

Expo 2005, Aichi, Japan — A614

No. 3516: a, Victoria Falls. b, Bald eagle. c, Caribbean coral reef. d, Childbirth. e, First man on the moon. f, Pollination.

2005, June 27   Perf. 12
3516 A614 $1.50 Sheet of 6, #a-f 6.75 6.75

Albert Einstein (1879-1955), Physicist — A615

No. 3517 — Einstein and country name in: a, Blue. b, Black. c, White. d, Red
$6, Einstein with pipe.

2005, June 27   Perf. 12¾
3517 A615 $2 Sheet of 4, #a-d 6.00 6.00
Souvenir Sheet
3518 A015 $6 multi 4.50 4.50

Souvenir Sheet

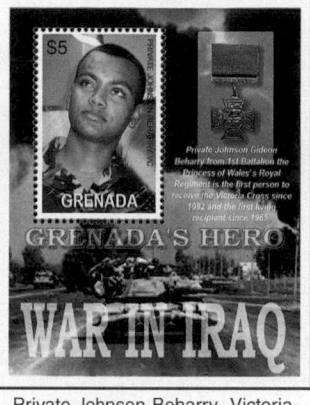

Private Johnson Beharry, Victoria Cross Recipient in Iraq War — A616

2005, July 11   Litho.
3519 A616 $5 multi 3.75 3.75

Hans Christian Andersen (1805-75), Author — A617

No. 3520: a, Andersen, with hands shown. b, Photograph of Andersen. c, Andersen, with white tie.
$6, Andersen's tombstone, Copenhagen.

2005, July 11
3520 A617 $3 Sheet of 3, #a-c 6.75 6.75
Souvenir Sheet
3521 A617 $6 multi 4.50 4.50

Friedrich von Schiller (1759-1805), Writer — A618

No. 3522, vert.: a, William Tell Memorial, Altdorf, Switzerland. b, Animated movie of William Tell. c, Stage production of William Tell.
$6, Scene from William Tell story.

2005, July 11   Perf. 14
3522 A618 $3 Sheet of 3, #a-c 6.75 6.75
Souvenir Sheet
3523 A618 $6 multi 4.50 4.50

Jules Verne (1828-1905), Writer — A619

No. 3524: a, Photograph of Verne. b, Photograph of Verne in oval. c, Drawing of Verne.
$6, From the Earth to the Moon.

2005, July 11   Perf. 12¾
3524 A619 $3 Sheet of 3, #a-c 6.75 6.75
Souvenir Sheet
3525 A619 $6 multi 4.50 4.50

Battle of Trafalgar, Bicent. — A620

No. 3526, vert.: a, Admiral Horatio Nelson. b, Napoleon Bonaparte. c, HMS Victory. d, The Nelson Touch.
$6, Sailors on ship.

2005, July 11   Perf. 12¾
3526 A620 $2 Sheet of 4, #a-d 6.00 6.00
Souvenir Sheet
3527 A620 $6 multi 4.50 4.50

Miniature Sheets

Dennis The Menace, Comic Strip by Hank Ketcham — A621

No. 3528, $2: a, "Grandpa got a new knee. . ." b, "Joey an' me don't have any money. . ." c, "Good news, Mrs. Wilson! . ." d, "I think the boy's. . ."
No. 3529, $2: a, "How 'bout a trade. . ." b, "It's not a good idea. . ." c, "I'll bet you were the top . ." d, "Boy, I'm glad I don't have to. . ."

2005, July 11   Perf. 14¼
Sheets of 4, #a-d
3528-3529 A621 Set of 2 12.00 12.00

Souvenir Sheet

Taipei 2005 Intl. Stamp Exhibition — A622

No. 3530: a, Shalom Meir Tower, Tel Aviv. b, Empire State Building, New York. c, Taipei 101 Building, Taipei. d, Eiffel Tower, Paris.

2005, Aug. 19   *Perf. 14*
3530 A622 $2 Sheet of 4, #a-d   6.00 6.00

Pope John Paul II (1920-2005) and Lech Walesa — A623

2005, Aug. 22   *Perf. 12¾*
3531 A623 $4 multi   3.00 3.00
Printed in sheets of 4.

Wedding of Prince Charles and Camilla Parker Bowles — A624

Various pictures of couple with oval in: No. 3532, $2, Lemon. No. 3533, $2, Light blue. No. 3534, $2, Pink, horiz.

2005, Sept. 7   *Perf. 13½*
3532-3534 A624   Set of 3   4.50 4.50
Each stamp printed in sheets of 4.

Christmas — A625

Designs: 25c, The Nativity, by Correggio. 75c, Virgin and Child, by Lorenzo Lotto. $1, The Holy Family, by Lotto. $5, Madonna and Child with the Saints, by Lotto. $6, Allegory of Music, by Fra Filippo Lippi.

2005, Nov. 15   *Perf. 12¾*
3535-3538 A625   Set of 4   5.25 5.25
Souvenir Sheet
3539 A625 $6 multi   4.50 4.50

Bird Type of 2000
2005   Litho.   *Perf. 12x11¾*
     Size:22x26mm
3540 A472 10c Purple-throated
       Carib   .20 .20

Miniature Sheets

Chelsea Soccer Team, Cent. — A626

Liverpool Soccer Team — A627

No. 3541: a, Stadium and field. b, Stadium, field, team emblem and years. c, Players holding English League Championship award. d, Players in bus with cup and flag. e, Fans with flag. f, Aerial view of bus carrying players. g, Players. h, Coach. i, Stadium, field, team emblem. j, Team with award.
No. 3542: a, Crowd watching bus carrying players near stadium. b, Player and coach holding UEFA Cup. c, Gate. d, Aerial view of stadium. e, Banner. f, Players waving. g, Fans. h, Soccer match. i, Players celebrating. j, Crowd cheering players in bus.

2005, Dec. 28   Litho.   *Perf. 13¼*
3541 A626 $1.50 Sheet of 10,
       #a-j   11.50 11.50
3542 A627 $1.50 Sheet of 10,
       #a-j   11.50 11.50

The Two Hounds, by Hui-Tsung A628

2006, Jan. 3
3543 A628 $1 shown   .75 .75
Souvenir Sheet
3544 A628 $4 Entire painting   3.00 3.00
No. 3544 contains one 50x37mm stamp.

Pope Benedict XVI — A629

2006, Jan. 10
3545 A629 $2 multi   1.50 1.50
Printed in sheets of 4.

A630

Elvis Presley (1935-77) — A631

No. 3546 — Movie posters: a, Girls! Girls! Girls! b, Jailhouse Rock. c, Paradise - Hawaiian Style. d, It Happened at the World's Fair.

2006   Litho.   *Perf. 13¼*
3546 A630 $3 Sheet of 4, #a-
     d   9.00 9.00
Litho. & Embossed
Die Cut Perf. 7¾
Without Gum
3547 A631 $20 shown   15.00 15.00
Issued: No. 3546, 7/11, No. 3547, 2/21.

Queen Elizabeth II, 80th Birthday — A632

No. 3548: a, Wearing necklace, no earrings. b, Wearing blue jacket. c, Portrait. d, Wearing jacket and earrings. $6, Wearing hat.

2006, Feb. 21   Litho.   *Perf. 13¼*
3548 A632 $3 Sheet of 4, #a-d   9.00 9.00
Souvenir Sheet
Perf. 12¼x12
3549 A632 $6 multi   4.50 4.50

Teams Competing in 2006 World Cup Soccer Championships, Germany — A633

Designs: No. 3550, $1.50, Angola. No. 3551, $1.50, Argentina. No. 3552, $1.50, Australia. No. 3553, $1.50, Brazil. No. 3554, $1.50, Costa Rica. No. 3555, $1.50, Croatia. No. 3556, $1.50, Czech Republic. No. 3557, $1.50, Ecuador. No. 3558, $1.50, England. No. 3559, $1.50, France. No. 3560, $1.50, Germany. No. 3561, $1.50, Ghana. No. 3562, $1.50, Iran. No. 3563, $1.50, Italy. No. 3564, $1.50, Ivory Coast. No. 3565, $1.50, Japan. No. 3566, $1.50, Mexico. No. 3567, $1.50, Netherlands. No. 3568, $1.50, Paraguay. No. 3569, $1.50, Poland. No. 3570, $1.50, Portugal. No. 3571, $1.50, Saudi Arabia. No. 3572,

---

$1.50, Serbia and Montenegro. No. 3573, $1.50, South Korea. No. 3574, $1.50, Spain. No. 3575, $1.50, Sweden. No. 3576, $1.50, Switzerland. No. 3577, $1.50, Togo. No. 3578, $1.50, Trinidad and Tobago. No. 3579, $1.50, Tunisia. No. 3580, $1.50, Ukraine. No. 3581, $1.50, United States.

2006, Mar. 29   *Perf. 12¼x12*
3550-3581 A633   Set of 32   36.00 36.00

Nos. 3550-3581 each printed in sheets of 6. Stamps other than Nos. 3550, 3553, 3554, 3560, 3561, 3566, 3575, 3579 and 3581, which have solid color backgrounds, have multicolored backgrounds that vary within the sheet.

Marilyn Monroe (1926-62), Actress — A634

2006, Mar. 30   *Perf. 13¼*
3582 A634 $3 multi   2.25 2.25
Printed in sheets of 4.

2006 Winter Olympics, Turin A635

Designs: No. 3583, Poster for 1980 Lake Placid Winter Olympics. No. 3583A, Poster for 2006 Turin Winter Olympics. No. 3584, Switzerland #B173. No. 3584A, Italy #2722. $2, Poster for 1948 St. Moritz Winter Olympics. $3, Switzerland #B172.

2006, May 10   *Perf. 14¼*
3583 A635 75c multicolored   .55 .55
3583A A635 75c multi   .55 .55
3584 A635 90c multicolored   .70 .70
3584A A635 90c multi   .70 .70
3585 A635 $2 multicolored   1.50 1.50
3586 A635 $3 multicolored   2.25 2.25
   Nos. 3583-3586 (6)   6.25 6.25

Rosa Parks (1913-2005), American Civil Rights Activist — A636

2006, May 27   *Perf. 11½x12*
3587 A636 $3 multi   2.25 2.25
Printed in sheets of 3.

Flags and Uniforms of World Cup Soccer Champions A637

Designs: 75c, Brazil, 2002. 90c, Germany, 1990. $3, France, 1998.

2006, June 9   *Perf. 13¼*
3588-3590   A637   Set of 3   3.50   3.50

World Cup Trophy — A638

2006, June 9
Self-Adhesive   *Die Cut*
3591   A638 $6 multi   4.50   4.50

Rembrandt (1606-69), Painter A639

Designs: 50c, The Little Jewish Bride. $1, Young Man in Velvet Cap. $1.50, Old Woman Sleeping. No. 3595, $3, Woman Reading. No. 3596, $6, Portrait of a Seated Man (70x100mm). No. 3597, $6, Portrait of a Scholar (70x100mm).
No. 3598, $3: a, Young Woman with Flowers in Her Hair. b, Portrait of a Seated Woman. c, Alijdt Adriaensor. d, Amalia van Solms.

Perf. 12, 12½x12¼ (#3596, 3597)
2006, June 16
3592-3597   A639   Set of 6   13.50   13.50
3597a   Imperf.   4.50   4.50
Miniature Sheet
Perf. 13x13¼
3598   A639 $3 Sheet of 4, #a-d   9.00   9.00

Souvenir Sheet

Wolfgang Amadeus Mozart (1756-91), Composer — A640

2006, June 22   *Perf. 12¾*
3599   A640 $6 multi   4.50   4.50

Souvenir Sheet

Ludwig Durr (1878-1956), Engineer, and Zeppelins — A641

No. 3600 — Durr and: a, Graf Zeppelin D-LZ-127. b, Graf Zeppelin LT. c, Graf Zeppelin L-26.

2006, June 22
3600   A641 $4 Sheet of 3, #a-c   9.00   9.00

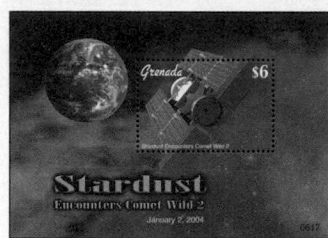

Space — A642

No. 3601, $2 — Sputnik 1: a, Sergei Korolev. b, Sputnik 1 in space. c, Inside Sputnik 1. d, Sputnik 1 capsule.
No. 3602, $2, vert. — Apollo-Soyuz: a, Apollo rocket. b, Apollo command module and adapter. c, Soyuz rocket on launchpad. d, Soyuz.
No. 3603 — Giotto Comet Probe: a, Halley's Comet, round head in yellow at right. b, Tip of Giotto Probe launcher Ariane V14. c, Halley's Comet, head at left, thin tail. d, Halley's Comet, head in white at right. e, Bottom of Giotto Probe launcher Ariane V14. f, Halley's Comet, head at left, wide tail.
No. 3604, $6, Stardust Comet Probe. No. 3605, $6, Comet Tempel 1 Deep Impact Mission. No. 3606, $6, Space Shuttle Discovery's return to space.

2006, Sept. 14   *Litho.*   *Perf. 12¾*
Sheets of 4, #a-d
3601-3602   A642   Set of 2   12.00   12.00
3603   A642 $2 Sheet of 6, #a-f   9.00   9.00
Souvenir Sheets
3604-3606   A642   Set of 3   13.50   13.50

Christopher Columbus (1451-1506), Explorer — A643

Designs: $1.50, Sinking of the Santa Maria. $2, Santa Maria, vert. $3, Columbus, sailor and ship, vert. $4, Columbus and ships, vert. $6, Fleet of ships, 1493.

2006, Oct. 26   *Perf. 12¾*
3607-3610   A643   Set of 4   8.00   8.00
Souvenir Sheet
3611   A643 $6 multi   4.50   4.50

Butterflies A644

Designs: 10c, Mourning cloak butterfly. 25c, Snout butterfly. $1, Tithorea pinthias. $2, Diadem butterfly. $4, Red satyr butterfly. $5, Taygetis chrysogone. $10, Pierella hortona. $20, Morpho aega.

2006, Dec. 1   *Litho.*   *Perf. 12½*
3612   A644   10c multi   .20   .20
3613   A644   25c multi   .20   .20
3614   A644 $1 multi   .75   .75
3615   A644 $2 multi   1.50   1.50
3616   A644 $4 multi   3.00   3.00
3617   A644 $5 multi   3.75   3.75
3618   A644 $10 multi   7.50   7.50
3619   A644 $20 multi   15.00   15.00
    Nos. 3612-3619 (8)   31.90   31.90

Princess Maxima of the Netherlands — A645

No. 3620: a, Head of Princess Maxima. b, Princess Maxima holding purse.

2006, Dec. 7   *Perf. 13½*
3620   A645 $1.50 Pair, #a-b   2.25   2.25
Printed in sheets containing 3 of each stamp.

Christmas — A646

Details of The Adoration of the Shepherds, by Peter Paul Rubens: 25c, Man with hat. 50c, Mary. 75c, Shepherd. $1, Baby Jesus.
No. 3625: a, Like 25c. b, Like 50c. c, Like 75c. d, Like $1.

2006, Dec. 21   *Perf. 14*
3621-3624   A646   Set of 4   1.90   1.90
Souvenir Sheet
3625   A646 $2 Sheet of 4, #a-d   6.00   6.00

Betty Boop — A647

No. 3626 — Betty Boop: a, Sitting on "E." b, With hands on thighs, between "Y" and "B." c, With one leg elevated. d, With hands clasped, Standing behind "E." e, With arms at side, standing in front of "Y." f, With arms raised upwards.
No. 3627: a, With hands clasped, blue circles. b, With arms at side, red and blue circles. c, With arms raised upwards, pink and blue circles. d, At microphone, blue circles.
No. 3628, $3: a, Holding mirror. b, Wearing fruited hat.
No. 3629, $3, horiz.: a, Head and upper torso. b, Lower torso.

2006, Dec. 22   *Perf. 14*
3626   A647 $1.50 Sheet of 6, #a-f   6.75   6.75
3627   A647 $2 Sheet of 4, #a-d   6.00   6.00
Souvenir Sheets of 2, #a-b
3628-3629   A647   Set of 2   9.00   9.00

Arsenal Soccer Team — A648

No. 3630: a, $1, Players and crowd. b, $1, Soccer field at night. c, $1, Fans in seats at end of stadium. d, $1, Emirates Stadium exterior. e, $1, Players. f, $2, Players. g, $2, Aerial view of stadium exterior. h, $2, Fans. i, $2, Soccer field and fans. j, $2, Stadium exterior at night.

2007, Jan. 16
3630   A648   Sheet of 10, #a-j   11.50   11.50

Concorde Test Pilots and Flags — A649

No. 3631: a, Amore Turcat, French flag. b, Brian Trubshaw, British flag.
Illustration reduced.

2007, Feb. 15
3631   A649 $2 Pair, #a-b   3.00   3.00
Printed in sheets containing three of each stamp.

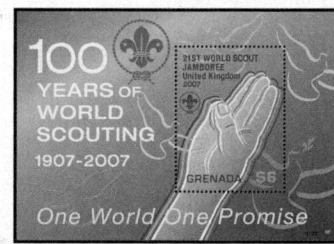

Scouting, Cent. — A650

No. 3632 — Scout sign and denomination in: a, Blue. b, Orange. c, Red violet. d, Green $6, Orange.

2007, Feb. 15
3632   A650 $3 Sheet of 4, #a-d   9.00   9.00
Souvenir Sheet
3633   A650 $6 multi   4.50   4.50

Pres. John F. Kennedy (1917-63) — A651

No. 3634, $2 — First meeting with Soviet Premier Nikita Khrushchev: a, Khrushchev at the Simferopol Space Control Center. b, Kennedy greeting Khrushchev. c, Kennedy and Khrushchev on sofa. d, Kennedy and Khrushchev at residence of US Ambassador in Vienna.
No. 3635, $2 — Cuban Missile Crisis: a, Khrushchev and Fidel Castro. b, Kennedy addressing nation. c, Completed SA-2 missile site. d, Kennedy and Khrushchev shaking hands in Vienna.

2007, Feb. 15
Sheets of 4, #a-d
3634-3635   A651   Set of 2   12.00   12.00

Souvenir Sheet

New Year 2007 (Year of the Pig) — A652

No. 3636 — Text "Traditional Chinese New Year Paper Cutting" in: a, $1, Black. b, $1, White. c, $2, Beige. d, $2, Yellow.

2007, Feb. 18   **Perf. 14**
3636   A652   Sheet of 4, #a-d   4.50   4.50

Pope Benedict XVI — A653

2007, June 4   **Litho.**   **Perf. 13¼**
3637   A653 $1 multi   .75   .75
Printed in sheets of 8.

2007 Cricket World Cup, East Indies — A654

Designs: $1, Cricket World Cup emblem, flag and map of Grenada. $2, Rawl Lewis. $3, Queen's Park, horiz. $6, Cricket World Cup emblem.

2007, June 18
3638-3640   A654   Set of 3   4.50   4.50
Souvenir Sheet
3641   A654 $6 multi   4.50   4.50

Wedding of Queen Elizabeth II and Prince Philip, 60th Anniv. — A655

No. 3642: a, Queen and Prince, orange panel. b, Queen, orange panel. c, Queen, light blue panel. d, Queen and Prince, light blue panel. e, Queen and Prince, lilac panel. f, Queen, lilac panel. $6, Queen and Prince, diff.

2007, June 25
3642   A655 $2 Sheet of 6, #a-f   9.00   9.00
Souvenir Sheet
3643   A655 $6 multi   4.50   4.50

Princess Diana (1961-97) — A656

No. 3644 — Diana with: a, Red dress. b, Light blue and white dress. c, White gown. d, Green and white dress.
No. 3645, $6, Scarf on head. No. 3646, $6, Red dress, horiz.

2007, June 25
3644   A656 $2 Sheet of 4, #a-d   6.00   6.00
Souvenir Sheets
3645-3646   A656   Set of 2   9.00   9.00

Intl. Polar Year — A657

No. 3647, vert.: a, Adult penguin with head raised. b, Three penguins in distance. c, Adult penguin with head lowered. d, Juvenile penguin, ball. e, Juvenile penguin with wings extended. f, Juvenile penguin with head raised.
$6, Penguin on skis.

2007, June 25
3647   A657 $2 Sheet of 6, #a-f   9.00   9.00
Souvenir Sheet
3648   A657 $6 multi   4.50   4.50

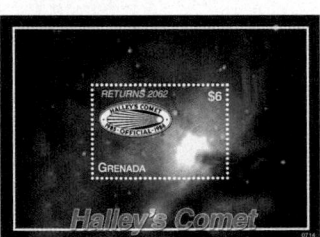

1986 Halley's Comet Merchandising Emblem — A658

No. 3649: a, Orange brown frame. b, Dark blue frame. c, Purple frame. d, Red frame. $6, Emblem, night sky.

2007, July 11
3649   A658 $2 Sheet of 4, #a-d   6.00   6.00
Souvenir Sheet
3650   A658 $6 multi   4.50   4.50

U.S. Presidents — A659

No. 3651: a, 1c, George Washington. b, 2c, John Adams. c, 3c, Thomas Jefferson. d, 4c, James Madison. e, 5c, James Monroe. f, 6c, John Quincy Adams. g, 7c, Andrew Jackson. h, 8c, Martin Van Buren. i, 9c, William Henry Harrison. j, 10c, John Tyler. k, 11c, James Knox Polk. l, 12c, Zachary Taylor. m, 13c, Millard Fillmore. n, 14c, Franklin Pierce. o, $4, Presidential seal.
No. 3652: a, 15c, James Buchanan. b, 16c, Abraham Lincoln. c, 17c, Andrew Johnson. d, 18c, Ulysses S. Grant. e, 19c, Rutherford B. Hayes. f, 20c, James A. Garfield. g, 21c, Chester A. Arthur. h, 22c, Grover Cleveland. i, 23c, Benjamin Harrison. j, 24c, Grover Cleveland. k, 25c, William McKinley. l, 26c, Theodore Roosevelt. m, 27c, William Howard Taft. n, 28c, Woodrow Wilson. o, $2, Capitol Dome.
No. 3653: a, 29c, Warren G. Harding. b, 30c, Calvin Coolidge. c, 31c, Herbert Hoover. d, 32c, Franklin D. Roosevelt. e, 33c, Harry S Truman. f, 34c, Dwight D. Eisenhower. g, 35c, John F. Kennedy. h, 36c, Lyndon B. Johnson. i, 37c, Richard M. Nixon. j, 38c, Gerald R. Ford. k, 39c, Jimmy Carter. l, 40c, Ronald Reagan. m, 41c, George H. W. Bush. n, 42c, William J. Clinton. o, 43c, George W. Bush.

2007, July 16   **Perf. 12**
3651   A659   Sheet of 15, #a-o   3.75   3.75
3652   A659   Sheet of 15, #a-o   3.75   3.75
3653   A659   Sheet of 15, #a-o   4.00   4.00
    Nos. 3651-3653 (3)   11.50   11.50

Worldwide Fund for Nature (WWF) — A660

No. 3654 — Clymene dolphins with denomination in: a, Orange. b, Bluish green. c, Yellow. d, Aquamarine.

2007, July 23   **Perf. 13¼**
3654   Strip of 4   3.75   3.75
   a.-d.   A660 $1.20 Any single   .90   .90
   e.   Miniature sheet, 2 each #3654a-3654d   7.50   7.50

Souvenir Sheet

St. George's University, 30th Anniv. — A661

2007, Oct. 26   **Perf. 12¾**
3655   A661 $6 multi   4.50   4.50

Souvenir Sheet

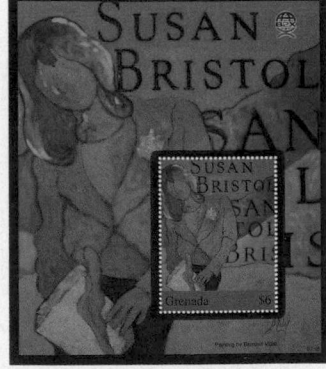

Susan Bristol, Painting by Bernard Vidal — A662

2007, Oct. 26   **Perf. 13¼**
3656   A662 $6 multi   4.50   4.50

Victoria Cross, 150th Anniv. — A663

No. 3657, vert.: a, Corporal Bryan Budd. b, Brigadier General James Forbes-Robertson. c, Private Johnson Beharry. d, Sergeant William J. Gordon. e, Private Henry Tandey. f, Private Jorgen Christian Jensen. $6, Seaman Jack Mantel.

2007, Oct. 26   **Litho.**
3657   A663 $1.50 Sheet of 6, #a-f   6.75   6.75
Souvenir Sheet
3658   A663 $6 multi   4.50   4.50

First Helicopter Flight, Cent. — A664

No. 3659, horiz.: a, S-65/RH-53D. b, Autogyro and bird. c, BK 117. d, AS-64. $6, AH-64 Apache.

2007, Oct. 26
3659   A664 $2 Sheet of 4, #a-d   6.00   6.00
Souvenir Sheet
3660   A664 $6 multi   4.50   4.50

Miniature Sheets

Intl. Holocaust Remembrance Day — A665

No. 3661 $1.40 — United Nations diplomats and delegates: a, Srgian Kerim, President of 62nd General Assembly. b, Andrei Dapkiunas, Belarus. c, Jean-Marie Ehouzou, Benin. d, Milos Prica, Bosnia & Herzegovina. e, Samuel O. Outlule, Botswana. f, Francis K. Butagira,

Uganda. g, Valeriy P. Kuchinsky, Ukraine. h, Jean Ping, President of 59th General Assembly.

No. 3662, $1.40: a, Erasmo Lara-Peña, Dominican Republic. b, Diego Cordovez, Ecuador. c, Carmen M Gallardo-Hernandez, El Salvador. d, Lino Sima Ekua Avomo, Equatorial Guinea. e, Tina Intelmann, Estonia. f, Dawit Yohannes, Ethiopia. g, Isikia Rabiei Savua, Fiji. h, Lars Wide, Chef de Cabinet of 60th General Assembly.

No. 3663, $1.40: a, Ángus Friday, Grenada. b, Alfredo Lopes Cabral, Guinea-Bissau. c, Samuel Rudolph Insanally, Guyana. d, Lèo Mérorès, Haiti. e, Ivan Romero-Martinez, Honduras. f, Gabor Brodi, Hungary. g, Hjalmar W. Hannesson, Iceland. h, Dan Gillerman, Israel.

No. 3664, $1.40: a, Colin Beck, Solomon Islands. b, Dumisani S. Kumalo, South Africa. c, Juan Antonio Yáñez-Barnueva, Spain. d, Anders Liden, Sweden. e, Peter Maurer, Switzerland. f, K. Laxanachantorn Laohaphan, Thailand. g, José Luis Guterres, East Timor. h, Fekitamoeloa 'Utoikamanu, Tonga.

2007, Oct. 26   **Litho.**
Sheets of 8, #a-h
3661-3664 A665   Set of 4   35.00 35.00

Christmas
A666

Various details from Nativity with the Annunciation to the Shepherds, by Follower of Jan Joest: 25c, 50c, 75c, $1.

2007, Nov. 1   **Perf. 14¾x14**
3665-3668 A666   Set of 4   1.90 1.90

New Year 2008 (Year of the Rat) A667

2007, Dec. 3   **Litho.**   **Perf. 13x13¼**
3669 A667 $2 multi   1.50 1.50
Printed in sheets of 4.

Souvenir Sheet

Breast Cancer Prevention — A668

2007, Dec. 11   **Perf. 14**
3670 A668 $6 multi   4.50 4.50

Princess Diana (1961-97) — A669

Serpentine Die Cut 7¾
2007, Dec. 11   **Litho. & Embossed**
Without Gum
3671 A669 $20 gold & multi   15.00 15.00

Miniature Sheets

A670

Elvis Presley (1935-77) — A671

No. 3672 — Presley: a, Holding guitar at neck. b, Singing, not touching microphone. c, Wearing green shirt. d, Facing right, playing guitar. e, Singing, holding microphone. f, Facing right, playing guitar.

No. 3673 — Presley: a, Holding microphone. b, Wearing necktie. c, Holding guitar over shoulder. d, And guitar head.

2008   **Litho.**   **Perf. 13¼**
3672 A670 $1.50 Sheet of 6, #a-f   6.75 6.75
3673 A671 $2 Sheet of 4, #a-d   6.00 6.00
Issued: No. 3672, 1/14; No. 3673, 6/13.

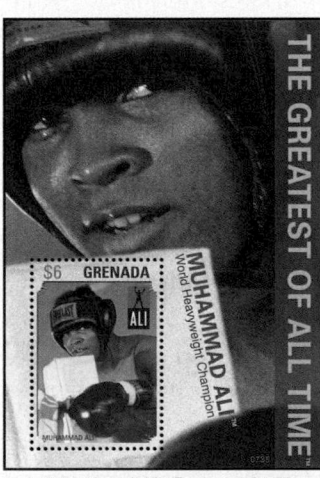
Muhammad Ali, Boxer — A672

No. 3674, $2 — Ali: a, With towel on head, bank of microphones at left. b, With towel on head, bank of microphone at right. c, With fist raised. d, With towel off head, bank of microphones at right.

No. 3675, $2, horiz. — Ali: a, With arms raised. b, Wearing robe. c, At punching bag. d, Boxing.

No. 3676, $6, Ali wearing protective headgear. No. 3677, $2, Ali with fan's hand on shoulder.

Perf. 12x11½, 11½ (#3675)
2008, Jan. 14
Sheets of 4, #a-d
3674-3675 A672   Set of 2   12.00 12.00
Souvenir Sheets
Perf. 13¼
3676-3677 A672   Set of 2   9.00 9.00

Paintings by Qi Baishi (1864-1957) — A673

No. 3678: a, Magnolias and Bees. b, Mother Hen, Chicks and Banana Leaves. c, Fish, Crabs and Watergrass. d, Crows Returning to Wintry Trees.
$4, Morning Glories.

2008, Feb. 6   **Perf. 12½**
3678 A673 $1 Sheet of 4, #a-d   3.00 3.00
Souvenir Sheet
Perf. 11¼x11½
3679 A673 $4 multi   3.00 3.00

Miniature Sheet

2008 Summer Olympics, Beijing — A674

No. 3680: a, Greece #123. b, Poster for 1896 Olympic Games, Athens. c, Germany #B88. d, Poster for 1936 Olympic Games, Berlin.

2008, Feb. 6   **Perf. 14¼**
3680 A674 $3 Sheet of 4, #a-d   9.00 9.00

Flora of Taiwan — A675

No. 3681, horiz.: a, Oolong tea. b, Pink lotus. c, Japanese maple. d, Bitter melon. e, Rice field. f, Lychees.
$5, Shitou Forest.

2008, May 8   **Perf. 11½**
3681 A675 $1 Sheet of 6, #a-f   4.50 4.50
Souvenir Sheet
Perf. 13½
3682 A675 $5 multi   3.75 3.75
No. 3681 contains six 40x30mm stamps. 2008 Taipei Intl. Stamp Exhibition.

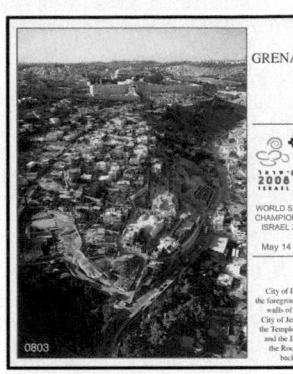
2008 World Stamp Championship, Israel — A676

2008, May 14   **Imperf.**
3683 A676 $6 multi   4.50 4.50

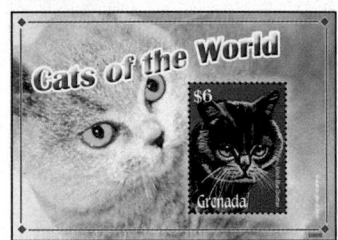
Cats — A677

No. 3684: a, Tortoiseshell. b, Korat. c, Turkish Van. d, Manx.
$6, British blue shorthair.

2008, June 18   **Perf. 11½**
3684 A677 $1.40 Sheet of 4, #a-d   4.25 4.25
Souvenir Sheet
3685 A677 $6 multi   4.50 4.50

Miniature Sheet

Players on 2008 Los Angeles Lakers Basketball Team — A678

No. 3686: a, Trevor Ariza. b, Jordan Farmar. c, Derek Fisher. d, Pau Gasol. e, Kobe Bryant. f, Lamar Odom. g, Vladimir Radmanovic. h, Sasha Vujacic. i, Luke Walton.

2008, June 17   **Litho.**   **Perf. 13½**
3686 A678 $1 Sheet of 9, #a-i   6.75 6.75

Miniature Sheet

Visit of Pope Benedict XVI to United States — A679

No. 3687 — Pope Benedict XVI and faded background showing: a, Bishop's red zucchetto under LL flourish. b, White ceiling tiles at top. c, Bishop's ear at UL. d, Bishop's hands at R.

2008, June 18   **Perf. 13½**
3687 A679 $2 Sheet of 4, #a-d   6.00 6.00

Miniature Sheet

Pres. John F. Kennedy (1917-63) — A680

No. 3688 — Kennedy and background designs of: a, Flag's white stripe and blue field. b, Flag's white and red stripes. c, Necktie. d, Flag's red and white stripes, with blue in UL corner.

2008, Oct. 10   **Perf. 11½x11¼**
3688 A680 $1.50 Sheet of 4, #a-d   4.50 4.50

Miniature Sheets

A681

A682

A683

A684

A685

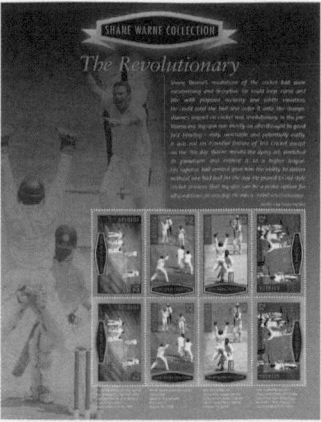

Shane Warne, Cricket Player — A686

No. 3689 — Warne: a, Holding ball, tan frame. b, Waving to crowd, tan frame. c, Close-up, tan frame. d, Wearing white shirt, green frame. e, As "b," green frame. f, As "c," green frame.

No. 3690 — Warne: a, Bowling in Australia uniform, tan frame. b, Holding trophy, tan frame. c, Celebrating, tan frame. d, As "a," green frame. e, As "b," green frame. f, As "c," green frame.

No. 3691 — Drawings of Warne by Phillip Howe: a, The Mastery (tan frame). b, The Revolutionary (tan frame). c, The Appeal (tan frame). d, The Natural (tan frame). e, As "a," green frame. f, As "b," green frame. g, As "c," green frame. h, As "d," green frame. Titles are in sheet margin.

No. 3692 — Warne bowling: a, Left arm horizontal, tan frame. b, Leg lifted, hands even, tan frame. c, Leg lifted, right hand higher than left hand, tan frame. d, Arm above head, tan frame. e, As "a," green frame. f, As "b," green frame. g, As "c," green frame. h, As "d," green frame.

No. 3693 — Warne: a, Celebrating and making fist, tan frame. b, With ball near ear, tan frame. c, After releasing ball, tan frame. d, With arm above head, umpire in background, tan frame. e, As "a," green frame. f, As "b," green frame. g, As "c," green frame. h, As "d," green frame.

No. 3694 — Match scenes: a, Warne bowling against Mike Gatting, tan frame, horiz. b, Warne taking 600th test wicket, tan frame. c, Warne capturing 533rd wicket. d, Warne taking 356th test wicket. e, As "a," green frame. f, As "b," green frame. g, As "c," green frame. h, As "d," green frame. Match descriptions are in sheet margin.

2008, Dec. 3   **Perf. 14x14½, 14½x14**
3689 A681 $2 Sheet of 6, #a-f   9.25 9.25
3690 A682 $2 Sheet of 6, #a-f   9.25 9.25
3691 A683 $2 Sheet of 8, #a-h   12.50 12.50
3692 A684 $2 Sheet of 8, #a-h   12.50 12.50
3693 A685 $2 Sheet of 8, #a-h   12.50 12.50
3694 A686 $2 Sheet of 8, #a-h   12.50 12.50
    Nos. 3689-3694 (6)   68.50 68.50

Miniature Sheet

Pope John Paul II (1920-2005) — A687

No. 3695 — Pope John Paul II: a, As child. b, At coronation. c, Holding books. d, With hands raised. e, Wearing biretta, hand on chin. f, Wearing zucchetto, hand touching face.

2008, Dec. 8   **Perf. 13½**
3695 A687 $2 Sheet of 6, #a-f   9.25 9.25

Coat of Arms — A688

2008, June 18   **Litho.**   **Perf. 14x15**
3696 A688 250c multi + label   1.90 1.90
  Printed in sheets of 8 + 8 labels.

Inauguration of US Pres. Barack Obama — A689

2009, Jan. 20   **Perf. 12¼x11¾**
3697 A689 $2.75 multi   2.10 2.10
  Printed in sheets of 4.

Miniature Sheets

Space Exploration, 50th Anniv. (in 2007) — A690

No. 3698, $2: a, Ultraviolet photograph of Sun. b, Buzz Aldrin on Moon. c, Crane lifting Space Shuttle Atlantis at Kennedy Vehicle Assembly Building. d, Mars Orbiter looking at Victoria Crater. e, Cassini Mission to Saturn. f, Engines being installed on Space Shuttle Atlantis.

No. 3699, $2: a, International Space Station. b, Concept for new lunar truck. c, Milky Way over Ontario. d, M16 and the Eagle Nebula. e, Astronaut in space on Expedition 16. f, Dextre robot working on the Space Station.

No. 3700, $2.50, vert.: a, Canadarm 2 (robotic arm on Space Station). b, Space Shuttle Atlantis on launch pad in daylight. c, Cat's Eye Nebula. d, Orion crew capsule.

No. 3701, $2.50, vert.: a, Space Shuttle Atlantis at Kennedy Space Center at night. b, International Space Station as seen from Space Shuttle Discovery. c, Aurora over Saturn. d, Kibo pressurized and logistic modules.

2009, Jan. 22   **Perf. 12**
    Sheets of 6, #a-f
3698-3699 A690   Set of 2   18.50 18.50
    Sheets of 4, #a-d
     Perf. 12½
3700-3701 A690   Set of 2   15.50 15.50

A691

A692

Birds — A693

Designs: $1, White-crowned pigeon. $2, Blue-winged warbler. $4, Bananaquit. $5, Monk parakeet.

No. 3706: a, Yellow-crowned amazon. b, Yellow-bellied sapsucker. c, Jamaican mango.

No. 3707: a, Tree swallow. b, Ringed kingfisher. c, Black-and-white warbler.

2009, Jan. 22   **Perf. 12½**
3702-3705 A691   Set of 4   9.25 9.25
3706 A692 $3 Sheet of 3, #a-c   7.00 7.00
     Perf. 12¾x13
3707 A693 $3 Sheet of 3, #a-c   7.00 7.00

New Year 2009
(Year of the
Ox) — A694

2009, Jan. 26   **Perf. 12**
3708 A694 $2.50 multi   1.90 1.90
   Printed in sheets of 4.

A695

Mushrooms — A696

Designs: 25c, Panaeolus papilionaceus. 50c, Panaeolus cyanescens. 75c, Panaeolus sphintrinus. 90c, Panaeolus fimicola. $1, Copelandia cyanescens. $4, Psilocybe cubensis.

No. 3715: a, Panaleus subbalteatus. b, Alboleptonia earlei. c, Porphyrellus portoricensis. d, Psilocybe caerulescens.

2009, Feb. 9   **Perf. 11½**
3709-3714 A695   Set of 6   5.75 5.75
3715 A696 $2.50 Sheet of 4, #a-d   7.75 7.75

    Miniature Sheet

Marilyn Monroe (1926-62),
Actress — A697

No. 3716 — Monroe: a, With arm extended. b, Touching wall. c, With chair in background. d, Resting on arms.

2009, Feb. 9
3716 A697 $2.50 Sheet of 4, #a-d   7.75 7.75

Flag of Grenada, and Designer
Anthony C. George — A698

Frame color: 10c, Blue green. 25c, Blue. 50c, Red. 75c, Yellow.
$6, Flag and George, vert.

2009, Feb. 25   **Perf. 13¼**
3717-3720 A698   Set of 4   1.25 1.25
     Souvenir Sheet
     Perf. 12
3721 A698 $6 multi   4.75 4.75
   No. 3721 contains one 30x40mm stamp.

Peony on
Vase — A699

2009, Apr. 10   **Perf. 13¼**
3722 A699 75c multi   .55 .55
     Souvenir Sheet
3723 A699 $5 Peony, diff.   3.75 3.75
   No. 3723 contains one 44x44mm stamp.
   No. 3722 was printed in sheets of 12.

    Miniature Sheet

Olympic Track and Field
Events — A700

No. 3724: a, Pole vault. b, Hurdles. c, Relay race. d, High jump.

2009, Apr. 29   **Perf. 12**
3724 A700 $1.40 Sheet of 4, #a-d   4.25 4.25
   China 2009 World Stamp Exhibition, Luoyang.

    Miniature Sheet

First Man on the Moon, 40th
Anniv. — A701

No. 3725: a, Proposed upper stages of Orion spacecraft, Wernher von Braun. b, Crew of Apollo 11. c, Lunar Orbiter. d, Ranger 7. e, Lunar Module, Pres. John F. Kennedy. f, Proposed Orion lunar module.

2009, Apr. 29   **Perf. 11½**
3725 A701 $2 Sheet of 6, #a-f   9.00 9.00

    Miniature Sheet

Joseph Haydn (1732-1809),
Composer — A702

No. 3726: a, Haydn's birthplace, Rohrau, Austria. b, Johann Peter Salomon, impresario. c, Austro-Hungarian Haydn Orchestra. d, Wolfgang Amadeus Mozart, composer. e, Haydn's house, Vienna. f, Ludwig van Beethoven, composer and student of Haydn.

2009, Apr. 29
3726 A702 $2.25 Sheet of 6,
      #a-f   10.00 10.00

    Miniature Sheet

Elvis Presley (1935-77) — A703

No. 3727 — Presley: a, With guitar strap on both sides. b, Facing left. c, With hand raised. d, With guitar strap at right.

2009, Apr. 29   **Perf. 13¼**
3727 A703 $2.50 Sheet of 4, #a-d   7.50 7.50

    Miniature Sheets

Dogs — A704

No. 3728, $2.30 — Golden retriever: a, On outdoor chair. b, On lawn, with pumpkin and gourds. c, On sofa. d, Two dogs in basket.
No. 3729, $2.50 — Beagle: a, On desktop. b, Face. c, On lawn. d, Near stone wall.

2009, Apr. 29   **Perf. 11½**
     Sheets of 4, #a-d
3728-3729 A704   Set of 2   14.50 14.50
   American Kennel Club, 125th anniv.

    Miniature Sheet

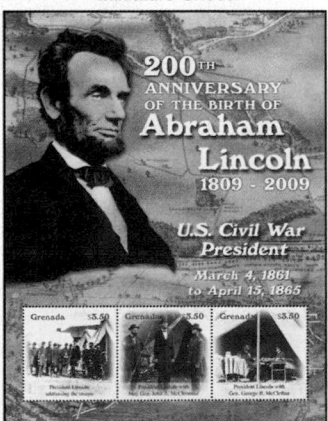

Pres. Abraham Lincoln (1809-65) — A705

No. 3730 — Lincoln: a, Addressing Union troops. b, With Major General John A. McClernand. c, With General George B. McClellan.

2009, July 21   **Litho.**   **Perf. 13½**
3730 A705 $3.50 Sheet of 3, #a-c   8.00 8.00

Miniature Sheet

Visit of Pope Benedict XVI to
Bethlehem — A706

No. 3731 — Pope Benedict and buildings in
Bethlehem, a, $1.50. b, $2. c, $2.50. d, $3.

2009, July 21   **Perf. 11½**
3731 A706   Sheet of 4, #a-d   6.75 6.75

Miniature Sheet

Charles Darwin (1809-82),
Naturalist — A707

No. 3732 — Darwin and: a, Bird. b, Wolf. c,
Fossil. d, Tortoise.

2009, July 21
3732 A707 $2.50 Sheet of 4, #a-
     d   7.50 7.50

Chinese Aviation, Cent. — A708

No. 3733: a, J-5. b, J-6. c, J-7G. d, J-7.
$6, JF-17.

2009, Nov. 13   **Litho.**   **Perf. 14**
3733 A708 $2 Sheet of 4, #a-d   6.50 6.50
      Souvenir Sheet
         Perf. 14¼
3734 A708 $6 multi   4.75 4.75
  2009 Aeropex, Beijing. No. 3733 contains
four 42x28mm stamps.

Miniature Sheet

Chinese Zodiac Animals — A709

No. 3735: a, Rat. b, Ox. c, Tiger. d, Rabbit.
e, Dragon. f, Snake. g, Horse. h, Ram. i, Monkey. j, Cock. k, Dog. l, Pig.

2010, Jan. 4   **Perf. 12**
3735 A709 60c Sheet of 12, #a-l   5.50 5.50

Miniature Sheet

Elvis Presley (1935-77) — A710

Various views of Presley's face.

2010, Jan. 7   **Perf. 13¼**
3736 A710 $2.75 Sheet of 4,
     #a-d   8.50 8.50

Christmas
2009
A711

Designs: $1, Fish wearing stocking caps.
$2, Christmas tree, lights, fruit. $4, Bells. $5,
Map of Grenada, stars, Christmas ornaments.

2010, Jan. 13   **Perf. 12½**
3737-3740 A711   Set of 4   9.25 9.25

Orchids — A712

Designs: $1.20, Brassia caudata. $1.80,
Epidendrum imatophyllum. No. 3743, $3,
Ionopsis utriculoides. $5, Habenaria
bractescens.
  No. 3745, horiz.: a, Vanilla pompona. b,
Caularthron bicornutum. c, Epidendrum noc-
turnum. d, Aspasia variegata.
  No. 3746, $3, horiz.: a, Epidendrum hartii.
b, Brassavola cucullata.

2010, Jan. 13   **Perf. 13¼x13**
3741-3744 A712   Set of 4   8.50 8.50
      Perf. 13x13¼
3745 A712 $2.75 Sheet of 4,
     #a-d   8.50 8.50
      Souvenir Sheet
3746 A712 $3 Sheet of 2,
     #a-b   4.75 4.75

Ferrari Automobiles and Their
Parts — A713

No. 3747, $1.25: a, Engine of 1989 F1-89.
b, 1989 F1-89.
  No. 3748, $1.25: a, Engine of 1994 F355
Berlinetta. b, 1994 F355 Berlinetta.
  No. 3749, $1.25: a, Wires and parts to 1997
355 F1 Berlinetta. b, 1997 355 F1 Berlinetta.
  No. 3750, $1.25: a, Steering wheel of 1997
F310 B. b, 1997 F310 B.

2010, Mar. 1   **Perf. 12**
    Vert. Pairs, #a-b
3747-3750 A713   Set of 4   7.75 7.75

Miniature Sheet

Pres. John F. Kennedy (1917-63),
50th Anniv. of Election — A714

No. 3751: a, Facing left, black and white
photograph. b, Standing, black and white photograph. c, Color photograph. d, With flag in
background, black and white photograph.

2010, Apr. 9   **Perf. 12x11½**
3751 A714 $2.75 Sheet of 4,
     #a-d   8.25 8.25

Miniature Sheets

A715

Princess Diana (1961-97) — A716

No. 3752: a, Wearing black hat, gray and
white along left margin of stamp. b, Wearing
blue hat, with black frame at LL over gray area.
c, As "b," with black frame at LL over white
area. d, As "a," with hand of Princess Diana
(from central illustration) touching black frame
at left.
  No. 3753: a, Wearing white hat, gray and
white along left margin. b, Wearing no hat,
with black frame at LL over red area (Diana's
jacket from central illustration). c, As "b," with
LL corner over gray area. d, As "a," with entire
left margin over red area (Diana's jacket from
central illustration).

2010, Apr. 9
3752 A715 $2.75 Sheet of 4,
     #a-d   8.25 8.25
3753 A716 $2.75 Sheet of 4,
     #a-d   8.25 8.25

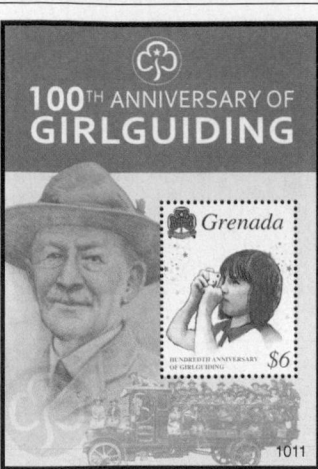

Girl Guides, Cent. — A717

No. 3754, horiz. - Girl Guides: a, Looking at
image taken by camera. b, With cameras. c,
With movie clapboard. d, Looking at image
take by camera with telephoto lens.
$6, Girl Guide with camera.

2010, June 11   **Perf. 13x13¼**
3754 A717 $2.75 Sheet of 4,
     #a-d   8.25 8.25
      Souvenir Sheet
       Perf. 13¼x13
3755 A717 $6 multi   4.50 4.50

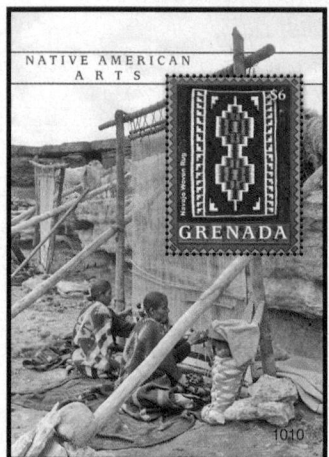

Native American Arts — A718

No. 3756: a, Apache woven basket. b, Sioux
beaded moccasins. c, Iroquois cornhusk
mask. d, Tlingit totem pole. e, Inuit hunter doll.
f, Hopi pottery.
$6, Navajo woven rug.

2010, June 11   **Perf. 13¼x13**
3756 A718 $2 Sheet of 6, #a-f   9.00 9.00
      Souvenir Sheet
3757 A718 $6 multi   4.50 4.50

       Souvenir Sheet

New Year 2010 (Year of the
Tiger) — A719

No. 3758 — Half of tiger's head with denomination at: a, UL. b, UR.

2010, Jan. 4   **Litho.**   **Perf. 12**
3758 A719 $5 Sheet of 2, #a-b   7.75 7.75

2010 World Cup Soccer
Championships, South Africa — A720

No. 3759, $1.50 — Group A first-round matches: a, South Africa vs. Mexico. b, Uruguay vs. France. c, Uruguay vs. South Africa. d, France vs. Mexico. e, Mexico vs. Uruguay. f, France vs. South Africa.
No. 3760, $1.50 — Group B first-round matches: a, South Korea vs. Greece. b, Argentina vs. Nigeria. c, South Korea vs. Argentina. d, Nigeria vs. Greece. e, Nigeria vs. South Korea. f, Greece vs. Argentina.
No. 3761, $1.50 — Group C first-round matches: a, England vs. United States. b, Algeria vs. Slovenia. c, United States vs. Slovenia. d, England vs. Algeria. e, Slovenia vs. England. f, Algeria vs. United States.
No. 3762, $1.50 — Group D first-round matches: a, Serbia vs. Ghana. b, Germany vs. Australia. c, Germany vs. Serbia. d, Ghana vs. Australia. e, Ghana vs. Germany. f, Australia vs. Serbia.
No. 3763, $3.50: a, Nelson Mandela Bay Stadium, Port Elizabeth. b, Cape Town Stadium, Cape Town.
No. 3764, $3.50: a, Soccer City Stadium, Johannesburg. b, Moses Mabhida Stadium, Durban.

2010, June 11 **Perf. 13¼**
Sheets of 6, #a-f
3759-3762 A720 Set of 4   27.00 27.00
Sheets of 2, #a-b
3763-3764 A720 Set of 2   10.50 10.50

Miniature Sheet

Carl Edwards, NASCAR Driver — A721

No. 3765 — Edwards: a, Wearing baseball cap, arms not visible. b, Without hat, arms raised. c, Wearing racing helmet. d, Wearing baseball cap, arms visible.

2010, July 26 **Perf. 12**
3765 A721 $2.75 Sheet of 4, #a-
d   8.25 8.25

Frédéric Chopin (1810-49),
Composer — A722

No. 3766: a, Sketch of Chopin facing left. b, George Sand, writer. c, Chopin, with arms folded. d, Chopin's birthplace.
$6, Chopin and musical notes.

2010, Sept. 1
3766 A722 $2.50 Sheet of 4, #a-
d   7.50 7.50
Souvenir Sheet
3767 A722 $6 multi   4.50 4.50

Henri Dunant (1828-1910), Founder of the Red Cross — A723

No. 3768 — Dunant and members of Red Cross "Committee of Five" founding members: a, Louis Appia. b, Gustave Moynier. c, Théodore Maunoir. d, Henri Dufour.
$6, Dunant and the First Geneva Convention, 1894.

2010, Sept. 1
3768 A723 $2.50 Sheet of 4, #a-
b   7.50 7.50
Souvenir Sheet
3769 A723 $6 multi   4.50 4.50

Miniature Sheet

Pope John Paul II (1920-
2005) — A724

No. 3770 — Pope John Paul II: a, With crucifix. b, Without crucifix.

2010, Nov. 4
3770 A724 $2.75 Sheet of 4,
#3770a, 3
#3770b   8.25 8.25

Boy Scouts of America, Cent. — A725

No. 3771, $2.75: a, Scout saluting. b, Scout rescuing child.
No. 3772, $2.75: a, Scout assisting woman with groceries. b, Scout reading from book.

2010, Nov. 4 **Perf. 12½**
Pairs, #a-b
3771-3772 Set of 2   8.25 8.25
Nos. 3771-3772 each were printed in sheets containing two pairs.

A726

Pres. Abraham Lincoln (1809-65) — A727

No. 3773 — Lincoln: a, With mouth to right of "resting." b, With mouth to right of "endure." c, Seated.
No. 3774 — Lincoln: a, Standing. b, With son, Tad. c, Seated.

2010, Nov. 4
3773 A726 $2 Horiz. strip of 3,
#a-c   4.50 4.50
3774 A727 $2 Horiz. strip of 3,
#a-c   4.50 4.50
Nos. 3773-3774 each were printed in sheets containing two strips.

Miniature Sheets

Pres. Barack Obama at Nuclear Security Summit — A728

Pres. Obama and Mexican President Felipe Calderón — A729

No. 3775 — Pres. Obama: a, Facing right. b, With Vice-President Joseph Biden. c, Facing left. d, Greeting person.
No. 3776: a, Obama and Calderón shaking hands. b, Calderón. c, Obama. d, Calderón and Obama standing together.

2010, Nov. 4 **Perf. 12**
3775 A728 $2.75 Sheet of 4, #a-
d   8.25 8.25
3776 A729 $2.75 Sheet of 4, #a-
d   8.25 8.25

SEMI-POSTAL STAMPS

Catalogue values for unused stamps in this section are for Never Hinged items.

Nos. 227-229 Overprinted

Type I   Type II

1968
Type I
B1A A38 2c + 3c on $2 multi .20 .20
B1B A38 3c + 3c on $3 multi .20 .20
Type II
B1C A38 1c + 3c on $2 multi .20 .20
B1D A38 2c + 3c on $3 multi 22.50 50.00
Nos. B1A-B1D (4)   23.10 50.60
Issued: B1A-B1B, 7/22; B1C-B1D, 8/19.

ESPANA '82 World Cup Soccer SP1

Players and Flags of Winning Countries.

Unwmk.
1981, Nov. 30 **Litho.** **Perf. 14**
B1 SP1 25c + 10c West Germany, 1974   .50 .50
B2 SP1 40c + 20c Argentina, 1978   .70 .70
B3 SP1 50c + 25c Brazil, 1970   1.00 1.00
B4 SP1 $1 + 50c Grt. Britain, 1966   1.75 1.75
Nos. B1-B4 (4)   3.95 3.95
Souvenir Sheet
B5 SP1 $5 + 50c World Cup, ESPANA '82   4.00 4.00
Nos. B1-B4 each issued in sheets of 12 with sheet background showing soccer ball.

1988 Seoul Olympics — SP2

1986, Dec. 1 **Litho.** **Perf. 15**
B6 SP2 10c + 5c Pole vault   .25 .30
B7 SP2 50c + 20c Balance beam   .55 .65
B8 SP2 70c + 30c Shot put   .85 .85
B9 SP2 $2 + $1 High jump   1.75 2.50
Nos. B6-B9 (4)   3.40 4.30
Souvenir Sheet
B10 SP2 $3 + $1 Swimming   3.50 3.50
Surtax for natl. Olympic team.

World Philatelic Programs SP3

Halley's Comet or Stamp Collecting emblem and: No. B11, Halley's initial work on nebulae, 1676. No. B12, Experiments at sea (tall ship, manned capsule). No. B13, Halley observes complete lunar cycle, 1720-1738. No. B14, Halley publishes Newton's Principia, 1687. No. B15, Halley charts the southern skies, 1676.

1989, Apr. 25 **Litho.** **Perf. 14**
B11 SP3 25c +5c multi   .75 .75
B12 SP3 75c +5c multi   1.25 1.25
B13 SP3 90c +5c multi   1.50 1.50
B14 SP3 $2 +5c multi   2.00 2.00

Size: 111x78mm
Imperf

B15	SP3	$5 +5c multi	4.25	4.25
	Nos. B11-B15 (5)		9.75	9.75

AIR POST STAMPS

> **Catalogue values for unused stamps in this section are for Never Hinged items.**

Nos. 428-429 Surcharged with New Value, Olympic Rings, "Air Mail" and: "WINTER OLYMPICS / FEB. 3-13, 1972 / SAPPORO, JAPAN"

Perf. 13½x14

1972, Feb. 3		Litho.	Unwmk.	
C1	A66	35c on ½c multi	.40	.40
C2	A66	50c on 1c multi	.60	.60

11th Winter Olympic Games, Sapporo, Japan, Feb. 3-13.

Nos. 294-300, 302A, 303-309 Surcharged Type "a" or Overprinted Type "b"

a

b

Perfs. as Before

1972, May 2			Photo.;	Litho.
C3	A45	5c violet & multi	.20	.20
C4	A45	8c multicolored	.20	.20
C5	A45	10c orange & multi	.20	.20
C6	A45	15c gray & multi	.20	.20
C7	A45	25c multicolored	.40	.30
C8	A45	30c on 1c multi	.50	.35
C9	A45	35c multicolored	.55	.40
C10	A45	40c on 2c multi	.60	.45
C11	A45	45c on 3c multi	.65	.50
C12	A45	50c multicolored	.70	.55
C13	A45	60c on 5c multi	.80	.70
C14	A45	70c on 6c multi	.95	.90
C15	A45	$1 multicolored	7.00	1.25
C16	A45	$1.35 on 8c multi	3.50	3.00
C17	A45	$2 multicolored	8.50	7.00
C18	A45	$3 multicolored	11.00	9.00
C19	A45	$5 multicolored	14.00	16.00
	Nos. C3-C19 (17)		49.95	41.20

"AIR MAIL" reading down on 5c, 15c, 25c, 35c, 60c and $5.

Olympic Type of Regular Issue

Olympic Rings and: 25c, 60c, $1, Boxing. 70c, Equestrian (not inscribed air mail).

1972, Sept. 8		Litho.	Perf. 14	
C20	A69	25c blue & multi	.50	.30
C21	A69	$1 green & multi	.90	.75

Souvenir Sheet

C22		Sheet of 2	1.50	1.50
a.		A69 60c blue & multi	.50	.50
b.		A69 70c deep yellow & multi	1.00	1.00

Nos. 409-412 Overprinted Vertically, Reading Up "AIR MAIL"

1972, Oct.		Litho.	Perf. 11	
C23	A62	5c multicolored	.60	.20
C24	A62	35c multicolored	1.50	.60
C25	A62	50c multicolored	1.75	1.00
C26	A62	75c multicolored	2.50	2.00
	Nos. C23-C26 (4)		6.35	3.80

Boy Scout Type of Regular Issue

Designs: 25c, Scout saluting. 35c, Two Scouts knotting ropes.

1972, Nov.			Perf. 14	
C27	A70	25c dp blue & multi	.40	.35
C28	A70	35c brn org & multi	.60	.55

John Hancock — AP1

Designs: 50c, Benjamin Franklin. 75c, John Adams. $1, Marquis de Lafayette.

1975, May 6		Litho.	Perf. 14½, 13	
C29	AP1	40c multicolored	.25	.20
C30	AP1	50c multicolored	.45	.20
C31	AP1	75c multicolored	.55	.20
C32	AP1	$1 multicolored	.65	.25
	Nos. C29-C32 (4)		1.90	.85

American Revolution Bicentennial. Nos. C29-C32 issued in sheets of 40. Each denomination was also printed in sheets of 5 plus label, perf. 13.

POSTAGE DUE STAMPS

D1   D2

1892		Typo.	Wmk. 2	Perf. 14	
J1	D1	1p black		30.00	2.75
J2	D1	2p black		190.00	3.25
J3	D1	3p black		190.00	4.00
	Nos. J1-J3 (3)			410.00	10.00

Black Surcharge

J4	D2	1p on 6p red lilac	92.50	2.25
a.		Tete beche pair	1,400.	1,800.
b.		Double surcharge		190.00
c.		Same as "b," tete beche Labels		
J5	D2	1p on 8p bister	875.00	6.00
a.		Tete beche pair	4,000.	1,600.
J6	D2	2p on 6p red lilac	190.00	4.50
a.		Tete beche pair	2,000.	1,275.
J7	D2	2p on 8p bister	3,200.	12.00
a.		Tete beche pair	7,500.	3,500.
	Nos. J4-J7 (4)		4,357.	24.75

Nos. J4-J7 were printed with alternate horizontal rows inverted.

1906-11			Wmk. 3	
J8	D1	1p black ('11)	3.75	5.00
J9	D1	2p black	12.50	3.75
J10	D1	3p black	15.00	6.50
	Nos. J8-J10 (3)		31.25	15.25

D3

1921-22			Wmk. 4	
J11	D3	1p black	1.40	1.40
J12	D3	1½p black	10.00	20.00
J13	D3	2p black	3.00	4.50
J14	D3	3p black	3.00	4.75
	Nos. J11-J14 (4)		17.40	30.65

Issued: 1½p, Dec. 15, 1922, others, Dec. 1921.

> **Catalogue values for unused stamps in this section, from this point to the end of the section, are for Never Hinged items.**

1952, Mar. 1				
J15	D3	2c black	.50	9.00
a.		Wmk. 4a (error)	25.00	

J16	D3	4c black	.50	9.00
a.		Wmk. 4a (error)	25.00	
J17	D3	6c black	.65	13.00
a.		Wmk. 4a (error)	42.50	
J18	D3	8c black	.60	11.00
a.		Wmk. 4a (error)	50.00	
	Nos. J15-J18 (4)		2.25	42.00

WAR TAX STAMPS

Nos. 80a, 80 Overprinted

1916		Wmk. 3	Perf. 14	
MR1	A21	1p carmine	2.50	2.00
a.		1p scarlet	3.00	3.00
b.		Double overprint	325.00	
c.		Inverted overprint	325.00	

No. 80 Overprinted

MR2	A21	1p scarlet	.30	.20

OFFICIAL STAMPS

> **Catalogue values for unused stamps in this section are for Never Hinged items.**

Nos. 1006-1018, 1020, 1051-1053 Overprinted: "P.R.G."

1982, July 15		Litho.	Perf. 14, 15	
O1	A141	5c multicolored	.20	.20
O2	A141	6c multicolored	.20	.20
O3	A141	10c multicolored	.20	.20
O4	A141	12c multicolored	.20	.20
O5	A141	15c multicolored	.20	.20
O6	A141	20c multicolored	.20	.20
O7	A141	25c multicolored	.20	.20
O8	A141	30c multicolored	.25	.25
O9	A141	40c multicolored	.30	.30
O10	A141	50c multicolored	.40	.40
O11	CD331	50c multicolored	.40	.40
O12	A141	90c multicolored	.75	.75
O13	A141	$1 multicolored	.80	.80
O14	CD331	$2 multicolored	2.00	2.00
O15	A141	$3 multicolored	2.50	2.50
O16	CD331	$4 multicolored	4.50	4.50
O17	A141	$10 multicolored	8.00	8.00
	Nos. O1-O17 (17)		21.30	21.30

PRG stands for People's Revolutionary Government.

GRENADA GRENADINES

grə-'nā-də ˌgre-nə-'dēnz

LOCATION — North of Grenada
GOVT. — Part of Grenada
CAPITAL — None

Main islands are Carriacou and Ronde.

Catalogue values for all unused stamps in this country are for Never Hinged items.

All stamps are a type of Grenada unless otherwise noted or illustrated. Nos. 15-58 have the additional inscription Grenadines.

Grenada Nos. 516-517a Overprinted

Perf. 13½x14

1973, Dec. 23	**Litho.**		**Wmk. 314**	
1	A77	25c dp orange & multi	.20	.20
2	A77	$2 green & multi	.60	.50
a.	Souvenir sheet of 2 (75c, $1)		.80	.50

Grenada Nos. 294-297, 299-301, 303, 306-309 Overprinted

Perf. 14x14½, 14½x14

1974, May 29	**Photo.**		**Unwmk.**	
		Size: 25x44mm		
3	A45	1c multicolored	.20	.20
4	A45	2c multicolored	.20	.20
5	A45	3c multicolored	.20	.20
6	A45	5c multicolored	.20	.20
7	A45	8c multicolored	.20	.20
8	A45	10c multicolored	.20	.20
9	A45	12c multicolored	.20	.20
10	A45	25c multicolored	.30	.30
		Size: 25x47mm		
11	A45	$1 multicolored	3.00	1.40
12	A45	$2 multicolored	4.75	2.00
13	A45	$3 multicolored	4.75	2.90
14	A45	$5 multicolored	5.50	3.50
		Nos. 3-14 (12)	19.70	11.50

World Cup Soccer Type

Designs: Soccer matches and flags. ½c, West Germany-Chile. 1c, East Germany-Australia. 2c, Yugoslavia-Brazil. 10c, Scotland-Zaire. 25c, Netherlands-Uruguay. 50c, Sweden-Bulgaria. 75c, Italy-Haiti. $1, Poland-Argentina. $2, Flags of participating nations.

1974, Sept. 17	**Litho.**		**Perf. 14½**	
15	A81	½c multicolored	.20	.20
16	A81	1c multicolored	.20	.20
17	A81	2c multicolored	.20	.20
18	A81	10c multicolored	.25	.20
19	A81	25c multicolored	.35	.20
20	A81	50c multicolored	.45	.25
21	A81	75c multicolored	.45	.25
22	A81	$1 multicolored	.50	.30
		Nos. 15-22 (8)	2.60	1.80
		Souvenir Sheet		
23	A81	$2 multicolored	2.25	2.25

UPU Centenary Type

UPU Emblem and: 8c, Mailboat *Caesar*, 1839, helicopter. 25c, German messenger, 1540, satellite. 35c, Biplanes, zeppelin, jet. No. 27, US Mail train, 19th cent., Concorde. No. 28a, Bellman, 18th cent., radar. $2, German postman, 18th cent., mail train, 1980's.

1974, Oct. 8			**Perf. 14½**	
24	A82	8c multicolored	.20	.20
25	A82	25c multicolored	.20	.20
26	A82	35c multicolored	.25	.20
27	A82	$1 multicolored	1.10	.50
		Nos. 24-27 (4)	1.75	1.10
		Souvenir Sheet		
		Perf. 13		
28		Sheet of 2	2.25	2.25
a.	A82	$1 multicolored	.50	.50
b.	A82	$2 multicolored	1.25	1.25

Churchill Type

Design: $2, Churchill, different portrait.

1974, Nov. 11			**Perf. 13½**	
29	A83	35c multicolored	.20	.20
30	A83	$2 multicolored	.50	.50
		Souvenir Sheet		
31		Sheet of 2	.80	.80
a.	A82	75c like 35c	.30	.30
b.	A82	$1 like $2	.35	.35

Christmas Type

Paintings of the Virgin and Child.

1974, Nov. 27			**Perf. 14½**	
32	A84	½c Botticelli	.20	.20
33	A84	1c Niccolo di Pietro	.20	.20
34	A84	2c Van der Weyden	.20	.20
35	A84	3c Bastiani	.20	.20
36	A84	10c Giovanni	.20	.20
37	A84	25c Van der Weyden, diff.	.20	.20
38	A84	50c Botticelli	.20	.20
39	A84	$1 Mantegna	.30	.25
		Nos. 32-39 (8)	1.70	1.65
		Souvenir Sheet		
		Perf. 13½		
40	A84	$2 Niccolo di Pietro	1.10	1.10

Big Game Fish Type

1975, Feb. 17			**Perf. 14½**	
41	A86	½c Sailfish	.20	.20
42	A86	1c Blue marlin	.20	.20
43	A86	2c White marlin	.20	.20
44	A86	10c Yellowfin tuna	.20	.20
45	A86	25c Wahoo	.25	.20
46	A86	50c Dolphin	.40	.20
47	A86	70c Grouper	.50	.30
48	A86	$1 Great barracuda	.75	.50
		Nos. 41-48 (8)	2.70	2.00
		Souvenir Sheet		
		Perf. 13		
49	A86	$2 Mako shark	2.50	2.50

Flowers of Grenada Type

1975, Mar. 11			**Perf. 14½**	
50	A87	½c Grandilla barbadine	.20	.20
51	A87	1c Bleeding heart	.20	.20
52	A87	2c Poinsettia	.20	.20
53	A87	3c Cocoa	.20	.20
54	A87	10c Gladioli	.20	.20
55	A87	25c Red head-yellow head	.20	.20
56	A87	50c Plumbago	.40	.35
57	A87	$1 Orange blossoms	.75	.55
		Nos. 50-57 (8)	2.35	2.10
		Souvenir Sheet		
		Perf. 13½		
58	A87	$2 Barbados gooseberry	1.75	1.75

Remainders of Grenada Grenadines stamps between Scott Nos. 59 and 269, except Nos. 109-128, 217-220, 237-240 and some souvenir sheets, were later canceled to order and sold at a fraction of their face value. Our used values for these stamps are for c-t-o examples. Postally used stamps are worth the same as unused, never hinged examples.

Christ Crowned with Thorns, by Titian — G1

Easter paintings of the Crucifixion by various artists.

1975, June 24			**Perf. 14½**	
59	G1	½c shown	.20	.20
60	G1	1c Giotto	.20	.20
61	G1	2c Tintoretto	.20	.20
62	G1	3c Cranach	.20	.20
63	G1	35c Caravaggio	.20	.20
64	G1	75c Tiepolo	.20	.20
65	G1	$2 Velasquez	.30	.20
		Nos. 59-65 (7)	1.50	1.40
		Souvenir Sheet		
		Perf. 13½		
66	G1	$1 Titian, diff.	1.25	1.25

Works by Michelangelo (1475-1564) — G2

Butterflies — G3

Designs: ½c, Dawn (sculpture, detail from Medici tomb). 1c, Delphic Sibyl. 2c, Giuliano de Medici (sculpture). 40c, The Creation. 50c, Lorenzo de Medici (sculpture). 75c, Persian Sibyl. $1, The Prophet Jeremiah. $2, Head of Christ (sculpture).

1975, July 16			**Perf. 14½**	
67	G2	½c violet & multi	.20	.20
68	G2	1c multicolored	.20	.20
69	G2	2c green & multi	.20	.20
70	G2	40c multicolored	.25	.20
71	G2	50c brt red & multi	.35	.20
72	G2	75c multicolored	.50	.20
73	G2	$2 brt blue & multi	.80	.20
		Nos. 67-73 (7)	2.50	1.40
		Souvenir Sheet		
		Perf. 13½		
74	G2	$1 multicolored	1.40	.75

1975, Aug. 12			**Perf. 15**	
75	G3	½c Emperor	.25	.20
76	G3	1c Queen	.25	.20
77	G3	2c Tiger pierid	.25	.20
78	G3	35c Cracker	.55	.20
79	G3	45c Scarlet bamboo page	.70	.20
80	G3	75c Apricot	1.25	.20
81	G3	$2 Purple king shoemaker	3.25	.20
		Nos. 75-81 (7)	6.50	1.40
		Souvenir Sheet		
		Perf. 13½		
82	G3	$1 Bamboo page	6.00	6.00

Jamboree Scenes and Badges G4

Nordjamb 75 Emblem and: ½c, Progress badge. 1c, Boating badge. 2c, Coxswain badge. 35c, Interpreter badge. 45c, Ambulance badge. 75c, Chief scout's award. $1, Venture award. $2, Queen's scout award.

1975, Aug. 22			**Perf. 15**	
83	G4	½c lemon yel & multi	.20	.20
84	G4	1c vio blue & multi	.20	.20
85	G4	2c green & multi	.20	.20
86	G4	35c dull vio & multi	.20	.20
87	G4	45c org brown & multi	.20	.20
88	G4	75c brown & multi	.30	.20
89	G4	$2 green & multi	.70	.20
		Nos. 83-89 (7)	2.00	1.40
		Souvenir Sheet		
		Perf. 13½		
90	G4	$1 dull vio & multi	1.25	.40

Nordjamb 75, 14th Boy Scout World Jamboree, Lillehammer, Norway, July 29-Aug. 7.

Surrender of Lord Cornwallis G5

Designs: 1c, Minuteman. 2c, Paul Revere's Ride. 3c, Battle of Bunker Hill. 5c, *Spirit of '76*. 45c, Backwoodsman. 75c, Boston Tea Party. No. 98, Naval engagement. No. 99, George Washington. No. 100, White House, flags.

1975, Sept. 30			**Perf. 14**	
		Size: 39x25mm		
91	G5	½c multicolored	.20	.20
92	G5	1c multicolored	.20	.20
93	G5	2c multicolored	.20	.20
94	G5	3c multicolored	.20	.20
95	G5	5c multicolored	.20	.20
96	G5	45c multicolored	.20	.20
97	G5	75c multicolored	.25	.20
98	G5	$2 multicolored	.55	.45
		Size: 59x39mm		
		Perf. 11		
99	G5	$2 multicolored, vert.	.55	.45
a.	Souvenir sheet of 1, imperf.		1.10	1.10
100	G4	$2 multicolored	.55	.45
a.	Souvenir sheet of 1, imperf.		1.10	1.10
		Nos. 91-100 (10)	3.10	2.75

American Revolution Bicentennial. Nos. 99a, 100a have simulated perfs.

Fencing G6

1975, Oct. 27			**Perf. 15**	
101	G6	½c shown	.20	.20
102	G6	1c Hurdling	.20	.20
103	G6	2c Pole vault	.20	.20
104	G6	35c Weightlifting	.20	.20
105	G6	45c Javelin	.20	.20
106	G6	75c Discus	.20	.20
107	G6	$2 Diving	.35	.25
		Nos. 101-107 (7)	1.55	1.45
		Souvenir Sheet		
108	G6	$1 Sprinter	.80	.20

Pan American Games, Mexico City, Oct. 12-26, 1975.

Type of 1975

Designs: ½c, Cruising Yachts, Point Saline. 1c, Yacht Club race, St. George's. 2c, Careenage Taxi. 3c, Working boats. 5c, Deep water dock, St. George's. 6c, Cocoa beans drying. 8c, Nutmegs. 10c, Rum distillery, River Antoine Estate. 12c, Cocoa tree. 15c, Landing catch at Fontenoy. 20c, Parliament building, St. George's. 25c, Fort George cannons. 35c, Pearls airport. 50c, General Post Office. 75c, Caribs Leap, Sauteurs Bay. $1, Careenage, St. George's. $2, St. George's harbor at night. $3, Grand Anse beach. $5, Canoe and Black Bays from Point Saline lighthouse. $10, Sugar Loaf Island from Levera beach.

1975-76			**Perf. 14½**	
		Size: 38x25mm		
109	A85	½c multicolored	.20	.35
110	A85	1c multicolored	.20	.20
111	A85	2c multicolored	.20	.20
112	A85	3c multicolored	.20	.20
113	A85	5c multicolored	.20	.20
114	A85	6c multicolored	.20	.20
115	A85	8c multicolored	.20	.20
116	A85	10c multicolored	.20	.20
117	A85	12c multicolored	.20	.20
118	A85	15c multicolored	.20	.20
119	A85	20c multicolored	.20	.65
120	A85	25c multicolored	.20	.20
121	A85	35c multicolored	1.00	.20
122	A85	50c multicolored	.25	1.00
		Perf. 13½x14		
		Size: 45x28mm		
123	A85	75c multicolored	.55	.65
124	A85	$1 multicolored	.85	.95
125	A85	$2 multicolored	1.25	2.25
126	A85	$3 multicolored	1.50	2.75
127	A85	$5 multicolored	1.75	5.50
128	A85	$10 multicolored	3.00	6.00
		Nos. 109-128 (20)	12.55	22.30

Issued: #109-127, 11/5/75; #128, 1/1/76. For overprints see Nos. 360-372.

Madonna and Child by Durer — G8

Christmas: Paintings showing Madonna and Child by various artists.

1975, Dec. 17   *Perf. 14*
129	G8	½c shown	.20	.20
130	G8	1c Durer, diff.	.20	.20
131	G8	2c Correggio	.20	.20
132	G8	40c Botticelli	.20	.20
133	G8	50c Niccolo da Cremona	.20	.20
134	G8	75c Correggio, diff.	.20	.20
135	G8	$2 Correggio, diff.	.35	.20
		Nos. 129-135 (7)	1.55	1.40

Souvenir Sheet
136	G8	$1 Bellini	.80	.60

Sea Shells G9

1976, Jan. 13
137	G9	½c Bleeding Tooth	.25	.20
138	G9	1c Wedge clam	.25	.20
139	G9	2c Hawk wing conch	.25	.20
140	G9	3c Distorsio clathrata	.25	.20
141	G9	25c Scotch bonnet	.55	.20
142	G9	50c King helmet	1.00	.20
143	G9	75c Queen conch	1.75	.20
		Nos. 137-143 (7)	4.30	1.40

Souvenir Sheet
144	G9	$2 Atlantic triton	3.00	1.00

Lignum Vitae G10

Designs: 1c, Cocoa thrush. 2c, Tarantula. 35c, Hooded tanager. 50c, Nyctaginaceae. 75c, Grenada dove. $1, Marine toad. $2, Blue-hooded euphonia.

1976, Feb. 4
145	G10	½c multicolored	.20	.20
146	G10	1c multicolored	.20	.20
147	G10	2c multicolored	.20	.20
148	G10	35c multicolored	1.25	.20
149	G10	50c multicolored	1.25	.20
150	G10	75c multicolored	2.50	.30
151	G10	$1 multicolored	2.50	.30
		Nos. 145-151 (7)	8.10	1.60

Souvenir Sheet
152	G10	$2 multicolored	5.75	1.25

Hooked Sailfish G11

Designs: 1c, Careened schooner, Carriacou. 2c, Annual regatta. 18c, Boat building. 22c, Workboat race. 75c, Cruising off Petit Martinique. $1, Water skiing. $2, Yacht racing.

1976, Feb. 17
153	G11	½c multicolored	.20	.20
154	G11	1c multicolored	.20	.20
155	G11	2c multicolored	.20	.20
156	G11	18c multicolored	.30	.20
157	G11	22c multicolored	.30	.20
158	G11	75c multicolored	.50	.20
159	G11	$1 multicolored	.65	.25
		Nos. 153-159 (7)	2.35	1.50

Souvenir Sheet
160	G11	$2 multicolored	1.00	1.00

Making a Camp Fire G12

50th anniv. of Girl Guides of Grenada: 1c, First aid. 2c, Nature study. 50c, Cooking. $1, Drawing. $2, Playing guitar.

1976, Mar. 17
161	G12	½c multicolored	.20	.20
162	G12	1c multicolored	.20	.20
163	G12	2c multicolored	.20	.20
164	G12	50c multicolored	.55	.20
165	G12	$1 multicolored	1.25	.30
		Nos. 161-165 (5)	2.40	1.10

Souvenir Sheet
166	G12	$2 multicolored	1.40	1.00

Christ Mocked by Bosch — G13

Easter Paintings: 1c, Christ Crucified by Messina. 2c, Adoration by Durer. 3c, Lamentation of Christ by Durer. 35c, The Entombment by Van Der Weyden. $2, Blood of the Redeemer by Bellini. $3, The Deposition by Raphael.

1976, Apr. 28
167	G13	½c multicolored	.20	.20
168	G13	1c multicolored	.20	.20
169	G13	2c multicolored	.20	.20
170	G13	3c multicolored	.20	.20
171	G13	35c multicolored	.20	.20
172	G13	$3 multicolored	.40	.30
		Nos. 167-172 (6)	1.40	1.30

Souvenir Sheet
173	G13	$2 multicolored	.90	.90

Frigate South Carolina G14

1c, Schooner Lee. 2c, HMS Roebuck. 35c, Andrew Doria. 50c, Sloop Providence. $1, Flagship Alfred. $2, Frigate Confederacy. $3. Cutter Revenge.

1976, May 18
174	G14	½c multicolored	.20	.20
175	G14	1c multicolored	.20	.20
176	G14	2c multicolored	.20	.20
177	G14	35c multicolored	.80	.20
178	G14	50c multicolored	1.00	.20
179	G14	$1 multicolored	1.60	.25
180	G14	$2 multicolored	2.50	.40
		Nos. 174-180 (7)	6.50	1.65

Souvenir Sheet
181	G14	$3 multicolored	3.00	1.25

American Revolution Bicentennial.

Piper Apache G15

Designs: 1c, Beech Twin Bonanza. 2c, de Havilland Twin Otter. 40c, Britten Norman Islander. 50c, de Havilland Heron. $2, Hawker Siddeley Avro 748. $3, BAC 1-11.

1976, June 10
182	G15	½c multicolored	.20	.20
183	G15	1c multicolored	.20	.20
184	G15	2c multicolored	.20	.20
185	G15	40c multicolored	.50	.20
186	G15	50c multicolored	.65	.20
187	G15	$2 multicolored	1.75	.30
		Nos. 182-187 (6)	3.50	1.30

Souvenir Sheet
188	G15	$3 multicolored	3.00	1.50

Olympic Games, Montreal G16

1976, July 1
189	G16	½c Cycling	.20	.20
190	G16	1c Gymnastics	.20	.20
191	G16	2c Hurdling	.20	.20
192	G16	35c Shot put	.20	.20
193	G16	45c Diving	.25	.20
194	G16	75c Sprinting	.25	.20
195	G16	$2 Rowing	.75	.30
		Nos. 189-195 (7)	2.00	1.50

Souvenir Sheet
196	G16	$3 Sailing	1.25	1.00

Virgin and Child by Cima — G17

Christmas: 1c, 2c, The Nativity by Romanino. 35c, Adoration of the Kings by Brueghel. 50c, Madonna and Child by Girolamo. 75c, Adoration of the Magi by Giorgione, horiz. $2, The Adoration of the Kings by Angelico, horiz. $3, The Holy Family by Garofalo.

1976, Oct. 19
197	G17	½c multicolored	.20	.20
198	G17	1c multicolored	.20	.20
199	G17	2c multicolored	.20	.20
200	G17	35c multicolored	.20	.20
201	G17	50c multicolored	.25	.20
202	G17	75c multicolored	.30	.25
203	G17	$2 multicolored	.90	.35
		Nos. 197-203 (7)	2.25	1.60

Souvenir Sheet
204	G17	$3 multicolored	1.75	1.75

Alexander Graham Bell, First Telephone G18

Portraits of Bell and Telephone from: 1c, 1895. 2c, 1900. 35c, 1915. 75c, 1920. $1, 1929. $2, 1963. $3, 1976.

1977, Jan. 28
205	G18	½c multicolored	.20	.20
206	G18	1c multicolored	.20	.20
207	G18	2c multicolored	.20	.20
208	G18	35c multicolored	.20	.20
209	G18	75c multicolored	.20	.20
210	G18	$1 multicolored	.35	.20
211	G18	$2 multicolored	.65	.25
		Nos. 205-211 (7)	2.00	1.45

Souvenir Sheet
212	G18	$3 multicolored	2.00	1.00

Centenary of 1st telephone conversation, Mar. 10, 1876.

Coronation Coach — G19

Royal Visit — G20

Designs: 50c, Crown of St. Edward. No. 214, Queen entering Abbey. No. 219, Queen and Prince Charles. $4, Queen is crowned. No. 216, Mall on Coronation Night. No. 220, Queen's Flag.

Litho. and Embossed

1977, Feb. 7   *Perf. 13½*
213	G19	35c multicolored	.20	.20
214	G19	$2 multicolored	.25	.20
215	G19	$4 multicolored	.35	.25
		Nos. 213-215 (3)	.80	.65

Souvenir Sheet

Perf. 14
216	G19	$5 multicolored	.90	.90

Booklet Stamps

Roulette x imperf.

Self-adhesive
217	G20	35c multicolored	.20	.20
a.		Booklet pane of 6	.75	
218	G20	50c multicolored	.35	.35
219	G20	$2 multicolored	.55	.55
220	G20	$5 multicolored	.65	.65
a.		Bklt. pane of 3, #218, #219, #220	1.25	

Reign of Queen Elizabeth II, 25th anniv. Nos. 213-215, perf. 11, have different background colors and come from sheetlets of 3 stamps plus label.
For overprints see Nos. 237-240.

Easter — G21   Adoration of Jesus by Correggio — G22

Paintings of the Crucifixion by various artists.

1977, July 5   **Litho.**   *Perf. 14*
221	G21	½c Fra Angelico	.20	.20
222	G21	1c Fra Angelico, diff.	.20	.20
223	G21	2c El Greco	.20	.20
224	G21	18c El Greco, diff.	.20	.20
225	G21	35c Fra Angelico, diff.	.20	.20
226	G21	50c Giottino	.20	.20
227	G21	$2 da Messina	.30	.25
		Nos. 221-227 (7)	1.50	1.45

Souvenir Sheet
228	G21	$3 Fra Angelico, diff.	1.25	.90

1977, Nov. 17   *Perf. 14*

Christmas: Paintings of the Madonna and Child by various artists.
229	G22	½c shown	.20	.20
230	G22	1c Giorgione	.20	.20
231	G22	2c Morales	.20	.20
232	G22	18c Raphael	.20	.20
233	G22	35c Van Dyck	.20	.20
234	G22	50c Filippo Lippi	.20	.20
235	G22	$2 Filippo Lippi, diff.	.30	.25
		Nos. 229-235 (7)	1.50	1.45

Souvenir Sheet
236	G22	$3 Ghirlandaio	1.25	.90

Nos. 213-216 Overprinted

1977, Nov. 23   *Perf. 13½*

237	G19	35c multicolored	.20	.20
238	G19	$2 multicolored	.30	.30
239	G19	$4 multicolored	.65	.65
		Nos. 237-239 (3)	1.15	1.15

Souvenir Sheet

240	G19	$5 multicolored	.90	.90

Caribbean visit of Queen Elizabeth II. Nos. 237-239 exist perf. 11.

Swimming and Life Saving G23

6th Caribbean Jamboree, Kingston, Jamaica, Aug. 5-14: 1c, Hiking. 2c, Ropes and Knots. 22c, Erecting Tent. 35c, Limbo dance. 75c, Cooking. $2, Pioneer bridge building. $3, Sea Scouts' race.

1977, Dec. 7   *Perf. 14*

241	G23	½c multicolored	.20	.20
242	G23	1c multicolored	.20	.20
243	G23	2c multicolored	.20	.20
244	G23	22c multicolored	.20	.20
245	G23	35c multicolored	.40	.20
246	G23	75c multicolored	.80	.20
247	G23	$3 multicolored	1.50	.40
		Nos. 241-247 (7)	3.50	1.60

Souvenir Sheet

248	G23	$2 multicolored	1.90	1.25

Space Shuttle Blast-off G24

Designs: 1c, Booster separation. 2c, External tank separation. 22c, Working in orbit. 50c, Re-entry. $2, Towing in. $3, Landing.

1978, Feb. 3

249	G24	½c multicolored	.20	.20
250	G24	1c multicolored	.20	.20
251	G24	2c multicolored	.20	.20
252	G24	22c multicolored	.20	.20
253	G24	50c multicolored	.20	.20
254	G24	$3 multicolored	1.50	.50
		Nos. 249-254 (6)	2.50	1.50

Souvenir Sheet

255	G24	$2 multicolored	1.00	1.00

US Space Shuttle.

Alfred Nobel, Medicine Medal G25

Alfred Nobel and: 1c, Physics, Chemistry Medal. 2c, Peace Medal. 22c, Nobel Institute, Oslo. 75c, Peace Prize committee. $2, Peace Medal, Nobel's will. $3, Literature Medal.

1978, Feb. 22

256	G25	½c multicolored	.20	.20
257	G25	1c multicolored	.20	.20
258	G25	2c multicolored	.20	.20
259	G25	22c multicolored	.35	.20
260	G25	75c multicolored	.80	.20
261	G25	$3 multicolored	2.75	.40
		Nos. 256-261 (6)	4.50	1.40

Souvenir Sheet

262	G25	$2 multicolored	2.75	.90

Nobel Prize awards.

Germany No. C37 — G26

15c, France #C43. 25c, Liechtenstein #C8 specimen. 35c, Panama #257. 50c, Russia #C15. 75c, US #C10. $2, Germany #C57. $3, Spain #C56.

1978, Mar. 15

263	G26	5c multicolored	.20	.20
264	G26	15c multicolored	.75	.20
265	G26	25c multicolored	.30	.20
266	G26	35c multicolored	.50	.20
267	G26	50c multicolored	.85	.20
268	G26	$3 multicolored	2.25	.40
		Nos. 263-268 (6)	4.85	1.40

Souvenir Sheet

269		Sheet of 2	2.75	1.25
a.	G26	75c multicolored	.60	.30
b.	G26	$2 multicolored	1.60	.80

50th anniv. of Lindbergh's solo trans-Atlantic flight. 75th anniv. of 1st Zeppelin flight.

Coronation Ring — G27

Designs: $2, Queen's Orb. $2.50, Imperial State Crown. $5, Queen Elizabeth II.

1978, Apr. 12   *Perf. 14*

270	G27	50c multicolored	.20	.20
271	G27	$2 multicolored	.25	.25
272	G27	$2.50 multicolored	.35	.35
		Nos. 270-272 (3)	.80	.80

Souvenir Sheet

273	G27	$5 multicolored	.90	.90

Nos. 270-272, perf 12, printed in sheets of 3 + label, have different background colors. Issue date; June 2, 1978.

G28

Designs: 18c, Drummer, Royal Regiment of Fusiliers. 50c, Drummer, Royal Anglian Regiment. $5, Drum Major, Queen's Regiment.

1978, Apr. 12   *Roulette x imperf.*

Booklet Stamps

Self-Adhesive

274		Souvenir booklet	2.50	3.00
a.	G28	Pane of 6 (3 ea 18c, 50c)	.75	.75
b.	G28	Pane of 1 ($5)	1.50	1.50

G29

1978, May 18   *Perf. 14*

Paintings by Rubens: 5c, Le Chapeau de Paille. 15c, Hector Killed by Achilles. 18c,

Helene Fourment and Her Children. 22c, Rubens and Isabella Brandt. 35c, Ildefonso Altarpiece. $2, Self-portrait. $3, Four Negro Heads.

275	G29	5c multicolored	.20	.20
276	G29	15c multicolored	.20	.20
277	G29	18c multicolored	.20	.20
278	G29	22c multicolored	.30	.20
279	G29	35c multicolored	.30	.20
280	G29	$3 multicolored	2.40	1.50
		Nos. 275-280 (6)	3.60	2.50

Souvenir Sheet

281	G29	$2 multicolored	1.60	1.60

400th birth anniv. of Rubens.

Wright Flyer G30

Designs: 15c, Orville Wright, vert. 18c, Wilbur Wright, vert. 25c, 35c, 75c, $2, $3, various Wright airplanes.

1978, Aug. 10

282	G30	5c multicolored	.20	.20
283	G30	15c multicolored	.20	.20
284	G30	18c multicolored	.20	.20
285	G30	25c multicolored	.20	.20
286	G30	35c multicolored	.20	.20
287	G30	75c multicolored	.25	.25
288	G30	$3 multicolored	1.00	1.00
		Nos. 282-288 (7)	2.25	2.25

Souvenir Sheet

289	G30	$2 multicolored	1.75	1.75

75th anniv. of first powered flight by the Wright brothers, Dec. 17, 1903.

Audubon's Shearwater G31   Players, Soccer Ball G32

10c, Northern ring-necked plover. 18c, Garnet-throated hummingbird. 22c, Black-bellied tree duck. 40c, Purple martin. $1, Yellow-bellied tropic bird. $2, Long-billed curlew. $5, Snowy egret.

1978, Sept. 28

290	G31	5c multi	1.00	.25
291	G31	10c multi	1.25	.25
292	G31	18c multi, horiz.	1.50	.30
293	G31	22c multi, horiz.	2.00	.30
294	G31	40c multi, horiz.	3.00	.50
295	G31	$1 multi	4.25	.60
296	G31	$2 multi	5.75	1.10
		Nos. 290-296 (7)	18.75	3.30

Souvenir Sheet

297	G31	$5 multicolored	17.00	17.00

1978, Nov. 2

Soccer players in action.

298	G32	15c multicolored	.20	.20
299	G32	35c multicolored	.20	.20
300	G32	50c multicolored	.25	.20
301	G32	$3 multicolored	.75	.75
		Nos. 298-301 (4)	1.40	1.35

Souvenir Sheet

302	G32	$2 multicolored	1.60	1.60

World Cup Soccer Championships, Argentina, June 1-25.

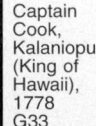

Captain Cook, Kalaniopu (King of Hawaii), 1778 G33

22c, Cook, Hawaiian native. 50c, Cook, death scene, 2/14/79. $3, Cook and offering ceremony. $4, Cook, HMS Resolution.

1978, Dec. 13

303	G33	18c multicolored	.55	.20
304	G33	22c multicolored	.70	.25
305	G33	50c multicolored	1.25	.50
306	G33	$3 multicolored	3.00	2.00
		Nos. 303-306 (4)	5.50	2.95

Souvenir Sheet

307	G33	$4 multicolored	3.50	3.50

250th birth anniv. of Captain James Cook and Bicentennial of his discovery of the Hawaiian Islands.

Durer Paintings — G34

Christmas: 40c, The Virgin at Prayer. 60c, Dresden Alterpiece. 90c, Madonna and Child. $2, Madonna and Child. $4, Salvator Mundi.

1978, Dec 20

308	G34	40c multicolored	.20	.20
309	G34	60c multicolored	.20	.20
310	G34	90c multicolored	.25	.25
311	G34	$3 multicolored	.80	.80
		Nos. 308-311 (4)	1.45	1.45

Souvenir Sheet

312	G34	$4 multicolored	1.50	1.50

Strelitzia Reginae — G35

1979, Feb. 15

313	G35	22c shown	.25	.25
314	G35	40c Euphorbia pulcherrima	.40	.40
315	G35	$1 Heliconia humilis	.80	.45
316	G35	$3 Thunbergia alata	1.40	.80
		Nos. 313-316 (4)	2.85	1.90

Souvenir Sheet

317	G35	$2 Bougainvillea glabra	2.10	2.10

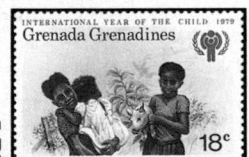

Children with Pig G36

International Year of the Child: 50c, Children with donkey. $1, Children with goats. $3, Children fishing. $4, Child with coconuts.

1979, Mar. 22

318	G36	18c multicolored	.20	.20
319	G36	50c multicolored	.20	.20
320	G36	$1 multicolored	.60	.60
321	G36	$3 multicolored	.80	.80
		Nos. 318-321 (4)	1.80	1.80

Souvenir Sheet

322	G36	$4 multicolored	1.10	1.10

150th Birth Anniv. of Jules Verne G37

Designs: 18c, 20,000 Leagues Under the Sea. 38c, From the Earth to the Moon. 75c, From the Earth to the Moon, diff. $3, Five Weeks in a Balloon. $4, Around the World in 80 Days.

1979, Apr. 20

323	G37	18c multicolored	.75	.20
324	G37	38c multicolored	.85	.25
325	G37	75c multicolored	1.00	.40
326	G37	$3 multicolored	2.00	2.00
		Nos. 323-326 (4)	4.60	2.85

Souvenir Sheet

327	G37	$4 multicolored	4.00	4.00

Sir Rowland Hill, Mail Truck — G38

Designs: $1, Ocean liner. $2, Mail train. $3, Concorde. $4, Sir Rowland Hill.

1979, July 30   *Perf. 14*

328	G38	15c multicolored	.20	.20
329	G38	$1 multicolored	.20	.20
330	G38	$2 multicolored	.75	.75
331	G38	$3 multicolored	1.10	1.10
		Nos. 328-331 (4)	2.25	2.25

Souvenir Sheet

332	G38	$4 multicolored	1.50	1.50

Death centenary of Sir Rowland Hill.
Nos. 328-331, perf. 12, printed in sheets of 5 + label, have different colored backgrounds.

Virgin and Child Enthroned (Byzantine Era, 11th Cent.) — G39

Christmas sculptures: 25c, Presentation in the Temple by Beauneveu c. 1390. 30c, Flight to Egypt (Utrecht, c. 1510). 40c, Madonna and Child by della Quercia, 1047-48. 90c, Madonna della Mela by della Robbia, c. 1455. $1, Madonna and Child by Rossellino, 1461-66. $2, Madonna (Antwerp, 1700). $4, Virgin (Krumau, c. 1390).

1979, Oct. 23   *Perf. 14*

333	G39	6c multicolored	.20	.20
334	G39	25c multicolored	.20	.20
335	G39	30c multicolored	.20	.20
336	G39	40c multicolored	.20	.20
337	G39	90c multicolored	.20	.20
338	G39	$1 multicolored	.25	.25
339	G39	$2 multicolored	.40	.40
		Nos. 333-339 (7)	1.65	1.65

Souvenir Sheet

340	G39	$4 multicolored	1.00	1.00

Great Hammerhead Shark — G40

Designs: 45c, Banded butterflyfish. 50c, Permit. 60c, Threaded turban. 70c, Milk conch. 75c, Great blue heron. 90c, Colored Atlantic natica. $1, Red footed booby. $2.50, Collared plover.

1979, Nov. 9

341	G40	40c multicolored	.55	.55
342	G40	45c multicolored	.60	.60
343	G40	50c multicolored	.70	.70
344	G40	60c multicolored	.80	.80
345	G40	70c multicolored	1.00	1.00
346	G40	75c multicolored	1.60	1.10
347	G40	90c multicolored	1.40	1.40
348	G40	$1 multicolored	2.00	2.00
		Nos. 341-348 (8)	8.65	8.15

Souvenir Sheet

349	G40	$2.50 multicolored	2.25	2.25

Doctor Goofy G41

International Year of the Child: 1c, Admiral Mickey Mouse. 2c, Fireman Goofy. 3c, Nurse Minnie Mouse. 4c, Drum Major Mickey Mouse. 5c, Policeman Donald Duck. 10c, Pilot Donald Duck. $2, Mailman Goofy, horiz. $2.50 Engineer Donald Duck, horiz. $3, Fireman Mickey Mouse.

1979, Dec. 12   *Perf. 11*

350	G41	½c multicolored	.20	.20
351	G41	1c multicolored	.20	.20
352	G41	2c multicolored	.20	.20
353	G41	3c multicolored	.20	.20
354	G41	4c multicolored	.20	.20
355	G41	5c multicolored	.25	.25
356	G41	10c multicolored	.25	.25
357	G41	$2 multicolored	2.50	2.50
358	G41	$2.50 multicolored	3.00	3.00
		Nos. 350-358 (9)	7.00	7.00

Souvenir Sheet
Perf. 13½

359	G41	$3 multicolored	3.50	3.50

Nos. 114, 117-128 Overprinted

1980, Mar. 10   *Perf. 15*

360	A85	6c multicolored	.20	.20
361	A85	12c multicolored	.20	.20
362	A85	15c multicolored	.20	.20
363	A85	20c multicolored	.20	.20
364	A85	25c multicolored	.20	.20
365	A85	35c multicolored	.20	.20
366	A85	50c multicolored	.30	.35

Perf. 13½x14

367	A85	75c multicolored	.35	.40
368	A85	$1 multicolored	.50	.60
369	A85	$2 multicolored	.75	.90
370	A85	$3 multicolored	1.40	1.60
371	A85	$5 multicolored	2.00	2.40
372	A85	$10 multicolored	3.25	3.75
		Nos. 360-372 (13)	9.75	11.20

Classroom G42

Rotary Intl., 75th anniv.: 30c, Rotary emblem, people. 60c, Rotary executive making contribution to physician. $3, Young patients, nurses. $4, Paul P. Harris, founder of Rotary.

1980, Mar. 12   *Perf. 14*

373	G42	6c multicolored	.20	.20
374	G42	30c multicolored	.25	.25
375	G42	60c multicolored	.45	.45
376	G42	$3 multicolored	2.10	1.60
		Nos. 373-376 (4)	3.00	2.50

Souvenir Sheet

377	G42	$4 multicolored	1.40	1.40

Yellow-bellied Seedeater — G43

40c, Blue-hooded euphonia. 90c, Yellow warbler. $2, Tropical mockingbird. $3, Barn owl.

1980, Apr. 14

378	G43	25c multicolored	.65	.20
379	G43	40c multicolored	.70	.25
380	G43	90c multicolored	1.60	.85
381	G43	$2 multicolored	2.25	1.60
		Nos. 378-381 (4)	5.20	2.90

Souvenir Sheet

382	G43	$3 multicolored	5.50	5.50

Running G44

Designs: 40c, Soccer. 90c, Boxing. $2, Wrestling. $4, Runners in silhouette.

1980, Apr. 21

383	G44	30c multicolored	.20	.20
384	G44	40c multicolored	.20	.20
385	G44	90c multicolored	.40	.40
386	G44	$2 multicolored	.85	.85
		Nos. 383-386 (4)	1.65	1.65

Souvenir Sheet

387	G44	$4 multicolored	.90	.90

22nd Summer Olympic Games, Moscow, July 19-Aug. 3.

Nos. 328-331 Overprinted

1980, May 6   *Perf. 12*

388	G38	15c multicolored	.20	.20
389	G38	$1 multicolored	1.10	.50
390	G38	$2 multicolored	2.25	1.75
391	G38	$3 multicolored	3.75	3.00
		Nos. 388-391 (4)	7.30	5.45

Issued in sheets of 5 + label.

Longspine Squirrelfish — G45

Designs: 1c, Blue chromis. 2c, Foureye butterflyfish. 4c, Sergeant major. 5c, Yellowtail snapper. 6c, Mutton snapper. 10c, Cocoa damselfish. 12c, Royal gramma. 15c, Cherubfish. 20c, Blackbar soldierfish. 25c, Comb grouper. 30c, Longsnout butterflyfish. 40c, Pudding wife. 50c, Midnight parrotfish. 90c, Redspotted hawkfish. $1, Hogfish. $3, Beau gregory. $5, Rock beauty. $10, Barred hamlet.

1980, Aug. 6   *Perf. 14*
No imprint date below design

392	G45	½c multicolored	.20	.20
a.		Perf. 12, inscribed 1982	10.00	10.00
393	G45	1c multicolored	.20	.20
394	G45	2c multicolored	.20	.20
395	G45	4c multicolored	.20	.20
396	G45	5c multicolored	.20	.20
397	G45	6c multicolored	.20	.20
398	G45	10c multicolored	.20	.20
a.		Inscribed "1984"	.30	.30
399	G45	12c multicolored	.20	.20
400	G45	15c multicolored	.20	.20
401	G45	20c multicolored	.20	.20
a.		Inscribed "1987"	1.25	1.25
402	G45	25c multicolored	.20	.20
403	G45	30c multicolored	.20	.20
404	G45	40c multicolored	.25	.25
405	G45	50c multicolored	.30	.35
406	G45	90c multicolored	.45	.50
407	G45	$1 multicolored	.55	.60
408	G45	$3 multicolored	1.50	1.75
409	G45	$5 multicolored	2.00	2.25
410	G45	$10 multicolored	3.25	3.75
		Nos. 392-410 (19)	10.70	11.85

Bambi with Mother — G46

Various scenes from Walt Disney's Bambi.

1980, Oct. 7   *Perf. 11*

411	G46	½c multicolored	.20	.20
412	G46	1c multicolored	.20	.20
413	G46	2c multicolored	.20	.20
414	G46	3c multicolored	.20	.20
415	G46	4c multicolored	.20	.20
416	G46	5c multicolored	.20	.20
417	G46	10c multicolored	.20	.20
418	G46	$2.50 multicolored	1.75	1.75
419	G46	$3 multicolored	1.75	1.75
		Nos. 411-419 (9)	4.90	4.90

Souvenir Sheet

420	G46	$4 multicolored	3.00	3.00

Christmas.

The Unicorn in Captivity by Unknown 15th Cent. Artist — G47

Designs: 10c, The Fighting Temeraire by J.M.W. Turner. 25c, Sunday Afternoon on the Ile De La Grande-Jatte by Seurat. 90c, Max Schmitt in a Single Scull by Eakins. $2, The Burial of the Count of Orgaz by El Greco. $3, George Washington by Stuart. $5, Kaiser Karl the Great by Durer. Nos. 425-427 are vert.

1981, Jan. 25   *Perf. 14*

421	G47	6c multicolored	.20	.20
422	G47	10c multicolored	.20	.20
423	G47	25c multicolored	.20	.20
424	G47	90c multicolored	.50	.50
425	G47	$2 multicolored	.90	.90
426	G47	$3 multicolored	1.25	1.25
		Nos. 421-426 (6)	3.25	3.25

Souvenir Sheet

427	G47	$5 multicolored	2.75	2.75

Disney Type of 1979

50th anniv. of Pluto character: $2, Mickey Mouse, Pluto and birthday cake. $4, Pluto.

1981, Jan. 26

428	A135a	$2 multicolored	1.10	1.10

Souvenir Sheet

429	A135a	$4 multicolored	2.75	2.75

No. 428 issued in sheets of 8.

Chip Coloring Easter Eggs — G48

Easter: Various Disney characters coloring Easter eggs.

1981, Apr. 14   *Perf. 11*

430	G48	35c multicolored	.25	.25
431	G48	40c multicolored	.25	.25
432	G48	$2 multicolored	1.10	1.10
433	G48	$2.50 multicolored	1.60	1.60
		Nos. 430-433 (4)	3.20	3.20

Souvenir Sheet
Perf. 14
434 G48 $4 multicolored 3.00 3.00

Bust of a
Woman — G49

Paintings by Pablo Picasso (1881-1973):
40c, Woman (Study for Les Demoiselles
d'Avignon). 90c, Nude with Raised Arms (The
Dancer of Avignon). $4, The Dryad. $5, Les
Demoiselles d'Avignon.

1981, May 5 Perf. 14
435 G49 6c multicolored .30 .30
436 G49 40c multicolored .30 .30
437 G49 90c multicolored .45 .45
438 G49 $4 multicolored 2.25 2.25

Size: 103x128mm
Imperf
439 G49 $5 multicolored 3.25 3.25
Nos. 435-439 (5) 6.55 6.55

Common Design Types
pictured following the introduction.

Royal Wedding Issue
Common Design Type
1981, June 16 Perf. 15
440 CD331a 40c Couple .20 .20
441 CD331a $2 Balmoral Castle .30 .30
442 CD331a $4 Charles .50 .50
Nos. 440-442 (3) 1.00 1.00

Souvenir Sheet
443 CD331a $5 Royal Coach 1.40 1.40
Sheets of 5 plus label contain 30c (like No.
440), 40c (like No. 441), or $4 in changed
colors, perf 15x14½.

Diana — G50

$1, Diana. $2, Charles. $5, Diana and
Charles.

Booklet
Self-Adhesive
*Roulette x imperf. (#444a), Imperf.
(#444b)*
1981, June 16
444 G50 Souvenir Booklet 4.00
a. Pane of 6 (3 each $1, $2) 2.25
b. Pane of 1, $5 1.75
Royal wedding.

Amy Johnson,
Pilot of 1st Britain-
Australia Solo
Flight by a
Woman, May
1930 — G51

Decade for Women: 70c, Mme. la Baronne
de Laroche, 1st qualified aviatrix, May 1910.
$1.10, Ruth Nichols. $3, Amelia Earhart, 1st
Atlantic solo flight by woman, May 1932. $5,
Valentina Tereshkova, 1st woman in space,
June 1963.

1981, Oct. 13 Perf. 14
445 G51 30c multicolored .45 .45
446 G51 70c multicolored .70 .70
447 G51 $1.10 multicolored .85 .85
448 G51 $3 multicolored 1.75 1.75
Nos. 445-448 (4) 3.75 3.75

Souvenir Sheet
449 G51 $5 multicolored 2.00 2.00

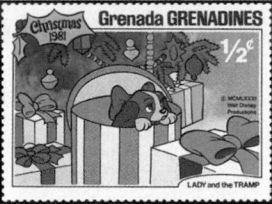

Lady and the Tramp — G52

Christmas. Various scenes from Walt Disney's film Lady and the Tramp.

1981, Nov. 2
450 G52 ½c multicolored .20 .20
451 G52 1c multicolored .20 .20
452 G52 2c multicolored .20 .20
453 G52 3c multicolored .20 .20
454 G52 4c multicolored .20 .20
455 G52 5c multicolored .20 .20
456 G52 10c multicolored .25 .20
457 G52 $2.50 multicolored 4.00 1.75
458 G52 $3 multicolored 4.00 2.25
Nos. 450-458 (9) 9.45 5.40

Souvenir Sheet
459 G52 $5 multicolored 7.25 6.25

747 Carrying Space Shuttle — G53

Designs: 40c, Re-entry. $1.10, External
tank separation. $3, Touchdown. $5, Lift-off.

1981, Nov. 2 Perf. 14½
460 G53 10c multicolored .40 .20
461 G53 40c multicolored .85 .30
462 G53 $1.10 multicolored 1.60 .80
463 G53 $3 multicolored 2.40 1.50
Nos. 460-463 (4) 5.25 2.80

Souvenir Sheet
464 G53 $5 multicolored 5.50 4.00

Soccer
Player — G54

World Cup Soccer Championships, Spain,
1982: Soccer players in various positions.

1981, Nov. 30 Perf. 14
465 G54 20c multicolored .20 .20
466 G54 40c multicolored .20 .20
467 G54 $1 multicolored .45 .30
468 G54 $2 multicolored .90 .60
Nos. 465-468 (4) 1.75 1.30

Souvenir Sheet
469 G54 $4 multicolored 1.75 1.50

Stagecoach, Mail Truck — G55

UPU Membership Cent.: 40c, UPU Emblem.
$2.50, Sailing ship, ocean liner. $4, Biplane,
Concorde. $5, Steam train, high-speed trains.

1982, Jan. 13 Perf. 15
470 G55 30c multicolored .40 .20
471 G55 40c multicolored .40 .20
472 G55 $2.50 multicolored 2.00 1.00
473 G55 $3 multicolored 3.25 2.00
Nos. 470-473 (4) 6.05 3.40

Souvenir Sheet
474 G55 $5 multicolored 5.25 4.50

Sprinting
G56

90c, Sea scouts sailing. $1.10, Hand crafts.
$3, Animal husbandry. $5, Music around
campfire.

1982, Feb. 19
475 G56 6c multicolored .20 .20
476 G56 90c multicolored .75 .60
477 G56 $1.10 multicolored 1.00 .70
478 G56 $3 multicolored 2.10 2.10
Nos. 475-478 (4) 4.05 3.60

Souvenir Sheet
479 G56 $5 multicolored 3.25 3.25
Boy Scouts, 75th anniv. Lord Baden-Powell,
125th birth anniv.

White
Peacock
G57

Designs: 40c, St. Vincent long-tail skipper.
$1.10, Painted lady. $3, Orion. $5, Silver spot.

1982, Mar. 24 Perf. 14
480 G57 30c multicolored 1.25 .60
481 G57 40c multicolored 1.25 .85
482 G57 $1.10 multicolored 3.00 2.25
483 G57 $3 multicolored 5.25 5.25
Nos. 480-483 (4) 10.75 8.95

Souvenir Sheet
484 G57 $5 multicolored 6.50 6.50

Princess Diana Issue
Common Design Type
1982, July 1 Perf. 14½x14
485 CD332 50c Blenheim Palace 1.25 1.25
486 CD332 60c Like 50c .75 .75
487 CD332 $1 Couple in field 1.75 1.75
488 CD332 $2 Like $1 1.90 1.90
489 CD332 $3 Diana 2.50 2.50
490 CD332 $4 Like $3 2.50 2.50
Nos. 485-490 (6) 10.65 10.65

Souvenir Sheet
491 CD332 $5 Diana, diff. 7.25 7.25
50c, $1, $3 issued in sheets of 5 plus label.

Overprinted

1982, Aug. 30
492 CD332 50c multicolored .75 .75
493 CD332 60c multicolored .80 .80
494 CD332 $1 multicolored 1.00 1.00
495 CD332 $2 multicolored 1.50 1.50
496 CD332 $3 multicolored 1.90 1.90
497 CD332 $4 multicolored 2.25 2.25
Nos. 492-497 (6) 8.20 8.20

Souvenir Sheet
498 CD332 $5 multicolored 5.25 5.25
Birth of Prince William of Wales, June 21.

Roosevelt Type of 1982
Designs: 30c, New Deal soil conservation.
40c, Roosevelt, George Washington Carver.
70c, Civilian Conservation Corps. $3,
Roosevelt, Liberian Pres. Edwin Barclay. $5,
Roosevelt addressing Howard University.

1982, July 27 Perf. 14
499 A154 30c multicolored .50 .20
500 A154 40c multicolored .50 .20
501 A154 70c multicolored .60 .30
502 A154 $3 multicolored 1.40 1.40
Nos. 499-502 (4) 3.00 2.10

Souvenir Sheet
503 A154 $5 multicolored 3.50 3.50

Presentation of
Christ in the
Temple — G58

Easter Paintings by Rembrandt: 60c,
Descent from the Cross. $2, Raising of the
Cross. $4, Resurrection of Christ. $5, The
Risen Christ.

1982, Sept. 2 Perf. 14½
504 G58 30c multicolored .55 .20
505 G58 60c multicolored .70 .20
506 G58 $2 multicolored 1.00 1.00
507 G58 $4 multicolored 1.75 1.75
Nos. 504-507 (4) 4.00 3.15

Souvenir Sheet
508 G58 $5 multicolored 3.50 3.50

G59

1982, Oct. 4 Perf. 15
509 G59 10c Santa Fe .70 .20
510 G59 40c Mistral 1.00 .30
511 G59 70c Rheingold 1.10 .65
512 G59 $1 ET 403 1.40 .70
513 G59 $1.10 Mallard 1.75 .75
514 G59 $2 Tokaido 2.00 1.25
Nos. 509-514 (6) 7.95 3.85

Souvenir Sheet
515 G59 $5 Settebello 3.75 3.75

Soccer
Players
G60

Italy, World Cup Soccer Champions: $4,
Soccer players, diff. $5, Map of Italy.

1982, Dec. 2 Perf. 14
516 G60 60c multicolored 1.00 .45
517 G60 $4 multicolored 3.00 3.00

Souvenir Sheet
518 G60 $5 multicolored 2.50 2.50

Christmas Type of 1982
Scenes from Walt Disney's film The
Rescuers.

1982, Dec. 14 Perf. 13½
519 A157 ½c multicolored .20 .20
520 A157 1c multicolored .20 .20
521 A157 2c multicolored .20 .20
522 A157 3c multicolored .20 .20
523 A157 4c multicolored .20 .20
524 A157 5c multicolored .20 .20
525 A157 10c multicolored .20 .20
526 A157 $2.50 multicolored 3.75 3.25
527 A157 $3 multicolored 3.75 3.25
Nos. 519-527 (9) 8.90 7.90

Souvenir Sheet
528 A157 $5 multicolored 7.25 6.25

Whales Type of 1982
Designs: 10c, Pilot whale. 60c, Dall porpoise. $1.10, Humpback whale. $3, Bowfin
whale. $5, Spotted dolphin.

1983, Jan. 10　　　　Perf. 14
529	A159	10c multicolored	1.25	1.10
530	A159	60c multicolored	3.00	2.75
531	A159	$1.10 multicolored	5.25	4.50
532	A159	$3 multicolored	8.50	7.00

Nos. 529-532 (4)　　18.00　15.35

Souvenir Sheet

| 533 | A159 | $5 multicolored | 9.00 | 7.50 |

Raphael Paintings Type

Designs: 25c, David and Goliath. 30c, David Sees Bathsheba. 90c, Triumph of David. $4, Anointing of Solomon. $5, Anointing of David.

1983, Feb. 15　　　　Perf. 14
534	A160	25c multicolored	.25	.25
535	A160	30c multicolored	.25	.25
536	A160	90c multicolored	.40	.40
537	A160	$4 multicolored	.90	.90

Nos. 534-537 (4)　　1.80　1.80

Souvenir Sheet

| 538 | A160 | $5 multicolored | 1.40 | 1.40 |

Audio and Video Communication — G61

World Communications Year: 60c, Ambulance. $1.10, Helicopters. $3, Satellite. $5, Diver, bottle-nose porpoise.

1983, Apr. 7　　　　Perf. 14
539	G61	30c multicolored	.25	.25
540	G61	60c multicolored	.45	.45
541	G61	$1.10 multicolored	.80	.80
542	G61	$3 blk, red & blue	1.50	1.50

Nos. 539-542 (4)　　3.00　3.00

Souvenir Sheet

| 543 | G61 | $5 multicolored | 3.50 | 3.00 |

For overprints see Nos. 629-630A.

Car Type of 1983

Designs: 10c, 1931 Chrysler Imperial Roadster. 30c, 1925 Doble Steam Car. 40c, 1965 Ford Mustang. 60c, 1930 Packard Tourer. 70c, 1913 Mercer Raceabout. 90c, 1963 Corvette Stingray. $1.10, 1935 Auburn 851 Supercharger Speedster. $2.50, 1933 Pierce Arrow Silver Arrow. $3, 1929 Duesenberg Dual Cowl Phaeton. $4, 1928 Mercedes-Benz SSK. $5, 1923 McFarlan Knickerbocker Cabriolet.

1983, May 4　　　　Perf. 14½
544	A163	10c multicolored	.20	.20
545	A163	30c multicolored	.35	.35
546	A163	40c multicolored	.35	.35
547	A163	60c multicolored	.50	.50
548	A163	70c multicolored	.50	.50
549	A163	90c multicolored	.50	.50
550	A163	$1.10 multicolored	.55	.55
551	A163	$2.50 multicolored	.90	.90
552	A163	$3 multicolored	1.10	1.00
553	A163	$4 multicolored	1.10	1.10

Nos. 544-553 (10)　　6.05　5.95

Souvenir Sheet

| 554 | A163 | $5 multicolored | 3.50 | 3.50 |

Anniversary of Manned Flight Type

Designs: 40c, Short Solent flying boat. 70c, Curtiss R3C-2 seaplane. 90c, Hawker Nimrod biplane. $4, Montgolfier balloon. $5, Victoria Luise airship.

1983, July 18　　　　Perf. 14
555	A164	40c multicolored	1.00	.25
556	A164	70c multicolored	1.25	.50
557	A164	90c multicolored	1.50	1.50
558	A164	$4 multicolored	3.75	3.25

Nos. 555-558 (4)　　7.50　5.50

Souvenir Sheet

| 559 | A164 | $5 multicolored | 3.50 | 3.50 |

Christmas
G62

Walt Disney characters in scenes from "Jingle Bells."

1983, Nov. 7　　　　Perf. 11
560	G62	½c multicolored	.20	.20
561	G62	1c multicolored	.20	.20
562	G62	2c multicolored	.20	.20
563	G62	3c multicolored	.20	.20
564	G62	4c multicolored	.20	.20
565	G62	5c multicolored	.20	.20
566	G62	10c multicolored	.20	.20
567	G62	$2.50 multicolored	5.75	5.75
568	G62	$3 multicolored	6.25	6.25

Nos. 560-568 (9)　　13.40　13.40

Souvenir Sheet
Perf. 13½

| 569 | G62 | $5 multicolored | 12.00 | 12.00 |

G63

1984, Jan. 9　　　　Perf. 14
570	G63	30c Weightlifting	.25	.20
571	G63	60c Gymnastics	.55	.50
572	G63	70c Archery	.75	.60
573	G63	$4 Sailing	2.75	2.75

Nos. 570-573 (4)　　4.30　4.05

Souvenir Sheet

| 574 | G63 | $5 Basketball | 4.00 | 4.00 |

Olympic Games, Los Angeles.

G64

1984, Apr. 9　　　　Perf. 15

Designs: 15c, Frangipani. 40c, Dwarf poinciana. 70c, Walking iris. $4, Lady's slipper. $5, Brazilian glory vine.

575	G64	15c multicolored	.20	.20
576	G64	40c multicolored	.30	.30
577	G64	70c multicolored	.75	.55
578	G64	$4 multicolored	2.75	2.75

Nos. 575-578 (4)　　4.00　3.80

Souvenir Sheet

| 579 | G64 | $5 multicolored | 3.75 | 3.75 |

For overprints see Nos. 598-600.

Easter
G65

Walt Disney characters with Easter hats.

1984, May 1　　　　Perf. 11
580	G65	½c multicolored	.20	.20
581	G65	1c multicolored	.20	.20
582	G65	2c multicolored	.20	.20
583	G65	3c multicolored	.20	.20
584	G65	4c multicolored	.20	.20
585	G65	5c multicolored	.20	.20
586	G65	10c multicolored	.20	.20
587	G65	$2 multicolored	2.00	2.00
588	G65	$4 multicolored	2.90	2.90

Nos. 580-588 (9)　　6.30　6.30

Souvenir Sheet

| 589 | G65 | $5 multicolored | 5.25 | 5.25 |

Bobolink
G66

Birds: 50c, Eastern kingbird. 60c, Barn swallow. 70c, Yellow warbler. $1, Rose-breasted grosbeak. $1.10, Yellowthroat. $2, Catbird. $5, Fork-tailed flycatcher.

1984, May 21　　　　Perf. 14
590	G66	40c multicolored	2.50	2.00
591	G66	50c multicolored	2.90	2.25
592	G66	60c multicolored	3.25	2.90
593	G66	70c multicolored	3.25	2.90
594	G66	$1 multicolored	3.50	3.50
595	G66	$1.10 multicolored	4.00	4.00
596	G66	$2 multicolored	5.00	5.00

Nos. 590-596 (7)　　24.40　22.55

Souvenir Sheet

| 597 | G66 | $5 multicolored | 11.00 | 11.00 |

Nos. 577-579
Overprinted

1984, June 19　　　　Perf. 15
| 598 | G64 | 70c multicolored | 1.25 | 1.25 |
| 599 | G64 | $4 multicolored | 5.50 | 5.50 |

Souvenir Sheet

| 600 | G64 | $5 multicolored | 5.00 | 5.00 |

Geeststar
G67

1984, July 16　　　　Perf. 15
601	G67	30c shown	.85	.85
602	G67	60c Daphne	1.10	1.10
603	G67	$1.10 Schooner Southwind	1.40	1.40
604	G67	$4 Oceanic	2.40	2.40

Nos. 601-604 (4)　　5.75　5.75

Souvenir Sheet

| 605 | G67 | $5 Privateer | 5.75 | 5.75 |

Correggio Paintings Type

Designs: 10c, The Hunt — Blowing the Horn. 30c, St. John the Evangelist, horiz. 90c, The Hunt — The Deer's Head. $4, The Virgin Crowned by Christ, horiz. $5, Martyrdom of the Four Saints.

1984, Aug. 22　　　　Perf. 14
606	A171a	10c multicolored	.20	.20
607	A171a	30c multicolored	.25	.25
608	A171a	90c multicolored	.70	.70
609	A171a	$4 multicolored	3.00	3.00

Nos. 606-609 (4)　　4.15　4.15

Souvenir Sheet

| 610 | A171a | $5 multicolored | 4.00 | 4.00 |

The Song of the
Dog — G68

Paintings by Edgar Degas: 70c, Cafe-Concert. $1.10, The Orchestra of the Opera. $3, The Dance Lesson. $5, Madame Camus at the Piano.

1984, Aug. 22
611	G68	25c multicolored	.45	.20
612	G68	70c multicolored	.75	.60
613	G68	$1.10 multicolored	1.60	1.60
614	G68	$3 multicolored	3.00	3.00

Nos. 611-614 (4)　　5.80　5.40

Souvenir Sheet

| 615 | G68 | $5 multicolored | 4.00 | 4.00 |

150th birth anniv. of Degas.

Queen
Victoria
Gardens
G69

$4, Ayers Rock. $5, Yarra River, Melbourne.

1984, Sept. 21
| 616 | G69 | $1.10 multicolored | .85 | .85 |
| 617 | G69 | $4 multicolored | 3.25 | 3.25 |

Souvenir Sheet

| 618 | G69 | $5 multicolored | 4.00 | 4.00 |

AUSIPEX International Stamp Exhibition, Melbourne, Australia.

Colonel
Steven's
Model,
"1825"
G70

Locomotives: 50c, Royal George, 1827. 60c, Stourbridge Lion, 1829. 70c, Liverpool, 1830. 90c, South Carolina, 1832. $1.10, Monster, 1836. $2, Lafayette, 1837. $4, Lion, 1838.

1984, Oct. 3　　　　Perf. 15
619	G70	20c multicolored	.80	.30
620	G70	50c multicolored	1.00	.60
621	G70	60c multicolored	1.10	.75
622	G70	70c multicolored	1.25	1.25
623	G70	90c multicolored	1.40	1.40
624	G70	$1.10 multicolored	1.40	1.40
625	G70	$2 multicolored	1.75	1.75
626	G70	$4 multicolored	2.25	2.25

Nos. 619-626 (8)　　10.95　9.70

Souvenir Sheets

| 627 | G70 | $5 Sequin's Engine, 1829 | 4.25 | 4.25 |
| 628 | G70 | $5 Der Adler, 1835 | 4.25 | 4.25 |

Nos. 539, 541, 543 Overprinted

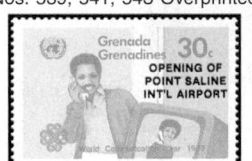

1984, Oct. 28　　　　Perf. 14
| 629 | G61 | 30c multicolored | .35 | .25 |
| 630 | G61 | $1.10 multicolored | 1.25 | .95 |

Souvenir Sheet

| 630A | G61 | $5 multicolored | 6.50 | 5.25 |

Opening of the Point Saline International Airport. No. 630A is overprinted in the margin.

Christmas Type of 1984

Scenes from various Donald Duck movies.

1984, Nov. 26　　Perf. 13½x14
631	A173	45c multicolored	.95	.55
632	A173	60c multicolored	1.10	.90
633	A173	90c multicolored	1.60	1.25
634	A173	$2 multi, perf. 12	2.50	2.50
635	A173	$4 multicolored	4.75	4.75

Nos. 631-635 (5)　　10.90　9.80

Souvenir Sheet

| 636 | A173 | $5 multicolored | 6.50 | 6.00 |

No. 634 issued in sheets of 8.

Audubon Type of 1985

Designs: 50c, Blue-winged teal. 90c, White ibis. $1.10, Swallow-tailed kite. $3, Common Gallinule. $5, Mangrove cuckoo.

1985, Feb. 11 — Perf. 14

637	A174	50c multicolored	2.25	.90
638	A174	90c multicolored	2.75	1.60
639	A174	$1.10 multicolored	3.75	2.10
640	A174	$3 multicolored	4.75	4.75
		Nos. 637-640 (4)	13.50	9.35

Souvenir Sheet

641	A174	$5 multicolored	6.25	6.25

See Nos. 732-736.

Motorcycle Centenary — G71

Anniv. emblem and: 30c, Kawasaki 750, 1972. 60c, Honda Goldwing GL1000, 1974, horiz. 70c, Kawasaki Z650, 1976, horiz. $4, Honda CBX, 1977. $5, BMW R100RS, 1978.

1985, Mar. 11

642	G71	30c multicolored	.75	.50
643	G71	60c multicolored	1.00	1.00
644	G71	70c multicolored	1.25	1.25
645	G71	$4 multicolored	5.00	5.00
		Nos. 642-645 (4)	8.00	7.75

Souvenir Sheet

646	G71	$5 multicolored	6.00	6.00

Intl. Youth Year G72

Designs: 50c, Folding bandages (health). 70c, Diver, turtle (environment). $1.10, Sailing (leisure). $3, Boys playing chess (education). $5, Hands touching globe.

1985, Apr. 15

647	G72	50c multicolored	.65	.45
648	G72	70c multicolored	1.00	.85
649	G72	$1.10 multicolored	1.50	1.40
650	G72	$3 multicolored	7.50	7.50
		Nos. 647-650 (4)	10.65	10.20

Souvenir Sheet

651	G72	$5 multicolored	5.00	5.00

Intl. Civil Aviation Org., 40th Anniv. G73

Designs: 5c, Lockheed Lodestar. 70c, Avro 748 Turboprop. $1.10, Boeing 727. $4, Boeing 707. $5, Pilatus Britten-Norman Islander.

1985, Apr. 30

652	G73	5c multicolored	.50	.20
653	G73	70c multicolored	2.25	.70
654	G73	$1.10 multicolored	2.75	1.10
655	G73	$4 multicolored	4.50	3.25
		Nos. 652-655 (4)	10.00	5.25

Souvenir Sheet

656	G73	$5 multicolored	5.75	5.00

Girl Guides Type

Designs: 30c, Lady Baden-Powell, Guide leaders. 50c, Botany field trip. 70c, Making camp, vert. $4, Sailing, vert. $5, Lord and Lady Baden-Powell, vert.

1985, May 30

657	A176	30c multicolored	.50	.25
658	A176	50c multicolored	1.25	.95
659	A176	70c multicolored	1.25	.55
660	A176	$4 multicolored	5.00	2.75
		Nos. 657-660 (4)	8.00	3.90

Souvenir Sheet

661	A176	$5 multicolored	5.50	5.50

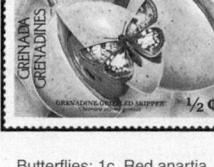

Grenadine Grizzled Skipper G74

Butterflies: 1c, Red anartia. 2c, Lesser Antillean giant hairstreak. 4c, Santa Domingo longtail skipper. 5c, Spotted Manuel's skipper. 6c, Grenada's polydamus swallowtail. 10c, Palmira sulphur. 12c, Pupillated orange sulphur. 15c, Migrant sulphur. 20c, St. Christopher's hairstreak. 25c, St. Lucia mestra. 30c, Insular gulf fritillary. 40c, Michael's Caribbean buckeye. 60c, Frampton's flambeau. 70c, Bamboo page. $1.10, Antillean cracker. $2.50, Red crescent hairstreak. $5, Single colored Antillean white. $10, Lesser whirlabout. $20, Blue night.

1985-86 — Perf. 14

662	G74	½c multicolored	.25	.25
663	G74	1c multicolored	.25	.25
664	G74	2c multicolored	.25	.25
665	G74	4c multicolored	.25	.25
666	G74	5c multicolored	.25	.25
667	G74	6c multicolored	.25	.25
668	G74	10c multicolored	.40	.25
669	G74	12c multicolored	.60	.25
670	G74	15c multicolored	.60	.25
671	G74	20c multicolored	.80	.25
672	G74	25c multicolored	.80	.25
673	G74	30c multicolored	.80	.30
674	G74	40c multicolored	1.00	.60
675	G74	60c multicolored	1.40	.95
676	G74	70c multicolored	1.60	1.00
677	G74	$1.10 multicolored	2.50	1.90
678	G74	$2.50 multicolored	4.50	3.75
679	G74	$5 multicolored	6.75	6.25
680	G74	$10 multicolored	11.00	11.00
681	G74	$20 multicolored	15.50	15.50
		Nos. 662-681 (20)	49.75	44.00

Issued: #662-679, 6/17; #680, 11/11; #681, 1/8/86.
For overprints see Nos. 737-738.

1986 — Perf. 12½x12

662a	G74	½c multicolored	.40	.40
663a	G74	1c multicolored	.40	.40
664a	G74	2c multicolored	.40	.40
665a	G74	4c multicolored	.40	.40
666a	G74	5c multicolored	.40	.40
667a	G74	6c multicolored	.40	.40
668a	G74	10c multicolored	.40	.40
669a	G74	12c multicolored	.40	.40
670a	G74	15c multicolored	.40	.40
671a	G74	20c multicolored	.40	.40
672a	G74	25c multicolored	.40	.40
673a	G74	30c multicolored	.60	.60
674a	G74	40c multicolored	.70	.70
675a	G74	60c multicolored	1.25	1.25
676a	G74	70c multicolored	1.25	1.25
677a	G74	$1.10 multicolored	2.00	2.00
678a	G74	$2.50 multicolored	7.00	7.00
679a	G74	$5 multicolored	12.00	12.00
680a	G74	$10 multicolored	20.00	20.00
681a	G74	$20 multicolored	26.00	26.00
		Nos. 662a-681a (20)	75.20	75.20

Issued: #662a-677a, 679a, 1986; #678a, 680a, 9/1986; #681a, 5/1989.

Queen Mother Birthday Type

$1, Portrait. $1.50, At Ascot, horiz. $2.50, Queen Mother, Prince Charles. $5, Portrait, diff.

1985, July 3 — Perf. 14

682	A181	$1 multicolored	.65	.65
683	A181	$1.50 multicolored	1.10	1.10
684	A181	$2.50 multicolored	1.75	1.75
		Nos. 682-684 (3)	3.50	3.50

Souvenir Sheet

685	A181	$5 multicolored	3.75	3.75

1986, Jan. 28 — Perf. 12x12½

686	A181	70c like #682	.60	.60
687	A181	$1.10 like #683	.75	.75
688	A181	$3 like #684	2.50	2.50
		Nos. 686-688 (3)	3.85	3.85

Issued in sheets of 5 plus label.

Water Sports Type

Designs: 15c, Scuba diving. 70c, Playing in waterfall. 90c, Water skiing. $4, Swimming. $5, Skin diver, sailboat.

1985, July 15 — Perf. 15

689	A179	15c multicolored	.20	.20
690	A179	70c multicolored	.55	.55
691	A179	90c multicolored	1.00	1.00
692	A179	$4 multicolored	3.50	3.50
		Nos. 689-692 (4)	5.25	5.25

Souvenir Sheet

693	A179	$5 multicolored	4.50	4.50

Queen Conch G75

Marine Life: 90c, Porcupine fish, fire coral. $1.10, Ghost crab. $4, West Indies spiny lobster. $5, Long-spined urchin.

1985, Aug. 1 — Perf. 14

694	G75	60c multicolored	.85	.70
695	G75	90c multicolored	1.50	1.00
696	G75	$1.10 multicolored	1.75	1.25
697	G75	$4 multicolored	4.25	4.25
		Nos. 694-697 (4)	8.35	7.20

Souvenir Sheet

698	G75	$5 multicolored	8.50	8.50

Bach Anniversary Type

Portrait, signature, music from Invention No. 9 and: 15c, Natural trumpet. 60c, Bass viol. $1.10, Flute. $3, Double flageolet. $5, Portrait.

1985, Sept. 3 — Perf. 14

699	A184	15c multicolored	.65	.20
700	A184	60c multicolored	1.10	.60
701	A184	$1.10 multicolored	2.00	1.00
702	A184	$3 multicolored	3.00	2.50
		Nos. 699-702 (4)	6.75	4.30

Souvenir Sheet

703	A184	$5 multicolored	4.50	4.50

Royal Visit Type

10c, Arms of Great Britain, Grenada. $1, Queen Elizabeth II. $4, HMY Britannia. $5, Map.

1985, Nov. 4 — Perf. 14½

704	A186	10c multicolored	.25	.20
705	A186	$1 multi, vert.	1.50	1.50
706	A186	$4 multicolored	4.50	4.50
		Nos. 704-706 (3)	6.25	6.20

Souvenir Sheet

707	A186	$5 multicolored	5.25	5.25

UN Anniversary Type

UN stamps and famous people: $1, #373, Neil Armstrong. $2, #221, Mahatma Gandhi. $2.50, #43, Maimonides. $5, Ralph Bunche.

1985, Nov. 22

708	A189	$1 multicolored	1.50	1.25
709	A189	$2 multicolored	4.25	4.25
710	A189	$2.50 multicolored	5.00	5.00
		Nos. 708-710 (3)	10.75	10.50

Souvenir Sheet

711	A189	$5 multicolored	5.25	5.25

Twain & Disney Type

Walt Disney characters in scenes from "Letters From Hawaii": 25c, Mickey, Minnie on beach. 50c, Donald Duck surfing. $1.50, Donald roasting marshmallow. $3, Mickey canoeing. $5, Mickey, cat.

1985, Nov. 27 — Perf. 14x13½

712	A185	25c multicolored	.85	.40
713	A185	50c multicolored	1.25	.90
714	A185	$1.50 multicolored	3.25	3.25
715	A185	$3 multicolored	5.50	5.50
		Nos. 712-715 (4)	10.85	10.05

Souvenir Sheet

716	A185	$5 multicolored	7.00	7.00

Brothers Grimm & Disney Type

Walt Disney characters in scenes from "The Elves and the Shoemaker": 30c, Mickey as shoemaker. 60c, Elves helping. 70c, Mickey, new shoes. $4, Minnie at sewing machine. $5, Minnie & Mickey.

1985, Nov. 27 — Perf. 13½x14

717	A187	30c multicolored	.85	.45
718	A187	60c multicolored	1.25	1.00
719	A187	70c multicolored	1.60	1.25
720	A187	$4 multicolored	5.25	5.25
		Nos. 717-720 (4)	8.95	7.95

Souvenir Sheet

721	A187	$5 multicolored	7.50	7.50

Madonna and Child by Titian — G76

Christmas paintings: 70c, Madonna and Child with St. Mary and John the Baptist by Bugiardini. $1.10, Adoration of the Magi by Di Fredi. $3, Madonna and Child with Young St. John the Baptist by Bartolomeo. $5, The Annunciation by Botticelli.

1985, Dec. 23 — Perf. 15

722	G76	50c multicolored	.60	.45
723	G76	70c multicolored	.75	.55
724	G76	$1.10 multicolored	1.25	.90
725	G76	$3 multicolored	2.40	2.40
		Nos. 722-725 (4)	5.00	4.30

Souvenir Sheet

726	G76	$5 multicolored	4.00	4.00

Statue of Liberty Type of 1985

Designs: 5c, Croton Reservoir, 1875. 10c, NY Public Library, 1986. 70c, Old Boathouse, Central Park, 1894. $4, Boating, Central Park, 1986. $5, Statue of Liberty, vert.

1986, Jan. 6 — Perf. 15

727	A191	5c multicolored	.20	.20
728	A191	10c multicolored	.20	.20
729	A191	70c multicolored	.40	.40
730	A191	$4 multicolored	2.75	2.75
		Nos. 727-730 (4)	3.55	3.55

Souvenir Sheet

731	A191	$5 multicolored	5.00	5.00

Audubon Type of 1985

Designs: 50c, Louisiana heron. 70c, Black-crowned night heron. 90c, Bittern. $4, Glossy ibis. $5, King eider.

1986, Jan. 28 — Perf. 12½x12

732	A174	50c multicolored	2.25	1.10
733	A174	70c multicolored	2.75	1.60
734	A174	90c multicolored	3.00	2.40
735	A174	$4 multicolored	5.50	5.50
		Nos. 732-735 (4)	13.50	10.60

Souvenir Sheet — Perf. 14

736	A174	$5 multicolored	8.00	8.00

Nos. 732-735 issued in sheets of 5 plus label.

Nos. 676, 679 Overprinted

1986, Feb. 20 — Perf. 14

737	G74	70c multicolored	1.50	1.50
738	G75	$5 multicolored	6.50	6.50

World Cup Soccer Championships, Mexico — G77

Various soccer plays.

1986, Mar. 18

739	G77	10c multicolored	.65	.40
740	G77	70c multicolored	1.90	1.40
741	G77	$1 multicolored	2.25	1.90
742	G77	$4 multicolored	5.50	5.50
		Nos. 739-742 (4)	10.30	9.20

Souvenir Sheet

743	G77	$5 multicolored	6.25	6.25

For overprints see Nos. 772-776.

Halley's Comet Type

Designs: 5c, Nicolaus Copernicus, Earl of Rossi's six foot reflector. 20c, Sputnik. 40c, Tycho Brahe's notes, sketch of comet of 1577. $4, Edmond Halley, comet of 1682. $5, Halley's comet. Captions on 40c and $4 are reversed.

1986, Mar. 26

744	A194	5c multicolored	.50	.50
745	A194	20c multicolored	.80	.50
746	A194	40c multicolored	1.00	.75
747	A194	$4 multicolored	5.00	5.00
		Nos. 744-747 (4)	7.30	6.75

Souvenir Sheet

748	A194	$5 multicolored	4.75	4.75

"Tycho," on 40c, and "Nicolaus" on 5c misspelled.
For overprints see Nos. 787-791. Compare No. 748 with No. 913.

Queen Elizabeth II, 60th Birthday
Common Design Type

Designs: 2c, At Windsor Park, 1933. $1.50, Queen Elizabeth II. $4, In Sydney, Australia, 1970. $5, Family portrait, Coronation Day, 1937.

1986, Apr. 21

749	CD339	2c yel & blk	.20	.20
750	CD339	$1.50 pale grn & multi	1.00	1.00
751	CD339	$4 dl lil & multi	2.75	2.75
		Nos. 749-751 (3)	3.95	3.95

Souvenir Sheet

752	CD339	$5 tan & blk	3.75	3.75

AMERIPEX '86 Type

Walt Disney characters visiting: 30c, Grand Canyon. 60c, Golden Gate Bridge. $1, Chicago Watertower. $3, The White House. $5, NY Harbor, Statue of Liberty.

1986, May 22　　　　　　　**Perf. 11**

753	A195	30c multicolored	.80	.50
754	A195	60c multicolored	1.20	1.20
755	A195	$1 multicolored	2.00	2.00
756	A195	$3 multicolored	4.00	4.00
		Nos. 753-756 (4)	8.00	7.70

Souvenir Sheet
Perf. 14

757	A195	$5 multicolored	6.25	6.25

Royal Wedding Issue, 1986
Common Design Type

Designs: 60c, Prince Andrew and Sarah Ferguson. 70c, Andrew. $4, Andrew in dress uniform, helicopter. $5, Couple, diff.

1986, July 1　　　　　　　**Perf. 14**

758	CD340	60c multicolored	.45	.45
759	CD340	70c multicolored	.55	.55
760	CD340	$4 multicolored	3.00	3.00
		Nos. 758-760 (3)	4.00	4.00

Souvenir Sheet

761	CD340	$5 multicolored	5.00	5.00

Mushrooms
G78

Seashells
G79

Designs: 15c, Hygrocybe firma. 50c, Xerocomus coccolobae. $2, Volvariella cubensis. $3, Lactarius putidus. $5, Leponia caeruleocapitata.

1986, July 15　　　　　　　**Perf. 15**

762	G78	15c multicolored	1.60	.80
763	G78	50c multicolored	3.75	2.40
764	G78	$2 multicolored	7.00	7.00
765	G78	$3 multicolored	9.00	9.00
		Nos. 762-765 (4)	21.35	19.20

Souvenir Sheet

766	G78	$5 multicolored	19.00	19.00

1986, Aug. 1

Designs: 15c, Giant Atlantic pyram. 50c, Beau's murex. $1.10, West Indian fighting

---

conch. $4, Alphabet coral. $5, Brown-lined paper bubble.

767	G79	15c multicolored	1.25	.60
768	G79	50c multicolored	3.00	1.75
769	G79	$1.10 multicolored	3.25	3.25
770	G79	$4 multicolored	5.75	5.75
		Nos. 767-770 (4)	13.25	11.35

Souvenir Sheet

771	G79	$5 multicolored	11.50	11.50

Nos. 739-743 Overprinted in Gold:
WINNERS / Argentina 3 / W.Germany 2

1986, Sept. 15　　　　　　　**Perf. 14**

772	G77	10c multicolored	.75	.45
773	G77	70c multicolored	1.50	1.25
774	G77	$1 multicolored	2.00	1.50
775	G77	$4 multicolored	4.75	4.75
		Nos. 772-775 (4)	9.00	7.95

Souvenir Sheet

776	G77	$5 multicolored	8.00	8.00

Manicou
G80

Wildlife.

1986, Sept. 15　　　　　　　**Perf. 15**

777	G80	10c shown	.25	.25
778	G80	30c Giant toad	.50	.50
779	G80	60c Land tortoise	1.00	1.00
780	G80	70c Murine opossum	1.10	1.10
781	G80	90c Burmese mongoose	1.25	1.25
782	G80	$1.10 Antillean armadillo	1.60	1.60
783	G80	$2 Agouti	2.50	2.50
784	G80	$3 Humpback whale	5.75	5.75
		Nos. 777-784 (8)	13.95	13.95

Souvenir Sheets

785	G80	$5 Mona monkey	7.00	7.00
786	G80	$5 Iguana	7.00	7.00

Nos. 744-748 Overprinted in Silver or Black

1986, Oct. 15　　　　　　　**Perf. 14**

787	A194	5c multicolored (Bk)	.90	.75
788	A194	20c multicolored	1.10	.65
789	A194	40c multicolored (Bk)	1.25	.75
790	A194	$4 multicolored	6.50	6.50
		Nos. 787-790 (4)	9.75	8.65

Souvenir Sheet

791	A194	$5 multicolored	8.50	8.50

Christmas Type of 1986

1986 Nov. 3　　　　　　　**Perf. 11**

792	A199	25c Chip 'n' Dale	.55	.25
793	A199	30c Mickey Mouse	.55	.30
794	A199	50c Piglet, Pooh, Jose Carioca	.70	.40
795	A199	60c Daisy	.80	.50
796	A199	70c A kiss under the mistletoe	.95	.60
797	A199	$1.50 Huey, Dewey, and Louie	1.75	1.75
798	A199	$3 Mickey Mouse, Morty	2.00	2.00
799	A199	$4 Kittens on the keys	3.50	3.50
		Nos. 792-799 (8)	10.80	9.30

Souvenir Sheets

800	A199	$5 Mickey Mouse	5.00	5.00
801	A199	$5 Bambi	5.00	5.00

Nos. 793, 795-796, 799 vert.

Automobile Centenary Type

Designs: 10c, 1984 Aston-Martin Volante. 30c, 1948 Jaguar Mk V. 60c, 1956 Nash Ambassador. 70c, 1984 Toyota Supra. 90c, 1985 Ferrari Testarossa. $1, 1955 BMW 501B. $2, 1968 Mercedes-Benz 280SL. $3, 1932 Austro-Daimler ADR8.

1986, Nov. 20　　　　　　　**Perf. 15**

802	A202	10c multicolored	.30	.30
803	A202	30c multicolored	.55	.55
804	A202	60c multicolored	.75	.75
805	A202	70c multicolored	.75	.75
806	A202	90c multicolored	.90	.90
807	A202	$1 multicolored	.90	.90
808	A202	$2 multicolored	1.25	1.25
809	A202	$3 multicolored	1.60	1.60
		Nos. 802-809 (8)	7.00	7.00

Souvenir Sheets

810	A202	$5 1977 Morgan +8	4.25	4.25
811	A202	$5 Checker Taxi	4.25	4.25

Chagall Type

Paintings: $1.10 — No. 812, The Mirror. No. 813, Dancer with a Fan. No. 814, The Acrobat. No. 815, Abraham's Sacrifice. No. 816, The Fruit Seller. No. 817, The Rooster. No. 818, The Wedding. No. 819, Horsewoman. No. 820, The Aged Lion from Fables of La Fontaine. No. 821, The Fruit Basket. No. 822, The Satyr and the Wayfarer. No. 823, Self-portrait with Seven Fingers. No. 824, Fruit and Flowers. No. 825, Lovers and Flowers. No. 826, The Wedded with an Angel. No. 827, In the Cafe, 1936. No. 828, The Equestrian. No. 829, Blue Violinist, 1947. No. 830, I and the Village. No. 831, Portrait of Vava, 1955. No. 832, To Russia, Asses and Cattle, 1911. No. 833, The Accordion Player. No. 834, The Violinist, 1913. No. 835, Mother and Child, 1968. No. 836, Sunday, 1953. No. 837, Red and Black World, 1951. No. 838, Double Portrait with Wineglass, 1917. No. 839, Homage to Apollinaire. No. 840, Time is a River without Banks, 1930. No. 841, The Rue de La Paix, 1953. No. 842, Bonjour Paris. No. 843, The Blue Home, 1926, horiz. No. 844, Still-life, 1912, horiz. No. 845, Autumn Village. No. 846, Aleko: Scene I (Costume Design). No. 847, The Jew in Pink, 1914. No. 848, The Clown Musician, 1927. No. 849, War, 1943. No. 850, The Artist Angel. No. 851, Woman at Window, 1961.

$5 — No. 852, Birthday, 1915. No. 853, Wheatfield on a Summer Afternoon, 1942. No. 854, The Nude above Vitebsk. No. 855, Aleko and Zemphira by Moonlight. No. 856, The Family Dinner. No. 857, Life. No. 858, The Flying Carriage, 1913. No. 859, The Studio. No. 860, Birth. No. 861, Rain.

1986-87　　　　　　　**Perf. 14x13½**

812-851	A203	Set of 40	70.00	70.00

Size: 110x95mm
Imperf

852-861	A203	Set of 10	37.50	37.50

Issued: Nos. 824-851, 855-861, 1987.

America's Cup Type

1987, Feb. 5　　　　　　　**Perf. 15**

862	A204	25c Defender, 1895	.85	.55
863	A204	45c Caleta, 1886	1.10	.85
864	A204	70c Azzurra, 1981	1.40	1.40
865	A204	$4 Australia II, 1983	3.00	3.00
		Nos. 862-865 (4)	6.35	5.80

Souvenir Sheet

866	A204	$5 Columbia, Shamrock, 1899	7.00	7.00

Discovery of America Type

1987, Apr. 27

867	A206	15c Columbus	.25	.25
868	A206	30c Queen Isabella	.25	.25
869	A206	50c Santa Maria	.40	.40
870	A206	60c Landing in New World	.45	.45
871	A206	90c Lesser Antilles	.75	.75
872	A206	$1 King Ferdinand	.80	.80
873	A206	$2 Fort of La Navidad	1.75	1.75
874	A206	$3 Galley off Hispaniola	2.50	2.50
a.		Sheet of 8	12.00	12.00
		Nos. 867-874 (8)	7.15	7.15

Souvenir Sheets

875	A207	$5 Native Canoe	6.00	6.00
876	A207	$5 Santa Maria at anchor	6.00	6.00

Transportation Innovations Type

Designs: 10c, Saunders Roe SR-N1 Hovercraft, 1959. 15c, Bugatti Royale, 1931. 30c, Aleksei Leonov, 1st space walk, 1965. 50c, CSS Hunley, submarine, 1864. 60c, Rolls Royce Flying Bedstead, VTOL aircraft, 1954. 70c, Jenny Lind, locomotive, 1854. 90c, Duryea, 1893. $1.50, Steam locomotive, London subway, 1863. $2, SS Great Britain, screw-driven steamship, 1843. $3, Budweiser rocket, 1979.

1987, May 18　　　　　　　**Perf. 14**

877	A209	10c multicolored	.55	.30
878	A209	15c multicolored	.60	.40
879	A209	30c multicolored	.80	.50
880	A209	50c multicolored	1.10	.75
881	A209	60c multicolored	1.25	.90
882	A209	70c multicolored	1.40	1.25
883	A209	90c multicolored	1.50	1.25

884	A209	$1.50 multicolored	2.25	2.25
885	A209	$2 multicolored	2.75	2.75
886	A209	$3 multicolored	3.00	3.00
		Nos. 877-886 (10)	15.20	13.35

Capex '87 Type

Fish.

1987, June 15

887	A208	6c Yellow chub	.25	.25
888	A208	30c Kingfish	.55	.40
889	A208	50c Mako shark	.75	.65
890	A208	60c Dolphinfish	.85	.85
891	A208	90c Bonito	1.10	1.10
892	A208	$1.10 Cobia	1.40	1.40
893	A208	$3 Great tarpon	3.25	3.25
894	A208	$4 Swordfish	3.50	3.50
		Nos. 887-894 (8)	11.65	11.40

Souvenir Sheets

895	A208	$5 Jewfish	5.00	5.00
896	A208	$5 Amberjack	5.00	5.00

Statue of Liberty Type

10c, Washing statue's face. 15c, Commemorative medals. 25c, Band facing right. 30c, Band facing forward. 45c, Liberty's face. 50c, Washing statue's hair, horiz. 60c, Commemorative statuettes, horiz. 70c, Boats in NY Harbor, horiz. $1, Re-opening. $1.10, Blimps, Liberty & Manhattan Islands. $2, Warship. $3, Commemorative flags.

1987, Aug. 5

897	A210	10c multicolored	.20	.20
898	A210	15c multicolored	.30	.30
899	A210	25c multicolored	.45	.45
900	A210	30c multicolored	.50	.50
901	A210	45c multicolored	.55	.55
902	A210	50c multicolored	.60	.60
903	A210	60c multicolored	.70	.70
904	A210	70c multicolored	.80	.80
905	A210	$1 multicolored	.95	.95
906	A210	$1.10 multicolored	1.00	1.00
907	A210	$2 multicolored	1.90	1.90
908	A210	$3 multicolored	2.10	2.10
		Nos. 897-908 (12)	10.05	10.05

Inventors Type

Designs: 60c, Isaac Newton, Newton Medal. $1, Louis Daguerre, inventor of Daguerreotype. $2, Antoine Lavoisier, French chemist, apparatus. $3, Rudolf Diesel, German engineer, Diesel engine. $5, Halley's comet.

1987, Sept. 9

909	A211	60c multicolored	.90	.70
910	A211	$1 multicolored	1.10	1.10
911	A211	$2 multicolored	2.25	2.25
912	A211	$3 multicolored	5.25	5.25
		Nos. 909-912 (4)	9.50	9.30

Souvenir Sheet

913	A211	$5 multicolored	7.25	7.25

No. 913 inscribed "Great Scientific Discoveries" in margin.
No. 912 incorrectly inscribed "James Watt, Steam Engine." See Grenada No. 1538.

US Constitution Bicentennial Type

10c, Constitutional Convention, Philadelphia. 50c, Georgia state flag. 60c, Capitol, vert. $4, Thomas Jefferson, vert. $5, Alexander Hamilton, vert.

1987, Nov. 1

914	A214	10c multicolored	.25	.20
915	A214	50c multicolored	.85	.75
916	A214	60c multicolored	.85	.80
917	A214	$4 multicolored	4.75	4.75
		Nos. 914-917 (4)	6.70	6.50

Souvenir Sheet

918	A214	$5 multicolored	4.25	4.25

Hafnia '87 Type

Walt Disney characters in adaptations of Hans Christian Andersen Fairy Tales: 25c, The Swineherd. 30c, What the Good Man Does is Always Right. 50c, Little Tuk. 60c, The World's Fairest Rose. 70c, The Garden of Paradise. $1.50, The Naughty Boy. $3, What the Moon Saw. $4, Thumbelina. No. 927, Hans Clodhopper. No. 928, Elder Tree Mother.

1987, Nov. 16

919	A215	25c multicolored	.55	.30
920	A215	30c multicolored	.60	.40
921	A215	50c multicolored	.80	.80
922	A215	60c multicolored	.80	.80
923	A215	70c multicolored	.85	.85
924	A215	$1.50 multicolored	2.25	2.25
925	A215	$3 multicolored	3.00	3.00
926	A215	$4 multicolored	3.50	3.50
		Nos. 919-926 (8)	12.35	11.90

Souvenir Sheets

927	A215	$5 multicolored	6.50	6.50
928	A215	$5 multicolored	6.50	6.50

Christmas — G81

Paintings by El Greco: 10c, Virgin and Child with Saints Martin and Agnes. 50c, Detail from Virgin and Child with Saints Martin and Agnes. 60c, The Annunciation. $4, Holy Family with St. Anne. $5, Adoration of the Shepherds.

1987, Dec. 15

929	G81	10c multicolored	.45	.20
930	G81	50c multicolored	1.40	.95
931	G81	60c multicolored	1.40	1.10
932	G81	$4 multicolored	5.50	5.50
		Nos. 929-932 (4)	8.75	7.75

Souvenir Sheet

933	G81	$5 multicolored	9.25	9.25

Wedding Anniv. Type

1988, Feb. 15

934	A218	20c Elizabeth, Anne	.25	.20
935	A218	30c Wedding portrait	.25	.25
936	A218	$2 Elizabeth, Charles, Anne	1.50	1.50
937	A218	$3 Elizabeth wearing tiara	2.25	2.25
		Nos. 934-937 (4)	4.25	4.20

Souvenir Sheet

938	A218	$5 Elizabeth in wedding gown	4.25	4.25

1988 Summer Olympics Type

Walt Disney characters in modern and ancient events.

1988, Apr. 13   *Perf. 13½x14, 14x13½*

939	A219	1c Rhythmic gymnastics	.20	.20
940	A219	2c Pankration	.20	.20
941	A219	3c Synchronized swimming	.20	.20
942	A219	4c Hoplite race	.20	.20
943	A219	5c Baseball	.20	.20
944	A219	10c Horse race	.25	.25
945	A219	$6 Windsurfing	5.00	5.00
946	A219	$7 Chariot race	5.75	5.75
		Nos. 939-946 (8)	12.00	12.00

Souvenir Sheet

947	A219	$5 Tennis	5.00	5.00
948	A219	$5 Pentathlon	5.00	5.00

Boy Scout Type

1988, May 3   *Perf. 14*

949	A220	50c Semaphore, vert.	.50	.50
950	A220	70c Canoeing, vert.	.60	.60
951	A220	$1 Cook-out	.90	.90
952	A220	$3 Campfire	2.75	2.75
		Nos. 949-952 (4)	4.75	4.75

Souvenir Sheet

953	A220	$5 Pitching tent	4.50	4.50

Bird Type

1988, May 31

954	A222	20c Yellow-crowned night heron	.30	.30
955	A222	25c Brown pelican	.30	.30
956	A222	45c Audubon's shearwater	.45	.40
957	A222	60c Red-footed booby	.65	.45
958	A222	70c Bridled tern	.65	.60
959	A222	90c Red-billed tropicbird	.90	.90
960	A222	$3 Blue-winged teal	2.50	2.50
961	A222	$4 Sora	3.50	3.50
		Nos. 954-961 (8)	9.25	8.95

Souvenir Sheets

962	A222	$5 Little blue heron	5.00	5.00
963	A222	$5 Purple-throated carib	5.00	5.00

Titian Type

Paintings by Titian: 15c, Man with Blue Eyes, 1545. 30c, The Three Ages of Man, 1512. 60c, Don Diego Mendoza, 1545. 75c, Emperor Charles V Seated, 1548. $1, A Young Man in a Fur, 1515. $2, Tobias and the Angel, 1543. $3, Pietro Bembo, 1540. $4, Pier Luigi Farnese, 1546. No. 972, Sacred and Profane Love. No. 973, Venus and Adonis.

1988, June 15   *Perf. 13½x14*

964	A224	15c multicolored	.20	.20
965	A224	30c multicolored	.25	.25
966	A224	45c multicolored	.40	.40
967	A224	75c multicolored	.55	.55

968	A224	$1 multicolored	.75	.75
969	A224	$2 multicolored	1.50	1.50
970	A224	$3 multicolored	2.25	2.25
971	A224	$4 multicolored	3.00	3.00
		Nos. 964-971 (8)	8.90	8.90

Souvenir Sheet

972	A224	$5 multicolored	5.25	5.25
973	A224	$5 multicolored	5.25	5.25

Airship Type

Historic flights: 10c, Hindenburg over Rio de Janeiro, 1937. 20c, Hindenburg over NYC, 1937. 30c, US Navy airships, WWII convoy to Europe, 1944. 40c, Hindenburg docking at Lakehurst, NJ, 1937, vert. 60c, Joint flight, Hindenburg and Graf Zeppelin, 1936, vert. 70c, DC-3, Hindenburg, Los Angeles at Lakehurst, 1936. $1, Graf Zeppelin II over England, 1939, vert. $2, Deutschland, 1st passenger flight, 1912. $3, Graf Zeppelin over Dome of the Rock, Jerusalem, 1931. $4, Hindenburg Olympic flight, 1936. No. 984, Graf Zeppelin over Vatican City, 1933, vert. No. 985, Graf Zeppelin Polar flight, 1931.

1988, July 1   *Perf. 14*

974	A225	10c multicolored	.20	.20
975	A225	20c multicolored	.20	.20
976	A225	30c multicolored	.25	.25
977	A225	40c multicolored	.35	.35
978	A225	60c multicolored	.80	.60
979	A225	70c multicolored	1.10	.80
980	A225	$1 multicolored	1.10	.90
981	A225	$2 multicolored	1.75	1.75
982	A225	$3 multicolored	2.50	2.50
983	A225	$4 multicolored	3.25	3.25
		Nos. 974-983 (10)	11.50	10.80

Souvenir Sheets

984	A225	$5 multicolored	6.00	6.00
985	A225	$5 multicolored	6.00	6.00

Fairy Tales Type
Miniature Sheets

Bambi: No. 986a, Newborn Bambi, mother and forest animals. b, Bambi, Flower and Thumper. c, Bambi and opossum family hanging from tree. d, Bambi, his mother, and Faline, a female fawn. e, Foraging in a snow storm. f, Meeting his father, the Great Stag. g, Competing for Faline's attention. h, The Great Stag leading animals to safety during forest fire. i, Bambi, grown, becomes the Great Stag.
The Fox and the Hound: No. 987a, Big Mama, consoling the orphaned baby fox, Tod. b, Widow Tweed feeding Tod. c, Tod playing with Copper, the hound. d, Copper leashed. e, Copper and Chief. f, Chief barking at Tod, Copper shocked. g, Porcupine. h, Vixey, a female fox. i, Bear attacking Copper.
101 Dalmatians: No. 988a, Pongo, Perdita and their masters. b, Pongo and Perdita, courting. c, Three puppies. d, Cruella de Ville and henchmen. e, Captain the Horse, Colonel the Sheepdog and Tibbs the Cat. f, Dalmatians following Tibbs to freedom. g, Cruella racing car in pursuit. h, Dalmatians disguised in soot. i, Nanny dusting off the soot.
Dumbo: No. 989a, Stork delivering Dumbo. b, Elephant making fun of Dumbo's large ears. c, Dumbo, Mrs. Jumbo performing. d, Timothy the Mouse. e, Timothy and Dumbo. f, Crows pushing Dumbo off a cliff. g, Dumbo flying away from burning building. h, Dumbo flying with the crows. i, Dumbo and Mrs. Jumbo on train.
Lady and the Tramp: No. 990a, Darling holding Lady. b, Lady meets the Tramp. c, Lady looking in bassinet. d, Siamese cats, Lady. e, Lady, Tramp, crocodiles. f, Tramp kisses Lady. g, Lady in dog catcher's carriage. h, Lady and Tramp attacking rat. i, Trusty and Jock overturning dog catcher's carriage where Tramp is imprisoned.
The Aristocats: No. 991a, Edgar driving Madame Mornfamille's carriage. b, Dutchess and kittens. c, Edgar feeding the cats cream spiked with sleeping pills. d, Edgar transporting cats on motorcycle. e, Walter O'Malley discovers the abandoned cats. f, Three geese. g, Scat Cat and friends holding a jam session. h, Edgar attacks O'Malley with a pitch fork. i, Frau-Frau kicking Edgar.
No. 992, Faline and newborn twin fawns. No. 993, Tod and Vixey. No. 994, Pongo, Perdita and puppies. No. 995, Dumbo flying with Timothy the Mouse. No. 996, Lady and Tramp's puppies. No. 997, Walter O'Malley, Dutchess and kittens.

1988, July 25   *Perf. 14x13½*

986		Sheet of 9	4.25	4.25
a.-i.	A212	30c any single	.40	.40
987		Sheet of 9	4.25	4.25
a.-i.	A212	30c any single	.40	.40
988		Sheet of 9	4.25	4.25
a.-i.	A212	30c any single	.40	.40
989		Sheet of 9	4.25	4.25
a.-i.	A212	30c any single	.40	.40
990		Sheet of 9	4.25	4.25
a.-i.	A212	30c any single	.40	.40
991		Sheet of 9	4.25	4.25
a.-i.	A212	30c any single	.40	.40
		Nos. 986-991 (6)	25.50	25.50

Souvenir Sheets

992-997	A212	$5 each	6.50	6.50

SYDPEX '88 Type

Walt Disney characters: 1c, Conducting at Sydney Opera House. 2c, Climbing Ayers Rock. 3c, Working at a sheep station. 4c, Visiting Lone Pine Koala Sanctuary. 5c, Playing Australian football. 10c, Racing camels. No. 1004, Lawn bowling. $6, America's Cup trophy and Australia II. No. 1006, The Great Barrier Reef. No. 1007, Beach party.

1988, Aug. 1   *Perf. 14x13½*

998	A226	1c multicolored	.20	.20
999	A226	2c multicolored	.20	.20
1000	A226	3c multicolored	.20	.20
1001	A226	4c multicolored	.20	.20
1002	A226	5c multicolored	.20	.20
1003	A226	10c multicolored	.20	.20
1004	A226	$5 multicolored	5.50	5.50
1005	A226	$6 multicolored	6.50	6.50
		Nos. 998-1005 (8)	13.20	13.20

Souvenir Sheets

1006	A226	$5 multicolored	5.00	5.00
1007	A226	$5 multicolored	5.00	5.00

Flowering Trees Type

1988, Sept. 30   *Perf. 14*

1008	A228	10c Potato tree, vert.	.20	.20
1009	A228	20c Wild cotton	.20	.20
1010	A228	30c Shower of gold, vert.	.25	.25
1011	A228	60c Napoleon's button, vert.	.50	.45
1012	A228	90c Geiger tree	.75	.65
1013	A228	$1 Fern tree	.85	.85
1014	A228	$2 French cashew	1.75	1.75
1015	A228	$4 Amherstia, vert.	3.00	3.00
		Nos. 1008-1015 (8)	7.50	7.35

Souvenir Sheets

1016	A228	$5 African tulip tree, vert.	3.75	3.75
1017	A228	$5 Swamp immortelle	3.75	3.75

Car Type
Miniature Sheets

Designs: No. 1018a, 1925 Doble Series E, US. b, 1926 Alvis 12/50, United Kingdom. c, 1927 Sunbeam 3-liter, UK. d, 1928 Franklin Airman, US. e, 1929 Delage D8S, France. f, 1897 Mors, France. g, 1904 Peerless Green Dragon, US. h, 1909 Pope-Hartford, US. i, 1920 Daniels Submarine Speedster, US. j, 1922 McFarlan 9.3 liter, US.
No. 1019a, 1949 Frazer Nash Lemans Replica, UK. b, 1953 Pegaso Z102, Spain. No. 1019c, 1953 Siata Spyder V-8, Italy. d, 1953 Kurtis-Offenhauser, US. No. 1019e, 1954 Kaiser-Darrin, US. f, 1930 Tracta, France. g, 1932 Maybach Zeppelin, Germany. h, 1934 Railton Light Sports, UK. i, 1936 Hotchkiss, France. j, 1939 Mercedes-Benz W163, Germany.
No. 1020a, 1982 Aston Martin Vantage V8, UK. b, 1982 Porsche 956, Germany. No. 1020c, 1983 Lotus Esprit Turbo, UK. d, 1984 McLaren MP4/2, UK. e, 1985 Mercedes-Benz 190E 2-3-16, Germany. f, 1963 Ferrari 250 GT Lusso, Italy. g, 1964 Porsche 904, Germany. h, 1967 Volvo P1800, Sweden. i, 1970 McLaren-Chevrolet M8D, US. j, 1981 Jaguar XJ6, UK.

1988, Oct. 7   *Perf. 13x13½*

1018		Sheet of 10	15.00	15.00
a.-j.	A223	$2 any single	1.50	1.50
1019		Sheet of 10	15.00	15.00
a.-j.	A223	$2 any single	1.50	1.50
1020		Sheet of 10	15.00	15.00
a.-j.	A223	$2 any single	1.50	1.50

Christmas and Mickey Mouse 60th Anniv. Type
Miniature Sheet

"Mickey's Christmas Parade": No. 1021a, Dumbo. b, Goofy. c, Minnie Mouse. d, Morty, Ferdy and Clarabelle Cow. e, Huey, Dewey and Louie. f, Donald Duck. g, Wooden soldiers marching. h, Mickey Mouse leading parade. No. 1022, Capt. Hook on float. No. 1023, Mickey and Donald on float.

1988, Dec. 1   *Perf. 13½x14*

1021		Sheet of 8	6.00	6.00
a.-h.	A229	$1 any single	.75	.75

Souvenir Sheets
Perf. 14x13

1022	A229	$7 multicolored	6.50	6.50
1023	A229	$7 multicolored	6.50	6.50

Japanese Painting Type

"The Fifty-three Stations on the Tokaido" by Hiroshige (1979-1858): 15c, Crossing the Oi at Shimada by Ferry. 20c, Daimyo and Entourage at Arai. 45c, Cargo Portage through Goyu. 75c, Snowfall at Fujigawa. $1, Horses for the Emperor at Chiryu. $2, Rainfall at Tsuchiyama. $3, At Inn of Ishibe. $4, On the Shore of Lake Biwa at Otsu. No. 1032, Pilgrimage to Atsuta Shrine at Miya. No. 1033, Fishing Village of Yokkaichi on the Mie.

1989, May 15   *Perf. 14x13½*

1024	A233	15c multicolored	.30	.30
1025	A233	20c multicolored	.35	.35
1026	A233	45c multicolored	.60	.60
1027	A233	75c multicolored	1.00	1.00
1028	A233	$1 multicolored	1.00	1.00
1029	A233	$2 multicolored	1.75	1.75
1030	A233	$3 multicolored	2.75	2.75
1031	A233	$4 multicolored	3.75	3.75
		Nos. 1024-1031 (8)	11.50	11.50

Souvenir Sheets

1032	A233	$5 multicolored	4.50	4.50
1033	A233	$5 multicolored	4.50	4.50

1988 Olympic Medalists Type

Designs: 15c, Henry Maske, East Germany, boxing (165 lbs.). 50c, Andreas Schroeder, East Germany, freestyle wrestling (286 lbs.). 60c, East German team, women's gymnastics. 75c, Greg Louganis, US, men's springboard and platform diving. $1, Mitsuru Sato, Japan, freestyle wrestling (115 lbs.). $2, West German team, 4x200m freestyle relay. $3, Dieter Baumann, West Germany, 5000m race. $4, Jackie Joyner-Kersee, US, heptathlon. No. 1042, Joachim Kunz, East Germany, weight lifting (149 lbs.). No. 1043, West German equestrian team, 3-day event.

1989, Apr. 13   *Perf. 14*

1034	A232	15c multicolored	.30	.20
1035	A232	50c multicolored	.40	.35
1036	A232	60c multicolored	.50	.40
1037	A232	75c multicolored	.70	.55
1038	A232	$1 multicolored	.85	.75
1039	A232	$2 multicolored	1.50	1.50
1040	A232	$3 multicolored	2.25	2.25
1041	A232	$4 multicolored	3.00	3.00
		Nos. 1034-1041 (8)	9.50	9.00

Souvenir Sheets

1042	A232	$6 multicolored	4.75	4.75
1043	A232	$6 multicolored	4.75	4.75

World Cup Soccer Championships,
Italy — G82

Designs: 15c, World Cup, vert. 45c, Kaiser Franz, West Germany, vert. 75c, Like 20c, flag of Italy, 1982 champions. $1, Pele, Brazil, vert. $2, Like 20c, flag of West Germany, 1974 champions. $3, Like 20c, flag of Brazil, 1970 champions. $4, Jules Rimet Cup, vert. No. 1052, Pele, Jules Rimet Cup, vert. No. 1053, Goalie.

1989, June 12

1044	G82	15c multicolored	.20	.20
1045	G82	20c multicolored	.20	.20
1046	G82	45c multicolored	.30	.30
1047	G82	75c multicolored	.55	.55
1048	G82	$1 multicolored	1.40	1.40
1049	G82	$2 multicolored	2.75	2.75
1050	G82	$3 multicolored	2.10	2.10
1051	G82	$4 multicolored	2.75	2.75
		Nos. 1044-1051 (8)	10.25	10.25

Souvenir Sheets

1052	G82	$6 multicolored	4.75	4.75
1053	G82	$6 multicolored	4.75	4.75

Car Type of 1988
Miniature Sheets

North American locomotives: No. 1054a, Morris & Essex, Dover, 1841. No. 1054b, B&O, Memnon No. 57, 1848. No. 1054c, Camden & Amboy, John Stevens, 1849. No. 1054d, Lawrence Machine Shop, Lawrence, 1853. No. 1054e, South Carolina, James S. Corry, 1859. No. 1054f, Mine Hill & Schuylkill Haven, Flexible Beam No. 3, 1860. No. 1054g, DL&W, Montrose, 1861. No. 1054h, Central Pacific, Pequop No. 68, 1868. No. 1054i, Boston & Providence, Daniel Nason, 1863. No. 1054j, Morris & Essex, Joe Scranton, 1870.
No. 1055a, Central Railroad of New Jersey, No. 124, 1871. No. 1055b, Baldwin Steam Motor for Street Railways, 1876. No. 1055c, Lackawanna & Bloomsburg, Luzerne, 1878. No. 1055d, Central Mexicano, No. 150, 1892. No. 1055e, Denver, South Park & Pacific, Breckenridge No. 15, 1879. No. 1055f, Miles Planting & Manufacturing Co., "Daisy" Plantation locomotive, 1894. No. 1055g, Central of Georgia, Baldwin 854 No. 1136, 1895. No. 1055h, Savannah, Florida & Western, No. 111, 1900. No. 1055i, Douglas, Gilmore & Co. No. 3, 1902. No. 1055j, Lehigh Valley Coal Co., Compressed Air locomotive No. 900, 1903.
No. 1056a, Morgan's Louisiana & Texas, McKeen Motorcar, 1908. No. 1056b, Clear Lake Lumber Co., Type B Climax, 1910. No. 1056c, Blue Jay Lumber Co., Heisler No. 10,

1912. No. 1056d, Stewartstown, Gasoline Engine No. 6, 1920's. No. 1056e, Bangor & Aroostook, Class G No. 186, 1921. No. 1056f, Hammond Lumber Co., No. 6, 1923. No. 1056g, Central Railroad of New Jersey, No. 1000, 1925. No. 1056h, Atchison, Topeka & Santa Fe, Super Chief No. 1-1A, 1935. No. 1056i, Norfolk & Western, Class Y-6, 1948. No. 1056i, Boston & Maine, Budd Railcar, 1949.

1989, June 28   *Perf. 13x13½*

1054		Sheet of 10	20.00	20.00
a.-j.	A223	$2 any single	1.75	1.75
1055		Sheet of 10	20.00	20.00
a.-j.	A223	$2 any single	1.75	1.75
1056		Sheet of 10	20.00	20.00
a.-j.	A223	$2 any single	1.75	1.75

PHILEXFRANCE '89 — G83

Walt Disney characters in Paris.

1989, July 7   *Perf. 14x13½, 13½x14*

1057	G83	1c Military school	.20	.20
1058	G83	2c Conciergerie	.20	.20
1059	G83	3c Hotel de Ville, vert.	.20	.20
1060	G83	4c Genie of the Bastille, vert.	.20	.20
1061	G83	5c The Opera	.20	.20
1062	G83	10c Gardens of Luxembourg	.25	.25
1063	G83	$5 Arche de la Defense, vert.	7.00	7.00
1064	G83	$6 Place Vendome, vert.	7.00	7.00
		Nos. 1057-1064 (8)	15.25	15.25

Souvenir Sheets

1065	G83	$6 Riding moped	7.00	7.00
1066	G83	$6 Hot air ballooning	7.00	7.00

Moon Landing Anniv. Type

Apollo 11 mission, 1969: 25c, Liftoff, vert. 50c, Splashdown. 60c, Spacecraft approaching moon, vert. 75c, Buzz Aldrin conducting experiment on lunar surface. $1, Leaving Earth orbit. $2, Transport of launch vehicle to pad, vert. $3, Lunar module liftoff. $4, Eagle lands on moon, vert. No. 1075, Footprint on moon. No. 1076, Armstrong stepping onto the moon, vert.

1989, July 20   *Perf. 14*

1067	A237	25c multicolored	.30	.30
1068	A237	50c multicolored	.50	.50
1069	A237	60c multicolored	.60	.60
1070	A237	75c multicolored	.75	.75
1071	A237	$1 multicolored	.90	.90
1072	A237	$2 multicolored	2.00	2.00
1073	A237	$3 multicolored	2.50	2.50
1074	A237	$4 multicolored	3.50	3.50
		Nos. 1067-1074 (8)	11.05	11.05

Souvenir Sheets

1075	A237	$5 multicolored	5.00	5.00
1076	A237	$5 multicolored	5.00	5.00

Mushroom Type

1989, Aug. 17

1078	A238	6c Collybia aurea	.40	.25
1079	A238	10c Podaxis pistillaris	.40	.25
1080	A238	20c Hygrocybe firma	.65	.50
1081	A238	30c Agaricus rufoaurantiacus	.75	.65
1082	A238	75c Leptonia howellii	1.60	1.60
1083	A238	$2 Marasmiellus purpureus	3.00	3.00
1084	A238	$3 Marasmius trinitatis	3.50	3.50
1085	A238	$4 Hygrocybe martinicensis	4.00	4.00
		Nos. 1078-1085 (8)	14.30	13.75

Souvenir Sheets

1086	A238	$6 Lentinus crinitus	8.00	8.00
1087	A238	$6 Agaricus purpurellus	8.00	8.00

Butterflies Type

1989, Oct. 2   *Perf. 14*

1088	A239	25c Androgeus swallowtail	.85	.85
1089	A239	35c Cloudless sulpher	1.00	1.00

1090	A239	45c Cracker	1.10	1.10
1091	A239	50c Painted lady	1.10	1.10
1092	A239	75c Great southern white	1.75	1.75
1093	A239	90c Little sulpher	1.90	1.90
1094	A239	$2 Migrant sulpher	4.25	4.25
1095	A239	$3 Mimic	5.00	5.00
		Nos. 1088-1095 (8)	16.95	16.95

Souvenir Sheets

1096	A239	$6 Giant hairstreak	8.50	8.50
1097	A239	$6 Red anartia	8.50	8.50

World Stamp Expo Type

Scenes from Walt Disney animated films and quotes from Poor Richard's Almanack by Benjamin Franklin: 1c, "Beware of little expenses, a small leak will sink a great ship." 2c, "Trust thyself and another shall not betray thee." 3c, "A spoonful of honey will catch more flies than a gallon of vinegar." 4c, "No gain without pain." 5c, "A true friend is the best possession." 6c, "Haste makes waste." 8c, "A quiet conscience sleeps in thunder, but rest and guilt live far asunder." 10c, "The muses love the morning." $5, "An egg today is better than a hen tomorrow." No. 1107, "He that riseth late, must trot all day." No. 1108, "If you'd be belov'd, make yourself amiable." No. 1109, "In Christmas feasting pray take care; let not your table be a snare; but with the poor God's bounty share. Adieu my friends! Till the next year," vert.

1989, Nov.   *Litho.*   *Perf. 14x13½*

1098	A242	1c multicolored	.20	.20
1099	A242	2c multicolored	.20	.20
1100	A242	3c multicolored	.20	.20
1101	A242	4c multicolored	.20	.20
1102	A242	5c multicolored	.20	.20
1103	A242	6c multicolored	.20	.20
1104	A242	8c multicolored	.20	.20
1105	A242	10c multicolored	.20	.20
1106	A242	$5 multicolored	4.50	4.50
1107	A242	$6 multicolored	5.50	5.50
		Nos. 1098-1107 (10)	11.60	11.60

Souvenir Sheet

1108	A242	$6 multicolored	7.50	7.50
1109	A242	$6 multicolored	7.50	7.50

World Stamp Expo '89, Washington, D.C.

Shakespearean Actors and Theater Masks — G84

15c, Ethel Barrymore (1879-1959). $1.10, Richard Burton (1925-1984). $2, John Barrymore (1882-1942). $3, Paul Robeson (1898-1976). $6, Bando Tamasaburo & Nakamura Kanzaburo.

1989, Oct. 9   *Litho.*   *Perf. 14*

1110	G84	15c multicolored	.40	.30
1111	G84	$1.10 multicolored	1.75	1.50
1112	G84	$2 multicolored	2.75	2.75
1113	G84	$3 multicolored	3.00	3.00
		Nos. 1110-1113 (4)	7.90	7.55

Souvenir Sheet

1114	G84	$6 multicolored	7.00	7.00

20th Century Musicians — G85

1989, Oct. 9

1115	G85	10c Buddy Holly	.40	.30
1116	G85	25c Jimi Hendrix	.65	.50
1117	G85	75c Mighty Sparrow	.95	.95
1118	G85	$4 Katsutoji Kineya	4.25	4.25
		Nos. 1115-1118 (4)	6.25	6.00

Souvenir Sheet

1119	G85	$6 Lotte Lenya, Kurt Weill	6.25	6.25

Jimi is spelled incorrectly as "Jimmy."

Discovery of America Type

1989, Oct. 16

1120	A241	15c Canoeing	.40	.30
1121	A241	75c Cooking	1.25	1.25
1122	A241	90c Using stone tools	1.75	1.75
1123	A241	$3 Eating	4.50	4.50
		Nos. 1120-1123 (4)	7.90	7.80

Souvenir Sheet

1124	A241	$6 Building fire	6.25	6.25

Christmas Type

Religious paintings by Rubens: 10c, The Annunciation. 15c, The Flight of the Holy Family into Egypt. 25c, The Presentation in the Temple. 45c, The Holy Family Under the Apple Tree. $2, Madonna and Child with Saints. $4, The Virgin and Child Enthroned with Saints. No. 1132, The Holy Family. No. 1132, Adoration of the Magi. No. 1133, Adoration of the Magi, diff.

1990, Jan. 4   *Perf. 14*

1125	A243	10c multicolored	.40	.20
1126	A243	15c multicolored	.45	.20
1127	A243	25c multicolored	.65	.20
1128	A243	45c multicolored	.85	.40
1129	A243	$2 multicolored	2.40	2.40
1130	A243	$4 multicolored	3.50	3.50
1131	A243	$5 multicolored	3.50	3.50
		Nos. 1125-1131 (7)	11.75	10.40

Souvenir Sheets

1132	A243	$5 multicolored	7.00	7.00
1133	A243	$5 multicolored	7.00	7.00

America Issue (Insects) G86

1990, Mar. 16   *Perf. 14*

1134	G86	35c Hercules beetle	.45	.45
1135	G86	40c Click beetle	.45	.45
1136	G86	50c Harlequin beetle	.60	.60
1137	G86	60c Gold rim butterfly	1.10	1.10
1138	G86	$1 Red skimmer dragonfly	1.25	1.25
1139	G86	$2 Buprestid beetle	2.40	2.40
1140	G86	$3 Mimic butterfly	3.50	3.50
1141	G86	$4 Scarab beetle	3.50	3.50
		Nos. 1134-1141 (8)	13.25	13.25

Souvenir Sheets

1142	G86	$6 Canna skipper butterfly	6.50	6.50
1143	G86	$6 Monarch butterfly	6.50	6.50

Orchids — G87

1990, Mar. 6   *Litho.*   *Perf. 14*

1144	G87	15c Brassocattleya thalie	.35	.35
1145	G87	20c Odontocidium tigersun	.35	.35
1146	G87	50c Odontioda hamburhen	.55	.55
1147	G87	75c Paphiopedium delrosi	.65	.65
1148	G87	$1 Vuylstekeara yokara	1.10	1.10
1149	G87	$2 Paphiopedilum geelong	2.10	2.10
1150	G87	$3 Wilsonara tigerwood	2.75	2.75
1151	G87	$4 Cymbidium ormolui	3.50	3.50
		Nos. 1144-1151 (8)	11.35	11.35

Souvenir Sheets

1152	G87	$6 Odontonia sappho	7.00	7.00
1153	G87	$6 Cymbidium vieux rose	7.00	7.00

EXPO '90 Intl. Garden and Greenery Exposition, Osaka, Japan.

Wildlife Type

1990, Apr. 3

1154	A247	5c West Indies giant rice rat	.30	.30
1155	A247	25c Agouti	.45	.45

1156	A247	30c Humpback whale	1.00	1.00
1157	A247	40c Pilot whale	1.00	1.00
1158	A247	$1 Spotted dolphin	1.25	1.25
1159	A247	$2 Mongoose	2.40	2.40
1160	A247	$3 Prehensile-tailed porcupine	3.25	3.25
1161	A247	$4 West Indies manatee	3.75	3.75
		Nos. 1154-1161 (8)	13.40	13.40

Souvenir Sheets

1162	A247	$6 Caribbean monk seal	7.00	7.00
1163	A247	$6 Mongoose	7.00	7.00

World War II Type

Designs: 6c, First British troops arrive in France, Sept. 6, 1939. 10c, British launch "Operation Crusader", Nov. 18, 1941. 20c, Rommel begins retreat from El Alamein, Nov. 4, 1942. 45c, US forces land on Aleutian Islands, May 11, 1943. 50c, US Marines land on Tarawa, Nov. 20, 1943. 60c, US 5th Army enters Rome, June 4, 1944. 75c, US troops reach River Seine, Aug. 19, 1944. $1, Battle of the Bulge, Dec. 16, 1944. $5, Allies launch final phase of Italian Campaign, Apr. 9, 1945. No. 1173, Atom bomb dropped on Hiroshima, Aug. 6, 1945. No. 1174, St. Paul's Cathedral during London blitz, Battle of Britain, 1940.

1990, Apr. 30

1164	A248	6c multicolored	.40	.40
1165	A248	10c multicolored	.40	.40
1166	A248	20c multicolored	.65	.65
1167	A248	45c multicolored	.70	.70
1168	A248	50c multicolored	.80	.80
1169	A248	60c multicolored	.85	.85
1170	A248	75c multicolored	.95	.95
1171	A248	$1 multicolored	1.25	1.25
1172	A248	$5 multicolored	4.00	4.00
1173	A248	$6 multicolored	5.00	5.00
		Nos. 1164-1173 (10)	15.00	15.00

Souvenir Sheet

1174	A248	$6 multicolored	7.50	7.50

Disney Type

Disney characters portraying Shakespearian characters: 15c, Daisy Duck at Ann Hathaway's Cottage, Shottery. 30c, Minnie Mouse and a young Shakespeare walking in Stratford birthplace, vert. 50c, Minnie as Mary Arden, Shakespeare's mother in Wilmcote, vert. 60c, Mickey in front of New Place, Stratford. $1, Mickey walking in Great Garden of New Place. $2, Mickey at Guild Chapel, Scholars Lane, vert. $4, Mickey at the Royal Shakespeare Theater, Stratford, vert. $5, Ludwig von Drake instructing Shakespeare. No. 1183, Mickey at Edge Hill, Stratford, vert. No. 1184, Mickey and Minnie rowing past Holy Trinity Church, Stratford-Upon-Avon.

1990, May   *Perf. 14x13½*

1175	A250	15c multicolored	.50	.25
1176	A250	30c multicolored	.65	.45
1177	A250	50c multicolored	.95	.85
1178	A250	60c multicolored	1.10	1.10
1179	A250	$1 multicolored	1.50	1.50
1180	A250	$2 multicolored	2.75	2.75
1181	A250	$4 multicolored	4.00	4.00
1182	A250	$5 multicolored	4.00	4.00
		Nos. 1175-1182 (8)	15.45	14.90

Souvenir Sheets

Perf. 14

1183	A250	$6 multicolored	8.00	8.00
1184	A250	$6 multicolored	8.00	8.00

Penny Black Type
Souvenir Sheet

1990, May 3   *Litho.*   *Perf. 14*

1185	A249	$6 Globe with South America	8.00	8.00

Stamp World London '90.

Queen Mother, 90th Birthday Type

1990, July 5

1186	A251	$2 Pink hat	1.60	1.60
1187	A251	$2 With Charles	1.60	1.60
1188	A251	$2 Blue outfit	1.60	1.60
		Nos. 1186-1188 (3)	4.80	4.80

Souvenir Sheet

1189	A251	$6 like #1187	4.75	4.75

Bird Type

1990, Sept. 10   *Litho.*   *Perf. 14*

1190	A255	25c Yellow-bellied seedeater	.45	.45
1191	A255	45c Carib grackle	.65	.65
1192	A255	50c Black-whiskered vireo	.75	.75
1193	A255	75c Bananaquit	.85	.85
1194	A255	$1 Collared swift	1.25	1.25
1195	A255	$2 Yellow-bellied elaenia	1.90	1.90

1196	A255	$3 Blue-hooded euphonia	2.50	2.50
1197	A255	$5 Eared dove	4.50	4.50
		Nos. 1190-1197 (8)	12.85	12.85

Souvenir Sheets

1198	A255	$6 Mangrove cuckoo	5.75	5.75
1199	A255	$6 Scaly-breasted thrasher	5.75	5.75

Crustaceans

1990, Sept. 17

1200	A256	10c Slipper lobster	.25	.25
1201	A256	25c Green reef crab	.35	.35
1202	A256	65c Caribbean lobsterette	.70	.70
1203	A256	75c Blind deep sea lobster	.80	.80
1204	A256	$1 Flattened crab	1.10	1.10
1205	A256	$2 Ridged slipper lobster	2.00	2.00
1206	A256	$3 Land crab	2.50	2.50
1207	A256	$4 Mountain crab	3.00	3.00
		Nos. 1200-1207 (8)	10.70	10.70

Souvenir Sheets

1208	A256	$6 Caribbean king crab	5.25	5.25
1209	A256	$6 Purse crab	5.25	5.25

G88 G89

Players from participating countries.

1990, Sept. 24

1210	G88	15c England	.25	.25
1211	G88	45c Argentina	.50	.50
1212	G88	$2 Sweden	2.00	2.00
1213	G88	$4 South Korea	3.25	3.25
		Nos. 1210-1213 (4)	6.00	6.00

Souvenir Sheets

1214	G88	$6 Yugoslavia	5.00	5.00
1215	G88	$6 United States	5.00	5.00

World Cup Soccer Championships, Italy.

1990, Nov. 11   Litho.   Perf. 14

1216	G89	10c Boxing	.20	.20
1217	G89	25c Olympic flame	.25	.25
1218	G89	50c Soccer	.55	.55
1219	G89	75c Discus	.75	.75
1220	G89	$1 Pole vault	1.00	1.00
1221	G89	$2 Equestrian 3-day event	2.25	2.25
1222	G89	$4 Women's basketball	4.25	4.25
1223	G89	$5 Men's gymnastics	3.75	3.75
		Nos. 1216-1223 (8)	13.00	13.00

Souvenir Sheets

1224	G89	$6 Sailboarding	6.50	6.50
1225	G89	$6 Decathlon	6.50	6.50

1992 Summer Olympics, Barcelona.

Rubens Type

Entire paintings or different details from: 5c, 25c, Adam and Eve, vert. 15c, Esther before Ahasuerus. 50c, Expulsion from Eden. $1, Cain Slaying Abel, vert. $2, Lot's Flight. $4, Samson and Delilah. $5, Abraham and Melchizedek. No. 1234, The Meeting of David and Abigail. No. 1235, Daniel in the Lions Den.

1991, Jan. 31   Litho.   Perf. 14

1226	A259	5c multicolored	.25	.20
1227	A259	15c multicolored	.40	.20
1228	A259	25c multicolored	.50	.25
1229	A259	50c multicolored	.85	.45
1230	A259	$1 multicolored	1.50	1.25
1231	A259	$2 multicolored	2.00	2.00
1232	A259	$4 multicolored	3.00	3.00
1233	A259	$5 multicolored	3.50	3.50
		Nos. 1226-1233 (8)	12.00	11.05

Souvenir Sheets

1234	A259	$6 multicolored	6.00	6.00
1235	A259	$6 multicolored	6.00	6.00

Fish Type of 1990

1991, Feb. 5

1236	A254	15c Barred hamlet	.55	.30
1237	A254	35c Squirrelfish	.90	.60
1238	A254	45c Red-spotted hawkfish	1.00	.70
1239	A254	75c Bigeye	1.60	1.25

1240	A254	$1 Spiny puffer	1.90	1.50
1241	A254	$2 Smallmouth grunt	2.75	2.75
1242	A254	$3 Harlequin bass	3.50	3.50
1243	A254	$4 Creole fish	3.75	3.75
		Nos. 1236-1243 (8)	15.95	14.35

Souvenir Sheets

1244	A254	$6 Fairy basslet	6.50	6.50
1245	A254	$6 Copper sweeper	6.50	6.50

Hummel Figurines — G90   Orchids — G91

1991, Mar. 1   Litho.   Perf. 14

1246	G90	10c Angel, star	.25	.20
1247	G90	15c Angel, guitar, Christ Child	.35	.20
1248	G90	25c Shepherd	.50	.20
1249	G90	50c Angel, lantern, horn	1.00	.55
1250	G90	$1 Angel, children, Christ Child	1.50	1.00
1251	G90	$2 Angel, candle, Christ Child	2.50	2.50
1252	G90	$4 Angel with baskets	3.50	3.50
1253	G90	$5 Angels singing	3.75	3.75
		Nos. 1246-1253 (8)	13.35	11.90

Souvenir Sheets

1254		Sheet of 4	5.00	5.00
a.	G90	5c like No. 1247	.20	.20
b.	G90	40c like No. 1249	.30	.30
c.	G90	60c like No. 1250	.50	.50
d.	G90	$3 like No. 1253	2.75	2.75
1255		Sheet of 4	8.00	8.00
a.	G90	20c like No. 1246	.20	.20
b.	G90	30c like No. 1248	.25	.25
c.	G90	75c like No. 1251	.70	.70
d.	G90	$6 like No. 1252	5.50	5.50

Christmas 1990.

1991-92   Litho.   Perf. 14

Designs: 5c, Brassia maculata. 10c, Oncidium lanceanum. 15c, Broughtonia sanguinea. 25c, Diacrium bicornutum. 35c, Cattleya labiata. 45c, Epidendrum fragrans. 50c, Oncidium papilio. 75c, Neocogniauxia monophylla. $1, Epidendrum polybulbon. $2, Spiranthes speciosa. $4, Epidendrum ciliare. $5, Phais tankervilliae. $10, Brassia caudata. $20, Brassavola cordata.

1256	G91	5c multicolored	.70	.70
1257	G91	10c multicolored	.70	.70
1258	G91	15c multicolored	.75	.30
1259	G91	25c multicolored	.90	.30
1260	G91	35c multicolored	.90	.30
1261	G91	45c multicolored	1.25	.45
1262	G91	50c multicolored	1.25	.50
1263	G91	75c multicolored	1.50	.80
1264	G91	$1 multicolored	2.00	1.25
1265	G91	$2 multicolored	3.25	3.25
1266	G91	$4 multicolored	5.25	5.25
1267	G91	$5 multicolored	5.50	5.50
1268	G91	$10 multicolored	10.50	10.50
1269	G91	$20 multicolored	21.00	21.00
		Nos. 1256-1269 (14)	55.45	50.80

Issued: $20, 6/92; others, 4/1/91.

Butterfly Type

Designs: 5c, Crimson-patched longwing. 10c, Morpho helena. 15c, Morpho sulkowskyi. 20c, Dynastor napoleon. 25c, Pieridae callinira. 30c, Anartia amathea. 35c, Heliconiidae dido. 45c, Papilionidae columbus. 50c, Nymphalidae praeneste. 60c, Panacea prola. 75c, Julia. $1, Papilionidae orthosilaus. $2, Pyrrhopyge cometes. $3, Papilionidae paeon. $4, Morpho cypris. $5, Choringa. No. 1286, Caligo idomenides. No. 1287, Monarch. No. 1287A, Nymphalidae amydon. No. 1287B, Papilio childrenae.

1991, Apr. 8   Litho.   Perf. 14

1270	A261	5c multicolored	.60	.45
1271	A261	10c multicolored	.60	.45
1272	A261	15c multicolored	.85	.50
1273	A261	20c multicolored	.95	.55
1274	A261	25c multicolored	.95	.60
1275	A261	30c multicolored	1.10	.70
1276	A261	35c multicolored	1.10	.70
1277	A261	45c multicolored	1.25	.95
1278	A261	50c multicolored	1.40	1.00
1279	A261	60c multicolored	1.60	1.10
1280	A261	75c multicolored	1.60	1.25
1281	A261	$1 multicolored	2.00	1.60
1282	A261	$2 multicolored	2.75	2.75
1283	A261	$3 multicolored	3.50	3.50

1284	A261	$4 multicolored	4.00	4.00
1285	A261	$5 multicolored	5.00	5.00
		Nos. 1270-1285 (16)	29.25	25.10

Souvenir Sheets

1286	A261	$6 multicolored	6.00	6.00
1287	A261	$6 multicolored	6.00	6.00
1287A	A261	$6 multicolored	6.00	6.00
1287B	A261	$6 multicolored	6.00	6.00

Save Our Planet — G100

Walt Disney characters and ecology themes: 10c, Daisy and Donald, alternate forms of transportation. 15c, Goofy saving water. 25c, Donald, Daisy camping simply. 45c, Donald protecting birds. $1, Donald holding ascending balloons. $2, Minnie, Daisy using natural coolers. $4, Mickey, nephews cleaning beaches. $5, Scrooge McDuck using pedal power. No. 1296, Little Hiawatha and Iron Eyes Cody viewing destroyed forest. No. 1297, Donald, recycling. No. 1298, Minnie, Mickey planting trees.

1991, Apr. 22   Litho.   Perf. 14

1288	G100	10c multicolored	.65	.20
1289	G100	15c multicolored	.75	.20
1290	G100	25c multicolored	1.00	.40
1291	G100	45c multicolored	1.40	.60
1292	G100	$1 multicolored	2.25	1.40
1293	G100	$2 multicolored	3.25	3.00
1294	G100	$4 multicolored	4.00	4.00
1295	G100	$5 multicolored	4.00	4.00
		Nos. 1288-1295 (8)	17.30	13.80

Souvenir Sheets

1296	G100	$6 multicolored	6.50	6.50
1297	G100	$6 multicolored	6.50	6.50
1298	G100	$6 multicolored	6.50	6.50

Voyages of Discovery Type

Discovery of America, 500th anniv. (in 1992).: 15c, Ferdinand Magellan, 1519-1521. 20c, Sir Francis Drake, 1577-1580. 50c, Capt. James Cook, 1768-1771. 60c, Douglas World Cruiser, 1924. $1, Sputnik, 1957. $2, Yuri Gagarin, 1961. $4, John Glenn, 1962. $5, Space Shuttle, 1981. No. 1307, Columbus' fleet. No. 1308, The Pinta, vert.

1991, Apr. 29   Litho.   Perf. 14

1299	A262	15c multicolored	.35	.20
1300	A262	20c multicolored	.25	.25
1301	A262	50c multicolored	.50	.50
1302	A262	60c multicolored	.60	.60
1303	A262	$1 multicolored	.95	.95
1304	A262	$2 multicolored	1.90	1.90
1305	A262	$4 multicolored	3.75	3.75
1306	A262	$5 multicolored	4.50	4.50
		Nos. 1299-1306 (8)	12.80	12.65

Souvenir Sheets

1307	A262	$6 multicolored	6.00	6.00
1308	A262	$6 multicolored	6.00	6.00

Disney Phila Nippon '91 Type

Walt Disney characters demonstrating arts, crafts and industries of Japan: 15c, Minnie, silkworms. 30c, Mickey, Minnie, Morty and Ferdie photographing the Torii. 50c, Donald, Mickey, origami. 60c, Mickey, Minnie diving for pearls. $1, Minnie modeling kimono. $2, Mickey making masks. $4, Donald, Mickey making paper. $5, Minnie, Pluto, pottery. #1317, Mickey making prints, vert. #1318, Mickey arranging flowers, vert. #1319, Mickey, tea ceremony, vert. #1320, Mickey carving ivory and wood into netsukes, vert.

1991, May 6

1309	A263	15c multi	.50	.20
1310	A263	30c multi	.85	.35
1311	A263	50c multi	1.00	.55
1312	A263	60c multi	1.10	.60
1313	A263	$1 multi	2.00	1.00
1314	A263	$2 multi	2.75	2.50
1315	A263	$4 multi	3.75	3.75
1316	A263	$5 multi	4.50	4.50
		Nos. 1309-1316 (8)	16.45	13.45

Souvenir Sheets

1317	A263	$6 multi	5.00	5.00
1318	A263	$6 multi	5.00	5.00
1319	A263	$6 multi	5.00	5.00
1320	A263	$6 multi	5.00	5.00

Mushrooms Type

1991, June 1   Litho.   Perf. 14

1321	A265	5c Pyrrhoglossum pyrrhum	.40	.25
1322	A265	45c Agaricus purpurellus	1.00	.55
1323	A265	50c Amanita crase-oderma	1.00	.60
1324	A265	90c Hygrocybe acutoconica	1.75	1.25
1325	A265	$1 Limacella guttata	1.75	1.25
1326	A265	$2 Lactarius hygropho-roides	2.50	2.50
1327	A265	$4 Boletellus cubensis	4.00	4.00
1328	A265	$5 Psilocybe caerulescens	4.00	4.00
		Nos. 1321-1328 (8)	16.40	14.40

Souvenir Sheets

1329	A265	$6 Marasmius haemato-cephalus	7.50	7.50
1330	A265	$6 Lepiota spicu-lata	7.50	7.50

Royal Family Birthday, Anniversary
Common Design Type

1991, July 5   Litho.   Perf. 14

1331	CD347	5c multi	.50	.30
1332	CD347	20c multi	.30	.30
1333	CD347	25c multi	.30	.20
1334	CD347	60c multi	1.25	.75
1335	CD347	$1 multi	1.25	1.00
1336	CD347	$2 multi	2.00	2.00
1337	CD347	$3 multi	3.25	3.25
1338	CD347	$5 multi	5.00	5.00
		Nos. 1331-1338 (8)	13.85	12.80

Souvenir Sheet

1339	CD347	$5 Elizabeth, Philip	6.00	6.00
1340	CD347	$5 Diana, Charles, with sons	6.00	6.00

5c, 60c, $1, Nos. 1338, 1340, Charles and Diana, 10th wedding anniversary. Others, Queen Elizabeth II, 65th birthday.

Van Gogh Painting Type

Designs: 5c, Two Thistles, vert. 10c, The Baby Marcelle Roulin, vert. 15c, Still Life: Basket with Six Oranges. 25c, Orchard in Blossom, vert. 45c, Portrait of Armand Roulin, vert. 50c, Wood Gatherers in the Snow (detail), vert. 60c, Almond Tree in Blossom, vert. $1, Portrait of an Old Man, vert. $2, The Seine Bridge at Asnieres. $3, Vase with Lilacs, Daisies & Anemones, vert. $4, Self-portrait. $5, Portrait of Patience Escalier, vert. No. 1353, Les Alyscamps. No. 1354, Quay with Men Unloading Sand Barges. No. 1355, Sunset: Wheat Fields Near Arles.

Perf. 13½x14, 14x13½

1991, Nov. 18   Litho.

1341	A264	5c multicolored	.35	.20
1342	A264	10c multicolored	.35	.20
1343	A264	15c multicolored	.35	.20
1344	A264	25c multicolored	.35	.20
1345	A264	45c multicolored	.45	.35
1346	A264	50c multicolored	.55	.45
1347	A264	60c multicolored	.60	.50
1348	A264	$1 multicolored	1.00	.90
1349	A264	$2 multicolored	1.75	1.75
1350	A264	$3 multicolored	2.25	2.25
1351	A264	$4 multicolored	3.25	3.25
1352	A264	$5 multicolored	3.75	3.75
		Nos. 1341-1352 (12)	15.00	14.00

Size: 102x127mm, 127x102mm
Imperf

1353	A264	$6 multicolored	5.00	5.00
1354	A264	$6 multicolored	5.00	5.00
1355	A264	$6 multicolored	5.00	5.00

Marine Life Type
Miniature Sheet

Marine life of the deeper reef: No. 1356a, Sargassum triggerfish. b, Tobaccofish. c, Longsnout butterflyfish. d, Cherubfish. e, Black jack head. f, Black jack tail, masked goby. g, Spotfin hogfish. h, Fairy basslet. i, Orangeback bass. j, Candy basslet. k, Blackcap basslet. l, Longspine squirrelfish. m, Jackknife fish. n, Bigeye. o, Short Bigeye. $6, Caribbean flashlight fish.

1991, Dec. 5   Litho.   Perf. 14

1356	A270	50c Sheet of 15, #a.-o.	20.00	20.00

Souvenir Sheet

1357	A270	$6 multicolored	14.00	14.00

Christmas Art Type

Details, entire paintings or engravings by Martin Schongauer of the Annunciation. 35c, Angel of the Annunciation. 50c, Madonna of the Rose Hedge. 50c, Madonna of the Rose Hedge, diff. 75c,

Nativity. $1, Adoration of the Shepherds. $2, Nativity, diff. $4, Nativity, diff. $5, Symbol of St. Matthew. No. 1366, Nativity, diff. No. 1367, Adoration of the Shepherds.

1991, Dec. 9   *Perf. 12*

1358	A271	10c multicolored	.45	.20
1359	A271	35c multicolored	.80	.25
1360	A271	50c multicolored	1.10	.45
1361	A271	75c multicolored	1.40	.75
1362	A271	$1 multicolored	1.50	1.25
1363	A271	$2 multicolored	2.40	2.40
1364	A271	$4 multicolored	3.00	3.00
1365	A271	$5 multicolored	3.00	3.00
		Nos. 1358-1365 (8)	13.65	11.30

Souvenir Sheets
Perf. 14½

1366	A271	$6 multicolored	6.75	6.75
1367	A271	$6 multicolored	6.75	6.75

Queen Elizabeth II's Accession to the Throne, 40th Anniv.
Common Design Type

1992, Feb. 6   Litho.   *Perf. 14*

1368	CD348	60c multicolored	.90	.35
1369	CD348	75c multicolored	1.00	.40
1370	CD348	$2 multicolored	2.10	1.60
1371	CD348	$4 multicolored	3.00	3.00
		Nos. 1368-1371 (4)	7.00	5.35

Souvenir Sheets

1372	CD348	$6 Queen, rural scene	5.00	5.00
1373	CD348	$6 Queen, harbor	5.00	5.00

Railways of the World Type

Steam locomotives: No. 1379a, Medoc Class, Switzerland, 1857. b, Sterling, Great Britain, 1870. c, No. 90, France, 1877. d, Standard, US, 1880. e, Vittorio Emanuel II, Italy, 1884. f, Johnson Single, Great Britain, 1887. g, No. 999, US, 1893. h, Q1 Class, Great Britain, 1896. i, Claud Hamilton, Great Britain, 1900.
No. 1380a, Class P8, Germany, 1906. b, Class P, Denmark, 1935. c, Class Ps, US, 1926. d, Class 4-4-0, Ireland, 1932. e, Class GS, US, 1937. f, Class 12, Belgium, 1938. g, Class J, US, 1941. h, PA series, US, 1946. i, Class 4E1, South Africa, 1954.
No. 1381a, Tee 4-car train, Europe, 1957. b, FL9B, US, 1960. c, Shin-Kansen 16-car train, Japan, 1964. d, Class 103.1, Germany 1970. e, RTG 4-car train set, France, 1972. f, ETR 401 Pendolino 4-car train, Italy, 1976. g, Class 370, Great Britain, 1981. h, LRC, Canada, 1982. i, Mav BZMOT 601 1B1, Hungary, 1983.
No. 1382, ETR 401 four-car train, Italy, 1976. No. 1382A, Werner von Siemens' first electric locomotive, Germany, 1879.

1992, Feb. 13   Litho.   *Perf. 14*
Sheets of 9

1379	A269	75c #a.-i.	6.25	6.25
1380	A269	$1 #a.-i.	8.25	8.25
1381	A269	$2 #a.-i.	17.00	17.00
		Nos. 1379-1381 (3)	31.50	31.50

Souvenir Sheets

1382	A269	$6 multicolored	5.50	5.50
1382A	A269	$6 multicolored	5.50	5.50

1992 Summer Olympics, Barcelona — G101

Designs: 10c, Women's 100-meter backstroke. 15c, Women's handball. 25c, 4x100-meter relay. 35c, Hammer throw. 50c, 110-meter hurdles. 75c, Pole vault. $1, Volleyball. $2, Weight lifting. $5, Stationary rings. $6, Soccer. No. 1393, Baseball. No. 1394, Finn class single-handed dinghy.

1992, Mar. 23   Litho.   *Perf. 14*

1383	G101	10c multicolored	.65	.30
1384	G101	15c multicolored	.70	.30
1385	G101	25c multicolored	.80	.30
1386	G101	35c multicolored	.85	.35
1387	G101	50c multicolored	1.00	.65
1388	G101	75c multicolored	1.40	.85
1389	G101	$1 multicolored	1.50	1.10
1390	G101	$2 multicolored	2.75	2.75
1391	G101	$5 multicolored	3.75	3.75
1392	G101	$6 multicolored	4.00	4.00
		Nos. 1383-1392 (10)	17.40	14.35

Souvenir Sheets

1393	G101	$15 multicolored	11.50	11.50
1394	G101	$15 multicolored	11.50	11.50

Spanish Art Type

Paintings: 10c, The Surrender of Seville, by Francisco de Zurbaran. 35c, The Liberation of Saint Peter by an Angel, by Antonio de Pereda. 50c, Joseph Explains the Dreams of the Pharaoh, by Antonio del Castillo Saavedra, horiz. 75c, The Flower Vase, by Juan de Arellano. $1, The Duke of Pastrana, by Juan Carreno de Miranda. $2, $4, The Annunciation (diff. details), by Francisco Rizi. $5, Old Woman Seated, attributed to Antonio Puga. No. 1403, The Triumph of Saint Hermenegildo, by Francisco de Herrera, the Younger, vert. No. 1404, Relief of Genoa by the Second Marquis of Santa Cruz, by de Pereda, horiz.

1992, Apr. 30   *Perf. 13*

1395	A273	10c multicolored	.30	.20
1396	A273	35c multicolored	.50	.35
1397	A273	50c multicolored	.75	.60
1398	A273	75c multicolored	1.00	.75
1399	A273	$1 multicolored	1.25	.90
1400	A273	$2 multicolored	2.00	2.00
1401	A273	$4 multicolored	3.00	3.00
1402	A273	$5 multicolored	3.00	3.00
		Nos. 1395-1402 (8)	11.80	10.80

Size: 95x110mm
Imperf

1403	A273	$6 multicolored	5.25	5.25
1404	A273	$6 multicolored	5.25	5.25

Granada '92.

Discovery of America, 500th Anniv. — G102

Designs: 10c, Don Isaac Abarbanel (1437-1508), Spanish Minister of Finance. 25c, Columbus. 35c, Crewman sighting land. 50c, King Ferdinand and Queen Isabella. 60c, Columbus and Queen Isabella. $5, Santa Maria and map. No. 1411, Portrait of Columbus. No. 1412, Columbus at first landfall.

1992, May 7   Litho.   *Perf. 14*

1405	G102	10c multicolored	.25	.25
1406	G102	25c multicolored	.35	.30
1407	G102	35c multicolored	.55	.45
1408	G102	50c multicolored	.85	.85
1409	G102	60c multicolored	1.00	1.00
1410	G102	$5 multicolored	7.00	7.00
		Nos. 1405-1410 (6)	10.00	9.85

Souvenir Sheets

1411	G102	$6 multicolored	5.25	5.25
1412	G102	$6 multicolored	5.25	5.25

World Columbian Expo '92, Chicago.

USO Anniv. Type of 1992

1992, May 7

1413	A277	10c James Cagney	.55	.25
1414	A277	15c Ann Sheridan	.55	.25
1415	A277	35c Jerry Colonna	.55	.25
1416	A277	50c Spike Jones	.65	.35
1417	A277	75c Edgar Bergen, Charlie McCarthy	.80	.50
1418	A277	$1 Andrews Sisters	1.25	.75
1419	A277	$2 Dinah Shore	1.90	1.90
1420	A277	$5 Bing Crosby	4.25	4.25
		Nos. 1413-1420 (8)	10.50	8.50

Souvenir Sheets

1421	A277	$6 Marlene Dietrich	5.25	5.25
1422	A277	$6 Fred Astaire	5.25	5.25

Hummingbird Type of 1992

Designs: 5c, Blue-headed male. 10c, Rufous-breasted hermit female. 20c, Blue-headed female. 45c, Green-throated carib male. 90c, Antillean crested male. $2, Purple-throated carib male. $4, Purple-throated carib female. $5, Antillean crested female. No. 1431, Rufous-breated hermit female. No. 1432, Green-throated carib female.

1992, May 7

1423	A276	5c multicolored	.25	.25
1424	A276	10c multicolored	.25	.25
1425	A276	20c multicolored	.25	.25
1426	A276	45c multicolored	.40	.40
1427	A276	90c multicolored	.85	.85
1428	A276	$2 multicolored	2.00	2.00
1429	A276	$4 multicolored	4.00	4.00
1430	A276	$5 multicolored	5.00	5.00
		Nos. 1423-1430 (8)	13.00	13.00

Souvenir Sheets

1431	A276	$6 multicolored	6.00	6.00
1432	A276	$6 multicolored	6.00	6.00

Genoa '92.

Discovery of America Type

1992   *Perf. 14½*

1433	A275	$1 Coming ashore	1.25	1.25
1434	A275	$2 Natives, ships	2.75	2.75

Walt Disney's Goofy, 60th Anniv. — G103

Scenes from Disney cartoon films: 5c, Father's Day Off, 1953. 10c, Cold War, 1951. 15c, Home Made Home, 1951. 25c, Get Rich Quick, 1951. 50c, Man's Best Friend, 1952. 75c, Aquamania, 1961. 90c, Tomorrow We Diet, 1951. $1, Teachers Are People, 1952. $2, The Goofy Success Story, 1955. $3, Double Dribble, 1946. $4, Hello Aloha, 1952. $5, Father's Lion, 1952. No. 1447, Father's Weekend, 1953, vert. No. 1448, Motor Mania, 1950. No. 1449, Hold That Pose, 1950, vert.

1992, Nov. 24   Litho.   *Perf. 14x13½*

1435	G103	5c multicolored	.20	.20
1436	G103	10c multicolored	.20	.20
1437	G103	15c multicolored	.20	.20
1438	G103	25c multicolored	.20	.20
1439	G103	50c multicolored	.40	.40
1440	G103	75c multicolored	.60	.60
1441	G103	90c multicolored	.70	.70
1442	G103	$1 multicolored	.75	.75
1443	G103	$2 multicolored	1.50	1.50
1444	G103	$3 multicolored	2.25	2.25
1445	G103	$4 multicolored	3.00	3.00
1446	G103	$5 multicolored	3.75	3.75
		Nos. 1435-1446 (12)	13.75	13.75

Souvenir Sheets
Perf. 13½x14

1447	G103	$6 multicolored	4.50	4.50
1448	G103	$6 multicolored	4.50	4.50
1449	G103	$6 multicolored	4.50	4.50

Model Trains Type of 1992

Designs: 15c, #2220 Switcher locomotive, 2-inch gauge, US, 1910. 25c, 0-4-0 Engine, Bridge Port Line, O gauge, US, 1907. 50c, First Ives Co. electric toy locomotive, O gauge, US, 1910. 75c, J. C. Penney Special, standard gauge, US, 1920. $1, Cast metal locomotive, O gauge, US, 1916. $2, Copper-plated cast iron locomotive & tender pull toy, US, 1900. $4, Chromium plated locomotive #4689, standard gauge, US, 1928. $5, Ives long cab locomotive of the Olympian set, standard gauge, US, 1929.
No. 1458, Clockwork model, O gauge, US, 1910. No. 1459, American Flyer Statesman passenger train.

1992, Oct. 22   Litho.   *Perf. 14*

1450	A279	15c multicolored	.25	.20
1451	A279	25c multicolored	.40	.20
1452	A279	50c multicolored	.70	.45
1453	A279	75c multicolored	.90	.65
1454	A279	$1 multicolored	1.00	.90
1455	A279	$2 multicolored	2.00	2.00
1456	A279	$4 multicolored	3.50	3.50
1457	A279	$5 multicolored	3.50	3.50
		Nos. 1450-1457 (8)	12.25	11.40

Souvenir Sheet
Perf. 13

1458	A279	$6 multicolored	5.25	5.25
1459	A279	$6 multicolored	5.25	5.25

Nos. 1458-1459 contain one 51x40mm stamp.

New York City Type
Souvenir Sheet

1992, Oct. 28   *Perf. 14*

1460	A280	$6 Brooklyn Bridge	5.00	5.00

Postage Stamp Mega Event '92, New York City.

Christmas Type of 1992

Details or entire paintings of The Annunciation by: 5c, Robert Campin. 15c, Melchior Broederlam. 25c, The Annunciation (2 panels), by Fra Filippo Lippi. 35c, Simone Martini. 50c, Fra Filippo Lippi, detail of angel. 75c, The Annunciation (Mary), by Fra Filippo Lippi. 90c, Albert Bouts. $1, D. Di Michelino. $2, Van der Weyden. $3, Sandro Botticelli, detail of angel. $4, Botticelli, detail of Mary. $5, Bernardo Daddi, horiz. No. 1472, Rogier Van der Weyden, vert. No. 1473, Hubert Van Eyck. No. 1474, Botticelli.

Perf. 13½x14, 14x13½

1992, Nov. 16

1461	A281	5c multicolored	.20	.20
1462	A281	15c multicolored	.30	.20
1463	A281	25c multicolored	.35	.20
1464	A281	35c multicolored	.45	.30
1464A	A281	50c multicolored	.65	.50
1465	A281	75c multicolored	.85	.70
1466	A281	90c multicolored	1.00	1.00
1467	A281	$1 multicolored	1.10	1.10
1468	A281	$2 multicolored	2.10	2.10
1469	A281	$3 multicolored	2.75	2.75
1470	A281	$4 multicolored	3.25	3.25
1471	A281	$5 multicolored	3.50	3.50
		Nos. 1461-1471 (12)	16.50	15.80

Souvenir Sheets

1472	A281	$6 multicolored	5.00	5.00
1473	A281	$6 multicolored	5.00	5.00
1474	A281	$6 multicolored	5.00	5.00

America's Cup Yacht Race — G104

Designs: 15c, Atalanta, Mischief, 1881. 25c, Valkyrie III, Defender. 35c, Shamrock IV, Resolute. 75c, Endeavour II, Ranger, 1937. $1, Sceptre, Columbia, 1958. $2, Australia II, Liberty. $4, Stars and Stripes, Kookaburra III. $5, New Zealand, Stars and Stripes, 1988. No. 1483, America, Aurora, 1851. No. 1484, Emblems of 1992 participants.

1992, Oct.   *Perf. 14*

1475	G104	15c multicolored	.55	.25
1476	G104	25c multicolored	.70	.25
1477	G104	35c multicolored	.85	.40
1478	G104	75c multicolored	1.25	.90
1479	G104	$1 multicolored	1.40	.90
1480	G104	$2 multicolored	2.00	2.00
1481	G104	$4 multicolored	3.00	3.00
1482	G104	$5 multicolored	3.25	3.25
		Nos. 1475-1482 (8)	13.00	10.70

Souvenir Sheets

1483	G104	$6 multicolored	6.00	6.00
1484	G104	$6 multicolored	6.00	6.00

Nos. 1483-1484 contains one 58x43mm stamp.

G105

Anniversaries and Events — G106

Designs: 25c, Zeppelin Viktoria Luise over Kiel Harbor. 50c, Space Shuttle Columbia. 75c, Flag, arms of Germany, Konrad Adenauer. $1.50, Giant anteater. No. 1489, Scarlet macaw, vert. No. 1490, Emblem of Intl. Conf. on Nutrition. $3, Wolfgang Amadeus Mozart. No. 1492, Berlin airlift. No. 1493, Space Shuttle Endeavour crew repairing Intelsat VI. $5, Hindenburg disaster. No.' 1495, Adm. Richard E. Byrd's Ford Trimotor flying over North Pole, 1926. No. 1496, Map of Federal Republic of Germany, vert. No. 1497, Zeppelin Z.4 above clouds. No. 1498, First flight of space shuttle Endeavour. No. 1499, Scene from "The Marriage of Figaro." No. 1500, Jaguar.

1992   Litho.   *Perf. 14*

1485	G105	25c multicolored	.65	.25
1486	G105	50c multicolored	.75	.35
1487	G105	75c multicolored	.75	.60
1488	G105	$1.50 multicolored	1.10	1.10
1489	G105	$2 multicolored	2.50	2.00
1490	G105	$2 multicolored	1.50	1.50
1491	G106	$3 multicolored	2.25	2.25
1492	G105	$4 multicolored	3.00	3.00

1493	G105	$4 multicolored	3.00	3.00
1494	G105	$5 multicolored	3.75	3.75
1495	G105	$5 multicolored	3.75	3.75

Nos. 1485-1495 (11)   23.00   21.55

Souvenir Sheets
Perf. 13½

1496	G105	$6 multicolored	4.75	4.75
1497	G105	$6 multicolored	4.75	4.75
1498	G105	$6 multicolored	4.75	4.75

Perf. 14

1499	G106	$6 multicolored	4.75	4.75
1500	G106	$6 multicolored	4.75	4.75

Count Zeppelin, 75th anniv. of death (#1485, 1494, 1497). Intl. Space Year (#1486, 1493). Konrad Adenauer, 25th anniv. of death (#1487, 1492, 1496).Earth Summit, Rio de Janeiro (#1488-1489, 1500). Intl. Conf. on Nutrition, Rome (#1490). Wolfgang Amadeus Mozart, bicent. of death (in 1991) (#1491, 1499). Intl. Lions Intl., 75th anniv. (#1495). Space Year (#1498).

Issue dates: Nos. 1491, 1499, Oct. Nos. 1485-1486, 1490, 1493-1495, 1497, Nov. Nos. 1487-1489, 1492, 1496, 1500, Dec.

No. 1496 contains one 39x50mm stamp, Nos. 1497-1498 one 50x39mm stamp, No. 1500 one 52x40mm stamp.

Miniature Sheet
Entertainers Type of 1992

Grammy award winners: No. 1501a, Leonard Bernstein. b, Ray Charles. c, Bob Dylan. d, Barbra Streisand. e, Frank Sinatra. f, Harry Belafonte. g, Aretha Franklin. h, Garth Brooks. No. 1502a, Johnny Cash. b, Willie Nelson. No. 1503a, Charlie Parker. b, Miles Davis.

1992, Nov. 19   **Perf. 14**

1501	A286	90c Sheet of 8, #a.-h.	17.50	17.50

Souvenir Sheets

1502	A286	$3 Sheet of 2, #a.-b.	6.50	6.50
1503	A286	$3 Sheet of 2, #a.-b.	6.50	6.50

Dogs — G107   Butterflies — G108

Designs: 35c, Irish Setter, Glendalough, Ireland. 50c, Boston terrier, State House, Boston, US. 75c, Beagle, Temple to Athena, Greece. $1, Weimaraner, Nesselwang, Germany. $3, Norwegian elkhound, Urnes Stave Church, Norway. $4, Mastiff, Great Sphinx, Egypt. No. 1510, Akita, Kyoto torii, Japan. No. 1511, Saluki, Rub'al Khali, Saudi Arabia. No. 1512, Shar pei, China. No. 1513, Bulldog, United Kingdom.

1993, Jan. 20   **Litho.**   **Perf. 14**

1504	G107	35c multicolored	.65	.35
1505	G107	50c multicolored	.90	.65
1506	G107	75c multicolored	1.25	.75
1507	G107	$1 multicolored	1.60	1.10
1508	G107	$3 multicolored	3.25	3.25
1509	G107	$4 multicolored	3.50	3.50
1510	G107	$5 multicolored	3.50	3.50
1511	G107	$5 multicolored	3.50	3.50

Nos. 1504-1511 (8)   18.15   16.60

Souvenir Sheets

1512	G107	$6 multicolored	4.75	4.75
1513	G107	$6 multicolored	4.75	4.75

Louvre Painting Type
Miniature Sheet

Details or entire paintings: No. 1514a, The Virgin and Child with Young St. John the Baptist, by Botticelli. b, The Buffet, by Chardin. c, The Provider, by Chardin. d, Erasmus, by Durer. e, Self-Portrait, by Durer. f, Jeanne of Aragon, by Raphael. g-h, La Belle Jardiniere (diff. details), by Raphael.

$6, Charles I, King of England, Hunting, by Van Dyck.

1993, Mar. 8   **Litho.**   **Perf. 12**

1514	A289	$1 Sheet of 8, #a.-h. + label	11.50	11.50

Souvenir Sheet
Perf. 14½

1515	A289	$6 multicolored	7.50	7.50

No. 1515 contains one 55x88mm stamp.

1993, Apr. 13   **Litho.**   **Perf. 14**

1516	G108	15c Polydamas swallowtail	.35	.35
1517	G108	35c Guaraguao skipper	.50	.50
1518	G108	45c Giant hairstreak	.55	.55
1519	G108	75c Malachite	1.00	1.00
1520	G108	$1 Cloudless sulphur	1.25	1.25
1521	G108	$2 Silver spot	2.50	2.50
1522	G108	$4 St. Christopher's hairstreak	5.00	5.00
1523	G108	$5 Common longtail skipper	6.50	6.50

Nos. 1516-1523 (8)   17.65   17.65

Souvenir Sheets

1524	G108	$6 Orion	8.00	8.00
1525	G108	$6 Zebra	8.00	8.00

Flowers Type of 1993

1993, May

1526	A291	35c Hibiscus	.65	.30
1527	A291	35c Columbine	.65	.30
1528	A291	45c Red ginger	.65	.35
1529	A291	75c Bougainvillea	.90	.60
1530	A291	$1 Crown imperial	1.00	.75
1531	A291	$2 Fairy orchid	1.75	1.75
1532	A291	$4 Heliconia	3.00	3.00
1533	A291	$5 Tulip	3.25	3.25

Nos. 1526-1533 (8)   11.85   10.30

Souvenir Sheets

1534	A291	$6 Balloonflower, horiz.	5.00	5.00
1535	A291	$6 Blackberry lily, horiz.	5.00	5.00

No. 1536 will not be assigned.

Coronation of Queen Elizabeth II Type of 1993
Miniature Sheet

Designs: a, 35c, Official coronation photograph. b, 50c, Ampulla, spoon. c, $2, Queen, following coronation. d, $4, Queen, Prince Charles and his family, c. 1984.

$6, Portrait, by Pietro Annigoni, 1954.

1993, June 2   **Litho.**   **Perf. 13½x14**

1537	A293	Sheet, 2 each #a.-d.	10.50	10.50

Souvenir Sheet
Perf. 14

1538	A293	$6 multicolored	5.50	5.50

No. 1538 contains one 28x42mm stamp.

Anniversaries and Events Types of 1993

Designs: 50c, Telescope. 75c, Willy Brandt, Lyndon Johnson, 1961. $4, Radio telescope. $5, Willy Brandt, Eleanor Hulles, 1957. No. 1543, Copernicus. No. 1544, Willy, Rut Brandt.

1993, July 1   **Litho.**   **Perf. 14**

1539	A294	50c multicolored	1.40	.50
1540	A295	75c multicolored	1.60	1.60
1541	A294	$4 multicolored	4.00	4.00
1542	A295	$5 multicolored	4.00	4.00

Nos. 1539-1542 (4)   11.00   10.10

Souvenir Sheets

1543	A294	$6 multicolored	5.50	5.50
1544	A295	$6 multicolored	5.50	5.50

Copernicus, 450th death anniv. (#1539, 1541, 1543). Willy Brandt, 1st death anniv. (#1540, 1542, 1544).

Songbird Type of 1993
Miniature Sheet

Designs: No. 1545a, 15c, Painted bunting. b, 15c, White-throated sparrow. c, 25c, Common grackle. d, 25c, Royal flycatcher. e, 35c, Swallow tanager. f, 35c, Vermilion flycatcher. g, 45c, Black headed bunting. h, 50c, Rosebreasted grosbeak. i, 75c, Corn bunting. j, 75c, Rosebreasted thrush tanager. k, $1, Buff-throated saltator. l, $4, Plush-capped finch.

No. 1546, Bohemian waxwing. No. 1547, Pine grosbeak.

1993, July 13

1545	A297	Sheet of 12, #a.-l.	13.00	13.00

Souvenir Sheets

1546	A297	$6 multicolored	6.50	6.50
1547	A297	$6 multicolored	6.50	6.50

Seashell Type of 1993
Miniature Sheet

Designs: No. 1548a, 15c, Hawk wing conch. b, 15c, Music volute. c, 25c, Globe vase, deltoid rock shell. d, 35c, Spiny vase. e, 35c, Common sundial, common purple snail. f, 45c, Caribbean donax, gaudy asaphis. g, 45c, Mouse cone. h, 50c, Gold-mouthed triton. i,

75c, Tulip mussel, trigonal tivela. j, 75c, Common dove shell, chestnut latirus. k, $1, Widemouthed purpura. l, $4, Atlantic thorny oyster, Atlantic wing oyster.

No. 1549, Turkey wing. No. 1550, Zebra periwinkle.

1993, July 19   **Litho.**   **Perf. 14**

1548	A298	Sheet of 12, #a.-l.	13.00	13.00

Souvenir Sheet

1549	A298	$6 multicolored	6.50	6.50
1550	A298	$6 multicolored	6.50	6.50

Picasso Type of 1993

Paintings: 15c, Painter and Model, 1928. $1, The Artist and His Model, 1963. $4, The Drawing Lession, 1925. $6, Picasso seated in front of canvas, 1956.

1993, July 1   **Litho.**   **Perf. 14**

1551	A299	15c multi, horiz.	.60	.35
1552	A299	$1 multi, horiz.	1.50	1.50
1553	A299	$4 multi, horiz.	3.75	3.75

Nos. 1551-1553 (3)   5.85   5.60

Souvenir Sheet

1554	A299	$6 multi, horiz.	5.00	5.00

Olympics Type of 1993

Design: $6, Emil Zografski, ski jump.

1993, July 1

1554A	A300	35c multi	.30	.30
1554B	A300	$5 multi	3.75	3.75
1555	A300	$6 multicolored	5.00	5.00

Nos. 1554A-1555 (3)   9.05   9.05

Polska '93 Type of 1993

Paintings: 75c, Gra w Gudziki, by Ludomir Slendzinski, 1928. $2, Pocalunek Mongoskiego Ksiecia, by S.I. Witkiewicz, 1915. $6, Allegory, by Jan Wydra, 1929.

1993, July 1

1556	A301	75c multi, horiz.	1.25	1.25
1557	A301	$2 multi, horiz.	3.50	3.50

Souvenir Sheet

1558	A301	$6 multicolored	5.25	5.25

Taipei '93 Type

Designs: 35c, Macao Palace, Hong Kong. 45c, Stone pixie, Ming Tomb, Nanjing. $1, Stone camels, Ming Tomb, Nanjing. $5, Stone lion and elephant, Ming Tomb, Nanjing. Sculpture: No. 1563a, Nesting quail incense burner. b, Standing quail incense burner. c, Seated qilin incense burner. d, Pottery horse, Han Dynasty. e, Seated caparisoned elephant. f, Cow (imitation delft).

No. 1564, Sumatran tiger.

1993   **Litho.**   **Perf. 14x13½**

1559	A302	35c multi, horiz.	.25	.25
1560	A302	45c multi, horiz.	.35	.35
1561	A302	$1 multi, horiz.	.75	.75
1562	A302	$5 multi, horiz.	3.75	3.75

Nos. 1559-1562 (4)   5.10   5.10

Miniature Sheet

1563	A302	$1.50 Sheet of 6, #a.-f.	11.00	11.00

Souvenir Sheet
Perf. 13½x14

1564	A302	$6 multicolored	7.50	7.50

Nos. 1563a-1563f are horiz.

With Bangkok '93 Emblem

Designs: 35c, Naga snakes, Chiang Mai's Temple, Thailand. 45c, Sri Mariamman Temple, Singapore. $1, Topiary, Hua Hin Resort, Thailand. $5, Pak Tai Temple, Cheung Chau Island.

Thai paintings: No. 1569a, Buddha's victory over Mara. b, Mythological elephant. c, Battle with Mara. d, Untitled work, by Panya Wijinthanasarn, 1984. e, Temple mural. f, Elephants in Pahcekha Buddha's Heaven.

No. 1570, Monkey.

1993   **Perf. 14x13½**

1565	A302	35c multi, horiz.	.25	.25
1566	A302	45c multi, horiz.	.35	.35
1567	A302	$1 multi, horiz.	.75	.75
1568	A302	$5 multi, horiz.	3.75	3.75

Nos. 1565-1568 (4)   5.10   5.10

Miniature Sheet

1569	A302	$1.50 Sheet of 6, #a.-f.	11.00	11.00

Souvenir Sheet
Perf. 13½x14

1570	A302	$6 multicolored	6.50	6.50

Nos. 1569a-1569f are horiz.

Indopex '93 Type

Designs: 35c, Natl. Museum, Central Jakarta, Indonesia. 45c, Sacred Wheel &

Deer, Monastery. $1, Ramayana relief, Panataran Temple. $5, Candi Tikus, Trawulan, East Java.

Paintings: No. 1575a, Bullock Carts, bu Batara Lubis, 1983. c, Self-portrait with Goat, by Kartika, 1987. b, Surat Irsa II, by A.D. Pirous, 1983. c, Self-portrait with Goat, by Kartika, 1987. c, The Cow-est Cow, by Ivan Sagito, 1987. e, Rain Storm, by Sudjana Kerton, 1984. f, Story of Pucuk Flower, by Effendi, 1972.

No. 1576, Banteng cattle.

1993, Aug. 13   **Litho.**   **Perf. 14x13½**

1571	A302	35c multicolored	.25	.25
1572	A302	45c multicolored	.35	.35
1573	A302	$1 multicolored	.75	.75
1574	A302	$5 multicolored	3.75	3.75

Nos. 1571-1574 (4)   5.10   5.10

Miniature Sheet

1575	A302	$1.50 Sheet of 6, #a.-f.	11.00	11.00

Souvenir Sheet

1576	A302	$6 multicolored	5.25	5.25

Nos. 1571-1576 are horiz.

1994 World Cup Soccer
Championships, US — G109

Designs: 15c, Stuart McCall, Carlos Verri. 25c, Carlos Verri, Diego Maradona. 35c, S. Schillaci, J.P. Saldana. 45c, Ruud Gullit, Mark Wright. $1, Carlos Verri, Diego Maradona. $2, Zubizarreta, Fernandez, Albert. $4, Gheorghe Hagi, Paul McGrath. $5, Alberto Gorriz, Enzo Scifo. No. 1585, Schaefer Stadium, Foxboro, MA. No. 1586, Rudi Voeller, vert.

1993, Sept. 7   **Litho.**   **Perf. 14**

1577	G109	15c multicolored	.45	.20
1578	G109	25c multicolored	.45	.20
1579	G109	35c multicolored	.45	.20
1580	G109	45c multicolored	.45	.40
1581	G109	$1 multicolored	.75	.75
1582	G109	$2 multicolored	1.50	1.50
1583	G109	$4 multicolored	3.00	3.00
1584	G109	$5 multicolored	3.75	3.75

Nos. 1577-1584 (8)   10.80   10.00

Souvenir Sheets

1585	G109	$6 multicolored	5.00	5.00
1586	G109	$6 multicolored	5.00	5.00

Mickey Mouse, 65th Anniv. Type

Movie clips: 15c, The Worm Turns, 1937. 35c, Mickey's Rival, 1936. 50c, The Pointer, 1939. 75c, Society Dog Show, 1939. $1, A Gentleman's Gentleman, 1941. $2, The Little Whirlwind, 1941. $4, Mickey Down Under, 1948. $5, R'coon Dawg, 1951.

No. 1595, Mickey's Garden, 1935, vert. No. 1596, Lonesome Ghosts, 1937.

Perf. 13½x14, 14x13½

1993, Nov. 11   **Litho.**

1587	A305	15c multicolored	.60	.25
1588	A305	25c multicolored	.80	.35
1589	A305	50c multicolored	1.00	.60
1590	A305	75c multicolored	1.40	1.00
1591	A305	$1 multicolored	1.60	1.10
1592	A305	$2 multicolored	2.25	2.25
1593	A305	$4 multicolored	3.25	3.25
1594	A305	$5 multicolored	3.25	3.25

Nos. 1587-1594 (8)   14.15   12.05

Souvenir Sheets

1595	A305	$6 multicolored	5.50	5.50
1596	A305	$6 multicolored	5.50	5.50

Christmas Type of 1993

Various details from Adoration of the Shepherds by Durer: 10c, 75c, $1, $4. No. 1605, $6, horiz.

Various details from Oddi Altarpiece by Raphael: 25c, 35c, 50c, $5. No. 1606, $6.

Perf. 13½x14, 14x13½ (#1605)

1993, Nov. 22   **Litho.**

1597-1604	A306	Set of 8	11.00 11.00

Souvenir Sheets

1605-1606	A306	Set of 2	11.00 11.00

Eckener Type of 1993

Designs: 50c, Graf Zeppelin over Rio De Janeiro. 75c, Dr. Hugo Eckener. $5, Eckener commanding Graf Zeppelin. $6, Eckener, Pres. Herbert Hoover.

1993, Dec. 21　　Litho.　　Perf. 14
1607-1609　A307　Set of 3　　　　5.25　5.25
Souvenir Sheet
1610　A307　$6 multicolored　　　5.00　5.00

Royal Air Force Anniv. Type of 1993

Designs: 15c, Avro Lancaster. $5, Short Sunderland. $6, Supermarine Spitfire.

1993, Dec. 21
1611　A308　15c multicolored　　　.35　.20
1612　A308　$5 multicolored　　　6.50　6.50
Souvenir Sheet
1613　A308　$6 multicolored　　　7.00　7.00

Automobile Anniv. Type

Designs: 25c, 1955 Mercedes Benz 300SLR. 45c, 1957 Ford Thunderbird. $4, 1929 Ford 150A Station Wagon. $5, Mercedes Benz 540K.
Each $6: No. 1618, 1929 Mercedes Benz SSK. No. 1619, 1924 Ford Model T.

1993, Dec. 21　　Litho.　　Perf. 14
1614-1617　A309　Set of 4　　　10.00　10.00
Souvenir Sheets
1618-1619　A309　Set of 2　　　11.00　11.00

1st Benz 4-wheel car, 1st Ford engine, cent.

First Gas Balloon Flight in America Type

Designs: 35c, Blanchard's balloon crossing Delaware River. $3, Blanchard delivering Washington's passport of introduction. $6, Balloon in flight, vert.

1993, Dec. 21　　Litho.　　Perf. 14
1620-1621　A310　Set of 2　　　3.50　3.50
Souvenir Sheet
1622　A310　$6 multicolored　　　5.00　5.00

Fine Art Type

Details or entire paintings by Rembrandt: 15c, Hendrickje Stoffels as Flora. 35c, Lady & Gentlemen in Black. 50c, Aristotle with Bust of Homer. $5, Christ & the Woman of Samaria. Details or entire paintings by Matisse: 75c, Interior: Flowers and Parakeets. $1, Goldfish. $2, The Girl with Green Eyes. $3, Still Life with a Plaster Figure.
Each $6: No. 1631, Anna Accused of Stealing the Kid, by Rembrandt. No. 1632, Tea in the Garden by Matisse, horiz.

Perf. 13½x14, 14x13½
1993, Dec. 31　　　　　Litho.
1623-1630　A311　Set of 8　　　11.00　11.00
Souvenir Sheets
1631-1632　A311　Set of 2　　　11.00　11.00

Hong Kong '94 Type

Designs: No. 1633, Hong Kong #426, jet at Kai Tak Airport. No. 1634, Junk, Kwaloon Bay, #975.
Chinese jade: No. 1635a, White jade brush washer. b. Archaic jade brush washer. c, Dark green jade brush washer. d, Green jade alms bowl. e, Archaic jade dog. f, Yellow jade brush washer.

1994, Feb. 18　　Litho.　　Perf. 14
1633　A313　40c multicolored　　　.90　.90
1634　A313　40c multicolored　　　.90　.90
　a.　Pair, #1633-1634　　　　2.40　2.40
Miniature Sheet
1635　A314　45c Sheet of 6, #a.-f.　5.00　5.00

Nos. 1633-1634 issued in sheets of of 5 pairs. No. 1634a is a continuous design. Nos. 1635a-1635f are horiz.
New Year 1994 (Year of the Dog) (#1635e).

Dinosaurs G110

15c, Spinosaurus. 35c, Apatosaurus. 45c, Tyrannosaurus rex. 55c, Triceratops. $1, Pachycephalosaurus. $2, Pteranodon. $4, Parasaurolophus. $5, Brachiosaurus.
Each $6: No. 1644, Brachiosaurus, vert. No. 1645, Tyrannosaurus, spinosaurus, vert.

1994　　　Litho.　　　Perf. 14
1636-1643　G110　Set of 8　　　12.50　12.50
Souvenir Sheets
1644-1645　G110　Set of 2　　　11.00　11.00

Mushrooms G111

Designs: 35c, Hygrocybe hypohaemacta. 45c, Cantherellus cinnabarinus. 50c, Marasmius haematocephalus. 75c, Mycena pura. $1, Gymnopilus russipes. $2, Galocybe cyanocephala. $4, Pleuteus chrysophlebius. $5, Chlorophyllum molybdites.
Each $6: No. 1654, Collybia fibrosipes. No. 1655, Xeromphalina tenuipes.

1994
1646-1653　G111　Set of 8　　　10.50　10.50
Souvenir Sheets
1654-1655　G111　Set of 2　　　9.50　9.50

D-Day Type of 1994

40c, Churchill bridgelayer in action. $2, Sherman "Firefly" attacks beach. $3, Churchill Crocodile flame thrower. $6, Sherman "Crab" flail tank.

1994, Aug. 4　　Litho.　　Perf. 14
1656-1658　A318　Set of 3　　　5.00　5.00
Souvenir Sheet
1659　A318　$6 multicolored　　　5.25　5.25

First Manned Moon Landing, 25th Anniv. Type of 1994
Miniature Sheet of 6

Tribute to Challenger crew: No. 1660a, Slidewire escape training. b, Christa A. McAuliffe. c, Challenger 51-L on pad LC39B. d, Gregory B. Jarvis. e, Ellison S. Onizuka. f, Ronald E. McNair.
$6, Judith A. Resnick, vert.

1994, Aug. 4
1660　A319　$1.10 #a.-f.　　　7.50　7.50
Souvenir Sheet
1661　A319　$6 multicolored　　　6.50　6.50

PHILAKOREA '94 Type

Designs: 40c, Onung Tomb, Korea. $1, Stone pagoda, Mt. Nansan, Kyongju. $4, Pusan Port.
Paintings, by Sin Yunbok, late Choson Dynasty, 1758: No. 1665a-1665b, Admiring spring in the Country. c-d, Women on Dano Day. e-f, Enjoying Lotuses While Listening to Music. g-h, Women by a Crystal Stream.
$6, Blacksmith's Shop, by Kim Duksin (1754-1822).

1994, Aug. 4　　Perf. 14, 13½ (#1665)
1662-1664　A320　Set of 3　　　4.25　4.25
Miniature Sheet of 8
1665　A321　$1 #a.-h.　　　　9.50　9.50
Souvenir Sheet
1666　A320　$6 multicolored　　　5.00　5.00

Orchid Type of 1994

15c, Cattleya aurantiaca. 25c, Blettia patula. 45c, Sobralia macrantha. 75c, Encyclia belizensis. $1, Sophrolaeliocattleya. $2, Encyclia frangrans. $4, Schombocattleya. $5, Brassolaeliocattleya.
Each $6: No. 1675, Brassavola nodosa. No. 1676, Ornithidium coccineum.

1994, Aug. 7　　　　　Perf. 14
1667-1674　A322　Set of 8　　　11.00　11.00
Souvenir Sheets
1675-1676　A322　Set of 2　　　10.00　10.00

1994 World Cup Soccer Type
Miniature Sheet of 6

Designs: No. 1677a, Steve Mark, Grenada. b, Jurgen Kohler, Germany. c, Almir, Brazil. d, Michael Windischmann, US. e, Guiseppe Giannini, Italy. f, Rashidi Yekini, Nigeria.
Each $6: No. 1678, Kemari. No. 1679, The World Cup.

1994, Aug. 11　　　　Perf. 14
1677　A323　75c #a.-f.　　　5.25　5.25
Souvenir Sheets
1678-1679　A323　Set of 2　　　9.50　9.50

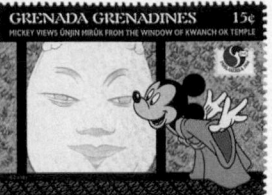

Disney's PHILAKOREA '94 — G112

15c, Mickey, Unjin Miruk, Kwanch Ok Temple. 35c, Goofy, statue of Admiral Yi, Chonju. 50c, Cousin Gus, Donald. 75c, Mickey playing flute. $1, Goofy, Tolharubang Grandfather statue. $2, Mickey, Minnie, Hyang-Wonjong. $4, Mickey, Unsan Pyolshin Festival. $5, Minnie, ceremonial fan.
Each $6: No. 1688, Minnie, Buk drum, vert. No. 1689, Mickey, Pugok Hawaii, vert.

1994, Aug. 16　Litho.　Perf. 14x13½
1680-1687　A312　Set of 8　　　15.00　15.00
Souvenir Sheets
Perf. 13½x14
1688-1689　G112　Set of 2　　　12.00　12.00

This set exists with very low face values.

Fish Type of 1994

Designs, each 75c: No. 1690a, Yellowtail snapper (b, e). b, Caribbean reef shark (a). c, Great barracuda. d, Redtail parrotfish. e, Blue tang. f, Queen angelfish. g, Red hind (h). h, Rock beauty. i, Queen parrotfish. j, Spanish hogfish. k, Spotted moray. l, Queen triggerfish (i).
Each 75c: No. 1691a, Pork fish (b). b, Blue chromis (a). c, Caribbean reef shark. d, Longspine squirrelfish. e, Foureye butterflyfish. f, Blue head. g, Royal gramma. h, Sharpnose puffer. i, Longsnout seahorse. j, Blackbar soldierfish (g, k). k, Redlip blenny. l, Rainbow wrasse.
Each $6: No. 1692, Rainbow wrasse, diff. No. 1693, Queen angelfish, diff.

1994, Sept. 1　　　　　Perf. 14
Miniature Sheets of 12
1690-1691　A324　Set of 2　　　24.00　24.00
Souvenir Sheets
1692-1693　A324　Set of 2　　　12.00　12.00

Intl. Olympic Committe Type of 1994

Designs: 50c, Silke Renk, Germany, javelin, 1992. $1.50, Mark Spitz, US, swimming, 1972. $6, Team Japan, Nordic combined, 1994.

1994　　　　　　　　　Perf. 14
1694　A325　50c multi, horiz.　.40　.40
1695　A325　$1.50 multi, horiz.　1.10　1.10
Souvenir Sheet
1696　A326　$6 multicolored　　　5.00　5.00

Intl. Year of the Family Type of 1994
1994
1697　A329　$1 Family of 5　　　.80　.80

Order of the Caribbean Community Type

Designs: 25c, Sir Shridath Ramphal, statesman, Guyana. 50c, William Demas, economist, Trinidad & Tobago. $2, Derek Walcott, writer, St. Lucia.

1994, Sept. 1
1698-1700　A330　Set of 3　　　3.00　3.00

Christmas Type of 1994

Paintings, by Bartolome Murillo: 15c, The Annunciation. 35c, The Adoration of the Shepherds. No. 1703, 50c, Flight into Egypt. No. 1704, 50c, Virgin and Child with St. Rose. 75c, Virgin and Child. $1, Virgin of the Rosary. $4, The Holy Family.
Each $6: No. 1708, Adoration of the Shepherds. No. 1709, The Holy Family with a Little Bird.

1994, Dec. 5　　Litho.　　Perf. 13½x14
1701-1707　A331　Set of 7　　　7.50　7.50
Souvenir Sheets
1708-1709　A331　Set of 2　　　10.00　10.00

Bird Type of 1995

25c, Ground dove. 50c, White-winged dove, horiz. $2, Inca dove. $4, Mourning dove, horiz.

1995, Jan. 10　　　　　Perf. 14
1710-1713　A332　Set of 4　　　9.50　9.50

English Touring Cricket, Cent. Type

Designs: 50c, M.A. Atherton, England, horiz. 75c, C.E.L. Ambrose, Leeward Isl./W. Indies. $1, B.C. Lara, Trinidad/W. Indies. $3, West Indies Team, horiz.

1995, Jan. 12
1714-1717　A333　Set of 3　　　4.00　4.00
Souvenir Sheet
1718　A333　$3 multicolored　　　4.00　4.00

Miniature Sheet of 10

Capitals of the World — G113

Designs: a, London. b, Cairo. c, Vienna. d, Paris. e, Rome. f, Budapest. g, Moscow. h, Beijing. i, Tokyo. j, Wasington.

1995, Mar. 10　　Litho.　　Perf. 14
1719　G113　$1 #a.-j.　　　10.00　10.00

New Year 1995 (Year of the Boar) — G114

Various stylized boars with different Chinese inscriptions: a, Smiling, purple legs. b, Smiling, red legs. c, Brown legs. d, Red legs.
$2, Two boars, horiz.

1995, Apr. 21　　Litho.　　Perf. 14½
1720　G114　75c Block or horiz.
　　　　　　strip of 4, #a.-d.　2.25　2.25
　e.　Souvenir sheet of 4, #1720a-
　　　1720d　　　　　　3.00　3.00
Souvenir Sheet
1721　G114　$2 multicolored　　　2.25　2.25

No. 1720 was issued in miniature sheets of 16 stamps.

VE Day Type of 1995
Miniature Sheets of 6 and 8

#1721A: b, Mitsubishi G4M1 "Betty." c, Aircraft carrying submarine I-14. d, Mitsubishi G3M1. e, Destroyer Akizuki. f, Battleship Kirishima. g, Cruiser Asigari.
Bombers: #1722: a, Avro Lancaster, Tallboy bomb. b, Junkers JU-88. c, B-25 Mitchell. d, B-17 Flying Fortress. e, Petlyakov Pe-2. f, Martin B-26 Marauder. g, Henkel He-111. h, Consolidated B-24 Liberator.
#1723, Pres. Truman displaying newspaper headline. #1723A, Aichi D3A1 "Val" dive bomber.

1995, May 8　　　　　Perf. 14
1721A　A336　$2 #b.-g. + label　9.50　9.50
1722　A336　$2 #a.-h. + label　13.00　13.00
Souvenir Sheets
1723　A336　$6 multicolored　　　5.25　5.25
1723A　A336　$6 multicolored　　　6.00　6.00

Inscription in central label of No. 1721A misidentifies a Yokosuka MXY-7 Okha kamikaze plane.
No. 1723 contains one 57x42mm stamp.

Scout Jamboree Type of 1995

a, 75c, Beach scene, scout. b, $1, Mountains, sea, scout with pole. c, $2, Flag, scout salute.
$6, Snorkeling, fish.

1995, May 8
1724　A337　Strip of 3, #a.-c.　3.00　3.00
Souvenir Sheet
1725　A337　$6 multicolored　　　5.50　5.50

No. 1724 was issued in sheets of 9 stamps.

UN, 50th Anniv. Type of 1995

Designs: a, 75c, Building, UN flag. b, $1, Trygve Lie (1896-1968), Norway, 1st Secretary General. c, $2, Flag, member of UN peacekeeping force.
$6, Dove, emblem.

1995, May 8

| 1726 | A338 | Strip of 3, #a.-c. | 3.00 | 3.00 |

Souvenir Sheet

| 1727 | A338 | $6 multicolored | 4.75 | 4.75 |

No. 1726 is a continuous design and was issued in sheets of 9 stamps.

Marine Life of the Caribbean — G115

No. 1728, each $1: a, Dolphins. b, Scorpion fish. c, Sea turtle, rock beauty. d, Butterflyfish, nurse shark. e, Angel fish. f, Grouper coney. g, Rainbow eel, moray eel. h, Sun flower-star, coral crab. i, Octopus.

No. 1729, each $1: a, Bull shark. b, Big white shark. c, Octopus. d, Barracuda (e). e, Moray eel (f, h, i). f, Spotted eagle ray. g, Gold-spotted snake. h, Stingray. i, Grouper.

$5, French angelfish. $6, Hammerhead shark.

1995, May 3   Litho.   Perf. 14

Miniature Sheets of 9, #a-i

| 1728-1729 | G115 | Set of 2 | 18.00 | 18.00 |

Souvenir Sheets

| 1730 | G115 | $5 multicolored | 4.25 | 4.25 |
| 1731 | G115 | $6 multicolored | 5.00 | 5.00 |

Domesticated Animals — G116

Horses: 15c, Suffolk punch. 25c, Shetland pony. $1, Arab. $3, Shire horse.

Dogs, each 75c: No. 1736a, Shetland sheepdog. b, Bull terrier. c, Afghan. d, Scottish terrier. e, Labrador retriever. f, English springer spaniel. g, Samoyed. h, Irish setter. i, Border collie. j, Pekingese. k, Dachshund. l, Weimaraner.

Cats, each 75c: No. 1737a, Blue persian. b, Sorrel abyssinian. c, White angora. d, Brown burmese. e, Red tabby exotic shorthair. f, Seal-point birman. g, Korat. h, Norwegian forest cat. i, Lilac-point Balinese. j, British shorthair. k, Red self longhair. l, Calico manx.

Each $6: No. 1738, English setter. No. 1739, Seal-point colorpoint.

1995, May 3

| 1732-1735 | G116 | Set of 4 | 3.50 | 3.50 |

Miniature Sheets of 12, #a-l

| 1736-1737 | G116 | | 14.00 | 14.00 |

Souvenir Sheets

| 1738-1739 | G116 | | 11.00 | 11.00 |

Sierra Club, Cent. G117

No. 1740, each $1: a, Brown pelican. b, Northern spotted owl. c, Northern spotted owl in winter. d, Jaguarundi. e, Central American spider monkeys facing forward. f, Two Central American spider monkeys. g, Central American spider monkey. h, Wood stork. i, Maned wolves.

No. 1741, each $1, vert: a, Northern spotted owl. b, Brown pelican. c, Brown pelican up close. d, Jaguarundi up close. e, Jaguarundi. f, Maned wolf. g, Wood stork facing right. h, Wood stork facing left. i, Maned wolf up close.

1995, May 5

Miniature Sheets of 9, #a-i

| 1740-1741 | G117 | Set of 2 | 25.00 | 25.00 |

FAO, 50th Anniv. — G118

No. 1742: a, 75c, Man working in field. b, $1, Woman working in field. c, $2, Two workers in field.

$6, Child with chopsticks.

1995, May 8

| 1742 | G118 | Strip of 3, #a.-c. | 3.00 | 3.00 |

Souvenir Sheet

| 1743 | G118 | $6 multicolored | 4.50 | 4.50 |

No. 1742 was issued in sheets of 9 stamps.

Rotary Intl., 90th Anniv. G119

1995, May 8

| 1744 | G119 | $5 Paul Harris, emblem | 3.75 | 3.75 |

Souvenir Sheet

| 1745 | G119 | $6 Old, new emblems | 4.50 | 4.50 |

Queen Mother, 95th Anniv. Type of 1995

No. 1746: a, Drawing. b, In black outfit. c, Formal portrait. d, In green outfit.

No. 1747, Speaking at Blitz Memorial.

1995, May 8

| 1746 | A344 | $1.50 Strip or block of 4, #a.-d. | 5.00 | 5.00 |

Souvenir Sheet

| 1747 | A344 | $6 multicolored | 5.00 | 5.00 |

No. 1746 was issued in sheets of 8 stamps.

Sheets of Nos. 1746-1747 exist with black border and text "In Memoriam - 1900-2002" in sheet margins.

1996 Summer Olympics Type

No. 1748, horiz: a, Rosemary Ackerman, East Germany, high jump. b, Li Ning, China, gymnastics. c, Denise Parker, US, archery.

No. 1749, horiz: a, Terry Carlisle, US, skeet shooting. b, Kathleen Nord, East Germany, 200-meter butterfly. c, Brigit Schmidt, East Germany, kayaking.

Each $6: No. 1750, George Foreman, US, boxing. No. 1751, Dan Gable US, Kikuo Wada, Japan, wrestling.

1995, June 23

| 1748 | A345 | 15c Strip of 3, #a.-c. | .60 | .60 |
| 1749 | A345 | $3 Strip of 3, #a.-c. | 9.50 | 9.50 |

Souvenir Sheets

| 1750-1751 | A345 | Set of 2 | 11.00 | 11.00 |

Designs: 10c, Brown pelican. 15c, Common stilt. 25c, Cuban trogan. 35c, Flamingo. 75c, Parrot. $1, Pintail duck. $2, Ringed kingfisher. $3, Strip-headed tanager.

No. 1760: a, Great blue heron. b, Jamaican tody. c, Laughing gull. d, Purple-throated carib. e, Red-legged thrush. f, Ruddy duck. g, Shoveler duck. h, West Indian red-bellied woodpecker.

Each $5: No. 1761, Blue-hooded Euphonia. No. 1762, Village weaver.

1995, Sept. 5   Litho.   Perf. 14

| 1752-1759 | G120 | Set of 8 | 8.00 | 8.00 |

Miniature Sheet of 8

| 1760 | G120 | $1 #a.-h. | 8.00 | 8.00 |

Souvenir Sheets

| 1761-1762 | G120 | Set of 2 | 10.50 | 10.50 |

Singapore '95 (#1760-1762). No. 1760d is mis-spelled.

Mickey's High Sea Adventure — G121

10c, Goofy carrying treasure chests, Donald. 35c, Mickey, Minnie at helm. 75c, Mickey, Donald, Goofy opening treasure chest. $1, Pirates confronting Mickey. $2, Mickey, Goofy, Donald in life boat. $5, Goofy using mop to fight enemy.

Each $6: No. 1769, Cannonballs being shot at Goofy, vert. No. 1770, Mickey on island, monkey pinching his nose, vert.

1995, Oct. 2   Litho.   Perf. 14x13½

| 1763-1768 | G121 | Set of 6 | 7.00 | 7.00 |

Souvenir Sheets
Perf. 13½x14

| 1769-1770 | G121 | Set of 2 | 10.00 | 10.00 |

Nobel Prize Recipients Type of 1995

No. 1770A, Derek Walcott, literature, 1992. No. 1770B, W. Arthur Lewis, economics, 1979.

No. 1771, each $1: a, Heike Kamerlingh Onnes, physics, 1913. b, Fridtjof Nansen, 1922. c, Sir Ronald Ross, physiology or medicine, 1902. d, Paul Müller, physiology or medicine, 1948. e, Allvar Gullstrand, physiology or medicine, 1911. f, Gerhart Hauptmann, literature, 1912. g, Hans Spemann, physiology or medicine, 1935. h, Cecil F. Powell, physics, 1950. i, Walther Bothe, physics, 1954.

No. 1772, each $1: a, Jules Bordet, physiology or medicine, 1919. b, René Cassin, peace, 1968. c, Verner von Heidenstam, literature, 1916. d, Jose Echegaray, literature, 1904. e, Otto Wallach, chemistry, 1910. f, Corneille Heymans, physiology or medicine, 1938. g, Ivar Giaever, physics, 1973. h, Sir William Cremer, peace, 1903. i, John W. Strutt, physics, 1904.

No. 1773, each $1: a, James Franck, physics, 1925. b, Tobias M.C. Asser, peace, 1911. c, Carl F.G. Spitteler, literature, 1919. d, Christiaan Eijkman, physiology or medicine, 1929. e, Ragnar Granit, physiology or medicine, 1967. f, Frederic Passy, peace, 1901. g, Louis Neel, physics, 1970. h, Sir William Ramsay, chemistry, 1904. i, Philip Noel-Baker, peace, 1959.

Each $6: No. 1774, Albert Schweitzer, peace, 1952. No. 1775, Willy Brandt, peace, 1971. No. 1776, Winston Churchill, literature, 1953.

1995, Oct. 18   Litho.   Perf. 14

| 1770A | A354 | 75c multicolored | .55 | .55 |
| 1770B | A354 | 75c multicolored | .55 | .55 |

Miniature Sheets of 9, #a-i

| 1771-1773 | A354 | Set of 3 | 20.00 | 20.00 |

Souvenir Sheets

| 1774-1776 | A354 | Set of 3 | 16.50 | 16.50 |

Motion Pictures, Cent. G122

Actresses, each $1: No. 1777a, Marion Davies. b, Marlene Dietrich. c, Lillian Gish. d, Bette Davis. e, Elizabeth Taylor. f, Veronica Lake. g, Ava Gardner. h, Grace Kelly. i, Kim Novak.

Romantic couples, each $1: No. 1778a, Nita Naldi, Rudolph Valentino. b, Ramon Novarro, Alice Terry. c, Frederic March, Joan Crawford.

d, Clark Gable, Vivien Leigh. e, Barbara Stanwyck, Burt Lancaster. f, Warren Beatty, Natalie Wood. g, Spencer Tracy, Katharine Hepburn. h, Humphrey Bogart, Lauren Bacall. i, Omar Sharif, Julie Christie.

Each $6: No. 1779, Sophia Loren. No. 1780, Greta Garbo, John Gilbert, horiz.

1995, Nov. 3   Perf. 13½x14

Miniature Sheets of 9, #a-i

| 1777-1778 | G122 | Set of 2 | 14.00 | 14.00 |

Souvenir Sheets
Perf. 13½x14, 14x13½

| 1779-1780 | G122 | Set of 2 | 10.00 | 10.00 |

Classic Racing Cars G123

Designs: 10c, 1990's Williams-Renault Formula 1. 25c, 1980's Le Mans Porsche 956. 35c, 1970's Lotus "John Player Special." 75c, 1960's Ford GT 40. $2, 1950's Mercedes Benz W196. $3, 1920's Mercedes SSK.

$6, 1971 Tyrrell-Ford Fourmula 1.

1995, Nov. 7   Perf. 14

| 1781-1786 | G123 | Set of 6 | 6.50 | 6.50 |

Souvenir Sheet

| 1787 | G123 | $6 multicolored | 6.00 | 6.00 |

Local Transportation — G124

1995, Nov. 7

| 1788 | G124 | 35c Donkey | .40 | .25 |
| 1789 | G124 | 75c Bus | 1.00 | .90 |

Miniature Sheet

Sailing Ships G125

Designs: No. 1790a, Preussen. b, Japanese junk. c, Pirate ship. d, Mayflower. e, Chinese junk. f, Santa Maria.

$5, Spanish galleon.

1995, Nov. 7

| 1790 | G125 | $1 Sheet of 6, #a.-f. | 6.00 | 6.00 |

Souvenir Sheet

| 1791 | G125 | $5 multicolored | 5.00 | 5.00 |

No. 1791 contains one 57x42mm stamp.

Christmas Type of 1995

Details or entire paintings: 10c, Immaculate Conception, by De Cosimo. 15c, St. Michel Dedicating Arms to the Madonna, by Le Nain. 35c, Annunciation, by de Credi. 50c, The Holy Family, by Jordaens. $3, Madonna and Child, by Lippi. $5, Madonna and Child with Ten Saints, by Fiorentino.

Each $6: No. 1798, Adoration of the Shepherds, by Van Oost. No. 1799, Holy Family, by Del Sart.

1995, Nov. 28   Perf. 13½x14

| 1792-1797 | A356 | Set of 6 | 8.00 | 8.00 |

Souvenir Sheets

| 1798-1799 | A356 | Set of 2 | 11.00 | 11.00 |

New Year 1996 (Year of the Rat) — G126

Stylized rats: No. 1800: a, blue & multi. b, violet & multi. c, red & multi. d, green & multi. $2, Two rats, horiz.

1996, Jan. 2　Litho.　Perf. 14½
1800 G126 75c Block of 4, #a.-d. 2.25 2.25
Miniature Sheet
1801 G126 75c Sheet of 1 #1800 2.25 2.25
Souvenir Sheet
1802 G126 $2 multicolored 1.75 1.75

No. 1800 was issued in sheets of 16 stamps.

Works by Dürer and Rubens Type of 1996

Details or entire work: 15c, The Centaur Family, by Dürer. 35c, Oriental Ruler Seated, by Dürer. 50c, The Entombment, by Dürer. 75c, Man in Armor, by Rubens. $1, Peace Embracing Plenty, by Rubens. $2, Departure of Lot, by Rubens. The Four Evangelists, by Rubens. No. 1810, $5, Knight, Death and Devil, by Dürer.

No. 1811, The Father of the Church, by Rubens. $6, St. Jerome, 1514 engraving, by Dürer.

1996, Jan. 29　Litho.　Perf. 14
1803-1810 A360 Set of 8 10.00 10.00
Souvenir Sheets
1811 A360 $5 multicolored 4.50 4.50
1812 A360 $6 multicolored 4.50 4.50

Disney Holidays — G127

Disney characters celebrating: 25c, New Year's Day, "Hopping John" Feast. 50c, May Day. 75c, Independence Day. 90c, Halloween. $3, Thanksgiving. $4, Hanukkah.

Each $6: No. 1819, Caribbean Carnival. No. 1820, St. Patrick's Day Parade, vert.

1996, Apr. 17　Litho.　Perf. 14x13½
1813-1818 G127 Set of 6 10.00 10.00
Perf. 14x13½, 13½x14
1819-1820 G127 Set of 2 13.00 13.00

Sites in China — G128

No. 1821, each $1: a, Entryway to hall, Imperial Palace. b, Great Wall's eastern end, Shanhaiguan. c, Fortress in Great Wall, Shanhaiguan. d, Gate of Heavenly Peace, Tiananmen, main entrance to Imperial City.

No. 1822, each $1: a, Mausoleum of Dr. Sun Yat-Sen, Nanjing. b, Summer Palace,

Beijing. c, Temple of Heaven, Beijing. d, Hall of Supreme Harmony, Forbidden City, Beijing. Each $6: No. 1823, Great Wall of China. No. 1824, Marble boat, Summer Palace, Beijing. Illustration reduced.

1996, May 8　　　　　Perf. 13
Sheets of 4, #a-d
1821-1822 G128 Set of 2 13.00 13.00
Souvenir Sheets
1823-1824 G128 Set of 2 10.50 10.50

China '96, 9th Asian Intl. Philatelic Exhibition (#1821-1822).
No. 1823 contains one 40x51mm stamp, No. 1824 one 51x40mm stamp.
See No. 1881.

Queen Elizabeth II, 70th Birthday Type of 1996

Designs: a, 35c, Portrait in blue dress. b, $2, Wearing crown. c, $4, Windsor Castle. $6, Standing in front of palace.

1996, May 8　Litho.　Perf. 13½x14
1825 A362 Strip of 3, #a.-c. 4.75 4.75
Souvenir Sheet
1826 A362 $6 multicolored 4.50 4.50

No. 1825 was issued in sheets of 9 stamps with each strip in a different order.

Flowers — G129

35c, Camellia "Apple Blossom." 90c, Camellia japonica "Extravaganza." $1, Chrysanthemum "Primrose Dorothy Else." $2, Dahlia "Brandaris."

No. 1831: a, Odontoglossum. b, Cattleya. c, Paphiopedilum "Venus's Slipper." d, Laeliocattleya "Marysville."

No. 1832: a, Fushcia "Citation." b, Fuchsia "Amy Lye." c, Clysonimus butterfly. d, Digitalis purpurea "Foxglove" (h). e, Lilium martagon "Martagon Lily." f, Tulip "Couleur Cardinal." g, Galanthus nivalis "Snowdrop." h, Rose "Superstar." i, Crocus "Dutch Yellow Mammouth." j, Lilium speciosum Japanese lily. k, Lilium "Joan Evans." l, Rose "Rosemary Harkness." $5, Narcissus "Rembrandt." $6, Gladiollus "Flowersong."

1996, June 12　Litho.　Perf. 14
1827-1830 G129 Set of 4 5.00 5.00
1831 G129 75c Strip of 4, #a.-d. 3.50 3.50
1832 G129 75c Sheet of 12, #a.-l. 9.00 9.00
Souvenir Sheets
1833 G129 $5 multicolored 4.50 4.50
1834 G129 $6 multicolored 5.00 5.00

No. 1831 issued in sheets of 12 stamps.

UNICEF, 50th Anniv. G130

Letters spelling UNICEF and: 75c, Child smiling. $2, Child eating. $3, Child reading. $6, Child on mother's back.

1996, June 26
1836-1838 G130 Set of 3 4.50 4.50
Souvenir Sheet
1839 G130 $6 multicolored 4.50 4.50
#1838 is unassigned.

Jerusalem, 3000th Anniv. G131

Flowers and: a, $1, Pool of Bethesda. b, $2, Damascus Gate. c, $3, Church of All Nations, Gethsemane. $6, Church of the Holy Sepulchre.

1996, June 26
1840 G131 Sheet of 3, #a.-c. 4.50 4.50
Souvenir Sheet
1841 G131 $6 multicolored 4.50 4.50

Radio, Cent. Type of 1996

Entertainers: 35c, Ed Wynn. 75c, Red Skelton. $1, Joe Penner. $3, Jerry Colonna. $6, Bob Elliott, Ray Goulding, horiz.

1996, June 26　　　　　Perf. 13½x14
1842-1845 A367 Set of 4 3.75 3.75
Souvenir Sheet
Perf. 14x13½
1846 A367 $6 multicolored 4.50 4.50

Olympics Type of 1996

35c, Memorial Coliseum, Los Angeles, 1994. 75c, Connie Carpenter-Phinney, US. $2, Mohamed Bouchighe, Algeria, vert. $3, Jackie Joyner-Kersee, US.

No. 1851, Gymnasts, vert, each $1: a, Julianne McNamara, US. b, Takuti Hayata, Japan. c, Nikolai Andrianov, Russia. d, Mitch Gaylord, US. e, Ludmilla Tourischeva, Russia. f, Karin Janz, Germany. g, Peter Kormann, US. h, Sawao Kato, Japan. i, Nadia Comaneci, Romania.

No. 1852, Equestrian participants, vert, each $1: a, Josef Neckermann, Germany. b, Harry Boldt, Germany. c, Elena Petouchkova, Russia. d, Alwin Schockemoehle, Germany. e, Hans Winkler, Germany. f, Joe Fargis, US. g, David Broome, Great Britain. h, Reiner Klimke, Germany. i, Richard Meade, Great Britain.

No. 1853, Young Japanese girl, vert. No. 1854, William Steinkraus, US.

1996, July 15　　　　　Perf. 14
1847-1850 A364 Set of 4 4.50 4.50
Sheets of 9, #a-i
1851-1852 A364 Set of 2 13.50 13.50
Souvenir Sheets
1853 A364 $5 multicolored 3.75 3.75
1854 A364 $6 multicolored 4.50 4.50

Classic Cars — G132

No. 1855: a, Delaunay-Belleville HB6, France. b, Bugatti Type-15, Italy. c, Mazda Type 800, Japan. d, Mercedes 24/100/140 Sport, Germany. e, MG K3 Rover, England. f, Plymouth Fury, US.

No. 1856: a, 35c, Chevrolet Belair Convertible, US. b, 75c, Rolls Royce Torpedo, England. c, $1, Nissan Type "Cepric," Japan. d, VIP car. e, Mercedes Benz 500k, Germany. f, Bugatti Type-13, Italy.

$5, Bugatti "Roadster" Type-55. $6, Lincoln Type-L, US.

1996, July 25　Litho.　Perf. 14
1855 G132 $1 Sheet of 6, #a.-f. 4.50 4.50
1856 G132 Sheet of 6, #a.-f. 5.75 5.75
Souvenir Sheets
1857 G132 $5 multicolored 3.75 3.75
1858 G132 $6 multicolored 4.50 4.50

Nos. 1857-1858 each contain one 51x39mm stamp.

Ships G133

Traditional Grenada schooners: 35c, Red and white. 75c, Blue and white.

No. 1861, Ancient ships, each $1: a, Athenian war trireme, 1000BC. b, Egyptian Nile trader, 3100BC. c, Bangladesh dinghi, 3100BC. d, Queen Hatshepsut warship, 1476BC. e, Chinese junk, 200BC. f, Polynesian voyager, 600BC.

No. 1862, Ocean liners, each $1: a, Europa, Germany, 1957. b, Lusitania, England, 1906.

c, Queen Mary, England, 1936. d, Bianca C, Italy. e, SS France, 1932. f, Orion, England, 1915.

$5, Queen Elizabeth 2, England, 1969. $6, Viking ship, 610BC.

1996, Aug. 14
1859 G133 35c multicolored .25 .25
1860 G133 75c multicolored .55 .55
Sheets of 6, #a-f
1861-1862 G133 Set of 2 9.00 9.00
Souvenir Sheets
1863 G133 $5 multicolored 3.75 3.75
1864 G133 $6 multicolored 4.50 4.50

No. 1863 contains one 51x42mm stamp, No. 1864 one 42x51mm stamp.

Famous Composers G134

Composer, work illustrated: No. 1865, each $1: a, Bèla Bartòk, "Mikrokosmos," 1926. b, Giacomo Puccini, "Madame Butterfly," 1904. c, George Gershwin, "Rhapsody in Blue," 1923. d, Leonard Bernstein, "West Side Story," 1957. e, Kurt Weill, "Three Penny Opera," 1928. f, John Cage, "Music of Changes," 1951. g, Aaron Copland, "El Salón Mexico," 1936. h, Sergei Prokofiev, "Peter and the Wolf," 1936. i, Igor Stravinsky, "Rite of Spring," 1913.

No. 1866, each $1: a, Felix Mendelssohn, overture to "Midsummer Night's Dream," 1826. b, Franz Schubert, "Die Forelle" (The Trout) D.550, 1817. c, Franz Joseph Haydn, "String Quartet in D Major," Op. 64 No. 5 (Lark), 1790. d, Robert Schumann, "Spring," Symphony No. 1, Op. 38, 1841. e, Ludwig Van Beethoven, "Moonlight" sonata Op. 27, No. 2. f, Gioacchino Rossini, "William Tell," 1829. g, George Frederick Handel, "Royal Fireworks Music," 1749. h, Peter Ilyich Tchaikovsky, "Swan Lake," Op.20, 1876. i, Frederic Chopin, "Fantasia," in F minor, Op. 49, 1840-41.

$5, Richard Strauss. $6, Mozart, "Jupiter" symphony in C major.

1996, Aug. 26
Sheets of 9, #a-i
1865-1866 G134 Set of 2 14.00 14.00
Souvenir Sheets
1867 G134 $5 multicolored 3.75 3.75
1868 G134 $6 multicolored 4.50 4.50

Trains G135

No. 1869, each $1.50: a, Pacific Blue Peter, British Eastern. b, Class P36 4-8-4, Russia. c, Class OJ 2-10-2, China. d, Class 12 4-4-2, Belgium. e, Challenger Class 4-6-6-4, US. f, Class 25 4-8-4 Condenser, South Africa.

No. 1870, each $1.50: a, Federal Railways Class 38 4-6-0, Germany. b, Duchess of Hamilton Class 4-6-2, London & Glasgow. c, Class WP 4-6-2, Indian State Railways. d, Class 141R "L'Americane" 282, France (American-built). e, Class A4 4-6-2 Mallard, England. f, Deutche Reichsbahn Class 18 4-6-2, Germany.

$5, Cornish Rivera Express, King Class 4-6-2, Britain. $6, Caledonian "Royal Scot Class," 4-6-0, Britain.

1996, Aug. 28
Sheets of 6, #a-f
1869-1870 G135 Set of 2 13.50 13.50
Souvenir Sheets
1871 G135 $5 multicolored 3.75 3.75
1872 G135 $6 multicolored 4.50 4.50

Christmas Type of 1996

Details of painting, Suffer Little Children to Come Unto Me, by Van Dyck: 15c, Child with beads over shoulder. 25c, Christ anointing head of child. $1, Mother holding infant, father, children. $1.50, Christ, disciples. $2, Father, infant. $4, Christ, children, family.

Each $6: No. 1879, Entire painting, horiz. No. 1880, Adoration of the Shepherds, by Bernaldo Strozzi, horiz.

1996, Nov. 18   Litho.   Perf. 13½x14
1873-1878 A377 Set of 6   7.00 7.00
Souvenir Sheets
1879-1880 A377 Set of 2   9.00 9.00

Souvenir Sheet

China '96 — G136

Painting depicting scene from "Hong Lou Meng." Illustration reduced.

1996, May 8   Litho.   Perf. 13x13½
1881 G136 $2 multicolored   4.00 4.00
No. 1881 was not available until March 1997.

Hong Kong Past and Present G137

No. 1882, Man Ho Temple, each $3: a, 1841. b, 1983.
No. 1883, City of Victoria with view of St. John's Cathedral, each $3: a, 1886. b, 1983.
No. 1884, Victoria Harbor, Hong Kong, each $3: a, 1858. b, 1983.
No. 1885, each $3: a, Treaty of Nanking, 1842. b, Margaret Thatcher signing Joint Declaration, 1984.
No. 1886, Victoria Harbor, each $3: a, Older black & white photograph. b, Modern photograph.

1997, Feb. 12   Litho.   Perf. 14
Sheets of 2, #a-b
1882-1886 G137 Set of 5   22.50 22.50

Hong Kong '97.

UNESCO Type of 1997

Designs: 15c, Kyoto, Japan. 25c, Roman ruins at Trier, Germany. $1, Mount Taishan, China. $1.50, Scandola Nature Reserve, France. $2, Fortress Wall, Dubrovnik, Croatia. $4, Angra Do Heroismo, Portugal.
No. 1893, vert, each $1: a, Sanctuary of Congonhas, Brazil. b, Cartagena, Colombia. c, City of Puebla, Mexico. d, Mayan Ruins, Copan, Honduras. e, Monastery of Popocatepetl, Mexico. f, Galapagos Islands, Ecuador. g, Waterfall, La Amistad Natl. Park, Costa Rica. h, Glaciares Natl. Park, Argentina.
No. 1894, vert, each $1: a, b, c, Kyoto, Japan. d, Ayutthaya, Thailand. e, Temple of Borobudur, Indonesia. f, Monuments, Pattadakal, India. g, Polonnaruwa, Sri Lanka. h, Sagarmatha Natl. Park, Nepal.
No. 1895, each $1.50: a, Cathedral of Notre Dame, France. b, Timbered house, Maulbronn, Germany. c, Himeji-Jo, Japan. d, Ruins, Delphi, Greece. e, Palace of Fontainebleau, France.
Each $6: No. 1896, Temple, Chengde, China. No. 1897, Pre-hispanic city of Teotihuacan, Mexico. No. 1898, Mont St. Michel, France.

1997, Apr. 3   Litho.   Perf. 14
1887-1892 A382 Set of 6   6.75 6.75
Sheets of 8
1893-1894 A382 Set of 2   12.00 12.00
Sheet of 5 + Label
1895 A382 #a.-e.   5.75 5.75
Souvenir Sheets
1896-1898 A382 Set of 3   15.00 15.00

Dogs and Cats G138

Dogs: 35c, Springer spaniel. 75c, Doberman pinscher. $1, Italian spinone, vert. $2, Cocker spaniel, vert.
No. 1903: a, Leonberger. b, Newfoundland. c, Boxer. d, St. Bernard. e, Silky terrier. f, Miniature schnauzer.
No. 1904, Golden retriever puppy.

1997, Apr. 10
1899-1902 G138 Set of 4   3.00 3.00
Sheet of 6
1903 G138 $1.50 #a.-f.   6.75 6.75
Souvenir Sheet
1904 G138 $6 multicolored   6.75 6.75

1997, Apr. 10

Cats: 45c, Abyssinian blue. 50c, Bermese cream, vert. 90c, Persian tortoiseshell and white. $3, Oriental shorthair red Agouti tabby, vert.
No. 1909: a, Siamese chocolate point. b, Oriental shorthair white. c, Burmese sable. d, Abyssinian tabby. e, Persian shaded silver. f, Tonkinese natural mink.

1905-1908 G138 Set of 4   3.75 3.75
Sheet of 6
1909 G138 $1.50 #a.-f.   6.75 6.75
Souvenir Sheet
1910 G138 $6 Sphinx, vert.   6.75 6.75

Prehistoric Animal Type of 1997

Designs: 45c, Stegosaurus. 90c, Diplodocus. $1, Pteranodon, vert. $2, Deinonychus, ankylasaurus, vert.
No. 1915: a, Rhamphorhynchus, brachiosaurus (c, d, e,). b, Archaeopteryx. c, Anurognathus. d, Albertosaurus (f). e, Herrerasaurus. f, Platyhystrix.
Each $6: No. 1916, Hypacrosaurus. No. 1917, Apatosaurus, allosaurus, vert.

1997, Apr. 15   Litho.   Perf. 14
1911-1914 A385 Set of 4   3.00 3.00
1915 A385 $1.50 Sheet of 6, #a.-
                  f.   6.75 6.75
Souvenir Sheets
1916-1917 A385 Set of 2   9.00 9.00

Queen Elizabeth II, Prince Philip, 50th Wedding Anniv. Type of 1997

No. 1918: a, Colored portrait. b, Royal Arms. c, Black and white portrait. d, Black and white portrait in royal attire. e, Sandringham House. f, Queen in blue dress, Prince in uniform.
$6, Wedding portrait.

1997, May 28   Litho.   Perf. 14
1918 A386a $1 Sheet of 6, #a.-f. 4.50 4.50
Souvenir Sheet
1919 A386a $6 multicolored   4.50 4.50

Paintings by Hiroshige Type of 1997

No. 1920: a, Koume Embankment. b, Azuma Shrine and the Entwined Camphor. c, Yanagishima. d, Inside Akiba Shrine, Ukeji. e, Distant View of Kinryuzan Temple and Azuma Bridge. f, Night View of Matsuchiyama and the San'ya Canal.
See: No. 1921, Five Pines, Onagi Canal. No. 1922, Spiral Hall, Five Hundred Rakan Temple.

1997, May 28   Perf. 13½x14
1920 A387 $1.50 Sheet of 6,
                  #a.-f.   8.50 8.50
Souvenir Sheets
1921-1922 A387 Set of 2   11.00 11.00

Heinrich von Stephan Type of 1997
1997, May 28   Litho.   Perf. 14

Portrait of Von Stephan and: No. 1923: a, The Pony Express, 1860-61. b, UPU emblem. c, Steam locomotive postal delivery, 1800's.
$6, Camel courier, Baghdad.

1923 A388 $1.50 Sheet of 3, #a.-
                  c.   2.50 2.50
Souvenir Sheet
1924 A388 $6 multicolored   4.50 4.50

PACIFIC 97.

Paul P. Harris Type of 1997
1997, May 28

Designs: $3, Women in Burkina Faso pumping well water, portrait of Harris. $6, Early Rotary parade float.

1925 A389 $3 multicolored   2.25 2.25
Souvenir Sheet
1926 A389 $6 multicolored   4.50 4.50

Grimm's Fairy Tale and Mother Goose Types of 1997
1997, May 28   Perf. 13½x14

Scenes from "The Fox and the Geese:" No. 1927: a, Fox, geese. b, Geese singing as fox waves knife, fork. c, Fox asleep, geese celebrating. No. 1928, Fox lurking in forest, horiz. No. 1929, Girl with black sheep.

1927 A391 $2 Sheet of 3, #a.-c.   4.50 4.50
Souvenir Sheets
Perf. 14x13½, 14
1928 A391 $6 multicolored   4.50 4.50
1929 A392 $6 multicolored   4.50 4.50

1998 Winter Olympic Games, Nagano G139

Designs: 90c, Downhill skier. $2, Luge. $3, Male figure skater. $5, Speed skater in blue hat.
No. 1934: a, Downhill skier in air. b, Freestyle skier. c, Curling. d, Ski jumper. e, Bobsled. f, Biathlon. g, Speed skater in yellow and red hat. h, Hockey. i, Cross-country skier.
Each $6: No. 1935, Luge, diff., vert. No. 1936, Female figure skater.

1997, June 26   Perf. 14
1930-1933 G139 Set of 4   8.25 8.25
1934 G139 $1 Sheet of 9, #a.-i.   6.75 6.75
Souvenir Sheets
1935-1936 G139 Set of 2   9.00 9.00

Return of Hong Kong to China Type

Chinese flag in foreground, "Hong Kong" in English and Chinese with city scene showing through words: $1, Night scene. $1.25, Daytime view of skyscrapers. $1.50, Skyline at night, horiz. $2, View of harbor, horiz.

1997, July 1
1937-1940 A394 Set of 4   4.50 4.50
Nos. 1937-1938 were issued in sheets of 4. Nos. 1939-1940 are 59x28mm and were issued in sheets of 3.

Fish G140

Designs: 10c, Wimplefish. 15c, Clown triggerfish. 25c, Ringed emperor angelfish. 35c, Hooded butterfly fish. 45c, Semicircle angelfish. 75c, Scribbled angelfish. 90c, Threadfin butterfly fish. $1, Clown surgeonfish.

1997, July 22   Litho.   Perf. 14
1941 G140 10c multicolored   .20   .20
1942 G140 15c multicolored   .20   .20
1943 G140 25c multicolored   .20   .20
1944 G140 35c multicolored   .25   .25
1945 G140 45c multicolored   .35   .35
1946 G140 75c multicolored   .55   .55
1947 G140 90c multicolored   .70   .70
1948 G140 $1 multicolored   .75   .75
      Nos. 1941-1948 (8)   3.20 3.20

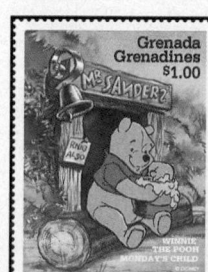

Winnie the Pooh G141

#1949: a, Winnie the Pooh. b, Kanga & Roo. c, Eeyore. d, Tigger. e, Piglet & Gopher. f, Rabbit.
$6, Christopher Robin.

1997, Aug. 7   Litho.   Perf. 13½x14
1949 G141 $1 Sheet of 6, #a.-f.   5.50 5.50
Souvenir Sheet
1950 G141 $6 multicolored   5.50 5.50

1998 World Cup Soccer Type of 1997

Team pictures: 10c, Italy, 1934. 20c, Angola. 45c, Brazil, 1958. $1, Uruguay, 1950. $1.50, West Germany, 1974. $5, Italy, 1938.
World Cup winners: No. 1951: a, England. b, W. Germany, 1954. c, Uruguay. d, West Germany, 1990. e, Argentina, 1986. f, Brazil. g, Argentina, 1978. h, W. Germany 1974.
Tournament stars, vert.: No. 1952: a, Ademir, Brazil. b, Kocsis, Hungary. c, Leonidas, Brazil. d, Nejedly, Czechoslovakia. e, Schiavio, Italy. f, Stabile, Uruguay. g, Pele, Brazil. h, Walter, W. Germany.
Each $6: No. 1953, Shearer, England, vert. No. 1954, Paulao, Angola.

1997, Aug. 11
1950A-1950F A397 Set of 6   6.25 6.25
Sheets of 8, #a-h
1951-1952 A397 Set of 2   12.00 12.00
Souvenir Sheets
1953-1954 A397 Set of 2   9.00 9.00

Fish Type of 1997

$2, Tursiops truncatus. $5, Balistes vetula. $10, Pterois volitans. $20, Equetus lanceolatus.

1997, July 22   Litho.   Perf. 14
1955 G140 $2 multicolored   1.50 1.50
1956 G140 $5 multicolored   3.75 3.75
1957 G140 $10 multicolored   7.50 7.50
1958 G140 $20 multicolored   15.00 15.00
      Nos. 1955-1958 (4)   27.75 27.75

Sealed with a Kiss — G142

Characters from Disney's classic animated films: No. 1959: a, Snow White, 1937. b, Pinocchio, 1940. c, Peter Pan, 1953. d, Cinderella, 1950. e, The Little Mermaid, 1989. f, Beauty and the Beast, 1991. g, Aladdin, 1992. h, Pocahontas, 1995. i, Hunchback of Notre Dame, 1996.
$5, The Aristocats, 1970, vert.

1997, Aug. 7   Litho.   Perf. 14x13½
1959 G142 $1 Sheet of 9, #a.-f.   6.75 6.75
Souvenir Sheet
Perf. 13½x14
1960 G142 $5 multicolored   3.75 3.75

Butterflies of the World G143

75c, Polyura dehaani. 90c, Polyura dolon. $1, Charaxes candiope. $1.50, Pantaporia punctata. $2, Charaxes etesippe. $3, Charaxes castor.
No. 1967, Euphaedra, each $1.50: a, Francina. b, Eleus. c, Harpalyce. d, Cyparissa. e, Gausape. f, Imperialis.
No. 1968, each $1.50: a, Euthalia confucius. b, Euthalia kardama. c, Limenitis albomaculata. d, Hestina assimilis. e, Kalima inachus. f, Euthalia teutoides.
Each $6: No. 1969, Charaxes numenes, vert. No. 1970, Charaxes nobilis, vert.

1997, Aug. 12   Perf. 14
1961-1966 G143 Set of 6   7.25 7.25
Sheets of 6, #a-f
1967-1968 G143 Set of 2   15.00 15.00
Souvenir Sheets
1969-1970 G143 Set of 2   10.00 10.00

James Dean
(1931-55),
Actor
G144

Various portraits.

1997, Aug. 22   *Perf. 14x13½*
1971 G144 $1 Sheet of 9, #a.-i.   6.75 6.75

Mushrooms — G145

Designs: 75c, Clitocybe metachroa. 90c, Clavulinopsis helvola. $1, Lycoperdon pyriforme. $1.50, Auricularia auricula-judae. $2, Clathrus archeri. $3, Lactarius trivialis.
No. 1978: a, Entoloma incanum. b, Coprinus atramentarius. c, Mycena polygramma. d, Lepista nuda. e, Pleurotis cornucopiae. f, Laccaria amethystina.
Each $6: No. 1979, Amanita muscaria. No. 1980, Morchella esculenta.

1997, Sept. 4   *Perf. 14*
1972-1977 G145   Set of 6   6.75 6.75
1978 G145 $1.50 Sheet of 6, #a.-
      f.   6.75 6.75
Souvenir Sheets
1979-1980 G145   Set of 2   9.00 9.00

G146   Orchids — G147

Designs: 35c, Symphyglossum sanguineum. 45c, Doritaenopsis "Mythic Beauty." 75c, Odontoglossum cervantesii. 90c, Cattleya "Pumpernickel." $1, Vanda "Patricia Law." $1.50, Odontonia "Debutante." $2, Laeliocattleya "Mini Purple." $3, Phragmipedium "Dominiarium."
No. 1989, each $1: a, Cymbidium "Showgirl." b, Disa "Blackii." c, Phalaenopsis aphrodite. d, Iwanagaara "Apple Blossum." e, Masdevallia "Copper Angel." f, Paphiopedilum micranthum. g, Paphiopedilum "Claire de Lune." h, Cattleya forbesii. i, Dendrobium "Dawn Maree."
No. 1990, each $1: a, Lycaste "Aquila." b, Brassolaeliocattleya "Dorothy Bertsch." c, Phalaenopsis "Zuma Urchin." d, Promenaea xanthina. e, Amesiella philippinensis. f, Brassocattleya "Angel Lace." g, Brassoepidsendrum "Peggy Ann." h, Miltonia seine. i, Sophralaeliocattleya "Precious Stones."
No. 1991, each $1.50: a, Miltoniosis "Jean Sabourin." b, Cymbididium "Red Beauty." c, Brassocattleya "Green Dragon." d, Phalaenopsis hybrid. e, Laelio cattleya "Mary Ellen Carter." f, Disa hybrid.
No. 1992, each $1.50: a, Lycaste macrobulbon. b, Cochleanthes discolor. c, Cymbidium "Nang Carpenter." d, Paphiopedilum "Clair de Lune." e, Masdevallia caudata. f, Cymbidum "Showgirl."
$5, Phalenopsis "Medford Star." $6, Brassolaeliocattleya "Mem. Dorothy Bertsch."

1997, Sept. 4
1981-1988 G146   Set of 8   7.50 7.50
Sheets of 9, #a-i
1989-1990 G147   Set of 2   13.50 13.50
Sheets of 6, #a-f
1991-1992 G146   Set of 2   13.50 13.50

Souvenir Sheets
1993 G146 $5 multicolored   3.75 3.75
1994 G146 $6 multicolored   4.50 4.50

Famous
Composers,
Musicians
G148

No. 1995, each $1: a, Beethoven. b, Tchaikovsky. c, J.S. Bach. d, Chopin. e, Stravinsky. f, Haydn. g, Mahler. h, Rossini.
Each $6: No. 1996, Mozart. No. 1997, Schubert.

1997, Oct. 10   *Litho.*   *Perf. 14½x14*
Sheet of 8
1995 G148   #a.-h. + label   6.00 6.00
Souvenir Sheets
1996-1997 G148   Set of 2   9.00 9.00

Diana,
Princess
of Wales
(1961-97)
G149

Various portraits of Diana wearing various hats, scenes following her death: No. 1998: a, Buckingham Palace. b, Island, Spencer Estate, Althorp. c, Westminster Abbey. d, Gate, Spencer Estate. e, Gate, Kensington Palace. g, Spencer Estate, Althorp.
$6, Diana smelling flowers in front of Kensington Palace.

1997, Nov. 10   *Perf. 14*
1998 G149 $1.50 Sheet of 6, #a.-
      f.   6.75 6.75
Souvenir Sheet
1999 G149 $6 multicolored   4.50 4.50
No. 1999 contains one 60x40mm stamp.

Christmas Art Type of 1997

Entire paintings, details, or sculptures: 20c, Choir of Angels, by Simon Marmion. 75c, The Annunciation, by Giotto. 90c, Festival of the Rose Garlands, by Albrecht Durer. $1.50, Madonna with Two Angels, by Hans Memling. $2, The Ognissanti Madonna, by Giotto. $3, Angel with Candlestick, by Michelangelo.
Each $6: No. 2006, Cupid Commemorating a Marriage by Incising on a Table, by Jean-Baptiste Huet, horiz. No. 2007, The Rising of the Sun, by Francois Boucher, horiz.

1997, Dec. 5   *Litho.*   *Perf. 14*
2000-2005 A402   Set of 6   12.50 12.50
Souvenir Sheets
2006-2007 A402   Set of 2   9.00 9.00

Marine Life Type of 1997

No. 2008, each $1: a, Holocanthus ciliaris. b, Ballstoides conspicillum. c, Chaetodon quadrimaculatus. d, Microspathodon chrysurus. e, Halichoeres garnoti. f, Gramma loreto. g, Liopropoma carmabi. h, Lactophrys triqueter. i, Cephalopolis miniatus.
Each $6: No. 2009, Carcharhinus melanopterus. No. 2010, Obistognathus aurifrons, vert.

1997, Dec. 12   *Litho.*   *Perf. 14*
2008 A386   Sheet of 9, #a.-i.   6.75 6.75
Souvenir Sheets
2009-2010 A386   Set of 2   9.00 9.00

New Year 1998
(Year of the
Tiger) — G150

Die Cut Perf. 11
1998, Feb. 10   Litho.
Self-Adhesive
2011 G150 $1.50 Hologram   3.00
Souvenir Sheet
2012 G150 $3 like #2011   5.00
No. 2011 was issued in sheets of 4. No. 2012 contains one 52x65mm stamp.

Great Ships, Shipwrecks — G151

Ships — #2013: a, CSS Alabama. b, Persia. c, Ariel. d, CSS Florida. e, Great Eastern. f, Jacob Bell. g, Star of India. h, Robert E. Lee. i, US Monitor Passaic. j, Madagascar. k, HMS Devastation. l, General Grant.
"Gone with the Wind," vert. — #2014: a, Clark Gable. b, Blockade runner wrecked on Sullivan's Island, North Carolina, 1863. c, Margaret Mitchell. d, George Alfred Trenholm, model for character Rhett Butler. e, Dock Street Theater, confiscated from Trenholm after Civil War. f, Howlet sinks off Charleston, South Carolina, 1865. g, USS Tecumseh sunk by Confederate gunboats, 1864. h, City jail, where Trenholm was imprisoned, 1865.
Each $6: No. 2015, Nashville sinks the Union clipper, Harvey Birch, vert. No. 2016, Dr. Lee Spence, expert on shipwrecks and sunken treasures, Alabama sinking Hatteras off Texas coast.

1998, May 7   *Litho.*   *Perf. 14*
2013 G151   75c Sheet of 12, #a.-
      l.   6.75 6.75
2014 G151 $1 Sheet of 8, #a.-h.   6.00 6.00
Souvenir Sheets
2015-2016 G151   Set of 2   9.00 9.00
#2015-2016 contain one 57x43mm stamp.

Modern,
Future
Aircraft
G152

70c, Concept strike fighter. 90c, Concept space shuttle. $2, Concept air & space jet. $3, V Jet II.
No. 2021: a, Velocity 173 RG Elite. b, Davis DA 9. c, Concorde. d, Voyager. e, Factimobile. f, RAF 2000. g, Boomerang. h, N1M Flying Wing.
Each $6: No. 2022, Gee-Bee replica. No. 2023, Concept Aeropod.

1998, May 13
2017-2020 G152   Set of 4   5.50 5.50
2021 G152 $1 Sheet of 8, #a.-h.   6.50 6.50
Souvenir Sheets
2022-2023 G152   Set of 2   9.00 9.00
No. 2022 is inscribed "Delmar."

Orchids — G153

Designs: $1, Laclia tenebrosa. $1.50, Phragmipedium besseae. $2, Pschopsis papilio. $3, Masdevallia coccinea.
No. 2028, each $1: a, Lycaste deppei. b, Dendrobium victoriae. c, Dendrobium nobile. d, Cymbidium danyanum. e, Cymbidium starbright. f, Cymbidium giganteum. g, Chysis aurea. h, Broughtonia sanguinea. i, Cattleya guttata.
No. 2029, each $1: a, Calanthe vestita. b, Cattleya bicolor. c, Laelia anceps. d, Epidendrum prismatocarpum. e, Coelogyne ochracea. f, Doritaenopsis eclantant. g, Laelia gouldiana. h, Encyclia vitellina. i, Maxillaria praestans.

Each $6: No. 2030, Masdevallia ignea. No. 2031, Encyclia brassavolae.

1998, May 19
2024-2027 G153   Set of 4   5.75 5.75
Sheets of 9, #a-i
2028-2029 G153   Set of 2   13.50 13.50
Souvenir Sheets
2030-2031 G153   Set of 2   9.00 9.00

Sea Birds Type of 1998

75c, Bonaparte's gull. 90c, Western sandpiper. $2, Great black-backed gull. $3, Dotterell.
No. 2036, each $1.50: a, Terns. b, Brown pelican. c, Black-legged kittiwake. d, Herring gull. e, Lesser noddy. f, Kittiwake.
No. 2037, each $1.50: a, Whimbrels. b, Golden white-tailed tropic bird. c, Arctic tern. d, Ruddy turnstones. e, Imperial shag. f, Magellan gull.
Each $5: No. 2038, Yellow-nosed albatross, vert. No. 2039, Broad-billed prion.

1998, June 30   *Litho.*   *Perf. 14*
2032-2035 A408   Set of 4   5.50 5.50
Sheets of 6, #a-f
2036-2037 A408   Set of 2   14.50 14.50
Souvenir Sheets
2038-2039 A408   Set of 2   8.50 8.50

Diana, Princess of Wales (1961-97) — G155

Diana in front of Kensington Palace: No. 2040, Wearing tiara, ruffled dress. No. 2041, Wearing white dress, pearls.

Litho. & Embossed
1998, July 14   *Die Cut 7½*
2040 G155 $20 gold
2041 G155 $20 gold & multi

Intl. Year of the Ocean Type

No. 2042: a, Great black-backed gull. b, Common dolphin. c, Seal. d, Amazonian catfish. e, Shark. f, Goldfish. g, Cyathopharynx. h, Whale. i, Telmatochromis. j, Crab. k, Octopus. l, Turtle.
No. 2043: a, Dolphins. b, Seal. c, Turtle. d, Leopard shark. e, Flame angelfish. f, Syndontis. g, Lamprologus. h, Kryptopterus bicirrhus. i, Pterophyllum scalare. j, Swimming pancake. k, Cowfish. l, Sea horse.
Each $6: No. 2044, Tetraodon mbu. No. 2045, Goldfish.

1998, Aug. 19   *Litho.*   *Perf. 14*
Sheets of 12
2042 A411   75c #a.-l.   6.75 6.75
2043 A411   90c #a.-l.   8.00 8.00
Souvenir Sheets
2044-2045 A411   Set of 2   9.00 9.00

Gandhi Type of 1998

Portraits of Gandhi.

1998, Sept. 15   *Litho.*   *Perf. 14*
2046 A413 $1 multicolored   .75 .75
Souvenir Sheet
2047 A413 $6 multicolored   4.50 4.50
No. 2046 was issued in sheets of 4.

Picasso Type of 1998

Paintings: 45c, Bust of a Woman, 1943, vert. $2, Three Musicians, 1921. $3, Studio at La Californie, 1956.
$5, Woman with a Blue Hat, 1901.

Perf. 14½x14, 14x14½
1998, Sept. 15
2048-2050 A414 Set of 3   4.25 4.25
Souvenir Sheet
2051 A414 $5 multicolored   3.75 3.75

Delacroix Type of 1998

Paintings — #2052: a, The Natchez. b, Christ and His Disciples Crossing the Sea of Galilee. c, Sunset. d, Moroccans Outside the Walls of Tangier. e, The Fireplace. f, Forest View with a Oak Tree. g, View of the Harbor at Dieppe. h, Arabs Skirmishing in the Mountains.
$5, Orphan Girl in a Cemetary, vert.

1998, Sept. 15   Litho.   Perf. 14
2052 A415 $1 Sheet of 8, #a.-h. 6.00 6.00
Souvenir Sheet
2053 A415 $5 multicolored   4.50 4.50

Organization of American States Type

1998, Sept. 15
2054 A416 $1 multicolored   .75 .75

Diana Type of 1998

1998   Perf. 14½
2055   A417 $1.50 multicolored   1.10 1.10
Self-Adhesive
Serpentine Die Cut Perf. 11½
Sheet of 1
Size: 53x65mm
2055A A417 $8 Diana, build-
                     ings

No. 2055 was issued in sheets of 6. Soaking in water may affect the multi-layer image of No. 2055A.
Issued: $1.50, 9/15; $8, 11/5/98.

Ferrari Type of 1998

No. 2056: a, 275 GTB. b, 340 MM. c, 250 GT SWB Berlinetta SEFAC "Hot Rod."
$5, First Ferrari Cabriolet (011-S).

1998, Sept. 15   Perf. 14
2056 A418 $2 Sheet of 3, #a.-c. 4.50 4.50
Souvenir Sheet
2057 A418 $5 multicolored   4.50 4.50

No. 2057 contains one 91x35mm stamp.

Scout Jamboree Type of 1998

Designs: 90c, Scout sign. $1.50, Lord Baden-Powell. $5, Scout salute.
$6, Lord Baden-Powell, diff., vert.

1998, Sept. 15
2058-2060 A419 Set of 3   5.75 5.75
Souvenir Sheet
2061 A419 $6 multicolored   4.50 4.50

Royal Air Force Type of 1998

No. 2062, each $2: a, Chinook. b, BAe Harrier GR5. c, Panavia Tornado F3 ADV. d, Chinook HC2 carrying 105mm light gun.
No. 2063, each $2: a, Tornado GR1. b, BAe Hawk TIA. c, Sepecat Jaguar GRI. d, Harrier GR7.
Each $6: No. 2064, Eurofighter 2000, Hunter. No. 2065, Biplane, hawk in flight. No. 2066, Head of hawk, biplane. No. 2067, Eurofighter 2000, Tornado.

1998, Sept. 15
Sheets of 4, #a-d
2062-2063 A420 Set of 2   12.00 12.00
Souvenir Sheets
2064-2067 A420 Set of 2   15.00 15.00

Disney Christmas Trains — G156

Silly Symphony Railroad — #2068, each $1: a, Santa in locomotive, rabbit. b, Giraffe, elephant, tiger. c, Wolf, Three Little Pigs. d, Robin Hood blowing horn, Jiminy Cricket, penguins, children. e, Geese, Indian boy, turtle in caboose.
Mickey's Toontown Christmas Train — #2069, each $1: a, Mickey in locomotive. b, Pluto, chipmunks in coal car. c, Donald, Daisy Duck in passenger car. d, Goofy leading Huey, Dewey, & Louie in caroling. e, Minnie in caboose.
Pooh's Railroad — #2070, each $1: a, Piglet as engineer. b, Winnie the Pooh shoveling honey. c, Rabbit, Owl. d, Kanga, Roo, Christopher Robin. e, Eeyore, Tigger.
Each $6: No. 2071, Santa setting up toy train under Christmas tree. No. 2072, Mickey as engineer. No. 2073, Winnie the Pooh reading paper, Rabbit, Piglet.

1998, Oct. 15   Perf. 14x13½
Sheets of 5, #a-e
2068-2070 G156 Set of 3   11.50 11.50
Souvenir Sheets
2071-2073 G156 Set of 3   13.50 13.50

New Year 1999 (Year of the Rabbit) Type

Various rabbits, color of country name: a, green. b, orange. c, red.

1999, Jan. 4 Litho. Die Cut Perf. 9
Self-Adhesive
Sheet of 3
2074 A425 $1.50 gold & multi
            #a.-c.   3.50 3.50

No. 2074b has point of triangle down.

Queen Elizabeth II and Prince Philip, 50th Wedding Anniv. — G157

Litho. & Embossed
1999, Jan. 8   Die Cut Perf. 7
Without Gum
2075 G157 $20 gold & multi

Australia '99, World Stamp Expo G158

Dinosaurs — #2076: a, Troodon. b, Camptosaurus. c, Parasaurolophus. d, Dryosaurus. e, Gallimimus. f, Camarasaurus (all vert.).
#2077: a, Duckbill. b, Lambeosaurus. c, Iguanodon. d, Euoplocephalus. e, Triceratops. f, Brachiosaurus. g, Ponoptosaurus. h, Stegosaurus.
Each $6: #2078, Edmontosaurus. #2079, Tyrannosaurus, vert. #2080, Halticosaurus, vert.

1999, Mar. 1   Litho.   Perf. 14
2076 G158 $1 Sheet of 6,
                    #a.-f.   4.50 4.50
2077 G158 $1.50 Sheet of 8,
                    #a.-h.   9.25 9.25
Souvenir Sheets
2078-2080 G158 Set of 3   13.50 13.50

Trains G159

Designs: 15c, India, 4-4-0 express passenger and mail engine. 75c, Ireland, 4-4-0. 90c, Canada, 4-6-0. $1.50, India, 4-4-0 express. $2, Australia, 4-6-2. $3, Great Britain, Stirling 0-4-2.
No. 2087, each 2: a, Belgium, type 4-4-0. b, Sweden, class "Cc" type 4-4-0. c, Chile, 0-6-4. d, Bolivia, Fairlie-type double engine.
No. 2088, each $2: a, Belgium, 4-cylinder 4-6-0. b, England, 4-cylinder 4-6-0. c, Northern Ireland, 2-cylinder compound 4-4-0. d, Holland, 4-4-0.
No. 2089, each $2: a, Switzerland, 0-8-0. b, Ireland, 0-6-0. c, US 4-6-0. d, Great Britain, Prince of Wales class 4-2-2.
No. 2090, each $2: a, Ireland, narrow gauge 2-4-2. b, Russia, 0-8-0. c, England, Ivatt large-boilered Atlantic. d, Germany, Atlantic type express.
No. 2091, each $2: a, France, 4-6-0. b, New Zealand, 2-6-4. c, Burma, 4-4-4. d, Malaya, 4-6-0.
Each $6: No. 2092, France, 4-4-0. No. 2093, Italy, 0-6-4.

1999, Apr. 12   Litho.   Perf. 14
2081-2086 G159 Set of 6   6.25 6.25
Sheets of 4, #a-d
2087-2091 G159 Set of 5   30.00 30.00
Souvenir Sheets
2092-2093 G159 Set of 2   9.00 9.00

Flora and Fauna Type of 1999

Designs: 75c, Porkfish. 90c, Leatherback turtle. $1.50, Ruby-throated hummingbird. $2, Theope eudocia.
No. 2098, vert., each $1: a, White-tailed tropicbird. b, Laughing gull. c, Palm tree. d, Humpback whale. e, Painted bunting. f, Common grackle. g, Green anole. h, Morpho peleides. i, Prepoua meandor.
No. 2099, vert., each $1: a, Common dolphin. b, Catonephele numiti. c, Sooty tern. d, Vermilion flycatcher. e, Blue grosbeak. f, Great egret. g, Actinote pellenea. h, Anteos clorinade. i, Common iguana.
Each $6: No. 2100, Bannaquit. No. 2101, Beay gregory.

1999, Apr. 26
2094-2097 A430 Set of 4   3.75 3.75
Sheets of 9, #a-i
2098-2099 A430 Set of 2   13.50 13.50
Souvenir Sheets
2100-2101 A430 Set of 2   9.00 9.00

Hokusai Type of 1999

Entire paintings or details, horiz. — #2102, each $1.50: a, A Breeze on a Fine Day. b, Ejiri. c, Horse drawings (kicking up hind legs). d, Horse drawings (with head down). e, View Along the Bank of the Sumida River. f, Thunderstorm Below the Mountain.
No. 2103. each $1.50: a, Fuchû. b, Doll Fair at Fikkendana. c, Sumo Wrestlers (with arms locked). d, Sumo Wrestlers (one head butting). e, Sôjô Henjô. f, Twin Gardens Gateway of the Asakusa Kannon Temple.
Each $6: No. 2104 Kôbô Daishi Exorcising Demon that Causes Sickness. No. 2105, Stretching Cloth.

1999, May 24   Litho.   Perf. 14x13½
Sheets of 6, #a-f
2102-2103 A431 Set of 2   13.50 13.50
Souvenir Sheet
2104-2105 A431 Set of 2   9.00 9.00

John H. Glenn's Return to Space G160

Portraits — #2106: a, Thumbs up, 1998 flight. b, Receiving NASA Service Award from Pres. Kennedy, 1962. c, Talking to Ground Control from Discovery, 1998. d, Climbing out of Friendship 7, 1962. e, Being checked for balance, 1998. f, Climbing into Friendship 7, 1962.
No. 2107, vert.: a, Portrait as Ohio Senator, 1974. b, Official portrait, 1962. c, Suit-up test, 1998. d, Suiting up for Discovery, 1998. e,

Meeting press after Discovery flight, 1998. f, Smiling aboard Discovery, 1998. g, Medical research, 1998. h, Official portrait, 1998.

1999, May 24   Perf. 14x14½
Sheets of 6 and 8
2106 G160 $1 #a.-f.   4.50 4.50
2107 G160 $1 #a.-h.   6.00 6.00

Goethe Type of 1999

No. 2108: a, Peasants dancing under the linden tree. b, Faust dreams of soaring above the mortal.
No. 2109, Portrait of Goethe.

1999, May 24   Perf. 14
2108 A432 $3 Sheet of 3, #a.-b.,
                Grenada #2858b 6.75 6.75
Souvenir Sheet
2109 A432 $6 multi   4.50 4.50

IBRA '99 World Stamp Expo Type of 1999

IBRA '99 emblem, Luckenbach sailing ship and: No. 2110, 35c, Thurn and Taxis #1. No. 2113, $3, North German Confederation #1. Emblem, Leipzig-Dresden Railway and: No. 2111, 45c, Schleswig-Holstein #1. No. 2112, $1.50, Oldenburg #4.
$6, Cover showing pair of Thurn & Taxis #1. Illustration reduced.

1999, May 24   Litho.   Perf. 14
2110-2113 A433 Set of 4   4.00 4.00
Souvenir Sheet
2114 A433 $6 multicolored   4.50 4.50

Philexfrance '99 Type

Souvenir Sheets
Designs, each $6: No. 2115, Co-co 7000 class high speed electric locomotive. No. 2116, Cha Pelon 4-8-0. Illustration reduced.

1999, May 24   Litho.   Perf. 14
2115-2116 A435 Set of 2   7.00 7.00

Beginning with Nos. 2117-2118, stamps from Grenada Grenadines will be inscribed GRENADA / Carriacou & Petite Martinique.

Wedding of Prince Edward and Sophie Rhys-Jones Type

No. 2117: a, Edward. b, Sophie, Edward. c, Sophie.
$6, Couple.

1999, June 18   Litho.   Perf. 13½
2117 A436 $3 Sheet of 3, #a.-c. 6.75 6.75
Souvenir Sheet
2118 A436 $6 multicolored   4.50 4.50

UN Rights of the Child Type of 1999

No. 2119: a, Boy. b, Liv Ullman, UNICEF's first woman ambassador. c, Woman.
$6, Maurice Pate, founding director of UNICEF.

1999, May 24   Litho.   Perf. 14
2119 A437 $3 Sheet of 3, #a.-c. 6.75 6.75
Souvenir Sheet
2120 A437 $6 multicolored   4.50 4.50

Queen Mother Type of 1999
Gold frames

No. 2121: a, Lady Elizabeth Bowles-Lyon. b, Queen Elizabeth in Rhodesia, 1957. c, Queen Elizabeth, Princess Elizabeth, and Princess Anne, 1950. d, Queen Mother, 1988.
$6, Queen Mother, Berlin.

1999, Aug. 16
Sheet of 4
2121 A440 $2 #a.-d. + label   6.00 6.00
Souvenir Sheet
2122 A440 $6 multicolored   4.50 4.50

No. 2122 contains one 38x50mm stamp. Margins of sheets are embossed. See Nos. 2369-2370.

Litho. & Embossed
Die Cut Perf. 8¾
Without Gum
2122A A440a $20 gold & multi

Famous People Type of 1999

Actors — #2123: a, George Raft (1895-1980). b, Raft in movie scene. c, Fatty Arbuckle (1887-1933) in movie scene. d, Portrait of Arbuckle. e, Buster Keaton (1895-

1966). f, Keaton in movie scene. g, Harold Lloyd (1893-1971) in movie scene. h, Portrait of Lloyd.

No. 2124: a, James Cagney (1899-1986). b, Cagney in movie scene. c, Edward G. Robinson (1893-1973). d, Robinson in movie scene. $6, Charlie Chaplin (1889-1977).

1999, Aug. 20   Litho.   Perf. 14
2123	A426	$1 Sheet of 8, #a.-h.	6.00	6.00
2124	A426	$2 Sheet of 4, #a.-d.	6.00	6.00

Souvenir Sheet
2125	A426	$6 multicolored	4.50	4.50

Space Exploration — G161

No. 2126, each $1.50: a, Sputnik I. b, Explorer I. c, Telstar I. d, Marisat I. e, Long Duration Exposure Facility. f, Hubble Space Telescope.

No. 2127, vert, each $1.50: a, X-15. b, Mercury Redstone 3 rocket, Freedom 7. c, Mercury Atlas 6 rocket, Friendship 7. d, Gemini 4, Edward H. White II. e, Saturn V rocket, Edwin Aldrin. f, Lunar rover.

Each $6: No. 2128, Space Shuttle Columbia. No. 2129, Mars Pathfinder.

1999, Oct. 8   Litho.   Perf. 14
Sheets of 6, #a.-f.
2126-2127	G161	Set of 2	13.50	13.50

Souvenir Sheets
2128-2129	G161	Set of 2	9.00	9.00

Christmas Type of 1999

Christmas plants: 15c, Poinsettia. 35c, Holly. 75c, Fir tree. $1.50, Ivy. $3, Geranium. $6, The Adoration of the Magi.

1999, Nov. 23   Litho.   Perf. 13¾
2130-2134	A444	Set of 5	4.25	4.25

Souvenir Sheet
2135	A444	$6 multicolored	4.50	4.50

Kirk Douglas (b. 1916), Actor G162

Douglas in various poses.

1999   Litho.   Perf. 13¾
2136	G162	$1.50 Sheet of 6, #a.-f.	6.75	6.75

Souvenir Sheet
2137	G162	$6 multi	4.50	4.50

Elvis Presley G163

Presley in various poses.

1999
Sheet of 6
2138	G163	$1.50 #a.-f.	6.75	6.75

Millennium Type of 2000

Highlights of 1970s — No. 2139: a, Salvador Allende elected Pres. of Chile. b, Earth Day. c, CAT scan introduced. d, Pres. Nixon

goes to China. e, Massacre at Olympics. f, Gas shortages. g, Sydney Opera House opens. h, Pres. Nixon resigns. i, New theory of black holes. j, US bicentennial. k, 1st "Test tube" baby. l, Pope John Paul II visits Poland. m, Iran's Islamic Revolution. n, Concorde makes 1st flight. o, Charles de Gaulle dies. p, Camp David agreements (60x40mm). q, Mother Teresa wins Nobel Peace Prize.

Highlights of 1300-1350 — No. 2140: a, Robert the Bruce crowned King of Scotland. b, Giotto paints frescoes. c, Mansa Musa rules Mali. d, Dante completes "The Divine Comedy." e, Noh theater developed in Japan. f, Tenochtitlan founded by Aztecs. g, Ibn Battutah journeys to Africa and Asia. h, Munich fire. i, Ivan I of Russia increases Moscow's importance. j, Hundred Years' War begins. k, First use of cannons in Europe. l, Black Death devastates Europe. m, Boccaccio begins writing "Decameron." n, Eyeglasses developed in Italy. o, Plate armor replaces chain mail. p, Grand Canal of China completed. (60x40mm). q, Migration of Maoris to New Zealand.

Sea Exploration — No. 2141: a, Ferdinand Magellan. b, Restless seas. c, Queen Elizabeth I. d, Albatrosses. e, Penguins. f, Tahiti. g, Breadfruit. h, Easter Island. i, Maori carving. j, Lobster. k, Orchid. l, Walrus. m, Kangaroo. n, The Beagle. o, Frigatebird. p, Strait of Magellan (60x40mm). q, Capt. James Cook.

2000   Litho.   Perf. 12¾x12½
Sheets of 17
2139	A450	20c #a.-q., + label	2.50	2.50
2140	A450	50c #a.-q., + label	6.25	6.25
2141	A450	50c #a.-q., + label	6.25	6.25

Issued: #2139, 3/28; #2140-2141, 2/1.

Souvenir Sheet

New Year 2000 (Year of the Dragon) — G164

2000, Feb. 5   Perf. 13¾
2142	G164	$4 multi	3.00 3.00

G165

Designs: 75c, Barn swallow. 90c, Caribbean coot. $2, Common moorhen. $3, Orange-winged parrot.

No. 2147, each $1: a, Red-collared lorikeet. b, Citron-crested cockatoo. c, Stella's lorikeet. d, Leadbeator's cockatoo. e, Golden conure. f, Red-spotted parakeet. g, Nobel macaw. h, Goffins cockatoo. i, Sun conure.

No. 2148, each $1: a, Turquoise parakeet. b, Scarlet-chested parakeet. c, Red-capped parakeet. d, Eastern rosella. e, Budgerigar. f, Orange-flanked parakeet. g, Mallee ringneck. h, Red-rumped parakeet. i, Yellow-fronted parakeet.

No. 2149, each $1.50: a, Puerto Rican emerald. b, Green mango. c, Red-legged

thrush. d, Red-crowned parrot. e, Hispaniolan parrot. f, Yellow-crowned parrot.

No. 2150, each $1.50: a, Yellow-shouldered blackbird. b, Troupial. c, Green-throated Carib. d, Black-hooded parakeet. e, Scarlet tanager. f, Yellow-crowned bishop.

Each $6: No. 2151, Puerto Rican lizard-cuckoo. No. 2152, Pin-tailed whydah, vert. No. 2153, Pennant's parakeet. No. 2154, Scarlet macaw, vert.

Illustration G166 reduced.

2000, Mar. 1   Litho.   Perf. 14
2143-2146	G165	Set of 4	5.50	5.50

Sheets of 9, #a.-i.
2147-2148	G166	Set of 2	15.00	15.00

Sheets of 6, #a.-f.
2149-2150	G165	Set of 2	15.00	15.00

Souvenir Sheets   Perf. 13¾
2151-2152	G165	Set of 2	9.50	9.50

Perf. 14
2153-2154	G166	Set of 2	9.50	9.50

No. 2151 contains one 48x32mm stamp; No. 2152 contains one 32x48mm stamp.

Tropical Fish G167

35c, Slender mbuna. 45c, Pygoplite diacanthus. #2157, 75c, Siamese fighting fish. #2158, 75c, Pomacanthus semicirclatus. 90c, Zanclus canescens. #2160, $1, Dwarf pencilfish. #2161, $1, Xiphophorus maculatus. #2162, $2, Wimplefish. #2163, $2, Gramma loreto. $3, Zebrasoma xanthurum.

#2165, each $1: a, Emperor angelfish. b, Strawberryfish. c, Jackknife fish. d, Flame angelfish. e, Clarke's anemonefish. f, Flashback dottyback. g, Coral trout. h, Foxface.

#2166, each $1: a, Bumblebee goby. b, Black-headed blenny. c, Boarfish. d, Achilles tang. e, Swordtail. f, Moorish idol. g, Banded pipefish. h, Striped sea catfish.

#2167, each $1.65: a, Bodianus rufus. b, Coris aygula. c, Centropyge bicolor. d, Balistoides conspicillum. e, Poecilia reticulata. f, Heniochus acuminatus.

#2168, each $1.65: a, Plectorhynchus chaetodonoids. b, Bodianus puchellus. c, Acanthurus leucosternon. d, Chromileptis altivelis. e, Pterophyllum scalare f, Premnas biaculeatus.

Each $6: #2169, Equetus punctatus. #2170, Harlequin tuskfish. #2171, Purplequeen. #2172, Pomacanthius imperator, vert.

2000, Mar. 28   Perf. 14
2155-2164	G167	Set of 10	9.00	9.00

Sheets of 8, #a.-h.
2165-2166	G167	Set of 2	12.00	12.00

Sheets of 6, #a.-f.
2167-2168	G167	Set of 2	15.00	15.00

Souvenir Sheets
2169-2172	G167	Set of 4	18.00	18.00

Van Dyck Painting Type of 2000

No. 2173, each $1.50: a, Cardinal Bentivoglio. b, Cardinal Infante Ferdinand. c, Cesare Alessandro Scaglia. d, A Roman Clergyman. e, Jean-Charles della Faille. f, Cardinal Domenico Rivarola.

No. 2174, each $1.50: a, Portrait of an Elderly Woman. b, Head of a Young Woman. c, Portrait of a Man. d, Jan van den Wouwer. e, Portrait of a Young Man. f, Portrait of Everhard Jabach.

No. 2175, each $1.50: a, A Man in Armor. b, Portrait of a Young General. c, Emanuele Filiberto, Prince of Savoy. d, Donna Polixena Spinola Guzman de Leganes. f, Luigia Cattaneo Gentile. f, Portrait of Giovanni Battista Cattaneo.

No. 2176, each $1.50: a, Marchesa Paolina Adorno Brignole-Sale, 1623-25. b, Marchesa Geronima Spinola. c, Marchesa Paolina Adorno Broignole-Sale, 1627. d, Marcello Durazzo. e, Marchesa Grimaldi Cattaneo with a Black Page. f, Young Man of the House of Spinola.

No. 2176G: h, A Man in Armor. i, Portrait of a Young General. j, Emanuele Filiberto, Prince of Savoy. k, Donna Polixena Spinola Guzman de Leganes. l, Luigia Cattaneo Gentile. m, Giovanni Battista Cattaneo.

Each $5: No. 2177, Portrait of Jacques le Roy. No. 2178, Hendrik van der Bergh.

Each $6: No. 2179, Frederik Hendrik, Prince of Orange. No. 2180, Justus van Meerstraeten. No. 2181, The Abbot Scaglia Adoring the Virgin and Child, horiz. No. 2182, Maria Louisa de Tassis, horiz.

2000, May 1   Perf. 13¾
Sheets of 6, #a.-f.
2173-2176	A449	Set of 4	27.00	27.00
2176G	A449	$1.50 Sheet of 6, #a-f	6.75	6.75

Souvenir Sheets
2177-2178	A449	Set of 2	7.50	7.50
2179-2182	A449	Set of 4	18.00	18.00

Prince William Type of 2000

No. 2183: a, Wearing scarf. b, Wearing suit with vest. c, Wearing casual shirt. d, Wearing gray suit.
$6, Wearing sweater.

2000, May 15   Litho.   Perf. 14
2183	A453	$1.50 Sheet of 4, #a-d	4.50	4.50

Souvenir Sheet   Perf. 13¾
2184	A453	$6 multi	4.50	4.50

No. 2183 contains four 28x42mm stamps.

Zeppelin Type of 2000

No. 2185 — Ferdinand von Zeppelin and: a, LZ-3. b, LZ-56. c, LZ-88.
$6, LZ-1.

2000, May 15   Perf. 14
2185	A454	$3 Sheet of 3, #a-c	6.75	6.75

Souvenir Sheet
2186	A454	$6 multi	4.50	4.50

No. 2185 contains three 42x28mm stamps.

Berlin Film Festival Type of 2000

No. 2187: a, James Stewart. b, Sachiko Hidari. c, Juliette Mayniel. d, Le Bonheur. e, La Notte. f, Lee Marvin.
$6, The Thin Red Line.

2000, May 15
2187	A455	$1.50 Sheet of 6, #a-f	6.75	6.75

Souvenir Sheet
2188	A455	$6 multi	4.50	4.50

Souvenir Sheets
Olympics Type of 2000

No. 2189: a, Frantz Reichel. b, Discus throw. c, Seoul Sports Complex and Korean flag. d, Ancient Greek wrestlers.

2000, May 15
2189	A457	$2 Sheet of 4, #a-d	6.00	6.00

Public Railways Type of 2000

No. 2190: a, Locomotion No. 1 and George Stephenson. b, Rocket.

2000, May 15
2190	A458	$3 Sheet of 2, #a-b	4.50	4.50

Bach Type of 2000
2000, May 15
2191	A459	$6 Statue of Bach	4.50	4.50

G168

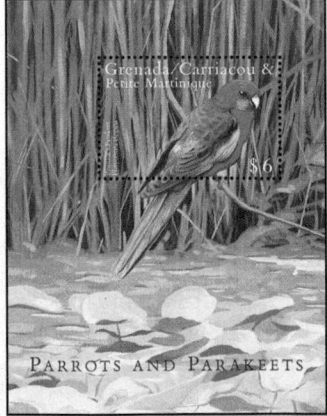

PARROTS AND PARAKEETS

Birds — G166

Butterflies and Moths — G169

No. 2192, each $1.50: a, Clara satin moth. b, Spanish festoon. c, Giant silkmoth. d, Oak eggar. e, Common wall. f, Large oak blue.

No. 2193, each $1.50: a, Jersey tiger. b, Boisduval's autumnal moth. c, Orange swallow-tailed moth. d, Regent skipper. e, Hoop pine moth. f, Coppery oysphania.

No. 2194, each $1.50: a, Grecian shoemaker. b, 88. c, Cramer's mesene. d, Salt marsh moth. e, Ruddy dagger wing. f, Blue night.

No. 2195, each $1.50: a, Heliconius charitonius. b, Tiger pierid. c, Hewiton's blue hairstreak. d, Esmeralda. e, California dogface. f, Orange theope.

No. 2196, each $2: a, Hummingbird gleariwing. b, Gold-drop helicopis. c, Great tiger moth. d, Staudinger's longtail.

No. 2197, each $2: a, Common map. b, Papilio machaon. c, Purple emperor. d, Red-lined geometrid.

Each $6: No. 2198, Peacock royal. No. 2199, Queen Alexandra's birdwing. No. 2200, Giant leopard moth. No. 2201, Robin moth, vert.

Illustrations reduced.

2000, May 29   **Perf. 14**
Sheets of 6, #a-f
2192-2193 G168 Set of 2   13.50 13.50
2194-2195 G169 Set of 2   13.50 13.50
Sheets of 4, #a-d
2196-2197 G168 Set of 2   12.00 12.00
Souvenir Sheets
2198-2199 G168 Set of 2   9.00 9.00
2200-2201 G169 Set of 2   9.00 9.00

Apollo-Soyuz Type

No. 2202, vert.: a, Thomas P. Stafford. b, Mission badge. c, Donald K. Slayton.
$6, Alexei Leonov, vert.

2000, May 15   **Litho.**   **Perf. 14**
2202 A456 $3 Sheet of 3, #a-c   6.75 6.75
Souvenir Sheet
2203 A456 $6 Alexei Leonov   4.50 4.50

Einstein Type
Souvenir Sheet
2000, May 15   **Perf. 14¼**
2204 A460 $6 multi   4.50 4.50

Space Type

Nos. 2205, each $1.50: a, Foton (green and orange background). b, Sub-satellite and comet tail. c, NEAR Eros (green background). d, Explorer 16 and sun. e, Astro Challenger (green and orange background). f, Giotto (green background).

No. 2206, each $1.50: a, Foton and asteroid. b, Sub-satellite and asteroid. c, NEAR Eros and asteroid. d, Explorer 16 and planet surface. e, Space Shuttle. f, Giotto (blue background).

Each $6: No. 2207, Lunar Prospector. No. 2208, Pegasus Saturn.

2000, May 15   **Perf. 14**
Sheets of 6, #a-f
2205-2206 A461 Set of 2   13.50 13.50
Souvenir Sheets
2207-2208 A461 Set of 2   9.00 9.00

Nos. 2205-2206 depict different satellites, but have the same inscriptions. World Stamp Expo 2000, Anaheim.

Trains
G170

Designs: 90c, Golsdorf 2-6-2, Vienna Metropolitan Railways. $1, Forrester 2-2-0, Dublin & Kingstown Railway. $2, Metro-Cammell Co, Nigerian Railways. $3, TGV 001, French Natl. Railways.

No. 2213, each $1.50: a, Braithwait 0-4-0, Eastern Counties Railway. b, The Philadelphia, Austria. c, Stephenson 2-2-2, Russia. d, L'aigle, Western Railway of France. e, Borsig Standard 2-2-2, Germany. f, The Ajax, Great Western Railway.

No. 2214, each $1.50: a, Co-Co locomotive, Norwegian State Railways. b, Diesel-electric locomotive, Jamaica Railway. c, Diesel-electric locomotive, Railway of the People's Republic of China. d, Electric locomotive, Portuguese Railways. e, Re 6/6, Swiss Federal Railways. f, Dual-purpose Electric locomotive, Turkish State Railways.

No. 2215, each $1.50: a, 4-4-0 engine, Perak Government Railway. b, 2-4-2 tank engine, Rhondda & Swansea Railway. c, 2-4-2 tank engine, Lancashire & Yorkshire Railway. d, 2-8-2 tank engine, Northwestern Railway of India. e, 4-2-2 Imperial Yellow Mail engine, Shanghai-Nanking Railway. f, 2-4-2 tank engine, Danish State Railway.

No. 2216, each $1.50: a, Electric railcar, South Jersey Transit. b, Metroliner, US. c, HSST Mag-lev train. d, E60C, Amtrak. e, TEE Express "Parsifal." f, 2-Co-Co-2 electric, Amtrak.

No. 2217, $6, The Experiment, US. No. 2218, 2-8-2 locomotive, Central South African Railway. No. 2219, $6, The Prospector, Western Australian Government Railways. No. 2220, Diesel-electric locomotive, South African Railways.

2000, June 13
2209-2212 G170 Set of 4   5.25 5.25
Sheets of 6, #a-f
2213-2216 G170 Set of 4   26.00 26.00
Souvenir Sheets
2217-2220 G170 Set of 4   18.00 18.00

European Soccer Championships Type

No. 2221, horiz., each $1.50 — Denmark: a, Tofting. b, Team photo. c, Michael Laudrup. d, Jorgensen. e, Philips Stadium, Eindhoven. f, Moller.

No. 2222, horiz., each $1.50 — France: a, Thuram. b, Team photo. c, Barthez. d, Zidane. e, Jan Breydel Stadium, Brugge. f, Michel Platini.

No. 2223, horiz., each $1.50 — Netherlands: a, Giovanni Van Bronckhorst. b, Team photo. c, Patrick Kluivert. d, Johan Cruyff. e, Amsterdam Arena Stadium. f, Zenden.

Each $6: No. 2224, Denmark coach Bo Johansson. No. 2225, France coach Roger Lemerre. No. 2226, Netherlands coach Frank Rijkaard.

2000, Aug. 8   **Perf. 13¾**
Sheets of 6, #a-f
2221-2223 A464 Set of 3   20.00 20.00
Souvenir Sheets
2224-2226 A464 Set of 3   13.50 13.50

Popes Type

No. 2227, each $1.50: a, Adrian VI, 1522-23. b, Paul II, 1464-71. c, Calixtus III, 1455-58. d, Eugenius IV, 1431-47.

2000, Aug. 22
2227 A467 Sheet of 4, #a-d   4.50 4.50
Souvenir Sheet
2228 A467 $6 Gregory IX, 1370-78   4.50 4.50

Monarchs Type

No. 2229, each $1.50: a, Louis XVI of France, 1774-92. b, Louis XVIII of France, 1814-24. c, Queen of Kublai Khan, China. d, Mary Tudor of England, 1553-58. e, Mohammed Ali of Iran, 1907-09. f, Ch'ien-lung (Qianlong, Hung-li) of China, 1735-96.
$6, Vladimir I, Grand Prince of Kiev, 980-1015.

2000, Aug. 22
2229 A468 Sheet of 6, #a-f   6.75 6.75
Souvenir Sheet
2230 A468 $6 Vladimir I   4.50 4.50

Fauna
G171

Designs: 75c, St. Lucia Amazon. 90c, Three-toed sloth. $1, Hispaniolan solenodon. $2, Thick-billed parrot.

No. 2235, each $1.50: a, Jaguarundi. b, Andean condor. c, Darwin's rhea. d, Central American tapir. e, Jaguar. f, Jamaican hutia.

No. 2236, each $1.50: a, Red vakari. b, San Andreas vireo. c, Golden lion tamarin. d, American crocodile. e, Spectacled caiman. f, Rhinoceros iguana.

Each $6: No. 2237, Pronghorn. No. 2238, Kemp Ridley sea turtle.

2000, Sept. 5   **Perf. 14**
2231-2234 G171 Set of 4   4.00 4.00
Sheets of 6, #a-f
2235-2236 G171 Set of 2   16.00 16.00
Souvenir Sheets
2237-2238 G171 Set of 2   11.00 11.00

The Stamp Show 2000, London (Nos. 2235-2238).

Souvenir Sheet

David Copperfield, Magician — G172

No. 2239, each $1.50: a, Copperfield's face at L, legs at R. b, Upper torso at L, face at R. c, Legs at L, face at R. d, Face at L, upper torso at R.

Illustration reduced.

2000, Sept. 14
2239 G172 Sheet of 4, #a-d   4.50 4.50

Prado Paintings Type

#2240, each $1.50: a, St. John the Baptist and the Franciscan Maestro Henricus Werl, by Robert Campin. b, Justice and Peace, by Corrado Giaquinto. c, St. Barbara, by Campin. d, John Fane, 10th Count of Westmoreland, by Thomas Lawrence. e, The Marchioness of Manzanedo, by Jean-Louis-Ernest Meissonier. f, Mr. Storer, by Martin Archer Shee.

#2241, each $1.50: a, Isabella Carla Eugenia, by Alonso Sánchez Coello. b, Portrait of a Nobleman with His Hand on His Chest, by El Greco. c, Philip III, by Juan Pantoja de la Cruz. d, Madonna & child from The Holy Family with Saints Ildefons & John the Evangelist, & the Master Alonso de Villegas, by Blas del Prado. e, The Last Supper, by Bartolomé Carducci. f, Man with goblet from The Holy Family with Saints Ildefons & John the Evangelist, & the Master Alonso de Villegas.

#2242, each $1.50: a, Dominic of Silos, by Bartolomé Bermejo. b, Head of a Prophet, by Jaime Huguet. c, Christ Giving His Blessing, by Fernando Gallego. d, The Mystic Marriage of St. Catherine, by Alonso Sánchez Coello. e, St. Catherine of Alexandria, by Fernando Yáñez de la Almedina. f, Virgin and Child, by Luis de Morales.

Each $6: #2243, The Holy Family with Saints Ildefons & John the Evangelist, & the Master Alonso de Villegas. #2244, The Last Supper, horiz. #2245, The Coronation of the Virgin, by El Greco, horiz.

2000, Oct. 19   **Perf. 12x12¼, 12¼x12**
Sheets of 6, #a-f
2240-2242 A470 Set of 3   20.00 20.00
Souvenir Sheets
2243-2245 A470 Set of 3   13.50 13.50

Espana 2000, Intl. Philatelic Exhibition.

Mushroom Type of 2000

No. 2246, $2: a, Cinnabar chanterelle. b, Blackening wax cap. c, Edible cort. d, Orange scaber-stalk bolete.

No. 2247, $2: a, Crab russula. b, Steel blue entoloma. c, Tiger lentinus. d, Yellow-white mycena.

No. 2248, $2, horiz.: a, Le Gal's bolete. b, Emetic russula. c, Silvery violet cort. d, Tree volvariella.

No. 2249, $6, Scaly vase chanterelle, horiz. No. 2250, $6, Common collybia, horiz.

2000, Mar. 3   **Litho.**   **Perf. 14**
Sheets of 4, #a-d
2246-2248 A448 Set of 3   18.00 18.00
Souvenir Sheets
2249-2250 A448 Set of 2   9.00 9.00

Dog Type of 2000

Designs: 45c, Irish setter. 90c, Dalmatian. $2, German shepherd.

No. 2254, $1.50: a, Alaskan malamute. b, Golden retriever. c, Afghan hound. d, Long-haired dachshund. e, Irish terrier. f, Miniature poodle.

No. 2255, $1.50: a, Great Dane. b, Newfoundland. c, Rottweiler. d, Bulldog. e, Japanese spitz. f, Bull terrier.

No. 2256, $6, Labrador retriever. No. 2257, $6, Basset hound, horiz.

2000, June 23
2251-2253 A473 Set of 3   2.50 2.50
Sheets of 6, #a-f
2254-2255 A473 Set of 2   13.50 13.50
Souvenir Sheets
2256-2257 A473 Set of 2   9.00 9.00

Cat Type of 2000

Designs: 75c, Blue point snowshoe. $3, Black and white Maine coon cat. $4, Brown tabby British shorthair.

No. 2261, $1.50: a, California spangled cat. b, Russian blue. c, Seal point Siamese. d, Black tabby British shorthair. e, Silver tabby British shorthair. f, Tricolor Japanese bobtail.

No. 2262, $1.50: a, British white shorthair. b, Blue cream American shorthair. c, Bombay. d, Red Burmese. e, Sorrel Abyssinian. f, Ocicat.

$5, Silver classic tabby Persian, horiz. No. 2263A, $5, Red-white bicolored British shorthair.

2000, June 23
2258-2260 A478 Set of 3   5.75 5.75
Sheets of 6, #a-f
2261-2262 A478 Set of 2   13.50 13.50
Souvenir Sheet
2263 A478 $5 multi   3.75 3.75
2263A A478 $5 multi   3.75 3.75

Battle of Britain Type of 2000

No. 2264, each $1: a, Women fire fighters, London. b, Family leaving after the Blitz. c, Searchlights, London. d, Winston Churchill in Coventry after German raid. e, Rescue after German bombing. f, Rescue after London bombing. g, Terror hits Buckingham Gate. h, After a German raid on Coventry.

No. 2265, each $1: a, Pilots scramble to their planes. b, Balloons to catch low-flying planes. c, Spitfire B. d, Speech by Princess Elizabeth. e, Fire Watchers, auxiliary fire service. f, Painting stripes to see at night. g, Bombed buildings in Britain. h, Air raid wardens, auxiliary police force.

Each $6: No. 2266, Hawker Hurricane. No. 2267, British family survives German bombing, vert.

2000, Oct. 30
Sheets of 8, #a-h
2264-2265 A471 Set of 2   12.00 12.00
Souvenir Sheets
2266-2267 A471 Set of 2   9.00 9.00

Queen Mother Type of 2000
2000, Oct. 30
2268 A479 $1.50 multi   1.10 1.10
Printed in sheets of 6.

Photomosaic Type of 1999

No. 2269, $1: Various flowers making up a photomosaic of the Queen Mother.
No. 2270, $1: Various photographs with religious theme making up a photomosaic of Pope John Paul II.

2000, Oct. 30   **Perf. 13¾**
2269-2270 A445 Set of 2   12.00 12.00

Harry Houdini, Magician — G173

2000		Litho.		Perf. 14
2271	G173	$1.50 multi		1.10 1.10

Issued in sheets of 4.

Souvenir Sheet

Barbara Taylor Bradford, Author — G174

Illustration reduced.

2000		Litho.		Perf. 12¼
2272	G174	$6 multi		4.50 4.50

Souvenir Sheet

Hong Kong Comic Strip "The Storm Riders" — G175

No. 2273: a, Character with arms folded. b, Character with sword. c, Character in brown cape. d, Character in green.
Illustration reduced.

2000			Perf. 13½
2273	G175	$4 Sheet of 4, #a-d	9.00 9.00

New Year 2001 (Year of the Snake) — G176

No. 2274: a, Rat snake. b, Mangrove snake. c, Boomslang. d, Emerald tree boa. e, African egg-eating snake. f, Chinese green tree viper.
Illustration reduced.

2001, Jan. 2			Perf. 14
2274	G176	90c Sheet of 6, #a-f	4.00 4.00

Souvenir Sheet

2275	G176	$4 King cobra	3.00 3.00

Rijksmuseum Type of 2001

No. 2276, $1.50: a, Person with red shirt from Dune Landcape, by Jan van Goyen. b, The Raampoortje, by Wouter Johannes van Troostwijk. c, House and horse from The Cattle Ferry, by Esaias van de Velde. d, The Departure of a Senior Functionary from Middleburg, by Adriaen van de Venne. e, Steeple and ferry from The Cattle Ferry. f, Four people near rock from Dune Landscape.

No. 2277, $1.50: a, Building, statue and dog from Garden Party, by Dirck Hals. b, Still Life with Gilt Cup, by Willem Claesz Heda. c, Cloud of smoke from Orestes and Pylades Disputing at the Altar, by Pieter Lastman. d, Buildings from Orestes and Pylades Disputing at the Altar. e, Self-portrait in a Yellow Robe, by Jan Lievens. f, Birds in sky from Garden Party.

No. 2278, $1.50: a, Beatrix from Marriage Portrait of Isaac Massa and Beatrix van der Laen, by Frans Hals. b, Winter Landscape With Ice Skaters, by Hendrick Avercamp. c, Man and woman from The Spendthrift, by Cornelis Troost. d, Men in brown from The Spendthrift. e, Man and woman from The Art Gallery of Jan Gildermeester Jansz, by Adriaan de Lelie. f, Three men from The Art Gallery of Jan Gildermeester Jansz.

No. 2279, $1.50: a, Man from A Music Party, by Rembrandt. b, Woman from A Music Party. c, Girl and boy from Rutger Jan Schimmelpennick With His Wife and Children, by Pierre-Paul Prud'hon. d, Girl from Rutger Jan Schimmelpennick With His Wife and Children. e, Two men from The Syndics, by Thomas de Keyser. f, Isaac and Beatrix from Marriage Portrait of Isaac Massa and Beatrix van der Laen.

No. 2280, $6, A Music Party. No. 2281, $6, Anna Accused by Tobit of Stealing a Kid, by Rembrandt. No. 2282, $6, Cleopatra's Banquet, by Gerard Lairesse, horiz. No. 2283, $6, View of Tivoli, by Isaac de Moucheron.

2001, Jan. 15			Perf. 13¾
Sheets of 6, #a-f			
2276-2279	A483	Set of 4	27.50 27.50
Souvenir Sheets			
2280-2283	A483	Set of 4	18.00 18.00

Pokémon Type of 2001

No. 2284, each $1.50: a, Bellsprout. b, Vulpix. c, Dewgong. d, Oddish. e, Dratini. f, Jigglypuff.

2001, Feb. 1			
2284	A484	Sheet of 6, #a-f	6.75 6.75
Souvenir Sheet			
2285	A484	$6 Pikachu	4.50 4.50

Animals of the Tropics G177

Designs: 75c, Greater flamingo, vert. 90c, Cuban crocodile. $1, Jaguarundi, vert. $2, Wedge-capped capuchin monkey.

No. 2290, $1.50, vert.: a, Cuban pygmy owl. b, Woody spider monkey. c, Bee hummingbirds. d, Dragonfly, poison dart frog. e, Red brocket deer. f, Cuban stream anole.

No. 2291, $1.50, vert.: a, Red-breasted toucan. b, Mexican black howler monkey. c, Fleck's pygmy boa. d, Red-eyed tree frog. e, Caiman. f, Jaguar.

No. 2292, $6, Ocelot, vert. No. 2293, $6, Western knight anole, vert.

2001, Feb. 1			Perf. 14
2286-2289	A177	Set of 4	4.00 4.00
Sheets of 6, #a-f			
2290-2291	G177	Set of 2	16.00 16.00
Souvenir Sheets			
2292-2293	G177	Set of 2	12.00 12.00

Hong Kong 2001 Stamp Exhibition.

Fish Type of 2000 with Added WWF Emblem

No. 2294: a, Sparisoma rubiripinne. b, Scarus vetula. c, Scarus taeniopterus. d, Sparisoma viride.

2001, Mar. 28		Litho.	Perf. 14
2294	G167	75c Strip of 4, #a-d	4.75 4.75

Waterfowl — G178

No. 2295, horiz, each $1.50: a, Falklands streamer duck. b, Black-crowned night heron. c, Muscovy duck. d, Ruddy duck. e, Black-necked screamer. f, White-faced whistling duck.

2001, Mar. 28			
2295	G178	Sheet of 6, #a-f	6.75 6.75
Souvenir Sheet			
2296	G178	$6 Great egret	4.50 4.50

Scenes From "The Littlest Rebel," Starring Shirley Temple — G179

Temple with — No. 2297, horiz.: a, Pointing soldier. b, Black woman. c, Soldier in carriage. d, Pres. Lincoln.
No. 2298: a, Spoon. b, Woman near tree. c, Soldier with hat. d, Woman. e, Black man and soldier. f, Man.
$6, Black man.

2001, Apr. 25			Perf. 13¾
2297	G179	$2 Sheet of 4, #a-d	6.00 6.00
2298	G179	$2 Sheet of 6, #a-f	9.00 9.00
Souvenir Sheet			
2299	G179	$6 multi	4.50 4.50

Clark Gable (1901-60) — G180

No. 2300, $1.50 — Color of photo: a, Purple. b, Sepia (wearing suit and tie). c, Yellow. d, Sepia (wearing sweater). e, Blue. f, Sepia (wearing bow tie).
No. 2301, $1.50 — Signature of Gable and Gable with: a, Cigar. b, Vest. c, Chair. d, Pen. e, Suit and tie. f, Pinstriped suit.
No. 2302, $6, Blue background. No. 2303, $6, Gable in uniform.

2001, Apr. 25			Perf. 14
Sheets of 6, #a-f			
2300-2301	G180	Set of 2	13.50 13.50
Souvenir Sheets			
2302-2303	G180	Set of 2	9.00 9.00

Betty Boop Type of 2000

No. 2304 — Boop: a, With comb. b, With veil. c, With lei. d, At carnival. e, With flower in hair. f, With cowboy hat. g, With beret. h, In automobile. i, As Statue of Liberty.
No. 2305, $6, In sari. No. 2306, $6, In gondola.

2001, Apr. 25			Perf. 13¾
2304	A481	$1 Sheet of 9, #a-i	6.75 6.75
Souvenir Sheets			
2305-2306	A481	Set of 2	9.00 9.00

Phila Nippon Type of 2001

Designs: 75c, Scenes of Daily Life in Edo, by Choshun Miyagawa. 90c, Twelve Famous Places in Japan, by Eisenin Naganobu Kano. $1, Scenery Along the Length of the Sumida River, by Kyuei Kano. $1.25, Cranes, by Eisenin Michinobu Kano. No. 2311, $2, A Courtesan of Yoshiwara, by Shunei Katsukawa. $3, Rite of Bear Killing: Praying to the Bear's Spirit, by unknown artist.

No. 2313, $2, vert. — Bodhisattva Samantabhadra from the Lotus Sutra with: a, Surrounding rings, yellow elephant. b, White elephant. c, Temple at left. d, Surrounding rings with rays.

No. 2314, $2 (85x28mm) — Chapter illustrations from Genji Monogatari Emaki, by Ryusetsu Hidenobu Kano: a, Kiritsubo. b, Akashi. c, Hatsune. d, E-Awase.

No. 2315, $6, A Sage Pointing at the Moon, by Ranseki Katagiri. No. 2316, $6, Frontispiece for Devadatta, Lotus Sutra, vert.

2001, May 1			Perf. 14
2307-2312	A487	Set of 6	6.75 6.75
Sheets of 4, #a-d			
2313-2314	A488	Set of 2	12.00 12.00
Souvenir Sheets			
2315-2316	A488	Set of 2	9.00 9.00

Marlene Dietrich Type of 2001

Dietrich with: a, Microphone. b, Robe. c, Flowered dress. d, Hat.

2001, May 15			Perf. 13¾
2317	A489	$2 Sheet of 4, #a-d	6.00 6.00

Queen Victoria Type of 2001

No. 2318 — Queen Victoria with: a, Scepter. b, Flower. c, Sash.
$6, Sash, diff.

2001, May 15			Perf. 14
2318	A490	$3 Sheet of 3, #a-c	6.75 6.75
Souvenir Sheet			
2319	A490	$6 multi	4.50 4.50

Queen Elizabeth II Type of 2001

No. 2320, each $1.25 — Predominant background colors: a, Brown and yellow. b, Green. c, Blue. d, Black. e, Red and violet. f, Red and light blue.
No. 2320G, each $2: h, Green background. i, Purple background. j, Brown background.
$6, Tan.

2001, May 15			Perf. 14
2320	A491	Sheet of 6, #a-f	5.75 5.75
2320G	A491	Sheet of 3, #h-j	4.50 4.50
Souvenir Sheet			
			Perf. 13¾
2321	A491	$6 multi	3.75 3.75

No. 2321 contains one 38x51mm stamp.

Ship Type of 2001

Designs: 90c, Creole. $1, Britannia. $2, Ariel. $3, Sindia.

No. 2326, $1.25: a, William Fawcett. b, Sirius. c, S.S. Great Britain. d, Oriental. e, Lightning. f, Great Eastern.

No. 2327, $1.25: a, Santa Maria and Christopher Columbus. b, Sao Gabriel and Vasco da Gama. c, Victoria and Ferdinand Magellan. d, Golden Hind and Sir Francis Drake. e, Endeavour and Capt. James Cook. f, HMS Erebus and John Franklin.

No. 2328, $1.25, vert.: a, Mayflower. b, Gabriel. c, Beagle. d, Challenger. e, Vega. f, Fram.

No. 2329, $6, Challenge. No. 2330, $6, Cutty Sark.

2001, June 18			Perf. 14
2322-2325	A497	Set of 4	5.25 5.25

Sheets of 6, #a-f
2326-2328 A497 Set of 3 17.00 17.00

Miniature Sheets
2329-2330 A497 Set of 2 9.00 9.00

Magician Type of Grenada Grenadines of 2000

Designs: No. 2331, $1.50, Howard Thurston. No. 2332, $1.50, Harry Kellar.

2001
2331-2332 G173 Set of 2 2.25 2.25

Issued in sheets of 4.

Mao Zedong Type of 2001

No. 2333, horiz.: a, Mao on stairs. b, Mao at right, with soldiers. c, Mao at left, with peasants. d, Mao seated, with officers.
$3, Portrait.

2001, May 15   **Litho.**   **Perf. 14**
2333 A493 $1.50 Sheet of 4,
    #a-d   4.50 4.50

Souvenir Sheet
2334 A493 $3 multi 2.25 2.25

Verdi Type of 2001

No. 2335 — Verdi and score: a, 25c. b, 75c. c, $2. d, $3.
$6, Portrait.

2001, May 15   **Perf. 14**
2335 A494 Sheet of 4, #a-d 4.50 4.50

Souvenir Sheet
2336 A494 $6 multi 4.50 4.50

Toulouse-Lautrec Type of 2001

No. 2337, horiz.: a, Helene V. b, The Clownesse. c, Madame Berthe Bady. d, The Woman With The Black Boa.
$6, Loie Fuller at the Folies Bergére.

2001, May 15   **Perf. 13¾**
2337 A495 $1 Sheet of 4, #a-d 3.00 3.00

Souvenir Sheet
2338 A495 $6 multi 4.50 4.50

Monet Type of 2001

No. 2339, horiz.: a, The Magpie. b, La Pointe de la Hève at Low Tide. c, Boats: Regatta at Argenteuil. d, La Grenouillère.
$6, Portrait of J. F. Jaquemart with Parasol.

2001, May 15
2339 A504 $1 Sheet of 4, #a-d 3.00 3.00

Souvenir Sheet
2340 A504 $6 multi 4.50 4.50

Orchids
G181

Designs: 25c, Vanda Singapore. 50c, Vanda Joan Warne. 75c, Vanda lamellata. $2, Vanda merrillii.
No. 2345, $1.50: a, Papilionanthe teres. b, Vanda flabellata. c, Vanda tessellata (name at LL). d, Vanda pumila. e, Rhynchostylis gigantea. f, Vandopsis gigantea.
No. 2346, $1.50: a, Vanda tessellata (name at center left). b, Vanda helvola. c, Vanda brunnea. d, Vanda stangeana. e, Vanda limbata. f, Vandopsis tricolor.
No. 2347, Vanda insignis. No. 2348, $6, Vandopsis lissochiloides.

2001, Oct. 15   **Perf. 14**
2341-2344 G181 Set of 4 2.60 2.60

Sheets of 6, #a-f
2345-2346 G181 Set of 2 13.50 13.50

Souvenir Sheets
2347-2348 G181 Set of 2 9.00 9.00

Souvenir Sheets

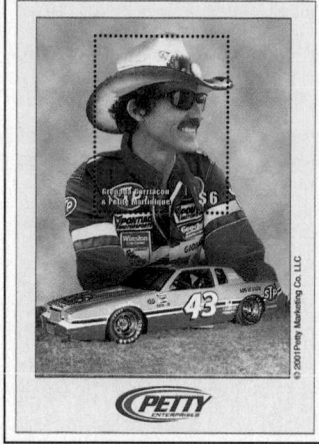

Richard Petty, Stock Car
Racer — G182

Designs: No. 2349, $6, shown. No. 2350, $6, Petty speaking into microphone.

2001, Oct. 15   **Perf. 13¾**
2349-2350 G182 Set of 2 9.00 9.00

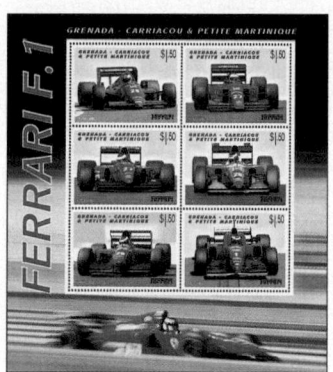

Ferrari Formula 1 Racing
Cars — G183

No. 2351: a, 1986 F1 86. b, 1989 F1 89. c, 1992 F92A. d, 1993 F1 93. e, 1994 412T1. f, 1996 F310.

2001, Nov. 19   **Perf. 13¾**
2351 G183 $1.50 Sheet of 6,
    #a-f   6.75 6.75

World Cup Soccer Championships Type of 2001

No. 2352, $1.50 — World Cup posters and badges from: a, 1950. b, 1954. c, 1958. d, 1962. e, 1966. f, 1970.
No. 2353, $1.50 — World Cup posters and badges from: a, 1978. b, 1982. c, 1986. d, 1990. e, 1994. f, 1998.
No. 2354, $6, World Cup poster and badge, 1930. No. 2355, $6, Head and globe from World Cup trophy.

2001, Nov. 29   **Perf. 13¾x14¼**

Sheets of 6, #a-f
2352-2353 A505 Set of 2 13.50 13.50

Souvenir Sheets
2354-2355 A505 Set of 2 9.00 9.00

Christmas — G184

Designs: 25c, Coronation of the Virgin, by Filippo Lippi. 75c, Virgin and Child, by Mantegna. $1.50, Madonna and Child, by Masaccio. $3, Madonna and Child, by Raphael.
$6, Virgin and child Enthroned with Angels, by Mantegna.

2001, Dec. 3   **Perf. 14**
2356-2359 G184 Set of 4 4.25 4.25

Souvenir Sheet
2360 G184 $6 multi 4.50 4.50

Royal Navy
Ships — G185

Designs: 75c, HMS Renown in Portsmouth Harbor, 1922. 90c, Battle of the Saintes, 1782. $2, Battle of Trafalgar, 1805. $3, Embarkation at Dover, 1520.
No. 2365, $1.50, horiz.: a, Battle of Solebay, 1672. b, HMS Royal Prince, 1679. c, Battle of Texel, 1673. d, Battle of Scheveningen, 1653. e, Barbary Pirates, 1600s. f, Royal Charles, 1667.
No. 2366, $1.50, horiz.: a, Skirmishing preceding the Battle of the First of June. b, Moonlight Battle, 1780. c, Great ships of the Jacobean Navy, 1623. d, Battle of the Gulf of Genoa, 1795. e, Battle of the Nile, 1798. f, St. Lucia, 1778.
No. 2367, $6, Battle of Navarino, 1827, horiz. No. 2368, $6, HMS Repulse, 1924, horiz.

2001, Dec. 10   **Litho.**
2361-2364 G185 Set of 4 5.00 5.00

Sheets of 6, #a-f
2365-2366 G185 Set of 2 13.50 13.50

Souvenir Sheets
2367-2368 G185 Set of 2 9.00 9.00

Queen Mother Type of 1999 Redrawn

No. 2369: a, Lady Elizabeth Bowles-Lyon. b, In Rhodesia, 1957. c, With Princesses Elizabeth and Anne, 1950. d, In 1988.
$6, In Berlin.

2001, Dec. 13   **Perf. 14**
Yellow Orange Frames
2369 A440 $2 Sheet of 4, #a-d, +
    label   6.00 6.00

Souvenir Sheet
Perf. 13¾
2370 A440 $6 multi 4.50 4.50

Queen Mother's 101st birthday. No. 2370 contains one 38x50mm stamp with a slightly darker appearance than that found on No. 2122. Sheet margins of Nos. 2369-2370 lack embossing and gold arms and frames found on Nos. 2121-2122.

Princess Diana Type of 2001
Souvenir Sheet

Diana in: a, Yellow dress. b, Red jacket. c, White pinstriped suit.

2001, Feb. 15   **Perf. 14**
2371 A509 $1.50 Sheet of 2 each
    #a-c   6.75 6.75

Pres. John F. Kennedy — G187

No. 2372, vert. — Pres. Kennedy: a, In boat. b, In chair. c, Profile. d, Close-up, smiling. e, Close-up. f, Looking down.
$6, With Nikita Khrushchev.

2001, Dec. 15   **Perf. 13¾**
2372 G187 $1.50 Sheet of 6,
    #a-f   6.75 6.75

Souvenir Sheet
2373 G187 $6 multi 4.50 4.50

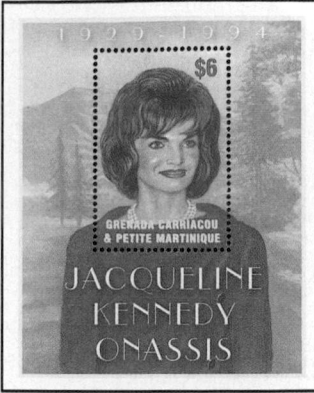

Jacqueline Kennedy Onassis (1929-94) — G188

No. 2374: a, Blue jacket, blue blouse. b, Red jacket, blue blouse. c, Green dress. d, Blue cape. e, Pink and blue jacket. f, Blue jacket, yellow blouse.
No. 2375, $6, Mountain in background. No. 2376, $6, Beige background.

2001, Dec. 15   **Perf. 14**
2374 G188 $1.50 Sheet of 6,
    #a-f   6.75 6.75

Souvenir Sheets
2375-2376 G188 Set of 2 9.00 9.00

G189

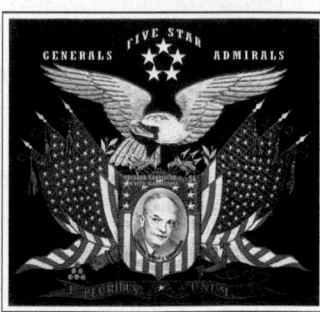

US Generals and Admirals — G190

No. 2377: a, Gen. Omar N. Bradley. b, Gen. George C. Marshall. c, Gen. Douglas MacArthur. d, Adm. William F. Halsey. e, Gen. Dwight D. Eisenhower. f, Adm. Chester Nimitz. g, Adm. William D. Leahy. h, Gen. Henry H. Arnold. i, Adm. Ernest J. King. j, Gen. George Washington. k, Gen. John J. Pershing.
No. 2378: a, Gen. George S. Patton, Jr. b, Gen. Joseph W. Stilwell. c, Adm. Thomas C. Kinkaid. d, Gen. Jonathan Wainwright. e, Lt. Gen. James H. Doolittle. f, Gen. Matthew B. Ridgway. g, Gen. Maxwell D. Taylor. h, Adm. Richmond Kelly Turner. i, Gen. Curtis E. LeMay. j, Gen. Hoyt S. Vandenberg. k, Gen. Carl Spaatz. l, Adm. Raymond Spruance.
No. 2379, $6, Eisenhower. No. 2380, $6, Douglas MacArthur.

2001, Dec. 15   **Perf. 14**
2377 G189 75c Sheet of 11, #a-
    k, + label   6.25 6.25
2378 G189 75c Sheet of 12, #a-l 6.75 6.75

Souvenir Sheets
Perf. 13¾
2379-2380 G190 Set of 2 9.00 9.00

Moths
G191

Designs: 75c, Pine emperor. 90c, Inquisitive monkey. $2, Oak eggar. $3, Madagascan sunset moth.

No. 2385, $1.50: a, Spanish moon moth. b, Coppery dysphania. c, Io moth. d, Large agarista. e, Millar's tiger. f, Tropical fruitpiercer.

No. 2386, $1.50: a, Indian moon moth. b, Beautiful tiger. c, Regal moth. d, Great tiger moth. e, Venus moth. f, Zodiac moth.

No. 2387, $6, Diva moth, vert. No. 2388, $6, African moon moth, vert.

2001, Dec. 17   *Perf. 14*
2381-2384 G191   Set of 4   5.00   5.00
Sheets of 6, #a-f
2385-2386 G191   Set of 2   13.50   13.50
Souvenir Sheets
2387-2388 G191   Set of 2   9.00   9.00
Vegaspex (#2386).

Reign of Queen Elizabeth II, 50th Anniv. Type of 2002

No. 2389: a, White hat. b, Red hat. c, Tiara. d, Hatless.
$6, With Princes Philip, Charles, Princess Anne.

2002, Feb. 6   *Perf. 14¼*
2389 A516 $2 Sheet of 4, #a-d   6.00   6.00
Souvenir Sheet
2390 A516 $6 multi   4.50   4.50

New Year 2002 (Year of the Horse) — G192

Various horses with background colors of — No. 2391: a, 75c, Light brown and light orange. b, $1.25, Light blue and olive green. c, $2, Tan and bister.
$6, Light orange and orange.

2002, Mar. 4   *Litho.*   *Perf. 13¾*
2391 G192   Sheet of 3, #a-c   3.00   3.00
Souvenir Sheet
2392 G192 $6 multi   4.50   4.50

United We
Stand — G193

2002, May 21   *Perf. 14*
2393 G193   80c multi   .60   .60
Printed in sheets of 4.

Chiune Sugihara Type of 2002
Souvenir Sheets
Sugihara and: No. 2394, $6, Map of Asia. No. 2395, $6, Pink background.

2002, July 1   *Perf. 13½x13¼*
2394-2395 A521   Set of 2   9.00   9.00

Winter Olympics Type of 2002
Montages of: No. 2396, $3, Skier in air, course flag, vert. No. 2397, $3, Skier, no flag, vert.

2002, July 1   *Perf. 13½x13¼*
2396-2397 A522   Set of 2   4.50   4.50
2397a   Souvenir sheet, #2396-2397   4.50   4.50

Intl. Year of Mountains Type of 2002
No. 2398: a, Mt. Kilimanjaro, Tanzania. b, Mt. Kenya, Kenya. c, Mauna Kea, Hawaii. d, Mt. Fuji, Japan.
$6, Koolau Mountains, Hawaii.

2002, July 1   *Perf. 13¼x13½*
2398 A523 $2 Sheet of 4, #a-d   6.00   6.00
Souvenir Sheet
2399 A523 $6 multi   4.50   4.50

Intl. Year of Ecotourism Type of 2002
No. 2400, horiz.: a, Tourists at waterfall. b, Bird. c, Butterfly. d, Fish. e, Cactus. f, Orchid.
$6, Birds, horiz.

2002, July 1   *Perf. 13¼x13½*
2400 A524 $1.50 Sheet of 6, #a-f   6.75   6.75
Souvenir Sheet
2401 A524 $6 multi   4.50   4.50
Nos. 2400-2401 were each overprinted in sheet margins "Hurricane Relief 2004" in 2005.

Scout Jamboree Type of 2002
No. 2402, horiz.: a, Campfire, Scout emblem. b, Scout with walking stick and backpack. c, Scout feeding calf. d, Girl giving Scout sign.
No. 2403, $6, Scout with hat.

2002, July 1   *Perf. 13¼x13½*
2402 A525 $2 Sheet of 4, #a-d   6.00   6.00
Souvenir Sheet
Perf. 13½x13¼
2403 A525 $2 multi   1.50   1.50

Amerigo Vespucci
(1454-1512),
Explorer — G194

Various portraits with background colors of: $1, Purple. $2, Orange brown. $3, Green.
$6, Vespucci and map.

2002, July 1   *Perf. 13½x13¼*
2404-2406 G194   Set of 3   4.50   4.50
Souvenir Sheet
2407 G194 $6 multi   4.50   4.50

Butterflies, Insects, Mushrooms and Whales Type of 2002
No. 2408, $1 — Whales: a, Sperm. b, Bottlenose. c, Sei. d, Killer. e, Humpback. f, Pygmy sperm.
No. 2409, $1 — Insects: a, Bumblebee. b, Dragonfly. c, Hercules beetle. d, Ladybug. e, Figure-of-eight butterfly. f, Praying mantis.
No. 2410, $2 — Butterflies: a, White peacock. b, Orange-barred sulphur. c, Blue night. d, Banded king shoemaker. e, Cramer's mesene. f, Common morpho.
No. 2411, $2 — Mushrooms: a, Shaggy mane. b, Shaggy parasol. c, Purple coincap. d, Sharp-scaled parasol. e, Thick-footed morel. f, Rosy-gill fairy helmet.
No. 2412, $6, Blue whale, horiz. No. 2413, $6, Dragonfly, horiz. No. 2414, $6, Blue night butterfly, horiz. No. 2415, $6, Death cap mushroom.

2002, Aug. 12   *Perf. 14*
Sheets of 6, #a-f
2408-2411 A538   Set of 4   27.50   27.50
Souvenir Sheets
2412-2415 A538   Set of 4   18.00   18.00

Elvis Presley Type of 2002 and

Elvis Presley — G195

No. 2416, Color portrait.
No. 2417: a, Wearing light plaid shirt. b, Holding microphone. c, Wearing dark shirt. d, Holding guitar with neck up. e, Wearing suit, holding guitar. f, Wearing short-sleeve shirt, holding guitar. g, Wearing shirt with flowers on shoulders. h, Wearing wrist watch and short-sleeve shirt. i, Wearing dark plaid shirt, holding guitar.

2002, Aug. 26   *Perf. 13¾*
2416 A527 $1 multi   .75   .75
2417 G195 $1 Sheet of 9, #a-i   6.75   6.75
No. 2416 printed in sheets of 9.

Dutch Nobel Prize Winners, Lighthouses and Women's Costumes Types of 2002
No. 2418 — Nobel Prize winners: a, Paul Crutzen, Chemistry, 1995. b, Nobel Medal for Physics, Chemistry, Physiology or Medicine, and Literature. c, Martinus J. G. Veltman, Physics, 1999. d, Hendrik A. Lorentz, Physics, 1902. e, Christiaan Eijkman, Physiology or Medicine, 1929. f, Gerardus 't Hooft, Physics, 1999.
No. 2419 — Lighthouses: a, Ameland. b, Vlieland. c, Julianadorp. d, Noordwijk. e, Hoek van Holland. f, Goeree.
No. 2420 — Women's costumes: a, Noord-Holland (woman with child). b, Overijssel (woman with blue dress and plaid neckerchief). c, Zeeland (woman with necklace).

2002, Aug. 29   *Perf. 13½x13¼*
2418 A532 $1.50 Sheet of 6, #a-f   6.75   6.75
2419 A533 $1.50 Sheet of 6, #a-f   6.75   6.75
Perf. 13¼
2420 A534 $3 Sheet of 3, #a-c   6.75   6.75
Amphilex 2002 Intl. Stamp Exhibition, Amsterdam.

Teddy Bear Centenary Types of 2002
No. 2421 — Bear with: a, 15c, Tasseled helmet. b, $2, Black hat with red bullseye. c, $3, Hat and neck ruffle. d, $4, Gray hat.
No. 2422 — Bear with: a, 50c, Happy birthday heart. b, $1, Flower, vest, hat, and violin case. c, $2, Hat and trench coat. d, $5, Shorts.

2002, Sept. 23   *Perf. 14*
2421 A529   Sheet of 4, #a-d   7.00   7.00
2422 A530   Sheet of 4, #a-d   6.50   6.50

Christmas Type of 2002
Carpaccio paintings: 15c, The Redeemer and the Four Apostles. 25c, The Miracle of the Relic of the Cross, vert. 50c, The Presentation in the Temple. $2, The Visitation. $3, The Birth of the Virgin.
$6, Madonna and Child and Two Angels, by Cimabue, vert.

2002, Nov. 4   *Perf. 14*
2423-2427 A541   Set of 5   4.50   4.50
Souvenir Sheet
2428 A541 $6 multi   4.50   4.50

World Cup Soccer Matches Type of 2002
No. 2429, $1.50: a, Oliver Neuville, Eddie Pope. b, Claudio Reyna, Miroslav Klose. c, Christian Ziege, Frankie Hejduk. d, Nadal, Jung Hwan Ahn. e, Luis Enrique, Chong Gug Song. f, Park Ji Sung, Mendieta Gaizka.
No. 2430, $1.50: a, Danny Mills, Ronaldo. b, Roque Junior, Emile Heskey. c, Sol Campbell, Rivaldo. d, Lamine Diatta, Hakan Sukur. e, Umit Davala, Khalilou Fadiga. f, El Hadji Diouf, Tugay Kerimoglu.
No. 2431, $3: a, Oliver Kahn. b, Brad Friedel.
No. 2432, $3: a, Chun Soo Lee. b, Juan Carlos Valeron.
No. 2433, $3: a, David Beckham, Roberto Carlos. b, Ronaldinho, Nicky Butt.
No. 2434, $3: a, Alpay Ozalan. b, Fadiga.

2002, Nov. 18   *Perf. 13¼*
Sheets of 6, #a-f
2429-2430 A542   Set of 2   13.50   13.50
Souvenir Sheets of 2, #a-b
2431-2434 A542   Set of 4   18.00   18.00

Dale Earnhardt Type of 2002
No. 2435: a, $2, 1980 photo. b, $2, 1986 photo. c, $2, 1987 photo. d, $2, 1990 photo. e, $2, 1991 photo. f, $2, 1993 photo. g, $2, 1994 photo. h, $4, Two cars (75x50mm).

2002   *Perf. 13½x13¾*
2435 A518   Sheet of 8, #a-h   13.50   13.50

New Year 2003
(Year of the
Ram) — G196

2003, Jan. 27   *Perf. 14*
2436 G196 $1.25 multi   .95   .95
Printed in sheets of 4.

G197

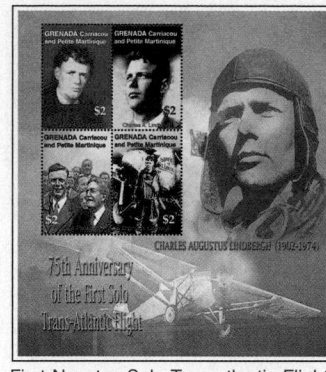

Coronation of Queen Elizabeth II, 50th Anniv. — G198

No. 2437: a, As child. b, In blue dress. c, On horse.
$6, Wearing sash and tiara.
$20, Wearing tiara.

2003   Litho.   *Perf. 14*
2437 G197 $3 Sheet of 3, #a-c   6.75 6.75

Souvenir Sheet
2438 G197 $6 multi   4.50 4.50

Miniature Sheet
Litho. & Embossed
Perf. 13¼x13
2439 G198 $20 gold & multi   15.00 15.00

Issued: Nos. 2437-2438, 8/25; No. 2439, 2/24.

Space Shuttle Columbia Type of 2003

No. 2440: a, Mission Specialist 1 David M. Brown. b, Commander Rick D. Husband. c, Mission Specialist 4 Laurel Blair Salton Clark. d, Mission Specialist 4 Kalpana Chawla. e, Payload Commander Michael P. Anderson. f, Pilot William C. McCool. g, Payload Specialist 4 Ilan Ramon.

2003, Apr. 7   Litho.   *Perf. 13¼*
2440 A549 $1 Sheet of 7, #a-g   5.25 5.25

Klimt Paintings Type of 2003

Designs: 15c, Le Chapeau de Plumes Noires. 25c, Le Schloss Kammer am Attersee. 50c, Malcesine sue le Lac de Garde. 75c, Ferme en Haute Autriche. $1.25, Portrait d'une Dame. $4, La Frise Beethoven.
No. 2447: a, Portrait de la Baronne Elisabeth Bachofen-Echt. b, Portrait d'une Dame, diff. c, Portrait d'Emilie Floge. d, Portrait d'Adele Bloch-Bauer.
$6, Le Baiser.

2003, Apr. 28   *Perf. 14¼*
2441-2446 A550 Set of 6   5.25 5.25
    Perf. 13¼
2447 A550 $2 Sheet of 4, #a-d   6.00 6.00

Size: 83x103mm
Imperf
2448 A550 $6 multi   4.50 4.50

Japanese Art Type of 2003

Paintings by Kunichika Toyohara: 50c, The Actor Danjuro Ichikawa IX as the Beggar Kagekiyo Akushichibyoe. 75c, The Actor Danjuro Ichikawa IX as the Female Demon Uwanari. $1.25, The Actor Tossho Sawamura II as Sutewakamaru. $3, The Actor Hikosaburo Bando V as Danjo Nikki.
No. 2453: a, The Actor Shikan Nakamura IV as Rokusuke Keyamura. b, The Actor Hikosaburo Bando V as Ichimisair No Musume Osono. c, The Actor Sadanji Ichikawa I as Wada No Shimobe Busuke. d, The Actor Sandanji Ichikawa I as Kiyomizu no Yoshitaka.
$6, The Actor Kikugoro Onoe V as Tsuneemon Torii Retruning to Mikawa, horiz.

2003, Apr. 28   *Perf. 14¼*
2449-2452 A551 Set of 4   4.25 4.25
2453 A551 $2 Sheet of 4, #a-d   6.00 6.00

Souvenir Sheet
2454 A551 $6 multi   4.50 4.50

Cranach Paintings Type of 2003

Details from paintings by Lucas Cranach the Elder: 25c, The St. Mary Altarpiece. $1, The St. Mary Altarpiece, diff., vert. $1.25, Duke John with St. James the Greater, from Altarpiece of the Princes, vert. $3, Frederick the Wise with St. Bartholomew, vert.

No. 2459: a, Judith at the Table of Holofernes. b, Central panel of St. Catherine Altarpeice. c, Judith Killing Holofernes. d, The Martyrdom of St. Catherine.
$6, Cardinal Albrecht of Brandenbourg as St. Jerome in the Wilderness, vert.

2003, Apr. 28
2455-2458 A552 Set of 4   4.25 4.25
2459 A552 $2 Sheet of 4, #a-d   6.00 6.00

Souvenir Sheet
2460 A552 $6 multi   4.50 4.50

Teddy Bear Type of 2003
2003, Apr. 29 Embroidered *Imperf.*
Self-Adhesive
2461 A553 $15 multi   11.50 11.50

Issued in sheets of 4.

Tour de France Type of 2003

No. 2462, $2: a, Ferdinand Kubler, 1950. b, Hugo Koblet, 1051. c, Fauoto Coppi, 1052. d, Louison Bobet, 1953.
No. 2463, $2: a, Bobet, 1954. b, Bobet, 1955. c, Roger Walkowiak, 1956. d, Jacques Anquetil, 1957.
No. 2464, $2: a, Gastone Nencini, 1960. b, Anquetil, 1961. c, Anquetil, 1962. d, Anquetil, 1963.
No. 2465, $6, Bobet, 1953-55. No. 2466, $6, Anquetil, 1957, diff. No. 2467, $6, Eddy Merckx, 1969.

2003, June 17   *Perf. 13¼*
Sheets of 4, #a-d
2462-2464 A555 Set of 3   18.00 18.00

Souvenir Sheets
2465-2467 A555 Set of 3   13.50 13.50

John F. Kennedy Type of 2002

No. 2468, $2: a, As Choate graduate, 1935. b, As congressman, 1946. c, With wife, Jacqueline, on tennis court. d, With son, John, Jr.
No. 2469, $2: a, With wife, Jacqueline. b, Announcing Cuban blockade, 1962. c, Seated in White House, 1962. d, Wife and children at funeral, 1963.

2003, July 1   *Perf. 14*
Sheets of 4, #a-d
2468-2469 A544 Set of 2   12.00 12.00

Intl. Year of Fresh Water Type of 2003

No. 2470 — Flag and: a, La Sagesse. b, Annadale Falls. c, Grand Etang.
$6, Flag and St. George, horiz.

2003, July 4   *Perf. 13½x13¼*
2470 A559 $2 Sheet of 3, #a-c   4.50 4.50

Souvenir Sheet
Perf. 13¼x13½
2471 A559 $6 multi   4.50 4.50

Circus Performers Type of 2003

No. 2472, $2 — Clowns: a, Anton Pilossian. b, Victor Vashnikov. c, Dan Rice. d, Tom Comet.
No. 2473, $2: a, Dog. b, Macaw. c, Monique. d, Vassily Trofimov.

2003, July 14   *Perf. 14*
Sheets of 4, #a-d
2472-2473 A560 Set of 2   12.00 12.00

Powered Flight Type of 2003

No. 2474, $2: a, Wright Brothers Flyer. b, NC-4. c, Douglas World Cruiser. d, Fokker Eindecker.
No. 2475, $2: a, Hawker Hart. b, Martin B-10. c, Armstrong Whitworth Siskin IIIA. d, Loening OL-8.
No. 2476, $2: a, Hansa-Brandenberg D.1. b, B.E. 2e. c, Handley Page 0/400. d, Avro 504.
No. 2477, $6, Wright Brothers No. 3 glider. No. 2478, $6, Wright Brothers Flyer No. 2. No. 2479, $6, Gloster Gamecock.

2003, July 14
Sheets of 4, #a-d
2474-2476 A556 Set of 3   18.00 18.00

Souvenir Sheets
2477-2479 A556 Set of 3   13.50 13.50

First Nonstop Solo Transatlantic Flight, 75th Anniv. — G199

No. 2480, $2: a, Charles Lindbergh (white denomination, blue background). b, Lindbergh (blue denomination, brown background. c, Lindbergh's arrival in Paris, 1927. d, Lindbergh and Spirit of St. Louis (white denomination, country name in blue)
No. 2481, $2: a, Lindbergh (blue denomination and background). b, Lindbergh and Spirit of St. Louis, blue denomination, red violet background). c, Lindbergh and Spirit of St. Louis (white denomination and country name). d, Lindbergh (white denomination, blue country name).

2003, July 14
Sheets of 4, #a-d
2480-2481 G199 Set of 2   12.00 12.00

Prince William Type of 2003

No. 2482, vert.: a, Looking right. b, Looking forward. c, Looking left.
$6, In ski jacket, vert.

2003, Sept. 22
2482 A562 $3 Sheet of 3, #a-c   6.75 6.75

Souvenir Sheet
2483 A562 $6 multi   4.50 4.50

Flowers Type of 2003

Designs: 75c, Wild rhododendron, vert. $1, Peony. $1.25, Camellia, vert. No. 2487, $2, Laurel, vert.
No. 2488, $2, vert.: a, Apple blossom. b, Mock orange. c, Wild rose. d, Hibiscus.
$6, Violets, vert.

2003, Oct. 23   *Perf. 13½*
2484-2487 A567 Set of 4   3.75 3.75
2488 A567 $2 Sheet of 4, #a-d   6.00 6.00

Souvenir Sheet
2489 A567 $6 multi   4.50 4.50

ASDA Postage Stamp Mega-event (#2489).

Fish Type of 2003

Designs: 25c, Domino damsel. 75c, Porcupine fish. $1.25, Damselfish. No. 2493, $2, Clownfish.
No. 2494, $2: a, Triggerfish. b, Half-and-half wrasse. c, Long-fin bannerfish. d, Butterflyfish.
$6, Blue-girdled angelfish.

2003, Oct. 23
2490-2493 A568 Set of 4   3.25 3.25
2494 A568 $2 Sheet of 4, #a-d   6.00 6.00

Souvenir Sheet
2495 A568 $6 multi   4.50 4.50

Birds Type of 2003

Designs: 25c, Rose-breasted grosbeak. No. 2497, 50c, Gray catbird. No. 2498, 50c, Bullock's oriole. $1, Blue grosbeak.
No. 2500, $2, vert.: a, Lazuli bunting. b, Indigo bunting. c, Broad-tailed hummingbird. d, Scarlet tanager.
$6, Barn swallow.

2003, Oct. 23
2496-2499 A569 Set of 4   1.75 1.75
2500 A569 $2 Sheet of 4, #a-d   6.00 6.00

Souvenir Sheet
2501 A569 $6 multi   4.50 4.50

Christmas Type of 2003

Designs: 35c, Madonna and Child, from Carnesecchi Tabernacle, by Domenico Veneziano. 75c, Madonna and Child, from Magnoli altarpiece, by Veneziano. 90c, Crevole Madonna, by Duccio di Buoninsegna. $3, Madonna and Child, by Veneziano.
$6, Madonna and Child by the Fireplace, by Robert Campin.

2003, Nov. 17   *Perf. 14¼*
2502-2505 A570 Set of 4   3.75 3.75

Souvenir Sheet
2506 A570 $6 multi   4.50 4.50

Hermitage Paintings Type of 2003

Designs: 75c, Abraham and Isaac, by Rembrandt, vert. $1, David and Jonathan, by Rembrandt, vert. $1.25, St. Onuphrius, by Jusepe de Ribera, vert. No. 2510, $2, Pope Paul III, by Titian, vert.
No. 2511, $2: a, Rest on the Flight into Egypt, by Bartolomé Estéban Murillo. b, Esther Before Ahasuerus, by Nicolas Poussin. c, Abraham's Servant and Rebecca, by Jacob Hogers. d, The Prophet Elisha and Naaman, by Lambert Jacobsz.
No. 2512, Hagar Flees Abram's House, by Peter Paul Rubens. No. 2513, The Building of Noah's Ark, by Guido Reni, vert.

2003, Dec. 8   *Perf. 13½*
2507-2510 A572 Set of 4   3.75 3.75
2511 A572 $2 Sheet of 4, #a-d   6.00 6.00

Imperf
Size: 78x65mm
2512 A572 $6 multi   4.50 4.50
Size: 67x78mm
2513 A572 $6 multi   4.50 4.50

Norman Rockwell Type of 2003

No. 2514, vert.: a, The Trumpeter. b, Waiting for the Vet. c, The Diving Board. d, The Discovery.
$6, Day in a Boy's Life.

2003, Dec. 8   Litho.   *Perf. 13¼*
2514 A571 $2 Sheet of 4, #a-d   6.00 6.00

Souvenir Sheet
2515 A571 $6 multi   4.50 4.50

Pablo Picasso Type of 2003

No. 2516: a, Jacqueline Sitting. b, Jacqueline with Flower. c, Seated Nude. d, Woman in Armchair.
$6, Head of a Woman.

2003, Dec. 8   *Perf. 13¼*
2516 A573 $2 Sheet of 4, #a-d   6.00 6.00
Imperf
2517 A573 $6 multi   4.50 4.50

No. 2516 contains four 37x50mm stamps.

New Year (Year of the Monkey) Type of 2004

No. 2518: a, White, blue and orange monkey. b, Blue monkey. c, Brown monkey. d, Monkey with orange face.

2004, Jan. 4   *Perf. 14*
2518 A574 $1.50 Sheet of 4, #a-d   4.50 4.50

Zhoa Mengfu (1254-1322), Artist — G200

No. 2519: a, The Mind Landscape of Xie Youyu. b, Scroll with green backround and large mountains at left and right. c, Twin Pines. d, Scroll with brown background and large mountain at left.
$6, Autumn.

2004, Jan. 29 Litho.   *Perf. 13½x13¼*
2519 G200 $2 Sheet of 4, #a-d   6.00 4.50

Souvenir Sheet
2520 G200 $6 multi   4.50 4.50

Arthur and Friends Type of 2004

No. 2521: a, Brain. b, Binky. c, Francine. d, Prunella. e, Arthur. f, Muffy.
No. 2522, $2: a, Francine, diff. b, Buster. c, Muffy, diff. d, Sue Ellen.
No. 2523, $2 a, Francine and butterfly. b, Binky and map. c, Brain and blackboard. d, Arthur and model of solar system.

2004, Jan. 29 — Perf. 13¼
2521 A577 $1.50 Sheet of 6,
　#a-f　　　　6.75　6.75
Sheets of 4, #a-d
2522-2523 A577　Set of 2　12.00 12.00

Olympics Type of 2004
Designs: 25c, Long jumper, 1924 Paris Olympics. 50c, Avery Brundage, Intl. Olympic Committee President, 1952-72. $1, Commemorative medal for 1972 Munich Olympics. $4, Paidotribai.

2004, Apr. 8 — Litho.
2524-2527 A579　Set of 4　4.50 4.50

Deng Xiaoping Type of 2004
Souvenir Sheet
2004, May 3 — Perf. 13½x13¼
2528 A582 $6 Wearing cap　4.50 4.50

Pope John Paul II Type of 2004
No. 2529: a, With Lech Walesa. b, With Meir Lau, Chief Rabbi of Israel. c, Blessing children. d, At computer. e, Wearing miter.

2004, May 3 — Perf. 13½
2529 A583 $2 Sheet of 5, #a-e　7.50 7.50

Marilyn Monroe Type of 2004
Designs: 50c, Portrait, diff.
No. 2531 — Various portraits with color and location of denomination of: a, Black, UL. b, Black, UR. c, White, UR. d, White, UL.

2004, May 3 — Perf. 13½x13¼
2530 A584 50c multi　　　.40　.40
2531 A584 $2 Sheet of 4, #a-d　6.00 6.00

No. 2530 was printed in sheets of 16.

D-Day Type of 2004
Designs: 25c, Admiral Sir Bertram Ramsay. 50c, Lt. Gen. Miles Dempsey. 75c, Bob Shrimpton, Submarine Detector on HMS Belfast. $4, Denis Edwards, 6th Airborne Division.
No. 2536, $2: a, Sir Winston Churchill without hat. b, Churchill with hat. c, British link up with Airborne troops. d, Link up at Orne River.
No. 2537, $2: a, US troops move inland. b, Troops move inland from Omaha Beach. c, Heavy fighting on Sword Beach. d, German generals meet.
No. 2538, $6, Assault landing craft head for invasion beaches. No. 2539, $6, Gunner in a British bomber.

2004, July 19 — Perf. 14
Stamps + Labels (#2532-2535)
2532-2535 A586　Set of 4　4.25 4.25
Sheets of 4, #a-d
2536-2537 A586　Set of 2　12.00 12.00
Souvenir Sheets
2538-2539 A586　Set of 2　9.00 9.00

Locomotives Type of 2004
No. 2540, $1: a, Liner V2 Class 2-6-2. b, Sudan Railways 2-8-2. c, China Railways DF4 Co-Co. d, LMS 2F 0-6-0 with Black 5 4-6-0. e, LMS Lickey Banker 0-10-0. f, LMS Princess Royal Pacific. g, LMS Reboilered Claughton Class 4-6-0. h, LMS Stanier 8F 2-8-0. i, Midland Railway Compound 4-4-0.
No. 2541, $1: a, Britannia Class 4-6-2. b, Indian Railways XD Class 2-8-2. c, China Railways KD6 2-8-0 (USATC S160). d, SE+CR 01 Class 0-6-0. e, Battle of Britain Light Pacific. f, SR King Arthur Class 4-6-0. g, SR Marsh 13 Class 4-4-2T. h, SR N Class 2-6-0. i, SR School Class 4-4-0.
No. 2542, $1: a, SR Merchant Navy Pacific 4-6-2. b, Gazira Cotton Railway, Sudan. c, Spanish Railways 4-8-4. d, LNER 04-1 Class 2-8-0. e, LNER A1 4-6-2 Pacific. f, LNER A3 Class 4-6-2. g, LNER A4 Class 4-6-2 Pacific. h, LNER B1 Class 4-6-0. i, LNER Ivatt Large Atlantic 4-4-2 A4 Pacific 4-6-2.
No. 2543, $6, Aberdeen to Penzance train. No. 2544, $6, London to Holyhead train. No. 2545, $6, Dublin to Tralee train.

2004, July 19 — Perf. 14
Sheets of 9, #a-i
2540-2542 A587　Set of 3　21.00 21.00
Souvenir Sheets
2543-2545 A587　Set of 3　13.50 13.50

Queen Juliana Type of 2004
2004, Aug. 25 — Litho. — Perf. 13¼
2546 A590 $2 1937 portrait　1.50 1.50

Printed in sheets of 6.

Carriacou Regatta Festival, 40th Anniv. — G201

Designs: 75c, Parade. 90c, People, boats in water. $1, Sailboats, vert.

2004, Oct. 11 — Perf. 14
2547-2549 G201　Set of 3　2.00 2.00

FIFA Type of 2004
No. 2550: a, David Beckham. b, Marcel Desailly. c, Guido Buchwald. d, Alfonso. $6, Bobby Charlton.

2004, Nov. 1 — Perf. 12¾x12½
2550 A595 $2 Sheet of 4, #a-d　6.00 6.00
Souvenir Sheet
2551 A595 $6 multi　4.50 4.50

Ocean Liners — G202

Designs: 25c, Titanic. 75c, Michelangelo. $1, America. $1.25, Vaterland. $2, Deutschland. $3, Mauritania.
$6, Ile de France.

2004, Nov. 29 — Perf. 14¼
2552-2557 G202　Set of 6　6.25 6.25
Souvenir Sheet
2558 G202 $6 multi　4.50 4.50

Elvis Presley Type of 2004
No. 2559, $2: a, Wearing purple shirt. b, Playing guitar, wearing polka dot shirt, "Elvis Presley" at right. c, With guitar hanging from neck, "Elvis Presley" at right. d, Wearing patterned shirt.
No. 2560, $2: a, Wearing brown shirt. b, Playing guitar, wearing polka dot shirt, "Elvis Presley" at left. c, With guitar hanging from neck, "Elvis Presley" at left. d, Wearing gray suit and black shirt, playing guitar.

2004, Nov. 29 — Perf. 13¼
Sheets of 4, #a-d
2559-2560 A588　Set of 2　12.00 12.00

Christmas Type of 2004
Paintings by Norman Rockwell: 35c, Follow Me in Merry Measure. 75c, The Merrie Old Coach Driver. 90c, Joy to the World. $3, Santa Reading His Mail.
$6, Wartime Santa.

2004, Dec. 9 — Perf. 12
2561-2564 A600　Set of 4　3.75 3.75
Size: 63x81mm
Imperf
2565 A600 $6 multi　4.50 4.50

Babe Ruth Type of 2004
No. 2566: a, Blue background. b, White background.
No. 2567: a, Swinging bat. b, Looking forward. c, Looking to right. d, With glove.

2004, Jan. 29 — Litho. — Perf. 14
2566 A598 50c Pair, #a-b　.75　.75
2567 A598 $2 Sheet of 4, #a-d　6.00 6.00

Moths — G202a

Designs: 75c, Scarlet-bodied wasp moth. 90c, Bella moth. $1, Sphinx moth. $3, Faithful beauty moth.
$6, Empyreuma affinis.

2004, Nov. 17 — Perf. 12¾
2568-2571 G202a　Set of 4　4.25 4.25
Souvenir Sheet
2572 G202a $6 multi　4.50 4.50

Ronald Reagan Type of 2004
No. 2573: a, With Press Secretary James Brady. b, With German Chancellor Helmut Kohl. c, With family. d, With Princess Diana.

2004, Nov. 29 — Perf. 13¼x13½
2573 A597 $2 Sheet of 4, #a-d　6.00 6.00

Year of the Rooster Type of 2005
Paintings by Ren Yi: 75c, Double Chickens and Peony. $3, A Rooster, horiz.

2005, Jan. 17 — Perf. 12¾x13
2574 A601 75c multi　　.60　.60
Souvenir Sheet
2575 A601 $3 multi　2.25 2.25

No. 2574 printed in sheets of 4. No. 2575 contains one 56x35mm stamp.

Intl. Year of Rice Type of 2005 and

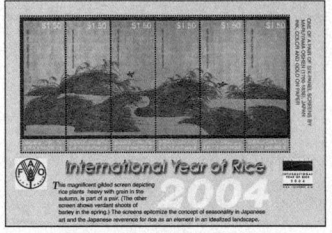

Screen Panels by Oshen Maruyama — G203

No. 2576 — Various panels depicting rice plants and birds.
$6, Rice Farming in Bali, by unknown artist, horiz.

2005, Feb. 10 — Perf. 14
2576 G203 $1.50 Sheet of 6, #a-f 6.75 6.75
Souvenir Sheet
2577 A602 $6 multi　4.50 4.50

Prehistoric Animals Type of 2005
No. 2578: a, Psittacosaurus. b, Deinonychus. c, Suchomimus. d, Smilodon.
$6, Tenotosaurus.

2005, Feb. 10 — Perf. 13¼x13½
2578 A604 $2 Sheet of 4, #a-d　6.00 6.00
Souvenir Sheet
2579 A604 $6 multi　4.50 4.50

See Nos. 2598-2601.

Reptiles and Amphibians — G204

No. 2580: a, Poison dart frog. b, Western Antillean anole. c, Black iguana. d, American crocodile.
$6, Anolis lizard.

2005, Feb. 10 — Perf. 12¾
2580 G204 $2 Sheet of 4, #a-d　8.00 8.00
Souvenir Sheet
2581 G204 $6 multi　6.00 6.00

Carnivorous Plants — G205

No. 2582: a, Heliamphora tatei. b, Sarracenia flava, Genlisea pygmaea. c, Nepenthes bicalcarata. d, Utricularia intermedia.
$6, Dionaea muscipula.

2005, Feb. 10
2582 G205 $2 Sheet of 4, #a-d　6.00 6.00
Souvenir Sheet
2583 G205 $6 multi　4.50 4.50

Elvis Presley Type of 2005
No. 2584, $1.50: a, With guitar, 1955. b, Singing, 1956. c, With hand on chin, 1958. d, In suit, 1962. e, With guitar, 1968. f, Singing, 1972.
No. 2585, $1.50: a, In Army uniform, 1958. b, Wearing Hawaiian shirt, 1961. c, Wearing cap, 1963. d, Wearing turban, 1965. e, Sitting on sports car, 1966. f, With stethoscope, 1969.

2005, Apr. 4 — Perf. 13½
Sheets of 6, #a-f
2584-2585 A607　Set of 2　13.50 13.50

Battle of Trafalgar, Bicent. — G206

Designs: 75c, Swiftsure. $1, British sail near Cape Trafalgar, horiz. $2, Capt. Alexander Ball. $3, Vice-Admiral Francedillaois Brueys d'Aigallieres.
$6, Admiral Aristide du Petit-Thouars.

2005, Apr. 4 — Perf. 14
2586-2589 G206　Set of 4　5.25 5.25
Souvenir Sheet
2590 G206 $6 multi　4.50 4.50

Yasujiro Ozu Type of 2005
No. 2591: a, A Mother Should Be Loved, 1934. b, An Inn in Tokyo, 1935. c, Dragnet Girl, 1933. d, There Was a Father, 1942.

2005, Apr. 8 — Perf. 14¼
2591 A608 $2 Sheet of 4, #a-d　6.00 6.00

Basketball Players Type of 2004
Designs: No. 2592, 75c, Steve Francis, Orlando Magic. No. 2593, 75c, Allan Houston, New York Knicks. No. 2594, 75c, Tracy McGrady, Houston Rockets. No. 2595, 75c, Steve Nash, Phoenix Suns. No. 2596, 75c, Shaquille O'Neal, Miami Heat. No. 2597, 75c, Chris Webber, Sacramento Kings.

2005, Mar. 8 — Litho. — Perf. 14
2592-2597 A596　Set of 6　3.50 3.50

Each stamp printed in sheets of 12.

Prehistoric Animals Type of 2005
No. 2598, $2: a, Eurypholis. b, Ichthyosaurus. c, Plesiosaur. d, Varnerxiphactinus.
No. 2599, $2: a, Pterosaurus. b, Archaeopteryx. c, Pterosaurian. d, Microraptor.
No. 2600, $6, Uintatherium. No. 2601, $6, Mammoth, vert.

Perf. 13¼x13¾, 13¾x13¼
2005, Apr. 15
Sheets of 4, #a-d
2598-2599 A604　Set of 2　12.00 12.00
Souvenir Sheets
2600-2601 A604　Set of 2　9.00 9.00

End of World War II Type of 2005

No. 2602, $2 — Battle of El Alamein: a, Field Marshal Bernard Montgomery directs troops forward. b, Field Marshal Erwin Rommel ready for battle. c, Troops move forward into battle. d, Line of German prisoners after battle.

No. 2603, $2 — Fall of Berlin: a, Russians at the gates of Berlin. b, German soldiers surrender. c, Berlin in ruins. d, Picking up the pieces. No. 2604, $6, Troops attacking. No. 2605, $6, Sign with quote by Adolf Hitler, vert.

2005, May 10

Sheets of 4, #a-d

2602-2603 A610 Set of 2   12.00 12.00

Souvenir Sheets

2604-2605 A610 Set of 2   9.00 9.00

Albert Einstein Type of 2005

No. 2606, vert.: a, Einstein, planet, diagram of Earth and Moon. b, Einstein. c, Israeli Prime Minister David Ben Gurion.

2005, June 27   **Perf. 13¼**

2606 A615 $3 Sheet of 3, #a-c   6.75 6.75

No. 2606 contains three 38x50mm stamps.

V-J Day Type of 2005

No. 2607, $2: a, P-38J Lightning. b, P-51D Mustang. c, F-4 fighter plane. d, Douglas C-47 Skytrain.

No. 2608, $2: a, Officer reads V-J Day message to his troops. b, Chaplain's prayer. c, Rejoicing the victory. d, USS Missouri in Tokyo Bay.

2005, July 11   **Perf. 12¾**

Sheets of 4, #a-d

2607-2608 A612 Set of 2   12.00 12.00

Rotary International Type of 2005

No. 2609, horiz.: a, People in front of National Polio Laboratory. b, People in National Polio Laboratory. c, Rotary International emblem.

2005, July 11   **Perf. 14**

2609 A613 $3 Sheet of 3, #a-c   6.75 6.75

Pope John Paul II (1920-2005) — G207

2005, Sept. 22   **Perf. 13¼x13½**

2610 G207 $3 multi   2.25 2.25

Printed in sheets of 6.

Maimonides (1135-1204), Philosopher — G208

2005   **Perf. 12**

2611 G208 $2 multi   1.50 1.50

Christmas Type of 2005

Designs: 35c, Madonna and Child, by Andrea del Sarto. 75c, Madonna Pesaro, by Titian. 90c, Madonna and Child, by Titian. $3, Madonna and Child, by Peter Paul Rubens. $6, Madonna and Child, by Domenico Veneziano.

2005   **Perf. 12¾**

2612-2615 A625 Set of 4   3.75 3.75

Souvenir Sheet

2616 A625 $6 multi   4.50 4.50

Dog, by Chang Dai-Chien G209

2006, Jan. 3   **Litho.**   **Perf. 11½x11¼**

2617 G209 $1 multi   .75 .75

New Year 2006 (Year of the Dog). Printed in sheets of 4.

Pope Benedict XVI Type of 2006

2006, Jan. 10   **Perf. 13¼**

2618 A629 $2 Pope, diff.   1.50 1.50

Printed in sheets of 4.

Elvis Presley Type of 2006

Variable Die Cut Perf.

2006, Feb. 21   **Litho. & Embossed**

Without Gum

2619 A631 $20 multi   15.00 15.00

Queen Elizabeth II, 80th Birthday Type of 2006

No. 2620: a, Queen wearing hat, sepia photograph. b, Queen wearing tiara. c, Queen with Princess Anne. d, Queen wearing hat, color photograph.

$6, Portrait of Queen in robe.

2006, Feb. 21   **Litho.**   **Perf. 13¼**

2620 A632 $3 Sheet of 4, #a-d   9.00 9.00

Souvenir Sheet

Perf. 12

2621 A632 $6 multi   4.50 4.50

Marilyn Monroe Type of 2006

2006, Mar. 30   **Perf. 13½**

2622 A634 $3 Monroe, diff.   2.25 2.25

Printed in sheets of 4.

Rembrandt Type of 2006

Designs: 75c, The Strolling Musicians. 90c, The Great Jewish Bride. $1, Old Haaringh. $4, Beggars Receiving Alms at the Door of a House. No. 2627, $6, Young Woman in a Pearl-trimmed Beret (70x100mm). No. 2628, $6, Portrait of a Boy (70x100mm).

No. 2629: a, Man from Lady and Gentleman in Black. b, Woman from Lady and Gentleman in Black. c, Man from The Shipbuilder and His Wife. d, Woman from The Shipbuilder and His Wife.

Perf. 12, 12½x12¼ (#2627-2628)

2006, June 16

2623-2628 A639 Set of 6   14.00 14.00

Miniature Sheet

2629 A639 $3 Sheet of 4, #a-d   9.00 9.00

Mozart Type of 2006

2006, June 22   **Litho.**   **Perf. 12¾**

2630 A640 $6 Don Giovanni   4.50 4.50

Space Type of 2006

No. 2631 — First Flight of Space Shuttle Columbia: a, Columbia on launchpad. b, Astronauts John W. Young and Robert L. Crippen. c, Liftoff of Columbia. d, Columbia in space. e, Crew in cabin. f, Columbia landing.

No. 2632, $3 — Apollo-Soyuz: a, Liftoff of Soyuz 19. b, Apollo-Soyuz crew. c, Crew in cabin. d, Soyuz 19.

No. 2633, $3 — Space Shuttle Discovery's return to space: a, Discovery on launchpad. b, Crew of Mission STS-114. c, Discovery and International Space Station. d, STS-114 space walk.

No. 2634, $6, Luna 9. No. 2635, $6, Venus Express. No. 2636, $6, Mars Reconnaissance Orbiter.

2006, Sept. 14

2631 A642 $2 Sheet of 6, #a-f   9.00 9.00

Sheets of 4, #a-d

2632-2633 A642 Set of 2   18.00 18.00

Souvenir Sheets

2634-2636 A642 Set of 3   13.50 13.50

Columbus Type of 2006

Designs: 75c, Pinta, vert. $1.50, Nina, Pinta and Santa Maria set sail. $2, Ship and map. $3, Columbus discovers San Salvador.

$6, Columbus.

2006, Oct. 26

2637-2640 A643 Set of 4   5.50 5.50

Souvenir Sheet

2641 A643 $6 multi   4.50 4.50

Christmas Type of 2006

Details of St. Willibrod in Adoration Before Mary, Mother of God, by Peter Paul Rubens: 25c, Man. 50c, Angels. 75c, Mary and Jesus. $1, St. Willibrod.

No. 2646: a, Like 25c. b, Like 50c. c, Like 75c. d, Like $1.

2006, Dec. 21   **Perf. 14**

2642-2645 A646 Set of 4   1.90 1.90

Souvenir Sheet

2646 A646 $2 Sheet of 4, #a-d   6.00 6.00

Souvenir Sheet

Airships — G210

No. 2647: a, LZ-127. b, Dining room of the Hindenburg. c, Marine airship L53.

2007, Jan. 16   **Perf. 13¼**

2647 G210 $3 Sheet of 3, #a-c   6.75 6.75

Souvenir Sheet

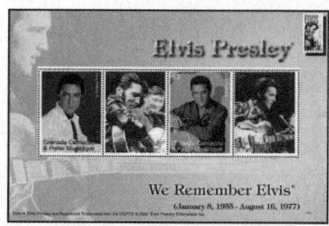

Elvis Presley (1935-77) — G211

No. 2648 — Various portraits with: a, Black denomination. b, Red denomination, playing guitar. c, White denomination. d, Red denomination, hands off guitar.

2007, Jan. 16   **Perf. 14¼**

2648 G211 $3 Sheet of 4, #a-d   9.00 9.00

Pres. John F. Kennedy (1917-63) — G212

No. 2649, $2: a, On crutches, running for Congress. b, Campaigning for Congress. c, Campaigning in New Hampshire. d, As president.

No. 2650, $2.50: a, Naru Island. b, As Navy lieutenant on Solomon Islands, wearing cap. c, As lieutenant on Solomon Islands, without cap. d, SOS coconut carved by Kennedy.

2007, Jan. 16   **Perf. 13½**

Sheets of 4, #a-d

2649-2650 G212 Set of 2   13.50 13.50

Scouting Type of 2007

Scout fleur-de-lis, "100," years "1907 / 2007," and background colors of: $2, Blue and green, horiz. $6, Orange and green, horiz.

2007, Jan. 16

2651 A650 $2 multi   1.50 1.50

Souvenir Sheet

2652 A650 $6 multi   4.50 4.50

No. 2651 printed in sheets of 4.

Year of the Pig Type of 2007

Miniature Sheet

No. 2653 — Wild Boar, by Liu Jiyou and painting name in: a, $1, Black. b, $1, Brown. c, $2, Black. d, $2, Red.

2007, Feb. 15   **Litho.**   **Perf. 14**

2653 A652 Sheet of 4, #a-d   4.50 4.50

G213

G214

Mushrooms — G215

Designs: 75c, Morchella semilibera. No. 2655, $1, Ganoderma resinaceum. No. 2656, $1, Helvella crispa. $4, Ganoderma sp.

No. 2658, $2: a, Russula sardonia. b, Amanita cruzii. c, Macrocybe titans. d, Amanita microspora.

No. 2659, $2: a, Aleuria aurantia. b, Boletus sp. c, Boletellus russellii. d, Otidea onotica.

No. 2660, $5, Amanita polypyramis. No. 2661, $5, Boletellus ananas. No. 2662, $5, Cantharellus cibarius.

2007, May 16   **Litho.**   **Perf. 14**

2654-2657 G213 Set of 4   5.25 5.25

Sheets of 4, #a-d

2658-2659 G214 Set of 2   12.00 12.00

Souvenir Sheets

2660 G214 $5 multi   3.75 3.75

2661-2662 G215 Set of 2   7.50 7.50

Birds — G216

Designs: 75c, Pied-billed grebe. No. 2664, $1, Black-crowned night heron. No. 2665, $1, Turkey vulture. $4, Green honeycreeper.

No. 2667, $2, horiz.: a, Caspian tern. b, Scarlet tanager. c, Common nighthawk. d, Osprey.

No. 2668, $2, horiz.: a, Hooded warbler. b, Northern flicker. c, Mockingbird. d, Blue tit.

No. 2669, $5, White-winged parakeet. No. 2670, $5, Blackpoll warbler, horiz. No. 2671, $5, Yellow-green vireo, horiz.

2007, May 16
2663-2666 G216 Set of 4 5.25 5.25

Sheets of 4, #a-d
2667-2668 G216 Set of 2 12.00 12.00

Souvenir Sheets
2669-2671 G216 Set of 3 11.50 11.50

Orchids — G217

Designs: 75c, Goodyera tesselata. $1.50, Oncidium floridanum. No. 2674, $2, Hexalectris spicata. $3, Pogonia ophioglossoides.
No. 2676, $2: a, Platanthera blephariglottis. b, Epipactis helleborine. c, Cypripedium alaskanum. d, Zeuxine strateumatica.
No. 2677, $2: a, Platanthera grandiflora. b, Platanthera peramoena. c, Cyrtopodium punctatum. d, Spiranthes odorata.
No. 2678, $6, Platanthera chapmanii. No. 2679, $6, Bletilla striata, horiz. No. 2680, $6, Macradenia lutescens, horiz.

2007, May 16 **Perf. 12¾**
2672-2675 G217 Set of 4 5.50 5.50

Sheets of 4, #a-d
2676-2677 G217 Set of 2 12.00 12.00

Souvenir Sheets
2678-2680 G217 Set of 3 13.50 13.50

Betty Boop in "Snow White" — G218

No. 2681, horiz.: a, Queen looking at ring in snow. b, Green witch looking at mirror, dog and clown. c, Dancing ghost. d, Betty Boop asleep, frozen skull.
No. 2682, horiz.: a, $1, Queen looking in mirror. b, $1, Angry queen. c, $1, Knights and tree stump. d, $2, Betty Boop with alarm clock. e, $2, Betty Boop with mirror, dog, clown. f, $2, Betty Boop in snow.
$6, Betty Boop running.

2007, June 4 **Perf. 13½**
2681 G218 $2 Sheet of 4, #a-d 6.00 6.00
2682 G218 Sheet of 6, #a-f 6.75 6.75

Souvenir Sheet
2683 G218 $6 multi 4.50 4.50

Intl. Polar Year Type of 2007

No. 2684, vert. — Royal penguins with: a, Country name at UR, denomination at LR. b, Country name at top, denomination at LR. c, Country name at LR, denomination at UL. d, Country name at bottom, denomination at UL. e, Country name at bottom, denomination at UR. f, Country name at UL, denomination at LR.
$6, African penguin, vert.

2007, June 25 **Perf. 13½**
2684 A657 $2 Sheet of 6, #a-f 9.00 9.00

Souvenir Sheet
2685 A657 $6 multi 4.50 4.50

First Helicopter Flight, Cent. Type of 2007

No. 2686, horiz.: a, BK 117. b, UH-1 Iroquois. c, S-65/RH-53D. d, UH-1B/C Iroquois. e, Autogyro. f, BO 105.
$6, AH-64 Apache, horiz.

2007, June 25
2686 A664 $1.50 Sheet of 6, #a-f 6.75 6.75

Souvenir Sheet
2687 A664 $6 multi 4.50 4.50

Pope Benedict XVI Type of 2007
2007, July 11
2688 A653 $1 Pope, diff. .75 .75
Printed in sheets of 8.

Christmas G219

Paintings: 25c, Virgin and Child with Saints Jerome and Bartholomew, by Alessandro Bonvicino. 50c, Virgin and Child Between Saints Thomas and Jerome, by Guido Reni. 75c, Virgin and Child, by Giovanni Batista Salvi. $1, Madonna of Decemviri, by Pietro Perugino.

2007, Oct. 26 **Perf. 14¼x14¾**
2689-2692 G219 Set of 4 1.90 1.90

Wedding of Queen Elizabeth II and Prince Philip, 60th Anniv. Type of 2007
Miniature Sheet

No. 2693 — Couple, denomination at left, dull maroon panel. b, Queen, denomination at right, dull maroon panel. c, Queen, denomination at left, maroon panel. d, Couple, denomination at right, maroon panel. e, Couple, denomination at left, maroon panel. f, Queen, denomination at right, maroon panel.

2007, June 25 **Litho.** **Perf. 13¼**
2693 A655 $1.50 Sheet of 6, #a-f 6.75 6.75

Year of the Rat Type of 2007
2007, Dec. 3 **Perf. 13x13¼**
2694 A667 $1 multi .75 .75
Printed in sheets of 4.

Princess Diana Type of 2007

No. 2695 — Diana wearing a, Plaid jacket. b, Purple feathered hat. c, Green dress. d, Plaid jacket, close-up in frame. e, Purple feathered hat, close-up in frame. f, Green dress, close-up in frame.
$6, Princess Diana, Prince Charles and infant, horiz.

2008, Jan. 14 **Perf. 13¼**
2695 A656 $1.50 Sheet of 6, #a-f 6.75 6.75

Souvenir Sheet
2696 A656 $6 multi 4.50 4.50

Elvis Presley Type of 2008

No. 2697 — Presley: a, Silhouette, holding microphone, gray background. b, Wearing green shirt. c, Silhouette, holding microphone, olive green background. d, Playing guitar. e, Silhouette, playing guitar. f, Wearing orange shirt.

2008, Jan. 14 **Perf. 13¼**
2697 A671 $1.50 Sheet of 6, #a-f 6.75 6.75

World Stamp Championship Type of 2008

Design: Aerial view of Jerusalem, horiz. (149x125mm).

2008, May 14 **Imperf.**
2698 A676 $6 multi 4.50 4.50

Basketball Type of 2008
Miniature Sheet

No. 2699 — Members of 2008 Boston Celtics basketball team: a, Ray Allen. b, Rajon Rondo. c, Paul Pierce. d, Kendrick Perkins. e, Kevin Garnett. f, Leon Powe. g, James Posey. h, Sam Cassell. i, P. J. Brown.

2008, June 17 **Litho.** **Perf. 13½**
2699 A678 $2 Sheet of 9, #a-i 6.75 6.75

Cats Type of 2008

No. 2700: a, Havana. b, Scottish Fold. c, American Curl. d, American Bobtail. e, Balinese. f, Singapura.
$6, Burmese, horiz.

2008, June 18 **Perf. 11½**
2700 A677 $1 Sheet of 6, #a-f 4.50 4.50

Souvenir Sheet
2701 A677 $6 multi 4.50 4.50

Elvis Presley Type of 2008
Miniature Sheet

No. 2702 — Presley: a, Wearing lei, holding microphone in right hand. b, Playing guitar, red striped background. c, Wearing lei, holding microphone in left hand, right arm extended with hand in fist. d, Playing guitar, olive green and black background. e, Wearing lei, holding microphone in left hand, right hand at side. f, Wearing red shirt.

2008, Oct. 10 **Perf. 13¼**
2702 A670 $1.50 Sheet of 6, #a-f 6.75 6.75

Christmas G220

Designs: 25c, Christmas ornament washing up on beach. 50c, Gift boxes hanging ornaments and electric Christmas lights. 75c, "Merry Christmas" written on beach. $1, Starfish and shells hanging ornaments, vert.

Perf. 14¾x14¼, 14¼x14¾
2008, Dec. 3 **Litho.**
2703-2706 G220 Set of 4 1.90 1.90

Space Exploration Type of 2009
Miniature Sheets

No. 2707, $2: a, Venus and Mercury. b, Jupiter. c, Earth and Mars. d, Saturn. e, Neptune. f, Uranus.
No. 2708, $2, vert. — Mariner 9: a, And the Valles Marineris on Mars. b, And technicians. c, And the Olympus Mons on Mars. d, Photograph of Valles Marineris. e, Lifting off on Atlas-Centaur rocket. f, And Phobos.
No. 2709, $2.50, vert. — Mariner 10: a, And Mars at UR. b, Lifting off on Atlas-Centaur rocket. c, And technicians. d, And Moon at UL.
No. 2710, $2.50, vert.: a, Pillars of Creation in Eagle Nebula. b, Orion Nebula. c, Crab Nebula. d, Horsehead Nebula.

2008, Dec. 24 **Perf. 14**

Sheets of 6, #a-f
2707-2708 A690 Set of 2 18.00 18.00

Sheets of 4, #a-d
2709-2710 A690 Set of 2 15.00 15.00

Fish G221

Designs: $1, Blue chromis. No. 2712, $2, Clown wrasse. No. 2713, $4, Orange-spotted filefish. $5, Palometa.
No. 2715, $2: a, Tiger grouper. b, Bluehead wrasse. c, Squirrel fish. d, Queen parrotfish. e, Yellowtail snapper. f, Barred hamlet.

2009, Jan. 9 **Perf. 12½**
2711-2714 G221 Set of 4 9.00 9.00
Perf. 12
2715 G221 $2 Sheet of 6, #a-f 9.00 9.00

G222

Shells — G223

Designs: 25c, True tulip. 50c Twisted plait olive. 75c, Junonia. $1, Royal comb venus.
No. 2720: a, Lion's paw. b, Banded tulip. c, Flame auger. d, Miniature melo, e, West Indian worm shell. f, Mouse cowry.

2009, Jan. 9 **Perf. 12½**
2716-2719 G222 Set of 4 1.90 1.90
Perf. 12
2720 G223 $2 Sheet of 6, #a-f 9.00 9.00

Obama Type of 2009

No. 2721 — Pres. Barack Obama: a, Pointing. b, Wearing blue tie, hands not shown. c, Touching thumb to index finger. d, Wearing red tie, hands not shown.
$10, Pres. Obama and US Capitol.

2009, Jan. 20 **Perf. 11½**
2721 A689 $2.75 Sheet of 4, #a-d 8.50 8.50

Souvenir Sheet
Perf. 13¼
2722 A689 $10 multi 7.75 7.75
No. 2722 contains one 38x51mm stamp.

New Year 2009 (Year of the Ox) — G224

2009, Jan. 26 **Perf. 11½**
2723 G224 $2.50 multi 1.90 1.90

Olympic Sports Type of 2009
Miniature Sheet

No. 2724, vert.: a, Archery. b, Track cycling. c, Wrestling. d, Boxing.

2009, Apr. 26 **Perf. 12**
2724 A700 $1.40 Sheet of 4, #a-d 4.25 4.25
China 2009 World Stamp Exhibition, Luoyang.

Miniature Sheet

Qianglong (1711-99), Chinese Emperor — G225

No. 2725: a, Qianglong as young man, with chop at UR. b, Qianglong, women, table and tree. c, Qianglong at desk. d, Qianglong as older man.

2009, Apr. 29 **Perf. 12**
2725 G225 $1.40 Sheet of 4, #a-d 4.25 4.25
China 2009 World Stamp Exhibition, Luoyang.

Elvis Presley Type of 2009
Miniature Sheet

No. 2726, horiz. — Presley: a, Singing, with hand raised near mouth, denimination in yellow brown. b, Holding microphone, denomination in purple. c, Holding microphone, diff., denomination in red violet. d, Singing and holding microphone, denomination in Prussian blue.

2009, Apr. 29 **Perf. 13½**
2726 A703 $2.50 Sheet of 4, #a-d 7.50 7.50

Worldwide Fund for Nature (WWF) — G226

No. 2727 — Various depictions of Caribbean spiny lobster with denomination in: a, Orange. b, Green. c, Pink. d, Yellow.

2009, June 23   **Perf. 13½**
2727	Strip of 4	9.00	9.00
a.-d.	G226 $3 Any single	2.25	2.25
e.	Sheet of 8 2 each #2727a-2727d	18.00	18.00

G227

G228

Mushrooms — G229

Designs: 25c, Psilocybe mexicana. $1, Crinipellis piceae. $2, Psilocybe subcubensis. $5, Psilocybe cubensis.
No. 2732: a, Panacolus fimicola. b, Psilocybe yungensis. c, Panacolus subbalteatus. d, Russula cremeolilacina.
No. 2733: a, Psilocybe guilartensis. b, Psilocybe aztecorum.

2009, July 2   **Perf. 14x14¾**
2728-2731	G227	Set of 4	6.25	6.25

Perf. 14¼x14¾
2732	G228	$2.50 Sheet of 4, #a-d	7.50	7.50

Souvenir Sheet
Perf. 14x14¾
2733	G229	$3 Sheet of 2, #a-b	4.50	4.50

Miniature Sheet

Pres. Abraham Lincoln (1809-65) — G230

No. 2734 — Photograph of Lincoln: a, Without beard, ear showing at right. b, Without beard, ear showing at left. c, With beard, wearing vest. d, With beard, without vest.

2009, July 21   **Litho.**   **Perf. 13¼**
2734	G230	$2.50 Sheet of 4, #a-d	7.50	7.50

Miniature Sheet

Visit of Pope Benedict XVI to Israel — G231

No. 2735: a, Pope Benedict XVI. b, Pope and Israeli President Shimon Peres. c, Pope at Temple Mount, Jerusalem. d, Pope and Heichal Shlomo.

2009, Sept. 15   **Perf. 11½x12**
2735	G231	$2.50 Sheet of 4, #a-d	7.50	7.50

Miniature Sheet

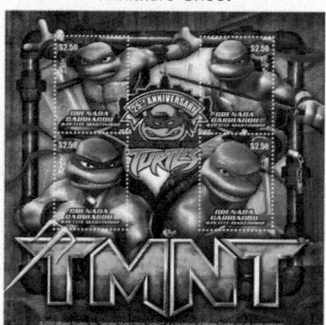

Teenage Mutant Ninja Turtles, 25th Anniv. — G232

No. 2736: a, Donatello. b, Leonardo. c, Raphael. d, Michelangelo.

2009, Sept. 15   **Perf. 12x11½**
2736	G232	$2.50 Sheet of 4, #a-d	7.50	7.50

Miniature Sheet

John F. Kennedy, Jr. (1960-99), Magazine Publisher — G233

No. 2737: a, As child, with father Pres. John F. Kennedy. b, With mother, Jacqueline. c, Alone. d, As child with mother, father and sister Caroline.

2009, Dec. 7   **Litho.**   **Perf. 11¼x11½**
2737	G233	$2.50 Sheet of 4, #a-d	7.75	7.75

First Man on the Moon, 40th Anniv. Type of 2009

No. 2738, vert.: a, Saturn, Titan and Voyager I. b, Apollo 11 Lunar Module. c, Voyager I, Europa, Jupiter, Io, Callisto and Ganymede. $6, Apollo 11 Lunar Module, diff., vert.

2009, Dec. 7   **Perf. 13¼**
2738	A701	$2 Horiz. strip of 3, #a-c	4.75	4.75

Souvenir Sheet
2739	A701	$6 multi	4.75	4.75

No. 2738 was printed in sheets containing 2 strips of three stamps.

G234

G235

G236

G237

Elvis Presley (1935-77) — G238

No. 2740 — Presley: a, Facing crowd, with guitar at right. b, Facing crowd, with guitar in front of him. c, Close-up with crowd in background. d, Holding microphone, no crowd.

2010, Jan. 7
2740	G234	$2.75 Sheet of 4, #a-d	8.50	8.50

Souvenir Sheets
2741	G235	$6 multi	4.75	4.75
2742	G236	$6 multi	4.75	4.75
2743	G237	$6 multi	4.75	4.75
2744	G238	$6 multi	4.75	4.75
	Nos. 2741-2744 (4)		19.00	19.00

Miniature Sheet

Awarding of 2009 Nobel Peace Prize to Pres. Barack Obama — G239

No. 2745 — Various photographs of Pres. Obama and gray map in background showing: a, Alaska, Western and Central United States. b, Greenland, Northeastern United States, Great Lakes. c, Southwestern United States, Mexico. d, Southeastern United States, Northern South America.

2010, Mar. 4   **Perf. 12x11½**
2745	G239	$2.50 Sheet of 4, #a-d	7.75	7.75

Orchids
G240

Designs: $1.20, Dendrophylax lindenii. $1.80, Scaphyglottis imbricata. No. 2748, $3, Encyclia ceratistes. $5, Scaphyglottis stellata.
No. 2750: a, Oncidium excavatum. b, Brassavola nodosa. c, Cattleya gaskelliana. d, Phalaenopsis cultivars.
No. 2751, $3: a, Lepanthopsis floripecten. b, Equitant oncidium.

Perf. 11½x11¼, 11½x12 (#2750)
2010, Mar. 4
2746-2749	G240	Set of 4	8.50	8.50

2750 G240 $2.50 Sheet of 4,
    #a-d   7.75   7.75

Souvenir Sheet

2751 G240 $3 Sheet of 2,
    #a-b   4.75   4.75

Miniature Sheets

G241

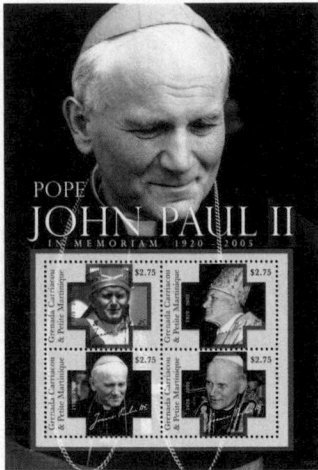

Pope John Paul II (1920-2005) — G242

No. 2752: a, Pope wearing zucchetto, country name over colored area. b, Pope wearing miter, white area under and below denomination. c, As "b," with colored area under and below denomination. d, As "a," country name over white area.

No. 2753: a, Pope wearing miter, looking forward. b, Pope wearing miter, looking left. c, Pope wearing zucchetto, looking right. d, Pope wearing zucchetto, looking left.

2010, Apr. 9   **Perf. 11½x12**

2752 G241 $2.75 Sheet of 4,
    #a-d   8.25   8.25

2753 G242 $2.75 Sheet of 4,
    #a-d   8.25   8.25

Girl Guides Type of 2010

No. 2754, horiz. — Girl Guides: a, And adult leader. b, In tent. c, Sitting in field of flowers. d, looking at young Girl Guide pointing.
$6, Girl Guides wearing hooded sweatshirts.

2010, June 11   **Perf. 13x13¼**

2754 A717 $2.75 Sheet of 4, #a-d   8.25   8.25

Souvenir Sheet
Perf. 13¼x13

2755 A717 $6 multi   4.50   4.50

World Cup Type of 2010

No. 2756, $1.50 — Group E first-round matches: a, Netherlands vs. Denmark. b, Japan vs. Cameroun. c, Netherlands vs. Japan. d, Denmark vs. Cameroun. e, Japan vs. Denmark. f, Cameroun vs. Netherlands.

No. 2757, $1.50 — Group F first-round matches: a, Italy vs. Paraguay. b, New Zealand vs. Slovakia. c, Slovakia vs. Paraguay. d, New Zealand vs. Italy. e, Slovakia vs. Italy. f, Paraguay vs. New Zealand.

No. 2758, $1.50 — Group G first-round matches: a, Ivory Coast vs. Portugal. b, Brazil vs. North Korea. c, Brazil vs. Ivory Coast. d, Portugal vs. North Korea. e, North Korea vs. Ivory Coast. f, Portugal vs. Brazil.

No. 2759, $1.50 — Group H first-round matches: a, Honduras vs. Chile. b, Spain vs. Switzerland. c, Chile vs. Switzerland. d, Honduras vs. Spain. e, Spain vs. Chile. f, Switzerland vs. Honduras.

No. 2760, $3.50: a, Ellis Park Stadium, Johannesburg. b, Mbombela Stadium, Nelspruit.

No. 2761, $3.50: a, Loftus Versfeld Stadium, Pretoria. b, Free State Stadium, Bloemfontein.

No. 2762, $3.50: a, Peter Mokaba Stadium, Polokwane. b, Royal Bafokeng Stadium, Rustenburg.

2010, June 11   **Litho.**   **Perf. 13¼**

Sheets of 6, #a-f

2756-2759 A720   Set of 4   27.00 27.00

Sheets of 2, #a-b

2760-2762 A720   Set of 3   16.00 16.00

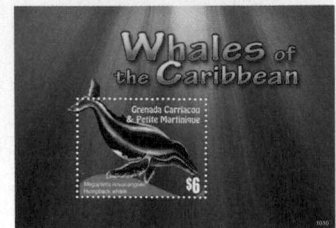

Whales — G243

No. 2763: a, Gervais's beaked whale. b, Cuvier's beaked whale. c, Pygmy sperm whale. d, Melon-headed whale. e, Bryde's whale. f, Sperm whale.
$6, Humpback whale.

2010, Sept. 1   **Perf. 12**

2763 G243 $2 Sheet of 6, #a-f   9.00   9.00

Souvenir Sheet

2764 G243 $6 multi   4.50   4.50

Leonardo da Vinci (1452-1519), Artist — G244

No. 2765, vert.: a, Reputed self-portrait. b, Statue of da Vinci outside of Uffizi Gallery, Florence. c, Vitruvian Man. d, La Scapigliata. e, Mona Lisa. f, Study of Horses.
$6, The Last Supper.

2010, Nov. 4

2765 G244 $2 Sheet of 6, #a-f   9.00   9.00

Souvenir Sheet

2766 G244 $6 multi   4.50   4.50

Miniature Sheets

G245

Elvis Presley (1935-77) — G246

No. 2767 — Presley: a, Standing behind microphone. b, With guitar, no microphone visible. c, Holding microphone, no guitar visible. d, With guitar, holding microphone.

No. 2768 — Presley: a, With guitar neck by face. b, Without microphone. c, Holding microphone. d, Playing guitar.

2010, Nov. 4

2767 G245 $2.75 Sheet of 4, #a-d   8.25   8.25

2768 G246 $2.75 Sheet of 4, #a-d   8.25   8.25

SEMI-POSTAL STAMPS

1988 Seoul Olympics Type

1986, Dec. 1   **Perf. 15**

B1 SP2 10c +5c Cycling   .90   .45
B2 SP2 50c +20c Sailing   .90   .90
B3 SP2 70c +30c Uneven Parallel Bars   .90   .90
B4 SP2 $2 +$1 Dressage   2.75   2.75
    Nos. B1-B4 (4)   5.45   5.00

Souvenir Sheet

B5 SP2 $3 +$1 Marathon   4.50   4.50

OFFICIAL STAMPS

Grenada Grenadines Nos. 396-408, 410, 440-442, 465-468 Overprinted "P.R.G."

1982, June   **Perf. 14, 15**

O1	G45	5c multicolored	.20	.20
O2	G45	6c multicolored	.20	.20
O3	G45	10c multicolored	.20	.20
O4	G45	12c multicolored	.20	.20
O5	G45	15c multicolored	.20	.20
O6	G45	20c multicolored	.20	.20
O7	G54	20c multicolored	.20	.20
O8	G45	25c multicolored	.20	.20
O9	G45	30c multicolored	.20	.20
O10	G45	40c multicolored	.25	.25
O11	CD331	40c multicolored	.25	.25
O12	G54	40c multicolored	.25	.25
O13	G45	50c multicolored	.30	.30
O14	G45	90c multicolored	.60	.60
O15	G45	$1 multicolored	.70	.70
O16	G54	$1 multicolored	.70	.70
O17	CD331	$2 multicolored	1.40	1.40
O18	G54	$2 multicolored	1.40	1.40
O19	G45	$3 multicolored	2.10	2.10
O20	CD331	$4 multicolored	2.75	2.75
O21	G45	$10 multicolored	7.00	7.00
		Nos. O1-O21 (21)	19.50	19.50

Royal Wedding stamps in changed colors, perf 15x14½ were also overprinted.

GRIQUALAND WEST

ˈgri-kwə-ˌland ˈwest

LOCATION — In South Africa west of the Orange Free State and north of the Orange River
GOVT. — British Crown Colony
AREA — 15,197 sq. mi.
POP. — 83,375 (1891)
CAPITAL — Kimberley

Originally a territorial division of the Cape of Good Hope Colony, Griqualand West was declared a British Crown Colony in 1873 and together with Griqualand East was annexed to the Cape Colony in 1880.

12 Pence = 1 Shilling

Beware of forgeries.

Stamps of Cape of Good Hope 1864-65 (Type I, 4p, 6p, 1sh) and 1871-76 (Type II, ½p, 1p, 4p, 5sh) Surcharged or Overprinted

Type I — With frame line around stamp.
Type II — Without frame line.

"Hope" — A1

Manuscript Surcharge in Dark Red

1874   **Wmk. 1**   **Perf. 14**

1 A1 1p on 4p blue (type I)   1,600.   2,500.

G. W.

Overprinted

1877   **Black Overprint**

2   1p rose   575.00   95.00
   a. Double overprint   2,500.

Red Overprint

3   4p blue (type II)   450.00   85.00

Overprinted

G

$$\underset{a}{G} \quad \underset{b}{G} \quad \underset{c}{G} \quad \underset{d}{G}$$

$$\underset{e}{G} \quad \underset{f}{G} \quad \underset{g}{G}$$

In Black on the One Penny, in Red on the Other Values

4	(a)	½p gray black	29.00	*30.00*
5	(a)	1p rose	30.00	26.00
6	(a)	4p blue (type I)	325.00	45.00
7	(a)	4p blue (type II)	250.00	32.50
8	(a)	6p dull violet	160.00	29.00
9	(a)	1sh green	190.00	27.50
a.		Inverted overprint		575.00
10	(a)	5sh orange	750.00	32.50
11	(b)	½p gray black	30.00	35.00
12	(b)	1p rose	30.00	22.50
13	(b)	4p blue (type I)	425.00	50.00
14	(b)	4p blue (type II)	275.00	30.00
15	(b)	6p dull violet	300.00	35.00
16	(b)	1sh green	375.00	27.50
17	(b)	5sh orange	1,000.	35.00
18	(c)	½p gray black	65.00	*75.00*
19	(c)	1p rose	70.00	42.50
20	(c)	4p blue (type I)	*750.00*	125.00
21	(c)	4p blue (type II)	*500.00*	80.00
22	(c)	6p dull violet	*350.00*	85.00
23	(c)	1sh green	*425.00*	65.00
24	(c)	5sh orange	*1,100.*	75.00
25	(d)	½p gray black	37.50	*42.50*
26	(d)	1p rose	37.50	29.00
27	(d)	4p blue (type I)	500.00	65.00
28	(d)	4p blue (type II)	375.00	37.50
29	(d)	6p dull violet	250.00	45.00
30	(d)	1sh green	350.00	37.50
31	(d)	5sh orange	950.00	45.00
32	(e)	½p gray black	70.00	*82.50*
33	(e)	1p rose	75.00	45.00
34	(e)	4p blue (type I)	775.00	135.00
35	(e)	4p blue (type II)	500.00	85.00
36	(e)	6p dull violet	375.00	90.00
37	(e)	1sh green	450.00	67.50
a.		Inverted overprint		950.00
38	(e)	5sh orange	1,250.	80.00
39	(f)	½p gray black	75.00	*82.50*
40	(f)	1p rose	80.00	50.00
41	(f)	4p blue (type I)	850.00	160.00
42	(f)	4p blue (type II)	625.00	110.00
43	(f)	6p dull violet	450.00	110.00
44	(f)	1sh green	550.00	82.50
45	(f)	5sh orange	1,750.	95.00
46	(g)	½p gray black	35.00	37.50
47	(g)	1p rose	30.00	21.00
48	(g)	4p blue (type I)	400.00	62.50
49	(g)	4p blue (type II)	350.00	37.50
50	(g)	6p dull violet	225.00	42.50
51	(g)	1sh green	325.00	32.50
a.		Inverted overprint	—	700.00
52	(g)	5sh orange	900.00	40.00

There are minor varieties of types e and f.

Overprinted in Black

G	G	G	G	G
i	k	l	m	n
G	G	G	G
o	p	q	r

1878

54	(g)	4p blue (type II)	400.00	70.00
55	(g)	6p dull violet	525.00	110.00
56	(i)	1p rose	32.50	21.00
57	(i)	4p blue (type II)	160.00	27.50
58	(i)	6p dull violet	300.00	60.00
a.		Double overprint		900.00
59	(k)	1p rose	70.00	36.00
60	(k)	4p blue (type II)	375.00	57.50
61	(k)	6p dull violet	500.00	95.00
62	(l)	1p rose	35.00	22.50
63	(l)	4p blue (type II)	175.00	29.00
64	(l)	6p dull violet	350.00	70.00
a.		Double overprint		950.00
65	(m)	1p rose	80.00	70.00
66	(m)	4p blue (type II)	400.00	82.50
67	(m)	6p dull violet	550.00	150.00
68	(n)	1p rose	85.00	75.00
69	(n)	4p blue (type II)	425.00	85.00
70	(n)	6p dull violet	625.00	150.00
a.		Double overprint		1,200.
71	(o)	1p rose	75.00	47.50
72	(o)	4p blue (type II)	400.00	75.00
73	(o)	6p dull violet	550.00	110.00
74	(p)	1p rose	80.00	67.50
75	(p)	4p blue (type II)	425.00	77.50
76	(p)	6p dull violet	550.00	140.00
77	(q)	1p rose	130.00	100.00
78	(q)	4p blue (type II)	650.00	160.00
79	(q)	6p dull violet	850.00	225.00
80	(r)	1p rose	450.00	325.00
81	(r)	4p blue (type II)	2,000.	475.00
82	(r)	6p dull violet	2,500.	650.00

There are two minor varieties of type i and one of type p.

Overprinted in Red

G	G
s	t

1878

83	(s)	½p gray black	17.50	17.50
a.		Double overprint	60.00	72.50
b.		Inverted overprint	19.00	19.00
c.		Double overprint, inverted	120.00	135.00
84	(s)	4p blue (type II)	400.00	120.00
a.		Inverted overprint	500.00	120.00
85	(t)	½p gray black	17.50	17.50
a.		Double overprint	95.00	95.00
b.		Inverted overprint	17.50	18.50
86	(t)	4p blue (type II)	—	100.00
a.		Inverted overprint	425.00	100.00

Black Overprint

87	(s)	½p gray black	250.00	130.00
a.		Inverted overprint	275.00	—
b.		With 2nd ovpt. (s) in red, invtd.	450.00	
c.		With 2nd ovpt. (t) in red, invtd.	225.00	
88	(s)	1p rose	18.00	13.50
a.		Double overprint	250.00	62.50
b.		Inverted overprint	18.00	17.50
c.		Double overprint, both inverted	250.00	82.50
d.		With second overprint (s) in red, both inverted	47.50	50.00
89	(s)	4p blue (type I)	—	175.00
90	(s)	4p blue (type II)	160.00	37.50
a.		Double overprint	200.00	
b.		Inverted overprint	275.00	97.50
c.		Double overprint, both inverted	—	350.00
91	(s)	6p dull violet	160.00	32.50
92	(t)	½p gray black	60.00	60.00
a.		Inverted overprint	130.00	87.50
b.		With 2nd ovpt. inverted	225.00	
93	(t)	1p rose	18.00	14.50
a.		Double overprint	—	105.00
b.		Inverted overprint	100.00	37.50
c.		Double overprint, both inverted	—	130.00
d.		With 2nd ovpt. (t) in red, both invtd.	100.00	100.00

94	(t)	4p blue (type I)		175.00
95	(t)	4p blue (type II)	180.00	17.50
a.		Double overprint		240.00
b.		Inverted overprint	300.00	37.50
c.		Double overprint, both inverted	—	325.00
96	(t)	6p dull violet		37.50

Overprinted in Black

97	½p gray black	20.00	8.75
a.	Double overprint	450.00	275.00
98	1p rose	22.50	6.75
a.	Double overprint	—	150.00
b.	Triple overprint	—	240.00
c.	Inverted overprint	—	92.50
99	4p blue (type II)	40.00	6.75
a.	Double overprint	—	125.00
100	6p brt violet	175.00	10.00
a.	Double overprint	800.00	190.00
b.	Inverted overprint	—	42.50
101	1sh green	150.00	7.00
a.	Double overprint	425.00	95.00
102	5sh orange	500.00	16.00
a.	Double overprint	700.00	92.50
b.	Triple overprint	—	325.00

These stamps were declared obsolete in 1880 and the remainders were used in Cape of Good Hope offices as ordinary stamps. Prices for used stamps are for examples with such cancels.

GUADELOUPE

ˈgwä-dəl-ˌüp

LOCATION — In the West Indies lying between Montserrat and Dominica
GOVT. — French colony
AREA — 688 sq. mi.
POP. — 271,262 (1946)
CAPITAL — Basse-Terre

Guadeloupe consists of two large islands, Guadeloupe proper and Grande-Terre, together with five smaller dependencies. Guadeloupe became an integral part of the Republic, acquiring the same status as the departments in metropolitan France, under a law effective Jan. 1, 1947.

100 Centimes = 1 Franc

> Catalogue values for unused stamps in this country are for Never Hinged items, beginning with Scott 168 in the regular postage section, Scott B12 in the semipostal section, Scott C1 in the airpost section, and Scott J38 in the postage due section.

> See France Nos. 850, 909, 1280, 1913 for French stamps inscribed "Guadeloupe."

Stamps of French Colonies Surcharged

1884 Unwmk. Imperf.

1	A8	20c on 30c brn, bis	72.50	60.00
a.		Large "2"	325.00	260.00
2	A8	25c on 35c blk, org	60.00	60.00
a.		Large "2"	325.00	260.00
a.		Large "5"	160.00	125.00

The 5c on 4c (French Colonies No. 40) was not regularly issued. Three examples exist. Value $42,500.

The 5c on 4c also exists as an essay, surcharge similar to the issued values. Value $1,000.

c   d

1889 Perf. 14x13½

Surcharged Type c

3	A9	3c on 20c red, grn	5.25	5.25
4	A9	15c on 20c red, grn	32.50	27.50
5	A9	25c on 20c red, grn	32.50	27.50
		Nos. 3-5 (3)	70.25	60.25

Surcharged Type d

6	A9	5c on 1c blk, lil bl	14.50	13.50
a.		Inverted surcharge		1,400.
b.		Double surcharge	450.00	450.00
7	A9	10c on 40c red, straw	40.00	35.00
a.		Double surcharge	475.00	475.00
8	A9	15c on 20c red, grn	32.50	30.00
a.		Double surcharge	475.00	475.00
9	A9	25c on 30c brn, bis	52.50	45.00
		Nos. 6-9 (4)	139.50	123.50

The word "centimes" in surcharges "b" and "c" varies from 10 to 12½mm.

Issue dates: No. 6, June 25; others, Mar. 22.

1891

10	A9	5c on 10c blk, lav	15.00	12.50
11	A9	5c on 1fr brnz grn, straw	17.00	12.50

Stamps of French Colonies Overprinted in Black

1891 Imperf.

12	A7	30c brn, yelsh	350.00	375.00
a.		Double overprint	725.00	725.00
13	A7	80c car, pnksh	1,100.	1,300.

Perf. 14x13½

14	A9	1c blk, lil bl	1.75	1.60
a.		Double overprint	40.00	40.00
b.		Inverted overprint	150.00	150.00
15	A9	2c brn, buff	2.60	2.00
a.		Double overprint	45.00	40.00
16	A9	4c claret, lav	6.00	5.25
17	A9	5c grn, grnsh	8.75	7.25
a.		Double overprint	45.00	40.00
b.		Inverted overprint	160.00	160.00
18	A9	10c blk, lavender	17.00	13.50
19	A9	15c blue	52.50	6.00
a.		Double overprint		110.00
20	A9	20c red, grn	45.00	30.00
a.		Double overprint	240.00	240.00
21	A9	25c blk, rose	47.50	5.25
a.		Double overprint	240.00	240.00
		Inverted overprint	225.00	225.00
22	A9	30c brn, bister	45.00	30.00
a.		Double overprint	240.00	240.00
23	A9	35c dp vio, org	87.50	72.50
a.		Double overprint	675.00	675.00
24	A9	40c red, straw	65.00	52.50
a.		Double overprint	675.00	675.00
25	A9	75c car, rose	130.00	125.00
26	A9	1fr brnz grn, straw	92.50	72.50
		Nos. 14-26 (13)	601.10	423.35

Navigation and Commerce — A7

Perf. 14x13½

1892-1901		Typo.		Unwmk.

Colony Name in Blue or Carmine

27	A7	1c blk, lil bl	1.40	1.40
28	A7	2c brn, buff	1.50	1.40
29	A7	4c claret, lav	1.75	1.50
30	A7	5c grn, grnsh	3.50	1.50
31	A7	5c yel grn ('01)	1.60	1.40
32	A7	10c blk, lavender	10.00	3.25
33	A7	10c red ('00)	8.75	2.40
a.		Imperf.	120.00	
34	A7	15c blue, quadrille paper	18.00	1.75

35	A7	15c gray, lt gray ('00)	13.00	1.60
36	A7	20c red, grn	11.00	6.50
37	A7	25c blk, rose	11.00	3.00
38	A7	25c blue ('00)	100.00	100.00
39	A7	30c brn, bister	24.00	15.00
40	A7	40c red, straw	24.00	15.00
41	A7	50c car, rose	32.50	16.00
42	A7	50c brn, az ('00)	45.00	42.50
43	A7	75c dp vio, org	32.50	22.50
44	A7	1fr brnz grn, straw	32.50	30.00
		Nos. 27-44 (18)	376.40	266.90

Perf. 13½x14 stamps are counterfeits.
For surcharges see Nos. 45-53, 83-85.

Nos. 39-41, 43-44 Surcharged in Black:

f   g

h

1903

45	A7	(f)	5c on 30c	4.00	4.00
a.		"C" instead of "G"	32.50	32.50
b.		Inverted surcharge	45.00	45.00
c.		Double surcharge	140.00	140.00
d.		Double surch., inverted	160.00	
46	A7	(g)	10c on 40c	9.50	9.50
a.		"C" instead of "G"	40.00	40.00
b.		"1" inverted	60.00	60.00
c.		Inverted surcharge	55.00	55.00
d.		Double surcharge	200.00	200.00
47	A7	(f)	15c on 50c	13.00	13.00
a.		"C" instead of "G"	40.00	40.00
b.		Inverted surcharge	110.00	110.00
c.		"15" inverted	375.00	375.00
48	A7	(g)	40c on 1fr	13.00	13.00
a.		"C" instead of "G"	52.50	52.50
b.		"4" inverted	120.00	120.00
c.		Inverted surcharge	110.00	110.00
d.		Double surcharge	240.00	240.00
e.		Triple surcharge	450.00	500.00
49	A7	(h)	1fr on 75c	42.50	42.50
a.		"C" instead of "G"	160.00	160.00
b.		"1" inverted	160.00	160.00
c.		Value above "G & D"	300.00	300.00
d.		Inverted surcharge	125.00	125.00
		Nos. 45-49 (5)	82.00	82.00

Letters and figures from several fonts were used for these surcharges, resulting in numerous minor varieties.

Nos. 48-49 With Additional Overprint "1903" in a Frame

1904, Mar.

Red Overprint

50	A7	(g)	40c on 1fr	65.00	72.50
b.		Inverted surcharge	425.00	425.00
c.		Double surcharge	1,250.	1,250.
51	A7	(h)	1fr on 75c	92.50	100.00
a.		Double surcharge	950.00	1,050.

Blue Overprint

52	A7	(g)	40c on 1fr	52.50	55.00
53	A7	(h)	1fr on 75c	87.50	95.00
		Nos. 50-53 (4)	297.50	322.50

The date "1903" may be found in 19 different positions and type faces within the frame. These stamps may also be found with the minor varieties of Nos. 48-49.

The 40c exists with black overprint. Value, $500 unused or used.

Harbor at Basse-Terre — A8

View of La Soufrière A9

Pointe-à-Pitre, Grand-Terre — A10

1905-27 Typo. Perf. 14x13½

54	A8	1c blk, *bluish*	.30	.30
55	A8	2c vio brn, *straw*	.30	.30
56	A8	4c bis brn, *az*	.30	.30
57	A8	5c green	2.40	.65
58	A8	5c dp blue ('22)	.25	.25
59	A8	10c rose	2.25	.65
60	A8	10c green ('22)	1.40	1.25
61	A8	10c red, *bluish* ('25)	.25	.25
62	A8	15c violet	.55	.50
63	A9	20c red, *grn*	.55	.40
64	A9	20c bl grn ('25)	.65	.65
65	A9	25c blue	.95	.55
66	A9	25c ol grn ('22)	.65	.65
67	A9	30c black	5.00	3.25
68	A9	30c rose ('22)	.70	.70
69	A9	30c brn ol, *lav* ('25)	.55	.55
70	A9	35c blk, *yel* ('06)	.80	.80
71	A9	40c red, *straw*	.80	.80
72	A9	45c ol gray, *lil* ('07)	1.40	.80
73	A9	45c rose ('25)	.80	.80
74	A9	50c gray grn, *straw*	5.50	4.00
75	A9	50c dp bl ('22)	1.25	1.10
76	A9	50c violet ('25)	.70	.70
77	A9	65c blue ('27)	.70	.70
78	A9	75c car, *bl*	.90	.80
79	A10	1fr blk, *green*	1.75	1.50
80	A10	1fr lt bl ('25)	1.00	.95
81	A10	2fr car, *org*	2.25	2.00
82	A10	5fr dp bl, *org*	7.50	7.50
		Nos. 54-82 (29)	42.40	33.65

Nos. 57, 59 and 82 exist imperf. Value, Nos. 57 and 59 each $60, No. 82 $140.
For surcharges see #86-95, 167, B1-B2.

Nos. 29, 39 and 40 Surcharged in Carmine or Black

1912, Nov.

83	A7	5c on 4c claret, *lav* (C)	1.50	1.50
84	A7	5c on 30c brn, *bis* (C)	2.00	2.00
85	A7	10c on 40c red, *straw*	2.25	2.25
		Nos. 83-85 (3)	5.75	5.75

Two spacings between the surcharged numerals are found on Nos. 83 to 85. For detailed listings, see the *Scott Classic Specialized Catalogue of Stamps and Covers.*

Stamps and Types of 1905-27 Surcharged with New Value and Bars

1924-27

86	A10	25c on 5fr dp bl, *org*	.75	.70
87	A10	65c on 1fr gray grn	1.40	1.25
88	A10	85c on 1fr gray grn	1.50	1.40
89	A9	90c on 75c dl red	1.40	1.25
90	A10	1.05fr on 2fr ver (Bl)	1.00	.85
91	A10	1.25fr on 1fr lt bl (R)	.65	.65
92	A10	1.50fr on 1fr dk bl	1.25	1.25
93	A10	3fr on 5fr org brn	1.50	1.50
94	A10	10fr on 5fr vio rose, *org*	11.00	11.00
95	A10	20fr on 5fr rose lil, *pnksh*	14.00	13.00
		Nos. 86-95 (10)	34.45	32.85

Years issued: Nos. 87-88, 1925. Nos. 90-91, 1926. Nos. 89, 92-95, 1927.

Sugar Mill — A11

Saints Roadstead A12

Harbor Scene A13

Perf. 14x13½

1928-40 Unwmk. Typo.

96	A11	1c yel & vio	.25	.25
97	A11	2c blk & lt red	.25	.25
98	A11	3c yel & red vio ('40)	.30	.25
99	A11	4c yel grn & org brn	.25	.25
100	A11	5c ver & grn	.25	.25
101	A11	10c bis brn & dp bl	.25	.25
102	A11	15c brn red & blk	.30	.25
103	A11	20c lil & ol brn	.50	.50
104	A12	25c grnsh bl & olvn	.55	.55
105	A12	30c gray grn & yel grn	.40	.40
106	A12	35c bl grn ('38)	.40	.40
107	A12	40c yel & vio	.40	.40
108	A12	45c vio brn & slate	.95	.80
109	A12	45c brn & dl grn ('40)	1.10	1.00
110	A12	50c dl grn & org	.30	.30
111	A12	55c ultra & car ('38)	1.40	1.25
112	A12	60c ultra & car ('40)	.65	.65
113	A12	65c gray blk & ver	.55	.55
114	A12	70c gray blk & ver ('40)	.70	.70
115	A12	75c dl red & bl grn	.70	.70
116	A12	80c car & brn ('38)	.85	.65
117	A12	90c dl red & dl rose	2.00	1.75
118	A12	90c rose red & bl ('39)	1.25	1.10
119	A13	1fr lt rose & lt bl	5.25	3.75
120	A13	1fr rose red & org ('38)	1.75	1.50
121	A13	1fr bl gray & blk brn ('40)	.70	.70
122	A13	1.05fr lt bl & rose	1.25	1.10
123	A13	1.10fr lt red & grn	4.00	2.75
124	A13	1.25fr bl gray & blk brn ('33)	.65	.65
125	A13	1.25fr brt rose & red org ('39)	.95	.95
126	A13	1.40fr lt bl & lil rose ('40)	.70	.70
127	A13	1.50fr dl bl & bl	.40	.40
128	A13	1.60fr lil rose & yel brn ('40)	.70	.70
129	A13	1.75fr lil rose & yel brn ('33)	5.75	3.25
130	A13	1.75fr vio bl ('38)	6.00	4.00
131	A13	2fr bl grn & dk brn	.40	.40
132	A13	2.25fr vio bl ('39)	1.25	1.25
133	A13	2.50fr pale org & grn ('40)	1.25	1.25
134	A13	3fr org brn & sl	.65	.65
135	A13	5fr dl bl & org	1.25	1.00
136	A13	10fr vio & ol brn	1.25	1.00
137	A13	20fr green & mag	1.50	1.40
		Nos. 96-137 (42)	50.20	40.95

Nos. 96-103, 110, 119, 123, 134, 137 exist imperf. Values each $30-$60.
For surcharges see Nos. 161-166.
For 10c, type A11, without "RF," see No. 163A.

Common Design Types
pictured following the introduction.

Colonial Exposition Issue
Common Design Types

1931, Apr. 13 Engr. Perf. 12½
Name of Country in Black

138	CD70	40c deep green	4.75	4.75
139	CD71	50c violet	4.75	4.75
140	CD72	90c red orange	4.75	4.75
141	CD73	1.50fr dull blue	4.75	4.75
		Nos. 138-141 (4)	19.00	19.00

Cardinal Richelieu Establishing French Antilles Co., 1635 — A14

Victor Hugues and his Corsairs — A15

1935 Perf. 13

142	A14	40c gray brown	10.00	10.00
143	A14	50c dull red	10.00	10.00
144	A14	1.50fr dull blue	10.00	10.00
145	A15	1.75fr lilac rose	10.00	10.00
146	A15	5fr dark brown	10.00	10.00
147	A15	10fr blue green	10.00	10.00
		Nos. 142-147 (6)	60.00	60.00

Tercentenary of the establishment of the French colonies in the West Indies.

Paris International Exposition Issue
Common Design Types

1937 Perf. 13

148	CD74	20c deep violet	1.90	1.90
149	CD75	30c dark green	1.75	1.75
150	CD76	40c car rose	1.50	1.50
151	CD77	50c dk brn & blk	1.50	1.50
152	CD78	90c red	1.50	1.50
153	CD79	1.50fr ultra	1.90	1.90
		Nos. 148-153 (6)	10.05	10.05

Colonial Arts Exhibition Issue
Souvenir Sheet
Common Design Type

1937 Imperf.

154	CD75	3fr dark blue	9.50	11.00

New York World's Fair Issue
Common Design Type

1939 Engr. Perf. 12½x12

155	CD82	1.25fr car lake	1.25	1.25
156	CD82	2.25fr ultra	1.25	1.25

For surcharges see Nos. 159-160.

La Soufrière View and Marshal Pétain A16

1941 Engr. Perf. 12½x12

157	A16	1fr lilac	.80	
158	A16	2.50fr blue	.80	

Nos. 157-158 were issued by the Vichy government in France, but were not placed on sale in Guadeloupe.
For surcharges, see Nos. B11A-B11B.

Nos. 155, 156, 113, 117 and 118 Surcharged with New Values in Black

1943 Perf. 14x13½, 12½x12

159	CD82	40c on 1.25fr	.80	.80
160	CD82	40c on 2.25fr	1.60	1.60
161	A12	50c on 65c	1.00	1.00
162	A12	1fr on 90c (#117)	1.40	1.40
163	A12	1fr on 90c (#118)	1.25	1.25
		Nos. 159-163 (5)	6.05	6.05

Type of 1928 Without "RF"

1943 Perf. 14x13½

163A	A11	10c bis brn & dp blue		.65

No. 163A was issued by the Vichy government in France, and was not placed on sale in Guadeloupe.

Nos. 104, 106, 113 and 90 Surcharged with New Values in Black

1944 Perf. 14x13½

164	A12	40c on 35c	1.10	1.10
165	A12	50c on 25c	.30	.30
166	A12	1fr on 65c	1.25	1.25
a.		Double surcharge	200.00	150.00
167	A10	4fr on 1.05fr on 2fr	1.75	1.75
		Nos. 164-167 (4)	4.40	4.40

The surcharge on No. 166 is spelled out.

> **Catalogue values for unused stamps in this section, from this point to the end of the section, are for Never Hinged items.**

Dolphins A17

1945 Unwmk. Photo. Perf. 11½

168	A17	10c chlky bl & red org	.30	.25
169	A17	30c lt yel grn & red	.30	.25
170	A17	40c lt bl & car	.85	.65

171	A17	50c red org & yel grn	.40	.30
172	A17	60c ol bis & lt bl	.40	.30
173	A17	70c lt gray & yel grn	.85	.65
174	A17	80c lt bl grn & yel	.85	.65
175	A17	1fr brn vio & grn	.40	.30
176	A17	1.20fr brt red vio & yel grn	.40	.30
177	A17	1.50fr dl brn & car	.90	.55
178	A17	2fr cer & bl	.90	.55
179	A17	2.40fr sal & yel grn	1.50	.95
180	A17	3fr gray brn & bl vio	.85	.55
181	A17	4fr ultra & buff	.70	.30
182	A17	4.50fr brn org & grn	.90	.65
183	A17	5fr dk vio & grn	1.10	.65
184	A17	10fr gray grn & red vio	1.10	.65
185	A17	15fr sl gray & org	1.50	.85
186	A17	20fr pale gray & dl org	2.50	1.00
		Nos. 168-186 (19)	16.70	10.25

Eboue Issue
Common Design Type

1945 Engr. Perf. 13

187	CD91	2fr black	.65	.50
188	CD91	25fr Prussian green	1.40	1.10

Basse-Terre Harbor and Woman A18

Cutting Sugar Cane — A19

Pineapple Bearer — A20

Guadeloupe Woman — A21

Gathering Coffee — A22

Guadeloupe Woman — A23

1947 Unwmk. Engr. Perf. 13

189	A18	10c red brown	.30	.25
190	A18	30c sepia	.30	.25
191	A18	50c blue grn	.40	.30
192	A19	60c black brn	.75	.50
193	A19	1fr dp carmine	1.00	.65
194	A19	1.50fr dk gray bl	1.50	.85
195	A20	2fr blue grn	1.50	.85
196	A20	2.50fr dp car	1.40	.95
197	A20	3fr deep blue	1.50	.95
198	A21	4fr violet	1.40	.95
199	A21	5fr blue grn	1.40	.95
200	A21	6fr red	1.40	.95
201	A22	10fr deep blue	1.50	1.00
202	A22	15fr dk vio brn	2.50	1.25
203	A22	20fr rose red	2.75	1.50
204	A23	25fr blue green	7.00	3.00
205	A23	40fr red	8.00	4.00
		Nos. 189-205 (17)	34.60	19.15

SEMI-POSTAL STAMPS

Nos. 59
and 62
Surcharged
in Red

1915-17 **Unwmk.** **Perf. 14 x 13½**
B1	A8	10c + 5c rose	5.25	3.50
B2	A8	15c + 5c violet	5.25	3.50
a.		Double surcharge	225.00	225.00
b.		Triple surcharge	240.00	240.00
c.		Inverted surcharge	240.00	240.00
d.		In pair with unovptd. stamp	275.00	

Curie Issue
Common Design Type
1938, Oct. 24 **Perf. 13**
B3	CD80	1.75fr + 50c brt ultra	11.00	10.50

French Revolution Issue
Common Design Type
Name and Value Typo. in Black
1939, July 5 **Photo.** **Perf. 13**
B4	CD83	45c + 25c green	10.00	10.00
B5	CD83	70c + 30c brown	10.00	10.00
B6	CD83	90c + 35c red org	10.00	10.00
B7	CD83	1.25fr + 1fr rose pink	10.00	10.00
B8	CD83	2.25fr + 2fr blue	10.00	10.00
		Nos. B4-B8 (5)	50.00	50.00

Common Design Type and

Colonial
Artillery
SP1

Colonial
Infantry — SP2

1941 **Photo.** **Perf. 13½**
B9	SP1	1fr + 1fr red	1.00
B10	CD86	1.50fr + 3fr maroon	1.00
B11	SP2	2.50fr + 1fr blue	1.50
		Nos. B9-B11 (3)	3.50

Nos. B9-B11 were issued by the Vichy government in France, but were not placed on sale in Guadeloupe.

Nos. 157-158
Surcharged in Black or Red

1944 **Engr.** **Perf. 12½x12**
B11A	50c + 1.50fr on 2.50fr blue (R)	.80
B11B	+ 2.50fr on 1fr lilac	.80

Colonial Development Fund.
Nos. B11A-B11B were issued by the Vichy government in France, but were not placed on sale in Guadeloupe.

Red Cross Issue
Common Design Type
1944 **Perf. 14½x14**
B12	CD90	5fr + 20fr ultra	1.40	1.00

The surtax was for the French Red Cross and national relief.

AIR POST STAMPS

Common Design Type
1945 **Unwmk.** **Photo.** **Perf. 14½x14**
C1	CD87	50fr green	1.50	1.00
C2	CD87	100fr deep plum	2.25	1.50

Victory Issue
Common Design Type
1946, May 8 **Engr.** **Perf. 12½**
C3	CD92	8fr redsh brn	1.25	1.00

Chad to Rhine Issue
Common Design Types
1946, June 6
C4	CD93	5fr dk slate grn	2.00	1.60
C5	CD94	10fr deep blue	2.00	1.60
C6	CD95	15fr brt violet	2.00	1.60
C7	CD96	20fr brown car	2.00	1.60
C8	CD97	25fr black	2.00	1.60
C9	CD98	50fr red brown	2.00	1.60
		Nos. C4-C9 (6)	12.00	9.60

Gathering Bananas — AP1

Seaplane at Roadstead — AP2

Pointe-a-Pitre Harbor and Guadeloupe
Woman — AP3

1947 **Unwmk.** **Perf. 13**
C10	AP1	50fr dk brown violet	6.00	2.75
C11	AP2	100fr deep blue	8.75	5.25
C12	AP3	200fr red	11.50	5.50
		Nos. C10-C12 (3)	26.25	13.50

AIR POST SEMI-POSTAL STAMPS

Mother & Nurse with
Children — SPAP1

1942, June 22 **Engr.** **Perf. 13**
CB1	SPAP1	1.50fr + 3.50fr green	1.00
CB2	SPAP1	2fr + 6fr brown & red	1.00

Native children's welfare fund.
Nos. CB1-CB2 were issued by the Vichy government in France, but were not placed on sale in Guadeloupe.

Colonial Education Fund
Common Design Type
1942, June 22
CB3	CD86a	1.20fr + 1.80fr blue & red	1.10

No. CB3 was issued by the Vichy government in France, but was not placed on sale in Guadeloupe.

POSTAGE DUE STAMPS

D1   D2   D3

1876 **Unwmk.** **Typeset** **Imperf.**
J1	D1	25c black	1,350.	925.
J2	D2	40c black, blue		37,500.
J3	D3	40c black	1,500.	1,200.

Twenty varieties of each.
Nos. J1 and J3 have been reprinted on thinner and whiter paper than the originals.

D4   D5

1879
J4	D4	15c black, blue	55.00	52.50
a.		Period after "c" omitted	175.00	175.00
J5	D4	30c black	110.00	87.50
a.		Period after "c" omitted	240.00	225.00

Twenty varieties of each.

1884
J6	D5	5c black	35.00	35.00
a.		Double impression	100.00	100.00
J7	D5	10c black, blue	75.00	65.00
a.		Double impression	150.00	150.00
J8	D5	15c black, violet	110.00	87.50
a.		Double impression	225.00	225.00
J9	D5	20c black, rose	160.00	100.00
a.		Italic "2" in "20"	1,000.	950.00
J10	D5	30c black, yellow	160.00	160.00
a.		Double impression	450.00	450.00
J11	D5	35c black, gray	60.00	52.50
a.		Double impression	225.00	225.00
J12	D5	50c black, green	32.50	27.50
a.		Double impression	200.00	200.00
		Nos. J6-J12 (7)	632.50	527.50

There are ten varieties of the 35c, and fifteen each of the other values, also numerous wrong font and missing letters.

Postage Due Stamps of
French Colonies
Surcharged in Black

Two surcharge types: I, wide font, "3" with rounded top; II, narrow font, "3" with flat top.

1903
Type I
J13	D1	30c on 60c brn,		
		cr	325.00	325.00
a.		Inverted surcharge	1,100.	1,100.
b.		Bee corner ornament turned	1,150.	1,150.
c.		As "b," inverted surcharge	1,700.	
d.		"G" omitted	800.00	800.00
e.		As "d," inverted surcharge	1,250.	
f.		Corrected surcharge, "30" over "33"	10,500.	10,500.
J14	D1	30c on 1fr rose,		
		cr	400.00	400.00
a.		Inverted surcharge	1,200.	1,200.
b.		"30" sideways	10,500.	10,500.
c.		As "b," inverted surcharge	10,500.	10,500.

Type II
J13A	D1	30c on 60c brn,		
		cr	1,000.	1,000.
a.		Inverted surcharge	1,100.	1,100.
b.		Bee corner ornament turned	1,600.	1,600.
c.		As "b," inverted surcharge	2,200.	
d.		"G" omitted	1,000.	1,000.
e.		As "d," inverted surcharge	1,500.	

f.		Corrected surcharge, "30" over "33"	10,500.	10,500.
J14A	D1	30c on 1fr rose,	400.00	400.00
a.		Inverted surcharge	1,200.	1,200.
b.		"30" sideways	10,500.	10,500.
c.		As "b," inverted surcharge	10,500.	10,500.

Gustavia   Avenue of
Bay — D6   Royal
         Palms — D7

1905-06 **Typo.** **Perf. 14x13½**
J15	D6	5c blue	.55	.55
J16	D6	10c brown	.55	.55
J17	D6	15c green	1.00	1.00
J18	D6	20c black, yel ('06)	1.00	1.00
J19	D6	30c rose	1.25	1.25
J20	D6	50c black	3.25	3.25
J21	D6	60c brown orange	1.75	1.75
J22	D6	1fr violet	3.25	3.25
		Nos. J15-J22 (8)	12.60	12.60

Type of 1905-06 Issue
Surcharged

1926-27
J23	D6	2fr on 1fr gray	2.00	2.00
J24	D6	3fr on 1fr ultra ('27)	2.75	2.75

1928, June 18
J25	D7	2c olive brn & lil	.25	.25
J26	D7	4c bl & org brn	.25	.25
J27	D7	5c gray grn & dk brn	.25	.25
J28	D7	10c dl vio & yel	.30	.30
J29	D7	15c rose & olive grn	.30	.30
J30	D7	20c brn org & ol grn	.50	.50
J31	D7	25c brn red & bl grn	.50	.50
J32	D7	30c slate & olivine	.80	.80
J33	D7	50c ol brn & lt red	.80	.80
J34	D7	60c dp bl & blk	.80	.80
J35	D7	1fr green & orange	3.00	2.60
J36	D7	2fr bis brn & lt red	2.25	1.90
J37	D7	3fr vio & bl blk	1.25	1.10
		Nos. J25-J37 (13)	11.25	10.35

Type of 1928 Without "RF"
1944
J37A	D7	60c dp bl & blk	.30
J37B	D7	1fr green & orange	.65
J37C	D7	2fr bis brn & lt red	.65
		Nos. J37A-J37C (3)	1.60

Nos. J37A-J37C were issued by the Vichy government in France, but were not placed on sale in Guadeloupe.

D8

Perf. 14x13
1947, June 2 **Unwmk.** **Engr.**
J38	D8	10c black	.30	.25
J39	D8	30c dull blue green	.40	.30
J40	D8	50c bright ultra	.40	.30
J41	D8	1fr dark green	.65	.50
J42	D8	2fr dark blue	.85	.70
J43	D8	3fr black brown	1.25	1.00
J44	D8	4fr lilac rose	1.40	1.25
J45	D8	5fr purple	1.90	1.60
J46	D8	10fr red	2.60	2.10
J47	D8	20fr dark violet	3.00	2.25
		Nos. J38-J47 (10)	12.75	10.25

GUATEMALA

ˌgwä-lə-ˈmä-lə

LOCATION — Central America, bordering on Atlantic and Pacific Oceans
GOVT. — Republic
AREA — 42,042 sq. mi.
POP. — 12,335,580 (1999 est.)
CAPITAL — Guatemala City

100 Centavos = 8 Reales = 1 Peso
100 Centavos de Quetzal = 1 Quetzal
(1927)

Catalogue values for unused stamps in this country are for Never Hinged items, beginning with Scott 316 in the regular postage section, Scott B5 in the semi-postal section, Scott C137 in the air post section, Scott CB5 in the air post semi-postal section and Scott E2 in the special delivery section.

Coat of Arms
A1   A2

Two types of 10c:
Type I — Both zeros in "10" are wide.
Type II — Left zero narrow.

Perf. 14x13½

1871, Mar. 1   Typo.   Unwmk.
1	A1	1c ocher	.80	10.50
a.		Imperf., pair	5.00	
b.		Printed on both sides, imperf.	75.00	
2	A1	5c lt bister brn	4.00	8.00
a.		Imperf. pair	35.00	
b.		Tête bêche pair	150.00	
c.		Tête bêche pair, imperf.	2,600.	
3	A1	10c blue (I)	5.00	8.00
a.		Imperf., pair (I)	45.00	
b.		Type II	8.00	10.50
c.		Imperf. pair (II)	60.00	
4	A1	20c rose	4.00	8.00
a.		Imperf., pair	45.00	
b.		20c blue (error)	125.00	125.00
c.		As "b," imperf.	800.00	
		Nos. 1-4 (4)	13.80	34.50

Forgeries exist. Forged cancellations abound. See No. C458.

1873   Litho.   Perf. 12
5	A2	4r dull red vio	325.00	85.00
6	A2	1p dull yellow	175.00	115.00

Forgeries exist.

Liberty
A3   A4

A5   A6

1875, Apr. 15   Engr.
7	A3	¼r black	1.00	3.50
8	A4	½r blue green	1.00	3.00
9	A5	1r blue	1.00	3.00
a.		Half used as ½r on cover		1,700.
10	A6	2r dull red	1.00	3.00
		Nos. 7-10 (4)	4.00	12.50

Nos. 7-10 normally lack gum. Unused values are for examples without gum.
Forgeries and forged cancellations exist.

Indian Woman — A7   Quetzal — A8

Typographed on Tinted Paper
1878, Jan. 10   Perf. 13
11	A7	½r yellow grn	.80	3.25
12	A7	2r carmine rose	1.25	4.00
13	A7	4r violet	1.25	4.75
14	A7	1p yellow	2.00	9.00
c.		Half used as 4r on cover		2,200.
		Nos. 11-14 (4)	5.30	21.00

Some sheets of Nos. 11-14 have papermaker's watermark, "LACROIX FRERES," in double-lined capitals appearing on six stamps.
Part perforate pairs of Nos. 11, 12 and 14 exist. Value for each, about $100.
Forgeries of Nos. 11-14 are plentiful. Forged cancellations exist.
For surcharges see Nos. 18, 20.

Imperf., Pairs
11a	A7	½r yellow green	50.00	
12a	A7	2r carmine rose	50.00	
13a	A7	4r violet	50.00	
14a	A7	1p yellow	50.00	

1879   Engr.   Perf. 12
15	A8	¼r brown & green	7.25	9.50
16	A8	1r black & green	10.50	13.50

For similar types see A11, A72, A103, A121, A146. For surcharges see Nos. 17, 19.

Nos. 11, 12, 15, 16
Surcharged in Black

1881   Perf. 12 and 13
17	A8	1c on ¼r brn & grn	12.00	16.00
a.		"ecntavo,"	40.00	47.50
b.		Pair, one without surcharge	200.00	
18	A7	5c on ½r yel grn	5.50	8.00
a.		"ecntavos,"	35.00	40.00
b.		"5" omitted	100.00	
c.		Double surcharge	95.00	120.00
19	A8	10c on 1r blk & grn	17.50	24.00
a.		"s" of "centavos" missing	75.00	75.00
b.		"ecntavos"	57.50	87.50
20	A7	20c on 2r car rose	32.50	87.50
a.		Horiz. pair, imperf. between	425.00	
		Nos. 17-20 (4)	67.50	135.50

The 5c had three settings.
Surcharge varieties found on Nos. 17-20 include: Period omitted; comma instead of period; "ecntavo." or "ecntavos."; "s" omitted; spaced "centavos."; wider "0" in "20."
Counterfeits of Nos. 17-20 are plentiful.

Quetzal — A11

1881, Nov. 7   Engr.   Perf. 12
21	A11	1c black & grn	3.00	2.00
22	A11	2c brown & grn	3.00	2.00
a.		Center inverted	400.00	250.00
23	A11	5c red & grn	6.00	2.60
a.		Center inverted	3,250.	1,300.
24	A11	10c gray vio & grn	2.75	2.00
25	A11	20c yellow & grn	2.75	2.40
a.		Center inverted	500.00	
		Nos. 21-25 (5)	17.50	11.00

Surcharged in Black

Gen. Justo Rufino Barrios — A12   A12a

A12b

1886, Mar. 6
26	A12	25c on 1p ver	.70	.70
a.		"centovos"	1.50	
b.		"centanos"	1.50	
c.		"255" instead of "25"	150.00	
d.		Inverted "S" in "Nacionales"	20.00	
f.		"cen avos"	20.00	
h.		"Corre cionales"	20.00	
i.		Inverted surcharge	75.00	
27	A12	50c on 1p ver	.70	.70
a.		"centovos"	1.50	
b.		"centanos"	1.50	
c.		"Carreos"	1.50	
d.		Inverted surcharge	50.00	
e.		Double surcharge	75.00	
f.		Inverted "S" in "Nacionales"	10.00	
g.		"centavo"	20.00	
h.		"cen avos"	20.00	
28	A12	75c on 1p ver	.70	.70
a.		"centovos"	1.50	
b.		"centanos"	1.50	
c.		"Carreos"	1.50	
d.		"50" for "75" at upper right	2.00	
e.		Inverted "S" in "Nacionales"	10.00	
f.		Double surcharge	75.00	
g.		"ales" inverted	100.00	
29	A12a	100c on 1p ver	1.40	1.40
a.		"110" at upper left and "á" at lower left, instead of "100"	5.00	
b.		Inverted surcharge	75.00	
c.		"Guatemala" bolder; 23mm instead of 18½mm wide	2.25	
d.		Double surcharge, one diagonal	100.00	
30	A12b	150c on 1p ver	1.40	1.40
a.		Inverted "G"	5.00	
b.		"Guetemala" and italic "5" in upper 4 numerals	5.00	
d.		Inverted surcharge	90.00	
e.		Pair, one without surcharge	100.00	
f.		Double surcharge	100.00	
		Nos. 26-30 (5)	4.90	4.90

There are many other minor varieties, such as wrong font letters, etc.
Used values of Nos. 26-30 are for canceled to order stamps. Postally used sell for much more.

National Emblem — A13

1886, July 1   Litho.   Perf. 12
31	A13	1c dull blue	5.00	2.00
32	A13	2c brown	5.00	3.00
33	A13	5c purple	37.50	.75
34	A13	10c red	10.00	.75
35	A13	20c emerald	15.00	1.25
36	A13	25c orange	15.00	1.50
37	A13	50c olive green	10.00	2.00
38	A13	75c carmine rose	10.00	2.00
39	A13	100c red brown	10.00	3.00
40	A13	150c dark blue	15.00	3.75
41	A13	200c orange yellow	18.50	4.75
		Nos. 31-41 (11)	151.00	25.75

Used values of Nos. 38-41 are for canceled to order stamps. Postally used sell for more.
See Nos. 43-50, 99-107. For surcharges see Nos. 42, 51-59, 75-85, 97-98, 108-110, 124-130.

No. 32 Surcharged in Black

Two settings:
I — "1886" (no period).
II — "1886." (period).

1886, Nov. 12
42	A13	1c on 2c brown, I	2.00	2.50
a.		Date inverted, I	75.00	
b.		Date double, I	75.00	
c.		Date omitted, I	60.00	
d.		Date double, one invtd., I	100.00	
e.		Date triple, one inverted, I	100.00	
f.		Setting II	1.50	1.00
g.		Inverted surcharge, II	4.00	
h.		Double surcharge, II	100.00	

Forgeries exist.

Type I   Type II

Two types of 5c:
I — Thin "5"
II — Larger, thick "5"

1886-95   Engr.   Perf. 12
43	A13	1c blue	.80	.20
44	A13	2c yellow brn	2.40	.20
a.		Half used as 1c on cover		100.00
45	A13	5c purple (I)	52.50	1.00
46	A13	5c vio (II) ('88)	1.60	.20
47	A13	6c lilac ('95)	.65	.20
48	A13	10c red ('90)	1.60	.20
49	A13	20c green ('93)	3.25	.75
50	A13	25c red org ('93)	8.00	1.25
		Nos. 43-44,46-50 (7)	18.30	3.00

The impression of the engraved stamps is sharper than that of the lithographed. On the engraved stamps the top four lines at left are heavier than those below them. (This is also true of the 1c litho., which is distinguished from the engraved only by a slight color difference and the impression.)
The "2" and "5" (I) are more open than the litho. numerals. The "10" of the engraved is wider. The 20c and 25c of the engraved have a vertical line at right end of the "centavos" ribbon.

No. 38 Surcharged in Blue Black

"1894" 14½mm wide

1894, Apr. 25
51	A13	10c on 75c car rose	4.50	4.50
a.		Double surcharge	75.00	
b.		Inverted surcharge	100.00	

Same on Nos. 38-41 in Blue or Red
"1894" 14mm wide

1894, June 13
52	A13	2c on 100c	7.50	4.25
53	A13	6c on 150c (R)	7.50	3.50
54	A13	10c on 75c	550.00	500.00
55	A13	10c on 200c	7.50	4.25
c.		Inverted surcharge	75.00	

Nos. 54-55 exist with thick or thin "1" in new value.

Same on Nos. 39-41 in Black or Red
"1894" 12mm wide

1894, July 14
52a	A13	2c on 100c red brn (Bk)	4.00	3.50
b.		Vert. pair, one without surcharge	150.00	
53a	A13	6c on 150c dk bl (R)	4.50	3.50
55a	A13	10c on 200c org yel (Bk)	5.00	3.50
d.		Inverted surcharge	100.00	
e.		Vert. pair, one without surcharge	150.00	

Nos. 44 and 46 Surcharged in Black, Blue Black, or Red:

b   c

d   e

1894-96
56	A13	(b) 1c on 2c (Bk)	.75	.30
a.		"Centav"	5.00	5.00
b.		Double surcharge	75.00	
c.		As "a," dbl. surcharge	150.00	
d.		Blue black surcharge	20.00	20.00
e.		Dbl. surch., one inverted	150.00	

57 A13 (c) 1c on 5c (R) .50 .20
('95)
  a. Inverted surcharge 3.00 3.00
  b. "1894" instead of "1895" 3.50 3.00
  c. Double surcharge 50.00
58 A13 (d) 1c on 5c (R) .75 .20
('95)
  a. Inverted surcharge 50.00 50.00
  b. Double surcharge 50.00 50.00
59 A13 (e) 1c on 5c (R) 1.25 .40
('96)
  a. Inverted surcharge 50.00 50.00
  b. Double surcharge 50.00 50.00
  Nos. 56-59 (4) 3.25 1.10

Nos. 56-58 may be found with thick or thin "1" in the new value.

National Arms and President J. M. Reyna Barrios
A21

1897, Jan. 1 **Engr.** **Unwmk.**
60 A21 1c blk, lil gray .55 .55
61 A21 2c blk, grnsh gray .55 .55
62 A21 6c blk, brn org .55 .55
63 A21 10c blk, dl bl .55 .55
64 A21 12c blk, rose red .55 .55
65 A21 18c blk, grysh white 9.50 9.50
66 A21 20c blk, scarlet 1.00 1.00
67 A21 25c blk, bis brn 1.60 1.00
68 A21 50c blk, redsh brn 1.00 1.00
69 A21 75c blk, gray 52.50 52.50
70 A21 100c blk, bl grn 1.00 1.00
71 A21 150c blk, dl rose 105.00 135.00
72 A21 200c blk, magenta 1.00 1.00
73 A21 500c blk, yel grn 1.00 1.00
  Nos. 60-73 (14) 176.35 205.75

Issued for Central American Exposition.
Stamps often sold as Nos. 65, 69 and 71 are examples with telegraph overprint removed.
Used values for Nos. 60-73 are for canceled-to-order stamps. Postally used examples are worth more.
The paper of Nos. 64 and 66 was originally colored on one side only, but has "bled through" on some examples.

No. 64 Surcharged in Violet

1897, Nov.
74 A21 1c on 12c rose red 1.00 1.00
  a. Inverted surcharge 30.00 30.00
  b. Pair, one without surcharge 75.00
  c. Dbl. surch., one invtd. 100.00

Stamps of 1886-93 Surcharged in Red

f   g

1898
75 (f) 1c on 5c violet 1.00 1.00
  a. Inverted surcharge 75.00
76 (f) 1c on 50c ol grn 1.50 1.25
  a. Inverted surcharge 100.00 100.00
77 (f) 6c on 5c violet 4.50 1.50
78 (f) 6c on 150c dk bl 4.50 3.25
79 (g) 10c on 20c emerald 5.00 4.00
  a. Double surch., one inverted 125.00 125.00
  Nos. 75-79 (5) 16.50 11.00

Black Surcharge
80 (f) 1c on 25c red org 2.00 2.00
81 (f) 1c on 75c car rose 1.50 1.50
  a. Double surcharge 100.00
82 (f) 6c on 10c red 10.00 9.00
83 (f) 6c on 20c emer 5.00 4.00
84 (f) 6c on 100c red brn 5.00 4.00
85 (f) 6c on 200c org yel 5.00 4.00
  a. Inverted surcharge 50.00 50.00
  Nos. 80-85 (6) 28.50 24.50

Information indicates that No. 77 inverted and double surcharges are counterfeits.

A24   A25

National Emblem
Revenue Stamp Overprinted or Surcharged in Carmine
Perf. 12, 12x14, 14x12

1898, Oct. 8 **Litho.**
86 A24 1c dark blue 1.40 1.40
  a. Inverted surcharge 12.50 12.50
87 A24 2c on 1c dk bl 2.25 2.25
  a. Inverted surcharge 12.50 12.50

Counterfeits exist.
See type A26.

Revenue Stamps Surcharged in Carmine

1898 **Engr.** **Perf. 12½ to 16**
88 A25 1c on 10c bl gray .75 .75
  a. "ENTAVO" 5.00 5.00
89 A25 2c on 5c pur 1.25 1.00
90 A25 2c on 10c bl gray 6.50 7.00
  a. Double surch., car & blk 100.00 75.00
91 A25 2c on 50c dp bl 9.25 9.25
  a. Double surch., car & blk 100.00 100.00
  Nos. 88-91 (4) 17.75 18.00

Black Surcharge
92 A25 2c on 1c lil rose 3.50 2.00
93 A25 2c on 25c red 7.50 8.00
94 A25 6c on 1p purple 4.00 4.50
95 A25 6c on 5p gray vio 7.50 7.50
96 A25 6c on 10p emer 7.50 7.50
  Nos. 92-96 (5) 30.00 29.50

Nos. 88 and 90 are found in shades ranging from Prussian blue to slate blue.
Varieties other than those listed are bogus. Counterfeits exist of No. 92.
Soaking in water causes marked fading.
See type A27.

No. 46 Surcharged in Red

1899, Sept. **Perf. 12**
97 A13 1c on 5c violet .40 .25
  a. Inverted surcharge 7.50 7.50
  b. Double surcharge 15.00 15.00
  c. Double surcharge, one inverted 15.00 15.00

No. 48 Surcharged in Black

1900, Jan.
98 A13 1c on 10c red .65 .50
  a. Inverted surcharge 10.00 10.00
  b. Double surcharge 75.00 75.00

Quetzal Type of 1886

1900-02 **Engr.**
99 A13 1c dark green .60 .25
100 A13 2c carmine .60 .25
101 A13 5c blue (II) 2.25 1.25
102 A13 6c lt green .75 .25
103 A13 10c bister brown 7.50 1.00
104 A13 20c purple 7.50 7.50
105 A13 20c bister brn ('02) 7.50 7.50
106 A13 25c yellow 7.50 7.50
107 A13 25c blue green ('02) 7.50 7.50
  Nos. 99-107 (9) 41.70 33.00

No. 49 Surcharged in Black

1901, May
108 A13 1c on 20c green .50 .50
  a. Inverted surcharge 22.50 22.50
  b. Double surch., one diagonal 50.00
109 A13 2c on 20c green 1.50 1.50

No. 50 Surcharged in Black

1901, Apr.
110 A13 1c on 25c red org .60 .60
  a. Inverted surcharge 25.00 25.00
  b. Double surcharge 50.00 50.00

A26   A27

Revenue Stamps Surcharged in Carmine or Black

1902, July **Perf. 12, 14x12, 12x14**
111 A26 1c on 1c dk blue 1.10 1.10
  a. Double surcharge 20.00
  b. Inverted surcharge 20.00
112 A26 2c on 1c dk blue 1.10 1.10
  a. Double surcharge 90.00
  b. Inverted surcharge 25.00

Perf. 14, 15
113 A27 6c on 25c red (Bk) 2.50 2.50
  a. Double surch., one invtd. 75.00 75.00
  Nos. 111-113 (3) 4.70 4.70

National Emblem — A28

Statue of Justo Rufino Barrios — A29

"La Reforma" Palace — A30

Temple of Minerva — A31   Lake Amatitlán — A32

Cathedral in Guatemala — A33

Columbus Theater — A34

Artillery Barracks — A35

Monument to Columbus — A36   School for Indians — A37

1902 **Engr.** **Perf. 12 to 16**
114 A28 1c grn & claret .20 .20
  a. Horiz. pair, imperf. vert. 100.00
115 A29 2c lake & blk .20 .20
  a. Horiz. or vert. pair, imperf btwn. 150.00
116 A30 5c blue & blk .30 .20
  a. 5c ultra & blk .75 .40
  b. Imperf., pair 100.00 100.00
  c. Horiz. pair, imperf. vert. 100.00
117 A31 6c bister & grn .30 .20
  a. Horiz. pair, imperf. vert. 150.00
118 A32 10c orange & bl .40 .40
  a. Horiz. pair, imperf. vert. 100.00
119 A33 20c rose lil & blk .60 .40
  a. Horiz. pair, imperf. vert. 100.00
120 A34 50c red brn & bl .45 .40
  a. Vert. pair, imperf. btwn. 350.00
121 A35 75c gray lil & blk .55 .40
  a. Horiz. pair, imperf. btwn. 150.00
  b. Horiz. pair, imperf. vert. 100.00
122 A36 1p brown & blk .85 .40
  a. Horiz. pair, imperf. btwn. 150.00
123 A37 2p ver & blk 1.00 .85
  Nos. 114-123 (10) 4.85 3.65

See Nos. 210, 212-214, 219, 223, 239-241, 243. For overprints and surcharges see Nos. 133, 135-139, 144-157, 168, 170-171, 178, 192-194, 298-299, 301, C19, C27, C123.

Issues of 1886-1900 Surcharged in Black or Carmine

1903, Apr. 18 **Perf. 12**
124 A13 25c on 1c dk grn 1.25 .55
  a. Inverted surcharge 50.00 50.00
125 A13 25c on 2c carmine 1.50 .55
126 A13 25c on 6c lt grn 2.50 1.75
  a. Inverted surcharge 40.00 40.00
127 A13 25c on 10c bis brn 7.50 7.00
128 A13 25c on 75c rose 10.00 10.00
129 A13 25c on 150c dk bl (C) 9.00 9.00
130 A13 25c on 200c yellow 10.00 10.00
  Nos. 124-130 (7) 41.75 38.85

Forgeries and bogus varieties exist.

Declaration of Independence A38

1907, Jan. 1 **Perf. 13½ to 15**
132 A38 12½c ultra & blk .45 .45
  a. Horiz. pair, imperf. btwn. 150.00

For surcharge see No. 134.

Nos. 118, 119 and 132 Surcharged in Black or Red

1908, May
133 A32 1c on 10c org & bl .30 .30
  a. Double surcharge 25.00
  b. Inverted surcharge 15.00 15.00
  c. Pair, one without surcharge 50.00
134 A38 2c on 12½c ultra & blk (R) .25 .25
  a. Horiz. or vert. pair, imperf. btwn. 100.00
  b. Inverted surcharge 15.00 10.00
  c. Double surcharge 30.00
135 A33 6c on 20c rose lil & blk .45 .25
  a. Inverted surcharge 20.00 20.00
  Nos. 133-135 (3) 1.00 .80

Similar Surcharge, Dated 1909, in Red or Black on Nos. 121 and 120

1909, Apr.
136	A35	2c on 75c (R)	.55	.55
137	A34	6c on 50c (R)	62.50	62.50
a.		Double surcharge	125.00	125.00
138	A34	6c on 50c (Bk)	.30	.30
		Nos. 136-138 (3)	63.35	63.35

Counterfeits exist of Nos. 137, 137a.

No. 123 Surcharged in Black

139	A37	12½c on 2p ver & blk	.30	.30
a.		Inverted surcharge	25.00	25.00
b.		Period omitted after "1909"	12.50	12.50

Counterfeits exist.

Gen. Miguel García Granados, Birth Cent. (in 1909) — A39

1910, Feb. 11   **Perf. 14**
140	A39	6c bis & indigo	.55	.40
a.		Imperf., pair	55.00	

Some sheets used for this issue contained a two-line watermark, "SPECIAL POSTAGE PAPER / LONDON." For surcharge see No. 143.

General Post Office — A40   Pres. Manuel Estrada Cabrera — A41

1911, June   **Perf. 12**
141	A40	25c bl & blk	.55	.25
a.		Center inverted	1,750.	900.00
142	A41	5p red & blk	.65	.65
a.		Center inverted	30.00	27.50

Nos. 116, 118 and 140 Surcharged in Black or Red:

h

i

j

1911   **Perf. 14**
143	A39 (h)	1c on 6c	25.00	9.75
a.		Double surcharge	75.00	75.00
144	A30 (i)	2c on 5c (R)	1.60	.85
145	A32 (j)	6c on 10c	1.25	1.25
a.		Double surcharge	50.00	
		Nos. 143-145 (3)	27.85	11.85

See watermark note after No. 140. Forgeries exist.

Nos. 119-121 Surcharged in Black:

k

---

l

m

1912, Sept.
147	A33 (k)	1c on 20c	.40	.40
a.		Inverted surcharge	12.50	12.50
b.		Double surcharge	15.00	15.00
148	A34 (l)	2c on 50c	.40	.40
a.		Inverted surcharge	12.50	12.50
b.		Double surcharge	12.50	
c.		Double inverted surcharge	25.00	
149	A35 (m)	5c on 75c	.80	.80
a.		"191" for "1912"	7.50	7.50
b.		Double surcharge	15.00	15.00
c.		Inverted surcharge	10.00	
		Nos. 147-149 (3)	1.60	1.60

Forgeries exist.

Nos. 120, 122 and 123 Surcharged in Blue, Green or Black:

n

o

p

1913, July
151	A34 (n)	1c on 50c (Bl)	.25	.25
a.		Inverted surcharge	10.00	
b.		Double surcharge	17.50	
c.		Horiz. pair, imperf. btwn.	100.00	
152	A36 (o)	6c on 1p (G)	.30	.30
153	A37 (p)	12½c on 2p (Bk)	.30	.30
a.		Inverted surcharge	15.00	15.00
b.		Double surcharge	40.00	
c.		Horiz. pair, imperf. btwn.	100.00	
		Nos. 151-153 (3)	.85	.85

Forgeries exist.

Nos. 114 and 115 Surcharged in Black:

q

r

s

t

1916-17
154	A28 (q)	2c on 1c ('17)	.25	.25
155	A28 (r)	6c on 1c	.25	.25
156	A28 (s)	12½c on 1c	.25	.25
157	A29 (t)	25c on 2c	.25	.25
		Nos. 154-157 (4)	1.00	1.00

Numerous errors of value and color, inverted and double surcharges and similar varieties are in the market. They were not regularly issued, but were surreptitiously made and sold.

Counterfeit surcharges abound.

"Liberty" and President Estrada Cabrera — A51

Estrada Cabrera and Quetzal — A52

1917, Mar. 15   **Perf. 14, 15**
158	A51	25c dp blue & brown	.25	.20

Re-election of President Estrada Cabrera.

1918   **Perf. 12**
161	A52	1.50p dark blue	.30	.25

Radio Station — A54   "Joaquina" Maternity Hospital — A55

"Estrada Cabrera" Vocational School — A56   National Emblem — A57

1919, May 3   **Perf. 14, 15**
162	A54	30c red & blk	2.75	.75
163	A55	60c ol grn & blk	.80	.50
164	A56	90c red brn & blk	.80	.75
165	A57	3p dp grn & blk	1.75	.50
		Nos. 162-165 (4)	6.10	2.50

See Nos. 215, 227. For surcharges see Nos. 166-167, 179-185, 188, 195-198, 245-246, C8-C11, C21-C22.

No. 162 Surcharged

Blue Overprint and Black Surcharge
1920, Jan.   **Unwmk.**
166	A54	2c on 30c red & blk	.30	.25
a.		Inverted surcharge	12.50	12.50
b.		"1920" double	10.00	10.00
c.		"1920" omitted	15.00	15.00
d.		"2 centavos" omitted	20.00	
e.		Imperf, pair	100.00	
f.		Pair, imperf. btwn.	100.00	

Nos. 123 and 163 Surcharged:

u

---

v

1920
167	A55	2c on 60c (Bk & R)	.25	.25
a.		Inverted surcharge	10.00	10.00
b.		"1920" inverted	7.50	7.50
c.		"1920" omitted	10.00	10.00
d.		"1920" only	10.00	
e.		Double surcharge	25.00	
168	A37	25c on 2p (Bk)	.30	.25
a.		"35" for "25"	10.00	10.00
b.		Large "5" in "25"	10.00	10.00
c.		Inverted surcharge	15.00	15.00
d.		Double surcharge	25.00	

A61

1920
169	A61	25c green	.25	.20
a.		Double overprint		50.00
b.		Double overprint, inverted	75.00	

See types A65-A66.

No. 119 Surcharged

1921, Apr.
170	A33	12½c on 20c	.25	.20
a.		Double surcharge	15.00	
b.		Inverted surcharge	15.00	

No. 121 Surcharged

1921, Apr.
171	A35	50c on 75c lil & blk	.50	.30
a.		Double surcharge	22.50	
b.		Inverted surcharge	25.00	25.00

Mayan Stele at Quiriguá — A62

Monument to President Granados — A63   "La Penitenciaria" Bridge — A64

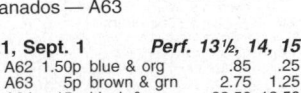

1921, Sept. 1   **Perf. 13½, 14, 15**
172	A62	1.50p blue & org	.85	.25
173	A63	5p brown & grn	2.75	1.25
174	A64	15p black & ver	22.50	12.50
		Nos. 172-174 (3)	26.10	14.00

See Nos. 216, 228, 229. For surcharges see Nos. 186-187, 189-191, 199-201, 207, 231, 247-251, C1-C5, C12, C23-C24.

A65   A66

Telegraph Stamps Overprinted or Surcharged in Black or Red

1921   *Perf. 14*
175	A65	25c green	.25 .20
176	A66	12½c on 25c grn (R)	.25 .20
177	A66	12½c on 25c grn	15.00 15.00
		Nos. 175-177 (3)	15.50 15.40

Nos. 119, 163 and 164 Surcharged in Black or Red:

w

x

1922, Mar.
178	A33(w)	12½c on 20c	.25 .25
a.		Inverted surcharge	10.00
179	A55(w)	12½c on 60c (R)	.50 .50
a.		Inverted surcharge	25.00
180	A56(w)	12½c on 90c	.50 .50
a.		Inverted surcharge	25.00
181	A55(x)	25c on 60c	1.00 1.00
a.		Inverted surcharge	20.00
182	A55(x)	25c on 60c (R)	125.00 125.00
183	A56(x)	25c on 90c	1.00 1.00
a.		Inverted surcharge	25.00
184	A56(x)	25c on 90c (R)	4.00 4.00
		Nos. 178-181,183-184 (6)	7.25 7.25

Counterfeits exist.

Nos. 165, 173-174 Surcharged in Red or Dark Blue

1922, May
185	A57	12½c on 3p grn & blk (R)	.25 .25
186	A63	12½c on 5p brn & grn	.50 .45
187	A64	12½c on 15p blk & ver	.50 .45
		Nos. 185-187 (3)	1.25 1.15

Nos. 165, 173-174 Surcharged in Red or Black

25 25 25 25
I   II   III   IV

1922
188	A57	25c on 3p (I) (R)	.20 .20
a.		Type II	.60 .60
b.		Type III	.60 .60
c.		Type IV	.30 .30
d.		Inverted surcharge	40.00
e.		Horiz. or vert. pair, imperf. btwn. (I)	125.00
189	A63	25c on 5p (I)	1.00 2.00
a.		Type II	2.00 3.00
b.		Type III	2.00 3.00
c.		Type IV	1.00 2.00
190	A64	25c on 15p (I)	1.00 1.50
a.		Type II	2.00 3.00
b.		Type III	2.00 3.00
c.		Type IV	1.00 1.50
191	A64	25c on 15p (I) (R)	22.50 22.50
a.		Type II	40.00 45.00
b.		Type III	45.00 45.00
c.		Type IV	30.00 35.00
		Nos. 188-191 (4)	24.70 33.70

Stamps of 1902-21 Surcharged in Dark Blue or Red

25 25 25
v   VI   VII

25 25
VIII   IX

1922, Aug.   **On Nos. 121-123**
192	A35	25c on 75c (V)	.40 .40
a.		Type VI	.40 .40
b.		Type VII	1.75 1.75
c.		Type VIII	5.50 4.75
d.		Type IX	6.50 6.00
193	A36	25c on 1p (V)	.30 .30
a.		Type VI	.30 .30
b.		Type VII	1.25 1.25
c.		Type VIII	2.50 2.50
d.		Type IX	4.00 3.50
e.		Inverted surcharge	40.00
194	A37	25c on 2p (V)	.45 .45
a.		Type VI	.45 .45
b.		Type VII	1.25 1.25
c.		Type VIII	4.00 4.00
d.		Type IX	6.50 6.50

On Nos. 162-165
195	A54	25c on 30c (V)	.45 .45
a.		Type VI	.45 .45
b.		Type VII	1.25 1.25
c.		Type VIII	5.50 5.50
d.		Type IX	6.50 6.50
196	A55	25c on 60c (V)	1.00 1.50
a.		Type VI	1.25 1.50
b.		Type VII	6.25 7.75
c.		Type VIII	8.50 9.50
d.		Type IX	10.00 11.00
197	A56	25c on 90c (V)	1.00 1.50
a.		Type VI	1.50 2.00
b.		Type VII	6.00 6.75
c.		Type VIII	8.50 9.50
d.		Type IX	10.00 11.00
198	A57	25c on 3p (R) (V)	.40 .40
a.		Type VI	.40 .40
b.		Type VII	1.25 1.00
c.		Type VIII	6.00 4.50
d.		Type IX	6.50 6.00
e.		Inverted surcharge	50.00

On Nos. 172-174
199	A62	25c on 1.50p (V)	.30 .30
a.		Type VI	.30 .30
b.		Type VII	1.25 1.00
c.		Type VIII	3.00 3.00
d.		Type IX	4.50 4.50
e.		Inverted surcharge	40.00
200	A63	25c on 5p (V)	.75 .90
a.		Type VI	.80 1.00
b.		Type VII	3.00 3.50
c.		Type VIII	5.50 6.00
d.		Type IX	8.00 8.50
201	A64	25c on 15p (V)	.85 .90
a.		Type VI	1.50 1.50
b.		Type VII	5.00 5.50
c.		Type VIII	6.50 6.50
d.		Type IX	12.00 12.00
		Nos. 192-201 (10)	5.90 7.10

Centenary Palace — A69

National Palace at Antigua — A70

1922   *Perf. 14, 14½*
Printed by Waterlow & Sons
202	A69	12½c green	.30 .20
a.		Horiz. or vert. pair, imperf. btwn.	100.00
203	A70	25c brown	.30 .20

See Nos. 211, 221, 234.

Columbus Theater A71

Quetzal A72

Granados Monument — A73

Litho. by Castillo Bros.
1924, Feb.   *Perf. 12*
204	A71	50c rose	.50 .20
a.		Imperf., pair	7.50
b.		Horiz. or vert. pair, imperf. btwn.	25.00
205	A72	1p dark green	2.25 .20
a.		Imperf. vertically	15.00
b.		Vert. pair, imperf. btwn.	20.00
c.		Imperf., pair	7.50
206	A73	5p orange	1.25 .50
a.		Imperf., pair	8.50
b.		Horiz. pair, imperf. btwn.	20.00
		Nos. 204-206 (3)	4.00 .90

For surcharges see Nos. 208-209.

Nos. 172 and 206 Surcharged

1924, July
207	A62	1p on 1.50p bl & org	.30 .20
208	A73	1.25p on 5p orange	.50 .50
a.		"UN PESO 25 Cents." omitted	40.00
b.		Horiz. pair, imperf. btwn.	25.00

#208 with two bars over "25 Cents."

1924
209	A73	1p on 5p orange	.50 .50

Types of 1902-22 Issues
Engr. by Perkins Bacon & Co.
1924, Aug.   Re-engraved   *Perf. 14*
210	A31	6c bister	.20 .20
211	A70	25c brown	.20 .20
212	A34	50c red	.25 .20
213	A36	1p orange brn	.25 .20
214	A37	2p orange	.35 .25
215	A57	3p deep green	2.00 .50
216	A64	15p black	5.00 2.75
		Nos. 210-216 (7)	8.25 4.30

The designs of the stamps of 1924 differ from those of the 1902-22 issues in many details which are too minute to illustrate. The re-engraved issue may be readily distinguished by the imprint "Perkins Bacon & Co. Ld. Londres."

Pres. Justo Rufino Barrios A74

Lorenzo Montúfar A75

1924, Aug.
217	A74	1.25p ultra	.20 .20
218	A75	2.50p dk violet	1.00 .25

See Nos. 224, 226. For surcharges see Nos. 232, C6, C20.

Aurora Park — A76

National Post Office — A77

National Observatory A78

Types of 1921-24 Re-engraved and New Designs Dated 1926
Engraved by Waterlow & Sons, Ltd.
1926, July-Aug.   *Perf. 12½*
219	A31	6c ocher	.20 .20
220	A76	12½c green	.20 .20
221	A70	25c brown	.20 .20
222	A77	50c red	.20 .20
223	A36	1p orange brn	.20 .20
224	A74	1.50p dk blue	.20 .20
225	A78	2p orange	1.25 1.00
226	A75	2.50p dk violet	1.50 1.25
227	A57	3p dark green	.45 .20
228	A63	5p brown vio	1.00 .40
229	A64	15p black	6.00 2.75
		Nos. 219-229 (11)	11.40 6.80

These stamps may be distinguished from those of the same designs in preceding issues by the imprint "Waterlow & Sons, Limited, Londres," the date, "1926," and the perforation. See Nos. 233, 242. For surcharge see No. 230.

Nos. 225-226, 228 Surcharged in Various Colors

1928
230	A78	½c on 2p (Bl)	.65 .50
a.		Inverted surcharge	12.50
231	A63	½c on 5p (Bk)	.35 .20
a.		Inverted surcharge	10.00 10.00
b.		Double surcharge	50.00
c.		Blue surcharge	45.00 45.00
d.		Blue and black surcharge	50.00 50.00
232	A75	1c on 2.50p (R)	.35 .20
b.		Double surcharge	50.00
		Nos. 230-232 (3)	1.35 .90

Barrios — A79

Montúfar — A80

General Orellana A82

Granados A81

Coat of Arms of Guatemala City — A83

Engraved by T. De la Rue & Co.
1929, Jan.   *Perf. 14*
233	A78	½c yellow grn	.75 .20
234	A70	1c dark brown	.25 .20
235	A79	2c deep blue	.25 .20
236	A80	3c dark violet	.20 .20
237	A81	4c orange	.25 .20
238	A82	5c dk carmine	.50 .20
239	A31	10c brown	.40 .20
240	A36	15c ultra	.50 .20
241	A29	25c brown org	1.00 .25
242	A76	30c green	.90 .30
243	A32	50c pale rose	2.00 .60
244	A83	1q black	3.00 .40
		Nos. 233-244 (12)	10.00 3.15

Nos. 233, 234 and 239 to 243 differ from the illustrations in many minor details, particularly in the borders.
See No. 300 for bisect of No. 235. For overprints and surcharges see Nos. 297, C13, C17-C18, C25-C26, C28, E1, RA17-RA18.

No. 227 Surcharged in Black or Red

1929, Dec. 28   **Perf. 12½, 13**
245	A57	3c on 3p dk grn (Bk)	1.25	1.90
a.		Inverted surcharge	15.00	15.00
246	A57	5c on 3p dk grn (R)	1.25	1.90
a.		Inverted surcharge	15.00	15.00

Inauguration of the Eastern Railroad connecting Guatemala and El Salvador.

No. 229 Surcharged in Red

1930, Mar. 30   **Unwmk.**
247	A64	1c on 15p black	1.25	1.40
248	A64	2c on 15p black	1.25	1.40
249	A64	3c on 15p black	1.25	1.40
250	A64	5c on 15p black	1.25	1.40
251	A64	15c on 15p black	1.25	1.40
		Nos. 247-251 (5)	6.25	7.00

Opening of Los Altos electric railway.

Hydroelectric Dam — A85

Los Altos Railway A86

Railroad Station A87

1930, Mar. 30   **Typo.**   **Perf. 12**
252	A85	2c brn vio & blk	1.40	1.90
a.		Horiz. pair, imperf. btwn.	125.00	
253	A86	3c dp red & blk	2.75	2.75
a.		Vert. pair, imperf. btwn.	125.00	
254	A87	5c buff & dk bl	2.75	2.75
		Nos. 252-254 (3)	6.90	7.40

Opening of Los Altos electric railway. Exist imperf.

Mayan Stele at Quiriguá — A91

1932, Apr. 8   **Engr.**
258	A91	3c carmine rose	1.90	.40

See Nos. 302-303.

Flag of the Race, Columbus and Tecum Uman A92

1933, Aug. 3   **Litho.**   **Perf. 12½**
259	A92	½c dark green	.75	.75
260	A92	1c dull brown	1.25	1.10
261	A92	2c deep blue	1.25	1.10
262	A92	3c dull violet	1.25	.75
263	A92	5c rose	1.25	1.10
		Nos. 259-263 (5)	5.75	4.80

Day of the Race and 441st anniv. of the sailing of Columbus from Palos, Spain, Aug. 3, 1492, on his 1st voyage to the New World. The 3c and 5c exist imperf.

Birthplace of Barrios A93

View of San Lorenzo A94

Justo Rufino Barrios A95

National Emblem and Locomotive A96

General Post Office — A97

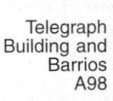

Telegraph Building and Barrios A98

Military Academy A99

National Police Headquarters — A100

Jorge Ubico and J. R. Barrios A101

1935, July 19   **Photo.**
264	A93	½c yel grn & mag	.40	.45
265	A94	1c org red & pck bl	.40	.45
266	A95	2c orange & blk	.40	.55
267	A96	3c car rose & pck bl	4.50	2.25
268	A97	4c pck bl & org red	4.50	10.00
269	A98	5c bl grn & brn	3.25	4.25
270	A99	10c slate grn & rose lake	4.50	5.50

271	A100	15c ol grn & org brn	4.50	4.75
272	A101	25c scarlet & bl	4.50	4.75
		Nos. 264-272 (9)	26.95	32.95

General Barrios. See Nos. C29-C31.

Lake Atitlán A102

Quetzal A103

Legislative Building — A104

1935, Oct. 10
273	A102	1c brown & crim	.25	.20
274	A103	3c rose car & pck grn	.70	.20
275	A103	3c red org & pck grn	.70	.20
276	A104	4c brt bl & dp rose	.35	.20
		Nos. 273-276 (4)	2.00	.80

See No. 277. For surcharges see Nos. B1-B3.

No. 273 perforated diagonally through the center

1936, June   **Perf. 12½x12**
277	A102	(½c) brown & crimson	.20	.20
a.		Unsevered pair	.50	.60

Bureau of Printing — A105

Map of Guatemala A106

1936, Sept. 24   **Perf. 12½**
278	A105	½c green & pur	.25	.20
279	A106	5c blue & dk brn	.90	.20

For surcharge see No. B4.

Quetzal A107

Union Park, Quezaltenango A108

Gen. Jorge Ubico on Horseback A109

1c, Tower of the Reformer. 3c, National Post Office. 4c, Government Building, Retalhuleu. 5c, Legislative Palace entrance. 10c, Custom House. 15c, Aurora Airport Custom House. 25c, National Fair. 50c, Residence of Presidential Guard. 1.50q, General Ubico, portrait standing, no cap.

1937, May 20
280	A107	½c pck bl & car rose	.70	.45
281	A107	1c ol gray & red brn	.70	.35

282	A108	2c vio & car rose	.60	.35
283	A108	3c brn vio & brt bl	.50	.25
284	A108	4c yel & dl ol grn	2.00	2.00
285	A107	5c crim & brt vio	2.10	1.75
286	A108	10c mag & brn blk	3.00	3.50
287	A108	15c ultra & cop red	2.50	3.50
288	A108	25c red org & vio	3.00	3.50
289	A108	50c dk grn & org red	4.50	5.50
290	A109	1q magenta & blk	22.50	22.50
291	A109	1.50q red brn & blk	22.50	22.50
		Nos. 280-291 (12)	64.60	66.40

Second term of President Ubico.

Mayan Calendar A119

Natl. Flower (White Nun Orchid) A120

Quetzal — A121

Map of Guatemala A122

1939, Sept. 7   **Perf. 13x12, 12½**
292	A119	½c grn & red brn	.85	.20
293	A120	2c bl & gray blk	5.00	1.00
294	A121	3c red org & turq grn	6.50	1.75
295	A121	3c ol bis & turq grn	6.50	1.75
296	A122	5c blue & red	5.75	5.75
		Nos. 292-296 (5)	24.60	10.45

For overprints see Nos. 324, C157.

No. 235 Surcharged with New Value in Red

1939, Sept.   **Perf. 14**
297	A79	1c on 2c deep blue	.25	.20

Stamps of 1929 Surcharged in Blue:

y

z

1940, June
298	A29 (y)	1c on 25c brn org	.25	.20
299	A32 (z)	5c on 50c pale rose (bar 10x¾mm)	.25	.20
a.		Bar 12½x2mm	.30	.20
b.		Bar 12½x1mm	50.00	5.00

No. 235 perforated diagonally through the center

1941, Aug. 16   **Perf. 14x11½**
300	A79	(1c) deep blue	.30	.20
a.		Unsevered pair	.80	.80

No. 241
Surcharged in
Black

1941, Dec. 24
301 A29 ½c on 25c brn org .30 .30

Type of 1932 Inscribed "1942"

1942 Engr. Perf. 12
302 A91 3c green .95 .25
303 A91 3c deep blue .95 .25

Issued to publicize the coffee of Guatemala.

Vase of
Guastatoya
A123

Home for the Aged
A124

1942, July 13 Unwmk.
304 A123 ½c red brown .35 .20
305 A124 1c carmine rose .35 .20

National Printing
Works
A125

Rafael Maria
Landivar
A126

1943, Jan. 25 Engr. Perf. 11, 12
307 A125 2c scarlet .25 .20
a. Vert. pair, imperf. horiz. 35.00

1943, Aug. Perf. 11
308 A126 5c brt ultra .25 .20

Death of Rafael Landivar, poet, 150th anniv.

National
Palace
A127

1944, June 30 Perf. 11
309 A127 3c dk blue green .30 .30

Inauguration of the Natl. Palace, Nov. 10, 1943.
See Nos. C137A-C139. For overprints see Nos. 311-311A, C133.

Ruins of
Zakuleu
A128

1945, Jan. 6
310 A128 ½c black brown .20 .20

Type of 1944 Overprinted in Blue

1945, Jan. 15
311 A127 3c deep blue .30 .25
Overprint Bar 1mm Thick
311A A127 3c deep blue 1.00 .70

Allegory of the
Revolution
A129

Torch
A130

1945, Feb. 20
312 A129 3c grayish blue .30 .25
Nos. 312,C128-C131 (5) 2.30 1.25

Revolution of 10/20/44.

1945, Oct. 20
313 A130 3c deep blue .25 .20

1st anniv. of the Revolution of Oct. 20, 1944.
See No. C135-C136.

José Milla y
Vidaurre
A131

Payo
Enriquez de
Rivera
A132

1945 Perf. 11, 12½
314 A131 1c deep green .20 .20
315 A132 2c dull lilac .20 .20
Nos. 314-315,C134-C134A (4) 2.10 1.70

See Nos. 343-346, 379, C137, C269, C311-C315.

Catalogue values for unused stamps in this section, from this point to the end of the section, are for Never Hinged items.

José Batres y
Montufar
A133

UPU Monument
Bern, Switzerland
A134

1946 Unwmk.
316 A133 ½c sepia .25 .20
317 A133 3c deep blue .25 .20
See Nos. 319, C142.

1946, Aug. 5 Photo. Perf. 14x13
318 A134 1c vio & gray brn .30 .20
Nos. 318,C140-C141 (3) 1.45 .75

Centenary of the first postage stamp.

Batres Type of 1946

1947, Nov. 11 Engr. Perf. 11, 12½
319 A133 3c dull green .25 .25

Symbolical of
Labor — A135

Bartolomé de
las Casas and
Indian — A136

1948, May 14 Unwmk. Perf. 11
320 A135 1c deep green .40 .25
a. Perf. 12½ 5.00
321 A135 2c sepia .40 .25
a. Perf. 12½ 5.00
322 A135 3c deep ultra .40 .25
a. Perf. 12½ 5.00
323 A135 5c rose carmine .40 .25
a. Perf. 12½ 5.00
Nos. 320-323 (4) 1.60 1.00

Labor Day, May 1, 1948. Other perfs. and compound perfs. exist.

No. 296 Overprinted "1948" in Carmine at Lower Right

1948, May 14 Perf. 12½
324 A122 5c blue & red .40 .30

1949, Oct. 8 Engr. Perf. 12½, 13½
325 A136 ½c red .25 .20
326 A136 1c black brown .25 .20
327 A136 2c dk blue grn .25 .20
a. 2c green, perf. 11, 11½ ('60) .25 .20
328 A136 3c rose pink .25 .20
a. 3c car, perf. 11, 12½, 13½ ('64) .30 .20
329 A136 4c ultra .25 .20
Nos. 325-329 (5) 1.25 1.00

See Nos. 384-386.

Gathering
Coffee — A137

1c, Poptun Agricultural Colony. 2c, Banana trees. 3c, Sugar cane field. 6c, Intl. Bridge.

1950, Feb. Photo. Perf. 14
330 A137 ½c vio bl, pink & ol gray .25 .20
331 A137 1c red brn, yel & grnsh gray .25 .20
332 A137 2c ol grn, pink & bl gray .25 .20
333 A137 3c pur, bl & org brn .25 .20
334 A137 6c dp org, aqua & vio .50 .20
Nos. 330-334 (5) 1.50 1.00

See Nos. 347-349.

Badge of Public
and Social
Assistance
Ministry — A138

Nurse — A139

Map Showing
Hospitals — A140

1950-51 Litho. Perf. 12, 12½x12
335 A138 1c car rose & bl .25 .20
336 A139 3c dl grn & rose red .35 .20
Perf. 12
337 A140 5c dk bl & choc ('51) .50 .25
a. Souvenir sheet, #335-337 8.00 8.00
Nos. 335-337 (3) 1.10 .65

Issued to publicize the National Hospitals Fund.
No. 337a exists perf. and imperf., same values.
A perforated souvenir sheet is known which is similar to No. 337a, but with the 5c stamp

like the basic stamp of No. C232 (with "BRIT-ISH HONDURAS" inscription).
See #C177-C180a. For overprint see #C232.

Motorcycle
Messenger
A141

1951, May 22 Perf. 14x12½
337B A141 4c bl grn & gray blk .55 .25

Issued for regular postage, although inscribed "Expreso." See No. E2.

Souvenir Sheet

A142

Typographed and Engraved
1951, Oct. 22 Imperf.
338 A142 Sheet of 2 5.00 5.00
a. 1c rose carmine 2.00 1.50
b. 10c deep ultramarine 2.00 1.50

75th anniv. (in 1949) of the UPU.
For overprint see No. 419.

A143

Modern
Model
Schools
A144

1951, Oct. 22 Photo. Perf. 13½x14
339 A143 ½c purple & sepia .35 .20
340 A144 1c brn car & dl grn .35 .20
341 A143 2c grnsh bl & red brn .35 .20
342 A144 4c blk brn & rose vio .35 .25
Nos. 339-342 (4) 1.40 .90

Enriquez de Rivera Type of 1945
Re-engraved

1952, June 4 Perf. 12½
343 A132 ½c violet .25 .20
344 A132 1c rose carmine .25 .20
345 A132 2c green .25 .20
346 A132 4c orange .45 .20
Nos. 343-346 (4) 1.20 .80

A panel containing the dates "1660-1951" has been added below the portrait.

Produce Type of 1950

Designs: ½c, Sugar cane field. 1c, Banana trees. 2c, Poptun Agricultural Colony.

1953, Feb. 11 Photo. Perf. 13½
347 A137 ½c dk brn & dp bl .70 .20
348 A137 1c red org & ol grn .70 .20
349 A137 2c dk car & gray blk .70 .20
Nos. 347-349 (3) 2.10 .60

Issued to publicize farming.

Rafael
Alvarez
Ovalle and
José
Joaquin
Palma
A145

1953, May 13
350	A145	½c purple & blk	.55	.40
351	A145	1c dk grn & org brn	.55	.40
352	A145	2c org brn & ol grn	.55	.40
353	A145	3c dk bl & ol brn	.55	.40
		Nos. 350-353 (4)	2.20	1.60

Authors of Guatemala's national anthem. For overprints see Nos. 374-378.

Quetzal — A146

1954, Sept. 27   Engr.   Perf. 12½, 11
354	A146	1c dp violet blue	1.00	.25

See Nos. 367-373, 380-382A, 434-444. For overprint see No. 395.

Mario Camposeco A147   Globe and Red Cross A148

10c, Carlos Aguirre Matheu. 15c, Goalkeeper.

1955-56   Unwmk.   Perf. 12½
355	A147	4c violet	1.00	.25
356	A147	4c carmine ('56)	1.00	.25
357	A147	4c blue grn ('56)	1.00	.25
358	A147	10c bluish grn	3.25	.75
359	A147	15c dark blue	3.25	2.00
		Nos. 355-359 (5)	9.50	3.50

50 years of Soccer in Guatemala.

1956, May 23   Perf. 13x12½
Designs: 3c, Red Cross, Telephone and "5110." 4c, Nurse, patient and Red Cross flag.
360	A148	1c brown & car	.25	.20
361	A148	3c dk green & red	.25	.20
362	A148	4c dk sl grn & red	.30	.20
		Nos. 360-362 (3)	.80	.60

Red Cross. See Nos. B5-B7, CB5-CB7. For surcharges see Nos. CB8-CB10.

Dagger-Cross of the Liberation — A149

1c, Map showing 2,000 km. (1,243 miles) of new roads. 3c, Oil production.

1956   Engr.   Perf. 12½
363	A149	½c violet	.20	.20
364	A149	1c dk blue grn	.20	.20

Perf. 11
365	A149	3c sepia	.20	.20
		Nos. 363-365 (3)	.60	.60

Liberation of 1954-55. Issue dates: ½c, 1c, July 27; 3c, Oct. 31. See Nos. C210-C218.

Quetzal Type of 1954
1957-58   Perf. 11, 12½
367	A146	2c violet	.55	.25
368	A146	3c carmine rose	.70	.25
369	A146	3c ultra	.70	.25
a.		3c dark blue, perf. 11½ ('72)	—	—
370	A146	4c orange	1.10	.25
371	A146	5c brown	1.50	.25
372	A146	5c org ver ('58)	1.50	.25
373	A146	6c yellow grn	2.00	.25
		Nos. 367-373 (7)	8.05	1.75

No. 368 is only perf. 12½. The 2c, 4c and No. 369 are found in perf. 11 and 12½. Other values are only perf. 11.

No. 350 Overprinted in Blue, Black, Carmine, Red Orange or Green:

1958, Nov.-Dec.   Photo.   Perf. 13½
374	A145	½c purple & blk (Bl)	.65	.65
375	A145	½c purple & blk (Bk)	.65	.65
376	A145	½c purple & blk (C)	.65	.65
377	A145	½c purple & blk (RO)	.65	.65
378	A145	½c purple & blk (G)	.65	.65
		Nos. 374-378 (5)	3.25	3.25

Cent. of the birth of Rafael Alvarez Ovalle, composer of Guatemala's national anthem.

Re-engraved Rivera Type of 1945
1959, Sept. 12   Engr.   Perf. 11, 12½
379	A132	4c gray blue	.30	.20

See note after No. 346.

Quetzal Type of 1954
1960-63   Unwmk.   Perf. 11
380	A146	2c brown ('61)	.55	.25
381	A146	4c lt violet	1.00	.25
382	A146	5c blue green	1.10	.25

Perf. 12½
382A	A146	5c slate gray ('63)	2.00	.40
		Nos. 380-382A (4)	4.65	1.15

Romulus and Remus Statue, Rome — A150   1871 Stamp — A151

1961   Photo.   Perf. 14
383	A150	3c blue	.65	.20

Inauguration of the Plaza Italia.

Las Casas Type of 1949
Perf. 11, 11½, 12½, 13½
1962-64   Engr.
384	A136	½c blue	.25	.20
385	A136	1c brt violet ('64)	.25	.20
386	A136	4c brown ('64)	.25	.20
		Nos. 384-386 (3)	.75	.60

1963-66   Unwmk.   Perf. 11
387	A151	10c carmine	.40	.25
388	A151	10c slate ('64)	.40	.25

Perf. 11½
389	A151	10c olive brn ('66)	.40	.25
390	A151	20c dp purple ('64)	.65	.30
391	A151	20c dk blue ('65)	.65	.30
		Nos. 387-391 (5)	2.50	1.35

For souvenir sheet, see No. C310.

Pedro Bethancourt Comforting Sick Man — A152

1964, Jan. 6   Engr.   Perf. 11
394	A152	2½c olive bister	.45	.25

Beatification (1962-63) of Pedro Bethancourt (1626-67). See Nos. C319-C322. For overprints see Nos. C381-C382.

Quetzal Type of 1957-58 Overprinted in Blue

1964, Dec. 29   Engr.   Perf. 12½
395	A146	4c orange	.45	.25

15th anniv. (in 1963) of the Intl. Soc. of Guatemala Collectors.

Map of Guatemala and British Honduras A153

1967, Apr. 28   Litho.   Perf. 14x13½
396	A153	4c ol, vio bl & dp rose	.55	.30
397	A153	5c ocher, vio bl & dp org	.45	.30
398	A153	6c dp org, vio bl & gray	.45	.30
		Nos. 396-398 (3)	1.45	.90

Issued to state Guatemala's claim to British Honduras.
For overprints see Nos. C411-C413.

Quetzal, Mayan Ball Game Goal — A154

Lithographed and Engraved
1968, Oct. 15   Perf. 11½
399	A154	1c blk, lt grn & red	.40	.20
400	A154	5c yel, lt grn & red	.55	.25
401	A154	8c org, lt grn & red	.65	.25
402	A154	15c bl, lt grn & red	1.10	.25
403	A154	30c lt vio, lt grn & red	2.00	1.10
		Nos. 399-403 (5)	4.70	2.05

19th Olympic Games, Mexico City, 10/12-27. The 1c, 5c, 8c, 15c also exist perf 12½, 1c, 8c, perf 13½.
See Nos. 412-415. For overprints see Nos. 408-411, C431-C435.

Child and Poinsettia — A155

1968-70   Typo.   Perf. 13½
404	A155	2½c grn, dp bis & car	.30	.20
405	A155	2½c grn, org & car ('70)	.45	.55
406	A155	5c green, gray & car	.45	.20
407	A155	21c green, lil & car	1.00	.85
		Nos. 404-407 (4)	2.20	1.80

Issued to help abandoned children.

Type of 1968 Overprinted in Black or Red

1970, Mar. 19   Litho.   Perf. 13½
408	A154	8c org, lt grn & red	.45	.20
409	A154	8c org, lt grn & red (R)	.45	.20

Perf. 12½
410	A154	15c bl, lt grn & red	.70	.25
411	A154	15c bl, lt grn & red (R)	.70	.25
		Nos. 408-411 (4)	2.30	.90

50th anniv. of ILO. Gold overprint believed to be a trial color.

Type of 1968
1971   Typo. & Engr.   Perf. 11½
412	A154	1c gray, yel grn & red	.30	.25

Typo.
413	A154	5c brt pink, yel grn & red	.55	.25
414	A154	5c brown, grn & red	.55	.25
415	A154	5c dk bl, grn & red	.55	.55
		Nos. 412-415 (4)	1.95	1.30

Mayas and CARE Package — A156

1971-72   Typo.   Perf. 13½
416	A156	1c black & multi	.25	.25

Perf. 11½
417	A156	1c violet & multi ('72)	.25	.25
418	A156	1c brown & multi ('72)	.25	.25
		Nos. 416-418 (3)	.75	.75

10th anniv. of CARE in Guatemala, a US-Canadian Cooperative for American Relief Everywhere. Exist imperf. See No. C459.

No. 338 (trimmed) Overprinted in Orange with Olympic Rings and: "JUEGOS OLIMPICOS / MUNICH 1972" Souvenir Sheet

1972, Oct. 23   Typo. & Engr.   Imperf.
419	A142	Sheet of 2	1.50	1.50
a.		1c rose carmine ("Munich")	.40	.40
b.		10c deep ultra ("1972")	.50	.50

20th Olympic Games, Munich, Aug. 26-Sept. 11. Commemorative inscriptions on No. 338 at left, top and right have been trimmed off. Size: 61x45mm (approximately). Many varieties exist. Gold overprints probably are proofs.

Pres. Carlos Arana Osorio A157

Designs: 3c, 5c, President Osorio seated, vert. 8c, Pres. Osorio standing, vert.

1973-74   Typo.   Perf. 12½
420	A157	2c blue & blk	.20	.20
421	A157	3c orange & brn	.25	.20
422	A157	5c rose car & blk	.30	.20
423	A157	8c black & brt grn	.55	.20
a.		Lithographed ('74)	.40	.20
		Nos. 420-423 (4)	1.30	.80

8th population and 3rd dwellings census, Mar. 26-Apr. 7, 1973.

Francisco Ximenez — A158

Typographed, Lithographed (#426)
1973-77   **Perf. 11½, 13½ (#426)**

424	A158	2c black & emer	.20	.20
425	A158	3c dk brn & org	.20	.20
426	A158	3c black & yellow	.45	.20
427	A158	6c black & brt bl	.45	.20
		Nos. 424-427 (4)	1.30	.80

Brother Francisco Ximenez, discoverer and translator of National Book of Guatemala. No. 427 issued for Intl. Book Year 1972.

Issued: 6c, 8/2; 2c, 1/14/75; #425, 3/5/75; #426, 9/26/77.

Sculpture of Christ, by Pedro de Mendoza, 1643 — A159

8c, Sculpture by Lanuza Brothers, 18th century.

1977, Apr. 4   Litho.   Perf. 11

428	A159	6c purple & multi	.40	.20
429	A159	8c purple & multi	.40	.20
		Nos. 428-429,C614-C619 (8)	4.65	2.70

Holy Week 1977.

INTERFER 77 Emblem — A160

1977, Oct. 31   Litho.   Perf. 11½

430	A160	7c black & multi	.40	.20

INTERFER 77, 4th International Fair, Guatemala, Oct. 31-Nov. 13.

Rotary Intl., 75th Anniv. A161

1980, July 31   Litho.   Perf. 11½

431	A161	4c shown	.80	.25
432	A161	6c Diamond and Quetzal	.80	.25
433	A161	10c Paul P. Harris	.95	.60
		Nos. 431-433 (3)	2.55	1.10

Quetzal Type of 1954

1984-86   Engr.   Perf. 12½

434	A146	1c deep green	.25	.20
435	A146	2c deep blue	.25	.20
436	A146	3c olive green	.20	.20
437	A146	3c sepia	.20	.20
438	A146	3c blue	.20	.20
439	A146	3c red	.20	.20
440	A146	3c orange	.20	.20
441	A146	3c vermilion	.25	.20
442	A146	4c lt red brn	.25	.20
443	A146	5c magenta	.25	.20
444	A146	6c deep blue	.30	.20
		Nos. 434-444 (11)	2.55	2.20

Issued: #436-439, 2/20; #441, 6c, 4/25/86; 1c, 4c, 5c, 2/16/87; 2c, 3/25/87.

Miguel Angel Asturias Cultural Center — A162

Perf. 12½, 11½ (5c, 9c), 12½x11½ (4c), 13x12½ (6c)
1987-96   Litho.

445	A162	1c light blue	.25	.20
446	A162	2c bister brown	.25	.20
447	A162	3c ultra	.25	.20
448	A162	4c bright pink	.25	.20
449	A162	5c orange	.25	.20
450	A162	6c pale green	.25	.20
451	A162	7c vermilion	.25	.20
452	A162	8c brt pink	.25	.20
453	A162	9c black	.25	.20
454	A162	10c pale green	.30	.20
		Nos. 445-454 (10)	2.55	2.00

Miguel Angel Asturias (1899-1974), 1967 Nobel laureate in literature.

Issued: 3c, 11/24; 7c, 11/17; 8c, 11/27; 10c, 12/8; 2c, 3/2/88; 5c, 3/23/90; 9c, 10/1/91; 4c, 6c, 3/16/93; 1c, 7/9/96.

For surcharge see No. 573.

Central American and Caribbean University Games A163

Toucan as a participant in various events.

1990   Litho.   Perf. 12½

455	A163	15c shown	.30	.20
456	A163	20c Torch bearer, vert.	.45	.20
457	A163	25c Volleyball	.65	.20
458	A163	30c Soccer	.70	.20
459	A163	45c Karate	1.10	.30
460	A163	1q Baseball	2.50	.70
461	A163	2q Basketball	4.50	1.50
462	A163	3q Hurdles	7.50	2.50
		Nos. 455-462 (8)	17.70	5.80

Issued: 20c, 8/22; 30c, 3q, 7/10; others, 4/25.

A164

A166

Oct. 20 Revolution, 50th Anniv. A165

Designs: 1q, Student holding book, rifle. 2q, Constitution, city buildings, San Carlos University, social security building.

1994, Nov. 8   Litho.   Perf. 11½

463	A164	40c multicolored	.30	.20
464	A165	60c multicolored	.50	.35
465	A164	1q multicolored	.95	.65
466	A166	2q multicolored	1.75	1.25
467	A166	3q multicolored	3.00	1.75
		Nos. 463-467 (5)	6.50	4.20

UNICEF, 50th Anniv. — A167

Designs: 10c, Soldier hugging child, vert. 20c, Children flying on doves.

1997, May 21   Litho.   Perf. 12½

468	A167	10c multicolored	.25	.20

Perf. 11½x12½

469	A167	20c multicolored	.25	.20

Landmark Buildings A168

Designs: 50c, Paraninfo University. 1q, Central American Services Building, vert.

1997, Mar. 6   Perf. 12½

470	A168	50c multicolored	.30	.30
471	A168	1q multicolored	.65	.65

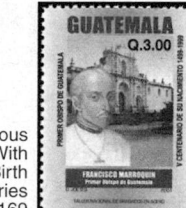

Famous Guatemalans With 1999 Birth Anniversaries A169

Designs: 3q, Francisco Marroquin (b. 1499), first Guatemalan bishop. 4q, Jacinto Rodriguez Diaz (b. 1899), aviator. 8.75q, Miguel Angel Asturias (1899-1974), 1967 Nobel Laureate for Literature. 10q, Cesar Brañas (b. 1899), writer.

2001, Oct. 9   Litho.   Perf. 12½x11½

472-475	A169	Set of 4	20.00	10.00

Visit of Pope John Paul II and Canonization of St. Peter of San José Betancur (1626-67) — A170

Designs: Nos. 476, 483a, 20c, Saint and churches, vert. Nos. 477, 483b, 25c, Saint and bell, vert. Nos. 478, 483c, 50c, Pope, Saint and church. Nos. 479, 483d, 1q, Saint, painting of nativity, and bell, vert. Nos. 480, 483e, 2q, Pope and Guatemala Archbishop Quezada Toruño. Nos. 481, 483f, 5q, Pope, fountain and church decoration. Nos. 482, 483g, 8.75q, Pope and churches.

2002, July 16   Litho.   Perf. 12½

476-482	A170	Set of 7	13.50	6.00

Souvenir Sheet

Rouletted 8½

483	A170	Sheet of 7, #a-g	13.50	13.50

Universal Postal Union, 125th Anniv. (in 1999) — A171

Designs: 20c, Quetzal, air mail envelopes, globe, flags. 2q, UPU emblem, quetzal, envelopes. 3q, Globe, quetzal, UPU emblem. 5q, Map of Guatemala, globe, envelopes and flags.

2002, Oct. 31   Litho.   Perf. 12½

484-487	A171	Set of 4	6.00	3.00

2001 Ascent of Mt. Everest by Jaime Viñals — A172

2002, Nov. 22

488	A172	3q multi	1.75	.85

Pan-American Health Organization, Cent. — A173

2002, Dec. 18

489	A173	4q multi	2.25	1.10

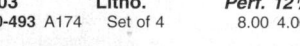

St. Josemaría Escrivá de Balaguer (1902-75) A174

Balaguer and: 20c, Farmer. 50c, Fisherman with boatful of fish. 3q, Fisherman, mountain. 10q, Church.

2003   Litho.   Perf. 12¼

490-493	A174	Set of 4	8.00	4.00

Masks for Dances — A175

Mask for: 20c, Dance of the Conquest. 2q, Dance of the Moors and Christians. 3q, Dance of the Deer. 4q, Dance of the Jaguar. 5q, Dance of Paabanc.

2003, July 9   Litho.   Perf. 12½

494-497	A175	Set of 4	6.00	2.75

Souvenir Sheet

Rouletted 8½

498	A175	5q multi	3.50	3.50

No. 498 was issued in sheets of 18 and has perf. 12½ margins.

Regional Sanitary Agricultural Organization, 50th Anniv. — A176

Designs: 20c, Banana picker. 1q, Hands in corn. 2q, Cow. 4q, Cultivated field. 5q, Sliced meat. 10q, Eye, map, ear of corn.
3q, Basket of vegetables.

2003, Dec. 8   **Litho.**   **Perf. 12½**
499-504 A176   Set of 6   11.00 5.25
Souvenir Sheet
Rouletted 8¼
505 A176 3q multi   1.50 .70

Tourist Attractions of Izabal Department A177

Designs: 20c, Punta de Manabique. 50c, Siete Altares. 1q, Las Escobas. 1.50q, View between Barrios and Pichilingo. 2q, Acropolis, Quiriguá. 3q, Livingston on the Río Dulce. No. 512, 4q, Castle of San Felipe. 5q, El Estor. 8.75q, Agua Caliente. 10q, Río Polochic.
No. 516, Quiriguá.

2004, Jan. 30   **Perf. 12½**
506-515 A177   Set of 10   18.00 8.00
Souvenir Sheet
Rouletted 6½
516 A177 4q multi   2.75 1.25

Elevation to Cardinal of Archbishop Rodolfo Quezada Toruño A178

Designs: 20c, Cardinal, cathedral. 25c, Cardinal holding crucifix, cathedral. 50c, Cardinal wearing biretta kneeling before Pope John Paul II. 1q, Cardinal wearing zucchetto kneeling before Pope. 2q, Cardinal holding biretta, wearing zucchetto. No. 522, 3q, Cardinal wearing zucchetto. 4q, Cardinal wearing miter. 5q, Cardinal kissing hand of Pope. 8.75q, Cardinal and bishops. 10q, Coat of arms
No. 527, 3q, Statue of Virgin Mary.

2004, Nov. 5   **Litho.**   **Perf. 12½**
517-526 A178   Set of 10   17.00 8.50
Souvenir Sheet
Rouletted 6½
527 A178 3q multi   1.50 .75

America Issue, Flora and Fauna — A179

Designs: 50c, Sarcoranphus papa. 3q, Heliconia collinsiana, vert. 5q, Felis concolor. 10q, Heliconius petiveranus.
12q, Tapirus vairdii.

2005, Apr. 29   **Litho.**   **Perf. 12½**
528 A179 50c multi   .25 .25
529 A179 3q multi   1.50 1.50
530 A179 5q multi   2.75 2.75
531 A179 10q multi   5.50 5.50
Souvenir Sheet
Rouletted 6½
532 A179 12q multi   6.50 6.50

Diplomatic Relations Between Guatemala and Japan A180

Flags of Guatemala and Japan and: 1q, Child, flowing well pipe, San Pedro La Laguna. 8q, Child, hospital, Puerto Barrios.
14q, Mt. Fuji.

2005, July 29   **Litho.**   **Perf. 12½**
533-534 A180   Set of 2   4.50 4.50
Souvenir Sheet
Rouletted 8½
535 A180 14q multi   7.00 7.00

Majolica A181

Designs: 1q, Incense burner. 2q, Jars. 6.50q, Bowls. 8q, Lantern.
12q, Covered jar and sugar bowls.

2005, Oct. 4   **Perf. 12½**
536-539 A181   Set of 4   8.50 8.50
Souvenir Sheet
Rouletted 8½
540 A181 12q multi   6.00 6.00

Rotary International, Cent. — A182

Designs: 2q, Emblem, handshake, Western Hemisphere. 6.50q, Emblem, Polio Plus emblem.
8q, Emblem.

2005, Nov. 15   **Perf. 12½**
541-542 A182   Set of 2   4.00 4.00
Souvenir Sheet
Rouletted 8½
543 A182 8q multi   4.00 4.00

America Issue, Fight Against Poverty — A183

No. 544, 50c: a, Open hands. b, Two children
No. 545, 5q: a, Clasped hands. b, Two children, diff.
Illustration reduced.

2006, Feb. 22   **Perf. 12½**
Horiz. Pairs, #a-b
544-545 A183   Set of 2   5.50 5.50

Prof. José Joaquín Pardo, Historian, Cent. of Birth — A184

2006, Feb. 28
546 A184 3q multi   1.50 1.50

Churches A185

Designs: 50c, Santa Cruz Hermitage, Antigua Guatemala. 1q, San Jacinto Church, Salcajá. 2q, San Andres Xecul Church, Totonicapan, vert. 3q, El Calvario Church,

---

Chichicastenango, vert. 4q, San Cristobal Acasaguastlán, El Progreso, vert. 5q, Antigua Cathedral, Antigua Guatemala. 8q, San Pedro Church and Hospital, Antigua Guatemala. 10q, San Pedro Las Huertas Church, Antigua Guatemala.
14q, Metropolitan Cathedral, Guatemala City.

2006, Mar. 15   **Perf. 12½**
547-554 A185   Set of 8   16.00 16.00
Souvenir Sheet
Rouletted 8½
555 A185 14q multi   7.00 7.00

Christmas A186

Various ceramic creche figurines: 20c, 6.50q.

2006, Nov. 27   **Litho.**   **Perf. 12½**
556-557 A186   Set of 2   3.25 3.25

Coffee Growing Regions A187

Designs: 50c, Acatenango. 1q, Antigua. 2q, Atitlán. 6.50q, Cobán. 8q, Fraijanes. 10q, Huehue.
No. 564: a, 5q, Oriente. b, 20q, San Marcos.

2006, Nov. 29   **Perf. 12½**
558-563 A187   Set of 6   14.00 14.00
Souvenir Sheet
Rouletted 6½
564 A187   Sheet of 2, #a-b   12.50 12.50

America Issue, Energy Conservation A188

Designs: 3q, Oil wells, gasoline pump nozzle. 10q, Light switch, solar panels.

2006, Dec. 7   **Perf. 12½**
565-566 A188   Set of 2   6.50 6.50

Diplomatic Relations Between Guatemala and Brazil, Cent. — A189

No. 567: a, Baile de la Conquista dancers. b, Maracatu dancers.

2006, Dec. 12
567 A189 4q Horiz. pair, #a-b   4.00 4.00

Nos. 453, C850-C852, C863, C865, C870-C871 Surcharged

Methods and Perfs As Before
2007, Jan. 23
568 AP186 50c on 40c #C850   .20 .20
569 AP188 50c on 40c #C863   .20 .20
570 AP186 1q on 60c #C851   .40 .40
571 AP191 2q on 80c #C871   .95 .95

---

572 AP188 3q on 60c #C865   1.50 1.50
573 A162   5q on 9c #453   3.00 3.00
574 AP186 8q on 80c #C852   4.00 4.00
575 AP191 10q on 60c #C870   4.75 4.75
Nos. 568-575 (8)   15.00 15.00
"Aereo" on Nos. 568-572, 574-575 is not obliterated.

Year of Transparency (in 2006) — A190

Designs: 20c, Hand holding ball with map of Guatemala. 6.50q, Magnifying glass, fingerprint (45x25mm)

2007, Jan. 23   **Litho.**   **Perf. 12½**
576-577 A190   Set of 2   3.25 3.25
Dated 2006.

Guatemala Philatelic Association, 75th Anniv. — A191

Designs: 1q, Guatemala #21. 3q, Guatemala #22. 6.50q, Guatemala #23. 8q, Guatemala #24.
25q, Guatemala #25.

2007, July 19   **Litho.**   **Perf. 12½**
578-581 A191   Set of 4   9.00 9.00
Souvenir Sheet
582 A191 25q multi   12.00 12.00

Diplomatic Relations Between Guatemala and Uruguay, Cent. — A192

No. 583: a, Santa Catarina Arch, Antigua, Guatemala. b, City gate, Colonia del Sacramento, Uruguay.

2007, Sept. 7
583 A192 4q Horiz. pair, #a-b   4.00 4.00
See Uruguay No. 2205.

America Issue, Education For All — A193

No. 584 — Stick figure children and: a, Blue panel. b, Red panel. c, Yellow orange panel. d, Green panel.

2007, Oct. 25
584 A193 4q Block of 4, #a-d   8.00 8.00

Christmas
A194

Scouting, Cent.
A195

Creche figures: 20c, Holy Family. 6.50q, Magi, horiz. (36x31mm).

2007, Dec. 4
585-586 A194   Set of 2   3.25 3.25

2007, Dec. 5
587 A195 20c multi   .20 .20

Institute For Municipal Development, 50th Anniv. (in 2007) — A196

2008, Jan. 30
588 A196 3q multi   1.50 1.50

Dated 2007.

Monsignor Juan Gerardi Conedera (1922-98) A197

2008, Apr. 25   Litho.   Perf. 12½
589 A197 8q multi   2.25 2.25

19th Cent. Defensive Bulwarks of Guatemala City — A198

No. 590: a, San Rafael de Matamoros. b, San José de Buena Vista.

2008, June 27
590 A198 1q Horiz. pair, #a-b   .55 .55

2008 Summer Olympics, Beijing — A199

Birds — A200

2008, Oct. 17   Litho.   Perf. 12½
591 A199 6.50q multi   1.75 1.75

2008, Nov. 14
Designs: 50c, Trogon violaceus braccatus. 1q, Amarilia beryllina viola. 2q, Turdus rufitorques. 4q, Glaucidium brasilianum ridgwayi. 20q, Brotogeris jugularis.

592-595 A200   Set of 4   2.10 2.10
Souvenir Sheet
596 A200 20q multi   6.25 6.25

Christmas — A201

Needlepoint: 20c, Flower. 8q, Christmas tree.

2008, Dec. 2   Litho.
597-598 A201   Set of 2   2.25 2.25

Franciscan Order, 800th Anniv. (in 2009) — A202

2008, Dec. 16
599 A202 3q multi   .85 .85

Consecration of Basilica of Esquipulus, 250th Anniv. A203

2009, Jan. 3
600 A203 50c multi   .20 .20

Natl. Marine Defense, 50th Anniv. A204

2009, Jan. 12
601 A204 1q multi   .30 .30

America Issue, National Festivals — A205

Designs: 50c, Dancers, Comalapa. 2q, All Saints Day Festival, Santiago Sacatepequez. 3q, Dancers and marimba players. 5q, Dancers.
8q, Cofrades y Capitanas.

2009, Feb. 6
602-605 A205   Set of 4   2.75 2.75
Souvenir Sheet
606 A205 8q multi   2.25 2.25

Native Costumes A206

Designs: 50c, San Juan Atitán man. 1q, San Juan Sacatepéquez woman. 2q, Tamahú woman. 3q, San Rafael Petzal woman. 4q, Totonicapán man. 5q, Patzicia woman. 8q, San Pedro San Marcos woman.
10q, San Juan Cotzal man and woman.

2009, Apr. 14   Litho.   Perf. 12½
607-613 A206   Set of 7   6.50 6.50
Souvenir Sheet
614 A206 10q multi   2.75 2.75

Marimbas A207

Designs: 3q, Gourd marimba. 4q, 18th cent. marimba. 5q, Double marimba. 8q, Concert marimba. 10q, Man playing marimba.

2009, Oct. 30
615-619 A207   Set of 5   8.25 8.25

Louis Braille (1809-52), Educator of the Blind — A208

2009, Nov. 13   Litho. & Embossed
620 A208 1q multi   .30 .30

Christmas A209

Beaded ornaments: 20c, Spheres. 50c, Reindeer. 1q, Angels. 6.50q, Star.

2009, Dec. 4   Litho.
621-624 A209   Set of 4   2.40 2.40

Battle of La Arada, 150th Anniv. (in 2011) — A210

No. 625: a, Sword and arms. b, Pres. Rafael Carrera.
10q, Carrera, vert.

2010, Feb. 12   Perf. 12½
625 A210 5q Horiz. pair, #a-b   2.60 2.60
Souvenir Sheet
626 A210 10q multi   2.60 2.60

America Issue A211

Traditional toys and games: 50c, Capitucho. 1q, Barillete (kite). 6.50q, Yo-yo. 8q, Trompo (top).

2010, Mar. 17
627-630 A211   Set of 4   4.25 4.25
Dated 2009.

SEMI-POSTAL STAMPS

Regular Issues of 1935-36 Surcharged in Blue or Red similar to illustration

1937, Mar. 15   Unwmk.   Perf. 12½
B1   A102 1c + 1c brn & crim   .75 1.00
B2   A103 3c + 1c rose car & pck grn   .75 1.00
B3   A103 3c + 1c red org & pck grn   .75 1.00
B4   A106 5c + 1c bl & dk brn (R)   .75 1.00
  Nos. B1-B4 (4)   3.00 4.00

1st Phil. Exhib. held in Guatemala, Mar. 15-20.

> Catalogue values for unused stamps in this section, from this point to the end of the section, are for Never Hinged items.

Type of Regular Issue, 1956

Designs: 5c+15c, Nurse, Patient and Red Cross Flag. 15c+50c, Red Cross, telephone and "5110." 25c+50c, Globe and Red Cross.

1956, June 19   Engr.   Perf. 13x12½
B5   A148 5c + 15c ultra & red   1.00 1.40
  a.   Imperf., pair   75.00
B6   A148 15c + 50c dk vio & red   2.25 2.75
B7   A148 25c + 50c bluish blk & car   2.25 2.75
  Nos. B5-B7 (3)   5.50 6.90

The surtax was for the Red Cross.

Jesus and Esquipulas Cathedral — SP1

1957, Oct. 29   Perf. 13
B8   SP1 1½c + ½c blk & brn   .55 .25

The surtax was for the Esquipulas highway. See Nos. CB12-CB14.

Type of Air Post Semi-Postal Stamps and

Arms — SP2

3c+3c, Wounded man, Battle of Solferino.

1960, Apr. 9   Photo.   Perf. 13½x14
Cross in Rose Red
B9   SP2   1c + 1c red brn & bl   .30 .25
B10 SPAP2 3c + 3c lil, bl & pink   .30 .25
B11 SP2   4c + 4c blk & bl   .30 .25
  Nos. B9-B11 (3)   .90 .75

Cent. (in 1959) of the Red Cross idea. The surtax went to the Red Cross. Exist imperf. See Nos. CB15-CB21.

AIR POST STAMPS

Surcharged in Red on No. 229

SERVICIO POSTAL AEREO AÑO DE 1928 Q0.03

1929, May 20   Unwmk.   Perf. 12½
C1   A64   3c on 15p blk   1.10 1.40
C2   A64   5c on 15p blk   .55 .45
C3   A64   15c on 15p blk   1.50 .45
  a.   Double surcharge (G & R)   100.00

C4 A64 20c on 15p blk   2.25 2.25
a. Inverted surcharge   100.00
b. Double surcharge   100.00

Surcharged in Red on No. 216
1929, May 20   **Perf. 14**
C5 A64 5c on 15p black   3.25 2.25
Nos. C1-C5 (5)   8.65 6.80

Surcharged in Black on No. 218

1929, Oct. 9
C6 A75 3c on 2.50p dk vio   1.00 1.00

Airplane and Mt. Agua AP3

1930, June 4   Litho.   Perf. 12½
C7 AP3 6c rose red   .60 .40
a. Double impression   25.00 25.00
b. Imperf., pair   350.00

For overprint see No. C14.

Nos. 227, 229 Surcharged in Black or Red

1930, Dec. 9   Perf. 12½
C8 A57 1c on 3p grn (Bk)   .40 .40
a. Double surcharge   100.00
C9 A57 2c on 3p grn (Bk)   1.10 1.50
C10 A57 3c on 3p grn (R)   1.10 1.50
C11 A57 4c on 3p grn (R)   1.10 1.50
C12 A64 10c on 15p blk (R)   5.00 5.00
a. Double surcharge   125.00
Nos. C8-C12 (5)   8.70 9.90

No. 237 Overprinted

1931, May 19   Perf. 14
C13 A81 4c orange   .40 .30
a. Double overprint   40.00 50.00

No. C7 Overprinted

Perf. 12½
C14 AP3 6c rose red   1.50 1.40
a. On No. C7a   30.00 30.00
b. Inverted overprint   7.00 7.00

Nos. 240, 242 Overprinted in Red

1931, Oct. 21   Perf. 14
C15 A36 15c ultra   2.00 .25
a. Double overprint   125.00 125.00
C16 A76 30c green   3.00 .95
a. Double overprint   75.00 75.00

Nos. 235-236 Overprinted in Red or Green

1931, Dec. 5
C17 A79 2c dp bl (R)   2.50 3.00
C18 A80 3c dk vio (G)   2.50 3.00

No. 240 Overprinted in Red

C19 A36 15c ultra   2.75 3.00

Nos. C17-C19 were issued in connection with the 1st postal flight from Barrios to Miami.

No. 224 Surcharged in Red

1932-33   Perf. 12½
C20 A74 2c on 1.50p dk bl   .80 .55

Nos. 227, 229 Surcharged in Violet, Red or Blue

C21 A57 3c on 3p grn (V)   .80 .25
a. Inverted surcharge   45.00 45.00
b. Vert. pair, imperf. horiz.   900.00
C22 A57 3c on 3p grn (R)   .80 .25
C23 A64 10c on 15p blk (R)   7.75 6.25
b. First "I" of "Interior" missing   10.00 10.00
C24 A64 15c on 15p blk (Bl)   9.00 8.50
a. First "I" of "Interior" missing   15.00 15.00
Nos. C20-C24 (5)   19.15 15.80

Issued: #C22, 1/1/33; others, 2/11/32.

No. 237 Overprinted in Green

1933, Jan. 1   Perf. 14
C25 A81 4c orange   .40 .35
a. Double overprint   40.00 40.00

Nos. 235, 238 and 240 Overprinted in Red or Black

1934, Aug. 7
C26 A82 5c dk car (Bk)   1.50 .25
C27 A36 15c ultra (R)   1.50 .25

Overprinted in Red

C28 A79 2c deep blue   .55 .20

View of Port Barrios — AP7

Designs: 15c, Tomb of Barrios. 30c, Equestrian Statue of Barrios.

1935, July 19   Photo.   Perf. 12½
C29 AP7 10c yel brn & pck grn   6.00 4.50
C30 AP7 15c gray & brn   1.50 1.75
C31 AP7 30c car rose & bl vio   1.50 1.25
Nos. C29-C31 (3)   9.00 7.50

Birth cent. of Gen. Justo Rufino Barrios.

Lake Amatitlán AP10

Designs: Nos. C36, C37, C45, C46. Different views of Lake Amatitlan. 3c, Port Barrios. No. C34, C35, Ruins of Fort San Felipe. 10c, Port Livingston. No. C39, C40, Port San Jose. No. C41, C42, View of Atitlan. No. C43, C44, Aurora Airport.

Overprinted with Quetzal in Green
1935-37   Size: 37x17mm
C32 AP10 2c org brn   .25 .20
C33 AP10 3c blue   .25 .20
C34 AP10 4c black   .25 .20
C35 AP10 4c ultra ('37)   .25 .20
C36 AP10 6c yel grn   .25 .20
C37 AP10 6c blk vio ('37)   4.00 .20
C38 AP10 10c claret   .50 .20
C39 AP10 15c red org   .65 .40
C40 AP10 15c yel grn ('37)   .65 .65
C41 AP10 30c olive grn   6.00 6.50
C42 AP10 30c ol bis ('37)   .75 .50
C43 AP10 50c rose vio   17.50 15.00
C44 AP10 50c Prus bl ('36)   4.00 3.00
C45 AP10 1q scarlet   17.50 20.00
C46 AP10 1q car ('36)   4.50 3.00
Nos. C32-C46 (15)   57.30 50.50

Issue dates follow No. C69.
For overprints and surcharges see Nos. C70-C79, CB1-CB2.

Central Park, Antigua AP11

Designs: 1c, Guatemala City. 2c, Central Park, Guatemala City. 3c, Monastery. Nos. C50-C51, Mouth of Dulce River. Nos. C52-C53, Plaza Barrios. Nos. C54-C55, Los Proceres Monument. No. C56, Central Park, Antigua. No. C57, Dulce River. Nos. C58-C59, Quezaltenango. Nos. C60-C61, Ruins at Antigua. Nos. C62-C63, Dock at Port Barrios. Nos. C64-C65, Port San Jose. Nos. C66-C67, Aurora Airport. 2.50q, Island off Atlantic Coast. 5q, Atlantic Coast view.

Overprinted with Quetzal in Green
Size: 34x15mm
C47 AP11 1c yel brn   .25 .20
C48 AP11 2c vermilion   .25 .20
C49 AP11 3c magenta   .25 .20
C50 AP11 4c org yel ('36)   1.75 1.40
C51 AP11 4c car lake ('37)   1.00 .75
C52 AP11 5c dl bl   .25 .20
C53 AP11 5c org ('37)   .25 .20
C54 AP11 10c red brn   .50 .35
C55 AP11 10c ol grn ('37)   .50 .30
C56 AP11 15c rose red   .25 .20
C57 AP11 15c ver ('37)   .25 .20
C58 AP11 20c ultra   2.50 3.00
C59 AP11 20c dp cl ('37)   .50 .25
C60 AP11 25c gray blk   3.00 3.50
C61 AP11 25c bl grn ('37)   .45 .25
a. Quetzal omitted   1,100.
C62 AP11 30c yel grn   1.50 1.50
C63 AP11 30c rose red ('37)   1.00 .50
C64 AP11 50c car rose   7.00 8.00
C65 AP11 50c pur ('36)   6.50 7.50
C66 AP11 1q dk bl   22.50 25.00
C67 AP11 1q grn ('36)   7.50 7.50
Size: 46x20mm
C68 AP11 2.50q rose red & ol grn ('36)   5.00 3.00
C69 AP11 5q org & ind ('36)   7.00 4.00
a. Quetzal omitted   1,500. 1,250.
Nos. C47-C69 (23)   70.20 67.95

Issued: #C32-C69, 11/1/35; 10/1/36; 1/1/37.
Value for No. C61a is for a sound stamp.
For overprints and surcharges see Nos. C80-C91, CB3-CB4.

Types of Air Post Stamps, 1935
Overprinted with Airplane in Blue

2c, Quezaltenango. 3c, Lake Atitlan. 4c, Progressive Colony, Lake Amatitlan. 6c, Carmen Hill. 10c, Relief map. 15c, National University. 30c, Espana Plaza. 50c, Police Station, Aurora Airport. 75c, Amphitheater, Aurora Airport. 1q, Aurora Airport.

1937, May 18
Center in Brown Black
C70 AP10 2c carmine   .25 .20
C71 AP10 3c blue   1.00 1.25
C72 AP10 4c citron   .25 .20
C73 AP10 6c yel grn   .35 .25
C74 AP10 10c red vio   2.00 2.25
C75 AP10 15c orange   1.50 1.00
C76 AP10 30c ol grn   3.75 3.00
C77 AP10 50c pck bl   5.00 4.25
C78 AP10 75c dk vio   10.00 11.00
C79 AP10 1q dp rose   11.00 12.00
Nos. C70-C79 (10)   35.10 35.40

Overprinted with Airplane in Black

1c, 7th Ave., Guatemala City. 2c, Los Proceres Monument. 3c, Natl. Printing Office. 5c, Natl. Museum. 10c, Central Park. 15c, Escuintla. 20c, Motorcycle Police. 25c, Slaughterhouse, Escuintla. 30c, Exhibition Hall. 50c, Barrios Plaza. 1q, Polytechnic School. 1.50q, Aurora Airport.

Size: 33x15mm
C80 AP11 1c yel brn & brt bl   .25 .20
C81 AP11 2c crim & dp vio   .25 .20
C82 AP11 3c red vio & red brn   .50 .50
C83 AP11 5c pck grn & cop red   4.00 3.00
C84 AP11 10c car & grn   1.25 1.00
C85 AP11 15c rose & dl ol grn   .50 .25
C86 AP11 20c ultra & blk   3.00 1.75
C87 AP11 25c dk gray & scar   2.50 2.50
C88 AP11 30c grn & dp vio   1.25 1.25
C89 AP11 50c magenta & ultra   10.00 12.00
Size: 42x19mm
C90 AP11 1q ol grn & red vio   10.00 12.00
C91 AP11 1.50q scar & ol brn   10.00 12.00
Nos. C80-C91 (12)   43.50 46.65

Second term of President Ubico.

Souvenir Sheet

AP12

1938, Jan. 10   Perf. 12½
C92 AP12 Sheet of 4   8.00 8.00
a. 15c George Washington   1.50 1.50
b. 4c Franklin D. Roosevelt   1.50 1.50
c. 4c Map of the Americas   1.50 1.50
d. 15c Pan American Union Building, Washington, DC   .75 .75

150th anniv. of US Constitution.

President Arosemena, Panama AP13

Flags of Central American Countries — AP19

Designs: 2c, Pres. Cortés Castro, Costa Rica. 3c, Pres. Somoza, Nicaragua. 4c, Pres. Carias Andino, Honduras. 5c, Pres. Martinez, El Salvador. 10c, Pres. Ubico, Guatemala.

1938, Nov. 20   **Unwmk.**

C93	AP13	1c org & ol brn	.25 .20
C94	AP13	2c scar, pale pink & sl grn	.30 .20
C95	AP13	3c grn, buff & ol brn	.40 .30
C96	AP13	4c dk cl, pale lil & brn	.55 .35
C97	AP13	5c bis, pale grn & ol brn	.50 .60
C98	AP13	10c ultra, pale bl & brn	1.00 1.25
		Nos. C93-C98 (6)	3.00 2.90

Souvenir Sheet

C99	AP19	Sheet of 6	8.00 8.00
a.		1c Guatemala	.80 .80
b.		2c El Salvador	.80 .80
c.		3c Honduras	1.10 1.10
d.		4c Nicaragua	1.40 1.40
e.		5c Costa Rica	1.40 1.40
f.		10c Panama	2.40 2.40

1st Central American Phil. Exhib., Guatemala City, Nov. 20-27.
For overprints see Nos. CO1-CO7.

La Merced Church, Antigua AP20

Designs: 2c, Ruins of Christ School, Antigua. 3c, Aurora Airport. 4c, Drill ground, Guatemala City. 5c, Cavalry barracks. 6c, Palace of Justice. 10c, Customhouse, San José. 15c, Communications Building, Retalhuleu. 30c, Municipal Theater, Quezaltenango. 50c, Customhouse, Retalhuleu. 1q, Departmental Building.

Inscribed "Aéreo Interior"
Overprinted with Quetzal in Green

1939, Feb. 14

C100	AP20	1c ol bis & chnt	.20 .20
C101	AP20	2c rose red & sl grn	.20 .20
C102	AP20	3c dl bl & bis	.25 .20
C103	AP20	4c rose pink & yel grn	.25 .20
C104	AP20	5c brn lake & brt ultra	.30 .20
C105	AP20	6c org & gray brn	.35 .20
C106	AP20	10c bis brn & gray blk	.50 .20
C107	AP20	15c dl vio & blk	.75 .20
C108	AP20	30c dp bl & dk car	1.10 .25
C109	AP20	50c org & brt vio	1.50 .40
a.		Quetzal omitted	1,750.
C110	AP20	1q yel grn & brt ultra	2.50 1.25
		Nos. C100-C110 (11)	7.90 3.50

See Nos. C111-C122. For overprint and surcharge see No. C124, C132.

1939, Feb. 14

Designs: 1c, Mayan Altar, Aurora Park. 2c, Sanitation Building. 3c, Lake Amatitlan. 4c, Lake Atitlan. 5c, Tamazulapa River bridge. 10c, Los proceres Monument. 15c, Palace of Captains General. 20c, Church on Carmen Hill. 25c, Barrios Park. 30c, Mayan Altar. 50c, Charles III fountain. 1q, View of Antigua.

Inscribed "Aérea International"
or "Aérea Exterior"
Overprinted with Quetzal in Green

C111	AP20	1c ol grn & gldn brn	.20 .20
C112	AP20	2c lt grn & blk	.30 .20
C113	AP20	3c ultra & cob bl	.20 .20
C114	AP20	4c org brn & yel grn	.20 .20
C115	AP20	5c sage grn & red org	.35 .20
C116	AP20	10c lake & sl blk	1.75 .20
C117	AP20	15c ultra & brt rose	1.75 .20
C118	AP20	20c yel grn & ap grn	.60 .20
C119	AP20	25c dl vio & lt ol grn	.60 .20
C120	AP20	30c dl rose & blk	.80 .20
C121	AP20	50c scar & brt yel	1.50 .20
C122	AP20	1q org & yel grn	2.50 .35
		Nos. C111-C122 (12)	10.75 2.55

No. 240 Overprinted in Carmine

1940, Apr. 14   **Perf. 14**

C123 A36 15c ultra   .60 .25

Pan American Union, 50th anniversary.

No. C112 Overprinted in Carmine

1941, Dec. 2   **Perf. 12½**

C124 AP20 2c lt grn & blk   .40 .25

Second Pan American Health Day.

San Carlos University, Antigua AP21

1943, June 25   **Engr.**   **Perf. 11**

C125	AP21	15c dk red brn	.55 .20
a.		Imperf., pair	100.00

Don Pedro de Alvarado AP22

Type I — Diagonal shading lines running from lower left to upper right at inner edges of commemorative tablet.
Type II — Additional diagonal shading lines running from upper left to lower right added throughout tablet, resulting in crosshatched lines at inner edges.

1943, Mar. 10   **Unwmk.**   **Perf. 11½**

C126	AP22	15c dp ultra (II)	.55 .25
a.		Type I	25.00 17.50

400th anniv. of the founding of Antigua.

National Police Building AP23

1943, Aug. 3   **Perf. 11**

C127 AP23 10c dp rose vio   .35 .20

Allegory of Revolution Type

1945, Apr. 27   **Engr.**

C128	A129	5c dp rose	.50 .25
C129	A129	6c dk bl grn	.50 .25
a.		Imperf., pair	110.00
C130	A129	10c violet	.50 .25
C131	A129	15c aqua	.50 .25
		Nos. C128-C131 (4)	2.00 1.00

No. C113 Surcharged in Red

1945, July 25   **Perf. 12½**

C132 AP20 2½c on 3c   1.50 1.50

The 1945 Book Fair.

Type of 1944 Overprinted "PALACIO NACIONAL" in Carmine

1945, Aug.   **Engr.**   **Perf. 11**

C133	A127	5c rose car	.30 .25
a.		Triple ovpt., one inverted	50.00 25.00
b.		Double ovpt., one inverted	65.00

See Nos. C137A-C139.

José Milla y Vidaurre Type

1945

C134	A131	7½c sepia	1.10 1.00
C134A	A131	7½c dark blue	.60 .30

Issued: #C134, Sept. 28; #C134A, Dec. 6.
For overprint see No. C230.

Torch Type

1945, Oct. 19

C135 A130 5c brt red vio   .40 .25

Souvenir Sheet
Imperf

C136	A130	Sheet of 2	5.00 4.00
a.		5c bright red violet	.40 .40

1st anniv. of the Revolution of Oct. 20, 1944.
See Nos. C147-C150.

> Catalogue values for unused stamps in this section, from this point to the end of the section, are for Never Hinged items.

Payo Enriquez de Rivera Type

1946, Jan. 22   **Unwmk.**   **Perf. 11**

C137 A132 5c rose pink   .50 .20

See Nos. C269, C311-C315.

Palace Type of 1944

1946-47

C137A	A127	5c rose car ('47)	.55 .25
C138	A127	10c deep lilac	.25 .25
a.		Imperf., pair	100.00
C139	A127	15c blue	.55 .25
a.		Imperf., pair	100.00
		Nos. C137A-C139 (3)	1.35 .75

See No. C133 for #C137A without overprint.

Sir Rowland Hill — AP30   Globes, Quetzal — AP31

1946, Aug. 5   **Photo.**   **Perf. 14x13**

C140	AP30	5c slate & brn (blk ovpt.)	.50 .25
a.		Without "AEREO" ovpt.	400.00 400.00
C141	AP31	15c car lake, ultra & emer	.65 .30

Centenary of the first postage stamp.

José Batres y Montufar — AP32

Signing the Declaration of Independence AP33

1946, Sept. 16   **Engr.**   **Perf. 11**

C142	AP32	10c Prus grn	.45 .25
a.		Perf. 12½	10.00 .20

1946, Dec. 19   **Perf. 11**

C143	AP33	5c rose car	.20 .20
C144	AP33	6c ol brn	.25 .20
C145	AP33	10c violet	.30 .25
C146	AP33	20c blue	.40 .25
		Nos. C143-C146 (4)	1.15 .90

125th anniv. of the signing of the Declaration of Independence.

Torch Type of 1945
Dated 1944-1946

1947, Feb. 3   **Engr.**

C147	A130	1c green	.40 .25
C148	A130	2c carmine	.40 .25
C149	A130	3c violet	.40 .25
C150	A130	5c dp bl	.40 .25
		Nos. C147-C150 (4)	1.60 1.00

Inscribed "II Aniversario de la Revolucion." "Aereo" in color on a white background.
2nd anniv. of the Revolution of 10/20/44.

Franklin D. Roosevelt — AP34

1947, June 6

C151	AP34	5c rose car	.25 .25
C152	AP34	6c blue	.25 .25
C153	AP34	10c dp ultra	.35 .25
C154	AP34	30c gray blk	1.60 .90
C155	AP34	50c lt violet	2.50 2.25
a.		Imperf., pair	125.00
C156	AP34	1q gray grn	4.25 3.75
a.		Imperf., pair	125.00
		Nos. C151-C156 (6)	9.20 7.65

No. 296 Overprinted in Carmine

1948, May 14   **Perf. 12½**

C157 A122 5c blue & red   .35 .25

Soccer Game AP35

1948, Aug. 31   **Engr.**
Center in Black

C158	AP35	3c brt carmine	.75 .30
C159	AP35	5c blue green	.90 .40
C160	AP35	10c dk violet	1.00 .95
C161	AP35	30c dp blue	2.25 3.50
C162	AP35	50c bister	4.50 4.50
		Nos. C158-C162 (5)	9.40 9.65

4th Central American and Caribbean Soccer Championship, Mar. 1948.

Seal, University of Guatemala — AP36

1949, Nov. 29   **Perf. 12½**
Center in Blue

C163	AP36	3c carmine	.70 .40
C164	AP36	10c green	1.00 .75
C165	AP36	50c yellow	3.75 3.25
		Nos. C163-C165 (3)	5.45 4.40

1st Latin American Cong. of Universities.

Lake Atitlan — AP37

Tecum Uman
Monument — AP38

Designs: 8c, San Cristobal Church. 13c,
Weaver. 35c, Momostenango Cliffs.

1950, Feb. 17   Photo.   *Perf. 14*
Multicolored Centers

C166	AP37	3c car rose	.35	.25
C167	AP38	5c red brn	.35	.25
C168	AP37	8c dk sl grn	.40	.25
C169	AP38	13c brown	.70	.25
C170	AP37	35c purple	2.50	3.00
	Nos. C166-C170 (5)		4.30	4.00

See No. C181.

Soccer — AP39

Pole
Vault — AP40

Designs: 3c, Foot race. 8c, Tennis. 35c,
Diving. 65c, Stadium.

1950, Feb. 25   Engr.   *Perf. 12½*
Center in Black

C171	AP39	1c purple	.65	.25
C172	AP39	3c carmine	.70	.25
C173	AP40	4c orange brn	.95	.30
C174	AP39	8c red violet	1.10	.40
C175	AP40	35c lt blue	2.50	3.25

Center in Green

C176	AP40	65c dk slate grn	5.00	5.50
	Nos. C171-C176 (6)		10.90	9.95

6th Central American and Caribbean Games.

Nurse
and
Patient
AP41

Designs: 10c, School of Nurses. 50c,
Zacapa Hospital. 1q, Roosevelt Hospital.

1950, Sept. 6   Litho.   *Perf. 12*
Quetzal in Blue Green

C177	AP41	5c rose vio & car	.25	.25
a.	Double impression (frame)		25.00	
C178	AP41	10c ol brn & emer	.70	.35
C179	AP41	50c ver & red vio	2.50	2.50
C180	AP41	1q org yel & sage grn	3.00	2.75
a.	Souv. sheet, #C177-C180		7.50	7.50
	Nos. C177-C180 (4)		6.45	5.85

National Hospital Fund.
Nos. C177-C180 exist with colors reversed,
perf. and imperf. These are proofs.

No. C168 perf. 12½ or 12 diagonally
through center

1951, Apr.   *Perf. 14*

C181	AP37	(4c) multi	15.00	9.00
a.	Unserveed pair		36.00	22.50

Counterfeits of diagonal perforation exist.

Ceremonial Stone
Ax — AP42

National Flag and
Emblem — AP43

1953, Feb. 11   Photo.   *Perf. 14x13½*

C182	AP42	3c dk bl & ol gray	.45	.45
C183	AP42	5c dk gray & hn brn	.55	.45
C184	AP42	10c dk pur & slate	.75	.45
	Nos. C182-C184 (3)		1.75	1.35

1953, Mar. 14   *Perf. 13½*
Multicolored Center

C185	AP43	1c maroon	.25	.20
C186	AP43	2c slate green	.25	.20
C187	AP43	4c dark brown	.30	.20
	Nos. C185-C187 (3)		.80	.60

Issued to mark the passing of the presidency from J. J. Arevalo to Col. Jacobo
Arbenz Guzman.

Regional
Dance — AP44

Horse
Racing
AP45

Designs: 4c, White nun — national flower.
5c, Allegory of the fair. 20c, Zakuleu ruins.
30c, Symbols of Agriculture. 50c, Champion
bull. 65c, Bicycle racing. 1q, Quetzal.

1953, Dec. 18   Engr.   *Perf. 12½*

C188	AP44	1c dp ultra & car	.25	.25
C189	AP44	4c org & grn	1.25	.30
C190	AP44	5c emer & choc	.80	.40
C191	AP45	15c choc & dk pur	1.10	1.00
C192	AP45	20c car & ultra	1.00	1.00
C193	AP44	30c dp ultra & choc	1.25	1.25
C194	AP45	50c pur & blk	1.25	1.25
C195	AP44	65c lt bl & dk grn	2.50	2.50
C196	AP44	1q dk bl grn & dk red	25.00	15.00
	Nos. C188-C196 (9)		34.40	22.95

National Fair, Oct. 20, 1953.

Indian — AP46

1954, Apr. 21   Unwmk.   *Perf. 12½*

C197	AP46	1c carmine	.25	.25
C198	AP46	2c dp blue	.30	.25
C199	AP46	4c yellow grn	.30	.25
C200	AP46	5c aqua	.55	.25
C201	AP46	6c orange	.55	.25
C202	AP46	10c violet	1.10	.30
C203	AP46	20c black brn	3.25	3.25
	Nos. C197-C203 (7)		6.35	4.80

Guatemala and
ODECA
Flags — AP47

Rotary Emblem,
Map of
Guatemala
AP48

1954, Oct. 13   Photo.   *Perf. 14x13½*

C204	AP47	1c multicolored	.55	.50
C205	AP47	2c multicolored	.55	.50
C206	AP47	4c multicolored	.55	.50
	Nos. C204-C206 (3)		1.65	1.50

3rd anniv. of the formation of the Organization of Central American States.

1956, Sept. 8   Engr.

C207	AP48	4c bl & dl yel	.30	.25
C208	AP48	6c lt bl grn & dl yel	.30	.20
C209	AP48	35c pur & dl yel	1.50	1.75
	Nos. C207-C209 (3)		2.10	2.20

50th anniv. of Rotary Intl. (in 1955).

Mayan Warrior
Holding Dagger
Cross of the
Liberation
AP49

4c, Family looking into the sun. 5c, The dagger of the Liberation destroying communist
symbols. 6c, Hands holding cogwheel & map
of Guatemala. 20c, Monument to the victims
of communism & flag. 30c, Champerico harbor.
65c, Radio tower, Mercury & map of Guatemala. 1q, Flags of the American nations. 5q,
Pres. Carlos Castillo Armas.

1956, Oct. 10   Photo.   *Perf. 14x13½*

C210	AP49	2c dp grn, red, bl & brn	.25	.25
C211	AP49	4c dp car & gray blk	.25	.25
C212	AP49	5c bl & red brn	.25	.25
C213	AP49	6c dk brn & dp ultra	.30	.25
C214	AP49	20c vio, brn & bl	1.40	1.75
C215	AP49	30c dp bl & ol	1.75	2.00
C216	AP49	65c chnt brn & grn	2.50	3.00
C217	AP49	1q dk brn & multi	3.50	4.00
C218	AP49	5q multi	14.00	15.00
	Nos. C210-C218 (9)		24.20	26.75

Liberation of 1954-55.
For overprints see Nos. C233, C243, C265-
C266, C417.

Red Cross,
Map and
Quetzal
AP50

Designs: 2c, José Ruiz Angulo and woman
with child, vert 3c, Pedro de Bethancourt with
sick man. 4c, Rafael Ayau.

Perf. 13½x14, 14x13½
1958, May 13   Unwmk.

C219	AP50	1c multicolored	.75	.40
C220	AP50	2c multicolored	.45	.20
C221	AP50	3c multicolored	.45	.20
C222	AP50	4c multicolored	.45	.20
	Nos. C219-C222 (4)		2.10	1.00

Issued in honor of the Red Cross.
For overprints and surcharges see Nos.
C235-C242, C251-C254, C283-C298, C390-
C394.

Col. Carlos
Castillo
Armas — AP51

Galleon of 1532
and Freighter
"Quezaltenango"
AP52

1959, Feb. 27   *Perf. 14x13½*
Center in Dark Blue and Yellow

C223	AP51	1c black	.30	.25
C224	AP51	2c rose red	.30	.25
C225	AP51	4c brown	.30	.25
C226	AP51	6c dk bl grn	.30	.25
C227	AP51	10c dk purple	.45	.30
C228	AP51	20c blue grn	1.25	.75
C229	AP51	35c gray	1.75	1.40
	Nos. C223-C229 (7)		4.65	3.45

Pres. Carlos Castillo Armas (1914-1957).

No. C134A
Overprinted in
Carmine

1959, Mar. 4   Engr.   *Perf. 11*

C230	A131	7½c dk blue	1.25	1.25

Issued to honor the United Nations.

1959, May 15   Litho.   *Perf. 11*

C231	AP52	6c ultra & rose red	1.00	.30

Issued to honor the formation of the Guate-
mala-Honduras merchant fleet.
For overprint see No. C467.

Type of 1950
Overprinted in Dark
Blue

1959, Oct. 9   *Perf. 12*

C232	A140	5c dk bl & lt brn	.65	.25
a.	Inverted overprint		200.00	35.00

Issued to state Guatemala's claim to British
Honduras. Overprint reads: "Belize is ours."
Map includes "BRITISH HONDURAS" and its
borderline, and excludes bit extending above
"A" of "GUATEMALA" on No. 337.
No. C232 is known without overprint in
multiples.

No. C213
Overprinted in
Red

1959, Oct. 26   Photo.   *Perf. 14x13½*

C233	AP49	6c dk brn & dp ultra	.60	.30

Centenary of coffee export.

Pres. and Mrs. Villeda of Honduras AP53

1959, Nov. 3   Litho.   Perf. 11
C234   AP53   6c pale brown   .40   .30
Visit of President Ramon Villeda Morales of Honduras, Oct. 12, 1958.
For overprint see No. C415.

Nos. C219-C222 Overprinted in Green, Violet, Blue or Brown

Perf. 13½x14, 14x13½
1960, Apr. 23   Photo.   Unwmk.
C235   AP50   1c multi (G)   2.00   1.75
C236   AP50   2c multi (V)   .95   .95
C237   AP50   3c multi (Bl)   .95   .95
C238   AP50   4c multi (Br)   .95   .95

Nos. C219-C222 Overprinted

C239   AP50   6c on 1c multi   5.00   2.50
C240   AP50   7c on 2c multi   2.50   2.25
C241   AP50   10c on 3c multi   4.00   4.25
C242   AP50   20c on 4c multi   4.50   4.50
     Nos. C235-C242 (8)   20.85 18.10
Nos. C235-C242 issued to publicize World Refugee Year, July 1, 1959-June 30, 1960.

No. C213 Overprinted in Red

1960, Apr. 30   Perf. 14x13½
C243   AP49   6c dk brn & dp ultra   1.25 1.25
Founding of the city of Melchor de Mencos.

UNESCO and Eiffel Tower, Paris AP54

1960, Nov. 4   Photo.   Perf. 12½
C244   AP54   5c dp mag & vio   .25   .25
C245   AP54   6c ultra & vio brn .25   .25
C246   AP54   8c emer & magenta .40   .25
C247   AP54   20c red brn & dl bl 1.40 1.40
     Nos. C244-C247 (4)   2.30 2.15
Issued to honor UNESCO.
For overprints see Nos. C258, C267-C268.

Abraham Lincoln — AP55

1960, Oct. 29   Engr.   Perf. 11
C248   AP55   5c violet blue   .20   .20
C249   AP55   30c violet   1.10 1.40
C250   AP55   50c gray   5.50 6.50
     Nos. C248-C250 (3)   6.80 8.10
Sesquicentenary of the birth of Abraham Lincoln.
An 8c was also printed, but was not issued and all copies were destroyed.

Nos. C219-C222 Overprinted in Green, Blue or Brown

Perf. 13½x14, 14x13½
1961, Apr. 20   Photo.   Unwmk.
C251   AP50   1c multi (G)   .60   .45
C252   AP50   2c multi (Bl)   .60   .45
C253   AP50   3c multi (Bl)   .60   .45
C254   AP50   4c multi (Br)   .60   .45
     Nos. C251-C254 (4)   2.40 1.80
Issued to honor the Red Cross.

Proclamation of Independence — AP56

1962   Engr.   Perf. 11
C255   AP56   4c sepia   .20   .20
C256   AP56   5c violet blue   .40   .20
C257   AP56   15c brt violet   1.40   .65
     Nos. C255-C257 (3)   2.00 1.05
140th anniv. of Independence (in 1961).
Issue dates: 4c, 5c, May 23; 15c, Aug. 10.

No. C245 Overprinted in Red

1962, Oct. 4   Photo.   Perf. 12½
C258   AP54   6c ultra & vio brn 1.00 1.40
WHO drive to eradicate malaria.

Dr. José Luna — AP57

Guatemalan physicians: 4c, Rodolfo Robles. 5c, Narciso Esparragoza y Gallardo. 6c, Juan J. Ortega. 10c, Dario Gonzalez. 20c, José Felipe Flores.

1962, Dec. 12   Photo.   Perf. 14x13½
C259   AP57   1c ol bis & dl pur .80   .20
C260   AP57   4c org yel & gray
                     ol   .80   .20
C261   AP57   5c pale bl & red
                     brn   .80   .20
C262   AP57   6c salmon & blk   .80   .20
C263   AP57   10c pale grn & red
                     brn   1.10   .20
C264   AP57   20c pale pink & bl 1.25   .80
     Nos. C259-C264 (6)   5.55 1.80

No. C213 Overprinted in Red: "PRESIDENTE/ YDIGORAS/ FUENTES/ RECORRE POR TIERRA/ CENTRO AMERICA/ 14 A 20 DIC. 1962"

1962, Dec.   Photo.   Perf. 14x13½
C265   AP49   6c dk brn & dp ultra 1.10   .80
Pres. Ydigoras' tour of Central America, Dec. 14-20, 1962.

No. C213 Overprinted in Vermilion

Perf. 14x13½
1963, Mar. 18   Unwmk.
C266   AP49   6c dk brn & dp ultra 6.00 3.00
Meeting of Pres. John F. Kennedy with the Presidents of the Central American Republics, San Jose, Costa Rica, Mar. 18-21.

Nos. C245-C246 Overprinted in Magenta or Black

1963, Mar. 14   Perf. 12½
C267   AP54   6c ultra & vio brn (M) .50   .20
C268   AP54   8c emerald & mag   .55   .20
Signing of the new charter of the Organization of Central American States (ODECA).

Enriquez de Rivera Type of 1946
Perf. 11, 11½, 12½
1963, Mar. 26   Engr.
C269   A132   5c olive bister   .30   .20

Woman Carrying Fruit Basket — AP58

1963, Mar. 14   Litho.   Perf. 11, 12½
C270   AP58   1c multicolored   .20   .20
Spring Fair, 1960.

Reaper — AP59

1963, July 25   Photo.   Perf. 14
C271   AP59   5c Prus green   .30   .20
C272   AP59   10c dark blue   .60   .30
FAO "Freedom from Hunger" campaign.

Ceiba Tree — AP60

1963   Unwmk.   Perf. 12
C273   AP60   4c brown & green   1.40   .20

Patzun Palace AP61

Buildings: 3c, Coban. 4c, Retalhuleu. 5c, San Marcos. 6c, Captains General of Antigua.

1964, Jan. 15   Perf. 13½x14
C274   AP61   1c rose red & brn   .50   .20
C275   AP61   3c rose cl & Prus grn .50 .20
C276   AP61   4c vio bl & rose lake .50 .20
C277   AP61   5c brown & blue   .65   .20
C278   AP61   6c green & slate   .65   .20
     Nos. C274-C278 (5)   2.80 1.00

City Hall, Guatemala City AP62

Design: 4c, Social Security Institute.

1964, Jan. 15   Photo.   Perf. 12x11½
C279   AP62   3c brt bl & brn   .40   .20
C280   AP62   4c brn & brt bl   .50   .20
See Nos. C281-C282A. For overprints see Nos. C360-C361, C421.

1964-65   Engr.   Perf. 11½
Designs: 3c, Social Security Institute. 4c, University administration building. No. C282, City Hall, Guatemala City. No. C282A, Engineering School.

Different Frames
C281   AP62   3c dull green   .55   .20
C281A   AP62   4c gray ('65)   .55   .20
C282   AP62   7c blue   .60   .20
C282A   AP62   7c olive bis ('65) .60   .20
     Nos. C281-C282A (4)   2.30   .80

Nos. C219-C222 Ovptd. in Green, Blue or Black

1964   Photo.   Perf. 13½x14, 14x13½
C283   AP50   1c multi (G)   1.25 1.40
C284   AP50   2c multi (Bl)   1.25 1.40
C285   AP50   3c multi (G)   1.25 1.40
C286   AP50   4c multi (Bk)   1.25 1.40
     Nos. C283-C286 (4)   5.00 5.60
18th Olympic Games, Tokyo, 10/10-25/64.

Nos. C219-C222 Surcharged in Green, Blue or Black

1964
C287   AP50   7c on 1c multi (G)   .30   .20
C288   AP50   9c on 2c multi (Bl)   .40   .40
C289   AP50   13c on 3c multi (Bl) .55   .45
C290   AP50   21c on 4c multi (Bk) 1.00   .85
     Nos. C287-C290 (4)   2.25 1.90

Nos. C219-C222 Ovptd. in Green, Blue or Black

1964, June 25
C291	AP50	1c multi (G)	.80	.85
C292	AP50	2c multi (Bl)	.80	.85
C293	AP50	3c multi (G)	.80	.85
C294	AP50	4c multi (Bk)	.80	.85
	Nos. C291-C294 (4)		3.20	3.40

New York World's Fair.

Nos. C219-C222 Overprinted in Green, Blue or Black: "VIII VUELTA / CICLISTICA"

1964
C295	AP50	1c multi (G)	1.60	1.40
C296	AP50	2c multi (Bl)	1.60	1.40
C297	AP50	3c multi (G)	1.60	1.40
C298	AP50	4c multi (Bk)	2.50	2.25
	Nos. C295-C298 (4)		7.30	6.45

Eighth Bicycle Race.

Pres. John F. Kennedy — AP63

1964   **Engr.**   **Perf. 11½**
C299	AP63	1c violet	1.10	.70
C300	AP63	2c yellow grn	1.10	.70
C301	AP63	3c brown	1.10	.70
C302	AP63	7c deep blue	1.10	.70
C303	AP63	50c dk gray	8.50	7.50
	Nos. C299-C303 (5)		12.90	10.30

Minute letters "TEOK" are in lower right corner of 1c, 2c, 3c and 50c.
Issue dates: 7c, July 10; others, Aug. 21.

Centenary Emblem — AP64

Perf. 11x12

1964, Sept. 9   **Unwmk.**   **Photo.**
C304	AP64	7c ultra, sil & red	.90	.25
C305	AP64	9c org, sil & red	.90	.40
C306	AP64	13c pur, sil & red	1.40	.55
C307	AP64	21c brt grn, sil & red	1.10	1.00
C308	AP64	35c brn, sil & red	2.10	1.40
C309	AP64	1q lem, sil & red	3.75	3.00
	Nos. C304-C309 (6)		10.15	6.60

Centenary (in 1963) of the Intl. Red Cross.
For overprints see Nos. C323-C327, C395-C400.

Type of Regular Issue 1963
Souvenir Sheet

1964   **Engr.**   *Imperf.*
C310	Sheet of 2	9.50	10.00
a.	A151 10c violet blue	4.00	4.00
b.	A151 20c carmine	4.00	4.00

15th UPU Congress, Vienna, May-June, 1964.

Enriquez de Rivera Type of 1946

1964, Dec. 18   **Engr.**   **Perf. 11½**
C311	A132	5c gray	.30	.20
C312	A132	5c orange	.30	.20
C313	A132	5c lt green	.30	.20
C314	A132	5c lt ultra	.30	.20
C315	A132	5c dull violet	.30	.20
	Nos. C311-C315 (5)		1.50	1.00

Bishop Francisco Marroquin AP65

Guatemalan Boy Scout Emblem — AP66

1965, Jan. 21   **Photo.**   **Unwmk.**
C316	AP65	4c lilac & brn	.20	.20
C317	AP65	7c gray & sepia	.60	.20
C318	AP65	9c vio bl & blk	.70	.20
	Nos. C316-C318 (3)		1.50	.60

Issued to honor Bishop Francisco Marroquin.

Bethancourt Type of Regular Issue, 1964

1965, Apr. 20   **Engr.**   **Perf. 11½**
C319	A152	2½c violet blue	.20	.20
C320	A152	3c orange	.20	.20
C321	A152	4c purple	.20	.20
C322	A152	5c yellow grn	.30	.20
	Nos. C319-C322 (4)		.90	.80

For overprints see Nos. C381-C382.

Nos. C304-C308 Overprinted in Red

1965, June 18   **Photo.**   **Perf. 11x12**
C323	AP64	7c ultra, sil & red	.45	.45
C324	AP64	9c org, sil & red	.55	.55
C325	AP64	13c pur, sil & red	.60	.55
C326	AP64	21c brt grn, sil & red	.85	.80
C327	AP64	35c brn, sil & red	1.00	1.25
	Nos. C323-C327 (5)		3.45	3.60

1966, Mar. 3   **Photo.**   **Perf. 14x13½**

Designs: 9c, Campfire and Scouts. 10c, Scout emblem and Scout carrying torch and flag. 15c, Scout emblem, flags and Scout giving Scout sign. 20c, Lord Baden-Powell.

C328	AP66	5c multicolored	.60	.55
C329	AP66	9c multicolored	.75	.70
C330	AP66	10c multicolored	.95	.85
C331	AP66	15c multicolored	1.25	1.10
C332	AP66	20c multicolored	1.75	1.50
	Nos. C328-C332 (5)		5.30	4.70

5th Interamerican Regional Training Conf., Guatemala City, Mar. 1-3.
For overprints see Nos. C376-C380.

Central American Independence Issue

Flags of Central American States — AP67

1966, Mar. 9   **Perf. 12½x13½**
C333	AP67	6c multicolored	.40	.20

Queen Nefertari Temple, Abu Simbel AP68

1966, Oct. 3   **Photo.**   **Perf. 12**
C334	AP68	21c violet & ocher	.85	.45

UNESCO world campaign to save historic monuments in Nubia.

Coat of Arms — AP69

1966-70   **Engr.**   **Perf. 13½**
C335	AP69	5c orange	.30	.20
C336	AP69	5c green	.30	.20
a.	5c yel grn, perf. 11½ ('69)		.30	.20

Perf. 11½
C337	AP69	5c blue ('67)	.30	.20
a.	5c dk bl, perf. 12½ ('69)		.30	.20

Perf. 12½
C338	AP69	5c gray ('67)	.30	.20
C339	AP69	5c purple ('67)	.30	.20
a.	5c bright violet ('69)		.30	.20

Perf. 11½
C339B	AP69	5c dp mag ('70)	.55	.20
C339C	AP69	5c grn, yel ('70)	.60	.20
	Nos. C335-C339C (7)		2.65	1.40

Issued: #C335, 10/31; #C336, 12/15/66; #C337, 2/9/67; #C338-C339, 4/28/67; #C336a, 12/3/69; #C339a, 12/11/69; #C339B, 7/8/70; #C339C, 10/16/70.

Msgr. Mariano Rossell y Arellano AP70

1966, Nov. 3   **Engr.**   **Perf. 13½**
C340	AP70	1c dp violet	.20	.20
C341	AP70	2c green	.30	.20
C342	AP70	3c brown	.30	.20
C343	AP70	7c blue	.45	.40
C344	AP70	50c dk gray	2.00	2.00
	Nos. C340-C344 (5)		3.25	3.00

Issued to honor Msgr. Mariano Rossell y Arellano, apostolic delegate.

Mario Mendez Montenegro AP71

1966-67   **Perf. 13½**
C345	AP71	2c rose red ('67)	.20	.20
C346	AP71	3c orange ('67)	.30	.20
C347	AP71	4c rose claret ('67)	.40	.20
C348	AP71	5c gray	.55	.20
C349	AP71	5c lt ultra ('67)	.55	.20
C350	AP71	5c green ('67)	.55	.20
C351	AP71	5c bluish blk ('67)	.55	.20
	Nos. C345-C351 (7)		3.10	1.40

Mario Mendez Montenegro (1910-65), founder of the Revolutionary Party.

Morning Glory and Map of Guatemala AP72

Flowers: 8c, Bird of paradise, horiz. 10c, White nun orchid, national flower, horiz. 20c, Nymphs of Amatitlan.

1967, Jan. 12   **Photo.**   **Perf. 12**
Flowers in Natural Colors
C352	AP72	4c orange	1.40	.60
C353	AP72	8c green	1.40	.60
C354	AP72	10c dk blue	1.60	1.00
C355	AP72	20c dk red	3.50	2.40
	Nos. C352-C355 (4)		7.90	4.70

Pan-American Institute Emblem — AP73

1967, Apr. 13   **Photo.**   **Perf. 13½**
C356	AP73	4c lt brn, lil & blk	.40	.20
C357	AP73	5c ol, bl & blk	.75	.20
C358	AP73	7c org yel, bl & blk	1.10	.40
	Nos. C356-C358 (3)		2.25	.80

8th Gen. Assembly of the Pan-American Geographical and Historical Institute in 1965.

No. C281 Overprinted

1967, Apr. 28   **Engr.**   **Perf. 11½**
C360	AP62	3c dull green	1.60	1.10

Guatemala's victory in the 3rd Norceca Soccer Games (Caribbean, Central and North American).

No. C281A Overprinted in Red

1967, June 28   **Engr.**   **Perf. 11½**
C361	AP62	4c gray	1.10	1.10

Meeting of American Presidents, Punta del Este, Apr. 10-12.

Handshake AP74

1967, June 28   **Photo.**   **Perf. 12**
C362	AP74	7c pink, brn & grn	.55	.25
C363	AP74	21c lt bl, grn & brn	.85	.55

"Peace and Progress through Cooperation."
For overprint see No. C416.

Church of
Santo
Domingo
AP75

1c, Yurrita Church, vert. 3c, Church of St. Francis. 4c, Antonio José de Irisarri, vert. 5c, Church of the Convent, vert. 7c, Mercy Church, Antigua. 10c, Metropolitan Cathedral.

1967, Aug. **Perf. 11½x12, 12x11½**
C364	AP75	1c grn, lt bl & dk brn	.40 .25
C365	AP75	2c plum, sal pink & brn	.45 .25
C366	AP75	3c brt rose, gray & blk	.45 .25
C367	AP75	4c mar, sl grn & org	.45 .25
C368	AP75	5c lil, pale grn & dk brn	.45 .25
C369	AP75	7c ultra, lil rose & blk	.55 .25
C370	AP75	10c pur, yel & blk	.95 .30
		Nos. C364-C370 (7)	3.70 1.80

Abraham Lincoln
(1809-1865)
AP76

1967 **Engr.** **Perf. 13½, 11½ (9c)**
C371	AP76	7c gray & dp org	.45 .25
C372	AP76	9c dk grn & grysh	.55 .25
C373	AP76	11c brn org & slate	.45 .30
C374	AP76	15c ultra & vio brn	.65 .40
C375	AP76	30c magenta & grn	1.50 1.50
		Nos. C371-C375 (5)	3.60 2.70

Issued: 7c, 9c, Oct. 9; others, Dec. 12. For surcharge see No. C554.

Nos. C328-C332
Overprinted

1967, Dec. 1 **Photo.** **Perf. 14x13½**
C376	AP66	5c multicolored	.40 .40
C377	AP66	9c multicolored	.65 .65
C378	AP66	10c multicolored	.85 .85
C379	AP66	15c multicolored	.85 .85
C380	AP66	20c multicolored	1.00 1.00
		Nos. C376-C380 (5)	3.75 3.75

Issued to commemorate the 8th Central American Boy Scout Camporee, Dec. 1-8.

Nos. C320-C321
Overprinted

1967, Dec. 11 **Engr.** **Perf. 11½**
C381	A152	3c orange	.55 .55
C382	A152	4c purple	.55 .55

Awarding of the Nobel Prize for Literature to Miguel Angel Asturias, Guatemalan writer.

Institute
Emblem — AP77

1967, Dec. 12 **Engr.** **Perf. 11½**
C383	AP77	9c black & grn	.80 .80
C384	AP77	25c car & brn	1.50 1.50
C385	AP77	1q ultra & bl	4.00 4.00
		Nos. C383-C385 (3)	6.30 6.30

Inter-American Agriculture Institute, 25th anniv.

UNESCO
Emblem
and
Children
AP78

1967, Dec. 12
C386	AP78	4c blue green	.30 .20
C387	AP78	5c blue	.35 .20
C388	AP78	7c gray	.50 .35
C389	AP78	21c brt rose lil	1.10 1.10
		Nos. C386-C389 (4)	2.25 1.85

20th anniv. (in 1966) of UNESCO.

Nos. C219-
C221 and
C304-C308
Ovptd. in
Black or
Yellow
Green

Perf. 13½x14, 14x13½, 11x12

1968, Jan. 23 **Photo.**
C390	AP50	1c multi	.80 .55
C391	AP50	1c multi (G)	.80 .80
C392	AP50	2c multi	.80 .80
C393	AP50	2c multi (G)	.80 .80
C394	AP50	3c multi	.80 .80
C395	AP64	3c multi (G)	.80 .80
C396	AP64	7c multi	.80 .80
C397	AP64	9c multi	1.10 1.10
C398	AP64	13c multi	1.60 1.10
C399	AP64	21c multi	2.25 1.10
C400	AP64	35c multi	1.90 1.90
		Nos. C390-C400 (11)	12.45 10.55

3rd meeting of Central American Presidents, Nov. 15-18, 1967.

Our Lady of the
Coro — AP79

Miguel Angel
Asturias, Flags of
Guatemala and
Sweden — AP80

1968-74 **Engr.** **Perf. 13½, 11½**
C403	AP79	4c ultra	.55 .25
C404	AP79	7c slate	.50 .25
C405	AP79	9c green	.50 .25
C406	AP79	9c lilac ('74)	.55 .25
C407	AP79	10c brick red	.95 .25
C408	AP79	10c gray	.60 .25
C408A	AP79	10c vio bl ('74)	.40 .20
C409	AP79	1q vio brn	4.00 3.50
C410	AP79	1q org yel	4.00 3.50
		Nos. C403-C410 (9)	12.05 8.70

Perf. 13½ applies to 4c and Nos. C407, C409-C410; perf. 11½ to 4c, 7c, 9c and Nos. C408, C408A.

Nos. 396-398
Overprinted

1968, Mar. 25 **Litho.** **Perf. 14x13½**
C411	A153	4c multicolored	.85 .85
C412	A153	5c multicolored	.85 .85
C413	A153	6c multicolored	.70 .70
		Nos. C411-C413 (3)	2.40 2.40

The 11th Bicycle Race.

1968, June 18 **Engr.** **Perf. 11½**
C414	AP80	20c ultra	1.10 .40

Awarding of the Nobel Prize for Literature to Miguel Angel Asturias.

No. C234 Overprinted in Carmine

1968, July 18 **Litho.** **Perf. 11**
C415	AP53	6c pale brown	.75 .40

International Human Rights Year.

No. C362
Overprinted

1968, July 18 **Photo.** **Perf. 12**
C416	AP74	7c pink, brn & grn	.65 .40

Issued to publicize forest conservation.

No. C213 Overprinted in Brown:
"Expedición / Científica / Nahakín / Guatemala-Peru / Ruta de los / Mayas"

1968, Aug. 23 **Photo.** **Perf. 14x13½**
C417	AP49	6c dk brn & dp ultra	.65 .65

Nahakin scientific expedition along the route of the Mayas undertaken jointly with Peru.

Views, Quetzal
and White Nun
Orchid — AP81

1968, Aug. 23 **Engr.** **Perf. 13½**
C418	AP81	10c dp cl & grn	.55 .25
C419	AP81	20c dp org & blk	.85 .60
C420	AP81	50c ultra & car	1.50 1.50
		Nos. C418-C420 (3)	2.90 2.35

Issued for tourist publicity.

No. C281A
Overprinted
in Carmine

1968, Nov. 4 **Perf. 11½**
C421	AP62	4c gray	.55 .55

20th anniv. of the Federation of Central American Universities.

Presidents
Gustavo
Diaz Ordaz
and Julio
Cesar
Mendez
Montenegro
AP82

1968, Dec. 3 **Litho.** **Perf. 14x13½**
C422	AP82	5c multicolored	.25 .25
C423	AP82	10c multicolored	.40 .25
C424	AP82	25c multicolored	.95 .85
		Nos. C422-C424 (3)	1.60 1.35

Mutual visits of the Presidents of Mexico and Guatemala.

ITU Emblem, Old and New
Communication Equipment — AP83

Engraved and Photogravure
1968-74 **Perf. 11½, 12½ (21c)**
C425	AP83	7c violet blue	.25 .20
C426	AP83	15c gray & emer	.45 .20
C426A	AP83	15c vio brn & org ('74)	.55 .25
C427	AP83	21c magenta	.70 .45
C428	AP83	35c rose red & emer	.95 .45
C429	AP83	75c green & red	2.40 2.40
C430	AP83	3q brown & red	9.25 7.75
		Nos. C425-C430 (7)	14.55 11.70

Cent. (in 1965) of the ITU.
Nos. C425, C427 are engr. only; on others denominations are photo. No. C426A is on thin, toned paper.
Issued: #C426A, 2/18/74; others 12/13/68.
For surcharges see Nos. C454, C516.

Nos. 399-403
Overprinted in Red,
Black or Gold

Lithographed and Engraved
1969 **Perf. 11½, 13½ (1c)**
C431	A154	1c blk, lt grn & red (R)	.80 .40
C432	A154	5c yel, lt grn & red	1.00 .55
C433	A154	8c org, lt grn & red	.95 .85
C434	A154	15c bl, lt grn & red	1.10 1.00
C435	A154	30c lt vio, lt grn & red (G)	1.60 1.40
		Nos. C431-C435 (5)	5.45 4.20

Dante
Alighieri — AP84

1969, July 17 Engr. Perf. 12½
C436 AP84 7c rose vio & ultra .40 .25
C437 AP84 10c dk blue .45 .25
C438 AP84 20c green .70 .25
C439 AP84 21c gray & brn 1.10 .80
C440 AP84 35c pur & brt grn 2.75 1.75
Nos. C436-C440 (5) 5.40 3.30

Dante Alighieri (1265-1321), Italian poet.

Map of Latin America — AP85

Design: 9c, Seal of University.

1969, Oct. 29 Typo. Perf. 13
Size: 44x27mm
C441 AP85 2c brt pink & blk .25 .20
Size: 35x27mm
C442 AP85 9c gray & blk .55 .25
Souvenir Sheet
Imperf
C443 AP85 Sheet of 2 1.40 1.40
a. 2c light blue & black .60 .60
b. 9c orange & black .60 .60

20th anniv. of the Union of Latin American Universities.

Moon Landing Issue

Moon Landing — AP86

1969-70 Engr. Perf. 11½
C444 AP86 50c maroon & blk 2.75 2.75
C445 AP86 1q ultra & blk 4.75 4.75
Souvenir Sheet
Imperf
C446 AP86 1q yel grn & ultra 6.75 6.75

See note after US No. C76. No. C446 contains one stamp with simulated perforations.
Issued: #C445-C446, 12/19/69; #C444, 1/6/70.

Giant Grebe Family on Lake Atitlan AP87

Designs: 4c, Lake Atitlan. 20c, Grebe chick, eggs atop floating nest, vert.

1970, Mar. 31 Litho. Perf. 13½
C447 AP87 4c red & multi .95 .25
C448 AP87 9c red & multi 1.40 .30
a. Souv. sheet of 2, #C447-C448 15.00 15.00
C449 AP87 20c red & multi 2.40 .85
Nos. C447-C449 (3) 4.75 1.40

Protection of zambullidor ducks.

Dr. Victor Manuel Calderon — AP88

Hand Holding Bible — AP89

1970 Litho. & Engr. Perf. 13, 12½
C450 AP88 1c lt bl & blk .20 .20
C451 AP88 2c pale grn & blk .25 .20
Perf. 13
C452 AP88 9c yellow & blk .55 .20
Nos. C450-C452 (3) 1.00 .60

Dr. Victor Manuel Calderon (1889-1969), who described microfilaria, a blood parasite.

1970 Litho. & Typo. Perf. 13x13½
C453 AP89 5c red & multi .30 .25

Fourth centenary of the Bible in Spanish.

No. C430 Surcharged

1971, Mar. 11 Engr. Perf. 11½
C454 AP83 50c on 3q brn & red 2.00 2.00

Arms of Guatemala, Newspapers — AP90

Official Decree of First Issue — AP91

1971 Litho. Perf. 11½, 12½
C455 AP90 2c dk bl & red .20 .20
C456 AP90 5c brn & red .20 .20
C457 AP90 25c brt bl & red .65 .40
Nos. C455-C457 (3) 1.05 .80
Souvenir Sheet
Lithographed and Engraved
Imperf
C458 AP91 Sheet of 5 2.00 2.00

Cent. of Guatemala's postage stamps.
Nos. C456-C457 have white value tablet.
No. C458 contains a litho. 4c black and engr. reproductions of Nos. 1-4 in colors similar to 1871 issue. Simulated perforations.
In 1974 No. C458 was overprinted "Conmemorativa / al Campeonato Mundial de Foot Ball / Munich 1974" and Munich Games emblem in black. Value $12. Overprint in gold or other colors was not authorized.
See Nos. C569-C570.

Mayas with CARE Package — AP92

1971 Typo. Perf. 11½
C459 AP92 5c multi .40 .40
a. Souv. sheet of 2 2.50 2.50

25th aniversary of CARE, a US-Canadian Cooperative for American Relief Everywhere. No. C459a contains imperf. stamps similar to Nos. 416 and C459.

J. Rufino Barrios, M. Garcia Granados, Map of Guatemala, Quetzal — AP93

1971, June 30 Perf. 11½
C460 AP93 2c multi, perf 13½ .80 .20
a. Value in pink ('72) .70 .20
C461 AP93 10c multi 1.50 .30
a. Value in pink, perf. 12½ ('72) 1.50 .30
C462 AP93 50c multi 8.00 3.25
C463 AP93 1q multi 12.00 6.50
Nos. C460-C463 (4) 22.30 10.25

Centenary of the liberal revolution of 1871.

Chavarry Arrué and León Bilak — AP94

Perf. 11½, 11x12½, 12½
1971-72 Engr.
C464 AP94 1c grn & blk ('72) .25 .20
C465 AP94 2c lt brn & blk ('72) .30 .25
C466 AP94 5c org & blk .45 .30
Nos. C464-C466 (3) 1.00 .75

Honoring J. Arnoldo Chavarry Arrué, stamp engraver; León Bilak, philatelist.

No. C231 Overprinted

1971, Oct. 25 Litho. Perf. 11½
C467 AP52 6c ultra & rose red .50 .20

INTERFER 71, Intl. Fair, Guatemala, Oct. 30-Nov. 21.

Flag and Map of Guatemala AP95

UNICEF Emblem and Mayan Figure — AP96

Perf. 13½ (1c); 12½ (3c, 9c); 11 (5c)
1971-75 Typo.
C468 AP95 1c blk, bl & lil .25 .25
a. Lithographed ('75) .25 .25
C469 AP95 3c brn, brt pink & bl .25 .25
C470 AP95 5c brn, org & bl .25 .25
a. Lithographed, perf. 12½ ('74) .25 .25
C471 AP95 9c blk, emer & bl .25 .25
Nos. C468-C471 (4) 1.00 1.00

Central American independence, sesqui.
Date of issue: #C469-C471, July 10, 1972.

1971-75 Engr. Perf. 11½
C472 AP96 1c yel grn .25 .25
C472A AP96 2c purple .25 .25
C473 AP96 50c vio brn 1.90 1.90
C474 AP96 1q ultra 3.00 3.00
Nos. C472-C474 (4) 5.40 5.40

25th anniv. UNICEF.
Issued: 2c, 2/24/75; others, 11/71.

Early Boeing Planes — AP97

Design: 10c, Bleriot's plane.

1972 Typo. Perf. 11½
C475 AP97 5c lt brn & brt bl .75 .30
C476 AP97 10c dark blue 1.25 .30

Military aviation in Guatemala, 50th anniv.

Arches, Antigua — AP98

1972-73 Typo. Perf. 11½
Dark Blue and Light Blue
C480 AP98 1c shown .25 .20
C481 AP98 1c Cathedral .25 .20
C482 AP98 1c Fountain, Central Park .25 .20
C483 AP98 1c Capuchin Monastery .25 .20
C484 AP98 1c Fountain and Santa Clara .25 .20
C485 AP98 1c Portal of San Francisco .25 .20
a. Block of 6, #C480-C485 1.75 1.60
Black, Lilac Rose, and Silver
C486 AP98 2½c shown .45 .20
C487 AP98 2½c Cathedral .45 .20
C488 AP98 2½c Fountain and Santa Clara .45 .20
C489 AP98 2½c Portal of San Francisco .45 .20
C490 AP98 2½c Fountain .45 .20
C491 AP98 2½c Capuchin Monastery .45 .20
a. Block of 6, #C3486-C491 3.00 1.60
Blue, Orange and Black
C492 AP98 5c shown .95 .25
C493 AP98 5c Cathedral .95 .25
C494 AP98 5c Santa Clara .95 .25
C495 AP98 5c Portal of San Francisco .95 .25
C496 AP98 5c Fountain .95 .25

C497	AP98	5c Capuchin Monastery	.95	.25
a.		Block of 6, #C492-C497	6.00	3.00

Nos. C492-C497 exist perf. 12½, same value.

Perf. 12½
Red, Blue and Black

C498	AP98	1q Fountain	4.75	2.50
C499	AP98	1q Capuchin Monastery	4.75	2.50
C500	AP98	1q shown	4.75	2.50
C501	AP98	1q Cathedral	4.75	2.50
C502	AP98	1q Fountain and Santa Clara	4.75	2.50
C503	AP98	1q Portal of San Francisco	4.75	2.50
a.		Block of 6, #C498-C503	27.50	15.00
		Nos. C480-C503 (24)	38.40	18.90

Earthquake ruins of Antigua. 1c printed se-tenant in sheets of 90 (10x9); 2½c, 5c se-tenant in sheets of 30 (5x6); 1q se-tenant in sheets of 6 (3x2).

On Nos. C498-C503 the inks were applied by a thermographic process giving a shiny raised effect.

Issued: #C480-C485, 12/14; #C486-C491, 1/22/73; #C492-C497, 3/12/73; #C498-C503, 8/22/73.

Nos. C480-C485 were overprinted "II Feria Internacional / INTERFER/73 / 31 Octubre — Noviembre 18 / 1973 / GUATEMALA" in black or lilac rose and issued 11/3/73. Value $3.

The same overprint exists in black on Nos. C480-C485, but these stamps were not decreed or issued.

See Nos. C528-C545, C770-C775F. For overprints see Nos. C517-C523.

Simon Bolivar and Map of Americas
AP99

1973-74   **Perf. 11½**

C504	AP99	3c brt lil rose & blk	.25	.25
C505	AP99	3c org & dk bl ('74)	.25	.25
C506	AP99	5c yel & multi	.25	.25
C507	AP99	5c brt grn & blk	.25	.25
		Nos. C504-C507 (4)	1.00	1.00

Indian with CARE Package, World Map
AP100

CARE Package
AP101

1973, June 14   **Typo.**   **Perf. 12½**

C508	AP100	2c blk & multi	.25	.20
C509	AP101	10c blk & multi	.55	.40
a.		Souvenir sheet of 2	1.50	1.50

25th anniversary of CARE (in 1971), a US-sponsored relief organization and 10th anniversary of its work in Guatemala.

No. C509a contains 2 stamps similar to Nos. C508-C509 with simulated perforations.

Guatemala No. 1, Laurel
AP102

1973-74   **Engr.**   **Perf. 12½, 11½ (1q)**

C510	AP102	1c yel brn ('74)	.25	.20
C511	AP102	1q rose claret	3.00	2.50

Centenary (in 1971) of Guatemala postage stamps. See Nos. C574-C576A.

Oak Wreath and Star
AP103

1973, Aug. 22   **Typo.**   **Perf. 12½**

C512	AP103	5c brn, yel & bl	.30	.25

Centenary of Escuela Politecnica, Guatemala's military academy.
See Nos. C552-C553.

Eleanor Roosevelt
AP104

Perf. 11½, 12½
1973, Sept. 11   **Engr.**

C513	AP104	7c blue	.40	.20

Eleanor Roosevelt (1884-1962), lecturer, writer, UN delegate.

Boys' School, Chiquimula
AP105

1973-74   **Typo.**   **Perf. 12½**

C514	AP105	3c blk & bl	.30	.25
C515	AP105	5c blk & dp lil rose	.30	.25

Centenary of the Instituto Varones in Chiquimula.
Issued: 5c, 12/5/73; 3c, 6/13/74.

No. C430 Surcharged in Red:
"Desvalorizadas a Q0.50" and Ornamental Obliteration of Old Denomination

1974   **Engr. & Photo.**   **Perf. 11½**

C516	AP83	50c on 3q brn & red	2.00	2.00

Nos. C480-C485 and C509a Overprinted with UPU Emblem, "UPU / HOMENAJE CENTENARIO / 1874 1974"

1974, June 13   **Typo.**   **Perf. 11½**

C517	AP98	1c dk bl & lt bl	.40	.30
C518	AP98	1c dk bl & lt bl	.40	.30
C519	AP98	1c dk bl & lt bl	.40	.30
C520	AP98	1c dk bl & lt bl	.40	.30
C521	AP98	1c dk bl & lt bl	.40	.30
C522	AP98	1c dk bl & lt bl	.40	.30
		Nos. C517-C522 (6)	2.40	1.80

Souvenir Sheet

C523		Sheet of 2	13.50	13.50

Centenary of Universal Postal Union.
No. C523 consists of an overprint on No. C509a, including "UNIVERSAL POSTAL UNION" instead of "UPU."
The overprint on No. C523 in red was not authorized by the Post Office. Value $28.

Antigua Type of 1972-73

1974, Oct. 8   **Typo.**   **Perf. 11½**
Black and Light Brown

C528	AP98	2c Capuchin Monastery	.25	.25
C529	AP98	2c Arches	.25	.25
C530	AP98	2c Cathedral	.25	.25
C531	AP98	2c Fountain and Santa Clara	.25	.25

C532	AP98	2c Portal of San Francisco	.25	.25
C533	AP98	2c Fountain	.25	.25
		Nos. C528-C533 (6)	1.50	1.50

1974, Sept. 24
Black and Yellow

C540	AP98	20c Capuchin Monastery	.55	.55
C541	AP98	20c Arches	.55	.55
C542	AP98	20c Cathedral	.55	.55
C543	AP98	20c Fountain and Santa Clara	.55	.55
C544	AP98	20c Portal of San Francisco	.55	.55
C545	AP98	20c Fountain	.55	.55
		Nos. C540-C545 (6)	3.30	3.30

Earthquake ruins of Antigua. Each group of six printed se-tenant in sheets of 30 (5x6). Value $2.

Nos. C528-C533 were printed in 1975 in black and bister se-tenant in sheets of 24 (4x6) on whiter paper. Value $5.

Generals Justo Rufino Barrios and M. Garcia Granados — AP106

Polytechnic School
AP107

1974-75   **Typo.**   **Perf. 12½, 11½ (25c)**

C552	AP106	6c red, gray & bl	.25	.25
C553	AP107	25c multi	.45	.30

Centenary (in 1973) of Escuela Politecnica, Guatemala's military academy.
Issued: 6c, 9/17; 25c, 1/1/75.

No. C373 Surcharged in Black and Green

1974, Dec. 3   **Engr.**   **Perf. 13½**

C554	AP76	10c on 11c multi	1.10	.50

Nature protection. The quetzal, Guatemala's national bird.

Costume San Martin Sacatepequez
AP108

Costumes of Women: 2c, Solola. 9c, Coban. 20c, Chichicastenango.

1974-75   **Typo.**   **Perf. 12½**

C556	AP108	2c car & multi	.25	.25
C557	AP108	2½c bl, car & brn	.20	.20
C559	AP108	9c bl & multi	.30	.25
a.		Perf. 12½x13½	.30	.25
C561	AP108	20c red & multi	.55	.25
		Nos. C556-C561 (4)	1.30	.95

Issue dates: 2½c, Dec. 16, 1974; 20c, Jan. 14, 1975; 2c, 9c, May 19, 1975.

Quetzals and Maya Quekchi Woman Wearing Huipil — AP109

1975, June 25   **Litho.**   **Perf. 13½**

C565	AP109	8c bl & multi	.70	.25
C566	AP109	20c red & multi	1.25	.40

International Women's Year 1975.

Rotary Emblem
AP110

1975-76   **Typo.**   **Perf. 13½**

C567	AP110	10c bl & multi	.40	.20

Perf. 11½

C568	AP110	15c bl & multi	.45	.20

Guatemala City Rotary Club, 50th anniv.
Issued: 10c, 10/1; 15c, 12/21/76.

Gaceta Type of 1971 Redrawn

1975-76   **Typo.**   **Perf. 12½**

C569	AP90	5c brn & red	.25	.25
C570	AP90	50c brt rose & brn	1.40	.55

The white background around numeral and on right of arms has been filled in.
Issued: 5c, 12/12; 50c, 12/1/76.

IWY Emblem and White Nun Orchid — AP111

1975-76   **Perf. 12½x13½, 11½ (8c)**

C571	AP111	1c multi	.30	.25
C572	AP111	8c yel & multi	.40	.25
C573	AP111	26c rose & multi	.95	.30
		Nos. C571-C573 (3)	1.65	.80

International Women's Year 1975.
Issued: 1c, 12/19; 8c, 12/12; 26c, 5/10/76.

Stamp Centenary Type of 1973

1975-77   **Engr.**   **Perf. 11½**

C574	AP102	6c orange	.25	.25
C575	AP102	6c green ('76)	.25	.25
C576	AP102	6c gray ('77)	.25	.25
C576A	AP102	6c vio bl ('77)	.25	.25
		Nos. C574-C576A (4)	1.00	1.00

Issued: #C574, 12/31; #C575, 5/10; others, 8/10.

Destroyed Joyabaj Village — AP112

Designs (Guatemala Flag and): 3c, Emergency food distribution. 5c, Jaguar Temple, Tikal. 10c, Destroyed bridge. 15c, Outdoors emergency hospital. 20c, Sugar cane harvest. 25c, Destroyed house. 30c, New building, Tecpan. 50c, Destroyed Cerro del Carmen church. 75c, Cleaning up debris. 1q, Military help. 2q, Lake Atitlan.

1976, June 4   Litho.   Perf. 12½

C577	AP112	1c red & multi	.20	.20
C578	AP112	3c multi	.20	.20
C579	AP112	5c pink & multi	.20	.20
C580	AP112	10c red & multi	.30	.20
C581	AP112	15c multi	.45	.20
C582	AP112	20c pink & multi	.45	.30
C583	AP112	25c red & multi	.80	.35
C584	AP112	30c multi	.95	.30
C585	AP112	50c red & multi	1.25	.45
C586	AP112	75c multi	2.00	1.00
C587	AP112	1q multi	3.00	1.25
C588	AP112	2q multi	5.75	3.00
	Nos. C577-C588 (12)		15.55	7.65

Earthquake of Feb. 4, 1976, and gratitude for foreign help. Inscriptions in colored panels vary. 3 imperf. souvenir sheets exist (50c, 1q, 2q). Size: 112x83mm. Value, each $15.

Allegory of Independence — AP113

Designs: 2c, Boston Tea Party. 3c, Thomas Jefferson, vert. 4c, 20c, 35c, Allegory of Independence (each different; 4c, 35c, vert.). 5c, Warren's Death at Bunker Hill. 10c, Washington at Valley Forge. 15c, Washington at Monmouth. 25c, The Generals at Yorktown. 30c, Washington Crossing the Delaware. 40c, Declaration of Independence. 45c, Patrick Henry, vert. 50c, Congress Voting Independence. 1q, Washington, vert. 2q, Lincoln, vert. 3q, Franklin, vert. 5q, John F. Kennedy, vert. The historical designs and portraits are after paintings.

1976, July 30   Litho.   Perf. 12½
Size: 46x27mm, 27x46mm

C592	AP113	1c multicolored	.25	.20
C593	AP113	2c multicolored	.20	.20
C594	AP113	3c multicolored	.20	.20
C595	AP113	4c multicolored	.25	.20
C596	AP113	5c multicolored	.25	.20
C597	AP113	10c multicolored	.25	.20
C598	AP113	15c multicolored	.30	.20
C599	AP113	20c multicolored	.45	.25
C600	AP113	25c multicolored	.45	.25
C601	AP113	30c multicolored	.80	.25
C602	AP113	35c multicolored	.85	.45
C603	AP113	40c multicolored	.85	.55
C604	AP113	45c multicolored	1.00	.65
C605	AP113	50c multicolored	1.40	.45
C606	AP113	1q multicolored	2.40	2.00
a.	Souvenir sheet		2.75	2.75
C607	AP113	2q multicolored	4.00	4.00
a.	Souvenir sheet		5.00	5.00
C608	AP113	3q multicolored	5.50	5.50
a.	Souvenir sheet		6.25	6.25

Size: 35x55mm

C609	AP113	5q multicolored	9.50	3.50
a.	Souvenir sheet		12.00	12.00
	Nos. C592-C609 (18)		28.85	19.25

American Bicentennial. Souvenir sheets contain one imperf. stamp each.

1974 Quetzal Coin AP114

Lithographed and Engraved
1976, Dec. 1   Perf. 11½

C610	AP114	8c org, blk & bl	.25	.20

Perf. 13½

C611	AP114	20c brt rose, bl & blk	.70	.25

50th anniv. of introduction of Quetzal currency.

Engineers at Work AP115

1976, Dec. 21   Engr.   Perf. 11½

C612	AP115	9c ultra	.30	.20
C613	AP115	10c green	.30	.20

School of Engineering, Guatemala City, centenary.

Holy Week Type of 1977

Designs: Sculptures of Christ from various Guatemalan churches. 4c, 7c, 9c, 20c, vert.

1977, Apr. 4   Litho.   Perf. 11

C614	A159	3c pur & multi	.40	.25
C615	A159	4c pur & multi	.40	.25
C616	A159	7c pur & multi	.40	.25
C617	A159	9c pur & multi	.45	.25
C618	A159	20c pur & multi	.95	.60
C619	A159	26c pur & multi	1.25	.70
	Nos. C614-C619 (6)		3.85	2.30

Souvenir Sheet
Roulette 7½

C620	A159	30c pur & multi	4.00	4.00

Holy Week 1977.

City Hall and Bank of Guatemala — AP116

Designs: 6c, Deed to original site, vert. 8c, Church and farm house, site of first legislative session. 9c, Coat of arms of Pedro Cortes, first archbishop. 22c, Arms of Guatemala City, vert.

Perf. 13½ (6c); 11½ (others)
1977, Aug. 10   Litho.

C621	AP116	6c multicolored	.40	.25
C622	AP116	7c multicolored	.40	.25
C623	AP116	8c multicolored	.40	.25
C624	AP116	9c multicolored	.55	.25
a.	Souvenir sheet		.80	.80
C625	AP116	22c multicolored	.85	.25
a.	Souvenir sheet		1.10	1.10
	Nos. C621-C625 (5)		2.60	1.25

Bicentenary of the founding of Nueva Guatemala de la Asuncion (Guatemala City). Nos. C624a-C625a contain one stamp each with simulated perforations.

Arms of Quetzaltenango AP117

City Hall and Torch AP118

1977, Sept. 11   Litho.   Perf. 11½

C626	AP117	7c blk & sil	.25	.20
C627	AP118	30c bl & yel	.85	.30

Founding of Quetzaltenango, 150th anniv.

Mayan Bas-relief — AP119

1977, Nov. 7

C628	AP119	10c brt car & blk	.30	.20

14th Intl. Cong. of Latin Notaries.

Children Bringing Gifts to Christ Child — AP120

Christmas: 1c, Mother and children, horiz. 4c, Guatemalan children's Nativity scene.

1977, Dec. 16   Litho.   Perf. 11½

C629	AP120	1c multicolored	.25	.25
C630	AP120	2c multicolored	.25	.25
C631	AP120	4c multicolored	.25	.25
	Nos. C629-C631 (3)		.75	.75

Almolonga Costume, Cancer League Emblem — AP121

Virgin of Sorrows, Antigua — AP122

Regional Costumes after Paintings by Carlos Mérida and Cancer League Emblem: 2c, Nebaj woman. 5c, San Juan Cotzal couple. 6c, Todos Santos couple. 20c, Regidores men. 30c, San Cristobal woman.

Perf. 14 (1c, 5c, No. C636); Perf. 12 (2c, 6c, No. C636a, 30c)
1978, Apr. 3   Litho.

C632	AP121	1c gold & multi	.20	.20
C633	AP121	2c gold & multi	.20	.20
C634	AP121	5c gold & multi	.20	.20
C635	AP121	6c gold & multi	.30	.20
C636	AP121	20c gold & multi	1.10	.25
a.	Souv. sheet of 1		3.00	3.00
C637	AP121	30c gold & multi	1.10	.30
	Nos. C632-C637 (6)		3.10	1.35

Part of proceeds from sale of stamps went to National League to Fight Cancer.

1978   Litho.   Perf. 11½

Statues from Various Churches: 4c, Virgin of Mercy, Antigua. 5c, Virgin of Anguish, Yurrita. 6c, Virgin of the Rosary, Santo Domingo. 8c, Virgin of Sorrows, Santo Domingo. 9c, Virgin of the Rosary, Quetzaltenango. 10c, Virgin of the Immaculate Conception, Church of St. Francis. 20c, Virgin of the Immaculate Conception, Cathedral Church.

C638	AP122	2c multicolored	.45	.30
C639	AP122	4c multicolored	.45	.30
C640	AP122	5c multicolored	.45	.30
C641	AP122	6c multicolored	.45	.30
C642	AP122	8c multicolored	.45	.30
C643	AP122	9c multicolored	.45	.30
C644	AP122	10c multicolored	.45	.30
C645	AP122	20c multicolored	1.25	.30
	Nos. C638-C645 (8)		4.40	2.40

Holy Week 1978. A 30c imperf. souvenir sheet shows the Pietà from Calvary Church, Antigua. Size: 71x101mm. Value $4.50.
Issued: 6c, 10c, 20c, 9/28; others, 5/22.

Soccer Player, Argentina '78 Emblem AP123

1978, July 3   Litho.   Perf. 12

C646	AP123	10c multicolored	.50	.20

11th World Cup Soccer Championship, Argentina, June 1-25.

Gymnastics AP124

1978, Sept. 4   Perf. 12

C647	AP124	6c shown	.25	.25
C648	AP124	6c Volleyball	.25	.25
C649	AP124	6c Target shooting	.25	.25
C650	AP124	6c Weight lifting	.25	.25
a.	Block of 4, #C647-C650		1.00	1.00
C651	AP124	8c Track & field	.25	.25
	Nos. C647-C651 (5)		1.25	1.25

13th Central American and Caribbean Games, Medellin, Colombia.

Cattleya Pachecoi AP125

Designs: Orchids.

1978, Dec. 7   Litho.   Perf. 12

C652	AP125	1c shown	1.40	1.25
C653	AP125	1c Sobralia	1.40	1.25
C654	AP125	1c Cypripedium	1.40	1.25
C655	AP125	1c Oncidium	1.40	1.25
a.	Block of 4, #C652-C655		20.00	20.00
C656	AP125	3c Cattleya bowrigiana	1.60	1.25
C657	AP125	3c Encyclia	1.60	1.25
C658	AP125	3c Epidendrum	1.60	1.25
C659	AP125	3c Barkeria	1.60	1.25
C660	AP125	8c Spiranthes	3.50	2.50
C661	AP125	20c Lycaste	12.50	10.50
	Nos. C652-C661 (10)		28.00	23.00

Seal of University AP126

Students of Different Departments AP127

Designs: 12c, Student in 17th cent. clothes. 14c, Students, 1978, and molecular model.

1978, Dec. 7

C662	AP126	6c multicolored	.20	.20
C663	AP127	7c multicolored	.25	.20
C664	AP126	12c multicolored	.30	.20
C665	AP126	14c multicolored	.45	.20
		Nos. C662-C665 (4)	1.20	.80

San Carlos University of Guatemala, tercentenary.

Brown and White Children
AP128

A Helping Hand — AP129

Designs: 7c, Child at play. 14c, Hands sheltering Indian girl.

1978, Dec. 7

C666	AP128	6c multicolored	.20	.20
C667	AP128	7c multicolored	.25	.20
C668	AP129	12c multicolored	.30	.20
C669	AP129	14c multicolored	.45	.20
		Nos. C666-C669 (4)	1.20	.80

Year of the Children of Guatemala.

Tree Planting and FAO Emblem — AP130

Forest protection: 8c, Burnt forest. 9c, Watershed, river and trees. 10c, Sawmill. 26c, Forests, river and cultivated terraces.

1979, Apr. 16   Litho.   Perf. 13½

C670	AP130	6c multicolored	.30	.25
C671	AP130	8c multicolored	.30	.25
C672	AP130	9c multicolored	.30	.25
C673	AP130	10c multicolored	.30	.25
C674	AP130	26c multicolored	.55	.25
a.		Souv. sheet of 5, #C670-C674	2.00	2.00
		Nos. C670-C674 (5)	1.75	1.25

Peten Wild Turkey — AP131

Clay Jar, 50-100 A.D. — AP132

Wildlife conservation: 3c, White-tailed deer, horiz. 5c, King buzzard. 7c, Horned owl. 9c, Young wildcat. 30c, Quetzal.

1979, June 14   Litho.   Perf. 13½

C675	AP131	1c multicolored	1.90	.70
C676	AP131	3c multicolored	1.10	.70
C677	AP131	5c multicolored	5.75	.70
C678	AP131	7c multicolored	12.50	2.75
C679	AP131	9c multicolored	2.75	.70
		Nos. C675-C679 (5)	24.00	5.55

Souvenir Sheet

C680	AP131	30c multicolored	16.00	16.00

1979, Sept. 19   Litho.   Perf. 13

Archaeological Treasures from Tikal: 3c, Mayan woman, ceramic head, 900 A.D. 4c, Earring, 50-100 A.D. 5c, vase, 700 A.D. 6c, Boy, 200-50 B.C. 7c, Bone carving, 700 A.D. 8c, Striped vase, 700 A.D. 10c, Covered vase on tripod, 450 B.C.

C681	AP132	2c multi	.40	.25
C682	AP132	3c multi	.55	.40
C683	AP132	4c multi	.80	.55
C684	AP132	5c multi	.95	.55
C685	AP132	6c multi	1.25	.80
C686	AP132	7c multi	1.25	.95
C687	AP132	8c multi	1.50	1.00
C688	AP132	10c multi	2.00	1.25
		Nos. C681-C688 (8)	8.70	5.75

Presidential Guard Patches
AP133

Presidential Guard, 30th anniv.: 10c, Guard Headquarters.

1979, Dec. 6   Litho.   Perf. 11½

C689	AP133	8c multi	.25	.25
C690	AP133	10c multi	.25	.25

National Coat of Arms — AP134

Arms of Guatemalan Municipalities.

1979, Dec. 27   Litho.   Perf. 13½

C691	AP134	8c shown	.45	.25
C692	AP134	8c Alta Verapaz	.45	.25
C693	AP134	8c Baja Verapaz	.45	.25
C694	AP134	8c Chimal Tenango	.45	.25
C695	AP134	8c Chiquimula	.45	.25
C696	AP134	8c Escuintla	.45	.25
C697	AP134	8c Flores	.45	.25
C698	AP134	8c Guatemala	.45	.25
C699	AP134	8c Huehuetenango	.45	.25
C700	AP134	8c Izabal	.45	.25
C701	AP134	8c Jalapa	.45	.25
C702	AP134	8c Jutiapa	.45	.25
C703	AP134	8c Mazatenango	.45	.25
C704	AP134	8c Progreso	.45	.25
C705	AP134	8c Quezaltenango	.45	.25
C706	AP134	8c Quiche	.45	.25
C707	AP134	8c Retalhuleu	.45	.25
C708	AP134	8c Sacatepequez	.45	.25
C709	AP134	8c San Marcos	.45	.25
C710	AP134	8c Santa Rosa	.45	.25
C711	AP134	8c Solola	.45	.25
C712	AP134	8c Totonicapan	.45	.25
C713	AP134	8c Zacapa	.45	.25
		Nos. C691-C713 (23)	10.35	5.75

Miniature Sheet
Imperf

C714	AP134	50c 1st & current natl. arms	3.50	3.50

No. C714 is horizontal.

The Creation of the World — AP135

Designs: Scenes from The Creation, Popul Vuh (Sacred Book of the Ancient Quiches of Guatemala): No. C716, Origin of the Twin Semi-gods. No. C717, Populating the earth. No. C718, Balam Quitze. No. C719, Quiche monarch Cotuha. No. C720, Birth of the Stick Men. No. C721, Princess Xquic's punishment. No. C722, Caha Paluma. No. C723, Cotuha and Iztayul invincible. No. C724, Odyssey of Hun Ahpu and Xbalanque. No. C725, Balam Acab. No. C726, Chief of all Nations. No. C727, Destruction of the Stick Men. No. C728, The Test in Xibalba. No. C729, Chomiha. No. C730, Warrior with captive. No. C731, Creation of the Corn Men. No. C732, Multiplication of the Prodigies. No. C733, Mahucutah. No. C734, Undefeatable king. No. C735, Thanksgiving. No. C736, Deification of Hun Ahpu and Xbalanque. No. C737, Tzununiha. No. C738, Greatness of the Quiches (battle scene).

1981   Litho.   Perf. 12

C715	AP135	1c multi	.20	.20
C716	AP135	1c multi	.20	.20
C717	AP135	2c multi	.20	.20
C718	AP135	2c multi	.20	.20
C719	AP135	3c multi	.20	.20
C720	AP135	4c multi	.25	.20
C721	AP135	4c multi	.25	.20
C722	AP135	4c multi	.25	.20
C723	AP135	4c multi	.25	.20
C724	AP135	6c multi	.30	.25
C725	AP135	6c multi	.30	.25
C726	AP135	6c multi	.30	.25
C727	AP135	8c multi	.45	.30
C728	AP135	8c multi	.45	.30
C729	AP135	8c multi	.45	.30
C730	AP135	8c multi	.45	.30
C731	AP135	10c multi	.55	.40
C732	AP135	10c multi	.55	.40
C733	AP135	10c multi	.55	.40
C734	AP135	10c multi	.55	.40
C735	AP135	22c multi	1.25	.85
C736	AP135	26c multi	1.40	.95
C737	AP135	30c multi	1.75	1.10
C738	AP135	50c multi	2.75	2.00
		Nos. C715-C738 (24)	14.05	10.25

Issued: #C715, C717, 3c, C727, C731, 22c, 1/29; #C716, C718, C721-C722, C724-C725, C728-C729, C732-C733, 26c, 30c, 3/16; others, 1981.

Thomas Edison (Phonograph Centenary) AP136

Talking Movies, 50th Anniv. — AP137

Telephone Centenary (1976) — AP138

Lindbergh's Atlantic Flight, 50th Anniv. (1977) AP139

12c, Jose Cecilio del Valle, patriot. 25c, Jesus Castillo (1877-1949), composer.

Perf. 11½, 12½ (25c)
1981, June 1   Litho.

C739	AP136	3c multi	.25	.25
C740	AP137	5c multi	.30	.25
C741	AP138	6c multi	.40	.25
C742	AP139	7c multi	.45	.30
C743	AP139	12c multi	.80	.45
C744	AP139	25c multi	1.50	1.00
		Nos. C739-C744 (6)	3.70	2.50

First Police Chief Roderico Toledo and Present Chief German Chupina
AP140

1981, Sept. 12   Litho.   Perf. 11½

C745	AP140	2c shown	.40	.25
C746	AP140	4c Headquarters	.40	.25

Mayan Rock of the Sun Calendar AP141

1981, Oct. 9

C747	AP141	1c multi	.25	.25

Gen. Jose Gervasio Artigas of Uruguay AP142

Liberators of the Americas: 2c, Bernardo O'Higgins (Chile). 4c, Jose de San Martin (Argentina). 10c, Miguel Garcia Granados. 2c, 4c, 10c, 31x47mm.

1982, Apr. 2   Litho.   Perf. 11½

C748	AP142	2c multi	.25	.25
C749	AP142	3c multi	.25	.25

Perf. 12½

C750	AP142	4c multi	.25	.25
C751	AP142	10c tan & blk	.25	.25
		Nos. C748-C751 (4)	1.00	1.00

Occidents Bank Centenary (1981) AP143

1c, Justo Rufino Barrios (1st pres.), Main Office, Quezaltenango. 2c, Main Office, 3c, Emblem, vert. 4c, Commemorative medals, vert.

1982, July 28   Litho.   Perf. 11½

C752	AP143	1c multi	.30	.25
C753	AP143	2c multi	.30	.25
C754	AP143	3c multi	.30	.25
C755	AP143	4c multi	.30	.25
		Nos. C752-C755 (4)	1.20	1.00

50th Anniv. of Natl. Mortgage Bank (1980) AP144

Various emblems. 5c vert.

1982, Oct. 18   Litho.   Perf. 11½
C756 AP144 1c multi   .30   .25
C757 AP144 2c multi   .30   .25
C758 AP144 5c multi   .30   .25
C759 AP144 10c multi   .30   .25
    Nos. C756-C759 (4)   1.20 1.00

AP145

AP146

1983, May 16   Litho.   Perf. 11½
C760 AP145 1c Portrait   .20   .20
C761 AP145 20c Aparition, horiz. .60   .40

20th Anniv. of Beatification of Pedro Bethancourt (1626-1667).

1983, July 25   Litho.   Perf. 11½
C762 AP146 10c multi   .30   .25

World Telecommunications and Health Day, May 17, 1981

Evangelical Church Centenary (1982) — AP147

1983, Aug. 9
C763 AP147 3c Hands holding bible   .40   .25
C764 AP147 5c Church   .40   .25

Natl. Railroad Centenary — AP148

10c, 1st locomotive crossing Puenta de Las Vacas. 25c, General Justo Rufino Barrios, Railroad Yard. 30c, Spanish Diesel, Amatitlan crossing.

1983, Sept. 28   Litho.   Perf. 11½
C765 AP148 10c multi   1.00   .80
C766 AP148 25c multi   2.75 1.75
C767 AP148 30c multi   3.00 2.00
    Nos. C765-C767 (3)   6.75 4.55

World Food Day AP149

1983, Oct. 16   Photo.   Perf. 11½
C768 AP149 8c Globe, wheat, vert.   .25   .20
C769 AP149 1q shown   2.75 1.75

Architecture Type of 1972

1984, Feb. 20   Typo.   Perf. 12½
Black and Green
C770 AP98 1c like #C480   .20   .20
C771 AP98 1c like #C481   .20   .20
C772 AP98 1c like #C482   .20   .20
C773 AP98 1c like #C483   .20   .20
C774 AP98 1c like #C484   .20   .20
C775 AP98 1c like #C485   .20   .20
    g. Strip of 6, #C770-C775 1.00 1.00
Black, Brown and Orange Brown
C775A AP98 5c like #C484   .25   .20
C775B AP98 5c like #C485   .25   .20
C775C AP98 5c like #C482   .25   .20
C775D AP98 5c like #C483   .25   .20
C775E AP98 5c like #C480   .25   .20
C775F AP98 5c like #C481   .25   .20
    h. Strip of 6, #C775A-C775F 1.75 1.75

Visit of Pope John Paul II, Mar. 8-9, 1983 AP150

1984, Mar. 26   Litho.   Perf. 11½
C776 AP150 4c Pope, arms   .45   .35
C777 AP150 8c Receiving Mayan indian .45   .35

Rafael Landivar (1731-93), Poet — AP151

Cardinal Mario Casariego y Acevedo AP152

1984, Aug. 6   Litho.   Perf. 11½
C778 AP151 2c Portrait, vert.   .30   .25
C779 AP151 4c Tomb   .30   .25

1984, Aug. 6
C780 AP152 10c 16th archbishop of Guat. (1909-83) .40   .25

Central American Bank for Economic Integration, 20th Anniv. — AP153

1984, Sept. 10   Litho.   Perf. 11½
C781 AP153 30c Bank emblem, map   1.10   .60

Coffee Production, 1870 AP154

Modern Coffee Production AP155

Designs: 1c, Planting coffee. 2c, Harvesting. 3c, Drying beans. 4c, Loading beans on steamer. 5c, Reyna plant grafting method. 10c, Picking beans, coffee cup. 12c, Drying unripened beans, Gardiola Freeze-drying machine. 25c, Cargo transports.

1984, Dec. 19   Perf. 11½
C782 AP154 1c sep & pale brn   .25   .25
C783 AP154 2c sep & pale org brn .25   .25
C784 AP154 3c sep & beige   .25   .25
C785 AP154 4c sep & pale yel brn .25   .25
C786 AP155 5c multi   .30   .25
C787 AP155 10c multi   .60   .40
C788 AP155 12c multi   .80   .45
C789 AP155 25c multi   1.50 1.00
    Nos. C782-C789 (8)   4.20 3.10

Natl. coffee production and export. An 86x112mm 25c stamp of Type AP154 and a 105x85mm 30c stamp of Type AP155 exist, value $110 and $140 respectively.

Natl. Scouting Assoc. — AP156

Scouting emblems and: 5c, Beaver scout, Pyramid of Tikal. 6c, Wolf scout, Palace of the Captains-General and Ahua Volcano. 8c, Scout, San Pedro Volcano and Marimba player. 10c, Rover scout and conquest mask dance. 20c, Lord Baden-Powell and Col. Carlos Cipriani, natl. founder.

1985, July 1
C792 AP156 5c multi   .30   .20
C793 AP156 6c multi   .40   .25
C794 AP156 8c multi   .45   .30
C795 AP156 10c multi   .45   .40
C796 AP156 20c multi   1.25   .85
    Nos. C792-C796 (5)   2.85 2.00

Inter-American Family Unity Year — AP157

Central American Aeronautics Admin., 25th Anniv. — AP158

1985, Oct. 16
C797 AP157 10c multi   .45   .30

1985, Nov. 11
C798 AP158 10c multi   .40   .25

Natl. Telegraph, Cent. — AP159

Portraits: Samuel Morse, telegraph inventor, and Justo Rufino Barrios, communications pioneer.

1985, Nov. 20   Perf. 12
C799 AP159 4c brn & blk   .25   .25

Intl. Olympic Committee, 90th Anniv. — AP160

Designs: 8c, Mayan bust of ancient sportsman. 10c, Baron Pierre de Coubertin (1863-1937), father of modern Games, 1st committee president.

1986, Jan. 28   Litho.   Perf. 11½
C800 AP160 8c multi   .55   .45
C801 AP160 10c multi   .75   .45

Volunteer Fire Department AP161

1986, Feb. 6   Litho.   Perf. 11½
C802 AP161 6c multi   .65   .25

Temple of Minerva — AP162

Quetzaltenango Coat of Arms, City Hall — AP163

1986, July 16   Litho.   Perf. 12½, 11½
C803 AP162 8c multi   .25   .20
C804 AP163 10c multi   .30   .25

Quetzaltenango Independence Fair, cent.

Volunteer Fire Department
AP164

1986, Oct. 10   Litho.   Perf. 11½
C805 AP164 8c Rescue   .85   .30
C806 AP164 10c Ruins   .85   .30

Assoc. of Telegraphers and Radio-Telegraph Operators, 25th Anniv. — AP165

1986, Oct. 10   Perf. 12
C807 AP165 6c multi   .50   .20

San Carlos University School of Architecture, 25th Anniv. — AP166

1987, Feb. 16   Litho.   Perf. 11½
C808 AP166 10c multi   .50   .20

ICAO, 40th Anniv. (in 1984) AP167

1987, Apr. 2   Litho.   Perf. 11½
C809 AP167 8c Aviateca Air-
          lines jet   .25   .20
C810 AP167 10c Jet, vert.   .30   .20

Chixoy Hydroelectric Power Plant — AP168

1987, May 18   Litho.   Perf. 11½
C811 AP168 2c multi   .40   .40
Nat'l. Electrification Institute inauguration (in 1985).

San Jose de los Infantes College, 200th Anniv. (in 1981) AP169

8c, Portrait of Archbishop Cayetano Francos y Monroy, founder. 10c, College crest.

1987, June 10
C812 AP169 8c multi, vert.   .25   .20
C813 AP169 10c multi   .30   .25

Promotion of Literacy in Latin America and Caribbean AP170

1987, Aug. 20   Litho.   Perf. 11½
C814 AP170 12c apple grn, blk &
          brt org   .40   .25

19th Natl. Folklore Carnival of Coban, Alta Verapaz, July 25 — AP171

1987, Oct. 12
C815 AP171 1q Three girls from
          Tamahu   5.50 2.00

1987, Dec. 8
C816 AP171 50c Girl weaving 2.75   .95
          See No. C831.

9th Pan American Games, Caracas AP172

1987, Nov. 5   Perf. 12½
C817 AP172 10c blk & sky blue .30   .20

Writers and Historians AP173

Esquipulas II — AP174

Designs: 1c, Flavio Herrera, poet, novelist. 2c, Rosendo Santa Cruz, novelist. 3c, Werner Ovalle Lopez, poet. 4c, Enrique A. Hidalgo, poet, humorist. 5c, Enrique Gomez Carrillo (1873-1927), novelist. 6c, Cesar Branas (1899-1976), journalist. 7c, Clemente Marroquin Rojas, historian. 8c, Rafael Arevalo Martinez (1884-1975), poet. 9c, Jose Milla y Vidaurre (1822-1882), historian. 10c, Miguel Angel Asturias, Nobel laureate for literature.

1987-90   Perf. 11½
C818 AP173 1c blk & lil   .30   .25
C819 AP173 2c blk & dl org   .30   .25
C820 AP173 3c blk & brt bl   .30   .25
C821 AP173 4c blk & ver   .30   .25
C822 AP173 5c blk & org brn .30   .25
C823 AP173 6c blk & org   .30   .25
C824 AP173 7c blk & grn   .30   .25
C825 AP173 8c blk & brt red .30   .25
C826 AP173 9c blk & brt rose lil .30   .25
C827 AP173 10c blk & yel   .30   .25
Nos. C818-C827 (10)   3.00 2.50
Issued: 6c, 8c, 9c, 11/5/87; 4c, 5c, 1/13/88; 7c, 3/23/90; 1c, 2c, 3c, 10c, 4/9/90.

1988, Jan. 15   Perf. 12½
C828 AP174 10c dark olive grn .40   .25
C829 AP174 40c plum   1.50 1.00
C830 AP174 60c deep blue vio 2.40 1.50
Nos. C828-C830 (3)   4.30 2.75
2nd Meeting of the Central American Peace Plan. Nos. C828-C829 horiz.

Folklore Festival Type of 1987
Souvenir Sheet

1988, Dec. 6   Litho.   Imperf.
C831 AP171 2q Music ensem-
          ble, horiz.   10.00 10.00

St. John Bosco (1815-1888), Educator AP175

1989, Feb. 1   Litho.   Perf. 11½
C832 AP175 40c gold & blk   .95   .55

French Revolution, Bicent. AP176

1989, Oct. 18   Litho.   Perf. 11½
C833 AP176 1q dark red, blk &
          deep blue   5.00 2.00

America Issue — AP177

UPAE emblem and: 10c, Detail of the *Madrid Codex.* 20c, Temple of the Gran Jaguar of Tikal, Tikal Natl. Park.

1990, Jan. 25   Litho.   Perf. 11½
C834 AP177 10c shown   1.75 1.10
C835 AP177 20c brown & multi 3.50 2.40

Institute of Nutrition of Central America and Panama, 40th Anniv. AP178

1990, May 18
C837 AP178 20c multicolored   .55   .25

Red Cross, Red Crescent Societies, 125th Anniv. AP179

1990, June 8
C838 AP179 50c multicolored 1.25   .40

Defense Ministry General Staff, Cent. AP180

1991, May 8   Litho.   Perf. 11½
C839 AP180 20c multicolored   .45   .20

America AP181

UPAE: 10c, Pacaya Volcano Erupting at Night. 60c, Lake Atitlan.

1991, July 30   Litho.   Perf. 11½
C840 AP181 10c multicolored   .25   .25
C841 AP181 60c multicolored 2.25   .50

America Issue AP182

Designs: 40c, Pinzon brothers, Nina. 60c, Columbus, Santa Maria, vert.

1992, July 27   Litho.   Perf. 11½
C842 AP182 40c green & black .95   .45
C843 AP182 60c green & black 1.40   .70

AP183

1992, Oct. 6   Litho.   Perf. 12½
C844 AP183 10c multicolored   .55   .25
Interamerican Institute for Agricultural Cooperation, 50th anniv.

1992, Dec. 1   Photo.   Perf. 11½
C845 AP184 1q multicolored   2.50   .80
World campaign against AIDS.

AP184

Orchids — AP185

20c, Phragmipedium caudatum. 50c, Encyclia cochleata. 1q, Encyclia vitellina. 1.50q, Odontoglossum laeve 2q, Odontoglossum uroskinneri.

1994, Aug. 9   Litho.   Perf. 11½

C845A	AP185	20c multi	.60	.60
C846	AP185	50c multi	1.10	.80
C847	AP185	1q multi	2.40	.80
C847A	AP185	1.50q multi	4.75	4.75
C848	AP185	2q multi	4.25	1.50
		Nos. C845A-C848 (5)	13.10	8.45

#C845A, C847A put on sale 8/16/96.

Tourism — AP186

Designs: 20c, Rafting. 40c, Water sports. 60c, Boats on Lake Atitlan, volcanic mountain. 80c, Tourist boat on Lake Atitlan. 1q, Mt. Pacaya erupting. 2q, Guatemala City. 3q, Macaws, vert. 4q, Temple of the Gran Jaguar, vert. 5q, Holy Week procession from Antigua, carpet of colored saw dust, vert.

1995-96   Litho.   Perf. 12½

C849	AP186	20c multicolored	.40	.25
C850	AP186	40c multicolored	.40	.25
C851	AP186	60c multicolored	.55	.30
C852	AP186	80c multicolored	.60	.40
C853	AP186	1q multicolored	.60	.30
C854	AP186	2q multicolored	1.25	.60
C855	AP186	3q multicolored	1.75	.85
C856	AP186	4q multicolored	2.50	1.25
C857	AP186	5q multicolored	3.00	1.75
		Nos. C849-C857 (9)	11.05	5.95

Issued: #C850, 7/5/96; #C852, 7/9/96.
For surcharges see Nos. 568-570, 574.

Visit of Pope John Paul II — AP187

Papal arms, quotation, Pope John Paul II: 10c, With arms outstreached, dove, "That all the people join hands for peace." 1q, Kissing infant, "Let the children come unto me." 1.75q, Holding crucifix, "The house of the Lord is my house." 1.90q, Looking forward, "Blessed is he who comes in the name of the Lord." 2.90q, Waving hand, "Remember that all men are our brothers."

1996, Jan. 5   Litho.   Perf. 12½

C858	AP187	10c multicolored	.20	.20
C859	AP187	1q multicolored	.45	.45
C860	AP187	1.75q multicolored	.85	.85
C861	AP187	1.90q multicolored	.95	.95
C862	AP187	2.90q multicolored	1.50	1.50
		Nos. C858-C862 (5)	3.95	3.95

Distinguished Guatemalans AP188

Designs: 40c, Carlos Merida (Self-portrait). 50c, José Eulalio Samayoa. 60c, Manuel Montufar y Coronado.

1996, Oct. 21   Litho.   Perf. 12½

C863	AP188	40c multicolored	.25	.25
C864	AP188	50c multicolored	.25	.25
C865	AP188	60c multicolored	.30	.30
		Nos. C863-C865 (3)	.80	.80

For surcharge see No. 572.

Mother Breastfeeding — AP190

1997, Mar. 6   Perf. 11½

C868	AP190	1q multicolored	.60	.60

Public Finance Projects — AP191

Designs: 20c, Education. 60c, Health care. 80c, Road construction. 1q, Family security.

1997, Oct. 6   Litho.   Perf. 11½x12½

C869	AP191	20c multicolored	.20	.20
C870	AP191	60c multicolored	.30	.25
C871	AP191	80c multicolored	.45	.40
C872	AP191	1q multicolored	.60	.45
		Nos. C869-C872 (4)	1.55	1.30

For surcharges see Nos. 571, 575.

Jorge Rybar and Machine — AP192

1998   Litho.   Perf. 12½

C873	AP192	10c multi	.25	.25

Plastics industry in Guatemala, 50th anniv.

Intl. Society of Guatemala Collectors, 50th Anniv. — AP193

1999, May 14   Litho.   Perf. 11½x12½

C874	AP193	1q Quetzel note	.60	.60

1993 Census AP194

2001, Dec. 6   Litho.   Perf. 11½

C875	AP194	10c multi	50.00	50.00

No. C875 was withdrawn from sale 12/11/01.

AIR POST SEMI-POSTAL STAMPS

Air Post Stamps of 1937 Surcharged in Red or Blue

1937, Mar. 15   Unwmk.   Perf. 12½

CB1	AP10	4c + 1c ultra (R)	.90	1.25
CB2	AP10	6c + 1c blk vio (R)	.90	1.25
CB3	AP11	10c + 1c ol grn (Bl)	.90	1.25
CB4	AP11	15c + 1c ver (Bl)	.90	1.25
		Nos. CB1-CB4 (4)	3.60	5.00

1st Phil. Exhib. held in Guatemala, Mar. 15-20.

> **Catalogue values for unused stamps in this section, from this point to the end of the section, are for Never Hinged items.**

Type of Regular Issue, 1956

Designs: 35c+1q, Red Cross, Ambulance and Volcano. 50c+1q, Red Cross, Hospital and Nurse. 1q+1q, Nurse and Red Cross.

Perf. 13x12½

1956, June 19   Engr.   Unwmk.

CB5	A148	35c + 1q red & ol grn	5.50	5.75
CB6	A148	50c + 1q ultra & red	5.50	5.75
CB7	A148	1q + 1q dk grn & dk red	5.50	5.75
		Nos. CB5-CB7 (3)	16.50	17.25

The surtax was for the Red Cross.

Nos. B5-B7 Overprinted

1957, May 11

CB8		5c + 15c	7.00	8.00
a.		Imperf., pair	225.00	
CB9		15c + 50c	7.00	8.00
a.		Overprint inverted	275.00	
CB10	A148	25c + 50c	7.00	8.00
		Nos. CB8-CB10 (3)	21.00	24.00

The surtax was for the Red Cross.

Type of Semi-Postal Stamps, 1957 and

Esquipulas Cathedral SPAP1

15c+1q, Cathedral & crucifix. 20c+1q, Christ with crown of thorns and part of globe. 25c+1q, Archbishop Mariano Rossell y Arellano.

Perf. 13½x14½, 13

1957, Oct. 29   Engr.   Unwmk.

CB11	SPAP1	10c + 1q choc & emer	7.00	7.50
CB12	SP1	15c + 1q dl grn & sep	7.00	7.50
CB13	SP1	20c + 1q bl gray & brn	7.00	7.50
CB14	SP1	25c + 1q lt vio & car	7.00	7.50
		Nos. CB11-CB14 (4)	28.00	30.00

The tax was for the Esquipulas highway.

Wounded Man, Battle of Solferino SPAP2

Designs: 6c+6c, 20c+20c, Flood disaster. 10c+10c, 25c+25c, Earth, moon and stars. 15c+15c, 30c+30c, Red Cross headquarters.

1960, Apr. 9   Photo.   Perf. 13½x14

CB15	SPAP2	5c + 5c multi	2.50	2.75
CB16	SPAP2	6c + 6c multi	2.50	2.75
CB17	SPAP2	10c + 10c multi	2.50	2.75
CB18	SPAP2	15c + 15c multi	2.50	2.75
CB19	SPAP2	20c + 20c multi	2.50	2.75
CB20	SPAP2	25c + 25c multi	2.50	2.75
CB21	SPAP2	30c + 30c multi	2.50	2.75
		Nos. CB15-CB21 (7)	17.50	19.25

Cent. (in 1959) of the Red Cross idea. The surtax went to the Red Cross. Exist imperf.

AIR POST OFFICIAL STAMPS

Nos. C93-C98 Overprinted in Black

1939, Apr. 29   Unwmk.   Perf. 12½

CO1	AP13	1c org & ol brn	1.10	1.10
CO2	AP13	2c multi	1.10	1.10
CO3	AP13	3c multi	1.10	1.10
CO4	AP13	4c multi	1.10	1.10
CO5	AP13	5c multi	1.10	1.10
CO6	AP13	10c multi	1.10	1.10
		Nos. CO1-CO6 (6)	6.60	6.60

No. C99 with Same Overprint on each Stamp

1939

CO7	AP19	Sheet of 6	3.75	3.75
a.		1c yel org, blue & blk	.60	.60
b.		2c lake, org, blue & blk	.60	.60
c.		3c olive, blue & orange	.60	.60
d.		4c dk claret, bl, org & blk	.60	.60
e.		5c grnsh bl, bl, red, org & blk	.60	.60
f.		10c olive bister, red & org	.60	.60

SPECIAL DELIVERY STAMPS

No. 237 Overprinted in Red

1940, June   Unwmk.   Perf. 14

E1	A81	4c orange	1.50	.35

No. E1 paid for express service by motorcycle messenger between Guatemala City and Coban.

> **Catalogue values for unused stamps in this section, from this point to the end of the section, are for Never Hinged items.**

Motorcycle Messenger SD1

Black Surcharge

1948, Sept. 3   Photo.   Perf. 14x12½

E2	SD1	10c on 4c bl grn & gray blk	3.25	.85

No. E2 without surcharge was issued for regular postage, not special delivery. See No. 337B.

OFFICIAL STAMPS

O1   National
Emblem — O2

1902, Dec. 18   Typeset   Perf. 12
O1	O1	1c green	5.50	3.50
O2	O1	2c carmine	5.50	3.50
O3	O1	5c ultra	5.50	2.75
O4	O1	10c brown violet	7.50	2.75
O5	O1	25c orange	7.50	2.75

a.   Horiz. pair, imperf. between   100.00
Nos. O1-O5 (5)   31.50 15.25

Nos. O1-O5 printed on thin paper with sheet watermark "AMERICAN LINEN BOND." Nos. O1-O3 also printed on thick paper with sheet watermark "ROYAL BANK BOND." Values are for copies that do not show the watermark. Counterfeits of Nos. O1-O5 exist.

During the years 1912 to 1926 the Post Office Department perforated the word "OFICIAL" on limited quantities of the following stamps: Nos. 114-123, 132, 141-149, 151-153, 158, 202, 210-229 and RA2. The perforating was done in blocks of four stamps at a time and was of two types.

A rubber handstamp "OFICIAL" was also used during the same period and was applied in violet, red, blue or black to stamps No. 117-118, 121-123, 163-165, 172 and 202-218.

Both perforating and handstamping were done in the post office at Guatemala City and use of the stamps was limited to that city.

1929, Jan.   Engr.   Perf. 14
O6	O2	1c pale grnsh bl	.30	.30
O7	O2	2c dark brown	.30	.30
O8	O2	3c green	.30	.30
O9	O2	4c deep violet	.40	.35
O10	O2	5c brown car	.40	.35
O11	O2	10c brown orange	.70	.70
O12	O2	25c dark blue	1.40	1.10

Nos. O6-O12 (7)   3.80 3.40

POSTAL TAX STAMPS

National
Emblem — PT1

Perf. 13½, 14, 15
1919, May 3   Engr.   Unwmk.
RA1 PT1 12½c carmine   .30 .20
Tax for rebuilding post offices.

G. P. O. and
Telegraph
Building — PT2

1927, Nov. 10   Typo.   Perf. 14
RA2 PT2 1c olive green   .55 .25
Tax to provide a fund for building a post office in Guatemala City.

No. RA2
Overprinted in
Green

1936, June 30
RA3 PT2 1c olive green   .70 .55
Liberal revolution, 65th anniversary.

No. RA2
Overprinted in
Blue

1936, Sept. 15
RA4 PT2 1c olive green   .55 .55
115th anniv. of the Independence of Guatemala.

No. RA2
Overprinted in
Red Brown

1936, Nov. 15
RA5 PT2 1c olive green   .55 .45
National Fair.

No. RA2
Overprinted in
Red

1937, Mar. 15
RA6 PT2 1c olive green   .55 .55

No. RA2
Overprinted in
Blue

1938, Jan. 10   Perf. 14x14½
RA7 PT2 1c olive green   .30 .25
a.   "1937-1939" omitted   110.00
150th anniv. of the US Constitution.

Arch of Communications Building
PT3   PT4
With Imprint Below Design
1942, June 3   Engr.   Perf. 11, 12x11
RA19 PT3 1c black brown   5.50 2.00

No imprint; Thin Paper
Perf. 11, 12x11, 11x12, 11x12x11x11
1942, July 18
RA20 PT3 1c black brown   .40 .25

1943   Perf. 11, 12x11, 12
RA21 PT4 1c orange   .40 .25

No. RA2
Overprinted in
Blue or Red

1938   Perf. 14
RA8 PT2 1c olive green (Bl)   .40 .30
RA9 PT2 1c olive green (R)   .40 .30

No. RA2
Overprinted in
Violet

1938, Nov. 20
RA10 PT2 1c olive green   .40 .25
1st Central American Philatelic Exposition.

No. RA2
Overprinted in
Green or Black

1939
RA11 PT2 1c olive green (G)   .40 .25
RA12 PT2 1c olive green (Bk)   .40 .25

No. RA2
Overprinted in
Violet or Brown

1940
RA13 PT2 1c olive green (V)   .40 .25
RA14 PT2 1c olive green (Br)   .40 .25

No. RA2
Overprinted in
Red

1940, Apr. 14
RA15 PT2 1c olive green   .40 .25
Pan American Union, 50th anniversary.

No. RA2
Overprinted in
Red

1941
RA16 PT2 1c olive green   .55 .25

No. 235 Surcharged
in Red

RA17 A79 1c on 2c deep blue   .30 .25

No. 235 Surcharged
in Carmine

1942, Jan.
RA18 A79 1c on 2c deep blue   .55 .25

PT5

Perf. 11, 12½ and Compound
1945, Feb.   Unwmk.
RA22 PT5 1c orange   .30 .25

1949   Perf. 12½
RA23 PT5 1c deep ultra   .30 .25

GUINEA
'gi-nē

LOCATION — Coast of West Africa, between Guinea-Bissau and Sierra Leone
GOVT. — Republic
AREA — 94,926 sq. mi.
POP. — 7,538,953 (1999 est.)
CAPITAL — Conakry

This former French Overseas Territory of French West Africa proclaimed itself an independent republic on October 2, 1958.

100 Centimes = 1 Franc
100 Caury = 1 Syli (1973)
100 Centimes = 1 Guinean Franc (1986)

> **Catalogue values for all unused stamps in this country are for Never Hinged items.**

Common Design Types pictured following the introduction.

French West Africa
No. 79 Overprinted

1959 Unwmk. Photo. Perf. 12x12½
168 CD104 10fr multi   4.00 2.50

French West Africa No. 78 Surcharged
in Red

Engr.
Perf. 13
169 A33 45fr on 20fr multi   4.50 2.25

Map, Dove
and Pres.
Sékou
Touré
A12

1959   Unwmk.   Engr.   Perf. 13
170	A12	5fr rose car	.40	.20
171	A12	10fr ultramarine	.60	.20
172	A12	20fr orange	1.00	.30
173	A12	65fr slate green	3.00	.95
174	A12	100fr violet	5.00	2.10

Nos. 170-174 (5)   10.00 3.75
Proclamation of independence, Oct. 2, 1958.

Bananas — A13

Flag Raising, Labé — A15

Fishing Boats and Tamara Lighthouse A14

1959   **Litho.**   *Perf. 11½*
175	A13	10fr shown	.20 .20
176	A13	15fr Grapefruit	.40 .20
177	A13	20fr Lemons	.70 .20
178	A13	25fr Avocados	.80 .20
179	A13	50fr Pineapple	1.75 .20
		Nos. 175-179 (5)	3.85 1.00

For overprints see Nos. 209-213.

1959   **Engr.**   *Perf. 13½*

5fr, Coco palms & sailboat, vert. 10fr, Launching fishing pirogue. 15fr, Elephant's head. 20fr, Pres. Sékou Touré & torch, vert. 25fr, Elephant.
180	A14	1fr rose	.20 .20
181	A14	2fr green	.20 .20
182	A14	3fr brown	.20 .20
183	A14	5fr blue	.80 .20
184	A14	10fr claret	.90 .20
185	A14	15fr light brn	1.10 .20
186	A14	20fr claret	1.60 .20
187	A14	25fr red brown	2.00 .20
		Nos. 180-187 (8)	7.00 1.60

1959   **Litho.**   *Perf. 12*
188	A15	50fr multicolored	1.10 .20
189	A15	100fr multicolored	2.40 .50

For overprints see Nos. 201-202.

UN Headquarters, New York, and People of Guinea — A16

1959   *Perf. 12*
190	A16	1fr vio blue & org	.20 .20
191	A16	2fr red lil & emer	.20 .20
192	A16	3fr brn & crimson	.20 .20
193	A16	5fr brn & grnsh bl	.20 .20
		Nos. 190-193,C22-C23 (6)	3.40 2.45

Guinea's admission to the UN, first anniv. For overprints see Nos. 205-208, C27-C28.

Uprooted Oak Emblem — A17

1960   **Photo.**   *Perf. 11½*
Granite Paper
194	A17	25fr multicolored	.80 .20
195	A17	50fr multicolored	1.10 .20

World Refugee Year, 7/1/59-6/30/60. For surcharges see Nos. B17-B18.

UPU Monument, Bern — A18

1960   **Granite Paper**   Unwmk.
196	A18	10fr gray brn & blk	.20 .20
197	A18	15fr lil & purple	.45 .20
198	A18	20fr ultra & dk blue	.75 .20
199	A18	25fr yel grn & sl grn	.95 .20
200	A18	50fr red org & brown	1.00 .20
		Nos. 196-200 (5)	3.35 1.00

Nos. 199-200 are vertical. Admission to the UPU, first anniv.

Nos. 188-189 Overprinted in Black, Orange or Carmine: "Jeux Olympiques Rome 1960" and Olympic Rings

1960   **Litho.**   *Perf. 12*
201	A15	50fr multi (Bk)	8.00 6.00
202	A15	100fr multi (O or C)	12.50 9.00
		Nos. 201-202,C24-C26 (5)	92.25 67.25

17th Olympic Games, Rome, 8/25-9/11.

Map and Flag of Guinea — A19

1960   **Photo.**   *Perf. 11½*
203	A19	25fr multicolored	.60 .30
204	A19	30fr multicolored	.80 .30

Second anniversary of independence.

Nos. 190-193 Overprinted

1961   **Litho.**   *Perf. 12*
205	A16	1fr vio blue & org	.20 .20
206	A16	2fr red lil & emer	.20 .20
207	A16	3fr brn & crimson	.20 .20
208	A16	5fr brn & grnsh bl	.20 .20

Nos. 175-179 Overprinted in Black or Orange

Perf. 11½
Fruits in Natural Colors
209	A13	10fr red	.20 .20
210	A13	15fr grn & pink	.40 .20
211	A13	20fr red brn & bl	.50 .20
212	A13	25fr bl & yel (O)	.50 .25
213	A13	50fr dk vio blue	1.00 .40
		Nos. 205-213,C27-C28 (11)	5.90 3.00

15th anniversary of United Nations.

Defassa Waterbuck A20

1961, Sept. 1   **Photo.**   *Perf. 11½*
Multicolored Design; Granite Paper
214	A20	5fr bright grn	.20 .20
215	A20	10fr emerald	.35 .20
216	A20	25fr lilac	.40 .20
217	A20	40fr orange	.75 .20

218	A20	50fr red orange	1.75 .30
219	A20	75fr ultramarine	2.50 .30
		Nos. 214-219 (6)	5.95 1.40

For surcharges see Nos. B19-B24.

Exhibition Hall — A21

1961, Oct. 2   *Perf. 11½*
Flag in Red, Yellow & Green Granite Paper
220	A21	5fr ultra & red	.30 .20
221	A21	10fr brown & red	.30 .20
222	A21	25fr gray grn & red	.30 .20
		Nos. 220-222 (3)	.90 .60

First Three-Year Plan.

Gray-breasted Helmet Guinea Fowl — A22

1961   **Unwmk.**   *Perf. 13x14*
223	A22	5fr rose lil, sepia & bl	.30 .20
224	A22	10fr dp org, sepia & bl	.35 .20
225	A22	25fr cerise, sepia & bl	.55 .20
226	A22	40fr ocher, sepia & bl	.95 .20
227	A22	50fr lemon, sepia & bl	1.25 .20
228	A22	75fr apple grn, sep & bl	2.50 .30
		Nos. 223-228 (6)	5.90 1.30

For surcharges see Nos. B30-B35.

Patrice Lumumba and Map of Africa — A23

1962, Feb. 13   **Photo.**   *Perf. 11½*
229	A23	10fr multicolored	.65 .25
230	A23	25fr multicolored	.80 .25
231	A23	50fr multicolored	.50 .25
		Nos. 229-231 (3)	1.95 .75

Death anniv. (on Feb. 12, 1961) of Patrice Lumumba, Premier of the Congo Republic.

King Mohammed V of Morocco and Map of Africa — A24

1962, Mar. 15   **Litho.**   *Perf. 13*
232	A24	25fr multicolored	1.10 .20
233	A24	75fr multicolored	2.75 .60

First anniv. of the conference of African heads of state at Casablanca. For surcharges see Nos. B36-B37.

African Postal Union Issue

Map of Africa and Post Horn — A25

1962, Apr. 23   **Photo.**   *Perf. 13½x13*
234	A25	25fr org, blk & grn	1.00 .20
235	A25	100fr deep brn & org	2.40 .55

Establishment of African Postal Union.

Bolon Player A26

Musical Instruments: 30c, 25fr, 50fr, Bote, vert. 1fr, 10fr, Flute, vert. 1.50fr, 3fr, Koni. 2fr, 20fr, Kora. 40fr, 75fr, Bolon.

Perf. 13½x13, 13x13½

1962, June 15
236	A26	30c bl, dk grn & red	.20 .20
237	A26	50c sal, brn & brt grn	.20 .20
238	A26	1fr yel grn, grn & lil	.20 .20
239	A26	1.50fr yel, red & bl	.20 .20
240	A26	2fr rose lil, red lil & grn	.20 .20
241	A26	3fr brn grn, grn & lil	.20 .20
242	A26	10fr org, brn & bl	.20 .20
243	A26	20fr ol, dk ol & car	.45 .20
244	A26	25fr ol, dk ol & lil	.55 .20
245	A26	40fr bl, grn & red lil	.80 .20
246	A26	50fr rose, dp rose & Prus bl	1.10 .25
247	A26	75fr dl yel, brn & Prus bl	1.50 .60
		Nos. 236-247,C32-C34 (15)	18.95 8.60

Hippopotamus — A27

25fr, 75fr, Lion. 30fr, 100fr, Leopard.

1962, Aug. 25   **Litho.**   *Perf. 13x13½*
248	A27	10fr org, grn & brn	.35 .20
249	A27	25fr emer, blk & brn	.90 .20
250	A27	30fr yel grn, dk brn & yel	1.00 .20
251	A27	50fr vio bl, dk brn & grn	1.25 .30
252	A27	75fr lil, lt lil & red brn	1.90 .40
253	A27	100fr grnsh bl, dk brn & yel	2.40 .60
		Nos. 248-253 (6)	7.80 1.90

See Nos. 340-345

Child at Blackboard — A28

Designs: 10fr, 20fr, Adult class.

1962, Sept. 19   **Photo.**   *Perf. 13½x13*
254	A28	5fr yel, dk brn & org	.20 .20
255	A28	10fr org & dk brn	.20 .20
256	A28	15fr yel grn, dk brn & red	.40 .20
257	A28	20fr bl & dk brn	.50 .20
		Nos. 254-257 (4)	1.30 .80

Campaign against illiteracy.

> **Imperforates**
> From late 1962 onward, most Guinea stamps exist imperforate.

Alfa Yaya — A29

1962, Oct. 2   **Perf. 13½**
30fr, King Behanzin. 50fr, King Ba Bemba. 75fr, Almamy Samory. 100fr, Tierno Aliou.

Gold Frame
258 A29 25fr brt bl & sepia .35 .20
259 A29 30fr yel & sepia .60 .20
260 A29 50fr brt pink & sepia .70 .30
261 A29 75fr yel grn & sepia 1.75 .45
262 A29 100fr org, red & sepia 2.10 .70
  Nos. 258-262 (5) 5.50 1.85

Heroes and martyrs of Africa.

Gray Parrot A30

Birds: 30c, 3fr, 50fr, Crowned crane (vert). 1fr, 20fr, Abyssinian ground hornbill. 1.50fr, 25fr, White spoonbill. 2fr, 40fr, Bateleur eagle.

1962, Dec.   **Perf. 13½x13, 13x13½**
263 A30 30c multicolored .20 .20
264 A30 50c multicolored .20 .20
265 A30 1fr multicolored .20 .20
266 A30 1.50fr multicolored .20 .20
267 A30 2fr multicolored .20 .20
268 A30 3fr multicolored .65 .20
269 A30 10fr multicolored .80 .20
270 A30 20fr multicolored .90 .20
271 A30 25fr multicolored .95 .20
272 A30 40fr multicolored 1.10 .20
273 A30 50fr multicolored 1.60 .35
274 A30 75fr multicolored 2.10 .50
  Nos. 263-274,C41-C43 (15) 29.60 11.10

Wheat Emblem and Globe A31

1963, Mar. 21   **Photo.**   **Perf. 13x14**
275 A31 5fr red & yellow .20 .20
276 A31 10fr emerald & yel .20 .20
277 A31 15fr brown & yel .20 .20
278 A31 25fr dark ol & yel .20 .20
  Nos. 275-278 (4) .80 .80

FAO "Freedom from Hunger" campaign.

Basketball — A32

50c, 4fr, 30fr, Boxing. 1fr, 5fr, Running. 1.50fr, 10fr, Bicycling. 2fr, 20fr, Single sculls.

1963, Mar. 16   **Unwmk.**   **Perf. 14**
279 A32 30c ver, dp claret &
     grn .20 .20
280 A32 50c lilac & blue .20 .20
281 A32 1fr dl org, sep & grn .20 .20
282 A32 1.50fr org, ultra & mag .20 .20

283 A32 2fr aqua, dk bl &
     mag .20 .20
284 A32 3fr ol, dp cl & grn .20 .20
285 A32 4fr car rose, pur &
     bl .20 .20
286 A32 5fr brt grn, ol &
     mag .20 .20
287 A32 10fr lil rose, ultra &
     mag .20 .20
288 A32 20fr red org, dk bl &
     crim .20 .20
289 A32 25fr emer, dp cl & dk
     grn .25 .20
290 A32 30fr gray, pur & bl .30 .20
  Nos. 279-290,C44-C46 (15) 18.05 8.95

For overprints and surcharges see Nos. 312-314, C58-C60.

A33

Various Butterflies.

1963, May 10   **Photo.**   **Perf. 12**
291 A33 10c dp rose, blk &
     gray .20 .20
292 A33 30c rose, blk & yel .20 .20
293 A33 40c yel grn, brn &
     yel .20 .20
294 A33 50c pale vio, blk &
     grn .20 .20
295 A33 1fr yel, blk & emer .40 .20
296 A33 1.50fr bluish grn, blk
     & sep .40 .20
297 A33 2fr multi .40 .20
298 A33 3fr multi 1.10 .20
299 A33 10fr rose lil, blk &
     grn 1.25 .20
300 A33 20fr gray, blk & grn 1.40 .20
301 A33 25fr yel grn, blk &
     gray 1.60 .20
302 A33 40fr multi 2.00 .45
303 A33 50fr ultra, blk & yel 2.50 .55
304 A33 75fr yel, blk & grn 3.25 .80
  Nos. 291-304,C47-C49 (17) 33.85 11.25

Handshake, Map and Dove — A34

1963, May 22   **Perf. 13½x14**
305 A34 5fr bluish grn & dk brn .20 .20
306 A34 10fr org yel & dk brn .20 .20
307 A34 15fr ol & dk brn .25 .20
308 A34 25fr bis brn & dk brn .30 .20
  Nos. 305-308 (4) .95 .80

Conference of African heads of state for African Unity, Addis Ababa.

Globe Encircled by Satellite — A35

1963, July 25   **Engr.**   **Perf. 10½**
309 A35 5fr green & car .20 .20
310 A35 10fr vio bl & car .40 .20
311 A35 15fr yellow & car .50 .20
  Nos. 309-311,C50 (4) 2.00 .80

Centenary of the International Red Cross.

Nos. 279-281 Surcharged in Carmine, Yellow or Orange: "COMMISSION PRÉPARATOIRE AUX JEUX OLYMPIQUES À CONAKRY," New Value and Olympic Rings

1963, Nov. 20   **Photo.**   **Perf. 14**
312 A32 40fr on 30c (C or Y) 1.40 1.10
313 A32 50fr on 50c (C or O) 2.10 1.75
314 A32 75fr on 1fr (C or O) 3.50 2.50
  Nos. 312-314,C58-C60 (6) 18.90 13.75

Meeting of the Olympic Games Preparatory Commission at Conakry. The overprint is in a circular line on #312, in 3 lines on each side on #313-314.

Jewelfish A36

Fish: 40c, 30fr, Golden pheasant. 50c, 40fr, Blue gularis. 1fr, 75fr, Banded Jewelfish. 1.50fr, African lyretail. 2fr, Six-barred epiplatys. 5fr, Jewelfish.

1964, Feb. 15   **Litho.**   **Perf. 14x13½**
315 A36 30c car rose & multi .20 .20
316 A36 40c pur & multi .20 .20
317 A36 50c car rose & multi .20 .20
318 A36 1fr blue & multi .20 .20
319 A36 1.50fr blue & multi .20 .20
320 A36 2fr pur & multi .60 .20
321 A36 5fr blue & multi .65 .20
322 A36 30fr grn & multi .85 .20
323 A36 40fr pur & multi 1.75 .40
324 A36 75fr multi 2.50 .55
  Nos. 315-324,C54-C55 (12) 17.35 4.50

John F. Kennedy A37

1964, Mar. 5   **Engr.**   **Perf. 10½**
Flag in Red and Blue
325 A37 5fr blk & pur .20 .20
326 A37 25fr grn & pur .40 .20
327 A37 50fr brn & pur .85 .30
  Nos. 325-327,C56 (4) 3.20 1.50

Issued in sheets of 20 with marginal quotations in English and French. Two sheets for each denomination. See No. C56.

Workers Welding Pipe — A38

5fr, Pipe line over mountains, vert. 10fr, Waterworks. 30fr, Transporting pipe. 50fr, Laying pipe.

1964, May 1   **Photo.**   **Perf. 11½**
328 A38 5fr deep mag .20 .20
329 A38 10fr bright pur .20 .20
330 A38 20fr org red .50 .20
331 A38 30fr ultra .65 .20
332 A38 50fr yel grn .75 .20
  Nos. 328-332 (5) 2.30 1.00

Completion of the water-supply pipeline to Conakry, Mar. 1964.

Ice Hockey — A39

1964, May 15   **Perf. 13x12½**
333 A39 10fr shown .40 .20
334 A39 25fr Ski jump .60 .20
335 A39 50fr Slalom 1.10 .40
  Nos. 333-335,C57 (4) 4.35 1.20

9th Winter Olympic Games, Innsbruck, Jan. 29-Feb. 9, 1964.

Eleanor Roosevelt Reading to Children — A40

1964, June 1   **Engr.**   **Perf. 10½**
336 A40 5fr green .25 .20
337 A40 10fr red org .25 .20
338 A40 15fr bright bl .25 .20
339 A40 25fr car rose .25 .20
  Nos. 336-339,C61 (5) 1.90 1.05

Eleanor Roosevelt, 15th anniv. of the Universal Declaration of Human Rights (in 1963).

Animal Type of 1962

Designs: 5fr, 30fr, Striped hyenas. 40fr, 300fr, Black buffaloes. 75fr, 100fr, Elephants.

1964, Oct. 8   **Litho.**   **Perf. 13x13½**
340 A27 5fr yellow & blk .20 .20
341 A27 30fr light bl & blk .45 .20
342 A27 40fr lil rose & blk 1.00 .25
343 A27 75fr yel grn & blk 2.25 .40
344 A27 100fr bister & blk 3.00 .75
345 A27 300fr orange & blk 8.00 2.75
  Nos. 340-345 (6) 14.90 4.55

Guinea Exhibit, World's Fair — A41

1964, Oct. 26   **Engr.**   **Perf. 10½**
346 A41 30fr vio & emerald .35 .20
347 A41 40fr red lil & emer .50 .20
348 A41 50fr sepia & emer .70 .20
349 A41 75fr rose red & dk bl 1.10 .25
  Nos. 346-349 (4) 2.65 .85

New York World's Fair, 1964-65.
See Nos. 372-375, C62-C63, C69-C70.

Queen Nefertari Crowned by Isis and Hathor — A42

Designs: 25fr, Ramses II in battle. 50fr, Submerged sphinxes, sailboat, Wadies-Sebua. 100fr, Ramses II holding crook and flail, Abu Simbel. 200fr, Feet and legs of Ramses statues, Abu Simbel.

1964, Nov. 19   **Photo.**   **Perf. 12**
350 A42 10fr dk bl, red brn &
     cit .20 .20
351 A42 25fr blk, dl red & brn .60 .20
352 A42 50fr dk brn, bl & vio .75 .20
353 A42 100fr dk brn, yel & pur 1.25 .40
354 A42 200fr pur, dl grn & buff 2.75 .75
  Nos. 350-354,C64 (6) 10.30 3.15

UNESCO campaign to preserve Nubian monuments.
For overprint see No. 415.

Weight Lifter and Caucasian, Japanese and Negro Children — A43

1965, Jan. 18　Photo.　Perf. 13x12½

10fr, Runner carrying torch. 25fr, Pole vaulting and flags. 40fr, Runners. 50fr, Judo. 75fr, Japanese woman, flags and stadium.

355	A43	5fr gold, claret & blk	.20	.20
356	A43	10fr gold, blk, ver & bl	.40	.20
357	A43	25fr gold, blk, yel grn & red	.45	.20
358	A43	40fr gold, blk, brn & yel	.50	.20
359	A43	50fr gold, blk & grn	.80	.30
360	A43	75fr gold & multi	1.50	.40
		Nos. 355-360,C65 (7)	5.60	1.85

18th Olympic Games, Tokyo, 10/10-25/64. For overprints see Nos. 410-414.

Doudou Mask, Boké — A44

Designs: 40c, 1fr, 15fr, Various Niamou masks, N'Zérékoré region. 60c, "Yoki," wood-carved statuette of a girl, Boke. 80c, Masked woman dancer from Guekedou. 2fr, Masked dancer from Macenta. 20fr, Beater from Tamtam. 60fr, Bird dancer from Macenta. 80fr, Bassari dancer from Koundara. 100fr, Sword dancer from Karana.

1965, Feb. 15　Unwmk.　Perf. 14

361	A44	20c multicolored	.20	.20
362	A44	40c multicolored	.20	.20
363	A44	60c multicolored	.20	.20
364	A44	80c multicolored	.20	.20
365	A44	1fr multicolored	.20	.20
366	A44	2fr multicolored	.20	.20
367	A44	15fr multicolored	.50	.20
368	A44	20fr multicolored	.55	.20
369	A44	60fr multicolored	1.25	.40
370	A44	80fr multicolored	1.25	.50
371	A44	100fr multicolored	1.75	.50
		Nos. 361-371,C68 (12)	12.75	5.75

World's Fair Type of 1964 Inscribed "1965"

1965, Mar. 24　Engr.　Perf. 10½

372	A41	30fr grn & orange	.40	.20
373	A41	40fr car & brt grn	.50	.20
374	A41	50fr brt grn & vio	.70	.25
375	A41	75fr brown & vio	1.00	.35
		Nos. 372-375 (4)	2.60	1.00

See Nos. C69-C70.

Blacksmith A45

Handicrafts: 20fr, Potter. 60fr, Cloth dyers. 80fr, Basketmaker.

1965, May 1　Photo.　Perf. 14

376	A45	15fr multicolored	.20	.20
377	A45	20fr multicolored	.50	.20
378	A45	60fr multicolored	.80	.30
379	A45	80fr multicolored	.95	.40
		Nos. 376-379,C71-C72 (6)	9.20	2.70

ITU Emblem, Old and New Communication Equipment — A46

1965, May 17　Unwmk.

380	A46	25fr yel, gray, gold & blk	.45	.20
381	A46	50fr yel, grn, gold & blk	.70	.25
		Nos. 380-381,C73-C74 (4)	5.40	1.50

ITU centenary.

Maj. Virgil I. Grissom — A47　　　Moon from 258mi. — A48

Sputnik Over Earth A49

American Achievements in Space: 10fr, Lt. Com. John W. Young. 25fr, Moon from 115mi. 30fr, Moon from 58mi. 100fr, Grissom and Young in Gemini 2 spaceship.

1965, July 19　Photo.　Perf. 13

Size: 21x29mm

382	A47	5fr dk red & multi	.20	.20
383	A47	10fr dk red & multi	.20	.20
384	A48	15fr gold, bl & dk bl	.20	.20

Size: 39x28mm

385	A48	25fr gold, bl & dk bl	.20	.20

Size: 21x29mm

386	A48	30fr gold, bl & dk bl	.20	.20

Size: 39x28mm

387	A47	100fr multi & dk red	.50	.40
a.		Sheet of 15, #382-387	9.00	

Russian Achievements in Space: 5fr, Col. Pavel Belyayev. 10fr, Lt. Col. Alexei Leonov. 15fr, Vostoks 3 & 4 in space. 30fr, Vostoks 5 & 6 over Earth. 100fr, Leonov floating in space.

Size: 21x29mm

388	A47	5fr bl & multi	.20	.20
389	A47	10fr bl & multi	.20	.20
390	A49	15fr bl & multi	.20	.20

Size: 39x28mm

391	A49	25fr bl & multi	.20	.20

Size: 21x29mm

392	A49	30fr bl & multi	.20	.20

Size: 39x28mm

393	A47	100fr blk, dk red & gold	.50	.40
a.		Sheet of 15, #388-393	9.00	
		Nos. 382-393 (12)	3.00	2.80

American and Russian achievements in space. Nos. 387a and 393a contain five triptychs each: four rows with 5fr, 100fr and 10fr, and a center row with 15fr, 25fr and 30fr stamps each.

ICY Emblem, UN Headquarters and Skyline, New York — A50

1965, Sept. 8　　　Perf. 10½

394	A50	25fr yel grn & ver	.35	.20
395	A50	45fr vio & orange	.40	.20
396	A50	75fr red brn & org	.65	.25
		Nos. 394-396,C75 (4)	2.65	1.00

Intl. Cooperation Year, 1965.

Polytechnic Institute, Conakry — A51

New Projects, Conakry: 30fr, Hotel Camayenne. 40fr, Gbessia Airport. 75fr, Stadium "28 September."

1965, Oct. 2　Photo.　Perf. 13½

397	A51	25fr multicolored	.30	.20
398	A51	30fr multicolored	.35	.20
399	A51	40fr multicolored	.60	.30
400	A51	75fr multicolored	.75	.40
		Nos. 397-400,C76-C77 (6)	10.10	5.10

Seventh anniversary of independence.

Photographing Far Side of Moon — A52

10fr, Trajectories of Ranger VII on flight to moon. 25fr, Relay satellite. 45fr, Vostoks I & II & globe.

1965, Nov. 15　Litho.　Perf. 14x13½

401	A52	5fr blk, pur & ocher	.20	.20
402	A52	10fr red brn, lt grn & yel	.20	.20
403	A52	25fr blk, bl & bis	.50	.20
404	A52	45fr blk, lt ultra & bis	1.00	.20
		Nos. 401-404,C78-C79 (6)	5.40	2.30

For overprints and surcharges see Nos. 529-530, C112-C112B.

Sword Dance, Karana — A53

Designs: 30c, Dancing girls, Lower Guinea. 50c, Behore musicians of Tiekere playing "Eyoro," horiz. 5fr, Doundouba dance of Kouroussa. 40fr, Bird man's dance of Macenta.

1966, Jan. 5　Photo.　Perf. 13½

Size: 26x36mm

405	A53	10c multicolored	.20	.20
406	A53	30c multicolored	.20	.20

Size: 36x28½mm

407	A53	50c multicolored	.45	.20

Size: 26x36mm

408	A53	5fr multicolored	.45	.20
409	A53	40fr multicolored	.75	.20
		Nos. 405-409,C80 (6)	3.55	1.50

Festival of African Art and Culture. See Nos. 436-441.

Engraved Overprint in Red or Orange on Nos. 355-356 and Nos. 358-360

1966, Mar. 14　　　Perf. 13x12½

410	A43	5fr multi (R)	.40	.20
411	A43	10fr multi (R)	.50	.20
412	A43	40fr multi (O)	.85	.20
413	A43	50fr multi (R)	1.10	.40
414	A43	75fr multi (R)	2.00	.65
		Nos. 410-414,C81 (6)	6.10	2.15

4th Pan Arab Games, Cairo, Sept. 2-11, 1965. The same overprint was also applied to imperf. sheets of No. 357.

Engraved Red Orange Overprint on No. 352: "CENTENAIRE DU TIMBRE CAIRE 1966"

1966, Mar. 14　　　Perf. 12

415	A42	50fr dk brn, bl & vio	1.00	.50

1st Egyptian postage stamps, cent. See #C82.

Vonkou Rock, Telimélé — A54

Views: 25fr, Artificial lake, Coyah. 40fr, Kalé waterfalls. 50fr, Forécariah bridge. 75fr, Liana bridge.

1966, Apr. 4　Photo.　Perf. 13½

416	A54	20fr multicolored	.20	.20
417	A54	25fr multicolored	.45	.20
418	A54	40fr multicolored	.50	.20
419	A54	50fr multicolored	.70	.20
420	A54	75fr multicolored	.90	.30
		Nos. 416-420,C83 (6)	4.15	1.70

See Nos. 475-478, C90-C91. For overprints see Nos. 482-488, C93-C95.

UNESCO Emblem A55

1966, May 2　Photo.　Unwmk.

421	A55	25fr multicolored	.70	.20

20th anniv. of UNESCO. See Nos. C84-C85.

Woman of Guinea and Morning Glory — A56　　　Symbolic Water Cycle and UNESCO Emblem — A57

Designs: Women and Flowers of Guinea.

1966, May 30　Photo.　Perf. 13½

Size: 23x34mm

422	A56	10c multicolored	.20	.20
423	A56	20c multicolored	.20	.20
424	A56	30c multicolored	.20	.20
425	A56	40c multicolored	.20	.20
426	A56	3fr multicolored	.20	.20
427	A56	4fr multicolored	.20	.20
428	A56	10fr multicolored	.20	.20
429	A56	25fr multicolored	.65	.20

Size: 28x43mm

430	A56	30fr multicolored	.80	.20
431	A56	50fr multicolored	1.00	.35
432	A56	80fr multicolored	1.50	.45
		Nos. 422-432,C86-C87 (13)	14.35	5.40

1966, Sept. 26　Engr.　Perf. 10½

433	A57	5fr bl & dp org	.30	.20
434	A57	25fr grn & dp org	.35	.20
435	A57	100fr brt rose lil & dp org	.95	.35
		Nos. 433-435 (3)	1.60	.75

Hydrological Decade (UNESCO), 1965-74.

Dance Type of 1966

Various folk dances. 25fr, 75fr, horizontal.

1966, Oct. 24   Photo.   Perf. 13½
Sizes: 26x36mm, 36x28½mm

436	A53	60c multicolored	.20	.20
437	A53	1fr multicolored	.20	.20
438	A53	1.50fr multicolored	.20	.20
439	A53	25fr multicolored	.75	.20
440	A53	50fr red & red	1.25	.20
441	A53	75fr multicolored	1.75	.50
		Nos. 436-441 (6)	4.35	1.50

Guinean National Dancers.

Child's Drawing and
UNICEF
Emblem — A58

Children's Drawings: 2fr, Elephant. 3fr, Girl. 20fr, Village, horiz. 25fr, Boy playing soccer. 40fr, Still life. 50fr, Bird in a tree.

1966, Dec. 12   Photo.   Perf. 13½

442	A58	2fr multicolored	.20	.20
443	A58	3fr multicolored	.20	.20
444	A58	10fr multicolored	.20	.20
445	A58	20fr multicolored	.20	.20
446	A58	25fr multicolored	.40	.20
447	A58	40fr multicolored	.45	.20
448	A58	50fr multicolored	.65	.20
		Nos. 442-448 (7)	2.30	1.40

20th anniv. of UNICEF. Printed in sheets of 10 stamps and 2 labels with ornamental borders and inscriptions.

Laboratory Technician — A59

WHO Emblem and: 50fr, Physician examining infant. 75fr, Pre-natal care & instruction. 80fr, WHO Headquarters, Geneva.

1967, Jan. 20   Photo.   Perf. 13½

449	A59	30fr multicolored	.30	.20
450	A59	50fr multicolored	.40	.20
451	A59	75fr multicolored	.60	.25
452	A59	80fr multicolored	.70	.35
		Nos. 449-452 (4)	2.00	1.00

Inauguration (in 1966) of WHO Headquarters, Geneva.

Niamou Mask,
N'Zerekore — A60

Designs: 10c, 1fr, 30fr, Small Banda mask, Kanfarade, Boké region. 1.50fr, 50fr, Like 30c. 50c, 5fr, 75fr, Bearded Niamou mask. 60c, 25fr, 100fr, Horned Yinadjinkele mask, Kankan region.

1967, Mar. 25   Photo.   Perf. 14x13

453	A60	10c org & multi	.20	.20
454	A60	30c cit & brn blk	.20	.20
455	A60	50c dp lil rose, blk & red	.20	.20
456	A60	60c dp org, blk & bis	.20	.20
457	A60	1fr yel grn & multi	.20	.20
458	A60	1.50fr sal pink & brn blk	.20	.20
459	A60	5fr ap grn, blk & red	.20	.20
460	A60	25fr red lil, blk & bis	.45	.20
461	A60	30fr bis & multi	.50	.20
462	A60	50fr grnsh bl & brn blk	.80	.20
463	A60	75fr yel, blk & red	1.25	.35
464	A60	100fr lt ultra, blk & bis	1.90	.55
		Nos. 453-464 (12)	6.30	2.90

Ball Python — A61

20c, Pastoria Research Institute. 50c, 75fr, Extraction of snake venom. 1fr, 50fr, Rock python. 2fr, Men holding rock python. 5fr, 30fr, Gaboon viper. 20fr, West African mamba.

1967, May 15   Litho.   Perf. 13½
Size: 43½x20mm

465	A61	20c multicolored	.20	.20
466	A61	30c multicolored	.20	.20
467	A61	50c multicolored	.20	.20
468	A61	1fr multicolored	.20	.20
469	A61	2fr multicolored	.20	.20
470	A61	5fr multicolored	.20	.20

Size: 56x26mm

471	A61	20fr multicolored	.65	.20
472	A61	30fr multicolored	1.10	.20
473	A61	50fr multicolored	1.25	.20
474	A61	75fr multicolored	2.00	.20
		Nos. 465-474,C88-C89 (12)	14.95	5.50

Research Institute for Applied Biology of Guinea (Pastoria). For souvenir sheet see No. C88a.

Scenic Type of 1966

Views: 5fr, Loos Island. 30fr, Tinkisso Waterfalls. 70fr, "The Elephant's Trunk" Hotel, Mt. Kakoulima. 80fr, Evening at the shore, Ratoma.

1967, June 20   Photo.   Perf. 13½

475	A54	5fr multicolored	.20	.20
476	A54	30fr multicolored	.20	.20
477	A54	70fr multicolored	.60	.20
478	A54	80fr multicolored	.85	.20
		Nos. 475-478,C90-C91 (6)	5.55	2.35

People's Palace, Conakry — A62

Elephant
A63

1967, Sept. 28   Photo.   Perf. 13½

479	A62	5fr silver & multi	.20	.20
480	A63	30fr silver & multi	.30	.20
481	A62	55fr gold & multi	.50	.20
		Nos. 479-481 (3)	1.00	.60

20th anniv. of the Democratic Party of Guinea and the opening of the People's Palace, Conakry. See No. C92.

Nos. 418-420 and 475-478
Overprinted with Lions Emblem and:
"AMITIE DES PEUPLES GRACE AU
TOURISME 1917-1967"

1967, Nov. 6

482	A54	5fr multicolored	.45	.20
483	A54	30fr multicolored	.90	.20
484	A54	40fr multicolored	.75	.20
485	A54	50fr multicolored	1.00	.20
486	A54	70fr multicolored	1.25	.30
487	A54	75fr multicolored	1.75	.20
488	A54	80fr multicolored	2.25	.50
		Nos. 482-488,C93-C95 (10)	18.35	5.40

50th anniversary of Lions International.

WHO Office for
Africa — A64

1967, Dec. 4   Photo.   Perf. 13½

| 489 | A64 | 30fr lt ol grn, bis & dk grn | .55 | .20 |
| 490 | A64 | 75fr red org, bis & dk bl | 1.10 | .30 |

Inauguration of the WHO Regional Office for Africa in Brazzaville, Congo.

Human Rights
Flame — A65

1968, Jan. 15   Photo.   Perf. 13½

| 491 | A65 | 30fr ocher, grn & dk car | .50 | .20 |
| 492 | A65 | 40fr vio, grn & car | .60 | .20 |

International Human Rights Year, 1968.

Coyah,
Dubréka
Region
A66

Homes and People: 30c, 30fr, Kankan Region. 40c, Kankan, East Guinea. 50c, 15fr, Woodlands Region. 60c, Fulahmori, Gaoual Region. 5fr, Cognagui, Kundara Region. 40fr, Fouta Djallon, West Guinea. 100fr, Labé, West Guinea.

1968, Apr. 1   Photo.   Perf. 13½x14
Size: 36x27mm

493	A66	20c gold & multi	.20	.20
494	A66	30c gold & multi	.20	.20
495	A66	40c gold & multi	.20	.20
496	A66	50c gold & multi	.20	.20

Perf. 14x13½
Size: 57x36mm

497	A66	60c gold & multi	.20	.20
498	A66	5fr gold & multi	.20	.20
499	A66	15fr gold & multi	.20	.20
500	A66	20fr gold & multi	.35	.20
501	A66	30fr gold & multi	.40	.20
502	A66	40fr gold & multi	.55	.20
503	A66	100fr gold & multi	1.50	.30
		Nos. 493-503,C100 (12)	8.70	3.55

The Storyteller — A67

African Legends: 15fr, The Little Genie of Mt. Nimba. No. 506, The Legend of the Moons and the Stars. No. 507, Lan, the Child Buffalo, vert. 40fr, Nianablas and the Crocodiles. 75fr, Leuk the Hare Playing the Drum, vert. 75fr, Leuk the Hare Selling his Sister, vert. 80fr, The Hunter and the Antelopewoman. The designs are from paintings by students of the Academy of Fine Arts in Bellevue.

1968   Photo.   Perf. 13½

504	A67	15fr multicolored	.20	.20
505	A67	25fr multicolored	.20	.20
506	A67	30fr multicolored	.25	.20
507	A67	30fr multicolored	.25	.20
508	A67	40fr multicolored	.40	.20
509	A67	40fr multicolored	.65	.20
a.		Souv. sheet of 4	5.50	5.50

510	A67	75fr multicolored	.65	.25
511	A67	80fr multicolored	1.10	.25
		Nos. 504-511,C101-C104 (12)	12.75	4.45

Issued in sheets of 10 plus 2 labels. No. 509a contains 4 imperf. stamps similar to Nos. 508-509, C101 and C104. "Poste Aerienne" omitted on the 70fr and 300fr of the souvenir sheet.
Issued: #505-506, 510-511, 5/16; #504, 507-509, 9/16.

Anubius Baboon — A68

African Animals: 10fr, Leopards. 15fr, Hippopotami. 20fr, Nile crocodile. 30fr, Ethiopian wart hog. 50fr, Defassa waterbuck. 75fr, Cape buffaloes.

1968, Nov. 25   Photo.   Perf. 13½
Size: 44x31mm

512	A68	5fr gold & multi	.20	.20
513	A68	10fr gold & multi	.60	.20
514	A68	15fr gold & multi	.65	.20
a.		Souv. sheet of 3, #512-514	1.50	1.50
515	A68	20fr gold & multi	.80	.20
516	A68	30fr gold & multi	1.00	.20
517	A68	50fr gold & multi	1.25	.20
a.		Souv. sheet of 3, #515-517	3.75	3.75
518	A68	75fr gold & multi	2.00	.30
a.		Souv. sheet of 3	10.50	10.50
		Nos. 512-518,C105-C106 (9)	14.00	4.15

No. 518a contains one No. 518 and one each similar to Nos. C105-C106 without "POSTE AERIENNE" inscription. The three souvenir sheets contain 3 stamps and one green and gold label inscribed "FAUNE AFRICAINE."

Senator
Robert F.
Kennedy
A69

Portraits: 75fr, Rev. Martin Luther King, Jr. 100fr, Pres. John F. Kennedy.

1968, Dec. 16

519	A69	30fr yel & multi	.55	.20
520	A69	75fr multicolored	1.25	.20
521	A69	100fr multicolored	1.75	.30
		Nos. 519-521,C107-C109 (6)	11.90	2.35

Robert F. Kennedy, John F. Kennedy and Martin Luther King, Jr., martyrs for freedom.
The stamps are printed in sheets of 15 (3x5) containing 10 stamps and five yellow-green and gold center labels. Sheets come either with English or French inscriptions on label.

Sculpture
and
Runner
A70

Sculpture and Soccer — A71

Designs (Sculpture and): 10fr, Boxing. 15fr, Javelin. 30fr, Steeplechase. 50fr, Hammer throw. 75fr, Bicycling.

1969, Feb. 18　Photo.　Perf. 13½

522	A70	5fr multicolored	.20	.20
523	A70	10fr multicolored	.20	.20
524	A70	15fr multicolored	.40	.20
525	A71	25fr multicolored	.40	.20
526	A70	30fr multicolored	.40	.20
527	A70	50fr multicolored	.65	.20
528	A70	75fr multicolored	.90	.20

Nos. 522-528,C110-C111A (10)　11.65　3.70

19th Olympic Games, Mexico City, 10/12-27.

No. 404 Surcharged and Overprinted in Red

1969, Mar. 17　Litho.　Perf. 14x13½

529	A52	30fr on 45fr multi	.60	.35
530	A52	45fr multicolored	.60	.35

Nos. 529-530,C112-C112B (5)　5.35　2.55

US Apollo 8 mission, the first men in orbit around the moon, Dec. 21-27, 1968.

Nos. 529-530 also exist with surcharge and overprint in black. These sell for about 10% more.

Tarzan — A72

Designs: 30fr, Tarzan sitting in front of Pastoria Research Institute gate. 75fr, Tarzan and his family. 100fr, Tarzan sitting in a tree.

1969, June 6　Photo.　Perf. 13½

531	A72	25fr orange & multi	.45	.20
532	A72	30fr bl grn & multi	.60	.20
533	A72	75fr yel grn & multi	1.25	.20
534	A72	100fr yellow & multi	1.90	.35

Nos. 531-534 (4)　4.20　.95

Tarzan was a Guinean chimpanzee with superior intelligence and ability.

Campfire A73

25fr, Boy Scout & tents. 30fr, Marching Boy Scouts. 40fr, Basketball. 45fr, Senior Scouts, thatched huts & mountain. 50fr, Guinean Boy Scout badge.

1969, July 1

535	A73	5fr gold & multi	.20	.20
536	A73	25fr gold & multi	.35	.20
537	A73	30fr gold & multi	.35	.20
538	A73	40fr gold & multi	.55	.20
539	A73	45fr gold & multi	.70	.20
540	A73	50fr gold & multi	.75	.20
	a.	Min. sheet of 6, #535-540	4.00	4.00

Nos. 535-540 (6)　2.90　1.20

Issued to honor the Boy Scouts of Guinea.

Launching Apollo 11 — A74

Designs: 30fr, Earth showing Africa as seen from moon. 50fr, Separation of lunar landing module and spaceship. 60fr, Astronauts and module on moon. 75fr, Module on moon and earth. 100fr, Module leaving moon. 200fr, Splashdown. "a" stamps are inscribed in French. "b" stamps are inscribed in English.

1969, Aug. 20　Photo.　Perf. 13½
Size: 34x55mm

541	A74	25fr Pair, #541a, 541b	.40	.20
542	A74	30fr Pair, #542a, 542b	.50	.20
543	A74	50fr Pair, #543a, 543b	.75	.20
544	A74	60fr Pair, #544a, 544b	1.25	.35
545	A74	75fr Pair, #545a, 545b	1.50	.40

Size: 34x71mm

546	A74	100fr Pair, #546a, 546b	2.50	.60

Size: 34x55mm

547	A74	200fr Pair, #547a, 547b	5.00	1.50

Nos. 541-547 (7)　11.90　3.45

Man's 1st landing on the moon, 7/20/69.

Harvest and ILO Emblem A75

ILO, 50th Anniv.: 25fr, Power lines and blast furnaces. 30fr, Women in broadcasting studio. 200fr, Potters.

1969, Oct. 28　Photo.　Perf. 13½

548	A75	25fr gold & multi	.20	.20
549	A75	30fr gold & multi	.30	.20
550	A75	75fr gold & multi	.75	.20
551	A75	200fr gold & multi	2.25	.60

Nos. 548-551 (4)　3.50　1.20

Mother and Sick Child — A76

25fr, Sick child. 40fr, Girl receiving vaccination. 50fr, Boy receiving vaccination. 60fr, Mother receiving vaccination. 200fr, Edward Jenner, M.D.

1970, Jan. 15　Photo.　Perf. 13½

552	A76	25fr multicolored	.20	.20
553	A76	30fr multicolored	.35	.20
554	A76	40fr multicolored	.40	.20
555	A76	50fr multicolored	.60	.20
556	A76	60fr multicolored	.70	.20
557	A76	200fr multicolored	2.40	1.00

Nos. 552-557 (6)　4.65　2.00

Campaign against smallpox and measles.

Map of Africa — A77

1970, Feb. 3　Litho.　Perf. 14½x14

558	A77	30fr lt bl & multi	.25	.20
559	A77	200fr lt vio & multi	1.75	.75

Meeting of statesmen of countries bordering on Senegal River: Mali, Guinea, Senegal and Mauritania.

Open Book and Radar A78

1970, July 6　Litho.　Perf. 14

560	A78	5fr lt bl & blk	.20	.20
561	A78	10fr rose & blk	.20	.20
562	A78	50fr yellow & blk	.60	.20
563	A78	200fr lilac & blk	2.10	.90

Nos. 560-563 (4)　3.10　1.50

International Telecommunications Day.

Lenin — A79

Designs: 20fr, Meeting with Lenin, by V. Serov. 30fr, Lenin Addressing Workers, by V. Serov. 40fr, Lenin with Red Guard Soldier and Sailor, by P. V. Vasiliev. 100fr, Lenin Speaking from Balcony, by P. V. Vasiliev. 200fr, Like 5fr.

1970, Nov. 16　Photo.　Perf. 13

564	A79	5fr gold & multi	.20	.20
565	A79	20fr gold & multi	.40	.20
566	A79	30fr gold & multi	.50	.20
567	A79	40fr gold & multi	.80	.20
568	A79	100fr gold & multi	1.60	.30
569	A79	200fr gold & multi	3.25	.75

Nos. 564-569 (6)　6.75　1.85

Lenin (1870-1924), Russian communist leader.

Phenecogrammus Interruptus — A80

Designs: Various fish from Guinea.

1971, Apr. 1　Photo.　Perf. 13

570	A80	5fr gold & multi	.20	.20
571	A80	10fr gold & multi	.25	.20
572	A80	15fr gold & multi	.30	.20
573	A80	20fr gold & multi	.30	.20
574	A80	25fr gold & multi	.45	.20
575	A80	30fr gold & multi	.65	.20
576	A80	40fr gold & multi	.85	.20
577	A80	45fr gold & multi	1.00	.20
578	A80	50fr gold & multi	1.40	.25
579	A80	75fr gold & multi	2.40	.55
580	A80	100fr gold & multi	3.25	.65
581	A80	200fr gold & multi	7.00	1.10

Nos. 570-581 (12)　18.05　4.15

Violet-crested Touraco — A81

Birds: 20fr, European golden oriole. 30fr, Blue-headed coucal. 40fr, Northern shrike. 75fr, Vulturine guinea fowl. 100fr, Southern ground hornbill.

1971, June 18　Photo.　Perf. 13
Size: 34x34mm

582	A81	5fr gold & multi	.20	.20
583	A81	20fr gold & multi	.45	.20
584	A81	30fr gold & multi	.70	.20
585	A81	40fr gold & multi	.85	.25
586	A81	75fr gold & multi	2.50	.55
587	A81	100fr gold & multi	3.25	.80

Nos. 582-587,C113-C113B (9)　18.10　4.65

UNICEF Emblem, Map of Africa — A82

1971, Dec. 24　Perf. 12x12½
Map in Olive

588	A82	25fr orange & blk	.20	.20
589	A82	30fr pink & black	.35	.20
590	A82	50fr gray grn & blk	.60	.20
591	A82	60fr gray bl & blk	.70	.20
592	A82	100fr lil rose & blk	1.10	.20

Nos. 588-592 (5)　2.95　1.00

UNICEF, 25th anniv.
For overprints see Nos. 625-629.

Imaginary Prehistoric Space Creature — A83

Various imaginary prehistoric space creatures.

1972, Apr. 1　Perf. 13½x13

593	A83	5fr multicolored	.20	.20
594	A83	20fr multicolored	.20	.20
595	A83	30fr multicolored	.45	.20
596	A83	40fr multicolored	.50	.20
597	A83	100fr multicolored	1.10	.35
598	A83	200fr multicolored	2.75	.75

Nos. 593-598 (6)　5.20　1.90

Black Boy, Men of 4 Races, Emblem — A84

Designs: 20fr, Oriental boy. 30fr, Indian youth. 50fr, Caucasian girl. 100fr, Men of 4 races and Racial Equality emblem.

1972, May 14　Perf. 13x13½

599	A84	15fr gold & multi	.20	.20
600	A84	20fr gold & multi	.20	.20
601	A84	30fr gold & multi	.35	.20

602 A84 50fr gold & multi .50 .20
603 A84 100fr gold & multi 1.00 .30
Nos. 599-603,C119 (6) 3.75 2.10

Intl. Year Against Racial Discrimination, 1971.

Map of Africa, Syncom Satellite — A85

Designs (Map of Africa and Satellites): 30fr, Relay. 75fr, Early Bird. 80fr, Telstar.

1972, May 17 **Litho.** *Perf. 13*
604 A85 15fr multicolored .20 .20
605 A85 30fr red org & multi .20 .20
606 A85 75fr grn & multi 1.00 .20
607 A85 80fr multicolored 1.10 .45
Nos. 604-607,C120-C121 (6) 6.90 3.15

4th World Telecommunications Day.

Carrier Pigeon, UPAF Emblem — A86

1972, July 10
608 A86 15fr brt bl & multi .20 .20
609 A86 30fr multicolored .20 .20
610 A86 75fr lil & multi .75 .20
611 A86 80fr multicolored .90 .45
Nos. 608-611,C122-C123 (6) 4.95 2.85

Book Year Emblem, Reading Child — A87

Designs (Book Year Emblem and): 15fr, Book as sailing ship. 40fr, Young woman with flower and book. 50fr, Book as key. 75fr, Man reading and globe. 200fr, Book and laurel.

1972, Aug. 2 **Photo.** *Perf. 14x13½*
612 A87 5fr red & multi .20 .20
613 A87 15fr multicolored .20 .20
614 A87 40fr yel & multi .45 .20
615 A87 50fr blue & multi .65 .20
616 A87 75fr dk red & multi 1.10 .45
617 A87 200fr org & multi 2.10 .90
Nos. 612-617 (6) 4.70 2.15

International Book Year 1972.

Javelin, Olympic Emblems, Arms of Guinea A88

1972, Aug. 26 **Photo.** *Perf. 13*
618 A88 5fr shown .20 .20
619 A88 10fr Pole vault .20 .20
620 A88 25fr Hurdles .40 .20
621 A88 30fr Hammer throw .60 .20
622 A88 40fr Boxing .75 .20
623 A88 50fr Vaulting .80 .25
624 A88 75fr Running 1.90 .45
Nos. 618-624,C124-C125 (9) 11.00 3.50

20th Olympic Games, Munich, 8/26-9/11.

Nos. 588-592 Overprinted

1972, Sept. 28 Photo. *Perf. 12x12½*
Map in Olive
625 A82 25fr org & blk .50 .20
626 A82 30fr pink & blk .70 .20
627 A82 50fr gray grn & blk 1.10 .25
628 A82 60fr gray bl & blk 1.75 .25
629 A82 100fr lil rose & blk 2.50 .80
Nos. 625-629 (5) 6.55 1.70

UN Conference on Human Environment, Stockholm, June 5-16.

Dimitrov at Leipzig Trial — A89

1972, Sept. 28 *Perf. 13*
Gold, Dark Green & Black
630 A89 5fr shown .20 .20
631 A89 25fr In Moabit Prison, 1933 .45 .20
632 A89 40fr Writing his memoirs .50 .20
633 A89 100fr Portrait 1.25 .30
Nos. 630-633 (4) 2.40 .90

George Dimitrov (1882-1949), Bulgarian Communist party leader and Premier.

Emperor Haile Selassie — A90

Design: 200fr, Emperor facing right.

1972, Oct. 2
634 A90 40fr blk & multi .55 .20
635 A90 200fr multicolored 2.75 .95

Syntomeida Epilais — A91

1973, Mar. 5 **Photo.** *Perf. 14x13½*
Designs: Various insects.
636 A91 5fr shown .35 .20
637 A91 15fr Ladybugs .45 .25
638 A91 30fr Green locust 1.50 .30
639 A91 40fr Honey bee 2.25 .40
640 A91 50fr Photinus pyralis 3.00 .60
641 A91 200fr Ancyluris formosissima 8.00 1.75
Nos. 636-641 (6) 15.55 3.50

Kwame Nkrumah A92

Various portraits of Kwame Nkrumah.

1973, May 25 **Photo.** *Perf. 13½*
642 A92 1.50s lt grn, gold & brn .20 .20
643 A92 2.50s lt grn, gold & brn .35 .20
644 A92 5s lt grn, gold & brn .60 .20
645 A92 10s gold & dark vio 1.75 .45
Nos. 642-645 (4) 2.90 1.05

OAU, 10th anniversary.

Institute for Applied Biology, Kindia A93

WHO Emblem and: 2.50s, Technicians inoculating egg. 3s, Filling vaccine into ampules. 4s, Sterilization of vaccine. 5s, Assembling of vaccine and vaccination gun. 10s, Inoculation of steer. 20s, Vaccination of woman.

1973, Nov. 16 **Photo.** *Perf. 13½*
Size: 40x36mm
646 A93 1s gold & multi .20 .20
647 A93 2.50s gold & multi .40 .20
648 A93 3s gold & multi .55 .20
649 A93 4s gold & multi .75 .20
Size: 47½x31mm
650 A93 5s gold & multi .90 .20
651 A93 10s gold & multi 1.40 .40
652 A93 20s gold & multi 3.25 1.00
Nos. 646-652 (7) 7.45 2.40

WHO, 25th anniversary.

Copernicus, Heliocentric System, Primeval Landscape — A94

Nicolaus Copernicus — A95

Designs (Copernicus and): 2s, Sun rising over volcanic desert, and spacecraft. 4s, Earth, moon and spacecraft. 5s, Moon scape and spacecraft. 10s, Jupiter and spacecraft. 20s, Saturn and heliocentric system.

1973, Dec. 17 **Photo.** *Perf. 13½*
653 A94 50c gold & multi .20 .20
654 A94 2s gold & multi .30 .20
655 A94 4s gold & multi .40 .20
656 A94 5s gold & multi .60 .20
657 A94 10s gold & multi 1.50 .40
658 A94 20s gold & multi 3.00 .90
Nos. 653-658 (6) 6.00 2.10

Souvenir Sheet
659 Sheet of 4 20.00 20.00
a. A95 20s Single stamp 3.25 3.25
Nicolaus Copernicus (1473-1543), Polish astronomer. No. 659 contains center label showing rocket and heliocentric system in gold margin.

Loading Bauxite on Freighter — A96

1974, Mar. 1 **Litho.** *Perf. 13½*
660 A96 4s shown .75 .20
661 A96 6s Freight train 2.00 .20
662 A96 10s Mining 3.25 .65
Nos. 660-662 (3) 6.00 1.05

Bauxite mining, Boke.

Clappertonia Ficifolia — A97

1974, May 20 **Photo.** *Perf. 13*
Size: 25x36mm
663 A97 50c shown .20 .20
664 A97 1s Rothmannia longiflora .20 .20
665 A97 2s Oncoba spinosa .20 .20
666 A97 3s Venidium fastuosum .40 .20
Size: 31x42mm
667 A97 4s Bombax costatum .50 .20
668 A97 5s Clerodendrum splendens .95 .20
669 A97 7.50s Combretuni grandiflorum 1.10 .30
670 A97 10s Mussaendra erythrophylla 1.25 .35
Size: 38x38mm (Diamond)
671 A97 12s Argemone mexicana 1.60 .45
Nos. 663-671,C127-C129 (12) 24.15 7.10

Drummers, Pigeon, UPAF and UPU Emblems — A98

Designs (Carrier Pigeon, African Postal Union and UPU Emblems): 6s, Runner with letter stick. 7.50s, Monorail and mail truck. No. 675, Jet and ocean liner. No. 676, Balloon and dugout canoe. 20s, Satellites over earth.

1974, Oct. 16 Photo. *Perf. 13½x14*
672 A98 5s mag & multi .60 .20
673 A98 6s grn & multi .80 .20
674 A98 7.50s ver & multi 1.25 .35
675 A98 10s Prus bl & multi 1.75 .60
Nos. 672-675 (4) 4.40 1.35

Souvenir Sheets
Perf. 13½
676 A98 10s ocher & multi 6.00 6.00
677 Sheet of 4, multi 12.00 12.00
a. A98 20s Single stamp 1.60 1.60

Centenary of Universal Postal Union. No. 676 contains one 70x60mm stamp.

Rope Bridge — A99

Designs (Pioneers): 2s, Field observation. 4s, Communication. 5s, Cooking in camp. 7.50s, Salute. 10s, Basketball.

1974, Nov. 22 Photo. Perf. 14x13½

678	A99	50c multicolored	.20	.20
679	A99	2s multicolored	.35	.20
680	A99	4s multicolored	.45	.20
681	A99	5s multicolored	.75	.20
682	A99	7.50s multicolored	1.10	.20
683	A99	10s multicolored	1.90	.45
a.		Souv. sheet of 2, #682-683	4.00	4.00
		Nos. 678-683 (6)	4.75	1.45

National Pioneer Movement.

Souvenir Sheet

Fruit — A100

1974, Nov. 22 Photo. Perf. 13x14

684		Sheet of 5	12.00	12.00
a.		4s Limes	1.00	.75
b.		4s Oranges	1.00	.85
c.		5s Bananas	1.50	1.25
d.		5s Mangos	1.50	1.25
e.		12s Pineapple	2.75	2.50

Chimpanzee — A101

1975, May 14 Photo. Perf. 13½

685	A101	1s shown	.45	.20
686	A101	2s Impala	.65	.20
687	A101	3s Wart hog	.75	.20
688	A101	4s Kobus defassa	.75	.20
a.		Souv. sheet of 4, #685-688	9.00	9.00
689	A101	5s Leopard	1.40	.20
690	A101	6s Greater kudu	1.40	.20
691	A101	6.50s Zebra	1.60	.25
692	A101	7.50s Cape buffalo	2.00	.25
a.		Souv. sheet of 4, #689-692	4.00	9.00
693	A101	8s Hippopotamus	3.25	.85
694	A101	10s Lion	3.25	.85
695	A101	12s Black rhinoceros	4.00	1.00
696	A101	15s Elephant	6.00	1.50
a.		Souv. sheet of 4, #693-696	26.50	26.50
		Nos. 685-696 (12)	25.50	5.90

Sheets exist perf. and imperf.
Stamps in Nos. 692a, 696a are inscribed "Poste Aerienne."

Lions, Pipe Line and ADB Emblem A102

Designs (African Development Bank Emblem, Pipe Line and): 7s, Elephants. 10s, Male lions. 20s, Elephant and calf.

1975, June 16 Photo. Perf. 13½

697	A102	5s gold & multi	.90	.20
698	A102	7s gold & multi	1.25	.20
699	A102	10s gold & multi	1.60	.35
700	A102	20s gold & multi	3.25	.70
		Nos. 697-700 (4)	7.00	1.45

African Development Bank, 10th anniv.

Women Musicians, IWY Emblem A103

IWY Emblem and: 7s, Women banjo & guitar players. 9s, Woman railroad shunter & train. 15s, Woman physician examining infant. 20s, Male & female symbols.

1976, Apr. 12 Photo. Perf. 13½

701	A103	5s multicolored	.60	.20
702	A103	7s multicolored	.90	.20
703	A103	9s blue & multi	1.50	.45
704	A103	15s multicolored	2.25	.75
a.		Souvenir sheet	3.00	3.00
705	A103	20s vio bl & multi	2.75	1.00
a.		Souvenir sheet of 4	13.00	13.00
		Nos. 701-705 (5)	8.00	2.60

International Women's Year 1975. No. 704a contains one stamp similar to No. 704 with gold frame. No. 705a contains 4 stamps similar to No. 705 with gold frame.

Woman Gymnast A104

Montreal Olympic Games Emblem and: 4s, Long jump. 5s, Hammer throw. 6s, Discus. 6.50s, Hurdles. 7s, Javelin. 8s, Running. 8.50s, Bicycling. 10s, High jump. 15s, Shot put. 20s, Pole vault. #717, Soccer. #718, Swimming.

1976, May 17 Photo. Perf. 13½

Size: 38x38mm

706	A104	3s multicolored	.40	.20
707	A104	4s grn & multi	.60	.20
708	A104	5s yel & multi	.60	.20
709	A104	6s multicolored	.70	.20
710	A104	6.50s plum & multi	.70	.20
711	A104	7s blue & multi	.95	.30
712	A104	8s ultra & multi	.95	.30
713	A104	8.50s org & multi	1.50	.35
714	A104	10s multicolored	1.60	.40
715	A104	15s multicolored	2.50	.75
716	A104	20s multicolored	3.25	.95
717	A104	25s grn & multi	3.75	1.00
		Nos. 706-717 (12)	17.50	5.05

Souvenir Sheet

718	A104	25s multicolored	5.00	5.00

21st Olympic Games, Montreal, Canada, July 17-Aug. 1. No. 718 contains one 32x32mm stamp. See No. C130.

A. G. Bell, Telephone, 1900 — A105

7s, Wall telephone, 1910. 12s, Syncom telecommunications satellite. #722, Telstar satellite. #723, Telephone switchboard operator, 1914.

1976, Nov. 15 Photo. Perf. 13

719	A105	5s multicolored	.65	.20
720	A105	7s multicolored	1.00	.20
721	A105	12s multicolored	1.60	.45
722	A105	15s multicolored	2.25	.60
a.		Souvenir sheet of 4, #719-722	7.00	7.00
		Nos. 719-722 (4)	5.50	1.45

Souvenir Sheet

723	A105	15s multicolored	2.50	2.50

Centenary of first telephone call by Alexander Graham Bell, Mar. 10, 1876.

Collybia Fusipes — A106

Mushrooms: 7s, Lycoperdon perlatum. 9s, Boletus edulis. 9.50s, Lactarius deliciosus. 11.50s, Agaricus campestris.

1977, Feb. 6 Photo. Perf. 13

Size: 48x26mm

724	A106	5s multicolored	1.90	.25
725	A106	7s multicolored	3.00	.25
726	A106	9s multicolored	3.50	.55
a.		Souvenir sheet of 2, #724, 726	7.50	7.50
727	A106	9.50s multicolored	3.50	.65

Size: 48x31mm

728	A106	11.50s multicolored	6.25	1.10
		Nos. 724-728,C131-C133 (8)	37.15	6.50

Hexaplex Hoplites — A107

Sea Shells: 2s, Perrona lineata. 4s, Marginella pseudofaba. 5s, Tympanotonos radula. 7s, Marginella strigata. 8s, Harpa doris. 10s, Demoulia pinguis. 20s, Bursa scrobiculator. 25s, Marginella adansoni.

1977, Apr. 25 Photo. Perf. 13

Size: 50x25mm

729	A107	1s gold & multi	.25	.20
730	A107	2s gold & multi	.40	.20
731	A107	4s gold & multi	1.00	.30
732	A107	5s gold & multi	1.50	.35
733	A107	7s gold & multi	2.10	.40
734	A107	8s gold & multi	2.50	.60

Size: 50x30mm

735	A107	10s gold & multi	3.25	.90
736	A107	20s gold & multi	6.50	1.25
737	A107	25s gold & multi	8.50	1.75
		Nos. 729-737 (9)	26.00	5.95

Farmers and Ox Plow A108

Designs: 5s, Pres. Touré addressing rally. 20s, Soldier driving farm tractor. 25s, Pres. Touré addressing UN General Assembly. 30s, 40s, Pres. Sékou Touré, vert.

1977, May 14 Perf. 13½x13, 13x13½

738	A108	5s gold & multi	.70	.20
739	A108	10s gold & multi	1.10	.40
740	A108	20s gold & multi	2.75	.90
741	A108	25s gold & multi	3.25	1.25
a.		Souvenir sheet of 4, #738-741	10.50	10.50
742	A108	30s gold & dk brn	4.00	1.25
743	A108	40s gold & sl grn	4.75	1.25
a.		Souvenir sheet of 2, #742-743	13.00	13.00
		Nos. 738-743 (6)	16.55	5.50

Democratic Party of Guinea, 30th anniv.

Nile Monitor — A109

Reptiles and Snakes: 4s, Frogs. 5s, Lizard (uromastix). 6s, Sand skink. 6.50s, Agama. 7s, Black-lipped spitting cobra. 8.50s, Ball python. 20s, Toads.

1977, Oct. 10 Photo. Perf. 13½

Size: 46x20mm

744	A109	3s multi	.65	.20
745	A109	4s multi	.95	.20
746	A109	5s multi	.95	.20

Size: 46x30mm

747	A109	6s multi	1.50	.25
748	A109	6.50s multi	1.90	.25
749	A109	7s multi	2.40	.55
750	A109	8.50s multi	2.75	.65
751	A109	20s multi	6.50	1.40
		Nos. 744-751,C134-C136 (11)	35.35	7.20

Eland — A110

Endangered Animals: 2s, Chimpanzee. 2.50s, Pygmy elephant. 3s, Lion. 4s, Palm squirrel. 5s, Hippopotamus. Each animal shown male, female and young.

1977, Dec. 12 Photo. Perf. 14x13½

752	A110	Strip of 3	1.10	.20
a.-c.		1s any single		.20
753	A110	Strip of 3	1.75	.25
a.-c.		2s any single		.40
754	A110	Strip of 3	2.25	.30
a.-c.		2.50s any single		.60
755	A110	Strip of 3	2.75	.40
a.-c.		3s any single		.70
756	A110	Strip of 3	3.50	.55
a.-c.		4s any single		1.10
757	A110	Strip of 3	4.50	.65
a.-c.		5s any single		1.40
		Nos. 752-757,C137-C142 (12)	58.10	22.35

Russian October Revolution, 60th Anniv. — A111

Designs: 2.50s, First Lenin debate, Moscow. 5s, Lenin speaking, 1917. 7.50s, Lenin and people. 8s, Lenin in first parade on Red Square.

1978, Feb. 27 Photo. Perf. 14

758	A111	2.50s gold & multi	.60	.20
759	A111	5s gold & multi	1.00	.20
760	A111	7.50s gold & multi	1.50	.30
761	A111	8s gold & multi	1.60	.35
		Nos. 758-761,C143-C144 (6)	15.45	3.95

Pres. Giscard d'Estaing at Microphones — A112

Pres. Valery Giscard d'Estaing of France and Pres. Sekou Toure of Guinea: 5s, 10s, In conference. 6.50s, Signing agreement. 7s, Attending official meeting. 8.50s, With their wives. 20s, Drinking a toast.

1979, Sept. 14   Photo.   Perf. 13
762	A112	3s lt brn & brn	.85	.20
763	A112	5s green & brn	1.50	.20
764	A112	6.50s red lil & brn	1.75	.25
765	A112	7s ultra & brn	1.90	.30
766	A112	8.50s dk red & brn	2.40	.55
767	A112	10s vio & brown	2.75	.80
768	A112	20s yel grn & brn	6.00	1.10
		Nos. 762-768,C145 (8)	24.15	5.40

Visit of Pres. Valery Giscard d'Estaing to Guinea.

Twenty Thousand Leagues Under the Sea — A113

Jules Verne Stories: 3s, Children of Capt. Grant. 5s, Mysterious Island. 7s, A Captain at Fifteen. 10s, The Borsac Mission.

1979, Nov. 8   Litho.   Perf. 12x12½
769	A113	1s multicolored	.40	.20
770	A113	3s multicolored	.45	.20
771	A113	5s multicolored	.85	.20
772	A113	7s multicolored	1.25	.30
773	A113	10s multicolored	1.75	.40
		Nos. 769-773,C146-C147 (7)	11.70	3.80

Jules Verne (1828-1905), French science fiction writer.

"Aerial Steam Carriage," 1842 — A114

Aviation Retrospect: 5s, Wright's Flyer 1 1903. 6.50s, Caudron, 1934. 7s, Spirit of St. Louis, 1927. 8.50s, Bristol Beaufighter, 1940. 10s, Bleriot XI, 1909. #780, Concorde. #781, Boeing 727, 1963.

1979, Nov. 22   Photo.   Perf. 14
774	A114	3s multi	.50	.20
775	A114	5s multi	.90	.20
776	A114	6.50s multi	1.10	.35
777	A114	7s multi	1.25	.45
778	A114	8.50s multi	1.50	.45
779	A114	10s multi	1.75	.45
780	A114	20s multi	3.50	.95
781	A114	20s multi	3.50	.95
		Nos. 774-781 (8)	14.00	3.90

Hafia Soccer Team — A115

Designs: 2s, Players and Sekou Touré cup, vert. 5s, Pres. Touré presenting cup. 7s, Pres.

Touré and player holding cup, vert. 8s, Sekou Touré cup, vert. 10s, Team captains and referees, vert. 20s, The winning goal.

Perf. 12½x12, 12x12½

1979, Dec. 18   Litho.
782	A115	1s multicolored	.20	.20
783	A115	2s multicolored	.20	.20
784	A115	5s multicolored	.80	.20
785	A115	7s multicolored	1.10	.35
786	A115	8s multicolored	1.25	.40
787	A115	10s multicolored	1.75	.45
788	A115	20s multicolored	3.25	.75
		Nos. 782-788 (7)	8.55	2.55

Hafia Soccer Team, African triple champions, 1977.

Train, IYC Emblem A116

IYC Emblem and: 2s, Children dancing around tree, vert. 4s, "1979" and leaves, vert. 7s, Village. 10s, Boy climbing tree. 25s, Boys of different races, flowers, sun.

1980, Jan. 14   Perf. 13x13½, 13½x13
789	A116	2s multicolored	.30	.20
790	A116	4s multicolored	.65	.20
791	A116	5s multicolored	.80	.20
792	A116	7s multicolored	1.00	.30
793	A116	10s multicolored	1.75	.40
794	A116	25s multicolored	4.00	1.10
		Nos. 789-794 (6)	8.50	2.40

International Year of the Child (1979).

Butterflyfish — A117

1980, Apr. 1   Perf. 12½x12, 12x12½
795	A117	1s shown	.30	.20
796	A117	2s Porgy	.70	.20
797	A117	3s Zeus conchifer, vert.	.75	.20
798	A117	4s Grouper	1.00	.25
799	A117	5s Sea horse, vert.	1.40	.25
800	A117	6s Hatchet fish	1.60	.35
801	A117	7s Pisodonophis semicinctus	1.75	.40
802	A117	8s Flying gurnard, vert.	2.25	.50
803	A117	9s Squirrelfish	2.75	.65
804	A117	10s Psettus sebae, vert.	3.00	.65
805	A117	12s Abudefuf hoeffleri	3.75	.75
806	A117	15s Triggerfish	5.50	1.00
		Nos. 795-806 (12)	24.75	5.40

Apollo 11 Take-Off — A118

1980, July 20   Photo.   Perf. 14
807	A118	1s shown	.20	.20
808	A118	2s Earth from moon	.20	.20
809	A118	4s Armstrong leaving module	.75	.20
810	A118	5s Armstrong on moon	.90	.20
811	A118	7s Collecting samples	1.25	.35
812	A118	8s Re-entry	1.40	.45
813	A118	12s Recovery	2.25	.75
814	A118	20s Crew	3.50	1.10
		Nos. 807-814 (8)	10.45	3.45

Apollo 11 moon landing, 10th anniv. (1979).

Intl. Palestinian Solidarity Day — A119

1981, Nov. 21   Photo.   Perf. 13½
815	A119	8s multicolored	1.50	.45
816	A119	11s multicolored	2.25	.60

Soccer — A120

1982   Litho.   Perf. 12½x12
817	A120	1s shown	.20	.20
818	A120	2s Basketball	.20	.20
819	A120	3s Diving	.50	.20
820	A120	4s Gymnast	.65	.20
821	A120	5s Boxing	.90	.20
822	A120	6s Pole vault	1.10	.30
823	A120	7s Running	1.25	.35
824	A120	8s Long jump	1.50	.40
		Nos. 817-824,C148-C152 (13)	20.80	6.00

22nd Summer Olympic Games, Moscow, July 19-Aug. 3, 1980.

5th Anniv. of West African Economic Community — A121

1982, May 14   Perf. 13½
825	A121	6s multicolored	1.10	.25
826	A121	7s multicolored	1.50	.35
827	A121	9s multicolored	2.00	.55
		Nos. 825-827 (3)	4.60	1.15

Kemal Ataturk Birth Centenary A122

1982, July 19   Photo.   Perf. 13½
828	A122	7s multi	1.25	.35
829	A122	10s multi, diff.	2.00	.45
830	A122	25s multi, horiz.	4.75	1.10
		Nos. 828-830,C153 (4)	13.00	3.15

1982 World Cup A123

Designs: Various soccer players.

1982, Aug. 23
831	A123	6s multicolored	1.25	.30
832	A123	8s multicolored	1.75	.40
833	A123	9s multicolored	1.90	.45
834	A123	10s multicolored	2.10	.45
		Nos. 831-834,C154-C156 (7)	21.60	7.40

Soccer Type of 1982
#831-834 Overprinted in Red and Green:
"CHAMPION ITALIE-11 JUILLET 1982" and Italian Flag

1982, Aug. 23   Photo.   Perf. 13½
835	A123	6s multicolored	1.25	.30
836	A123	8s multicolored	1.75	.40
837	A123	9s multicolored	1.90	.45
838	A123	10s multicolored	2.10	.45
		Nos. 835-838,C157-C159 (7)	20.40	6.10

Italy's victory in 1982 World Cup.

23rd Olympic Games, Los Angeles, July 28-Aug. 12, 1984 A124

1983, July 1   Litho.   Perf. 13½
839	A124	5s Wrestling	1.50	.20
840	A124	7s Weightlifting	1.90	.30
841	A124	10s Gymnastics	2.75	.55
842	A124	15s Discus	4.25	.95
843	A124	20s Kayak	6.00	1.40
844	A124	25s Equestrian	6.75	1.60
		Nos. 839-844 (6)	23.15	5.00

Litho. & Embossed
Size: 39x58mm
844A	A124	100s Running	45.00	37.50

Souvenir Sheets
Litho.
845	A124	30s Show jumping	5.00	1.60

Litho. & Embossed
845A	A124	100s Show jumping	15.00	12.50

Nos. 844A, 845A are airmail. No. 845A contains one 58x39mm stamp.

First Manned Balloon Flight, 200th Anniv. — A125

Designs: 5s, Marquis D'Arlandes, Pilatre de Rozier. 7s, Marie Antoinette Balloon, Rozier. 10s, Dirigible, Dupuy De Lome, horiz. 15s, Dirigible, Major A. Perseval, horiz.

1983, Aug. 1   Litho.   Perf. 13½
846	A125	5s multicolored	.80	.20
847	A125	7s multicolored	1.10	.30
848	A125	10s multicolored	1.50	.55
849	A125	15s multicolored	2.40	.65
		Nos. 846-849,C160-C161 (6)	12.80	4.70

Intl. Year of the Handicapped — A126

1983, Aug. 24   **Litho.**
850 A126 10s multicolored   3.75 .80
851 A126 20s multicolored   7.75 1.40

Dr. Robert Koch (1843-1910), TB Bacillus A127

Various phases of research.

1983, Aug. 24   **Litho.**
852 A127   6s multicolored   1.75 .25
853 A127 10s multicolored   2.75 .40
854 A127 11s multicolored   3.00 .40
855 A127 12s multicolored   3.50 .80
856 A127 15s multicolored   4.50 .95
857 A127 20s multicolored   6.00 1.10
858 A127 25s multicolored   6.75 1.40
    Nos. 852-858 (7)   28.25 5.30

Mosque, Conakry A128

1983, Oct. 2   **Litho.**   **Perf. 13½**
859 A128   1s multicolored   .40 .20
860 A128   2s multicolored   .55 .20
861 A128   5s multicolored   .95 .20
862 A128 10s multicolored   1.90 .55
    Nos. 859-862 (4)   3.80 1.15

Souvenir Sheet
863 A128 25s multicolored   4.00 1.90

Natl. independence, 25th anniv. No. 863 airmail.

Mano River Union, 10th Anniv. A129

2s, Development program graduates. 7s, Emblem. 8s, Pres. Toure of Guinea, Stevens of Sierra Leone, Doe of Liberia. 10s, 20s, Signing treaty.

1983, Oct. 3
864 A129   2s multicolored   .40 .20
865 A129   7s multicolored   .85 .20
866 A129   8s multicolored   1.25 .30
867 A129 10s multicolored   1.50 .35
    Nos. 864-867 (4)   4.00 1.05

Souvenir Sheet
868 A129 20s multicolored   3.25 1.75

No. 868 airmail.

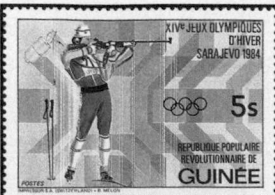

14th Winter Olympics, Sarajevo, Feb. 8-19, 1984 — A130

1983, Dec. 5   **Litho.**   **Perf. 13½**
869 A130   5s Biathlon   .75 .20
870 A130   7s Bobsledding   .95 .30
871 A130 10s Downhill skiing   1.40 .40
872 A130 15s Speed skating   2.25 .65
873 A130 20s Ski jumping   3.00 .85
874 A130 25s Figure skating   3.50 1.10
    Nos. 869-874 (6)   11.85 3.50

Litho. & Embossed
Size: 58x39mm
874A A130 100s Downhill skiing   40.00 32.50

Souvenir Sheets
Litho.
875 A130 30s Hockey   5.00 1.60

Litho. & Embossed
875A A130 100s 4-man bobsled   15.00 12.50

Nos. 873-875A airmail. No. 875A contains one 58x39mm stamp.

Self-portrait and Virgin with Blue Diadem, by Raphael A131

Designs: 7s, Self-portrait and Holy Family, by Rubens. 10s, Self-portrait and Portrait of Saskia, by Rembrandt. 15s, Portrait of Goethe and scene from Young Werther. 20s, Scouting Year. 25s, Paul Harris, Rotary emblem. 30s, J.F. Kennedy, Apollo XI. 100s, Paul Harris, 3 other men in Rotary meeting.

1984, Jan 2   **Litho.**   **Perf. 13**
876 A131   5s multicolored   2.00 .35
877 A131   7s multicolored   2.50 .45
878 A131 10s multicolored   3.00 .60
879 A131 15s multicolored   3.00 .75
880 A131 20s multicolored   3.00 .85
881 A131 25s multicolored   4.00 1.25
    Nos. 876-881 (6)   17.50 4.25

Souvenir Sheets
882 A131 30s multicolored   6.00 2.75

Litho. & Embossed
Perf. 13½
882A A131 100s gold & multi   12.00 8.00

Nos. 880-882A airmail. No. 882A contains one 51x42mm stamp.
For overprints see Nos. C164-C165.

Transportation — A132

1984, May 7   **Litho.**   **Perf. 13½**
883 A132   5s Congo River steamer   .75 .20
884 A132   7s Graf Zeppelin LZ 127   1.25 .20
885 A132 10s Daimler automobile, 1886   1.60 .30
886 A132 15s E. African RR Beyer-Garrat   2.25 .50
887 A132 20s Latecoere 28, 1929   3.25 .65

888 A132 25s Sial Marchetti S.M. 73, 1934   4.25 .85
    Nos. 883-888 (6)   13.35 2.70

Souvenir Sheet
889 A132 30s Series B locomotive   6.00 3.00

Nos. 887-889 airmail.

Anniversaries and Events — A133

Famous men: 5s, Abraham Lincoln, log cabin, the White House. 7s, Jean-Henri Dunant, Red Cross at Battle of Solferino. 10s, Gottlieb Daimler, 1892 Motor Carriage. 15s, Louis Bleriot, monoplane. 20s, Paul Harris, Rotary Intl. 25s, Auguste Piccard, bathyscaphe Trieste. 30s, Anatoly Karpov, world chess champion, chessboard and knight. 100s, Paul Harris, Rotary Intl. emblem.

1984, Aug. 20   **Litho.**   **Perf. 13½**
890 A133   5s multicolored   .80 .20
891 A133   7s multicolored   1.10 .20
892 A133 10s multicolored   1.60 .35
893 A133 15s multicolored   2.40 .60
894 A133 20s multicolored   3.00 .65
895 A133 25s multicolored   4.00 .80
    Nos. 890-895 (6)   12.90 2.70

Litho. & Embossed
Size: 60x30mm
895A A133 100s gold & multi
   b.   Min. sheet of 1, 91x70mm   60.00 —
   c.   Min. sheet of 1, 121x70mm   16.00 12.50

Souvenir Sheet
896 A133 30s multicolored   6.00 2.40

Nos. 894-896 are airmail.
For overprints see Nos. C163, C166.

The Holy Family, by Durer — A134

Painting details: 5s, The Mystic Marriage of St. Catherine and St. Sebastian, by Correggio. 10s, The Veiled Woman, by Raphael. 15s, Portrait of a Young Man, by Durer. 20s, Portrait of Soutine, by Modigliani. 25s, Esterhazy Madonna, by Raphael. 30s, Impannata Madonna, by Raphael.

1984, Aug. 23
897 A134   5s multicolored   .75 .20
898 A134   7s multicolored   1.25 .30
899 A134 10s multicolored   1.75 .35
900 A134 15s multicolored   2.25 .75
901 A134 20s multicolored   3.50 1.10
902 A134 25s multicolored   4.50 1.25
    Nos. 897-902 (6)   14.00 3.95

Souvenir Sheet
903 A134 30s multicolored   6.00 2.40

Nos. 901-903 airmail.

1984 Winter Olympics, Sarajevo A135

Gold medalists: 5s, East German two-man bobsled. 7s, Thomas Wassberg, Sweden, 50-kilometer cross-country. 10s, Gaetan Boucher, Canada, 1000 and 1500-meter speed skating. 15s, Katarina Witt, DDR, singles figure skating. 20s, Bill Johnson, US, men's downhill. 25s, Soviet Union, ice hockey. 30s, Jens Weissflog, DDR, 70-meter ski jump.

No. 909A, Phil Mahre, US, slalom skiing. No. 910A, Jayne Torvill & Christopher Dean, Great Britain, ice dancing.

1985, Sept. 23   **Litho.**   **Perf. 13½**
904 A135   5s multicolored   .75 .20
905 A135   7s multicolored   .95 .20
906 A135 10s multicolored   1.50 .30
907 A135 15s multicolored   2.10 .45
908 A135 20s multicolored   2.75 .60
909 A135 25s multicolored   3.75 .75
    Nos. 904-909 (6)   11.80 2.50

Litho. & Embossed
Size: 51x36mm
909A A135 100s gold & multi   60.00 30.00

Souvenir Sheets
Litho.
910 A135 30s multicolored   6.00 2.10

Litho. & Embossed
910A A135 100s gold & multi   18.00 15.00

Nos. 908A-910A are airmail. No. 910A contains one 51x36mm stamp.

1984 Los Angeles Summer Olympics — A136

Medalists and various satellites: 5s, T. Ruiz and C. Costie, US, synchronized swimming. 7s, West Germany, team dressage. 10s, US, yachting, flying Dutchman class. 15s, Mark Todd, New Zealand, individual 3-day equestrian event. 20s, Daley Thompson, G.B., decathlon. 25s, US, team jumping. 30s, Carl Lewis, US, long jump, 100 and 200-meter run, 4x100 relay.

1985, Mar. 18   **Litho.**   **Perf. 13½**
911 A136   5s multicolored   .45 .20
912 A136   7s multicolored   .70 .20
913 A136 10s multicolored   .90 .25
914 A136 15s multicolored   1.40 .40
915 A136 20s multicolored   1.60 .45
916 A136 25s multicolored   2.40 .60
    Nos. 911-917 (1)   .45 .20

Souvenir Sheet
917 A136 30s multicolored   6.00 2.10

Nos. 915-917 airmail.

Fungi — A137

1985, Mar. 21   **Litho.**   **Perf. 13½**
918 A137   5s Rhodophyllus callidermus   .90 .20
919 A137   7s Agaricus niger   1.60 .20
920 A137 10s Thermitomyces globulus   2.25 .45
921 A137 15s Amanita robusta   3.50 .60
922 A137 20s Lepiota subradicans   4.75 .90
923 A137 25s Cantharellus rhodophyllus   6.00 1.25
    Nos. 918-923 (6)   19.00 3.60

Souvenir Sheet
924 A137 30s Phlebopus sylvaticus   7.00 4.00

Nos. 922-924 airmail.
For surcharges see Nos. 962-968.

Scientist Herman J. Oberth, and Two-Stage Rocket A138

Space achievements: 10s, Lunik 1, USSR, 1959. 15s, Lunik 2 on the Moon, 1959. 20s, Lunik 3 photographing the Moon, 1959. 30s, US astronauts Armstrong, Aldrin, Collins and Apollo 11, 1969. 35s, Sally Ride, 1st American woman in space, 1983. 50s, Recovering a Palapa B satellite, 1984. No. 930A, Guion S. Bluford, 1st black American astronaut. No. 931A, Viking probe on Mars.

1985, May 26   Litho.   Perf. 13½

925	A138	7s multicolored	1.10	.20
926	A138	10s multicolored	1.40	.25
927	A138	15s multicolored	2.10	.40
928	A138	20s multicolored	2.40	.45
929	A138	30s multicolored	4.75	.85
930	A138	35s multicolored	5.50	.90
	Nos. 925-930 (6)		17.25	3.05

Litho. & Embossed
Size: 51x36mm

| 930A | A138 | 200s gold & multi | 47.50 | — |

Souvenir Sheet
Litho.

| 931 | A138 | 50s multicolored | 8.00 | 3.25 |

Litho. & Embossed

| 931A | A138 | 200s gold & multi | 32.50 | — |

Nos. 929-931A are airmail. No. 931A contains one 51x36mm stamp.

Maimonides (1135-1204), Jewish Scholar, Cordoba Jewish Quarter — A139

Anniversaries and events: 10s, Christopher Columbus departing from Palos for New World, 1492. 15s, Frederic Auguste Bartholdi (1834-1904), sculptor, architect, and Statue of Liberty, cent. 20s, Queen Mother, 85th birthday. 30s, Ulf Merbold, German physicist, US space shuttle Columbia. 35s, Wedding of Prince Charles and Lady Diana, 1981. 50s, Charles, Diana, Princes Henry and William. 100s, Queen Mother Elizabeth's 85th birthday.

1985, Sept. 23

932	A139	7s multicolored	1.00	.20
933	A139	10s multicolored	1.40	.25
934	A139	15s multicolored	2.10	.40
935	A139	20s multicolored	2.75	.55
936	A139	30s multicolored	4.00	.80
937	A139	35s multicolored	5.00	.90
	Nos. 932-937 (6)		16.25	3.10

Litho. & Embossed
Size: 42x51mm

| 937A | A139 | 100s gold & multi | 16.00 | 12.50 |

Souvenir Sheet
Litho.

| 938 | A139 | 50s multicolored | 8.00 | 3.25 |

Nos. 936-938 airmail. No. 938 contains one 51x36mm stamp. Nos. 934 and 937A exist in souvenir sheets of one.

Audubon Birth Bicent. — A140

Illustrations of bird species from Birds of America.

1985, Sept. 23   Litho.   Perf. 13½

939	A140	7s Coccyzus erythrophthalmus	.90	.20
940	A140	10s Conuropsis carolinensis	1.40	.30
941	A140	15s Anhinga anhinga	2.40	.50
942	A140	20s Buteo lineatus	3.00	.70
943	A140	30s Otus asio	5.00	1.25
944	A140	35s Toxostoma rufum	5.25	1.50
	Nos. 939-944 (6)		17.95	4.45

Souvenir Sheet

| 945 | A140 | 50s Zenaidura macroura | 7.50 | 3.00 |

Nos. 941, 944 vert. Nos. 943-945 are airmail. No. 945 contains one 51x36mm stamp. Nos. 939-944 exist in souvenir sheets of one. Value, set $90.

1986 World Cup Soccer Championships, Mexico — A141

Famous soccer players: 7s, Bebeto, Brazil. 10s, Rinal Dassaev, USSR. 15s, Phil Neal, Great Britain. 20s, Jean Tigana, France. 30s, Fernando Chalana, Portugal. 35s, Michel Platini, France. 50s, Karl Heinz Rummenigge, West Germany.

1985, Oct. 26

946	A141	7s multicolored	1.10	.20
947	A141	10s multicolored	1.50	.25
948	A141	15s multicolored	2.25	.40
949	A141	20s multicolored	3.00	.60
950	A141	30s multicolored	4.25	.85
951	A141	35s multicolored	5.25	.95
	Nos. 946-951 (6)		17.35	3.25

Souvenir Sheet

| 952 | A141 | 50s multicolored | 7.50 | 3.00 |

Nos. 950-952 airmail.

Cats and Dogs A142

1985, Oct. 26

953	A142	7s Blue-point Siamese	1.10	.20
954	A142	10s Cocker spaniel	1.50	.25
955	A142	15s Poodles	2.25	.40
956	A142	20s Blue Persian	3.00	.60
957	A142	25s European red-and-white tabby	3.75	.70
958	A142	30s German shepherd	4.25	.85
959	A142	35s Abyssinians	5.50	.95
960	A142	40s Boxer	6.50	1.25
	Nos. 953-960 (8)		27.85	5.20

Souvenir Sheet

| 961 | A142 | 50s Pyrenean mountain dog, chartreux cat | 7.50 | 3.00 |

Nos. 958-961 airmail. No. 961 contains one 51x30mm stamp.

Nos. 918-924 Surcharged with 4 Bars

1985, Nov. 15

962	A137	1s on 5s multi	.80	.20
963	A137	2s on 7s multi	.85	.20
964	A137	8s on 10s multi	1.75	.40
965	A137	30s on 15s multi	7.00	1.60
966	A137	35s on 20s multi	8.50	2.25
967	A137	40s on 25s multi	10.00	2.75
	Nos. 962-967 (6)		28.90	7.40

Souvenir Sheet

| 968 | A137 | 50s on 30s multi | 9.50 | 4.00 |

Nos. 966-968 airmail.

Locomotives — A143

Designs: 7s, 8F Class steam, Great Britain. 15s, Bobo 5500 Series III electric, German Fed. Railways. 25s, Pacific A Mazout No. 270, African Railways. 35s, Serie 420 electric train set, Suburban S-Bahn, Germany. 50s, ICE high-speed train, German Fed. Railways.

1985, Dec. 18   Litho.   Perf. 13½

969	A143	7s multicolored	1.10	.20
970	A143	15s multicolored	2.40	.70
971	A143	25s multicolored	4.50	.90
972	A143	35s multicolored	6.00	1.25
	Nos. 969-972 (4)		14.00	3.05

Souvenir Sheet

| 973 | A143 | 50s multicolored | 8.00 | 3.25 |

Nos. 972-973 airmail.
For surcharges see Nos. 991-995.

Columbus Discovering America, 1492 — A144

1985, Dec. 18

974	A144	10s Pinta	1.40	.25
975	A144	20s Santa Maria	3.00	.65
976	A144	30s Nina	4.75	.95
977	A144	40s Santa Maria, sighting land	6.75	1.25
	Nos. 974-977 (4)		15.90	3.10

Souvenir Sheet

| 978 | A144 | 50s Columbus and Nina | 7.50 | 3.00 |

Nos. 976-979 airmail.

Intl. Youth Year — A145

1986, Jan. 21

979	A145	10s Chopin	1.40	.40
980	A145	20s Botticelli	2.75	.85
981	A145	25s Picasso	3.50	1.10
982	A145	35s Rossini	5.00	1.50
	Nos. 979-982 (4)		12.65	3.85

Souvenir Sheet

| 983 | A145 | 50s Michelangelo | 7.50 | 3.00 |

Nos. 981, 983 airmail.
For surcharges see Nos. 996-1000.

Halley's Comet — A146

Sightings: 5fr, Bayeux Tapestry (detail), c. 1092, France. 30fr, Arab, astrolabe, 1400. 40fr, Montezuma II, Aztec deity. 50fr, Edmond Halley, trajectory diagram. 300fr, Halley, Sir Isaac Newton. 500fr, Giotto, Soviet and NASA space probes, comet. 600fr, Hally commemorative medal, Giotto probe.

1986, July 1   Litho.   Perf. 13½
5fr-500fr Surcharged with New Currency in Silver or Black

984	A146	5fr multi	.20	.20
985	A146	30fr multi	.35	.20
986	A146	40fr multi	.40	.20
987	A146	50fr multi	.50	.20
988	A146	300fr multi	2.75	1.00
989	A146	500fr multi	4.75	1.75
	Nos. 984-989 (6)		8.95	3.55

Souvenir Sheet

| 990 | A146 | 600fr multi | 6.50 | 2.50 |

Nos. 988-990 are airmail. Nos. 984-989 not issued without surcharge.

Nos. 969-973 Surcharged in Black or Black on Silver

1986, Aug. 25   Litho.   Perf. 13½

991	A143	2fr on 7s multi (B on S)	.55	.20
992	A143	25fr on 15s multi	.65	.20
993	A143	50fr on 25s multi	1.00	.20
994	A143	90fr on 35s multi	1.75	.55
	Nos. 991-994 (4)		3.95	1.15

Souvenir Sheet

| 995 | A143 | 500fr on 50s multi | 6.00 | 2.10 |

Nos. 979-983 Surcharged

1986, Aug. 25

996	A145	5fr on 10s multi	.40	.20
997	A145	35fr on 20s multi	.50	.20
998	A145	50fr on 25s multi	.75	.20
999	A145	90fr on 35s multi	1.25	.40
	Nos. 996-999 (4)		2.90	1.00

Souvenir Sheet

| 1000 | A145 | 500fr on 50s multi | 6.00 | 2.10 |

Locomotives — A147

Designs: 20fr, Dietrich 640 CV. 100fr, T.13 7906. 300fr, Vapeur 01220. 400fr, ABH Type 3 5020. 600fr, Renault ABH 3 (300 CV).

1986, Nov. 1

1001	A147	20fr multi	.35	.20
1002	A147	100fr multi	1.00	.35
1003	A147	300fr multi	3.00	.95
1004	A147	400fr multi	4.25	1.25
	Nos. 1001-1004 (4)		8.60	2.75

Souvenir Sheet

| 1005 | A147 | 600fr multi | 7.00 | 2.50 |

Nos. 1004-1005 are airmail.

Discovery of America, 500th Anniv. (in 1992) — A148

Designs: 40fr, Columbus at Ft. Navidad construction, Santa Maria, 1492. 70fr, Landing at Hispaniola, 2nd voyage, 1494. 200fr, Aboard ship, 3rd voyage, 1498. 500fr, Trading with Indians. 600fr, At court of Ferdinand and Isabella, 1493.

1986, Nov. 1

1006	A148	40fr multi	.50	.20
1007	A148	70fr multi	.80	.20
1008	A148	200fr multi	2.25	.70
1009	A148	500fr multi	5.50	1.75
	Nos. 1006-1009 (4)		9.05	2.85

Souvenir Sheet

| 1010 | A148 | 600fr multi | 7.00 | 2.50 |

Nos. 1009-1010 are airmail.

Anniversaries
& Events
A149

30fr, Prince Charles and Diana, 5th wedding
anniv. 40fr, Alain Prost, San Marino, 1985
Formula 1 Grand Prix world champion. 100fr,
Wedding of Prince Andrew and Sarah Ferguson. 300fr, Elvis Presley. 500fr, Michael Jackson. 600fr, M. Dassault (1892-1986), aerospace engineer.

1986, Nov. 12
1011	A149	30fr multi	.40	.20
1012	A149	40fr multi	.55	.20
1013	A149	100fr multi	1.25	.40
1014	A149	300fr multi	3.50	1.25
1015	A149	500fr multi	6.00	2.40
		Nos. 1011-1015 (5)	11.70	4.45

Souvenir Sheet
1016	A149	600fr multi	8.00	2.75

Nos. 1015-1016 are airmail.

1986 World Cup Soccer
Championships — A150

Various players and final scores.

1986, Nov. 12
1017	A150	100fr Pfaff	1.00	.35
1018	A150	300fr Platini	3.00	.95
1019	A150	400fr Matthaus	4.00	1.50
1020	A150	500fr D. Maradona	5.00	2.10
		Nos. 1017-1020 (4)	13.00	4.90

Souvenir Sheet
1021	A150	600fr Maradona, tro-phy	7.00	2.50

Nos. 1020-1021 are airmail. No. 1021 contains one 51x42mm stamp.
For surcharge see No. 1182A.

1988 Summer Olympics,
Seoul — A151

Pierre de Coubertin (1863-1937),
Seoul Stadium, Telecommunications
Satellite — A151a

1987, Jan. 17   Litho.   Perf. 13½
1022	A151	20fr Judo	.20	.20
1023	A151	30fr High jump	.35	.20
1024	A151	40fr Team hand-ball	.45	.20
1025	A151	100fr Women's gymnastics	1.00	.20
1026	A151	300fr Javelin	3.00	.90
1027	A151	500fr Equestrian	5.00	2.10
		Nos. 1022-1027 (6)	10.00	3.80

Souvenir Sheet
1028	A151a	600fr multi	7.00	2.50

Dated 1986. Nos. 1026-1028 are airmail.

1988 Winter Olympics,
Calgary — A152

1987, Mar. 23   Litho.   Perf. 13½
1029	A152	50fr on 40fr Biathlon	.50	.20
1030	A152	100fr Cross-country skiing	1.00	.35
1031	A152	400fr Ski jumping	4.00	2.50
1032	A152	500fr Two-man bob-sled	5.00	2.10
		Nos. 1029-1032 (4)	10.50	5.15

Souvenir Sheet
1033	A152	600fr Woman skater, satellite	7.00	2.50

No. 1029 not issued without overprint. Nos.
1031-1033 are airmail.

1988
Winter
Olympics,
Calgary
A153

Telecommunications satellite, athletes and
emblem.

1987, May 1
1034	A153	25fr Women's sla-lom	.30	.20
1035	A153	50fr Hockey	.50	.20
1036	A153	100fr Men's figure skating	.95	.30
1037	A153	150fr Men's downhill skiing	1.50	.45
1038	A153	300fr Speed skating	3.00	1.25
1039	A153	500fr Four-man bob-sled	4.75	2.10
		Nos. 1034-1039 (6)	11.00	4.50

Souvenir Sheet
1040	A153	600fr Ski jumping	7.00	2.50

Nos. 1038-1040 are airmail.

Famous
Men — A154

Intl. Cardiology Congresses in
Chicago, Washington and New
York — A155

Designs: 50fr, Lafayette, military leader during American and French revolutions. 100fr,
Ettore Bugatti (1881-1947), Italian automobile
manufacturer. 200fr, Garri Kasparov, Russian
chess champion. 300fr, George Washington.
400fr, Boris Becker, 1987 Wimbledon tennis
champion. 500fr, Sir Winston Churchill.

1987, Nov. 1   Litho.   Perf. 13½
1041	A154	50fr multi	.45	.20
1042	A154	100fr multi	1.00	.40
1043	A154	200fr multi	1.90	.80
1044	A154	300fr multi	2.75	1.25
1045	A154	400fr multi	3.75	1.50
1046	A154	500fr multi	4.75	2.00
		Nos. 1041-1046 (6)	14.60	6.25

Souvenir Sheet
1047	A155	1500fr multi	16.00	12.50

Nos. 1045-1047 are airmail. Stamp in No.
1047 divided into three sections by simulated
perforations.
For surcharge see No. 1182B.

Cave
Bear — A156

Prehistoric Animals — A157

1987, Nov. 1
1048	A156	50fr Dimetrodon	.80	.20
1049	A156	100fr Iguanodon	1.60	.50
1050	A156	200fr Tylosaurus	3.25	1.00
1051	A156	300fr shown	4.75	1.50
1052	A156	400fr Saber-tooth tiger	6.25	2.10
1053	A156	500fr Stegosaurus	8.25	2.50
		Nos. 1048-1053 (6)	24.90	7.80

Souvenir Sheet
1054	A157	600fr Triceratops	8.00	2.75

Nos. 1052-1054 are airmail.
For surcharge see No. 1182C.

1988 Summer
Olympics,
Seoul — A158

Male and female tennis players in action.

1987, Nov. 28
1055	A158	50fr multi	.45	.20
1056	A158	100fr multi, diff.	1.00	.35
1057	A158	150fr multi, diff.	1.50	.60
1058	A158	200fr multi, diff.	1.90	.75
1059	A158	300fr multi, diff.	3.00	1.25
1060	A158	500fr multi, diff.	5.00	1.90
		Nos. 1055-1060 (6)	12.85	5.05

Souvenir Sheet
1061	A158	600fr multi	7.00	2.75

Reintroduction of tennis as an Olympic
event. Nos. 1059-1061 are airmail.

1992
Summer
Olympics,
Barcelona
A159

Athletes participating in events, Barcelona
highlights: 50fr, Discus, courtyard of St. Croix
and St. Paul Hospital. 100fr, High jump, Pablo
Casals playing cello. 150fr, Long jump, Labyrinth of Horta. 170fr, Javelin, lizard from Guell
Park. 400fr, Gymnastics, Mercy Church. 500fr,
Tennis, Picasso Museum. 600fr, Running, tapestry by Miro.

1987, Dec. 28   Litho.   Perf. 13½
1062	A159	50fr multi	.50	.20
1063	A159	100fr multi	1.00	.35
1064	A159	150fr multi	1.50	.55
1065	A159	170fr multi	1.75	.60
1066	A159	400fr multi	3.75	1.40
1067	A159	500fr multi	5.00	1.75
		Nos. 1062-1067 (6)	13.50	4.85

Souvenir Sheet
1068	A159	600fr multi	6.50	4.50

Nos. 1066-1068 are airmail.
For surcharges see Nos. 1182D-1182E.

Wildlife
A160

1987, Dec. 28
1069	A160	50fr African wild dog pups	1.75	.75
1070	A160	70fr Adult	2.25	1.00
1071	A160	100fr Adults circling gazelle	2.75	1.25
1072	A160	170fr Chasing ga-zelle	3.25	1.50
1073	A160	400fr Crown cranes	4.75	1.40
1074	A160	500fr Derby elands	5.75	2.50
		Nos. 1069-1074 (6)	20.50	8.40

Souvenir Sheet
1075	A160	600fr Vervet monkeys	9.00	7.00

Nos. 1069-1072 picture World Wildlife Fund
emblem; Nos. 1073, 1075, picture Scouting
trefoil and No. 1074 pictures Rotary Intl.
emblem. Nos. 1073-1075 are airmail.
For surcharges see Nos. 1182F-1182G.

Reconciliation Summit Conference, July 11-12, 1986 — A161

Heads of state and natl. flags: Dr. Samuel Kanyon Doe of Liberia, Colonel Lansana Conte of Guinea and Maj.-Gen. Joseph Saidu Momoh of Sierra Leone.

1987		**Litho.**	**Perf. 13½**	
1076	A161	40fr multi	.40	.20
1077	A161	50fr multi	.55	.20
1078	A161	75fr multi	.90	.40
1079	A161	100fr multi	1.10	.55
1080	A161	150fr multi	1.75	.85
	Nos. 1076-1080 (5)		4.70	2.20

Space Exploration — A162

1988, Apr. 16				
1081	A162	50fr Galaxie-Grasp	.60	.20
1082	A162	150fr Energia Mir	1.50	.50
1083	A162	200fr NASA Space Station	2.00	.70
1084	A162	300fr Ariane 5-E.S.A.	3.00	1.00
1085	A162	400fr Mars-Rover	3.75	1.40
1086	A162	450fr Venus-Vega	5.00	1.60
	Nos. 1081-1086 (6)		15.85	5.40

Souvenir Sheet

1087	A162	500fr Mars-Phobos	8.00	6.00

Nos. 1085-1087 are airmail.

A163

A163a

Boy Scouts watching birds and butterflies.

1988, July 5		**Litho.**	**Perf. 13½**	
1088	A163	50fr Spermophaga ruficapilla	.60	.20
1089	A163	100fr Medon nymphalidae	1.25	.35
1090	A163	150fr Euplecte orix	1.75	.60
1091	A163	300fr Nectarinia pulchella	3.50	1.25
1092	A163	400fr Sophia nymphalidae	4.50	1.50
1093	A163	450fr Rumia nymphalidae	5.25	1.75
	Nos. 1088-1093 (6)		16.85	5.65

Souvenir Sheet

1094	A163	750fr Opis nymphalidae, Psittacula krameri	9.00	6.50

1990, Aug. 3	**Litho. & Embossed**		
1094A	A163a	1500fr Druya antimachus	20.00	12.50

Nos. 1092-1094A are airmail. No. 1094 contains one 35x50mm stamp.
#1094A exists in souvenir sheet of 1. Value $45.
For surcharge and overprints see Nos. 1182H, 1240-1246.

A164

Famous People: 200fr, Queen Elizabeth II, Prince Philip and crown jewels. 250fr, Fritz von Opel (1899-1971), German automotive industrialist, and 1928 RAK 2 Opel. 300fr, Wolfgang Amadeus Mozart, composer, and Masonic emblem. 400fr, Steffi Graf, tennis champion. 450fr, Buzz Aldrin and Masonic emblem. 500fr, Paul Harris, Rotary Intl. founder, and organization emblem. 750fr, Thomas Jefferson, horiz.

1988, July 5				
1095	A164	200fr multi	2.00	.75
1096	A164	250fr multi	2.50	.95
1097	A164	300fr multi	3.25	1.25
1098	A164	400fr multi	4.25	1.50
1099	A164	450fr multi	4.75	1.60
1100	A164	500fr multi	5.25	1.90
	Nos. 1095-1100 (6)		22.00	7.95

Souvenir Sheet

1101	A164	750fr multi	8.00	2.75

40th wedding anniv. of Queen Elizabeth II and Prince Philip (200fr).
Nos. 1099-1101 are airmail. No. 1101 contains one 42x36mm stamp.
For surcharges see Nos. 1182I, 1182Q.

1988 Winter Olympics Gold Medalists A165

Designs: 50fr, Vreni Schneider, Switzerland, women's giant slalom and slalom. 100fr, Frank-Peter Roetsch, East Germany, 10 and 20-kilometer biathlon. 150fr, Matti Nykaenen, Finland, 70 and 90-meter ski jumping. 250fr, Marina Kiehl, West Germany, women's downhill. 400fr, Frank Piccard, France, super giant slalom. 450fr, Katarina Witt, East Germany, women's figure skating. 750fr, Pirmin Zurbriggen, Switzerland, men's downhill.

1988, Oct. 2		**Litho.**	**Perf. 13½**	
1102	A165	50fr multi, vert.	.45	.20
1103	A165	100fr multi, vert.	.90	.35
1104	A165	150fr multi, vert.	1.50	.60
1105	A165	250fr multi, vert.	2.50	.95
1106	A165	400fr multi, vert.	3.75	1.50
1107	A165	450fr multi, vert.	4.50	1.60
	Nos. 1102-1107 (6)		13.60	5.20

Souvenir Sheet

1108	A165	750fr multi	8.00	2.75

Nos. 1103, 1107-1108 are airmail.
For surcharge see No. 1182J.

African Postal Union, 25th Anniv. A165a

1988		**Litho.**	**Perf. 13½**	
1108A	A165a	50fr multicolored	.45	.20
1108B	A165a	75fr multicolored	.75	.35
1108C	A165a	100fr multicolored	1.00	.40
1108D	A165a	150fr multicolored	1.60	.65
	Nos. 1108A-1108D (4)		3.80	1.60

World Health Day — A165b

1988, Oct. 2		**Litho.**	**Perf. 13½**	
1108E	A165b	50fr Medical research	.50	.20
1108F	A165b	150fr Immunization	1.50	.65
1108G	A165b	500fr Dentistry	4.75	2.25
	Nos. 1108E-1108G (3)		6.75	3.10

For surcharge see No. 1182K.

Opening of MT 20 Intl. Communications Center — A165c

1988, Dec. 8		**Litho.**	**Perf. 13½**	
1108H	A165c	50fr multicolored	.50	.20
1108I	A165c	100fr multicolored	1.00	.20
1108J	A165c	150fr multicolored	1.50	.65

Pierre de Coubertin, Founder of Intl. Olympic Committee A165d

1988		**Litho.**	**Perf. 13½y**	
1108K	A165d	50fr multi	.45	.40
1108L	A165d	100fr multi	.95	.80
1108M	A165d	150fr multi	1.50	1.40
1108N	A165d	500fr multi	5.00	4.00
	Nos. 1108K-1108N (4)		7.90	6.60

For surcharge see No. 1182L.

1992 Summer Olympics, Barcelona — A166

1989, May 3		**Litho.**	**Perf. 13½**	
1109	A166	50fr Diving	.55	.20
1110	A166	100fr Running, vert.	1.25	.55
1111	A166	150fr Shooting	2.10	.95
1112	A166	250fr Tennis, vert.	3.25	1.50
1113	A166	400fr Soccer	5.25	2.40
1114	A166	500fr Equestrian, vert.	6.50	3.00
	Nos. 1109-1114 (6)		18.90	8.60

Souvenir Sheet

1115	A166	750fr Yachting, vert.	7.50	2.50

Nos. 1113-1115 are airmail.
For surcharge see No. 1182M.

French Revolution, Bicent. — A167

Personalities of and scenes from the revolution: 250fr, Jean-Sylvain Bailly (1736-1793) leading proceedings in Tennis Court, June 20, 1789. 300fr, Count Mirabeau (1749-1791) at royal session, June 23, 1789. 400fr, Lafayette (1757-1834), federation anniversary celebration, July 18, 1790. 450fr, Jerome Petion de Villeneuve (1756-1794), king's arrest at Varennes-en-Argonne, June 21, 1791. 750fr, Camille Desmoulins (1760-1794), destruction of the Bastille, July 1789.

1989, July 7		**Litho.**	**Perf. 13½**	
1116	A167	250fr multi	3.00	.80
1117	A167	300fr multi	3.50	1.00
1118	A167	400fr multi	4.50	1.40
1119	A167	450fr multi	5.00	1.50
	Nos. 1116-1119 (4)		16.00	4.70

Souvenir Sheet

1120	A167	750fr multi	8.00	2.50

Nos. 1119-1120 airmail.
Nos. 1116-1119 exist in souvenir sheets of 1. Sold for 100fr extra.
For surcharge and overprints see Nos. 1182N, 1216-1220.

Planting A168

1989		**Litho.**	**Perf. 13½**	
1121	A168	25fr shown	.25	.20
1122	A168	50fr Irrigation	.50	.20
1123	A168	75fr Milking	.70	.25
1124	A168	100fr Fishing	.95	.35
1125	A168	150fr Farmers in corn field	1.40	.55
1126	A168	300fr Public well	3.00	1.10
	Nos. 1121-1126 (6)		6.80	2.65

Natl. Campaign for Self-sufficiency in Food Production and 10th anniv. of the Intl. Fund for Agricultural Development (in 1988). Dated 1988.

African Development Bank, 25th Anniv. — A169

1989, Nov. 4		**Litho.**	**Perf. 13½**	
1127	A169	300fr multicolored	3.00	1.10

Mano River Union, 15th Anniv. A170

Design: 300fr, Map of Guinea, Sierra Leone and Liberia, leaders' portraits.

1989, Nov. 4				
1128	A170	150fr multicolored	1.50	.65
1129	A170	300fr multicolored	3.00	1.25

World Cup Soccer, Italy — A171

Various soccer plays and: 200fr, Spire of San Domenico, Naples. 250fr, Piazza San Carlo, Turin. 300fr, Church of San Cataldo. 450fr, Church of San Francesco, Utine. 750fr, Statue of Dante, Florence and World Cup Soccer Trophy.

1990, Aug. 3 — Litho. — Perf. 13½

1130	A171	200fr multicolored	1.90 .80
1131	A171	250fr multicolored	2.50 1.00
1132	A171	300fr multicolored	3.25 1.25
1133	A171	450fr multicolored	5.00 1.90
		Nos. 1130-1133 (4)	12.65 4.95

Souvenir Sheet

1134	A171	750fr multicolored	7.25 2.75

No. 1133-1134 airmail.
For overprints see Nos. 1221-1225.

Concorde, TGV Atlantic — A172

1990, Aug. 3

1135	A172	400fr multicolored	4.00 1.50

No. 1135 exists in a souvenir sheet of 1.
For surcharge see No. 1182O.

Pope John Paul II, Pres. Gorbachev — A173

1990, Aug. 3

1136	A173	300fr multicolored	3.25 1.10

Summit Meeting, Dec. 2, 1989. No. 1136 exists in a souvenir sheet of 1. Value $10.

1992 Winter Olympics, Albertville — A174

1990, Aug. 3

1137	A174	150fr Downhill skiing	1.40 .65
1138	A174	250fr Cross country skiing	2.50 1.10
1139	A174	400fr Two-man bobsled	3.75 1.60
1140	A174	500fr Speedskating	5.00 2.00
		Nos. 1137-1140 (4)	12.65 5.35

Souvenir Sheet

1141	A174	750fr Slalom skiing	8.00 3.00

Nos. 1140-1141 airmail. Nos. 1137-1140 exist in souvenir sheets of 1.
For overprints and surcharge see Nos. 1182P, 1225-1230.

Pres. Bush, Pres. Gorbachev — A175

1990, Aug. 3 — Litho. — Perf. 13½

1142	A175	200fr multicolored	1.75 .75

Summit Meeting Dec. 3, 1989. No. 1142 exists in a souvenir sheet of 1.

De Gaulle's Call for French Resistance, 50th Anniv. — A176

1990

1143	A176	250fr multi	2.50 1.00

No. 1143 exists in a souvenir sheet of 1.

A177

World Cup Soccer Championships, Italy 1990 — A178

No. 1152, Player, Chateau Saint-Ange.

1991, Apr. 1 — Litho. — Perf. 13½

1144	A177	200fr Rudi Voller	1.75 .80
1145	A177	250fr Uwe Bein	2.25 1.00
1146	A177	300fr Pierre Littbarski	2.75 1.25
1147	A177	400fr Jurgen Klinsmann	4.00 1.90
1148	A177	450fr Lothar Matthaus	4.00 1.90
1149	A177	500fr Andreas Brehme	4.50 2.00
		Nos. 1144-1149 (6)	19.25 8.85

Litho. & Embossed

1150	A178	1500fr gold & multi	24.00 18.00

Souvenir Sheets

Litho.

1151	A177	750fr Brehme, diff.	8.00 3.00

Litho. & Embossed

1152	A178	1500fr gold & multi	16.00 12.50

Nos. 1148-1152 are airmail. Nos. 1144-1150 exist in souvenir sheets of 1.

Christmas A179

Paintings by Raphael: 50fr, Della Tenda Madonna. 100fr, Cowper Madonna. 150fr, Tempi Madonna. 250fr, Niccolini Madonna. 300fr, Orleans Madonna. 500fr, Solly Madonna. 750fr, Madonna of the Fish.

1991, Apr. 1 — Litho.

1153	A179	50fr multi	.50 .20
1154	A179	100fr multi	.85 .45
1155	A179	150fr multi	1.40 .65
1156	A179	250fr multi	2.25 1.00
1157	A179	300fr multi	2.75 1.25
1158	A179	500fr multi	4.50 2.00
		Nos. 1153-1158 (6)	12.25 5.55

Souvenir Sheet

1159	A179	750fr multi	8.00 3.00

Nos. 1157-1159 are airmail. Nos. 1153-1158 exist in souvenir sheets of 1.

A180

World War II Battles — A181

Designs: No. 1160, Sinking of the Bismarck, May 27, 1941, Adm. Raeder and Adm. Tovey. No. 1161, Battle of Midway, June 3, 1942, Adm. Yamamoto and Adm. Nimitz. 200fr, Guadalcanal, Oct. 7, 1942, Adm. Kondo and Adm. Halsey. 250fr, Battle of El Alamein, Oct. 23, 1942, Field Marshal Erwin Rommel, Field Marshal Montgomery. 300fr, Battle of the Bulge, Dec. 16, 1944, Gen. Guderian and Gen. Patton. 450fr, Sinking of the Yamato, Apr. 7, 1945, Adm. Kogo and Gen. MacArthur. No. 1166, Review of Free French Forces, July 14, 1940, Gen. Charles De Gaulle. 750fr, Boeing B-17G, Gen. Dwight Eisenhower. No. 1168, De Gaulle's Call for French Resistance, June 18, 1940.

1991, Apr. 8 — Litho. — Perf. 13½

1160	A180	100fr multicolored	.90 .45
1161	A180	150fr multicolored	1.25 .70
1162	A180	200fr multicolored	1.75 .90
1163	A180	250fr multicolored	2.25 1.10
1164	A180	300fr multicolored	2.75 1.25
1165	A180	450fr multicolored	6.00 3.00
a.		Sheet of 6, #1160-1165	16.00 8.00

Litho. & Embossed

1166	A181	1500fr gold & multi	17.00 11.00

Souvenir Sheets

Litho.

1167	A180	750fr multicolored	8.00 3.00

Litho. & Embossed

1168	A181	1500fr gold & multi	15.00 10.00

Nos. 1164-1168 are airmail. No. 1160-1166 exist in souvenir sheets of 1. Value, set $32.
For overprint see No. C177.

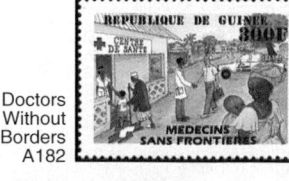

Doctors Without Borders A182

1991, Feb. 22 — Litho. — Perf. 13½

1169	A182	300fr multicolored	3.25 1.50

Telecom '91 A183

1991, Jan. 15

1170	A183	150fr multi, vert.	1.50 1.25
1171	A183	300fr shown	2.75 2.40

6th World Forum and Exposition on Telecommunications, Geneva, Switzerland.

American Entertainers and Films — A184

Designs: 100fr, Nat King Cole Trio. 150fr, Yul Brynner, The Magnificent Seven. 250fr, Judy Garland, The Wizard of Oz. 300fr, Steve McQueen, Papillon. 500fr, Gary Cooper, Sergeant York. 600fr, Bing Crosby, High Society. 750fr, John Wayne, How the West Was Won.

1991, Oct. 2 — Litho. — Perf. 13½

1172	A184	100fr multicolored	.75 .45
1173	A184	150fr multicolored	1.10 .60
1174	A184	250fr multicolored	2.00 1.00
1175	A184	300fr multicolored	2.40 1.25
1176	A184	500fr multicolored	4.00 2.00
1177	A184	600fr multicolored	8.75 4.25
		Nos. 1172-1177 (6)	19.00 9.55

Souvenir Sheet

1178	A184	750fr multicolored	8.00 3.00

Nos. 1176-1178 are airmail. No. 1172-1177 exist in souvenir sheets of 1.

Care Bears Promoting Environmental Protection — A184a

Designs: 50fr, Care Bears circling earth, vert. 100fr, Save water, vert. 200fr, Recycle, vert. 300fr, Control noise, vert. 400fr, Elephant. 500fr, Care Bear emblem, end of rainbow. 600fr, Scout, tent, Lord Baden-Powell.

1991 — Litho. — Perf. 13½

1178A	A184a	50fr multi	.40 .20
1178B	A184a	100fr multi	.85 .40
1178C	A184a	200fr multi	1.75 .85
1178D	A184a	300fr multi	2.50 1.25
1178E	A184a	400fr multi	3.50 1.75
		Nos. 1178A-1178E (5)	9.00 4.50

Souvenir Sheets

1178F	A184a	500fr multi	4.25 2.25
1178G	A184a	600fr multi	5.00 2.50

Nos. 1178F-1178G each contain one 39x27mm stamp. No. 1178G is airmail.

African Tourism Year A185

1991, Aug. 16 — Litho. — Perf. 13½

1179	A185	100fr Dancer, vert.	1.25 .60
1180	A185	150fr Baskets	2.00 .90
1181	A185	250fr Drum	3.25 1.25
1182	A185	300fr Flute player, vert.	3.50 1.60
		Nos. 1179-1182 (4)	10.00 4.35

Stamps of 1986-92 Surcharged in Black or Silver (#1182A-1182B, 1182D, 1182H-1182I, 1182M-1182N, 1182P)

1991 — Litho. — Perfs. as Before

1182A	A150	100fr on 400fr #1019	.85 .40
1182B	A154	100fr on 400fr #1045	.85 .40
1182C	A156	100fr on 400fr #1052	.85 .40
1182D	A159	100fr on 170fr #1065	.85 .40
1182E	A159	100fr on 400fr #1066	.85 .40

1182F	A160	100fr on 170fr #1072	125.00	—
1182G	A160	100fr on 400fr #1073	4.00	1.00
1182H	A163	100fr on 400fr #1092	.85	.40
1182I	A164	100fr on 400fr #1098	.85	.40
1182J	A165	100fr on 400fr #1106	.85	.40
1182K	A165b	100fr on 500fr #1108G	.85	.40
1182L	A165d	100fr on 500fr #1108N	.85	.40
1182M	A166	100fr on 400fr #1113	.85	.40
1182N	A167	100fr on 250fr #1116	.85	.40
1182O	A172	100fr on 400fr #1135	.85	.40
1182P	A174	100fr on 400fr #1139	.85	.40
1182Q	A164	300fr on 450fr #1099	2.50	1.25
1182R	AP14	300fr on 450fr #C170	2.50	1.25
Nos. 1182A-1182R (18)			145.90	9.10

Nos. 1182B-1182C, 1182E, 1182G, 1182M, 1182Q-1182R are airmail.

Visit by Pope John Paul II — A185a

1992, Feb. 24   Litho.   Perf. 13½

1182S	A185a	150fr multicolored	3.50	1.75

1994 World Cup Soccer, US — A186

A186a

Player, World Cup Trophy and scenes of Atlanta: 100fr, Little Five Points. 300fr, Fulton County Stadium. 400fr, Inman Park. 500fr, High Museum of Art. 1000fr, Intelsat VI, Capitol.
#1187A, Player in white shirt. #1187B, Player in red.

1992, Apr. 27   Litho.   Perf. 13½

1183	A186	100fr multi	1.25	.40
1184	A186	300fr multi	4.00	1.40
1185	A186	400fr multi	5.75	1.75
1186	A186	500fr multi	7.00	2.25
Nos. 1183-1186 (4)			18.00	5.65

Souvenir Sheet

1187	A186	1000fr multi	10.00	6.00

Litho. & Embossed

1187A	A186a	1500fr gold & multi	24.00	14.00

Souvenir Sheet

1187B	A186a	1500fr gold & multi	20.00	12.00

Nos. 1186-1187B are airmail. Nos. 1183-1186A exist in souvenir sheets of 1.

Lions Intl., 75th Anniv. — A187

1992, May 22   Litho.   Perf. 13½

1188	A187	150fr blue & multi	1.50	.75
1188A	A187	400fr lilac rose & multi	4.00	2.00

Anniversaries and Events — A188

Designs: 100fr, Satellite ERS-1 in orbit. 150fr, Vase with Fourteen Sunflowers, by Vincent van Gogh. 200fr, Napoleon Bonaparte. 250fr, Henri Dunant, Red Cross workers. 300fr, Brandenburg Gate. 400fr, Pope John Paul II. 450fr, Garry Kasparov, Anatoly Karpov, chess pieces. 500fr, African child, dove, emblems of Rotary and Lions Clubs.

1992, Nov. 10   Litho.   Perf. 13½

1189	A188	100fr multicolored	1.00	.45
1190	A188	150fr multicolored	1.50	.75
1191	A188	200fr multicolored	2.25	1.00
1192	A188	250fr multicolored	2.50	1.25
1193	A188	300fr multicolored	3.25	1.50
1194	A188	400fr multicolored	4.25	2.10
1195	A188	450fr multicolored	4.75	2.25
1196	A188	500fr multicolored	5.50	2.50
Nos. 1189-1196 (8)			25.00	11.80

Intl. Space Year (#1189). Vincent van Gogh, cent. of death (in 1990) (#1190). Napolean Bonaparte, 170th anniv. of death (in 1991) (#1191). Founding of Red Cross (in 1864) (#1192). Brandenburg Gate, bicent. (#1193). Pope John Paul II's visit to Africa in 1989 (#1194). World Chess Championships (#1195). Lions Intl., 75th anniv. (#1196).
Nos. 1195-1196 are airmail. Nos. 1189-1196 exist in souvenir sheets of one.
For overprint see No. C178.

Anniversaries and Events — A189

Designs: 200fr, The Devil and Kate, Antonin Dvorak. 300fr, Antonio Vivaldi. 350fr, Graf Zeppelin, flying boat, Count Ferdinand von Zeppelin. 400fr, English Channel Euro-Tunnel Train. 450fr, Konrad Adenauer, Brandenburg Gate. 500fr, Japanese naval ensign, Emperor Hirohito. 750fr, Tunnel Train, diff.

1992, Nov. 10

1197	A189	200fr multicolored	2.25	.90
1198	A189	300fr multicolored	3.25	1.40
1199	A189	350fr multicolored	3.75	1.50
1200	A189	400fr multicolored	4.00	1.90

1201	A189	450fr multicolored	5.00	2.00
a.	Souvenir sheet of 2, #1199, 1201		8.00	3.25
1202	A189	500fr multicolored	5.50	2.25
Nos. 1197-1202 (6)			23.75	9.95

Souvenir Sheet

1203	A189	750fr multicolored	8.00	3.75

Antonin Dvorak, 90th anniv. of death (in 1994) (#1197). Antonio Vivaldi, 250th anniv. of death (in 1991) (#1198). Count Ferdinand von Zeppelin, 75th anniv. of death (#1199). Opening of English Channel Tunnel (in 1994) (#1200, 1203). Konrad Adenauer, 25th anniv. of death, Brandenburg Gate, bicent. (#1201). Death of Emperor Hirohito (in 1989) (#1202).
Nos. 1201-1203 are airmail. Nos. 1197-1202 exist imperf. and in souvenir sheets of one. No. 1203 exists imperf. and contains one 60x42mm stamp.

Anniversaries and Events A190

Designs: 50fr, Modern Times, film by Charlie Chaplin. 100fr, Expo '92 Seville, Columbus. 150fr, St. Peter's Square, Rome. 200fr, Marlene Dietrich, roses. 250fr, Michael Schumacher, Benetton Ford B192. 300fr, Mercury rocket, John Glenn. 400fr, Bill Koch, America 3. 450fr, Mark Rypien, quarterback of Washington Redskins. 500fr, Rescue of Intelsat VI by shuttle Endeavour.

1992, Dec. 3

1204	A190	50fr multicolored	.45	.20
1205	A190	100fr multicolored	.90	.40
1206	A190	150fr multicolored	1.40	.65
1207	A190	200fr multicolored	1.90	.85
1208	A190	250fr multicolored	2.25	1.10
1209	A190	300fr multicolored	2.75	1.25
1210	A190	400fr multicolored	3.50	1.75
1211	A190	450fr multicolored	4.00	1.90
1212	A190	500fr multicolored	4.50	2.10
Nos. 1204-1212 (9)			21.65	10.20

Discovery of America, 500th anniv. (#1205). First US orbital space flight, 30th anniv. (#1209). Americas Cup yacht race (#1210). Super Bowl XXVI football game (#1211).
Nos. 1210-1212 are airmail. Nos. 1204-1212 exist in souvenir sheets of one.

Intl. Conference on Nutrition, Rome — A191

1992, Nov. 10   Litho.   Perf. 13½

1213	A191	150fr multi	1.50	.70
1214	A191	400fr multi	3.50	1.90
1215	A191	500fr multi	4.50	2.25
Nos. 1213-1215 (3)			9.50	4.85

Nos. 1116-1120 Ovptd. in Silver "BICENTENAIRE / DE L'AN I / DE LA REPUBLIQUE / FRANCAISE"

1992, Feb. 24   Litho.   Perf. 13½

1216	A167	250fr multicolored	3.00	1.10
1217	A167	300fr multicolored	3.75	1.40
1218	A167	400fr multicolored	5.00	1.75
1219	A167	450fr multicolored	5.75	2.00
Nos. 1216-1219 (4)			17.50	6.25

Souvenir Sheet

1220	A167	750fr multicolored	9.00	4.50

Nos. 1219-1220 are airmail. Nos. 1216-1219 exist in souvenir sheets of 1. Sold for 100fr extra.

Nos. 1130-1134 Ovptd. in Gold "1. ALLEMAGNE / 2. ARGENTINE / 3. ITALIE"

1992, Feb. 24   Litho.   Perf. 13½

1221	A171	200fr multicolored	2.00	.80
1222	A171	250fr multicolorcd	2.50	1.00
1223	A171	300fr multicolored	3.00	1.25
1224	A171	450fr multicolored	5.00	2.00
Nos. 1221-1224 (4)			12.50	5.05

Souvenir Sheet

1225	A171	750fr multicolored	8.00	3.00

Nos. 1137-1141 Ovptd. in Gold

1992   Litho.   Perf. 13½

1226	A174	150fr multicolored	1.75	.70
1227	A174	250fr multicolored	2.50	1.10
1228	A174	400fr multicolored	4.00	1.75
1229	A174	500fr multicolored	5.25	2.10
Nos. 1226-1229 (4)			13.50	5.65

Souvenir Sheet

1230	A174	750fr multicolored	6.25	3.00

Overprints read: 150fr, 750fr, "SLALOM GEANT / Alberto Tomba, Italie." 250fr, "SKI NORDIQUE / Vegard Ulvang, Norvege." 400fr, "BOB A DEUX / G. Weder / D Acklin, Suisse." 500fr, "PATINAGE DE VITESSE / Olaf Zinke 1000m., Allemagne."

A192

1994 World Cup Soccer Championships, US — A192a

Soccer player, city skyline: 100fr, San Francisco. 300fr, Washington, DC. 400fr, Detroit. 500fr, Dallas. 1000fr, New York.

1993, Sept. 24   Litho.   Perf. 13½

1233	A192	100fr multicolored	1.10	.45
1234	A192	300fr multicolored	3.50	1.50
1235	A192	400fr multicolored	4.50	1.90
1236	A192	500fr multicolored	5.75	2.40
Nos. 1233-1236 (4)			14.85	6.25

Souvenir Sheet

1237	A192	750fr multicolored	10.00	5.50

Litho. & Embossed

1237A	A192a	1500fr gold & multi	16.00	12.50

Nos. 1236-1237A are airmail. No. 1237A exists in a souvenir sheet of 1.

Miniature Sheet

Dinosaurs — A193

No. 1238: a, 50fr, Euparkeria. b, 50fr, Plateosaurus. c, 50fr, Anchisaurus. d, 50fr,

Ornithosuchus. e, 100fr, Megalosaurus. f, 100fr, Scelidosaurus. g, 100fr, Camptosaurus. h, 100fr, Ceratosaurus. i, 250fr, Ouranosaurus. j, 250fr, Dicraeosaurus. k, 250fr, Tarbosaurus. l, 250fr, Gorgosaurus. m, 250fr, Polacanthus. n, 250fr, Deinonychus. o, 250fr, Corythosaurus. p, 250fr, Spinosaurus. 1000fr, Tyrannosaurus rex.

1993, Oct. 27
1238   A193   Sheet of 16, #a.-p.   30.00   15.00

Souvenir Sheet
1239   A193   1000fr multicolored   10.00   4.50

No. 1239 is airmail and contains one 50x60mm stamp.

Nos. 1088-1094 Ovptd. in Silver "50eme ANNIVERSAIRE DE LA MORT DE BADEN POWEL"

1993, Feb. 24   Litho.   Perf. 13½
1240   A163   50fr multicolored   .45   .20
1241   A163   100fr multicolored   1.10   .50
1242   A163   150fr multicolored   1.75   .65
1243   A163   300fr multicolored   3.25   1.40
1244   A163   400fr multicolored   3.75   1.90
1245   A163   450fr multicolored   4.75   2.00
    Nos. 1240-1245 (6)   15.05   6.65

Souvenir Sheet
1246   A163   750fr multicolored   8.00   3.25

Nos. 1244-1246 are airmail.

A194

1994 Winter Olympic Games, Lillehammer A195

Views of Lillehammer: 150fr, Ice hockey. 250fr, Bobsled. 400fr, Biathlon. 450fr, Ski jump. 1000fr, Slalom skiing. 1500fr, Ice skating.

1993, July 16   Litho.   Perf. 13½
1247   A194   150fr multicolored   1.25   .65
1248   A194   250fr multicolored   2.75   1.25
1249   A194   400fr multicolored   4.25   2.10
1250   A194   450fr multicolored   4.75   2.25
    Nos. 1247-1250 (4)   13.00   6.25

Souvenir Sheet
1251   A194   1000fr multicolored   10.00   5.00

Litho. & Embossed
1252   A195   1500fr gold & multi   16.00   12.50

Nos. 1249-1252 are airmail.
For overprints see #1267A-1267E.

A196

1996 Summer Olympic Games, Atlanta — A197

Event, scenes of Atlanta: 150fr, Soccer, "Little White House." 250fr, Cycling, Georgia World Congress Center. 400fr, Basketball, underground Atlanta. 500fr, Baseball, new Georgia Railroad.
1000fr, Table tennis, Atlanta at night. 1500fr, Running, Georgia State Capitol, Olympic torch.

1993, July 16   Litho.   Perf. 13½
1253   A196   150fr multi   1.50   .65
1254   A196   250fr multi   2.75   1.25
1255   A196   400fr multi   4.75   2.10
1256   A196   500fr multi   6.00   2.50
    Nos. 1253-1256 (4)   15.00   6.50

Souvenir Sheet
1257   A196   1000fr multi   10.00   5.00

Litho. & Embossed
1257A   A197   1500fr gold & multi   16.00   12.50

Nos. 1256-1257A are airmail.
#1253-1256 exist in souvenir sheets of 1.

First Manned Moon Landing, 25th Anniv. — A197a

d, Luna 3, 1959. e, Ranger 7, 1964. f, Luna 9, 1966. g, Surveyor 1, 1966. h, Lunar Orbiter 1, 1966. i, Launch of Apollo 11, Neil Armstrong, 1969. j, Michael Collins, Apollo 11 command module. k, Apollo 11 landing on Moon, "Buzz" Aldrin. l, Apollo 12, 1969. m, Apollo 13, 1969. n, Luna 16, 1970. o, Luna 17, 1970. p, Apollo 14, 1971. q, Apollo 15, 1971. r, Apollo 16, 1972. s, Apollo 17, 1972.

1993, July 27   Litho.   Perf. 13½
Sheet of 16
1257B   A197a   150fr #d.-s.   25.00   12.25

D-Day Landings, Normandy, 50th Anniv. — A198

Battle scenes and: No. 1258a, 150fr, Field Marshal Irwin Rommel (1891-1944), Germany. b, 600fr, Gen. Dwight D. Eisenhower (1890-1969), Allies. c, 150fr, Gen. George S. Patton, Jr. (1885-1945), Allies.
Battle of the Bulge, 1944: No. 1259a, 150fr, Lt. Gen. William H. Simpson. b, 600fr, Battle scene. c, 150fr, Gen. Heinz Guderian (1888-1954).
Austerlitz, Dec. 2, 1805: No. 1260a, 150fr, John I, Prince of Liechtenstein (1760-1836). b, 600fr, Napoleon I. c, 150fr, Marshal Joachim Murat (1767-1815).
Battle of Borodino, Sept. 7, 1812: No. 1261a, 150fr, Marshal Michael Ney (1769-1815). b, 600fr, Battle scene. c, 150fr, Prince Pyotr Ivanovich Bagration (1765-1812).

1994, Jan. 26   Litho.   Perf. 13½
1258   A198   Strip of 3, #a.-c.   11.00   4.75
1259   A198   Strip of 3, #a.-c.   11.00   4.75
1260   A198   Strip of 3, #a.-c.   11.00   4.75
1261   A198   Strip of 3, #a.-c.   11.00   4.75
    Nos. 1258-1261 (4)   44.00   19.00

No. 1258b, 1259b, 1260b, 1261b are 60x46mm. Nos. 1258-1261 are each a continuous design.

Astronomers and Spacecraft A199

Designs: a, 300fr, Johannes Kepler, Pluto probe. b, 500fr, Copernicus, Galileo probe. b, 300fr, Sir Isaac Newton, Voyager.

1994, Jan. 26
1262   A199   Strip of 3, #a.-c.   15.00   6.75

No. 1262b is 60x46mm. No. 1262 has a continuous design.

Nos. 1233-1237 Ovptd. in Silver "1. BRESIL / 2. ITALIE / 3. SUEDE"

1994, Sept. 14   Litho.   Perf. 13½
1263   A192   100fr multicolored   1.00   .50
1264   A192   300fr multicolored   3.00   1.75
1265   A192   400fr multicolored   4.00   2.25
1266   A192   500fr multicolored   4.75   2.50
    Nos. 1263-1266 (4)   12.75   7.00

Souvenir Sheet
1267   A192   1000fr multicolored   10.00   5.00

Nos. 1266-1267 are airmail.

Nos. 1247-1251 Overprinted in Gold

1994, Sept. 14   Litho.   Perf. 13½
1267A   A194   150fr multi   1.25   .65
1267B   A194   250fr multi   2.40   1.25
1267C   A194   400fr multi   3.75   1.90
1267D   A194   450fr multi   4.50   2.10
    Nos. 1267A-1267D (4)   11.90   5.90

Souvenir Sheet
1267E   A194   1000fr multi   10.00   5.00

Overprints read: 150fr, MEDAILLE D'OR / SUEDE. 250fr, G. WEDER / D. ACKLIN / SUISSE. 400fr, F.B. LUNDBERG / NORVEGE. 450fr, J. WEISSFLOG / ALLEMAGNE. 1000fr, T. MOE / U.S.A.
Nos. 1267C-1267E are airmail.

Birds — A200

150fr, Carduelis carduelis. 250fr, Luscinia megarhynchos. #1270, Serinus canaria. #1271, Fringilla coelebs. #1272, Carduelis chloris. No. 1273, Erithacus rubecula.

1995, Aug. 31   Litho.   Perf. 13
1268   A200   150fr multicolored   .50   .25
1269   A200   250fr multicolored   .80   .35
1270   A200   500fr multicolored   1.60   .80
1271   A200   500fr multicolored   1.60   .80
1272   A200   500fr multicolored   1.60   .80
    Nos. 1268-1272 (5)   6.10   3.00

Souvenir Sheet
1273   A200   1000fr multicolored   6.00   3.00

No. 1273 contains one 32x40mm stamp.

1996 Summer Olympics, Atlanta — A201

1995, Aug. 5
1274   A201   150fr Javelin   .50   .25
1275   A201   250fr Boxing   .80   .40
1276   A201   500fr Basketball   1.60   .80
1277   A201   500fr Weight lifting   1.60   .80
1278   A201   500fr Soccer   1.60   .80
    Nos. 1274-1278 (5)   6.10   3.05

Souvenir Sheet
1279   A201   1000fr Archery   4.75   2.50

No. 1279 contains one 32x40mm stamp.

African Animals A202

Designs: 150fr, Cercopithecus mona, vert. 250fr, Cercopithecus aethiops, vert. No. 1282, Galagoides demidovi, vert. No. 1283, Manis gigantea. No. 1284, Lepus crawshayi. 1000fr, Aonyx capensis, vert.

1995, Sept. 25
1280   A202   150fr multicolored   .50   .25
1281   A202   250fr multicolored   .80   .35
1282   A202   500fr multicolored   1.60   .80
1283   A202   500fr multicolored   1.60   .80
1284   A202   500fr multicolored   1.60   .80
    Nos. 1280-1284 (5)   6.10   3.00

Souvenir Sheet
1285   A202   1000fr multicolored   6.00   3.00

1998 World Cup Soccer Championships, France — A203

Opposing two players wearing: No. 1288, Yellow shirt & blue shorts, red shirt & white shorts. No. 1289, Red & white uniform, red shirt & white shorts. No. 1290, Striped shirt & blue shorts, red & yellow shirt & green shorts.

1000fr, Three players.

1995, Oct. 30   Litho.   Perf. 13
1286	A203	150fr multicolored	.50	.25
1287	A203	250fr multicolored	.80	.35
1288	A203	500fr multicolored	1.60	.80
1289	A203	500fr multicolored	1.60	.80
1290	A203	500fr multicolored	1.60	.80
		Nos. 1286-1290 (5)	6.10	3.00

Souvenir Sheet
1291	A203	1000fr multicolored	6.00	3.00

No. 1291 contains one 32x40mm stamp.

Domestic Cats
A204

150fr, Tortoiseshell. 250fr, Tabby and white. #1294, Tortoiseshell and white longhair. #1295, Red tabby. #1296, Smoke long-haired. 1000fr, Chinchilla.

1995, July 25
1292	A204	150fr multicolored	.80	.40
1293	A204	250fr multicolored	1.25	.55
1294	A204	500fr multicolored	2.50	1.25
1295	A204	500fr multicolored	2.50	1.25
1296	A204	500fr multicolored	2.50	1.25
		Nos. 1292-1296 (5)	9.55	4.70

Souvenir Sheet
Perf. 12½
1297	A204	1000fr multicolored	6.00	3.00

No. 1297 contains one 40x32mm stamp.

Production of Electrical Power — A205

Designs: 100fr, Banéa Dam. 150fr, Water Chamber, Donkea. 200fr, Tinkisso Spillway, vert. 250fr, Cascades of Grand Falls. 500fr, Building, Kinkon.

1995, July 18   Perf. 12½
1298	A205	100fr multicolored	.50	.25
1299	A205	150fr multicolored	.75	.35
1300	A205	200fr multicolored	1.00	.50
1301	A205	250fr multicolored	1.25	.65
1302	A205	500fr multicolored	2.50	1.25
		Nos. 1298-1302 (5)	6.00	3.00

FAO, 50th Anniv. A206

Designs: 200fr, Man, oxen, boy. 750fr, Instructing women, children on nutrition.

1995, Oct. 16   Perf. 13
1303	A206	200fr multicolored	1.00	.55
1304	A206	750fr multicolored	4.00	2.00

Light Aircraft — A207

100fr, Pup-150, UK. 150fr, Gardan GY-80 Horizon, France. 250fr, Piper Cub J-3, US. No. 1308, Valmet L-90TP Redigo, Finland. No. 1309, Pilatus PC-6 Porter, Switzerland. No. 1310, Piper PA-28 Cherokee Arrow, US. 1000fr, Stol DO-27, Germany.

1995, Oct. 1   Perf. 12½
1305	A207	100fr multicolored	.45	.20
1306	A207	150fr multicolored	.75	.35
1307	A207	250fr multicolored	1.25	.65
1308	A207	500fr multicolored	2.40	1.10
1309	A207	500fr multicolored	2.40	1.10
1310	A207	500fr multicolored	2.40	1.10
		Nos. 1305-1310 (6)	9.65	4.50

Souvenir Sheet
1311	A207	1000fr multicolored	5.50	2.75

No. 1311 contains one 40x32mm stamp.

Flowers — A208

100fr, Sprekelia formosissima. 150fr, Rudbeckia purpurea. 250fr, Meconopsis betonicifolia. #1314, Gail Borden rose. #1315, Lathyrus odoratus. #1316, Iris starshine. 1000fr, Cypripedium alma gaevert.

1995, Oct. 12
1312	A208	100fr multicolored	.45	.20
1313	A208	150fr multicolored	.75	.35
1314	A208	250fr multicolored	1.25	.60
1315	A208	500fr multicolored	2.40	1.10
1316	A208	500fr multicolored	2.40	1.10
1317	A208	500fr multicolored	2.40	1.10
		Nos. 1312-1317 (6)	9.65	4.45

Souvenir Sheet
1318	A208	1000fr multicolored	5.50	2.75

No. 1318 contains one 32x40mm stamp.

Historic Buses — A209

250fr, 1832 Omnibus. 300fr, 1898 Daimler. 400fr, 1904 V.H. Bussing. 450fr, 1906 Autobus M.A.N. 500fr, 1904 Autocar M.A.N.

1995, Dec. 3   Litho.   Perf. 12½
1319	A209	250fr multicolored	.75	.35
1320	A209	300fr multicolored	.90	.45
1321	A209	400fr multicolored	1.25	.60
1322	A209	450fr multicolored	1.40	.70
1323	A209	500fr multicolored	1.50	.75
		Nos. 1319-1323 (5)	5.80	2.85

Arabian Horses A210

Various horses.

1995
Background Colors
1324	A210	100fr dk bl, vert.	.30	.20
1325	A210	150fr tan, vert.	.55	.20
1326	A210	250fr lt bl, vert.	.90	.40
1327	A210	500fr pink, vert.	1.75	.90
1328	A210	500fr lilac, vert.	1.75	.90
1329	A210	500fr sage	1.75	.90
		Nos. 1324-1329 (6)	7.00	3.50

Souvenir Sheet
1330	A210	1000fr white & gray	6.00	3.00

No. 1330 contains one 32x40mm stamp.

Mushrooms
A211

150fr, Leccinum nigrescens. 250fr, Boletus rhodoxanthus. #1333, Paxillus involutus. #1334, Cantharellus lutescens. #1335, Xerocomus rubellus. 1000fr, Gymnopilus junonius.

1995   Litho.   Perf. 12½
1331	A211	150fr multicolored	.45	.20
1332	A211	250fr multicolored	.75	.40
1333	A211	500fr multicolored	1.50	.75
1334	A211	500fr multicolored	1.50	.75
1335	A211	500fr multicolored	1.50	.75
		Nos. 1331-1335 (5)	5.70	2.85

Souvenir Sheet
1336	A211	1000fr multicolored	6.00	3.00

No. 1336 contains one 32x40mm stamp.

Tourism — A212

1996, Sept. 5   Litho.   Perf. 12½
1337	A212	200fr Mountain cliff	1.00	.50
1338	A212	750fr Young child	3.75	1.75
1339	A212	1000fr Women carrying wood	4.75	2.50
		Nos. 1337-1339 (3)	9.50	4.75

Dogs — A213

1996, Oct. 20
1340	A213	200fr Bull terrier	.85	.50
1341	A213	250fr Elkhound	1.10	.70
1342	A213	300fr Akita	1.40	.75
1343	A213	400fr Collie	1.75	1.00
1344	A213	450fr Rottweiler	2.00	1.00
1345	A213	500fr Boxer	2.40	1.10
		Nos. 1340-1345 (6)	9.50	5.05

Souvenir Sheet
Perf. 13
1346	A213	1000fr German pointer	5.00	2.50

No. 1346 contains one 32x40mm stamp.

Mushrooms
A214

1996, Dec. 20   Litho.   Perf. 12½
1347	A214	200fr Chestnut	.85	.45
1348	A214	250fr Granular	1.10	.55
1349	A214	300fr Destroying angel	1.40	.70
1350	A214	400fr Milky blue	1.75	.95
1351	A214	450fr Violet cortinarius	2.00	1.00
1352	A214	500fr Rough-stemmed	2.40	1.10
		Nos. 1347-1352 (6)	9.50	4.75

Souvenir Sheet
Perf. 13
1353	A214	1000fr Hygrophorus	5.00	2.50

No. 1353 contains one 32x40mm stamp.

Locomotives — A215

Designs: 200fr, Tom Thumb, 1829. 250fr, Genf, 1858. 300fr, Dübs and Company, 1873. 400fr, W.G. Bagnall of Castle Engine Works, 1932. 450fr, Werner von Siemens, 1879. 500fr, North London Tramways Co., 1885-89. 1000fr, General, 1862.

1996, Aug. 30   Perf. 12½
1354	A215	200fr multicolored	.85	.45
1355	A215	250fr multicolored	1.10	.60
1356	A215	300fr multicolored	1.40	.70
1357	A215	400fr multicolored	2.00	.95
1358	A215	450fr multicolored	2.25	1.00
1359	A215	500fr multicolored	2.40	1.10
		Nos. 1354-1359 (6)	10.00	4.80

Souvenir Sheet
1360	A215	1000fr multicolored	5.50	2.75

Nos. 1355, 1358 are each 68x27mm. No. 1360 contains one 40x32mm stamp.

Cats
A216

200fr, Tortoiseshell short-hair. 250fr, Black and white short-hair. 300fr, Japanese. 400fr, Himalayan. 450fr, Brown long-hair. 500fr, Blue Persian. 1000fr, Tortoiseshell long-hair.

1996, Nov. 15   Perf. 12½
1361	A216	200fr multicolored	.85	.45
1362	A216	250fr multicolored	1.10	.60
1363	A216	300fr multicolored	1.40	.70
1364	A216	400fr multicolored	2.00	.95
1365	A216	450fr multicolored	2.25	1.00
1366	A216	500fr multicolored	2.40	1.10
		Nos. 1361-1366 (6)	10.00	4.80

Souvenir Sheet
1367	A216	1000fr multicolored	5.00	2.50

No. 1367 contains one 32x40mm stamp.

Birds — A217

Designs: 200fr, Carduelis cucullata. 250fr, Uraeginthus bengalus. 300fr, Lonchura castaneothorax. 400fr, Amadina erythrocephala. 450fr, Chloebia gouldiae. 500fr, Euplectes orix. 1000fr, Poephila guttata.

1996, Sept. 28   Perf. 12½
1368	A217	200fr multicolored	.85	.45
1369	A217	250fr multicolored	1.10	.60
1370	A217	300fr multicolored	1.40	.70
1371	A217	400fr multicolored	2.00	.95
1372	A217	450fr multicolored	2.25	1.00
1373	A217	500fr multicolored	2.40	1.10
		Nos. 1368-1373 (6)	10.00	4.80

Souvenir Sheet
1374	A217	1000fr multicolored	5.00	2.50

No. 1374 contains one 32x40mm stamp.

Orchids
A218

Designs: 200fr, Paphiopedilum millmoore. 250fr, Paphiopedilum ernest read. 300fr, Paphiopedilum harrisianum. 400fr, Paphiopedilum gaudianum. 450fr, Paphiopedilum papa röhl. 500fr, Paphiopedilum sea cliffl. 1000fr, Paphiopedilum gowenanum.

1997, Mar. 3	Litho.	Perf. 12½		
1375	A218	200fr multicolored	.90	.50
1376	A218	250fr multicolored	1.10	.60
1377	A218	300fr multicolored	1.25	.65
1378	A218	400fr multicolored	1.75	.90
1379	A218	450fr multicolored	2.25	1.00
1380	A218	500fr multicolored	2.50	1.10
		Nos. 1375-1380 (6)	9.75	4.75

Souvenir Sheet

1381	A218	1000fr multicolored	5.00	2.50

No. 1381 contains one 32x40mm stamp.

1998 World Cup Soccer Championships, France — A219

Various soccer plays.

1997, Jan. 15				
1382	A219	200fr multi, vert.	.90	.50
1383	A219	250fr multi, vert.	1.10	.60
1384	A219	300fr multi, vert.	1.25	.65
1385	A219	400fr multicolored	1.75	.90
1386	A219	450fr multicolored	2.25	1.00
1387	A219	500fr multicolored	2.50	1.10
		Nos. 1382-1387 (6)	9.75	4.75

Souvenir Sheet

1388	A219	1000fr Goalie at net	5.00	2.50

No. 1388 contains one 32x40mm stamp.

Wild Animals A220

Designs: 200fr, Giraffa camelopardalis. 250fr, Cerothoterium simun, vert. 300fr, Phacochoerus aethiopicus. 400fr, Acinonyx jubatus. 450fr, Loxodonta africana, vert. 500fr, Choeropsis liberiensis. 1000fr, Okapia johnstoni.

1997, Apr. 15	Litho.	Perf. 12½		
1389	A220	200fr multicolored	.95	.45
1390	A220	250fr multicolored	1.25	.65
1391	A220	300fr multicolored	1.40	.75
1392	A220	400fr multicolored	1.90	.95
1393	A220	450fr multicolored	2.10	1.00
1394	A220	500fr multicolored	2.40	1.25
		Nos. 1389-1394 (6)	10.00	4.95

Souvenir Sheet

1395	A220	1000fr multicolored	10.00	4.00

19th Century Warships — A221

Designs: 200fr, Captain, England, 1870. 250fr, Konig Wilhelm, Germany, 1869. 300fr, Téméraire, England, 1877. 400fr, Mouillage, Italy, 1866. 450fr, Inflexible, England, 1881. 500fr, Magenta, France, 1862. 1000fr, Redoutable, France, 1878.

1997, May 20	Litho.	Perf. 12½		
1396	A221	200fr multicolored	.95	.45
1397	A221	250fr multicolored	1.10	.55
1398	A221	300fr multicolored	1.40	.75
1399	A221	400fr multicolored	1.90	.95
1400	A221	450fr multicolored	2.10	1.00
1401	A221	500fr multicolored	2.40	1.10
		Nos. 1396-1401 (6)	9.85	4.80

Souvenir Sheet

1402	A221	1000fr multicolored	5.00	2.50

No. 1402 contains one 32x40mm stamp.

Fish A222

Designs: 200fr, Siganus trispilos. 250fr, Scarus niger. 300fr, Choerodon fasciata. 400fr, Naso lituratus. 450fr, Hypoplectrus gemma. 500fr, Acanthurus achilles. 1000fr, Zebrasoma flavescens.

1997, June 15	Litho.	Perf. 13		
1403	A222	200fr multicolored	.50	.25
1404	A222	250fr multicolored	1.10	.50
1405	A222	300fr multicolored	1.40	.60
1406	A222	400fr multicolored	2.00	.80
1407	A222	450fr multicolored	2.25	.90
1408	A222	500fr multicolored	2.25	.95
		Nos. 1403-1408 (6)	9.50	4.00

Souvenir Sheet
Perf. 12½

1409	A222	1000fr multicolored	5.00	2.50

No. 1409 contains one 40x32mm stamp.

Chess Pieces A222a

200fr, Thailand, 14th cent. 250fr, China, 1930. 300fr, Portugal, 1920. 400fr, Germany. 450fr, Russia. 500fr, Pieces by Max Ernst. 1000fr, France, 18th cent.

1997, Oct. 20	Litho.	Perf. 13		
1409A	A222a	200fr multi	.95	.45
1409B	A222a	250fr multi	1.10	.55
1409C	A222a	300fr multi	1.40	.70
1409D	A222a	400fr multi	1.75	.90
1409E	A222a	450fr multi	2.10	1.00
1409F	A222a	500fr multi	2.25	1.10
		Nos. 1409A-1409F (6)	9.55	4.70

Souvenir Sheet
Perf. 12½

1409G	A222a	1000fr multi	5.50	2.75

No. 1409G contains one 32x40mm stamp.

Dogs A223

1997, Nov. 10	Litho.	Perf. 12½		
Stamp plus Label				
1410	A223	200fr Siberian husky	.70	.35
1411	A223	250fr Dachshund	.85	.45
1412	A223	300fr Boston terrier	1.00	.50
1413	A223	400fr Basset hound	1.40	.70

1414	A223	450fr Dalmatian	1.50	.75
1415	A223	500fr Rottweiler	1.70	.85
		Nos. 1410-1415 (6)	7.15	3.60

Souvenir Sheet

1416	A223	1000fr Golden retriever	5.50	2.75

Nos. 1410-1415 are each printed with se-tenant label.

Prehistoric Animals — A224

200fr, Dilophosaurus. 250fr, Psittacosaurus. 300fr, Dromiceiomimus. 400fr, Stenonychosaurus. 450fr, Opisthocoelicaudia. 500fr, Ornitholestes. 1000fr, Anchiceratops.

1997		Litho.	Perf. 12½		
1417	A224	200fr multi	.75	.40
1418	A224	250fr multi, vert.	.90	.50
1419	A224	300fr multi	1.10	.55
1420	A224	400fr multi, vert.	1.50	.75
1421	A224	450fr multi	1.60	.80
1422	A224	500fr multi	1.90	.90
		Nos. 1417-1422 (6)	7.75	3.90

Souvenir Sheet

1423	A224	1000fr multicolored	4.25	2.10

No. 1423 contains one 40x32mm stamp.

UNICEF — A224a

Design: 200fr, Children at school, horiz. 300fr, Baby receiving inoculation, horiz. 750fr, Mother nursing child. 1500fr, Women reading, horiz.

1997		Litho.	Perf. 13¼		
1423A	A224a	200fr multi	—	—
1423B	A224a	300fr multi	—	—
1423C	A224a	750fr multi	—	—
1423D	A224a	1500fr multi	—	—

Butterflies — A225

200fr, Eueides cleobaea. 250fr, Danaus cleophile. 300fr, Dryas julia. 400fr, Dismorphia cubana. 450fr, Pyrrhocalles antiga. 500fr, Phoebis orbis. 1000fr, Morpho adonis.

1998					
1424	A225	200fr multicolored	.75	.40
1425	A225	250fr multicolored	.90	.50
1426	A225	300fr multicolored	1.10	.55
1427	A225	400fr multicolored	1.50	.75
1428	A225	450fr multicolored	1.60	.80
1429	A225	500fr multicolored	1.90	.90
		Nos. 1424-1429 (6)	7.75	3.90

Souvenir Sheet

1430	A225	1000fr multicolored	4.25	2.10

No. 1430 contains one 40x32mm stamp.

Environmental Protection Week

Mount Nimba and frame in: 200fr, Brown. 300fr, Blue. 750fr, Green.

1998		Litho.	Perf. 13¼x13½		
1430A-1430C	A225a	Set of 3	—	—

Domestic Cats — A226

200fr, English shorthair bicolor. 250fr, Scottish fold. 300fr, Birman. 400fr, American coarse hair. 450fr, Snowshoe. 500fr, Maine coon. 1000fr, Malaysian.

1998		Litho.	Perf. 12½		
1431	A226	200fr multicolored	.65	.30
1432	A226	250fr multicolored	1.00	.45
1433	A226	300fr multicolored	1.10	.60
1434	A226	400fr multicolored	1.50	.75
1435	A226	450fr multicolored	1.75	.90
1436	A226	500fr multicolored	2.00	1.00
		Nos. 1431-1436 (6)	8.00	4.00

Souvenir Sheet
Perf. 13

1437	A226	1000fr multicolored	4.25	2.10

No. 1437 contains one 32x40mm stamp.

Diana, Princess of Wales (1961-97) A227

Various portraits.

1998		Litho.	Perf. 13½		
Sheets of 9					
1438	A227	200fr #a.-i.	8.00	4.00
1439	A227	300fr #a.-i.	12.00	6.00
1440	A227	750fr #a.-i.	30.00	15.00

Souvenir Sheets

1441	A227	1500fr multicolored	10.00	5.00
1442	A227	2000fr multicolored	10.00	5.00

Dated 1997.

1998 World Cup Soccer Championships, France — A228

Various soccer plays.

1998		Litho.	Perf. 12½		
1443	A228	200fr multi, vert.	.75	.40
1444	A228	250fr multi, vert.	.90	.50
1445	A228	300fr multi, vert.	1.10	.55
1446	A228	400fr multi, vert.	1.50	.75
1447	A228	450fr multi	1.60	.80
1448	A228	500fr multi	1.90	.90
		Nos. 1443-1448 (6)	7.75	3.90

Souvenir Sheet
Perf. 13
1449 A228 1000fr multi   5.50 2.75

No. 1449 contains one 32x40mm stamp.

Old Germanic Military Uniforms
A228a

Designs: 200fr, Officer, Von Witerfeldt's Regiment. 250fr, Non-commissioned officer, Von Kanitz's Regiment. 300fr, Private, Prince Franz von Anhalt-Dessau's Regiment. 400fr, Private, Von Kalnein's Regiment. 450fr, Grenadier, Duke Ferdinand of Brunswick's Regiment. 500fr, Musician, Rekow's Guards Battalion.
1000fr, Pioneer.

1997, Aug. 17   Litho.   Perf. 12½
1449A-1449F A228a Set of 6   10.00 5.00

Souvenir Sheet
1449G   A228a 1000fr multi   5.00 2.25

No. 1449G contains one 32x40mm stamp.

Steam Locomotives — A229

200fr, Baldwin Locomotive Works, 0-4-2. 250fr, American Locomotive Co., 0-6-0. 300fr, Vulcan Iron Works, 0-6-0. 400fr, Baldwin Locomotive Works, 0-6-0. 450fr, H.K. Porter Co., 0-6-0. 500fr, Vulcan Iron Works, 0-6-0, diff.
1000fr, Baldwin Locomotive Works, 0-6-0, diff.

1997, Sept. 10   Litho.   Perf. 12½
1450-1455 A229 Set of 6   10.00 4.75

Souvenir Sheet
1456 A229 1000fr multicolored   7.00 3.50

No. 1456 contains one 40x32mm stamp.

Nectophrynoides Occidentalis — A230

Color of border: 200fr, green. 300fr, blue. 750fr, pale rose.

1998   Perf. 13½
1457-1459 A230 Set of 3   5.50 2.75

Intl. Year of the Ocean
A231

Marine life — #1460: a, Physeter macrocephalus, neophova cinerea. b, Melanogrammus aeglefinus. c, Delphinapterus leucas. d, Megaptera novaengliae. e, Notorhynchus cependianus. f, Manta birostris. g, Delphinaterusleucas, macrozoarces americanus. h, Physalia physalis, pollachius virens. i, Manta birostris. j, Odontapis taurus. k, Thalassoma ruppelli, octopus vulgaris. l, Sebestes marinus.
1500fr, Megaptera novaengliae, diff.

1998
1460 A231 200fr Sheet of 12, #a.-l.   8.00 4.00

Souvenir Sheet
1461 A231 1500fr multicolored   9.00 4.25

Antique Cars A232

200fr, 1932 Chrysler, 8 cylinders, US. 300fr, 1907 Napier, 60HP, England. 450fr, 1903 Mercedes, 60HP, Germany. 750fr, 1925 Fiat 509, Italy.
No. 1466: a, 1929 Alfa Romeo 6C 1750 Zagato, Italy. b, 1932 Hispano-Suiza Type 68, Spain. c, 1931 Horsch V12, Germany. d, 1909 Rolland Pilain, 16hp, France. e, 1920 McLaughlin, Canada. f, 1930 Walter 6B, Czechoslovakia.
No. 1467: a, 1914 Fischer SS, Switzerland. b, 1922 Excelsior Adex C, Belgium. c, 1912 Pilain Torpedo, France. d, 1932 Franklin, 6 cylinders, US. e, 1912 Abadal 18/24hp, Spain. f, 1923 Alvis 12/50, England.
Each 1500fr: No. 1468, 1925 Rolls Royce Phantom 1, England. No. 1468A, 1932 Ford V8, US.

1998, Aug. 21
1462-1465 A232 Set of 4   8.50 4.25

Sheets of 6
1466 A232 450fr #a.-f.   13.00 6.50
1467 A232 750fr #a.-f.   24.00 11.50

Souvenir Sheets
1468-1468A A232 Set of 2   18.00 8.50

Nos. 1468-1468A each contain one 56x42mm stamp.

Greenpeace — A233

Designs: a, Albatross looking left. b, Albatross in flight. c, Stern of Greenpeace ship, helicopter. d, Bow of Greenpeace ship. e, Albatross nesting. f, Albatross looking right.
2000fr, Albatross with chick.

1998   Litho.   Perf. 13½
1469 A233 450fr Sheet of 6, #a.-f.   10.00 8.00

Souvenir Sheet
1470 A233 2000fr multicolored   9.50 4.75

No. 1470 contains one 40x46mm stamp.

Endangered Species — A234

Designs, vert: 200fr, Lynx pardellus. 300fr, Lepilemur mustelinus. 450fr, Canis rufus. 750fr, Bison bonasus.
No. 1475: a, Leopard. b, Civet (f. c, Bird (d). d, Hawk. e, Rhinoceros, impala. f, Okapi (e, h, i). g, Lion. h, Chimpanzee. i, Gorilla. j, Bird (long, curved beak). k, Hippopotamus (l). l, Antelope (h).
No. 1476: a, Falco pereginus. b, Acinonyx jubatus. c, Antilocapre americana. d, Mustela nigripes. e, Ursus maritimus. f, Rhinoceros unicornis.
No. 1477: a, Gymnobelideus leadbeater. b, Felis concolor. c, Felis pardalis. d, Panthera pardus. e, Felis pardalis. f, Bufo hemiophyrs. Mustela rutorius.
Each 1500fr: No. 1478, Muscardinus avellanarius. No. 1479, Aepyceros melampus, vert. No. 1480, Panthera uncia.

1998, Sept. 8
1471-1474 A234 Set of 4   9.00 4.50
Sheets of 12 & 6
1475 A234 200fr #a.-l.   10.00 5.00
1476 A234 450fr #a.-f.   12.00 5.75
1477 A234 750fr #a.-f.   18.00 9.00
Souvenir Sheets
1478-1480 A234 Set of 3   24.00 12.00

Locomotives of the World — A235

No. 1481: a, Sir Nigel Gresley, England. b, Switzerland. c, Canada. d, EMU 102-6 Tobu Railway Spacia, Japan. e, Krauss Maffei V200, Germany. f, IC 580 Portugal. g, Amtrak No. 5, US. h, TGV, France.
No. 1482: a, Nippon Pacific No. 82, Middle East. b, Russia. c, Freight train, Albania. d, Dart No. 8319, Ireland. e, No. 141-F-177, France. f, EMU No. 69625, Norway. g, Bo-Bo, New Zealand. h, Azusa, Japan.
No. 1483: a, Syrian Railways 2-8-0, Iraq. b, The Irish Mail, England. c, Four car EMU, Italy. d, Sprinter, England. e, Van Golu Express, Turkey. f, No. 11.2110, Norway. g, Two-car EMU, New Zealand. h, Grey Mouse, France.
No. 1484: a, The Flying Scotman, United Kingdom. b, National Railways, Japan. c, North Africa. d, F-40M Winnebago, US. e, Federal Railways Class 10, three cylinder 4-6-2, Germany. f, DX5500, New Zealand. g, CIE, Ireland. h, Intercity class 43, England.
Each 1500fr: No. 1485, D2157, New Zealand. No. 1486, 140.7410, German Railways. No. 1487, JR Shinkansen 221-204, Japan. No. 1488, Egyptian Railways, Bo-Bo.

1998, Oct. 30
Sheets of 8
1481 A235 200fr #a.-h.   8.00 3.75
1482 A235 300fr #a.-h.   12.00 5.75
1483 A235 450fr #a.-h.   16.00 7.75
1484 A235 750fr #a.-h.   24.00 12.00
Souvenir Sheets
1485-1488 A235 Set of 4   30.00 15.00

Aircraft A236

Amphibians & flying boats — #1489: a, Boeing Model 1, 1916. b, Grumman G-21 Goose, 1937. c, Latecoere 631, 1942. d, Cessna Model 205. e, Sikorsky S-42, 1934. f, Boeing Model 314 Clipper. g, De Havilland Canada DHC-2 Beaver, 1947. h, Lake Buccaneer, 1979.
Balloons and Dirigibles — #1490: a, Henri Giffard, 1852. b, Santos-Dumont "Baladeuse," 1903. c, Zeppelin L37. d, R101, 1930. e, Santos-Dumont, 1898. f, Baldwin, 1908. g, Norge, 1926. h, Hindenburg, 1936.
Helicopters — #1491: a, Sikorsky VS-300, 1940. b, Sikorsky S-61, 1957. c, Bell Long Ranger, 1966. d, Dauphin SA 365, 1972. e, Bell 47, 1946. f, Boeing Vertol 243LR, 1958. g, Aerospatial SA 315 Blama. h, Bell Model 222, 1981.
Spacecraft — #1492: a, Mercury Capsule, 1961. b, Gemini 8, 1966. c, Apollo Lunar Module, 1968. d, Soviet Vostok, 1961. e, Apollo Command Module, 1968. f, Soviet Soyuz, 1975.
Each 1500fr: No. 1493, Cessna 208 Caravan, 1980. No. 1494, Goodyear Blimp. No. 1495, Miles Mi-26, 1983. No. 1496, Space Shuttle Columbia, 1981.

1998, Oct. 30
Sheets of 8 & 6
1489 A236 200fr #a.-h.   9.00 4.25
1490 A236 300fr #a.-h.   13.00 6.25
1491 A236 450fr #a.-h.   18.00 9.00
1492 A236 750fr #a.-f.   22.50 11.00
Souvenir Sheets
1493-1496 A236 Set of 4   20.00 10.00

No. 1489a incorrectly inscribed "1961."

Dinosaurs A237

No. 1497: a, Dicraeosaurus. b, Parasaurolophus. c, Sauronithoides. d, Dilophosaurus. e, Titanosaurus, bagaceratops. f, Iguanodon. g, Tenontosaurus. h, Dryosaurus. i, Ceratosaurus.
1500fr, Yangchuanosaurus, brachiosaurus.

1998   Litho.   Perf. 13½
1497 A237 750fr Sheet of 9, #a.-i.   27.50 13.50
Souvenir Sheet
1498 A237 1500fr multicolored   6.00 3.00

Minerals — A238

a, Calcite. b, Wolframite. c, Spodumene. #1500D: e, Psilomelane. f, Heterosite. g, Columbo-tantalite.

1998   Litho.   Perf. 13½
Strip of 3
1499 A238 750fr Green background, #a.-c.   10.50 5.25
Souvenir Sheets of 3
1500 A238 750fr Gray blue background, #a.-c.   10.50 5.25
1500D A238 1500fr #e-g   21.00 21.00

Sailing Ships — A239

No. 1501, each 450fr: a, "Theseus." b, "Euphrates." c, Phoenician War Galley. d, Chinese Junk.
No. 1502, each 450fr: a, "Juan Sebastian." b, "Santa Maria." c, Frigate. d, Madurese Jukung rig.
No. 1503, vert, each 750fr: a, Windjammer, "Wavertree." b, British frigate, "Rose." c, Tromp's flagship, "Golden Leeuw." d, Danish Timber Barque.
No. 1504, vert, each 750fr: a, Kraeck. b, Clipper ship, "Golden State." c, English ship, "Resolution." d, "Eagle."
Each 1500fr: No. 1505, British barque, "Garthpool." No. 1506, HMS Victory.

1998, Nov. 10   Perf. 14
Sheets of 4, #a.-d.
1501-1502 A239 Set of 2   16.00 7.75
1503-1504 A239 Set of 2   30.00 15.00
Souvenir Sheets
1505-1506 A239 Set of 2   15.00 15.00

Novotel Hotel, Conakry — A239a

1998　　Litho.　　Perf. 13x13½
1506A A239a 200fr multi — —
1506B A239a 750fr multi — —

The editors suspect that additional stamps may have been issued in this set and would like to examine any examples. Numbers may change.

Modern Guinean Arts

A239b

A239c

A239d

A239e

A239f

A239g

A239h

A239i

1998, Dec. 8　Litho.　Perf. 13¼x13
1506D A239b 750fr Dance — —
1506E A239c 750fr Painting — —
1506F A239d 750fr Ceramics — —
1506G A239e 750fr Sculpture — —
1506H A239f 750fr Sculpture — —
1506I A239g 750fr Dance — —
1506J A239h 750fr Painting — —
1506K A239i 750fr Painting — —

Horses
A240

Designs: 150fr, Trotteur Russe. 200fr, Brabant. 300fr, Camargue. No. 1510, 450fr, Unidentified breed. No. 1511, 450fr, Dales pony. No. 1512, 750fr, Fjord.
No. 1513, vert.: a, Kabardin. b, Shire. c, Arabian. d, Mustang. e, Quarter horse. f, Appaloosa.
No. 1514, vert.: a, Thoroughbred. b, Lipizzaner. c, Belgian. d, Palomino. e, Haflinger. f, Fjord, diff.
Each 1500fr: No. 1515, Mustang, diff. No. 1516, Thorougbred colt.

1999, May 1　Litho.　Perf. 14
1507-1512 A240 Set of 6　11.00 11.00

Sheets of 6
1513 A240 450fr #a.-f.　12.00 12.00
1514 A240 750fr #a.-f.　21.00 21.00

Souvenir Sheets
1515-1516 A240 Set of 2　17.00 17.00

Guinea — People's Republic of China Diplomatic Relations, 40th Anniv. — A240a

Designs: 200fr, Shown. 300fr, Building with flat roof, horiz. 750fr, Building with slanted roof, horiz.

1999　　Litho.　　Perf. 13¼x13
1516A A240a 200fr multi — —
1516B A240a 300fr multi — —
1516C A240a 750fr multi — —

Dogs
A241

Designs: 200fr, Newfoundland. No. 1518, 750fr, St. Bernard.
No. 1519, vert.: a, Bulldog. b, Miniature schnauzer. c, Dachshund. d, Beagle. e, Bloodhound. f, Miniature pinscher.
1500fr, Irish setter.

1999, May 1
1517-1518 A241 Set of 2　5.00 5.00

Sheet of 6
1519 A241 750fr #a.-f.　18.00 18.00

Souvenir Sheet
1520 A241 1500fr multi　8.00 8.00

Modern Guinean Sculptures — A241a

Various sculptures.

1999, Aug. 9　Litho.　Perf. 13¼x13
1520A A241a 200fr multi　2.40 2.40
1520B A241a 250fr multi　2.40 2.40
1520C A241a 300fr multi　2.40 2.40
1520D A241a 500fr shown　2.40 2.40
1520E A241a 750fr multi　2.40 2.40

PhilexFrance '99.

A242

Dinosaurs & Prehistoric Animals — A243

Designs: 300fr, Ouranosaurus. No. 1522, 450fr, Centrosaurus. No. 1523, 450fr, Dilophosaurus, vert.
No. 1524: a, Cymbospondylus. b, Kronosaurus. c, Ichthyosaurus. d, Eurhinosaurus. e, Stenopterygius. f, Ophthalmosaurus. g, Shonisaurus. h, Temnodontosaurus. i, Mixosaurus.
No. 1525, vert.: a, Eudimorphodon. b, Sordes. c, Dimorphodon. d, Albertosaurus. e, Triceratops. f, Alioramus. g, Mesosaurus. h, Labidosaurus. i, Struthiomimus.
No. 1526: a, Saltosaurus. b, Corythosaurus. c, Protoceratops. d, Baryonyx. e, Pachycephalosaurus. f, Maiasaurus. g, Spinosaurus. h, Lambeosaurus.
2500fr, Elasmosaurus, vert. No. 1528, Tyrannosaurus Rex. No. 1529, Utahraptor. No. 1530, Parasaurolophus, vert.

1999, Aug. 12
1521-1523 A242 Set of 3　5.00 5.00

Sheets of 9
1524 A243 350fr #a.-i.　15.00 15.00
1525 A243 450fr #a.-i.　18.00 18.00

Sheet of 8
1526 A242 450fr #a.-h　18.00 18.00

Souvenir Sheets
1527 A243 2500fr multi　13.00 13.00
1528 A243 3000fr multi　13.00 13.00
1529-1530 A242 3000fr Set of 2　28.00 28.00

No. 1527 contains one 42x56mm stamp. No. 1528 contains one 56x42mm stamp.

Return of Macao to People's Republic of China, Dec. 20, 1999
A244

No. 1531, each 650fr: a, Current view of Nam Van (tall buildings). b, Nam Van in 1850s (hilltop and bay). c, Current view of Largo de Senado. d, Largo de Senado in 1900s.
No. 1532, each 650fr: a, Current view of Nam Van (highway). b, Nam Van in 1850s (buildings at water's edge). c, Current view of Nam Van (boat). d, Nam Van in 1850s (ships).

1999, Aug. 20　Perf. 14¼x14½
Sheets of 4, #a.-d.
1531-1532 A244 Set of 2　24.00 24.00

China 1999 World Philatelic Exhibition.

Paintings of Zhang Daqian (1899-1983) — A245

No. 1533: a, Ink Lotus. b, Ink Peony. c, Red Cliff Excursion at Night. d, Poetic Landscape. e, Landscape in the Evening. f, Spring Landscape. g, Chatting at Leisure in Mountains. h, Pine Nesting. i, Pine in Thunder. j, Blue and Green Landscape.
No. 1534: a, Landscape. b, Versing in the Landscape.

1999, Aug. 20　Litho.　Perf. 13¼
1533 A245 330fr Sheet of 10, #a.-j.　15.00 15.00

Souvenir Sheet of 2
Perf. 13
1534 A245 1150fr #a.-b.　4.50 4.50

No. 1534 contains two 51x39mm stamps. China 1999 World Philatelic Exhibition

First French Postage Stamp, 150th Anniv. — A245a

Litho. with Hologram Applied
1999, Sept. 10　Perf. 13
1534C A245a 750fr multi　4.75 4.75

Trains
A246

100fr, Diesel TGV, East Germany. No. 1536, 200fr, 1900 horsepower Diesel-electric, Finland. No. 1537, 200fr, Type MLW 3000 horsepower Diesel-electric. No. 1538, 250fr, A-4, Britain. No. 1539, 250fr, Class R 4-6-4. No. 1540, 250fr, Class M, 4-6-2, Tasmania. No. 1541, 450fr, Class 68000 Diesel-electric, France. No. 1542, 450fr, 4-8-4 Daylight Express. No. 1543, 450fr, Electric TGV, Italy. No. 1544, 450fr, Western Class Hydraulic-Diesel.
No. 1545: a, Class 10 3-cylinder 4-6-2. b, SD18 Diesel-electric. c, Hikari Super Express Train, Japan. d, Diesel-electric No. 10000. e, PA-1 Diesel-electric. f, 2500 horsepower experimental gas turbine locomotive.
No. 1546: a, YP Class, India. b, Class 47, Standard Type 4 Diesel-electric. c, DSI Class 2-8-2, Japan. d, Class D-341 Diesel-electric. e, S1 Class 2-6-4. f, 3600 horsepower electric, India.
No. 1547: a, 2000 horsepower GP-20 Diesel-electric. b, Class C-53 3-cylinder, Japan. c, Multiple-unit Diesel, Japan. d, Royal Scot Class 4-6-0. e, Deltic electric prototype. f, W.P. Standard 4-6-2.
No. 1548: 2500fr, Class 40 electric, England.
Each 3000fr: No. 1549, GP-40 Diesel-electric. No. 1550, 9780 horsepower DM-3, Sweden. No. 1551, 1750 horsepower Diesel-electric, Denmark.

1999, Oct. 25　Perf. 14
1535-1544 A246 Set of 10　13.00 13.00

Sheets of 6
1545 A246 300fr #a.-f.　8.50 8.50
1546 A246 450fr #a.-f.　12.00 12.00
1547 A246 750fr #a.-f.　21.00 21.00

Souvenir Sheets
1548 A246 2500fr multi　11.00 11.00
1549-1551 A246 Set of 3　40.00 40.00

Mushrooms and Insects — A247

Mushrooms and unidentified insects: No. 1552, 100fr, Lentinellus cochleatus. No. 1553, 100fr, Lactarius blennius. No. 1554, Lactarius sanguifluus. No. 1555, 150fr, Leucocortinarius bulbiger. No. 1556, 300fr, Clitocybe phyllophila. No. 1557, 300fr, Calocybe ionides. No. 1558, 300fr, Lactarius porninsis. No. 1559, 300fr, Cystoderma amianthinum. No. 1560, 300fr, Limacella guttata. No. 1561, 450fr, Suillus placidus. No. 1562, 450fr, Suillus grevillei. No. 1563, 450fr, Suillus luteus. No. 1564, 450fr, Suillus granulatus. No. 1565, 450fr, Pleurotus cornucopiae. No. 1566, 450fr, Calocybe carnea. No. 1567, 450fr, Panus tigrinus.

Mushrooms and insects — No. 1568: a, Hygrocybe nigreseens, Argynnis paphia. b, Hygrocybe subglobispora, Pterophoridae. c, Oudemansiella mucida, Tettigonia viridissima. d, Amanita rubescens, unidentified insect. e, Amanita muscaria, Oedipoda caerulescens. f, Suillus luteus, Happarchia fagi. g, Coprinus picaceus, Aphantopus hyperantus. h, Gymnopilus junonius, Ourapteryx sambucaria. i, Amanita muscaria, Catocala nupta.

No. 1569: a, Macrolepiota procera, Pieris brassicae. b, Lactarius britannicus, Pyrochroa cocci. c, Cortinarius sanguineus, Tabicina haematodes. d, Amanita muscaria, Sympetrum. e, Aerocomus badius, Issoria lathonia. f, Laccaria amethystea, Sympetrum. g, Paxillus atrotomentosus, Inachis io. h, Armillaria mellea, Chrystoxum cautum. i, Amanita echinocephala, Vanessa atalanta.

Each 2500fr: No. 1570, Lactarius brittanicus, Coccinella punctala. No. 1571, Amanita phalloides, Ochlodes venatus. No. 1572, Coprinus atramentarius, unidentified insect.

Each 3000fr: No. 1573, Amanita citrina, unidentified insect. No. 1574, Amanita pantherina, Aperia syringaria.

1999, Nov. 11
1552-1567	A247	Set of 16	24.00	24.00

Sheets of 9
1568	A247	300fr #a.-i.	12.00	12.00
1569	A247	450fr #a.-i.	18.00	18.00

Souvenir Sheets
1570-1572	A247	Set of 3	35.00	35.00
1573-1574	A247	Set of 2	24.00	24.00

Birds
A248   A249

Designs: No. 1575, 200fr, Catamblyrhychus diadema. No. 1576, 200fr, Tichodrome. No. 1577, 300fr, Turtle dove. No. 1578, 300fr, Flamingo. No. 1579, 300fr, Duck. No. 1580, 300fr, Woodpecker. No. 1581, 450fr, Warbler. No. 1582, 450fr, Bullfinch.

No. 1583: a, Wild turkey. b, Ring-necked pheasant. c, Gray partridge. d, Woodcock. e, Capercaillie. f, Rock partridge.

No. 1584: a, Cuban hummingbird. b, Rufous-breated hermit. c, Green-throated hummingbird. d, Bee-eater. e, Puerto Rican hummingbird. f, Antillean hummingbird.

No. 1585: a, Gould's finch. b, Oriole. c, Psarismus dalhousiae. d, Woodchat shrike. e, Pitta guajana. f, Neodreponis coruscans.

No. 1586, horiz.: a, Purple-throated Carib. b, Bahamas hummingbird. c, Blue-bearded hummingbird. d, Green hummingbird. e, Jamaican hummingbird. f, Vervaine.

Each 2500fr: No. 1587, Spotted waxwing. No. 1588, Red-banded bee-eater.

Each 2500fr: No. 1589, Bahamas hummingbird, horiz. No. 1590, Antillean crested hummingbird.

No. 1591, 3000fr, Emerald hummingbird.

1999, Nov. 22
1575-1582	A248	Set of 8	10.00	10.00

Sheets of 6
1583	A248	450fr #a.-f.	12.00	12.00
1584	A249	500fr #a.-f.	15.00	15.00
1585	A248	600fr #a.-f.	16.00	16.00
1586	A249	750fr #a.-f.	20.00	20.00

Souvenir Sheets
1587-1588	A248	Set of 2	24.00	24.00
1589-1590	A249	Set of 2	24.00	24.00
1591	A249	3000fr multi	14.00	14.00

Butterflies
A250

Designs: No. 1592, 300fr, Acraea acerata. No. 1593, 300fr, Charaxes protoclea. No. 1594, 300fr, Charaxes hadrianus. No. 1595, 300fr, Colotis halimede. No. 1596, 300fr, Colotis eucharis. No. 1597, Papilio dardanus.

No. 1598, vert.: a, Papilio charopus. b, Papilio dardanus. c, Acraea zetes. d, Hypolimnas salmacis. e, Cymothoe beckeri. f, Papilio nobilis.

No. 1599, vert.: a, Iolaus lalos. b, Graphium gudenusi. c, Hewitsonia boisduvali. d, Graphium ucalegon. e, Danaus chrysippus. f, Acraea satis.

Each 2500fr: No. 1600, Euxanthe tiberius. No. 1601, Colotis danae.

1999, Nov. 22
1592-1597	A250	Set of 6	7.50	7.50

Sheets of 6
1598	A250	450fr #a.-f.	12.00	12.00
1599	A250	750fr #a.-f.	20.00	20.00

Souvenir Sheets
1600-1601	A250	Set of 2	24.00	24.00

Wedding of Prince Edward and Sophie Rhys-Jones
A251

No. 1602: a, Edward in blue striped shirt. b, Sophie with scarf. c, Edward looking left. d, Sophie looking right. e, Edward with blue checked shirt. f, Sophie with black blouse.

3000fr, Couple.

1999, Dec. 6
1602	A251	750fr Sheet of 6, #a.-f.	21.00	21.00

Souvenir Sheet
1603	A251	3000fr multi	14.00	14.00

Hokusai Paintings
A252

No. 1604, each 750fr: a, Actor Ichikawa Ebizo. b, Drawings (man with fan). c, Actor Sakata Hangoro. d, Geisha and Madam. e, Drawings (man with sword). f, Kabuki Actor Hanshiro IV.

No. 1605, each 750fr: a, Kintaro and Wild Animals. b, Drawings (man with clasped hands). c, Lady Walking in the Snow. d, Lady and Maiden on an Outing. e, Drawings (man with incense burner). f, Girls at Their Toilette.

Each 3000fr: No. 1606, Sumo Wrestlers. No. 1607, Geisha House and Madam at Leisure with Child.

1999, Dec. 6
Perf. 12¼
Sheets of 6, #a.-f.
1604-1605	A252	Set of 2	35.00	35.00

Souvenir Sheets
1606-1607	A252	Set of 2	27.50	27.50

Johann Wolfgang von Goethe (1749-1832), German Poet — A253

No. 1608, each 1000fr: a, Mephistopheles tempts Faust with Margaret. b, Goethe and Friedrich von Schiller. c, The witches' kitchen, a potion brewed.

3000fr, Euphorion.

1999, Dec. 6
Perf. 14
1608	A253	Sheet of 3, #a.-c.	14.00	14.00

Souvenir Sheet
1609	A253	3000fr multi	14.00	14.00

A254

A255

Space Exploration — A256

Designs: No. 1610, 300fr, Pioneer 10. No. 1611, 300fr, Viking 1.

No. 1612: a, Takao Doi. b, Frank Borman. c, Alan B. Shepard, Jr. d, M. Scott Carpenter. e, Ulf Merbold. f, David R. Scott. g, Mamoru Mohri. h, Gherman Titov. i, Sally K. Ride. j, Walter M. Schirra. k, John L. Swigert, Jr. l, Yuri A. Gagarin.

No. 1613, each 500fr: a, Venus. b, Neptune. c, Jupiter. d, Uranus. e, Saturn. f, Mercury.

No. 1614, each 500fr: a, Mariner 4. b, HL-20. c, Mariner 2. d, Voyager 1. e, Venture Star. f, Phobos.

No. 1615, each 750fr: a, 1961 drawing of lunar ferry. b, 1960 drawing of lunar lander. c, 1959 drawing of lunar lander. d, 1962 drawing of lunar lander. e, 1962 drawing of lunar lander trainer. f, 1961 drawing of lunar lander.

No. 1616, vert., each 750fr: a, Apollo 5. b, Apollo 6, c, Apollo 7. d, Apollo escape test. e, Apollo "Little Joe." f, Apollo 4.

No. 1617, 1500fr, John Glenn.

Each 1500fr: No. 1618, Apollo 11 command module, vert. No. 1619, Collecting moon rocks.

Each 3000fr: No. 1620, Viking, diff. No. 1621, Mars Global Surveyor. No. 1622, Sojourner.

1999, Dec. 9
1610-1611	A254	Set of 2	3.00	3.00

Sheet of 12, #a.-l.
1612	A255	450fr multi	27.50	27.50

Sheets of 6, #a.-f.
1613-1614	A254	Set of 2	24.00	24.00
1615-1616	A256	Set of 2	40.00	40.00

Souvenir Sheets
1617	A255	1500fr multi	8.00	8.00
1618-1619	A256	Set of 2	15.00	15.00
1620-1622	A256	Set of 3	26.50	26.50

Nos. 1620-1622 each contain one 50x37mm stamp.

Queen Mother (b. 1900) — A257

No. 1623: a, In 1934. b, With tiara. c, Lady of the Garter. d, In 1997.

3000fr, With tiara, diff.

1999, Dec. 6
Perf. 14
1623	A257	1000fr Sheet of 4, #a.-d., + label	19.00	19.00

Souvenir Sheet
Perf. 13¾
1624	A257	3000fr multi	14.00	14.00

No. 1624 contains one 38x50mm stamp.

Cats
A257a

Designs: 300fr, Ragdoll. No. 1626, 400fr, Egyptian Mau.

No. 1627, vert.: a, Tonkinese. b, Korat. c, Siamese. d, British Shorthair. e, Bengal. f, Persian.

1500fr, Calico Shorthair, vert.

1999
Perf. 14
1625-1626	A257a	Set of 2	3.25	3.25

Sheet of 6
1627	A257a	450fr #a.-f.	12.00	12.00

Souvenir Sheet
1628	A257a	1500fr multi	8.00	8.00

Romance of the Three Kingdoms
A258

No. 1629, each 460fr: a, Archer and four men. b, Two men and tea pot. c, Spear carrier, man, woman. d, Horsemen jousting. e, Four men.

No. 1630, each 460fr: a, Swordsman on white horse. b, Spear carrier on black horse. c, Bed chamber. d, Man being speared. e, At sea.

2000fr, Three men with tea cups.

1999
Perf. 13¼
Sheets of 5, #a.-e.
1629-1630	A258	Set of 2	20.00	20.00

Souvenir Sheet
1631	A258	2000fr multi	9.00	9.00

No. 1631 contains one 48x58mm stamp.

Millennium — A354

No. 1823 — Marco Polo's Voyages: a, Young Marco Polo. b, Piazza San Marco. c, Polo's ship. d, Priest buying incense. e, Houses in Syria. f, Ruins of Saveh. g, Persian ventilator. h, Moncia costume. i, Ulan Bator Abbey. j, Buddha, 5th cent. k, Great Wall of China. l, Warrior of Kublai Khan's Army. m, Ship on the Yangtze. n, Japanese archer. o, Golden plate. p, Medallion of Marco Polo, horiz. (60x40mm). q, Kublai Khan.

No. 1824 — Expansion of Knowledge: a, Election of King Sigismund I of Hungary as Holy Roman Emperor, 1411. b, Filippo Brunelleschi wins architectural contest to build the dome of the Santa Maria de Fiore, 1420. c, Lorenzo Ghiberti sculpts human forms on doors of the Florence Baptistry, 1425. d, Death of Juliana of Norwich, c. 1443. e, Chinese Ming capital moves from Nanjing to Beijing, 1420. f, Europeans begin to use Chinese method of black printing, 1423. g, King Henry V of England defeats French at Battle of Agincourt, 1415. h, Tamerlane defeats Ottomans at Battle of Ankyra, 1402. i, Joan of Arc leads French forces at Siege of Orleans, 1429. j, Korea prospers under rule of King Sejong, 1419. k, Thomas à Kempis writes *The Imitation of Christ*, 1427. l, King Casimir IV of Poland unites Polish Kingdom with Grand Duchy of Lithuania, 1447. m, End of the Great Schism, 1417. n, John Hus burnt at the stake, 1415. o, Medici family dominates the government of Florence, 1434. p, Chaucer completes *Canterbury Tales*, 1400, horiz. (60x40mm). q, Shogun Yoshima Ashikaga begins rule in Japan, 1449.

No. 1825 — Across the Continents: a, Engraving, c. 1598. b, Caribbean warriors. c, Viking ship, 12th cent. d, Ship of Vasco da Gama. e, Detail from Italian engraving. f, Columbus's letter of 1493. g, Kokyboom tree, h, Megalzinga virens. i, Details from a map, Moon between Earth and Sun. j, Details from a map, Earth between Sun and Moon. k, Maori wood carving. l, Astrolabes. m, Frilled lizard (inscribed "Gila monster"). n, White ibises. o, Tahitian utensils. p, Ocean monsters, horiz. (60x40mm). q, Samoan boat.

Perf. 12¾x12½
2000, Feb. 18   **Litho.**
Sheets of 17, #a-q, + Label

1823	A354	200fr multi	16.00	16.00
1824	A354	250fr multi	21.00	21.00
1825	A354	300fr multi	24.00	24.00
	Nos. 1823-1825 (3)		61.00	61.00

New Year 2000 (Year of the Dragon) — A355

No. 1826 — Dragon with background in: a, Red, claws near "Office." b, Green. c, Blue. d, Red, tail near "Office."
2000fr, Light blue.

2000, Feb. 18   **Perf. 13¾**

1826	A355	400fr Sheet of 4, #a-d	7.50	7.50

Souvenir Sheet

1827	A355	2000fr multi	9.50	9.50

No. 1826 contains four 48x32mm stamps.

Miniature Sheet

Vacation Photographs — A356

No. 1828: Various photographs making up a photomosaic of the Titanic.

2000, Feb. 18

1828	A356	750fr Sheet of 8, #a-h	27.50	27.50

2000 Summer Olympics, Sydney — A357

No. 1829: a, Women's discus. b, Javelin. c, Men's discus. d, Shot put. e, Hammer throw.

No. 1830: a, Women's volleyball. b, Water polo. c, Women's beach volleyball. d, Handball. e, Women's soccer.

No. 1831: a, Women's judo. b, Wrestling. c, Men's judo. d, Boxing, pink background. e, Boxing, green background.

No. 1832: a, Women's diving. b, Synchronized swimming. c, Women's swimming. d, Women's sailing. e, Kayaking.

No. 1833: a, Badminton. b, Field hockey. c, Baseball. d, Fencing. e, Weight lifting.

No. 1834: a, Dressage. b, Archery. c, Show jumping. d, Rifle shooting. e, Pistol shooting.

No. 1835: a, Table tennis, two men. b, Table tennis, one man, blue and purple background. c, Table tennis, one man, green and yellow background. d, Women's table tennis. e, Table tennis, four players.

No. 1836: a, Women's tennis, blue background. b, Men's tennis, green background. c, Women's tennis, bister background. d, Men's tennis, gray background. e, Men's tennis, blue background.

No. 1837: a, Women's basketball. b, Men's basketball (Michael Jordan dunking basketball). c, Men's basketball, two players. d, Men's basketball (Jordan dribbling). e, Men's basketball, blue background.

No. 1838: a, Cycling Road Race (Route). b, Cycling Sprint Race (Vitesse). c, Cycling Team Pursuit. d, Cycling Points Race (Kilometre). e, Cycling Time Trial (Contre la montre).

2000, Nov. 14   **Perf. 13¼**
Sheets of 5, #a-e, + Label

1829	A357	150fr multi	3.50	3.50
1830	A357	150fr multi	3.50	3.50
1831	A357	200fr multi	4.50	4.50
1832	A357	200fr multi	4.50	4.50
1833	A357	300fr multi	7.00	7.00
1834	A357	300fr multi	7.00	7.00
1835	A357	600fr multi	13.50	13.50

1836	A357	600fr multi	13.50	13.50
1837	A357	750fr multi	17.00	17.00
1838	A357	750fr multi	17.00	17.00
	Nos. 1829-1838 (10)		91.00	91.00

Sports and Chess — A358

No. 1839 — Golf: a, Golfer with purple cap. b, Golfer with white pants. c, Golfer with white cap. d, Golfer with green shirt.

No. 1840 — Soccer: a, Marcel Dessally. b, Zinedine Zidane. c, Youri Djorkaeff. d, Thierry Henry.

No. 1841 — Auto racing: a, Ayrton Senna. b, Mika Hakkinen. c, Alain Prost. d, Michael Schumacher.

No. 1842 — Chess: a, Player with hands on forehead. b, Player with blue jacket. c, Player with gray jacket. d, Female player.

2000, Nov. 14
Sheets of 4, #a-d

1839	A358	450fr multi	8.00	8.00
1840	A358	450fr multi	8.00	8.00
1841	A358	750fr multi	14.00	14.00
1842	A358	750fr multi	14.00	14.00
	Nos. 1839-1842 (4)		44.00	44.00

Locomotives — A359

No. 1843, horiz.: a, De Witt Clinton. b, American 220. c, Triplet Mallet. d, Philadelphia & Reading 422 Baldwin. e, Mason Bogie. f, Promontory Point 220 No. 119. g, Mogul. h, Best Friend of Charleston. i, John Bull.

No. 1844, horiz.: a, Union Pacific Bo-Bo-Bo-Bo. b, Bipolar No. 2. c, Burlington Northern-Series SD 40-2 No. 7044. d, Amtrak Metroliner No. 880. e, Rio Grande Western Series F. f, Union Pacific Series DD 40AX. g, Lake Superior & Ishpeming Co-Co 025C No. 2500. h, Chicago, Milwaukee, St. Paul & Pacific Bipolar 3000V No. 4. i, Southern Pacific Krauss-Maffei C-C No. 9006.

No. 1845, horiz.: a, Southern Pacific GM-EMD Series F No. 98. b, Union Pacific M-10001. c, Union Pacific Switcher No. 4466. d, Chesapeake & Ohio Series M No. 500. e, Amtrak Series P32 No. 513. f, Southern Pacific EMD SD 40-2 No. 9368. g, Great Northern Series W-1 No. 5018. h, Grand Canyon 140. i, Pennsylvania Railroad 6100.

No. 1846, horiz.: a, Burlington Northern Santa Fe No. 4326. b, Conrail Series GP EMD No. 8194. c, Kansas City Southern No. 6639. d, Southern Pacific No. 9800. e, Pennsylvania Railroad 661 No. 4835. f, Union Pacific No. 8182. g, Burlington Northern No. 2917. h, Gulf, Mobile & Ohio Railroad Series F. i, Santa Fe No. 627.

No. 1847, horiz.: a, Norfolk Southern No. 6627. b, Grand Trunk No. 6219. c, Soo Line No. 6401. d, Santa Fe BNSF No. 2512. e, Chessie System No. 6035. f, Utah Railway No. 9010. g, Chicago & Northwestern No. 6866. h, Norfolk Southern No. 3328. i, Canadian National No. 4634.

No. 1848, horiz.: a, Canadian Pacific Budd Autorail Diesel No. 9112. b, New York Central 2-Do-2 No. 113. c, British Columbia Railway Series C630 No. 703. d, Chesapeake & Ohio Series GP9 No. 6137. e, Amtrak 661 No. 902. f, Santa Fe GP9 No. 2293. g, Trainmaster Type Co-Co. h, Chicago, Burlington & Quincy Pioneer Zephyr. i, Denver & Rio Grande Western No. 5350.

No. 1849, 2000fr, Tom Thumb, 2-2-0. No. 1850, 2000fr, Norfolk & Western Class J. No.

1851, 2000fr, Royal Gorge CC No. 403. No. 1852, 2000fr, Hudson 4-6-4 No. 490.

2000, Dec. 7
Sheets of 9, #a-i

1843	A359	200fr multi	8.00	8.00
1844	A359	300fr multi	12.50	12.50
1845	A359	350fr multi	15.00	15.00
1846	A359	400fr multi	16.00	16.00
1847	A359	450fr multi	18.00	18.00
1848	A359	500fr multi	21.00	21.00
	Nos. 1843-1848 (6)		90.50	90.50

Souvenir Sheets

1849-1852	A359	Set of 4	32.50	32.50

Nos. 1843-1848 each contain nine 51x36mm stamps.

A360

First Zeppelin flight, Cent. — A361

No. 1853: a, Zeppelin LZ-11 Viktoria Luise. b, E. T. Willows. c, Hindenburg. d, Astra-Torres 1. e, Beta. f, Schutte-Lanz SL3.

No. 1854: a, Gross-Basenach M1. b, Schutte-Lanz SL1. c, Parseval PL25. d, Siemens-Schuckert. e, Delta. f, Parseval PL VIII.

No. 1855: a, LZ-9. b, LZ-10 Schwaben. c, LZ-11 Viktoria Luise, diff. d, LZ-127 Graf Zeppelin. e, LZ-129 Hindenburg. f, LZ-130.

No. 1856: a, LZ-1. b, LZ-2. c, LZ-3. d, LZ-4. e, LZ-5. f, LZ-6.

No. 1857, Graf Zeppelin and airplane. No. 1858, LZ-1, diff.

2000, Dec. 11   **Perf. 14**
Sheets of 6, #a-f

1853	A360	300fr multi	8.50	8.50
1854	A360	450fr multi	12.00	12.00
1855	A361	1000fr multi	27.50	27.50
1856	A361	1000fr multi	27.50	27.50
	Nos. 1853-1856 (4)		75.50	75.50

Souvenir Sheets

1857	A360	4000fr multi	20.00	20.00
1858	A361	4000fr multi	20.00	20.00

Miniature Sheet

Flowers — A362

No. 1859: Various photographs making up a photomosaic of Queen Mother Elizabeth.

2000, Dec. 11
1859 A362 750fr Sheet of 8,
#a-h 26.00 26.00

Prince William of Wales, 18th Birthday — A363

No. 1860: a, Wearing red tie. b, Wearing black and white checked tie. c, With Prince Harry. d, Wearing blue sweater.
4000fr, Wearing scarf.

2000, Dec. 11 *Perf. 14*
1860 A363 1000fr Sheet of 4,
#a-d 18.00 18.00
Souvenir Sheet
Perf. 13¾
1861 A363 4000fr multi 19.00 19.00

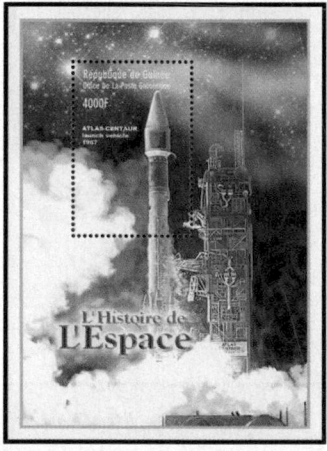

History of Space Exploration — A364

No. 1862, 200fr: a, Discovery of gunpowder. b, Fire arrows. c, Wan Hu's rocket glider. d, Konstantin Tsiolkovsky. e, Telescope of William Herschel. f, Galileo Galilei. g, Nicolaus Copernicus. h, Robert H. Goddard. i, Paper hot air balloons. j, Wernher von Braun. k, Launch of first rocket by Goddard. l, V-1 missile buzz-bomb.

No. 1863, 200fr: a, First American spacewalk by Ed White, Gemini 4. b, First man on the Moon, Apollo 11. c, Space Shuttle Atlantis. d, Voskhod 2. e, Sputnik 1. f, Apollo-Soyuz. g, John Glenn, first American to orbit Earth. h, Valentina Tereshkova, first woman in space. i, Yuri Gagarin, first man in space. j, Apollo 17. k, Robotic lunar explorer. l, Hubble Space Telescope.

No. 1864, 4000fr, Atlas-Centaur launch vehicle. No. 1865, 4000fr, International Space Station.

2000, Dec. 11 *Perf. 14*
Sheets of 12, #a-l
1862-1863 A364 Set of 2 ...... 17.00 17.00
Souvenir Sheets
1864-1865 A364 Set of 2 ...... 12.00 12.00

Apollo-Soyuz Mission, 25th Anniv. — A365

No. 1866, 1000fr: a, Saturn IB rocket. b, Apollo 18 command and service modules with docking adapter. c, Apollo 18 Commander Thomas P. Stafford. d, A-2 Soyuz rocket. e, Soyuz 19 spacecraft. f, Soyuz 19 Commander Alexei Leonov.

No. 1867, 1000fr, vert.: a, Lunar Module Eagle, upside-down. b, Lunar Module Eagle, with thrusters firing. c, Apollo 11 command module Columbia. d, Edwin E. Aldrin, Jr. on lunar module ladder. e, Apollo 11 Saturn V rocket. f, Re-entry of Apollo 11 capsule.
4000fr, Aldrin and lunar module on Moon.

2000, Dec. 11
Sheets of 6, #a-f
1866-1867 A365 Set of 2 ...... 42.50 42.50
Souvenir Sheet
1868 A365 4000fr multi 6.00 6.00

Marine Life — A367

Designs: No. 1873, 400fr, Coral grouper. No. 1874, 400fr, Candy cane sea star. 450fr, Hippocampus kuda.
No. 1876, 750fr: a, Chromis caerulea. b, Brittle star. c, Calloplesiops altivelis. d, Ewa blenny. e, Coral polyp. f, Butterflyfish.
No. 1877, 750fr: a, Chelonia mydas. b, Ptereleotris evides. c, Halichoeres iridis. d, Sea fan. e, Florometra serratissima. f, Gramma loreto.
No. 1878, 5000fr, Clownfish. No. 1879, 5000fr, Bigeye scad, horiz.

Perf. 13½x13¼, 13¼x13½
2001, Feb. 28
1873-1875 A367 Set of 3 ...... 5.50 5.50
Sheets of 6, #a-f
1876-1877 A367 Set of 2 ...... 40.00 40.00
Souvenir Sheets
1878-1879 A367 Set of 2 ...... 42.50 42.50

Marine Life A368

Designs: No. 1880, 400fr, Chaetodon semilarvatus. No. 1881, 400fr, Amphiprion ocellarus. No. 1882, 450fr, Gramma malacara. No. 1883, 450fr, Amphiprion bicinctuc.
No. 1884, 200fr: a, Diodon hystrix. b, Synchiropus splendidos. c, Lactoria cornuta. d, Canthigaster solandri. e, Gymnothorax tesselatus. f, Gramma loreto.
No. 1885, 200fr: a, Synchiropus picturatus. b, Pygoplytes diacanthus. c, Pomacanthus imperator. d, Holocanthus ciliaris. e, Phinecanthus aculeatus. f, Lienardella fasciatus.
No. 1886, 5000fr, Pterois antennata, vert. No. 1887, 5000fr, Hippocampus kuda, vert.

Perf. 13¼x13½, 13½x13¼
2001, Feb. 28
1880-1883 A368 Set of 4 ...... 7.50 7.50
Sheets of 6, #a-f
1884-1885 A368 Set of 2 ...... 11.00 11.00
Souvenir Sheets
1886-1887 A368 Set of 2 ...... 42.50 42.50

Marine Life — A369

No. 1888, 1000fr: a, Jackknife fish. b, Requiem shark. c, Great white shark (Grand blanc). d, Holocanthus ciliaris. e, Brain coral. f, Bluehead wrasse.
No. 1889, 1000fr: a, Sergeant major. b, Bottlenose dolphin. c, Swordfish. d, Sea horse. e, Slate pencil urchin. f, Gold-spotted snake eel.
No. 1890, 1000fr: a, Great white shark (Grand requin blanc). b, Baird's beaked whale. c, Butterflyfish. d, Turtle. e, Solenostomus paradoxus. f, Australian pineapple fish.
No. 1891, 1000fr: a, Hawksbill turtle. b, Killer whale. c, Manta ray. d, Filefish. e, Graysby. f, Striped-eel catfish.
No. 1892, 5000fr, Smooth trunkfish. No. 1879, 5000fr, Dolphin.

2001, Feb. 28 *Perf. 13¼x13½*
Sheets of 6, #a-f
1888-1891 A369 Set of 4 ...... 100.00 100.00
Souvenir Sheets
1892-1893 A369 Set of 2 ...... 42.50 42.50

Flora and Fauna — A370

No. 1894, 300fr — Bears: a, Spectacled bear. b, Giant panda. c, Silver bear. d, Cannelle (Pyreneean bear). e, Syrian bear. f, Grizzly bear.
No. 1895, 300fr — Primates: a, Howler monkey. b, Macaque. c, Drill. d, Yellow baboon. e, Anubis baboon. f, Gelada.
No. 1896, 300fr, vert. — Lemurs: a, Crowned lemur (couronné). b, Black lemur (macao). c, Albifrons lemur. d, Mongoz lemur. e, Sanfordi lemur. f, Fulvus lemur.
No. 1897, 300fr, vert. — Fish: a, Sebastes nigrocinctus. b, Lampris guttatus. c, Cyclopterus lumpus. d, Carnegiella strigata. e, Parosphromenus dreissneri. f, Syncniropus splendidus.
No. 1898, 300fr, vert. — Flowers: a, Peony (Pivoine des rocheuses). b, Hypericum richeri. c, Flamboyant. d, Bird of paradise (oiseau du paradis). e, Hesperantha petitiana. f, Moraea neopavonia.
No. 1899, 750fr — Lemurs: a, Lepilemur leucopus. b, Wooly avahi (avahi laineux). c, Black lemur (macao). d, Verreaux's sifaka (Propithecus verreauxi deckeni). e, Phaner. f, Verreaux's sifaka (Propithecus verrauxi majori).
No. 1900, 750fr — Flowers: a, Thunia alba. b, Eulophia guineensis. c, Polystacha bella. d, Oeceoclades maculata. e, Serapias cordigera. f, Angraecum distichum.
No. 1901, 750fr — Birds: a, Black cockatoo. b, Rosalbin cockatoo. c, Leadbetter's cockatoo. d, Goffin's cockatoo. e, Gray parrot. f, Senegal parrot.
No. 1902, 750fr, vert. — Owls: a, Hibou des marais. b, Hibou petit duc. c, Grand duc Americain. d, Chouette chevechette perlée. e, Hibou grand duc. f, Harphang des neiges.
No. 1903, 750fr, vert. — Insects: a, Giant Himalayan bee. b, Phyllium. c, Magicicada septemdecim. d, Petasida ephippigera. e, Graphosoma semipunctatum. f, Honeybee.

2001, Mar. 28 *Litho.* *Perf. 13¼*
Sheets of 6, #a-f
1894-1903 A370 Set of 10 ...... 140.00 140.00

Guinean Railways Locomotive A371

Design: 200fr, Front view. 300fr, Side view, horiz. 750fr, Rear view.

2001, May 16
1904-1906 A371 Set of 3 ...... 5.50 5.50
Nos. 1904-1906 each exist in souvenir sheets of 1, containing stamps lacking printer's inscription.

Locomotives — A372

Designs: 300fr, Union Pacific Jupiter. 400fr, No. 7200 Philadelphia. 600fr, C-28 Type 2-8-0. 800fr, Wainwright P Type 0-6-0. 1300fr, Union Pacific Rogers 119. 1600fr, Northwestern 4-6-0 steam engine.
No. 1913, 950fr: a, Oliver Cromwell. b, Big Boy 4-8-8-4 No. 4019. c, 1858 Rogers. d, Gray Lady. e, Old No. 1. f, Jones Goods 4-6-0.
No. 1914, 950fr: a, Jubilee Type No. SS96. b, Iron Horse. c, 4-6-0. d, Type OS2 2-10-0. e, Single Driver 1887 Johnson. f, King George V 4-6-0.
No. 1915, 950fr: a, Hardwicke Western 2-4-0, No. 790. b, High-wheeled Pacific, Texas State Railroad. c, Longhorne. d, City of Truro 4-4-0 No. 3440. e, Leander Type Jubilee. f, The American.
No. 1916, 4000fr, Stanier Black 5-4-6-0. No. 1917, 4000fr, LMS 5305. No. 1918, 4000fr, Duchess of Hamilton.

2001, June 8 *Perf. 13¼x13½*
1907-1912 A372 Set of 6 ...... 21.00 21.00
Sheets of 6, #a-f
1913-1915 A372 Set of 3 ...... 70.00 70.00
Souvenir Sheets
1916-1918 A372 Set of 3 ...... 55.00 55.00

Locomotives — A373

Designs: 500fr, Ae 6/6 Co-Co electric. 750fr, Hikari Super Express. 1000fr, Krauss-Maffei V200 Diesel-electric. 1250fr, 46 Type electric.
No. 1923, 950fr: a, EW Type Bo-Bo-Bo electric. b, 68000 Type Diesel-electric. c, Type Ge 6/6 electric. d, 19,000 horsepower Diesel-electric. e, Express Co-Co electric. f, AL6 Bo-Bo electric.
No. 1924, 950fr: a, 1,750 horsepower Diesel-electric. b, 7000 Co-Co electric. c, Type E10 Bo-Bo electric. d, D341 Type Diesel-electric. e, Diesel-hydraulic express. f, 5E1 electric.
No. 1925, 4000fr, Santa Fe F9 Diesel-electric. No. 1926, 4000fr, Type SSI Co-Co electric. No. 1918, 4000fr, Union Pacific electric.

2001, June 8
1919-1922 A373 Set of 4 ...... 15.00 15.00
Sheets of 6, #a-f
1923-1924 A373 Set of 2 ...... 45.00 45.00
Souvenir Sheets
1925-1927 A373 Set of 3 ...... 55.00 55.00
Belgica 2001 Intl. Stamp Exhibition, Brussels.

Locomotives — A374

Designs: 750fr, Type 18 4-6-2. 1000fr, ICE. 1250fr, Type G.
No. 1931, 950fr: a, Type WP 4-6-2. b, ETR 450. c, EU-07 Bo-Bo. d, Type 25 4-8-4. e, TGV. f, Type 345 Bo-Bo.
No. 1932, 950fr: a, Type SY 2-6-2. b, GM F7 War Bonnet. c, Type 4-4-0. d, Type A2/1 4-6-2. e, Type BB 22200. f, Type OL-49 4-6-2.
No. 1933, 4000fr, VT601. No. 1934, 4000fr, Type QJ 2-10-2.

2001, June 8
1928-1930 A374 Set of 3   13.00 13.00
Sheets of 6, #a-f
1931-1932 A374 Set of 2   45.00 45.00
Souvenir Sheets
1933-1934 A374 Set of 2   37.50 37.50
Belgica 2001 Intl. Stamp Exhibition, Brussels.

Famous People — A375

No. 1935 — Explorers: a, Vasco da Gama. b, Sir Francis Drake. c, Ferdinand Magellan. d, Capt. James Cook. e, Jacques Cartier. f, Christopher Columbus.
No. 1936: a, Albert Einstein. b, Albert Schweitzer. c, Henri Dunant. d, Sir Alexander Fleming. e, Marie Curie. f, Louis Pasteur.
No. 1937 — Space pioneers: a, Yuri Gagarin. b, John Glenn. c, Edward White. d, Neil Armstrong. e, John Young. f, Thomas Stafford and Alexei Leonov.
No. 1938 — Pope John Paul II: a, As baby, with mother and dove. b, Wearing miter and holding crucifix. c, In garden. d, Kneeling. e, Holding crucifix, with dove. f, With arms raised.
No. 1939 — Lord Robert Baden-Powell, Scouts and: a, Psittacus enthacus. b, Charaxes eupale. c, Pluvianus aegyptius. d, Catacroptera cloanthe. e, Merops albicollis. f, Euphaedra eupalus.

2001, June 14   **Perf. 13¼**
Sheets of 6, #a-f
1935 A375 350fr multi   10.00 10.00
1936 A375 450fr multi   12.00 12.00
1937 A375 475fr multi   13.00 13.00
1938 A375 600fr multi   16.00 16.00
1939 A375 750fr multi   21.00 21.00
     Nos. 1935-1939 (5)   72.00 72.00
Nos. 1936a-1936f and 1939a-1939f each exist in souvenir sheets of one.

Birds — A377

Designs: 200fr, Guinea fowl (pintade vulturine). 250fr, African fish eagle (pygarve vocifer). 300fr, Striped hoopoe (huppe fasciée). 350fr, Jacana. 400fr, Secretary bird (serpentaire). 450fr, Wild Guinea fowl (pintade sauvage).
No. 1948, 950fr: a, Verreaux's eagle (aigle de verreaux). b, White pelican. c, Swallow (hirondelle de rivage). d, Egyptian geese (ouette d'Egype). e, Crane (grue cendrée). f, Heron.

No. 1949, 950fr: a, Swallow (hirondelle de fenetre). b, Dwarf bee-eater (guepier nain). c, Blue rock thrush (merle solitaire rouge). d, Senegal jabiru. e, Ibis. f, Purple swamphen (talève sultane).
No. 1950, 950fr: a, Vulture (vautour chaugoun). b, Red and yellow barbet (barbican à tete rouge). c, Buzzard (buse rounoir). d, Tufted lark (cochevis). e, Gray wagtail (bergeronnette des ruisseaux). f, Red-heades shrike (pie grieche à tete rouge).
No. 1951, 4000fr, Flamingo (petit flamant). No. 1952, 4000fr, Anhinga. No. 1953, 4000fr, Marabout. No. 1954, 4000fr, Ostrich (autriche).

2001, Aug. 27   **Perf. 13½x13¼**
1942-1947 A377 Set of 6   8.50 8.50
Sheets of 6, #a-f
1948-1950 A377 Set of 3   52.50 52.50
Souvenir Sheets
1951-1954 A377 Set of 4   16.50 16.50
Phila Nippon '01, Japan (#1948-1954).

Birds — A378

Designs: 200fr, Heron. 300fr, Ibis. 500fr, Stonechat (tarier patre). 550fr, Sparrow (hirondelle striée). 600fr, Egyptian courser (pluvian fluviatile). 650fr, Jacana.
No. 1961, 750fr: a, Variable sunbird (souimanga à ventre jaune). b, Long-tailed sunbird (soui-manga à longue queue). c, Scarletchested sunbird (soui-manga à poitrine rouge). d, Abyssinian roller (rollier d'Abyssinie). e, Blue-breasted roller (rollier à ventre bleu). f, Broad-billed roller (rolle violet).
No. 1962, 750fr: a, Black bee-eater (guepier noir). b, Blue-headed bee-eater (guepier à tete bleue). c, White-throated bee-eater (guepier à gorge blanche). d, Red-throated bee-eater (guepier à gorge rouge). e, Rosy bee-eater (guepier gris-rose). f, Carmine bee-eater (guepier supreme).
No. 1963, 750fr: a, Blue-breasted kingfisher (martin-chasseur à poitrine bleue). b, Grayheaded kingfisher (martin-chasseur à tete grise). c, Chocolate-backed kingfisher (martin-chasseur marron). d, Dwarf kingfisher (martin-pécheur à tete rousse). e, Malachite kingfisher (martin-pécheur huppé). f, Giant kingfisher (alcyon géant).
No. 1964, 4000fr, Touraco. No. 1965, 4000fr, White-faced whistling duck (dendrocygne veuf). No. 1966, 4000fr, Denham's bustard (outarde du Denham).

2001, Aug. 27
1955-1960 A378 Set of 6   11.00 11.00
Sheets of 6, #a-f
1961-1963 A378 Set of 3   55.00 55.00
Souvenir Sheets
1964-1966 A378 Set of 3   52.50 52.50
Phila Nippon '01, Japan (#1961-1966).

A379

Butterflies — A380

Designs: 700fr, Icolotis zoe. 750fr, Catopsilia florella. 800fr, Kallimoides rumia. 850fr, Charaxes eupale. No. 1971, 950fr, Physcaeneura leda. 1000fr, Mylothris chloris.
No. 1973, 900fr: a, Papilio demodocus. b, Anaphaeis auroto. c, Charaxes superbus. d, Amauris echeria. e, Euxanthe wakefieldi. f, Papilio dardanus.
No. 1974, 900fr: a, Hypolimnas salmacis. b, Myrena silenus. c, Charaxes smagardus. d, Papilio zalmoxis. e, Salamis parnassus. f, Charaxes bohemani.
No. 1975, 900fr: a, Charaxes fournierae. b, Eurema floricola. c, Mimacraea marshalli. d, Charaxes candiope. e, Catacroptera cloanthe. f, Danaus chrysippus.
No. 1976, 950fr: a, Castalius isis. b, Axioceres amanga. c, Eurema brenda. d, Epamera stenogrammica. e, Pseudaletis agrippina. f, Alaena margaritalea.
No. 1977, 950fr: a, Papilio dardanus, diff. b, Charaxes eupale, diff. c, Acraea cerasa. d, Precis clelia. e, Colotis celimene. f, Pseudacraea poggei.
No. 1978, 4000fr, Papilio antimachus. No. 1979, 4000fr, Acraea zetes. No. 1980, 4000fr, Colotis danae.
No. 1981, 4000fr, Hypolimnas deceptor. No. 1982, 4000fr, Euphaedra perseis.

2001, Aug. 27   **Perf. 13¼x13½**
1967-1972 A379 Set of 6   20.00 20.00
Sheets of 6, #a-f
1973-1975 A379 Set of 3   21.00 21.00
1976-1977 A380 Set of 2   35.00 35.00
Souvenir Sheets
1978-1980 A379 Set of 3   52.50 52.50
1981-1982 A380 Set of 2   35.00 35.00
Phila Nippon '01, Japan (#1973-1982). Rectangles replace the accented "e's" on all stamps of type A280.

Hummingbirds — A387

Designs: No. 2038, 900fr, Anthracothorax manga. No. 2039, 900fr, Eulampis holosericeus. No. 2040, 1000fr, Archilochus colubris. No. 2041, 1000fr, Chlorostilbon ricordii.
No. 2042, 1000fr: a, Selasphorus rufus. b, Mellisuga helenae. c, Eutoxeres aquila. d, Anthracothorax viridis. e, Allamanda cathartica. f, Orthorhynchus cristatus.
No. 2043, 1000fr: a, Archilochus alexandri. b, Calliphlox evelynae. c, Chlorostilbon maugaeus. d, Musta ornata. e, Phaethornis superciliosus. f, Eulampis jugularis.
No. 2044, 1000fr: a, Cyanophaia bicolor. b, Glaucis hirsuta. c, Chlorostilbon swainsonn. d, Heliconia. e, Heliconia bihai. f, Anthracothorax dominicus.
No. 2045, 4000fr, Amazilia violiceps. No. 2046, 4000fr, Trochilus scitulus. No. 2047, 4000fr, Trochilus polytmus, vert.

Perf. 13¼x13½, 13½x13¼
2001   **Litho.**
2038-2041 A387 Set of 4   14.00 14.00
Sheets of 6, #a-f
2042-2044 A387 Set of 3   65.00 65.00
Souvenir Sheets
2045-2047 A387 Set of 3   47.50 47.50

Trains of Africa
A390

Designs: No. 2050, 750fr, 0-6-4, Z.A.S.M, Transvaal, 1858. No. 2051, 750fr, 4-6-2, Central South Africa, 1858. No. 2052, 750fr, 4-4-0, Cape Province, 1903. No. 2053, 750fr, 4-8-2 Class 12, South Africa, 1920. No. 2054, 750fr, 4-6-2 Class 10 RB, South Africa, 1950. No. 2055, 750fr, 4-8-2, Benguela, 1951. No. 2056, 750fr, 4-6-4+4-6-4 Class 15A, South Africa, 1952. No. 2057, 750fr, 4-8-4 Class 25 NC, South Africa, 1953.
No. 2058, 200fr: a, Cape Province locomotive, 1895. b, 2-8-2, Central South Africa, 1920. c, 4-4-2, Cape Province, 1898. d, 4-8-2 Class 23, South Africa, 1930. e, Natal Province locomotive, 1901. f, 2-8-4 Class 24, South Africa, 1940.
No. 2059, 300fr: a, 4-6-2 Class 16E, South Africa, 1935. b, 4-8-4 Class 25, South Afirca,

1953. c, 2-D-1+1-D-2 Class 20, South Africa, 1954. d, 4-8-2+2-8-4 Class 59, East Africa, 1955. e, 1-Co-Co-1 Class 92, East Africa, 1971. f, 2-D-2 Class 26, South Africa, 1982.
No. 2060, 750fr: a, 4-8-2 Class 15F, South Africa, 1948. b, 4-8-2+2-8-4 GEA Beyer-Garret, South Africa, 1950. c, 4-8-2 Class 11, South Africa, 1951. d, 4-8-2+2-8-4 GEA Beyer-Garret, South Africa, 1954. e, 1-Co-Co-1 Class 4E, South Africa, 1954. f, Co-Co Class 9E, South Africa, 1978.
No. 2061, 4000fr, Umtali-Salisbury Class 4-4-0, 1897. No. 2062, 4000fr, Bo-Bo Class 5E, Blue Train, South Africa, 1969.

2002, Feb. 8 Litho. Perf. 13¼x13½
2050-2057 A390 Set of 8   21.00 21.00
Sheets of 6, #a-f
2058-2060 A390 Set of 3   26.50 26.50
Souvenir Sheets
2061-2062 A390 Set of 2   12.00 12.00

Watercraft — A391

Designs: No. 2063, 750fr, Three-masted schooner, 1866. No. 2064, 750fr, Two-masted schooner, 1932. No. 2065, 750fr, Bark, 1968. No. 2066, 750fr, Sailboard. No. 2067, 750fr, Galleass, 16th cent., horiz. No. 2068, 750fr, Sailboat, horiz.
No. 2069, 750fr: a, Galleon, 16th cent. b, 17th cent. ship. c, Corvette, 18th cent. d, Gaffrig yacht. e, Dinghy. f, Catamaran.
No. 2070, 4000fr, Full-rigged ship, 20th cent., horiz. No. 2071, 4000fr, Pinnace, 17th cent., horiz.

Perf. 13½x13¼, 13¼x13½
2002, Feb. 8
2063-2068 A391 Set of 6   16.00 16.00
2069 A391 750fr Sheet of 6,
           #a-f   17.00 17.00
Souvenir Sheets
2070-2071 A391 Set of 2   12.00 12.00
Nos. 2070-2071 each contain one 56x42mm stamp.

Airplanes and Ships — A392

No. 2072, 750fr: a, Wright Brothers Flyer. b, Super Sabre F-100. c, Junkers J1. d, De Havilland Comet. e, Douglas DC-3. f, Boeing 747.
No. 2073, 750fr: a, Egyptian wooden boat. b, 18th cent. sailboat. c, Viking longboat. d, Great Eastern. e, Spanish galleon, 16th cent. f, Savannah.
No. 2074, 4000fr, Concorde. No. 2075, 4000fr, Ocean Princess.

2002, Feb. 8   **Perf. 13¼x13½**
Sheets of 6, #a-f
2072-2073 A392 Set of 2   9.25 9.25
Souvenir Sheets
2074-2075 A392 Set of 2   8.25 8.25

First Zeppelin Flight, Cent. — A393

No. 2076: a, LZ-3. b, LZ-5. c, USS Macon. d, Zeppelin NT.
No. 2077, 4000fr, LZ-4. No. 2078, 4000fr, LZ-129.

2002, Feb. 8
2076 A393 750fr Sheet of 4,
#a-d   12.00 12.00
Souvenir Sheets
2077-2078 A393 Set of 2   12.00 12.00

Airplanes — A394

No. 2079: a, Lockheed Streamliner. b, Dornier Do-X. c, Lockheed Vega. d, Boeing 707. e, Douglas DC-3. f, De Havilland Comet. 4000fr, Concorde.

2002, Feb. 8
2079 A394 750fr Sheet of 6,
#a-f   17.00 17.00
Souvenir Sheet
2080 A394 4000fr multi   6.00 6.00

Airplanes A395

Designs: No. 2081, 750fr, Tupelov TU-144. No. 2082, 750fr, Tri-star L-1011. No. 2083, 750fr, Airbus A-300-B. No. 2084, 750fr, Boeing 777-200.
No. 2085, 750fr: a, Junkers G-24. b, Armstrong Whitworth XV Atalanta. c, Aerospatiale SE 210 Caravelle III. d, De Havilland D. H. 106 Comet 4B. e, Armstrong Whitworth 650 Argosy 100. f, Douglas DC-9.
No. 2086, 750fr: a, Wright Brothers Flyer. b, Vickers Vimy. c, Spirit of St. Louis. d, Junkers G-38. e, Douglas DC-3. f, Vickers-Armstrong Viscount 700.
No. 2087, 4000fr, Boeing 747. No. 2088, 4000fr, Airbus A-3XX.

2002, Feb. 8
2081-2084 A395 Set of 4   11.00 11.00
Sheets of 6, #a-f
2085-2086 A395 Set of 2   32.50 32.50
Souvenir Sheets
2087-2088 A395 Set of 2   12.00 12.00

Military Aircraft A396

Designs: No. 2089, 750fr, Sopwith Camel. No. 2090, 750fr, Fokker Dr-1. No. 2091, 750fr, Messerschmitt Bf-109 E. No. 2092, 750fr, Mitsubishi Zero. No. 2093, 750fr, Northrop F-20 Tigershark. No. 2094, 750fr, Dassault-Breguet Mirage 2000.
No. 2095, 750fr: a, S.E. 5A. b, Fokker D-VII. c, Thomas Morse S4C. d, De Havilland D.H. 2. e, Boeing PW-9D. f, Spad XIII.
No. 2096, 750fr: a, Mustang P-51. b, Junkers Ju-87R. c, Curtiss Hawk 75A. d, Hawker Hurricane. e, Nakajima Ki-43 Hayabusa. f, Macchi M.C. 200 Saetta.
No. 2097, 750fr: a, Panavia Tornado Gr. Mk1. b, Mikoyan-Gurevich MiG-15. c, Vought

A-7D Corsair 11. d, BAe Sea Harrier FRS Mk1. e, General Dynamics F-111. f, Dassault/Breguet Dornier Alpha Jet.
No. 2098, 4000fr, Saab Draken J35. No. 2099, 4000fr, Supermarine Spitfire.

2002, Feb. 8
2089-2094 A396 Set of 6   16.00 16.00
Sheets of 6, #a-f
2095-2097 A396 Set of 3   52.50 52.50
Souvenir Sheets
2098-2099 A396 Set of 2   12.00 12.00

Antique Automobiles — A397

No. 2100, 1000fr: a, 1920 Rolls-Royce. b, 1896 Ford. c, 1930 Hispano-Suiza. d, 1924 Stoewer Allemagne D10 D12. e, 1924 Chrysler. f, 1912 Hudson.
No. 2101, 1000fr: a, 1930 Bugatti SIA. b, 1901 Mercedes. c, 1926 Jordan Playboy. d, 1936 Cadillac V-16. e, 1914 Stutz Bearcat. f, 1904 Daimler.
No. 2102, 4000fr, 1886 Daimler-Benz. No. 2103, 4000fr, 1903 Ford Model A.

2002, Feb. 8   *Perf. 13¼x13½*
Sheets of 6, #a-f
2100-2101 A397 Set of 2   42.50 42.50
Souvenir Sheets
2102-2103 A397 Set of 2   12.00 12.00

Race Cars A398

Designs: No. 2104, 750fr, Marmon Wasp, 1911 Indianapolis 500. No. 2105, 750fr, Ferrari Dino 246, 1958 French Grand Prix. No. 2106, 750fr, Lotus 49, 1967 German Grand Prix. No. 2107, Tyrell 003, 1971 American Grand Prix.
No. 2108, 750fr: a, Mercedes, 1914 French Grand Prix. b, Duesenberg, 1921 French Grand Prix. c, Bugatti, 1924 French Grand Prix. d, Alfa Romeo P3, 1934 French Grand Prix. e, Auto Union, 1937 Nürburgring Rally. f, Maserati 8C, 1939 German Grand Prix.
No. 2109, 750fr: a, Vanwall, 1957 British Grand Prix. b, Cooper T43, 1958 Argentine Grand Prix. c, Lotus 25, 1965 British Grand Prix. d, Brabham-Repro BT-19, 1966 French Grand Prix. e, Renault RS 01, 1977 British Grand Prix. f, Ferrari 640, 1989 Brazilian Grand Prix.
No. 2110, 4000fr, Coventry Daimler, 1899 Paris-Ostende Race. No. 2111, 4000fr, Penske PC-23, 1994 Portland Race.

2002, Feb. 8
2104-2107 A398 Set of 4   11.00 11.00
Sheets of 6, #a-f
2108-2109 A398 Set of 2   17.00 17.00
Souvenir Sheets
2110-2111 A398 Set of 2   12.00 12.00

Pres. John F. Kennedy (1917-63) — A400

No. 2113: a, With ship's wheel. b, With doves. c, With arch.
4000fr, At podium with flag and map.
Illustration reduced.

Perf. 13½x13¼
2002, Feb. 20   Litho.
2113 A400 750fr Horiz. strip of
3, #a-c   8.00 8.00
Souvenir Sheet
2114 A400 4000fr multi   7.00 7.00
No. 2113 printed in sheets of 2 strips.

Pres. Ronald Reagan (1911-2004) — A401

No. 2115: a, With stars. b, With curtain. c, With US Capitol.
4000fr, With Statue of Liberty and Presidential seal.
Illustration reduced.

2002, Feb. 20
2115 A401 750fr Horiz. strip of
3, #a-c   8.00 8.00
Souvenir Sheet
2116 A401 4000fr multi   7.00 7.00
No. 2115 printed in sheets of 2 strips.

Princess Diana (1961-97) — A402

No. 2117: a, Wearing tiara. b, Holding flowers. c, Wearing hat.
4000fr, Wearing black dress.
Illustration reduced.

2002, Feb. 20
2117 A402 750fr Horiz. strip of
3, #a-c   8.00 8.00
Souvenir Sheet
2118 A402 4000fr multi   7.00 7.00
No. 2117 printed in sheets of 2 strips.

Prince William of Wales — A403

No. 2119, 750fr: a, Wearing brown checked shirt. b, Wearing jacket and bow tie. c, Wearing green sweater. d, Wearing lilac sweater. e, Wearing brown suit, white shirt and blue tie. f, Wearing brown suit, striped shirt and blue gray tie.
No. 2120, 750fr: a, Wearing blue shirt. b, Wearing blue suit, blue background. c, Wearing riding helmet. d, Wearing blue suit, white background. e, Wearing blue sweater. f, Wearing ski gear.
No. 2121, 4000fr, With Prince Harry. No. 2122, 4000fr, With Prince Charles, horiz.

Perf. 13½x13¼, 13¼x13½
2002, Feb. 20
Sheets of 6, #a-f
2119-2120 A403 Set of 2   32.50 32.50
Souvenir Sheets
2121-2122 A403 Set of 2   14.00 14.00

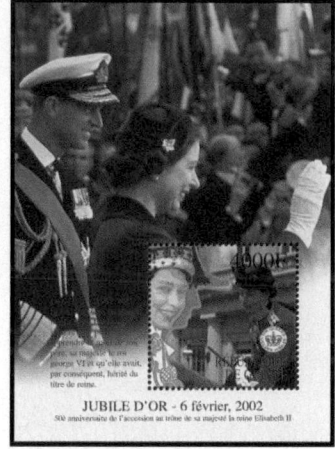

Queen Elizabeth II, 50th Anniv. of Reign — A404

No. 2123: a, Wearing blue coat and gloves. b, With Prince Philip. c, Wearing gray coat and hat. d, Wearing yellow suit and hat. 4000fr, Wearing red uniform.

2002, Feb. 20   *Perf. 14¼*
2123 A404 1400fr Sheet of 4,
#a-d   12.00 12.00
Souvenir Sheet
2124 A404 4000fr multi   7.00 7.00

A405

A406

Elvis Presley (1935-77) — A407

No. 2125 — Background color: a, Blue. b, Yellow. c, Red. d, Pink. e, Lilac. f, Yellow green.
No. 2126: a, Red and white shirt. b, Blue shirt. c, Black and brown shirt. d, Purple shirt. e, Red jacket with neckerchief. f, Red shirt.
No. 2127: a, Wearing red and white shirt with scarf. b, Wearing black jacket and gray shirt. c, Holding guitar on shoulder. d, With

hands resting on guitar. e, Singing. f, Wearing army uniform.

2002, Feb. 20   **Perf. 13½x13¼**
2125	A405	750fr Sheet of 6, #a-f	18.00	18.00
2126	A406	750fr Sheet of 6, #a-f	18.00	18.00
2127	A407	750fr Sheet of 6, #a-f	18.00	18.00

Nobel Prize Physics
Laureates — A408

No. 2128, each 750fr: a, Hendrik Lorentz, 1902. b, Pieter Zeeman, 1902. c, Sir Joseph Thomson, 1906. d, Gabriel Lippman, 1908. e, Max von Laue, 1914. f, Jean B. Perrin, 1926.
No. 2129, each 750fr: a, Owen Richardson, 1928. b, Sir Chandrasekhara Venkata Raman, 1930. c, Victor F. Hess, 1936. d, Carl D. Anderson, 1936. e, Sir George Thompson, 1937. f, Clinton Davisson, 1937.
No. 2130, each 750fr: a, Enrico Fermi, 1938. b, Ernest Lawrence, 1939. c, Isidor I. Rabi, 1944. d, Patrick Blackett, 1948. e, Fritz Zernike, 1953. f, Donald A. Glaser, 1960.
No. 2131, each 750fr: a, Alfred Kastler, 1966. b, Luis W. Alvarez, 1968. c, Murray Gell-Mann, 1969. d, John Bardeen, 1972. e, Leon N. Cooper, 1972. f, John R, Schrieffer, 1972.
No. 2132: 4000fr, Wilhelm Röntgen, 1901. No. 2133, 4000fr, Marie Curie, 1903. No. 2134, 4000fr, Pierre Curie, 1903. No. 2135, 4000fr, Antoine Henri Becquerel, 1903.

2002, Feb. 20   **Litho.**
Sheets of 6, #a-f
2128-2131	A408	Set of 4	72.50	72.50

Souvenir Sheets
2132-2135	A408	Set of 4	27.50	27.50

Nobel Prizes, cent. (in 2001).

Albert Einstein (1879-1955),
Physicist — A409

No. 2136: a, Smoking pipe. b, Wearing black jacket and tie, facing left. c, Wearing blue sweater. d, Wearing black jacket and tie, facing right. e, Wearing black sweater. f, Wearing brown jacket.
4000fr, With wife, Elsa.

2002, Feb. 20
2136	A409	750fr Sheet of 6, #a-f	17.00	17.00

Souvenir Sheet
2137	A409	4000fr multi	7.00	7.00

Pres. Theodore Roosevelt (1858-
1919) — A410

No. 2138: a, As Assistant Navy Secretary. b, In Cuba, 1898. c, In Yellowstone Park, 1903. d, As President, 1901-09. e, Campaigning for war preparedness, 1916. f, In 1917.
4000fr, As colonel in Rough Riders.

2002, Feb. 20   **Perf. 13¼**
2138	A410	950fr Sheet of 6, #a-f	21.00	21.00

Souvenir Sheet
2139	A410	4000fr multi	7.00	7.00

Jacqueline
Kennedy Onassis
(1929-94), First
Lady — A411

Designs: No. 2140, 1000fr, Wearing white blouse, yellow background. 2000fr, With Pres. John F. Kennedy, horiz. No. 2142, 4000fr, Wearing Inaugural Ball gown.
No. 2143: a, Wearing necklace, shoulders showing, green background. b, Wearing hat. c, Facing left, green background. d, Wearing necklace, orange background. e, Wearing necklace, shoulders covered, green background. f, Wearing sunglasses.
No. 2144, 4000fr, As child.

Perf. 13½x13¼, 13¼x13½
2002, Feb. 20
2140-2142	A411	Set of 3	26.00	26.00
2143	A411	1000fr Sheet of 6, #a-f	24.00	24.00

Souvenir Sheet
2144	A411	4000fr multi	7.00	7.00

Famous
People — A412

Designs: No. 2145, 750fr, Pres. John F. Kennedy (1917-63). No. 2146, 750fr, Pres. Ronald Reagan (1911-2004). No. 2147, 750fr, Chiune Sugihara, Japanese diplomat who saved Jews in World War II. No. 2148, 750fr, Queen Elizabeth II as younger woman, denomination at right. No. 2149, 750fr, Queen Elizabeth II wearing tiara, denomination at left. No. 2150, 750fr, Princess Diana (1961-97). No. 2151, 750fr, Queen Mother Elizabeth (1900-2002). No. 2152, 750fr, Prince William of Wales, denomination in red. No. 2153, 750fr, Prince William of Wales, denomination

---

in yellow. No. 2154, 750fr, Prince William of Wales, denomination in violet. No. 2155, 750fr, Hereditary Prince Haakon and Princess Mette-Marie of Norway, horiz. No. 2156, 750fr, Prince Philippe and Princess Mathilde of Belgium, horiz.

2002, Feb. 20   **Perf. 14**
2145-2156	A412	Set of 12	32.50	32.50

2002
Winter
Olympic
Games,
Salt Lake
City
A413

Designs: No. 2157, 750fr, Biathlon. No. 2158, 750fr, Luge. No. 2159, 750fr, Skiing. No. 2160, 750fr, Snowboarding, vert.

Perf. 13¼x13½, 13½x13¼
2002, Feb. 20
2157-2160	A413	Set of 4	11.00	11.00

Japanese Entertainment — A414

No. 2161, 750fr — Film stars: a, Miyoshi Umeki. b, Kimiko Ikegami. c, Masahiro Takashima. d, Sessue Hayakawa. e, Toshiro Mifune. f, Kaho Minami.
No. 2162, 750fr — Kabuki actors: a, Shinnosuke as Sukeroku. b, Kikugoro as Genkuro Kitsune. c, Ganjiro as Izaemon. d, Kikunosuke as Shiratama. e, Kikunosuke as Keisei. f, Shinnosuke as Matsuomaru.
No. 2163, 4000fr, Akira Kurosawa, film director. No. 2164, 4000fr, Danjuro as Kampei and Tamasaburo as Okaru, horiz.

Perf. 13½x13¼, 13¼x13½
2002, Feb. 20
Sheets of 6, #a-f
2161-2162	A414	Set of 2	32.50	32.50

Souvenir Sheets
2163-2164	A414	Set of 2	14.00	14.00

Scouts — A422

No. 2208 — Scouts and shells: a, 200fr, Cypraea caurica. b, 300fr, Olivella nana. c, 5000fr, Marginella persicula.
No. 2209 — Scouts and sea mammals: a, 200fr, Balaena mysticetus. b, 300fr, Tursiops truncatus. c, 5000fr, Delphinus delphis.
No. 2210 — Scouts and dinosaurs: a, 200fr, Spinosaurus. b, 300fr, Ouranosaurus. c, 5000fr, Kentrosaurus.
No. 2211 — Scouts and dogs: a, 200fr, Bouvier Bernois. b, 750fr, Chihuahua. c, 5000fr, Irish wolfhound.
No. 2212 — Scouts and meteorites from: a, 200fr, Tatahouine. b, 750fr, Gao-Guenie. c, 5000fr, Great Sand Sea.
No. 2213 — Scouts and cats: a, 300fr, Japanese bobtail. b, 750fr, Egyptian Mau. c, 5000fr, Bombay.
No. 2214 — Scouts and minerals: a, 300fr, Anglesite. b, 750fr, Brucite. c, 5000fr, Beudantite.

No. 2215 — Scouts and mushrooms: a, 300fr, Aseroe rubra. b, 750fr, Boletus edulis. c, 5000fr, Hygrocybe punicea.
No. 2216 — Scouts and butterflies: a, 300fr, Anaphe panda. b, 750fr, Eurema brigitta. c, 5000fr, Acraea zetes.

2002, Dec. 27   **Litho.**   **Perf. 13¼**
Sheets of 3, #a-c
2208-2216	A422	Set of 9	62.50	62.50

Each stamp exists in souvenir sheet of 1.

Nicolaus
August
Otto
(1832-91),
Engineer
A423

Wright
Brothers
and Wright
Flyer
A424

Astronaut Spacewalking — A425

Pierre de
Coubertin (1863-
1937), Intl.
Olympic
Committee
President
A426

Winston
Churchill,
Franklin D.
Roosevelt
and
Joseph
Stalin
A427

Newspaper
Mastheads
A428

Ferris
Wheels on
Film
A429

2002   **Perf. 13½x13¼, 13¼x13½**
2217	A423	200fr multi	1.60	1.60
2218	A424	300fr multi	1.60	1.60
2219	A425	750fr multi	1.60	1.60
2220	A426	1000fr multi	1.60	1.60
2221	A427	1250fr multi	1.60	1.60
2222	A428	1500fr multi	1.60	1.60
2223	A429	2000fr multi	1.60	1.60

Space — A430

Designs: No. 2224, 3000fr, Multi-scout Mars Lander. No. 2225, 3000fr, Stardust Probe. No. 2226, 3000fr, Mars Rover. No. 2227, 3000fr, Ceres-Vesta Probe. No. 2228, 3000fr, Deep Space Probe. No. 2229, 3000fr, NGST Space Telescope. No. 2230, 3000fr, Rosetta Probe. No. 2231, 3000fr, NEAR Probe.

No. 2232, 1500fr, horiz.: a, Newton Space Telescope. b, Darwin Space Telescope. c, Kepler Space Telescope. d, Herschel Space Telescope. e, Plank Space Telescope. f, Xeus Space Telescope. g, Mars Orbiter. h, Net Lander.

No. 2233, 1500fr, horiz.: a, Mission Specialist 4 Kalpana Chawla. b, Payload Commander Michael P. Anderson. c, Mission Specialist 1 David M. Brown. d, Pilot William C. McCool. e, Mission Specialist 4 Laurel B. Clark. f, Payload Specialist 4 Ilan Ramon. g, Commander Rick D. Husband. h, Columbia Space Shuttle.

No. 2234, 3000fr, Chawla, diff. No. 2235, 3000fr, Anderson, diff. No. 2236, 3000fr, Brown, diff. No. 2237, 3000fr, McCool, diff. No. 2238, 3000fr, Clark, diff. No. 2239, 3000fr, Ramon, diff. No. 2240, 3000fr, Husband, diff. No. 2241, 3000fr, Columbia Space Shuttle, diff. No. 2242, 6000fr, Corot Space Telescope, horiz. No. 2243, 6000fr, Crew of ill-fated Columbia Space Shuttle mission STS-107, horiz.

2003, Mar. 3			**Perf. 13¼**	
2224-2231	A430	Set of 8	25.00	25.00
	Sheets of 8, #a-h			
2232-2233	A430	Set of 2	30.00	30.00
	Souvenir Sheets			
2234-2243	A430	Set of 10	37.50	37.50

Nos. 2242 and 2243 each contain one 50x41mm stamp. Nos. 2224-2231 each exist in souvenir sheets of 1.

2004 Summer Olympics, Athens — A431

Designs: No. 2244, 750fr, No. 2252, 3000fr, Triathlon and Pentathlon. No. 2245, 750fr, No. 2253, 3000fr, Archery. No. 2246, 1500fr, No. 2254, 3000fr, Table tennis. No. 2247, 1500fr, No. 2255, 3000fr, Taekwondo and Judo. No. 2248, 1500fr, No. 2256, 3000fr, Equestrian. No. 2249, 1500fr, No. 2257, 3000fr, Women's tennis. No. 2250, 1500fr, No. 2258, 3000fr, Swimming. No. 2251, 1500fr, No. 2259, 3000fr, Track and field. No. 2260, 6000fr, Soccer.

2003, Nov. 12			**Perf. 13¼**	
2244-2251	A431	Set of 8	15.00	15.00
	Souvenir Sheets			
2252-2260	A431	Set of 9	30.00	30.00
2259a		Souvenir sheet, #2252, 2257-2259	12.00	12.00

No. 2260 contains one 36x51mm stamp.

Pope John Paul II (1920-2005) — A433

Pope: 100fr, Hugging man. 150fr, In vestments, with open arms. 200fr, Face. 300fr, Praying at microphone. 450fr, Blessing bishop. 500fr, Kissing ground and with arms raised. 550fr, With Black Madonna of Czestochowa. 600fr, Wounded in assassination attempt.

650fr, With man. 1000fr, With children and Virgin Mary. 1500fr, Handshake. 2000fr, With Lech Walesa. 2500fr, With people tearing down Berlin Wall. 7500fr, With crowd.

2004		**Litho.**	**Perf. 13x13¼**	
2263-2276	A433	Set of 14	12.50	12.50

SEMI-POSTAL STAMPS

Eye Examination — SP1

Microscopic Examination SP2

#B13, Medical laboratory. #B14, Insect control. #B16, Surgical operation.

Engraved and Lithographed

1960		**Unwmk.**	**Perf. 11½**	
B12	SP1	20fr + 10fr ultra & car	1.25	.60
B13	SP1	30fr + 20fr brn org & violet	1.25	.60
B14	SP1	40fr + 20fr rose lil & blue	1.60	.80
B15	SP2	50fr + 50fr grn & brn	2.50	1.25
B16	SP2	100fr + 100fr lil & grn	3.00	1.50
		Nos. B12-B16 (5)	9.60	4.75

Issued for national health propaganda. For overprints see Nos. B25-B29.

Nos. 194-195 Surcharged "1961" and New Value in Red or Orange

1961, June 6			**Photo.**	
B17	A17	25fr + 10fr (R or O)	7.00	3.50
B18	A17	50fr + 20fr (R or O)	7.00	3.50

Nos. B17-B18 exist with orange surcharges transposed: "1961 + 10FRS." on 50fr and "1961 + 20FRS." on 25fr.

Nos. 214-219 Surcharged in Green, Lilac, Orange or Blue: "POUR LA PROTECTION DE NOS ANIMAUX +5 FRS"

Photo., Surcharge Engr.

1961, Dec. 8				
	Multicolored Design; Granite Paper			
B19	A20	5fr + 5fr brt grn (G)	.40	.20
B20	A20	10fr + 5fr emer (G)	.50	.20
B21	A20	25fr + 5fr lilac (L)	.75	.35
B22	A20	40fr + 5fr org (O)	1.00	.45
B23	A20	50fr + 5fr red org (O)	1.40	.65
B24	A20	75fr + 5fr ultra (B)	2.00	.90
		Nos. B19-B24 (6)	6.05	2.75

The surtax was for animal protection.

Nos. B12-B16 Overprinted in Red or Orange

Engr. & Litho.

1962, Feb.			**Perf. 11½**	
B25	SP1	20fr + 10fr (R or O)	.50	.25
B26	SP1	30fr + 20fr (R or O)	.70	.35
B27	SP1	40fr + 20fr (R or O)	.80	.40
B28	SP2	50fr + 50fr (R or O)	1.60	.80
B29	SP2	100fr + 100fr (R or O)	3.25	1.60
		Nos. B25-B29 (5)	6.85	3.40

WHO drive to eradicate malaria. No. B25 also exists with black overprint.

Nos. 223-228 Surcharged in Red: "POUR LA PROTECTION DE NOS OISEAUX + 5 FRS"

Photo., Surcharge Engr.

1962, May 14			**Perf. 13x14**	
B30	A22	5fr + 5fr multi	.40	.20
B31	A22	10fr + 5fr multi	.50	.20
B32	A22	25fr + 5fr multi	.65	.20
B33	A22	40fr + 5fr multi	.90	.45
B34	A22	50fr + 5fr multi	1.50	.75
B35	A22	75fr + 5fr multi	3.50	1.75
		Nos. B30-B35 (6)	7.45	3.55

The surtax was for bird protection.

Nos. 232-233 Surcharged in Orange or Red and Overprinted: "Aide aux Réfugiés Algeriens"

1962, Nov. 1		**Litho.**	**Perf. 13**	
B36	A24	25fr + 15fr multi	.90	.45
B37	A24	75fr + 25fr multi	1.75	.90

Issued to help Algerian refugees.

Astronomers and Space Phenomena — SP3

1989, Mar. 7		**Litho.**	**Perf. 13½**	
B38	SP3	100fr +25fr Helical nebula	1.00	.40
B39	SP3	150fr +25fr Orion nebula	1.50	.80
B40	SP3	200fr +25fr Eagle nebula	2.25	1.00
B41	SP3	250fr +25fr Trifide nebula	2.75	1.10
B42	SP3	300fr +25fr Eta-carinae nebula	3.25	1.50
B43	SP3	500fr +25fr NGC-2264 nebula	5.25	2.40
		Nos. B38-B43 (6)	16.00	7.20
	Souvenir Sheet			
B44	SP3	750fr +50fr Horse's Head nebula	7.25	3.00

Nos. B42-B44 are airmail.

AIR POST STAMPS

Lockheed Constellation — AP1

Design: 500fr, Plane on ground.

Lithographed and Engraved

1959, July 13		**Unwmk.**	**Perf. 11½**	
	Size: 52½x24mm			
C14	AP1	100fr dp car, ultra & emer	2.75	1.00
C15	AP1	200fr emer, brn & lil	3.75	2.00
	Size: 56½x26mm			
C16	AP1	500fr multicolored	9.50	3.50
		Nos. C14-C16 (3)	16.00	6.50

For overprints see Nos. C24-C26, C52-C53.

Doves with Letter and Olive Twig — AP2

1959, Oct. 16		**Engr.**	**Perf. 13½**	
C17	AP2	40fr blue	.40	.20
C18	AP2	50fr emerald	.80	.40
C19	AP2	100fr dk car rose	1.40	1.00
C20	AP2	200fr rose red	2.50	1.75
C21	AP2	500fr red orange	7.00	3.00
		Nos. C17-C21 (5)	12.10	6.35

For overprints see Nos. C35-C38.

Admission to UN Type of 1959

Engr. & Litho.

1959, Dec. 12			**Perf. 12**	
	Size: 44x26mm			
C22	A16	50fr multicolored	1.10	.75
C23	A16	100fr multicolored	1.50	.90

For overprints see Nos. C27-C28.

Nos. C14-C16 Overprinted in Carmine, Orange or Blue: "Jeux Olympiques Rome 1960" and Olympic Rings

1960		**Litho. & Engr.**	**Perf. 11½**	
	Size: 52½x24mm			
C24	AP1	100fr multi (C or O)	9.75	4.25
C25	AP1	200fr multi (Bl)	17.00	8.00
	Size: 56½x26mm			
C26	AP1	500fr multi (C or O)	45.00	40.00
		Nos. C24-C26 (3)	71.75	52.25

17th Olympic Games, Rome, 8/25-9/11.

Nos. C22-C23 Overprinted

Engr. & Litho.

1961, Oct. 24			**Perf. 12**	
C27	A16	50fr multicolored	1.00	.40
C28	A16	100fr multicolored	1.50	.55

United Nations, 15th anniversary.

Mosquito and Malaria Eradication Emblem AP3

1962, Apr. 7		**Engr.**	**Perf. 10½**	
C29	AP3	25fr orange & blk	.65	.20
C30	AP3	50fr car rose & blk	1.00	.35
C31	AP3	100fr green & blk	1.75	.60
		Nos. C29-C31 (3)	3.40	1.15

WHO drive to eradicate malaria.

A souvenir sheet exists containing a 100fr green & sepia stamp, imperf. Sepia coat of arms in margin. Size: 102x76mm. Value $10.

Musician Type of Regular Issue

Musical Instruments: 100fr, 200fr, Kora. 500fr, Balafon.

1962, June 15		**Photo.**	**Perf. 13x13½**	
C32	A26	100fr brt pink, dk car & Prus bl	1.40	.50
C33	A26	200fr lt & dk ultra & car rose	2.75	1.25
C34	A26	500fr dl org, pur & Prus bl	9.00	4.00
		Nos. C32-C34 (3)	13.15	5.75

Nos. C17-C20 Overprinted in Carmine, Orange or Black: "La Conquête De L'Espace"

Perf. 13½

1962, Nov. 15		**Unwmk.**	**Engr.**	
C35	AP2	40fr blue (C or O)	.80	.25
C36	AP2	50fr emer (C or O)	.80	.35
C37	AP2	100fr dk car rose (B)	1.75	.70
C38	AP2	200fr rose red (B)	3.00	1.25
		Nos. C35-C38 (4)	6.35	2.55

The conquest of space. Two types of overprint: Straight lines on 40fr and 50fr in carmine, 100fr (black). Curved lines on 40fr and 50fr in orange, 200fr (black).

Bird Type of Regular Issue

Birds: 100fr, Hornbill. 200fr, White spoonbill. 500fr, Bateleur eagle.

1962, Dec.		**Photo.**	**Perf. 13x13½**	
C41	A30	100fr multicolored	3.00	1.10
C42	A30	200fr multicolored	5.00	2.40
C43	A30	500fr multicolored	12.50	4.75
		Nos. C41-C43 (3)	20.50	8.25

Sports Type of Regular Issue, 1963

Designs: 100fr, Running. 200fr, Bicycling. 500fr, Single sculls.

1963, Mar. 16 **Perf. 14**
C44 A32 100fr dp rose, sep &
grn   2.00   .80
C45 A32 200fr ol bis, ultra &
mag   4.50   2.00
C46 A32 500fr ocher, dk bl &
red   9.00   3.75
Nos. C44-C46 (3)   15.50   6.55

Butterfly Type of Regular Issue

Various Butterflies.

1963, May 10   Unwmk.   Perf. 12
C47 A33 100fr cit, dk brn &
gray   2.00   .35
C48 A33 200fr sal pink, blk &
green   6.25   2.40
C49 A33 500fr multicolored   10.50   4.50
Nos. C47-C49 (3)   18.75   7.25

Red Cross Type of Regular Issue

1963, July 25   Engr.   Perf. 10½
C50 A35 25fr black & car   .90   .20

Souvenir Sheet
Imperf
C51 A35 100fr green & car   4.00   3.00

Nos. C14-C15 Overprinted

Lithographed and Engraved
1963, Oct. 28   Perf. 11½
C52 AP1 100fr dp car, ultra &
emer   1.90   .70
C53 AP1 200fr emer, brn & lil   4.50   1.25

1st Pan American air service from Conakry to New York, July 30, 1963.

Fish Type of Regular Issue, 1964

100fr, African lyretail. 300fr, Six-barred epiplatys.

1964, Feb. 15   Litho.   Perf. 14x13½
C54 A36 100fr grn & multi   2.25   .55
C55 A36 300fr brn & multi   7.75   1.40

Kennedy Type of Regular Issue, 1964

1964, Mar. 5   Engr.   Perf. 10½
C56 A37 100fr multicolored   1.75   .80
See note after No. 327.

Olympic Type of Regular Issue

Design: 100fr, Women's ice skating.

1964, May 15   Photo.   Perf. 13x12½
C57 A39 100fr gold, brn org &
ind   2.25   .40

Nos. C44-C46 Overprinted in Carmine or Orange: "Jeux Olympiques Tokyo 1964" and Olympic Rings

1964, May 15   Unwmk.   Perf. 14
C58 A32 100fr (C or O)   1.90   1.40
C59 A32 200fr (C or O)   3.00   2.00
C60 A32 500fr (C or O)   7.00   5.00
Nos. C58-C60 (3)   11.90   8.40

18th Olympic Games, Tokyo, Oct. 10-25.

Mrs. Roosevelt Type of Regular Issue

1964, June 1   Engr.   Perf. 10½
C61 A40 50fr violet   .90   .25

Souvenir Sheets

Unisphere, "Rocket Thrower" and Guinea Pavilion — AP4

1964, Oct. 26   Engr.   Imperf.
C62 AP4 100fr dk bl & org   1.60   .80
C63 AP4 200fr rose red & emer   3.75   1.90
NY World's Fair, 1964-65. See Nos. C69-C70.

Nubian Monuments Type of Regular Issue

300fr, Queen Nefertari, Abu Simbel.

1964, Nov. 19   Photo.   Perf. 12
C64 A42 300fr gold, dl red brn &
sal   4.75   1.40
For overprint see No. C82.

Japanese
Hostess,
Plane and
Map of
Africa
AP5

1965, Jan. 18   Perf. 12½x13
C65 AP5 100fr gold, blk & red lil 1.75 .35
18th Olympic Games, Tokyo, Oct. 10-25, 1964. Two multicolored souvenir sheets (200fr vert. and 300fr horiz.) exist, showing different views of Mt. Fuji. Sizes: 86x119mm, 119x86mm. Value, both: $12.50 perf; $40 imperf.
For overprint see No. C81.

Mask Type of Regular Issue

300fr, Niamou mask from N'Zérékoré.

1965, Feb. 15   Photo.   Perf. 14
C68 A44 300fr multicolored   6.25   2.75

World's Fair Type of 1964 Souvenir Sheets

1965, Mar. 24   Engr.   Imperf.
C69 AP4 100fr green & brn   2.40   1.00
C70 AP4 200fr grn & car rose   4.75   2.50

Handicraft Type of Regular Issue

100fr, Cabinetmaker. 300fr, Ivory carver.

1965, May 1   Photo.   Perf. 14
C71 A45 100fr multicolored   1.50   .35
C72 A45 300fr multicolored   5.25   1.25

ITU Type of Regular Issue, 1965

1965, May 17   Unwmk.
C73 A46 100fr multicolored   1.25   .30
C74 A46 200fr multicolored   3.00   .75
Exist imperf.

ICY Type of Regular Issue, 1965

1965, Sept. 8   Engr.   Perf. 10½
C75 A50 100fr bl & yel org   1.25   .35

West Facade, Polytechnic Institute — AP6

Design: 200fr, North facade.

1965, Oct. 2   Photo.   Perf. 13½
C76 AP6 200fr gold & multi   2.10   1.00
C77 AP6 500fr gold & multi   6.00   3.00
Seventh anniversary of independence.

For overprints see Nos. C84-C85.

Moon Type of 1965

100fr, Ranger VII approaching moon, vert. 200fr, Launching of Ranger VII, Cape Kennedy, vert.

1965, Nov. 15   Litho.   Perf. 13½x14
C78 A52 100fr rose red, yel & dk
brown   1.00   .50
C79 A52 200fr multicolored   2.50   1.00
For overprints & surcharge see #C112-C112B.

Dancer Type of Regular Issue, 1966

100fr, Kandia Kouyate, national singer.

1966, Jan. 5   Photo.   Perf. 13½
Size: 36x28½mm
C80 A53 100fr multi, horiz.   1.50   .50

Engraved
Overprint
on No. C65

1966, Mar. 14   Photo.   Perf. 12½x13
C81 AP5 100fr gold, blk & red lil 1.25 .45
Fourth Pan Arab Games, Cairo, Sept. 2-11, 1965. The same overprint was applied to two souvenir sheets noted after No. C65 (red ovpt. on 200fr, black ovpt. on 300fr).

Engraved Dark Blue Overprint on No. C64: "CENTENAIRE DU TIMBRE / CAIRE 1966"

1966, Mar. 14   Perf. 12
C82 A42 300fr gold, dl red brn &
sal   2.75   1.50
Centenary of first Egyptian postage stamp.

Scenic Type of Regular Issue

View: Boulbinet Lighthouse.

1966, Apr. 4   Perf. 13½
C83 A54 100fr multicolored   1.40   .60
See #C90-C91. For overprints see #C93-C95.

Nos. C76-C77 Ovptd. in Blue or Yellow

1966, May 2   Photo.   Perf. 13½
C84 AP6 200fr multi (Bl)   2.25   1.10
C85 AP6 500fr multi (Y)   5.75   2.75
UNESCO, 20th anniv.

Woman-Flower Type of Regular Issue

Designs: Women and flowers of Guinea.

1966, May 30   Photo.   Perf. 13½
Size: 28x34mm
C86 A56 200fr multicolored   3.50   .70
C87 A56 300fr multicolored   5.50   2.10

Snake Type of Regular Issue

Designs: 200fr, Pastoria Research Institute. 300fr, Men holding rock python.

1967, May 15   Photo.   Perf. 13½
Size: 56x20mm
C88 A61 200fr multicolored   3.25   1.25
a.   Souv. sheet of 3, #471, 474, C88 9.00 6.50
C89 A61 300fr multicolored   5.50   2.25

Scenic Type of Regular Issue

Views: 100fr, House of explorer Olivier de Sanderval. 200fr, Conakry.

1967, June 20   Photo.   Perf. 13½
C90 A54 100fr multicolored   .95   .45
C91 A54 200fr multicolored   2.75   1.10
For overprints see Nos. C94-C95.

Elephant Type of Regular Issue, 1967

1967, Sept. 28   Photo.   Perf. 13½
C92 A63 200fr gold & multi   1.60   .75

Nos. C83 and C90-C91 Overprinted with Lions Emblem and: "AMITIE DES PEUPLES GRACE AU TOURISME 1917-1967"

1967, Nov. 6
C93 A54 100fr multi (#C83)   2.50   .90
C94 A54 100fr multi (#C90)   2.50   .90
C95 A54 200fr multi (#C91)   5.00   1.50
Nos. C93-C95 (3)   10.00   3.30
50th anniversary of Lions International.

Detail from Mural by José Vela Zanetti — AP7

Family, Mural by Per Krohg — AP8

The designs of the 30fr, 50fr and 200fr show mankind's struggle for a lasting peace after the mural in the lobby of the UN Conference Building, NY. The designs of the 100fr and of Nos. C98a-C98b show mankind's hope for the future after a mural in the UN Security Council Chamber.

1967, Nov. 11
C96 AP7 30fr multicolored   .40   .20
C97 AP7 50fr multicolored   .50   .20
C98 AP8 100fr multicolored   1.10   .35
a.   Souv. sheet of 3, English inscrip-
tion   3.00   3.00
b.   As "a," French inscription 3.00   3.00
C99 AP7 200fr multi   2.50   .50
Nos. C96-C99 (4)   4.50   1.25

Nos. C98a and C98b each contain a 100fr stamp similar to No. C98 and two 50fr stamps showing festival scenes. The 50fr stamps have not been issued individually.

People and Dwellings Type of Regular Issue

Design: 300fr, People and village of Les Bassari, Kundara Region.

1968, Apr. 1   Photo.   Perf. 14x13½
Size: 57x36mm
C100 A66 300fr gold & multi   4.50   1.25

Legends Type of Regular Issue

70fr, The Girl and the Hippopotamus. 100fr, Old Faya's Inheritance, vert. 200fr, Soumangourou Kante Killed by Djegue (woman on horseback). 300fr, Little Gouné, Son of the Lion, vert.

1968   Photo.   Perf. 13½
C101 A67 70fr multicolored   .90   .20
C102 A67 100fr multicolored   1.40   .30
C103 A67 200fr multicolored   2.75   1.00
a.   Souv. sheet of 4   7.00   7.00
C104 A67 300fr multicolored   4.00   1.25
Nos. C101-C104 (4)   9.05   2.75

Issued in sheets of 10 plus 2 labels. No. C103a contains 4 imperf. stamps similar to Nos. 510-511 and C102-C103.;
For souvenir sheet see No. 509a.
Issued: #C102-C103, 5/16; #C101, C104, 9/16.

African Animal Type of Regular Issue

1968, Nov. 25   Photo.   Perf. 13½
Size: 49x35mm
C105 A68 100fr Lions   2.75   .55
C106 A68 200fr Elephant   4.75   2.10
For souvenir sheet see No. 518a.

Robert F. Kennedy Type of Regular Issue, 1968

Portraits: 50fr, Senator Robert F. Kennedy. 100fr, Rev. Martin Luther King, Jr. 200fr, Pres. John F. Kennedy.

1968, Dec. 16

C107	A69	50fr yel & multi	1.10	.20
C108	A69	100fr multicolored	2.25	.20
C109	A69	200fr multicolored	5.00	1.25
		Nos. C107-C109 (3)	8.35	1.65

The stamps are printed in sheets of 15 (3x5) containing 10 stamps and five green and gold center labels. Sheets come either with English or French inscriptions on label.

Olympic Type of Regular Issue

Sculpture &: 100fr, Gymnast on vaulting horse. 200fr, Gymnast on rings. 300fr, High jump.

1969, Feb. 1   Photo.   Perf. 13½

C110	A71	100fr multicolored	1.25	.30
C111	A71	200fr multicolored	2.75	.90
C111A	A71	300fr multicolored	4.50	1.10
		Nos. C110-C111A (3)	8.50	2.30

Nos. C78-C79 Surcharged and Overprinted in Red

1969, Mar. 17   Litho.   Perf. 13½x14

C112	A52	25fr on 200fr multi	.50	.20
C112A	A52	100fr multicolored	1.25	.65
C112B	A52	200fr multicolored	2.40	1.00
		Nos. C112-C112B (3)	4.15	1.85

See note after No. 530.
Nos. C112-C112B also exist with surcharge and overprint in orange (25fr, 200fr) or black (100fr). These sell for a small premium.

Bird Type of Regular Issue

Birds: 50fr, Violet-crested touraco. 100fr, European golden oriole. 200fr, Vulturine guinea fowl.

1971, June 18   Photo.   Perf. 13
Size: 41x41mm

C113	A81	50fr gold & multi	1.40	.40
C113A	A81	100fr gold & multi	2.75	.80
C113B	A81	200fr gold & multi	6.00	1.25
		Nos. C113-C113B (3)	10.15	2.45

John and Robert Kennedy, Martin Luther King, Jr. — AP9

Embossed on Metallic Foil

1972   Die Cut Perf. 10½

C114	AP9	300fr silver	35.00	35.00

Embossed & Typo.

C114A	AP9	1500fr gold, cream & green	55.00	55.00

Jules Verne, Moon Rocket — AP10

Embossed on Metallic Foil

1972   Die Cut Perf. 10½

C115	AP10	300fr silver	35.00	35.00
C115A	AP10	1200fr gold	85.00	85.00

Richard Nixon — AP11

Nixon and Mao — AP12

Nixon's Trip to People's Republic of China: a, Nixon. b, Chinese table tennis player. c, American table tennis player, Capitol dome. d, Mao Tse-tung.

Embossed on Metallic Foil

1972   Die Cut Perf. 10½

C116	AP11	90fr Block of 4, #a.-d., silver	27.50	27.50
C117	AP11	290fr Block of 4, #a.-d., gold	45.00	45.00

Embossed & Typo.

C118	AP12	1200fr gold & red	70.00	70.00

Perforations within blocks of 4 are perf. 11.

Racial Equality Year Type of Regular Issue

Design: 100fr, Men of 4 races and racial equality emblem (like No. 603).

1972, May 14   Photo.   Perf. 13x13½

C119	A84	100fr gold & multi	1.50	1.00

Satellite Type of Regular Issue

Designs: 100fr, Map of Africa and Relay. 200fr, Map of Africa and Early Bird.

1972, May 17   Litho.   Perf. 13

C120	A85	100fr yel & multi	1.40	.70
C121	A85	200fr multicolored	3.00	1.40

African Postal Union Type of Regular Issue

Air mail envelope and UPAF emblem.

1972, July 10

C122	A86	100fr multicolored	1.00	.55
C123	A86	200fr multicolored	1.90	1.25

Olympic Type of Regular Issue

1972, Aug. 26   Photo.   Perf. 13

C124	A88	100fr Gymnast on rings	2.40	.60
C125	A88	200fr Bicycling	3.75	1.10

Souvenir Sheet

C126	A88	300fr Soccer	7.00	7.00

Flower Type of 1974

1974, May 20   Photo.   Perf. 13
Size: 38x38mm (Diamond)

C127	A97	20s Thunbergia alata	3.50	.95
C128	A97	25s Diascia barberae	4.25	1.10
C129	A97	50s Kigelia africana	10.00	2.75
		Nos. C127-C129 (3)	17.75	4.80

Olympic Games Type of 1976
Souvenir Sheet

1976, May 17   Photo.   Perf. 13½

C130		Sheet of 4	16.00	12.50
a.		A104 25s Soccer	2.50	2.50

No. C130 contains 32x32mm stamps.

Mushroom Type of 1977

Mushrooms: 10s, Morchella esculenta. 12s, Lepiota procera. 15s, Cantharellus cibarius.

1977, Feb. 6   Photo.   Perf. 13
Size: 48x31mm

C131	A106	10s multicolored	4.50	.70
C132	A106	12s multicolored	6.25	.90
C133	A106	15s multicolored	8.25	2.10
		Nos. C131-C133 (3)	19.00	3.70

Reptile Type of 1977

Reptiles: 10s, Flap-necked chameleon. 15s, Nile crocodiles. 25s, Painted tortoise.

1977, Oct. 10   Photo.   Perf. 13½
Size: 46x30mm

C134	A109	10s multicolored	4.25	.80
C135	A109	15s multicolored	5.50	1.10
C136	A109	25s multicolored	8.00	1.60
		Nos. C134-C136 (3)	17.75	3.50

Animal Type of 1977

Endangered Animals: 5s, Eland. 8s, Pygmy elephant. 9s, Hippopotamus. 10s, Chimpanzee. 12s, Palm squirrel. 13s, Lion. Male, female and young of each animal shown.

1977, Dec. 12   Photo.   Perf. 14x13½

C137	A110	Strip of 3	4.00	1.75
a.-c.		5s any single	1.10	
C138	A110	Strip of 3	6.25	2.75
a.-c.		8s any single	1.90	
C139	A110	Strip of 3	6.75	3.00
a.-c.		9s any single	2.00	
C140	A110	Strip of 3	7.00	3.50
a.-c.		10s any single	2.10	
C141	A110	Strip of 3	8.50	4.00
a.-c.		12s any single	2.50	
C142	A110	Strip of 3	9.75	5.00
a.-c.		13s any single	3.00	
		Nos. C137-C142 (6)	42.25	20.00

Russian Revolution Type, 1978

10s, Russian ballet. 30s, Pushkin Monument.

1978, Feb. 27   Photo.   Perf. 14

C143	A111	10s gold & multi	2.75	.80
C144	A111	30s gold & multi	8.00	2.10

Giscard d'Estaing Type of 1979

Pres. Valery Giscard d'Estaing of France, vert.

1979, Sept. 14   Photo.   Perf. 13

C145	A112	25s multicolored	7.00	2.00

Jules Verne Type of 1979

Designs: 20s, Five Weeks in a Balloon. 25s, Robur the Conqueror.

1979, Nov. 8   Litho.   Perf. 12x12½

C146	A113	20s multicolored	3.50	1.25
C147	A113	25s multicolored	3.50	1.25

Olympic Type of 1982

1982   Litho.   Perf. 12½x12, 12x12½

C148	A120	9s Fencing	1.60	.45
C149	A120	10s Soccer, vert.	1.90	.45
C150	A120	11s Basketball, vert.	2.25	.45
C151	A120	20s Diving, vert.	4.00	1.10
C152	A120	25s Boxing, vert.	4.75	1.50
		Nos. C148-C152 (5)	14.50	3.95

Ataturk Type of 1982

1982, July 19   Photo.   Perf. 13½

C153	A122	25s like #830	5.00	1.25

World Cup Type of 1982

Designs: Various soccer players.

1982, Aug. 23

C154	A123	10s multicolored	2.60	.95
C155	A123	20s multicolored	5.50	2.10
C156	A123	25s multicolored	6.50	2.75
		Nos. C154-C156 (3)	14.60	5.80

Nos. C154-C156 Overprinted like #835-838

1982, Aug. 23   Photo.   Perf. 13½

C157	A123	10s multicolored	2.40	.75
C158	A123	20s multicolored	5.00	1.75
C159	A123	25s multicolored	6.00	2.00
		Nos. C157-C159 (3)	13.40	4.50

Location of flag in overprint varies.

Balloon Type

Designs: 20s, Graf Zeppelin, Airship, horiz. 25s, Double Eagle II, L. Newman, B. Abruzzo, M. Anderson. 30s, Le Geant Hot Air Balloon, Nadar; Dirigible, Dumont.

1983, Aug. 1   Litho.   Perf. 13½

C160	A125	20s multicolored	3.25	1.25
C161	A125	25s multicolored	3.75	1.75

Souvenir Sheet

C162	A125	30s multicolored	5.00	1.90

Nos. 894, 880-881 and 896 Overprinted

1985, Nov. 5   Litho.   Perf. 13½

C163	A133	20s "80c Anniversaire / 1905-1985"	2.75	1.25
C164	A131	20s "Rassemblement / Jambville-1985"	2.75	1.25
C165	A131	25s "80e Anniversaire / 1905-1985"	3.50	1.50
		Nos. C163-C165 (3)	9.00	4.00

Souvenir Sheet

C166	A133	30s "Kasparov / champion / du Monde"	15.00	10.00

US Space Shuttle Challenger Explosion, Jan. 28, 1986 — AP13

Designs: 100fr, Lift-off, crew names. 170fr, Shuttle design, Christa McAuliffe holding shuttle model. 600fr, Lift-off, vert.

1986, July 1
100fr, 170fr Surcharged in Silver and Black

C167	AP13	100fr multicolored	1.10	.30
C168	AP13	170fr multicolored	1.90	.50

Souvenir Sheet

C169	AP13	600fr multicolored	7.00	2.75

#C167-C168 not issued without surcharge. Souvenir sheets of one exist containing Nos. C167 and C168.

Robin Yount, Milwaukee Brewers Baseball Player — AP14

1990, Aug. 3   Litho.   Perf. 13½

C170	AP14	450fr multicolored	5.00	2.10

No. C170 exists in a souvenir sheet of 1. For surcharge see No. 1182R.

Souvenir Sheet

Armstrong, Aldrin, Collins and Apollo 11 Emblem — AP15

1990, Aug. 3   Litho.   Perf. 13½

C171	AP15	750fr multicolored	8.00	3.25

Galileo Spacecraft — AP16

1990, Aug. 3
C172 AP16 500fr multicolored　　5.25　2.25
No. C172 exists as a souvenir sheet of 1.

Pope John
Paul II,
Visit to
Africa
AP18

Portrait and: No. C174, Raising hand in benediction. No. C175, Child.

Litho. & Embossed
1992, Oct. 26　　　　　**Perf. 13½**
C174 AP18 1500fr gold & multi　24.00　19.00
Souvenir Sheet
C175 AP18 1500fr gold & multi　18.00　15.00
No. C175 exists imperf.

Elvis Presley, 15th Anniv. of
Death — AP19

1992, Nov. 10
C176 AP19 1500fr gold & multi　24.00　20.00
No. C176 exists in miniature sheet of one.

De Gaulle Type of 1991 Overprinted
"6 JUNE 1944 / DEBARQUEMENT"

1994　Litho. & Embossed　Perf. 13½
C177 A181 1500fr like #1168　15.00　12.50

No. 1195 Ovptd. in Silver
"RENCONTHE / FISCHER-SPASSKY /
4 SEPT au 5 NOV 1992 /
AU MONTENEGRO"

1993, Feb. 24　Litho.　Perf. 13½
C178 A188 450fr multicolored　　4.50　2.25
No. C178 exists in souvenir sheet of 1.

POSTAGE DUE STAMPS

　D5　　　　　　　D6

1959　　Unwmk.　Litho.　Perf. 11½
J36 D5 1fr emerald　　　　.30　.20
J37 D5 2fr lilac rose　　　　.30　.20
J38 D5 3fr brown　　　　　.55　.20
J39 D5 5fr blue　　　　　1.40　.20

J40 D5 10fr orange　　　　2.10　.55
J41 D5 20fr rose lilac　　　4.25　.95
　　Nos. J36-J41 (6)　　　8.90　2.30

1960　　Engr.　　Perf. 13½
J42 D6 1fr dark carmine　　.20　.20
J43 D6 2fr brown orange　　.20　.20
J44 D6 3fr dark car rose　　.30　.20
J45 D6 5fr bright green　　　.70　.35
J46 D6 10fr dark brown　　1.50　.50
J47 D6 20fr dull blue　　　3.00　1.25
　　Nos. J42-J47 (6)　　　5.90　2.75

GUINEA-BISSAU

'gi-nē-bi-'sau,ⁿ,

LOCATION — West coast of Africa
between Senegal and Guinea
GOVT. — Republic
AREA — 13,948 sq. mi.
POP. — 1,234,555 (1999 est.)
CAPITAL — Bissau

Guinea-Bissau, the former Portuguese Guinea, attained independence September 10, 1974. The state includes the Bissagos Islands.

100 Centavos = 1 Escudo
100 Centavos = 1 Peso

**Catalogue values for all unused
stamps in this country are for
Never Hinged items.**

Amilcar Cabral, Map of Africa and
Flag — A27

Design: Flag of the PAIGC (African Party of Independence of Guinea-Bissau and Cape Verde) shows location of Guinea-Bissau on map of Africa.

Perf. 11x10½
1974, Sept. 10　Litho.　Unwmk.
345 A27 1p brown & multi　1.00　.55
346 A27 2.50p brown & multi　1.40　.80
347 A27 5p brown & multi　15.00　7.50
348 A27 10p brown & multi　3.75　2.10
　　Nos. 345-348 (4)　　21.15　10.95

First anniv. of Proclamation of Independence, Sept. 24, 1973.

WMO
Emblem — A28

Portuguese Guinea No. 344
Overprinted in Black

1975　　Litho.　　Perf. 13
349 A28 2c brown & multi　1.40　1.40
No. 349 exists with overprint in brown. Value, $5.

Amilcar Cabral, Map of Africa,
Flag — A29

1975, Sept.　Litho.　Perf. 11
350 A29 1p brown & multi
351 A29 2.50p brown & multi
352 A29 5p brown & multi
353 A29 10p brown & multi
　　Nos. 350-353 (4)　　14.00　7.50

Nos. 350-353 are dated Sept. 24, 1973, in the design. Also exist dated Sept. 21, 1973. Value of latter set, $10.

Flag and Arms of Guinea-Bissau and
Amilcar Cabral — A30

Flag, Arms and: 2e, #358, Family. 3e, 5e, Pres. Luiz Cabral. #359, like 1e.

1975, Sept.　　　Perf. 14
354 A30 1e yel & multi　2.00　1.00
355 A30 2e multicolored　2.00　1.25
356 A30 3e red & multi　3.00　1.50
357 A30 5e yel & multi　8.00　4.00
358 A30 10e red & multi　12.00　5.00
359 A30 10e brt grn & multi　12.00　5.00
　　Nos. 354-359 (6)　　39.00　17.75

Amilcar Cabral's 51st birth anniv. (1e, No. 359); African Party of Independence of Guinea-Bissau and Cape Verde, 19th anniv. (2e, No. 358); Proclamation of Independence, 2nd anniv. (3e, 5e).
For surcharges see Nos. 367-367E.

Henry Knox, Cannons of
Ticonderoga — A30a

Designs: 10e, Israel Putnam, Battle of Bunker Hill. 15e, Washington crossing the Delaware. 20e, Tadeusz Kosciuszko, Battle of Saratoga. 30e, Von Steuben, winter at Valley Forge. 40e, Lafayette, Washington rallying troops at Monmouth. 50e, Signing the Declaration of Independence.

1976, May 5　Litho.　Perf. 13½
360 A30a 5e multicolored
360A A30a 10e multicolored
360B A30a 15e multicolored
360C A30a 20e multicolored
360D A30a 30e multicolored
360E A30a 40e multicolored
　　Nos. 360-360E (6)　　12.00　3.75
Souvenir Sheet
360F A30a 50e multicolored　16.00

American Revolution, bicentennial. Nos. 360D-360F are airmail. Nos. 360-360E exist in miniature sheets of 1, perf. and imperf. No. 360F contains one 75x45mm stamp and exists imperf.
See Nos. 371-371A.

Masked
Dancer
A30b

1976, May 10　　　Perf. 11
**Denomination in Black on Silver
Block**
361 A30b 2p shown
361A A30b 3p Dancer, drummer
361B A30b 5p Dancers on stilts

361C A30b 10p Dancer with
　　　　　　spear, bow
361D A30b 15p Masked dancer,
　　　　　　diff.
361E A30b 20p Dancer with
　　　　　　striped cloak
　　Nos. 361-3601 (6)　　9.00　3.00
Souvenir Sheet
361F A30b 50p Like No. 361E　8.00　8.00
Nos. 361C-361F are airmail. Silver block obliterates original denomination. Not issued without surcharge.

Nos. 361-361F Ovptd. in Black

1976, June 8　　　Perf. 11
362 A30b 2p on No. 361
362A A30b 3p on No. 361A
362B A30b 5p on No. 361B
362C A30b 10p on No. 361C
362D A30b 15p on No. 361D
362E A30b 20p on No. 361E
　　Nos. 362-362E (6)　　9.50　2.80
Souvenir Sheet
362F A30b 50p on No. 361F　5.00　5.00
Nos. 362C-362F are airmail. UPU cent. (in 1974). Nos. 362-362F exist imperf, and Nos. 362-362E in imperf miniature sheets of 1, all with black or red overprints.

Cabral, Guinean
Mother and
Children — A31

1976, Aug.　Litho.　Perf. 13½
363 A31 3p multicolored　.20　.20
364 A31 5p multicolored　.20　.20
365 A31 6p multicolored　.55　.20
366 A31 10p multicolored　.70　.20
　　Nos. 363-366 (4)　　1.65　.80

3rd anniv. of assassination of Amilcar Cabral (1924-1973), revolutionary leader.

Nos. 354-359 Surcharged in Black on
Silver

1976, Sept. 12　Litho.　Perf. 14
367 A30 1p on 1e No. 354
367A A30 2p on 2e No. 355
367B A30 3p on 3e No. 356
367C A30 5p on 5e No. 357
367D A30 10p on 10e No. 358
367E A30 10p on 10e No. 359
　　Nos. 367-367E (6)　　6.50　1.40

1876 Bell Telephone and Laying First
Trans-Atlantic Cable — A31a

Telephones of: 3p, France, 1890, and first
telephone booth, 1893. 5p, Germany, 1903,
and automatic telephone, 1898. 10p, England,
1910, and relay station, 1963. 15p, France,
1924, and communications satellite. 20p,
Modern telephone, 1970, and Molniya satellite. 50p, Picture phone.

1976, Oct. 18 *Perf. 13½*
368 A31a 2p multicolored
368A A31a 3p multicolored
368B A31a 5p multicolored
368C A31a 10p multicolored
368D A31a 15p multicolored
368E A31a 20p multicolored
 Nos. 368-368E (6)   6.00 2.75
Souvenir Sheet
368F A31a 50p multicolored   6.00 6.00

Nos. 368C-368F are airmail. No. 368F contains one 68x42mm stamp. No. 368F exists
imperf. Nos. 368-368E exist in souvenir sheets
of one, perf. and imperf.

1976 Winter Olympics,
Innsbruck — A31b

1976, Nov. 3 *Perf. 14x13½*
369 A31b 1p Women's figure
    skating
369A A31b 3p Ice hockey
369B A31b 5p Two-man bobsled
369C A31b 10p Pairs figure skat-
    ing
369D A31b 20p Cross country
    skiing
369E A31b 30p Speed skating
 Nos. 369-369E (6)   7.50 2.50
Souvenir Sheet
369F A31b 50p Downhill skiing   5.50 5.50

Nos. 369C-369F are airmail. No. 369F
exists imperf. Nos. 369-369E exist in souvenir
sheets of one, perf. and imperf.

1976
Summer
Olympics,
Montreal
A31c

1976, Nov. 24 *Perf. 13½*
370 A31c 1p Soccer
370A A31c 3p Pole vault
370B A31c 5p Women's hurdles
370C A31c 10p Discus
370D A31c 20p Sprinting
370E A31c 30p Wrestling
 Nos. 370-370E (6)   7.00 2.25
Souvenir Sheet
370F A31c 50p Cycling, horiz.   6.50 6.50

Nos. 370E-370F are airmail. No. 370F contains one 47x38mm stamp. No. 370F exists
imperf. Nos. 370-370E exist in souvenir sheets
of one, perf. and imperf.

American Revolution Type of 1976

Designs: 3.50p, Crispus Attucks, Boston
Massacre. 5p, Martin Luther King, US Capitol.

1977, Jan. 27 *Perf. 13½*
**Denomination in Black on Gold
Block**
371 A30a 3.50p multicolored
371A A30a 5p multicolored
 Nos. 371-371A (2)   .80 .40

Gold block obliterates original denomination. Not issued without surcharge. Exist in
souvenir sheets of one, perf. and imperf.

Cabral Addressing UN General
Assembly — A32

Design: 50c, Cabral and guerrilla fighters.

1977, July *Litho.* *Perf. 13½*
372 A32 50c multicolored   .20 .20
373 A32 3.50p multicolored   .30 .20

For surcharges see Nos. C12-C13.

Henri
Dunant,
Nobel
Peace
Prize,
1901
A32a

Nobel Prize Winners: 5p, Einstein, Physics,
1921. 6p, Irene and Frederic Joliot-Curie,
Chemistry, 1935. 30p, Fleming, Medicine,
1945. 35p, Hemingway, Literature, 1954. 40p,
J. Tinbergen, Economics, 1969. 50p, Nobel
Prize Medal.

1977, July 27
374 A32a 3.50p multicolored
374A A32a 5p multicolored
374B A32a 6p multicolored
374C A32a 30p multicolored
374D A32a 35p multicolored
374E A32a 40p multicolored
 Nos. 374-374E (6)   15.00 5.25
Souvenir Sheet
374F A32a 50p multicolored   5.50 5.50

Nos. 374D-374F are airmail. No. 374F contains one 57x39mm stamp. No. 374F exists
imperf. Nos. 374-374E exist in souvenir sheets
of one, perf. and imperf.

Postal Runner, Telstar
Satellite — A32b

UPU Centenary (in 1974): 5p, Biplane,
satellites encircle globe. 6p, Mail truck, satellite
control room. 30p, Stagecoach, astronaut canceling letters on Moon. 35p, Steam locomotive, communications satellite. 40p, Space
shuttle, Apollo-Soyuz link-up. 50p, Semaphore
signalling system, satellite dish.

1977, Sept. 30
375 A32b 3.50p multicolored
375A A32b 5p multicolored
375B A32b 6p multicolored
375C A32b 30p multicolored
375D A32b 35p multicolored
375E A32b 40p multicolored
 Nos. 375-375E (6)   10.00 4.25
Souvenir Sheet
375F A32b 50p multicolored   5.00 5.00

Nos. 375D-375F are airmail. No. 375F
exists imperf. Nos. 375-375E exist in souvenir
sheets of one, perf. and imperf.

Torch and Party
Emblem — A33

1977, Sept. *Litho.* *Perf. 14*
376 A33 3p yel & multi   .25 .20
377 A33 15p sal & multi   1.25 .60
378 A33 50p lt grn & multi   3.00 1.50
 Nos. 376-378 (3)   4.50 2.30

African Party of Independence of Guinea-
Bissau and Cape Verde, 20th anniversary.

Queen Elizabeth II, Silver
Jubilee — A33a

Designs: 5p, Coronation ceremony. 10p,
Yeoman of the Guard, Crown Jewels. 20p,
Trumpeter. 25p, Royal Horse Guard. 30p,
Royal Family. 50p, Queen Elizabeth II.

1977, Oct. 15
379 A33a 3.50p multicolored
379A A33a 5p multicolored
379B A33a 10p multicolored
379C A33a 20p multicolored
379D A33a 25p multicolored
379E A33a 30p multicolored
 Nos. 379-379E (6)   11.00 2.75
Souvenir Sheet
379F A33a 50p multicolored   5.00 5.00

Nos. 379D-379F are airmail. No. 379F contains one 42x39mm stamp. No. 379F exists
imperf. Nos. 379-379E exist in souvenir sheets
of one, perf. and imperf.

Massacre of
the Innocents
by Rubens
A33b

Paintings by Peter Paul Rubens: 5p, Rape of
the Daughters of Leukippos. 6p, Lamentation
of Christ, horiz. 30p, Francisco IV Gonzaga,
Prince of Mantua. 35p, The Four Continents.
40p, Marquise Brigida Spinola Doria. 50p, The
Wounding of Christ.

1977, Nov. 15
380 A33b 3.50p multicolored
380A A33b 5p multicolored
380B A33b 6p multicolored
380C A33b 30p multicolored
380D A33b 35p multicolored
380E A33b 40p multicolored
 Nos. 380-380E (6)   11.00 5.00
Souvenir Sheet
380F A33b 50p multicolored   5.50 5.50

Nos. 380D-380F are airmail. Nos. 380-380F
exist imperf. Nos. 380-380E exist in souvenir
sheets of one, perf. and imperf.

Congress
Emblem — A34

1977, Nov. 15 *Litho.* *Perf. 14*
381 A34 3.50p multicolored   .30 .20

3rd PAIGC Congress, Bissau, Nov. 15-20.

Santos-Dumont's Airship,
1901 — A34a

Airships: 5p, R-34 crossing the Atlantic,
1919. 10p, Norge over North Pole, 1926. 20p,
Graf Zeppelin over Abu Simbel, 1931. 25p,
Hindenburg over New York, 1937. 30p, Graf
Zeppelin, Concorde, space shuttle. 50p, Ferdi-
nand von Zeppelin, horiz.

1978, Feb. 27
382 A34a 3.50p multicolored
382A A34a 5p multicolored
382B A34a 10p multicolored
382C A34a 20p multicolored
382D A34a 25p multicolored
382E A34a 30p multicolored
 Nos. 382-382E (6)   8.00 3.75
Souvenir Sheet
382F A34a 50p multicolored   5.00 5.00

Nos. 382D-382F are airmail. No. 382F
exists imperf. Nos. 382-382E exist in souvenir
sheets of one, perf. and imperf.

World Cup Soccer Championships,
Argentina — A34b

Soccer players and posters from previous
World Cup Championships: 3.50p, 1930. 5p,
1938. 10p, 1950. 20p, 1962. 25p, 1970. 30p,
1974. 50p, Argentina '78 emblem.

1978, Mar. 15
383 A34b 3.50p multicolored
383A A34b 5p multicolored
383B A34b 10p multicolored
383C A34b 20p multicolored
383D A34b 25p multicolored
383E A34b 30p multicolored
 Nos. 383-383E (6)   8.00 3.75
Souvenir Sheet
383F A34b 50p multicolored   5.00 5.00

Nos. 383D-383F are airmail. Nos. 383-383F
exist imperf. Nos. 383-383E exist in miniature
sheets of one, perf. and imperf.
For surcharges see Nos. 393-393F.

Endangered Species — A34c

1978, Apr. 17
384	A34c	3.50p	Black antelope		
384A	A34c	5p	Fennec		
384B	A34c	6p	Secretary bird		
384C	A34c	30p	Hippopotami		
384D	A34c	35p	Cheetahs		
384E	A34c	40p	Gorillas		
		Nos. 384-384E (6)		13.00	6.00

Souvenir Sheet
384F	A34c	50p	Cercopithecus erythotis	6.50	6.50

Nos. 384D-384F are airmail. No. 384F contains one 39x42mm stamp. No. 384F exists imperf. Nos. 384-384E exist in souvenir sheets of one, perf. and imperf.

Antenna, ITU Emblem A35

1978, May 17   Litho.   Perf. 13½
385	A35	3.50p	silver & multi	.20	.20
386	A35	10p	gold & multi	.90	.30

10th World Telecommunications Day.

Boy — A36

3p, Infant and grandfather. 5p, Boys. 30p, Girls.

1978   Perf. 14
387	A36	50c	yel grn & dk bl	.20	.20
388	A36	3p	claret & car rose	.20	.20
389	A36	5p	ocher & brown	.40	.20
390	A36	30p	car & ocher	2.10	.80
		Nos. 387-390 (4)		2.90	1.40

Children's Day.

Queen Elizabeth II, Silver Jubilee A36a

Elizabeth, Imperial State Crown — A36b

Designs: 5p, Queen, Prince Philip in Coronation Coach. 10p, Queen, Prince Philip. 20p, Mounted drummer. 25p, Imperial State Crown,

St. Edward's Crown. 30p, Queen holding orb and scepter. 50p, Queen on Throne flanked by Archbishops. No. 391H, Coronation Coach.

1978, June 15
391	A36a	3.50p	multicolored		
391A	A36a	5p	multicolored		
391B	A36a	10p	multicolored		
391C	A36a	20p	multicolored		
391D	A36a	25p	multicolored		
391E	A36a	30p	multicolored		
		Nos. 391-391E (6)		7.00	2.75

Litho. & Embossed
391F	A36b	100p	gold & multi	20.00	—

Souvenir Sheets
391G	A36a	50p	multicolored	5.00	5.00

Litho. & Embossed
391H	A36b	100p	gold & multi	14.00	—

Nos. 391D-391H are airmail. Nos. 391-391E exist in souvenir sheets of one, perf. and imperf. Nos. 391F-391H exist imperf.

History of Aviation — A36c

1978, June 15   Litho.   Perf. 13½
392	A36c	3.50p	Wright Brothers		
392A	A36c	10p	Santos-Dumont		
392B	A36c	15p	Bleriot		
392C	A36c	20p	Lindbergh, Spirit of St. Louis		
392D	A36c	25p	Lunar module		
392E	A36c	30p	Space shuttle		
		Nos. 392-392E (6)		8.50	3.25

Souvenir Sheet
392F	A36c	50p	Concorde	5.50	5.50

Nos. 392D-392F are airmail. Nos. 392-392E exist in souvenir sheets of one, perf. and imperf. No. 392F exists imperf.

Nos. 383-383F Ovptd. in Gold

1978, Oct. 2
393	A34b	3.50p	on No. 383		
393A	A34b	5p	on No. 383A		
393B	A34b	10p	on No. 383B		
393C	A34b	20p	on No. 383C		
393D	A34b	25p	on No. 383D		
393E	A34b	30p	on No. 383E		
		Nos. 393-393E (6)		8.00	

Souvenir Sheet
393F	A34b	50p	on No. 383F	5.00	5.00

Nos. 393D-393F are airmail. Nos. 393-393F exist imperf. Nos. 393-393E exist in miniature sheets of 1 perf. and imperf. No. 393F exists overprinted in silver.

Virgin and Child by Albrecht Durer — A36d

Different Paintings of the Virgin and Child (Virgin only on 30p) by Durer.

1978, Nov. 14
394	A36d	3.50p	multicolored		
394A	A36d	5p	multicolored		
394B	A36d	6p	multicolored		
394C	A36d	30p	multicolored		
394D	A36d	35p	multicolored		
394E	A36d	40p	multicolored		
		Nos. 394-394E (6)		10.00	4.00

Souvenir Sheet
394F	A36d	50p	multicolored	5.50	5.50

Nos. 394D-394F are airmail. No. 394F contains one 51x56mm stamp. Nos. 394-394E exist in souvenir sheets of one, perf. and imperf. No. 394F exists imperf.

Sir Rowland Hill (1795-1879), Wurttemberg No. 53 — A36e

Hill and: 5p, Belgium #1. 6p, Monaco #10. 30p, Spain 2r stamp of 1851 in blue. 35p, Switzerland #5. 40p, Two Sicilies #8. 50p, Portuguese Guinea #13 in brown.

1978, Dec. 15
395	A36e	3.50p	multicolored		
395A	A36e	5p	multicolored		
395B	A36e	6p	multicolored		
395C	A36e	30p	multicolored		
395D	A36e	35p	multicolored		
395E	A36e	40p	multicolored		
		Nos. 395-395E (6)		17.00	2.00

Souvenir Sheet
395F	A36e	50p	multicolored	5.50	5.50

Nos. 395D-395F are airmail. No. 395F contains one 51x42mm stamp. Nos. 395-395E exist in souvenir sheets of one, perf. and imperf. No. 395F exists imperf.

Intl. Day of the Child — A36f

1979, Jan. 15   Perf. 14
396	A36f	3.50p	shown		
396A	A36f	10p	Children drinking		
396B	A36f	15p	Child with book		
396C	A36f	20p	Space plane		
396D	A36f	25p	Skylab		
396E	A36f	30p	Children playing chess		
		Nos. 396-396E (6)		10.00	3.50

Souvenir Sheet
396F	A36f	50p	Children watching spaceship	5.50	5.50

Nos. 396C-396F are airmail. Nos. 396-396E exist in souvenir sheets of one, perf. and imperf. No. 396F exists imperf.

A36g

A36h

1979   Litho.   Perf. 13
397	A36g	4.50p	multicolored	.45	.20

Massacre of Pindjiguiti, 20th anniv.

1979   Litho.   Perf. 14
397A	A36h	50c	shown	.20	.20
397B	A36h	4p	People, rainbow, diff.	.30	.20

World Telecommunications Day.

Family A37

1979, May   Litho.   Perf. 12x11½
398	A37	50c	multicolored	.45	.20
399	A37	2p	multicolored	.95	.20
400	A37	4p	multicolored	.45	.20
		Nos. 398-400 (3)		1.85	.60

General population census, Apr. 16-30.

Cassaca Conference, 16th Anniv. — A37a

1980, Feb. 13   Litho.   Perf. 14x14¼
400A	A37a	3.50p	multi	—	—
400B	A37a	6.50p	multi	—	—

An additional stamp was issued in this set. The editors would like to examine any examples.

Ernst Udet and Fokker D.VII — A38

1980   Litho.   Perf. 13½
401	A38	3.50p	shown	.45	.20
401A	A38	5p	Charles Nungesser, Nieuport 17	.45	.20
401B	A38	6p	von Richthofen, Fokker DR.1	.55	.20
401C	A38	30p	Francesco Baracca, Spad XIII	2.25	.70
		Nos. 401-401C, C14-C14A (6)		10.20	3.55

Lake Placid Emblem, Speed Skating — A39

1980
402	A39	3.50p	shown	.45	.20
402A	A39	5p	Downhill skiing	.45	.20
402B	A39	6p	Luge	.55	.20
402C	A39	30p	Cross-country skiing	2.25	.70
		Nos. 402-402C, C15-C16 (6)		9.95	3.55

13th Winter Olympic Games, Lake Placid, NY, Feb. 12-24.

Shot-put A40

1980, Aug. **Litho.** **Perf. 13½**
403	A40	3.50p shown	.30	.20
403A	A40	5p Athlete on rings	.70	.20
403B	A40	6p Running	.90	.25
403C	A40	30p Fencing	3.50	.70
		Nos. 403-403C,C18-C19 (6)	14.65	3.60

22nd Summer Olympic Games, Moscow, 7/19-8/3.

Pres. Luis Cabral, Children and Workers A41

5p, Pres. Cabral holding books.

1980, Aug. **Litho.** **Perf. 13½**
404	A41	3.50p multicolored	.45	.20
405	A41	5p multicolored	.75	.20

Literacy campaign. See Nos. C21-C22.

Cooperation Among Developing Countries — A42

1980, Aug.
406	A42	3.50p multicolored	.80	.20
407	A42	6p multicolored	.80	.20
408	A42	10p multicolored	1.60	.20
		Nos. 406-408 (3)	3.20	.60

Baskets — A43

1980, Aug. **Litho.** **Perf. 13½**
409	A43	3p Bird, family wood statues, vert.	.35	.20
410	A43	6p shown	.35	.20
411	A43	20p Head, doll carvings	1.25	.45
		Nos. 409-411 (3)	1.95	.85

Infant and Toy Train, Locomotive, IYC Emblem A44

1980
412	A44	6p Classroom, horiz.	.50	.30
412A	A44	10p Boy reading Jules Verne story	.90	.55
412B	A44	25p shown	1.75	.80

412C	A44	35p Archer, boy with bow	2.75	1.25
		Nos. 412-412C (4)	5.90	2.90

Souvenir Sheet
412D	A44	50p Students in lab	4.50	4.50

International Year of the Child (1979).

Columbia Space Shuttle and Crew — A45

Space Exploration: 3.50p, Galileo, satellites. 5p, Wernher von Braun. 6p, Jules Verne, rocket.

1981, May **Litho.** **Perf. 13½**
413	A45	3.50p multicolored	.40	.20
413A	A45	5p multicolored	.45	.20
413B	A45	6p multicolored	.50	.20
413C	A45	30p multicolored	2.50	.90
		Nos. 413-413C,C23-C24 (6)	11.10	4.25

Soccer Players, World Cup, Argentina '78 and Espana '82 Emblems — A46

Soccer scenes and famous players: 3.50p, Platini, France. 5p, Bettega, Italy. 6p, Rensenbrink, Netherlands. 30p, Rivelino, Brazil.

1981, May
414	A46	3.50p multicolored	.40	.25
414A	A46	5p multicolored	.45	.25
414B	A46	6p multicolored	.50	.25
414C	A46	30p multicolored	2.50	.80
		Nos. 414-414C,C26-C27 (6)	11.10	4.30

Prince Charles and Lady Diana, St. Paul's Cathedral A47

Royal Wedding (Couple and): 3.50p, Diana leading horse. 5p, Charles crowned Prince of Wales. 6p, Diana with kindergarten children.

1981 **Litho.** **Perf. 13½**
415	A47	3.50p multicolored	.40	.20
415A	A47	5p multicolored	.55	.20
415B	A47	6p multicolored	.60	.20
415C	A47	30p multicolored	2.10	.90
		Nos. 415-415C,C29-C30 (6)	12.40	4.25

Woman Before a Mirror, by Picasso (1881-1973) A48

Picasso Birth Cent.: Various paintings.

1981, Dec. **Litho.** **Perf. 13½**
416	A48	3.50p multi	.50	.20
417	A48	5p multi	.65	.20
418	A48	6p multi	.75	.20
419	A48	30p multi	3.75	.90
		Nos. 416-419,C32-C33 (6)	18.15	4.35

Henrique Vermelho and his Ship, Drakkar A49

Navigators and their ships: 5p, Vasco de Gama, St. Gabriel. 6p, Ferdinand Magellan, Victoria. 30p, Jacques Cartier, Emerillon.

1981 **Litho.** **Perf. 13½**
420	A49	3.50p multicolored	.30	.20
421	A49	5p multicolored	.45	.20
422	A49	6p multicolored	.65	.20
423	A49	30p multicolored	3.00	1.00
		Nos. 420-423,C35-C36 (6)	13.15	4.75

Christmas — A50

Designs: Virgin and Child paintings.

1981
424	A50	3.50p Mantegna	.30	.20
425	A50	5p Bellini	.45	.20
426	A50	6p Mantegna, diff.	.65	.20
427	A50	25p Correggio	3.00	1.00
		Nos. 424-427,C38-C39 (6)	13.15	4.75

Scouting Year — A51

1982, June 9 **Litho.** **Perf. 13½**
428	A51	3.50p Archery	.40	.20
429	A51	5p First aid training	.40	.20
430	A51	6p Bugler	.55	.20
431	A51	30p Cub scouts	3.00	.65
		Nos. 428-431,C41-C42 (6)	12.10	3.35

1982 World Cup — A52

Various soccer players and cup.

1982, June 13 **Litho.** **Perf. 13½**
432	A52	3.50p Keegan	.40	.20
433	A52	5p Rossi	.40	.20
434	A52	6p Zico	.55	.20
435	A52	30p Arconada	3.00	.65
		Nos. 432-435,C44-C45 (6)	12.10	3.35

21st Birthday of Princess Diana — A53

Portraits and scenes of Diana.

1982
436	A53	3.50p multicolored	.40	.20
437	A53	5p multicolored	.40	.20
438	A53	6p multicolored	.55	.20
439	A53	30p multicolored	3.00	.65
		Nos. 436-439,C47-C48 (6)	12.10	3.35

For overprints see Nos. 450-456.

Visit by Portuguese President Eanes — A54

4.50p, Portugal and Guinea-Bissau flags.

1982 **Litho.** **Perf. 13½**
440	A54	4.50p multicolored	.40	.20
441	A54	20p multicolored	1.60	1.10

Manned Flight Bicentenary — A55

Various hot air balloons.

1983, Jan. 15 **Litho.** **Perf. 11**
442	A55	50c multicolored	.20	.20
443	A55	2.50p multicolored	.20	.20
444	A55	3.50p multicolored	.40	.20
445	A55	5p multicolored	.65	.20
446	A55	10p multicolored	.70	.20
447	A55	20p multicolored	1.75	.35
448	A55	30p multicolored	2.50	.45
		Nos. 442-448 (7)	6.40	1.80

Souvenir Sheet
Perf. 12½
449	A55	50p multicolored	5.50	.90

No. 449 contains one 47x47mm stamp.

Nos. 436-439, C47-C48, C49A-C49B
Overprinted: "21 DE JULHO .
GUILHERMO ARTUR FILIPE LUIS
PRINCIPE DE GALES"

1982 **Litho.** **Perf. 13½**
450	A53	3.50p multicolored	.70	.20
451	A53	5p multicolored	.80	.20
452	A53	6p multicolored	.95	.20
453	A53	30p multicolored	4.25	.65
454	A53	35p multicolored	5.25	.80
455	A53	40p multicolored	5.75	1.10
		Nos. 450-455 (6)	17.70	3.15

Souvenir Sheet
456	A53	50p multicolored	9.00	1.25

Litho. & Embossed
456A	A53a	200p gold & multi	18.00	

Souvenir Sheet
456B	A53a	200p gold & multi, vert.	40.00	

Nos. 454-456A are airmail.

African Apes
and Monkeys
A56

1983, Mar. 15   Litho.   Perf. 13½
457	A56	1p	Comopithecus hamadryas	.20 .20
458	A56	1.50p	Gorilla gorilla	.20 .20
459	A56	3.50p	Theropithecus gelada	.45 .20
460	A56	5p	Mandrillus sphinx	.55 .20
461	A56	8p	Pan trogladytes	1.25 .20
462	A56	20p	Colobus abyssinicus	2.00 .30
463	A56	30p	Cercopithecus diana	2.75 .45
			Nos. 457-463 (7)	7.40 1.75

Souvenir Sheet

TEMBAL '83, Stamp Exhibition,
Basel — A57

1983, May 21
464	A57	50p	Space shuttle	6.00 1.10

A58

Designs: Various telecommunications satellites and space shuttles.

1983, May 25   Litho.   Perf. 13½
465	A58	1p	multicolored	.20 .20
466	A58	1.50p	multicolored	.20 .20
467	A58	3.50p	multicolored	.20 .20
468	A58	5p	multicolored	.40 .20
469	A58	8p	multicolored	.60 .20
470	A58	20p	multicolored	1.50 .40
471	A58	30p	multicolored	2.25 .65
			Nos. 465-471 (7)	5.35 2.05

Souvenir Sheet
472	A58	50p	multicolored	4.50 .90

History of
Chess — A59

Early Chess Game — A60

Various chess pieces.

1983, June 13   Litho.   Perf. 12
473	A59	1p	multicolored	.20 .20
474	A59	1.50p	multicolored	.20 .20
475	A59	3.50p	multicolored	.20 .20
476	A59	5p	multicolored	.45 .20
477	A59	10p	multicolored	.95 .20
478	A59	20p	multicolored	1.75 .20
479	A59	40p	multicolored	4.25 .60
			Nos. 473-479 (7)	8.00 1.80

Souvenir Sheet
480	A60	50p	brown & blk	5.50 .85

Raphael,
500th Birth
Anniv.
A61

Various paintings.

1983, June 30   Litho.   Perf. 12½
481	A61	1p	gold & multi	.20 .20
482	A61	1.50p	gold & multi	.20 .20
483	A61	3.50p	gold & multi	.20 .20
484	A61	5p	gold & multi	.50 .20
485	A61	8p	gold & multi	.65 .20
486	A61	15p	gold & multi	1.25 .20
487	A61	30p	gold & multi	2.40 .45
			Nos. 481-487 (7)	5.40 1.65

Souvenir Sheet
488	A61	50p	gold & multi	4.50 1.25

1984 Summer
Olympics, Los
Angeles — A62

1983, July 20   Litho.   Perf. 12½
489	A62	1p	Swimming	.20 .20
490	A62	1.50p	Jumping	.20 .20
491	A62	3.50p	Fencing	.50 .20
492	A62	5p	Weightlifting	.50 .20
493	A62	10p	Running	.65 .20
494	A62	20p	Equestrian	1.40 .25
495	A62	40p	Bicycling	2.75 .70
			Nos. 489-495 (7)	6.20 1.95

Souvenir Sheet
496	A62	50p	Stadium	4.50 1.25

Souvenir Sheet

BRASILIANA '83, Philatelic
Exhibition — A63

1983, July 29   Litho.   Perf. 13
497	A63	50p	multicolored	10.00 7.50

Local Fish — A64

Perf. 12x11½, 11½x12
1983, Dec. 8   Litho.
498	A64	1p	Monodactylus sebae, vert.	.20 .20
499	A64	1.50p	Botia macracanthus	.20 .20
500	A64	3.50p	Ctenopoma acutirostre	.45 .20
501	A64	5p	Roloffia bertholdi	.50 .20
502	A64	8p	Aphyosemion bualanum	.75 .20
503	A64	10p	Aphyosemion bivittatum	1.10 .20
504	A64	30p	Aphyosemion australe	3.25 .95
			Nos. 498-504 (7)	6.45 2.15

1984 Winter
Olympics,
Sarajevo — A65

1983, Oct. 10   Litho.   Perf. 13
505	A65	1p	Speed skating	.20 .20
506	A65	1.50p	Ski jumping	.20 .20
507	A65	3p	Biathlon	.50 .20
508	A65	5p	Bobsledding	.65 .20
509	A65	10p	Hockey	.75 .20
510	A65	15p	Figure skating	1.50 .20
511	A65	20p	Luge	2.00 .30
			Nos. 505-511 (7)	5.80 1.50

Souvenir Sheet
512	A65	50p	Downhill skiing	6.00 6.00

No. 512 contains one 31x40mm stamp.

A66

A67

1983, Nov. 7   Perf. 12½
513	A66	4.50p	Emblem	.60 .20
514	A66	7.50p	Woman, flag	.80 .20
515	A66	9p	Sewing	1.10 .20
516	A66	12p	Farm workers	1.50 .20
			Nos. 513-516 (4)	4.00 .80

First anniv. of Women's Federation.

1983, Nov. 12   Litho.   Perf. 13

Designs: Local flowers.
517	A67	1p	Canna coccinea	.20 .20
518	A67	1.50p	Bouganville litoralis	.20 .20
519	A67	3.50p	Euphorbia milii	.30 .20
520	A67	5p	Delonix regia	.40 .20
521	A67	8p	Bauhinia variegata	.70 .20
522	A67	10p	Spathodea campanulata	.95 .20
523	A67	30p	Hibiscus rosa sinensis	2.75 .80
			Nos. 517-523 (7)	5.50 2.00

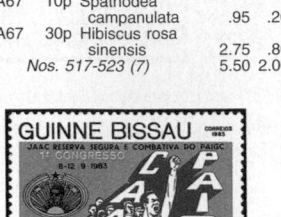

JAAC Congress, Sept. 8-12 — A68

1983, Sept. 1   Litho.   Perf. 13
524	A68	4p	shown	1.25 .20
524A	A68	5p	Emblem	1.25 .20

World
Food
Day
A69

1983, Oct. 16   Litho.   Perf. 12½x12
525	A69	1.50p	multicolored	.20 .20
526	A69	2p	multicolored	.35 .20
527	A69	4p	multicolored	.50 .20

Imperf
Size: 61x62mm
528	A69	10p	Hoeing	3.00 1.00
			Nos. 525-528 (4)	4.05 1.60

1984 Winter
Olympics,
Sarajevo
A70

1984, Feb. 8   Perf. 12
529	A70	50c	Ski jumping	.20 .20
530	A70	2.50p	Speed skating	.50 .20
531	A70	3.50p	Hockey	.65 .20
532	A70	5p	Biathlon	.75 .20
533	A70	6p	Downhill skiing	.80 .20
534	A70	20p	Figure skating	2.25 .40
535	A70	30p	Bobsledding	3.75 .45
			Nos. 529-535 (7)	8.90 1.85

Souvenir Sheet
Perf. 11½
536	A70	50p	Skiing	8.50 3.25

No. 536 contains one 32x43mm stamp.

World Communications Year — A71

1983, Aug. 30   Litho.   Perf. 12½
537	A71	50c	Rowland Hill	.40	.20
538	A71	2.50p	Samuel Morse	.50	.20
539	A71	3.50p	H.R. Hertz	.60	.20
540	A71	5p	Lord Kelvin	.75	.20
541	A71	10p	Alex. Graham Bell	1.50	.20
542	A71	20p	G. Marconi	3.00	.60
543	A71	30p	V. Zworykin	4.25	.75
		Nos. 537-543 (7)		11.00	2.35

Souvenir Sheet
| 544 | A71 | 50p | Satellites | 8.50 | 3.25 |

No. 544 contains one stamp 31x39mm.

Vintage Cars A72

1984, Mar. 20   Perf. 12
545	A72	5p	Duesenberg, 1928	.45	.20
546	A72	8p	MG Midget, 1932	.80	.20
547	A72	15p	Mercedes, 1928	1.10	.20
548	A72	20p	Bentley, 1928	1.25	.30
549	A72	24p	Alfa Romeo, 1929	1.50	.35
550	A72	30p	Datsun, 1932	2.10	.50
551	A72	35p	Lincoln, 1932	2.50	.55
		Nos. 545-551 (7)		9.70	2.30

Souvenir Sheet
| 552 | A72 | 100p | Gottlieb Daimler | 11.00 | 4.25 |

No. 552 contains one stamp 50x42mm.

Madonna and Child, by Morales — A73

Paintings by Spanish Artists (Espana '84): 6p, Dona Tadea Arias de Enriquez, by Goya. 10p, Santa Cassilda, by Zurbaran. 12p, Saints Andrew and Francis, by El Greco. 15p, Infanta Isabel Clara Eugenia, by Coello. 35p, Queen Maria of Austria, by Velazquez. 40p, Holy Trinity, by El Greco. 100p, Clothed Maja, by Goya.

1984, Apr. 20
553	A73	3p	multicolored	.35	.20
554	A73	6p	multicolored	.55	.20
555	A73	10p	multicolored	.85	.20
556	A73	12p	multicolored	1.10	.20
557	A73	15p	multicolored	1.40	.25
558	A73	35p	multicolored	3.50	.60
559	A73	40p	multicolored	4.25	.65
		Nos. 553-559 (7)		12.00	2.30

Souvenir Sheet
| 560 | A73 | 100p | multicolored | 11.00 | 4.75 |

No. 560 contains one stamp 29x50mm.

Carnivorous Animals — A74

1984, June 28
561	A74	3p	Panthera tigris	.40	.20
562	A74	6p	Panthera leo	.60	.20
563	A74	10p	Neofelis nebulosa	.70	.20
564	A74	12p	Acinonyx jubatus	.85	.20
565	A74	15p	Lynx lynx	.95	.20
566	A74	35p	Panthera pardus	2.50	.45
567	A74	40p	Uncia uncia	2.75	.45
		Nos. 561-567 (7)		8.75	1.90

Intl. Civil Aviation Org., 40th Anniv. — A75

1984, Apr. 4   Litho.   Perf. 12½
568	A75	8p	Caravelle	.75	.20
569	A75	22p	DC-6B	1.50	.35
570	A75	80p	IL-76	5.25	1.25
		Nos. 568-570 (3)		7.50	1.80

1984 Summer Olympics, Los Angeles — A76

1984, May 24   Perf. 12
571	A76	6p	Soccer	.45	.20
572	A76	8p	Dressage	.55	.20
573	A76	15p	Yachting	1.10	.20
574	A76	20p	Field hockey	1.40	.25
575	A76	22p	Women's team handball	1.50	.25
576	A76	30p	Canoeing	2.25	.40
577	A76	40p	Boxing	2.75	.80
		Nos. 571-577 (7)		10.00	2.30

Souvenir Sheet
Perf. 11½
| 578 | A76 | 100p | Windsurfing | 10.00 | 3.75 |

World Heritage — A77

Wood sculptures: 3p, Pearl throne, Cameroun and Central Africa. 6p, Antelope, South Sudan. 10p, Kneeling woman, East Africa. 12p, Mask, West African coast. 15p, Leopard, Guinea coast. 35p, Standing woman, Zaire. 40p, Funerary statues, Southeast Africa and Madagascar.

1984, Aug. 15   Perf. 12½
579	A77	3p	multicolored	.65	.20
580	A77	6p	multicolored	.75	.20
581	A77	10p	multicolored	.85	.20
582	A77	12p	multicolored	1.40	.25
583	A77	15p	multicolored	1.75	.30
584	A77	35p	multicolored	3.50	.65
585	A77	40p	multicolored	3.75	.70
		Nos. 579-585 (7)		12.65	2.50

Amilcar Cabral, 60th Birth Anniv. — A78

1984, Sept. 12   Perf. 13
586	A78	5p	Public speaking	.85	.20
587	A78	12p	In combat fatigues	.95	.20
588	A78	20p	Memorial building, Bafata	1.75	.35
589	A78	50p	Mausoleum, Bissau	4.25	.80
		Nos. 586-589 (4)		7.80	1.55

Independence, 11th Anniv. — A79

1984, Sept. 24
590	A79	3p	Mechanic	.60	.20
591	A79	6p	Student	.70	.20
592	A79	10p	Mason	.90	.20
593	A79	12p	Health care, vert.	1.25	.30
594	A79	15p	Seamstress, vert.	1.50	.30
595	A79	35p	Telecommunications	2.75	.70
596	A79	40p	PAIGC building	3.25	.75
		Nos. 590-596 (7)		10.95	2.65

Whales A80

1984, Sept. 30   Perf. 12
597	A80	5p	Eschrichtius gibbosus	.80	.20
598	A80	8p	Balaenoptera musculus	1.10	.20
599	A80	10p	Tursiops truncatus	1.60	.35
600	A80	20p	Physeter macrocephalus	2.25	.35
601	A80	24p	Orcinus orca	3.00	.45
602	A80	30p	Balaena mysticetus	3.50	.55
603	A80	35p	Balaenoptera borealis	3.75	.60
		Nos. 597-603 (7)		16.00	2.70

Butterflies A81

1984, Oct. 6   Perf. 12½x13
604	A81	3p	Hypolimnas dexithea	.50	.20
605	A81	6p	Papilio arcturus	.65	.20
606	A81	10p	Morpho menelaus terrestris	.75	.20
607	A81	12p	Apaturina erminea papuana	1.00	.25
608	A81	15p	Prepona praeneste	1.25	.35
609	A81	35p	Ornithoptera paradisea	2.10	.65
610	A81	40p	Morpho hecuba obidona	2.75	.75
		Nos. 604-610 (7)		9.00	2.60

1984 Olympic Winners — A82

National flag, medal and: 6p, Carl Lewis, 4x100 relay, US. 8p, Koji Gushiken, gymnastics, Japan. 15p, Reiner Klimke, equestrian,

Federal Republic of Germany. 20p, Tracie Ruiz, synchronized swimming, US. 22p, Mary Lou Retton, gymnastics, US. 30p, Michael Gross, swimming, Federal Republic of Germany. 40p, Edwin Moses, hurdler, US. 100p, Daley Thompson, decathlon, Great Britain.

1984, Nov. 27   Perf. 13
611	A82	6p	multicolored	.45	.20
612	A82	8p	multicolored	.65	.20
613	A82	15p	multicolored	1.00	.25
614	A82	20p	multicolored	1.50	.25
615	A82	22p	multicolored	1.60	.30
616	A82	30p	multicolored	2.50	.45
617	A82	40p	multicolored	3.25	.65
		Nos. 611-617 (7)		10.95	2.30

Souvenir Sheet
Perf. 12½
| 618 | A82 | 100p | multicolored | 10.00 | 3.75 |

No. 618 contains one stamp 32x40mm.

Locomotives — A83

1984, Dec. 15   Perf. 13
619	A83	5p	White Mountain Central No. 4	.60	.20
620	A83	8p	Kessler 2-6-OT, 1886	.70	.20
621	A83	15p	Langen tram, 1901	.95	.30
622	A83	20p	Gurjao No. 6	1.25	.35
623	A83	24p	Achenseebahn	1.50	.40
624	A83	30p	Vitznau-Rigi steam locomotive	1.90	.55
625	A83	35p	Riggenbach rackrail, 1873	2.10	.85
		Nos. 619-625 (7)		9.00	2.85

Souvenir Sheet
Perf. 12½
| 625A | A83 | 100p | like #621 | 9.50 | 3.25 |

No. 625A contains one stamp 40x32mm.

Native Crafts — A83a

LUBRAPEX '84: a, Numbe mask. b, Sono statue. c, Erande statue. d, Kokumba arms. e, Oma mask. f, Koni mask.

1984   Litho.   Perf. 13½
| 626 | A83a | 7.50p | Strip of 6, #a.-f. | 5.50 | 3.50 |

Motorcycle Cent. — A84

1985, Feb. 20   Perf. 13x12½
627	A84	5p	Harley-Davidson	.65	.20
628	A84	8p	Kawasaki	.95	.20
629	A84	15p	Honda	1.40	.25
630	A84	20p	Yamaha	2.25	.35
631	A84	25p	Suzuki	3.25	.40
632	A84	30p	BMW	3.75	.55
633	A84	35p	Moto Guzzi	5.75	.60
		Nos. 627-633 (7)		18.00	2.55

Souvenir Sheet
Perf. 12½
| 634 | A84 | 100p | Daimler Motorized Bicycle, 1885, vert. | 16.00 | 5.50 |

No. 634 contains one 32x40mm stamp.

Miniature Sheet

Mushrooms
A85

1985, May 15   **Perf. 13**

635		Sheet of 6	8.00	2.10
a.	A85	7p Clitocybe gibba	.50	.20
b.	A85	9p Morchella elata	.55	.25
c.	A85	12p Lepista nuda	.75	.30
d.	A85	20p Lactarius deliciosus	1.25	.35
e.	A85	30p Russula virescens	1.75	.45
f.	A85	35p Chroogomphus rutilus	2.00	.55

Henri Dunant (1828-1910), Red Cross
Founder, Plane — A87

1985, June 12   **Perf. 12½**

643	A87	20p shown	.90	.20
644	A87	25p Ambulance	1.10	.20
645	A87	40p Helicopter	2.25	.45
646	A87	80p Speed boat	4.75	.65
		Nos. 643-646 (4)	9.00	1.50

Cats — A88

1985, July 5   **Perf. 13**

647	A88	7p multicolored	.20	.20
648	A88	10p multicolored	.30	.20
649	A88	12p multicolored	.50	.20
650	A88	15p multicolored	.80	.20
651	A88	20p multicolored	1.10	.20
652	A88	40p multicolored	1.60	.25
653	A88	45p multicolored	2.50	.40
		Nos. 647-653 (7)	7.00	1.65

Souvenir Sheet

654	A88	100p multicolored	7.50	5.50

ARGENTINA '85. No. 654 contains one
40x32mm stamp.

Composers
and Musical
Instruments
A89

Designs: 4p, Vincenzo Bellini (1801-1835),
harp, 1820, and descant viol, 16th cent. 5p,
Schumann (1810-1856) and Viennese pyramid piano, 1829. 7p, Chopin (1810-1849) and
piano-forte, 1817. 12p, Luigi Cherubini (1760-
1842) and 18th cent. Baryton violin and
Quinton viol. 20p, G. B. Pergolesi (1710-1736)
and double-manual harpsichord, 1734. 30p,
Handel (1685-1759), valve trumpet, 1825, and
timpani drum, 18th cent. 50p, Heinrich Schutz
(1585-1672), bass viol and two-stop oboe,
17th cent. 100s, Bach (1685-1750) and St.
Thomas Church organ, Leipzig.

1985, Aug. 5   **Perf. 12**

655	A89	4p multicolored	.45	.20
656	A89	5p multicolored	.55	.20
657	A89	7p multicolored	.75	.20
658	A89	12p multicolored	1.25	.20
659	A89	20p multicolored	1.75	.20
660	A89	30p multicolored	2.75	.30
661	A89	50p multicolored	4.50	.60
		Nos. 655-661 (7)	12.00	1.90

Souvenir Sheet
Perf. 11½

662	A89	100p multicolored	11.00	4.25

No. 662 contains one 30x50mm stamp.

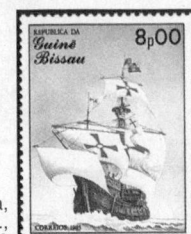

Santa Maria,
15th Cent.,
Spain — A90

Ships: 15p, Carack, 16th cent., Netherlands.
20p, Mayflower, 17th cent., Great Britain. 30p,
St. Louis, 17th cent., France. 35p, Royal Sovereign, 1635, Great Britain. 45p, Soleil Royal,
17th cent., France. 80p, English brig, 18th-
19th cent.

1985, Sept. 12   **Perf. 13**

663	A90	8p multicolored	.50	.20
664	A90	15p multicolored	.75	.20
665	A90	20p multicolored	1.00	.20
666	A90	30p multicolored	1.60	.30
667	A90	35p multicolored	1.90	.30
668	A90	45p multicolored	2.50	.45
669	A90	80p multicolored	4.75	.75
		Nos. 663-669 (7)	13.00	2.40

UN, 40th
Anniv.
A91

1985, Oct. 17

670	A91	10p Emblem, doves, vert.		.80
671	A91	20p Emblem, 40		1.60

Venus and
Mars, by
Sandro Botticelli
(1445-1510)
A92

Botticelli paintings (details): 7p, Virgin with
Child and St. John. 12p, St. Augustine in the
Work Hall. 15p, Awakening of Spring. 20p,
Virgin and Child. 40p, Virgin with Child and St.
John, diff. 45p, Birth of Venus. 100p, Virgin
and Child with Two Angels.

1985, Oct. 25   **Perf. 12½x13**

672	A92	7p multicolored	.50	.20
673	A92	10p multicolored	.55	.20
674	A92	12p multicolored	.70	.20
675	A92	15p multicolored	.80	.20
676	A92	20p multicolored	1.10	.20
677	A92	40p multicolored	2.25	.40
678	A92	45p multicolored	2.75	.45

Size: 73x106mm
Imperf

679	A92	100p multicolored	8.50	5.50
		Nos. 672-679 (8)	17.15	7.35

ITALIA '85.

Intl.
Youth
Year
A93

1985, Nov. 29   **Litho.**   **Perf. 12½**

680	A93	7p Dance	.45	.20
681	A93	13p Wind surfing	.55	.20
682	A93	15p Rollerskating	.60	.20
683	A93	25p Hang gliding	1.10	.20
684	A93	40p Surfing	1.75	.30
685	A93	50p Skateboarding	2.25	.50
686	A93	80p Parachuting	3.75	.70
		Nos. 680-686 (7)	10.45	2.30

Souvenir Sheet
Perf. 13

687	A93	100p Self-defense	7.50	5.50

No. 687 contains one 40x32mm stamp.

Miniature Sheet

Halley's Comet — A94

1986 World Cup Soccer
Championships, Mexico — A95

24th
Summer
Olympics,
Seoul,
1988
A96

Italian
Automobile
Industry,
Cent.
A97

German
Railways,
150th
Anniv.
A98

Discovery
of America,
500th
Anniv. (in
1992)
A99

First American Manned Space Flight,
25th Anniv. — A100

1986 Wimbledon Tennis
Championships — A101

1986 Masters Tennis
Championships — A102

Giotto Space Probe — A103

Designs: a, Comet tail. b, Comet. c, Trophy.
d, Trophy base. e, Five-ring Olympic emblem.
f, Alfa Tourer, Italy, c. 1905. g, Railway station,
Frankfurt-on Main, c. 1914. h, Barcelona, site
of Discovery of America exhibition and 1992
Olympics. i, Space station solar panels and
tanks. j, Space station. k, Removing cargo
from space shuttle. l, Docking facility, station
panels. m, Boris Becker swinging tennis
racket. n, Becker, diff. o, Ivan Lendl holding
racket. p, Lendl, diff.

1986, Dec. 30   **Litho.**   **Perf. 13½**

688	Sheet of 16	125.00	
a.-p.	A94-A102 15p any single	7.50	3.25

Souvenir Sheet

689	A103	100p multicolored	14.00	10.00

Nos. 688a-688b, 688c-688d, 688i-688l,
688m-688n, 688o-688p are se-tenant in continuous designs. Inscription on Nos. 688i-688l
incorrect; should read "TRIPULADO MER-
CURY / 5-5-1961."

Discovery of
America, 500th
Anniv. (in
1992) — A104

Designs: No. 690, Christopher Columbus
aboard caravelle. No. 691, Guadalquivir Port,
Seville, c. 1490. No. 692, Pedro Alvars Cabral
landing at Bahia, Brazil. No. 693, Bridge over
the Guadalquivir River, Seville. No. 694, Port,
Lisbon, 15th cent.

1987, Feb. 27

690	A104	50p multicolored	4.00	1.00
691	A104	50p multicolored	4.00	1.00
692	A104	50p multicolored	4.00	.70
693	A104	50p multicolored	4.00	1.00
		Nos. 690-693 (4)	16.00	3.70

Souvenir Sheet

| 694 | A104 | 150p multicolored | 18.00 | 10.00 |

No. 694 exists with pink or yellow anniv.
emblem pictured in vignette. Values are the
same.

Portuguese Guinea Nos. 306-309,
313, 316-317, Ovptd., Guinea-Bissau
No. 349 Surcharged

1987, July   Litho.   Perf. 13½

696	A21	100p on 20c #306	1.75	.60
697	A21	200p on 35c #307	3.25	1.25
698	A21	300p on 70c #308	5.00	1.60
699	A21	400p on 80c #309	5.50	2.00
700	A21	500p on 3.50e #313	7.75	2.75
701	A21	1000p on 15e #316	20.00	5.50
702	A21	2000p on 20e #317	40.00	13.50
		Perf. 13		
703	CD61	2500p on 2e #349	50.00	14.50
		Nos. 696-703 (8)	133.25	41.70

Placement of "Bissau," new denomination
and obliterating bar varies.

1988 Winter Olympics,
Calgary — A106

1988, Jan. 15   Litho.   Perf. 13

704	A106	5p Pairs figure skating	.50	.20
705	A106	10p Luge	.80	.20
706	A106	50p Skiing	1.00	.20
707	A106	200p Slalom skiing	1.25	.35
708	A106	300p Skibobbing	2.25	.50
709	A106	500p Ski jumping, vert.	3.25	.65
710	A106	800p Speed skating, vert.	5.75	2.25
		Nos. 704-710 (7)	14.80	4.35

Souvenir Sheet

| 710A | A106 | 900p Two-man luge | 9.00 | 3.25 |

No. 710A contains one 40x32mm stamp.

Soccer — A107

Various soccer plays.

1988, Apr. 14   Litho.   Perf. 13

711	A107	5p multi	.20	.20
712	A107	10p multi, diff.	.20	.20
713	A107	50p multi, diff.	.75	.20
714	A107	200p multi, diff.	1.60	.40
715	A107	300p multi, diff.	2.50	.50
716	A107	500p multi, diff.	3.50	.65
717	A107	800p multi, diff.	6.00	1.60
		Nos. 711-717 (7)	14.75	3.75

Souvenir Sheet

| 718 | A107 | 900p multi, diff. | 11.00 | 4.25 |

ESSEN '88 stamp exhibition. No. 718 contains one 32x40mm stamp.

1988 Summer Olympics,
Seoul — A108

Perf. 12½x12, 12x12½

1988, Feb. 26   Litho.

719	A108	5p Yachting, vert.	.20	.20
720	A108	10p Equestrian	.20	.20
721	A108	50p High jump	.50	.20
722	A108	200p Shooting	1.60	.40
723	A108	300p Long jump, vert.	2.50	.50
724	A108	500p Tennis, vert.	3.75	.65
725	A108	800p Women's archery, vert.	6.25	1.25
		Nos. 719-725 (7)	15.00	3.40

Souvenir Sheet

Perf. 12½

| 726 | A108 | 900p Soccer | 7.00 | 2.25 |

No. 726 contains one 40x32mm stamp.

Ancient Ships — A109

Designs: 5p, Egyptian, c. 3300 B.C. 10p,
Pharaoh Sahure's ship, c. 2700 B.C. 50p,
Queen Hatsepsowe's ship, c. 1500 B.C. 200p,
Ramses III's ship, c. 1200 B.C. 300p, Greek
trireme, 480 B.C. 500p, Etruscan bireme, 600
B.C. 800p, Venetian galley, 12th cent.

1988   Litho.   Perf. 13x12½

727	A109	5p multi	.20	.20
728	A109	10p multi	.20	.20
729	A109	50p multi	.65	.20
730	A109	200p multi	1.50	.20
731	A109	300p multi	2.10	.30
732	A109	500p multi	3.50	.50
733	A109	800p multi	5.75	.85
		Nos. 727-733 (7)	13.90	2.45

FINLANDIA
'88 — A110

Chess champions, board and chessmen.

1988   Litho.   Perf. 12x12½

734	A110	5p Philidor	.20	.20
735	A110	10p Staunton	.20	.20
736	A110	50p Anderssen	.70	.20
737	A110	200p Morphy	1.75	.20
738	A110	300p Steinitz	2.25	.30
739	A110	500p Lasker	4.25	.40
740	A110	800p Capablanca	6.25	.65
		Nos. 734-740 (7)	15.60	2.15

Souvenir Sheet

Perf. 13

| 741 | A110 | 900p Ruy Lopez | 12.00 | 4.50 |

No. 741 contains one 40x32mm stamp.

Dogs
A111

1988   Perf. 13x12½

742	A111	5p Basset hound	.35	.20
743	A111	10p Great blue of Gascony	.45	.20
744	A111	50p Sabujo of Italy	.45	.20
745	A111	200p Yorkshire terrier	1.10	.55
746	A111	300p Small musterlander	1.75	.80
747	A111	500p Pointer	2.75	1.40
748	A111	800p German setter	4.50	2.25
		Nos. 742-748 (7)	11.35	5.60

Souvenir Sheet

Perf. 12½

| 749 | A111 | 900 German shepherd | 7.00 | 2.50 |

No. 749 contains one 40x32mm stamp.

Intl. Red Cross and Red Crescent
Organizations, 125th Annivs. — A112

1988   Perf. 13

750	A112	10p Jean-Henri Dunant	.70	.20
751	A112	50p Dr. T. Maunoir	.30	.20
752	A112	200p Dr. Louis Appia	1.25	.20
753	A112	800p Gustave Moynier	5.75	.65
		Nos. 750-753 (4)	8.00	1.25

Maps and Fauna — A113

1988   Perf. 12½x13, 13x12½

754	A113	5p *Panthera leo*	.20	.20
755	A113	10p *Glaucidium brasilianum*	.20	.20
756	A113	50p *Upupa epops*	.70	.20
757	A113	200p *Equus burchelli antiquorum*	1.50	.20

758	A113	300p *Loxodonta africana*	2.25	.30
759	A113	500p *Acryllium vulturinum*	3.50	1.60
760	A113	800p *Diceros bicornis*	6.00	.65
		Nos. 754-760 (7)	14.35	3.35

Nos. 754-755, 758-760 vert. The genus
"Upupa" is misspelled on the 50p and "Loxodonta" is misspelled on the 300p.

Samora Machel
(1933-1986),
Pres. of
Mozambique
A114

1988   Perf. 13

761	A114	10p shown	.20	.20
762	A114	50p Raising fist	.45	.20
763	A114	200p With sentry	1.50	.20
764	A114	300p Wearing earphones at UN	2.50	.25
		Nos. 761-764 (4)	4.65	.85

Mushrooms — A115

1988   Litho.   Perf. 13x12½

765	A115	370p *Peziza aurantia*	2.50	.35
766	A115	470p *Morchella*	3.00	.40
767	A115	600p *Amanita caesarea*	4.50	.60
768	A115	780p *Amanita muscaria*	6.50	.70
769	A115	800p *Amanita phalloides*	6.50	.70
770	A115	900p *Agaricus bisporus*	7.75	.90
771	A115	945p *Cantharellus cibarius*	7.25	.95
		Nos. 765-771 (7)	38.00	4.60

1992 Winter Olympics,
Albertville — A116

1989, Oct. 12   Litho.   Perf. 12½x12

772	A116	50p Speed skating	.70	.20
773	A116	100p Women's figure skating	.90	.20
774	A116	200p Ski jumping	1.75	.20
775	A116	350p Skiing	2.10	.40
776	A116	500p Skiing, diff.	3.50	.55
777	A116	800p Bobsled	5.50	.95
778	A116	1000p Ice hockey	7.00	1.10
		Nos. 772-778 (7)	21.45	3.60

Souvenir Sheet

Perf. 12½

| 779 | A116 | 1500p Ice hockey, diff. | 11.00 | 5.00 |

No. 779 contains one 32x40mm stamp.

World Cup Soccer Championships,
Italy — A117

Various soccer players.

1989		Litho.	Perf. 12½	
780	A117	50p multicolored	.20	.20
781	A117	100p multicolored	.65	.20
782	A117	200p multicolored	.90	.20
783	A117	350p multicolored	1.50	.35
784	A117	500p multicolored	1.75	.45
785	A117	800p multicolored	3.50	.80
786	A117	1000p multicolored	4.50	.90
		Nos. 780-786 (7)	13.00	3.10

Souvenir Sheet
Perf. 13

786A	A117	1500p multicolored	7.50	2.75

No. 786A contains one 40x32mm stamp.

Lilies (Lilium) — A118

1989			Perf. 12½	
787	A118	50p Limelight	.20	.20
788	A118	100p Candidum	.50	.20
789	A118	200p Pardalinum	.90	.35
790	A118	350p Auratum	1.50	.65
791	A118	500p Canadense	1.75	.70
792	A118	800p Enchantment	3.50	1.50
793	A118	1000p Black Dragon	4.50	1.90
		Nos. 787-793 (7)	12.85	5.50

Souvenir Sheet

794	A118	1500p Lilium pyrenaicum	7.50	2.75

No. 794 contains one 32x40mm stamp.

Trains A119

Various railroad engines.

1989, May 24		Litho.	Perf. 13	
795	A119	50p multicolored	.20	.20
796	A119	100p multicolored	.45	.20
797	A119	200p multicolored	.75	.35
798	A119	350p multicolored	1.60	.70
799	A119	500p multicolored	2.25	.95
800	A119	800p multicolored	3.25	1.60

Perf. 12½
Size: 68x27mm

801	A119	1000p multicolored	4.00	.85
		Nos. 795-801 (7)	12.50	4.85

Souvenir Sheet
Perf. 12½

802	A119	1500p multicolored	7.00	3.25

No. 802 contains one 32x40mm stamp.

La Marseillaise by Francois Rude — A120

Paintings: 100p, Armed mob. 200p, Storming the Bastille. 350p, Lafayette, Liberty, vert. 500p, Dancing around the Liberty tree. 800p, Rouget de Lisle singing La Marseillaise by Pils. 1000p, Storming the Bastille, diff. 1500p, Arms of the Republic of France.

Perf. 12½, 12x12½ (350p)

1989, July 5				
803	A120	50p shown	.20	.20
804	A120	100p multicolored	.40	.20
805	A120	200p multicolored	.80	.40
806	A120	350p multicolored, 27x44mm	1.60	.75
807	A120	500p multicolored	2.25	1.00
808	A120	800p multicolored	3.50	1.60
809	A120	1000p multicolored	4.25	2.00
		Nos. 803-809 (7)	13.00	6.15

Souvenir Sheet
Perf. 13

810	A120	1500p multicolored	7.50	2.75

Birds A121

Designs: 50p, Alectroenas pulcherrima. 100p, Streptopelia senegalensis. 200p, Oena capensis. 350p, Claravis mondetoura. 500p, Streptopelia roseogrisea. 800p, Otidiphaps nobilis. 1000p, Chalcophaps indica. 1500p, Reinwardtoena Reinwardtsi.

1989		Litho.	Perf. 12½	
811	A121	50p multicolored	.20	.20
812	A121	100p multicolored	.45	.20
813	A121	200p multicolored	.85	.40
814	A121	350p multicolored	1.50	.65
815	A121	500p multicolored	2.25	.90
816	A121	800p multicolored	3.50	1.60
817	A121	1000p multicolored	4.25	1.90
		Nos. 811-817 (7)	13.00	5.85

Souvenir Sheet

818	A121	1500p multicolored	6.50	3.50

Pioneers Organization — A122

1989			Perf. 13	
819	A122	10p Children presenting flag, vert.	.20	.20
820	A122	50p Children saluting, vert.	.60	.20
821	A122	200p shown	2.50	.95
822	A122	300p Children playing ball	3.50	1.50
		Nos. 819-822 (4)	6.80	2.85

Town of Cacheu, 400th Anniv. A123

1989, Nov. 30				
823	A123	10p Monument, vert.	.20	.20
824	A123	50p shown	.20	.20
825	A123	200p Old building	1.00	.20
826	A123	300p Church	1.60	.30
		Nos. 823-826 (4)	3.00	.90

Dated 1988.

A124

Designs: Prehistoric creatures.

Perf. 13, 12½x12 (100p)

1989, Sept. 15				
827	A124	50p Trachodon	.20	.20
828	A124	100p Edaphosaurus, 68x27mm	.50	.20
829	A124	200p Mesosaurus	.90	.35
830	A124	350p Elephas primigenius	1.60	.65
831	A124	500p Tyrannosaurus	2.75	.90
832	A124	800p Stegosaurus	4.25	1.50
833	A124	1000p Cervus megaceros	4.75	1.75
		Nos. 827-833 (7)	14.95	5.55

Nos. 828, 831-833 horiz.

A125

1989, Apr. 10		Litho.	Perf. 13	

Designs: Musical instruments.

834	A125	50p Bombalon	.40	.20
835	A125	100p Flauta	.60	.20
836	A125	200p Tambor	1.25	.30
837	A125	350p Dondon	2.00	.40
838	A125	500p Balafon	2.50	.45
839	A125	800p Kora	3.00	.60
840	A125	1000p Nhanhero	3.25	.70
		Nos. 834-840 (7)	13.00	2.85

A126

1989, July 13			Perf. 12x12½	

Designs: Indian artifacts.

841	A126	50p Teotihuacan	.25	.20
842	A126	100p Mochica	.40	.20
843	A126	200p Jaina	.75	.35
844	A126	350p Nayarit	1.60	.70
845	A126	500p Inca	2.25	1.00
846	A126	800p Hopewell	3.50	1.60
847	A126	1000p Taina	4.25	1.90
		Nos. 841-847 (7)	13.00	5.95

Souvenir Sheet
Perf. 12½

848	A126	1500p Indian statuette	7.50	2.50

Brasiliana '89 Philatelic Exhibition. Nos. 841-847 printed se-tenant with multicolored label showing scenes of colonization. No. 848 contains one 32x40mm stamp.

1992 Summer Olympics, Barcelona A127

1989, June 3			Perf. 12½x13	
849	A127	50p Hurdles	.30	.20
850	A127	100p Boxing	.55	.20
851	A127	200p High jump	.80	.20
852	A127	350p Sprinters in the blocks	1.25	.35
853	A127	500p Woman sprinter	2.10	.55
854	A127	800p Gymnastics	3.25	.95
855	A127	1000p Pole vault	4.25	1.25
		Nos. 849-855 (7)	12.50	3.70

Souvenir Sheet

856	A127	1500p Soccer	6.50	2.40

No. 856 contains one 32x40mm stamp.

Wild Animals — A128

1989, Nov. 24			Perf. 12½	
857	A128	50p Syncerus caffer	.45	.20
858	A128	100p Equus quagga	.70	.20
859	A128	200p Diceros bicornis	.95	.25
860	A128	350p Okapia johnstoni	1.50	.40
861	A128	500p Macaca mulatta	2.00	.60
862	A128	800p Hippopotamus amphibius	3.25	1.00
863	A128	1000p Acinonyx jubatus	3.75	1.25
864	A128	1500p Panthera leo	5.75	1.75
		Nos. 857-864 (8)	18.35	5.65

Christmas A129

Paintings of the Madonna and Child (50p) and the Adoration of the Magi.

1989, Dec. 10			Perf. 13	
865	A129	50p Fra Filippo Lippi	.60	.20
866	A129	100p Pieter Brueghel	.80	.20
867	A129	200p Mostaert	1.10	.20
868	A129	350p Durer	1.75	.35
869	A129	500p Rubens	3.00	.60
870	A129	800p Van der Weyden	4.75	.90
871	A129	1000p Francia, horiz.	6.00	1.25
		Nos. 865-871 (7)	18.00	3.70

Womens' Hairstyles A130

Various hairstyles.

1989, Mar. 8			Perf. 12½x13	
872	A130	50p multicolored	.20	.20
873	A130	100p multicolored	.55	.20
874	A130	200p multicolored	.85	.35
875	A130	350p multicolored	1.50	.65
875A	A130	500p multicolored	2.00	.90
876	A130	800p multicolored	3.50	1.50
877	A130	1000p multicolored	4.25	1.75
		Nos. 872-877 (7)	12.85	5.55

Vegetables — A131

1989, May 20   *Perf. 12½*
878	A131	50p	Capisium annum	.20 .20
879	A131	100p	Solanium	.20 .20
880	A131	200p	Curcumis peco	.85 .20
881	A131	350p	Solanium licopersicum	1.50 .40
882	A131	500p	Solanium itiopium	2.10 .60
883	A131	800p	Hibiscus esculentus	3.25 .95
884	A131	1000p	Oseille de guine	4.25 1.25
		Nos. 878-884 (7)		12.35 3.80

Visit of Pope John Paul II — A132

1990, Jan. 27   **Litho.**   *Perf. 13½*
885	A132	500p	shown	2.25 1.60
886	A132	1000p	multi, diff.	4.50 3.25

Souvenir Sheet
887	A132	1500p	multi, diff., vert.	7.50 6.25

Souvenir Sheet

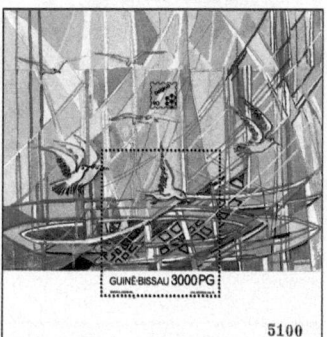

Belgica '90 — A133

1990, June 1   *Perf. 14½*
888	A133	3000p	multicolored	7.00 3.50

World Meteorology Day — A134

1990, Oct. 1   **Litho.**   *Perf. 13*
889	A134	1000p	Radar weather map	1.75 .70
890	A134	3000p	Heliograph	7.25 2.50

LUBRAPEX '90 — A135

1990, Sept. 21   *Perf. 14*
891	A135	500p	Rooster, hen	1.10 .50
892	A135	800p	Turkey	1.90 .75
893	A135	1000p	Duck, ducklings	2.50 .90
		Nos. 891-893 (3)		5.50 2.15

Souvenir Sheet
Perf. 13½
894	A135	1500p	Rooster, turkey, ducks	6.00 2.40

UN Development Program, 40th Anniv. — A136

1990   **Litho.**   *Perf. 14*
895	A136	1000p	multicolored	2.50 .75

Fight against AIDS.

Textile Manufacturing A137

No. 896: a, Gossypium hirsutum. b, Processing cotton. c, Spinning thread. d, Picking cotton. e, Moth, silkworms. f, Dyeing thread. g, Weaving. h, Animal design. i, Multicolored stripes design. j, Stripes, dots design.

1990
896			Sheet of 10	2.00
a.-j.	A137	150p	any single	.25 .25
897	A137	400p	like #896a	.35 .20
898	A137	500p	like #896g	.45 .20
899	A137	600p	like #896h	.55 .35
		Nos. 896-899 (4)		3.35 .75

Carnival Masks A138

1990   **Litho.**   *Perf. 14*
900	A138	200p	Mickey Mouse	.45 .20
901	A138	300p	Hippopotamus	.65 .20
902	A138	600p	Bull	1.25 .35
903	A138	1200p	Bull, diff.	2.50 .50
		Nos. 900-903 (4)		4.85 1.25

Fish A139

Designs: 300p, Pentanemus quinquarius. 400p, Psettias sabae. 500p, Chaetodipterus goreensis. 600p, Trachinotus goreensis.

1991, Mar. 10   **Litho.**   *Perf. 14*
904	A139	300p	multicolored	.65 .35
905	A139	400p	multicolored	1.00 .45
906	A139	500p	multicolored	1.10 .55
907	A139	600p	multicolored	1.25 .70
		Nos. 904-907 (4)		4.00 2.05

Fire Trucks A140

1991, Aug. 19   **Litho.**   *Perf. 14*
908	A140	200p	shown	.40 .20
909	A140	500p	Ladder truck	.85 .45
910	A140	800p	Rescue vehicle	1.25 .70
911	A140	1500p	Ambulance	2.50 1.25
		Nos. 908-911 (4)		5.00 2.60

Birds — A141

Designs: 100p, Kaupifalco monogrammicus. 250p, Balearica pavonina. 350p, Bucorvus abyssinicus. 500p, Ephippiorhynchus senegalensis. 1500p, Kaupifalco monogrammicus, diff.

1991, Sept. 10
912	A141	100p	multicolored	.75 .20
913	A141	250p	multicolored	1.10 .20
914	A141	350p	multicolored	1.75 .55
915	A141	500p	multicolored	2.40 .75
		Nos. 912-915 (4)		6.00 1.70

Souvenir Sheet
Perf. 14½
916	A141	1500p	multicolored	5.00 5.00

No. 916 contains one 40x50mm stamp.

Messages A142

1991, Oct. 28   **Litho.**   *Perf. 14*
917	A142	250p	Congratulations	.40 .20
918	A142	400p	With love	.75 .40
919	A142	800p	Happiness	1.25 .80
920	A142	1000p	Seasons Greetings	1.60 .95
		Nos. 917-920 (4)		4.00 2.35

Fruits — A143

Designs: 500p, Landolfia owariensis. 1500p, Dialium guineensis. 2000p, Adansonia digitata. 3000p, Parkia biglobosa.

1992, Mar. 25   **Litho.**   *Perf. 14*
921	A143	500p	multicolored	.30 .30
922	A143	1500p	multicolored	.75 .75
923	A143	2000p	multicolored	1.10 1.10
924	A143	3000p	multicolored	1.75 1.75
		Nos. 921-924 (4)		3.90 3.90

Healthy Hearts — A144

1992, Apr. 7

Designs: 1500p, Cigarette butts, healthy heart. 4000p, Heart running over junk food.
925	A144	1500p	multicolored	1.75 .80
926	A144	4000p	multicolored	3.75 2.10

Traditional Costumes A145

Designs: a, 400p, Fula. b, 600p, Balanta. c, 1000p, Fula, diff. d, 1500p, Manjaco.

1992, Feb. 28   **Litho.**   *Perf. 14*
927	A145	Strip of 4, #a.-d.		3.00 2.10

Canoes A146

Designs: Nos. 928-931, Various types of canoes. No. 932, Alcedo cristata galerita.

1992, May 10
928	A146	750p	multicolored	.40 .40
929	A146	800p	multicolored	.55 .55
930	A146	1000p	multicolored	.70 .70
931	A146	1300p	multicolored	.90 .90
		Nos. 928-931 (4)		2.55 2.55

Souvenir Sheet
Perf. 13½
932	A146	1500p	multicolored	6.00 6.00

Trees — A147

a, 100p, Cassia alata. b, 400p, Perlebia purpurea. c, 1000p, Caesalpina pulcherrima. d, 1500p, Adenanthera pavonina. 3000p, Caesalpina pulcherrima, diff.

1992, May 8   *Perf. 14*
933	A147	Block of 4, #a.-d.		5.50 5.50

Souvenir Sheet
Perf. 13½
934	A147	3000p	multicolored	5.00 5.00

1992 Summer Olympics, Barcelona A148

1992, July 28   **Litho.**   *Perf. 14*
935	A148	600p	Basketball	.25 .20
936	A148	1000p	Volleyball	.60 .20
937	A148	1500p	Team handball	.90 .20
938	A148	2000p	Soccer	1.25 .20
		Nos. 935-938 (4)		3.00 .80

Trees
A149

Designs: 1000p, Afzelia africana Smith. 1500p, Kaya senegalenses. 2000p, Militia regia. 3000p, Pterocarpus erinaceus.

1992, Sept. 11 | | | **Perf. 12**
939 A149 1000p multicolored | .50 | .45
940 A149 1500p multicolored | .65 | .60
941 A149 2000p multicolored | .95 | .80
942 A149 3000p multicolored | 1.40 | 1.25
Nos. 939-942 (4) | 3.50 | 3.10

Souvenir Sheet

Discovery of America, 500th
Anniv. — A150

1992, Sept. 18
943 A150 5000p multicolored | 3.50 | 3.50
Genoa '92.

Procolobus
Badius
Temminckii
A151

Designs: a, Pair in tree. b, Adult seated in vegetation c, Adult seated in tree fork. d, Female with young.

1992 **Litho.** **Perf. 12x11½**
944 A151 2000p Strip of 4, #a.-d. 5.25 5.25
World Wildlife Fund.

Reptiles
A152

1993, May 18 **Litho.** **Perf. 14**
945 A152 1500p Bitis sp. | .50 | .25
946 A152 3000p Osteolaemus te-traspis | 1.10 | .55
947 A152 4000p Varanus niloticus | 1.50 | .70
948 A152 5000p Agama agama | 1.90 | .85
a. Souvenir sheet of 4, #945-948 | 6.00 | 2.50
Nos. 945-948 (4) | 5.00 | 2.35

Souvenir Sheet

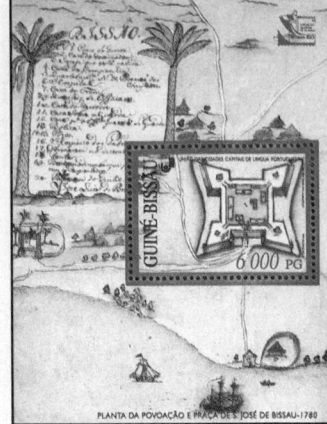

Union of Portuguese Speaking
Capitals — A153

1993, July 30 **Litho.** **Perf. 13½**
949 A153 6000p Fort 1.50 1.50
Brasiliana '93.

Tourism — A154

Designs: a, 1000p. b, 2000p. c, 4000p. d, 5000p. Illustration reduced.

1993, Nov. 15 **Litho.** **Perf. 14**
950 A154 Block of 4, #a.-d. 4.00 4.00

Traditional
Jewelry
A155

1993, Nov. 30 **Perf. 14½**
951 A155 1500p Bracelet | .45 | .20
952 A155 3000p Mask pendant | 1.10 | .50
953 A155 4000p Circle pendant | 1.50 | .65
954 A155 5000p Filigree pendant | 1.75 | .80
Nos. 951-954 (4) | 4.80 | 2.15

1994, Nov. 30
Souvenir Sheet
955 A155 18,000p like #952 8.00 8.00
Hong Kong '94 (No. 955). No. 955 has continuous design.

1994 World Cup Soccer
Championships, US — A156

Various stylized designs of player, ball, net.

1994, June 17 **Litho.** **Perf. 14**
956 A156 4000p multicolored | 1.50 | .85
957 A156 5000p multicolored | 2.00 | 1.10
958 A156 5500p multicolored | 2.50 | 1.25
959 A156 6500p multicolored | 3.00 | 1.60
Nos. 956-959 (4) | 9.00 | 4.80

Flowering
Plants — A157

Designs: 2000p, Erythrina senegalensis. 3000p, Cassia occidentalis. 4000p, Gardenia ternifolia. 6000p, Cochlospermum tinctorium.

1994, May 30 **Litho.** **Perf. 14**
960 A157 2000p multicolored | .90 | .45
961 A157 3000p multicolored | 1.25 | .70
962 A157 4000p multicolored | 1.60 | .90
963 A157 6000p multicolored | 2.75 | 1.50
Nos. 960-963 (4) | 6.50 | 3.55

Snakes — A158

#964: a, Dasypeltis scabra. b, Philothamnus. c, Naja melanoleuca. d, Python sebae. 15,000p, Thelotornis kirtlandii.

1994, Aug. 16 **Litho.** **Perf. 14**
964 A158 5000p Block of 4, #a.-d. 8.00 8.00

Souvenir Sheet
Perf. 13½
965 A158 15,000p multicolored 6.50 6.50
PHILAKOREA '94, SINGPEX '94. No. 965 contains one 60x50mm stamp.

Palmeira
Dendem — A159

3000p, Climbing tree to pick fruit. 6500p, Hand processing palm fruit into baskets. 7500p, Mechanical processing. 8000p, Palm oil, uses.

1995, Feb. 27 **Litho.** **Perf. 14**
966 A159 3000p multicolored | .75 | .35
967 A159 6500p multicolored | 1.50 | .70
968 A159 7500p multicolored | 1.75 | .80
969 A159 8000p multicolored | 2.00 | .85
Nos. 966-969 (4) | 6.00 | 2.70

FAO, 50th
Anniv.
A160

1995 **Litho.** **Perf. 13½**
970 A160 3000p Net fishing | .75 | .45
971 A160 6500p Disking field | 1.50 | .85
972 A160 7500p Hands holding fruit | 1.75 | 1.00
973 A160 8000p Vendors along road | 2.00 | 1.10
a. Souvenir sheet of 2, #972-973 | 4.50 | 2.25
Nos. 970-973 (4) | 6.00 | 3.40

UN, 50th
Anniv. — A161

1995, Oct. 24 **Litho.** **Perf. 13½**
974 A161 4000p shown | 1.00 | .55
975 A161 5500p UN flag | 1.25 | .75
976 A161 7500p Natl. flag | 1.75 | 1.00
977 A161 8000p Hand on dove | 2.00 | 1.10
Nos. 974-977 (4) | 6.00 | 3.40

Souvenir Sheet
978 A161 15,000p UN emblem 5.00 5.00

100 Centimes = 1 Franc (1997)

Endangered Animals — A166

No. 995: a, 5000p, Hippopotamus. b, 7500p, Crocodile. c, 10,000p, Chelonia mydas. d, 12,000p, Trichechus senegalensis.

1997 **Litho.** **Perf. 12x11¾**
995 A166 Block of 4, #a-d
Despite change to franc currency on May 2, 1997, Nos. 995-997 have denominations in pesos.

Venomous Animals — A167

No. 996: a, 7500p, Pandinus imperator. b, 8000p, Naja nigricollis. c, 10,000p, Scolopendra morsitans. d, 11,000p, Lycosa tarentula.

1997
996 A167 Block of 4, #a-d — —

Economic Community of West African
States, 20th Anniv. (in 1995) — A168

1997, Dec. 26
997 A168 25,000p multi — —

Native
Foods
A169

Designs: 100fr, Caldo branco. 120fr, Siga. 160fr, Caldo de amendoin. 190fr, Caldo de chabeu.

1998, June 1
998-1001 A169 Set of 4 — —

No. 1001 Overprinted in Brown

1998, Sept. 4   Litho.   Perf. 12x11¾
1002 A169 190fr on No. 1001 — —

Maritime Discoveries — A170

1998, Oct. 9   Perf. 12x11¾
1003 A170 200fr multi — —
 a.   Souvenir sheet of 1, perf. 12½ — —

Marine Life A171

Designs: 150fr, Cultellus tenuis. 170fr, Penaeus keraethurus. 200fr, Periophthalmus papilio. 250fr, Istiophorus albicans.

1998, Dec. 28   Perf. 12x11¾
1004-1007 A171 Set of 4 — —
1007a   Souvenir sheet, #1004-1007, perf. 12½ — —

Souvenir Sheet

España 2000 World Philatelic Exhibition — A174

2000   Litho.   Perf. 13x12¾
1016 A174 1000fr multi — —

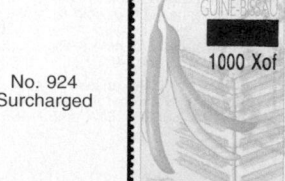

No. 924 Surcharged

Methods and Perfs As Before 2000 ?
1027 A143 1000fr on 3000p #924 —
 At least 12 other surcharges were issued in this set. The editors would like to examine any examples.

AIR POST STAMPS

Liftoff of Soyuz Spacecraft AP1

Apollo-Soyuz mission: 10p, Launch of Apollo spacecraft. 15p, Leonov, Stafford and meeting in space. 20p, Eclipse of the sun. 30p, Infra-red photo of Earth. 40p, Return to Earth. 50p, Apollo and Soyuz docked, horiz.

1976, Oct. 4   Perf. 13½
C10   AP1   5p multicolored
C10A   AP1   10p multicolored
C10B   AP1   15p multicolored
C10C   AP1   20p multicolored
C10D   AP1   30p multicolored
C10E   AP1   40p multicolored
 Nos. C10-C10E (6)   11.50   6.50

Souvenir Sheet
C10F   AP1   50p multicolored   5.00   5.00
 No. C10F contains one 60x42mm stamp. Nos. C10-C10E exist in souvenir sheets of one, perf. and imperf.

Viking Spacecraft Orbiting Mars AP2

35p, Viking gathering Martian soil samples.

1977, Jan. 27
C11   AP2   25p multicolored   2.50   1.00
C11A   AP2   35p multicolored   2.50   1.00

Nos. 372-373 Surcharged with New Value and "CORREIO AEREO" in Black on Silver Panels

1978   Litho.   Perf. 13½
C12 A32 15p on 3.50p multi   1.10   .40
C13 A32 30p on 50c multi   1.50   .60

History of Aviation Type of 1980

1980   Litho.   Perf. 13½
C14 A38 35p Willy de Houthulst, Hanriot HD.1   2.75   1.00
C14A A38 40p Charles Guynemer, Spad S. VII   3.75   1.25

Souvenir Sheet
C14B A38 50p Comdr. de Rose, Nieuport   6.50   4.50
 No. C14B contains one stamp 37x55mm.

Winter Olympics Type of 1980

1980
C15 A39 35p Slalom   2.75   1.00
C16 A39 40p Figure skating 3.50   1.25

Souvenir Sheet
C17 A39 50p Ice hockey, horiz.   7.00   4.50

Summer Olympics Type of 1980
1980, Aug.   Litho.   Perf. 13½
C18 A40 35p Somersault   4.25   1.00
C19 A40 40p Running   5.00   1.25

Souvenir Sheet
C20 A40 50p Emblem   7.00   4.50

Literacy Type of 1980
1980, Aug.   Litho.   Perf. 13½
C21 A41 15p like #404   2.25   .50
C22 A41 25p like #405   3.75   .60

Space Type of 1981
35p, Viking 1 & 2. 40p, Apollo-Soyuz craft & crew. 50p, Apollo 11 crew, craft & emblem.

1981, May   Litho.   Perf. 13½
C23 A45 35p multicolored   3.50   1.25
C24 A45 40p multicolored   3.75   1.50

Souvenir Sheet
C25 A45 50p multicolored   9.00   6.00
 No. C25 contains one stamp 60x42mm.

Soccer Type of 1981
Designs: 35p, Rummenigge, Germany. 40p, Kempes, Argentina. 50p, Juanito, Spain.

1981, May
C26 A46 35p multicolored   3.50   1.25
C27 A46 40p multicolored   3.75   1.50

Souvenir Sheet
C28 A46 50p multicolored   11.00   7.25
 No. C28 contains one stamp 56x40mm.

Royal Wedding Type of 1981
1981   Litho.   Perf. 13½
C29 A47 35p Palace   4.00   1.25
C30 A47 40p Prince of Wales arms   4.75   1.50

Souvenir Sheet
C31 A47 50p Couple   9.00   6.00

Picasso Type of 1981
1981, Dec.   Litho.   Perf. 13½
C32 A48 35p multicolored   5.50   1.25
C33 A48 40p multicolored   7.00   1.60

Souvenir Sheet
C34 A48 50p multicolored   9.00   6.00
 No. C34 contains one stamp 41x50mm.

Navigator Type of 1981
35p, Francis Drake, Golden Hinde. 40p, James Cook, Endeavor. 50p, Columbus, Santa Maria.

1981   Litho.   Perf. 13½
C35 A49 35p multicolored   3.75   1.40
C36 A49 40p multicolored   5.00   1.75

Souvenir Sheet
C37 A49 50p multicolored   12.00   7.50

Christmas Type of 1981
1981
C38 A50 30p Memling   4.00   1.40
C39 A50 35p Bellini, diff. 4.75   1.75

Souvenir Sheet
C40 A50 50p Fra Angelico   9.00   6.00
 No. C40 contains one 35x59mm stamp.

Scout Type of 1982
1982, June 9   Litho.   Perf. 13½
C41 A51 35p Canoeing   3.50   .85
C42 A51 40p Flying model planes   4.25   1.25

Souvenir Sheet
C43 A51 50p Playing chess   18.00   8.25
 No. C43 contains one 48x38mm stamp.

Soccer Type of 1982
1982, June 13   Litho.   Perf. 13½
C44 A52 35p Kempes   3.50   .85
C45 A52 40p Kaltz   4.25   1.25

Souvenir Sheet
C46 A52 50p Stadium   9.00   3.75

Diana Type of 1982 and

Princess Diana, 21st Birthday — AP3

1982
C47 A53 35p multicolored   3.50   .85
C48 A53 40p multicolored   4.25   1.25

Souvenir Sheet
C49 A53 50p multi, vert.   9.00   3.75

1982, Oct. 1   Litho. & Embossed
C49A AP3 200p gold & multi   18.00

Souvenir Sheet
C49B AP3 200p gold & multi, vert.   40.00
 For overprints see Nos. 456A-456B.

Audubon Birth Bicent. — AP4

1985, Apr. 16   Litho.   Perf. 12
C50 AP4 5p Brown pelican   1.00
C51 AP4 10p American white pelican   1.60
C52 AP4 20p Great blue heron   2.10
C53 AP4 40p American flamingo   4.25
 Nos. C50-C53 (4)   8.95

GUYANA

gī-'a-nə

LOCATION — Northeast coast of South America
GOVT. — Republic
AREA — 83,000 sq. mi.
POP. — 705,156 (1999 est.)
CAPITAL — Georgetown

The former Crown Colony of British Guiana became an independent member of the British Commonwealth May 26, 1966, taking the name Guyana. On February 23, 1970, Guyana became a republic, remaining a Commonwealth nation.

100 Cents = 1 Dollar

Catalogue values for all unused stamps in this country are for Never Hinged items.

Watermark

Wmk. 364 — Lotus Bud Multiple

British Guiana #254-256, 258-260, 267 Overprinted

Perf. 12½x13, 13

1966, May 26		**Wmk. 4**		**Engr.**	
1	A60	2c dark green		.50	.30
1A	A60	3c red brn & ol		4.75	5.00
2	A61	4c violet		2.75	.75
3	A60	6c yellow green		.75	.20
4	A60	8c ultra		2.50	1.00
5	A61	12c brn & blk		3.00	1.00
6	A61	$5 blk & ultra		40.00	57.50
		Nos. 1-6 (7)		54.25	65.75

Same Overprint on British Guiana Stamps and Types of 1954
Engr.; Center Litho. on $1

1966-67			**Wmk. 314 Upright**	
7	A60	1c black ('67)	.35	.40
8	A60	3c red brn & ol (#279)	2.00	.30
9	A61	4c violet ('67)	.35	.75
10	A60	5c blk & red (#280)	.50	.30
10A	A60	6c yel green ('67)	.35	.30
11	A60	8c ultra ('67)	.90	1.75
12	A61	12c brn & blk (#281)	.35	.30
13	A60	24c org & blk (#282)	7.25	.50
14	A60	36c blk & rose (#283)	.75	.60
15	A61	48c red brn & ultra (#284)	6.75	8.00
16	A61	72c emer & rose (#285)	1.00	1.00
17	A60	$1 blk & multi (#286)	4.25	.90
18	A60	$2 mag (#287)	3.75	1.60
19	A61	$5 black & ultra	3.00	5.00
		Nos. 7-19 (14)	31.55	21.70

For surcharges see Nos. 543, 544A, 625-626, 1446.

1966-67			**Wmk. 314 Sideways**	
7a	A60	1c black	.95	.45
9a	A61	4c violet	.95	.45
11a	A60	8c ultramarine	.95	.45
12a	A61	12c brown & black ('67)	.95	.45
13a	A60	24c orange & black	4.75	1.25
14a	A60	36c black & rose ('67)	.80	3.00
15a	A61	48c red brown & ultra	.80	.55
16a	A61	72c emerald & rose ('67)	4.00	6.75
17a	A60	$1 black & multi ('67)	5.00	6.75
18a	A60	$2 magenta ('67)	5.75	6.75
19a	A61	$5 black & ultra ('67)	4.00	6.75
		Nos. 7a-19a (11)	28.90	33.60

See Nos. 32-32T and note. For surcharges see Nos. 544, 627-628, 1447.

Flag and Map of Guyana — A1

Designs: 25c, $1, Arms of Guyana.

Unwmk.

1966, May 26		**Photo.**	**Perf. 14**	
20	A1	5c violet & multi	.30	.30
21	A1	15c dk red brown & multi	.30	.30
22	A1	25c brt blue & multi	.35	.35
23	A1	$1 sepia & multi	1.25	1.25
		Nos. 20-23 (4)	2.20	2.20

Guyana's independence, May 26, 1966.

Bank of Guyana A2

1966, Oct. 11			**Perf. 13½x14**	
24	A2	5c yel grn, blue, blk & gold	.30	.20
25	A2	25c blue, black & gold	.30	.20

Establishment of the Bank of Guyana.

British Guiana No. 13 — A3

1967, Feb. 23		**Litho.**	**Perf. 12½**	
26	A3	5c multicolored	.25	.20
a.		*Imperf., pair*		
27	A3	25c multicolored	.25	.20

Issued to honor the unique British Guiana 1c black on magenta stamp of 1856.

Canceled to Order

Remainders of Nos. 26-30, 33-38 and 54-67 were canceled and sold by the Post Office in 1969. Values are for these canceled to order stamps. Postally used examples do not command a significant premium.

Chateau Margot — A4

Designs: 15c, Independence Arch. 25c, Guyana Fort, Fort Island, horiz. $1, Parliament, National Assembly Hall, horiz.

Perf. 14, 14½x14, 14x14½

1967, May 26		**Photo.**	**Unwmk.**	
28	A4	6c multicolored	.20	.20
29	A4	15c multicolored	.20	.20
30	A4	25c multicolored	.20	.20
31	A4	$1 multicolored	.30	.20
		Nos. 28-31 (4)	.90	.80

First anniversary of independence.

British Guiana Stamps and Types of 1954 Locally Overprinted

1967			**Wmk. 4**	
32	A60	1c black	.20	.20
32A	A60	2c dark green	.20	.20
32B	A60	3c red brown & ol	.90	.20
32C	A61	4c violet	.30	.20
32D	A60	6c yellow green	.30	.20
32E	A60	8c ultramarine	.30	.20
32F	A61	12c brown & black	.30	.20
32G	A60	$2 magenta	3.25	2.50
32H	A61	$5 black & ultra	4.25	2.75
		Nos. 32-32H (9)	10.00	6.65

The 24c with Wmk. 4 also exists with this overprint. Value $325.

1967-68			**Wmk. 314 Upright**	
32I	A60	1c black ('68)	.20	.70
32J	A60	2c dk green ('68)	.45	1.40
32K	A60	3c red brown & ol	.35	.20
32L	A60	4c violet ('68)	.20	1.25
32M	A60	5c black & red	1.50	2.00
32N	A60	6c yel green ('68)	.40	.90
32O	A60	24c orange & blk	3.25	.45
32P	A60	36c black & rose	1.25	.20
32Q	A61	48c red brn & ultra	1.25	.75
32R	A61	72c emer & rose	2.50	.85
32S	A61	$1 black & multi	4.75	1.00
32T	A60	$2 magenta	5.00	4.00
		Nos. 32I-32T (12)	21.10	13.50

The 1c, 4c, 6c, 8c and $5 with Wmk. 314 were not issued without overprint.
For surcharges see Nos. 540, 542, 543A.

"Millie," the Bilingual Macaw — A5

Wicketkeeper, Emblem of West Indies Cricket Team — A6

Christmas Issues

1967, Nov. 6			**Perf. 14½x14**	
33	A5	5c olive green & multi	.30	.20
33A	A5	25c purple & multi	.40	.20

1968, Jan. 22				
34	A5	5c red & multi	.20	.20
35	A5	25c yel green & multi	.30	.20

1968, Jan. 8		**Photo.**	**Perf. 14**	

Designs: 6c, Batsman and emblem of Marylebone Cricket Club. 25c, Bowler and emblem of West Indies Cricket Team.

36	A6	5c multicolored	.25	.20
37	A6	6c multicolored	.25	.20
38	A6	25c multicolored	.50	.20
a.		*Strip of 3, #36-38*	1.25	1.25

Visit of the Marylebone Cricket Club to the West Indies, Jan.-Feb. 1968. Printed in sheets of 9.

Pike Cichlid — A7

Marail Guan — A8

Christ of St. John of the Cross, by Salvador Dali — A9

Designs: 2c, Piranha. 3c, Cichla ocellaris (fish). 5c, Armored catfish. 6c, Two-spotted cichlid. 15c, Harpy eagle. 20c, Hoatzin. 25c, Andean cock-of-the-rock. 40c, Great kiskadee. 50c, Agouti. 60c, Peccary. $1, Paca. $2, Armadillo. $5, Ocelot.

Perf. 14x14½, 14½x14

1968, Mar. 4		**Photo.**	**Unwmk.**	
39	A7	1c chalky blue & multi	.25	.20
40	A7	2c gray & multi	.25	.20
41	A7	3c grnsh bl & multi	.25	.20
42	A7	5c ultra & multi	.25	.20
43	A7	6c brt olive & multi	.80	.20
44	A8	10c yel green & multi	.90	.20
45	A8	15c green & multi	1.90	.20
46	A8	20c ap grn & multi	1.00	.20
47	A8	25c brt green & multi	1.00	.20
48	A8	40c pale brn & multi	1.75	.80
49	A7	50c rose brn & multi	1.40	.75
50	A7	60c lilac rose & multi	1.50	.25
51	A7	$1 dp orange & multi	1.90	.25
52	A7	$2 ocher & multi	2.50	3.50
53	A7	$5 red & multi	3.50	4.25
		Nos. 39-53 (15)	19.15	11.60

See Nos. 68-82.
For overprints & surcharges see #357, 410-413, 603, 752, 756, 761a, 1463, 1501, 1839, 2045.

1968, Mar. 25			**Perf. 14x14½**	
54	A9	5c car rose & multi	.20	.20
55	A9	25c brt violet & multi	.30	.20

Easter.

"Efficiency Year" — A10

Designs: 30c, 40c, "Savings bonds."

1968, July 22		**Litho.**	**Perf. 14**	
56	A10	6c green & multi	.20	.20
57	A10	25c fawn & multi	.20	.20
58	A10	30c multicolored	.20	.20
59	A10	40c multicolored	.20	.20
		Nos. 56-59 (4)	.80	.80

Issued to promote the sale of savings bonds and to publicize Efficiency Year.

Open Koran A11

Perf. 14x13½

1968, Oct. 9		**Photo.**	**Unwmk.**	
60	A11	6c sal pink, gold & blk	.20	.20
61	A11	25c pale vio, gold & blk	.20	.20
62	A11	30c pale yel grn, gold & blk	.20	.20
63	A11	40c pale blue, gold & blk	.20	.20
		Nos. 60-63 (4)	.80	.80

Koran's 1400th anniversary.
For overprints & surcharges see #354, 355, 441, 445, 487-488, 575, 630, 1464-1465.

Dish Aerials, Thomas Lands, Guyana — A12

Designs: 30c, 40c, Map showing connection between Guyana and Trinidad. All stamps are inscribed: "Guyana Sends Christmas Greetings to the World."

Wmk. 364

1968, Nov. 11   Litho.   Perf. 14
64 A12 6c blue, gray, ocher & emer   .20 .20
65 A12 25c brt rose lil, brn & emer   .20 .20
66 A12 30c blue grn & dk blue grn   .20 .20
67 A12 40c blue grn & red   .20 .20
    Nos. 64-67 (4)   .80 .80

Christmas; communications link with Trinidad by the tropospheric scatter system.

Types of 1968
Designs as before.

Perf. 14x14½, 14½x14
1968   Photo.   Wmk. 364
68 A7 1c chalky bl & multi   .20 .20
69 A7 2c gray & multi   .20 .25
70 A7 3c grnsh bl & multi   .20 .55
71 A7 5c ultra & multi   .20 .20
72 A7 6c brt olive & multi   .20 .55
73 A8 10c yel grn & multi   .65 .55
74 A8 15c green & multi   .65 .20
75 A8 20c apple grn & multi   .65 .65
76 A8 25c brt green & multi   .65 .20
77 A8 40c pale brn & multi   1.25 .65
78 A7 50c rose brn & multi   .70 .20
79 A7 60c lilac rose & multi   .75 .90
80 A7 $1 dp org & multi   1.50 1.10
81 A7 $2 ocher & multi   2.10 3.00
82 A7 $5 red & multi   2.10 4.50
    Nos. 68-82 (15)   12.00 13.70

For overprints & surcharges see #373, 376-377, 413D, 565-566, 633, 635, 704-705, 744, 749, 752a, 757-758, 761-762, 1862-1863, 1981, O2.

Celebrants Spraying Perfumed Powder — A13

Phagwah (Holi) Hindu Festival: 25c, 40c, Two celebrants spraying colored water.

1969, Feb. 26   Litho.   Perf. 13½
83 A13 6c multicolored   .25 .20
84 A13 25c multicolored   .25 .20
85 A13 30c multicolored   .25 .20
86 A13 40c multicolored   .25 .20
    Nos. 83-86 (4)   1.00 .80

The Last Supper, by Salvador Dali A14

1969, Mar. 10   Photo.   Perf. 13
87 A14 6c dp carmine & multi   .20 .20
88 A14 25c green & multi   .20 .20
89 A14 30c org brown & multi   .20 .20
90 A14 40c dp violet & multi   .20 .20
    Nos. 87-90 (4)   .80 .80

Easter. For overprints and surcharges see Nos. 393-394, 482-485, 572, 576, 634, 765, 772, 1407-1410, 1813, 1815-1817, 2050.

Map of Caribbean — A15   Prow of Aluminum Ship — A16

Design: 25c, "Strength in Unity," horiz.

Wmk. 364
1969, Apr. 30   Litho.   Perf. 13½
91 A15 6c violet blue & multi   .20 .20
92 A15 25c brt rose, yel & brown   .20 .20

1st anniv. of CARIFTA (Caribbean Free Trade Area).

1969, Apr. 30   Perf. 12x11, 11x12
50th Anniv. of the ILO: 40c, Bauxite processing plant, horiz.
93 A16 30c black, blue & silver   .40 .20
94 A16 40c multicolored   .50 .25

Flag Raising A17

Designs: 8c, 30c, Campfire.

1969, Aug. 13   Litho.   Perf. 13½x13
95 A17 6c pale green & multi   .20 .20
96 A17 8c orange & multi   .20 .20
97 A17 25c pale brown & multi   .20 .20
98 A17 30c multicolored   .20 .20
99 A17 50c rose & multi   .20 .20
    Nos. 95-99 (5)   1.00 1.00

60th anniv. of Scouting in Guyana; 3rd Caribbean Scout Jamboree, Georgetown, Aug. 13-22. For overprints and surcharges see Nos. 392, 395, 397, 402, 404-405, 453.

Gandhi and Spinning Wheel A18

1969, Oct. 1   Perf. 14½x14
100 A18 6c olive, blk & lt brn   .30 .65
101 A18 15c rose lilac, blk & lt brn   1.00 .65

Mohandas K. Gandhi (1868-1948), leader in India's fight for independence.

Mother Sally Troupe — A19   City Hall, Georgetown — A20

1969, Nov. 17   Perf. 14x13½
102 A19 5c multicolored   .20 .20
103 A20 6c blue & multi   .20 .20
104 A19 25c multicolored   .20 .20
105 A20 60c orange & multi   .20 .20
    Nos. 102-105 (4)   .80 .80

Christmas. The 5c, 6c, and 25c exist without the "Christmas 1969" overprint.

Prime Minister Forbes Burnham and Map — A21   Descent from the Cross, by Rubens — A22

6c, "Rural Self Help Project" (man & woman building house). 15c, University of Guyana, horiz. 25c, President's Residence, horiz.

1970, Feb. 23   Litho.   Perf. 14
106 A21 5c blue, brn & ocher   .20 .20
107 A21 6c blue, blk ocher & brn   .20 .20
108 A21 15c apple grn & multi   .20 .20
109 A21 25c multicolored   .20 .20
    Nos. 106-109 (4)   .80 .80

Issued for Republic Day, Feb. 23, 1970.

1970, Mar. 24   Perf. 14x14½
Easter: 6c, 25c, Christ on the Cross, by Rubens.
110 A22 5c blue & multi   .20 .20
111 A22 6c rose lilac & multi   .20 .20
112 A22 15c dark red & multi   .20 .20
113 A22 25c yellow & multi   .30 .20
    Nos. 110-113 (4)   .90 .80

"Peace" and UN Emblem A23

UN 25th Anniv.: 6c, 25c, UN emblem, panning for gold and drilling for minerals.

1970, Oct. 26   Perf. 14½x14
114 A23 5c red & multi   .20 .20
115 A23 6c blue & multi   .20 .20
116 A23 15c multicolored   .20 .20
117 A23 25c brown & multi   .20 .20
    Nos. 114-117 (4)   .80 .80

Mother and Child, by Philip Moore — A24

1970, Dec. 8   Litho.   Perf. 13½
118 A24 5c violet & multi   .20 .20
119 A24 6c brown & multi   .20 .20
120 A24 15c dk green & multi   .20 .20
121 A24 25c maroon & multi   .20 .20
    Nos. 118-121 (4)   .80 .80

Christmas.

National Cooperative Bank — A25

1971, Feb. 23   Wmk. 364   Perf. 14
122 A25 6c red & multi   .20 .20
123 A25 15c yellow & multi   .20 .20
124 A25 25c ultra & multi   .20 .20
    Nos. 122-124 (3)   .60 .60

Republic Day.

"Togetherness, Vision, Understanding" A26

Volunteer Felling Tree, by John Criswick — A27

1971, Mar. 22   Perf. 14½x14
125 A26 5c yel grn & multi   .20 .20
126 A26 6c lil rose & multi   .20 .20
127 A26 15c multicolored   .20 .20
128 A26 25c yellow & multi   .20 .20
    Nos. 125-128 (4)   .80 .80

Intl. year against racial discrimination.

1971, July 19   Perf. 14
129 A27 5c blue & multi   .20 .20
130 A27 20c green & multi   .20 .20
131 A27 25c yellow & multi   .20 .20
132 A27 50c brown & multi   .40 1.25
    Nos. 129-132 (4)   1.00 1.85

1st anniv. of the Natl. Self-help Road Project.

Yellow Allamanda — A28

Flora: 1c, Pitcher plant of Mt. Roraima. 3c, Hanging heliconia. 5c, Annatto tree. 6c, Cannonball tree. 10c, Cattleya violacea. 15c, Christmas orchid. 20c, Paphinia cristata. 25c, Gongora quinquinervis. 40c, Tiger beard. 50c, Guzmania lingulata. 60c, Soldier's cap. $1, Chelonanthus uliginoides. $2, Norantea guianensis. $5, Odontadenia grandiflora.

1971-76   Litho.   Perf. 13x13½
133 A28 1c multi ('72)   .20 .20
134 A28 2c lilac & multi   .20 .20
135 A28 3c multicolored   .20 .20
136 A28 5c lt blue & multi   .20 .20
137 A28 6c dull rose & multi   .20 .20

Perf. 13½
138 A28 10c multi ('72)   4.25 .20
a.   Perf. 13   5.25 .20
139 A28 15c multi ('72)   1.00 .20
a.   Perf. 13 ('76)   .75 .20
140 A28 20c multi ('72)   4.00 .40
a.   Perf. 13   7.00 .40
141 A28 25c multi, 25c at center ('72)   6.50 9.00
141A A28 25c multi, 25c right of center ('73)   .45 .55
b.   Perf. 13 ('76)   .45 .30
142 A28 40c multi ('72)   4.50 .20
143 A28 50c multi ('73)   .50 .80
144 A28 60c multi ('73)   .40 .65
145 A28 $1 multi ('73)   .40 .40
146 A28 $2 multi ('73)   .60 .60
147 A28 $5 multi ('73)   1.00 1.00
    Nos. 133-147 (16)   24.60 15.00

No. 141 has 2 blossoms at left, 3 at right; this is reversed on No. 141A.
The overprint "REVENUE / ONLY" between rules was applied to Nos. 134-136, 141A, 142-147 in 1975. Postal use was permitted in Nov.-Dec., 1975. Value, set $20.
See Nos. 433-434, 731-732.
For overprints and surcharges see Nos. 192, 209, 234, 331-335, 351, 358-359, 367, 370, 372, 374-375A, 379-383, 385-390A, 401, 407, 422-425, 433-434, 438-440, 447, 450, 451, 457-458, 460-461, 464-466, 497-500, 545-546, 550, 563-564, 597, 602, 618, 631-632, 641-642, 666-667, 727, 747-748, 750-751, 753-754, 759-760, 803, 805, 807-808, 810-812, 847-848, 910-911, 995, 1361, 1382-1383, 1385-1386, 1391-1392, 1452, 1454, 1456-1460, 1466, 1499, 1778-1779, 1781-

1784, 1837-1838, 1870-1872, 1898-1900, 2046-2049, 2225-2227, C2-C4, O1, O3-O5, O7, O13-O14, Q1-Q4, QO1.

The Lord's Prayer, by School Girl Veronica Bassoo — A29

Guyana Masker, by School Boy Michael Austin — A30

Perf. 13½x14, 14x13½

1971, Nov. 15   Litho.   Wmk. 364
148	A29	5c brt green & multi	.20	.20
149	A29	20c brt green & multi	.20	.20
150	A30	25c multicolored	.20	.20
151	A30	50c multicolored	.30	.30
		Nos. 148-151 (4)	.90	.90

Christmas.

Guyana Dollar — A31

Handclasp and Mosque — A32

1972, Feb. 23   Litho.   Perf. 14½x14
152	A31	5c blk, dp org & silver	.20	.20
153	A31	20c blk, dp lil rose & sil	.20	.20
154	A31	25c black, ultra & silver	.20	.20
155	A31	50c black, emerald & silver	.35	.35
		Nos. 152-155 (4)	.95	.95

Republic Day.

1972, Apr. 3   Perf. 14
156	A32	5c brown & multi	.20	.20
157	A32	25c blue & multi	.20	.20
158	A32	30c green & multi	.20	.20
159	A32	60c yellow brn & multi	.30	.30
		Nos. 156-159 (4)	.90	.90

Youman Nabi (Peaceful Prophet), Mohammedan festival.

Map of South America, Emblem of Non-aligned Countries — A33

CARIFESTA '72 Emblem — A34

1972, July 20
160	A33	8c violet & multi	.20	.20
161	A33	25c yellow grn & multi	.20	.20
162	A33	40c orange & multi	.20	.20
163	A33	50c red brown & multi	.25	.25
		Nos. 160-163 (4)	.85	.85

Conf. of Foreign Ministers of Nonaligned Countries, Georgetown, Aug. 7-12.
For overprints & surcharges see #573, 611, O17.

1972, Aug. 25
164	A34	8c orange & multi	.20	.20
165	A34	25c orange & multi	.20	.25
166	A34	40c orange & multi	.20	.25
167	A34	50c orange & multi	.25	.35
		Nos. 164-167 (4)	.85	1.00

Caribbean Festival of Arts (CARIFESTA), Georgetown, Aug. 25-Sept. 15.

Holy Family — A35

1972, Oct. 18   Litho.   Perf. 13x13½
168	A35	8c blue & multi	.20	.20
169	A35	25c blue & multi	.20	.20
170	A35	40c blue & multi	.20	.25
171	A35	50c blue & multi	.20	.30
		Nos. 168-171 (4)	.80	.95

Christmas.

Umana Yana (Meeting Place of Wai Wai Chiefs) — A36

1973, Feb. 23   Litho.   Perf. 14x14½

Designs: 25c, 40c, Bethel Chapel.
172	A36	8c brt blue & multi	.25	.20
173	A36	25c rose red & multi	.25	.20
174	A36	40c emerald & multi	.25	.20
175	A36	50c black & multi	.35	.25
		Nos. 172-175 (4)	1.10	.85

Republic Day.

Pomegranate, Fertility and Church Symbol — A37

Map of Guyana and People Looking to the Cross — A38

1973, Apr. 19   Perf. 14x14½, 13½
176	A37	8c pink & multi	.20	.20
177	A38	25c yellow & multi	.20	.20
178	A38	40c ultra & multi	.20	.20
179	A37	50c yellow & multi	.20	.20
		Nos. 176-179 (4)	.80	.80

Easter.

Symbolic of Blood Donation — A39

Perf. 14x14½

1973, Oct. 1   Wmk. 364
180	A39	8c red & black	.20	.20
181	A39	25c red & lilac	.25	.20
182	A39	40c red & vio blue	.40	.50
183	A39	50c red & brown	.65	.90
		Nos. 180-183 (4)	1.50	1.80

Guyana Red Cross, 25th anniversary.

Steel Band, Star, Pegasus Hotel — A40

Madonna and Child, St. Philip's Anglican Church, Georgetown A41

1973, Nov. 20   Litho.   Perf. 14x14½
184	A40	8c lilac & multi	.20	.20
185	A40	25c lilac & multi	.25	.20

Perf. 13½x14
186	A41	40c violet blue & multi	.40	.70
187	A41	50c violet blue & multi	.40	.70
		Nos. 184-187 (4)	1.25	1.80

Christmas.

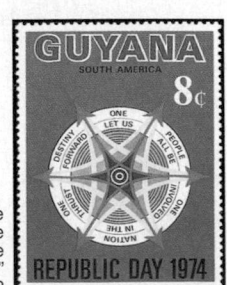

"One People, One Nation, One Destiny" A42

Designs: 25c, 50c, Wai Wai Indian.

1974, Feb. 23   Litho.   Perf. 13½
188	A42	8c multicolored	.20	.20
189	A42	25c multicolored	.20	.20
190	A42	40c multicolored	.20	.30
191	A42	50c multicolored	.20	.40
		Nos. 188-191 (4)	.80	1.10

Republic Day.

No. 137 Surcharged with New Value and 2 Bars

Perf. 13x13½

1974, Mar. 18   Wmk. 364
192	A28	8c on 6c multi	.50	.50

For overprints and surcharges see Nos. 424, 459, 474-478, 1453, 1500, 1780.

Crucifix Super-imposed on Eddy Bow Kite — A43

Crucifix in Pre-Columbian Timehri Style — A44

1974, Apr. 8   Perf. 13½x14
193	A43	8c green & multi	.50	.20
194	A44	25c black, green & gray	.50	.20
195	A44	40c black, gray & car	.50	.20
196	A43	50c gold & multi	.50	.20
		Nos. 193-196 (4)	2.00	.80

Easter.

UPU Emblem and British Guiana Type of 1863 — A45

Mailman and UPU Emblem A46

1974, June 18   Litho.   Perf. 14, 14½
197	A45	8c rose & multi	.50	.25
198	A46	25c yellow green & multi	.60	.25
199	A45	40c blue & multi	.60	.40
200	A46	50c yellow green & multi	.80	.55
		Nos. 197-200 (4)	2.50	1.45

Centenary of Universal Postal Union.

Girl Guides Holding Banner A47

Designs: 25c, 40c, Guides in camp cooking and carrying water. 50c, Like 8c.

1974, Aug. 1   **Perf. 14½**
201	A47 8c multicolored	.25	.20
202	A47 25c multicolored	.35	.20
203	A47 40c multicolored	.60	.40
204	A47 50c multicolored	.60	.50
a.	Souvenir sheet of 4, #201-204	2.50	2.50
	Nos. 201-204 (4)	1.80	1.30

Girl Guides of Guyana, 50th anniv. For overprints see Nos. 574, 1352.

Buck Toyeau — A48

Christmas (Fruit): 35c, Carambola (starfruit) and awaras. 50c, Pawpaw and tangerine. $1, Pineapple and sapodillas.

1974, Nov. 18   **Litho.**   **Perf. 14x13½**
205	A48 8c multicolored	.25	.20
206	A48 35c multicolored	.25	.20
207	A48 50c multicolored	.30	.20
208	A48 $1 multicolored	.50	.75
a.	Souvenir sheet of 4, #205-208	2.25	4.50
	Nos. 205-208 (4)	1.30	1.35

For overprints & surcharges see #551, 612, 716.

No. 135 Surcharged with New Value and Two Bars

1975, Jan. 20   **Litho.**   **Perf. 13x13½**
209	A28 8c on 3c multi	.50	.50

For surcharge see No. 423.

Golden Arrow of Courage — A49

Republic Day: 35c, Cacique's Crown of Honour. 50c, Cacique's Crown of Valour. $1, Order of Excellence.

1975, Feb. 23   **Perf. 13x13½**
210	A49 10c brown & multi	.30	.20
211	A49 35c brown red & multi	.30	.20
212	A49 50c green & multi	.30	.35
213	A49 $1 violet bl & multi	.50	.65
	Nos. 210-213 (4)	1.40	1.40

For overprints and surcharges see Nos. 360, 368, 398, 637, 1359.

Old Sluice Gate — A50

Modern Sluice Gate A51

1975, May 2   **Perf. 14**
214	A50 10c bister & multi	.35	.20
215	A50 35c brown & multi	.35	.20
216	A50 50c bister & multi	.35	.40
217	A51 $1 green & multi	.60	.75
a.	Souvenir sheet of 4, #214-217	2.50	4.00
	Nos. 214-217 (4)	1.65	1.55

Intl. Commission on Irrigation and Drainage, 25th anniv.
For overprints see Nos. 361, 592, 794-795, 1374-1375.

IWY Emblem, Symbolic Man and Woman A52

Designs: IWY emblem and petroglyph designs of men and women.

1975, July 1   **Litho.**   **Wmk. 364**
218	A52 10c yellow & dull grn	.25	.25
219	A52 35c Prus blue & pur	.25	.25
220	A52 50c orange & dk blue	.30	.30
221	A52 $1 ultra & brown	.50	.50
a.	Souvenir sheet of 4, #218-221, perf. 14½	2.50	4.25
	Nos. 218-221 (4)	1.30	1.30

Intl. Women's Year. For overprints and surcharges see Nos. 362, 399, 555.

Freedom Monument, Georgetown A53

"GNS," Flower and Clasped Hands A54

Designs: Various views of Freedom Monument, Georgetown.

1975, Aug. 26   **Litho.**   **Perf. 14**
222	A53 10c gray & multi	.25	.25
223	A53 35c yellow & multi	.25	.25
224	A53 50c lilac & multi	.30	.30
225	A53 $1 olive & multi	.45	.45
	Nos. 222-225 (4)	1.25	1.25

Namibia Day (independence for South-West Africa).
For overprints and surcharges see Nos. 330, 582, 593, 619, 1360.

1975, Oct. 2   **Wmk. 364**   **Perf. 14**

"GNS" and Clasped hands: 35c, Wheel. 50c, Soccer ball. $1, Uniform cap.

226	A54 10c violet, yel & grn	.25	.25
227	A54 35c brt bl, org & grn	.25	.25
228	A54 50c lt brn, brt bl & grn	.30	.30
229	A54 $1 grn, vio & brt grn	.40	.40
a.	Souvenir sheet of 4, #226-229	2.75	4.00
	Nos. 226-229 (4)	1.20	1.20

Guyana National Service, 1st anniv. For overprint & surcharges see #448, 636, 638.

Foresters' Building and Badge A55

35c, Rock painting of hunter. 50c, Crossed axes and hunting horn. $1, Bow and arrow.

1975, Nov. 14   **Litho.**   **Wmk. 364**
230	A55 10c red, black & gold	.25	.25
231	A55 35c red, black & gold	.25	.25
232	A55 50c gold & multi	.30	.30
233	A55 $1 gold & multi	.45	.45
a.	Souvenir sheet of 4, #230-233	2.50	4.25
	Nos. 230-233 (4)	1.25	1.25

Ancient Order of Foresters, centenary.
For overprints and surcharges see Nos. 356, 363, 400, 422, 583.

No. 144 Surcharged

1976, Feb. 10   **Perf. 13½**
234	A28 35c on 60c multi	.60	.60

For overprints see Nos. 703-703b, 852.

St. John Ambulance Emblem — A56

Independence Arch, 1966 — A57

1976, Mar. 29   **Litho.**   **Perf. 14**
235	A56 8c black, lil rose & sil	.25	.25
236	A56 15c black, orange & sil	.25	.25
237	A56 35c black, emer & silver	.25	.25
238	A56 40c black, blue & sil	.30	.30
	Nos. 235-238 (4)	1.05	1.05

Guyana St. John Ambulance, 50th anniv. For surcharges see Nos. 715, 717, 1411.

1976, May 25   **Perf. 13½**

Stylized Designs: 15c, Victoria regia. 35c, Letter "S" for socialism. 40c, Worker with pitchfork.

239	A57 8c silver & multi	.20	.20
240	A57 15c silver & multi	.20	.20
241	A57 35c silver & multi	.20	.20
242	A57 40c silver & multi	.20	.20
a.	Souvenir sheet of 4, #239-242, perf. 14	1.00	1.50
	Nos. 239-242 (4)	.80	.80

10th anniv. of independence. For surcharges see Nos. 567, 639, 1444.

Map of West Indies, Bats, Wicket and Ball A57a

Prudential Cup — A57b

Unwmk.
1976, Aug. 3   **Litho.**   **Perf. 14**
243	A57a 15c light blue & multi	1.25	1.75
244	A57b 15c lilac rose & black	1.25	1.75

World Cricket Cup, won by West Indies Team, 1975.
For overprints & surcharges see #352-353, 653-654.

Lamp — A58

Guitar-Sitar, Benin Head — A59

Designs: 15c, Hand and flame. 35c, Flame. 40c, Lakshmi, Hindu goddess of wealth.

1976, Oct. 21   **Perf. 14**
245	A58 8c multicolored	.20	.20
246	A58 15c orange & multi	.20	.20
247	A58 35c purple & multi	.25	.25
248	A58 40c ultra & multi	.30	.30
a.	Souvenir sheet of 4, #245-248	1.40	1.75
	Nos. 245-248 (4)	.95	.95

Deepavali, Hindu Festival of Lights.
For surcharges see Nos. 719-721.

1977, Feb. 1   **Litho.**   **Perf. 14½**
249	A59 10c gold & multi	.20	.20
250	A59 35c gold & multi	.20	.20
251	A59 50c gold & multi	.35	.35
252	A59 $1 gold & multi	.50	.50
a.	Souvenir sheet of 4, #249-252	1.60	3.50
	Nos. 249-252 (4)	1.25	1.25

2nd World Black and African Festival, Lagos, Nigeria, Jan. 15-Feb. 12. Nos. 249-252a were not issued without black bar.
For overprints see Nos. 364, 369, 584.

1c and 5c Coins A60

Coins (Obverse): 15c, 10c and 25c. 35c, 50c and $1. 40c, $5 and $10. $1, $50 and $100. $2, Reverse, Coat of arms.

1977, May 26   **Perf. 14**
253	A60 8c multicolored	.35	.35
254	A60 15c multicolored	.40	.40
255	A60 35c multicolored	.70	.70
256	A60 40c multicolored	.85	.85
257	A60 $1 multicolored	1.25	1.25
258	A60 $2 multicolored	2.00	2.00
	Nos. 253-258 (6)	5.55	5.55

New coinage. For overprints and surcharges see Nos. 539, 541A, 568, 594, O18, O20, Q5.

Hand Pump, c. 1850 A61

National Fire Prevention Week: 15c, Steam engine, c. 1860. 35c, Fire engine, c. 1930. 40c, Fire engine, 1977.

     Perf. 14x14½
1977, Nov. 15   **Litho.**   **Wmk. 364**
259	A61 8c multicolored	1.25	.20
260	A61 15c multicolored	2.00	.20
261	A61 35c multicolored	2.25	1.10
262	A61 40c multicolored	2.50	1.25
	Nos. 259-262 (4)	8.00	2.75

For surcharges see Nos. 1370-1371.

Cuffy Monument — A62

8c, 35c, Cuffy statue from monument.

1977, Dec. 7   Litho.   Perf. 14
263 A62   8c multicolored   .20   .20
264 A62 15c multicolored   .20   .20
265 A62 35c multicolored   .20   .20
266 A62 40c multicolored   .20   .20
      Nos. 263-266 (4)   .80   .80

Cuffy, Guyana's national hero, led a slave revolution in 1763. The monument was unveiled in 1976. For overprints see Nos. 446, 569, 613.

Wildlife Protection — A63

1978, Feb. 15   Perf. 14
267 A63   8c Manatee   1.25   .25
268 A63 15c Giant sea turtle   1.50   .40
269 A63 35c Harpy eagle   6.25 2.75
270 A63 40c Iguana   6.00 2.75
      Nos. 267-270 (4)   15.00 6.15

8c, 15c are horiz. For overprints and surcharges see Nos. 443, 722-723, 1416.

Parliament and Prime Minister Burnham — A64

Prime Minister and: 15c, Student and school children. 35c, Bauxite mine. 40c, Cooperative village.

1978, Apr. 27   Litho.   Perf. 13½x14
271 A64   8c violet & black   .20   .20
272 A64 15c gray, blk & bl   .20   .20
273 A64 35c multicolored   .20   .20
274 A64 40c gray, blk & org   .20   .20
   a.   Souvenir sheet of 4, #271-274   1.10 1.75
      Nos. 271-274 (4)   .80   .80

Prime Minister Linden Forbes Burnham, 25th anniv. of his entry into parliament. For surcharges see Nos. 648-649.

Dr. George Giglioli, Anopheles Mosquito — A65

Agrias Claudina — A66

30c, Institute of Applied Science & Technology, proposed for University of Guyana. 50c, Map of Guyana & National Science Research Council emblem. 60c, Commonwealth Science Council emblem.

Perf. 13½x14, 14x13½
1978, Sept. 4   Litho.   Wmk. 364
275 A65 10c multi   .30   .30
276 A65 30c multi, horiz.   .30   .30
277 A65 50c multi   .40   .40
278 A65 60c multi, horiz.   .50   .50
      Nos. 275-278 (4)   1.50 1.50

For overprints see Nos. 577, 585, 590.

1978-80   Perf. 14x13½
Size: 22x16mm
279 A66   5c Prepona pheridamas   2.50   .25
280 A66 10c Archonias bellona   2.50   .25
281 A66 15c Eryphanis polyxena   2.50   .25

282 A66 20c Helicopis cupido   2.50   .25
283 A66 25c Nessaea batesli   2.50   .25
283A A66 30c Nymphidium mantus ('80) 2.00 3.25
284 A66 35c Siderone galanthis   2.50   .25
285 A66 40c Morpho rhetenor, male   2.50   .25
286 A66 50c Hamadryas amphinone   2.50   .30
286A A66 60c Papilio androgeus ('80) 2.25 1.75

Perf. 13½x13
287 A66 $1 Agrias claudina   6.00   .35
288 A66 $2 Morpho rhetenor, female 8.75   .70
289 A66 $5 Morpho deidamia   9.75 1.50
289A A66 $10 Elbella patrobas, perf. 14 ('80)   7.50 6.25
      Nos. 279-289A (14)   56.25 15.85

Issued: #279-283, 284-286, 287-289, 10/1/78. For overprints and surcharges see Nos. 391, 406, 436-436A, 481, 486, 554, 668-670, 733-743, 871, 936-939, 944, 969, 1373, 1418, 1455, 1786, 1812, 1814, 1832-1833, 1873, 1901, 1912-1913, 1984-1988, 2051, 2053, 2054C, 2055, 2057, 2057B-2057C, 2058-2059, 2082-2111, C5-C6, O15-O16, O23-O29.

Indian Making Stone Chip Grater — A67

UNESCO Emblem and: 30c, Arawak Cassiri jar and decorated Amerindian jar. 50c, Gate to old Dutch fort, Kykover-al. 60c, Fort Island, Dutch ruins.

1978, Dec. 27   Wmk. 364   Perf. 14
290 A67 10c green & multi   .25   .25
291 A67 30c green & multi   .25   .25
292 A67 50c green & multi   .30   .30
293 A67 60c green & multi   .30   .30
      Nos. 290-293 (4)   1.10 1.10

National and International Heritage Year. For surcharges see Nos. 604-606.

Earth Station at Dawn, Georgetown A68

Designs: 30c, Earth Station in daylight, Georgetown. 50c, Intelsat V. $3, Intelsat IVa.

1979, Feb. 7   Litho.   Perf. 14x14½
294 A68 10c multicolored   .20   .20
295 A68 30c multicolored   .25   .20
296 A68 50c multicolored   .40   .20
297 A68 $3 multicolored   1.40 1.40
      Nos. 294-297 (4)   2.25 2.00

For surcharges see Nos. 384, 655, 714, 1376-1377, 1380, O9.

British Guyana No. 5 — A69

Designs: 30c, British Guiana No. 13, vert. 50c, British Guiana No. 152. $3, Printing press used for 1c Magenta, vert.

1979, June 11   Wmk. 364   Perf. 14
298 A69 10c multicolored   .20   .20
299 A69 30c multicolored   .30   .20
300 A69 50c multicolored   .40   .20
301 A69 $3 multicolored   .60   .60
      Nos. 298-301 (4)   1.50 1.20

Sir Rowland Hill (1795-1879), originator of penny postage.
For overprints & surcharges see #409, 426, 428, 449, 479, 480, 578, 586, 598, 614, O6.

"Fun with the Fowls" and IYC Emblem — A70

Children's Drawings and IYC Emblem: 10c, "Me and my sister," vert. 50c, "Two boys catching ducks." $3, "Mango season."

1979, Aug. 20   Litho.   Perf. 13½
302 A70 10c multicolored   .25   .25
303 A70 30c multicolored   .25   .25
304 A70 50c multicolored   .45   .45
305 A70 $3 multicolored   1.25 1.75
      Nos. 302-305 (4)   2.20 2.70

Intl. Year of the Child. For overprints and surcharges see Nos. 435, 579, 587, 599, 615, 943.

H. N. Critchlow, Worker Hauling Sack — A71

Critchlow and: 30c, Baker, horiz. 50c, Flag and crowd. $3, Portrait only.

1979, Sept. 27   Litho.   Perf. 14
306 A71 10c multicolored   .20   .20
307 A71 30c multicolored   .20   .20
308 A71 50c multicolored   .25   .25
309 A71 $3 multicolored   .60   .90
      Nos. 306-309 (4)   1.25 1.55

Guyana Labor Union, 60th anniversary. For surcharges see Nos. 403, 429, 718.

Cooperative Republic, 10th Anniv. — A72

Wmk. 364
1980, Feb. 23   Litho.   Perf. 14
313 A72 10c shown   .20   .20
314 A72 35c Demerara River Bridge   .30   .20
315 A72 60c Kaieteur Falls   .50   .20
316 A72 $3 Makanaima, American Indian   .75   .75
      Nos. 313-316 (4)   1.75 1.35

For overprints and surcharges see Nos. 365, 371, 450A, 442, 591, 656.

Miniature Sheet

Snoek, London 1980 Emblem A73

London 80 Emblem and Fish; a, Snoek. b, Haimara. c, Electric eel. d, Golden rivulus. e, Pencil fish. f, Four-eyed fish. g, Pirai. h, Smoking hassar. i, Devil ray. j, Flying patwa. k, Arapaima. l, Lukanani.

1980, May 6   Wmk. 373   Perf. 14
317   Sheet of 12   6.00 6.00
   a.-l. A73 35c any single   .40   .40

London 1980 Intl. Stamp Exhib., May 6-14. For overprints & surcharges see #444, 725-726, 1414.

Children's Convalescent Home, Rotary Emblem — A74

Rotary International, 75th anniversary (Emblem and): 30c, Georgetown club emblem. 50c, District 404 emblem (hibiscus), vert. $3, Anniversary emblem, vert.

Perf. 14x14½, 14½x14
1980, June 23   Litho.   Wmk. 364
318 A74 10c multicolored   .20   .20
319 A74 30c multicolored   .20   .20
320 A74 50c multicolored   .45   .50
321 A74 $3 multicolored   1.25 1.25
      Nos. 318-321 (4)   2.10 2.15

For overprints and surcharges see Nos. 552, 580, 601, C1.

Emblem and Caduceus A75

Wmk. 364
1980, Sept. 23   Litho.   Perf. 13½
322 A75 10c shown   .20   .20
323 A75 60c Scientist, beach scene   .60   .30
324 A75 $3 Emblems over island   1.50 1.25
      Nos. 322-324 (3)   2.30 1.75

Commonwealth Caribbean Medical Research Council, 25th anniversary. For overprints and surcharges see Nos. 366, 427, 430, 494, 553.

Virola Surinamensis (Christmas 1980) — A76

1980, Nov. 1   Wmk. 373   Perf. 14
325 A76 10c shown   .25   .20
326 A76 30c Hymenaea courbaril   .40   .20
327 A76 50c Mora excelsa   .60   .35
328 A76 $3 Peltogyne venosa 1.75 1.60
      Nos. 325-328 (4)   3.00 2.35

For overprints and surcharges see Nos. 431, 773, 790, 792-793.

Miniature Sheet

A77

Designs: a, Tree porcupine. b, Howler monkeys. c, Squirrel monkeys. d, Two-toed sloth. e, Tapir. f, Collared peccary. g, Six-banded armadillo. h, Anteater. i, Great anteaters. j, Mouse opossums. k, Four-eyed opossum. l, Orange-rumped agouti.

1981, Mar. 2   Wmk. 364   Perf. 14
329   Sheet of 12   8.75 8.75
   a.-l. A77 30c any single   .65   .65
   m.   As #329g, perf. 12   3.25   .40

For overprints see #581, 819, 1399, 1503, 1844.

During 1981-91, there were numerous sources creating stamps for Guyana, with as many as 5-7 parties being active at any given time.

No. 222 Surcharged

1981, May 4
330 A53 $1.05 on 10c multi 1.75

For surcharges see Nos. 396, 620.

Nos. 135, 146-147 Surcharged

Nos. 145 and 147 Surcharged in Blue or Black

1981 Litho. Wmk. 364 Perf. 13½
331 A28 60c on 3c #135 .... 1.25
332 A28 75c on $5 #147 .... 1.00
333 A28 $1.10 on $5 #146 .... 1.00
334 A28 $3.60 on $5 #147 (Blk) 3.50
  a. Blue overprint 3.50
335 A28 $7.20 on $1 #145 (Bl) 3.50
  a. Black overprint 5.00

No. 333 is airmail. Issue dates: $3.60, $7.20, May 6. Others July 22. Diagonal overprint on No. 332. Vertical overprint on No. 333. Location of surcharge varies.

See Nos. 621, 666-667, Q4, QO5. For overprints and surcharges see Nos. 378, 489-496, 547, 549, 646, 818, 867-868, O11, Q3, QO3.

Map of Guyana — A78

1981, May 11 Photo. Perf. 13½
336 A78 10c on 3c multi 1.00
337 A78 30c on 2c multi 1.00
338 A78 50c on 2c multi 1.00
339 A78 60c on 3c multi 1.00
340 A78 75c on 3c multi 5.00
  Nos. 336-340 (5)

Revenue stamps surcharged for postal use. For similar stamp, see #934a. For surcharge see #503.

Nos. J5-J8 Surcharged in Red, Black, or Brown

a   b

1981, June 8 Typo. Perf. 13½x14
       Type "a"
341 D1 10c on 2c #J6
342 D1 15c on 12c #J8 (Blk)
343 D1 20c on 1c #J5
344 D1 45c on 2c #J6
345 D1 55c on 4c #J7
346 D1 60c on 4c #J7 (Brn)
347 D1 65c on 2c #J6
348 D1 70c on 4c #J7
349 D1 80c on 4c #J7
    Nos. 341-349 (9) 11.00
       Type "b"
341a D1 10c on 2c #J6
342a D1 15c on 12c #J8 (Blk)
343a D1 20c on 1c #J5
344a D1 45c on 2c #J6
345a D1 55c on 4c #J7
347a D1 65c on 2c #J6
348a D1 70c on 4c #J7

349a D1 80c on 4c #J7
    Nos. 341a-349a
    (8) 11.00
Pairs with types a and b exist for all values except the 60c.

Nos. 48, 61-62, 74, 139, 142-143, 145-147, 212-213, 216, 220, 231-232, 243-244, 251-252, 315-316, and 323 Overprinted in Black or Red

1981 Perfs. as Before
Watermarks & Printing Methods as Before
350 A8 15c on #74 (R) 17.50
351 A28 15c on #139
  a. Red overprint 7.00
  b. On #139a, red overprint 8.00
352 A57a 15c on #243 .... 8.50
353 A57b 15c on #244 .... 5.00
354 A11 25c on #61 (R) .... .75
355 A11 30c on #62 (R) .... .75
356 A55 35c on #231 (R) 3.00
357 A8 40c on #48 .... 12.00
358 A28 40c on #142
359 A28 50c on #143 .... 4.00
360 A49 50c on #212 .... 3.25
361 A50 50c on #216 .... 1.50
362 A52 50c on #220 .... 27.50
363 A55 50c on #232 .... 3.25
364 A59 50c on #251 .... 15.00
365 A72 60c on #315 .... .90
366 A75 60c on #323 .... .90
367 A28 $1 on #145 .... 3.50
  a. Red overprint 2.00
368 A49 $1 on #213 .... 7.50
369 A59 $1 on #252 .... 6.50
370 A28 $2 on #146 .... 8.00
  a. Red overprint 2.00
  b. Black ovpt. with serifs 25.00
371 A72 $3 on #316 .... 3.00
372 A28 $5 on #147 .... 4.25
    Nos. 350-372
    (23) 50.00

Issued: #354-356, 367, 6/8; #350, 357, 370, 7/1; #351-353, 359-366, 368-369, 371-372, 7/7.
Location and size of overprint varies. Refer to second paragraph in footnote following No. 147 for Nos. 358-359.
For surcharges and overprints see Nos. 556, 607, 659, 745, 849-850, 1362.

Nos. 68, 135-136, 139, 145-147, 297, 333 Surcharged or Overprinted

1981 Litho. Perfs. as Before
Watermarks & Printing Methods as Before
373 A7 15c on 1c #68 .... 1.10
374 A28 50c on 5c #136 .... 2.50
375 A28 75c on 5c #136 .... 30.00
375A A28 80c on 15c #139
376 A7 100c on 1c #68 .... 1.00
377 A7 110c on 1c #68 .... 1.00
  a. Strip of 3, #373, 376-377 .... 7.00
378 A28 $1.10 on #333 .... 17.50
379 A28 120c on $1 #145 .... 2.50
380 A28 140c on $1 #145 .... 2.50
381 A28 150c on $2 #146 .... 2.50
382 A28 210c on $5 #147 .... 30.00
383 A28 220c on 5c #136 .... 30.00
384 A68 220c on $3 #297 .... 4.50
385 A28 250c on $5 #147 .... 2.75
386 A28 280c on $5 #147 .... 2.75
387 A28 360c on $2 #146 .... 3.50
388 A28 375c on $5 #147 .... 3.00
389 A28 $7.20 on 3c #135 .... 110.00
390 A28 720c on 60c #144 .... 3.75
390A A28 $20 on 5c #136

Location and size of surcharge and obliterator varies. Obliterator is an "X" on Nos. 381-388, 390, two solid boxes on Nos. 379-380, and five bars on No. 389. Numeral "7" is placed before 5 make surcharge on No. 375. "Royal Wedding 1981" obliterated by three bars on No. 378. New denomination on No.

375A does not have cent sign. Obliterator on No. 390A is three horizontal bars.
Refer to second paragraph in footnote following No. 147 for Nos. 381, 387 and 390. Nos. 376-378 are airmail.
Issued: #375, 382, 6/8; #373-374, 376-388, 390, 7/1.
For overprint and surcharges see Nos. 408, 788, 859-860, 863-864, 1379, 1417.

No. 281 Overprinted "ESSEQUIBO / IS OURS"

1981, July Litho. Perf. 14x13½
391 A66 15c on #281 .... 6.75
  a. Ovpt. without serifs

Nos. 87, 95-96, 142, 146, 210, 218, 230, 309, 330, O15 Surcharged

1981 Perfs. as Before
Watermarks & Printing Methods as Before
392 A17 55c on 6c #95 .... 4.50
393 A14 70c on 6c #87 .... 1.25
394 A14 100c on 6c #87 .... 1.50
395 A17 100c on 8c #96 .... 4.50
396 A53 100c on #330 .... 40.00
  (surcharge reading down)
  a. Surcharge reading up 50.00
397 A17 110c on 6c #95 .... 3.00
398 A49 110c on 10c #210 .... 3.00
399 A52 110c on 10c #218 .... 7.25
400 A55 110c on 10c #230 .... 7.25
401 A28 125c on $2 #146 .... 16.50
402 A17 180c on 6c #95 .... 4.50
403 A71 240c on $3 #309 .... 10.50
404 A17 400c on 6c #95 .... 4.50
405 A17 $4.40 on 6c #95 .... 2.25
  a. Fours same size 11.00
406 A66 550c on $10 #O15 .... 10.00
407 A28 625c on 40c #142 .... 17.50

Issued: #392, 394-395, 397-399, 405, 405a, 407, July 7; #393, 402-404, 406, Sept. 15. Refer to 2nd paragraph in footnote following #147 for #407. For overprints and surcharges see #651-652, 996, 1858-1859, 1861, O8, O10, O12.

No. 383 Ovptd. "Espana 82"
No. 301 Surcharged "1831-1981 / Von Stephan"

Perfs. as Before
1981, July 22 Litho. Wmk. 364
408 A28 220c on #383 .... 3.75
409 A69 330c on $3 #301 .... 4.50

For surcharges see Nos. 616, 622.

Nos. 43, 72 Surcharged

1981 Photo. Unwmk. Perf. 14x14½
410 A7 12c on 12c on 6c #43
411 A7 Pair, #a.-b.
  a. 15c on 10c on 6c #43
  b. 15c on 30c on 6c #43
412 A7 Pair, #a.-b.
  a. 15c on 50c on 6c #43
  b. 15c on 60c on 6c #43
413 A7 Strip of 3, #a.-c.
  a. 12c on 6c #43
  b. 50c on 6c #43
  c. $1 On 6c #43
  Wmk. 364
413D A7 Strip of 3, #e.-g.
  e. 12c on 6c #72
  f. 50c on 6c #72
  g. $1 on 6c #72

Issue dates: Nos. 410-412, Aug. 24. No. 413-413D, Nov. 10.
Nos. 410-412 were not issued without large numeral surcharges. Obliterator is black box on Nos. 410-412, "X" on Nos. 413a & 413De. Nos. 413b-413c, 413Df-g are airmail.
For overprints and surcharges see Nos. 728-728a, 914, 994, 994a, 1400-1401.

16th Anniv. of the Guyana Defense Force — A79

1981, Oct. 1 Wmk. 364 Perf. 13½
414 A79 15c on 10c Armed Ranger, 1772 .... .30 .25
415 A79 50c Private, Foot Regiment, 1825 .... .75 .45
416 A79 $1 on 30c Marine Private, 1775 .... 1.40 1.40
417 A79 $1.10 on $3 Defense Force officers, 1966 .... 1.60 1.60
    Nos. 414-417 (4) 4.05 3.70

Nos. 414, 416-417 not issued without surcharge. For overprints see Nos. 570, 588, 595, 1368-1369.

Louis Braille and Boy Reading Braille — A80

Intl. Year of the Disabled: 50c, Helen Keller and Rajkumari Singh. $1, Beethoven and Sonny Thomas. $1.10, Renoir and painting.

1981, Nov. 2 Perf. 13½x14
418 A80 15c on 10c multi .... .20 .20
419 A80 50c multi .... .50 .40
420 A80 $1 on 60c multi .... .90 .80
421 A80 $1.10 on $3 multi 1.10 1.10
    Nos. 418-421 (4) 2.70 2.50

Nos. 418, 420-421 not issued without surcharge. For overprints and surcharge see #571, 589, 596, 1913A.

Nos. 192, 209, 230, 298, 301, 309, 322, 324, 328, O1 Surcharged in Blue or Red

1981, Nov. 14   *Perfs. as Before*
Watermarks & Printing Methods as Before

422	A55	110c on 10c #230	5.00
423	A28	110c on #209	5.00
424	A28	110c on #192	5.00
425	A28	110c on #O1	3.75
426	A69	110c on 10c #298 (R)	2.75
427	A75	110c on 10c #322	15.00
428	A69	110c on $3 #301 (R)	2.50
429	A71	110c on $3 #309	8.00
430	A75	110c on $3 #324	3.00
a.		Red surcharge	8.00
431	A76	110c on $3 #328	6.00
a.		Red surcharge	55.00
		Nos. 422-431 (10)	56.00

Nos. 423-424 were issued with two 110c surcharges of different sizes. Refer to second paragraph in footnote below No. 147 for No. 425. For overprints and surcharges see Nos. 791, 820, 855, 1000, 1364-1366.

Flower Type of 1971-76 Surcharged
1981, Nov. 24   **Photo.**   *Perf. 15x14*
Size: 20x23mm
Coil Stamps

433	A28	15c on 2c like #134	.35
434	A28	15c on 8c Mazaruni Pride	.35
a.		Pair, #433-434	1.10

Nos. 433-434 were not issued without surcharge. See Nos. 731-732.

No. 305 Surcharged
"U.N.I.C.E.F. / 1946-1981"
Wmk. 364
1981, Nov. 14   **Litho.**   *Perf. 13½*

435	A70	125c on $3 #305	3.25

For surcharge see No. 942.

No. 279 Surcharged "Nov. 81" (#436) or "Cancun 81" (#436A)
1981, Nov. 14   *Perf. 14x13½*

436	A66	50c on 5c #279	
436A	A66	50c on 5c #279	6.50

Conversion to Metric System, Jan. 2 — A81

a, Tape measure. b, Juggler. c, Man, envelope. d, Baby on scale. e, Canje Bridge. f, Liter bucket.

Perf. 14½x14
1982, Jan. 18   **Wmk. 364**

437	A81	15c Sheet of 6, #a.-f.	3.25 3.25

For surcharge see No. 557.

Nos. 61, 63, 139, 140, 141A, 143-144, 146-147, 228, 266, 269, 300, 314 and 316-317 Ovptd. "1982" Vertically or Horizontally in Blue or Violet

1982-83   *Perfs. as Before*
Watermarks & Printing Methods as Before

438	A28	15c on #139	8.00
a.		On #139a	65.00
439	A28	20c on #140	4.00
440	A28	25c on #141A	6.50
441	A11	25c on #61 (V)	2.00
442	A72	35c on #314	1.00
443	A63	35c on #269	6.00
444	A73	35c on block of 6, #317a-317f	20.00
445	A11	40c on #63 (V)	1.00
446	A62	40c on #266	1.00
447	A28	50c on #143	3.00
448	A54	50c on #228	2.00
449	A69	50c on #300	1.00
449A	A28	60c on #464	7.00
450	A28	$2 on #146	1.50
450A	A72	$3 on #316	2.25
451	A28	$5 on #147	1.50
		Nos. 438-451 (16)	67.75

Issued: #439-441, 2/8; #450-451, 4/23; #445-446, 4/27; #438, 6/17; #443-444, 8/16; #442, 9/15; #447-449, 10/11; #449A, 7/1/83; #450A, 11/3/83.
For other stamps overprinted "1982" only, see Nos 482-483, 555.

For overprints and surcharges see Nos. 806, 809, 813-814, 851, 999, 1354, 1415.

Nos. 97, O3, O4, O9-O10 Ovptd. "POSTAGE" in Blue
1982   *Perfs. as Before*
Watermarks and Printing Methods as Before

452	A28	15c on #O3	10.00
453	A17	25c on #97	6.00
454	A28	50c on #O4	1.50
455	A68	100c on #O9	2.50
456	A17	110c on #O10	3.00

For surcharge see No. 853. For similar overprints see Nos. 729-730. Refer to second paragraph in footnote following No. 147 for No. 454.

Nos. 133, 137, 142, and 192 Surcharged in Blue or Green

Perfs. as Before
1982   **Litho.**   **Wmk. 364**

457	A28	20c on 6c #137	.90
458	A28	20c on 6c #137 (G)	.90
459	A28	125c on #192	.90
460	A28	180c on #142 ovpt. "1982"	5.75
461	A28	220c on 1c #133	2.00
		Nos. 457-461 (5)	10.45

No. 458 has no obliterator, "20c" is 23mm long.
Issued: #457-459, 2/8; #460, 4/8; #461, 4/23.
Refer to 2nd paragraph in footnote following #147 for #460.
For overprints see #755, 856, 862.

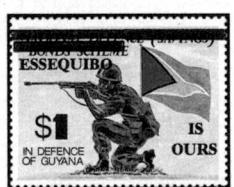

Savings Campaign A81a

1982   **Litho.**   *Perf. 14½*

462	A81a	$1 Soldier & flag	.60
463	A81a	$1.10 on $5, two soldiers, flag	7.00
a.		Inverted comma before "OURS"	

Size of obliterator differs on Nos. 463 and 463a. Nos. 462-463a are revenue stamps ovptd. for postal use.
Issued: #462, 2/8; #463, 3/3; #463a, 7/13.

Nos. 134, 136, & 192 Surcharged in Black or Green
"BADEN-POWELL / 1857-1982" (#464a, 465a, 466a)
"Scout Movement / 1907-1982" (#464b, 465b, 466b)
"1907-1982" (#464c, 465c, 466c)
"1857-1982" (#464d, 465d, 466d)
"1982" (#464e, 465e, 466e)

Perf. 13x13½
1982, Feb. 22   **Litho.**   **Wmk. 364**
Sheets of 25

464		8 #a.-b., 4 #c.-d., 1 #e.	9.00
a.-e.		A28 15c on 2c #134, any single	.40
465		8 #a.-b., 4 #c.-d., 1 #e.	20.00
a.-e.		A28 110c on 5c #136, any single	.80
466		8 #a.-b., 4 #c.-d., 1 #e.	20.00
a.-e.		A28 125c on #192, any single (G)	.80

Lord Robert Baden-Powell, 125th anniv. of birth. Boy Scout Movement, 75th anniv.
For overprints and surcharges see Nos. 558, 778-784, 836-837, 1347.

Nos. 289, 299, 301 Surcharged or Overprinted in Black or Blue

 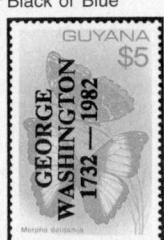

Perfs. as Before
1982, Feb. 15   **Litho.**   **Wmk. 364**

479	A69	100c on $3 #301	1.75	.50
480	A69	400c on 30c #299	2.50	2.00
481	A66	$5 on #289 (Bl)	11.50	7.50
		Nos. 479-481 (3)	15.75	10.00

For surcharges see Nos. 617, 904-906, 937-939, O22-O29.

Nos. 88-89 Ovptd. "1982" in Blue and Nos. 87, 90 Surcharged in Blue or Red
1982, Mar. 15   **Photo.**   *Perf. 13*

482	A14	25c on #88	
483	A14	30c on #89	
484	A14	45c on 6c #87	
485	A14	75c on 40c #90 (R)	
		Nos. 482-485 (4)	2.50

For overprints see Nos. 766-767.

Nos. 60, 284, 324, and 331-333 Surcharged in Black or Blue

1982   *Perfs. as Before*
Watermarks & Printing Methods as Before

486	A66	20c on 35c #284	7.50
487	A11	80c on 6c #60 (Bl)	3.00
488	A11	85c on 6c #60 (Bl)	3.00
489	A28	85c on #331	5.00
490	A28	130c on #331	3.00
491	A28	160c on #333 (Bl)	3.00
a.		Black surcharge	
492	A28	170c on #333	15.00
493	A28	210c on #332 (Bl)	3.00
494	A75	210c on $3 #324 (Bl)	4.00
495	A28	235c on #332	4.00
a.		Blue surcharge	9.00
496	A28	330c on #333	3.50
		Nos. 486-496 (11)	54.00

Nos. 491-491a, 492, & 496 are airmail. Obliterators differ.
Issue dates: #486, Mar. 15. Others, Apr. 27.
For surcharges see Nos. 647, 1367.

Nos. 135, 137, 144 & 145 Overprinted or Surcharged in Blue or Black "ESPANA / 1982" or "ESPANA / 1982" and "ITALY" (#499)
Wmk. 364
1982, May 15   **Litho.**   *Perf. 13½*

497	A28	$1 on #145 (Blk)	1.50
498	A28	110c on #135	1.50
499	A28	$2.35 on 180c on 60c #144	14.00
500	A28	250c on 6c #137	2.00

Refer to second paragraph in footnote below No. 147 for No. 499.
#499 not issued without $2.35 surcharge.
See No. 597 for stamp with one-line Espana 1982 overprint. For surcharges see #774-777.

Map Revenue Type A78 Surcharged in Black, Blue, or Red
1982-83   **Photo.**   **Wmk. 364**   *Perf. 13*

501	A78	15c on 2c (Bl)	
502	A78	20c on 2c (Bl)	
503	A78	20c on 10c #336 (Bl)	
504	A78	25c on 2c	
a.		Blue surcharge	
b.		Red surcharge	1.00

505	A78	30c on 2c (Bl)	
506	A78	40c on 2c	
a.		Blue surcharge	
507	A78	45c on 2c (Bl)	
508	A78	50c on 2c (Bl)	
509	A78	60c on 2c (Bl)	
510	A78	75c on 2c (Bl)	
511	A78	80c on 2c (Bl)	
512	A78	85c on 2c (Bl)	
513	A78	$1.00 on 3c	
514	A78	$1.10 on 3c	
515	A78	$1.20 on 3c	
516	A78	$1.25 on 3c	
517	A78	$1.30 on 3c	
518	A78	$1.50 on 3c	
519	A78	$1.60 on 3c	
520	A78	$1.70 on 3c	
521	A78	$1.75 on 3c	
522	A78	$1.80 on 3c	
523	A78	$2.00 on 3c	
524	A78	$2.10 on 3c	
525	A78	$2.20 on 3c	
526	A78	$2.35 on 3c	
527	A78	$2.40 on 3c	
528	A78	$2.50 on 3c	
529	A78	$3.00 on 3c	
530	A78	$3.30 on 3c	
531	A78	$3.75 on 3c	
532	A78	$4.00 on 3c	
533	A78	$4.40 on 3c	
534	A78	$5.00 on 3c	
535	A78	$5.50 on 3c	
536	A78	$6.25 on 3c	
537	A78	$15 on 2c (R)	
538	A78	$20 on 2c (R)	
		Nos. 501-538 (38)	210.00

Revenue stamps surcharged for postal use. Issue dates: Nos. 501-502, 504-538, May 17, 1982; No. 503, Mar. 14, 1983.
For surcharge see No. 935.

British Guiana Nos. 254, 255, 279, Guyana 10A, 13, 13a, 32J, 32K, 32N Surcharged "H.R.H. / Prince William / 21st June 1982" in Blue

British Guiana stamps also have "GUYANA."

1982, July 12   *Perfs. as Before*
Watermarks & Printing Methods as Before

539	A60	50c on 2c #254	1.00	.45
540	A60	50c on 2c #32J	20.00	4.50
541	A66	$1.10 on 5c #279	3.00	.65
541A	A60	$1.10 on 3c #255	2.00	.55
542	A60	$1.10 on 3c #32K	32.50	4.50
543	A60	$1.25 on 6c #10A		
543A	A60	$1.25 on 6c #32N	.85	.85
544	A60	$2.20 on 24c #13a	3.00	
544A	A60	$2.20 on 24c #13	2.00	2.00

For surcharges see Nos. 797-800.

Nos. 133-134 Surcharged "C.A. & CARIB / Games / 1982"
Perf. 13x13½
1982, Aug. 16   **Litho.**   **Wmk. 364**

545	A28	50c on #134	2.25	.40
546	A28	60c on 1c #133	2.75	.25
		Nos. 545-546 (2)	5.00	

Central American and Caribbean Games, Havana. For overprint see No. 816.

Nos. 331, C2 Surcharged
1982, Sept. 15

547	A28	130c on #331	2.25
548	A28	170c on #C2	2.75
549	A28	440c on #331 ovptd. "1982"	3.50
a.		Without "1982"	80.00
		Nos. 547-549 (3)	8.50

For surcharge see No. 802.

No. 137 Surcharged "Commonwealth / GAMES / AUSTRALIA / 1982" in Blue
1982, Sept. 27

550	A28	$1.25 on 6c #137	2.25	.50

For surcharge see No. 789.

No. 207 Ovptd. "INT. / FOOD DAY / 1982" in Dark Blue
No. 320 Ovptd. "INT. YEAR / OF THE / ELDERLY" in Dark Blue
No. 323 Ovptd. "Dr. R. KOCH / CENTENARY / TBC BACILLUS / DISCOVERY" in Dark Blue
No. 287 Ovptd. "F.D. ROOSEVELT / 1882-1982 " in Green
No. 221 Ovptd. "1982" in Blue
No. 332 Surcharged "GAC Inaug. Flight / Georgetown- / Boa Vista, Brasil" in Blue and "1982" in Blue Green

1982, Oct. 15   Perfs. as Before
Watermarks & Printing Methods as Before

551	A48	50c on #207	21.00	1.00
552	A74	50c on #320	14.00	1.00
553	A75	60c on #323	5.00	.55
554	A66	$1 on #287	6.00	1.00
555	A52	$1 on #221	6.00	1.25
556	A28	200c on #332	20.00	2.75
		Nos. 551-556 (6)	72.00	7.55

For surcharges see Nos. 895, 902, 936, 1363.

No. 437 Surcharged "CARICOM / Heads of Gov't / Conference / July 1982"
Perf. 14½x14
1982, Jan. 18   Litho.   Wmk. 364

557		Sheet of 6	15.00	12.50
a.-f.	A81	50c on 15c, any single	2.25	.50

Nos. 464 Ovptd. "CHRISTMAS / 1982" in Red
Perf. 13x13½
1982, Dec. 1

558		Sheet of 25, 8 #a.-b., 4 #c.-d., 1 #e.	32.50	32.50
a.-b.	A28	15c on #464a-464b, either single	.90	.45
c.-d.	A28	15c on #464c-464d, either single	2.10	.45
e.	A28	15c on #464e	24.00	24.00

Nos. 134, 137 Surcharged

Perf. 13x13½
1982-83   Litho.   Wmk. 364

563	A28	15c on 2c #134 (Bl)	.50
a.		Red surcharge	2.00
b.		Black surcharge	.75
564	A28	20c on 6c #137 (Bk)	.50
a.		Green surcharge	.75

Issued: #563, Dec. 15; #564, Jan. 5, 1983. Compare No. 564 with Nos. 631-632. For surcharges see Nos. 846, 846a, 846b.

No. 72 Surcharged
1982, Dec. 15   Photo.   Perf. 14x14½

565	A7	50c on 6c #72	.75	.25
566	A7	$1.00 on 6c #72	1.25	.45
		Nos. 565-566 (2)	2.00	.70

Nos. 62, 88-89, 144, 161, 202, 217, 224-225, 232, 240, 251, 254, 257, 264, 276-278, 299-301, 303-305, 315, 319, 321, 329m, 414-416, and 418-420 Ovptd. "1983" Vertically or Horizontally
1983   Perfs. as Before
Watermarks & Printing Methods as Before

567	A57	15c on #240	6.00
568	A60	15c on #254	1.50
569	A62	15c on #264	1.00
570	A79	15c on 10c #414	1.00
571	A80	15c on 10c #418	.25
572	A14	25c on #88	.50
573	A33	25c on #161	14.00
574	A47	25c on #202	
575	A11	30c on #62	1.50
576	A14	30c on #89	.50
577	A65	30c on #276	12.50
578	A69	30c on #299	5.00
579	A70	30c on #303	10.00
580	A74	30c on #319	6.00
581	A77	30c on #329m	3.00
582	A53	50c on #224	2.00
583	A55	50c on #232	5.00
584	A59	50c on #251	7.00
585	A65	50c on #277	5.00
586	A69	50c on #300	2.00
587	A70	50c on #304	30.00
588	A79	50c on #415	1.00
589	A80	50c on #419	2.00
590	A65	60c on #278	5.50
591	A72	60c on #315	7.00
592	A51	$1 on #217	10.00
593	A53	$1 on #225	10.00
594	A60	$1 on #257	6.00
595	A79	$1 on 30c #416	2.75
596	A80	$1 on 60c #420	7.50
597	A28	180c on 60c #144	2.00
598	A69	$3 on #301	12.00

599	A70	$3 on #305	15.00
601	A74	$3 on #321	75.00
602	A28	360c on $2 #146	2.25

Issued: #567-571, 583, 585-586, 2/1; #596, 3/7; #573, 3/11; #572, 576, 3/17; #582, 584, 587, 588, 589, 592-595, 598-599, 601, 4/1; #574, 5/23; #575, 577-580, 590-591, 7/1; #602, 11/3; #581, 11/15; #597, 12/14.
Refer to the second paragraph in footnote under No. 147 for Nos. 597 & 602. No. 597 contains unissued overprint, "ESPANA 1982." For overprints and surcharges see Nos. 724, 901, 940, 943A.

No. O2 Ovptd. "POSTAGE" in Red
Perf. 14½x14
1983, Feb. 1   Photo.   Wmk. 364

603	A8	15c on #O2	16.00	.50

For surcharge see Nos. 746-746a.

Nos. 291-293, 356 Surcharged in Blue or Black
Wmk. 364
1983, Feb. 8   Litho.   Perf. 14

604	A67	90c on 30c #291 (Blk)	2.00	1.00
605	A67	90c on 50c #292	1.25	.30
606	A67	90c on 60c #293	2.00	1.00
607	A55	90c on #356	4.75	.50
		Nos. 604-607 (4)	10.00	2.80

For overprints and surcharges see Nos. 763-764, 768-769, 770-771.

Flag A82

Cooperative Youth Palace — A83

1983, Feb. 19   Perf. 14½x14

608	A82	Pair	.60	.60
a.		25c Flag flying right	.30	.30
b.		25c Flag flying left	.30	.30
609	A83	$1.30 shown	1.00	1.00
		Size: 43x25mm		
		Perf. 14½		
610	A83	$6 Map	3.25	3.25

60th birthday of Pres. Linden Forbes Burnham. No. 608a inscribed for birthday; No. 608b for Burnham's 30th anniv. of election to parliament.
See #660, 913. For overprints & surcharges see #826-835, 924-926, 1404-1406.

Nos. 160, 205, 222, 263, 298, 302, 330, 333, 408-409, 480, C4, O1 and Q3 Ovptd. in Blue or Red
1983   Litho.   Perfs. as Before
Watermarks & Printing Methods as Before

611	A33	50c on 8c #160 (R)	25.00
612	A48	50c on 8c #205	2.25
613	A62	50c on 8c #263	8.00
614	A69	50c on 10c #298 (R)	1.50
615	A70	50c on 10c #302	4.00
616	A69	50c on #409	4.50
617	A69	50c on #480	2.00
618	A28	50c on #O1	5.00
619	A53	$1 on #222	8.50
620	A53	$1 on #330	5.00
621	A28	$1 on #333	5.00
622	A28	$1 on #408	10.00
623	A28	$1 on #C4	1.50
624	A28	$1 on #Q3	25.00

#621 has Royal Wedding ovpt. similar to #331. #624 also ovptd. "1982." See #648-649 for similar surcharges. For overprint see #815,

941. Issued: #614, 617, 619-624, 3/7; #611, 3/11; others, 4/1.

Nos. 10A, 13a Surcharged "Commonwealth / Day / 14 March 1983" and Emblem in Blue or Black
Wmk. 314 Upright
1983, Mar. 14   Engr.   Perf. 12½x13

625	A60	25c on 6c #10A	
626	A60	$1.20 on 6c #10A (Bl)	
		Wmk. 314 Sideways	
627	A60	$1.30 on 24c #13a	
628	A60	$2.40 on 24c #13a (Bl)	
		Nos. 625-628 (4)	5.00

For overprints see Nos. 1823-1825.

Intl. Maritime Organization, 25th Anniv. — A84

Perf. 14
1983, Mar. 17   Typo.   Wmk. 3
Red Overprint on British Guiana Revenue Stamp

629	A84	$4.80 grn & blue	9.00

Nos. 60, 72, 87 & 137 Surcharged in Black or Blue
1983   Perfs. as Before
Watermarks & Printing Methods as Before

630	A11	15c on 6c #60	.75
a.		Blue surcharge	1.00
631	A28	20c on 6c #137, two obliterators	1.00
632	A28	20c on 6c #137	1.00
633	A7	50c on #72	.75
634	A14	50c on #87	1.00
		Nos. 630-634 (5)	4.50

Issued: #630, 632-633, 5/23; #630a, 631, 634, 5/2.
Surcharge on No. 632 has "c" after value. No. 564 does not.
For surcharge see No. 916.

No. 72 Surcharged in Black or Red
Perf. 14x14½
1983   Photo.   Wmk. 364

635	A7	$1 on 6c #72	1.60
a.		Red overprint, 4mm high	6.50

Issue dates: #635, May 2. #635a, May 23.
For surcharge see No. 916A.

Nos. 142, 147, 211, 226-227, 239 & 249 Surcharged in Blue
1983   Perfs. as Before
Watermarks & Printing Methods as Before

636	A54	110c on 10c #226	3.00
637	A49	120c on 35c #211	4.50
638	A54	120c on 35c #227	4.50
639	A57	120c on 8c #239	4.50
640	A59	120c on 10c #249	4.50
641	A28	250c on 40c #142	12.00
642	A28	400c on $5 #147	9.00
		Nos. 636-642 (7)	42.00

Issue dates: Nos. 636, 641-642, May 2. Others, July 1. For surcharge see No. 865.

Nos. 332, 495a, C3 Surcharged in Red or Blue
"ITU / 1983" or (#643)
"WHO / 1983" or (#644)
"17 MAY '83 / ITU/WHO /" (#645)
"ITU/WHO / 17 MAY / 1983" (#646-647)
1983, May 17   Perfs. as Before
Watermarks & Printing Methods as Before

643	A28	25c on #C3	4.00	.90
644	A28	25c on #C3	4.00	.90
645	A28	25c on #C3	4.00	.90
a.		Strip of 3, #643-645	22.50	10.00
646	A28	$4.50 on #332 (Bl)	16.00	2.00
647	A28	$4.50 on #495a (Bl)		

Nos. 643-645 issued in sheets of 25 with 8 each Nos. 643-644 and 9 No. 645.

Nos. 272, 274 Surcharged in Dark Blue
Perf. 13½x14
1983, May 18   Litho.   Wmk. 364

648	A64	$1 on 15c #272	7.50	1.00
649	A64	$1 on 40c #274	12.50	1.00
		Nos. 648-649 (2)	20.00	2.00

Surcharge on No. 648 also contains overprint "1983."

Nos. 402, 404, O8 Surcharged or Overprinted "CANADA 1983"
1983, June 15   Perf. 13½x13

650	A17	$1.30 on #O8	4.50	3.00
651	A17	180c on #402	4.50	4.50
652	A17	$3.90 on #404	10.00	10.00
		Nos. 650-652 (3)	19.00	17.50

For surcharge see No. 1860.

Nos. 243-244 Surcharged
1983, June 22   Unwmk.   Perf. 14

653	A57a	60c on 15c #243	15.00	1.00
654	A57b	$1.50 on 15c #244	22.50	2.50
		Nos. 653-654 (2)	37.50	3.50

Nos. 297, 313 Surcharged
1983, July 1   Perfs. as Before   Wmk. 364

655	A68	120c on #297	7.50	1.25
656	A72	120c on 10c #313 (R)	7.50	1.25

No. 655 has unissued surcharge, "INTERNATIONAL / SCIENCE YEAR / 375."

British Guiana No. J1 and Guyana No. J5 Surcharged "120 / GUYANA" in Dark Blue
1983, July 1   Wmk. 4   Perf. 13½x14

657	D1	120c on 1c #J1	6.00	1.25
		Wmk. 364		
658	D1	120c on 1c #J5	6.00	1.25

No. 371 Surcharged in Red "CARICOM DAY 1983"
1983, July 1   Wmk. 364   Perf. 14

659	A72	60c on $3 #371	3.00

Type A82 Without Inscription
1983, July 1   Litho.   Perf. 14½x14

660	A82	Pair	.30	.30
a.		25c, Flag flying right	.20	.20
b.		25c, Flag flying left	.20	.20

River Steamers A85

1983, July 11   Litho.   Perf. 14

661	A85	30c Kurupukari	.20	.20
662	A85	60c Makouria	.40	.40
a.		Tete-beche pair		
663	A85	120c Powis	.85	.85
a.		Tete-beche pair		
664	A85	130c Pomeroon	.95	.95
665	A85	150c Lukanani	1.10	1.10
		Nos. 661-665 (5)	3.50	3.50

No. 146 Surcharged in Dark Blue
1983, July 22   Perf. 13½

666	A28	$2.30 on $1.10 on $2		
667	A28	$3.20 on $1.10 on $2		
		Nos. 666-667 (2)	6.50	

Nos. 666-667 have unissued surcharge of "$1.10 / Royal Wedding / 1981" similar to No. 331.

Nos. 282-283 & 283A Overprinted as Shown or with Various Initials in Red or Blue

Overprints: No. 668a, BW. b, LM. c, GY 1963 / 1983. d, JW. e, CU. f, Mont Golfier / 1783-1983.

No. 669a, BGI. b, GEO. c, MIA. d, BVB. e, PBM. f, Mont Golfier / 1783-1983. g, POS. h, JFK.

No. 670a, AHL. b, BCG. c, BMJ. d, EKE. e, GEO. f, GFO. g, IBM. h, Mont Golfier / 1783-1983. i, KAI. j, KAR. k, KPG. l, KRG. m, KTO. n, LTM. o, MHA. p, MWI. q, MYM. r, NAI. s, ORJ. t, USI. u, VEG.

1983, Sept. 5   *Perf. 14x13½*
Sheets of 25

668	A66	20c 4 each #a.-e., 5 #f	
			30.00
669	A66	25c 2 each #a., c.-e., g.-h., 8 #b., 5 #f.	45.00
670	A66	30c #a.-e., g.-u., 5 #f., (BI)	40.00

Manned flight, bicentennial and Guyana Airways, 20th anniv. For ovpts. see #871, 969.

No. 234 Surcharged in Dark Blue

1983, Sept. 14   *Perf. 13½*

703	A28	240c on #234	3.00	1.25
a.		"4" with serif	3.50	1.50

Nos. 703, 703a appear in same sheet.

Nos. 68, 70 Surcharged "FAO 1983" in Red

Perf. 14x14½

1983, Sept. 15   Photo.   Wmk. 364

704	A7	30c on 1c #68	.50	.20
705	A7	$2.60 on 3c #70	2.25	2.25
		Nos. 704-705 (2)	2.75	2.45

For overprints see Nos. 1497-1498.

Great Britain, Postal Use in British Guiana, 150th Anniv. — A86

Stamps: a, #20. b, #26. c, #27. d, #28.

1983, Oct. 1   Litho.   *Perf. 14*
Inscribed in Black

706	A86	25c #20	.25	.25
707	A86	30c #26	.25	.25
708	A86	60c #27	.45	.45
709	A86	120c #28	1.00	1.00

Inscribed in Blue

710		Block of 4	.80	.80
a.-d.	A86 25c any single		.20	.20
711		Block of 4	1.00	1.00
a.-d.	A86 30c any single		.20	.20
712		Block of 4	1.75	1.75
a.-d.	A86 45c any single		.40	.40
713		Block of 4	5.00	5.00
a.	A86 120c #20		.80	.80
b.	A86 130c #26, Demerara		.85	.85
c.	A86 150c #27, Berbice		1.00	1.00
d.	A86 200c #28, Essequibo		1.50	1.50
	Nos. 706-713 (8)		10.50	10.50

Nos. 706-709 printed in sheets with bottom two rows inverted. Nos. 710-712 printed in sheets of 60. No. 713 printed in sheets with blue marginal text.

For overprints and surcharges see Nos. 796, 903, 912, 1448, 1982.

#235 & 238 Surcharged
#297 Surcharged "INT. / COMMUNICATIONS / YEAR"
#206 Surcharged "Int. Food Day / 1983"
#309 Surcharged "1918-1983 / I.L.O."

1983, Oct. 15   *Perfs. as Before*
Watermarks & Printing Methods as Before

714	A68	50c on 375c on $3 #297	6.00
715	A56	75c on 8c #235	7.00
716	A41	$1.20 on 35c #206	1.75
717	A56	$1.20 on 40c #238	7.00
718	A71	240c on $3 #309	2.00
		Nos. 714-718 (5)	23.75

No. 714 was not issued without 375c surcharge. For overprint see No. 821.

Nos. 245, 247-248 Surcharged

Unwmk.

1983, Nov. 1   Litho.   *Perf. 14*

719	A58	20c on 8c #245	.35	.20
720	A58	$1.50 on 35c #247	2.40	1.00
721	A58	$1.50 on 40c #248	1.25	1.00
		Nos. 719-721 (3)	4.00	2.20

Nos. 268 & 270 Surcharged

1983, Nov. 15   Wmk. 364

722	A63	60c on 15c #268	2.50	.50
723	A63	$1.20 on 40c #270	2.50	.90

No. 601 Ovptd. "Human Rights / Day"

1983, Dec. 1   *Perf. 14½x14*

724	A74	$3 on #601	3.25	1.75

For surcharge see footnote following No. 998.

Nos. 317 and 726 Surcharged "LOS ANGELES / 1984"

1983, Dec. 6   Wmk. 373

725		Sheet of 12	8.00
a.-l.	A73 55c on 125c on 35c #726a-726l, any single		.65
726		Sheet of 12	
a.-l.	A73 125c on 35c #317a-317l, any single		

For surcharge see No. 1897.

No. 133 Surcharged "COMMONWEALTH / HEADS OF GOV'T / MEETING--INDIA / 1983"

Perf. 13½x13½

1983, Dec. 14   Litho.   Wmk. 364

727	A28	150c on 1c #133	4.00	1.00

Nos. 413a, 413e Surcharged "CHRISTMAS / 1983"

1983, Dec. 14   Photo.   *Perf. 14x14½*
Watermarks as before

728	A7	20c on #413a	1.50	.20
		20c on #413De	.50	.20

Nos. 146, O15 Ovptd. "POSTAGE" in Blue

1984, Jan. 8   *Perfs. as before*

729	A28	$2 on #146	4.25	1.00
730	A66	550c on $10 #O15	22.00	1.00

Refer to second paragraph in footnote following No. 147 for No. 729.

Flower Type of 1971-76 Surcharged in Blue

Perf. 15x14

1984, Jan.   Photo.   Unwmk.
Size: 20x23mm
Coil Stamps

731	A28	17c on 2c, like #134	4.50	2.75
732	A28	17c on 8c, Mazaruni Pride	4.50	2.75
a.		Pair, #731-732	10.00	10.00

Nos. 731-732 were intended for use on 8c envelopes to increase postage rate to 25c and were not issued without surcharge.

Nos. 284, 286A Surcharged in Black or Overprinted in Dark Blue
(1) "ALL / OUR HERITAGE"
(2) "1984" 7mm long
(3) "REPUBLIC / DAY"
(4) "BERBICE"
(5) "DEMERARA"
(6) "ESSEQUIBO"
(7) "1984" 18mm long

Perf. 14x13½

1984, Feb. 24   Litho.   Wmk. 364

733	A66	25c on 35c (1)	.75	.20
734	A66	25c on 35c (2)	1.25	.50
735	A66	25c on 35c (3)	1.25	.50
736	A66	25c on 35c #284	1.25	.50
737	A66	25c on 35c (4)	6.00	4.50
738	A66	25c on 35c (5)	6.00	4.50
739	A66	25c on 35c (6)	6.00	4.50
740	A66	25c on 35c (7)	14.00	14.00
741	A66	60c on #286A (1) (DBI)	3.50	1.00
742	A66	60c on #286A (3) (DBI)	3.50	1.00
743	A66	60c on #286A (2) (DBI)	3.50	1.00

Nos. 733-740 were issued in sheets of 25, 6 #733, 4 each #734-736, 2 each #737-739, 1 #740. Nos. 741-743 were issued in sheets of 25, 8 each #741-742, 9 #743.

Nos. 49-50, 52, 73-74, 77-80, 82, 139, 141A-143, 350, 603 Surcharged or Overprinted in Black and/or Blue "Protecting Our Heritage"

1984, Mar. 5   *Perfs. as Before*
Watermarks & Printing Methods as Before

744	A8	20c on 15c #74	8.50	.50
a.		Blue surcharge (value and words)	20.00	

745	A8	20c on 15c #350	8.50	.50
746	A8	20c on 15c #603 (BI)	17.50	2.00
a.		"Protecting our Heritage" in black		
747	A28	25c on #141A	14.50	.50
		25c on #141b	65.00	.60
748	A28	30c on 15c #139	24.00	.60
749	A8	40c on #77	12.50	.60
750	A28	50c on #143	1.50	.60
751	A28	50c on #143 (Revenue Ovpt.)	1.50	.60
752	A7	60c on #50	18.50	.60
a.		60c on #79	100.00	
753	A28	90c on 40c #142	19.50	.90
754	A28	90c on 40c #142 (Revenue ovpt.)	140.00	
755	A28	180c on #460	14.50	1.50
756	A7	$2 on #52	80.00	2.25
757	A8	225c on 10c on #73	25.00	1.75
758	A7	260c on $1 #80	17.50	1.50
759	A28	320c on 40c #142	17.50	3.25
760	A28	350c on 40c #142	24.00	4.25
761	A7	390c on 50c #78	9.50	4.00
a.		390c on #49	125.00	
762	A7	450c on $5 #82	12.50	4.00
		Nos. 744-762 (19)	467.00	

Nos. 748, 753-754, 759-760 use row of "X", 6mm high, as obliterator. Nos. 744-746, 757 have new value printed vertically over old value. No. 758, 761-762 have new value printed horizontally over old value. Refer to second paragraph in footnote under No. 147 for Nos. 751, 754-755.

Nos. 89, 484-485, 606 Overprinted or Surcharged in Dark Blue "1984"
No. 87 Surcharged
No. 606 Surcharged "INT. / CHESS / FED. / 1924-1984" in Dark Blue (#764a, 769a, 771a)

1984   *Perfs. as Before*
Watermarks & Printing Methods as Before

763	A67	25c on #606	2.00
764	A67	25c on #606	4.00
a.		Pair, #763-764	10.00
765	A14	30c on #89	.50
766	A14	45c on 6c #484	.50
767	A14	75c on 40c #485	.50
768	A67	75c on #606	1.00
769	A67	75c on #606	3.00
a.		Pair, #768-769	8.00
770	A67	90c on #606	1.00
771	A67	90c on #606	3.00
a.		Pair, #770-771	9.00
772	A14	130c on 6c #87	.50
773	A76	$3 on #328	3.00
		Nos. 763-773 (11)	19.00

Issued: #765-767, 772, Mar. 17; #773, June 15; #763-764, 768-769, 770-771, July 20.
No. 767 exists with surcharge either above old value or in center of stamp.

Nos. 497-500 Surcharged

1984, Apr. 2   Litho.   *Perf. 13½*

774	A28	75c on #497	11.00	.55
775	A28	75c on #498	13.00	.55
776	A28	225c on #500	3.50	1.75
777	A28	230c on #499	4.00	1.25
		Nos. 774-777 (4)	31.50	4.10

Nos. 464e, 465a, 465b, 465e, 466a, 466b, 466e Surcharged Like No. 748

1984, May 2

778	A28	20c on #464e	2.25	.50
779	A28	75c on #465e	11.50	1.00
780	A28	90c on #465a	7.00	1.25
781	A28	90c on #465b	9.50	1.25
782	A28	120c on #466a	11.00	1.50
783	A28	120c on #466e	11.00	1.50
784	A28	120c on #466b	3.50	1.50

No. C3 Surcharged "ITU DAY / 1984" (#785)
No. C3 Surcharged "WHO DAY / 1984" (#786)
Nos. C3, 386 Surcharged "ITU/WHO / DAY / 1984" (#787-788)

1984, May 17

785	A28	25c on #C3	1.60	1.60
786	A28	25c on #C3	1.60	1.60
787	A28	25c on #C3	1.60	1.60
788	A28	$4.50 on #386	2.50	2.50
		Nos. 785-788 (4)	7.30	7.30

The surcharge is vertical on Nos. 785-787, horizontal on No. 788.

No. 550 Surcharged

1984, June 11

789	A28	120c on #550	8.75	1.00

Nos. 325-327, 431 Surcharged in Blue or Black

Wmk. 373

1984, June 15   Litho.   *Perf. 14*

790	A76	55c on 30c #326 (Blk)	5.00	.50
791	A76	75c on #431	1.10	.75
792	A76	160c on 50c #327	1.50	1.50
793	A76	260c on 10c #325	2.50	1.75
		Nos. 790-793 (4)	10.10	4.25

No. 214 Surcharged

1984, June 18   Litho.   Wmk. 364

794	A50	55c on 110c on 10c	1.25	.50
795	A50	90c on 110c on 10c	1.50	.75

No. 214 surcharged 110c only was never issued.

No. 713 Ovptd. "UPU / Congress 1984 / Hamburg"

1984, June 19

796		Block of 4	5.00	5.00
a.	A86 120c on #713a		.75	.75
b.	A86 130c on #713b		.90	.90
c.	A86 150c on #713c		1.00	1.00
d.	A86 200c on #713d		1.25	1.25

Nos. 539, 541, 543-544 Surcharged in Black, Blue or Dark Green

1984, June 21   *Perfs. as Before*
Watermarks & Printing Methods as Before

797	A60	45c on #539	.50	.50
798	A66	75c on #541 (DkG)	2.50	.60
a.		60c on British Guiana #255 (DkG)		
799	A60	120c on #543	.75	.55
800	A60	200c on #544 (BI)	6.75	1.50
		Nos. 797-800 (4)	10.50	3.15

Nos. 135, 548, C2-C3 Surcharged in Blue or Black
No. C4 Overprinted "1984"

Perf. 13x13½

1984, June 30   Litho.   Wmk. 364

801	A28	75c on #C2 (Blk)	1.50	.50
802	A28	120c on #548 (Blk)	1.90	.75
803	A28	150c on #135	1.60	.80
804	A28	200c on #C3	17.50	2.50
804A	A28	330c on #C4	3.00	3.00
		Nos. 801-804A (5)	25.50	7.55

Surcharge on Nos. 801-802, 804 is like No. 748. Surcharge on No. 803 is like No. 457.

No. 135 Surcharged "CARICOM / HEADS OF GOV'T / CONFERENCE / JULY 1984"
No. 450A Surcharged "CARICOM DAY 1984"

1984, June 30   *Perfs. as Before*
Watermarks & Printing Methods as Before

805	A28	60c on 3c #135	1.40	.60
806	A72	60c on #450A	1.40	.60

Nos. 140-141, 141A, 329, 334, 427, 439a-440, 546, 611, 718, O13 Ovptd. "1984" in Black or Blue

1984   *Perfs. as Before*
Watermarks & Printing Methods as Before

807	A28	20c on #140	12.50	
a.		On #140a	150.00	
808	A28	20c on #140	55.00	
a.		On #140a	150.00	
809	A28	20c on #439, 1984 omitted	60.00	
810	A28	25c on #141	100.00	
a.		1984 omitted	100.00	
811	A28	25c on #141 (Revenue Only)	6.00	
812	A28	25c on #141A		
813	A28	25c on #141, 1982 ovpt., 1984 omitted	40.00	
814	A28	25c on #440, 1984 omitted		
815	A33	50c on #611 (BI)	10.00	
816	A28	60c on #546 (BI)	1.00	
817	A28	$2 on #O13 (BI)	2.50	
818	A28	$3.60 on #334	4.00	
c.		As #818, fleur-de-lis omitted	10.00	
d.		On #334a (BI)	4.00	
e.		As "d," fleur-de-lis omitted	5.00	
819		Sheet of 12	4.00	
a.-l.	A77 30c on #329a-329l, any single		
820	A71	240c on #429	4.75	
821	A71	240c on #418	4.75	

Overprint on Nos. 808-814, 818 contains fleur-de-lis. Refer to second paragraph in footnote below No. 147 for Nos. 811-812, 817.

Issued: #819, Sept. 15; #820-821, Oct. 15.

Teachers' Assoc. Centenary — A87

1984, July 16   **Wmk. 364**   *Perf. 14*
822	A87	25c Children dancing	.25	.25
823	A87	25c Torch, graduate	.25	.25
824	A87	25c Torch concentric circles	.25	.25
825	A87	25c Teachers, school	.25	.25
a.		Block of 4	1.00	1.00

No. 609 Surcharged in Blue:
"CYCLING" (#826, 831)
"TRACK / AND / FIELD" (#827, 832)
"OLYMPIC / GAMES / 1984" (#828, 833)
"BOXING" (#829, 834)
"OLYMPIC / GAMES / 1984 / LOS ANGELES" (#830, 835)

Perf. 14½x14
1984, July 28   **Litho.**   **Wmk. 364**
826	A83	25c on $1.30	1.00	.80
827	A83	25c on $1.30	1.00	.80
828	A83	25c on $1.30	1.00	.80
829	A83	25c on $1.30	3.75	2.00
830	A83	25c on $1.30	3.75	2.25
831	A83	$1.20 on $1.30	3.00	2.50
832	A83	$1.20 on $1.30	3.00	2.50
833	A83	$1.20 on $1.30	3.00	2.50
834	A83	$1.20 on $1.30	5.50	3.00
835	A83	$1.20 on $1.30	5.50	4.00

Nos. 826-828 and 831-833 exist in strips of 3. Nos. 827, 829-830 and 832, 834-835 exists in booklets.

Nos. 465-466 Surcharged "GIRL / GUIDES / 1924-1984" in Blue

1984, Aug. 15   *Perf. 13x13½*
Sheets of 25
836		8 #a.-b., 4 #c.-d., 1 #e.	
a.-e.		A28 25c on #465a-465e, any single	
837		8 #a.-b., 4 #c.-d., 1 #e.	
a.-e.		A28 25c on #466a-466e, any single	
		Nos. 836-837 (2)	35.00

Nos. 138-139, 234, 335, 351, 378, 380, 388, 401, 423, 438, 452, 459, 461, 563, 642, O3, O11-O12, O14 Surcharged

1984   *Perfs. as Before*
Watermarks & Printing Methods as Before
846	A28	20c on #563	1.00
a.		20c on #563a (Blk over R)	1.00
b.		20c on #563b (Blk over Bl)	1.00
847	A28	25c on #138	27.50
a.		25c on #138a	55.00
848	A28	25c on #139	150.00
849	A28	25c on #351a	20.00
a.		25c on #351	70.00
850	A28	25c on #351b	8.50
851	A28	25c on #438	8.00
a.		25c on #438a	150.00
852	A28	25c on #234	100.00
853	A28	25c on #452	8.00
854	A28	25c on #O3	8.00
855	A28	60c on #423, two obliterators, small 110 only	45.00
a.		Single obliterator, small 110 only	
856	A28	120c on #459	5.00
857	A28	120c on #401	35.00
858	A28	120c on #O12	2.00
859	A28	120c on #380	6.00
860	A28	130c on #378	100.00
861	A28	130c on #O11	12.50
862	A28	200c on #461	5.00
863	A28	320c on #378	5.50
864	A28	350c on #388	5.00
865	A28	390c on #642	6.00
866	A28	450c on #O14	5.75
867	A28	600c on #335	15.00
a.		600c on #335a	17.50
868	A28	600c on #335	3.00
a.		600c on #335a	4.00
		Nos. 846-868 (23)	581.75

Nos. 860-861 are airmail. Obliterator on Nos. 846, 856-859, 862-866 is row of "X", on Nos. 847, 850, 852 is single line, on Nos. 848-849, 851, 853-854 is fleur-de-lis, on No. 855 is a block of 6 lines, on No. 867 is 3 lines, on No. 868 is 3 lines and fleur-de-lis.

Nos. 556, 670, C4 Overprinted in Blue or Surcharged in Blue and Black

Overprints: #a-f, ICAO on #670a-670f. g, IMB/ICAO on #g. h, KCV/ICAO on #h. i, KAI/ICAO on #i. j-k, ICAO on #670j-670k. l, 1984 on #h. m, KPM/ICAO on #670 l-670n. n-p, ICAO on #670o-670u. q, PMT/ICAO on #h. r-x, ICAO on #670o-670u.

Perf. 14x13½
1984, Sept. 6   **Litho.**   **Wmk. 364**
871	A66	30c Sheet of 25, #a.-k., m.-x., 2 #l	65.00	65.00
895	A28	200c ICAO on #556	5.50	2.25
896	A28	200c ICAO on #C4 (Bl & Blk)	3.00	2.00

No. 896 is airmail with unissued "GAC" overprint. For surcharge see No. 1470.

Nos. J3-J4, J7-J8 Surcharged "120 / GUYANA" in Blue

Perf. 13½x14
1984, Oct. 1   **Typo.**   **Wmk. 314**
897	D1	120c on 4c #J3	3.00	.80
898	D1	120c on 12c #J4	3.00	.80

Wmk. 364
899	D1	120c on 4c #J7	8.00	.80
900	D1	120c on 12c #J8	28.50	1.25
		Nos. 897-900 (4)	42.50	3.65

Nos. 551, 571 Surcharged in Black or Blue

Perfs. as Before
1984, Oct. 15   **Wmk. 364**
901	A80	$1.50 on #571 (Bl)	14.00	1.50
902	A48	150c on 50c #551	4.00	1.00

Obliterator is "X" on No. 901. Surcharge on No. 902 places "1" before existing 50c value, obliterates "1982" and adds "1984."

Nos. 712, 479-481 Surcharged

1984, Oct. 22   *Perf. 14*
903		Block of 4	1.25	1.25
a.-d.		A06 25c on 45c on #712a-712d, any single	.20	.20
904	A69	120c on #479	9.50	.75
905	A69	120c on #480	1.25	.75
906	A66	320c on #481	20.00	2.75
		Nos. 903-906 (4)	32.00	5.50

Nos. 135-136 Surcharged "MAHA SABHA / 1934-1984" in Blue

1984, Nov. 1   *Perf. 13x13½*
910	A28	25c on 5c #136	.75	.20
911	A28	$1.50 on 3c #135	4.25	1.50
		Nos. 910-911 (2)	5.00	1.70

No. 713 Ovptd. "Philatelic Exhibition / New York 1984" in Red

1984, Nov. 15   *Perf. 14*
912		Block of 4	5.00	5.00
a.		A86 120c on No. 713a	1.00	.80
b.		A86 130c on No. 713b	1.10	.90
c.		A86 150c on No. 713c	1.25	1.00
d.		A86 200c on No. 713d	1.50	1.25

Type A83 Inscribed with Olympic Rings and "OLYMPIC GAMES 1984 / LOS ANGELES"

1984, Nov. 16   *Perf. 13½*
913	A83	$1.20 multicolored	5.00	5.00

Copies with numbers stamped on back are coils.
For similar stamp overprinted see No. 923.
For surcharges see Nos. 1953-1957.

Nos. 410, 413e, 633, 635a Surcharged

1984, Nov. 24   **Photo.**   *Perf. 14x14½*
Watermarks as Before
914	A7	20c on #410	1.00	.20
915	A7	20c on #413De	92.50	7.50
916	A7	25c on #633	.50	.20
916A	A7	60c on #635a	.70	.45

No. 914 has an "X" obliterating a "1" and no obliterating lines. No. 1400 has obliterating lines and small "20" in UR.

Elanoides
Forficatus
A88

Designs: a, Pair in tree. b, Landing on branch. c, In flight, wings up. d, In flight, wings down. e, In flight, wings outstretched.

1984, Dec. 3   **Wmk. 364**   *Perf. 14½*
917	A88	60c Strip of 5, #a.-e.	22.50	22.50

Inscribed "Christmas 1982."
For surcharges see Nos. 1502, 1840.

High Street Architecture — A89

Designs: 25c, St. George's Cathedral, 1892, Colonial Life Insurance Co. 60c, No. 920a, Demerara Mutual Life Assurance Soc., Ltd. No. 920b, 200c, Town Hall, 1888, City Engineers Office. No. 920c, 300c, Victoria Law Courts, 1887.

1985, Feb. 8   *Perf. 14*
918	A89	25c multi	.20	.20
919	A89	60c multi	.40	.40
920		Triptych	1.40	1.40
a.-c.		A89 120c, any single	.45	.45
d.		Triptych, unwmkd.	1.75	1.75
o.-g.		As "d," any single	.60	.60
921	A89	200c multi	1.25	1.25
922	A89	300c multi	1.75	1.75
		Nos. 918-922 (5)	5.00	5.00

For surcharge see No. 1850.

Type A83 Ovptd. "INTERNATIONAL / YOUTH YEAR 1985"

Wmk. 364
1985, Feb. 15   **Litho.**   *Perf. 14½*
923	A83	$1.20 multi	3.00	.75

Bars obliterate Olympic Games inscription with second line spelled "LOS ANGELES." No. 913 spells "Los Angeles" correctly.

Nos. 608, 610 Ovptd. in Red "Republic / Day / 1970-1985" or "1970 / 1985 / Republic / Day"

1985, Feb. 22   *Perfs. as Before*
924	A82	25c on #608		
925	A83	120c on $6 #610		
926	A83	130c on $6 #610		
		Nos. 924-926 (3)	3.00	2.25

Ocelot Cub
Xica — A90

Macaw
Nena — A90a

Perf. 12½x13
1985, Mar. 11   **Wmk. 364**
927	A90	25c multi	2.00	.30
928	A90	60c multi	.60	.60
929		Triptych	3.50	3.50
a.-c.		A90 120c, like #927-928, 930	1.10	1.10
930	A90	130c multi	1.25	1.25

Perf. 14½
931	A90a	320c shown	4.25	2.00
932	A90a	330c Cub on hind legs	2.50	2.00
		Nos. 927-932 (6)	14.10	9.65

No. 929, perf. 14, inscribed "1986," were from the liquidation of stock held by the printer, value 75c.
For overprints see #1903-1905, 1983, 2032.

Map Revenue Type A78 and Nos. 481, 501, 554, O6 Surcharged in Black or Blue

1985   *Perfs as Before*
Watermarks & Printing Methods as Before
933	A69	30c on 50c on #O6 (Bl)	1.00	.20
934	A78	55c on 2c multi	1.00	.25
a.		"ESSEQUIBO IS OURS" omitted	15.00	
935	A78	55c on #501	1.00	.40
936	A66	90c on #554 (Bl)	7.00	.65

937	A66	225c on #481	10.00	2.00
938	A66	230c on #481 (Bl)	10.00	2.25
939	A66	260c on #481 (Bl)	10.00	2.50
		Nos. 933-939 (7)	40.00	8.25

Issued: #933-936, 938-939, 3/11; #937, 4/11.
Obliterator on Nos. 934-935 is fleur-de-lis.

Nos. 305, 435, 587, 599, & 615 Ovptd. "INTERNATIONAL / YOUTH YEAR / 1985" in Blue

Wmk. 364
1985, Apr. 15   **Litho.**   *Perf. 13½*
940	A70	50c on #587	2.00	.30
941	A70	50c on #615	7.00	.30
942	A70	120c on #435	2.25	.55
943	A70	$3 on #305	10.00	—
943A	A70	$3 on #599	2.25	1.25
		Nos. 940-943A (5)	23.50	2.40

No. 280 Surcharged with Names of 1860 Post Offices or Postal Agencies in Blue

Overprints: a, Airy Hall. b, Belfield / Arab. Coast. c, Delfield / E.C. Dem. d, Belladrum. e, Beterver- / wagting. f, Blairmont / Ferry. g, Boeraserie. h, Brahn. i, Bushlot. j, De / Kinderen. k, Fort / Wellington. l, Georgetown. m, Hague. n, Leguan. o, Mahaica. p, Mahaicony. q, New / Amsterdam. r, Plaisance. s, No. 6 Police / Station. t, Queenstown. u, Vertenoegen. v, Vigilance. w, Vreed-en- / Hoop. x, Wakenaam. y, Windsor / Castle.

Perf. 14x13½
1985, May 2   **Litho.**   **Wmk. 364**
Sheet of 25
944	A66	25c on 10c, #a.-y.	27.50	27.50

Colonial Post Office, 125th anniv.

Nos. 670 Ovptd. "1985" or with Letters in Red

Overprints: a-f, 1985 on #670a-670f. g, I on #670g. h, T on #670h. i, U on #670i. j-k, 1985 on #670j-670k. l, W on #670h. m, H on #670h. n, O on #670h. o-p, 1985 on #670 l-670m. q, D on #670n. r, A on #670h. s, Y on #670o. t-y, 1985 on #670p-670u.

1985, May 17
Sheet of 25
969	A66	30c #a.-y.	20.00	20.00

Nos. 413a & 413e Surcharged

1985, May 21   **Photo.**   *Perf. 14x14½*
Watermarks as Before
994	A7	20c on #413a	10.00	1.00
a.		20c on #413De	14.00	2.00

#994a has "20" at left and 11 obliterating lines. #1401 has "20" at right and 12 lines.

No. 135 Surcharged "CARDI / 1975-1985"

Perf. 13x13½
1985, May 29   **Litho.**   **Wmk. 364**
995	A28	60c on 3c #135	1.75	.40

Caribbean Agricultural Research Development Institute, 10th anniv.

No. 407 Surcharged

1985, June 3
996	A28	600c on #407	40.00	5.00

Nos. 288, 724, C1 Surcharged "ROTARY / INTERNATIONAL / 1905-1985" in Red

1985, June 21   *Perfs. as Before*
Watermarks & Printing Methods as Before
997	A74	120c on #C1	14.50	1.00
998	A66	300c on #288	10.00	3.50

No. 724 with a similar surcharge is usually found on first day covers.

No. 450A Surcharged "CARICOM DAY / 1985" and
No. 426 Surcharged "135th Anniversary / Cotton Reel / 1850-1985" in Red

1985, June 28   *Perfs. as Before*
Watermarks & Printing Methods as Before
999	A72	60c on #450A	1.00	.50
1000	A69	120c on #426	1.00	.50

Orchids from Reichenbachia, by
Sanders — A91

1985-87　　　　　　　*Perf. 14*
**Wmk. 364 (#1027, 1031, 1036, 1046,
1049, 1052, 1054, 1071, 1074,
1076, 1079, 1084, 1091, 1108),
Unwmkd.**

Series 1

1021	A91	120c Plate No. 1	.90	.60
1022	A91	60c Plate No. 2	.40	.40
1023	A91	130c Plate No. 3	1.00	.65
1024	A91	200c Plate No. 4	1.75	1.00
1025	A91	60c Plate No. 5	.50	.50
1026	A91	75c like #1025	.50	.50
a.		Wmk. 364 ('87)	11.00	11.00
1027	A91	100c Plate No. 6	.80	.80
1028	A91	130c like #1027	1.00	.65
a.		Wmk. 364 ('86)	1.25	1.25
1029	A91	60c Plate No. 7	.50	.50
1030	A91	25c Plate No. 8	.50	.50
1031	A91	50c Plate No. 9	.50	.50
1032	A91	55c like #1031	.50	.50
a.		Wmk. 364 ('86)	.50	.50
1033	A91	60c Plate No. 10	.50	.50
1034	A91	120c Plate No. 11	.90	.60
1035	A91	25c Plate No. 12	.50	.50
1036	A91	100c Plate No. 13	.80	.80
1037	A91	130c like #1036	1.00	.65
a.		Wmk. 364 ('86)	5.00	3.00
1038	A91	200c Plate No. 14	1.75	1.00
1039	A91	55c Plate No. 15	.50	.50
1040	A91	180c like #1039	1.60	.90
a.		Wmk. 364 ('87)	11.00	9.00
		Nos. 1021-1040 (20)	16.40	12.55

Issued: #1022-1024, 1028-1029, 1033,
1035, 1037, 7/9; #1032, 8/12; #1021, 1030,
1034, 1038, 9/16; #1026, 2/26/86; #1040,
7/24/86; #1025, 1027, 1031, 1036, 1039,
8/21/86.
Nos. 1021, 1034 horiz.

1041	A91	130c Plate No. 16	1.00	.65
1042	A91	55c Plate No. 17	.50	.50
a.		Wmk. 364 ('87)	6.00	6.00
1043	A91	80c like #1042	.60	.60
1044	A91	130c Plate No. 18	1.00	.65
1045	A91	60c Plate No. 19	.50	.50
1046	A91	100c Plate No. 20	.80	.80
1047	A91	130c like #1046	1.00	.65
a.		Wmk. 364 ('86)	3.00	2.00
1048	A91	200c Plate No. 21	1.75	1.00
1049	A91	50c Plate No. 22	.50	.50
1050	A91	55c like #1049	.50	.50
a.		Wmk. 364 ('86)	.50	.50
1051	A91	25c Plate No. 23	.50	.50
1052	A91	50c Plate No. 24	.50	.50
1053	A91	225c like #1052	2.00	1.10
a.		Wmk. 364 ('86)	5.00	2.75
1054	A91	100c Plate No. 25	.80	.80
1055	A91	130c like #1054	1.00	.65
a.		Wmk. 364 ('86)	6.00	3.75
1056	A91	150c Plate No. 26	1.40	.75
1057	A91	90c Plate No. 27	.90	.60
1058	A91	120c Plate No. 28	.90	.60
1059	A91	130c Plate No. 29	1.00	.65
1060	A91	130c Plate No. 30	1.00	.65
		Nos. 1041-1060 (20)	18.15	13.15

Issued: #1044-1045, 1047, 1055, 1057,
1059-1060, 7/9; #1041, 1050, 8/12; #1048,
1051, 1058, 9/16; #1042, 1053, 1056, 7/10/86;
#1046, 1049, 1052, 1054, 8/21/86; #1043,
11/25/86.
Nos. 1048, 1058 horiz.

1061	A91	60c Plate No. 31	.50	.50
1062	A91	150c Plate No. 32	1.25	.75
1063	A91	200c Plate No. 33	1.75	1.00
1064	A91	150c Plate No. 34	1.40	.75
1065	A91	150c Plate No. 35	1.40	.75
1066	A91	90c Plate No. 36	.90	.60
1067	A91	120c Plate No. 37	.90	.60
1068	A91	90c Plate No. 38	.90	.65
1069	A91	80c Plate No. 39	.80	.60
1070	A91	260c like #1069	2.50	1.25
a.		Wmk. 364 ('87)	6.00	5.50
1071	A91	100c Plate No. 40	.80	.80
1072	A91	150c like #1071	1.25	.75
a.		Wmk. 364 ('86)	6.00	3.50
1073	A91	150c Plate No. 41	1.25	.75
1074	A91	100c Plate No. 42	.75	.75
1075	A91	150c like #1075	1.25	.75
a.		Wmk. 364 ('86)	6.00	3.50
1076	A91	100c Plate No. 43	.80	.80
1077	A91	200c like #1076	1.75	1.00
a.		Wmk. 364 ('86)	6.00	3.25
1078	A91	60c Plate No. 44	.90	.90
1079	A91	100c Plate No. 45	.90	.90

1080	A91	150c like #1079	1.25	.75
a.		Wmk. 364 ('86)	6.00	3.50
		Nos. 1061-1080 (20)	23.00	15.60

Issued: #1061, 7/9; #1062, 1064-1066,
1068, 1073, 1078, 8/12; #1072, 1075, 1077,
1080, 9/16; #1063, 1067, 1070, 7/10/86;
#1069, 1071, 1074, 1076, 1079, 8/21/86.
Nos. 1063, 1071-1072, 1074-1077, 1079-
1080 horiz.

1081	A91	120c Plate No. 46	.80	.60
1082	A91	60c Plate No. 47	.50	.50
1083	A91	150c Plate No. 48	1.25	.75
1084	A91	150c Plate No. 49	1.25	1.25
1085	A91	55c like #1084	.50	.50
a.		Wmk. 364 ('86)	3.00	3.00
1086	A91	60c Plate No. 50	.50	.50
1087	A91	320c like #1086	4.00	2.10
a.		Wmk. 364 ('87)	10.00	9.50
1088	A91	25c Plate No. 51	.50	.50
1089	A91	25c Plate No. 52	.90	.90
1090	A91	30c Plate No. 53	.50	.50
a.		Wmk. 364 ('86)	3.00	3.00
1091	A91	50c like #1090	.50	.50
1092	A91	45c Plate No. 54	.50	.50
a.		Wmk. 364 ('87)	10.00	10.00
1093	A91	60c like #1092	.50	.50
1094	A91	50c Plate No. 55	1.10	1.10
1095	A91	60c like #1094	1.40	1.40
1096	A91	75c like #1094	.50	.50
a.		Wmk. 364	3.00	3.00
1097	A91	120c Plate No. 56	1.00	.70
1098	A91	60c Plate No. 57	.50	.50
1099	A91	120c Plate No. 58	1.00	.70
1100	A91	25c Plate No. 59	.50	.50
a.		Dark red flowers ('86)	3.00	3.00
		Nos. 1081-1100 (20)	18.20	15.60

Issued: #1082-1083, 1085, 1089, 8/12;
#1088, 9/16; #1095, 10/7; #1087, 1092,
2/26/86; #1081, 1090, 1096-1100, 7/10/86;
#1086, 1091, 1093, 8/21/86; #1084, 12/22/86;
#1094, 1/16/87.
No. 1098 horiz.

1101	A91	75c Plate No. 60	.60	.60
1102	A91	225c like #1101	2.00	1.10
a.		Wmk. 364 ('87)	13.00	13.00
1103	A91	25c Plate No. 61	.50	.50
1104	A91	150c Plate No. 62	1.25	.75
1105	A91	25c Plate No. 63	.50	.50
1106	A91	50c Plate No. 64	1.10	1.10
a.		Wmk. 364	—	—
1107	A91	55c like #1106	.50	.50
a.		Wmk. 364 ('86)	4.00	4.00
1108	A91	50c Plate No. 65	.50	.50
1109	A91	100c like #1108	.50	.50
a.		Wmk. 364	4.00	4.00
1110	A91	130c Plate No. 66	1.00	.65
1111	A91	120c Plate No. 67	.90	.60
1112	A91	40c Plate No. 68	1.00	1.00
1113	A91	100c like #1112	.50	.50
a.		Wmk. 364 ('87)	6.00	6.00
1114	A91	60c Plate No. 69	.50	.50
1115	A91	120c like #1114	.90	.60
a.		Wmk. 364 ('87)	14.00	14.00
1116	A91	25c Plate No. 70	.50	.50
1117	A91	25c like #1117	.20	.20
a.		Wmk. 364 ('87)	14.00	14.00
1118	A91	60c like #1117	.60	.60
1119	A91	25c Plate No. 72	.60	.60
1120	A91	60c Plate No. 73	.60	.60
		Nos. 1101-1120 (20)	14.75	12.40

Issued: #1104, 1107, 8/12; #1103, 1105,
1116, 1119, 9/16; #1102, 1115, 1117, 4/4/86;
#1109-1111, 1113, 1120, 7/10/86; #1101,
1108, 1114, 1118, 8/21/86; #1112, 11/25/86.
No. 1114-1115, 1117-1118, 1120 horiz.

1121	A91	80c Plate No. 74	.60	.60
1122	A91	250c like #1121	2.25	1.25
a.		Wmk. 364 ('87)	6.00	6.00
1123	A91	60c Plate No. 75	.50	.50
1124	A91	65c Plate No. 76	.50	.50
1125	A91	150c like #1124	1.25	.75
a.		Wmk. 364 ('87)	14.00	14.00
1126	A91	40c Plate No. 77	.50	.50
a.		Wmk. 364 ('87)	12.00	12.00
1127	A91	45c like #1126	.50	.50
1128	A91	45c Plate No. 78	.50	.50
1129	A91	150c like #1128	1.25	.75
a.		Wmk. 364 ('87)	13.00	13.00
1130	A91	60c Plate No. 79	.50	.50
1131	A91	200c like #1130	1.75	1.00
a.		Wmk. 364 ('87)	13.00	13.00
1132	A91	65c Plate No. 80	.50	.50
1133	A91	330c like #1132	3.00	1.60
a.		Wmk. 364 ('87)	14.00	14.00
1134	A91	45c Plate No. 81	.50	.50
a.		Wmk. 364 ('87)	14.00	14.00
1135	A91	55c like #1134	.50	.50
1136	A91	55c Plate No. 82	.50	.50
1137	A91	320c like #1136	3.00	1.60
a.		Wmk. 364 ('87)	15.00	15.00
1138	A91	75c Plate No. 83	.60	.60
1139	A91	300c like #1138	2.75	1.50
a.		Wmk. 364 ('87)	15.00	15.00
1140	A91	45c Plate No. 84	.50	.50
1141	A91	90c like #1140	.50	.50
a.		Wmk. 364 ('87)	13.00	13.00
		Nos. 1121-1141 (21)	22.45	15.65

Issued: #1126, 1129, 1131, 1139, 1141,
2/26/86; #1122-1123, 7/10/86; #1125, 1133-
1134, 1137, 7/24/86; #1121, 1124, 1127-1128,
1130, 1132, 1135-1136, 1138, 1140, 8/21/86.
No. 1123 horiz.

1142	A91	45c Plate No. 85	.50	.50
1143	A91	360c like #1142	3.00	1.75
a.		Wmk. 364 ('87)	14.00	14.00
1144	A91	30c Plate No. 86	.50	.50
a.		Wmk. 364 ('87)	6.50	6.50
1145	A91	40c like #1144	1.10	1.10
1146	A91	60c like #1144	.50	.50

1147	A91	150c like #1146	1.25	.75
a.		Wmk. 364 ('87)	17.00	17.00
1148	A91	65c Plate No. 88	.50	.50
1149	A91	100c like #1148	.60	.60
a.		Wmk. 364 ('87)	14.00	14.00
1150	A91	55c Plate No. 89	.50	.50
1151	A91	90c like #1150	.50	.50
a.		Wmk. 364 ('87)	14.00	14.00
1152	A91	40c Plate No. 90	.50	.50
1153	A91	375c like #1152	2.50	2.50
a.		Wmk. 364 ('87)	7.00	7.00
1154	A91	40c Plate No. 91	2.10	2.10
1155	A91	130c like #1154	1.25	.65
a.		Wmk. 364 ('87)	6.50	6.50
1156	A91	50c Plate No. 92	.50	.50
a.		Wmk. 364 ('87)	14.00	14.00
1157	A91	75c like #1156	.60	.60
1158	A91	60c Plate No. 93	.50	.50
a.		Wmk. 364 ('87)	6.50	6.50
1159	A91	80c like #1158	.60	.60
1160	A91	60c Plate No. 94	.50	.50
a.		Wmk. 364 ('87)	14.00	14.00
1161	A91	350c like #1160	3.25	1.75
1162	A91	60c Plate No. 95	.60	.60
a.		Wmk. 364 ('87)	14.00	14.00
1163	A91	75c like #1162	.60	.60
1164	A91	40c Plate No. 96	.50	.50
a.		Wmk. 364 ('87)	14.00	14.00
1165	A91	65c like #1164	.60	.60
		Nos. 1142-1165 (24)	23.55	19.70

See note below #1341. Issued: #1143,
1156, 1162, 2/26/86; #1147, 1161, 4/4/86;
#1144, 1153, 1155, 1158, 7/10/86; #1149,
1151, 1164, 7/24/86; #1142, 1146, 1148,
1150, 1152, 1157, 1159-1160, 1163, 1165,
8/21/86; #1154, 9/26/86; #1145, 10/23/86.
Some stamps printed in sheets of 25, blocks
of 4 each of different stamps separated by
gutter containing 2 #1337 and strip of 5 #1339.
Margin contains separation marks for #1337,
1339.
Nos. 1146-1147, 1160-1161 horiz.
Nos. 1025, 1027, 1031, 1036, 1039, 1046,
1049, 1052, 1054, 1071, 1074, 1076,
1079, 1086, 1091, 1093, 1101, 1108, 1114,
1118, 1121, 1124, 1127-1128, 1130, 1132,
1135-1136, 1138, 1140, 1142, 1146, 1148,
1150, 1152, 1157, 1159-1160, 1163, 1165
sold as singles in booklets only. Two booklets
of 48 stamps each contain these numbers and
previous values issued in the series. Value,
each booklet, $80.
See #1372. For overprints and surcharges
see #1342-1346, 1393, 1402-1403, 1412-
1413, 1494, 1511-1670F, 1731-1740, 1742-
1750, 1755-1759, 1761, 1764-1773, 1785,
1845-1849, 1906-1909, 1914-1933, 1939-
1941, 1943-1947, 1958-1959, 1960-1979,
2000, C7, C9-C12, E2, E4.

1986-89　　**Litho.**　**Unwmk.**　*Perf. 14*
Series 2

1166	A91	175c Plate No. 1	1.50	.65
1167	A91	560c like #1166	4.50	1.60
1168	A91	90c Plate No. 2	1.25	1.25
1169	A91	200c like #1168	2.25	1.25
1170	A91	50c Plate No. 3	.50	.50
1171	A91	90c like #1170	.60	.60
1172	A91	90c Plate No. 4	.60	.60
1173	A91	140c like #1172	1.25	.50
1174	A91	130c Plate No. 5	1.10	.50
1175	A91	160c like #1174	1.50	.80
1176	A91	50c Plate No. 6	.50	.50
1177	A91	390c like #1176	3.50	2.00
1178	A91	30c Plate No. 7	.50	.50
1179	A91	40c like #1178	.50	.50
1180	A91	70c Plate No. 8	.50	.50
1181	A91	75c like #1180	.60	.60
1182	A91	70c Plate No. 9	.50	.50
1183	A91	200c like #1182	1.75	1.00
1184	A91	90c Plate No. 10	1.25	1.25
1185	A91	320c like #1184	3.00	1.75
		Nos. 1166-1185 (20)	27.65	17.35

Issued: #1172, 1175, 1181, 1183, 9/23;
#1184, 10/23; #1177, 1185, 10/31; #1169,
11/25; #1171, 1179, 12/27; #1168, 1/5/87;
#1167, 4/24/87; #1166, 1170, 1173-1174,
1176, 1178, 1180, 1182, 8/23/88.
Nos. 1174-1175 horiz.

1186	A91	200c Plate No. 11	1.75	.75
1187	A91	70c Plate No. 12	.50	.50
1188	A91	320c like #1187	2.75	1.60
1189	A91	50c Plate No. 13	1.50	1.50
1190	A91	90c like #1189	.60	.60
1191	A91	30c Plate No. 14	.60	.60
1192	A91	120c like #1191	1.00	.60
1193	A91	50c Plate No. 15	4.25	4.25
1194	A91	85c like #1193	.50	.50
1195	A91	260c like No. 16	2.25	.60
1196	A91	320c like #1195	3.25	1.40
1197	A91	45c Plate No. 17	.50	.50
1198	A91	70c like #1197	.50	.50
1199	A91	85c Plate No. 18	.60	.60
1200	A91	320c like #1199	3.00	1.60
1201	A91	175c Plate No. 19	1.50	.65
1202	A91	450c like #1201	3.75	1.25
1203	A91	25c Plate No. 20	.50	.50
1204	A91	50c like #1203	.50	.50
1205	A91	100c Plate No. 21	2.00	2.00
		Nos. 1186-1205 (20)	31.80	21.00

Issued: #1188, 1205, 9/23; #1190, 1197,
10/31; #1189, 12/3; #1192, 1194, 1200, 1203,
12/27; #1193, 1199, 1/5/87; #1202, 4/24/87;
#1196, 6/13/88; #1186-1187, 1191, 1198, 1201,
1204, 6/1/88; #1195, 7/7/89.
Nos. 1201-1202, 1205, horiz.

1206	A91	30c Plate No. 22	.50	.50
1207	A91	150c like #1206	1.25	.75
1208	A91	200c Plate No. 23	1.75	.75
1209	A91	85c Plate No. 24	1.60	1.60
1210	A91	225c like #1209	4.75	4.75
1211	A91	140c Plate No. 25	1.25	.55
1212	A91	230c like #1211	2.25	.70
1213	A91	200c Plate No. 26	1.75	.75
1214	A91	60c Plate No. 27	.50	.50
1215	A91	90c like #1214	1.10	1.10
1216	A91	30c Plate No. 28	.50	.50
1217	A91	330c like #1216	3.00	1.60
1218	A91	130c like No. 29	1.00	.50
1219	A91	350c like #1218	3.25	1.75
1220	A91	30c Plate No. 30	3.25	3.25
1221	A91	875c Plate No. 31	6.00	3.50
1222	A91	50c Plate No. 32	.50	.50
1223	A91	130c like #1222	1.00	.50
1224	A91	50c Plate No. 33	.50	.50
1225	A91	90c like #1224	.90	.90
		Nos. 1206-1225 (20)	36.60	25.60

Issued: #1219, 1220, 9/23; #1214, 1224,
10/31; #1210, 11/25; #1209, 1215, 12/15;
#1207, 1217, 1223, 12/27; #1212, 2/14/87;
#1221, 6/15/88; #1206, 1208, 1211, 1213,
1216, 1218, 1222, 1225, 8/23/88.
Nos. 1218-1219 horiz.

1226	A91	140c Plate No. 34	1.10	.50
1227	A91	360c like #1226	3.00	1.75
1228	A91	380c Plate No. 35	3.25	1.40
1229	A91	525c Plate No. 36	4.00	2.25
1230	A91	175c Plate No. 37	1.25	.65
1231	A91	390c like #1230	3.00	1.25
1232	A91	130c Plate No. 38	1.00	.65
1233	A91	140c like #1232	1.10	.50
1234	A91	175c Plate No. 39	1.50	.75
1235	A91	260c like #1234	2.00	.75
1236	A91	250c Plate No. 40	4.50	1.90
1237	A91	$10 like #1236	7.50	5.75
1238	A91	140c like No. 41	1.10	.50
1239	A91	180c like #1238	1.40	.45
1240	A91	80c Plate No. 42	.50	.50
1241	A91	130c like #1240	1.10	.50
1242	A91	200c Plate No. 43	1.75	.55
1243	A91	100c like No. 44	.80	.80
1244	A91	200c like #1243	1.75	1.00
1245	A91	35c Plate No. 45	.50	.50
1246	A91	85c like #1245	.60	.60
		Nos. 1226-1246 (21)	42.70	23.40

Issued: #1227, 1232, 1240, 9/23; #1244,
1246, 10/31; #1245, 1/5/87; #1239, 2/14/87;
#1231, 1235, 4/24/87; #1242, 9/29/87; #1237,
3/24/88; #1229, 6/1/88; #1226, 1228, 1230,
1233-1234, 1236, 1238, 1241, 1243, 8/23/88.
Nos. 1230-1231, 1240-1241 horiz.

1247	A91	225c Plate No. 46	1.50	.80
1248	A91	175c Plate No. 47	1.25	.65
1249	A91	240c like #1248	1.75	.70
1250	A91	200c Plate No. 48	1.40	.55
1251	A91	200c Plate No. 49	1.40	.55
1252	A91	720c like #1251	5.00	3.75
1253	A91	160c Plate No. 50	1.00	.55
1254	A91	300c like #1253	2.00	1.50
1255	A91	175c Plate No. 51	1.10	.60
1256	A91	500c like #1255	3.00	1.50
1257	A91	140c Plate No. 52	1.00	.40
1258	A91	590c like #1257	3.25	1.60
1259	A91	200c Plate No. 53	1.25	.55
1260	A91	290c like #1259	2.00	1.25
1261	A91	175c Plate No. 54	1.25	.60
1261A	A91	460c like #1261	2.75	1.40
1262	A91	120c Plate No. 55	.90	.35
1263	A91	75c Plate No. 56	.50	.50
1264	A91	100c like #1263	.50	.50
1265	A91	225c Plate No. 57	1.25	.50
		Nos. 1247-1265 (20)	34.05	18.90

Issued: #1254, 1263, 10/31; #1258, 2/14/87;
#1249, 1256, 1261A, 4/24/87; #1250, 9/29/87;
#1252, 1260, 11/23/87; #1247-1248, 8/23/88;
#1253, 1255, 11/3/88; #1251, 1257, 1259,
1261-1262, 1264-1265, 1/3/89.
Nos 1261, 1261A horiz.

1266	A91	175c Plate No. 58	1.25	.50
1267	A91	275c like #1266	2.00	.85
1268	A91	775c Plate No. 59	4.00	3.25
1269	A91	200c Plate No. 60	1.50	.55
1270	A91	575c like #1269	2.75	1.50
1271	A91	255c Plate No. 61	2.00	1.00
1272	A91	280c Plate No. 62	1.40	.95
1273	A91	700c like #1272	4.75	4.25
1274	A91	285c Plate No. 63	1.40	.60
1275	A91	200c Plate No. 64	1.00	.55
1276	A91	680c like #1275	3.75	3.25
1277	A91	140c Plate No. 65	.70	.40
1278	A91	650c like #1277	3.00	1.60
1279	A91	280c Plate No. 66	1.25	.75
1280	A91	750c like #1279	4.75	4.25
1281	A91	280c Plate No. 67	1.25	.75
1282	A91	$15 like #1281	8.50	7.50
1283	A91	325c Plate No. 68	1.75	.85
1284	A91	530c Plate No. 69	3.00	2.75
1285	A91	550c Plate No. 70	3.75	3.75
		Nos. 1266-1285 (20)	53.75	40.25

Issued: #1278, 2/14/87; #1267, 4/24/87;
#1270, 1283, 10/26/87; #1271, 1280,
11/23/87; #1282, 1284, 6/1/88; #1268, 1273,
6/15/88; #1285, 8/15/88; #1272, 1274,
11/3/88; #1266, 1269, 1275, 1277, 1279,
1281, 1/3/89.
No. 1266-1267, 1283, 1285 horiz.

1286	A91	670c Plate No. 71	4.50	4.25
1287	A91	300c Plate No. 72	1.50	.80
1288	A91	$25 like #1287	9.50	8.50
1289	A91	130c Plate No. 73	.80	.25
1290	A91	475c like #1289	2.75	2.50

1291	A91	350c Plate No. 74	2.25	2.00
1291A	A91	900c like #1291	6.50	6.00
1291B	A91	600c on 900c #1291A		
1292	A91	200c Plate No. 75	1.00	.70
1293	A91	250c Plate No. 76	1.25	.65
1294	A91	850c like #1293	4.75	4.25
1295	A91	300c Plate No. 77	1.50	.80
1296	A91	480c like #1295	2.25	1.25
1297	A91	280c Plate No. 78	1.40	.75
1298	A91	950c like #1298	6.50	6.00
1299	A91	250c Plate No. 79	1.25	.90
1300	A91	800c like #1299	5.00	4.00
1301	A91	300c Plate No. 80	1.50	.80
1302	A91	400c like #1301	2.00	1.10
1303	A91	305c Plate No. 81	1.50	.80
1304	A91	250c Plate No. 82	1.25	.65
1305	A91	330c like #1304	1.25	.65

Nos. 1286-1291A,1292-1305
(21) 60.55 47.80

Issued: #1305, 2/14/87; #1288, 1296, 1302, 7/22/87; #1291A-1291B, 10/9/87; #1294, 1300, 11/23/87; #1290, 6/1/88; #1298, 6/15/88; #1291, 6/22/88; #1286, 8/15/88; #1292, 1299, 11/3/88; #1287, 1293, 1295, 1297, 1301, 1303-1304, 1/3/89; #1289, 7/7/89. No. 1286 horiz.

1306	A91	350c Plate No. 83	1.75	.95
1307	A91	$20 like #1306	7.50	5.25
1308	A91	360c Plate No. 84	2.25	2.00
1309	A91	250c Plate No. 85	1.25	.65
1310	A91	300c like #1309	1.50	.75
1311	A91	350c Plate No. 86	1.75	.95
1312	A91	500c like #1311	2.25	1.25
1313	A91	250c Plate No. 87	1.25	.65
1314	A91	425c like #1313	2.00	1.00
1315	A91	250c Plate No. 88	1.25	.65
1316	A91	440c like #1315	2.00	1.10
1317	A91	350c Plate No. 89	1.75	.95
1318	A91	520c like #1317	2.60	1.40
1319	A91	270c Plate No. 90	1.25	1.25
1320	A91	250c Plate No. 91	1.10	.65
1321	A91	$12 like #1320	7.50	7.00
1322	A91	200c Plate No. 92	1.00	.55
1323	A91	200c Plate No. 93	1.00	.70
1324	A91	300c Plate No. 94	1.50	.80
1325	A91	600c like #1324	2.75	1.60
1326	A91	420c Plate No. 95	2.25	1.40
1327	A91	200c Plate No. 96	1.00	.40
1328	A91	375c like #1327	1.75	.95

Nos. 1306-1328 (23) 50.70 33.90

Issued: #1310, 1314, 1316, 2/14/87; #1307, 1312, 1318, 6/2/87; #1325, 7/22/87; #1322, 9/29/87; #1326, 10/26/87; #1328, 11/23/87; #1321, 3/24/88; #1308, 1319, 8/15/88; #1323, 11/3/88; #1306, 1309, 1311, 1313, 1315, 1317, 1320, 1324, 1/3/89; #1327, 7/7/89. No. 1326 horiz.

Nos. 1166, 1170, 1174, 1176, 1178, 1180, 1182, 1187, 1191, 1193, 1198, 1201, 1204, 1206, 1211, 1216, 1218, 1222, 1225-1226, 1230, 1233-1234, 1236, 1238, 1248, 1257, 1261, 1264, 1266, 1277, 1279, 1281, 1287, 1293, 1295, 1297, 1301, 1304, 1306, 1308-1309, 1311, 1313, 1315, 1317, 1320, 1324 sold as singles in booklets only. Two booklets of 48 stamps each contain these numbers and previous values issued in the series. Value, each booklet, $80.

Miniature Sheets of 4

Designs: Nos. 1329a, 1330b, 1331b, like #1303. Nos. 1329b, 1330a, 1332a, like #1265. Nos. 1329c, 1330c, 1332b, like #1247. Nos. 1330d, 1331a, 1332c, like #1262.

1329		A91 1262, 1329a-1329c	4.50	4.50
a.-c.	A91	120c any single	1.00	1.00
1330		#a.-d.	4.50	4.50
a.-d.	A91	150c any single	1.00	1.00
1331		#1247, 1265, 1331a-1331b	5.00	5.00
a.-b.	A91	225c any single	.95	.95
1332		A91 1303, 1332a-1332c	5.00	5.00
a.-c.	A91	305c any single	.95	.95
1333			7.00	7.00
a.	A91	320c like #1262	1.25	1.25
b.	A91	330c like #1247	1.25	1.25
c.	A91	350c like #1303	1.50	1.50
d.	A91	500c like #1265	2.40	2.40
1334			7.00	7.00
a.	A91	320c like #1247	1.25	1.25
b.	A91	330c like #1247	1.25	1.25
c.	A91	350c like #1303	1.50	1.50
d.	A91	500c like #1303	2.40	2.40
1335			7.00	7.00
a.	A91	320c like #1303	1.25	1.25
b.	A91	330c like #1265	1.25	1.25
c.	A91	350c like #1262	1.50	1.50
d.	A91	500c like #1247	2.40	2.40
1336			7.00	7.00
a.	A91	320c like #1265	1.25	1.25
b.	A91	330c like #1303	1.25	1.25
c.	A91	350c like #1303	1.50	1.50
d.	A91	500c like #1262	2.40	2.40

Issued: #1329-1332, 7/7/89; others, 2/26/88.
For surcharges & overprints see #1671-1727, 1776-1777, 1834-1835, 1942, 1948-1949, 1998-1999, 2031, 2033-2044, 2064, 2907A-2907G, 2928-2928D, E3, E5, O40-O56.

Natl. Arms — A92

1985-87 **Perf. 14 Vert.**

1337	A92	25c multi	.20	.50
1338	A92	25c multi ('87)	1.25	.75

Perf. 14 Horiz.

1339	A92	25c multi	.20	.20
1340	A92	25c multi ('87)	1.25	.75

Nos. 1337-1340 (4) 2.90 2.20

Perf. 14

1341	A92	25c multi		

Nos. 1337-1340 were cut from orchid sheet gutters. Stamps vary considerably in size.
Nos. 1338, 1340 are Nos. 1337 and 1339 redrawn to include black border.
Issue dates: Nos. 1337, 1339, 1341, July 1985. No. 1338, 1340 June 2, 1987.
See Nos. 1467-1468. For surcharges see Nos. 1777A-1777C.

Nos. 1024, 1044, 1047, 1059, 1060 Surcharged or Overprinted in Blue or Black "QUEEN MOTHER 1900-1985" on 1 or 2 Lines

1985 **Perfs. as Before**

1342	A91 130c on #1044		
1343	A91 130c on #1059		
1344	A91 130c on #1060		

Nos. 1342-1344 (3) 6.25

Miniature sheets

1345	Sheet of 4		7.50
a.-d.	A91 200c on #1024, any single		
1346	Sheet of 4		11.00
a.-d.	A91 200c on 130c #1047, any single (Bk)		

Issued: #1342-1345, July 9; #1346, Sept. 12.
Nos. 1345a, 1346a overprinted "LADY BOWES-LYON 1900-1923". Nos. 1345b, 1346b overprinted "DUCHESS OF YORK 1923-1937". Nos. 1345c, 1346c overprinted "QUEEN ELIZABETH 1937-1952". Surcharge on No. 1346 sans serif.
For overprints see #1741, 1751-1754, 1774-1775.

Nos. 465 Surcharged in Red "INTERNATIONAL / YOUTH YEAR / 1985"

Perf. 13x13½

1985, July 18 **Litho.** **Wmk. 364**

1347	Sheet of 25, 8 #a.-b., 4 #c.-d., 1 #e.		175.00
a.-e.	A28 25c on #465a-465e, any single		

No. 203 Surcharged

No. 443 Surcharged

1985, July 26 **Perfs. as Before**
Watermarks & Printing Methods as Before

1352	A47 225c on #203	30.00	4.00
1354	A63 240c on #443	20.00	5.00

Girl Guides, 75th anniv. (#1352), John J. Audubon, bicentennial of birth. No. 203 surcharged only with 350c, $2.25 or surcharged with both was not issued.

Abolition of Slavery, Sesquicent. — A93

Designs: 25c, Revolution leaders, 1763. 60c, Damon's execution, 1834. 130c, Demerara Uprising, 1823. 150c Den Arendt slave ship.

Unwmk.

1985, July 29 **Litho.** **Perf. 14**

1355	A93	25c gray & black	.25	.25
1356	A93	60c pink & black	.65	.65
1357	A93	130c blue grn & blk	1.40	1.40
1358	A93	150c lilac & blk	1.60	1.60

Nos. 1355-1358 (4) 3.90 3.90

See Nos. 1994-1997 for changed colors.

No. 210 Surcharged "Guyana/Libya / Friendship 1985"
No. 223 Surcharged in Brown
No. 135 Surcharged "Mexico / 1986"

1985, Aug. 16 **Perfs. as Before**
Watermarks and Printing Methods as Before

1359	A49	150c on #210	9.00	3.00
1360	A53	150c on #223	2.75	.85
1361	A28	275c on 3c #135	9.00	1.75

Nos. 1359-1361 (3) 20.75 5.60

Refer to 2nd paragraph under No. 147 for No. 1361. See No. 1452 for 225c Mexico 1986 surcharge.

Nos. 366, 427, 430, 430a, 494, & 553 Ovptd. or Surcharged "1955-1985" Vertically or Horizontally

Wmk. 364

1985, Sept. 23 **Litho.** **Perf. 13½**

1362	A75	60c on #366	.50	.50
1363	A75	60c on #553	.50	.50
1364	A75	120c on #427	1.00	1.00
1365	A75	120c on #430	1.00	1.00
1366	A75	120c on #430a	1.00	1.00
1367	A75	120c on #494	1.00	1.00

Nos. 1362-1367 (6) 5.00 5.00

No. 417 Surcharged "1965-1985" Vertically

1985, Sept. 30

1368	A79	25c on #417	.75	.30
1369	A79	225c on #417	2.50	1.50

Nos. 260 & 262 Surcharged "1985"

1985, Oct. 5 **Litho.** **Perf. 14x14½**

1370	A61	25c on 40c #262	11.00	.40
1371	A61	320c on 15c #260	20.00	3.75

Orchid Type of 1985 Surcharged in Red "CRISTOBAL COLON / 1492-1992"

1985, Oct. 12 **Perf. 14**

1372	A91	350c on 120c like #1108	8.75	3.25

No. 1372 not issued without surcharge. For overprint see No. E1. For surcharge see No. 1591A.

No. 288 Overprinted "SIR WINSTON CHURCHILL / 1965-1985"

1985, Oct. 15 **Perf. 13½x13**

1373	A66	$2 on #288	12.00	3.75

No. 214 Surcharged "1950-1985"

1985, Oct. 15 **Perf. 14**

1374	A50	25c on 110c on 10c	.40	.25
1375	A50	200c on 110c on 10c	1.40	1.40

#214 with 110c surcharge only was not issued.

Nos. 295-297, 384, and O9 Overprinted or Surcharged "United / Nations / 1945-1985"

1985, Oct. 28 **Perf. 14x14½**

1376	A68	30c on #295	1.75	.20
1377	A68	50c on #296	1.75	.30
1378	A68	100c on #O9	1.75	.50
1379	A68	225c on #384	18.50	1.25
1380	A68	$3 on #297	4.00	2.75

Nos. 1376-1380 (5) 27.75 5.00

Nos. 142-144, 289A, O4-O5, O7, O15, and QO1-QO2 Ovptd. "POSTAGE"

1985, Oct. 29 **Perfs. as Before**
Watermarks and Printing Methods as Before

1381	A28	30c on #O4	1.00	.30
1382	A28	40c on #142	60.00	.90
1383	A28	50c on #143	1.00	.90
1384	A28	50c on #O5	1.00	.40
1385	A28	60c on #144	4.25	.50
1386	A28	60c on #144 (Revenue Only)	1.50	.35
1387	A28	60c on #O7	3.75	.40
1388	A66	$10 on #O15	17.50	7.00
1389	A28	$15 on #QO1	17.50	12.00
1390	A28	$20 on #QO2	17.50	13.00

Nos. 1381-1390 (10) 125.00 35.35

Refer to 2nd paragraph in footnote following No. 147 for Nos. 1381, 1384, 1386-1387.

Nos. 133-134 Surcharged "Deepavali / 1985"

1985, Nov. 1

1391	A28	25c on 2c #134	1.00	.35
1392	A28	150c on 1c #133	3.00	1.00

Miniature Sheet No. 1050 Ovptd. in Red

Overprinted: a, "Christmas 1985." b, "Happy New Year." c, "Merry Christmas." d, "Happy Holidays."

1985, Nov. 3 **Unwmk.** **Perf. 14**

1393	A91	55c Sheet of 4, #a.-d.	12.00	7.00

For surcharge see No. 1670F.

Clive Lloyd, Cricketer — A94

Lloyd Holding Intl. Cup — A95

Designs: #a, $2.25, Lloyd playing cricket. #b, $1.30, Lloyd, bat and wicket. #c, 60c, Gloves, wicket, bat, natl. flag.

1985, Nov. 7 **Perf. 14½x14**

1394		Triptych	.75	.75
a.-c.	A94	25c any single	.20	.20

Size: 30x38mm
Perf. 14½x14½

1395	A94	60c multi	.45	.45
1396	A94	$1.30 multi	.90	.90
1397	A94	$2.25 multi	1.60	1.60
1398	A95	$3.50 multi	2.60	2.60

Nos. 1394-1398 (5) 6.30 6.30

For surcharge see No. 1504.

Miniature Sheet No. 329 Ovptd. "1985" in Red

Wmk. 364

1985, Nov. 15 **Litho.** **Perf. 14**

1399	A77	30c Sheet of 12, #a.-l.	17.50	17.50

Nos. 410 and 413e Surcharged

1985, Dec. 23 **Photo.** **Perf. 14x14½**
Watermarks as Before

1400	A7	20c on #410	6.00	.50
1401	A7	20c on #413De	6.00	.50

Compare No. 1400 with No. 914 and 1401 with No. 994a.

Nos. 1075, 1077 Ovptd. "REICHENBACHIA 1886-1986" in Purple

1986, Jan. 13	**Litho.**		***Perf. 14***	
1402	A91	150c on #1075	9.00	1.00
1403	A91	200c on #1077	9.00	1.10

For surcharge and overprints see Nos. 1553, 1760, 1762-1763.

Nos. 608, 610 Surcharged "Republic Day / 1986"

Perfs. as Before			
1986, Feb. 22		**Wmk. 364**	
1404	A82	25c on #608	
1405	A83	120c on $6 #610	
1406	A83	225c on $6 #610	
Nos. 1404-1406 (3)		2.00	

No. 87 Surcharged "1986"

1986, Mar. 24	**Photo.**		***Perf. 13***	
1407	A14	25c on 6c #87	.30	.25
1408	A14	50c on 6c #87	.50	.45
1409	A14	100c on 6c #87	.90	.85
1410	A14	200c on 6c #87	1.75	1.50
Nos. 1407-1410 (4)			3.45	3.05

No. 237 Surcharged "1926 / 1986"

1986, Mar. 27	**Litho.**		***Perf. 14***	
1411	A56	150c on 35c #237	5.50	1.00

St. John Ambulance, 60th anniv.

Nos. 1028, 1037 Surcharged "Queen Elizabeth / 1926 1986"

1986, Apr. 21			**Unwmk.**	
1412	A91	Sheet of 4	8.50	8.50
a.		130c on 130c #1028	2.00	1.50
b.		200c on 130c #1028	2.00	1.50
c.		260c on 130c #1028	2.00	1.50
d.		330c on 130c #1028	2.00	1.50
1413	A91	130c on #1037	2.00	.75

Location of overprint on No. 1413 differs from No. 1412.

For overprints & surcharges see #1670A, 1738B.

Nos. 267, 317g-317 l, 444a-444f Surcharged "Protect the"

		Wmk. 373		
1986, May 3	**Litho.**		***Perf. 14***	
1414	A73	60c on 35c #317g-317l, #a.-f.		
		block of 6, #a.-f.	3.00	3.00
1415	A73	60c on 35c #444, block of 6, #a.-f.	50.00	17.50
		Wmk. 364		
1416	A63	$6 on 8c #267	4.00	3.75

No. 390 Surcharged

1986, May 5	**Litho.**		***Perf. 13***	
1417	A28	600c on #390	15.00	1.25

No. 283A Surcharged

Overprints: a, Abary. b, Anna Regina. c, Aurora. d, Bartica Grove. e, Bel Air. f, Belle Plaine. g, Clonbrook. h, T.P.O. Dem. / Railway. i, Enmore. j, Fredericks / burg. k, Good Success. l, 1986. m, Mariabba. n, Massaruni. o, Nigg. p, No. 50. q, No. 63 / Benab. r, Philadelphia. s, Sisters. t, Skeldon. u, Suddie. v, Taymouth / Manor. w, Wales. x, Whim.

Perf. 14x13½			
1986, May 15	**Litho.**	**Wmk. 364**	
1418	Sheet of 25, #a.-k., m.-x., 2 #l	27.50	27.50
a.-x.	A66 25c on 30c, any single	1.00	.75

British Guiana No. 254 Surcharged "GUYANA / INDEPENDENCE 1966-1986"

Nos. 10A and 13a Surcharged "1986"

No. 237 Surcharged

No. 713a-713d Surcharged "INDEPENDENCE / 1966-1986"

1986, May 26		***Perfs. as Before***	
Watermarks and Printing Methods as Before			
1443	A60	25c on 2c British Guiana #254	.25	.20
1444	A57	25c on 35c #241	.25	.20
1445	A60	60c on 2c British Guiana #254	.45	.30
1446	A60	120c on 6c #10A	.50	.35
1447	A60	130c on 24c #13a	9.00	.75
1448		Block of 4	1.75	1.75
a.	A86 25c on 120c #713a	.35	.20
b.	A86 25c on 130c #713b	.35	.20
c.	A86 25c on 150c #713c	.35	.20
d.	A86 225c on 200c #713d	.70	.70
Nos. 1443-1448 (6)		12.20	

No. 135 Surcharged "MEXICO / 1986" in Blue

Perf. 13x13½			
1986, May 31	**Litho.**	**Wmk. 364**	
1452	A28	225c on 3c #135	20.00	3.75

World Cup Soccer Championships, Mexico City.

Nos. 135 and 192 Surcharged "CARICOM HEADS OF GOV'T / CONFERENCE / JULY 1986" in Blue
No. 286A Ovptd. "CARICOM / DAY 1986" in Blue

1986		***Perfs. as Before***	
Watermarks and Printing Methods as Before			
1453	A28	25c on #192	2.75	.75
1454	A28	60c on 3c #135	3.50	.30
1455	A66	60c on #286A	11.00	.75
Nos. 1453-1455 (3)		17.25	

Issued: #1455, June 28; #1453-1454, July 1.

Nos. 133 and 137 Surcharged "INT. YEAR / OF PEACE" in Black or Blue

1986, July 14	**Litho.**		***Perf. 13x13½***	
1456	A28	25c on 1c #133 (Bl)	.75	.45
1457	A28	60c on 6c #137	1.75	1.75
1458	A28	120c on 6c #137	1.75	1.75
1459	A28	130c on 6c #137	1.75	1.75
1460	A28	150c on 6c #137	1.75	1.75
Nos. 1456-1460 (5)			7.75	

Halley's Comet — A96

Designs: a, Br. Guiana #172. b, Guyana #931.

1986, July 19		***Perf. 14***	
1461	A96	320c Pair, #a.-b.	3.00	3.00
c.	Imperf.		7.50	

No. 1461 has continuous design. No. 1461 exists imperf. between. Most were overprinted.

For overprints and surcharges see Nos. 1822, 1836, 2029, E5-E6, E11, E14.

No. 43 Surcharged

1986, July 28	**Photo.**		***Perf. 14x14½***	
1463	A7	20c on 6c #43	8.00	.40

Nos. 60-61 Surcharged "GUSIA / 1936-1986"

Perf. 14x13½			
1986, Aug. 15	**Photo.**	**Unwmk.**	
1464	A11	25c on #61	5.25	.45
1465	A11	$1.50 on 6c #60	10.00	3.25

No. 136 Surcharged "REGIONAL / PHARMACY / CONFERENCE / 1986" in Blue

Perf. 13x13½			
1986, Aug. 15	**Litho.**	**Wmk. 364**	
1466	A28	130c on 5c #136	12.00	1.75

Nos. 1337, 1339, 1341 Inscribed "1966-1986"

Perfs. as Before			
1986, Sept. 23		**Unwmk.**	
1467	A92	25c on #1337	2.50	.30
1468	A92	25c on #1339	2.50	.30
1469	A92	25c on #1341	2.50	.30
Nos. 1467-1469 (3)		7.50	.90

No. 871 Surcharged

Perf. 14x13½			
1986, Oct. 1	**Litho.**	**Wmk. 364**	
	Sheet of 25		
1470	#a.-k., m.-x., 2 #l	55.00	40.00
a.-x.	A66 120c any single	2.00	1.25

No. 1145 Surcharged "12th World Orchid Conference" / "TOKYO JAPAN MARCH 1987"

		Unwmk.		
1986, Oct. 6	**Litho.**		***Perf. 14***	
1494	A91	650c on 40c #1145	17.50	6.00

For overprint see No. 1851.

Orchid Type like No. 1052 Surchd. "1492-1992" and "CHRISTOPHER COLUMBUS" in Black and Red or Red

1986, Oct.				
1495	A91	320c on 150c	11.50	3.00
1496	A91	320c on 150c (R)	11.50	3.00

Issued: #1495, 10/10; #1496, 10/30. #1495-1496 not issued without surcharge.

Nos. 704 and 705 Surcharged "1986"

Perf. 14x14½			
1986, Oct. 15	**Photo.**	**Wmk. 364**	
1497	A7	50c on #704	4.75	.60
1498	A7	225c on #705	13.50	3.25

Nos. 134, 192 Surcharged "Deepavali /1986"

1986, Nov. 3	**Litho.**		***Perf. 13x13½***	
1499	A28	25c on 2c #134	3.00	.50
1500	A28	200c on #192	10.00	3.00

No. 43 Surcharged "CHRISTMAS / 1986" in Red
No. 917 Surcharged in Red

1986, Nov. 26		***Perfs. as Before***		
Watermarks and Printing Methods as Before				
1501	A7	20c on 6c #43	4.75	.30
Miniature Sheet				
1502	A88	120c on 60c on #a.-e.	8.50	8.50

No. 1502 is surcharged on an unissued miniature sheet containing No. 917.

No. 329 Ovptd. "1986" in Blue

		Wmk. 364		
1986, Nov. 26	**Litho.**		***Perf. 14***	
1503	A77	30c Sheet of 12, #a.-l.	25.00	25.00

No. 1398 Surcharged in Red

1986, Dec. 1	**Litho.**		***Perf. 14x14½***	
1504	A95	$15 on $3.50 #1398	45.00	20.00

L.F.S. Burnham, President 1980-85 A97

1986, Dec. 13	**Litho.**		***Perf. 12½x13***	
1505	A97	25c Tomb	.20	.20
1506	A97	120c Flags, map	.35	.35
1507	A97	130c Government building	.45	.45
1508	A97	$6 Portrait, necklace, vert.	2.00	2.00
Nos. 1505-1508 (4)			3.00	3.00

Orchid Type of 1985-87 Surcharged "GPOC / 1977 - 1987"

1987, Jan. 19			***Perf. 14***	
1509	A91	225c on 25c like #1090	4.50	1.00
1510	A91	$10 on 50c like #1052	11.00	11.00

Nos. 1509-1510 not issued without surcharge. No. 1509 adds "2" to 25c value, No. 1510 uses flower as obliterator.

Stamps of Type A91 Surcharged in Black or Red

a

b

c

d

e

f

g

h

i

j

k

l

1987-89   *Perfs. as Before*
Design A91
Series 1
(Plate Number in Parentheses)
On Nos. 1022-1039

1511	(a)	120c on 60c (2)	2.75
1512	(b)	120c on 60c (2)	1.10
1513	(a)	120c on 60c (5)	2.10
1514	(c)	200c on 60c (5)	1.10
1515	(c)	200c on 75c (5)	1.10

Obliterator invtd. in surch. on #1514-1515.

1516	(d)	200c on 60c (7)	1.10
1517	(d)	200c on 25c (8)	1.60
1518	(e)	200c on 25c (8)	1.10
1519	(a)	120c on 50c (9)	1.10
1520	(b)	120c on 50c (9)	
1521	(f)	120c on 50c (9)	1.10
1522	(g)	120c on 50c (9)	
1523	(a)	120c on 55c (9)	2.25
1524	(h)	120c on 55c (9)	1.60
a.		120c on 55c #1032a	2.00
1525	(g)	120c on 55c (9)	1.10
1526	(a)	120c on 60c (10)	2.25
1527	(d)	200c on 60c (10)	1.10
1528	(h)	$2 on 25c (12)	1.10

Surcharge on No. 1528 lacks obliterator.

1529	(f)	120c on 55c (15)	1.40
1530	(a)	200c on 55c (15)	5.50

Issued: #1518, 1528, 3/6; #1514-1515, 3/17; #1516-1517, 1522, 1525, 1527, 3/87; #1521, 1524, 1529, 7/87; #1511, 1513, 1519, 1523, 1526, 1530, 9/87; #1512, 1520, 7/88.

On Nos. 1042-1061

1531	(b)	120c on 55c (17)	1.10
1532	(d)	200c on 55c (17)	1.60
1533	(a)	600c on 80c (17)	3.25
1534	(a)	120c on 60c (19)	2.25
1535	(d)	200c on 60c (19)	1.10
1536	(a)	120c on 50c (22)	
1537	(b)	120c on 50c (22)	
1538	(f)	120c on 50c (22)	1.10
1539	(c)	200c on 50c (22)	1.10
1540	(i)	225c on 50c (22)	1.60
1541	(a)	120c on 55c #1050a (22)	2.25
1542	(f)	120c on 55c #1050a (22)	1.75
1543	(c)	200c on 55c #1050a (22)	1.10
1544	(h)	$2 on 25c (23)	1.40
1545	(a)	120c on 60c (24)	2.25
1546	(a)	120c on 50c (24)	
1547	(d)	200c on 50c (24)	1.10
1548	(a)	120c on 60c (31)	2.25
1549	(d)	200c on 60c (31)	1.10

Issued: #1544, 3/6; #1539, 1543, 3/17; #1532, 1535, 1547, 1549, 3/87; #1540, 6/87; #1538, 1542, 7/87; #1533-1534, 1536, 1541, 1545-1546, 1548, 9/87; #1531, 1537, 7/88.

On Nos. 1069-1091

1550	(b)	120c on 80c (39)	
1551	(a)	600c on 80c (39)	3.25
1552	(g)	$15 on 80c (39)	4.50
1553	(i)	225c on #1402 (42)	1.60
1554	(d)	200c on 60c (44)	1.10
1555	(d)	200c on 60c (47)	1.10
1556	(a)	120c on 50c (49)	
1557	(f)	120c on 50c (49)	
1558	(a)	120c on 55c #1085a (49)	2.25
1559	(f)	120c on 55c #1085a (49)	1.40
a.		120c on 55c on #1085a	2.50
1560	(d)	200c on 55c #1085a (49)	1.25
a.		200c on 55c on #1085a	4.50
1561	(a)	120c on 60c (50)	2.25
1562	(b)	120c on 60c (50)	
1563	(e)	200c on 25c (51)	1.40
1564	(d)	200c on 25c (52)	1.10
1565	(a)	120c on 30c (53)	
a.		120c on 30c on #1090a	
1566	(a)	120c on 50c (53)	2.25
1567	(d)	200c on 30c #1090a (53)	1.10
1568	(a)	200c on 50c (53)	
1569	(d)	200c on 50c (53)	1.10
1570	(g)	$15 on 25c (53)	3.25
1571	(g)	$25 on 25c (53)	6.50

Surcharge on #1571 lacks obliterator and places a "$" in front of original denomination. #1570-1571 not issued without surcharge.
Issued: #1563, 3/6; #1552, 1554-1555, 1560, 1564, 1567, 1569-1571, 3/87; #1553, 6/87; #1557, 1559, 7/87; #1551, 1556, 1558, 1561, 1566, 1568, 9/87; #1550, 1562, 1565, 7/88.

On Nos. 1092-1108, 1372

1572	(b)	120c on 45c (54)	
1573	(a)	120c on 60c (54)	2.25
1574	(b)	120c on 60c (54)	1.10
1575	(a)	120c on 50c (55)	
1576	(i)	225c on 60c (55)	1.60
1577	(b)	120c on 60c (57)	1.10
a.		New value at bottom	
1578	(d)	200c on 60c (57)	1.10
1579	(b)	120c on 25c (59)	1.10
1580	(b)	120c on 75c (60)	2.25
1581	(c)	200c on 75c (60)	2.75
1582	(b)	120c on 25c (61)	
1583	(b)	120c on 25c (63)	1.10
1584	(a)	120c on 50c (64)	
1585	(f)	120c on 50c (64)	1.60

1586	(a)	120c on 55c, wmkd. (64)	2.25
1587	(f)	120c on 55c (64)	1.10
a.		120c on 55c on #1107a	1.40
1588	(g)	120c on 55c (64)	1.10
a.		120c on 55c on #1107a	1.25

Surcharge on Nos. 1522, 1525, 1588-1588a does not contain date.

Issued: #1581, 3/17; #1578, 1588, 1591, 3/87; #1576, 6/87; #1585, 1587, 7/87; #1573, 1575, 1580, 1584, 1586, 1589-1590, 9/87; #1591A, 10/9/87; #1572, 1574, 1577, 1579, 1582-1583, 7/88.

On Nos. 1112-1124

1592	(b)	120c on 40c (68)	1.10
a.		New value at LL	
1593	(c)	200c on 40c (68)	1.10
a.		Obliterator inverted	1.25
1594	(a)	225c on 40c (68)	2.75
1595	(a)	120c on 60c (69)	
1596	(b)	120c on 60c (69)	1.10
1597	(b)	120c on 25c (70)	
1598	(b)	120c on 25c (71)	
1599	(a)	120c on 60c (71)	2.25
1600	(d)	200c on 25c (71)	1.10
1601	(d)	200c on 60c (71)	1.10
1602	(j)	120c on 25c (72)	
1603	(d)	200c on 25c (72)	1.10
1604	(b)	120c on 60c (73)	
1605	(d)	200c on 60c (73)	.80
1606	(b)	120c on 80c (74)	
1607	(a)	600c on 80c (74)	3.25
1608	(g)	$12 on 80c (74)	3.75
1609	(b)	120c on 60c (75)	
a.		New value at bottom	
1610	(d)	200c on 60c (75)	1.10
1611	(a)	225c on 65c (76)	2.75

Issued: #1593, 3/17; #1600-1601, 1603, 1605, 1608, 1610, 3/87; #1594-1595, 1599, 1611, 9/87; #1592, 1596-1598, 1604, 1606-1607, 1609, 7/88; #1602, 9/88.

On Nos. 1126-1142

1612	(b)	120c on 40c (77)	
a.		New value at UL	
1613	(d)	200c on 40c (77)	1.10
1614	(a)	200c on 45c (77)	3.25
1615	(d)	200c on 45c (77)	1.10
1616	(d)	200c on 45c (78)	3.25
1617	(d)	200c on 45c (78)	1.10
1618	(a)	120c on 60c (79)	3.25
1619	(b)	120c on 60c (79)	
1620	(a)	225c on 65c (80)	3.25
1621	(b)	120c on 45c (81)	
1622	(f)	120c on 55c (81)	1.40
1623	(d)	200c on 45c (81)	1.10
1624	(a)	200c on 55c (81)	4.50
1625	(f)	120c on 55c (82)	1.75
1626	(a)	200c on 55c (82)	11.50
1627	(a)	120c on 75c (83)	3.25
1628	(b)	120c on 90c (84)	
1629	(a)	200c on 45c (84)	3.25
1630	(a)	200c on 45c (85)	3.25
1631	(a)	200c on 45c (85)	1.10

Issued: #1613, 1615, 1617, 1623, 1631, 3/87; #1622, 1625, 7/87; #1614, 1616, 1620, 1624, 1626-1627, 1629-1630, 9/87; #1612, 1619, 1621, 1628, 7/88.

On Nos. 1144-1153

1632	(b)	120c on 30c (86)	
1633	(b)	120c on 40c (86)	1.10
1634	(d)	200c on 30c (86)	1.10
1635	(d)	200c on 40c (86)	
1636	(a)	225c on 40c (86)	3.25
a.		Inscribed "ONTOGLOS- SUM"	2.75
1637	(a)	120c on 60c (87)	2.25
a.		Surcharge reading up	
1638	(d)	200c on 60c (87)	1.10
1639	(a)	225c on 65c (08)	2.75
1640	(f)	120c on 55c (89)	1.40
1641	(b)	120c on 90c (89)	
1642	(a)	200c on 55c (89)	5.25
1643	(a)	225c on 90c (89)	1.10
1644	(a)	120c on 40c (90)	2.25
1645	(b)	120c on 40c (90)	1.10
1646	(c)	200c on 40c (90)	1.10
1647	(d)	200c on 40c (R) (90)	1.40
1648	(c)	200c on 375c (90)	1.10
a.		200c on 375c #1153a	4.50
1649	(a)	225c on 40c (90)	2.75
1650	(i)	225c on 40c (90)	1.75
1651	(k)	260c on 375c (90)	1.10

Issued: #1647, 2/9/87; #1646, 1648, 3/17/87; #1634-1635, 1638, 1643, 3/87; #1650, 6/87; #1640, 7/87; #1636-1637, 1639, 1642, 1644, 1649, 9/87; #1632-1633, 1641, 1645, 7/88; #1651, 10/88.
Surcharge on #1651 is placed over original value and has no obliterator.

On Nos. 1154-1165

1652	(a)	120c on 40c (91)	2.25
1653	(a)	120c on 40c (91)	1.10
a.		New value at LR	
1654	(a)	225c on 40c (91)	3.25
1655	(i)	225c on 40c (91)	1.60
1656	(b)	120c on 50c (92)	
1657	(a)	120c on 75c (92)	2.75
1658	(c)	200c on 50c (92)	
1659	(c)	200c on 75c (92)	1.10

1660	(b)	120c on 60c (93)	
1661	(b)	120c on 80c (93)	
1662	(i)	225c on 60c (93)	1.75
1663	(i)	225c on 80c (93)	1.75
1664	(a)	600c on 80c (93)	
1665	(a)	120c on 60c (94)	
1666	(b)	120c on 60c (94)	
1667	(b)	120c on 60c (95)	1.10
1668	(a)	120c on 75c (95)	3.50
1669	(b)	120c on 40c (96)	
1670	(a)	225c on 65c (96)	2.75

Miniature Sheets

1670A		Sheet of 4	27.50
b.	(a)	600c on 130c #1412a (6)	
c.	(a)	600c on 200c #1412b (6)	
d.	(a)	600c on 260c #1412c (6)	
e.	(a)	600c on 330c #1412d (6)	
1670F		Sheet of 4	15.00
g.	(i)	225c on #1393a (22)	
h.	(i)	225c on #1393b (22)	
i.	(i)	225c on #1393c (22)	
j.	(i)	225c on #1393d (22)	

Issued: #1658-1659, 3/17/87; #1655, 1662-1663, 6/87; #1652, 1654, 1657, 1664-1665, 1668, 1670, 9/87; #1670F, 11/9/87; #1670A, 11/20/87; #1653, 1656, 1660-1661, 1667, 1669, 7/88.
For overprints see Nos. 1975, 1979.

Series 2
On Nos. 1168-1204

1671	(b)	120c on 90c (2)	1.10
1672	(b)	120c on 50c (3)	1.10
1673	(f)	120c on 50c (3)	1.10
1674	(b)	200c on 90c (4)	
1675	(b)	120c on 50c (6)	1.10
1676	(f)	120c on 50c (6)	1.10
1677	(b)	120c on 30c (7)	1.10
1678	(b)	120c on 70c (8)	1.10
1679	(b)	120c on 70c (9)	1.10
a.		New value at LR	
1680	(b)	120c on 90c (10)	1.10
1681	(b)	120c on 70c (12)	1.10
a.		New value at LL	
1682	(b)	120c on 50c (13)	1.10
1683	(b)	120c on 90c (13)	
1684	(b)	120c on 30c (14)	1.10
a.		New value at UR	
1685	(b)	120c on 50c (15)	1.10
1686	(b)	120c on 85c (15)	
1687	(b)	120c on 70c (17)	13.50
1688	(b)	120c on 85c (18)	1.10
1689	(c)	200c on 85c (18)	
1690	(b)	120c on 50c (20)	1.10
1691	(f)	120c on 50c (20)	1.75

Issued: #1689, 3/17/87; #1673, 1676, 1691, 7/87; #1671-1672, 1674-1675, 1677-1688, 1690, 7/88.

On Nos. 1205-1240

1692	(b)	120c on 45c (21)	1.10
1693	(b)	120c on 30c (22)	1.10
1694	(l)	350c on 330c #O52 (23)	1.10
1695	(b)	120c on 85c (24)	1.10
1696	(j)	120c on 140c (R) (25)	1.10
1697	(l)	250c on 225c #O46 (26)	1.10
a.		New value at UL	
1698	(b)	120c on 60c (27)	2.25
1699	(b)	120c on 90c (27)	
1700	(b)	120c on 30c (28)	1.10
a.		New value at UL	2.25
1701	(b)	120c on 30c (30)	1.10
1702	(k)	240c on 140c (30)	1.10

No. 1702 not issued without surcharge.

1703	(l)	150c on 175c #O44 (31)	1.10
1704	(b)	120c on 50c (32)	1.10
1705	(f)	120c on 50c (32)	1.10
1706	(k)	240c on 140c (34)	1.10
1707	(l)	125c on 140c #O42 (36)	1.10
1708	(k)	120c on 140c (38)	1.10
1709	(k)	120c on 140c (41)	1.10
1710	(b)	200c on 80c (42)	1.10
1711	(l)	150c on #O43 (43)	1.10

Issued: #1705, 7/87; #1692-1693, 1695, 1698-1701, 1704, 1710, 7/88; #1702, 1706, 10/88; #1696, 1708-1709, 2/22/89; #1694, 1697, 1703, 1707, 1711, 3/89.

On Nos. 1245-1314

1712	(b)	120c on 35c (45)	1.10
1713	(b)	120c on 85c (45)	1.10
1714	(j)	120c on 140c (R) (52)	1.10
1715	(k)	300c on 290c (53)	1.10
1716	(j)	120c on 175c (R) (54)	1.10
1717	(k)	170c on 175c (58)	1.10
1718	(j)	250c on #O48 (59)	1.10
1719	(j)	120c on 140c (R) (65)	1.10
1720	(k)	250c on 280c (66)	1.10
1721	(k)	250c on 280c (67)	1.10
1722	(k)	250c on 230c #O47 (68)	1.10
1723	(l)	250c on 260c #O49 (69)	1.10
a.		New value at UR	1.10
1724	(l)	600c on #O54 (70)	1.10
1725	(l)	$12 on #O55 (71)	1.10

1726	(I)	$15 on #O56 (84)	1.10
1727	(k)	240c on 425c (87)	1.10
1728	(I)	300c on 275c #O50 (90)	1.10
1729	(I)	125c on 130c #O41 (92)	1.10
1730	(I)	350c on #O53 (95)	1.10

On No. 1730 "Postage" reads up or down.
Issued: #1712-1713, 7/88; #1727, 10/88; #1714, 1716, 1719, 2/22/89; #1715, 1717-1718, 1720-1726, 1728-1730, 3/89.
Obliterator on Nos. 1708-1709, 1715, 1717, 1720-1721 has two thick bars.

Stamps of Type A91 Overprinted

m

n

o

p

1987 — Perfs. as Before
Series 1
1731	(m)	120c on #1021 (1)	5.25	
1732	(n)	130c on #1023 (3)	2.50	
1733	(n)	130c on #1028a (6)	5.00	
1734	(n)	130c on #1028 (6)	2.50	
a.		130c on #1028a	2.50	
1735	(m)	120c on #1034 (11)	3.25	
1736	(m)	130c on #1037a (13)	3.25	
1737	(m)	130c on #1413 (13)	5.00	
1738	(o)	130c on #1037 (13)	1.10	
a.		130c on #1037a	1.10	
1738B	(p)	130c on #1413 (13)	1.10	
1739	(n)	200c on #1038 (14)	2.50	
1740	(n)	130c on #1041 (16)	1.10	
1741	(n)	130c on #1342 (18)	1.10	
1742	(p)	130c on #1342 (18)	1.10	
1743	(n)	130c on #1047a (20)	2.25	
1744	(n)	130c on #1047a (20)	2.50	
a.		130c on #1047	4.00	
1745	(m)	200c on #1048 (21)	2.25	
1746	(n)	200c on #1048 (21)		
1747	(n)	130c on #1055a (25)	4.50	
1748	(o)	130c on #1055 (25)	1.10	
a.		130c on #1055a	1.10	

1749	(p)	150c on #1056 (26)	1.10
1750	(m)	120c on #1058 (28)	5.00
1751	(m)	130c on #1343 (29)	1.10
1752	(p)	130c on #1343 (29)	1.10

Issued: #1732, 1734, 1737-1741, 1744, 1746, 1748, 1751, Mar; #1731, 1733, 1735-1736, 1743, 1745, 1747, 1750, July; #1738B, Nov. 20; #1742, 1749, 1752, Dec.

1753	(m)	130c on #1344 (30)	1.10
1754	(p)	130c on #1344 (30)	1.10
1755	(m)	200c on #1063 (33)	1.10
1756	(m)	120c on #1067 (37)	1.60
1757	(m)	260c on #1070 (39)	2.25
1758	(m)	150c on #1072a, ovpt. reading up (40)	2.00
a.		150c on #1072	3.25
1759	(m)	150c on #1075a (42)	3.50
1760	(m)	150c on #1402 (42)	5.50
1761	(m)	200c on #1077a (43)	5.50
1762	(m)	200c on #1403 (43)	5.50
1763	(m)	200c on #1403 (43)	3.50
1764	(m)	150c on #1080 reading down (45)	2.25
a.		150c on #1080a reading up	3.25
1765	(m)	120c on #1081 (46)	8.50
1766	(m)	120c on #1097 (56)	3.25
1767	(m)	120c on #1099 (58)	3.25
1768	(n)	130c on #1110 (66)	3.25
1769	(p)	130c on #1110 (66)	1.10
1770	(p)	120c on #1111 (67)	1.10
1771	(n)	250c on #1122 (74)	1.40
1772	(n)	200c on #1131 (79)	1.10
1773	(o)	130c on #1155 (91)	1.60

Miniature Sheets of 4
| 1774 | (n) | 200c on #1345 (4) | 4.00 |
| 1775 | (n) | 200c on #1346 (20) | 5.50 |

Series 2
| 1776 | (n) | 200c on #1169 (2) | 7.00 |
| 1777 | (n) | 200c on #1183 (9) | 1.75 |

Issued: #1753, 1755, 1757, 1763, 1768, 1771-1777, Mar.; #1756, 1758, 1759-1762, 1764-1767, July. #1754, 1769-1770, Dec.
Overprint reads up on #1759, 1761. Overprint reads down on #1731, 1735, 1745, 1750, 1755, 1758a, 1760, 1762, 1763.
See Nos. 1813-1814, 1844 for other stamps overprinted "1987" only.

Nos. 1337, 1339, 1341 Surcharged
1987, Mar. 6 — Perfs. as Before
1777A	A92	200c on #1337	6.00	2.00
1777B	A92	200c on #1339	6.00	2.00
1777C	A92	200c on #1341	6.00	2.00
		Nos. 1777A-1777C (3)	18.00	6.00

See note following No. 1341.

Nos. 134, 136, 139a, and 192 Surcharged "Post Office / Corp. / 1977-1987" in Blue
Perfs. as Before
1987, Feb. 17 — Litho. — Wmk. 364
1778	A28	25c on 2c #134	.25	.20
1779	A28	25c on 5c #136	.25	.20
1780	A28	25c on #192	.25	.20
1781	A28	25c on 15c #139a	5.00	.50
1782	A28	60c on 15c #139a	10.00	.40
1783	A28	$1.20 on 2c #134	.85	.85
1784	A28	$1.30 on 15c #139a	11.00	2.75
		Nos. 1778-1784 (7)	27.60	5.10

Nos. 1032, 1032a Surcharged "12th World Orchid Conference" and "TOKYO JAPAN"
1987, Mar. 12 — Unwmk. — Perf. 14
| 1785 | A91 | 650c on 55c #1032 | 11.00 | 6.50 |
| a. | | 650c on 55c #1032a | 12.00 | 7.00 |

No. 280 Surcharged with Names of Post Offices Operating in 1885
Overprints: a, AGRICOLA. b, BAGOTVILLE. c, BOURDA. d, BUXTON. e, CABACABURI. f, CAR- / MICHAEL STREET. g, COTTON / TREE. h, DUNOON. i, FELLOW- / SHIP. j, GROVE. k, HACKNEY. l, LEONORA. m, 1987. n, MALLALI. o, PROVI- / DENCE. p, RELI- ANCE. q, SPARTA. r, STEWART- / VILLE. s, TARLOGY. t, T.P.O. / BERBICE RIV. u, T.P.O. / DEM. RIV. v, T.P.O. / ESSEQ. RIV. w, T.P.O. / MASSARUNI / RIV. x, TUSCHEN / (De / VRIENDEN). y, ZORG.

Perf. 14x13½
1987, Mar. 17 — Wmk. 364
| 1786 | | Sheet of 25, #a.-y. | 42.50 | 35.00 |
| a.-y. | A66 | 25c on 10c, any single | 1.50 | 1.25 |

British Guiana Post Office, 125th Anniv.

Columbus' Discovery of America, 500th Anniv. (in 1992) — A98

Paintings: 120c, Discovery of America, by Dali. 225c, Preparations Before the Journey, by unknown artist. 360c, Catholic Kings from Prado Museum. $6, Columbus' Fleet, by R. Monleon.

1987, Mar. 30 — Perf. 13½
1787	A98	120c multicolored	1.75	1.00
1788	A98	225c multicolored	4.00	3.00
1789	A98	360c multicolored	6.25	3.00
a.		Strip of 3, #1787-1789	13.50	13.50

Souvenir Sheet
| 1790 | A98 | $6 gold & multi | 15.00 | 15.00 |

No. 1790 exists with silver border.

No. 289A Ovptd. "28 MARCH 1927 / PAA / GEO-POS"
1987, Mar. 28 — Perf. 13½x13
| 1811 | A66 | $10 on #289A | 24.00 | 13.00 |

First Georgetown to Port-of-Spain Flight, 50th Anniv.

No. 285 Surcharged
1987, Apr. 6 — Perf. 14x13½
| 1812 | A66 | 25c on 40c #285 | 12.50 | .40 |

Nos. 87-88, 90, 287 Surcharged or Overprinted "1987"
1987, Apr. — Perfs. as Before
Watermarks and Printing Methods as Before
1813	A14	25c on #88	.75	.10
1814	A14	$1 on #287	15.00	1.00
1815	A14	120c on 6c #87	.90	.20
1816	A14	320c on 6c #87	1.50	.75
1817	A14	500c on 40c #90	2.00	1.40
		Nos. 1813-1817 (5)	20.15	3.45

Issued: #1813, 1815-1817, Apr. 21; #1814, Apr.

No. 1461 Ovptd. "CAPEX '87"
1987, June 10 — Litho. — Perf. 14
| 1822 | A96 | 320c Pair, #a.-b. | 5.50 | 5.50 |
| c. | | on #1461, imperf. between | 11.00 | |

For surcharges see Nos. 2030, E15.

Nos. 626-628 Ovptd. "1987"
Wmk. 314 Upright
1987, July 15 — Engr. — Perf. 12½x13
| 1823 | A60 | $1.20 on #626 | .90 | .25 |

Wmk. 314 Sideways
1824	A60	$1.30 on #627	10.00	.75
1825	A60	$2.40 on #628	12.00	3.75
		Nos. 1823-1825 (3)	22.90	4.75

A99

A100

Locomotives — A101

#1826a, 1827a, Alexandra 4. #1826b, 1827b, Diesel locomotive facing right. #1826c, 1827c, Steam locomotive facing right. #1826d, 1827d, Diesel locomotive No. 21 facing left.
#1829a, 1830b, Alexandra 4. #1829b, 1830a, Diesel locomotive facing right. #1829c, 1830d, Steam locomotive facing right. #1829d, 1830c, Diesel locomotive No. 21. #1830e, Photograph of trains in Georgetown Station. #1831, Steam locomotive pulling cattle cars, map of routes from Parika to Vreedenhoop and from Georgetown to Rosignol.

1987, Aug. 3 — Perf. 15
1826		Block of 4	2.00	2.00
a.-d.	A99	$1.20 green, any single	.40	.40
1827		Block of 5	5.00	5.00
a.-d.	A99	$3.20 blue, any single	.85	.85
e.	A100	$3.20 blue	.85	.85
1828	A101	$12 shown	4.00	4.00
		Nos. 1826-1828 (3)	11.00	11.00

1987, Dec. 4
1829		Block of 4	2.40	2.40
a.-d.	A99	$1.20 rose lake, any single	.50	.50
1830		Block of 5	6.25	6.25
a.-d.	A99	$3.30 blk, any single	1.10	1.10
e.	A100	$3.30 black	1.10	1.10
1831	A101	$10 multi	4.50	4.50
		Nos. 1829-1831 (3)	13.15	13.15

Sizes: #1827e, 1830e, 84x57mm. #1828, 1831, 90x40mm.
For surcharges see #E12-E13. For overprints see #1910-1911, 1935-1938, 2024-2028F, 2054, 2056.

No. 287 Ovptd. "FAIREY NICHOLL / 15 AUG 1927 / GEO-MAB" or "FAIREY NICHOLL / 8 AUG 1927 / GEO-MAZ"
1987, Aug. 7 — Litho. — Perf. 13½x13
1832	A66	$1 "MAB" on #287	12.00	11.00
1833	A66	$1 "MAZ" on #287	12.00	11.00
a.		Pair, #1832-1833	30.00	27.50

No. 1291A Surcharged "CRISTOVAO COLOMBO / 1492 — 1992" (#1834) or "CHRISTOPHE COLOMB / 1492 — 1992" (#1835)
No. 1461c Surcharged "THE PASSING OF HALLEY'S COMET: / PROPHESY OF THE ARRIVAL OF / HERNAN CORTES 1519. / V CENTENARY OF THE LANDING OF / CHRISTOPHER COLUMBUS / IN THE AMERICAS"
Unwmk.
1987, Oct. 9 — Litho. — Perf. 14
1834	A91	950c on 900c #1291A	3.00	3.00
1835	A91	950c on 900c #1291A	3.00	3.00
a.		Pair, #1834-1835	7.00	7.00

Imperf
| 1836 | A96 | $20 on 320c #1461c | 8.50 | 8.50 |

Nos. 135-136 Surcharged "DEEPAVALI / 1987"
1987, Nov. 2 — Litho. — Perf. 13x13½
| 1837 | A28 | 25c on 3c #135 | 2.25 | .40 |
| 1838 | A28 | $3 on 5c #136 | 8.00 | 3.50 |

No. 43 Surcharged "CHRISTMAS / 1987" in Red
No. 1502 Surcharged "1987" in Blue
1987, Nov. 9 — Perfs. as Before
Watermarks and Printing Methods as Before
| 1839 | A7 | 20c on 6c #43 | | |

Miniature Sheet
| 1840 | A88 | 120c on 60c #1502 | | |

No. 329 Overprinted "1987"
No. 920 Surcharged "Protect Our Heritage '87" in Red
Nos. 1037, 1040, 1056, 1110-1111, 1494 Surcharged "PROTECT OUR HERITAGE '87"
1987, Dec. 9 — Perfs. as Before
Watermarks and Printing Methods as Before
1844	A77	30c Sheet of 12, #a.-l. on #329	7.00	7.00
1845	A91	120c on #1111	1.50	1.50
1846	A91	130c on #1110	1.75	1.75

1847	A91	150c on #1056	2.25 2.25
1848	A91	180c on #1040	2.50 2.50
1849	A91	320c on #1137	3.00 3.00
1850	A89	320c Triptych, #a.-c., on 120c #920	9.00 9.00
1851	A91	650c on #1494	5.00 5.00
		Nos. 1844-1851 (8)	32.00 32.00

1988 Summer Olympics, Seoul — A102

1987, Dec. 30   Litho.   Perf. 13½x14

1852	A102	$2 Jumping	2.50 2.25
1853	A102	$3 Discus	3.75 3.25
1854	A102	$5 Vase	6.50 5.50
a.		Strip of 3, #1852-1854	13.50 13.50

Souvenir Sheet

Perf. 14

1855	A102	$3.50 Olympic Rings, horiz.	10.00 10.00

Christmas 1987 — A103

Paintings: #a, The Virgin of the Rocks, by Da Vinci. #b, Virgin with Grapes, by Mignard. #c, Sacred Family, by Raphael. #d, Virgin Mary, by Lucas Cranach. No. 1857, Adoration of Three Kings, by Rubens.

1988, Jan. 7   Litho.   Perf. 14

1856	A103	$2 Strip of 4, #a.-d.	7.75 7.75

Souvenir Sheet

1857	A103	$10 Sheet of 1	13.50 13.50

Dated 1987.

Nos. 397, 405 and 651 Ovptd. or Surcharged "*AUSTRALIA* / 1987 JAMBOREE 1988" in Red

1988, Jan. 7   Litho.   Perf. 13½x13

1858	A17	$4.40 on #405	
1859	A17	$10 on #397	
1860	A17	$10 on #651	
1861	A17	$10 on #405	
a.		$10 on #405a	
		Nos. 1858-1861 (4)	10.00

Obliterator on Nos. 1859-1861 is red fleur-de-lis. Size and location of overprint varies.

Nos. 68 and 70 Surcharged "IFAD / For a World / Without Hunger"

Perf. 14x14½

1988, Jan. 26   Photo.   Wmk. 364

1862	A7	25c on 1c #68	2.00 .30
1863	A7	$5 on 3c #70	7.00 3.00
		Nos. 1862-1863 (2)	9.00 3.30

No. 1862 uses new denomination as obliterator and No. 1863 uses "X."

Flora and Fauna — A104

Mushrooms — #1864: a, Corprinus comatus. b, Amanita muscaria. c, Pholiota aurivella. d, Laccaria amethstina.
Birds — #1865: a, Starling. b, Reed warbler. c, Kingfisher. d, Goldcrest.
Cats — #1866: a, Himalayan. b, American shorthaired. c, Maine coon. d, Abyssinian.
Cactus flowers — #1866: e, Sulcorebutia densiseta. f, Subutia hyalacantha. g, Echinopsis. h, Lobivia polycephala.
Nos. 1866a-1866h horiz.

1988, Jan. 28   Perf. 14

1864	A104	$2 Strip of 4, #a.-d.	10.50 10.50
1865	A104	$2 Strip of 4, #a.-d.	9.50 9.50

Miniature Sheet

Perf. 14x13½

1866	A104	$2 Sheet of 8, #a.-h.	13.00 13.00

Dated 1987.

Santa Maria — A105

Ships: a, Santa Maria. b, Grande Francoise. #1869, San Martin, horiz.

1988, Feb. 10   Litho.   Perf. 13½x14

1867	A105	$7 Pair, #a.-b., pale yel & multi	6.00 6.00
1868	A105	$7 Pair, #a.-b., bl & multi	6.00 6.00

Souvenir Sheet

Perf. 14

1869	A105	$7 silver & multi	12.00 12.00

Discovery of America, 500th anniv. (in 1992). Nos. 1867-1868 printed checkerboard with se-tenant labels describing ship dimensions. No. 1869 exists with gold border.

Nos. 136, 139a, and 146 Surcharged "Republic / Day / 1988" in Blue

Perfs. as Before

1988, Feb. 23   Wmk. 364

1870	A28	25c on 5c #136	.20 .20
1871	A28	120c on 15c #139a	6.50 .75
1872	A28	$10 on $2 #146	2.00 2.00
		Nos. 1870-1872 (3)	8.70 2.95

No. 283A Surcharged with Names of Post Offices Operating in 1900

Overprints: a, Albouystown. b, Anns Grove. c, Amacura. d, Arakaka. e, Baramanni. f, Cuyuni. g, Hope Placer. h, HMPS. i, Kitty. j, M'M'Zorg. k, Maccaseema. l, 1988. m, Morawhanna. n, Naamryck. o, Purini. p, Potaro / Landing. q, Rockstone. r, Rosignol. s, Stanleytown. t, Santa Rosa. u, Tumatumari. v, Weldaad. w, Wismar. x, TPO Berbice / Railway.

1988, Apr. 5   Perf. 14x13½

1873	A66	25c Sheet of 25, #a.-k., m.-x., 2 #l.	32.50 32.50

British Guiana Post Office, 125th Anniv.

No. 725 Surcharged "Olympic / Games / 1988"

Perf. 14½x14

1988, May 3   Litho.   Wmk. 373

1897	A73	120c Sheet of 12, #a.-l.	18.00 18.00

Nos. 136-137 and 146 Surcharged "Caricom Day / 1988"

Perf. 13x13½

1988, June 15   Litho.   Wmk. 364

1898	A28	25c on 5c #136	.90 .20
1899	A28	$1.20 on 6c #137	.90 .20
1900	A28	$10 on $2 #146	4.50 4.00
		Nos. 1898-1900 (3)	6.30 4.40

No. 286A Overprinted

Overprints: a, 1988. b, WHO / 1948-1988.

1988, June 17   Litho.   Perf. 14x13½

1901		Sheet of 25, 24 #a.,	
		1 #b.	27.50 25.00
a.		A28 60c any single	.40 .20
b.		A28 60c	17.50 17.50

World Health Day, 40th anniv.

No. 929d Overprinted as Indicated
Nos. 1053a, 1063, 1131, and 1161 Overprinted "CONSERVE / WATER"

Overprints: No. 1903, "CONSERVE TREES" on ocher stamp, "CONSERVE ELECTRICITY on green stamp, "CONSERVE WATER on brown stamp. No. 1904, "CONSERVE ELECTRICITY" on ocher stamp, "CONSERVE WATER on green stamp, "CONSERVE TREES" on brown stamp. No. 1905, "CONSERVE WATER" on ocher stamp, "CONSERVE TREES on green stamp, "CONSERVE ELECTRICITY on brown stamp.

Perfs. as Before

1988, July 15   Litho.

Watermarks as Before

1903		Triptych	3.50 3.50
a.-c.		A90 120c any single	.90 .60
1904		Triptych	3.50 3.50
a.-c.		A90 120c any single	.90 .60
1905		Triptych	3.50 3.50
a.-c.		A90 120c any single	.90 .90
1906	A91	200c on #1063	1.10 1.10
1907	A91	200c on #1131	1.10 1.10
1908	A91	225c on #1053a	1.10 1.10
1909	A91	350c on #1161	1.10 1.10
		Nos. 1903-1909 (7)	14.90 14.90

Location and size of overprint varies.

Nos. 1826a and 1829a Ovptd. "BEWARE / OF ANIMALS" (a.)
Nos. 1826b and 1829b Ovptd. "BEWARE / OF CHILDREN" (b.)
Nos. 1826c and 1829c Ovptd. "DRIVE SAFELY" (c.)
Nos. 1826d and 1829d Ovptd. "DO NOT / DRINK AND DRIVE" (d.)

Unwmk.

1988, July 15   Litho.   Perf. 15

Block of 4, #a.-d.

1910	A99	$1.20 on #1826	7.50 7.50
1911	A99	$1.20 on #1829	7.50 7.50
		Nos. 1910-1911 (2)	15.00 15.00

No. 287 Ovptd. or Surcharged

Perf. 13½x13

1988, July   Litho.   Wmk. 364

1912	A66	$1 "1988" on #287	8.00 1.50
1913	A66	120c on $1 #287	8.00 1.50

No. 421 Surcharged with New Value and "1988"

1988?   Litho.   Perf. 13½x14

1913A	A80	$1.20 on $1.10 on $3 #421	

Nos. 1037a, 1047a, 1056-1057, 1066-1068, 1097, 1099, 1109-1109a, 1110-1111, 1113, 1115, 1122, 1125, 1129, 1147, 1149, and 1155 Ovptd. "CONSERVE / OUR RESOURCES"

1988, July   Perf. 14

Watermarks as Before

Series 1

Plate Numbers in Parentheses

1914		130c on #1037a (13)	1.00 .75
a.		Overprint inverted	7.50

#1914a probably is as common as #1914.

1915	A91	130c on #1047a (20)	1.00 .75
1916	A91	150c on #1056 (26)	1.00 .75
1917	A91	120c on #1057 (27)	1.00 .75
1918	A91	120c on #1066 (36)	1.00 .75
1919	A91	120c on #1067 (37)	1.00 .75
1920	A91	130c on #1068 (38)	1.00 .75
1921	A91	120c on #1097 (56)	1.00 .75
1922	A91	120c on #1099 (58)	1.00 .75
1923	A91	100c on #1109 (65)	1.00 .75
a.		100c on #1109a	
1924	A91	130c on #1110 (66)	1.00 .75
1925	A91	120c on #1111 (67)	1.00 .75
1926	A91	100c on #1113 (68)	1.00 .75
1927	A91	120c on #1115 (69)	1.00 .75
1928	A91	250c on #1122 (74)	1.00 .75
1929	A91	150c on #1125 (76)	1.00 .75
1930	A91	150c on #1129 (78)	1.00 .75
1931	A91	150c on #1147 (87)	1.00 .75
1932	A91	100c on #1149 (88)	1.00 .75
1933	A91	130c on #1155 (91)	1.00 .75

Nos. 1827a-1827d and 1830a-1830d Ovptd. with Red Cross

1988, Aug. 3   Litho.   Perf. 15

1935	A99	$3.20 Pair, #a.-b., on #1827a,	
		1827c	3.50 3.50
1936	A99	$3.20 Pair, #a.-b., on #1827b,	
		1827d	3.50 3.50
1937	A99	$3.30 Pair, #a.-b., on #1830a,	
		1830c	3.50 3.50
1938	A99	$3.30 Pair, #a.-b., on #1830b,	
		1830d	3.50 3.50
		Nos. 1935-1938 (4)	14.00 14.00

Nos. 1038, 1131 Ovptd. and Nos. 1147, 1175 Surcharged "1928-1988 / CRICKET / JUBILEE"

1988, Sept. 5   Litho.   Perf. 14

Watermarks as Before

Plate Numbers in Parentheses

1939	A91	200c on #1038 (14)	22.50 22.50
1940	A91	200c on #1131 (79)	1.25 .50
1941	A91	800c on 150c #1147 (87)	9.50 9.50
1942	A91	800c on 160c #1175 (5)	3.75 3.75
		Nos. 1939-1942 (4)	37.00 36.25

Series 1

Plate Numbers in Parentheses

Nos. 1063, 1081, 1139, 1147, 1161, 1185, 1219, 1232, and 1305 Ovptd. and No. 1227 Surcharged "OLYMPIC GAMES / 1988"

1988, Sept. 16   Unwmk.

1943	A91	200c on #1063 (33)	.70 .70
1944	A91	120c on #1081 (46)	.70 .70
1945	A91	300c on #1139 (83)	.70 .70
1946	A91	150c on #1147 (87)	.70 .70
1947	A91	350c on #1161 (94)	.90 .90

Series 2

1948	A91	320c on #1185 (10)	.90 .90
1949	A91	350c on #1219 (34)	.90 .90
1950	A91	300c on 360c #1227 (34)	.90 .90
1951	A91	130c on #1232 (38)	.90 .90
1952	A91	330c on #1305 (82)	.90 .90

Overprint reads up on No. 1947.

Type A83 Ovptd. or Surcharged "OLYMPICS 1988" (a.) or "KOREA 1988" (b.)

1988   Litho.   Wmk. 364   Perf. 13½

1953	A83	$1.20 Pair, #a.-b.	1.25 1.25
1954	A83	130c on $1.20, pair, #a.-b.	1.25 1.25
1955	A83	150c on $1.20, pair, #a.-b.	1.25 1.25
1956	A83	200c on $1.20, pair, #a.-b.	1.50 1.50
1957	A83	350c on $1.20, pair, #a.-b.	1.75 1.75
c.		Strip of 5, #1953a-1957a	7.00 7.00
d.		Strip of 5, #1953b-1957b	7.00 7.00

Overprint obliterates inscription spelled "LOS ANGELES."

No. 1087 Ovptd. and No. 1143 Surcharged "V CENTENARY OF / THE LANDING OF / CHRISTOPHER COLUMBUS / IN THE AMERICAS"

Unwmk.

1988, Oct. 12   Litho.   Perf. 14

1958	A91	320c on #1087	2.75 .75
1959	A91	$15 on 360c #1143	5.00 5.00
		Nos. 1958-1959 (2)	7.75 5.75

Nos. 1027, 1036, 1040, 1046, 1054, 1062, 1070, 1071, 1074, 1076, 1079, 1102, 1104, 1133, 1137 and 1143 Surcharged "SEASON'S / GREETINGS" in Blue or Black
Nos. 1053, 1053a, 1102, 1591A and 1670F Ovptd. or Surcharged "SEASON'S / GREETINGS / 1988" in Blue

1988, Nov. 10   Perfs. as Before

Watermarks and Printing Methods as Before

Plate Numbers in Parentheses

1960	A91	120c on 100c #1027 (6)	2.00
1961	A91	120c on 100c #1036 (13)	2.00
1962	A91	240c on 180c #1040 (15) (Bk)	1.00
1963	A91	120c on 100c #1046 (20)	2.00
1964	A91	225c on 100c #1053 (24)	2.00
a.		225c on #1053a	2.50
1965	A91	120c on 100c #1054 (25)	2.00
1966	A91	150c on #1062 (32) (Bk)	1.00
1967	A91	260c on #1070 (39) (Bk)	1.00
1968	A91	120c on 100c #1071 (40)	2.00

1969	A91	120c on 100c #1074 (42)		2.00
1970	A91	120c on 100c #1076 (43)		2.00
1971	A91	120c on 100c #1079 (45)		2.00
1972	A91	225c on #1102 (60) (Bk)		1.00
1973	A91	225c on #1102 (60) (Bk)		1.00
1974	A91	150c on #1104 (62) (Bk)		1.00
1975	A91	225c on #1591A (65)		1.50
1976	A91	330c on #1133 (80) (Bk)		1.00
1977	A91	320c on #1137 (82) (Bk)		1.00
1978	A91	360c on #1143 (85) (Bk)		1.00
		Nos. 1960-1978 (19)		27.50

Miniature Sheet

1979	A91	225c on #1670F (22)	4.75	4.75

Size and location of overprint varies.

Nos. 72, 713 and 932 Surcharged or Ovptd. "CHRISTMAS / 1988" in Red or Black

1988, Nov. 16   **Perfs. as Before**
Watermarks and Printing Methods as Before

1981	A7	20c on #72	.30	.20
1982	A86	Block of 4 (Bk)	2.25	2.25
a.		120c on #713a	.50	.50
b.		120c on 130c #713b	.50	.50
c.		120c on 150c #713c	.50	.50
d.		120c on 200c #713d	.50	.50
1983	A90a	500c on 330c #932	2.50	2.50
		Nos. 1981-1983 (3)	5.05	4.95

Overprint reads up on No. 1983.

Nos. 288, 289, and 289A Surcharged or Ovptd. for Prevention of AIDS

Beginnning of overprint reads: Nos. 1984a, 1985e, "Get information..." Nos. 1984b, 1985a, "Get the facts..." Nos. 1984c, 1985b, "Say no to drugs..." Nos. 1984d, 1985c, $2, $5, $10, "Protect yourself..." Nos. 1984e, 1985d, "Be compassionate..."

Perf. 13½x13

1988, Dec. 1		**Litho.**		**Wmk. 364**
1984	A66	120c Strip of 5, #a.-e., on #289	18.50	18.50
1985	A66	120c Strip of 5, #a.-e., on #289A	18.50	18.50
1986	A66	$2 on #288	12.00	3.00
1987	A66	$5 on #289	14.00	7.50
1988	A66	$10 on #289A	16.00	12.00
		Nos. 1984-1988 (5)	79.00	59.50

1988 Winter Olympics, Calgary A106

Design: $3.50, Olympic rings.

1988, Dec. 1				**Perf. 14**
1989	A106	$7 Downhill skiing	11.00	11.00

Souvenir Sheet

1990	A106	$3.50 Sheet of 1	6.00	6.00

No. 1989 exists in souvenir sheet of 1. Value $40.

Christmas — A107

Paintings: No. 1991a, Virgin and Child Between St. George and St. Catherine, by Titian. b, Adoration of the Magi, by Titian.
No. 1992a, Holy Family, by Rubens. b, Adoration of the Shepherds, by Rubens.
$8, The Madonna, by Titian.

Perf. 14x13½, 13½x14

1988, Dec. 15		**Litho.**		
1991	A107	$2 Pair, #a.-b.	7.00	7.00
1992	A107	$2 Pair, #a.-b.	7.00	7.00

Souvenir Sheet
Perf. 13½x14

1993	A107	$8 multicolored	17.50	17.50

Nos. 1991a-1991b, 1992a-1992b exist in souvenir sheets of 1.

Abolition of Slavery Type of 1985

1988, Dec. 16   **Litho.**   **Perf. 14**
Designs as Before

1994	A93	25c brown & black	.25	.25
1995	A93	60c magenta & black	.50	.50
1996	A93	130c green & black	1.00	1.00
1997	A93	150c blue & black	1.25	1.25
		Nos. 1994-1997 (4)	3.00	3.00

Nos. 1087, 1167, and 1200 Surcharged "SALUTING WINNERS / OLYMPIC GAMES / 1988"

Unwmk.

1989, Jan. 3		**Litho.**		**Perf. 14**
1998	A91	$5.50 on 560c #1167	1.75	1.25
1999	A91	$9 on 320c #1200	2.25	2.25
2000	A91	$10.50 on 320c #1087	3.00	3.00
		Nos. 1998-2000 (3)	7.00	6.50

Miniature Sheets

Red Cross, 125th Anniv. — A108

Designs: No. 2001, Henri Dunant, vert. No. 2002, First maritime ambulance. No. 2003, Red Cross hospital ship in African War. No. 2004, Red Cross air ambulance. No. 2005, Red Cross train.
Nos. 2001-2004 printed with red cross in center of sheet. Each stamp contains part of the red cross at the: a, LR. b, LL. c, UR. d, UL.

Perf. 13½x14, 14x13½

1989, Jan. 5		**Litho.**		
2001	A108	$2 Sheet of 4, #a.-d.	10.00	10.00
2002	A108	$2 Sheet of 4, #a.-d.	10.00	10.00
2003	A108	$2 Sheet of 4, #a.-d.	10.00	10.00
2004	A108	$2 Sheet of 4, #a.-d.	10.00	10.00
		Nos. 2001-2004 (4)	40.00	40.00

Souvenir Sheet
Perf. 14x13½

2005	A108	$7 Sheet of 1	11.00	11.00

Dated 1988.

Trains — A109

Designs: a, Hernalser sleeping carriage. b, 5 Forney locomotive. c, Austrian sleeping carriage. d, Pacific 231 locomotive.
$10, First Japanese imperial train.

1989, Jan. 5		**Litho.**		**Perf. 14**
2006	A109	$2 Sheet of 4, #a.-d.	15.00	15.00

Souvenir Sheet

2007	A109	$10 multicolored	11.00	11.00

Nos. 2006a-2006d exist in souvenir sheets of 1, each $3.75.
Dated 1988.

Naval Airship LZ 92, 1916 — A110

#2008: a, Astronaut on moon. b, Graf Zeppelin over San Francisco Bay, 1929. c, Testu-Brissy on horseback ascending in balloon, 1798.
#2009, Graf Zeppelin LZ 127.

1989, Jan. 26				**Perf. 14**
2007A	A110	$2 black	3.00	3.00
2008	A110	$2 Strip of 3, #a.-c.	8.00	8.00

Souvenir Sheet

2009	A110	$2 Sheet of 1	10.00	6.00

Nos. 2007A, 2008b, 2009, Ferdinand von Zeppelin, 150th birth anniv. in 1988. No. 2008a, 1st moon landing, 20th anniv. in 1989. The inscriptions on Nos. 2007A and 2009 are in error. Dated 1988.

Mushrooms — A111

#2010: a, Cortinarius bolaris. b, Cortinarius laniger. c, Tricholoma sulphureum. d, Lepiota cristata.
#2011, Sarcoscypha coccinea, vert.

1989, Feb. 1				**Perf. 14x13½**
2010	A111	$2 Block of 4, #a.-d.	15.00	15.00

Souvenir Sheet
Perf. 13½x14

2011	A111	$5 Sheet of 1	11.00	11.00

Dated 1988.

Boy Scout Jamboree, Australia — A112

Design: $8, Scouts of different races.

1989, Feb. 10				
2012	A112	$10 grn, black & yel	15.00	15.00

Souvenir Sheet

2013	A112	$8 Sheet of 1	15.00	15.00

Dated 1988. #2012 exists in souvenir sheet of 1.

1988 Summer Olympics, Seoul — A113

Emblem of South American Soccer Federation — A113a — 2020

Designs: No. 2014, Florence Griffith-Joyner. No. 2015, Carl Lewis. No. 2016, Equestrian. No. 2017, Runners, horiz. No. 2018, City skyline, Olympic Rings, horiz. No. 2019, 1988 & 1992 Olympic mascots, horiz. No. 2022, Griffith-Joyner, Lewis, horiz. No. 2023, Cosmic Athlete by Dali, horiz.

1989, Feb. 15		**Litho.**		**Perf. 14**
2014	A113	$2 multicolored	3.50	3.50
2015	A113	$2 multicolored	3.50	3.50
2016	A113	$2 multicolored	3.50	3.50
2017	A113	$2 multicolored	3.50	3.50
2018	A113	$2 multicolored	3.50	3.50
2019	A113	$2 multicolored	3.50	3.50
2020	A113a	$2 multicolored	3.50	3.50

Souvenir Sheets

2022	A113	$3.50 multicolored	15.00	15.00
2023	A113	$3.50 multicolored	15.00	15.00

No. 2023 exists with gold border and inscriptions. Nos. 2014-2020 inscribed 1988.
An additional stamp was issued in this set. The editors would like to examine any examples.

Nos. 1826, 1829 and 1831 Ovptd. "REPUBLIC DAY 1989" in Red

1989, Feb. 22		**Litho.**		**Perf. 15**
2024	A99	$1.20 Block of 4, #a.-d., on #1826	4.50	4.50
2025	A99	$1.20 Block of 4, #a.-d., on #1829	4.50	4.50
2026	A101	$10 on #1831	7.50	7.50
		Nos. 2024-2026 (3)	16.50	16.50

Nos. 1827a-1827d and 1830a-1830d Surcharged in Red

1989, Feb. 22				
2027	A99	$5 Pair, #a.-b., on $3.20 #a., c.	7.50	7.50
2028	A99	$5 Pair, #a.-b., on $3.20 #a., c.	7.50	7.50
2028C	A99	$5 Pair, #d.-e., on $3.30 #a., c.	7.50	7.50
2028F	A99	$5 Pair, #g-h., on $3.30 #b., d.	7.50	7.50

Nos. 1461, 1822 Surcharged in Red

1989, Feb. 22		**Litho.**		**Perf. 14**
2029	A96	$10 #a.-b. on #1461	10.00	10.00
2030	A96	$10 #a.-b. on #1822	10.00	10.00

No. 1188 Surcharged "EASTER"

1989, Mar. 22				**Perf. 14**
2031	A91	Sheet of 4 on #1188	5.00	5.00
a.		125c on 320c #1188	.50	.50
b.		250c on 320c #1188	1.00	1.00
c.		300c on 320c #1188	1.25	1.25
d.		350c on 320c #1188	1.50	1.50

No. 927 Surcharged

1989, Mar.		**Wmk. 364**		**Perf. 14**
2032	A90	250c on 25c #927	6.00	1.25

Inscribed "1986."

No. 1197 Surcharged "RED CROSS / 1948 / 1988"

1989, Apr.		**Unwmk.**		**Perf. 14**
2033	A91	375c on 45c #1197	5.50	5.50
2034	A91	425c on 45c #1197	5.50	5.50

Guyana Red Cross, 40th anniv.

#1263 & 1252 Surcharged in Pairs "ALL FOR / HEALTH" (a.) or "HEALTH / FOR ALL" (b.)

1989, Apr. 3				
2035	A91	250c on 75c #1263 (56), pair	8.00	8.00
2036	A91	675c on 720c #1252 (49), pair	10.00	10.00

For surcharge see No. 2052.

Nos. 1224-1225, and 1254
Overprinted or Surcharged
"BOY SCOUTS / 1909 1989" (a.)
or
"GIRL GUIDES / 1924 1989" (b.)
Nos. 1272-1273 Surcharged "LADY
BADEN POWELL / 1889-1989"

1989, Apr. 11

2037	A91	250c on 100c, pair, #a.-b.	5.00	5.00
2038	A91	$2.50 on 50c, pair, #a.-b.	5.00	5.00
2039	A91	300c Pair, #a.-b.	5.00	5.00
c.		Pair, #d.-e., Prussian bl ovpt.		
2040	A91	$25 on 280c #1272	7.00	7.00
a.		Prussian blue overprint		
2041	A91	$25 on 700c #1273	7.00	7.00
a.		Prussian blue overprint		
		Nos. 2037-2041 (5)	29.00	29.00

Nos. 2037-2039, Boy Scouts in Guyana, 80th anniversary and Girl Guides, 65th anniversary. Nos. 2040-2041, Lady Baden Powell, birth centenary.

No. 1177 Surcharged
"PHOTOGRAPHY / 1839-1989"

1989, Apr. 15

2042	A91	550c on 390c	7.00	7.00
2043	A91	650c on 390c, 2 bar obliterator	7.00	7.00
a.		6 bar obliterator	7.00	7.00
		Nos. 2042-2043, 2043a (3)	21.00	21.00

Nos. 2042-2043 printed in sheets of 4 with alternating overprints.

No. 1263 Surcharged
"I.L.O. / 1919-1989"

1989, May 2

2044	A91	300c on 75c #1263	12.00	2.25

Intl. Labor Organization, 70th anniversary.

Nos. 43, 87, 134-137, 279-280, 284-285, and 286A 288, 1827, 1830, and 2035-2036 Surcharged in Black or Blue

q

s

r

t

1989-92 *Perfs. as Before*
Watermarks and Printing Methods as Before

2045	A7(q)	80c on 6c #43	.60	.35
a.		A7 80c on 6c #43	.60	.35
2046	A28(q)	$1 on 2c #134	.60	.35
a.		A28(r) $1 on 2c #134	.60	.35
2047	A28(q)	$2.05 on 3c #135	.60	.35
a.		A28(q) $2.05 on 3c #135	.60	.35
2048	A28(q)	$2.55 on 5c #136	.60	.35
a.		A28(r) $2.55 on 5c #136	.60	.35
2049	A28(q)	$3.25 on 6c #137	.60	.40
a.		A28(r) $3.25 on 6c #137	.60	.40

2050	A14(q)	$5 on 6c #87	.60	.35
a.		A14(s) $5 on 6c #87	.60	.35
b.		A14(r) $5 on 6c #87	.60	—
2051	A66(q)	$6 on 5c #279		
2052	A91	640c Pair, #2036	5.00	5.00
2053	A66(q)	$6.40 on 10c #280	6.00	.90
a.		A66 $6.40 on 10c #280	6.00	.90
b.		A66(r) $6.40 on 10c #280	6.00	.90
2054		Block of 5, #a.-e. on #1830	42.50	42.50
a.-d.		A99(t) $6.40 on $3.30 #a.-d.	5.00	2.00
		A100(t) $190 on $3.30 #e.	22.50	20.00
2054F	A66(r)	$7.65 on 35c #284	7.25	1.50
2055	A66	$7.65 on 40c #285	8.25	1.50
2056		Block of 5, #a.-e. on #1827	42.50	42.50
a.-d.		A99(t) $7.65 on $3.20 #a.-d.	5.00	2.00
		A100(t) $225 on $3.20 #e.	22.50	20.00
2057	A66(q)	$8.90 on 60c #286A	9.00	1.50
a.		A66 $8.90 on 60c #286A	9.00	1.50
2057B	A66(q)	$30 on 10c #280		
2057C	A66(q)	$35 on 35c #284		
2058	A66(r)	$50 on $2 #288 (Bl)	20.00	10.00
2059	A66(r)	$100 on $2 #288	27.50	20.00

Issued: #2045a, 2053-2053a, 2054F, 2055, May 18; #2057, May 26; #2058-2059, June 5; #2045, 2049, 2046a, 2048a, 2049a, June 15; #2050-2050a, 2051, 2052, 2054, 2056, Aug. 16; #2050b, 1992.

Nos. 2045a, 2053a, 2055, 2057a have no obliterator. New denominations are larger on Nos. 2045a, 2053a and 2057a. No. 2045a has no cent sign. Denomination on No. 2050b is above "X" obliterator.

Nos. 2054e, 2056b additionally overprinted "SPECIAL DELIVERY."

No. 1244 Surcharged "CARICOM / DAY"

Unwmk.

1989, June 26 Litho. Perf. 14

2064	A91	125c on 200c #1244, 2 bar obliterator	8.00	1.50
a.		6 bar obliterator	10.00	1.75

No. 280 Ovptd. in Gold or Silver for Gold Medalists at 1988 Summer Olympics

Overprints read: Nos. 2082a, 2083a, "SEOUL / OLYMPICS." Nos. 2082b, 2083b, "Men's 800M / Ereng / Kenya." Nos. 2082c, 2083c, "KOREA." Nos. 2082d, 2083d, "Men's / Gymnastics / Artemov / USSR." Nos. 2082e, 2083e, "Men's / Swimming / Louganis / USA." Nos. 2082f, 2083f, "Woman's / Swimming / Otto / DDR." Nos. 2082g, 2083g, "Men's Fencing / Lamour / France." Nos. 2082h, 2083h, "Men's / Gymnastics / Lou / China." Nos. 2082i, 2083i, "Men's / Cycling / Knol / Holland." Nos. 2082j, 2083j, "Men's / Swimming / Szabo / Hungary." Nos. 2082k, 2083k, "1988." Nos. 2082l, 2083l, "Men's / Swimming / Nesty / Suriname." Nos. 2082m, 2083m, "Men's Boxing / Lewis / Canada." Nos. 2082n, 2083n, "Men's Javelin / Korjus / Finland." Nos. 2082o, 2083o, "Basketball / USA." Nos. 2082p, 2083p, "Men's / Equestrian / Klimke / W. Germany." Nos. 2082q, 2083q, "Men's Boxing / Park / Korea." Nos. 2082r, 2083r, "Women's / Marathon / Mota / Portugal." Nos. 2082s, 2083s, "Men's / Swimming / Suzuki / Japan." Nos. 2084a, 2085a, "Men's 100M / Lewis / USA." Nos. 2084b, 2085b, "Men's / Pole Vault / Bubka / USSR." Nos. 2084c, 2085c, "Women's / 100-200m / Joyner / USA." Nos. 2084d, 2085d, "Men's Pentathlon / Martinek / Hungary." Nos. 2084e, 2085e, "Men's Wrestling / Sako / Japan." Nos. 2084f, 2085f, "Men's Judo / Saito / Japan." Nos. 2084g, 2085g, "Women's 800M / Wodars / DDR." Nos. 2084h, 2085h, "Men's Boxing / Gross / W. Germany." Nos. 2084i, 2085i, "Men's Boxing / Maske / DDR." Nos. 2084j, 2085j, "Men's Boxing / Kim / Korea." Nos. 2084k, 2085k, "Woman's / Swimming / Evans / USA." Nos. 2084l, 2085l, "Soccer / USSR." Nos. 2084m, 2085m, "Woman's / Gymnastics / Silivas / Romania." Nos. 2084n, 2085n, "Men's Boxing / Mercer / USA." Nos. 2084o, 2085o, "Men's Marathon / Bordin / Italy." Nos. 2084p, 2085p, "Women's Tennis / Graf / W. Germany."

Perf. 14x13½

1989, Apr. Litho. Wmk. 364
Sheets of 25

2082		5 #a., 3 #c., #b., d.-s.	12.50	12.50
a.-s.		A66 10c on #280, any single	.45	.45
2083		5 #a., 3 #c., #b., d.-s. (S)	12.50	12.50
a.-s.		A66 10c on #280, any single	.45	.45
2084		8 #a.-b., 6 #c., 2 #d. #e.	12.50	12.50
a.-e.		A66 10c on #280, any single	.45	.45
2085		8 #a.-b., 6 #c., 2 #d. #e. (S)	12.50	12.50
a.-e.		A66 10c on #280, any single	.45	.45

No. 280 Ovptd. in Gold or Silver for Gold Medalists at 1988 Winter Olympics

Overprints read: Nos. 2086a, 2087a, "Gold Medal / Winners." Nos. 2086b, 2087b, "Ice Hockey / USSR." Nos. 2086c, 2087c, "CALGARY / OLYMPICS." Nos. 2086d, 2087d, "Bobsled / Kipours-Kozlov / USSR." Nos. 2086e, 2087e, "Women's Skating / 1500-3000-5000M / Gennip / Netherlands." Nos. 2086f, 2087f, "Men's / Speed / Skating / 5000-10000M / Gustafson / Sweden." Nos. 2086g, 2087g, "Men's / Figure / Skating / Boitano / USA." Nos. 2086h, 2087h, "Women's / 500M Skating / Blair / USA." Nos. 2086i, 2087i, "Women's / Figure Skating / Witt / DDR." Nos. 2086j, 2087j, "Men's Giant / Slalom / Tomba / Italy." Nos. 2086k, 2087k, "CANADA." Nos. 2086l, 2087l, "Men's Super / Giant Slalom / Picard / France." Nos. 2086m, 2087m, "Women's / Downhill Skiing / Kiehl / W. Germany." Nos. 2086n, 2087n, "Men's 50m Skiing Svan / Sweden." Nos. 2086o, 2087o, "Men's Nordic / Combined Skiing / Mueller-Pohl / Schwarz / W. Germany." Nos. 2086p, 2087p, "Women's / Giant Slalom / Schneider / Switzerland." Nos. 2086q, 2087q, "Women's / 5-km Skiing / Matikainen / Finland." Nos. 2086r, 2087r, "Men's Downhill / Alpine Skiing / Zurbriggen / Switzerland." Nos. 2086s, 2087s, "Men's Ski / Jumping / Nykanen / Finland."

1989, Apr.

2086		4 #a., 3 #c., #b., d.-s., #2082k	12.50	12.50
a.-s.		A66 10c on #280, any single	.45	.45
2087		4 #a., 3 #c., #b., d.-s., #2083k (S)	12.50	12.50
a.-s.		A66 10c on #280, any single	.45	.45

No. 281 Ovptd. in Gold or Silver in Memory of Hirohito, Emperor of Japan

Overprints read: Nos. 2088a, 2089a, "Emperor / Hirohito." Nos. 2088b, 2089b, "Showa / Era." Nos. 2088c, 2089c, "Chrysanthemum / Dynasty." Nos. 2088d, 2089d, "Emperor / of Japan." Nos. 2088e, 2089e, "1901." Nos. 2088f, 2089f, "1989." Nos. 2088g, 2089g, "Emperor / Hirohito / 1901-1989."

1989, Apr.

2088		5 #a., 4 #c.-d., 9 #b., #e.-g.	12.50	12.50
a.-g.		A66 15c on #281, any single	.45	.45
2089		5 #a., 4 #c.-d., 9 #b., #e.-g. (S)	12.50	12.50
a.-g.		A66 15c on #281, any single	.45	.45

No. 280 Ovptd. in Gold or Silver for Enthronment of Akihito, Emperor of Japan

Overprints reads: Nos. 2090a, 2091a, "Honoring / His / Majesty." Nos. 2090b, 2091b, "Emperor / of Japan." Nos. 2090c, 2091c, "1989." Nos. 2090d, 2091d, "HEISI / ERA."

1989, Apr.

2090		12 #a, 8 #b., 4 #c., #d.	12.50	12.50
a.-d.		A66 10c on #280, any single	.45	.45
2091		12 #a., 8 #b., 4 #c., #d. (S)	12.50	12.50
a.-d.		A66 10c on #280, any single	.45	.45

Overprint is 10mm long on #2090c, 2091c.

Nos. 280-281 and 283 Ovptd. with Emblems of Scouts, Rotary Intl., and Lions Intl. in Gold, Silver, Metallic Red, Metallic Green and Black

Overprints: Nos. 2092a, 2093a, 2094a, 2095a, 2096b, 2097b, 2098b, 2099b, 2100c, 2101c, 2102c, 2103c, Scouting emblem. Nos. 2092b, 2093b, 2094b, 2095b, 2096a, 2097a, 2098a, 2099a, 2100b, 2101b, 2102b, 2103b, Rotary emblem. Nos. 2092c, 2093c, 2094c, 2095c, 2096c, 2097c, 2098c, 2099c, 2100a, 2101a, 2102a, 2103a, Lions emblem. Nos. 2092d 2093d 2094d 2095d 2096d 2097d 2098d 2099d 2100d 2101d 2102d 2103d, "1989." Nos. 2092e, 2093e, 2094e, 2095e, Large scouting emblem. Nos. 2096e, 2097e, 2098e, 2099e, Large Rotary emblem. Nos. 2100e, 2101e, 2102e, 2103e, Large Lions emblem.

1989, Apr.

2092		8 #a.-b., 6 #c., 2 #d., #e.	12.50	12.50
a.-e.		A66 10c on #280, any single	.45	.45
2093		8 #a.-b., 6 #c., 2 #d., #e. (S)	12.50	12.50
a.-e.		A66 10c on #280, any single	.45	.45
2094		8 #a.-b., 6 #c., 2 #d., #e. (R)	12.50	12.50
a.-e.		A66 10c on #280, any single	.45	.45

2095		8 #a.-b., 6 #c., 2 #d., #e. (Bk)	12.50	12.50
a.-e.		A66 10c on #280, any single	.45	.45
2096		8 #a.-b., 6 #c., 2 #d., #e.	12.50	12.50
a.-e.		A66 15c on #281, any single	.45	.45
2097		8 #a.-b., 6 #c., 2 #d., #e. (S)	12.50	12.50
a.-e.		A66 15c on #281, any single	.45	.45
2098		8 #a.-b., 6 #c., 2 #d., #e. (R)	12.50	12.50
a.-e.		A66 15c on #281, any single	.45	.45
2099		8 #a.-b., 6 #c., 2 #d., #e. (Gr)	12.50	12.50
a.-e.		A66 15c on #281, any single	.45	.45
2100		8 #a.-b., 6 #c., 2 #d., #e.	12.50	12.50
a.-e.		A66 25c on #283, any single	.45	.45
2101		8 #a.-b., 6 #c., 2 #d., #e. (S)	12.50	12.50
a.-e.		A66 25c on #283, any single	.45	.45
2102		8 #a.-b., 6 #c., 2 #d., #e. (R)	12.50	12.50
a.-e.		A66 25c on #283, any single	.45	.45
2103		8 #a.-b., 6 #c., 2 #d., #e. (Gr)	12.50	12.50
a.-e.		A66 25c on #283, any single	.45	.45

"1989" overprints are 7½mm long.

No. 280 Ovptd. in Gold or Silver for Halley's Comet

Overprints read: Nos. 2104a, 2105a, "Halley's / Comet." Nos. 2104b, 2105b, "Famous / Space Event." Nos. 2104c, 2105c, "Edmund / Halley / 1656-1742." Nos. 2104d, 2105d, "1910." Nos. 2104e, 2105e, "1986."

1989, Apr.

2104		11 #a., 6 #b., 4 #c., 2 #d.-e.	12.50	12.50
a.-e.		A66 10c on #280, any single	.45	.45
2105		11 #a., 6 #b., 4 #c., 2 #d.-e. (S)	12.50	12.50
a.-e.		A66 10c on #280, any single	.45	.45

No. 280 Ovptd. in Gold or Silver for Space Achievements

Overprints read: Nos. 2106a, 2107a, "Sputnik I / Oct. 4, 1957." Nos. 2106b, 2107b, "Explorer I / Jan. 31, 1958." Nos. 2106c, 2107c, "Sputnik II / Laika / Spacedog / Nov. 3, 1957." Nos. 2106d, 2107d, "Alan Shepard, Jr. / Mercury III / May 5, 1961." Nos. 2106e, 2107e, "Yuri Gagarin / Vostok I / April 12, 1961." Nos. 2106f, 2107f, "John Glenn / Mercury VI / Feb. 20, 1962." Nos. 2106g, 2107g, "Vostok III / Vostok IV / Aug. 12, 1962." Nos. 2106h, 2107h, "Grissom-Young / Gemini III / March 23, 1965." Nos. 2106i, 2107i, "Luna III / Oct. 4, 1959." Nos. 2106j, 2107j, "Edward H. White II / Gemini IV / June 3, 1965." Nos. 2106k, 2107k, "V. Tereshkova / First Woman / in Space / June 16-19, 1963." Nos. 2106 l, 2107 l, "Surveyor I / June 2, 1966." Nos. 2106m, 2107m, "Space / Achievements." Nos. 2106n, 2107n, "Voskod I / First 3 Man Crew / Oct. 12-13, 1964." Nos. 2106o, 2107o, "Apollo I / Jan. 27, 1967." Nos. 2106p, 2107p, "Alexei A. Leonov / First Walk in Space / March 18-19, 1965." Nos. 2106q, 2107q, "Apollo VIII / Dec. 21-27, 1968." Nos. 2106r, 2107r, "V. Komarov / Soyuz I / April 24, 1967." Nos. 2106s, 2107s, "Apollo XI / First Man on Moon / July 20, 1969." Nos. 2106t, 2107t, "Lunokhod I / Dec. 10, 1970." Nos. 2106u, 2107u, "Apollo XIII / April 11-17, / 1970." Nos. 2106v, 2107v, "Soyuz XI / June 30, 1971." Nos. 2106w, 2107w, "Viking I / July 20, 1976." Nos. 2106x, 2107x, "Vega I / March 6, 1986." Nos. 2106y, 2107y, "Columbia Sts-1 / April 12-14, / 1981."

1989, Apr.

2106		#a.-y.	12.50	12.50
a.-y.		A66 10c on #280, any single	.45	.45
2107		#a.-y. (S)	12.50	12.50
a.-y.		A66 10c on #280, any single	.45	.45

No. 280 Ovptd. in Gold or Silver

Overprints read: Nos. 2108a, 2109a, "1969-/ 1989." Nos. 2108b, 2109b, "Apollo XI." Nos. 2108c, 2109c, "First Man / on Moon." Nos. 2108d, 2109d, "USA." Nos. 2108e, 2109e, "Neil A. / Armstrong." Nos. 2108f, 2109f, "Col. Edwin E. / Aldrin, Jr." Nos. 2108g, 2109g, "Lt. Col. / Michael / Collins."

1989, Apr.

2108		5 #a, 7 b, 4 c, 6 d, e-g	12.50	12.50
a.-g.		A66 10c on #280, any single	.45	.45
2109		5 #a, 7 b, 4 c, 6 d, e-g (S)	12.50	12.50
a.-g.		A66 10c on #280, any single	.45	.45

Moon Landing, 20th anniv.

No. 281 Ovptd. in Gold or Silver for Space Shuttle Program

Overprints read: Nos. 2110a, 2111a, "Enterprise / Aug. 12, 1977." Nos. 2110b, 2111b, "Columbia / April 12, 1981." Nos. 2110c, 2111c, "Space / Shuttles." Nos. 2110d, 2111d, "Discovery / Aug. 30, 1984." Nos. 2110e, 2111e, "Atlantis / Oct. 3, 1985." Nos. 2110f, 2111f, "Challenger / Heroes." Nos. 2110g, 2111g, "Resnik / McAuliffe / Jarvis." Nos. 2110h, 2111h, "In Memoriam / Challenger /

Jan. 28, 1986." Nos. 2110i, 2111i, "Onizuka / Smith / McNair / Scobee."

1989, Apr.

2110		4 #a.-e., 2 #g.-i.		12.50	12.50
a.-i.		A66 15c on #281, any single		.45	.45
2111		4 #a.-e., 2 #f., #g.-i. (S)		12.50	12.50
a.-i.		A66 15c on #281, any single		.45	.45

Butterflies — A115   A116

1989, Sept. 7   Litho.   *Perf. 14*

2208	A115	80c	Stalachtis calliope	.50	.25
2209	A115	$2.25	Morpho rhetenor	.60	.25
2210	A115	$5	Agrias claudia	.75	.40
2211	A115	$6.40	Marpesia marcella	.85	.70
2212	A115	$7.65	Papilio zagreus	1.00	.90
2213	A115	$8.90	Chorinea faunus	1.25	1.10
2214	A115	$25	Cepheuptychia cephus	4.00	3.00
2215	A115	$100	Nessaea regina	13.50	12.50
		Nos. 2208-2215 (8)		22.45	19.10

See Nos. E16-E17. For overprints see Nos. 2251-2254, 2256-2257, 2260-2261, 2283-2290, E19-E22, E24, E26-E27, E31.

1989, Nov. 8

Women in Space, 25th Anniv. (in 1988): $6.40, Kathryn Sullivan, 1st US woman to walk in space. $12.80, Svetlana Savitskaya, 1st Soviet woman to walk in space. $15.30, Judy Resnik & Christa McAuliffe, astronauts killed in Challenger explosion. $100, Sally Ride, 1st US woman astronaut.

2216	A116	$6.40	multicolored	1.00	.25
2217	A116	$12.80	multicolored	1.75	1.25
2218	A116	$15.30	multicolored	2.00	1.50
2219	A116	$100	multicolored	11.50	11.50
		Nos. 2216-2219 (4)		16.25	14.50

See No. E18. For overprints see Nos. 2255, 2258-2259, 2262, E23, E25, E28, E32.

1990 World Cup Soccer Championships, Italy — A117

Various soccer players.

Perf. 14x13½, 13½x14

1989, Nov. 20

2220	A117	$2.55	shown	5.00	5.00
2221	A117	$2.55	Yellow shirt, vert.	5.00	5.00
2222	A117	$2.55	Goalie	5.00	5.00
2223	A117	$2.55	Green shirt, vert.	5.00	5.00
		Nos. 2220-2223 (4)		20.00	20.00

Souvenir Sheet

2224	A117	$20	Championships emblem, vert.	17.50	17.50

#2220-2223 exist in souvenir sheets of 1. For surcharges see Nos. 2263-2267.

No. 134-136 Surcharged "AHMADIYYA / CENTENARY / 1889-1989"

Perf. 13x13½

1989, Nov. 22   Litho.   Wmk. 364

2225	A28	80c	on 2c #134	4.50	.60
2226	A28	$6.40	on 3c #135	13.50	5.50
2227	A28	$8.90	on 5c #136	15.00	8.00
		Nos. 2225-2227 (3)		33.00	14.10

1992 Summer Olympics, Barcelona A118

1989, Dec. 5   *Perf. 13½x14, 14x13½*

2228	A118	$2.55	shown	4.00	4.00
2229	A118	$2.55	Boxing, horiz.	4.00	4.00
2230	A118	$2.55	Chariot racing, horiz.	4.00	4.00
2231	A118	$2.55	Javelin, horiz.	4.00	4.00
2232	A118	$2.55	Running, horiz.	4.00	4.00
2233	A118	$2.55	Wrestling	4.00	4.00
		Nos. 2228-2233 (6)		24.00	24.00

Souvenir Sheets

2234	A118	$10	Running, horiz., diff.	15.00	15.00
2235	A118	$10	Columbus Walk by Picasso	15.00	15.00
		Nos. 2234-2235 (2)		30.00	30.00

#2228-2233 exist in souvenir sheets of 1.

Christmas — A119

Paintings: No. 2236, Child Declaring in Favor of His Mother, by Titian. No. 2237, The Sacred Family, by Rubens. No. 2238, Saint Anne, the Virgin and Child, by Durer. No. 2239, Madonna Enthroned, Surrounded by Saints, by Rubens. $20, Saint Ildefonso, by Rubens.

1989, Dec. 26   *Perf. 14x13½, 13½x14*

2236	A119	$2.55	multi	4.00	4.00
2237	A119	$2.55	multi, vert.	4.00	4.00
2238	A119	$2.55	multi, vert.	4.00	4.00
2239	A119	$2.55	multi, vert.	4.00	4.00
		Nos. 2236-2239 (4)		16.00	16.00

Souvenir Sheet

2240	A119	$20	multi, vert.	20.00	20.00

#2236-2239 exist in souvenir sheets of 1.

Harpy Eagle — A120

Channel-billed Toucan — A121

1990, Jan. 23   Litho.   *Perf. 14*

2241	A120	$2.25	Eagle's head	1.25	.50
2242	A120	$5	Eagle with prey	1.75	.75
2243	A120	$8.90	Eagle facing right	2.75	1.00
2244	A121	$15	shown	1.75	.90
2245	A121	$25	Blue & yellow macaw	2.25	1.00
2246	A120	$30	Eagle facing left	5.25	4.50
2247	A121	$50	Wattled jacana, horiz.	4.00	3.00
2248	A121	$60	Hoatzin, horiz.	4.50	3.25
		Nos. 2241-2248 (8)		23.50	14.90

Souvenir Sheets

2249	A121	$100	Great kiskadee, horiz.	7.00	7.00
2250	A121	$100	Amazon kingfisher, horiz.	7.00	7.00

Nos. 2241-2243, 2246, World Wildlife Fund.

Nos. 2208-2184 Ovptd. in Silver with Rotary Emblem and "ROTARY INTERNATIONAL 1905-1990" on 2 or 3 Lines

1990, Mar. 15

2251	A115	80c	on #2208	
2252	A115	$2.25	on #2209	
2253	A115	$5	on #2210	
2254	A115	$6.40	on #2211	
2255	A116	$6.40	on #2216	
2256	A115	$7.65	on #2212	
2257	A115	$8.90	on #2213	
2258	A116	$12.80	on #2217	
2259	A116	$15.30	on #2218	
2260	A115	$25	on #2214	
2261	A115	$100	on #2215	
2262	A116	$100	on #2219	
		Nos. 2251-2262 (12)		37.50

Nos. 2220-2222, 2224 Surcharged "GERMANY / CHAMPION"
No. 2223 Surcharged "GERMANY / CHAMPION / ARGENTINA / SUB-CHAMPION"

1990   *Perfs. as Before*

2263	A117	$75	on #2220	
2264	A117	$75	on #2221	
2265	A117	$75	on #2222	
2266	A117	$75	on #2223	
		Nos. 2263-2266 (4)		10.00

Souvenir Sheet

2267	A117	$225	on #2224	8.00

#2263-2266 exist in souvenir sheets of 1.

Miniature Sheets

Penny Black, 150th Anniv., 500th Anniv. of Thurn & Taxis Postal Service A122

No. 2268: a, Banghy Post runner, 1832. b, Penny Black, Sir Rowland Hill. c, Dutch mail ship. d, Paddle steamer Monarch, 1830. e, Paddle steamer Hindostan, 1842. f, Mail steamer Chusan. g, Sailing ship Madagascar, 1853. h, Paddle steamer Orinoco, 1855. i, Packet Orpheus, 1835.

No. 2269: a, Imperial postal messenger. b, Swiss messenger, 1499. c, River messenger, 15th century. d, Russian courier, Middle Ages. e, Oldenburg postilions, 1820. f, Indian mail coach, 1829. g, Baden mail coach postilions, 1820. h, Pony Express, 1860. i, Camel rider.

No. 2270: a, Mail coach, 1840. b, Danish Ball Post, 1815. c, Australian Bush mailman, 1838. d, Japanese postmen, 1870. e, Mail cart, 1857. f, Russian mail troika. g, Wells, Fargo Overland Express. h, Phantoms of the Night, 1853. i, Cobb & Co. coach, Australia.

No. 2271: a, Postilions, 1850. b, Mounted postilion, Holland. c, Paddle steamer Arctic, 1850. d, Peruvian swimming couriers. e, First London post box, 1855. f, Indian mail cart, 1870. g, Balloon post, 1870. h, Bath Mail Coach. i, Postrider, 1837.

No. 2272: a, Northeastern Railway post office. b, Traveling post office, 1838. c, American Express. d, Graf Zeppelin. e, Columbia Post airplane, 1925. f, Calcutta flying boat. g, Junkers JU-52/3M mail plane. h, Douglas M2 mail plane. i, US air mail service, DH-4.

No. 2273: a, First Atlantic Airways. b, Morris post office van, 1931. c, Swiss post-passenger bus. d, Westland-Sikorsky S51 helicopter mail flight. e, Union Pacific Railway. f, Boeing Model 314 flying boat, Yankee Clipper. g, Boeing 747. h, Concorde. i, Apollo 11, US #C76.

No. 2274, Mounted postilion. No. 2275, Thurn & Taxis #7. No. 2276, Thurn & Taxis #45.

1990, May 3

2268	A122	$15.30	Sheet of 9, #a.-i.	9.00	9.00
2269	A122	$15.30	Sheet of 9, #a.-i.	9.00	9.00
2270	A122	$15.30	Sheet of 9, #a.-i.	9.00	9.00
2271	A122	$17.80	Sheet of 9, #a.-i.	10.00	10.00
2272	A122	$20	Sheet of 9, #a.-i.	11.00	11.00
2273	A122	$20	Sheet of 9, #a.-i.	11.00	11.00
		Nos. 2268-2273 (6)		59.00	59.00

Souvenir Sheets

2274	A122	$150	multi	7.50	7.50
2275	A122	$150	multi	7.50	7.50
2276	A122	$150	multi	7.50	7.50

For overprint see No. 2551.

Nos. 1028, 1032, 1055, 1085, 1107 Surcharged "ROTARY / DISTRICT 405 / 9th CONFERENCE / MAY 1990 / GEORGETOWN"

Unwmk.

1990, May 8   Litho.   *Perf. 14*

Design A91

Plate Numbers in Parentheses

2277		80c	on 55c #1032 (9)	
2278		80c	on 55c #1085 (49)	
2279		80c	on 55c #1107 (64)	
2280		$6.40	on 130c #1028 (6)	
2281		$6.40	on 130c #1055 (25)	
2282		$7.65	on 130c #1055 (25)	
		Nos. 2277-2282 (6)		10.00

Nos. 2208-2215 Overprinted

90th Birthday
H.M. The Queen Mother

1990, June 8   Litho.   *Perf. 14*

2283	A115	80c	on #2208	1.75	.45
2284	A115	$2.25	on #2209	2.00	.45
2285	A115	$5	on #2210	2.50	.65
2286	A115	$6.40	on #2211	2.75	.65
2287	A115	$7.65	on #2212	3.00	.90
2288	A115	$8.90	on #2213	3.25	1.00
2289	A115	$25	on #2214	6.00	6.00
2290	A115	$100	on #2215	15.00	15.00
		Nos. 2283-2290 (8)		36.25	25.10

See Nos. E26-E27.

Locomotives — A123

1990, July 15   *Perf. 14x13½*

2291	A123	$2.55	Class 3F	
2292	A123	$2.55	Class A4	
2293	A123	$2.55	Liner Class A34	
2294	A123	$2.55	Pacific Class	
2295	A123	$2.55	Grange Class	
		Nos. 2291-2295 (5)		13.50

Souvenir Sheets

Perf. 13½x14, 14x13½

2296	A123	$20	Castle Class, vert.	
2297	A123	$20	Southern Railway	
		Nos. 2296-2297 (2)		22.50

Still Life with Guitar, by Picasso — A124

Paintings: No. 2299, Horseman, by Velazquez. No. 2300, Sunflowers, by Van Gogh, vert. No. 2301, Man Wearing Striped Shirt, by Miro, vert. No. 2302, Franz von Taxis, by Durer, vert. No. 2303, Virgin and Child, by Titian, vert. No. 2304, Presentation of Marie de Medici, by Rubens, vert.

Perf. 14x13½, 13½x14

1990, Aug. 1 **Litho.**

2298	A124	$2.55	multicolored	
2299	A124	$2.55	multicolored	
2300	A124	$2.55	multicolored	
2301	A124	$2.55	multicolored	
2302	A124	$2.55	multicolored	
		Nos. 2298-2302 (5)		11.50

Souvenir Sheets

2303	A124	$20	multicolored	
2304	A124	$20	multicolored	
		Nos. 2303-2304 (2)		18.00

Postal System of Thurn and Taxis, 500th anniv. (#2302). Titian, 500th birth anniv. (#2303). Rubens, 350th death anniv. (#2304).

Birds — A125

Designs: 80c, Guiana partridge, horiz. $2.55, Collared trogon. $3.25, Derby aracari. $5, Black-necked aracari. $5.10, Green aracari. $5.80, Ivory-billed aracari. $6.40, Guiana toucanet. $6.50, Sulphur-breasted toucan. $7.55, Red-billed toucan. $7.65, Toco toucan. $8.25, Natterers toucanet. $8.90, Welcome trogon. $9.75, Doubtful trogon. $11.40, Banded aracari. $12.65, Golden-headed train bearer. $12.80, Rufus-breasted hermit. $13.90, Band-tail barbthroat. $15.30, White-tipped sickle bill. $17.80, Black jacobin. $19.20, Fiery topaz. $22.95, Tufted coquette. $26.70, Ecuadorian pied-tail. $30, Quetzal. $50, Green-crowned brilliant. $100, Emerald-chinned hummingbird. $190, Lazuline sabrewing. $225, Berylline hummingbird.

1990, Sept. 12 **Litho.** **Perf. 14**

2305	A125	80c	multi	.25	.25
2306	A125	$2.55	multi	.25	.25
2307	A125	$3.25	multi	.25	.25
2308	A125	$5	multi	.25	.25
2309	A125	$5.10	multi	.25	.25
2310	A125	$5.80	multi	.25	.25
2311	A125	$6.40	multi	.25	.25
2312	A125	$6.50	multi	.25	.25
2313	A125	$7.55	multi	.35	.35
2314	A125	$7.65	multi	.45	.45
2315	A125	$8.25	multi	.55	.55
2316	A125	$8.90	multi	.65	.65
2317	A125	$9.75	multi	.65	.65
2318	A125	$11.40	multi	.70	.70
2319	A125	$12.65	multi	.75	.75
2320	A125	$12.80	multi	.80	.80
2321	A125	$13.90	multi	.90	.90
2322	A125	$15.30	multi	1.10	1.10
2323	A125	$17.80	multi	1.25	1.25
2324	A125	$19.20	multi	1.40	1.40
2325	A125	$22.95	multi	1.60	1.60
2326	A125	$26.70	multi	1.90	1.90
2327	A125	$30	multi	2.00	2.00
2328	A125	$50	multi	3.25	3.25
2329	A125	$100	multi	6.00	6.00
2330	A125	$190	multi	11.50	11.50
2331	A125	$225	multi	14.00	14.00
		Nos. 2305-2331 (27)		51.80	51.80

Butterflies — A126

No. 2340: a, Thecla falerina. b, Pheles heliconides. c, Echenais leucocyana. d, Heliconius xanthocles. e, Mesopthalma idotea. f, Parides aeneas. g, Heliconius numata. h, Thecla critola. i, Themone pais. j, Nymula agle. k, Adelpha cocala. l, Anaea eribotes. m, Prepona demophon. n, Selenophanes cassiope. o, Consul hippona. p, Antirrhaea avernus.

No. 2341: a, Thecla telemus. b, Thyridia confusa. c, Heliconius burneyi. d, Parides lysander. e, Eunica orphise. f, Adelpha melona. g, Morpho menelaus. h, Nymula phylleus. i, Stalachtis phlegia. j, Theope barea. k, Morpho perseus. l, Lycorea ceres. m, Archonias bellona. n, Caerois chorinaeus. o, Vila azeca. p, Nessaea batesii.

No. 2342: a, Heliconius silvana. b, Eunica alcmena. c, Mechanitis polymnia. d, Mesosemia ephyne. e, Thecla erema. f, Callizona acesta. g, Stalachtis phaedusa. h, Battus belus. i, Nymula philiasus. j, Parides childrenae. k, Stalachtis euterpe. l, Dysmathia portia. m, Tithorea hermias. n, Prepona pheridamas. o, Dismorphia fortunata. p, Hamadryas amphinome.

No. 2343: a, Heliconius vetustus. b, Mesosemia eumene. c, Parides phosphorus. d, Polystichtis emylius. e, Xanthocleis aedesia. f, Doxocopa agathina. g, Adelpha plesaure. h, Heliconius wallacei. i, Notheme eumeus. j, Melinaea mediatrix. k, Theritas coronata. l, Dismorphia orise. m, Phyciodes ianthe. n, Morpho aega. o, Zaretis isidora. p, Pierella lena.

Nos. 2340-2341 are horiz.

1990, Sept. 26 **Litho.** **Perf. 14**

2332	A126	80c	Melinaea idae	.85	.85
2333	A126	$2.55	Rhetus dysonii	.85	.85
2334	A126	$5	Actinote anteas	.85	.85
2335	A126	$6.40	Heliconius tales	.85	.85
2336	A126	$7.65	Thecla telemus	.85	.85
2337	A126	$8.90	Theope eudocia	1.10	1.10
2338	A126	$50	Heliconius vicini	4.50	4.50
2339	A126	$100	Amarynthis meneria	9.50	9.50
		Nos. 2332-2339 (8)		19.35	19.35

Miniature Sheets

2340	A126	$10	Sheet of 16, #a.-p.	16.00 16.00
2341	A126	$10	Sheet of 16, #a.-p.	16.00 16.00
2342	A126	$10	Sheet of 16, #a.-p.	16.00 16.00
2343	A126	$10	Sheet of 16, #a.-p.	16.00 16.00

Souvenir Sheets

2344	A126	$150	Heliconius aoede	10.00 10.00
2345	A126	$150	Phyciodes clio, horiz.	10.00 10.00
2346	A126	$190	Nymphidium caricae	15.00 15.00
2347	A126	$190	Thecla hemon	15.00 15.00

For surcharges see #2415-2425, 2596-2606.

Mushrooms A127

1990, Oct. 12

2348	A127	$2.55	Oudemanseilla mucida	
2349	A127	$2.55	Phollota squarosa	
2350	A127	$2.55	Coprinus comatus	
2351	A127	$2.55	Anellaria semiovaja	
		Nos. 2348-2351 (4)		14.00

Souvenir Sheet

2352	A127	$20	Phallus impudicus	14.00

Sailing Ships — A128

1990, Oct. 12

2353	A128	$2.55	Brig century	
2354	A128	$2.55	Dutch marine ship	
2355	A128	$2.55	Galleon, 1588	
2356	A128	$2.55	Warship, 16th cent.	
2357	A128	$2.55	Hulk, 17th cent.	
		Nos. 2353-2357 (5)		13.00

Souvenir Sheet

2358	A128	$20	Dutch ships, 16th-17th cent.	14.00

No. 2358 printed in continuous design. Discovery of America, 500th anniv. (in 1992).

Flora — A129

Orchids: $7.65, Vanilla inodora. $8.90, Epidendrum ibaguense. No. 858, Maxillaria parkeri. $15.30, Epidendrum nocturnum. $17.80, Catasetum discolor. $20, Scuticaria hadwenii. $25, Epidendrum fragrans. $100, Epistephium parviflorum.

No. 2367: a, Dichea muricata. b, Octomeria erosilabia. c, Spiranthes orchiodes. d, Brassavola nodosa. e, Epidendrum rigidum. f, Brassia caudata. g, Pleurothallis diffusa. h, Aspasia variegata. i, Stenia pallida. j, Cyrtopodium punctatum. k, Cattleya deckeri. l, Cryptarrhena lunata. m, Cattleya violacea. n, Caularthron bicornutum. o, Oncidium carthagenense. p, Galeandra devoniana.

No. 2368: a, Bifrenaria aurantiaca. b, Epidendrum ciliare. c, Dichaea picta. d, Scaphyglottis violacea. e, Cattleya percivaliana. f, Map of Guyana (no flower). g, Epidendrum difforme. h, Eulophia maculata. i, Spiranthes tenuis. j, Peristeria guttata. k, Pleurothallis pruinosa. l, Cleistes rosea. m, Maxillaria variabilis. n, Brassavola cucullata. o, Epidendrum moyobambae. p, Oncidium orthostates.

No. 2369: a, Brassavola martiana. b, Paphinia cristata. c, Aganisia pulchella. d, Oncidium lanceanum. e, Lockhartia imbricata. f, Caularthron bilamellatum. g, Oncidium nanum. h, Pleurothallis ovalifolia. i, Galeandra dives. j, Cycnoches loddigesii. k, Ada aurantiaca. l, Catasetum barbatum. m, Palmorchis pubescens. n, Epidendrum anceps. o, Huntleya meleagris. p, Sobralia sessilis.

No. 2370: a, Maxillaria camaridii. b, Vanilla pompona. c, Stanhopea grandiflora. d, Oncidium pusillum. e, Polycycnis vittata. f, Cattleya lawrenceana. g, Menadenium labiosum. h, Rodriguezia secunda. i, Mormodes buccinator. j, Otostylis brachystalix. k, Maxillaria discolor. l, Liparis elata. m, Gongora maculata. n, Koellensteinia graminea. o, Rudolfiella aurantiaca. p, Scuticaria steelei.

Flowering Trees: No. 2371: a, Cochlospermum vitifolium. b, Eugenia malaccensis. c, Plumiera rubra. d, Erythrina glauca. e, Spathodea campanulata. f, Jacaranda filicifolia. g, Samanea saman. h, Cassia fistula. i, Abutilon integrimum. j, Lagerstroemia speciosa. k, Tabebuia serratifolia. l, Guaiacum officinale. m, Solanum macranthum. n, Peltophorum roxburghii. o, Bauhinia variegata. p, Plumiera alba.

Flowering Vines: No. 2372: a, Gloriosa rothschildiana. b, Pseudocalymma alliaceum. c, Callichlamys latifolia. d, Distictis riversii. e, Maurandya barclaiana. f, Beaumontia fragrans. g, Phaseolus caracalla. h, Mandevilla splendens. i, Solandra longiflora. j, Passiflora coccinea. k, Allamanda cathartica. l, Bauhinia galpini. m, Verbena maritima. n, Mandevilla suaveolens. o, Phryganocydia corymbosa. p, Jasminum sambac.

1990, Oct. 16 **Litho.** **Perf. 14**

2359	A129	$7.65	multicolored	.40	.40
2360	A129	$8.90	multicolored	.55	.55
2361	A129	$12.80	multicolored	.85	.85
2362	A129	$15.30	multicolored	.90	.90
2363	A129	$17.80	multicolored	1.00	1.00
2364	A129	$20	multicolored	1.25	1.25
2365	A129	$25	multicolored	1.50	1.50
2366	A129	$100	multicolored	6.50	6.50
		Nos. 2359-2366 (8)		12.95	12.95

Miniature Sheets

2367	A129	$10	Sheet of 16, #a.-p.	8.00 8.00
2368	A129	$10	Sheet of 16, #a.-p.	8.00 8.00
2369	A129	$12.80	Sheet of 16, #a.-p.	12.00 12.00
2370	A129	$12.80	Sheet of 16, #a.-p.	12.00 12.00
2371	A129	$12.80	Sheet of 16, #a.-p.	12.00 12.00
2372	A129	$12.80	Sheet of 16, #a.-p.	12.00 12.00
		Nos. 2367-2372 (6)		64.00 64.00

Souvenir Sheets

2373	A129	$150	Coleandra devoniana	9.00 9.00
2374	A129	$150	Delonix regia	9.00 9.00
2375	A129	$150	Hexisea bidentata	9.00 9.00
2376	A129	$150	Lecythis ollaria	9.00 9.00
2377	A129	$190	Ionopsis utricularioides	11.00 11.00
		Nos. 2373-2377 (5)		47.00 47.00

Nos. 2370-2375 are horiz. For surcharges see Nos. 2593-2595.

Souvenir Sheet

Cenozoic Era Wildlife — A130

Designs: a, Palaelodus. b, Archaeotrogon. c, Vulture. d, Bradyrus tridactylus. e, Natalus stramineus bat. f, Cebidae. g, Cuvieronius. h, Phororhacos. i, Smilodectes. j, Megatherium. k, Titanotylopus. l, Teleoceras. m, Macrauchenia. n, Mylodon. o, Smilodon. p, Glyptodon. q, Protohydrocherus. r, Archaeohyrax. s, Pyrotherium. t, Platypittamys.

1990, Nov. 6

2378	A130	$12.80	Sheet of 20, #a.-t.	15.00 15.00

Miniature Sheets

Endangered Wildlife — A131

#2379: a, Ivory-billed woodpecker. b, Cauca guan. c, Sun conure. d, Quetzal. e, Long-wattled umbrellabird. f, Banded cotinga. g, Blue-chested parakeet. h, Rufous-bellied chachalaca. i, Yellow-faced amazon. j, Toucan barbet. k, Red siskin. l, Cock-of-the-rock. m, Hyacinth macaw. n, Yellow cardinal. o, Bare-necked umbrellabird. p, Saffron toucanette. q, Red-billed curassow. r, Spectacled parrotlet. s, Lovely cotinga. t, Black-breasted gnateater.

#2380: a, Swallow-tailed kite. b, Hoatzin. c, Ruby topaz hummingbird. d, Black vulture. e, Rufous-tailed jacamar. f, Scarlet macaw. g, Rose-breasted thrush tanager. h, Toco toucan. i, Bearded bellbird. j, Blue-crowned motmot. k, Green oropendola. l, Pompadour cotinga. m, Vermilion flycatcher. n, Blue and yellow macaw. o, White-barred piculet. p, Great razor-billed curassow. q, Ruddy quail-dove. r, Paradise tanager. s, Anhinga. t, Greater flamingo.

#2381: a, Harpy eagle. b, Andean condor. c, Amazonian umbrellabird. d, Spider monkeys. e, Hyacinth macaw, diff. f, Red siskin, diff. g, Toucan barbet, diff. h, Three-toed sloth. i, Guanaco. j, Spectacled bear. k, White-lipped peccary. l, Maned wolf. m, Jaguar. n, Spectacled caiman. o, Giant armadillo. p, Giant anteater. q, South American river otter. r, Yapok. s, Central American river turtle. t, Cauca guan, diff.

Perf. 14x13½, 13½x14

1990, Nov. 6 **Litho.**

2379	A131	$12.80	Sheet of 20, #a.-t.	22.50 22.50
2380	A131	$12.80	Sheet of 20, #a.-t.	22.50 22.50
2381	A131	$12.80	Sheet of 20, #a.-t.	22.50 22.50

#2381a-2381t are horiz. #2380s incorrectly inscribed Anhigna. See #E29-E30.

Numbers have been reserved for additional values in this set.

Independence, 25th Anniv. — A132

Illustration reduced.

1991, June 25   Litho.   Imperf.
2389 A132 $225 multicolored   10.00 10.00

Miniature Sheets

Olympic
Gold
Medal
Winners
A133

No. 2390: a, Ramon Fonst. b, Lucien Gaudin. c, Ole A. Lilloe-Olsen. d, Morris Fisher. e, Ray C. Ewry. f, Hubert Van Innes. g, Alvin Kraenzlein. h, Johnny Weissmuller. i, Hans Winkler.

No. 2391: a, Viktor Chukarin. b, Agnes Keleti. c, Barbel Wochel. d, Eric Heiden. e, Alvodar Gerevich. f, Guiseppe Delfino. g, Alexander Tikhonov. h, C.F. Pahud de Mortanges. i, Patricia McCormick.

No. 2392: a, Nelli Kim. b, Viktor Krovopuskov. c, Viktor Sidiak. d, Nikolai Andrianov. e, Nadia Comaneci. f, Mitsuo Tsukahara. g, Yelena Novikova-Belova. h, John Naber. i, Kornelia Ender.

No. 2393: a, Olga Korbut. b, Lyudmila Turischeva. c, Lasse Viren. d, George Miez. e, Roland Matthes. f, Pal Kovaks. g, Jesse Owens. h, Mark Spitz. i, Eduardo Mangiarotti.

No. 2394: a, Sawao Kato. b, Rudolf Karpati. c, Jeno Fuchs. d, Emil Zatopek. e, Fanny Blankers-Koen. f, Melvin Sheppard. g, Gert Fredriksson. h, Paul Elvstrom. i, Harrison W. Dillard.

No. 2395: a, Lydia Skoblikova. b, Ivar Ballangrud. c, Clas Thunberg. d, Anton Heida. e, Akinori Nakayama. f, Sixten Jernberg. g, Yevgeniy Grischin. h, Paul Radmilovic. i, Charles Daniels.

No. 2396: a, Betty Cuthbert. b, Vera Caslavska. c, Galina Kulakova. d, Yukio Endo. e, Vladimir Morozov. f, Boris Shaklin. g, Don Schollander. h, Gyozo Kulscar. i, Christian D'Oriola.

No. 2397: a, Al Oerter. b, Polina Astakhova. c, Takashi Ono. d, Valentin Muratov. e, Henri St. Cyr. f, Iain Murray Rose. g, Larissa Latynina. h, Carlo Pavesi. i, Dawn Fraser.

No. 2398, Paavo Nurmi, vert. No. 2399, Johannes Kolehmainen, vert. $190. Nedo Nadi, vert.

1991, Aug. 12   Litho.   Perf. 14x13½
2390 A133 $15.30 Sheet of 9,
                    #a.-i.   5.75   5.75
2391 A133 $17.80 Sheet of 9,
                    #a.-i.   6.75   6.75
2392 A133 $20 Sheet of 9,
                    #a.-i.   7.25   7.25
2393 A133 $20 Sheet of 9,
                    #a.-i.   7.25   7.25
2394 A133 $25 Sheet of 9,
                    #a.-i.   9.50   9.50
2395 A133 $25 Sheet of 9,
                    #a.-i.   9.50   9.50
2396 A133 $30 Sheet of 9,
                    #a.-i.   11.50 11.50
2397 A133 $30 Sheet of 9,
                    #a.-i.   11.50 11.50
      Nos. 2390-2397 (8)   69.00 69.00

Souvenir Sheets
Perf. 13x13½
2398 A133 $150 multicolored   5.50   5.50
2399 A133 $150 multicolored   5.50   5.50
2400 A133 $190 multicolored   7.00   7.00

For overprints see Nos. 2552-2557.

Discovery of America, 500th Anniv. (in 1992) — A134

Birds: $6.40, Phoenicopterus ruber. $7.65, Ostinops decumanus. $50, Falco peregrinus. $100, Nymphicus hollandicus. $190, Vultur feriphus. $260, Merganetta armata, horiz.

1991, Sept. 15   Litho.   Perf. 13½x14
2401 A134 $6.40 multicolored
2402 A134 $7.65 multicolored
2403 A134 $50 multicolored
2404 A134 $100 multicolored
2405 A134 $190 multicolored
      Nos. 2401-2405 (5)   16.50

Souvenir Sheet
Perf. 14x13½
2406 A134 $260 multicolored 15.00

A135

Various orchids.

Perf. 13½x14, 14x13½
1991, Sept. 30
2407 A135 $6.40 multicolored
2408 A135 $7.65 multi, horiz.
2409 A135 $50 multicolored
2410 A135 $100 multicolored
2411 A135 $190 Odontoglossum
      Nos. 2407-2411 (5)   8.00

Souvenir Sheets
2412 A135 $360 multicolored
2413 A135 $360 Cycnoches
                  ventricosum
2414 A135 $360 Miltonia
                  hibrida,
                  horiz.
      Nos. 2412-2414 (3)   22.50

Nos. 2332-2339, 2343-2345 Ovptd. or Surcharged

Overprints: 80c, $2.55, Nos. 2421-2422, 2423a, 2423p, Rotary emblem and "1905-1990." $5.00, $6.40, $7.65, Nos. 2420, 2423d, 2423m, Rotary emblem and "Paul Percy Harris Founder 1868-1947" on 2 or 3 lines. Nos. 2423b, 2423l, 2423n, Boy Scout emblem and "1907-1992." Nos. 2423c, 2423i, 2423o, Lions Intl. emblem and "1917-1992." Nos. 2423e, 2423h, Red Cross emblem and "125 Years / Red Cross." Nos. 2423f-2423g, 2423j-2423k have parts of larger Rotary emblem. Nos. 2424-2425 ovptd. with service emblems in sheet margins.

1991, Oct. 29   Perfs. as Before
2415 A126 80c on #2332   .25   .25
2416 A126 $2.55 on #2333   .25   .25
2417 A126 $5 on #2334   .25   .25
2418 A126 $6.40 on #2335   .25   .25
2419 A126 $7.65 on #2336   .25   .25
2420 A126 $100 on $8.90
                  #2337   2.75   2.75
2421 A126 $190 on $50
                  #2338   5.00   5.00
2422 A126 $225 on $100
                  #2339   5.75   5.75
      Nos. 2415-2422 (8)   14.75 14.75

Miniature Sheet
2423 A126   Sheet of 16   12.00 12.00
  a.-l. $10 any single   .25   .25
  m. $50 on $10 #2343m   1.25   1.25
  n. $75 on $10 #2343n   1.75   1.75
  o. $100 on $10 #2343o   2.25   2.25
  p. $190 on $10 #2343p   4.25   4.25

Souvenir Sheets
2424 A126 $400 on $150
                  #2344   12.00 12.00
2425 A126 $500 on $150
                  #2345   14.00 14.00

Swiss Confederation, 700th Anniv. — A136

Designs: $6.40, Painting by Diego Giacometti. $7.65, Swiss puppets. $50, Man in top hat by Goya. $100, Stained glass window of Mary & Joseph. $190, Stained glass window of Jesus healing the sick. No. 2431, Ship's cross-section, by Le Corbusier. No. 2432, Portrait of Giovanna Tornabuoni.

1991, Oct. 30   Perf. 13½x14
2426 A136 $6.40 multicolored
2427 A136 $7.65 multicolored
2428 A136 $50 multicolored
2429 A136 $100 multicolored
2430 A136 $190 multicolored
  a.   Sheet of 5 + label, #2426-
        2430   12.00

Souvenir Sheets
2431 A136 $360 multicolored
2432 A136 $360 multicolored
      Nos. 2431-2432 (2)   25.00

Phila Nippon '91 — A137

Trains: $6.40, Class 581 12-car. $7.65, Class EF-81. $50, Class 381 9-car. $100, Kodama 8-car. $190, Shin-Kansen 16-car. No. 2438, Shin-Kansen 16-car, diff. No. 2439, Japanese locomotives in Calcutta.

1991, Nov. 16   Perf. 14x13½
2433 A137 $6.40 multicolored
2434 A137 $7.65 multicolored
2435 A137 $50 multicolored
2436 A137 $100 multicolored
2437 A137 $190 multicolored
      Nos. 2433-2437 (5)   16.50

Souvenir Sheets
2438 A137 $360 multicolored
2439 A137 $360 multicolored
      Nos. 2438-2439 (2)   32.50

Swiss Confederation, 700th anniv., #2439.

Common Design Types pictured following the introduction.

Royal Family Birthday, Anniversary
Common Design Type

1991, Nov.   Litho.   Perf. 14
2440 CD347 $8.90 multi   .35   .20
2441 CD347 $12.80 multi   .35   .30
2442 CD347 $15.30 multi   .35   .30
2443 CD347 $50 multi   1.25   1.10
2444 CD347 $75 multi   1.75   1.75
2445 CD347 $100 multi   2.50   2.50
2446 CD347 $130 multi   3.00   3.00
2447 CD347 $150 multi   3.75   3.75
2448 CD347 $190 multi   5.00   5.00
2449 CD347 $200 multi   5.25   5.25
      Nos. 2440-2449 (10)   23.55 23.15

Souvenir Sheets
2450 CD347 $225 Elizabeth   6.50   6.50
2451 CD347 $225 Charles,
                  Diana,
                  sons   7.00   7.00

$8.90, $50, $75, $190, No. 2451, Charles and Diana, 10th wedding anniversary. $130, $150, Prince Philip, 70th birthday. Others, Queen Elizabeth II, 65th birthday.

Japanese Attack on Pearl Harbor, 50th Anniv. A138

No. 2452: a, Akagi launches attack planes. b, Sakamaki's midget submarine beached. c, Mistubishi ASM Zero fighter. d, USS Arizona under attack. e, Aichi D3A1 Val dive bomber. f, USS California. g, P40 defends Pearl Harbor. h, USS Cassin and Downes hit at dry dock. i, B17 crash lands at Bellows Point. j, USS Nevada burns at Hospital Point.

1991, Dec. 7   Perf. 14½x15
2452 A138 $50 Sheet of 10,
                  #a.-j.   17.00 17.00

1992 Winter Olympics, Albertville — A139

Walt Disney characters at the Olympics: $6.40, Gus Gander playing ice hockey. $7.65, Mickey, Minnie in bobsled. $8.90, Huey, Dewey, Louie pretending to luge. $12.80, Goofy freestyle skiing. $50, Goofy ski jumping. $100, Donald, Daisy Duck speed skating. $130, Pluto cross-country skiing. $190, Mickey, Minnie ice dancing. No. 2461, Scrooge McDuck slalom skiing. No. 2462, Huey curling.

1991, Dec. 12   Perf. 13½x13
2453 A139 $6.40 multi   .40   .40
2454 A143 $7.65 multi   .45   .45
2455 A143 $8.90 multi   .50   .50
2456 A143 $12.80 multi   .70   .70
2457 A143 $50 multi   1.50   1.50
2458 A139 $100 multi   2.50   2.50
2459 A139 $130 multi   3.00   3.00
2460 A143 $190 multi   4.50   4.50
      Nos. 2453-2460 (8)   13.55 13.55

Souvenir Sheets
2461 A139 $225 multi   7.00   7.00
2462 A143 $225 multi   7.00   7.00

Mushrooms — A140

Designs: $6.40, Boletus satanoides. $7.65, Russula nigricans. $50, Cortinarius glaucopus. $100, Lactarius camphoratus. $190, Cortinarius callisteus. No. 2468, Russula integra. No. 2469, Coprinus micaceus, vert.

1991, Dec. 16   Litho.   Perf. 14x13½
2463 A140 $6.40 multicolored
2464 A140 $7.65 multicolored
2465 A140 $50 multicolored
2466 A140 $100 multicolored
2467 A140 $190 multicolored
      Nos. 2463-2467 (5)   16.00 16.00

Souvenir Sheets
Perf. 14x13½, 13½x14
2468 A140 $360 multicolored
2469 A140 $360 multicolored
      Nos. 2468-2469 (2)   30.00

Walt Disney Christmas Cards — A141

Designs and year of issue: 80c, Mickey, friends singing carols, 1989. $2.55, Mickey, friends riding trolley car, 1962. $5, Donald, Pluto wrapping package, 1971. $6.40, Mickey holding candle, 1948. $7.65, Mickey with Santa mask, 1947. $8.90, Pinocchio's shadow, 1939. $50, Three Little Pigs, dancing on wolf's back, 1933. $200, Mickey, mice singing carols, 1949.

No. 2478: a, Conductor, Donald. b, Elephant with book. c, Goofy, centaurs. d, Snow White, dwarfs. e, Pluto, dinosaur.

No. 2479: a, Mickey in sleigh. b, Three little pigs, Winnie-the-Pooh, Bambi. c, Dalmatian, bear, monkey, Lady and the Tramp. d, Alice, Goofy, Mad Hatter. e, Pinocchio, Tinker Bell, Peter Pan, Seven Dwarfs, Donald Duck. f, Pluto, 1974.

No. 2480, Mickey and friends riding in coach, 1932. No. 2481, Mickey, Pluto greeting friends, 1935. No. 2482, Donald, Jose Carioca, 1944. No. 2483, Couple dancing, baseball batter, 1945. No. 2484, Mickey, Donald, Goofy, 1946. No. 2485, Santa in chimney, 1969. No. 2486, Portrait of Winnie-the-Pooh hanging on wall, 1969. No. 2487, Mickey, 1978.

1991, Dec. 17			**Perf. 14x13½**		
2470	A141	80c multi		.25	.20
2471	A141	$2.55 multi		.25	.20
2472	A141	$5 multi		.25	.25
2473	A141	$6.40 multi		.35	.25
2474	A141	$7.65 multi		.35	.25
2475	A141	$8.90 multi		.35	.25
2476	A141	$50 multi		1.40	1.40
2477	A141	$200 multi		5.25	5.25
2478	A141	$50 Strip of 5,		7.00	7.00
		#a.-e.			
2479	A141	$50 Strip of 6,		8.50	8.50
		#a.-f.			
	Nos. 2470-2479 (10)			23.95	23.55
	Souvenir Sheets				
2480	A141	$260 multi		6.00	6.00
2481	A141	$260 multi		6.00	6.00
2482	A141	$260 multi		6.00	6.00
2483	A141	$260 multi		6.00	6.00
2484	A141	$260 multi		6.00	6.00
2485	A141	$260 multi		6.00	6.00
2486	A141	$260 multi		6.00	6.00
2487	A141	$260 multi		6.00	6.00
	Nos. 2480-2487 (8)			48.00	48.00

Nos. 2478a-2478e, 2479a-2479f, 2480-2481, 2485 and 2487 are vert.

No. 2377 Surcharged

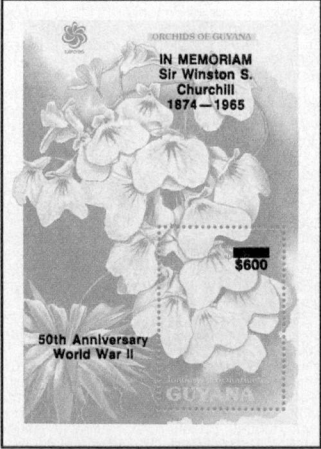

1991, Dec. 19		**Litho.**		**Perf. 14**	
2487B	A129	$600 on $190 #2377			

An additional sheet was issued in this set. The editors would like to examine it.

Christmas
A142

Paintings: $6.40, Madonna and Child with Angels, by Titian, horiz. $7.65, Madonna and Child with Angels, by Rubens. $50, Madonna and Child, by Raphael. $100, Madonna and Child, by Durer. $190, Madonna, by Durer. No. 2493, Madonna and Child by Rubens, horiz. No. 2494, Madonna, by Durer, diff.

1991, Dec. 30	**Perf. 14x13½, 13½x14**			
2488	A142	$6.40 multicolored		
2489	A142	$7.65 multicolored		
2490	A142	$50 multicolored		
2491	A142	$100 multicolored		
2492	A142	$190 multicolored		
	Nos. 2488-2 92(5)		15.00	
	Souvenir Sheets			
2493	A142	$360 multicolored		
2494	A142	$360 multicolored		
	Nos. 2493-2494 (2)		35.00	

Brandenburg Gate, Bicent. — A143

Designs: $10, Map of Berlin. $25, US Pres. George Bush, Polish Pres. Lech Walesa. $100, German Chancellor Helmut Kohl, Foreign Minister Hans-Dietrich Genscher. $190, Armored helmet.

1991, Dec.			**Perf. 14**		
2495	A143	$10 multicolored		.40	.40
2496	A143	$25 multicolored		.90	.90
2497	A143	$100 multicolored		3.25	3.25
	Nos. 2495-2497 (3)			4.55	4.55
	Souvenir Sheet				
2498	A143	$190 multicolored		6.50	6.50

Wolfgang Amadeus Mozart, Death Bicent. A144

Portrait of Mozart and: $75, Laxenburg. $80, Death of Leopold II. $100, Mozart's birthplace, Salzburg.

1991, Dec.					
2499	A144	$75 multicolored		2.50	2.50
2500	A144	$80 multicolored		2.75	2.75
2501	A144	$100 multicolored		3.00	3.00
	Nos. 2499-2501 (3)			8.25	8.25
	Souvenir Sheet				
2502	A144	$190 Bust of Mozart, vert.		6.00	6.00

17th World Scout Jamboree, Korea — A145

Designs: $30, Scouts hiking. $40, Emblems, flag. $100, Lord Baden-Powell, vert. $190, Rocket cover with US No. 1145.

1991, Dec.					
2503	A145	$25 multicolored		1.00	1.00
2504	A145	$30 multicolored		1.10	1.10
2505	A145	$40 multicolored		1.25	1.25
2506	A145	$100 multicolored		3.25	3.25
	Nos. 2503-2506 (4)			6.60	6.60
	Souvenir Sheet				
2507	A145	$190 multicolored		6.50	6.50

Charles de Gaulle
A146

De Gaulle: $60, In Venice, 1944. $75, With Khrushchev, 1960. $80, In Algiers, 1958. $100, With Pope Paul VI, 1967.

1991, Dec.					
2508	A146	$60 multicolored		2.00	2.00
2509	A146	$75 multicolored		2.50	2.50
2510	A146	$80 multicolored		2.75	2.75
2511	A146	$100 multicolored		3.25	3.25
	Nos. 2508-2511 (4)			10.50	10.50
	Souvenir Sheets				
2512	A146	$150 Portrait, vert.		7.50	7.50
2513	A146	$190 Portrait, diff, vert.		9.75	9.75

Anniversaries and Events — A147

Designs: No. 2515, Caroline Herschel, astronomer, Old Town Hall, Hanover. No. 2516, Map of Switzerland, woman in traditional dress. $80, Otto Lilienthal's glider No. 3. $100, Locomotive. $190, Arms of Bern and Solothurn.

1991, Dec.					
2515	A147	$75 multicolored		4.00	4.00
2516	A147	$75 multicolored		3.25	3.25
2517	A147	$80 multicolored		3.75	3.75
2518	A147	$100 multicolored		5.00	5.00
	Nos. 2515-2518 (4)			16.00	16.00
	Souvenir Sheet				
2519	A147	$190 multicolored		5.75	5.75

Hanover, 750th anniv. (#2515), Swiss Confederation, 700th anniv. (#2516, 2519), first glider flight, cent. (#2517), Trans-Siberian Railway, cent. (#2518).

Discovery of America, 500th Anniv. A148

Designs: $6.40, Columbus lands on Trinidad. $7.65, Columbus, globe. $8.90, Ships blown off course by hurricane. $12.80, Map, hands in chains. $15.30, Land sighted. $50, Nina, Pinta. $75, Santa Maria. $100, Columbus trading with natives. $125, Superstitions & sea monsters. $130, Map, Columbus ashore. $140, Priest & natives. $150, Columbus kneeling before King Ferdinand and Queen Isabella. #2532, Map of New World. #2533, One of Columbus' ships, vert. #2534, Columbus.

1992, Jan. 2			**Perf. 14**		
2520	A148	$6.40 multi		.40	.35
2521	A148	$7.65 multi		.45	.40
2522	A148	$8.90 multi		.50	.45
2523	A148	$12.80 multi		.55	.50
2524	A148	$15.30 multi		.60	.55
2525	A148	$50 multi		1.75	1.75
2526	A148	$75 multi		2.25	2.25
2527	A148	$100 multi		3.00	3.00
2528	A148	$125 multi		3.75	3.75
2529	A148	$130 multi		4.00	4.00
2530	A148	$140 multi		4.25	4.25
2531	A148	$150 multi		4.50	4.50
	Nos. 2520-2531 (12)			26.00	25.75
	Souvenir Sheets				
2532	A148	$280 multi		8.50	8.50
2533	A148	$280 multi		8.50	8.50
2534	A148	$280 multi		8.50	8.50

Movie Posters — A149

Designs: $8.90, The Great K & A Train Robbery. $12.80, Cimarron. $15.30, Buzzin' Around. $25, Adventures of Captain Marvel. $30, The Mummy. $50, A Sainted Devil. $75, A Tale of Two Cities. $100, A Tugboat Romeo. $130, Thief of Bagdad. $150, Bacon Grabbers. $190, A Night at the Opera. $200, Citizen Kane. No. 2547, She Done Him Wrong. No. 2548, The Circus. No. 2549, Babe Comes Home. No. 2550, Zeppelin, horiz.

1992, Mar. 11	**Litho.**		**Perf. 14**		
2535	A149	$8.90 multi		.60	.50
2536	A149	$12.80 multi		.65	.55
2537	A149	$15.30 multi		.70	.65
2538	A149	$25 multi		.80	.75
2539	A149	$30 multi		.90	.85
2540	A149	$75 multi		1.50	1.40
2541	A149	$75 multi		2.25	2.00
2542	A149	$100 multi		3.00	2.75
2543	A149	$130 multi		3.75	3.50
2544	A149	$150 multi		4.50	4.25
2545	A149	$190 multi		5.75	5.50
2546	A149	$200 multi		6.00	5.75
	Nos. 2535-2546 (12)			30.40	28.45
	Size: 70x100mm, 100x70mm				
	Imperf				
2547	A149	$225 multi		6.75	6.75
2548	A149	$225 multi		6.75	6.75
2549	A149	$225 multi		6.75	6.75
2550	A149	$225 multi		6.75	6.75

No. 2273 Overprinted or Surcharged with Olympic Rings and "ALBERTVILLE '92" or "XVIth Olympic Winter / Games in Albertville" (No. 2551e)

1992		**Perfs. as Before**	
2551	A122	Sheet of 9	
a.-f.		$20 on $20 #2273a-2273f	
g.		$70 on $20 #2273g	
h.		$100 on $20 #2273h	
i.		$190 on $20 #2273i	

Nos. 2391g, 2395c, 2396c, 2398, 2400 Ovptd. "ALBERTVILLE '92"
No. 2399 Ovptd. "Barcelona '92" and emblems in Sheet Margin

1992			**Perfs. as Before**		
2552	A133	$17.80 on #2391g		12.00	12.00
2553	A133	$25 on #2395c		12.00	12.00
2554	A133	$30 on #2396c		12.00	12.00
	Souvenir Sheets				
2555	A133	$150 on #2398		7.00	7.00
2556	A133	$150 on #2399		7.00	7.00
2557	A133	$190 on #2400		7.00	7.00

Nos. 2552-2554 printed in sheets of 9, overprint applied to only one stamp per sheet. Overprint on Nos. 2555, 2557 applied to sheet margin.

Easter
A150

Various details from paintings by Durer: $6.40, $12.80, $50, $130, No. 2567, The Martyrdom of Ten Thousand. $7.65, $15.30, $100, $190, No. 2566, Adoration of the Trinity.

1992	**Litho.**		**Perf. 13½x14**		
2558	A150	$6.40 multi		.30	.20
2559	A150	$7.65 multi		.30	.20
2560	A150	$12.80 multi		.45	.25
2561	A150	$15.30 multi		.55	.45
2562	A150	$50 multi		1.50	1.25
2563	A150	$100 multi		2.75	2.75
2564	A150	$130 multi		3.75	3.75
2565	A150	$190 multi		5.75	5.75
	Nos. 2558-2565 (8)			15.35	14.60

Souvenir Sheets

2566	A150	$225 multi	6.75	6.75
2567	A150	$225 multi	6.75	6.75

Queen Elizabeth II's Accession to the Throne, 40th Anniv.
A151

Queen Elizabeth II: $8.90, With Prince Philip. $12.80, In uniform. $100, At coronation. $130, Wearing black cape and hat. No. 2572, Coronation portrait. No. 2573, Fortieth anniv. portrait.

1992   **Litho.**   **Perf. 14**

2568	A151	$8.90 multicolored	1.00	.50
2569	A151	$12.80 multicolored	1.50	.60
2570	A151	$100 multicolored	5.25	4.00
2571	A151	$130 multicolored	6.25	5.00
		Nos. 2568-2571 (4)	14.00	10.10

Souvenir Sheets

2572	A151	$225 multicolored	7.25	7.25
2573	A151	$225 multicolored	7.25	7.25

Diocese of Guyana, 150th Anniv. A152

Designs: $6.40, Holy Cross Church, Annai Bupununi. $50, St. Peter's Church. $100, St. George's Cathedral, interior, vert. $190, Map, vert. $225, Religious symbols.

1992   **Litho.**   **Perf. 14**

2574	A152	$6.40 multicolored	.40	.30
2575	A152	$50 multicolored	1.25	1.10
2576	A152	$100 multicolored	2.75	2.75
2577	A152	$190 multicolored	4.50	4.50
		Nos. 2574-2577 (4)	8.90	8.65

Souvenir Sheet

2578	A152	$225 multicolored	7.00	7.00

Miniature Sheet

Horses — A153

No. 2579: a, Palomino. b, Appaloosa. c, Clydesdale. d, Arab. e, Morgan. f, Friesian. g, Pinto. h, Thoroughbred. No. 2580, Lipizzaner.

1992, Aug. 10

2579	A153	$190 Sheet of 8, #a.-h.	37.50	37.50

Souvenir Sheet

2580	A153	$190 multicolored	8.00	8.00

No. 2580 contains one 58x29mm stamp.

Cats — A154

No. 2588A: b, Russian blue. c, Havana brown. d, Himalayan. e, Manx. f, Cornish rex. g, Black Persian. h, Scottish fold. i, Siamese.

1992, Aug. 10   **Perf. 14½x14**

2581	A154	$5 Burmese	.30	.20
2582	A154	$6.40 Turkish van	.30	.20
2583	A154	$12.80 American shorthair	.40	.35
2584	A154	$15.30 Egyptian	.55	.50
2585	A154	$50 Egyptian mau	1.75	1.50
2586	A154	$100 Japanese bobtail	3.25	3.25
2587	A154	$130 Abyssinian	4.00	4.00
2588	A154	$225 Oriental shorthair	7.50	7.50
		Nos. 2581-2588 (8)	18.05	17.50

Miniature Sheet
Perf. 14x13½

2588A	A154	$50 Sheet of 8, #b.-i.	12.00	12.00

Souvenir Sheets
Perf. 14x14½

2589	A152	$250 Chartreuse, vert.	7.25	7.25
2590	A154	$250 Turkish angora	7.25	7.25
2591	A154	$250 Maine coon	7.25	7.25
2592	A154	$250 Chinchilla	7.25	7.25

No. 2589 has continuous design. Nos. 2590-2592 are vert. and have continous design.

Nos. 2368-2369 Surcharged on 4 stamps and Overprinted in Red "PHILA NIPPON '91 / WORLD STAMP EXHIBITION NIPPON '91" and Show Emblem in Sheet Margin No. 2376 Surcharged in Red

1992   **Perfs. as Before**

2593	A129	Sheet of 12, #a.-d., #2368a-2368l	19.00
	a.	$25 on $10 #2368m	
	b.	$50 on $10 #2368n	
	c.	$75 on $10 #2368o	
	d.	$130 on $10 #2368p	
2594	A129	Sheet of 16, #a.-d., 2369a-2369l	19.00
	a.	$25 on $12.80 #2369m	
	b.	$50 on $12.80 #2369n	
	c.	$75 on $12.80 #2369o	
	d.	$100 on $12.80 #2369p	

Souvenir Sheet

2595	A129	$250 on $150 #2376	

Nos. 2332-2340, 2346-2347 Overprinted or Surcharged

Overprints: 80c, $2.55, Nos. 2602-2603, Lions emblem and "Lions International / 1917-1992." $5, $6.40, $7.65, Nos. 2601, 2604d, 2604m, Lions emblem and "Melvin Jones Founder 1880-1961" on 2 or 3 lines. Nos. 2604a, 2604p, Lions emblem and "1917-1992." Nos. 2604b, 2604i, 2604o, Rotary emblem and "1905-1990." Nos. 2604c, 2604l, 2604n, Boy Scout emblem and "1907-1992." Nos. 2604e, 2604h, Red Cross emblem and "125 Years Red Cross." Nos. 2604f-2604g, 2604j-2604k have parts of larger Lions emblem. Nos. 2605-2606 have service organization emblems in sheet margins.

1992   **Perfs. as Before**

2596	A126	80c on #2332	
2597	A126	$2.55 on #2333	
2598	A126	$5 on #2334	
2599	A126	$6.40 on #2335	
2600	A126	$7.65 on #2336	
2601	A126	$100 on #8.90 #2337	
2602	A126	$190 on $50 #2338	
2603	A126	$225 on $100 #2339	

Miniature Sheet

2604		Sheet of 16	45.00
	a.-l.	A126 $10 any single	
	m.	A126 $50 on $10 #2340m	
	n.	A126 $75 on $10 #2340n	
	o.	A126 $100 on $10 #2340o	
	p.	A126 $190 on $10 #2340p	

Souvenir Sheets

2605	A126	$400 on $190 #2346	
2606	A126	$500 on $190 #2347	

Elephants — A155

No. 2607: a, Mammoth, Oligocene Epoch. b, Stegodon, mid- Miocene Epoch. c, Mammoth, Pliocene Epoch. d, Hannibal's army crossing Alps. e, Royal elephant of the Maharaja of Mysore, India. f, Elephant pulling tree trunks, Burma. g, Tiger hunt, India. h, Elephant towing raft on River Kwai, Thailand. $225, African elephants, Kenya.

1992, Aug. 10   **Litho.**   **Perf. 14**

2607	A155	$50 Sheet of 8, #a.-h.	16.00	16.00

Souvenir Sheet

2608	A155	$225 multicolored	11.00	11.00

No. 2607 has continuous design.

Animals of Guyana A156

1992, Aug. 10

2609	A156	$8.90 Red howler monkey	.25	.20
2610	A156	$12.80 Ring-tailed coati	.30	.25
2611	A156	$15.30 Jaguar	.40	.35
2612	A156	$25 Two-toed sloth	.65	.60
2613	A156	$50 Giant armadillo	1.40	1.25
2614	A156	$75 Giant anteater	2.00	2.00
2615	A156	$100 Capybara	2.75	2.75
2616	A156	$130 Ocelot	3.50	3.50
		Nos. 2609-2616 (8)	11.25	10.90

Souvenir Sheets

2617	A156	$225 Wooly opossum, vert.	7.00	7.00
2618	A156	$225 Night monkey, vert.	7.00	7.00

Souvenir Sheet

Statue of Liberty, New York — A157

1992, Oct. 28

2619	A157	$325 multicolored	11.00	11.00

Postage Stamp Mega Event '92, New York City.

Miniature Sheets

Model Trains A158

Marklin toy locomotives: No. 2620a, 2-4-4-2 Crocodile locomotive, 1 gauge, 1933. b, French prototype streetcar, 1 gauge, 1933. c, British prototype Flatiron 2-4-4 tank engine, O gauge, 1913. d, German National Railways 0-6-0 switching engine, Z gauge, 1970. e, Smoking/non-smoking third class car, 1 gauge, 1909. f, American style 0-4-0 locomotive, O gauge, 1904. g, Zurich, Switzerland prototype streetcar, O gauge, 1928. h, Central London Railway Bo-Bo, 1 gauge, 1904. i, "The Great Bear" Pacific, 1 gauge, 1909.

No. 2621: a, 0-4-4 American style locomotive, 2 gauge, 1907. b, German first and second class passenger car, 1 gauge, 1908. c, British Great Eastern Railway 4-4-0, 1 gauge, 1908. d, English prototype steeplecab, O gauge, 1904. e, Santa Fe Railroad diesel, 1962. f, British Great Northern 4-4-0, 3 gauge, live steam model, 1903. g, Caledonian Railway "Cardean" of Scotland, 1 gauge, 1904. h, British LNWR passenger car, 1 gauge, 1903. i, Swiss Gotthard Rwy. 0-4-0 locomotive, O gauge, 1920.

No. 2622: a, British LB & SCR tank engine, O gauge, 1920. b, German National Railways, tunnel locomotive, 1 gauge, 1904. c, "Borsig" 4-6-4 streamliner, O gauge, 1935. d, French PLM first class car, 1 gauge, 1929. e, American style 0-4-0 locomotive #1021, 1 gauge, 1904. f, "Paris-Orsay" long-nose steeplecab, 1 gauge, 1920. g, British "Cock O' The North," 1 gauge, 1936. h, Prussian State Railways P8 4-6-0 live steam model, 1 gauge, 1975. i, 1937 German "Schnell Treibwagen," O gauge, 1937.

No. 2623: a, Marklin North British Railway "Atlantic," 1 gauge, 1913. b, Bing British London & Western Railway 4-4-2 "Precursor," O gauge, clockwork model, 1916. c, Marklin British Great Western "King George V," O gauge, 1937. d, Marklin passenger car, "Kaiser Train," 1 gauge, 1901. e, Bing 4-4-0 side tank engine, 1 gauge, live steam model, 1904. f, Marklin short-nose steeplecab, 1 gauge, 1912. g, Marklin "Der Adler," 1 gauge, 1935. h, Bing British Great Western Railway "County of Northampton," 1 gauge, live steam model, 1909. i, Bing British Midland Railway "Black Prince," 3 gauge, live steam model, 1908.

Bing toy locomotives: No. 2624: a, Midland Railway "Deeley Type" 4-4-0, 1 gauge clockwork model, 1909. b, No. 2631, British Midland Railway 0-4-0, 3 gauge clockwork model, 1903. c, German 4-6-2 Pacific, O gauge clockwork model, 1927. d, British Great Western Railway, third class coach, O gauge, 1926. e, British London & Southwestern "M7" 0-4-4, 1 gauge clockwork model, 1909. f, "Pilot" 4-4-0 side tank engine, 3 gauge live steam model, 1901. g, British London & Northwestern Railway Webb "Cauliflower," O gauge clockwork model, 1912. h, No. 112, 4-4-0 side tank locomotive, 1 gauge live steam model, 1910. i, British Great Northern Railway, "Stirling Single," 2 gauge live steam model, 1904.

Carette toy locomotives: No. 2625: a, Lithographed tin "Penny Bazaar" train, 1904. b, Winteringham 0-4-0 locomotive, O gauge, 1917. c, British Northeastern Railway, Smith Compound, 3 gauge, 1905. d, SE & CR 2-2-4 steam railcar, 1 gauge, live steam model, 1908. e, No. 776 British Great Northern Railway Stirling "Single," 3 gauge, live steam model, 1903. f, British Midland Railway 4-4-0, O gauge, clockwork model, 1911. g, London Metropolitan Railway "Westinghouse," 1 gauge, 1908. h, Clestory coach, 1 gauge, 1907. i, Steam railcar No. 1, O gauge, live steam model, 1906.

Marklin toy locomotives: No. 2626: a, LMS "Precursor" 4-4-2 tank engine, O gauge clockwork model, 1923. b, American "Congressional Limited" passenger car, 1 gauge, 1908. c, Swiss prototype "Ae 3/6" locomotive, O gauge, 1934. d, German National Railways class 80, 0-6-0, 1 gauge, 1975. e, British Southern Railway third class coach, O gauge, 1926. f, "Bowen-Cooke" 4-6-2 tank engine, O gauge, 1913. g, First electric prototype model, "Two Penny Tube," London, 1 gauge clockwork model, 1901. h, "Paris-Orsay" steeplecab, 1 gauge, 1920. i, 0-2-2 Passenger engine, O gauge clockwork model, 1895.

Bing toy locomotives: No. 2627: a, 2-2-0 engine and tender, 2 gauge live steam model, 1895. b, British Midland Railway "single," O gauge clockwork model, 1913. c, #524/510 reversible express passenger locomotive, 1 gauge, 1916. d, "Kaiser Train" passenger car with Gothic windows, 1 gauge, 1902. e, Tinplate model, British rural station, 1 gauge, 1915. f, British LSMR "M7" side tank locomotive, O gauge clockwork model, 1909. g, 4-4-4 "Windcutter," 1 gauge live steam model, 1912. h, British Great Central Railway "Sir Sam Fay," 1 gauge clockwork model, 1914. i, "Dunalastair" locomotive Caledonian Railway, 1 gauge clockwork model, 1910.

No. 2628, German National Railroad class 0-1 Pacific, O gauge, 1937. No. 2629, Bing 0-4-0 Contractor's locomotive, 4 gauge, 1904. No. 2630, Rack Railway "Steeplecab" locomotive, 2 gauge, 1908. No. 2631, Bing Pabst Blue Ribbon Beer refrigerator car, O gauge, 1925. No. 2632, Marklin "Commodore Vanderbilt," O gauge, 1937. No. 2633, Bing British Great Western Railway "County of Northampton," 1 gauge, live steam model, 1909. No. 2634,

Marklin French Prototype PLM Pacific, 1 gauge, live steam model, 1912. No. 2635, Marklin "Mountain Etat" second series, O gauge, 1933.

1992, Nov. 19 — Perf. 14

2620	A158	$45 Sheet of 9, #a.-i.	8.00	8.00
2621	A158	$45 Sheet of 9, #a.-i.	8.00	8.00
2622	A158	$45 Sheet of 9, #a.-i.	8.00	8.00
2623	A158	$45 Sheet of 9, #a.-i.	8.00	8.00
2624	A158	$45 Sheet of 9, #a.-i.	8.00	8.00
2625	A158	$45 Sheet of 9, #a.-i.	8.00	8.00
2626	A158	$45 Sheet of 9, #a.-i.	8.00	8.00
2627	A158	$45 Sheet of 9, #a.-i.	8.00	8.00

Souvenir Sheets

2628	A158	$350 multicolored	7.00	7.00
2629	A158	$350 multicolored	7.00	7.00

Perf. 14x13½

2630	A158	$350 multicolored	7.00	7.00

Perf. 13x13½, 13½x13

2631	A158	$350 multicolored	7.00	7.00
2632	A158	$350 multicolored	7.00	7.00
2633	A158	$350 multicolored	7.00	7.00
2634	A158	$350 multicolored	7.00	7.00
2635	A158	$350 multicolored	7.00	7.00

Genoa '92. Nos. 2628-2635 each contain one 50x39mm stamp.

While Nos. 2622-2623 & 2631 have the issue date as Nos. 2620-2621 & 2628-2630, the face value of of Nos. 2622-2623 & 2631 was lower when they were released.

Anniversaries and Events — A159

Designs: $12.80, Zeppelin over Lake Constance, 1909. No. 2638, Voyager 1, Jupiter. No. 2639, Konrad Adenauer, John F. Kennedy. No. 2640, Aeromedical airlift. No. 2641, Amazon dolphins. No. 2642, Lift-off of Voyager 1, 1977. No. 2643, Baby gorilla. No. 2644, America's Cup yacht Stars and Stripes. No. 2644A, Eye screening van, doctor with patient. $190, Adenauer, Charles de Gaulle. $225, Zeppelin preparing for takeoff. No. 2647, Count Zeppelin, vert. No. 2648 View of Earth from space, vert. No. 2649, Konrad Adenauer, vert. No. 2650, Tree frog, vert.

1993, Jan. — Litho. — Perf. 14

2637	A159	$12.80 multi	.75	.75
2638	A159	$50 multi	1.75	1.75
2639	A159	$50 multi	2.00	2.00
2640	A159	$100 multi	4.50	4.50
2641	A159	$100 multi	3.00	3.00
2642	A159	$130 multi	4.25	4.25
2643	A159	$130 multi	3.75	3.75
2644	A159	$130 multi	4.75	4.75
2644A	A159	$130 multi	4.75	4.75
2645	A159	$190 multi	6.00	6.00
2646	A159	$225 multi	6.50	6.50
		Nos. 2637-2646 (11)	42.00	42.00

Souvenir Sheets

2647	A159	$225 multi	7.50	7.50
2648	A159	$225 multi	7.00	7.00
2649	A159	$225 multi	7.00	7.00
2650	A159	$225 multi	7.00	7.00

Count Zeppelin, 75th anniv. of death (#2637, 2646-2647). Intl. Space Year (#2638, 2642, 2648). Konrad Adenauer, 25th anniv. of death (#2639, 2645, 2649). World Health Organization (#2640). Earth Summit, Rio (#2641, 2643, 2650). America's Cup Yacht Race (#2644). Lions Intl., 75th anniv. (#2644A).

Miniature Sheet

Biblical Story of David and Goliath — A160

No. 2651: a, City of Jerusalem, two birds in flight. b, City, bird in flight at right. c, City, sun above. d, City, bird in flight at left. e, City with clouds above. f, Philistine army (i-k, q-r). g, Goliath. h, Goliath's arm, spear shaft (b, i, n). l,

Goliath's leg (m, q-s), shield. n, David (r-t, w) with slingshot. o, Jewish soldiers with spears or swords (p-y).

1992, Dec. 29 — Litho. — Perf. 14

2651	A160	$25 Sheet of 25, #a.-y.	19.00	19.00

No. 2651 has a continuous design.

Parrots A161

1993, Mar. 10

2652	A161	80c Hyacinth macaw	.35	.20
2653	A161	$6.40 Scarlet macaw	.60	.30
2654	A161	$7.65 Green macaw, vert.	.60	.30
2655	A161	$15.30 Tovi parakeet	.80	.60
2656	A161	$50 Blue & yellow macaw	1.25	.95
2657	A161	$100 Military macaw, vert.	2.50	2.40
2658	A161	$130 Red & green macaw, vert.	3.25	3.25
2659	A161	$190 Severa macaw	3.75	3.75
		Nos. 2652-2659 (8)	13.10	11.75

Souvenir Sheet

2660	A161	$225 Scarlet macaw, diff.	6.00	6.00
2661	A161	$225 Green parakeet, vert.	6.00	6.00

While Nos. 2654-2656, 2659, 2661 have the same issue date as Nos. 2652-2653, 2657-2658, 2660, the value of Nos. 2654-2656, 2659, 2661 was lower when released.

Miniature Sheets

Dinosaurs — A162

No. 2662: a, Archaeopteryx. b, Pteranodon. c, Quetzalcoatlus. d, Protoavis. e, Dicraeosaurus. f, Moschops. g, Lystrosaurus. h, Dimetrondon. i, Staurikosaurus. j, Cacops. k, Diarthrognathus. l, Estemmenosuchus.

No. 2663: a, Pteranodon. b, Cearadactylus. c, Eudimorphodon. d, Pterodactylus. e, Stauirkosaurus. f, Euoplocephalus. g, Tuojiangosaurus. h, Oviraptor. i, Protoceratops. j, Panaoplosaurus. k, Psittacosaurus. l, Corythosaurus.

No. 2664: a, Sordes. b, Quetzalcoatlus. c, Archaeopteryx. d, Rhamphorynchus. e, Spinosaurus. f, Anchisaurus. g, Stegosaurus. h, Leaellynasaurus. i, Minmi. j, Heterdontosaurus. k, Lesothosaurus. l, Deninonychus.

1993, Mar. 10 — Litho. — Perf. 14

2662	A162	$30 Sheet of 12, #a.-l.	8.75	8.75
2663	A162	$30 Sheet of 12, #a.-l.	8.75	8.75
2664	A162	$30 Sheet of 12, #a.-l.	8.75	8.75

Miniature Sheet

Signs of the Zodiac A163

No. 2665: a, Aquarius. b, Pisces. c, Aries. d, Taurus. e, Gemini. f, Cancer. g, Leo. h, Virgo. i, Libra. j, Scorpio. k, Sagittarius. l, Capricorn.

1992, Dec. 29 — Litho. — Perf. 14x13½
Sheet of 12

2665	A163	$30 Sheet of 12, #a.-l.	19.00	19.00

Caribbean Manatee A164

Designs: $6.40, Adult sticking head out of water. $7.65, Adult, eating, with young. $8.90, Adult swimming underwater. $50, Adult swimming with young.

1993, Mar. 10 — Litho. — Perf. 15x14½

2666	A164	$6.40 multicolored	1.25	1.10
2667	A164	$7.65 multicolored	1.25	1.10
2668	A164	$8.90 multicolored	1.25	1.10
2669	A164	$50 multicolored	4.75	4.75
		Nos. 2666-2669 (4)	8.50	8.05

World Wildlife Federation. Exists imperf. Value, set $36.

Fauna — A165

No. 2670: a, Southern tamandua. b, Three-toed sloth. c, Red howler monkey. d, Four-eyed opossum. e, Black spider monkey. f, Giant otter. g, Red brocket. h, Tree porcupine. i, Tayra. j, Tapir. k, Ocelot. l, Giant armadillo.

No. 2671: a, Crimson topaz hummingbird. b, Bearded bellbird (f). c, Amazonian umbrelabird. d, Paradise jacamar (h). e, Paradise tanager. f, White-tailed trogon (i-j). g, Scarlet macaw (k). h, Red fan parrot. i, Red-billed toucan. j, White plumed antbird. k, Crimson-hooded manakin. l, Guyanan cock-of-the-rock.

No. 2672, Paca. No. 2673, Tufted coquettes, horiz.

1993, Mar. 10 — Perf. 14

2670	A165	$50 Sheet of 12, #a.-l.	14.00	14.00
2671	A165	$50 Sheet of 12, #a.-l.	13.75	13.75

Souvenir Sheets

2672	A165	$325 multicolored	8.25	8.25
2673	A165	$325 multicolored	9.00	9.00

Coronation of Queen Elizabeth II, 40th Anniv. A166

No. 2674: a, $25, Official coronation photograph. b, $50, Gems from royal collection. c, $75, Queen, Duke of Edinburgh. d, $130, Queen opening Parliament.

$325, State Portrait, by Sir James Gunn, 1954-56.

1993, June 2 — Litho. — Perf. 13½x14

2674	A166	Sheet, 2 each #a.-d.	16.00	16.00

Souvenir Sheet
Perf. 14

2675	A166	$325 multicolored	10.00	10.00

No. 2675 contains one 28x42mm stamp. For overprints see Nos. 2793-2795.

A167

Famous People A168

Athletes: No. 2676: a, O. J. Simpson, football. b, Rohan B. Kanhai, cricket. c, Gabriela Sabatini, tennis. d, Severiano Ballesteros, golf. e, Peace dove, blue background. f, Franz Beckenbauer, soccer. g, Pele, soccer. h, Wilt Chamberlain, basketball, i, Nadia Comaneci, gymnastics.

Scientists: No. 2677: a, Louis Leakey, archaeology. b, Jonas Salk, polio vaccine. c, Hideyo Noguchi, yellow fever. d, Karl Landsteiner, blood transfusions. e, Peace dove, blue green background. f, Sigmund Freud, psychoanalysis. g, Louis Pasteur. h, Madame Curie, radium tubes. i, Jean Baptiste Perrin, physics.

Artists, entertainers: No. 2678: a, Gabriel Marquez, writer. b, Pablo Picasso, artist. c, Cecil DeMille, film director. d, Martha Graham, dance. e, Peace dove, purple background. f, Charles Chaplin, actor. g, Paul Robeson, singer. h, Rudolph Dunbar, musician. i, Louis Armstrong, musician.

Politicians: No. 2679: a, Jawaharlal Nehru. b, Dr. Eric Williams, first prime minister of Trinidad and Tobago. c, John F. Kennedy. d, Hugh Desmond Hoyte, president of Guyana. e, Peace dove over map. f, Friedrich Ebert. g, Franklin D. Roosevelt. h, Mikhail Gorbachev. i, Winston Churchill.

Humanitarians: No. 2680: a, Gandhi. b, Dalai Lama. c, Michael Manley, prime minister of Jamaica. d, Javier Perez de Cuellar, former UN Secretary General. e, Peace dove, globe. f, Mother Teresa. g, Martin Luther King, Jr. h, Nelson Mandela. i, Raoul Wallenberg.

Transportation, communication: No. 2681: a, DC-3 cargo plane. b, Space shuttle. c, Concorde. d, Ferdinand von Zeppelin. e, Peace dove. f, Guglielmo Marconi. g, Adrian Thompson, mountaineer. h, Bullet train, Japan. i, John von Neumann, mathematician.

No. 2682, UN Flag, natl. flags. No. 2683, Jackie Robinson. No. 2684, Einstein's formula. No. 2685, Elvis Presley. No. 2686, Nobel Peace Prize certificate. No. 2687, Apollo Moon Landing.

1993, July 26 — Litho. — Perf. 14

2676	A167	$50 Sheet of 9, #a.-i.	16.00	16.00
2677	A167	$50 Sheet of 9, #a.-i.	16.00	16.00
2678	A167	$50 Sheet of 9, #a.-i.	16.00	16.00
2679	A168	$100 Sheet of 9, #a.-i.	16.00	16.00
2680	A168	$100 Sheet of 9, #a.-i.	16.00	16.00
2681	A168	$100 Sheet of 9, #a.-i.	16.00	16.00

Souvenir Sheets

2682	A168	$250 multi, vert.	8.00	8.00
2683	A167	$250 multi, vert.	8.00	8.00
2684	A167	$250 multi, vert.	8.00	8.00
2685	A167	$250 multi, vert.	8.00	8.00
2686	A168	$250 multi, vert.	8.00	8.00
2687	A168	$250 multi	8.00	8.00

Willy Brandt (1913-1992), German Chancellor — A169

Designs: $25, Brandt, Golda Meir, 1969. $190, Brandt at steel mill, 1969. $325, Brandt.

1993, Aug. 16 — Litho. — Perf. 14

2688	A169	$25 multicolored	.90	.90
2689	A169	$190 multicolored	6.50	6.50

Souvenir Sheet

2690	A169	$325 multicolored	9.00	9.00

Armillary
Sphere — A170

Copernicus (1473-1543): $190, Satellite antenna. $300, Copernicus.

1993, Aug. 16
2691	A170	$50 multicolored	1.75	1.75
2692	A170	$190 multicolored	6.25	6.25

Souvenir Sheet
2693	A170	$300 multicolored	8.00	8.00

Georg Hackl, Luge
Gold Medalist,
1992 — A171

1993, Aug. 16
1994 Winter Olympics, Lillehammer, Norway: $130, Karen Magnussen, figure skater, 1972. $325, German bobsled team, 1992.

2694	A171	$50 multicolored	1.75	1.75
2695	A171	$130 multicolored	4.25	4.25

Souvenir Sheet
2696	A171	$325 multicolored	9.50	9.50

A172

World War
II — A173

Designs: $6.40, Audie Murphy. $7.65, British, US forces link up in France, June 8, 1944. $8.90, Monte Cassino falls to Allies, May 18, 1944. $12.80, Battleship Yamato attacked by US in Battle of East China Sea, Apr. 7, 1945. $15.30, St. Basil's Cathedral, Moscow, Foreign Ministers Conf., Oct. 19, 1943. $50, US forces cross Rhine River, Mar. 7, 1945. $100, B-29s begin bombing raids on Japan from China, June 15, 1944. $130, Gen. George S. Patton, Jr., Battle of Sicily ends, Aug. 17, 1943. $190, Battleship Tirpitz sunk, Nov. 12, 1944. $200, US Sherman tank, US forces enter Brittany after taking Normandy, Aug. 1, 1944. $225, End of fighting in Italy, May 2, 1945.

No. 2708 — War at Sea, 1943: a, Adm. Yamamoto launches air offensive, Apr. 7. b, PT-109 in Blackett Strait, Aug. 1. c, USS Enterprise. d, Allied ships attack Rabaul, Oct. 12. e, US troops land at Cape Gloucester, Dec. 26. f, USS Bogue enters service, Feb. g, Wildcat fighters sink U-118. h, Battle of Atlantic reaches peak, U-boats sink 108 ships. i, Italian fleet surrenders at Malta, Sept. 10. j, Battleship Duke of York sinks Scharnhorst, Dec. 26.

No. 2709 — War in the Air, 1943: a, Royal Australian Air Force Beaufighter, Battle of Bismark Sea, Mar. 2-4. b, P-38 Lightening shoots down Adm. Yamamoto's plane over Bougainville, Apr. 7. c, B-24 Liberators bomb Tarawa prior to landings, Sept. 17-19. d, B-25 Mitchell of Fifth Air Force bombs Rabaul, Oct. 12. e, US Navy aircraft attack Makin, Nov. 19. f, US Army Air Force's first daylight raid over Germany, Jan. 27. g, Royal Air Force Mosquito bombers make first daylight raid on Berlin, Jan. 30. h, Allies devastate Hamburg with first firestorm, July 24-30. i, B-24 bombers raid Ploesti oil refineries in Romania, Aug. 1. j, Battle of Berlin begins, Nov. 18.

No. 2710, $325, US, Russian infantry meeting at Elbe River, Apr. 25, 1945.

1993, Oct. 18 — Litho. — Perf. 14
2697	A172	$6.40 multicolored	.80	.30
2698	A172	$7.65 multicolored	.85	.35
2699	A172	$8.90 multicolored	.90	.40
2700	A172	$12.80 multicolored	.95	.60
2701	A172	$15.30 multicolored	1.00	.70
2702	A172	$50 multicolored	1.75	1.25
2703	A172	$100 multicolored	2.75	2.50
2704	A172	$130 multicolored	4.00	4.00
2705	A172	$190 multicolored	5.50	5.50
2706	A172	$200 multicolored	5.75	5.75
2707	A172	$225 multicolored	6.50	6.50
Nos. 2697-2707 (11)			30.75	27.85

Miniature Sheets
Perf. 15
2708	A173	$50 Sheet of 10, #a.-j.	14.00	14.00
2709	A172	$50 Sheet of 10, #a.-j.	14.00	14.00

Nos. 2709a-2709j are 35½x22mm.

Souvenir Sheet
Perf. 14
2710	A172	$325 multicolored	12.00	12.00

1994 World Cup
Soccer
Championships,
U.S. — A174

Player, country: $5, Stuart Pearce, England. $6.40, Ronald Koeman, Holland. $7.65, Gianluca Vialli, Italy. $12.80, McStay, Scotland, Alemao, Brazil. $15.30, Ceulemans, Belgium, Butcher, England. $50, Dragan Stojkovic, Yugoslavia. $100, Ruud Gullit, Holland. $130, Miloslav Kadlec, Czechoslovakia. $150, Ramos, Uruguay, Berthold, Germany. $190, Baggio, Italy; Wright, England. $200, Yarentchuck, Russia, Renquin, Belgium. $225, Timofte, Romania; Aleinikov, Russia. No. 2724, Rene Higuita, Colombia. No. 2723, Salvatore Schillaci, Italy, horiz.

1993, Oct. 18 — Litho. — Perf. 14
2711	A174	$5 multicolored	.25	.25
2712	A174	$6.40 multicolored	.25	.25
2713	A174	$7.65 multicolored	.35	.25
2714	A174	$12.80 multicolored	.40	.25
2715	A174	$15.30 multicolored	.45	.30
2716	A174	$50 multicolored	1.60	.90
2717	A174	$100 multicolored	2.50	2.50
2718	A174	$130 multicolored	3.00	3.00
2719	A174	$150 multicolored	3.50	3.50
2720	A174	$190 multicolored	4.25	4.25
2721	A174	$200 multicolored	5.00	5.00
2722	A174	$225 multicolored	5.25	5.25
Nos. 2711-2722 (12)			26.80	25.70

Souvenir Sheets
2723	A174	$325 multicolored	8.50	8.50
2724	A174	$325 multicolored	8.50	8.50

Order of the
Caribbean
Community
A175

1993, Sept. 27 — Litho. — Perf. 14
2725	A175	$7.65 William Demas	1.00	.75
2726	A175	$7.65 Derek Walcott	1.00	.75
2727	A175	$7.65 Sir Shridath Ramphal	2.00	1.00
Nos. 2725-2727 (3)			4.00	2.50

Christmas
A176

Details from Holy Family Under the Apple Tree, by Rubens: No. 2728, $6.40, No. 2730, $12.80, No. 2733, $130, No. 2734, $190.
Details from The Virgin in Glory, by Durer: No. 2729, $7.65, No. 2731, $15.30, No. 2732, $50, No. 2735, $250.
No. 2736, Holy Family Under the Apple Tree (entire). No. 2737, The Virgin in Glory (entire).

1993, Dec. 1 — Perf. 13½x14
2728-2735	A176	Set of 8	14.00	14.00

Souvenir Sheets
2736	A174	$325 multicolored	7.00	7.00
2737	A174	$325 multicolored	7.00	7.00

Louvre
Museum,
Bicent.
A177

Details or entire paintings: No. 2738, Mona Lisa, by Da Vinci.
No. 2739, $50: a, La Femme à la Puce, by Crespi. b, La Femme Hydropique, by Dou. c, Portrait d'un Couple, by Ittenbach. d, Cléopâtre Assise, Demi Face, sur un Trône Elevé, by Moreau. e, La Richesse, by Vouet. f, Vieillard et Jeune Garçon, by Ghirlandaio. g, Louis XIV, by Rigaud. h, La Buveuse, by Pieter De Hooch.
No. 2740, $50: a, Autoportrait aux Besicles, by Chardin. b, L'Infante Marie-Thérèse, by Velasquez. c, Le Printemps, by Arcimboldo. d, La Vierge de Douleur, by Bouts. e, L'Etude, by Fragonard. f, François 1er, by Clouet. g, Le Condottière, by Antonello Da Messina. h, La Bohémienne, by Hals.
No. 2741, $50: a, La Femme à la Puce, entire, by Crespi. b, Autoportrait au Chevalet, by Rembrandt. c, Femmes d'Alger dans Leur Appartement, by Delacroix. d, Tête de Jeune Homme, by Raphael. e, Vénus et les Grâces, by Botticelli. f, Nature Morte à l'Echiquier, by Lubin Baugin. g, Lady MacBeth Somnambule, by Fussli. h, La Tabagie, by Chardin.
Nos. 2742, $50: a-c, L'Accordée de Village (left, center, right), by Greuze. d, Autoportrait, by Melendez. e, Le Chevalier, La Jeune Fille et La Mont, by Baldung-Grien. f, Le Jeune Mendiant, by Murillo. g-h, Les Pèlerins d'Emmaus (left, right), by Mathieu Le Nain.
No. 2743, $50: a-b, Le Vierge au Lapin (diff. details), by Titian. c, La Belle Jardinière, by Raphael. d, La Dentellière, by Vermeer. e, Jeanne d'Aragon, by Raphael. f, L'Astronome, by Vermeer. g, Le Pont du Rialto, by Canaletto. h, Sigismond Malatesta, by Piero Della Francesca.
No. 2744, $325, Cour de Ferme, by Jan Brueghel, the Younger. No. 2745, $325, Le Pont du Rialto, by Canaletto. No. 2746, $325, Le Sacre de Napoléon 1er, by David. No. 2747, $325, Details and painting of Mona Lisa. No. 2748, $325, Le Diseuse de Bonne Aventure, by Caravaggio. No. 2749, $325, Les Noces de Cana, by Veronese.

1993, Dec. 6 — Litho. — Perf. 13½x14
2738	A177	$50 multicolored	.90	.90
a.		Sheet of 8 + label	8.00	8.00

Sheets of 8, #a-h, + Label
2739-2743	A177	Set of 5	40.00	40.00

Souvenir Sheets
Perf. 12
2744-2749	A177	Set of 6	37.50	37.50

Nos. 2744-2746 each contain one 80x47mm stamp. Nos. 2747-2749 one 80x53mm stamp.

Christmas
A177a

Entire paintings or details: $7.65, St. Anne with Mary and the Child Jesus, by Dürer. $8.90, Mary Being Crowned by Two Angels, by Dürer. $50, Pentecost, by Titian. $100, Samson and Delilah, by Rubens. $250, Origin of the Milky Way, by Rubens.
No. 2749F, $500, The Descent from the Cross, by Rubens, horiz. No. 2749G, $500, The Descent from the Cross, by Dürer, horiz.

1993 — Litho. — Perf. 13½x14, 14x13½
2749A-2749E	A177a	Set of 5	13.50	13.50

Souvenir Sheets
2749F-2749G	A177a	Set of 2	16.00	16.00

Polska '93 (Paintings) — A178

Designs: $50, $130, Pantaloons, by Tadeusz Brzozowski, 1966. $75, Photo of fortress in Miedzyrecz. $325, Children in the Garden, by Wladyslaw Podkowinski, 1892, horiz.

1993 — Perf. 14
2750	A178	$50 multicolored	1.75	1.75
2751	A178	$75 multicolored	2.25	2.25
2752	A178	$130 multicolored	4.00	4.00
a.		Pair, #2750 #2752	6.00	6.00
Nos. 2750-2752 (3)			8.00	8.00

Souvenir Sheet
2753	A178	$325 multicolored	8.00	8.00

Picasso
(Paintings) — A179

Designs: $15.30, Bather, Paris, 1909. $100, Two Nudes, 1906. $190, Nude Seated on a Rock, 1921. $325, The Rescue, 1922.

1993, Nov. — Litho. — Perf. 14
2754	A179	$15.30 multicolored	.40	.40
2755	A179	$100 multicolored	2.60	2.60
2756	A179	$190 multicolored	5.00	5.00
Nos. 2754-2756 (3)			8.00	8.00

Souvenir Sheet
2756A	A179	$325 multicolored	8.00	8.00

Rebirth of
Democracy, 1st
Anniv. — A180

Designs: $6.40, Dr. Cheddie B. Jagan, Guyana Pres. $325, Sunburst, "REBIRTH OF DEMOCRACY," horiz.

1993, Dec. 17 Litho. Perf. 13½x14
2757 A180 $6.40 multicolored .80 .80

Souvenir Sheet
Perf. 13
2757A A180 $325 multicolored 7.50 7.50

Aladdin — A181

Nos. 2758: a-h, Various characters from Disney animated film, vert.
Nos. 2759: a-i, Various film scenes.
Nos. 2760: a-i, Various scenes from Disney animated film.
No. 2761, Genie, Jasmine, and Aladdin. No. 2762, Aladdin, the Genie, Abu, Magic Carpet. No. 2763, Aladdin as Prince Ali Ababwa. No. 2764, Aladdin, Abu, Jasmine.

1993, Dec. 20 Litho. Perf. 14x13½
2758 A181 $7.65 Sheet of 8,
  #a.-h. 2.00 2.00
2759 A181 $50 Sheet of 9,
  #a.-i. 12.00 12.00
2760 A181 $65 Sheet of 9,
  #a.-i. 14.00 14.00
  Nos. 2758-2760 (3) 28.00 28.00

Souvenir Sheets
2761 A181 $325 multicolored 7.50 7.50
2762 A181 $325 multicolored 7.50 7.50
2763 A181 $325 multicolored 7.50 7.50
2764 A181 $325 multicolored 7.50 7.50

A182

Hong Kong '94 — A183

Stamps, photograph of Happy Valley Horse Race Course: No. 2765, Hong Kong #437, scoreboard. No. 2766, Track, horses, #2545.
No. 2767 — Snuff boxes, Qing Dynasty: a, Painted enamel in shape of bamboo. b, Painted enamel with human figure. c, Amber with lions playing ball. d, Agate in shape of two gourds. e, Glass overlay with dog. f, Glass, foliage design.
No. 2768 — Porcelain, Ch'ing Dynasty: a, Covered jar with dragon. b, Rotating brush holder. c, Covered jar with horses. d, Amphora vase with bats & peaches. e, Tea caddy with Fo dogs. f, Vase with wild camellia & peaches.

1994, Feb. 18 Perf. 14
2765 A182 $50 multicolored .80 .80
2766 A182 $50 multicolored .80 .80
  a. Pair, #2765-2766 1.60 1.60

Miniature Sheets
2767 A183 $20 Sheet of 6, #a.-f. 8.00 8.00
2768 A183 $20 Sheet of 6, #a.-f. 8.00 8.00

Nos. 2765-2766 issued in sheets of 5 pairs. No. 2766a is continuous design.
New Year 1994 (Year of the Dog) (#2767e, #2768e).

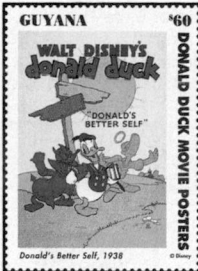

Vintage Donald Duck — A184

No. 2769, $60 — Movie posters: a, Donald's Better Self, 1938. b, Donald's Golf Game, 1938. c, Sea Scouts, 1939. d, Donald's Penguin, 1939. e, A Good Time for a Dime, 1941. f, Truant Officer Donald. g, Orphan's Benefit, 1941. h, Chef Donald, 1941.
No. 2770, $60: a, The Village Smithy, 1942. b, Donald's Snow Fight, 1942. c, Donald's Garden, 1942. d, Donald's Gold Mine, 1942. e, The Vanishing Private, 1942. f, Sky Trooper, 1942. g, Bellboy Donald, 1942. h, The New Spirit, 1942.
No. 2771, $60: a, Saludos Amigos, 1943. b, The Eyes Have It, 1945. c, Donald's Crime, 1945. d, Straight Shooters, 1947. e, Donald's Dilemma, 1947. f, Bootle Beetle, 1947. g, Daddy Duck, 1948. h, Soup's On, 1948.
No. 2772 — Story boards from Pirate Gold, horiz.: a, Pirate ship. b, Carrying treasure chest. c, Donald Duck with map. d, Donald, souvenir shop. e, Donald following Aracuan bird. f, Angry Donald.
No. 2773, $80 — Movie posters: a, Donald's Happy Birthday, 1949. b, Sea Salts, 1949. c, Honey Harvester, 1949. d, All in a Nutshell, 1949. e, The Greener Yard, 1949. f, Slide, Donald, Slide, 1949. g, Lion Around, 1950. h, Trailer Horn, 1950.
No. 2774, $80: a, Bee at the Beach, 1950. b, Out on a Limb, 1950. c, Corn Chips, 1951. d, Test Pilot Donald, 1951. e, Lucky Number, 1951. f, Out of Scale, 1951. g, Bee on Guard, 1951. h, Let's Stick Together, 1952.
No. 2775, $80: a, Trick or Treat, 1952. b, Don's Fountain of Youth, 1953. c, Rugged Bear, 1953. d, Canvas Back Duck, 1953. e, Dragon Around, 1954. f, Grin and Bear It, 1954. g, The Flying Squirrel, 1954. h, Up a Tree, 1955.
No. 2776, Studio Fan Card, Melody Time, 1948.
No. 2777, $500, Scene from picture book of first movie, The Wise Little Hen, 1944, horiz. No. 2778, $500, Sketch for closing scene of Timber, 1941. No. 2779, $500, Donald Duck, horiz. No. 2780, $500, Studio fan card, The Three Caballeros, 1945, horiz.
Movie posters contained in No. 2780A are listed as designs for Nos. 2769-2771, 2774-2775, 2777, 2780.

Perf. 14x13½, 13½x14
1993, Dec. 6 Litho.
Sheets of 8, #a-h
2769-2771 A184 Set of 3 28.50 28.50
2772 A184 $80 Sheet of 6,
  #a.-f. 9.00 9.00

Sheets of 8, #a-h
2773-2775 A184 Set of 3 34.50 34.50

Size: 130x104mm
Imperf
2776 A184 $500 multi 10.00 10.00

Souvenir Sheets
Perf. 14x13½, 13½x14
2777-2780 A184 Set of 4 40.00 40.00

Imperf
Self-Adhesive
Size: 64x89mm
2780A A184 $60 Set of 50 70.00

No. 2780A exists with backing labels printed in English or French. Value is for either set. No. 2780A was printed on thin card and sold in sealed cellophane packages containing 10 stamps. To affix stamps, backing containing film information must be removed.
#2769-2771, 2773-2775 exist in sheets of 7 $5 stamps + label. The label replaces #2769f, 2770b, 2771h, 2773a, 2774d, 2775e. These sheets became available Nov. 20, 1996.

Tropical Flowers A185

Designs: $6.40, Cestrum parqui. $7.65, Brunfelsia calycina. $12.80, Datura rosei. $15.30, Ruellia macrantha. No. 2785, $50, Portlandia albiflora. $130, Pachystachys coccinea. $190, Beloperone guttata. $250, Ferdinandusa speciosa.
No. 2789, $50: a, Clusia grandiflora. b, Begonia haageana. c, Fuchsia simplicicaulis. d, Guaiacum officinale (a). e, Pithecoctenium cynanchoides. f, Sphaeralcea umbellata. g, Erythrina poeppigiana. h, Steriphoma paradoxa. i, Allemanda violacea (f). j, Centropogon cornutus (g). k, Passiflora quadrangularis. l, Victoria amazonica.
No. 2790, $50: a, Cobaea scandens. b, Pyrostegia venusta (c). c, Petrea kohautiana (b). d, Hippobroma longiflora (a). e, Cleome hassleriana (b, d, f, h, i). f, Verbena peruviana (c). g, Tropaeolum peregrinum. h, Plumeria rubra (g, i). i, Selenicereus grandiflorus. j, Mandevilla splendens (g). k, Pereskia aculeata. l, Ipomoea learii.
No. 2791, $325, Columnea fendleri. No. 2792, $325, Lophospermum erubescens.

1994, Feb. 10 Litho. Perf. 13½
2781-2788 A185 Set of 8 13.75 13.75

Sheets of 12, #a-l
Perf. 14
2789-2790 A185 Set of 2 27.00 27.00

Souvenir Sheets
Perf. 13
2791-2792 A185 Set of 2 14.00 14.00

Nos. 2674-2675 Ovptd. "ROYAL VISIT FEB 19-22, 1994" in One or Two Lines

1994 Litho. Perf. 13½x14
2793 A166 Sheet, 2 each #a.-
  d. 14.00 14.00

Souvenir Sheet
Perf. 14
2794 A166 $325 multicolored 9.00 9.00

Hummel Figurines — A186

Designs: No. 2795, $20, No. 2803a, $30, Girl holding basket and heart. No. 2796, $25, Boy holding heart. No. 2797, $35, No. 2804a, $20, Chef holding dessert. No. 2798, $50, No. 2804b, $130, Girl holding planter of mushrooms. No. 2799, $60, Girl holding plant, horiz. No. 2800, $130, No. 2803b, $6, Four girls. No. 2801, $190, Two girls, boy and puppy. No. 2802, $250, No. 2804c, $35, Boy holding covered dish, puppy.

1994, May 5 Litho. Perf. 14
2795-2802 A186 Set of 8 18.00 18.00

Souvenir Sheets
2803 A186 Sheet of 4, #a.-b,
  #2796, 2801 5.50 5.50
2804 A186 Sheet of 4, #a.-c,
  #2799 5.50 5.50

Sierra Club, Cent. A187

No. 2805 — Various animals or scenic places: a-b, American alligator. c-d, Italian Alps. e-f, Mono Lake.
No. 2806: a, Red kangaroo. b-d, Whooping crane. e-f, Alaskan brown bear. g, Bald eagle. h, Giant panda.
No. 2807, vert.: a-b, Red kangaroo. c, American alligator. d, Alaskan brown bear. e-f, Bald eagle. g-h, Giant panda.
No. 2808, vert.: a-c, Sea lion. d, Mono Lake. e, Sierra Club centennial emblem. f, Italian Alps. g-i, Matterhorn.

1994, May 20 Litho. Perf. 14
2805 A187 $70 Sheet of 6,
  #a.-f. 8.50 8.50
2806 A187 $70 Sheet of 8,
  #a.-h. 11.50 11.50
2807 A187 $70 Sheet of 8,
  #a.-h. 11.50 11.50

2808 A187 $70 Sheet of 9,
  #a.-i. 14.50 14.50
  Nos. 2805-2808 (4) 46.00 46.00

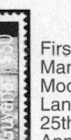

First Manned Moon Landing, 25th Anniv. A188

No. 2809, $60: a, Robert R. Gilruth, Apollo 16. b, Ernst Stuhlinger, Apollo 17. c, Christopher C. Kraft, X-30 National Aero-Space Plane. d, Rudolf Opitz, Me-163, July 24, 1943. e, Clyde W. Tombaugh, "Face on Mars." f, Hermann Oberth, Scene from "The Girl in the Moon."
No. 2810, $60: a, Werner von Braun, Apollo 11. b, Rocco A. Petrone, Apollo 11. c, Eberhard Rees, Apollo 12. d, Allies breach Gustav Line, May 19. d, Thomas O. Paine, Apollo 14. f, A.F. Staats, Apollo 15.
No. 2811, $60: a, Walter Dornberger, 1st A-4 launch. b, Rudolph Nebel, Surveyor 1. c, Robert H. Goddard, Apollo 7. d, Kurt Debus, Apollo 8. e, James T. Webb, Apollo 9. f, George E. Mueller, Apollo 10.
No. 2812, Frank J. Everest, Jr.

1994, July 20 Litho. Perf. 14
Sheets of 6, #a-f
2809-2811 A188 Set of 3 22.00 22.00

Souvenir Sheet
2812 A188 $325 multicolored 8.50 8.50

A189

World War II — A190

Designs: $6, Photo reconnaissance Spitfire. $35, 226 Squadron B-25. $190, 76 Squadron P-47 Thunderbolts.
No. 2816 — Europe and North Africa, 1944: a, Allied landings, Anzio, Jan. 22. b, RAF bombs Amiens prison, Feb. 18. c, Sevastopol falls to Red Army, May 9. d, Allies breach Gustav Line, May 19. e, D-Day, June 6. f, V-1 attacks on London begin, June 13. g, Cease fire declared for Paris, Aug. 19. h, Germany launches V-2 rockets, Sept. 8. i, German battleship Tirpitz sunk, Nov. 12. j, Siege of Bastogne lifted, Dec. 29.
No. 2817 — D-Day: a, Paratroops drop behind enemy lines. b, Glider-born commandos land behind enemy lines. c, USS Arkansas shells Omaha beach defenses. d, Allied aircraft attack enemy movements. e, Allied landing craft hit the beach. f, Allied troops pinned down by enemy fire. g, Commandos exit landing craft. h, Specialized Allied tanks destroy enemy mines. i, Allies break through beach defenses. j, Consolidation of position.
No. 2818, RAF Lancaster bomber.

1994, June 20 Perf. 14
2813 A189 $6 multicolored .40 .40
2814 A189 $35 multicolored 1.10 1.10
2815 A189 $190 multicolored 5.00 5.00
  Nos. 2813-2815 (3) 6.50 6.50

Perf. 13
2816 A190 $60 Sheet of 10,
  #a.-j. 14.00 14.00
2817 A190 $60 Sheet of 10,
  #a.-j. 14.00 14.00

Souvenir Sheet
Perf. 14
2818 A189 $325 multicolored 9.00 9.00

A191

Butterflies
A192

Designs: $6, Heliconius melpomene. $20, Helicopius cupido. $25, Agrias claudina. $30, Parides coelus. $50, Heliconius hecale. $60, Morpho diana. $190, Dismorphia orise. $250, Morpho deidamia.

No. 2827: a, Anaea marthesia. b, Brassolis astyra. c, Heliconius melpomene. d, Haetera piera. e, Morpho diana dixey. f, Parides coelus. g, Catagramma pitheas. h, Nessaea obrinus. i, Automeris janus. j, Papilio torquatus. k, Eunica sophonisba. l, Ceratinia nise. m, Panacea procilla. n, Pyrrhogyra neaerea. o, Morpho deidamia. p, Dismorphia orise.

No. 2829, $325, Eunica sophonisba. No. 2830, $325, Anaea eribotes.

No. 2831, $325, Hamadryas velutina. No. 2832, $325, Agrias claudina.

1994, July 5　　Litho.　　Perf. 14
2819-2826　A191　Set of 8　　16.00 16.00
2827　A192　$50 Sheet of 16,
　　　　#a.-p.　　　　　　22.00 22.00
Souvenir Sheets
2829-2830　A191　Set of 2　　15.00 15.00
2831-2832　A192　Set of 2　　15.00 15.00

Nos. 2829-2830 each contain one 43x28mm stamp.

Bible
Stories — A193

No. 2833 — Story of Ruth and Naomi: a-f: Ruth & Naomi preparing to leave Moab & return to Israel. g-l: Ruth harvesting grain in fields of Boaz. m-r: Boaz receives a man's sandal, finalizing sale of Naomi's field. s-x: Naomi, Boaz, Ruth and Obed, who was David's grandfather.

No. 2834 — Story of Joseph: a-d, Jacob made Joseph a coat of many colors. e-h, Joseph's brothers take his coat and cast him into pit. i-l, Joseph is sold to the Ishmaelites. m-p, Joseph is accused by Potiphar's wife and thrown into prison. q-t, Joseph interprets Pharoah's dreams. u-x, Joseph is reunited with his brothers.

No. 2835 — Parting of the Red Sea: a-x, Moses leading Israelites through sea, Pharoah's army drowning.

No. 2836 — Daniel and the Lions: a-x, Daniel in lion's den surrounded by various animals, angel.

1994, Aug. 4　　Litho.　　Perf. 14
Sheets of 24, #a-x
2833-2836　A193　$20 Set of 4　52.00 52.00

Nos. 2835-2836 have continuous design.

A194　　　　　　A195

Philakorea '94: $6, Statues of socialist ideals, Pyongyang. $25, Statue of Adm. Yi Sunsin. $120, Sokkat'ap Pagoda, Pulguksa. $130, Village guardian, Chejudo Island.

No. 2841, $60 — Ten-fold screens: a, Shown. b-e, Cranes. h-i, Deer. j, Deer, mushrooms, waterfall.

No. 2842, $60: b-d, Cranes. f-h, Deer. c, h, Waterfalls. i-j, Mushrooms.

No. 2843, $60, Falled Rock, horiz. No. 2844, $325, Westerners at Korean Court, horiz.

1994, June 20　　Litho.　　Perf. 14
2837-2840　A194　Set of 4　　6.00 6.00
Sheets of 10, #a-j
Perf. 13
2841-2842　A195　Set of 2　　26.00 26.00
Souvenir Sheets
Perf. 14
2843-2844　A194　Set of 2　　14.00 14.00

Nos. 2841-2842 have continuous design.

Entertainers of Takarazuka Revue, Japan
A196

No. 2845: a, $60, Mira Anju. b, $60, Yuki Amami. c, $60, Maki Ichiro. d, $60, Yu Shion. e, $20, Miki Maya. f, $20, Fubuki Takane. g, $20, Seika Juze. h, $20, Saki Asaji.

1994　　　　　　　　Perf. 14½
2845　A196　Sheet of 8, #a.-h. +
　　　　4 labels　　　9.00 9.00

Nos. 2845a-2845d are 34x47mm.

A197

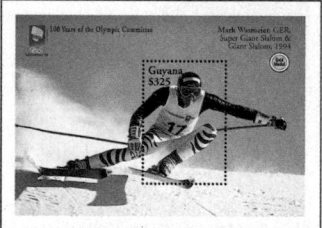

Intl. Olympic Committee, Cent. — A198

Designs: $20, Nancy Kerrigan, US, figure skating, 1994. $35, Sawao Kato, Japan, gymnastics, 1976. $130, Florence Griffith-Joyner, US, 100-, 200-meters, 1988.

$325, Mark Wasmeier, Germany, super giant & giant slalom, 1994.

1994, June 20
2846-2848　A197　Set of 3　　4.50 4.50
Souvenir Sheet
2849　A198　$325 multicolored　8.00 8.00

1994 World Cup Soccer Championships, U.S. — A199

Player, country: $6, Paulo Futre, Portugal. $35, Lyndon Hooper, Canada. $60, Enzo Francescoli, Uruguay. $190, Freddy Rincon, Colombia.

No. 2854, $60: a, Paolo Maldini, Italy. b, Guyana player. c, Bwalya Kalusha, Zambia. d, Diego Maradona, Argentina. e, Andreas Brehme, Germany. f, Eric Wynalda, US.

No. 2855, $60: a, John Doyle, US. b, Eric Wynalda, US, diff. c, Thomas Dooley, US. d, Ernie Stewart, US. f, Marcelo Balboa, US. g, Coach Bora Milutinovic, US.

No. 2856, $325, 1994 World Cup program cover. No. 2857, $325, Oiler Watson.

1994, Aug. 8
2850-2853　A199　Set of 4　　7.00 7.00

Sheets of 6, #a-f
2854-2855　A199　Set of 2　　18.00 18.00
Souvenir Sheets
2856-2857　A199　Set of 2　　17.00 17.00

Birds — A200

No. 2858, $35: a, Goshawk. b, Lapwing. c, Ornate umbrellabird. d, Slatey-headed parakeet. e, Regent bowerbird. f, Egytian goose. g, White-winged crossbill. h, Waxwing. i, Ruff. j, Hoopoe. k, Superb starling. l, Great jacamar.

No. 2859, $35: a, Peregrine falcon. b, Great spotted woodpecker. c, White-throated kingfisher. d, Peruvian cock-of-the-rock. e, Yellowheaded Amazon. f, Victoria crowned pigeon. g, Little owl. h, Pheasant. i, Goldfinch. j, Jay. k, Sulphur-brasted toucan. l, Japanese blue flycatcher.

No. 2860, $325, Gould's violet-ear. No. 2861, $325, Bald eagle.

1994, Sept. 15
Sheets of 12, #a.-i.
2858-2859　A200　Set of 2　　22.00 22.00
Souvenir Sheets
2860-2861　A200　Set of 2　　19.00 19.00

PHILAKOREA '94.

1996 Summer Olympics, Atlanta — A201

1994, Sept. 28

German athletes: $6, Anja Fichtel, fencing, 1988, horiz. $25, Annegret Richter, 100-meter dash, 1976. $30, Heike Henkel, high jump, 1982. $35, Armin Hary, 100-meter dash, 1960. $50, Heide Rosendahl, long jump, 1972. $60, Josef Neckermann, equestrian grand prix, 1968. $130, Heike Drechsler, long jump, 1988. $190, Ulrike Mayfarth, high jump, 1984. $250, Michael Gross, swimming, 1984, horiz.

No. 2870A: b, $135, Markus Wasmeier, skiing, 1994. c, $190, Katja Seizinger, skiing, 1994.

No. 2871, $325, Franziska van Almsick, swimming, 1992. No. 2872, $325, Steffi Graf, tennis, 1994.

2862-2870　A201　Set of 9　　18.00 18.00
Souvenir Sheets
2870A　A201　Sheet of 2, #b.-c.　7.25 7.25
2871-2872　A201　Set of 2　　14.50 14.50

Space Missions, First Manned Moon Landing, 25th Anniv.
A202

No. 2873, $60: a, Laika, first dog in space. b, Yuri Gagarin, first man in space. c, John Glenn, first American to orbit earth. d, Edward White, first American to walk in space. e, Neil Armstrong, first to step foot onto moon. f, Luna 16. g, Luna 17. h, Skylab 1. i, 1975 Apollo-Soyuz.

No. 2874, $60 — Unmanned probes: a, Mars 3, Mars. b, Mariner 10, Mercury. c, Voyager, planetary grand tour. d, Pioneer, Venus. e, Giotto, Halley's Comet. f, Megellan, Venus.

g, Galileo, Jupiter. h, Ulysses, Sun. i, Cassini, Titan.

No. 2875, $325, "Buzz" Aldrin, Neil Armstrong, Michael Collins. No. 2876, $325, Pioneer 1, 2.

1994, Nov. 10　　Litho.　　Perf. 13½
Sheets of 9, #a-i
2873-2874　A202　Set of 2　　26.00 26.00
Souvenir Sheets
2875-2876　A202　Set of 2　　17.00 17.00

Steam Locomotives — A203

Designs: No. 2877, $25, South Eastern Railway #285, 1882. No. 2878, $25, West Point Foundry, 1830. No. 2879, $300, Mt. Washington Cog Railway, 1886. No. 2880, $300, Stroudley-Brighton, 1872.

No. 2881, $30: a, "John Bull," 1831. b, Stephenson, 1837. c, "Atlantic," 1832. d, Stourbridge Lion, 1829. e, Polonceau, 1854. f, Rogers, 1856. g, "Vulcan," 1858. h, "Namur," 1846.

No. 2882, $30: a, West Point Foundry, 1832. b, Sequin, 1830. c, Stephenson's Planet, 1830. d, Norris 4-2-0, 1840. e, Union Iron Works os San Francisco, 1867. f, Andrew Jackson, 1832. g, Herald, 1831. h, Cumberland, 1845.

No. 2883, $30: a, Pennsylvania's Class K, 1880. b, Cooke, 1885. c, John B. Turner, 1867. d, Baldwin, 1871. e, Richard Trevithick, 1804. f, John Stephens, 1825. g, John Blenkinsop, 1803. h, Pennsylvania, 1803.

$250, Est Railway, 1878. $300, "Claud Hamilton," 1840.

1994, Nov. 15　　　　　Perf. 14
2877-2880　A203　Set of 4　　15.00 15.00
Sheets of 8, #a-h, + Label
2881-2883　A203　Set of 3　　19.00 19.00
Souvenir Sheets
2884　A203　$250 multicolored　8.00 8.00
2885　A203　$300 multicolored　10.00 10.00

English Touring Cricket, Cent.
A204

Designs: $20, C.H. Lloyd, Guyana/West Indies, vert. $35, C.W. Hooper, Guyana/West Indies, Wisden Trophy. $60, G.A. Hick, England, Wisden Trophy.

$200, First English Team, 1895.

1994, June 20　　Litho.　　Perf. 14
2886-2888　A204　Set of 3　　4.00 4.00
Souvenir Sheet
2889　A204　$200 multicolored　6.00 6.00

Christmas
A205

Paintings: $6, Joseph with the Christ Child, by Guido Reni. $20, Adoration of the Christ Child, by Girolamo Romanino. $25, Adoration of the Christ Child with St. Barbara and St. Martin, by Raffaello Botticini. $30, Holy Family, by Pompeo Girolam Batoni. $35, Flight into Egypt, by Bartolommeo Carducci. $60, Holy Family and the Baptist, by Andrea del Sarto. $120, Sacred Conversation, by Cesare de Sesto. $190, Madonna and Child with Sts. Joseph & John the Baptist, by Pontormo.

No. 2898, $325, Holy Family and St. Elizabeth and St. John the Baptist, by Francisco Primaticcio. No. 2899, $325, Presentation of Christ in the Temple, by Fra Bartolommeo.

1994, Dec. 5 — **Perf. 13½x14**
2890-2897 A205 Set of 8 — 13.50 13.50

Souvenir Sheets
2898-2899 A205 Set of 2 — 18.00 18.00

Order of the Caribbean Community — A206

First award recipients: No. 2900, $60, Sir Shridath Ramphal, statesman, Guyana. No. 2901, $60, William Demas, economist, Trinidad & Tobago. No. 2902, $60, Derek Walcott, writer, St. Lucia.

1994 — **Perf. 14**
2900-2902 A206 Set of 3 — 5.00 5.00

Motion Picture, Star Trek Generations A207

A207a

No. 2903, "Boldly Go," Starship Enterprise.
No. 2904, $100: a, Capt. Picard. b, Cmdr. Riker. c, Capt. Kirk. d, Villain with phaser. e, Kirk, Picard on horseback. f, Klingons L'rsa and B'tor. g, Kirk, Picard, diff. h, Counselor Troi. i, Picard, Lt. Cmdr. Data.
No. 2905, $100: a, Troi, Riker. b, Worf. c, Picard. d, Worf, Lt. Cmdr. LaForge. e, Sailing ship, Enterprise. f, Picard, Riker. g, Data. h, Worf. i, Dr. Crusher.
No. 2906, Like No. 2903, horiz.
$1000, Kirk and Picard.
No. 2906D: e, Capt. Picard. f, Capt. Kirk. Illustration A207a reduced.

1994 — **Litho.** — **Perf. 13½x14**
2903 A207 $100 multicolored — 3.25 3.25

Sheets of 9, #a-i
2904-2905 A207 Set of 2 — 58.50 58.50

Souvenir Sheet
Perf. 14x13½
2906 A207 $500 multicolored — 12.00 12.00

Litho. & Embossed
Die Cut Perf. 9
2906C A207a $1000 gold & multi — 30.00 30.00

Souvenir Sheet
Die Cut Perf. 9 on Outside
2906D A207a $500 Sheet of 2, #e.-f. — 30.00 30.00

Issued: No. 2906C, 11/18, others 12/7. No. 2903 was issued in sheets of 9. Nos. 2906e-2906f are imperf.

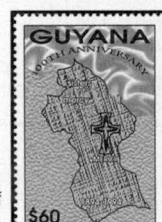

Sisters of Mercy of Guyana, Cent. — A208

1994, Dec. 12 — **Perf. 14**
2907 A208 $60 multicolored — 1.90 1.90

Nos. 1037a, 1097, 1099 Surcharged "ILO / 75th Anniversary / 1919-1994"
Perfs & Printing Methods as Before
1994
2907A A91 $6 on 130c #103/a
2907B A91 $30 on 120c #1099
2907C A91 $35 on 120c #1097

Nos. 1063, 1098, 1120, 1123 Surcharged in Blue "CENTENARY / Sign For The / MAHDI / 1894-1994"
Perfs. & Printing Methods as Before
1994
2907D A91 $6 on 60c #1120
2907E A91 $20 on 200c #1063
2907F A91 $30 on 60c #1098
2907G A91 $35 on 60c #1123

Cricket A209

Designs: $20, Sobers congratulates Lara. $30, Brian Lara setting world record, vert. $375, Lara, Chanderpaul.
$300, Brian Lara walking under "avenue of bats," vert.

1995, Feb. 3 — **Litho.** — **Perf. 14**
2908-2910 A209 Set of 3 — 8.25 8.25

Souvenir Sheet
2911 A209 $300 multicolored — 7.00 7.00

A210

A211

Babe Ruth (1895-1948) — A212

Type A211 various portraits like #2914. $2000, Portrait, Ruth holding bat, vert.

Type A212 illustration reduced.

1995, Feb. 6 — **Litho.** — **Perf. 14**
2912 A210 $65 multi — 1.40 1.40

Self-Adhesive (#2913)
Size: 64x89mm (#2913)
2913 A211 $350 Set of 12 — 70.00 70.00

Litho. & Embossed
Perf. 12
2914 A212 $1000 gold & sep 25.00

Embossed
2914A A212 $2000 gold — 29.00

Litho.
Perf. 14
2915 A211 $65 Sheet of 12, #a.-l. — 14.00 14.00

Souvenir Sheet
2916 A211 $500 like #2912a, horiz. — 12.00 12.00

No. 2912 issued in sheets of 9. Portraits of Babe Ruth in No. 2913 are same as in No. 2915, but surrounded by gold frame, gold autograph, baseballs, and simulated perfs. No. 2913 was sold in sealed cellophane package. To affix stamps, backing containing biographical information must be removed.

Disney Characters at Work — A213

No. 2917, $30 — Animal workers: a, Veterinarian. b, Animal trainer. c, Animal psychiatrist. d, Ornithologist. e, Dog groomer. f, Herpetologist. g, Pet shop keeper. h, Park ranger. i, Aquarist.
No. 2918, $30 — Arts & crafts: a, Mickey the animator, Pluto. b, Goofy the tailor, Mickey. c, Pete the glass blower, Morty. d, Clarabelle modeling for Minnie the artist. e, Daisy sculpts Donald. f, Donald, nephews working with clay. g, Watchmakers, Chip & Dale. h, Locksmith Donald, nephews. i, Grandma Duck makes a quilt.
No. 2919, $30 — Medical group: a, Family doctor. b, Optometrist. c, Nurse. d, Psychiatrist. e, Physical therapist. f, Dentist. g, Radiologist. h, Pharmacist. i, Chiropractor.
No. 2920, $35 — Hard hat & company, vert.: a, Mickey, Pluto in truck. b, Mickey at work. c, Goofy jackhammer. d, Minnie at work. e, Forklifters. f, Construction contractor. g, Carpenter. h, Bulldozer.
No. 2921, $35 — Home services, vert.: a, Mickey, plumber. b, Mickey, paperboy. c, Huey, Dewey, Louie, moving service. d, Pete, handyman. e, Donald, nephews' house painting service. f, Goofy, washer repairman. g, Minnie, babysitter. h, Daisy cares for Grandma Duck.
No. 2922, $35 — Public service workers, vert.: a, Policeman. b, Fireman. c, Ambulance driver. d, Crossing guard. e, Museum docent. f, Census taker. g, Street maintenance workers. h, Sanitation worker.
No. 2923, $200, Goofy, zoo keeper. No. 2924, $200, Camera, Pluto, vert. No. 2925, $200, Goofy, surgeon. No. 2926, $200, Minnie, pups, tool chest. No. 2927, $200, Minnie, maid. No. 2928, $200, Horace, politician.

1995, Feb. 23 — **Litho.** — **Perf. 13½x14**
Sheets of 9, #a-i
2917-2919 A213 Set of 3 — 18.00 18.00

Sheets of 8, #a-h
Perf. 14x13½
2920-2922 A213 Set of 3 — 19.00 19.00

Souvenir Sheets
2923-2928 A213 Set of 6 — 39.00 39.00

Nos. 2917-2922 exist in sheets of 7 or 8 $5 stamps + label. The label replaces Nos. 2917e, 2918e, 2919g, 2920h, 2921h, 2922e. These sheets became available Nov. 20, 1996.

Nos. 1022, 1033, 1045, 1061 Surcharged in Red "SALVATION / ARMY / 1895-1995"
1995, Apr. 24 — **Litho.** — **Perf. 14**
2928A A91 $6 on 60c #1033
2928B A91 $20 on 60c #1045
2928C A91 $30 on 60c #1022
2928D A91 $35 on 60c #1061

New Year 1995 (Year of the Boar) — A214

No. 2929 — Stylized boars: a, $20. b, $30. c, $50, Facing forward. denomination LR. d, $100. f, $50, "Abundant Year of the Pig." g, $50, "Fortunate Year of the Pig." h, $50, Facing forward, denomination LL. $150, Face, Chinese inscriptions.

1995, May 4 — **Litho.** — **Perf. 14½**
2929 A214 Block of 4, #a.-d. — 6.00 6.00
e. Souvenir sheet of 4, #c, f.-h. — 8.00 8.00

Souvenir Sheet
2930 A214 $150 multicolored — 6.00 6.00

No. 2929 was issued in miniature sheets of 4.

A215

Birds: $5, Goshawk. $6, Lapwing. $8, Ornate umbrellabird. $15, Slatey-headed parakeet. $19, Regent bowerbird. $20, Egyptian goose. $25, White-winged crossbill. $30, Waxwing. $35, Ruff. $60, Hoopoe. $100, Superb starling. $500, Great jacamar.

1995, May 8 — **Litho.** — **Perf. 14½x13½**
2931 A215 $5 multicolored — .25 .25
2932 A215 $6 multicolored — .30 .25
2933 A215 $8 multicolored — .35 .25
2934 A215 $15 multicolored — .45 .30
2935 A215 $19 multicolored — .55 .30
2936 A215 $20 multicolored — .60 .40
2937 A215 $25 multicolored — .70 .45
2938 A215 $30 multicolored — .80 .50
2939 A215 $35 multicolored — 1.00 .60
2940 A215 $60 multicolored — 1.25 1.10
2941 A215 $100 multicolored — 2.00 2.00
2942 A215 $500 multicolored — 9.00 8.50
Nos. 2931-2942 (12) — 17.25 14.90

Nolan Ryan, Baseball Player — A216

No. 2943: a, Looking left, Mets. b, With bat, Mets. c, Pitching, Mets. d, Looking toward home plate, Angels. e, Pitching, Angels. f, Without hat, Angels. g, In red cap, Astros. h, Pitching, Astros. i, In black cap, Astros. j,

Pitching, Rangers. k, Getting ready to pitch, Rangers. l, Up close, Rangers.

1995   **Litho.**   *Imperf.*
Self-Adhesive
Size: 64x89mm
2943 A216 $350 Set of 12,
     #a.-l.   70.00 70.00

Nos. 2943a-2943l are printed on thin cards, distributed in boxed sets containing certificate of aunthenticity and sealed in celophane packages. To affix stamps, backing containing biographical information must be removed.

Miniature Sheets of 12

Singapore '95 — A217

No. 2944, $35 — Dogs: a, Gordon setter. b, Long-haired chihuahua. c, Dalmation. d, Afghan. e, English bulldog. f, Miniature schnauzer. g, Clumber spaniel. h, Pekingese. i, St. Bernard. j, English cocker spaniel. k, Alaskan malamute. l, Rottweiler.
No. 2945, $35 — Cats: a, Norwegian forest cat. b, Scottish fold. c, Red burmese. d, British blue-hair. e, Abyssinian. f, Siamese. g, Exotic shorthair. h, Turkish van cat. i, Black Persian. j, Black-tipped burmilla. k, Singapura. l, Calico shorthair.
No. 2946, $35 — Horses: a, Chestnut thoroughbred colt. b, Liver chestnut quarter horse. c, Black Freisian. d, Chestnut Belgian. e, Appaloosa. f, Lipizzanas. g, Chestnut hunter. h, British shire. i, Palomino. j, Seal brown point. k, Arab. l, Afghanistan Kabardin.
No. 2947, $300, Golden retriever. No. 2948, $300, Maine coon. No. 2949, $300, American Anglo-Arab.

1995, June 1   *Perf. 14*
Sheets of 12, #a-l
2944-2946 A217 Set of 3   30.00 30.00
Souvenir Sheets
2947-2949 A217 Set of 3   18.00 18.00

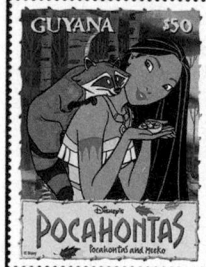

Pocahontas A218

No. 2950 — Characters from Disney animated film: a, Pocahontas, Meeko. b, John Smith. c, Chief Powhatan. d, Kocoum. e, Ratcliffe. f, Wiggins. g, Nakoma. h, Thomas.
No. 2951, Meeko, horiz.

1995, June 23   **Litho.**   *Perf. 13½x14*
2950 A218 $50 Sheet of 8,
     #a.-h.   17.00 17.00
Souvenir Sheet
Perf. 14x13½
2951 A218 $300 multicolored   10.00 10.00
See Nos. 2985-2990.

UN, 50th Anniv. — A219

No. 2952 — Map of: a, $35, North, South America. b, $60, Europe, Africa. c, $200, Asia, Australia.

$300, Secretary General Boutros Boutros-Ghali.

1995, July 6   *Perf. 14*
2952 A219   Strip of 3, #a.-c. 5.50 5.50
Souvenir Sheet
2953 A219 $300 multicolored   5.00 5.00

End of World War II, 50th Anniv. A220

No. 2954: a, P61 Black Widow. b, PT boat. c, B26 Marauder. d, Cruiser USS San Juan. e, US Gato class submarine. f, US destroyer.
No. 2955: a, Jan. 1945, Battle of Bulge is over. b, Sigfried Line is breached. c, Liberation of concentration camps. d, Operation "Manna," Allies drop food to starving Dutch. e, GIs looking for snipers at end of Italian campaign. f, Newspaper headline announces Hitler's suicide. g, Soviet tanks pour into Berlin. h, U-858, first German warship to surrender in US waters.
No. 2956, $300, Battleship, aircraft carrier. No. 2957, $300, Top of Brandenburg Gate.

1995, July 6
2954 A220 $60 Sheet of 6,
     #a.-f. + label 7.25 7.25
2955 A220 $60 Sheet of 8,
     #a.-h. + label   9.50 9.50
Souvenir Sheets
2956-2957 A220   Set of 2   10.00 10.00
No. 2957 contains one 57x42mm stamp.

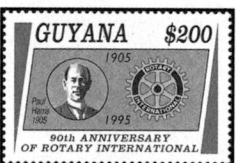

FAO, 50th Anniv. — A221

No. 2958: a, $35, Girl carrying sack on head. b, $60, Man carrying sack, woman sorting sacks. c, $200, Woman lifting sack.
$300, Pouring from ladle into bowl.

1995, July 6   **Litho.**   *Perf. 14*
2958 A221   Strip of 3, #a.-c.   5.75 5.75
Souvenir Sheet
2959 A221 $300 multicolored   5.00 5.00
No. 2958 is a continuous design.

Rotary Intl., 90th Anniv. A222

Designs: $200, Paul Harris, Rotary emblem. $300, Old, new Rotary emblems.

1995, July 6
2960 A222 $200 multicolored   4.50 4.50
Souvenir Sheet
2961 A222 $300 multicolored   5.25 5.25

1995 Boy Scout Jamboree, Netherlands — A223

Slogan, emblem, and: $20, Campfire. $25, Scout, beach. $30, Hiking. $35, Snorkeling. $60, Natl. flag, scout salute. $200, Fishing from boat.
No. 2968, $300, Canoeing. No. 2969, $300, Camping.

1995, July 6
2962-2967 A223   Set of 6   7.00 7.00
Souvenir Sheets
2968-2969 A223   Set of 2   10.00 10.00

Queen Mother, 95th Birthday A224

No. 2970: a, Drawing. b, Violet hat. c, Formal portrait. d, Green blue hat.
$325, As younger woman.

1995, July 6   *Perf. 13½x14*
2970 A224 $100 Strip or block of
     4, #a.-d.   8.25 8.25
Souvenir Sheet
2971 A224 $325 multicolored   7.00 7.00
No. 2970 issued in sheets of 2.
Sheets of Nos. 2970 and 2971 exist with black border in margin with text "In Memoriam/1900-2002."

Holidays of the World A225

No. 2972: a, Thanksgiving, US. b, Christmas, Germany. c, Hanukkah, Israel. d, Easter, Spain. e, Carnivale, brazil. f, Bastill Day, France. g, Independence Day, India. h, St. Patrick's Day, Ireland.
$300, Chinese New Year, China.

1995, Aug. 8   **Litho.**   *Perf. 14*
2972 A225 $60 Sheet of 8, #a.-
     h.   9.75 9.75
Souvenir Sheet
2973 A225 $300 multicolored   5.00 5.00

Marine Life A226

No. 2974, vert: a, Cocoa damselfish. b, Sergeant major. c, Beau gregory. d, Yellowtail damselfish.
No. 2975: a, $30, Butterflyfish. b, $35, Bluehead. c, $60, Yellow damselfish. d, $200, Clown wrasse.
No. 2976: a, $30, Lemon shark. b, $35, Green turtle. c, $60 Sawfish. d, $200, Stingray.
No. 2977, $60: a, Tiger shark. b, Needlefish. c, Horse-eye jack. d, Princess parrotfish. e, Yellowtail snapper. f, Spotted snake eel. g, Trunkfish. h, Cherubfish. i, French angelfish.
No. 2978, $60: a, Sei whale. b, Barracuda. c, Mutton snapper. d, Hawksbill turtle. e, Spanish hogfish. f, Queen angelfish. g, Porkfish. h, Trumpetfish. i, Electric ray.
No. 2979, $300, Carcharodon carcharias. No. 2980, $300, Dermochelys coriacea.

1995, Sept. 5   **Litho.**   *Perf. 14*
2974 A226 $80 Strip of 4, #a.-
     d.   6.00 6.00
Sheets of 4, #a-d
2975-2976 A226   Set of 2   12.00 12.00
Sheets of 9, #a-i
2977-2978 A226   Set of 2   26.00 26.00
Souvenir Sheets
2979-2980 A226   Set of 2   16.00 16.00
No. 2974 was issued in sheets of 4.

Miniature Sheets of 8

1996 Summer Olympics, Atlanta — A227

No. 2981 $60: a, Shot put. b, Relay. c, Balance beam. d, Cycling. e, Synchronized swimming. f, Hurdles. g, Pommel horse. h, Discus thrower, head down.
No. 2982, $60: a, Pole vault. b, Long jump. c, Track. d, Wrestling. e, Discus thrower, head up. f, Basketball. g, Boxing. h, Weight lifting.
No. 2983, $300, Long jump. No. 2984, $300, Runners.

1995, Oct. 2   **Litho.**   *Perf. 14*
Sheets of 8, #a-h
2981-2982 A227   Set of 2   16.00 16.00
Souvenir Sheets
2983-2984 A227   Set of 2   10.00 10.00

Pocahontas Type of 1995
Miniature Sheets

Nos. 2985-2987: Various scenes from Disney animated film, horiz.
No. 2988, $325, Pocahontas behind tree branch, horiz. No. 2989, Pocahontas, Powhatan, horiz. No. 2990, $325, Pocahontas kneeling.

Perf. 14x13½, 13½x14 (#2990)
1995, Oct. 9   **Litho.**
2985 A218 $8 Sheet of 9,
     #a.-i.   3.50 3.50
2986 A218 $30 Sheet of 9,
     #a.-i.   11.50 11.50
2987 A218 $35 Sheet of 9,
     #a.-i.   15.00 15.00
Souvenir Sheets
2988-2990 A218 Set of 3   32.50 32.50

Fauna — A228

No. 2991: a, $35, House martin. b, $60. Hobby. c, $20, Sand martin (a). d, $200, Long-tailed skua (b).
No. 2992: a, Olive colobus. b, Violet-backed starling. c, Diana monkey. d, African palm civet. e, Giraffe, zebras. f, African linsang. g, Royal antelope (fawn). h, Royal antelope (adult, fawn) (g. i). i, Palm squirrel.
No. 2993, $300, Brush pig. No. 2994, $300, Chimpanzee.

1995, Oct. 18   **Litho.**   *Perf. 14*
2991 A228   Block of 4, #a.-d.   7.00 7.00
2992 A228 $60 Sheet of 9,
     #a.-i.   9.00 9.00
Souvenir Sheets
2993-2994 A228   Set of 2   10.00 10.00
No. 2991 was issued in sheets of 16 stamps.

Queenstown Holy Mosque, Georgetown, Cent. — A229

1995, Dec. 1   **Litho.**   *Perf. 14*
2995 A229 $60 multicolored   1.00 1.00

Christmas
A230

New Year 1996
(Year of the
Rat) — A237

Prehistoric Animals — A241

Details or entire paintings, by Carracci: $25, The Angel of Annunciation. $30, Annunciation of the Virgin. $35, Assumption of the Virgin. $60, Baptism of Christ. $100, Madonna and Child. $300, Birth by the Virgin.
No. 3002, $325, Madonna and Ten Saints, by Fiorentino. No. 3003, $325, Mystical Marriage of St. Catherine, by Carracci.

1995, Dec. 4   *Perf. 13½x14*
2996-3001 A230 Set of 6   9.25 9.25
Souvenir Sheets
3002-3003 A230 Set of 2   11.00 11.00

Guyana Defense
Force, 30th
Anniv. — A231

1995, Dec. 7   *Perf. 14*
3004 A231 $6 Woman with gun   .20   .20
3005 A231 $60 Man with gun   .90   .90

John Lennon
(1940-80) — A232

1995
3006 A232 $35 multicolored   1.00 1.00
No. 3006 was issued in sheets of 16.

Nobel Prize Fund
Established,
Cent. — A233

No. 3007, $35: a, Henri Becquerel, physics, 1903. b, Igor Tamm, physics, 1958. c, Georges Köhler, medicine, 1984. d, Gerhard Domagk, medicine, 1939. e, Yasunari Kawabata, literature, 1968. f, Maurice Allais, economics, 1988. g, Aristide Briand, peace, 1926. h, Pavel Cherenkov, physics, 1958. i, Feodor Lynen, medicine, 1964.
No. 3008 $35: a, Adolf von Baeyer, chemistry, 1905. b, Hideki Yukawa, physics, 1949. c, George W. Beadle, medicine, 1958. d, Edwin M. McMillian, chemistry, 1951. e, Samuel C.C. Ting, physics, 1976. f, Saint-John Perse, literature, 1960. g, John F. Enders, medicine, 1954. h, Felix Bloch, physics, 1952. i, P.B. Medawar, medicine, 1960.
No. 3009, $35: a, Albrecht Kossel, medicine, 1910. b, Arthur H. Compton, physics, 1927. c, N.M. Butler, peace, 1931. d, Charles Laveran, medicine, 1907. e, George R. Minot, medicine, 1934. f, Henry H. Dale, medicine, 1936. g, Jacques Monod, medicine, 1965. h, Alfred Hershey, medicine, 1969. i, Pär Lagerkvist, literature, 1951.
No. 3010, $35: a, Francis Crick, medicine, 1962. b, Manne Siegbahn, physics, 1924. c,

Eisaku Sato, peace, 1974. d, Robert Koch, medicine, 1905. e, Edgar D. Adrian, medicine, 1932. f, Erwin Neher, medicine, 1991. g, Henry Taube, chemistry, 1983. h, Norman Angell, peace, 1933. i, Robert Robinson, chemistry, 1947.
No. 3011 $35: a, Nikolai Basov, physics, 1964. b, Klas Arnoldson, peace, 1908. c, René Sully-Prudhomme, literature, 1901. d, Robert W. Wilson, physics, 1978. e, Hugo Theorell, medicine, 1955. f, Nelly Sachs, literature, 1966. g, Hans von Euler-Chelpin, chemistry, 1929. h, Mairead Corrigan, peace, 1976. i, Willis E. Lamb, Jr, physics, 1955.
No. 3012 $35: a, Norman F. Ramsey, physics, 1989. b, Chen Ning Yang, physics, 1957. c, Earl W. Sutherland, Jr., medicine, 1971. d, Paul Karrer, chemistry, 1937. e, Harmut Michel, chemistry, 1988. f, Richard Kuhn, chemistry, 1938. g, P.A.M. Dirac, physics, 1933. h, Victor Grignard, chemistry, 1912. i, Richard Willstätter, chemistry, 1915.
No. 3013, $300, Le Duc Tho, peace, 1973. No. 3014, $300, Yasunari Kawabata, literature, 1968. No. 3015, $300, Heinrich Böll, literature, 1972. No. 3016, $300, Henry Kissinger, peace, 1973. No. 3017, $300, Kenichi Fukui, chemistry, 1981. No. 3018, $300, Lech Walesa, peace, 1983.

1995, Dec. 20   *Litho.*   *Perf. 14*
Sheets of 9, #a-i
3007-3012 A233 Set of 6   57.00 57.00
Souvenir Sheets
3013-3018 A233 Set of 6   36.00 36.00

Caribbean Development Bank, 25th
Anniv. — A234

1995, Dec. 29   *Litho.*   *Perf. 14*
3019 A234 $60 multicolored   1.00 1.00

Marilyn
Monroe
(1926-62)
A235

No. 3020, Various portraits. No. 3021, Portrait, horiz.

1995, Dec. 29   *Perf. 13½x14*
3020 A235 $60 Sheet of 9, #a.-
            i.   9.00 9.00
Souvenir Sheet
Perf. 14x13½
3021 A235 $300 multicolored   5.00 5.00

David
Copperfield,
Magician
A236

Nos. 3022-3023, Various portraits, magic acts.

1995, Dec. 29   *Perf. 13½x14*
3022 A236 $60 Sheet of 9,
            #a.-i.   10.00 10.00
Souvenir Sheet
3023 A236 $300 multicolored   5.00 5.00

No. 3024 — Stylized rats: a, $20. b, $30. c, $50, light brown & multi. d, $100.
No. 3025: a, Like #3024a, b, Like #3024b. c, Like #3024c, darker brown & multi. d, Like #3024d.
No. 3026, Rat facing forward.

1996, Jan. 2   *Perf. 14½*
3024 A237 Block of 4, #a.-d.   4.00 4.00
Miniature Sheet
3025 A237 $50 Sheet of 4, #a.-
            d.   3.50 3.50
Souvenir Sheet
3026 A237 $150 multicolored   3.50 3.50
No. 3024 was issued in sheets of 16 stamps.

UNICEF,
50th
Anniv.
A238

No. 3027: a, Children, building in background. b, Man, boy, tree in background. c, Children behind tree. d, Man, children.

1996, Jan. 2   *Perf. 14*
3027 A238 $1100 Sheet of 4,
            #a.-d.   70.00 70.00
No. 3027 is a continuous design.

Paintings by
Peter Paul
Rubens
A239

Details or entire paintings: $6, The Garden of Love. $10, Two Sleeping Children. $20, All Saints Day. $25, Sacrifice of Abraham. $30, The Last Supper. $35, The Birth of Henry of Navarre. $40, Standing Female Saint Study. $50, $60, The Garden of Love, each diff. No. 3037, $200, The Martyrdom of St. Livinus. No. 3038, $200, Der Heilige Franz Von Paula. $300, The Union of Maria de Medici and Henry IV.
No. 3039, $325, The Three Crosses. No. 3040, $325, Decius Mus Addressing the Legions, horiz. No. 3041, $325, Triumph of Henry IV, horiz.

1996, Jan. 29   *Litho.*   *Perf. 14*
3028-3038A A239 Set of 11   19.00 19.00
Souvenir Sheets
3039-3041 A239 Set of 3   18.50 18.50
Nos. 3039-3041 each contain one 57x85mm or 85x57mm stamp.

Miniature Sheets

A240

No. 3042: a, Tarbosaurus. b, Hadrosaurus. c, Polacanthus. d, Psittacosaurus. e, Ornitholestes. f, Yangchuanosaurus. g, Scelidosaurus. h, Kentrosaurus. i, Coelophysis. j, Lesothosaurus. k, Plateosaurus. l, Staurikosaurus.
No. 3043, $35: a, Eudimorphodon. b, Criorynchus. c, Elasmosaurus. d, Rhomaleosaurus. e, Ceresiosaurus. f, Mesosaurus. g, Grendelius. h, Nothosaurus. i, Mixosaurus. j, Placodus. k, Coelacanth. l, Mosasaurus.
No. 3044, $35: a, Ornithomimus. b, Pteranodon. c, Rhamphorynchus. d, Ornitholestes. e, Brachiosaurus. f, Parasaurolophus. g, Ceratosaurus. h, Camarasaurus. i, Euoplocephalus. j, Scutellosaurus. k, Compsognathus. l, Stegoceras.
No. 3045, $35: a, Apatosaurus. b, Archaeopteryx. c, Dimorphodon. d, Deinonychus. e, Coelophysis. f, Tyrannosaurus. g, Triceratops. h, Anatosaurus. i, Saltasaurus. j, Allosaurus. k, Oviraptor. l, Stegosaurus.
No. 3046, $60: a, Heterodontosaurus (b). b, Compsognathus (c). c, Ornithomimus (b).
No. 3047, $60: a, Saurolophus. b, Muttaburrasaurus (a). c, Dicraeosaurus (b).
No. 3048, $300, Apatosaurus, allosaurus, horiz. No. 3049, $300, Tyrannosaurus rex. No. 3050, $300, Quetzalcoatlus. No. 3051, $300, Lagosuchus. No. 3052, $300Struthiomimus.

1996, Feb. 12
3042 A240 $35 Sheet of 12,
            #a.-l.   8.00 8.00
Sheets of 12, #a-l
3043-3045 A241 Set of 3   24.00 24.00
Sheets of 3, #a-c
3046-3047 A240 Set of 2   7.00 7.00
Souvenir Sheets
3048-3049 A240 Set of 2   12.00 12.00
3050-3052 A241 Set of 3   18.00 18.00

Pandas — A242

No. 3053 — In tree: a, Lying on back, looking right. b, Arms, legs around branch. c, Paws holding onto tree. d, Sitting, looking left.
No. 3054 — On rocks by stream: a, Standing. b, Sitting, holding bamboo stick. c, Holding bamboo to mouth. d, Lying on stomach.

1996, Apr. 12   *Litho.*   *Perf. 14*
3053 A242 $60 Sheet of 4, #a.-d. 5.00 5.00
3054 A242 $60 Sheet of 4, #a.-d. 5.00 5.00
China '96, 9th Asian Intl. Philatelic Exhibtion.

Mushrooms,
Insects and
Coral — A243

Designs: $20, Yellow morce, leaf beetle. $25, Green spored mushroom. $30, Leaf beetle, common mushroom. $35, Monarch caterpillars, pine cone mushroom.
No. 3059, $60: a, Green-beaded jelly club. b, Aspic puffball. c, Stalkless paxillus. d, Stoutstalked amanita.
No. 3060, $60: a, Fly agaric. b, Graying yellow russula, click beetle. c, Netted stinkhorn, housefly. d, Butterfly hunter, stropharia.
No. 3061, $60: a, Cockle-shell lentinus. b, Parasitic volvariella. c, Deadly lepiota. d, Shaggy-stalked boleta.

No. 3062: a, Armillauella mellea. b, Sealy vase chanterelle. c, Bitter pholiota. d, Flute white helvella. e, Fading scarlet waxy cap. f, Jask's lantern. g, Hygzocybe acutoconica. h, Mycena viscosa.

No. 3063, $300, Orange mycena. No. 3064, $300, Violet-branched coral, Red raspberry slime, yellow-tipped coral, horiz.

1996, May 3   Litho.   Perf. 14

3055-3058	A243	Set of 4	3.50	3.50

Strips of 4, #a-d

3059-3061	A243	Set of 3	13.50	13.50
3062	A243	$60 Sheet of 8, #a.-h.	9.00	9.00

Souvenir Sheets

3063-3064	A243	Set of 2	11.50	11.50

Nos. 3059-3061 were issued in sheets of 8 stamps.

Deng Xiaoping, Chinese Communist Leader — A244

No. 3065: a, Painting inscription. b, With dignitaries, waving. c, Signing autograph. d, Waving.
$300, Wearing white shirt, vert.

1996   Perf. 13

3065	A244	$30 Strip or block of 4, #a.-d.	2.00	2.00

Souvenir Sheet

3066	A244	$300 multicolored	5.00	5.00

No. 3065 issued in sheets of 16 stamps.

Queen Elizabeth II, 70th Birthday A245

No. 3067: a, Portrait wearing blue dress. b, Wearing blue green dress, hat. c, On throne, opening Parliament.
$325, In ceremonial attire.

1996, May 3   Litho.   Perf. 13½x14

3067	A245	$100 Strip of 3, #a.-c.	5.00	5.00

Souvenir Sheet

3068	A245	$325 multicolored	5.25	5.25

No. 3067 was issued in sheets of 9 stamps, with each strip having a different order.

Jerusalem, 3000th Anniv. — A246

No. 3069: a, $30. The Hulda Gates. b, $35, Old City, View from Mt. of Olives. c, $200, Absalom's Memorial, Kidron Valley.
$300, Children's Memorial.

1996   Litho.   Perf. 14

3069	A246	Sheet of 3, #a.-d.	5.00	5.00

Souvenir Sheet

3070	A246	$300 multicolored	5.00	5.00

Birds — A247

No. 3071: a, Blue & yellow macaw. b, Andean condor. c, Crested eagle. d, White-tailed trogon. e, Toco toucan. f, Great horned owl. g, Andean cock-of-the-rock. h, Great curassow.

No. 3071I — Hummingbirds: j, Long-billed starthroat. k, Velvet-purple coronet. l, Racket-tailed coquette. m, Violet-tailed sylph. n, Broad-tailed hummingbird. o, Blue-tufted star-throat. p, White-necked jacobin. q, Ruby-throated hummingbird.

No. 3072, Ornate hawk eagle, horiz. No. 3073, Gould's violet-ear.

1996, July 10

3071	A247	$60 Sheet of 8, #a.-h.	7.50	7.50
3071I	A247	$60 Sheet of 8, #j.-q.	7.50	7.50

Souvenir Sheets

3072	A247	$300 multicolored	5.50	5.50
3073	A247	$300 multicolored	5.50	5.50

Radio, Cent. A248

Entertainers: $20, Frank Sinatra. $35, Gene Autry. $60, Groucho Marx. $200, Red Skelton. $300, Burl Ives.

1996, July 25

3074-3077	A248	Set of 4	5.00	5.00

Souvenir Sheet

3078	A248	$300 multicolored	5.00	5.00

1996 Summer Olympic Games, Atlanta A249

Designs: $20, Pancratium. $30, Olympic Stadium, 1956. $60, Leonid Spirin, 20k walk, 1956, vert. $200, Lars Hall, modern pentathlon, 1952, 1956, vert.

No. 3083, $50, vert.: a, Florence Griffith-Joyner. b, Ines Geissler. c, Nadia Comaneci. d, Tatiana Gutsu. e, Olga Korbut. f, Barbara Krause. g, Olga Bryzgina. h, Fanny Blankers-Koen. i, Irena Szewinska.

No. 3084, $50, vert.: a, Gerd Wessig. b, Jim Thorpe. c, Norman Read. d, Lasse Viren. e, Milt Campbell. f, Abebe Bikila. g, Jesse Owens. h, Viktor Saneev. i, Waldemer Cierpinski.

No. 3085, $50, vert.: a, Dietmar Schmidt. b, Pam Shriver. c, Zina Garrison. d, Hyun Jung-Hwa. e, Steffi Graf. f, Michael Jordan. g, Karch Kiraly. h, "Magic" Johnson. i, Ingolf Wiegert.

No. 3086, $50: a, Volleyball. b, Basketball. c, Tennis. d, Table tennis. e, Baseball. f, Handball. g, Field hockey. h, Water polo. i, Soccer.

No. 3087, $50, vert.: a, Cycling. b, Hurdles. c, High jump. d, Diving. e, Weight lifting. f, Canoeing. g, Wrestling. h, Gymnastics. i, Running.

No. 3088, $300, Carl Lewis, track and field gold medalist. No. 3089, $300, US defeats Korea for gold medal in baseball, 1988.

1996, July 25

3079-3082	A249	Set of 4	5.00	5.00

Sheets of 9, #a-i

3083-3087	A249	Set of 5	35.00	35.00

Souvenir Sheets

3088-3089	A249	Set of 2	9.75	9.75

Olymphilex '96 (#3088).

Disney Cartoons — A250

No. 3090 — Mickey outdoors: a, Mickey's Bait Shop. b, Ol' Mickey, The Lumbercamp Legend and Pluto the Yellow Dog. c, For All Men Are Equal Before Fish.

No. 3091, vert. — Super sports: a, BMX Championships. b, Goofy, Hockey Superstar. c, Malibu Surf City.

No. 3092, vert. — Nautical Mickey: a, The Path to Adventure is Shown in the Stars. b, Captain Mickey's Steamship School. c, Ahoy, Follow the Wind on Waves of Fortune.

No. 3093, $250, M. Mouse, ESQ, Lawman, vert.: No. 3094, $250, All Aboard, Ride the Great American Transcontinental Railroad. No. 3095, $250, Mouse and Pinkerton, Wild West Detective Agency, vert. $300, Donald's Rock & Ice Mountaineers. $325, Guided by The Great Spirit, vert.

1996, July 26   Perf. 14x13½, 13½x14

3090	A250	$60 Strip of 3, #a.-c.	4.50	4.50
3091	A250	$80 Strip of 3, #a.-c.	6.00	6.00
3092	A250	$100 Strip of 3, #a.-c.	8.50	8.50

Souvenir Sheets

3093-3095	A250	Set of 3	22.50	22.50
3096	A250	$300 multi	7.50	7.50
3097	A250	$325 multi	8.50	8.50

Nos. 3090-3092 were issued in sheets of 9 stamps.

Disney Antique Toys — A251

No. 3098: a, Two-Gun Mickey. b, Wood-jointed Mickey doll. c, Donald Jack-in-the Box. d, Rocking Minnie. e, Fireman Donald Duck. f, Long-billed Donald Duck. g, Painted wood Mickey doll. h, Wind-up Jiminy Cricket.

No. 3099, $300, Mickey doll. No. 3100, $300, Carousel train.

1996, July 26   Perf. 13½x14

3098	A251	$6 Sheet of 8, #a.-h.	7.00	7.00

Souvenir Sheets

3099-3100	A251	Set of 2	18.00	18.00

Domestic Cats A253

No. 3102, $60: a, Birman. b, American curl. c, Turkish Angora. d, European shorthair. e, Persian. f, Scottish fold. g, Sphynx. h, Malayan. i, Cornish rex.

No. 3103, $60, vert: a, Norwegian forest. b, Russian shorthair. c, European shorthair. d, Birman. e, Ragdoll. f, Egyptian mau. g, Persian. h, Angora. i, Siamese.

No. 3104, $300, Maine coon, vert. No. 3105, $300, Himalayan.

1996, Sept. 18   Perf. 14

Sheets of 9, #a-i

3102-3103	A253	Set of 2	19.00	19.00

Souvenir Sheets

3104-3105	A253	Set of 2	11.00	11.00

Deep Ocean Exploration — A254

No. 3106: a, Goblin shark, coelacanth. b, Remote operated vehicle, JASON. c, Deep water invertebrates. d, Submarine NR1 (e). e, Giant squid (b, c, f, g, h, j, m). f, Sperm whale (b, c). g, Volcanic vents, submersible ALVIN. h, Air-recycling pressure suit, shipwreck. i, Bacteria survey, submersible SHINKAI 6500. j, Giant tube worms. k, Anglerfish. l, Six-gill shark (k). m. Autonomous underwater vehicle ABE. n, Viperfish. o, Swallower, hatchetfish. $300, Sea anemone.

1996, Dec. 2   Litho.   Perf. 14

3106	A254	$30 Sheet of 15, #a.-o.	7.50	7.50

Souvenir Sheet

3107	A254	$300 multicolored	5.25	5.25

Characters from Disney's Snow White in Christmas Scenes A255

Designs: $6, Snow White. $20, Doc. $25, Dopey, Sneezy. $30, Sleepy, Happy, Bashful. $35, Dopey, Santa. $60, Dopey, fireplace. $100, Dopey, Grumpy. $200, Dopey as Santa.

No. 3116, $300, Snow White looking at squirrel in box. No. 3117, $300, Dopey placing star on tree.

1996, Dec. 16   Perf. 13½x14

3108-3115	A255	Set of 8	17.50	17.50

Souvenir Sheets

3116-3117	A255	Set of 2	22.00	22.00

Marine Life A256

No. 3118: a, Red gorgonians. b, Plexaura homomalla, butterflyfish (a, c). c, Dendronephtbya. d, Common clownfish, anemone, mushroom coral (a). e, Anemone, horse-eyed jack (d, g-h). f, Slender snappers (c), splendid coral trout. g, Anemones. h, Brain coral, Indo-Pacific hard coral. i, Cup coral (f, h).

Elvis Presley's First "Hit" Year, 40th Anniv. A252

Various portraits.

1996, Sept. 8   Litho.   Perf. 13½x14

3101	A252	$100 Sheet of 6, #a.-f.	11.00	11.00

1996, Dec. 2   **Litho.**   *Perf. 14*
3118 A256 $60 Sheet of 9,
   #a.-i.   11.00 11.00

New Year 1997
(Year of the
Ox) — A257

No. 3119 — Denomination at: a, $20, LR. b,
$30, LL. c, $35, UR. d, $50, UL.
No. 3120: a, Like #3119a. b, Like #3119b. c,
Like #3119c.
$150, Ox, facing.

1997, Jan. 2   **Litho.**   *Perf. 14½*
3119 A257   Block of 4, #a.-d.   3.75 3.75
3120 A257 $50 Sheet of 4, #a.-
   c. + #3119d   4.00 4.00
     Souvenir Sheet
3121 A257 $150 multicolored   3.00 3.00

No. 3119 was issued in sheets of 16 stamps.

Mickey and Friends Celebrate Chinese
Lunar New Year — A258

No. 3122: a, $6, Mickey. b, $20, Home visit.
c, $25, Fortune lantern. d, $30, Silhouette. e,
$35, Flower market. f, $60, Harmonious man,
woman.
No. 3123: a, Red-pocket money. b, Lion
dance. c, Calligraphy. d, Surplus every year. e,
Fireworks. f, Ox.
$150, Mickey marching, vert. $200, Mickey,
ox.

1997, Jan. 2   *Perf. 14x13½*
3122 A258   Sheet of 6, #a.-
   f.   6.00 6.00
3123 A258 $30 Sheet of 6, #a.-
   f.   6.50 6.50
     Souvenir Sheets
     Perf. 13½x14, 14x13½
3124 A258 $150 multicolored   5.50 5.50
3125 A258 $200 multicolored   6.00 6.00

Marine
Life
A259

No. 3126, $6, Angelfish. No. 3127, $6, Hyed
snapper. $20, Box fish. $25, Golden damselfish. $35, Clown triggerfish. $200, Harlequin tuskfish.
$300, Caribbean flower coral.

1996   **Litho.**   *Perf. 14*
3126-3131 A259 Set of 6   8.50 8.50
     Souvenir Sheet
3132 A259 $300 multicolored   7.00 7.00

Hotel Tower, 50th Anniv. — A260

1996, Dec. 28
3133 A260 $30 multicolored   1.00 1.00

Souvenir Sheet

The Summer Palace, Beijing — A261

Illustration reduced.

1996, Apr. 12   **Litho.**   *Perf. 13*
3134 A261 $60 multicolored   2.00 2.00
China '96. No. 3134 was not available until
March 1997.

Transfer of Hong Kong — A262

No. 3135, $80: a, Tortoise. b, Dragon. c,
Unicorn. d, Phoenix.
No. 3136, $80, vert.: a, Swallow & willow. b,
Kingfisher & chrysanthemum. c, Crane & pine.
d, Peacock & peony.
No. 3137, $80, vert.: a-d, Various kites.
No. 3138, vert.: a-b, Paintings of mountains
and lakes.

1997, Feb. 12   *Perf. 14*
     Sheets of 4 , #a-d
3135-3137 A262 Set of 3   15.00 15.00
3138 A262 $200 Sheet of 2,
   #a.-b.   6.00 6.00

Hong Kong '97. No. 3138 contains two
70x44mm stamps.

Motion
Pictures,
Cent.
A263

No. 3139 — Movie star, World War II films:
a, Burgess Meredith, "The Story of GI Joe." b,
M.E. Clifton-James, "I Was Monty's Double." c,
Audie Murphy, "To Hell and Back." d, Gary
Cooper, "The Story of Dr. Wassell." e, James
Mason, "The Desert Fox." f, Manart Kippen,
"Mission to Moscow." g, Robert Taylor, "Above
and Beyond." h, James Cagney, "The Gallant
Hours." i, John Garfield, "Pride of the
Marines."
$300, George C. Scott, "Patton," horiz.

1997, Feb. 21   *Perf. 13½x14*
3139 A263 $50 Sheet of 9,
   #a.-i.   10.00 10.00
     Souvenir Sheet
     Perf. 14x13½
3140 A263 $300 multicolored   9.00 9.00

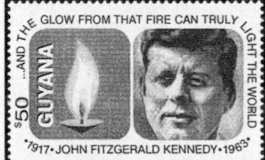

Pres. John F. Kennedy (1917-
63) — A264

1997, Mar. 14   **Litho.**   *Perf. 14*
3141 A264 $50 blue   1.25 1.25

George
Washington
A265

Designs from works of art: No. 3142: a,
Washington in battle. b, Washington taking
oath. c, Washington Seated in Armchair, from
engraving after Chappel. d, Col. Washington
of Virginia Militia, by Charles W. Peale. e,
George Washington, by Rembrandt Peale. f,
Washington Addressing Constitutional Convention, by Junius Brutus Stearns. g, Washington on His Way to the Continental Congress. h, Washington on a White Charger, by
John Faed. i, Washington as a Surveyor, from
an engraving by G.R. Hall after Darley's draw-
ing. j, Bas-relief of Washington Praying at Valley Forge. k, Death of Gen. Mercer at Battle of
Princeton, by John Trumbull. l, Washington
Taking Command of the Continental Army at
Cambridge. m, George Washington, by Gilbert
Stuart.
No. 3143: a, Washington Before the Battle
of Trenton, by John Trumbull. b, Washington,
His Family at Mt. Vernon, by Alonzo Chappel.
c, Inauguration of Washington in New York
City, by Chappel. d, Washington, by Adolph
Ulrich Wertmuller. e, Washington Accepts His
Commission as Commander-in-Chief, June
1775, Currier & Ives lithograph. f, Washington
from a mezzotint by Sartain. g, On the Lawn at
Mt. Vernon after the War. h, Washington Con-
versing with a Farmhand During the Baling
Season with Nelly and Washington Custus
Playing Nearby, from anonymous print after
Junius Brutus Stearns. i, Nellie Custis' Wed-
ding on Washington's Last Birthday, by
Ogden. j, Washington Crossing the Delaware,
by Leutze. k, Washington Receives Orders
from Mortally Wounded Gen. Braddock at
1755 Battle of Monongahela. l, Washington
Birthplace (supposed) on the Potomac, Currier
& Ives lithograph. m, Washington at Yorktown,
by James Peale.

1997, Mar. 14   **Litho.**   *Perf. 14*
3142   Sheet of 13   17.50 17.50
  a.-l.   A265 $60 any single   1.00 1.00
  m.   A265 $300 imperf.   5.00 5.00
3143   Sheet of 13   17.50 17.50
  a.-l.   A265 $60 any single   1.00 1.00
  m.   A265 $300 imperf.   5.00 5.00

Nos. 3142m, 3143m are each 66x91mm
and have simulated perforations.
No. 3142m exists perf. 14½.

Mushrooms
A266

Designs: $6, Morchella hortensis. $20,
Boletus chrysenteron. $25, Hygrophorus
agathosmus. $30, Cortinarius violaceus. $35,
Acanthocystis geogenius. $60, Mycena
polygramma. $200, Hebeloma radicosum.
$300, Coprinus comatus.
No. 3152, $80: a, Coprinus picaceus. b,
Stropharia umbonatescens. c, Paxillus
involutus. d, Amanita inaurata. e, Lepiota
rhacodes. f, Russula amoena.
No. 3153, $80: a, Volvaria volvacea. b, Psal-
liota augusta. c, Tricholoma aurantium. d,
Pholiota spectabilis. e, Cortinarius armillatus.
f, Agrocybe dura.
No. 3154, $300, Pholiota mutabilis. No.
3155, $300, Amanita muscaria.

1997, Apr. 2   **Litho.**   *Perf. 14*
3144-3151 A266 Set of 8   10.50 10.50
     Sheets of 6, #a-f
3152-3153 A266 Set of 2   16.00 16.00
     Souvenir Sheets
3154-3155 A266 Set of 2   10.00 10.00

Flowers — A267

Designs: No. 3156, $6, Pineapple lily. No.
3157, $6, Blue columbine. $20, Petunia. $25,
Lily of the Nile. $30, Bird of Paradise. $35,
African daisy. $60, Cape daisy. $80, Gazania.
$100, Cape water lily. $200, Insigne lady's
slipper.
No. 3166: a, Monarch supperwart. b, Passion flower. c, Butterfly iris. d, Red-hot poker.
e, Dir. G.T. Moore water lily. f, Superbissima
painted tongue. g, Orchid. h, Annual
chrysanthemum.
No. 3167: a, Tulips. b, Liatris. c, Roses. d,
Gerber daisies. e, Sunflowers. f,
Chrysanthemums.
No. 3168, Petunia.

1997, Apr. 2
3156-3165 A267 Set of 10   9.00 9.00
3166 A267 $60 Sheet of 8, #a.-
   h.   8.50 8.50
3167 A267 $80 Sheet of 6, #a.-
   f.   8.50 8.50
     Souvenir Sheet
3168 A267 $300 multicolored   5.00 5.00

Deng Xiaoping (1904-97) — A268

Illustration reduced.

1997, May 1
3169 A268 $100 shown   1.75 1.75
     Souvenir Sheet
3170 A268 $150 Portrait, diff.   2.75 2.75

No. 3169 was issued in sheets of 3.

UNESCO, 50th Anniv. — A269

Designs: $20, Horyu-Ji, Japan. $25,
Scandola Nature Reserve, France. $30, Great
Wall Defenses, China. $35, Wurzburg, Ger-
many. $60, Monastery of Batalha, Portugal.
$200, Dubrovnik, Croatia.
No. 3177, $60, vert. — Sites in Germany: a,
Cathedral of Aquisgran, Aachen. b, Cathedral
at Trier. c, Column of Augusta Treveror, Trier.
d, f, Residences, Wurzburg. e, Church interior,
Wurzburg. g, House of the River at Inselstadt,
Bamberg. h, Cathedral interior, Speyer.
No. 3178, $60, Sites in Greece, vert: No.
3178: a, Monastery of Thessaloniki. b, d, e,
Monastery at Mystras. c, Church of Santa
Sofia, Thessaloniki. f, City, Thessaloniki. g,
Painting, Mystras. h, Museum of Byzantine
Art, Thessaloniki.
No. 3179, $60, vert.: a, Monastery of Poblet
Catalonia, Spain. b, Old City of Salamanca,
Spain. c, Toledo, Spain. d, Cathedral of Flo-
rence, Italy. e, Tower of Pisa, Italy. f, g, h,
Convent of Christ, Tomar, Portugal.
No. 3180, $80 — Sites in Japan: a, d,
Horyu-Ji. b, c, Kyoto.
No. 3181, $80 — Sites in the Americas: a,
Cuzco, Peru. b, Potosi, Bolivia. c, Fortress,
San Lorenzo, Panama. d, Sangay Natl. Park,

Ecuador. e, Los Glaciares Natl. Park, Argentina.

No. 3182, $80 — Sites in US: a, Monticello. b, Yosemite Natl. Park. c, Yellowstone Natl. Park. d, Olympic Natl. Park. e, Everglades.

No. 3183, $300, Mount Taishan Shrine, China. No. 3184, $300, Monastery of Batalha, Portugal. No. 3185, $300, Bamberg Cathedral (detail), Germany. No. 3186, $300, Monastery, Mount Athos, Greece.

1997, May 20
3171-3176 A269 Set of 6   9.00 9.00

Sheets of 8, #a-h + Label
3177-3179 A269 Set of 3   22.50 22.50

Sheets of 5
3180-3182 A269 Set of 3   17.50 17.50

Souvenir Sheets
3183-3186 A269 Set of 4   18.50 18.50

Queen Elizabeth II, Prince Philip, 50th Wedding Anniv. A270

No. 3187: a, Queen. b, Royal Arms. c, Wedding portrait. d, Queen, Prince. e, Broadlands House. f, Prince Philip.
$300, Queen Elizabeth II.

1997, May 20   Litho.   Perf. 14
3187 A270 $60 Sheet of 6, #a.-
      f.   7.00 7.00

Souvenir Sheet
3188 A270 $300 multicolored   5.50 5.50

Paintings, by Hiroshige (1797-1858) A271

No. 3189: a, Oumayagashi. b, Ryogoku Ekoin & Moto-Yanagibashi Bridge. c, Pine of Success and Oumayagashi Asakusa River. d, Fireworks at Ryogoku. e, Dyers' Quarter, Kanda. f, Cotton-goods Lane, Odenma-cho.
No. 3190, $300, Suruga-cho. No. 3191, $300, Yatsukoji, inside Sujikai Gate.

1997, May 20   Perf. 13½x14
3189 A271 $80 Sheet of 6,
      #a.-f.   6.75 6.75

Souvenir Sheets
3190-3191 A271 Set of 2   10.00 10.00

Heinrich von Stephan (1831-97), Founder of UPU A272

No. 3192: a, Frieze of Roman post service. b, UPU emblem. c, Cable car, Boston, 1907. $300, Von Stephan, Egyptian messenger.

1997, May 20   Litho.   Perf. 14
3192 A272 $100 Sheet of 3,
      #a.-c.   8.00 8.00

Souvenir Sheet
3193 A272 $300 multicolored   9.00 9.00
PACIFIC 97.

Paul P. Harris (1868-1947), Founder of Rotary, Intl. — A273

Designs: $200, Health, hunger and humanity, portrait of Harris. $300, Mutual respect among all faiths, races and cultures.

1997, May 20
3194 A273 $200 multicolored   2.75 2.75

Souvenir Sheet
3195 A273 $300 multicolored   4.25 4.25

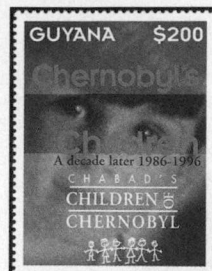

Chernobyl Disaster, 10th Anniv. A274

Designs: No. 3196, Chabad's Children of Chernobyl. No. 3197, UNESCO.

1997, May 20   Perf. 13½x14
3196 A274 $200 multicolored   3.00 3.00
3197 A274 $200 multicolored   3.00 3.00

Grimm's Fairy Tales — A275

Mother Goose — A276

Scenes from "Hansel & Gretel:" No. 3198: a, Hansel & Gretel in forest. b, Gingerbread house. c, Wicked witch. $500, Witch trying to capture Gretel, horiz.
$300, Rooster from "Cock-A-Doodle-Doo."

1997, May 20   Perf. 13½x14
3198 A275 $100 Sheet of 3,
      #a.-c.   5.50 5.50

Souvenir Sheets
Perf. 14, 14x13½
3199 A276 $300 multicolored   5.00 5.00
3200 A275 $500 multicolored   8.25 8.25

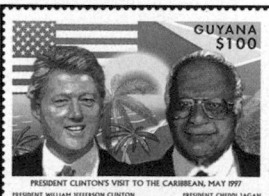

US Pres. Bill Clinton's Visit to Caribbean, May 1997 — A277

Designs: $30, Guyana Pres. Cheddi Jagan, Pres. Clinton, map of Caribbean, vert. $100, Clinton, Jagan, flags of US, Guyana, palm trees, beach.

Perf. 13½x14, 14x13½
1997, June 23
3201 A277 $30 multicolored   .50 .50
3202 A277 $100 multicolored   1.50 1.50
Nos. 3201-3202 each issued in sheets of 9. See Nos. 3237-3238.

1998 Winter Olympic Games, Nagano
A278   A279

Medalists: $30, Georg Thoma. $35, Katja Seizinger. $60, Georg Hackl. $200, Katarina Witt.

No. 3207, $60: a, Gunda Niemann, 3000- & 5000-m speed skating, 1992. b, Tony Nash, Robin Dixon, 2-man bobsled, 1964. c, Switzerland 4-man bobsled, 1988. d, Piet Kleine, speed skating, 1976.

No. 3208, $60: a, Oksana Baiul, figure skating, 1994. b, Cathy Turner, 500-m short track speed skating, 1994. c, Brian Boitano, figure skating, 1988. d, Nancy Kerrigan, figure skating, 1994.

No. 3209: a, Markus Wasmeier. b, Jens Weissflog. c, Erhard Keller. d, Rosi Mittermaier. e, Gunda Niemann. f, Peter Angerer.

No. 3210, Swiss 4-Man bobsled team.

No. 3211, $300, Jean-Claude Killy, slalom, 1968. No. 3212, $300, Chen Lu, figure skating, 1992.

1997, July 1   Perf. 14
3203-3206 A278   Set of 4   4.75 4.75

Strips or Blocks of 4, #a-d
3207-3208 A279   Set of 2   12.00 12.00
3209 A278 $30 Sheet of 6,
              #a.-f.   3.00 3.00

Souvenir Sheets
3210 A278 $300 multicolored   6.00 6.00
3211-3212 A279 Set of 2   12.00 12.00
Nos. 3207-3208 issued in sheets of 8 stamps.

Souvenir Sheet

Return of Hong Kong to China — A280

Litho. & Embossed
1997, July 1   Perf. 14
3213 A280 $500 gold & multi   7.50 7.50

Domestic Cats A281

Designs, vert.: $30, Norwegian forest cat. $35, Oriental spotted tabby. $200, Asian smoke.

No. 3217: a, Abyssinian. b, Chocolate colorpoint shorthair. c, Silver tabby. d, Persian. e, Maine coon cat & kitten. f, Brown shaded Burmese. g, Persian kitten. h, Siamese. i, British shorthair.
$300, Manx, vert.

1997, July 29
3214-3216 A281 Set of 3   4.25 4.25
3217 A281 $60 Sheet of 9, #a.-
      i.   8.50 8.50

Souvenir Sheet
3218 A281 $300 multi   5.50 5.50

Birds A282

Designs: $25, Verdin. $30, Wood thrush, vert. $60, Rofous-sided towhee. $200, Pygmy nuthatch, vert.

No. 3223, $80: a, Groove-billed ani. b, Green honeycreeper. c, Toucanet. d, Wire-tailed manakin. e, Hoatzin. f, Tiger heron.

No. 3224, $80 — Hummingbirds: a, Magenta-throated woodstar. b, Long-tailed hermit. c, Red-footed plumeleteer. d, Anna's. e, White-tipped sicklebill. f, Fiery-throated.

No. 3225, $300, Pinnated bittern. No. 3226, $300, Keel-billed toucan.

1997, Aug. 12   Litho.   Perf. 14
3219-3222 A282 Set of 4   6.00 6.00

Sheets of 6, #a-f
3223-3224 A282 Set of 2   16.00 16.00

Souvenir Sheets
3225-3226 A282 Set of 2   12.00 12.00

Dogs — A283

Designs: $20, Chihuahua. $25, Norfolk terrier. $60, Welsh terrier.

No. 3230: a, Shar-pei. b, Chihuahua. c, Chow chow. d, Sealyham terrier. e, Collie. f, German shorthair pointer. g, Bulldog. h, German shepherd. i, Old English sheepdog.
$300, Tibetan spaniel.

1997, July 29   Litho.   Perf. 14
3227-3229 A283 Set of 3   3.75 3.75
3230 A283 $60 Sheet of 9, #a.-
      i.   8.50 8.50

Souvenir Sheet
3231 A283 $300 multicolored   5.50 5.50

Pres. Cheddi Jagan's 1st Election to Parliament, 50th Anniv. — A284

1997, Oct. 6   Litho.   Perf. 14
3232 A284 $6 green & multi   .20 .20
3233 A284 $30 pale yellow &
              multi   4.25 4.25
Nos. 3232-3233 each issued in sheets of 9.

Diana, Princess of Wales (1961-97) — A285

No. 3234: a-f, Various portraits.
No. 3235, $300, Wearing red dress. No. 3236, $300, With longer hair.

1997, Oct. 15
3234 A285 $80 Sheet of 6, #a.-f.   8.25 8.25

Souvenir Sheets
Perf. 14½
3235-3236 A285 Set of 2   10.00 10.00

Nos. 3235-3236 each contain one 34x52mm stamp.

US Pres. Bill Clinton's Visit Type of 1997

Designs: $6, Like #3201. No. 3238, Clinton, Jagan, flags, sun on horizon.

Perf. 13½x14, 14x13½
1997, Nov. 10
3237 A277 $6 multi   .20 .20
3238 A277 $30 multi   .50 .50

Nos. 3237-3238 each issued in sheets of 9.

Souvenir Sheets

Chinese Pres. Jiang Zemin's Visit to New York — A286

Pres. Zemin, New York skyline, and: $200, Flags of China, UN, US. $300, Flags of China, US.

1997, Nov. 10   **Perf. 14**
3239 A286 $200 multicolored   3.00 3.00
3240 A286 $300 multicolored   4.50 4.50

Buildings in Guyana — A287

1997, Dec. 8   **Litho.**   **Perf. 14**
3241 A287 $6 W. Fogarty #1   .20 .20
3242 A287 $30 Public building   .60 .60

Christmas A288

Entire paintings, details, or sculptures: $24, $30, Diff. angels from The Triumph of Galatea,

by Raphael. $35, Primavera, by Botticelli. $60, Angel Musicians, by Agostino di Duccio, (bas relief). $100, From cover of Life Magazine, #1212, 1906. $200, Madonna and Saints, by Rosso Fiorentino.
No. 3249, $300, The Gardens of Love, by Rubens. No. 3250, $300, Cherubs, by Philippe de Champaigne.

1997, Dec. 8
3243-3248 A288 Set of 6   7.50 7.50

Souvenir Sheets
3249-3250 A288 Set of 2   12.00 12.00

Historical Events A289

Designs: No. 3251, $60, Explorers discover tomb of Tutankhamun, 1922. No. 3252, $60, Lincoln Memorial dedicated, Washington, DC, 1922. No. 3253, $60, Alexander Graham Bell dies, 1922. No. 3254, $60, Calvin Coolidge becomes President, 1923. No. 3255, $60, John L. Baird develops 1st experimental television, 1923. No. 3256, $60, Warren G. Harding dies, 1923. No. 3257, $60, First Winter Olympic Games, Chamonix, France, 1924. No. 3258, $60, Tennessee bans teaching of evolution in schools, 1925. No. 3259, $60, Chinese leader Sun Yat-Sen dies, 1925. No. 3260, $60, Robert Goddard launches 1st liquid fuel rocket, 1926. No. 3261, $60, Richard E. Byrd is 1st to fly over North Pole, 1926. No. 3262, $60, Sesquicentennial Exposition, Philadelphia, 1926.

1997. Dec. 8
3251-3262 A289 Set of 12   12.50 12.50

New Year 1998 (Year of the Tiger) — A290

No. 3263 — Various stylized tigers with denomination in: a, LR. b, LL. c, UR. d, UL. $150, Tiger, red background.

1998, Jan. 5   **Litho.**   **Perf. 14½**
3263 A290 $50 Sheet of 4, #a.- d.   5.00 5.00

Souvenir Sheet
3264 A290 $150 multicolored   4.25 4.25

Prehistoric Wildlife — A291

Designs: $25, Kentrosaurus. $30, Lesothosaurus. $35, Stegoceras. $60, Lagosuchus. $100, Herrerasaurus. $200, Iguanodon.
No. 3271, $55: a, Quetzalcoatlus (d). b, Pteranodon (a, c). c, Peteinosaurus. d, Criorhychus (g). e, Pterodaustro. f, Eudimorphodon. g, Archeopteryx. h, Dimorphodon. i, Sharovipteryx.
No. 3272, $55: a, Ceresiosaurus. b, Nothosaurus. c, Rhomaleosaurus. d, Grendelius. e, Mixosaurus. f, Mesosaurus. g, Placodus. h, Stethacanthus. i, Coelacanth.
No. 3273, $300, Styracosaurus, vert. No. 3274, $300, Yangchuanosaurus, vert.

1998, Feb. 23   **Litho.**   **Perf. 14**
3265-3270 A291 Set of 6   7.00 7.00

Sheets of 9, #a-i
3271-3272 A291 Set of 2   16.00 16.00

Souvenir Sheets
3273-3274 A291 Set of 2   8.50 8.50

1998 World Cup Soccer Championships, France — A292

Group A: No. 3275, $30, Brazil. No. 3276, $30, Morocco. No. 3277, $30, Norway. No. 3278, $30, Scotland.
Group B: No. 3279, $30, Austria. No. 3280, $30, Cameroun. No. 3281, $30, Chile. No. 3282, $30, Italy.
Group C: No. 3283, $30, Denmark. No. 3284, $30, France. No. 3285, $30, Saudi Arabia. No. 3286, $30, South Africa.
Group D: No. 3287, $30, Bulgaria. No. 3288, $30, Nigeria. No. 3289, $30, Paraguay. No. 3290, $30, Spain.
Group E: No. 3291, $30, Belgium. No. 3292, $30, Holland. No. 3293, $30, S. Korea. No. 3294, $30, Mexico.
Group F: No. 3295, $30, Germany. No. 3296, $30, Iran. No. 3297, $30, US. No. 3298, $30, Yugoslavia.
Group G: No. 3299, $30, Colombia. No. 3300, $30, England. No. 3301, $30, Romania. No. 3302, $30, Tunisia.
Group H: No. 3303, $30, Argentina. No. 3304, $30, Croatia. No. 3305, $30, Jamaica. No. 3306, $30, Japan.
Japanese players, vert.: No. 3306A, $300, Okada. No. 3306B, $300, Nakata.

1998, Apr. 8   **Litho.**   **Perf. 14x13½**
3275-3306 A292 Set of 32   14.00 14.00

Perf. 13½x14
Souvenir Sheets
3306A- A292 Set of 2
3306B   8.50 8.50

Nos. 3275-3306 were each issued in sheets of 8 + 1 label.
For overprints see Nos. 3317-3324.

The Titanic A293

No. 3307: a, J. Bruce Ismay, managing director, White Star Line. b, Jack Phillips, radio operator. c, Margaret "Unsinkable Molly" Brown, passenger. d, Capt. Edward J. Smith. e, Frederick Fleet, lookout. f, Thomas Andrews, managing director of Harland and Wolff.
$300, Titanic sinking.

1998, June 17   **Litho.**   **Perf. 14**
3307 A293 $80 Sheet of 6, #a.- f.   6.75 6.75

Souvenir Sheet
3308 A293 $300 multicolored   4.25 4.25

Sailing Ships A294

No. 3309, $80: a, Viking double-ended ship, 14th cent. b, Portuguese caravel, "Nina." d, Fannie, 1896. e, "Victoria," 1519. f, Arab sambook.
No. 3310, $80: a, "Dutch Fluyt." b, "Alastor." c, "Falcon." d, "Red Rover." e, "British Anglesey." f, "Archibald Russel."
No. 3311, $300, Oseberg ship. No. 3312, $300, "Half Moon," 1609.

1998, June 17   **Litho.**   **Perf. 14**
Sheets of 6, #a-f
3309-3310 A294 Set of 2   13.50 13.50

Souvenir Sheets
3311-3312 A294 Set of 2   8.50 8.50

Diana, Princess of Wales (1961-97) — A295

Designs: No. 3313, $1500, Diana in black and brown fur trimmed hat and coat. No. 3314, $1500, Diana wearing suit and hat.

Litho. & Embossed
1998, Aug. 3   **Die Cut 7½**
3313-3314 A295 $1500 Set of 2   150.00

Queen Mother A296

1998, Aug. 4   **Perf. 13½**
3315 A296 $90 multicolored   1.40 1.40

CARICOM, 25th Anniv. — A297

1998, July 4   **Litho.**   **Perf. 13½**
3316 A297 $20 multicolored   .40 .40

Nos. 3275, 3282-3286, 3289, 3304 Ovptd. "FRANCE WINNERS" in Gold

1998, Aug. 20   **Litho.**   **Perf. 14x13½**
3317   A292 $30 on #3275   .45 .45
3318   A292 $30 on #3282   .45 .45
3319   A292 $30 on #3283   .45 .45
3320   A292 $30 on #3284   .45 .45
3321   A292 $30 on #3285   .45 .45
3322   A292 $30 on #3286   .45 .45
3323   A292 $30 on #3289   .45 .45
3324   A292 $30 on #3304   .45 .45
Nos. 3317-3324 (8)   3.60 3.60

Nos. 3317-3324 were each issued in sheets of 8+label. Each sheet contains additional overprints in sheet margins.

National Hockey League Players — A298

No. 3325: a, Bryan Berard. b, Ray Bourque. c, Martin Brodeur. d, Pavel Bure. e, Chris Chelios. f, Sergei Fedorov. g, Peter Forsberg. h, Wayne Gretzky. i, Dominik Hasek. j, Brett Hull. k, Jarome Iginla. l, Jaromir Jagr. m, Paul Kariya. n, Saku Koivu. o, John LeClair. p, Brian Leetch. q, Eric Lindros. r, Patrick Marleau. s, Mark Messier. t, Mike Modano. u, Chris Osgood. v, Zigmund Palffy. w, Felix Potvin. x, Jeremy Roenick. y, Patrick Roy. z, Joe Sakic. aa, Sergei Samsonov. ab, Teemu Selanne. ac, Brendan Shanahan. ad, Ryan Smyth. ae, Jocelyn Thibault. af, Joe Thornton. ag, Keith Tkachuk. ah, John Vanbiesbrouck. ai, Steve Yzerman. aj, Dainius Zubrus.

1998, Apr. 1   Litho.   Perf. 13½
3325 A298 $35 Sheet of 36,
                  #a.-aj.   18.00 18.00

Aircraft
A299

No. 3326, $80 — Military aircraft: a, A7K Corsair II. b, A6E Intruder. c, U2 Spy plane. d, Blackhawk. e, F-16. f, Phantom II.
No. 3327, $80 — Pioneers of aviation: a, Wright Brothers, 1903. b, Bleriot, 1911. c, Curtiss Jenny, 1919. d, Airship Schwaben, 1911. e, W-8B, 1923. f, DH-66, 1926.
No. 3328, $300, A-10 Warthog. No. 3329, $300HH-65A Dolphin.

1998, Sept. 28   Perf. 14
Sheets of 6, #a-f
3326-3327 A299 Set of 2   13.50 13.50
Souvenir Sheets
3328-3329 A299 Set of 2   8.50 8.50

Endangered
Species — A300

Nos. 3330, $80, 3332, $300, Various pictures of the giant panda.
Nos. 3331, $80, 3333, $300, Various pictures of the mountain gorilla.

1998, Oct. 8
Sheets of 6, a-f
3330-3331 A300 Set of 2   17.00 17.00
Souvenir Sheets
3332-3333 A300 Set of 2   18.00 18.00

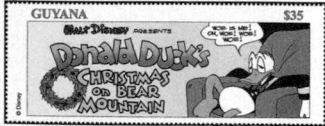

Donald Duck Adventures, Christmas
on Bear Mountain — A301

No. 3334 — Cartoon panels: a, 1-8. b, 9-16. c, 17-24. d, 25-32. e, 33-40. f, 41-48. g, 49-56. h, 57-64. i, 65-72. j, 73-80. k, Pane of 2, Carl Barks, vert., bears and duck.
Illustration reduced.

1998, Oct. 15   Perf. 14x13½, 13½x14
3334   Complete booklet   45.00 45.00
  a.-j. A301 $35 Any pane of 4   2.75 2.75
     k. A301 $300 Pane of 2   10.00 10.00

Disney's Uncle Scrooge, by Carl Barks, 50th anniv.

Organization of American States, 50th Anniv.
A302

1998, Oct. 29   Perf. 14
3335 A302 $40 multicolored   .55 .55

Ferrari Automobiles — A302a

No. 3335A: c, 212 Export. d, 410 Superamerica chassis. e, 125 S. $300, 512 S Racer.
Illustration reduced.

1998, Oct. 29   Litho.   Perf. 14
3335A A302a $100 Sheet of 3,
                   #c-e   5.00 5.00
Souvenir Sheet
3335B A302a $300 multi   5.00 5.00
No. 3335A contains three 39x25mm stamps.

Diana, Princess of Wales (1961-97)
A303

1998, Oct. 29
3336   A303 $60 multicolored   1.00 1.00
Self-Adhesive
Serpentine Die Cut Perf. 11½
Sheet of 1
Size: 53x65mm
3336A A303 $300 Diana, buildings, bridge   65.00

No. 3336 was issued in sheets of 6.
Soaking in water may affect the multi-layer image of No. 3336A.
Issued: $60, 10/29; $300, 11/5/98.

Grand Prix Champion Racing Cars and Drivers—A304 — 3337

No. 3337, $80: a, 1914 Grand Prix Mercedes, Christian Lautenschlager. b, 1930 Bugati Type 35B, P. Etancelin. c, 1934 Alfa Romeo P3, Louis Chiron. d, 1938 Mercedes Benz W154, Richard Seaman. e, 1938 Auto Union D Type, Tazio Nuvolari. f, 1951 Alfa Romeo 158, Juan Manuel Fangio.
No. 3338, $80: a, 1955 Mercedes Benz W196, Stirling Moss. b, 1960 Ferrari Dino 246, Phil Hill. c, 1966 Brabham-Repco BT19, Jack Brabham. d, 1970 Lotus Ford 72, John Miles. e, 1983 Renault RE40, Alain Prost. f, 1998 McLaren Mercedes MP4/13, David Coulthard.
No. 3339, $300, 1906 Grand Prix Renault, Ferenc Szisz. No. 3340, $300, 1956 Maserati 250F, Stirling Moss.

1998, Oct. 29
Sheets of 6, #a-f
3337-3338 A304 Set of 2   13.50 13.50
Souvenir Sheets
3339-3340 A304 Set of 2   8.50 8.50
Nos. 3339-3340 contain one 57x42mm stamp.

Tigger's Happy New Year — A304a

No. 3340A, vert. — Tigger: d, Giving gift to Winnie the Pooh. e, With fireworks. f, Giving flowers to Kanga. g, With Piglet. h, At door. i, With Eeyore.
No. 3340B, $300, Tigger beating drum. No. 3340C, $300, Tigger carrying staff for dragon.

1998, Oct. 29   Litho.   Perf. 13¼
3340A A304a $60 Sheet of 6, #a-
                   f   5.75 5.75
Souvenir Sheets
3340B-3340C A304a Set of 2   8.50 8.50

Gandhi — A305

No. 3341: a, Age 37, 1906. b, Age 77, 1946. c, Age 78, 1948. d, Age 77, 1947. $300, Age 76, 1946, horiz.

1998, Oct. 29
3341   A305 $100 Sheet of 4, #a-
                   d   5.50 5.50
Souvenir Sheet
3342   A305 $300 multicolored   4.25 4.25
No. 3341b-3341c are each 53x38mm.

Pablo Picasso
A306

Paintings, details: $25, Sleeping Peasants, 1919. $60, Large Nude in Red Armchair, 1929, vert. $200, Sculpture, "Female Head," 1931, vert.
$300, Man and Woman, 1971, vert.

1998, Oct. 29   Perf. 14½
3343-3345 A306 Set of 3   4.00 4.00
Souvenir Sheet
3346   A306 $300 multicolored   4.50 4.50

Royal Air Force, 80th Anniv.
A307

No. 3347, $100: a, Avro Lancaster B2. b, PBY-5A Catalina Amphibian. c, BAe Hawk TIA trainers (Red Arrows). d, Avro Lancaster, DeHavilland Mosquito.
No. 3348, $100: a, BAe Hawk TIA. b, C130 Hercules. c, Panavia Tornado GRI. d, BAe Hawk 200.

No. 3349, $150: a, BAe Nimrod RIP. b, Panavia Tornado F3 ADV. c, CH-47 Chinook helicopter. d, Panavia Tornado GRIA.
No. 3350, $200, Biplane, hawks in flight. No. 3351, $200, Eurofighter, Spitfire. No. 3352, $300, Eurofighters. No. 3353, $300, Head of hawk, hawk spreading wings, biplane. No. 3354, $300, Tiger Moth, Eurofighter. No. 3355, $300, Hawk spreading wings, biplane.

1998, Oct. 29   Perf. 14
Sheets of 4, #a.-d.
3347-3349 A307 Set of 3   20.00 20.00
Souvenir Sheets
3350-3355 A307 Set of 6   22.50 22.50

1998 World Scout Jamboree, Chile — A308

No. 3356: a, James E. West, 1st scout executive with early Eagle Scouts. b, Pres. Kennedy greets Explorers, 51st Scouts anniv., 1961. c, Astronaut Walter Schirra receives a special merit badge, 1962.

1998, Oct. 29   Litho.   Perf. 14
3356   A308 $160 Sheet of 3,
                   #a.-c.   7.00 7.00

Paintings by Eugene Delacroix (1798-1863)
A309

No. 3357, $60: a, The Sultan of Morocco Receives the Count de Mornay. b, Armed Indian with a Gurkha Scimitar. c, Portrait presumed to be of the Singer Baroihet in Turkish Dress. d, Moroccan Notebook: Studies of Jewish Women. e, Arab Horseman Giving a Signal. f, Arab Cavalry Practicing a Charge. g, A Seated Moor. h, Jewish Woman in Traditional Dress.
No. 3358, $60: a, Corner of the Studio; the Stove. b, Room in the Apartment the Count de Mornay. c, Hamlet and Horatio in the Graveyard. d, George Sand. e, The Bride of Abydos. f, Elysian Fields. g, A Lioness Standing by a Tree. h, Monsieur Alfred Bruyas.
No. 3359, $300, Moroccan Jewish Wedding, horiz. No. 3360, $300, Death of Sardanapulus, horiz.

1998, Oct. 29
Sheets of 8, #a.-h.
3357-3358 A309 Set of 2   13.50 13.50
Souvenir Sheets
3359-3360 A309 Set of 2   8.50 8.50

St. Andrew's Church, Georgetown, 180th Anniv. — A310

Various views of front of church: $6, $30, $60.

1998   Litho.   Perf. 14
3361-3363 A310 Set of 3   1.25 1.25

New Year 1999
(Year of the
Rabbit) — A311

No. 3364 — Various stylized rabbits with denomination at: a, LR. b, LL. c, UR. d, UL. $150, Red background, Chinese inscription.

1999, Jan. 4   Litho.   Perf. 14½
3364 A311 $50 Sheet of 4, #a.-
               d.   3.00 3.00

Souvenir Sheet
3365 A311 $150 multicolored   2.25 2.25

Disney
Characters
in Sporting
Activities
A312

No. 3366, $80 — Skateboarding: a, Huey. b, Mickey. c, Dewey. d, Louie. e, Goofy. f, Donald.

No. 3367, $80 — Rollerblading: a, Minnie. b, Goofy. c, Daisy. d, Baby Duck. e, Donald. f, Mickey.

No. 3368, $80 — Skateboarding, rollerblading, red, white & blue background:: a, Baby Duck. b, Daisy. c, Mickey. d, Goofy. e, Dewey. f, Donald.

No. 3369, $300, Dewey. No. 3370, $300, Daisy. No. 3371, $300, Goofy, horiz.

Perf. 13½x14, 14X13½
1999, Mar. 1   Litho.
Sheets of 6, #a-f
3366-3368 A312 Set of 3   25.00 25.00

Souvenir Sheets
3369-3371 A312 Set of 3   18.50 18.50

Mickey Mouse, 70th anniv.

Disney Characters in Trains — A313

No. 3372, $100 — 101 Dalmatians Express: a, Locomotive. b, Flatcar. c, Car with pillars. d, "Basket" car. e, Caboose.

No. 3373, $100 — Robin Hood Train: a, Engine. b, Marian, Robin Hood. c, Royal coach. d, Flatcar. e, Caboose.

No. 3374, $100 — Snow White, Diamond Mine Railroad: a, Engine. b, Flatcar. c, Snow White, Prince Charming. d, Passenger car. e, Pump car.

No. 3375, $100 — Little Mermaid Railroad: a, Engine. b, Fish holding pearls. c, Little Mermaid. d, Various marine life in car. e, "Bah Hum Bug!"

No. 3376: a, Dwarf from Diamond Mine Railroad driving locomotive. b, Dwarf on pump car.

No. 3377, $300, Bandits, Cruela De Vil. No. 3378, $300, Robin Hood, Bear. No. 3379, $300, Little Mermaid kissing Prince under mistletoe. No. 3380, $300, Little Mermaid holding starfish.

1999, Mar. 1   Perf. 13½x14
Sheets of 5, #a-e
3372-3375 A313 Set of 4   36.00 36.00
3376   A313 $200 Sheet of 2,
                  #a.-b.   9.00 9.00

Souvenir Sheets
3377-3380 A313 Set of 4   22.00 22.00

Caribbean Butterflies — A314

No. 3381, $80: a, Scarce Bamboo Page. b, Spicebush swallowtail. c, Isabella. d, The mosaic. e, Gulf fritillary. f, Figure-of-eight.

No. 3382, $80: a, Hewitson's blue hairstreak. b, Polydamas swallowtail. c, Common morpho. d, Blue-green reflector. e, Malachite. f, Grecian shoemaker.

No. 3383, $300, Giant swallowtail, vert. No. 3384, $300, Pipevine swallowtail, vert.

1999, Mar. 15   Perf. 14
Sheets of 6, #a-f
3381-3382 A314 Set of 2   14.50 14.50

Souvenir Sheets
3383-3384 A314 Set of 2   9.00 9.00

Flowers
A315

No. 3385, $60: a, Geranium. b, Oncidium macranthum. c, Bepi orchidglades. d, Sunflowers (2). e, Cattleya walkeriana. f, Cattleya frasquita. g, Helianthus maximilani (one). h, Paphiopedilum insigne sanderae, lily. i, Lily (2).

No. 3386, $60: a, Dendrobium nobile. b, Phalaenopsis schilleriana. c, Cymbidium alexette. d, Rhododendron. e, Phragmipedium besseae, laelia cinnabarina. f, Masdevallia veitchiana. g, Calochortus nuttallii. h, Brassolaeliocattleya pure gold. i, Laelia cinnabarina.

No. 3387: a, Leptotes bicolor, masdevallia ignea. b, Sophrolaeliocattleya, anguloa clowesii. c, Laelia pumila. d, Masdevallia ignea. e, Dendrobium phalaenopsis.

No. 3388, $300, Asocentrum miniatum, vert. No. 3389, $300, Iris pseudacorus.

1999, Mar. 15   Litho.   Perf. 14
Sheets of 9, #a-i
3385-3386 A315 Set of 2   16.00 16.00
3387   A315 $90 Sheet of 6,
                  #a.-f.   7.50 7.50

Souvenir Sheet
3388-3389 A315 Set of 2   8.50 8.50

Akira Kurosawa (1910-98), Film Director — A316

No. 3390 — Films, vert.: a, "The Dream." b, "Rashomon." c, "Kagemusha." d, "Red Beard." e, "Seven Samurai." f, "Yojimbo."

No. 3391 — Portraits: a, Pointing. b, Hand on face. c, Standing. d, With camerman. $300, Scene from "Dreams."

1999, Mar. 22
3390 A316 $80 Sheet of 6, #a.-
            f.   6.75 6.75
3391 A316 $130 Sheet of 4, #a.-
            d.   7.25 7.25

Souvenir Sheet
3392 A316 $300 multicolored   4.25 4.25

Mushrooms
A317

Designs: $25, Coprinus atramentarius. $35, Hebeloma crustuliniforme. $100, Russula nigricans. $200, Tricholoma aurantium.

No. 3397, $60: a, Boletus aereus. b, Coprinus comatus. c, Inocybe godeyi. d, Morchella crassipes. e, Lepiota acutesquamosa. f, Amanita phalloides. g, Boletus spadiceus. h, Cortinarius collinitus. i, Lepiota procera.

No. 3398, $60: a, Russula ochroleuca. b, Hygrophorus hypothelus. c, Amanita rubescens. d, Boletus satanas. e, Amanita echinocephala. f, Amanita muscaria. g, Boletus badius. h, Hebeloma radicosum. i, Mycena polygramma.

No. 3399, $300, Lepiota acutequamosa. No. 3400, $300, Pluteus cervinus.

1999, May 6   Litho.   Perf. 14
3393-3396 A317 Set of 4   4.25 4.25

Sheets of 9, #a-i
Perf. 14½
3397-3398 A317 Set of 2   16.50 16.50

Souvenir Sheet
3399-3400 A317 Set of 2   9.00 9.00

Nos. 3397-3398 each contain nine 32x41mm stamps. Nos. 3399-3400 each contain one 32x41mm stamp.

Trains — A318

No. 3401, $80: a, Burlington Northern GP 39-2, 1974. b, CSX GP40-2, 1967. c, Erie Lackawana Railroad GP 9, 1956. d, Amtrak P 42 Genesis, 1993. e, Erie Railroad S-2, 1948. f, Pennsylvania Railroad S-1, 1947.

No. 3402, $80: a, Northern and Western #610, c. 1933. b, Pennsylvania Railroad M1B Mountain, 1930. c, Reading Railroad FP7A, 1951. d, New York Central 2-8-4, c. 1940. e, Union Pacific Challenger Big Boy, 1963. f, GP 15-15-1, 1956.

No. 3403, $80: a, Shinkansen Bullet 100 series, 1984, Japan. b, Ukranian Diesel ZMGR, 1983, Russia. c, Rhatische Bahn GE 6/6 II, Germany. d, Eurostar TGV, 1986, France. e, Atlantique TGV, 1989, France. f, Class 86-6, UK.

No. 3404, $80: a, Joseph Clark 0-4-0, 1868. b, Diamond Stack Bethel 4-4-0, 1863. c, New York Central #999, 1890. d, Boston & Maine Ballardville 0-4-0, 1876. e, Atlantic 4-4-0 Portland Rochester Railroad, 1863. f, America 4-4-0 Baltimore & Ohio Railroad, 1881.

Railroad pioneers: No. 3405, $300, George Stephen, vert. No. 3406, $300, Alfred de Glehn, vert. No. 3407, $300, George Nagelmackers, vert. No. 3408, $300, R.F. Trevithick, vert.

1999, May 10   Perf. 14
Sheets of 6, #a.-f.
3401-3404 A318 Set of 4   29.00 29.00

Souvenir Sheets
3405-3408 A318 Set of 4   17.00 17.00

Australia '99 World Stamp Expo.

Wedding of Prince Edward and Sophie Rhys-Jones — A319

Various portraits: Nos. 3409, $150, 3411, $300, rose lilac sheet margin. Nos. 3410, $150, 3412, $300, yellow brown sheet margin.

1999, June 19   Litho.   Perf. 14¼
Sheets of 4, #a.-d.
3409-3410 A319 Set of 2   17.00 17.00

Souvenir Sheets
3411-3412 A319 Set of 2   8.50 8.50

Nos. 3411-3412 are horiz.

Johann Wolfgang von Goethe (1749-1832), Poet — A320

No. 3413: a, Lynceus sings from the watchtower. b, Portaits of Von Goethe and Friedrich von Schiller (1759-1805), poet. c, The fallen Icarus.

$300, Mephistopheles appears as salamander, vert.

1999, June 22   Litho.   Perf. 14
3413 A320 $150 Sheet of 3, #a.-
            c.   6.25 6.25

Souvenir Sheet
3414 A320 $300 multicolored   4.25 4.25

IBRA '99, World Philatelic Exhibition, Nuremberg — A321

Designs: $60, Class E10 Bo-bo electric locomotive, BMW offices, Munich, 1952, vert. $200, Class 01, 4-6-2 steam express train, 1926.
Illustration reduced.

1999, June 22
3415 A321 $60 multicolored   .90 .90
3416 A321 $200 multicolored   2.75 2.75

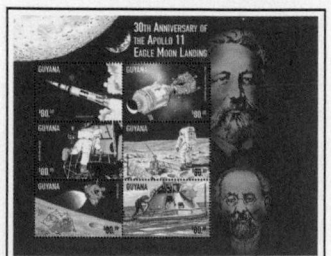

Apollo 11 Moon Landing, 30th Anniv. — A322

No. 3417, $80: a, Blast off. b, Command Module docked with Lunar Lander. c, First man on moon. d, Seismic experiments package. e, Back to the orbiter. f, Astronauts being picked up.

No. 3418, $80, vert: a, Sputnik, 1959, Konstantin Tsiolkovsky. b, Apollo 11 liftoff. c, On the moon. d, Collecting samples of lunar rocks. e, Apollo 11 Lunar Module. f, Splashdown.

No. 3419, $300, Salute to the flag. No. 3420, $300, Michael Collins.

1999, June 22
Sheets of 6, #a-f
3417-3418 A322 Set of 2   13.00 13.00
Souvenir Sheet
3419-3420 A322 Set of 2   8.50 8.50

Souvenir Sheets

PhilexFrance '99, World Philatelic Exhibition — A323

Designs: No. 3421, $300, Co-Co 7000 Class High Speed 1949-55. No. 3422, $300, 241-P Class 4-8-2 Express 1947-49. Illustration reduced.

1999, June 22
3421-3422 A323 Set of 2   9.00 9.00

Paintings by Hokusai (1760-1849) — A324

No. 3423, $80: a, Travelers Climbing a Mountain Path. b, Washing in a River. c, The Blind (eyes & mouth open). d, The Blind (eyes & mouth shut). e, Convolvulus and Tree-Frog. f, Fishermen Hauling a Net.

No. 3424, $80: a, Hibiscus and Sparrow. b, Hydrangea and Swallow. c, The Blind (eyes shut, mouth open). d, The Blind (eyes open, mouth shut). e, Irises. f, Lilies.

No. 3425, $300, Flowering Cherries at Mount Yoshino, vert. No. 3426, $300, A View of a Stone Causeway, vert.

1999, June 22 Litho. Perf. 14x13¾
Sheets of 6, #a-f
3423-3424 A324 Set of 2   13.50 13.50
Souvenir Sheets
Perf. 13¾x14
3425-3426 A324 Set of 2   8.50 8.50

Pope John Paul II — A325

1999, June 22   **Perf. 14**
3427 A325 $80 Sheet of 6, #a.-f. 7.50 7.50

John Glenn's Return to Space — A326

No. 3428: a, In space suit, 1962. b, After landing, 1962. c, As Senator. d, With helmet, 1998. e, Without helmet, 1998.

1999, June 22   **Perf. 14½x14¼**
3428 A326 $100 Sheet of 5, #a.-e. 7.00 7.00

Parrots and Parakeets — A327

No. 3429, $60: a, Hyacinth macaw. b, Blue and gold macaw. c, Blue-fronted Amazon parrot. d, Amazon parrot. e, Sun Conure. f, Tivi parakeet. g, Bavaria's conure. h, Fairy lorikeet.

No. 3430, $60: a, Marron macaw. b, Thick-billed parrot. c, Golden-crowned canure. d, Yellow-naped macaw. e, Double yellow-headed parrot. f, Golden-fronted parakeet. g, Maroon-billed conure. h, Nandaya conure.

No. 3431, $300, Jendaya conure, horiz. No. 3432, $300, Gray-cheeked parakeet.

1999, Aug. 3   **Perf. 14**
Sheets of 8, #a.-h.
3429-3430 A327 Set of 2   14.00 14.00
Souvenir Sheets
3431-3432 A327 Set of 2   8.50 8.50

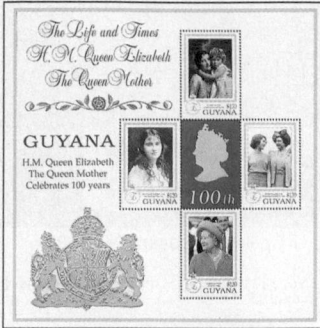

Queen Mother, 100th Birthday (in 2000) — A328

No. 3433: a, Duchess of York, Princess Elizabeth, 1928. b, Lady Elizabeth Bowles-Lyon, 1914. c, Queen Elizabeth, Princess Elizabeth, 1940. d, Queen Mother, Venice, 1984. e, $400, Queen Mother, Canada, 1988.

1999, Aug. 4
Gold Frames
3433 A328 $130 Sheet of 4, #a.-d. + label 8.00 8.00
Souvenir Sheet
Perf. 13¾
3434 A328 $400 multicolored 5.50 5.50

No. 3434 contains one 38x50mm stamp. Margins of sheets are embossed. See Nos. 3689-3690.

China Soccer League Superstars — A329

Nos. 3435a-3435g, 3436a-3436g, Various players. Nos. 3435h, 3436h, League emblem.

1999, Aug. 16   **Perf. 14½x14¼**
3435 A329 $50 Sheet of 8, #a.-h. 5.25 5.25
3436 A329 $60 Sheet of 8, #a.-h. 6.25 6.25

Rights of the Child — A330

No. 3437: a, Denomination at LL, flag at UR. b, Denomination at UL, flag at LL. c, Denomination at UL, flag at UR.
$300, Prince Talal.

1999, June 22 Litho. Perf. 14
3437 A330 $150 Sheet of 3, #a.-c. 5.50 5.50
Souvenir Sheet
3438 A330 $300 multicolored 4.00 4.00

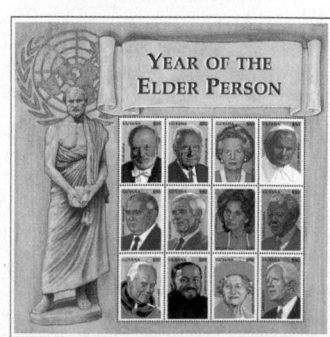

Intl. Year of the Elderly — A331

No. 3439: a, Kurt Masur. b, Rupert Murdoch. c, Margaret Thatcher. d, Pope John Paul II. e, Mikhail Gorbachev. f, Ted Turner. g, Sophia Loren. h, Nelson Mandela. i, John Glenn. j, Luciano Pavarotti. k, Queen Mother. l, Jimmy Carter.

No. 3440 — Ronald Reagan: a, As young man. b, In uniform. c, Feeding chimp. d, With campaign poster. e, With cowboy hat. f, With wine glass.
$300, Reagan in star.

1999, June 22   Litho.   Perf. 14
3439 A331 $50 Sheet of 12, #a.-l. 8.50 8.50
3440 A331 $100 Sheet of 6, #a.-f. 7.00 7.00
Souvenir Sheet
3441 A331 $300 multicolored 3.50 3.50

Souvenir Sheet

Mei Lan Fang, Chinese Actor — A332

1999, Aug. 16   Litho.   Perf. 13¾
3442 A332 $400 multicolored 4.50 4.50

First Balloon Flight Around the World — A333

No. 3443: a, Orbiter 3. b, Emblem. c, Bertrand Piccard. d, Brian Jones.
$300, Orbiter 3, flight path.

1999, Aug. 16   Litho.   Perf. 14
3443 A333 $150 Sheet of 4, #a.-d. 7.25 7.25
Souvenir Sheet
3444 A333 $300 multicolored 4.00 4.00

The Kennedy Family A334

No. 3445: a, Jacqueline and John, Jr. b, John and John, Jr. c, John and Jacqueline. d, Jacqueline. e, John, Jr. and Caroline. f, John.
No. 3445G: h, John, Jr. as adult and child. i, John, Jr. and Jacqueline. j, John Jr.

1999, Oct. 4   Litho.   Perf. 13¾
3445   A334 $80 Sheet of 6, #a.-f. 6.25 6.25
3445G A334 $160 Sheet of 3, #h.-j. 5.75 5.75

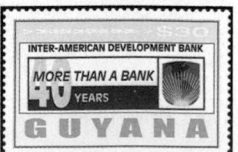

Inter-American Development Bank, 40th Anniv. — A335

1999, Nov. 15   Litho.   Perf. 14
3446 A335 $30 multicolored .40 .40

Ferrari Automobiles — A336

Designs: $30, 312 T2. $35, 553 F.1. $60, D 50. $200, 246 F.1. $300, 126/C2. $400, 312/B2.

1999	Litho.		Perf. 14
3447-3452	A336	Set of 6	11.50 11.50

Sidney Sheldon, Novelist — A337

1999	Litho.		Perf. 14
3453	A337	$80 multicolored	1.00 1.00

Issued in sheets of 4.

A338

No. 3454: a, During World War II. b, Wedding photo. c, As child. d, At coronation of George VI. e, In 1971. f, In 1991. g, in 1914. h, In 1988. i, At Royal Agricultural show. j, On 60th birthday.
$1,000, Portrait.

1999	Litho.		Perf. 12
3454	A338	$60 Sheet of 10, #a.-j.	8.75 8.75

Imperf
Size: 51x76mm

3455	A338	$1000 multicolored	12.00 12.00

Sheets of #3454 exist with black border in margin with text "In Memoriam/1900-2002."

Queen Mother (b. 1900) — A339

Litho. & Embossed

1999, Aug. 4		Die Cut Perf. 8¾
3456	A339	$1500 gold & multi	35.00

Millennium
A340

No. 3457, Founding of first university, 1088.
No. 3458 — Highlights of the 11th Century: a, Anasazi trade center. b, "Black Virgin." c, Seljuk warrior. d, Appearance of Halley's Comet. e, Battle of Hastings. f, William of Normandy crowned King of England. g, Power of the Fujiwara is checked. h, Holy Roman Emperor Henry IV. i, Muslims build Timbuktu. j, Like No. 3457. k, Gondolas come into use in Venice. l, El Cid. m, First crusade. n, Crusaders capture Jerusalem. o, Chinese statue of Guanyin (60x40mm). p, Rubiayat of Omar Khayyam (60x40mm). q, Syrian storage jar.
No. 3459 — Highlights of the 1910s: a, Manet and Post-impressionists show, Grafton Gallery, London. b, Standard Oil loses Supreme Court antitrust suit. c, Harriet Quimby, 1st female pilot in US. d, US enters World War I. e, Titanic sinks. f, Pu Yi resigns as Chinese Emperor. g, Grand Central Station built in NYC. h, Assassination of Archduke Francis Ferdinand. i, Panama Canal opens. j, Lawrence of Arabia. k, Easter Uprising, Ireland. l, 1917 Russian Revolution. m, Execution of the Romanovs. n, Treaty of Versailles ends World War I. o, Influenza epidemic. p, Leo Tolstoy & Mark Twain die (60x40mm). q, Bauhaus opens, Weimar, Germany.

1999, Dec. 20	Litho.		Perf. 13¼x13
3457	A340	$35 multi	.50 .50
		Perf. 12¾x12½	
3458	A340	$35 Sheet of 17, #a.-q.	7.50 7.50
3459	A340	$35 Sheet of 17, #a.-q., + label	7.50 7.50

Flowers — A341

#3460: Various flowers making up a photomosaic of Princess Diana.
#3461: Various details of paper money of the world making up a photomosaic of George Washington's portrait on $1 bill.

1999-2000	Litho.		Perf. 13¾
3460	A341	$80 Sheet of 8, #a.-h.	12.00 12.00
3461	A341	$80 Sheet of 8, #a.-h.	10.00 10.00

Issued: #3460, 12/31; #3461, 3/27/00.
See Nos. 3568-3569.

New Year 2000 (Year of the Dragon) — A342

No. 3462 — Dragons with denomination in: a, LR. b, LL. c, UR, d, UL.
$300, LR.

2000, Feb. 5		Perf. 14¾
3462	A342	$100 Sheet of 4, #a.-d.	5.00 5.00
	Souvenir Sheet	
3463	A342	$300 multi	3.50 3.50

A343

Automobiles — A344

No. 3464, $100: a, Nicholas Cugnot's steam-powered Fardier, 1769. b, Siegfried Marcus's motor carriage, 1875. c, Karl Benz's Velo, 1894. d, Virgilio Bordino's steam carriage, 1854. e, 1886 Benz. f, 1908 Ford Model T.
No. 3465, $100: a,1926 Duesenberg Model A Phaeton. b, 1927 Mercedes-Benz Model K. c, 1928, Rolls-Royce Phantom I limousine. d, 1935 Auburn 851 Speedster. e, 1936 Mercedes-Benz 540K Cabriolet B. f, 1949, Volkswagen Cabriolet Beetle.
No. 3466, $100: a, 1957 Ford Thunderbird. b, 1957 Jaguar XK150. c, 1968 Chevrolet Corvette Stingray. d, 1973 BMW 2002 Turbo. e, 1975 Porsche 911 Turbo. f, 1999 Volkswagen Beetle.
No. 3467, $100: a, 1886 Daimler motor car. b, 1898 Opel Luzman. c, 1899 Benz Landaulet coupe. d, 1892 Peugeot Vis-a-vis. e, 1886 Benz. f, 1894 Benz Velo, diff.
No. 3468, $100: a, 1896 Ford. b, 1903 De Dion-Bouton Populare. c, 1900 Vauxhall. e, 1908 Rolls-Royce Silver Ghost. f, 1908 Ford Model T, diff.
No. 3469, $400, 1904 Mercedes-Benz 60/70. No. 3470, $400, 1939 Mercedes-Benz Type 320 Cabriolet. No. 3471, $400, 1954 Mercedes-Benz 300SL Gullwing.
No. 3472, $400, 1904 Turner-Miesse. No. 3473, $400, 1910 Runabout.

2000, Mar. 13	Litho.		Perf. 13½
	Sheets of 6, #a.-f.		
3464-3466	A343	Set of 3	22.00 22.00
	Perf. 14		
3467-3468	A344	Set of 2	14.00 14.00

Souvenir Sheets

	Perf. 14½		
3469-3471	A343	Set of 3	13.50 13.50
	Perf. 14¼		
3472-3473	A344	Set of 2	9.00 9.00

Size of stamps from Nos. 3463-3466, 41x25mm; from Nos. 3467-3468, 42x28mm.

Marine Life
A345

Designs: $30, Lachnolaimus maximus. $35, Cyphoma gibbosum. $60, Trachinotus falcatus. $100, Bodianus pulchellus. $200, Anisotremus virginicus. $300, Etheostoma spectabile.
No. 3480, $80: a, Hypoplectrus indigo. b, Chlamys hastata. c, Sebastes rubrivinctus. d, Selene vomer. e, Marginella carnea. f, Phoca vitulina. g, Coryphaena hippurus. h, Epinephelus fulvus.
No. 3481, $80: a, Sphyraena barracuda. b, Saccopharynx sp. c, Chromodoris amoena. d, Makaira nigricans. e, Orcinus orca. f, Hippocampus reidi. g, Chelonia mydas. h, Emblemaria pandionis.
No. 3482, $80, vert.: a, Pteros volitans. b, Tursiops truncatus. c, Dipulmaris antarctica. d, Pomacanthus arcuatus. e, Aetobatus narinari. f, Carcharhinus amblyrhynchos. g, Sacura margaritacea. h, Octopus dolfeini.
No. 3483, $400, Asteroschema tenue, vert. No. 3484, $400, Apodichthys flavidus, vert. No. 3485, $400, Periclimenes pederseni.

2000, May 15		Perf. 14
3474-3479	A345	Set of 6	8.50 8.50
	Sheets of 8, #a.-h.		
3480-3482	A345	Set of 3	25.00 25.00
	Souvenir Sheets		
3483-3485	A345	Set of 3	14.00 14.00

No. 3485 contains one 57x42mm stamp.

Souvenir Sheet

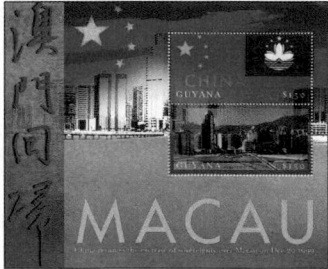

1999 Return of Macao to People's Republic of China — A346

No. 3486: a, Flag. b, Skyline.
Illustration reduced.

2000, May 15		
3486	A346	$150 Sheet of 2, #a.-b.	3.75 3.75

100th Test Match at Lord's Ground — A347

Designs: $100, Rohan Kanhai. $300, Clive Lloyd.
$400, Lord's Ground, horiz.

2000, May 15	Litho.		Perf. 14
3487-3488	A347	Set of 2	5.00 5.00
	Souvenir Sheet		
3489	A347	$400 multi	5.25 5.25

Prince William, 18th Birthday — A348

No. 3490: a, With Prince Harry. b, Wearing sweater. c, In profile. d, In suit.
$400, In ski wear.
Illustration reduced.

2000, May 15   *Perf. 14*
3490 A348 $100 Sheet of 4, #a-d   5.50 5.50
Souvenir Sheet
Perf. 13¾
3491 A348 $400 multi   5.25 5.25
No. 3490 contains four 28x42mm stamps. It exists imperf.

First Zeppelin Flight, Cent. — A349

No. 3492 — Ferdinand von Zeppelin and: a, LZ-1. b, LZ-2. c, LZ-9.
$400, LZ-127.

2000, May 15   *Perf. 14*
3492 A349 $200 Sheet of 3, #a-c   7.25 7.25
Souvenir Sheet
3493 A349 $400 multi   4.75 4.75
No. 3492 contains three 40x24mm stamps.

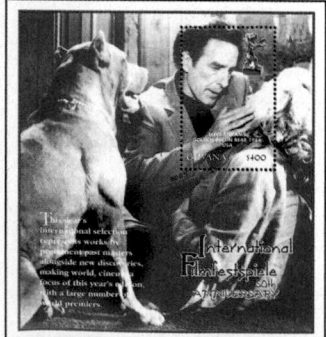

Berlin Film Festival, 50th Anniv. — A350

No. 3494: a, Das Boot Ist Voll. b, David. c, Hong Gao Liang (Red Sorghum). d, Die Ehe der Maria Braun. e, Edith Evans. f, Michel Simon.
$400, Love Streams.
Illustration reduced.

2000, May 15
3494 A350 $100 Sheet of 6, #a-f   7.00 7.00
Souvenir Sheet
3495 A350 $400 multi   4.50 4.50

Apollo-Soyuz Mission, 25th Anniv. — A351

No. 3496: a, Vance D. Brand, Thomas P. Stafford. b, Apollo 18, docking adapter. c, Stafford, Valeri Kubasov.
$400, Stafford, Donald K. Slayton.
Illustration reduced.

2000, May 15
3496 A351 $200 Sheet of 3, #a-c   7.25 7.25
Souvenir Sheet
3497 A351 $400 multi   4.50 4.50

Souvenir Sheets

2000 Summer Olympics, Sydney — A352

No. 3498: a, Henry Robert Pearce. b, Volleyball. c, Olympic Park, Montreal, and Canadian flag. d, Ancient Greek runners.
Illustration reduced.

2000, May 15
3498 A352 $160 Sheet of 4, #a-d   7.50 7.50

Public Railways, 175th Anniv. — A353

No. 3499: a, Timothy Hackworth. b, Sans Pareil. c, Branhope Tunnel.
Illustration reduced.

2000, May 15
3499 A353 $200 Sheet of 3, #a-c   7.00 7.00

Johann Sebastian Bach (1685-1750) — A354

Illustration reduced.

2000, May 15
3500 A354 $400 multi   4.75 4.75
Souvenir Sheet

Albert Einstein (1879-1955) — A355

Illustration reduced.

2000, May 15   Litho.   Perf. 14¼
3501 A355 $400 multi   5.00 5.00

Space — A356

No. 3502, $100: a, Amsat IIIc. b, SRET. c, Inspector. d, Stardust. e, Temisat. f, Arsene.
No. 3503, $100, horiz.: a, Sun and Echo satellite (inscribed Apollo 11). b, Saturn, and-Pioneer. c, Moon and Apollo 11 (inscribed Echo satellite). d, Mars and Mars Explorer. e, Space Shuttle, Intl. Space Station. f, Halley's Comet and Giotto.
No. 3504, $100, horiz.: a, Cesar, Argentine, Spanish flags. b, Sirio 2, Italian flag. c, Taos S.80, French flag. d, Viking, Swedish flag. e, SCD 1, Brazilian flag. f, Offeq 1, Israeli flag.
No. 3505, $400, Clementine. No. 3506, $400, Solar Max, horiz.
Illustration reduced.

2000, May 15   Litho.   Perf. 14
Sheets of 6, #a-f
3502-3504 A356 Set of 3   22.00 22.00
Souvenir Sheets
3505-3506 A356 Set of 2   9.25 9.25
World Stamp Expo 2000, Anaheim.

The Three Stooges — A357

No. 3507: a, Shemp, Moe, Larry, man with glasses. b, Skeleton, Larry, Moe. c, Shemp. d, Stooges with fingers in mouths. e, Stooges reading book. f, Stooges attacking man. g, Stooges with candle. h, Stooges, man, fire bucket. i, Moe, Shemp, man in window.
No. 3508, $400, Moe in doorway. No. 3509, $400, Larry, skeleton.
Illustration reduced.

2000, July 27   *Perf. 13¾*
3507 A357 $80 Sheet of 9, #a-i   8.75 8.75
Souvenir Sheets
3508-3509 A357 Set of 2   9.00 9.00
See Nos. 3542-3544.

Betty Boop — A358

No. 3510: a, In striped blouse. b, With shopping bags. c, On cushion. d, As belly dancer. e, In red lingerie. f, In cutoff shorts. g, With musical notes. h, In flowered pants. i, In black dress.
No. 3511, $400, In fur coat. No. 3512, $400, In polka dot bathing suit, with flamingos.
Illustration reduced.

2000, July 27   *Perf. 13¾*
3510 A358 $80 Sheet of 9, #a-i   9.00 9.00
Souvenir Sheets
3511-3512 A358 Set of 2   9.00 9.00
See Nos. 3545-3552.

Third Annual
Caribbean Media
Conference
A359

2000, Aug. 14   *Perf. 14*
3513 A359 $100 multi   1.25 1.25

European Soccer
Championships — A360

No. 3514, $80, horiz.: a, Denmark. b, Germany. c, Italy. d, Netherlands. e, Portugal. f, Romania. g, Czech Republic. h, Norway.
No. 3515, $80, horiz.: a, Turkey. b, Slovenia. c, Yugoslavia. d, Sweden. e, Belgium. f, Spain. g, France. h, England.
No. 3516, $400, Jurgen Klinsmann. No. 3517, $400, Stefan Kuntz.
Illustration reduced.

2000, Aug. 21   *Perf. 13¾*
Sheets of 8, #a-h, + label
3514-3515 A360 Set of 2   16.00 16.00
Souvenir Sheets
3516-3517 A360 Set of 2   9.50 9.50

Mushrooms — A361

No. 3518, $100, horiz.: a, Sealy vase chanterelle. b, Caesar's mushroom. c, Greenheaded jelly club. d, Salmon unicorn entoloma. e, White oysterette. f, Variable cort.
No. 3519, $100, horiz.: a, Coccora. b, Winter polypore. c, Turpentine waxy cap. d, Aeryginosa. e, Fly agaric. f, Honey mushroom.
No. 3520, $100, horiz: a, Salmon waxy cap. b, Shellfish-scented russula. c, Scarlet waxy cap. d, Stuntz's blue legs. e, Netted rhodotus. f, Indigo milky.
No. 3521, $400, Tiny volvariella. No. 3522, $400, Turkey tail, horiz. No. 3523, $400, Pinwheel marasmius, horiz.
Illustration reduced.

2000, Oct. 4   *Perf. 14*
Sheets of 6, #a-f
3518-3520 A361 Set of 3   22.50 22.50
Souvenir Sheets
3521-3523 A361 Set of 3   14.00 14.00
The Stamp Show 2000, London.

A362

Flowers — A363

Designs: No. 3524, $35, Bougainvillea spectabilis. No. 3525, $60, Euphorbia milii. No. 3526, $200, Catharanthus roseus. No. 3527, $300, Ipomoea carnea.
No. 3528, $35, Russelia equisetiformis. No. 3529, $60, Sprekelia formosissima. No. 3530, $200, Passiflora quadrangularis. No. 3531, $300, Mirabilis jalapa.
No. 3532, $100: a, Lantana camara. b, Jatropha integerrima. c, Plumeria alba. d, Strelitzia reginae. e, Clerodendrum splendens. f, Thunbergia grandiflora.
No. 3533, $100, vert.: a, Cordia sebestena. b, Heliconia wagneriana. c, Dendrobium phalaenopsis. d, Passiflora caerulea. e, Oncidium nubigenum. f, Hibiscus rosa-sinensis.
No. 3534, $100: a, Ipomoea tricolor. b, Lantana camara (inscribed canara). c, Cantua buxifolia. d, Fuchsia. e, Eichornia crassipes. f, Cosmos sulphureus.
No. 3535, $100: a, Bignonia capreolata. b, Calceolaria herbeo-hybrida. c, Canna generalis. d, Bauhinia grandiflora. e, Amaranthus caudatus. f, Abutilon megapotamicum.
No. 3536, $400, Guzmania lingulata. No. 3537, $400, Cattleya granulosa, vert.
No. 3538, $400, Tacsonia van-volxemii. No. 3539, $400, Oeceoclades maculata.

2000, Oct. 30   *Perf. 14*
3524-3527 A362 Set of 4   6.75 6.75
3528-3531 A363 Set of 4   6.75 6.75
Sheets of 6, #a-f
3532-3533 A362 Set of 2   14.00 14.00
3534-3535 A363 Set of 2   14.00 14.00
Souvenir Sheets
3536-3537 A362 Set of 2   9.50 9.50
3538-3539 A363 Set of 2   9.50 9.50

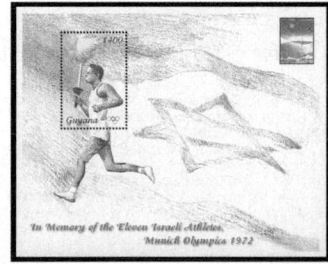

Munich Olympics Massacre — A364

No. 3540: a, Yaakov Springer. b, Andrei Schpitzer. c, Amitsur Shapira. d, David Berger. e, Ze'ev Friedman. f, Joseph Gottfreund. g, Moshe Weinberg. h, Kahat Shor. i, Mark Slavin. j, Eliezer Halfin. k, Joseph Romano. l, Poster of Munich Olympics.
Illustration reduced.

2000, Oct. 30
3540 A364 $40 Sheet of 12,
       #a-l   7.00 7.00
Souvenir Sheet
3541 A364 $400 Torch bearer   5.50 5.50

Three Stooges Type of 2000

No. 3542: a, Moe with seltzer bottle, Shemp, Larry. b, As cave men trying to break rock. c, Moe with cow. d, Two women, Shemp, Moe. e, Moe, Shemp, seated. f, As cave men, Shemp holding large rock. g, Stooges wearing pith helmets. h, Stooges, picture frames. i, Stooges with fake beards.
No. 3543, $400, Larry, woman, vert. No. 3544, $400, Moe in plaid shirt, vert.

2000, July 27   *Litho.*   *Perf. 13¾*
3542 A357 $80 Sheet of 9, #a-i   8.75 8.75
Souvenir Sheets
3543-3544 A357 Set of 2   9.00 9.00

Betty Boop Type of 2000
Souvenir Sheets

#3545, At football field. #3546, With tennis racquet. #3547, With ankh earrings, winking. #3548, With red swimsuit. #3549, As portrait

of queen. #3550, As Can-can girl. #3551, Standing on shell. #3552, As Mona Lisa, horiz.

2000, July 27
3545-3552 A358 $400 Set of 8   40.00 40.00

I Love Lucy — A365

No. 3553: a, Lucy reading book. b, Ricky, Lucy with book. c, Ricky kissing Lucy. d, Lucy near window. e, Lucy grabbing Ethel. f, Ricky holding scarf, Lucy in bed. g, Ethel, Lucy, frying pan. h, Ricky with frying pan. i, Lucy, Ethel, coffee table.
No. 3554, $400, Lucy in pink robe. No. 3555, $400, Lucy with garbage can lid.
Illustration reduced.

2000, July 27
3553 A365 $60 Sheet of 9, #a-i   6.75 6.75
Souvenir Sheets
3554-3555 A365 Set of 2   9.00 9.00

FIN. K. L — A366

No. 3556: a, Lee Hyo-Ri. b, Ok Ju-Hyun. c, Lee Jin. d, Lee Jin. e, Group. f, Sung Yu-Ri. g, Lee Hyo-Ri. h, Sung Yu-Ri. i, Ok Ju-Hyun. #d, f, i, full color, others, sepia tone.

2000, Sept. 7   *Perf. 13½*
3556 A366 $80 Sheet of 9, #a-i   9.00 9.00

Queen Mother,
100th
Birthday — A367

2000, Dec. 1   *Perf. 14*
3557 A367 $100 multi   1.40 1.40
Printed in sheets of 6.

Christmas — A368

$60, #3562b, Heads of 2 angels, org background. $90, #3562a, 2 full angels, bl background. $120, #3562c, Heads of 2 angels, bl background. $400, #3562d, 2 full angels, org background.
No. 3563, Baby Jesus, horiz.

2000, Dec. 18
3558-3561 A368   Set of 4   8.50 8.50
3562 A368 $180 Sheet of 4, #a-d   8.25 8.25
Souvenir Sheet
3563 A368 $400 multi   4.75 4.75

New Year 2001 (Year of the
Snake) — A369

No. 3564: a, Green snake head. b, Red snake head. c, Blue snake head. d, Yellow snake head.
$250, Purple snake head, vert.
Illustration reduced.

2001, Jan. 2   *Litho.*   *Perf. 13½x13*
3564 A369 $80 Sheet of 4, #a-d   4.25 4.25
Souvenir Sheet
       Perf. 13x13½
3565 A369 $250 multi   3.00 3.00

Tourist Attractions — A370

Designs: No. 3566, $90, Prime Minister's residence. No. 3567, $90, Kaiteur Falls, vert.

2001, Jan. 30   *Perf. 13¼*
3566-3567 A370 Set of 2   2.25 2.25

Flower Photomosaic Type of 1999

No. 3568, $80: Various photographs of flowers making up a photomosaic of the Queen Mother.
No. 3569, $100: Various photographs of religious sites making up a photomosaic of Pope John Paul II.

2001, Feb. 13   *Perf. 13¾*
Sheets of 8, #a-h
3568-3569 A341 Set of 2   19.00 19.00
Souvenir Sheet

Chow Yun-Fat, Actor — A371

Background color: a, Blue green. b, Dark red. c, Olive brown. d, Red violet. e, Dark blue. f, Purple.

2001, Feb. 13   *Perf. 13¾x13¼*
3570 A371 $60 Sheet of 6, #a-f   4.25 4.25

Pokémon — A372

No. 3571: a, Staryu. b, Seaking. c, Tentacool. d, Magikarp. e, Seadra. f, Goldeen. Illustration reduced.

2001, Feb. 13   **Perf. 13¾**
3571 A372 $100 Sheet of 6, #a-f   7.50 7.50

Souvenir Sheet

3572 A372 $400 Horsea   4.50 4.50

Betty Boop Type of 2000

Designs: No. 3573, $400, In pink hat. No. 3574, $400, As singer on stage. No. 3575, $400, With red top and necklace, on beach. No. 3576, $400, In orange and black hat, horiz.

2001 ?   **Litho.**   **Perf. 13¾**
3573-3576 A358   Set of 4   18.00 18.00

I Love Lucy Type of 2000

Designs: No. 3577, $400, Dressed like Carmen Miranda. No. 3578, $400, With blue hat and gloves. No. 3579, $400, As knife thrower's target. No. 3580, $400, At table, wearing blue hat. No. 3581, $400, Wearing glasses with thick black frames.

2001 ?
3577-3581 A365   Set of 5   22.50 22.50

A373

A374

Cats and Dogs — A375

Designs: No. 3582, $35, Boxer. No. 3583, $60, Cinnamon ocicat. No. 3584, $100, Smooth dachshund. $300, White Manx.
No. 3586, $35, Chihuahua. No. 3587, $60, Persian tabby. No. 3588, $100, Colorpoint shorthair. $200, Cocker spaniel.
No. 3590 — Names of dogs (border color and location of denomination), $100: a, Pup (pink, bottom). b, Yogi (orange, bottom). c, Hooch (yellow, bottom) d, Huxley Blu (orange, top) e, Snowflake (yellow, top). f, Red (pink, top).
No. 3591 — Names of cats (border color and location of denomination), $100: a, Tom (orange, bottom). b, Puff (yellow, bottom). c, Jag (pink, bottom). d, Fritz (yellow, top). e, Smokey (pink, top). f, Thor, (orange, top).
No. 3592, $60: a, Devon rex. b, Egyptian mau. c, Turkish angora. d, Sphynx. e, Persian. f, American wirehair. g, Exotic shorthair. h, American curl.
No. 3593, $80: a, Airedale terrier. b, Greyhound. c, Afghan hound. d, Samoyed. e, Field spaniel. f, Scottish terrier. g, Brittany spaniel. h, Boston terrier.
No. 3594, $80: a, American shorthair. b, Somali. c, Singapura. d, Balinese. e, Egyptian mau. f, Scottish fold. g, Sphynx. h, Korat.
No. 3595, $80: a, Rottweiler. b, German shepherd. c, Bernese mountain dog. d, Sharpei. e, Dachshund. f, Jack Russell terrier. g, Boston terrier. h, Welsh corgi.
No. 3596, $400, Dalmatian. No. 3597, $400, Birman. No. 3598, $400, Abyssinian. No. 3599, $400, Beagle. No. 3600, $400, German shepeherd named Baron of Fillmore. No. 3601, $400, Cat named Spike.

2001, Mar. 1   **Perf. 14**
3582-3585 A373   Set of 4   6.25 6.25
3586-3589 A374   Set of 4   5.25 5.25

Sheets of 6, #a-f

3590-3591 A375   Set of 2   16.00 16.00

Sheets of 8, #a-h

3592-3593 A373   Set of 2   15.00 15.00
3594-3595 A374   Set of 2   16.50 16.50

Souvenir Sheets

3596-3597 A373   Set of 2   9.50 9.50
3598-3599 A374   Set of 2   9.50 9.50
3600-3601 A375   Set of 2   9.50 9.50

Hong Kong 2001 Stamp Exhibition (Nos. 3592-3593, 3596-3597).

Souvenir Sheets

Hello Kitty — A376

Western children's stories with Hello Kitty characters: No. 3602, $400, Cinderella. No. 3603, $400, The Wizard of Oz. No. 3604, $400, Little Red Riding Hood. No. 3605, $400, Peter Pan. No. 3606, $400, Heidi. No. 3607, $400, Alice in Wonderland.
Oriental children's stories with Hello Kitty characters: No. 3608, $400, The Fishermen. No. 3609, $400, In the Snow. No. 3610, $400, Bamboo Princess. No. 3611, $400, Three in a

Boat. No. 3612, $400, Up a Tree. No. 3613, $400, On a Bear.

2001, Mar. 28   **Litho.**   **Perf. 13¾**
3602-3613 A376   Set of 12   55.00 55.00

Phila Nippon '01, Japan — A377

Designs: No. 3614, $25, Hanaogi with Maidservant, by Eisho Chokosai. No. 3615, $25, Girl at a Hot Spring Resort, by Goyo Hashiguchi. No. 3616, $30, Morokoshi of the Echizenya, by Eiri Rekisentei. No. 3617, $30, Courtesan Receiving Letter of Invitation, by Harunobu Suzuki. No. 3618, $35, Two Girls on Their Way to or from the Bathhouse, by Suzuki. No. 3619, $35, Mother and Daughter on an Outing, by Utamaro. No. 3620, $60, Matron in Love, by Utamaro. No. 3621, $60, Girl and Frog, by Suzuki. No. 3622, $100, The Courtesan Midorigi, by Eisho Chokosai. No. 3623, $100, Three Beauties of High Fame, by Utamaro. No. 3624, $200, Maiko, by Bakusen Tsuchida. No. 3625, $200, Girl Breaking Off the Branch of a Flowering Tree, by Suzuki.
No. 3626 — Paintings by Jakuchu Ito (28x84mm): a, Insects, Reptiles and Amphibians at a Pond. b, Rose Mallows and Fowl. c, Rooster, Sunflower and Morning Glories. d, A Group of Roosters. e, Black Rooster and Nandina. f, Birds and Autumn Maples. g, Wagtail and Roses. h, Cockatoos in a Pine.
No. 3627 — Predominate features of sections of Procession to the Shugakuin Imperial Villa, by Sesshin Kakimoto (28x84mm): a, Bridge. b, High mountain, road and bridge. c, Large tree in foreground. d, Small island in foreground. e, Building at bottom. f, Building and large tree at bottom.
No. 3628 — Paintings of Women (28x84mm): a, Girls After the Bath, by Utamaro. b, Summer Evening on the Riverbank at Hama-cho, by Kiyonaga Torii. c, A Beauty in the Wind, by Ando Kaigetsudo. d, Sisters by Shoen Uemura. e, Kasamori Osen, by Suzuki.
No. 3629 — Details from Backstage at a Kabuki Theater, by Moronobu Hishikawa (30x38mm): a, Top of screen. b, Man with red kimono. c, Man with stringed instrument. e, Man on chair.
No. 3630, $400, Portrait of Senseki Takami, by Kazan Watanabe. No. 3631, $400, Fish and Octopus From the Colorful Realm of Living Beings, by Ito. No. 3632, $400, Woman Holding a Flower, by Hisako Kajiwara, horiz. No. 3633, $400, Palace of Immortals in an Autumn Valley, by Yako Okochi, horiz. No. 3634, $400, Wintry Sky, by Hosen Higashibara, horiz.

2001, June 18   **Perf. 14**
3614-3625 A377   Set of 12   11.00 11.00
3626 A377 $80 Sheet of 8, #a-h   8.25 8.25
3627 A377 $100 Sheet of 6, #a-f   7.50 7.50
3628 A377 $120 Sheet of 5, #a-e   6.75 6.75
3629 A377 $160 Sheet of 4, #a-d   7.50 7.50

Sizes: 90x120mm, 120x90mm

Imperf

3630-3634 A377   Set of 5   22.50 22.50

Giuseppe Verdi (1813-1901), Opera Composer — A378

No. 3635: a, Verdi, score at LR. b, Actor, score from Rigoletto. c, Actor, score from Ernani. d, Verdi, scores at left. $400, Verdi and scores.

2001, June 18   **Perf. 14**
3635 A378 $160 Sheet of 4, #a-d   8.25 8.25

Souvenir Sheet

3636 A378 $400 multi   5.50 5.50

Toulouse-Lautrec Paintings — A379

No. 3637, horiz.: a, Maurice Joyant in the Baie de Somme. b, Monsieur Boileau. c, Monsieur, Madame and the Dog.
$300, Man from Monsieur, Madame and the Dog.

2001, June 18   **Perf. 13¾**
3637 A379 $160 Sheet of 3, #a-c 5.50 5.50

Souvenir Sheet

3638 A379 $300 multi   5.25 5.25

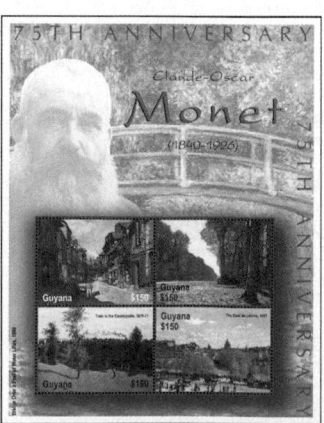

Monet Paintings — A380

No. 3639, horiz.: a, Village Street in Normandy, Near Honfleur. b, The Road to Chailly. c, Train in the Countryside. d, The Quai du Louvre.
$400, Flowering Garden.

2001, June 18
3639 A380 $150 Sheet of 4, #a-d 7.50 7.50
Souvenir Sheet
3640 A380 $400 multi 5.25 5.25

Queen Victoria (1819-1901) — A381

Pictures of Victoria from — No. 3641, $200: a, 1829. b, 1837. c, 1840. d, 1897 (with crown).
No. 3642, $200: a, 1850. b, 1843. c, 1859. d, 1897 (with hat).
No. 3643, $400, 1885 (with crown). No. 3644, $400, Undated.

2001, June 18 **Perf. 14**
Sheets of 4, #a-d
3641-3642 A381 Set of 2 19.00 19.00
Souvenir Sheets
3643-3644 A381 Set of 2 9.50 9.50

Queen Elizabeth II, 75th Birthday — A382

No. 3645: a, Pink hat. b, Red hat. c, White hat. d, Tiara.

2001, June 18 **Perf. 14**
3645 A382 $150 Sheet of 4, #a-d 7.50 7.50
Souvenir Sheet
Perf. 13¾
3646 A382 $400 shown 5.25 5.25
No. 3645 contains four 28x42mm stamps.

Photomosaic of Queen Elizbeth II — A383

2001, June 18 **Perf. 14**
3647 A383 $80 multi .90 .90
Printed in sheets of 8, with and without inscription reading "In Celebration of the 50th Anniversary of H.M. Queen Elizabeth II's Accession to the Throne."

Flower Photomosaic Type of 1999-2000
No. 3648: Various pictures of American scenes making up a photomosaic of Pres. John F. Kennedy.

2001, June 18
3648 A341 $80 Sheet of 8, #a-h 7.50 7.50

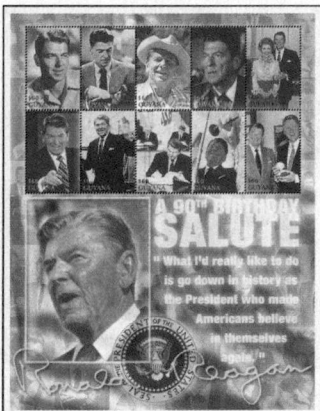

Pres. Ronald Reagan — A384

Reagan: a, In checked shirt. b, With Bonzo. c, With cowboy hat. d, With dark tie. e, With wife, Nancy. f, With striped tie. g, Waving. h, Signing treaty with Mikhail Gorbachev. i, With hammer and chisel. j, With Pres. Clinton.

2001, June 18
3649 A384 $60 Sheet of 10, #a-j 8.25 8.25

Betty Boop Type of 2000
Designs: No. 3650, $400, With swimsuit and sunglasses. No. 3651, $400, With lilac headdress. No. 3652, $400, With purple top and pirate's hat. No. 3653, $400, Dancing on radio, horiz.

2001 **Perf. 13¾**
3650-3653 A358 Set of 4 18.00 18.00

Betty Boop Type of 2000
Designs: No. 3654, $400, In orange and yellow polka dot swimsuit, holding gift. No. 3655, $400, Holding on anchor. No. 3556, $400, In red bikini, surfing. No. 3557, $400, Wearing birthday hat, horiz.

2001 **Litho.** **Perf. 13¾**
3654-3657 A358 Set of 4 18.00 18.00

Historical Events Type of 1997
No. 3658: a, Securities and Exchange Commission formed, 1934. b, Herbert Hoover is elected president, 1928. c, The Jazz Singer is first talking movie, 1927. d, J. Edgar Hoover becomes director of FBI, 1924. e, Alexander Fleming discovers penicillin, 1928. f, FCC established to regulate broadcasting, 1934. g, Lindbergh becomes first to fly solo across Atlantic, 1927. h, Albert Einstein is awarded Nobel Prize for Physics, 1921. i, Hindenburg dies and Hitler becomes German Führer, 1934. j, Social Security Act provides safety for Americans, 1935. k, Earhart is first to fly solo from Hawaii to California, 1935. l, Marcus Garvey's prison sentence is commuted, 1927.

2001, Mar. 28 **Perf. 14¼x14¾**
3658 A289 $60 Sheet of 12, #a-l 9.50 9.50

Prehistoric Animals — A385

Designs: $20, Allosaurus. $30, Spinosaurus. $35, Pteranodon. $60, Cetiosaurus. $200, Archaeopteryx. $300, Parasaurolophus.
No. 3665, $100, horiz.: a, Alamosaurus. b, Archaeopteryx, diff. c, Pachycephalosaurus. d, Parasaurolophus, diff. e, Edmontosaurus. f, Triceratops.
No. 3666, $100, horiz.: a, Brachiosaurus and two palm trees. b, Dimorphodon. c, Coelophysis. d, Velociraptor. e, Antrodemus. f, Euparkeria.
No. 3667, $100, horiz.: a, Ichthyostega. b, Eryops. c, Ichthyosaur. d, Pliosaur. e, Dunklosteus. f, Eogyrinus.
No. 3668, $100, horiz.: a, Brachiosaurus and palm tree. b, Pteranodon, diff. c, Compsognathus. d, Corythosaurus. e, Allosaurus, diff. f, Torosaurus.
No. 3669, $400, Brachiosaurus, diff. No. 3670, $400, Torosaurus, diff., horiz. No. 3671, $400, Ichthyosaur, diff., horiz. No. 3672, $400, Pteranodon, diff., horiz.

2001, Oct. 15 **Perf. 14**
3659-3664 A385 Set of 6 7.25 7.25
Sheets of 6, #a-f
3665-3668 A385 Set of 4 27.50 27.50
Souvenir Sheets
3669-3672 A385 Set of 4 18.00 18.00
Vegaspex (#3665-3672).

Animals of Tropical Rainforests A386

Designs: $35, Mandrill, vert. $100, Leaf cutting ants.
No. 3675, $80: a, Elephant. b, Impala. c, Leopard. d, Gray parrot. e, Hippopotamus. f, Pygmy chimp. g, African green python. h, Mountain gorilla.
No. 3676, $80: a, Three-toed sloth. b, Lion tamarin. c, Ringtail lemur. d, Sugar glider. e, Toucan. f, Trogons. g, Pygmy marmoset. h, Poison arrow frog.
No. 3677, $400, Tapir, vert. No. 3678, $400, Sable antelope, vert.

2001, Oct. 15
3673-3674 A386 Set of 2 1.50 1.50
Sheets of 8, #a-h
3675-3676 A386 Set of 2 14.50 14.50
Souvenir Sheets
3677-3678 A386 Set of 2 9.00 9.00

Tropical Birds — A387

No. 3679, $100, horiz.: a, Rainbow lorikeet. b, King bird of paradise. c, Yellow-chevroned parakeet. d, Masked lovebird. e, Scarlet ibis. f, Toco toucan.
No. 3680, $100, horiz.: a, Hyacinth macaw. b, Wire-tailed manakin. c, Scarlet macaw. d,

Sun parakeet. e, Roseate spoonbill. f, Red-billed toucan.
No. 3681, $400, Eclectus parrot. No. 3682, $400, Sulfur-crested cockatoo.

2001, Oct. 15 **Litho.**
Sheets of 6, #a-f
3679-3680 A387 Set of 2 15.00 15.00
Souvenir Sheets
3681-3682 A387 Set of 2 11.00 11.00

New Year 2002 (Year of the Horse) — A388

No. 3683 — Evolution of Chinese character for "horse": a, Two characters outside, one character inside parentheses at UR. b, Three characters outside, one character inside parentheses at UR. c, Four characters outside, one character inside parentheses at UR. d, Three characters outside, two characters inside parentheses at UR.
No. 3684 — Figure on horse: a, Denomination at UL. b, Denomination at UR.

2001, Oct. 15 **Perf. 13**
3683 A388 $100 Sheet of 4, #a-d 6.50 6.50
Perf. 13¼
3684 A388 $150 Sheet of 2, #a-b 5.50 5.50
No. 3684 contains two 38x50mm stamps.

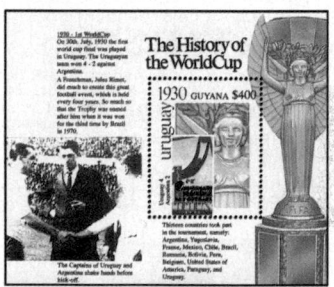

2002 World Cup Soccer Championships, Japan and Korea — A389

No. 3685, $100 — Posters from: a, 1950, and player. b, 1954, and Jules Rimet. c, 1958, Pelé and teammates. d, 1962, and Zito scoring goal. e, 1966, and English players celebrating. f, 1970, and Jairzinho.
No. 3686, $100 — Posters from: a, 1978, and Daniel Passarella. b, 1982, and Paolo Rossi. c, 1986, and Diego Maradona. d, 1990, and German players celebrating. e, 1994, and Brazilian players celebrating. f, 1998, and Zinedine Zidane.
No. 3687, $400, 1930 poster, head from Jules Rimet Trophy. No. 3688, $400, Head and globe from World Cup trophy.

2001, Dec. 26 **Perf. 13¾x14¼**
Sheets of 6, #a-f
3685-3686 A389 Set of 2 14.00 14.00
Souvenir Sheets
Perf. 14¼
3687-3688 A389 Set of 2 9.00 9.00

Queen Mother Type of 1999 Redrawn
No. 3689: a, With Princess Elizabeth, 1928. b, Lady Elizabeth-Bowles Lyon, 1914. c, With Princess Elizabeth, 1950. d, In Venice, 1984. $400, In Canada, 1988.

2001, Dec. Perf. 14
Yellow Orange Frames
3689 A328 $130 Sheet of 4, #a-d, + label 5.75 5.75

Souvenir Sheet
Perf. 13¾
3690 A328 $400 multi 4.50 4.50

Queen Mother's 101st birthday. No. 3690 contains one 38x50mm stamp with a bluer cast than that found on No. 3434. Sheet margins of Nos. 3689-3690 lack embossing and gold arms and frames found on Nos. 3433-3434.

I Love Lucy Type of 2000
Souvenir Sheets

Designs: No. 3691, $400, Lucy wearing leis, with hands up. No. 3692, $400, Lucy with checked shirt and apron, with mouth open.

2001 ? Perf. 13¾
3691-3692 A365 Set of 2 9.00 9.00

Wedding of Netherlands Prince Willem-Alexander and Máxima Zorreguieta — A390

No. 3693: a, Couple (Máxima at left), flag colors at left. b, Couple (heads apart), flag colors at right. c, Couple (Máxima at right), flag colors at left. d, Couple (heads together), flag colors at right. e, Willem-Alexander. f, Máxima.

2002, Jan. 7 Litho. Perf. 14¾x14¼
3693 A390 $120 Sheet of 6, #a-f 8.00 8.00

United We Stand — A391

2002, Feb. 6 Perf. 13½x13¼
3694 A391 $200 multi 2.25 2.25

Printed in sheets of four.

Reign of Queen Elizabeth II, 50th Anniv. — A392

No. 3695: a, Blue hat. b, Feathered hat. c, Waving. d, With horse at right. $400, With horse at left.

2002, Feb. 6 Perf. 14½
3695 A392 $150 Sheet of 4, #a-d 6.75 6.75

Souvenir Sheet
3696 A392 $400 multi 4.50 4.50

Flower Photomosaic Type of 1999-2000

No. 3697: Various science photographs making up a photomosaic of Albert Einstein.

2002, Feb. 25 Perf. 13¾
3697 A341 $80 Sheet of 8, #a-h 7.25 7.25

Nobel Prizes, Cent. (in 2001) — A393

No. 3698, $100 — Chemistry laureates: a, Harold C. Urey, 1934. b, Willard F. Libby, 1960. c, Frederick Sanger, 1958 and 1980. d, Theodor Svedberg, 1926. e, Cyril N. Hinshelwood, 1956. f, Nikolai Semenov, 1956.

No. 3699, $100: a, Alexander Todd, Chemistry, 1957. b, John Steinbeck, Literature, 1962. c, Edward C. Kendall, Physiology or Medicine, 1950. d, Frederick G. Banting, Physiology or Medicine, 1923. e, Charles Nicolle, Physiology or Medicine, 1928. f, Charles Richet, Physiology or Medicine, 1913.

No. 3700, $400, International Red Cross, Peace, 1917. No. 3701, $400, John J. R. MacLeod, Physiology or Medicine, 1923. No. 3702, $400, Derek H. R. Barton, Chemistry, 1969.

2002, Feb. 25 Perf. 14
Sheets of 6, #a-f
3698-3699 A393 Set of 2 13.50 13.50

Souvenir Sheets
3700-3702 A393 Set of 3 13.50 13.50

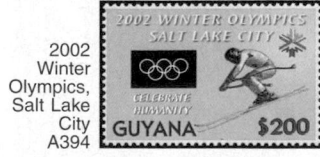

2002 Winter Olympics, Salt Lake City A394

Designs: No. 3703, $200, Skier. No. 3704, $200, Figure skater.

2002, July 1 Litho. Perf. 13¼x13½
3703-3704 A394 Set of 2 4.50 4.50
  a. Souvenir sheet, #3703-3704 4.50 4.50

Guyana — People's Republic of China Diplomatic Relations, 30th Anniv. — A395

Designs: No. 3705, $100, Chinese flag, Kaieteur Falls, Guyana. No. 3706, $100, Guyanese flag, Great Wall of China.

2002, July 1 Perf. 14
3705-3706 A395 Set of 2 2.25 2.25

Intl. Volunteers Year (in 2001) A396

Emblem, Guyanese flag and: $35, Person on ladder touching Guyana on map. $60, Map of Guyana and IVY emblem. $300, People.

2002, July 1
3707-3709 A396 Set of 3 4.50 4.50

Intl. Year of Ecotourism — A397

No. 3710: a, Owl. b, Waterfall and tourists. c, Baboon. d, Butterfly. e, Flower. f, Otter. $400, Leopard.

2002, July 1 Perf. 13¼x13
3710 A397 $100 Sheet of 6, #a-f 6.75 6.75

Souvenir Sheet
3711 A397 $400 multi 4.50 4.50

Intl. Year of Mountains — A398

No. 3712: a, Devil's Tower, US. b, Schreckhorn, Switzerland. c, Mt. Rainier, US. d, Mt. Everest, Nepal and Tibet. No. 3713: Mt. McKinley. U.S.

2002, July 1 Perf. 13½x13¼
3712 A398 $200 Sheet of 4, #a-d 14.00 14.00

Souvenir Sheet
3713 A398 $400 multi 7.00 7.00
  See Nos. 3848-3851.

20th World Scout Jamboree, Thailand — A399

No. 3714: a, Environmental Science merit badge. b, Citizenship in the World merit badge. c, Life Saving merit badge. $400, Mascot, Scout emblem.

2002, July 1
3714 A399 $200 Sheet of 3, #a-c 6.75 6.75

Souvenir Sheet
3715 A399 $400 multi 4.50 4.50

Flora and Fauna — A400

No. 3716, $100 — Butterflies: a, Sweet oil. b, Swallowtail. c, Southern white admiral. d, Prepona pheridamas. e, Plain tiger. f, Common eggfly.

No. 3717, $100 — Moths: a, Burgena varia. b, Lime hawkmoth. c, Spurge hawkmoth. d, Eligma laetipicta. e, Io moth. f, Pine hawkmoth.

No. 3718, $100 — Birds: a, Flycatcher. b, Barbary shrike. c, Red-faced mousebird. d, Red-footed booby. e, White-fronted goose. f, Great crested grebe.

No. 3719, $100 — Whales: a, Sperm. b, Pygmy sperm. c, Blue. d, Bottlenose. e, Killer. f, True's beaked.

No. 3720, $100, vert. — Orchids: a, Masdevallia tovarensis. b, Encyclia vitellina. c, Dendrobium nobile. d, Masdevallia falcata. e, Calanthe vestita. f, Brassolaeliacattleya Rising Sun.

No. 3721, $400, Zebra butterfly. No. 3722, $400, Callimorpha quadripuntaria. No. 3723, $400, Whiskered tern. No. 3724, $400, Beluga whale. No. 3725, $400, Brassavola nodosa.

2002, Aug. 7 Perf. 14
Sheets of 6, #a-f
3716-3720 A400 Set of 5 47.50 47.50

Souvenir Sheets
3721-3725 A400 Set of 5 35.00 35.00

Elvis Presley (1935-77) A401

Designs: No. 3726, $60, In army uniform. No. 3727, $60, Singing.

2002, Aug. 16 Perf. 13¾
3726-3727 A401 Set of 2 2.25 2.25

Each stamp was printed in a sheet of nine.

Popeye — A402

No. 3728: a, Popeye. b, Olive Oyl. c, Wimpy. d, Jeep. e, Swee'Pea and Olive Oyl. f, Swee'Pea.
$400, Popeye, diff.

2002, Oct. 7   **Perf. 14**
3728 A402 $100 Sheet of 6, #a-f 8.50 8.50
Souvenir Sheet
3729 A402 $400 multi   6.50 6.50

New Year 2003 (Year of the Ram) — A403

Rams and background color of: a, Red. b, Orange. c, Bright pink. d, Yellow green.

2003, Jan. 27 Litho.   **Perf. 14¼x14½**
3730 A403 $100 Sheet of 4, #a-d 6.50 6.50

Pres. John F. Kennedy (1917-63) — A404

No. 3731, vert.: a, Pres. Kennedy, Presidential seal. b, Pres. Kennedy, Dr. Martin Luther King, Jr. c, Pres. Kennedy, space capsule. d, Pres. Kennedy, US flag, White House. e, Pres. Kennedy, map of Cuba, missile. f, Jacqueline and John F. Kennedy, Jr., US flag.
$400, Pres. Kennedy and wife, Jacqueline.

2003, Jan. 27   **Perf. 14**
3731 A404 $100 Sheet of 6, #a-f 8.00 8.00
Souvenir Sheet
3732 A404 $400 multi   6.50 6.50

Pres. Ronald Reagan — A405

No. 3733, vert. — Pres. Reagan: a, And eagle. b, As actor. c, And Mt. Rushmore. d, And wife Nancy. e, And White House. f, Riding horse.
$400, With Mikhail Gorbachev.

2003, Jan. 27
3733 A405 $100 Sheet of 6, #a-f 8.00 8.00
Souvenir Sheet
3734 A405 $400 multi   7.00 7.00

Princess Diana (1961-97) — A406

No. 3735: a-f, Various depictions of Princess wearing tiaras or bridal veils.
$400, Wearing pink and yellow dress.

2003, Jan. 27
3735 A406 $100 Sheet of 6, #a-f 7.00 7.00
Souvenir Sheet
3736 A406 $400 multi   5.00 5.00

Paintings of Lucas Cranach the Elder (1472-1553) A407

Designs: $35, Portrait of a Man. $60, Portrait of a Woman. $100, Duchess Catherine of Mecklenburg. $200, Portrait of Duke Henry of Saxony.
No. 3741: a, The Virgin, c. 1518. b, The Virgin and Child Under the Apple Tree. c, The Virgin, c. 1535. d, The Virgin, c. 1525.
$400, The Virgin and Child Holding a Piece of Bread.

2003, June 17 Litho.   **Perf. 14¼**
3737-3740 A407 Set of 4   4.50 4.50
3741 A407 $150 Sheet of 4, #a-d 6.75 6.75
Souvenir Sheet
3742 A407 $400 multi   4.50 4.50

Art by Kunichika Toyohara (1835-1900) A408

Designs: $60, The Actor Shikan Nakamura IV. $80, The Actor Danjuro Ichikawa IX as Sukeroku, 1883. $100, The Actor Tatsunosuke Onoe. $300, The Actor Sadanji Ichikawa I as Kyusuke.
No. 3747: a, The Actor Sansho Kawarazaki as Watonai. b, The Actor Danjuro Ichikawa IX as Gongoru Kagemasa Kamakura. c, The Actor Sadanji Ichikawa I as Sadakuro. d, The Actor Danjuro Ichikawa IX as Sukeroku, 1898.
$400, The Actor Danjuro Ichikawa IX as Shukeigashira Kiyomasa Kato, horiz.

2003, June 17
3743-3746 A408 Set of 4   6.00 6.00
3747 A408 $150 Sheet of 4, #a-d 6.75 6.75
Souvenir Sheet
3748 A408 $400 multi   4.50 4.50

Paintings by Wassily Kandinsky (1866-1944) A409

Designs: $25, Tension in Red. $30, Black Accompaniment. $35, Calm Tension. $60, Hard and Soft. $100, Yellow Point, horiz. $300, Composition VIII, horiz.
No. 3755: a, Red Oval. b, On the White II. c, Mutual Agreement. d, Inclination.
No. 3756, $400, White Center, horiz. No. 3757, $400, Black Weft, horiz.

2003, June 17
3749-3754 A409 Set of 6   6.25 6.25
3755 A409 $150 Sheet of 4, #a-d 6.75 6.75

Size: 104x84mm
Imperf
3756-3757 A409 Set of 2   9.00 9.00

Caribbean Community, 30th Anniv. — A410

Anniversary emblem and: $20, Map of Guyana, vert. $60, Bank of Guyana Building. $100, Hands with torch, vert. $160, Stethoscope and AIDS ribbon, vert.

2003, July 7   **Perf. 14**
3758-3761 A410 Set of 4   3.75 3.75

A411

Teddy Bears, Cent. (in 2002) — A412

No. 3762 — Background color: a, Lilac. b, Dull greenish blue. c, Light blue. d, Dull yellow green. e, Dull blue green. f, Dull gray green. h, Gray. i, Dull green. j, Gray blue.
No. 3763 — Bear with: a, Red dress. b, Menorah. c, Christmas lights. d, Blue dress.

2003, Aug. 25
3762 A411 $80 Sheet of 9, #a-i 8.50 8.50
3763 A412 $150 Sheet of 4, #a-d 7.00 7.00

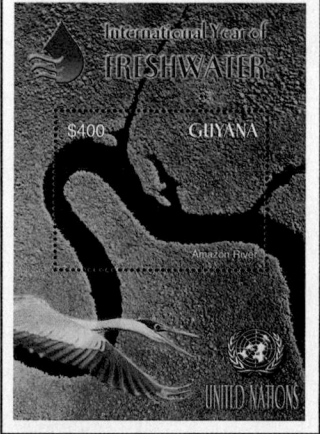

Intl. Year of Fresh Water — A413

No. 3764 — Kaieteur Falls: a, Top. b, Middle. c, Base.
$400, Amazon River.

2003, Aug. 25   **Perf. 13¾**
3764 A413 $200 Sheet of 3, #a-c 8.25 8.25
Souvenir Sheet
3765 A413 $400 multi   6.00 6.00

Tour de France Bicycle Race, Cent. — A414

No. 3766: a, Jacques Anquetil, 1964. b, Felice Gimondi, 1965. c, Lucien Aimar, 1966. d, Roger Pingeon, 1967.
$400, Jan Janssen, 1968.

2003, Aug. 25   **Perf. 13½x13**
3766 A414 $150 Sheet of 4, #a-d 7.25 7.25
Souvenir Sheet
3767 A414 $400 multi   5.00 5.00

Coronation of Queen Elizabeth II, 50th Anniv. — A415

No. 3768: a, Wearing tiara. b, Wearing dark blue dress. c, Wearing lilac dress.
$400, Wearing crown.

2003, Aug. 25   **Perf. 14**
3768 A415 $200 Sheet of 3, #a-c 6.75 6.75
Souvenir Sheet
3769 A415 $400 multi   4.50 4.50

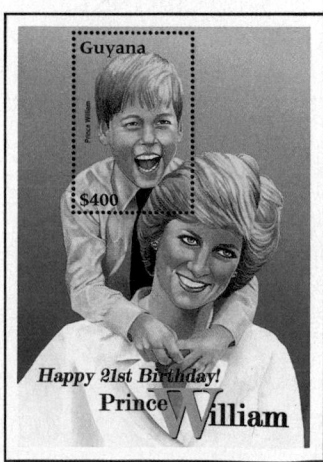

Prince William, 21st Birthday — A416

No. 3770: a, As toddler. b, As adult. c, As infant.
$400, As young boy.

2003, Aug. 25
3770 A416 $200 Sheet of 3, #a-c 7.00 7.00
Souvenir Sheet
3771 A416 $400 multi   5.50 5.50

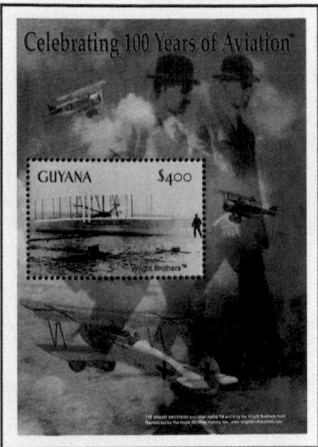

Powered Flight, Cent. — A417

Designs: $100, Airplane of Sir Alliot Verdon Roe. $160, Airplane of Samuel Franklin Cody.
No. 3772, $150: a, Wright Flyer. b, Spad 13. c, Sopwith F-1. d, Albatros D.II.
No. 3773, $150: a, Nieuport 17. b, S. E. 5a. c, D. H. 4. d, German biplane.
No. 3774, $400, Wright Flyer making first flight. No. 3775, $400, Fokker D.VIIs.

2003, Aug. 25
3771A	A417	$100 multi	1.10	1.10
3771B	A417	$160 multi	1.75	1.75

Sheets of 4, #a-d
3772-3773	A417	Set of 2	13.50	13.50

Souvenir Sheets
3774-3775	A417	Set of 2	10.00	10.00

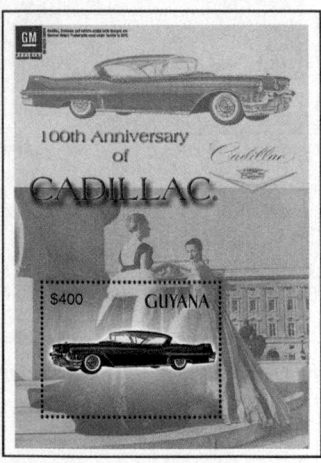

General Motors Automobiles — A418

No. 3776, $150 — Cadillacs: a, 1948 Sixty Special. b, 1966 Fleetwood Sixty Special. c, 1967 Eldorado. d, 1976 Eldorado convertible.
No. 3777, $150 — Corvettes: a, 1964 Stingray. b, 1963 Stingray. c, 1966 Stingray. 4. d, 1969.
No. 3778, $400, Undescribed Cadillac (1957 Coupe de Ville). No. 3779, $400, 1971 Corvette.

2003, Aug. 25 **Sheets of 4, #a-d**
3776-3777	A418	Set of 2	14.50	14.50

Souvenir Sheets
3778-3779	A418	Set of 2	9.50	9.50

Butterflies — A419

Designs: $20, Grecian shoemaker. $55, Clorinde. $80, Orange-barred sulphur. $100, Atala. $160, White peacock. $200, Polydamus swallowtail. $300, Giant swallowtail. $400, Banded king shoemaker. $500, Blue night. $1000, Orange theope. $2000, Small lacewing. $3000, Common morpho.

2003, Nov. 4   Litho.   Perf. 13¼
3780	A419	$20 multi	.30	.30
3781	A419	$55 multi	.85	.85
3782	A419	$80 multi	1.25	1.25
3783	A419	$100 multi	1.50	1.50
3784	A419	$160 multi	2.25	2.25
3785	A419	$200 multi	3.00	3.00
3786	A419	$300 multi	4.25	4.25
3787	A419	$400 multi	5.75	5.75
3788	A419	$500 multi	7.25	7.25
3789	A419	$1000 multi	13.50	13.50
3790	A419	$2000 multi	27.50	27.50
3791	A419	$3000 multi	40.00	40.00
		Nos. 3780-3791 (12)	107.40	107.40

Worldwide Fund for Nature (WWF) A420

No. 3792: a, Head of channel-billed toucan. b, Two toco toucans on branch. c, Channel-billed toucan on branch. d, Toco toucan and chick.

2003, Dec. 1   Perf. 14
3792		Horiz. strip of 4, #a-d	5.00	5.00
a.-d.		A420 $100 Any single	1.20	1.20
e.		Souvenir sheet, 2 each #3792a-3792d	10.50	10.50

Mushrooms — A421

Designs: No. 3793, $20, Clitocybe gibba. No. 3794, $20, Clitocybe clavipes. $30, Calocybe carnea. $300, Marasmius.
No. 3797: a, Amanita spissa. b, Boletus aestivalis. c, Boletus rubellus. d, Clathrus archeri.
$400, Volvariella bombycina.

2003, Dec. 1
3793-3796	A421	Set of 4	4.50	4.50
3797	A421	$150 Sheet of 4, #a-d	7.25	7.25

Souvenir Sheet
3798	A421	$400 multi	5.75	5.75

Mammals A422

Designs: $25, Common tenrec. $60, Humboldt's woolly monkey, vert. $100, Gundi. $200, Harbor seal.
No. 3803: a, Prevost's squirrel. b, Mountain tapir. c, Sea otter. d, Indus dolphin.
$400, Peter's disk-winged bat, vert.

2003, Dec. 1
3799-3802	A422	Set of 4	4.25	4.25
3803	A422	$150 Sheet of 4, #a-d	6.75	6.75

Souvenir Sheet
3804	A422	$400 multi	4.50	4.50

Flowers — A423

Designs: $20, Begonia sedeni. $30, Dahlia. $35, Eschecholzia californica. $300, Lupinus perennis.
No. 3809: a, Agapanthus africanus. b, Hyacinth cultivars. c, Protea linearis. d, Hippestrum aulicum.
$400, Crocus sativus, horiz.

2003, Dec. 1
3805-3808	A423	Set of 4	4.25	4.25
3809	A423	$150 Sheet of 4, #a-d	6.75	6.75

Souvenir Sheet
3810	A423	$400 multi	5.00	5.00

Fish A424

Designs: $25, Regal tang. $60, Pajama tang. $100, Coral beauty. $200, Emperor angelfish.
No. 3815: a, High hat. b, Regal angelfish. c, Fire clown. d, Domino damselfish.
$400, Tomato clown.

2003, Dec. 1
3811-3814	A424	Set of 4	4.75	4.75
3815	A424	$150 Sheet of 4, #a-d	9.00	9.00

Souvenir Sheet
3816	A424	$400 multi	5.50	5.50

Guyana — Brazil Diplomatic Relations, 35th Anniv. A425

2003, Dec. 18
3817	A425	$20 multi	.20	.20

New Year 2004 (Year of the Monkey) — A426

No. 3818: a, Dark brown monkey with orange face. b, Dark brown and white monkey with brown face. c, Brown monkey with orange monkey with black face.

2004, Jan. 5
3818	A426	$100 Sheet of 4, #a-d	4.75	4.75

Paintings by Tang Yin (1470-1524) — A427

No. 3819, vert.: a, Concubines of Emperor Chu. b, Lady. c, Untitled painting depicting woman. d, Untitled painting depicting landscape.
$400, Mountain Scene.

2004, Jan. 21   Litho.   Perf. 13¼
3819	A427	$150 Sheet of 4, #a-d	6.75	6.75

Souvenir Sheet
3820	A427	$400 multi	4.50	4.50

Birth of Princess Catherina Amalia of the Netherlands — A428

No. 3821: a, Princess, one hand shown. b, Princess and father, Prince Willem-Alexander. c, Princess, two hands shown.

2004, Feb. 15   Perf. 14¼
3821	A428	$200 Sheet of 3, #a-c	7.00	7.00

FIFA (Fédération Internationale de Football Association), Cent. — A429

World Cup championship teams: No. 3822, $80, Uruguay, 1930. No. 3823, $80, Italy, 1934. No. 3824, $80, Italy, 1938. No. 3825, $80, Uruguay, 1950. No. 3826, $80, Germany, 1954. No. 3827, $80, Brazil, 1958. No. 3828, $80, Brazil, 1962. No. 3829, $80, England, 1966. No. 3830, $80, Brazil, 1970.

2004, Feb. 16   Perf. 13¼
3822-3830	A429	Set of 9	8.25	8.25

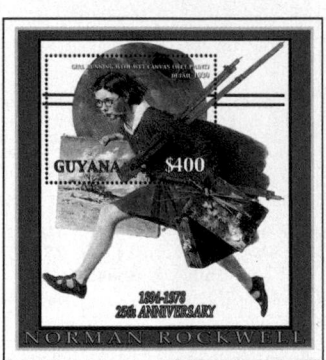

Paintings by Norman Rockwell (1894-1978) — A430

No. 3831, vert.: a, Doctor and Doll. b, Babysitter with Screaming Infant. c, Girl with Black Eye. d, Checkup.
$400, Girl Running with Wet Canvas (Wet Paint).

2004, Feb. 16   Perf. 14¼
3831	A430	$150 Sheet of 4, #a-d	6.75	6.75

Souvenir Sheet
3832	A430	$400 multi	4.50	4.50

Paintings by Pablo Picasso (1881-1973) — A431

No. 3833: a, Woman in Yellow Hat. b, Seated Woman, 1962. c, Head of a Woman. d, Large Profile.
$400, Seated Woman, 1971.

2004, Feb. 16 **Perf. 14¼**
3833 A431 $150 Sheet of 4, #a-d 6.75 6.75
Imperf
3834 A431 $400 multi 4.50 4.50
No. 3833 contains four 38x50mm stamps.

Rembrandt Paintings A432

Designs: $35, A Woman Bathing. $60, Flora. $100, The Poet, Jan Hermansz Krul. $200, Portrait of a Young Man.
No. 3839: a, The Apostle James. b, The Apostle Bartholemew. c, The Evangelist Matthew Inspired by an Angel. d, The Apostle Peter Standing.
$400, Balaam and the Ass.

2004, Feb. 16 **Perf. 14¼**
3835-3838 A432 Set of 4 4.50 4.50
3839 A432 $150 Sheet of 4, #a-d 6.75 6.75
Souvenir Sheet
3840 A432 $400 multi 4.75 4.75

Paintings in the Hermitage, St. Petersburg, Russia — A433

Designs: $35, Mercury Giving Bacchus to Nymphs to Raise, by Laurent de La Hyre. $60, Satyr and Bacchante, by Nicolaus Poussin, vert. $100, Parting of Abelard and Eloisa, by Angelica Kauffmann. $200, Pastoral Scene, by François Boucher.
No. 3845, vert.: a, The Union of Earth and Water, by Peter Paul Rubens. b, Hercules Between Love and Wisdom, by Pompeo Girolano Batoni. c, Innocence Choosing Love Over Wealth, by Pierre-Paul Prud'hon. d, Mars and Venus, by Joseph Marie Vien.
No. 3846, Allegory of Virtuous Life, by Hendrik Van Balen. No. 3847, Statue of Ceres, by Rubens, vert.

2004, Feb. 16 **Perf. 14¼**
3841-3844 A433 Set of 4 4.50 4.50
3845 A433 $150 Sheet of 4, #a-d 7.00 7.00

Imperf
Size: 77x55mm
3846 A433 $400 multi 5.50 5.50
Size: 56x77mm
3847 A433 $400 multi 5.50 5.50

Intl. Year of Mountains Type of 2002
Designs: $80, Mt. Kosciuszko, Australia. $100, Mt. Elbrus, Russia. $150, Mt. Vinson, Antarctica.
$400, Mt. Everest, Nepal.

2004 **Perf. 14**
3848-3850 A398 Set of 3 3.75 3.75
Souvenir Sheet
3851 A398 $400 multi 4.50 4.50

Miniature Sheet

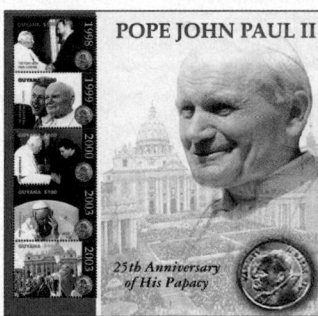

Election of Pope John Paul II, 25th Anniv. (in 2003) — A434

No. 3852: a, With Fidel Castro, 1998. b, With Pres. Bill Clinton, 1999. c, With bishop and man, 2000. d, With hands on head, 2003. e, In Popemobile, 2003.

2004, Sept. 27 **Litho.** **Perf. 14**
3852 A434 $100 Sheet of 5, #a-e 5.75 5.75

2004 Summer Olympics, Athens A435

Designs: $60, Poster for 1912 Stockholm Olympics. $80, High jump, 1932 Los Angeles Olympics, horiz. $100, Commemorative medal for 1932 Olympics. $200, Ancient Greek runners, horiz.

2004, Sept. 27 **Perf. 14¼**
3853-3856 A435 Set of 4 6.75 6.75

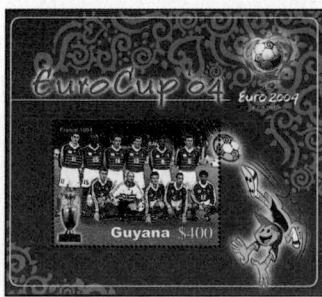

European Soccer Championships, Portugal — A436

No. 3857, vert.: a, Michel Platini. b, Luis Arconada. c, Bruno Bellone. d, Parc des Princes, Paris.
$400, 1984 France team.

2004, Sept. 27 **Litho.**
3857 A436 $150 Sheet of 4, #a-d 8.00 8.00
Souvenir Sheet
3858 A436 $400 multi 5.00 5.00
No. 3857 contains four 28x47mm stamps.

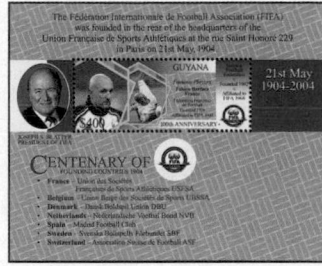

FIFA (Fédération Internationale de Football Association), Cent. — A437

No. 3859: a, Alf Ramsey. b, Pele. c, Lothar Matthaus. d, Dennis Bergkamp.
$400, Fabien Barthez.

2004, Sept. 27 **Perf. 12¾x12½**
3859 A437 $150 Sheet of 4, #a-d 7.00 7.00
Souvenir Sheet
3860 A437 $400 multi 5.00 5.00

A438

D-Day, 60th Anniv. — A439

No. 3861, $150: a, Operation Overlord begins. b, Troops in landing craft storm the beaches of Normandy. c, Troops deep behind enemy lines. d, Churchill announces landings a success.
No. 3862, $150: a, Royal Scots Fusiliers. b, 2nd Company, 101st Heavy Tank Battalion. c, Anti-tank gun of 7th Green Howards. d, 229th Engineer Combat Battalion.
No. 3863, $150, vert.: a, Michael Wittmann. b, Lt. Robert Edlin. c, CSM Stanley Hollis. d, Kurt Meyer.
No. 3864, vert.: a, Rear Admiral John L. Hall. b, Rear Admiral Carlton F. Bryant. c, General Dwight D. Eisenhower. d, General Hap Arnold.
No. 3865, $400, Tank battle, Cotentin Peninsula. No. 3866, $400, Seaforth Highlanders of Canada. No. 3867, $400, Sgt. Clifton Barker. No. 3868, Major General Maxwell D. Taylor.

2004, Sept. 27 **Perf. 13½**
Sheets of 4, #a-d
3861-3863 A438 Set of 3 21.00 21.00
3864 A439 $150 Sheet of 4, #a-d 7.00 7.00
Souvenir Sheets
3865-3867 A438 Set of 3 15.00 15.00
3868 A439 $400 multi 5.00 5.00

A440

A441

A442

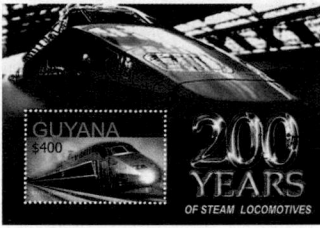

Locomotives — A443

No. 3869: a, Santa Fe Depot. b, LD Porta. c, D9000 Royal Scots Gray. d, TGV.
No. 3870, $150: a, Hercules 4-4-0. b, Sterling 8 ft Single Class 4-2-2. c, Class YP 4-6-2. d, Class 01.10 4-6-2.
No. 3871, $150: a, GWR King Class 4-6-0. b, 4500 Class 4-6-2. c, Class F 4-6-2. d, Class 231C 4-6-2.
No. 3872, $150: a, Western Railway, France, 1856. b, Dutch State Railway, 1880. c, Southern Railway, England, 1890. d, Madras and Southern Mahratta Railway, India, 1891.
No. 3873, $150: a, Baltimore and Ohio Railroad, US, 1856. b, Utica and Schenectady Railroad, US, 1837. c, Great Southern Railway, Spain, 1913. d, Victorian Government Railway, Australia, 1906.
No. 3874, $150: a, Shantung Railway, China, 1919. b, Great Indian Peninsula Railway, 1898. c, Cumberland Valley Railroad, US, 1851. d, Central Pacific Railroad, US, 1863.
No. 3875, $150: a, Great Northern Railway, Ireland, 1876. b, London and Northwestern Railways, 1873. c, Shanghai-Nanking Railway, China, 1910. d, London, Brighton and South Coast Railway, 1846.
No. 3876, $400, No. 990, 4-4-0. No. 3877, $400, Northumbrian 0-2-2, vert.
No. 3878, $400, Netherlands State Railway, 1888. No. 3879, $400, Austrian State Railway, 1868. No. 3880, $400, London, Midland and Scottish Railway, 1923. No. 3881, $400, Pennsylvania Railroad, 1848.
No. 3882, TGV Atlantique.

2004, Sept. 27 **Perf. 13½**
3869 A440 $150 Sheet of 4, #a-d 7.00 7.00
Sheets of 4, #a-d
3870-3871 A441 Set of 2 14.00 14.00
3872-3875 A442 Set of 4 30.00 30.00
Souvenir Sheets
3876-3877 A441 Set of 2 10.00 10.00
3878-3881 A442 Set of 4 20.00 20.00
3882 A443 $400 multi 5.00 5.00

Souvenir Sheet

Deng Xiaoping (1904-97), Chinese Leader — A444

2004   *Perf. 14*
3883 A444 $400 multi   4.75 4.75

South American Reptiles, Fish, Bats and Flowers — A445

No. 3884, $160 — Reptiles: a, Red-foot tortoise. b, Emerald tree boa. c, Green iguana. d, Cuvier's dwarf caiman.
No. 3885, $160 — Fish: a, Velvet cichlid. b, Freshwater sting ray. c, Splash tetra. d, Red piranha.
No. 3886, $160 — Bats: a, Mexican funnel-eared bat. b, Greater bulldog bat. c, Vampire bat. d, Doffroy's tailless bat.
No. 3887, $160, vert. — Flowers: a, Blue passion flower. b, Scarlet passion flower. c, Passion vine. d, Bromeliad flower.
No. 3888, $400, Eyelash viper. No. 3889, $400, Tambaqui, vert. No. 3890, $400, Short-tailed fruit bat, vert. No. 3891, $400, Epiphytic blueberry, vert.

Perf. 13¼x13½, 13½x13¼
2005, Jan. 10   Litho.
Sheets of 4, #a-d
3884-3887 A445 Set of 4   36.00 36.00
Souvenir Sheets
3888-3891 A445 Set of 4   19.50 19.50

New Year 2005 (Year of the Rooster) — A446

No. 3892: a, Rooster with dark feathers. b, Rooster with white feathers.
Illustration reduced.

2005, Jan. 24   *Perf. 12¾*
3892 A446 $50 Pair, #a-b   1.40 1.40
Printed in sheets containing two pairs.

Prehistoric Animals — A447

No. 3893, $150: a, Eustreptospondylus. b, Rhamphorhynchus. c, Utahraptor. d, Entelodonts.
No. 3894, $150: a, Moeritherium. b, Deinonychus. c, Ophthalmosaurus. d, Grendelius.
No. 3895, $150: a, Spinosaurus. b, Tarbosaurus. c, Coelophysis. d, Sinosauropteryx prima.
No. 3896, $400, Velociraptor babies. No. 3897, $400, Ophthalmosaurus baby. No. 3898, $400, Iguanodon bernissartensis, vert.

2005, Jan. 24   Litho.   *Perf. 12¾*
Sheets of 4, #a-d
3893-3895 A447 Set of 3   20.00 20.00
Souvenir Sheets
3896-3898 A447 Set of 3   15.00 15.00

Eddy Grant, Musician — A448

Designs: $20, Grant at UR. $80, Grant at UL.
No. 3901 — Portrait in: a, Blue. b, Yellow green. c, Blue violet. d, Red violet.
$400, Grant with guitar.

2005, Feb. 17   *Perf. 12¾*
3899-3900 A448 Set of 2   1.25 1.25
3901 A448 $190 Sheet of 4, #a-d 9.75 9.75
Souvenir Sheet
3902 A448 $400 multi   4.75 4.75

Pope John Paul II (1920-2005) and Pres. Ronald Reagan (1911-2004) A449

2005, Aug. 12   Litho.   *Perf. 13½*
3903 A449 $300 multi   3.25 3.25

Battle of Trafalgar, Bicent. A450

Designs: $25, Vice-admiral Cuthbert Collingwood. $35, Admiral Horatio Nelson injured at Battle of Santa Cruz. $60, Nelson's funeral car arriving at St. Paul's Cathedral, horiz. $80, Nelson and Flag Captain Thomas M. Hardy. $100, First shots of Battle of Trafalgar, horiz. $300, British ship hoists signals to begin pincer movement. $400, Nelson.

2005, Aug. 12   *Perf. 13¼*
3904-3909 A450 Set of 6   6.50 6.50
Souvenir Sheet
Perf. 12
3910 A450 $400 multi   5.00 5.00

V-E Day, 60th Anniv. — A451

No. 3911, horiz.: a, Neville Chamberlain makes peace with Adolf Hitler, 1938. b, The Royal Air Force hits back. c, Victory, 1945. $400, Netherlands #277.

2005, Aug. 12   *Perf. 12¾*
3911 A451 $200 Sheet of 3, #a-c 7.25 7.25
Souvenir Sheet
3912 A451 $400 multi   5.00 5.00

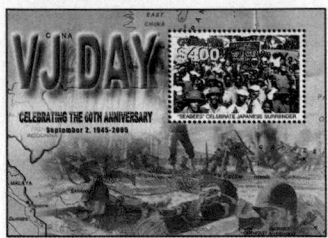

V-J Day, 60th Anniv. — A452

No. 3913: a, Japan attacks Pearl Harbor, 1941. b, Iwo Jima War Memorial, Harlington, Texas. c, Newspaper announcing Japanese surrender, 1945.
$400, Seebees celebrate Japanese surrender.

2005, Aug. 12
3913 A452 $200 Sheet of 3, #a-c 7.25 7.25
Souvenir Sheet
3914 A452 $400 multi   5.00 5.00

Rotary International, Cent. — A453

No. 3915: a, Dentist examining patient's mouth. b, 2005 Rotary President-elect Carl-Wilhelm Stenhammar. c, Rotary District of Guyana first couple.
$400, Homer Wood, founder of second Rotary Club.

2005, Aug. 12
3915 A453 $150 Sheet of 3, #a-c 6.25 6.25
Souvenir Sheet
3916 A453 $400 multi   4.75 4.75

Friedrich von Schiller (1759-1805), Writer — A454

Designs: $400, Schiller and Ludwig van Beethoven.
No. 3918: a, Schiller. b, Schiller and his house. c, Beethoven.
Illustration reduced.

2005, Aug. 12
3917 A454 $400 multi   4.75 4.75
Souvenir Sheet
3918 A454 $200 Sheet of 3, #a-c 7.00 7.10
No. 3918 contains three 42x28mm stamps.

Hans Christian Andersen (1805-75), Author — A455

No. 3919: a, The Traveling Companion. b, The Shadow. c, The Drop of Water.
$400, The Emperor's New Suit.

2005, Aug. 12   *Perf. 12¾*
3919 A455 $200 Sheet of 3, #a-c 7.00 7.00
Souvenir Sheet
Perf. 12
3920 A455 $400 multi   4.75 4.75
No. 3919 contains three 42x28mm stamps.

Jules Verne (1828-1905), Writer — A456

No. 3921, vert.: a, Verne. b, Book illustration. c, Space capsule as imagined by Verne. d, Space capsule.
$400, Man on the Moon.

2005, Aug. 12   *Perf. 12¾*
3921 A456 $150 Sheet of 4, #a-d 6.50 6.50
Souvenir Sheet
3922 A456 $400 multi   5.00 5.00

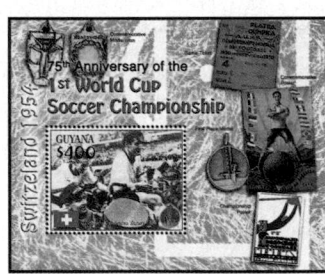

World Cup Soccer Championships, 75th Anniv. — A457

No. 3923: a, 1954 Germany team. b, Final goal in 1954 German victory over Hungary. c, Wankdorf Stadium. d, Helmut Rahn.
$400, German players celebrating victory.

2005, Aug. 12   *Perf. 12*
3923 A457 $150 Sheet of 4, #a-d 8.00 8.00
Souvenir Sheet
3924 A457 $400 multi   4.75 4.75

Space — A458

No. 3925: a, Luna 9 in space. b, Luna 9 capsule. c, Oceanus Procellarum region of Moon. d, Sergei Korolev. e, First images of the Moon. f, Launch of Molniya 8K78M rocket.

No. 3926, $200: a, Space Shuttle Discovery docked with International Space Station Destiny Laboratory, b, Astronaut Stephen K. Robinson attached to Canadarm 2. c, View of Discovery during docking operation. d, Discovery and stairway truck.

No. 3927, $200, vert.: a, First launch of Space Shuttle Columbia. b, Astronaut Robert C. Crippen. c, Astronaut John W. Young. d, Mission control.

No. 3928, $200, vert.: a, Launch vehicle MV-5 rocket. b, Hayabusa satellite. c, Composite color image of Itokawa asteroid. d, Projected return to Earth of satellite.

No. 3929, $400, Venus Express. No. 3930, $400, Lunar Reconnaissance Orbiter. No. 3931, $400, Calipso satellite. No. 3932, $400, Hayabusa satellite over Itokawa asteroid.

2006   **Litho.**   **Perf. 14**
3925 A458 $160 Sheet of 6,
     #a-f   12.50 12.50
Sheets of 4, #a-d
3926-3928 A458 Set of 3   28.00 28.00
Souvenir Sheets
3929-3932 A458 Set of 4   17.00 17.00
   Issued: Nos. 3925, 3926, 3930, 7/10, Nos. 3928, 3932, 7/27.

Souvenir Sheet

"Penny Magenta" Stamp, 150th Anniv. — A459

2006, July 27   **Perf. 12x11½**
3933 A459 $400 multi   4.50 4.50
Souvenir Sheet

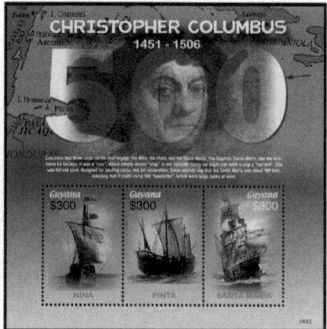

Christopher Columbus (1451-1506), Explorer — A460

No. 3934: a, Nina. b, Pinta. c, Santa Maria.

2006, July 27   **Perf. 13¼**
3934 A460 $300 Sheet of 3,
     #a-c   11.00 11.00

Airships — A461

No. 3935: a, De Beers Zeppelin NT. b, Lockheed Martin LTA 2004. c, Strattelite concept airship.
$400, Skybus Airship.

2006, July 27   **Perf. 13¼**
3935 A461 $200 Sheet of 3, #a-c   7.25 7.25
Souvenir Sheet
3936 A461 $400 multi   4.50 4.50

Rembrandt (1606-69), Painter — A462

No. 3937 — Details from The Music Makers: a, Man with viola. b, Woman with shawl. c, Man with harp. d, Woman with tiara.
$400, Old Man with a Jewelled Cross.

2006, July 27   **Perf. 13¼**
3937 A462 $160 Sheet of 4, #a-d   8.25 8.25
Imperf
3938 A462 $400 shown   4.50 4.50
No. 3937 contains four 37x50mm stamps.

Queen Elizabeth II, 80th Birthday — A463

No. 3939: a, Queen and Guyana Parliament Building. b, Queen wearing black and white hat.
$400, Queen and flags of Guyana and Great Britain.
Illustration reduced.

2006, July 27   **Perf. 13¼**
3939 A463 $200 Pair, #a-b   4.50 4.50
Souvenir Sheet
3940 A463 $400 multi   5.25 5.25
No. 3939 printed in sheets containing two pairs.

Souvenir Sheet

2006 World Cup Soccer Championships, Germany — A464

No. 3941 — 2006 World Cup emblem, World Cup and: a, $80, Man in Japanese

clothing. b, $100, Kemari players. c, $160, Tsuchu players. d, $300, People's Republic of China #2073.

2006, Sept. 14   **Litho.**   **Perf. 13¼**
3941 A464 Sheet of 4, #a-d   7.00 7.00

Betty Boop — A465

No. 3942, vert.: a, With top hat and cane. b, Holding mirror. c, Holding flower bouquet. d, In city. e, At microphone. f, Lifting dress.
No. 3943: a, Sitting with legs crossed. b, In car.

2006, Dec. 14   **Litho.**   **Perf. 14**
3942 A465 $100 Sheet of 6, #a-f   6.50 6.50
Souvenir Sheet
3943 A465 $200 Sheet of 2, #a-b   4.25 4.25

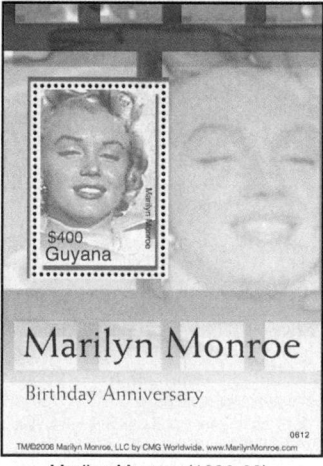

Marilyn Monroe (1926-62), Actress — A466

No. 3944: a, Wearing beret. b, Wearing red dress, horizontal post at both sides of neck. c, Wearing red dress, horizontal post at left of neck. d, With eyes closed.
$400, With eyes partially closed.

2007, Feb. 15   **Perf. 13¼**
3944 A466 $200 Sheet of 4, #a-d   8.00 8.00
Souvenir Sheet
3945 A466 $400 multi   4.00 4.00

Dogs — A467

No. 3946: a, Papillon. b, Dogue de Bordeaux. c, Cavalier King Charles spaniel. d, Neapolitan mastiff.
$400, Basset hound.

2007, Feb. 15   **Perf. 14**
3946 A467 $160 Sheet of 4, #a-d 6.50 6.50
Souvenir Sheet
3947 A467 $400 multi   4.00 4.00

Cats A468

Designs: $25, Chartreux. $35, Seal snowshoe. $60, Maine coon cat. $300, Turkish Angora.
$400, Blue Burmese, vert.

2007, Feb. 15
3948-3951 A468 Set of 4   4.25 4.25
Souvenir Sheet
3952 A468 $400 multi   4.00 4.00

Birds A469

Designs: $25, Summer tanager. $35, Graycheeked thrush. $60, Blackpoll warbler. $300, Thick-billed parrot.
No. 3957, vert.: a, Golden-tailed warbler. b, Blue-crowned parakeet. c, White-winged parakeet. d, Yellow-green vireo.
No. 3958, $400, Pacific golden plover, vert.
No. 3959, $400, Bobolink, vert.

2007, Feb. 15
3953-3956 A469 Set of 4   4.25 4.25
3957 A469 $160 Sheet of 4, #a-d 6.50 6.50
Souvenir Sheets
3958-3959 A469 Set of 2   8.00 8.00
   For overprint, see No. 4025.

Butterflies A470

Designs: $25, Morpho vitrea. $35, Rothschildia hesperus. $60, Anaea nessus. $300, Dryas iulia.
No. 3964: a, Callithea sapphira. b, Prepona buckleyana. c, Lycorea pasinutia. d, Danaus eresimus.
No. 3965, $400, Cithaerias aurorina. No. 3966, $400, Eurytides protesilaus.

2007, Feb. 15
3960-3963 A470 Set of 4 4.25 4.25
3964 A470 $160 Sheet of 4, #a-d 6.50 6.50

Souvenir Sheets
3965-3966 A470 Set of 2 8.00 8.00

Orchids — A471

Designs: $25, Bletia florida. $35, Basiphyl-laea corallicola. $60, Calopogon multiflorus. $300, Bletia purpurea.
No. 3971: a, Cypripedium acaule. b, Calopogon tuberosus. c, Calopogon pallidus. d, Bletia patula.
$400, Cypripedium reginae.

2007, Feb. 15
3967-3970 A471 Set of 4 4.25 4.25
3971 A471 $160 Sheet of 4, #a-d 6.50 6.50

Souvenir Sheet
3972 A471 $400 multi 4.00 4.00

Souvenir Sheet

New Year 2007 (Year of the Pig) — A472

No. 3973 — Pig at: a, $55, Right. b, $80, Left. c, $100, Right. d, $160, Left.

2007, Mar. 21 Perf. 13¼
3973 A472 Sheet of 4, #a-d 4.00 4.00

Souvenir Sheet

Wolfgang Amadeus Mozart (1756-91), Composer — A473

No. 3974 — Mozart: a, In 1770. b, In 1762. c, Circa 1789. d, Portrait by Joseph Grassi.

2007, Mar. 21
3974 A473 $190 Sheet of 4, #a-d 7.50 7.50

Scouting, Cent. — A474

No. 3975, horiz.: a, Lord Robert Baden-Powell and dove. b, Scouts on raft. c, Scouts pulling tug-of-war rope.
$400, Dove and hand of Baden-Powell.

2007, Mar. 21
3975 A474 $180 Sheet of 3, #a-c 5.50 5.50

Souvenir Sheet
3976 A474 $400 multi 4.00 4.00

Souvenir Sheets

Pres. John F. Kennedy (1917-63) — A475

No. 3977: a, $80, Taking oath of office. b, $100, Giving inaugural speech. c, $160, Portrait. d, $190, With wife at inaugural ball.
No. 3978: a, $80, Peace Corps. b, $100, Space program. c, $160, Civil rights. d, $190, Portrait, diff.

2007, Mar. 21 Perf. 13¼
Sheets of 4, #a-d
3977-3978 A475 Set of 2 10.50 10.50

Elvis Presley (1935-77) — A476

No. 3979, $160: a, Wearing glasses, blue panel at top. b, Without glasses, red background.
No. 3980, $160: a, Without glasses, orange panel at bottom. b, With glasses, red background.

2007, Mar. 21 Perf. 14
Pairs, #a-b
3979-3980 A476 Set of 2 6.50 6.50
Nos. 3979-3980 each were printed in sheets containing two pairs.

2007 Cricket World Cup, West Indies — A477

Designs: $100, Cricket World Cup emblem, map and flag of Guyana. $200, Guyana cricket team, horiz.
$500, Cricket World Cup emblem.

2007, Mar. 28 Perf. 13¼
3981-3982 A477 Set of 2 3.00 3.00

Souvenir Sheet
3983 A477 $500 multi 5.00 5.00

A478

Pope Benedict XVI — A479

Illustration A479 reduced.

2007, Apr. 17 Litho. Perf. 13¼
3984 A478 $80 multi .80 .80

Litho. & Embossed
Serpentine Die Cut
Without Gum
3985 A479 $1500 multi 15.00 15.00
No. 3984 was printed in sheets of 8.

Concorde A480

No. 3986, $100: a, Concorde Prototype 002 and towing vehicle. b, Concorde Prototype 002 and stairway.
No. 3987, $100: a, Concorde and Royal Air Force Red Arrows. b, Concorde, Red Arrows and Queen Elizabeth 2.

2007, Apr. 17 Litho. Perf. 13¼
Pairs, #a-b
3986-3987 A480 Set of 2 4.00 4.00
Nos. 3986-3987 were each printed in sheets containing 3 pairs.

Miniature Sheet

2008 Summer Olympics, Beijing — A481

No. 3988: a, Field hockey. b, Basketball. c, Judo. d, Shooting.

2008, Apr. 22 Litho. Perf. 13¼x13
3988 A481 $100 Sheet of 4, #a-d 4.00 4.00

10th Caribbean Festival of Arts — A482

Map in: $20, Yellow and white, frame in red. $55, White, frame in green. $80, Yellow and white, frame in blue green. $160, Green, frame in white and yellow.

2008, Aug. 19 Perf. 14¼
3989-3992 A482 Set of 4 3.25 3.25

Jesuits in Guyana, 150th Anniv. A483

Designs: $80, St. Stanislaus College. $100, Sacred Heart Church. $160, Father Cuthbert Cary-Elwes, missionary, and indigenous people.

2008, Aug. 25 Litho. Perf. 13x13¼
3993-3995 A483 Set of 3 3.50 3.50

Souvenir Sheet

Sir James Douglas (1803-77), First Governor of British Columbia — A484

2008, Aug. 25 Perf. 13¼
3996 A484 $160 multi 1.60 1.60

Peony A485

2009, Apr. 10 Litho.
3997 A485 $80 multi .80 .80
Printed in sheets of 8.

Miniature Sheet

Elvis Presley (1935-77) — A486

No. 3998 — Presley with: a, Red and blue jacket, bright yellow face, holding microphone. b, Brown jacket, holding microphone. c, White jacket and red shirt. d, Tan and white shirt. e, Gray face, holding microphone. f, With hand open.

2009, July 7   **Perf. 12**
3998 A486 $160 Sheet of 6, #a-f   9.50 9.50

Miniature Sheet

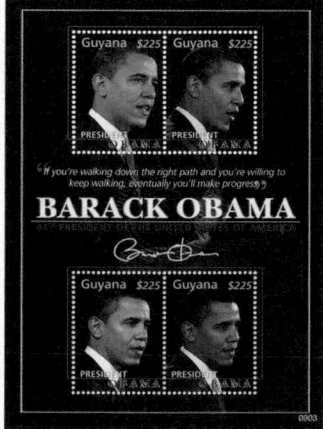

US Pres. Barack Obama — A487

No. 3999: — Pres. Obama with: a, Gray tie, with "O" on jacket and shirt collar and "B" on shirt collar and tie. b, Gray tie, with "O" on jacket and shirt collar and "B" on tie and jacket. c, Red tie. d, Gray tie, with "O" on jacket and "B" on tie and shirt collar.

2009, July 7
3999 A487 $225 Sheet of 4, #a-d   9.00 9.00

Miniature Sheet

China 2009 World Stamp Exhibition, Luoyang — A488

No. 4000 — Unnamed works of art by Wang Hui (1632-1717): a, Flowers. b, Mountain at right. c, Mountain at left in clouds, part of show emblem at LR. d, Mountain in center, part of show emblem at LL.

2009, Apr. 10   **Litho.**   **Perf. 12**
4000 A488 $100 Sheet of 4, #a-d   4.00 4.00

Miniature Sheet

Georgetown Rotary Club, 50th Anniv. — A489

No. 4001 — Map of Guyana, Rotary International emblem and: a, $80, 50th anniversary commemorative magazine. b, $80, Santa Claus visiting the elderly. c, $160, Poster showing people in wheelchairs. d, $160, Man and boy in front of canopy.

2009, July 22   **Perf. 11½**
4001 A489   Sheet of 4, #a-d   4.75 4.75

Miniature Sheet

Ferrari Race Cars — A490

No. 4002: a, 1952 500 F2. b, 1953, 500 F2. c, 1958, 246 F1. d, 1976 312 T2.

2009, July 22   **Perf. 14¼**
4002 A490 $200 Sheet of 4, #a-d   8.00 8.00

Souvenir Sheet

Takutu Bridge — A491

2009, Sept. 14   **Perf. 13¼**
4003 A491 $400 multi   4.00 4.00

Scouting A492

Designs: No. 4004, $55, Parade for Guyana Scouting centenary. No. 4005, $55, Scout shooting arrow at 14th Caribbean Jamboree, vert. No. 4006, $80, Scout leader, Scout and tent. No. 4007, $80, Scouts lashing logs together. No. 4008, $160, Guyana Scouting Centenary emblem. No. 4009, $160, Emblem of 14th Caribbean Jamboree.

Perf. 14¾x14, 14x14¾
2009, Sept. 29
4004-4009 A492   Set of 6   5.75 5.75

Miniature Sheets

A493

Michael Jackson (1958-2009), Singer — A494

No. 4010: a, Wearing jacket with red collar. b, Wearing hat. c, Wearing black jacket, with microphone at mouth. d, Wearing red and black shirt, with microphone at mouth.
No. 4011: a, Facing forward, with microphone at mouth. b, Facing right, with microphone at waist. c, Facing left, with microphone at mouth. d, Facing forward with arms at side, with microphone at waist.

2009, Oct. 9   **Perf. 11½x11¼**
4010 A493 $180 Sheet of 4, #a-d   7.25 7.25
         Perf. 11¼x11½
4011 A494 $180 Sheet of 4, #a-d   7.25 7.25

Miniature Sheets

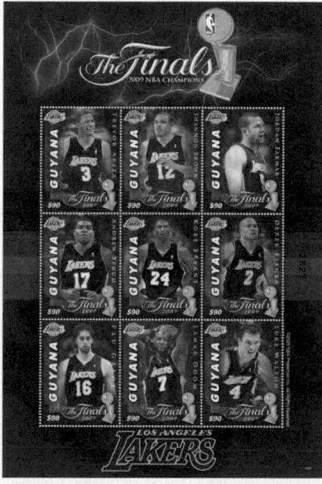

Teams in 2009 National Basketball Association Finals — A495

No. 4012, $90 — Los Angeles Lakers: a, Trevor Ariza. b, Shannon Brown. c, Jordan Farmar. d, Andrew Bynum. e, Kobe Bryant. f, Derek Fisher. g, Pau Gasol. h, Lamar Odom. i, Luke Walton.
No. 4013, $90 — Orlando Magic: a, Rafer Alston. b, Marcin Gortat. c, Rashard Lewis. d, Courtney Lee. e, Dwight Howard. f, Jameer Nelson. g, Mickael Pietrus. h, J. J. Redick. i, Hedo Türkoglu.

2009, Oct. 9   **Perf. 14¼**
     Sheets of 9, #a-i
4012-4013 A495   Set of 2   16.00 16.00

British Commonwealth, 60th Anniv. — A496

2009, Nov. 25   **Litho.**   **Perf. 12x11½**
4014 A496 $60 multi   .60 .60
    Printed in sheets of 6.

Miniature Sheet

National Library, Cent. — A497

No. 4015: a, Building exterior, black and white photograph. b, Building exterior, color photograph. c, Interior, color photograph. d, Interior, black and white photograph.

2009, Dec. 15   **Perf. 11½x12**
4015 A497 $100 Sheet of 4, #a-d   4.00 4.00

Chinese Aviation, Cent. — A498

No. 4016: a, J-8II. b, J-11. c, J-10 with landing gear visible. d, J-10 with landing gear retracted.
    $100, J-10, diff.

2009, Dec. 15   **Perf. 14**
4016 A498 $150 Sheet of 4, #a-d   6.00 6.00
     Souvenir Sheet
       Perf. 14¼
4017 A498 $100 multi   1.00 1.00
  Aeropex 2009, Beijing. No. 4016 contains four 42x28mm stamps.

Pope Benedict XVI and Pope John Paul II — A499

No. 4018 — Pope Benedict XVI (while Cardinal) and Pope John Paul II with: a, Part of dome of St. Peter's Basilica at LL. b, Upper section of Basilica entablature at bottom. c, Columns of Basilica at bottom, with dark grayish yellow area next to denomination. d, As "c," with smaller light grayish yellow area next to denomination.

No. 4019: a, Pope Benedict XVI (while Cardinal). b, Pope John Paul II.

2009, Dec. 15   *Perf. 11½*
4018 A499 $200 Sheet of 4, #a-d 8.00 8.00

Souvenir Sheet
Perf. 11½x12
4019 A499 $400 Sheet of 2, #a-b 8.00 8.00

Miniature Sheet

Chinese Zodiac Animals — A500

No. 4020: a, Rat. b, Ox. c, Tiger. d, Rabbit. e, Dragon. f, Snake. g, Horse. h, Ram. i, Monkey. j, Cock. k, Dog. l, Pig.

2010, Jan. 4   *Perf. 12*
4020 A500 $45 Sheet of 12, #a-l 5.25 5.25

Miniature Sheet

Republic of Guyana, 40th Anniv. — A501

No. 4021: a, 2010 Republic Day emblem. b, Masqueraders. c, Mash float parade. d, Children's costume parade.

2010, Mar. 17   *Perf. 11½x12*
4021 A501 $80 Sheet of 4, #a-d 3.25 3.25

Personalizable Stamp — A502

2010, Apr. 26   **Litho.**   *Perf. 14¾x14*
4022 A502 $160 gray & black 1.60 1.60

The image shown is generic. No. 4022 was available in sheets of 12 without any image ("Guyana $160" only), and vignette portions could be personalized.

Pope Benedict XVI — A503

Litho. & Embossed
2010, Apr. 26   *Die Cut Perf. 8½*
Without Gum
4023 A503 $2000 multi 20.00 20.00

Souvenir Sheet

Presidents of the United States and People's Republic of China — A504

No. 4024: a, Pres. Barack Obama. b, Pres. Hu Jintao.

2010, Apr. 26   **Litho.**   *Perf. 11½*
4024 A504 $300 Sheet of 2, #a-b 6.00 6.00

Miniature Sheet

No. 3957 Overprinted

Methods and Perfs As Before
2010, Apr. 26
4025 A469 $160 Sheet of 4, #a-d 6.25 6.25

Miniature Sheets

Princess Diana (1961-97) — A505

No. 4026, $225 — Diana wearing: a, Tiara. b, Red and black hat. c, Blouse with red collar and cuffs. d, Sailor's hat.
No. 4027, $225 — Diana wearing: a, Black hat. b, Beige hat. c, White dress. d, Blue hat.

2010, Apr. 26   **Litho.**   *Perf. 12*
Sheets of 4, #a-d
4026-4027 A505   Set of 2   18.00 18.00

Souvenir Sheets

A506

A507

A508

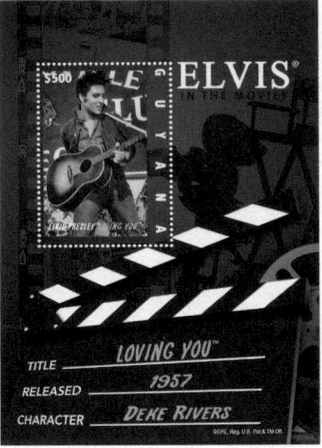

Elvis Presley (1935-77) — A509

2010, Apr. 26   *Perf. 13¼*
4028 A506 $500 multi 5.00 5.00
4029 A507 $500 multi 5.00 5.00
4030 A508 $500 multi 5.00 5.00
4031 A509 $500 multi 5.00 5.00
   Nos. 4028-4031 (4) 20.00 20.00

Souvenir Sheet

New Year 2010 (Year of the Tiger) — A510

No. 4032 — Tiger with denomination in: a, Green. b, White.

2010, Jan. 4   **Litho.**   *Perf. 12*
4032 A510 $450 Sheet of 2, #a-b 9.00 9.00

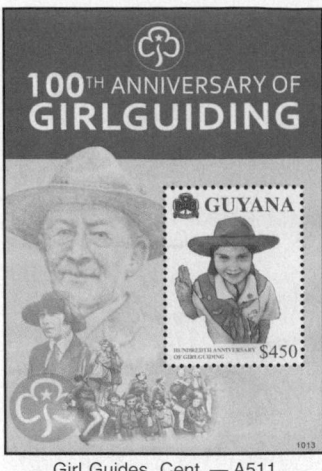

Girl Guides, Cent. — A511

No. 4033, horiz.: a, Three Girl Guides wearing rabbit ears. b, Two Girl Guides. c, Three Girl Guides wearing blue uniforms. d, Four Girl Guides holding rope.
$450, Girl Guide saluting.

2010, July 14   *Perf. 11½x12*
4033 A511 $275 Sheet of 4,
   #a-d 11.00 11.00

Souvenir Sheet
Perf. 11¼x11½
4034 A511 $450 multi 4.50 4.50

Miniature Sheet

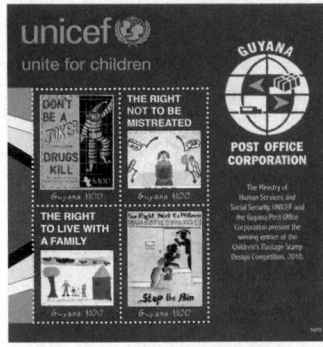

Winning Entries In Children's Postage Stamp Design Contest — A512

No. 4035 — Slogan: a, Don't Be a Joker - Drugs Kill. b, The Right Not to be Mistreated. c, The Right to Live With a Family. d, Your Right Not to Witness Domestic Violence.

2010, Sept. 2   *Perf. 12*
4035 A512 $100 Sheet of 4, #a-d 4.00 4.00

Miniature Sheet

Porkknocker Day, 10th Anniv. — A513

No. 4036: a, Map of area near Bartica. b, Cyrilda de Jesus, female porkknocker (miner). c, Dick Manning, male porkknocker. d, Mazaruni diamonds and gold nuggets.

2010, Oct. 14
4036 A513 $100 Sheet of 4, #a-d 4.00 4.00

AIR POST STAMPS

No. 321 Surcharged in Blue "HUMAN RIGHTS / DAY / 1981 / 110 AIR"

1981, Nov. 14   *Perfs. as Before*
C1 A74 110c on $3 No. 321   3.50

For surcharge see No. 997.

Nos. 133, 136 and 146 Surcharged in Red, Black or Blue "AIR / Princess / of Wales / 1961-1982"

1982, June 25   *Perfs. as Before*
Printing Methods as Before
C2 A28 110c on 5c No. 136
(R)   2.50   .40
C3 A28 220c on 1c No. 133   2.75   1.00
C4 A28 330c on $2 No. 146
(Bl)   2.75   1.60
Nos. C2-C4 (3)   7.25

For surcharges see Nos. 623, 785-787, 801, 004-004A, O19, O21, O30-O39.

No. 287 Surcharged in Dark Blue "UNICEF / 1946-1986 / AIR" or "UNESCO / 1946-1986 / AIR"

    Perfs. as Before
1986, Oct. 24   *Litho.*
C5 A66 120c on $1 UNICEF   11.00
C6 A66 120c on $1 UNESCO   11.00
a.   Pair, #C5-C6   24.00

Nos. 1026, 1095, 1096, 1096a, 1100, 1138, 1163 Surcharged "AIR"

1987-88   *Litho.*   *Perf. 14*
Design A91
Plate Numbers in Parentheses
C7   75c on 25c No. 1100 (59)   13.50   1.50
C8   60c on No. 1095 (55)   11.00   10.00
C9   75c on No. 1026 (5)   1.25   .65
C10   75c on No. 1096 (55)   1.25   .65
a.   75c on No. 1096a
C11   75c on No. 1138 (83)   1.25   .65
C12   75c on No. 1163 (95)   1.25   .65

Issued: #C7, 11/87; #C8, 12/87; #C9-C12, 8/88.

SPECIAL DELIVERY STAMPS

Orchid Type of 1985 Overprinted or Surcharged "EXPRESS"

1986-87   *Litho.*   *Perf. 14*
Plate Numbers in Parentheses
E1 A91 $12 on #1372 (65)   12.00   12.00
E2 A91 $15 on 40c #1145
(86)   12.00   12.00
E3 A91(p) $15 on #E2 (86)   11.00   11.00
E4 A91 $25 on 25c like
#1090 (53)   15.00   15.00
Nos. E1-E4 (4)   50.00

Issue dates: $12, $25, #E2, Nov. 10. #E3, Dec. 1987. #E4 not issued without surcharge.

No. 1461c Surcharged "EXPRESS"

1986-87   *Litho.*   *Imperf.*
E5 A96 $20 on 320c #1461c   12.00   12.00

No. E5 Ovptd. with Maltese Cross
1987, Mar. 3
E6 A96 $20 on No. E5   12.00   12.00

Orchid Type of 1985 Inscribed "Express"

1987-88   *Litho.*   *Perf. 14*
Series 2
Plate Numbers in Parentheses
E7 A91 $15 like #1186 (11)   4.00   4.00
E8 A91 $20 like #1323 (93)   7.50   7.50
E9 A91 $25 like #1274 (63)   6.50   6.50
E10 A91 $45 like #1228 (35)   12.00   12.00
Nos. E7-E10 (4)   30.00   30.00

Issued: $45, 9/1; $15, 9/29; $25, 10/26; $20, 5/17/88.

No. "1461" Surcharged "EXPRESS / FORTY DOLLARS"

1987, Nov.   *Perf. 14*
E11 A96 $40 on 320c No.
1461, imperf.
btwn.   15.00   15.00

A five-pointed star appears between the lines of the surcharge on #E11. See #E14.

Nos. 1827e, 1830e Surcharged in Red "SPECIAL DELIVERY"

1988, Aug. 10   *Perf. 15*
E12 A100 $40 on $3.20
#1827e   12.00   12.00
E13 A100 $45 on $3.30
#1830e   12.00   12.00

See Nos. 2054b, 2056b.

Nos. "1461," 1822c Surcharged in Red "EXPRESS / FORTY DOLLARS"

1989, Mar.   *Perf. 14*
E14 A96 $40 on 320c #1461, im-
perf. btwn.   7.00   7.00
E15 A96 $40 on 320c #1822c,
imperf. btwn.   7.00   7.00

Butterflies Type of 1989 Inscribed "EXPRESS"
Souvenir Sheets

1989, Sept. 7   *Litho.*   *Perf. 14*
E16 A115 $130 Pharoas
coeleste   7.75   7.75
E17 A115 $190 Papilio tor-
quatus   12.50   12.50

For overprints see #E19-E22, E24, E26-E27, E31.

Women in Space Type of 1989 Inscribed "EXPRESS"
Souvenir Sheets

1989, Nov. 8
E18 A116 $190 Valentina Ter-
eshkova   12.50   12.50

For overprints see No. E23, E25, E28, E32.

Nos. E16-E17 Ovptd. with World Stamp Expo '89 Emblem

1989, Nov. 17
E19 A115 $130 on No. E16   7.00   7.00
E20 A115 $190 on No. E17   7.00   7.00

Nos. E16-E18 Ovptd. in Sheet Margin "Stamp World London 90" and Show Emblem

1990, May 3
E21 A115 $130 on No. E16
E22 A115 $190 on No. E17
E23 A116 $190 on No. E18
Nos. E21-E23 (3)   30.00

Nos. E17-E18 Ovptd. in Sheet Margin with Rotary Emblem and "ROTARY / INTERNATIONAL / 1905-1990"

1990, Mar.
E24 A115 $190 on No. E17
E25 A116 $190 on No. E18
Nos. E24-E25 (2)   22.50

Nos. E16-E18 Ovptd. in Sheet Margin "90th BIRTHDAY / H.M. THE / QUEEN MOTHER"

1990, June 8   *Litho.*   *Perf. 14*
E26 A115 $130 on No. E16   7.75   7.75
E27 A115 $190 on No. E17   12.50   12.50
E28 A116 $190 on No. E18   12.50   12.50
Nos. E26-E28 (3)   32.75   32.75

Endangered Wildlife Type
Souvenir Sheets

1990, Nov. 6   *Litho.*   *Perf. 14*
E29 A131 $130 Harpy eagle   7.00   7.00
E30 A131 $150 Ocelot   7.50   7.50

Nos. E29-E30 each contain one 43x57mm stamp.

Nos. E16, E18 Ovptd. in Sheet Margin with "BELGICA PHILATELIC / EXPOSITION 1990" and Scout, Lions, Rotary and Show Emblems

1990, June 2
E31 A115 $130 on No. E16   7.50   7.50
E32 A116 $190 on No. E18   7.50   7.50

No. E31 has Scout and Lions emblems. No. E32 has Scout and Rotary emblems.

POSTAGE DUE STAMPS

Type of British Guiana Inscribed "Guyana"

    Perf. 13½x14
1967-68   *Wmk. 314*   *Typo.*
J2 D1 2c black ('68)   .75   .75
J3 D1 4c ultramarine   .30   .30
J4 D1 12c carmine   .50   .50
Nos. J2-J4 (3)   1.55   1.55

For surcharges see Nos. 897-898.

1973   *Wmk. 364*
J5 D1 1c green   .35   2.00
J6 D1 2c black   .35   2.00
J7 D1 4c ultramarine   .35   2.00
J8 D1 12c carmine   .40   2.00
Nos. J5-J8 (4)   1.45   8.00

For surcharges see #341-349, 658, 899-900.

OFFICIAL STAMPS

Nos. 74, 139, 141, 143-144, 146-147, 289A, 297, 300, 333, 395, 397, 401 Surcharged in Black, Red, or Black and Red

1981-82   *Perfs. as Before*
Printing Methods as Before
O1 A28 10c on 25c #141
(Bk & R)   4.00   2.25
O2 A8 15c on #74   10.00   2.00
O3 A28 15c on #139   13.50   1.00
O4 A28 30c on $2 #146 (Bk
& R)   1.00   .50
O5 A28 50c on #143 (R)   2.00   .75
O6 A69 50c on #300   1.50   .40
O7 A28 60c on #144 (R)   1.50   .25
O8 A17 100c on #395   2.00   2.00
O9 A68 100c on $3 #297 (Bk
& R)   3.50   .75
O10 A17 110c on #397   3.50   2.00
O11 A28 $1.10 on #333 (R)
O12 A28 125c on #401 (R)   1.50   .80
O13 A28 $2 on #146 (R)   12.50
O14 A28 $5 on #147 (R)   3.00   3.00
O15 A66 $10 on #289A   17.50

Issued: #O1, O5, O7, O15, 6/8; #O2, O4, O9, O11-O12, 7/1; #O13, 7/12/82; others, 7/7. Surcharge on Nos. O3, O6, O8, O10, O13-O14 have no obliterator. No. O11 is airmail.
Refer to 2nd paragraph in footnote following #147 for #O1, O4-O5, O7 and O13.
For overprints and surcharges see No. 406, 425, 452, 454-456, 603, 618, 650, 817, 854, 861, 866, 933, 1378, 1381, 1384, 1387-1388.

Nos. 162, 256, 258, 282, 480, C2-C3 Surcharged in Blue or Black

1982   *Perfs. as Before*
Printing Methods as Before
O16 A66 20c on #282   10.00   1.25
O17 A33 40c on #162   1.50   .75
O18 A60 40c on #256   2.00   1.00
O19 A28 110c on #C2 (Bk)   3.00   1.00
O20 A60 $2 on #258   18.00   3.50
O21 A28 220c on #C3   3.00   .80
O22 A69 250c on #480   1.75   .80
Nos. O16-O22 (7)   39.25

Issue dates: 110c, Sept. 15; others, May 17. Nos. O19, O21 are airmail.

No. 481 Surcharged "OPS" Reading Up in Blue Violet or Blue Violet and Black

1984, Apr. 2   *Perfs. as Before*
O23 A66 150c on $5   6.00   3.00
O24 A66 200c on $5   6.50   3.25
O25 A66 225c on $5 (BV &
Bk)   6.50   3.25
O25A A66 230c on $5   6.75   3.50
O26 A66 260c on $5   7.00   3.75
O27 A66 320c on $5   7.00   3.75
O28 A66 350c on $5   7.50   3.75
O29 A66 600c on $5   8.00   4.25
Nos. O23-O29 (8)   10.00   6.00

Nos. C2-C3 Surcharged "OPS" in Black and Blue, Black or Blue

1984, June 25   *Perfs. as Before*
O30 A28 25c on No. C2 (Bk)   1.00   .50
O31 A28 30c on No. C2   1.00   .50
O32 A28 45c on No. C3   1.25   .50
O33 A28 55c on No. C2 (Bk)   1.25   .60
O34 A28 60c on No. C3   1.50   .60
O35 A28 75c on No. C3   2.00   .70
O36 A28 90c on No. C3 (Bl)   2.00   .70
O37 A28 120c on No. C3   2.25   .90
O38 A28 130c on No. C3 (Bl)   2.25   1.25
O39 A28 330c on No. C3 (Bl)   4.00   1.25
Nos. O30-O39 (10)   17.25

Overprint reads up on No. O39.

Orchid Type of 1985

1987-88   *Litho.*   *Unwmk.*   *Perf. 14*
Series 2
Plate Numbers in Parentheses
O40 A91 120c like #1250 (48)   1.50   .40
O41 A91 130c like #1322 (92)   1.50   .40
O42 A91 140c like #1229 (36)   1.00   .40
O43 A91 150c like #1242 (43)   1.50   .50
O44 A91 175c like #1221 (31)   1.00   .50
O45 A91 200c like #1271 (61)   1.50   .60
O46 A91 225c like #1213 (26)   1.50   .60
O47 A91 230c like #1283 (68)   .75   .60
O48 A91 250c like #1268 (59)   .75   .60
O49 A91 260c like #1284 (69)   .75   .60
O50 A91 275c like #1319 (90)   1.75   .75
O51 A91 320c like #1292 (75)   1.75   .85
O52 A91 330c like #1208 (23)   2.00   1.00
O53 A91 350c like #1326 (95)   1.00   1.00
O54 A91 600c like #1285 (70)   1.50   1.50
O55 A91 $12 like #1286 (71)   2.50   2.50
O56 A91 $15 like #1308 (84)   3.00   3.00
Nos. O40-O56 (17)   25.25   15.80

Nos. O47, O53-O56 horiz.

Issued: #O42, O44, O48, O49, 10/5/88; others, 10/5/88.
For overprints & surcharges see #1694, 1697, 1703, 1707, 1722-1726, 1728-1730.

PARCEL POST STAMPS

No. 145 Surcharged "PARCEL POST"

1981, June 8   *Litho.*   *Perf. 13½*
Q1 A28 $15 on $1 No. 145   19.50   3.50
Q2 A28 $20 on $1 No. 145   19.00   7.00
Nos. Q1-Q2 (2)   38.00

For overprints see Nos. QO1-QO2.

No. 333 Surcharged "PARCEL POST" in Blue

1983, Jan. 15
Q3 A28 $12 on No. 333   12.50   2.00

For surcharge see No. 624.

No. 146 Surcharged "Parcel Post"

1983, Sept. 14
Q4 A28 $12 on $1.10 on $2   2.50   2.50

No. Q4 has a horizontal Royal Wedding / 1981 surcharge similar to No. 331. For overprint see No. QO5.

No. 255 Surcharged in Red "TWENTY FIVE DOLLARS / PARCEL POST 25.00"

1985, Apr. 25   *Perf. 14*
Q5 A60 $25 on 35c No. 255   33.00   27.50

PARCEL POST OFFICIAL STAMPS

Nos. Q1-Q2 Overprinted "OPS" in Red

1981, June 8
QO1 A28 $15 on Q1   18.00   2.50
QO2 A28 $20 on Q2   17.00   3.25

For surcharges see Nos. 1389-1390.

No. 333 Surcharged in Blue
"OPS / 1982 / Parcel Post / $12.00"

1983, Jan. 15
QO3 A28 $12 on No. 333   115.00   20.00

No. QO3 Overprinted "OPS" in Black

1983, Aug. 22
QO4 A28 $12 on No. QO3   42.50   4.00

No. Q4 Overprinted "OPS" in Blue

1983, Nov. 3
QO5 A28 $12 on No. Q4   15.00   4.00

HAITI

'hā-tē

LOCATION — Western part of Hispaniola
GOVT. — Republic
AREA — 10,714 sq. mi.
POP. — 6,884,264 (1999 est.)
CAPITAL — Port-au-Prince

100 Centimes = 1 Piaster (1906)
100 Centimes = 1 Gourde

> Catalogue values for unused stamps in this country are for Never Hinged items, beginning with Scott 370 in the regular postage section, Scott B2 in the semipostal section, Scott C33 in the air post section, Scott CB9 in the air post semi-postal section, Scott CO6 in the air post official section, Scott CQ1 in the air post parcel post seciton, Scott E1 in the special delivery section, Scott J21 in the postage due section, Scott Q1 in the parcel post section, Scott RA1 in the postal tax section, and Scott RAC1 in the air post postal tax section.

ISSUES OF THE REPUBLIC
Watermark

Wmk. 131 — RH

Liberty Head — A1

A3   A4

On A3 (#18, 19) there are crossed lines of dots on face. On A4 the "5" is 3mm wide, on A1 2½mm wide.

1881   **Unwmk.**   **Typo.**   **Imperf.**
1	A1	1c vermilion, *yelsh*	9.00	5.50
2	A1	2c violet, *pale lil*	11.00	5.50
3	A1	3c gray bister, *pale bis*	20.00	8.00
4	A1	5c yel green, *grnsh*	32.50	16.00
5	A1	7c deep blue, *grysh*	22.00	4.00
6	A1	20c red brown, *yelsh*	82.50	30.00
		Nos. 1-6 (6)	177.00	69.00

Nos. 1-6 were printed from plate I, Nos. 7-13 from plates II and III.

1882   **Perf. 13½**
7	A1	1c dp ver, *dp yelsh* ('83)	5.75	2.10
a.		Vert. pair imperf. btwn.	200.00	160.00
c.		As "b," vert. pair, imperf between	200.00	160.00
8	A1	2c dp purple, *pale lil* ('83)	11.00	3.25
a.		2c dark violet, *white* ('84)	12.00	6.50
b.		As "a," vert. pair, imperf between	175.00	160.00
c.		As "a.," horiz. pair, imperf between	175.00	160.00
d.		2c red violet, *pale lilac* ('85)	7.25	2.60
e.		As "d," vert. pair, imperf between	175.00	175.00
f.		As "d," horiz. pair, imperf between	175.00	175.00
9	A1	3c gray bister, *pale bis*	11.50	3.25
b.		As "a," horiz. pair, imperf between	125.00	125.00
10	A1	5c blue grn, *grnsh*	8.25	1.60
a.		5c yellow green, *greenish* ('85)	7.75	1.40
b.		5c deep green, *greenish* ('85)	7.75	1.40
c.		As "b," horiz. pair, imperf between	190.00	175.00
11	A1	7c deep blue, *grysh* ('85)	10.50	2.10
a.		Horiz. pair, imperf. between	150.00	140.00
12	A1	7c ultra, *grysh* ('85)	16.00	3.25
a.		Vert. pair, imperf. between	150.00	140.00
13	A1	20c pale brn, *yelsh* ('86)	15.00	4.50
a.		Vert. pair, imperf between	175.00	175.00
b.		20c red brown, *yellowish* ('84)	20.00	8.00
c.		As "b," vert. pair, imperf between	150.00	140.00
d.		As "b," horiz. pair, imperf between	150.00	140.00
		Nos. 7-13 (7)	78.00	20.05

Stamps perf. 14, 16 are postal forgeries.

1886-87   **Perf. 13½**
18	A3	1c vermilion, *yelsh*	5.75	2.00
a.		Horiz. pair, imperf. vert.		175.00
b.		Horiz. pair, imperf. between	200.00	190.00
19	A3	2c dk violet, *lilac*	42.50	7.00
20	A4	5c green ('87)	20.00	2.75
		Nos. 18-20 (3)	68.25	11.75

General Louis Etienne Félicité Salomon — A5

1887   **Engr.**   **Perf. 14**
21	A5	1c lake	.40	.30
22	A5	2c violet	1.00	.70
23	A5	3c blue	.70	.45
24	A5	5c green	25.00	.55
a.		Double impression	200.00	
		Nos. 21-24 (4)	27.10	2.00

Imperfs. of Nos. 21-24 are plate proofs. Value per pair, $50.

No. 23 Handstamp Surcharged in Red

1890
25	A5	2c on 3c blue	1.75	1.50
a.		Inverted surcharge	6.00	8.00
b.		Double surcharge	6.00	7.00
c.		Double surcharge, one inverted		10.00

Missing letters are frequently found. This applies to succeeding surcharged issues.

Coat of Arms A7

Coat of Arms (Leaves Drooping) A9

1891   **Perf. 13**
26	A7	1c violet	1.00	.30
27	A7	2c blue	1.50	.30
28	A7	3c gray lilac	2.00	.55
a.		3c slate	1.75	.55

29	A7	5c orange	5.50	.50
30	A7	7c red	20.00	2.75
		Nos. 26-30 (5)	30.00	4.30

Nos. 26-30 exist imperf. Value of unused pairs, each $50.
The 2c, 3c and 7c exist imperf. vertically.

No. 28 Surcharged Like No. 25 in Red

1892
31	A7	2c on 3c gray lilac	1.40	.95
a.		2c on 3c slate	1.60	1.00
b.		Inverted surcharge	12.00	
c.		Double surcharge	16.00	
d.		Pair, one without surcharge	16.00	

1892-95   **Engr., Litho. (20c)**   **Perf. 14**
32	A9	1c lilac	.40	.20
b.		Double impression		
33	A9	2c deep blue	.50	.20
34	A9	3c gray	.70	.45
35	A9	5c orange	2.75	.50
36	A9	7c red	.50	.20
a.		Imperf., pair	30.00	
37	A9	20c brown	1.40	1.00
		Nos. 32-37 (6)	6.25	2.55

Nos. 32, 33, 35 exist in horiz. pairs, imperf. vert., Nos. 33, 35, in vert. pairs, imperf. horiz. No. 32 exists imperf. It is a proof.

1896   **Engr.**   **Perf. 13½**
38	A9	1c light blue	.55	.70
39	A9	2c red brown	.65	1.20
40	A9	3c lilac brown	.55	1.20
41	A9	5c slate green	.65	1.20
42	A9	7c dark gray	.90	1.75
43	A9	20c orange	1.10	2.25
		Nos. 38-43 (6)	4.40	8.30

Nos. 32-37 are 23¾mm high, Nos. 38-43 23¼mm to 23½mm. The "C" is closed on Nos. 32-37, open on Nos. 38-43. Other differences exist. The stamps of the two issues may be readily distinguished by their colors and perfs. Nos. 38-43 exist imperf. and in horiz. pairs, imperf. vert. The 1c, 3c, 5c, 7c exist in vert. pairs, imperf. horiz. or imperf. between. The 5c, 7c exist in horiz. pairs, imperf. between. Value of unused pairs, $9 and up.

#37, 43 Surcharged Like #25 in Red

1898
44	A9	2c on 20c brown	1.40	3.00
a.		Inverted surcharge	14.00	
b.		Double surcharge	16.00	
45	A9	2c on 20c orange	.90	.65
a.		Inverted surcharge	9.00	
b.		Double surcharge	14.00	
c.		Double surcharge, one inverted	17.00	

No. 45 exists in various part perf. varieties.

Coat of Arms — A11

1898   **Wmk. 131**   **Perf. 11**
46	A11	1c ultra	2.50	2.50
47	A11	2c brown carmine	.55	.40
48	A11	3c dull violet	2.50	2.50
49	A11	5c dark green	.55	.40
a.		Double impression		
50	A11	7c gray	5.00	5.00
51	A11	20c orange	10.00	10.00
		Nos. 46-51 (6)	21.10	20.80

All values exist imperforate. They are plate proofs.

Pres. T. Augustin Simon Sam — A12

Coat of Arms — A13

1898-99   **Unwmk.**   **Perf. 12**
52	A12	1c ultra	.20	.20
53	A13	1c yel green ('99)	.20	.20
54	A12	2c deep orange	.20	.20
55	A13	2c car lake ('99)	.20	.20
56	A12	3c green	.20	.20
57	A13	4c red	.20	.20
58	A12	5c red brown	.20	.20
59	A13	5c pale blue ('99)	.20	.20
60	A12	7c gray	.20	.20
61	A13	8c carmine	.20	.20
62	A13	10c orange red	.20	.20
63	A13	15c olive green	.60	.45

64	A12	20c black	.60	.45
65	A12	50c rose brown	1.00	.50
66	A12	1g red violet	2.25	2.00
		Nos. 52-66 (15)	6.65	5.60

For overprints see Nos. 67-81, 110-124, 169, 247-248.

Stamps of 1898-99 Handstamped in Black

1902
67	A12	1c ultra	.60	.45
a.		Inverted overprint	1.75	
b.		Pair, one without overprint	9.00	
68	A13	1c yellow green	.45	.30
a.		Inverted overprint	1.75	
b.		Double overprint	6.00	
c.		Pair, one without overprint	9.00	
69	A12	2c deep orange	.80	.70
a.		Inverted overprint	2.00	
b.		Double overprint	6.00	
c.		Pair, one without overprint	9.50	
70	A13	2c carmine lake	.45	.30
a.		Inverted overprint	2.00	
b.		Double overprint	6.00	
71	A12	3c green	.45	.45
a.		Inverted overprint	2.00	
72	A13	4c red	.60	.55
a.		Inverted overprint	2.00	
b.		Double overprint	6.00	
73	A12	5c red brown	1.25	1.10
a.		Inverted overprint	6.00	
74	A13	5c pale blue	.45	.45
a.		Inverted overprint	2.00	
b.		Double overprint	6.00	
75	A12	7c gray	.95	.90
a.		Inverted overprint	2.50	
b.		Double overprint	6.00	
76	A13	8c carmine	.95	.90
a.		Inverted overprint	5.00	
b.		Double overprint	6.00	
77	A13	10c orange red	.95	.90
a.		Inverted overprint	6.00	
b.		Double overprint	6.00	
78	A13	15c olive green	4.50	4.50
a.		Inverted overprint	8.00	
b.		Double overprint	10.00	
79	A12	20c black	4.50	4.50
a.		Inverted overprint	14.00	
b.		Double overprint	16.00	
80	A12	50c rose brown	14.50	14.50
a.		Inverted overprint	20.00	
81	A12	1g red violet	20.00	20.00
a.		Inverted overprint	40.00	
b.		Pair, one without overprint	45.00	
		Nos. 67-81 (15)	51.40	50.50

Many forgeries exist of this overprint.

Centenary of Independence Issues

Coat of Arms A14   Pierre D. Toussaint L'Ouverture A15

Emperor Jean Jacques Dessalines A16   Pres. Alexandre Sabes Pétion A17

1903, Dec. 31   **Engr.**   **Perf. 13¼, 14**
82	A14	1c green	.35	.35

Center Engr., Frame Litho.
83	A15	2c rose & blk	.60	1.75
84	A15	5c dull blue & blk	.60	1.75
85	A16	7c plum & blk	.60	1.75
86	A16	10c yellow & blk	.60	1.75
87	A17	20c slate & blk	.60	1.75
88	A17	50c olive & blk	.60	1.75
		Nos. 82-88 (7)	3.95	10.85

Nos. 82 to 88 exist imperforate. Some are known with head omitted.
Nos. 83-88 exist with centers inverted.
Forgeries exist both perforated and imperf and constitute the great majority of Nos. 83-88 offered in the marketplace. Stamps perforated

13½ are forgeries. Many forgeries exist with heads lithographed instead of engraved.

Same Handstamped in Blue

1904

89	A14	1c green	.50	1.50
90	A15	2c rose & blk	.50	1.50
91	A15	5c dull blue & blk	.50	1.50
92	A16	7c plum & blk	.50	1.50
93	A16	10c yellow & blk	.50	1.50
94	A17	20c slate & blk	.50	1.50
95	A17	50c olive & blk	.50	1.50
		Nos. 89-95 (7)	3.50	10.50

Two dies were used for the handstamped overprint on Nos. 89-95. Letters and figures are larger on one than on the other. All values exist imperforate.

Pres. Pierre Nord-Alexis — A18

1904   Engr.   Perf. 13¼, 14

96	A18	1c green	.35	.35
97	A18	2c carmine	.35	.35
98	A18	5c dark blue	.35	.35
99	A18	10c orange brown	.35	.35
100	A18	20c orange	.35	.35
101	A18	50c claret	.35	.35
a.		Tête bêche pair	350.00	
		Nos. 96-101 (6)	2.10	2.10

Used values are for c-t-o's. Postally used examples are worth considerably more.
Nos. 96-101 exist imperforate. Value, set $10.
This issue, and the overprints and surcharges, exist in horiz. pairs, imperf. vert., and in vert. pairs, imperf. horiz.
For overprints and surcharges see Nos. 102-109, 150-161, 170-176, 217-218, 235-238, 240-242, 302-303.
Forgeries of Nos. 96, 101, 101a exist.
Reprints or very accurate imitations of this issue exist, including No. 101a. Some are printed in very bright colors on very white paper and are found both perforated and imperforate. The original stamps are perf. 13¼ or 14, the reprints (forgeries) perf 13½, as well as numerous other perforations, including compound perfs.

Same Handstamped in Blue like #89-95

1904

102	A18	1c green	.60	1.50
103	A18	2c carmine	.60	1.50
104	A18	5c dark blue	.60	1.50
105	A18	10c orange brown	.60	1.50
106	A18	20c orange	.60	1.50
107	A18	50c claret	.60	1.50
		Nos. 102-107 (6)	3.60	9.00

The note after No. 95 applies also to Nos. 102-107. All values exist imperf.
Forgeries exist.

Regular Issue of 1904 Handstamp Surcharged in Black

1906, Feb. 20

108	A18	1c on 20c orange	.35	.20
a.		1c on 50c claret	950.00	
109	A18	2c on 50c claret	.35	.20

No. 108a is known only with inverted surcharge.
Forgeries exist.

Nos. 52-66 Handstamped in Red

1906

110	A12	1c ultra	1.25	.85
111	A13	1c yellow green	.65	.65
112	A12	2c deep orange	2.25	2.10
113	A13	2c carmine lake	1.25	1.10
114	A13	3c green	1.25	1.10
115	A13	4c red	5.25	4.00
116	A13	5c red brown	6.50	5.00
117	A13	5c pale blue	.95	.55
118	A12	7c gray	4.50	4.00
119	A13	8c carmine	.95	.90
120	A13	10c orange red	1.75	1.10
121	A13	15c olive green	2.25	1.10
122	A12	20c black	5.25	4.00
123	A12	50c rose brown	5.00	3.25
124	A12	1g red violet	10.50	6.50
		Nos. 110-124 (15)	49.55	36.20

Forgeries of this overprint are plentiful.

Coat of Arms — A19

President Nord-Alexis A20

Market at Port-au-Prince A21

Sans Souci Palace — A22

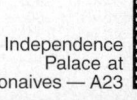

Independence Palace at Gonaives — A23

Entrance to Catholic College at Port-au-Prince A24

Monastery and Church at Port-au-Prince A25

Seat of Government at Port-au-Prince A26

Presidential Palace at Port-au-Prince A27

For Foreign Postage (centimes de piastre)

1906-13   Perf. 12

125	A19	1c de p green	.35	.20
126	A20	2c de p ver	.45	.20
127	A21	3c de p brown	.60	.25
128	A21	3c de p org yel		
		('11)	6.00	4.00
129	A22	4c de p car lake	.60	.35
130	A22	4c de p lt ol grn		
		('13)	12.50	9.00
131	A20	5c de p dk blue	2.50	.30
132	A23	7c de p gray	1.75	.85
133	A23	7c de p org red		
		('13)	32.50	22.50
134	A24	8c de p car rose	1.75	.80
135	A24	8c de p ol grn		
		('13)	25.00	19.00
136	A25	10c de p org red	1.25	.30
137	A25	10c de p red brn		
		('13)	25.00	19.00
138	A26	15c de p sl grn	2.25	.90
139	A26	15c dp p yel ('13)	13.00	7.50
140	A20	20c de p blue grn	2.25	.90
141	A19	50c de p red	3.25	2.25
142	A19	50c de p yel		
		('13)	13.00	7.50
143	A27	1p claret	7.25	4.50
144	A27	1p red ('13)	13.00	11.00
		Nos. 125-144 (20)	164.25	111.30

All 1906 values exist imperf. These are plate proofs.
For overprints and surcharges see Nos. 177-195, 213-216, 239, 245, 249-260, 263, 265-277, 279-284, 286-301, 304.

Nord-Alexis A28

Coat of Arms — A29

For Domestic Postage (centimes de gourde)

1906-10

145	A28	1c de g blue	.35	.20
146	A29	2c de g org yel	.45	.20
147	A29	2c de g lemon ('10)	.65	.25
148	A28	3c de g slate	.40	.20
149	A29	7c de g green	1.25	.45
		Nos. 145-149 (5)	3.10	1.30

For overprints see Nos. 196-197.

Regular Issue of 1904 Handstamp Surcharged in Red like #108-109

1907

150	A18	1c on 5c dk bl	.40	.35
151	A18	1c on 20c org	.40	.20
152	A18	2c on 10c org brn	.40	.40
153	A18	2c on 50c claret	.50	.40

Black Surcharge

154	A18	1c on 5c dk bl	.50	.40
155	A18	1c on 10c org brn	.50	.20
156	A18	2c on 20c org	.40	.40

Brown Surcharge

157	A18	1c on 5c dk bl	1.50	1.25
158	A18	1c on 10c org brn	1.50	1.25
159	A18	2c on 20c org	5.00	4.00
160	A18	2c on 50c claret	27.50	22.50

Violet Surcharge

161	A18	1c on 20c org	150.00	

The handstamps are found sideways, diagonal, inverted and double.
Forgeries exist.

A30

President Antoine T. Simon — A31

For Foreign Postage

1910

162	A30	2c de p rose red &		
		blk	.65	.50
163	A30	5c de p bl & blk	13.00	1.00
164	A30	20c de p yel grn & blk	12.50	7.50

For Domestic Postage

165	A31	1c de g lake & blk	.30	.20
		Nos. 162-165 (4)	26.45	9.20

For overprint and surcharges see Nos. 198, 262, 278, 285.

A32   A33

Pres. Cincinnatus Leconte — A34

1912

166	A32	1c de g car lake	.40	.40
167	A33	2c de g dp org	.50	.40

For Foreign Postage

168	A34	5c de p dp blue	.90	.40
		Nos. 166-168 (3)	1.80	1.20

For overprints see Nos. 199-201.

Stamps of Preceding Issues Handstamped Vertically

1914

On No. 61

169	A13	8c carmine	13.00	10.00

On Nos. 96-101

170	A18	1c green	35.00	30.00
171	A18	2c carmine	35.00	30.00
172	A18	5c dk blue	.65	.40
173	A18	10c orange brn	.65	.40
174	A18	20c orange	1.10	.50
175	A18	50c claret	2.50	1.25
		Nos. 170-175 (6)	74.90	62.55

Perforation varieties of Nos. 172-175 exist.
No. 175 overprinted "T. M." is a revenue stamp. The letters are the initials of "Timbre Mobile."

On No. 107

176	A18	50c claret	10,000.	13,000.

Horizontally on Stamps of 1906-13

177	A19	1c de p green	.50	
178	A20	2c de p ver	.65	.40
179	A21	3c de p brown	1.10	.60
180	A21	3c de p org yel	.50	.40
181	A22	4c de p car lake	1.10	.60
182	A22	4c de p lt ol grn	2.75	1.40
183	A23	7c de p gray	2.50	2.40
184	A23	7c de p org red	6.50	6.00
185	A24	8c de p car rose	4.50	4.00
186	A24	8c de p ol grn	8.25	8.00
187	A25	10c de p org red	1.30	.60
188	A25	10c de p red brn	3.50	2.10
189	A26	15c de p sl grn	3.75	3.25
190	A26	15c de p yellow	2.75	1.40
191	A20	20c de p bl grn	3.25	1.25
192	A19	50c de p red	5.75	5.50
193	A19	50c de p org yel	9.75	9.00
194	A27	1p claret	5.75	5.50
195	A27	1p red	10.50	9.75

196	A29	2c de g lemon	.50 .40
197	A28	3c de g slate	.50 .40
		Nos. 177-197 (21)	75.65 63.35

On No. 164
198	A30	20c de p yel grn & blk	3.75 3.50

Vertically on Nos. 166-168
199	A32	1c de g car lake	.50 .40
200	A33	2c de g dp org	.65 .50
201	A34	5c de p dp blue	1.10 .40
		Nos. 199-201 (3)	2.25 1.30

Two handstamps were used for the overprints on Nos. 169-201. They may be distinguished by the short and long foot of the "L" of "GL" and the position of the first "1" in "1914" with regard to the period above it. Both handstamps are found on all but #176, 294, 295, 306, 308.

Handstamp Surcharged

On Nos. 141 and 143
213	A19	1c de p on 50c de p red	.50 .40
214	A27	1c de p on 1p claret	.65 .50

On Nos. 142 and 144
215	A19	1c de p on 50c de p org yel	.65 .50
216	A27	1c de p on 1p red	.65 .50

Handstamp Surcharged

On Nos. 100 and 101
217	A18	7c on 20c orange	.50 .20
218	A18	7c on 50c claret	.45 .20

The initials on the preceding handstamps are those of Gen. Oreste Zamor; the date is that of his triumphal entry into Port-au-Prince.

Pres. Oreste Zamor

Coat of Arms

Pres. Tancrède Auguste

Owing to the theft of a large quantity of this 1914 issue, while in transit from the printers, the stamps were never placed on sale at post offices. A few stamps have been canceled through carelessness of favor. Value, set of 10, $8.50.

Preceding Issues Handstamp Surcharged in Carmine or Blue

On Nos. 98-101
1915-16
235	A18	1c on 5c dk bl (C)	2.00 2.25
236	A18	1c on 10c org brn	.60 .75
237	A18	1c on 20c orange	.60 .75
238	A18	1c on 50c claret	.60 .75

On No. 132
239	A23	1c on 7c de p gray (C)	.60 .75

On Nos. 106-107
240	A18	1c on 20c orange	1.50 1.50
241	A18	1c on 50c claret	3.50 1.50
242	A18	1c on 50c cl (C)	45.00 35.00
		Nos. 235-242 (8)	54.40 43.25

Nos. 240-242 are known with two types of the "Post Paye" overprint. No. 237 with red surcharge and any stamps with violet surcharge are unofficial.

> Values for Nos. 245-308 are for examples with the boxed "Gourde" surcharge partially on the stamp. Examples upon which this surcharge is fully present on the stamp command substantial premiums.

No. 143 Handstamp Surcharged in Red

1917-19
245	A27	2c on 1p claret	.50 .50

Stamps of 1906-14 Handstamp Surcharged in Various Colors

1c, 5c

On Nos. 123-124
247	A12	1c on 50c (R)	35.00 30.00
248	A12	1c on 1g (R)	35.00 30.00

On #127, 129, 134, 136, 138, 140-141
249	A22	1c on 4c de p (Br)	.65 .75
250	A25	1c on 10c de p (Bl)	.65 .75
252	A20	1c on 20c de p (R)	.65 .75
253	A20	1c on 20c de p (Bk)	.65 .75
254	A19	1c on 50c de p (R)	.65 .75
255	A19	1c on 50c de p (Bk)	.65 .75
256	A21	2c on 3c de p (R)	.65 .75
257	A24	2c on 8c de p (R)	.65 .75
258	A24	2c on 8c de p (Bk)	.65 .75
259	A26	2c on 15c de p (R)	.65 .75
260	A20	2c on 15c de p (R)	.65 .75
		Nos. 249-260 (11)	7.15 8.25

The 1c on 10c de p stamp in black is actually a blue ink which bled into the stamps.

On Nos. 164, 128
262	A30	1c on 20c de p (Bk)	3.75 3.50
263	A21	2c on 3c de p (R)	.60 .75

On #130, 133, 135, 137, 139, 142, 144
265	A22	1c on 4c de p (R)	.60 .75
266	A23	1c on 7c de p (Br)	.60 .75
267	A26	1c on 15c de p (R)	.60 .75
268	A19	1c on 50c de p (Bk)	2.00 2.50
269	A27	1c on 1p (Bk)	2.00 2.50
270	A24	2c on 8c de p (R)	.60 .75
271	A25	2c on 10c de p (Br)	.60 .75
272	A26	2c on 15c de p (R)	.60 .75
273	A25	5c on 10c de p (Bl)	2.00 2.50
274	A25	5c on 10c de p (VBk)	.60 .75
275	A26	5c on 15c de p (R)	5.00 6.00
		Nos. 265-275 (11)	15.20 18.75

"O. Z." Stamps of 1914 Handstamp Surcharged in Red or Brown

276	A26	1c on 15c de p sl grn	.60 .75
277	A20	1c on 20c de p bl grn	.60 .75
278	A30	1c on 20c de p yel grn & blk	.60 .75
279	A27	1c on 1p claret (Br)	.60 .75
280	A27	1c on 1p claret	2.00 2.50
281	A27	5c on 1p red (Br)	.60 .75
		Nos. 276-281 (6)	5.00 6.25

"O. Z." Stamps of 1914 Handstamp Surcharged in Violet, Green, Red, Magenta or Black
1 ct and 2 cts as in 1917-19 and

1919-20
282	A22	2c on 4c de p car lake (V)	.60 .75
283	A24	2c on 8c de p car rose (G)	.60 .75
284	A24	2c on 8c de p ol grn (R)	.60 .75
285	A30	2c on 20c de p yel grn & blk (R)	.75 1.00
286	A19	2c on 50c de p red (G)	.60 .75
288	A19	2c on 50c de p red (R)	.60 .75
289	A19	2c on 50c de p org yel (R)	.60 .75
290	A27	2c on 1pi claret (R)	3.00 3.50
291	A27	2c on 1pi red (R)	2.00 2.50
292	A21	3c on 3c de p brn (R)	.60 .75
293	A23	3c on 7c de p org red (R)	.60 .75
294	A21	3c on 3c de p brn (R)	.60 .75
295	A21	5c on 3c de p org yel (R)	2.00 2.50
296	A22	5c on 4c de p car lake (R)	.60 .75
297	A22	5c on 4c de p ol grn (R)	.60 .75
298	A23	5c on 7c de p gray (V)	.60 .75
299	A23	5c on 7c de p org red (V)	.60 .35
300	A25	5c on 10c de p org red (V)	.60 .75
301	A26	5c on 15c de p yel (M)	.60 .75
		Nos. 282-301 (19)	16.75 20.35

Nos. 217 and 218 Handstamp Surcharged with New Value in Magenta
302	A18	5c on 7c on 20c orange	.60 .75
303	A18	5c on 7c on 50c claret	3.50 4.00

No. 187 Handstamp Surcharged in Magenta
304	A25	5c de p on 10c de p	.60 .75

Postage Due Stamps of 1906-14 Handstamp Surcharged in Black or Magenta (#308)

On Stamp of 1906
305	D2	5c on 50c ol gray	15.00 15.00

On Stamp of 1914
306	D2	5c on 50c ol violet	.60 .75
307	D2	5c on 50c olive gray	.60 .75
308	D2	5c on 50c ol gray (M)	2.50 2.00
		Nos. 305-308 (4)	18.70 18.50

Nos. 299 with red surcharge and 306-307 with violet are trial colors or essays.

Allegory of Agriculture A40

Allegory of Commerce A41

1920, Apr.	Engr.		Perf. 12
310	A40	3c deep orange	.40 .40
311	A40	5c green	.40 .40
312	A41	10c vermilion	.50 .40
313	A41	15c violet	.50 .40
314	A41	25c deep blue	.65 .50
		Nos. 310-314 (5)	2.45 2.10

Nos. 311-313 overprinted "T. M." are revenue stamps. The letters are the initials of "Timbre Mobile."

President Louis J. Borno — A42

Christophe's Citadel — A43

Old Map of West Indies — A44

Borno — A45

National Capitol — A46

1924, Sept. 3			
315	A42	5c deep green	.40 .20
316	A43	10c carmine	.40 .20
317	A44	20c violet blue	.90 .40
318	A45	50c orange & blk	.90 .40
319	A46	1g olive green	1.60 .50
		Nos. 315-319 (5)	4.20 1.70

For surcharges see Nos. 359, C4A.

Coffee Beans and Flowers — A47

1928, Feb. 6
320 A47 35c deep green 3.75 .60
For surcharge see No. 337.

Pres. Louis Borno — A48

1929, Nov. 4
321 A48 10c carmine rose .50 .40

Signing of the "Frontier" treaty between Haiti and the Dominican Republic.

Presidents Salomon and Vincent — A49

Pres. Sténio Vincent — A50

1931, Oct. 16
322 A49 5c deep green 1.30 .50
323 A50 10c carmine rose 1.30 .50

50th anniv. of Haiti's joining the UPU.

President Vincent — A52

Aqueduct at Port-au-Prince A53

Fort National — A54

Palace of Sans Souci — A55

Christophe's Chapel at Milot — A56

King's Gallery Citadel — A57

Vallières Battery — A58

1933-40
325 A52 3c orange .30 .20
326 A52 3c dp ol grn ('39) .30 .20
327 A53 5c green .30 .20
a. 5c emerald ('38) .30 .20
b. 5c bright green ('39) .30 .20
c. 5c brown olive ('40) .50 .20
329 A54 10c rose car .50 .20
a. 10c vermilion .65 .20
330 A54 10c red brn ('40) .50 .20
331 A55 25c blue .90 .20
332 A56 50c brown 2.50 .55
333 A57 1g dark green 2.50 .55
334 A58 2.50g olive bister 4.50 .90
Nos. 325-334 (9) 12.30 3.20

For surcharges see Nos. 357-358, 360.

Alexandre Dumas, His Father and Son — A59

1935, Dec. 29 **Litho.** **Perf. 11½**
335 A59 10c rose pink & choc .90 .40
336 A59 25c blue & chocolate 1.60 .50
Nos. 335-336,C10 (3) 7.00 3.40

Visit of a delegation from France to Haiti.
No. 335 exists imperf and in horiz. pair, imperf. between. #336 exists as pair, imperf horiz.

No. 320 Surcharged in Red

1939, Jan. 24 **Perf. 12**
337 A47 25c on 35c dp grn .90 .40

Statue of Liberty, Map of Haiti and Flags of American Republics A60

1941, June 30 **Engr.** **Perf. 12**
338 A60 10c rose carmine 1.00 .50
339 A60 25c dark blue .90 .40
Nos. 338-339,C12-C13 (4) 8.40 2.40

3rd Inter-American Caribbean Conf., held at Port-au-Prince.

Patroness of Haiti, Map and Coat of Arms — A61

1942, Dec. 8
Size: 26x36¼mm
340 A61 3c dull violet .40 .20
341 A61 5c brt green .50 .20
342 A61 10c rose car .50 .20
343 A61 15c orange .65 .50
344 A61 20c brown .65 .50
345 A61 25c deep blue 1.40 .50
346 A61 50c red orange 1.75 .70
347 A61 2.50g olive black 4.75 1.10
Size: 32x45mm
348 A61 5g purple 11.50 4.50
Nos. 340-348,C14-C18 (14) 27.80 10.40

Issued in honor of Our Lady of Perpetual Help, patroness of Haiti.
For surcharges see Nos. 355-356.

Adm. Hammerton Killick and Destruction of "La Crête-à-Pierrot" — A62

1943, Sept. 6
349 A62 3c orange .40 .20
350 A62 5c turq green .50 .40
351 A62 10c carmine rose .50 .40
352 A62 25c deep blue .65 .40
353 A62 50c olive 1.40 .50
354 A62 5g brown black 5.75 3.00
Nos. 349-354,C22-C23 (8) 11.45 6.90

Nos. 343 and 345 Surcharged with New Value and Bars in Red

1944, July 19
355 A61 10c on 15c orange .40 .20
356 A61 10c on 25c dp blue .40 .20

Nos. 319, 326 and 334 Surcharged with New Values and Bars in Red

1944-45
357 A52 2c on 3c dp ol grn .30 .20
358 A52 5c on 3c dp ol grn .40 .40
359 A46 10c on 1g ol grn .50 .40
a. Surcharged "01.0" 1.50
360 A58 20c on 2.50g ol bis .50 .40
Nos. 357-360 (4) 1.70 1.40

Nurse and Wounded Soldier on Battlefield — A63

1945, Feb. 20
Cross in Rose
361 A63 3c gray black .20 .20
362 A63 5c dk blue grn .20 .20
363 A63 10c red orange .30 .20
364 A63 20c black brn .30 .20
365 A63 25c deep blue .40 .20
366 A63 35c orange .50 .20
367 A63 50c car rose .50 .20
368 A63 1g olive green .90 .40
369 A63 2.50g pale violet 2.50 .50
Nos. 361-369,C25-C32 (17) 18.65 7.00

Issued to honor the Intl. Red Cross.
20c, 1g, 2.50g, Aug. 14. Others, Feb. 20.
For overprints and surcharges see Nos. 456-457, C153-C160.

Catalogue values for unused stamps in this section, from this point to the end of the section, are for Never Hinged items.

Col. François Capois A64

Jean Jacques Dessalines A65

Unwmk.
1946, July 18 **Engr.** **Perf. 12**
370 A64 3c red orange .25 .20
371 A64 5c Prus green .25 .20
372 A64 10c red .25 .20
373 A64 20c olive black .25 .20
374 A64 25c deep blue .30 .20
375 A64 35c orange .40 .20
376 A64 50c red brown .50 .40
377 A64 1g olive brown .50 .40
378 A64 2.50g gray 1.30 .50
Nos. 370-378,C35-C42 (17) 9.50 5.60

For surcharges see Nos. 383, 392, C43-C45, C49-C51, C61-C62.

1947-54
379 A65 3c orange yel .20 .20
380 A65 5c green .20 .20
380A A65 5c dp vio ('54) .65 .20
381 A65 10c carmine rose .25 .20
382 A65 25c deep blue .40 .20
Nos. 379-382,C46 (6) 2.10 1.20

No. 375 Surcharged with New Value and Rectangular Block in Black

1948
383 A64 10c on 35c orange .40 .20

Arms of Port-au-Prince A66

Engraved and Lithographed
1950, Feb. 12 **Perf. 12½**
384 A66 10c multicolored .40 .20
Nos. 384,C47-C48 (3) 2.20 1.20

200th anniv. (in 1949) of the founding of Port-au-Prince.

Nos. RA10-RA12 and RA16 Surcharged or Overprinted in Black

1950, Oct. 4 **Unwmk.** **Perf. 12**
385 PT2 3c on 5c ol gray .20 .20
386 PT2 5c green .40 .20
387 PT2 10c on 5c car rose .40 .20
388 PT2 20c on 5c blue .50 .20
Nos. 385-388,C49-C51 (7) 4.25 3.40

75th anniv. (in 1949) of the UPU.
Exist with inverted or double surcharge and 10c on 5c green.

Cacao — A67

Pres. Paul E. Magloire and Day Nursery, Saline — A68

1951, Sept. 3   Photo.   Perf. 12½
389   A67   5c dark green   .40   .20
    Nos. 389,C52-C54 (4)   27.15   4.70

1953, May 4   Engr.   Perf. 12
    Design: 10c, Applying asphalt.
390   A68   5c green   .20   .20
391   A68   10c rose carmine   .30   .20
    Nos. 390-391,C57-C60 (6)   3.75   2.15

No. 375 Surcharged in Black

1953, Apr. 7
392   A64   50c on 35c orange   .50   .40
    Gen. Pierre Dominique Toussaint L'Ouverture, 1743-1803, liberator.

J. J. Dessalines and Paul E. Magloire — A69

Alexandre Sabes Pétion — A70   Battle of Vertieres — A71

Design: No. 395, Larmartiniere. No. 396, Boisrond-Tonnerre. No. 397, Toussaint L'Ouverture. No. 399, Capois. No. 401, Marie Jeanne and Lamartiniere leading attack.

1954, Jan. 1   Photo.   Perf. 11½
    Portraits in Black
393   A69   3c blue gray   .20   .20
394   A70   5c yellow green   .30   .20
395   A70   5c yellow green   .30   .20
396   A70   5c yellow green   .40   .30
397   A70   5c yellow green   .30   .20
398   A69   10c crimson   .30   .20
399   A70   15c rose lilac   .40   .20
    Perf. 12½
400   A71   25c dark gray   .40   .20
401   A71   25c deep orange   .40   .20
    Nos. 393-401 (9)   3.00   1.90
    Nos. 393-401,C63-C70,C71-C74 (21)   14.90   10.45

150th anniv. of Haitian independence. See Nos. C95-C96.

Mme. Yolette Magloire — A72

1954, Jan. 1   Perf. 11½
402   A72   10c orange   .30   .20
403   A72   10c blue   .30   .20
    Nos. 402-403,C75-C80 (8)   6.70   5.05

Henri Christophe, Paul Magloire and Citadel A73

Tomb and Arms of Henri Christophe — A74

Perf. 13½x13
1954, Dec. 6   Litho.   Unwmk.
404   A73   10c carmine   .25   .20
    Perf. 13
405   A74   10c red, blk & car   .30   .20
    Nos. 404-405,C81-C90 (12)   15.10   8.65
    Restoration of Christophe's Citadel.

J. J. Dessalines A75   Pres. Magloire and Dessalines Memorial, Gonaives A76

1955-57   Photo.   Perf. 11½
406   A75   3c ocher & blk   .20   .20
407   A75   5c pale vio & blk ('56)   .20   .20
408   A75   10c rose & blk   .25   .20
   a.   10c salmon pink & black ('57)   .20   .20
409   A75   25c chalky bl & blk ('56)   .30   .20
   a.   25c blue & black ('57)   .30   .20
    Nos. 406-409,C93-C94 (6)   1.45   1.20
    For surcharges, see Nos. 454-455.

1955, Aug. 1
410   A76   10c deep blue & blk   .40   .20
411   A76   10c crimson & blk   .40   .20
    Nos. 410-411,C97-C98 (4)   2.10   .80
    21st anniv. of the new Haitian army. Nos. 410-411 were printed in a single sheet of 20 (5x4). The two upper rows are of No. 410, the two lower No. 411, providing five se-tenant pairs. Value 85 cents.

Flamingo A77   Mallard A78

1956, Apr. 14   Photo.   Perf. 11½
    Granite Paper
412   A77   10c blue & ultra   2.25   .30
413   A78   25c dk grn & bluish grn   3.25   .45
    Nos. 412-413,C99-C104 (8)   43.40   6.80

Immanuel Kant — A79

1956, July 19   Perf. 12
    Granite Paper
414   A79   10c brt ultra   .30   .20
    Nos. 414,C105-C107 (4)   2.45   1.30
    10th anniv. of the 1st Inter-American Philosophical Congress.

Zim Waterfall A80   J. J. Dessalines and Dessalines Memorial, Gonaives A81

1957, Dec. 16   Unwmk.   Perf. 11½
    Granite Paper
415   A80   10c orange & blue   .30   .20
    Nos. 415,C108-C111 (5)   4.70   2.90
    For surcharge & overprint see #CB49, CQ2.

1958, July 1   Photo.
416   A81   5c yel grn & blk   .25   .20
    Bicentenary of birth of J. J. Dessalines. See Nos. 470-471, C112, C170. For overprints see Nos. 480-482, C183-C184, CQ1, Q1-Q3.

"Atomium" — A82

View of Brussels Exposition A83

Perf. 13x13½, 13½x13
1958, July 22   Litho.   Unwmk.
417   A82   50c brown   .40   .20
418   A82   75c brt green   .40   .20
419   A82   1g purple   .75   .20
420   A83   1.50g red orange   .75   .40
    Nos. 417-420,C113-C114 (6)   5.05   2.35
    Issued for the Universal and International Exposition at Brussels.
    For surcharges see Nos. B2-B3, CB9.

Sylvio Cator — A84   U. S. Satellite — A85

1958, Aug. 16   Photo.   Perf. 11½
    Granite Paper
421   A84   5c green   .20   .20
422   A84   10c brown   .20   .20
423   A84   20c lilac   .25   .20
    Nos. 421-423,C115-C118 (7)   4.05   2.25
    30th anniversary of the world championship record broad jump of Sylvio Cator.

1958, Oct. 8   Perf. 14x13½
    Designs: 20c, Emperor penguins. 50c, Modern observatory. 1g, Ocean exploration.
424   A85   10c brt bl & brn red   .30   .20
425   A85   20c black & dp org   1.40   .50
426   A85   50c grn & rose brn   .75   .30
427   A85   1g black & blue   .80   .30
    Nos. 424-427,C119-C121 (7)   9.35   2.70
    Issued for the International Geophysical Year 1957-58.

President François Duvalier — A86

Engraved and Lithographed
1958, Oct. 22   Unwmk.   Perf. 11½
    Commemorative Inscription in Ultramarine
428   A86   10c blk & dp pink   .30   .20
429   A86   50c blk & lt grn   .40   .20
430   A86   1g blk & brick red   .50   .40
431   A86   5g blk & sal   2.40   1.50
    Nos. 428-431,C122-C125 (8)   10.90   6.35
    1st anniv. of the inauguration of Pres. Dr. François Duvalier. See note on souvenir sheets after No. C125.

1958 Nov. 20
    Without Commemorative Inscription
432   A86   5c blk & lt vio bl   .20   .20
433   A86   10c blk & dp pink   .20   .20
434   A86   20c blk & yel   .20   .20
435   A86   50c blk & lt grn   .30   .20
436   A86   1g blk & brick red   .50   .40
437   A86   1.50g blk & rose pink   .65   .50
438   A86   2.50g blk & gray vio   .90   .50
439   A86   5g blk & sal   1.60   1.10
    Nos. 432-439,C126-C132 (15)   13.20   7.90
    For surcharges see Nos. B13, B22-B24.

Map of Haiti — A87

1958, Dec. 5   Photo.   Perf. 11½
    Granite Paper
440   A87   10c rose pink   .20   .20
441   A87   25c green   .30   .20
    Nos. 440-441,C133-C135 (5)   1.80   1.20
    Tribute to the UN. See No. C135a. For overprints and surcharges see Nos. 442-443, B4-B5, CB11-CB12.

    Nos. 440-441 Overprinted "10th ANNIVERSARY OF THE / UNIVERSAL DECLARATION / OF HUMAN RIGHTS" in English (a), French (b), Spanish (c) or Portuguese (d)

1959, Jan. 28
442   Block of 4   .35   .35
   a.-d.   A87 10c any single   .20   .20
443   Block of 4   .90   .70
   a.-d.   A87 25c any single   .20   .20
    Nos. 442-443,C136-C138 (5)   14.75   14.55
    10th anniv. of the signing of the Universal Declaration of Human Rights.

Pope Pius XII and Children — A88

    50c, Pope praying. 2g, Pope on throne.

1959, Feb. 28   Photo.   Perf. 14x13½
444   A88   10c vio bl & ol   .20   .20
445   A88   50c green & dp brn   .40   .20
446   A88   2g dk claret & dk brn   .90   .50
    Nos. 444-446,C139-C141 (6)   3.40   1.90
    Issued in memory of Pope Pius XII. For surcharges see Nos. B6-B8.

Abraham Lincoln — A89

1959, May 12   Photo.   *Perf. 12*
447 A89 50c lt bl & deep claret   .40 .20
   Nos. 447,C142-C144 (4)   2.50 1.50

Sesquicentennial of the birth of Abraham Lincoln. Imperf. pairs exist.
For surcharges see #B9, CB16-CB18.

Chicago's Skyline and Dessables House — A90

Jean Baptiste Dessables and Map of American Midwest, c. 1791 — A91

Design: 50c, Discus thrower and flag of Haiti.

1959, Aug. 27   Unwmk.   *Perf. 14*
448 A90 25c blk brn & lt bl   .40 .20
449 A90 50c multicolored   .50 .40
450 A90 75c brown & blue   .65 .50
   Nos. 448-450,C145-C147 (6)   4.70 2.25

3rd Pan American Games, Chicago, 8/27-9/7.
For surcharges see #B10-B12, CB19-CB21.

No. 449 Overprinted

1960, Feb. 29
451 A90 50c multicolored   1.60 1.20
   Nos. 451,C148-C150 (4)   7.65 7.25

8th Olympic Winter Games, Squaw Valley, Calif., Feb. 18-29, 1960.

Uprooted Oak Emblem and Hands — A92

1960, Apr. 7   Litho.   *Perf. 12½x13*
452 A92 10c salmon & grn   .20 .20
453 A92 50c violet & mag   .40 .20
   Nos. 452-453,C151-C152 (4)   1.50 1.00

World Refugee Year, July 1, 1959-June 30, 1960. See Nos. 489-490, C191-C192. For surcharges see Nos. B14-B17, B28-B29, CB24-CB27, CB45-CB46.

No. 406 Surcharged with New Values

1960, Apr. 27   Photo.   *Perf. 11½*
454 A75 5c on 3c ocher & blk   .25 .20
455 A75 10c on 3c ocher & blk   .35 .20

No. 369 Surcharged or Overprinted in Red: "28eme ANNIVERSAIRE"

1960, May 8   Engr.   *Perf. 12*
Cross in Rose
456 A63 1g on 2.50g pale vio   .90 .50
457 A63 2.50g pale violet   1.40 1.00
   Nos. 456-457,C153-C160 (10)   7.30 5.30

28th anniversary of the Haitian Red Cross.

Claudinette Fouchard, Miss Haiti, Sugar Queen — A93

Sugar Queen and: 20c, Sugar harvest. 50c, Beach. 1g, Sugar plantation.

Perf. 11½
1960, May 30   Photo.   Unwmk.
Granite Paper
458 A93 10c ol bis & vio   .25 .20
459 A93 20c red brn & blk   .30 .20
460 A93 50c brt bl & brn   .75 .20
461 A93 1g green & brn   1.75 .20
   Nos. 458-461,C161-C162 (6)   6.20 1.50

Haitian sugar industry.

Olympic Victors, Athens, 1896, Melbourne Stadium and Olympic Torch A94

Designs: 20c, Discus thrower and Rome stadium. 50c, Pierre de Coubertin and victors, Melbourne, 1956. 1g, Athens stadium, 1896.

1960, Aug. 18   Photo.   *Perf. 12*
462 A94 10c black & org   .20 .20
463 A94 20c dk blue & crim   .20 .20
464 A94 50c green & ocher   .65 .20
465 A94 1g dk brn & grnsh bl   .80 .65
   Nos. 462-465,C163-C165 (7)   5.50 2.30

17th Olympic Games, Rome, Aug. 25-Sept. 11. For surcharges see Nos. B18-B19, CB28-CB29.

Occide Jeanty and Score from "1804" A95

20c, Occide Jeanty and National Capitol.

1960, Oct. 19   *Perf. 14x14½*
466 A95 10c orange & red lilac   .25 .20
467 A95 20c blue & red lilac   .35 .20
468 A95 50c brown & sepia   .50 .40
   Nos. 466-468,C166-C167 (5)   2.35 1.25

Cent. of the birth of Occide Jeanty, composer. Printed in sheets of 12 (3x4) with commemorative inscription and opening bars of "1804," Jeanty's military march, in top margin.

UN Headquarters, NYC — A96

1960, Nov. 25   Engr.   *Perf. 10½*
469 A96 1g green & blk   .50 .40
   Nos. 469,C168-C169 (3)   1.40 1.00

15th anniv. of the UN. For surcharges see Nos. B20-B21, CB30-CB31, CB35-CB36. Exists with center inverted.

Dessalines Type of 1958
Perf. 11½
1960, Nov. 5   Unwmk.   Photo.
Granite Paper
470 A81 10c red org & blk   .25 .20
471 A81 25c ultra & blk   .35 .20
   Nos. 470-471,C170 (3)   .85 .60

Alexandre Dumas Père and Musketeer — A97

5c, Map of Haiti & birthplace of General Alexandre Dumas, horiz. 50c, Alexandre Dumas, father & son, French & Haitian flags, horiz.

1961, Feb. 10   *Perf. 11½*
Granite Paper
472 A97 5c lt blue & choc   .20 .20
473 A97 10c rose, blk & sep   .20 .20
474 A97 50c dk blue & crim   .40 .20
   Nos. 472-474,C177-C179 (6)   3.25 1.40

Gen. Dumas (Alexandre Davy de la Pailleterie), born in Jeremie, Haiti, and his son and grandson, French authors.

Three Pirates — A98

Tourist publicity: 5c, Map of Tortuga. 15c, Pirates. 20c, Privateer in battle. 50c, Pirate with cutlass in rigging.

1961, Apr. 4   Litho.   *Perf. 12*
475 A98 5c blue & yel   .20 .20
476 A98 10c lake & yel   .20 .20
477 A98 15c ol grn & org   .20 .20
478 A98 20c choc & org   .30 .20
479 A98 50c vio bl & org   .40 .20
   Nos. 475-479,C180-C182 (8)   2.60 1.85

For surcharges and overprints see Nos. 484-485, C186-C187.

Nos. 416, 470-471 and 378 Overprinted: "Dr. F. Duvalier / Président / 22 Mai 1961"

1961, May 22   Photo.   *Perf. 11½*
480 A81 5c yel grn & blk   .20 .20
481 A81 10c red org & blk   .20 .20
482 A81 25c ultra & blk   .25 .20

Engr.
Perf. 12
483 A64 2.50g gray   1.10 .60
   Nos. 480-483,C183-C185 (7)   2.60 2.00

Re-election of Pres. Francois Duvalier.

No. 475 Surcharged: "EXPLORATION SPATIALE JOHN GLENN," Capsule and New Value

1962, May 10   Litho.
484 A98 50c on 5c bl & yel   .50 .40
485 A98 1.50g on 5c bl & yel   1.40 1.00
   Nos. 484-485,C186-C187 (4)   3.80 2.80

U.S. achievement in space exploration and for the 1st orbital flight of a US astronaut, Lt. Col. John H. Glenn, Jr., Feb. 20, 1962.

Malaria Eradication Emblem — A99

Design: 10c, Triangle pointing down.

Unwmk.
1962, May 30   Litho.   *Perf. 12*
486 A99 5c crimson & dp bl   .20 .20
487 A99 10c red brn & emer   .20 .20
488 A99 50c blue & crimson   .40 .20
   Nos. 486-488,C188-C190 (6)   1.90 1.40

WHO drive to eradicate malaria. Sheets of 12 with marginal inscription. For surcharges see Nos. B25-B27, CB42-CB44.

WRY Type of 1960 Dated "1962"
1962, June 22   *Perf. 12½x13*
489 A92 10c lt blue & org   .20 .20
490 A92 50c rose lil & dl grn   .40 .40
   Nos. 489-490,C191-C192 (4)   1.35 1.25

Issued to publicize the plight of refugees. For souvenir sheet see note after #C191-C192.

Haitian Scout Emblem — A100

5c, 50c, Scout giving Scout sign. 10c, Lord and Lady Baden-Powell, horiz.

Perf. 14x14½, 14½x14
1962, Aug. 6   Photo.
491 A100 3c blk, ocher & pur   .20 .20
492 A100 5c cit, red brn & blk   .20 .20
493 A100 10c ocher, blk & grn   .20 .20
494 A100 25c maroon, ol & bl   .25 .20
495 A100 50c violet, grn & red   .40 .20
   Nos. 491-495,C193-C195 (8)   2.60 2.00

22nd anniv. of the Haitian Boy Scouts. For surcharges and overprints see Nos. B31-B34, C196-C199.

TIMBRE MOBILE, etc.
From 1970 through 1979 postage and airmail stamps were overprinted for use as revenue stamps. The overprints used were: "TIMBRE MOBILE," "TIMBRE DE SOLIDARITE," "SOLIDARITE," "TIMBRE SOLIDARITE," "OBLIGATION PELIGRE."

Space Needle, Space Capsule and Globe — A101

1962, Nov. 19   Litho.   Perf. 12½
496 A101 10c red brn & lt bl   .20   .20
497 A101 20c vio bl & pink   .20   .20
498 A101 50c emerald & yel   .40   .20
499 A101 1g car & lt grn   .50   .40
  Nos. 496-499,C200-C202 (7)   3.00 2.00

"Century 21" International Exposition, Seattle, Wash., Apr. 21-Oct. 21.
For overprints see #503-504, C206-C207.

Plan of Duvalier Ville and Stamp of 1904 — A102

1962, Dec. 10   Photo.   Perf. 14x14½
500 A102 5c vio, yel & blk   .20   .20
501 A102 10c car rose, yel & blk   .20   .20
502 A102 25c bl gray, yel & blk   .35   .20
  Nos. 500-502,C203-C205 (6)   3.15 1.70

Issued to publicize Duvalier Ville.
For surcharge see No. B30.

Nos. 498-499 with Vertical Overprint in Black Similar to

1963, Jan. 23   Litho.   Perf. 12½
503 A101 50c emerald & yel   .65   .40
  a.   Claret overprint, horiz.   .65   .40
504 A101 1g car & lt grn   1.40   .50
  a.   Claret overprint, horiz.   1.40   .50
  Nos. 503-504,C206-C207 (4)   5.20 2.60
  Nos. 503a-504a,C206a-C207a (4) 5.20 2.60

"Peaceful Uses of Outer Space." The black vertical overprint has no outside frame lines and no broken shading lines around capsule. Nos. 503a and 504a were issued Feb. 20.

Symbolic Harvest
A103

1963, July 12   Photo.   Perf. 13x14
505 A103 10c orange & blk   .20   .20
506 A103 20c bluish grn & blk   .20   .20
  Nos. 505-506,C208-C209 (4)   1.30 1.00

FAO "Freedom from Hunger" campaign.

J. J. Dessalines
A104

Weight Lifter
A105

1963, Oct. 17   Perf. 14x14½
507 A104 5c tan & ver   .25   .20
508 A104 10c yellow & blue   .25   .20
  Nos. 507-508,C214-C215 (4)   1.00   .80

For overprints see Nos. 509, C216-C217.

No. 508 Overprinted: "FETE DES MERES / 1964"

1964, July 22
509 A104 10c yellow & blue   .25   .20
  Nos. 509,C216-C218 (4)   1.65 1.00

Issued for Mother's Day, 1964.

1964, Nov. 12   Photo.   Perf. 11½
Granite Paper

Design: 50c, Hurdler.

510 A105 10c lt bl & dk brn   .20   .20
511 A105 25c salmon & dk brn   .25   .20
512 A105 50c pale rose lil & dk
             brn   .40   .20
  Nos. 510-512,C223-C226 (7)   2.80 1.90

18th Olympic Games, Tokyo, Oct. 10-25. Printed in sheets of 50 (10x5), with map of Japan in background extending over 27 stamps.
For surcharges see #B35-B37, CB51-CB54.

Madonna of Haiti and International Airport, Port-au-Prince
A106

1964, Dec. 15   Perf. 14½x14
513 A106 10c org yel & blk   .20   .20
514 A106 25c bl grn & blk   .25   .20
515 A106 50c brt yel grn & blk   .40   .20
516 A106 1g vermilion & blk   .50   .40
  Nos. 513-516,C227-C229 (7)   3.80 2.25

Same Overprinted "1965"
1965, Feb. 11
517 A106 10c org, yel & blk   .20   .20
518 A106 25c blue grn & blk   .25   .20
519 A106 50c brt yel grn & blk   .40   .20
520 A106 1g vermilion & blk   .50   .40
  Nos. 517-520,C230-C232 (7)   3.40 2.30

Unisphere, NY World's Fair — A107

1965, Mar. 22   Photo.   Perf. 13½

20c, "Rocket Thrower" by Donald De Lue.

521 A107 10c grn, yel ol & dk
             red   .20   .20
522 A107 20c plum & orange   .25   .20
523 A107 50c dk brn, dk red, yel
             & grn   .40   .20
  Nos. 521-523,C233-C235 (6)   4.15 3.10

New York World's Fair, 1964-65.

Merchantmen — A108

1965, May 13   Unwmk.   Perf. 11½
524 A108 10c blk, lt grn & red   .20   .20
525 A108 50c blk, lt bl & red   .40   .20
  Nos. 524-525,C236-C237 (4)   1.75 1.10

The merchant marine.

ITU Emblem, Old and New Communication Equipment — A109

1965, Aug. 16   Litho.   Perf. 13½
526 A109 10c gray & multi   .20   .20
527 A109 25c multicolored   .40   .20
528 A109 50c multicolored   .50   .20
  Nos. 526-528,C242-C245 (7)   4.50 2.30

Cent. of the ITU.
For overprints see #537-539, C255-C256.

Statue of Our Lady of the Assumption
A110

Designs: 5c, Cathedral of Port-au-Prince, horiz. 10c, High altar.

Perf. 14x13, 13x14
1965, Nov. 19   Photo.
Size: 39x29mm, 29x39mm
529 A110 5c multicolored   .20   .20
530 A110 10c multicolored   .25   .20
531 A110 25c multicolored   .30   .20
  Nos. 529-531,C246-C248 (6)   4.55 3.45

200th anniv. of the Metropolitan Cathedral of Port-au-Prince.

Passionflower
A111

Flowers: 5c, 15c, American elder. 10c, Okra.

1965, Dec. 20   Photo.   Perf. 11½
Granite Paper
532 A111 3c dk vio, lt vio bl &
             grn   .20   .20
533 A111 5c grn, lt bl & yel   .20   .20
534 A111 10c multicolored   .20   .20
  a.   "0.10" omitted
535 A111 15c grn, pink & yel   .70   .20
536 A111 50c dk vio, yel & grn   1.40   1.10
  Nos. 532-536,C249-C254 (11)   15.30 6.80

For surcharges see Nos. 566, B38-B40, CB55-CB56.

Nos. 526-528 Overprinted in Red: "20e. Anniversaire / UNESCO"
1965, Aug. 27   Litho.   Perf. 13½
537 A109 10c gray & multi   .30   .20
538 A109 25c yel brn & multi   .35   .35
539 A109 50c pale grn & multi   .70   .70
  Nos. 537-539,C255-C256 (5)   5.35 2.60

20th anniversary of UNESCO.

Amulet — A112

Ceremonial Stool — A113

Perf. 14x½x14, 14x14½
1966, Mar. 14   Photo.   Unwmk.
540 A112 5c grnsh bl, blk & yel   .20   .20
541 A113 10c multi   .20   .20
542 A112 50c scar, yel & blk   .40   .20
  Nos. 540-542,C257-C259 (6)   3.35 2.15

For overprints and surcharges see Nos. 543, 567-570, C260-C261, C280-C281.

No. 541 Overprinted in Red: "Hommage / a Hailé Sélassiéler / 24-25 Avril 1966"

1966, Apr. 24
543 A113 10c multi   .30   .20
  Nos. 543,C260-C262 (4)   2.35 1.60

Visit of Emperor Haile Selassie of Ethiopia, Apr. 24-25.

Space Rendezvous of Gemini VI and VII, Dec. 15, 1965
A114

1966, May 3   Perf. 13½
544 A114 5c vio bl, brn & lt bl   .20   .20
545 A114 10c pur, brn & lt bl   .20   .20
546 A114 25c grn, brn & lt bl   .30   .20
547 A114 50c dk red, brn & lt bl   .40   .20
  Nos. 544-547,C263-C265 (7)   2.65 1.90

Walter M. Shirra, Thomas P. Stafford, Frank A. Borman, James A. Lovell and Gemini VI.
For overprint see No. 584.

Soccer Ball within Wreath and Pres. Duvalier
A115

Design: 10c, 50c, Soccer player within wreath and Duvalier.

Lithographed and Photogravure
1966, June 16   Perf. 13x13½
Portrait in Black; Gold Inscription; Green Commemorative Inscription in Two Lines
548 A115 5c pale sal & grn   .20   .20
549 A115 10c lt ultra & grn   .20   .20
550 A115 15c lt grn & grn   .25   .20
551 A115 50c pale lil rose & grn   .40   .20

Green Commemorative Inscription in 3 Lines; Gold Inscription Omitted
552 A115 5c pale sal & grn   .20   .20
553 A115 10c lt ultra & grn   .20   .20
554 A115 15c lt grn & grn   .20   .20
555 A115 50c pale lil rose & grn   .40   .20
  Nos. 548-555,C266-C269 (12)   4.15 3.20

Caribbean Soccer Festival, June 10-22. Nos. 548-551 also for the Natl. Soccer Championships, May 8-22.
For surcharges and overprint see Nos. 578-579, C288, CB57.

"ABC," Boy and Girl — A116

10c, Scout symbols. 25c, Television set, book and communications satellite, horiz.

Perf. 14x13½, 13½x14

1966, Oct. 18   Litho. & Engr.
556 A116 5c grn, sal pink & brn .20 .20
557 A116 10c red brn, lt brn & blk .20 .20
558 A116 25c grn, bl & dk vio .25 .20
    Nos. 556-558,C270-C272 (6) 2.20 1.70

Issued to publicize education through literacy, Scouting and by audio-visual means.

Dr. Albert Schweitzer, Maps of Alsace and Gabon — A117

Designs: 10c, Dr. Schweitzer and pipe organ. 20c, Dr. Schweitzer and Albert Schweitzer Hospital, Deschapelles, Haiti.

Perf. 12½x13

1967, Apr. 20   Photo.   Unwmk.
559 A117 5c pale lil & multi .20 .20
560 A117 10c buff & multi .20 .20
561 A117 20c gray & multi .40 .20
    Nos. 559-561,C273-C276 (7) 3.35 2.60

Issued in memory of Dr. Albert Schweitzer (1875-1965), medical missionary to Gabon, theologian and musician.

Watermelon and J. J. Dessalines — A118

1967, July 4   Photo.   Perf. 12½
562 A118 5c shown .20 .20
563 A118 10c Cabbage .20 .20
564 A118 20c Tangerine 1.25 .20
565 A118 50c Chayote 2.00 .20
    Nos. 562-565,C277-C279 (7) 11.15 5.50

No. 532 Surcharged

1967, Aug. 21   Photo.   Perf. 11½
566 A111 50c on 3c multi .30 .20
    Nos. 566,B38-B40,CB55-CB56 (6) 2.15 1.70

12th Boy Scout World Jamboree, Farragut State Park, Idaho, Aug. 1-9.

Nos. 540-542 Overprinted and Surcharged

Perf. 14½x14, 14x14½

1967, Aug. 30   Photo.
567 A112 5c grnsh bl, blk & yel .20 .20
568 A113 10c multi .20 .20
569 A112 50c scar, yel & blk .25 .20
570 A112 1g on 5c multi .50 .40
    Nos. 567-570,C280-C281 (6) 2.50 1.95

EXPO '67 Intl. Exhibition, Montreal, 4/28-10/27.

Pres. Duvalier and Brush Turkey A119

1967, Sept. 22   Photo.   Perf. 14x13
571 A119 5c car rose & gold .20 .20
572 A119 10c ultra & gold .20 .20
573 A119 25c dk red brn & gold .25 .20
574 A119 50c dp red lil & gold .40 .20
    Nos. 571-574,C282-C284 (7) 3.30 2.40

10th anniversary of Duvalier revolution.

Writing Hands A120

Designs: 10c, Scout emblem and Scouts, vert. 25c, Audio-visual teaching of algebra.

1967, Dec. 11   Litho.   Perf. 11½
575 A120 5c multicolored .20 .20
576 A120 10c multicolored .20 .20
577 A120 25c dk grn, lt bl & yel .25 .20
    Nos. 575-577,C285-C287 (6) 2.05 1.70

Issued to publicize the importance of education.
For surcharges see Nos. CB58-CB60.

Nos. 552 and 554 Surcharged

Lithographed and Photogravure

1968, Jan. 18   Perf. 13x13½
578 A115 50c on 15c .85 .20
579 A115 1g on 5c 1.00 .85
    Nos. 578-579,C288,CB57 (4) 6.50 4.55

19th Olympic Games, Mexico City, Oct. 12-27.
The 1968 date is missing on 2 stamps in every sheet of 50.

Caiman Woods, by Raoul Dupoux A121

1968, Apr. 22   Photo.   Perf. 12
Size: 36x26mm
580 A121 5c multi .20 .20
581 A121 10c rose red & multi .20 .20
582 A121 25c multi .20 .20
583 A121 50c dl lil & multi .40 .20
    Nos. 580-583,C289-C295 (11) 6.45 4.70

Caiman Woods ceremony during the Slaves' Rebellion, Aug. 14, 1791.

No. 547 Overprinted

1968, Apr. 19   Photo.   Perf. 13½
584 A114 50c dk red, brn & lt bl .90 .80
    Nos. 584,C296-C298 (4) 5.40 2.90

10th Winter Olympic Games, Grenoble, France, Feb. 6-18, 1968.

Monument to the Unknown Maroon — A122

Palm Tree and Provincial Coats of Arms — A123

Madonna, Papal Arms and Arms of Haiti — A124

1968, May 22   Perf. 11½
Granite Paper
585 A122 5c bl & blk .20 .20
586 A122 10c rose brn & blk .20 .20
587 A122 20c vio & blk .20 .20
588 A122 25c lt ultra & blk .25 .20
589 A122 50c brt bl grn & blk .40 .20
    Nos. 585-589,C299-C301 (8) 2.95 2.10

Unveiling of the monument to the Unknown Maroon, Port-au-Prince.
For surcharges see Nos. C324-C325.

Perf. 13x14, 12½x13½

1968, Aug. 16   Photo.

Design: 25c, Cathedral, arms of Pope Paul VI and arms of Haiti.

590 A123 5c grn & multi .20 .20
591 A124 10c brn & multi .20 .20
592 A124 25c multi .25 .20
    Nos. 590-592,C302-C305 (7) 3.55 2.80

Consecration of the Bishopric of Haiti, 10/28/66.

Air Terminal, Port-au-Prince — A125

1968, Sept. 22   Photo.   Perf. 11½
Portrait in Black
593 A125 5c brn & lt ultra .20 .20
594 A125 10c brn & lt bl .20 .20
595 A125 25c brn & pale lil .25 .20
    Nos. 593-595,C306-C308 (6) 2.60 2.10

Inauguration of the Francois Duvalier Airport in Port-au-Prince.

Slave Breaking Chains, Map of Haiti, Torch, Conch — A126

1968, Oct. 28   Litho.   Perf. 14½x14
596 A126 5c brn, lt bl & brt pink .20 .20
597 A126 10c brn, lt ol & brt pink .20 .20
598 A126 25c brn, bis & brt pink .25 .20
    Nos. 596-598,C310-C313 (7) 3.00 2.30

Slaves' Rebellion, of 1791.

Children Learning to Read A127

10c, Children watching television. 50c, Hands setting volleyball and sports medal.

1968, Nov. 14   Perf. 11½
599 A127 5c multi .20 .20
600 A127 10c multi .20 .20
601 A127 50c multi .40 .20
    Nos. 599-601,C314-C316 (6) 2.35 1.70

Issued to publicize education through literacy, audio-visual means and sport.
For surcharges see #B41-B42, CB61-CB62.

Winston Churchill — A128

Churchill: 5c, as painter. 10c, as Knight of the Garter. 15c, and soldiers at Normandy. 20c, and early seaplane. 25c, and Queen Elizabeth II. 50c, and Big Ben, London.

1968, Dec. 23   Photo.   Perf. 13
602 A128 3c gold & multi .20 .20
603 A128 5c gold & multi .20 .20
604 A128 10c gold & multi .20 .20
605 A128 15c gold & multi .20 .20
606 A128 20c gold & multi .20 .20
607 A128 25c gold & multi .25 .20
608 A128 50c gold & multi .40 .20
    Nos. 602-608,C319-C322 (11) 4.00 3.10

Exist imperf. For surcharge see No. 828.

1968 Winter Olympics, Grenoble A128a

Designs: 5c, 1.50g, Peggy Fleming, US, figure skating. 10c, Harold Groenningen, Norway, cross-country skiing. 20c, Belousova & Protopopov, USSR, pairs figure skating. 25c, Toini Gustafsson, Sweden, cross country skiing. 50c, Eugenio Monti, Italy, 4-man bobsled. 2g, Erhard Keller, Germany, speed skating. 4g, Jean-Claude Killy, France, downhill skiing.

1968, Nov. 11   Litho.   Perf. 14x13½
609   A128a 5c brt bl & multi .20 .20
609A A128a 10c bl grn & multi .20 .20

609B	A128a	20c brt rose & multi	.20	.20
609C	A128a	25c sky bl & multi	.25	.20
609D	A128a	50c ol bis & multi	.45	.30
609E	A128a	1.50g vio & multi	1.10	.65

Size: 36x65mm
Perf. 12x12½

609F	A128a	2g emer grn & multi	2.25	2.25
	Nos. 609-609F (7)		4.65	4.00

Souvenir Sheet

609G	A128a	4g brn & multi	20.00	20.00

No. 609G contains one 36x65mm stamp. Nos. 609F-609G are airmail. No. 609G exists imperf. with green, brown and blue margin.

No. 589 Surcharged with New Value and Rectangle

1969, Feb. 21   Photo.   Perf. 11½

610	A122	70c on 50c	.50	.40
	Nos. 610,C324-C325 (3)		1.80	1.30

Blue-headed Euphonia — A129

Birds of Haiti: 10c, Hispaniolan trogon. 20c, Palm chat. 25c, Stripe-headed tanager. 50c, Like 5c.

1969, Feb. 26   Perf. 13½

611	A129	5c lt grn & multi	2.00	.50
612	A129	10c yel & multi	2.00	.50
613	A129	20c cream & multi	2.25	.50
614	A129	25c lt lil & multi	2.50	.60
615	A129	50c lt gray & multi	3.50	.60
	Nos. 611-615,C326-C329 (9)		28.50	9.45

For overprints see Nos. C344A-C344D.

Olympic Marathon Winners, 1896-1968 — A130

Designs: Games location, date, winner, country and time over various stamp designs. Souvenir sheets do not show location, date, country or time.

1969, May 16   Perf. 12½x12
Size: 66x35mm (Nos. 616, 616C, 616F, 616O)

616	A130	5c like Greece #124	.20	.20
616A	A130	10c like France #124	.25	.20
616B	A130	15c US #327	.25	.20
616C	A130	20c like Great Britain #142	.50	.25
616D	A130	20c Sweden #68	.50	.25
616E	A130	25c Belgium #B49	.80	.35
616F	A130	25c like France #198	.80	.35
616G	A130	25c Netherlands #B30	.80	.35
616H	A130	30c US #718	.90	.40
616I	A130	50c Germany #B86	1.40	.60
616J	A130	60c Great Britain #274	1.75	.85
616K	A130	75c like Finland #B110	2.50	1.25
616L	A130	75c like Australia #277	2.50	1.25
616M	A130	90c Italy #799	2.75	1.40
616N	A130	1g like Japan #822	3.75	1.60
616O	A130	1.25g like Mexico #C328	5.00	2.50
	Nos. 616-616O (16)		24.65	12.00

Souvenir Sheets

616P	A130	1.50g US #718, diff.	16.00	9.00

Imperf

616Q	A130	1.50g Germany #B86, diff.	16.00	9.00

Nos. 616H-616O are airmail. Nos. 616P-616Q contain one 66x35mm stamp. A 2g souvenir sheet exists, perf. & imperf. Value, each $9.

Power Lines and Light Bulb — A131

1969, May 22   Litho.   Perf. 13x13½

617	A131	20c lilac & blue	.20	.20

Issued to publicize the Duvalier Hydroelectric Station. See Nos. C338-C340.

Learning to Write — A132

Designs: 10c, children playing, vert. 50c, Peace poster on educational television, vert.

1969, Aug. 12   Litho.   Perf. 13½

618	A132	5c multi	.20	.20
619	A132	10c multi	.20	.20
620	A132	50c multi	.25	.20
	Nos. 618-620,C342-C344 (6)		2.25	1.70

Issued to publicize national education.

ILO Emblem A133

1969, Sept. 22   Perf. 14

621	A133	5c bl grn & blk	.20	.20
622	A133	10c brn & blk	.20	.20
623	A133	20c vio bl & blk	.20	.20
	Nos. 621-623,C345-C347 (6)		2.95	1.70

50th anniv. of the ILO.

Apollo Space Missions — A133a

Designs: 10c, Apollo 7 rendezvous of command module, third stage. 15c, Apollo 7, preparation for re-entry. 20c, Apollo 8, separation of third stage. 25c, Apollo 8, mid-course correction. 70c, Apollo 8, approaching moon. 1g, Apollo 8, orbiting moon, Christmas 1968, vert. 1.25, Apollo 8, leaving moon. 1.50g, Apollo 8, crew, vert. 1.75g, 2g, Apollo 11, first lunar landing.

1969, Oct. 6   Perf. 12x12½

624	A133a	10c brt rose & multi	.20	.20
624A	A133a	15c vio & multi	.20	.20
624B	A133a	20c ver & multi	.25	.20
624C	A133a	25c emer grn & multi	.25	.20
624D	A133a	70c brt bl & multi	.25	.20
624E	A133a	1g bl grn & multi	.55	.30
624F	A133a	1.25g dk bl & multi	.65	.40
624G	A133a	1.50g dp rose lil & multi	.80	.50

Souvenir Sheets

624H	A133a	1.75g grn & multi	12.00	8.00
624I	A133a	2g sky bl & multi	12.00	8.00
	Nos. 624-624I (10)		27.15	18.20

Nos. 624D-624I are airmail. Nos. 624-624I exist imperf. in different colors.

Papilio Zonaria — A134

Butterflies: 20c, Zerene cesonia cynops. 25c, Papilio machaonides.

1969, Nov. 14   Photo.   Perf. 13½

625	A134	10c pink & multi	3.50	.75
626	A134	20c gray & multi	6.00	2.00
627	A134	25c lt bl & multi	9.00	2.10
	Nos. 625-627,C348-C350 (6)		93.50	15.60

Martin Luther King, Jr. A135

1970, Jan. 12   Litho.   Perf. 12½x13½

628	A135	10c bis, red & blk	.20	.20
629	A135	20c grnsh bl, red & blk	.20	.20
630	A135	25c brt rose, red & blk	.20	.20
	Nos. 628-630,C351-C353 (6)		3.05	2.25

Martin Luther King, Jr. (1929-1968), American civil rights leader.

Laeliopsis Dominguensis A136   UPU Monument and Map of Haiti A137

Haitian Orchids: 20c, Oncidium Haitiense. 25c, Oncidium calochilum.

1970, Apr. 3   Litho.   Perf. 13x12½

631	A136	10c yel, lil & blk	.20	.20
632	A136	20c lt bl grn, yel & brn	2.00	2.00
633	A136	25c bl & multi	2.50	2.00
	Nos. 631-633,C354-C356 (6)		15.45	10.40

1970, June 23   Photo.   Perf. 11½

Designs: 25c, Propeller and UPU emblem, vert. 50c, Globe and doves.

634	A137	10c blk, brt grn & ol bis	.20	.20
635	A137	25c blk, brt rose & ol bis	.20	.20
636	A137	50c blk & bl	.35	.25
	Nos. 634-636,C357-C359 (6)		2.70	1.95

16th Cong. of the UPU, Tokyo, Oct. 1-Nov. 16, 1970.
For overprints see Nos. 640, C360-C362.

Map of Haiti, Dam and Generator A138

Design: 25c, Map of Haiti, dam and pylon.

1970   Litho.   Perf. 14x13½

637	A138	20c lt grn & multi	.20	.20
638	A138	25c lt bl & multi	.25	.20

François Duvalier Central Hydroelectric Plant.
For surcharges see #B43-B44, RA40-RA41.

Apollo 12 — A138a

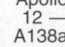

1970, Sept. 7   Perf. 13½x14

639	A138a	5c Lift-off	.20	.20
639A	A138a	10c 2nd stage ignition	.20	.20
639B	A138a	15c Docking preparations	.25	.20
639C	A138a	20c Heading for moon	.35	.20
639D	A138a	25c like 639B	.45	.20
639E	A138a	25c Lunar exploration	.25	.20
639F	A138a	30c Landing on Moon	.65	.25
639G	A138a	30c Lift-off from Moon	.45	.25
639H	A138a	40c 3rd stage separation	.90	.35
639I	A138a	40c Lunar module, crew	.55	.35
639J	A138a	50c Lunar orbital activities	1.10	.35
639K	A138a	50c Leaving Moon orbit	.65	.35
639L	A138a	75c In Earth orbit	1.10	.40
639M	A138a	1g Re-entry	1.50	.50
639N	A138a	1.25g Landing at sea	2.25	.75
639O	A138a	1.50g Docking with lunar module	2.40	.75
	Nos. 639-639O (16)		13.25	5.40

Nos. 639E, 639G, 639I, 639K-639O are airmail. Nos. 639-639O exist imperf. with brighter colors. Value, unused $16.
For overprints see Nos. 656-656O.

No. 636 Overprinted in Red with UN Emblem and: "XXVe ANNIVERSAIRE / O.N.U."

1970, Dec. 14   Photo.   Perf. 11½

640	A137	50c blk & bl	.35	.20
	Nos. 640,C360-C362 (4)		2.30	1.50

UN, 25th anniv.

Fort Nativity, Drawing by Columbus — A139   Ascension, by Castera Bazile — A140

1970, Dec. 22

641	A139	3c dk brn & buff	.20	.20
642	A139	5c dk grn & pale grn	.30	.20

Christmas 1970.

1971, Apr. 29   Litho.   Perf. 12x12½

Paintings: 5c, Man with Turban, by Rembrandt. 20c, Iris in a Vase, by Van Gogh. 50c, Baptism of Christ, by Castera Bazile. No. 647, Young Mother Sewing, by Mary Cassatt. No. 648, The Card Players, by Cezanne.

Size: 20x40mm

643	A140	5c multi	.20	.20
644	A140	10c multi	.20	.20

Perf. 13x12½
Size: 25x37mm

645	A140	20c multi	.20	.20

Perf. 12x12½
Size: 20x40mm

646	A140	50c multi	.50	.20
	Nos. 643-646,C366-C368 (7)		3.50	2.45

Souvenir Sheets
Imperf

647	A140	3g multi	5.00	5.00
648	A140	3g multi	5.00	5.00

No. 647 contains one stamp, size: 20x40mm. No. 648 size: 25x37mm.
Nos. 643-646, C366-C368 exist imperf. in changed colors.

Soccer Ball — A141

Design: No. 651, 1g, 5g, Jules Rimet cup.

1971, June 14   Photo.   Perf. 11½
649	A141	5c salmon & blk	.20	.20
650	A141	50c tan & blk	.50	.35
651	A141	50c rose pink, blk & gold	.50	.35
652	A141	1g lil, blk & gold	.65	.45
653	A141	1.50g gray & blk	.80	.55
654	A141	5g gray, blk & gold	2.40	1.60
		Nos. 649-654 (6)	5.05	3.50

Souvenir Sheet
Imperf
655		Sheet of 2	12.00	8.50
a.	A141	70c light violet & black	4.00	3.00
b.	A141	1g light green, blue & gold	4.00	3.00

9th World Soccer Championships for the Jules Rimet Cup, Mexico City, May 30-June 21, 1970. The surface tint of the sheets of 50 (10x5) of Nos. 649-654 includes a map of Brazil covering 26 stamps. Positions 27, 37 and 38 inscribed "Brasilia," "Santos," "Rio de Janeiro" respectively. On soccer ball design the 4 corner stamps are inscribed "Pele."

Nos. 655a and 655b have portions of map of Brazil in background; No. 655a inscribed "Pele" and "Santos," No. 655b "Brasilia."

Nos. 639-639O Ovptd. in Gold

1971, Mar. 15
656	A138a	5c multi	.20	.20
656A	A138a	10c multi	.20	.20
656B	A138a	15c multi	.25	.20
656C	A138a	20c multi	.35	.20
656D	A138a	25c multi	.45	.20
656E	A138a	25c multi	.25	.20
656F	A138a	30c multi	.65	.25
656G	A138a	30c multi	.45	.25
656H	A138a	40c multi	.90	.35
656I	A138a	40c multi	.55	.35
656J	A138a	50c multi	1.10	.35
656K	A138a	50c multi	.65	.35
656L	A138a	75c multi	1.10	.40
656M	A138a	1g multi	1.50	.50
656N	A138a	1.25g multi	2.25	.75
656O	A138a	1.50g multi	2.40	.75
		Nos. 656-656O (16)	13.25	5.50

Nos. 656E, 656G, 656I, 656K-656O are airmail.
Exist overprinted in silver. Value, unused $16.

J. J. Dessalines — A142

1972, Apr. 28   Photo.   Perf. 11½
657	A142	5c grn & blk	.20	.20
658	A142	10c brt bl & blk	.20	.20
659	A142	25c org & blk	.20	.20
		Nos. 657-659,C378-C379 (5)	2.05	1.45

See Nos. 697-700, C448-C458, 727, C490-C493, C513-C514. For surcharges see Nos. 692, 705-709, 724-726, C438, C512.

"Sun" and EXPO '70 Emblem — A143

1972, Oct. 27   Photo.   Perf. 11½
660	A143	10c ocher, brn & grn	.20	.20
661	A143	25c ocher, brn & mar	.20	.20
		Nos. 660-661,C387-C390 (6)	2.90	1.95

EXPO '70 International Exposition, Osaka, Japan, Mar. 15-Sept. 13, 1970.

Gold Medalists, 1972 Summer Olympics, Munich — A143a

Designs: 5c, L. Linsenhoff, dressage, W. Ruska, judo. 10c, S. Kato, gymnastics, S.Gould, women's swimming. 20c, M. Peters, women's pentathlon, K. Keino, steeplechase. 25c, L. Viren, 5,000, 10,000m races, R. Milburn, 110m hurdles. No. 662D, D. Morelon, cycling, J. Akii-Bua, 400m hurdles. No. 662E, R. Williams, long jump. 75c, G. Mancinelli, equestrian. 1.50g, W. Nordwig, pole vault. 2.50g, K. Wolferman, javelin. 5g, M. Spitz, swimming.

1972, Dec. 29   Perf. 13½
662	A143a	5c multicolored	.20	.20
662A	A143a	10c multicolored	.20	.20
662B	A143a	20c multicolored	.20	.20
662C	A143a	25c multicolored	.20	.20
662D	A143a	50c multicolored	.25	.20
662E	A143a	50c multicolored	.70	.20
662F	A143a	75c multicolored	1.00	.20
662G	A143a	1.50g multicolored	1.50	.70
662H	A143a	2.50g multicolored	3.00	1.10
662I	A143a	5g multicolored	5.75	1.60
		Nos. 662-662I (10)	13.00	4.80

Nos. 662E-662I are airmail.

Basket Vendors A144

Designs: 80c, 2.50g, Postal bus.

1973, Jan.   Photo.   Perf. 11½
665	A144	50c blk & multi	.35	.20
666	A144	80c blk & multi	.45	.35
667	A144	1.50g blk & multi	.70	.45
668	A144	2.50g blk & multi	1.50	.80
		Nos. 665-668 (4)	3.00	1.80

20th anniv. of Caribbean Travel Assoc.

Space Exploration
A set of 12 stamps for US-USSR space exploration, the same overprinted for the centenary of the UPU and 3 overprinted in silver for Apollo 17 exist but we have no evidence that they were printed with the approval of the Haitian postal authorities. Value, $10 and $6, respectively.

Micromelo Undata A145

Designs: Marine life; 50c horizontal.

1973, Sept. 4   Litho.   Perf. 14
669	A145	5c shown	.25	.20
670	A145	10c Nemaster rubiginosa	.25	.20
671	A145	25c Cyerce cristallina	.50	.20
672	A145	50c Desmophyllum riisei	1.00	.20
		Nos. 669-672,C395-C398 (8)	8.90	1.90

For surcharge see No. C439.

Gramma Loreto — A146

1973   Perf. 13½
673	A146	10c shown	.50	.20
674	A146	50c Acanthurus coeruleus	.65	.50
		Nos. 673-674,C399-C402 (6)	8.00	4.50

For surcharges see Nos. 693, C440.

Soccer Stadium A147

Design: 20c, Haiti No. 654.

1973, Nov. 29   Perf. 14x13
675	A147	10c bis, blk & emer	.20	.20
676	A147	20c rose lil, blk & tan	.20	.20
		Nos. 675-676,C407-C410 (6)	5.40	3.65

Caribbean countries preliminary games of the World Soccer Championships, Munich, 1974.

Jean Jacques Dessalines A148   Nicolaus Copernicus A149

1974, Apr. 22   Photo.   Perf. 14
677	A148	10c lt bl & emer	.20	.20
678	A148	20c rose & blk	.20	.20
679	A148	25c yel & vio	.20	.20
		Nos. 677-679,C411-C414 (7)	2.90	2.15

For surcharges see Nos. 694, C443.

1974, May 24   Litho.   Perf. 14x13½
Design: 10c, Symbol of heliocentric system.
680	A149	10c multi	.20	.20
681	A149	25c brt grn & multi	.20	.20
		Nos. 680-681,C415-C419 (7)	3.05	2.15

For overprint and surcharges see Nos. 695, C444, C460-C463.

Pres. Jean-Claude Duvalier — A151

1974   Photo.   Perf. 14x13½
689	A151	10c grn & gold	.25	.20
690	A151	20c car rose & gold	.30	.20
691	A151	50c bl & gold	.40	.20
		Nos. 689-691,C421-C426 (9)	7.40	4.40

For surcharge and overprints see Nos. C445, C487-C489.

Audubon Birds
In 1975 or later various sets of bird paintings by Audubon were produced by government employees without official authorization. They were not sold by the Haiti post office and were not valid for postage. The first set consisted of 23 values and was sold in 1975. A second set containing some of the original stamps and some new stamps appeared unannounced several years later. More sets may have been printed as there are 75 different stamps. These consist of 5 denominations each for the 15 designs.
Perf and imperf souvenir sheets picturing Audubon were also produced.

Nos. 659, 673 and 679-680 Surcharged with New Value and Bar
Perf. 11½, 13½, 14, 14x13½
1976   Photo.; Litho.
692	A142	80c on 25c	.55	.35
693	A146	80c on 10c	.55	.35
694	A148	80c on 25c	.55	.35
695	A149	80c on 10c	.55	.35
		Nos. 692-695 (4)	2.20	1.40

Haiti No. C11 and Bicentennial Emblem — A152

1976, Apr. 22   Photo.   Perf. 11½
Granite Paper
696	A152	10c multi	.25	.20
		Nos. 696,C434-C437 (5)	4.70	3.20

American Bicentennial.

Dessalines Type of 1972
1977   Photo.   Perf. 11½
697	A142	10c rose & blk	.20	.20
698	A142	20c lemon & blk	.20	.20
699	A142	50c vio & blk	.35	.20
700	A142	50c tan & blk	.35	.20
		Nos. 697-700 (4)	1.10	.80

Dessalines Type of 1972 Surcharged in Black or Red
1978   Photo.   Perf. 11½
705	A142	1g on 20c (#698)	.65	.35
706	A142	1g on 1.75g (#C454)	.65	.35
707	A142	1.25g on 75c (#C448)	.65	.35
708	A142	1.25g on 1.50g (#C453)	.65	.35
709	A142	1.25g on 1.50g (#C453; R)	.65	.35
		Nos. 705-709 (5)	3.25	1.75

Rectangular bar obliterates old denomination on Nos. 705-709 and "Par Avion" on Nos. 706-709.

J. C. Duvalier Earth
Telecommunications Station — A153

Designs: 20c, Video telephone. 50c, Alexander Graham Bell, vert.

1978, June 19   Litho.   Perf. 13½
710 A153 10c multi .25 .20
711 A153 20c multi .25 .20
712 A153 50c multi .35 .20
Nos. 710-712,C466-C468 (6) 2.70 1.95

Centenary of first telephone call by Alexander Graham Bell, Mar. 10, 1876.

Athletes'
Inaugural
Parade — A154

1978, Sept. 4   Litho.   Perf. 13½x13
713 A154 5c shown .20 .20
714 A154 25c Bicyclists .20 .20
715 A154 50c Pole Vault .40 .20
Nos. 713-715,C469-C471 (6) 6.50 3.95

21st Olympic Games, Montreal, 7/17-8/1/76.

Mother Nursing
Child — A155

Mother Feeding
Child — A156

1979, Jan. 15   Photo.   Perf. 14x14½
716 A155 25c multi .25 .20
Nos. 716,C472-C473 (3) 1.60 1.10

Inter-American Children's Inst., 50th anniv.

1979, May 11   Photo.   Perf. 11½
717 A156 25c multi .20 .20
718 A156 50c multi .35 .20
Nos. 717-718,C474-C476 (5) 3.55 2.45

30th anniversary of CARE (Cooperative for American Relief Everywhere).

Human Rights
Emblem — A157

1979, July 20   Litho.   Perf. 14
719 A157 25c multi .30 .20
Nos. 719,C477-C479 (4) 3.30 2.25

30th anniversary of declaration of human rights.

Anti-Apartheid
Year Emblem,
Antenor
Firmin, "On
the Equality of
Human
Races"
A158

1979, Nov. 22   Photo.   Perf. 12x11½
720 A158 50c tan & black .50 .20
Nos. 720,C480-C482 (4) 4.35 2.25

Anti-Apartheid Year (1978).

Children
Playing, IYC
Emblem
A159

1979, Dec. 19   Photo.   Perf. 12
721 A159 10c multi .25 .20
722 A159 25c multi .25 .20
723 A159 50c multi .40 .20
Nos. 721-723,C483-C486 (7) 8.50 4.50

International Year of the Child.

Nos. C379, C449,
C454 Surcharged

1980   Photo.   Perf. 11½
Granite Paper
724 A142 1g on 2.50g lil & blk .55 .45
725 A142 1.25g on 80c emer &
blk .65 .55
726 A142 1.25g on 1.75g rose &
blk .65 .55
Nos. 724-726 (3) 1.85 1.55

Dessalines Type of 1972

1980, Aug. 27   Photo.   Perf. 11½
Granite Paper
727 A142 25c org yel & blk .30 .20
Nos. 727,C490-C493 (5) 5.10 3.65

Henry Christophe Citadel — A160

1980, Dec. 2   Litho.   Perf. 12½x12
728 A160 5c shown .20 .20
729 A160 25c Sans Souci Palace .20 .20
730 A160 50c Vallieres market .35 .20
Nos. 728-730,C494-C498 (8) 5.50 4.10

World Tourism Conf., Manila, Sept. 27.
For surcharges see Nos. 738, C511.

Soccer Players, World Cup, Flag of
Uruguay (1930 Champion) — A161

1980, Dec. 30   Litho.   Perf. 14
731 A161 10c shown .20 .20
732 A161 20c Italy, 1934 .20 .20
733 A161 25c Italy, 1938 .20 .20
Nos. 731-733,C499-C506 (11) 10.10 6.70

World Cup Soccer Championship, 50th anniv.
For surcharges see Nos. 741, 829.

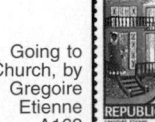

Going to
Church, by
Gregoire
Etienne
A162

Paintings: 5c, Woman with Birds and Flowers, by Hector Hyppolite, vert. 20c, Street Market, by Petion Savain. 25c, Market Vendors, by Michele Manuel.

1981, May 12   Photo.   Perf. 11½
734 A162 5c multi .20 .20
735 A162 10c multi .20 .20
736 A162 20c multi .20 .20
737 A162 25c multi .20 .20
Nos. 734-737,C507-C510 (8) 5.45 4.00

For surcharges see Nos. 739-740.

Nos. 728, 734-735, 732 Surcharged
Perf. 12½x12, 14, 11½
1981, Dec. 30   Litho., Photo.
738 A160 1.25g on 5c multi .65 .55
739 A162 1.25g on 20c multi .65 .55
740 A162 1.25g on 10c multi .65 .55
741 A161 1.25g on 20c multi .65 .55
Nos. 738-741,C511-C512 (6) 4.45 3.60

10th Anniv. of
Pres. Duvalier
Reforms — A163

1982, June 21   Photo.   Perf. 11½x12
Granite Paper
742 A163 25c yel grn & blk .20 .20
743 A163 50c olive & blk .35 .20
744 A163 1g rose & blk .55 .45
745 A163 1.25g bl & blk .65 .55
746 A163 2g org red & blk 1.10 .85
747 A163 5g org & blk 2.40 1.60
Nos. 742-747 (6) 5.25 3.85

Nos. 742, 744-746 Overprinted in
Blue: "1957-1982 / 25 ANS DE
REVOLUTION"
1982, Nov. 29   Photo.   Perf. 11½x12
Granite Paper
748 A163 25c yel grn & blk .20 .20
749 A163 1g rose & blk .55 .45
750 A163 1.25g blue & blk .65 .55
751 A163 2g org red & blk 1.10 .85
Nos. 748-751 (4) 2.50 2.05

25th anniv. of revolution.

Scouting
Year
A164

Perf. 13½x14, 14x13½
1983, Feb. 26   Litho.
752 A164 5c Building campfire .20 .20
753 A164 10c Baden-Powell,
vert. .20 .20
754 A164 25c Boat building .20 .20
755 A164 50c like 10c .50 .20
756 A164 75c like 25c 1.25 .25
757 A164 1g like 5c 1.50 .30
758 A164 1.25g like 25c 2.00 .35
759 A164 2g like 10c 2.75 .60
Nos. 752-759 (8) 8.60 2.30

Nos. 756-759 airmail.
For surcharge see No. 827.

Patroness of Haiti — A165

1983, Mar. 9   Litho.   Perf. 14
760 A165 10c multi .20 .20
761 A165 20c multi .20 .20
762 A165 25c multi .20 .20
763 A165 50c multi .20 .20
764 A165 75c multi .35 .20
765 A165 1g multi .60 .20
766 A165 1.25g multi .70 .30
767 A165 1.50g multi 1.00 .35
768 A165 1.75g multi 1.40 .40

769 A165 2g multi 1.75 .50
770 A165 5g multi 2.75 1.00
  a. Souvenir sheet, 116x90mm 11.00 11.00
  j. Souvenir sheet, 90x116mm 11.00 11.00
Nos. 760-770 (11) 9.35 3.75

Centenary of the Miracle of Our Lady of Perpetual Help. Nos. 764-770 airmail.
For surcharge see No. 875.

UPU
Admission,
100th
Anniv.
A165a

1983, June 10   Litho.   Perf. 15x14
770B A165a 5c shown .50 .20
770C A165a 10c L.F. Salomon, J.C.
Duvalier .50 .20
770D A165a 25c No. 1, UPU
emblem .50 .20
770E A165a 50c like 10c .50 .20
770F A165a 75c like 10c .60 .25
770G A165a 1g like 5c .80 .25
770H A165a 1.25g like 25c 1.00 .30
770I A165a 2g like 25c 1.60 .40
Nos. 770B-770I (8) 6.00 2.00

Nos. 770F-770I airmail.
For surcharge see No. 825.

1982 World
Cup — A166

Games and scores. Nos. 776-780 airmail, horiz.

1983, Nov. 22   Litho.   Perf. 14
771 A166 5c Argentina, Belgium .20 .20
772 A166 10c Northern Ireland, Yugoslavia .20 .20
773 A166 20c England, France .20 .20
774 A166 25c Spain, Northern Ireland .20 .20
775 A166 50c Italy (champion) .35 .20
776 A166 1g Brazil, Scotland .55 .45
777 A166 1.25g Northern Ireland, France .65 .55
778 A166 1.50g Poland, Cameroun .95 .65
779 A166 2g Italy, Germany 1.10 .85
780 A166 2.50g Argentina, Brazil 1.40 1.10
Nos. 771-780 (10) 5.80 4.60

For surcharge see No. 826.

Haiti Postage Stamp
Centenary — A167

1984, Feb. 28   Litho.   Perf. 14½
781 A167 5c #1 .30 .20
782 A167 10c #2 .30 .20
783 A167 25c #3 .30 .20
784 A167 50c #5 .30 .25
785 A167 75c Liberty, Salomon .45 .25
786 A167 1g Liberty, Salomon .60 .35
787 A167 1.25g Liberty, Duvalier .70 .40
788 A167 2g Liberty, Duvalier 1.10 .75
Nos. 781-788 (8) 4.05 2.60

Nos. 785-788 airmail.
For surcharge see No. 826A.

A168

A169

1984, May 30   Photo.   Perf. 11½
Granite Paper
789	A168	25c Broadcasting equipment, horiz.	.20	.20
790	A168	50c like 25c	.35	.30
791	A168	1g Drum	.55	.45
792	A168	1.25g like 1g	.65	.55
793	A168	2g Globe	1.10	.85
794	A168	2.50g like 2g	1.40	1.10
		Nos. 789-794 (6)	4.25	3.35

World Communications Year.

1984, July 27
Granite Paper
795	A169	5c Javelin, running, pole vault, horiz.	.20	.20
796	A169	10c like 5c	.20	.20
797	A169	25c Hurdles, horiz.	.20	.20
798	A169	50c like 25c	.75	.20
799	A169	1g Long jump	1.25	.95
800	A169	1.25g like 1g	1.75	1.25
801	A169	2g like 1g	2.40	1.75
		Nos. 795-801 (7)	6.75	4.75

Souvenir Sheet
802	A169	2.50g multi	8.00	4.25

1984 Summer Olympics. No. 802 exists imperf. Value $15.
For surcharge see No. 874.

Arrival of Europeans in America, 500th Anniv. — A170

The Unknown Indian, detail or full perspective of statue. Nos. 807-809 are vert. and airmail.

1984, Dec. 5   Litho.   Perf. 14
803	A170	5c multi	.45	.35
804	A170	10c multi	.45	.35
805	A170	25c multi	.45	.35
806	A170	50c multi	.75	.50
807	A170	1g multi	.90	.60
808	A170	1.25g multi	1.40	.75
809	A170	2g multi	5.00	2.50
a.		Souvenir sheet of #806, 809	15.00	15.00
		Nos. 803-809 (7)	9.40	5.40

For surcharge see No. 881.

Simon Bolivar and Alexander Petion — A171

Designs: 25c, 1.25g, 7.50g, Portraits reversed. 50c, 4.50g, Bolivar, flags of Grand Colombian Confederation member nations.

1985, Aug. 30   Perf. 13½x14
810	A171	5c multi	.30	.25
811	A171	25c multi	.30	.25
812	A171	50c multi	.35	.25
813	A171	1g multi	.55	.30
814	A171	1.25g multi	.60	.45
815	A171	2g multi	1.10	.85
816	A171	7.50g multi	3.25	2.10
		Nos. 810-816 (7)	6.45	4.45

Souvenir Sheet
Imperf
817	A171	4.50g multi	3.50	2.50

Nos. 813-817 airmail.
For surcharge see No. 876.

Arrival of Europeans in America, 500th Anniv. — A172

Designs: 10c, 25c, 50c, Henri, cacique of Bahoruco, hero of the Spanish period, 1492-1625. 1g, 1.25g, 2g, Henri in tropical forest.

1986, Apr. 11   Litho.   Perf. 14
818	A172	10c multi	.85	.20
819	A172	25c multi	.85	.20
820	A172	50c multi	.85	.20
821	A172	1g multi	1.50	.35
822	A172	1.25g multi	2.00	.40
823	A172	2g multi	3.00	.60
		Nos. 818-823 (6)	9.05	1.95

Nos. 821-823 are airmail. A 3g souvenir sheet exists picturing Henri in tropical forest. Value $16.
For surcharge see No. 883.

Nos. 770B, 771, 781, 756, C322, C500 Surcharged

1986, Apr. 18
825	A165a	25c on 5c No. 770B	.30	.20
826	A166	25c on 5c No. 771	.30	.20
826A	A167	25c on 5c No. 781	.30	.20
827	A164	25c on 75c No. 756	.30	.20
828	A128	25c on 1.50g No. C322	.30	.20
829	A161	25c on 75c No. C500	.30	.20
		Nos. 825-829 (6)	1.80	1.20

Intl. Youth Year — A173

UNESCO, 40th Anniv. (in 1986) — A174

1986, May 20   Litho.   Perf. 14x15
830	A173	10c Afforestation	.20	.20
831	A173	25c IYY emblem	.20	.20
832	A173	50c Girl Guides	.35	.20
833	A173	1g like 10c	.55	.45
834	A173	1.25g like 25c	.65	.55
835	A173	2g like 50c	1.10	.85
		Nos. 830-835 (6)	3.05	2.45

Souvenir Sheet
836	A173	3g multi	12.50	12.50

Nos. 833-836 are airmail.
For surcharge see No. 873.

1987, May 29   Photo.   Perf. 11½
Granite Paper
837	A174	10c multi	.20	.20
838	A174	25c multi	.20	.20
839	A174	50c multi	.35	.20
840	A174	1g multi	.55	.45
841	A174	1.25g multi	.70	.55
842	A174	2.50g multi	1.40	1.10
		Nos. 837-842 (6)	3.40	2.70

Souvenir Sheet
Granite Paper
843	A174	2g multi	3.00	3.00

Nos. 840-842 are airmail.
For surcharge see No. 882.

Charlemagne Peralte, Resistance Leader — A175

1988, Oct. 18   Litho.   Perf. 14
844	A175	25c multi	.20	.20
845	A175	50c multi	.35	.20
846	A175	1g multi	.55	.45
847	A175	2g multi	1.10	.85
a.		Souvenir sheet of 1	7.50	7.50
848	A175	3g multi	1.75	1.40
		Nos. 844-848 (5)	3.95	3.10

Nos. 846-848, 847a are airmail.

Slave Rebellion, 200th Anniv. A176

Design: 1g, 2g, 3g, Slaves around fire, vert.

1991, Aug. 22   Litho.   Perf. 12x11½
849	A176	25c brt green & multi	.60	.30
850	A176	50c pink & multi	1.00	.50

Perf. 11½x12
851	A176	1g blue & multi	2.00	1.00
852	A176	2g yellow & multi	4.00	2.00
a.		Souv. sheet of 2, #850 & 852	27.50	27.50
853	A176	3g buff & multi	7.50	3.50
		Nos. 849-853 (5)	15.10	7.30

Nos. 851-853 are airmail.

Discovery of America, 500th Anniv. A177

Designs: 25c, 50c, Ships at anchor, men coming ashore, native. 1g, 2g, 3g, Ships, beached long boats, vert.

1993, July 30   Litho.   Perf. 11½
854	A177	25c green & multi	.50	.20
855	A177	50c yellow & multi	.75	.30
856	A177	1g blue & multi	1.00	.60
857	A177	2g pink & multi	2.25	1.00
a.		Souvenir sheet of 2, #856-857	—	—
858	A177	3g orange yellow & multi	5.00	3.00
		Nos. 854-858 (5)	9.50	5.10

Nos. 856-858, 857a are airmail.

25th Genl. Assembly of the Organization of American States A178

Designs: 50c, 75c, 7.50g, Emblem, map of Haiti. 1g, 2g, 3g, 5g, Emblems, map of North, South America, vert.

Perf. 14x12½, 12½x14
1995, June 25   Litho.
859	A178	50c violet & multi	.40	.20
860	A178	75c green & multi	.60	.30
861	A178	1g gray blue & multi	.75	.45
862	A178	2g lilac rose & multi	1.50	.85
863	A178	3g green & multi	2.00	1.40
864	A178	5g violet & multi	3.25	1.90
		Nos. 859-864 (6)	8.50	5.10

Souvenir Sheet
Imperf
865	A178	7.50g green blue & multi	10.00	10.00

UN, 50th Anniv. A179

Designs: 50c, 75c, Dove holding UN, Haitian flags. 1g, 2g, 3g, 5g, Haitian, UN flags, dove carrying olive branch.

1995, Nov. 24   Litho.   Perf. 12x11½
866	A179	50c blue & multi	.50	.30
867	A179	75c lilac & multi	.75	.40
868	A179	1g apple green & multi	1.00	.60
869	A179	2g yellow & multi	2.25	1.00
870	A179	3g orange brown & multi	3.50	1.50
871	A179	5g blue green & multi	5.75	3.00
		Nos. 866-871 (6)	13.75	6.80

Souvenir Sheet
872	A179	5g multicolored	16.50	16.50

Nos. 868-872 are airmail.

Nos. 766, 800, 814, 834 Surcharged

1996   Perfs., Etc., as Before
873	A173	1g on 1.25g #834	.75	.60
874	A169	2g on 1.25g #800	1.50	1.00
875	A165	3g on 1.25g #766	2.25	1.50
876	A171	3g on 1.25g #814	2.50	1.50
		Nos. 873-876 (4)	7.00	4.60

Size and location of surcharge varies. Nos. 873, 875-876 are airmail.

1996 Summer Olympic Games, Atlanta — A180

1996, Aug. 2   Litho.   Perf. 14
877	A180	3g Hurdler	.75	.45
878	A180	10g Athlete up close	2.50	1.60

Volleyball Federation, 1996 Summer Olympics, Atlanta — A181

#879: a, 50c, Three players in yellow shirts. b, 75c, Three players in red shirts. c, 1g, Two players in white shirts, torch. d, 2g, Players in yellow, in red.
15g, Player in red.

1996, Aug. 2
879	A181	Sheet of 4, #a.-d.	17.50	17.50

Souvenir Sheet
880	A181	15g multicolored	17.50	17.50

Volleyball, cent. (#880).

Nos. 803, 818, 837 Surcharged

1996, Nov. Litho. Perfs. as Before
881 A170 1g on 5c #803 .75 .60
882 A174 4g on 10c #837 3.00 2.00
883 A172 6g on 10c #818 4.00 3.00
Nos. 881-883 (3) 7.75 5.60
Size and location of surcharge varies.

Christmas
A182

Paintings: 2g, The Virgin and Infant, by Jacopo Bellini. 3g, Adoration of the Shepherds, by Strozzi. 6g, Virgin and the Infant, by Giovanni Bellini. 10g, Virgin and the Infant, by Francesco Mazzola. #888, Adoration of the Magi, by Gentile da Fabriano.
#889 The Nativity, by Jan de Beer, horiz.

1996, Dec. 16 Litho. Perf. 13½x14
884 A182 2g multicolored .50 .30
885 A182 3g multicolored .75 .60
886 A182 6g multicolored 1.50 1.25
887 A182 10g multicolored 3.00 1.50
888 A182 25g multicolored 6.50 4.25
Nos. 884-888 (5) 12.25 7.90

Souvenir Sheet
Perf. 14x13½
889 A182 25g multicolored 10.00 10.00

UNICEF, 50th Anniv. — A183

1997, Jan. 28 Perf. 14
890 A183 4g green & multi 1.25 .75
891 A183 5g pink & multi 1.75 1.00
892 A183 6g blue & multi 2.25 1.50
893 A183 10g brown & multi 3.75 2.00
894 A183 20g bister & multi 7.00 3.50
Nos. 890-894 (5) 12.25 7.35
Nos. 890-894 (5) 16.00 8.75

Souvenir Sheet
895 A183 25g like #890-894, vert. 10.00 10.00

#890-894 were each issued in sheets of 6.

Grimm's Fairy
Tales — A184

2g, #902a, Sleeping Beauty. 3g, #902b, Snow White. 4g, #902c, Prince awakening Sleeping Beauty. 6g, #902d, Old man sleeping from "The Drink of Life." 10g, #902e, Cinderella. 20g, #902f, Old man awakened after taking drink.
No. 903, Cottage of the Seven Dwarfs, horiz.

1998, Jan. 5 Litho. Perf. 13½
896-901 A184 Set of 6 30.00 30.00

Size: 38x50mm
Perf. 14
902 A184 Sheet of 6, #a.-f. 35.00 35.00
Souvenir Sheet
903 A184 25g multicolored 27.50 27.50

Abstract
paintings
A185

1998, Oct. 30 Litho. Perf. 12½
2g, "Coconut on Pastel Stairs," by Luce Turnier. 3g, "Ogou," by Rose Marie Desruisseau. 5g, "Lantern," by Hilda Williams. 6g, Woman using artist's brush and palette.
15g, Fish, flower and geometric design with faces, snakes by Philippe Dodar.

904 A185 2g multicolored 3.00 1.50
905 A185 3g multicolored 5.00 2.00
906 A185 5g multicolored 7.00 2.75
907 A185 6g multicolored 12.00 4.00
Nos. 904-907 (4) 27.00 10.25

Souvenir Sheet
Perf. 13
908 A185 15g multicolored 40.00 35.00
Tourism. Nos. 904-907 exist in imperf. souvenir sheet of 4. No. 908 contains one 28x36mm stamp.

Birds
A186

Designs: 2g, Priotelus roseigaster. 4g, Xenoligeo mantana. 10g, Phoenicophilus poliocephalus. 20g, Phoenicopterus ruber.

1999, Aug. 27 Litho. Perf. 14
909 A186 2g multicolored .75 .75
910 A186 4g multicolored 1.50 1.50
911 A186 10g multicolored 4.00 4.00
912 A186 20g multicolored 7.00 7.00
a. Souvenir sheet, #909-912 15.00 15.00
Nos. 909-912 (4) 13.25 13.25

Nos. 911-912 are airmail.

Worldwide Fund for Nature — A187

No. 913: a, 2g, Hyla vasta. b, 4g, Head of Hyla vasta. c, 2g, Cyclura ricordii. d, 4g, Head of Cyclura ricordii.

1999, Aug. 27 Litho. Perf. 14
913 A187 Block of 4, #a.-d. 3.00 3.00
Issued in sheets of 16 (4x4) and 8 (2x4).

Souvenir Sheet

Protection of Natural
Resources — A188

1999 Litho. Perf. 13¾
914 A188 20g multicolored 7.50 7.50

Christmas
A188a A188b

1999 Photo. Perf. 11¾
Panel Color
914A A188a 1g Prussian blue .20 .20
914B A188a 3g red brown .50 .50
914C A188a 5g dark blue 1.50 1.50
914D A188b 10g dk purple 3.00 3.00
914E A188b 15g red 3.75 3.75
914F A188b 20g blue 5.50 5.50
Nos. 914A-914F (6) 11.20 11.20
Nos. 914A-914F (6) 14.45 14.45
914Fg Souvenir sheet, #915A-915F 14.00 14.00
Nos. 914D-914F are airmail.

Chinese Inventions — A189

No. 915, 2g, Movable type. No. 916, 3g, Paper. No. 917, 6g, Gunpowder, cannon. No. 918, 10g, Compass.

1999, Dec. 20 Litho. Perf. 13¾
915-918 A189 Set of 4 15.00 15.00
a. Souv. sheet, #915-918 20.00 20.00
UPU, 125th anniv.

Tourism
A190

Designs: 2g, Pirogue. 3g, Smiling girl. 4g, Zim Pond, vert. 5g, Ardardins Island, vert. 6g, Gingerbread House. 10g, National Palace.20g, Peligre Reservoir, vert.

Perf. 14¼x14½, 14½x14¼
2000, June 5 Litho.
919-925 A190 Set of 7 11.00 11.00
a. Souv. sheet, #919-925 + label 12.50 12.50
Souvenir Sheet
926 A190 25g Boat "Pays," vert. 12.00 12.00

1801
Constitution,
Bicent.
A191

Designs: 1g, 2g, 5g, 10g, 25g, 50g, Toussaint L'Ouverture and 1801 Constitution.
No. 933: a, Toussaint L'Ouverture. b, 1801 Constitution.

2001 Litho. Perf. 13¾x13¼
927 A191 1g multi — —
928 A191 2g multi — —
929 A191 5g multi — —
930 A191 10g multi — —
931 A191 25g multi — —
932 A191 50g multi — —
Souvenir Sheet
Perf. 12¾
933 A191 25g Sheet of 2, #a-b — —
Nos. 929-932 are airmail. No. 933 contains two 25x29mm stamps.

Toussaint
L'Ouverture
(c. 1743-
1803)
A192

Background color: 1g, Green. 2g, Brown. 3g, Yellow green. 5g, Red brown. 6g, blue. 10g, Violet.

2003, Apr. 7 Litho. Perf. 13
934-939 A192 Set of 6 30.00 30.00
Souvenir Sheet
Imperf
940 A192 15g multi 15.00 15.00

Pope John Paul II and Pope Benedict XVI Stamps

In 2005 a set of 8 face-different stamps with the image of John Paul II and 8 face different stamps with the image of Benedict XVI were printed without official authorization. They were printed in sheetlets numbered 1-40, with either three or six stamps per sheet. Selvage of various sheets containing the same stamps bear text in either French, English, Latin, Polish, Italian or Spanish. They were not sold by the Haiti post office and were not valid for postage.

The following items inscribed "Republic of Haiti" have been declared "illegal" by Haitian postal authorities:
Sheets of six 8g stamps depicting Pope John Paul II, and Pope Benedict XVI.
Sheets of six 10g stamps depicting Pope John Paul II, and Pope Benedict XVI.
Sheets of six 15g stamps depicting Pope John Paul II, and Pope Benedict XVI.
Sheet of three 20g stamps depicting Pope John Paul II.
Sheet of three 30g stamps depicting Pope John Paul II.
Sheets of two 25g stamps depicting Pope Benedict XVI (2 different).

A sheet of seven stamps of various denominations and two labels and a sheet of eight 25g stamp and one label commemorating the Jan. 12, 2010 Haiti earthquake have been determined to be bogus issues.

SEMI-POSTAL STAMPS

Pierre de Coubertin
SP1

Engraved & Litho (flag)
1939, Oct. 3   Unwmk.   Perf. 12
B1 SP1 10c + 10c multi   27.50 27.50
Nos. B1,CB1-CB2 (3)   77.50 77.50

Pierre de Coubertin, organizer of the modern Olympic Games. The surtax was used to build a Sports Stadium at Port-au-Prince.

Catalogue values for unused stamps in this section, from this point to the end of the section, are for Never Hinged items.

Nos. 419-420
Surcharged in Deep Carmine

Perf. 13x13½, 13½x13
1958, Aug. 30   Litho.   Unwmk.
B2 A82 1g + 50c purple   2.50 2.40
B3 A83 1.50g + 50c red org   2.50 2.40
Nos. B2-B3,CB9 (3)   7.50 7.20

The surtax was for the Red Cross. Overprint arranged horizontally on No. B3.

Similar Surcharge in Red on One Line on Nos. 440-441
1959, Apr. 7   Photo.   Perf. 11½
Granite Paper
B4 A87 10c + 25c rose pink   .40 .25
B5 A87 25c + 25c green   .40 .35

Nos. 444-446 Surcharged Like Nos. B2-B3 in Red
Perf. 14x13½
B6 A88 10c + 50c vio bl & ol   .75 .50
B7 A88 25c + 50c dp brn   .75 .60
B8 A88 2g + 50c dp cl & dk brn   1.25 1.00
Nos. B6-B8,CB10-CB15 (9)   7.65 7.00

The surtax was for the Red Cross.

No. 447 Surcharged Diagonally

Unwmk.
1959, July 23   Photo.   Perf. 12
B9 A89 50c + 20c lt bl & dp cl   .85 .85
Nos. B9,CB16-CB18 (4)   4.05 4.05

Issued for the World Refugee Year, July 1, 1959-June 30, 1960.

Nos. 448-450 Surcharged in Dark Carmine

1959, Oct. 30   Perf. 14
B10 A90 25c + 75c blk brn & lt bl   .65 .60
B11 A90 50c + 75c multi   .90 .60
B12 A91 75c + 75c brn & bl   .90 .60
Nos. B10-B12,CB19-CB21 (6)   5.45 4.80

The surtax was for Haitian athletes. On No. B12, surcharge lines are spaced to total depth of 16mm.

No. 436 Surcharged in Red: "Hommage a l'UNICEF +G. 0,50"
Engraved and Lithographed
1960, Feb. 2   Perf. 11½
B13 A86 1g + 50c blk & brick red   .90 .90
Nos. B13,CB22-CB23 (3)   3.65 3.65

UNICEF.

Nos. 452-453 Surcharged with Additional Value and Overprinted "ALPHABETISATION" in Red or Black
Perf. 12½x13
1960, July 12   Litho.   Unwmk.
B14 A92 10c + 20c sal & grn (R)   .35 .20
B15 A92 10c + 30c sal & grn (R)   .40 .20
B16 A92 50c + 20c vio & mag (R)   .40 .20
B17 A92 50c + 30c vio & mag   .55 .50
Nos. B14-B17,CB24-CB27 (8)   4.55 3.55

Olympic Games Issue
Nos. 464-465 Surcharged with Additional Value
1960, Sept. 9   Photo.   Perf. 12
B18 A94 50c + 25c grn & ocher   .40 .20
B19 A94 1g + 25c dk brn & grnsh bl   .50 .40
Nos. B18-B19,CB28-CB29 (4)   1.95 1.40

No. 469 Surcharged: "UNICEF +25 centimes"
1961, Jan. 14   Engr.   Perf. 10½
B20 A96 1g + 25c grn & blk   .50 .40
Nos. B20,CB30-CB31 (3)   1.55 1.20

UNICEF.

No. 469 Surcharged: "OMS SNEM +20 CENTIMES"
1961, Dec. 11
B21 A96 1g + 20c grn & blk   .55 .50
Nos. B21,CB35-CB36 (3)   4.40 4.35

Haiti's participation in the UN malaria eradication drive.

Nos. 434, 436 and 438 Surcharged in Black or Red:

(Surcharge arranged to fit shape of stamp.)
1961-62   Engr. & Litho.   Perf. 11½
B22 A86 20c + 25c blk & yel   .30 .20
B23 A86 1g + 50c blk & brick red (R) ('62)   .50 .50
B24 A86 2.50g + 50c blk & gray vio (R) ('62)   .90 .60
Nos. B22-B24,CB37-CB41 (8)   5.15 5.15

The surtax was for the benefit of the urban rehabilitation program in Duvalier Ville.

Nos. 486-488 Surcharged: "+25 centimes"
1962, Sept. 13   Litho.   Perf. 12
B25 A99 5c + 25c crim & dp bl   .30 .20
B26 A99 10c + 25c red brn & emer   .30 .20
B27 A99 50c + 25c bl & crim   .40 .20
Nos. B25-B27,CB42-CB44 (6)   2.15 1.40

Nos. 489-490 Surcharged in Red: "+0.20"
1962   Unwmk.   Perf. 12½x13
B28 A92 10c + 20c bl & org   .30 .20
B29 A92 50c + 20c rose lil & ol grn   .40 .40
Nos. B28-B29,CB45-CB46 (4)   1.60 1.40

No. 502 Surcharged: "ALPHABETISATION" and "+0,10"
1963, Mar. 15   Photo.   Perf. 14x14½
B30 A102 25c + 10c bl gray, yel & blk   .25 .20
Nos. B30,CB47-CB48 (3)   1.15 .80

Nos. 491-494 Surcharged and Overprinted in Black or Red With Olympic Emblem and: "JEUX OLYMPIQUES / D'HIVER / INNSBRUCK 1964"
Perf. 14x14½, 14½x14
1964, July 27   Unwmk.
B31 A100 10c + 10c on 3c (R)   .60 .40
B32 A100 50c + 10c on 5c   .60 .40
B33 A100 50c + 10c on 10c (R)   .60 .40
B34 A100 50c + 10c on 25c   .60 .40
Nos. B31-B34,CB49 (5)   3.30 2.40

9th Winter Olympic Games, Innsbruck, Austria, Jan. 20-Feb. 9, 1964. The 10c surtax went for charitable purposes.

Nos. 510-512 Surcharged: "+ 5c." in Black
1965, Mar. 15   Photo.   Perf. 11½
Granite Paper
B35 A105 10c + 5c lt bl & dk brn   .20 .20
B36 A105 25c + 5c sal & dk brn   .30 .20
B37 A105 50c + 5c pale rose lil & dk brn   .50 .40
Nos. B35-B37,CB51-CB54 (7)   3.10 2.25

Nos. B35-B37 and CB51-CB54 also exist with this surcharge (without period after "c") in red. They also exist with a similar black surcharge which lacks the period and is in a thinner, lighter type face.

Nos. 533 and 535-536 Surcharged and Overprinted with Haitian Scout Emblem and "12e Jamboree / Mondial 1967" Like Regular Issue
1967, Aug. 21   Photo.   Perf. 11½
B38 A111 10c + 10c on 5c multi   .20 .20
B39 A111 15c + 10c multi   .20 .20
B40 A111 50c + 10c multi   .30 .20
Nos. B38-B40,CB55-CB56 (5)   1.85 1.50

12th Boy Scout World Jamboree, Farragut State Park, Idaho, Aug. 1-9. The surcharge on No. B38 includes 2 bars through old denomination.

Nos. 600-601 Surcharged in Red with New Value, Red Cross and: "50ème. Anniversaire / de la Ligue des / Sociétés de la / Croix Rouge"
1969, June 25   Litho.   Perf. 11½
B41 A127 10c + 10c multi   .20 .20
B42 A127 50c + 20c multi   .50 .40
Nos. B41-B42,CB61-CB62 (4)   2.10 1.50

50th anniv. of the League of Red Cross Societies.

Nos. 637-638 Surcharged with New Value and: "INAUGURATION / 22-7-71"
1971, Aug. 3   Litho.   Perf. 14x13½
B43 A138 20c + 50c multi   .45 .35
B44 A138 25c + 1.50g multi   .80 .45

Inauguration of the François Duvalier Central Hydroelectric Plant, July 22, 1971.

AIR POST STAMPS

Plane over Port-au-Prince — AP1

1929-30   Unwmk.   Engr.   Perf. 12
C1 AP1 25c dp grn ('30)   .50 .40
C2 AP1 50c dp vio   .65 .40
C3 AP1 75c red brn ('30)   1.75 1.25
C4 AP1 1g dp ultra   1.90 1.60
Nos. C1-C4 (4)   4.80 3.65

AP1a

Red Surcharge
1933, July 6
C4A AP1a 60c on 20c blue   75.00 80.00

Non-stop flight of Capt. J. Errol Boyd and Robert G. Lyon from New York to Port-au-Prince.

Plane over Christophe's Citadel — AP2

1933-40
C5 AP2 50c org brn   5.25 1.00
C6 AP2 50c ol grn ('35)   4.00 1.00
C7 AP2 50c car rose ('37)   3.50 2.00
C8 AP2 50c blk ('38)   2.00 1.00
C8A AP2 60c choc ('40)   1.10 .50
C9 AP2 1g ultra   1.75 .50
Nos. C5-C9 (6)   17.60 6.00

For surcharge see No. C24.

Dumas Type of Regular Issue
1935, Dec. 29   Litho.   Perf. 11½
C10 A59 60c brt vio & choc   4.50 2.50

Visit of delegation from France to Haiti.

Arms of Haiti and Portrait of George Washington — AP4

1938, Aug. 29   Engr.   Perf. 12
C11 AP4 60c deep blue   .70 .40

150th anniv. of the US Constitution.

Caribbean Conference Type of Regular Issue
1941, June 30
C12 A60 60c olive   3.25 .85
C13 A60 1.25g purple   3.25 .65

Madonna Type of Regular Issue
1942, Dec. 8   Perf. 12
C14 A61 10c dk olive   .40 .20
C15 A61 25c brt ultra   .50 .40
C16 A61 50c turq grn   .90 .40
C17 A61 60c rose car   1.40 .50
C18 A61 1.25g black   2.50 .50
Nos. C14-C18 (5)   5.70 2.00

Souvenir Sheets
C19 A61 Sheet of 2, #C14, C16   5.00 5.00
a.   Imperf   25.00 25.00

C20 A61 Sheet of 2, #C15,
C17 5.00 5.00
a. Imperf. 25.00 25.00
C21 A61 Sheet of 1, #C18 5.00 5.00
a. Imperf. 25.00 25.00

Our Lady of Perpetual Help, patroness of Haiti.

Killick Type of Regular Issue
1943, Sept. 6
C22 A62 60c purple .65 .20
C23 A62 1.25g black 1.60 1.60

No. C8A Surcharged with New Value and Bars in Red
1944, Nov. 25
C24 AP2 10c on 60c choc .50 .40
a. Bars at right vertical 2.40
b. Double surcharge 65.00

Red Cross Type of Regular Issue
1945   **Cross in Rose**
C25 A63 20c yel org .40 .20
C26 A63 25c brt ultra .40 .20
C27 A63 50c ol blk .40 .20
C28 A63 60c dl vio .50 .20
C29 A63 1g yellow 1.40 .40
C30 A63 1.25g carmine 1.25 .40
C31 A63 1.35g green 1.25 .50
C32 A63 5g black 7.25 2.50
Nos. C25-C32 (8) 12.85 4.70

Issue dates: 1g, Aug. 14; others, Feb. 20.
For surcharges see Nos. C153-C160.

> Catalogue values for unused stamps in this section, from this point to the end of the section, are for Never Hinged items.

Franklin D. Roosevelt — AP11

1946, Feb. 5   Unwmk.   Perf. 12
C33 AP11 20c black .40 .20
C34 AP11 60c black .50 .20

Capois Type of Regular Issue
1946, July 18   Engr.
C35 A64 20c car rose .20 .20
C36 A64 25c dk grn .20 .20
C37 A64 50c orange .25 .20
C38 A64 60c purple .40 .20
C39 A64 1g gray blk .50 .20
C40 A64 1.25g red vio .75 .40
C41 A64 1.35g black .80 .50
C42 A64 5g rose car 2.40 1.20
Nos. C35-C42 (8) 5.50 3.10

For surcharges see Nos. C43-C45, C49-C51, C61-C62.

Nos. C37 and C41 Surcharged with New Value and Bar or Block in Red or Black
1947-48
C43 A64 5c on 1.35g (R) ('48) .60 .40
C44 A64 30c on 50c .50 .40
C45 A64 30c on 1.35g (R) .50 .40
Nos. C43-C45 (3) 1.60 1.20

Dessalines Type of 1947-54 Regular Issue
1947, Oct. 17   Engr.
C46 A65 20c chocolate .40 .20

Christopher Columbus and Fleet — AP14

Pres. Dumarsais Estiméand Exposition Buildings — AP15

1950, Feb. 12   Perf. 12½
C47 AP14 30c ultra & gray .90 .50
C48 AP15 1g black .90 .50

200th anniversary (in 1949) of the founding of Port-au-Prince.

Nos. C36, C39 and C41 Surcharged or Overprinted in Carmine

1950, Oct. 4   Perf. 12
C49 A64 30c on 25c dk grn .40 .30
a. 30c on 1g gray black 75.00
C50 A64 1g gray blk .60 .50
a. "P" of overprint omitted 65.00 60.00
C51 A64 1.50g on 1.35g blk 1.75 1.50
Nos. C49-C51 (3) 2.75 2.30

75th anniv. (in 1949) of the UPU.

Bananas AP16

Coffee AP17

Sisal AP18

Isabella I AP19

1951, Sept. 3   Photo.   Perf. 12½
C52 AP16 30c dp org 2.25 .40
C53 AP17 80c dk grn & sal pink 5.50 .60
C54 AP18 5g gray 19.00 3.50
Nos. C52-C54 (3) 26.75 4.50

For surcharge see No. C218.

1951, Oct. 12   Perf. 13
C55 AP19 15c brown .30 .20
C56 AP19 30c dull blue .40 .40

Queen Isabella I of Spain, 500th birth anniv.

Type of Regular Issue
1953, May 4   Engr.   Perf. 12
20c, Cap Haitien Roadstead. 30c, Workers' housing, St. Martin. 1.50g, Restored cathedral. 2.50g, School lunchroom.

C57 A68 20c dp bl .25 .20
C58 A68 30c red brn .40 .20
C59 A68 1.50g gray blk .85 .50
C60 A68 2.50g violet 1.75 .85
Nos. C57-C60 (4) 3.25 1.75

Nos. C38 and C41 Surcharged in Black

1953, May 18
C61 A64 50c on 60c pur .40 .20
a. Double surcharge 50.00 50.00
C62 A64 50c on 1.35g blk .40 .20
a. Double surcharge 50.00

150th anniv. of the adoption of the natl. flag.

Dessalines and Magloire Type and:

Henri Christophe — AP21

1954, Jan. 1   Photo.   Perf. 11½
C63 AP21 50c shown .50 .25
C64 AP21 50c Toussaint L'Ouverture .50 .25
C65 AP21 50c Dessalines .50 .25
C66 AP21 50c Petion .50 .25
C67 AP21 50c Boisrond-Tonerre .50 .25
C68 AP21 1g Petion .80 .50
C69 AP21 1.50g Lamartiniere 1.50 1.00
C70 A69 7.50g shown 5.50 5.00
Nos. C63-C70 (8) 10.30 7.75

See Nos. C95-C96.

Marie Jeanne and Lamartinière Leading Attack — AP23

Design: Nos. C73, C74, Battle of Vertieres.

1954, Jan. 1   Perf. 12½
C71 AP23 50c black .40 .20
C72 AP23 50c carmine .40 .20
C73 AP23 50c ultra .40 .20
C74 AP23 50c sal pink .40 .20
Nos. C71-C74 (4) 1.60 .80

150th anniv. of Haitian independence.

Mme. Magloire Type of Regular Issue
1954, Jan. 1   Perf. 11½
C75 A72 20c red org .20 .20
C76 A72 50c brown .40 .40
C77 A72 1g gray grn .50 .40
C78 A72 1.50g crimson .75 .50
C79 A72 2.50g bl gray 1.25 .90
C80 A72 5g gray 3.00 2.25
Nos. C75-C80 (6) 6.10 4.65

Christophe Types of Regular Issue
1954, Dec. 6   Litho.   Perf. 13½x13
Portraits in Black
C81 A73 50c orange .40 .20
C82 A73 1g blue .80 .50
C83 A73 1.50g green 1.10 .65
C84 A73 2.50g gray 1.75 .90
C85 A73 5g rose car 3.25 1.90

Perf. 13
Flag in Black and Carmine
C86 A74 50c orange .40 .20
C87 A74 1g bl bl .75 .45
C88 A74 1.50g bl grn 1.10 .65
C89 A74 2.50g gray 1.75 .90
C90 A74 5g red org 3.25 1.90
Nos. C81-C90 (10) 14.55 8.25

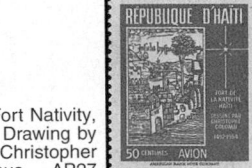

Fort Nativity, Drawing by Christopher Columbus — AP27

1954, Dec. 14   Engr.   Perf. 12
C91 AP27 50c dk rose car .65 .60
C92 AP27 50c dk gray .65 .50

Dessalines Type of 1955-57 Issue
Perf. 11½
1955, July 14   Unwmk.   Photo.
C93 A75 20c org & blk .25 .20
C94 A75 20c yel grn & blk .25 .20

For overprint see No. C183a.

Portrait Type of 1954
Dates omitted
Design: J. J. Dessalines.

1955, July 19
Portrait in Black
C95 AP21 50c gray .40 .20
C96 AP21 50c blue .40 .20

Dessalines Memorial Type of Regular Issue
1955, Aug. 1
C97 A76 1.50g gray & blk .65 .20
C98 A76 1.50g grn & blk .65 .20

Types of 1956 Regular Issue and

Car and Coastal View — AP30

Designs: No. C100, 75c, Plane, steamship and Haiti map. 1g, Car and coastal view. 2.50g, Flamingo. 5g, Mallard.

1956, Apr. 14   Unwmk.   Perf. 11½
Granite Paper
C99 AP30 50c hn brn & lt bl .70 .25
C100 AP30 50c blk & gray .45 .25
C101 AP30 75c dp grn & bl grn .95 .50
C102 AP30 1g ol grn & lt bl .80 .30
C103 A77 2.50g dp org & org 14.00 1.75
C104 A78 5g red & buff 21.00 3.00
Nos. C99-C104 (6) 37.90 6.05

For overprint see No. C185.

Kant Type of Regular Issue
1956, July 19   Photo.   Perf. 12
Granite Paper
C105 A79 50c chestnut .40 .20
C106 A79 75c dp yel grn .50 .40
C107 A79 1.50g dp magenta 1.25 .50
a. Miniature sheet of 3 8.00 5.00
Nos. C105-C107 (3) 2.15 1.10

No. C107a exists both perf. and imperf. Each sheet contains Nos. C105, C106 and a 1.25g gray black of same design.

Waterfall Type of Regular Issue
1957, Dec. 16   Perf. 11½
Granite Paper
C108 A80 50c grn & grnsh bl .25 .20
C109 A80 1.50g ol grn & grnsh bl .65 .40
C110 A80 2.50g dk bl & brt bl 1.00 .60
C111 A80 5g bluish blk & saph 2.50 1.50
Nos. C108-C111 (4) 4.40 2.70

For surcharge and overprint see Nos. CB49, CQ2.

Dessalines Type of Regular Issue
1958, July 2
C112 A81 50c org & blk .65 .40

For overprints see Nos. C184, CQ1.

Brussels Fair Types of Regular Issue, 1958
Perf. 13x13½, 13½x13
1958, July 22   Litho.   Unwmk.
C113 A82 50c pale car rose 1.25 .50
C114 A83 5g bright blue 1.50 .85
a. Souv. sheet of 2, #C113-C114, imperf. 5.50 5.00

For surcharge see No. CB9.

Sylvio Cator — AP33

1958, Aug. 16   Photo.   Perf. 11½
Granite Paper
C115 AP33 50c green .25 .20
C116 AP33 50c blk brn .25 .20
C117 AP33 1g org brn .50 .40
C118 AP33 5g gray 2.40 .85
Nos. C115-C118 (4) 3.40 1.65

30th anniversary of the world championship record broad jump of Sylvio Cator.

IGY Type of Regular Issue, 1958

Designs: 50c, US Satellite. 1.50g, Emperor penguins. 2g, Modern observatory.

1958, Oct. 8   *Perf. 14x13½*

C119	A85	50c dp ultra & brn red	.60	.25
C120	A85	1.50g brn & crim	3.25	.75
C121	A85	2g dk bl & crim	2.25	.40
a.		Souv. sheet of 4, #427, C119-C121, imperf.	8.00	7.50
		Nos. C119-C121 (3)	6.10	1.40

President Francois Duvalier AP34

Engraved and Lithographed
1958, Oct. 22   **Unwmk.**   *Perf. 11½*
Commemorative Inscription in Ultramarine

C122	AP34	50c blk & rose	1.00	.40
C123	AP34	2.50g blk & ocher	1.40	.60
C124	AP34	5g blk & rose lil	1.90	1.25
C125	AP34	7.50g blk & lt bl grn	3.00	2.00
		Nos. C122-C125 (4)	7.30	4.05

See note after No. 431.
Souvenir sheet of 3 exist, perf. and imperf., containing one each of Nos. C124-C125 and No. 431. Sheets measure 132x77mm. with marginal inscription in ultramarine. Value, $6.25 each.
For surcharges see Nos. CB37-CB39.

Same Without Commemorative Inscription
1958, Nov. 20

C126	AP34	50c blk & rose	.40	.20
C127	AP34	1g blk & vio	.50	.25
C128	AP34	1.50g blk & pale brn	.75	.40
C129	AP34	2g blk & rose pink	1.00	.40
C130	AP34	2.50g blk & ocher	1.00	.50
C131	AP34	5g blk & rose lil	2.00	1.25
C132	AP34	7.50g blk & lt bl grn	3.00	2.00
		Nos. C126-C132 (7)	8.65	4.60

For surcharges see #CB22-CB23, CB40-CB41.

Type of Regular Issue and

Flags of Haiti and UN — AP35

Perf. 11½
1958, Dec. 5   **Unwmk.**   **Photo.**
Granite Paper

C133	AP35	50c pink, car & ultra	.40	.20
C134	A87	75c brt bl	.40	.20
C135	A87	1g brown	.50	.40
a.		Souv. sheet of 2, #C133, imperf.	3.50	3.50
		Nos. C133-C135 (3)	1.30	.80

For surcharges see Nos. CB10-CB12.

Nos. C133-C135 Overprinted: "10th ANNIVERSARY OF THE UNIVERSAL DECLARATION OF HUMAN RIGHTS,"
in English (a), French (b), Spanish (c) or Portuguese (d)
1959, Jan. 28

C136		Block of 4	2.75	2.75
a.-d.		AP35 50c any single	.60	.60
C137		Block of 4	3.75	3.75
a.-d.		A87 75c any single	.80	.80
C138		Block of 4	7.00	7.00
a.-d.		A87 1g any single	1.50	1.50
		Nos. C136-C138 (3)	13.50	13.50

Pope Pius XII — AP36

1.50g, Pope praying. 2.50g, Pope on throne.

1959, Feb. 28   **Photo.**   *Perf. 14x13½*

C139	AP36	50c grn & lil	.25	.20
C140	AP36	1.50g ol & red brn	.65	.40
C141	AP36	2.50g pur & dk bl	1.00	.40
		Nos. C139-C141 (3)	1.90	1.00

Issued in memory of Pope Pius XII.
For surcharges see Nos. CB13-CB15.

Lincoln Type of Regular Issue, 1959
Designs: Various Portraits of Lincoln.

1959, May 12   *Perf. 12*

C142	A89	1g lt grn & chnt	.50	.40
C143	A89	2g pale lem & sl grn	.75	.50
C144	A89	2.50g buff & vio bl	.85	.40
a.		Min. sheet of 4, #447, C142-C144, imperf.	3.00	2.75
		Nos. C142-C144 (3)	2.10	1.30

Imperf. pairs exist.
For surcharges see Nos. CB16-CB18.

Pan American Games Types of Regular Issue
Designs: 50c, Jean Baptiste Dessables and map of American Midwest, c. 1791. 1g, Chicago's skyline and Dessables house. 1.50g, Discus thrower and flag of Haiti.

Unwmk.
1959, Aug. 27   **Photo.**   *Perf. 14*

C145	A91	50c hn brn & aqua	.75	.25
C146	A90	1g lil & aqua	1.00	.40
C147	A90	1.50g multi	1.40	.50
		Nos. C145-C147 (3)	3.15	1.15

For surcharges see Nos. CB19-CB21.

Nos. C145-C147 Overprinted like No. 451
1960, Feb. 29

C148	A91	50c hn brn & aqua	1.40	1.40
C149	A90	1g lil & aqua	1.90	1.90
C150	A90	1.50g multi	2.75	2.75
		Nos. C148-C150 (3)	6.05	6.05

WRY Type of Regular Issue, 1960
1960, Apr. 7   **Litho.**   *Perf. 12½x13*

C151	A92	50c bl & blk	.40	.20
C152	A92	1g lt grn & mar	.50	.40
a.		Souv. sheet of 4, #452-453, C151-C152, imperf.	6.50	6.00

See Nos. C191-C192. For surcharges see Nos. CB24-CB27, CB45-CB46.

Nos. C31, C28 and 369 Surcharged or Overprinted in Red: "28ème ANNIVERSAIRE"
1960, May 8   **Engr.**   *Perf. 12*
Cross in Rose

C153	A63	20c on 1.35g grn	.40	.20
C154	A63	50c on 60c dl vio	.65	.40
C155	A63	50c on 1.35g grn	.40	.40
C156	A63	50c on 2.50g pale vio	.40	.40
C157	A63	60c dl vio	.40	.40
C158	A63	1g on 1.35g grn	.70	.50
C159	A63	1.35g green	.65	.50
C160	A63	2g on 1.35g grn	1.40	1.00
		Nos. C153-C160 (8)	5.00	3.80

28th anniv. of the Haitian Red Cross. Additional overprint "Avion" on No. C156.

Sugar Type of Regular Issue
Miss Fouchard &: 50c, Harvest. 2.50g, Beach.

Perf. 11½
1960, May 30   **Unwmk.**   **Photo.**
Granite Paper

C161	A93	50c lil rose & brn	.90	.20
C162	A93	2.50g ultra & brn	2.25	.50

Olympic Type of Regular Issue
Designs: 50c, Pierre de Coubertin, Melbourne stadium and torch. 1.50g, Discus thrower and Rome stadium. 2.50g, Victors' parade, Athens, 1896, and Melbourne, 1956.

1960, Aug. 18   *Perf. 12*

C163	A94	50c mar & bis	.65	.20
C164	A94	1.50g rose car & yel grn	1.40	.40
C165	A94	2.50g sl grn & mag	1.60	.45
a.		Souv. sheet of 2, #465, C165, imperf.	5.50	5.50
		Nos. C163-C165 (3)	3.65	1.05

For surcharges see Nos. CB28-CB29.

Jeanty Type of Regular Issue
50c, Occide Jeanty and score from "1804." 1.50g, Occide Jeanty and National Capitol.

1960, Oct. 19   *Perf. 14x14½*

C166	A95	50c yel & bl	.50	.20
C167	A95	1.50g lil rose & sl grn	.75	.25

Printed in sheets of 12 (3x4) with inscription and opening bars of "1804," Jeanty's military march, in top margin.

UN Type of Regular Issue, 1960
1960, Nov. 25   **Engr.**   *Perf. 10½*

C168	A96	50c red org & blk	.40	.20
C169	A96	1.50g dk bl & blk	.50	.40
a.		Souv. sheet of 3, #469, C168-C169, imperf.	3.25	3.25

For surcharges see #CB30-CB31, CB35-CB36.
Nos. C168-C169 exist with centers inverted.

Dessalines Type of Regular Issue
1960, Nov. 5   **Photo.**   *Perf. 11½*
Granite Paper

C170	A81	20c gray & blk	.25	.20

For overprint see No. C183.

Sud-Caravelle Jet Airliner and Orchid — AP37

Designs: 50c, Boeing 707 jet airliner, facing left, and Kittyhawk. 1g, Sud-Caravelle jet airliner and Orchid. 1.50g, Boeing 707 jet airliner and air post stamp of 1933.

1960, Dec. 17   **Photo.**   **Unwmk.**
Granite Paper

C171	AP37	20c dp ultra & car	.20	.20
C172	AP37	50c rose brn & grn	.50	.25
C173	AP37	50c brt grnsh bl & ol grn	.50	.25
C174	AP37	50c gray & grn	.50	.25
C175	AP37	1g gray ol & ver	1.60	.25
C176	AP37	1.50g brt pink & dk bl	1.25	.30
a.		Souv. sheet of 3, #C174-C176, imperf.	4.00	4.00
		Nos. C171-C176 (6)	4.55	1.50

Issued for Aviation Week, Dec. 17-23.
#C172-C174 are dated 17 Decembre 1903.
For overprints and surcharges see Nos. CB32-CB34, CO1-CO5.

Dumas Type of Regular Issue.
Designs: 50c, The Three Musketeers and Dumas père, horiz 1g, The Lady of the Camellias and Dumas fils. 1.50g, The Count of Monte Cristo and Dumas père.

1961, Feb. 10   **Photo.**   *Perf. 11½*
Granite Paper

C177	A97	50c brt bl & blk	.60	.20
C178	A97	1g blk & red	.75	.25
C179	A97	1.50g brt grn & bl blk	1.10	.35
		Nos. C177-C179 (3)	2.45	.80

Type of Regular Issue, 1961
Tourist publicity: 20c, Privateer in Battle. 50c, Pirate with cutlass in rigging. 1g, Map of Tortuga.

1961, Apr. 4   **Litho.**   *Perf. 12*

C180	A98	20c dk bl & yel	.30	.20
C181	A98	50c brt pur & org	.55	.25
C182	A98	1g Prus grn & yel	.45	.40
		Nos. C180-C182 (3)	1.30	.85

For overprint and surcharge see #C186-C187.

Nos. C170, C112 and C101 Overprinted: "Dr. F. Duvalier Président 22 Mai 1961"
1961, May 22   **Photo.**   *Perf. 11½*

C183	A81	20c gray & blk	.20	.20
a.		On No. C93		
C184	A81	50c org & blk	.25	.20
C185	AP30	75c dp grn & bl blk	.40	.40
		Nos. C183-C185 (3)	.85	.80

Re-election of Pres. Francois Duvalier.

No. C182 Overprinted or Surcharged: "EXPLORATION SPATIALE JOHN GLENN" and Capsule
1962, May 10   **Litho.**   *Perf. 12*

C186	A98	1g Prus grn & yel	.50	.40
C187	A98	2g on 1g Prus grn & yel	1.40	1.00

See note after No. 485.

Malaria Type of Regular Issue
Designs: 20c, 1g, Triangle pointing down. 50c, Triangle pointing up.

1962, May 30   **Unwmk.**

C188	A99	20c lilac & red	.20	.20
C189	A99	50c emer & rose car	.40	.20
C190	A99	1g org & dk vio	.50	.40
a.		Souv. sheet of 3	3.00	3.00
		Nos. C188-C190 (3)	1.10	.80

Sheets of 12 with marginal inscription.
No. C190a contains stamps similar to Nos. 488 and C189-C190 in changed colors and imperf. Issued July 16.
A similar sheet without the "Contribution . . ." inscription was issued May 30.
For surcharges see Nos. CB42-CB44.

WRY Type of 1960 Dated "1962"
1962, June 22   *Perf. 12½x13*

C191	A92	50c lt bl & red brn	.35	.25
C192	A92	1g bister & blk	.40	.40

A souvenir sheet exists containing one each of #489-490, C191-C192, imperf Value, $5.50.
For surcharges see Nos. CB45-CB46.

Boy Scout Type of 1962
Designs: 20c, Scout giving Scout sign. 50c, Haitian Scout emblem. 1.50g, Lord and Lady Baden-Powell, horiz.

Perf. 14x14½, 14½x14
1962, Aug. 6   **Photo.**   **Unwmk.**

C193	A100	20c multi	.20	.20
C194	A100	50c multi	.50	.40
C195	A100	1.50g multi	.65	.40
		Nos. C193-C195 (3)	1.35	1.00

A souvenir sheet contains one each of Nos. C194-C195 imperf. Value, $5.50.
A similar sheet inscribed in gold, "Epreuves De Luxe," was issued Dec. 10. Value $3.

Nos. 495 and C193-C195 Overprinted: "AEROPORT INTERNATIONAL 1962"
1962, Oct. 26   *Perf. 14x14½, 14½x14*

C196	A100	20c multi, #C193	.25	.20
C197	A100	50c multi, #495	.40	.20
C198	A100	50c multi, #C194	.40	.20
C199	A100	1.50g multi, #C195	.60	.40
		Nos. C196-C199 (4)	1.65	1.00

Proceeds from the sale of Nos. C196-C199 were for the construction of new airport at Port-au-Prince. The overprint on No. C197 has "Poste Aérienne" added.

Seattle Fair Type of 1962
Design: Denomination at left, "Avion" at right.

1962, Nov. 19   **Litho.**   *Perf. 12½*

C200	A101	50c blk & pale lil	.40	.20
C201	A101	1g org brn & gray	.60	.40
C202	A101	1.50g red lil & org	.70	.40
		Nos. C200-C202 (3)	1.70	1.00

An imperf. sheet of two exists containing one each of Nos. C201-C202 with simulated gray perforations. Size: 133x82mm. Value, $5.50.

Street in Duvalier Ville and Stamp of 1881 — AP38

1962, Dec. 10   **Photo.**   *Perf. 14x14½*
Stamp in Dark Brown

C203	AP38	50c orange	.50	.20
C204	AP38	1g blue	.90	.40
C205	AP38	1.50g green	1.00	.50
		Nos. C203-C205 (3)	2.40	1.10

Issued to publicize Duvalier Ville.
For surcharges see Nos. CB47-CB48.

Nos. C201-C202 Overprint in Black

1963, Jan. 23   Litho.   Perf. 12½
C206 A101   1g org brn & gray   1.40   .60
  a.   Claret overprint, horiz.   1.40   .60
C207 A101 1.50g red lil & org   1.75   1.10
  a.   Claret overprint, horiz.   1.75   1.10

"Peaceful Uses of Outer Space." The black vertical overprint has no outside frame lines and no broken shading lines around capsule. Nos. C206a and C207a were issued Feb. 20.

Hunger Type of Regular Issue
Perf. 13x14

1963, July 12   Unwmk.   Photo.
C208 A103 50c lil rose & blk   .40   .20
C209 A103   1g lt ol grn & blk   .50   .40

Dag Hammarskjold and UN Emblem — AP39

Lithographed and Photogravure
1963, Sept. 28   Perf. 13½x14
Portrait in Slate
C210 AP39   20c buff & brn   .20   .20
C211 AP39   50c lt bl & car   .40   .20
  a.   Souvenir sheet of 2   3.50   3.50
C212 AP39   1g pink & bl   .40   .20
C213 AP39 1.50g gray & grn   .65   .50
  Nos. C210-C213 (4)   1.65   1.10

Dag Hammarskjold, Sec. Gen. of the UN, 1953-61. Printed in sheets of 25 (5x5) with map of Sweden extending over 9 stamps in second and third vertical rows. No. C211a contains 2 imperf. stamps: 50c blue and carmine and 1.50g ocher and brown with map of southern Sweden in background.
For overprints see Nos. C219-C222, C238-C241, CB50.

Dessalines Type of Regular Issue, 1963

1963, Oct. 17   Photo.   Perf. 14x14½
C214 A104 50c bl & lil rose   .25   .20
C215 A104 50c org & grn   .25   .20

Nos. C214-C215 and C53 Overprinted in Black or Red: "FETE DES MERES / 1964"

1964, July 22   Perf. 14x14½, 12½
C216 A104   50c bl & lil rose   .40   .20
C217 A104   50c org & grn   .40   .20
C218 AP17 1.50g on 80c dk grn
      & sal pink (R)   .60   .40
  Nos. C216-C218 (3)   1.40   .80

Issued for Mother's Day, 1964.

Nos. C210-C213 Overprinted in Red

Lithographed and Engraved
1964, Oct. 2   Perf. 13½x14
Portrait in Slate
C219 AP39   20c buff & brn   .40   .20
C220 AP39   50c lt bl & car   .40   .20
C221 AP39   1g pink & bl   .60   .40
C222 AP39 1.50g gray & grn   .70   .40
  Nos. C219-C222,CB50 (5)   3.50   2.55

Cent. (in 1963) of the Intl. Red Cross.

Olympic Type of Regular Issue
#C223, Weight lifter. #C224-C226, Hurdler.

1964, Nov. 12   Photo.   Perf. 11½
Granite Paper
C223 A105   50c pale lil & dk
        brn   .40   .20
C224 A105   50c pale grn & dk
        brn   .40   .20
C225 A105   75c buff & dk brn   .50   .40
C226 A105 1.50g gray & dk brn   .65   .50
  a.   Souv. sheet of 4   2.60   2.50
  Nos. C223-C226 (4)   1.95   1.30

Printed in sheets of 50 (10x5), with map of Japan in background extending over 27 stamps.
No. C226a contains four imperf. stamps similar to Nos. C223-C226 in changed colors and with map of Tokyo area in background.
For surcharges see Nos. CB51-CB54.

Airport Type of Regular Issue, 1964
1964, Dec. 15   Perf. 14½x14
C227 A106   50c org & blk   .40   .20
C228 A106 1.50g brt lil rose &
        blk   .65   .45
C229 A106 2.50g lt vio & blk   1.40   .60
  Nos. C227-C229 (3)   2.45   1.25

Same Overprinted "1965"
1965, Feb. 11   Photo.
C230 A106   50c org & blk   .40   .20
C231 A106 1.50g brt lil rose &
        blk   .65   .40
C232 A106 2.50g lt vio & blk   1.00   .70
  Nos. C230-C232 (3)   2.05   1.30

World's Fair Type of Regular Issue, 1965
Designs: 50c, 1.50g, "Rocket Thrower" by Donald De Lue. 5g, Unisphere, NY World's Fair.

1965, Mar. 22   Unwmk.   Perf. 13½
C233 A107   50c dp bl & org   .40   .20
C234 A107 1.50g gray & org   .50   .40
C235 A107   5g multi   2.40   1.90
  Nos. C233-C235 (3)   3.30   2.50

Merchant Marine Type of Regular Issue, 1965
1965, May 13   Photo.   Perf. 11½
C236 A108   50c blk, lt grnsh bl
        & red   .40   .20
C237 A108 1.50g blk, lt vio & red   .75   .50

Nos. C210-C213 Overprinted

Lithographed and Photogravure
1965, June 26   Perf. 13½x14
Portrait in Slate
C238 AP39   20c buff & brn   .20   .20
C239 AP39   50c lt bl & car   .40   .20
C240 AP39   1g pink & bl   .50   .40
C241 AP39 1.50g gray & grn   .65   .50
  Nos. C238-C241 (4)   1.75   1.30

20th anniversary of the United Nations.

ITU Type of Regular Issue
Perf. 13½
1965, Aug. 16   Unwmk.   Litho.
C242 A109   50c multi   .40   .20
C243 A109   1g multi   .50   .40
C244 A109 1.50g bl & multi   1.00   .50
C245 A109   2g pink & multi   1.50   .60
  Nos. C242-C245 (4)   3.40   1.70

A souvenir sheet, released in 1966, contains 50c and 2g stamps resembling Nos. C242 and C245, with simulated perforations. Value $15.00.
For overprints see Nos. C255-C256.

Cathedral Type of Regular Issue, 1965
Designs: 50c, Cathedral, Port-au-Prince, horiz. 1g, High Altar. 7.50g, Statue of Our Lady of the Assumption.

Perf. 14x13, 13x14
1965, Nov. 19   Photo.
Size: 39x29mm, 29x39mm
C246 A110   50c multi   .40   .20
C247 A110   1g multi   .65   .40
Size: 38x52mm
C248 A110 7.50g multi   2.75   2.25
  Nos. C246-C248 (3)   3.80   2.85

Flower Type of Regular Issue
#C249, 5g, Passionflower. #C250, C252, Okra. #C251, C253, American elder.

1965, Dec. 20   Photo.   Perf. 11½
Granite Paper
C249 A111   50c dk vio, yel &
        grn   1.10   .20
C250 A111   50c multi   1.10   .20
C251 A111   50c grn, gray &
        yel   1.10   .20
C252 A111 1.50g multi   1.90   1.40
C253 A111 1.50g grn, tan & yel   1.90   1.40
C254 A111   5g dk vio, yel grn
        & grn   5.50   1.50
  Nos. C249-C254 (6)   12.60   4.90

For surcharges see Nos. CB55-CB56.

Nos. C242-C243 Overprinted in Red: "20e. Anniversaire / UNESCO"

1965, Aug. 27   Litho.   Perf. 13½
C255 A109 50c lt vio & multi   1.40   .50
C256 A109   1g citron & multi   2.60   .85

20th anniversary of UNESCO.
The souvenir sheet noted below No. C245 was also overprinted "20e. Anniversaire / UNESCO" in red. Value, $20.

Culture Types of Regular Issue and

Modern Painting — AP40

Designs: 50c, Ceremonial stool. 1.50g, Amulet.

Perf. 14x14½, 14½x14, 14
1966, Mar. 14   Photo.   Unwmk.
C257 A113   50c lil, brn & brnz   .40   .20
C258 A112 1.50g brt rose lil, yel
        & blk   .65   .50
C259 AP40 2.50g multi   1.50   .85
  Nos. C257-C259 (3)   2.55   1.55

For overprints and surcharge see Nos. C260-C262, C280-C281.

Nos. C257-C259 Overprinted in Black or Red: "Hommage / a Hailé Sélassiéler / 24-25 Avril 1966"

1966, Apr. 24
C260 A112   50c (R)   .40   .20
C261 A113 1.50g (vert. ovpt.)   .65   .50
C262 AP40 2.50g (R)   1.00   .70
  Nos. C260-C262 (3)   2.05   1.40

See note after No. 543.

Walter M. Schirra, Thomas P. Stafford, Frank A. Borman, James A. Lovell and Gemini VI and VII — AP41

1966, May 3   Perf. 13½
C263 AP41   50c vio bl, brn & lt
        bl   .40   .20
C264 AP41   1g grn, brn & lt bl   .50   .40
C265 AP41 1.50g car, brn & bl   .65   .50
  Nos. C263-C265 (3)   1.55   1.10

See No. 547.
For overprints see Nos. C296-C298.

Portrait in Black; Gold Inscription; Green Commemorative Inscription in Two Lines
Soccer Type of Regular Issue

Designs: 50c, Pres. Duvalier and soccer ball within wreath. 1.50g, President Duvalier and soccer player within wreath.

Lithographed and Photogravure
1966, June 16   Perf. 13x13½
C266 A115   50c lt ol grn & plum   .40   .20
C267 A115 1.50g rose & plum   .65   .50

Green Commemorative Inscription in 3 Lines; Gold Inscription Omitted
C268 A115   50c multi   .40   .40
C269 A115 1.50g rose & plum   .65   .50
  Nos. C266-C269 (4)   2.10   1.60

Caribbean Soccer Festival, June 10-22. Nos. C266-C267 also for the National Soccer Championships, May 8-22.
For overprint and surcharge see Nos. C288, CB57.

Education Type of Regular Issue
Designs: 50c, "ABC", boy and girl. 1g, Scout symbols. 1.50g, Television set, book and communications satellite.

Perf. 14x13½, 13½x14
Litho. and Engraved
1966, Oct. 18
C270 A116 50c grn, yel & brn   .40   .20
C271 A116   1g dk brn, org &
        blk   .50   .40
C272 A116 1.50g grn, bl grn &
        dk bl   .65   .50
  Nos. C270-C272 (3)   1.55   1.10

Schweitzer Type of Regular Issue
Designs (Schweitzer and): 50c, 1g, Albert Schweitzer Hospital, Deschapelles, Haiti. 1.50g, Maps of Alsace and Gabon. 2g, Pipe organ.

Perf. 12½x13
1967, Apr. 20   Photo.   Unwmk.
C273 A117   50c multi   .50   .40
C274 A117   1g multi   .50   .40
C275 A117 1.50g lt bl & multi   .65   .50
C276 A117   2g multi   .90   .70
  Nos. C273-C276 (4)   2.55   2.00

Fruit-Vegetable Type of Regular Issue, 1967
1967, July 4   Photo.   Perf. 12½
C277 A118   50c Watermelon   2.00   .20
C278 A118   1g Cabbage   2.50   2.00
C279 A118 1.50g Tangerine   3.00   2.50
  Nos. C277-C279 (3)   7.50   4.70

No. C258 Overprinted or Surcharged Like EXPO '67 Regular Issue
1967, Aug. 30   Photo.   Perf. 14½x14
C280 A112 1.50g multi   .60   .40
C281 A112   2g on 1.50g multi   .75   .55

Issued to commemorate EXPO '67 International Exhibition, Montreal, Apr. 28-Oct. 27.

Duvalier Type of Regular Issue, 1967
1967, Sept. 22   Photo.   Perf. 14x13
C282 A119   1g brt grn & gold   .50   .40
C283 A119 1.50g vio & gold   .65   .50
C284 A119   2g org & gold   1.10   .70
  Nos. C282-C284 (3)   2.25   1.60

Education Type of Regular Issue, 1967
50c, Writing hands. 1g, Scout emblem and Scouts, vert. 1.50g, Audio-visual teaching of algebra.

1967, Dec. 11   Litho.   Perf. 11½
C285 A120   50c multi   .25   .20
C286 A120   1g multi   .50   .40
C287 A120 1.50g multi   .65   .50
  Nos. C285-C287 (3)   1.40   1.10

For surcharges see Nos. CB58-CB60.

No. C269 Overprinted

Lithographed and Photogravure

1968, Jan. 18   **Perf. 13x13½**
C288 A115 1.50g rose & plum   1.40   1.00
See note after No. 579.

Caiman Woods Type of Regular Issue

1968, Apr. 22   **Photo.**   **Perf. 12**
Size: 36x26mm
C289 A121   50c multi   .40   .20
C290 A121   1g multi   .50   .40

Perf. 12½x13½
Size: 49x36mm
C291 A121   50c multi   .40   .20
C292 A121   1g multi   .50   .40
C293 A121   1.50g multi   .75   .60
C294 A121   2g gray & multi   .90   .70
C295 A121   5g multi   2.00   1.40
    Nos. C289-C295 (7)   5.45   3.90

Nos. C263-
C265
Overprinted

1968, Apr. 19   **Perf. 13½**
C296 AP41   50c multi   .70   .40
C297 AP41   1g multi   1.40   .60
C298 AP41   1.50g multi   2.40   1.10
    Nos. C296-C298 (3)   4.50   2.10
See note after No. 584.

Monument Type of Regular Issue

1968, May 22   **Perf. 11½**
Granite Paper
C299 A122   50c ol bis & blk   .40   .20
C300 A122   1g brt rose & blk   .50   .40
C301 A122   1.50g org & blk   .80   .50
    Nos. C299-C301 (3)   1.70   1.10
For surcharges see Nos. C324-C325.

Types of Regular Bishopric Issue

50c, Palm tree & provincial coats of arms.
1g, 2.50g, Madonna, papal arms & arms of
Haiti. 1.50g, Cathedral, arms of Pope Paul VI
& arms of Haiti.

Perf. 13x14, 12½x13½
1968, Aug. 16   **Photo.**
C302 A123   50c lil & multi   .40   .20
C303 A124   1g multi   .50   .40
C304 A124   1.50g multi   .65   .50
C305 A124   2.50g multi   1.40   1.10
    Nos. C302-C305 (4)   2.95   2.20

Airport Type of Regular Issue

50c, 1.50g, 2.50g, Front view of air terminal.

1968, Sept. 22   **Photo.**   **Perf. 11½**
Portrait in Black
C306 A125   50c rose lake &
           pale vio   .40   .20
C307 A125   1.50g rose lake & bl   .65   .50
C308 A125   2.50g rose lake & lt
           grnsh bl   .90   .80
    Nos. C306-C308 (3)   1.95   1.50

Pres. Francois Duvalier — AP42

Embossed & Typo. on Gold Foil

1968, Sept. 22   **Die Cut Perf. 14**
C309 AP42 30g black & red   40.00   35.00

Freed Slaves' Type of Regular Issue

1968, Oct. 28   **Litho.**   **Perf. 14½x14**
C310 A126   50c brn, lil & brt
           pink   .40   .20
C311 A126   1g brn, yel grn &
           brt pink   .50   .40
C312 A126   1.50g brn, lt vio bl &
           brt pink   .65   .50
C313 A126   2g brn, lt grn & brt
           pink   .80   .60
    Nos. C310-C313 (4)   2.35   1.70

Education Type of Regular Issue, 1968

50c, 1.50g, Children watching television.
1g, Hands throwing ball, and sports medal.

1968, Nov. 14   **Perf. 11½**
C314 A127   50c multi   .40   .20
C315 A127   1g multi   .50   .40
C316 A127   1.50g multi   .65   .50
    Nos. C314-C316 (3)   1.55   1.10
For surcharges see Nos. CB61-CB62.

Jan Boesman and
his Balloon — AP43

1968, Nov. 28   **Litho.**   **Perf. 13½**
C317 AP43   70c lt yel grn & se-
           pia   .65   .50
C318 AP43   1.75g grnsh bl & se-
           pia   1.40   1.00
Dr. Jan Boesman's balloon flight, Mexico
City, Nov. 1968.

Miniature Sheet

Cachet of May 2,
1925
Flight — AP44

1968, Nov. 28   **Litho.**   **Perf. 13½x14**
Black Cachets, Magenta
Inscriptions
and Rose Lilac Background
C318A   Sheet of 12   13.00   13.00
   b.   AP44 70c 2 Mai 1925   .70   .80
   c.   AP44 70c 2 Septembre
          1925   .70   .80
   d.   AP44 70c 28 Mars 1927   .70   .80
   e.   AP44 70c 12 Juillet 1927   .70   .80
   f.   AP44 70c 13 Septembre
          1927   .70   .80
   g.   AP44 70c 6 Février 1928   .70   .80
Galiffet's 1784 balloon flight and pioneer
flights of the 1920's. No. C318A contains 2
each of Nos. C318b-C318g. The background
of the sheet shows in white outlines a balloon
and the inscription "BALLON GALIFFET
1784." The design of each stamp shows a different airmail cachet, date of a special flight
and part of the white background design.

Churchill Type of Regular Issue

Churchill: 50c, and early seaplane. 75c, and
soldiers at Normandy. 1g, and Queen Elizabeth II. 1.50g, and Big Ben, London. 3g, and
coat of arms, horiz.

1968, Dec. 23   **Photo.**   **Perf. 13**
C319 A128   50c gold & multi   .40   .20
C320 A128   75c gold & multi   .50   .40
C321 A128   1g gold & multi   .65   .50
C322 A128   1.50g gold & multi   .80   .60
    Nos. C319-C322 (4)   2.35   1.70
Souvenir Sheet
Perf. 12½x13, Imperf.
C323 A128   3g sil, blk & red   6.00   6.00
Nos. C319-C322 exist imperf. Value, $6.
No. C323 contains one horizontal stamp,
For surcharge, see No. C515. size:
38x25½mm.

Nos. C299-C300 Surcharged with New Value and Rectangle

1969, Feb. 21   **Photo.**   **Perf. 11½**
C324 A122   70c on 50c   .50   .40
C325 A122   1.75g on 1g   .80   .50

Bird Type of Regular Issue

Birds of Haiti: 50c, Hispaniolan trogon. 1g,
Black-cowled oriole. 1.50g, Stripe-headed
tanager. 2g, Striated woodpecker.

1969, Feb. 26   **Perf. 13½**
C326 A129   50c multi   3.00   .85
C327 A129   1g lt bl & multi   3.75   1.40
C328 A129   1.50g multi   4.50   2.00
C329 A129   2g gray & multi   5.00   2.50
    Nos. C326-C329 (4)   16.25   6.75
For overprints see Nos. C344A-C344D.

Electric Power Type of 1969

1969, May 22   **Litho.**   **Perf. 13x13½**
C338 A131   20c dk bl & lil   .25   .20
C339 A131   25c grn & rose red   .25   .20
C340 A131   25c rose red & grn   .25   .20
    Nos. C338-C340 (3)   .75   .60

Education Type of 1969

Designs: 50c, Peace poster on educational
television, vert. 1g, Learning to write. 1.50g,
Playing children, vert.

1969, Aug. 12   **Litho.**   **Perf. 13½**
C342 A132   50c multi   .30   .20
C343 A132   1g multi   .50   .40
C344 A132   1.50g multi   .80   .50
    Nos. C342-C344 (3)   1.60   1.10

Nos. C326-C329
Overprinted

1969, Aug. 29   **Photo.**   **Perf. 13½**
C344A A129   50c multi   1.25   1.25
C344B A129   1g lt bl & multi   2.40   2.40
C344C A129   1.50g multi   4.50   4.50
C344D A129   2g gray & mul-
          ti   5.75   5.75
    Nos. C344A-C344D (4)   13.90   13.90

ILO Type of Regular Issue

1969, Sept. 22   **Perf. 14**
C345 A133   25c red & blk   .30   .20
C346 A133   70c org & blk   .65   .20
C347 A133   1.75g brt pur & blk   1.40   .70
    Nos. C345-C347 (3)   2.35   1.10

Butterfly Type of Regular Issue

50c, Danaus eresimus kaempfferi. 1.50g,
Anaea marthesia nemesis. 2g, Prepona
antimache.

1969, Nov. 14   **Photo.**   **Perf. 13½**
C348 A134   50c multi   12.50   2.50
C349 A134   1.50g multi   25.00   3.25
C350 A134   2g yel & multi   37.50   5.00
    Nos. C348-C350 (3)   102.50   10.75

King Type of Regular Issue

1970, Jan. 12   **Litho.**   **Perf. 12½x13½**
C351 A135   50c emer, red & blk   .45   .20
C352 A135   1g brick red, red &
          blk   .80   .60
C353 A135   1.50g brt bl, red & blk   1.20   .85
    Nos. C351-C353 (3)   2.45   1.65

Orchid Type of Regular Issue

Haitian Orchids: 50c, Tetramicra elegans.
1.50g, Epidendrum truncatum. 2g, Oncidium
desertorum.

1970, Apr. 3   **Litho.**   **Perf. 13x12½**
C354 A136   50c buff, brn &
          mag   2.00   .20
C355 A136   1.50g multi   3.50   2.50
C356 A136   2g lilac & multi   5.25   3.50
    Nos. C354-C356 (3)   10.75   6.20

UPU Type of Regular Issue

Designs: 50c, Globe and doves. 1.50g,
Propeller and UPU emblem, vert. 2g, UPU
Monument and map of Haiti.

1970, June 23   **Photo.**   **Perf. 11½**
C357 A137   50c blk & vio   .35   .20
C358 A137   1.50g multi   .65   .45
C359 A137   2g multi   .95   .65
   a.   Souvenir sheet of 3, #C357-
          C359, imperf.   2.50   2.25
    Nos. C357-C359 (3)   1.95   1.30

Nos. C357-C359a Overprinted in Red with UN Emblem and: "XXVe ANNIVERSAIRE / O.N.U."

1970, Dec. 14   **Photo.**   **Perf. 11½**
C360 A137   50c blk & vio   .35   .20
C361 A137   1.50g multi   .65   .45
C362 A137   2g multi   .95   .65
   a.   Souvenir sheet of 3   3.50   3.00
    Nos. C360-C362 (3)   1.95   1.30
United Nations, 25th anniversary.

Haitian
Nativity
AP45

1970, Dec. 22
C363 AP45   1.50g sepia & multi   .65   .45
C364 AP45   1.50g ultra & multi   .65   .45
C365 AP45   2g multi   1.10   .65
    Nos. C363-C365 (3)   2.40   1.55
Christmas 1970.

Painting Type of Regular Issue

Paintings: 50c, Nativity, by Rigaud Benoit.
1g, Head of a Negro, by Rubens. 1.50g,
Ascension, by Castera Bazile (like No. 648).

1971, Apr. 29   **Litho.**   **Perf. 12x12½**
Size: 20x40mm
C366 A140   50c multi   .50   .20
C367 A140   1g multi   .80   .65
C368 A140   1.50g multi   1.10   .80
    Nos. C366-C368 (3)   2.40   1.65
Nos. C366-C368 exist imperf in changed
colors.

Balloon and Haiti No. C2 — AP46

No. C370, as #C369. No. C373, Haiti #C2.
1g, 1.50g, Supersonic transport & Haiti #C2.

1971, Dec. 22   **Photo.**   **Perf. 11½**
C369 AP46   20c bl, red org &
          blk   .30   .20
C370 AP46   50c ultra, red org &
          blk   .50   .25
C371 AP46   1g org & blk   1.25   .35
C372 AP46   1.50g lil rose & blk   1.90   .45
    Nos. C369-C372 (4)   3.95   1.25
Souvenir Sheet
Imperf
C373 AP46   50c brt grn & blk   9.00   4.50
40th anniv. (in 1969) of air post service in
Haiti.
For overprints see #C374-C377, C380-
C386.

Nos. C369-C372 Overprinted

1972, Mar. 17   **Perf. 11½**
C374 AP46   20c multi   .20   .20
C375 AP46   50c multi   .35   .35
C376 AP46   1g org & blk   .55   .45
C377 AP46   1.50g lil rose & blk   .65   .55
    Nos. C374-C377 (4)   1.75   1.55
14th INTERPEX, NYC, Mar. 17-19.

Dessalines Type of Regular Issue

1972, Apr. 28   **Photo.**   **Perf. 11½**
C378 A142   50c yel grn & blk   .35   .20
C379 A142   2.50g lil & blk   1.10   .65
For surcharge see No. C438.

Nos. C369-C372 Overprinted

1972, May 4
C380	AP46	20c multi	.20	.20
C381	AP46	50c multi	.35	.20
C382	AP46	1g org & blk	.45	.45
C383	AP46	1.50g lil rose & blk	.65	.45
		Nos. C380-C383 (4)	1.65	1.20

HAIPEX, 5th Congress.

Nos. C370-C372 Overprinted

1972, July
C384	AP46	50c multi	.35	.20
C385	AP46	1g org & blk	.45	.35
C386	AP46	1.50g lil rose & blk	.65	.45
		Nos. C384-C386 (3)	1.45	1.00

Belgica '72, International Philatelic Exhibition, Brussels, June 24-July 9.

Tower of the Sun, EXPO '70 Emblem AP47

1972, Oct. 27
C387	AP47	50c bl, plum & dk bl	.35	.20
C388	AP47	1g bl, plum & red	.55	.35
C389	AP47	1.50g bl, plum & blk	.65	.45
C390	AP47	2.50g bl, plum & grn	.95	.55
		Nos. C387-C390 (4)	2.50	1.55

EXPO '70 International Exposition, Osaka, Japan, Mar. 15-Sept. 13, 1970.
For surcharges see Nos. C447-C447A.

Souvenir Sheets

1972 Summer Olympics, Munich — AP47a

Designs: 2.50g, Israeli delegation, opening ceremony in Munich Stadium. 5g, Assassinated Israeli athlete David Berger.

1973   *Perf. 13½*
C390A	AP47a	2.50g multi	2.00	2.00
C390B	AP47a	5g multi	2.25	1.50

No. C390B contains one 22½x34mm stamp.

Headquarters and Map of Americas — AP48

1973, May 11   Litho.   *Perf. 14½*
C391	AP48	50c dk bl & multi	.35	.20
C392	AP48	80c multi	.50	.35
C393	AP48	1.50g vio & multi	.60	.45
C394	AP48	2g brn & multi	.85	.55
		Nos. C391-C394 (4)	2.30	1.55

70th anniversary (in 1972) of the Panamerican Health Organization.

Marine Life Type of Regular Issue

50c, 1.50g horizontal.

1973, Sept. 4   *Perf. 14*
C395	A145	50c Platypodia spectabilis	1.00	.20
C396	A145	85c Goniaster tessellatus	1.40	.20
C397	A145	1.50g Stephanocyathus diadema	2.00	.30
C398	A145	2g Phyllangia americana	2.50	.40
		Nos. C395-C398 (4)	6.90	1.10

For surcharge see No. C439.

Fish Type of Regular Issue

Designs: Tropical fish.

1973   *Perf. 13½*
C399	A146	50c Gramma melacara	.65	.50
C400	A146	85c Holacanthus tricolor	.80	.65
C401	A146	1.50g Liopropoma rubre	1.40	.75
C402	A146	5g Clepticus parrai	4.00	1.90
		Nos. C399-C402 (4)	6.85	3.80

For surcharge see No. C440.

Haitian Flag AP49

Nos. C404, C405, Haitian flag and coat of arms. No. C406, Flag and Pres. Jean-Claude Duvalier.

1973, Nov. 18   *Perf. 14½x14*
Size: 35x22½mm
C403	AP49	80c blk & red	.45	.35
C404	AP49	80c red & blk	.45	.35

Perf. 14x13½
Size: 42x27mm
C405	AP49	1.85g blk & red	.95	.65
C406	AP49	1.85g red & blk	.95	.65
		Nos. C403-C406 (4)	2.80	2.00

For overprints and surcharges see Nos. C427-C428, C432-C433, C441-C442.

Soccer Type of Regular Issue

50c, 80c, Soccer Stadium. 1.75g, 10g, Haiti #654.

1973, Nov. 29   *Perf. 14x13*
C407	A147	50c multi	.35	.20
C408	A147	80c multi	.45	.35
C409	A147	1.75g multi	.95	.45
C410	A147	10g multi	3.25	2.25
		Nos. C407-C410 (4)	5.00	3.25

Dessalines Type of 1974

1974, Apr. 22   Photo.   *Perf. 14*
C411	A148	50c brn & grnsh bl	.35	.20
C412	A148	80c gray & brn	.45	.35
C413	A148	1g lt grn & mar	.55	.45
C414	A148	1.75g lil & ol brn	.95	.55
		Nos. C411-C414 (4)	2.30	1.55

For surcharge see No. C443.

Copernicus Type of 1974

Designs: No. C415, 80c, 1.50g, 1.75g, Symbol of heliocentric system. No. C416, 1g, 2.50g, Nicolaus Copernicus.

1974, May 24   Litho.   *Perf. 14x13½*
C415	A149	50c org & multi	.35	.20
C416	A149	50c yel & multi	.35	.20
C417	A149	80c multi	.45	.35
C418	A149	1g multi	.55	.45
C419	A149	1.75g brn & multi	.95	.55
		Nos. C415-C419 (5)	2.65	1.75

Souvenir Sheet
Imperf
C420		Sheet of 2	2.50	2.50
a.		A149 1.50g light green & multi	.90	.90
b.		A149 2.50g deep orange & multi	1.40	1.40

For overprint and surcharges see Nos. C444, C460-C463.

Pres. Duvalier Type of 1974

1974   Photo.   *Perf. 14x13½*
C421	A151	50c vio brn & gold	.35	.20
C422	A151	80c rose red & gold	.45	.35
C423	A151	1g red lil & gold	.65	.45
C424	A151	1.50g Prus bl & gold	1.00	.65

C425	A151	1.75g brt vio & gold	1.25	.65
C426	A151	5g ol grn & gold	2.75	1.50
		Nos. C421-C426 (6)	6.45	3.80

For surcharge and overprints see Nos. C445, C487-C489.

Nos. C405-C406 Surcharged in Violet Blue

1975, July 15   Litho.   *Perf. 14x13½*
C427	AP49	80c on 1.85g, #C405	1.50	1.50
C428	AP49	80c on 1.85g, #C406	1.50	1.50

Nos. C405-C406 Overprinted in Blue

1975, July 15   Litho.   *Perf. 14x13½*
C432	AP49	1.85g blk & red	.95	.65
C433	AP49	1.85g red & blk	.95	.65

Centenary of Universal Postal Union. "100 ANS" in 2 lines on No. C433.

Names of Haitian Participants at Siege of Savannah — AP50

1976, Apr. 22   Photo.   *Perf. 11½*
Granite Paper
C434	AP50	50c multi	.35	.20
C435	AP50	80c multi	.55	.35
C436	AP50	1.50g multi	.80	.55
C437	AP50	7.50g multi	2.75	1.90
		Nos. C434-C437 (4)	4.45	3.00

American Bicentennial.

Stamps of 1972-74 Surcharged with New Value and Bar in Black or Violet Blue

Photogravure; Lithographed
1976   *Perf. 11½, 13½, 14x13½, 14*
C438	A142	80c on 2.50g, #C379	.55	.35
C439	A145	80c on 85c, #C396	.55	.35
C440	A146	80c on 85c, #C400	.55	.35
C441	AP49	80c on 1.85g, #C405	.55	.35
C442	AP49	80c on 1.85g, #C406	.55	.35
C443	A148	80c on 1.75g, #C414 (VB)	.55	.35
C444	A149	80c on 1.75g, #C419 (VB)	.55	.35
C445	A151	80c on 1.75g, #C425	.55	.35
C446	AP50	80c on 1.50g, #C436	.55	.35
C447	AP47	80c on 1.50g, #C389	.55	.35
C447A	AP47	80c on 2.50g #C390	.55	.35
		Nos. C438-C447A (11)	6.05	3.85

Black surcharge of Nos. C441-C442 differs from the violet blue surcharge of Nos. C427-C428 in type face, arrangement of denomination and bar, and size of bar (10x6mm).

Dessalines Type of 1972

1976-77   Photo.   *Perf. 11½*
Granite Paper
C448	A142	75c yel & blk	.35	.35
C449	A142	80c emer & blk	.35	.35
C450	A142	1g bl & blk	.45	.45
C451	A142	1g red brn & blk	.55	.45

C452	A142	1.25g yel grn & blk	.45	.35
C453	A142	1.50g bl gray & blk	.45	.35
C454	A142	1.75g rose & blk	.55	.45
C455	A142	2g yel & blk	.65	.55
C457	A142	5g bl grn & blk	1.75	1.10
C458	A142	10g ocher & blk	3.50	2.10
		Nos. C448-C458 (10)	9.05	6.40

Issued: 75c, 80c, #C451, 1.75g, 5g, 10g, 1977.

Nos. C415-C416, C418-C419 Overprinted or Surcharged in Black, Dark Blue or Green

1977, July 6   Litho.   *Perf. 14x13½*
C460	A149	1g (Bk)	.45	.35
C461	A149	1.25g on 50c (DB)	.55	.45
C462	A149	1.25g on 50c (G)	.55	.45
C463	A149	1.25g on 1.75g (Bk)	.55	.45
		Nos. C460-C463 (4)	2.10	1.70

Charles A. Lindbergh's solo transatlantic flight from NY to Paris, 50th anniv.

Telephone Type of 1978

Designs: 1g, Telstar over globe. 1.25g, Duvalier Earth Telecommunications Station. 2g, Wall telephone, 1890, vert.

1978, June 19   Litho.   *Perf. 13½*
C466	A153	1g multi	.45	.35
C467	A153	1.25g multi	.55	.45
C468	A153	2g multi	.85	.55
		Nos. C466-C468 (3)	1.85	1.35

Olympic Games Type of 1978

Montreal Olympic Games' Emblem and: 1.25g, Equestrian. 2.50g, Basketball. 5g, Yachting.

1978, Sept. 4   Litho.   *Perf. 13½x13*
C469	A154	1.25g multi	.70	.60
C470	A154	2.50g multi	1.50	1.25
C471	A154	5g multi	3.50	1.50
		Nos. C469-C471 (3)	5.70	3.35

Children's Institute Type, 1979

Designs: 1.25g, Mother nursing child. 2g, Nurse giving injection.

1979, Jan. 15   Photo.   *Perf. 14x14½*
C472	A155	1.25g multi	.55	.35
C473	A155	2g multi	.80	.55

Haitians Spinning Cotton, CARE Workshop AP51

1979, May 11   Photo.   *Perf. 11½*
C474	AP51	1g multi	.65	.55
C475	AP51	1.25g multi	.95	.65
C476	AP51	2g multi	1.40	.85
		Nos. C474-C476 (3)	3.00	2.05

30th anniversary of CARE.

Human Rights Type of 1979

1979, July 20   Litho.   *Perf. 14*
C477	A157	1g multi	.65	.55
C478	A157	1.25g multi	.95	.65
C479	A157	2g multi	1.40	.85
		Nos. C477-C479 (3)	3.00	2.05

Anti-Apartheid Year Type of 1979

1979, Nov. 22   Photo.   *Perf. 12x11½*
C480	A158	1g yel grn & blk	1.00	.55
C481	A158	1.25g bl & blk	1.10	.65
C482	A158	2g gray olive	1.75	.85
		Nos. C480-C482 (3)	3.85	2.05

IYC Type of 1979

1979, Dec. 19   Photo.   *Perf. 12*
C483	A159	1g multi	.65	.55
C484	A159	1.25g multi	.95	.65
C485	A159	2.50g multi	2.50	1.10
C486	A159	5g multi	3.50	1.60
		Nos. C483-C486 (4)	7.60	3.90

Nos. C421, C424-C425 Overprinted

1980, May 17 Photo. Perf. 14x13½
C487	A151	50c multi	.35	.20
C488	A151	1.50g multi	.95	.45
C489	A151	1.75g multi	1.20	.55
		Nos. C487-C489 (3)	2.50	1.20

Wedding of Pres. Duvalier, May 27.

Dessalines Type of 1972
1980, Aug. 27 Photo. Perf. 11½
Granite Paper
C490	A142	1g gray vio & blk	.55	.45
C491	A142	1.25g sal pink & blk	.65	.55
C492	A142	2g pale grn & blk	1.20	.85
C493	A142	5g lt bl & blk	2.40	1.60
		Nos. C490-C493 (4)	4.80	3.45

For surcharge see No. C512.

Tourism Type
1980, Dec. 2 Litho. Perf. 12½x12
C494	A160	1g like #728	.55	.45
C495	A160	1.25g like #729	.65	.55
C496	A160	1.50g Carnival dancers	.95	.55
C497	A160	2g Vendors	1.20	.85
C498	A160	2.50g like #C497	1.40	1.10
		Nos. C494-C498 (5)	4.75	3.50

For surcharge see No. C511.

Soccer Type of 1980
1980, Dec. 30 Litho. Perf. 14
C499	A161	50c Uruguay, 1950	.35	.20
C500	A161	75c Germany, 1954	.45	.35
C501	A161	1g Brazil, 1958	.65	.45
C502	A161	1.25g Brazil, 1962	.80	.55
C503	A161	1.50g Gt. Britain, 1966	1.10	.65
C504	A161	1.75g Brazil, 1970	1.25	.85
C505	A161	2g Germany, 1974	1.40	.95
C506	A161	5g Argentina, 1978	3.50	2.10
		Nos. C499-C506 (8)	9.50	6.10

Painting Type of 1981
1981, May 12 Photo. Perf. 11½
C507	A162	50c like #734	.35	.20
C508	A162	1.25g like #735	.65	.55
C509	A162	2g like #736	1.25	.85
C510	A162	5g like #737	2.40	1.60
		Nos. C507-C510 (4)	4.65	3.20

Nos. C496, C493 Surcharged
Perf. 12½x12, 11½
1981, Dec. 30 Litho., Photo.
C511	A160	1.25g on 1.50g multi	.65	.55
C512	A142	2g on 5g multi	1.20	.85

Dessalines Type of 1972
1982, Jan. 25 Photo. Perf. 11½
Granite Paper
C513	A142	1.25g lt brn & blk	.65	.55
C514	A142	2g lilac & blk	1.20	.85

No. C320 Surcharged

2000? Photo. Perf. 13
C515	A128	3g on 75c #C320	— —

AIR POST SEMI-POSTAL STAMPS

Coubertin Semipostal Type of 1939
Unwmk.
1939, Oct. 3 Engr. Perf. 12
CB1	SP1	60c + 40c multi	25.00	25.00
CB2	SP1	1.25g + 60c multi	25.00	25.00

Mosquito and National Sanatorium — SPAP2
1949, July 22 Cross in Carmine
CB3	SPAP2	20c + 20c sep	11.00	6.00
CB4	SPAP2	30c + 30c dp grn	11.00	6.00
CB5	SPAP2	45c + 45c lt red brn	11.00	6.00
CB6	SPAP2	80c + 80c pur	11.00	6.00
CB7	SPAP2	1.25g + 1.25g car rose	11.00	6.00
a.		Souvenir sheet	40.00	25.00
CB8	SPAP2	1.75g + 1.75g bl	11.00	6.00
a.		Souvenir sheet	40.00	25.00
		Nos. CB3-CB8 (6)	66.00	36.00

The surtax was used for fighting tuberculosis and malaria.

> **Catalogue values for unused stamps in this section, from this point to the end of the section, are for Never Hinged items.**

No. C113 Surcharged in Deep Carmine

1958, Aug. 30 Litho. Perf. 13x13½
CB9	A82	2.50g + 50c	2.50	2.40

The surtax was for the Red Cross.

Similar Surcharge in Red on One Line on Nos. C133-C135
1959, Apr. 7 Photo. Perf. 11½
Granite Paper
CB10	AP35	50c + 25c pink, car & ultra	.40	.40
CB11	A87	75c + 25c brt bl	.50	.50
CB12	A87	1g + 25c brn	.75	.75

Nos. C139-C141 Surcharged Like No. CB9 in Red
CB13	AP36	50c + 50c grn & lil	1.00	1.00
CB14	AP36	1.50g + 50c ol & red brn	1.00	1.00
CB15	AP36	2.50g + 50c pur & dk bl	1.25	1.25
		Nos. CB10-CB15 (6)	4.90	4.90

Surtax for the Red Cross.

Nos. C142-C144 Surcharged Diagonally

1959, July 23 Unwmk. Perf. 12
CB16	A89	1g + 20c	1.00	1.00
CB17	A89	2g + 20c	1.10	1.10
CB18	A89	2.50g + 20c	1.10	1.10
		Nos. CB16-CB18 (3)	3.20	3.20

World Refugee Year, July 1, 1959-June 30, 1960. A similar surcharge of 50c was applied horizontally to stamps in No. C144a. Value $25.

C145-C147 Surcharged in Dark Carmine

1959, Oct. 30 Photo. Perf. 14
CB19	A91	50c + 75c hn brn & aqua	1.00	1.00
CB20	A90	1g + 75c lil & aqua	1.00	1.00
CB21	A90	1.50g + 75c multi	1.00	1.00
		Nos. CB19-CB21 (3)	3.00	3.00

The surtax was for Haitian athletes. On No. CB19, surcharge lines are spaced to total depth of 16mm.

Nos. C129-C130 Surcharged in Red: "Hommage a l'UNICEF +G. 0,50"
Engraved and Lithographed
1960, Feb. 2 Perf. 11½
CB22	AP34	2g + 50c	1.00	1.00
CB23	AP34	2.50g + 50c	1.75	1.75

Issued to honor UNICEF.

Nos. C151-C152 Surcharged and Overprinted: "ALPHABETISATION" in Red or Black.
1960, July 12 Litho. Perf. 12½x13
CB24	A92	50c + 20c (R)	.40	.40
CB25	A92	50c + 30c	.65	.50
CB26	A92	1g + 20c (R)	.90	.75
CB27	A92	1g + 30c	.90	.75
		Nos. CB24-CB27 (4)	2.85	2.45

Olympic Games Issue
Nos. C163-C164 Surcharged
1960, Sept. 9 Photo. Perf. 12
CB28	A94	50c + 25c	.40	.25
CB29	A94	1.50g + 25c	.65	.55

Nos. C168-C169 Surcharged: "UNICEF +25 centimes"
1961, Jan. 14 Engr. Perf. 10½
CB30	A96	50c + 25c red org & blk	.40	.25
CB31	A96	1.50g + 25c dk bl & blk	.65	.55

Nos. C171, C175-C176 Surcharged with Additional Value, Scout Emblem and: "18e Conference Internationale du Scoutisme Mondial Lisbonne Septembre 1961"
1961, Sept. 30 Photo. Perf. 11½
CB32	AP37	20c + 25c	.40	.30
CB33	AP37	1g + 25c	.50	.40
CB34	AP37	1.50g + 25c	.60	.60
		Nos. CB32-CB34 (3)	1.50	1.30

Issued to commemorate the 18th Boy Scout World Conference, Lisbon, Sept. 19-24, 1961. The surtax was for the Red Cross. Additional proceeds from the sale of Nos. CB32-CB34 benefited the Port-au-Prince airport project.
The same surcharge was also applied to No. C176a. Value $3.

Nos. C168-C169 Surcharged: "OMS SNEM +20 CENTIMES"
1961, Dec. 11 Engr. Perf. 10½
CB35	A96	50c + 20c	1.60	1.60
CB36	A96	1.50g + 20c	2.25	2.25

Issued to publicize Haiti's participation in the UN malaria eradication drive.

Nos. C123, C126-C127 and C131-C132 Surcharged in Black or Red

Engraved and Lithographed
1961-62 Perf. 11½
CB37	AP34	50c + 25c	.25	.25
CB38	AP34	1g + 50c	.35	.35
CB39	AP34	2.50g + 50c (R) ('62)	.65	.65
CB40	AP34	5g + 50c	1.10	1.10
CB41	AP34	7.50g + 50c (R) ('62)	1.50	1.50
		Nos. CB37-CB41 (5)	3.85	3.85

The surtax was for the benefit of the urban rehabilitation program in Duvalier Ville.

Nos. C188-C190 Surcharged: "+25 centimes"
1962, Sept. 13 Litho. Perf. 12
CB42	A99	20c + 25c	.25	.20
CB43	A99	50c + 25c	.40	.20
CB44	A99	1g + 25c	.50	.40
		Nos. CB42-CB44 (3)	1.15	.80

#C191-C192 Surcharged in Red: "+0.20"
1962 Perf. 12½x13
CB45	A92	50c + 20c	.40	.40
CB46	A92	1g + 20c	.50	.40

Nos. C203 and C205 Surcharged: "ALPHABETISATION" and "+0, 10"
1963, Mar. 15 Photo. Perf. 14x14½
CB47	AP38	50c + 10c	.40	.40
CB48	AP38	1.50g + 10c	.50	.40

No. C110 Surcharged in Red with Olympic Emblem and: "JEUX OLYMPIQUES / D'HIVER / INNSBRUCK 1964"
1964, July 27 Photo. Perf. 11½
CB49	A80	2.50g + 50c + 10c	.90	.80

See note after No. B34. The 50c+10c surtax went for charity.

No. C213 Surcharged in Red

Engraved and Photogravure
1964, Oct. 2 Perf. 13½x14
CB50	AP39	2.50g + 1.25g on 1.50g	1.40	1.25

Issued to commemorate the centenary (in 1963) of the International Red Cross.

Nos. C223-C226 Surcharged: "+ 5c."
1965, Mar. 15 Photo. Perf. 11½
CB51	A105	50c + 5c pale lil & dk brn	.40	.20
CB52	A105	50c + 5c pale grn & dk brn	.40	.20
CB53	A105	75c + 5c buff & dk brn	.50	.40
CB54	A105	1.50g + 5c gray & dk brn	.80	.65
		Nos. CB51-CB54 (4)	2.10	1.45

The souvenir sheet No. C226a was surcharged "+25c." Value, $8.
See note following No. B37.

Nos. C251 and C253 Surcharged and Overprinted with Haitian Scout Emblem and "12e Jamboree / Mondial 1967" Like Regular Issue
1967, Aug. 21 Photo. Perf. 11½
CB55	A111	50c + 10c multi	.50	.40
CB56	A111	1.50g + 50c multi	.65	.50

See note after No. B40.

No. C269 Surcharged Like Regular Issue

Lithographed and Photogravure

1968, Jan. 18		**Perf. 13x13½**		
CB57	A115	2.50g + 1.25g on		
		1.50g	3.25	2.50

See note after No. 579.

#C285-C287 Surcharged "CULTURE + 10"

1968, July 4		**Perf. 11½**		
CB58	A120	50c + 10c multi	.40	.20
CB59	A120	1g + 10c multi	.50	.40
CB60	A120	1.50g + 10c multi	.65	.50
		Nos. CB58-CB60 (3)	1.55	1.10

Nos. C314 and C316 Surcharged in Red with New Value, Red Cross and: "50ème. Anniversaire / de la Ligue des / Sociétés de la / Croix Rouge"

1969, June 25		**Litho.**	**Perf. 11½**	
CB61	A127	50c + 20c multi	.50	.40
CB62	A127	1.50g + 25c multi	.90	.50

League of Red Cross Societies, 50th anniv.

AIR POST OFFICIAL STAMPS

Nos. C172-C176 and C176a Overprinted: "OFFICIEL"

Perf. 11½

1961, Mar.	**Unwmk.**		**Photo.**
CO1	AP37	50c rose brn & grn	.60
CO2	AP37	50c brt grnsh bl & ol grn	.60
CO3	AP37	50c gray & grn	.60
CO4	AP37	1g gray ol & ver	.85
CO5	AP37	1.50g brt pink & dk bl	1.40
a.		Sheet of 3	3.75
		Nos. CO1-CO5 (5)	4.05

Nos. CO1-CO5a only available canceled.

Catalogue values for unused stamps in this section, from this point to the end of the section, are for Never Hinged items.

Jean Jacques Dessalines — OA1

1962, Mar. 7	**Photo.**		**Perf. 14x14½**	
		Size: 20½x38mm		
CO6	OA1	50c dk bl & sepia	.50	.40
CO7	OA1	1g lt bl & maroon	.80	.50
CO8	OA1	1.50g bister & bl	1.00	.70
		Size: 30x40mm		
CO9	OA1	5g rose & ol grn	2.75	2.40
		Nos. CO6-CO9 (4)	5.05	4.00

Inscription at bottom of #CO9 is in 2 lines.

AIR POST PARCEL POST STAMPS

Catalogue values for unused stamps in this section are for Never Hinged items.

Nos. C112 and C111 Overprinted in Red

Perf. 11½

1960, Nov. 21	**Unwmk.**		**Photo.**
CQ1	A81	50c orange & black	.50	.40
CQ2	A80	5g bluish blk & saph	3.50	2.60

Type of Parcel Post Stamps, 1961 Inscribed "Poste Aerienne"

1961, Mar. 24			**Perf. 14**	
CQ3	PP1	2.50g yel grn & mar	2.00	1.40
CQ4	PP1	5g org & green	2.50	1.60

SPECIAL DELIVERY STAMP

The catalogue value for the unused stamp in this section is for Never Hinged.

Postal Administration Building — SD1

Unwmk.

1953, May 4		**Engr.**	**Perf. 12**	
E1	SD1	25c vermilion	.70	.50

POSTAGE DUE STAMPS

    D1   D2

1898, May	**Unwmk.**	**Engr.**	**Perf. 12**	
J1	D1	2c black	1.00	.75
J2	D1	5c brown	1.50	1.00
J3	D1	10c brown orange	2.00	1.50
J4	D1	50c slate	3.00	2.50
		Nos. J1-J4 (4)	7.50	5.75

For overprints see Nos. J5-J9, J14-J16.

Stamps of 1898 Handstamped like #67-81

1902		**Black Overprint**		
J5	D1	2c black	2.50	1.50
J6	D1	5c red brown	2.50	1.50
J7	D1	10c brown orange	2.50	1.50
J8	D1	50c slate	12.00	7.00
		Red Overprint		
J9	D1	2c black	3.50	3.50
		Nos. J5-J9 (5)	23.00	15.00

1906				
J10	D2	2c dull red	1.50	1.00
J11	D2	5c ultra	2.75	2.50
J12	D2	10c violet	2.75	2.50
J13	D2	50c olive gray	11.50	7.50
		Nos. J10-J13 (4)	18.50	13.50

For surcharges and overprints see Nos. 305-308, J17-J20.

Preceding Issues Handstamped like #169-201

1914		**On Stamps of 1898**		
J14	D1	5c red brown	1.50	1.10
J15	D1	10c brown orange	1.50	1.10
J16	D1	50c slate	6.00	5.50
		Nos. J14-J16 (3)	9.00	7.70
		On Stamps of 1906		
J17	D2	2c dull red	1.25	1.00
J18	D2	5c ultra	2.25	2.25
J19	D2	10c violet	7.50	5.50
J20	D2	50c olive gray	35.00	35.00
		Nos. J17-J20 (4)	46.00	43.75

The note after No. 201 applies to Nos. J14-J20 also.

Unpaid Letter — D3

1951, July		**Litho.**	**Perf. 11½**	
J21	D3	10c carmine	.20	.20
J22	D3	20c red brown	.25	.20
J23	D3	40c green	.40	.40
J24	D3	50c orange yellow	.50	.50
		Nos. J21-J24 (4)	1.35	1.30

PARCEL POST STAMPS

Catalogue values for unused stamps in this section are for Never Hinged items.

Nos. 416, 470-471 and 378 Overprinted in Red

Photogravure, Engraved
Perf. 11½, 12

1960, Nov. 21			**Unwmk.**	
Q1	A81	5c yel grn & blk	.20	.20
Q2	A81	10c red org & blk	.20	.20
Q3	A81	25c ultra & black	.40	.25
Q4	A64	2.50g gray	2.75	2.40
		Nos. Q1-Q4 (4)	3.55	3.05

Coat of Arms — PP1

Unwmk.

1961, Mar. 24		**Photo.**	**Perf. 14**	
Q5	PP1	50c bister & black	.50	.40
Q6	PP1	1g pink & dark blue	.80	.50

See Nos. CQ3-CQ4.

POSTAL TAX STAMPS

Catalogue values for unused stamps in this section, are for Never Hinged items.

Haitian Woman, War Invalids and Ruined Buildings PT1

Unwmk.

1944, Aug. 16		**Engr.**	**Perf. 12**	
RA1	PT1	5c dull purple	1.40	.60
RA2	PT1	5c dark blue	1.40	.60
RA3	PT1	5c olive green	1.40	.60
RA4	PT1	5c black	1.40	.60
1945, Dec. 17				
RA5	PT1	5c dark green	1.40	.60
RA6	PT1	5c sepia	1.40	.60
RA7	PT1	5c red brown	1.40	.60
RA8	PT1	5c rose carmine	1.40	.60
		Nos. RA1-RA8 (8)	11.20	4.80

The proceeds from the sale of Nos. RA1 to RA8 were for United Nations Relief.

George Washington, J.J. Dessalines and Simón Bolívar — PT2

1949, Sept. 20				
RA9	PT2	5c red brown	.50	.40
RA10	PT2	5c olive gray	.50	.40
RA11	PT2	5c blue	.50	.40
RA12	PT2	5c green	.50	.40
RA13	PT2	5c violet	.50	.40
RA14	PT2	5c black	.50	.40
RA15	PT2	5c orange	.50	.40
RA16	PT2	5c carmine rose	.50	.40
		Nos. RA9-RA16 (8)	4.00	3.20

Bicentenary of Port-au-Prince.
For overprint and surcharges see #385-388.

Helicopter Inspection of Hurricane Damage PT3   Helicopter PT4

1955, Jan. 3		**Photo.**	**Perf. 11½**	
RA17	PT3	10c bright green	.25	.20
RA18	PT3	10c bright blue	.25	.20
RA19	PT3	10c gray black	.25	.20
RA20	PT3	10c orange	.25	.20
RA21	PT3	20c rose carmine	.35	.20
RA22	PT3	20c deep green	.35	.20
		Nos. RA17-RA22 (6)	1.70	1.20

1955, May 3				
RA23	PT4	10c black, *gray*	.25	.20
RA24	PT4	20c violet blue, *blue*	.30	.20

The surface tint of the sheets of 50, (10x5) of #RA23-RA24, RAC1-RAC2 includes a map of Haiti's southern peninsula which extends over the three center rows of stamps.
The tax was for reconstruction.
See Nos. RAC1-RAC2.

PT5

1959-60	**Unwmk.**	**Photo.**	**Perf. 11½**	
		Size: 38x22½mm		
RA25	PT5	5c green	.20	.20
RA26	PT5	5c black ('60)	.20	.20
RA27	PT5	10c red	.20	.20
		Nos. RA25-RA27 (3)	.60	.60
1960-61				
		Size: 28x17mm		
RA28	PT5	5c green	.20	.20
RA29	PT5	10c red	.20	.20
RA30	PT5	10c blue ('61)	.20	.20
		Nos. RA28-RA30 (3)	.60	.60

PT6

1963, Sept.			**Perf. 14½x14**	
		Size: 13½x21mm		
RA31	PT6	10c red orange	.20	.20
RA32	PT6	10c bright blue	.20	.20
RA33	PT6	10c olive	.20	.20
		Nos. RA31-RA33, RAC6-RAC8 (6)	1.20	1.20

1966-69 Photo. Perf. 14x14½
Size: 17x25mm

RA34	PT6	10c bright green	.20	.20
RA35	PT6	10c violet	.20	.20
RA36	PT6	10c violet blue	.20	.20
RA37	PT6	10c brown ('69)	.20	.20
Nos. RA34-RA37,RAC9-RAC15				
(11)			2.20	2.20

Nos. RA25-RA37 represent a tax for a literacy campaign.
See Nos. RA42-RA45, RAC20-RAC22.

Duvalier de Peligre
Hydroelectric
Works — PT7

1970-72

RA38	PT7	20c violet & olive	.20	.20
RA39	PT7	20c ultra & blk ('72)	.20	.20

See Nos. RA46, RAC16-RAC19, RAC23.

Nos. 637-638 Surcharged:
"ALPHABETISATION +10"

1971, Dec. 23 Litho. Perf. 14x13½

RA40	A138	20c + 10c multi	.35	.20
a.	Inverted surcharge			2.00
RA41	A138	25c + 10c multi	.35	.20

Tax was for the literacy campaign.

"CA" Type of 1963

1972-74 Photo. Perf. 14x14½
Size: 17x25mm

RA42	PT6	5c violet blue	.20	.20
RA43	PT6	5c deep carmine	.20	.20
RA44	PT6	5c ultra ('74)	.20	.20
RA45	PT6	5c carmine rose ('74)	.20	.20
Nos. RA42-RA45 (4)			.80	.80

Tax was for literacy campaign.

Hydroelectric Type of 1970

1980 Photo. Perf. 14x14½

RA46	PT7	25c choc & green	.25	.20

AIR POST POSTAL TAX STAMPS

> Catalogue values for unused stamps in this section, are for Never Hinged items.

Helicopter Type of 1955

1955 Unwmk. Photo. Perf. 11½

RAC1	PT4	10c red brn, pale sal	.30	.20
RAC2	PT4	20c rose pink, pink	.35	.20

See note after No. RA24.

Type of Postal Tax Stamps, 1960-61

1959
Size: 28x17mm

RAC3	PT5	5c yellow	.20	.20
RAC4	PT5	10c dull salmon	.20	.20
RAC5	PT5	10c blue	.20	.20
Nos. RAC3-RAC5 (3)			.60	.60

Type of Postal Tax Stamps, 1963

1963, Sept. Perf. 14½x14
Size: 13½x21mm

RAC6	PT6	10c dark gray	.20	.20
RAC7	PT6	10c violet	.20	.20
RAC8	PT6	10c brown	.20	.20
Nos. RAC6-RAC8 (3)			.60	.60

1966-69 Perf. 14x14½
Size: 17x25mm

RAC9	PT6	10c orange	.20	.20
RAC10	PT6	10c sky blue	.20	.20
RAC11	PT6	10c yellow ('69)	.20	.20
RAC12	PT6	10c carmine ('69)	.20	.20
RAC13	PT6	10c gray grn ('69)	.20	.20
RAC14	PT6	10c lilac ('69)	.20	.20
RAC15	PT6	10c dp claret ('69)	.20	.20
Nos. RAC9-RAC15 (7)			1.40	1.40

Nos. RAC3-RAC15, RAC20-RAC21 represent a tax for a literacy campaign.

Hydroelectric Type of 1970

1970-74

RAC16	PT7	20c tan & slate	.20	.20
RAC17	PT7	20c brt bl & dl vio	.20	.20
RAC18	PT7	25c sal & bluish blk ('74)	.25	.20

RAC19	PT7	25c yel ol & bluish blk ('74)	.25	.20
Nos. RAC16-RAC19 (4)			.90	.80

"CA" Type of 1963

1973 Photo. Perf. 14x14½
Size: 17x26mm

RAC20	PT6	10c brn & blue	.35	.20
RAC21	PT6	10c brn & green	.35	.20
RAC22	PT6	10c brn & orange	.35	.20
Nos. RAC20-RAC22 (3)			1.05	.60

Hydroelectric Power Type of 1970

1979(?) Photo. Perf. 14x14½

RAC23	PT7	25c blue & vio brn	.25	.20

HATAY

hä-'tī

LOCATION — Northwest of Syria, bordering on Mediterranean Sea
GOVT. — Semi-independent republic
AREA — 10,000 sq. mi. (approx.)
POP. — 273,350 (1939)
CAPITAL — Antioch

Alexandretta, a semi-autonomous district of Syria under French mandate, was renamed Hatay in 1938 and transferred to Turkey in 1939.

100 Santims = 1 Kurush
40 Paras = 1 Kurush (1939)

Stamps of Turkey, 1931-38, Surcharged in Black:

On A77   On A78

1939 Unwmk. Perf. 11½x12

1	A77	10s on 20pa dp org	1.50	.35
a.	"Sent" instead of "Sant"		125.00	22.50
2	A78	25s on 1ku dk sl grn	1.75	.35
a.	Small "25"		12.50	1.50
3	A78	50s on 2ku dk vio	1.75	.35
a.	Small "50"		6.00	2.00
4	A77	75s on 2½ku green	1.50	.40
5	A78	1ku on 4ku slate	9.50	.25
6	A78	1ku on 5ku rose red	5.00	1.40
7	A78	1½ku on 3ku brn org	2.50	.80
8	A78	2½ku on 4ku slate	3.50	1.00
9	A78	5ku on 8ku brt blue	5.50	1.25
10	A77	12½ku on 20ku ol grn	6.50	2.00
11	A77	20ku on 25ku Prus bl	12.00	7.00
Nos. 1-11 (11)			51.00	19.15
Set, never hinged			130.00	

Map of
Hatay — A1

Lions of
Antioch
A2

Flag of
Hatay
A3

Post Office
A4

1939 Unwmk. Typo. Perf. 12

12	A1	10p orange & aqua	2.50	.75
13	A1	30p lt vio & aqua	2.50	.75
14	A1	1½ku olive & aqua	2.50	.75
15	A2	2½ku turq grn	3.00	1.00
16	A2	3ku light blue	3.00	1.00
17	A2	5ku chocolate	3.00	1.00
18	A3	6ku brt blue & car	3.75	1.25
19	A3	7½ku dp green & car	4.25	1.40
20	A3	12ku violet & car	5.00	1.40
21	A3	12½ku dk blue & car	4.00	1.50
22	A4	17½ku brown car	8.00	3.00
23	A4	25ku olive brn	9.00	3.50
24	A4	50ku slate blue	18.00	8.50
Nos. 12-24 (13)			68.50	25.80
Set, never hinged			175.00	

Stamps of 1939
Overprinted in
Black

1939

25	A1	10p orange & aqua	1.75	.75
a.	Overprint reading up		22.50	
26	A1	30p lt vio & aqua	1.75	.75
27	A1	1½ku ol & aqua	2.50	.80
28	A2	2½ku turq grn	2.50	.80
29	A2	3ku light blue	2.75	.80
30	A2	5ku chocolate	3.50	1.25
a.	Overprint inverted		22.50	
31	A3	6ku brt bl & car	3.75	1.25
32	A3	7½ku dp grn & car	4.00	1.25
33	A3	12ku vio & car	4.00	1.25
34	A3	12½ku dk bl & car	4.50	1.25
35	A4	17½ku brn car	5.50	2.25
a.	Overprint inverted		22.50	
36	A4	25ku olive brn	9.00	4.25
37	A4	50ku slate blue	19.00	10.00
Nos. 25-37 (13)			64.50	26.65
Set, never hinged			150.00	

The overprint reads "Date of annexation to the Turkish Republic, June 30, 1939."
On Nos. 25-27, the overprint reads down. On Nos. 28-37, it is horizontal.

POSTAGE DUE STAMPS

Postage Due Stamps of
Turkey, 1936,
Surcharged or
Overprinted in Black

1939 Unwmk. Perf. 11½

J1	D6	1ku on 2ku lt bl	3.25	.45
J2	D6	3ku bright violet	3.75	.90
J3	D6	4ku on 5ku Prus bl	3.75	.90
J4	D6	5ku on 12ku brt rose	4.25	.90
J5	D6	12ku bright rose	50.00	27.50
Nos. J1-J5 (5)			65.00	30.65
Set, never hinged			170.00	

Castle at
Antioch
D1

1939 Typo. Perf. 12

J6	D1	1ku red orange	4.00	1.00
J7	D1	3ku dk olive brown	4.50	1.25
J8	D1	4ku turqoise green	5.00	1.75
J9	D1	5ku slate black	5.75	2.50
Nos. J6-J9 (4)			19.25	6.50
Set, never hinged			42.50	

Nos. J6-J9 Overprinted in Black like Nos. 25-37

1939

J10	D1	1ku red orange	3.75	1.25
J11	D1	3ku dk olive brown	4.50	1.50
J12	D1	4ku turqoise green	4.50	1.75
J13	D1	5ku slate black	6.50	2.00
a.	Overprint inverted		22.50	
Nos. J10-J13 (4)			19.25	6.50
Set, never hinged			52.50	

HELIGOLAND

'he-lə-gō-ˌland

LOCATION — An island in the North Sea near the northern coast of Germany
GOVT. — Former British Possession
AREA — ¼ sq. mi.
POP. — 2,307 (1900)

Great Britain ceded Heligoland to Germany in 1890. It became part of Schleswig-Holstein province. Stamps of Heligoland were superseded by those of the German Empire.

16 Schillings = 1 Mark
100 Pfennig = 1 Mark = 1 Schilling (1875)

> **REPRINTS**
> Most Heligoland issues were extensively reprinted between 1875 and 1895, and these comprise the great majority of Heligoland stamps in the marketplace. Such reprints sell for much less than the originals, usually for $1-$2 each. Expertization of Heligoland issues is strongly recommended by the editors.

Queen Victoria
A1   A2

A3   A4

HALF SCHILLING
A1: Curl below chignon is rounded.
A2: Curl resembles hook or comma.

Typo., Head Embossed

1867-68 Unwmk. Rouletted

1	A1	½sch bl grn & rose	325.00	1,000.
1A	A2	½sch bl grn & rose	800.00	1,700.
2	A1	1sch rose & dp grn	190.00	200.00
4	A3	2sch rose & pale grn		14.50	60.00
4	A3	6sch gray grn & rose		16.50	475.00

Reprints of No. 2 lack the large curl, those of No. 1A are not in blue green, and those of Nos. 3 and 4 are on slightly porous paper and the colors are either too deep or too bright. The 2sch and 6sch perforated exist only as reprints.

1869-71 Perf. 13½x14½
Thick Soft Paper

5	A2	½sch ol grn & car	125.00	160.00
a.	½sch blue green & rose		240.00	250.00
b.	½sch yellow green & rose		475.00	450.00
6	A2	1sch rose & yel grn	175.00	300.00

Reprints are on thinner paper and in too dark colors.

1873　　　　　　　　　**Thick Quadrille Paper**

7	A4	¼sch pale rose & pale grn	32.50	2,250.
a.		¼sch deep rose & pale grn	325.00	2,250.
8	A4	¼sch yel grn & rose	135.00	3,600.
9	A2	½sch brt grn & rose	125.00	210.00
10	A4	¾sch gray grn & pale rose	35.00	2,250.
a.		¾sch gray green & dp rose	35.00	2,250.
11	A2	1sch rose & pale grn	210.00	425.00
12	A4	1½sch yel grn & rose	72.50	325.00

Reprints are never on quadrille paper.

1874　　　　　　　　　**Thin Wove Paper**

| 13 | A4 | ¼sch rose & yel grn | 17.50 | |

Originals have the large curl. The early reprints have the small curl. The later reprints are on thin hard paper with smooth white gum and the colors are too bright.

A5

A6

A7

Coat of Arms — A8

1875　　　　　　　　　**Wove Paper**

14	A5	1pf dk rose & dk grn	14.50	600.00
15	A5	2pf yel grn & dk rose	14.50	875.00
16	A6	5pf dk rose & dk grn	20.00	21.00
17	A6	10pf blue grn & red	13.00	37.50
a.		10pf yel green & dark rose	110.00	27.50
b.		10pf lt green & pale red	140.00	25.00
18	A7	25pf rose & dk green	16.50	30.00
a.		25pf dk rose & dk green	16.50	30.00
19	A7	50pf dk grn & brick red	22.50	85.00
a.		50pf dl grn & dk rose	65.00	37.50

The 1pf and 2pf have been reprinted on very white paper with white gum. The colors are too bright and too light.

1876-88　　　　　　　　　**Typo.**

20	A8	3pf dp grn & dl red	275.00	1,600.
a.		3pf green & bright red ('77)	175.00	1,000.
21	A8	20pf ver & brt grn ('88)	14.50	32.50
a.		20pf brn org & grn ('87)	425.00	47.50
b.		20pf vio car & yel grn ('80)	240.00	125.00
c.		20pf anil rose & dk grn ('85)	425.00	65.00
d.		20pf lil rose & dk grn ('76)	240.00	125.00
e.		20pf rose red & dk grn ('80)	240.00	125.00

The coat-of-arms on Nos. 20, 21 and subvarieties is printed in three colors: varying shades of yellow, red and green.
The 3pf has been reprinted. The colors are usually too pale, especially the red, which is either orange or orange red.

A9

A10

1879　　　　　　　　　**Typo.**

22	A9	1m dp green & car	225.00	225.00
a.		1m blue green & salmon	225.00	240.00
b.		1m dark green & ver	80.00	
23	A10	5m blue grn & sal	190.00	1,200.

Perf. 11½

24	A9	1m dp grn & car	1,700.	5,500.
25	A10	5m bl grn & rose red	1,700.	12,000.
a.		Horiz. pair, imperf. vert.	5,000.	

Nos. 13, 20a, 22b, 24 and 25 were never placed in use. Forged cancellations of Nos. 1-23 are plentiful.
Heligoland stamps were replaced by those of the German Empire in 1890.

HONDURAS

hän-'dur-əs

LOCATION — Central America, between Guatemala on the north and Nicaragua on the south
GOVT. — Republic
AREA — 43,277 sq. mi.
POP. — 5,997,327 (1999 est.)
CAPITAL — Tegucigalpa

8 Reales = 1 Peso
100 Centavos = 1 Peso (1878)
100 Centavos = 1 Lempira (1933)

> **Catalogue values for unused stamps in this country are for Never Hinged items, beginning with Scott 344 in the regular postage section, Scott B1 in the semipostal section, Scott C144 in the airpost section, Scott CB5 in the airpost semi-postal section, Scott CE3 in the airpost special delivery section, Scott CO110 in the airpost official section, and Scott RA6 in the postal tax section.**

Values for unused stamps are for examples with original gum as defined in the catalogue introduction. Very fine examples of the locally printed Nos. 95-110, 127, 140, 151-210C, and 218-279 will have margins clear of the perforations but will be noticeably off center.

Watermark

Wmk. 209 — Multiple Ovals

Coat of Arms — A1

1865, Dec.　Unwmk.　Litho.　Imperf.

| 1 | A1 | 2r black, *green* | .65 | — |
| 2 | A1 | 2r black, *pink* | .65 | — |

Comayagua

Tegucigalpa

Medio real = ½ real
Un real = 1 real
Dos reales = 2 reales

Comayagua Issue
1877, May

Red Surcharge

| 3 | A1 | ½r on 2r blk, *grn* | 70.00 | |

Blue Surcharge

| 5 | A1 | 2r on 2r blk, *grn* | 150.00 | |
| 6 | A1 | 2r on 2r blk, *pink* | 475.00 | — |

Black Surcharge

7	A1	1r on 2r blk, *grn*	150.00	
8	A1	2r on 2r blk, *grn*	800.00	
9	A1	2r on 2r blk, *pink*	500.00	

No. 5 may exist only as the base for No. 13a.

Tegucigalpa Issue
1877, July

Black Surcharge

13	A1	1r on 2r blk, *grn*	15.00	35.00
a.		Surcharged on #5	1000.	
14	A1	1r on 2r blk, *pink*	80.00	
16	A1	2r on 2r blk, *pink*		

Blue Surcharge

18	A1	½r on 2r blk, *grn*	80.00	
19	A1	½r on 2r blk, *pink*	25.00	
20	A1	1r on 2r blk, *pink*	35.00	
23	A1	2r on 2r blk, *pink*	15.00	25.00

Red Surcharge

| 24 | A1 | ½r on 2r blk, *grn* | 15.00 | 35.00 |
| 25 | A1 | ½r on 2r blk, *pink* | 60.00 | |

Only the stamps valued or dashed used are known to have been postally used. Nos. 3 and 7 may have been postally used, but to date no examples are recorded used. The other listed stamps were sold as remainders. No covers bearing Nos. 3 to 25 are known.
The blue surcharges range from light blue to violet black. The black surcharge has no tinge of blue. The red surcharges range from light to dark carmine. Some exist double or inverted, but genuine errors are rare. Normal cancel is a blue or black 7-bar killer. Target cancels on Nos. 1-24 are forgeries. Surcharges and cancels have been extensively forged.

Regular Issue

President Francisco Morazán — A4

Thin, hard paper, colorless gum
Various Frames

1878, July　Engr.　Perf. 12
Printed by National Bank Note Co. of N.Y.

30	A4	1c violet	.50	.50
31	A4	2c brown	.50	.50
32	A4	½r black	5.00	.50
33	A4	1r green	25.00	.50
34	A4	2r deep blue	3.00	5.00
35	A4	4r vermilion	5.00	10.00
36	A4	1p orange	6.00	25.00
		Nos. 30-36 (7)	45.00	42.00

Various counterfeit cancellations exist on Nos. 30-36. Most used copies of Nos. 35-36 offered are actually 35a-36a with fake or favor cancels.

Re-Issue
Soft paper, yellowish gum
Various Frames

1889
Printed by American Bank Note Co. of N.Y.

30a	A4	1c deep violet	10.00	
31a	A4	2c red brown	.25	
32a	A4	½r black	.25	
33a	A4	1r blue green	.25	
34a	A4	2r ultramarine	5.00	
35a	A4	4r scarlet vermilion	.25	
36a	A4	1p orange yellow	.25	
		Nos. 30a-36a (7)	16.25	

Although Nos. 30a-36a were not intended for postal use, they were valid, and genuine cancels are known on Nos. 31a-34a.

Arms of Honduras — A5

1890, Jan. 6

40	A5	1c yellow green	.30	.30
41	A5	2c red	.30	.30
42	A5	5c blue	.30	.30
43	A5	10c orange	.35	.40
44	A5	20c ocher	.35	.40
45	A5	25c rose red	.35	.40
46	A5	30c purple	.50	.60
47	A5	40c dark blue	.50	.80
48	A5	50c brown	.55	.80

49	A5	75c blue green	.55	2.00
50	A5	1p carmine	.70	2.25
		Nos. 40-50 (11)	4.75	8.55

The tablets and numerals of Nos. 40 to 50 differ for each denomination.
For overprints see Nos. O1-O11.

Used values of Nos. 1-110 are for stamps with genuine cancellations applied while the stamps were valid. Various counterfeit cancellations exist.

A6

President Luis Bográn — A7

1891, July 31

51	A6	1c dark blue	.30	.30
52	A6	2c yellow brown	.30	.30
53	A6	5c blue green	.30	.30
54	A6	10c vermilion	.30	.30
55	A6	20c brown red	.30	.30
56	A6	25c magenta	.40	.55
57	A6	30c slate	.40	.55
58	A6	40c blue green	.40	.55
59	A6	50c black brown	.50	.80
60	A6	75c purple	.50	1.25
61	A6	1p brown	.75	1.60
62	A6	2p brn & black	2.25	5.00
a.		Head inverted	225.00	
63	A7	5p pur & black	2.00	5.75
a.		Head inverted	60.00	
64	A7	10p green & blk	2.00	5.75
a.		Head inverted	75.00	
		Nos. 51-64 (14)	10.70	23.30

#62, 64 exist with papermakers watermark.
For overprints see Nos. O12-O22.

Columbus Sighting Honduran Coast — A8

General Trinidad Cabanas — A9

1892, July 31

65	A8	1c slate	.40	.45
66	A8	2c deep blue	.40	.45
67	A8	5c yellow green	.40	.45
68	A8	10c blue green	.40	.45
69	A8	20c red	.40	.45
70	A8	25c orange brown	.50	.55
71	A8	30c ultramarine	.50	.60
72	A8	40c orange	.50	.90
73	A8	50c brown	.60	.85
74	A8	75c lake	.60	1.25
75	A8	1p purple	.60	1.40
		Nos. 65-75 (11)	5.30	7.80

Discovery of America by Christopher Columbus, 400th anniv.

1893, Aug.

76	A9	1c green	.25	1.50
77	A9	2c scarlet	.25	1.50
78	A9	5c dark blue	.25	1.50
79	A9	10c orange brn	.25	1.50
80	A9	20c brown red	.25	1.50
81	A9	25c dark blue	.30	1.50
82	A9	30c red orange	.50	1.50
83	A9	40c black	.50	1.50
84	A9	50c olive brn	.50	1.50
85	A9	75c purple	.75	1.50
86	A9	1p deep magenta	.75	1.75
		Nos. 76-86 (11)	4.55	16.75

"Justice"
A10

President Celio
Arias
A11

1895, Feb. 15
87	A10	1c vermilion	.30	.30
88	A10	2c deep blue	.30	.30
89	A10	5c slate	.35	.50
90	A10	10c brown rose	.45	.50
91	A10	20c violet	.45	.50
92	A10	50c deep violet	.45	.85
93	A10	50c olive brown	.55	1.25
94	A10	1p dark green	.60	1.60
		Nos. 87-94 (8)	3.45	5.80

The tablets and numerals of Nos. 76-94 differ for each denomination.

1896, Jan. 1 Litho. Perf. 11½
95	A11	1c dark blue	.30	.35
96	A11	2c yellow brn	.30	.35
97	A11	5c purple	1.10	.30
a.		5c red violet	.60	1.10
98	A11	10c vermilion	.40	.40
a.		10c red	4.50	4.50
99	A11	20c emerald	.75	.50
a.		20c deep green		
100	A11	30c ultramarine	.65	.70
101	A11	50c rose	.90	1.00
102	A11	1p black brown	1.25	1.50
		Nos. 95-102 (8)	5.65	5.10

Counterfeits are plentiful. Nos. 95-102 exist imperf. between horiz. or vertically.

Originals of Nos. 95 to 102 are on both thin, semi-transparent paper and opaque paper; reprints are on thicker, opaque paper and usually have a black cancellation "HONDURAS" between horizontal bars.

Railroad
Train — A12

1898, Aug. 1
103	A12	1c brown	.50	.20
104	A12	2c rose	.50	.20
105	A12	5c dull ultra	1.00	.25
b.		5c red violet (error)	1.50	.70
106	A12	6c red violet	.90	.25
b.		6c dull rose (error)		
107	A12	10c dark blue	1.00	.30
108	A12	20c dull orange	1.25	1.25
109	A12	50c orange red	2.00	1.25
110	A12	1p blue green	4.00	3.00
		Nos. 103-110 (8)	11.15	6.20

Excellent counterfeits of Nos. 103-110 exist.
For overprints see Nos. O23-O27.

Laid Paper
103a	A12	1c	1.00	.50
104a	A12	2c	1.25	.50
105a	A12	5c	1.60	.50
106a	A12	6c	1.60	.75
107a	A12	10c	1.60	1.00
		Nos. 103a-107a (5)	7.05	3.25

General Santos
Guardiola
A13

President José
Medina
A14

1903, Jan. 1 Engr. Perf. 12
111	A13	1c yellow grn	.35	.20
112	A13	2c carmine rose	.35	.30
113	A13	5c blue	.35	.30
114	A13	6c dk violet	.35	.30
115	A13	10c brown	.40	.20
116	A13	20c dull ultra	.45	.40
117	A13	50c vermilion	1.25	1.10
118	A13	1p orange	1.25	1.10
		Nos. 111-118 (8)	4.75	4.00

"PERMITASE" handstamped on stamps of 1896-1903 was applied as a control mark by the isolated Pacific Coast post office of Amapala to prevent use of stolen stamps.

1907, Jan. 1 Perf. 14
119	A14	1c dark green	.20	.20
120	A14	2c scarlet	.25	.25
120A	A14	2c carmine	9.00	5.50
121	A14	5c blue	.30	.30
122	A14	6c purple	.35	.30
a.		6c dark violet	.80	.60
123	A14	10c gray brown	.40	.35
124	A14	20c ultra	.90	.85
a.		20c blue violet	110.00	110.00
125	A14	50c deep lake	1.10	1.10
126	A14	1p orange	1.50	1.50
a.		1p orange yellow	—	
		Nos. 119-126 (9)	14.00	10.35

All values of the above set exist imperforate, imperforate horizontally and in horizontal pairs, imperforate between. No. 124a imperf is worth only 10% of the listed perforated variety. For surcharges see Nos. 128-130.

1909 Typo. Perf. 11½
127	A14	1c green	1.25	1.00
a.		Imperf., pair	4.00	4.00
b.		Printed on both sides	7.50	10.00

The 1909 issue is roughly typographed in imitation of the 1907 design. It exists pin perf. 8, 13, etc.

No. 124 Handstamp Surcharged in Black, Green or Red:

1910, Nov. Perf. 14
128	A14	1c on 20c ultra	8.50	6.00
129	A14	5c on 20c ultra (G)	8.50	6.00
130	A14	10c on 20c ultra (R)	8.50	6.00
		Nos. 128-130 (3)	25.50	18.00

As is usual with handstamped surcharges inverts and double exist.

Honduran
Scene — A15

1911, Jan. Litho. Perf. 14, 12 (1p)
131	A15	1c violet	.35	.20
132	A15	2c green	.35	.20
a.		Perf. 12	5.00	1.25
133	A15	5c carmine	.40	.20
a.		Perf. 12	8.00	3.50
134	A15	6c ultramarine	.50	.30
135	A15	10c blue	.60	.40
136	A15	20c yellow	.60	.50
137	A15	50c brown	2.00	1.75
138	A15	1p olive green	2.50	2.00
		Nos. 131-138 (8)	7.30	5.55

For overprints and surcharges see Nos. 139, 141-147, O28-O47.

No. 132a
Overprinted in Red

1911, Sept. 19 Perf. 12
139	A15	2c green	20.00	18.00
a.		Inverted overprint	24.00	22.50

90th anniversary of Independence.

Counterfeit overprints on perf. 14 stamps exist.

President Manuel
Bonilla — A16

1912, Feb. 1 Typo. Perf. 11½
140	A16	1c orange red	12.00	12.00

Election of Pres. Manuel Bonilla.

Stamps of 1911 Surcharged in Black, Red or Blue:

a   b

1913 Litho. Perf. 14
141	A15(a)	2c on 1c violet	1.25	.75
a.		Double surcharge		3.25
b.		Inverted surcharge	4.50	
c.		Double surch., one invtd.	6.75	
d.		Red surcharge	40.00	40.00
142	A15(b)	2c on 1c violet	7.00	5.75
a.		Inverted surcharge	14.00	
143	A15(b)	2c on 10c blue	2.75	2.25
a.		Double surcharge	5.75	5.75
b.		Inverted surcharge		
144	A15(b)	2c on 20c yellow	7.00	6.75
145	A15(b)	5c on 1c violet	2.50	.75
146	A15(b)	5c on 10c bl (Bl)	2.75	1.50
147	A15(b)	6c on 1c violet	2.75	2.25
		Nos. 141-147 (7)	26.00	20.00

Counterfeit surcharges exist.

Terencio
Sierra — A17

Bonilla — A18

ONE CENTAVO:
Type I — Solid border at sides below numerals.
Type II — Border of light and dark stripes.

1913-14 Typo. Perf. 11½
151	A17	1c dark brn, I	.20	.20
a.		1c brown, type II	.75	.45
152	A17	2c carmine	.25	.20
153	A18	5c blue	.40	.20
154	A18	5c ultra ('14)	.40	.20
155	A18	6c gray vio	.50	.25
156	A18	6c purple ('14)	.40	.25
a.		6c red lilac	.60	.35
157	A17	10c blue	.75	.75
158	A17	10c brown ('14)	1.25	.50
159	A17	20c brown	1.00	.75
160	A18	50c rose	2.00	2.00
161	A18	1p gray green	2.25	2.25
		Nos. 151-161 (11)	9.40	7.55

For overprints and surcharges see Nos. 162-173, O48-O57.

Surcharged in Black
or Carmine

1914
162	A17	1c on 2c carmine	.75	.75
163	A17	5c on 2c carmine	1.25	.90
164	A18	5c on 6c gray vio	2.00	2.00
165	A17	10c on 2c carmine	2.00	2.00
166	A18	10c on 6c gray vio	2.00	2.00
a.		Double surcharge	10.00	
167	A18	10c on 6c gray vio (C)	2.00	2.00
168	A18	10c on 50c rose	6.50	5.00
		Nos. 162-168 (7)	16.50	14.65

No. 158 Surcharged
173ovpt

1915
173	A17	5c on 10c brown	2.50	1.75

Ulua
Bridge — A19

Bonilla
Theater — A20

1915-16 Typo.
174	A19	1c chocolate	.20	.20
175	A19	2c carmine	.20	.20
a.		Tête bêche pair	1.00	1.00
176	A20	5c bright blue	.25	.20
177	A20	6c deep purple	.35	.20
178	A19	10c dull blue	.75	.20
179	A19	20c red brown	1.25	1.00
a.		Tête bêche pair	4.00	4.00
180	A20	50c red	1.50	1.50
181	A20	1p yellow grn	2.50	2.50
		Nos. 174-181 (8)	7.00	6.00

For overprints & surcharges see #183, 231-232, 237, 239-240, 285, 292, C1-C13, C25, C28, C31, C36, C57, CO21, CO30-CO32, CO42, O58-O65.

Imperf., Pairs
174a	A19	1c	2.00	2.00
175b	A19	2c	2.00	2.00
176a	A20	5c	3.50	
178a	A19	10c	3.50	
179b	A19	20c	5.25	
180b	A20	50c	7.00	
181a	A20	1p	8.75	8.75

Francisco
Bertrand — A21

1916, Feb. 1
182	A21	1c orange	2.00	2.00

Election of Pres. Francisco Bertrand.
Unauthorized reprints exist.

Official Stamp No.
O60 Overprinted

1918
183	A20	5c bright blue	2.00	1.50
a.		Inverted overprint	5.00	5.00

Statue to Francisco
Morazán — A22

1919 Typo.
184	A22	1c brown	.20	.20
a.		Printed on both sides	2.00	
b.		Imperf., pair	.70	
185	A22	2c carmine	.25	.20
186	A22	5c lilac rose	.25	.20
187	A22	6c brt violet	.25	.20
188	A22	10c dull blue	.25	.25
189	A22	15c light blue	.75	.20
190	A22	15c dark violet	.60	.20
191	A22	20c orange brn	1.00	.30
a.		20c gray brown	10.00	
b.		Imperf., pair	2.75	
192	A22	50c light brown	4.00	2.50
a.		Imperf. pair	15.00	
193	A22	1p yellow green	7.50	20.00
a.		Imperf., pair	20.00	
b.		Printed on both sides	9.00	
c.		Tête bêche pair	15.00	
		Nos. 184-193 (10)	15.05	24.25

See note on handstamp following No. 217.
Unauthorized reprints exist.
For overprints and surcharges see Nos. 201-210C, 230, 233, 235-236, 238, 241-243,

287, 289, C58, C61, CO23, CO25, CO33,
CO36-CO38, CO39, CO40, O66-O74.

"Dawn of
Peace" — A23

1920, Feb. 1
Size: 27x21mm

194	A23	2c rose	2.50	2.50
a.		Tête bêche pair	15.00	12.50
b.		Imperf., pair	15.00	12.50

Size: 51x40mm

195	A23	2c gold	10.00	10.00
196	A23	2c silver	10.00	10.00
197	A23	2c bronze	10.00	10.00
198	A23	2c red	12.00	12.00
		Nos. 194-198 (5)	44.50	44.50

Assumption of power by Gen. Rafael Lopez
Gutierrez.
Nos. 195-198 exist imperf.
Unauthorized reprints of #195-198 exist.

Type of 1919, Dated "1920"

1921

201	A22	6c dark violet	10.00	5.00
a.		Tête bêche pair	15.00	
b.		Imperf., pair	15.00	

Unauthorized reprints exist.

No. 185 Surcharged
in Antique Letters

1922

202	A22	6c on 2c carmine	.40	.40
a.		"ALE" for "VALE"	2.00	2.00
b.		Comma after "CTS"	2.00	2.00
c.		Without period after "CTS"	2.00	2.00
d.		"CT" for "CTS"	2.00	2.00
e.		Double surcharge	4.25	
f.		Inverted surcharge	4.25	

Stamps of 1919
Surcharged in Roman
Figures and Antique
Letters in Green

1923

203	A22	10c on 1c brown	1.50	1.50
204	A22	50c on 2c carmine	2.00	2.00
a.		Inverted surcharge	10.00	10.00
b.		"HABILTADO"	6.00	6.00

Surcharged in Black
or Violet Blue

205	A22	1p on 5c lil rose (Bk)	3.50	3.50
a.		"PSEO"	20.00	20.00
b.		Inverted surcharge	20.00	20.00
206	A22	1p on 5c lil rose		
		(VB)	20.00	20.00
a.		"PSEO"	70.00	

On Nos. 205-206, "Habilitado Vale" is in
Antique letters, "Un Peso" in Roman.

No. 185 Surcharged
in Roman Letters in
Green

207	A22	6c on 2c carmine	3.50	2.75

Nos. 184-185
Surcharged in Roman
Letters in Green

208	A22	10c on 1c brown	1.75	1.25
a.		"DIES"	6.00	
b.		"DEIZ"	6.00	
c.		"DEIZ CAS"	6.00	
d.		"TTS" for "CTS"	6.00	
e.		"HABILTADO"	6.00	
f.		"HABILTAD"	6.00	
g.		"HABILITA"	6.00	
h.		Inverted surcharge	30.00	
209	A22	50c on 2c carmine	3.75	2.75
a.		"CAT" for "CTA"	10.00	
b.		"TCA" for "CTA"	10.00	
c.		"TTS" for "CTS"	10.00	
d.		"CAS" for "CTS"	10.00	
e.		"HABILTADO"	10.00	

Surcharge on No. 209 is found in two spacings between value and HABILITADO: 5mm
(illustrated) and 1 ½mm.

No. 186 Surcharged
in Antique Letters in
Black

$ 1.00
HABILITADO
VALE
UN PESO

210	A22	1p on 5c lil rose	25.00	25.00
a.		"PFSO"	75.00	

In the surcharges on Nos. 202 to 210 there
are various wrong font, inverted and omitted
letters.

No. 184 Surcharged in
Large Antique Letters
in Green

$ 0.10
HABILITADO
VALE
DIEZ CTS

210C	A22	10c on 1c brown	15.00	15.00
d.		"DIFZ"	55.00	55.00

Dionisio de
Herrera
A24

Pres. Miguel
Paz Baraona
A25

1924, June　Litho.　Perf. 11, 11½

211	A24	1c olive green	.30	.20
212	A24	2c deep rose	.35	.20
213	A24	4c red violet	.40	.20
214	A24	10c blue	.40	.20
215	A24	20c yellow brn	.80	.35
216	A24	50c vermilion	1.75	1.10
217	A24	1p emerald	4.00	2.75
		Nos. 211-217 (7)	8.00	5.00

In 1924 a facsimile of the signatures of San-
tiago Herrera and Francisco Caceres, covering
four stamps, was handstamped in violet to pre-
vent the use of stamps that had been stolen
during a revolution.
Imperfs exist.
For overprints and surcharges see Nos.
280-281, 290-291, C14-C24, C26-C27, C29-
C30, C32-C35, C56, C60, C73-C76, CO1-
CO5, CO22, CO24, CO28-CO29, CO34-
CO35, CO38A, CO39A, CO41, CO43, O75-
O81.

1925, Feb. 1　Typo.　Perf. 11½

218	A25	1c dull blue	2.00	2.00
a.		1c dark blue	2.00	2.00
219	A25	1c car rose	5.00	5.00
a.		1c brown carmine	5.00	5.00
220	A25	1c olive brn	14.00	14.00
a.		1c orange brown	14.00	14.00
b.		1c dark brown	14.00	14.00
c.		1c black brown	14.00	14.00
221	A25	1c buff	12.00	12.00
222	A25	1c red	60.00	60.00
223	A25	1c green	40.00	40.00
		Nos. 218-223 (6)	133.00	133.00

Imperf

225	A25	1c dull blue	5.50	5.50
a.		1c dark blue	5.50	5.50
226	A25	1c car rose	8.75	8.75
a.		1c brown carmine	8.75	8.75
227	A25	1c olive brn	8.75	8.75
a.		1c orange brown	8.75	8.75
b.		1c deep brown	8.75	8.75
c.		1c black brown	8.75	8.75

228	A25	1c buff	8.75	8.75
229	A25	1c red	60.00	60.00
229A	A25	1c green	27.50	27.50
		Nos. 225-229A (6)	119.25	119.25

Inauguration of President Baraona.
Counterfeits and unauthorized reprints exist.

No. 187 Overprinted
in Black and Red

1926, June　　　Perf. 11½

230	A22	6c bright violet	1.50	1.25

Many varieties of this two-part overprint
exist: one or both inverted or double, and various combinations. Value, each $10.

Nos. 177 and 187
Overprinted in Black
or Red

1926

231	A20	6c deep pur (Bk)	2.00	2.00
a.		Inverted overprint	5.50	5.50
b.		Double overprint	5.50	5.50
232	A20	6c deep pur (R)	2.50	2.50
a.		Double overprint	5.00	5.00
233	A22	6c lilac (Bk)	.60	.60
a.		6c violet	.75	.75
b.		Inverted overprint	5.00	5.00
c.		Double overprint	5.00	5.00
d.		Double ovpt., one inverted	5.00	5.00
e.		"192"	7.50	7.50
f.		Double ovpt., both inverted	7.50	7.50

Same Overprint on No. 230

235	A22	6c violet	20.00	20.00
a.		"1926" inverted	20.00	20.00
b.		"Habilitado" triple, one invtd.	20.00	20.00

No. 188 Surcharged
in Red or Black

236	A22	6c on 10c blue (R)	.50	.20
c.		Double surcharge	5.00	4.00
d.		Without bar		
e.		Inverted surcharge	4.00	3.50
f.		"Vale" omitted		
g.		"6cts" omitted		
h.		"cts" omitted		
k.		Black surcharge	55.00	55.00

Nos. 175 and 185
Overprinted in
Green

237	A19	2c carmine	.20	.20
a.		Tête bêche pair	4.00	4.00
b.		Double overprint	2.00	1.40
c.		"HARILITADO"	2.00	1.40
d.		"1926" only	2.75	2.75
e.		Double overprint, one inverted	2.75	2.75
f.		"1926" omitted	3.50	3.50
g.		Triple overprint, two inverted	5.25	5.25
h.		Double on face, one on back	5.25	5.25
238	A22	2c carmine	.20	.20
a.		"HARILITADO"	.90	.90
b.		Double overprint	1.40	1.40
c.		Inverted overprint	2.00	2.00

No. 177
Overprinted in Red

Large Numerals, 12x5mm

1927

239	A20	6c deep purple	25.00	25.00
a.		"1926" over "1927"	35.00	35.00
b.		Invtd. ovpt. on face of stamp, normal ovpt. on back	30.00	

No. 179 Surcharged

1927

240	A19	6c on 20c brown	.75	.75
a.		Tête bêche pair	2.75	2.75
c.		Inverted overprint	2.50	2.50
d.		Double surcharge	8.50	8.50

Nos. 8 and 10 in the setting have no period
after "cts" and No. 50 has the "t" of "cts"
inverted.

Same Surcharge on Nos. 189-191

241	A22	6c on 15c blue	27.50	27.50
242	A22	6c on 15c vio	.70	.70
a.		Double surcharge	1.75	1.75
b.		Double surch., one invtd.	2.00	2.00
c.		"L" of "Vale" omitted		
243	A22	6c on 20c yel brn	.60	.60
a.		6c on 20c deep brown		
b.		"6" omitted	1.75	1.75
c.		"Vale" and "cts" omitted	3.50	3.50
		Nos. 240-243 (4)	29.55	29.55

On No. 242 and 243 stamps Nos. 12, 16
and 43 in the setting have no period after "cts"
and No. 34 often lacks the "s." On No. 243 the
"c" of "cts" is missing on stamp No. 38. On No.
241 occur the varieties "ct" or "ts" for "cts." and
no period.

Southern
Highway — A26

Ruins of
Copán — A27

Pine Tree — A28

Presidential
Palace — A29

Ponciano
Leiva — A30

Pres. M.A.
Soto — A31

Lempira — A32

Map of
Honduras — A33

President Juan
Lindo — A34

Statue of
Columbus — A35

1927-29 Typo. Wmk. 209

244	A26	1c ultramarine	.30	.20
a.		1c blue	.30	.20
245	A27	2c carmine	.30	.20
246	A28	5c dull violet	.30	.20
247	A28	5c bl gray ('29)	25.00	7.00
248	A29	6c blue black	.75	.50
a.		6c gray black	.75	.50
249	A29	6c dark bl ('29)	.40	.20
a.		6c light blue	.40	.20
250	A30	10c blue	.70	.20
251	A31	15c deep blue	1.00	.50
252	A32	20c dark blue	1.25	.60
253	A33	30c dark brown	1.50	1.00
254	A34	50c light blue	2.50	1.50
255	A35	1p red	5.00	2.50
		Nos. 244-255 (12)	39.00	14.60

In 1929 a quantity of imperforate sheets of No. 249 were stolen from the Litografia Nacional. Some of them were perforated by sewing machine and a few copies were passed through the post. To prevent the use of stolen stamps of the 1927-29 issues they were declared invalid and the stock on hand was overprinted "1929 a 1930."

For overprints and surcharges see Nos. 259-278, CO19-CO20B.

Pres. Vicente Mejia Colindres and Vice-Pres. Rafael Diaz Chávez — A36

President Mejia Colindres — A37

1929, Feb. 25

256	A36	1c dk carmine	3.00	3.00
257	A37	2c emerald	3.00	3.00

Installation of Pres. Vicente Mejia Colindres. Printed in sheets of ten.

Nos. 256 and 257 were surreptitiously printed in transposed colors. They were not regularly issued.

Stamps of 1927-29 Overprinted in Various Colors

1929, Oct.

259	A26	1c blue (R)	.20	.20
a.		1c ultramarine (R)	.50	.20
b.		Double overprint	2.50	1.75
c.		As "a", double overprint	2.50	1.75
260	A26	1c blue (Bk)	6.50	6.50
a.		1c ultramarine (Bk)		
261	A27	2c car (R Br)	3.50	3.50
a.		Double overprint		
262	A27	2c car (Bl Gr)	1.00	1.00
a.		Double overprint		
263	A27	2c car (Bk)	1.00	.50
264	A27	2c car (V)	.50	.25
a.		Double overprint		
b.		Double ovpt., one inverted		
265	A27	2c org red (R)	1.50	
266	A28	5c dl vio (R)	.40	.30
a.		Double overprint (R+V)		
267	A28	5c bl gray (R)	1.00	.75
a.		Double overprint (R+Bk)		
269	A29	6c gray blk (R)	2.50	2.00
a.		Double overprint	6.00	6.00
272	A29	6c dk blue (R)	.40	.20
a.		6c light blue (R)	.40	.20
b.		Double overprint	2.00	2.00
c.		Double overprint (R+V)		
273	A30	10c blue (R)	.40	.20
a.		Double overprint	2.50	1.75
274	A31	15c dp blue (R)	.50	.25
a.		Double overprint	3.50	2.50
275	A32	20c dark bl (R)	.50	.35
276	A33	30c dark brn (R)	.75	.60
a.		Double overprint	3.50	2.50
277	A34	50c light bl (R)	2.00	1.00
278	A35	1p red (V)	5.00	2.50
		Nos. 259-278 (17)	27.65	20.10

Nos. 259-278 exist in numerous shades. There are also various shades of the red and violet overprints. The overprint may be found reading upwards, downwards, inverted, double, triple, tête bêche or combinations.

Status of both 6c stamps with overprint in black is questioned.

A38

1929, Dec. 10

279	A38	1c on 6c lilac rose	.70	.70
a.		"1992" for "1929"		
b.		"9192" for "1929"		
c.		Surcharge reading down	8.00	
d.		Dbl. surch., one reading down		

Varieties include "1992" reading down and pairs with one surcharge reading down, double or with "1992."

No. 214 Surcharged in Red

Perf. 11, 11½

1930, Mar. 26 Unwmk.

280	A24	1c on 10c blue	.35	.30
a.		"1093" for "1930"	1.40	
b.		"tsc" for "cts"	1.40	
281	A24	2c on 10c blue	.35	.30
a.		"tsc" for "cts"	2.00	
b.		"Vale 2" omitted		

Official Stamps of 1929 Overprinted in Red or Violet

1930, Mar. Wmk. 209 Perf. 11½

282	O1	1c blue (R)	.50	.50
a.		Double overprint	2.00	2.00
284	O1	2c carmine (V)	.90	.90

Stamps of 1915-26 Overprinted in Blue

On No. 174

1930, July 19 Unwmk.

285	A19	1c chocolate	.30	.25
a.		Double overprint	1.00	1.00
b.		Inverted overprint	1.40	1.40
c.		Dbl. ovpt., one inverted	1.40	1.40

On No. 184

287	A22	1c brown	15.00	15.00
a.		Double overprint		
c.		Inverted overprint		

On No. 204

289	A22	50c on 2c carmine	100.00	90.00
b.		Inverted surcharge		

On Nos. 211 and 212

290	A24	1c olive green	.20	.20
a.		Double overprint	1.75	1.75
b.		Inverted overprint	1.75	1.75
d.		On No. O75	12.00	
291	A24	2c carmine rose	.25	.25
a.		Double overprint	1.75	1.75
b.		Inverted overprint	1.75	1.75

On No. 237

292	A19	2c car (G & Bl)	100.00	100.00

From Title Page of Government Gazette, First Issue — A39

1930, Aug. 11 Typo. Wmk. 209

295	A39	2c orange	2.00	2.00
296	A39	2c ultramarine	2.00	2.00
297	A39	2c red	2.00	2.00
		Nos. 295-297 (3)	6.00	6.00

Publication of the 1st newspaper in Honduras, cent. The stamps were on sale and available for postage on Aug. 11th, 1930, only. Not more than 5 examples of each color could be purchased by an applicant.

Nos. 295-297 exist imperf. and part-perforate. Unauthorized reprints exist.

For surcharges see Nos. CO15-CO18A.

Paz Baraona — A40

Manuel Bonilla — A41

Lake Yojoa — A42

View of Palace at Tegucigalpa A43

City of Amapala A44

Mayan Stele at Copán A45

Christopher Columbus A46

Discovery of America A47

Loarque Bridge A48

Unwmk.

1931, Jan. 2 Engr. Perf. 12

298	A40	1c black brown	.75	.20
299	A41	2c carmine rose	.75	.20
300	A42	5c dull violet	1.00	.20
301	A43	6c deep green	1.00	.20
302	A44	10c brown	1.50	.25
303	A45	15c dark blue	2.00	.30
304	A46	20c black	3.50	.40
305	A47	50c olive green	4.50	1.50
306	A48	1p slate black	9.00	2.50
		Nos. 298-306 (9)	24.00	5.75

Regular Issue of 1931 Overprinted in Black or Various Colors

1931

307	A40	1c black brown	.40	.30
308	A41	2c carmine rose	.60	.30
309	A45	15c dark blue	1.00	.30
310	A46	20c black	2.50	.40

Overprinted

311	A42	5c dull violet	.50	.30
312	A43	6c deep green	.50	.30
315	A44	10c brown	1.50	.35
316	A47	50c olive green	8.00	5.00
317	A48	1p slate black	10.00	7.50
		Nos. 307-317 (9)	25.00	14.75
		Nos. 307-317,C51-C55 (14)	50.00	35.75

The overprint is a control mark. It stands for "Tribunal Superior de Cuentas" (Superior Tribunal of Accounts).

Overprint varieties include: inverted; double; double, one or both inverted; on back; pair, one without overprint; differing colors (6c exists with overprint in orange, yellow and red).

President Carías and Vice-President Williams — A49

1933, Apr. 29

318	A49	2c carmine rose	.50	.35
319	A49	6c deep green	.75	.40
320	A49	10c deep blue	1.00	.50
321	A49	15c red orange	1.25	.75
		Nos. 318-321 (4)	3.50	2.00

Inauguration of Pres. Tiburico Carias Andino and Vice-Pres. Abraham Williams, Feb. 1, 1933.

Columbus' Fleet and Flag of the Race — A50

Wmk. 209

1933, Aug. 3 Typo. Perf. 11½

322	A50	2c ultramarine	1.00	.65
323	A50	6c yellow	1.00	.65
324	A50	10c lemon	1.40	.85

Perf. 12

325	A50	15c violet	2.00	1.50
326	A50	50c red	4.00	3.50
327	A50	1 l emerald	7.00	7.00
		Nos. 322-327 (6)	16.40	14.15

"Day of the Race," an annual holiday throughout Spanish-American countries. Also for the 441st anniv. of the sailing of Columbus to the New World, Aug. 3, 1492.

Masonic Temple, Tegucigalpa — A51

Designs: 2c, President Carias. 5c, Flag. 6c, Tomás Estrada Palma.

Unwmk.

1935, Jan. 12 Engr. Perf. 12

328	A51	1c green	.40	.20
329	A51	2c carmine	.40	.20
330	A51	5c dark blue	.40	.25
331	A51	6c dark brown	.40	.25
a.		Vert. pair, imperf. btwn.	20.00	20.00
		Nos. 328-331 (4)	1.60	.90
		Nos. 328-331,C77-C83 (11)	15.15	6.25

Gen. Carías Bridge — A55

1937, June 4
332	A55	6c car & ol green	.90	.40
333	A55	21c grn & violet	1.50	.65
334	A55	46c orange & brn	2.10	1.50
335	A55	55c ultra & black	3.00	2.40
		Nos. 332-335 (4)	7.50	4.95

Prolongation of the Presidential term to Jan. 19, 1943.

Seal of Honduras A56

Central District Palace — A57

Designs: 3c, Map of Honduras. 5c, Bridge of Choluteca. 8c, Flag.

1939, Mar. 1   *Perf. 12½*
336	A56	1c orange yellow	.20	.20
337	A57	2c red orange	.20	.20
338	A57	3c carmine	.30	.20
339	A57	5c orange	.30	.20
340	A56	8c dark blue	.50	.20
		Nos. 336-340 (5)	1.50	1.00
		Nos. 336-340,C89-C98 (15)	15.30	8.45

Nos. 336-340 exist imperf.
For overprints see #342-343.

Nos. 336 and 337 Overprinted in Green

1944   *Perf. 12½*
342	A56	1c orange yellow	.30	.30
a.		Inverted overprint	5.00	5.00
343	A57	2c red orange	1.25	.75
a.		Inverted overprint	5.00	5.00

> **Catalogue values for unused stamps in this section, from this point to the end of the section, are for Never Hinged items.**

International Peace Movement — A58

1984, Feb. 15   Litho.   *Perf. 12*
344	A58	78c multi	.85	.65
345	A58	85c multi	.95	.30
346	A58	95c multi	1.00	.35
347	A58	1.50 l multi	1.75	.55
348	A58	2 l multi	2.10	.70
349	A58	5 l multi	5.50	1.75
		Nos. 344-349 (6)	12.15	4.30

Central American Aeronautics Corp., 25th Anniv. — A59

Designs: 2c, Edward Warner Award issued by the Intl. Civil Aviation Organization, vert. 5c, Corp. emblem, flags of Guatemala, Honduras, El Salvador, Costa Rica and Panama. 60c, Transmission tower, plane. 75c, Corp. emblem, vert. 1 l, 1.50 l, Emblem, flags, diff.

1987, Feb. 26   Litho.   *Perf. 12*
350	A59	2c multi	.20	.20
351	A59	5c multi	.20	.20
352	A59	60c multi	.75	.35
353	A59	75c multi	.95	.40
354	A59	1 l multi	1.25	.55
		Nos. 350-354 (5)	3.35	1.70

Souvenir Sheet
355	A59	1.50 l multi	3.00	3.00

Housing Institute (INVA), 30th Anniv. A60

1987, Oct. 9   Litho.   *Perf. 13½*
356	A60	5c shown	.30	.20
357	A60	95c Map, emblem, text	1.00	.40

EXFILHON '88 — A61

1988, Sept. 11   Litho.   *Imperf.*
358	A61	3 l dull red brn & brt ultra	4.50	4.50

1988 Summer Olympics, Seoul — A62

1988, Sept. 30   Litho.   *Imperf.*
359	A62	4 l multi	4.75	4.75
		Nos. 359,C772-C773 (3)	7.05	5.65

Luis Bogran Technical Institute, Cent. A63

85c, Cogwheel, map, flag of Honduras.

1990, Sept. 28   Litho.   *Perf. 10½*
360	A63	20c multicolored	.20	.20
361	A63	85c multicolored	.65	.40

Size: 114x82mm
Imperf
362	A63	2 l like #360	2.00	1.40
		Nos. 360-362 (3)	2.85	2.00

Nos. 360-361 are airmail.

America Issue A64

UPAE emblem, land and seascapes showing produce and fish.

1990, Oct. 31   Litho.   *Perf. 13½*
363	A64	20c multi, vert.	.30	.20
364	A64	1 l multicolored	.80	.30

A65

A66

1992, Feb. 17
365	A65	50c shown	.40	.20
366	A65	3 l Cross-country skiing	2.00	1.25

1992 Winter Olympics, Albertville.

1992, May 21   Litho.   *Perf. 13½*

Mother's Day (Paintings): 20c, Saleswoman, by Manuel Rodriguez. 50c, The Grandmother and Baby, by Rodriguez. 5 l, Saleswomen, by Maury Flores.
367	A66	20c shown	.25	.20
368	A66	50c multicolored	.40	.20
369	A66	5 l multicolored	3.25	2.00
		Nos. 367-369 (3)	3.90	2.40

Butterflies A67

Designs: 25c, Melitaeinae chlosyne janais. 85c, Heliconiinae agrilus vanillae. 3 l, Morphinae morpho granadensis. 5 l, Heliconiinae dryadula phalusa.

1992, June 22
370	A67	25c multicolored	.50	.20
371	A67	85c multicolored	1.25	.40
372	A67	3 l multicolored	4.50	1.25

Size: 108x76mm
Imperf
373	A67	5 l multicolored	6.00	5.25
		Nos. 370-373 (4)	12.25	7.10

1992 Summer Olympics, Barcelona — A68

1992, Mar. 16   Litho.   *Perf. 13½*
374	A68	20c Running	.20	.20
375	A68	50c Tennis	.30	.20
376	A68	85c Soccer	.55	.40
		Nos. 374-376 (3)	1.05	.80

Japanese Overseas Cooperation Volunteers in Honduras, 20th Anniv. — A69

Designs: 1.40 l, Volunteers working on Japanese letter, vert. 4.30 l, Folding screen showing Mayan Gods. 5.40 l, Men, women of Honduras in traditional costumes, volunteer.

1995, Sept. 20   Litho.   *Perf. 13½*
377	A69	1.40 l multicolored	.50	.40
378	A69	4.30 l multicolored	1.50	1.25
379	A69	5.40 l multicolored	1.75	1.50
		Nos. 377-379 (3)	3.75	3.15

Nos. 378-379 are airmail.

Birds — A70

Designs: 1.40 l, Buteo jamaicensis. 1.50 l, Ramphastos sulfuratus. 2 l, Dendrocygna autumnalis. 2.15 l, Micrastur semitorguatus. 3 l, Polyporus plancus. 5.40 l, 10 l, Sacroamphus papa.

1997, Apr. 29   Litho.   *Perf. 13½*
380	A70	1.40 l multicolored	.55	.55
381	A70	1.50 l multicolored	.60	.60
382	A70	2 l multicolored	.80	.80
383	A70	2.15 l multicolored	.90	.90
a.		Pair, #382, 383	3.00	3.00
384	A70	3 l multicolored	1.25	1.25
a.		Pair, #380, 384	3.00	3.00
385	A70	5.40 l multicolored	2.00	2.00
a.		Pair, #381, 385	4.00	4.00
		Nos. 380-385 (6)	6.10	6.10

Size: 50x73mm
Imperf
386	A70	20 l multicolored	6.50	6.00

Nos. 380-385 were printed in panes of 30 (5x6), with one value compring the top three rows and another the bottom three rows. Thus, each pane contains five setenant pairs.
No. 386 is airmail.

No. RA8 Surcharged in Gold

1999, June 25   Litho.   *Perf. 13½*
387	PT6	2.60 l on 1c	.65	.35
388	PT6	7.85 l on 1c	1.90	.95
389	PT6	10.65 l on 1c	2.60	1.25
390	PT6	11.55 l on 1c	2.75	1.40
391	PT6	12.45 l on 1c	3.00	1.50
392	PT6	13.85 l on 1c	3.50	1.75
		Nos. 387-392 (6)	14.40	7.20

For surcharges, see C1199//C1206.

SEMI-POSTAL STAMPS

> **Catalogue values for unused stamps in this section are for Never Hinged items.**

Indigenous
Musical
Instruments
SP1

No. B1: a, Garífuna drum. b, Flutes. c, Tol-
tec drum. d, Hornpipe. e, Maya drum. f, Conch
shell.

2000, Apr. 7	Litho.	Perf. 13¼	
B1	Sheet of 6, "Pro filate-lia" in black	16.00	16.00
a.-f.	SP1 10 l + 1 l Any single	2.50	2.50
g.	As #B1, "Pro filatelia" in gold	17.50	17.50

See Nos. C1073, C1209.

AIR POST STAMPS

Regular Issue of
1915-16
Overprinted in
Black, Blue or Red

1925		Unwmk.	Perf. 11½	
C1	A20	5c lt blue (Bk)	87.50	87.50
C2	A20	5c lt blue (Bl)	300.00	300.00
a.		Inverted overprint	400.00	
b.		Vertical overprint	600.00	
c.		Double overprint	800.00	
C3	A20	5c lt blue (R)	7,250.	

Value for No. C3 is for an example without
gum.

C4	A19	10c dk blue (R)	175.00	
a.		Inverted overprint	325.00	
b.		Overprint tête bêche, pair	800.00	
C5	A19	10c dk blue (Bk)	1,100.	
C6	A19	20c red brn (Bk)	175.00	175.00
a.		Inverted overprint	250.00	
b.		Tête bêche pair	400.00	
c.		Overprint tête bêche, pair	725.00	
d.		"AFRO"	1,400.	
e.		Double overprint	600.00	
C7	A19	20c red brn (Bl)	175.00	175.00
a.		Inverted overprint	700.00	
b.		Tête bêche pair	1,000	
c.		Vertical overprint	900.00	
C8	A20	50c red (Bk)	450.00	300.00
a.		Inverted overprint	550.00	
b.		Overprint tête bêche, pair	900.00	
C9	A20	1p yel grn (Bk)	600.00	600.00

Surcharged in Black
or Blue

C10	A19	25c on 1c choc	125.00	125.00
a.		Inverted surcharge	700.00	
C11	A20	25c on 5c lt bl (Bl)	225.00	225.00
a.		Inverted surcharge	700.00	
b.		Double inverted surcharge	675.00	
C12	A19	25c on 10c dk bl	125,000.	
C13	A19	25c on 20c brn (Bl)	200.00	200.00
a.		Inverted surcharge	325.00	
b.		Tête bêche pair	450.00	

Counterfeits of Nos. C1-C13 are plentiful.

Monoplane
and
Lisandro
Garay
AP1

1929, June 5	Engr.	Perf. 12	
C13C	AP1 50c carmine	2.00	1.75

No. 216 Surcharged
in Blue

1929		Perf. 11, 11½	
C14	A24 25c on 50c ver	5.00	3.50

In the surcharges on Nos. C14 to
C40 there are various wrong font and
defective letters and numerals, also
periods omitted.

Nos. 215-217
Surcharged in Green,
Black or Red

1929, Oct.			
C15	A24 5c on 20c yel brn (G)	1.40	1.40
a.	Double surcharge (R+G)	45.00	
C16	A24 10c on 50c ver (Bk)	2.25	1.90
C17	A24 15c on 1p emer (R)	3.50	3.50
	Nos. C15-C17 (3)	7.15	6.80

a   b

Nos. 214 and 216 Surcharged
Vertically in Red or Black

1929, Dec. 10			
C18	A24(a) 5c on 10c bl (R)	.60	.60
C19	A24(b) 20c on 50c ver	1.00	1.00
a.	"1299" for "1929"	190.00	
b.	"cts. cts." for "cts. oro."	190.00	
c.	"r" of "Aereo" omitted	2.00	
d.	Horiz. pair, imperf. btwn.	20.00	

Nos. 214, 215 and
180 Surcharged in
Various Colors

1930, Feb.			
C20	A24 5c on 10c (R)	.50	.50
a.	"1930" reading down	3.50	
b.	"1903" for "1930"	3.50	
c.	Surcharge reading down	10.00	
d.	Double surcharge	14.00	
e.	Dbl. surch., one downward	14.00	
C21	A24 5c on 10c (Y)	450.00	450.00
C22	A24 5c on 20c (Bl)	125.00	125.00
C23	A24 10c on 20c (Bk)	.70	.70
a.	"0" for "10"	3.50	
b.	Double surcharge	8.75	
c.	Dbl. surch., one downward	12.00	
d.	Horiz. pair, imperf. btwn.	70.00	
C24	A24 10c on 20c (V)	750.00	750.00
a.	"0" for "10"	1,600.	
C25	A20 25c on 50c (Bk)	.95	.95
a.	"Internaoicnal"	3.50	
b.	"o" for "oro"	3.50	
c.	Inverted surcharge	17.50	
d.	As "a," invtd. surch.	175.00	
e.	As "b," invtd. surch.	175.00	

Surcharge on Nos. C20-C24 are vertical.

Nos. 214, 215 and
180 Surcharged

1930, Apr. 1			
C26	A24 5c on 10c blue	.50	.50
a.	Double surcharge	9.50	
b.	"Servicioa"	3.50	
C27	A24 15c on 20c yel brn	.55	.55
a.	Double surcharge	7.00	
C28	A20 20c on 50c red, surch. reading down	.95	.95
a.	Surcharge reading up	7.00	
	Nos. C26-C28 (3)	2.00	2.00

Nos. C22 and C23
Surcharged Vertically
in Red

1930			
C29	A24 10c on 5c on 20c (Bl+R)	.90	.90
a.	"1930" reading down	9.00	9.00
b.	"1903" for "1930"	9.00	9.00
c.	Red surcharge, reading down	14.00	
C30	A24 10c on 10c on 20c (Bk+R)	87.50	87.50
a.	"0" for "10"	190.00	

No. 181 Surcharged
as No. C25 and Re-
surcharged

C31	A20 50c on 25c on 1p grn	4.25	4.25
a.	"Internaoicnal"	7.00	
b.	"o" for "oro"	7.00	
c.	25c surcharge inverted	17.50	17.50
d.	50c surcharge inverted	17.50	17.50
e.	As "a" and "c"		
f.	As "a" and "d"		
g.	As "b" and "c"		
h.	As "b" and "d"		
	Nos. C29-C31 (3)	92.65	92.65

No. 215 Surcharged
in Dark Blue

1930, May 22			
C32	A24 5c on 20c yel brn	1.25	1.00
a.	Double surcharge	5.25	5.25
b.	Horiz. pair, imperf. btwn.	60.00	60.00
c.	Vertical pair, imperf. between	20.00	20.00

Nos. O78-O80 Surcharged like Nos.
C20 to C25 in Various Colors

1930			
C33	A24 5c on 10c (R)	450.00	350.00
a.	"1930" reading down	1,500.	
b.	"1903" for "1930"	1,500.	
C34	A24 5c on 20c (Bl)	400.00	400.00
C35	A24 25c on 50c (Bk)	225.00	225.00
a.	55c on 50c vermilion	325.00	325.00

No. C35 exists with inverted surcharge.

No. O64 Surcharged like No. C28

C36	A20 20c on 50c red, surcharge reading down	350.00	350.00
a.	Surcharge reading up	350.00	350.00
b.	Dbl. surch., reading down	350.00	350.00
c.	Dbl. surch., reading up	350.00	350.00

No. O87
Overprinted

1930, Feb. 21	Wmk. 209	Perf. 11½	
C37	O1 50c yel, grn & blue	1.40	1.25
a.	"Internacional"	5.25	
b.	"Iuternacional"	5.25	
c.	Double overprint	5.25	

Nos. O86-O88
Overprinted in
Various Colors

1930, May 23			
C38	O1 20c dark blue (R)	1.10	.85
a.	Double overprint	8.75	
b.	Triple overprint	12.00	
C39	O1 50c org, grn & bl (Bk)	1.10	.90
C40	O1 1p buff (Bl)	1.40	1.25
a.	Double overprint	10.50	
	Nos. C38-C40 (3)	3.60	3.00

National
Palace
AP3

1930, Oct. 1	Engr.	Perf. 12		
		Unwmk.		
C41	AP3 5c yel orange	.50	.30
C42	AP3 10c carmine	.75	.60
C43	AP3 15c green	1.00	.75
C44	AP3 20c dull violet	1.25	.60
C45	AP3 1p light brown	4.00	4.00
	Nos. C41-C45 (5)	7.50	6.25

Same Overprinted in Various Colors

1931		Perf. 12	
C51	AP3 5c yel orange (R)	2.00	1.50
C52	AP3 10c carmine (Bk)	3.00	2.50
C53	AP3 15c green (Br)	5.00	4.00
C54	AP3 20c dull vio (O)	5.00	4.25
C55	AP3 1p lt brown (G)	10.00	8.75
	Nos. C51-C55 (5)	25.00	21.00

See note after No. 317.

Stamps of Various
Issues Surcharged in
Blue or Black (#C59)

1931, Oct.		Perf. 11½	
	On No. 215		
C56	A24 15c on 20c yel brn	3.50	2.75
a.	Horiz. pair, imperf. btwn.	42.50	
b.	Green surcharge	20.00	20.00
	On No. O64		
C57	A20 15c on 50c red	4.25	3.50
a.	Inverted surcharge	10.50	10.50
	On No. O72		
C58	A22 15c on 20c brn	4.25	4.25
a.	Vert. pair, imperf. between	12.00	

On Nos. C57 and C58 the word "OFICIAL"
is canceled by two bars.

	On No. O88		
	Wmk. 209		
C59	O1 15c on 1p buff	4.25	4.25
a.	Vert. pair, imperf. horiz.	25.00	
b.	"Servicio"	14.00	14.00

The varieties "Vaie" for "Vale," "aereo" with
circumflex accent on the first "e" and "Interior"
with initial capital "I" are found on #C56, C58-
C59. #C57 is known with initial capital in
"Interior."

A similar surcharge, in slightly larger letters
and with many minor varieties, exists on Nos.
215, O63, O64 and O73. The authenticity of
this surcharge is questioned.

Nos. 215, O73, O87-
O88 Surcharged in
Green, Red or Black

1931, Nov.		Unwmk.	
C60	A24 15c on 20c (G)	3.50	2.75
a.	Inverted surcharge	6.25	
b.	"XI" omitted	6.25	
c.	"X" for "XI"	6.25	
d.	"PI" for "XI"	6.25	
C61	A22 15c on 50c (R)	3.50	2.75
a.	"XI" omitted	6.75	
b.	"PI" for "XI"	6.75	
c.	Double surcharge	20.00	20.00

On No. C61 the word "OFICIAL" is not
barred out.

	Wmk. 209		
C62	O1 15c on 50c (Bk)	2.75	2.50
a.	"1391" for "1931"	10.50	10.50
b.	Double surcharge	8.75	8.75
C63	O1 15c on 1p (Bk)	2.50	2.25
a.	"1391" for "1931"	12.50	
b.	Surcharged on both sides	7.00	

Nos. O76-O78
Surcharged in Black or
Red

1932   **Unwmk.**   *Perf. 11, 11½*

C73	A24	15c on 2c	.80	.80
a.		Double surcharge	5.50	
b.		Inverted surcharge	4.25	
c.		"Ae" of "Aero" omitted	1.00	
d.		On No. 212 (no "Official")		
C74	A24	15c on 6c	.80	.80
a.		Double surcharge	3.50	
b.		Horiz. pair, imperf. btwn.	17.50	
c.		"Aer" omitted		
d.		"A" omitted	1.00	
e.		Inverted surcharge	3.50	
C75	A24	15c on 10c (R)	.80	.80
a.		Double surcharge	5.50	
b.		Inverted surcharge	3.50	
c.		"r" of "Aereo" omitted	1.00	

Same Surcharge on No. 214 in Red

C76	A24	15c on 10c dp bl	150.00	100.00

There are various broken and missing letters in the setting.
A similar surcharge with slightly larger letters exists.

Post
Office
and
National
Palace
AP4

View of Tegucigalpa — AP5

Designs: 15c, Map of Honduras. 20c, Mayol Bridge. 40c, View of Tegucigalpa. 50c, Owl. 1 l, Coat of Arms.

1935, Jan. 10   *Perf. 12*

C77	AP4	8c blue	.20	.20
C78	AP5	10c gray	.25	.20
C79	AP5	15c olive gray	.40	.20
C80	AP5	20c dull green	.50	.20
C81	AP5	40c brown	.70	.20
C82	AP4	50c yellow	8.25	1.60
C83	AP4	1 l green	3.25	2.75
		Nos. C77-C83 (7)	13.55	5.35

Flags of US and Honduras — AP11

Engr. & Litho.
1937, Sept. 17   **Unwmk.**

C84	AP11	46c multicolored	2.75	1.40

US Constitution, 150th anniv.

Comayagua
Cathedral
AP12

Founding of
Comayagua
AP13

Alonzo
Cáceres and
Pres.
Carías — AP14

Lintel of Royal
Palace
AP15

1937, Dec. 7   **Engr.**

C85	AP12	2c copper red	.20	.20
C86	AP13	8c dark blue	.35	.20
C87	AP14	15c slate black	.70	.70
C88	AP15	50c dark brown	4.25	2.75
		Nos. C85-C88 (4)	5.50	3.85

City of Comayagua founding, 400th anniv.
For surcharges see Nos. C144-C146.

Mayan Stele at
Copán
AP16

Mayan
Temple,
Copán
AP17

Designs: 15c, President Carias. 30c, José C. de Valle. 40c, Presidential House. 46c, Lempira. 55c, Church of Our Lady of Suyapa. 66c, J. T. Reyes. 1 l, Hospital at Choluteca. 2 l, Ramón Rosa.

1939, Mar. 1   *Perf. 12½*

C89	AP16	10c orange brn	.20	.20
C90	AP16	15c grnsh blue	.30	.20
C91	AP17	21c gray	.50	.20
C92	AP16	30c dk blue grn	.55	.20
C93	AP17	40c dull violet	1.00	.25
C94	AP16	46c dk gray brn	1.00	.65
C95	AP16	55c green	1.25	1.00
a.		Imperf., pair	22.50	
C96	AP16	66c black	1.75	1.25
C97	AP16	1 l olive grn	3.00	1.00
C98	AP16	2 l henna red	4.25	2.50
		Nos. C89-C98 (10)	13.80	7.45

For surcharges see Nos. C118-C119, C147-C152.

Souvenir Sheets

AP26

14c, Francisco Morazan. 16c, George Washington. 30c, J. C. de Valle. 40c, Simon Bolivar.

1940, Apr. 13   **Engr.**   *Perf. 12*
Centers of Stamps Lithographed

C99	AP26	Sheet of 4	10.00	10.00
a.		14c black, yellow, ultra & rose	1.40	1.40
b.		16c black, yellow, ultra & rose	1.75	1.75
c.		30c black, yellow, ultra & rose	2.40	2.40

d.		40c black, yellow, ultra & rose	2.75	2.75
		Imperf		
C100	AP26	Sheet of 4	16.00	16.00
a.		14c black, yellow, ultra & rose	2.25	2.25
b.		16c black, yellow, ultra & rose	2.75	2.75
c.		30c black, yellow, ultra & rose	4.00	4.00
d.		40c black, yellow, ultra & rose	4.50	4.50

Pan American Union, 50th anniv.
For overprints see Nos. C153-C154, C187.

Air Post
Official
Stamps of
1939
Overprinted in
Red

1940, Oct. 12   *Perf. 12½*

C101	OA2	2c dp bl & green	.20	.20
C102	OA2	5c dp blue & org	.25	.25
C103	OA2	8c deep bl & brn	.30	.30
C104	OA2	15c dp blue & car	.50	.50
C105	OA2	46c dp bl & ol grn	.80	.80
C106	OA2	50c dp bl & vio	.90	.90
C107	OA2	1 l dp bl & red brn	3.75	3.75
C108	OA2	2 l dp bl & red org	7.50	7.50
		Nos. C101-C108 (8)	14.20	14.20

Erection and dedication of the Columbus Memorial Lighthouse.

Air Post
Official
Stamps of
1939
Overprinted in
Black

1941, Aug. 2

C109	OA2	5c deep bl & org	3.00	.25
C110	OA2	8c dp blue & brn	5.00	.25
a.		Overprint inverted		225.00

Nos. CO44,
CO47-CO51
Surcharged in
Black

1941, Oct. 28

C111	OA2	3c on 2c	.40	.20
C112	OA2	8c on 2c	.50	.50
C113	OA2	8c on 15c	.50	.50
C114	OA2	8c on 46c	.60	.60
C115	OA2	8c on 1 l	.75	.50
C116	OA2	8c on 1 l	1.25	.70
C117	OA2	8c on 2 l	2.00	1.50
		Nos. C111-C117 (7)	6.00	4.20

Once in each sheet a large "h" occurs in "ocho."

Nos. C90, C94
Surcharged in
Red

1942, July 14

C118	AP16	8c on 15c	.70	.30
a.		"Cerreo"	2.00	2.00
b.		Double surcharge	25.00	25.00
c.		As "a," double surcharge	175.00	
C119	AP16	16c on 46c	.70	.30
a.		"Cerreo"	2.00	2.00

Plaque
AP27

Morazán's Tomb,
San
Salvador — AP28

Designs: 5c, Battle of La Trinidad. 8c, Morazán's birthplace. 16c, Statue of Morazán. 21c, Church where Morazán was baptized. 1 l, Arms of Central American Federation. 2 l, Gen. Francisco Morazán.

1942, Sept. 15   *Perf. 12*

C120	AP27	2c red orange	.20	.20
C121	AP27	5c turq green	.20	.20
C122	AP27	8c sepia	.20	.20
C123	AP28	14c black	.40	.30
C124	AP27	16c olive gray	.25	.20
C125	AP27	21c light blue	1.00	.65
C126	AP27	1 l brt ultra	3.00	2.25
C127	AP28	2 l dl ol brn	7.50	7.25
		Nos. C120-C127 (8)	12.75	11.25

Gen. Francisco Morazan (1799-1842).
For surcharges see Nos. C349-C350.

Coat of
Arms
AP35

Cattle
AP36

Bananas — AP37   Pine Tree — AP38

Tobacco
Plant
AP39

Orchid
AP40

Coco
Palm — AP41

Map of
Honduras
AP42

Designs: 2c, Flag. 8c, Rosario. 16c, Sugar cane. 30c, Oranges. 40c, Wheat. 1 l, Corn. 2 l, Map of Americas.

1943, Sept. 14 — Perf. 12½

C128	AP35	1c light grn	.20	.20
C129	AP35	2c blue	.20	.20
C130	AP36	5c green	.30	.20
C131	AP37	6c dark bl grn	.25	.20
C132	AP36	8c lilac	.30	.20
C133	AP38	10c lilac brn	.30	.20
C134	AP39	15c dp claret	.35	.20
C135	AP38	16c dark red	.35	.20
C136	AP40	21c deep blue	.75	.20
C137	AP39	30c org brown	.60	.20
C138	AP40	40c red orange	.60	.20
C139	AP41	55c black	1.10	.60
C140	AP41	1 l dark olive	1.75	1.40
C141	AP37	2 l brown red	5.25	4.00
C142	AP42	5 l orange	13.00	13.00
a.		Vert. pair, imperf. btwn.	150.00	
		Nos. C128-C142 (15)	25.30	21.20

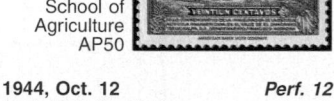

Pan-American School of Agriculture
AP50

1944, Oct. 12 — Perf. 12

C143	AP50	21c dk blue grn	.40	.20

Inauguration of the Pan-American School of Agriculture, Tegucigalpa.

> **Catalogue values for unused stamps in this section, from this point to the end of the section, are for Never Hinged items.**

Air Post Stamps of 1937-39 Surcharged in Red or Green

1945, Mar. 13 — Perf. 11, 12½

C144	AP15	1c on 50c dk brn	.20	.20
C145	AP12	2c on 2c cop red	.20	.20
C146	AP14	8c on 15c sl blk	.25	.20
C147	AP16	10c on 10c org brown (G)	.45	.30
C148	AP16	15c on 15c grnsh blue (G)	.30	.25
C149	AP17	30c on 21c gray (G)	4.50	3.00
C150	AP17	40c on 40c dull violet (G)	2.25	1.25
C151	AP16	1 l on 46c dk gray brown (G)	2.25	1.75
C152	AP16	2 l on 66c blk (G)	4.50	3.00
		Nos. C144-C152 (9)	14.90	10.15

Souvenir Sheets

Nos. C99 and C100 Overprinted in Red

"VICTORIA DE LAS NACIONES UNIDAS, ALEMANIA SE RINDE INCONDICIONALMENTE 8 DE MAYO DE 1945. ACDO. No. 1231 QUE AUTORIZA LA CONTRAMARCA"

1945, Oct. 1 — Perf. 12

C153	AP26	Sheet of 4	4.00	3.00

Imperf

C154	AP26	Sheet of 4	6.50	4.25

Allied Nations' victory and Germany's unconditional surrender, May 8, 1945.

Seal of Honduras
AP51

Arms of Gracias and Trujillo
AP52

Franklin D. Roosevelt ("F.D.R." under Column)
AP53

Arms of San Miguel de Heredia de Tegucigalpa
AP54

Designs (Coats of Arms): 5c, Comayagua and San Jorge de Olancho. 15c, Province of Honduras and San Juan de Puerto Caballas. 21c, Comayagua and Tencoa. 1 l, Jerez de la Frontera de Choluteca and San Pedro de Zula.

1946, Oct. 15 — Perf. 12½ — Unwmk. Engr.

C155	AP51	1c red	.20	.20
a.		Vert. pair, imperf. between	17.50	
b.		Imperf., pair	70.00	
C156	AP52	2c red orange	.20	.20
a.		Imperf., pair	70.00	
C157	AP52	5c violet	.45	.20
C158	AP53	8c brown	1.60	.50
a.		Horiz. pair, imperf. btwn.	70.00	
C159	AP52	15c sepia	.80	.20
C160	AP52	21c deep blue	.90	.30
a.		Horiz. pair, imperf. btwn.	15.00	
b.		Imperf., pair	70.00	
C161	AP52	1 l green	3.25	1.25
C162	AP54	2 l dark grn	5.00	2.00
		Nos. C155-C162 (8)	12.40	4.85

No. C158 commemorates the death of Franklin D. Roosevelt and the Allied victory over Japan in World War II.

Type AP53 Redrawn ("Franklin D. Roosevelt" under Column)
AP59

1947, Oct. — Perf. 12½

C163	AP59	8c brown	.50	.35
a.		Vert. pair, imperf. between	87.50	
b.		Horiz. pair, imperf. btwn.	175.00	
c.		Perf. 12x6	175.00	

Map, Ancient Monuments and Conference Badge
AP60

1947, Oct. 20 — Perf. 11x12½
Various Frames

C164	AP60	16c green	.40	.20
C165	AP60	22c orange yel	.30	.20
C166	AP60	40c orange	.65	.35
C167	AP60	1 l deep blue	1.10	.90
C168	AP60	2 l lilac	4.00	3.50
C169	AP60	5 l brown	10.50	8.00
		Nos. C164-C169 (6)	16.95	13.15

1st Intl. Archeological Conf. of the Caribbean.
For overprints and surcharges see Nos. C181-C186, C351, C353-C354, C379, C544.

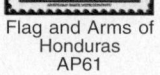

Flag and Arms of Honduras
AP61

Juan Manuel Galvez
AP62

J. M. Galvez, Gen. Tiburcio Carias A. and Julio Lozano
AP63

National Stadium
AP64

Designs: 5c, 15c, Julio Lozano. 9c, Juan Manuel Galvez. 40c, Custom House. 1 l, Recinto Hall. 2 l, Gen. Tiburcio Carias A. 5 l, Galvez and Lozano.

Various frames inscribed: "Conmemorativa de la Sucesion Presidencial para el Periodo de 1949-1955."

1949, Sept. 17 — Engr. — Perf. 12

C170	AP61	1c deep blue	.20	.20
C171	AP62	2c rose car	.20	.20
C172	AP62	5c deep blue	.20	.20
C173	AP62	9c sepia	.20	.20
C174	AP62	15c red brown	.25	.20
C175	AP63	21c gray black	.45	.20
C176	AP64	30c olive gray	.60	.20
C177	AP64	40c slate gray	.90	.20
C178	AP61	1 l red brown	1.40	.40
C179	AP62	2 l violet	3.25	1.50
C180	AP64	5 l rose car	9.25	5.50
		Nos. C170-C180 (11)	16.90	9.00

Presidential succession for the 1949-1955 term.
For overprints and surcharges see Nos. C188-C197, C206-C208, C346, C355, C419-C420, C478, C545.

Nos. C164-C169 Overprinted in Carmine

1951, Feb. 26 — Perf. 11x12½

C181	AP60	16c green	.50	.40
a.		Inverted overprint	45.00	45.00
C182	AP60	22c orange yel	.65	.55
a.		Inverted overprint	45.00	
C183	AP60	40c orange	.65	.55
C184	AP60	1 l deep blue	2.00	1.75
C185	AP60	2 l lilac	3.75	3.25
a.		Inverted overprint	60.00	
C186	AP60	5 l brown	32.50	29.00
		Nos. C181-C186 (6)	40.05	35.50

Souvenir Sheets
Same Overprint in Carmine on Nos. C99 and C100
Perf. 12

C187	AP26	Sheet of 4	8.00	4.75
a.		Imperf.	250.00	250.00

UPU, 75th anniv. (in 1949).

Nos. C170 to C179 Overprinted in Carmine

1951, Feb. 27 — Perf. 12

C188	AP61	1c deep blue	.20	.20
C189	AP62	2c rose car	.20	.20
C190	AP62	5c deep blue	.20	.20
C191	AP62	9c sepia	.20	.20
C192	AP62	15c red brown	.20	.20
C193	AP63	21c gray black	.25	.20
C194	AP64	30c olive gray	.60	.30
C195	AP64	40c slate gray	.90	.60
C196	AP61	1 l red brown	2.25	1.50
C197	AP62	2 l violet	7.25	5.00
		Nos. C188-C197 (10)	12.25	8.60

Founding of Central Bank, July 1, 1950.

Discovery of America
AP65

Queen Isabella I — AP66

2c, 1 l, Columbus at court. 8c, Surrender of Granada. 30c, Queen Isabella offering her jewels.

1952, Oct. 11 — Perf. 13½x14, 14x13½ — Engr. Unwmk.

C198	AP65	1c red org & blk	.20	.20
C199	AP65	2c bl & red brn	.20	.20
C200	AP65	8c dk grn & dk brown	.20	.20
C201	AP66	16c dk bl & blk	.40	.25
C202	AP65	30c pur & dk grn	.70	.70
C203	AP65	1 l dp car & blk	1.75	1.40
C204	AP65	2 l brn & vio	4.25	3.50
C205	AP66	5 l rose lil & ol	9.25	8.75
		Nos. C198-C205 (8)	16.95	15.20

500th birth anniv. of Isabella I of Spain.
For overprints and surcharges see Nos. C209-C221, C377-C378, C404-C406, C489, CO52-CO59.

No. C175 Surcharged in Carmine

1953, May 13 — Perf. 12

C206	AP63	5c on 21c gray blk	.25	.20
C207	AP63	8c on 21c gray blk	.55	.20
C208	AP63	16c on 21c gray blk	.95	.20
		Nos. C206-C208 (3)	1.75	.60

Nos. CO52-CO54 Surcharged "HABILITADO 1953" and New Value in Red

1953, Dec. 8 — Perf. 13½x14, 14x13½

C209	AP65	10c on 1c	.20	.20
a.		Inverted surcharge	50.00	50.00
C210	AP65	12c on 1c	.20	.20
C211	AP65	15c on 2c	.30	.20
C212	AP65	20c on 2c	.50	.30
C213	AP65	24c on 2c	.50	.30
a.		Inverted surcharge	50.00	50.00
C214	AP65	25c on 2c	.50	.30
C215	AP65	30c on 8c	.60	.30
C216	AP65	35c on 8c	.70	.45
C217	AP65	50c on 8c	.80	.45
C218	AP65	60c on 8c	1.00	.90

Same Overprint on Nos. CO57-CO59

C219	AP65	1 l dk grn & dk brown	3.00	2.25
C220	AP65	2 l bl & red brn	6.75	5.50
C221	AP66	5 l red org & blk	16.00	13.00
a.		Date inverted	150.00	
		Nos. C209-C221 (13)	31.05	24.35

Flags of UN and Honduras
AP67

2c, UN emblem. 3c, UN building. 5c, Shield. 15c, Juan Manuel Galvez. 30c, UNICEF. 1 l, UNRRA. 2 l, UNESCO. 5 l, FAO.

Engraved; Center of 1c Litho.
1953, Dec. 18 — *Perf. 12½*
Frames in Black
C222	AP67	1c ultra & vio bl	.20	.20
C223	AP67	2c blue	.20	.20
C224	AP67	3c rose lilac	.20	.20
C225	AP67	5c green	.25	.20
C226	AP67	15c red brown	.40	.25
C227	AP67	30c brown	.85	.90
C228	AP67	1 l dp carmine	6.75	4.50
C229	AP67	2 l orange	8.75	6.25
C230	AP67	5 l blue green	19.00	15.00
		Nos. C222-C230 (9)	36.60	27.30

Issued to honor the United Nations.
For overprints and surcharges see Nos. C231-C249, C331-C335, C472, C490, CO60-CO68.

Nos. CO60-CO66
Overprinted in
Red

1955, Feb. 23   Unwmk.   Perf. 12½
Frames in Black
C231	AP67	1c ultra & vio bl	.20	.20
C232	AP67	2c dp blue grn	.20	.20
C233	AP67	3c orange	.20	.20
C234	AP67	5c dp carmine	.25	.20
C235	AP67	15c dk brown	.35	.35
C236	AP67	30c purple	1.00	.90
C237	AP67	1 l olive gray	20.00	15.00

Overprint exists inverted on 1c, 3c.

Nos. C231 to C233 Surcharged in Black

C238	AP67	8c on 1c	.20	.20
C239	AP67	10c on 2c	.20	.20
C240	AP67	12c on 3c	.20	.20
		Nos. C231-C240 (10)	22.80	17.70

50th anniv. of the founding of Rotary International (Nos. C231-C240).

Nos. CO60-CO63, C226-C230
Overprinted

1956, July 14   Unwmk.   Perf. 12½
Frames in Black
C241	AP67	1c ultra & vio bl	.20	.20
C242	AP67	2c dp bl grn	.20	.20
C243	AP67	3c orange	.25	.20
C244	AP67	5c dp car	.30	.25
C245	AP67	15c red brn	.35	.30
C246	AP67	30c brown	.55	.40
C247	AP67	1 l dp car	4.00	2.75
C248	AP67	2 l orange	5.75	4.75
C249	AP67	5 l bl grn	15.00	14.00
		Nos. C241-C249 (9)	26.60	23.05

10th anniv. of UN (in 1955). The red "OFICIAL" overprint was not obliterated.
The "ONU" overprint exists inverted on 1c, 3c, 5c and 1-lempira.

Basilica of
Suyapa
AP68

Pres. Julio Lozano
Diaz — AP69

3c, Southern Highway. 4c, Genoveva Guardiola de Estrada Palma. 5c, Maria Josefa Lastiri de Morazan. 8c, Landscape and cornucopia (5-Year Plan). 10c, National Stadium. 12c, US School. 15c, Central Bank. 20c, Legislative Palace. 25c, Development Bank (projected). 30c, Toncontin Airport. 40c, Juan Ramon Molina Bridge. 50c, Peace Monument. 60c, Treasury Palace. 1 l, Blood bank. 2 l, Communications Building. 5 l, Presidential Palace.

Engraved; #C255 Litho.
1956, Oct. 3   Perf. 13x12½, 12½x13
C250	AP68	1c black & vio bl	.20	.20
C251	AP69	2c black & dk bl	.20	.20
C252	AP68	3c black & brown	.20	.20
C253	AP69	4c black & lilac	.20	.20
C254	AP69	5c black & dk red	.20	.20
C255	AP68	8c brown & multi	.20	.20
C256	AP69	10c black & emer	.20	.20
C257	AP68	12c black & green	.20	.20
C258	AP69	15c dk red & blk	.30	.20
C259	AP68	20c black & ultra	.30	.20
C260	AP69	24c black & lil	.35	.20
C261	AP68	25c black & green	.40	.25
C262	AP68	30c black & car rose	.40	.25
C263	AP68	40c black & red brn	.50	.25
C264	AP69	50c black & bl grn	.60	.35
C265	AP68	60c black & orange	.80	.45
C266	AP68	1 l black & rose vio	2.00	1.00
C267	AP69	2 l black & mag	3.75	2.25
C268	AP69	5 l black & brn car	9.00	5.00
		Nos. C250-C268 (19)	20.00	12.00

Issued to publicize the Five-Year Plan.
For overprints and surcharges see Nos. C414-C418, C491-C493, C537-C538, C542, C550.
Types AP68 and AP69 in different colors, overprinted "OFICIAL," see Nos. CO69-CO87.

Flag of Honduras
AP70

Designs: 2c, 8c, Monument and mountains. 10c, 15c, 1 l, Lempira. 30c, 2 l, Coat of arms.

1957, Oct. 21   Litho.   Perf. 13
Frames in Black
C269	AP70	1c buff & ultra	.20	.20
C270	AP70	2c org, pur & emerald	.20	.20
C271	AP70	5c pink & ultra	.20	.20
C272	AP70	8c org, vio & ol	.20	.20
C273	AP70	10c violet & brown	.20	.20
C274	AP70	12c lt grn & ultra	.25	.20
C275	AP70	15c green & brown	.30	.20
C276	AP70	30c pink & slate	.45	.25
C277	AP70	1 l blue & brown	2.00	1.50
C278	AP70	2 l lt grn & slate	3.75	3.00
		Nos. C269-C278 (10)	7.75	6.15

First anniv. of the October revolution.
For overprints and surcharge, see Nos. C551, CO88-CO97.

Control marks were handstamped in violet on many current stamps in July and August, 1958, following fire and theft of stamps at Tegucigalpa in April.
All post offices were ordered to honor only stamps overprinted with the facsimile signature of their departmental revenue administrator. Honduras has 18 departments.

Flags of
Honduras and
US — AP71

1958, Oct. 2   Engr.   Perf. 12
Flags in National Colors
C279	AP71	1c light blue	.20	.20
C280	AP71	2c red	.20	.20
C281	AP71	5c green	.20	.20
C282	AP71	10c brown	.25	.20
C283	AP71	20c orange	.40	.20
C284	AP71	30c deep rose	.45	.20
C285	AP71	50c gray	.60	.40
C286	AP71	1 l orange yel	1.25	1.00
C287	AP71	2 l gray olive	2.40	2.00
C288	AP71	5 l vio blue	5.50	4.00
		Nos. C279-C288 (10)	11.45	8.65

Honduras Institute of Inter-American Culture. The proceeds were intended for the Binational Center, Tegucigalpa.
For overprints see Nos. C320-C324.

Abraham
Lincoln — AP72

Lincoln's
Birthplace
AP73

Designs: 3c, 50c, Gettysburg Address. 5c, 1 l, Freeing the slaves. 10c, 2 l, Assassination. 12c, 5 l, Memorial, Washington.

1959, Feb. 12   Unwmk.   Perf. 13½
Flags in National Colors
C289	AP72	1c green	.20	.20
C290	AP73	2c dark blue	.20	.20
C291	AP73	3c purple	.25	.20
C292	AP73	5c dk carmine	.25	.20
C293	AP73	10c black	.30	.20
C294	AP73	12c dark brown	.30	.20
C295	AP72	15c red orange	.40	.25
C296	AP73	25c dull pur	.60	.40
C297	AP73	50c ultra	.75	.65
C298	AP73	1 l red brown	1.50	1.40
C299	AP73	2 l gray olive	2.40	1.75
C300	AP73	5 l ocher	5.50	5.00
a.		Miniature sheet	10.00	10.00
		Nos. C289-C300 (12)	12.65	10.65

Birth sesquicentennial of Abraham Lincoln.
No. C300a contains one each of the 1c, 3c, 10c, 25c, 1 l and 5 l, imperf.
For overprints and surcharges see Nos. C316-C319, C325-C330, C345, C347-C348, C352, C356-C364, C494-C495, C539-C541, C552-C555.
Types AP72 and AP73 in different colors, overprinted "OFICIAL," see Nos. CO98-CO109.

Constitution
AP74

Designs: 2c, 12c, Inauguration of Pres. Villeda Morales, horiz. 3c, 25c, Pres. Ramon Villeda Morales. 5c, 50c, Allegory of Second Republic (Torch and olive branches).

Engr.; Seal Litho. on 1c, 10c
1959, Dec. 21   Perf. 13½
C301	AP74	1c red brn, car & ultra	.20	.20
C302	AP74	2c bister brn	.20	.20
C303	AP74	3c ultra	.20	.20
C304	AP74	5c orange	.20	.20
C305	AP74	10c dull green, car & ultra	.25	.20
C306	AP74	12c rose red	.35	.20
C307	AP74	25c dull lilac	.85	.20
C308	AP74	50c dark blue	1.40	.50
		Nos. C301-C308 (8)	3.65	1.90

Second Republic of Honduras, 2nd anniv.
For surcharge see No. C543.

King
Alfonso XIII
and Map
AP75

Designs: 2c, 1906 award of King Alfonso XIII of Spain. 5c, Arbitration commission delivering its award, 1907. 10c, Intl. Court of Justice. 20c, Verdict of the Court, 1960. 50c, Pres. Morales, Foreign Minister Puerto and map. 1 l, Pres. Davila and Pres. Morales.

1961, Nov. 18   Engr.   Perf. 14½x14
C309	AP75	1c dark blue	.20	.20
C310	AP75	2c magenta	.20	.20
C311	AP75	5c deep green	.20	.20
C312	AP75	10c brn orange	.20	.20
C313	AP75	20c vermilion	.40	.35
C314	AP75	50c brown	1.00	.50
C315	AP75	1 l vio black	1.50	1.00
		Nos. C309-C315 (7)	3.70	2.70

Judgment of the Intl. Court of Justice at The Hague, Nov. 18, 1960, returning a disputed territory to Honduras from Nicaragua.

Nos. C295-C297
and CO105
Surcharged

1964, Apr. 7   Perf. 13½
Flags in National Colors
C316	AP72	6c on 15c red org	.25	.20
C317	AP73	8c on 25c dull pur	.25	.20
C318	AP73	10c on 50c ultra	.30	.20
C319	AP73	20c on 25c black	.75	.40
		Nos. C316-C319 (4)	1.55	1.00

The red "OFICIAL" overprint on No. C319 was not obliterated.
See Nos. C345-C355, C419-C421.

Nos. C279-C281, C284 and C287
Overprinted: "FAO / Lucha Contra / el Hambre"

1964, Mar. 23   Unwmk.   Perf. 12
Flags in National Colors
C320	AP71	1c light blue	.20	.20
C321	AP71	2c red	.20	.20
C322	AP71	5c green	.25	.20
C323	AP71	30c deep rose	1.10	.75
C324	AP71	2 l gray olive	5.75	5.50
		Nos. C320-C324 (5)	7.50	6.85

FAO "Freedom from Hunger Campaign" (1963).

Nos. CO98-CO101, CO104 and CO106 Overprinted in Blue or Black: "IN MEMORIAM / JOHN F. KENNEDY / 22 NOVEMBRE 1963"

1964, May 29   Perf. 13½
Flags in National Colors
C325	AP72	1c ocher (Bl)	.20	.20
C326	AP73	2c gray ol (Bl)	.20	.20
C327	AP73	3c red brn (Bl)	.35	.20
C328	AP73	5c ultra (Bk)	.50	.30
C329	AP72	15c dk brn (Bl)	2.00	1.25
C330	AP73	50c dk car (Bl)	10.50	6.25
		Nos. C325-C330 (6)	13.75	8.40

Pres. John F. Kennedy (1917-63). The red "OFICIAL" overprint was not obliterated. The same overprint was applied to the stamps in miniature sheet No. C300a and seal of Honduras and Alliance for Progress emblem added in margin. Value $65.

Nos. C222-C224, C226 and CO67
Overprinted with Olympic Rings and "1964"

Engr.; Center of 1c Litho.
1964, July 23   Perf. 12½
Frames in Black
C331	AP67	1c ultra & vio bl	.20	.20
C332	AP67	2c blue	.20	.20
C333	AP67	3c rose lilac	.25	.25
C334	AP67	15c red brown	.50	.50
C335	AP67	2 l lilac rose	6.25	6.25
		Nos. C331-C335 (5)	7.40	7.40

18th Olympic Games, Tokyo, Oct. 10-25. The red "OFICIAL" overprint on No. C335 was not obliterated.

Nos. C520-C523 Overprinted in Bright
Green: "1949-1974 SOS Kinderdorfer
International Honduras-Austria"

1974, July 25   Photo.
C546	AP90	10c grn, gold & brn	.20	.20
C547	AP90	15c grn, gold & brn	.20	.20
C548	AP90	30c grn, gold & brn	.25	.25
C549	AP90	40c grn, gold & brn	.35	.35
		Nos. C546-C549 (4)	1.00	1.00

25th anniversary of Children's Villages in
Honduras. Overprint in 6 lines on 10c and
30c, in 4 lines on 15c and 40c.

Stamps of 1956-73 Surcharged

1975, Feb. 24   Litho.; Engr.
C550	AP68	16c on 1c (#C250)	.20	.20
C551	AP70	16c on 1c (#C269)	.20	.20
C552	AP72	16c on 1c (#C289)	.20	.20
C553	AP72	16c on 1c (#CO98)	.20	.20
C554	AP78	16c on 1c (#C369)	.30	.30
C555	AP85	18c on 12c (#C456)	.40	.25
C556	AP90	18c on 10c (#C520)	.25	.20
C557	AP91	18c on 10c (#C525)	.25	.20
C558	AP91	18c on 12c (#C526)	.25	.20
C559	AP92	18c on 8c (#C527)	.25	.20
C560	AP90	50c on 30c (#C522)	.75	.50
C561	AP90	1 l on 30c (#C522)	1.25	1.00
		Nos. C550-C561,CE5 (13)	5.50	4.20

Denominations not obliterated on Nos.
C551, C553-C558, C560-C561; "OFICIAL"
overprint not obliterated on No. C553.
For surcharges, see Nos. C1197, C1198,
C1200.

Flags of
Germany
and Austria
AP93

Designs (Flags): 2c, Belgium & Denmark.
3c, Spain & France. 4c, Hungary & Russia.
5c, Great Britain & Italy. 10c, Norway & Sweden. 12c, Honduras. 15c, US & Switzerland.
20c, Greece & Portugal. 30c, Romania & Serbia. 1 l, Egypt & Netherlands. 2 l, Luxembourg & Turkey.

1975, June 18   Litho.   Perf. 13
Gold & Multicolored; Colors Listed
are for Shields
C562	AP93	1c lilac	.20	.20
C563	AP93	2c gold	.20	.20
C564	AP93	3c rose gray	.20	.20
C565	AP93	4c light blue	.20	.20
C566	AP93	5c yellow	.20	.20
C567	AP93	10c gray	.20	.20
C568	AP93	12c lilac rose	.25	.25
C569	AP93	15c bluish green	.35	.35
C570	AP93	20c bright blue	.40	.40
C571	AP93	30c pink	.75	.75
C572	AP93	1 l salmon	1.75	1.75
C573	AP93	2 l yellow green	3.75	3.75
		Nos. C562-C573 (12)	8.45	8.45

Souvenir Sheet
C574	AP93	Sheet of 12	12.00	12.00

UPU, cent. (in 1974). No. C574 contains 12
stamps similar to Nos. C562-C573 with
shields in different colors.

Humuya
Youth
Center and
Mrs.
Arellano
AP94

Designs (Portrait of First Lady, Gloria de
Lopez Arellano, IWY Emblem and): 16c,
Jalteva Youth Center. 18c, Mrs. Arellano (diff.
portrait) and IWY emblem. 30c, El Carmen de
San Pedro Sula Youth Center. 55c, Flag of
National Social Welfare Organization, vert. 1 l,
La Isla sports and recreational facilities. 2 l,
Women's Social Center.

1976, Mar. 5   Litho.   Perf. 13½
C575	AP94	8c sal & multi	.20	.20
C576	AP94	16c yel & multi	.20	.20
C577	AP94	18c pink & multi	.20	.20
C578	AP94	30c org & multi	.45	.45
C579	AP94	55c multicolored	.70	.70
C580	AP94	1 l multicolored	1.50	1.50
C581	AP94	2 l multicolored	2.75	2.75
		Nos. C575-C581 (7)	6.00	6.00

International Women's Year (1975).
For surcharges see #C736-C737, C781,
C798, C885, C887, C919, C1203.

"CARE"
and Globe
AP95

Designs: 1c, 16c, 30c, 55c, 1 l, Care package and globe, vert. Others like 5c.

1976, May 24   Litho.   Perf. 13½
C582	AP95	1c blk & lt blue	.20	.20
C583	AP95	5c rose brn & blk	.20	.20
C584	AP95	16c black & org	.20	.20
C585	AP95	18c lemon & blk	.25	.25
C586	AP95	30c blk & blue	.35	.35
C587	AP95	50c yel grn & blk	.50	.50
C588	AP95	55c blk & buff	.50	.50
C589	AP95	70c brt rose & blk	.70	.70
C590	AP95	1 l blk & lt grn	1.25	1.25
C591	AP95	2 l ocher & blk	2.40	2.40
		Nos. C582-C591 (10)	6.55	6.55

20th anniversary of CARE in Honduras.
For surcharges see Nos. C735, C738,
C788, C888, C922, C1105.

Fawn in Burnt-out
Forest — AP96

"Sons of
Liberty" — AP97

Forest Protection: 16c, COHDEFOR
emblem (Corporacion Hondureña de
Desarollo Forestal). 18c, Forest, horiz. 30c,
2 l, Live and burning trees. 50c, like 10c. 70c,
Emblem. 1 l, Young forest, horiz.

1976, May 28   Litho.   Perf. 13½
C592	AP96	10c multicolored	.20	.20
C593	AP96	16c multicolored	.25	.20
C594	AP96	18c multicolored	.25	.20
C595	AP96	30c grn & multi	.50	.20
C596	AP96	50c multicolored	.75	.30
C597	AP96	70c brn & multi	1.00	.40
C598	AP96	1 l yel & multi	2.00	.75
C599	AP96	2 l vio & multi	3.50	3.50
		Nos. C592-C599,CE6 (9)	9.20	6.25

For surcharges see Nos. C784, C787,
C917, C1100.

1976, Aug. 29   Litho.   Perf. 12
American Bicentennial: 2c, Raising flag of
"Liberty and Union." 3c, Bunker Hill flag. 4c,
Washington's Cruisers' flag. 5c, 1st Navy
Jack. 6c, Flag of Honduras over Presidential
Palace, Tegucigalpa. 18c, US flag over Capi-
tol. 55c, Grand Union flag. 2 l, Bennington
flag. 3 l, Betsy Ross and her flag.

C601	AP97	1c multicolored	.20	.20
C602	AP97	2c multicolored	.20	.20
C603	AP97	3c multicolored	.20	.20
C604	AP97	4c multicolored	.20	.20
C605	AP97	5c multicolored	.20	.20
C606	AP97	6c multicolored	.20	.20
C607	AP97	18c multicolored	.30	.35
C608	AP97	55c multicolored	.75	.70
a.		Souv. sheet of 4, #C603,		
		C606-C608	2.00	2.00
C609	AP97	2 l multicolored	2.25	2.25
a.		Souv. sheet of 3, #C601,		
		C604, C609	4.50	4.50
C610	AP97	3 l multicolored	4.75	4.75
a.		Souv. sheet of 3, #C602,		
		C605, C610	5.50	5.50
		Nos. C601-C610 (10)	9.25	9.25

For surcharges see Nos. C883-C884, C885,
C889, C1102.

King Juan Carlos
of Spain — AP98

Designs: 16c, Queen Sophia. 30c, Queen
Sophia and King Juan Carlos. 2 l, Arms of
Honduras and Spain, horiz.

1977, Sept. 13   Litho.   Perf. 14
C611	AP98	16c multicolored	.20	.20
C612	AP98	18c multicolored	.20	.20
C613	AP98	30c multicolored	.30	.20
C614	AP98	2 l multicolored	2.10	2.10
		Nos. C611-C614 (4)	2.80	2.75

Visit of King and Queen of Spain.
For surcharges see Nos. C890, C918,
C1107.

Mayan Steles,
Exhibition
Emblems
AP99

Designs: 18c, Giant head. 30c, Statue. 55c,
Sun god. 1.50 l, Mayan pelota court.

1978, Apr. 28   Litho.   Perf. 12
C615	AP99	15c multi	.20	.20
C616	AP99	18c multi	.45	.45
C617	AP99	30c multi	.65	.65
C618	AP99	55c multi	1.25	1.25

Imperf
C619	AP99	1.50 l multi	4.00	4.00
		Nos. C615-C619 (5)	6.55	6.55

Honduras '78 Philatelic Exhibition.
For overprints and surcharges see Nos.
C642-C645, C786, C920, C924, CB6.

Del Valle's
Birthplace
AP100

Designs: 14c, La Merced Church,
Choluteca, where del Valle was baptized. 15c,
Baptismal font, vert. 20c, Del Valle reading
independence acts. 25c, Portrait, documents,
map of Central America. 40c, Portrait, vert.
1 l, Monument, Central Park, Choluteca, vert.
3 l, Bust, vert.

1978, Apr. 11   Litho.   Perf. 14
C620	AP100	8c multicolored	.20	.20
C621	AP100	14c multicolored	.20	.20
C622	AP100	15c multicolored	.20	.20
C623	AP100	20c multicolored	.20	.20
C624	AP100	25c multicolored	.30	.30
C625	AP100	40c multicolored	.40	.40
C626	AP100	1 l multicolored	1.25	1.25
C627	AP100	3 l multicolored	4.00	4.00
		Nos. C620-C627 (8)	6.75	6.75

Bicentenary of the birth of José Cecilio del
Valle (1780-1834), Central American patriot
and statesman.
For surcharges see Nos. C739, C793,
C795, C886A, C1098.

Rural
Health
Center
AP101

Designs: 6c, Child at water pump. 10c, Los
Laureles Dam, Tegucigalpa. 20c, Rural

aqueduct. 40c, Teaching hospital, Tegucigalpa. 2 l, Parents and child. 3 l, National vaccination campaign. 5 l, Panamerican Health
Organization Building, Washington, DC.

1978, May 10   Litho.   Perf. 14
C628	AP101	5c multicolored	.20	.20
C629	AP101	6c multicolored	.20	.20
C630	AP101	10c multicolored	.20	.20
C631	AP101	20c multicolored	.25	.25
C632	AP101	40c multicolored	.45	.45
C633	AP101	2 l multicolored	1.90	1.90
C634	AP101	3 l multicolored	3.00	3.00
C635	AP101	5 l multicolored	4.50	4.50
		Nos. C628-C635 (8)	10.70	10.70

75th anniv. of Panamerican Health Organization (in 1977).
For surcharges see Nos. C783, C783A.

Luis Landa
and his
"Botanica"
AP102

Designs (Luis Landa and): 16c, Map of
Honduras showing St. Ignacio. 18c, Medals
received by Landa. 30c, Landa's birthplace in
St. Ignacio. 2 l, Brassavola (orchid), national
flower. 3 l, Women's Normal School.

1978, Aug. 29   Photo.   Perf. 13x13½
C636	AP102	14c multicolored	.20	.20
C637	AP102	16c multicolored	.20	.20
C638	AP102	18c multicolored	.20	.20
C639	AP102	30c multicolored	.40	.20
C640	AP102	2 l multicolored	3.00	1.00
C641	AP102	3 l multicolored	3.50	3.50
		Nos. C636-C641 (6)	7.50	5.30

Prof. Luis Landa (1875-1975), botanist.
For surcharges see Nos. C740, C794,
C888A, C923, C1099.

Nos. C615-C618 Overprinted in Red
with Argentina '78 Soccer Cup
Emblem and:
"Argentina Campeon / Holanda Sub-
Campeon / XI Campeonato Mundial /
de Football"

1978, Sept. 6   Litho.   Perf. 12
C642	AP99	15c multicolored	.20	.20
C643	AP99	18c multicolored	.35	.20
C644	AP99	30c multicolored	.45	.40
C645	AP99	55c multicolored	1.00	.65
		Nos. C642-C645 (4)	2.00	1.45

Argentina's victory in World Cup Soccer
Championship. Same overprint was applied to
No. C619. Value $45.
For surcharges, see No. C924, C1079.

Central University and Coat of
Arms — AP103

Designs show for each denomination a 19th
century print and a contemporary photograph
of same area (except 1.50 l, 5 l): No. C647,
University City. 8c, Manuel Bonilla Theater.
No. C650, Court House, vert. No. C651, North
Boulevard highway intersection, vert. No.
C652, Natl. Palace. No. C653, Presidential
Palace. 20c, Hospital. 40c, Cathedral. 50c,
View of Tegucigalpa. 1.50 l, Aerial view of
Tegucigalpa. No. C660, Arms of San Miguel
de Tegucigalpa, 18th cent., vert. No. C661,
Pres. Marco Aurelio Soto (1846-1908) (paint-
ing), vert.

1978, Sept. 29
C646	AP103	6c black & brn	.20	.20
C647	AP103	6c multicolored	.20	.20
a.		Pair, #C646-C647	.20	.20
C648	AP103	8c black & brn	.20	.20
C649	AP103	8c multicolored	.20	.20
a.		Pair, #C648-C649	.25	.25
C650	AP103	10c black & brn	.20	.20
C651	AP103	10c multicolored	.20	.20
a.		Pair, #C650-C651	.30	.30
C652	AP103	16c black & brn	.25	.20
C653	AP103	16c multicolored	.25	.20
a.		Pair, #C652-C653	.50	.50
C654	AP103	20c black & brn	.30	.20
C655	AP103	20c multicolored	.30	.20
a.		Pair, #C654-C655	.60	.60

C656 AP103 40c black & brn .75 .45
C657 AP103 40c multicolored .75 .45
  a. Pair, #C656-C657 1.60 1.60
C658 AP103 50c black & brn 1.00 .50
C659 AP103 50c multicolored 1.00 .50
  a. Pair, #C658-C659 2.10 2.10
C660 AP103 5 l black & brn 6.75 6.75
C661 AP103 5 l multicolored 6.75 6.75
  a. Pair, #C660-C661 14.00 14.00
  Nos. C646-C661 (16) 19.30 17.40

Souvenir Sheet

C662 AP103 1.50 l multi 2.75 2.75

400th anniv. of the founding of Tegucigalpa. In the listing the first number is for the 19th cent. design, the second for the 20th cent. design.
For overprints and surcharges see #C724-C725, C740A-C746, C766-C769, C779-C780, C1094-C1095, C1103-C1104.

Goalkeeper — AP104

Designs: Various soccer scenes.

1978, Nov. 26   **Litho.**   ***Perf. 12***
C663 AP104 15c multi, vert. .20 .20
C664 AP104 30c multi .30 .30
C665 AP104 55c multi, vert. .60 .60
C666 AP104 1 l multi 1.40 1.40
C667 AP104 2 l multi 2.50 2.50
  Nos. C663-C667 (5) 5.00 5.00

7th Youth Soccer Championship, Nov. 26. For surcharge see No. C797.

UPU Emblem — AP105

2c, Postal emblem of Honduras. 25c, Dr. Ramon Rosa, vert. 50c, Pres. Marco Aurelio Soto, vert.

1979, Apr. 1   **Litho.**   ***Perf. 12***
C668 AP105 2c multicolored .20 .20
C669 AP105 15c multicolored .20 .20
C670 AP105 25c multicolored .20 .20
C671 AP105 50c multicolored .40 .40
  Nos. C668-C671 (4) 1.00 1.00

Centenary of Honduras joining UPU.

Rotary Emblem and "50" AP106

1979, Apr. 26   **Litho.**   ***Perf. 14***
C672 AP106 3c multi .20 .20
C673 AP106 5c multi .20 .20
C674 AP106 50c multi .50 .50
C675 AP106 2 l multi 1.75 1.75
  Nos. C672-C675 (4) 2.65 2.65

Rotary Intl. of Honduras, 50th anniv. For surcharge see No. C884A, C1096.

Map of Caratasca Lagoon AP107

Designs: 10c, Fort San Fernando de Omoa. 24c, Institute anniversary emblem, vert. 5 l, Map of Santanilla islands.

1979, Sept. 15   **Litho.**   ***Perf. 13½***
C676 AP107 5c multi .20 .20
C677 AP107 10c multi .20 .20
C678 AP107 24c multi .25 .20
C679 AP107 5 l multi 4.00 4.00
  Nos. C676-C679 (4) 4.65 4.60

Panamerican Institute of History and Geography, 50th anniversary. For surcharge see No. C891.

General Post Office, 1979 — AP108

UPU Membership Cent.: 3 l, Post Office, 19th cent.

1980, Feb. 20   **Litho.**   ***Perf. 12***
C680 AP108 24c multi .20 .20
C681 AP108 3 l multi 2.75 2.75

For surcharge see No. C925.

Workers in the Field, IYC Emblem AP109

1980, Dec. 9   **Litho.**   ***Perf. 14½***
C682 AP109 1c shown .20 .20
C683 AP109 5c Landscape, vert. .20 .20
C684 AP109 15c Sitting boy, vert. .20 .20
C685 AP109 20c IYC emblem, vert. .25 .25
C686 AP109 30c Beach scene .45 .45
  Nos. C682-C686 (5) 1.30 1.30

Souvenir Sheet

C687 AP109 1 l UNICEF and IYC emblems, horiz. 1.50 1.50

International Year of the Child (1979).

Maltese Cross, Hill AP110

1980, Dec. 17
C688 AP110 1c shown .25 .25
C689 AP110 2c Penny Black .25 .25
C690 AP110 5c Honduras type A1 .25 .25
C691 AP110 10c Honduras type A1 .25 .25

Size: 47x34mm

C692 AP110 15c Postal emblem .25 .25
C693 AP110 20c Flags of Honduras, Gt. Britain .25 .25
  Nos. C688-C693 (6) 1.50 1.50

Souvenir Sheet

C694 AP110 1 l Honduras #C402 2.50 2.50

Sir Rowland Hill (1795-1879), originator of penny postage. No. C694 contains one stamp 47x34mm.

Intibucana Mother and Child — AP111

Inter-American Women's Commission, 50th Anniv.: 2c, Visitacion Padilla, Honduras Section founder. 10c, Maria Trinidad del Cid, Section member. 1 l, Emblem, horiz.

1981, June 15   **Litho.**   ***Perf. 14½***
C695 AP111 2c multicolored .20 .20
C696 AP111 10c multicolored .20 .20
C697 AP111 40c multicolored .30 .30
C698 AP111 1 l multicolored .80 .80
  Nos. C695-C698 (4) 1.50 1.50

Bernardo O'Higgins, by Jose Gil de Castro — AP112

1981, June 29

Paintings of O'Higgins: 16c, Liberation of Chile, by Cosme San Martin, horiz. 20c, Portrait of Ambrosio O'Higgins (father). 1 l, Abdication of Office, by Antonio Caro, horiz.

C699 AP112 16c multicolored .20 .20
C700 AP112 20c multicolored .20 .20
C701 AP112 30c multicolored .25 .25
C702 AP112 1 l multicolored 1.00 .50
  Nos. C699-C702 (4) 1.65 1.15

For surcharges see Nos. C785, C888B, C1106.

CONCACAF 81 Soccer Cup — AP113

1981, Dec. 30   **Litho.**   ***Perf. 14***
C703 AP113 20c Emblem .60 .25
C704 AP113 50c Player 1.25 .35
C705 AP113 70c Flags 1.90 1.00
C706 AP113 1 l Stadium 2.75 1.50
  Nos. C703-C706 (4) 6.50 3.10

Souvenir Sheet

C707 AP113 1.50 l like #C703 1.75 1.75

For overprint see No. C797.

50th Anniv. of Air Force (1981) AP114

Designs: 3c, Curtiss CT-32 Condor. 15c, North American NA-16. 25c, Chance Vought F4U-5. 65c, Douglas C47. 1 l Cessna A37-B. 2 l, Super Mister SMB-11.

1983, Jan. 14   **Litho.**   ***Perf. 12***
C708 AP114 3c multi .20 .20
C709 AP114 15c multi .20 .20
C710 AP114 25c multi .35 .20
C711 AP114 65c multi .65 .35
C712 AP114 1 l multi 1.00 .50
C713 AP114 2 l multi 2.00 1.75
  Nos. C708-C713 (6) 4.40 3.20

Souvenir Sheet

C714 AP114 1.55 l Helicopter 4.00 4.00

For surcharges see Nos. C884B, C1097.

UPU Executive Council Membership, 3rd Anniv. — AP115

1983, Jan. 14
C715 AP115 16c UPU monument .20 .20
C716 AP115 18c 18th UPU Congress emblem .20 .20
C717 AP115 30c Natl. Postal Service emblem .35 .35
C718 AP115 55c Rio de Janeiro .50 .50
C719 AP115 2 l Dove on globe 2.00 2.00
  Nos. C715-C719 (5) 3.25 3.25

Souvenir Sheet

C720 AP115 1 l like 2 l 2.50 2.50

For surcharges see Nos. C921, C1204.

Natl. Library and Archives Centenary (1980) AP116

1983, Feb. 11   **Litho.**   ***Perf. 12***
C721 AP116 9c Library .30 .20
C722 AP116 1 l Books 1.10 .40

For surcharge see No. C1101.

Intl. Year of the Disabled (1979) AP117

1983, Feb. 11

C723 AP117 25c Emblem .40 .25

No. C657a Overprinted in Red: "CONMEMORATIVA DE LA VISITA / DE SS. JUAN PABLO II / 8 de marzo de 1983"

1983, Mar. 8
C724 AP103 40c multicolored 3.00 2.50
C725 AP103 40c multicolored 3.00 2.50
  a. Pair, #C724-C725 6.00 5.00

Visit of Pope John Paul II.

Literacy Campaign (1980) — AP118

World Food Day, Oct. 16, 1981 — AP119

1983, May 18   **Litho.**   ***Perf. 12***
C726 AP118 40c Hands, open book .50 .45
C727 AP118 1.50 l People holding books 2.00 1.90

1983, May 18
C728 AP119 65c Produce, emblem 1.00 1.00

20th Anniv. of Inter-American Development Bank (1980) — AP120

1983, June 17 Litho. Perf. 12
C729 AP120 1 l Comayagua River Bridge 1.50 .50
C730 AP120 2 l Luis Bogran Technical Institute of Physics 2.75 1.00

2nd Anniv. of Return to Constitutional Government — AP121

1984, Jan. 27 Litho. Perf. 12
C731 20c Arms, text .20 .20
C732 20c Pres. Suazo Cordova .20 .20
a. AP121 Pair, #C731-C732 .65 .55

La Gaceta Newspaper Sesquicentenary (1980) — AP122

1984, May 25 Litho. Perf. 12
C733 AP122 10c multicolored .35 .35
C734 AP122 20c multicolored .35 .35

Nos. C582 and C575-C576 Surcharged

1985, June 26 Litho. Perf. 13½
C735 AP95 5c on 1c #C582 .20 .20
C736 AP94 10c on 8c #C575 .20 .20
C737 AP94 20c on 16c #C576 .20 .20
C738 AP95 1 l on 1c #C582 1.00 .40
Nos. C735-C738 (4) 1.60 1.00

Nos. C621, C636, C647a Surcharged
Litho., Photo. (No. C740)
1986, Aug. 21 Perfs. as before
C739 AP100 50c on 14c #C621 .45 .25
C740 AP102 60c on 14c #C636 .55 .30
C740A AP103 85c on 6c #C646 .80 .55
C740B AP103 85c on 6c #C647 .80 .55
c. Pair, #C740A-C740B 1.75 1.50
C741 AP103 95c on 6c #C646 .90 .60
C742 AP103 95c on 6c #C647 .90 .60
a. Pair, #C741-C742 2.00 1.75
Nos. C739-C742 (6) 4.40 2.85

Black bar obliterating old values on #C739-C740 also cover "aereo."

Nos. C656-C657 Ovptd. in Red "EXFILHON '86," "MEXICO '86" and:
No. C743 "ARGENTINA CAMPEON"
No. C744 "ALEMANIA FEDERAL Sub Campeon"
No. C745 "FRANCIA TERCER LUGAR"
No. C746 "BELGICA CUARTO LUGAR"

1986, Sept. 12 Litho. Perf. 12
C743 AP103 40c No. C656 .40 .20
C744 AP103 40c No. C657 .40 .20
C745 AP103 40c No. C657 .40 .20
C746 AP103 40c No. C656 .40 .20
a. Block of 4, #C743-C746 2.00

AP123

San Fernando de Omoa Castle — AP124

20c, Phulapanzak Falls. 78c, Bahia Isls. beach. 85c, Bahia Isls. cove. 95c, Yojoa Lake. 1 l, Woman painting pottery.

Perf. 13½x14, 14x13½
1986, Nov. 10 Litho.
C747 AP123 20c multi, vert. .20 .20
C748 AP123 78c multi 1.10 .55
C749 AP123 85c multi 1.25 .55
C750 AP123 95c multi, vert. 1.40 .65
C751 AP123 1 l multi 1.50 .70

Size: 84x59mm
Imperf
C752 AP124 1.50 l multi 2.75 2.75
Nos. C747-C752 (6) 8.20 5.40
For overprint see No. C782.

AP125

Flora — AP126

1987, Feb. 2 Litho. Perf. 13½
National flag, Pres. Jose Azcona Hoyo.
C753 AP125 20c multicolored .30 .25
C754 AP125 85c multicolored 1.25 .85
Democratic government, 1st anniv.

1987, July 8 Litho. Perf. 13½x14
C755 AP126 10c Eupatorium cyrillinelsonii .25 .25
C756 AP126 20c Salvia ernestivargasii .45 .45
C757 AP126 95c Robinsonella erasmi-sosae 1.40 .75
Nos. C755-C757 (3) 2.10 1.45

Birds — AP127

AP128

1987, Sept. 10 Litho. Perf. 13½x14
C758 AP127 50c Eumomota superciliosa 1.75 .50
C759 AP127 60c Ramphastos sulfuratus 2.00 .50

C760 AP127 85c Amazona autumnalis 3.50 1.10
Nos. C758-C760 (3) 7.25 2.10

1987, Dec. 10 Litho. Perf. 13½
C761 AP128 1 l blk, brt yel & dark red 1.25 .50
Natl. Autonomous University of Honduras, 30th anniv.

AP129

AP130

1987, Dec. 23 Litho. Perf. 13½
C762 AP129 20c red & dk ultra .50 .20
Natl. Red Cross, 50th anniv.

1988, Jan. 27 Litho. Perf. 13½
C763 AP130 95c brt blue & org yel 1.10 .45
17th regional meeting of Lions Intl.

Atlantida Bank, 75th Anniv. AP131

Main offices: 10c, La Ceiba, Atlantida, 1913. 85c, Tegucigalpa, 1988.

1988, Feb. 10
C764 AP131 10c multi .25 .20
C765 AP131 85c mutli .90 .40
a. Souv. sheet of 2, #358-359, imperf. 1.25 1.25
No. C765a sold for 1 l.

No. C649a Surcharged

No. C647a Surcharged

1988, June 9 Litho. Perf. 12
C766 AP103 20c on 8c #C648 .90 .90
C767 AP103 20c on 8c #C649 .90 .90
a. Pair, #C766-C767 2.00 2.00

1988, July 8 Litho. Perf. 12
C768 AP103 5c on 6c #C646 .30 .30
C769 AP103 5c on 6c #C647 .30 .30
a. Pair, #C768-C769 .80 .80

Postman AP132

Tegucigalpa Postmark on Stampless Cover, 1789 — AP133

1988, Sept. 11 Litho. Perf. 13½
C770 AP132 85c dull red brn 1.10 .40
C771 AP133 2 l dull red brn & ver 2.50 1.00
EXFILHON '88.

Summer Olympics Type of 1988
1988, Sept. 30 Litho. Perf. 13½
Size: 28x33mm
C772 A62 85c Running, vert. 1.10 .40
Size: 36x27mm
C773 A62 1 l Baseball, soccer, basketball 1.20 .50

Discovery of America, 500th Anniv. (in 1992) AP134

Pre-Colombian pottery artifacts: 10c, Footed vase, vert. 25c, Bowl. 30c, Footed bowl. 50c, Pitcher, vert. 1 l, Rectangular footed bowl.

1988 Litho. Perf. 13½
C774 AP134 10c multicolored .30 .20
C775 AP134 25c multicolored .75 .25
C776 AP134 30c multicolored .90 .30
C777 AP134 50c multicolored 1.50 .50
Nos. C774-C777 (4) 3.45 1.25
Size: 115x83mm
Imperf
C778 AP134 1 l multicolored 3.25 3.25

Nos. C653a and C576 Surcharged
1988 Litho. Perf. 12, 13½
C779 AP103 10c on 16c #C652 .20 .20
C780 AP103 10c on 16c #C653 .25 .20
a. Pair, #C779-C780 .50 .50
C781 AP94 50c on 16c #C576 .80 .40
Nos. C779-C781 (3) 1.25 .80
Nos. C779-C780 exist with double surcharge.
Issued: 10c, Apr. 7, 50c, May 25.

No. C752 Overprinted

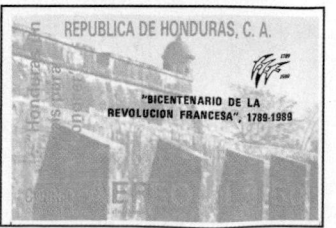

1989, July 14 Litho. Imperf.
C782 AP124 1.50 l multi 2.75 2.75
French revolution, bicent.

Nos. C629 and C593 Surcharged

I

II

1989 Litho. Perf. 14, 13½
C783 AP101 15c on 6c, I .40 .20
C783A AP101 15c on 6c, II 1.00 .20
C784 AP96 1 l on 16c 1.25 .95
    Nos. C783-C784 (3) 2.65 1.35
    Issue date: 1 l, June 15.

Nos. C699 and C616 Surcharged

1989, Dec. 15 Litho. Perf. 14½, 12
C785 AP112 20c on 16c #C699 .40 .20
C786 AP99 95c on 18c #C616 1.40 .50
    No. C786 exists with inverted surcharge.
    Issued: #C785, Dec. 15; #C786, Dec. 28.

Nos. C594 and C585 Surcharged with
New Denomination and "IV Juegos /
Olimpicos / Centroamericanos"

1990, Jan. 12 Litho. Perf. 13½
C787 AP96 75c on 18c #C594
    (S) 1.10 .85
C788 AP95 85c on 18c #C585 1.25 .95
    No. C787 exists with double and inverted
surcharge.

World Wildlife
Fund — AP135

Various *Mono ateles.*

1990, Apr. 18 Litho. Perf. 13½
C789 AP135 10c shown 3.75 2.50
C790 AP135 10c Adult, young 3.75 2.50
C791 AP135 20c Adult hang-
    ing, diff. 6.00 4.00
C792 AP135 20c Adult, young,
    diff. 6.50 4.50
    Nos. C789-C792 (4) 20.00 13.50

No. C621 Surcharged

1990, Feb. 8 Litho. Perf. 14
C793 AP100 20c on 14c multi .25 .20

Nos. C621 and C636 Surcharged "50
Aniversario / IHCI" / 1939-1989

1990, Mar. 29
C794 AP102 20c on 14c No. 636 .25 .20
C795 AP100 1 l on 14c No. 621 .65 .40

No. C665 Surcharged

1990, June 14 Litho. Perf. 12
C796 AP104 1 l on 55c multi .75 .40
World Cup Soccer Championships, Italy.

No. C707 Ovptd. in Margin
"CAMPEONATO MUNDIAL DE
FUTBOL Italia '90," and Character
Trademark
Souvenir Sheet

1990, June 14 Perf. 14
C797 AP113 1.50 l multi .80 .80

No. C577 Surcharged in Black

1990, Feb. 22 Litho. Perf. 13½
C798 AP94 20c on 18c multi .40 .20

FAO, 45th
Anniv. — AP136

1990, Oct. 16 Litho. Perf. 13½
C799 AP136 95c yel, blk, bl, grn .85 .75

17th Interamerican Congress of
Industry and Construction — AP137

1990, Nov. 21 Litho. Perf. 13½
C800 AP137 20c Map, vert. .25 .20
C801 AP137 1 l Jose Cecilio
    Del Valle Pal-
    ace .65 .45

AP138

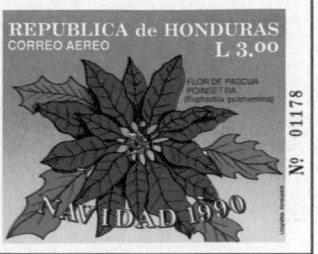

Christmas — AP139

1990, Nov. 30 Litho. Perf. 13½
C802 AP138 20c shown .40 .20
C803 AP138 95c Madonna and
    Child, vert. .80 .40
    Size: 112x82mm
    Imperf
C804 AP139 3 l Poinsettia 2.50 2.00
    Nos. C802-C804 (3) 3.70 2.60

Salesian
Order in
Honduras,
80th Anniv.
AP140

1990, Dec. 28 Litho. Perf. 13½
C805 AP140 75c St. John Bosco .50 .30
C806 AP140 1 l Natl. Youth
    Sanctuary .70 .50

Pres. Rafael
Leonardo
Callejas — AP141

1991, Jan. 31
C807 AP141 30c Taking oath .20 .20
C808 AP141 2 l Portrait 1.25 .90

Moths and
Butterflies
AP142

1991, Feb. 28 Litho. Perf. 13½
C809 AP142 85c Strymon me-
    linus 1.25 .40
C810 AP142 90c Diorina sp. 1.50 .50
C811 AP142 1.50 l Hyalophora
    cecropia 2.50 .70
    Size: 114x82mm
    Imperf
C812 AP142 5 l Papilio polix-
    enes 4.00 4.00
    Nos. C809-C812 (4) 9.25 5.60

Notary
Day — AP143

1991, May 22 Litho. Perf. 13½
C813 AP143 50c multicolored .40 .25

Rafael Heliodoro
Valle, Birth
Cent. — AP144

1991, July 26 Litho. Perf. 13½
C815 AP144 2 l pale pink & blk 1.40 .90

Churches
AP145

Discovery of America, 500th Anniv. emblem
and: 30c, Church of St. Manuel of Colohete,
Gracias. 95c, Church of Our Lady of Mercy,
Gracias. 1 l, Comayagua Cathedral.

1991, Aug. 30 Litho. Perf. 13½
C816 AP145 30c multicolored .20 .20
C817 AP145 95c multicolored .70 .20
C818 AP145 1 l multicolored .85 .45
    Nos. C816-C818 (3) 1.75 .85

Latin
American
Institute,
25th Anniv.
AP146

1991, June 20
C819 AP146 1 l multicolored .70 .40

Flowers
AP147

1991, Apr. 30
C820 AP147 30c Rhyncholaelia
    glauca .25 .20
C821 AP147 50c Oncidium
    splendidum,
    vert. .50 .40
C822 AP147 95c Laelia
    anceps, vert. .75 .70
C823 AP147 1.50 l Cattleya skin-
    neri 1.25 1.10
    Nos. C820-C823 (4) 2.75 2.40

Espamer
'91,
Buenos
Aires
AP148

1991, July 1
C824 AP148 2 l multicolored 2.25 .80
    Size: 101x82mm
    Imperf
C825 AP148 5 l like #C824 3.50 3.50
Discovery of America, 500th anniv. (in 1992).

11th Pan
American
Games,
Havana
AP149

1991, Aug. 8
C826 AP149 30c Equestrian   .25   .20
C827 AP149 85c Judo   .60   .40
C828 AP149 95c Men's swim-
                  ming   .75   .40

Size: 114x83mm
Imperf
C829 AP149 5 l Women's swim-
                  ming   3.50 3.50
      Nos. C826-C829 (4)   5.10 4.50

Pre-Columbian Culture — AP150

UPAEP emblem, artifacts and: 25c, ears of corn. 40c, ear of corn, map. 1.50 l, map.

1991, Sept. 30   Litho.   Perf. 13½
C830 AP150 25c multicolored   .25   .20
C831 AP150 40c multicolored   .75   .40
C832 AP150 1.50 l multicolored   1.50   .60
      Nos. C830-C832 (3)   2.50 1.20

4th Intl. Congress on Control of Insect Pests AP151

Designs: 30c, Tactics to control pests. 75c, Integration of science. 1 l, Cooperation between farmers and scientists. 5 l, Pests and biological controls.

1991, Nov. 22
C833 AP151 30c multicolored   .40   .20
C834 AP151 75c multicolored   1.10   .55
C835 AP151 1 l multicolored   2.10   .85

Size: 115x83mm
Imperf
C836 AP151 5 l multicolored   3.25 3.25
      Nos. C833-C836 (4)   6.85 4.85

America Issue AP152

1992, Jan. 27   Litho.   Perf. 13½
C837 AP152 90c Sighting land   .75   .60
C838 AP152 1 l Columbus'
                  ships   .85   .75
C839 AP152 2 l Ship, map,
                  birds   1.60 1.25
      Nos. C837-C839 (3)   3.20 2.60

Christmas AP153

1991, Dec. 19
C840 AP153 1 l shown   .65   .40
C841 AP153 2 l Poinsettias in
                  rooster vase   1.40   .90

Honduran Savings Insurance Company, 75th Anniv. AP154

1992, Jan. 17
C842 AP154 85c multicolored   .55   .30
C843 AP154 1 l Priest saying
                  mass   .65   .40

Size: 115x83mm
Imperf
C844 AP154 5 l like #C842   3.25 3.25
      Nos. C842-C844 (3)   4.45 3.95

First mass in New World, 490th anniv. (No. C843). Taking possession of new continent, 490th anniv. (Nos. C842, C844).

Pres. Rafael Leonardo Callejas, 2nd Year in Office AP155

Callejas with: 20c, Italian president Francesco Cossiga. 2 l, Pope John Paul II.

1992, Jan. 27   Litho.   Perf. 13½
C845 AP155 20c black & purple   .25   .20
C846 AP155 2 l black & multi   1.40   .80

Flowers AP156

1992, July 25   Litho.   Perf. 13½
C847 AP156 20c Bougainvillea
                  glabra   .25   .20
C848 AP156 30c Canna indica   .25   .20
C849 AP156 75c Epiphyllum   .70   .45
C850 AP156 95c Sobralia
                  macrantha   .90   .65
      Nos. C847-C850 (4)   2.10 1.50

Gen. Francisco Morazan Hydroelectric Complex — AP157

1992, Aug. 17
C851 AP157 85c Dam face, vert.   .50   .30
C852 AP157 4 l Rear of dam   2.40 1.60

AP158

1992, Aug. 24
C853 AP158 95c black & multi   .65   .55
C854 AP158 95c multicolored   .65   .55

Intl. Conference on Agriculture, 50th anniv.

AP159

1992, Sept. 18   Litho.   Perf. 13½
Gen. Francisco Morazan (1792-1842): 5c, Morazan mounted on horseback. 10c, Statue of Morazan. 50c, Watch and sword, horiz. 95c,

Portrait of Josefa Lastiri de Morazan. 5 l, Portrait of Morazan in uniform.

C855 AP159 5c   multicolored   .20   .20
C856 AP159 10c multicolored   .20   .20
C857 AP159 50c multicolored   .35   .20
C858 AP159 95c multicolored   .60   .30

Size: 76x108mm
Imperf
C859 AP159 5 l multicolored   3.00 2.25
      Nos. C855-C859 (5)   4.35 3.15

Children's Day — AP160

Paintings of children: 25c, Musicians. 95c, Boy, dog standing in doorway. 2 l, Flower girl.

1992, Sept. 7
C860 AP160 25c multicolored   .20   .20
C861 AP160 95c multicolored   .60   .30
C862 AP160 2 l multicolored   1.25   .80
      Nos. C860-C862 (3)   2.05 1.30

Intl. Conference on Nutrition AP161

1992, Sept. 30   Litho.   Perf. 13½
C863 AP161 1.05 l multicolored   .70   .45

Pan-American Agricultural School, 50th Anniv. — AP162

1992, Oct. 9
C864 AP162 20c Bee keepers   .20   .20
C865 AP162 85c Woman, goats   .50   .30
C866 AP162 1 l Plowing   .60   .40
C867 AP162 2 l Man with tool,
                  vert.   1.25   .80
      Nos. C864-C867 (4)   2.55 1.70

Exfilhon '92 — AP163

Birds: 1.50 l, F. triquilidos. 2.45 l, Ara macao. 5 l, Quetzal pharomachrus mocinno.

1992, Oct. 2
C868 AP163 1.50 l multicolored   1.75 1.50
C869 AP163 2.45 l multicolored   2.75 2.40

Size: 76x108mm
Imperf
C870 AP163 5 l multicolored   3.25 3.25
      Nos. C868-C870 (3)   7.75 7.15

Discovery of America, 500th anniv.

America Issue — AP164

Discovery of America, 500th Anniv. — AP165

UPAEP emblem and: 35c, Native settlement. 5 l, Explorers meeting natives in boats.

1992, Oct. 30   Litho.   Perf. 13½
C871 AP164 35c multicolored   .20   .20
C872 AP164 5 l multicolored   2.75 2.00

Printed on both thick and thin paper.

1992, Oct. 30
Details from First Mass, by Roque Zelaya: 95c, Ships off-shore. 1 l, Holding services with natives, horiz. 2 l, Natives, countryside, temples, horiz.

C873 AP165 95c multicolored   .50   .40
C874 AP165 1 l multicolored   .65   .45
C875 AP165 2 l multicolored   1.25 1.00
      Nos. C873-C875 (3)   2.40 1.85

City of El Progreso, Cent. AP166

1992, Oct. 17
C876 AP166 1.55 l multicolored   .90   .55

First Road Conservation Congress of Panama and Central America — AP167

1992, Nov. 16   Perf. 13½
C878 AP167 20c shown   .20   .20
C879 AP167 85c Bulldozer on
                  highway   .45   .30

Pan-American Health Organization, 90th Anniv. — AP168

1992, Nov. 27
C880 AP168 3.95 l multicolored   2.25 1.75

Christmas AP169

Paintings by Roque Zelaya: 20c, Crowd watching people climb pole in front of church, vert. 85c, Nativity scene.

1992, Nov. 24
C881 AP169 20c multicolored   .20 .20
C882 AP169 85c multicolored   .65 .30

Surcharges on:

No. C601

Nos. C606-C607

Nos. C584, C612, C637

Nos. C672, C678, C708

Nos. C575-C576, C603, C620, C699

1992-93
Perfs. and Printing Methods as Before

C883 AP97 20c on 1c #C601   .40 .20
C884 AP97 20c on 3c #C603   .40 .20
C884A AP106 20c on 3c #C672   .40 .20
C884B AP114 20c on 3c #C708   .40 .20
C885 AP97 20c on 6c #C606   .40 .20
C886 AP94 20c on 8c #C575   .40 .20
C886A AP100 20c on 8c #C620   .25 .20
C887 AP94 50c on 16c #C576   .40 .20
C888 AP95 50c on 16c #C584   .40 .20
C888A AP102 50c on 16c #C637   .40 .20
C888B AP112 50c on 16c #C699   .40 .20
C889 AP97 85c on 18c #C607   .50 .30
C890 AP98 85c on 18c #C612   .50 .30
C891 AP107 85c on 24c #C678   .40 .30
      Nos. C883-C891 (14)   5.65 3.10

Size and location of surcharge varies.
Issued: #C883, 12/18/92; #C889, 1/22/93; #C885, 3/8/93; #C888A, 9/7/93; #C888, 9/13/93; #C890, 9/24/93; #C891, 10/1/93; #C884A, 10/5/93; #C884B, 10/8/93; #C884, C886A, 10/21/93; #C886, 10/29/93; #C887, C888B, 11/3/93.

Intl. Court of Justice Decision on Border Dispute Between Honduras & El Salvador
AP170

Designs: 90c, Pres. of El Salvador and Pres. Callejas of Honduras, vert. 1.05 l, Country flags, map of Honduras and El Salvador.

1993, Feb. 24   Litho.   Perf. 13½
C893 AP170 90c multicolored   .50 .30
C894 AP170 1.05 l multicolored .65 .40
      Third year of Pres. Callejas' term.

Mother's Day — AP171

Endangered Animals — AP172

Paintings of a mother and child, by Sandra Pendrey.

1993, May 5   Litho.   Perf. 13½
C895 AP171 50c Red blanket   .30 .20
C896 AP171 95c Green blanket   .55 .30

1993, May 14   Perf. 13½
C897 AP172 85c Manatee, horiz. .65 .50
C898 AP172 2.45 l Puma, horiz. 1.75 1.25
C899 AP172 10 l Jaguar   6.50 4.00
      Nos. C897-C899 (3)   8.90 5.75

Natl. Symbols AP173

1993, June 25   Litho.   Perf. 13½
C900 AP173 25c Ara macao   1.10 .95
C901 AP173 95c Odocoileus virginianus 1.50 1.25

First Brazilian Postage Stamps, 150th Anniv. AP174

1993, Sept. 10   Litho.   Perf. 13½
C902 AP174 20c Brazil No. 1   .20 .20
C903 AP174 50c Brazil No. 2   .30 .20
C904 AP174 95c Brazil No. 3   .55 .40
      Nos. C902-C904 (3)   1.05 .80

Departments in Honduras — AP175

Various scenes, department name: No. C905a, Atlantida. b, Colon. c, Cortes. d, Choluteca. e, El Paraiso. f, Francisco Morazan.
No. C906a, Comayagua. b, Copan. c, Intibuca. d, Islas de la Bahia. e, Lempira. f, Ocotepeque.
No. C907a, La Paz. b, Olancho. c, Santa Barbara. d, Valle. e, Yoro. f, Gracias a Dios.

1993, Sept. 20   Litho.   Perf. 13½
C905 AP175 20c Strip of 6, #a.-f.   .65 .65
C906 AP175 50c Strip of 6, #a.-f.   1.50 1.50
C907 AP175 1.50 l Strip of 6, #a.-f. 4.25 4.25
      Nos. C905-C907 (3)   6.40 6.40
      No. C906 is vert.

Endangered Birds — AP176

UN Development Program AP177

1993, Oct. 11   Litho.   Perf. 13½
C908 AP176 20c Spizaetus ornatus   .25 .20
C909 AP176 80c Cairina moschata, horiz. 1.00 .50
C910 AP176 2 l Harpia harpija, horiz.   2.25 1.50
      Nos. C908-C910 (3)   3.50 2.20

1993, Oct. 19
C911 AP177 95c multicolored   .50 .35

Christmas AP178

1993, Nov. 5
C912 AP178 20c Church   .25 .20
C913 AP178 85c Woman, flowers   .45 .30

Nos. C577, C585, C593, C611, C616, C638, C643, C680, C716 Surcharged

1993
Perfs. and Printing Methods as Before

C917 AP96 50c on 16c #C593   .25 .25
C918 AP98 50c on 16c #C611   .25 .25
C919 AP94 50c on 18c #C577   .25 .25
C920 AP99 50c on 18c #C616   .25 .25
C921 AP115 50c on 18c #C716   .40 .40
C922 AP95 85c on 18c #C585   .40 .40
C923 AP102 85c on 18c #C638   .40 .40
C924 AP99 85c on 18c #C643   .40 .40
C925 AP108 85c on 24c #C680   .40 .40
      Nos. C917-C925 (9)   3.00 3.00

Size and location of surcharge varies.
Issued: #C917-C918, 11/12; #C920, C924, 11/23; #C921, C925, 11/30; #C922-C923, 12/3; #C919, 12/10.

Fish AP179

1993, Dec. 7   Litho.   Perf. 13½
C931 AP179 20c Pomacanthus arcuatus   .30 .20
C932 AP179 85c Holacanthus ciliaris   .80 .50
C933 AP179 3 l Chaetodon striatus   2.50 1.90
      Nos. C931-C933 (3)   3.60 2.60

Famous Men — AP180

1993, Nov. 17
C934 AP180 25c Ramon Rosa   .20 .20
C935 AP180 65c Jesus Aguilar Paz   .30 .25
C936 AP180 85c Augusto C. Coello   .40 .30
      Nos. C934-C936 (3)   .90 .75

Pres. Rafael Leonardo Callejas, 4th Year in Office AP181

95c, Wife, Norma, planting tree, vert.

1994, Jan. 21   Litho.   Perf. 13½
C937 AP181 95c multicolored   .45 .30
C938 AP181 1 l multicolored   .50 .30

AP182

AP183

1994, Mar. 8   Litho.   Perf. 13 ½
C939 AP182 1 l multicolored   .45   .30
Intl. Year of the Family.

1994, Oct. 24   Litho.   Perf. 13½
C940 AP183 1 l multicolored   .45   .30
Intl. Conference on Peace and Development
in Central America, Tegucigalpa.

Christmas
AP184

UN, 50th
Anniv. — AP185

Paintings by Gelasio Gimenez: 95c,
Madonna and Child. 1 l, Holy Family.

1994, Dec. 15   Litho.   Perf. 13½
C941 AP184 95c multicolored   .45   .30
C942 AP184 1 l multicolored   .55   .40

1995, Jan. 17
Designs: 1 l, The Sowing: Ecological Family,
by Elisa Dulcey. 2 l, Family Scene, by Delmer
Mejia. 3 l, UN emblem, "50."

C943 AP185 1 l multicolored   .50   .50
C944 AP185 2 l multicolored   .85   .85
C945 AP185 3 l multicolored   1.25   1.25
Nos. C943-C945 (3)   2.60   2.60

Pres.
Carlos
Roberto
Reina, 1st
Anniv. of
Taking
Office
AP186

Designs: 80c, Beside flag, vert. 1 l, Summit
meeting of area presidents & vice presidents.

1995, Jan. 27
C946 AP186 80c multicolored   .30   .30
C947 AP186 95c multicolored   .35   .35
C948 AP186 1 l multicolored   .40   .40
Nos. C946-C948 (3)   1.05   1.00

America
Issue
AP187

Postal vehicles.

1995, Feb. 28   Litho.   Perf. 13½
C949 AP187 1.50 l Van   .65   .55
C950 AP187 2 l Motorcycle   .80   .70

Miniature Sheet of 30

Mushrooms
AP188

1 l: a, Marasmius cohaerens. b, Lepista
nuda. c, Polyporus pargamenus. d, Fomes. e,
Paneolus sphinctrinus. f, Hygrophorus
aurantiaca.
1.50 l, vert: g, Psathyrella. h, Amanita
rubescens. i, Boletellus russelli. j, Boletus fros-
tii. k, Marasmius spegazzinii. l, Fomes
annosus.
2 l, vert: m, Craterellus cornucopioides. n,
Amanita. o, Auricularia delicata. p, Psllocybe
cubensis. q, Clavariadelphus pistilaris. r, Boletus regius.
2.50 l: s, Scleroderma aurantium. t, Amanita
praegraveolens. u, Cantharellus cibarius. v,
Geastrum triplex. w, Russula emetica. x, Boletus pinicola.
3 l: y, Fomes versicolor. z, Cantharellus
pupurascens. aa, Lyophyllum decastes. ab,
Pleurotus ostreatus. ac, Boletus ananas. ad,
Amanita caesarea.

1995, Apr. 7
C951 AP188 Sheet of 30, #a.-
ad.   35.00   35.00

FAO, 50th
Anniv.
AP189

1995, May 25   Litho.   Perf. 13½
C952 AP189 3 l multicolored   .70   .40

CARE,
50th Anniv.
AP190

Designs: 1.40 l, Family, farm. No. C954,
Orchid, wildlife, couple working in soil. No.
C955, Couple in vegetable garden.

1995, Aug. 4   Litho.   Perf. 13½
C953 AP190 1.40 l multicolored   .50   .50
C954 AP190 5.40 l multicolored   2.10   2.10
C955 AP190 5.40 l multicolored   2.10   2.10
Nos. C953-C955 (3)   4.70   4.70

El Puente Archaeological
Park — AP191

Illustration reduced.

1995, Aug. 8   Imperf.
C956 AP191 20 l multicolored   6.25   6.25

America
Issue
AP192

1.40 l, Kinosternon scorpioides. 4.54 l,
Alpinia purpurata, vert. 10 l, Polyborus
plancus, vert.

1995, Oct. 10   Litho.   Perf. 13½
C957 AP192 1.40 l multicolored   .50   .50
C958 AP192 4.54 l multicolored   1.60   1.60
C959 AP192 10 l multicolored   3.50   3.50
Nos. C957-C959 (3)   5.60   5.60

Reptiles
AP193

1995, Nov. 10   Litho.   Perf. 13
C960 AP193 5.40 l Iguana igua-
na   2.10   2.00
C961 AP193 5.40 l Agalychnis   2.10   2.00

Christmas
AP194

1995, Dec. 4   Litho.   Perf. 13½
C962 AP194 1.40 l Bell, vert.   .50   .60
C963 AP194 5.40 l Nativity figu-
rines   2.25   2.25
C964 AP194 6.90 l Carved deer,
vert.   2.50   2.50
Nos. C962-C964 (3)   5.25   5.35

Integration
System of
Central
America
AP195

1.40 l, Map of Central America, Tegucigalpa
Protocol, 1991. 4.30 l, Functions listed, 1993.
5.40 l, 17th Summit of Presidents of Central
America.

1996, Feb. 19   Litho.   Perf. 13½
C965 AP195 1.40 l multicolored   .50   .50
C966 AP195 4.30 l multicolored   1.60   1.60
C967 AP195 5.40 l multicolored   2.00   2.00
Nos. C965-C967 (3)   4.10   4.10

UN Fight
Against
Drug
Trafficking
and Abuse,
10th Anniv.
AP196

Designs: 1.40 l, Stylized picture of minds on
drugs. 5.40 l, Person with butterfly for brain,
vert. 10 l, Musical score, "Viva la Vida."

1996, May 3
C968 AP196 1.40 l multicolored   .40   .40
C969 AP196 5.40 l multicolored   1.75   1.75
C970 AP196 10 l multicolored   2.75   2.75
Nos. C968-C970 (3)   4.90   4.90

Arrival of
the
Garifunas
in
Honduras,
Bicent.
AP197

Designs: 1.40 l, Headdress, vert. 5.40 l,
Dancers, men playing drums. 10 l, Drums.

1996, June 13   Litho.   Perf. 13½
C971 AP197 1.40 l multicolored   .40   .20
C972 AP197 5.40 l multicolored   1.50   1.00
C973 AP197 10 l multicolored   2.75   1.50
Nos. C971-C973 (3)   4.65   2.70

EXFILHON
'96, 7th
Philatelic
Exhibition
AP198

1996, July 12   Litho.   Perf. 13½
C974 AP198 5.40 l Steam locomotive   2.00   2.00
C975 AP198 5.40 l Passenger
railcar   2.00   2.00

73x52mm
Imperf
C976 AP198 20 l +2 l like
#C974   7.50   7.50
Nos. C974-C976 (3)   11.50   11.50

6th Central
American
Games
AP199

1996, Aug. 30   Litho.   Perf. 13½
C977 AP199 4.30 l Soccer   1.40   .60
C978 AP199 4.54 l Volleyball   1.40   .65
C979 AP199 5.40 l Mascot, vert.   1.60   .75
Nos. C977-C979 (3)   4.40   2.00

Scouting in
Honduras,
75th Anniv.
AP200

1996, Oct. 25   Litho.   Perf. 13½
C980 AP200 2.15 l Emblems   .50   .20
C981 AP200 5.40 l Emblem, vert.   1.40   .60
C982 AP200 6.90 l Scout feeding
deer, vert.   2.10   .80
Nos. C980-C982 (3)   4.00   1.60

Christmas
AP201

Poinsettia and: 1.40 l, Candles. 5.40 l, Candles, vert.

1996, Dec. 23   Litho.   Perf. 13½
C983 AP201 1.40 l multicolored   .65   .20
C984 AP201 3 l shown   1.25   .50
C985 AP201 5.40 l multicolored   2.10   .95
Nos. C983-C985 (3)   4.00   1.65

Traditional
Costumes
AP202

America issue: 4.55 l, Man in costume.
5.40 l, Woman in costume. 10 l, Couple in
costumes.

1997, Jan. 17   Litho.   Perf. 13½
C986 AP202 4.55 l multicolored   1.10   .50
C987 AP202 5.40 l multicolored   1.40   .65
C988 AP202 10 l multicolored   3.50   1.10
Nos. C986-C988 (3)   6.00   2.25

Honduras Plan, 20th Anniv., Intl. Plan, 60th Anniv. AP203

Children's paintings: 1.40 l, Outdoor scene, children swimming, vert. 5.40 l, Girl standing beside lake, fish. 9.70 l, People working between buildings.

1997, Feb. 7   Litho.   Perf. 13½
C989   AP203 1.40 l multicolored   .50   .20
C990   AP203 5.40 l multicolored   1.50   .70
C991   AP203 9.70 l multicolored   3.00 2.50
    Nos. C989-C991 (3)   5.00 3.40

Heinrich von Stephan (1831-97) AP205

1997, May 9   Litho.   Perf. 13½
C995   AP205 5.40 l multicolored   1.25   .55

World Population Day AP206

Designs: 6.90 l, Child's drawing of people outside, trees, houses.

1997, July 11   Litho.   Perf. 13½
C996   AP206 1.40 l shown   .50   .50
C997   AP206 6.90 l multicolored 2.50 1.25

Butterflies AP207

Designs: 1 l, Rothchildia forbesi. 1.40 l, Parides photinus. 2.15 l, Morpho peleides. 3 l, Eurytides marcellus. 4.30 l, Parides iphidamas. 5.40 l, Danaus plexippus. 20 l+2 l, Hamadryas arinome.

1997, July 31
C998   AP207   1 l multi   .50   .20
C999   AP207 1.40 l multi   .50   .20
C1000 AP207 2.15 l multi   .90   .20
C1001 AP207   3 l multi   1.25   .20
C1002 AP207 4.30 l multi   1.60   .65
C1003 AP207 5.40 l multi   2.25   .85
        Imperf
        Size: 80x53mm
C1004 AP207 20 l +2 l multi   7.50 5.50
    Nos. C998-C1004 (7)   14.50 7.80

For surcharge see No. C1175.

St. Teresa of Jesus, Death Cent. — AP208

1997, Aug. 20   Litho.   Perf. 13½
C1005 AP208 1.40 l shown   .30   .30
C1006 AP208 5.40 l Portrait, diff. 1.25   .60

Astronomical Observatory AP209

Designs: 5.40 l, Statue of Father Jose Trinidad Reyes. 10 l, Woman with book leading child up steps.

1997, Sept. 19   Litho.   Perf. 13½
C1007 AP209 1.40 l multicolored   .30   .20
C1008 AP209 5.40 l multicolored 1.25   .60
C1009 AP209   10 l   multicolored 2.25 1.10
    Nos. C1007-C1009 (3)   3.80 1.90

Alma Mater Foundation, 150th anniv., Autonomous University, 40th anniv.

Alcoholics Anonymous in Honduras, 37th anniv. — AP210

1997, Oct. 27
C1010 AP210 5.40 l multicolored 1.60   .60

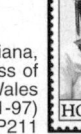

Diana, Princess of Wales (1961-97) AP211

1.40 l, Portrait, vert. 5.40 l, Diana dressed to walk through mine field, warning sign. 20 l, Mother Teresa, Princess Diana.

1997, Oct. 15
C1011 AP211 1.40 l multi   .40   .20
C1012 AP211 5.40 l multi   1.60   .70
        Size: 51x78mm
        Imperf
C1013 AP211 20 l   multi-
                    ticolored   6.00 4.25
    Nos. C1011-C1013 (3)   8.00 5.15

Christmas AP212

1997, Dec. 2   Litho.   Perf. 13½
C1014 AP212 1.40 l Christ of Pi-
                     cacho   .40   .40
C1015 AP212 5.40 l Virgin of
                     Suyapa   1.60   .85

Mascot — AP213

C1016: a, Basketball. b, At bat, baseball. c, Soccer. d, Racquetball. e, Spiking volleyball. f, Setting volleyball. g, Bowling. h, Table tennis. i, Rings over map of Central America. j, Pitching, baseball.

No. C1017: a, Kicking, karate. b, Chopping, karate. c, Bowing, karate. d, Wrestling. e, Weight lifting. f, Boxing. g, Body building. h, Fencing. i, Program cover. j, Shooting.

No. C1018: a, Riding bicycle. b, Riding bicycle by shoreline. c, Swimming. d, Water polo. e, Hurdles. f, Gymnastics. g, Riding horse. h, Tennis. i, Program cover with mascot. j, Chess.

1997
        Sheets of 10
C1016 AP213 1.40 l #a.-j.   3.50 3.50
C1017 AP213 1.50 l #a.-j.   3.75 3.75
C1018 AP213 2.15 l #a.-j.   5.00 5.00

6th Central American Games, San Pedro Sula.

Fish AP214

1.40 l, Cichlasoma dovii. 2 l, Cichlasoma spilurum. 3 l, Cichlasoma spilurum facing right. 5.40 l, Astyanay fasciatus.

1997   Litho.   Perf. 13½
C1019 AP214 1.40 l multicolored   .30   .30
C1020 AP214   2 l   multicolored   .40   .40
C1021 AP214   3 l   multicolored   .60   .50
C1022 AP214 5.40 l multicolored 1.10   .90
    Nos. C1019-C1022 (4)   2.40 2.10

Marine Life, Islas de la Bahía (Bay Islands) — AP215

Designs: a, Balistes vetula. b, Haemudon plumieri. c, Pomacanthus paru. d, Juvenile halichoeres garnoti. e, Pomacanthus arcuatus. f, Holacanthus ciliaris. g, Diver's face, pseud opterogorgia. h, Diver's oxygen tanks, pseud opterogorgia. i, Dendrogya cylindrus. j, Holocentrus adscensionis. k, Dendrogya cylindrus, diff. l, Stegastes fuscus. m, Gorgonia mariae. n, Pillar coral. o, Pomacanthus arcuatus, diff. p, Holocentrus adscensionis, diff. q, Eusmilia fastigiata. r, Scarus coelestinus. s, Pillar coral, diff. t, Lachnolaimus masimus.

1998, Mar. 13   Litho.   Perf. 13½
        Sheet of 20
C1023 AP215 2.50 l #a.-t.   16.00 16.00
        Bancahsa, 50th anniv.
        Exists imperf.

America Issue AP216

1998, May 29   Litho.   Perf. 13½
C1024 AP216 5.40 l Post Office
                     headquar-
                     ters   1.60   .80
C1025 AP216 5.40 l Postman on
                     motorcycle   1.60   .80

Maya Artifacts — AP217

Designs: 1 l, Large carving on temple. 1.40 l, Stele of Mayan king. 2.15 l, Large stelae. 5.40 l, Small ornamental carving.

20 l, Maya Ruins, Copán.

1998, June 19   Litho.   Perf. 13½
C1026 AP217   1 l   multi   .20   .20
C1027 AP217 1.40 l multi   .55   .20
C1028 AP217 2.15 l multi   .90   .20
C1029 AP217 5.40 l multi   2.10   .55
        Size: 78x52mm
        Imperf
C1030 AP217   20 l   mul-
                     ticolored   6.50 3.00
    Nos. C1026-C1030 (5)   10.25 4.15

1998 World Cup Soccer Championships, France — AP218

No. C1033: a, Stadium, Tegucigalpa. b, St. Denis Stadium, France.

1998, July 3   Litho.   Perf. 13½
C1031 AP218 5.40 l shown   1.50   .70
C1032 AP218   10 l   Players,
                     vert.   3.00 1.50
        Imperf
C1033 AP218   10 l   Pair, #a.-
                     b.   8.25 7.00

No. C1033 contains two 53x42mm stamps. No. C1033 also issued rouletted between the stamps; value the same.

Reptiles AP219

Designs: 1.40 l, Green iguana. 2 l, Rattlesnake. 3 l, Two iguanas. 5.40 l, Coral snake. 20 l + 2 l, Marine turtle.

1998, July 31   Litho.   Perf. 13½
C1034 AP219 1.40 l multi   .40   .35
C1035 AP219   2 l   multi   .75   .60
C1036 AP219   3 l   multi   .95   .75
C1037 AP219 5.40 l multi   1.90 1.25
        Size: 77x52mm
        Imperf
C1038 AP219 20 l +2 l multi   7.00 4.50
    Nos. C1034-C1038 (5)   11.00 7.45

Christmas AP220

Designs: 3 l, Girl taking ornament from bird, vert. 5.40 l, Christ Child asleep on bed of holly, dove, stars. 10 l, Boy with lantern leading donkey, cabin in the snow, vert.

1998, Dec. 8   Litho.   Perf. 13½
C1039 AP220   3 l   multicolored   .70   .30
C1040 AP220 5.40 l multicolored 1.25   .60
C1041 AP220   10 l   multicolored 2.25 1.25
    Nos. C1039-C1041 (3)   4.20 2.15

Pres. Carlos Roberto Flores, 1st Anniv. of Taking Office AP221

Designs: 5.40 l, Pres. and Mrs. Flores, Pope John Paul II. 10 l, Portrait of Pres., Mrs. Flores, vert.

1999, Jan. 27   Litho.   Perf. 13½
C1042 AP221 5.40 l multicolored 1.10   .55
C1043 AP221   10 l   multicolored 2.00 1.00

Hurricane Mitch — AP222

No. C1044: a, Men working to clean up. b, Helicopter distributing aid. c, Vehicles under water, North Zone. d, Tipper Gore, Mary de Flores cleaning. e, Working to save banana crop. f, Destruction of Tegucigalpa. g, Cars, buses, trucks blocked by rock slide. h, Destruction of Comayagüela. i, Streets of Comayagüela. j, Oriental Zone. k, Loading debris, help from Mexico. l, Streets of Limpieza. m, Pres. Flores with Pres. Chirac of Fance. n, Business district of Comayagüela. o, Flooding, Tegucigalpa. p, Car in street, Comayagüela.

No. C1045: a, Central Zone. b, South Zone. c, Prince Felipe de Borbon, Mary de Flores. d, Small child crying. e, Cleaning up debris, Comayagüela. f, Families, man carrying baby, North Zone. g, Two men looking at destruction of building, Tegucigalpa. h, Man, child, woman wading in water, North Zone. i, Destruction in rural area. j, Cars piled up, concrete abutment along roadway. k, Cars, buildings along roadway. l, Mexican troops, airplane. m, Boys swimming. n, Pres. & Mrs. Flores, Hillary Clinton. o, People walking over rubble and debris, South Zone. p, Pres. Flores, former US Pres. George Bush.

Illustration reduced.

1999, Feb. 19   *Rouletted*
Sheets of 16
C1044 AP222 5.40 l #a.-p.   18.00 18.00
C1045 AP222 5.40 l #a.-p.   18.00 18.00
For surcharges, see Mos. C1207, C1208.

Famous Honduran Women — AP223

America Issue: 2.60 l, Maria del Pilar Salinas (b. 1914), scholar. 7.30 l, Clementina Suarez (1902-91), poet, writer. 10.65 l, Mary Flake de Flores, first lady of Honduras.

1999, Apr. 20   **Litho.**   *Perf. 13½*
C1046 AP223 2.60 l multi   .55 .25
C1047 AP223 7.30 l multi   1.50 .75
C1048 AP223 10.65 l multi   2.25 1.10
    Nos. C1046-C1048 (3)   4.30 2.10
       Dated 1998.

Mother's Day AP224

Designs: 20 l, Police officer Orellana breastfeeding baby, vert. 30 l, Paphiopedilum urbanianum. 50 l, Miltoniopsis vexillaria.

1999, May 14   **Litho.**   *Perf. 13½*
C1049 AP224 20 l multicolored   4.25 3.50
C1050 AP224 30 l multicolored   6.25 4.25
C1051 AP224 50 l multicolored   10.50 7.25
    Nos. C1049-C1051 (3)   21.00 15.00

Endangered Birds — AP225

No. C1052, 5 l: a, Sarcorampohus papa. b, Leucopternis albicollis. c, Harpia harpyja. d, Pulsatrix perspicallata. e, Spizaetus ornatus. f, Pharomarchrus mocinno. g, Aulacorhynchus prasinus. h, Amazilia luciae. i, Ara macao. j, Centurus pygmaeus.

3 l: k, Aratinga canicularis. l, Amazona albifrons. m, Amazona auropalliata. n, Amazona autumnalis. o, Eurypyga helias. p, Crax rubra. q, Brotogeris jugularis. r, Pionus senilis. s, Aratinga rubritorques. t, Tinamus major.

No. C1053: a, Jaberu mycteria. b, Chondrohierax uncinatus. c, Pharomachrus mocinno. d, Ramphastos sulfuratus.

1999, July 8
C1052 AP225   Sheeet of 20, #a.-t.   17.50 17.50
C1053 AP225 10 l Sheet of 4, #a.-d.   9.00 7.50

    Banco Sogerin, 30th anniv.

Inter-American Development Bank, 40th Anniv. — AP226

1999, Nov. 22   **Litho.**   *Perf. 13½*
C1054 AP226 18.30 l multi   3.75 2.00
For surcharge see No. C1249.

Blessed Josemaría Escrivá de Balaguer (1902-75), Founder of Opus Dei — AP227

1999, Nov. 29
C1055 AP227 2.60 l multi   .60 .30
C1056 AP227 16.40 l multi   3.25 2.00

Millennium AP228

Designs: 2 l, Salvador Moncada, discoverer of nitric oxide in blood, vert. 8.65 l, Albert Einstein, vert. 10 l, Wilhelm Röntgen, vert. 14.95 l, George Stephenson and locomotive "Rocket."

1999, Oct. 18
C1057 AP228 2 l multi   .40 .20
C1058 AP228 8.65 l multi   1.60 .80
C1059 AP228 10 l multi   1.90 .95
C1060 AP228 14.95 l multi   2.75 1.40
    Nos. C1057-C1060 (4)   6.65 3.35

National Congress, 175th Anniv. AP229

Designs: 4.30, Statue of Francisco Morazán. 10 l, Congress President Rafael Pineda Ponce, Congress Building.

1999, Dec. 17   **Litho.**   *Perf. 13¼*
C1061 AP229 4.30 l multi   1.00 .50
C1062 AP229 10 l multi   2.25 1.10

AP230

Holy Year 2000 — AP231

Holy Year Emblem and: 4 l, Pope John Paul II, people. 4.30 l, St. Peter. 6.90 l, Jesus, Jerusalem, horiz. 7.30 l, John Paul II, crowd, horiz. 10 l, John Paul II giving blessing. 14 l, Pres. Carlos Roberto Flores, John Paul II.

2000, Jan. 1   **Litho.**   *Perf. 13¼*
C1063 AP230 4 l multi   .90 .40
C1064 AP230 4.30 l shown   1.40 .70
C1065 AP230 6.90 l multi   1.50 .80
C1066 AP230 7.30 l multi   1.60 .85
C1067 AP230 10 l multi   2.25 1.10
C1068 AP231 14 l shown   4.25 1.75
Nos. C1064, C1068 Redrawn
C1069 AP230 4.30 l multi   1.25 .50
C1070 AP231 14 l multi   3.50 1.50
    Nos. C1063-C1070 (8)   16.65 7.60

#C1067 issued in sheets of 6, with picture of John Paul II in selvage. #C1069 has "HONDURAS" in yellow; #C1064 in white. #C1070 has "HONDURAS" at right, reading up; #C1068 at top.

2nd Anniv. of Inauguration of Pres. Flores — AP232

Pres. Flores and: 10 l, Conference delegates. 10.65 l, Mario Hung Pacheco.

2000, Jan. 27
C1071 AP232 10 l multi   2.50 1.25
C1072 AP232 10.65 l multi   3.00 1.40

Musical Instruments Type of Semi-postals of 2000

No. 1073, vert.: a, 1.40 l, Marimba, denomination at L. b, 1.40 l, Marimba, denomination at L c, 1.40 l, Ayotl. d, 10 l, Maya drum. e, 10 l, Teponaxtle. f, 2.60 l, Maracas. g, 2.60 l, Güiro. h, 2.60 l, Chinchín. i, 2.60 l, Raspador. j, 2.60 l, Horse's jawbone. k, 3 l, Green zoomorphic whistle. l, 3 l, Aztec drum. m, 3 l, One-tone zoomorphic whistle. n, 3 l, Two-tone zoomorphic whistle. o, 3 l, Tun. p, 4 l, Gourd. q, 4 l, Deer hide drum. r, 4 l, Guacalitos. s, 4 l, Five musicians, marimba. t, 4 l, Four musicians, marimba.

2000, Apr. 7   **Litho.**   *Perf. 13¼*
C1073 SP1 Sheet of 20, #a-t   21.00 21.00

Paintings of Pablo Zelaya Sierra — AP233

No. C1074: a, 2 l, Green City (building and tree). b, 2 l, Old Woman With Rosary. c, 2 l, Rural Women (women with jars). d, 2 l, Woman With Green Robe. e, 2 l, City. f, 1.40 l, Shoulders of a Man. g, 1.40 l, Goat. h, 1.40 l, Spanish City. i, 1.40 l, Woman With Chignon. j, 1.40 l, Woman With Calabash. k, 2.60 l, Goat and Birds. l, 2.60 l, Tree Trunks. m, 2.60 l, Nuns. n, 2.60 l, Archers. o, 2.60 l, Moon and Boats. p, 2.60 l, Bust. q, 10 l, Still-life. r, 10 l, Composition With Books. s, 2.60 l, Landscape. t, 2.60 l, Head, Fan and Book.

2000, July 1
C1074 AP233 Sheet of 20, #a-t   22.50 22.50

Airmail Anniv. Type of Semi-postals

Designs: 7.30 l, #C12. 10 l, Thomas Canfield Pounds, owner of Central American Airline, vert. 10.65 l, Pres. Rafael López Gutiérrez, signer of first airmail contract, vert.

2000, July 7
    Size: 35x25mm
C1075 SP2 7.30 l multi   1.60 .85
    Size: 25x35mm
C1076 SP2 10 l multi   2.25 1.10
C1077 SP2 10.65 l multi   2.40 1.25
    Nos. C1075-C1077 (3)   6.25 3.20

America Issue, A New Millennium Without Arms — AP234

Designs: 10 l, Sobralia macrantha, No guns, vert. 10.65 l, Peace dove, No soldiers, vert. 14 l, Train, No bombs, no more terrorism.

2000, July 28   **Litho.**   *Perf. 13¼*
C1078-C1080 AP234 Set of 3   9.00 7.00

2000 Summer Olympics, Sydney AP235

Designs: 2.60 l, Soccer players Ivan Guerrero, Mario Chirinos. 10.65 l, Swimmer Ramon Valle. 12.45 l, Runner Gina Coello.

No. C1084: a, 4.30 l, Swimmer. b, 4.30 l, Soccer player Danilo Turcios. c, 10.65 l, Runner Pedro Ventura. d, 12.45 l, Soccer player David Suazo.

2000, Sept. 13
C1081-C1083 AP235 Set of 3   10.00 8.50
    Souvenir Sheet
C1084 AP235 Sheet of 4, #a-d   11.00 11.00
No. C1084 exists imperf.

Intl. Voluntarism Year — AP236

Emblem, people and: 2.60 l, White-crowned parrot. 10.65 l, Telipogon ampliflorus.

2000, Dec. 5
C1085-C1086 AP236 Set of 2   3.25 2.25

Christmas
AP237

Designs: 2.60 l, Madonna and child. 7.30 l, Nativity, vert. 14 l, Carpet painter.

2000, Dec. 18
C1087-C1089 AP237 Set of 3   5.00 3.25

America Issue,
Birds — AP238

Designs: 2.60 l, Amazona auropalliata caribea. 4.30 l, Columbina passerina, horiz. 10.65 l, Ara macao. 20 l, Aguila harpia.

2001, Feb. 16   **Litho.**   *Perf. 13¼*
C1090-C1093 AP238 Set of 4   10.00 8.25

Nos. C584,
C593, C606,
C611, C646-
C647, C652-
C653, C699
Surcharged — c

Nos. C620, C672, C708, C721
Surcharged — d

No. C637 Surcharged — e

Methods and Perfs. as Before
2001

C1094	AP103(c)	2 l on 16c	
		#C652	.35 .20
C1095	AP103(c)	2 l on 16c	
		#C653	.35 .20
a.	Pair, #C1094-C1095		.70 .35
C1096	AP106(d)	2.60 l on 3c	
		#C672	.45 .20
C1097	AP114(d)	2.60 l on 3c	
		#C708	.45 .20
C1098	AP100(d)	2.60 l on 8c	
		#C620	.45 .20
C1099	AP102(e)	2.60 l on 16c	
		#C637	.45 .20
C1100	AP96(c)	3 l on 16c	
		#C593	.55 .25
C1101	AP116(d)	4 l on 9c	
		#C721	.70 .35
C1102	AP97(c)	4.30 l on 6c	
		#C606	.75 .35
C1103	AP103(c)	7.30 l on 6c	
		#C646	1.25 .60
C1104	AP103(c)	7.30 l on 6c	
		#C647	1.25 .60
a.	Pair, #C1103-C1104		2.50 1.20

C1105	AP95(c)	10 l on 16c	
		#C584	1.75 .90
C1106	AP112(c)	10.65 l on 16c	
		#C699	1.90 .95
C1107	AP98(c)	14 l on 16c	
		#C611	3.00 1.25
	Nos. C1094-C1107 (14)		13.65 6.45

Size and location of surcharge varies.
Issued: Nos. C1096-C1099, 3/26; others, 4/3.

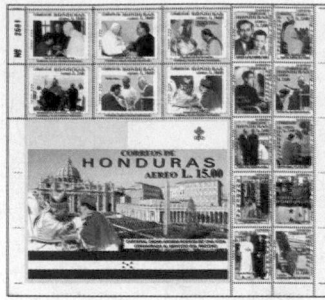

Oscar Cardinal Rodriguez — AP239

No. C1108: a, 2.60 l, With father, 1946. b, 2.60 l, In Sanctuary of Our Lady of Suyapa. c, 2.60 l, As seminarian, 1964. d, 2.60 l, Installation as archbishop. e, 2.60 l, Ordination, 1960. f, 2.60 l, At Vatican, Feb. 21, 2001. g, 2.60 l, At mass in Guatemala, 1970. h, 2.60 l, Standing behind Honduran flag. i, 2.60 l, With Pope John Paul II, 1993. j, 2.60 l, Returning to Honduras as Cardinal, Mar. 10, 2001. k, 2.60 l, Giving address as Cardinal, Mar. 10, 2001. l, 10.65 l, With Pope and woman, 1993. m, 10.65 l, Papal audience, Feb. 23, 2001. n, 10.65 l, Celebration of the Eucharist. o, 10.65 l, Kneeling before Pope, 1993. p, 10.65 l, Installation as Cardinal, Feb. 21, 2001. q, 15 l, Installation as Cardinal, St. Peter's Square.

2001, May 9   **Litho.**   *Perf. 13¼*
C1108 AP239 Sheet of 17,
   #a-q   30.00 30.00

Stamp sizes: Nos. C1108a-C1108j, 29x40mm; C1108k-C1108p, 49x40mm; C1108q, 163x131mm. No. C1108 exists imperf. Value $30.

Banco de Occidente, S.A., 50th
Anniv. — AP240

Mayan ceramics: a, 2 l, Flower pot. b, 2 l, Anthropomorphic jar. c, 2 l, Anthropomorphic cover. d, 2 l, Cylindrical vase. e, 2 l, Censer tripod. f, 3 l, Scribe. g, 3 l, Cylindrical jar with anthropomorphic figures. h, 3 l, Three-part container. i, 3 l, Ceramic face. j, 3 l, Anthropomorphic jar, diff. k, 5 l, Three-legged vessel. l, 5 l, Pot with handles. m, 5 l, Censer. n, 5 l, Anthropomorphic cover. o, 5 l, Anthropomorphic jar, diff. p, 6.90 l, Pot with handles, diff. q, 6.90 l, Anthropomorphic cover, diff. r, 6.90 l, Anthropomorphic jar, diff. s, 6.90 l, Red cylindrical container. t, 6.90 l, Decorated container.

2001, Sept. 1   **Litho.**   *Perf. 13¼*
C1109 AP240 Sheet of 20,
   #a-t   26.00 26.00

UN High Commissioner for Refugees,
50th Anniv. — AP241

Designs: 2.60 l, Refugee and child, vert. 10.65 l, Refugees running.

2001
C1110-C1111 AP241 Set of 2   4.00 3.00

Souvenir Sheet

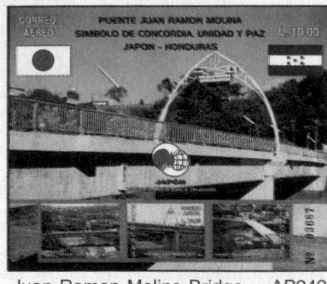

Juan Ramon Molina Bridge — AP242

No. C1112: a, 2.60 l, Aerial view from end. b, 10 l, Close-up view from side. c, 10.65 l, Aerial view from side. d, 13.65 l, Side view showing river.

2001, Dec. 20   **Litho.**   *Rouletted 6½*
C1112 AP242 Sheet of 4, #a-
   d   15.00 15.00

Stamp sizes: No. C1112b, 152x93mm; others, 40x30mm.

America
Issue —
Wildlife
AP243

Designs: 10 l, Bird, Yojoa Lake. 10.65 l, Iguana, Cisne Islands. 20 l, Chrysina quetzalcoatli, Morpho sp., Pulaphanzhak Cataracts.

2002, Jan. 31   *Perf. 13¼*
C1113-C1115 AP243 Set of 3   13.00 13.00

Pan-American Health Organization,
Cent. — AP244

2002, Apr. 7
C1116 AP244 10 l multi   3.25 3.25

Miguel R. Pastor, Central District
Mayor — AP245

Central District emblem and: a, 1.40 l, Cathedral of San Miguel, statues, birds (57x35mm). b, 1.40 l, Chimpanzee throwing banana peel in trash can (57x35mm). c, 1.40 l, Municipal building (57x35mm). d, 2.60 l, Mayor Pastor, flags (27x35mm). e, 2.60 l, Mayor Pastor under tree (27x35mm). f, 2.60 l, Mayor Pastor with old woman (27x35mm). g, 2.60 l, Mayor Pastor with crowd (27x35mm). h, 2.60 l, Mayor Pastor planting seedling (27x35mm). i, 2.60 l, Mayor Pastor and family (27x35mm). j, 10 l, Municipal council (57x35mm). k, 10 l, Mayor with guests (57x35mm). l, 10.65 l, Cathedral of San Miguel, statues, birds (114x75mm).

2002, June 13   **Litho.**   *Perf. 13¼*
C1117 AP245 Sheet of 12,
   #a-l   16.00 16.00

Souvenir Sheet

Discovery of Honduras, 500th
Anniv. — AP246

No. C1118: a, 10.65 l, Boat on shore, jungle. b, 12.45 l, Natives on shore. c, 13.65 l, Spaniards coming ashore. d, 20 l, Spanish ship.

2002, Aug. 14
C1118 AP246 Sheet of 4, #a-d   9.00 9.00

Exfilhon 2002.

Souvenir Sheet

Christianity in Honduras, 500th
Anniv. — AP247

No. C1119: a, 2.60 l, Natives and cross. b, 3 l, Santa Barbara Trujillo Fort. c, 10 l, 400 Years of History, by Mario Castillo. d, 10 l, Spaniards on shore, ships at sea.

2002, Aug. 14
C1119 AP247 Sheet of 4, #a-d   5.00 5.00

America issue.

Banco del
Pais, 10th
Anniv.
AP248

2002, Sept. 5   **Litho.**   *Perf. 13¼*

C1120	AP248	2 l multi	.25 .25
a.		Block of 10	3.00 3.00
C1121	AP248	2.60 l multi	.50 .50
a.		Block of 10	4.25 4.25
C1122	AP248	10 l multi	1.75 1.75
a.		Sheet of 30	45.00 45.00
C1123	AP248	10.65 l multi	2.00 2.00
a.		Sheet of 30	50.00 50.00
	Nos. C1120-C1123 (4)		4.50 4.50

Backgrounds of Nos. C1120-C1123 show a flag on a staff and clouds in the blocks and and the flag on the sheets, giving each stamp a different background.

Orchids
AP249

Designs: 1.40 l, Vanilla planifolia. 2.60 l, Lycaste viriginalis. 3 l, Coelia bella. 4.30 l, Chysis laevis. 8.65 l, Myrmecophila bryslana. 10 l, Rhyncolaelia digbyana. 20 l, Mormodes aromatica.

2002, Sept. 25   **Litho.**   *Perf. 13¼*
C1124-C1129 AP249 Set of 6   7.00 7.00

Size: 96x66mm
Imperf

C1130 AP249 20 l multi   6.00 6.00
for surcharges see Nos. C1241, C1243, C1252-C1253.

Christmas
AP250

Designs: 2.60 l, Creche scene. 10.65 l, Holy Family. 14 l, People at recreation of nativity scene.

2002, Nov. 25
C1131-C1133 AP250 Set of 3   4.00 4.00

National Children's Foundation
AP251

Designs: 2.60 l, Children. 10 l, Elderly people. 10.65 l, Symbols of Honduras, vert.

2002, Dec. 6
C1134-C1136 AP251 Set of 3   3.50 3.50

Insects — AP252

No. C1137: a, 2 l, Chrysina spectabilis. b, 2 l, Chrysina strasseni. c, 2 l, Viridimicus omoaensis. d, 2 l, Hoplopyga liturata. e, 2.60 l, Chrysina cusuquensis. f, 2.60 l, Calomacraspis haroldi. g, 2.60 l, Pelidnota strigosa. h, 2.60 l, Odontocheila tawahka. i, 3 l, Chrysina cavei. j, 3 l, Macropoides crassipes. k, 3 l, Pelidnota velutipes. l, 3 l, Tragidion cyanovestis. m, 4 l, Chrysina pastori. n, 4 l, Platycoelia humeralis. o, 4 l, Phanaeus eximius. p, 4 l, Acanthoderes cavei. q, 10.65 l, Chrysina quetzalcoatli. r, 10.65 l, Cyclocephala abrelata. s, 10.65 l, Aegithus rufipennis. t, 10.65 l, Callipogon barbatum.
No. C1138 — Chrysina spp.: a, Eggs. b, Larva. b, Pupa.

2003, Feb. 20
C1137 AP252 Sheet of 20, #a-t   17.00 17.00
Souvenir Sheet
C1138 AP252 10 l Sheet of 3, #a-c   6.00 6.00

Banco Atlantida, 90th anniv. (#C1137).

World Food Program
AP253

Designs: 2.60 l, Children with food. 6.90 l, Child with food. 10.65 l, Child with bowl and spoon.

2003, May 15
C1139-C1141 AP253 Set of 3   3.50 3.50
For surcharge see No. C1196.

Souvenir Sheet

Pontificate of John Paul II, 25th Anniv., and 20th Anniv. of Visit to Honduras — AP254

No. C1142: a, 13.65 l, Pope giving blessing. b, 14.55 l, Pope at airport. c, 15.45 l, Pope with staff. d, 16.65 l, Pope with rosary beads.

2003, Oct. 10   **Perf. 10½**
C1142 AP254 Sheet of 4, #a-d   11.00 11.00

Regional Sanitary Agricultural Organization, 50th Anniv. — AP255

Designs: 2.60 l, Eggs, sliced meat. 10 l, Eye, map of Central America, corn. 10.65 l, Emblem, map of Central America. 14 l, Vegetables. 20 l, Corn, tomato, fish.

2003, Oct. 24   **Perf. 13¼**
C1143-C1147 AP255 Set of 5 10.00 10.00

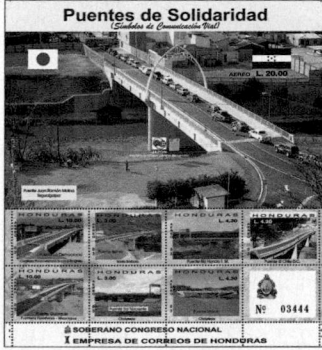

Bridges Built by Japan — AP256

No. C1148: a, 3 l, Ilama Bridge, Santa Bárbara. b, 3 l, Sol Naciente Bridge, Choluteca. c, 4.30 l, Río Hondo Bridge, Francisco Morazán. d, 4.30 l, El Chile Bridge, Central District. e, 4.30 l, Iztoca Bridge, Choluteca. f, 10 l, La Democracia Bridge, near El Progreso. g, 10 l, Guasaule Bridge, Honduras-Nicaragua border. 20 l, Juan Ramón Molina Bridge, Tegucigalpa (168x109mm).

2003, Nov. 25   **Litho.**   **Perf. 13¼**
C1148 AP256 Sheet of 7, #a-h + label   10.00 10.00

Telethon Honduras
AP257

Telethon emblem and: 1.40 l, Flag on staff. 2.60 l, Hand, flag in light blue. 7.30 l, Hand, flag in dark blue. 10 l, Map.

2003, Dec. 4
C1149-C1152 AP257 Set of 4   3.50 3.50
For surcharges see Nos. C1244-C1245, C1247.

Christmas
AP258

Designs: 10.65 l, Angel. 14 l, Holy Family in manger.

2003, Dec. 8
C1153-C1154 AP258 Set of 2   4.00 4.00

Souvenir Sheet

Endangered Birds — AP259

No. C1155: a, 10 l, Arantinga strenua. b, 10.65 l, Falco deiroleucus. c, 14 l, Spizaetus melanoleucos. d, 20 l, Amazona xantholora.

2004, May 13
C1155 AP259 Sheet of 4, #a-d   10.00 10.00
Exfilhon 2004.

Endangered Animals — AP260

Designs: 85c, Pecari tajacu. 1.40 l, Mazama americana. 2 l, Tamandua mexicana, vert. 2.60 l, Felis concolor. No. C1160, Tamandua mexicana, vert. No. C1161, Felis concolor. No. C1162, Mazama americana. No. C1163, Bradypus variegatus. 4.30 l, Pecari tajacu. 7.85 l, Agalychnis challidryas, vert. 10.65 l, Bradypus variegatus. 14.95 l, Agalchinis challidryas, vert.
No. C1168, vert.: a, Mono titi. b, Cebus capucinus. c, Ateles geoffroyi. d, Alouatta palliata.

2004, May 24   **Litho.**   **Perf. 13¼**
C1156	AP260	85c multi	.20	.20
C1157	AP260	1.40 l multi	.20	.20
C1158	AP260	2 l multi	.40	.40
C1159	AP260	2.60 l multi	.45	.45
C1160	AP260	3 l multi	.55	.55
C1161	AP260	3 l multi	.55	.55
C1162	AP260	4 l multi	.60	.60
C1163	AP260	4 l multi	.60	.60
C1164	AP260	4.30 l multi	.65	.65
C1165	AP260	7.85 l multi	1.40	1.40
C1166	AP260	10.65 l multi	2.10	2.10
C1167	AP260	14.95 l multi	3.00	3.00
	Nos. C1156-C1167 (12)		10.70	10.70
C1168	AP260	10 l Sheet of 4, #a-d	7.50	7.50

Nos. C1156-C1158, C1161, C1163, and C1165 were each printed in souvenir sheets of 4.
For surcharges see Nos. C1239-C1240, C1242, C1254-C1255.

Shells
AP261

Designs: Nos. C1169, C1174f, Voluta polypleura. Nos. C1170, C1174d, Strombus gallus. Nos. C1171, C1174a, Charonia variegata, Terebra taurina. Nos. C1172, C1174e, Spondylus americanus. Nos. C1173, C1174c, Strombus raninus. No. C1174b, Man blowing conch shell.

2004, July 19   **Litho.**   **Perf. 13¼**
C1169	AP261	85c multi	.20	.20
C1170	AP261	1.40 l multi	.20	.20
C1171	AP261	2 l multi	.20	.20
C1172	AP261	2.60 l multi	.55	.55
C1173	AP261	10.65 l multi	2.10	2.10
	Nos. C1169-C1173 (5)		3.25	3.25

Miniature Sheet
C1174	Sheet of 6		11.00	11.00
a.-b.	AP261 4 l Either single		.75	.75
c.-d.	AP261 5 l Either single		.95	.95
e.-f.	AP261 20 l Either single		3.75	3.75

For surcharges see Nos. C1246, C1248, C1250-C1251.

No. C1004 Surcharged in Red

Illustration reduced.

2004, Aug. 13   **Litho.**   **Imperf.**
C1175 AP207 50 l on 20 l+2 l multi   9.00 9.00

Miniature Sheet

Banco Fichosa, Sponsor of National Soccer Team — AP262

No. C1176: a, 4.30 l, Players, Honduras flag. b, 10.65 l, Team. c, 14 l, Saúl Martinez, David Suazo. d, 20 l, Amado Guevara.

2004, Sept. 3   **Litho.**   **Perf. 13¼**
C1176 AP262 Sheet of 4, #a-d 6.50 6.50

Christmas
AP263

Designs: 2.60 l, Flight into Egypt. 7.85 l, Santa Claus on ornament. 10.65 l, Three Kings. 20 l, Holy Family.

2004, Nov. 23   **Litho.**   **Perf. 13¼**
C1177-C1180	AP263	Set of 4	7.50	7.50
C1178a		Sheet of 4 #C1178	6.50	6.50

For surcharges see Nos. C1224-C1227.

AP264

National
Unity — AP265

2005, Feb. 3
C1181 AP264 10 l multi   1.10 1.10
C1182 AP265 20 l multi   2.25 2.25

Rotary International, Cent. — AP266

Rotary International emblem and: 2.60 l, Rafael Díaz Chávez, Paul Harris and Jorge Fidel Durón. 5 l, "100 años," vert. 8 l, Globe and arrows. 10.65 l, Map of Honduras, PolioPlus emblem. 14 l, Mayan sculpture.

2005, Feb. 23
C1183-C1187 AP266 Set of 5   5.25 5.25

Pope John Paul
II (1920-2005)
AP267

Pope: 10 l, Wearing white vestments. 15 l, Wearing colored vestments.
20 l, Holding crucifix.

2005, Apr. 15   Litho.   Perf. 13¼
C1188-C1189 AP267 Set of 2   3.25 3.25
  Souvenir Sheet
C1190   Sheet of 2 #C1190a   5.25 5.25
  a. AP267 20 l multi, 29x42mm   2.50 2.50

Honduran
Medical Review,
75th
Anniv. — AP268

Designs: 3 l, House. 5 l, Bird. 12 l, Jaguar. 30 l, Flowers.
No. C1195: a, Macaws. b, Macaw in banana tree. c, Rooster. d, Turkeys and hens.

2005, May 18
C1191-C1194 AP268 Set of 4   6.50 6.50
  Souvenir Sheet
C1195 AP268 25 l Sheet of 4,
     #a-d   13.00 13.00

Nos. 390-392, B1, C550, C552, C553, C576, C715, C1044-C1045, C1140 and RA8 Surcharged

"X" Obliterators — f

Box Obliterator
and "Aereo" —
g

Box Obliterator — h

Illustration "h" reduced.

Methods and Perfs as Before
2005, June 3
C1196 AP253(f)   3 l on 6.90 l
    #C1140   .30   .30
C1197 AP72(f)   5 l on 16c
     on 1c
    #C552   .55   .55
C1198 AP72(f)   5 l on 16c
     on 1c
    #C553   .55   .55
C1199 PT6(g)   10 l on 13.85
     l on 1c
    #392   1.10 1.10
C1200 AP68(f)   14 l on 16c
     on 1c
    #C550   1.50 1.50
C1201 PT6(g)   20 l on 13.85
     l on 1c
    #392   2.10 2.10
C1202 PT6(g)   25 l on 11.55
     l on 1c
    #390   2.75 2.75
C1203 AP94(f)   30 l on 16c
    #C576   3.25 3.25
C1204 AP115(f)   35 l on 16c
    #C715   3.75 3.75
C1205 PT6(g)   40 l on 11.55
     l on 1c
    #390   4.25 4.25
C1206 PT6(g)   50 l on 12.45
     l on 1c
    #391   5.50 5.50
  Nos. C1196-C1206 (11)   25.60 25.60
  Sheets
C1207   Sheet of 16
    (#C1044)   15.00 15.00
  a.-p. AP222(h) 8 l on 5.40 l any
    single   .90   .90
C1208   Sheet of 16
    (#C1045)   15.00 15.00
  a.-p. AP222(h) 8 l on 5.40 l any
    single   .90   .90
C1209   Sheet of 6 (#B1)   10.00 10.00
  a.-f. SP1(f) 15 l on 10 l +1 l any
    single   1.60 1.60
  g. As No. C1209, on No. B1a   10.00 10.00
Size, location and font of surcharges and obliterators vary on types "f" and "h."

Honduras
— Japan
Diplomatic
Relations,
70th Anniv.
AP269

Designs: 8 l, Actors in play. 15 l, Emblem of Japanese-Central American Year. 30 l, National Congress, Japanese Princess Sayako.
No. C1213: a, Japanese ceramics. b, Flowers. c, Mayan ceramics. d, Mount Fuji, Japan and Pico Bonito National Park, Honduras.

2005, Aug. 9   Litho.   Perf. 13¼
C1210-C1212 AP269 Set of 3   7.00 7.00
  Souvenir Sheet
C1213 AP269 25 l Sheet of 4,
    #a-d   13.00 13.00

Gen. José
Trinidad Cabañas
(1805-71)
AP270

Cabañas: 3 l, With green panel at bottom. 8 l, With university buildings, horiz. 15 l, In oval frame.

2005, Sept. 12
C1214-C1216 AP270 Set of 3   3.25 3.25

Honduras, Water
Capital — AP271

Water droplet and: 30 l, Heart, butterfly, Sanaa and Ras-hon emblems. 50 l, Heart.

2005, Sept. 28
C1217 AP271 30 l multi   4.00 4.00
  Souvenir Sheet
C1218 AP271 50 l multi   7.00 7.00

Souvenir Sheet

America Issue — Endangered
Mushrooms — AP272

No. C1219: a, 20 l, Hygrophorus marzuolus. b, 25 l, Lactarius deliciosus. c, 30 l, Boletus pinophilus. d, 50 l, Gyromitra esculenta.

2005
C1219 AP272   Sheet of 4, #a-
    d   17.00 17.00

AP273

Mail
Transport
AP274

Designs: 5 l, Charles Lindbergh, PAA emblem. 25 l, Postal rail car, 1920. 30 l, First Honduran postal car, 1914.

---

50 l, Sikorsky S-38 airplane, PAA emblem, horiz.

2005, Dec. 6   Litho.   Perf. 13¼
C1220 AP273   5 l multi   .65   .65
C1221 AP274   25 l multi   3.00 3.00
C1222 AP274   30 l multi   3.75 3.75
  Nos. C1220-C1222 (3)   7.40 7.40
  Imperf
  Size: 89x64mm
C1223 AP273 50 l multi   6.50 6.50

Nos. C1177-
C1179
Surcharged

2005   Litho.   Perf. 13¼
C1224 AP263   3 l on 2.60 l
    #C1177   .35   .35
C1225 AP263   15 l on 7.85 l
    #C1178   1.90 1.90
C1226 AP263   25 l on 7.85 l
    #C1178   3.50 3.50
C1227 AP263   50 l on 10.65 l
    #C1179   6.75 6.75
  Nos. C1224-C1227 (4)   12.50 12.50
No. C1226 has a thick wavy line obliterator and was issued in sheets of four.

2006 Winter
Olympics,
Turin — AP275

Skier and: 20 l, Turin Olympics emblem, Olympic rings. 50 l, Olympic rings.

2006, Jan. 24
C1228-C1229 AP275 Set of 2   9.00 9.00

Forgiveness of Honduran Debts by
Foreign Nations — AP276

Designs: 14 l, Structure 4, Copán Ruins. 15 l, Flags of nations forgiving debts. 30 l, Honduras Pres. Ricardo Maduro, vert.

2006, Jan. 26
C1230-C1232 AP276 Set of 3   12.50 12.50

Cortés Chamber
of Commerce
and Industry,
75th
Anniv. — AP277

Anniversary and Chamber of Commerce emblem and: 20 l, Gears. 35 l, The Forger, sculpture by J. Zelaya, horiz. 50 l, El Industrial, mural by A. Martínez.

2006
C1233-C1235 AP277 Set of 3   13.00 13.00

Diplomatic Relations Between Honduras and Brazil, Cent. AP278

Designs: 20 l, Flags of Honduras and Brazil. 30 l, Baron of Rio Branco (1845-1912) Brazilian diplomat, vert.

2006   Litho.   Perf. 13¼
C1236-C1237 AP278 Set of 2   6.50 6.50

Miniature Sheet

Honduran Friendship With Japan — AP279

No. C1238: a, 10 l, Children learning about Chagas disease. b, 15 l, Teacher and children. c, 20 l, Japanese naval vessels and flag. d, 25 l, Sailors in dress uniforms.

2006
C1238 AP279 Sheet of 4, #a-d   7.50 7.50

Nos. C1054, C1124-C1125, C1127-C1128, C1149-C1151, C1159, C1162, C1164, C1166-C1167, C1169-C1170, C1172-C1173 Surcharged

Methods and Perfs As Before

2007 ?
C1239	AP260	2 l on 2.60 l #C1159	.25	.25
C1240	AP260	2 l on 4 l #C1162	.25	.25
C1241	AP249	2 l on 8.65 l #C1128	.25	.25
C1242	AP260	2 l on 10.65 l #C1166	.25	.25
C1243	AP249	3 l on 1.40 l #C1124	.35	.35
C1244	AP257	3 l on 1.40 l #C1149	.35	.35
C1245	AP257	3 l on 2.60 l #C1150	.35	.35
C1246	AP261	3 l on 2.60 l #C1172	.35	.35
C1247	AP257	3 l on 7.30 l #C1151	.35	.35
C1248	AP261	3 l on 10.65 l #C1173	.35	.35
C1249	AP226	3 l on 18.30 l #C1054	.35	.35
C1250	AP261	5 l on 85c #C1169	.55	.55
C1251	AP261	5 l on 1.40 l #C1170	.55	.55
C1252	AP249	5 l on 2.60 l #C1125	.55	.55
C1253	AP249	5 l on 4.30 l #C1127	.55	.55
C1254	AP260	5 l on 4.30 l #C1164	.55	.55
C1255	AP260	5 l on 14.95 l #C1167	.55	.55
		Nos. C1239-C1255 (17)	6.75	6.75

Constitution, 25th Anniv. — AP280

Designs: 5 l, Leaders of the Legislative, Executive and Judicial branches of government. 10 l, 1824 Constituent Assembly Building. 15 l, Presidential House, 1922-91, vert. 20 l, Legislative Building.

2007   Litho.   Perf. 13¼
C1256-C1259 AP280 Set of 4   5.50 5.50

Miniature Sheet

Central Bank of Honduras, 50th Anniv. — AP281

No. C1260 — Central Bank of Honduras emblem and paintings: a, 5 l, Holocausto, by César Rendón. b, 10 l, La Novia, by Miguel Angel Ruiz Matute. c, 15 l, Ayer, Hoy y Mañana, by Felipe Bouchard. d, 20 l, Paisaje de Tegucigalpa, by Mario Castillo. e, 25 l, Dinamismo, by Benigno Gómez. f, 30 l, Guitarras en Descanso, by Dante Lazzaroni.

2007
C1260 AP281 Sheet of 6, #a-f 11.50 11.50

Adjudication of "Four Cardinal Points" Police Torture Case — AP282

2007, Oct. 18   Litho.   Perf. 13¼
C1261 AP282 50 l multi   5.50 5.50
     Printed in sheets of 2.

Miniature Sheets

Launch of Sputnik I, 50th Anniv. — AP283

No. C1262: a, 25 l, Sputnik launch vehicle, pale blue background (30x40mm). b, 35 l, Sputnik I, yellow background (30x40mm). c, 50 l, Sputnik orbiting Earth, pale green background (60x40mm).
No. C1263: a, 25 l, As #C1262a, pale green background. b, 35 l, As #C1262b, pale blue background. c, 50 l, As #C1262c, yellow background.

2007, Nov. 30
C1262	AP283	Sheet of 3, #a-c	12.00	12.00
C1263	AP283	Sheet of 3, #a-c	12.00	12.00

Miniature Sheet

Paintings by Gaye-Darléne Bidart de Satulsky — AP284

No. C1264: a, 3 l, Medusa de las Islas. b, 3 l, Nido de Amor. c, 3 l, Guitarrista Isleño. d, 5 l, "M" Hombre Cruz. e, 5 l, Amor a Martillazos. f, 5 l, Sor María Rosa. g, 5 l, Isleña, Luna y Mar. h, 5 l, Clementina Suárez. i, 5 l, La Naranjera.

2008
C1264 AP284 Sheet of 9, #a-i   4.25 4.25

Miniature Sheet

America Issue — AP285

No. C1265: a, 2 l, Factory workers and sewing machine. b, 3 l, Energy savings mascot. c, 5 l, School children. d, 10 l, Children in native costumes.

2008
C1265 AP285 Sheet of 4, #a-d 2.10 2.10

2008 Summer Olympics, Beijing AP286

Designs: 3 l, Olympic torch. No. C1267, 5 l, Judo. No. C1268, 5 l, Runners. 25 l, Soccer.

2008, July 30
C1266-C1269 AP286 Set of 4 4.00 4.00

Juan Ramón Molina (1875-1908), Poet — AP287

Designs: 10 l, Molina, mermaid and ship. 25 l, Molina.

2008, Oct. 30
C1270-C1271 AP287 Set of 2 3.75 3.75

Miniature Sheet

Treaty of Amity, Commerce and Navigation Between Honduras and Mexico, Cent. — AP288

No. C1272: a, 5 l, Sailor and ship. b, 10 l, Hands, flags and maps. c, 15 l, Handshake, double helix of flags, horiz. d, 20 l, Flags and "100 Años de Amistad." c, 25 l, "100" and colors of flags, horiz. f, 50 l, Parrot and eagle, horiz.

2008   Litho.   Perf. 13¼
C1272 AP288 Sheet of 6, #a-f + 3 labels   13.50 13.50

España Normal School, Villa Ahumada, 58th Anniv. AP289

Designs: 2 l, School. 5 l, School emblem.

2009, Aug. 28   Litho.   Perf. 13¼
C1273-C1274 AP289 Set of 2 .75 .75

America Issue AP290

Traditional toys and games: 3 l, Hopscotch. 10 l, Kite. 20 l, Top. 50 l, Children playing soccer, jumping rope and flying kite.

2009, Aug. 28
C1275-C1278 AP290 Set of 4 8.75 8.75

President's House AP291

Dove, Map of Honduras AP292

Interim President Roberto Michaletti Baín — AP293

2009, Dec. 3
C1279	AP291	3 l multi	.35	.35
C1280	AP292	15 l multi	1.60	1.60
C1281	AP293	20 l multi	2.10	2.10
		Nos. C1279-C1281 (3)	4.05	4.05

2010 World Cup Soccer
Championships, South Africa — AP294

Designs: 5 l, Child playing soccer. 20 l, Honduras soccer team. 25 l, Emblem of Honduras soccer team.

2009, Dec. 3
C1282-C1284 AP294 Set of 3 5.25 5.25

AIR POST SEMI-POSTAL STAMPS

No. C13C Surcharged with Plus Sign
and Surtax in Black

Unwmk.
1929, June 5 Engr. Perf. 12
CB1 AP1 50c + 5c carmine .65 .30
CB2 AP1 50c + 10c carmine .70 .35
CB3 AP1 50c + 15c carmine .95 .55
CB4 AP1 50c + 20c carmine 1.40 .75
Nos. CB1-CB4 (4) 3.70 1.95

Catalogue values for unused stamps in this section, from this point to the end of the section, are for Never Hinged items.

Souvenir Sheet

Airmail Pilot Sumner B. Morgan and
Airplane — SP2

2000, July 7
CB5 SP2 50 l + 5 l multi 11.00 11.00
First airmail flight in Honduras, 75th anniv., EXFILHON 2000. See Nos. C1075-C1077.

No. C619 Surcharged With New Value
in Black and 2000 Sydney Olympics
Emblem in Red

2000, Sept. 13 Litho. Imperf.
CB6 AP99 48.50 l +1.50 l multi 10.00 10.00

AIR POST SPECIAL DELIVERY STAMPS

No. CO52
Surcharged
in Red

Perf. 13½x14
1953, Dec. 8 Engr. Unwmk.
CE1 AP65 20c on 1c 3.00 1.50

Transport
Plane
APSD1

1956, Oct. 3 Perf. 13x12½
CE2 APSD1 20c black & red .80 .50
Surcharges on No. CE2 (see Nos. C421, C477) eliminate its special delivery character.

Catalogue values for unused stamps in this section, from this point to the end of the section, are for Never Hinged items.

Stamp Centenary Type of Air Post
Issue

Design: 20c, Mailman on motorcycle.

1966, May 31 Litho. Perf. 14x14½
CE3 AP81 20c bis brn, brn & gold 1.00 .50
Centenary (in 1965) of the first Honduran postage stamp.
The "HABILITADO" overprint on No. CE3 (see No. C479) eliminates its special delivery character.

Independence Type of Air Post Issue
1972, May 19 Litho. Perf. 13
CE4 AP89 20c Corsair plane .70 .35

Same Surcharged
1975
CE5 AP89 60c on 20c 1.00 .65

Forest Protection Type of Air Post
1976, May 28 Litho. Perf. 13½
CE6 AP96 60c Stag in forest .75 .50

AIR POST OFFICIAL STAMPS

Official Stamps Nos.
O78 to O81
Overprinted in Red,
Green or Black

OA1

1930 Perf. 11, 11½
CO1 A24 10c deep blue (R) 1.25 1.25
CO2 A24 20c yellow brown 1.25 1.25
a. Vert. pair, imperf. btwn. 14.00
CO3 A24 50c vermilion (Bk) 1.40 1.40
CO4 A24 1p emerald (R) 1.25 1.25
Nos. CO1-CO4 (4) 5.15 5.15

Green Surcharge
CO5 OA1 5c on 6c red vio 1.00 1.00
a. "1910" for "1930" 2.75 2.75
b. "1920" for "1930" 2.75 2.75
The overprint exists in other colors and on other denominations but the status of these is questioned.

Official
Stamps of
1931
Overprinted

1931 Unwmk. Perf. 12
CO6 O2 1c ultra .35 .35
CO7 O2 2c black brown .85 .85
CO8 O2 5c olive gray 1.00 1.00
CO9 O2 6c orange red 1.00 1.00
a. Inverted overprint 24.00 24.00

CO10 O2 10c dark green 1.25 1.25
CO11 O2 15c olive brown 2.00 1.75
a. Inverted overprint 20.00 20.00
CO12 O2 20c red brown 2.00 1.75
CO13 O2 50c gray violet 1.40 1.40
CO14 O2 1p deep orange 2.00 1.75
Nos. CO6-CO14 (9) 11.85 11.10

In the setting of the overprint there are numerous errors in the spelling and punctuation, letters omitted and similar varieties.
This set is known with blue overprint. A similar overprint is known in larger type, but its status has not been fully determined.

Postage Stamps of 1918-30
Surcharged Type "a" or Type "b"
(#CO22-CO23) in Green, Black, Red
and Blue

a

b

1933 Wmk. 209, Unwmk.
CO15 A39 20c on 2c #295 (G) 3.25 3.25
CO16 A39 20c on 2c #296 (G) 3.25 3.25
CO17 A39 20c on 2c #297 (G) 3.25 3.25
CO17A A39 40c on 2c #295 2.00 2.00
CO18 A39 40c on 2c #297 (G) 7.00 7.00
CO18A A39 40c on 2c #297 4.25 4.25
CO19 A28 40c on 5c #246 4.25 4.25
CO19A A28 40c on 5c #247 7.00 7.00
CO20 A28 40c on 5c #266 15.00 15.00
CO20A A28 40c on 5c #267 9.00 9.00
CO20B A28 40c on 5c #267 (R) 14.00 14.00
CO21 A20 70c on 5c #183 3.00 3.00
CO22 A24 70c on 10c #214 (R) 3.25 3.25
CO23 A22 1 l on 20c #191 (Bl) 3.25 3.25
CO24 A24 1 l on 50c #216 (Bl) 14.00 14.00
CO25 A22 1.20 l on 1p #193 (Bl) 1.00 1.00
Nos. CO15-CO25 (16) 96.75 96.75

**Official Stamps of 1915-29
Surcharged Type "a" or Type "b"
(#CO28-CO29, CO33-CO41, CO43) in
Black,
Red, Green, Orange, Carmine or
Blue**
CO26 O1 40c on 5c #O84 (Bk) 1.00 1.00
CO27 O1 40c on 5c #O84 (R) 25.00 25.00
CO28 A24 60c on 6c #O77 (Bk) .70 .70
CO29 A24 60c on 6c #O77 (G) 25.00 25.00
CO30 A20 70c on 5c #O60 (Bk) 5.25 5.25
CO31 A19 70c on 10c #O62 (R) 9.00 9.00
CO32 A19 70c on 10c #O62 (Bk) 7.75 7.75
CO33 A22 70c on 10c #O70 (R) 4.50 4.00
CO34 A24 70c on 10c #O78 (O) 3.50 3.50
CO35 A24 70c on 10c #O78 (C) 4.50 4.50
CO36 A22 70c on 10c #O71 (R) 87.50 87.50
CO37 A22 90c on 10c #O70 (R) 5.25 5.25
CO38 A22 90c on 15c #O71 (R) 8.00 8.00
CO38A A24 1 l on 2c #O76 1.40 1.40
CO39 A22 1 l on 20c #O72 2.50 2.50
CO39A A24 1 l on 20c #O79 3.75 3.75
CO40 A22 1 l on 50c #O73 1.90 1.90
CO41 A24 1 l on 50c #O80 4.25 4.25
CO42 A20 1.20 l on 1p #O65 9.00 7.00
CO43 A24 1.20 l on 1p #O81 3.00 3.00
Nos. CO26-CO43 (20) 212.75 210.25

Varieties of foregoing surcharges exist.

Merchant Flag
and Seal of
Honduras
OA2

1939, Feb. 27 Unwmk. Perf. 12½
CO44 OA2 2c dp blue & grn .20 .20
CO45 OA2 5c dp blue & org .20 .20
CO46 OA2 8c dp blue & brn .20 .20
CO47 OA2 15c dp blue & car .30 .20
CO48 OA2 46c dp blue & ol grn .40 .40
CO49 OA2 50c dp blue & vio .50 .30
CO50 OA2 1 l dp blue & red brn 1.75 1.25
CO51 OA2 2 l dp blue & red org 3.75 2.25
Nos. CO44-CO51 (8) 7.30 4.90

For overprints and surcharges see #C101-C117.

Types of Air Post Stamps of 1952
Overprinted in Red

Perf. 13½x14, 14x13½
1952 Engr. Unwmk.
CO52 AP65 1c rose lil & ol .20 .20
CO53 AP65 2c brown & vio .20 .20
CO54 AP65 8c dp car & blk .20 .20
CO55 AP66 16c pur & dk grn .25 .25
CO56 AP65 30c dk bl & blk .50 .50
CO57 AP65 1 l dk grn & dk brown 1.75 1.75
CO58 AP65 2 l bl & red brn 3.50 3.50
CO59 AP66 5 l red org & blk 8.50 8.50
Nos. CO52-CO59 (8) 15.10 15.10

Queen Isabella I of Spain, 500th birth anniv.
For overprints and surcharge, see Nos. CE1, CO110.

No. C222 and
Types of Air Post
Stamps of 1953
Overprinted in
Red

Engraved; Center of 1c Litho.
1953, Dec. 18 Perf. 12½
Frames in Black
CO60 AP67 1c ultra & vio bl .20 .20
CO61 AP97 2c dp blue grn .20 .20
CO62 AP67 3c orange .20 .20
CO63 AP67 5c dp carmine .20 .20
CO64 AP67 15c dk brown .25 .20
CO65 AP67 30c purple .45 .35
CO66 AP67 1 l olive gray 4.00 2.25
CO67 AP67 2 l lilac rose 5.00 3.00
CO68 AP67 5 l ultra 11.50 7.00
Nos. CO60-CO68 (9) 22.00 13.60

Issued to honor the United Nations.

Types of Air
Post Stamps
Overprinted in
Red

Engraved; 8c Lithographed
1956, Oct. 3 Perf. 13x12½
CO69 AP68 1c blk & brn car .20 .20
CO70 AP69 2c black & mag .20 .20
CO71 AP68 3c blk & rose vio .20 .20
CO72 AP69 4c black & org .20 .20
CO73 AP69 5c black & bl grn .20 .20
CO74 AP68 8c violet & multi .20 .20
CO75 AP68 10c blk & red brn .20 .20
CO76 AP68 12c blk & car rose .20 .20
CO77 AP68 15c carmine & blk .20 .20
CO78 AP69 20c black & ol brn .20 .20
CO79 AP69 24c black & blue .20 .20
CO80 AP68 25c blk & rose vio .20 .20
CO81 AP68 30c black & grn .20 .20
CO82 AP69 40c blk & red org .25 .25
CO83 AP69 50c blk & brn red .30 .30
CO84 AP68 60c blk & rose vio .40 .40
CO85 AP68 1 l black & brn 1.40 1.10

CO86	AP69	2 l black & dk bl	2.75	2.25
CO87	AP69	5 l black & vio bl	5.75	5.25
		Nos. CO69-CO87 (19)	13.45	12.15

Nos. C269-C278 Overprinted Vertically in Red (Horizontally on Nos. CO89 and CO91)

1957, Oct. 21   Litho.   Perf. 13
Frames in Black

CO88	AP70	1c buff & aqua	.20	.20
CO89	AP70	2c org, pur & emer	.20	.20
CO90	AP70	5c pink & ultra	.20	.20
a.		Inverted overprint		
CO91	AP70	8c orange, vio & ol	.20	.20
CO92	AP70	10c violet & brn	.20	.20
CO93	AP70	12c lt grn & ultra	.20	.20
CO94	AP70	15c green & brn	.20	.20
CO95	AP70	30c pink & sl	.55	.25
CO96	AP70	1 l blue & brn	1.40	1.00
CO97	AP70	2 l lt grn & sl	2.75	2.25
		Nos. CO88-CO97 (10)	6.10	4.90

Types of Lincoln Air Post Stamps 1959 Overprinted in Red

1959   Engr.   Perf. 13½
Flags in National Colors

CO98	AP72	1c ocher	.20	.20
CO99	AP73	2c gray olive	.20	.20
a.		Inverted overprint		
CO100	AP73	3c red brown	.20	.20
CO101	AP73	5c ultra	.20	.20
CO102	AP73	10c dull purple	.20	.20
a.		Overprint omitted		
CO103	AP73	12c red orange	.20	.20
CO104	AP72	15c dark brown	.20	.20
CO105	AP73	25c black	.20	.20
CO106	AP73	50c dark car	.30	.25
CO107	AP73	1 l purple	.75	.65
CO108	AP73	2 l dark blue	1.40	1.10
a.		Min. sheet of 6, 2c, 5c, 12c, 15c, 50c, 2 l, imperf.	3.00	3.00
CO109	AP73	5 l green	4.50	3.75
		Nos. CO98-CO109 (12)	8.55	7.35

Catalogue values for unused stamps in this section, from this point to the end of the section, are for Never Hinged items.

No. CO55 Overprinted: "IN MEMORIAM / Sir Winston / Churchill / 1874-1965"

1965, Dec. 20   Perf. 14x13½
| CO110 | AP66 | 16c purple & dk grn | 1.00 | 1.00 |

See note after No. C379.

Nos. C336-C344 Overprinted in Red:

1965   Photo.   Perf. 14
Black Design and Inscription

CO111	AP76	1c yellow green	.20	.20
CO112	AP76	2c pale rose lil	.20	.20
CO113	AP76	5c light ultra	.20	.20
CO114	AP76	8c bluish grn	.25	.25
CO115	AP76	10c buff	.30	.30
CO116	AP76	12c lemon	.35	.35
CO117	AP76	1 l light ocher	4.00	4.00
CO118	AP76	2 l pale olive grn	8.75	8.75
CO119	AP76	3 l rose	11.00	11.00
		Nos. CO111-CO119 (9)	25.25	25.25

OFFICIAL STAMPS

Type of Regular Issue of 1890 Overprinted in Red

1890   Unwmk.   Perf. 12
O1	A5	1c pale yellow	.25
O2	A5	2c pale yellow	.25
O3	A5	5c pale yellow	.25
O4	A5	10c pale yellow	.25
O5	A5	20c pale yellow	.25
O6	A5	25c pale yellow	.25
O7	A5	30c pale yellow	.25
O8	A5	40c pale yellow	.25
O9	A5	50c pale yellow	.25
O10	A5	75c pale yellow	.25
O11	A5	1p pale yellow	.25
		Nos. O1-O11 (11)	2.75

Type of Regular Issue of 1891 Overprinted in Red

1891
O12	A6	1c yellow	.25
O13	A6	2c yellow	.25
O14	A6	5c yellow	.25
O15	A6	10c yellow	.25
O16	A6	20c yellow	.25
O17	A6	25c yellow	.25
O18	A6	30c yellow	.25
O19	A6	40c yellow	.25
O20	A6	50c yellow	.25
O21	A6	75c yellow	.25
O22	A6	1p yellow	.25
		Nos. O12-O22 (11)	2.75

Nos. O1 to O22 were never placed in use. Cancellations were applied to remainders. They exist with overprint inverted, double, triple and omitted; also, imperf. and part perf.

Regular Issue of 1898 Overprinted

1898-99   Perf. 11½
O23	A12	5c dl ultra	.40
O24	A12	10c dark bl	.80
O25	A12	20c dull org	1.25
O26	A12	50c org red	2.40
O27	A12	1p blue grn	3.00
		Nos. O23-O27 (5)	7.85

Counterfeits of basic stamps and of overprint exist.

Regular Issue of 1911 Overprinted

1911-15   Perf. 12, 14
Carmine Overprint

O28	A15	1c violet	1.50	.65
a.		Inverted overprint	2.40	2.40
b.		Double overprint	2.00	
O29	A15	6c ultra	2.50	2.00
a.		Inverted overprint	2.75	2.75
O30	A15	10c blue	1.50	1.25
a.		"OFICAIL"	2.50	
b.		Double overprint	3.50	
O31	A15	20c yellow	15.00	12.00
O32	A15	50c brown	8.00	7.00
O33	A15	1p ol grn	12.00	10.00
		Nos. O28-O33 (6)	40.50	32.90

Black Overprint
O34	A15	2c green	1.00	.70
a.		"CIFICAIL"	5.00	
O35	A15	5c carmine	1.50	1.00
a.		Perf. 12	7.50	5.00
O36	A15	6c ultra	4.50	4.50
O37	A15	10c blue	4.00	4.00
O38	A15	20c yellow	5.00	5.00
O39	A15	50c brown	5.00	5.00
		Nos. O34-O39 (6)	21.50	19.20

Counterfeits of overprint of Nos. O28-O39 exist.

With Additional Surcharge

1913-14
O40	A15	1c on 5c car	1.75	1.50
O41	A15	2c on 5c car	2.00	1.50
O42	A15	10c on 1c vio	4.00	3.50
a.		"OFICIAL" inverted	7.50	
O43	A15	20c on 1c vio	3.00	2.50
		Nos. O40-O43 (4)	10.75	9.00

On No. O40 the surcharge reads "1 cent."
Nos. O40-O43 exist with double surcharge.

No. O43 Surcharged Vertically in Black, Yellow or Maroon

1914
O44	A15	10c on 20c on 1c	20.00	20.00
a.		Maroon surcharge	20.00	20.00
O45	A15	10c on 20c on 1c (Y)	40.00	40.00

No. O35 Surcharged

1915
| O46 | A15 | 10c on 5c car | 20.00 | 20.00 |

No. O39 Surcharged

| O47 | A15 | 20c on 50c brn | 5.00 | 5.00 |

Regular Issues of 1913-14 Overprinted in Red or Black

1915   Perf. 11½
O48	A17	1c brn (R)	.40	.40
a.		"OFICIAL"	5.00	
O49	A17	2c car (Bk)	.40	.40
a.		"OFICIAL"	5.00	
b.		Double overprint	4.00	
O50	A18	5c ultra (Bk)	.45	.45
a.		"OFIC"	4.00	
O51	A18	5c ultra (R)	1.00	1.00
a.		"OFIC"		
b.		"OFICIAL"	5.00	
O52	A18	6c pur (Bk)	1.50	1.50
a.		6c red lil (Bk)		
O53	A17	10c brn (Bk)	1.25	1.25
O54	A17	20c brn (Bk)	3.00	3.00
O55	A17	20c brn (R)	3.00	3.00
a.		Double overprint (R+Bk)	10.00	
b.		"OFICIAL"	5.00	
O56	A18	50c rose (Bk)	6.00	6.00
		Nos. O48-O56 (9)	17.00	17.00

The 10c blue has the overprint "OFICIAL" in different type from the other stamps of the series. It is stated that forty stamps were overprinted for the Postmaster General but the stamp was never put in use or on sale at the post office.

No. 152 Surcharged

O57	A17	1c on 2c car	2.00	2.00
a.		"0.10" for "0.01"	4.25	4.25
b.		"0.20" for "0.01"	4.25	4.25
c.		Double surcharge	8.50	8.50
d.		As "a," double surcharge	77.50	
e.		As "b," double surcharge	77.50	

Regular Issue of 1915-16 Overprinted in Black or Red.

1915-16
O58	A19	1c choc (Bk)	.20	.20
O59	A19	2c car (Bk)	.20	.20
a.		Tête bêche pair	1.25	1.25
b.		Double overprint	2.00	
c.		Double overprint, one inverted	2.00	
d.		"b" and "c" in tête bêche pair		
O60	A20	5c brt blue (R)	.30	.30
a.		Inverted overprint	3.00	
O61	A20	6c deep pur (R)	.40	.40
a.		Black overprint	3.00	
b.		Inverted overprint	2.00	2.00
O62	A19	10c dl bl (R)	.40	.40
O63	A19	20c red brn (Bk)	.60	.60
a.		Tête bêche pair	2.50	
O64	A20	50c red (Bk)	1.75	1.75
O65	A20	1p yel grn (C)	3.75	3.75
		Nos. O58-O65 (8)	7.60	7.60

The 6c, 10c and 1p exist imperf.

Regular Issue of 1919 Overprinted

1921
O66	A22	1c brown	2.25	2.25
a.		Inverted overprint	3.00	3.00
O67	A22	2c carmine	6.50	6.50
a.		Inverted overprint	3.00	3.00
O68	A22	5c lilac rose	6.50	6.50
a.		Inverted overprint	3.00	
O69	A22	6c brt vio	.50	.50
a.		Inverted overprint		
O70	A22	10c dull blue	.60	.60
a.		Double overprint		
O71	A22	15c light blue	.70	.70
a.		Inverted overprint	2.00	
b.		Double overprint, one inverted	4.00	
O72	A22	20c brown	1.00	1.00
O73	A22	50c light brown	1.50	1.50
O74	A22	1p yellow green	3.00	3.00
		Nos. O66-O74 (9)	22.55	22.55

Regular Issue of 1924 Overprinted

1924   Perf. 11, 11½
O75	A24	1c olive brn	.20	.20
O76	A24	2c deep rose	.20	.20
O77	A24	6c red vio	.30	.30
O78	A24	10c red bl	.45	.45
O79	A24	20c yel brn	.60	.60
O80	A24	50c vermilion	1.25	1.25
O81	A24	1p emerald	2.00	2.00
		Nos. O75-O81 (7)	5.00	5.00

J. C. del Valle — O1

Designs: 2c, J. R. Molina. 5c, Coffee tree. 10c, J. T. Reyes. 20c, Tegucigalpa Cathedral. 50c, San Lorenzo Creek. 1p, Radio station.

HONDURAS (continued)

1929 Litho. Wmk. 209 Perf. 11½
O82	O1	1c blue	.20	.20
O83	O1	2c carmine	.20	.20
a.		2c rose		.20
O84	O1	5c purple	.35	.35
O85	O1	10c emerald	.50	.35
O86	O1	20c dk bl	.60	.60
O87	O1	50c org, grn & bl	1.00	1.00
O88	O1	1p buff	1.75	1.75
		Nos. O82-O88 (7)	4.60	4.45

Nos. O82-O88 exist imperf.
For overprints and surcharges see Nos. 282, 284, C37-C40, C59, C62-C63, CO26-CO27.

View of
Tegucigalpa
O2

1931 Unwmk. Engr. Perf. 12
O89	O2	1c ultra	.30	.20
O90	O2	2c black brn	.30	.20
O91	O2	5c olive gray	.35	.35
O92	O2	6c orange red	.40	.30
O93	O2	10c dark green	.50	.45
O94	O2	15c olive brn	.65	.40
O95	O2	20c red brown	.75	.20
O96	O2	50c gray vio	1.00	.65
O97	O2	1p dp orange	1.75	1.75
		Nos. O89-O97 (9)	6.00	4.60

For overprints see #CO6-CO14, O98-O105.

Official Stamps of 1931 Overprinted in
Black

1936-37
O98	O2	1c ultra	.25	.25
O99	O2	2c black brn	.25	.25
a.		Inverted overprint	10.00	
O100	O2	5c olive gray	.30	.30
O101	O2	6c red orange	.40	.40
O102	O2	10c dark green	.40	.40
O103	O2	15c olive brown	.50	.50
a.		Inverted overprint	5.00	
O104	O2	20c red brown	1.00	1.00
a.		"1938-1935"		
O105	O2	50c gray violet	4.00	3.00
		Nos. O98-O105 (8)	7.10	6.10

Double overprints exist on 1c and 2c. No.
O97 with this overprint is fraudulent.

POSTAL TAX STAMPS

Red Cross
PT1

Francisco
Morazán
PT2

Engr.; Cross Litho.
1941, Aug. 1 Unwmk. Perf. 12
RA1	PT1	1c blue & carmine	.25	.20

Obligatory on all domestic or foreign mail,
the tax to be used by the Honduran Red
Cross.

1941, Aug. 1 Engr.
RA2	PT2	1c copper brown	.40	.20

Francisco Morazan, 100th anniv. of death.

Mother and
Child — PT3

Henri
Dunant — PT4

1945 Engr.; Cross Litho.
RA3	PT3	1c ol brn, car & bl	.25	.20

The tax was for the Honduran Red Cross.

Similar to Type of 1945
Large Red Cross

1950
RA4	PT3	1c olive brn & red	.25	.20

The tax was for the Honduran Red Cross.

1959 Perf. 13x13½
RA5	PT4	1c blue & red	.25	.20

The tax was for the Red Cross.

> **Catalogue values for unused stamps in this section, from this point to the end of the section, are for Never Hinged items.**

Henri
Dunant — PT5

No. RA7, as PT5, but redrawn; country
name panel at bottom, value at right, "El poder
. . ." at top.

1964, Dec. 15 Litho. Perf. 11
RA6	PT5	1c brt grn & red	.25	.20
RA7	PT5	1c brown & red	.25	.20

The tax was for the Red Cross.

Nurse and
Patient — PT6

1969, June Litho. Perf. 13½
RA8	PT6	1c light blue & red	.25	.20

The tax was for the Red Cross.
For surcharges see Nos. 387-391, C1199,
C1201-C1202, C1205-C1206.

HONG KONG

ˈhäŋˌkäŋ

LOCATION — A peninsula and island in
southeast China at the mouth of the
Canton River
GOVT. — Special Administrative Area
of China (PRC) (as of 7/1/97)
AREA — 426 sq. mi.
POP. — 6,847,125 (1999 est.)
CAPITAL — Victoria

100 Cents = 1 Dollar

> **Catalogue values for unused stamps in this country are for Never Hinged items, beginning with Scott 174 in the regular postage section, Scott B1 in the semipostal section and Scott J13 in the postage due section.**

Watermark

Wmk. 340

Values for unused stamps are for
examples with original gum as defined
in the catalogue introduction. Very fine
examples of Nos. 1-25, 29-48, 61-66d
and 69-70a will have perforations touching the design on at least one side due
to the narrow spacing of the stamps on
the plates. Stamps with perfs clear of
the design on all four sides are scarce
and will command higher prices.

Queen Victoria — A1

Unwmk.
1862, Dec. 8 Typo. Perf. 14
1	A1	2c pale brown	550.00	125.00
a.		2c deep brown	700.00	150.00
2	A1	8c buff	775.00	85.00
3	A1	12c blue	700.00	72.50
4	A1	18c lilac	700.00	67.50
5	A1	24c green	1,200.	140.00
6	A1	48c rose	3,000.	400.00
7	A1	96c gray	4,000.	525.00

1863-80 Wmk. 1
8	A1	2c brown ('65)	145.00	8.50
a.		2c deep brown ('64)	350.00	35.00
9	A1	2c dull rose ('80)	200.00	30.00
a.		2c rose	225.00	32.50
10	A1	4c slate	135.00	8.25
a.		4c greenish grey	350.00	55.00
b.		4c bluish slate	525.00	25.00
11	A1	5c ultra ('80)	600.00	55.00
12	A1	6c lilac	475.00	18.50
a.		6c violet	600.00	18.50
13	A1	8c org buff ('65)	575.00	12.50
a.		8c bright orange	475.00	13.00
b.		8c brownish orange	525.00	13.00
14	A1	10c violet ('80)	675.00	19.00
15	A1	12c light blue	37.50	7.50
a.		12c light greenish blue	1,100.	37.50
b.		12c deep blue	300.00	14.00
16	A1	16c yellow ('77)	2,200.	77.50
17	A1	18c lilac ('66)	7,750.	350.00
18	A1	24c green ('65)	575.00	12.50
a.		24c deep green	1,000.	32.50
19	A1	30c vermilion	850.00	17.50
20	A1	30c violet ('71)	300.00	7.00
21	A1	48c rose carmine	1,100.	55.00
22	A1	48c brown ('80)	1,600.	120.00
23	A1	96c bister ('65)	85,000.	800.00
24	A1	96c gray ('66)	1,750.	65.00

Imperfs. are plate proofs.

1874 Perf. 12½
25	A1	4c slate	13,500.	300.00

See #36-49. For surcharges or overprints on
stamps of type A1 see #29-35B, 51-56, 61-66,
69-70.

A2

A3

A4

1874 Engr. Wmk. 1 Perf. 15½x15
26	A2	$2 sage green	400.00	70.00
27	A3	$3 violet	375.00	55.00
28	A4	$10 rose	8,250.	800.00

Nos. 26-28 are revenues which were used
postally. Used values are for postally canceled
copies. Black "Paid All" cancels are fiscal
usage.
See Nos. 57-59. For surcharges see Nos.
50, 67. For type surcharged see No. 60.

Nos. 17 and 20 Surcharged in Black:

1876 Perf. 14
29	A1	16c on 18c lilac	2,500.	185.00
30	A1	28c on 30c violet	1,750.	62.50

Stamps of 1863-80
Surcharged in Black

1879-80
31	A1	5c on 8c org ('80)	1,100.	110.00
a.		Inverted surcharge		18,500.
b.		Double surcharge		20,000.
32	A1	5c on 18c lilac	1,050.	70.00
33	A1	10c on 12c blue	1,100.	65.00
34	A1	10c on 16c yellow	4,750.	55.00
a.		Inverted surcharge		85,000.
b.		Double surcharge		85,000.
35	A1	10c on 24c green ('80)	1,550.	95.00

Most examples of No. 31a are damaged.

Nos. 16-17, 35B Surcharged in Black

A5

A6

1879
35A	A5	3c on 16c on card	425.	2,200.
		Stamp off card		475.
35B	A5	5c on 18c on card	425.	2,600.
		Stamp off card		550.
35C	A6	3c on 5c on 18c on card	8,000.	9,500.
		Stamp off card	6,500.	8,250.

Nos. 35A-35C were sold affixed to postal
cards. Most used examples are found off card
so values are given for these.

Type of 1862
1882-1902 Wmk. 2 Perf. 14
36b	A1	2c carmine ('84)	50.00	2.75
37	A1	2c green ('00)	32.50	1.10
38	A1	4c slate ('96)	16.00	2.75
39	A1	4c car rose ('00)	22.50	1.25
40	A1	5c ultramarine	36.00	1.25
41	A1	5c yellow ('00)	27.50	8.00
42	A1	10c lilac	925.00	20.00
43	A1	10c green	160.00	2.25
a.		10c blue green	2,000.	45.00
44	A1	10c vio, red ('91)	37.50	2.25
45	A1	10c ultra ('00)	57.50	2.50
46	A1	12c blue ('02)	55.00	67.50
47	A1	30c gray grn ('91)	100.00	27.50
a.		30c yellow green	150.00	45.00
48	A1	30c brown ('01)	60.00	27.50
		Nos. 36b-48 (13)	1,499.	154.85

No. 47 has fugitive ink. Both colors will turn
dull green upon soaking.
The 2c rose, perf 12, is a proof.

No. 28 Surcharged in Black

1880   Wmk. 1   Perf. 15½x15

50	A4	12c on $10 rose	1,000.	375.00

Surcharged in Black

1885-91   Wmk. 2   Perf. 14

51	A1	20c on 30c ver	200.00	7.00
a.		Double surcharge		—
52	A1	20c on 30c gray grn ('91)	125.00	175.00
a.		20c on 30c yellow green	200.00	200.00
53	A1	50c on 48c brown	450.00	45.00
54	A1	50c on 48c lil ('91)	300.00	325.00
55	A1	$1 on 96c ol gray	825.00	90.00
56	A1	$1 on 96c vio, red ('91)	900.00	400.00

For overprints see Nos. 61-63.

Types of 1874 and

A7

1890-1902   Wmk. 2   Perf. 14

56A	A7	2c dull purple	150.00	30.00

Wmk. 1

57	A2	$2 gray green	475.00	300.00
58	A3	$3 lilac ('02)	625.00	525.00
59	A4	$10 gray grn ('92)	12,000.	12,000.

Due to a shortage of 2c postage stamps, No. 56A was authorized for postal use December 24-30, 1890.

Fake postmarks are known on No. 59. Beware also of fiscal cancels altered to resemble postal cancels.

For surcharge see No. 68.

Type of 1874 Surcharged in Black

1891, Jan. 1   Wmk. 2

60	A4	$5 on $10 vio, red	360.00	115.00

Nos. 36b, 44 Overprinted

a   b

1891, Jan. 1

60A	A1	2c carmine (a)	1,100.	425.00
60B	A1	2c carmine (b)	1,050.	425.00
a.		Inverted overprint		6,500.
60C	A1	10c vio, red (a)	1,900.	475.00

Nos. 60A-60C were overprinted for use as fiscal stamps, "S.O." denoting "Stamp Office" and "S.D." denoting "Stamp Duty." They were authorized for postal use Jan. 1, 1891-1893. Examples of No. 60A with "O" changed to "D" in manuscript are known.

Forged overprints are often encountered. Expertization is required.

Nos. 52, 54 and 56 Handstamped with Chinese characters

61	A1	(g) 20c on 30c	45.00	8.50
a.		20c on 30c dull green	62.50	11.00
b.		"20 CENTS" double		
62	A1	(h) 50c on 48c	95.00	6.25
63	A1	(i) $1 on 96c	525.00	27.50

No. 61 may be found with Chinese character 2mm, 2½mm or 3mm high.

The handstamped Chinese surcharges on Nos. 61-63 exist in several varieties including inverted, double, triple, misplaced, omitted and (on #63) on both front and back.

Nos. 43 and 20 Surcharged

1891

64	A1	7c on 10c green	82.50	9.00
a.		Double surcharge	6,500.	1,500.

Wmk. 1

65	A1	14c on 30c violet	190.00	80.00

Beware of faked varieties.

No. 36 Overprinted in Black

1891, Jan. 22   Wmk. 2

66	A1	2c rose	575.00	140.00
a.		Double overprint	17,500.	13,000.
b.		"U" of "JUBILEE" shorter	800.00	200.00
c.		"J" of "JUBILEE" shorter	800.00	200.00
d.		Tall "K" in "KONG"	1,300.	500.00

50th anniversary of the colony. Beware of faked varieties.

No. 26 Surcharged (Chinese Handstamped)

1897, Sept.   Wmk. 1   Perf. 15½x15

67	A2	$1 on $2 sage green	300.00	150.00
a.		Without Chinese surcharges	5,000.	4,500.
b.		Diagonal Chinese surcharge omitted		33,000.

On No. 57   Perf. 14

68	A2	$1 on $2 gray green	300.00	150.00
a.		Without Chinese surcharges	2,100.	2,000.
b.		Diagonal Chinese surcharge omitted		16,000.
c.		Vertical Chinese surcharge omitted		

Handstamp Surcharged in Black

1898   Wmk. 2

69	A1	10c on 30c gray grn	60.00	87.50
a.		Large Chinese surcharge	1,600.	1,600.
b.		Without Chinese surcharge	600.00	1,200.
70	A1	$1 on 96c black	200.00	32.50
a.		Without Chinese surcharge	3,000.	4,000.

The Chinese surcharge is added separately. See notes below Nos. 61-63. The small Chinese surcharge is illustrated.

King Edward VII — A10

1903   Wmk. 2

71	A10	1c brown & lilac	2.25	.55
72	A10	2c gray green	16.00	1.60
73	A10	4c violet, red	20.00	.45
74	A10	5c org & gray grn	17.50	10.00
75	A10	8c violet & black	12.00	1.75
76	A10	10c ultra & lil, bl	50.00	2.00
77	A10	12c red vio & gray grn, yel	10.00	5.25
78	A10	20c org brn & blk	52.50	4.00
79	A10	30c blk & gray grn	57.50	24.00
80	A10	50c red vio & gray green	60.00	50.00
81	A10	$1 olive grn & lil	100.00	25.00
82	A10	$2 scar & black	325.00	300.00
83	A10	$3 dp blue & blk	400.00	400.00
84	A10	$5 blue grn & lil	550.00	550.00
85	A10	$10 org & blk, bl	1,300.	900.00
		Nos. 71-85 (15)	2,972.	1,874.

1904-11   Wmk. 3
Ordinary or Chalky Paper

86	A10	1c brown ('10)	6.75	1.10
a.		Booklet pane of 4		
87	A10	2c gray green	16.00	2.25
88	A10	2c deep green	32.50	1.90
a.		Booklet pane of 4		
b.		Booklet pane of 12		
89	A10	4c violet, red	21.00	.50
90	A10	4c carmine	15.00	.50
a.		Booklet pane of 4		
b.		Booklet pane of 12		
91	A10	5c org & gray grn	32.50	10.00
92	A10	6c red vio & org ('07)	27.50	5.25
93	A10	8c vio & blk ('07)	16.00	2.25
94	A10	10c ultra & lil, bl	27.50	1.50
95	A10	10c ultramarine	40.00	.50
96	A10	12c red vio & gray grn, yel ('07)	18.00	6.00
97	A10	20c org brn & blk	50.00	3.00
98	A10	20c ol grn & vio ('11)	50.00	50.00
99	A10	30c blk & gray grn	50.00	25.00
100	A10	30c org & vio ('11)	60.00	32.50
101	A10	50c red vio & gray green	90.00	12.50
102	A10	50c blk, grn ('11)	47.50	18.00
103	A10	$1 ol grn & lil	150.00	32.50
104	A10	$2 scar & black	290.00	130.00
105	A10	$2 blk & car ('10)	360.00	360.00
106	A10	$3 dp bl & blk	325.00	250.00
107	A10	$5 bl grn & lil	525.00	425.00
108	A10	$10 org & blk, bl	2,000.	1,300.
		Nos. 86-108 (23)	4,250.	2,670.

Nos. 86, 88, 90, 94 and 95 are on ordinary paper only. Nos. 92, 93, 96, 98, 100, 102, 105, 106 and 107 are on chalky paper and the others of the issue are on both papers.

The 4c, 5c, 8c, 12c 20c, 50c, $2 and $5 denominations of type A10 are expressed in colored letters or numerals and letters on a colorless background.

King George V
A11   A12

A13   A14

A15

Type I No. 117   Type II No. 128

Two Types of 25c:

I: A short vertical stroke crosses the bottom of the top Chinese character in the left label.

II: The vertical stroke is absent from the character.

1912-14   Ordinary Paper

109	A11	1c brown	4.00	.60
a.		Booklet pane of 12		
110	A11	2c deep green	11.50	.40
a.		Booklet pane of 12		
111	A12	4c carmine	6.50	.40
a.		Booklet pane of 12		
b.		Booklet pane of 4		
112	A13	6c orange	6.00	2.25
113	A12	8c gray	27.50	8.00
114	A11	10c ultramarine	37.50	.35

Chalky Paper

115	A14	12c vio, yel	9.00	10.00
116	A14	20c ol grn & vio	12.00	1.50
117	A15	25c red vio & dl vio (I) ('14)	32.50	32.50
118	A13	30c org & violet	29.00	9.00
119	A14	50c black, bl grn, white back	25.00	2.00
a.		50c black, emerald	27.50	10.00
b.		50c black, bl grn, ol back	1,400.	32.50
c.		50c black, emer, ol back	32.50	10.00
120	A11	$1 blue & vio, bl	55.00	6.00
121	A14	$2 black & red	180.00	70.00
122	A13	$3 vio & green	275.00	100.00
123	A14	$5 red & grn, grn	725.00	400.00
a.		$5 red & grn, bl grn, ol back	1,300.	375.00
124	A13	$10 blk & vio, red	675.00	95.00
		Nos. 109-124 (16)	2,110.	738.00

For overprints see British Offices in China #1-27.

1914, May   Surface-colored Paper

125	A14	12c violet, yel	10.00	18.00
126	A14	50c black, green	25.00	5.00
127	A14	$5 red & grn, grn	675.00	350.00
		Nos. 125-127 (3)	710.00	373.00

Stamp of 1912-14 Redrawn (Type II)

1919, Aug.   Chalky Paper

128	A15	25c red vio & dl vio	225.00	80.00

Types of 1912-14 Issue

1921-37   Wmk. 4   Ordinary Paper

129	A11	1c brown	1.10	.50
130	A11	2c deep green	3.50	.75
131	A11	2c gray ('37)	22.50	8.00
132	A12	3c gray ('31)	10.00	1.50
133	A12	4c rose red	5.50	1.00
134	A12	5c violet ('31)	18.00	.40
135	A12	8c gray	21.00	40.00
136	A12	8c orange	5.75	2.00
137	A11	10c ultramarine	7.50	.45

Chalky Paper

138	A14	12c vio, yel ('33)	20.00	4.00
139	A14	20c ol grn & dl vio	8.50	.40
140	A15	25c red vio & dl vio, redrawn	7.50	1.50
141	A13	30c yel & violet	12.00	1.75
142	A14	50c blk, emerald	24.00	.45
143	A11	$1 ultra & vio, bl	45.00	.60
144	A14	$2 black & red	140.00	7.50
145	A13	$3 dl vio & grn ('26)	200.00	70.00
146	A14	$5 red & grn, emer ('25)	550.00	85.00
		Nos. 129-146 (18)	1,101.	225.80

Common Design Types pictured following the introduction.

Silver Jubilee Issue
Common Design Type

1935, May 6   Engr.   Perf. 11x12

147	CD301	3c black & ultra	4.00	4.00
148	CD301	5c indigo & grn	10.00	3.00
149	CD301	10c ultra & brn	22.50	4.00
150	CD301	20c brn vio & ind	40.00	10.00
		Nos. 147-150 (4)	76.50	21.00
		Set, never hinged		200.00

Coronation Issue
Common Design Type
1937, May 12   **Perf. 11x11½**

151	CD302	4c deep green	4.00	4.00
152	CD302	15c dark carmine	8.75	4.00
153	CD302	25c deep ultra	11.25	4.50
	Nos. 151-153 (3)		24.00	12.50
	Set, never hinged		35.00	

King George VI — A16

1938-48   **Typo.**   **Perf. 14**
Ordinary Paper

154	A16	1c brown	.75	1.00
155	A16	2c gray	1.25	.25
156	A16	4c orange	2.50	3.25
157	A16	5c green	1.10	.20
157B	A16	8c brown red ('41)	1.00	2.75
c.		Imperf., pair	30,000.	
158	A16	10c violet	3.50	.60
159	A16	15c carmine	1.00	.30
159A	A16	20c gray ('46)	.60	.30
159B	A16	20c rose red ('48)	3.75	.45
160	A16	25c ultramarine	17.00	3.50
160A	A16	25c gray ol ('46)	2.25	2.75
161	A16	30c olive bister	110.00	4.00
161B	A16	30c lt ultra ('46)	3.50	.20

Chalky Paper

162	A16	50c red violet	4.50	.40
b.		Ordinary paper	32.50	.75
162C	A16	80c lilac rose ('48)	2.50	1.00
163	A16	$1 lilac & ultra	4.50	3.75
a.		Ordinary paper	8.00	17.50
163B	A16	$1 dp org & grn ('46)	27.50	1.25
c.		Ordinary paper	12.50	.35
164	A16	$2 dp org & grn	52.50	27.50
164A	A16	$2 vio & red ('46)	25.00	1.10
b.		Ordinary paper	25.00	8.25
165	A16	$5 lilac & red	40.00	50.00
165A	A16	$5 grn & vio ('46)	60.00	4.75
b.		Ordinary paper	45.00	16.00
166	A16	$10 grn & vio	325.00	130.00
166A	A16	$10 vio & ultra ('46)	110.00	20.00
b.		Ordinary paper	80.00	50.00
	Nos. 154-166A (23)		799.70	259.30
	Set, never hinged		1,200.	

Coarse Impressions
Ordinary Rough-Surfaced Paper
1941-46   **Perf. 14½x14**

155a	A16	2c gray	1.50	6.00
156a	A16	4c orange ('46)	3.00	3.25
157a	A16	5c green	1.75	5.25
158a	A16	10c violet	6.00	.20
161a	A16	30c dull olive bister	18.00	9.50
162a	A16	50c red lilac	20.00	2.00
	Nos. 155a-162a (6)		50.25	26.20
	Set, never hinged		85.00	

A17

1938, Jan. 11   **Wmk. 4**

167	A17	5c green	50.00	20.00

No. 167 is a revenue stamp officially authorized to be sold and used for postal purposes. Used Jan. 11-20, 1938. The used price is for the stamp on cover. CTO covers exist.

Street Scene — A18

Hong Kong Bank — A22

Liner and Junk — A19

University of Hong Kong — A20

Harbor — A21

China Clipper and Seaplane A23

Perf. 13½x13, 13x13½
1941, Feb. 26   **Engr.**   **Wmk. 4**

168	A18	2c sepia & org	3.50	2.00
169	A19	4c rose car & vio	4.00	4.50
170	A20	5c yel grn & blk	1.75	.35
171	A21	15c red & black	4.00	2.50
172	A22	25c dp blue & dk brn	9.00	8.00
173	A23	$1 brn org & brt bl	29.00	12.00
	Nos. 168-173 (6)		51.25	29.35
	Set, never hinged		100.00	

Centenary of British rule.

> Catalogue values for unused stamps in this section, from this point to the end of the section, are for Never Hinged items.

Peace Issue

Phoenix Rising from Flames A24

1946, Aug. 29   **Perf. 13x12½**

174	A24	30c car & dp blue	4.00	2.00
175	A24	$1 car & brown	6.25	1.00
	Set, hinged		5.00	

Return to peace after WWII.

Silver Wedding Issue
Common Design Types
Perf. 14x14½
1948, Dec. 22   **Photo.**   **Wmk. 4**

178	CD304	10c purple	3.50	1.00

Engr.; Name Typo.
Perf. 11½x11

179	CD305	$10 rose car	400.00	110.00
	Set, hinged		275.00	

UPU Issue
Common Design Types
Engr.; Name Typo. on 20c & 30c
1949, Oct. 10   **Perf. 13½, 11x11½**

180	CD306	10c violet	4.25	1.00
181	CD307	20c deep car	18.00	4.50
182	CD308	30c indigo	15.00	4.25
183	CD309	80c red violet	35.00	10.00
	Nos. 180-183 (4)		72.25	19.75
	Set, hinged		25.00	

Coronation Issue
Common Design Type
1953, June 2   **Engr.**   **Perf. 13½x13**

184	CD312	10c purple & black	7.00	.35
	Hinged		2.50	

Elizabeth II A25

Arms of University A26

1954-60   **Typo.**   **Perf. 13½x14**

185	A25	5c orange	1.75	.20
a.		Imperf., pair	1,350.	
186	A25	10c violet	2.50	.20
187	A25	15c green	4.50	1.00
188	A25	20c brown	6.00	.30
189	A25	25c rose red	4.75	3.00
190	A25	30c gray	5.00	.20
191	A25	40c blue	6.00	.40
192	A25	50c red violet	6.50	.25
193	A25	65c lt gray ('60)	21.00	13.00
194	A25	$1 org & green	8.00	.20
195	A25	$1.30 bl & ver ('60)	26.50	.85
196	A25	$2 violet & red	13.50	.50
197	A25	$5 green & vio	90.00	2.50
198	A25	$10 violet & ultra	75.00	10.00
	Nos. 185-198 (14)		271.00	32.60
	Set, hinged		125.00	

Nos. 185-187 are on ordinary paper; Nos. 188-198 on chalky paper.

Perf. 11½x12
1961, Sept. 11   **Photo.**   **Wmk. 314**

199	A26	$1 bl, blk, red, grn & gold	8.00	2.00
a.		Gold omitted	2,000.	

University of Hong Kong, 50th anniv.

Queen Victoria Statue, Victoria Park, Hong Kong — A27

Queen Elizabeth II — A28

1962, May 4   **Perf. 14**

200	A27	10c car rose & black	.65	.20
201	A27	20c blue & black	2.00	2.25
202	A27	50c bister & black	4.50	.45
	Nos. 200-202 (3)		7.15	2.90

1st postage stamps of Hong Kong, cent.

Wmk. 314 Upright
1962, Oct. 4   **Photo.**   **Perf. 14½x14**
Size: 17x21mm

203	A28	5c red orange	.80	.60
a.		Booklet pane of 4	3.00	
204	A28	10c purple	1.50	.20
a.		Booklet pane of 4	6.50	
205	A28	15c green	3.50	2.75
206	A28	20c red brown	2.50	.20
a.		Booklet pane of 4	13.00	
207	A28	25c lilac rose	3.25	4.00
208	A28	30c dark blue	2.50	.20
209	A28	40c Prus green	4.00	.70
210	A28	50c crimson	1.75	.30
a.		Booklet pane of 4	25.00	
211	A28	65c ultramarine	18.50	2.00
212	A28	$1 dark brown	19.00	.40

Perf. 14x14½
Size: 25½x30½mm
Portrait in Natural Colors

213	A28	$1.30 sky blue	5.00	.20
a.		Ocher (sash) omitted	42.50	
b.		Yellow omitted	57.50	
214	A28	$2 fawn	7.00	1.00
a.		Yellow and ocher (sash) omitted	225.00	
b.		Yellow omitted	57.50	
215	A28	$5 orange	17.50	1.50
a.		Ocher (sash) omitted	57.50	
216	A28	$10 green	30.00	3.00
217	A28	$20 violet blue	150.00	27.50
	Nos. 203-217 (15)		266.80	44.55

1966-72   **Wmk. 314 Sideways**

203b	A28	5c ('67)	.60	.60
204b	A28	10c ('67)	.75	.50
205a	A28	15c ('67)	2.00	2.00
206b	A28	20c	1.75	2.50
207a	A28	25c ('67)	3.00	3.00
208a	A28	30c ('70)	10.00	4.00
209a	A28	40c ('67)	4.00	3.00
210b	A28	50c ('67)	3.00	2.00
211a	A28	65c ('67)	8.00	2.75
212a	A28	$1 ('67)	18.50	1.75
213c	A28	$1.30 ('72)	11.00	2.75
214c	A28	$2 ('71)	18.00	3.00

215b	A28	$5 ('71)	75.00	24.50
217a	A28	$10 ('72)	200.00	75.00
	Nos. 203b-217a (14)		355.60	127.35

Freedom from Hunger Issue
Common Design Type
Perf. 14x14½
1963, June 4   **Photo.**   **Wmk. 314**

218	CD314	$1.30 green	57.50	8.75

Red Cross Centenary Issue
Common Design Type
1963, Sept. 2   **Litho.**   **Perf. 13**

219	CD315	10c black & red	4.50	.35
220	CD315	$1.30 ultra & red	35.00	8.50

ITU Issue
Common Design Type
1965, May 17   **Perf. 11x11½**

221	CD317	10c red lil & yel	4.50	.30
222	CD317	$1.30 apple grn & turq blue	27.50	4.25

Intl. Cooperation Year Issue
Common Design Type
1965, Oct. 25   **Perf. 14½**

223	CD318	10c blue grn & cl	3.50	.35
224	CD318	$1.30 lt violet & grn	22.50	3.75

Churchill Memorial Issue
Common Design Type
1966, Jan. 24   **Photo.**   **Perf. 14**
Design in Black, Gold and Carmine Rose

225	CD319	10c bright blue	3.00	.25
226	CD319	50c green	3.50	.40
227	CD319	$1.30 brown	24.00	3.50
228	CD319	$2 violet	37.50	8.00
	Nos. 225-228 (4)		68.00	12.15

WHO Headquarters Issue
Common Design Type
1966, Sept. 20   **Litho.**   **Perf. 14**

229	CD322	10c multicolored	3.25	.30
230	CD322	$1.30 multicolored	11.00	2.00

UNESCO Anniversary Issue
Common Design Type
1966, Dec. 1   **Litho.**   **Perf. 14**

231	CD323	10c "Education"	4.00	.25
232	CD323	50c "Science"	20.00	1.25
233	CD323	$2 "Culture"	65.00	18.50
	Nos. 231-233 (3)		89.00	20.00

Three Rams' Heads A29

Lunar New Year: $1.30, Three rams.

1967, Jan. 17   **Photo.**   **Perf. 14**

234	A29	10c red, citron & grn	2.50	.60
235	A29	$1.30 red, cit & brt grn	37.50	11.00

Outline of Telephone with Map of South East Asia and Australia A30

1967, Mar. 30   **Photo.**   **Perf. 12½**

236	A30	$1.30 dk red & blue	21.00	4.75

Completion of the Hong Kong-Malaysia link of the South East Asia Commonwealth Cable, SEACOM.

Monkeys A31

Lunar New Year: $1.30, Two monkey families.

1968, Jan. 23   Wmk. 314   Perf. 14
237 A31 10c crim, blk & gold   2.25   .50
238 A31 $1.30 crim, blk & gold   37.50   8.50

Liner and
New Sea
Terminal
A32

Seacraft: 20c, Pleasure launch and sailing
cruiser. 40c, Vehicle ferry. 50c, Passenger
ferry. $1, Sampan. $1.30, Junk.

Perf. 13x12½
1968, Apr. 24   Litho.   Unwmk.
239 A32 10c multicolored   2.25   .25
240 A32 20c sky blue, bis &
                black   3.75   .80
241 A32 40c org, rose lil &
                black   11.00   9.00
242 A32 50c brt red, emer
                & black   7.50   .65
243 A32 $1 yel, cop red &
                black   17.50   5.50
244 A32 $1.30 dk bl, brt pink
                & black   47.50   5.50
       Nos. 239-244 (6)   89.50 21.70

Bauhinia
Blakeana — A33

Perf. 14x14½
1968, Sept. 25   Photo.   Wmk. 314
245 A33 65c shown   11.00   .60
  a.   Wmkd. sideways ('72)   55.00 17.50
246 A33 $1 Coat of Arms   11.00   .55
  a.   Wmkd. sideways ('71)   11.00   2.50

Human
Rights
Flame and
"Lamp of
Life"
A34

1968, Nov. 20   Litho.   Perf. 13½
247 A34 10c green, org & blk   2.25   .85
248 A34 50c magenta, yel & blk   6.50   2.50

International Human Rights Year.

Cock
A35

Design: $1.30, Cock, vert.

Perf. 13x13½, 13½x13
1969, Feb. 11   Photo.   Unwmk.
249 A35 10c brown, blk, org
                & red   8.00   1.25
  a.   Red omitted   350.00
250 A35 $1.30 ocher, blk, org
                & red   70.00 15.00

Lunar New Year, Feb. 17, 1969.

Chinese
University
Seal — A36

1969, Aug. 26   Unwmk.   Perf. 13
251 A36 40c multicolored   9.00   4.00

Chinese University of Hong Kong, founded
1963.

Radar,
Globe and
Satellite
A37

Perf. 14x14½
1969, Sept. 24   Photo.   Wmk. 314
252 A37 $1 scar, blk, sil & bl   27.50   5.50

Opening of the satellite earth station (connected through the Indian Ocean satellite
Intelsat III) on Stanley Peninsula, Hong Kong.

Chow — A38   Emblem — A39

Lunar New Year (Year of the Dog): $1.30,
Chow, horiz.

1970, Jan. 28   Perf. 14
253 A38 10c black & multi   5.00   .60
254 A38 $1.30 green & multi   70.00 13.00

Perf. 13½x13, 13x13½
1970, Mar. 14   Litho.   Wmk. 314
25c, Emblem and Chinese junks, horiz.
255 A39 15c multicolored   .90   .90
256 A39 25c multicolored   2.00   2.00

EXPO '70 Intl. Exposition, Osaka, Japan,
Mar. 15-Sept. 13.

"A Compassionate Ship on the Bitter
Sea" — A40

1970, Apr. 9   Photo.   Perf. 14
257 A40 10c yel green & multi   1.25   .30
258 A40 50c scarlet & multi   4.50   1.75

Centenary of the Tung Wah Group of Hospitals (including schools and various charitable
organizations).

A.P.Y.
Emblem — A41

1970, Aug. 5   Litho.   Wmk. 314
259 A41 10c yellow & multi   1.50   .65

Issued for Asian Productivity Year.

Boar
A42

Perf. 13x13½
1971, Jan. 20   Photo.   Unwmk.
260 A42 10c yel grn, gold &
                black   6.00   1.25
261 A42 $1.30 vio, gold & blk   40.00 12.00

Lunar New Year.

Scout Emblem and "60" — A43

Perf. 14x14½
1971, July 23   Litho.   Wmk. 314
262 A43 10c red, yellow &
                black   .90   .20
263 A43 50c blue, emer &
                black   4.25   1.25
264 A43 $2 vio, lil rose & blk   25.00 12.00
       Nos. 262-264 (3)   30.15 13.45

60th anniversary of Hong Kong Boy Scouts.

Festival   Symbolic Flower
Emblem   A45
A44

Festival of Hong Kong: 50c, Dancers, horiz.

1971, Nov. 2   Perf. 14
265 A44 10c lilac & orange   1.75   .20

Perf. 14½
266 A45 50c lilac & multi   3.50   1.10
267 A45 $1 lilac & multi   10.00   7.75
       Nos. 265-267 (3)   15.25   9.05

Rats
A46

Perf. 13½x13
1972, Feb. 8   Photo.   Unwmk.
268 A46 10c black, red &
                gold   4.00   .60
269 A46 $1.30 black, gold &
                red   37.50 13.50

Lunar New Year.

Cross Harbor Tunnel Entrance — A47

Perf. 14x14½
1972, Oct. 20   Litho.   Wmk. 314
270 A47 $1 multicolored   7.50   2.25

Inauguration of Cross Harbor Tunnel linking
Victoria and Kowloon.

Silver Wedding Issue, 1972
Common Design Type

Design: Queen Elizabeth II, Prince Philip,
phoenix and dragon.

1972, Nov. 20   Photo.   Perf. 14x14½
271 CD324 10c citron & multi   1.10   .20
272 CD324 50c gray & multi   1.00   1.50

Ox
A48

Lunar New Year: 10c, Ox, vert.

1973, Feb. 3   Perf. 14
273 A48 10c dk brown & red   3.50   .60
274 A48 $1.30 dk brn, yel & org 10.00   8.00

Elizabeth II — A49

**Wmk. 314 Upright; Sideways (15c,
30c, 40c)**
1973, June 12   Photo.   Perf. 14½x14
Size: 20x24mm
275 A49 10c orange   1.00   .60
  d.   Watermark sideways (coil) 1.75   1.75
276 A49 15c olive green   8.00   8.00
277 A49 20c bright purple   1.75   .30
278 A49 25c deep brown   12.50   8.00
279 A49 30c ultramarine   1.10   .90
280 A49 40c blue green   3.25   3.25
281 A49 50c red   1.50   .60
282 A49 65c dp bister   16.50 12.50
283 A49 $1 dk slate green   2.50   .75

Perf. 14x14½
Wmk. 314 Sideways
Size: 28x32mm
284 A49 $1.30 dk pur & yel   7.75   .75
285 A49 $2 dp brn & lt grn   9.00   1.25
286 A49 $5 dk vio bl &
                rose   14.00   3.50

Photo. & Embossed
287 A49 $10 dk sl green &
                pink   20.00   9.00
288 A49 $20 black & rose   32.50 32.50
       Nos. 275-288 (14)   131.35 81.75

1975-78   Wmk. 373   Perf. 14½x14
Size: 20x24mm
275a A49 10c orange   .50   .30
  c.   Booklet pane of 4 ('76) 2.00
276a A49 15c olive green   17.50 13.00
  c.   Booklet pane of 4   70.00
277a A49 20c bright purple   .50   .20
  c.   Booklet pane of 4 ('76) 2.00
278a A49 25c deep brown   20.00 17.50
279a A49 30c ultramarine   .75   .70
280a A49 40c blue green   1.25   1.25
281a A49 50c red   2.75   .75
  c.   Booklet pane of 4   11.00
           Complete booklet, 2 #275c,
           276c, 2 #277c, 281c   90.00
282a A49 65c deep bister   22.50 12.50
283a A49 $1 dark slate green   3.50   1.00

Perf. 14x14½
Size: 28x32mm
284a A49 $1.30 dark purple &
                yel   3.00   .90
285a A49 $2 dp brn & lt grn   5.00   1.60
286a A49 $5 dk vio bl & rose
                ('78)   12.50   3.00
287a A49 $10 dk sl grn & pink
                ('78)   14.50   7.50
288a A49 $20 black & rose
                ('78)   17.50 14.00
       Nos. 275a-288a (14)   121.75 74.20

No. 288a exists imperf. Value, pair $750.
See Nos. 316-327.

Princess Anne's Wedding Issue
Common Design Type
Wmk. 314
1973, Nov. 14   Litho.   Perf. 14
289 CD325 50c ocher & multi   .75   .20
290 CD325 $2 lilac & multi   2.50   2.00

Chinese Character "Hong" — A50

Designs: 50c, "Kong." $1, "Festival."

1973, Nov. 23 Litho. Perf. 14½x14
291	A50	10c red & green	.60 .20
292	A50	50c plum & red	2.50 1.00
293	A50	$1 emerald & plum	5.50 4.00
		Nos. 291-293 (3)	8.60 5.20

Festival of Hong Kong 1973.

Tiger A51

Lunar New Year: $1.30, Tiger, vert.

Perf. 14½x14, 14x14½
1974, Jan. 8   Wmk. 314
294	A51	10c green & multi	3.00 .50
295	A51	$1.30 lilac & multi	13.00 12.00

Chinese Opera Mask — A52

Designs: Chinese opera masks.

1974, Feb. 1 Photo. Perf. 12x12½
296	A52	10c black, red & org	.60 .25
297	A52	$1 multicolored	6.00 4.50
298	A52	$2 black, org & gold	12.00 9.50
a.		Souvenir sheet of 3, #296-298, perf. 14x13	65.00 55.00
		Nos. 296-298 (3)	18.60 14.25

Hong Kong Arts Festival.

Carrier Pigeons A53

Cent. of UPU: 50c, Symbolic globe in envelope. $2, Hands holding letters.

1974, Oct. 9   Litho.   Perf. 14
299	A53	10c blue, grn & blk	.50 .20
a.		Unwatermarked	35.00
300	A53	50c magenta & multi	2.25 .40
301	A53	$2 violet & multi	5.50 4.00
		Nos. 299-301 (3)	8.25 4.60

Rabbit A54

Lunar New Year: $1.30, Two rabbits.

1975, Feb. 5   Wmk. 314   Perf. 14
302	A54	10c silver & red	1.50 1.00
a.		Unwatermarked	1.60 1.00
303	A54	$1.30 gold & green	7.75 7.75
a.		Unwatermarked	8.00 11.00

Queen Elizabeth II, Prince Philip, Hong Kong Arms — A55

Wmk. 373
1975, Apr. 30   Litho.   Perf. 13½
304	A55	$1.30 blue & multi	3.50 1.50
305	A55	$2 yellow & multi	4.75 4.50

Royal Visit 1975.

Mid-Autumn Festival — A56

Brown Laughing Thrush — A57

Abstract Designs: $1, Dragon Boat Festival (boats). $2, Tin Hau Festival (ships with flags).

1975, July 31   Unwmk.   Perf. 14
306	A56	50c rose lil & multi	3.00 .75
307	A56	$1 brt grn & multi	11.00 2.75
308	A56	$2 orange & multi	32.50 11.00
a.		Souv. sheet of 3, #306-308	125.00 65.00
		Nos. 306-308 (3)	46.50 14.50

Hong Kong Festivals, 1975.

1975, Oct. 29   Litho.   Wmk. 373

Birds: $1.30, Chinese bulbul. $2, Black-capped kingfisher.

309	A57	50c lt blue & multi	2.75 .75
310	A57	$1.30 pink & multi	11.00 6.00
311	A57	$2 yellow & multi	19.50 12.50
		Nos. 309-311 (3)	33.25 19.25

Dragon A58

Lunar New Year: $1.30, like 20c, pattern reversed.

1976, Jan. 21   Litho.   Perf. 14½
312	A58	20c gold, pur & lilac	1.25 .50
313	A58	$1.30 gold, red & grn	8.00 3.50

Queen Elizabeth Type of 1973
Wmk. 373 (#320-323), Unwmkd.
1976-81   Photo.   Perf. 14½x14
Size: 20x24mm
316	A49	20c bright purple	3.50 1.25
318	A49	30c ultramarine	8.00 2.25
320	A49	60c lt violet ('77)	1.75 1.75
321	A49	70c yellow ('77)	1.75 .75
322	A49	80c brt magenta ('77)	2.25 2.25
323	A49	90c sepia ('81)	9.00 2.25

Size: 28x32mm
Perf. 14x14½
324	A49	$2 dp brn & lt grn	10.50 4.00
325	A49	$5 dk vio bl & rose	14.00 7.50

Photo. & Embossed
326	A49	$10 dk sl grn & pink	90.00 40.00
327	A49	$20 black & rose	175.00 60.00
		Nos. 316-327 (10)	315.75 122.00

"60" and Girl Guides Emblem A59

$1.30, "60," tents and Girl Guides emblem.

1976, Apr. 23   Wmk. 314   Perf. 14½
328	A59	20c silver & multi	1.25 .25
329	A59	$1.30 silver & multi	6.50 4.50

60th anniv. of Hong Kong Girl Guides.

"Postal Services" (in Chinese) — A60

Designs: $1.30, General Post Office, 1911-1976. $2, New G.P.O., 1976.

1976, Aug. 11   Litho.   Wmk. 373
330	A60	20c gray, green & black	.90 .20
331	A60	$1.30 gray, red & black	4.00 1.75
332	A60	$2 gray, yel & black	7.00 4.00
		Nos. 330-332 (3)	11.90 5.95

Opening of new GPO building.

Snake A61

Lunar New Year: $1.30, Snake & branch face left.

1977, Jan. 6   Perf. 13½
333	A61	20c multicolored	.90 .25
334	A61	$1.30 multicolored	5.75 4.00

Queen Dotting Eye of Dragon, 1975 Visit — A62

20c, Presentation of the orb. $2, Orb, vert.

1977, Feb. 7   Litho.
335	A62	20c multicolored	.60 .25
336	A62	$1.30 multicolored	1.50 1.00
337	A62	$2 multicolored	2.00 1.50
		Nos. 335-337 (3)	4.10 2.75

25th anniv. of the reign of Elizabeth II.

Streetcars — A63

Designs: 60c, Star ferryboat. $1.30, Funicular railway. $2, Junk and sampan.

1977, June 30   Wmk. 373   Perf. 13½
338	A63	20c multicolored	.70 .20
339	A63	60c multicolored	1.75 1.75
340	A63	$1.30 multicolored	3.25 2.25
341	A63	$2 multicolored	3.75 3.25
		Nos. 338-341 (4)	9.45 7.45

Tourist publicity.

Buttercup Orchid — A64

1977, Oct. 12   Litho.   Perf. 14

$1.30, Lady's-slipper. $2, Susan orchid.
342	A64	20c blue & multi	1.50 .35
343	A64	$1.30 yellow & multi	4.50 1.75
344	A64	$2 green & multi	7.50 4.50
		Nos. 342-344 (3)	13.50 6.60

Horse and Chinese Character "Ma" — A65

1978, Jan. 26   Litho.   Perf. 14½
345	A65	20c multicolored	.75 .20
346	A65	$1.30 multicolored	5.00 4.50

Lunar New Year.

Elizabeth II — A66

1978, June 2   Litho.   Perf. 14x14½
347	A66	20c carmine & dk blue	.50 .20
348	A66	$1.30 dk blue & carmine	1.75 1.75

25th anniv. of coronation of Elizabeth II.

Boy and Girl A67

Design: $1.30, Ring-around-a-rosy.

1978, Nov. 8   Wmk. 373   Perf. 14½
349	A67	20c multicolored	.25 .20
350	A67	$1.30 multicolored	1.50 1.00

Centenary of Po Leung Kuk, society for help and education of orphans and poor children.

Electronics — A68

Industries: $1.30, Toy (bear and drum). $2, Garment (mannequins).

1979, Jan. 9   Litho.   Perf. 14½
351	A68	20c multicolored	.30 .20
352	A68	$1.30 multicolored	1.10 1.00
353	A68	$2 multicolored	1.25 1.25
		Nos. 351-353 (3)	2.65 2.45

Precis Orithya — A69

Butterflies: $1, Graphium sarpedon. $1.30, Heliophorus epicles phoenicoparyphus. $2, Danaus genutia.

1979, June 20   Photo.   Unwmk.
354	A69	20c multicolored	1.10 .25
355	A69	$1 multicolored	2.00 .85
356	A69	$1.30 multicolored	2.25 1.90
357	A69	$2 multicolored	2.50 2.50
		Nos. 354-357 (4)	7.85 5.50

Cross
Section
of
Station
A70

Mass Transit Railroad: $1.30, Front, rear
and side views of train. $2, Map of routes.

1979, Oct. 1　　Litho.　　Perf. 13½
358	A70	20c multicolored	.50	.20
359	A70	$1.30 multicolored	1.75	.55
360	A70	$2 multicolored	2.25	2.50
		Nos. 358-360 (3)	4.50	3.25

Ching Chung Koon Temple, Tuen
Mun — A71

Rural Architecture: 20c, Tsui Shing Lau
Pagoda, Sheung Cheung Wai, vert. $1.30, Vil-
lage house, Sai O.

Perf. 13x13½, 13½x13
1980, May 14　Litho.　Wmk. 373
361	A71	20c multicolored	.35	.20
362	A71	$1.30 multicolored	1.40	1.10
363	A71	$2 multicolored	1.75	1.75
		Nos. 361-363 (3)	3.50	3.05

**Queen Mother Elizabeth Birthday
Issue**
Common Design Type
1980, Aug. 4　　Litho.　　Perf. 14
364	CD330	$1.30 multicolored	1.10	1.00

Botanical
Gardens — A72

1980, Nov. 12　　Litho.　　Perf. 13½
365	A72	20c shown	.30	.25
366	A72	$1 Ocean Park	.65	.35
367	A72	$1.30 Kowloon Park	.75	.75
368	A72	$2 Country Park	1.40	1.40
		Nos. 365-368 (4)	3.10	2.75

Epinephelus Akaara — A73

1981, Jan. 28　　Litho.　　Perf. 13½
369	A73	20c shown	.25	.20
370	A73	$1 Nemipterus vir-		
		gatus	.65	.45
371	A73	$1.30 Choerodon azurio	.80	.60
372	A73	$2 Scarus ghobban	1.25	1.25
		Nos. 369-372 (4)	2.95	2.50

Royal Wedding Issue
Common Design Type
1981, July 29　　Photo.　　Perf. 14
373	CD331	20c Bouquet	.20	.20
374	CD331	$1.30 Charles	.55	.35
375	CD331	$5 Couple	2.50	2.50
		Nos. 373-375 (3)	3.25	3.05

Public Housing
Development
A74

Various public housing developments.

1981, Oct. 14　　Litho.　　Perf. 13½
376	A74	20c multicolored	.25	.20
377	A74	$1 multicolored	.70	.40
378	A74	$1.30 multicolored	1.00	.65
379	A74	$2 multicolored	1.25	1.25
a.		Souvenir sheet of 4, #376-379	6.50	6.50
		Nos. 376-379 (4)	3.20	2.50

Port of
Hong
Kong
A75

Various views of Port of Hong Kong.

1982, Jan. 12　　Litho.　　Perf. 14½
380	A75	20c multicolored	.60	.25
381	A75	$1 multicolored	1.75	1.10
382	A75	$1.30 multicolored	2.00	1.60
383	A75	$2 multicolored	2.25	2.25
		Nos. 380-383 (4)	6.60	5.20

Five-banded Civet — A76

1982, May 4　　Litho.　　Perf. 14½
384	A76	20c shown	.30	.20
385	A76	$1 Pangolin	.60	.45
386	A76	$1.30 Chinese porcu-		
		pine	1.25	.85
387	A76	$5 Barking deer	3.50	3.50
		Nos. 384-387 (4)	5.65	5.00

Queen Elizabeth II
A77　　　　　A78

Perf. 14½x14
1982, Aug. 30　　Photo.　　Wmk. 373
388	A77	10c yellow & dk red	.80	.60
389	A77	20c blue vio & vio	1.00	1.00
390	A77	30c orange & pur	1.50	.30
391	A77	40c lt blue & red	1.50	.30
392	A77	50c pale grn & brn	1.50	.30
393	A77	60c gray & brt mag	2.75	2.00
394	A77	70c brt org & dk grn	2.75	.90
395	A77	80c gray ol & brn ol	2.75	3.00
396	A77	90c grnsh bl & grn	4.50	.60
397	A77	$1 brt pink & brn org	2.50	.30
398	A77	$1.30 rose vio & dk bl	4.00	.30
399	A77	$2 buff & blue	6.50	1.00

Photo. & Embossed
Perf. 14x14½
400	A78	$5 lemon & lake	8.00	2.50
401	A78	$10 brn & blk brn	9.00	5.00
402	A78	$20 lt blue & lake	15.00	15.00
403	A78	$50 gray & lake	36.00	30.00
		Nos. 388-403 (16)	100.05	63.10

Nos. 388 and 397 also issued in coils.

1985-87　　　　　　　　　Unwmk.
388a	A77	10c	.75	.75
389a	A77	20c	18.50	10.00
391a	A77	40c	1.00	1.00
392a	A77	50c	1.00	.30
393a	A77	60c	1.60	1.00
394a	A77	70c	3.50	.50
395a	A77	80c	3.75	2.75
396a	A77	90c	4.25	.40
397a	A77	$1	1.90	.40

398b	A77	$1.30	2.50	.35
398A	A77	$1.70 brt yel grn &		
		dp bl	4.25	1.50
399a	A77	$2	4.00	1.50
400a	A78	$5	9.00	3.00
401a	A78	$10	9.00	4.00
402a	A78	$20	11.00	7.00
403a	A78	$50	32.50	25.00
		Nos. 388a-403a (16)	108.50	59.55

Issued: $1.30, 6/13/86; $1.70, 9/2/86; 20c,
6/87; others, 10/10/85.

3rd Far
East and
South
Pacific
Games
for the
Disabled
A79

Perf. 14x14½
1982, Oct. 31　　Litho.　　Wmk. 373
404	A79	30c Table tennis	.50	.20
405	A79	$1 Racing	1.10	1.00
406	A79	$1.30 Basketball	3.25	1.75
407	A79	$5 Archery	5.25	5.25
		Nos. 404-407 (4)	10.10	8.20

Performing
Arts — A80

1983, Jan. 26　　Litho.　　Perf. 14½x14
408	A80	30c Dancing	.50	.20
409	A80	$1.30 Theater	2.00	1.50
410	A80	$5 Music	5.25	5.25
		Nos. 408-410 (3)	7.75	6.95

A81

1983, Mar. 14　　　　Perf. 14½x13½
411	A81	30c Aerial view	.75	.25
412	A81	$1 Liverpool Bay	1.75	1.10
413	A81	$1.30 Flag	2.00	1.00
414	A81	$5 Queen Elizabeth		
		II	4.50	4.50
		Nos. 411-414 (4)	9.00	7.10

Commonwealth Day.

Views by
Night
A82

1983, Aug. 17　　Litho.　　Perf. 14½
415	A82	30c Victoria Harbor	1.50	.75
416	A82	$1 Space Museum	4.50	2.50
417	A82	$1.30 Chinese New		
		Year Fireworks	5.50	2.50
418	A82	$5 Jumbo Restau-		
		rant	16.50	14.00
		Nos. 415-418 (4)	28.00	19.50

Royal Observatory Centenary — A83

1983, Nov. 23　　Litho.　　Perf. 14½
419	A83	40c Technical facili-		
		ties	.90	.30
420	A83	$1 Wind measure-		
		ment	2.50	1.50
421	A83	$1.30 Temperature		
		measurement	2.75	1.75
422	A83	$5 Earthquake		
		measurement	8.50	8.50
		Nos. 419-422 (4)	14.65	12.05

Training
Plane,
Dorado
A84

1984, Mar. 7　　Wmk. 373　　Perf. 13½
423	A84	40c shown	1.50	.30
424	A84	$1 Hong Kong		
		Clipper sea-		
		plane	2.75	1.75
425	A84	$1.30 Jumbo jet, Kai		
		Tak Airport	3.00	1.75
426	A84	$5 Baldwin Broth-		
		ers balloon,		
		vert.	8.50	8.50
		Nos. 423-426 (4)	15.75	12.30

Map of
Hong
Kong,
19th
Cent.
A85

Various maps.

1984, June 21　　Litho.　　Perf. 14
427	A85	40c multicolored	1.25	.35
428	A85	$1 multicolored	2.00	1.40
429	A85	$1.30 multicolored	3.25	2.00
430	A85	$5 multicolored	11.00	11.00
		Nos. 427-430 (4)	17.50	14.75

Chinese
Lanterns
A86

1984, Sept. 6　　Litho.　　Perf. 13½x13
431	A86	40c Rooster	1.25	.50
432	A86	$1 Bull	3.00	1.75
433	A86	$1.30 Butterfly	4.00	2.00
434	A86	$5 Fish	12.00	12.00
		Nos. 431-434 (4)	20.25	16.25

Jockey Club Centenary — A87

1984, Nov. 21　　Litho.　　Perf. 14½
435	A87	40c Supporting		
		health care	1.50	.50
436	A87	$1 Supporting dis-		
		abled	3.00	1.50
437	A87	$1.30 Supporting the		
		arts	4.00	2.25
438	A87	$5 Supporting		
		Ocean Park	9.00	9.00
a.		Souvenir sheet of 4, #435-438	30.00	30.00
		Nos. 435-438 (4)	17.50	13.25

Historic
Buildings
A88

Perf. 13½
1985, Mar. 14　　Unwmk.　　Litho.
439	A88	40c Hung Sing		
		Temple	1.00	.30
440	A88	$1 St. John's Ca-		
		thedral	2.00	1.75
441	A88	$1.30 Old Supreme		
		Court Building	2.50	2.00
442	A88	$5 Wan Chai Post		
		Office	7.00	7.00
		Nos. 439-442 (4)	12.50	11.05

Intl. Dragon Boat Festival
A89

Perf. 13½x13

1985, June 19	**Wmk. 373**		**Litho.**	
443	A89	40c multicolored	.75	.30
444	A89	$1 multicolored	2.25	1.50
445	A89	$1.30 multicolored	3.50	1.75
446	A89	$5 multicolored	11.00	9.00
a.		Strip of 4, #443-446	32.50	30.00
b.		Souvenir sheet of 4, #443-446, perf. 13x12½	32.50	32.50
		Nos. 443-446 (4)	17.50	12.55

Nos. 443-446 when placed together form a continuous design.

Queen Mother 85th Birthday Issue
Common Design Type

1985, Aug. 7	**Litho.**	**Perf. 14½x14**		
447	CD336	40c At Glamis Castle, age 9	.65	.25
448	CD336	$1 On balcony with Princes William and Charles	1.60	1.25
449	CD336	$1.30 Photograph by Cecil Beaton,1980	2.25	1.25
450	CD336	$5 Holding Prince Henry	5.75	5.75
		Nos. 447-450 (4)	10.25	8.50

Indigenous Flowers — A90

1985, Sept. 25	**Litho.**	**Perf. 13½**		
451	A90	40c Melastoma	2.00	.60
452	A90	50c Chinese lily	2.25	.70
453	A90	60c Grantham's camellia	2.75	1.75
454	A90	$1.30 Narcissus	3.75	1.75
455	A90	$1.70 Bauhinia	4.25	2.00
456	A90	$5 Chinese New Year flower	8.00	8.00
		Nos. 451-456 (6)	23.00	14.80

See No. 898.

Modern Architecture — A91

1985, Nov. 27		**Perf. 15**		
457	A91	50c Hong Kong Academy for Performing Arts	.80	.30
458	A91	$1.30 Exchange Square, vert.	1.50	1.00
459	A91	$1.70 Hong Kong Bank Hdqtrs., vert.	2.25	1.25
460	A91	$5 Hong Kong Coliseum	7.50	7.50
		Nos. 457-460 (4)	12.05	10.05

Halley's Comet
A92

1986, Feb. 26	**Litho.**	**Perf. 13½x13**		
461	A92	50c Comet, solar system	1.50	.25
462	A92	$1.30 Edmond Halley	2.25	1.25
463	A92	$1.70 Hong Kong, trajectory	3.50	1.50
464	A92	$5 Comet, Earth	10.00	10.00
a.		Souvenir sheet of 4, #461-464	32.50	32.50
		Nos. 461-464 (4)	17.25	13.00

Queen Elizabeth II 60th Birthday
Common Design Type

Designs: 50c, At the wedding of Cecillia Bowes-Lyon, Brompton Parish Church, 1939. $1, Most Noble Order of the Garter, service at St. George's Chapel, Windsor Castle, 1977. $1.30, State visit, 1975. $1.70, Queen Mother's 80th birthday celebration, Royal Lodge, Windsor, 1980. $5, Visiting Crown Agents' offices, 1983.

1986, Apr. 21		**Perf. 14½**		
465	CD337	50c scar, blk & sil	.50	.20
466	CD337	$1 ultra & multi	1.10	.35
467	CD337	$1.30 green & multi	1.40	.50
468	CD337	$1.70 violet & multi	1.60	.75
469	CD337	$5 rose vio & multi	5.00	5.00
		Nos. 465-469 (5)	9.60	6.80

EXPO '86, Vancouver — A93

1986, July 18	**Litho.**	**Perf. 13½**		
470	A93	50c Transportation	1.00	.30
471	A93	$1.30 Finance	1.75	1.00
472	A93	$1.70 Trade	2.75	1.50
473	A93	$5 Communications	7.50	7.50
		Nos. 470-473 (4)	13.00	10.30

Fishing Vessels
A94

1986, Sept. 24		**Litho.**		
474	A94	50c Hand-liner sampan	.90	.30
475	A94	$1.30 Stern trawler	1.75	1.25
476	A94	$1.70 Long liner junk	3.50	1.50
477	A94	$5 Junk trawler	7.50	7.50
		Nos. 474-477 (4)	13.65	10.55

19th Cent. Paintings — A95

50c, Possibly, Second puan khequa, by Spoilum. $1.30, Chinese woman, artist unknown. $1.70, Self-portrait at age 52, by Kwan Kiu Chin. $5, Possibly, Wife of a merchant, by George Chinnery.

1986, Dec. 9		**Litho.**	**Perf. 14**	
478	A95	50c multicolored	.50	.20
479	A95	$1.30 multicolored	1.60	1.25
480	A95	$1.70 multicolored	1.90	1.50
481	A95	$5 multicolored	5.25	5.25
		Nos. 478-481 (4)	9.25	8.20

New Year (Year of the Hare)
A96

Embroideries of various rabbits.

1987, Jan. 21	**Litho.**	**Perf. 13½x14**		
482	A96	50c multicolored	1.00	.30
483	A96	$1.30 multicolored	1.60	1.25
484	A96	$1.70 multicolored	2.00	1.25
485	A96	$5 multicolored	7.00	7.00
a.		Souvenir sheet of 4, #482-485	45.00	45.00
		Nos. 482-485 (4)	11.60	9.80

19th Century Paintings in the Hong Kong Museum of Art and Shanghai Banking Corp.
A97

Scenes: 50c, A Village Square, Hong Kong Island, 1838, by Auguste Borget (1809-1877). $1.30, Boat Dwellers in Kowloon Bay, 1838, by Borget. $1.70, Flagstaff House, Lt. Governor D'Aguilar's Residence, 1846, by Murdoch Bruce. $5, A View of Wellington Street, late 19th century, by C. Andrasi.

1987, Apr. 23	**Litho.**	**Perf. 14**		
486	A97	50c multicolored	1.00	.25
487	A97	$1.30 multicolored	2.50	1.40
488	A97	$1.70 multicolored	3.00	1.50
489	A97	$5 multicolored	9.00	9.00
		Nos. 486-489 (4)	15.50	12.15

Elizabeth II, Hong Kong Waterfront
A98

Queen, Natl. Landmarks
A99

Type I — Darker Shading Under Chin

Type II — Lighter Shading Under Chin

Designs: $5, Tsim Shah Tsui, Kowloon. $10, Victoria Harbor. $20, Legislative Council Building. $50, Government House.

1987, July 13	**Litho.**	**Perf. 14½x14**		
Type I				
No date inscription below design				
490	A98	10c yel grn, gray & blk	.50	.20
491	A98	40c bluish grn, lt yel & blk	1.25	.20
492	A98	50c brn org, buff & blk	1.00	.20
493	A98	60c lt blue, pale rose & blk	1.00	.20
494	A98	70c vio, pale rose & blk	1.25	.25
495	A98	80c brt rose lil, lt blue & blk	1.50	1.00
496	A98	90c pink, pale beige & blk	1.25	1.00
497	A98	$1 brt lem & blk	1.25	.40
498	A98	$1.30 rose claret, brt yel grn & blk	1.25	1.25
499	A98	$1.70 lt blue & blk	1.25	.80
500	A98	$2 yel grn, cream & blk	1.40	.70
			Perf. 14	
501	A99	$5 grn, lt grn & blk	3.50	2.00
502	A99	$10 brn, yel brn & blk	8.00	5.00
503	A99	$20 rose vio, lil & blk	17.50	10.00
504	A99	$50 sep, gray & blk	42.50	32.50
		Nos. 490-504 (15)	84.40	55.70

1988, Sept. 1				
Type II				
No date inscription below design				
490a	A98	10c	.60	.20
491a	A98	40c	1.25	.20
492a	A98	50c	1.25	.20
493a	A98	60c	1.25	.25
494a	A98	70c	1.50	1.00
495a	A98	80c	1.50	1.00
496a	A98	90c	1.50	1.00
497a	A98	$1	1.50	.45
498a	A98	$1.30	2.25	1.50
499a	A98	$1.70	1.50	1.00
500a	A98	$2	1.75	.75
501a	A99	$5	5.50	2.25
502a	A99	$10	10.00	6.00
503a	A99	$20	20.00	12.00
504a	A99	$50	45.00	35.00
		Nos. 490a-504a (15)	96.35	62.80

See Nos. 532-533, 592-593, 629.

1989, Aug. 1				
Inscribed "1989"				
490b	A98	10c	.75	1.00
491b	A98	40c	1.75	2.00
492b	A98	50c	1.25	.55
493b	A98	60c	1.60	.30
494b	A98	70c	2.00	1.60
495b	A98	80c	2.00	1.25
496b	A98	90c	1.50	1.00
497b	A98	$1	2.00	.65
498b	A98	$1.30	3.75	4.00
500b	A98	$2	2.25	.75
501b	A99	$5	5.50	2.25
502b	A99	$10	8.00	6.50
503b	A99	$20	13.50	12.00
504b	A99	$50	21.00	22.50
		Nos. 490b-504b (14)	66.85	56.35

1990				
Inscribed "1990"				
490c	A98	10c	.75	1.00
491c	A98	40c	1.75	2.00
492c	A98	50c	1.25	.55
493c	A98	60c	1.60	.30
494c	A98	70c	2.00	1.60
495c	A98	80c	2.00	1.25
496c	A98	90c	1.50	1.00
497c	A98	$1	2.00	.65
498c	A98	$1.30	3.75	4.00
500c	A98	$2	2.25	.75
501c	A99	$5	5.50	2.25
502c	A99	$10	8.00	6.50
a.		Souv. sheet of 1	110.00	
503c	A99	$20	13.50	12.00
504c	A99	$50	21.00	22.50
		Nos. 490c-504c (14)	66.85	56.35

No. 502ca was issued in conjunction with the New Zealand 1990 World Stamp Exhibition with NZ 1990 inscriptions and related design in the sheet selvage.
No. 502ca issued 8/24.

1991				
Inscribed "1991"				
490d	A98	10c	1.10	1.00
492d	A98	50c	2.00	.55
493d	A98	60c	2.50	.30
494d	A98	70c	3.25	1.60
495d	A98	80c	3.25	1.25
496d	A98	90c	2.40	1.00
497d	A98	$1	3.25	.65
499d	A98	$1.70	2.40	1.00
500d	A98	$2	3.50	.75
501d	A99	$5	8.75	2.25
502d	A99	$10	13.00	6.50
a.		Souv. sheet of 1, PHILANIPPON selvage	55.00	30.00
b.		As "a," Olympics selvage	27.50	17.50
c.		As "a," World Columbian selvage	6.25	7.00
503d	A99	$20	22.50	12.00
504d	A99	$50	22.50	22.50
		Nos. 490d-504d (13)	90.40	53.85

Nos. 502da-502dc were were issued to commemorate Hong Kong's participation in PHILANIPPON ' and the sponsorship of the 1992 Olympics Games by the Hong Kong Post Office, respectively. The selvage of each sheets bears a distinctive design and inscriptions. See No. 629.
Issued: No. 502da, 11/16; 502db, 12/4.

Nethersole Hospital, Cent. — A100

1987, Sept. 8		**Perf. 14½**		
505	A100	50c Hospital, 1887	1.25	.20
506	A100	$1.30 Patients, staff	2.75	1.40
507	A100	$1.70 Technology, 1987	3.25	1.50
508	A100	$5 Treatment	10.00	10.00
		Nos. 505-508 (4)	17.25	13.10

Natl. Flag
A101

Map of Hong Kong
A101a

Coil Stamps

1987, July 13		**Perf. 15x14**		
No date inscription below design				
509	A101	10c shown	1.75	1.75
b.		Inscribed "1990"	1.50	1.50
c.		Inscribed "1991"	1.50	1.50
510	A101a	50c blk, dull olive & lake	2.00	2.00

See Nos. 611-614.

1989, Aug. 1
Inscribed "1989"
509a	A101	10c multicolored	1.00	1.25
510a	A101a	50c multicolored	1.75	1.25

Folk Costumes — A102

1987, Nov. 18 — Perf. 13½
511	A102	50c multicolored	.65	.20
512	A102	$1.30 multi, diff.	1.75	1.25
513	A102	$1.70 multi, diff.	2.00	1.60
514	A102	$5 multi, diff.	6.25	6.25
		Nos. 511-514 (4)	10.65	9.30

New Year (Year of the Dragon) A103

1988, Jan. 27 — Litho. — Perf. 13½
515	A103	50c multicolored	.90	.30
516	A103	$1.30 multi, diff.	2.25	1.00
517	A103	$1.70 multi, diff.	2.50	1.50
518	A103	$5 multi, diff.	5.00	5.00
a.		Souv. sheet of 4, #515-518	20.00	20.00
		Nos. 515-518 (4)	10.65	7.80

See No. 838e.

Indigenous Birds — A104

Indigenous Trees — A105

1988, Apr. 20 — Perf. 13½x14
519	A104	50c White-breasted kingfisher	1.25	.30
520	A104	$1.30 Fukien niltava	2.50	1.50
521	A104	$1.70 Black kite	3.00	1.75
522	A104	$5 Pied kingfisher	6.50	6.50
		Nos. 519-522 (4)	13.25	10.05

1988, June 16 — Litho. — Perf. 13½
523	A105	50c Chinese banyan	.35	.20
524	A105	$1.30 Bauhinia blakeana	1.10	.75
525	A105	$1.70 Cotton tree	1.40	.85
526	A105	$5 Schima	3.75	3.75
a.		Souv. sheet of 4, #523-526	16.00	12.00
		Nos. 523-526 (4)	6.60	5.55

See No. 923. See note after No. 940.

Peak Tramway, Victoria, Cent. — A106

Catholic Cathedral, Caine Road, Cent. — A107

Various views of Hong Kong and the tram line.

1988, Aug. 4 — Litho. — Perf. 15
527	A106	50c multicolored	.55	.20
528	A106	$1.30 multi, diff.	1.10	1.00
529	A106	$1.70 multi, diff.	1.25	1.25
530	A106	$5 multi, diff.	3.75	3.75
a.		Souvenir sheet of 4, #527-530	12.00	12.00
		Nos. 527-530 (4)	6.65	6.20

1988, Sept. 30 — Litho. — Perf. 14
531	A107	60c multicolored	1.60	1.60

Queen and Waterfront Type of 1987
Type II

1988, Sept. 1 — Litho. — Perf. 14½x14
No date inscription below design
532	A98	$1.40 multicolored	3.00	.60
a.		Inscribed "1989"	3.00	.60
b.		Inscribed "1990"	3.00	.60
533	A98	$1.80 multicolored	4.50	.75
a.		Inscribed "1989"	4.50	.75
b.		Inscribed "1990"	4.50	.75
c.		Inscribed "1991"	4.50	.75

Issued: No. 532a, 533a, 8/1/89; 532b, 533b, 1990; No. 533c, 4/2/91.

New Year (Year of the Snake) A108

1989, Jan. 18 — Litho. — Perf. 13½x14
534	A108	60c multicolored	.75	.20
535	A108	$1.40 multi, diff.	1.75	.70
536	A108	$1.80 multi, diff.	2.00	.90
a.		Bklt. pane, 5 each #534, 536	14.00	
537	A108	$5 multi, diff.	6.25	6.25
a.		Souv. sheet of 4, #534-537	18.00	13.00
		Nos. 534-537 (4)	10.75	8.05

See No. 838g.

Cheung Chau Bun Festival — A109

1989, May 4 — Unwmk. — Perf. 13½
538	A109	60c Girl, doll	.65	.20
539	A109	$1.40 Girl	1.40	.80
540	A109	$1.80 Festival paper god	1.90	.90
541	A109	$5 Bun tower gate	4.75	4.75
		Nos. 538-541 (4)	8.70	6.65

Modern Art — A110

Hong Kong People — A111

60c, Twin, sculpture by Cheung Yee (b. 1936). $1.40, Figures, painted by Luis Chan (b. 1905). $1.80, Lotus, sculpture by Van Lau (b. 1933). $5, Zen, painted by Lui Shou-kwan (1919-1975).

1989, July 19 — Perf. 12x13
542	A110	60c multicolored	.65	.25
543	A110	$1.40 multicolored	1.50	.80
544	A110	$1.80 multicolored	1.90	.95
545	A110	$5 multicolored	4.00	4.00
		Nos. 542-545 (4)	8.05	6.00

1989, Sept. 6 — Perf. 13x14½
Designs: 60c, Youth holding autumn festival decoration, lunar year festival dragon. $1.40, Shadow boxer, horse racing. $1.80, Office and construction workers. $5, Two women, two men (ethnic multiplicity).

546	A111	60c multicolored	.75	.25
547	A111	$1.40 multicolored	2.25	.80
548	A111	$1.80 multicolored	2.50	.90
549	A111	$5 multicolored	5.25	5.25
		Nos. 546-549 (4)	10.75	7.20

See No. 762.

Construction Projects A112

1989, Oct. 5 — Unwmk. — Perf. 13
550	A112	60c University of Science and Technology	.55	.20
551	A112	70c Cultural center	.60	.40
552	A112	$1.30 Eastern Harbor Crossing	1.10	1.10
553	A112	$1.40 Bank of China	1.25	.85
554	A112	$1.80 Convention center	1.40	1.25
555	A112	$5 Light rail transit	6.50	6.50
		Nos. 550-555 (6)	11.40	10.30

Visit of the Prince and Princess of Wales — A113

Portraits and view of Hong Kong: 60c, Charles and Diana. $1.40, Diana. $1.80, Charles. $5, Couple wearing formal attire.

1989, Nov. 8 — Wmk. 340 — Perf. 14½
556	A113	60c multicolored	1.50	.30
557	A113	$1.40 multicolored	2.50	1.10
558	A113	$1.80 multicolored	1.90	1.10
559	A113	$5 multicolored	7.50	7.50
a.		Souvenir sheet of 1	17.50	15.00
		Nos. 556-559 (4)	13.40	10.00

New Year 1990 (Year of the Horse) A114

Perf. 13½x12½
1990, Jan. 23 — Unwmk.
560	A114	60c multicolored	.90	.35
561	A114	$1.40 multi, diff.	2.00	.80
562	A114	$1.80 multi, diff.	2.25	1.25
a.		Bkt. pane, 3 each 60c, $1.80	15.00	
		Complete booklet, 2 #562a	30.00	
563	A114	$5 multi, diff.	6.50	6.50
a.		Souvenir sheet of 4, #560-563	20.00	15.00
		Nos. 560-563 (4)	11.65	9.35

Examples of No. 562a ovptd. with marginal inscription were released on May 3 to publicize Stamp World London '90.
See No. 838k.

Intl. Cuisine — A115

Pollutants — A116

1990, Apr. 26 — Litho. — Perf. 12½x13
564	A115	60c Chinese	.70	.25
565	A115	70c Indian	.70	.50
566	A115	$1.30 Chinese, diff.	1.25	1.25
567	A115	$1.40 Thai	1.25	.70
568	A115	$1.80 Japanese	1.50	1.10
569	A115	$5 French	4.75	4.75
		Nos. 564-569 (6)	10.15	8.55

Wmk. 340
1990, June 5 — Litho. — Perf. 14½
570	A116	60c Air	.45	.20
571	A116	$1.40 Noise	.95	.80
572	A116	$1.80 Water	1.60	.80
573	A116	$5 Land	3.50	3.50
		Nos. 570-573 (4)	6.50	5.30

World Environment Day.

Electrification of Hong Kong, Cent. — A117

Views of Hong Kong and streetlights.

1990, Oct. 2 — Litho. — Perf. 14½
574	A117	60c 1890	.60	.20
575	A117	$1.40 1940	1.40	1.00
576	A117	$1.80 1960	1.50	1.00
577	A117	$5 1980	3.25	3.25
a.		Souvenir sheet of 2, #575, 577	7.50	7.50
		Complete booklet, 4 #577a	30.00	
		Nos. 574-577 (4)	6.75	5.45

Christmas — A118

1990, Nov. 8
578	A118	50c shown	.30	.20
579	A118	60c Dove, holly	.40	.20
580	A118	$1.40 Skyline, snowman	1.00	.45
581	A118	$1.80 Santa Claus' hat, skyscraper	1.10	.55
582	A118	$2 Children, Santa Claus	1.60	1.40
583	A118	$5 Candy cane, skyline	3.75	3.75
		Nos. 578-583 (6)	8.15	6.55

New Year 1991 (Year of the Sheep) A119

Different embroidered rams.

1991, Jan. 24 Litho. *Perf. 13½x12½*
584	A119	60c multicolored	.40	.20
585	A119	$1.40 multicolored	.95	.60
586	A119	$1.80 multicolored	1.10	.75
a.		Bklt. pane, 3 each #584, 586	7.50	
		Complete booklet, 2 #586a	15.00	
587	A119	$3.50 multicolored	3.50	3.50
a.		Souv. sheet of 4, #584-587	9.00	9.00
		Nos. 584-587 (4)	5.95	5.05

See No. 838j.

Education — A120

Perf. 13½x13
1991, Apr. 18 Litho. Unwmk.
588	A120	80c Kindergarten	.40	.25
589	A120	$1.80 Primary & secondary	1.25	.80
590	A120	$2.30 Vocational	1.50	1.25
591	A120	$5 Tertiary	4.00	4.00
		Nos. 588-591 (4)	7.15	6.30

Queen and Waterfront Type of 1987
Type II
1991, Apr. 2 Litho. *Perf. 14½x14*
592	A98	$1.20 multicolored	.45	.30
593	A98	$2.30 multicolored	.90	.60

Transportation
A121

1991, June 6 Unwmk. *Perf. 14*
594	A121	80c Rickshaw	.55	.50
595	A121	90c Bus	.75	.60
596	A121	$1.70 Ferry	1.25	1.00
597	A121	$1.80 Tram	1.50	.80
598	A121	$2.30 Mass transit railway	2.25	2.00
599	A121	$5 Hydrofoil	4.25	3.75
		Nos. 594-599 (6)	10.55	8.45

A122

Historic
Landmarks
A123

Royal postboxes with contemporary envelopes: 80c, Stamp of Type A1, Queen Victoria. $1.70, Stamps of Type A10, King Edward VII. $1.80, #149, King George V. $2.30, Stamps of Type A16, King George VI. $5, $10, Stamp of Type A98, Queen Elizabeth II.

1991, Aug. 25 Litho. *Perf. 14*
600	A122	80c multicolored	.60	.30
601	A122	$1.70 multicolored	1.25	1.00
602	A122	$1.80 multicolored	1.75	.80
603	A122	$2.30 multicolored	1.50	1.25
604	A122	$5 multicolored	4.00	3.00
		Nos. 600-604 (5)	9.10	6.35

Souvenir Sheet
605	A122	$10 multicolored	15.00	15.00

Hong Kong Post Office, 150th anniv.
See No. 792.

1991, Oct. 24
606	A123	80c Bronze Buddha	.65	.25
607	A123	$1.70 Peak Pavilion	1.10	.55
608	A123	$1.80 Clock Tower	1.25	.60
609	A123	$2.30 Catholic Cathedral	1.75	.75
610	A123	$5 Wong Tai Sin Temple	4.25	1.75
		Nos. 606-610 (5)	9.00	3.90

Map of Hong Kong Type
1992, Mar. 26 Photo. *Perf. 14½x14*
Coil Stamps
Color of Map
611	A101a	80c red lilac	.50	.40
612	A101a	90c blue	.75	.60
613	A101a	$1.80 brt yel grn	1.40	1.00
614	A101a	$2.30 red brown	1.60	1.40
		Nos. 611-614 (4)	4.25	3.40

Inscribed 1991.

New
Year
1992
(Year of
the
Monkey)
A125

Various embroidery designs of monkeys.

1992, Jan. 22 Litho. *Perf. 14½*
615	A125	80c multicolored	.35	.25
616	A125	$1.80 multicolored	.90	.50
617	A125	$2.30 multicolored	1.50	.75
a.		Bklt. pane, 3 ea #615, 617	6.25	
		Complete booklet, 2 #617a	14.00	
618	A125	$5 multicolored	3.50	3.00
a.		Sheet of 4, #615-618	10.50	12.00
		Nos. 615-618 (4)	6.25	4.50

See No. 838i.

**Queen Elizabeth II's Accession to
the Throne, 40th Anniv.**
Common Design Type
Unwmk.
1992, Feb. 11 *Perf. 14*
619	CD349	80c multicolored	.35	.20
620	CD349	$1.70 multicolored	.70	.35
621	CD349	$1.80 multicolored	.75	.40
622	CD349	$2.30 multicolored	1.10	.55
623	CD349	$5 multicolored	2.75	1.10
		Nos. 619-623 (5)	5.65	2.60

1992 Summer Olympics,
Barcelona — A126

1992, Apr. 2 Litho. *Perf. 14½*
Black Inscription
624	A126	80c Running	.40	.20
625	A126	$1.80 Swimming and javelin	1.00	.80
626	A126	$2.30 Cycling	1.50	1.25
627	A126	$5 High jump	3.00	2.50
		Nos. 624-627 (4)	5.90	4.75

Souvenir Sheet
628		Sheet of 4	7.50	7.50
a.	A126	80c red inscription	.20	.20
b.	A126	$1.80 green inscription	.60	.60
c.	A126	$2.30 blue inscription	1.00	1.00
d.	A126	$5 orange yellow inscription	1.75	1.75
e.		Sheet of 4 with inscription in margin	5.75	5.75

Issue date: No. 628e, July 25. New inscription on No. 628e sheet margin reads "To Commemorate the Opening of the 1992 Summer Olympic Games 25 July 1992" in English and Chinese.

Queen and Landmarks Type of 1987
Souvenir Sheet
Perf. 14
1992, May 22 Litho. Type II
629	A99	$10 lt violet & black	6.00	4.75

World Columbian Stamp Expo '92.

A127

Perf. 15x14
1992-97 Photo. Unwmk.
Color of Chinese Inscription
630	A127	10c pink	.30	.30
630A	A127	20c black	1.00	1.00
631	A127	50c red orange	.30	.25
632	A127	60c blue	1.50	.40
633	A127	70c red lilac	1.50	.55
634	A127	80c rose	.30	.20
635	A127	90c gray green	.30	.20
636	A127	$1 orange brown	.35	.20
637	A127	$1.10 carmine	1.00	.45
638	A127	$1.20 violet	.35	.20
639	A127	$1.30 dark blue	1.50	.65
640	A127	$1.40 apple green	1.00	.25
641	A127	$1.50 brown	1.00	.80
642	A127	$1.60 green	1.00	.45
643	A127	$1.70 ultramarine	.80	.80
644	A127	$1.80 rose lilac	1.50	.55
645	A127	$1.90 green	.80	.80
646	A127	$2 blue green	1.00	.50
647	A127	$2.10 claret	1.50	1.10
648	A127	$2.30 gray	1.50	.65
649	A127	$2.40 dark blue	2.50	1.25
650	A127	$2.50 olive green	1.00	.55
a.		Sheet of 6, 2 #647, 4 #650	9.00	
d.		Booklet pane, 2 #647, 4 #650	7.50	
651	A127	$2.60 dark brown	1.50	1.50
651A	A127	$3.10 salmon	1.25	.65
l.		Sheet of 6, 2 #642, 4 #651A	8.00	
o.		Booklet pane, 2 #642, 4 #651A	7.50	
651B	A127	$5 bright green	3.00	2.00
k.		Souvenir sheet of 1	7.00	2.00
m.		Sheet of 6, 4 #639, 2 #651B	12.50	
n.		Booklet pane, 4 #639, 2 #651B	18.00	
p.		Souvenir booklet, 2 #650d, 651Ao, 651Bn	35.00	

Size: 25x30mm
Perf. 14½x14
651C	A127	$10 brown	4.00	2.50
h.		Souvenir sheet of 1	6.00	2.50
651D	A127	$20 orange red	6.00	4.00
651E	A127	$50 gray	12.50	10.00
		Nos. 630-651E (28)	50.25	32.75

Issued: 20c, $1.30, $1.90, $2.40, 11/1/93; #651Bk, 2/18/94; #651Ch, 8/16/94; $1.10, $1.50, $2.10, $2.60, 6/1/95; $1.40, $1.60, $2.50, $3.10, 9/2/96; #651Bp, 2/14/97; others, 6/16/92.

10c, 50c, 80c, 90c, $1, $1.20, $1.30, $1.50, $1.60, $1.80, $1.90, $2.10, 2.30, $2.40, $2.50, $2.60, $3.10 also issued in coils. These have numbers on the back of every fifth stamp.

No. 651Bk issued for Hong Kong '94; No. 651Ch for Conference of Commonwealth Postal Administrations.

Nos. 650a, 651Al, 651Bm are 130x85mm.

Nos. 650d, 651Ao, 651Bn are 180x130mm and are rouletted at left.

See Nos. 656, 677-678, 683, 688, 724, 729, 738, 743, 756-757.

1993-96 Litho. *Perf. 15x14*
636a	A127	$1 Litho.	.75	.75
b.		As "a," bklt. pane of 10	7.50	
638a	A127	$1.20 Litho.	.75	.75
b.		As "a," bklt. pane of 10	7.50	
		Complete booklet, #638b	7.50	
639a	A127	$1.30 Litho.	.50	.50
b.		As "a," booklet pane of 10	5.00	
645a	A127	$1.90 Litho.	1.00	1.00
b.		As "a," bklt. pane of 10	10.00	
647a	A127	$2.10 Litho.	1.00	1.00
b.		As "a," bklt. pane of 10	10.00	
		Complete booklet, #647b	10.00	
649a	A127	$2.40 Litho.	1.00	1.00
b.		As "a," bklt. pane of 10	10.00	
650b	A127	$2.50 Litho.	1.00	1.00
c.		As "b," booklet pane of 10	10.00	
651f	A127	$2.60 Litho.	1.00	1.00
g.		As "f," bklt. pane of 10	10.00	
		Complete booklet, #651g	10.00	
651Ai	A127	$3.10 Litho.	1.00	1.00
j.		As "i," booklet pane of 10	10.00	
		Nos. 636a-651Ai (9)	8.00	8.00

Chinese characters on Nos. 636a, 638a, 645a, 647a, 649a, 651f are lighter in shade and contrast less with the background color than characters on Nos. 636, 638, 645, 647, 649, 651.

Issued: #636a, 12/14/93; #645a, 649a, 12/23/93; 647a, 651f, 6/1/95; #639a, 650a, 651Ai, 9/2/96.

Stamp Collecting — A128

Stamps and: 80c, Perforation gauge, #559, 586a. $1.80, Canceler, #66, stamp tongs. $2.30, Magnifying glass, #174, 180, 181. $5, Watermark detector, Type A1.

1992, July 15 Litho. *Perf. 14½*
652	A128	80c multicolored	.35	.20
653	A128	$1.80 multicolored	.75	.40
654	A128	$2.30 multicolored	1.10	.90
655	A128	$5 multicolored	2.25	1.75
		Nos. 652-655 (4)	4.45	3.25

See note after No. 940.

Queen Type of 1992
Souvenir Sheet
Perf. 14½x14
1992, Sept. 1 Photo. Unwmk.
Background Color
656	A127	$10 blue	6.50	6.50

Kuala Lumpur Philatelic Exhibition '92.
Size of stamp: 25x30mm.

Chinese
Opera — A129

1992, Sept. 24 Litho. *Perf. 13½*
657	A129	80c Principal male role	1.10	.30
658	A129	$1.80 Martial role	1.90	1.40
659	A129	$2.30 Principal female role	2.25	1.60
660	A129	$5 Comic role	4.25	3.25
		Nos. 657-660 (4)	9.50	6.55

Greetings Stamps — A130

1992, Nov. 19 Litho. *Perf. 14½*
661	A130	80c Hearts	.35	.20
662	A130	$1.80 Stars	.70	.35
663	A130	$2.30 Presents	.80	.80
664	A130	$5 Balloons	1.90	1.40
a.		Bklt. pane of 6, #662-664, 3 #661	6.00	5.00
		Complete booklet, 2 #664a	12.00	
		Nos. 661-664 (4)	3.75	2.75

New
Year
1993
(Year of
the
Rooster)
A131

Various embroidery designs of a rooster.

1993, Jan. 7 Litho. *Perf. 13½*
665	A131	80c multicolored	.25	.20
666	A131	$1.80 multicolored	.65	.50
667	A131	$2.30 multicolored	1.10	.90
a.		Bklt. pane, 3 ea #665, 667	4.75	
		Complete booklet, 2 #667a	9.50	
668	A131	$5 multicolored	2.75	2.75
a.		Souvenir sheet of 4, #665-668	8.50	8.50
		Nos. 665-668 (4)	4.75	4.45

See No. 838h.

Chinese String Instruments A132

1993, Apr. 14   Litho.   Perf. 14½
669 A132   80c Pipa   .40   .20
670 A132 $1.80 Erhu   .75   .70
671 A132 $2.30 Ruan   1.10 1.00
672 A132 $5 Gehu   2.25 2.00
    Nos. 669-672 (4)   4.50 3.90

Coronation of Queen Elizabeth II, 40th Anniv. A133

Different views of Hong Kong with portraits of Queen that appear on Types A25, A28, A49 and A127.

1993, June 3   Litho.   Perf. 14
673 A133   80c multicolored   .40   .20
674 A133 $1.80 multicolored   .80   .75
675 A133 $2.30 multicolored 1.25 1.10
676 A133 $5 multicolored   3.00 2.50
    Nos. 673-676 (4)   5.45 4.55

Queen Type of 1992
Souvenir Sheets
1993, July 6   Litho.   Perf. 14½x14
Background Color
677 A127 $10 brown   7.00 7.00

1993, Aug. 12   Background Color
678 A127 $10 bright blue   6.50 6.50

Hong Kong '94 Stamp Exhibition. Nos. 677-678 contain a 25x30mm stamp.
No. 678 exists with gold, silver or red overprints with the Hong Kong Philatelic Society emblem and Chinese characters. These sheets were sold only at various philatelic exhibitions.

Science and Technology — A134

Designs: 80c, Education, Hong Kong University of Science and Technology. $1.80, Public presentation, Hong Kong Science Museum. $2.30, Achievement reqognition, Governor's Award. $5, World class telecommunications, telecommunications industry.

1993, Sept. 8   Perf. 14½
679 A134   80c multicolored   .25   .20
680 A134 $1.80 multicolored   .60   .50
681 A134 $2.30 multicolored   .80   .70
682 A134 $5 multicolored   1.90 1.40
    Nos. 679-682 (4)   3.55 2.80

Queen Type of 1992
Souvenir Sheet
1993, Oct. 5   Litho.   Perf. 14½x14
Background Color
683 A127 $10 bright green   4.00 4.50

Bangkok '93 Stamp Exhibition.
No. 683 contains one 25x30mm stamp.

Goldfish A135

1993, Nov. 17   Litho.   Perf. 14½
684 A135 $1 Red calico egg-fish   .40   .35
685 A135 $1.90 Red cap oranda   .80   .50
686 A135 $2.40 Red & white fringetail   1.25 1.10
687 A135 $5 Black & gold dragon-eye   2.75 2.50
a.   Souvenir sheet of 4, #684-687   10.00 10.00
    Nos. 684-687 (4)   5.20 4.45

Queen Type of 1992
Perf. 15x14
1994, Jan. 27   Photo.   Wmk. 373
688 Souvenir booklet   20.00 20.00
a.   A127 Sheet of #630, 5 #646 6.50 6.50
b.   A127 Sheet of #643, 5 #644 6.50 6.50
c.   A127 Sheet of 5 #636, #651B 6.50 6.50

First Hong Kong stamps, 130th anniv. No. 688 sold for $38.

Year of the Dog A136

Various embroidery designs of dogs.

1994, Jan. 27   Litho.   Perf. 14½
689 A136 $1 multicolored   .35   .20
690 A136 $1.90 multicolored   .75   .50
691 A136 $2.40 multicolored 1.00   .80
a.   Bkt. pane, 3 ea #689, 691 6.50
      Complete booklet, 2 #691a 13.00
692 A136 $5 multicolored   2.25 2.00
a.   Souvenir sheet of 4, #689-692 12.00 12.00
    Nos. 689-692 (4)   4.35 3.50

See No. 838f.

Royal Hong Kong Police Force, 150th Anniv. — A137

Designs: $1, Traffic policeman, woman. $1.20, Marine policeman. $1.90, Male, female officers of 1950. $2, Policeman holding M-16. $2.40, Policemen, 1906, pre-1920. $5, Policemen, 1900.

1994, May 4   Litho.   Perf. 13½
693 A137 $1 multicolored   .35   .30
694 A137 $1.20 multicolored   .45   .35
695 A137 $1.90 multicolored   .65   .55
696 A137 $2 multicolored   1.00   .60
697 A137 $2.40 multicolored 1.50 1.25
698 A137 $5 multicolored   3.25 3.00
    Nos. 693-698 (6)   7.20 6.05

Traditional Chinese Festivals — A138

Designs: $1, Dragon Boat Festival. $1.90, Lunar New Year. $2.40, Seven Sisters Festival. $5, Mid-Autumn Festival.

1994, June 8   Litho.   Perf. 14
699 A138 $1 multicolored   .35   .25
700 A138 $1.90 multicolored   .75   .75
701 A138 $2.40 multicolored 1.25 1.25
702 A138 $5 multicolored   2.25 2.25
    Nos. 699-702 (4)   4.60 4.50

XV Commonwealth Games, Victoria, BC, Canada — A139

Unwmk.
1994, Aug. 25   Litho.   Perf. 14
703 A139 $1 Swimming   .25   .25
704 A139 $1.90 Lawn bowling   .90   .50
705 A139 $2.40 Gymnastics   1.10   .60
706 A139 $5 Weight lifting   2.00 1.25
    Nos. 703-706 (4)   4.25 2.60

Dr. James Legge (1815-97), Religious Leader, Translator — A140

1994, Oct. 5   Litho.   Perf. 14
707 A140 $1 multicolored   .65   .65

Corals — A141

1994, Nov. 17   Litho.   Perf. 14
708 A141 $1 Alcyonium   .30   .20
709 A141 $1.90 Zoanthus   .50   .45
710 A141 $2.40 Tubastrea   .65   .55
711 A141 $5 Platygyra   1.50 1.10
a.   Souv. sheet of 4, #708-711 6.50 6.50
    Nos. 708-711 (4)   2.95 2.30

See No. 916.

New Year 1995 (Year of the Boar) A142

Various embroidery designs of pigs.

1995, Jan. 17   Litho.   Perf. 14½
712 A142 $1 multicolored   .40   .35
713 A142 $1.90 multicolored   .85   .65
714 A142 $2.40 multicolored 1.10   .75
a.   Bkt. pane, 3 each #712, 714 6.00
      Complete booklet, 2 #714a 12.00
715 A142 $5 multicolored   2.50 2.50
a.   Souvenir sheet of 4, #712-715 7.50 7.50
    Nos. 712-715 (4)   4.85 4.25

See No. 838d.

Intl. Sporting Events A143

Designs: $1, Hong Kong Rugby Sevens. $1.90, China Sea Race. $2.40, Intl. Dragon Boat Races. $5, Hong Kong Intl. Horse Races.

1995, Mar. 22   Litho.   Perf. 14½
716 A143 $1 multicolored   .50   .20
717 A143 $1.90 multicolored   .80   .80
718 A143 $2.40 multicolored 1.25 1.25
719 A143 $5 multicolored   2.50 2.50
    Nos. 716-719 (4)   5.05 4.75

Traditional Buildings — A144

Litho. & Engr.
1995, May 24   Perf. 13½
720 A144 $1 Tsui Shing Lau   .40   .20
721 A144 $1.90 Sam Tung UK   .75   .45
722 A144 $2.40 Lo Wai   .85   .50
723 A144 $5 Man Shek Tong   2.00 1.10
    Nos. 720-723 (4)   4.00 2.25

Queen Type of 1992
Souvenir Sheet
1995, Aug. 25   Litho.   Perf. 14
Background Color
724 A127 $10 carmine   6.00 2.50

Singapore '95 World Stamp Exhibition. No. 724 contains one 25x30mm stamp.

Royal Hong Kong Regiment (1854-1995) — A145

$1.20, Modern Regimental Badge, vert. $2.10, Current flag. $2,60, Former flag. $5, Royal Hong Kong Defense Force, 1951 soldier's badge, vert.

1995, Aug. 16   Litho.   Perf. 14½
725 A145 $1.20 multicolored   .30   .30
726 A145 $2.10 multicolored   .50   .50
727 A145 $2.60 multicolored   .80   .80
728 A145 $5 multicolored   2.00 2.00
    Nos. 725-728 (4)   3.60 3.60

Queen Type of 1992
Souvenir Sheet
1995, Oct. 9   Litho.   Perf. 14
Background Color
729 A127 $10 brown   6.75 6.75

End of World War II, 50th anniv. No. 729 contains one 25x30mm stamp.

Hong Kong Movie Stars A146

1995, Nov. 15   Litho.   Perf. 13½
730 A146 $1.20 Bruce Lee   2.00 1.00
731 A146 $2.10 Leung Sing-Por 3.00 1.50
732 A146 $2.60 Yam Kim-Fai   4.00 2.50
733 A146 $5 Lin Dai   7.50 7.50
    Nos. 730-733 (4)   16.50 12.50

New Year 1996 (Year of the Rat) A147

Various embroidery designs of rats.

1996, Jan. 31   Litho.   Perf. 13½
734 A147 $1.20 multicolored   .30   .30
735 A147 $2.10 multicolored   .55   .55
736 A147 $2.60 multicolored   .70   .70
a.   Bkt. pane, 3 ea #734, 736 3.75
      Complete booklet, 2 #736a 7.50
737 A147 $5 multicolored   1.25 1.25
a.   Souvenir sheet of 4, #734-737 5.00 5.00
    Nos. 734-737 (4)   2.80 2.80

See No. 838a.

Queen Type of 1992
Souvenir Sheet
Unwmk.
1996, Feb. 23 **Litho.** *Perf. 14*
738 A127 $10 org & grn 7.00 7.00
Hong Kong '97 Stamp Exhibition. No. 738 contains one 25x30mm stamp.

1996 Summer Olympics, Atlanta — A148

1996, Mar. 20 **Litho.** *Perf. 13½*
739 A148 $1.20 Gymnastics .30 .30
740 A148 $2.10 Diving .70 .70
741 A148 $2.60 Running .90 .90
742 A148 $5 Basketball 1.60 1.60
Nos. 739-742 (4) 3.50 3.50

Souvenir Sheet
742A Sheet of 4, #742b-742e 4.00 4.00
f. As #742A, different sheet margin 4.75 4.75
No. 742Af shows Olympic gold medal at top of sheet margin.
Nos. 748-751 have denominations in color and Olympic rings in gold. Nos. 739-742 have denominations in black, Olympic rings in different colors. No. 742Ab-742Ae have gold Olympic rings.
No. 742f issued 7/19/96.

Queen Type of 1992
Souvenir Sheet
Unwmk.
1996, May 18 **Litho.** *Perf. 14*
743 A127 $10 brt grn & bl vio 4.00 4.00
Hong Kong '97 Stamp Exhibition. No. 743 contains one 25x30mm stamp.

Archaeological Finds — A149

1996, June 26 **Litho.** *Perf. 13½*
744 A149 $1.20 Painted pottery basin .30 .30
745 A149 $2.10 Stone "Yue" .55 .55
746 A149 $2.60 Stone "GE" .80 .80
747 A149 $5 Pottery tripod 1.50 1.50
Nos. 744-747 (4) 3.15 3.15

1996 Summer Olympic Games Type
1996, July 19 *Perf. 14x14½*
Color of Denomination
748 A148 $1.20 like #739, red .30 .20
749 A148 $2.10 like #740, blue .40 .40
750 A148 $2.60 like #741, green .75 .75
751 A148 $5 like #742, org 1.50 1.50
Nos. 748-751 (4) 2.95 2.85
Nos. 748-751 have denominations in color and Olympic rings in gold. Nos. 739-742 have denominations in black, Olympic rings in different colors.

Mountains in Hong Kong — A150

Unwmk.
1996, Sept. 24 **Litho.** *13½x14*
752 A150 $1.30 Pat Sing Leng .50 .45
Perf. 14x14½, 14½x14
753 A150 $2.50 Ma On Shan 1.00 1.00
754 A150 $3.10 Lion Rock, vert. 1.25 1.25

Perf. 14x13½
755 A150 $5 Lantau Peak, vert. 1.90 1.90
Nos. 752-755 (4) 4.65 4.60
No. 753 is 40x36mm, No. 754 36x40mm.
See #899, 905.

Queen Type of 1992
Souvenir Sheets
1996 **Photo.** **Unwmk.** *Perf. 14*
756 A127 $10 red & grn 3.50 3.50
757 A127 $10 brn & dk brn 4.00 4.00
Issued: No. 756, 10/16; No. 757, 10/29. Visit Hong Kong '97 Stamp Exhibition (#756). 1996 Summer Olympic Games, Atlanta (#757). Nos. 756-757 each contain one 25x30mm stamp.

Urban Heritage A151

Designs: $1.30, Main building, University of Hong Kong, 1912. $2.50, Western Market, 1906. $3.10, Old Pathological Institute, 1905. $5, Flagstaff House, 1846.

Litho. & Engr.
1996, Nov. 20 *Perf. 13½*
758 A151 $1.30 multicolored .45 .45
759 A151 $2.50 multicolored .75 .75
760 A151 $3.10 multicolored .90 .90
761 A151 $5 multicolored 1.50 1.50
Nos. 758-761 (4) 3.60 3.60

Hong Kong People Type of 1989
Souvenir Sheet
Perf. 13x13½
1997, Jan. **Photo.** **Unwmk.**
762 A111 $5 like No. 549 1.50 1.50
No. 762 contains one 23x33mm stamp that has darker colors and a different perf. than No. 549.

Panoramic Views of Hong Kong Skyline — A152

#763-775: Various daytime views from harbor.
#776-778, Various nighttime views from harbor.

Perf. 13½x13
1997, Jan. 26 **Litho.** **Unwmk.**
Background Color
763 A152 10c pink .20 .20
764 A152 20c vermilion .20 .20
765 A152 50c orange .20 .20
766 A152 $1 orange yellow .25 .25
767 A152 $1.20 olive .30 .30
768 A152 $1.30 apple green .35 .35
a. Booklet pane of 10 3.50
    Complete booklet, #768a 3.50
769 A152 $1.40 green .35 .35
770 A152 $1.60 blue green .40 .40
771 A152 $2 green blue .55 .55
772 A152 $2.10 blue .55 .55
773 A152 $2.50 purple .65 .65
a. Booklet pane of 10 6.50
    Complete booklet, #773a 6.50
774 A152 $3.10 rose .80 .80
a. Booklet pane of 10 8.00
    Complete booklet, #774a 8.00
c. Sheet of 4, #771-774 2.50 2.50
775 A152 $5 orange 1.25 1.25
a. Sheet of 13, #763-775 5.75 5.75

Size: 28x33mm
Perf. 14x13½
776 A152 $10 blue 2.50 2.50
a. Souv. sheet of 1 (Series #4) 8.00
b. Souv. sheet of 1 (Series #5) 8.00
c. Souv. Sheet of 1 (Sheet #12) 3.00 3.00
d. Souv. sheet of 1, perf14x13¼ (Sheet #14) 2.60 2.60
777 A152 $20 bl, pur & rose 5.25 5.25
778 A152 $50 purple & rose 13.00 13.00
a. Sheet of 3, #776-778 21.00
Nos. 763-778 (16) 26.80 26.80
Hong Kong '97 (#776a-776b). 1996 Atlanta Paralympic Games (#776c). 13th Asian Games, Bangkok, Thailand (#774c). China 1999 World Philatelic Exhibition (#776d). Perforations are alternating small and large holes.
#775a and 778a are continuous designs.

Issued: #776a, 2/12; #776b, 2/16; #774c, 3/27/99; #776d, 8/21/99.
See note after No. 940.

Coil Stamps
Photo. *Perf. 14½x14*
763a A152 10c .25 .25
765a A152 50c .25 .25
768b A152 $1.30 .45 .45
770a A152 $1.60 .50 .50
773b A152 $2.50 .80 .80
774b A152 $3.10 1.00 1.00
Nos. 763a-774b (6) 3.25 3.25
These have numbers on back of every fifth stamp. Perforations are the same size.

New Year 1997 (Year of the Ox) A153

Various designs of oxen.

Perf. 14½
1997, Feb. 27 **Litho.** **Unwmk.**
Background Color
780 A153 $1.30 pink .30 .30
781 A153 $2.50 orange yellow .65 .65
782 A153 $3.10 green .80 .80
a. Booklet pane, 3 each #780a, 782b 6.00
    Complete booklet, 2 #782a 12.00
783 A153 $5 blue 1.25 1.25
a. Souvenir sheet of 4, #780-783 4.50 4.50
Nos. 780-783 (4) 3.00 3.00
See Nos. 838b, 838c.

Perf. 13½
780a A153 $1.30 .50 .50
781a A153 $2.50 .90 .90
782b A153 $3.10 1.10 1.10
783b A153 $5 1.75 1.75
c. Souvenir sheet of 4, #780a-781a, 782b-783b 4.50 4.50

Migratory Birds — A154

$1.30, Yellow-breasted bunting. $2.50, Great knot. $3.10, Falcated teal. $5, Black-faced spoonbill.

Perf. 13½
1997, Apr. 27 **Unwmk.** **Photo.**
784 A154 $1.30 multicolored .30 .30
785 A154 $2.50 multicolored .65 .65
786 A154 $3.10 multicolored .80 .80
787 A154 $5 multicolored 1.25 1.25
Nos. 784-787 (4) 3.00 3.00

Landmarks — A155

$1.30, Hong Kong Stadium. $2.50, The Peak Tower. $3.10, Hong Kong Convention & Exhibition Center. $5, The Lantau Link (bridge).

1997, May 18 *Perf. 13½*
788 A155 $1.30 multicolored .30 .30
789 A155 $2.50 multicolored .75 .75
790 A155 $3.10 multicolored 1.00 1.00
791 A155 $5 multicolored 1.75 1.75
a. Souvenir sheet of 4 2.25 2.25
Nos. 788-791 (4) 3.80 3.80
Opening of the Lantau Link (bridge) (#791a). Nos. 788-791 and 791a also exist perf 14x14½. Values are the same.

Royal Postbox Type of 1991
Souvenir Sheet
1997, June 30 **Litho.** *Perf. 11½*
792 A122 $5 like No. 604 1.50 1.50
No. 792 contains one 19x29mm stamp.

Special Administrative Region of People's Republic of China

First Issue Under Chinese Administration A156

Sights and symbols of Hong Kong: $1.30, Chinese architecture. $1.60, Modern buildings, methods of transportation. $2.50, Skyscrapers, Hong Kong Convention & Exhibition Center. $2.60, Cargo ship entering port. $3.10, Chinese junks, dolphins jumping in water. $5, Hibiscus flower.

1997, July 1 **Litho.** *Perf. 12x12½*
793 A156 $1.30 multicolored .35 .35
794 A156 $1.60 multicolored .40 .40
795 A156 $2.50 multicolored .65 .65
796 A156 $2.60 multicolored .70 .70
797 A156 $3.10 multicolored .80 .80
798 A156 $5 multicolored 1.25 1.25
a. Souvenir sheet of 1 1.25 1.25
Nos. 793-798 (6) 4.15 4.15

1997 World Bank Group/Intl. Monetary Fund Annual Meetings — A157

Designs: $1.30, Finance, banking. $2.50, Investment, stock exchange. $3.10, Trade, telecommunications. $5, Infrastructure, transport.

Perf. 14½
1997, Sept. 21 **Litho.** **Unwmk.**
799 A157 $1.30 multicolored .30 .30
800 A157 $2.50 multicolored .65 .65
801 A157 $3.10 multicolored .80 .80
802 A157 $5 multicolored 1.25 1.25
Nos. 799-802 (4) 3.00 3.00

Shells — A158

1997, Nov. 9 **Photo.** *Perf. 13½*
803 A158 $1.30 Clam .35 .35
804 A158 $2.50 Cowrie .65 .65
805 A158 $3.10 Cone .80 .80
806 A158 $5 Murex 1.25 1.25
Nos. 803-806 (4) 3.05 3.05

New Year 1998 (Year of the Tiger) A159

Various embroidery designs of tigers.

1998, Jan. 4 **Litho.** *Perf. 13½*
807 A159 $1.30 multicolored .30 .30
808 A159 $2.50 multicolored .65 .65
809 A159 $3.10 multicolored .80 .80
a. Bklt. pane, 6 ea #807, 809 7.00
    Complete booklet, #809a 7.00
810 A159 $5 multicolored 1.25 1.25
a. Souvenir sheet of 4, #807-810 3.50 3.50
Nos. 807-810 (4) 3.00 3.00
See No. 838.

Star Ferry, Cent.
A160

Star Ferry during: $1.30, 1900's. $2.50, 1910's-1920's. $3.10, 1920's-1950's. $5, Mid-1950's on.

1998, Apr. 26 Photo. Perf. 13½
811	A160	$1.30 multicolored	.30	.30
812	A160	$2.50 multicolored	.65	.65
813	A160	$3.10 multicolored	.80	.80
814	A160	$5 multicolored	1.25	1.25
		Nos. 811-814 (4)	3.00	3.00

Nos. 811-814 also exist perf 14½ from a booklet of one each sold only at "Australia '99" International Stamp Exhibition for $25.

Souvenir Sheet

The Closing of Kai Tak Airport — A161

Illustration reduced.

1998, July 5 Photo. Perf. 13½
815	A161	$5 multicolored	1.50	1.50

New Hong Kong Airport A162

$1.30, Passengers on terminal's moving sidewalks. $1.60, Couple entering Automated People Mover. $2.50, Airport Railway, Tsing Ma Bridge. $2.60, Terminal building, Airmail Center. $3.10, Aircraft gates. $5, Terminal departure level.

1998, July 5 Perf. 14
816	A162	$1.30 multicolored	.35	.35
817	A162	$1.60 multicolored	.40	.40
818	A162	$2.50 multicolored	.65	.65
819	A162	$2.60 multicolored	.70	.70
820	A162	$3.10 multicolored	.80	.80
821	A162	$5 multicolored	1.25	1.25
a.		Souvenir sheet of 1	1.50	1.50
b.		Block of 6, #816-821	4.75	4.75

See note after No. 940.

A163   A164

Scouting in Hong Kong: Rope tied in various knots, different scouting divisions: $1.30, Grasshopper Scouts, Cub Scouts. $2.50, Tower, tents, Boy Scouts, Girl Scouts. $3.10, Helicopter, sailboats, Venture Scouts. $5, City buildings, Rover Scouts, adult leaders.

Unwmk.
1998, July 26 Litho. Perf. 14
822	A163	$1.30 multicolored	.30	.30
823	A163	$2.50 multicolored	.65	.65
824	A163	$3.10 multicolored	.80	.80
825	A163	$5 multicolored	1.25	1.25
		Nos. 822-825 (4)	3.00	3.00

1998, Sept. 20 Litho. Perf. 13½
Hong Kong designs.
826	A164	$1.30 Graphic	.35	.35
827	A164	$2.50 Product	.65	.65
828	A164	$3.10 Interior	.85	.85
829	A164	$5 Fashion	1.25	1.25
		Nos. 826-829 (4)	3.10	3.10

Kites — A165

1998, Nov. 15 Litho. Perf. 13½
830	A165	$1.30 Dragonfly	.30	.30
831	A165	$2.50 Dragon	.65	.65
832	A165	$3.10 Butterfly	.80	.80
833	A165	$5 Goldfish	1.25	1.25
a.		Souvenir sheet, #830-833	3.00	3.00
		Nos. 830-833 (4)	3.00	3.00

A166

1999, Jan. 31 Photo. Perf. 14x13½
New Year 1999 (Year of the Rabbit): White rabbit with flower designs in various positions.
834	A166	$1.30 yel org & multi	.35	.35
		Scratched panel		.35
a.		Sheet of 10	3.50	
835	A166	$2.50 green & multi	.65	.65
		Scratched panel		.35
a.		Sheet of 10	6.50	
836	A166	$3.10 orange & multi	.80	.80
		Scratched panel		.35
a.		Sheet of 10	8.00	
837	A166	$5 red lilac & multi	1.25	1.25
		Scratched panel		.35
a.		Sheet of 10	12.50	
		Nos. 834-837 (4)	3.05	3.05

Nos. 834-837 are printed with a layering of gold "scratch off" ink, which, when removed, reveals a Chinese greeting.

New Year Types of 1987-98
Designs: a, Like #734. b, Like #780. c, Like #783. d, Like #712. e Like 515. f, Like #691. g, Like #534. h, Like #668. i, Like #615. j, Like #584. k, Like #560. #a.-k. have 4 Chinese characters at UL instead of crown and ER.

1999, Feb. 21 Litho. Perf. 13½
Sheet of 12
838		$1.30 #a.-k, #807 + label	6.00	6.00

Design in label and sheet selvage is engraved.

Intl. Year of Older Persons — A167

Perf. 14½
1999, Mar. 14 Litho. Unwmk.
839	A167	$1.30 Calligraphy	.35	.35
840	A167	$2.50 Bird raising	.65	.65
841	A167	$3.10 Playing Go	.80	.80
842	A167	$5 Voluntary services	1.25	1.25
		Nos. 839-842 (4)	3.05	3.05

Souvenir Sheet

Giant Pandas in Hong Kong — A168

Illustration reduced.

1999, Apr. 25 Litho. Perf. 14¼
843	A168	$10 multicolored	2.75	2.75

No. 843 contains one circular stamp 38mm in diameter.

Public Transport — A169

1999, May 23
844	A169	$1.30 Bus	.35	.35
845	A169	$2.40 Minibus	.70	.70
846	A169	$2.50 Tram	.75	.75
847	A169	$2.60 Taxi	.80	.80
848	A169	$3.10 Airport express	.90	.90
		Nos. 844-848 (5)	3.50	3.50

Hong Kong and Singapore Tourism — A170

Designs: $1.20, Hong Kong Harbor. $1.30, Singapore Skyline. $2.50, Giant Buddha, Hong Kong. $2.60, Merlion, Sentosa Island, Singapore. $3.10, Hong Kong street scene. $5, Bugis Junction, Singapore.

Perf. 13¼
1999, July 1 Litho. Unwmk.
849	A170	$1.20 multicolored	.35	.35
850	A170	$1.30 multicolored	.40	.40
851	A170	$2.50 multicolored	.70	.70
852	A170	$2.60 multicolored	.70	.70
853	A170	$3.10 multicolored	.85	.85
854	A170	$5 multicolored	1.50	1.50
a.		Souvenir sheet, #849-854	4.50	4.50
		Nos. 849-854 (6)	4.50	4.50

See Singapore Nos. 896-902.

People's Republic of China, 50th Anniv. — A171

Designs: $1.30, Flags of People's Republic and Hong Kong Special Administrative District. $2.50 Bauhinia blakeana flower, Hong Kong skyline. $3.10, Dragon dance. $5, Fireworks.

Perf. 14¼ Syncopated
1999, Oct. 1 Photo.
Granite Paper
855	A171	$1.30 multicolored	.40	.40
856	A171	$2.50 multicolored	.75	.75
857	A171	$3.10 multicolored	.85	.85
858	A171	$5 multicolored	1.50	1.50
a.		Block or strip of 4, #855-858	3.50	3.50

Issued in sheets of 4 blocks or strips and individually in sheets of 20.

Landmarks — A172

10c, Museum of Tea Ware. 20c, St. John's Cathedral. 50c, Legislative Council building. $1, Tai Fu Tai. $1.20, Wong Tai Sin Temple. $1.30, Victoria Harbor. $1.40, Hong Kong Railway Tower. $1.60, Tsim Sha Tsui Clock Tower. $2, Happy Valley Racecourse. $2.10, Kowloon-Canton Railway. $2.50, Chi Lin Nunnery. $3.10, Buddha at Po Lin Monastery. $5, Aw Boon Haw Gardens. $10, Tsing Ma Bridge. $20, Hong Kong Convention & Exhibition Center. $50, Hong Kong Intl. Airport.

Perf. 13x13¾ Syncopated
1999, Oct. 18 Photo.
Granite Paper
859	A172	10c blue & multi	.20	.20
a.		Booklet pane of 1	.20	
860	A172	20c blue & multi	.20	.20
a.		Booklet pane of 1	.20	
861	A172	50c blue & multi	.20	.20
a.		Booklet pane of 1	.25	
862	A172	$1 blue & multi	.25	.25
a.		Booklet pane of 1	.50	
863	A172	$1.20 blue & multi	.30	.30
a.		Booklet pane of 1	.60	
864	A172	$1.30 blue & multi	.35	.35
a.		Booklet pane of 1	.70	
865	A172	$1.40 blue & multi	.35	.35
a.		Booklet pane of 1	.70	
b.		Booklet pane of 10	3.50	—
		Booklet, #865b	3.50	
866	A172	$1.60 blue & multi	.40	.40
a.		Booklet pane of 1	.80	
867	A172	$2 blue & multi	.50	.50
a.		Booklet pane of 1	1.00	
868	A172	$2.10 blue & multi	.55	.55
a.		Booklet pane of 1	1.10	
869	A172	$2.50 blue & multi	.60	.60
a.		Booklet pane of 1	1.25	
870	A172	$3.10 blue & multi	.75	.75
a.		Booklet pane of 1	1.50	
871	A172	$5 blue & multi	1.25	1.25
a.		Booklet pane of 1	2.50	
		Souv. booklet, #859a-871a	12.00	
b.		Sheet of 13, #859-871	5.50	5.50
c.		Souvenir sheet of 1 (Definitive #4)	1.25	1.25
d.		Souv. sheet of 1 (Definitive #6)	1.25	1.25

Size: 26x32mm
Perf. 13¼
872	A172	$10 blue & multi	2.50	2.50
a.		Souv. sheet of 1 (Exhibition #1)	2.50	2.50
b.		Souv. sheet of 1 (Exhibition #1)	3.50	3.50
c.		Souv. sheet of 1 (Definitive #2)	2.50	2.50
d.		Souv. sheet of 1 (Definitive #2)	2.50	2.50
e.		Souv. sheet of 1 (Definitive #5)	2.50	2.50
873	A172	$20 blue & multi	5.00	5.00
874	A172	$50 blue & multi	12.50	12.50
a.		Sheet of 3, #872-874	20.00	20.00
		Nos. 859-874 (16)	25.90	25.90

Coil Stamps
Perf. 13¾x13¼ Syncopated
Size: 18x22mm
874B	A172	10c blue & multi	.20	.20
874C	A172	50c blue & multi	.20	.20
874D	A172	$1.30 blue & multi	.35	.35
874E	A172	$1.60 blue & multi	.40	.40
874F	A172	$2.50 blue & multi	.60	.60
874G	A172	$3.10 blue & multi	.75	.75
		Nos. 874B-874G (6)	2.50	2.50

#872a-872b are Syncopated perf 14x14¼. #872c is Syncopated perf 13¼x13. #872d is Syncopated perf 14x14½. No. 872e is Syncopated perf. 13¼x13.

Issued: #872a, 1/31/00; #872b, 2/10/00; #872c, 4/15/00; #872d, 12/2/00; #871c, 4/21/01; #872e, 8/1/01; #874B-874E, 874G, 10/18/99; #874F, 10/18/99; #871d, 1/19/02. #865b, 4/1/02.

See note after No. 940.
See also Nos. 917, 965-973, 991-993, 1083

Chinese White Dolphin — A173

Various views of dolphin.

1999, Nov. 14   Litho.   *Perf. 14½*
Granite Paper
875	A173	$1.30 green & multi	.60	.60
876	A173	$2.50 bl grn & multi	1.00	1.00
877	A173	$3.10 blue & multi	1.25	1.25
878	A173	$5 pur & multi	1.75	1.75

Souvenir Sheet
879	Sheet of 4, #a.-d.		3.25	3.25

Nos. 875-878 have Worldwide Fund for Nature (WWF) emblem; Nos. 879a-879d do not.
See No. 900.

Souvenir Sheet

Millennium — A174

No. 880: a, Dragon boat races, skyline. b, Bridge, birds.
Illustration reduced.

Perf. 14¼ Syncopated
1999, Dec. 31   Photo.
Granite Paper
880	A174	$5 Sheet of 2, #a.-b.	3.00	3.00

New Millennium Children's Stamp Design Contest Winners — A175

Designs: $1.30, Scales. $2.50, Children planting tree on planet. $3.10, Planets. $5, Inhabited planets, space shuttle, rocket.

2000, Jan. 1   Granite Paper
881	A175	$1.30 multi	.40	.30
882	A175	$2.50 multi	.75	.75
883	A175	$3.10 multi	.85	.85
884	A175	$5 multi	1.50	1.50
	Nos. 881-884 (4)		3.50	3.40

Victoria Harbor
A176

Litho. & Embossed with Foil Application
2000, Jan. 1   *Perf. 13¼*
885	A176	$50 gold & multi	18.00	18.00

New Year 2000
(Year of the
Dragon) — A177

Various dragons.

Perf. 14¼ Syncopated
2000, Jan. 23   Litho.
Granite Paper
886	A177	$1.30 multi	.35	.35
887	A177	$2.50 multi	.65	.65
888	A177	$3.10 multi	.75	.75

889	A177	$5 multi	1.25	1.25
a.	Souvenir sheet of 1, imperf.		13.50	13.50
b.	Souvenir sheet, #886-889		3.75	3.75
	Nos. 886-889 (4)		3.00	3.00

Museums and Libraries — A178

Designs: $1.30, Heritage Museum. $2.50, Central Library. $3.10, Museum of Coastal Defense. $5 Museum of History.
Illustration reduced.

Perf. 14½x14¼
2000, Mar. 26   Photo.
Granite Paper
890	A178	$1.30 multi	.70	.35
891	A178	$2.50 multi	1.25	.95
892	A178	$3.10 multi	1.50	1.00
893	A178	$5 multi	2.25	2.25
a.	Block, #890-893		6.00	6.00
	Nos. 890-893 (4)		5.70	4.55

Nos. 890-893 issued in sheets of 24. No. 893a issued only in sheet containing 4 blocks.

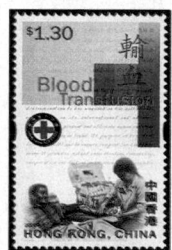

Red Cross — A179

Designs: $1.30, Blood transfusion. $2.50, Special education. $3.10, Disaster relief. $5, Voluntary service.

Perf. 14¼ Syncopated
2000, May 7   Photo.
Granite Paper
894	A179	$1.30 multi	.40	.30
895	A179	$2.50 multi	.75	.75
896	A179	$3.10 multi	.85	.85
897	A179	$5 multi	1.50	1.50
a.	Souvenir sheet, #894-897		3.50	3.50
	Nos. 894-897 (4)		3.50	3.40

Flower Type of 1989, Mountain Type of 1996 Inscribed "Hong Kong, China," and Dolphin Type of 1999
Perf. 14¼ Syncopated
2000, June 17   Photo.
Granite Paper
898	A90	$5 Booklet pane of 1, like #455	3.00	3.00
899	A150	$5 Booklet pane of 1, like #755	3.00	3.00
900	A173	$5 Booklet pane of 1, like #879d	3.00	3.00
	Booklet, #898-900		9.00	

Hong Kong 2001 Stamp Exhibition. Booklet sold for $35.

Insects — A180

Designs: $1.30, Pyrops candelarius. $2.50, Macromidia ellenae. $3.10, Troides helena spilotia. $5, Chiridopsis bowringi.

Perf. 13½x13¼ Syncopated
2000, July 16   Litho.
Granite Paper
901-904	A180	Set of 4	3.50	3.00
904a	Souvenir sheet, #901-904		3.50	3.50

Mountain Type of 1996 Inscribed "Hong Kong, China"
Souvenir Sheet
Perf. 13¼ Syncopated
2000, Aug. 12   Photo.
Granite Paper
905	A150	$10 Like #754	3.00	2.50

Hong Kong 2001 Stamp Exhibition.

2000 Summer
Olympics,
Sydney — A181

Designs: $1.30, Cycling, badminton. $2.50, Table tennis, running. $3.10, Judo, rowing. $5, Swimming, sailboarding.

Perf. 14¼ Syncopated
2000, Aug. 27   Litho.
Granite Paper
906-909	A181	Set of 4	3.75	3.00

Birds
A182

2000, Sept. 30   Photo.
Granite Paper
910		Booklet pane of 2	2.00	
a.	A182 $1.30 Yellow-breasted bunting		.70	.70
b.	A182 $2.50 Great knot		1.25	1.25
911		Booklet pane of 2	4.25	
a.	A182 $3.10 Falcated teal		1.60	1.60
b.	A182 $5 Black-faced spoonbill		2.60	2.60
	Booklet, #910-911		6.25	

Booklet containing Nos. 910-911 sold for $25.

Chinese General Chamber of Commerce, Cent. — A183

Designs: $1.30, Hong Kong in 1900. $2.50, Headquarters buildings. $3.10, People reading notice for distribution of relief funds. $5, Hand with computer mouse, currency symbols.

Perf. 13¾ Syncopated
2000, Oct. 22   Litho.
Granite Paper
912-915	A183	Set of 4	3.75	3.00

Coral Type of 1994 Inscribed "Hong Kong, China"
Souvenir Sheet
Perf. 13¼ Syncopated
2000, Nov. 25   Photo.
Granite Paper
916	A141	$10 Like #709	3.50	2.50

Landmarks Type of 1999
Souvenir Sheet
Litho. & Holography
2000, Dec. 31
917	A172	$20 Like #873	5.00	5.00

Soaking in water may affect hologram.

New Year 2001
(Year of the
Snake) — A184

Various snakes. Denominations: $1.30, $2.50, $3.10, $5.

Perf. 14½ Sync.
2001, Jan. 1   Photo.
918-921	A184	Set of 4	3.50	3.00
921a	Souvenir sheet of 1, imperf.		1.75	1.75
921b	Souvenir sheet, #918-921		4.00	4.00

Souvenir Sheet

Opening of Hong Kong 2001 Stamp Exhibition — A185

No. 922: a, Year of the Dragon. b, Year of the Snake.

Litho. & Embossed with Foil Application
2001, Feb. 1   *Perf. 13¼*
922	A185	$50 Sheet of 2, #a-b	35.00	35.00

Indiginous Trees Type of 1988 Inscribed "Hong Kong, China"
2001   Photo.   *Perf. 14¼ Syncopated*
Granite Paper
923	A105	$5 multi, sheetlet #5	1.75	1.75
a.	Sheetlet #6		1.75	1.75
b.	Sheetlet #7		1.75	1.75
c.	Sheetlet #8		1.75	1.75

Issued: No. 923, 2/2; No. 923a, 2/3; No. 923b, 2/4; No. 923c, 2/5. No. 923b with gold overprint in margin reading "To commemorate the FIAP Day of HONG KONG 2001 Stamp Exhibition on 4th February, 2001" is a private emission.
See note after No. 940 for unsyncopated stamp.

Greetings — A186

Designs: $1.30, Maple leaves. $1.60, Swans. $2.50, Chicks. $2.60, Cherry blossoms. $3.10, Bamboo. $5, Snow-covered plant.

2001, Feb. 1   Photo.
Granite Paper
Stamps + Labels
924-929	A186	Set of 6	5.00	4.00

See note after Nos. 934-937.

Hong Kong Water
Supply, 150th
Anniv. — A187

Designs: $1.30, Tai Tam Tuk Reservoir. $2.50, Plover Cove Reservoir. $3.10, Pipelines. $5, Beakers, chemical symbols.

2001, Mar. 18   Litho. & Embossed
Granite Paper

| 930-933 | A187 | Set of 4 | 4.00 | 3.00 |
| *a.* | | Block of 4, #930-933 | 4.00 | 4.00 |

Movie
Stars
A188

Designs: $1.30, Ng Cho-fan (1911-93) and Pak Yin (1920-87). $2.50, Sun Ma Si-tsang (1916-97) and Tang Bik-wan (1926-91). $3.10, Cheung Wood-yau (1910-85) and Wong Manlei (1913-98). $5, Mak Bing-wing (1915-84) and Fung Wong-nui (1925-92).

2001, Apr. 8   Litho.
Granite Paper

| 934-937 | A188 | Set of 4 | 4.00 | 3.00 |
| *a.* | | Block of 4, #934-937 | 4.00 | 4.00 |

Values are for stamps with surrounding selvage.

On June 12, 2001 Hong Kong sold for $120 limited numbers of a sheet containing 18 examples of the $1.30 stamp, No. 924. The 18 labels to the right of the stamps on this sheet differ from those found on examples of No. 924 sold on the stamp's original date of issue, and the 18 labels to the left of the stamps depict Chinese celebrities.

Dragon Boat
Races
A189

Dragon boats and: No. 938, $5, Sydney Opera House. No. 939, Hong Kong Convention and Exhibition Center.

2001, June 25   Litho.   Perf. 14x14½
Granite Paper

| 938-939 | A189 | Set of 2 | 3.50 | 2.50 |
| *a.* | | Souvenir sheet, #938-939 | 3.50 | 3.50 |

See Australia Nos. 1977-1978.

Emblem of 2008 Summer Olympics,
Beijing — A190

2001, July 14   Photo.   Perf. 13x13¼

| 940 | A190 | $1.30 multi + label | .35 | .35 |

No. 940 printed in sheets of 12 stamp + label pairs with one large central label. See People's Republic of China No. 3119, Macao No. 1067. No. 940 with different label is from People's Republic of China No. 3119a.

On July 21, 2001 Hong Kong sold a booklet containing stamps with a face value of $12.40 for $30. The stamps are the Indigenous Trees type of 1988 with the inscription "Hong Kong, China." The first pane in the booklet contained $1.30 and $2.50 stamps, and those on the second pane contained $3.10 and $5 stamps.

On Aug. 25, 2001 Hong Kong sold a booklet containing stamps with a face value of $30 for $65. The first pane in the booklet contained four stamps with a face value of $1.80 of the Stamp Collecting type of 1992 with the inscription "Hong Kong, China." The second pane contained two $3.10 perf. 13½x13 stamps on granite paper of type A152, and two $3.10 perf. 13¾ syncopated stamps on granite paper of type A172. The third pane contained four $2.60 perf. 14¼ stamps on granite paper of type A162.

Tea Culture — A191

Various tea services and background colors of: $1.30, Lilac. $2.50, Orange brown. $3.10, Bright orange. $5, Green.

Perf. 14¼x14½ Syncopated
2001, Sept. 9   Litho.

| 944-947 | A191 | Set of 4 | 3.50 | 3.00 |

Herbs — A192

Designs: $1.30, Centella asiatica. $2.50, Lobelia chinensis. $3.10, Gardenia jasminoides. $5, Scutellaria indica.

Perf. 14½ Syncopated
2001, Oct. 7   Litho.
Granite Paper

| 948-951 | A192 | Set of 4 | 3.75 | 3.00 |

Children's Stamp
Coloring
Contest — A193

Designs: $1.30, Bear. $2.50, Penguin. $3.10, Flower. $5, Bee.

Die Cut Perf. 13¾x13¼ Sync.
2001, Nov. 18
Granite Paper
Self-Adhesive

| 952-955 | A193 | Set of 4 | 4.00 | 3.00 |
| *a.* | | Souvenir sheet, #952-955 | 4.00 | 4.00 |

New Year 2002
(Year of the
Horse) — A194

Various horses. Denominations: $1.30, $2.50, $3.10, $5.

2002, Jan. 13   Perf. 14½ Syncopated
Granite Paper

956-959	A194	Set of 4	3.50	3.00
a.		Souvenir sheet of 1, imperf.	2.00	2.00
b.		Souvenir sheet, #956-959	4.00	4.00

Souvenir Sheet

New Year 2002 (Year of the
Horse) — A195

No. 960: a, Snake. b, Horse.

Litho. & Embossed with Foil
Application

2002, Feb. 9   Perf. 13¼

| 960 | A195 | $50 Sheet of 2, #a-b | 35.00 | 35.00 |

Works of
Art — A196

Details from: $1.30, Lines in Motion, by Chui Tze-hung. $2.50, Volume and Time, by Hon Chi-fun. $3.10, Bright Sun, by Aries Lee. $5, Midsummer, by Irene Chou.

Perf. 14½ Syncopated
2002, Feb. 24   Litho.
Granite Paper

| 961-964 | A196 | Set of 4 | 4.00 | 3.00 |

Landmarks Type of 1999

Designs: $1.40, Hong Kong Railway Museum. $1.80, Hong Kong Stadium. $1.90, Western Market. $2.40, Kwun Yam statue, Repulse Bay. $3, Peak Tower. $13, Hong Kong Cultural Center.

Perf. 13x13¾ Syncopated
2002, Apr. 1   Photo.
Granite Paper

965	A172	$1.80 blue & multi	.45	.45
966	A172	$1.90 blue & multi	.50	.50
967	A172	$2.40 blue & multi	.60	.60
a.		Booklet pane of 10	6.00	
		Booklet, #967a	6.00	
968	A172	$3 blue & multi	.75	.75
a.		Booklet pane of 10	7.50	
		Booklet, #968a	7.50	

Size: 26x32mm
Perf. 13¼ Syncopated

| 969 | A172 | $13 blue & multi | 3.50 | 3.50 |
| | | Nos. 965-969 (5) | 5.80 | 5.80 |

Coil Stamps
Size: 18x22mm
Perf. 14¾x13¼ Syncopated

970	A172	$1.40 blue & multi	.35	.35
971	A172	$1.80 blue & multi	.45	.45
972	A172	$2.40 blue & multi	.60	.60
973	A172	$3 blue & multi	.75	.75
		Nos. 970-973 (4)	2.15	2.15

Cyberindustry
in Hong
Kong — A197

Designs: $1.40, Innovation. $2.40, Connectivity. $3, Trend. $5, Strength.

Perf. 13¾ Syncopated
2002, Apr. 14   Litho.
Granite Paper

| 974-977 | A197 | Set of 4 | 3.50 | 3.00 |
| *a.* | | Block of 4, #974-977 | 3.50 | 3.50 |

A booklet of two panes, one containing one each of Nos. 974 and 976, and another containing one each of Nos. 975 and 977, sold for $30. Value, $11.

2002 World Cup Soccer
Championships, Japan and
Korea — A198

No. 978: a, Goalie. b, Crowd and players.

Perf. 12 Syncopated
2002, May 16   Photo.

| 978 | | Horiz. pair, with central label | 1.00 | 1.00 |
| *a.-b.* | A198 | $1.40 Either single | .50 | .50 |

No. 978 was printed in sheets of 5 pairs and five different labels.

A souvenir sheet containing Nos. 978a-978b, People's Republic of China No. 3198, and Macao Nos. 1091a-1091b exists.

Corals
A199

Designs: $1.40, North Atlantic pink tree, Pacific orange cup, and North Pacific horn corals. $2.40, North Atlantic giant orange tree, and Black corals. $3, Dendronepthea gigantea and Dendronepthea corals. $5, Tubastrea and Echinogorgia corals.

Perf. 13¾x14 Syncopated
2002, May 19   Litho.
Granite Paper

| 979-982 | A199 | Set of 4 | 3.50 | 3.00 |
| *a.* | | Souvenir sheet, #979-982 | 3.50 | 3.50 |

On May 10, 2003, Hong Kong sold a booklet with a face value of $11.80 for $25. The first pane contains Nos. 979-980 perf 13¼x13. The second pane contains Nos. 981-982, perf 13¼x13.

See Canada Nos. 1948-1951.

Beijing
—
Kowloon
Through
Trains
A200

Train and: $1.40, Hong Kong commercial buildings. $2.40, Wuhan-Changjiang Bridge, Wuchang. $3, Shaolin Monastery Pagodas, Zhengzhou. $5, Temple of Heaven, Beijing.

2002, June 9   Perf. 14¼ Syncopated
Granite Paper

| 983-986 | A200 | Set of 4 | 3.50 | 3.00 |
| *a.* | | Horiz. strip of 4, #983-986 | 3.50 | 3.50 |

Hong Kong Special Administrative
Region, 5th Anniv. — A201

Designs: $1.40, White dolphins, corals.
$2.40, Students, bauhinia flowers. $3, Flying
cranes, Hong Kong International Airport. $5,
Flags of Hong Kong and People's Republic of
China, fireworks over skyline.

2002, July 1   **Granite Paper**
987-990 A201   Set of 4   3.50 3.00
   a.   Souvenir sheet, #987-990   3.50 3.50

**Landmarks Type of 1999 with Pink
Denomination and Country Name**
Souvenir Sheet

Design: Tsing Ma Bridge.

Perf. 13¼ Syncopated
2002, July 27   **Photo.**
Granite Paper
991 A172 $10 pink & multi   2.75 2.50
Philakorea 2002.

**Landmarks Type of 1999 With Olive
Green Denomination and Country
Name**
Souvenir Sheet

Design: Tsing Ma Bridge.

Perf. 13¼ Syncopated
2002, Aug. 24   **Photo.**
Granite Paper
992 A172 $10 ol green & multi   3.00 2.50
Amphilex 2002 Intl. Stamp Exhibition,
Amsterdam.

**Landmarks Type of 1999 With Buff
Background**
Souvenir Sheet

Design: Tsing Ma Bridge.

2002, Sept. 7
993 A172 $10 blue, buff & multi   2.75 2.50

Rocks
A202

Designs: $1.40, Ping Chau (siltstone).
$2.40, Port Island (conglomerate). $3, Po Pin
Chau (tuff). $5, Lamma Island (granite).

Perf. 13¼x12¾
2002, Sept. 15   **Litho.**
994-997 A202   Set of 4   3.50 3.00
   a.   Souvenir sheet, #994-997   3.50 3.50

Portions of the designs were applied by a
thermographic process, producing a shiny,
raised effect.

Eastern and
Western
Cultures
A203

Designs: 10c, Radar screen, luopan. 20c,
Calculator, abacus. 50c, Incense coil, stained
glass window. $1, Chair, Chinese bed. $1.40,
Dim sum, loaves of bread. $1.80, Silverware,
chopsticks and spoon. $1.90, Canned drinks,
tea caddies. $2, Western and Eastern wed-
ding cakes. $2.40, Erhu, violin. $2.50, Letter
boxes, internet. $3, Sailboats, dragon boat.
$5, Tiled roof, glass wall. $10, Ballet, Chinese
opera. $13, Chess, Xiangqi. $20, Christmas
decorations, lanterns. $50, Eastern and West-
ern sculptures.

Perf. 13¼x13 Syncopated
2002, Oct. 14   **Photo.**
Granite Paper
998 A203   10c multi   .20 .20
999 A203   20c multi   .20 .20
1000 A203   50c multi   .20 .20
1001 A203 $1 multi   .25 .25

1002 A203 $1.40 multi   .35 .25
   a.   Booklet pane of 10   3.50
     Booklet, #1002a   3.50
1003 A203 $1.80 multi   .45 .25
   a.   Booklet pane of 10 ('03)   4.75
     Complete booklet, #1003a   4.75 —
1004 A203 $1.90 multi   .50 .25
1005 A203 $2 multi   .50 .25
1006 A203 $2.40 multi   .60 .25
   a.   Booklet pane of 10   6.00
     Booklet, #1006a   6.00
1007 A203 $2.50 multi   .65 .30
1008 A203 $3 multi   .75 .35
   a.   Booklet pane of 10   7.50
     Booklet, #1008a   7.50
1009 A203 $5 multi   1.25 .40
   a.   Souvenir sheet, #998-1009   5.75 5.75
   b.   Booklet pane, #998-1009   5.75
     Booklet, #1009b   5.75

Size: 40x24mm
Perf. 14¾ Syncopated
1010 A203 $10 multi   2.75 .25
1011 A203 $13 multi   3.50 .75
1012 A203 $20 multi   6.00 1.00
1013 A203 $50 multi   15.00 4.00
    Souvenir sheet #1010-1013   27.50 27.50
    Nos. 998-1013 (16)   33.15 9.15

Coil Stamps
Size: 22x19mm
Perf. 13¼x14¾ Syncopated
1014 A203 $1.40 multi   .35 .35
1015 A203 $1.80 multi   .45 .45
1016 A203 $2.40 multi   .60 .60
1017 A203 $3 multi   .75 .75
    Nos. 1014-1017 (4)   2.15 2.15

No. 1003a issued 10/7/04.

Christmas — A204

Designs: $1.40, Christmas tree. $2.40,
Ornament. $3, Snowman. $5, Bell.

Photo. with Hologram Applied
Perf. 13½ Syncopated
2002, Nov. 24
Granite Paper
1018-1021 A204   Set of 4   3.50 3.00
   a.   Block or strip of 4,
     #1018-1021   3.50 3.50

Perforations within the stamp outline the
designs.

Hong Kong
Disneyland
A205

Designs: $1.40, Main Street. $2.40,
Fantasyland. $3, Adventureland. $5,
Tomorrowland.

Perf. 13¾ Syncopated
2003, Jan. 12   **Litho. & Embossed**
Granite Paper
1022-1025 A205   Set of 4   3.50 3.00
   a.   Souvenir sheet, #1022-1025   3.50 3.50

New Year 2003
(Year of the
Ram) — A206

Various rams: $1.40, $2.40, $3, $5.

Perf. 14¼ Syncopated
2003, Jan. 19   **Litho.**
Granite Paper
1026-1029 A206   Set of 4   3.50 3.00
   a.   Souvenir sheet of 1, im-
     perf.   2.00 2.00
   b.   Souvenir sheet, #1026-
     1029   3.50 3.50

New Year Types of 2000-03
2003, Jan. 19   Litho.   **Perf. 12¾x13¼**
Flocked Paper
1030   Block of 4   10.50 10.50
   a.   A177 $10 Like #888   2.60 2.60
   b.   A184 $10 Like #920   2.60 2.60
   c.   A194 $10 Like #957   2.60 2.60
   d.   A206 $10 Like #1029   2.60 2.60

Souvenir Sheet

New Year 2003 (Year of the
Ram) — A207

No. 1031: a, Horse. b, Ram.

**Litho. & Embossed with Foil
Application**
2003, Jan. 19   **Perf. 13¼**
1031 A207 $50 Sheet of 2,
     #a-b   27.50 27.50

Traditional Trades and
Handicrafts — A208

Designs: $1.40, Letter writing. $1.80, Bird
cage making, vert. $2.40, Qipao tailoring.
$2.50, Hairdressing, vert. $3, Dough figurine
making, vert. $5, Olive selling.

**Perf. 13½x14 Syncopated, 13½
Syncopated (vert. stamps)**
2003, Mar. 13   **Litho.**
Granite Paper
1032-1037 A208   Set of 6   5.25 4.25
1037a   Souvenir sheet, #1032-1037   5.25 5.25

Souvenir Sheet

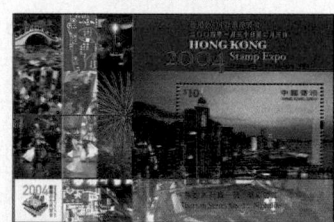

Hong Kong 2004 Stamp Expo — A209

2003, Apr. 8   **Perf. 13¼ Syncopated**
Granite Paper
1038 A209 $10 multi   3.00 2.50

Souvenir Sheet

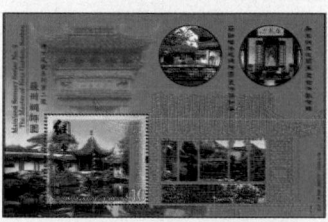

Master-of-Nets Garden,
Suzhou — A210

2003, June 27   **Granite Paper**
1039 A210 $10 multi   3.50 3.00

Miniature Landscapes — A211

Plants: $1.40, Fukien tea. $2.40, Hedge
sageretia. $3, Fire-thorn, vert. $5, Chinese
hackberry, vert.

**Perf. 13¾x12¾ Syncopated,
12¾x13¾ Syncopated**
2003, July 17   **Photo.**
Granite Paper
1040-1043 A211   Set of 4   3.50 3.00

Aquarium
Fish
A212

Various fish: $1.40, $2.40, $3, $5.

2003, Aug. 7   **Perf. 14¼ Syncopated**
Granite Paper
With Fish-Shaped Holes in Paper
1044-1047 A212   Set of 4   3.50 3.00
   a.   Block of 4, #1044-1047   3.50 3.50

A213

Heartwarming
A214

Perf. 13¾ Syncopated
2003, Sept. 10   **Litho.**
Inscribed "Local Mail Postage"
Granite Paper
1048 A213 ($1.40) multi   .40 .35
1049 A214 ($1.40) multi   .40 .35
   a.   Sheet of 16 + 17 labels
     ('04)   13.00 13.00

Inscribed "Air Mail Postage"
1050 A213   ($3) multi   1.10 .80
1051 A214   ($3) multi   1.10 .80
   a.   Sheet, 4 each #1048-1051,
     + 17 labels   12.00 12.00
    Nos. 1048-1051 (4)   3.00 2.30

No. 1049a issued 10/7/04. No. 1049a sold
for $50 and has a 2004 Olympic Games theme
on the labels. A similar sheet issued in 2005
with labels having a Lions Club Convention
theme, sold for $108 in conjunction with other
items, and was not available separately.

Birds
A215

Designs: $1.40, Pied avocet. $2.40, Horned
grebe. $3, Black-throated diver. $5, Great
crested grebe.

Perf. 12½ Syncopated
2003, Oct. 4   **Litho. & Engr.**
Granite Paper
1052-1055 A215   Set of 4   3.50 3.00
1055a   Booklet pane #1052-1055   3.50
     Complete booklet, 2 #1055a   7.00

See Sweden No. 2469.

Souvenir Sheet

Hong Kong 2004 Stamp Expo — A216

Perf. 13¼ Syncopated

2003, Oct. 14　　　　　　　　　Litho.
Granite Paper

1056	A216 $10 multi		3.00	2.00
1056a	Sheet, 2 each #1038,			
	1056, + 2 labels		21.00	21.00

No. 1056a was issued 1/30/04 and sold for $80. Labels could be personalized.

Percussion
Instruments — A217

Designs: $1.40, Drum. $2.40, Clappers. $3, Cymbals. $5, Gongs. $13, Chimes.

Perf. 13½x13¼ Syncopated

2003, Nov. 6　　　　　　　　　Photo.

1057-1060	A217	Set of 4	3.50	3.00

Souvenir Sheet

Perf. 13¾x13¼ Syncopated

1061	A217 $13 multi		4.00	3.50

No. 1061 contains one 35x45mm stamp.

Launch of First Manned Chinese
Spacecraft — A218

No. 1062: a, Astronaut, Shenzhou spacecraft. b, Rocket lift-off.
Illustration reduced.

2003, Oct. 16 Photo.　*Perf. 13x13¼*

1062	A218 $1.40 Pair, #a-b	1.25	.75

A booklet containing No. 1062, People's Republic of China No. 3314 and Macao No. 1128a exists. The booklet sold for a premium over face value.

UNESCO World Heritage Sites in
People's Republic of China — A219

Designs: $1.40, Potala Palace, vert. (27x75mm). $1.80, Imperial Palace of the Ming and Qing Dynasties. $2.40, Mausoleum of the First Qin Emperor. $2.50, Mount Huangshan, vert. $3, Old Town of Lijiang, vert. $5, Jiuzhaigou Valley (75x27mm).

Perf. 13¼ Syncopated

2003, Nov. 25　　　　　　　　Litho.
Granite Paper

1063	A219 $1.40 multi	.45	.40
a.	Perf. 13¼x13¼x13¼x13		
	Syncopated	.45	.40

Perf. 13x13¼ Syncopated

1064	A219 $1.80 multi	.55	.50
a.	Perf. 13x13¼x12½x13¼		
	Syncopated	.55	.50
1065	A219 $2.40 multi	.65	.60
a.	Perf. 12½x13¼ Syncopated	.65	.60

Perf. 13 Syncopated

1066	A219 $2.50 multi	.75	.65
a.	Perf. 13¼x13x13¼ Synco-		
	pated	.75	.65
b.	Perf. 13¼x13x13x13 Synco-		
	pated	.75	.65
c.	Perf. 13¼x13x13¼x13¼ Syn-		
	copated	.75	.65
1067	A219 $3 multi	.90	.80
a.	Perf. 12½x13x13 Synco-		
	pated	.90	.80

Perf. 13x12¾ Syncopated

1068	A219 $5 multi	1.40	1.25
a.	Perf. 13x12¾x13 and		
	13¼x13 Syncopated	1.40	1.25
b.	Perf. 13 Syncopated	1.40	1.25
c.	Miniature sheet (see note		
	below)	14.00	14.00
	Nos. 1063-1068 (6)	4.70	4.20

No. 1068c contains one each of Nos. 1063a, 1064, 1065, 1066a, 1066b, 1066c, 1067a, 1068b and two each of Nos. 1063, 1064a, 1065a, 1067 and 1068a. Perfs for the minor varieties are for the measurement that comprises the longest part of each side, as the sides of some stamps have sections with varying perf measurements. Approximately one half of the bottom row of perfs on No. 1068a is perf. 13 while the other half is perf. 13¼.

Development of Public
Housing — A220

Various buildings.

Perf. 13¼x13 Syncopated

2003, Dec. 11　　　　　　　　Photo.
Granite Paper

1069	A220 $1.40 org & multi	.50	.40
a.	Tete-beche pair	1.00	.80
1070	A220 $2.40 yel & multi	.75	.60
a.	Tete-beche pair	1.50	1.20
1071	A220 $3 pur & multi	1.25	.80
a.	Tete-beche pair	2.50	1.60
1072	A220 $5 red & multi	2.00	1.25
a.	Tete-beche pair	4.00	2.50
	Nos. 1069-1072 (4)	4.50	3.05

New Year 2004
(Year of the
Monkey) — A221

Various monkeys: $1.40, $2.40, $3, $5.

Perf. 13½x13¼ Syncopated

2004, Jan. 4　　　　　　　　　Litho.
Granite Paper

1073-1076	A221	Set of 4	3.00	3.00
1076a	Souvenir sheet of 1, imperf.		1.50	1.50
1076b	Souvnir sheet, #1073-1076		3.00	3.00

Souvenir Sheet

New Year 2004 (Year of the
Monkey) — A222

No. 1077: a, Ram. b, Monkey.

**Litho. & Embossed with Foil
Application**

2004, Jan. 4　　　　　　　*Perf. 13¼*

1077	A222 $50 Sheet of 2,		
	#a-b	35.00	35.00

Souvenir Sheets

New Year Puddings and
Greeting — A223

New Year Puddings With Two
Greetings — A224

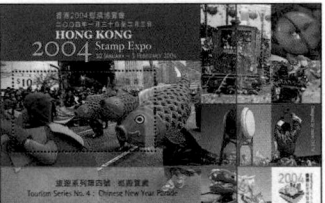

New Year Parade — A225

Jade — A226

Fire Dragon Dance — A227

No. 1079: a, Same Chinese text as on No. 1078 when viewed from directly above (top character with long curved line at bottom). b, Text different from that on No. 1078 when viewed from directly above.

2004 Litho. *Perf. 13¼ Syncopated*
Granite Paper

1078	A223 $10 multi	2.60	2.60
1079	A224 $10 Sheet of 2,		
	#a-b	5.25	5.25
1080	A225 $10 multi	2.60	2.60
1081	A226 $10 multi	2.60	2.60
1082	A227 $10 multi	2.60	2.60
	Nos. 1078-1082 (5)	15.65	15.65

2004 Hong Kong Stamp Expo. Issued: Nos. 1078-1079, 1/30; No. 1080, 1/31; No. 1081, 2/1; No. 1082, 2/2.

Nos. 1079a and 1079b show the same two Chinese texts, but the texts appear different depending on the angle at which one views the stamps. Under magnification it can be seen that the two Chinese texts are printed differently to achieve this effect.

**Landmarks Type of 1999 With Red
Violet Denomination and Country
Name**

No. 1083: a, Museum of Tea Ware. b, St. John's Cathedral. c, Legislative Council Building. d, Tai Fu Tai. e, Wong Tai Sin Temple. f, Victoria Harbor. g, Hong Kong Railway Museum. h, Tsim Sha Tsui Clock Tower. i, Hong Kong Stadium. j, Western Market. k, Happy Valley Racecourse. l, Kowloon-Canton Railway. m, Repulse Bay. n, Chi Lin Nunnery. o, Peak Tower. p, Buddha at Po Lin Monastery. q, Aw Boon Haw Gardens. r, Tsing Ma Bridge. s, Hong Kong Cultural Center. t, Hong Kong Convention and Exhibition Center. u, Hong Kong Intl. Airport.

Perf. 13x13¾ Syncopated

2004, Feb. 3　　　　　　　　　Photo.
Granite Paper

1083	Sheet of 21	7.75	7.75
a.-u.	A172 $1.40 Any single, red vio &		
	multi (23x27mm)	.35	.35

2004 Hong Kong Stamp Expo.

Rugby
Sevens
A228

Designs: $1.40, Hong Kong Sevens. $2.40, New Zealand Sevens. $3, Hong Kong Stadium. $5, Westpac Stadium, Wellington, New Zealand.

Perf. 13¼x14¼ Syncopated

2004, Feb. 25　　　　　　　　Litho.
Granite Paper

1084-1087	A228	Set of 4	3.00	3.00
1087a	Block of 4, #1084-1087		3.00	3.00

Children's Games and
Activities — A229

Designs: $1.40, Scissors, Paper, Stone. $2.40, Chinese chess. $3, Blowing bubbles. $5, Hopscotch.

2004, Apr. 7　　　　　　**Granite Paper**

1088-1091	A229	Set of 4	3.00	2.50
1091a	Block of 4, #1088-1091		3.00	3.00

Souvenir Sheet

Chen Clan Academy — A230

Perf. 13½x13¼ Syncopated

2004, May 6

1092	A230 $10 multi	3.00	2.50

Trams in Hong Kong, Cent. — A231

Various trams and tickets: $1.40, Green ticket. $2.40, Brown ticket. $3, Blue ticket. No. 1096, $5, Yellow ticket.
No. 1097, Olive ticket.

2004, May 27   Granite Paper

| 1093-1096 | A231 | Set of 4 | 3.00 | 2.50 |
| *1096a* | | Souvenir sheet, #1093-1096 | 3.00 | 3.00 |

Souvenir Sheet

| 1097 | A231 | $5 multi | 1.25 | 1.25 |

People's Liberation Army Forces of Hong Kong — A232

Inscriptions: $1.40, The Powerful and Civilized Military Force. $1.80, Social Services. $2.40, Open Day. $2.50, Army. $3, Navy. $5, Air Force.

Perf. 13¼x14 Syncopated

2004, June 30   Litho.

Granite Paper

1098	A232	$1.40 multi	.35	.35
a.		Booklet pane of 4	2.00	
1099	A232	$1.80 multi	.50	.50
a.		Booklet pane of 4	2.50	
1100	A232	$2.40 multi	.60	.60
a.		Booklet pane of 4	3.25	
1101	A232	$2.50 multi	.65	.65
a.		Booklet pane of 4	3.50	
1102	A232	$3 multi	.80	.80
a.		Booklet pane of 4	4.25	
1103	A232	$5 multi	1.25	1.25
a.		Booklet pane of 4	6.50	
		Complete booklet, #1098a-1103a	22.00	
		Nos. 1098-1103 (6)	4.15	4.15

Complete booklet sold for $85.

Relay Race — A233

Diving — A234

Volleyball — A235

Cycling — A236

Badminton — A237

No. 1104: a, Runners in blocks. b, Runners. c, Runner taking baton. d, Runner at finish.
No. 1105: a, Diver on board. b, Diver with legs tucked in. c, Diver with arms and legs extended. d, Diver entering water.
No. 1106: a, Player making save. b, Player leaping to get ball. c, Player striking ball above net. d, Player trying to block ball.
No. 1107: a, Cyclists, denomination at left. b, Cyclist at right, denomination at left. c, Cyclists, denomination at right. d, Cyclist with arms extended.
No. 1108: a, Bird above head, racquet at shoulder level. b, Bird at shoulder level, racquet at knee level. c, Bird and racquet above head. d, Player with face covered by arm.
Illustrations reduced.

Perf. 13½x13¼ Syncopated

2004, July 20

Granite Paper

1104	A233	$1.40 Horiz. strip of 4, #a-d	1.50	1.50
1105	A234	$1.40 Horiz. strip of 4, #a-d	1.50	1.50
1106	A235	$1.40 Horiz. strip of 4, #a-d	1.50	1.50
1107	A236	$1.40 Horiz. strip of 4, #a-d	1.50	1.50
1108	A237	$1.40 Horiz. strip of 4, #a-d	1.50	1.50
e.		Miniature sheet, #1104-1108	7.50	7.50

Souvenir Sheet

2004 Summer Olympics, Athens — A238

No. 1109: a, Runner without clothes. b, Runner with clothes.

2004, Aug. 13   Granite Paper

| 1109 | A238 | $5 Sheet of 2, #a-b | 2.60 | 2.60 |

Deng Xiaoping (1904-97), Chinese Leader — A239

No. 1110: a, Saluting flags. b, Watching fireworks.
$10, Three photographs.
Illustration reduced.

2004, Aug. 22   *Perf. 13x13¼*

| 1110 | A239 | $1.40 Horiz. pair, #a-b | .75 | .75 |

Souvenir Sheet

| 1111 | A239 | $10 multi | 2.60 | 2.60 |

Hong Kong Currency — A240

Obverse and reverse of: $1.40, 1863 one mil bronze coin. $2.40, 1866 twenty cent silver coin. $3, 1935 one dollar banknotes. No. 1115, $5, 1997 one thousand dollar gold coin commemorating establishment of Special Administrative Region.
No. 1116, $5, 1993 ten dollar coin.

Perf. 13¼x14 Syncopated

2004, Sept. 2

Granite Paper

| 1112-1115 | A240 | Set of 4 | 3.00 | 3.00 |
| *1115a* | | Miniature sheet, #1112-1115 | 3.00 | 3.00 |

Souvenir Sheet

| 1116 | A240 | $5 multi | 1.25 | 1.25 |

Pearl River Delta Region Development — A241

Designs: $1.40, Men and bridge. $2.40, Men and crane. $3, Tourist attractions. $5, Men and buildings.

2004, Oct. 19   Granite Paper

| 1117-1120 | A241 | Set of 4 | 3.00 | 3.00 |
| *1120a* | | Block of 4, #1117-1120 | 3.00 | 3.00 |

No. 1120a printed in sheets of 4 blocks.

Mushrooms — A242

Designs: $1.40, Straw mushrooms. $2.40, Red-orange mushrooms. $3, Violet marasmius. No. 1124, $5, Lingzhi mushrooms.
No. 1125, Hexagon fungi.

Perf. 13½x13¼ Syncopated

2004, Nov. 23

Granite Paper

| 1121-1124 | A242 | Set of 4 | 3.00 | 3.00 |
| *1124a* | | Souvenir sheet, #1121-1124 | 3.00 | 3.00 |

Souvenir Sheet

| 1125 | A242 | $5 multi | 1.25 | 1.25 |

Letters of the Alphabet — A243

Nos. 1126 and 1127 — Upper half of letters made with common household items: a, Clothespin. b, Scissors. c, Lamp. d, Plastic cap for glue bottle. e, Steaming rack. f, Caliper with ruler. g, Bolt of padlock. h, Bamboo ladder. i, Flashlight. j, Toilet brush. k, Stapler. l, Sock. m, Draftsman's triangle. n, Nail clippers. o, Rubber band. p, Strainer. q, Link from chain. r, Sunglasses. s, Clothes hanger. t, Wooden broom. u, Sandals. v, Compass. w, Corkscrew. x, Faucet. y, Fork. z, Paint roller.

Perf. 13¼x13 Syncopated

2005, Jan. 4   Litho.

Granite Paper (#1126)

| 1126 | A243 | Sheet of 30 (see footnote) | 11.00 | 11.00 |
| *a.-z.* | | $1.40 Any single | .35 | .35 |

Self-Adhesive

Serpentine Die Cut 12½ Syncopated

| 1127 | A243 | Sheet of 30 (see footnote) | 11.00 | |
| *a.-z.* | | $1.40 Any single | .35 | .35 |

Each sheet contains one of each letter and an additional example of a, e, i and o stamps. Covers were prepared in 2006 with se-tenant strips spelling "KUNG," "HEI," "FAT" and "CHOY," which are not found in No. 1126.

New Year 2004 (Year of the Rooster) — A244

Various roosters with background colors of: $1.40, Orange. $2.40, Green. $3, Dark red. $5, Blue.

2005, Jan. 30   *Perf. 14¼ Syncopated*

Granite Paper

1128-1131	A244	Set of 4	3.00	3.00
1131a		Souvenir sheet of 1, imperf.	1.50	1.50
1131b		Souvenir sheet, #1128-1131	3.00	3.00

Souvenir Sheet

New Year 2005 (Year of the Rooster) — A245

No. 1132: a, Monkey. b, Rooster.

Litho. & Embossed With Foil Application

2005, Jan. 30   *Perf. 13¼*

| 1132 | A245 | $50 Sheet of 2, #a-b | 27.50 | 27.50 |

Fairy Tales by Hans Christian Andersen (1805-75) — A246

Designs: $1.40, The Ugly Duckling. $2.40, The Little Mermaid. $3, The Little Match Girl. $5, The Emperor's New Clothes.

Perf. 13¾ Syncopated

2005, Mar. 22   Litho. & Embossed

Granite Paper

1133-1136	A246	Set of 4	4.00	4.00
1133a		Souvenir sheet of 4	1.75	1.75
1134a		Souvenir sheet of 4	3.00	3.00
1135a		Souvenir sheet of 4	4.00	4.00
1136a		Souvenir sheet of 4	6.50	6.50

Souvenir Sheet

Hong Kong Skyline, Sydney Opera House — A247

Perf. 13½ Syncopated

2005, Apr. 21   Litho.

Granite Paper

| 1137 | A247 | $10 multi | 2.60 | 2.60 |

Pacific Explorer 2005 World Stamp Expo, Sydney.

Goldfish
A248

Designs: $1.40, Variegated pearl-scale. $2.40, Red and white swallow-tail. $3, Pale bronze egg-phoenix. No. 1141, $5, Blue wenyu. No. 1142, $5, Red and white dragon-eye.

Perf. 13¼x14 Syncopated
2005, May 12
Granite Paper

1138-1141	A248	Set of 4	3.00	3.00
1141a		Souvenir sheet, #1138-1141	3.00	3.00

Souvenir Sheet

1142	A248	$5 multi	1.25	1.25

No. 1142 contains one 45x35mm stamp.

Maritime Expeditions of Zheng He, 600th Anniv. A249

No. 1143 — Ships and: a, Zheng He (1371-1433), explorer. b, Giraffe, ceramics. c, Compass wheel. $10, Zheng He on ship.

2005, June 28   **Perf. 13x13¼**

1143		Horiz. strip of 3	1.10	1.10
a.-c.	A249	$1.40 Any single	.35	.35

Souvenir Sheet
Perf. 13¼

1144	A249	$10 multi	2.60	2.60

No. 1144 contains one 50x30mm stamp.

Creative Industries A250

Designs: $1.40, Circles, squares and triangles (advertising). $2.40, Numerals, letters and symbols (computer and digital industries). $3, Vertical and horizontal lines (broadcasting industries). $5, Curved brushstrokes (arts and crafts).

Perf. 14x14¼ Syncopated
2005, July 21   **Litho.**
Granite Paper

1145-1148	A250	Set of 4	3.00	3.00
1148a		Block of 4 with selvage, #1145-1148	3.00	3.00
1148b		Booklet pane, 2 #1148a	6.00	
		Complete booklet, 2 #1148b	12.00	

Each block of 4 in the booklet has a different arrangement. Rouletting separates the blocks within each booklet pane.

Great Inventions of Ancient China — A251

Designs: $1.40, Compass. $2.40, Printing. $3, Gunpowder. $5, Papermaking.

Perf. 13¼x14¼ Syncopated
2005, Aug. 18

1149-1152	A251	Set of 4	3.00	3.00
1152a		Miniature sheet, 4 each #1149-1152	12.00	12.00

Opening of Hong Kong Disneyland A252

Designs: $1.40, Mickey and Minnie Mouse. $2.40, Dumbo. $3, Simba and Nala. No. 1156, $5, Pluto. Nos. 1157, 1158, Mickey Mouse.

Perf. 13¾x13½ Syncopated
2005, Sept. 12   **Litho.**
Granite Paper (#1153-1157)

1153-1156	A252	Set of 4	3.00	3.00
1156a		Souvenir sheet, #1153-1156	3.00	3.00

Souvenir Sheets

1157	A252	$5 multi	1.25	1.25

Litho. & Embossed with Foil Application

1158	A252	$50 gold & multi	13.00	13.00

Souvenir Sheet

Qiantang Tidal Bore — A253

Perf. 13¼ Syncopated
2005, Sept. 16   **Litho.**

1159	A253	$10 multi	2.60	2.60

Fishing Villages A254

Designs: $1.40, Tai O, Hong Kong. $2.40, Aldeia da Carrasqueira, Portugal. $3, Tai O, diff. $5, Aldeia da Carrasqueira, diff.

Perf. 14¼x14 Syncopated
2005, Oct. 18

1160-1163	A254	Set of 4	3.00	3.00
1163a		Miniature sheet, 4 each #1160-1163	12.00	12.00

See Portugal Nos. 2767-2768.

Popular Singers — A255

Designs: $1.40, Wong Ka Kui. $1.80, Danny Chan. $2.40, Roman Tam. $3, Leslie Cheung. $5, Anita Mui.

Perf. 13½x13¼ Syncopated
2005, Nov. 8
Granite Paper

1164-1168	A255	Set of 5	3.50	3.50

Because of concerns about the licensing of the images of the singers in foreign countries, the philatelic bureau did not make Nos. 1164-1168 available by mail order to foreign customers. The stamps were freely available to any purchasers over the counter.

New Year 2006 (Year of the Dog) — A256

Designs: $1.40, Golden retriever. $2.40, Pekingese. $3, German shepherd. $5, Beagle.

Perf. 13½x13¼ Syncopated
2006, Jan. 15   **Litho.**
Granite Paper

1169-1172	A256	Set of 4	3.00	3.00
1172a		Souvenir sheet of #1172, imperf.	2.00	2.00
1172b		Souvenir sheet of #1169-1172	3.50	3.50

Souvenir Sheet

New Year 2006 (Year of the Dog) — A257

No. 1173: a, Rooster. b, Dog.

Litho. & Embossed with Foil Application
2006, Jan. 15   **Perf. 13½x13¼**

1173	A257	$50 Sheet of 2, #a-b	35.00	35.00

Chinese Lanterns — A258

No. 1174: a, $1.40, Lotus Fairy lantern. $1.80, Narcissus lantern. $2.40, Peacock lantern. $5, Boys holding Dragon lantern.

Perf. 12¾x13¼ Syncopated
2006, Feb. 12   **Litho.**
Granite Paper (#1174)

1174	A258	Horiz. strip of 3, #a-c	1.50	1.50

Souvenir Sheet
Perf. 13¼ Syncopated

1175	A258	$5 multi	1.25	1.25

No. 1175 contains one 35x46mm stamp.

Teddy Bears in Costumes A259

Teddy bears in various costumes.

Perf. 13¾ Syncopated
2006, Mar. 30
Granite Paper

1176	A259	$1.40 multi	.35	.35
1177	A259	$1.80 multi	.50	.50
a.		Booklet pane, #1176-1177	1.60	
1178	A259	$2.40 multi	.60	.60
1179	A259	$2.50 multi	.65	.65
a.		Booklet pane, #1178-1179	2.40	

1180	A259	$3 multi	.80	.80
1181	A259	$5 multi	1.25	1.25
a.		Booklet pane, #1180-1181	3.75	
		Complete booklet, #1177a, 1179a, 1181a	7.75	
b.		Souvenir sheet, #1176-1181, + central label	4.25	4.25

Complete booklet sold for $30.

Souvenir Sheet

Gongbei Rock, Mount Taishan — A260

2006, May 4   **Perf. 14¼ Syncopated**
Granite Paper

1182	A260	$10 multi	2.60	2.60

Souvenir Sheet

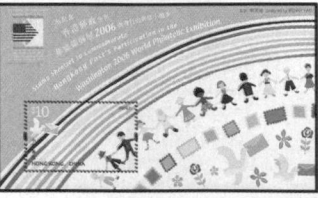

Washington 2006 World Philatelic Exhibition — A261

Perf. 13¼x12¾ Syncopated
2006, May 27
Granite Paper

1183	A261	$10 multi	2.60	2.60

Chinese Idioms A262

Idioms: $1.40, Respect makes successful marriage. $2.40, Reading is always rewarding. $3, Prepare for success. $5, All in the same boat.

Perf. 13¾ Syncopated
2006, June 15
Granite Paper

1184-1187	A262	Set of 4	3.00	3.00
1187a		Souvenir sheet, #1184-1187	3.00	3.00

Attractions in Hong Kong's Districts — A263

Designs: No. 1188, $1.40, Central Police Station Historical Compound, Peak Tram, International Finance Center, Central and Western District. No. 1189, $1.40, Victoria Park, Island Eastern Corridor, Hong Kong Museum of Coastal Defense, Eastern District. No. 1190, $1.40, Floating restaurant, Murray House, Ocean Park, Southern District. No. 1191, $1.40, Hong Kong Convention and Exhibition Center, Old Wan Chai Post Office, Lovers' Rock, Wan Chai District. No. 1192, $1.40, Hong Kong Cultural Center, Temple Street, Yuen Po Bird Garden, Yau Tsim Mong District. No. 1193, $1.40, Wong Tai Sin Temple, Lion Rock, Chi Lin Nunnery, Wong Tai Sin District. No. 1194, $1.40, Lei Yue Mun Seafood Bazaar, buildings, Child-giving Rocks, Kwun Tong District. No. 1195, $1.40, Computer shopping center, Lingnan Garden, Festival Walk, Sham Shui Po District. No. 1196, $1.40, Kowloon Walled City Park, Wonderful Worlds of Whampoa, Sung Wong Toi, Kowloon City District. No. 1197, $1.40, Seafood Street, Tai Long Wan, Lions Nature Education Center Shell House, Sai Kung District. No. 1198,

$1.40, Lantau Link View Point, Kwai Chung Container Terminals, Tsing Ma Bridge, Kwai Tsing District. No. 1199, $1.40, Lookout Tower, Lam Tsuen Wishing Tree, Tai Po Waterfront Park, Tai Po District. No. 1200, $1.40, Fung Ying Seen Koon, Chung Ying Street, Pak Hok Lam, North District. No. 1201, $1.40, Sam Tung Uk Museum, Yuen Yuen Institute, Tai Mo Shan Country Park, Tsuen Wan District. No. 1202, $1.40, Amah Rock, Shing Mun River Promenade, Che Kung Temple, Sha Tin District. No. 1203, $1.40, Hong Kong Gold Coast, Ching Chung Koon, Tsing Shan Monastery, Tuen Mun District. No. 1204, $1.40, Mai Po Nature Reserve, birds over farm, Chinese cakes, Yuen Long District. No. 1205, $1.40, Tian Tan Buddha, Cheung Chau Bun Festival, Tai O, Islands District.

2006, July 18   Perf. 13½ Syncopated
Granite Paper

| 1188-1205 | A263 | Set of 18 | 6.50 | 6.50 |
| *1205a* | | Souvenir sheet, #1188-1205 | 6.50 | 6.50 |

Fireworks
A264

Designs: No. 1206, $5, No. 1208a, $50, Fireworks over Hong Kong Harbor. No. 1207, $5, No. 1208b, $50, Fireworks over Prater Ferris Wheel, Vienna, Austria.

2006, Aug. 22   Litho.   Perf. 14

| 1206-1207 | A264 | Set of 2 | 2.60 | 2.60 |

Souvenir Sheet
Photo. With Glass Beads Affixed

| 1208 | A264 | $50 Sheet of 2, #a-b | 26.00 | 26.00 |
| *c.* | | Sheet, Austria #2060b, Hong Kong #1208a | 32.50 | 32.50 |

See Austria No. 2060.
No. 1208c sold for €12.40 in Austria and for $120 in Hong Kong, and is identical to Austria No. 2060c.

Intl. Day of
Peace — A265

Chinese characters and: $1.40, Flower and "Love." $1.80, Origami crane and "Peace." $2.40, Four-leaf clover and "Hope." $3, Tree and "Caring." $5, Earth and "Harmony."

Perf. 13½x13¼ Syncopated
2006, Sept. 21   Litho.
Granite Paper

| 1209-1213 | A265 | Set of 5 | 3.50 | 3.50 |
| *1213a* | | Souvenir sheet, #1209-1213 | 3.50 | 3.50 |

Government Vehicles — A266

Designs: $1.40, Correctional Services security bus. $1.80, Customs Department X-ray scanning vehicle. $2.40, Fire Department hydraulic platform pumper truck. $2.50, Government Flying Service Super Puma helicopter. $3, Police Department traffic patrol motorcycle. $5, Immigration Department launch.

Perf. 13¼x14½ Syncopated
2006, Oct. 19   Litho.
Granite Paper

| 1214-1219 | A266 | Set of 6 | 5.00 | 5.00 |
| *1219a* | | Sheet, 3 each #1214-1219 | 15.00 | 15.00 |

Dr. Sun Yat-sen (1866-1925), Republic of China President — A267

Photographs from: $1.40, 1883. $2.40, 1912. $3, 1916. No. 1223, $5, 1922. No. 1224, $5, 1924 (hands visible).

Perf. 13¼x13 Syncopated
2006, Nov. 12
Granite Paper

| 1220-1223 | A267 | Set of 4 | 4.00 | 4.00 |

Souvenir Sheet

| 1224 | A267 | $5 multi | 2.00 | 2.00 |

A booklet containing two panes, one containing Nos. 1220-1221, and one containing Nos. 1222-1223 sold for $25.

Heartwarming
A268

Perf. 13½ Syncopated
2006, Nov. 28
Granite Paper
Inscribed "Local Mail Postage"

1225	A268	($1.40) Hearts	.35	.35
1226	A268	($1.40) Bottles	.35	.35
a.		Sheet of 20 + 21 labels	12.50	12.50

Inscribed "Air Mail Postage"

1227	A268	($3) Flowers	.80	.80
1228	A268	($3) Drink glasses	.80	.80
a.		Sheet, 5 each #1225-1228, + 21 labels	11.50	11.50
b.		Sheet of 20 + 21 labels	27.50	27.50
		Nos. 1225-1228 (4)	2.30	2.30

Nos. 1226a, 1228b issued 5/2/08. Labels on Nos. 1226a and 1228b could not be personalized. Nos. 1226a and 1228b sold as a set for $154.

Birds — A269

Designs: 10c, White-bellied sea eagle. 20c, Collared scops owl. 50c, Scarlet minivet. $1, Common kingfisher. $1.40, Fork-tailed sunbird. $1.80, Roseate tern. $1.90, Black-faced spoonbill. $2, Little egret. $2.40, Greater painted snipe. $2.50, Barn swallow. $3, Red-whiskered bulbul. $5, Long-tailed shrike. $10, White wagtail. $13, Northern shoveler. $20, Common magpie. $50, Dalmatian pelican.

Perf. 13x13¾ Syncopated
2006, Dec. 31   Photo.
Granite Paper
Size: 22x26mm

1229	A269	10c multi	.20	.20
1230	A269	20c multi	.20	.20
1231	A269	50c multi	.20	.20
1232	A269	$1 multi	.25	.25
1233	A269	$1.40 multi	.35	.35
a.		Booklet pane of 10	3.50	—
		Complete booklet, #1233a	3.50	
1234	A269	$1.80 multi	.45	.45
a.		Booklet pane of 10	4.50	
		Complete booklet, #1234a	4.50	
1235	A269	$1.90 multi	.50	.50
1236	A269	$2 multi	.55	.55
1237	A269	$2.40 multi	.60	.60
a.		Booklet pane of 10	6.00	
		Complete booklet, #1237a	6.00	
1238	A269	$2.50 multi	.65	.65
1239	A269	$3 multi	.80	.80
a.		Booklet pane of 10	8.00	
		Complete booklet, #1239a	8.00	
1240	A269	$5 multi	1.40	1.40
a.		Miniature sheet, #1229-1240	6.25	6.25
b.		Booklet pane, #1229-1240	6.25	
		Complete booklet, #1240b	6.25	

Size: 25x30mm
Perf. 13½x13¼ Syncopated

1241	A269	$10 multi	2.60	2.60
a.		Souvenir sheet of 1	2.60	2.60
1242	A269	$13 multi	3.50	3.50
1243	A269	$20 multi	5.25	5.25
1244	A269	$50 multi	13.00	13.00
a.		Souvenir sheet, #1241-1244	25.00	25.00
		Nos. 1229-1244 (16)	30.50	30.50

Coil Stamps
Size: 17x21mm
Perf. 14¾x13½ Syncopated

1245	A269	$1.40 multi	.35	.35
1246	A269	$1.80 multi	.45	.45
1247	A269	$2.40 multi	.60	.60
1248	A269	$3 multi	.80	.80
		Nos. 1245-1248 (4)	2.20	2.20

Nos. 1241-1244 have microperforations around denominations.
Issued: No. 1241a, 9/21/10.

New Year 2007
(Year of the
Pig) — A270

Various pigs with background colors of: $1.40, Brown. $2.40, Orange red. $3, Green. $5, Rose.

2007, Feb. 4   Perf. 13½ Syncopated
Granite Paper

1249-1252	A270	Set of 4	3.25	3.25
1252a		Souvenir sheet of #1252, imperf.	2.00	2.00
1252b		Souvenir sheet, #1249-1252	3.75	3.75

New Year Types of 2004
2007, Feb. 4   Litho.   Perf. 13x13½
Flocked Paper

1253		Block of 4	10.50	10.50
a.	A221	$10 Like #1075	2.60	2.60
b.	A244	$10 Like #1128	2.60	2.60
c.	A256	$10 Like #1170	2.60	2.60
d.	A270	$10 Like #1251	2.60	2.60

Souvenir Sheet

New Year 2007 (Year of the
Pig) — A271

No. 1254: a, Beagle. b, Pig and piglet.

Litho. & Embossed With Foil Application
2007, Feb. 4   Perf. 13¼

| 1254 | A271 | $50 Sheet of 2, #a-b | 26.00 | 26.00 |

Scouting, Cent. — A272

Designs: $1.40, Campfire, Lord Robert Baden-Powell. $2.40, Hong Kong Scouting emblem, compass. $3, Backpack, knot. $5, Scouts, tent.

Litho. With Foil Application
Perf. 13¼x14¼ Syncopated
2007, Mar. 1
Granite Paper

| 1255-1258 | A272 | Set of 4 | 3.50 | 3.50 |
| *1258a* | | Souvenir sheet, #1255-1258 | 3.50 | 3.50 |

Children's
Games and
Puzzles
A273

Designs: $1.40, Find the difference between the two rabbits. $1.80, Color in the dotted areas. $2.40, Maze. $2.50, Follow lines to hunt for Easter Eggs. $3, Find the ten rabbits. $5, Look for a star.

Perf. 13¾ Syncopated
2007, Mar. 22   Litho.
Granite Paper

| 1259-1264 | A273 | Set of 6 | 4.25 | 4.25 |
| *1264a* | | Souvenir sheet, #1259-1264 | 4.25 | 4.25 |

A booklet containing three panes, containing Nos. 1259-1260, 1261-1262, and 1263-1264 respectively, sold for $36.

Souvenir Sheet

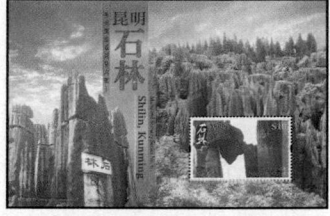

Stone Forest, Shilin — A274

Perf. 13¼x14¼ Syncopated
2007, May 3
Granite Paper

| 1265 | A274 | $10 multi | 2.60 | 2.60 |

Chinese
Martial
Arts
A275

Designs: $1.40, Southern Lion Dance. $2.40, Nanquan. $3, Northern Lion Dance. $5, Beitui.

Litho. with Foil Application
2007, May 22

| 1266-1269 | A275 | Set of 4 | 3.00 | 3.00 |
| *1269a* | | Souvenir sheet, #1266-1269 | 3.00 | 3.00 |

Butterflies — A276

Designs: $1.40, Faunis eumeus. $1.80, Prioneris philonome. $2.40, Polyura nepenthes. $3, Tajuria maculata. $5, Acraea issoria.

Perf. 13½ Syncopated
2007, June 14   Litho.
Granite Paper

| 1270-1274 | A276 | Set of 5 | 3.50 | 3.50 |

A booklet containing two panes, one containing Nos. 1270-1272 and the other containing Nos. 1273-1274, sold for $38.

Return of Hong Kong to China, 10th Anniv. A277

Perf. 13x12¾ Syncopated

2007, July 1   Photo.
1275 A277 $1.40 multi   .35 .35

A souvenir sheet containing No. 1275 and People's Republic of China Nos. 3594-3596 sold for $12.95.

A278

Hong Kong Special Administrative Region, 10th Anniv. — A279

Designs: $1.40, Ten children with joined hands. $1.80, Banner on Hong Kong Heritage Museum. $2.40, Vehicles on Tsing Ma Bridge. $2.50, Ten birds over Hong Kong Wetland Park. $3, Two International Finance Center Building and Moon. $5, Fireworks over Hong Kong.

No. 1282: a, "7" over Bank of China Tower, fireworks over Cheung Kong Center. b, Fireworks over smaller buildings. c, Fireworks over smaller buildings, Two International Finance Center Building at right.

Perf. 13½x14¼ Syncopated

2007, July 1   Litho.
Granite Paper
1276-1281 A278 Set of 6   4.25 4.25
Litho. With Foil Application and Hologram
Perf. 13½
1282 A279 $10 Sheet of 3, #a-c   7.75 7.75

Souvenir Sheet

Bangkok 2007 Asian International Stamp Exhibition — A280

Perf. 13½x14¼ Syncopated

2007, Aug. 3   Litho.
Granite Paper
1283 A280 $10 multi   2.60 2.60

Civic Education A281

Designs: $1.40, Human rights. $2.40, Rule of law. $3, Social participation. $5, Corporate citizenship.

2007, Aug. 23   **Perf. 13 Syncopated**
Granite Paper
1284-1287 A281 Set of 4   3.00 3.00
1287a   Miniature sheet, 4 each   #1284-1287   12.00 12.00

Declared Monuments — A282

Designs: $1.40, Tin Hau Temple, Causeway Bay. $1.80, Old Wan Chai Post Office. $2.40, Former Central Police Station Compound. $2.50, Former Yamen Building of Kowloon Walled City. $3, Kun Lung Gate Tower, Lung Yeuk Tau. $5, Tang Lung Chau Lighthouse.

Litho. & Engr.
2007, Sept. 20   **Perf. 14x13¼**
Granite Paper
1288-1293 A282 Set of 6   4.25 4.25
1293a   Miniature sheet, #1288-1293   4.25 4.25

Christmas — A283

Designs: $1.40, Stocking. $2.40, Gingerbread man-shaped egg tart. $3, Bell decorated with neon lights. $5, Snowman with Chinese vest.

2007, Oct. 11   **Litho.**   **Perf. 13x13½**
Granite Paper
1294-1297 A283 Set of 4   3.00 3.00

Woodwork — A284

Designs: No. 1298, $5, Zitan armchair with dragon design, China, denomination at left. No. 1299, $5, Modern Finnish bowls, denomination at right.

Perf. 13½x14¼ Syncopated
2007, Nov. 2
Granite Paper
1298-1299 A284 Set of 2   2.60 2.60
1299a   Souvenir sheet, #1298-1299   2.60 2.60

See Finland No. 1298.

Heartwarming A285

Designs: No. 1300, Birds and flowers. No. 1301, Firecrackers. No. 1302, Gifts and balloons. No. 1303, Slippers.

Perf. 13½ Syncopated
2007, Dec. 28   Litho.
Granite Paper
Inscribed "Local Mail Postage"
1300 A285 ($1.40) multi   .35 .35
1301 A285 ($1.40) multi   .35 .35
Inscribed "Air Mail Postage"
1302 A285 ($3) multi   .80 .80
1303 A285 ($3) multi   .80 .80
  a.   Sheet, 5 each #1300-1303   + 21 labels   11.50 11.50

New Year 2008 (Year of the Rat) — A286

Various rats with background colors of: $1.40, Blue. $2.40, Green. $3, Orange red. $5, Brown.

Perf. 13½x13¼ Syncopated
2008, Jan. 26   Litho.
Granite Paper
1304-1307 A286 Set of 4   3.00 3.00
1307a   Souvenir sheet of #1307,   imperf.   1.25 1.25
1307b   Souvenir sheet, #1304-1307   3.00 3.00

Souvenir Sheet

New Year 2008 (Year of the Rat) — A287

No. 1308: a, Pig. b, Rat.

Litho. & Embossed With Foil Application
2008, Jan. 26   **Perf. 13¼**
1308 A287 $50 Sheet of 2, #a-b   26.00 26.00

Souvenir Sheet

Huanglong — A288

Perf. 14¼ Syncopated
2008, Feb. 28   Litho.
Granite Paper
1309 A288 $10 multi   2.60 2.60

Flowers A289

Designs: $1.40, Chinese hibiscus. $1.80, Tree cotton. $2.40, Allamandas. $2.50, Azaleas. $3, Indian lotus. $5, Morning glories.

Perf. 13½x13¼ Syncopated
2008, Mar. 14
Granite Paper
1310-1315 A289 Set of 6   4.25 4.25
1315a   Souvenir sheet, #1310-1315   4.25 4.25

Paper Folding Art — A290

Designs: $1.40, Bauhinia blossoms. $1.80, Bear, horiz. $2.40, Lunar New Year decorations. $2.50, Lotus flowers and rainbow, horiz. $3, Koalas, monkey with banana. $5, Christmas party scene, horiz.

Perf. 14¼x13½, 13½x14¼ Syncopated
2008, May 22
1316-1321 A290 Set of 6   4.25 4.25
1321a   Souvenir sheet, #1316-1321   4.25 4.25

Jellyfish — A291

Designs: $1.40, Flower hat jellyfish. $1.80, Octopus jellyfish, horiz. $2.40, Brown sea nettle. $2.50, Moon jellyfish, horiz. $3, Lion's mane jellyfish. $5, Pacific sea nettle.

Perf. 14¼ Syncopated
2008, June 12   Litho.
Granite Paper
1322-1327 A291 Set of 6   4.25 4.25
1327a   Souvenir sheet, #1322-1327   4.25 4.25

Stamps have a glow-in-the dark coating on the jellyfish illustrations. A booklet containing panes of Nos. 1322-1323, 1324-1325, and 1326-1327, sold for $36.

Giant Pandas A292

Designs: $1.40, Ying Ying, Le Le, and hearts. $2.40, Ying Ying and leaves. $3, Le Le and panda heads. $5, Ying Ying, Le Le, and circles.

2008, July 1   **Perf. 13¾ Syncopated**
Granite Paper
1328-1331 A292 Set of 4   3.00 3.00
1331a   Sheet, 2 each # 1328-1331, +   4 labels   6.00 6.00

Hong Kong, Venue for 2008 Summer Olympic Equestrian Events — A293

Designs: $1.40, Horse and rider jumping fence. $2.40, Dressage. $3, Horse and rider jumping over water obstacle. $5, Horse and rider at medal stand.

Perf. 13¼x14 Syncopated
2008, Aug. 9
Granite Paper
1332-1335 A293 Set of 4   3.00 3.00
1335a   Souvenir sheet, #1332-1335   3.00 3.00

Souvenir Sheet

Praga 2008 World Stamp
Exhibition — A294

Perf. 13¼x14¼ Syncopated
2008, Sept. 12   Litho.
Granite Paper
1336 A294 $10 multi   2.60 2.60

Big Head
Buddha Mask,
Hong
Kong — A295

Chwibari Mask,
Korea — A296

Perf. 13¼x14 Syncopated
2008, Nov. 6
Granite Paper
1337 A295 $5 multi   1.40 1.40
1338 A296 $5 multi   1.40 1.40
  a.   Souvenir sheet, #1337-1338   3.00 3.00
See South Korea No. 2299.

The
Judiciary
A297

Designs: $1.40, Statue of Justice. $2.40,
Court of Final Appeal. $3, Judicial robes for
various courts. $5, Chief Justice's mace.

Perf. 13¾ Syncopated
2008, Nov. 27
Granite Paper
1339-1342 A297 Set of 4   3.00 3.00
  1342a   Souvenir sheet, #1339-1342   3.00 3.00

New Year 2009
(Year of the
Ox) — A298

Various oxen with background colors of:
$1.40, Purple. $2.40, Brown. $3, Green. $5,
Blue.

Perf. 13½x13¼ Syncopated
2009, Jan. 17   Litho.
Granite Paper
1343-1346 A298 Set of 4   3.00 3.00
  1346a   Souvenir sheet of #1346, im-
           perf.   1.25 1.25
  1346b   Souvenir sheet, #1343-1346   3.00 3.00

Souvenir Sheet

New Year 2009 (Year of the
Ox) — A299

No. 1347: a, Rat. b, Ox.

**Litho. & Embossed With Foil
Application**
2009, Jan. 17   Perf. 13¼
1347 A299 $50 Sheet of 2, #a-
            b   26.00 26.00

Souvenir Sheet

Mount Tianshan — A300

Perf. 14¼ Syncopated
2009, Feb. 24   Litho.
Granite Paper
1348 A300 $10 multi   2.60 2.60

Souvenir Sheet

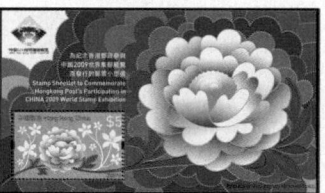

Peony and Bauhinia Flowers — A301

2009, Apr. 7   *Perf. 13¼ Syncopated*
               Granite Paper
1349 A301 $5 multi   1.40 1.40
  China 2009 World Stamp Exhibition,
Luoyang.

Souvenir Sheet

Tangram Figure — A302

2009, May 14   Perf. 13¼
Granite Paper
1350 A302 $50 multi + 2 labels 13.00 13.00
  Hong Kong 2009 Intl. Stamp Exhibition.

Items in Hong Kong
Museums — A303

Designs: $1.40, Poem by Wang Duo, Hong
Kong Museum of Art. $1.80, Landscape,
painting by Wang Yuanqi, Hong Kong Museum
of Art. $2.40, Calligraphy by Wang Xizhi, Art
Museum of the Chinese University of Hong
Kong. $2.50, Bird in Moonlight, painting by
Gao Qifeng, Hong Kong Heritage Museum.
$3, Flower and Butterfly, fan painting by Ju
Lian, Hong Kong Heritage Museum, horiz.
(50x30mm). $5, Drawing by Gu Huai, Univer-
sity Museum and Art Gallery of the University
of Hong Kong, horiz. (50x30mm).

Perf. 13½x13¼ Syncopated
2009, May 16
Granite Paper
1351-1356 A303 Set of 6   4.25 4.25
  1356a   Souvenir sheet, #1351-
           1356   4.25 4.25

Heartwarming
A304

Designs: No. 1357, Flowers. No. 1358, Lion.
No. 1359, Birthday hats. No. 1360, Butterflies
and heart.

Perf. 13½ Syncopated
2009, June 25
Granite Paper
Inscribed "Local Mail Postage"
1357 A304 ($1.40) multi   .35 .35
1358 A304 ($1.40) multi   .35 .35
Inscribed "Air Mail Postage"
1359 A304 ($3) multi   .80 .80
1360 A304 ($3) multi   .80 .80
  a.   Sheet of 12, 3 each #1357-
        1360, + 12 labels   7.00 7.00
  Nos. 1357-1360 (4)   2.30 2.30
Labels on No. 1360a could not be
personalized.

Customs
and
Excise
Service,
Cent.
A305

Designs: $1.40, Officer with drug-sniffing
dog and baggage inspectors of 1960s. $2.40,
Mobile x-ray vehicle scanner and Sheng Shui
Customs Station, 1935. $3, Patrol boats. $5,
Officers raising flag.

Perf. 13¼x13 Syncopated
2009, Sept. 17   Litho.
Granite Paper
1361-1364 A305 Set of 4   3.00 3.00
  1364a   Souvenir sheet, #1361-
           1364   3.00 3.00
A booklet containing two panes, one with
Nos. 1361-1362, and the other with Nos.
1363-1364, sold for $36.

A306

People's Republic of China, 60th
Anniv. — A307

Designs: $1.40, Cogwheels, Victoria Har-
bor, Hong Kong and Tiananmen Square, Beij-
ing. $1.80, Flag of People's Republic of China,
Forever Blooming Bauhinia statue, Hong
Kong. $2.40, Dove, Olympic Stadium, Beijing.
$2.50, Shenzhou-7 on launch pad. $3, Doves,
Temple of Heaven. $5, Dragon, Great Wall of
China.
  No. 1371: a, Emblem of People's Republic
of China, Tiananmen Square. b, Emblem of
Hong Kong, Hong Kong skyline at night.

2009, Oct. 1   Perf. 13¼
Granite Paper (A306)
1365-1370 A306 Set of 6   4.50 4.50
  1370a   Souvenir sheet, #1365-
           1370   5.00 5.00
Souvenir Sheet
Perf. 13
1371 A307 $5 Sheet of 2, #a-b 3.00 3.00

Soccer
A308

Soccer player from: $1.40, Hong Kong.
$2.40, Hong Kong, diff. $3, Brazil. $5, Brazil,
diff.

Perf. 13¼x14¼ Syncopated
2009, Nov. 5
Granite Paper
1372-1375 A308 Set of 4   3.00 3.00
  1375a   Souvenir sheet, #1372-
           1375   3.00 3.00
See Brazil No. 3114.

2009
East
Asia
Games,
Hong
Kong
A309

Designs: No. 1376, $1.40, Judo, rowing and
rugby. No. 1377, $1.40, Wushu, track, bad-
minton and shooting. No. 1378, $2.40,
Squash, basketball, field hockey and swimming. No. 1379, $2.40, Cycling, weight lifting
and tennis. No. 1380, $3, Bowling, windsurf-
ing, soccer and taekwondo. No. 1381, $3,
Dancing, table tennis, volleyball and billiards.

Litho. With Foil Application
2009, Dec. 5   *Perf. 14¼ Syncopated*
               Granite Paper
1376-1381 A309 Set of 6   3.50 3.50
  1381a   Souvenir sheet, #1376-
           1381   3.50 3.50

Stonecutters
Bridge — A310

Designs: $1.40, View of bridge tower from
water level. $2.40, Aerial view of bridge, horiz.
$3, View of bridge from water level, horiz. $5,
Aerial view of bridge tower.

Perf. 14½x14 Syncopated, 14x14½ Syncopated
2009, Dec. 17
Granite Paper   Litho.

1382-1385	A310	Set of 4	3.00	3.00
1385a		Souvenir sheet, #1382-1385	3.00	3.00

New Year 2010 (Year of the Tiger) — A311

Various tigers with background colors of: $1.40, Red. $2.40, Green. $3, Blue. $5, Orange.

Perf. 13½x13¼ Syncopated
2010, Feb. 6
Granite Paper

1386-1389	A311	Set of 4	3.00	3.00
1389a		Souvenir sheet of #1389, imperf.	1.25	1.25
1389b		Souvenir sheet, #1386-1389	3.00	3.00

Souvenir Sheet

New Year 2010 (Year of the Tiger) — A312

No. 1390: a, Ox. b, Tiger.

Litho. & Embossed With Foil Application
2010, Feb. 6   Perf. 13¾

1390	A312	$50 Sheet of 2, #a-b	26.00	26.00

Souvenir Sheet

Fujian Tulou UNESCO World Heritage Site — A313

Perf. 13¼ Syncopated
2010, Mar. 18
Granite Paper   Litho.

1391	A313	$10 multi	2.60	2.60

Expo 2010, Shanghai — A314

Designs: $1.40, Dragon dance. $2.40, Hong Kong on green leaf. $3, Tsing Ma Bridge, Hong Kong. $5, Smart Card chip, head, Hong Kong skyline.

2010, Apr. 27   Perf. 13¼ Syncopated
Granite Paper

1392-1395	A314	Set of 4	3.00	3.00
1395a		Souvenir sheet #1392-1395	3.00	3.00

No. 1395a was printed in sheet containing four souvenir sheets.

Souvenir Sheet

London 2010 Intl. Philatelic Exhibition — A315

2010, May 8   Litho.
Granite Paper

1396	A315	$10 multi	2.60	2.60

Hong Kong Street Scenes — A316

Designs: No. 1397, $1.40, Pottinger Street. No. 1398, $1.40, Nathan Road. No. 1399, $2.40, Hollywood Road. No. 1400, $2.40, Temple Street. No. 1401, $3, Des Voeux Road West. No. 1402, $3, Stanley Market.

Perf. 13¾ Syncopated
2010, June 24
Granite Paper

1397-1402	A316	Set of 6	3.50	3.50
1402a		Souvenir sheet, #1397-1402	3.50	3.50

Intl. Year of Biodiversity — A317

Designs: $1.40, Macropodus hongkongensis. $2.40, Liuixalus romeri. $3, Sinopora hongkongensis. $5, Fukienogomphus choifongae.

Perf. 13¼x14¼ Syncopated
2010, July 15
Granite Paper   Litho.

1403-1406	A317	Set of 4	3.00	3.00
1406a		Souvenir sheet, #1403-1406	3.00	3.00

Railways in Hong Kong, Cent. — A318

Designs: $1.40, Steam train, Hong Kong Railway Museum. $1.80, Diesel train, clock tower of Kowloon-Canton Railway Terminus. $2.40, Electric train, Hung Hom Terminus. $2.50, Mass Transit Railway train, International Finance Center. $3, Kowloon-Guangzhou through train, Mass Transit Railway Hung Hom Station. $5, Airport Express train, aerial view of Hong Kong International Airport.

$20, Steam train, Hong Kong Railway Museum, diff.

Perf. 13½x13¼ Syncopated
2010, Sept. 28
Granite Paper   Litho.

1407-1412	A318	Set of 6	4.25	4.25
1412a		Souvenir sheet, #1407-1412	4.25	4.25

Souvenir Sheet
Litho. With Three-Dimensional Plastic Affixed

1413	A318	$20 multi	5.25	5.25

No. 1413 contains one 37x51mm stamp.
A booklet containing three panes, containing Nos. 1407-1408, 1409-1410, and 1411-1412 respectively, sold for $36.

Winning Entries in Children's Stamp Design Contest — A319

Designs: $1.40, "Harbor of Hong Kong." $2.40, "Beautiful Hong Kong." $3, "Hong Kong is Fun." $5, "City Beat."

Perf. 13¼x13½ Syncopated
2010, Oct. 21
Granite Paper   Litho.

1414-1417	A319	Set of 4	3.00	3.00
1417a		Souvenir sheet, #1414-1417	3.00	3.00

Renovation of Old Neighborhoods — A320

Designs: $1.40, Rehabilitation. $2.40, Revitalization. $3, Preservation. $5, Redevelopment.

Perf. 13¾ Syncopated
2010, Nov. 16
Granite Paper

1418-1421	A320	Set of 4	3.00	3.00
1421a		Souvenir sheet, #1418-1421	3.00	3.00

SEMI-POSTAL STAMPS

> Catalogue values for unused stamps in this section are for Never Hinged items.

Community Chest of Hong Kong — SP1

1988, Nov. 30   Litho.   Perf. 14½

B1	SP1	60c +10c Girl	.60	.35
B2	SP1	$1.40 +20c Elderly woman	.75	.70
B3	SP1	$1.80 +30c Blind youth	1.75	1.00
B4	SP1	$5 +$1 Mother and child	4.25	2.75
		Nos. B1-B4 (4)	7.35	4.80

Surtax for the social welfare organization.

POSTAGE DUE STAMPS

Scales Showing Letter Overweight — D1

1923, Dec. Typo. Wmk. 4   Perf. 14

J1	D1	1c brown	2.75	.70
a.		Chalky paper, wmkd. sideways	1.60	3.50
J2	D1	2c green	13.00	5.25
J3	D1	4c red	37.50	7.50
J4	D1	6c orange	35.00	15.00
J5	D1	10c ultramarine	30.00	9.00
		Nos. J1-J5 (5)	118.25	37.45
		Set, never hinged	300.00	

No. J1a issued Mar. 21, 1956.

1938-47   Perf. 14

J6	D1	2c gray	1.40	10.00
J7	D1	4c orange yellow	2.50	10.00
J8	D1	6c carmine	10.00	6.00
J9	D1	8c fawn ('46)	6.00	32.50
J10	D1	10c violet	17.50	7.50
J11	D1	20c black ('46)	12.50	3.50
J12	D1	50c black ('47)	40.00	16.00
		Nos. J6-J12 (7)	89.90	85.50
		Set, never hinged	190.00	

Nos. J6-J7 and J10 exist on both ordinary and chalky paper.

> Catalogue values for unused stamps in this section, from this point to the end of the section, are for Never Hinged items.

Wmk. 314 Sideways
1965-69   Perf. 14

J13	D1	4c orange yellow	9.00	30.00
J14	D1	5c orange ver ('69)	3.75	5.25
a.		5c carmine, wmk. upright ('67)	4.00	5.00
J15	D1	10c purple ('67)	4.75	7.50
J16	D1	20c black	10.00	4.50
J17	D1	50c dark blue	37.50	7.00
a.		Wmk. upright ('70)	50.00	11.50
		Nos. J13-J17 (5)	65.00	52.75

Size of 5c, 21x18mm.; others, 22x18mm.

Wmk. 314 Upright
1972-74   Perf. 13½x14
Glazed Ordinary Paper

J18	D1	5c red brown ('74)	3.00	6.00

Perf. 14x14½

J19	D1	10c lilac	7.00	5.00
J20	D1	20c black	8.50	7.00
J21	D1	50c dull blue	6.00	11.00
		Nos. J18-J21 (4)	24.50	29.00

1978   Wmk. 373

J22	D1	10c lilac	1.00	5.50
f.		Chalk-surfaced paper	1.00	2.25
J22A	D1	20c black	1.50	7.50
g.		Chalk-surfaced paper	1.75	2.25
J22B	D1	50c dull blue	1.50	6.00
h.		Chalk-surfaced paper	1.75	3.00
J22C	D1	$1 yellow	14.00	14.00
i.		Chalk-surfaced paper	1.50	4.25
		Nos. J22-J22C (4)	18.00	33.00

Size of $1, 20½x17mm; others, 22x18mm.
Issued: Nos. J22-J22C, 3/19; J22f-J22i, 12/15.

1986, Jan. 11   Unwmk.
Chalk-surfaced Paper

J22D	D1	50c dull blue	2.25	5.75
J22E	D1	$1 yellow	3.00	8.00

D2

Perf. 14x15
1986, Mar. 25   Litho.   Unwmk.

J23	D2	10c light green	.20	.50
J24	D2	20c dark red brown	.20	.50
J25	D2	50c lilac	.20	.20
J26	D2	$1 light orange	.20	.20
J27	D2	$5 grayish blue	1.00	1.75
J28	D2	$10 rose red	2.00	3.50
		Nos. J23-J28 (6)	3.80	6.65

D3

Perf. 14x14¾

2004, Sept. 23		Litho.	Unwmk.	
J29	D3	10c dark blue	.20	.50
J30	D3	20c blue	.20	.50
J31	D3	50c orange	.30	.20
J32	D3	$1 pink	.65	.75
J33	D3	$5 olive green	1.60	1.75
J34	D3	$10 cerise	3.50	3.50
		Nos. J29-J34 (6)	6.45	7.20

OCCUPATION STAMPS

Issued under Japanese Occupation

War Factory Girl — A144

Gen. Maresuke Nogi — A84

Admiral Heihachiro Togo — A86

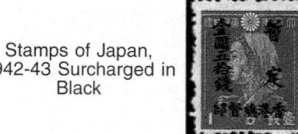

Stamps of Japan, 1942-43 Surcharged in Black

Wmk. 257

1945, Apr.		Typo.	Perf. 13	
N1	A144	1½y on 1s org brn	40.00	35.00
N2	A84	3y on 2s ver	14.00	30.00
N3	A86	5y on 5s brn lake	975.00	175.00
		Nos. N1-N3 (3)	1,029.	240.00

No. N1 has eleven characters.

HORTA

'hor-tə

LOCATION — An administrative district of the Azores, consisting of the islands of Pico, Fayal, Flores and Corvo
GOVT. — A district of the Republic of Portugal
AREA — 305 sq. mi.
POP. — 49,000 (approx.)
CAPITAL — Horta

1000 Reis = 1 Milreis

King Carlos
A1   A2
Chalk-surfaced Paper

Perf. 11½, 12½, 13½

1892-93		Typo.	Unwmk.	
1	A1	5r yellow	2.00	1.50
2	A1	10r reddish violet	2.00	1.75
3	A1	15r chocolate	2.00	2.00
4	A1	20r lavender	3.00	3.00
5	A1	25r dp grn, perf. 11½	4.50	1.00
a.		Perf. 13½	5.00	3.75
6	A1	50r blue	6.25	3.00
a.		Perf. 13½	9.00	5.25
7	A1	75r carmine	6.50	4.00
8	A1	80r yellow green	9.00	6.00
9	A1	100r brn, yel ('93)	35.00	10.00
a.		Perf. 12½	125.00	90.00

10	A1	150r car, rose ('93)	45.00	32.50
11	A1	200r dk bl, bl ('93)	45.00	32.50
12	A1	300r dark blue ('93)	45.00	35.00
		Nos. 1-12 (12)	205.25	132.25

Bisects of No. 1 were used in Aug. 1894. Value, on newsprint, $16.

The reprints have shiny white gum and clean-cut perforation 13½. The white paper is thinner than that of the originals. Value unused, $12 each.

1897-1905   Perf. 11½
Name and Value in Black Except 500r

13	A2	2½r gray	.50	.30
14	A2	5r orange	.50	.30
15	A2	10r lt green	.50	.30
16	A2	15r brown	4.50	2.50
17	A2	15r gray grn ('99)	1.25	.80
18	A2	20r gray violet	1.75	.85
19	A2	25r sea green	2.25	.45
20	A2	25r car rose ('99)	.90	.50
21	A2	50r blue	3.00	.70
22	A2	50r ultra ('05)	12.00	7.00
23	A2	65r slate blue ('98)	.70	.55
24	A2	75r rose	1.90	.95
25	A2	75r brn, yel ('05)	15.00	10.00
26	A2	80r violet	1.25	1.10
27	A2	100r dk blue, bl	1.75	.95
28	A2	115r org brn, pink ('98)	3.00	1.50
29	A2	130r gray brn, buff ('98)	3.00	1.50
30	A2	150r lt brn, buff	3.00	1.50
31	A2	180r sl, pnksh ('98)	3.00	1.75
32	A2	200r red vio, pale lil	5.50	4.00
33	A2	300r dk blue, rose	9.00	6.75
34	A2	500r blk & red, bl	12.00	8.50
		Nos. 13-34 (22)	86.25	52.75

Stamps of Portugal replaced those of Horta.

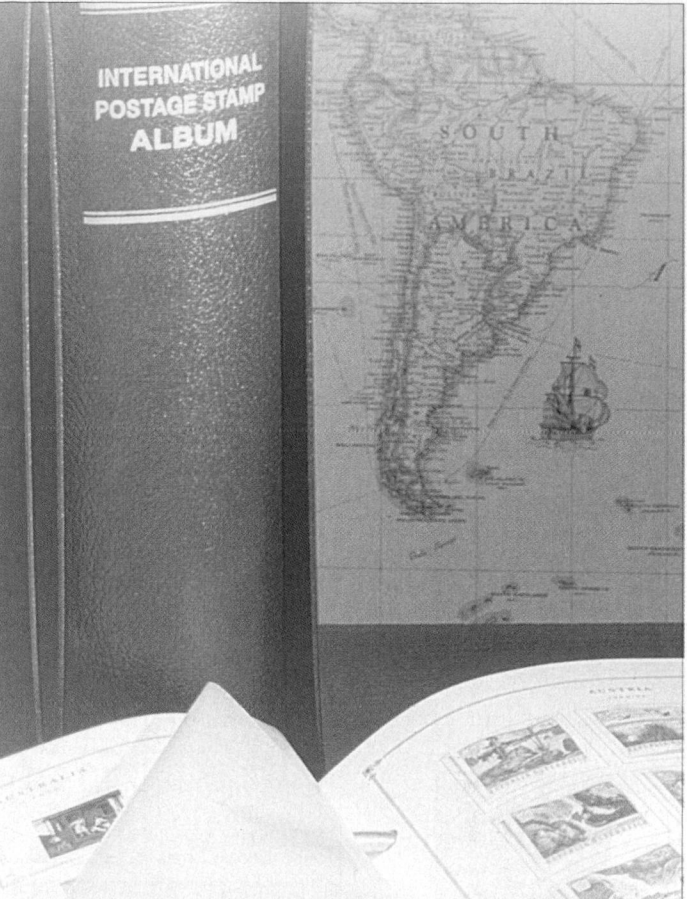

HUNGARY

ˈhəŋ-g.ə-ˌrē

LOCATION — Central Europe
GOVT. — Republic
AREA — 35,911 sq. mi.
POP. — 10,186,372 (1999 est.)
CAPITAL — Budapest

Prior to World War I, Hungary together with Austria comprised the Austro-Hungarian Empire. The Hungarian post became independent on May 1, 1867. During 1850-1871 stamps listed under Austria were also used in Hungary. Copies showing clear Hungarian cancels sell for substantially more.

100 Krajczár (Kreuzer) = 1 Forint 100 Fillér = 1 Korona (1900) 100 Fillér = 1 Pengö (1926) 100 Fillér = 1 Forint (1946)

Catalogue values for unused stamps in this country are for Never Hinged items, beginning with Scott 503 in the regular postage section, Scott B92 in the semipostal section, Scott C35 in the airpost section, Scott CB1 in the airpost semi-postal section, Scott F1 in the registrtation section, Scott J130 in the postage due section, and Scott Q9 in the parcel post section.

Watermarks

Wmk. 91 — "ZEITUNGS-MARKEN" in Double-lined Capitals across the Sheet

Wmk. 106 — Multiple Star

Wmk. 132 — kr in Oval

Wmk. 133 — Four Double Crosses

Wmk. 135 — Crown in Oval or Circle, Sideways

Wmk. 136   Wmk. 136a

Wmk. 137 — Double Cross

Wmk. 210 — Double Cross on Pyramid

Wmk. 266 — Double Barred Cross, Wreath and Crown

Wmk. 283 — Double Barred Cross on Shield, Multiple

Watermarks 132, 135, 136 and 136a can be found normal, reversed, inverted, or reversed and inverted.

Values for unused stamps are for examples with original gum as defined in the catalogue introduction. Very fine examples of Nos. 1-12 will have perforations touching the framelines on one or two sides due to imperfect perforating methods. Stamps with perfs clear on all four sides are very scarce and will command substantial premiums.

Issues of the Monarchy

Franz Josef I — A1

1871		**Unwmk.**	**Litho.**	**Perf. 9½**

1	A1	2k orange	225.00	90.00
a.		2k yellow	1,300.	225.00
2	A1	3k lt green	725.00	550.00
3	A1	5k rose	300.00	20.00
a.		5k brick red	600.00	75.00
4	A1	10k blue	700.00	90.00
a.		10k pale blue	950.00	150.00
5	A1	15k yellow brn	750.00	100.00
6	A1	25k violet	750.00	175.00
a.		25k bright violet	850.00	275.00

The first printing of No. 1, in dark yellow, was not issued because of spots on the King's face. A few stamps were used at Pest in 1873. Value, $3,500.

1871-72				**Engr.**
7	A1	2k orange	37.50	7.50
a.		2k yellow	150.00	17.00
b.		Bisect on cover	—	
8	A1	3k green	85.00	25.00
a.		3k blue green	110.00	30.00
9	A1	5k rose	50.00	1.75
a.		5k brick red	125.00	8.00
10	A1	10k deep blue	200.00	10.00
11	A1	15k brown	225.00	15.00
a.		15k copper brown	—	900.00
b.		15k black brown	875.00	85.00
12	A1	25k lilac	140.00	40.00
		Nos. 7-12 (6)	737.50	99.25

Reprints are perf. 11½ and watermarked "kr" in oval. Value, set $225.

Crown of St. Stephen
A2   A3

Design A3 has an overall burelage of dots. Compare with design N3.

1874-76				**Perf. 13**
13	A2	2k red violet	50.00	4.00
a.		2k violet	60.00	5.00
14	A2	3k yellow green	50.00	4.00
a.		3k blue green	70.00	5.00
15	A2	5k red	15.00	.80
a.		5k brick red	40.00	2.00
b.		5k lilac red	25.00	1.50
c.		5k rose	12.00	.50
16	A2	10k blue	65.00	1.50
17	A2	20k grnsh gray	575.00	14.00
a.		20k gray	600.00	15.00
		Nos. 13-17 (5)	755.00	24.30

				Perf. 11½
13b	A2	2k red violet	70.00	10.00
c.		2k violet	75.00	12.00
d.		2k rose lilac	110.00	9.00
e.		2k gray blue	90.00	9.50
14b	A2	3k yellow green	80.00	8.00
c.		3k blue green	90.00	10.00
15d	A2	5k red	90.00	2.00
e.		5k rose	80.00	1.50
16a	A2	10k blue	110.00	10.00
17b	A2	20k gray	1,500.	42.50

				Perf. 13x11½
13f	A2	2k red violet	150.00	25.00
g.		2k rose lilac	165.00	30.00
14d	A2	3k yellow green	100.00	4.25
15f	A2	5k lilac red	125.00	12.00
g.		5k rose	150.00	15.00
16b	A2	10k blue	200.00	5.75
17c	A2	20k gray	600.00	47.50

				Perf. 11½x13
13h	A2	2k red violet	100.00	4.75
f.		2k rose lilac	165.00	4.00
g.		2k gray blue	125.00	3.50
15h	A2	5k red	125.00	1.00

17d	A2	20k gray	—	95.00
				Perf. 9½
14e	A2	3k green	3,000.	2.000.

All examples of the 5k perf 9½ are counterfeit.

1881		**Wmk. 132**		**Perf. 11½**
18	A2	2k lilac	7.00	.80
a.		2k violet	7.00	.80
b.		2k gray blue	9.00	1.00
19	A2	3k blue green	7.00	.80
a.		3k yellow green	9.00	1.20
20	A2	5k rose	5.00	.30
21	A2	10k blue	12.00	.80
a.		10k pale blue	14.00	1.20
22	A2	20k gray	9.00	1.25
a.		20k greenish gray	10.00	1.50
		Nos. 18-22 (5)	40.00	3.95

				Perf. 13
18c	A2	2k violet	150.00	18.00
d.		2k gray blue	120.00	9.50
19b	A2	3k blue green	90.00	3.75
c.		3k yellow green	100.00	5.00
20a	A2	5k rose	120.00	3.75
21b	A2	10k blue	75.00	4.75
22b	A2	20k gray	350.00	15.00

				Perf. 13x11½
18e	A2	2k violet	—	40.00
19d	A2	3k blue green	200.00	6.00
e.		3k yellow green	—	8.00
20b	A2	5k rose	—	15.00
21c	A2	10k blue	—	8.00
22c	A2	20k gray	600.00	40.00

				Perf. 11½x13
18f	A2	2k violet	180.00	9.00
g.		2k gray blue	150.00	7.00
19f	A2	3k blue green	—	60.00
g.		3k yellow green	—	75.00
20c	A2	5k rose	75.00	1.00
21d	A2	10k blue	1,400.	2.00
22d	A2	20k gray	—	40.00

				Perf. 12x11½
18h	A2	2k lilac	1.00	.25
i.		2k violet	12.50	1.20
19h	A2	3k blue green	1.00	.25
20d	A2	5k rose	2.50	.25
21e	A2	10k blue	3.00	.25
22e	A2	20k gray	300.00	7.50

1888-98		**Typo.**	**Perf. 11½, 12x11½**	
		Numerals in Black		
22A	A3	1k black, one plate	.55	.40
c.		"1" printed separately	10.50	.90
23	A3	2k red violet	.80	.35
a.		Perf. 11½	725.00	50.00
24	A3	3k green	2.00	.50
a.		Perf. 11½	50.00	15.00
25	A3	5k rose	2.00	.30
a.		Perf. 11½	65.00	1.75
26	A3	8k orange	7.00	.80
a.		"8" double	150.00	
27	A3	10k blue	5.50	1.40
a.		Perf. 11½	450.00	325.00
28	A3	12k brown & green	14.00	1.00
29	A3	15k claret & blue	11.00	.40
30	A3	20k gray	8.50	2.25
a.		Perf. 11½	1,400.	600.00
31	A3	24k brn vio & red	25.00	1.25
32	A3	30k ol grn & brn	27.50	.45
33	A3	50k red & org	45.00	1.40
		Numerals in Red		
34	A3	1fo gray bl & sil	185.00	2.50
a.		Perf. 11½	190.00	3.50
35	A3	3fo lilac brn & gold	18.00	11.00
		Nos. 22A-35 (14)	351.85	24.00

1898-99				**Perf. 12x11½**
		Numerals in Black		
		Wmk. 135 (Oval)		
35A	A3	1k black	1.50	.50
36	A3	2k violet	6.00	.50
37	A3	3k green	4.00	.60
38	A3	5k rose	5.00	.40
39	A3	8k orange	17.50	4.00
40	A3	10k blue	5.00	1.00
41	A3	12k red brn & grn	75.00	9.00
42	A3	15k rose & blue	5.00	.75
43	A3	20k gray	35.00	2.00
44	A3	24k vio brn & red	6.00	4.75
45	A3	30k ol grn & brn	40.00	1.50
46	A3	50k dull red & org	100.00	15.00
		Nos. 35A-46 (12)	300.00	40.00

				Perf. 11½
35Ab	A3	1k black	40.00	7.50
36a	A3	2k violet	125.00	20.00
37a	A3	3k green	100.00	15.00
38a	A3	5k rose	140.00	15.00
39a	A3	8k orange	250.00	120.00
40a	A3	10k blue	150.00	60.00
41a	A3	12k red brn & grn	300.00	75.00
42a	A3	15k rose & blue	180.00	45.00
43a	A3	20k gray	275.00	60.00
44a	A3	24k vio brn & red	350.00	140.00
45a	A3	30k ol grn & brn	200.00	50.00
46a	A3	50k dull red & org	400.00	150.00

		Wmk. 135 (Circle)		
				Perf. 12x11½
35Ac	A3	1k black	14.00	7.50
36b	A3	2k violet	7.50	.75
37b	A3	3k green	8.50	1.25
38b	A3	5k rose	10.00	.50
39b	A3	8k orange	50.00	15.00
41b	A3	12k red brn & grn	60.00	22.50
42b	A3	15k rose & blue	200.00	3.00
43b	A3	20k gray	5.00	3.50
44b	A3	24k vio brn & red	900.00	40.00
45b	A3	30k ol grn & brn	5.00	4.00

46b	A3	50k dull red & org		15.00	30.00

Perf. 11½

35Ad	A3	1k black		50.00	15.00
36c	A3	2k violet		200.00	25.00
37c	A3	3k green		200.00	40.00
38c	A3	5k rose		100.00	15.00
39c	A3	8k orange		80.00	12.50
40c	A3	10k blue		350.00	80.00
41c	A3	12k red brn & grn		550.00	300.00
42c	A3	15k rose & blue		375.00	200.00
43c	A3	20k gray		1,200.	350.00
44c	A3	24k vio brn & red		1,500.	400.00
45c	A3	30k ol grn & brn		600.00	150.00
46c	A3	50k dull red & org		375.00	275.00

In the watermark with circles, a four-pointed star and "VI" appear four times in the sheet in the large spaces between the intersecting circles. The paper with the circular watermark is often yellowish and thinner than that with the oval watermark.

"Turul" and Crown of St. Stephen — A4

Franz Josef I Wearing Hungarian Crown — A5

1900-04   Wmk. 135   Perf. 12x11½
Numerals in Black

47	A4	1f gray		.60	.40
a.		1f dull lilac		.65	.40
48	A4	2f olive yel		.70	.25
49	A4	3f orange		.55	.25
50	A4	4f violet		.60	.20
a.		Booklet pane of 6		60.00	
51	A4	5f emerald		2.75	.20
a.		Booklet pane of 6		35.00	
52	A4	6f claret		.95	.60
a.		6f violet brown		1.75	.60
53	A4	6f bister ('01)		12.00	1.20
54	A4	6f olive grn ('02)		4.00	.60
55	A4	10f carmine		3.00	.25
a.		Booklet pane of 6		35.00	
56	A4	12f violet ('04)		1.50	1.25
57	A4	20f brown ('01)		1.90	.60
58	A4	25f blue		3.25	.65
a.		Booklet pane of 6		60.00	
59	A4	30f orange brn		22.50	.25
60	A4	35f red vio ('01)		12.50	.40
a.		Booklet pane of 6		100.00	
61	A4	50f lake		13.00	1.25
62	A4	60f green		44.00	.55
63	A5	1k brown red		45.00	.70
64	A5	2k gray blue ('01)		275.00	22.50
65	A5	3k sea green		85.00	4.50
66	A5	5k vio brown ('01)		85.00	30.00
		Nos. 47-66 (20)		613.80	66.60

The watermark on Nos. 47 to 66 is always the circular form of Wmk. 135 described in the note following No. 46.

Pairs imperf between of Nos. 47-49, 51 were favor prints made for an influential Budapest collector. Value, $90 each.

For overprints & surcharges see #B35-B52, 2N1-2N3, 6N1-6N6, 6NB127N1-7N6, 7NB1, 10N1.

Perf. 11½

47b	A4	1f gray		90.00	17.50
48a	A4	2f olive yel		90.00	12.50
49a	A4	3f orange		22.50	2.25
50b	A4	4f violet		70.00	1.50
51b	A4	5f emerald		5.50	1.40
52b	A4	6f claret		110.00	12.50
53a	A4	6f bister ('01)		80.00	22.50
54a	A4	6f olive grn ('02)		160.00	90.00
55b	A4	10f carmine		90.00	3.00
56a	A4	12f violet ('04)		70.00	27.50
57a	A4	20f brown ('01)		140.00	45.00
58b	A4	25f blue		140.00	15.00
59a	A4	30f orange brn		150.00	35.00
60b	A4	35f red vio ('01)		190.00	80.00
61a	A4	50f lake		190.00	80.00
62a	A4	60f green		250.00	20.00
63a	A5	1k brown red		45.00	3.25
64a	A5	2k gray blue ('01)		550.00	120.00
65a	A5	3k sea green			1,500.
66a	A5	5k vio brown ('01)		550.00	225.00

1908-13   Wmk. 136   Perf. 15

67	A4	1f slate		.35	.20
68	A4	2f olive yellow		.30	.20
69	A4	3f orange		.35	.20
70	A4	5f emerald		.35	.20
c.		Booklet pane of 6		100.00	
71	A4	6f olive green		.35	.20
72	A4	10f carmine		.45	.20
c.		Booklet pane of 6		100.00	
73	A4	12f violet		.40	.20
74	A4	16f gray green ('13)		.20	.40
75	A4	20f dark brown		3.50	.20
76	A4	25f blue		2.25	.20
77	A4	30f orange brown		2.50	.20
78	A4	35f red violet		3.75	.20
79	A4	50f lake		1.75	.30
80	A4	60f green		4.00	.20
81	A5	1k brown red		7.25	.25
82	A5	2k gray blue		50.00	.35
83	A5	5k violet brown		75.00	7.50
		Nos. 67-83 (17)		152.75	11.40

Nos. 67-73, 75-83 exist imperf. Value, set $1,000.

1904-05   Wmk. 136a   Perf. 12x11½

67a	A4	1f slate		1.20	1.75
68a	A4	2f olive yellow		3.50	.40
69a	A4	3f orange		.90	.25
70a	A4	5f emerald		2.50	.20
71a	A4	6f olive green		1.25	.45
72a	A4	10f carmine		3.75	.20
73a	A4	12f violet		2.25	1.60
75a	A4	20f dark brown		12.00	.85
76a	A4	25f blue		18.00	.80
77a	A4	30f orange brown		4.50	.40
78a	A4	35f red violet		14.00	.80
79a	A4	50f lake		10.50	2.50
c.		50f magenta		.60	4.00
80a	A4	60f green		200.00	.75
81a	A5	1k brown red		150.00	2.00
82a	A5	2k gray blue		550.00	60.00
c.		Perf. 11½		575.00	87.50
83a	A5	5k violet brown		175.00	80.00
		Nos. 67a-83a (16)		1,149.	152.95

1906   Perf. 15

67b	A4	1f slate		.75	.45
68b	A4	2f olive yellow		.40	.20
69b	A4	3f orange		.70	.20
70b	A4	5f emerald		.35	.20
71b	A4	6f olive green		.90	.20
72b	A4	10f carmine		.75	.20
73b	A4	12f violet		1.10	.20
75b	A4	20f dark brown		2.25	.30
76b	A4	25f blue		2.75	.20
77b	A4	30f orange brown		3.00	.20
78b	A4	35f red violet		13.00	.20
79b	A4	50f lake		2.25	.50
80b	A5	60f green		30.00	.65
81b	A5	1k brown red		30.00	.65
82b	A5	2k gray blue		100.00	8.00
		Nos. 67b-82b (15)		188.20	12.15

1913-16   Wmk. 137 Vert.   Perf. 15

84	A4	1f slate		.30	.20
85	A4	2f olive yellow		.20	.20
86	A4	3f orange		.20	.20
87	A4	5f emerald		.50	.20
88	A4	6f olive green		.20	.20
89	A4	10f carmine		.20	.20
90	A4	12f violet, yel		.20	.20
91	A4	16f gray green		.35	.50
92	A4	20f dark brown		.75	.20
93	A4	25f ultra		.85	.20
94	A4	30f orange brown		.75	.20
95	A4	35f red violet		.75	.20
96	A4	50f lake, blue		.35	.20
a.		Cliché of 35f in plate of 50f		250.00	—
97	A4	60f green		4.25	2.25
98	A4	60f green, salmon		.60	.30
99	A4	70f red brn, grn ('16)		.30	.20
100	A4	80f dull violet ('16)		.30	.20
101	A5	1k dull red		1.25	.20
102	A5	2k dull blue		2.75	.30
103	A5	5k violet brown		9.00	2.00
		Nos. 84-103 (20)		24.05	8.35

Nos. 89-97, 99-103 exist imperf. Value, set $1,200.

For overprints and surcharges see Nos. 2N1-2N3, 6N1-6N6, 6NB12, 7N1-7N6, 7NB1, 10N1.

Wmk. 137 Horiz.

84a	A4	1f slate		.80	1.25
85a	A4	2f olive yellow		2.10	.60
87a	A4	5f emerald		.50	.60
88a	A4	6f olive green		1.00	.60
89b	A4	10f carmine		1.10	.35
90a	A4	12f violet, yellow		2.10	.45
92a	A4	20f dark brown		6.25	.50
94a	A4	30f orange brown		42.50	.35
95a	A4	35f red violet		150.00	.50
96b	A4	50f lake, blue		10.50	9.50
97a	A4	60f green		3.75	2.50
98a	A4	60f green, salmon		1.60	.30
101a	A5	1k dull red		16.00	.50
102a	A5	2k dull blue		75.00	2.50
		Nos. 84a-102a (14)		313.20	20.50

A5a — 103A

1916, July 1   Perf. 15

103A	A5a	10f violet brown		.80	.50

Although issued as a postal savings stamp, No. 103A was also valid for postage. Used value is for postal usage.

Exists imperf. Value $12.

For overprints and surcharges see Nos. 2N59, 5N23, 6N50, 8N13, 10N42.

Queen Zita — A6

Charles IV — A7

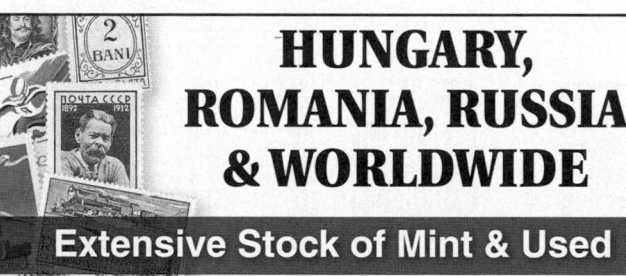
1916, Dec. 30

104	A6	10f violet		1.00	.85
105	A7	15f red		1.00	.85

Coronation of King Charles IV and Queen Zita on Dec. 30, 1916.

Exist imperf. Value, set $25.

During 1921-24 the two center rows of panes of various stamps then current were punched with three holes forming a triangle. These were sold at post offices. Collectors and dealers who wanted the stamps unpunched would have to purchase them through the philatelic agency at a 10% advance over face value.

Harvesting (White Numerals) — A8

1916

106	A8	10f rose		.75	.30
107	A8	15f violet		.75	.30

Exist imperf. Value, set $25.

For overprints and surcharges see Nos. B56-B57, 2N4-2N5, 5N1.

Harvesting Wheat — A9

Parliament Building at Budapest — A10

1916-18   Perf. 15

108	A9	2f brown orange		.20	.20
109	A9	3f red lilac		.20	.20
110	A9	4f slate gray ('18)		.20	.20
111	A9	5f green		.20	.20
112	A9	6f grnsh blue		.20	.20
113	A9	10f rose red		1.75	.20
114	A9	15f violet		.20	.20
115	A9	20f gray brown		.20	.20
116	A9	25f dull blue		.50	.20
117	A9	35f brown		.20	.20
118	A9	40f olive green		.20	.20

Perf. 14

119	A10	50f red vio & lil		.25	.20
120	A10	75f brt bl & pale bl		.25	.20
121	A10	80f grn & pale grn		.25	.20
122	A10	1k red brn & claret		.25	.20
123	A10	2k ol brn & bister		.25	.20
124	A10	3k dk vio & indigo		1.50	.20
125	A10	5k dk brn & lt brn		1.50	.20
126	A10	10k vio brn & vio		2.75	.20
		Nos. 108-126 (19)		11.05	3.80

Nos. 108-126 exist imperf. Value, set $120.

See Nos. 335-377, 388-396. For overprints and surcharges see Nos. 153, 167, C1-C5, J76-J99, 1N1-1N21, 1N26-1N30, 1N33, 1N36-1N39, 2N6-2N27, 2N33-2N38, 2N41, 2N43-2N48, 4N1-4N4, 5N2-5N17, 6N7-6N24, 6N29-6N39, 7N7-7N30, 7N38, 7N41-7N42, 8N1-8N4, 9N1-9N2, 9N4, 10N2-10N16, 10N25-10N29, 10N31, 10N33-10N41, 11N1-15, 11N20-24, 11N27, 11N30, 11N32-33.

Charles IV — A11

Queen Zita — A12

1918   **Perf. 15**

127	A11	10f scarlet	.20	.20
128	A11	15f deep violet	.30	.75
129	A11	20f dark brown	.20	.20
130	A11	25f brt blue	.20	.20
131	A12	40f olive green	.20	.20
132	A12	50f lilac	.20	.35
		Nos. 127-132 (6)	1.30	2.05

Exist imperf. Value, set $35.
For overprints see Nos. 168-173, 1N32, 1N34-1N35, 2N28-2N32, 2N39-2N40, 2N42, 2N49-2N51, 5N18-5N22, 6N25-6N28, 6N40-6N43, 7N31-7N37, 7N39-7N40, 8N5, 9N3, 10N17-10N21, 10N30, 10N32, 11N16-19, 11N25-26, 11N28-29, 11N31.

Issues of the Republic

Hungarian Stamps of 1916-18 Overprinted in Black

1918-19   **Wmk. 137**   **Perf. 15, 14**
On Stamps of 1916-18

153	A9	2f brown orange	.20	.20
154	A9	3f red lilac	.20	.20
155	A9	4f slate gray	.20	.20
156	A9	5f green	.20	.20
157	A9	6f grnsh blue	.20	.20
158	A9	10f rose red	.20	.20
159	A9	20f gray brown	.20	.20
162	A9	40f olive green	.20	.20
163	A10	1k red brn & claret	.25	.25
164	A10	2k ol brn & bis	.25	.25
165	A10	3k dk violet & ind	.50	.50
166	A10	5k dk brn & lt brn	1.50	1.50
167	A10	10k vio brn & vio	.90	.90

On Stamps of 1918

168	A11	10f scarlet	.20	.20
169	A11	15f deep violet	.20	.20
170	A11	20f dark brown	.20	.20
171	A11	25f brt blue	.20	.20
172	A12	40f olive green	.25	.25
173	A12	50f lilac	.25	.25
		Nos. 153-173 (19)	6.30	6.20

Nos. 153-164 exist imperf. Value, set $90.
Nos. 153-162, 168-173 exist with overprint inverted. Value, each $6.

A13   A14

1919-20   **Perf. 15**

174	A13	2f brown orange	.20	.20
176	A13	4f slate gray	.20	.20
177	A13	5f yellow grn	.20	.20
178	A13	6f grnsh blue	.20	.20
179	A13	10f red	.20	.20
180	A13	15f violet	.20	.20
181	A13	20f dark brown	.20	.20
182	A13	20f green ('20)	.20	.20
183	A13	25f dull blue	.20	.20
184	A13	40f olive green	.20	.20
185	A13	40f rose red ('20)	.20	.20
186	A13	45f orange	.20	.20

Perf. 14

187	A14	50f brn vio & pale vio	.20	.20
188	A14	60f brown & bl ('20)	.20	.20
189	A14	95f dk bl & bl	.20	.20
190	A14	1k red brn	.20	.20
191	A14	1k dk bl & dull bl ('20)	.20	.20
192	A14	1.20k dk grn & grn	.20	.20
193	A14	1.40k yellow green	.20	.20
194	A14	2k ol brn & bis	.20	.20
195	A14	3k dk vio & ind	.20	.20
196	A14	5k dk brn & brn	.20	.60
197	A14	10k vio brn & red vio	.50	.75
		Nos. 174-197 (23)	4.90	5.55

The 3f red lilac, type A13, was never regularly issued without overprint (Nos. 204 and 312). In 1923 a small quantity was sold by the Government at public auction. Value $4.
For overprints see Nos. 203-222, 306-330, 1N40, 2N52-2N58, 6N44-6N49, 8N6-8N12, 10N22-10N24, 11N34-35.
Nos. 174, 177-179, 181-197 exist imperf. Value set $70.

Issues of the Soviet Republic

Karl Marx — A15

Sándor Petöfi — A16

Ignác Martinovics — A17

György Dózsa — A18

Friedrich Engels — A19

Wmk. 137 Horiz.
1919, June 14   **Litho.**   **Perf. 12½x12**

198	A15	20f rose & brown	1.00	1.00
199	A16	45f brn org & dk grn	1.00	1.00
200	A17	60f blue gray & brn	5.00	5.00
201	A18	75f claret & vio brn	5.00	5.00
202	A19	80f olive db & blk brn	5.00	5.00
		Nos. 198-202 (5)	17.00	17.00

Used values are for favor cancels.
Exist imperf. Value, Set $175.

Wmk. Vertical

198a	A15	20f	13.00
199a	A16	45f	13.00
200a	A17	60f	13.00
201a	A18	75f	13.00
202a	A19	80f	27.50
		Nos. 198a-202a (5)	79.50

Nos. 198a-202a were not used postally. "Canceled" examples exist. Same values.

Stamps of 1919 Overprinted in Red

1919, July 21   **Typo.**   **Perf. 15**

203	A13	2f brown orange	.20	.20
204	A13	3f red lilac	.20	.20
205	A13	4f slate gray	.20	.20
206	A13	5f yellow green	.20	.20
207	A13	6f grnsh blue	.20	.20
208	A13	10f red	.20	.20
209	A13	15f violet	.20	.20
210	A13	20f dark brown	.20	.20
211	A13	25f dull blue	.20	.20
212	A13	40f olive green	.20	.20
213	A13	45f orange	.20	.20

Overprinted in Red

Perf. 14

214	A14	50f brn vio & pale vio	.25	.25
215	A14	95f dk blue & blue	.25	.25
216	A14	1k red brown	.25	.25
217	A14	1.20k dk grn & grn	.25	.25
218	A14	1.40k yellow green	.25	.25
219	A14	2k ol brn & bister	.80	.80
220	A14	3k dk vio & ind	.65	.65
221	A14	5k dk brn & brn	.50	.50
222	A14	10k vio brn & red vio	1.00	1.00
		Nos. 203-222 (20)	6.40	6.40

"Magyar Tanacsköztarsasag" on Nos. 198 to 222 means "Hungarian Soviet Republic."
Nos. 203-218, 221-222 exist imperf. Value, set $150.

Issues of the Kingdom

Stamps of 1919 Overprinted in Black

1919, Nov. 16

306	A13	5f green	.65	.65
307	A13	10f rose red	.65	.65
308	A13	15f violet	.65	.65
309	A13	20f gray brown	.65	.65
310	A13	25f dull blue	.65	.65
		Nos. 306-310 (5)	3.25	3.25

Issued to commemorate the Romanian evacuation. The overprint reads: "Entry of the National Army-November 16, 1919."
Forged overprints exist.

Nos. 203 to 213 Overprinted in Black

1920, Jan. 26   **Perf. 15**

311	A13	2f brown orange	1.10	1.10
312	A13	3f red lilac	.20	.20
313	A13	4f slate gray	1.10	1.10
314	A13	5f yellow green	.20	.20
315	A13	6f blue green	.30	.30
316	A13	10f red	.20	.20
317	A13	15f violet	.20	.20
318	A13	20f dark brown	.20	.20
319	A13	25f dull blue	.20	.20
320	A13	40f olive green	1.40	1.40
321	A13	45f orange	1.40	1.40

Nos. 214 to 222 Overprinted in Black

Perf. 14

322	A14	50f brn vio & pale vio	1.50	1.50
323	A14	95f dk bl & bl	1.50	1.50
324	A14	1k red brown	1.50	1.50
325	A14	1.20k dk grn & grn	1.60	1.60
326	A14	1.40k yellow green	1.60	1.60
327	A14	2k ol brn & bis	7.50	7.50
328	A14	3k dk vio & ind	8.00	8.00
329	A14	5k dk brn & brn	.40	.40
330	A14	10k vio brn & red vio	9.00	9.00
		Nos. 311-330 (20)	39.10	39.10

Counterfeit overprints exist.

Types of 1916-18 Issue Denomination Tablets Without Inner Frame on Nos. 350 to 363

1920-24   **Wmk. 137**   **Perf. 15**

335	A9	5f brown orange	.20	.20
336	A9	10f red violet	.20	.20
337	A9	40f rose red	.20	.20
338	A9	50f yellow green	.20	.20
339	A9	50f blue vio ('22)	.20	.20
340	A9	60f black	.20	.20
341	A9	1k green ('22)	.20	.20
342	A9	1½k brown vio ('22)	.20	.20
343	A9	2k grnsh blue ('22)	.20	.20
344	A9	2½k dp green ('22)	.20	.20
345	A9	3k brown org ('22)	.20	.20
346	A9	4k lt red ('22)	.20	.20
347	A9	4½k dull violet ('22)	.40	.20
348	A9	5k dp brn ('22)	.20	.20
349	A9	6k dark blue ('22)	.20	.20
350	A9	10k brown ('23)	.20	.20
351	A9	15k slate ('23)	.20	.20
352	A9	20k red vio ('23)	.20	.20
353	A9	25k orange ('23)	.20	.20
354	A9	40k gray grn ('23)	.20	.20
355	A9	50k dark blue ('23)	.20	.20
356	A9	100k claret ('23)	.25	.20
357	A9	150k dark green ('23)	.35	.20
358	A9	200k green ('23)	.35	.20
359	A9	300k rose red ('24)	.50	.20
360	A9	350k violet ('23)	1.25	.20
361	A9	500k dark gray ('24)	1.50	.20
362	A9	600k olive bis ('24)	1.50	.20
363	A9	800k org yel ('24)	2.10	.20

Perf. 14

364	A10	2.50k bl & gray bl	.25	.20
365	A10	3.50k gray	.25	.20
366	A10	10k brown ('22)	.60	.20
367	A10	15k dk gray ('22)	.25	.20
368	A10	20k red vio ('22)	.25	.20
369	A10	25k orange ('22)	.25	.20
370	A10	30k claret ('22)	.25	.20
371	A10	40k gray grn ('22)	.25	.20
372	A10	50k dp blue ('22)	.25	.20
373	A10	100k yel brn ('22)	.25	.20
374	A10	400k turq bl ('23)	.85	.30
375	A10	500k brt vio ('23)	.80	.20
376	A10	1000k lilac ('24)	.90	.20
377	A10	2000k car ('24)	2.00	.20
		Nos. 335-377 (43)	19.60	8.70

Nos. 372 to 377 have colored numerals.
Nos. 335-338, 340, 350-365, 368, 370, 372-377 exist imperf. Value, set $200.

Madonna and
Child — A23

1921-25   Typo.   Perf. 12
378 A23 50k dk brn & bl .20 .20
379 A23 100k ol bis & yel
brn .30 .20

Wmk. 133
380 A23 200k dk bl & ul-
tra .35 .20
381 A23 500k vio brn &
vio .65 .25
382 A23 1000k vio & red
vio .90 .30
383 A23 2000k grnsh bl &
vio 1.25 .45
384 A23 2500k ol brn &
buff 1.50 .35
385 A23 3000k brn red &
vio 1.50 .35
386 A23 5000k dk grn &
yel grn 1.50 .35
 a. Center inverted 15,000. 8,000.
387 A23 10000k gray vio
& pale
bl 1.50 1.25
Nos. 378-387 (10) 9.65 3.90

Nos. 380-387 exist imperf. Value, set of 8
$200.
Issue dates: 50k, 100k, Feb. 27, 1921;
2500k, 10,000k, 1925; others, 1923.

Types of 1916-18
Denomination Tablets Without Inner
Frame on Nos. 388-394
1924   Wmk. 133   Perf. 15
388 A9 100k claret .25 .20
389 A9 200k yellow grn .20 .20
390 A9 300k rose red .25 .20
391 A9 400k deep blue .25 .20
392 A9 500k dark gray .30 .20
393 A9 600k olive bister .40 .25
 a. "800" in upper right corner 140.00 140.00
394 A9 800k org yel .45 .20

Perf. 14½x14
395 A10 1000k lilac 1.10 .20
396 A10 2000k carmine 1.60 .20
Nos. 388-396 (9) 4.80 1.85
Nos. 395 and 396 have colored numerals.
Exist imperf. Value, set $40.

Maurus Jókai
(1825-1904),
Novelist
A24

1925, Feb. 1   Unwmk.   Perf. 12
400 A24 1000k dp grn & blk
brn 7.50 7.50
401 A24 2000k lt brn & blk brn 3.00 1.00
402 A24 2500k dk bl & blk brn 7.50 7.50
Nos. 400-402 (3) 18.00 16.00
Exist imperf. Value, set $100.

Crown of St.
Stephen
A25

Matthias
Cathedral
A26

Palace at
Budapest — A27

Perf. 14x14¼, 15
1926-27   Wmk. 133   Litho.
403 A25 1f dk gray .45 .20
404 A25 2f lt blue .50 .20
405 A25 3f orange .50 .20
406 A25 4f violet .60 .20

407 A25 6f lt green .65 .20
408 A25 8f lilac rose 1.40 .20

Typo.
409 A26 10f deep blue 1.75 .20
410 A26 16f dark violet 1.75 .20
411 A26 20f carmine 2.10 .20
412 A26 25f lt brown 1.90 .20

Perf. 14¼x14
413 A27 32f dp vio & brt vio 4.50 .20
414 A27 40f dk blue & blue 5.75 .20
Nos. 403-414 (12) 21.85 2.40

See Nos. 428-436. For surcharges see Nos.
450-456, 466-467.
Nos. 403-414, 418-421 exist imperf. Value,
set $250.

Madonna and
Child — A28

1926-27   Engr.   Perf. 14
415 A28 1p violet 25.00 .80
416 A28 2p red 20.00 1.25
417 A28 5p blue ('27) 25.00 6.00
Nos. 415-417 (3) 70.00 8.05

Exist imperf. Value, set $450.

Palace at Budapest
A29

St. Stephen
A30

1926-27   Typo.   Perf. 14x14¼
418 A29 30f blue grn ('27) 4.00 .20
419 A29 46f ultra ('27) 5.25 .30
420 A29 50f brown blk ('27) 6.00 .20
421 A29 70f scarlet 9.75 .20
Nos. 418-421 (4) 25.00 .90

For surcharge see No. 480.

1928-29   Engr.   Perf. 15
422 A30 8f yellow grn .65 .30
423 A30 8f rose lake ('29) .65 .30
424 A30 16f orange red .85 .30
425 A30 16f violet ('29) .85 .30
426 A30 32f ultra 2.25 1.10
427 A30 32f bister ('29) 2.25 1.10
Nos. 422-427 (6) 7.50 3.40

890th death anniversary of St. Stephen, the
first king of Hungary.
Exist imperf. Value, set $350.

Types of 1926-27 Issue
Perf. 14x14¼, 15
1928-30   Typo.   Wmk. 210
428 A25 1f black .25 .20
429 A25 2f blue .35 .20
430 A25 3f orange .35 .20
431 A25 4f violet .35 .20
432 A25 6f blue grn .60 .20
433 A25 8f lilac rose 1.10 .20
434 A26 10f dp blue ('30) 4.50 .20
435 A26 16f violet 1.75 .20
436 A26 20f dull red 1.75 .20
Nos. 428-436 (9) 11.00 1.80

On #428-433 the numerals have thicker
strokes than on the same values of the 1926-
27 issue.
Exist imperf. Value, set $110.

Palace at
Budapest — A31

Type A31 resembles A27 but the steamer is
nearer the right of the design.

1928-31   Perf. 14¼x14
437 A31 30f emerald ('31) 3.25 .20
438 A31 32f red violet 4.00 .30
439 A31 40f deep blue 4.75 .20

440 A31 46f apple green 4.00 .20
441 A31 50f ocher ('31) 4.00 .20
Nos. 437-441 (5) 20.00 1.10
Exist imperf. Value, set $110.

Admiral Nicholas
Horthy — A32

1930, Mar. 1   Litho.   Perf. 15
445 A32 8f myrtle green .75 .30
446 A32 16f purple 1.00 .35
447 A32 20f carmine 6.00 1.10
448 A32 32f olive brown 4.00 3.75
449 A32 40f dull blue 7.75 1.65
Nos. 445-449 (5) 19.50 7.15

10th anniv. of the election of Adm. Nicholas
Horthy as Regent, Mar. 1, 1920.
Exist imperf. Value, set, $225.

Stamps of 1926-28
Surcharged

1931, Jan. 1   Perf. 14¼, 15
450 A25 2f on 3f orange 1.00 .40
451 A25 6f on 8f magenta 1.00 .20
 a. Perf. 14x14¼ 25.00 50.00
452 A26 10f on 16f violet .90 .20

Wmk. 133
453 A25 2f on 3f orange 3.50 3.00
 a. Perf. 14x14¼ 3.50 6.00
454 A25 6f on 8f magenta 2.75 3.00
 a. Perf. 14x14¼ 40.00 80.00
455 A26 10f on 16f dk vio 2.25 1.50
 a. Perf. 14x14¼ 3.00 4.00

456 A26 20f on 25f lt brn 2.25 1.25
 a. Perf. 14x14¼ 2.25 2.25
Nos. 450-456 (7) 13.65 9.55

For surcharges see Nos. 466-467.

St. Elizabeth
A33

Ministering to
Children
A34

Wmk. 210
1932, Apr. 21   Photo.   Perf. 15
458 A33 10f ultra 1.25 .65
459 A33 20f scarlet 1.25 .65

Perf. 14
460 A34 32f deep violet 4.00 2.75
461 A34 40f deep blue 3.00 1.75
Nos. 458-461 (4) 9.50 5.80

700th anniv. of the death of St. Elizabeth of
Hungary.
Exist imperf. Value, set $120.

Madonna, Patroness of Hungary — A35

1932, June 1   *Perf. 12*
462	A35	1p yellow grn	24.00	2.00
463	A35	2p carmine	26.00	3.00
464	A35	5p deep blue	95.00	10.00
465	A35	10p olive bister	140.00	60.00
		Nos. 462-465 (4)	285.00	75.00

Exist imperf. Value, set $1,100.

Nos. 451 and 454 Surcharged

1932, June 14   **Wmk. 210**   *Perf. 15*
466	A25	2f on 6f on 8f mag	1.50	.40

Wmk. 133
467	A25	2f on 6f on 8f mag	50.00	40.00

Imre Madách — A36

Designs: 2f, Janos Arany. 4f, Dr. Ignaz Semmelweis. 6f, Baron Roland Eotvos. 10f, Count Stephen Szechenyi. 16f, Ferenc Deak. 20f, Franz Liszt. 30f, Louis Kossuth. 32f, Stephen Tisza. 40f, Mihaly Munkacsy. 50f, Alexander Csoma. 70f, Farkas Bolyai.

1932   **Wmk. 210**   *Perf. 15*
468	A36	1f slate violet	.20	.20
469	A36	2f orange	.20	.20
470	A36	4f ultra	.20	.20
471	A36	6f yellow grn	.20	.20
472	A36	10f Prus green	.20	.20
473	A36	16f dull violet	.25	.20
474	A36	20f deep rose	.20	.20
475	A36	30f brown	.45	.20
476	A36	32f brown vio	.70	.45
477	A36	40f dull blue	.70	.20
478	A36	50f deep green	1.10	.20
479	A36	70f cerise	1.50	.20
		Nos. 468-479 (12)	5.90	2.65
		Set, never hinged	11.50	

Issued in honor of famous Hungarians. Exist imperf. Value $100. See Nos. 509-510.

No. 421 Surcharged

1933, Apr. 15   **Wmk. 133**   *Perf. 14*
480	A29	10f on 70f scarlet	3.00	.25
		Never hinged	6.00	

Leaping Stag and Double Cross — A47

Wmk. 210
1933, July 10   **Photo.**   *Perf. 15*
481	A47	10f dk green	1.50	1.25
482	A47	16f violet brn	2.00	2.50
483	A47	20f car lake	3.00	1.25
484	A47	32f yellow	5.00	4.00
485	A47	40f deep blue	6.00	4.00
		Nos. 481-485 (5)	17.50	13.00
		Set, never hinged	35.00	

Boy Scout Jamboree at Gödöllö, Hungary, July 20 - Aug. 20, 1933. Exists imperf. Value, set $175.

Souvenir Sheet

Franz Liszt — A48

1934, May 6   *Perf. 15*
486	A48	20f lake	60.00	100.00
		Never hinged	160.00	

2nd Hungarian Phil. Exhib., Budapest, and Jubilee of the 1st Hungarian Phil. Soc. Sold for 90f, including entrance fee. Size: 64x76mm. Exists imperf. Value $2,500.

Francis II Rákóczy (1676-1735), Prince of Transylvania A49

1935, Apr. 8   *Perf. 12*
487	A49	10f yellow green	.70	.35
488	A49	16f brt violet	4.00	3.00
489	A49	20f dark carmine	1.00	1.00
490	A49	32f brown lake	5.00	5.00
491	A49	40f blue	6.75	6.75
		Nos. 487-491 (5)	17.45	16.10
		Set, never hinged	35.00	

Exists imperf. Value, set $450.

Cardinal Pázmány — A50

Signing the Charter — A51

1935, Sept. 25
492	A50	6f dull green	1.10	1.00
493	A51	10f dark green	.40	.35
494	A50	16f slate violet	1.50	1.25
495	A50	20f magenta	.45	.40
496	A51	32f deep claret	3.50	1.60
497	A51	40f dark blue	3.00	1.60
		Nos. 492-497 (6)	9.95	6.20
		Set, never hinged	18.00	

Tercentenary of the founding of the University of Budapest by Peter Cardinal Pázmány. Exists imperf. Value, set $450.

Ancient City and Fortress of Buda — A52

Guardian Angel over Buda — A53

Shield of Buda, Cannon and Massed Flags — A54

First Hungarian Soldier to Enter Buda — A55

1936, Sept. 2   *Perf. 11½x12½*
498	A52	10f dark green	.80	.45
499	A53	16f deep violet	3.00	3.50
500	A54	20f car lake	.80	.65
501	A53	32f dark brown	3.00	4.25
502	A52	40f deep blue	3.00	5.00
		Nos. 498-502 (5)	10.60	13.85
		Set, never hinged	20.00	

250th anniv. of the recapture of Budapest from the Turks. Exists imperf. Value, set $450.

> **Catalogue values for unused stamps in this section, from this point to the end of the section, are for Never Hinged items.**

Budapest International Fair — A56

1937, Feb. 22   *Perf. 12*
503	A56	2f deep orange	.20	.20
504	A56	6f yellow green	.40	.20
505	A56	10f myrtle green	.55	.20
506	A56	20f deep cerise	1.25	.40
507	A56	32f dark violet	2.25	.85
508	A56	40f ultra	1.75	.90
		Nos. 503-508 (6)	6.40	2.75

Exist imperf. Value, set $500.

Portrait Type of 1932

5f, Ferenc Kolcsey. 25f, Mihaly Vorosmarty.

1937, May 5   *Perf. 15*
509	A36	5f brown orange	.80	.25
510	A36	25f olive green	1.50	.25

Exist imperf. Value, set $400.

Pope Sylvester II, Archbishop Astrik — A59

Designs: 2f, 16f, Stephen the Church builder. 4f, 20f, St. Stephen enthroned. 5f, 25f, Sts. Gerhardt, Emerich, Stephen. 6f, 30f, St. Stephen offering holy crown to Virgin Mary. 10f, same as 1f. 32f, 50f, Portrait of St. Stephen. 40f, Madonna and Child. 70f, Crown of St. Stephen.

See designs A75-A77 for smaller stamps of designs similar Nos. 521-524, but with slanted "MAGYAR KIR POSTA."

1938, Jan. 1   *Perf. 12*
511	A59	1f deep violet	.40	.20
512	A59	2f olive brown	.40	.20
513	A59	4f brt blue	.80	.20
514	A59	5f magenta	1.25	.25
515	A59	6f dp yel grn	1.60	.25
516	A59	10f red orange	1.25	.25
517	A59	16f gray violet	2.00	.25
518	A59	20f car lake	1.25	.60
519	A59	25f dark green	1.60	.50
520	A59	30f olive bister	2.50	.20
521	A59	32f dp claret, *buff*	2.50	.90
522	A59	40f Prus green	3.50	.25
523	A59	50f rose vio, *grnsh*	5.00	.25
524	A59	70f ol grn, *bluish*	6.25	.75
		Nos. 511-524 (14)	30.30	5.05

900th anniv. of the death of St. Stephen. Exists imperf. Value, set $550. For overprints see Nos. 535-536.

Admiral Horthy — A67

1938, Jan. 1   *Perf. 12½x12*
525	A67	1p peacock green	4.50	.25
526	A67	2p brown	5.25	.35
527	A67	5p sapphire blue	8.25	2.25
		Nos. 525-527 (3)	18.00	2.85

Exist imperf. Value, set $475.

Souvenir Sheet

St. Stephen — A68

1938, May 22   **Wmk. 210**   *Perf. 12*
528	A68	20f carmine lake	32.50	25.00

3rd Hungarian Phil. Exhib., Budapest. Sheet sold only at exhibition with 1p ticket. Exists imperf. Value $4,500.

College of Debrecen A69

Three Students — A71

George Marothy — A73

10f, 18th cent. view of College. 20f, 19th cent. view of College. 40f, Stephen Hatvani.

Perf. 12x12½, 12½x12
1938, Sept. 24   **Wmk. 210**
529	A69	6f deep green	.55	.20
530	A69	10f brown	.55	.20
531	A71	16f brown car	.55	.30
532	A69	20f crimson	.65	.25
533	A73	32f slate green	1.10	.75
534	A73	40f brt blue	1.10	.60
		Nos. 529-534 (6)	4.50	2.30

Founding of Debrecen College, 400th anniv. Exists imperf. Value $350.

Types of 1938 Overprinted in Blue (#535) or Carmine (#536):

a

b

1938   Perf. 12
535	A59(a)	20f salmon pink	2.00	1.50
536	A59(b)	70f brn, grnsh	2.25	1.50
a.		Overprint omitted	12,000.	8,000.

Restoration of the territory ceded by Czechoslovakia.
Exists imperf. Value $135.
Forgeries exist of No. 536a.

Crown of St. Stephen A75

St. Stephen A76

Madonna, Patroness of Hungary A77

Coronation Church, Budapest A78

Reformed Church, Debrecen A79

Cathedral, Esztergom A80

Deak Square Evangelical Church, Budapest — A81

Cathedral of Kassa — A82

Wmk. 210
1939, June 1   Photo.   Perf. 15
537	A75	1f brown car	.20	.20
538	A75	2f Prus green	.20	.20
539	A75	4f ocher	.20	.20
540	A75	5f brown violet	.20	.20
541	A75	6f yellow green	.20	.20
542	A75	10f bister brn	.20	.20
543	A75	16f rose violet	.20	.20
544	A76	20f rose red	.20	.20
545	A77	25f blue gray	.20	.20

Perf. 12
546	A78	30f red violet	.55	.20
547	A79	32f brown	.40	.20
548	A80	40f greenish blue	.55	.20
549	A81	50f olive	.60	.20
550	A82	70f henna brown	.60	.20
		Nos. 537-550 (14)	4.50	2.80

See #521-524, 578-596. For overprints see #559-560.
Exists imperf. Value, set $350.

Girl Scout Sign and Olive Branch — A83

6f, Scout lily, Hungary's shield, Crown of St. Stephen. 10f, Girls in Scout hat & national headdress. 20f, Dove & Scout emblems.

1939, July 20   Photo.   Perf. 12
551	A83	2f brown orange	.50	.35
552	A83	6f green	.50	.35
553	A83	10f brown	.80	.40
554	A83	20f lilac rose	1.25	.80
		Nos. 551-554 (4)	3.05	1.90

Girl Scout Jamboree at Gödöllö.
Exists imperf. Value, set $400.

Admiral Horthy at Szeged, 1919 — A87

Admiral Nicholas Horthy A88

Cathedral of Kassa and Angel Ringing "Bell of Liberty" A89

1940, Mar. 1
555	A87	6f green	.30	.20
556	A88	10f ol blk & ol bis	.35	.25
557	A89	20f brt rose brown	.85	.60
		Nos. 555-557 (3)	1.50	1.05

20th anniversary of the election of Admiral Horthy as Regent of Hungary.
Exists imperf. Value, set $135.

Crown of St. Stephen A90

1940, Sept. 5
558	A90	10f dk green & yellow	.20	.20

Issued in commemoration of the recovery of northeastern Transylvania from Romania.
Exists imperf. Value $35.

Nos. 542, 544 Overprinted in Red or Black

1941, Apr. 21   Perf. 15
559	A75	10f bister brn (R)	.25	.20
560	A76	20f rose red (Bk)	.25	.20

Return of the Bacska territory from Yugoslavia.
Exist imperf. Value, set $70.

Admiral Nicholas Horthy — A92

Wmk. 210
1941, June 18   Photo.   Perf. 12
570	A92	1p dk green & buff	.25	.20
571	A92	2p dk brown & buff	.50	.40
572	A92	5p dk rose vio & buff	2.25	1.00
		Nos. 570-572 (3)	3.00	1.60

Exist imperf. Value, set $100.
See Nos. 597-599.

Count Stephen Széchenyi A93

Count Széchenyi and Royal Academy of Science A94

Representation of the Narrows of Kazán — A95

Chain Bridge, Budapest A96

Mercury, Train and Boat — A97

1941, Sept. 21
573	A93	10f dk olive grn	.25	.20
574	A94	16f olive brown	.25	.20
575	A95	20f carmine lake	.30	.20
576	A96	32f red orange	.65	.25
577	A97	40f royal blue	.65	.25
		Nos. 573-577 (5)	2.10	1.10

Count Stephen Szechenyi (1791-1860).
Exist imperf. Value, set $350.

Types of 1939
Perf. 12x12½, 12½x12, 15
1941-43   Wmk. 266
578	A75	1f rose lake ('42)	.20	.20
579	A75	3f dark brown	.20	.20
580	A75	5f violet gray ('42)	.20	.20
581	A75	6f lt green ('42)	.20	.20
582	A75	8f slate grn	.20	.20
583	A75	10f olive brn ('42)	.20	.20
584	A75	12f red orange	.20	.20
585	A76	20f rose red ('42)	.20	.20
586	A76	24f brown violet	.20	.20
587	A78	30f lilac ('42)	.20	.20
588	A82	30f rose red ('43)	.20	.20
589	A80	40f blue green ('42)	.20	.20
590	A79	40f gray black ('43)	.20	.20
591	A81	50f olive grn ('42)	.20	.20
592	A80	50f brt blue ('43)	.20	.20
593	A82	70f copper red ('42)	.20	.20
594	A81	70f gray green ('43)	.20	.20
595	A77	80f brown bister	.20	.20
596	A78	80f bister brn ('43)	.20	.20
		Nos. 578-596 (19)	3.80	3.80

Exist imperf. Value, set $350.

Horthy Type of 1941
Perf. 12x12½
1941, Dec. 18   Wmk. 266
597	A92	1p dk green & buff	.90	.25
598	A92	2p dk brown & buff	.40	.25
599	A92	5p dk rose vio & buff	.70	.35
		Nos. 597-599 (3)	2.00	.85

Exist imperf. Value, set $70.

Stephen Horthy — A98

1942, Oct. 15   Perf. 12
600	A98	20f black	.20	.20

Death of Stephen Horthy (1904-42), son of Regent Nicholas Horthy, who died in a plane crash.
Exists imperf. Value $55.

Arpád — A99

A109

Portraits: 2f, King Ladislaus I. 3f, Miklós Toldi. 4f, János Hunyadi. 5f, Paul Kinizsi. 6f, Count Miklós Zrinyi. 8f, Francis II Rákóczy. 10f, Count Andrew Hadik. 12f, Arthur Görgei. 18f, 24f, Virgin Mary, Patroness of Hungary.

1943-45   Perf. 15
601	A99	1f grnsh black	.20	.20
602	A99	2f red orange	.20	.20
603	A99	3f ultra	.20	.20
604	A99	4f brown	.20	.20
605	A99	5f vermilion	.20	.20
606	A99	6f slate blue	.20	.20
607	A99	8f dk ol grn	.20	.20
608	A99	10f brown	.20	.20
609	A99	12f dp blue grn	.20	.20
610	A99	18f dk gray	.20	.20
611	A109	20f chestnut brn	.20	.20
612	A109	24f rose violet	.20	.20
613	A109	30f brt carmine	.20	.20
614	A109	50f blue	.20	.20
615	A109	80f yellow brn	.20	.20
616	A109	1p green	.30	.20
616A	A109	2p brown ('45)	.50	.60
616B	A109	5p dk red violet ('45)	.85	1.00
		Nos. 601-616B (18)	4.65	4.80

Exist imperf. Value, set $175.
For overprints and surcharges see Nos. 631-658, 660-661, 664, 666-669, 671-672, 674-677, 679, 680, 682, 685-689, 691-698, 801-803, 805-806, 810-815, F2, Q2-Q3, Q7.

Message to the Shepherds A110

St. Margaret — A113

20f, Nativity. 30f, Adoration of the Magi.

1943, Dec. 1   Perf. 12x12½
617	A110	4f dark green	.20	.20
618	A110	20f dull blue	.20	.20
619	A110	30f brown orange	.20	.20
		Nos. 617-619 (3)	.60	.60

Exist imperf. Value, set $175.

1944, Jan. 19   Perf. 15
620	A113	30f deep carmine	.20	.20

Canonization of St. Margaret of Hungary.
Exists imperf. Value $55.
For surcharges see Nos. 662, 673A.

Kossuth with Family — A114

Lajos Kossuth — A117

Honvéd Drummer A115

Design: 30f, Kossuth orating.

1944, Mar. 20 *Perf. 12½x12, 12x12½*
621	A114	4f yellow brown	.20	.20
622	A115	20f dk olive grn	.20	.20
623	A115	30f henna brown	.20	.20
624	A117	50f slate blue	.20	.20
		Nos. 621-624 (4)	.80	.80

Louis (Lajos) Kossuth (1802-94).
Exist imperf. Value, set $225.
For surcharges see Nos. B175-B178.

St. Elizabeth — A118

Portraits: 24f, St. Margaret. 30f, Elizabeth Szilágyi. 50f, Dorothy Kanuizsai. 70f, Susanna Lóránttfy. 80f, Ilona Zrinyi.

1944, Aug. 1 *Perf. 15*
625	A118	20f olive	.20	.20
626	A118	24f rose violet	.20	.20
627	A118	30f copper red	.20	.20
628	A118	50f dark blue	.20	.20
629	A118	70f orange red	.20	.20
630	A118	80f brown car	.20	.20
		Nos. 625-630 (6)	1.20	1.20

Exist imperf. Value, set $160.
For overprints and surcharges see Nos. 659, 663, 665, 670, 673, 678, 681, 683-684, 690, 804, 807-809, F1, F3, Q1, Q4-Q6, Q8.

Issues of the Republic

Types of Hungary, 1943 Surcharged in Carmine

1945, May 1 *Wmk. 266*
Blue Surface-tinted Paper
631	A99	10f on 1f grnsh blk	1.50	1.50
632	A99	20f on 3f ultra	1.50	1.50
633	A99	30f on 4f brown	1.50	1.50
634	A99	40f on 6f slate bl	1.50	1.50
635	A99	50f on 8f dk ol grn	1.50	1.50
636	A99	1p on 10f brown	1.50	1.50
637	A99	150f on 12f dp bl grn	1.50	1.50
638	A99	2p on 18f dk gray	1.50	1.50
639	A109	3p on 20f chnt brn	1.50	1.50
640	A109	5p on 24f rose vio	1.50	1.50
641	A109	6p on 50f blue	1.50	1.50
642	A109	10p on 80f yel brn	1.50	1.50
643	A109	20p on 1p green	1.50	1.50

Yellow Surface-tinted Paper
644	A99	10f on 1f grnsh blk	1.50	1.50
645	A99	20f on 3f ultra	1.50	1.50
646	A99	30f on 4f brown	1.50	1.50
647	A99	40f on 6f slate bl	1.50	1.50
648	A99	50f on 8f dk ol grn	1.50	1.50
649	A99	1p on 10f brown	1.50	1.50
650	A99	150f on 12f dp bl grn	1.50	1.50
651	A99	2p on 18f dk gray	1.50	1.50
652	A109	3p on 20f chnt brn	1.50	1.50
653	A109	5p on 24f rose vio	1.50	1.50
654	A109	6p on 50f blue	1.50	1.50
655	A109	10p on 80f yel brn	1.50	1.50
656	A109	20p on 1p green	1.50	1.50
		Nos. 631-656 (26)	39.00	39.00

Hungary's liberation.

Types of Hungary, 1943-45, Surcharged in Carmine or Black

1945
Blue Surface-tinted Paper
657	A99	10f on 4f brn (C)	.20	.20
658	A99	10f on 10f brn (C)	.45	.45
659	A118	20f on 20f ol (C)	.20	.20
660	A99	28f on 5f ver	.20	.20
661	A109	30f on 30f brt car	.20	.20
662	A113	30f on 30f dp car	.20	.20
663	A118	30f on 30f cop red	.20	.20
664	A99	40f on 10f brown	.20	.20
665	A118	1p on 70f org red	.25	.25
666	A109	1p on 80f yel brn (C)	.20	.20
667	A99	2p on 4f brown	.20	.20
668	A109	2p on 2p brn (C)	.20	.20
669	A109	4p on 30f brt car	.20	.20
670	A118	8p on 20f olive	.20	.20
671	A99	10p on 2f red org	12.00	12.00
672	A109	10p on 80f yel brn	.20	.20
673	A118	20p on 30f cop red	.20	.20

Same Surcharge with Thinner Unshaded Numerals of Value
673A	A113	300p on 30f dp car	.20	.20

Surcharged as Nos. 657-673
Yellow Surface-tinted Paper
674	A99	10f on 12f dp bl grn (C)	.20	.20
675	A99	20f on 1f grnsh blk (C)	.20	.20
676	A99	20f on 18f dk gray (C)	.20	.20
a.		Double surcharge		
677	A99	40f on 24f rose vio (C)	.20	.20
678	A118	40f on 24f rose vio (C)	.20	.20
679	A109	42f on 20f chnt brn (C)	.20	.20
680	A109	50f on 50f bl (C)	.20	.20
681	A118	50f on 50f dk bl (C)	.20	.20
682	A99	60f on 8f dk ol grn (C)	.20	.20
683	A118	80f on 24f rose vio	.20	.20
684	A118	80f on 80f brn car (C)	.20	.20
685	A109	1p on 20f chnt brn	.20	.20
686	A109	1p on 1p grn (C)	.20	.20
687	A99	150f on 6f sl bl (C)	.90	.90
688	A99	1.60p on 12f dp bl grn	.20	.20
689	A99	3p on 3f ultra (C)	.30	.30
690	A118	3p on 50f dk bl	.20	.20
691	A99	5p on 8f dk ol grn	.20	.20
692	A109	5p on 5p dk red vio (C)	.25	.25
693	A109	6p on 50f blue	.20	.20
694	A109	7p on 1p grn	.20	.20
695	A99	9p on 1f grnsh blk	.20	.20

Same Surcharge with Thinner, Unshaded Numerals of Value
696	A99	40p on 8f dk ol grn	.20	.20
697	A99	60p on 18f dk gray	.20	.20
698	A99	100p on 12f dp bl grn	.20	.20
		Nos. 657-698 (43)	21.55	21.55

Various shades and errors of overprint exist on Nos. 657-698.
These surface-tinted stamps exist without surcharge, but were not so issued.

Construction A124

Designs: 1.60p, Manufacturing. 2p, Railroading. 3p, Building. 5p, Agriculture. 8p, Communications. 10p, Architecture. 20p, Writing.

Wmk. 266
1945, Sept. 11 *Photo.* *Perf. 12*
700	A124	40f gray black	7.50	7.50
701	A124	1.60p olive bis	7.50	7.50
702	A124	2p slate green	7.50	7.50
703	A124	3p dark purple	7.50	7.50
704	A124	5p dark red	7.50	7.50
705	A124	8p brown	7.50	7.50
706	A124	10p deep claret	7.50	7.50
707	A124	20p slate blue	7.50	7.50
		Nos. 700-707 (8)	60.00	60.00

World Trade Union Conf., Paris, Sept. 25 to Oct. 10, 1945.
Exist imperf. Value, set $500.

"Reconstruction" — A132

1945-46
708	A132	12p brown olive	.25	.25
709	A132	20p brt green	.20	.20
710	A132	24p orange brn	.25	.25
711	A132	30p gray black	.20	.20
712	A132	40p olive green	.20	.20
713	A132	60p red orange	.20	.20
714	A132	100p orange yel	.20	.20
715	A132	120p brt ultra	.20	.20
716	A132	140p brt red	.40	.40
717	A132	200p olive brn	.20	.20
718	A132	240p brt blue	.20	.20
719	A132	300p dk carmine	.20	.20
720	A132	500p dull green	.20	.20
721	A132	1000p red violet	.20	.20
722	A132	3000p brt red ('46)	.20	.20
		Nos. 708-722 (15)	3.30	3.30

#708-721 exist tête bêche. Value: $12.50.
Exist imperf. Value, set $275.

"Liberation" A133

1946, Feb. 12
723	A133	3ez p dark red	.20	.20
724	A133	15ez p ultra	.20	.20

Exist imperf. Value, set $55.

Postrider — A134

Photo.; Values Typo.
1946 *Perf. 15*
725	A134	4ez p brown org	.20	.20
726	A134	10ez p brt red	.20	.20
727	A134	15ez p ultra	.20	.20
728	A134	20ez p dk brown	.20	.20
729	A134	30ez p red violet	.20	.20
730	A134	50ez p gray black	.20	.20
731	A134	80ez p brt ultra	.20	.20
732	A134	100ez p rose car	.20	.20
733	A134	160ez p gray green	.20	.20
734	A134	200ez p yellow grn	.20	.20
735	A134	500ez p red	.20	.20
736	A134	640ez p olive bis	.20	.20
737	A134	800ez p rose violet	.20	.20
		Nos. 725-737 (13)	2.60	2.60

Exist imperf. Value, set $80.

Abbreviations:
Ez (Ezer) = Thousand
Mil (Milpengo) = Million
Mlrd (Milliard) = Billion
Bil (Billio-pengo) = Trillion

Arms of Hungary — A135

1946 *Wmk. 210*
738	A135	1mil p vermilion	.20	.20
a.		"1" in center omitted	600.00	
739	A135	2mil p ultra	.20	.20
740	A135	3mil p brown	.20	.20
741	A135	4mil p slate gray	.20	.20
742	A135	5mil p rose violet	.20	.20
743	A135	10mil p green	.20	.20
744	A135	20mil p carmine	.20	.20
745	A135	50mil p olive	.20	.20

Arms and Post Horn
A136   A137
746	A136	100mil p henna brn	.20	.20
747	A136	200mil p henna brn	.20	.20
748	A136	500mil p henna brn	.20	.20
749	A136	1000mil p henna brn	.20	.20
750	A136	2000mil p henna brn	.20	.20
751	A136	3000mil p henna brn	.20	.20
752	A136	5000mil p henna brn	.20	.20
753	A136	10,000mil p henna brn	.20	.20
754	A136	20,000mil p henna brn	.20	.20
755	A136	30,000mil p henna brn	.20	.20
756	A136	50,000mil p henna brn	.25	.25

Denomination in Carmine
757	A137	100mlrd p olive	.20	.20
758	A137	200mlrd p olive	.20	.20
759	A137	500mlrd p olive	.20	.20

Dove and Letter — A138

Denomination in Carmine
760	A138	1bil p grnsh blk	.20	.20
761	A138	2bil p grnsh blk	.20	.20
763	A138	5bil p grnsh blk	.20	.20
764	A138	10bil p grnsh blk	.20	.20
765	A138	20bil p grnsh blk	.20	.20
766	A138	50bil p grnsh blk	.20	.20
767	A138	100bil p grnsh blk	.20	.20
768	A138	200bil p grnsh blk	.20	.20
769	A138	500bil p grnsh blk	.20	.20
770	A138	1000bil p grnsh blk	.20	.20
771	A138	10,000bil p grnsh blk	.20	.20
772	A138	50,000bil p grnsh blk	.25	.25
773	A138	100,000bil p grnsh blk	.25	.25
774	A138	500,000bil p grnsh blk	.25	.25

Denomination in Black
775	A137	5ez ap green	.20	.20
776	A137	10ez ap green	.20	.20
777	A137	20ez ap green	.20	.20
778	A137	50ez ap green	.20	.20
779	A137	80ez ap green	.20	.20
780	A137	100ez ap green	.20	.20
781	A137	200ez ap green	.20	.20
782	A137	500ez ap green	.20	.20
783	A137	1mil ap vermilion	.20	.20
784	A137	5mil ap vermilion	.20	.20
		Nos. 738-784 (46)	9.40	9.40

Denominations are expressed in "ado" or "tax" pengos.
Nos. 738-784 exist imperf. Value, set $500.

Early Steam Locomotive A139

Designs: 20,000ap, Recent steam locomotive. 30,000ap, Electric locomotive. 40,000ap, Diesel locomotive.

1946, July 15 *Wmk. 266* *Perf. 12*
785	A139	10,000ap vio brn	5.00	5.00
786	A139	20,000ap dk blue	5.00	5.00
787	A139	30,000ap dp yel grn	5.00	5.00
788	A139	40,000ap rose car	5.00	5.00
b.		"40,000 ap" omitted	3,000.	
		Nos. 785-788 (4)	20.00	20.00

Centenary of Hungarian railways.
Exist imperf. Value, set $950.

Industry A143

Agriculture A144

1946 *Wmk. 210* *Photo.* *Perf. 15*
788A	A143	8f henna brn	.20	.20
789	A143	10f henna brn	.30	.20
790	A143	12f henna brn	.25	.20
791	A143	20f henna brn	.30	.20
792	A143	30f henna brn	.40	.20
793	A143	40f henna brn	.40	.20

794	A143	60f henna brn	.40	.20
795	A144	1fo dp yel grn	.85	.20
796	A144	1.40fo dp yel grn	.85	.20
797	A144	2fo dp yel grn	1.50	.20
798	A144	3fo dp yel grn	5.75	.20
799	A144	5fo dp yel grn	1.75	.20
800	A144	10fo dp yel grn	3.00	.35
		Nos. 788A-800 (13)	15.95	2.75

For surcharges see Nos. Q9-Q11.
Exist imperf. Value, set $200.

Stamps and Types of 1943-45
Overprinted in Carmine or Black to Show Class of Postage for which Valid

"Any." or "Nyomtatv." = Printed Matter.
"Hl" or "Helyi levél" = Local Letter.
"Hlp." or "Helyi lev.-lap" = Local Postcard.
"Tl." or "Távolsági levél" =Domestic Letter.
"Tlp." or "Távolsági lev.-lap" = Domestic Postcard.

a   b

1946   **Wmk. 266**

801	A99(a)	"Any 1." on 1f (#601;C)	.20	.20
802	A99(a)	"Any 2," on 1f (#601;C)	.20	.20
803	A99(b)	"Nyomtatv. 20gr" on 60f on 8f (#682;Bk + C)	.20	.20
804	A118(a)	"Hl. 1" on 50f (#628;C)	.20	.20
805	A99(a)	"Hl. 2" on 40f on 10f (#664;C + Bk)	.20	.20
806	A99(b)	"Helyi levél" on 10f brn, bl (Bk)	.20	.20
807	A118(a)	"Hlp.1" on 8p on 20f (#670;C + Bk)	.20	.20
808	A118(a)	"Hlp.2." on 8p on 20f (#670;C + Bk)	.20	.20
809	A118(b)	"Helyi lev.-lap" on 20f ol, bl (C)	.20	.20
810	A99(a)	"Tl.1" on 10f (#608;Bk)	.20	.20
811	A99(a)	"Tl.2." on 10f on 4f (#657;Bk + C)	.20	.20
812	A99(b)	"Tavolsagi level" on 18f (#610;C)	.20	.20
813	A99(a)	"Tlp.1." on 4f (#604;Bk)	.20	.20
814	A99(a)	"Tlp.2." on 4f (#604;Bk)	.20	.20
815	A99(b)	"Tavolsagi lev.-lap" on 4f (#604;Bk)	.20	.20
		Nos. 801-815 (15)	3.00	3.00

Nos. 806, 809 not issued without overprint.

György Dózsa — A145

Designs: 10f, Antal Budai-Nagy. 12f, Tamas Esze. 20f, Ignac Martinovics. 30f, Janos Batsanyi. 40f, Lajos Kossuth. 60f, Mihaly Tancsics. 1fo, Alexander Petöfi. 2fo, Andreas Ady. 4fo, Jozsef Attila.

1947, Mar. 15   **Photo.**   **Wmk. 210**

816	A145	8f rose brown	.40	.20
817	A145	10f deep ultra	.40	.20
818	A145	12f dark brown	.40	.20
819	A145	20f dk yel grn	.40	.20
820	A145	30f dk ol bis	.50	.20
821	A145	40f brown car	.50	.20
822	A145	60f cerise	.70	.20
823	A145	1fo dp grnsh bl	1.00	.20
824	A145	2fo dk violet	2.25	.35
825	A145	4fo grnsh black	3.00	.70
		Nos. 816-825 (10)	9.55	2.65

Exist imperf. Value, set $200.

Peace and Agriculture A155   Postal Savings Emblem A156

1947, Sept. 22   **Perf. 12**

826	A155	60f bright red	1.00	.20
a.		"60f." omitted	2,250.	

Peace treaty.
Exists imperf. Value, set $120.

1947, Oct. 31

60f, Postal Savings Bank, Budapest.

827	A156	40f rose brown	.20	.20
828	A156	60f brt rose car	.80	.20

Savings Day, Oct. 31, 1947.
Exist imperf. Value, set $70.

Hungarian Flag — A157

1848 Printing Press A158

Barred Window and Dove — A159

1848 Shako, Sword and Trumpet A160

"On your feet Hungarian, the Homeland is Calling!" A161

Arms of Hungary — A162

Perf. 12½x12, 12x12½

1948   **Wmk. 283**   **Photo.**

829	A157	8f dk rose red	.40	.20
830	A158	10f ultra	.45	.20
831	A159	12f copper brn	.80	.25
832	A160	20f deep green	1.60	.20
833	A161	30f olive brown	1.00	.20
834	A157	40f dk vio brn	1.25	.20
835	A161	60f carmine lake	1.50	.20
a.		Printed on both sides	1,000.	
836	A162	1fo brt ultra	1.60	.20
837	A162	2fo red brown	2.75	.25
838	A162	3fo green	4.75	.60
839	A162	4fo scarlet	7.00	.80
		Nos. 829-839 (11)	23.10	3.30

Cent. of the beginning of Hungary's war for independence.
#834 is inscribed "Kossuth," #835 "Petofi."
Exist imperf. Value, set $320.

Baron Roland Eötvös A163

1948, July 27

840	A163	60f deep red	1.60	.30

Roland Eötvös, physicist, birth cent.
Exists imperf. Value $100.

Hungarian Workers — A164

1948, Oct. 17   **Wmk. 283**   **Perf. 12**

841	A164	30f dk carmine rose	1.00	.30
a.		Sheet of 4	32.50	27.50

The 17th Trade Union Congress, Budapest, October 1948. No. 841a was sold for 2 forint.
Exist imperf. Value: single $40; sheet of 4 $2,000.

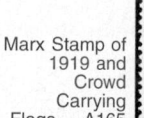

Marx Stamp of 1919 and Crowd Carrying Flags — A165

Petöfi Stamp of 1919 and Flags — A166

1949, Mar. 19   **Flags in Carmine**

842	A165	40f brown	.85	.40
843	A166	60f olive gray	.85	.40

1st Hungarian Soviet Republic, 30th anniv.
Exist imperf. Value, set $55.

Workers of the Five Continents and Flag — A167

1949, June 29   **Perf. 12x12½**
Flag in Red

844	A167	30f yellow brown	3.25	3.00
845	A167	40f brown violet	3.25	3.00
846	A167	60f lilac rose	3.25	3.00
847	A167	1fo violet blue	3.25	3.00
		Nos. 844-847 (4)	13.00	12.00

2nd Congress of the World Federation of Trade Unions, Milan, 1949.
Exist imperf. Value, set $145.

Sándor Petöfi — A168   Youth of Three Races — A169

Perf. 12½x12
1949, July 31   **Engr.**   **Unwmk.**

848	A168	40f claret	.65	.30
849	A168	60f dark red	.50	.20
850	A168	1fo deep blue	.60	.20
		Nos. 848-850 (3)	1.75	.70

Cent. of the death of Sándor Petöfi, poet.
Exist imperf. Value, set $35.
See Nos. 867-869.

Perf. 12½x12
1949, Aug. 14   **Photo.**   **Wmk. 283**

Designs: 30f, Three fists. 40f, Soldier breaking chain. 60f, Soviet youths carrying flags. 1fo, Young workers displaying books.

851	A169	20f dk violet brn	1.00	.70
a.		20f blue green	3.25	3.00
852	A169	30f blue green	1.25	.80
a.		30f violet brown	3.25	3.00

853	A169	40f olive bister	1.40	1.00
a.		40f ultramarine	3.25	3.00
854	A169	60f rose pink	1.40	1.00
855	A169	1fo ultra	2.25	1.50
a.		1fo olive bister	3.75	3.50
b.		Souv. sheet of 5, #851a-853a, 854, 855a	32.50	27.50
		Nos. 851-855 (5)	7.30	5.00

World Festival of Youth and Students, Budapest, Aug. 14-28, 1949.
Exist imperf. Value, set $110. No. 855b imperf, $2,200.

Arms of Hungarian People's Republic A170

1949   **Wmk. 283**
Arms in Bister, Carmine, Blue and Green

856	A170	20f green	1.40	.50
a.		Unwatermarked	1.75	.80
857	A170	60f carmine	1.40	.30
a.		Unwatermarked	1.10	.30
858	A170	1fo blue	2.75	1.10
a.		Unwatermarked	1.40	.60
		Nos. 856-858 (3)	5.55	1.90

Adoption of the Hungarian People's Republic constitution.
Nos. 856-858 exist imperf. Value, set $220. Nos. 856-858 exist with papermaker's watermark. These sell for the same.

Symbols of the UPU — A171

1949, Nov. 1   **Perf. 12x12½**

859	A171	60f rose red	.70	.50
a.		Booklet pane of 6	10.00	
860	A171	1fo blue	.70	.50
a.		Booklet pane of 6	14.00	
		Nos. 859-860,C63 (3)	2.80	2.00

75th anniv. of the UPU.
Nos. 859 and 860 exist imperf. and stamps from 859a and 860a in horiz. pairs, imperf. between. Values: set $15; pairs, imperf between $10.
See No. C63, C81.

Chain Bridge A172

1949, Nov. 20   **Wmk. 283**

861	A172	40f blue green	.45	.35
862	A172	60f red brown	.45	.20
863	A172	1fo blue	.60	.25
		Nos. 861-863,C64-C65 (5)	4.00	3.30

Cent. of the opening of the Chain Bridge at Budapest to traffic.
Exist imperf. Value, set $12.
For souvenir sheet see No. C66.

Joseph V. Stalin — A173

Perf. 12½x12
1949, Dec. 21   **Engr.**

864	A173	60f dark red	1.00	.20
865	A173	1fo deep blue	1.00	.30
866	A173	2fo deep blue	2.75	1.00
		Nos. 864-866 (3)	4.75	1.00

70th anniv. of the birth of Joseph V. Stalin.
Exist imperf. Value, set $20.

See Nos. 1034-1035.

Petőfi Type of 1949

1950, Feb. 5   *Perf. 12½x12*
867	A168	40f brown	.80	.35
868	A168	60f dark carmine	.45	.20
869	A168	1fo dark green	.45	.25
		Nos. 867-869 (3)	1.70	.80

Value, set $35.

Philatelic Museum, Budapest A174

Perf. 12x12½

1950, Mar. 12   **Photo.**   **Wmk. 283**
870	A174	60f gray & brown	8.00	8.00

20th anniv. of the establishment of the Hungarian PO Phil. Museum.
Exists imperf. Value $90.
See No. C68.

Coal Mining A175

Designs: 10f, Heavy industry. 12f, Power production. 20f, Textile industry. 30f, "Cultured workers." 40f, Mechanized agriculture. 60f, Village cooperative. 1fo, Train. 1.70fo, "Holiday." 2fo, Defense. 3fo, Shipping. 4fo, Livestock. 5fo, Engineering. 10fo, Sports.

1950   **Wmk. 283**
871	A175	8f gray	.60	.20
872	A175	10f claret	.60	.20
873	A175	12f orange ver	1.00	.35
874	A175	20f blue green	.60	.20
875	A175	30f rose violet	1.00	.20
876	A175	40f sepia	1.00	.20
877	A175	60f red	1.25	.20
878	A175	1fo gray brn, yel & lil	3.50	.25
879	A175	1.70fo dk grn & yel	8.00	.40
880	A175	2fo vio brn & cr	3.50	.20
881	A175	3fo slate & cream	8.00	.20
882	A175	4fo blk brn & sal	45.00	5.00
883	A175	5fo rose vio & yel	20.00	2.50
884	A175	10fo dk brn & yel	70.00	11.00
		Nos. 871-884 (14)	164.05	21.10
		Hinged set	80.00	

Issued to publicize Hungary's Five Year Plan.
Exist imperf. Value, set $575.
See Nos. 945-958.

Citizens Welcoming Liberators — A176

1950, Apr. 4   **Unwmk.**   *Perf. 12*
885	A176	40f gray black	1.10	.55
886	A176	60f rose brown	.90	.20
887	A176	1fo deep blue	1.10	.25
888	A176	2fo brown	1.40	.65
		Nos. 885-888 (4)	4.50	1.65

Fifth anniversary of Hungary's liberation.
Exist imperf. Value, set $60.

Chess Players A177

Design: 1fo, Iron Workers Union building and chess emblem.

1950, Apr. 9   **Wmk. 106**
889	A177	60f deep magenta	2.50	.50
890	A177	1fo deep blue	4.00	1.25
		Nos. 889-890,C69 (3)	12.50	3.85

World Chess Championship Matches, Budapest.
Exist imperf. Value, set (3) $265.

Workers Symbolizing International Proletariat — A178

Design: 60f, Blast furnace, tractor, workers holding Maypole.

1950, May 1
891	A178	40f orange brown	2.00	.65
892	A178	60f rose carmine	1.75	.30
893	A178	1fo deep blue	2.00	.50
		Nos. 891-893 (3)	5.75	1.45

Issued to publicize Labor Day, May 1, 1950.
Exist imperf. Value, set $85.

Liberty, Cogwheel, Dove and Globes — A179

Inscribed: "1950. V. 10.-24."
Design: 60f, Three workers and flag.

1950, May 10   **Photo.**   *Perf. 12x12½*
894	A179	40f olive green	1.75	.60
895	A179	60f dark carmine	1.50	.40
		Nos. 894-895,C70 (3)	4.85	1.65

Meeting of the World Federation of Trade Unions, Budapest, May 1950.
Exist imperf. Value, set $80.

Doctor Inspecting Baby's Bath — A180

Children's Day: 30f, Physical Culture. 40f, Education. 60f, Boys' Camp. 1.70fo, Model plane building.

1950, June 4   **Wmk. 106**
896	A180	20f gray & brn	2.00	1.10
897	A180	30f brn & rose lake	.60	.20
898	A180	40f indigo & dk grn	.60	.20
899	A180	60f SZABAD	1.00	.20
a.		UTANPOTLASUNK . .	1,000.	950.00
900	A180	1.70fo dp grn & gray	1.75	.80
		Nos. 896-900 (5)	5.95	2.50

Exist imperf. Value, set $60.

Youths Marching on Globe — A181

Working Man and Woman — A182

30f, Foundry worker. 60f, Workers on Mt. Gellert. 1.70fo, Worker, peasant & student; flags.

Inscribed: Budapest 1950. VI. 17-18.

Perf. 12x12½, 12½x12

1950, June 17
901	A181	20f dark green	1.40	.45
902	A181	30f deep red org	.40	.20
903	A182	40f dark brown	.40	.20
904	A182	60f deep claret	.80	.25
905	A182	1.70fo dark olive grn	1.50	.55
		Nos. 901-905 (5)	4.50	1.65

Issued to publicize the First Congress of the Working Youth, Budapest, June 17-18, 1950.
Exist imperf. Value, set $65.

Peonies — A183

Designs: 40f, Anemones. 60f, Pheasant's-eye. 1fo, Geraniums. 1.70fo, Bluebells.

Engraved and Lithographed
Perf. 12½x12

1950, Aug. 20   **Unwmk.**
906	A183	30f rose brn, rose pink & grn	1.25	.40
907	A183	40f dk green, lil & yel	1.60	.40
908	A183	60f red brn, yel & grn	2.00	.50
909	A183	1fo purple, red & grn	4.50	2.00
910	A183	1.70fo dk violet & grn	4.00	1.00
		Nos. 906-910 (5)	13.35	4.30

Exist imperf. Value, set $70.

Miner — A184

Designs: 60f, High speed lathe. 1fo, Prefabricated building construction.

Perf. 12x12½

1950, Oct. 7   **Photo.**   **Wmk. 106**
911	A184	40f brown	1.75	.60
912	A184	60f carmine rose	1.40	.30
913	A184	1fo brt blue	1.75	.45
		Nos. 911-913 (3)	4.90	1.35

2nd National Exhibition of Inventions.
Exist imperf. Value, set $35.

Gen. Josef Bem and Battle at Piski A185

Perf. 12½x12

1950, Dec. 10   **Engr.**   **Unwmk.**
914	A185	40f dark brown	1.25	.60
915	A185	60f deep carmine	1.00	.30
916	A185	1fo deep blue	1.75	.65
		Nos. 914-916 (3)	4.00	1.55

Gen. Josef Bem, death centenary.
Exist imperf. Value, set $35.
See No. C80.

Signing Petition A186

Peace Demonstrator Holding Dove — A187

1fo, Mother and Children with soldier.

Wmk. 106

1950, Nov. 23   **Photo.**   *Perf. 12*
917	A186	40f ultra & red brn	9.25	7.00
918	A187	60f red org & dk grn	2.25	2.25
919	A186	1fo ol grn & dk brn	10.00	7.00
		Nos. 917-919 (3)	21.50	16.25

Exist imperf. Value, set $80.

Women Swimmers A188

Designs: 20f, Vaulting. 1fo, Mountain climbing. 1.70fo, Basketball. 2fo, Motorcycling.

1950, Dec. 2   *Perf. 12x12½*
920	A188	10f blue & gray	.45	.20
921	A188	20f salmon & dk brn	.45	.20
922	A188	40f olive & brn	.90	.45
923	A188	1fo olive & grn	1.50	.55
924	A188	2fo salmon & pur	2.50	1.25
		Nos. 920-924,C82-C86 (10)	15.55	6.30

Exist imperf. Value, set (10) $120.

Canceled to Order

The government stamp agency started about 1950 to sell canceled sets of new issues. Values in the second ("used") column are for these canceled-to-order stamps. Postally used stamps are worth more.

The practice was to end Apr. 1, 1991.

A189

Worker, Peasant, Soldier and Party Flag — A190

60f, Matthias Rakosi & allegory. 1fo, House of Parliament, columns of workers & banner.

Inscribed: "Budapest * 1951 * Februar 24."

1951, Feb. 24   *Perf. 12½x12, 12x12½*
925	A189	10f yellow green	.70	.35
926	A190	30f brown	.80	.40
927	A190	60f carmine rose	.80	.50
928	A189	1fo blue	1.00	.60
		Nos. 925-928 (4)	3.30	1.85

2nd Congress of the Hungarian Workers' Party.
Exist imperf. Value, set $55.

Mare and Foal — A191

Designs: 30f, Sow and shoats. 40f, Ram and ewe. 60f, Cow and calf.

1951, Apr. 5   **Perf. 12x12½**
929	A191	10f ol bis & rose brn	1.10	.25
930	A191	30f rose brn & ol bis	1.25	.55
931	A191	40f dk green & brn	1.25	.55
932	A191	60f brown org & brn	1.50	.35
		Nos. 929-932,C87-C90 (8)	18.35	5.10

Issued to encourage increased livestock production.
Exist imperf. Value, set (8) $100.

Flags of Russia and Hungary — A192

Russian Technician Teaching Hungarians A193

1951, Apr. 4   **Perf. 12½x12, 12x12½**
933	A192	60f brnsh carmine	1.40	.25
934	A193	1fo dull violet	1.40	.40

Issued to publicize the "Month of Friendship" between Hungary and Russia, 1951.
Exist imperf. Value, set $32.50.

Worker Holding Olive Branch and Mallet A194

Workers Carrying Flags — A195

1fo, Workers approaching Place of Heroes.

Perf. 12x12½, 12½x12
1951, May 1   **Photo.**   **Wmk. 106**
935	A194	40f brown	1.00	.50
936	A195	60f scarlet	.80	.20
937	A194	1fo blue	1.00	.25
		Nos. 935-937 (3)	2.80	.95

Issued to publicize Labor Day, May 1, 1951.
Exist imperf. Value, set $32.50.

Leo Frankel — A196

Paris Street Fighting, 1871 — A197

1951, May 20
938	A196	60f dark brown	1.00	.25
939	A197	1fo blue & red	1.25	.40

80th anniv. of the Commune of Paris.
Exist imperf. Value, set $28.

Children of Various Races — A198

1951, June 3   **Perf. 12½x12**

Designs: 40f, Boy and girl at play. 50f, Street car and Girl Pioneer. 60f, Chemistry students. 1.70fo, Pioneer bugler.

Inscribed:
"Nemzetkozi Gyermeknap 1951"
940	A198	30f dark brown	.60	.20
941	A198	40f green	.60	.20
942	A198	50f brown red	.60	.25
943	A198	60f plum	.85	.35
944	A198	1.70fo blue	1.10	1.00
		Nos. 940-944 (5)	3.75	2.00

International Day of Children, 6/3/51.
Exist imperf. Value, set $45.

5-Year-Plan Type of 1950

Designs as before.

1951-52   **Wmk. 106**   **Perf. 12x12½**
945	A175	8f gray	.60	.20
946	A175	10f claret	.35	.20
947	A175	12f orange ver	.35	.20
948	A175	20f blue green	.35	.20
949	A175	30f rose violet	.35	.20
950	A175	40f sepia	.65	.20
951	A175	60f red	.75	.20
952	A175	1fo gray brn, yel & lil	.85	.20
953	A175	1.70fo dk grn & yel	2.00	.20
954	A175	2fo vio brn & cr	3.00	.20
955	A175	3fo slate & cream	4.25	.25
956	A175	4fo blk brn & sal	5.25	.35
957	A175	5fo rose vio & yel ('52)	5.75	.75
958	A175	10fo dk brn & yel ('52)	13.00	3.00
		Nos. 945-958 (14)	37.50	6.35

Maxim Gorky — A199

Perf. 12½x12½
1951, June 17   **Engr.**   **Unwmk.**
959	A199	60f copper red	.60	.25
960	A199	1fo deep blue	.75	.35
961	A199	2fo rose violet	1.10	.75
		Nos. 959-961 (3)	2.45	1.35

15th anniversary of the death of Gorky.
Exist imperf. Value, set $30.

Budapest Buildings

Railroad Workshop A200

Building in Lehel Street A201

Suburban Bus Terminal A202

Rakosi House of Culture A203

George Kilian Street School A204

Central Construction Headquarters A205

Design Size: 22x18mm

1951   **Wmk. 106**   **Photo.**   **Perf. 15**
962	A200	20f green	.55	.20
963	A201	30f red orange	.70	.20
964	A202	40f brown	.70	.20
965	A203	60f red	1.00	.20
966	A204	1fo blue	1.50	.20
967	A205	3fo deep plum	3.00	.20
		Nos. 962-967 (6)	7.45	1.20

Exist imperf. Value, set $110.
See Nos. 1004-1011, 1048-1056C.

Design Size: 21x17mm

1958
962a	A200	20f green	.65	.20
963a	A201	30f red orange	1.10	.20
964a	A202	40f brown	.95	.20
965a	A203	60f red	1.40	.20
966a	A204	1fo blue	1.40	.20
967a	A205	3fo deep plum	3.00	.20
		Nos. 962a-967a (6)	8.50	1.20

Tractor Manufacture A206

30f, Fluoroscope examination. 40f, Checking lathework. 60f, Woman tractor operator.

1951, Aug. 20   **Perf. 12x12½**
968	A206	20f black brown	.20	.20
969	A206	30f deep blue	.25	.20
970	A206	40f crimson rose	.65	.20
971	A206	60f brown	.80	.25
		Nos. 968-971,C91-C93 (7)	5.45	2.20

The successful conclusion of the first year under Hungary's 5-year plan.
Exist imperf. Value, set $60.

Soldiers of the People's Army — A207

1951, Sept. 29
972	A207	1fo brown	1.60	.30

Issued to publicize Army Day, Sept. 29, 1951. See No. C94.
Exist imperf. Value (with C94) $32.50.

Stamp of 1871, Portrait Replaced by Postmark A208

Cornflower A209

Perf. 12½x12
1951, Sept. 12   **Engr.**   **Unwmk.**
973	A208	60f olive green	2.00	1.50
		Nos. 973,B207-B208 (3)	22.00	20.00

80th anniv. of Hungary's 1st postage stamp.
See Nos. C95, CB13-CB14.
Exist imperf. Value, set (3) $70.

1951, Nov. 4   **Engr. & Litho.**
974	A209	30f shown	.90	.20
975	A209	40f Lily of the Valley	3.25	.75
976	A209	60f Tulip	1.00	.40
977	A209	1fo Poppy	1.75	.80
978	A209	1.70fo Cowslip	2.75	2.40
		Nos. 974-978 (5)	9.65	4.55

Exist imperf. Value, set $70.

Storming of the Winter Palace A210

Designs: 60f, Lenin speaking to soldiers. 1fo, Lenin and Stalin.

Perf. 12x12½
1951, Nov. 7   **Photo.**   **Wmk. 106**
979	A210	40f gray green	.90	.65
980	A210	60f deep blue	1.00	.20
981	A210	1fo rose lake	1.10	.45
		Nos. 979-981 (3)	3.00	1.30

34th anniversary of the Russian Revolution.
Exist imperf. Value, set $45.

Marchers Passing Stalin Monument — A211

1951, Dec. 16   **Wmk. 106**
982	A211	60f henna brown	1.50	.60
983	A211	1fo deep blue	1.50	.60

Joseph V. Stalin, 72nd birthday.
Exist imperf. Value, set $32.50.

Grand Theater, Moscow A212

Views of Moscow: 1fo, Lenin Mausoleum. 1.60fo, Kremlin.

1952, Feb. 20   **Perf. 12**
984	A212	60f ol grn & rose brn	.65	.20
985	A212	1fo lil rose & ol brn	1.00	.35
986	A212	1.60fo red brn & ol	2.00	.65
		Nos. 984-986 (3)	3.65	1.20

Hungarian-Soviet Friendship Month.
Exist imperf. Value, set $32.50.

Rakosi and Farmers A213

Matyas Rakosi — A214

Design: 2fo, Rakosi and Workers.

Perf. 12x12½, 12½x12
1952, Mar. 9   **Engr.**   **Unwmk.**
987	A213	60f deep plum	1.00	.35
988	A214	1fo dk red brown	1.00	.40
989	A213	2fo dp violet blue	2.25	.80
		Nos. 987-989 (3)	4.25	1.55

60th anniv. of the birth of Matyas Rakosi, communist leader.

Exist imperf. Value, set $35.

Lajos Kossuth and Speech at Debrecen A215

Designs: 30f, Sándor Petöfi. 50f, Gen. Josef Bem. 60f, Mihaly Tancsics. 1fo, Gen. János Damjanich. 1.50fo, Gen. Alexander Nagy.

1952, Mar. 15   Perf. 12x12½

990	A215	20f green	.20	.20
991	A215	30f rose violet	.20	.20
992	A215	50f grnsh blk	.45	.20
993	A215	60f brown car	.50	.20
994	A215	1fo blue	.80	.25
995	A215	1.50fo redsh brown	1.10	.60
		Nos. 990-995 (6)	3.25	1.65

Heroes of the 1848 revolution.
Exist imperf. Value, set $32.50.
Nos. 990-995 also exist perf 12. Value, set $300.

No. B204 Surcharged in Black with Bars Obliterating Inscription and Surtax
Perf. 12½x12

1952, Apr. 27   Photo.   Wmk. 283
996   SP121   60f magenta   37.50   32.50

Budapest Philatelic Exhibition. Counterfeits exist.

Girl Drummer Leading Parade A216

Designs: 60f, Workers and soldier. 1fo, Worker, flag-encircled globe and dove.

Perf. 12x12½

1952, May 1   Photo.   Wmk. 106

997	A216	40f dk grn & dull red	1.75	.60
998	A216	60f dk red brn & dull red	1.00	.50
999	A216	1fo sepia & dull red	1.75	.80
		Nos. 997-999 (3)	4.50	1.90

Issued to publicize Labor Day, May 1, 1952.
Exist imperf. Value, set $175.

Runner — A217

Designs: 40f, Swimmer. 60f, Fencer. 1fo, Woman gymnast.

1952, May 26   Perf. 11

1000	A217	30f dark red brown	.70	.20
1001	A217	40f deep green	.70	.20
1002	A217	60f deep lilac rose	1.00	.25
1003	A217	1fo deep blue	1.40	.50
		Nos. 1000-1003,C107-C108 (6)	8.40	3.40

Issued to publicize Hungary's participation in the Olympic Games, Helsinki, 1952.
Exist imperf. Value, set (6) $100.

Building Types of 1951

Buildings: 8f, School, Stalinvarost. 10f, Szekesfeharvar Station. 12f, Building, Ujpest. 50f, Metal works, Inotai. 70f, Grain elevator, Hajdunanas. 80f, Tiszalok dam. 4fo, Miners' union headquarters. 5fo, Workers' apartments, Ujpest.

Design Size: 22x18mm

1952   Wmk. 106   Perf. 15

1004	A202	8f green	.45	.20
1005	A200	10f purple	.45	.20
1006	A202	12f carmine	.45	.20
1007	A202	50f gray blue	.65	.20
1008	A202	70f yellow brn	1.00	.20
1009	A202	80f maroon	1.25	.20
1010	A202	4fo olive grn	2.75	.20
1011	A202	5fo gray black	3.75	.20
		Nos. 1004-1011 (8)	10.75	1.60

Exist imperf. Value, set $140.

Design Size: 21x17mm

1958

1004a	A202	8f green	.45	.20
1005a	A200	10f purple	2.00	.20
1006a	A202	12f carmine	.50	.20
1007a	A202	50f gray blue	.65	.20
1008a	A202	70f yellow brn	.80	.20
1009a	A202	80f maroon	1.25	.20
1010a	A202	4fo olive grn	2.75	.20
1011a	A202	5fo gray black	4.00	.20
		Nos. 1004a-1011a (8)	12.40	1.60

Approaching Train — A218

Railroad Day: 1fo, Railroad Construction.

1952, Aug. 10   Perf. 12x12½

1012	A218	60f red brown	1.10	.35
1013	A218	1fo deep olive grn	1.40	.40

Exist imperf. Value, set $30.

Coal Excavator A219

Miners' Day: 1fo, Coal breaker.

1952, Sept. 7

1014	A219	60f brown	.90	.25
1015	A219	1fo dark green	1.50	.30

Exist imperf. Value, set $30.

Lajos Kossuth — A220   Janos Hunyadi — A221

Design: 60f, Kossuth statue.

1952, Sept. 19   Perf. 12½x12

1016	A220	40f ol brn, pink	.85	.40
1017	A220	60f black brn, bl	.85	.40
1018	A220	1fo purple, citron	.85	.65
		Nos. 1016-1018 (3)	2.55	1.45

150th anniv. of the birth of Lajos Kossuth.
Exist imperf. Value, set $40.

1952, Sept. 28   Engr.   Unwmk.

Portraits: 30f, Gyorgy Dozsa. 40f, Miklos Zrinyi. 60f, Ilona Zriuyi. 1fo, Bottyan Vak. 1.50fo, Aurel Stromfeld.

1019	A221	20f purple	.25	.20
1020	A221	30f dark green	.25	.20
1021	A221	40f indigo	.25	.20
1022	A221	60f dk violet brn	.55	.30
1023	A221	1fo dk blue grn	.80	.40
1024	A221	1.50fo dark brown	1.90	1.00
		Nos. 1019-1024 (6)	4.00	2.30

Army Day, Sept. 28, 1952.
Exist imperf. Value, set $55.

Lenin and Conference at Smolny Palace A222

Designs: 60f, Stalin and Cavalry Attack. 1fo, Marx, Engels, Lenin and Stalin.

1952, Nov. 7   Wmk. 106
Portraits in Olive Gray

1025	A222	40f deep claret	2.25	.70
1026	A222	60f gray	1.00	.25
1027	A222	1fo rose red	2.25	.40
		Nos. 1025-1027 (3)	5.50	1.35

Russian Revolution, 35th anniversary.
Exist imperf. Value, set $55.

Peasant Woman Holding Wheat — A223

Peace Meeting A224

Perf. 12½x12, 12x12½

1952, Nov. 22

1028	A223	60f brn red, citron	1.25	.25
1029	A224	1fo brown, blue	1.25	.75

Third Hungarian Peace Congress, 1952.
Exist imperf. Value, set $30.

Subway Construction A225

Design: 1fo, Station and map.

1953, Jan. 19   Photo.   Perf. 12x12½

1030	A225	60f dk slate green	1.25	.50
1031	A225	1fo brown red	1.60	.55

Completion of the Budapest subway extension.
Exist imperf. Value, set $30.

Tank and Flag — A226

Stalin — A227

60f, Map of Central Europe and Soldier.

1953, Feb. 18

1032	A226	40f dark car rose	1.25	.25
1033	A226	60f chocolate	1.25	.45

Battle of Stalingrad, 10th anniversary.
Exist imperf. Value, set $30.

Perf. 12x11½

1953   Engr.   Wmk. 106
1034   A227   60f pur blk   1.25   .20

Souvenir Sheet

1035   A227   2fo purple black   27.50   22.50

Death of Joseph Stalin (1879-1953).
Exist imperf. Values: 60f $20; 2fo $175.
Issue dates: #1034, Mar. 27; #1035, Mar. 9.

Workers' Rest Home, Galyateto A228

Designs: 40f, Home at Mecsek. 50f, Parad Mineral Baths. 60f, Home at Kekes. 70f, Balatonfured Mineral Baths.

1953, Apr.   Photo.   Perf. 12x12½

1036	A228	30f fawn	.60	.20
1037	A228	40f deep blue	.60	.20
1038	A228	50f dk olive bis	.60	.20
1039	A228	60f dp yellow grn	.60	.20
1040	A228	70f scarlet	.60	.25
		Nos. 1036-1040,C121-C122 (7)	4.90	1.70

Exist imperf. Value, set (7) $70.

Young Workers with Red Flags — A229   Karl Marx — A230

1953, May 1   Perf. 12½x12
1041   A229   60f brn & red, yel   1.00   .20

Issued to publicize Labor Day, May 1, 1953.
Exist imperf. Value $27.50.

1953, May 1   Engr.   Perf. 11½x12
1042   A230   1fo black, pink   1.50   .20

70th anniv. of the death of Karl Marx. See No. 1898.
Exist imperf. Value $32.50.

Insurgents in the Forest — A231

30f, Drummer & fighters. 40f, Battle scene. 60f, Cavalry attack. 1fo, Francis Rákóczy II.

1953, June 14   Photo.   Perf. 11

1043	A231	20f dk ol grn & org red, grnsh	.60	.45
1044	A231	30f vio brn & red org	1.00	.60
1045	A231	40f gray bl & red org, pink	1.25	.65
1046	A231	60f dk ol brn & org, yel	2.25	1.25
1047	A231	1fo dk red brn & org red, yel	3.50	2.00
		Nos. 1043-1047 (5)	8.60	4.95

250th anniv. of the insurrection of 1703.
Exist imperf. Value $55.

Building Types of 1951

Buildings: 8f, Day Nursery, Ozd. 10f, Medical research institute, Szombathely. 12f, Apartments, Komlo. 20f, Department store, Ujpest. 30f, Brick factory, Maly. 40f, Metropolitan hospital. 50f, Sports building, Stalinvaros. 60f, Post office, Csepel. 70f, Blast furnace, Diosgyor. 1.20fo, Agricultural school, Ajkacsinger Valley. 1.70fo, Iron Works School, Csepel. 2fo, Optical works house of culture.

Design Size: 22x18mm

1953   Wmk. 106   Perf. 15

1048	A204	8f olive green	.35	.20
1049	A204	10f purple	.45	.20
1050	A205	12f rose carmine	.65	.20
1051	A204	20f dark green	.50	.20
1052	A204	30f orange	.80	.20
1053	A204	40f dark brown	1.20	.20
1054	A205	50f blue violet	1.50	.20
1055	A205	60f rose red	1.20	.20
1056	A204	70f yellow brown	1.60	.20

1056A	A205	1.20fo red	3.25	.20
1056B	A204	1.70fo blue	2.50	.20
1056C	A204	2fo green	4.00	.20
		Nos. 1048-1056C (12)	18.00	2.40

Exist imperf. Value, set $185.

Design Size: 21x17mm

1958

1048a	A204	8f olive green	.70	.20
1049a	A204	10f purple	—	.45
1050a	A205	12f rose carmine	1.20	.20
1051a	A204	20f dark green	1.20	.20
1052a	A204	30f orange	1.10	.20
1053a	A204	40f dark brown	1.40	.20
1054a	A205	50f blue violet	1.40	.20
1055a	A204	60f rose red	1.40	.20
1056a	A204	70f yellow brown	2.00	.20
1056Aa	A205	1.20fo red	2.75	.20
1056Ba	A204	1.70fo blue	1.80	.20
1056Ca	A204	2fo green	3.25	.20
		Nos. 1048a-1056Ca (12)	18.20	2.65

Exist imperf. Value, set $160.

Bicycling — A232

1953, Aug. 20 — *Perf. 11*

1057	A232	20f shown	.40	.25
1058	A232	30f Swimming	.40	.20
1059	A232	40f Calisthenics	.40	.20
1060	A232	50f Discus	.60	.20
1061	A232	60f Wrestling	.75	.20
		Nos. 1057-1061,C123-C127 (10)	14.05	5.00

Opening of the People's Stadium, Budapest.
Exist imperf. Value, set (10) $120.

Kazar Costume A233

Lenin — A234

Provincial Costumes: 30f, Ersekcsanad. 40f, Kalocsa. 60f, Sioagard. 1fo, Sarkoz. 1.70fo, Boldog. 2fo, Orhalom. 2.50fo, Hosszuheteny.

1953, Sept. 12 — *Engr.* — *Perf. 12*

1062	A233	20f blue green	1.25	.40
1063	A233	30f chocolate	1.50	.40
1064	A233	40f ultra	2.00	.40
1065	A233	60f red	2.50	1.50
1066	A233	1fo grnsh blue	3.25	1.50
1067	A233	1.70fo brt green	4.25	2.25
1068	A233	2fo carmine rose	6.00	3.00
1069	A233	2.50fo purple	8.50	6.00
		Nos. 1062-1069 (8)	29.25	15.45

Exist imperf. Value, set $135.
See No. 1189.

1954, Jan. 21 — **Wmk. 106** — *Perf. 12*

Designs: 60f, Lenin and Stalin at meeting. 1fo, Lenin, facing left.

1073	A234	40f dk blue grn	1.75	.80
1074	A234	60f black brown	1.75	.30
1075	A234	1fo dk car rose	2.25	1.00
		Nos. 1073-1075 (3)	5.75	2.10

30th anniversary, death of Lenin.
Exist imperf. Value, set $55.

Worker Reading A235

Revolutionary and Red Flag — A236

Design: 1fo, Soldier.

Perf. 12x12½, 12½x12

1954, Mar. 21 — **Photo.**

1076	A235	40f gray blue & red	4.25	.75
1077	A236	60f brown & red	4.25	.75
1078	A235	1fo gray & red	4.25	.75
		Nos. 1076-1078 (3)	12.75	2.25

35th anniversary of the "First Hungarian Communist Republic."
Exist imperf. Value, set $80.

Blood Test — A237

Maypole — A238

Designs: 40f, Mother receiving newborn baby. 60f, Medical examination of baby.

1954, Mar. 8 — *Perf. 12*

1079	A237	30f brt blue	.25	.20
1080	A237	40f brown bister	.45	.20
1081	A237	60f purple	.55	.25
		Nos. 1079-1081,C146-C148 (6)	6.05	2.80

Exist imperf. Value, set $80.

1954, May 1 — *Perf. 12½x12*

Design: 60f, Flag bearer.

1082	A238	40f olive	.50	.20
1083	A238	60f orange red	.50	.20

Issued to publicize Labor Day, May 1, 1954.
Exist imperf. Value, set $27.50.

Farm Woman with Fruit A239

1954, May 24 — *Perf. 12*

1084	A239	60f red orange	.80	.25

3rd Congress of the Hungarian Workers Party, Budapest, May 24, 1954.

Exists imperf. Value, set $22.

Natl. Museum, Budapest — A240

Peppers A241

Designs: 60f, Arms of People's Republic. 1fo, Dome of Parliament Building.

1954, Aug. 20 — *Perf. 12½x12*

1085	A240	40f brt blue	1.25	.25
1086	A240	60f redsh brown	1.25	.30
1087	A240	1fo dark brown	1.50	.55
		Nos. 1085-1087 (3)	4.00	1.50

People's Republic Constitution, 5th anniv.
Exist Imperf. Value, set $35.

1954, Sept. 11 — **Engr., Fruit Litho.**

Fruit: 50f, Tomatoes. 60f, Grapes. 80f, Apricots. 1fo, Apples. 1.20fo, Plums. 1.50fo, Cherries. 2fo, Peaches.

Fruit in Natural Colors

1088	A241	40f gray blue	.80	.25
1089	A241	50f plum	.80	.25
1090	A241	60f gray blue	.95	.25
1091	A241	80f chocolate	1.00	.25
1092	A241	1fo rose violet	1.40	.40
1093	A241	1.20fo dull blue	1.75	.45
1094	A241	1.50fo plum	1.50	1.25
1095	A241	2fo gray blue	4.00	.65
		Nos. 1088-1095 (8)	12.20	3.75

National agricultural fair.
Exist imperf. Value, set $70.

Maurus Jokai — A242

1954, Oct. 17 — **Engr.**

1096	A242	60f dk brown olive	1.25	.35
1097	A242	1fo deep claret	1.50	.90

50th anniv. of the death of Maurus Jokai, writer.
Exist imperf. Value, set $30.
No. 1097 in violet blue is from the souvenir sheet, No. C157.

Janos Apacai Csere A243

1954, Dec. 5 — **Photo.** — *Perf. 12x12½*

Scientists: 10f, Csoma Sandor Korosi. 12f, Anyos Jedlik. 20f, Ignaz Semmelweis. 30f, Janos Irinyi. 40f, Frigyes Koranyi. 50f, Armin Vambery. 60f, Karoly Than. 1fo, Otto Herman. 1.70fo, Tivadar Puskas. 2fo, Endre Hogyes.

1098	A243	8f dk vio brn, *yel*	.20	.20
1099	A243	10f brn, car, *pink*	.20	.20
1100	A243	12f gray, *bl*	.20	.20
1101	A243	20f brn, *yel*	.20	.20
1102	A243	30f vio bl, *pink*	.20	.20
1103	A243	40f dk grn, *yel*	.20	.20
1104	A243	50f red brn, *pale grn*	.20	.20
1105	A243	60f blue, *pink*	.20	.20
1106	A243	1fo olive	.55	.20

1107	A243	1.70fo rose brn, *yel*	.80	.25
1108	A243	2fo blue green	1.00	.45
		Nos. 1098-1108 (11)	3.95	2.50

Exist imperf. Value, set $55.

Readers in Industrial Library — A244

Industry A245

1fo, Agriculture. 2fo, Liberation monument.

1955, Apr. 4 — *Perf. 12½x12, 12x12½*

1109	A244	40f dk car & ol brn	.65	.25
1110	A245	60f dk green & red	.65	.25
1111	A245	1fo choc & grn	1.00	.45
1112	A244	2fo blue grn & brn	1.40	.80
		Nos. 1109-1112 (4)	3.70	1.75

10th anniversary of Hungary's liberation.
Exist imperf. Value, set $50.

Date, Flags, Grain Elevator and Tractor A246

1955, May 1 — *Perf. 12x12½*

1113	A246	1fo rose carmine	.80	.20

Labor Day, May 1, 1955.
Exist imperf. Value, set $22.

Government Printing Plant — A247

1955, May 28 — **Wmk. 106**

1114	A247	60f gray grn & hn brn	.50	.20

Centenary of the establishment of the government printing plant.
Exist imperf. Value, set $22.

Young Citizens and Hungarian Flag — A248

1955, June 15 — *Perf. 12*

1115	A248	1fo red brown	.65	.25

Issued to publicize the second national congress of the Hungarian Youth Organization.
Exist imperf. Value, set $22.

Truck Farmer A249

10f, Fisherman. 12f, Bricklayer. 20f, Radio assembler. 30f, Woman potter. 40f, Railwayman & train. 50f, Clerk & scales. 60f, Postman emptying mail box. 70f, Cattle & herdsman. 80f, Textile worker. 1fo, Riveter.

1.20fo, Carpenter. 1.40fo, Streetcar conductor. 1.70fo, Herdsman & pigs. 2fo, Welder. 2.60fo, Woman tractor driver. 3fo, Herdsman in national costume & horse. 4fo, Bus driver. 5fo, Lineman. 10fo, Coal miner.

1955   Wmk. 106   Perf. 12x12½

1116	A249	8f chestnut	.20	.20
1117	A249	10f Prus green	.25	.20
1118	A249	12f red orange	.25	.20
1119	A249	20f olive green	.40	.20
1120	A249	30f dark red	.35	.20
1121	A249	40f brown	.40	.20
1122	A249	50f violet bl	.40	.20
1123	A249	60f brown red	.50	.20
1124	A249	70f olive	.80	.20
1125	A249	80f purple	.50	.20
1126	A249	1fo blue	1.00	.20
1127	A249	1.20fo olive bis	1.20	.20
1128	A249	1.40fo deep green	1.00	.20
1129	A249	1.70fo purple	1.00	.20
1130	A249	2fo rose brown	1.00	.20
1131	A249	2.60fo vermilion	1.50	.20
1132	A249	3fo green	2.25	.20
1133	A249	4fo peacock blue	2.00	.20
1134	A249	5fo orange brown	2.00	.25
1135	A249	10fo violet	1.75	.55
		Nos. 1116-1135 (20)	18.75	4.40

Exist imperf. Value, set $140.
For surcharges see Nos. B211-B216.

Postrider Blowing Horn — A250

1955, June 25   Perf. 12½x12
1136	A250	1fo rose violet	.50	.20

Hungarian Postal Museum, 25th anniv.
Exists tete-beche. Value: 2½ times the value of a single.
Exists imperf. Value $27.50.

Mihaly Csokonai Vitez A251

1fo, Mihaly Vorosmarty. 2fo, Attila József.

1955, July 28   Perf. 12
1137	A251	60f olive black	1.25	.30
1138	A251	1fo dark blue	1.25	.40
1139	A251	2fo rose brown	1.50	.65
		Nos. 1137-1139 (3)	4.00	1.35

Issued to honor three Hungarian poets.
Exist imperf. Value $40.

Bela Bartok — A252

1955, Oct. 9
1140	A252	60f light brown	1.25	.50
		Nos. 1140,C168-C169 (3)	6.75	3.75

10th anniversary of the death of Bela Bartok, composer.
Exist imperf. Value, set (3) $35.

Diesel Train A253

Designs: 60f, Bus. 80f, Motorcycle. 1fo, Truck. 1.20fo, Steam locomotive. 1.50fo, Dump truck. 2fo, Freighter.

1955, Dec. 20   Perf. 14½
1141	A253	40f grn & vio brn	.20	.20
1142	A253	60f dp grn & ol	.20	.20
1143	A253	80f ol grn & brn	.35	.20
1144	A253	1fo ocher & grn	.70	.30
1145	A253	1.20fo salmon & blk	1.25	.35
1146	A253	1.50fo grnsh blk & red brn	1.40	.50
1147	A253	2fo aqua & brown	1.90	.75
		Nos. 1141-1147 (7)	6.00	2.50

Exist imperf. Value, set $60.

Puli (Sheepdog) — A254

Puli and Steer A255

Hungarian Pointer — A256

Hungarian Dogs: 60f, Pumi (sheepdog). 1fo, Retriever with fowl. 1.20fo, Kuvasz (sheepdog). 1.50fo, Komondor (sheepdog) and cottage. 2fo, Komondor (head).

Perf. 11x13 (A254), 12
1956, Mar. 17   Engr. & Litho.
1148	A254	40f yel, blk & red	.20	.20
1149	A255	50f blue, bis & blk	.20	.20
1150	A254	60f yel grn, blk & red	.35	.20
1151	A256	80f bluish grn, ocher & blk	.40	.25
1152	A256	1fo turq, ocher & blk	.45	.30
1153	A254	1.20fo salmon, blk & chnt	.75	.35
1154	A255	1.50fo ultra, blk & buff	1.40	.45
1155	A254	2fo cerise, blk & chnt	2.25	.95
		Nos. 1148-1155 (8)	6.00	2.90

Exist imperf. Value, set $55.

Pioneer Emblem A257

Perf. 12x12½
1956, June 2   Photo.   Wmk. 106
1156	A257	1fo red	.50	.20
1157	A257	1fo gray	.50	.20

Pioneer movement, 10th anniversary.
Exist imperf. Value, set $27.50.

Janos Hunyadi Statue — A258

Miner — A259

1956, Aug. 12   Perf. 12
1158	A258	1fo brown, yelsh	1.00	.35

500th anniv. of the defeat of the Turks at the battle of Pecs under Janos Hunyadi.
Printed in sheets of 50 with alternate vertical rows inverted and center row of perforation omitted, providing 25 tête bêche pairs, of which 5 are imperf. between. Values for tete-beche pairs: unused $1.25; used $.70. Values for tete-beche pairs, imperf between: unused $2; used $11.50.
Exists imperf. Value $40. Tête bêche pair also exists imperf. Value, $110.

1956, Sept. 2
1159	A259	1fo dark blue	.50	.20

Issued in honor of Miners' Day 1956.
Exists imperf. Value $30.

Kayak Racer A260

Sports: 30f, Horse jumping hurdle. 40f, Fencing. 60f, Women hurdlers. 1fo, Soccer. 1.50fo, Weight lifting. 2fo, Gymnastics. 3fo, Basketball.

1956, Sept. 25   Wmk. 106   Perf. 11
Figures in Brown Olive
1160	A260	20f lt blue	.20	.20
1161	A260	30f lt olive grn	.20	.20
1162	A260	40f deep orange	.20	.20
1163	A260	60f bluish grn	.20	.20
1164	A260	1fo vermilion	.35	.20
1165	A260	1.50fo blue violet	.65	.25
1166	A260	2fo emerald	.80	.30
1167	A260	3fo rose lilac	1.40	.40
		Nos. 1160-1167 (8)	4.00	1.95

16th Olympic Games at Melbourne, Nov. 22-Dec. 8, 1956.
Exist imperf. Value, set $100.

Franz Liszt A261

Portrait: 1fo, Frederic Chopin facing left.

1956, Oct. 7   Photo.   Perf. 12x12½
1168	A261	1fo violet blue	2.00	2.00
1169	A261	1fo magenta	2.00	2.00
a.		Pair, #1168-1169	6.00	6.00

29th Day of the Stamp. Sold only at the Philatelic Exhibition together with entrance ticket for 4fo.
Exist imperf. Value, pair $30.

Janos Arany — A262

1957, Sept. 15   Wmk. 106   Perf. 12
1170	A262	2fo bright blue	.60	.20

75th anniv. of the death of Janos Arany, poet.
Exists imperf. Value $15.

Arms of Hungary A263

1957, Oct. 1
1171	A263	60f brt red	.75	.20
1172	A263	1fo dp yellow grn	.75	.20

Exists imperf. Value, set $27.50.

Trade Union Congress Emblem A264

1957, Oct. 4
1173	A264	1fo dk carmine	.50	.20

4th Intl. Trade Union Cong., Leipzig, 10/4-15.
Exists imperf. Value $20.

Dove and Colors of Communist Countries — A265

Design: 1fo, Lenin.

1957, Nov. 7   Litho.   Perf. 12
1174	A265	60f gray, blk & multi	.50	.20
1175	A265	1fo ol bis & indigo	.50	.20

Russian Revolution, 40th anniversary.
Exist imperf. Value, set $35.

Komarom Tumbler Pigeons A266

Pigeons: 40f, Two short-beaked Budapest pigeons. 60f, Giant domestic pigeon. 1fo, Three Szeged pigeons. 2fo, Two Hungarian fantails.

Perf. 12x12½
1957-58   Photo.   Wmk. 106
1176	A266	30f yel grn, cl & ocher	.25	.20
1177	A266	40f ocher & blk	.25	.20
1178	A266	60f blue & gray	.25	.20
1179	A266	1fo gray & red brn	.25	.20
1180	A266	2fo brt pink & gray	.60	.40
		Nos. 1176-1180,C175 (6)	2.50	1.70

Intl. Pigeon Exhibition, Budapest, 12/14-16.
Exist imperf. Value, set (6) $40.
Issued: 30f, 1/12/58; others, 12/14/57.

Television
Station — A267

1958, Feb. 22   Engr.   Perf. 11
1181 A267 2fo rose violet   1.25   .65
  a.   Perf. 12   7.50   7.50

Souvenir Sheet
1182 A267 2fo green   42.50 42.50
Issued to publicize the television industry. No. 1182 sold for 25fo.
Exist imperf. Values: single $25; souvenir sheet $175.

Mother
and Child
A268

Designs: 30f, Old man feeding pigeons. 40f, School boys. 60f, "Working ants and fiddling grasshopper." 1fo, Honeycomb and bee. 2fo, Handing over money.

1958, Mar. 9   Photo.   Perf. 12
1183 A268 20f yel grn & ol gray   .20   .20
1184 A268 30f lt olive & mar   .20   .20
1185 A268 40f yel bis & brn   .20   .20
1186 A268 60f rose car & grnsh
                blk   .30   .20
1187 A268 1fo ol gray & dk brn   .60   .35
1188 A268 2fo org & ol gray   1.50   .50
     Nos. 1183-1188 (6)   3.00   1.65
Issued to publicize the value of savings and insurance.
Exist imperf. Value, set $45.

**Kazar Costume Type of 1953
Souvenir Sheet**
1958, Apr. 17   Engr.   Perf. 12
1189 A233 10fo magenta   27.50 27.50
Issued for the Universal and International Exposition at Brussels.
Exists imperf. Value $80.

Arms of
Hungary
A269

1958, May 23   Litho.   Wmk. 106
Arms in Original Colors
1190 A269 60f lt red brn & red   .20   .20
1191 A269 1fo gray grn & grn   .50   .20
1192 A269 2fo gray & dk brn   .80   .20
     Nos. 1190-1192 (3)   1.50   .60
1st anniv. of the law amending the constitution.
Exist imperf. Value, set $22.

Youth Holding Book — A270

1958, June 14   Photo.   Perf. 12½x12
1193 A270 1fo brown carmine   .45   .20
5th Hungarian Youth Festival at Keszthely.

Printed with alternating label, inscribed: V. IFJUSAGI TALALKOZO KESZTHELY 1958. Exists imperf. Value, with label $20.

Post Horn and Town
Hall,
Prague — A271

1958, June 30
1194 A271 60f green   .20   .20
  a.   Pair, #1194, C184   .80   .80
Conference of Postal Ministers of Communist Countries at Prague, June 30-July 8.
Exists imperf. Value, $9. In pair with #C184 imperf, value $20.

Dolomite Flax — A272

Hungarian
Thistles — A273

30f, Kitaibelia vitifolia. 60f, Crocuses. 1fo, Hellebore. 2fo, Lilies. 2.50fo, Pinks. 3fo, Dog roses.

Perf. 11x13, 12½x12 (A273)
1958, Aug. 12   Photo.   Wmk. 106
1195 A272 20f red vio & yel   1.00   .20
1196 A272 30f blue, yel &
                grn   .20   .20
1197 A273 40f brown & bis   .25   .20
1198 A273 60f bl grn & pink   .30   .20
1199 A273 1fo rose car &
                yel grn   .55   .25
1200 A273 2fo grn & yel   .95   .20
1201 A272 2.50fo vio bl & pink   1.10   .45
1202 A272 3fo green & pink   1.90   .70
  a.   Souv. sheet of 4, perf. 12 35.00 35.00
     Nos. 1195-1202 (8)   6.25   2.40

No. 1202a and a similar imperf. sheet were issued for the International Philatelic Congress at Brussels, Sept. 15-17, 1958. They contain the triangular 20f, 30f, 2.50fo and 3fo stamps printed in different colors. Sheets measure 111x111mm. and are printed on unwatermarked, linen-finish paper. Background of stamps, marginal inscriptions and ornaments in green. No. 1202a also exists perf. 11. Value, $47.50.
Exist imperf. Value, set $40. Value of 1202a imperf, $100.

Paddle,
Ball and
Olive
Branch
A274

Designs: 30f, Table tennis player, vert. 40f, Wrestlers, vert. 60f, Wrestlers, horiz. 1fo, Water polo player, vert. 2.50fo, High dive, vert. 3fo, Swimmer.

1958, Aug. 30   Wmk. 106   Perf. 12
1203 A274 20f rose red,
                pnksh   .20   .20
1204 A274 30f olive, grnsh   .20   .20
1205 A274 40f mag, yel   .25   .20
1206 A274 60f brown, bluish   .40   .20
1207 A274 1fo ultra, bluish   .45   .20

1208 A274 2.50fo dk red, yel   1.10   .30
1209 A274 3fo grnsh bl, grnsh   1.40   .50
     Nos. 1203-1209 (7)   4.00   1.80
Intl. Wrestling and European Swimming and Table Tennis Championships, held at Budapest.
Exist imperf. Value, set $32.50.

Red Flag — A275

Design: 2fo, Hand holding newspaper.

1958, Nov. 21   Perf. 12½x12
1210 A275 1fo brown & red   .20   .20
1211 A275 2fo dk gray bl & red   .55   .20
40th anniversary of the founding of the Hungarian Communist Party and newspaper.
Exist imperf. Value, set $17.

Satellite,
Sputnik
and
American
Rocket
A276

Designs: 10f, Eötvös Torsion Balance and Globe. 20f, Deep sea exploration. 30f, Icebergs, penguins and polar light. 40f, Soviet Antarctic camp and map of Pole. 60f, "Rocket" approaching moon. 1fo, Sun and observatory.

1959, Mar. 14   Perf. 12x12½
Size: 32x21mm
1212 A276 10f car rose & sepia   .35   .20
1213 A276 20f brt blue & gray   .25   .20
1214 A276 30f dk slate grn & bis .40   .20
Perf. 12
Size: 35x26mm
1215 A276 40f slate bl & lt bl   .25   .20
Perf. 15
Size: 58x21mm
1216 A276 60f Prus bl & lemon   .45   .20
Perf. 12
Size: 35x26mm
1217 A276 1fo scarlet & yel   .70   .30
1218 A276 5fo brn & red brn   1.60   .80
     Nos. 1212-1218 (7)   4.00   2.10
Intl. Geophysical Year. See No. 1262.
Exist imperf. Value, set $30.

"Revolution" — A277

1959, Mar. 21   Perf. 12½x12
1219 A277 20f vio brn & red   .20   .20
1220 A277 60f blue & red   .20   .20
1221 A277 1fo brown & red   .45   .20
     Nos. 1219-1221 (3)   .85   .60
40th anniv. of the proclamation of the Hungarian Soviet Republic.
Exist imperf. Value, set $17.

Rose — A278

1959, May 1   Photo.   Perf. 11
1222 A278 60f lilac, dp car & grn .40   .20
1223 A278 1fo lt brn, dl red &
                grn   .60   .20
Issued for Labor Day, May 1, 1959.
Exist imperf. Value, set $20.

Early Locomotive — A279

Designs: 30f, Diesel coach. 40f, Early semaphore, vert. 60f, Csonka automobile. 1fo, Icarus bus. 2fo, First Lake Balaton steamboat. 2.50fo, Stagecoach.

1959, May 26   Litho.   Perf. 14½x15
1224 A279 20f multi   .20   .20
1225 A279 30f multi   .20   .20
1226 A279 40f multi   .25   .20
1227 A279 60f multi   .30   .20
1228 A279 1fo multi   .45   .20
1229 A279 2fo multi   .80   .20
1230 A279 2.50fo multi   .95   .30
     Nos. 1224-1230,C201 (8)   5.15   2.75
Transport Museum, Budapest.
Exist imperf. Value, set (8) $30.

Perf. 10½x11½
1959, May 29   Wmk. 106
1231 A279 2.50fo multi   2.00   2.00
Designer's name on No. 1231. Printed in sheets of four with four labels to commemorate the congress of the International Federation for Philately in Hamburg. Value $16.
Exist imperf. Values: paid with label $20; sheetlet $120.

Post Horn and World Map — A280

1959, June 1   Photo.   Perf. 12
1232 A280 1fo cerise   .75   .30
Postal Ministers Conference, Berlin.
Printed in sheets of 25 stamps with 25 alternating gray labels showing East Berlin Opera House.
Exists imperf. Value: in pair with label, $15.

Great
Cormorant
A281

Warrior, 10th Century — A282

Birds: 20f, Little egret and nest. 30f, Purple heron and nest. 40f, Great egret. 60f, White spoonbill. 1fo, Gray heron. 2fo, Squacco heron and nest. 3fo, Glossy ibis.

1959, June 14
1233	A281	10f green & indigo	.20	.20
1234	A281	20f gray bl & ol grn	.20	.20
1235	A281	30f org, grnsh blk & vio	.20	.20
1236	A281	40f dark grn & gray	.20	.20
1237	A281	60f dp cl & pale rose	.35	.20
1238	A281	1fo dp bl grn & blk	.50	.20
1239	A281	2fo dp orange & gray	.85	.30
1240	A281	3fo bister & brn lake	1.50	.70
		Nos. 1233-1240 (8)	4.00	2.20

Exist imperf. Value, set $40.

1959, July 11

Designs: 20f, Warrior, 15th century. 30f, Soldier, 18th century. 40f, Soldier, 19th century. 60f, Cavalry man, 19th century. 1fo, Fencer, assault. 1.40fo, Fencer on guard. 3fo, Swordsman saluting.

1241	A282	10f gray & blue	.20	.20
1242	A282	20f gray & dull yel	.20	.20
1243	A282	30f gray & gray vio	.20	.20
1244	A282	40f gray & ver	.20	.20
1245	A282	60f gray & rose lil	.20	.20
1246	A282	1fo ind & lt bl grn	.30	.20
1247	A282	1.40fo orange & blk	.60	.25
1248	A282	3fo blk & ol grn	.90	.70
		Nos. 1241-1248 (8)	2.80	2.15

24th World Fencing Championships, Budapest.
Exist imperf. Value, set $35.

Sailboat, Lake Balaton — A283

40f, Vintager & lake, horiz. 60f, Bathers. 1.20fo, Fishermen. 2fo, Summer guests & ship.

1959, July 11   Photo.   Wmk. 106
1249	A283	30f blue, *yel*	.20	.20
1250	A283	40f carmine rose	.20	.20
1251	A283	60f dp red brown	.20	.20
1252	A283	1.20fo violet	.30	.20
1253	A283	2fo red org, *yel*	.60	.50
		Nos. 1249-1253,C202-C205 (9)	2.60	2.20

Issued to publicize Lake Balaton and the opening of the Summer University.
Exist imperf. Value, set (9) $35.

Haydn's Monogram A284

Esterhazy Palace A285

Haydn and Schiller Monograms — A286

Design: 1fo, Joseph Haydn and score.

1959, Sept. 20   Wmk. 106   Perf. 12
1254	A284	40f dp claret & yel	.20	.20
1255	A285	60f Prus bl, gray & yel	.75	.75
1256	A284	1fo dk vio, lt brn & org	.65	.20

Designs: 40f, Schiller's monogram. 60f, Pegasus rearing from flames. 1fo, Friedrich von Schiller.

1257	A284	40f olive grn & org	.20	.20
1258	A285	60f violet bl & lil	.40	.20
1259	A284	1fo dp cl & org brn	.80	.20
		Nos. 1254-1259 (6)	3.00	1.75

Souvenir Sheet

Imperf
1260	A286	Sheet of 2	17.50	17.50
a.		3fo magenta	3.50	3.50
b.		3fo green	3.50	3.50

150th anniv. of the death of Joseph Haydn, Austrian composer, Nos. 1254-1256; 200th anniv. of the birth of Friedrich von Schiller, German poet and dramatist, Nos. 1257-1259; No. 1260 honors both Haydn and Schiller.
Nos. 1254-1260 exist imperf. Value, set $25.
No. 1260 exists imperf. Value $22.

Shepherd — A287

1959, Sept. 25   Engr.   Perf. 12
1261	A287	2fo deep claret	1.50	1.50
a.		With ticket	2.25	2.25

Day of the Stamp and Natl. Stamp Exhib. Issued in sheets of 8 with alternating ticket. The 4fo sale price marked on the ticket was the admission fee to the Natl. Stamp Exhib.
Exist imperf. Values: single $8; single with ticket $20.

Type of 1959 Overprinted in Red

1959, Sept. 24   Photo.   Perf. 15
1262	A276	60f dull bl & lemon	.50	.25
a.		Overprint omitted	3,000.	

Landing of Lunik 2 on moon, Sept. 14.
Exists imperf. Value $12.

Handing over Letter A288

1959, Oct. 4   Litho.   Perf. 12
1263	A288	60f multicolored	.50	.20

Intl. Letter Writing Week, Oct. 4-10.
Exists imperf. Value $15.

Szamuely and Lenin — A289

Designs: 40f, Aleksander Pushkin. 60pf, Vladimir V. Mayakovsky. 1fo, Hands holding peace flag.

1959, Nov. 14   Photo.   Wmk. 106
1264	A289	20f dk red & bister	.20	.20
1265	A289	40f brn & rose lil, *bluish*	.20	.20
1266	A289	60f dk blue & bis	.20	.20
1267	A289	1fo bl, car, buff, red & grn	.40	.30
		Nos. 1264-1267 (4)	1.00	.90

Soviet Stamp Exhibition, Budapest.
Exists imperf. Value $25.

European Swallowtail A290

Butterflies: 30f, Arctia hebe, horiz. 40f, Lysandra hylas, horiz. 60f, Apatura ilia.

Perf. 11½x12, 12x11½

1959, Nov. 20

Butterflies in Natural Colors
1268	A290	20f blk & yel grn	.20	.20
1269	A290	30f lt blue & blk	.35	.20
1270	A290	40f dk gray & org brn	.35	.20
1271	A290	60f dk gray & dl yel	.45	.20
		Nos. 1268-1271,C206-C208 (7)	6.00	2.10

Exist imperf. Value, set (7) $40.

Worker with Banner — A291

Design: 1fo, Congress flag.

1959, Nov. 30   Perf. 14½
1272	A291	60f brown, grn & red	.25	.20
1273	A291	1fo brn, red, red & grn	.25	.20

Issued to commemorate the 7th Congress of the Hungarian Socialist Workers' Party.
Exist imperf. Value, set $17.

Teacher Reading Fairy Tales — A292

Fairy Tales: 30f, Sleeping Beauty. 40f, Matt, the Goose Boy. 60f, The Cricket and the Ant. 1fo, Mashenka and the Three Bears. 2fo, Hansel and Gretel. 2.50fo, Pied Piper. 3fo, Little Red Riding Hood.

1959, Dec. 15   Litho.   Perf. 11½

Designs in Black
1274	A292	20f gray & multi	.20	.20
1275	A292	30f brt pink	.20	.20
1276	A292	40f lt blue grn	.20	.20
1277	A292	60f lt blue	.20	.20
1278	A292	1fo yellow	.35	.25
1279	A292	2fo brt yellow grn	.55	.25
1280	A292	2.50fo orange	.70	.40
1281	A292	3fo crimson	1.10	.60
		Nos. 1274-1281 (8)	3.50	2.30

Exist imperf. Value, set $30.

Sumeg Castle — A293

Castles: 20fr, Tata. 30f, Diosgyor. 60f, Saros-Patak. 70f, Nagyvazsony. 1.40fo, Siklos. 1.70fo, Somlo. 3fo, Csesznek, vert. 5fo, Koszeg, vert. 10fo, Sarvar, vert.

Wmk. 106

1960, Feb. 1   Photo.   Perf. 14½

Size: 21x17½mm
1282	A293	8f purple	.20	.20
1283	A293	20f dk yel grn	.20	.20
1284	A293	30f orange brn	.20	.20
1285	A293	60f rose red	.25	.20
1286	A293	70f emerald	.25	.20

Perf. 12x11½, 11½x12

Size: 28x21mm, 21x28mm
1287	A293	1.40fo ultra	.35	.20
1288	A293	1.70fo dl vio, "Somlo"	.45	.20
b.		"Somlyo"	1.25	.20
1289	A293	3fo red brown	.80	.30
1290	A293	5fo yellow green	1.50	.40
1291	A293	10fo carmine rose	3.00	1.00
		Nos. 1282-1291 (10)	7.20	3.10

Exist imperf. Value, set $100.

Tinted Paper

Perf. 14½

Size: 21x17½mm
1282a	A293	8f pur, *bluish*	.20	.20
1283a	A293	20f dk yel grn, *grnsh*	.20	.20
1284a	A293	30f org brn, *yel*	.35	.20
1285a	A293	60f rose red, *pnksh*	.25	.20
1286a	A293	70f emer, *bluish*	.65	.20

Perf. 12x11½

Size: 28x21mm
1287a	A293	1.40fo ultra, *bluish*	.70	.25
1288a	A293	1.70fo dull vio, *bluish*	.90	.25
		Nos. 1282a-1288a (7)	3.25	1.50

Exist imperf. Value, set $35.
See Nos. 1356-1365, 1644-1646.

Halas Lace — A294

Cross-country Skier — A295

Designs: Various Halas lace patterns.

Wmk. 106

1960, Feb. 15   Litho.   Perf. 11½
Sizes: 20f, 60f, 1fo, 3fo: 27x37mm
30f, 40f, 1.50fo, 2fo: 37½x43½mm

Inscriptions in Orange
1292	A294	20f brown black	.20	.20
1293	A294	30f violet	.25	.20
1294	A294	40f Prus blue	.40	.20
1295	A294	60f dark brown	.50	.25
1296	A294	1fo dark green	.80	.30
1297	A294	1.50fo green	1.00	.40
1298	A294	2fo dark green	1.75	.60
1299	A294	3fo dk carmine	3.00	.80
		Nos. 1292-1299 (8)	7.90	2.95

Exist imperf. Value, set $30.
See Nos. 1570-1577.

Souvenir Sheet

Design as on No. 1299.

1960, Sept. 3
Inscriptions in Orange

1300	Sheet of 4 + 4 labels	16.00	16.00
a.	3fo brown olive	3.25	3.25
b.	3fo bright violet	3.25	3.25
c.	3fo emerald	3.25	3.25
d.	3fo bright blue	3.25	3.25

Fédération Internationale de Philatélie Congress, Warsaw, Sept. 3-11. No. 1300 contains 4 stamps and 4 alternating labels, printed in colors of adjoining stamps.
Exists imperf. Value $120.

1960, Feb. 29 **Photo.** **Perf. 11½x12**

Sports: 40f, Ice hockey player. 60f, Ski jumper. 80f, Woman speed skater. 1fo, Downhill skier. 1.20fo, Woman figure skater.

Inscriptions and Figures in Bister

1301	A295	30f deep blue	.20	.20
1302	A295	40f brt green	.20	.20
1303	A295	60f scarlet	.20	.20
1304	A295	80f purple	.20	.20
1305	A295	1fo brt grnsh blue	.60	.60
1306	A295	1.20fo brown red	.70	.45
	Nos. 1301-1306,B217 (7)		3.00	1.80

8th Olympic Winter Games, Squaw Valley, Calif., Feb. 18-29, 1960.
Exists imperf. Value $25.

Clara Zetkin — A296

Portraits: No. 1308, Kato Haman. No. 1309, Lajos Tüköry. No. 1310, Giuseppe Garibaldi. No. 1311, István Türr. No. 1312, Ottó Herman. No. 1313, Ludwig van Beethoven. No. 1314, Ferenc Mora. No. 1315, Istvan Toth Bucsoki. No. 1316, Donat Banki. No. 1317, Abraham G. Pattantyus. No. 1318, Ignaz Semmelweis. No. 1319, Frédéric Joliot-Curie. No. 1320, Ferenc Erkel. No. 1321, Janos Bolyai. No. 1322, Lenin.

1960 **Photo.** **Perf. 10½**

1307	A296	60f lt red brn	.25	.20

Engr.

1308	A296	60f pale purple	.25	.20
1309	A296	60f rose red	.25	.20
1310	A296	60f violet	.25	.20
1311	A296	60f blue green	.25	.20
1312	A296	60f blue	.25	.20
1313	A296	60f gray brown	.25	.20
1314	A296	60f salmon pink	.25	.20
1315	A296	60f gray	.25	.20
1316	A296	60f rose lilac	.25	.20
1317	A296	60f green	.25	.20
1318	A296	60f violet blue	.25	.20
1319	A296	60f brown	.25	.20
1320	A296	60f rose brown	.25	.20
1321	A296	60f grnsh blue	.25	.20
1322	A296	60f dull red	.25	.20
	Nos. 1307-1322 (16)		4.00	3.20

Nos. 1307-1308 commemorate International Women's Day, Mar. 8.
Exists imperf. Value $65.

Flower and Quill — A297

Wmk. 106

1960, Apr. 2 **Photo.** **Perf. 12**

1323	2fo brn, yel & grn	1.25	1.25
a.	A297 With ticket	1.50	1.50

Issued for the stamp show of the National Federation of Hungarian Philatelists. The olive green 4fo ticket pictures the Federation's headquarters and served as entrance ticket to

the show. Printed in sheets of 35 stamps and 35 tickets.
Exists imperf. Value, stamp + ticket, $20.

Soviet Capt. Ostapenko Statue — A298

Perf. 12½x11½, 11½x12½

1960, Apr. 4

Designs: 60f, Youth holding flag, horiz.

1324	A298 40f dp carmine & brn	.20	.20
1325	A298 60f red brn, red & grn	.20	.20

Hungary's liberation from the Nazis, 15th anniv.
Exist imperf. Value, set $15.

Boxers — A299

Sports: 10f, Rowers. 30f, Archer. 40f, Discus thrower. 50f, Girls playing ball. 60f, Javelin thrower. 1fo, Rider. 1.40fo, Wrestlers. 1.70fo, Swordsmen. 3fo, Hungarian Olympic emblem.

1960, Aug. 21 **Perf. 11½x12**
Designs in Ocher and Black

1326	A299	10f blue	.20	.20
1327	A299	20f salmon	.20	.20
1328	A299	30f lt violet	.20	.20
1329	A299	40f yellow	.20	.20
1330	A299	50f deep pink	.20	.20
1331	A299	60f gray	.20	.20
1332	A299	1fo pale brn vio	.25	.20
1333	A299	1.40fo lt violet bl	.25	.20
1334	A299	1.70fo ocher	.45	.20
1335	A299	3fo multi	1.00	.50
	Nos. 1326-1335,B218 (11)		3.90	2.60

17th Olympic Games, Rome, 8/25-9/11.
Exist imperf. Value, set $30.

Souvenir Sheet

Romulus and Remus Statue and Olympic Flame — A300

1960, Aug. 21

1336	A300 10fo multicolored	17.50	16.00

Winter and Summer Olympic Games, 1960.
Exists imperf. Value $55.

Woman of Mezokovesd Writing Letter — A301

1960, Oct. 15 **Photo.** **Wmk. 106**

1337	A301 2fo multicolored	1.40	1.40
a.	With ticket	1.75	1.75

Day of the Stamp and Natl. Stamp Exhib. Issued in sheets of 8 with alternating ticket. The 4fo sale price marked on the ticket was the admission fee to the Natl. Stamp Exhib.
Exists imperf. Value, stamp + ticket, $15.

The Turnip, Russian Fairy Tale — A302

Brown Bear — A303

Fairy Tales: 30f, Snow White and the Seven Dwarfs. 40f, The Miller, His Son and the Donkey. 60f, Puss in Boots. 80f, The Fox and the Raven. 1fo, The Maple-Wood Pipe. 1.70fo, The Fox and the Stork. 2fo, Momotaro (Japanese).

1960, Dec. 1 **Perf. 11½x12**

1338	A302	20f multi	.20	.20
1339	A302	30f multi	.20	.20
1340	A302	40f multi	.20	.20
1341	A302	60f multi	.20	.20
1342	A302	80f multi	.20	.20
1343	A302	1fo multi	.35	.20
1344	A302	1.70fo multi	.65	.35
1345	A302	2fo multi	1.00	.50
	Nos. 1338-1345 (8)		3.00	2.05

Exist imperf. Value, set $25.

1961, Feb. 24 **Perf. 11½x12**

Animals: 20f, Kangaroo. 30f, Bison. 60f, Elephants. 80fr, Tiger with cubs. 1fo, Ibex. 1.40fo, Polar bear. 2fo, Zebra and young. 2.60fo, Bison cow with calf. 3fo, Main entrance to Budapest Zoological Gardens. 30f, 60f, 80f, 1.40fo, 2fo, 2.60fo are horizontal.

1346	A303	20f orange & blk	.20	.20
1347	A303	30f yel grn & blk brn	.20	.20
1348	A303	40f org brn & brn	.20	.20
1349	A303	60f lil rose & gray	.20	.20
1350	A303	80f gray & yel	.20	.20
1351	A303	1fo blue grn & brn	.20	.20
1352	A303	1.40fo grnsh bl, gray & blk	.35	.20
1353	A303	2fo pink & black	.50	.25
1354	A303	2.60fo brt vio & brn	.70	.40
1355	A303	3fo multicolored	1.25	.75
	Nos. 1346-1355 (10)		4.00	2.80

Issued for the Budapest Zoo.
Exist imperf. Value, set $30.

Castle Type of 1960

10f, Kisvárda. 12f, Szigliget. 40f, Simon Tornya. 50f, Füzér. 80f, Egervár. 1fo, Vitány. 1.20fo, Sirok. 2fo, Boldogkö. 2.60fo, Hollókö. 4fo, Eger.

1961, Mar. 3 **Photo.** **Perf. 14½**
Size: 21x17½mm

1356	A293	10f orange brn	.20	.20
1357	A293	12f violet blue	.20	.20
1358	A293	40f brt green	.20	.20

1359	A293	50f brown	.20	.20
1360	A293	80f dull claret	.20	.20

Perf. 12x11½
Size: 28x21mm

1361	A293	1fo brt blue	.20	.20
1362	A293	1.20fo rose violet	.25	.20
1363	A293	2fo olive bister	.40	.20
1364	A293	2.60fo dull blue	.60	.20
1365	A293	4fo brt violet	.75	.20
	Nos. 1356-1365 (10)		3.20	2.00

Exist imperf. Value, set $75.

Child Chasing Butterfly A304

Ferenc Rozsa, Journalist A305

40f, Man on operating table. 60f, Ambulance & stretcher. 1fo, Traffic light & scooter. 1.70fo, Syringe. 4fo, Emblem of Health Information Service (torch & serpent).

1961, Mar. 17 **Litho.** **Perf. 10½**
Cross in Red
Size: 18x18mm

1366	A304	30f org brn & blk	.20	.20
1367	A304	40f bl grn, bl & sepia	.20	.20

Size: 25x30mm

1368	A304	60f multi	.20	.20
1369	A304	1fo multi	.20	.20
1370	A304	1.70fo multi	.45	.20
1371	A304	4fo gray & yel grn	1.25	.50
	Nos. 1366-1371 (6)		2.50	1.50

Health Information Service.
Exist imperf. Value, set $30.

Wmk. 106, Unwmk.
1961 **Photo.** **Perf. 12**

Portraits: No. 1373, Gyorgy Kilian. No. 1374, Jozsef Rippl-Ronai. No. 1375, Sandor Latinka. No. 1376, Maté Zalka. No. 1377, Jozsef Katona.

1372	A305	1fo red brown	.25	.20
1373	A305	1fo greenish blue	.25	.20
1374	A305	1fo rose brown	.25	.20
1375	A305	1fo olive bister	.25	.20
1376	A305	1fo olive green	.25	.20
1377	A305	1fo maroon	.25	.20
	Nos. 1372-1377 (6)		1.50	1.20

Press Day (#1372); the inauguration of the Gyorgy Kilian Sports Movement (#1373); birth cent. of Jozsef Rippl-Ronai, painter (#1374); Sandor Latinka, revolutionary leader, 75th death anniv. (#1375); Mate Zalka, author and revolutionist (#1376); Jozsef Katona, dramatist (#1377).
Nos. 1374, 1375, 1377 are unwmkd. Others in this set have wmk. 106.
Exist imperf. Value, set $40.

Yuri A. Gagarin and Vostok 1 A306

Roses — A307

Design: 1fo, Launching Vostok 1.

Perf. 11½x12

1961, Apr. 25   **Wmk. 106**
1381	A306	1fo dk bl & bis brn	.55	.25
1382	A306	2fo dp ultra & bis brn	2.50	2.00

1st man in space, Yuri A. Gagarin, 4/12/61.
Exist imperf. Value, set $80.

1961, Apr. 29   *Perf. 12½x11½*

Design: 2fo, as 1fo, design reversed.
1383	A307	1fo grn & dp car	.20	.20
1384	A307	2fo grn & dp car	.80	.20
a.		Pair, #1383-1384	1.50	.30

Issued for May Day, 1961.
Exist imperf. Value, No. 1384a $25.

"Venus" and Moon A308

Designs: Various Stages of Rocket.

1961, May 24   **Wmk. 106**   *Perf. 14½*
1385	A308	40f grnsh bl, bis & blk	.30	.20
1386	A308	60f brt bl, bis & blk	.40	.20
1387	A308	80f ultra & blk	.50	.50
1388	A308	2fo violet & yel	1.25	1.25
		Nos. 1385-1388 (4)	2.45	2.15

Soviet launching of the Venus space probe, Feb. 12, 1961. Exist imperf. Value, set $35. No. 1388 was also printed in sheets of four, perf. and imperf. Size: 130x76mm. Value: perf $10; imperf $275.

Warsaw Mermaid, Letter and Sea, Air and Land Transport — A309

Mermaid and: 60f, Television screen and antenna. 1fo, Radio.

1961, June 19   **Photo.**   *Perf. 13½*
1389	A309	40f red org & blk	.20	.20
1390	A309	60f lilac & blk	.20	.20
1391	A309	1fo brt blue & blk	.60	.20
		Nos. 1389-1391 (3)	1.00	.60

Conference of Postal Ministers of Communist Countries held at Warsaw. Exist imperf. Value, set $20.

Flag and Parliament — A310

Designs: 1.70fo, Orchid. 2.60fo, Small tortoise-shell butterfly. 3fo, Goldfinch.

1961, June 23   *Perf. 11*
Background in Silver
1392	A310	1fo green, red & blk	.40	.35
1393	A310	1.70fo red & multi	.50	.45
1394	A310	2.60fo purple & multi	.75	.75
1395	A310	3fo blue & multi	1.00	1.00

1961, Aug. 19
Background in Gold
1396	A310	1fo green & blk	.35	.30
1397	A310	1.70fo red & multi	.50	.40
1398	A310	2.60fo purple & multi	.75	.75
1399	A310	3fo blue & multi	1.00	1.00
		Nos. 1392-1399 (8)	5.25	5.00

Issued to publicize the International Stamp Exhibition, Budapest, Sept. 23-Oct. 3, 1961. #1392-1399 each printed in sheets of 4. In gold background issue the top left inscription is changed on 1fo and 3fo. Exist imperf. Values: set $50; sheetlet set $270.

George Stephenson A311   Winged Wheel, Steering Wheel and Road A312

Design: 2fo, Jenö Landler.

Perf. 12½x11½

1961, July 4   **Photo.**   **Wmk. 106**
1400	A311	60f yellow olive	.20	.20
1401	A312	1fo blue & bister	.25	.20
1402	A312	2fo yellow brown	.25	.20
		Nos. 1400-1402 (3)	.70	.60

Conference of Transport Ministers of Communist Countries held at Budapest. Exist imperf. Value, set $22.

Soccer A313

1961, July 8   **Unwmk.**   *Perf. 14½*
1403	A313	40f shown	.20	.20
1404	A313	60f Wrestlers	.20	.20
1405	A313	1fo Gymnast	.20	.20
		Nos. 1403-1405 (3)	.60	.60

50th anniv. of the Steel Workers Sport Club (VASAS). See No. B219. Exist imperf. Value, set of 4 (with B219) $22.

Galloping Horses — A314

40f, Hurdle Jump. 60f, Two trotters. 1fo, Three trotters. 1.70fo, Mares & foals. 2fo, Race horse "Baka." 3fo, Race horse "Kincsem."

1961, July 22
1406	A314	30f multi	.20	.20
1407	A314	40f multi	.20	.20
1408	A314	60f multi	.35	.20
1409	A314	1fo multi	.35	.20
1410	A314	1.70fo multi	.50	.20
1411	A314	2fo multi	.90	.30
1412	A314	3fo multi	1.00	.40
		Nos. 1406-1412 (7)	3.50	1.70

Exist imperf. Value, set $35.

Keyboard, Music and Liszt Silhouette A315

Liszt Monument, Budapest A316

Designs: 2fo, Academy of Music, Budapest, and bar of music. 10fo, Franz Liszt.

1961, Oct. 2   **Unwmk.**   *Perf. 12*
1413	A315	60f gold & blk	.20	.20
1414	A315	1fo dark gray	.35	.20
1415	A315	2fo dk bl & gray grn	.50	.40
		Nos. 1413-1415 (3)	1.05	.80

Souvenir Sheet
1416	A316	10fo multi	8.50	7.00

150th anniv. of the birth, and the 75th anniv. of the death of Franz Liszt, composer. Exist imperf. Value: set $25; souvenir sheet $40.

Lenin — A317

Monk's Hood — A318

1961, Oct. 22   *Perf. 11½*
1417	A317	1fo deep brown	.25	.20

22nd Congress of the Communist Party of the USSR, Oct. 17-31. Exist imperf. Value $6.

Wmk. 106

1961, Nov. 4   **Photo.**   *Perf. 12*
1418	A318	20f shown	.20	.20
1419	A318	30f Centaury	.20	.20
1420	A318	40f Blue iris	.20	.20
1421	A318	60f Thorn apple	.20	.20
1422	A318	1fo Purple hollyhock	.30	.20
1423	A318	1.70fo Hop	.40	.20
1424	A318	2fo Poppy	.40	.30
1425	A318	3fo Mullein	.60	.50
		Nos. 1418-1425 (8)	2.50	2.00

Exist imperf. Value, set $30.

Nightingale A319   Mihaly Karolyi A320

Birds: 40f, Great titmouse. 60f, Chaffinch, horiz. 1fo, Eurasian jay. 1.20fo, Golden oriole. 1.20fo, European blackbird, horiz. 2fo, Yellowhammer, 3fo, Lapwing, horiz.

1961, Dec. 18   **Unwmk.**   *Perf. 12*
1426	A319	30f multi	.20	.20
1427	A319	40f multi	.20	.20
1428	A319	60f multi	.20	.20
1429	A319	1fo multi	.20	.20
1430	A319	1.20fo multi	.20	.20
1431	A319	1.50fo multi	.45	.20
1432	A319	2fo multi	.55	.25
1433	A319	3fo multi	.75	.35
		Nos. 1426-1433 (8)	2.75	1.80

Exist imperf. Value, set $30.

1962, Mar. 18
1434	A320	1fo black	.20	.20

Mihaly Karolyi, (1875-1955), Prime Minister of Hungarian Republic (1918-19). Exists imperf. Value $5.

1962, Mar. 29

Portrait: No. 1435, Ferenc Berkes.
1435	A320	1fo red brown	.20	.20

Fifth Congress of the Hungarian Cooperative Movement, and to honor Ferenc Berkes, revolutionary. See Nos. 1457, 1459. Exists imperf. Value $5.

Map of Europe, Train Signals and Emblem — A321

1962, May 2   **Photo.**
1436	A321	1fo blue green	.20	.20

14th Intl. Esperanto Cong. of Railway Men. Exists imperf. Value $5.

Xiphophorus Helleri A322

Tropical Fish: 30f, Macropodus opercularis. 40f, Lebistes reticulatus. 60f, Betta splendens. 80f, Puntius tetrazona. 1fo, Pterophyllum scalare. 1.20fo, Mesogonistius chaetodon. 1.50fo, Aphyosemion australe. 2fo, Hyphessobrycon innesi. 3fo, Symphysodon aequifasciata haraldi.

1962, May 5   *Perf. 11½x12*
Fish in Natural Colors, Black Inscriptions
1437	A322	20f blue	.20	.20
1438	A322	30f citron	.20	.20
1439	A322	40f lt blue	.20	.20
1440	A322	60f lt yellow grn	.20	.20
1441	A322	80f blue green	.30	.20
1442	A322	1fo brt bl grn	.20	.20
1443	A322	1.20fo blue green	.20	.20
1444	A322	1.50fo grnsh blue	.25	.20
a.		"1962" twice in design	2.00	2.00
1445	A322	2fo green	.50	.25
1446	A322	3fo gray grn & yel	.75	.50
		Nos. 1437-1446 (10)	3.00	2.35

On No. 1444a, the year date appears both to the left and below the value inscription. On No. 14444, it appears only to the left of the value. Exist imperf. Value, set $30.

Globe, Soccer Ball and Flags of Colombia and Uruguay — A323

Goalkeeper — A324

Flags of: 40f, USSR and Yugoslavia. 60f, Switzerland and Chile. 1fo, Germany and Italy. 1.70fo, Argentina and Bulgaria. 3fo, Brazil and Mexico.

Unwmk.
1962, May 21   Photo.   Perf. 11
Flags in National Colors

1447	A323	30f rose & bis	.20	.20
1448	A323	40f pale grn & bis	.20	.20
1449	A323	60f pale lil & bis	.20	.20
1450	A323	1fo blue & bis	.75	.40
1451	A323	1.70fo ocher & bis	.55	.25
1452	A323	3fo pink & blue bis	1.50	.40

Nos. 1447-1452,B224,C209A (8)   7.00   2.05

Souvenir Sheet
Perf. 12

1453	A324	10fo multicolored	6.50	6.50

World Cup Soccer Championship, Chile, May 30-June 17.
Exist imperf. Value: set (8) $30; souvenir sheet $30.

Type of 1961 and

Johann Gutenberg A325

#1456, Miklós Misztófalusi Kis, Hungarian printer (1650-1702). #1457, Jozsef Pach. #1458, András Cházár. #1459, Dr. Ferenc Hutyra. #1460, Gábor Egressy & National Theater.

1962   Unwmk.   Photo.   Perf. 12

1455	A325	1fo blue black	.20	.20
1456	A325	1fo red brown	.20	.20
1457	A320	1fo blue	.20	.20
1458	A325	1fo violet	.20	.20
1459	A320	1fo deep blue	.30	.20
1460	A325	1fo rose red	.40	.20

Nos. 1455-1460 (6)   1.50   1.20

Cent. of Printers' and Papermakers' Union (Nos. 1455-1456). 75th anniv. of founding, by Joszef Pech, of Hungarian Hydroelectric Service (No. 1457). András Cházár, founder of Hungarian deaf-mute education (No. 1458). Dr. Ferenc Hutyra, founder of Hungarian veterinary medicine (No. 1459). 125th anniv. of National Theater (No. 1460).
Exist imperf. Value, set $25.

Malaria Eradication Emblem — A327

1962, June 25   Perf. 15

1461	A327	2.50fo lemon & blk	.50	.40
a.		2.50fo grn & blk, sheet of 4, perf. 11	4.00	3.75

WHO drive to eradicate malaria.
Imperfs exist. Values: single (lemon) $9; single (green) $10; green sheetlet of 4 $50.
Imperf. sheets with control numbers exist.

Sword-into-Plowshare Statue, United Nations, NY — A328

1962, July 7   Perf. 12
1462	A328	1fo brown	.20	.20

World Congress for Peace and Disarmament, Moscow, July 9-14.
Exists imperf. Value $5.

Floribunda Rose — A329   Festival Emblem — A330

1962   Perf. 12½x11½
Various Roses in Natural Colors

1465	A329	20f orange brn	.20	.20
1466	A329	40f slate grn	.20	.20
1467	A329	60f violet	.20	.20
1468	A329	80f rose red	.20	.20
1469	A329	1fo dark green	.25	.20
1470	A329	1.20fo orange	.30	.20
1471	A329	2fo dk blue grn	.50	.45
1472	A330	3fo multi	.75	.35

Nos. 1465-1472 (8)   2.60   2.00

No. 1472 was issued for the 8th World Youth Festival, Helsinki, July 28-Aug. 6.
Exist imperf. Value, set $40.

Weight Lifter — A331

Oil Derrick and Primitive Oil Well — A332

1962, Sept. 16   Perf. 12
1473	A331	1fo copper red	.30	.20

European Weight Lifting Championships.
Exists imperf. Value $7.

Perf. 12x11½
1962, Oct. 8   Photo.   Unwmk.
1474	A332	1fo green	.20	.20

25th anniv. of the Hungarian oil industry.
Exists imperf. Value $7.

Racing Motorcyclist — A333

Designs: 30f, Stunt racing. 40f, Uphill race. 60f, Cyclist in curve. 1fo, Start. 1.20fo, Speed racing. 1.70fo, Motorcyclist with sidecar. 2fo, Motor scooter. 3fo, Racing car.

1962, Dec. 28   Perf. 11

1475	A333	20f multi	.20	.20
1476	A333	30f multi	.20	.20
1477	A333	40f multi	.20	.20
1478	A333	60f multi	.20	.20
1479	A333	1fo multi	.20	.20
1480	A333	1.20fo multi	.20	.20
1481	A333	1.70fo multi	.35	.20
1482	A333	2fo multi	.50	.25
1483	A333	3fo multi	.75	.40

Nos. 1475-1483 (9)   2.80   2.05

Exist imperf. Value, set $24.

Ice Skater — A334

Designs: 20f-3fo, Various figure skating and ice dancing positions. 20f, 3fo horiz. 10fo, Figure skater and flags of participating nations.

Perf. 12x11½, 11½x12
1963, Feb. 5   Photo.   Unwmk.

1484	A334	20f multi	.20	.20
1485	A334	40f multi	.20	.20
1486	A334	60f multi	.20	.20
1487	A334	1fo multi	.45	.20
1488	A334	1.40fo multi	.45	.20
1489	A334	2fo multi	.50	.25
1490	A334	3fo multi	1.00	.50

Nos. 1484-1490 (7)   3.00   1.75

Souvenir Sheet
Perf. 11½x12

1491	A334	10fo multi	5.00	5.00

European Figure Skating and Ice Dancing Championships, Budapest, Feb. 5-10.
Exist imperf. Value: set $24; souvenir sheet $110.

János Batsányi (1763-1845) — A335

#1493, Helicon Monument. #1494, Actors before Szeged Cathedral. #1495, Leo Weiner, composer. #1496, Ferenc Entz,horticulturist. #1497, Ivan Markovits, inventor of Hungarian shorthand,1863. #1498, Dr. Frigyes Koranyi. #1499, Ferenc Erkel (1810-93), composer. #1500, Geza Gardonyi (1863-1922), writer of Hungarian historical novels for youth. #1501, Pierre de Coubertin, Frenchman, reviver of Olympic Games. #1502, Jozsef Eötvös,

author, philosopher, educator. #1503, Budapest Industrial Fair emblem. #1504, Stagecoach and Arc de Triomphe, Paris. #1505, Hungary map and power lines. #1506, Roses.

1963   Unwmk.   Perf. 11

1492	A335	40f dk car rose	.20	.20
1493	A335	40f blue	.20	.20
1494	A335	40f violet blue	.20	.20
1495	A335	40f olive	.20	.20
1496	A335	40f emerald	.20	.20
1497	A335	40f dark blue	.20	.20
1498	A335	60f dull violet	.20	.20
1499	A335	60f bister brn	.20	.20
1500	A335	60f gray green	.20	.20
1501	A335	60f red brown	.40	.20
1502	A335	60f lilac	.20	.20
1503	A335	1fo purple	.20	.20
1504	A335	1fo rose red	.25	.20
1505	A335	1fo gray	.25	.20
1506	A335	2fo multi	.50	.20

Nos. 1492-1506 (15)   3.60   3.00

#1493, 10th Youth Festival, Keszthely. #1494, Outdoor plays, Szeged. #1495, Budapest Music Competition. #1496, Cent. of professional horticultural training. #1498, 50th anniv. of the death of Prof. Koranyi, pioneer in fight against tuberculosis. #1499, Erkel Memorial Festival, Gyula. #1501, 10th anniv. of the People's Stadium, Budapest. #1502, 150th anniv. of birth of Jozsef Eötvös, organizer of modern public education in Hungary. #1504, Paris Postal Conf., 1863. #1505, Rural electrification. #1506, 5th Natl. Rose Show.
Exist imperf. Value, set $80.

Ship and Chain Bridge, Budapest — A336

Bus and Parliament A337

20f, Trolley. 30f, Sightseeing bus & Natl. Museum. 40f, Bus & trailer. 50f, Railroad tank car. 60f, Trolley bus. 70f, Railroad mail car. 80f, Motorcycle messenger. #1516, Mail plane, vert. #1517, Television transmitter, Miskolc, vert. 1.40fo, Mobile post office. 1.70fo, Diesel locomotive. 2fo, Mobile radio transmitter & stadium. 2.50fo, Tourist bus. 2.60fo, Passenger train. 3fo, P.O. parcel conveyor. 4fo, Television transmitters, Pecs, vert. 5fo, Hydraulic lift truck & mail car. 6fo, Woman teletypist. 8fo, Map of Budapest & automatic dial phone. 10fo, Girl pioneer &woman letter carrier.

1963-64   Photo.   Perf. 11

1507	A336	10f brt blue	.20	.20
1508	A336	20f dp yellow grn	.20	.20
1509	A336	30f violet	.20	.20
1510	A336	40f orange	.20	.20
1511	A336	50f brown	.20	.20
1512	A336	60f crimson	.20	.20
1513	A336	70f olive gray	.20	.20
1514	A336	80f red brn ('64)	.25	.20

Perf. 12x11½, 11½x12

1515	A337	1fo rose claret	.20	.20
1516	A337	1.20fo orange brn	.80	.60
1517	A337	1.20fo dp vio ('64)	.20	.20
1518	A337	1.40fo dp yel grn	.20	.20
1519	A337	1.70fo maroon	.25	.20
1520	A337	2fo grnsh blue	.30	.20
1521	A337	2.50fo lilac	.35	.20
1522	A337	2.60fo olive	.35	.20
1523	A337	3fo dk blue ('64)	.25	.20
1524	A337	4fo blue ('64)	.35	.20
1525	A337	5fo ol brn ('64)	.45	.20
1526	A337	6fo dk ol bis ('64)	.55	.20
1527	A337	8fo red lilac ('64)	.80	.20
1528	A337	10fo emerald ('64)	.80	.40

Nos. 1507-1528 (22)   7.50   5.00

Size of 20f, 60f: 20½-21x16¾-17mm.
Minute inscription in lower margin includes year date, number of stamp in set and designer's name (Bokros F. or Legrady S.).
Exist imperf. Value, set $60.
See Nos. 1983-1983B, 2196-2204.

Coil Stamps

1965-67   Perf. 14
Size: 21½x16½mm

1508a	A336	20f deep yellow green	.30	.20
1512a	A336	60f crimson ('67)	.50	.20

Black control number on back of every 3rd stamp.

Motorboat — A338

Girl, Steamer and Castle — A339

Design: 60f, Sailboat.

1963, July 13   *Perf. 11*

1529	A338	20f sl grn, red & blk	.20	.20
1530	A339	40f multicolored	.20	.20
1531	A338	60f bl, blk, brn & org	.60	.25
		Nos. 1529-1531 (3)	1.00	.65

Centenary of the summer resort Siofok.
Exist imperf. Value, set $25.

Child with Towel and Toothbrush — A340

Karancsság Woman — A341

Designs: 40f, Child with medicines. 60f, Girls of 3 races. 1fo, Girl and heart. 1.40fo, Boys of 3 races. 2fo, Medical examination of child. 3fo, Hands shielding plants.

1963, July 27   *Perf. 12x11½*

1532	A340	30f multi	.20	.20
1533	A340	40f multi	.20	.20
1534	A340	60f multi	.20	.20
1535	A340	1fo multi	.20	.20
1536	A340	1.40fo multi	.20	.20
1537	A340	2fo multi	.25	.25
1538	A340	3fo multi	.50	.40
		Nos. 1532-1538 (7)	1.75	1.65

Centenary of the International Red Cross.
Exist imperf. Value, set $20.

1963, Aug. 18   **Engr.**   *Perf. 11½*

Provincial Costumes: 30f, Kapuvár man. 40f, Debrecen woman. 60f, Hortobágy man. 1fo, Csököly woman. 1.70fo, Dunántúl man. 2fo, Buják woman. 2.50fo, Alföld man. 3fo, Mezőkövesd bride.

1539	A341	20f claret	.20	.20
1540	A341	30f green	.20	.20
1541	A341	40f brown	.25	.20
1542	A341	60f brt blue	.25	.20
1543	A341	1fo brown red	.30	.20
1544	A341	1.70fo purple	.40	.20
1545	A341	2fo dk blue grn	.25	.20
1546	A341	2.50fo dk carmine	.55	.25
1547	A341	3fo violet blue	.85	.45
		Nos. 1539-1547 (9)	3.25	2.10

Popular Art Exhibition in Budapest.
Exist imperf. Value, set $50.

Slalom and 1964 Olympic Emblem — A342

Sports: 60f, Downhill skiing. 70f, Ski jump. 80f, Rifle shooting on skis. 1fo, Figure skating pair. 2fo, Ice hockey. 2.60fo, Speed ice skating. 10fo, Skier and mountains, vert.

1963-64   **Photo.**   *Perf. 12*
1964 Olympic Emblem in Black and Red

1548	A342	40f yel grn & bis	.20	.20
1549	A342	60f violet & bis	.20	.20
1550	A342	70f ultra & bis	.20	.20
1551	A342	80f emerald & bis	.20	.20
1552	A342	1fo brn org & bis	.20	.20
1553	A342	2fo brt blue & bis	.40	.20
1554	A342	2.60fo rose lake & bis	.60	.40
		Nos. 1548-1554,B234 (8)	2.70	1.90

Souvenir Sheet
Perf. 11½x12

1555	A342	10fo grnsh bl, red & brn ('64)	4.25	4.00

9th Winter Olympic Games, Innsbruck, Austria, Jan. 29-Feb. 9, 1964.
Exist imperf. Value: set (8) $25; souvenir sheet $30.

Four-Leaf Clover — A343

Good Luck Symbols: 20f, Calendar and mistletoe, horiz. 30f, Chimneysweep and clover. 60f, Top hat, pig and clover. 1fo, Clown with balloon and clover, horiz. 2fo, Lanterns, mask and clover.

Perf. 12x11½, 11½x12
1963, Dec. 12   **Photo.**   **Unwmk.**
Sizes: 28x22mm (20f, 1fo);
22x28mm (40f);
28x39mm (30f, 60f, 2fo)

1556	A343	20f multi	.20	.20
1557	A343	30f multi	.20	.20
1558	A343	40f multi	.20	.20
1559	A343	60f multi	.20	.20
1560	A343	1fo multi	.20	.20
1561	A343	2fo multi	.45	.20
		Nos. 1556-1561,B235-B236 (8)	2.65	1.80

New Year 1964.
Exist imperf. Value, set $20.
The 20f and 40f issued in booklet panes of 10, perf. and imperf.; sold for 2 times and 1½ times face respectively.

Moon Rocket — A344

U.S. & USSR Spacecraft: 40f, Venus space probe. 60f, Vostok I, horiz. 1fo, Friendship 7. 1.70fo, Vostok III & IV. 2fo, Telstar 1 & 2, horiz. 2.60fo, Mars I. 3fo, Radar, rockets and satellites, horiz.

1964, Jan. 8   *Perf. 11½x12, 12x11½*

1562	A344	30f grn, yel & brnz	.20	.20
1563	A344	40f pur, bl & sil	.20	.20
1564	A344	60f bl, blk, yel, sil & red	.20	.20
1565	A344	1fo dk brn, red & sil	.20	.20
1566	A344	1.70fo vio bl, blk, tan & red	.30	.20
1567	A344	2fo sl grn, yel & sil	.40	.20
1568	A344	2.60fo dp bl, yel & brnz	.60	.30
1569	A344	3fo dp vio, lt bl & brnz	.75	.50
		Nos. 1562-1569 (8)	2.85	2.00

Achievements in space research.
Exist imperf. Value, set $20.

Lace Type of 1960

Various Halas Lace Designs.
Sizes: 20f, 2.60fo: 38x28mm. 30f, 40f, 60f, 1fo, 1.40fo: 38x45mm.

Engr. & Litho.
1964, Feb. 28   *Perf. 11½*

1570	A294	20f emerald & blk	.20	.20
1571	A294	30f dull yel & blk	.20	.20
1572	A294	40f deep rose & blk	.20	.20
1573	A294	60f olive & blk	.20	.20
1574	A294	1fo red org & blk	.35	.20
1575	A294	1.40fo blue & blk	.45	.20
1576	A294	2fo bluish grn & blk	.55	.25
1577	A294	2.60fo lt vio & blk	.85	.45
		Nos. 1570-1577 (8)	3.00	1.90

Exist imperf. Value, set $35.

Special Anniversaries-Events Issue

Imre Madach (1823-64) — A345

Shakespeare A346

Karl Marx and Membership Card of International Working Men's Association — A347

Michelangelo — A348

Lajos Kossuth and György Dózsa — A349

Budapest Fair Buildings — A350

#1579, Ervin Szabo. #1580, Writer Andras Fay (1786-1864). #1581, Aggtelek Cave scene. #1582, Excavating bauxite. #1584, Equestrian statue, Szekesfehervar. #1585, Bowler. #1586, Waterfall and forest. #1587, Architect Miklos Ybl (1814-91) and Budapest Opera. #1590, Armor, saber, sword & foil.

#1592, Galileo Galilei. #1593, Women basketball players. #1595, Two runners breaking tape.

Perf. 11½x12, 12x11½, 11
1964   **Photo.**   **Unwmk.**
Inscribed: "ÉVFORDULÓK-ESEMÉNYEK"

1578	A345	60f brt purple	.20	.20
1579	A345	60f olive	.20	.20
1580	A345	60f olive grn	.20	.20
1581	A346	60f bluish grn	.20	.20
1582	A347	60f Prus blue	.20	.20
1583	A347	60f rose red	.20	.20
1584	A348	60f slate blue	.20	.20
1585	A345	1fo car rose	.20	.20
a.		With Olympic rings bottom tab	1.00	1.00
1586	A348	1fo dull blue grn	.20	.20
1587	A348	1fo orange brn	.20	.20
1588	A349	1fo ultra	.20	.20
1589	A350	1fo brt green	.20	.20
1590	A345	2fo yellow brn	.20	.20
1591	A346	2fo magenta	.35	.20
1592	A346	2fo red brown	.25	.20
1593	A346	2fo brt blue	.25	.20
1594	A348	2fo gray brown	.30	.20
1595	A348	2fo brown red	.25	.20
		Nos. 1578-1595 (18)	4.00	3.60

No. 1579, Municipal libraries, 60th anniv., and librarian Szabo (1877-1918). No. 1582, Bauxite mining in Hungary, 30th year. No. 1583, Cent. of 1st Socialist Intl. No. 1584, King Alba Day in Székesfehérvár. No. 1585, 1st European Bowling Championship, Budapest.

No. 1586, Cong. of Natl. Forestry Federation. No. 1588, City of Cegléd, 600th anniv. No. 1589, Opening of 1964 Budapest Intl. Fair. No. 1590, Hungarian Youth Fencing Association, 50th anniv. Nos. 1591-1592, Shakespeare and Galileo, 400th birth anniversaries. No. 1593, 9th European Women's Basketball Championship. No. 1594, Michelangelo's 400th death anniv. No. 1595, 50th anniv. of 1st Hungarian-Swedish athletic meet.

Exists imperf. Value, set $100. No. 1585a imperf value $350.

Eleanor Roosevelt — A351

Design, horiz.: a, d, Portrait at right. b, c, Portrait at left.

1964, Apr. 27   *Perf. 12½*

1596	A351	2fo gray, black & buff	.30	.20

Miniature Sheet
Perf. 11

1597		Sheet of 4	3.00	2.75
a.	A351	2fo dp claret, brn & blk	.65	.65
b.	A351	2fo dk bl, brn & blk	.65	.65
c.	A351	2fo grn, brn & blk	.65	.65
d.	A351	2fo olive, brn & blk	.65	.65

Exist imperf. Value: single $9; souvenir sheet $25.

Fencing — A352

Sport: 40f, Women's gymnastics. 60f, Soccer. 80f, Equestrian. 1fo, Running. 1.40fo, Weight lifting. 1.70fo, Gymnast on rings. 2fo, Hammer throw and javelin. 2.50fo, Boxing.

1964, June 12   **Photo.**   *Perf. 11*
Multicolored Design and Inscription

1598	A352	30f lt ver	.20	.20
1599	A352	40f blue	.20	.20
1600	A352	60f emerald	.20	.20
1601	A352	80f tan	.20	.20
1602	A352	1fo yellow	.20	.20
1603	A352	1.40fo bis brn	.20	.20

1604	A352	1.70fo bluish gray	.30	.20
1605	A352	2fo gray grn	.35	.20
1606	A352	2.50fo vio gray	.55	.40

Nos. 1598-1606,B237 (10) 3.00 2.75

18th Olympic Games, Tokyo, Oct. 10-25.
Exist imperf. Value, set (10) $25.

Elberta
Peaches
A353

Peaches: 40h, Blossoms (J. H. Hale). 60h,
Magyar Kajszi. 1fo, Mandula Kajszi. 1.50fo,
Borsi Rozsa. 1.70fo, Blossoms (Alexander).
2fo, Champion. 3fo, Mayflower.

1964, July 24   Perf. 11½

1607	A353	40f multi	.20	.20
1608	A353	60f multi	.20	.20
1609	A353	1fo multi	.20	.20
1610	A353	1.50fo multi	.20	.20
1611	A353	1.70fo multi	.25	.20
1612	A353	2fo multi	.35	.20
1613	A353	2.60fo multi	.45	.30
1614	A353	3fo multi	.65	.50

Nos. 1607-1614 (8) 2.50 2.00

National Peach Exhibition, Szeged.
Exist imperf. Value, set $35.

Crossing Street in Safety
Zone — A354

60f, "Watch out for Children" (child & ball).
1fo, "Look before Crossing" (mother & child).

1964, Sept. 27   Perf. 11

1615	A354	20f multicolored	.20	.20
1616	A354	60f multicolored	.20	.20
1617	A354	1fo lilac & multi	.60	.20

Nos. 1615-1617 (3) 1.00 .60

Issued to publicize traffic safety.
Exist imperf. Value, set $25.

Souvenir Sheet

Voskhod 1 and Globe — A355

1964, Nov. 6   Perf. 12x11½

1618	A355	10fo multicolored	3.75	3.50

Russian space flight of Vladimir M.
Komarov, Boris B. Yegorov and Konstantine
Feoktistov.
Exists imperf. Value $45.

Arpad Bridge — A356

Danube Bridges, Budapest: 30f, Margaret
Bridge. 60f, Chain Bridge. 1fo, Elizabeth
Bridge. 1.50fo, Freedom Bridge. 2fo, Petőfi
Bridge. 2.50fo, Railroad Bridge.

1964, Nov. 21   Photo.   Perf. 11x11½

1619	A356	20f multi	.20	.20
1620	A356	30f multi	.20	.20
1621	A356	60f multi	.20	.20
1622	A356	1fo multi	.25	.20
1623	A356	1.50fo multi	.30	.20
1624	A356	2fo multi	.50	.20
1625	A356	2.50fo multi	.85	.40

Nos. 1619-1625 (7) 2.50 1.60

Opening of the reconstructed Elizabeth
Bridge. See No. C250.
Exist imperf. Value, set $40.

Ring-necked Pheasant and Hunting
Rifle — A357

Designs: 30f, Wild boar. 40f, Gray partridges. 60f, Varying hare. 80f, Fallow deer.
1fo, Mouflon. 1.70fo, Red deer. 2fo, Great bustard. 2.50fo, Roebuck and roe deer. 3fo,
Emblem of National Federation of Hungarian
Hunters (antlers).

1964, Dec. 30   Photo.   Perf. 12x11½

1626	A357	20f multi	.20	.20
1627	A357	30f multi	.20	.20
1628	A357	40f multi	.20	.20
1629	A357	60f multi	.20	.20
1630	A357	80f multi	.20	.20
1631	A357	1fo multi	.20	.20
1632	A357	1.70fo multi	.25	.20
1633	A357	2fo multi	.30	.20
1634	A357	2.50fo multi	.50	.30
1635	A357	3fo multi	.75	.50

Nos. 1626-1635 (10) 3.00 2.40

Exist imperf. Value, set $40.

Castle Type of 1960

3fo, Czesznek, vert. 4fo, Eger. 5fo, Koszeg,
vert.

1964   Perf. 11½x12, 12x11½
Size: 21x28mm, 28x21mm

1644	A293	3fo red brown	1.00	.20
1645	A293	4fo brt violet	1.50	.20
1646	A293	5fo yellow grn	1.50	.20

Nos. 1644-1646 (3) 4.00 .60

Equestrian, Gold and Bronze
Medals — A358

Medals: 30f, Women's gymnastics, silver &
bronze. 50f, Small-bore rifle, gold & bronze.
60f, Water polo, gold. 70f, Shot put, bronze.
80f, Soccer, gold. 1fo, Weight lifting, 1 bronze,
2 silver. 1.20fo, Canoeing, silver. 1.40fo, Hammer throw, silver. 1.50fo, Wrestling, 2 gold.
1.70fo, Javelin, 2 silver. 3fo, Fencing, 4 gold.

1965, Feb. 20   Perf. 12
Medals in Gold, Silver or Bronze

1647	A358	20f lt ol grn & dk brn	.20	.20
1648	A358	30f violet & dk brn	.20	.20
1649	A358	50f olive & dk brn	.20	.20
1650	A358	60f lt bl & red brn	.20	.20
1651	A358	70f lt gray & red brn	.20	.20
1652	A358	80f yel grn & dk brn	.20	.20
1653	A358	1fo lil, vio & red brn	.20	.20
1654	A358	1.20fo lt bl, ultra & red brn	.20	.20
1655	A358	1.40fo gray & red brn	.20	.20
1656	A358	1.50fo tan, lt brn & red brn	.25	.20
1657	A358	1.70fo pink & red brn	.50	.25
1658	A358	3fo grnsh blue & brn	.70	.55

Nos. 1647-1658 (12) 3.25 2.80

Victories by the Hungarian team in the 1964
Olympic Games, Tokyo, Oct. 10-25.
Exist imperf. Value, set $30.

Arctic
Exploration
A359

Chrysan-
themums
A360

Designs: 30f, Radar tracking rocket, ionosphere research. 60f, Rocket and earth with
reflecting layer diagrams, atmospheric
research. 80f, Telescope and map of Milky
Way, radio astronomy. 1.50fo, Earth, compass
rose and needle, earth magnetism. 1.70fo,
Weather balloon and lightning, meteorology.
2fo, Aurora borealis and penguins, arctic
research. 2.50fo, Satellite, earth and planets,
space research. 3fo, IQSY emblem and world
map. 10fo, Sun with flares and corona, snow
crystals and rain.

Perf. 11½x12
1965, Mar. 25   Photo.   Unwmk.

1659	A359	20f blue, org & blk	.20	.20
1660	A359	30f gray, blk & emer	.20	.20
1661	A359	60f lilac, blk & yel	.20	.20
1662	A359	80f lt grn, yel & blk	.20	.20
1663	A359	1.50fo lemon, bl & blk	.20	.20
1664	A359	1.70fo blue, pink & blk	.20	.20
1665	A359	2fo ultra, sal & blk	.25	.20
1666	A359	2.50fo org brn, yel & blk	.40	.20
1667	A359	3fo lt bl, cit & blk	.70	.40

Nos. 1659-1667 (9) 2.55 2.00

Souvenir Sheet

1668	A359	10fo ultra, org & blk	2.50	2.50

Intl. Quiet Sun Year, 1964-65.
Exist imperf. Value: set $20; souvenir sheet
$30.

1965, Apr. 4

30f, Peonies. 50f, Carnations. 60f, Roses.
1.40fo, Lilies. 1.70fo, Anemones. 2fo, Gladioli.
2.50fo, Tulips. 3fo, Mixed flower bouquet.

Flowers in Natural Colors

1669	A360	20f gold & gray	.20	.20
1670	A360	30f gold & gray	.20	.20
1671	A360	50f gold & gray	.20	.20
1672	A360	60f gold & gray	.20	.20
1673	A360	1.40fo gold & gray	.20	.20
1674	A360	1.70fo gold & gray	.20	.20
1675	A360	2fo gold & gray	.20	.20
1676	A360	2.50fo gold & gray	.30	.20
1677	A360	3fo gold & gray	.60	.50

Nos. 1669-1677 (9) 2.30 2.10

20th anniversary of liberation from the Nazis.
Exist imperf. Value, set $20.

"Head of a
Combatant" by
Leonardo da
Vinci — A361

Perf. 11½x12
1965, May 4   Photo.   Unwmk.

1678	A361	60f bister & org brn	.30	.20

Issued to publicize the First International
Renaissance Conference, Budapest.
Exists imperf. Value $9.

Nikolayev, Tereshkova and View of
Budapest — A362

1965, May 10   Perf. 11

1679	A362	1fo dull blue & brn	.25	.20

Visit of the Russian astronauts Andrian G.
Nikolayev and Valentina Tereshkova (Mr. &
Mrs. Nikolayev) to Budapest.
Exists imperf. Value $10.

ITU Emblem,
Old and New
Communication
Equipment
A363

1965, May 17

1680	A363	60f violet blue	.20	.20

Cent. of the ITU.
Exists imperf. Value $7.

Souvenir Sheet

Austrian WIPA Stamp of
1933 — A363a

1965, June 4   Photo.   Perf. 11

1681	A363a	Sheet of 2 + 2 labels	3.50	3.50
a.		2fo gray & deep ultra	1.50	1.50

1965 Vienna Intl. Phil. Exhib. WIPA, 6/4-13.
Exists imperf. Value $30.

Marx and Lenin,
Crowds with
Flags — A364

ICY Emblem
and
Pulley — A365

1965, June 15   Perf. 11½x12

1682	A364	60f red, blk & yel	.20	.20

6th Conference of Ministers of Post of
Socialist Countries, Peking, June 21-July 15.
Exists imperf. Value $9.

1965, June 25

1683	A365	2fo dark red	.20	.20
a.		Min. sheet of 4, perf. 11	2.25	2.25

Intl. Cooperation Year, 1965. No. 1683a contains rose red, olive, Prussian green and violet stamps.
Exists imperf. Value: single $6; sheetlet of 4 $30.

Musical Clown — A366

Dr. Semmelweis A367

Circus Acts: 20f, Equestrians. 40f, Elephant. 50f, Seal balancing ball. 60f, Lions. 1fo, Wildcat jumping through burning hoops. 1.50fo, Black leopards. 2.50fo, Juggler. 3fo, Leopard and dogs. 4fo, Bear on bicycle.

1965, July 26   Photo.   Perf. 11½x12

1684	A366	20f multi	.20	.20
1685	A366	30f multi	.20	.20
1686	A366	40f multi	.20	.20
1687	A366	50f multi	.20	.20
1688	A366	60f multi	.20	.20
1689	A366	1fo multi	.20	.20
1690	A366	1.50fo multi	.25	.20
1691	A366	2.50fo multi	.35	.20
1692	A366	3fo multi	.40	.20
1693	A366	4fo multi	.50	.40
		Nos. 1684-1693 (10)	2.70	2.20

Exist imperf. Value, set $20.

1965, Aug. 20   Photo.   Unwmk.

1694	A367	60f red brown	.20	.20

Dr. Ignaz Philipp Semmelweis (1818-1865), discoverer of the cause of puerperal fever and introduced antisepsis into obstetrics.
Exists imperf. Value $6.

Runner — A368

Sport: 30f, Swimmer at start. 50f, Woman diver. 60f, Modern dancing. 80f, Tennis. 1.70fo, Fencing. 2fo, Volleyball. 2.50fo, Basketball. 4fo, Water polo. 10fo, People's Stadium, Budapest, horiz.

1965, Aug. 20   Perf. 11
Size: 38x38mm

1695	A368	20f multi	.20	.20
1696	A368	30f blue & red brn	.20	.20
1697	A368	50f bl grn, blk & red brn	.20	.20
1698	A368	60f vio, blk & red brn	.20	.20
1699	A368	80f tan, ol & red brn	.20	.20
1700	A368	1.70fo multi	.25	.20
1701	A368	2fo multi	.30	.20
1702	A368	2.50fo gray, blk & red brn	.45	.25

1703	A368	4fo bl, red brn & blk	.75	.45
		Nos. 1695-1703 (9)	2.75	2.10

Souvenir Sheet
Perf. 12x11½

1704	A368	10fo bis, red brn & gray		3.00 2.75

Intl. College Championships, "Universiade," Budapest. No. 1704 contains one 38x28mm stamp.
Exist imperf. Value: set $25; souvenir sheet $30.

Hemispheres and Warsaw Mermaid — A369

1965, Oct. 8   Photo.   Perf. 12x11½

1705	A369	60f brt blue	.20	.20

Sixth Congress of the World Federation of Trade Unions, Warsaw.
Exists imperf. Value $6.

Phyllocactus Hybridus A370

Flowers from Botanical Gardens: 30f, Cattleya Warszewiczii (orchid). 60f, Rebutia calliantha. 70f, Paphiopedilum hybridium. 80f, Opuntia cactus. 1fo, Laelia elegans (orchid). 1.50fo, Christmas cactus. 2fo, Bird-of-paradise flower. 2.50fo, Lithops Weberi. 3fo, Victoria water lily.

1965, Oct. 11   Perf. 11½x12

1706	A370	20f gray & multi	.20	.20
1707	A370	30f gray & multi	.20	.20
1708	A370	60f gray & multi	.20	.20
1709	A370	70f gray & multi	.20	.20
1710	A370	80f gray & multi	.20	.20
1711	A370	1fo gray & multi	.20	.20
1712	A370	1.50fo gray & multi	.25	.20
1713	A370	2fo gray & multi	.25	.20
1714	A370	2.50fo gray & multi	.40	.25
1715	A370	3fo gray & multi	.60	.35
		Nos. 1706-1715 (10)	2.70	2.20

Exist imperf. Value, set $22.

"The Black Stallion" A371

Tales from the Arabian Nights: 30f, Shahriar and Scheherazade. 50f, Sinbad's Fifth Voyage (ship). 60f, Aladdin, or The Wonderful Lamp. 80f, Harun al-Rashid. 1fo, The Flying Carpet. 1.70fo, The Fisherman and the Genie. 2fo, Ali Baba and the Forty Thieves. 3fo, Sinbad's Second Voyage (flying bird).

1965, Dec. 15   Litho.   Perf. 11½

1716	A371	20f multi	.20	.20
1717	A371	30f multi	.20	.20
1718	A371	50f multi	.20	.20
1719	A371	60f multi	.20	.20
1720	A371	80f multi	.20	.20
1721	A371	1fo multi	.20	.20
1722	A371	1.70fo multi	.35	.20
1723	A371	2fo multi	.45	.20
1724	A371	3fo multi	.75	.50
		Nos. 1716-1724 (9)	2.75	2.10

Exist imperf. Value, set $25.

Congress Emblem A372

Callimorpha Dominula A373

1965, Dec. 9   Photo.   Perf. 11½x12

1725	A372	2fo dark blue	.30	.20

Fifth Congress of the International Federation of Resistance Fighters (FIR), Budapest.
Exists imperf. Value $6.

1966, Feb. 1   Photo.   Perf. 11½x12
Various Butterflies in Natural Colors;
Black Inscription

1726	A373	20f lt aqua	.20	.20
1727	A373	60f pale violet	.20	.20
1728	A373	70f tan	.20	.20
1729	A373	80f lt ultra	.20	.20
1730	A373	1fo gray	.20	.20
1731	A373	1.50fo emerald	.40	.20
1732	A373	2fo dull rose	.30	.20
1733	A373	2.50fo bister	.45	.30
1734	A373	3fo blue	.70	.50
		Nos. 1726-1734 (9)	2.85	2.20

Exist imperf. Value, set $30.

Lal Bahadur Shastri A374

Designs: 60f, Bela Kun. 2fo, Istvan Széchenyi and Chain Bridge.

Lithographed; Photogravure (#1736)
1966   Perf. 11½x12, 12x11½

1735	A374	60f red & black	.20	.20
1736	A374	1fo brt violet	.20	.20
1737	A374	2fo dull yel, buff & sepia	.25	.20
		Nos. 1735-1737 (3)	.65	.60

Kun (1886-1939), communist labor leader; Shastri (1904-66), Indian Prime Minister; Count Istvan Széchenyi (1791-1860), statesman.
Exist imperf. Value, set $15.
See Nos. 1764-1765, 1769-1770.

Luna 9 — A375

Design: 3fo, Luna 9 sending signals from moon to earth, horiz.

Crocus — A376

1966, Mar. 12   Photo.   Perf. 12

1738	A375	2fo violet, blk & yel	.45	.20
1739	A375	3fo lt ultra, blk & yel	.85	.60

1st soft landing on the moon by the Russian satellite Luna 9, Feb. 3, 1966.
Exist imperf. Value, set $15.

1966, Mar. 12   Perf. 11

Flowers: 30f, Cyclamen. 60f, Ligularia sibirica. 1.40fo, Lilium bulbiferum. 1.50fo, Snake's head. 3fo, Snapdragon and emblem of Hungarian Nature Preservation Society.

Flowers in Natural Colors

1740	A376	20f brown	.20	.20
1741	A376	30f aqua	.20	.20
1742	A376	60f rose claret	.20	.20
1743	A376	1.40fo gray	.30	.20
1744	A376	1.50fo ultra	.45	.25
1745	A376	3fo mag & sepia	.65	.40
		Nos. 1740-1745 (6)	2.00	1.45

Exist imperf. Value, set $25.

1966, Apr. 16

Designs: 20f, Barn swallows. 30f, Longtailed tits. 60f, Red crossbill and pine cone. 1.40fo, Middle spotted woodpecker. 1.50fo, Hoopoe feeding young. 3fo, Forest preserve, lapwing and emblem of National Forest Preservation Society.

Birds in Natural Colors

1746	A376	20f brt green	.20	.20
1747	A376	30f vermilion	.25	.20
1748	A376	60f brt green	.40	.20
1749	A376	1.40fo vio blue	1.00	.25
1750	A376	1.50fo blue	1.25	.50
1751	A376	3fo brn, mag & grn	2.00	1.00
		Nos. 1746-1751 (6)	5.10	2.35

Nos. 1740-1751 issued to promote protection of wild flowers and birds.
Exist imperf. Value, set $30.

Locomotive, 1847; Monoplane, 1912; Autobus, 1911; Steamer, 1853, and Budapest Railroad Station, 1846 — A377

Designs: 2fo, Transportation, 1966: electric locomotive V.43; turboprop airliner IL-18; Ikarusz autobus; Diesel passenger ship, and Budapest South Railroad Station.

1966, Apr. 2   Photo.   Perf. 12

1752	A377	1fo yel, brn & grn	.20	.20
1753	A377	2fo pale grn, bl & brn	.35	.20

Re-opening of the Transport Museum, Budapest.
Exist imperf. Value, set $17.

Bronze Order of Labor — A378

Decorations: 30f, Silver Order of Labor. 50f, Banner Order, third class. 60f, Gold Order of Labor. 70f, Banner Order, second class. 1fo, Red Banner Order of Labor. 1.20fo, Banner Order, first class. 2fo, Order of Merit. 2.50fo, Hero of Socialist Labor. Sizes: 20f, 30f, 60f, 1fo, 2fo, 2.50fo: 19½x38mm. 50f: 21x29mm. 70f, 25x31mm. 1.20fo: 28x38mm.

1966, Apr. 2   Unwmk.   Perf. 11
Decorations in Original Colors

1754	A378	20f dp ultra	.20	.20
1755	A378	30f lt brown	.20	.20
1756	A378	50f blue green	.20	.20
1757	A378	60f violet	.20	.20
1758	A378	70f carmine	.20	.20
1759	A378	1fo violet bl	.20	.20
1760	A378	1.20fo brt blue	.20	.20
1761	A378	2fo olive	.25	.20
1762	A378	2.50fo dull blue	.35	.20
		Nos. 1754-1762 (9)	2.00	1.80

Exist imperf. Value, set $20.

Portrait Type of 1966 and

Dubna Nuclear Research Institute — A379

WHO Headquarters, Geneva — A380

Designs: No. 1764, Pioneer girl. No. 1765, Tamás Esze (1666-1708), military hero. No. 1767, Old view of Buda and UNESCO emblem. No. 1768, Horse-drawn fire pump and emblem of Sopron Fire Brigade. No. 1769, Miklos Zrinyi (1508-66), hero of Turkish Wars. No. 1770, Sandor Koranyi (1866-1944), physician and scientist.

1966   Litho.   Perf. 11½x12

1763	A379	60f blue grn & blk	.20	.20
1764	A374	60f multicolored	.20	.20
1765	A374	60f brt bl & blk	.20	.20
1766	A380	2fo lt ultra & blk	.20	.20
1767	A380	2fo lt blue & pur	.25	.20
1768	A380	2fo orange & blk	.25	.20
1769	A374	2fo ol bis & brn	.20	.20
1770	A374	2fo multicolored	.20	.20
		Nos. 1763-1770 (8)	1.70	1.60

No. 1763, 10th anniv. of the United Institute for Nuclear Research, Dubna, USSR; No. 1764, 20th anniv. of Pioneer Movement; No. 1766, Inauguration of the WHO Headquarters, Geneva; No. 1767, 20th anniv. of UNESCO and 72nd session of Executive Council, Budapest, May 30-31; No. 1768, Cent. of Volunteer Fire Brigade.

Exist imperf. Value, set $50.

Hungarian Soccer Player and Soccer Field — A381

Jules Rimet, Cup and Soccer Ball — A382

Designs (Views of Soccer play): 30f, Montevideo 1930 (Uruguay 4, Argentina 2). 60f, Rome 1934 (Italy 2, Czechoslovakia 1). 1fo, Paris 1938 (Italy 4, Hungary 2). 1.40fo, Rio de Janeiro 1950 (Uruguay 2, Brazil 1). 1.70fo, Bern 1954 (Germany 3, Hungary 2). 2fo, Stockholm 1958 (Brazil 5, Sweden 2). 2.50fo, Santiago 1962 (Brazil 3, Czechoslovakia 1).

Souvenir Sheet

1966, May 16   Photo.   Perf. 11½x12
1771	A381	10fo multi	3.25	3.00

Exists imperf. Value $30.

1966, June 6   Perf. 12x11½

1772	A382	20f blue & multi	.25	.20
1773	A382	30f orange & multi	.25	.20
1774	A382	60f multi	.20	.20
1775	A382	1fo multi	.20	.20
1776	A382	1.40fo multi	.20	.20
1777	A382	1.70fo multi	.20	.20
1778	A382	2fo multi	.25	.20
1779	A382	2.50fo multi	.60	.40
		Nos. 1772-1779,B258 (9)	2.75	2.30

World Cup Soccer Championship, Wembley, England, July 11-30.
Exist imperf. Value, set (9) $22.75.

European Red Fox — A383

Hunting Trophies: 60f, Wild boar. 70f, Wildcat. 80f, Roebuck. 1.50fo, Red deer. 2.50fo, Fallow deer. 3fo, Mouflon.

1966, July 4   Photo.   Perf. 11½x12
Animals in Natural Colors

1780	A383	20f gray & lt brn	.20	.20
1781	A383	60f buff & gray	.20	.20
1782	A383	70f lt bl & gray	.20	.20
1783	A383	80f pale grn & yel bis	.25	.20
1784	A383	1.50fo pale lem & brn	.35	.20
1785	A383	2.50fo gray & brn	.60	.35
1786	A383	3fo pale pink & gray	.95	.50
		Nos. 1780-1786 (7)	2.75	1.85

The 80f and 1.50fo were issued with and without alternating labels, which show date and place when trophy was taken; the 2.50fo was issued only with labels, 20f, 60f, 70f and 3fo without labels only.

Nos. 1780-1786 exist imperf. Value, set $30.

Discus Thrower and Matthias Cathedral A384

30f, High jump & Agriculture Museum. 40f, Javelin (women's) & Parliament. 50f, Hammer throw, Mt. Gellert & Liberty Bridge. 60f, Broad jump & view of Buda. 1fo, Shot put & Chain Bridge. 2fo, Pole vault & Stadium. 3fo, Long distance runners & Millenium Monument.

1966, Aug. 30   Photo.   Perf. 12x11½

1787	A384	20f grn, brn & org	.20	.20
1788	A384	30f multi	.30	.20
1789	A384	40f multi	.20	.20
1790	A384	50f multi	.20	.20
1791	A384	60f multi	.20	.20
1792	A384	1fo multi	.25	.20
1793	A384	2fo multi	.50	.20
1794	A384	3fo multi	.75	.50
		Nos. 1787-1794 (8)	2.60	1.90

8th European Athletic Championships, Budapest, Aug. 30-Sept. 4. See No. C261.
Exist imperf. Value, set $20.

Girl in the Forest by Miklos Barabas A385

Paintings: 1fo, Mrs. Istvan Bitto by Miklos Barabas (1810-98). 1.50fo, Hunyadi's Farewell by Gyula Benczur (1844-1920). 1.70fo, Reading Woman by Gyula Benczur, horiz. 2fo, Woman with Fagots by Mihaly Munkacsi (1844-1900). 2.50fo, Yawning Boy by Mihaly Munkacsi. 3fo, Lady in Violet by Pal Szinyei Merse (1845-1920). 10fo, Picnic in May by Pal Szinyei Merse, horiz.

1966, Dec. 9   Perf. 12½
Gold Frame

1795	A385	60f multi	.20	.20
1796	A385	1fo multi	.25	.20
1797	A385	1.50fo multi	.40	.20
1798	A385	1.70fo multi	.40	.20
1799	A385	2fo multi	.40	.20
1800	A385	2.50fo multi	.45	.20
1801	A385	3fo multi	.90	.80
		Nos. 1795-1801 (7)	3.00	2.00

Souvenir Sheet

1802	A385	10fo multi	6.00	6.00

Issued to honor Hungarian painters. Size of stamp in No. 1802: 56x51mm.
Exist imperf. Value: set $20; souvenir sheet $30.

Vostoks 3 and 4 — A386

Space Craft: 60f, Gemini 6 and 7. 80f, Vostoks 5 and 6. 1fo, Gemini 9 and target rocket. 1.50fo, Alexei Leonov walking in space. 2fo, Edward White walking in space. 2.50fo, Voskhod. 3fo, Gemini 11 docking Agena target.

1966, Dec. 29   Perf. 11

1803	A386	20f multi	.20	.20
1804	A386	60f multi	.20	.20
1805	A386	80f multi	.20	.20
1806	A386	1fo multi	.20	.20
1807	A386	1.50fo multi	.30	.20
1808	A386	2fo multi	.30	.20
1809	A386	2.50fo multi	.50	.30
1810	A386	3fo multi	.75	.50
		Nos. 1803-1810 (8)	2.65	2.00

American and Russian twin space flights.

Exist imperf. Value, set $20.

Pal Kitaibel and Kitaibelia Vitifolia — A387

Flowers of the Carpathian Basin: 60f, Dentaria glandulosa. 1fo, Edraianthus tenuifolius. 1.50fo, Althaea pallida. 2fo, Centaurea mollis. 2.50fo, Sternbergia colchiciflora. 3fo, Iris Hungarica.

1967, Feb. 7   Photo.   Perf. 11½x12
Flowers in Natural Colors

1811	A387	20f rose, blk & gold	.20	.20
1812	A387	60f green	.20	.20
1813	A387	1fo violet gray	.20	.20
1814	A387	1.50fo blue	.20	.20
1815	A387	2fo light olive	.25	.20
1816	A387	2.50fo gray grn	.45	.30
1817	A387	3fo yellow grn	.75	.50
		Nos. 1811-1817 (7)	2.25	1.80

Pal Kitaibel (1757-1817), botanist, chemist and physician.
Exist imperf. Value, set $20.

Militiaman A388

1967, Feb. 18   Photo.   Perf. 11½x12
1818	A388	2fo blue gray	.40	.20

Workers' Militia, 10th anniversary.
Exists imperf. Value $12.

Mme. Du Barry and Louis XV, by Gyula Benczur (1844-1920) — A390

Souvenir Sheet

Painting: 10fo, Milton dictating "Paradise Lost" to his daughters, by Soma Orlai Petrics.

1967, May 6   Photo.   Perf. 12½
1819	A390	10fo multi	4.75	4.50

Exists imperf. Value $30.

1967, June 22

Paintings: 60f, Franz Liszt by Mihaly Munkacsi (1844-1900). 1fo, Samuel Lanyi, self-portrait, 1840. 1.50fo, Lady in Fur-lined Jacket by Jozsef Borsos (1821-83). 1.70fo, The Lovers, by Pal Szinyei Merse (1845-1920). 2fo, Portrait of Szidonia Deak, 1861, by Alajos Gyorgyi (1821-63). 2.50fo, National Guardsman, 1848, by Jozsef Borsos.

Gold Frame

1820	A390	60f multi	.20	.20
1821	A390	1fo multi	.20	.20
1822	A390	1.50fo multi	.20	.20
1823	A390	1.70fo multi, horiz.	.30	.20
1824	A390	2fo multi	.35	.20

1825	A390	2.50fo multi	.45 .20
1826	A390	3fo multi	.75 .70

Nos. 1820-1826 (7) 2.45 1.90

Issued to honor Hungarian painters. No. 1819 commemorates AMPHILEX 67 and the F.I.P. Congress, Amsterdam, May 11-21. No. 1819 contains one 56x50mm stamp.
Exist imperf. Value, set $20.
See #1863-1870, 1900-1907, 1940-1947.

Map of Hungary, Tourist Year Emblem, Plane, Train, Car and Ship
A391

1967, May 6   **Perf. 12x11½**
1827 A391 1fo brt blue & blk   .20 .20

International Tourist Year, 1967.
Exists imperf. Value $6.

S.S. Ferencz Deak, Schönbüchel
Castle, Austrian Flag — A392

Designs: 60f, Diesel hydrobus, Bratislava Castle and Czechoslovak flag. 1fo, Diesel ship Hunyadi, Buda Castle and Hungarian flag. 1.50fo, Diesel tug Szekszard, Golubac Fortress and Yugoslav flag. 1.70fo, Towboat Miskolc, Vidin Fortress and Bulgarian flag. 2fo, Cargo ship Tihany, Galati shipyard and Romanian flag. 2.50fo, Hydrofoil Siraly I, Izmail Harbor and Russian flag.

1967, June 1   **Perf. 11½x12**
Flags in National Colors

1828	A392	30f lt blue grn	.35 .20
1829	A392	60f orange brn	.35 .20
1830	A392	1fo grnsh blue	.75 .50
1831	A392	1.50fo lt green	1.00 .30
1832	A392	1.70fo blue	1.25 .45
1833	A392	2fo rose lilac	2.25 .75
1834	A392	2.50fo lt olive grn	5.25 1.10

Nos. 1828-1834 (7) 11.20 3.25

25th session of the Danube Commission.
Exists imperf. Value, set $375.

Poodle
A393

Collie — A394

1fo, Hungarian pointer. 1.40fo, Fox terriers. 2fo, Pumi, Hungarian sheep dog. 3fo, German shepherd. 4fo, Puli, Hungarian sheep dog.

1967, July 7   **Litho.**   **Perf. 12**

1835	A393	30f multi	.25 .20
1836	A394	60f multi	.25 .20
1837	A393	1fo multi	.20 .20
1838	A394	1.40fo multi	.25 .20
1839	A393	2fo multi	.35 .20
1840	A394	3fo multi	.60 .50
1841	A393	4fo multi	.95 .60

Nos. 1835-1841 (7) 2.85 2.00

Exist imperf. Value, set $30.

Sterlets
A395

Fish: 60f, Pike perch. 1fo, Carp. 1.70fo, European catfish. 2fo, Pike. 2.50fo, Rapfin.

1967, Aug. 22   **Photo.**   **Perf. 12x11½**

1842	A395	20f multi	.20 .20
1843	A395	60f bister & multi	.20 .20
1844	A395	1fo multi	.20 .20
1845	A395	1.70fo multi	.20 .20
1846	A395	2fo green & multi	.30 .20
1847	A395	2.50fo gray & multi	.75 .55

Nos. 1842-1847,B263 (7) 2.75 2.00

14th Cong. of the Intl. Federation of Anglers (C.I.P.S.), Dunaujvaros, Aug. 20-28.
Exist imperf. Value, set $20.

Prince Igor, by Aleksandr
Borodin — A396

Opera Scenes: 30f, Freischütz, by Karl Maria von Weber. 40f, The Magic Flute, by Mozart. 60f, Prince Bluebeard's Castle, by Bela Bartok. 80f, Carmen, by Bizet, vert. 1fo, Don Carlos, by Verdi, vert. 1.70fo, Tannhäuser, by Wagner, vert. 3fo. Laszlo Hunyadi, by Ferenc Erkel, vert.

1967, Sept. 26   **Photo.**   **Perf. 12**

1848	A396	20f multi	.20 .20
1849	A396	30f multi	.20 .20
1850	A396	40f multi	.20 .20
1851	A396	60f multi	.20 .20
1852	A396	80f multi	.20 .20
1853	A396	1fo multi	.20 .20
1854	A396	1.70fo multi	.45 .30
1855	A396	3fo multi	1.00 .70

Nos. 1848-1855 (8) 2.65 2.20

Exist imperf. Value, set $20.

Teacher, Students and Stone from Pecs University, 14th Century
A397

1967, Oct. 9   **Photo.**   **Perf. 11½x12**
1856 A397 2fo gold & dp grn   .40 .20

600th anniv. of higher education in Hungary; University of Pecs was founded in 1367.
Exists imperf. Value $6.

Eötvös University, and Symbols of
Law and Justice — A398

1967, Oct. 12   **Perf. 12x11½**
1857 A398 2fo slate   .40 .20

300th anniv. of the School of Political Science and Law at the Lorand Eötvös University, Budapest.
Exists imperf. Value $6.

Lenin as Teacher, by Sandor Legrady
A399

Paintings by Sandor Legrady: 1fo, Lenin. 3fo, Lenin on board the cruiser Aurora.

1967, Oct. 31   **Perf. 12½**

1858	A399	60f gold & multi	.20 .20
1859	A399	1fo gold & multi	.20 .20
1860	A399	3fo gold & multi	.60 .25

Nos. 1858-1860 (3) 1.00 .65

50th anniv. of the Russian October Revolution.
Exist imperf. Value, set $17.50.

Venus 4 Landing on Venus — A400

1967, Nov. 6   **Perf. 12**
1861 A400 5fo gold & multi   1.25 1.10

Landing of the Russian automatic space station Venus 4 on the planet Venus.
Exists imperf. Value $10.

Souvenir Sheet

19th Century Mail Coach and Post
Horn — A401

Photogravure; Gold Impressed
1967, Nov. 21   **Perf. 12½**
1862 A401 10fo multicolored   3.25 3.00

Hungarian Postal Administration, cent.
Exists imperf. Value $35.

Painting Type of 1967

Paintings: 60f, Brother and Sister by Adolf Fenyes (1867-1945). 1fo, Wrestling Boys by Oszkar Glatz (1872-1958). 1.50fo, "October" by Karoly Ferenczy (1862-1917). 1.70fo, Women at the River Bank by Istvan Szönyi (1894-1960), horiz. 2fo, Godfather's Breakfast by Istvan Csok (1865-1961). 2.50fo, "Eviction Notice" by Gyula Derkovits (1894-1934). 3fo, Self-portrait by M. T. Czontvary Kosztka (1853-1919). 10fo, The Apple Pickers by Bela Uitz (1887-).

1967, Dec. 21   **Photo.**   **Perf. 12½**

1863	A390	60f multi	.20 .20
1864	A390	1fo multi	.20 .20
1865	A390	1.50fo multi	.20 .20
1866	A390	1.70fo multi	.20 .20
1867	A390	2fo multi	.30 .20
1868	A390	2.50fo multi	.40 .25
1869	A390	3fo multi	.70 .45

Nos. 1863-1869 (7) 2.20 1.70

Miniature Sheet
1870 A390 10fo multi   2.75 2.50

Issued to honor Hungarian painters.
Exists imperf. Value: set $20; souvenir sheet $22.

Biathlon — A402

Sport (Olympic Rings and): 60f, Figure skating, pair. 1fo, Bobsledding. 1.40fo, Slalom. 1.70fo, Women's figure skating. 2fo, Speed skating. 3fo, Ski jump. 10fo, Ice hockey.

1967, Dec. 30   **Photo.**   **Perf. 12½**
Souvenir Sheet
1871 A402 10fo lilac & multi   2.50 2.00

Exists imperf. Value $18.

1968, Jan. 29   **Perf. 11**

1872	A402	30f multi	.20 .20
1873	A402	60f multi	.20 .20
1874	A402	1fo multi	.20 .20
1875	A402	1.40fo rose & multi	.20 .20
1876	A402	1.70fo multi	.20 .20
1877	A402	2fo multi	.30 .20
1878	A402	3fo ol & multi	.80 .30

Nos. 1872-1878,B264 (8) 2.80 1.80

10th Winter Olympic Games, Grenoble, France, Feb. 6-18. No. 1871 contains one 43x43mm stamp.
Exist imperf. Value, set (8) $20.

Kando Statue, Miskolc, Kando
Locomotive and Map of Hungary
A403

1968, Mar. 30   **Photo.**   **Perf. 11½x12**
1879 A403 2fo dark blue   .40 .20

Kalman Kando (1869-1931), engineer, inventor of Kando locomotive.
Exists imperf. Value $9.

Domestic Cat
A404

1968, Mar. 30   **Perf. 11**

1880	A404	20f shown	.20 .20
1881	A404	60f Cream Persian	.20 .20
1882	A404	1fo Smoky Persian	.20 .20
1883	A404	1.20fo Domestic kitten	.20 .20
1884	A404	1.50fo White Persian	.30 .20
1885	A404	2fo Brown-striped Persian	.30 .20
1886	A404	2.50fo Siamese	.60 .25
1887	A404	5fo Blue Persian	1.25 .55

Nos. 1880-1887 (8) 3.25 2.00

Exist imperf. Value, set $30.

Zoltan Kodaly, by Sandor Légrády A405

1968, Apr. 17 Photo. Perf. 12½
1888 A405 5fo gold & multi 1.00 .75
Kodaly (1882-1967), composer & musicologist.
Exists imperf. Value $10.

White Storks A406

Birds: 50f, Golden orioles. 60f, Imperial eagle. 1fo, Red-footed falcons. 1.20fo, Scops owl. 1.50fo, Great bustard. 2fo, European bee-eaters. 2.50fo, Graylag goose.

1968, Apr. 25
Birds in Natural Colors
1889 A406 20f ver & lt ultra .20 .20
1890 A406 50f ver & gray .20 .20
1891 A406 60f ver & lt bl .20 .20
1892 A406 1fo ver & yel grn .25 .20
1893 A406 1.20fo ver & brt grn .25 .20
1894 A406 1.50fo ver & lt vio .25 .20
1895 A406 2fo ver & pale lil .55 .30
1896 A406 2.50fo ver & lt brn grn 1.10 .50
Nos. 1889-1896 (8) 3.00 2.00
International Bird Preservation Congress.
Exists imperf. Value, set $30.

City Hall, Kecskemét A407

Student and Agricultural College A408

1968, Apr. 25 Perf. 12x11½
1897 A407 2fo brown orange .30 .20
600th anniversary of Kecskemét.
Exists imperf. Value $5.

Marx Type of 1953
1968, May 5 Engr. Perf. 12
1898 A230 1fo claret .20 .20
Karl Marx (1818-1883).
Exists imperf. Value $6.

1968, May 24 Photo. Perf. 12x11½
1899 A408 2fo dk olive green .30 .20
150th anniv. of the founding of the Agricultural College at Mosonmagyaróvár.
Exists imperf. Value $5.

Painting Type of 1967
Paintings: 40f, Girl with Pitcher, by Goya (1746-1828). 60f, Head of an Apostle, by El Greco (c. 1541-1614). 1fo, Boy with Apple Basket and Dogs, by Pedro Nunez (1639-1700), horiz. 1.50fo, Mary Magdalene, by El Greco. 2.50fo, The Breakfast, by Velazquez

(1599-1660), horiz. 4fo, The Virgin from The Holy Family, by El Greco. 5fo, The Knife Grinder, by Goya. 10fo, Portrait of a Girl, by Palma Vecchio (1480-1528).

1968, May 30 Perf. 12½
1900 A390 40f multi .20 .20
1901 A390 60f multi .20 .20
1902 A390 1fo multi .20 .20
1903 A390 1.50fo multi .20 .20
1904 A390 2.50fo multi .50 .20
1905 A390 4fo multi .70 .20
1906 A390 5fo multi 1.00 .35
Nos. 1900-1906 (7) 3.00 1.55
Souvenir Sheet
1907 A390 10fo multi 3.25 3.00
Issued to publicize art treasures in the Budapest Museum of Fine Arts and to publicize an art exhibition.
Exist imperf. Values: set of 7, $20; souvenir sheet $30.

Lake Balaton at Badacsony A409

Views on Lake Balaton: 40f like 20f. 60f, Tihanyi Peninsula. 1fo, Sailboats at Almadi. 2fo, Szigliget Bay.

1968-69 Litho. Perf. 12
1908 A409 20f multi .20 .20
1908A A409 40f multi ('69) .20 .20
 b. Bklt. pane, #1909, 1911, 2
  each #1908A, 1910 .75
 c. Bklt. pane, #1909-1911, 3
  #1908A .75
 d. Bklt. pane, #1911, 3 #1908A,
  2 #1909 .75
1909 A409 60f multi .20 .20
1910 A409 1fo multi .20 .20
1911 A409 2fo multi .45 .20
Nos. 1908-1911 (5) 1.25 1.00
Exist imperf. Value, set $30.

Locomotive, Type 424 — A410

1968, July 14 Photo. Perf. 12x11½
1912 A410 2fo gold, lt bl & slate .60 .20
Centenary of the Hungarian State Railroad.
Exists imperf. Value $8.

Horses Grazing — A411

Designs: 40f, Horses in storm. 60f, Horse race on the steppe. 80f, Horsedrawn sleigh. 1fo, Four-in-hand and rainbow. 1.40fo, Farm wagon drawn by 7 horses. 2fo, One rider driving five horses. 2.50fo, Campfire on the range. 4fo, Coach with 5 horses.

1968, July 25 Perf. 11
1913 A411 30f multi .20 .20
1914 A411 40f multi .20 .20
1915 A411 60f multi .20 .20
1916 A411 80f multi .20 .20
1917 A411 1fo multi .20 .20
1918 A411 1.40fo multi .30 .20
1919 A411 2fo multi .30 .20
1920 A411 2.50fo multi .40 .25
1921 A411 4fo multi .75 .45
Nos. 1913-1921 (9) 2.75 2.10
Horse breeding on the Hungarian steppe (Puszta).
Exist imperf. Value $50.

Mihály Tompa (1817-68), Poet — A412

1968, July 30 Photo. Perf. 12x11½
1922 A412 60f blue black .20 .20
Exists imperf. Value $5.

Festival Emblem, Bulgarian and Hungarian National Costumes — A413

1968, Aug. 3 Litho. Perf. 12
1923 A413 60f multicolored .30 .20
Issued to publicize the 9th Youth Festival for Peace and Friendship, Sofia, Bulgaria.
Exists imperf. Value $6.

Souvenir Sheet

Runners and Aztec Calendar Stone — A414

1968, Aug. 21 Photo. Perf. 12½
1924 A414 10fo multicolored 2.50 2.25
19th Olympic Games, Mexico City, 10/12-27.
Exists imperf. Value $30.

Scientific Society Emblem — A415

Perf. 12½x11½
1968, Dec. 10 Photo.
1925 A415 2fo brt blue & blk .35 .20
Society for the Popularization of Scientific Knowledge.
Exists imperf. Value $5.50.

Hesperis A416

Garden Flowers: 60f, Pansy. 80f, Zinnias. 1fo, Morning-glory. 1.40fo, Petunia. 1.50fo, Portulaca. 2fo, Michaelmas daisies. 2.50fo, Dahlia.

1968, Oct. 29 Perf. 11½x12
Flowers in Natural Colors
1926 A416 20f gray .20 .20
1927 A416 60f lt green .20 .20
1928 A416 80f bluish lilac .25 .20
1929 A416 1fo buff .25 .20
1930 A416 1.40fo lt grnsh bl .20 .20
1931 A416 1.50fo lt blue .25 .20
1932 A416 2fo pale pink .30 .25
1933 A416 2.50fo lt blue .60 .40
Nos. 1926-1933 (8) 2.25 1.85
Exist imperf. Value, set $20.

Pioneers Saluting Communist Party — A417

Children's Paintings: 60f, Four pioneers holding banner saluting Communist Party. 1fo, Pioneer camp.

1968, Nov. 16 Photo. Perf. 12x11½
1934 A417 40f buff & multi .20 .20
1935 A417 60f buff & multi .20 .20
1936 A417 1fo buff & multi .30 .20
Nos. 1934-1936 (3) .70 .60
50th anniv. of the Communist Party of Hungary. The designs are from a competition among elementary school children.
Exist imperf. Value, set $20.

Workers, Monument by Z. Olcsai-Kiss — A418

Design: 1fo, "Workers of the World Unite!" poster by N. Por, vert.

Perf. 11½x12, 12x11½
1968, Nov. 24 Photo.
1937 A418 1fo gold, red, & blk .20 .20
1938 A418 1fo gold & multi .20 .20
Communist Party of Hungary, 50th anniv.
Exist imperf. Value, set $17.

Human Rights Flame — A419

1968, Dec. 10 Perf. 12½x11½
1939 A419 1fo dark red brown .25 .20
International Human Rights Year.
Exists imperf. Value $5.

Painting Type of 1967

Italian Paintings: 40f, Esterhazy Madonna, by Raphael. 60f, The Annunciation, by Bernardo Strozzi. 1fo, Portrait of a Young Man, by Raphael. 1.50fo, The Three Graces, by Battista Naldini. 2.50fo, Portrait of a Man, by Sebastiano del Piombo. 4fo, The Doge Marcantonio Trevisani, by Titian. 5fo, Venus, Cupid and Jealousy, by Angelo Bronzino. 10fo, Bathsheba Bathing, by Sebastiano Ricci, horiz.

1968, Dec. 10   Photo.   Perf. 12½

1940	A390	40f multi	.20	.20
1941	A390	60f multi	.20	.20
1942	A390	1fo multi	.20	.20
1943	A390	1.50fo multi	.20	.20
1944	A390	2.50fo multi	.30	.20
1945	A390	4fo multi	.60	.25
1946	A390	5fo multi	.80	.35
		Nos. 1940-1946 (7)	2.50	1.60

Miniature Sheet
Perf. 11

1947	A390	10fo multi	2.75	2.50

Issued to publicize art treasures in the Budapest Museum of Fine Arts. No. 1947 contains one stamp size of stamp: 62x45mm.
Exist imperf. Value: set $22; souvenir sheet $25.

1869 and 1969 Emblems of Athenaeum Press — A420

1969, Jan. 27   Perf. 12½x11½

1948	A420	2fo gold, gray, lt bl & blk	.30	.20

Centenary of Athenaeum Press, Budapest.
Exists imperf. Value $4.50.

Endre Ady (1877-1919), Lyric Poet — A421

1969, Jan. 27   Perf. 11½x12

1949	A421	1fo multicolored	.20	.20

Exists imperf. Value $5.

Olympic Medal and Women's Javelin — A422

Olympic Medal and: 60f, Canadian singles (canoeing). 1fo, Soccer. 1.20fo, Hammer throw. 2fo, Fencing. 3fo, Greco-Roman Wrestling. 4fo, Kayak single. 5fo, Equestrian. 10fo, Head of Mercury by Praxiteles and Olympic torch.

1969, Mar. 7   Photo.   Perf. 12

1950	A422	40f multi	.20	.20
1951	A422	60f multi	.20	.20
1952	A422	1fo multi	.20	.20
1953	A422	1.20fo multi	.20	.20
1954	A422	2fo multi	.20	.20
1955	A422	3fo multi	.30	.20
1956	A422	4fo multi	.70	.20
1957	A422	5fo multi	.75	.45
		Nos. 1950-1957 (8)	2.75	1.85

Souvenir Sheet
Litho.   Perf. 11½

1958	A422	10fo multi	2.75	2.75

Victories won by the Hungarian team in the 1968 Olympic Games, Mexico City, Oct. 12-

27, 1968. No. 1958 contains one 45x33mm stamp.
Exist imperf. Value: set $22; souvenir sheet $25.

1919 Revolutionary Poster — A423

Revolutionary Posters: 60f, Lenin. 1fo, Man breaking chains. 2fo, Industrial worker looking at family and farm. 3fo, Militia recruiter. 10fo, Shouting revolutionist with red banner, horiz.

1969, Mar. 21   Photo.   Perf. 11½x12
Gold Frame

1960	A423	40f red & black	.20	.20
1961	A423	60f red & black	.20	.20
1962	A423	1fo red & black	.20	.20
1963	A423	2fo black, gray & red	.25	.20
1964	A423	3fo multicolored	.35	.20
		Nos. 1960-1964 (5)	1.20	1.00

Souvenir Sheet
Perf. 12½

1965	A423	10fo red, gray & blk	1.50	1.50

50th anniv. of the proclamation of the Hungarian Soviet Republic.
Exist imperf. Value: set $17.50; souvenir sheet $17.50.
The 60f red lilac with 4-line black printing on back was given away by the Hungarian PO. Value 75c, mint or cancelled.
No. 1965 contains one 51x38½mm stamp.

Jersey Tiger A424

Designs: Various Butterflies and Moths.

1969, Apr. 15   Litho.   Perf. 12

1966	A424	40f shown	.20	.20
1967	A424	60f Eyed hawk moth	.20	.20
1968	A424	80f Painted lady	.20	.20
1969	A424	1fo Tiger moth	.20	.20
1970	A424	1.20fo Small fire moth	.25	.20
1971	A424	2fo Large blue	.35	.20
1972	A424	3fo Belted oak egger	.65	.45
1973	A424	4fo Peacock	.90	.50
		Nos. 1966-1973 (8)	2.95	2.15

Exist imperf. Value, set $30.

ILO Emblem A426

1969, May 22   Photo.   Perf. 12x11½

1974	A426	1fo car lake & lake	.20	.20

50th anniv. of the ILO.
Exist imperf. Value $7.

Black Pigs, by Paul Gauguin A427

French Paintings: 60f, These Women, by Toulouse-Lautrec, horiz. 1fo, Venus in the Clouds, by Simon Vouet. 2fo, Lady with Fan, by Edouard Manet, horiz. 3fo, La Petra Camara (dancer), by Théodore Chassériau. 4fo, The Cowherd, by Constant Troyon, horiz. 5fo, The Wrestlers, by Gustave Courbet. 10fo, Pomona, by Nicolas Fouché.

1969, May 28   Photo.   Perf. 12½

1975	A427	40f multicolored	.20	.20
1976	A427	60f multicolored	.20	.20
1977	A427	1fo multicolored	.20	.20
1978	A427	2fo multicolored	.30	.20
1979	A427	3fo multicolored	.50	.20
1980	A427	4fo multicolored	.70	.25
1981	A427	5fo multicolored	1.00	.50
		Nos. 1975-1981 (7)	3.10	1.75

Miniature Sheet

1982	A427	10fo multicolored	4.00	4.00

Art treasures in the Budapest Museum of Fine Arts. No. 1982 contains one 40x62mm stamp.
Exist imperf. Value: set $20; souvenir sheet $25.

Hotel Budapest A428

Budapest Post Office 100 A429

1969, May   Photo.   Perf. 11

1983	A428	1fo brown	.30	.20

Exists imperf. Value $20.

Coil Stamps

1970, Aug. 3   Perf. 14

1983A	A428	40f gray	.40	.20
1983B	A428	1fo brown	.50	.20

Black control number on back of every 5th stamp.

Arms and Buildings of Vac A430

Towns of the Danube Bend: 1fo, Szentendre. 1.20fo, Visegrad. 3fo, Esztergom.

1969, June 9   Litho.   Perf. 12

1984	A430	40f multi	.20	.20
a.		Bklt. pane, #1985, 1987, 4 #1984		2.75
b.		Bklt. pane, #1986, 3 #1984, 2 #1985		2.75
1985	A430	1fo multi	.20	.20
1986	A430	1.20fo multi	.20	.20
1987	A430	3fo multi	.30	.25
		Nos. 1984-1987 (4)	.90	.85

Stamps in booklet panes Nos. 1984a-1984b come in two arrangements.
Exist imperf. Value, set $17.50.

"PAX" and Men Holding Hands — A431

1969, June 17   Photo.   Perf. 11½x12

1988	A431	1fo lt bl, dk bl & gold	.20	.20

20th anniversary of Peace Movement.
Exists imperf. Value $6.

The Scholar, by Rembrandt A432

1969, Sept. 15   Perf. 11½x12

1989	A432	1fo sepia	.20	.20

Issued to publicize the 22nd International Congress of Art Historians, Budapest.
Exists imperf. Value $7.

Fossilized Zelkova Leaves — A433

1969, Sept. 21   Photo.

Designs: 60f, Greenockit calcite sphalerite crystals. 1fo, Fossilized fish, clupea hungarica. 1.20fo, Quartz crystals. 2fo, Ammonite. 3fo, Copper. 4fo, Fossilized turtle, placochelys placodonta. 5fo, Cuprite crystals.

1990	A433	40f red, gray & sep	.20	.20
1991	A433	60f violet, yel & blk	.20	.20
1992	A433	1fo blue, tan & brn	.20	.20
1993	A433	1.20fo emer, gray & lil	.20	.20
1994	A433	2fo olive, tan & brn	.20	.20
1995	A433	3fo orange, brt & dk grn	.30	.20
1996	A433	4fo dull blk grn, brn & blk	.55	.30
1997	A433	5fo multicolored	.90	.40
		Nos. 1990-1997 (8)	2.75	1.90

Centenary of the Hungarian State Institute of Geology.
Exists imperf. Value, set $20.

Steeplechase — A434

Designs: 60f, Fencing. 1fo, Pistol shooting. 2fo, Swimmers at start. 3fo, Relay race. 5fo, Pentathlon.

1969, Sept. 15   Photo.   Perf. 12x11½

1998	A434	40f blue & multi	.20	.20
1999	A434	60f multi	.20	.20
2000	A434	1fo multi	.20	.20
2001	A434	2fo violet & multi	.30	.20
2002	A434	3fo lemon & multi	.50	.30
2003	A434	5fo bluish grn, gold & dk red	.75	.50
		Nos. 1998-2003 (6)	2.15	1.60

Hungarian Pentathlon Championships.
Exists imperf. Value, set $20.

First Hungarian Postal Card — A435

1969, Oct. 1
2004 A435 60f ver & ocher .20 .20
Centenary of the postal card. Hungary and Austria both issued cards in 1869.
Exists imperf. Value $6.

Mahatma Gandhi — A436

1969, Oct. 1   **Perf. 11½x12**
2005 A436 5fo green & multi 1.25 .70
Mohandas K. Gandhi (1869-1948), leader in India's fight for independence.
Exists imperf. Value $9.

World Trade Union Emblem A437

1969, Oct. 17   **Photo.**   **Perf. 12x11½**
2006 A437 2fo fawn & dk blue .30 .20
Issued to publicize the 7th Congress of the World Federation of Trade Unions.
Exists imperf. Value $6.

Janos Balogh Nagy, Self-portrait A438

1969, Oct. 17   **Perf. 11½x12**
2007 A438 5fo gold & multi 1.50 .80
Janos Balogh Nagy (1874-1919), painter.
Exists imperf. Value $9.

St. John the Evangelist, by Anthony Van Dyck — A439

Dutch Paintings: 60f, Three Fruit Pickers (by Pieter de Molyn?). 1fo, Boy Lighting Pipe, by Hendrick Terbrugghen. 2fo, The Feast, by Jan Steen. 3fo, Woman Reading Letter, by Pieter de Hooch. 4fo, The Fiddler, by Dirk Hals. 5fo, Portrait of Jan Asselyn, by Frans Hals. 10fo,

Mucius Scaevola before Porsena, by Rubens and Van Dyck.

1969-70   **Photo.**   **Perf. 12½**
2008 A439 40f multi .20 .20
2009 A439 60f multi .20 .20
2010 A439 1fo multi .20 .20
2011 A439 2fo multi .25 .20
2012 A439 3fo multi .40 .20
2013 A439 4fo multi .50 .30
2014 A439 5fo multi 1.00 .50
Nos. 2008-2014 (7) 2.75 1.80
Miniature Sheet
2015 A439 10fo multi 3.25 3.25
Treasures in the Museum of Fine Arts, Budapest and the Museum in Eger.
Exist imperf. Value: set $20; souvenir sheet $35.
Issued: 40f-5fo, 12/2/69; 10fo, 1/70.

Kiskunfelegyhaza Circling Pigeon — A440

1969, Dec. 12   **Photo.**   **Perf. 11½x12**
2016 A440 1fo multicolored .20 .20
Issued to publicize the International Pigeon Show, Budapest, Dec. 1969.
Exists imperf. Value $6.50.

Subway A441

1970, Apr. 3   **Photo.**   **Perf. 12**
2017 A441 1fo blk, lt grn & ultra .30 .20
Opening of new Budapest subway.
Exists imperf. Value $9.

Souvenir Sheet

Panoramic View of Budapest 1945 and 1970, and Soviet Cenotaph — A442

1970, Apr. 3   **Perf. 12x11½**
2018 A442 Sheet of 2 2.75 2.50
   a. 5fo "1945" 1.00 1.00
   b. 5fo "1970" 1.00 1.00
25th anniv. of the liberation of Budapest.
Exists imperf. Value $30.

Cloud Formation, Satellite, Earth and Receiving Station — A443

1970, Apr. 8   **Litho.**   **Perf. 12**
2019 A443 1fo dk bl, yel & blk .20 .20
Centenary of the Hungarian Meteorological Service.
Exists imperf. Value $6.

Lenin Statue, Budapest — A444

Design: 2fo, Lenin portrait.

1970, Apr. 22   **Photo.**   **Perf. 11**
2020 A444 1fo gold & multi .25 .20
2021 A444 2fo gold & multi .25 .20
Lenin (1870-1924), Russian communist leader.
Exist imperf. Value, set $12.

Franz Lehar and "Giuditta" Music — A445

1970, Apr. 30   **Photo.**   **Perf. 12**
2022 A445 2fo multicolored .50 .20
Franz Lehar (1870-1948), composer.
Exists imperf. Value $9.

Samson and Delilah, by Michele Rocca A446

Paintings: 60f, Joseph Telling Dream, by Giovanni Battista Langetti. 1fo, Clio, by Pierre Mignard. 1.50fo, Venus and Satyr, by Sebastiano Ricci, horiz. 2.50fo, Andromeda, by Francesco Furini. 4fo, Venus, Adonis and Cupid, by Luca Giordano. 5fo, Allegorical Feast, by Corrado Giaquinto. 10fo, Diana and Callisto, by Abraham Janssens, horiz.

1970, June 2   **Photo.**   **Perf. 12½**
2023 A446 40f gold & multi .20 .20
2024 A446 60f gold & multi .20 .20
2025 A446 1fo gold & multi .20 .20
2026 A446 1.50fo gold & multi .25 .20
2027 A446 2.50fo gold & multi .30 .20
2028 A446 4fo gold & multi .60 .30
2029 A446 5fo gold & multi .75 .50
Nos. 2023-2029 (7) 2.50 1.80
Miniature Sheet
Perf. 11
2030 A446 10fo gold & multi 3.50 3.00
No. 2030 contains one 63x46mm horizontal stamp.
Exist imperf. Values: set $20; souvenir sheet $30.

Beethoven Statue, by Janos Pasztor, at Martonvasar A447

1970, June 27   **Litho.**   **Perf. 12**
2031 A447 1fo plum, gray grn & org yel .75 .20
Ludwig van Beethoven, composer. The music in the design is from his Sonatina No. 1.
Exists imperf. Value $10.

Foundryman A448

King Stephen I — A449

1970, July 28   **Litho.**   **Perf. 12**
2032 A448 1fo multicolored .25 .20
200th anniversary of the first Hungarian steel foundry at Diosgyor, now the Lenin Metallurgical Works.
Exists imperf. Value $6.

1970, Aug. 19   **Photo.**   **Perf. 11½x12**
2033 A449 3fo multicolored 1.00 .50
Millenary of the birth of Saint Stephen, first King of Hungary.
Exists imperf. Value $6.

Women's Four on Lake Tata and Tata Castle — A450

1970, Aug. 19   **Litho.**   **Perf. 12**
2034 A450 1fo multicolored .35 .20
17th European Women's Rowing Championships, Lake Tata.
Exists imperf. Value $6.

Mother Giving Bread to her Children, FAO Emblem — A451

1970, Sept. 21   **Litho.**   **Perf. 12**
2035 A451 1fo lt blue & multi .20 .20
7th European Regional Cong. of the UNFAO, Budapest, Sept. 21-25.
Exists imperf. Value $6.

Boxing and Olympic Rings
A452

Designs (Olympic Rings and): 60f, Canoeing. 1fo, Fencing. 1.50fo, Water polo. 2fo, Woman gymnast. 2.50fo, Hammer throwing. 3fo, Wrestling. 5fo, Swimming, butterfly stroke.

1970, Sept. 26   Photo.   Perf. 11

2036	A452	40f lt violet & multi	.20	.20
2037	A452	60f sky blue &		
		multi	.20	.20
2038	A452	1fo orange & multi	.20	.20
2039	A452	1.50fo multi	.20	.20
2040	A452	2fo multi	.25	.20
2041	A452	2.50fo multi	.30	.20
2042	A452	3fo multi	.40	.25
2043	A452	5fo multi	.60	.40
		Nos. 2036-2043 (8)	2.35	1.85

75th anniv. of the Hungarian Olympic Committee. The 5fo also publicizes the 1972 Olympic Games in Munich.
Exist imperf. Value, set $20.

Flame and Family
A453

1970, Sept. 28   Litho.   Perf. 12

2044	A453	1fo ultra, org & emer	.20	.20

5th Education Congress, Budapest.
Exists imperf. Value $6.

Chalice, by Benedek Suky, 1440 — A454

Hungarian Goldsmiths' Art: 60f, Altar burette, 1500. 1fo, Nadasdy goblet, 16th century. 1.50fo, Coconut goblet, 1600. 2fo, Silver tankard, by Mihaly Toldalaghy, 1623. 2.50fo, Communion cup of Gyorgy Rakoczy I, 1670. 3fo, Tankard, 1690. 4fo, Bell-flower cup, 1710.

1970, Oct.   Photo.   Perf. 12

2045	A454	40f gold & multi	.20	.20
2046	A454	60f gold & multi	.20	.20
2047	A454	1fo gold & multi	.20	.20
2048	A454	1.50fo gold & multi	.20	.20
2049	A454	2fo gold & multi	.20	.20
2050	A454	2.50fo gold & multi	.25	.20
2051	A454	3fo gold & multi	.40	.30
2052	A454	4fo gold & multi	.60	.40
		Nos. 2045-2052 (8)	2.25	1.90

Exist imperf. Value $20.

Virgin and Child, by Giampietrino — A455

Paintings from Christian Museum, Esztergom: 60f, "Love" (woman with 3 children), by Gregorio Lazzarini. 1fo, Legend of St. Catherine, by Master of Bat. 1.50fo, Adoration of the Shepherds, by Francesco Fontebasso, horiz. 2.50fo, Adoration of the Kings, by Master of Aranyosmarot. 4fo, Temptation of St. Anthony the Hermit, by Jan de Cock. 5fo, St. Sebastian, by Marco Palmezzano. 10fo, Lady with the Unicorn, by Painter of Lombardy.

1970, Dec. 7   Photo.   Perf. 12½

2053	A455	40f silver & multi	.20	.20
2054	A455	60f silver & multi	.20	.20
2055	A455	1fo silver & multi	.20	.20
2056	A455	1.50fo silver & multi	.20	.20
2057	A455	2.50fo silver & multi	.40	.20
2058	A455	4fo silver & multi	.65	.30
2059	A455	5fo silver & multi	.90	.40
		Nos. 2053-2059 (7)	2.75	1.70

Souvenir Sheet

2060	A455	10fo silver & multi	3.00	2.75

No. 2060 contains one 50½x56mm stamp.
Exist imperf. Values: set $20; souvenir sheet $20.

Monument to Hungarian Martyrs, by A. Makrisz — A456

1970, Dec. 30   Photo.   Perf. 12x11½

2061	A456	1fo ultra & sepia	.20	.20

The 25th anniversary of the liberation of the concentration camps at Auschwitz, Mauthausen and Dachau.
Exists imperf. Value $6.

"Souvenir Sheets"
Beginning in 1971, the government stamp agency, as well as a number of other state sanctioned organizations, have created souvenir sheets that do not have postal validity. These are not listed in this catalogue.

Marseillaise, by Francois Rude — A457

1971, Mar. 18   Litho.   Perf. 12

2062	A457	3fo bister & green	.40	.20

Centenary of the Paris Commune.
Exists imperf. Value $6.

Béla Bartók (1881-1945), Composer
A458

1971

Design: No. 2064, András L. Achim (1871-1911), peasant leader.

2063	A458	1fo gray & dk car	.55	.20
2064	A458	1fo gray & green	.20	.20

Issued: #2063, Mar. 25; #2064, Apr. 17.
Exist imperf. Value, set $13.

Györ Castle, 1594
A459

1971, Mar. 27

2065	A459	2fo lt blue & multi	.40	.20

700th anniversary of Györ.
Exists imperf. Value $6.

Bison Hunt — A460

Designs: 60f, Wild boar hunt. 80f, Deer hunt. 1fo, Falconry. 1.20fo, Felled stag and dogs. 2fo, Bustards. 3fo, Net fishing. 4fo, Angling.

1971, May   Photo.   Perf. 12

2066	A460	40f ver & multi	.20	.20
2067	A460	60f plum & multi	.20	.20
2068	A460	80f multi	.20	.20
2069	A460	1fo lilac & multi	.20	.20
2070	A460	1.20fo multi	.25	.20
2071	A460	2fo multi	.25	.20
2072	A460	3fo multi	.40	.30
2073	A460	4fo green & multi	.55	.40
		Nos. 2066-2073 (8)	2.25	1.90

World Hunting Exhibition, Budapest, Aug. 27-30. See No. C313.
Exist imperf. Value, set $30.

Souvenir Sheet

Portrait of a Man, by Dürer — A461

1971, May 21   Perf. 12½

2074	A461	10fo gold & multi	2.75	2.50

Albrecht Dürer (1471-1528), German painter and etcher.
Exists imperf. Value $25.

Carnation and Pioneers' Emblem — A462

1971, June 2   Photo.   Perf. 12

2075	A462	1fo dark red & multi	.20	.20

Hungarian Pioneers' Organization, 25th anniv.
Exists imperf. Value $6.

FIR Emblem, Resistance Fighters — A463

1971, July 3

2076	A463	1fo brown & multi	.30	.20

International Federation of Resistance Fighters (FIR), 20th anniversary.
Exists imperf. Value $6.

Walking in Garden, Tokyo School
A464

Japanese Prints from Museum of East Asian Art, Budapest: 60f, Geisha in Boat, by Yeishi (1756-1829). 1fo, Woman with Scroll, by Yeishi. 1.50fo, Courtesans, by Kiyonaga (1752-1815). 2fo, Awabi Fisher Women, by Utamaro (1753-1806). 2.50fo, Seated Courtesan, by Harunobu (1725-1770). 3fo, Peasant Woman Carrying Fagots, by Hokusai (1760-1849). 4fo, Women and Girls Walking, by Yeishi.

1971, July 9 — Perf. 12½

2077	A464	40f gold & multi	.20	.20
2078	A464	60f gold & multi	.20	.20
2079	A464	1fo gold & multi	.20	.20
2080	A464	1.50fo gold & multi	.20	.20
2081	A464	2fo gold & multi	.25	.20
2082	A464	2.50fo gold & multi	.30	.20
2083	A464	3fo gold & multi	.50	.25
2084	A464	5fo gold & multi	.75	.45
		Nos. 2077-2084 (8)	2.60	1.90

Exist imperf. Value, set $20.

Locomotive, Map of Rail System and Danube — A465

1971, July 15 — Litho. — Perf. 12
2086	A465	1fo multi	.30	.20

125th anniversary of first Hungarian railroad between Pest and Vac.
Exists imperf. Value $9.

Griffin Holding Ink Balls A466

1971, Sept. 11 — Photo. — Perf. 12x11½
2087	A466	1fo multicolored	1.00	.75

Centenary of stamp printing in Hungary. Printed se-tenant with 2 labels showing printing presses of 1871 and 1971 and Hungary Nos. P1 and 1171. Value unused, $1.
Exists imperf. Value, strip $15.

OIJ Emblem and Printed Page — A467

1971, Sept. 21 — Perf. 11½x12
2088	A467	1fo dk bl, bl & gold	.25	.20

25th anniversary of the International Organization of Journalists (OIJ).
Exists imperf. Value $7.

Josef Jacob Winterl and Barren Strawberry — A468

Plants: 60f, Bromeliaceae. 80f, Titanopsis calcarea. 1fo, Periwinkle. 1.20fo, Gymnocalycium. 2fo, White water lily. 3fo, Iris arenaria. 5fo, Peony.

1971, Oct. 29 — Litho. — Perf. 12
2089	A468	40f lt vio & multi	.20	.20
2090	A468	60f gray & multi	.20	.20
2091	A468	80f multi	.20	.20
2092	A468	1fo multi	.20	.20
2093	A468	1.20fo lilac & multi	.20	.20
2094	A468	2fo gray & multi	.30	.20
2095	A468	3fo multi	.50	.25
2096	A468	5fo multi	.75	.40
		Nos. 2089-2096 (8)	2.55	1.85

Bicentenary of Budapest Botanical Gardens.
Exist imperf. Value, set $25.

Galloping — A469

Equestrian Sports: 60f, Trotting. 80f, Horses fording river. 1fo, Jumping. 1.20fo, Start. 2fo, Polo. 3fo, Steeplechase. 5fo, Dressage.

1971, Nov. 22 — Photo. — Perf. 12
2097	A469	40f blue & multi	.20	.20
2098	A469	60f ocher & multi	.20	.20
2099	A469	80f olive & multi	.20	.20
2100	A469	1fo red & multi	.20	.20
2101	A469	1.20fo multi	.25	.20
2102	A469	2fo multi	.30	.20
2103	A469	3fo violet & multi	.50	.30
2104	A469	5fo blue & multi	.75	.50
		Nos. 2097-2104 (8)	2.60	2.00

Exist imperf. Value, set $20.

Beheading of Heathen Chief Koppany A470

Designs: 60f, Samuel Aba pursuing King Peter. 1fo, Basarad's victory over King Charles Robert. 1.50fo, Strife between King Salomon and Prince Geza. 2.50fo, Founding of Obuda Church by King Stephen I and Queen Gisela. 4fo, Reconciliation of King Koloman and his brother Almos. 5fo, Oradea Church built by King Ladislas I. 10fo, Funeral of Prince Emeric and blinding of Vazul.

1971, Dec. 10 — Litho.
2105	A470	40f buff & multi	.20	.20
2106	A470	60f buff & multi	.20	.20
2107	A470	1fo buff & multi	.20	.20
2108	A470	1.50fo buff & multi	.20	.20
2109	A470	2.50fo buff & multi	.25	.20
2110	A470	4fo buff & multi	.50	.30
2111	A470	5fo buff & multi	.75	.50
		Nos. 2105-2111 (7)	2.30	1.80

Miniature Sheet
Perf. 11½
2112	A470	10fo buff & multi	3.00	2.75

History of Hungary, from miniatures from Illuminated Chronicle of King Louis the Great, c. 1370. No. 2112 contains one stamp (size 44½x52mm).
Exist imperf. Value: set $20; souvenir sheet $25.

Equality Year Emblem A471

1971, Dec. 30 — Litho. — Perf. 12
2113	A471	1fo bister & multi	.30	.20

Intl. Year Against Racial Discrimination.
Exists imperf. Value $6.

Ice Hockey and Sapporo '72 Emblem — A472

Sport and Sapporo '72 Emblem: 60f, Men's slalom. 80f, Women's figure skating. 1fo, Ski jump. 1.20fo, Long-distance skiing. 2fo, Men's figure skating. 3fo, Bobsledding. 4fo, Biathlon. 10fo, Buddha.

1971, Dec. 30 — Perf. 12
2114	A472	40f black & multi	.20	.20
2115	A472	60f black & multi	.20	.20
2116	A472	80f black & multi	.20	.20
2117	A472	1fo black & multi	.20	.20
2118	A472	1.20fo black & multi	.25	.20
2119	A472	2fo black & multi	.35	.20
2120	A472	3fo black & multi	.50	.30
2121	A472	4fo black & multi	.75	.50
		Nos. 2114-2121 (8)	2.65	2.00

Souvenir Sheet
Perf. 11½
2122	A472	10fo gold & multi	2.75	2.50

11th Winter Olympic Games, Sapporo, Japan, Feb. 3-13, 1972. No. 2122 contains one 86x48mm stamp.
Exist imperf. Value: set $20; souvenir sheet $25.

Hungarian Locomotive — A473

Locomotives: 60f, Germany. 80f, Italy. 1fo, Soviet Union. 1.20fo, Japan. 2fo, Great Britain. 4fo, Austria. 5fo, France.

1972, Feb. 23 — Photo. — Perf. 12x11½
2123	A473	40f multi	.20	.20
2124	A473	60f ocher & multi	.20	.20
2125	A473	80f multi	.20	.20
2126	A473	1fo olive & multi	.20	.20
2127	A473	1.20fo ultra & multi	.35	.30
2128	A473	2fo ver & multi	.20	.20
2129	A473	4fo multi	.50	.25
2130	A473	5fo multi	.90	.45
		Nos. 2123-2130 (8)	2.75	2.00

Exist imperf. Value, set $30.

Janus Pannonius, by Andrea Mantegna A474

1972, Mar. 27 — Litho. — Perf. 12
2131	A474	1fo gold & multi	.25	.20

Janus Pannonius (Johannes Czezmiczei, 1434-1472), humanist and poet.
Exists imperf. Value $6.

Mariner 9 — A475

Design: No. 2133, Mars 2 and 3 spacecraft.

1972, Mar. 30 — Photo. — Perf. 11½x12
2132	A475	2fo dk blue & multi	.45	.45
2133	A475	2fo multi	.45	.45
a.		Strip #2132-2133 + label	1.25	1.25

Exploration of Mars by Mariner 9 (US), and Mars 2 and 3 (USSR). Issued in sheets containing 4 each of Nos. 2132-2133 and 4 labels inscribed in Hungarian, Russian and English. Exist imperf. Values: strip $12; sheetlet $40.

13th Century Church Portal — A476

1972, Apr. 11
2134	A476	3fo greenish black	.40	.20

Centenary of the Society for the Protection of Historic Monuments.
Exists imperf. Value $10.

Hungarian Greyhound — A477

Hounds: 60f, Afghan hound (head). 80f, Irish wolfhound. 1.20fo, Borzoi. 2fo, Running greyhound. 4fo, Whippet. 6fo, Afghan hound.

1972, Apr. 14 — Litho. — Perf. 12
2135	A477	40f multi	.20	.20
2136	A477	60f brown & multi	.20	.20
2137	A477	80f multi	.20	.20
2138	A477	1.20fo multi	.20	.20
2139	A477	2fo multi	.30	.20
2140	A477	4fo multi	.70	.20
2141	A477	6fo multi	1.10	.60
		Nos. 2135-2141 (7)	2.90	1.80

Exist imperf. Value, set $35.

József Imre, Emil Grósz, László Blaskovics (Ophthalmologists) — A478

Design: 2fo, Allvar Gullstrand, V. P. Filatov, Jules Gonin, ophthalmologists.

1972, Apr. 17
2142	A478	1fo red, brn & blk	.40	.20
2143	A478	2fo blue, brn & blk	.95	.45

First European Ophthalmologists' Congress, Budapest.
Exist imperf. Value, set $20.

Girl Reading and UNESCO Emblem A479

Roses — A480

1972, May 27 Photo. Perf. 11½x12
2144 A479 1fo multicolored .40 .20
International Book Year 1971.
Exists imperf. Value $6.

1972, June 1
2145 A480 1fo multicolored .40 .20
15th Rose Exhibition, Budapest.
Exists imperf. Value $6.

George Dimitrov A481

1972, June 18 Litho. Perf. 12
2146 A481 3fo black & multi .40 .20
90th anniversary, birth of George Dimitrov (1882-1949), communist leader.
Exists imperf. Value $6.

Souvenir Sheet

St. Martin and the Beggar, Stained-glass Window — A482

1972, June 20 Perf. 10½
2147 A482 10fo multi 2.75 2.50
Belgica 72, International Philatelic Exhibition, Brussels, June 24-July 9.
Exists imperf. Value $30.

Gyorgy Dozsa (1474-1514), Peasant Leader — A483

1972, June 25 Photo. Perf. 11½x12
2148 A483 1fo red & multi .20 .20
Exists imperf. Value $6.

Olympic Rings, Soccer — A484

Designs (Olympic Rings and): 60f, Water polo. 80f, Javelin, women's. 1fo, Kayak, women's. 1.20fo, Boxing. 2fo, Gymnastics, women's. 5fo, Fencing.

1972, July 15 Perf. 11
2149 A484 40f multi .20 .20
2150 A484 60f multi .20 .20
2151 A484 80f multi .20 .20
2152 A484 1fo lilac & multi .20 .20
2153 A484 1.20fo blue & multi .20 .20
2154 A484 2fo multi .40 .25
2155 A484 5fo green & multi .75 .50
Nos. 2149-2155,B299 (8) 2.65 2.05
20th Olympic Games, Munich, Aug. 26-Sept. 11. See No. C325.
Exist imperf. Value, set $25.

Prince Geza Selecting Site of Székesfehérvár — A485

Designs: 60f, St. Stephen, first King of Hungary. 80f, Knights (country's defense). 1.20fo, King Stephen dictating to scribe (legal organization). 2fo, Sculptor at work (education). 4fo, Merchants before king (foreign relations). 6fo, View of castle and town of Székesfehérvár, 10th century. 10fo, King Andreas II presenting Golden Bull to noblemen.

1972, Aug. 20 Photo. Perf. 12
2156 A485 40f slate & multi .20 .20
2157 A485 60f multi .20 .20
2158 A485 80f lilac & multi .20 .20
2159 A485 1.20fo multi .20 .20
2160 A485 2fo bister & multi .40 .20
2161 A485 4fo blue & multi .55 .25
2162 A485 6fo purple & multi .75 .50
Nos. 2156-2162 (7) 2.50 1.75

Souvenir Sheet
Perf. 12½
2163 A485 10fo black & multi 3.00 3.00
Millennium of the town of Székesfehérvár; 750th anniv. of the Golden Bull granting rights to lesser nobility. #2163 contains one 94x45mm stamp.
Exist imperf. Value: set $20; souvenir sheet $20.

Parliament, Budapest A486

Design: 6fo, Session room of Parliament.

1972, Aug. 20 Litho.
2164 A486 5fo dk blue & multi .60 .25
2165 A486 6fo multicolored .75 .30
Constitution of 1949.
Exist imperf. Value, set $15.

Eger, 17th Century View, and Bottle of Bull's Blood — A487

Design: 2fo, Contemporary view of Tokay and bottle of Tokay Aszu.

1972, Aug. 21 Litho. Perf. 12
2166 A487 1fo buff & multi .30 .20
2167 A487 2fo green & multi .65 .20
1st World Wine Exhibition, Budapest, Aug. 1972.
Exist imperf. Value, set $15.

Georgikon Emblems, Grain, Potato Flower — A488

1972, Sept. 3
2168 A488 1fo multi .20 .20
175th anniv. of the founding of the Georgikon at Keszthely, the 1st scientific agricultural academy.
Exists imperf. Value $6.

Covered Candy Dish — A489

Herend Porcelain: 40f, Vase with bird. 80f, Vase with flowers and butterflies. 1fo, Plate with Mexican landscape. 1.20fo, Covered dish. 2fo, Teapot, cup and saucer. 4fo, Plate with flowers. 5fo, Baroque vase showing Herend factory.

1972, Sept. 15
Sizes: 23x46mm (40f, 80f, 2fo, 5fo);
33x36mm, others
2169 A489 40f gray & multi .20 .20
2170 A489 60f ocher & multi .20 .20
2171 A489 80f multi .20 .20
2172 A489 1fo multi .20 .20
2173 A489 1.20fo green & multi .20 .20
2174 A489 2fo multi .30 .20
2175 A489 4fo red & multi .50 .30
2176 A489 5fo multi .70 .50
Nos. 2169-2176 (8) 2.50 2.00
Herend china factory, founded 1839.
Exist imperf. Value, set $20.

UIC Emblem and M-62 Diesel Locomotive — A490

1972, Sept. 19 Photo. Perf. 11½x12
2177 A490 1fo dark red .35 .20
50th anniversary of International Railroad Union Congress, Budapest, Sept. 19.
Exist imperf. Value $15.

"25" and Graph — A491

1972, Sept. Perf. 11½x12
2178 A491 1fo yellow & brown .35 .20
Planned national economy, 25th anniv.
Exists imperf. Value $8.

Budapest, 1972 — A492

#2179, View of Obuda, 1872. #2181, Buda, 1872. #2183, Pest, 1872. #2182, 2184, Budapest, 1972.

1972, Sept. 26 Perf. 12x11½
2179 A492 1fo Prus bl & rose car .20 .20
2180 A492 1fo rose car & Prus bl .20 .20
a. Pair, #2179-2180 .40 .20
2181 A492 2fo ocher & olive .30 .20
2182 A492 2fo olive & ocher .30 .20
a. Pair, #2181-2182 .75 .35
2183 A492 3fo green & lt brn .40 .20
2184 A492 3fo lt brown & grn .40 .20
a. Pair, #2183-2184 1.25 .50
Nos. 2179-2184 (6) 1.80 1.20
Centenary of unification of Obuda, Buda and Pest into Budapest.
Exist imperf. Value, set in pairs $30.

Ear and Congress Emblem A493

1972, Oct. 3 Perf. 11½x12
2185 A493 1fo brown, yel & blk .20 .20
11th Intl. Audiology Cong., Budapest.
Exists imperf. Value $8.

Flora Martos — A494

1972 Photo. Perf. 11½x12
Portrait: No. 2187, Miklós Radnóti.
2186 A494 1fo green & multi .20 .20
2187 A494 1fo brown & multi .20 .20
Flora Martos (1897-1938), Hungarian Labor Party leader, & Miklós Radnóti (1909-44), poet.
Exist imperf. Value, set $8.
Issued: #2186, Nov. 5; #2187, Nov. 11.

Muses, by
Jozsef Rippl-
Ronai
A495

Stained-glass Windows, 19th-20th Centuries: 60f, 16th century scribe, by Ferenc Sebesteny. 1fo, Flight into Egypt, by Karoly Lotz and Bertalan Székely. 1.50fo, Prince Arpad's Messenger, by Jenö Percz. 2.50fo, Nativity, by Lili Sztehlo. 4fo, Prince Arpad and Leaders, by Karoly Kernstock. 5fo, King Matthias and Jester, by Jenö Haranghy.

1972, Nov. 15   **Perf. 12**
2188	A495	40f multi	.20	.20
2189	A495	60f multi	.20	.20
2190	A495	1fo multi	.20	.20
2191	A495	1.50fo multi	.20	.20
2192	A495	2.50fo multi	.35	.20
2193	A495	4fo multi	.65	.30
2194	A495	5fo multi	1.10	.50
		Nos. 2188-2194 (7)	2.90	1.80

Exist imperf. Value, set $20.

Weaver, Cloth and Cogwheel — A496

1972, Nov. 27   **Litho.**   **Perf. 12**
2195	A496	1fo silver & multi	.25	.20

Opening of Museum of Textile Techniques, Budapest.
Exists imperf. Value $7.

Main Square,
Szarvas — A497

Designs: 1fo, Modern buildings, Salgotarjan. 3fo, Tokay and vineyard. 4fo, Esztergom Cathedral. 7fo, Town Hall, Kaposvar. 20fo, Veszprem.

1972   **Litho.**   **Perf. 11**
2196	A497	40f brown & orange	.20	.20
2197	A497	1fo dk & lt blue	.20	.20

Exist imperf. Value, set $20.

Church and
City Hall,
Vac — A498

1973   **Perf. 12x11½**
2198	A498	3fo dk & lt green	.40	.20
2199	A498	4fo red brn & org	.50	.20
2200	A498	7fo blue vio & lil	1.00	.20
2200A	A498	20fo multicolored	2.50	.40
		Nos. 2196-2200A (6)	4.80	1.40

Exist imperf. Value, set $45.
See Nos. 2330-2335.

Coil Stamps
Type of 1963-64

Designs as before.

1972, Nov.   **Photo.**   **Perf. 14**
Size: 21½x17½mm, 17½x21½mm
2201	A336	2fo blue green	.40	.20
2202	A336	3fo dark blue	.55	.20
2203	A336	4fo blue, vert.	.75	.25
2204	A336	6fo bister	1.10	.35
		Nos. 2201-2204 (4)	2.80	1.00

Black control number on back of every 5th stamp.

Minute inscription centered in lower margin: "Legrady Sandor."

Arms of Soviet
Union — A498a

1972, Dec. 30   **Photo.**   **Perf. 11½x12**
2205	A498a	1fo multicolored	.20	.20

50th anniversary of Soviet Union.
Exists imperf. Value $15.

Petöfi
Speaking at
Pilvax Cafe
A499

2fo, Portrait. 3fo, Petöfi on horseback, 1848-49.

1972, Dec. 30   **Engr.**   **Perf. 12**
2206	A499	1fo rose carmine	.20	.20
2207	A499	2fo violet	.35	.20
2208	A499	3fo Prus green	.45	.25
		Nos. 2206-2208 (3)	1.00	.65

Sesquicentennial of the birth of Sandor Petöfi (1823-49), poet and revolutionary.
Exist imperf. Value, set $20.

Postal Zone Map of Hungary and
Letter-carrying Crow — A500

1973, Jan. 1   **Litho.**   **Perf. 12**
2209	A500	1fo red & black	.20	.20

Introduction of postal code system.
Exists imperf. Value $7.

Imre Madách
(1823-64), Poet
and Dramatist
A501

1973, Jan. 20   **Photo.**   **Perf. 11½x12**
2210	A501	1fo multicolored	.20	.20

Exists imperf. Value $8.

Busho
Mask — A502

Designs: Various Busho masks.

1973, Feb. 17   **Litho.**   **Perf. 12**
2211	A502	40f tan & multi	.20	.20
2212	A502	60f dull grn & multi	.20	.20
2213	A502	80f lilac & multi	.20	.20
2214	A502	1.20fo multi	.20	.20
2215	A502	2fo tan & multi	.30	.20
2216	A502	4fo multi	.50	.30
2217	A502	6fo lilac & multi	.75	.40
		Nos. 2211-2217 (7)	2.35	1.70

Busho Walk at Mohacs, ancient ceremony to drive out winter.
Exist imperf. Value, set $20.

Nicolaus
Copernicus
A503

1973, Feb. 19   **Engr.**   **Perf. 12**
2218	A503	3fo bright ultra	.75	.50

Printed with alternating label showing heliocentric system and view of Torun.
Exists imperf. Value $15.

Vascular
System and
WHO Emblem
A504

1973, Apr. 16   **Photo.**   **Perf. 12**
2219	A504	1fo sl grn & brn red	.25	.20

25th anniv. of WHO.
Exists imperf. Value $7.

Tank,
Rocket,
Radar,
Plane,
Ship
and
Soldier
A505

1973, May 9   **Litho.**   **Perf. 12**
2220	A505	3fo blue & multi	.50	.20

Philatelic Exhibition of Military Stamp Collectors of Warsaw Treaty Member States. No. 2220 was printed with alternating label showing flags of Warsaw Treaty members.
Exists imperf. Value $15.

Hungary No. 1396 and IBRA '73
Emblem — A506

1973, May 11   **Litho.**   **Perf. 12**
2221	A506	40f shown	.20	.20
2222	A506	60f No. 1397, POLSKA '73	.20	.20
2223	A506	80f No. 1398, IBRA '73	.20	.20
2224	A506	1fo No. 1399, POLSKA	.20	.20
2225	A506	1.20fo No. B293a, IBRA	.20	.20
2226	A506	2fo No. B293b, POLSKA	.25	.20
2227	A506	4fo No. B293c, IBRA	.50	.30
2228	A506	5fo No. B293d, POLSKA	.75	.40
		Nos. 2221-2228 (8)	2.50	1.90

Publicity for IBRA '73 International Philatelic Exhibition, Munich, May 11-20; and POLSKA '73, Poznan, Aug. 15-Sept. 2. See No. C345.
Exist imperf. Value, set $20.

Typesetting,
from "Orbis
Pictus," by
Comenius
A507

3fo, Printer & wooden screw press, woodcut from Hungarian translation of Gospels.

1973, June 5   **Photo.**   **Perf. 11½x12**
2229	A507	1fo black & gold	.20	.20
2230	A507	3fo black & gold	.40	.20

500th anniv. of book printing in Hungary.
Exist imperf. Value $12.

Storm over Hortobagy Puszta, by
Csontvary — A508

Paintings: 60f, Mary's Well, Nazareth. 1fo, Carriage Ride by Moonlight in Athens, vert. 1.50fo, Pilgrimage to Cedars of Lebanon, vert. 2.50fo, The Lonely Cedar. 4fo, Waterfall at Jajce. 5fo, Ruins of Greek Theater at Taormina. 10fo, Horseback Riders on Shore.

1973, June 18   **Perf. 12½**
2231	A508	40f gold & multi	.20	.20
2232	A508	60f gold & multi	.20	.20
2233	A508	1fo gold & multi	.20	.20
2234	A508	1.50fo gold & multi	.20	.20
2235	A508	2.50fo gold & multi	.40	.20
2236	A508	4fo gold & multi	.65	.35
2237	A508	5fo gold & multi	.80	.50
		Nos. 2231-2237 (7)	2.65	1.85

Souvenir Sheet
2238	A508	10fo gold & multi	3.50	3.00

Paintings by Tividar Kosztka Csontvary (1853-1919). No. 2238 contains one stamp (size: 90x43mm).
Exist imperf. Value: set $20; souvenir sheet $30.

Hands Holding Map of Europe — A509

Flowers — A510

1973, July 3   Photo.   Perf. 11½x12
2239 A509 2.50fo blk & gldn
                brn   3.00   3.00
  a. Sheetlet of 4 + 2 labels   10.00   9.00

Conference for European Security and Cooperation. Helsinki, July 1973. No. 2239 was printed in a sheetlet of 4 stamps and 2 blue labels showing conference sites.
Exists imperf. Value, sheetlet $200.

1973, Aug. 4
2240 A510 40f   Provence roses   .20   .20
2241 A510 60f   Cyclamen   .20   .20
2242 A510 80f   Lungwort   .20   .20
2243 A510 1.20fo English daisies   .20   .20
2244 A510 2fo   Buttercups   .30   .20
2245 A510 4fo   Violets   .70   .30
2246 A510 6fo   Poppies   1.00   .50
      Nos. 2240-2246 (7)   2.80   1.80

Exist imperf. Value, set $20.

"Let's be Friends in Traffic" — A511

Designs: 60f, "Not even one drink." 1fo, "Light your bicycle."

1973, Aug. 18   Photo.   Perf. 12x11½
2247 A511 40f   green & orange   .20   .20
2248 A511 60f   purple & orange   .20   .20
2249 A511 1fo   indigo & orange   .20   .20
      Nos. 2247-2249 (3)   .60   .60

To publicize traffic rules.
Exist imperf. Value $17.

Adoration of the Kings A512

Paintings: 60f, Angels playing violin and lute. 1fo, Adoration of the Kings. 1.50fo, Annunciation. 2.50fo, Angels playing organ and harp. 4fo, Visitation of Mary. 5fo, Legend of St. Catherine of Alexandria. 10fo, Nativity.

1973, Nov. 3   Photo.   Perf. 12½
2250 A512 40f   gold & multi   .20   .20
2251 A512 60f   gold & multi   .20   .20
2252 A512 1fo   gold & multi   .20   .20
2253 A512 1.50fo gold & multi   .25   .20
2254 A512 2.50fo gold & multi   .40   .25
2255 A512 4fo   gold & multi   .60   .30
2256 A512 5fo   gold & multi   .80   .50
      Nos. 2250-2256 (7)   2.65   1.85

Souvenir Sheet
Perf. 11
2257 A512 10fo gold & multi   3.00   2.75

Paintings by Hungarian anonymous early masters from the Christian Museum at Esztergom. No. 2257 contains one 49x74mm stamp.
Exist imperf. Value: set $20; souvenir sheet $20.

Mihaly Csokonai Vitez — A513

1973, Nov. 17   Photo.   Perf. 11½x12
2258 A513 2fo bister & multi   .35   .20

Mihaly Csokonai Vitez (1773-1805), poet.
Exists imperf. Value $6.

José Marti and Cuban Flag — A514

1973, Nov. 30
2259 A514 1fo dk brn, red & bl   .20   .20

Marti (1853-95), Cuban natl. hero and poet.
Exists imperf. Value $6.

Barnabas Pesti (1920-44), Member of Hungarian Underground Communist Party — A515

1973, Nov. 30
2260 A515 1fo blue, brn & buff   .20   .20

Exists imperf. Value $6.

Women's Double Kayak — A516

Designs: 60f, Water polo. 80f, Men's single kayak. 1.20fo, Butterfly stroke. 2fo, Men's fours kayak. 4fo, Men's single canoe. 6fo, Men's double canoe.

1973, Dec. 29   Litho.   Perf. 12x11
2261 A516 40f   red & multi   .20   .20
2262 A516 60f   blue & multi   .20   .20
2263 A516 80f   multicolored   .20   .20
2264 A516 1.20fo green & multi   .25   .20
2265 A516 2fo   car & multi   .35   .20
2266 A516 4fo   violet & multi   .45   .30
2267 A516 6fo   multicolored   .50   .50
      Nos. 2261-2267 (7)   2.15   1.80

Hungarian victories in water sports at Tampere and Belgrade.
Exist imperf. Value, set $25.

Souvenir Sheet

Map of Europe — A517

1974, Jan. 15   Photo.   Perf. 12x11½
2268   Sheet of 2 + label   8.50   8.00
  a. A517 5fo multicolored   2.25   2.25

European Peace Conference (Arab-Israeli War), Geneva, Jan. 1974.
Exists imperf. Value $150.

Lenin — A518

1974, Jan. 21   Photo.   Perf. 11½x12
2269 A518 2fo gold, dull bl & brn .50   .20

50th anniv. of the death of Lenin (1870-1924).
Exists imperf. Value $7.

Jozsef Boczor, Imre Békés, Tamás Elek — A519

1974, Feb. 21   Perf. 12½
2270 A519 3fo brown & multi   .25   .20

30th anniversary of the death in France of Hungarian resistance fighters.
Exists imperf. Value $7.

Comecon Building, Moscow and Flags A520

1974, Feb. 26   Photo.   Perf. 12x11½
2271 A520 1fo multicolored   .25   .20

25th anniversary of the Council of Mutual Economic Assistance.
Exists imperf. Value $9.

Bank Emblem, Coins and Banknote A521

1974, Mar. 1   Perf. 11½x12
2272 A521 1fo lt green & multi   .25   .20

25th anniversary of the State Savings Bank.
Exists imperf. Value $6.

Spacecraft on Way to Mars — A522

Designs: 60f, Mars 2 over Mars. 80f, Mariner 4. 1fo, Mars and Mt. Palomar Observatory. 1.20fo, Soft landing of Mars 3. 5fo, Mariner 9 with Mars satellites Phobos and Deimos.

1974, Mar. 11   Photo.   Perf. 12½
2273 A522 40f   gold & multi   .20   .20
2274 A522 60f   silver & multi   .20   .20
2275 A522 80f   gold & multi   .20   .20
2276 A522 1fo   silver & multi   .20   .20
2277 A522 1.20fo gold & multi   .25   .20
2278 A522 5fo   silver & multi   .75   .40
      Nos. 2273-2278,C347 (7)   2.55   1.90

Exploration of Mars. See No. C348.
Exist imperf. Value, set (7) $20.

Salvador Allende (1908-73), Pres. of Chile — A523

1974, Mar. 27   Photo.   Perf. 11½x12
2279 A523 1fo black & multi   .20   .20

Exists imperf. Value $6.

Mona Lisa, by Leonardo da Vinci A524

1974, Apr. 19   Perf. 12½
2280 A524 4fo gold & multi   6.25   6.00

Exists imperf. Value $20. Exhibition of the Mona Lisa in Asia.
Printed in sheets of 6 stamps and 6 labels with commemorative inscription. Value, $65.
Exist imperf. Value: single with labels $30; sheetlet $200.

Souvenir Sheet

Issue of 1874 and Flowers — A525

a, Mallow. b, Aster. c, Daisy. d, Columbine.

1974, May 11   Litho.   Perf. 11½
2281 A525 Sheet of 4   2.75   2.75
  a.-d. 2.50fo any single   .50   .50

Centenary of the first issue inscribed "Magyar Posta" (Hungarian Post).
Exists imperf. Value, sheet of 4 $30.

Carrier Pigeon, World Map, UPU Emblem — A526

1974, May 22   Litho.   Perf. 12
2282	A526	40f shown	.20	.20
2283	A526	60f Mail coach	.20	.20
2284	A526	80f Old mail automobile	.25	.20
2285	A526	1.20fo Balloon post	.35	.20
2286	A526	2fo Mail train	.45	.20
2287	A526	4fo Mail bus	1.00	.40
		Nos. 2282-2287,C349 (7)	3.20	2.00

Centenary of the Universal Postal Union.
Exist imperf. Value, set $25.

Dove of Basel, Switzerland No. 3L1, 1845 — A527

1974, June 7   Photo.   Perf. 11½x12
2288	A527	3fo gold & multi	1.25	1.25

INTERNABA 1974 Philatelic Exhibition, Basel, June 7-16. No. 2288 issued in sheets of 3 stamps and 3 labels showing Internaba 1974 emblem. Size: 104x125mm.
Exist imperf. Values: single $12; sheet $35.

Chess Players, from 13th Century Manuscript A528

Designs: 60f, Chess players, 15th century English woodcut. 80f, Royal chess party, 15th century Italian chess book. 1.20fo, Chess players, 17th century copper engraving by Selenus. 2fo, Farkas Kempelen's chess playing machine, 1769. 4fo, Hungarian Grand Master Geza Maroczy (1870-1951). 6fo, View of Nice and emblem of 1974 Chess Olympiad.

1974, June 6   Litho.   Perf. 12
2289	A528	40f multi	.20	.20
2290	A528	60f multi	.20	.20
2291	A528	80f multi	.25	.20
2292	A528	1.20fo multi	.30	.20
2293	A528	2fo multi	.45	.20
2294	A528	4fo multi	1.10	.30
2295	A528	6fo multi	1.75	.50
		Nos. 2289-2295 (7)	4.25	1.80

50th anniv. of Intl. Chess Federation and 21st Chess Olympiad, Nice, June 6-30.
Exist imperf. Value, set $170.

Souvenir Sheet

Cogwheel Railroad — A529

Designs: a, Passenger train, 1874. b, Freight train, 1874. c, Electric train, 1929-73. d, Twin motor train, 1973.

1974, June 25   Litho.   Perf. 12
2296	A529	Sheet of 4	3.50	3.25
a.-d.		2.50fo, any single	.50	.50

Cent. of Budapest's cogwheel railroad.
Exist imperf. Value, sheet $40.

Congress Emblem (Globe and Parliament) — A530

1974, Aug. 18   Photo.   Perf. 12
2297	A530	2fo silver, dk & lt bl	.35	.20

4th World Congress of Economists, Budapest, Aug. 19-24.
Exists imperf. Value $5.50.

Bathing Woman, by Károly Lotz A531

Paintings of Nudes: 60f, Awakening, by Károly Brocky. 1fo, Venus and Cupid, by Brocky, horiz. 1.50fo, After the Bath, by Lotz. 2.50fo, Resting Woman, by Istvan Csok, horiz. 4fo, After the Bath, by Bertalan Szekely. 5fo, "Devotion," by Erzsebet Korb. 10fo, Lark, by Pál Szinyei Merse.

1974, Aug.   Perf. 12½
2298	A531	40f gold & multi	.20	.20
2299	A531	60f gold & multi	.20	.20
2300	A531	1fo gold & multi	.20	.20
2301	A531	1.50fo gold & multi	.30	.20
2302	A531	2.50fo gold & multi	.35	.20
2303	A531	4fo gold & multi	.70	.25
2304	A531	5fo gold & multi	.90	.40
		Nos. 2298-2304 (7)	2.85	1.65

Souvenir Sheet
Perf. 11
2305	A531	10fo gold & multi	3.25	3.00

No. 2305 contains one stamp (45x70mm).
Exist imperf. Value: set $30; souvenir sheet $30.

Mimi, by Béla Czóbel A532

1974, Sept. 4
2306	A532	1fo multicolored	.50	.20

91st birthday of Béla Czóbel, Hungarian painter.
Exists imperf. Value $8.

Intersputnik Tracking Station — A533

High Voltage Line "Peace" and Pipe Line "Friendship" A534

Perf. 11½x12, 12x11½
1974, Sept. 5   Litho.
2307	A533	1fo blue & violet	.20	.20
2308	A534	3fo multicolored	.60	.20

Technical assistance and cooperation between Hungary and USSR, 25th anniv.
Exist imperf. Value, set $12.

Pablo Neruda — A535

1974, Sept. 11   Photo.   Perf. 11½x12
2309	A535	1fo multicolored	.20	.20

Pablo Neruda (Neftali Ricar do Reyes, 1904-1973), Chilean poet.
Exists imperf. Value $6.

Sweden No. 1 and Lion from Royal Palace, Stockholm A536

1974, Sept. 21   Perf. 12x11½
2310	A536	3fo ultra, yel grn & gold	1.50	1.50

Stockholmia 74 Intl. Philatelic Exhibition, Stockholm, Sept. 21-29. No. 2310 issued in sheets of 3 stamps and 3 labels showing Stockholmia emblem. White margin inscribed "UPU" multiple in white. Size: 126x104mm. Value $6.50.
Exists imperf. Value: single $10; sheetlet $30.

Tank Battle and Soldier with Anti-tank Grenade — A537

1974, Sept. 28   Litho.   Perf. 12
2311	A537	1fo gold, orange & blk	.20	.20
		Nos. 2311,C351-C352 (3)	.90	.60

Army Day.
Exist imperf. Value (3) $17.

Segner and Segner Crater on Moon A538

1974, Oct. 5
2312	A538	3fo multicolored	.75	.25

270th anniversary of the birth of Janos Andras Segner, naturalist. No. 2312 printed se-tenant with label arranged checkerwise in sheet. Label shows Segner wheel.
Exists imperf. Value, with label $15.

Rhyparia Purpurata — A539

Lepidoptera: 60f, Melanargia galathea. 80f, Parnassius Apollo. 1fo, Celerio euphorbia. 1.20fo, Catocala fraxini. 5fo, Apatura iris. 6fo, Palaeochrysophanus hyppothoe.

1974, Nov. 11   Photo.   Perf. 12½
2313	A539	40f multicolored	.20	.20
2314	A539	60f violet & multi	.20	.20
2315	A539	80f multicolored	.20	.20
2316	A539	1fo brown & multi	.20	.20
2317	A539	1.20fo blue & multi	.25	.25
2318	A539	5fo purple & multi	.75	.30
2319	A539	6fo multicolored	1.00	.40
		Nos. 2313-2319 (7)	2.80	1.75

Exist imperf. Value, set $25.

Motherhood A540

1974, Dec. 24   Litho.   Perf. 12
2320	A540	1fo lt blue, blk & yel	.25	.20

Exists imperf. Value $6.

Robert Kreutz — A541

1974, Dec. 24
2321	A541	1fo shown	.30	.20
2322	A541	1fo István Pataki	.30	.20

30th death anniv. of anti-fascist martyrs Kreutz (1923-44) and Pataki (1914-44).
Exist imperf. Value, set $12.

Puppy
A542

Young Animals: 60f, Siamese kittens, horiz. 80f, Rabbit. 1.20fo, Foal, horiz. 2fo, Lamb. 4fo, Calf, horiz. 6fo, Piglet.

1974, Dec. 30
2323	A542	40f lt blue & multi	.20	.20
2324	A542	60f multicolored	.20	.20
2325	A542	80f olive & multi	.20	.20
2326	A542	1.20fo green & multi	.20	.20
2327	A542	2fo brown & multi	.30	.20
2328	A542	4fo orange & multi	.70	.30
2329	A542	6fo violet & multi	1.10	.50
		Nos. 2323-2329 (7)	2.90	1.80

Exist imperf. Value, set $20.
See Nos. 2403-2409.

Building Type of 1972

4fo, Szentendre. 5fo, View of Szolnok across Tisza River. 6fo, Skyscraper, Dunaújváros. 8fo, Church and city hall, Vac. 10fo, City Hall, Kiskunfélegyháza. 50fo, Church (Turkish Mosque), Hunyadi Statue & TV tower, Pecs.

1974-80   Litho.   Perf. 12x11½
2330	A498	4fo red brn & pink	.60	.20
2331	A498	5fo dk blue & ultra	.75	.20
2332	A498	6fo dk brn & org	.90	.20
2333	A498	8fo dk & brt grn	1.25	.20
2334	A498	10fo brown & yel	1.75	.20
2335	A498	50fo multi	6.00	1.25
		Nos. 2330-2335 (6)	11.25	2.25

Exist imperf. Value, set $90.
Issued: 8fo, 12/7; 10fo, 50fo, 12/30; 5fo, 3/8/75; 6fo, 6/10/75; 4fo, 6/20/80.

Hospital, Lambarene — A544

60f, Dr. Schweitzer, patient & microscope. 80f, Patient arriving by boat. 1.20fo, Hospital supplies arriving by ship. 2fo, Globe, Red Cross, carrier pigeons. 4fo, Nobel Peace Prize medal. 6fo, Portrait & signature of Dr. Schweitzer, organ pipes & "J. S. Bach."

1975, Jan. 14   Photo.   Perf. 12
2340	A544	40f gold & multi	.20	.20
2341	A544	60f gold & multi	.20	.20
2342	A544	80f gold & multi	.20	.20
2343	A544	1.20fo gold & multi	.20	.20
2344	A544	2fo gold & multi	.25	.20
2345	A544	4fo gold & multi	.60	.30
2346	A544	6fo lil & multi	.80	.45
		Nos. 2340-2346 (7)	2.45	1.75

Dr. Albert Schweitzer (1875-1965), medical missionary and musician, birth centenary.
Exist imperf. Value, set $20.

Farkas
Bolyai — A545

1975, Feb. 7   Litho.   Perf. 11½x12
| 2347 | A545 | 1fo gray & red brown | .20 | .20 |

Bolyai (1775-1856), mathematician.
Exists imperf. Value $8.

Mihály Károlyi
A546

1975, Mar. 4   Litho.   Perf. 12
| 2348 | A546 | 1fo lt blue & brown | .20 | .20 |

Birth centenary of Count Mihály Károlyi (1875-1955), prime minister, 1918-1919.
Exists imperf. Value $5.50.

Woman, IWY Emblem A547

1975, Mar. 8   Perf. 12x11½
| 2349 | A547 | 1fo aqua & black | .20 | .20 |

International Women's Year 1975.
Exists imperf. Value $5.50.

"Let us Build up the Railroads" — A548

Posters: 60f, "Bread starts here." 2fo, "Hungarian Communist Party-a Party of Action." 4fo, "Heavy Industry-secure base of Three-year Plan." 5fo, "Our common interest-a developed socialist society."

1975, Mar. 17   Photo.   Perf. 11
2350	A548	40f red & multi	.20	.20
2351	A548	60f red & multi	.20	.20
2352	A548	2fo red & multi	.20	.20
2353	A548	4fo red & multi	.40	.20
2354	A548	5fo red & multi	.50	.30
		Nos. 2350-2354 (5)	1.50	1.10

Hungary's liberation from Fascism, 30th anniv.
Exist imperf. Value, set $20.

Arrow, 1915, Pagoda and Mt. Fuji — A549

Antique Cars: 60f, Swift, 1911, Big Ben and Tower of London. 80f, Model T Ford, 1908, Capitol and Statue of Liberty. 1fo, Mercedes, 1901, Towers of Stuttgart. 1.20fo, Panhard Levassor, 1912, Arc de Triomphe and Eiffel Tower. 5fo, Csonka, 1906, Fishermen's Bastion and Chain Bridge. 6fo, Emblems of Hungarian Automobile Club, Alliance Internationale de Tourisme and Federation Internationale de l'Automobile.

1975, Mar. 27   Litho.   Perf. 12
2355	A549	40f lt blue & multi	.20	.20
2356	A549	60f lt green & multi	.20	.20
2357	A549	80f pink & multi	.20	.20
2358	A549	1fo lilac & multi	.20	.20
2359	A549	1.20fo orange & multi	.20	.20
2360	A549	5fo ultra & multi	.65	.30
2361	A549	6fo lilac rose & multi	1.00	.50
		Nos. 2355-2361 (7)	2.65	1.80

Hungarian Automobile Club, 75th anniv.
Exist imperf. Value, set $25.

The Creation of Adam, by Michelangelo — A550

1975, Apr. 23   Photo.   Perf. 12½
| 2362 | A550 | 10fo gold & multi | 3.50 | 3.25 |

Michelangelo Buonarroti (1475-1564), Italian painter, sculptor and architect.
Exists imperf. Value $28.

Academy of Science A551

Designs: 2fo, Dates "1975 1825." 3fo, Count Istvan Szechenyi.

1975, May 5   Litho.   Perf. 12
2363	A551	1fo green & multi	.20	.20
2364	A551	2fo green & multi	.30	.20
2365	A551	3fo green & multi	.50	.30
		Nos. 2363-2365 (3)	1.00	.70

Sesquicentennial of Academy of Science, Budapest, founded by Count Istvan Szechenyi.
Exists imperf. Value, set $20.

Emblem of 1980 Olympics and Proposed Moscow Stadium — A553

1975, May 8   Photo.   Perf. 11½x12
| 2366 | A553 | 5fo lt blue & multi | 1.50 | 1.25 |

Socflex 75 Intl. Philatelic Exhibition, Moscow, 5/8-18. #2366 issued in sheets of 3 stamps and 3 labels showing Socfilex 75 emblem (War Memorial, Berlin-Treptow).
Exists imperf. Value: single with label $17.50; sheetlet $55.

France No. 1100 and Venus of Milo — A554

1975, June 3   Photo.   Perf. 11½x12
| 2367 | A554 | 5fo lilac & multi | 1.50 | 1.25 |

ARPHILA 75 International Philatelic Exhibition, Paris, June 6-16. No. 2367 issued in sheets of 3 stamps and 3 labels showing ARPHILA 75 emblem.
Exists imperf. Value: single with label $15; sheetlet $40.

Early Transformer, Kando Locomotive, 1902, Pylon — A555

1975, June 10   Litho.   Perf. 12
| 2368 | A555 | 1fo multicolored | .30 | .20 |

Hungarian Electrotechnical Association, 75th anniversary.
Exists imperf. Value $15.

Epée, Saber, Foil and Globe — A556

1975, July 11
| 2369 | A556 | 1fo multicolored | .25 | .20 |

32nd World Fencing Championships, Budapest, July 11-20.
Exists imperf. Value $12.

Souvenir Sheet

Whale Pavilion, Oceanexpo 75 — A557

1975, July 21   Photo.   Perf. 12½
| 2370 | A557 | 10fo gold & multi | 3.00 | 2.75 |

Oceanexpo 75, International Exhibition, Okinawa, July 20, 1975-Jan. 1976.
Exists imperf. Value $40.

Dr. Agoston Zimmermann (1875-1963), Veterinarian A558

1975, Sept. 4   Litho.   Perf. 12
| 2371 | A558 | 1fo brown & blue | .20 | .20 |

Exists imperf. Value $8.

Symbolic of 14 Cognate Languages A559

1975, Sept. 9
| 2372 | A559 | 1fo gold & multi | .20 | .20 |

International Finno-Ugrian Congress.

Exists imperf. Value $7.

Voters — A560

Design: No. 2374, Map of Hungary with electoral districts.

1975, Oct. 1
| 2373 | A560 | 1fo multicolored | .30 | .20 |
| 2374 | A560 | 1fo multicolored | .30 | .20 |

Hungarian Council System, 25th anniv.
Exist imperf. Value, set $12.

Fish and Waves (Ocean Pollution) A561

Designs: 60f, Skeleton hand reaching for rose in water glass. 80f, Fish gasping for raindrop. 1fo, Carnation wilting in polluted soil. 1.20fo, Bird dying in polluted air. 5fo, Sick human lung and smokestack. 6fo, "Stop Pollution" (raised hand protecting globe from skeleton hand).

1975, Oct. 16   Litho.   Perf. 11½
2375	A561	40f multi	.20	.20
2376	A561	60f multi	.20	.20
2377	A561	80f multi	.20	.20
2378	A561	1fo multi	.20	.20
2379	A561	1.20fo multi	.25	.20
2380	A561	5fo multi	.60	.30
2381	A561	6fo multi	.85	.40
		Nos. 2375-2381 (7)	2.50	1.70

Environmental Protection.
Exist imperf. Value, set $20.

Mariska Gárdos (1885-1973) A562

Portraits: No. 2383, Imre Mezö (1905-56). No. 2384, Imre Tarr (1900-37).

1975, Nov. 4   Litho.   Perf. 12
2382	A562	1fo black & red org	.25	.20
2383	A562	1fo black & red org	.25	.20
2384	A562	1fo black & red org	.25	.20
		Nos. 2382-2384 (3)	.75	.60

Famous Hungarians, birth anniversaries.
Exist imperf. Value, set $20.

Treble Clef, Organ and Orchestra — A563

1975, Nov. 14
| 2385 | A563 | 1fo multicolored | .40 | .20 |

Franz Liszt Musical Academy, centenary.
Exists imperf. Value $12.

Szigetcsep Icon — A564

Virgin and Child, 18th Century Icons: 60f, Graboc. 1fo, Esztergom. 1.50fo, Vatoped. 2.50fo, Tottos. 4fo, Gyor. 5fo, Kazan.

1975, Nov. 25   Photo.   Perf. 12½
2386	A564	40f	gold & multi	.20	.20
2387	A564	60f	gold & multi	.20	.20
2388	A564	1fo	gold & multi	.20	.20
2389	A564	1.50fo	gold & multi	.20	.20
2390	A564	2.50fo	gold & multi	.35	.20
2391	A564	4fo	gold & multi	.70	.30
2392	A564	5fo	gold & multi	.90	.60
		Nos. 2386-2392 (7)		2.75	1.90

Exist imperf. Value, set $20.

Members' Flags, Radar, Mother and Child — A565

1975, Dec. 15   Litho.   Perf. 12
| 2393 | A565 | 1fo multicolored | .30 | .20 |

20th anniversary of the signing of the Warsaw Treaty (Bulgaria, Czechoslovakia, German Democratic Rep., Hungary, Poland, Romania, USSR).
Exists imperf. Value $7.

Ice Hockey, Winter Olympics' Emblem — A566

Designs (Emblem and): 60f, Slalom. 80f, Ski race. 1.20fo, Ski jump. 2fo, Speed skating. 4fo, Cross-country skiing. 6fo, Bobsled. 10fo, Figure skating, pair.

1975, Dec. 29   Photo.   Perf. 12x11½
2394	A566	40f silver & multi	.20	.20
2395	A566	60f silver & multi	.20	.20
2396	A566	80f silver & multi	.20	.20
2397	A566	1.20fo silver & multi	.20	.20
2398	A566	2fo silver & multi	.35	.20
2399	A566	4fo silver & multi	.70	.30
2400	A566	6fo silver & multi	.90	.50
		Nos. 2394-2400 (7)	2.75	1.80

Souvenir Sheet
Perf. 12½
| 2401 | A566 | 10fo silver & multi | 3.25 | 3.00 |

12th Winter Olympic Games, Innsbruck, Austria, Feb. 4-15, 1976. No. 2401 contains one stamp (59x36mm).
Exist imperf. Value: set $20; souvenir sheet $20.

"P," 5-pengö and 500-pengö Notes — A567

1976, Jan. 16   Litho.   Perf. 12
| 2402 | A567 | 1fo multicolored | .25 | .20 |

Hungarian Bank Note Co., 50th anniversary.
Exists imperf. Value $10.

Animal Type of 1974

Young Animals: 40f, Wild boars, horiz. 60f, Squirrels. 80f, Lynx, horiz. 1.20fo, Wolves. 2fo, Foxes, horiz. 4fo, Bears. 6fo, Lions, horiz.

1976, Jan. 26
2403	A542	40f multi	.20	.20
2404	A542	60f blue & multi	.20	.20
2405	A542	80f multi	.20	.20
2406	A542	1.20fo multi	.20	.20
2407	A542	2fo violet & multi	.30	.20
2408	A542	4fo yellow & multi	.65	.30
2409	A542	6fo multi	.75	.40
		Nos. 2403-2409 (7)	2.50	1.70

Exist imperf. Value, set $20.

A.G. Bell, Telephone, Molniya I and Radar — A568

1976, Mar. 10   Litho.   Perf. 11½x12
| 2410 | A568 | 3fo multicolored | .75 | .75 |

Centenary of first telephone call by Alexander Graham Bell, Mar. 10, 1876. Issued in sheets of 4.
Exists imperf. Value: single $5.50; sheetlet $20.

Battle of Kuruc-Labantz — A569

Paintings: 60f, Meeting of Rakoczi and Tamas Esze, by Endre Veszprem. 1fo, Diet of Onod, by Mor Than. 2fo, Camp of the Kurucs. 3fo, Ilona Zrinyi (Rakoczi's mother), vert. 4fo, Kuruc officers, vert. 5fo, Prince Francis II Rakoczy, by Adam Manyoki, vert. Painters of 40f, 2fo, 3fo, 4fo, are unknown.

1976, Mar. 27   Photo.   Perf. 12½
2411	A569	40f gold & multi	.20	.20
2412	A569	60f gold & multi	.20	.20
2413	A569	1fo gold & multi	.30	.20
2414	A569	2fo gold & multi	.60	.20
2415	A569	3fo gold & multi	.85	.25
2416	A569	4fo gold & multi	1.25	.30
2417	A569	5fo gold & multi	1.60	.50
		Nos. 2411-2417 (7)	5.00	1.85

Francis II Rakoczy (1676-1735), leader of Hungarian Protestant insurrection, 300th birth anniversary.
Exist imperf. Value $30.

Standard Meter, Hungarian Meter Act — A570

2fo, Istvan Krusper, his vacuum balance, standard kilogram. 3fo, Interferometer & rocket.

1976, Apr. 5   Perf. 11½x12
2418	A570	1fo multicolored	.20	.20
2419	A570	2fo multicolored	.30	.20
2420	A570	3fo multicolored	.50	.30
		Nos. 2418-2420 (3)	1.00	.70

Introduction of metric system in Hungary, cent.
Exist imperf. Value, set $22.

US No. 1353 and Independence Hall, Philadelphia — A571

Photogravure and Foil Embossed
1976, May 29   Perf. 11½x12
| 2421 | A571 | 5fo blue & multi | 1.40 | 1.25 |

Interphil 76 International Philatelic Exhibition, Philadelphia, Pa., May 29-June 6. No. 2421 issued in sheets of 3 stamps and 3 labels showing bells. Size: 115x125mm.
Exists imperf. Value: single with label $10; sheetlet $35.

"30" and Various Pioneer Activities — A572

1976, June 5   Litho.   Perf. 12
| 2422 | A572 | 1fo multicolored | .30 | .20 |

Hungarian Pioneers, 30th anniversary.
Exists imperf. Value $7.

Trucks, Safety Devices, Trade Union Emblem — A573

1976, June   Perf. 12½
| 2423 | A573 | 1fo multicolored | .20 | .20 |

Labor safety.
Exists imperf. Value $7.

Intelstat 4, Montreal Olympic Emblem, Canadian Flag — A574

Designs: 60f, Equestrian. 1fo, Butterfly stroke. 2fo, One-man kayak. 3fo, Fencing. 4fo, Javelin. 5fo, Athlete on vaulting horse.

1976, June 29 Photo. Perf. 11½x12
2424 A574 40f dk blue & multi .20 .20
2425 A574 60f slate grn & multi .20 .20
2426 A574 1fo blue & multi .20 .20
2427 A574 2fo green & multi .35 .20
2428 A574 3fo brown & multi .45 .30
2429 A574 4fo bister & multi .60 .30
2430 A574 5fo maroon & multi .75 .40
Nos. 2424-2430 (7) 2.75 1.70

21st Olympic Games, Montreal, Canada, July 17-Aug. 1. See No. C365.
Exist imperf. Value, set $30.

Denmark No. 2 and Mermaid, Copenhagen — A575

1976, Aug. 19 Photo. Perf. 11½x12
2431 A575 3fo multicolored 1.25 1.25

HAFNIA 76 Intl. Phil. Exhib., Copenhagen, Aug. 20-29. No. 2431 issued in sheets of 3 stamps and 3 labels showing HAFNIA emblem.
Exists imperf. Value: single with label $7; sheetlet $25.

Souvenir Sheet

Discovery of Body of Lajos II, by Bertalan Székely — A576

1976, Aug. 27 Photo. Perf. 12½
2432 A576 20fo multicolored 3.00 2.75
450th anniversary of the Battle of Mohacs against the Turks.
Exists imperf. Value $25.

Flora, by Titian A577

1976, Aug. 27
2433 A577 4fo gold & multi .75 .25
Titian (1477-1576), Venetian painter.
Exists imperf. Value $10.

Hussar, Herend China — A578

1976, Sept. 28 Litho. Perf. 12
2434 A578 4fo multicolored .75 .25
Herend China manufacture, sesqui.
Exists imperf. Value $8.

Daniel Berzsenyi (1776-1836), Poet — A579

1976, Sept. 28
2435 A579 2fo black, gold & yel .25 .20
Exists imperf. Value $6.

Pal Gyulai (1826-1909), Poet and Historian A580

1976, Sept. 28
2436 A580 2fo orange & black .25 .20
Exists imperf. Value $6.

Tuscany No. 1 and Emblem — A581

1976, Oct. 13 Photo. Perf. 11½x12
2437 A581 5fo orange & multi 1.75 1.75

ITALIA 76 International Philatelic Exhibition, Milan, Oct. 14-24. No. 2437 issued in sheets of 3 stamps and 3 labels showing Italia 76 emblem. Size: 106x127mm.

Exists imperf. Value: single with label $12; sheetlet $35.

Jozsef Madzsar, M.D. — A582

Labor leaders: No. 2439, Ignac Bogar (1876-1933), secretary of printers' union. No. 2440, Rudolf Golub (1901-44), miner.

1976, Nov. 4 Litho. Perf. 12
2438 A582 1fo deep brown & red .20 .20
2439 A582 1fo deep brown & red .20 .20
2440 A582 1fo deep brown & red .20 .20
Nos. 2438-2440 (3) .60 .60
Exist imperf. Value, set $15.

Science and Culture House, Georgian Dancer, Hungarian and USSR Flags A583

1976, Nov. 4 Perf. 12½x12
2441 A583 1fo multicolored .40 .20
House of Soviet Science and Culture, Budapest, 2nd anniversary.
Exists imperf. Value $6.

Koranyi Sanitarium and Statue — A584

1976, Nov. 11 Perf. 12
2442 A584 2fo multicolored .35 .20
Koranyi TB Sanitarium, founded by Dr. Frigyes Koranyi, 75th anniversary.
Exists imperf. Value $6.

Locomotive, 1875, Enese Station — A585

Designs: 60f, Steam engine No. 17, 1885, Rabatamasi Station. 1fo, Railbus, 1925, Fertoszentmiklos Station. 2fo, Express steam engine, Kapuvar Station. 3fo, Engine and trailer, 1926, Gyor Station. 4fo, Eight-wheel express engine, 1934, and Fertoboz Station. 5fo, Raba-Balaton engine, Sopron Station.

1976, Nov. 26 Litho. Perf. 12
2443 A585 40f multicolored .20 .20
2444 A585 60f multicolored .20 .20
2445 A585 1fo multicolored .20 .20
2446 A585 2fo multicolored .30 .20
2447 A585 3fo multicolored .50 .20
2448 A585 4fo multicolored .70 .35
2449 A585 5fo multicolored .90 .50
Nos. 2443-2449 (7) 3.00 1.85

Gyor-Sopron Railroad, centenary.
Exist imperf. Value, set $25.

Poplar, Oak, Pine and Map of Hungary A586

1976, Dec. 14
2450 A586 1fo multicolored .25 .20
Millionth hectare of reforestation.
Exists imperf. Value $8.

Weight Lifting and Wrestling, Silver Medals — A587

60f, Kayak, men's single & women's double. 1fo, Horse vaulting. 4fo, Women's fencing. 6fo, Javelin. 20fo, Water polo.

1976, Dec. 14 Photo. Perf. 11½x12
2451 A587 40f multicolored .20 .20
2452 A587 60f multicolored .20 .20
2453 A587 1fo multicolored .20 .20
2454 A587 4fo multicolored .75 .30
2455 A587 6fo multicolored .90 .50
Nos. 2451-2455 (5) 2.25 1.40

Souvenir Sheet
Perf. 12½x11½
2456 A587 20fo multicolored 3.25 3.25

Hungarian medalists in 21st Olympic Games.
Exist imperf. Value: set $20; souvenir sheet $20.

Spoonbills — A588

Birds: 60f, White storks. 1fo, Purple herons. 2fo, Great bustard. 3fo, Common cranes. 4fo, White wagtails. 5fo, Garganey teals.

1977, Jan. 3 Litho. Perf. 12
2457 A588 40f multicolored .20 .20
2458 A588 60f multicolored .20 .20
2459 A588 1fo multicolored .25 .20
2460 A588 2fo multicolored .40 .20
2461 A588 3fo multicolored .45 .30
2462 A588 4fo multicolored .90 .40
2463 A588 5fo multicolored 1.10 .50
Nos. 2457-2463 (7) 3.50 2.00

Birds from Hortobagy National Park.
Exist imperf. Value, set $25.

1976 World Champion Imre Abonyi Driving Four-in-hand — A589

Designs: 60f, Omnibus on Boulevard, 1870. 1fo, One-horse cab at Budapest Railroad Station, 1890. 2fo, Mail coach, Buda to Vienna route. 3fo, Covered wagon of Hajduszoboszlo. 4fo, Hungarian coach, by Jeremias Schemel, 1563. 5fo, Post chaise, from a Lübeck wood panel, 1430.

1977, Jan. 31   Litho.   Perf. 12x11½

2464	A589	40f multicolored	.20	.20
2465	A589	60f multicolored	.20	.20
2466	A589	1fo multicolored	.20	.20
2467	A589	2fo multicolored	.30	.20
2468	A589	3fo multicolored	.30	.20
2469	A589	4fo multicolored	.50	.35
2470	A589	5fo multicolored	.70	.45
		Nos. 2464-2470 (7)	2.40	1.80

History of the coach.
Exist imperf. Value, set $25.

Peacock
A590

Birds: 60f, Green peacock. 1fo, Congo peacock. 3fo, Argus pheasant. 4fo, Impeyan pheasant. 6fo, Peacock pheasant.

1977, Feb. 22   Litho.   Perf. 12

2471	A590	40f multicolored	.20	.20
2472	A590	60f multicolored	.20	.20
2473	A590	1fo multicolored	.20	.20
2474	A590	2fo multicolored	.40	.20
2475	A590	4fo multicolored	.60	.30
2476	A590	6fo multicolored	.90	.50
		Nos. 2471-2476 (6)	2.50	1.60

Exist imperf. Value, set $25.

Newspaper Front Page, Factories A591

1977, Mar. 3   Litho.   Perf. 12

2477	A591	1fo gold, black & ver	.25	.20

Nepszava newspaper, centenary.
Exists imperf. Value $6.

Flowers, by Mihaly Munkacsy A592

Flowers, by Hungarian Painters: 60f, Jakab Bogdany. 1fo, Istvan Csok, horiz. 2fo, Janos Halapy. 3fo, Jozsef Rippl-Ronai, horiz. 4fo, Janos Tornyai. 5fo, Jozsef Koszta.

1977, Mar. 18   Photo.   Perf. 12½

2478	A592	40f gold & multi	.20	.20
2479	A592	60f gold & multi	.20	.20
2480	A592	1fo gold & multi	.20	.20
2481	A592	2fo gold & multi	.30	.20
2482	A592	3fo gold & multi	.40	.20
2483	A592	4fo gold & multi	.55	.30
2484	A592	5fo gold & multi	.75	.50
		Nos. 2478-2484 (7)	2.60	1.80

Exist imperf. Value, set $25.

Newton and Double Convex Lens A593

1977, Mar. 31   Litho.   Perf. 12

2485	A593	3fo tan & multi	1.00	.80

Isaac Newton (1643-1727), natural philosopher and mathematician, 250th death anniversary. No. 2485 issued in sheets of 4 stamps and 4 blue and black labels showing illustration from Newton's "Principia Mathematica," and Soviet space rocket.
Exists imperf. Value: single with label $8; sheetlet $30.

Janos Vajda (1827-97), Poet — A594

1977, May 2   Litho.   Perf. 12

2486	A594	1fo green, cream & blk	.20	.20

Exists imperf. Value $6.

Netherlands No. 1 and Tulips — A595

1977, May 23   Photo.   Perf. 11½x12

2487	A595	3fo multicolored	1.25	1.25

AMPHILEX '77, Intl. Stamp Exhib., Amsterdam, May 26-June 5. Issued in sheets of 3 stamps + 3 labels showing Amphilex poster.
Exist imperf. Value: single with label $7; sheetlet $25.

Scene from "Wedding at Nagyrede" A596

1977, June 14   Litho.   Perf. 12

2488	A596	3fo multicolored	.50	.20

State Folk Ensemble, 25th anniversary.
Exists imperf. Value $7.

Souvenir Sheet

Bath of Bathsheba, by Rubens — A597

1977, June 14   Photo.   Perf. 11

2489	A597	20fo multicolored	3.75	3.50

Peter Paul Rubens (1577-1640), Flemish painter.
Exists imperf. Value $60.

Medieval View of Sopron, Fidelity Tower, Arms A598

1977, June 25   Litho.   Perf. 12x11½

2490	A598	1fo multicolored	1.40	1.40

700th anniv. of Sopron. Printed se-tenant with label showing European Architectural Heritage medal awarded Sopron in 1975.
Exists imperf. Value, single with label $20.

Race Horse Kincsem A599

1977, July 16   Litho.   Perf. 12

2491	A599	1fo multicolored	1.00	.90

Sesquicentennial of horse racing in Hungary. Printed se-tenant with label showing portrait of Count Istvan Szechenyi and vignette from his 1827 book "Rules of Horse Racing in Hungary."
Exists imperf. Value, single with label $20.

German Democratic Republic No. 370 — A600

1977, Aug. 18   Photo.   Perf. 12x11½

2492	A600	3fo multicolored	1.25	1.10

SOZPHILEX 77 Philatelic Exhibition, Berlin, Aug. 19-28. No. 2492 issued in sheets of 3 stamps and 3 labels showing SOZPHILEX emblem.
Exist imperf. Value: single with label $7; sheetlet $20.

Scythian Iron Bell, 6th Century B.C. — A601

Panel, Crown of Emperor Constantin Monomakhos — A602

Designs: No. 2494, Bronze candlestick in shape of winged woman, 12th-13th centuries. No. 2495, Centaur carrying child, copper aquamanile, 12th century. No. 2496, Gold figure of Christ, from 11th century Crucifix. Designs show art treasures from Hungarian National Museum, founded 1802.

1977, Sept. 3   Litho.   Perf. 12

2493	A601	2fo multicolored	.75	.75
2494	A601	2fo multicolored	.75	.75
2495	A601	2fo multicolored	.75	.75
2496	A601	2fo multicolored	.75	.75
a.		Horiz. strip of 4, #2493-2496	3.00	3.00

Souvenir Sheet

2497	A602	10fo multicolored	3.50	3.00

50th Stamp Day.
Exist imperf. Value: strip of 4 $20; souvenir sheet $22.

Sputnik A603

Spacecraft: 60f, Skylab. 1fo, Soyuz-Salyut 5. 3fo, Luna 24. 4fo, Mars 3. 6fo, Viking.

1977, Sept. 20

2498	A603	40f multicolored	.20	.20
2499	A603	60f multicolored	.20	.20
2500	A603	1fo multicolored	.20	.20
2501	A603	3fo multicolored	.40	.20
2502	A603	4fo multicolored	.65	.35
2503	A603	6fo multicolored	.90	.45
		Nos. 2498-2503 (6)	2.55	1.60

Space explorations, from Sputnik to Viking. See No. C375.
Exist imperf. Value, set $20.

Janos Szanto Kovacs (1852-1908), Agrarian Movement Pioneer A604

Ervin Szabo (1877-1918), Revolutionary Workers' Movement Pioneer — A605

1977, Nov. 4 Litho. Perf. 12
2504 A604 1fo red & black .30 .20
2505 A605 1fo red & black .30 .20
Exist imperf. Value, set $12.

Monument to Hungarian October Revolutionists, Omsk — A606

1977, Nov. 4
2506 A606 1fo black & red .20 .20
60th anniv. of Russian October Revolution.
Exists imperf. Value $5.50.

Hands and Feet Bathed in Thermal Spring — A607

1977, Nov. 1
2507 A607 1fo multicolored .25 .20
World Rheumatism Year.
Exists imperf. Value $8.

Endre Ady — A608

1977, Nov. 22 Engr. Perf. 12
2508 A608 1fo violet blue .35 .35
Endre Ady (1877-1919), lyric poet. Issued in sheets of 4.
Exists imperf. Value $7. Sheetlet $35.

Lesser Panda — A609

Designs: 60f, Giant panda. 1fo, Asiatic black bear. 4fo, Polar bear. 6fo, Brown bear.

1977, Dec. 16 Litho. Perf. 11½x12
2509 A609 40f yellow & multi .20 .20
2510 A609 60f yellow & multi .20 .20
2511 A609 1fo yellow & multi .35 .20

2512 A609 4fo yellow & multi .75 .30
2513 A609 6fo yellow & multi 1.00 .50
Nos. 2509-2513 (5) 2.50 1.40
Exist imperf. Value $25.

Souvenir Sheet

Flags and Ships along Intercontinental Waterway — A610

Flags: a, Austria. b, Bulgaria. c, Czechoslovakia. d, France. e, Luxembourg. f, Yugoslavia. g, Hungary. h, Fed. Rep. of Germany. i, Romania. j, Switzerland. k, USSR.

1977, Dec. 28 Litho. Perf. 12
2514 A610 Sheet of 11 8.00 7.75
a.-k. 2fo, any single 1.00 1.00
European Intercontinental Waterway: Danube, Main and Rhine.
Exists imperf. Value $170.

Lancer, 17th Century A611

Hussars: 60f, Kuruts, 1710. 1fo, Baranya, 1762. 2fo, Palatine officer, 1809. 4fo, Sandor, 1848. 6fo, Trumpeter, 5th Honved Regiment, 1900.

1978, Jan. Litho. Perf. 11½x12
2515 A611 40f lilac & multi .20 .20
2516 A611 60f yel grn & multi .20 .20
2517 A611 1fo red & multi .20 .20
2518 A611 2fo dull bl & multi .35 .20
2519 A611 4fo olive bis & multi .70 .20
2520 A611 6fo gray & multi 1.10 .50
Nos. 2515-2520 (6) 2.75 1.60
Exist imperf. Value, set $20.

School of Arts and Crafts A612

1978, Mar. 31 Litho. Perf. 12
2521 A612 1fo multicolored .20 .20
School of Arts and Crafts, 200th anniv.
Exists imperf. Value $7.

Soccer Players, Flags of West Germany and Poland — A613

Designs (Various Soccer Scenes and Flags): No. 2523, Hungary and Argentina. No. 2524, France and Italy. No. 2525, Tunisia and Mexico. No. 2526, Sweden and Brazil. No. 2527, Spain and Austria. No. 2528, Peru and Scotland. No. 2529, Iran and Netherlands.

Flags represent first round of contestants. 20fo, Argentina '78 emblem.

1978, May 25 Litho. Perf. 12
2522 A613 2fo multicolored .20 .20
2523 A613 2fo multicolored .20 .20
2524 A613 2fo multicolored .20 .20
2525 A613 2fo multicolored .20 .20
2526 A613 2fo multicolored .25 .20
2527 A613 2fo multicolored .25 .20
2528 A613 2fo multicolored .55 .30
2529 A613 2fo multicolored .90 .40
Nos. 2522-2529 (8) 2.75 1.90
Souvenir Sheet
Perf. 11½
2530 A613 20fo multicolored 3.75 3.75
Argentina '78 11th World Cup Soccer Championships, Argentina, June 2-25.
Exist imperf. Values: set $20; souvenir sheet $25.

Vase, Star and Glass Blower's Tube A614

1978, May 20 Litho. Perf. 12
2531 A614 1fo multicolored .20 .20
Ajka Glass Works, centenary.
Exist imperf. Value $7.

Canada No. 1 and Trillium — A615

1978, June 2
2532 A615 3fo multicolored 1.00 .90
CAPEX '78, Canadian International Philatelic Exhibition, Toronto, Ont., June 9-18. Issued in sheets of 3 stamps and 3 labels showing CAPEX '78 emblem.
Exists imperf. Value: single with label $7; sheetlet $20.

Souvenir Sheets

Leif Ericson and his Ship — A616

Explorers and their ships: #2533b, Columbus. c, Vasco da Gama. d, Magellan. #2534a, Drake. b, Hudson. c, Cook. d, Peary.

1978, June 10 Litho. Perf. 12x11½
2533 Sheet of 4 3.25 3.00
a.-d. A616 2fo, any single .70 .70
2534 Sheet of 4 3.25 3.00
a.-d. A616 2fo, any single .70 .70
Exist imperf. Value: set of 2 sheets $100.

Diesel Train, Pioneer's Kerchief — A617

Congress Emblem as Flower — A618

1978, June 10 Perf. 12
2535 A617 1fo multicolored .20 .20
30th anniversary of Pioneer Railroad.
Exists imperf. Value $8.

1978, June
Design: No. 2537, Congress emblem, "Cuba" and map of Cuba.
2536 A618 1fo multi .25 .20
2537 A618 1fo multi .25 .20
a. Pair, #2536-2537 .50 .30
11th World Youth Festival, Havana.
Exist imperf. Value $15.

WHO Emblem, Stylized Body and Heart — A619

Clenched Fist, Dove and Olive Branch — A620

1978, Aug. 21 Litho. Perf. 12
2538 A619 1fo multicolored .20 .20
Drive against hypertension.
Exists imperf. Value $8.

1978, Sept. 1 Litho. Perf. 12
2539 A620 1fo gray, red & black .20 .20
Publication of review "Peace and Socialism," 20th anniversary.
Exists imperf. Value $6.

Train, Telephone, Space Communication — A621

1978, Sept. 8 Litho. Perf. 12
2540 A621 1fo multicolored .25 .20
20th anniv. of Organization for Communication Cooperation of Socialist Countries.
Exists imperf. Value $6.

"Toshiba" Automatic Letter Sorting
Machine — A622

1978, Sept. 15   Litho.   Perf. 11½x12
2541 A622 1fo multicolored   .50   .20
Introduction of automatic letter sorting. No.
2541 printed with se-tenant label showing bird
holding letter.
Exists imperf. Value: single with label $15.

Eros
Offering
Grapes,
Villa
Hercules
A623

Roman Mosaics Found in Hungary: No.
2543, Tiger (Villa Hercules, Budapest). No.
2544, Bird eating berries (Balacapuszta). No.
2545, Dolphin (Aquincum). 10fo, Hercules
aiming at Centaur fleeing with Deianeira (Villa
Hercules).

Photogravure and Engraved
1978, Sept. 16   Perf. 11½
2542 A623 2fo multicolored   1.50   1.25
2543 A623 2fo multicolored   1.50   1.25
2544 A623 2fo multicolored   1.50   1.25
2545 A623 2fo multicolored   1.50   1.25
  Nos. 2542-2545 (4)   6.00   5.00

Souvenir Sheet
2546 A623 10fo multicolored   9.00   8.50
Stamp Day. No. 2546 contains one stamp
(52x35mm).
Exist imperf. Value: set $80; souvenir sheet
$170.

Count Imre
Thököly — A624

1978, Oct. 1   Photo.   Perf. 12½
2547 A624 1fo black & yellow   .25   .20
300th anniv. of Hungary's independence
movement, led by Imre Thököly (1657-1705).
Exists imperf. Value $6.

Souvenir Sheet

Hungarian Crown Jewels — A625

1978, Oct. 10
2548 A625 20fo gold & multi   5.50   5.25
Return of Crown Jewels from US, 1/6/78.
Exists imperf. Value $40.

"The
Red
Coach"
A626

1978, Oct. 21   Litho.   Perf. 12
2549 A626 3fo red & black   .50   .20
Gyula Krudy, 1878-1933, novelist.
Exists imperf. Value $7.

St. Ladislas I
Reliquary,
Györ
Cathedral
A627

1978, Nov. 15   Perf. 11½x12½
2550 A627 1fo multicolored   .20   .20
Ladislas I (1040-1095), 900th anniversary of
accession to throne of Hungary.
Exists imperf. Value $7.

Miklos Jurisics Statue, Köszeg — A628

1978, Nov. 15   Perf. 12
2551 A628 1fo multicolored   .30   .20
650th anniversary of founding of Köszeg.
Exists imperf. Value $6.

Samu Czaban and Gizella
Berzeviczy — A629

Photogravure and Engraved
1978, Nov. 24   Perf. 11½x12
2552 A629 1fo brown, buff & red   .50   .20
Samu Czaban (1878-1942) and Gizella
Berzeviczy (1878-1954), Communist teachers
during Soviet Republic (1918-1919).
Exists imperf. Value $6.

Communist
Party Emblem
A630

1978, Nov. 24   Litho.   Perf. 12
2553 A630 1fo gray, red & blk   .20   .20
Hungarian Communist Party, 60th anniv.
Exists imperf. Value $6.

Woman
Cutting Bread
A631

Ceramics by Margit Kovacs (1902-1976):
2fo, Woman with pitcher. 3fo, Potter.

1978, Nov. 30   Litho.   Perf. 11½x12
2554 A631 1fo multicolored   .20   .20
2555 A631 2fo multicolored   .30   .20
2556 A631 3fo multicolored   .70   .60
  Nos. 2554-2556 (3)   1.20   1.00

Exist imperf. Value, set $20.

Virgin
and
Child, by
Dürer
A632

Dürer Paintings: 60f, Adoration of the Kings,
horiz. 1fo, Self-portrait, 1500. 2fo, St. George.
3fo, Nativity, horiz. 4fo, St. Eustatius. 5fo, The
Four Apostles. 20fo, Dancing Peasant Couple,
1514 (etching).

1979, Jan. 8   Photo.   Perf. 12½
2557 A632 40f gold & multi   .20   .20
2558 A632 60f gold & multi   .20   .20
2559 A632 1fo gold & multi   .20   .20
2560 A632 2fo gold & multi   .30   .20
2561 A632 3fo gold & multi   .35   .20
2562 A632 4fo gold & multi   .70   .30
2563 A632 5fo gold & multi   .80   .60
  Nos. 2557-2563 (7)   2.75   1.90

Souvenir Sheet
Litho.
2564 A632 20fo buff & brown   3.50   3.25
Albrecht Dürer (1471-1528), German
painter and engraver.
Exist imperf. Value: set $20; souvenir sheet
$50.

Human Rights
Flame — A633

1979, Feb. 8   Litho.   Perf. 11½x12
2565 A633 1fo dk & lt blue   1.25   1.25
Universal Declaration of Human Rights,
30th anniversary. No. 2565 issued in sheets of
12 stamps (3x4) and 4 labels. Alternating horizontal rows inverted.
Exists imperf. Value $12. Strip of 3 $45,
Sheetlet $100.

Child at
Play — A634

IYC Emblem and: No. 2567, Family. No.
2568, 3 children (international friendship).

1979, Feb. 26   Perf. 12
2566 A634 1fo multicolored   .75   .75
2567 A634 1fo multicolored   .75   .75
2568 A634 1fo multicolored   6.50   5.50
  Nos. 2566-2568 (3)   8.00   7.00

Exist imperf. Value, set $30.

Soldiers
of the
Red
Army,
by Bela
Uitz
A635

1979, Mar. 21   Litho.   Perf. 12
2569 A635 1fo silver, blk & red   .20   .20
60th anniv. of Hungarian Soviet Republic.
Exists imperf. Value $6.

Calvinist Church,
Nyirbator — A636

1979, Mar. 28   Perf. 11
2570 A636 1fo brown & yellow   .20   .20
700th anniv. of Nyirbator. See No. 2601.
Exists imperf. Value $12.

Chessmen, Gold Cup, Flag — A637

1979, Apr. 12   Litho.   Perf. 12
2571 A637 3fo multicolored   1.00   .50
Hungarian victories in 23rd Chess Olympiad, Buenos Aires, 1978.
Exists imperf. Value $20.

Alexander Nevski Cathedral, Sofia,
Bulgaria No. 1 — A638

1979, May 18   Litho.   Perf. 11½x12
2572 A638 3fo multicolored   .75   .75
Philaserdica '79 Philatelic Exhibition, Sofia,
Bulgaria, May 18-27. No. 2572 issued in
sheets of 3 stamps and 3 labels showing Philaserdica emblem and arms of Sofia.
Exist imperf. Value: single with label $7;
sheetlet $25.

Stephenson's Rocket, 1829, IVA '79 Emblem — A639

Railroad Development: 60f, Siemens' first electric locomotive, 1879. 1fo, "Pioneer," Chicago & Northwestern Railroad, 1836. 2fo, Orient Express, 1883. 3fo, Trans-Siberian train, 1898. 4fo, Express train on Tokaido line, 1964. 5fo, Transrapid-O5 train, exhibited 1979. 20fo, Map of European railroad network.

1979, June 8   Litho.   Perf. 12x11½
2573	A639	40f multi	.20	.20
2574	A639	60f multi	.20	.20
2575	A639	1fo multi	.20	.20
2576	A639	2fo multi	.30	.20
2577	A639	3fo multi	.45	.25
2578	A639	4fo multi	.60	.45
2579	A639	5fo multi	.90	.50
	Nos. 2573-2579 (7)		2.85	2.00

Souvenir Sheet
Perf. 12½x11½
2580	A639	20fo multi	4.00	3.75

Intl. Transportation Exhibition (IVA '79), Hamburg. #2580 contains one 47x32mm stamp.
Exist imperf. Value: set $25; souvenir sheet $50.

Natural Gas Pipeline and Compressor A640

2fo, Lenin power station & dam, Dniepropetrovsk & pylon. 3fo, Comecon Building, Moscow, & star symbolizing 10 member states.

1979, June 26   Perf. 11½x12
2581	A640	1fo multi	.20	.20
2582	A640	2fo multi	.25	.20
2583	A640	3fo multi	.40	.20
	Nos. 2581-2583 (3)		.85	.60

30th anniversary of the Council of Mutual Economic Assistance, Comecon.
Exist imperf. Value, set $17.

Zsigmond Moricz (1879-1942), Writer, by Jozsef Ripple-Ronai A641

1979, June 29   Perf. 12
2584	A641	1fo multi	.20	.20

Exists imperf. Value $6.

Town Hall, Helsinki, Finnish Flag, Moscow '80 Emblem A642

Designs (Moscow '80 Emblem and): 60f, Colosseum, Rome, Italian flag. 1fo, Asakusa Temple, Tokyo, Japanese flag. 2fo, Mexico City Cathedral, Mexican flag. 3fo, Our Lady's Church, Munich, German flag. 4fo, Skyscrapers, Montreal, Canadian flag. 5fo, Lomonosov University, Misha the bear and Soviet flag.

1979, July 31   Perf. 12x11½
2585	A642	40f multi	.20	.20
2586	A642	60f multi	.20	.20
2587	A642	1fo multi	.20	.20
2588	A642	2fo multi	.20	.20
2589	A642	3fo multi	.30	.25
2590	A642	4fo multi	.40	.30
2591	A642	5fo multi	.70	.45
	Nos. 2585-2591 (7)		2.20	1.80

Pre-Olympic Year.
Exist imperf. Value, set $24.

Boy with Horse and Greyhounds, by Janos Vaszary — A643

Paintings of Horses: 60f, Coach and Five, by Karoly Lotz. 1fo, Boys on Horseback, by Celesztin Pallya. 2fo, Farewell, by Lotz. 3fo, Horse Market, by Pallya. 4fo, Wanderer, by Bela Ivanyi-Grunwald. 5fo, Ready for the Hunt, by Karoly Sterio.

1979, Aug. 11   Photo.   Perf. 12½
2592	A643	40f multi	.20	.20
2593	A643	60f multi	.20	.20
2594	A643	1fo multi	.20	.20
2595	A643	2fo multi	.25	.20
2596	A643	3fo multi	.40	.20
2597	A643	4fo multi	.50	.30
2598	A643	5fo multi	.75	.40
	Nos. 2592-2598 (7)		2.50	1.70

Exist imperf. Value, set $30.

Sturgeons, Map of Danube, "Calypso" — A644

1979, Aug. 11
2599	A644	3fo multi	.50	.20

Environmental protection of rivers and seas.
Exists imperf. Value $7.

Pentathlon A645

1979, Aug. 12   Litho.   Perf. 12
2600	A645	2fo multi	.50	.20

Pentathlon World Championship, Budapest, Aug. 12-18.
Exists imperf. Value $6.

Architecture Type of 1979
Design: Vasvar Public Health Center.

1979, Aug. 15   Litho.   Perf. 11
2601	A636	40f multi	.20	.20

700th anniversary of Vasvar.
Exists imperf. Value $12.

Denarius of Stephen I, 1000-1038, Reverse A646

Hungarian Coins: 2fo, Copper coin of Bela III, 1172-1196. 3fo, Golden groat of King Louis the Great, 1342-1382. 4fo, Golden forint of Matthias I, 1458-1490. 5fo, Silver gulden of Wladislaw II, 1490-1516.

Engraved and Photogravure
1979, Sept. 3   Perf. 12x11½
2602	A646	1fo multi	.20	.20
2603	A646	2fo multi	.25	.20
2604	A646	3fo multi	.35	.25
2605	A646	4fo multi	.50	.40
2606	A646	5fo multi	1.00	.70
	Nos. 2602-2606 (5)		2.30	1.75

9th International Numismatic Congress, Berne, Switzerland.
Exist imperf. Value, set $20.

Souvenir Sheet

Unofficial Stamp, 1848 — A647

1979, Sept. 15   Litho.   Perf. 12
2607	A647	10fo dk brown, blk & red	2.75	2.50

Stamp Day.
Exists imperf. Value $30.

Souvenir Sheet

Gyor-Sopron-Ebenfurt rail service, cent. — A648

Designs: a, Elbel Locomotive. b, Type 424 steam engine. c, "War Locomotive." d, Hydraulic diesel locomotive.

1979, Oct. 19   Litho.   Perf. 12
2608	A648	Sheet of 4	3.25	3.00
a.-d.	A648	5fo any single	.65	.65

Exists imperf. Value $37.50

Vega-Chess, by Victor Vasarely A649

1979, Oct. 29
2609	A649	1fo multi	.20	.20

Exists imperf. Value $20.

International Savings Day — A650

1979, Oct. 29   Litho.   Perf. 12
2610	A650	1fo multi	.20	.20

Exists imperf. Value $6.

Otter — A651

Wildlife Protection: 60f, Wild cat. 1fo, Pine marten. 2fo, Eurasian badger. 4fo, Polecat. 6fo, Beech marten.

1979, Nov. 20
2611	A651	40f multi	.20	.20
2612	A651	60f multi	.20	.20
2613	A651	1fo multi	.20	.20
2614	A651	2fo multi	.30	.20
2615	A651	4fo multi	.60	.25
2616	A651	6fo multi	.90	.60
	Nos. 2611-2616 (6)		2.40	1.65

Exist imperf. Value, set $20.

Tom Thumb, IYC Emblem A652

IYC Emblem and Fairy Tale Scenes: 60f, The Ugly Duckling. 1fo, The Fisherman and the Goldfish. 2fo, Cinderella. 3fo, Gulliver's Travels. 4fo, The Little Pigs and the Wolf. 5fo, Janos the Knight. 20fo, The Fairy Ilona.

1979, Dec. 29   Litho.   Perf. 12x11½
2617	A652	40f multi	.20	.20
2618	A652	60f multi	.20	.20
2619	A652	1fo multi	.20	.20
2620	A652	2fo multi	.35	.20
2621	A652	3fo multi	.50	.30
2622	A652	4fo multi	.70	.30
2623	A652	5fo multi	1.00	.60
	Nos. 2617-2623 (7)		3.15	2.00

Souvenir Sheet
2624	A652	20fo multi	3.75	3.50

Exist imperf. Value: set $25; souvenir sheet $30.

Trichodes Apairius and Yarrow — A653

Insects Pollinating Flowers: 60f, Bumblebee and blanketflower. 1fo, Red admiral butterfly and daisy. 2fo, Cetonia aurata and rose. 4fo, Graphosoma lineatum and petroselinum hortense. 6fo, Chlorophorus varius and thistle.

1980, Jan. 25   Litho.   Perf. 12
2625 A653 40f multi   .20   .20
2626 A653 60f multi   .20   .20
2627 A653 1fo multi   .25   .20
2628 A653 2fo multi   .35   .20
2629 A653 4fo multi   .50   .25
2630 A653 6fo multi   .75   .30
      Nos. 2625-2630 (6)   2.25   1.35
      Exist imperf. Value, set $20.

Hanging Gardens of Semiramis, 6th Century B.C., Map showing Babylon — A654

Seven Wonders of the Ancient World (and Map): 60f, Temple of Artemis, Ephesus, 6th century B.C. 1fo, Zeus, by Phidias, Olympia. 2fo, Tomb of Maussolos, Halikarnassos, 3rd century B.C. 3fo, Colossos of Rhodes. 4fo, Pharos Lighthouse, Alexandria, 3rd century B.C. 5fo, Pyramids, 26th-24th centuries B.C.

1980, Feb. 29   Litho.   Perf. 12x11½
2631 A654 40f multi   .20   .20
2632 A654 60f multi   .20   .20
2633 A654 1fo multi   .20   .20
2634 A654 2fo multi   .30   .20
2635 A654 3fo multi   .40   .25
2636 A654 4fo multi   .60   .35
2637 A654 5fo multi   .85   .60
      Nos. 2631-2637 (7)   2.75   2.00
      Exist imperf. Value, set $25.

Tihany Benedictine Abbey and Deed — A655

1980, Mar. 19   Litho.   Perf. 12
2638 A655 1fo multi   .20   .20
      Benedictine Abbey, Tihany, 925th anniversary of deed (oldest document in Hungarian).
      Exists imperf. Value $6.

Gabor Bethlen, Copperplate Print — A656

1980, Mar. 19
2639 A656 1fo multi   .20   .20
      Gabor Bethlen (1580-1629), Prince of Transylvania (1613-29) and King of Hungary (1620-29).
      Exists imperf. Value $6.

Easter Casket of Garamszentbenedek, 15th Century (Restoration) — A657

1980, Mar. 19
2640 A657 1fo shown   .20   .20
2641 A657 2fo Three Marys   .25   .25
2642 A657 3fo Apostle James   .35   .35
2643 A657 4fo Thaddeus   .55   .55
2644 A657 5fo Andrew   .75   .55
      Nos. 2640-2644 (5)   2.10   1.90
      Exist imperf. Value, set $20.

Liberation from Fascism, 35th Anniversary A658

1980, Apr. 3   Litho.   Perf. 12
2645 A658 1fr multi   .20   .20
      Exists imperf. Value $6.

Jozsef Attila, Poet and Lyricist — A659

1980, Apr. 11
2646 A659 1fo rose car & olive   .20   .20
      Exists imperf. Value $6.
      See No. 2675.

Hungarian Postal Museum, 50th anniv. — A660

1980, Apr. 28   Perf. 11½x12
2647 A660 1fo multi   1.90   1.50
      Features Hungary No. 386a.
      Exists imperf. Value $30.

Two Pence Blue, Mounted Guardsman, London 1980 Emblem — A661

1980, Apr. 30   Perf. 11½x12
2648 A661 3fo multi   1.00   1.00
      London 1980 International Stamp Exhibition, May 6-14. No. 2648 issued in sheets of 3 stamps and 3 labels showing London 1980 emblem and arms of city. Size: 104x125mm.
      Exists imperf. Value: single with label $6; sheetlet $20.

Norway No. B51, Mother with Child, by Gustav Vigeland — A662

1980, June 9   Litho.   Perf. 11½x12
2649 A662 3fo multi   1.00   1.00
      NORWEX '80 Stamp Exhibition, Oslo, June 13-22. No. 2649 issued in sheets of 3 stamps and 3 labels showing NORWEX emblem. Size: 108x125mm.
      Exists imperf. Value: single with label $6; sheetlet $19.

Margit Kaffka (1880-1918), Writer — A663

1980, June 9   Perf. 12
2650 A663 1fo blk & pur, cr   .25   .20
      Exists imperf. Value $7.

Zoltan Schönherz (1905-42), Anti-fascist Martyr — A664

1980, July 25   Litho.
2652 A664 1fo multi   .20   .20
      Exists imperf. Value $6.

Dr. Endre Hogyes and Congress Emblem A665

1980, July 25
2653 A665 1fo multi   .20   .20
      28th International Congress of Physiological Sciences, Budapest, Dr. Hogyes (1847-1906) first described equilibrium reflex-curve and modified Pasteur's rabies vaccine.
      Exists imperf. Value $6.

Decanter, c. 1850 — A666

1980, Sept.   Litho.   Perf. 12
2654 A666 1fo shown   .25   .25
2655 A666 2fo Decorated glass   .35   .35
2656 A666 3fo Stem glass   .65   .65
      Nos. 2654-2656 (3)   1.25   1.25
      Souvenir Sheet
2657 A666 10fo Pecs glass   2.50   2.25
      53rd Stamp Day.
      Exist imperf. Value: set $15; souvenir sheet $20.

Bertalan Por, Self-portrait A667

1980, Nov. 4   Litho.   Perf. 12
2658 A667 1fo Artist (1880-1964)   .35   .20
      Exists imperf. Value $4.

Graylag Goose — A668

1980, Nov. 11   Perf. 11½x12
2659 A668 40f shown   .20   .20
2660 A668 60f Black-crowned
                 night heron   .20   .20
2661 A668 1fo Shoveler   .20   .20
2662 A668 2fo Chlidonias
                 leucopterus   .30   .20
2663 A668 4fo Great crested
                 grebe   .60   .30
2664 A668 6fo Black-necked stilt 1.00   .50
      Nos. 2659-2664 (6)   2.50   1.60
      Souvenir Sheet
2665 A668 20fo Great white her-
                 on   4.25   4.00
      European Nature Protection Year. No. 2665 contains one stamp (37x59mm).
      Exist imperf. Value: set $30; souvenir sheet $40.

Souvenir Sheet

Dove on Map of Europe — A669

1980, Nov. 11   **Perf. 12½x11½**
2666 A669 20fo multi   4.50 4.00
European Security and Cooperation Conference, Madrid.
Exists imperf. Value $40.

Johannes Kepler and Model of his Theory — A670

1980, Nov. 21   **Litho.**   **Perf. 12**
2667 A670 1fo multi   .35 .20
Johannes Kepler (1571-1630), German astronomer, 350th anniversary of death. No. 2667 printed se-tenant with label showing rocket and satellites orbiting earth.
Exists imperf. Value, single with label $15.

Karoly Kisfaludy (1788-1830), Poet and Dramatist A671

1980, Nov. 21
2668 A671 1fo brn red & dull brn   .20 .20
Exists imperf. Value $6.

UN Headquarters, New York — A672

UN membership, 25th anniversary.

Photogravure and Engraved
1980, Dec. 12   **Perf. 11½x12**
2669 A672 40f shown   .20 .20
2670 A672 60f Geneva head-
    quarters   .20 .20
2671 A672 1fo Vienna headquar-
    ters   .25 .20
2672 A672 2fo UN & Hungary
    flags   .30 .20
2673 A672 4fo UN, Hungary
    arms   .55 .35
2674 A672 6fo World map   .90 .55
    Nos. 2669-2674 (6)   2.40 1.70
Exist imperf. Value, set $30.

Attila Type of 1980
Ferenc Erdei (1910-71), economist & statesman.

1980, Dec. 23   **Litho.**   **Perf. 12**
2675 A659 1fo dk green & brown   .20 .20
Exists imperf. Value $6.

Bela Szanto — A674

Count Lajos Batthyany A675

1981, Jan. 31   **Litho.**   **Perf. 12**
2676 A674 1fo multi   .20 .20
Bela Szanto (1881-1951), labor movement leader.
Exists imperf. Value $6.
See Nos. 2698, 2724, 2767.

1981, Feb. 14
2677 A675 1fo multi   .20 .20
Count Lajos Batthyany (1806-1849), prime minister, later executed.
Exists imperf. Value $7.

Bela Bartok (1881-1945), Composer A677

Design: b, Cantata Profana illustration.

1981, Mar. 25   **Litho.**   **Perf. 12½**
2685   Sheet of 2   2.50 2.50
    a.-b. A677 10fo any single   1.25 1.25
Exists imperf. Value $30.

Telephone Exchange System Cent. — A678

1981, Apr. 29   **Litho.**   **Perf. 12**
2686 A678 2fo multi   .25 .20
Exists imperf. Value $6.

Belling Stag — A679

1981, Apr. 29
2687 A679 2fo multi   .25 .20
Exists imperf. Value $6.

Flag of the House of Arpad, 11th Cent. A680

1981, Apr. 29
2688 A680 40f shown   .20 .20
2689 A680 60f Hunyadi family,
    15th cent.   .20 .20
2690 A680 1fo Gabor Bethlen,
    1600   .20 .20
2691 A680 2fo Ferenc Rakoczi II,
    1716   .25 .20
2692 A680 4fo Honved, 1848   .60 .25
2693 A680 6fo Troop flag, 1919   .80 .35
    Nos. 2688-2693 (6)   2.25 1.40
Exist imperf. Value, set $20.

Red Cross and Ambulance Vehicles A681

Map of Europe and J. Henry Dunant (Red Cross Founder) — A682

1981, May 4
2694 A681   2fo multi   .25 .20

Souvenir Sheet
Perf. 12½x11½
2695 A682 20fo multi   2.50 2.50
Hungarian Red Cross cent. (2fo); 3rd European Red Cross Conf., Budapest, May 4-7 (20fo).
Exist imperf. Value: single $6; souvenir sheet $30.

Souvenir Sheet

1933 WIPA Exhibition Seals — A683

1981, May 15   **Perf. 12x12½**
2696   Sheet of 4   2.75 2.75
    a.-d. A683 5fo any single   .65 .65
WIPA 1981 Phil. Exhib., Vienna, May 22-31.
Exists imperf. Value $30.

Stephenson and his Nonpareil — A684

1981, June 12   **Litho.**   **Perf. 12**
2697 A684 2fo multi   .25 .20
George Stephenson (1781-1848), British railroad engineer, birth bicentenary.
Exists imperf. Value $7.

Famous Hungarians Type
Bela Vago (1881-1939), anti-fascist martyr.

1981, Aug. 7   **Litho.**   **Perf. 12**
2698 A674 2fo ocher & brn ol   .25 .20
Exists imperf. Value $6.

Alexander Fleming (1881-1955), Discoverer of Penicillin — A686

1981, Aug. 7
2699 A686 2fo multi   .25 .20
Exists imperf. Value $8.

Bridal Chest A687

Designs: Bridal chests.

1981, Sept. 12   **Litho.**   **Perf. 12**
2700 A687 1fo Szentgal, 18th
    cent.   .20 .20
2701 A687 2fo Hodmezovasar-
    hely, 19th cent.   .30 .20

Souvenir Sheet
2702 A687 10fo Bacs County,
    17th cent.   1.75 1.75
54th Stamp Day. No. 2702 contains one stamp (44x25mm).
Exist imperf. Values: Nos. 2700-2701 $15; No. 2702 $25.

Calvinist College, Papa, 450th Anniv. A688

1981, Oct. 3   **Litho.**   **Perf. 12**
2703 A688 2fo multi   .25 .20
Exists imperf. Value $6.

World Food Day — A689

1981, Oct. 16
2704 A689 2fo multi   .25 .20
Exists imperf. Value $7.

Passenger Ship Rakoczi, 1964, No. 1834 — A690

Sidewheelers and Hungarian stamps.

1981, Nov. 25   **Perf. 12x11½**
2705 A690 1fo Franz I, #1828   .20 .20
2706 A690 1fo Arpad, #1829   .20 .20
2707 A690 2fo Szechenyi,
    #1830   .30 .20
2708 A690 2fo Grof Szechenyi
    Istvan, #1831   .30 .20

2709	A690	4fo	Sofia, #1832	.65	.30
2710	A690	6fo	Felszabadulas, #1833	.95	.50
2711	A690	8fo	shown	1.25	.65
			Nos. 2705-2711 (7)	3.85	2.25

Souvenir Sheet
Perf. 13

2712	A690	20fo	Hydrofoil Solyom, #1830	3.00	3.00

European Danube Commission, 125th anniv.
Exist imperf. Value: set $30; souvenir sheet $35.

Souvenir Sheet

Slovakian Natl. Costumes — A691

Perf. 12½x11½

1981, Nov. 18				**Litho.**	
2713			Sheet of 4	2.00	1.90
a.	A691	1fo	shown	.20	.20
b.	A691	2fo	German	.40	.35
c.	A691	3fo	Croatian	.60	.60
d.	A691	4fo	Romanian	.80	.75

Exists imperf. Value $30.

Christmas 1981 — A692

Sculptures: 1fo, Mary Nursing the Infant Jesus, by Margit Kovacs. 2fo, Madonna of Csurgo.

1981, Dec. 4				**Perf. 12½x11½**	
2714	A692	1fo	multi	.20	.20
2715	A692	2fo	multi	.40	.20

Exist imperf. Value, set $12.

Pen Pals, by Norman Rockwell A693

1981, Dec. 29				**Perf. 11½x12**	

Norman Rockwell Illustrations.

2716	A693	1fo	shown	.20	.20
2717	A693	2fo	Courting Under the Clock at Midnight	.20	.20
2718	A693	2fo	Maiden Voyage	.20	.20
2719	A693	4fo	Threading the Needle	.45	.25
			Nos. 2716-2719,C435-C437 (7)	3.10	2.50

Exist imperf. Value, set (7) $25.

Souvenir Sheet

La Toilette, by Pablo Picasso (1881-1973) — A694

1981, Dec. 29			**Litho.**	**Perf. 11½**	
2720	A694	20fo	multicolored	3.50	3.50

Exists imperf. Value $70.

25th Anniv. of Worker's Militia A695

1982, Jan. 26			**Litho.**	**Perf. 12**	
2721	A695	1fo	Shooting practice	.20	.20
2722	A695	4fo	Members, 3 generations	.50	.35

Exist imperf. Value, set $12.

10th World Trade Union Congress — A696

1982, Feb. 12			**Litho.**	**Perf. 12x11½**	
2723	A696	2fo	multicolored	.25	.20

Exists imperf. Value $6.

Famous Hungarians Type

Gyula Alpri (1882-1944), anti-fascist martyr.

1982, Mar. 24				**Perf. 12**	
2724	A674	2fo	multicolored	.25	.20

Exists imperf. Value $6.

Robert Koch — A698

1982, Mar. 24			**Litho.**	**Perf. 12**	
2725	A698	2fo	multicolored	.25	.20

TB Bacillus centenary.
Exists imperf. Value $7.

1982 World Cup — A699

Designs: Hungary in competition with other World Cup teams.
#2733: a, Barcelona Stadium. b, Madrid Stadium.

1982, Apr. 16				**Perf. 11**	
2726	A699	1fo	Egypt, 1934	.20	.20
2727	A699	1fo	Italy, 1938	.20	.20
2728	A699	2fo	Germany, 1954	.20	.20
2729	A699	2fo	Mexico, 1958	.20	.20
2730	A699	4fo	England, 1962	.45	.25
2731	A699	6fo	Brazil, 1966	.70	.40
2732	A699	8fo	Argentina, 1978	.90	.55
			Nos. 2726-2732 (7)	2.85	2.00

Souvenir Sheet

2733			Sheet of 2	3.00	3.00
a.-b.	A699	10fo	any single	1.40	1.40

No. 2733 contains 44x44mm stamps.
Exist imperf. Value: set $22.75; souvenir sheet $30.

European Table Tennis Championship, Budapest, Apr. 17-25 — A700

1982, Apr. 16			**Litho.**	**Perf. 11½x12**	
2734	A700	2fo	multi	.25	.20

Exists imperf. Value $5.50.

Roses A701

1982, Apr. 30				**Perf. 12**	
2735	A701	1fo	Pascali	.20	.20
2736	A701	1fo	Michele Meilland	.20	.20
2737	A701	2fo	Diorama	.30	.20
2738	A701	2fo	Wendy Cussons	.30	.20
2739	A701	3fo	Blue Moon	.40	.25
2740	A701	3fo	Invitation	.40	.25
2741	A701	4fo	Tropicana	.60	.30
			Nos. 2735-2741 (7)	2.40	1.60

Souvenir Sheet

2742	A701	10fo	Bouquet	2.50	2.50

No. 2742 contains one stamp (34x59mm, perf. 11).
Exist imperf. Value: set $25; souvenir sheet $40.

25 Years of Space Travel — A702

1982, May 18			**Photo.**	**Perf. 11½**	
2743	A702	1fo	Columbia shuttle, 1981	.20	.20
2744	A702	1fo	Armstrong, Apollo 11, 1969	.20	.20
2745	A702	2fo	A. Leonov, Voskhod 2, 1965	.30	.20
2746	A702	2fo	Yuri Gagarin, Vostok	.30	.20
2747	A702	4fo	Laika, Sputnik 2, 1957	.55	.35
2748	A702	4fo	Sputnik I, 1957	.55	.35
2749	A702	6fo	Space researcher K.E. Tsiolkovsky	.90	.50
			Nos. 2743-2749 (7)	3.00	2.00

Exist imperf. Value, set $20.

A703

1982, May 7			**Litho.**	**Perf. 12**	
2750	A703	2fo	multi	.50	.20

George Dimitrov (1882-1947), 1st prime minister of Bulgaria. SOZPHILEX '82 Stamp Exhib., Sofia, Bulgaria, May. No. 2750 se-tenant with label showing Bulgarian 1300th anniv. emblems.
Exists imperf. Value, with label $15.

Diosgyor paper mill, bicent. — A704

1982, May 27			**Litho.**	**Perf. 12x11½**	
2751	A704	2fo	multi	.25	.20

Exists imperf. Value $6.

First Rubik's Cube World Championship, Budapest, June 5 — A705

1982, June 4				**Perf. 11½x12**	
2752	A705	2fo	multi	.25	.20

Exists imperf. Value $8.

Souvenir Sheet

George Washington, by F. Kemmelmeyer — A706

Washington's 250th Birth Anniv.: a, Michael Kovats de Fabricy (1724-1779), Cavalry Commandant, by Sandor Finta.

1982, July 2			**Litho.**	**Perf. 11**	
2753	A706		Sheet of 2	2.50	2.50
a.-b.		5fo	any single	.75	.75

Exists imperf. Value $25.

World Hematology Congress, Budapest — A707

Zirc Abbey, 800th Anniv. — A708

1982, July 30   **Perf. 12½x11½**
2754 A707 2fo multi   .25 .20
Exists imperf. Value $7.

1982, Aug. 19   **Perf. 11½x12**
2755 A708 2fo multi   .25 .20
Exists imperf. Value $6.

KNER Printing Office, Gyoma, Centenary — A709

1982, Sept. 23 Litho.   **Perf. 12x11½**
2756 A709 2fo Emblem   .25 .20
Exists imperf. Value $6.

AGROFILA '82 Intl. Agricultural Stamp Exhibition, Godollo — A710

1982, Sept. 24   **Perf. 11½x12**
2757 A710 5fo Map   1.00 .95
Issued in sheets of 3 stamps and 3 labels showing Godollo Agricultural University, emblem. Size: 109x127mm.
Exist imperf. Value: single with label $6; sheetlet $20.

Public Transportation Sesquicentennial — A711

1982, Oct. 5 Litho.   **Perf. 12x11½**
2758 A711 2fo multi   .25 .20
Exists imperf. Value $20.

Vuk and a Bird — A712

Scenes from Vuk the Fox Cub, Cartoon by Attila Dargay.

1982, Nov. 11   **Perf. 12½**
2759 A712 1fo shown   .20 .20
2760 A712 1fo Dogs   .20 .20
2761 A712 2fo Rooster   .25 .20
2762 A712 2fo Owl   .25 .20
2763 A712 4fo Geese   .50 .30
2764 A712 6fo Frog   .70 .55
2765 A712 8fo Master fox   1.00 .70
Nos. 2759-2765 (7)   3.10 2.35
Exist imperf. Value, set $22.

Engineering Education Bicentenary A713

1982, Oct. 13   **Perf. 12**
2766 A713 2fo Budapest Poly-technical Univ.   .25 .20
Exists imperf. Value $7.

Famous Hungarians Type

Gyorgy Boloni (1882-1959), writer and journalist.

1982, Oct. 29
2767 A674 2fo multi   .25 .20
Exists imperf. Value $6.

October Revolution, 65th Anniv. — A715

1982, Nov. 5 Litho.   **Perf. 11½x12**
2768 A715 5fo Lenin   .75 .40
Exists imperf. Value $7.

Works of Art in Hungarian Chapel, Vatican — A716

1982, Nov. 30   **Perf. 12x11½**
Designs: No. 2769, St. Stephen, first King of Hungary (1001-1038). No. 2770, Pope Sylvester II making donation to St. Stephen. No. 2771, Pope Callixtus III ordering noon victory bell ringing by St. John of Capistrano, 1456. No. 2772, Pope Paul VI showing Cardinal Lekai location of Hungarian Chapel. No. 2773, Pope John Paul II consecrating chapel, 1980. No. 2774, Madonna and Child. Nos. 2769, 2774 sculptures by Imre Varga; others by Amerigo Tot. Nos. 2770-2773, size 37x18mm,

in continuous design in block of 4 between Nos. 2769 and 2774.
2769 A716 2fo multi   .40 .40
2770 A716 2fo multi   .40 .40
2771 A716 2fo multi   .40 .40
2772 A716 2fo multi   .40 .40
2773 A716 2fo multi   .40 .40
2774 A716 2fo multi   .40 .40
  a.   Block of 6, #2769-2774   2.60 2.60
Exist imperf. Value, block $20.

Souvenir Sheet

Zoltan Kodaly (1882-1967), Composer — A717

1982, Dec. 16   **Perf. 11½**
2775 A717 20fo multi   2.75 2.75
Exists imperf. Value $25.

A718

Perf. 12½x11½
1982, Dec. 16   **Litho.**
2776 A718 2fo multi   .35 .20
New Year 1983.
Exists imperf. Value $6.

A719

1982, Dec. 29   **Perf. 11½x12½**
Design: Johann Wolfgang Goethe (1749-1832), German poet, by Heinrich Kolbe.

Souvenir Sheet
2777 A719 20fo multi   2.75 2.75
Exists imperf. Value $37.50.

10th Anniv. of Postal Code — A720

1983, Jan. 24   **Perf. 11½x12**
2778 A720 2fo multi   .25 .20
Exists imperf. Value $6.

3rd Budapest Spring Festival, Mar. 18-27 A721

1983, Mar. 18 Litho.   **Perf. 12x11½**
2779 A721 2fo Ship of Peace, by Engre Szasz   .25 .20
Exists imperf. Value $6.

Gyula Juhasz (1883-1937), Poet — A722

1983, Apr. 15   **Perf. 12**
2780 A722 2fo multi   .25 .20
Exists imperf. Value $6.

City of Szentgotthard, 800th Anniv. — A723

1983, May 4 Litho.   **Perf. 11½**
2781 A723 2fo Monastery, seal, 1489   .25 .20
Exists imperf. Value $6.

Malomto Lake, Tapolca — A724

1983, May 17   **Perf. 11½x12**
2782 A724 5fo multi   .80 .80
TEMBAL '83 Intl. Topical Stamp Exhibition, Basel, May 21-29. Issued in sheets of 3 stamps and 3 labels.
Exists imperf. Value: single with label $5.50; sheetlet $20.

Souvenir Sheet

5th Interparliamentary Union Conference on European Cooperation, Budapest, May 30-June 5 — A725

1983, May 30   **Litho.**   **Perf. 12½**
2783 A725 20fo Budapest Parliament   3.50 3.25
    Exists imperf. Value $25.

Jeno Hamburger (1883-1936) A726

1983, May 31   **Perf. 12**
2784 A726 2fo multi   .45 .20
    Exists imperf. Value $6.

Lady with Unicorn, by Raphael (1483-1517) A727

Paintings: No. 2786, Joan of Aragon. No. 2787, Granduca Madonna. No. 2788, Madonna and Child with St. John. 4fo, La Muta. 6fo, La Valeta. 8fo, La Fornarina. 20fo, Esterhazy Madonna.

Perf. 11½x12½
1983, June 29   **Litho.**
2785 A727 1fo multi   .20 .20
2786 A727 1fo multi   .20 .20
2787 A727 2fo multi   .25 .20
2788 A727 2fo multi   .25 .20
2789 A727 4fo multi   .45 .30
2790 A727 6fo multi   .65 .30
2791 A727 8fo multi   .75 .45
    Nos. 2785-2791 (7)   2.75 1.85

Souvenir Sheet

2792 A727 20fo multi   3.00 3.00
    No. 2792 contains one stamp (24x37mm).
    Exist imperf. Value: set $25; souvenir sheet $25.

Simon Bolivar (1783-1830) A728

1983, July 22   **Litho.**   **Perf. 12**
2793 A728 2fo multi   .25 .20
    Exists imperf. Value $6.

Istvan Vagi (1883-1940), Anti-fascist Martyr A729

1983, July 22   **Perf. 11½x12½**
2794 A729 2fo multi   .45 .20
    Exists imperf. Value $6.

68th World Esperanto Congress, Budapest, July 30-Aug. 6 — A730

1983, July 29   **Perf. 12**
2795 A730 2fo multi   .25 .20
    Exists imperf. Value $6.

Souvenir Sheet

Martin Luther (1483-1546) — A731

1983, Aug. 12   **Perf. 12½**
2796 A731 20fo multi   2.75 2.50
    Exists imperf. Value $25.

Birds — A732

Designs: Protected birds of prey and World Wildlife Fund emblem

1983, Aug. 18   **Perf. 11½x12**
2797 A732 1fo Aquila heliaca   .20 .20
2798 A732 1fo Aquila pomarina   .20 .20
2799 A732 2fo Haliaetus albicilla   .25 .20
2800 A732 2fo Falco vespertinus   .25 .20
2801 A732 4fo Falco cherrug   .45 .30
2802 A732 6fo Buteo lagopus   .75 .35
2803 A732 8fo Buteo buteo   .90 .75
    Nos. 2797-2803 (7)   3.00 2.20
    Exist imperf. Value, set $20.

29th Intl. Apicultural Congress, Budapest, Aug. 25-31 — A733

1983, Aug. 25   **Perf. 12**
2804 A733 1fo Bee collecting pollen   .20 .20
    Exists imperf. Value $7.

Fruit, by Bela Czobel (1883-1976) — A734

1983, Sept. 15   **Litho.**   **Perf. 12x11½**
2805 A734 2fo multi   .25 .20
    Exists imperf. Value $6.

World Communications Year — A735

No. 2806, Telecommunications, Earth Satellite. No. 2807, Intersputnik Earth Station. 2fo, TMM-81 Telephone Service. 3fo, Intelligent Terminal System. 5fo, OCR Optical Reading Instrument. 8fo, Teletext. 20fo, Molniya Communications Satellite.

1983, Oct. 7   **Litho.**   **Perf. 11½x12**
2806 A735 1fo multi   .20 .20
2807 A735 1fo multi   .20 .20
2808 A735 2fo multi   .25 .20
2809 A735 3fo multi   .40 .25
2810 A735 5fo multi   .70 .40
2811 A735 8fo multi   1.10 .65
    Nos. 2806-2811 (6)   2.85 1.90

Souvenir Sheet
Perf. 12x12½

2812 A735 20fo multi   3.00 3.00
    Exist imperf. Value: set $20; souvenir sheet $25.

34th Intl. Astronautical Federation Congress — A736

1983, Oct. 10   **Photo.**   **Perf. 12**
2813 A736 2fo multi   .75 .20
    Exists imperf. Value $6.

SOZPHILEX 83, Moscow — A737

1983, Oct. 14   **Litho.**   **Perf. 12**
2814 A737 2fo Kremlin   .50 .50
    Issued in sheets of 3 stamps and 3 labels showing emblem. Size: 101x133mm.
    Exists imperf. Value: single with label $6; sheetlet $20.

Mihaly Babits (1883-1941), Poet and Translator — A738

1983, Nov. 25
2815 A738 2fo multi   .25 .20
    Exists imperf. Value $6.

Souvenir Sheet

European Security and Cooperation Conference, Madrid — A739

Perf. 12½x11½
1983, Nov. 10   **Litho.**
2816 A739 20fo multi   3.75 3.75
    Exists imperf. Value $23.

1984 Winter Olympics, Sarajevo — A740

Designs: Ice dancers representing the seven phases of a figure cut.

1983, Dec. 22   **Litho.**   **Perf. 12x12½**
2817 A740 1fo Emblem upper right   .20 .20
2818 A740 1fo Emblem upper left   .20 .20
2819 A740 2fo Arms extended   .25 .20
2820 A740 2fo Arms bent   .25 .20
2821 A740 4fo Man looking down   .55 .30
2822 A740 4fo Girl looking up   .55 .30
2823 A740 6fo multi   .85 .45
    a. Strip of 7, #2817-2823   3.00 2.00

Souvenir Sheet
Perf. 12½

2824 A740 6fo multi   3.00 3.00
    No. 2824 contains one 49x39mm stamp.
    Exist imperf. Value: strip $25; souvenir sheet $25.

Christmas A741

Resorts and Spas — A742

Designs: 1fo, Madonna with Rose, Kassa, 1500. 2fo, Altar piece, Csikmenasag, 1543.

1983, Dec. 13 Litho. Perf. 11½x12
2825 A741 1fo multi .25 .20
2826 A741 2fo multi .50 .20
Exist imperf. Value, set $12.

1983, Dec. 18
2827 A742 1fo Zanka, Lake Bala- ton .20 .20
2828 A742 2fo Hajduszoboszlo .30 .20
2829 A742 5fo Heviz .70 .35
Nos. 2827-2829 (3) 1.20 .75
Exist imperf. Value, set $20.

Virgin with Six Saints, by Giovanni Battista Tiepolo — A743

Rest During Flight into Egypt, by Giovanni Domenico Tiepolo — A744

Paintings Stolen and Later Recovered, Museum of Fine Arts, Budapest: b, Esterhazy Madonna, by Raphael. c, Portrait of Giorgione, 16th cent. d, Portrait of a Woman, by Tintoretto. e, Pietro Bempo, by Raphael. f, Portrait of a Man, by Tintoretto.

1984, Feb. 16 Perf. 12½x12
2839 Sheet of 7 3.75 3.75
a.-f. A743 2fo multi .35
g. A744 8fo multi 1.50
Exists imperf. Value $50.

Energy Conservation A745

1984, Mar. 30 Litho. Perf. 11½x12
2840 A745 1fo multi .25 .20
Exists imperf. Value $7.

Sandor Korosi Csoma (1784-1842), Master of Tibetan Philology A746

1984, Mar. 30 Perf. 11½x12½
2841 A746 2fo multi .25 .20
Stamps with silver inscription and with back inscription "Gift of the Hungarian Post" issued to members of Natl. Fed. of Hungarian Philatelists. Value $1.50.
Exists imperf. Value $6.

Miniature Sheet

No. 1900 — A747

Designs: b, No. 1346. c, No. 1259.

1984, Apr. 20 Litho. Perf. 12x11½
2842 Sheet of 3 + 3 labels 2.75 2.75
a.-c. A747 4fo multi .70
Espana '84; Ausipex '84; Philatelia '84.
Exists imperf. Value $25.

Post-Roman Archaeological Discoveries — A748

#2843, Round gold disc hair ornaments, Rakamaz. #2844, Saber belt plates, Szolnok-Strazsahalom and Galgocz. #2845, Silver disc hair ornaments, Sarospatak. #2846, Swords. 4fo, Silver and gold bowl, Ketpo. 6fo, Bone walking stick handles, Hajdudorog and Szabadbattyan. 8fo, Ivory saddle bow, Izsak; bit, stirrups, Muszka.

1984, May 15 Perf. 12
2843 A748 1fo dk brn & tan .20 .20
2844 A748 1fo dk brn & tan .20 .20
2845 A748 2fo dk brn & tan .25 .20
2846 A748 2fo dk brn & tan .25 .20
2847 A748 4fo dk brn & tan .50 .20
2848 A748 6fo dk brn & tan .75 .30
2849 A748 8fo dk brn & tan 1.00 .40
Nos. 2843-2849 (7) 3.15 1.70
Exist imperf. Value, set $20.

View of Cracow — A749

1984, May 21 Litho. Perf. 12½x11½
2850 A749 2fo multi .25 .20
Permanent Committee of Posts and Telecommunications, 25th Session, Cracow.
Exists imperf. Value $6.

Butterflies A750

1984, June 7 Perf. 11½x12
2851 A750 1fo Epiphille dilecta .20 .20
2852 A750 1fo Agra sara .20 .20
2853 A750 2fo Morpho cypris .25 .20
2854 A750 2fo Ancylusis formos- sissima .25 .20
2855 A750 4fo Danaus chrysip- pus .50 .20
2856 A750 6fo Catagramma cy- nosura .75 .30

2857 A750 8fo Ornithoptera paradisea 1.00 .45
Nos. 2851-2857 (7) 3.15 1.75
Exist imperf. Value, set $25.

A751   A752

Archer, by Kisfaludy Strobl (1884-1975).

1984, July 26 Litho. Perf. 12½x11½
2858 A751 2fo multicolored .25 .20
Exists imperf. Value $4.

1984, July 26
2859 A752 2fo multicolored .25 .20
Akos Hevesi (1884-1937), revolutionary. See Nos. 2884-2885, 2910, 2915, 2962.
Exists imperf. Value $6.

Kepes Ujsag Peace Festival A753

Aerobatic Championship A754

1984, Aug. 3 Litho. Perf. 12½x11½
2860 A753 2fo Map, building .25 .20
Exists imperf. Value $5.50.

1984, Aug. 14
2861 A754 2fo Plane, map .25 .20
Exists imperf. Value $6.

Horse Team World Championship, Szilvasvarad, Aug. 17-20 — A755

1984, Aug. 17 Perf. 12
2862 A755 2fo Horse-drawn wag- on .25 .20
Exists imperf. Value $6.

Budapest Riverside Hotels — A756

1984, Sept.
2863 A756 1fo Atrium Hyatt .20 .20
2864 A756 2fo Duna Interconti- nental .25 .20
2865 A756 4fo Forum .50 .25
2866 A756 4fo Thermal Hotel, Margaret Isld. .50 .25
2867 A756 5fo Hilton .70 .35
2868 A756 8fo Gellert 1.00 .50
Nos. 2863-2868 (6) 3.15 1.75

Souvenir Sheet
2869 A756 20fo Hilton, diff. 2.75 2.75
Exist imperf. Value: set $20; souvenir sheet $25.

14th Conference of Postal Ministers, Budapest — A757

1984, Sept. 10 Perf. 12½x11½
2870 A757 2fo Building, post horn .25 .20
Exists imperf. Value $6.

57th Stamp Day A758

1984, Sept. 21 Perf. 12
2871 A758 1fo Four-handled vase, Zsolnay .20 .20
2872 A758 2fo Platter, vert. .80 .20

Souvenir Sheet
2872A A758 10fo #19 on cover 1.75 1.75
No. 2872A contains one stamp (44x27mm, perf. 11).
Exist imperf. Value: set $15; souvenir sheet $25.

Edible Mushrooms A759

Photogravure and Engraved
1984, Oct. Perf. 12x11½
2873 A759 1fo Boletus edulis .35 .20
2874 A759 1fo Marasmius oreades .35 .20
2875 A759 2fo Morchella es- culenta .60 .20
2876 A759 2fo Agaricus campester .60 .20
2877 A759 3fo Macrolepiota procera .90 .25
2878 A759 3fo Cantharellus cibarius .90 .25
2879 A759 4fo Armillariella mel- lea 1.25 .30
Nos. 2873-2879 (7) 4.95 1.60
Exist imperf. Value, set $20.

Budapest Opera House Centenary — A760

1984, Sept. 27 Perf. 12x11½
2880 A760 1fo Fresco by Mor Than .20 .20
2881 A760 2fo Hallway .25 .20
2882 A760 5fo Auditorium .65 .30
Nos. 2880-2882 (3) 1.10 .70

Souvenir Sheet
2883 A760 20fo Building 2.75 2.75
No. 2883 contains one stamp (49x40mm, perf. 12½).
Exist imperf. Value: set $20; souvenir sheet $25.

Famous Hungarians Type of 1984

#2884, Bela Balazs, writer (1884-1949); #2885, Kato Haman, labor leader (1884-1936).

1984, Dec. 3 Litho. Perf. 12½x11½
2884 A752 2fo multi   .25   .20
2885 A752 2fo multi   .25   .20

Exist imperf. Value, set $12.

Madonna and Child, Trensceny A763

1984, Dec. 17 Litho. Perf. 11½x12
2886 A763 1fo multi   .30   .30

Exists imperf. Value $6.

Owls — A764

Photogravure and Engraved
1984, Dec. 28 Perf. 12½x11½
2887 A764 1fo Athene Noctua   .20   .20
2888 A764 1fo Tyto alba   .20   .20
2889 A764 2fo Strix aluco   .25   .20
2890 A764 2fo Asio otus   .25   .20
2891 A764 4fo Nyctea scadiaca   .45   .30
2892 A764 6fo Strix uralensis   .75   .40
2893 A764 8fo Bubo bubo   .90   .50
  Nos. 2887-2893 (7)   3.00   2.00

Exist imperf. Value, set $20.

Torah Crown, Buda — A765

19th Cent. Art from Jewish Museum, Budapest.

1984, Dec. Litho. Perf. 12
2894 A765 1fo shown   .20   .20
2895 A765 1fo Chalice, Moscow   .20   .20
2896 A765 2fo Torah shield, Vienna   .25   .20
2897 A765 2fo Chalice, Warsaw   .25   .20
2898 A765 4fo Container, Augsburg   .55   .20
2899 A765 6fo Candlestick holder, Warsaw   .80   .35
2900 A765 8fo Money box, Pest   1.10   .45
  Nos. 2894-2900 (7)   3.35   1.80

Exist imperf. Value, set $20.

Souvenir Sheet

Hungarian Olympic Committee, 90th Anniv. — A766

1985, Jan. 2 Photo. Perf. 12x12½
2901 A766 20fo Long jump   2.75   2.75

Exists imperf. Value $25.

Novi Sad, Yugoslavia — A767

Danube Bridges: No. 2903, Baja. No. 2904, Arpad Bridge, Budapest. No. 2905, Bratislava, Czechoslovakia. 4fo, Reichsbrucke, Vienna. 6fo, Linz, Austria. 8fo, Regensburg, Federal Rep. of Germany. 20fo, Elizabeth Bridge, Budapest, and map.

1985, Feb. 12 Litho. Perf. 12x11½
2902 A767 1fo multi   .20   .20
2903 A767 1fo multi   .20   .20
2904 A767 2fo multi   .25   .20
2905 A767 2fo multi   .25   .20
2906 A767 4fo multi   .50   .25
2907 A767 6fo multi   .75   .40
2908 A767 8fo multi   1.00   .45
  Nos. 2902-2908 (7)   3.15   1.90

Souvenir Sheet
Perf. 12½
2909 A767 20fo multi   3.00   3.00

Exist imperf. Value: set $20; souvenir sheet $25.

Famous Hungarians Type of 1984

Design: Laszlo Rudas (1885-1950), communist philosopher.

1985, Feb. 21 Perf. 12½x11½
2910 A752 2fo gold & brn   .25   .20

Exists imperf. Value $6.

Intl. Women's Day, 75th Anniv. A769

1985, Mar. 5 Photo. Perf. 11½x12½
2911 A769 2fo gold & multi   .25   .20

Exists imperf. Value $6.

OLYMPHILEX '85, Lausanne A770

1985, Mar. 14 Litho. Perf. 11½x12
2912 A770 4fo No. B81   .50   .25
2913 A770 5fo No. B82   .65   .30

Exist imperf. Value, set $12.

Souvenir Sheet

Liberation of Hungary From German Occupation Forces, 40th Anniv. — A771

Design: Liberty Bridge, Budapest and silhouette of the Liberation Monument on Gellert Hill illuminated by fireworks.

1985, Mar. 28 Perf. 12½
2914 A771 20fo multi   2.75   2.75

Exists imperf. Value $30.

Famous Hungarians Type of 1984

Design: Gyorgy Lukacs (1885-1971) communist philosopher, educator.

1985, Apr. 12 Perf. 12½x11½
2915 A752 2fo gold & brn   .25   .20

Exists imperf. Value $6.

Totfalusi Bible, 300th Anniv. — A773

1985, Apr. 25 Perf. 12
2916 A773 2fo gold & black   .25   .20

1st Bible printed in Hungarian by Nicolas Totfalusi Kis (1650-1702), publisher, in 1685. Exists imperf. Value $6.

Lorand Eotvos Univ., 350th Anniv. — A774

Design: Archbishop Peter Pazmany (1570-1637), founder.

1985, May 14
2917 A774 2fo magenta & gray   .50   .20

No. 2917 printed se-tenant with label picturing obverse and reverse of university commemorative medal.
Exists imperf. Value, with label $15.

26th European Boxing Championships, Budapest — A775

1985, May 25
2918 A775 2fo multi   .25   .20

Exists imperf. Value $6.

Intl. Youth Year — A776

1985, May 29 Perf. 11½x12
2919 A776 1fo Girl's soccer   .20   .20
2920 A776 2fo Windsurfing   .20   .20
2921 A776 2fo Aerobic exercise   .20   .20
2922 A776 4fo Karate   .45   .20
2923 A776 4fo Go-kart racing   .45   .20
2924 A776 5fo Hang gliding   .65   .25
2925 A776 6fo Skateboarding   .70   .35
  Nos. 2919-2925 (7)   2.85   1.60

Exist imperf. Value, set $20.

Electro-magnetic High-speed Railway — A777

EXPO '85, Tsukuba, Japan: futuristic technology.

1985, May 29 Perf. 12x11½
2926 A777 2fo shown   .30   .20
2927 A777 4fo Fuyo (robot) Theater   .70   .20

Exist imperf. Value, set $15.

Audubon Birth Bicentenary A778

Audubon illustrations

1985, June 19 Perf. 12
2928 A778 2fo Colaptes cafer   .30   .20
2929 A778 2fo Bombycilla garrulus   .30   .20
2930 A778 2fo Dryocopus pileatus   .30   .20
2931 A778 4fo Icterus galbula   .55   .30
  Nos. 2928-2931,C446-C447 (6)   2.90   1.75

Exist imperf. Value set (6) $25.

Mezohegyes Stud Farm, Bicent. — A779

Horses: No. 2932, Nonius-36, 1883, a dark chestnut. No. 2933, Furioso-23, 1889, a light chestnut. No. 2934, Gidrian-1, 1935, a blond breed. No. 2935, Ramses-3, 1960, gray sporting horse. No. 2936, Krozus-1, 1970, chestnut sporting horse.

1985, June 28

2932	A779	1fo multi	.20	.20
2933	A779	2fo multi	.25	.20
2934	A779	4fo multi	.55	.20
2935	A779	4fo multi	.55	.20
2936	A779	6fo multi	.85	.35
	Nos. 2932-2936 (5)		2.40	1.15

Exist imperf. Value, set $20.

Prevention of Nuclear War — A780

Design: Illustration of a damaged globe and hands, by Imre Varga (b. 1923), 1973 Kossuth prize-winner.

1985, June 28   *Perf. 11½x12*

2937	A780	2fo multi	.20	.20

Intl. Physician's Movement for the Prevention of Nuclear War, 5th Congress.
Exists imperf. Value $7.

European Music Year — A781

1985, July 10   *Perf. 11*

Composers and instruments: 1fo, George Frideric Handel (1685-1759), kettle drum, horn. 2fo, Johann Sebastian Bach (1685-1750), Thomas Church organ. No. 2940, Luigi Cherubini (1760-1842), harp, bass viol, baryton. No. 2941, Frederic Chopin (1810-1849), piano, 1817. 5fo, Gustav Mahler (1860-1911), pardessus de viole, kettle drum, double horn. 6fo, Erkel Ferenc (1810-1893), bass tuba, violin.

2938	A781	1fo multi	.20	.20
2939	A781	2fo multi	.25	.20
2940	A781	4fo multi	.50	.20
2941	A781	4fo multi	.50	.20
2942	A781	5fo multi	.65	.25
2943	A781	6fo multi	.75	.30
	Nos. 2938-2943 (6)		2.85	1.35

Exist imperf. Value, set $22.75.

Souvenir Sheet

12th World Youth Festival, Moscow — A782

1985, July 22   *Perf. 12½*

2944	A782	20fo Emblem, Red Square	2.75	2.50

Exists imperf. Value $37.50.

Souvenir Sheet

Helsinki Agreement, 10th Anniv. — A783

1985, Aug. 1   *Perf. 11*

2945	A783	20fo Finlandia Hall, Helsinki	3.00	3.00

Exists imperf. Value $37.50.

World Tourism Day — A784

    Perf. 12½x11½

1985, Sept. 27   **Litho.**

2946	A784	2fo Key, globe, heart	.25	.20

Exists imperf. Value $6.

COMNET '85 — A785

1985, Oct. 1   *Perf. 11½*

2947	A785	4fo Computer terminal	.60	.30

3rd Computer Sciences Conference, Budapest, Oct. 1-4.
Exists imperf. Value $6.

Souvenir Sheet

Danube River, Budapest Bridges — A786

1985, Oct. 15   *Perf. 12*

2948	A786	20fo multi	3.25	3.25

European Security and Cooperation Conference and Cultural Forum, Budapest, Oct. 15-Nov. 25. Exists inscribed "Kuturalis Forum Resztvevoi Tiszteletere" in gold on front and "Gift of the Hungarian Post" on back. Not valid for postage.
Exists imperf. Value $40.

16-17th Century Ceramics — A787

1fo, Faience water jar and dispenser, 1609. 2fo, Tankard, 1670. 10fo, Hexagonal medicine jar, 1774.

1985, Oct. 18   *Perf. 12½x11½*

2949	A787	1fo multi	.20	.20
2950	A787	2fo multi	.80	.20

Souvenir Sheet

2951	A787	10fo multi	1.75	1.75

EUROPHILEX '85, Oct. 14-31.
Exist imperf. Value: set $12; souvenir sheet $25.

Italy No. 799, view of Rome — A788

1985, Oct. 21   *Perf. 12x11½*

2952	A788	5fo multi	.90	.90

Italia '85, Rome, Oct. 25-Nov. 3.
Issued in sheets of 3 stamps and 3 labels showing emblem.
Exists imperf. Value: single with label $7.50; sheetlet $22.75.

UN, 40th Anniv. — A789

1985, Oct. 24   *Perf. 11½x12*

2953	A789	4fo Dove, globe, emblem	.50	.30

Exists imperf. Value $6.

Indigenous Lilies — A790

Photogravure and Engraved

1985, Oct. 28   *Perf. 12x11½*

2954	A790	1fo Lilium bulbiferum	.20	.20
2955	A790	2fo Lilium martagon	.25	.20
2956	A790	2fo Erythronium dens-canis	.25	.20
2957	A790	4fo Fritillaria meleagris	.55	.20
2958	A790	4fo Lilium tigrinum	.55	.20
2959	A790	5fo Hemerocallis lilio-asphodelus	.70	.30
2960	A790	6fo Bulbocodium vernum	.85	.35
	Nos. 2954-2960 (7)		3.35	1.65

Exist imperf. Value, set $20.

Christmas 1985 — A791

1985, Nov. 6   **Litho.**   *Perf. 13½x13*

2961	A791	2fo Youths caroling	.25	.20

Exists imperf. Value $7.

Famous Hungarians Type of 1984

Design: Istvan Ries (1885-1950), Minister of Justice (1949), labor movement.

1985, Nov. 11   *Perf. 12½x11½*

2962	A752	2fo gold & ol brn	.25	.20

Exists imperf. Value $6.

Motorcycle Centenary — A793

Photogravure & Engraved

1985, Dec. 28   *Perf. 11½x12*

2963	A793	1fo Fantic Sprinter, 1984	.20	.20
2964	A793	2fo Suzuki Katana GSX, 1983	.20	.20
2965	A793	2fo Harley-Davidson Duo-Glide, 1960	.20	.20
2966	A793	4fo Rudge-Whitworth, 1935	.45	.20
2967	A793	4fo BMW R47, 1927	.45	.20
2968	A793	5fo NSU, 1910	.60	.20
2969	A793	6fo Daimler, 1885	.70	.25
	Nos. 2963-2969 (7)		2.80	1.45

Exist imperf. Value, set $20.

Bela Kun (1886-1939), Communist Party Founder — A794

Perf. 12½x11½

1986, Feb. 20   **Litho.**
2970 A794 4fo multi   .50   .30

Exist imperf. Value $6.

Souvenir Sheet

US Shuttle Challenger — A795

1986, Feb. 21   *Perf. 11½*
2971 A795 20fo multi   3.25 3.25

Memorial to the US astronauts who died when the Challenger exploded during takeoff, Jan. 28.
Exist imperf. Value $25.

Halley's Comet — A796

#2972, US Ice satellite, dinosaurs. #2973, USSR Vega and Bayeaux tapestry detail, 1066, France. #2974, Japanese Suisei and German engraving, 1507. #2975, European Space Agency Giotto and The Three Magi, tapestry by Giotto. #2976, USSR Astron and Apianis constellation, 1531. #2977, US space shuttle and Edmond Halley.

Perf. 11½x13½

1986, Feb. 14   **Litho.**
2972 A796 2fo multi   .25   .20
2973 A796 2fo multi   .25   .20
2974 A796 2fo multi   .25   .20
2975 A796 4fo multi   .45   .20
2976 A796 4fo multi   .45   .20
2977 A796 6fo multi   .80   .35
    Nos. 2972-2977 (6)   2.45 1.35

Exist imperf. Value, set $19.

Seeing-eye Dog, Red Cross A797   Soccer Players in Blue and Red Uniforms A798

Perf. 12½x11½

1986, Mar. 20   **Litho.**
2978 A797 4fo multi   .50   .20

Assistance for the blind.
Exists imperf. Value $15.

1986, Apr. 2   *Perf. 11*
Color of Uniforms
2979 A798 2fo shown   .25   .20
2980 A798 2fo blue & green   .25   .20
2981 A798 4fo red & black   .55   .20
2982 A798 4fo yellow & red   .55   .20
2983 A798 4fo yellow & green   .55   .20
2984 A798 6fo orange & white   .75   .30
    Nos. 2979-2984 (6)   2.90 1.30

Souvenir Sheet
Perf. 12½

2985 A798 20fo Victors   3.50 3.50

1986 World Cup Soccer Championships, Mexico. No. 2979 contains one stamp (size: 41x32mm). Also exists with added inscription "In honor of the winner . . ." and red control number.
Exist imperf. Value: set $25; souvenir sheet $25.

Buda Castle Cable Railway Station Reopening — A799

1986, Apr. 30   *Perf. 11½x12*
2986 A799 2fo org, brn & pale yel   .40   .20

Exists imperf. Value $6.

A800

A801

AMERIPEX '86, Chicago, May 22-June 1: a, Yankee doodle rose. b, America rose. c, George Washington, statue by Gyula Bezeredy (1858-1935), Budapest.

1986, Apr. 30   *Perf. 12½x11½*
Souvenir Sheet
2987   Sheet of 3   3.25 3.00
a.-b.   A800 5fo any single   .75   .75
c.   A800 10fo multi   1.50 1.50

Size of No. 2987c: 27x74mm.
Exists imperf. Value $35.

1986, May 6   *Perf. 11½x12*
2988 A801 4fo Folk dolls   .50   .30

Hungary Days in Tokyo.
Exists imperf. Value $6.

Andras Fay (1786-1864), Author, Politician — A802

Lithographed and Engraved
1986, May 29   *Perf. 12*
2989 A802 4fo beige & fawn   .65   .30

Printed se-tenant with label picturing First Hungarian Savings Bank Union, founded by Fay.
Exists imperf. Value, with label $15.

Automobile, Cent. A803

#2990, 1961 Ferrari Tipo 156, 1985 race car. #2991, 1932 Alfa Romeo Tipo B, 1984 race car. #2992, 1936 Volkswagen, 1986 Porsche 959. #2993, 1902 Renault 14CV, 1985 Renault 5 GT Turbo. #2994, 1899 Fiat 3½, 1985 Fiat Ritmo. 6fo, 1886 Daimler, 1986 Mercedes-Benz 230SE.

1986, July 24   **Litho.**   *Perf. 12*
2990 A803 2fo multi   .25   .20
2991 A803 2fo multi   .25   .20
2992 A803 2fo multi   .25   .20
2993 A803 4fo multi   .55   .20
2994 A803 4fo multi   .55   .20
2995 A803 6fo multi   .85   .35
    Nos. 2990-2995 (6)   2.70 1.35

Exists imperf. Value, set $22.

Wasa, 1628, Warship — A804

1986, Aug. 15   **Litho.**   *Perf. 11½x12*
2996 A804 2fo multi   .50   .50

STOCKHOLMIA '86, 8/28-9/7. Printed se-tenant with label (size: 27x34mm) picturing exhibition emblem. Printed in sheets of 3.
Exists imperf. Value: single with label $7; sheetlet $25.

14th Intl. Cancer Congress, Budapest — A805

Design: Moritz Kaposi (1837-1902), Austrian cancer researcher.

1986, Aug. 21   *Perf. 12½x11½*
2997 A805 4fo multicolored   .50   .30

Exists imperf. Value $10.

Recapture of Buda Castle, by Gyula Benczur (1844-1920) — A806

1986, Sept. 2   *Perf. 12*
2998 A806 4fo multicolored   .50   .30

Recapture of Buda from the Turks, 300th anniv.
Exists imperf. Value $7.

Tranquility — A807

Hope — A808

Stamp Day: Paintings by Endre Szasz.

1986, Sept. 5
2999 A807 2fo shown   .40   .20
3000 A807 2fo Confidence   .40   .20

Souvenir Sheet
Perf. 11½
3001 A808 10fo shown   1.75 1.75

Exist imperf. Value: set $20; souvenir sheet $30.

5th Intl. Conference on Oriental Carpets, Vienna and Budapest A809

1986, Sept. 17   **Litho.**   *Perf. 11*
3002 A809 4fo Anatolia crivelli, 15th cent.   .60   .30

Exists imperf. Value $5.50.

Franz Liszt, Composer A810

1986, Oct. 21   **Engr.**   *Perf. 12*
3003 A810 4fo grayish green   .50   .30

Exists imperf. Value $6.

Intl. Peace Year — A811

1986, Oct. 24   **Litho.**
3004 A811 4fo multicolored   .75   .30

No. 3004 printed se-tenant with label. Exists imperf. Value, with label $22.

Souvenir Sheet

Hofburg Palace, Vienna, and Map — A812

1986, Nov. 4   **Perf. 11**
3005 A812 20fo multicolored   3.00 2.75

European Security and Cooperation Conference, Vienna.
Exists imperf. Value $35.

Fruits A813

Photogravure & Engraved
1986, Nov. 25   **Perf. 12x11½**
3006 A813 2fo Sour cherries   .25 .20
3007 A813 2fo Apricots   .25 .20
3008 A813 4fo Peaches   .50 .25
3009 A813 4fo Raspberries   .50 .25
3010 A813 4fo Apples   .50 .25
3011 A813 6fo Grapes   .80 .35
    Nos. 3006-3011 (6)   2.80 1.50

Exist imperf. Value, set $20.

Natl. Heroes — A814

Designs: No. 3012, Jozseph Pogany (1886-1939), journalist, martyr. No. 3013, Ferenc Munnich (1886-1967), prime minister, 1958-61.

1986   **Litho.**   **Perf. 12½x11½**
3012 A814 4fo multi   .65 .30
3013 A814 4fo multi   .65 .30

   Issued: #3012, Nov. 6; #3013, Nov. 14.
Exist imperf. Value, set $12.

World Communist Youth Fed., 12th Congress A815

1986, Nov. 21   **Perf. 12**
3014 A815 4fo multi   .50 .30

Exist imperf. Value $6.

Castles — A816

Festetics Castle, Keszthely A816a

2fo, Forgach, Szecseny. 3fo, Savoya, Rack-eve. 4fo, Batthyany, Kormend. 5fo, Szechenyi, Nagycenk. 6fo, Rudnyanszky, Nagyteteny. 7fo, Esterhazy, Papa. 8fo, Szapary, Buk. 10fo, Festetics, Keszthely. 12fo, Dory Castle, Mihalyi. 20fo, Brunswick, Martonvasar. 30fo, De la Motte, Nosvaj. 40fo, L'Huillier-Coborg, Edeleny. 50fo, Teleki-Degenfeld, Szirak. 70fo, Magochy, Pacin. 100fo, Eszterhazy, Fertod.

Perf. 12x11½, 11½x12½ (7fo)
1986-91   **Litho.**
3015 A816 2fo multi   .20 .20
3016 A816 3fo multi   .20 .20
3017 A816 4fo multi   .20 .20
3018 A816 5fo multi   .30 .20
3019 A816 6fo multi   .35 .20
3020 A816 7fo multi   .50 .30
3021 A816 8fo multi   .50 .30
3022 A816 10fo multi   .85 .40
3023 A816 12fo multi   .90 .50
3024 A816 20fo multi   1.75 .75
3025 A816 30fo multi   2.25 1.10
3026 A816 40fo multi   3.00 1.60
3027 A816 50fo multi   4.00 1.90
3028 A816 70fo multi   5.00 2.75
3029 A816 100fo multi   8.00 4.00
  Nos. 3015-3029 (15)   28.00 14.60

The 7fo, 12fo are inscribed "Magyarország."
  Issued: 2-6, 8fo, 11/28; 10, 20-30, 100fo, 5/28/87; 40-60fo, 7/30/87; 7fo, 6/27/91; 12fo, 9/6/91.
Exist imperf. Value, set $190.
For overprint see No. 3320.

1989-92   **Litho. & Engr.**   **Perf. 12**
3030 A816a 10fo multi   1.50 .85

Litho.
3031 A816a 15fo multi   1.10 .65

The 15fo is inscribed "Magyarorszag."
  Issued: 10fo, Feb. 28; 15fo, Mar. 27, 1992.
No. 3030 exist imperf. Value $12.

Wildlife Conservation A817

1986, Dec. 15   **Perf. 12**
3035 A817 2fo Felis silvestris   .30 .20
3036 A817 2fo Lutra lutra   .30 .20
3037 A817 2fo Mustela erminea   .30 .20
3038 A817 4fo Sciurus vulgaris   .55 .30
3039 A817 4fo Erinaceus concolor   .55 .30
3040 A817 6fo Emys orbicularis   .80 .40
  Nos. 3035-3040 (6)   2.80 1.60

Exist imperf. Value, set $20.

Portraits of Hungarian Kings in the Historical Portrait Gallery — A818

King and reign: No. 3041, St. Steven, 997-1038. No. 3042, Geza I, 1074-1077. No. 3043, St. Ladislas, 1077-1095. No. 3044, Bela III, 1172-1196. No. 3045, Bela IV, 1235-1270.

1986, Dec. 10   **Perf. 11½x12**
3041 A818 2fo multi   .30 .20
3042 A818 2fo multi   .30 .20
3043 A818 4fo multi   .60 .30
3044 A818 4fo multi   .60 .30
3045 A818 6fo multi   .90 .45
  Nos. 3041-3045 (5)   2.70 1.45

Exist imperf. Value, set $20.
See Nos. 3120-3122.

Fungi — A819

Lithographed and Engraved
1986, Dec. 30   **Perf. 11½**
3046 A819 2fo Amanita phalloides   .30 .20
3047 A819 2fo Inocybe patouillardi   .30 .20
3048 A819 2fo Amanita muscaria   .30 .20
3049 A819 4fo Omphalotus olearius   .55 .30
3050 A819 4fo Amanita pantherina   .55 .30
3051 A819 6fo Gyromitra esculenta   .80 .40
  Nos. 3046-3051 (6)   2.80 1.60

Exist imperf. Value, set $20.

Saltwater Fish — A820

1987, Jan. 15   **Photo.**   **Perf. 11½**
3052 A820 2fo Colisa fasciata   .30 .20
3053 A820 2fo Pseudotropheus zebra   .30 .20
3054 A820 2fo Iriatherina werneri   .30 .20
3055 A820 4fo Aphyosemion multicolor   .55 .30
3056 A820 4fo Papiliochromis ramirezi   .55 .30
3057 A820 6fo Hyphessobrycon erythrostigma   .80 .40
  Nos. 3052-3057 (6)   2.80 1.60

Exist imperf. Value, set $25.

Seated Woman, 1918, by Bela Uitz (1887-1972), Painter A821

Abstract, 1960, by Lajos Kassak (1887-1967) A822

1987, Mar. 6   **Litho.**   **Perf. 12**
3058 A821 4fo multicolored   .50 .30

Exists imperf. Value $6.

1987, Mar. 20
3059 A822 4fo black & red   .50 .30

Exists imperf. Value $6.

Medical Pioneers — A823

Designs: 2fo, Hippocrates (460-377 B.C.), Greek physician. No. 3061, Avicenna or Ibn Sina (A.D. 980-1037), Islamic pharmacist, diagnostician. No. 3062, Ambroise Pare (1510-1590), French surgeon. No. 3063, William Harvey (1578-1657), English physician, anatomist. 6fo, Ignaz Semmelweis (1818-1865), Hungarian obstetrician.

1987, Mar. 31
3060 A823 2fo black & dk red brn   .30 .20
3061 A823 4fo black & dk grn   .55 .30
3062 A823 4fo black & steel bl   .55 .30
3063 A823 4fo black & olive blk   .55 .30
3064 A823 6fo black & grn blk   .80 .40
  Nos. 3060-3064 (5)   2.75 1.50

Exists imperf. Value, set $20.

Neolithic and Copper Age Artifacts — A824

1987, Apr. 15   **Litho.**   **Perf. 12**
Designs: 2fo, Urn, Hodmezovasarhely. No. 3066, Altar, Szeged. No. 3067, Deity, Szegvar-Tuzkoves. 5fo, Vase, Center.

3065 A824 2fo pale bl grn & sep   .25 .20
3066 A824 4fo buff & sepia   .55 .30
3067 A824 4fo pale org & sepia   .55 .30
3068 A824 5fo pale yel grn & sep   .80 .40
  Nos. 3065-3068 (4)   2.15 1.20

Exists imperf. Value, set $20.

Souvenir Sheet

Esztergom Cathedral Treasury Reopening — A825

1987, Apr. 28   **Perf. 11**
3069 A825 20fo Calvary of King Matthias   3.50 3.50

No. 3069 margin pictures the Horn Chalice of King Sigismund, Rhineland, 1408 (UL), Crozier of Archbishop Miklos Olah, Hungary, c. 1490 (UR), Monstrance of Imre Eszterhazy, by Gaspar Meichl, Vienna, 1728 (LL), and the Chalice of Matthias, Hungary, c. 1480.
Exists imperf. Value $30.

Hungarian First
Aid Assoc.,
Cent. — A826

1987, May 5   *Perf. 11½x12*
3070 A826 4fo Ambulances,
                   1887-1987   .50   .30
   Exists imperf. Value $6.

Souvenir Sheet

CAPEX
'87,
Toronto
A827

   Stamp exhibitions: b, OLYMPHILEX '87,
Rome. c, HAFNIA '87, Copenhagen.

1987, May 20   Litho.   Perf. 11
3071   Sheet of 3 + 3 labels   3.50   2.75
 a.-c. A827 5fo any single   1.25   .90
   Exists imperf. Value $20.

Jozsef Marek (1886-1952),
Veterinarian — A828

1987, May 25   *Perf. 12x11½*
3072 A828 4fo multicolored   .50   .30
   Veterinary education, bicent.
   Exists imperf. Value $6.

Teleki's African Expedition,
Cent. — A829

1987, June 10
3073 A829 4fo multicolored   .50   .30
   Samuel Teleki (1845-1916), explorer.
   Exists imperf. Value $6.

Woodcut by
Abraham von
Werdt, 18th
Cent. — A830

Litho. & Engr.
1987, June 25   *Perf. 12*
3074 A830 4fo beige & sepia   .50   .30
   Hungarian Printing, Paper and Press Workers' Union, 125th anniv.
   Exists imperf. Value $6.

Antarctic
Research, 75th
Anniv. — A831

Helicopter Landing, Mirnij Research
Station — A832

1987, June 30   **Litho.**
   Map, explorer and scene: No. 3075, James
Cook (1728-1779) and ship. No. 3076, Fabian
von Bellingshausen (1778-1852) and seals.
No. 3077, Ernest H. Shackleton (1874-1922)
and penguins. No. 3078, Roald Amundsen
(1872-1928) discovering South Pole, dog
team. No. 3079, Robert F. Scott (1868-1912)
and ship. No. 3080, Richard E. Byrd (1888-
1957) and Floyd Bennett monoplane.

3075 A831 2fo multi   .30   .20
3076 A831 2fo multi   .30   .20
3077 A831 2fo multi   .30   .20
3078 A831 4fo multi   .55   .30
3079 A831 4fo multi   .55   .30
3080 A831 6fo multi   .80   .40
         Nos. 3075-3080 (6) 2.80   1.60
Souvenir Sheet
Perf. 11½
3081 A832 20fo multi   3.00   3.00
   Exist imperf. Value: set $25; souvenir sheet
$50.

Railway Officers
Training Institute,
Cent. — A833

1987, Sept. 4   Litho.   Perf. 11½x12
3082 A833 4fo blue & black   .75   .50
   Exists imperf. Value $6.

Stamp Day, 60th
Anniv. — A834

Litho. & Engr.
1987, Sept. 18   *Perf. 12*
   Masonry of the medieval Buda Castle: 2fo,
Flowers, dolphin. 4fo, Arms of King Matthias.
10fo, "ONDIDIT/GENEROSVM" inscribed on
capital.

3083 A834 2fo multi   .35   .20
3084 A834 4fo multi   .70   .45
Souvenir Sheet
Perf. 11
3085 A834 10fo multi   1.75   1.75
   Exist imperf. Value: set $15; souvenir sheet
$30.

A835

1987, Sept. 30   Litho.   Perf. 12
3086 A835 4fo multi   .80   .50
 a.   Se-tenant with label   .80   .50
   No 3086 printed in sheet of 50 and in sheet
of 25 plus 25 labels picturing 13th cent. church
at Gyongyospata which houses the altar.
   Exists imperf. Value $12; with label $40.

A836

Orchids
A837

1987, Oct. 29   Litho.   Perf. 11
3087 A836 2fo Cypripedium
                    calceolus   .35   .25
3088 A836 2fo Orchis purpurea   .35   .25
3089 A836 4fo Himantoglossum
                    hircinum   .60   .50
3090 A836 4fo Ophrys scolopax
                    cornuta   .65   .50
3091 A836 5fo Cephalanthera
                    rubra   .75   .60
3092 A836 6fo Epipactis
                    atrorubens   .80   .75
         Nos. 3087-3092 (6) 3.50   2.85
Miniature Sheet
3093 A837 20fo shown   3.50   3.25
   Exist imperf. Value: set $25; souvenir sheet
$40.

1988 Winter
Olympics,
Calgary — A838

1987, Nov. 24
3094 A838 2fo Speed skating   .35   .25
3095 A838 2fo Cross-country
                    skiing   .35   .25
3096 A838 4fo Biathlon   .65   .40
3097 A838 4fo Ice hockey   .65   .40
3098 A838 4fo 4-Man bobsled   .65   .40
3099 A838 6fo Ski-jumping   1.00   .65
         Nos. 3094-3099 (6) 3.65   2.35
Souvenir Sheet
3100 A838 20fo Slalom   3.50   3.25
   Exist imperf. Value: set $25; souvenir sheet
$22.

Souvenir Sheet

U.S.-Soviet Summit, Dec. 7-
10 — A839

1987, Dec. 7   *Perf. 12*
3101 A839 20fo Shaking hands 3.50   3.25
   Meeting of Gen. Secretary Gorbachev and
Pres. Reagan to discuss and sign nuclear
arms reduction treaty.
   Exists imperf. Value $22.

Fairy
Tales — A840

   Designs: No. 3102, The White Crane, from
Japan. No. 3103, The Fox and the Crow,
Aesop's Fables. No. 3104, The Tortoise and
the Hare, Aesop's Fables. No. 3105, The Ugly
Duckling, by Hans Christian Andersen. No.
3106, The Steadfast Tin Soldier, by Andersen.

1987, Dec. 11
3102 A840 2fo multi   .40   .25
3103 A840 2fo multi   .40   .25
3104 A840 4fo multi   .75   .50
3105 A840 4fo multi   .75   .50
3106 A840 6fo multi   1.00   .75
         Nos. 3102-3106 (5) 3.30   2.25
   Exist imperf. Value, set $20.

Count Ferdinand von Zeppelin (1838-
1917), Designer of Dirigibles — A841

1988, Jan. 29   Litho.   Perf. 12
3107 A841 2fo LZ-2, 1905   .40   .25
3108 A841 4fo LZ-4, 1908   .80   .45
3109 A841 4fo LZ-10, Schwaben,
                    1911   .90   .45
3110 A841 8fo LZ-127, Graf
                    Zeppelin, 1928   1.50   1.00
         Nos. 3107-3110 (4) 3.60   2.15
   Exist imperf. Value, set $22.

1988 World Figure Skating
Championships, Budapest — A842

   Various athletes wearing period costumes.

1988, Feb. 29   Photo.   Perf. 11½
3111 A842 2fo Male, 20th cent.   .35   .25
3112 A842 2fo Male, (cap), 19th
              cent.   .35   .25
3113 A842 4fo Male (hat), 18th
              cent.   .60   .40
3114 A842 4fo Woman, c. 1930   .60   .40
3115 A842 5fo Woman (contem-
              porary)   .75   .50
3116 A842 6fo Pair   1.00   .65
       Nos. 3111-3116 (6)   3.65 2.45

Souvenir Sheet
Perf. 12x11½
3117 A842 20fo Death spiral   3.50 3.25
  No. 3117 contains one 37x52mm stamp.
  Exist imperf. Value: set $20; souvenir
sheet $25.

Illes Monus (1888-
1944), Party
Leader — A843

1988, Mar. 11   Litho.   Perf. 11½x12
3118 A843 4fo multi   .75   .50
  Exists imperf. Value $4.
  See Nos. 3152, 3160.

Miniature Sheet

Postmaster's Coat, Hat and Post Horn,
18th Cent. — A844

1988, Mar. 18   Litho.   Perf. 13
3119 A844 4fo + 4 labels   1.25 1.25
  Intl. stamp exhibitions, 1988. No. 3119 con-
tains 4 labels picturing exhibition emblems:
JUVALUX '88, Luxembourg, Mar. 29-Apr. 4
(UL), SYDPEX '88, Sydney, Australia, July 30-
Aug.7 (UR), FINLANDIA '88, Helsinki, Finland,
June 1-12 (LR), and PRAGA '88, Prague,
Czechoslovakia, Aug. 26-Sept. 4 (LL).
  Exists imperf. Value $30.

King Type of 1986
  Portraits of Hungarian kings in the Historical
Portrait Gallery. King and reign: 2fo, Charles
Robert (1308-1342). 4fo, Louis I (1342-1382).
6fo, Sigismund (1387-1437).

1988, Mar. 31   Perf. 11½x12
3120 A818 2fo pale grn, sep &
              red   .30   .20
3121 A818 4fo pale ultra, sep &
              red   .60   .45
3122 A818 6fo pale vio, sep &
              red   .90   .65
       Nos. 3120-3122 (3)   1.80 1.30
  Exists imperf. Value, set $20.

1988 Summer
Olympics,
Seoul — A845

1988, Apr. 20   Litho.   Perf. 13½x13
3123 A845 2fo Rowing   .30   .20
3124 A845 4fo Hurdling   .60   .45
3125 A845 4fo Fencing   .60   .45
3126 A845 6fo Boxing   .90   .65
       Nos. 3123-3126 (4)   2.40 1.75

Souvenir Sheet
Perf. 12½
3127 A845 20fo Tennis   3.75 3.25
  Exist imperf. Value: set $20; souvenir sheet
$30.

Computer
Animation
A846

1988, May 12   Perf. 12
  Design: Graphic from the computer-
animated film *Dilemma*, 1972, by graphic artist
Janos Kass (b. 1927) and cartoon film director
John Halas (b. 1912).
3128 A846 4fo black, pur & ver   .75   .50
  Exists imperf. Value $7.

Eurocheck Congress, June 10,
Budapest — A847

1988, June 10   Litho.   Perf. 12
3129 A847 4fo multicolored   .75   .50
  Eurocheck as legal tender, 20th anniv.
  Exists imperf. Value $7.

*Sovereign of
the
Seas* — A848

1988, June 30
3130 A848 2fo shown   .35   .20
3131 A848 2fo *Santa Maria*   .35   .25
3132 A848 2fo *Mayflower*   .35   .25
3133 A848 4fo *Jylland*   .75   .50
3134 A848 6fo *St. Jupat*   1.10   .80
       Nos. 3130-3134 (5)   2.90 2.00
  Exist imperf. Value, set $20.

Fight Drug
Abuse — A849

1988, July 7   Litho.   Perf. 12
3135 A849 4fo multicolored   .75   .50
  Exists imperf. Value $7.

Ducks
A850

1988, July 29   Litho.   Perf. 13x13½
3136 A850 2fo Anas crecca   .30   .20
3137 A850 2fo Bucephala
              clangula   .30   .20

3138 A850 4fo Anas penelope   .65   .45
  a.   Pane of 10 #3136 + 10 #3138
          with gutter btwn.   12.00
          Complete booklet, #3138a,
          with text and cover in either
          English or German   12.00
3139 A850 4fo Netta rufina   .65   .50
3140 A850 6fo Anas strepera   1.10   .65
       Nos. 3136-3140 (5)   3.00 2.00

Souvenir Sheet
Perf. 12½x11½
3141 A850 20fo Anas
              platyrhynchos   4.75 3.50
  No. 3141 contains one 52x37mm stamp.
  Exist imperf. Value: set $25; souvenir sheet
$40.
  For surcharges see Nos. 3199-3200.

Antique
Toys — A851

1988, Aug. 12   Perf. 12
3142 A851 2fo Train   .30   .25
3143 A851 2fo See-saw   .30   .25
3144 A851 4fo +2fo Pecking
              chickens   1.00   .65
3145 A851 5fo String-manipulat-
              ed soldier   .85   .55
       Nos. 3142-3145 (4)   2.45 1.70
  Surtax for youth philately programs.
  Exist imperf. Value, set $20.

Calvinist College,
Debrecen, 450th
Anniv. — A852

1988, Aug. 16   Litho.   Perf. 13½x13
3146 A852 4fo multi   .75   .50
  Exists imperf. Value $6.

58th American Society of Travel
Agents World Congress, Oct. 23-29,
Budapest
A853

1988, Aug. 30   Perf. 12
3147 A853 4fo multi   .75   .50
  Exists imperf. Value $8.

P.O. Officials Training
School,
Cent. — A854

1988, Sept. 9   Litho.   Perf. 12
3148 A854 4fo Badge on collar   .75   .50
  Exists imperf. Value $7.

Gabor Baross (1848-1892), Minister of
Commerce and
Communication — A855

  Portrait and: 2fo, Postal Savings Bank,
Budapest, emblem and postal savings stamp.
4fo, Telephone and telegraph apparatus,
registration label and cancellations. 10fo, East
Railway Station, Budapest.

1988, Sept. 16
3149 A855 2fo multi   .30   .25
3150 A855 4fo multi   .65   .50

Souvenir Sheet
Perf. 11½
3151 A855 10fo multi   2.25 2.00
  No. 3151 contains one 50x29mm stamp.
  Exist imperf. Value: set $15; souvenir sheet
$50.

Famous Hungarians Type of 1988
  Gyula Lengyel (1888-1941), political writer.

1988, Oct. 7   Perf. 11½x12
3152 A843 4fo multi   .75   .50
  Exists imperf. Value $6.

Christmas — A857

Perf. 12½x11½
1988, Nov. 10   Litho.
3153 A857 2fo multi   .40   .25
  Exists imperf. Value $6.

Nobel Prize
Winners — A858

  Designs: No. 3154, Richard Adolf
Zsigmondy (1865-1929), Germany, chemistry
(1925). No. 3155, Robert Barany (1876-1936),
Austria, medicine (1914). No. 3156, Georg von
Hevesy (1885-1966), Hungary, chemistry
(1943). No. 3157, Albert Szent-Gyorgyi (1893-
1986), Hungary-US, medicine (1937). No.
3158, Georg von Bekesy (1899-1972), US,
medicine (1961). 6fo, Denis Gabor (1900-
1979), Great Britain, physics (1971).

Litho. & Engr.
1988, Nov. 30   Perf. 12
3154 A858 2fo red brown   .35   .25
3155 A858 2fo green   .35   .25
3156 A858 2fo deep claret   .35   .25
3157 A858 4fo rose lake   .60   .40
3158 A858 4fo steel blue   .60   .40
3159 A858 6fo sepia   .75   .65
       Nos. 3154-3159 (6)   3.00 2.20
  Exist imperf. Value, set $30.

Famous Hungarians Type of 1988
  Arpad Szakasits (1888-1965), party leader.

1988, Dec. 6   Perf. 11½x12
3160 A843 4fo multicolored   .75   .50
  Exists imperf. Value $6.

Souvenir Sheet

Medals Won by Hungarian Athletes at the 1988 Seoul Olympic Games — A860

1988, Dec. 19 **Litho.** **Perf. 12**
3161 A860 20fo multicolored 3.75 3.50
Exists imperf. Value $30.

Silver and Cast Iron — A861

1988, Dec. 28 **Litho. & Engr.**
3162 A861 2fo Teapot, Pest, 1846 .35 .25
3163 A861 2fo Coffee pot, Buda, 18th cent. .35 .25
3164 A861 4fo Sugar bowl, Pest, 1822 .65 .45
3165 A861 5fo Cast iron plate, Romania, 1850 .85 .55
Nos. 3162-3165 (4) 2.20 1.50
Exist imperf. Value, set $20.

Postal Savings Bank Inauguration — A862

1989, Jan. 20 **Litho.** **Perf. 12x11½**
3166 A862 5fo royal blue, blk & silver .90 .55
Exists imperf. Value $6.

Kalman Wallisch (1889-1934), Labor Leader — A863

1989, Feb. 28 **Litho.** **Perf. 12**
3167 A863 3fo dk red & brt bl .55 .35
Exists imperf. Value $6.
See No. 3170.

World Indoor Sports Championships, Budapest, Mar. 3-5 — A864

1989, Mar. 3 **Perf. 13x13½**
3168 A864 3fo multicolored .55 .35
Exists imperf. Value $6.

Souvenir Sheet

Interparliamentary Union Cent. and 81st Session, Budapest, Mar. 13-18 — A865

a, Parliament, Big Ben & Tower Bridge, London. b, Parliament & Chain Bridge, Budapest.

1989, Mar. 13 **Litho.** **Perf. 11**
3169 A865 Sheet of 2 3.75 3.50
a.-b. 10fo any single 1.75 1.60
Exists with red inscriptions and control number. Value $75.
Exists imperf. Value $25.

Famous Hungarians Type of 1989

Janos Gyetvai (1889-1967), journalist, diplomat.

1989, Apr. 7 **Litho.** **Perf. 12**
3170 A863 3fo dark red & brt grn .55 .35
Exists imperf. Value $6.

Stud Farm at Babolna, 200th Anniv. A867

Horses: a, O Bajan. b, Meneskari Csikos. c, Gazal II.

1989, May 18 **Litho.** **Perf. 12**
3171 Strip of 3 1.75 1.10
a.-c. A867 3fo any single .55 .35
Exists imperf. Value, strip $20.

ART '89, May 23-27, Budapest A868

1989, May 23 **Perf. 12x11½**
3172 A868 5fo multi .90 .55
Exhibition for disabled artists.
Exists imperf. Value $6.

Flower Arrangements — A869

1989, May 31 **Perf. 12**
3173 A869 2fo multi, vert. .35 .25
3174 A869 3fo multi, vert. .40 .30
3175 A869 3fo shown .40 .30
3176 A869 5fo multi, diff. .85 .50
3177 A869 10fo multi, vert. 1.50 1.00
Nos. 3173-3177 (5) 3.50 2.35
Exist imperf. Value, set $20.

French Revolution, Bicent. A870

1989, June 1 **Perf. 12**
3178 A870 5fo brt blue, blk & red .75 .50

Souvenir Sheet
Perf. 11½
3179 A870 20fo like 5fo 3.50 3.25
No. 3179 contains one 50x30mm stamp. Exist imperf. Value: single $15; souvenir sheet $30.

Medieval Church of the Csolts Near Veszto — A871

Photography, 150th Anniv. — A872

1989, June 15 **Litho.** **Perf. 12**
3180 A871 3fo multi .50 .30
Exists imperf. Value $6.

1989, June 15
3181 A872 5fo multi .80 .50
Exists imperf. Value $6.

Old Mills — A873

Designs: 2fo, Water mill, Turistvandi, 18th cent. 3fo, Horse-driven mill, Szarvas, 1836. 5fo, Windmill, Kiskunhalas, 18th cent. 10fo, Water wheel on the Drava River.

1989, June 20
3182 A873 2fo multi .30 .20
3183 A873 3fo multi .45 .30
3184 A873 5fo multi .75 .50
3185 A873 10fo multi 1.50 1.00
Nos. 3182-3185 (4) 3.00 2.00
Exist imperf. Value, set $20.

Souvenir Sheet

1st Moon Landing, 20th Anniv. — A874

1989, July 12 **Litho.** **Perf. 12½**
3186 A874 20fo multi 3.75 3.50
Exists imperf. Value $25.

Gliders — A875

1989, July 20 **Perf. 12**
3187 A875 3fo Futar .45 .30
3188 A875 5fo Cimbora .80 .60
17th Intl. Old Timers Rally, Budakeszi Airport, and 60th anniv. of glider flying in Hungary.
Exist imperf. Value, set $20.

Reptiles A876

1989, July 26 **Perf. 11**
3189 A876 2fo Lacerta agilis .25 .20
3190 A876 3fo Lacerta viridis .45 .25
3191 A876 5fo Vipera rakosiensis .70 .40
3192 A876 5fo Natrix natrix .70 .40
3193 A876 10fo Emys orbicularis 1.25 .75
Nos. 3189-3193 (5) 3.35 2.00
Exist imperf. Value, set $30.

31st Modern Pentathlon World Championships, Aug. 30-Sept. 4, Budapest — A877

1989, July 31 **Perf. 13½x13**
3194 A877 5fo multi .80 .50
Exists imperf. Value $6.

Caves — A878

10th World Speleology Congress, Aug. 13-20, Sofia.

1989, Aug. 14   **Litho.**   *Perf. 11*
3195	A878	3fo Baradla	.30	.20
3196	A878	5fo Szemlohegy	.55	.40
3197	A878	10fo Anna	.90	.70
3198	A878	12fo Lake Cave of Tapolca	1.25	.80
		Nos. 3195-3198 (4)	3.00	2.10

Exist imperf. Value, set $20.

Nos. 3136 and 3138 Surcharged

1989, Aug. 14   *Perf. 13x13½*
3199	A850	3fo on 2fo #3136	2.00	1.75
3200	A850	5fo on 4fo #3138	2.00	1.75
a.		Pane of 10 #3199 + pane of 10 #3200 with gutter between	20.00	
		Complete booklet, #3200a, with text and cover in either English or German	35.00	

A879

1989, Aug. 24   *Perf. 12*
3201	A879	5fo multi	.80	.45

Third World Two-in-Hand Carriage-driving Championships, Balatonfenyves, Aug. 24-27.
Exists imperf. Value $6.

A880

1989, Sept. 8   **Litho.**   *Perf. 12*

Nurses: 5fo, Zsuzsanna Kossuth (1820-1854) and emblem. 10fo, Florence Nightingale (1820-1910) and medal awarded in her name by the Red Cross.

3202	A880	5fo multi	.65	.40
3203	A880	10fo multi	1.10	.75

Stamp Day. See No. B341.
Exist imperf. Value, set $15.

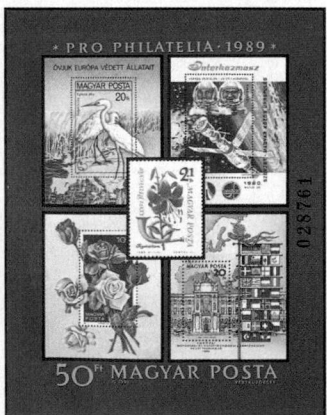

Pro-Philatelia 1989 — A881

1989, Oct. 10   **Litho.**   **Imperf.**
3204	A881	50fo #2665, C426, 2742, 3005, B233	6.25	5.75

Dismantling of the Electronic Surveillance System (Iron Curtain) on the Hungary-Austria Border — A882

1989, Oct. 30   *Perf. 11*
3205	A882	5fo multi	1.00	.50

Exists imperf. Value $7.

Conquest of Hungary, by Mor Than — A883

1989, Oct. 31
3206	A883	5fo multi	.75	.45

Arpad, chief who founded the 1st Magyar dynasty of Hungary in 889.
Exists imperf. Value $6.

Christmas — A884

1989, Nov. 10   **Litho.**   *Perf. 11½x12*
3207	A884	3fo Flight to Egypt	.45	.25

Exists imperf. Value $6.

Jawaharlal Nehru — A885

Litho. & Engr.

1989, Nov. 14   *Perf. 12*
3208	A885	3fo buff & rose brn	.45	.25

Jawaharlal Nehru, 1st prime minister of independent India.
Exists imperf. Value $6.

Modern Art (Paintings) A886

3fo, *Mike,* by Dezso Korniss. 5fo, *Sunrise,* by Lajos Kassak. 10fo, *Grotesque Burial,* by Endre Balint. 12fo, *Memory of Toys,* by Tihamer Gyarmathy.

1989, Dec. 18   **Litho.**   *Perf. 12*
3209	A886	3fo multicolored	.35	.25
3210	A886	5fo multicolored	.65	.50
3211	A886	10fo multicolored	1.40	.95
3212	A886	12fo multicolored	1.60	1.10
		Nos. 3209-3212 (4)	4.00	2.80

Exist imperf. Value, set $30.

Medical Pioneers — A887

1989, Dec. 29   **Engr.**   *Perf. 12*

#3213, Galen (129-c.199), Greek physician. #3214, Paracelsus (1493-1541), German alchemist. 4fo, Andreas Vesalius (1514-64), Belgian anatomist. 6fo, Rudolf Virchow (1821-1902), German pathologist. 10fo, Ivan Petrovich Pavlov (1849-1936), Russian physiologist.

3213	A887	3fo olive gray	.40	.25
3214	A887	3fo brown	.40	.25
3215	A887	4fo black	.70	.45
3216	A887	6fo intense black	.85	.55
3217	A887	10fo brown violet	1.40	.80
		Nos. 3213-3217 (5)	3.75	2.30

Exist imperf. Value, set $25.

Hungarian Savings Bank, 150th Anniv. — A888

1990, Jan. 11   **Litho.**
3218	A888	5fo multicolored	.75	.45

Exists imperf. Value $8.

A889   A890

1990, Jan. 15   *Perf. 12*
3219	A889	5fo brown & sepia	.75	.45

Singer Sewing Machine, 25th anniv.
Exists imperf. Value $7.

1990, Jan. 29

3fo, Telephone, Budapest Exchange. 5fo, Mailbox and main p.o., Budapest, c. 1900.

3220	A890	3fo multicolored	.40	.20
3221	A890	5fo multicolored	.60	.30

Coil Stamps
Size: 17x22mm
Perf. 14
Photo.

3222	A890	3fo shown	.40	.20
3223	A890	5fo multi	.60	.30
		Nos. 3220-3223 (4)	2.00	1.00

Nos. 3220-3221 inscribed "Pj 1989." Nos. 3222-3223 inscribed "1989."
Nos. 3220-3221 exist imperf. Value, set $20.

A891

A892

Designs: Protected bird species.

1990, Feb. 20   **Litho.**   *Perf. 11½x12*
3224	A891	3fo *Alcedo atthis*	.45	.30
3225	A891	3fo *Pyrrhula pyrrhula*	.45	.30
3226	A891	3fo *Dendrocopos syriacus*	.45	.30
3227	A891	5fo *Upupa epops*	.75	.50
3228	A891	5fo *Merops apiaster*	.75	.50
3229	A891	10fo *Coracias garrulus*	1.50	1.00
		Nos. 3224-3229 (6)	4.35	2.90

Exist imperf. Value, set $30.

1990, Mar. 14   **Litho.**   *Perf. 12*

Flowers of the continents (Africa).

3230	A892	3fo *Leucadendron*	.40	.25
3231	A892	3fo *Protea compacta*	.40	.25
3232	A892	3fo *Leucadendron spissifolium*	.40	.25
3233	A892	5fo *Protea barbigera*	.70	.40
3234	A892	5fo *Protea lepidocarpodendron*	.70	.40
3235	A892	10fo *Protea cynaroides*	1.25	.85
		Nos. 3230-3235 (6)	3.85	2.40

Souvenir Sheet
Perf. 12½x12
3236	A892	20fo Montage of African flowers	3.75	3.75

No. 3236 contains one 27x38mm stamp. See Nos. 3278-3283, 3371-3375, 3377-3381, 3451-3455.
Exist imperf. Value: set $30; souvenir sheet $40.

A893

Portraits of Hungarian kings in the Historical Portrait Gallery. King and reign: No. 3237, Janos Hunyadi (c. 1407-1409). No. 3238, Matthias Hunyadi (1443-1490).

1990, Apr. 6   **Litho.**   *Perf. 11½x12*
3237	A893	5fo multicolored	.70	.40
3238	A893	5fo multicolored	.70	.40
a.		Pair, #3237-3238	1.40	1.00

Exist imperf. Value, pair $15.

Souvenir Sheet

A894

Litho. & Engr.

1990, Apr. 17   *Perf. 12½x12*
3239	A894	20fo black & buff	3.75	3.25

Penny Black 150th anniv., Stamp World London '90.
Exists imperf. Value $25.

Karoli Bible, 400th Anniv. — A895

1990, Apr. 24   **Litho.**
3240 A895 8fo Gaspar Karoli   1.00 .70

No. 3240 printed se-tenant with label picturing Bible frontispiece.
Exists imperf. Value, with label $15.

1990 World Cup Soccer Championships, Italy — A896

Various athletes.

1990, Apr. 27   **Perf. 11½x12**
3241 A896 3fo Dribble   .30 .20
3242 A896 5fo Heading the ball   .55 .35
3243 A896 5fo Kick   .55 .35
3244 A896 8fo Goal attempt   .80 .55
3245 A896 8fo Dribble, diff.   .80 .55
3246 A896 10fo Dribble, diff.   1.00 .75
    Nos. 3241-3246 (6)   4.00 2.75

Souvenir Sheet
Perf. 12½
3247 A896 20fo Dribble, diff.   3.50 3.50

No. 3247 contains one 32x42mm stamp.
Exist imperf. Value: set $30; souvenir sheet $25.

Kelemen Mikes (1690-1761), Writer — A897

1990, May 31   **Litho.**   **Perf. 13½x13**
3248 A897 8fo black & gold   1.10 .75
    Exists imperf. Value $6.

Noemi and Beni Ferenczy, Birth Cent. — A898

Designs: 3fo, Painting by Noemi Ferenczy. 5fo, Sculpture by Beni Ferenczy.

1990, June 18   **Litho.**   **Perf. 12**
3249 A898 3fo multicolored   .30 .20
3250 A898 5fo multicolored   .50 .30
    Exist imperf. Value, set $12.

Ferenc Kazinczy (1759-1831), Hungarian Language Reformer A899

1990, July 18   **Litho.**   **Perf. 12**
3251 A899 8fo multicolored   .60 .40
    Exists imperf. Value $10.

Ferenc Kolcsey (1790-1838), Poet — A900

1990, Aug. 3
3252 A900 8fo multicolored   .60 .40
    Exists imperf. Value $10.

New Coat of Arms A901

1990, Aug. 17   **Litho.**   **Perf. 13½x13**
3253 A901 8fo multicolored   .60 .40

Souvenir Sheet
Perf. 11
3254 A901 20fo multicolored   4.00 4.00

No. 3254 contains one 34x50mm stamp.
A souvenir sheet like No. 3254 was released with a hologram as the stamp. The sheet exists with black or red control numbers on the reverse. Values: with black numbers $175; with red numbers $300.
Exist imperf. Value: single $16; souvenir sheet $40.

Grapes and Wine Producing Areas — A902

Grapes and Growing Area: 3fo, Cabernet franc, Hajos-Vaskut. 5fo, Cabernet sauvignon, Villany-Siklos. No. 3257, Italian Riesling, Badacsony. No. 3258, Kadarka, Szekszard. No. 3259, Leanyka, Eger. 10fo, Furmint, Tokaj-Hegyalja.

1990, Aug. 31   **Perf. 13x13½**
3255 A902 3fo multicolored   .25 .20
3256 A902 5fo multicolored   .45 .30
3257 A902 8fo multicolored   .65 .45
3258 A902 8fo multicolored   .65 .45
3259 A902 8fo multicolored   .65 .45
3260 A902 10fo multicolored   .85 .60
    Nos. 3255-3260 (6)   3.50 2.45

    Exist imperf. Value, set $30.
See Nos. 3580-3582, 3656-3657, 3704-3705, 3773-3774, 3832-3833, 3938-3939, 4037-4039.

Paintings by Endre Szasz A903

1990, Oct. 12   **Litho.**   **Perf. 12**
3261 A903 8fo Feast   .70 .45
3262 A903 12fo Message   1.10 .65

Stamp Day. See No. B344.
Exist imperf. Value, set $20.

Prehistoric Animals A904

1990, Nov. 16   **Litho.**   **Perf. 12**
3263 A904 3fo Tarbosaurus   .25 .20
3264 A904 5fo Brontosaurus   .40 .25
3265 A904 5fo Stegosaurus   .40 .25
3266 A904 5fo Dimorphodon   .40 .25
3267 A904 8fo Platybelodon   .70 .35
3268 A904 10fo Mammoth   .85 .40
    Nos. 3263-3268 (6)   3.00 1.70

    Exist imperf. Value, set $30.

Intl. Literacy Year — A905

1990, Nov. 21   **Perf. 13x13½**
3269 A905 10fo multicolored   1.00 .65
    Exist imperf. Value $6.

Budapest Stamp Museum, 60th Anniv. — A906

1990, Nov. 23   **Perf. 12½**
3270 A906 5fo brn red & grn   .50 .30
    Exist imperf. Value $6.

Souvenir Sheet

Thurn & Taxis Postal System, 500th Anniv. — A907

Illustration reduced.

1990, Nov. 30   **Litho.**   **Perf. 12½x12**
3271 A907 50fo multicolored   6.75 5.00

Antique Clocks — A908

1990, Dec. 14   **Perf. 12**
3272 A908 3fo Travelling clock, 1576   .25 .20
3273 A908 5fo Table clock, 1643   .45 .30
3274 A908 5fo Mantel clock, 1790   .45 .30
3275 A908 10fo Table clock, 1814   .85 .60
    Nos. 3272-3275 (4)   2.00 1.40

    Exist imperf. Value, set $20.

Madonna with Child by Botticelli — A909

1990, Dec. 14   **Perf. 12½x11½**
3276 A909 5fo multicolored   .45 .25
    Exists imperf. Value $5.50.

Lorand Eotvos (1848-1919) and Torsion Pendulum A910

1991, Jan. 31   **Litho.**   **Perf. 11**
3277 A910 12fo multicolored   1.10 .65
    Exists imperf. Value $12.

Flowers of the Continents Type
Flowers of the Americas.

1991, Feb. 28   **Litho.**   **Perf. 12**
3278 A892 5fo Mandevilla splendens   .35 .20
3279 A892 7fo Lobelia cardinalis   .45 .30
3280 A892 7fo Cobaea scandens   .45 .30
3281 A892 12fo Steriphoma paradoxa   .75 .50
3282 A892 15fo Beloperone guttata   1.00 .70
    Nos. 3278-3282 (5)   3.00 2.00

Souvenir Sheet
Perf. 11
3283 A892 20fo Flowers of the Americas   3.50 1.75

No. 3283 contains one 27x44mm stamp.
Exist imperf. Value: set $25; souvenir sheet $60.

Post Office, Budapest A911

Designs: 7fo, Post Office, Pecs.

Perf. 11½x12½

1991, Mar. 22   Litho.
3284	A911	5fo multicolored	5.50	4.00
3285	A911	7fo multicolored	6.50	4.50
a.		Pair, #3284-3285	13.00	11.00

Admission to CEPT.
Exist imperf. Value, pair $50.

Europa — A912

1991, Apr.   Litho.   **Perf. 12½**
3286	A912	12fo Ulysses probe	4.00	2.00
3287	A912	30fo Cassini-Huygens probe	8.00	6.00

Exist imperf. Value, set $50.

Budapest Zoological and Botanical
Gardens, 125th Anniv. — A913

1991, May 15   **Perf. 13½x13**
3288	A913	7fo Gorilla	.60	.35
3289	A913	12fo Rhinoceros	.85	.60
3290	A913	12fo Toucan	.85	.60
3291	A913	12fo Polar bear	.85	.60
3292	A913	20fo Orchid	1.40	1.00
		Nos. 3288-3292 (5)	4.55	3.15

Exist imperf. Value, set $22.

A914

A915

1991, May 24   Litho.   **Perf. 12**
3293	A914	12fo multi	1.00	.60

Count Pal Teleki (1879-1941), politician.
Exists imperf. Value $5.50.

1991, June 13   **Perf. 13x13½**
3294	A915	12fo multicolored	1.00	.60

44th World Fencing Championships,
Budapest.
Exists imperf. Value $9.

Images of the Virgin and Child in Hungarian Shrines A916

Designs: 7fo, Mariapocs. No. 3296,
Mariagyud. No. 3297, Celldomolk. No. 3298,
Mariaremete. 20fo, Esztergom.

1991, June 17   **Perf. 12½**
3295	A916	7fo multicolored	.55	.35
3296	A916	12fo multicolored	.85	.60
3297	A916	12fo multicolored	.85	.60
3298	A916	12fo multicolored	.85	.60
3299	A916	20fo multicolored	1.40	1.00
		Nos. 3295-3299 (5)	4.50	3.15

Compare with design A927.
Exist imperf. Value, set $25.

Souvenir Sheet

Visit of Pope John Paul II, Aug. 16-20,
1991 — A917

1991, July 15   Litho. & Engr.   **Perf. 12**
3300	A917	50fo multicolored	4.50	3.50

Exists imperf. Value $25.

Karoly Marko (1791-1860),
Painter — A918

1991, June 17   **Perf. 12**
3301	A918	12fo multicolored	1.25	.75

Exists imperf. Value $9.

Basketball,
Cent. — A919

1991, June 27   Litho.   **Perf. 12**
3302	A919	10fo multicolored	1.25	.75

Exists imperf. Value $9.

Otto Lilienthal's First Glider Flight,
Cent. — A920

Aircraft of aviation pioneers.

1991, June 27
3303	A920	7fo Otto Lilienthal	.50	.35
3304	A920	12fo Wright Brothers	.80	.65
3305	A920	20fo Alberto Santos-Dumont	1.40	1.00
3306	A920	30fo Aladar Zselyi	2.00	1.50
		Nos. 3303-3306 (4)	4.70	3.50

Exist imperf. Value, set $25.

3rd Intl.
Hungarian
Philological
Congress
A921

1991, Aug. 12   Litho.   **Perf. 13½x13**
3307	A921	12fo multicolored	1.10	.65

Exists imperf. Value $7.

A922

A923

1991, Sept. 6   Engr.   **Perf. 12**
3308	A922	12fo dark red	.65	.45

Count Istvan Szechenyi (1791-1860),
founder of Academy of Sciences.
Exists imperf. Value $7.

1991, Sept. 6   Litho.

Wolfgang Amadeus Mozart (1756-91).
3309	A923	12fo As child	1.00	.50
3310	A923	20fo As adult	2.00	.80

Souvenir Sheet
3311	A923	30fo +15fo, in red coat	4.00	2.50

Stamp Day. No. 3311 contains one
30x40mm stamp.
Exist imperf. Value: set $30; souvenir sheet
$60.

Telecom '91 — A924

1991, Sept. 30   Litho.   **Perf. 12**
3312	A924	12fo multicolored	.90	.50

6th World Forum and Exposition on Telecommunications, Geneva, Switzerland. Exists
imperf. Value $8.

A925

A926

1991, Oct. 30   Litho.   **Perf. 13½x13**
3313	A925	12fo multicolored	.90	.50

Sovereign Order of the Knights of Malta.
Exists imperf. Value, set $8.

1991, Oct. 30   **Perf. 12**

Early explorers and Discovery of America,
500th anniv. (in 1992): 7fo, Sebastian Cabot,
Labrador Peninsula, Nova Scotia. No. 3315,
Amerigo Vespucci, South American region.
No. 3316, Hernando Cortez, Mexico. 15fo,
Ferdinand Magellan, Straits of Magellan. 20fo,
Francisco Pizarro, Peru, Andes Mountain
region. 30fo, Christopher Columbus and coat
of arms.

3314	A926	7fo multicolored	.50	.25
3315	A926	12fo multicolored	.80	.45
3316	A926	12fo multicolored	.80	.45
3317	A926	15fo multicolored	1.00	.60
3318	A926	20fo multicolored	1.40	.75
		Nos. 3314-3318 (5)	4.50	2.50

Souvenir Sheet
3319	A926	30fo multicolored	2.50	2.00

No. 3319 contains one 26x37mm stamp.
Exist imperf. Value: set $30; souvenir sheet
$65.

No. 3023
Overprinted in
Brown

1991, Oct. 22   Litho.   **Perf. 12x11½**
3320	A816	12fo multi	1.25	.45

Anniversary of Hungarian revolution, 1956.

Christmas — A927

Images of the Virgin and Child from: 7fo,
Mariapocs. 12fo, Mariaremete.

1991, Nov. 20   *Perf. 13½x13*
3322 A927 7fo multicolored   .65   .25
3323 A927 12fo multicolored   1.10   .45

Nos. 3322-3323 issued in sheets of 20 plus 20 labels.
Exist imperf. Value, set $16.

A928

1991, Nov. 20   *Perf. 12*
3324 A928 12fo multicolored   .90   .45

Fight for human rights. Exist imperf. Value $24.

A929

1991, Dec. 6   *Perf. 13½x13*
3325 A929 7fo Cross-country skiing   .35   .20
3326 A929 12fo Slalom skiing   .70   .30
3327 A929 15fo Four-man bobsled   .80   .45
3328 A929 20fo Ski jump   1.10   .60
3329 A929 30fo Hockey   1.60   .85
     Nos. 3325-3329 (5)   4.55   2.40

Souvenir Sheet
Perf. 12½x11½
3330 A929 30fo Pairs figure skating   2.50   2.00

1992 Winter Olympics, Albertville.
Exist imperf. Value: set $30; souvenir sheet $22.

Souvenir Sheet

First Hungarian Postage Stamp, 120th Anniv. — A930

1991, Dec. 20   **Litho.**   *Perf. 12x12½*
3331 A930 50fo No. 6   4.00   3.00

Piarist Order in Hungary, 350th Anniv. — A931

1992, Jan. 22   *Perf. 13½x13*
3332 A931 10fo multicolored   .85   .40

World Heritage Village of Holloko A932

1992, Jan. 22   *Perf. 12*
3333 A932 15fo multicolored   1.10   .60

1992 Summer Olympics, Barcelona — A933

1992, Feb. 26   **Litho.**   *Perf. 13½x13*
3334 A933 7fo Swimming   .60   .40
3335 A933 9fo Cycling   .80   .50
3336 A933 10fo Gymnastics   1.40   .60
3337 A933 15fo Running   2.75   1.40
     Nos. 3334-3337 (4)   5.55   2.90

Discovery of America, 500th Anniv. — A934

Expo '92, Seville: No. 3338, Map shaped as Indian, Columbus' fleet. No. 3339, Face-shaped map of ocean, sailing ship. No. 3340, Map shaped as European face, ship. No. 3341, Map, square, protractor, compass.

1992, Mar. 27   **Litho.**   *Perf. 12*
3338 A934 10fo multicolored   .60   .35
3339 A934 10fo multicolored   .60   .35
3340 A934 15fo multicolored   1.00   .55
3341 A934 15fo multicolored   1.00   .55
     Nos. 3338-3341 (4)   3.20   1.80

Jozsef Cardinal Mindszenty (1892-1975), Leader of Hungarian Catholic Church — A935

1992, Mar. 27   *Perf. 12½x11½*
3342 A935 15fo red, brn & buff   1.10   .60

A936

1992, Mar. 27   *Perf. 13½x13*
3343 A936 15fo multicolored   1.10   .60

Jan Amos Komensky (Comenius), writer, 400th birth anniv.

A937

1992, Apr. 14   **Litho.**   *Perf. 13½x13*
3344 A937 15fo Maya Indian sculpture   2.50   1.00
3345 A937 40fo Indian sculpture, diff.   7.25   3.00

Europa. Discovery of America, 500th anniv..

European Gymnastics Championships, Budapest — A938

1992, May 15   **Litho.**   *Perf. 12*
3346 A938 15fo multicolored   1.10   .60

A939

1992, June 26   **Litho.**   *Perf. 13½x13*
3347 A939 15fo multicolored   1.00   .50

St. Margaret, 750th Anniv. (in 1991). No. 3347 printed with se-tenant label.

A940

1992, June 26   *Perf. 13x13½*

Protected birds.

3348 A940 9fo Falco cherrug   .40   .20
3349 A940 10fo Hieraaetus pennatus   .60   .20
3350 A940 15fo Circaetus gallicus   .85   .50
3351 A940 40fo Milvus milvus   1.60   1.00
     Nos. 3348-3351 (4)   3.45   1.90

Raoul Wallenberg, Swedish Diplomat, 80th Anniv. of Birth — A941

1992, July 30   **Litho.**   *Perf. 12*
3352 A941 15fo gray & red   1.25   .45

Theodore von Karman (1881-1963), Physicist and Aeronautical Engineer — A942

Design: 40fo, John von Neumann (1903-1957), mathematician.

1992, Aug. 3   **Litho.**   *Perf. 12x11½*
3353 A942 15fo multicolored   .45   .25
3354 A942 40fo multicolored   1.90   .70

3rd World Congress of Hungarians A943

1992, Aug. 3   *Perf. 13½x13*
3355 A943 15fo multicolored   .80   .35

Telecom '92 — A945

1992, Oct. 6   **Litho.**   *Perf. 12½x11½*
3360 A945 15fo multicolored   .80   .35

Stamp Day — A946

1992, Sept.4   *Perf. 12*
3361 A946 10fo +5fo Coat of arms, vert.   .85   .80
3362 A946 15fo shown   .85   .40
3363 A946 15fo +5fo like #3362, inscribed "65. Belyegnap"   1.10   .85
     Nos. 3361-3363 (3)   2.80   2.05

Souvenir Sheet
3364 A946 50fo +20fo Postilion   4.50   3.25

Eurofilex '92 (#3361, 3363-3364). Nos. 3361, 3363 printed with se-tenant label. No. 3364 contains one 40x30mm stamp.

Famous Men — A947

Postal Uniforms — A948

Designs: 10fo, Stephen Bathory (1533-1586), Prince of Transylvania and King of

Poland. 15fo, Stephen Bocskay (1557-1606), Prince of Transylvania. 40fo, Gabriel Bethlen (1580-1629), Prince of Transylvania and King of Hungary.

1992, Oct. 28   Litho.   Perf. 12
3365 A947 10fo multicolored   .40   .20
3366 A947 15fo multicolored   .70   .30
3367 A947 40fo multicolored   1.25   .85
     Nos. 3365-3367 (3)   2.35   1.35

1992, Nov. 20   Perf. 13½x13
Designs: 10fo, Postrider, 1703-1711. 15fo, Letter carrier, 1874.
3368 A948 10fo multicolored   .65   .30
3369 A948 15fo multicolored   1.00   .50

Christmas A949

Litho. & Engr.
1992, Nov. 20   Perf. 12
3370 A949 15fo blue & black   1.00   .50

Flowers of the Continents Type of 1990
Flowers of Australia: 9fo, Clianthus formosus. 10fo, Leschenaultia biloba. 15fo, Anigosanthos manglesii. 40fo, Comesperma ericinum. 50fo, Bouquet of flowers.

1992, Nov. 20   Litho.
3371 A892   9fo multicolored   .50   .25
3372 A892 10fo multicolored   .55   .40
3373 A892 15fo multicolored   .75   .50
3374 A892 40fo multicolored   1.75   1.25
     Nos. 3371-3374 (4)   3.55   2.40

Souvenir Sheet
Perf. 12½
3375 A892 50fo multicolored   5.00   3.75
No. 3375 contains one 32x41mm stamp.

1992 European Chess Championships A950

1992, Oct. 28   Perf. 11
3376 A950 15fo multicolored   1.10   .35

Flowers of the Continents Type of 1990
Flowers of Asia: No. 3377, Dendrobium densiflorum. No. 3378, Arachnis flos-aeris. No. 3379, Lilium speciosum. No. 3380, Meconopsis aculeata. 50fo, Bouquet of flowers.

1993, Jan. 27   Litho.   Perf. 13½x13
3377 A892 10fo multicolored   .45   .25
3378 A892 10fo multicolored   .45   .25
3379 A892 15fo multicolored   1.00   .50
3380 A892 15fo multicolored   1.00   .50
     Nos. 3377-3380 (4)   2.90   1.50

Souvenir Sheet
Perf. 12½
3381 A892 50fo multicolored 11.00   3.25
No. 3381 contains one 32x41mm stamp.

Scythian Archaeological Artifacts — A951

1993, Feb. 25   Litho.   Perf. 13x13½
3382 A951 10fo Horse standing   .50   .20
3383 A951 17fo Horse lying down 1.00   .25

Hungarian Rowing Association, Cent. — A952

1993, Feb. 25   Litho.   Perf. 12
3384 A952 17fo multicolored   .75   .20

Missale Romanum of Matthias Corvinus (Matyas Hunyadi, King of Hungary) — A953

Design: 40fo, Illuminated page.

1993, Mar. 12   Litho.   Perf. 12
3385 A953 15fo multicolored   .75   .25

Souvenir Sheet
3386 A953 40fo multicolored   5.00   4.00
Illustration reduced. No. 3386 contains one 60x38mm stamp.
See Belgium Nos. 1474, 1476.

Motocross World Championships A954

1993, May 5   Litho.   Perf. 11½x12
3387 A954 17fo multicolored   .60   .25

Europa — A955

Buildings designed by Imre Makovecz: 17fo, Roman Catholic Church, Paks. 45fo, Hungarian Pavilion, Expo '92, Seville.

1993, May 5   Perf. 13x13½
3388 A955 17fo multicolored   1.50   .50
3389 A955 45fo multicolored   2.75   1.25

Heliocentric Solar System, Copernicus — A956

1993, May 5   Perf. 12
3390 A956 17fo multicolored   .90   .25
Polska '93. No. 3390 issued in sheets of 8 + 4 labels.

Edible Mushrooms A957

1993, June 18   Litho.   Perf. 13½x13
3391 A957 10fo Ramaria botrytis   .40   .20
3392 A957 17fo Craterellus
                 cornucopioides   .70   .25
3393 A957 45fo Amanita caesa-
                 rea   2.25   .80
     Nos. 3391-3393 (3)   3.35   1.25

St. Christopher, by Albrecht Durer — A958

1993, June 18   Perf. 12
3394 A958 17fo sil, blk & buff   .65   .20
Year of the Elderly.

City of Mohacs, 900th Anniv. — A959

1993, June 18   Perf. 13½x13
3395 A959 17fo buff, mar & red
                 brn   .65   .20

Hungarian State Railways, 125th Anniv. — A960

1993, June 18   Perf. 13x13½
3396 A960 17fo lt blue & blue   .65   .20

Comedians A961

1993, July 28   Litho.   Perf. 12
3397 A961 17fo Kalman Latabar   .70   .25
3398 A961 30fo Charlie Chaplin 1.10   .65

Butterflies A962

1993, July 28   Perf. 13½x13
3399 A962 10fo Limenitis populi   .30   .20
3400 A962 17fo Aricia artaxerxes   .70   .25
3401 A962 30fo Plebejides py-
                 laon   1.25   .65
     Nos. 3399-3401 (3)   2.25   1.10

Souvenir Sheet

Helsinki Conference on European Security and Cooperation, 20th Anniv. — A963

1993, July 28   Perf. 12
3402 A963 50fo multicolored   2.75   2.50

Intl. Solar Energy Society Congress, Budapest — A964

Perf. 12½x11½
1993, Aug. 23   Litho.
3403 A964 17fo multicolored   .60   .30
No. 3403 printed se-tenant with label.

Writers — A965

1993, Aug. 23   Perf. 12
Designs: No. 3404, Laszlo Nemeth (1901-75). No. 3405, Dezso Szabo (1879-1945). No. 3406, Antal Szerb (1901-45).
3404 A965 17fo blue   .45   .20
3405 A965 17fo blue   .45   .20
3406 A965 17fo blue   .45   .20
     Nos. 3404-3406 (3) 1.35   .60

School of Agronomy, Pannon Agricultural Univ., 175th Anniv. — A966

1993, Oct. 22   Litho.   Perf. 12
3407 A966 17fo multicolored   .60   .30

Ships A967

1993, Oct. 27   Perf. 13x13½
3408 A967 10fo Steamer with
                 sails   .35   .20
3409 A967 30fo Battleship   1.00   .50
  a. Pair, #3408-3409   1.60   .70

Prehistoric Man — A968

1993, Oct. 27   **Perf. 13½x13**
3410 A968 17fo Skull fragment   .60   .30
3411 A968 30fo Stone tool   1.00   .50

Souvenir Sheet

Roman Roads — A969

1993, Oct. 27   **Perf. 11**
3412 A969 50fo multicolored   2.75 1.50

Christmas A970

Altarpiece: 10fo, Virgin and Christ Child, Cathedral of Szekesfehervar, by F. A. Hillebrant.

1993, Nov. 24   **Perf. 13½x13**
3413 A970 10fo multicolored   .35   .20

Sights of Budapest — A971

Designs: 17fo, Szechenyi Chain Bridge. 30fo, Opera House. 45fo, Matthias Church, vert. Illustration reduced.

Photo. & Engr.
1993, Dec. 16   **Perf. 12**
3414 A971 17fo lt grn & dk grn   1.10   .55
3415 A971 30fo lt mag & dk mag   1.75   .65
3416 A971 45fo lt brn & dk brn   2.75 1.50
    Nos. 3414-3416 (3)   5.60 2.70

Expo '96.

Josef Antall (1932-93) — A972

1993   **Litho.**   **Perf. 11**
3417 A972 19fo multicolored   .80   .40
  a.   Souvenir sheet of 1   1.50 1.50

For surcharge, see No. 4167.

ICAO, 50th Anniv. A973

1994, Jan. 13   **Perf. 13x13½**
3418 A973 56fo multicolored   1.90   .95

1994 Winter Olympics, Lillehammer — A974

1994, Jan. 13   **Perf. 12**
3419 A974 12fo Downhill skiing   .40   .20
3420 A974 19fo Ice hockey   .70   .30

A975

Easter: 12fo, Golgotha, by Mihaly Munkacsy.

1994, Feb. 17   **Litho.**   **Perf. 11½x12**
3421 A975 12fo multicolored   .40   .20

A976

1994, Feb. 17

Artists: 12fo, Gyula Benczur (1844-1920). 19fo, Mihaly Munkacsy (1844-1900).

3422 A976 12fo multicolored   .40   .20
3423 A976 19fo multicolored   .65   .30

Lajos Kossuth (1802-94) A977

1994, Feb. 17
3424 A977 19fo multicolored   .65   .30

Gen. Joseph Bem (1794-1850) A978

1994, Mar. 10   **Perf. 12**
3425 A978 19fo multicolored   .65   .30

Otis Tarda — A979

World Wildlife Fund: No. 3426, Female, male with feathers ruffled in mating dance. No. 3427, Nestlings, female on nest. No. 3428, Nestlings, female standing. No. 3429, Three flying.

1994, Mar. 14
3426 A979 10fo multicolored   .75   .40
3427 A979 10fo multicolored   .75   .40
3428 A979 10fo multicolored   .75   .40
3429 A979 10fo multicolored   .75   .40
  a.   Block of 4, #3426-3429   3.50 3.00

A980

Europa: 19fo, Sailing steamer Tegetthoff, Franz-Joseph Land, Julius Payer (1842-1915), Austrian explorer. 50fo, Mark Aurel Stein (1862-1943), explorer, archeologist, geographer, Asian scenes.

1994, Apr. 1   **Litho.**   **Perf. 13x13½**
3430 A980 19fo multicolored   1.75   .50
3431 A980 50fo multicolored   2.75 1.25

Austro-Hungarian Arctic Expedition, 120th anniv. (#3430).

A981

#3432, Baron Miklos Josika (1794-1865), Novelist. #3433, Balint Balassi (1551-94), poet.

1994, May 19   **Litho.**   **Perf. 12**
3432 A981 19fo gray   .65   .30
3433 A981 19fo rose lake   .65   .30

Creation of Magyar Hungary, 1100th Anniv. (in 1996) — A982

Designs: No. 3434, Two soldiers on horseback. No. 3435, Soldier on white horse, others in background with flags. No. 3436, Soldier on black horse, others in background. No. 3437, Man with staff, oxen pulling carts. No. 3438, Oxen pulling royal cart. No. 3439, Man with staff on shoulder, oxen with packs. No. 3440,

Minstrels, bard celebrating. No. 3441, Soldiers preparing to sacrifice white horse. No. 3442, Shaman before fire, headsman.

1994-96
3434 A982 19fo multicolored   .65   .30
3435 A982 19fo multicolored   .65   .30
3436 A982 19fo multicolored   .65   .30
  a.   Strip of 3, #3434-3436   2.00 2.00
3437 A982 22fo multicolored   .65   .30
3438 A982 22fo multicolored   .65   .30
3439 A982 22fo multicolored   .65   .30
  a.   Strip of 3, #3437-3439   2.00 2.00
3440 A982 24fo multicolored   .55   .30
3441 A982 24fo multicolored   .55   .30
3442 A982 24fo multicolored   .55   .30
  a.   Strip of 3, #3440-3442   1.65   .90
    Nos. 3434-3442 (9)   5.55 2.70

Nos. 3436a, 3439a, 3442a are continuous design. #3436a sold for 59fo.
Nos. 3435, 3438, 3441 are 60x40mm.
Issued: #3434-3436, 5/19/94; #3437-3439, 2/23/95; #3440-3442, 2/29/96.

Souvenir Sheet

1996, Apr. 18
3442B A982 195fo multicolored 20.00 16.00

Nos. 3436a, 3439a, 3442a are continuous design. #3436a sold for 59fo. No. 3442B contains one each of Nos. 3436a, 3439a, 3442a.

Intl. Olympic Committee, Cent. — A985

Designs: 12fo, 1896, 1992 medals. No. 3444, Flag, runners, Olympic flame. No. 3445, Athens Stadium, 1896. 35fo, Pierre de Coubertin (1863-1937), first president.

1994, June 16   **Litho.**   **Perf. 12½**
3443 A985 12fo multicolored   .45   .20
3444 A985 19fo multicolored   .65   .30
3445 A985 19fo multicolored   .65   .30
3446 A985 35fo multicolored   1.25   .60
    Nos. 3443-3446 (4)   3.00 1.40

1994 World Cup Soccer Championships, US — A986

US flag, soccer players and: No. 3447, Elvis Presley. No. 3448, Marilyn Monroe. No. 3449, John Wayne.

1994, June 16   **Perf. 12**
3447 A986 19fo multicolored   .65   .30
3448 A986 19fo multicolored   .65   .30
3449 A986 35fo multicolored   1.25   .60
    Nos. 3447-3449 (3)   2.55 1.20

Intl. Year of the Family A987

1994, July 21   **Litho.**   **Perf. 11**
3450 A987 19fo multicolored   .65   .30

Flowers of the Continents Type of 1990

Flowers of Europe: 12fo, Leucojum aestivum. 19fo, Helianthemum nummularium. 35fo, Eryngium alpinum. 50fo, Thlaspi rotundifolium. 100fo, Bouquet of European flowers.

1994, Aug. 18   **Litho.**   **Perf. 11½x12**
3451 A892 12fo multicolored   .40   .20
3452 A892 19fo multicolored   .65   .35
3453 A892 35fo multicolored   1.25   .60
3454 A892 50fo multicolored   1.60   .85
    Nos. 3451-3454 (4)   3.90 2.00

Souvenir Sheet
Perf. 12½

3455 A892 100fo multicolored   4.00 2.50

No. 3455 contains one 32x41mm stamp.

UPU, 120th Anniv. A988

UPU emblem and: 19fo, Heinrich Von Stephan (1831-97). 35fo, Mihaly Gervay (1819-96).
#3458: a, Von Stephan, vert. b, Gervay, vert.

1994, Sept. 9   **Litho.**   **Perf. 12**
3456 A988 19fo multicolored   .55 .30
3457 A988 35fo multicolored   1.00 .50

Souvenir Sheet of 2
3458 A988 50fo +25fo, #a.-b.   4.50 2.25

Stamp Day, 67th anniv.

Folk Designs — A989

Various ornate designs.

1994-96   **Litho.**   **Perf. 11½x12**
3459 A989 1fo bl vio & blk   .20 .20
3460 A989 2fo multi   .20 .20
3461 A989 3fo multi   .20 .20
3461A A989 9fo multi   .20 .20
3462 A989 11fo multi   .35 .20
3463 A989 12fo multi   .35 .20
3463A A989 13fo grn, red & blk   .20 .20
3464 A989 14fo multi   .25 .20
3465 A989 16fo bl, red & blk   .30 .20
3466 A989 17fo red & blk   .30 .20
3467 A989 19fo multi   .50 .25
3468 A989 22fo multi   .35 .20
3469 A989 24fo multi   .40 .20
3470 A989 32fo multi   .95 .50
3471 A989 35fo multi   1.00 .50
3472 A989 38fo multi   .65 .30
3473 A989 40fo multi   1.40 .55
3474 A989 50fo multi   1.75 .70
3475 A989 75fo multi   1.50 .65
3476 A989 80fo multi   1.75 .70
3477 A989 300fo multi   6.25 2.60
3478 A989 500fo multi   10.00 4.50
Nos. 3459-3478 (22)   29.05 13.65

Issued: 11fo, 12fo, 19fo, 32fo, 35fo, 40fo, 50fo, 10/10/94; 1fo, 1/10/95; 2fo, 3fo, 9fo, 14fo, 22fo, 38fo, 4/3/95; 13fo, 16fo, 17fo, 24fo, 75fo, 80fo, 7/1/96.
See #3561, 3615, 3630, 3644-3646, 3649-3650. For surcharge see #3583.

Souvenir Sheet

Summit Meeting of the Conference for European Security & Cooperation — A990

1994, Sept. 10   **Litho.**   **Perf. 12**
3479 A990 100fo Budapest   3.00 2.50

Holocaust, 50th Anniv. — A991

1994, Oct. 20
3480 A991 19fo multicolored   .55 .30

Buildings in Budapest A992

#3481, Vajdahunyadvar Castle. #3482, Nemzeti Museum. #3483, Muszaki Palace.

1994, Nov. 17   **Engr.**
3481 A992 19fo violet   .55 .30
3482 A992 19fo green   .55 .30
3483 A992 19fo brown   .55 .30
Nos. 3481-3483 (3)   1.65 .90

Christmas — A993

1994, Nov. 17   **Litho.**
3484 A993 12fo shown   .40 .20
3485 A993 35fo Flight into Egypt   1.25 .60

Hungarian Shipping Co., Cent. — A994

Design: 22fo, Early steamer Francis Joseph I, cargo ship Baross.

1995, Jan. 24   **Litho.**   **Perf. 13**
3486 A994 22fo multicolored   .65 .30

Easter — A995

1995, Mar. 7   **Perf. 12**
3487 A995 14fo black & lilac   .45 .25

Hungarian Shipping — A996

Designs: 14fo, Tug-wheeled steamship, map of first navigable section of the Tisza, view of Szeged. 60fo, Pal Vasarhelyi, Tisza survey ship, surveyor.

1995, Mar. 7   **Perf. 13**
3488 A996 14fo multicolored   .45 .25
3489 A996 60fo multicolored   2.00 1.00

Natl. Meteorological Service, 125th Anniv. — A997

1995, Apr. 7   **Perf. 12**
3490 A997 22fo multicolored   .65 .30

FAO, 50th Anniv. — A998

1995, Apr. 7
3491 A998 22fo multicolored   .65 .30

European Nature Conservation Year — A999

#3492, Crane, frog, flowers. #3493, Squirrel, insect. #3494, Bird, berries, flowers. #3495, Butterfly, hedgehog, flowers.

1995, May 9   **Litho.**   **Perf. 13½x13**
3492 A999 14fo multicolored   .55 .25
3493 A999 14fo multicolored   .55 .25
3494 A999 14fo multicolored   .55 .25
3495 A999 14fo multicolored   .55 .25
   a.   Strip of 4, #3492-3495   3.00 2.50

Peace & Liberty — A1000

1995, May 9
3496 A1000 22fo multicolored   2.25 .40

Europa.

Hungarian Olympic Committee, Cent. — A1001

22fo, Diver, Pierre de Coubertin. 60fo, Javelin. 100fo, Fencing.

1995, June 12   **Litho.**   **Perf. 12**
3497 A1001 22fo multicolored   .60 .30
3498 A1001 60fo multicolored   1.60 .80
3499 A1001 100fo multicolored   2.75 1.40
Nos. 3497-3499 (3)   4.95 2.50

St. Ladislas I (1040?-1095) A1002

1995, June 12
3500 A1002 22fo multicolored   .60 .30

Laszlo Almasy, Sahara Researcher, Birth Cent. — A1003

1995, Aug. 22   **Litho.**   **Perf. 13x13½**
3501 A1003 22fo multicolored   .75 .30

Odon Lechner, Architect, 150th Birth Anniv. — A1004

Design: 22fo, Museum of Applied Arts, Lechner. Illustration reduced.

Litho. & Engr.
1995, Aug. 22   **Perf. 12**
3502 A1004 22fo multicolored   .75 .30

Contemporary Paintings A1005

No. 3503, Abstract, by Laszlo Moholy-Nagy (1895-1946). No. 3504, Woman with a violin, by Aurel Bernath (1895-1982).

1995, Sept. 18   **Litho.**
3503 A1005 22fo multicolored   .75 .30
3504 A1005 22fo multicolored   .75 .30

Eotvos College, Cent. — A1006

60fo, Eotvos College, Josef Eotvos (1813-71), statesman, writer, educational leader.

1995, Sept. 18
3505 A1006 60fo red brn, blk   1.60 .80

Stamp Day A1007

Designs: 22fo, Horse-drawn mail chaise. 40fo, Jet, map. 100fo + 30fo, Man, boys looking at stamp album, vert.

1995, Sept. 29   Litho.   Perf. 13½x13
3506 A1007 22fo multicolored   .60   .30
3507 A1007 40fo multicolored   1.10   .55

Souvenir Sheet
Perf. 12x12½
3508 A1007 100fo +30fo multi   3.50 2.50

Buildings of Budapest
A1008

#3509, Nyugati Palyaudvar. #3510, Vigado.

1995   Engr.   Perf. 12
3509 A1008 22fo dark olive brn   1.00   .30
3510 A1008 22fo deep claret   1.00   .30

UN, 50th Anniv.
A1009

1995, Oct. 24   Litho.   Perf. 11
3511 A1009 60fo multicolored   1.60   .80

Christmas — A1010

1995, Nov. 16   Perf. 12
Children's designs: 14fo, Spark thrower. 60fo, The Three Magi.
3512 A1010 14fo multicolored   .40   .20
3513 A1010 60fo multicolored   1.60   .80

Nobel Prize Fund Established, Cent. — A1011

1995, Nov. 16
3514 A1011 100fo Medals   2.75 1.40

No. 3514 is printed se-tenant with label.

St. Elizabeth of Hungary Bathing Lepers — A1012

1995, Nov. 16   Perf. 13
3515 A1012 22fo multicolored   .60   .30

No. 3515 is printed se-tenant with label.

A1013

Archaeological Finds from Karos: a, Gold and silver saber. b, Badge.

1996, Mar. 14   Litho.   Perf. 13½x13
3516 A1013 24fo #a.-b. + 2 labels 2.00   .55

Souvenir Sheet

Pannonhalma, Benedictine Monastery, 1000th Anniv. — A1014

1996, Mar. 21   Engr.   Perf. 12
3517 A1014 100fo deep violet   5.50 3.50

Sheet margin is litho. and multicolored.

1996 Summer Olympics, Atlanta
A1015

1996, Apr. 18   Litho.   Perf. 11½x12
3518 A1015 24fo Swimming   .55   .30
3519 A1015 50fo Tennis   1.10   .60
3520 A1015 75fo Kayak   1.75   .85
      Nos. 3518-3520 (3)   3.40 1.75

National Productivity
A1016

1996, Apr. 18   Litho.   Perf. 12
3521 A1016 24fo multicolored   .55   .30

Natl. Writers Assoc., Cent. — A1017

1996, Apr. 18   Perf. 12x11½
3522 A1017 50fo multicolored   1.10   .60

Budapest Subway, Cent. — A1018

1996, May 2   Perf. 12
3523 A1018 24fo multicolored   .80   .30

Famous Women
A1019

Europa: 24fo, Queen Gizella. 75fo, Bavarian Princess Elisabeth Wittelsbach.

1996, May 2   Litho.   Perf. 12
3524 A1019 24fo multicolored   1.00   .50
3525 A1019 75fo multicolored   3.00 1.25

Pannonhalma, Benedictine Monastery, 1000th Anniv. A1020

Designs: 17fo, Entrance to cathedral. 24fo, Monks in northern wing.

1996, June 21   Engr.   Perf. 12
3526 A1020 17fo red brown   .60   .20
3527 A1020 24fo dark blue   .90   .30

See Nos. 3536-3537.

Intl. Anti-Drug Day — A1021

1996, June 21   Litho.   Perf. 14
3528 A1021 24fo multicolored   .55   .30

Hungarian Developers of Technolgy — A1022

Inventor, invention: 24fo, Denes Mihaly (1894-1953), Telehor. 50fo, Jozsef Biro Laszlo (1899-1985), mass-produced ball-point pen. 75fo, Zoltan Bay (1900-92), lunar radar set.

1996, June 21   Perf. 12x11½
3529 A1022 24fo multicolored   .55   .30
3530 A1022 50fo multicolored   1.10   .60
3531 A1022 75fo multicolored   1.75   .85
      Nos. 3529-3531 (3)   3.40 1.75

Hungarian Railways, 150th Anniv. — A1023

Designs: 17fo, 303-Series steam tender locomotive. No. 3533, 325-Series locomotive . No. 3534, "Pest," steam locomotive made by Cokerill and Co.

1996, July 12   Perf. 13½x13
3532 A1023 17fo multicolored   .55   .20
3533 A1023 24fo multicolored   .70   .20
3534 A1023 24fo multicolored   1.50   .30
      Nos. 3532-3534 (3)   2.75   .80

Second European Congress of Mathematicians
A1024

1996, July 12   Perf. 12
3535 A1024 24fo multicolored   .55   .30

Pannonhalma, Benedictine Monastery, Type of 1996

Designs: 17fo, Refectory. 24fo, Main library.

1996, Aug. 12   Engr.   Perf. 12
3536 A1020 17fo dark brown   .60   .20
3537 A1020 24fo dark green   .90   .20

Nature Expo '96
A1025

1996, Aug. 12   Litho.   Perf. 12x11½
3538 A1025 13fo Egretta alba   .20   .20
3539 A1025 13fo Iris sibirica   .20   .20
3540 A1025 13fo Lynx lynx   .20   .20
3541 A1025 13fo Ropalopus ungaricus 1.20 1.20
   a. Block of 4, #3538-3541   2.00 2.00

A1026   A1027

1996, Aug. 12   Perf. 12
3542 A1026 24fo No. 4   1.00   .20

Hungarian postage stamps, 125th anniv.
Issued in miniature sheets of 6 stamps in two columns of 3 separated by a column of labels. Values, stamp plus label $1.50, miniature sheet $7.50.

1996, Aug. 21   Litho.   Perf. 11½x12
Stamp Day, Budapest '96: 17fo, Prince Arpad, people from 14th cent. "Vienna Picture Chronicle," man stirring liquid in pot. 24fo, Prince on horseback, archer.
150fo+50fo, #601, first page from "The Deeds of Hungarians."
3543 A1027 17fo multicolored   .60   .20
3544 A1027 24fo multicolored   .90   .20

Souvenir Sheet
Perf. 12x12½
3545 A1027 150fo +50fo multi   5.50 3.00

Steamships on Lake Balaton, 150th
Anniv. — A1028

Steamer Kisfaludy.

1996, Sept. 17   Litho.   Perf. 12
3548 A1028 17fo multicolored   .60   .20

Hungarian Revolution, 40th
Anniv. — A1029

Newspaper clippings and: 13fo, People
marching. 16fo, Troops on back of truck. 17fo,
Two men with guns. 24fo, Imre Nagy addressing people.
40fo, Nagy Cabinet.

1996, Oct. 23   Litho.   Perf. 12
3549 A1029 13fo multicolored   .35   .20
3550 A1029 16fo multicolored   .40   .20
3551 A1029 17fo multicolored   .40   .20
3552 A1029 24fo multicolored   .60   .20
      Nos. 3549-3552 (4)   1.75   .80

Souvenir Sheet
3553 A1029 40fo multicolored   4.00 2.25

Souvenir Sheet

1996 Summer Olympic Games,
Atlanta — A1030

Illustration reduced.

1996, Oct. 22
3554 A1030 150fo multicolored   4.50 2.25

A1036

1996, Nov. 14   Litho.   Perf. 11½x12
3555 A1036 24fo multicolored   .40   .20

Miklos Wesselenyi (1796-1850), writer.

A1037

1996, Nov. 14   Perf. 13½x13
3556 A1037 24fo multicolored   .40   .20

UNICEF, 50th anniv.

Christmas
A1038

Paintings: 17fo, Mary with Infant Jesus and
Two Angels, by Matteo di Giovanni. 24fo, Ado-
ration of the Kings, by unknown painter of
Salsburg.

1996, Nov. 14   Perf. 12
3557 A1038 17fo multicolored   .35   .20
3558 A1038 24fo multicolored   .65   .20

Hungarian Literature — A1039

Designs: No. 3559, Scenes from "The
Umbrella of St. Peter," Kalman Mikszath
(1847-1910). No. 3560, Scenes of men and
dogs from "Abel in the Vast Trackless Forest"
and "Matthias the Ice-breaker," Aron Tamasi
(1897-1966).

1997, Jan. 16   Litho.   Perf. 12x11½
3559 A1039 27fo multicolored   .50   .25
3560 A1039 27fo multicolored   .50   .25

Folk Art Type of 1994

1997, Mar. 26   Perf. 11½x12
3561 A989 27fo multicolored   .50   .25

Coat of Arms of Budapest and
Counties — A1040

No. 3562: a, Hajdú-Bihar. b, Baranya. c,
Bács-Kiskun. d, Békés. e, Borsod-Abaúj-
Zemplén.
No. 3563: a, Fejér. b, Györ-Moson-Sopron.
c, Heves. d, Jász-Nagykun-Szolnok. e,
Komárom-Esztergom. f, Nógrád.
No. 3564: a, Pest. b, Somogy. c, Toina. d,
Vas. e, Veszprém. f, Zala.
No. 3565: a, Budapest. b, Csongrád. c,
Szaboics-Szatmár-Bereg.

1997, Mar. 26   Perf. 11½x12
3562 A1040 27fo Sheet of 5,
                   #a.-e. + label   5.00 3.25
3563 A1040 27fo Sheet of 6,
                   #a.-f.   6.25 4.25
3564 A1040 27fo Sheet of 6,
                   #a.-f.   6.25 4.25
3564G A1040 27fo Hajdu-Bihar   .75   .75

Size: 51x33mm
3565 A1040 27fo Sheet of 3,
                   #a.-c.   2.25 1.75

No. 3564G is 51x33mm and has the same
design as No. 3562a which has a se-tenant
label, but lacks the perforations separating
these items. Nos. 3262a-3262e, 3563a-3563f,
3564a-3564f, 3565a-3565c were also printed

in individual sheets. Value, set of singles (20):
mint $11; used $4.

Youth Stamps — A1042

Designs: 20fo, Scouting emblem, tents, sailboat, waterfall. 27fo+10fo, Knights on horseback from "Toldi," by Janos Arany.

1997, Apr. 23   Perf. 12
3566 A1041 20fo multicolored   .50   .20
3567 A1042 27fo +10fo multi   1.25   .35

A1043

1997, Apr. 23   Perf. 13½x13
3568 A1043 90fo multicolored   1.60   .80

World Meeting of Custom Directors.

A1044

1997, Apr. 23   Engr.   Perf. 12
3569 A1044 80fo deep violet   1.75   .70

St. Adalbert (956-997). See Germany No.
1964, Poland No. 3307, Czech Republic No.
3012, Vatican City No. 1040..

Stories and
Legends
A1045

Europa: 27fo, Hunters on horseback shooting bow and arrow at deer. 90fo, Preparing
body in sarcophagus of Prince Geza.

1997, May 5   Litho.   Perf. 13x13½
3570 A1045 27fo multicolored   1.00   .40
3571 A1045 90fo multicolored   2.25   .90

African
Animals
A1046

16fo, Oryx gazella. #3573, Equus burchelli.
#3574, Diceros bicornis. 27fo, Panthera leo.
90fo, Loxodonta africana.

1997, May 5   Perf. 12
3572 A1046 16fo multicolored   .25   .20
3573 A1046 20fo multicolored   .55   .20
3574 A1046 20fo multicolored   .55   .20
3575 A1046 27fo multicolored   .90   .30
      Nos. 3572-3575 (4)   2.25   .90

Souvenir Sheet
3576 A1046 90fo multicolored   4.50 3.00

A1047

1997, June 8   Litho.   Perf. 12
3577 A1047 90fo multicolored   1.60   .70

Polish Queen Jadwiga (1373-99).

A1048

World Congress on Stress, Budapest: Janos
(Hans) Selye (1907-82), founder of theory of
stress, face of person under stress.

1997, July 1
3578 A1048 90fo multicolored   1.60   .70

Indigenous
Fish
A1049

Designs: a, Gymnocephalus schraetzer. b,
Cottus gobio. c, Alburnoides bipunctatus. d,
Cobitis taenia.

1997, June 6   Litho.   Perf. 13x13½
3579 A1049 20fo Strip of 4, #a.-
                   d.   2.50 1.25

**Grapes and Wine Producing Areas
Type of 1990**

Grapes and growing area: No. 3580, Nemes
kadarka, Great Kiskoros. No. 3581, Teitfürtü
ezerjo, Mor. No. 3582, Harslevelu, Gyongyos.

1997, Aug. 12   Litho.   Perf. 13x13½
3580 A902 27fo multicolored   .40   .20
3581 A902 27fo multicolored   .40   .20
3582 A902 27fo multicolored   .90   .20
      Nos. 3580-3582 (3)   1.70   .60

No. 3469 Surcharged in Red

1997, July 10   Litho.   Perf. 11½x12
3583 A989 60fo on 24fo multi   .90   .45

Christmas
A1050

20fo, Holy family. 27fo, Adoration of the Magi.

1997, Oct. 31   **Litho.**   **Perf. 13x13½**
3584 A1050 20fo multicolored   .40 .20
3585 A1050 27fo multicolored   .60 .20

World Weight Lifting Championships, Thailand
A1051

1997, Nov. 12   **Perf. 12**
3586 A1051 90fo multicolored   1.60 .65

Zsigmond Szechenyi, African Explorer
A1052

1998, Jan. 22   **Litho.**   **Perf. 12**
3587 A1052 60fo multicolored   1.60 .45

Natl. Anthem by Ferenc Kolcsey, 175th Anniv.
A1053

1998, Jan. 22
3588 A1053 75fo multicolored   1.60 .55

1998 Winter Olympic Games, Nagano — A1054

1998, Jan. 22   **Perf. 13½x13**
3589 A1054 30fo Downhill skiing   .65 .30
3590 A1054 100fo Snowboarding   1.10 .85

Valentine's Day — A1055

1998, Feb. 11   **Perf. 11½x12**
3591 A1055 24fo multi   .55 .20

A1056   A1057

1998, Feb. 11   **Perf. 12**
3592 A1056 50fo multicolored   1.75 .50

Leo Szilard (1898-1964), physicist.

1998, Feb. 11   **Perf. 11½x12**

Balint Postas (Post Office Mascot) in front of printed material: 23fo, Holding letter. 24fo, Bowing. 30fo, Standing straight with arms outstretched. 65fo, Flying.

3593 A1057 23fo multicolored   .50 .20
3594 A1057 24fo multicolored   .50 .20
3595 A1057 30fo multicolored   .65 .30
3596 A1057 65fo multicolored   1.40 .65
    Nos. 3593-3596 (4)   3.05 1.35

Easter
A1058   A1059

1998, Mar. 13   **Litho.**   **Perf. 13½x13**
3597 A1058 24fo Stylized egg   .55 .20
       Perf. 11
3598 A1059 30fo Christ's resurrection   .65 .20

1848-49 Revolution, War of Independence, 150th Anniv. — A1060

23fo, Sandor Petofi (1823-49), poet, handwriting, tricolor. 24fo, Mihaly Tancsics, writer & politician, ink well. 30fo, Lajos Kossuth (1802-94), seal.

1998, Mar. 13   **Perf. 12**
3599 A1060 23fo multicolored   .40 .20
3600 A1060 24fo multicolored   .50 .20
3601 A1060 30fo multicolored   .60 .20
    Nos. 3599-3601 (3)   1.50 .60

See Nos. 3640-3643.

Art Nouveau — A1061

Ceramics: 20fo, Vase with relief design of young girl picking flowers, 1899. 24fo, Flower holder with peacock-eyed butterflies, 1901. 30fo, Vase with tulip stems, 1899. 95fo, Round container with legs, 1912.

1998, Mar. 31   **Litho.**   **Perf. 12**
3602 A1061 20fo multi, vert.   .35 .20
    Complete booklet, 10 #3602   3.25
3603 A1061 24fo multi   .40 .20
    Complete booklet, 10 #3603   3.75
3604 A1061 30fo multi, vert.   .50 .25
    Complete booklet, 10 #3604   4.75
3605 A1061 95fo multi   1.50 .70
    Nos. 3602-3605 (4)   2.75 1.35

Postal Regulation, 250th Anniv. — A1062

Designs: 24fo+10fo, Courier of 1748, detail of postal route connecting counties of Zala and Gyor. 30fo+10fo, Mounted courier, blowing post horn, script of regulation. 150fo, Horse-drawn postal coach, detail of postal route.

1998, Apr. 10
3606 A1062 24fo +10fo multi   .75 .45
3607 A1062 30fo +10fo multi   1.25 .60
    Souvenir Sheet
3608 A1062 150fo multicolored   5.00 2.50

Stamp Day.

Animals of the Americas
A1063

23fo, Bison bison. #3610, Ursus horribilis. #3611, Alligator mississippiensis. 30fo, Leopardus pardalis. 150fo, Loddigesia mirabilis.

1998, Apr. 30
3609 A1063 23fo multicolored   .70 .35
3610 A1063 24fo multicolored   .70 .35
3611 A1063 24fo multicolored   .70 .35
3612 A1063 30fo multicolored   .90 .45
    Nos. 3609-3612 (4)   3.00 1.50
    Souvenir Sheet
3613 A1063 150fo multicolored   5.00 2.50

Gyorgy Jendrassik, Engineer, Birth Cent.
A1064

1998, May 4   **Engr.**
3614 A1064 100fo dark blue   1.50 .75

Folk Designs Type of 1994

1998, June 5   **Litho.**   **Perf. 11½x12**
3615 A989 5fo multicolored   .20 .20

1998 Canoe-Kayak World Championships, Szeged — A1065

1998, June 5   **Perf. 12**
3616 A1065 30fo multicolored   .45 .20

1998 World Cup Soccer Championships, France — A1066

Different soccer players.

1998, June 5
3617 A1066 30fo multicolored   .45 .20
3618 A1066 110fo multicolored   1.60 .80
   a.   Pair, 3617-3618   2.10 1.00

1998 European Track & Field Championships, Budapest — A1067

1998, June 5   **Perf. 12x11**
3619 A1067 24fo Hurdles   .35 .20
3620 A1067 65fo Pole vault   .95 .50
3621 A1067 80fo Hammer throw   1.25 .60
    Nos. 3619-3621 (3)   2.55 1.30

Gabor Baross (1848-92), Postal Administrator
A1068

1998, June 5   **Perf. 12**
3622 A1068 60fo multicolored   .90 .45

A1069

1998, July 31   **Litho.**   **Perf. 12**
3623 A1069 24fo multicolored   .60 .25
    Complete booklet, 10 #3623   10.00

Széchenyi Hill Children's Railway, 50th anniv.

A1070

1998, July 31   **Perf. 12x11½**
3624 A1070 65fo multicolored   .95 .50

World Congress of Computer Technology, Budapest.

Natl. Holidays — A1071

Europa: 50fo, Sculptures, Festival of the 1956 Revolution, Proclamation of the Republic, 1989, October 23. 60fo, Sheaf of grain, Natl. arms, National Day, August 20.

1998, Aug. 19   **Litho.**   **Perf. 12**
3625 A1071 50fo multicolored   1.50 .65
3626 A1071 60fo multicolored   2.25 .85

A1072

1998, Aug. 19
3627 A1072 100fo multicolored   1.40 .70
World Federation of Hungarians, 60th Anniv.

National Parks
A1073

Various flora, fauna, explorer of given region: 24fo, Dr. Miklós Udvardy, Hortobágy Natl. Park. 70fo, Adám Boros, Kiskunság Natl. Park.

1998, Oct. 6   Litho.   Perf. 12
3628 A1073 24fo multicolored   .50 .20
3629 A1073 70fo multicolored   1.25 .50
See Nos. 3654-3655, 3689-3690, 3745-3747, 3689-3690, 4072.

Folk Designs Type of 1994
1998   Litho.   Perf. 11½x12
3630 A989 200fo multicolored   5.00 .70

Christmas
A1074

Designs: 20fo, Painting, "Visit of the Shepherds," by Agnolo Bronzino (1503-72). 24fo, Artwork, "Mary Upon the Throne with the Infant," by Carlo Crivelli (1430?-94?), vert.

1998, Oct. 30   Perf. 12x11½, 11½x12
3631 A1074 20fo multicolored   .40 .20
  Complete booklet, 10 #3631   3.75
3632 A1074 24fo multicolored   .45 .20
  Complete booklet, 10 #3632   6.50
See No. 3676.

Easter
A1075

1999, Feb. 11   Litho.   Perf. 12
3633 A1075 27fo Decorated eggs   .35 .20
3634 A1075 32fo Shroud of Turin   .75 .20
No. 3634 is 38x53mm.

Intl. Year of the Elderly
A1076

1999, Feb. 11   Perf. 12½x13½
3635 A1076 32fo multicolored   .75 .20

Sailing Ships
A1077

1999, Feb. 11   Perf. 12
3636 A1077 32fo Novara   .40 .20
3637 A1077 79fo Phoenix   1.00 .50
3638 A1077 110fo Galley, 15th
      cent.   1.40 .70
  Nos. 3636-3638 (3)   2.80 1.40

Souvenir Sheet

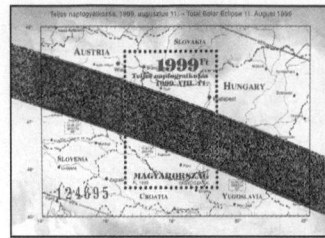

Total Solar Eclipse, Aug. 11 — A1078

Illustration reduced.

1999, Feb. 11
3639 A1078 1999fo multi   22.00 22.00
No. 3639 contains a holographic image. Soaking in water may affect the hologram.

Revolution of 1848-49 Type of 1998
24fo, Sword, Artúr Görgey (1818-1916), general. 27fo, Military decoration, Lajos Batthyány (1806-49), premier of 1st Hungarian ministry. 32fo, Military decoration, Jósef Bem (1794-1850), Polish General who joined Hungarian army.
100fo, Battle scene.

1999, Mar. 12
3640 A1060 24fo multicolored   .45 .20
3641 A1060 27fo multicolored   .55 .20
3642 A1060 32fo multicolored   .60 .20
  Nos. 3640-3642 (3)   1.60 .60

Souvenir Sheet
3643 A1060 100fo multicolored   4.00 2.00
No. 3643 contains one 45x28mm stamp.

Folk Designs Type of 1994
1999   Litho.   Perf. 12½
3644 A989 24fo multicolored   .40 .20
3645 A989 65fo red & black   1.10 .30
3646 A989 90fo multicolored   2.00 .55
  Nos. 3644-3646 (3)   3.50 1.05
Nos. 3644-3646 are inscribed "1999."

Entrance into NATO — A1079

1999, Mar. 12   Litho.   Perf. 12x11½
3647 A1079 110fo multicolored   1.60 .55

Souvenir Sheet

1999 Modern Pentathlon World Championships, Budapest — A1080

Illustration reduced.

1999, Mar. 24   Perf. 12½
3648 A1080 100fo multicolored   3.50 1.75

Folk Designs Type of 1994
Various ornate designs.

1999, Apr. 19   Litho.   Perf. 11½x12
3649 A989 79fo multicolored   1.60 .45
3650 A989 100fo multicolored   2.40 .60

A1081

A1082

1999, May 3   Perf. 12
3651 A1081 50fo slate & bister   .85 .30
Ferenc Pápai Páriz (1649-1716).

1999, May 3
3652 A1082 100fo multicolored   1.50 .65
Ferencvárosi Torna Sport Club, cent.

World Science Conference
A1082a

1999, May 3   Litho.   Perf. 11½x12½
3652A A1082a 65fo multicolored   2.00 .60

Council of Europe, 50th Anniv.
A1083

1999, May 4   Perf. 13x13¼
3653 A1083 50fo multicolored   1.75 .50

National Parks Type of 1998
Europa: 27fo, Aggteleki National Park. 32fo, Bükki National Park.

1999, May 6   Perf. 12
3654 A1073 27fo multicolored   3.50 1.40
3655 A1073 32fo multicolored   5.00 3.25

Grapes and Wine Producing Areas Type of 1990
Grapes, growing area and: 24fo, Castle ruins, Somló region. 27fo, 17th cent. view of Sopron.

1999, May 6   Litho.   Perf. 12¼x12½
3656 A902 24fo multi, horiz.   .70 .20
3657 A902 27fo multi, horiz.   1.10 .30

Animals of Asia
A1085

Designs: 27fo, Tigris regalis. 32fo, Ailuropodus melanoleucus. 52fo, Panthera pardus. 79fo, Pongo pygmaeus. 100fo, Aix galericulata.

1999, May 6   Perf. 12
3658 A1085 27fo multicolored   .50 .25
3659 A1085 32fo multicolored   .65 .30
3660 A1085 52fo multicolored   .95 .40
3661 A1085 79fo multicolored   1.90 .50
  Nos. 3658-3661 (4)   4.00 1.45

Souvenir Sheet
3662 A1085 100fo multicolored   6.50 5.00
No. 3662 contains one 50x30mm stamp.

Queen Maria Theresa's Introduction of Mail Coach Service, 250th Anniv.
A1086

Stamp Day: 32fo+15fo, Decree by Maria Theresa, coach, street. 52fo+20fo, People entering coach, woman with letters, portion of decree.
150fo, Horse-drawn coach arriving a station.

1999, May 21   Litho.   Perf. 12½x12¼
3663 A1086 32fo +15fo multi   .80 .75
3664 A1086 52fo +20fo multi   1.40 1.00

Souvenir Sheet
3665 A1086 150fo multicolored   4.50 4.00
#3665 contains one 32x42mm stamp.

Red Poppy — A1087

1999, July 7   Litho.   Perf. 12x11½
3666 A1087 27fo shown   1.00 .40
3667 A1087 32fo Stalkless gentian   1.50 .70
See Nos. 3805-3806.

George Cukor (1899-1983), Film Director — A1088

1999, July 7   Litho.   Perf. 12
3668 A1088 50fo multicolored   1.25 .40

UPU, 125th Anniv.
A1089

1999, Aug. 13   Litho.   Perf. 12
3669 A1089 32fo multicolored   1.25 .85
Issued in sheets of 3. Value $4.50.

Frankfurt Book Fair — A1090

1999, Sept. 9   Litho.   Perf. 12
3670 A1090 40fo multicolored   1.75 .25

Antique
Furniture
A1091

Designs: 10fo, Chair, 17th cent, vert. 20fo, Chair by Károly Lingel, 1915, vert. 50fo, Chair by Pál Esterházy, vert. 70fo, Upholstered chair, vert. 100fo, Couch by Lajos Kozma.

Perf. 11½x12, 12x11½

1999, Oct. 7			Litho.	
3671	A1091	10fo bister & dk brn	.20	.20
3672	A1091	20fo green & dk grn	.40	.20
3673	A1091	50fo blue & dk bl	.80	.30
3674	A1091	70fo red & dk red	1.25	.35
3675	A1091	100fo brown & dk brn	1.75	.50
		Nos. 3671-3675 (5)	4.40	1.55

Nos. 3671-3673, 3675 exist dated "2001."
See Nos. 3711-3721, 3737-3743, 3790-3791, 3821-3823, 3960-3965, 4134.

Bronzino Christmas Painting Type of 1998 and

Magi — A1092

Madonna and Child, Stained Glass by Miksa Róth — A1093

1999, Oct. 15			Perf. 12x11½, 11½x12	
3676	A1074	24fo multi	.65	.20
		Complete booklet, 10 #3676	10.00	
3677	A1092	27fo multi	.85	.20
		Complete booklet, 10 #3677	9.50	
3678	A1093	32fo multi	1.00	.20
		Complete booklet, 10 #3678	10.00	
		Nos. 3676-3678 (3)	2.50	.60

Jenö Wigner
(1902-95), Winner
of 1963 Nobel
Physics
Prize — A1094

1999, Nov. 3			Perf. 12	
3679	A1094	32fo blue	1.00	.30

Souvenir Sheet

Chain Bridge, 150th Anniv. — A1095

Illustration reduced.

1999, Nov. 3				
3680	A1095	150fo multi	3.25	2.25

Hungarian
Millennium
A1096

Designs: 28fo, 30fo, Coronation scepter. 34fo, 40fo, Millennium flag.

2000			Litho.	Perf. 12x11½	
3681	A1096	28fo multi		.80	.20
3682	A1096	30fo multi		.80	.20
3683	A1096	34fo multi		.80	.20
3684	A1096	40fo multi		1.10	.20
		Nos. 3681-3684 (4)		3.50	.80

Coronation of Stephen I, Hungarian conversion to Christianity, 1000th anniv.
Issued: 30fo, 40fo, 1/1; 28fo, 24fo, 2/24.
No. 3681 exists dated 2001.
See No. 3744.

Souvenir Sheet

Famous Hungarians
A1097

No. 3685: a, 30fo, Miklós Misztófalusi Kis (1650-1702), scientist. b, 40fo, Anyos Jedlik (1800-95), physicist. c, 50fo, Jeno Kvassay (1850-1919), engineer. d, 80fo, Jeno Barcsay (1900-88), painter.

2000, Jan. 11			Perf. 11½x12	
3685	A1097	Sheet of 4, #a.-d.	4.00	3.75

Souvenir Sheet of 5

Literary and
Theatrical
Personalities
A1098

No. 3686: a, Mihály Vörösmarty (1800-55), dramatist. b, Mari Jászai (1850-1926), actress. c, Sándor Márai (1900-89), writer. d, Lujza Blaha (1850-1926), actress. e, Lorinc Szabó (1900-57), writer.

2000, Feb. 24			Perf. 12	
3686	A1098	50fo #a.-e.	4.00	3.50

A1099

Easter — A1100

2000, Mar. 20				
3687	A1099	26fo multi	.50	.20
3688	A1100	28fo multi	.75	.30

National Parks Type of 1998

Designs: 29fo, Bluethroat, Siberian iris, ornithologist György Breuer (1887-1955), Ferto-Hanság Park. 34fo, Black stork, fritillary, scientist Pál Kitaibel (1757-1817), Duna-Dráva Park.

2000, Mar. 20			Litho.	Perf. 12	
3689	A1073	29fo multi		.60	.20
		Complete booklet, 10 #36892		5.50	
3690	A1073	34fo multi		1.00	.35
		Complete booklet, 10 #3690		7.50	

Ferihegy
Airport, 50th
Anniv. — A1101

2000, May 3			Perf. 12x11½	
3691	A1101	136fo multi	2.00	1.00

István Türr (1825-1908) and Canal Boat — A1102

2000, May 9			Perf. 12	
3692	A1102	80fo multi	1.50	.70

Expo 2000, Hanover.

Australian
Wildlife — A1103

2000, May 9				
3693	A1103	26fo shown	.30	.20
3694	A1103	28fo Opossum	.35	.20
3695	A1103	83fo Koala	1.10	.30
3696	A1103	90fo Red kangaroo	1.00	.35
		Nos. 3693-3696 (4)	2.75	1.05

Souvenir Sheet

3697	A1103	110fo Platypus	4.00	2.25

Souvenir Sheet

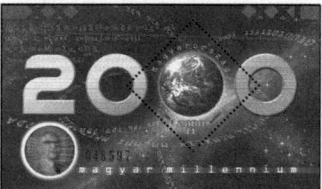

Millennium — A1104

Litho., Hologram in Margin

2000, May 9				
3698	A1104	2000fo multi	25.00	25.00

Soaking in water may affect the hologram.

Europa, 2000
Common Design Type and

A1105

2000, May 9			Litho.	
3699	A1105	34fo multi	2.75	.75
3700	CD17	54fo multi	3.75	1.75

Stamp
Day — A1106

26fo, Queen Gisela in coronation gown. 28fo, King Stephen I in coronation gown.

2000, May 18				
3701	A1106	26fo multi	.75	.45
3702	A1106	28fo multi	1.25	.65

Austria No.
4 and
Bisect
A1107

2000, May 18				
3703	A1107	110fo multi	1.75	1.75

WIPA 2000 Philatelic Exhibition, Vienna.

Grapes and Wine Producing Areas Type of 1990

Grapes and: 29fo, Winery building, Balatonfüred-Csopak region, horiz. 34fo, Storage containers, Aszár-Neszmély region, horiz.

2000, May 25			Perf. 13¼x13	
3704	A902	29fo multi	.60	.35
3705	A902	34fo multi	1.00	.40

Houses of
Worship
A1108

Designs: No. 3706, 30fo, Abbey Church, Ják. No. 3707, 30fo, Reformed Church, Tákos. No. 3708, 30fo, St. Antal's Church, Eger. No. 3709, 30fo, Deák Evangelical Church, Budapest. 120fo, Dohany Synagogue, Budapest.

2000			Litho.	Perf. 12	
3706-3710	A1108	Set of 5		3.00	3.00

Issued: 120fo, 9/19; others 6/30. See Israel No. 1416.

Furniture Type of 1999

Designs: 2fo, Wooden chair, 1838, vert. 3fo, 19th cent. chair, vert. 4fo, Chair by Géza Maróti, 1900, vert. 5fo, Chair by Odon Farago, 1900, vert. 6fo, Chair by Márton Kovács, 1893, vert. 9fo, 18th cent. chair from Dunapataj, vert. 26fo, 1850 chair, vert. 29fo, 19th cent. chair with animal designs, vert. 30fo, Chair by Károly Nagy, 1935, vert. 80fo, 1840-50 chair, vert. 90fo, Chair by Lajos Kozma, 1928, vert.

2000			Perf. 11½x12	
3711-3721	A1091	Set of 11	4.50	2.00

Issued: 2fo, 3fo, 9fo, 26fo, 29fo, 30fo, 6/30; others, 10/9.

Hungarian
Aviation, 90th
Anniv.
A1109

2000, Aug. 18			Perf. 12¾x12¼	
3722	A1109	120fo multi	1.75	1.50

Souvenir Sheets

Hungarian
History
A1110

No. 3723: a, King with orb, knights. b, St. Laszlo with sword. c, St. Elizabeth, Mongol invasion. d, King Sigismund, knight on horseback. e, Janos Hunuyadi and Janos Kapisztran.

No. 3724: a, King Matthias. b, Crucifixion scene, Miklos Zrinyi. c, Trumpeter on horseback, battle scenes. d, Gabor Bethlen (in black hat). e, Peer Parmany, university.

2000, Aug. 18　　　　　　**Perf. 12**
3723　　Sheet of 5　　　　5.00　3.50
　a.-e. A1110 50fo Any single　.70　.35
3724　　Sheet of 5　　　　5.00　3.50
　a.-e. A1110 50fo Any single　.70　.35

A1111

A1112

Christmas
A1113

2000, Oct. 16　　　　　**Perf. 12¼x11½**
3725 A1111 26fo shown　　　.40　.20

　　　　　　　　Perf. 13¼x13
3726 A1112 28fo shown　　　.65　.20
　　　Booklet, 10 #3726　　7.00
3727 A1112 29fo Christmas tree　.65　.20

　　　　　　　　Perf. 12
3728 A1113 34fo shown　　　.70　.20
　　　Booklet, 10 #3728　　8.00
　　　Nos. 3725-3728 (4)　　2.40　.80

European Convention on Human
Rights, 50th Anniv. — A1114

2000, Nov. 3　　　　　**Perf. 12½**
3729 A1114 50fo multicolored　.75　.50

2000
Summer
Olympics,
Sydney
A1115

Sports and total of medals won: 30fo, Shooting, three bronzes. 40fo, Weight lifting, six silvers. 80fo, Men's rings, eight golds. 120fo, Rowing, total count.

2000, Nov. 22　　　　　**Perf. 12**
3730-3732 A1115　Set of 3　1.50　1.50
　　　　　Souvenir Sheet
3733 A1115 120fo multi　　3.00　1.75

European
Language
Year
A1116

2001, Jan. 15　**Litho.**　**Perf. 13x13¼**
3734 A1116 100fo multi　　1.25　1.25

Souvenir Sheet

Greetings — A1117

No. 3735: a, Bugler on pig. b, Man, woman, flower. c, Baby in cradle. d, Clown. e, Mother and child.

2001, Feb. 9　　　　　**Perf. 11½x12**
3735 A1117 36fo Sheet of 5, #a-f 2.50 2.00

World Speed Skating Championships,
Budapest — A1118

2001, Feb. 9　**Litho.**　　**Perf. 13**
3736 A1118 140fo multi　　1.75　1.75

Furniture Type of 1999

Designs: 1fo, Three-legged stool, by János Vincze, 1910, vert. 7fo, 1853 chair, vert. 8fo, 19th cent. chair, vert. 31fo, Like No. 3717, vert. 40fo, Armchair by Ignác Alpár, 1896, vert. 60fo, Armchair by Ferenc Steindl, 1840, vert. 200fo, Settee by Sebestyén Vogel, 1810.

2001　　　　**Perf. 11½x12, 12x11½**
3737-3743 A1091　Set of 7　4.25　1.50
　　Issued: 31fo, 3/5; others, 2/9.

Hungarian Millennium Type of 2000
2001, Mar. 5　　　　**Perf. 12x11½**
3744 A1096 36fo Millennium flag 1.00　.25

National Parks Type of 1998

Designs: 28fo, Balaton. 36fo, Körös-maros. 70fo, Duna-Ipoly.

2001, Mar. 5　　　　　**Perf. 12**
3745-3747 A1073　Set of 3　1.75　1.50

Easter
A1119

2001, Mar. 5　　　　　**Perf. 13**
3748 A1119 28fo multi　　　.50　.20

Locomotives — A1120

Designs: 31fo, Mk. 48. 36fo, 490. 100fo, 394. 150fo, C50.

2001, Apr. 13　　　　**Perf. 13¼x13**
3749-3752 A1120　Set of 4　3.25　3.25

Esztergom Archbishopric, 1000th
Anniv. — A1121

2001, Apr. 18　　　　　**Perf. 12**
3753 A1121 124fo multi　　1.50　1.25

Organizations — A1122

No. 3754: a, 70fo, Emblems of European and Mediterranean Plant Protection Organization and Intl. Plant Protection Convention. b, 80fo, UN High Commissioner for Refugees, 50th anniv.
Illustration reduced.

2001, Apr. 18　　　　**Perf. 13¼x13**
3754 A1122　Horiz. pair, #a-b　1.75　1.50

Europa
A1123

Designs: 36fo, Open chest with water. 90fo, Split globe with water.

2001, May 9　　　　　**Perf. 12**
3755-3756 A1123　Set of 2　3.25　1.75

Animals
A1124

Designs: 28fo, Phoca hispida. 36fo, Canis lupus. 70fo, Testudo hermanni. 90fo, Alcedo atthis ispida.
200fo, Cervus elaphus.

2001, May 9　　　　　**Perf. 12**
3757-3760 A1124　Set of 4　2.50　2.50
　　　　　Souvenir Sheet
3761 A1124 200fo multi　　3.00　2.25

A1125

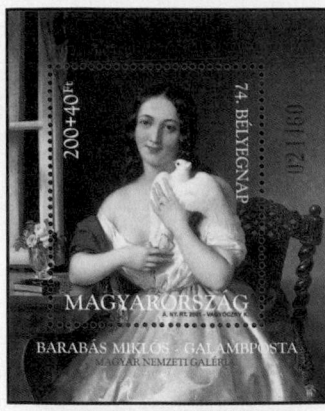

Stamp Day — A1126

Designs: 36fo, #N2. 90fo, #2. 200fo+40fo, Pigeon Post, by Miklos Barabás.

2001, May 25　　　　**Perf. 12¼x11½**
3762-3763 A1125　Set of 2　1.75　1.50
　a. Sheet, 6 each # 3762-3763　10.50　9.00
　　　　　Souvenir Sheet
　　　　　　　Perf. 12½
3764 A1126 200fo +40fo multi　3.50　2.75

European Water
Polo
Championships
A1127

2001, June 14　　　　**Perf. 13½x13**
3765 A1127 150fo multi　　2.00　1.00

Intl. Scouting Conference — A1128

2001, June 21　　　　　**Perf. 12**
3766 A1128 150fo multi　　2.00　1.00

World Youth Track and Field
Championships, Debrecen — A1129

2001, July 12　**Litho.**　**Perf. 13x13¼**
3767 A1129 140fo multi　　1.50　1.00

Artist's Colony,
Gödöllő,
Cent. — A1130

Fészek Arts Club, Cent. — A1131

2001, July 12   *Perf. 12*
3768   A1130   100fo multi   1.00   .50
3769   A1131   150fo blue & blk   1.50   .75

Hungarian History Type of 2000
Souvenir Sheets

No. 3770: a, Prince Francis II Rákóczy, swordsman on horseback, Ilona Zrinyi. b, Rider from Royal Horse Guard, Castle at Munkács, Queen Maria Theresa. c, Count Stephen Széchenyi, Chain Bridge. d, Lajos Kossuth, Artúr Görgey with sword on horseback, battle scene. e, Poet János Arany, Parliament building.
No. 3771: a, World War I soldier on horseback, outline map of Hungary and lost parts of empire, Hungarian people. b, Albert Szent-Gyorgi and chemistry equipment. c, Chain Bridge, World War II soldiers, Bishop Vilmos Apor. d, Pictures of 1956 revolution, Polish-Hungarian Solidarity banner. e, Barbed wire, children representing Hungary's future, Hungarian millennium flag.

2001, Aug. 15
3770   Sheet of 5   5.00   2.50
   a.-e.   A1110   50fo Any single   1.00   .35
3771   Sheet of 5   5.00   2.50
   a.-e.   A1110   50fo Any single   1.00   .35

Souvenir Sheet

Crown of St. Stephen — A1132

Litho. & Embossed
2001, Aug. 15   *Perf. 13x12¾*
3772   A1132   2001fo multi   22.00   22.00

Grapes and Wine Producing Areas Type of 1990

Grapes and: 60fo, Pannonhalma Abbey, Pannonhalma-Sokoróalja region, horiz. 70fo, Spherical observatory and Red Chapel, Balatonboglár, horiz.

2001, Aug. 17   Litho.   *Perf. 13¼x13*
3773-3774   A902   Set of 2   1.50   .75

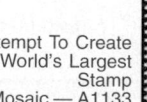

Attempt To Create World's Largest Stamp Mosaic — A1133

2001, Oct. 9   *Perf. 12*
3775   A1133   10fo multi   .30   .20

Maria Valeria Bridge Reconstruction — A1134

2001, Oct. 11   *Perf. 13¼x13*
3776   A1134   36fo multi   .50   .50
     See Slovakia No. 388.

Christmas A1135

2001, Oct. 16   *Perf. 12*
3777   A1135   36fo multi   .50   .20

State Printers, 150th Anniv. — A1136

2001, Nov. 23   Litho.   *Perf. 13¼x13*
3778   A1136   150fo multi   1.75   .75

2002 Winter Olympics, Salt Lake City — A1137

2002, Feb. 8   Litho.   *Perf. 12*
3779   A1137   160fo multi   2.50   .90

Souvenir Sheet

History of the Bicycle — A1138

No. 3780: a, Large-wheeled bicycle and rider, c. 1880. b, Tricycle, early 1900s. c, Károly Iszer (1860-1929), Budapest Sport Club chairman and bicycle. d, Tandem bicycle.

2002, Feb. 20   *Perf. 11½x12¼*
3780   A1138   40fo Sheet of 4,
       #a-d   2.50   1.75

Souvenir Sheet

Hungarian — Ottoman Battles of 1552 — A1139

No. 3781: a, 50fo, Siege of Eger Castle (25x30mm). b, 50fo, Battle of Temesvár (25x30mm). c, 100fo+50fo, Battle of Drégely Castle (40x30mm).

2002, Feb. 20   *Perf. 12*
3781   A1139   Sheet of 3, #a-c   4.00   2.75

Easter — A1140

2002, Mar. 14   *Perf. 11½x12¼*
3782   A1140   30fo multi   .50   .20

Airplanes Designed by Hungarians — A1141

Designs: 180fo, Libelle, by János adorján, 1910. 190fo, Magyar Lloyd, by Tibor Melczer, 1914.

2002, Mar. 14   *Perf. 12½*
3783-3784   A1141   Set of 2   4.00   2.25
    See Nos. 3831-3832, 3968-3969.

Famous Hungarians A1142

Designs: 33fo, Lajos Kossuth (1802-94), leader of Hungarian independence movement. 134fo, János Bolyai (1802-60), mathematician. 150fo, Gyula Illyés (1902-83), writer.

2002, Mar. 14   *Perf. 13x13½*
3785-3787   A1142   Set of 3   4.00   1.75

Souvenir Sheet

Parliament Building, Cent. — A1143

2002, Mar. 14   *Perf. 11½x12¼*
3788   A1143   500fo multi   6.50   5.50

Souvenir Sheet

Opening of National Theater — A1144

2002, Mar. 14
3789   A1144   500fo multi   6.00   5.25

Furniture Type of 1999

Designs: 33fo, Chair, 1809, vert. 134fo, Theater armchair, 1900.

2002, Mar. 28   *Perf. 11½x12, 12x11½*
3790-3791   A1091   Set of 2   2.50   1.00

Environmental Protection — A1145

2002, Mar. 28   *Perf. 12*
3792   A1145   158fo multi   1.60   .80

Souvenir Sheet

Founding of Hungarian National Museum and National Széchényi Library, Bicent. — A1146

No. 3793: a, Mihály Apafi psalter, 1686. b, Illuminated letter from Graduale Pars II. c, Standard of the Civil Guard of Pest, 1848. d, Basin for holy water, 12th cent.

2002, Apr. 29
3793   A1146   150fo Sheet of 4,
       #a-d   7.50   7.50

Halas Lace, Cent. — A1147

Designs: 100fo, Tablecloth with Two Deer, by Mrs. Béla Bazala, 1916. 110fo, Swan Tablecloth, by Erno Stepanek, 1930. 140fo, Jancsi and Iluska, by Antal Tar, 1935.

Litho. & Embossed
2002, May 3   *Perf. 12*
3794-3796   A1147   Set of 3   4.00   1.75

Europa A1148

2002, May 9   Litho.   *Perf. 11*
3797   A1148   62fo multi   1.50   1.50

2002 World Cup Soccer Championships, Japan and Korea — A1149

2002, May 9   *Perf. 13x13½*
3798   A1149   160fo multi + label   2.00   1.60

Fauna A1150

Designs: 30fo, Felis sylvestris. 38fo, Podarcis taurica. 110fo, Garrulus glandarius. 160fo, Rosalia alpina. 500fo, Acipenser ruthenus.

2002, May 9   *Perf. 12*
3799-3802   A1150   Set of 4   4.00   1.75
Souvenir Sheet
3803   A1150   500fo multi   6.00   5.00

Greetings — A1151

No. 3804: a, Etesd meg! b, Megszülettem! c, Sok boldogságot! d, Ontözd meg! e, Ennyire szeretlek!

Serpentine Die Cut 12¼x12¾
2002, May 29
     Self-Adhesive
3804   Booklet pane of 5   2.50
   a.-e.   A1151   38fo Any single   .50   .20

Flower Type of 1999

Designs: 30fo, Red poppy. 38fo, Stalkless gentian.

2002, June 24		Perf. 12¼x11½
3805-3806 A1087	Set of 2	1.00 .35

Art — A1152

Designs: 62fo, Kodobálók, by Károly Ferenczy. 188fo, Táncosno, sculpture by Ferenc Megyessy, vert.

	Perf. 12¾x12¼, 12¼x12¾
2002, June 24	
3807-3808 A1152 Set of 2	3.00 1.25

UNESCO World Heritage Sites — A1153

Designs: 100fo, Budapest. 150fo, Hollóko. 180fo, Caves of Aggtelek Karst, horiz.

2002, June 24		Perf. 12
3809-3811 A1153	Set of 3	4.50 2.25

See Nos. 3881-3882, 4073.

Kalocsa Archbishopric, 1000th Anniv. — A1154

2002, Aug. 1 Litho.	Perf. 13¼x12½
3812 A1154 150fo multi	1.50 .75

Medical Congresses A1155

No. 3813: a, 100fo, 38th European Diabetes Association Congress. b, 150fo, 16th European Arm and Shoulder Surgeons Congress.

2002, Aug. 23	Perf. 13x13¼
3813 A1155 Vert. pair, #a-b	3.00 2.50

Printed in sheets of two pairs. Value $5.50.

Ceramics by Margit Kovács — A1156

No. 3814: a, 33fo, Madonna and Child, 1938. b, 38fo, Mother and Children, 1953. 400fo+200fo, St. George, 1936.

2002, Oct. 3		Perf. 13¼x13
3814 A1156	Pair, #a-b	1.00 .35

Souvenir Sheet
Perf. 12¼x11½

3815 A1156 400fo +200fo multi	6.00 6.00

Stamp Day. No. 3814 printed in sheets of two pairs. Value $1.75. No. 3815 contains one 25x36mm stamp.

Christmas A1157

Designs: 30fo, Adoration of the Magi. 38fo, Bethlehem.

Litho. with Foil Application

2002, Oct. 30		Perf. 12
3816-3817 A1157	Set of 2	1.25 .35

See No. 4006.

World Gymnastics Championships, Debrecen — A1158

2002, Nov. 20 Litho.	Perf. 13x13¼
3818 A1158 160fo multi	1.60 .80

Hungarian and Turkish Buildings — A1159

Designs: 40fo, Rakoczi House, Tekirdag, Turkey. 110fo, Gazi Kassim Pasha Mosque, Pécs, Hungary.

2002, Dec. 2 Litho.		Perf. 13½x13¼
3819-3820 A1159	Set of 2	1.50 .75

See Turkey No. 2844.

Furniture Type of 1999

Designs: 32fo, Wooden chair with carved back, 19th cent., vert. 35fo, Armchair, 18th cent., vert. 65fo, Armchair with carved back, 1920, vert.

2003, Jan. 30		Perf. 11½x12¼
3821-3823 A1091	Set of 3	1.75 .70

Scientists A1160

Designs: 32fo, John von Neumann (1903-57), mathematician, and computer pioneer. 40fo, Rezsö Soó (1903-80), botanist. 60fo, Károly Zipernowsky (1853-1942), electrical engineer.

2003, Feb. 12	Perf. 13x13¼
3824 A1160 32fo multicolored	.35 .25
3825 A1160 40fo multicolored	6.00 6.00
3826 A1160 60fo multicolored	.60 .60
Nos. 3824-3826 (3)	6.95 6.85

Souvenir Sheet

Herend Porcelain — A1161

No. 3827: a, Platter with floral design, Frankenthal coffee set. b, Vase with floral design, coffee set. c, Vase with ram's head handles. d, Shell-shaped bowl, pitcher.

2003, Feb. 12		Perf. 12
3827 A1161 150fo Sheet of 4, #a-d		6.00 6.00

Defeat of Royal Hungarian Army, 60th Anniv. — A1162

2003, Feb. 15	Perf. 12¼x12½
3828 A1162 40fo multi	.60 .25

Easter — A1163

2003, Mar. 14	
3829 A1163 32fo multi	.50 .20

Nemzeti Sport, Cent. — A1164

Illustration reduced.

2003, Mar. 14	Perf. 13x13¼
3830 A1164 150fo multi + label	2.00 .75

Airplanes Type of 2002

Designs: 142fo, Gerle 13, by Antal Bánhidi, 1933. 160fo, L-2 Róma, by Árpád Lampich, 1925.

2003, Mar. 20		Perf. 12½
3831-3832 A1141	Set of 2	3.50 1.50

Hotels — A1165

Designs: 110fo, Rogner Hotel, Héviz. 120fo, Hélia Hotel, Budapest.

2003, Mar. 20		
3833-3834 A1165	Set of 2	2.50 1.10

See Nos. 3883-3884.

Souvenir Sheet

Extreme Sports — A1166

No. 3835: a, 100fo, BMX cycling. b, 100fo, Snowboarding. c, 100fo, Parachuting. d, 100fo+50fo, Kayaking.

2003, Mar. 20		Perf. 12
3835 A1166	Sheet of 4, #a-d	4.50 4.50

Greetings A1167

No. 3836: a, Church. b, Two flowers. c, One flower. d, Easter eggs. e, Candles in window, Christmas tree.

Serpentine Die Cut 12¾

2003, Mar. 20
Self-Adhesive

3836	Booklet pane of 5	2.00
a.-e. A1167 40fo Any single		.40 .20

Souvenir Sheet

Space Shuttle Columbia — A1168

2003, Apr. 9	Perf. 12
3837 A1168 500fo multi	5.00 2.50

World Ice Hockey Championships, Budapest — A1169

Illustration reduced.

2003, Apr. 10	Perf. 13x13¼
3838 A1169 110fo multi + label	1.10 .55

Budapest Sports Arena — A1170

Illustration reduced.

2003, Apr. 10	
3839 A1170 120fo multi + label	1.25 .60

Souvenir Sheet

Ratification of European Union Accession Treaty — A1171

2003, Apr. 14	Perf. 12
3840 A1171 500fo multi	7.50 7.50

Policeman on Motorcycle and Emergency Phone Number A1172

2003, Apr. 24
3841 A1172 65fo multi .65 .35

Stamp Day — A1173

Designs: 35fo, Statue of woman with legs crossed. 40fo, Statue of woman with hand on chin.
400fo+100fo, Fountain.

2003, May 6 *Perf. 13¼x13*
3842-3843 A1173 Set of 2 .75 .40
Souvenir Sheet
Perf. 12¾x13
3844 A1173 400fo +100fo multi 7.00 5.00
No. 3844 contains one 31x40mm stamp.

Souvenir Sheet

Uprising Against Hapsburgs of Ferenc Rákóczi II, 400th Anniv. — A1174

No. 3845: a, Swords and scabbards. b, Coins. c, Bannor, pipes and drums. d, Guns.

2003, May 6 *Perf. 12*
3845 A1174 120fo Sheet of 4, #a-d 6.50 5.50

Europa — A1175

2003, May 9
3846 A1175 65fo multi 1.75 1.75

Fauna A1176

Designs: 35fo, Mustela eversmanni. 40fo, Calandrella brachydactyla. 100fo, Hyla arborea. 110fo, Misgurnus fossilis.
500fo, Eresus cinnabarinus.

2003, May 9
3847-3850 A1176 Set of 4 4.00 1.75
Souvenir Sheet
3851 A1176 500fo multi 6.00 5.00

Grapes and Wine Producing Areas Type of 1990

Grapes and: 60fo, Bükkalja region, horiz. 130fo, Balaton-felvidéki region, horiz.

2003, June 6 *Perf. 13¼x12½*
3852-3853 A902 Set of 2 2.50 1.00

Souvenir Sheet

Robe of St. László — A1177

2003, June 13 *Perf. 12*
3854 A1177 300fo multi 4.25 3.00

Art A1178

Designs: 32fo, Sculpture by Imre Varga, vert. 60fo, Mostar Bridge, by Tivadar Csontváry Kosztka.

Perf. 12½x13¼, 13¼x12½
2003, July 18
3855-3856 A1178 Set of 2 1.50 .50

Souvenir Sheet

Sports History — A1179

No. 3857: a, Ferenc Puskás Stadium Budapest, 50th anniv. b, Hungary vs. England soccer match, 50th anniv.

2003, July 18 *Perf. 11½x12¼*
3857 A1179 250fo Sheet of 2, #a-b 5.75 5.00

European Union Membership A1180

2003 **Litho.** *Perf. 12x11½*
3858 A1180 115fo shown 1.40 .60
3859 A1180 130fo Clock at 11:35 1.60 .70
Issued: 115fo, 9/16; 130fo, 10/18.
See Nos. 3877-3878.

Nutrition A1181

2003, Sept. 16 *Perf. 12*
3860 A1181 120fo multi 1.50 .60

European Automobile-free Day — A1182

2003, Sept. 16
3861 A1182 150fo multi 1.50 .75

Reszo Soó (1903-80), Botanist A1183

2003, Sept. 23
3862 A1183 44fo multi .55 .25

Book Printing — A1184

Designs: No. 3863, 44fo, Hungarian Illuminated Chronicle, 1358. No. 3864, 44fo, Ritual of Zhou, China.

2003, Sept. 30
3863-3864 A1184 Set of 2 1.40 .45
See People's Republic of China Nos. 3309-3310.

Souvenir Sheet

Ferenc Deák (1803-76), Statesman — A1185

2003, Oct. 18
3865 A1185 500fo multi 6.00 5.00

Christmas — A1186

Designs: 35fo, Reindeer. 44fo, Angels, Christmas tree, houses.

2003, Oct. 31 *Perf. 11½x12*
3866-3867 A1186 Set of 2 1.00 .40

Souvenir Sheet

World Science Forum, Budapest — A1187

2003, Nov. 7 **Litho.** *Perf. 12*
3868 A1187 500fo multi 6.00 5.00

Locomotives Type of 2001
Designs: 120fo, Muki Diesel locomotive, Kemence Forest Railway. 150fo, Rezét steam locomotive, Gemenc Forest Railway.

2004, Feb. 4 *Perf. 13¼x13*
3869-3870 A1120 Set of 2 3.00 3.00

Famous Men — A1188

Designs: 40fo, Bálint Balassi (1554-94), poet. 44fo, József Bajza (1804-58), poet. 80fo, János András Segner (1704-77), physicist.

2004, Feb. 4 *Perf. 13*
3871-3873 A1188 Set of 3 2.25 .85

Souvenir Sheet

Dogs — A1189

No. 3874: a, 100fo, Puli. b, 100fo, Hungarian greyhound. c, 100fo, Mudi. d, 100fo+50fo, Vizsla.

2004, Feb. 19 *Perf. 12*
3874 A1189 Sheet of 4, #a-d 5.50 4.50
Surtax on No. 3874d for youth philately.

Souvenir Sheet

Festivals — A1190

No. 3875: a, Busójárás Carnival. b, Virágkarnevál (Flower Carnival). c, Borfesztivál (Wine Festival). d, Fesztiválok Karneválok (Festivals and Carnivals).

2004, Feb. 19
3875 A1190 60fo Sheet of 4, #a-d 3.25 2.40

European Ministerial Conference on the Information Society — A1191

No. 3876 — Color of panel and "e:" a, Red violet. b, Dark blue. c, Green. d, Orange. Illustration reduced.

2004, Feb. 26 *Perf. 13¼x13*
3876 A1191 40fo Block of 4, #a-d 3.00 2.25

European Union Membership (Clock) Type of 2003

2004 *Perf. 12x11½*
3877 A1180 100fo Clock at 11:48 1.25 .50
3878 A1180 190fo Clock at 11:57 2.25 .90
Issued: 100fo, 3/5; 190fo, 4/19.

Tenth World Indoor Track and Field Championships, Budapest A1192

2004, Mar. 5   *Perf. 13x13¼*
3879 A1192 120fo multi   1.50 .60

Easter — A1193

2004, Mar. 18   **Litho.**
3880 A1193 48fo multi   .50 .25

World Heritage Sites Type of 2002

Designs: 150fo, Abbey of Pannonhalma. 170fo, Hortobágy National Park, horiz.

2004, Mar. 18   *Perf. 12*
3881-3882 A1153 Set of 2   3.75 1.60

Hotels Type of 2003

Designs: 120fo, Bük Thermal and Sports Hotel, Bükfürdő. 150fo, Aqua-Sol Hotel, Hajdúszoboszló.

2004, Mar. 18
3883-3884 A1165 Set of 2   3.25 1.25

Holocaust, 60th Anniv. A1194

2004, Apr. 16   *Perf. 13x13¼*
3885 A1194 160fo multi   1.90 .75

Souvenir Sheet

Zsolnay Porcelain, 150th Anniv. — A1195

No. 3886: a, Vase with handles. b, Small vase, vessel with horse and rider top. c, Vase. d, Mocha set.

2004, Apr. 20   **Litho.**   *Perf. 12*
3886 A1195 160fo Sheet of 4,
    #a-d   7.00 7.00

Police Boat and Emergency Phone Number A1196

2004, Apr. 23   **Litho.**   *Perf. 13x13¼*
3887 A1196 48fo multi   .60 .35

Souvenir Sheet

Admission to European Union — A1197

2004, Apr. 30   *Perf. 12*
3888 A1197 500fo multi   5.25 5.25

Expansion of the European Union — A1198

No. 3889: a, 120fo, Stars and flowers. b, 150fo, Stars, map of Europe, flags of nations entering European Union.
Illustration reduced.

2004, May 1   **Litho.**
3889 A1198 Horiz. pair, #a-b   3.25 2.75

European Parliament Elections A1199

2004, May 7   *Perf. 12½x13½*
3890 A1199 150fo multi   1.75 .70

Europa A1200

2004, May 7   *Perf. 12*
3891 A1200 160fo multi   2.25 1.00

Fauna A1201

Designs: 48fo, Nannospalax leucodon. 65fo, Panurus biarmicus. 90fo, Ablepharus kitaibelii fitzingeri. 120fo, Huso huso. 500fo, Anthaxia hungarica.

2004, May 7
3892-3895 A1201 Set of 4   4.00 1.50

Souvenir Sheet
3896 A1201 500fo multi   5.25 5.25

Stamp Day — A1202

Designs: 48fo, Walls and Doors, sculpture by Erzsébet Schaár. 65fo, Translucent Red Circle, painting by Tihamér Gyarmathy. 400fo+200fo, The Wasp King, painting by Béla Kondor.

2004, May 7   **Litho.**   *Perf. 12¼x12¾*
3897-3898 A1202 Set of 2   2.10 .55
Souvenir Sheet
    Perf. 12¾x12¼
3899 A1202 400fo +200fo multi   7.25 5.75
No. 3899 contains one 41x31mm stamp.

FIFA (Fédération Internationale de Football Association), Cent. — A1203

2004, May 21   **Litho.**   *Perf. 13¼x13*
3900 A1203 100fo multi   1.25 .45

Central European Catholics' Day — A1204

No. 3901: a, Basilica, Mariazell, Austria. b, Statue of Madonna, Mariazell. c, Statue of Madonna and Child, Mariazell. d, Statue of Madonna, Celldömölk, Hungary. e, Framed painting of Madonna and Child, Mariazell. f, Statue of Mary of Kiscell, Obuda Parish, Hungary.

2004, May 21   **Litho.**   *Perf. 11½x12*
3901 A1204 100fo Sheet of 6,
    #a-f   6.50 5.75

Information Technology A1205

2004, June 28   *Perf. 13x13¼*
3902 A1205 120fo multi   1.25 .60

Theodor Herzl (1860-1904), Zionist Leader A1206

2004, July 6   **Litho.**   *Perf. 12*
3903 A1206 150fo multi   2.25 .75
See Austria No. 1960, Israel No. 1566.

2004 Summer Olympics, Athens — A1207

Designs: 90fo, Canoeing. 130fo, Volleyball. 150fo, Running.

2004, July 13
3904-3906 A1207 Set of 3   3.75 1.75

A1208

A1209

A1210

A1211

A1212

A1213

A1214

Folkloriada Festival — A1215

Illustrations reduced.

2004, Aug. 12
3907   Block of 10 + 10 labels   10.00 10.00
  a. A1208 65fo dark blue   .75 .40
  b. A1208 65fo orange   .75 .40
  c. A1209 65fo orange brown   .75 .40
  d. A1209 65fo purple   .75 .40
  e. A1210 65fo carmine   .75 .40
  f. A1211 65fo orange brown   .75 .40
  g. A1212 65fo orange brown   .75 .40
  h. A1213 65fo Prussian blue   .75 .40
  i. A1214 65fo green   .75 .40
  j. A1215 65fo orange brown   .75 .40
  k. Sheet, #3907   32.00 32.00

No. 3907k has labels that could be personalized. The personalized sheet sold for 1600fo.

Chess History — A1216

No. 3908 — Beginning of text, square color, piece (if any): a, A sakkjáték, tan, black rook. b, A magyaroknak, brown. c, A magyar történelem, tan, black bishop. d, A magyar sakkirodalom, brown, black king. e, A XVIII. században, tan, black queen. f, Az elso, brown. g, Az 1839-ben, tan, black knight. h, A XIX. század, brown, black rook. i, A magyar sakkfeladványszerok, brown, black pawn. j, Három, a XIX. század, tan, black pawn. k, Maróczy Géza, brown, black pawn. l, Két kiváló, tan, black pawn. m, A levelezási, brown, black bishop. n, A sakkélet, tan, black pawn. o, A férfi országos, brown, black pawn. p, A II. világháború tan után sokáig, black pawn. q, A nol sakkozás, tan. r, 1958-ban már, brown. s, A sakkozók, tan, black knight. t, 1951-ben indult, brown. u, A XX. századnak, tan. v, A II. világháború utá feladvány, brown. w, A XX. században, tan. x, A XX. század elején, brown. y, A világ sakkéletét, brown. z, A két világháború között, tan. aa, A háború után, brown. ab, A férfi sakkolimpián, tan. ac, A nemzetek közti, brown, black pawn. ad, 1957-ben a hollandiai, tan. ae, A noi sakkolimpiákon, brown. af, A XIX. és XX. században, tan. ag, Sakkirodalom nélkül, tan. ah, A XX. század magyar, brown. ai, a széles sakkozó, tan, white bishop. aj, A Magyar Sakkszövetség, brown. ak, Barcza Gedeon, tan, white pawn. al, Szábo László, brown. am, Portisch Lajos, tan. an, Adorján András, brown. ao, Sax Gyula, brown. ap, Ribli Zoltán, tan. aq, Lékó Péter, brown. ar, Almási Zoltán, tan. as, Bilek, István, brown. at, A két világháború közti, tan, white knight. au, Az olimpiákon többször, brown. av, Sok kiváló magyar, tan. aw, Polgár Zsuzsa, tan, white pawn. ax, Polgár Judit, brown, white pawn. ay, Polgár Zsófia, tan, white pawn. az, Lángos Józsa, brown, white pawn. ba, Veroci Zsuzsa, tan. bb, Ivánka Mária, brown, white pawn. bc, Mádl Ildikó, tan, white pawn. bd, Országos bajnoki, brown, white pawn. be, Sakkozásunk a XXI. századot, brown, white rook. bf, A sakkozással, tan, white knight. bg, A magyar sakkozás, brown, white bishop. bh, Minden összefoglaló,tan, white king. bi, A jelen munkában, brown, white queen. bj, Elek Ferenc, tan. bk, Katkó (Regos) Imre, brown. bl, Gróf Pongrácz Arnold, tan, white rook.

2004, Sept. 24
3908   Sheet of 64   42.50   42.50
a.-bl.   A1216 50fo Any single   .60   .40

Souvenir Sheet

Admission to European Union — A1217

No. 3909 — Large stars and time of small clock: a, 11:20. b, 11:35. c, 11:48. d, 11:57.

2004, Oct. 8   *Perf. 12x11½*
3909   A1217 100fo Sheet of 4,   5.50   4.00
     #a-d

Istvan Bocskay (1557-1606), Leader of 1604-06 Rebellion — A1218

2004, Nov. 11   Litho.   *Perf. 11½x12*
3910   A1218 120fo multi   1.25   .60

Intl. Organization of Supreme Audit Institutions, 18th Congress, Budapest
A1219

2004, Oct. 11   *Perf. 11¼*
3911   A1219 150fo multi   1.50   .75

Christmas Type of 2002 and

A1220

A1221

A1222

A1223

A1224

A1225

A1226

A1227

A1228

A1229

A1230

A1231

A1232

A1233

A1234

Christmas — A1235

No. 3915: Various Christmas cookies. Illustration reduced.

Litho. With Foil Application
2004   *Perf. 12*
3912   A1157 48fo Bethlehem   .50   .25

Litho.
Perf. 11¼
3913   Sheet of 20 + 20 labels   30.00   16.50
a.   A1220 48fo multi + label   1.25   .40
b.   A1221 48fo multi + label   1.25   .40
c.   A1222 48fo multi + label   1.25   .40
d.   A1223 48fo multi + label   1.25   .40
e.   A1224 48fo multi + label   1.25   .40
f.   A1225 48fo multi + label   1.25   .40

3914   Sheet of 20 + 20 labels   30.00   16.50
a.   A1226 48fo multi + label   1.25   .40
b.   A1227 48fo multi + label   1.25   .40
c.   A1228 48fo multi + label   1.25   .40
d.   A1229 48fo multi + label   1.25   .40
e.   A1230 48fo multi + label   1.25   .40
f.   A1231 48fo multi + label   1.25   .40
g.   A1232 48fo multi + label   1.25   .40
h.   A1233 48fo multi + label   1.25   .40
i.   A1234 48fo multi + label   1.25   .40
3915   A1235 48fo Sheet of 20,   30.00   16.50
     #a-t, + 20 labels

Issued: No. 3912, 10/28; Nos. 3913-3915, 11/3.

No. 3913 contains 5 #3913b, 3 #3913c, 4 each #3913a, 3913e, 2 each #3913d, 3913f. Background colors on some stamps differ slightly.

No. 3914 contains #3914d, 3914e, 4 each #3914a, 3914b, 2 each #3914c, 3914f, 3914g, 3914h, 3914i.

Nos. 3913-3915 could be personalized, with each sheet selling for 2000fo.

Sándor Korösi Csoma (1784-1842), Philologist and Sir Marc Aurel Stein (1862-1943), Archaeologist
A1236

2004, Nov. 3   Litho.   *Perf. 13x13¼*
3916   A1236 80fo multi   1.25   .40

Natura 2000 — A1237

2004, Dec. 3   *Perf. 11½x12*
3917   A1237 100fo multi   1.10   .55

Zodiac — A1238

No. 3918: a, Capricorn (goat). b, Aquarius (water bearer). c, Pisces (fish). d, Aries (ram). e, Taurus (bull). f, Gemini (twins). g, Cancer (crab). h, Leo (lion). i, Virgo (virgin). j, Libra (scales). k, Scorpio (scorpion). l, Sagittarius (archer).

2005, Jan. 3   Litho.   *Perf. 11¼*
3918   A1238 50fo Sheet of 12,   10.00   7.50
     #a-l
m.   Sheet of 20 #3918a + 20 labels   29.00   —
n.   Sheet of 20 #3918b + 20 labels   29.00   —
o.   Sheet of 20 #3918c + 20 labels   29.00   —
p.   Sheet of 20 #3918d + 20 labels   29.00   —
q.   Sheet of 20 #3918e + 20 labels   29.00   —
r.   Sheet of 20 #3918f + 20 labels   29.00   —
s.   Sheet of 20 #3918g + 20 labels   29.00   —
t.   Sheet of 20 #3918h + 20 labels   29.00   —
u.   Sheet of 20 #3918i + 20 labels   29.00   —
v.   Sheet of 20 #3918j + 20 labels   29.00   —
w.   Sheet of 20 #3918k + 20 labels   29.00   —
x.   Sheet of 20 #3918l + 20 labels   29.00   —

Nos. 3918m-3918x each sold for 2100fo and had labels that could be personalized.

Rotary International, Cent. — A1239

2005, Feb. 4   *Perf. 13¼x13*
3919 A1239 130fo multi   1.60 .70

Souvenir Sheet

Cats — A1240

No. 3920: a, 100fo, Siamese, silhouette of cat sitting. b, 100fo, Maine Coon cat, silhouette of cat with arched back and thin tail. c, 100fo, Persian, silhouette of cat with large tail. d, 100fo+50fo, Domestic cat, silhouette of cat walking.

2005, Feb. 4   *Perf. 12x11½*
3920 A1240   Sheet of 4, #a-d   4.75 4.75

Easter — A1241

2005, Feb. 21   *Perf. 12*
3921 A1241 50fo multi   .55 .25

Intl. Weight Lifting Federation, Cent. A1242

2005, Mar. 3   *Perf. 12¼x12½*
3922 A1242 170fo multi   1.90 .95

Sándor Iharos (1930-96), Runner A1243

2005, Mar. 10   *Perf. 13x13¼*
3923 A1243 90fo multi   1.00 .50

Souvenir Sheet

Opening of Palace of Arts, Budapest — A1244

2005, Mar. 10   *Perf. 12*
3924 A1244 500fo multi   5.50 5.50

World Theater Day — A1245

2005, Mar. 21   *Perf. 11¼*
3925 A1245 50fo multi   .80 .25

Compass and Map of Hungary — A1246

No. 3926: a, Compass at right, map of western Hungary. b, Compass at left, map of eastern Hungary.

2005, Apr. 1   Litho.   *Perf. 11¼*
3926 A1246 50fo Pair, #a-b, + 2 labels   2.00 1.10
   c.   Sheet of 20, 10 each #3926a-3926b, + 20 labels   40.00

No. 3926c sold for 2100fo. Labels on sheets of 3926 and 3926c could be personalized. Compare with No. 4054.

Writers A1247

Designs: 90fo, Jeno Rejto (1905-43), novelist, playwright. 140fo, Attila József (1905-37), poet.

2005, Apr. 11   Litho.   *Perf. 13x13¼*
3927-3928 A1247   Set of 2   2.75 1.25

Police Helicopter and Emergency Phone Number A1248

2005, Apr. 22   *Perf. 13x13¼*
3929 A1248 85fo multi   .90 .45

End of World War II, 60th Anniv. A1249

2005, May 6   *Perf. 13*
3930 A1249 150fo multi   1.60 .80

Farm Animals A1250

Designs: 50fo, Hungarian gray bull. 70fo, Hungarian spotted cow. 100fo, Hortobágy Racka sheep. 110fo, Cigája sheep. 500fo, Mangalica pigs.

2005, May 9   *Perf. 13x13¼*
3931-3934 A1250   Set of 4   3.75 1.60
Souvenir Sheet
3935 A1250 500fo multi   6.50 5.00

No. 3935 contains one 41x32mm stamp.

Souvenir Sheet

Europa — A1251

No. 3936 — Plate of Chicken Paprika and Dumplings with: a, Flowers at UR. b, Flowers at UL.

2005, May 9   *Perf. 12*
3936 A1251 160fo Sheet, 2 each
   #a-b   7.75 6.25

The top and bottom rows of stamps in the sheet are tete-beche.

Souvenir Sheet

Pope John Paul II (1920-2005) — A1252

2005, May 18
3937 A1252 500fo multi   6.00 5.00

Grapes and Wine Producing Areas Type of 1990

Designs: 120fo, Pintes grapes, Zala region, horiz. 140fo, Kunleány grapes, Csongrád region, horiz.

2005, May 25   *Perf. 13¼x12½*
3938-3939 A902   Set of 2   3.25 1.40

Church, Ják, and Ornament From Cluny Abbey, France A1253

2005, May 25   *Perf. 13x13¼*
3940 A1253 110fo multi   1.60 .55

Souvenir Sheet

Consecration of St. Stephen's Basilica, Budapest, Cent. — A1254

2005, May 25   *Perf. 12¾x13*
3941 A1254 500fo multi   6.00 5.00

Miniature Sheet

Budapest Tourist Attractions — A1255

No. 3942: a, Hallway and exhibits, Postal Museum. b, #386a and die of vignette, Stamp Museum, horiz. c, Agriculture Museum, Vajdahunyad Castle. d, Ethnographic Museum, horiz. e, Sándor Palace, horiz.

Perf. 11½x12, 12x11½ (horiz. stamps)
2005, May 25
3942 A1255 100fo Sheet of 5, #a-e, + 5 labels   6.50 5.00

First Hungarian in Space, 25th Anniv. — A1256

2005, May 26   *Perf. 12½*
3943 A1256 130fo multi   1.25 .65

A1257

Formula I Auto Racing in Hungary, 20th Anniv. (in 2006) A1258

Designs: Nos. 3944, 3947, Hungaroring Race Track. No. 3945, Car No. 12. No. 3946, Driver in red car.

2005   Litho.   *Perf. 11¼*
3944 A1257 50fo multi + label   .50 .25
      Perf. 13x13¼
3945 A1258 50fo multi   .75 .25
3946 A1258 90fo multi   1.25 .45
Souvenir Sheet   *Perf. 13x12¾*
3947 A1258 500fo +200fo multi   7.75 7.00

78th Stamp Day (Nos. 3945-3947). Issued: Nos. 3944, 3947, 7/18; Nos. 3945-3946, 6/17. Labels on No. 3944 could be personalized.

Souvenir Sheet

Enameled Pictures on St. Stephen's
Crown — A1259

No. 3948: a, 100fo, St. Thomas (20x26mm)
. b, 100fo, King Géza I (in square panel with
black lettering) (20x26mm). c, 100fo, Byzantine Emperor Michael Ducas (in arched panel
with red lettering) (20x26mm). d, 100fo,
Byzantine Emperor Constantine (in square
panel with red lettering) (20x26mm). e, 100fo,
Jesus Christ (in arched panel with no lettering)
(20x26mm). f, 500fo, St. Stephen's Crown
(30x36mm).

2005, Aug. 19   Litho.   Perf. 12x11½
3948 A1259 Sheet of 6, #a-f 11.50 10.50

First
Hungarian
Mail Vehicle,
Cent.
A1260

2005, Sept. 15   Perf. 11¼x11
3949 A1260 50fo multi   .50 .25

Trash
Recycling
A1261

2005, Sept. 15   Perf. 13x13¼
3950 A1261 140fo multi   1.75 .70

World Wrestling Championships,
Budapest — A1262

2005, Sept. 26   Perf. 13
3951 A1262 150fo multi   1.75 .75

Ferenc Farkas (1905-2000),
Composer — A1263

2005, Sept. 30   Perf. 13x13¼
3952 A1263 100fo multi   1.75 .50

World Science
Forum,
Budapest
A1264

2005, Sept. 30
3953 A1264 120fo multi   1.75 .60
         See No. 4052.

Hungarian
University
of Craft
and
Design,
125th
Anniv.
A1265

2005, Oct. 19   Perf. 12
3954 A1265 90fo multi   1.25 .45

The Three
Magi — A1266

Christmas
A1267

No. 3956: a, Candle. b, Apple. c, Heart-
shaped ornament. d, Teddy bear.

Litho. with Foil Application
2005, Oct. 19   Perf. 12¾x12¼
3955 A1266 50fo blue   .75 .25
Self-Adhesive
Litho.
Serpentine Die Cut 12¾
3956   Booklet pane of 4   3.25
a.-d. A1267 50fo Any single   .80 .25

House of
the Future
A1268

2005, Dec. 16   Litho.   Perf. 12
3957 A1268 100fo multi   1.25 .45

Hungarian News Agency, 125th
Anniv. — A1269

2006, Jan. 1   Litho.   Perf. 12x11½
3958 A1269 90fo multi   1.10 .45

2006 Winter
Olympics,
Turin
A1270

2006, Feb. 10   Perf. 13¼
3959 A1270 200fo multi   3.25 1.00

Furniture Type of 1999

Designs: 52fo, Like #3790, vert. 75fo, Chair
with heart carved in back, 1893, vert. 212fo,
Like #3791. 300fo, Settee, 18th cent. 500fo,
Rococo settee, c. 1880. 1000fo, Vassily chair,
by Marcel Breuer, 1925.

2006   Perf. 11½x12¼
3960 A1091 52fo bl & dk bl   .50 .25
3961 A1091 75fo org brn &
                brn   .70 .35
Perf. 12¼x11½
3962 A1091 212fo grn & dk
                grn   2.00 1.00
Perf. 12¾x12¼
3963 A1091 300fo red & dk
                red   3.00 1.50
3964 A1091 500fo bl & dk bl   5.00 2.50
3965 A1091 1000fo ol & dk ol 10.00 5.00
        Nos. 3960-3965 (6)   21.20 10.60

Issued: 52fo, 75fo, 212fo, 3/16; others, 5/19.

World Heritage
Sites — A1271

Designs: 52fo, Early Christian Necropolis,
Pecs. 90fo, Ferto-Neuseidler Lake Cultural
Landscape, horiz.

2006, Mar. 16   Perf. 12
3966-3967 A1271 Set of 2   1.75 .75

Airplanes Type of 2002

Designs: 120fo, Boeing 767-200ER. 140fo,
Lockheed Sirius 8A.

2006, Mar. 16
3968-3969 A1141 Set of 2   3.25 1.40

Easter — A1272

2006, Mar. 22
3970 A1272 52fo multi   .50 .25

Union of
European
Football
Associations
Congress,
Budapest
A1273

2006, Mar. 22   Perf. 13x13¼
3971 A1273 170fo multi   2.25 .85

Sándor Légrády (1906-87), Stamp
Designer, and Vignette of Unissued
Stamp — A1274

2006, Mar. 30   Litho.   Perf. 12x11½
3972 A1274 75fo multi   1.00 .35

Ilona Sasváriné-Paulik (1954-99),
Paralymic Athlete — A1275

2006, Mar. 30   Perf. 13x13¼
3973 A1275 185fo multi   2.00 .85

László Detre (1906-74),
Astronomer — A1276

2006, Mar. 30   Perf. 12
3974 A1276 212fo multi   2.75 1.00

Wi-fi
Technology
A1277

2006, Mar. 30   Perf. 13x13¼
3975 A1277 240fo multi   2.50 1.10

Orchid — A1278

Rose — A1279

Lily — A1280

Tulip — A1281

Gerbera Daisy — A1282

Rose — A1283

Rose — A1284

Rose — A1285

Butterfly and Wedding Rings — A1286

Butterfly and Rose — A1287

Daisy and Rubber Duck — A1288

Daisy and Blue Booties — A1289

Daisy and Pink Booties — A1290

Daisy and Rattle — A1291

Rose — A1292

Clematis — A1293

2006	Litho.	Perf. 11¼	
3976	Vert. strip of 5 + 5 labels	12.50	12.50
a.	A1278 52fo multi + label	2.00	.35
b.	A1279 52fo multi + label	2.00	.35
c.	A1280 52fo multi + label	2.00	.35
d.	A1281 52fo multi + label	2.00	.35
e.	A1282 52fo multi + label	2.00	.35
	Sheet, 4 each #3976a-3976e	45.00	45.00
3977	Strip of 3 + 3 labels	2.50	.50
a.	A1283 52fo multi + label	.75	.50
b.	A1284 52fo multi + label	.75	.50
c.	A1285 52fo multi + label	.75	.50
	Sheet, 7 each #3977a-3977b, 6 #3977c	20.00	20.00
3978	Pair + 2 labels	2.00	2.00
a.	A1286 52fo multi + label	1.00	.50
b.	A1287 52fo multi + label	1.00	.50
	Sheet, 10 each #3978a-3978b	20.00	20.00
3979	Block or strip of 4 + 4 labels	12.00	12.00
a.	A1288 52fo multi + label	2.00	.50
b.	A1289 52fo multi + label	2.00	.50
c.	A1290 52fo multi + label	2.00	.50
d.	A1291 52fo multi + label	2.00	.50
	Sheet, 3 each #3979b-39779c, 7 each #3977a, 3977d	55.00	
3980	Pair + 2 labels	5.00	5.00
a.	A1292 90fo multi + label	2.00	.50
b.	A1293 90fo multi + label	2.00	.50
	Sheet, 10 each #3980a-3980b	60.00	—
	Nos. 3976-3980 (5)	34.00	32.00

Issued: Nos. 3976, 3977, 5/4, others, 5/19. Background colors of stamps in full sheets varies. Labels could be personalized for an additional fee.
Compare with No. 4092.

Battle of Belgrade, 550th Anniv. — A1294

2006, May 9   **Perf. 13½x12½**
3981 A1294 120fo multi   1.75   .65

2006 World Cup Soccer Championships, Germany — A1295

2006, May 9   **Perf. 13x13¼**
3982 A1295 170fo multi   3.50   .90

Europa — A1296

2006, May 9   **Perf. 12**
3983 A1296 190fo multi   2.25 1.10
Printed in sheets of 4, with each stamp rotated 90 degrees to create circle of faces. Value $9.50.

Horses A1297

Breeds: 75fo, Shagya Arab. 90fo, Furioso (Mezohegyes halfbreed). 140fo, Gidran. 160fo, Nonius.
No. 3988: a, Huçul. b, Lippizaner. c, Kisbér halfbreed.

2006, May 9
3984-3987 A1297 Set of 4   5.50 2.25
Souvenir Sheet
3988 A1297 200fo Sheet of 3, #a-c   7.00 3.00
Margin of No. 3988 is embossed.

Composers — A1298

Designs: No. 3989, 90fo, George Enescu (1881-1955), and Romanian flag. No. 3990, 90fo, Béla Bartók (1881-1945) and Hungarian flag.

2006, June 8   **Perf. 13x13¼**
3989-3990 A1298 Set of 2   2.25   .85
See Romania No. 4838.

Miskolc Intl. Opera Festival A1299

2006, June 15   **Perf. 13¼x13**
3991 A1299 190fo multi   2.25   .85

Souvenir Sheet

Budapest Museum of Fine Arts, Cent. — A1300

No. 3992: a, Esterházy Madonna, by Raphael. b, Mary Magdalene, by El Greco. c, Equestrian statue, by Leonardo da Vinci, horiz. d, Three Fishing Boats, by Claude Monet, horiz.

2006, June 23   **Litho.**   **Perf. 12**
3992 A1300 200fo Sheet of 4, #a-d   9.00 4.00

The Four Virtues, Frescoes From Castle Museum, Esztergom — A1301

Iconostasis, Szentendre Cathedral — A1302

No. 3993: a, Bölcsesség and Mértékletesség. b, Allhatatosság and Igazságosság.

2006, June 23   **Perf. 13¼x13**
3993 A1301 52fo Horiz. pair, #a-b   1.50   .50
Souvenir Sheet
Perf. 12
3994 A1302 400fo +200fo multi   6.50 5.50
Stamp Day.

Emblem of Border Guard and Falcon A1303

2006, June 27   **Perf. 12**
3995 A1303 170fo multi   1.75   .80

European Swimming Championships, Budapest — A1304

Designs: 90fo, Synchronized swimmers and diver. 180fo, Swimmers and fish.

2006, July 27   **Perf. 13x13¼**
3996-3997 A1304 Set of 2   2.75 1.25

Contemporary Art — A1305

Designs: 120fo, Child with Model Aircraft, by László Fehér. 140fo, Circle Dance, sculpture by István Haraszty, vert. 160fo, Aequilibrium, tapestry by Zsuzsa Péreli, vert.

2006, July 27   Perf. 13x13¼, 13¼x13
3998-4000 A1305 Set of 3   4.50 2.00

Hungaroring Race Track, 20th Anniv. — A1306

2006, Aug. 3   **Perf. 13x13¼**
4001 A1306 75fo multi   1.00   .40

Souvenir Sheet

Budapest Zoo, 140th Anniv. — A1307

2006, Aug. 9   **Litho.**   **Perf. 12**
4002 A1307 500fo multi   5.50 2.40

Souvenir Sheet

Consecration of Esztergom Basilica, 150th Anniv. — A1308

2006, Aug. 18
4003 A1308 500fo multi   5.50 2.40

Miniature Sheet

Enamel Paintings on St. Stephen's Crown — A1309

No. 4004: a, St. John (scsiohs inscription at top). b, St. Andrew (scsandreas) c, St. Peter (scspetrvs). d, God. e, St. Paul (scspavlus). f, St. Philip (scsphilipvs). g, St. Jacob (scsiacobvs).

Litho. (Foil Application on Sheet Margin)
2006, Aug. 18   **Perf. 12x11½**
4004 A1309 100fo Sheet of 7,
#a-g   8.00 4.00

Souvenir Sheet

1956 Revolution, 50th Anniv. — A1310

2006, Oct. 20   **Litho.**   **Perf. 13x12¾**
4005 A1310 500fo multi   5.50 3.00
No. 4005 has a die cut hole in the middle of the flag.

Christmas Type of 2002
Litho. With Foil Application
2006, Oct. 27   **Perf. 12**
4006 A1157 52fo Adoration of the Magi   .60 .25

Souvenir Sheet

1956 Melbourne Summer Olympics, 50th Anniv. — A1311

2006, Nov. 13   **Litho.**   **Perf. 12**
4007 A1311 500fo László Papp   5.25 2.60

Hungarian Red Cross, 125th Anniv. A1312

2006, Nov. 24   **Perf. 12¼x11½**
4008 A1312 100fo multi   1.10 .55

Launch of Sputnik 1 and Sputnik 2, 50th Anniv. — A1313

2007, Feb. 6   **Litho.**   **Perf. 12**
4009 A1313 350fo multi   3.75 1.90

Easter — A1314

2007, Feb. 9   **Perf. 12¼x12¾**
4010 A1314 62fo multi   .65 .30

Famous Men — A1315

Designs: 107fo, János Ferencsik (1907-84), conductor. 135fo, Count Lajos Batthyány (1807-49), prime minister.

2007, Feb. 9   **Perf. 12**
4011-4012 A1315 Set of 2   2.50 1.25

Rural Life — A1316

Designs: 62fo, Man with bottle and woman with glass. 95fo, Girl with flowers and birds. 242fo, Man cooking fish over fire.

2007, Feb. 9   **Perf. 12¼x11½**
4013-4015 A1316 Set of 3   4.25 2.10

Customs and Finance Guards, 140th Anniv. A1317

2007, Mar. 10   **Perf. 12**
4016 A1317 180fo multi   2.00 1.00

Diets A1318

Designs: 210fo, Prince John Sigismund of Transylvania and Torda Church. 230fo, Prince Ferenc Rákóczi II and Marosvásárhely Castle

2007, Apr. 10   **Perf. 13¼x12½**
4017-4018 A1318 Set of 2   5.00 2.50
Diet of Torda, 450th anniv.; Diet of Marosvásárhely, 300th anniv.

Souvenir Sheet

The Boys of Paul Street, Novel by Ferenc Molnár (1878-1952) — A1319

No. 4019: a, 160fo, Molnar. b, 160fo, Posted handbill. c, 160fo+30fo, Boy in red shirt. d, 160fo+30fo, Boy in green shirt.

2007, Apr. 10   **Perf. 12**
4019 A1319 Sheet of 4, #a-d   8.00 8.00

A1320

A1321

A1322

A1323

A1324

A1325

A1326

A1327

A1328

A1329

A1330

A1331

Graduation — A1332

No. 4020: a, Two hot air balloons. b, Graduate pulled by balloon, arch of books, diploma, hot air balloon. c, Graduation cap, hot air balloon, graduate. d, Three graduates, hot air balloon. e, Hot air balloon, graduate pulled by balloon, two graduates standing on books. f, Graduate on path, graduate holding portfolio. g, Diploma, two graduates standing on books. h, Diploma on path, bottom half of graduate at upper right. i, Three graduates on path. j, Arch of books, diploma, inkwell, quill pen, path. k, Two graduates on path. l, Inkwell, quill pen, three books. m, Graduate with magnifying glass, path. n, Graduate with magnifying glass. o, Diploma on path, legs of two graduates, path. p, Graduate carrying portfolio, diploma on arch of books. q, Arch of books, diploma, inkwell, quill pen. r, Arch of books, diploma. s, Inkwell, quill pen, graduate. t, Diploma on path, graduate at right, legs of graduate at top.

2007, Apr. 16	**Litho.**		**Perf. 11¼**
4020	A1320 (62fo) Sheet of 20, #a-t, + 20 labels	20.00	14.00
4021	Block of 8 + 8 labels	8.00	8.00
a.	A1321 (62fo) multi + label	1.00	.50
b.	A1322 (62fo) multi + label	1.00	.50
c.	A1323 (62fo) multi + label	1.00	.50
d.	A1324 (62fo) multi + label	1.00	.50
e.	A1325 (62fo) multi + label	1.00	.50
f.	A1326 (62fo) multi + label	1.00	.50
g.	A1327 (62fo) multi + label	1.00	.50
h.	A1328 (62fo) multi + label	1.00	.50
	Sheet, 3 each #4021a-4021d, 2 each #4021e-4021h, + 20 labels	20.00	20.00
4022	Pair + 2 labels	2.00	2.00
a.	A1329 (62fo) multi + label	1.00	.50
b.	A1330 (62fo) multi + label	1.00	.50
	Sheet, 10 each #4022a-4022b, + 20 labels	20.00	20.00
4023	Pair + 2 labels	2.10	2.10
a.	A1331 (95fo) multi + label	1.00	.50
b.	A1332 (95fo) multi + label	1.00	.50
	Sheet, 10 each #4023a-4023b, + 20 labels	21.00	21.00

Labels on Nos. 4020-4023 could be personalized for an additional fee.

Stamp Day
A1333

Designs: 62fo, St. Elizabeth of Hungary (1207-31) caring for the sick. 95fo, St. Elizabeth caring for poor.
500fo+200fo, St. Emeric (1007-31) praying.

2007, Apr. 27	**Litho.**		**Perf. 13**
4024-4025	A1333 Set of 2	1.75	.85
	Souvenir Sheet		
	Perf. 13x12¾		
4026	A1333 500fo +200fo multi	8.00	8.00

No. 4026 contains one 40x32mm stamp.

Television Broadcasting in Hungary, 50th Anniv. — A1334

2007, May 9		**Perf. 13x13½**
4027	A1334 160fo multi	1.75	.85

Souvenir Sheet

Europa — A1335

No. 4028: a, Scouts in canoe. b, Scouts and Brownsea Island commemorative stone.

2007, May 9		**Perf. 12**
4028	A1335 210fo Sheet, 2 each #a-b	9.25	4.50

Scouting, cent.

Dogs
A1336

Designs: 62fo, Komondor. 150fo, Transylvanian hound. 180fo, Kuvasz. 240fo, Pumis. 600fo, Hungarian vizsla.

2007, May 9		**Perf. 13x13½**
4029-4032	A1336 Set of 4	7.00	3.50
	Souvenir Sheet		
	Perf. 12		
4033	A1336 600fo multi	6.50	3.25

11th Intl. Cave Rescue Conference, Aggtelek-Jósvafo — A1337

2007, May 15	**Litho.**		**Perf. 12**
4034	A1337 200fo multi	2.25	1.10

Academy of Music Building, Budapest, Cent. — A1338

2007, May 18		
4035	A1338 250fo multi	2.75	1.40

Souvenir Sheet

National Gallery, 50th Anniv. — A1339

No. 4036: a, The Mystical Betrothal of St. Catherine, c. 1490. b, View of Rome, by Károly Markó the Elder, 1835. c, October, by Károly Ferenczy, 1903. d, Picnic in May, by Pál Szinyei Merse, 1873, horiz.

2007, May 23		**Perf. 12**
4036	A1339 150fo Sheet of 4, #a-d	6.50	3.25

Grapes and Wine Producing Areas Type of 1990

Designs: 95fo, Cirfandli grapes, Pecs region. 140fo, Ezerfürtü grapes, Etyek-Buda region. 260fo, Zenit grapes, Tolna region.

2007, May 25		**Perf. 12½x13¼**
4037-4039	A902 Set of 3	5.50	2.75

Emblem of Border Guard and German Shepherd
A1340

2007, June 27	**Litho.**		**Perf. 12**
4040	A1340 107fo multi	1.25	.60

Personalized Stamp Types of 2004-05 Redrawn With "Belföld" Instead of Denomination and

Pens — A1341

A1342

A1343

A1344

A1345

A1346

A1347

A1348

A1349

A1350

Doorknockers
A1351

Chain Bridge, Budapest — A1352

Parliament, Budapest — A1353

Buda Castle, Budapest — A1354

Heroes Square, Budapest — A1355

Fisherman's Bastion, Budapest — A1356

No. 4043: a, Quill pen, open inkwell, ink spots, green background. b, Brown fountain pen with point on flourish of "M," brown background. c, Open and closed black and gold fountain pens, green background. d, Black and gold fountain pen with point on flourish of "M," green background. e, Ball-point pen, pen point at LL, pink background. f, Cap of black and gold pen, green background. g, Brown fountain head with flat circular tip on nib, open inkwell, brown background. h, Black and gold pen with pen point at UL, pink background. i, Black and gold fountain pen, pen point at LR, green background. j, Ball-point pen, pen point at LR, pink background. k, Fountain pen and quill, green background. l, Fountain pen, pen point at LR, brown background. m, Brown fountain pen, inkwell, brown background. n, Inkwell, quill, fountain pen, ink spots, green background. o, Plunger and clip of black ball-point pen, pink background. p, Quills, quill pen, ink spots, green background. q, Closed inkwell, pen nib, quill, ink spots, green background. r, Two fountain pens, brown background. s, Black and gold fountain pen and cap, green background. t, Tip of ball-point pen with point on flourish of "M," pink background. Illustration A1341 is reduced.

2007	**Litho.**		**Perf. 11¼**
4041	Sheet of 20 + 20 labels	20.00	20.00
a.	A1220 (62fo) multi + label	1.00	.80
b.	A1221 (62fo) multi + label	1.00	.80
c.	A1222 (62fo) multi + label	1.00	.80
d.	A1223 (62fo) multi + label	1.00	.80
e.	A1224 (62fo) multi + label	1.00	.80
f.	A1225 (62fo) multi + label	1.00	.80
4042	Block or horiz. strip of 4 + 4 labels	4.00	4.00
a.	A1288 (62fo) multi + label	1.00	.80
b.	A1289 (62fo) multi + label	1.00	.80

c.	A1290 (62fo) multi + label	1.00	.80
d.	A1291 (62fo) multi + label	1.00	.80
	Sheet of 20, 7 each #4042a,		
	4042d, 3 each #4042b,		
	4042c, + 20 labels	20.00	20.00
4043	A1341 Sheet of 20 +		
	20 labels	20.00	20.00
a.-t.	(62fo) Any single + label	1.00	.80
4044	Block of 10 + 10 la-		
	bels	10.00	10.00
a.	A1342 (62fo) multi + label	1.00	.80
b.	A1343 (62fo) multi + label	1.00	.80
c.	A1344 (62fo) multi + label	1.00	.80
d.	A1345 (62fo) multi + label	1.00	.80
e.	A1346 (62fo) multi + label	1.00	.80
f.	A1347 (62fo) multi + label	1.00	.80
g.	A1348 (62fo) multi + label	1.00	.80
h.	A1349 (62fo) multi + label	1.00	.80
i.	A1350 (62fo) multi + label	1.00	.80
j.	A1351 (62fo) multi + label	1.00	.80
	Sheet of 20, 2 each #4044a-		
	4044j, + 20 labels	20.00	20.00
4045	Vert. strip of 5 + 5		
	labels	5.00	5.00
a.	A1352 (62fo) multi + label	1.00	.80
b.	A1353 (62fo) multi + label	1.00	.80
c.	A1354 (62fo) multi + label	1.00	.80
d.	A1355 (62fo) multi + label	1.00	.80
e.	A1356 (62fo) multi + label	1.00	.80
	Sheet of 20, 4 each #4045a-		
	4045e, + 20 labels	20.00	20.00
	Nos. 4041-4045 (5)	59.00	59.00

Issued: No. 4041, 9/27; others, 7/16.
No. 4041 contains 4 each #4041a, 4041e, 2 each #4041d, 4041f, 5 #4041b and 3 #4041c. Background colors on some stamps differ slightly. Labels could be personalized for an additional fee.

Zoltán Kodály (1882-1967), Composer — A1357

2007, July 16   **Perf. 13x13¼**
4046 A1357 200fo multi   2.25 1.10

Hungarian University Sports Federation, Cent. — A1358

2007, July 30   **Perf. 11½x12**
4047 A1358 360fo multi   4.00 2.00

Dolomite Flax — A1359   Pasque Flower — A1360

Serpentine Die Cut 10¾x10½
2007, Aug. 1
Self-Adhesive
Booklet Stamps
4048	A1359 (230fo) multi	2.50	1.25
a.	Booklet pane of 4 + 4 eti-		
	quettes	10.00	
4049	A1360 (260fo) multi	3.00	1.50
a.	Booklet pane of 4 + 4 eti-		
	quettes	12.00	

Souvenir Sheet

Enamel Paintings on St. Stephen's Crown — A1361

No. 4050: a, St. Cosmas (light blue robe). b, St. George (holding spear and shield). c, Archangel Michael (holding staff).

Litho. (Litho. With Foil Application in Sheet Margin)
2007, Aug. 17   **Perf. 12x11½**
4050 A1361 300fo Sheet of 3,
       #a-c   10.00 5.00

János Selye (1907-82), Stress Researcher — A1362

Perf. 13¼x12¾
2007, Aug. 23   **Litho.**
4051 A1362 400fo multi   4.50 2.25
Second World Stress Conference, Budapest.

World Science Forum Type of 2005 Redrawn
2007, Sept. 27   **Perf. 13x13¼**
4052 A1264 230fo multi   2.60 1.25

Christmas — A1363

No. 4053: a, Annunciation. b, Holy Family and Shepherds. c, Adoration of the Magi. Illustration reduced.

2007, Oct. 19   **Perf. 12**
4053 A1363 62fo Horiz. strip of
     3, #a-c   2.50 1.25

Compass and Map Type of 2005 Redrawn With "Belföld" Instead of Denomination

No. 4054: a, Compass at right, map of western Hungary. b, Compass at left, map of eastern Hungary.

2008, Feb. 8   **Litho.**   **Perf. 11¼**
4054	A1246 (70fo) Pair, #a-b, + 2		
	labels	1.60	1.60
	Sheet of 18 #4054a, 17		
	#4054b, + 35 labels	28.00	—

Labels could be personalized.

Easter A1364

2008, Feb. 27   **Perf. 12**
4055 A1364 70fo multi   .80 .40

King Matthias, 550th Anniv. of Election — A1365

King Matthias, arms and: 70fo, Fountain. 100fo, Castle and horses. 600fo+200fo, King and Queen on throne.

2008, Mar. 13
4056-4057 A1365 Set of 2   2.10 1.10
Souvenir Sheet
4058 A1365 600fo +200fo multi 10.00 10.00
Stamp Day. No. 4058 contains one 40x30mm stamp.

General Károly Knezich (1808-49) A1366

2008, Mar. 14   **Perf. 13x12½**
4059 A1366 380fo multi   4.75 2.40

Miniature Sheet

Transportation — A1367

No. 4060: a, 150fo, Automobile. b, 150fo, Ship. c, 150fo+30fo, Train. d, 150fo+30fo, Airplane.

2008, Mar. 14   **Perf. 12**
4060 A1367   Sheet of 4, #a-d   8.25 8.25

Romany Dancer and Musicians A1368

German Dancer and Accordion A1369

2008   **Perf. 13½x13**
4061 A1368 260fo multi   3.25 1.60
4062 A1369 275fo multi   3.50 1.75
Hungarian ethnic minorities. Issued: 260fo, 4/8; 275fo, 5/9.

2008 Summer Olympics, Beijing A1370

Designs: 70fo, Water polo. 100fo, Wrestling. 170fo, Fencing.

2008, Apr. 16   **Perf. 13x13¼**
4063-4065 A1370 Set of 3   4.25 2.10

Miniature Sheet

Europa — A1371

No. 4066: a, 100fo, Letter in envelope, capital "A." b, 230fo, Pen nib.

2008, May 9   **Perf. 12**
4066 A1371   Sheet, 2 each #a-
     b   8.25 4.25
Stamps on bottom row are tete-beche in relation to the top row.

Indigenous Animals A1372

Designs: 145fo, Hungarian giant rabbit. 150fo, Hungarian domestic goat. 170fo, Cikta sheep. 310fo, Hungarian donkey. 600fo, Water buffalo.

2008, May 9
4067-4070 A1372   Set of 4   9.50 4.75
Souvenir Sheet
4071 A1372 600fo multi   7.50 3.75

National Parks Type of 1998
Design: Orség National Park.
2008, May 16
4072 A1073 220fo multi   3.00 1.50

UNESCO World Heritage Sites Type of 2002
Design: Tokaj Wine Region.
2008, May 16
4073 A1153 290fo multi   3.75 1.90

UEFA Euro 2008 Soccer Championships, Austria and Switzerland A1373

2008, May 16   **Perf. 13½x13**
4074 A1373 250fo multi   3.25 1.60

Vacation Vouchers, 10th Anniv. A1374

2008, May 20   **Perf. 12x11½**
4075 A1374 70fo multi   .90 .45

A1375

A1376

A1377

A1378

A1379

Philavillage
A1380

2008   **Perf. 12, 13¼x13 (#4077)**
4076	A1375	100fo multi	1.40	.70
4077	A1376	100fo multi	1.40	.70
4078	A1377	100fo multi	1.40	.70
4079	A1378	100fo multi	1.40	.70
4080	A1379	100fo multi	1.40	.70
4081	A1380	100fo multi	1.40	.70
	Nos. 4076-4081 (6)		8.40	4.20

Issued: Nos. 4076-4077, 6/6; Nos. 4078-4079, 6/20; Nos. 4080-4081, 7/10. Stamps also served as game pieces for Philavillage board game.

A1381

A1382

A1383

A1384

A1385

Philavillage
A1386

2008   **Litho.**   **Perf. 12**
4082	A1381	100fo multi	1.25	.60
4083	A1382	100fo multi	1.25	.60

Perf. 13x13¼, 13¼x13 (#4086)
4084	A1383	100fo multi	1.10	.55
4085	A1384	100fo multi	1.10	.55
4086	A1385	100fo multi	.95	.50
4087	A1386	100fo multi	.95	.50
	Nos. 4082-4087 (6)		6.60	3.30

Issued: Nos. 4082-4083, 9/2; Nos. 4084-4085, 10/9; Nos. 4086-4087, 11/5. Stamps also served as game pieces for Philavillage board game.

Hungarian Illuminated Chronicle, 650th Anniv. — A1387

Litho. & Embossed With Foil Application
2008, June 20   **Perf. 12**
4088	A1387	400fo multi	5.50	2.75

Souvenir Sheet

Debrecen and Veszprém Zoos, 50th Anniv. — A1388

No. 4089: a, Giraffes, cranes, hippopotamus, camel (Debrecen). b, Camel, crane, lion, zebra, rhinoceros, flamingo (Veszprém).

2008, Aug. 14   **Litho.**   **Perf. 12**
4089	A1388	260fo Sheet of 2, #a-b	6.50	3.25

Souvenir Sheet

Enamel Paintings on St. Stephen's Crown — A1389

No. 4090: a, Archangel Gabriel (holding staff). b, St. Demeter (with shield and spear). c, St. Damian (with beard).

Litho. (Litho. With Foil Application in Sheet Margin)
2008, Aug. 19   **Perf. 12x11½**
4090	A1389	300fo Sheet of 3, #a-c	11.50	5.75

Miklós Zrinyi (1508-66), Military Leader A1390

2008, Sept. 5   **Litho.**   **Perf. 13x13¼**
4091	A1390	190fo multi	2.25	1.10

Flowers Types of 2006 Redrawn With "Belföld" Instead of Denomination
2008, Sept. 2   **Litho.**   **Perf. 11¼**
4092		Vert. strip of 5 + 5 labels	4.25	4.25
a.	A1278	(70fo) multi + label	.85	.85
b.	A1279	(70fo) multi + label	.85	.85
c.	A1280	(70fo) multi + label	.85	.85
d.	A1281	(70fo) multi + label	.85	.85
e.	A1282	(70fo) multi + label	.85	.85
		Sheet, 4 each #4092a-4092e, + 20 labels	17.00	—

Background colors of stamps in full sheets varies. Labels could be personalized for an additional fee.

Archangel Gabriel, Sculpture by György Zala (1858-1937) A1391

2008, Sept. 25   **Litho.**   **Perf. 13¼x13**
4093	A1391	200fo multi	2.25	1.10

Synagogues A1392

Designs: 200fo, Synagogue, Szeged. 250fo, Synagogue of the Jewish Theological Seminary, Budapest.

2008, Sept. 25   **Perf. 12½x13¼**
4094-4095	A1392	Set of 2	5.00	2.50

Cat — A1393

Bear — A1394

Rabbit — A1395

Lion — A1396

Giraffe — A1397

2008, Oct. 9   **Perf. 11¼**
4096		Vert. strip of 5 + 5 labels	3.75	3.75
a.	A1393	(70fo) multi	.75	.40
b.	A1394	(70fo) multi	.75	.40
c.	A1395	(70fo) multi	.75	.40
d.	A1396	(70fo) multi	.75	.40
e.	A1397	(70fo) multi	.75	.40
		Sheet, 4 each #4096a-4096e, + 20 labels	15.00	15.00

Labels on No. 4096 could be personalized for an additional fee.

Souvenir Sheet

Ferenc Puskás (1927-2006), Player on 1952 Hungarian Olympic Soccer Team — A1398

2008, Oct. 28   **Perf. 12**
4097	A1398	600fo multi	6.00	3.00

Christmas A1399

Art by György Konecsni (1908-70): 70fo, Nativity. 100fo, Adoration of the Magi.

2008, Oct. 28   **Perf. 12¼x11½**
4098-4099	A1399	Set of 2	1.75	.85

Edward Teller (1908-2003), Nuclear
Physicist — A1400

2008, Nov. 3   **Perf. 13x13¼**
4100 A1400 250fo multi   2.40 1.25

Ludovika
Academy, 200th
Anniv. — A1401

2008, Nov. 5   **Perf. 13¼x13**
4101 A1401 300fo multi   3.00 1.50

Crocus — A1402   Scilla — A1403

2009, Feb. 24 Litho.   Perf. 11½x12
4102 A1402 (75fo) multi   .65 .30
4103 A1403 (100fo) multi   .85 .40
Self-Adhesive
Serpentine Die Cut 10x10¼
4104 A1403 (75fo) multi   .65 .30
    Nos. 4102-4104 (3)   2.15 1.00

Easter — A1404

2009, Feb. 24   **Perf. 12x12½**
4105 A1404 75fo multi   .65 .30

Franciscan Order, 800th
Anniv. — A1405

2009, Feb. 24   **Perf. 12**
4106 A1405 100fo multi   .85 .40

1909 Flights of Louis Blériot,
Cent. — A1406

No. 4107: a, Flight across English Channel.
b, Flight at Kisrákoson, Hungary.
Illustration reduced.

2009, Mar. 12
4107 A1406 105fo Horiz. pair,
             #a-b, + cen-
             tral label   2.00 1.00

Souvenir Sheet

Budapest Research Reactor, 50th
Anniv. — A1407

2009, Mar. 25   **Perf. 11¼**
4108 A1407 1000fo multi   9.25 4.50

Preservation of Polar Regions and
Glaciers — A1408

Designs: Nos. 4109, 4113, 75fo, Ursus
maritimus and walruses. Nos. 4110, 4114,
130fo, Ovibos moschatus. Nos. 4111, 4115,
145fo, Uncia uncia. Nos. 4112, 4116, 275fo,
Aptenodytes patagonicus.
    No. 4117: a, Ursus maritimus. b, Alopex
lagopus.

2009, Mar. 27 Litho.   Perf. 12½x12
4109-4112 A1408 Set of 4   5.75 3.00
Litho. & Silk-screened
4113-4116 A1408 Set of 4   5.75 3.00
Souvenir Sheet
4117 A1408 260fo Sheet of 2,
             #a-b   4.75 2.40
Portions of the designs of Nos. 4113-4117
that were applied by the silk-screen process
have a silvery shine when viewed at an angle.

Joseph Haydn (1732-1809),
Composer — A1409

2009, Apr. 2 Litho.   Perf. 13x13¼
4118 A1409 300fo red & black   2.75 1.40

Locomotives — A1410

Designs: 75fo, Mk48 Diesel locomotive.
100fo, C 50 Diesel locomotive. 125fo, MD 40
Diesel locomotive. 275fo, Morgó steam
locomotive.

2009, Apr. 2   **Perf. 13¼x13**
4119-4122 A1410 Set of 4   5.25 2.60

Souvenir Sheet

Ferenc Kazinczy (1759-1831),
Writer — A1411

2009, Apr. 2   **Perf. 13x12¾**
4123 A1411 600fo multi   5.50 2.75

Miniature Sheet

Elek Benedek (1859-1929), Fable
Writer and Translator — A1412

No. 4124: a, 100fo, Arabian man, chicken
and bees. b, 100fo, Three pigs. c, 100fo+50fo,
Cat in king's robes. d, 100fo+50fo, Benedek.

2009, Apr. 2   **Perf. 12x12½**
4124 A1412 Sheet of 4, #a-d   4.75 2.40

Miklós Radnóti (1909-44),
Poet — A1413

2009, May 5   **Perf. 13¼x13**
4125 A1413 280fo multi   2.60 1.25

Souvenir Sheet

Europa — A1414

No. 4126: a, 100fo, Galileo Galilei and
Galileo space probe. b, 230fo, Planets.

2009, May 8   **Perf. 12**
4126 A1414 Sheet, 2 each #a-
             b   6.25 6.25
Intl. Year of Astronomy.

John Calvin
(1509-64),
Theologian and
Religious
Reformer
A1415

2009, May 22   **Perf. 13¼x13**
4127 A1415 200fo multi   2.00 1.00

Donát Bánki (1859-1922), Inventor of
Carburetor — A1416

2009, June 5
4128 A1416 300fo multi   3.00 1.50

Visegrád,
1000th
Anniv.
A1417

Designs: 75fo, Column and entableture.
100fo, Solomon Tower, octagonal column,
carved head.
    600fo+200fo, Summer Palace, fountain,
monument, Madonna and Child.

2009, June 5   **Perf. 13x13¼**
4129-4130 A1417 Set of 2   1.75 .85
Souvenir Sheet
4131 A1417 600fo +200fo multi   7.75 4.00
Stamp Day.

Discovery of Statue
of Virgin Mary,
Máriabesnyo, 250th
Anniv. — A1418

2009, Aug. 14   **Perf. 13¼x12**
4132 A1418 200fo multi   2.10 1.10

Bishopric of Pécs, 1000th
Anniv. — A1419

2009, Aug. 19   **Perf. 12**
4133 A1419 100fo multi   1.10 .55

Furniture Type of 1999
Design like #3791.

2009, Sept. 4 Litho.   Perf. 12¼x11½
4134 A1091 230fo blue green   2.40 1.25

Building, Pecs — A1420

Calvary Hill, Pecs — A1421

City Hall, Szechenyi Square, Pecs — A1422

Sts. Peter and Paul Cathedral, Pecs — A1423

Building, Pecs — A1424

Hungarian Academy of Sciences, Sculpture, Pecs — A1425

Synagogue, Pecs — A1426

Sts. Peter and Paul Cathedral, Pecs — A1427

Door Knocker and Handle, Pecs — A1428

Klimó Library, Pecs — A1429

National Theater, Pecs — A1430

Zsolnay Fountain, Pecs — A1431

Roof, Pecs — A1432

Street, Pecs — A1433

Necropolis, Pecs — A1434

Post Office Roof, Pecs — A1435

Mosque, Pecs — A1436

Barbican, Pecs — A1437

Mosque and Minaret, Pecs — A1438

Sculpture, Pecs — A1439

2009, Sept. 4   Litho.   Perf. 11¼

4135		Sheet of 20 + 20 labels	16.00	16.00
a.	A1420	(75fo) multi + label	.80	.80
b.	A1421	(75fo) multi + label	.80	.80
c.	A1422	(75fo) multi + label	.80	.80
d.	A1423	(75fo) multi + label	.80	.80
e.	A1424	(75fo) multi + label	.80	.80
f.	A1425	(75fo) multi + label	.80	.80
g.	A1426	(75fo) multi + label	.80	.80
h.	A1427	(75fo) multi + label	.80	.80
i.	A1428	(75fo) multi + label	.80	.80
j.	A1429	(75fo) multi + label	.80	.80
k.	A1430	(75fo) multi + label	.80	.80
l.	A1431	(75fo) multi + label	.80	.80
m.	A1432	(75fo) multi + label	.80	.80
n.	A1433	(75fo) multi + label	.80	.80
o.	A1434	(75fo) multi + label	.80	.80
p.	A1435	(75fo) multi + label	.80	.80
q.	A1436	(75fo) multi + label	.80	.80
r.	A1437	(75fo) multi + label	.80	.80
s.	A1438	(75fo) multi + label	.80	.80
t.	A1439	(75fo) multi + label	.80	.80

Labels could be personalized for an additional fee.

Opening of Border Between Austria and Hungary, 20th Anniv. A1440

2009, Sept. 10   Litho.   Perf. 12
4136 A1440 210fo multi   2.40 1.25
See Austria No. 2219, Germany No. 2548.

Rainbow, by József Egry (1883-1951) — A1441

2009, Sept. 10   Perf. 13¼x12½
4137 A1441 275fo multi   3.00 1.50

Louis Braille (1809-52), Educator of the Blind — A1442

Litho. & Embossed
2009, Oct. 15   Perf. 13¼x13
4138 A1442 200fo multi   2.25 1.10

A1443

Christmas A1444

2009, Oct. 15   Litho.   Perf. 12
4139 A1443 75fo multi   .80 .40
Perf. 12x11½
4140 A1444 100fo blue & yel org   1.10 .55

Miniature Sheet

Hungarian-Japanese Jubilee Year — A1445

No. 4141: a, Hungarian flask. b, Mount Fuji, horiz. c, Jar from Japanese tea service. d,

Matyo folk embroidery, Hungary. e, Elizabeth Bridge, Hungary, horiz. f, Crane and leaves fabric pattern from Japanese kimono.

2009, Oct. 16   Perf. 12
4141 A1445 260fo Sheet of 6,
    #a-f   17.00 8.50
See Japan No. 3167.

Ajka Crystal — A1446

2009, Oct. 28
4142 A1446 300fo multi   3.25 1.60

World Science Forum, Budapest A1447

2009, Nov. 5   Perf. 13x13¼
4143 A1447 100fo multi   1.10 .55

Filaclub Characters A1448

No. 4144: a, Bogi Fila. b, Levi Fila. c, Pötyi Fila.

2009, Dec. 4
4144   Horiz. strip of 3   .70 .35
a.-c. A1448 20fo Any single   .20 .20
Promotion of children's philately.

Hassan Jakovali Mosque, Pecs — A1449

Calvary Hill, Pecs — A1450

National Theater, Pecs — A1451

Hungarian Academy of Sciences, Pecs — A1452

Barbican,
Pecs — A1453

Synagogue,
Pecs — A1454

Statue of St.
Francis of Assisi,
by György
Bársony,
Pecs — A1455

Interior of
National Theater,
Pecs — A1456

Statue of Janus
Pannonius, by
Sándor Rétfalvi,
Pecs — A1457

County Hall,
Pecs — A1458

Post Office,
Pecs — A1459

St. Peter and
Paul Cathedral,
Pecs — A1460

St. Peter and
Paul Cathedral,
Pecs — A1461

Statue of the
Holy Trinity, by
György Kiss,
Pecs — A1462

Mosque of Pasha
Gazi Kasim,
Pecs — A1463

University Gate,
Pecs — A1464

Necropolis,
Pecs — A1465

Zsolnay
Fountain,
Pecs — A1466

Klimó Library,
Pecs — A1467

Statue of Tivadar
Csontváry
Kosztka, Zsolnay
Vase,
Pecs — A1468

Reformed
Church,
Pecs — A1469

Tettye Ruins,
Pecs — A1470

Lutheran Church,
Pecs — A1471

City Hall,
Pecs — A1472

Symbol
Sculpture, by
Victor Vasarely,
Pecs — A1473

2010, Jan. 10   **Litho.**   **Perf. 12**

4145	Sheet of 25		20.00	10.00
a.	A1449	(75fo) multi	.80	.40
b.	A1450	(75fo) multi	.80	.40
c.	A1451	(75fo) multi	.80	.40
d.	A1452	(75fo) multi	.80	.40
e.	A1453	(75fo) multi	.80	.40
f.	A1454	(75fo) multi	.80	.40
g.	A1455	(75fo) multi	.80	.40
h.	A1456	(75fo) multi	.80	.40
i.	A1457	(75fo) multi	.80	.40
j.	A1458	(75fo) multi	.80	.40
k.	A1459	(75fo) multi	.80	.40
l.	A1460	(75fo) multi	.80	.40
m.	A1461	(75fo) multi	.80	.40
n.	A1462	(75fo) multi	.80	.40
o.	A1463	(75fo) multi	.80	.40
p.	A1464	(75fo) multi	.80	.40
q.	A1465	(75fo) multi	.80	.40
r.	A1466	(75fo) multi	.80	.40
s.	A1467	(75fo) multi	.80	.40
t.	A1468	(75fo) multi	.80	.40
u.	A1469	(75fo) multi	.80	.40
v.	A1470	(75fo) multi	.80	.40
w.	A1471	(75fo) multi	.80	.40
x.	A1472	(75fo) multi	.80	.40
y.	A1473	(75fo) multi	.80	.40

Pecs, 2010 European Cultural Capital.

2010
Winter
Olympics,
Vancouver
A1474

2010, Feb. 5

4146	A1474	260fo multi	2.60	1.40

Izidor Kner (1860-1935),
Publisher — A1475

2010, Feb. 5   **Perf. 12x13¼**

4147	A1475	295fo multi	3.00	1.50

Budapest
Landmarks
A1476

Designs: 295fo, Tympanum of Humanities
Building, Loránd Eötvös University, Budapest.
400fo, Elisabeth Tower, Budapest.

2010, Feb. 19   **Perf. 12½x12**

4148-4149	A1476	Set of 2	7.00	3.50

Loránd Eötvös University, 375th anniv., Elisabeth Tower, cent.

Easter
A1477

2010, Mar. 1

4150	A1477	80fo multi	.85	.40

Republican
Guard
Regiment,
250th
Anniv.
A1478

2010, Mar. 1   **Perf. 13x13¼**

4151	A1478	320fo multi	3.25	1.60

Souvenir Sheet

Ferenc Erkel (1810-93),
Composer — A1479

2010, Mar. 26   **Perf. 12**

4152	A1479	500fo multi	5.25	2.60

Stamp
Day — A1480

Sites in Sopron: 80fo, Saint Ursula's
Church, Church of the Virgin Mary. 105fo,
Sculpture of the Virgin Mary, Gates of Faith,
horiz.
500fo+200fo, Statue of the Holy Trinity.

2010, Mar. 26   **Perf. 12x12½, 12½x12**

4153-4154	A1480	Set of 2	1.90	.95

Souvenir Sheet

4155	A1480	500fo +200fo multi	7.25	3.50

Surtax on No. 4155 for Natl. Association of
Hungarian Stamp Collectors.

Hungarian
Documents
on Paper,
700th
Anniv.
A1481

2010, Apr. 8   **Perf. 13x13¼**

4156	A1481	140fo multi	1.40	.70

*Chronicle of the
Ways of the
Hungarians,* by
Gáspár Heltai (c.
1510-74),
Writer — A1482

2010, Apr. 8   **Perf. 13¼x13**

4157	A1482	240fo multi	2.50	1.25

Expo 2010, Shanghai — A1483

Gömböc in various positions with stamps numbered in lower left: Nos. 4158a, 4158ae, 1. Nos. 4158b, 4158af, 2. Nos. 4158c, 4158ag, 3. Nos. 4158d, 4158ah, 2 squared (4). Nos. 4158e, 4158ai, 5. Nos. 4158f, 4158aj, 2*3 (6). Nos. 4158g, 4158ak, 7. Nos. 4158h, 4158al, 2 cubed (8). Nos. 4158i, 4158am, 3 squared (9). Nos. 4158j, 4158an, 2*5 (10). Nos. 4158k, 4158ao, 11. Nos. 4158l, 4158ap, 2 squared * 3 (12). Nos. 4158m, 4158aq, 13. Nos. 4158n, 4158ar, 2*7 (14). Nos. 4158o, 4158as, 3*5 (15). Nos. 4158p, 4158at, 2 to the fourth power (16). Nos. 4158q, 4158au, 17. Nos. 4158r, 4158av, 2*9 (18). Nos. 4158s, 4158aw, 19. Nos. 4158t, 4158ax, 2 squared * 5 (20). Nos. 4158u, 4158ay, 3*7 (21). Nos. 4158v, 4158az, 2*11 (22). Nos. 4158w, 4158ba, 23. Nos. 4158x, 4158bb, 2 cubed * 3 (24). Nos. 4158y, 4158bc, 5 squared (25). Nos. 4158z, 4158bd, 2*13 (26). Nos. 4158aa, 4158be, 3 cubed (27). Nos. 4158ab, 4158bf, 2 squared * 7 (28). Nos. 4158ac, 4158bg, 29. Nos. 4158ad, 4158bh, 2*3*5 (30).

2010, Apr. 30   Litho.   Perf. 12
4158   Sheet of 30   30.00 30.00
a.-ad.   A1483 100fo Any single   1.00   .50
ae.-bh. A1483 100fo Any booklet
         single, perf. 12 horiz. at
         top   1.00   .50
         Complete booklet,
         #4158ae-4158bh   30.00

Miniature Sheet

The Tragedy of Man, Play by Imre Madách, 150th Anniv. — A1484

No. 4159 — Scenes from play: a, 105fo, Adam and Eve in Garden of Eden (denomination in white). b, 105fo, Men and women in London (denomination in black). c, 105fo+50fo, Men and women in Rome (denomination at bottom in white). d, 105fo+50fo, Woman in Prague (denomination at top in white).

2010, May 3   Perf. 13x13¼
4159 A1484 Sheet of 4, #a-d   4.75 2.40
Surtax for supporting youth stamp collecting.

2010 World Cup Soccer Championships, South Africa — A1485

2010, May 7   Perf. 11
4160 A1485 325fo multi   3.00 1.50

Intl. Year of Biodiversity A1486

Designs: 80fo, Spermophilus citellus. 110fo, Phyllomorpha lacinata. 215fo, Parus caeruleus. 350fo, Vipera ursinii rakosiensis. 500fo, Iris aphylla ssp. hungarica.

2010, May 7   Perf. 12½x12
4161-4164 A1486 Set of 4   7.00 3.50

Souvenir Sheet
Perf. 12
4165 A1486 500fo multi   4.75 2.40

Miniature Sheet

Europa — A1487

No. 4166 — Vackor the Bear: a, Holding plant. b, Picking fruit.

2010, May 7   Perf. 12
4166 A1487 150fo Sheet, 2 each
         #a-b   5.50 2.75

No. 3417a Surcharged in Red

Method and Perf. As Before
2010, June 18
4167 A972 200fo on 19fo multi
         (R)   1.75   .90
Election of Prime Minister József Antall, 20th anniv.

Frédéric Chopin (1810-49), Composer — A1488

2010, June 18   Litho.   Perf. 12½
4168 A1488 240fo multi   2.10 1.10

Self-Portrait of Miklós Barabás (1810-98) A1489

2010, June 18   Perf. 12½x13¼
4169 A1489 365fo multi   3.25 1.60

World Triathlon Championships, Budapest — A1490

2010, July 2   Litho.   Perf. 13x13¼
4170 A1490 280fo multi   2.50 1.25

European Swimming League Championships, Budapest and Lake Balaton — A1491

2010, July 2   Perf. 13¼x13
4171 A1491 300fo multi   2.60 1.40

25th Hungarian Formula 1 Grand Prix — A1492

2010, July 30   Perf. 12
4172 A1492 230fo multi   2.10 1.10

Synagogues A1493

Designs: 110fo, Nagykoros Synagogue. 175fo, New Synagogue, Szolnok.

2010, Sept. 6   Perf. 12½x13¼
4173-4174 A1493 Set of 2   2.60 1.40

Hungarian Gymnastics Federation, 125th Anniv. — A1494

2010, Sept. 24 Litho. Perf. 12x12½
4175 A1494 140fo multi   1.40   .70

Christmas A1495

Designs: 80fo, Madonna and Child. 105fo, Angels making music, horiz.

Litho. With Foil Application
2010, Oct. 28   Perf. 12
4176-4177 A1495 Set of 2   1.90   .95

Embroidery — A1496

Designs: 80fo, Termeh embroidery designs, Yazd, Iran. 240fo, Jazgyian embroidery designs, Hungary.

2010, Nov. 10 Litho. Perf. 12½x12
4178-4179 A1496 Set of 2   3.25 1.60
         See Iran Nos.

Souvenir Sheet

Rudolf Kárpáti (1920-99), Fencing Gold Medalist at 1960 Summer Olympics — A1497

2010, Dec. 10   Perf. 12
4180 A1497 500fo multi   4.75 2.40

Sándor Püski (1911-2009), Book Publisher A1498

2011, Feb. 4   Litho.   Perf. 12x12½
4181 A1498 270fo multi   2.75 1.40

Hungarian Presidency of the Council of the European Union — A1499

2011, Feb. 7   Perf. 12
4182 A1499 90fo multi   .90   .45

Visegrád Group, 20th Anniv. — A1500

2011, Feb. 15
4183 A1500 240fo multi   2.40 1.25
         See Czech Republic No. , Poland No. , Slovakia No.

SEMI-POSTAL STAMPS

Issues of the Monarchy

"Turul" and St. Stephen's Crown — SP1

Franz Josef I Wearing Hungarian Crown — SP2

Wmk. Double Cross (137)

1913, Nov. 20   Typo.   Perf. 14

B1	SP1	1f slate	.25	.20
B2	SP1	2f olive yellow	.25	.20
B3	SP1	3f orange	.25	.20
B4	SP1	5f emerald	.25	.20
B5	SP1	6f olive green	.25	.20
B6	SP1	10f carmine	.30	.20
B7	SP1	12f violet, *yellow*	.60	.20
B8	SP1	16f gray green	.90	.20
B9	SP1	20f dark brown	2.40	.40
B10	SP1	25f ultra	1.50	.25
B11	SP1	30f orange brown	1.75	.25
B12	SP1	35f red violet	1.75	.25
B13	SP1	50f lake, *blue*	3.00	.60
B14	SP1	60f green, *salmon*	3.00	.50
B15	SP2	1k dull red	26.00	2.00
B16	SP2	2k dull blue	78.00	40.00
B17	SP2	5k violet brown	30.00	30.00
	Nos. B1-B17 (17)		150.45	75.85

Nos. B1-B17 were sold at an advance of 2f over face value, as indicated by the label at bottom. The surtax was to aid flood victims.
For overprints see Nos. 5NB1-5NB10, 6NB1-6NB11.
Exist imperf. Value, set $1,050.

Semi-Postal Stamps of 1913 Surcharged in Red, Green or Brown:

a   b

1914

B18	SP1(a)	1f slate	.25	.20
B19	SP1(a)	2f olive yel	.25	.20
B20	SP1(a)	3f orange	.25	.20
B21	SP1(a)	5f emerald	.25	.20
B22	SP1(a)	6f olive green	.25	.20
B23	SP1(a)	10f carmine (G)	.35	.20
B24	SP1(a)	12f violet, *yel*	.25	.20
B25	SP1(a)	16f gray green	.30	.20
B26	SP1(a)	20f dark brown	1.00	.20
B27	SP1(a)	25f ultra	1.00	.20
B28	SP1(a)	30f orange brn	1.40	.25
B29	SP1(a)	35f red violet	2.25	.20
B30	SP1(a)	50f lake, *bl*	1.75	.50
B31	SP1(a)	60f green, *salmon*	2.50	.55
B32	SP2(b)	1k dull red (Br)	55.00	25.00
B33	SP2(b)	2k dull blue	40.00	26.00
B34	SP2(b)	5k violet brn	30.00	21.00
	Nos. B18-B34 (17)		137.05	75.50

Exist imperf. Value, set $850.

Regular Issue of 1913 Surcharged in Red or Green:

c   d

1915, Jan. 1

B35	A4(c)	1f slate	.20	.20
B36	A4(c)	2f olive yel	.20	.20
B37	A4(c)	3f orange	.20	.20
B38	A4(c)	5f emerald	.20	.20
B39	A4(c)	6f olive grn	.20	.20
B40	A4(c)	10f carmine (G)	.20	.20
B41	A4(c)	12f violet, *yel*	.20	.20
B42	A4(c)	16f gray green	.25	.25
B43	A4(c)	20f dark brown	.30	.30
B44	A4(c)	25f ultra	.20	.20
B45	A4(c)	30f orange brn	.40	.20
B46	A4(c)	35f red violet	.45	.20
B47	A4(c)	50f lake, *bl*	.65	.25
a.		On No. 96a	5,500.	
B48	A4(c)	60f green, *salmon*	.85	.30
B49	A5(d)	1k dull red	1.25	3.00
B50	A5(d)	2k dull blue	3.25	7.50
B51	A5(d)	5k violet brown	9.00	17.50

Surcharged as Type "c" but in Smaller Letters

B52	A4	60f green, *salmon*	2.40	1.00
	Nos. B35-B52 (18)		20.40	32.10

Nos. B18-B52 were sold at an advance of 2f over face value. The surtax to aid war widows and orphans.
Exist imperf. Value, set $225.

Soldiers Fighting
SP3   SP4

Eagle with Sword
SP5

Harvesting
SP6

1916-17   Perf. 15

B53	SP3	10f + 2f rose red	.20	.20
B54	SP4	15f + 2f dull violet	.20	.20
B55	SP5	40f + 2f brn car ('17)	.20	.20
	Nos. B53-B55 (3)		.60	.60

Exist imperf. Value, set $15.
For overprints and surcharge see Nos. B58-B60. 1NB1-1NB3, 2NB1-2NB6, 4NJ1, 5NB11-5NB13, 6NB13-6NB15, 7NB2-7NB3, 9NB1, 10NB1-10NB4, 11NB1-B4.

1917, Sept. 15
Surcharge in Red

B56	SP6	10f + 1k rose	.35	.50
B57	SP6	15f + 1k violet	.35	.50

Nos. B56 and B57 were issued in connection with the War Exhibition of Archduke Josef.

Issues of the Republic

Semi-Postal Stamps of 1916-17 Overprinted in Black

1918

B58	SP3	10f + 2f rose red	.20	.20
B59	SP4	15f + 2f dull violet	.20	.20
B60	SP5	40f + 2f brown car	.20	.20
	Nos. B58-B60 (3)		.60	.60

Nos. B58-B60 exist with inverted overprint.
Exist imperf. Value, set $15.

> Postally used examples of Nos. B69-B174 sell for more.

Issues of the Kingdom

Released Prisoner Walking Home — SP7

Prisoners of War — SP8

Homecoming of Soldier — SP9

Wmk. 137 Vert. or. Horiz.

1920, Mar. 10   Perf. 12

B69a	SP7	40f + 1k dull red	1.75	3.50
B70a	SP8	60f + 2k gray brown	3.00	6.00
B71	SP9	1k + 5k dk blue	1.75	3.50
	Nos. B69a-B71 (3)		6.50	13.00
	Set, never hinged		18.50	

The surtax was used to help prisoners of war return home from Siberia.
Exist imperf. Value, set $120.

Statue of Petöfi — SP10

Griffin — SP11

Sándor Petöfi — SP12

Petöfi Dying — SP13

Petöfi Addressing People — SP14

1923, Jan. 23   Perf. 14 (10k, 40k), 12

B72	SP10	10k slate green	.50	1.00
B73	SP11	15k dull blue	1.50	2.75
B74	SP12	25k gray brown	.50	1.00
B75	SP13	40k brown violet	1.75	2.75
B76	SP14	50k violet brown	1.75	2.75
	Nos. B72-B76 (5)		6.00	10.25
	Set, never hinged		12.00	

Birth centenary of the Hungarian poet Sándor Petöfi. The stamps were on sale at double face value, for a limited time and in restricted quantities, after which the remainders were given to a charitable organization.
Exist imperf. Value, set $120.

Child with Symbols of Peace — SP15

Mother and Infant — SP16

 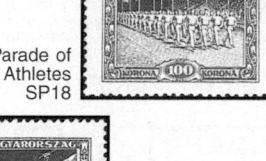

Instruction in Archery — SP17

Wmk. 133

1924, Apr. 8   Engr.   Perf. 12

B77	SP15	300k dark blue	1.75	2.75
a.		Perf. 11½	35.00	30.00
B78	SP16	500k black brown	1.75	2.75
B79	SP17	1000k black green	2.00	4.00
	Nos. B77-B79 (3)		5.50	9.50
	Set, never hinged		12.00	

Each stamp has on the back an inscription stating that it was sold at a premium of 100 per cent over the face value.
Exist imperf. Value, set $100.

Parade of Athletes SP18

Skiing — SP19

Skating — SP20

Diving — SP21

Fencing SP22

Scouts Camping — SP23

Soccer SP24

Hurdling — SP25

Perf. 12, 12½ and Compound

			Unwmk.	
1925		**Typo.**		
B80	SP18	100k bl grn & brn	3.50	4.00
B81	SP19	200k lt brn & myr grn	4.00	5.00
B82	SP20	300k dark blue	5.00	6.00
B83	SP21	400k dp bl & dp grn	5.75	8.00
B84	SP22	500k purple brown	7.50	10.00
B85	SP23	1000k red brown	8.50	11.00
B86	SP24	2000k brown violet	10.00	12.00
B87	SP25	2500k olive brown	12.00	14.00
		Nos. B80-B87 (8)	56.25	70.00
		Set, never hinged	115.00	

These stamps were sold at double face value, plus a premium of 10 per cent on orders sent by mail. They did not serve any postal need and were issued solely to raise funds to aid athletic associations. An inscription regarding the 100 per cent premium is printed on the back of each stamp.

Exist imperf. Value, set $425.

St. Emerich SP26

Sts. Stephen and Gisela SP27

St. Ladislaus SP28

Sts. Gerhardt and Emerich SP29

1930, May 15   Wmk. 210   Perf. 14

B88	SP26	8f + 2f deep green	.45	.40
B89	SP27	16f + 4f brt violet	.50	.70
B90	SP28	20f + 4f deep rose	1.75	2.50
B91	SP29	32f + 8f ultra	2.50	3.75
		Nos. B88-B91 (4)	5.20	7.35
		Set, never hinged	11.00	

900th anniv. of the death of St. Emerich, son of Stephen I, king, saint and martyr.
Exist imperf. Value, set $160.

> **Catalogue values for unused stamps in this section, from this point to the end of the section, are for Never Hinged items.**

St. Ladislaus — SP30

Holy Sacrament SP31

SP32

1938 May 16   Photo.   Perf. 12

B92	SP30	16f + 16f dull slate bl	3.00	3.00
B93	SP31	20f + 20f dk car	3.00	3.00

Souvenir Sheet

B94	SP32	Sheet of 7	50.00	32.50
a.		6f + 6f St. Stephen	4.00	3.00
b.		10f + 10f St. Emerich	4.00	3.00
c.		16f + 16f slate blue (B92)	4.00	3.00
d.		20f + 20f dark carmine (B93)	4.00	3.00
e.		32f + 32f St. Elizabeth	4.00	3.00
f.		40f + 40f St. Maurice	4.00	3.00
g.		50f + 50f St. Margaret	4.00	3.00

Printed in sheets measuring 136½x155mm. Nos. B94c and B94d are slightly smaller than B92 and B93.
Eucharistic Cong. in Budapest, May, 1938.
Exist imperf. Value: set $170; souvenir sheet $4,000.

St. Stephen, Victorious Warrior SP33

St. Stephen, Offering Crown SP34

SP35

1938, Aug. 12   Perf. 12

B95	SP33	10f + 10f violet brn	3.00	3.00
B96	SP34	20f + 20f red org	3.00	3.00

Souvenir Sheet

B97	SP35	Sheet of 7	32.50	20.00
a.		6f + 6f St. Stephen the Missionary	3.25	2.00
b.		10f + 10f violet brown (B95)	3.25	2.00
c.		16f + 16f Seated Upon Throne	3.25	2.00
d.		20f + 20f red orange (B96)	3.25	2.00
e.		32f + 32f Receives Bishops and Monks	3.25	2.00
f.		40f + 40f St. Gisela, St. Stephen and St. Emerich	3.25	2.00
g.		50f + 50f St. Stephen on Bier	3.25	2.00

Death of St. Stephen, 900th anniversary.
No. B97 is on brownish paper, Nos. B95-B96 on white.
Nos. B95-B97 exist imperf. Values: Nos. B95-B96 $150; No. B97 $4,500.

Statue Symbolizing Recovered Territories SP36

Castle of Munkács SP37

Admiral Horthy Entering Komárom SP38

Cathedral of Kassa SP39

Girl Offering Flowers to Soldier — SP40

1939, Jan. 16

B98	SP36	6f + 3f myrtle grn	.60	.35
B99	SP37	10f + 5f olive grn	.25	.20
B100	SP38	20f + 10f dark red	.25	.20
B101	SP39	30f + 15f grnsh blue	1.10	.60
B102	SP40	40f + 20f dk bl gray	1.10	.65
		Nos. B98-B102 (5)	3.30	2.00

The surtax was for the aid of "Hungary for Hungarians" patriotic movement.
Exist imperf. Value, set $250.

Memorial Tablets SP41

Gáspár Károlyi, Translator of the Bible into Hungarian SP42

Albert Molnár de Szenci, Translator of the Psalms SP43

Prince Gabriel Bethlen — SP44

Susanna Lórántffy — SP45

Perf. 12x12½, 12½x12

			Wmk. 210	
1939		**Photo.**		
B103	SP41	6f + 3f green	.70	.55
B104	SP42	10f + 5f claret	.70	.55
B105	SP43	20f + 10f copper red	.80	.75
B106	SP44	32f + 16f bister	1.25	1.00
B107	SP45	40f + 20f chalky blue	1.40	1.00
		Nos. B103-B107 (5)	4.85	3.85

Souvenir Sheets
Perf. 12

B108	SP44	32f olive & vio brn	15.00	15.00

Imperf

B109	SP44	32f bl grn, cop red & gold	15.00	15.00

National Protestant Day. The surtax was used to erect an Intl. Protestant Institute.
The souvenir sheets sold for 1.32p each.
Nos. B103-B108 exist imperf. Values: Nos. B103-B107 $350; No. B108 $4,000.
Issue dates: Nos. B103-B107, Oct. 2. Nos. B108-B109, Oct. 27.

Boy Scout Flying Kite — SP47

Allegory of Flight — SP48

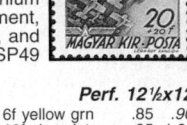

Archangel Gabriel from Millennium Monument, Budapest, and Planes — SP49

1940, Jan. 1   Perf. 12½x12

B110	SP47	6f + 6f yellow grn	.85	.90
B111	SP48	10f + 10f chocolate	.95	1.00
B112	SP49	20f + 20f copper red & gold	1.25	1.40
		Nos. B110-B112 (3)	3.05	3.30

The surtax was used for the Horthy National Aviation Fund.
Exist imperf. Value, set $170.

SP50

Soldier Protecting Family from Floods SP51

Souvenir Sheet
Wmk. 210

1940, May 6   Photo.   Perf. 12

B113	SP50	20f + 1p dk blue grn	6.00	6.00

Exist imperf. Value $4,250.

1940, May

B114	SP51	10f + 2f gray brown	.40	.25
B115	SP51	20f + 4f orange red	.40	.40
B116	SP51	20f + 50f red brown	1.25	1.25
		Nos. B114-B116 (3)	2.05	1.75

The surtax on Nos. B113-B116 was used to aid flood victims.

Exist imperf. Value, set $170.

Hunyadi Coat of
Arms
SP52

King Matthias
SP54

Hunyadi
Castle
SP53

Equestrian
Statue of
King Matthias
SP55

Corvin
Codex — SP56

Equestrian Statue of King
Matthias — SP57

1940   *Perf. 12½x12, 12x12½*
B117 SP52   6f + 3f blue grn   .60   .60
B118 SP53 10f + 5f gldn brn   .60   .60
B119 SP54 16f + 8f dk ol bis   .80   .80
B120 SP55 20f + 10f brick red   .80   .80
B121 SP56 32f + 16f dk gray   1.25   1.10
   Nos. B117-B121 (5)   4.05   3.90

Souvenir Sheet

B122 SP57 20f + 1p dk bl grn &
                    pale grn   6.00   6.00

King Matthias (1440-1490) at Kolozsvar,
Transylvania. The surtax was used for war
relief.
   Nos. B117-B122 exist imperf. Values: Nos.
B117-B121 $220; No. B122 $4,250.
   Issued: #B117-B121, July 1. #B122. Nov. 7.

Hungarian
Soldier — SP58

20f+50f, Virgin Mary and Szekley, symbol-
izing the return of transylvania. 32f+50f,
Szekley Mother Offering Infant Son to the
Fatherland.

1940, Dec. 2   Photo.   *Perf. 12½x12*
B123 SP58 10f + 50f dk blue grn   .95   .95
B124 SP58 20f + 50f brown car   1.00   1.00
B125 SP58 32f + 50f yellow brn   1.25   1.25
   Nos. B123-B125 (3)   3.20   3.20

   Occupation of Transylvania. The surtax was
for the Pro-Transylvania movement.
   Exist imperf. Value, set $200.

Symbol for
Drama
SP61

Symbol for
Sculpture — SP62

Symbols: 16f+16f, Art. 20f+20f, Literature.

1940, Dec. 15   *Perf. 12x12½, 12½x12*
B126 SP61   6f + 6f dark green   1.40   1.25
B127 SP62 10f + 10f olive bis   1.40   1.25
B128 SP62 16f + 16f dk violet   1.40   1.25
B129 SP61 20f + 20f fawn   1.40   1.25
   Nos. B126-B129 (4)   5.60   5.00

Souvenir Sheet

1941, Jan. 5   *Imperf.*
B130   Sheet of 4   6.00   6.00
   a.   SP61 6f + 6f olive brown   1.25   1.25
   b.   SP62 10f + 10f henna brown   1.25   1.25
   c.   SP62 16f + 16f dk blue green 1.25   1.25
   d.   SP61 20f + 20f rose violet   1.25   1.25

   Surtax on #B126-B130 was used for the
Pension and Assistance Institution for Artists.
Nos. B126-B129 exist imperf. Value, set
$70.

Winged Head
of
Pilot — SP66

   Designs: 10f+10f, Boy Scout with model
plane. 20f+20f, Glider in flight. 32f+32f, Our
Lady of Loreto, patroness of Hungarian pilots.

1941, Mar. 24   *Perf. 12x12½*
B131 SP66   6f + 6f grn olive   .55   .50
B132 SP66 10f + 10f dp claret   .55   .50
B133 SP66 20f + 20f org ver   .65   .60
B134 SP66 32f + 32f turq blue   1.60   1.50
   Nos. B131-B134 (4)   3.35   3.10

   The surtax was used to finance civilian and
army pilot training through the Horthy National
Aviation Fund.
   Exist imperf. Value, set $270.

Infantry
SP70

   12f+18f, Heavy artillery. 20f+30f, Plane and
tanks. 40f+60f, Cavalryman and cyclist.

1941, Dec. 1   Photo.   Wmk. 266
Inscribed: "Honvedeink
Karacsonyara 1941"
B135 SP70   8f + 12f dk green   .50   .50
B136 SP70 12f + 18f olive grn   .50   .50
B137 SP70 20f + 30f slate   .60   .60
B138 SP70 40f + 60f red brown   .60   .60
   Nos. B135-B138 (4)   2.20   2.20

   The surtax was for the benefit of the Army.
Exist imperf. Value, set $275.

Soldier and
Emblem
SP74

1941, Dec. 1
B139 SP74 20f + 40f dark red   2.25 2.25

   The surtax was for the soldiers' Christmas.
Exists imperf. Value $70.

Aviator and
Plane — SP75

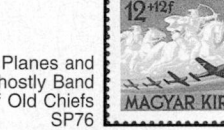

Planes and
Ghostly Band
of Old Chiefs
SP76

Plane and
Archer
SP77

Aviators and
Plane — SP78

1942, Mar. 15   *Perf. 12½x12, 12x12½*
B140 SP75   8f + 8f dark green   .80   .80
B141 SP76 12f + 12f sapphire   .80   .80
B142 SP77 20f + 20f brown   .80   .80
B143 SP78 30f + 30f dark red   .80   .80
   Nos. B140-B143 (4)   3.20   3.20

   The surtax aided the Horthy National Aviation Fund.
   Exist imperf. Value, set $270.

Blood
Transfusion — SP79

   Designs: 8f+32f, Bandaging wounded soldier. 12f+50f, Radio and carrier pigeons.
20f+1p, Widows and orphans.

1942, Sept. 1   *Perf. 12½x12*
B144 SP79   3f + 18f dk ol & red   1.60   1.50
B145 SP79   8f + 32f dp brn &
                    red   1.60   1.50
B146 SP79 12f + 50f dp cl & red   1.60   1.50
B147 SP79 20f + 1p slate bl &
                    red   1.60   1.50
   Nos. B144-B147 (4)   6.40   6.00

   The surtax aided the Hungarian Red Cross.
Sheets of 10. Value set $85.
   Exist imperf. Value, set $300.

Widow of Stephen
Horthy — SP83

Red Cross
Nurse Aiding
Soldier
SP84

Magdalene
Horthy Mother of
Stephen
Horthy — SP85

1942, Dec. 1   *Perf. 13, Imperf.*
B148 SP83   6f + 1p vio bl &
                    red   3.00   3.00
   a.   Sheet of 4   27.50 27.50
B149 SP84   8f + 1p dk ol grn
                    & red   3.00   3.00
   a.   Sheet of 4   27.50 27.50
B150 SP85 20f + 1p dk red
                    brn & red   3.00   3.00
   a.   Sheet of 4   27.50 27.50
   Nos. B148-B150 (3)   9.00   9.00

   The surtax aided the Hungarian Red Cross.

King Ladislaus I
    SP86   SP87

1942, Dec. 21   Wmk. 266   *Perf. 12*
B151 SP86   6f + 6f olive gray   .80   1.00
B152 SP87   8f + 8f green   .80   1.00
B153 SP86 12f + 12f dull violet   .80   1.00
B154 SP87 20f + 20f Prus green   .80   1.00
B155 SP86 24f + 24f brown   .80   1.00
B156 SP87 30f + 30f rose car   .80   1.00
   Nos. B151-B156 (6)   4.80   6.00

   900th anniv. of the birth of St. Ladislaus
(1040-95), the 700th anniv. of the beginning of
the country's reconstruction by King Béla IV
(1206-70) and the 600th anniv. of the accession of King Lajos the Great (1326-82).
   The surtax aided war invalids and their
families.
   Exist imperf. Value, set $350.

Archer on
Horseback
SP92

Knight with Sword
and
Shield — SP93

Old Magyar
Arms — SP94

Designs: 3f+1f, 4f+1f, Warrior with shield
and battle ax. 12f+2f, Knight with lance,
20f+2f, Musketeer. 40f+4f, Hussar. 50f+6f,
Artilleryman.

1943
B157	SP92	1f + 1f dk gray	.20	.35
B158	SP93	3f + 1f dull violet	.50	.80
B159	SP93	4f + 1f lake	.20	.35
B160	SP93	8f + 2f green	.20	.35
B161	SP93	12f + 2f bister brn	.20	.35
B162	SP93	20f + 2f dp claret	.20	.35
B163	SP93	40f + 4f gray vio	.20	.35
B164	SP93	50f + 6f org brn	.25	.35
B165	SP94	70f + 8f slate blue	.40	.35
		Nos. B157-B165 (9)	2.35	3.60

The surtax aided war invalids.
Exist imperf. Value, set $270.

Model
Glider — SP101

Gliders — SP102

White-tailed Sea
Eagle and
Planes — SP103

ME-109E Fighter
and
Gliders — SP104

1943, July 17
B166	SP101	8f + 8f green	.80	1.00
B167	SP102	12f + 12f royal blue	.80	1.00
B168	SP103	20f + 20f chestnut	.80	1.00
B169	SP104	30f + 30f rose car	.80	1.00
		Nos. B166-B169 (4)	3.20	4.00

The surtax aided the Horthy National Aviation Fund.
Exist imperf. Value, set $270.

Stephen
Horthy
SP105

1943, Aug. 16
B170	SP105	30f + 20f dp rose vio	.55	.50

The surtax aided the Horthy National Aviation Fund.
Exists imperf. Value $70.

Nurse and
Soldier
SP106

Designs: 30f+30f, Soldier, nurse, mother
and child. 50f+50f, Nurse keeping lamp alight.
70f+70f, Wounded soldier and tree shoot.

1944, Mar. 1
Cross in Red
B171	SP106	20f + 20f brown	.55	.40
B172	SP106	30f + 30f henna	.55	.40
B173	SP106	50f + 50f brown vio	.65	.40
B174	SP106	70f + 70f Prus blue	.65	.40
		Nos. B171-B174 (4)	2.40	1.60

The surtax aided the Hungarian Red Cross.
Exist imperf. Value, set $270.

Issues of the Republic
Types of 1944 Surcharged in Red or
Black:

a

b

1945, July 23　　Wmk. 266　　Perf. 12
B175	A115(a)	3p + 9p on 20f dk ol grn, *yel*	.40	1.00
B176	A114(b)	4p + 12p on 4f yel brn, *bl* (Bk)	.40	1.00
B177	A117(b)	8p + 24p on 50f sl bl, *yel*	.40	1.00
B178	A115(a)	10p + 30p on 30f hn brn, *bl* (Bk)	.40	1.00
		Nos. B175-B178 (4)	1.60	4.00

The surtax was for the Peoples Universities.
"Béke" means "peace".

Imre Sallai
and Sandor
Fürst
SP110

Designs: 3p+3p, L. Kabok and Illes Monus.
4p+4p, Ferenc Rozsa and Zoltan Schonerz.
6p+6p, Anna Koltai and Mrs. Paul Knurr.
10p+10p, George Sarkozi and Imre Nagy.
15p+15p, Vilmos Tartsay and Jeno Nagy.
20p+20p, Janos Kiss and Andreas Bajcsy-
Zsilinszky. 40p+40p, Endre Sagvari and Otto
Hoffmann.

1945, Oct. 6　　　　　　Photo.
B179	SP110	2p + 2p yel brn	1.75	1.75
B180	SP110	3p + 3p deep red	1.75	1.75
B181	SP110	4p + 4p dk pur	1.75	1.75
B182	SP110	6p + 6p dk yel grn	1.75	1.75
B183	SP110	10p + 10p dp car	1.75	1.75
B184	SP110	15p + 15p dk sl grn	1.75	1.75
B185	SP110	20p + 20p dk brn	1.75	1.75
B186	SP110	40p + 40p dp bl	1.75	1.75
		Nos. B179-B186 (8)	14.00	14.00

The surtax was for child welfare.
Exist imperf. Value, set $150.

Andreas Bajcsy-Zsilinszky and
Eagle — SP111

1945, May 27
B187	SP111	1p + 1p dk brn vio	.90	.90

1st anniv. of the death of Andreas Bajcsy-
Zsilinszky, hanged by the Nazis for anti-fascist
activities.
Exists imperf. Value $135.

Lion with
Broken
Shackles
SP112

1946, May 1
B188	SP112	500ez + 500ez p p	2.25	2.25
B189	SP112	1mil p + 1mil p	2.25	2.25
B190	SP112	1.5mil p + 1.5mil p	2.25	2.25
B191	SP112	2mil p + 2mil p	2.25	2.25
		Nos. B188-B191 (4)	9.00	9.00

75th anniv. of Hungary's 1st postage stamp.
The surtax was for the benefit of postal
employees.
Exist imperf. Value, set $135.

"Agriculture"
Holding
Wheat — SP113

Physician with
Syringe — SP114

1946, Sept. 7　　　　　　Photo.
B192	SP113	30f + 60f dp yel grn	5.00	7.00
B193	SP113	60f + 1.20fo rose brn	5.00	7.00
B194	SP113	1fo + 2fo dp blue	5.00	7.00
		Nos. B192-B194 (3)	15.00	21.00

1st Agricultural Congress and Exhibition.
Exist imperf. Value, set $325.

Perf. 12½x12
1947, May 16　　　　　　Wmk. 210
Designs: 12f+50f, Physician examining X-
ray picture. 20f+50f, Nurse and child. 60f+50f,
Prisoner of war starting home.
B195	SP114	8f + 50f ultra	3.75	5.00
B196	SP114	12f + 50f choc	3.75	5.00
B197	SP114	20f + 50f dk grn	3.75	5.00
B198	SP114	60f + 50f dk red	1.00	1.25
		Nos. B195-B198 (4)	12.25	16.25

The surtax was for charitable purposes.
Exist imperf. Value, set $400.

Franklin D.
Roosevelt
and Freedom
of Speech
Allegory
SP115

Pres. F. D. Roosevelt and Allegory: 12f+12f,
Freedom of Religion. 20f+20f, Freedom from
Want. 30f+30f, Freedom from Fear.

1947, June 11　Photo.　Perf. 12x12½
Portrait in Sepia
B198A	SP115	8f + 8f dark red	4.00	5.25
B198B	SP115	12f + 12f deep green	4.00	5.25
B198C	SP115	20f + 20f brown	4.00	5.25
B198D	SP115	30f + 30f blue	4.00	5.25
		Nos. B198A-B198D,CB1-CB1C (8)	33.00	42.00

Exist imperf. Value, set $250.
Nos. B198A-B198D and CB1-CB1C were
also printed in sheets of 4 of each denomination (size: 117x96mm). Value, set of 8, $700.
Exist imperf. Value $900.
A souvenir sheet exists, containing one
each of Nos. B198A-B198D with border
inscriptions and decorations in brown. Size:
161x122mm. Value $125. Exists imperf. Size
$250.

Lenin — SP118

XVI Century
Mail Coach
SP119

Designs: 60f+60f, Soviet Cenotaph, Budapest. 1fo+1fo, Joseph V. Stalin.

1947, Oct. 29　Photo.　Wmk. 283
B199	SP118	40f + 40f ol grn & org brn	4.50	5.50
B200	SP118	60f + 60f red & sl bl	2.00	2.00
B201	SP118	1fo + 1fo vio & brn blk	4.50	5.50
		Nos. B199-B201 (3)	11.00	13.00

The surtax was for the Hungarian-Soviet
Cultural Association.
Exist imperf. Value, set $475.

1947, Dec. 21　　　　　Perf. 12x12½
B202	SP119	30f (+ 50f) hn brn	9.50	10.00
		Sheet of 4	55.00	55.00

Stamp Day. The surtax paid admission to a
philatelic exhibition in any of eight Hungarian
towns, where the stamps were sold.
No. B202 exists imperf. Values: single $800;
sheetlet of 4 $4,000.

Globe and
Carrier
Pigeon — SP120

Woman
Worker — SP121

1948, Oct. 17　　　　　Perf. 12½x12
B203	SP120	30f (+ 1fo) grnsh bl	5.00	5.00
		Sheet of 4	40.00	40.00

5th Natl. Hungarian Stamp Exhib., Budapest. Each stamp sold for 1.30 forint, which
included admission to the exhibition.
Exists imperf. Value: single $450; sheetlet
$2,250.

1949, Mar. 8
B204	SP121	60f + 60f magenta	2.50	2.50

Intl. Woman's Day, Mar. 8, 1949. The surtax
was for the Democratic Alliance of Hungarian
Women.
Exists imperf. Value $70.

Aleksander S.
Pushkin — SP122

SP123

1949, June 6   **Photo.**
B205 SP122 1fo + 1fo car lake   9.00   9.00

Souvenir Sheet
Perf. 12½x12,
Imperf

B206 SP123 1fo + 1fo red vio
     & car lake   15.00   15.00

150th anniversary of the birth of Aleksander S. Pushkin. The surtax was for the Hungarian-Russian Culture Society.
No. B205 exists imperf. Value $220.

IMPERFORATE STAMPS
    Through 1991, most semi-postal stamps were also issued imperforate. Where these items form part of a larger set with regular issues, values for imperfs will be included in that of the sets to which they belong, footnoted in the Regular Issues section. For Nos. B207-B345, values for imperfs will be given only for those items not included in sets with regular issues.

1st Stamp Type
Perf. 12½x12
1951, Oct. 6   **Engr.**   **Unwmk.**
B207 A208 1fo + 1fo red   7.50   7.00
B208 A208 2fo + 2fo blue   12.50   11.50
     Exists imperf.

Postwoman
Delivering
Mail — SP124

1953, Nov. 1   **Wmk. 106**   **Perf. 12**
B209 SP124 1fo + 1fo blue grn   4.00   1.25
B210 SP124 2fo + 2fo rose vio   4.00   1.25
     Stamp Day, Nov. 1, 1953.
     Exist imperf. Value. $60.

Stamps of
1955
Surcharged
in Red or
Lake

1957, Jan. 31   **Photo.**   **Perf. 12x12½**
B211 A249 20f + 20f olive grn   .20   .20
B212 A249 30f + 30f dk red (L)   .25   .25
    a.   Red (cross) inverted   450.00
B213 A249 40f + 40f brown   .30   .25
B214 A249 60f + 60f brn red
     (L)   .50   .50
B215 A249 1fo + 1fo blue   .75   .50
B216 A249 2fo + 2fo rose brn   1.00   .90
     Nos. B211-B216 (6)   3.00   2.40
The surtax was for the Hungarian Red Cross.
    Exist imperf. Value, set $135.

Winter Olympic Type of 1960
Design: Olympic Games emblem.

Perf. 11½x12
1960, Feb. 29   **Wmk. 106**
B217 A295 2fo + 1fo multi   .90   .35
     Exists imperf.

Olympic Type of 1960
Design: 2fo+1fo, Romulus and Remus.

Perf. 11½x12
1960, Aug. 21   **Photo.**   **Wmk. 106**
B218 A299 2fo + 1fo multi   .75   .30
     Exists imperf.

Sport Club Type of 1961
Sport: 2fo+1fo, Sailboats.

1961, July 8   **Unwmk.**   **Perf. 14½**
B219 A313 2fo + 1fo multi   .35   .20
     Exists imperf.

St. Margaret's Island and
Danube — SP125

Views of Budapest: No. B221, Fishermen's Bastion. No. B222, Coronation Church and Chain Bridge. No. B223, Mount Gellert.

Unwmk.
1961, Sept. 24   **Photo.**   **Perf. 12**
B220 SP125 2fo + 1fo multi   .70   .70
B221 SP125 2fo + 1fo multi   .70   .70
B222 SP125 2fo + 1fo multi   .70   .70
B223 SP125 2fo + 1fo multi   .70   .70
    a.   Horiz. strip of 4, #B220-B223   3.00   3.00
Stamp Day, 1961, and Budapest Intl. Stamp Exhibition.
No. B223a has a continuous design.
Exist imperf. Value, strip $32.
Miniature presentation sheets, perf. and imperf., contain one each of Nos. B220-B223; size: 204x66½mm. Value for both sheets, $2,000.

Soccer Type of Regular Issue, 1962
Design: Flags of Spain and Czechoslovakia.

1962, May 21   **Perf. 11**
Flags in Original Colors
B224 A323 4fo + 1fo lt grn & bister   2.50   .30
     Exists imperf.

Austrian Stamp of
1850 with Pesth
Postmark
SP126

Stamps: No. B226, #201. No. B227, #C164. No. B228, #C208.

Lithographed and Engraved
1962, Sept. 22   **Unwmk.**   **Perf. 11**
Design and Inscription
in Dark Brown
B225 SP126 2fo + 1fo yellow   .55   .55
B226 SP126 2fo + 1fo pale
     pink   .55   .55
B227 SP126 2fo + 1fo pale
     blue   .55   .55
B228 SP126 2fo + 1fo pale yel
     grn   .55   .55
    a.   Horiz. strip of 4, #B225-B228   2.50   2.25
    b.   Souv. sheet of 4, #B225-B228   6.00   6.00
35th Stamp Day and 10th anniv. of Mabeosz, the Hungarian Phil. Fed.
    Exist imperf. Value: strip $23; souvenir sheet $45.

Emblem, Cup
and Soccer
Ball — SP127

1962, Nov. 18   **Photo.**   **Perf. 11½x12**
B229 SP127 2fo + 1fo multi   .60   .50
Winning of the "Coupe de l'Europe Centrale" by the Steel Workers Sport Club (VASAS) in the Central European Soccer Championships.
Exists imperf. Value $7.

Stamp
Day — SP128

1963, Oct. 24   **Perf. 11½x12**
Size: 32x43mm
B230 SP128 2fo + 1fo Hyacinth   .50   .50
B231 SP128 2fo + 1fo Narcissus   .50   .50
B232 SP128 2fo + 1fo Chrysanthemum   .50   .50
B233 SP128 2fo + 1fo Tiger lily   .50   .50
    a.   Horiz. strip of 4, #B230-B233   3.00   3.00
    b.   Min. sheet of 4, #B230-B233   3.50   3.50
#B233b contains 25x32mm stamps, perf. 11.
    Exist imperf. Value: strip $25; miniature sheet $40.

Winter Olympic Type of 1963
Design: 4fo+1fo, Bobsledding.

1963, Nov. 11   **Perf. 12**
B234 A342 4fo + 1fo grnsh bl & bis   .70   .30
     Exists imperf.

New Year Type of Regular Issue
Good Luck Symbols: 2.50fo+1.20fo, Horseshoe, mistletoe and clover. 3fo+1.50fo, Pigs, clover and balloon, horiz.

Perf. 12x11½, 11½x12
1963, Dec. 12   **Photo.**   **Unwmk.**
Sizes: 28x39mm (#B235); 28x22mm
(#B206)
B235 A343 2.50fo + 1.20fo multi   .50   .25
B236 A343 3fo + 1.50fo multi   .70   .35
The surtax was for the modernization of the Hungarian Postal and Philatelic Museum.
Exist imperf.

Olympic Type of Regular Issue
Design: 3fo+1fo, Water polo.

1964, June 12   **Perf. 11**
B237 A352 3fo + 1fo multi   .60   .75
     Exists imperf.

Exhibition Hall — SP129

1964, July 23   **Photo.**
B238 SP129 3fo + 1.50fo blk, red org & gray   .60   .35
Tennis Exhibition, Budapest Sports Museum.
Exists imperf. Value $10.

Twirling Woman
Gymnast
SP130

1964, Sept. 4   **Perf. 11½x12**
Size: 27x38mm
B239 SP130 2fo + 1fo Lilac   .45   .45
B240 SP130 2fo + 1fo Mallards   .45   .45
B241 SP130 2fo + 1fo Gymnast   .45   .45
B242 SP130 2fo + 1fo Rocket & globe   .45   .45
    a.   Horiz. strip of 4, #B239-B242   2.25   2.25
    b.   Souv. sheet of 4, #B239-B242   3.25   3.25
37th Stamp Day and Intl. Topical Stamp Exhib., IMEX. No. B242b contains 4 20x28mm stamps, perf. 11.
    Exist imperf. Value: strip $20; souvenir sheet $37.50.

13th
Century
Tennis
SP131

History of Tennis: 40f+10f, Indoor tennis, 16th century. 60f+10f, Tennis, 18th century. 70f+30f, Tennis court and castle. 80f+40f, Tennis court, Fontainebleau (buildings). 1fo+50f, Tennis, 17th century. 1.50fo+50f, W. C. Wingfield, Wimbledon champion 1877, and Wimbledon Cup. 1.70fo+50f, Davis Cup, 1900. 2fo+1fo, Bela Kehrling (1891-1937), Hungarian champion.

Lithographed and Engraved
1965, June 15   **Unwmk.**   **Perf. 12**
B243 SP131 30f + 10f mar, dl org   .20   .20
B244 SP131 40f + 10f blk, pale lil   .20   .20
B245 SP131 60f + 10f grn, ol   .20   .20
B246 SP131 70f + 30f lil, brt grn   .25   .20
B247 SP131 80f + 40f dk bl, lt vio   .25   .20
B248 SP131 1fo + 50f grn, yel   .25   .20
B249 SP131 1.50fo + 50f sep, lt ol grn   .30   .25
B250 SP131 1.70fo + 50f ind, lt bl   .35   .25
B251 SP131 2fo + 1fo dk red, lt grn   .50   .30
     Nos. B243-B251 (9)   2.50   2.00
    Exist imperf. Value, set $25.

Flood
Scene
SP132

10fo+5fo, Relief commemorating 1838 flood.

1965, Aug. 14   **Photo.**   **Perf. 12x11½**
B252 SP132 1fo + 50f org brn & bl   .30   .30

Souvenir Sheet
B253 SP132 10fo + 5fo gldn brn & buff   2.75   2.75
Surtax for aid to 1965 flood victims.
Exist imperf. Value: No. B252 $7; No. B253 $25.

Geranium
Stamp of
1950 (No.
909)
SP133

Stamp Day: No. B255, #120. No. B256, #1489. No. B257, #1382.

Perf. 12x11½
1965, Oct. 30 Photo. Unwmk.
Stamps in Original Colors

B254	SP133 2fo + 1fo gray & dk bl	.65	.60
B255	SP133 2fo + 1fo gray & red	.65	.60
B256	SP133 2fo + 1fo gray & ocher	.65	.60
B257	SP133 2fo + 1fo gray & vio	.65	.60
a.	Horiz. strip of 4, #B254-B257	3.00	3.00
b.	Souv. sheet of 4, #B254-B257	3.50	3.25

#B254b contains 32x23mm stamps, perf. 11.
Exist imperf. Value: No. B257a $20; No. B257b $30.

Soccer Type of Regular Issue

Design: 3fo+1fo, Championship emblem and map of Great Britain showing cities where matches were held.

1966, June 6 Photo. Perf. 12x11½
B258	A382 3fo + 1fo multi	.60	.50

Exists imperf.

Woman Archer and Danube at Visegrad SP134

Stamp Day: No. B260, Gloria Hungariae grapes and Lake Balaton. No. B261, Red poppies and ruins of Diosgyor Castle. No. B262, Russian space dogs Ugolek and Veterok.

1966, Sept. 16 Photo. Perf. 12x11½
B259	SP134 2fo + 50f multi	.60	.60
B260	SP134 2fo + 50f multi	.60	.60
B261	SP134 2fo + 50f multi	.60	.60
B262	SP134 2fo + 50f multi	.60	.60
a.	Horiz. strip of 4, #B259-B262	2.75	2.75
b.	Souv. sheet of 4, #B259-B262	2.75	2.75

#B262b contains 4 29x21mm stamps, perf. 11.
Exist imperf. Value: B262a $20; B262b $35.

Anglers, C.I.P.S. Emblem and View of Danube SP135

1967, Aug. 22 Photo. Perf. 12x11½
B263	SP135 3fo + 1fo multi	.90	.45

See note after No. 1847.
Exists imperf.

Olympic Type of Regular Issue
Indoor stadium & Winter Olympics emblem.

1968, Jan. 29 Photo. Perf. 11
B264	A402 4fo + 1fo multi	.70	.30

Exists imperf.

Jug, Western Hungary, 1618 SP136

Hungarian Earthenware: No. B266, Tiszafüred vase, 1847. No. B267, Toby jug, 1848. No. B268, Decorative Baja plate, 1870. No. B269a, Jug, Northern Hungary, 1672. No. B269b, Decorative Mezöcsat plate, 1843. No. B269c, Decorative Moragy plate, 1860. No. B269d, Pitcher, Debrecen, 1793.

1968, Oct. 5 Litho. Perf. 12
B265	SP136 1fo + 50f ultra & multl	.50	.50
B266	SP136 1fo + 50f sky bl & multi	.50	.50
B267	SP136 1fo + 50f sepia & multi	.50	.50
B268	SP136 1fo + 50f yel brn & multi	.50	.50
	Nos. B265-B268 (4)	2.00	2.00

Miniature Sheet
B269	Sheet of 4	2.75	2.50
a.	SP136 2fo + 50f ultra & multi	.45	.40
b.	SP136 2fo + 50f yel brn & multi	.45	.40
c.	SP136 2fo + 50f olive & multi	.45	.40
d.	SP136 2fo + 50f brt rose & multi	.45	.40

Issued for 41st Stamp Day. No. B269 contains 4 25x36mm stamps. See Nos. B271-B275.
Exist imperf. Value: Nos. B265-B268 $20; No. B269 $20.

Suspension Bridge, Buda Castle and Arms of Budapest — SP137

Lithographed and Engraved
1969, May 22 Perf. 12
B270	SP137 5fo + 2fo sep, pale yel & gray	1.00	1.00

Budapest 71 Philatelic Exposition.
Exists imperf. Value $9.

Folk Art Type of 1968
Hungarian Wood Carvings: No. B271, Stirrup cup from Okorag, 1880. No. B272, Jar with flower decorations from Felsötiszavidek, 1898. No. B273, Round jug, Somogyharsagy, 1935. No. B274, Two-legged jug, Alföld, 1740. No. B275a, Carved panel (farm couple), Csorna, 1879. No. B275b, Tankard, Okany, 1914. No. B275c, Round jar with soldiers, Sellye, 1899. No. B275d, Square box with 2 women, Lengyeltoti, 1880.

1969, Sept. 13 Litho. Perf. 12
B271	SP136 1fo + 50f rose cl & multi	.60	.60
B272	SP136 1fo + 50f dp bis & multi	.60	.60
B273	SP136 1fo + 50f bl & multi	.60	.60
B274	SP136 1fo + 50f lt bl grn & multi	.60	.60
	Nos. B271-B274 (4)	2.40	2.40

Miniature Sheet
B275	Sheet of 4	2.75	2.50
a.	SP136 2fo + 50f ultra & multi	.50	.45
b.	SP136 2fo + 50f brn org & multi	.50	.45
c.	SP136 2fo + 50f lt brn & multi	.50	.45
d.	SP136 2fo + 50f bl grn & multi	.50	.45

Issued for the 42nd Stamp Day. No. B275 contains 4 stamps (size: 25x36mm).
Exists imperf. Value: B271-B274 $20; B275 $20.

Fishermen's Bastion, Coronation Church and Chain Bridge — SP138

Designs: No. B277, Parliament and Elizabeth Bridge. No. B278, Castle and Margaret Bridge.

1970, Mar. 7 Litho. Perf. 12
B276	SP138 2fo + 1fo gldn brn & multi	.60	.60
B277	SP138 2fo + 1fo bl & multi	.60	.60
B278	SP138 2fo + 1fo lt vio & multi	.60	.60
	Nos. B276-B278 (3)	1.80	1.80

Budapest 71 Philatelic Exhibition, commemorating the centenary of Hungarian postage stamps.
Exist imperf. Value, set $20.

King Matthias I Corvinus SP139

Initials and Paintings from Bibliotheca Corvina: No. B280, Letter "A." No. B281, Letter "N." No. B282, Letter "O." No. B283a, Ransanus Speaking before King Matthias. No. B283b, Scholar and letter "Q." No. B283c, Portrait of Appianus and letter "C." No. B283d, King David and letter "A."

1970, Aug. 22 Photo. Perf. 11½x12
B279	SP139 1fo + 50f multi	.40	.40
B280	SP139 1fo + 50f multi	.40	.40
B281	SP139 1fo + 50f multi	.40	.40
B282	SP139 1fo + 50f multi	.40	.40
	Nos. B279-B282 (4)	1.60	1.60

Miniature Sheet
B283	Sheet of 4	2.75	2.50
a.-d.	SP139 2fo + 50f, any single	.50	.45

Issued for the 43rd Stamp Day. No. B283 contains 4 stamps (size: 22½x32mm).
Exist imperf. Value: Nos. B279-B282 $20; B283 $25.

View of Buda, 1470 — SP140

#B285, Buda, 1600. #B286, Buda and Pest, about 1638. #B287, Buda and Pest, 1770. #B288a, Buda, 1777. #B288b, Buda, 1850. #B288c, Buda, 1895. #B288d, Budapest, 1970.

1971, Feb. 26 Litho. Perf. 12
B284	SP140 2fo + 1fo blk & yel	.60	.60
B285	SP140 2fo + 1fo blk & pink	.60	.60
B286	SP140 2fo + 1fo blk & pale grn	.60	.60
B287	SP140 2fo + 1fo blk & pale sal	.60	.60
	Nos. B284-B287 (4)	2.40	2.40

Souvenir Sheet
Perf. 10½
B288	Sheet of 4	2.50	2.25
a.	SP140 2fo + 1fo blk & pale sal	.50	.45
b.	SP140 2fo + 1fo blk & pale grn	.50	.45
c.	SP140 2fo + 1fo blk & lilac	.50	.45
d.	SP140 2fo + 1fo blk & pink	.50	.45

Budapest 71 Intl. Stamp Exhib. for the cent. of Hungarian postage stamps, Budapest, Sept. 4-12. No. B288 contains 4 stamps, size: 39½x18mm.
Exist imperf. Value: Nos. B284-B287 $17.50; No. B288 $20.

Iris and #P1 SP141

Designs: No. B290, Daisy and #199. No. B291, Poppy and #391. No. B292, Rose and #B128. No. B293a, Carnations and #200. No. B293b, Dahlia and #1068. No. B293c, Tulips and #C196. No. B293d, Anenomes and #C251.

1971, Sept. 4 Photo. Perf. 12x11½
B289	SP141 2fo + 1fo sil & multi	.70	.70
B290	SP141 2fo + 1fo sil & multi	.70	.70
B291	SP141 2fo + 1fo sil & multi	.70	.70
B292	SP141 2fo + 1fo sil & multi	.70	.70
	Nos. B289-B292 (4)	2.80	2.80

Souvenir Sheet
Perf. 11½
B293	Sheet of 4	2.75	2.50
a.-d.	SP141 2fo + 1fo, any single	.50	.45

Cent. of 1st Hungarian postage stamps and in connection with Budapest 71 Intl. Stamp Exhib., Sept. 4-12.
Exist imperf. Value: Nos. B289-B292 $20; No. B293 $35.

Miskólcz Postmark, 1818-43 — SP142

Postmarks: No. B295, Szegedin, 1827-48. No. B296, Esztergom, 1848-51. No. B297, Budapest 1971 Exhibition. No. B298a, Paar family signet, 1593. No. B298b, Courier letter, 1708. No. B298c, First well-known Hungarian postmark "V. TOKAI," 1752. No. B298d, Letter, 1705.

1972, May Perf. 12x11½
B294	SP142 2fo + 1fo blue & blk	.70	.70
B295	SP142 2fo + 1fo yel & blk	.70	.70
B296	SP142 2fo + 1fo yel grn & blk	.70	.70
B297	SP142 2fo + 1fo ver & multi	.70	.70
	Nos. B294-B297 (4)	2.80	2.80

Souvenir Sheet
B298	Sheet of 4	2.50	2.25
a.	SP142 2fo + 1fo yel grn & multi	.50	.45
b.	SP142 2fo + 1fo brn & multi	.50	.45
c.	SP142 2fo + 1fo ultra & multi	.50	.45
d.	SP142 2fo + 1fo red & multi	.50	.45

9th Congress of National Federation of Hungarian Philatelists (Mabeosz). No. B298 contains 4 stamps (size: 32x23mm).
Exist imperf. Value: Nos. B294-B297 $20; No. B298 $22.

Olympic Type of Regular Issue
Design: Wrestling and Olympic rings.

1972, July 15 Photo. Perf. 11
B299	A484 3fo + 1fo multi	.50	.30

Exists imperf.

Historic Mail Box, Telephone and Molnya Satellite — SP143

Design: No. B301, Post horn, Tokai postmark, and Nos. 183, 1802, 1809.

1972, Oct. 27 Litho. Perf. 12
B300	SP143 4fo + 2fo grn & multi	.80	.70
B301	SP143 4fo + 2fo bl & multi	.80	.70

Reopening of the Post and Philatelic Museums, Budapest.
Exist imperf. Value, set $17.50.

Bird on Silver Disk, 10th Century SP144

Treasures from Hungarian Natl. Museum. No. B303, Ring with serpent's head, 11th cent. No. B304, Lovers, belt buckle, 12th cent. No. B305, Flower, belt buckle, 15th cent. No. B306a, Opal pendant, 16th cent. No. B306b, Jeweled belt buckle, 18th cent. No. B306c, Flower pin, 17th cent. No. B306d, Rosette pendant, 17th cent.

1973, Sept. 22   Litho.   Perf. 12

B302 SP144 2fo + 50f brn & multi .65 .65
B303 SP144 2fo + 50f brt rose lil & multi .65 .65
B304 SP144 2fo + 50f dk bl & multi .65 .65
B305 SP144 2fo + 50f grn & multi .65 .65

Nos. B302-B305 (4) 2.60 2.60

Souvenir Sheet

B306 Sheet of 4 2.50 2.50
a. SP144 2fo + 50f brown & multi .35 .35
b. SP144 2fo + 50f car & multi .35 .35
c. SP144 2fo + 50f ol grn & multi .35 .35
d. SP144 2fo + 50f brt bl & multi .35 .35

46th Stamp Day. No. B306 contains 4 stamps (size: 25x35mm).
Exist imperf. Value: Nos. B302-B305 $20; No. B306 $25.

Gothic Wall Fountain SP145

Visegrad Castle and Bas-reliefs — SP146

Designs: No. B308, Wellhead, Anjou period. No. B309, Twin lion-head wall fountain. B310, Fountain with Hercules riding dolphin. No. B311a, Raven panel. No. B311b, Visegrad Madonna. B311c, Lion panel. No. B311d, Visegrad Castle. Designs show artworks from Visegrad Palace of King Matthias Corvinus I, 15th century. Illustration SP146 is reduced.

1975, Sept. 13   Litho.   Perf. 12
Multicolored and:

B307 SP145 2fo + 1fo green 2.00 2.00
B308 SP145 2fo + 1fo ver 2.00 2.00
B309 SP145 2fo + 1fo blue 2.00 2.00
B310 SP145 2fo + 1fo lilac 2.00 2.00
a. Horizontal strip of 4 9.00 8.50

Souvenir Sheet

B311 SP146 Sheet of 4 10.00 10.00
a. 2fo + 1fo 21x32mm 1.40 1.40
b. 2fo + 1fo 47x32mm 1.40 1.40
c. 2fo + 1fo 21x32mm 1.40 1.40
d. 2fo + 1fo 99x32mm 1.40 1.40

European Architectural Heritage Year 1975 and 48th Stamp Day.
Exist imperf. Value: Nos. B307-B310 $250; No. B311 $250.

Knight SP147

Gothic Sculptures, Buda Castle — SP148

Gothic sculptures from Buda Castle.

1976   Photo.   Perf. 12

B312 SP147 2.50 + 1fo shown .60 .60
B313 SP147 2.50 + 1fo Armor-bearer .60 .60
B314 SP147 2.50 + 1fo Apostle .60 .60
B315 SP147 2.50 + 1fo Bishop .60 .60
a. Horizontal strip of 4, #B312-B315 2.75 2.75

Souvenir Sheet

Designs: a, Man with hat. b, Woman with wimple. c, Man with cloth cap. d, Man with fur hat.

B316 Sheet of 4 3.00 3.00
a.-d. SP148 2.50 + 1fo any single .55 .55

49th Stamp Day.
No. B316 issued in connection with 10th Congress of National Federation of Hungarian Philatelists (Mabeosz).
Exist imperf. Value: Nos. B312-B315 $20; No. B316 $25.
Issued: #B316, May 22; #B312-B315, Sept. 4.

Young Runners SP149

1977, Apr. 2   Litho.   Perf. 12
B317 SP149 3fo + 1.50fo multi .85 .85

Sports promotion among young people.
Exists imperf. Value $7.

Young Man and Woman, Profiles SP150

1978, Apr. 1   Litho.   Perf. 12
B318 SP150 3fo + 1.50fo multi .90 .90

Hungarian Communist Youth Movement, 60th anniversary.
Exists imperf. Value $12.

"Generations," by Gyula Derkovits SP151

1978, May 6   Litho.   Perf. 12
B319 SP151 3fo + 1.50fo multi .90 .90

Szocfilex '78, Szombathely. No. B319 printed in sheets of 3 stamps and 3 labels showing Szocfilex emblem.
Exists imperf. Value: single $7; sheetlet $22.50.

Girl Reading Book, by Ferenc Kovacs SP152

1979, Mar. 31   Litho.   Perf. 12
B320 SP152 3fo + 1.50fo blk & ultra .45 .45

Surtax was for Junior Stamp Exhibition, Bekescsaba.
Exists imperf. Value $7.

Watch Symbolizing Environmental Protection SP153

1980, Apr. 3   Litho.   Perf. 12
B321 SP153 3fo + 1.50fo multi .70 .70

Surtax was for Junior Stamp Exhibition, Dunaujvaros.
Exists imperf. Value $5.50.

International Year of the Disabled SP154

Youths and Factory SP155

1981, May 15   Litho.   Perf. 12
B322 SP154 2fo + 1fo multi .45 .45

Exists imperf. Value $7.

1981, May 29   Perf. 12x11½
B323 SP155 4fo + 2fo multi .80 .80

Young Communist League, 10th Congress, Budapest, May 29-31.
Exists imperf. Value $9.

European Junior Tennis Cup, July 25-Aug. 1 — SP156

1982, Apr. 2   Litho.   Perf. 12x11½
B324 SP156 4fo + 2fo multi .80 .80

Exists imperf. Value $8.

Souvenir Sheet

SP157

Perf. 12½x11½
1982, June 11   Litho.
B325 SP157 20fo + 10fo multi 4.00 4.00

PHILEXFRANCE '82 Stamp Exhibition, Paris, June 11-21.
Exists imperf. Value $20.

55th Stamp Day — SP158

Budapest Architecture and Statues: No. B326, Fishermen's Bastion, Janos Hunyadi (1403-1456). No. B327, Parliament, Ferenc Rakoczi the Second (1676-1735).

1982, Sept. 10   Litho.   Perf. 12
B326 SP158 4fo + 2fo multi .90 .90
B327 SP158 4fo + 2fo shown .90 .90

Exist imperf. Value, set $17.50.

Souvenir Sheet

Parliament, Chain Bridge, Buda Castle, Budapest — SP159

Illustration reduced.

1982, Sept. 10   Perf. 11½
B328 SP159 20fo + 10fo multi 3.75 3.75

European Security and Cooperation Conference, 10th anniv.
Exists imperf. Value $24.

21st Junior Stamp Exhibition, Baja, Mar. 31-Apr. 9 — SP160

1983, Mar. 31   Litho.   Perf. 12x11½
B329 SP160 4fo + 2fo multi .90 .90

Surtax was for show.
Exists imperf. Value $7.

56th Natl. Stamp Day SP161

Budapest Architecture (19th Cent. Engravings by): Rudolph Alt, H. Luders (No. B331).

1983, Sept. 9   Litho.   Perf. 12
B330 SP161 4fo + 2fo Old Natl. Theater .90 .90
B331 SP161 4fo + 2fo Municipal Concert Hall .90 .90

Souvenir Sheet
Lithographed and Engraved
Perf. 11
B332 SP161 20fo + 10fo Holy Trinity Square 3.75 3.75

No. B332 contains one stamp (28x45mm). Exist imperf. Value: Nos. B330-B331 $25; No. B332 $30.

SP162

1984, Apr. 2   Litho.   Perf. 12½x11½
B333 SP162 4fo + 2fo Mother & Child .75 .75

Surtax was for children's foundation. Exists imperf. Value $12.

SP163

Little Red Riding Hood, by the Brothers Grimm.

1985, Apr. 2   Litho.   Perf. 11½x12
B334 SP163 4fo + 2fo multi .75 .75

Jacob (1785-1863) and Wilhelm (1786-1859) Grimm, fabulists and philologists. Exists imperf. Value $10.

Natl. SOS Children's Village Assoc., 3rd Anniv. SP164

1985, Dec. 10   Litho.   Perf. 11
B335 SP164 4fo + 2fo multi .75 .75

Surtax for natl. SOS Children's Village. Exists imperf. Value $10.

Natl. Young Pioneers Org., 40th Anniv. SP165

1986, May 30   Perf. 11½x12½
B336 SP165 4fo + 2fo multi .75 .60

Exists imperf. Value $8.

Souvenir Sheet

Budapest Natl. Theater — SP166

Lithographed and Engraved
1986, Oct. 10   Perf. 11
B337 SP166 20fo + 10fo tan, brn & buff 4.00 4.00

Surtax benefited natl. theater construction. Exists imperf. Value $30.

Natl. Communist Youth League, 30th Anniv. — SP167

1987, Mar. 20   Perf. 13½x13
B338 SP167 4fo + 2fo multi .60 .60

Exists imperf. Value $8.

Souvenir Sheet

SOCFILEX '88, Aug. 12-21, Kecskemet — SP168

1988, Mar. 10   Litho.   Perf. 11½
B339 SP168 20fo +10fo multi 4.00 4.00

Surtax for SOCFILEX '88. Exists imperf. Value $30.

Sky High Tree, a Tapestry by Erzsebet Szekeres SP169

1989, Apr. 12   Litho.   Perf. 12
B340 SP169 5fo + 2fo multi 1.50 1.50

Surtax to promote youth philately. Exist imperf. Value, set $10.

Souvenir Sheet

Battle of Solferino, by Carlo Bossoli — SP170

1989, Sept. 8   Litho.   Perf. 10½
B341 SP170 20fo +10fo multi 3.75 3.75

Stamp Day. Exists imperf. Value $50.

Souvenir Sheet

Martyrs of Arad, Arad, Romania, 1849 — SP171

1989, Oct. 6   Perf. 11½x12½
B342 SP171 20fo +10fo multi 3.75 3.75

Surtax to fund production of another statue. Exists imperf. Value $30.

Teacher's Training High School, Sarospatak Municipal Arms — SP172

1990, Mar. 30   Litho.   Perf. 12x11½
B343 SP172 8fo +4fo multi 1.75 1.75

28th Youth Stamp Exhib., Sarospatak, Apr. 6-22. Exists imperf. Value $12.

Souvenir Sheet

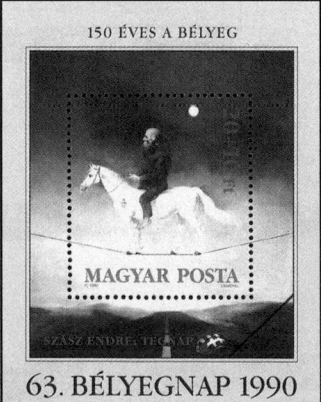

Yesterday, by Endre Szasz — SP173

1990, Oct. 12   Litho.   Perf. 12
B344 SP173 20fo +10fo multi 3.75 3.75

Stamp Day. Surtax for National Federation of Hungarian Philatelists. Exists imperf. Value $37.50.

Tapestry, Peter and the Wolf, by Gabriella Hajnal — SP174

1991, Apr. 30   Litho.   Perf. 12
B345 SP174 12fo +6fo multi 1.50 .80

Surtax to promote youth philately. Exists imperf. Value $9.

Children's Drawings SP175

Designs: 9fo + 4fo, Girl holding flower, vert. 10fo + 4fo, Child standing beneath sun. 15fo + 4fo, Boy wearing crown, vert.

1992, May 15   Litho.   Perf. 12
B346 SP175 9fo +4fo multi 1.10 1.10
B347 SP175 10fo +4fo multi 1.25 1.25
B348 SP175 15fo +4fo multi 1.65 1.65
Nos. B346-B348 (3) 4.00 4.00

Surtax for children's welfare.

Souvenir Sheet

1992 Summer Olympics, Barcelona — SP176

1992, Sept. 4   Litho.   Perf. 12
B349 SP176 50fo +20fo multi 3.50 3.00

Textile Art, by Erzsebet Szekeres SP177

1993, Apr. 14   Litho.   Perf. 12
B350 SP177 10fo +5fo Outdoor scene .60 .40
B351 SP177 17fo +8fo Tree of life 1.60 1.00

Stamp Day SP178

Stamp designers, stamps: 10fo + 5fo, Zoltan Nagy (1916-1987), #1062. 17fo + 5fo, Sandor

Legrady (1906-1987), #523. 50fo + 20fo,
Ferenc Helbing (1870-1959), #465.

1993, Sept. 10   Litho.   Perf. 12
B352 SP178 10fo +5fo multi   .75   .30
B353 SP178 17fo +5fo multi   1.00   .45
Souvenir Sheet
B354 SP178 50fo +20fo multi   3.25   1.75
No. B354 contains one 35x27mm stamp.

The Little Prince,
by Antoine de
Saint-Exupery
SP179

1994, Apr. 1   Litho.   Perf. 13½x13
B355 SP179 19fo +5fo multi   1.00   .60
Surtax for children's welfare.

Poem, "John
the Hero,"
150th Anniv.
SP180

1995, Apr. 7   Litho.   Perf. 12
B356 SP180 22fo +10fo multi   1.00   .60
Surtax to promote youth philately.

Olympiafila '95, Budapest — SP181

1995, June 12   Litho.   Perf. 11
B357 SP181 22fo +11fo yellow
  rings   1.10   .50
B358 SP181 22fo +11fo purple
  rings   1.10   .50
  a.   Pair, #B357-B358   2.50   1.50
No. B358a also sold in a strip of 3 pairs in a booklet.

World Festival
of Puppet
Players,
Budapest
SP182

Laszlo Vitez puppet and ghost puppet.

1996, June 21   Litho.   Perf. 12
B359 SP182 24fo +10fo multi   1.00   .75

Oder River
Flood of
1997
SP183

1997, Sept. 12   Litho.   Perf. 12
B360 SP183 27fo +100fo flower
  in water   1.90   .95
Surtax is for aid to flood victims.

Stamp Day
SP184

Early postman using: 27fo + 5fo, Motorized tricycle. 55fo + 5fo, Experimental registered letter-receiving machine, vert. 90fo + 30fo, Postal van.

1997, Sept. 19
B361 SP184 27fo +5fo multi   .75   .25
B362 SP184 55fo +5fo multi   1.50   .45
Souvenir Sheet
B363 SP184 90fo +30fo multi   7.00   3.75

Souvenir Sheet

Revolution of 1848 — SP185

Design: Seven members of movement, newspaper *Nemzeti dal.* Illustration reduced.

1998, Mar. 13   Litho.   Perf. 12
B364 SP185 150fo +50fo multi   4.50   1.75
Surtax to promote youth philately.

Youth
Stamp
SP186

1999, Mar. 12   Litho.   Perf. 12
B365 SP186 52fo +25fo multi   1.50   .75

István Fekete
(1900-70),
Writer — SP187

2000, Jan. 11   Litho.   Perf. 12
B366 SP187 60fo +30fo multi   1.50   1.00
Surtax for youth philately.

Hunphilex
2000
Stamp
Exhibition,
Budapest
SP188

2000, Jan. 11
B367 SP188 200fo +100fo multi   4.00   3.00
Surtax to support stamp exhibition.

Souvenir Sheet

Hunphilex 2000 Stamp Exhibition,
Budapest — SP189

2000, Aug. 18   Litho.   Perf. 12
B368 SP189 200fo +100fo Coronation robe   3.75   2.75
  a.   Sheet of 2   9.00   5.75

Star Over Eger,
by Geza
Gardonyi
SP190

2001, Jan. 15   Litho.   Perf. 13¼x13
B369 SP190 60fo +30fo multi   1.75   .50
Surtax for youth philately.

Campaign Against
Breast
Cancer — SP191

2005, Sept. 29   Litho.   Perf. 12
B370 SP191 90fo +50fo multi   2.00   1.00

Victory in First Grand Prix Race by
Ferenc Szisz (1873-1944) — SP192

2006, May 9   Litho.   Perf. 13x13¼
B371 SP192 120fo +50fo multi   2.00   2.00

Smile, by
Zita Zagyi
SP193

2008, May 20   Litho.   Perf. 13x13¼
B372 SP193 100fo + 50fo multi   1.90   1.90
Design was a winner in a children's art contest. Surtax for Hungarian Ambulance Service.

Togetherness — SP194

2009, Aug. 31
B373 SP194 75fo +50fo multi   1.40   1.40
Surtax for Crisis Foundation.

Hungarian Red
Cross — SP195

2010, Mar. 1   Litho.   Perf. 12¼x12¾
B374 SP195 105fo + 55fo multi   1.75   1.75
Surtax for Red Cross.

Interlocking Hands — SP196

2010, Nov. 24   Litho.   Perf. 13x13¼
B375 SP196 (80fo) +100fo multi   1.75   1.75
Surtax for victims of Hungarian Red Sludge disaster of Oct. 4, 2010.

AIR POST STAMPS

Issues of the Monarchy

Nos. 120, 123
Surcharged in
Red or Blue

Wmk. 137
1918, July 4   Typo.   Perf. 14
C1   A10   1k 50f on 75f (R)   25.00   27.50
C2   A10   4k 50f on 2k (Bl)   25.00   27.50
Counterfeits exist.
Exist imperf. Value, set $350.

No. 126
Surcharged

1920, Nov. 7
C3   A10   3k on 10k (G)   1.40   2.25
C4   A10   8k on 10k (R)   1.40   2.25
C5   A10   12k on 10k (Bl)   1.40   2.25
Nos. C3-C5 (3)   4.20   6.75
Set, never hinged   7.50

Icarus — AP3

1924-25   Perf. 14
C6   AP3   100k red brn & red   1.50   2.50
C7   AP3   500k bl grn & yel grn   1.50   2.50
C8   AP3   1000k bis brn & brn   1.50   2.50
C9   AP3   2000k dk bl & lt bl   1.50   2.50

Wmk. 133

C10	AP3	5000k dl vio & brt vio	2.25	2.50
C11	AP3	10000k red & dl vio	2.50	4.00
		Nos. C6-C11 (6)	10.75	16.50
		Set, never hinged	20.00	

Issue dates: 100k-2000k, Apr. 11, 1924. Others, Apr. 20, 1925.
Exist imperf. Value, set $120.
Forgeries exist.
For surcharges see Nos. J112-J116.

Mythical "Turul" — AP4

"Turul" Carrying Messenger
AP5   AP6

1927-30   Engr.   Perf. 14

C12	AP4	4f orange ('30)	.40	.40
C13	AP4	12f deep green	.75	.55
C14	AP4	16f red brown	.75	.60
C15	AP4	20f carmine	.75	.60
C16	AP4	32f brown vio	2.40	2.00
C17	AP4	40f dp ultra	2.40	1.25
C18	AP5	50f claret	2.40	1.25
C19	AP5	72f olive grn	2.40	1.40
C20	AP5	80f dp violet	2.75	1.60
C21	AP5	1p emerald ('30)	4.00	1.25
C22	AP5	2p red ('30)	5.00	3.50
C23	AP5	5p dk blue ('30)	16.50	27.50
		Nos. C12-C23 (12)	40.50	41.90
		Set, never hinged	65.00	

Exist imperf. Value, set $275.

1931, Mar. 27   Overprinted

C24	AP6	1p orange (Bk)	47.50	65.00
C25	AP6	2p dull vio (G)	47.50	65.00
		Set, never hinged	160.00	

Exist imperf. Value, set $420.

Monoplane over Danube Valley — AP7

Worker Welcoming Plane, Double Cross and Sun Rays — AP8

Spirit of Flight on Plane Wing
AP9

"Flight" Holding Propeller
AP10

Wmk. 210
1933, June 20   Photo.   Perf. 15

C26	AP7	10f blue green	2.90	.20
C27	AP7	16f purple	2.00	.25

Perf. 12½x12

C28	AP8	20f carmine	4.50	.20
C29	AP8	40f blue	4.00	1.25
C30	AP9	48f gray black	9.50	1.50
C31	AP9	72f bister brn	20.00	2.75
C32	AP10	1p yellow grn	25.00	2.50

C33	AP10	2p violet brn	47.50	17.50
C34	AP10	5p dk gray	82.50	140.00
		Nos. C26-C34 (9)	197.90	166.15
		Set, never hinged	375.00	

Exist imperf. Value, set $2,600.

> **Catalogue values for unused stamps in this section, from this point to the end of the section, are for Never Hinged items.**

Fokker F VII over Mail Coach AP11

Plane over Parliament AP12

Airplane AP13

1936, May 8   Perf. 12½x12½

C35	AP11	10f brt green	.80	.40
C36	AP11	20f crimson	.80	.40
C37	AP11	36f brown	.90	.40
C38	AP12	40f brt blue	.90	.40
C39	AP12	52f red org	3.25	.85
C40	AP12	60f brt violet	20.00	2.00
C41	AP12	80f dk sl grn	4.00	.60
C42	AP13	1p dk yel grn	4.75	.55
C43	AP13	2p brown car	7.50	2.00
C44	AP13	5p dark blue	24.00	19.50
		Nos. C35-C44 (10)	66.90	27.10
		Set, hinged	27.50	

Exist imperf. Value, set $675.

Issues of the Republic

Loyalty Tower, Sopron — AP14

Designs: 20f, Cathedral of Esztergom. 50f, Liberty Bridge, Budapest. 70f, Palace Hotel, Lillafüred. 1fo, Vajdahunyad Castle, Budapest. 1.40fo, Visegrád Fortress on the Danube. 3fo, Lake Balaton. 5fo, Parliament Building, Budapest.

Perf. 12½x12
1947, Mar. 5   Photo.   Wmk. 210

C45	AP14	10f rose lake	1.00	.25
C46	AP14	20f gray green	.35	.20
C47	AP14	50f copper brn	.40	.20
C48	AP14	70f olive grn	.40	.20
C49	AP14	1fo gray blue	.75	.25
C50	AP14	1.40fo brown	.90	.40
C51	AP14	3fo green	2.00	.25
C52	AP14	5fo rose violet	5.25	3.25
		Nos. C45-C52 (8)	11.05	5.00

Exist imperf. Value, set $280.

Johannes Gutenberg and Printing Press AP22

Designs: 2f, Columbus. 4f, Robert Fulton. 5f, George Stephenson. 6f, David Schwarz and Ferdinand von Zeppelin. 8f, Thomas A. Edison. 10f, Louis Bleriot. 12f, Roald Amundsen. 30f, Kalman Kando. 40f, Alexander S. Popov.

Perf. 12x12½
1948, May 15   Wmk. 283

C53	AP22	1f orange red	.25	.20
C54	AP22	2f dp magenta	.25	.20
C55	AP22	4f blue	.25	.20
C56	AP22	5f orange brn	.35	.35
C57	AP22	6f green	.35	.35
C58	AP22	8f dp red vio	.35	.35
C59	AP22	10f brown	.50	.45
C60	AP22	12f blue grn	.50	.45
C61	AP22	30f brown rose	1.75	1.50
C62	AP22	40f blue violet	2.25	1.75
		Nos. C53-C62 (10)	6.80	5.80

Explorers and inventors.
Exist imperf. Value, set $120.
See Nos. CB3-CB12.

> **IMPERFORATE STAMPS**
> Through 1991, most air post stamps stamps were also issued imperforate. Where these items form part of a larger set with regular issues, values for imperfs will be included in that of the sets to which they belong, footnoted in the Regular Issues section. For Nos. C63-C452, values for imperfs will be given only for those items not included in sets with regular issues.

UPU Type
1949, Nov. 1

C63	A171	2fo orange brn	1.40	1.00
a.		Booklet pane of 6	37.50	

75th anniv. of the UPU. See No. C81.
Exists imperf.

Chain Bridge Type and

Symbols of Labor — AP25

1949, Nov. 20

C64	A172	1.60fo scarlet	1.25	1.25
C65	A172	2fo olive	1.25	1.25

Souvenir Sheet
Perf. 12½x12

C66	AP25	50fo car lake	350.00	350.00

Opening of the Chain Bridge, Budapest, cent.
No. C66 exists imperf. Value $4,500.

Postman and Mail Carrying Vehicles AP26

1949, Dec. 11   Perf. 12

C67	AP26	50f lilac gray	6.00	6.00
		Sheet of 4	40.00	30.00

Stamp Day, 1949.
Exists imperf. Value: single $100; sheet $525.

Plane, Globe, Stamps and Stagecoach — AP27

1950, Mar. 12   Perf. 12x12½

C68	AP27	2fo red brn & yel	9.50	9.50

20th anniv. of the establishment of the Hungarian Post Office Philatelic Museum.
Exists imperf. Value $50.

Chess Emblem, Globe and Plane AP28

1950, Apr. 9   Wmk. 106   Perf. 12

C69	AP28	1.60fo brown	6.00	2.10

World Chess Championship Matches, Budapest.
Exists imperf.

Globes, Parliament Building and Chain Bridge — AP29

1950, May 16   Perf. 12x12½

C70	AP29	1fo red brown	1.60	.65

Meeting of the World Federation of Trade Unions, Budapest, May 1950.
Exists imperf.

Statue of Liberty and View of Budapest — AP30

Designs: 30f, Crane and apartment house. 70f, Steel mill. 1fo, Stalinyec tractor. 1.60fo, Steamship. 2fo, Reaping-threshing machine. 3fo, Passenger train. 5fo, Matyas Rakosi Steel Mill, Csepel. 10fo, Budaörs Airport.

Perf. 12½x12

			Engr.	Unwmk.
C71	AP30	20f claret	.65	.25
C72	AP30	30f blue vio	.65	.20
C73	AP30	70f violet brn	.25	.20
C74	AP30	1fo yellow brn	.25	.20
C75	AP30	1.60fo ultra	.70	.40
C76	AP30	2fo red org	.75	.25
C77	AP30	3fo olive blk	1.00	.40
C78	AP30	5fo gray blue	2.00	1.25
C79	AP30	10fo chestnut	6.25	1.75
		Nos. C71-C79 (9)	12.50	4.90

See Nos. C167 and C172.
Exist imperf. Value, set $100.

Bem Type
Souvenir Sheet
1950, Dec. 10   Engr.   Imperf.

C80	A185	2fo deep plum	42.50	42.50

Stamp Day and Budapest Stamp Exhibition.

UPU Type of 1949
Perf. 12x12½, Imperf.
1950, July 2   Photo.   Wmk. 106

C81	A171	3fo dk car & dk brn	27.50	27.50
		Sheet of 4	525.00	525.00

Exists imperf. Value: single $80; sheet of 4 $600.

Sports Type

Designs: 30f, Volleyball. 40f, Javelin-throwing. 60f, Sports badge. 70f, Soccer. 3fo, Glider meet.

1950, Dec. 2

C82	A188	30f lilac & magenta	.50	.20
C83	A188	40f olive & indigo	.75	.25
C84	A188	60f ol, dk brn & org red	1.25	.40
C85	A188	70f gray & dk brn	2.75	.55
C86	A188	3fo buff & dk brn	4.50	2.25
		Nos. C82-C86 (5)	9.75	3.65

Exist imperf.

Livestock Type

1951, Apr. 5   Photo.   Perf. 12x12½

C87	A191	20f Mare & foal	2.00	.30
C88	A191	70f Sow & shoats	2.25	.70
C89	A191	1fo Ram & ewe	3.75	.90
C90	A191	1.60fo Cow & calf	5.25	1.50
		Nos. C87-C90 (4)	13.25	3.40

Exist imperf.

Telegraph
Linemen
AP34

Tank
Column — AP35

Designs: 1fo, Workers on vacation. 2fo, Air view of Stalin Bridge.

1951, Aug. 20

C91	AP34	70f henna brown	.85	.30
C92	AP34	1fo blue green	.95	.35
C93	AP34	2fo deep plum	1.75	.70
		Nos. C91-C93 (3)	3.55	1.35

Successful conclusion of the 1st year under Hungary's 5-year plan.
Exist imperf.

1951, Sept. 29   Perf. 12½x12

C94	AP35	60f deep blue	.85	.25

Army Day, Sept. 29, 1951.
Exists imperf.

1st Stamp Type
Souvenir Sheet

1951, Oct. 6   Engr.   Unwmk.

C95	A208	80f olive green	75.00	65.00

Stamp exhibition to commemorate the 80th anniv. of Hungary's 1st postage stamp.
Exists imperf. Value $200.
Twelve hundred copies in rose lilac, perf. and imperf., were presented to exhibitors and members of the arranging committee of the exhibition. Value, each $1,600.

Avocet — AP37

Hungarian Birds: 30f, White stork. 40f, Golden oriole. 50f, Kentish plover. 60f, Black-winged stilt. 70f, Lesser gray shrike. 80f, Great bustard. 1fo, Redfooted falcon. 1.40fo, European bee-eater. 1.60fo, Glossy ibis. 2.50fo, Great white egret.

Perf. 13x11

1952, Mar. 16   Photo.   Wmk. 106
Birds in Natural Colors

C96	AP37	20f emer, *grnsh*	.20	.20
C97	AP37	30f sage grn, *grysh*	.25	.20
C98	AP37	40f brown, *cr*	.35	.20
C99	AP37	50f orange, *cr*	.40	.20
C100	AP37	60f deep carmine	.50	.25
C101	AP37	70f red org, *cr*	.60	.35
C102	AP37	80f olive, *cr*	.80	.45
C103	AP37	1fo dp blue, *bluish*	1.00	.50
C104	AP37	1.40fo gray, *grysh*	2.00	.65
C105	AP37	1.60fo org brn, *cr*	2.50	.85
C106	AP37	2.50fo rose vio, *cr*	3.50	1.35
		Nos. C96-C106 (11)	12.10	5.15

Exist imperf. Value, set $100.

Olympic Games Type

Designs: 1.70fo, hammer thrower; 2fo, Stadium, Budapest.

1952, May 26   Perf. 11

C107	A217	1.70fo dp red orange	2.10	1.00
C108	A217	2fo olive brown	2.50	1.25

Issued to publicize Hungary's participation in the Olympic Games, Helsinki, 1952.
Exists imperf.

Leonardo da
Vinci — AP39

1952, June 15   Perf. 12½x12

C109	AP39	1.60fo shown	1.50	1.00
C110	AP39	2fo Victor Hugo	1.50	1.00

Exist imperf. Value, set $35.

AP40

AP41

1953, Mar. 4   Perf. 12x12½

C111	AP40	20f Red squirrel	.50	.20
C112	AP41	30f Hedgehog	.65	.25
C113	AP41	40f Hare	.65	.30
C114	AP40	50f Beech marten	.80	.40
C115	AP41	60f Otter	1.00	.45
C116	AP41	70f Red fox	1.00	.50
C117	AP40	80f Fallow deer	1.25	.75
C118	AP41	1fo Roe deer	1.60	1.00
C119	AP41	1.50fo Boar	4.00	1.25
C120	AP40	2fo Red deer	4.50	1.50
		Nos. C111-C120 (10)	15.95	6.60

Exist imperf. Value, set $75.

Type of Regular Issue

Designs: 1fo, Children at Balaton Lake. 1.50fo, Workers' Home at Lillafured.

1953, Apr. 19   Perf. 12

C121	A228	1fo brt grnsh blue	.65	.25
C122	A228	1.50fo dp red lilac	1.25	.40

Exist imperf.

People's Stadium Type

1953, Aug. 20   Perf. 11

C123	A232	80f Water polo	1.00	.20
C124	A232	1fo Boxing	2.00	.25
C125	A232	2fo Soccer	2.25	.80
C126	A232	3fo Track	2.50	.95
C127	A232	5fo Stadium	3.75	1.75
		Nos. C123-C127 (5)	11.50	3.40

Exist imperf.

No. C125 Overprinted in Black

1953, Dec. 3

C128	A232	2fo green & brown	20.00	16.00

Hungary's success in the soccer matches at Wembley, England, Nov. 25, 1953. Counterfeits exist.
Exists imperf. Value $300.

Janos Bihari
and Scene
from
Verbunkos
AP44

Portraits: 40f, Ferenc Erkel. 60f, Franz Liszt. 70f, Mihaly Mosonyi. 80f, Karl Goldmark. 1fo, Bela Bartok. 2fo, Zoltan Kodaly.

1953, Dec. 5   Photo.   Perf. 12
Frames and Portraits in Brown

C129	AP44	30f blue gray	.35	.20
C130	AP44	40f orange	.35	.25
C131	AP44	60f green	.55	.25
C132	AP44	70f red	.45	.30
C133	AP44	80f gray blue	.50	.40
C134	AP44	1fo olive bis	1.00	.60
C135	AP44	2fo violet	1.50	1.25
		Nos. C129-C135 (7)	4.70	3.25

Hungarian composers.
Exists imperf. Value, set $40.

Carrot
Beetle — AP45

May (or
June) Beetle
AP46

Designs: Various beetles. 60f, Bee.

Perf. 12½x12, 12x12½

1954, Feb. 6   Wmk. 106

C136	AP45	30f dp org & dk brn	.50	.20
C137	AP46	40f grn & dk brn	.60	.20
C138	AP46	50f rose brn & blk	.85	.30
C139	AP46	60f vio, dk brn & yel	.85	.45
C140	AP45	80f grnsh gray, pur & rose	1.25	.70
C141	AP45	1fo ocher & blk	1.75	.80
C142	AP46	1.20fo dl grn & dk brn	2.10	1.00
C143	AP46	1.50fo ol brn & dk brn	3.25	1.25
C144	AP46	2fo hn brn & dk brn	4.25	1.50
C145	AP45	3fo bl grn & dk brn	5.50	2.00
		Nos. C136-C145 (10)	20.90	8.40

Exists imperf. Value, set $110.

Lunchtime at
the Nursery
AP47

Designs: 1.50fo, Mother taking child from doctor. 2fo, Nurse and children.

1954, Mar. 8   Perf. 12

C146	AP47	1fo olive green	1.00	.40
C147	AP47	1.50fo red brown	1.40	.50
C148	AP47	2fo blue green	2.40	1.25
		Nos. C146-C148 (3)	4.55	2.00

Exist imperf.

Model Glider Construction — AP48

Boy
Flying
Model
Glider
AP49

Designs: 60f, Gliders. 80f, Pilot leaving plane. 1fo, Parachutists. 1.20fo, Biplane. 1.50fo, Plane over Danube. 2fo, Jet planes.

1954, June 25   Perf. 11

C149	AP48	40f brn, ol & dk bl gray	.30	.20
C150	AP49	50f gray & red brn	.40	.20
C151	AP48	60f red brn & dk bl gray	.40	.20
C152	AP48	80f violet & sep	.45	.20
C153	AP48	1fo brn & dk bl gray	.65	.20
C154	AP49	1.20fo olive & sep	1.00	.25
C155	AP48	1.50fo cl & dk bl gray	1.25	.50
C156	AP49	2fo blue & dk brn	1.90	.50
		Nos. C149-C156 (8)	6.35	2.25

Exist imperf. Value, set $75.

Jokai Type
Souvenir Sheet

1954, Oct. 17   Engr.   Perf. 12½x12

C157	A242	1fo violet blue	37.50	37.50

Stamp Day. Exists imperforate. Value $90.

Children on
Sled — AP51

Skaters
AP52

50f, Ski racer. 60f, Ice yacht. 80f, Ice hockey. 1fo, Ski jumper. 1.50fo, Downhill ski racer. 2fo, Man and woman exhibition-skating.

1955		Photo.	Perf. 12	
C158	AP51	40f multi	1.25	.20
C159	AP52	50f multi	.30	.20
C160	AP51	60f multi	.30	.20
C161	AP51	80f multi	.50	.20
C162	AP51	1fo multi	1.25	.30
C163	AP52	1.20fo multi	1.25	.30
C164	AP52	1.50fo multi	1.75	.60
C165	AP52	2fo multi	2.40	.50
	Nos. C158-C165 (8)		9.00	2.50

Exist imperf. Value, set $75.
Issued: 1.20fo, 2fo, Jan. 27; others Feb. 26.

Government Printing Plant Type
Souvenir Sheet

1955, May 28		Perf. 12x12½
C166	A247	5fo hn brn & gray grn	32.50	32.50

Cent. of the establishment of the government printing plant.
Exists imperf. Value $160.

No. C78 Printed on Aluminum Foil

Perf. 12½x12

1955, Oct. 5		Engr.	Unwmk.
C167	AP30	5fo gray blue	15.00	12.50

Intl. Cong. of the Light Metal Industry and for 20 years of aluminum production in Hungary.
Exists imperf. Value $100.

Bartok Type
Wmk. 106

1955, Oct. 9		Photo.	Perf. 12
C168	A252	1fo gray green	2.00	1.25
C169	A252	1fo violet brn	3.50	2.00
a.		With ticket	15.00	12.50

10th anniv. of the death of Bela Bartok, composer. No. C169a was issued for the Day of the Stamp, Oct. 16, 1955. The 5fo sales price, marked on the attached ticket, was the admission fee to any one of 14 simultaneous stamp shows.
Exist imperf. Value, set with ticket, $135.

"Esperanto" — AP55

Lazarus Ludwig Zamenhof AP56

1957, June 8

| C170 | AP55 | 60f red brown | .50 | .25 |
| C171 | AP56 | 1fo dark green | .50 | .30 |

10th anniversary of the death of L. L. Zamenhof, inventor of Esperanto.
Exist imperf. Value $32.50.

Type of 1950

Design: 20fo, Budaörs Airport.

Perf. 12½x12

1957, July 18		Engr.	Unwmk.
C172	AP30	20fo dk slate grn	8.00	4.00
		Punched 3 holes	9.25	4.50

A few days after issuance, stocks of No. C172 were punched with three holes and used on domestic surface mail.
Exist imperf. Value $70.

Courier and Fort Buda AP57

Design: No. C174, Plane over Budapest.

Wmk. 106

1957, Oct. 13		Photo.	Perf. 12
C173	AP57	1fo ol bis & brn, buff	.75	.75
C174	AP57	1fo ol bis & dp cl, buff	.75	.75
a.		Strip of #C173-C174 + label	2.25	2.25

Stamp Day, Oct. 20th. The triptych sold for 6fo.
Exists imperf. Value, strip $30.

Type of Regular Pigeon Issue

Design: 3fo, Two carrier pigeons.

1957, Dec. 14		Perf. 12x12½
C175	A266	3fo red, grn, gray & blk	.90	.50

Exists imperf.

Hungarian Pavilion, Brussels — AP58

Designs: 40f, Map, lake and local products. 60f, Parliament. 1fo, Chain Bridge, Budapest. 1.40fo, Arms of Hungary and Belgium. 2fo, Fountain, Brussels, vert. 3fo, City Hall, Brussels vert. 5fo, Exposition emblem.

Perf. 14½x15

1958, Apr. 17		Litho.	Wmk. 106
C176	AP58	20f red org & red brn	.20	.20
C177	AP58	40f lt blue & brn	.20	.20
C178	AP58	60f crimson & sep	.20	.20
C179	AP58	1fo bis & red brn	.20	.20
C180	AP58	1.40fo dull vio & multi	.20	.20
C181	AP58	2fo gldn brn & dk brn	.35	.20
C182	AP58	3fo bl grn & sep	.80	.40
C183	AP58	5fo gray ol, blk, red, bl & yel	1.50	.60
	Nos. C176-C183 (8)		3.65	2.20

Universal and Intl. Exposition at Brussels.
Exist imperf. Value $30.

View of Prague and Morse Code AP59

1958, June 30 Photo. Perf. 12x12½

| C184 | AP59 | 1fo rose brown | .35 | .20 |

See No. 1194a for se-tenant pair.
Conference of Postal Ministers of Communist Countries at Prague, June 30-July 8.
Exists imperf.

Post Horn, Pigeon and Pen AP60

No. C185, Stamp under magnifying glass.

1958, Oct. 25		Wmk. 106	Perf. 12
C185	AP60	1fo dp car & bis	.55	.55
C186	AP60	1fo yel grn & bis	.55	.55
a.		Strip, #C185-C186 + label	2.00	2.00

Natl. Stamp Exhib., Budapest, 10/25-11/2.
#C185 inscribed: "XXXI Belyegnap 1958."
Exist imperf. Value, strip $30.

1958, Oct. 26

Designs: 60f, as No. C186. 1fo, Ship, plane, locomotive and pen surrounding letter.

| C187 | AP60 | 60f dp plum & grysh buff | .40 | .20 |
| C188 | AP60 | 1fo bl & grysh buff | .60 | .20 |

Issued for Letter Writing Week.
Exist imperf. Value, set $20.

Plane over Heroes' Square Budapest — AP61

Design: 5fo, Plane over Tower of Sopron.

Perf. 12½x12

1958, Nov. 3		Engr.	Wmk. 106
C189	AP61	3fo gray, rose vio & red	1.25	.60
C190	AP61	5fo gray, dk bl & red	1.50	.90

40th anniv. of Hungarian air post stamps.
Exist imperf. Value, set $25.

Same Without Commemorative Inscription

Plane over: 20f, Szeged. 30f, Sarospatak. 70f, Gyor. 1fo, Budapest, Opera House. 1.60fo, Veszprém. 2fo, Budapest, Chain Bridge. 3fo, Sopron. 5fo, Heroes' Square, Budapest. 10fo, Budapest, Academy of Science and Parliament. 20fo, Budapest.

1958, Dec. 31		Engr.	Wmk. 106
		Yellow Paper	
		and Vermilion Inscriptions	
C191	AP61	20f green	.20	.20
C192	AP61	30f violet	.20	.20
C193	AP61	70f brown vio	.25	.20
C194	AP61	1fo blue	.40	.20
C195	AP61	1.60fo purple	.40	.20
C196	AP61	2fo Prus green	.50	.25
C197	AP61	3fo brown	1.00	.25
C198	AP61	5fo olive green	1.50	.25
C199	AP61	10fo dark blue	2.25	.35
C200	AP61	20fo brown	3.75	.75
	Nos. C191-C200 (10)		10.45	2.85

Exist imperf. Value, set $70.

Transport Type of Regular Issue

Design: 3fo, Early plane.

1959, May		Litho.	Perf. 14½x15
C201	A279	3fo dl lil, blk, yel & brn	2.00	1.25

Exist imperf.

Tihany — AP62

Designs: 70f, Ship. 1fo, Heviz and water lily. 1.70fo, Sailboat and fisherman statue.

1959, July 15		Photo.	Perf. 11½x12
C202	AP62	20f brt green	.20	.20
C203	AP62	70f brt blue	.20	.20
C204	AP62	1fo ultra & car rose	.20	.20
C205	AP62	1.70fo red brn, yel	.50	.30
	Nos. C202-C205 (4)		1.10	.90

Issued to publicize Lake Balaton and the opening of the Summer University.
Exist imperf.

Moth-Butterfly Type of 1959

Butterflies: 1fo, Lycaena virgaureae. 2fo, Acherontia atropos, horiz. 3fo, Red admiral.

Perf. 11½x12, 12x11½

1959, Nov. 20			Wmk. 106
		Butterflies in Natural Colors	
C206	A290	1fo black & lt bl grn	.90	.20
C207	A290	2fo black & lilac	1.50	.35
C208	A290	3fo dk gray & emer	2.25	.75
	Nos. C206-C208 (3)		4.65	1.30

Exist imperf.

Souvenir Sheet

Rockets in Orbit, Gagarin, Titov & Glenn — AP63

Perf. 11, Imperf.

1962, Mar. 29			Unwmk.
C209	AP63	10fo multi	9.50	7.50

Cosmonants Yuri A. Gagarin and Gherman Titov, USSR and astronaut John H. Glenn, Jr., US.
Exists imperf. Value $50.

Soccer Type of 1962

Flags of Hungary and Great Britain.

1962, May 21		Photo.	Perf. 11
		Flags in National Colors	
C209A	A323	2fo greenish bister	1.10	.30

Exists imperf.

Glider and Lilienthal's 1898 Design — AP64

Designs: 30f, Icarus and Aero Club emblem. 60f, Light monoplane and 1912 aerobatic plane. 80f, Airship GZ-1 and Montgolfier balloon. 1fo, IL-18 Malev and Wright 1903 plane. 1.40fo, Stunt plane and Nyesterov's 1913 plane. 2fo, Helicopter and Asboth's 1929 helicopter. 3fo, Supersonic bomber and Zhukovski's turbomotor. 4fo, Space rocket and Tsiolkovsky's rocket.

1962, July 19		Unwmk.	Perf. 15
C210	AP64	30f blue & dull yel	.20	.20
C211	AP64	40f yel grn & ultra	.20	.20
C212	AP64	60f ultra & ver	.20	.20
C213	AP64	80f grnsh bl & sil	.20	.20
C214	AP64	1fo lilac, sil & bl	.20	.20
C215	AP64	1.40fo blue & org	.20	.20
C216	AP64	2fo bluish grn & brn	.25	.20
C217	AP64	3fo vio, sil & bl	.50	.25
C218	AP64	4fo grn, sil & blk	.80	.35
	Nos. C210-C218 (9)		2.75	2.00

Issued to show flight development: "From Icarus to the Space Rocket."
Exist imperf. Value, set $25.

Earth, TV Screens and Rockets — AP65

Design: 2fo, Andrian G. Nikolayev, Pavel R. Popovich and rockets.

1962, Sept. 4			Perf. 12
C219	AP65	1fo dk bl & org brn	.70	.35
C220	AP65	2fo dk bl & org brn	.80	.55
a		Pair, #C219-C220	1.75	.90

First group space flight of Vostoks 3 and 4, Aug. 11-15, 1962. Printed in alternating horizontal rows.
Exist imperf. Value $20.

John H. Glenn, Jr. AP66

Astronauts: 40f, Yuri A. Gagarin. 60f, Gherman Titov. 1.40fo, Scott Carpenter. 1.70fo, Andrian G. Nikolayev. 2.60fo, Pavel R. Popovich. 3fo, Walter Schirra.

1962, Oct. 27   Perf. 12x11½
Portraits in Bister

C221	AP66	40f purple	.20 .20
C222	AP66	60f dark green	.20 .20
C223	AP66	1fo dark bl grn	.20 .20
C224	AP66	1.40fo dark brown	.20 .20
C225	AP66	1.70fo deep blue	.30 .25
C226	AP66	2.60fo violet	.65 .30
C227	AP66	3fo red brown	1.10 .45
		Nos. C221-C227 (7)	2.85 1.80

Issued to honor the first seven astronauts and in connection with the Astronautical Congress in Paris.
Exist imperf. Value, set $20.

Eagle Owl — AP67

Birds: 40f, Osprey. 60f, Marsh harrier. 80f, Booted eagle. 1fo, African fish eagle. 2fo, Lammergeier. 3fo, Golden eagle. 4fo, Kestrel.

1962, Nov. 18   Litho.   Perf. 11½
Birds in Natural Colors

C228	AP67	30f yel grn & blk	.20 .20
C229	AP67	40f org yel & blk	.20 .20
C230	AP67	60f bister & blk	.20 .20
C231	AP67	80f lt grn & blk	.20 .20
C232	AP67	1fo ol bis & blk	.20 .20
C233	AP67	2fo bluish grn & blk	.35 .20
C234	AP67	3fo lt vio & blk	.65 .30
C235	AP67	4fo dp org & blk	1.25 .50
		Nos. C228-C235 (8)	3.25 2.00

Exist imperf. Value, set $30.

Radio Mast and Albania No. 623 AP68

Designs (Communication symbols and rocket stamps of various countries): 30f, Bulgaria #C77, vert. 40f, Czechoslovakia #1108. 50f, Communist China #380. 60f, North Korea. 80f, Poland #875. 1fo, Hungary #1386. 1.20fo, Mongolia #189, vert. 1.40fo, DDR #580. 1.70fo, Romania #1200. 2fo, Russia #2456, vert. 2.60fo, North Viet Nam.

Perf. 12x11½, 11½x12
1963, May 9   Photo.   Unwmk.
Stamp Reproductions in Original Colors

C236	AP68	20f olive green	.20 .20
C237	AP68	30f rose lake	.20 .20
C238	AP68	40f violet	.20 .20
C239	AP68	50f brt blue	.20 .20
C240	AP68	60f orange brn	.20 .20
C241	AP68	80f ultra	.20 .20
C242	AP68	1fo dull red brn	.20 .20
C243	AP68	1.20fo aqua	.20 .20
C244	AP68	1.40fo olive	.25 .20
C245	AP68	1.70fo brown olive	.25 .20
C246	AP68	2fo rose lilac	.30 .20
C247	AP68	2.60fo bluish green	.60 .40
		Nos. C236-C247 (12)	3.00 2.60

5th Conference of Postal Ministers of Communist Countries, Budapest.
Exist imperf. Value, set $30.

Souvenir Sheet

Globe and Spaceships — AP69

Perf. 11½x12, Imperf.
1963, July 13   Unwmk.
C248	AP69	10fo dk & lt blue	8.00 7.00

Space flights of Valeri Bykovski, June 14-19, and Valentina Tereshkova, June 16-19, 1963, 1st woman cosmonaut.
Exists imperf. Value $30.

Souvenir Sheet

Mt. Fuji and Stadium — AP70

1964, Sept. 22 Photo.   Perf. 11½x12
C249	AP70	10fo multi	4.00 3.50

18th Olympic Games, Tokyo, Oct. 10-24.
Exists imperf. Value $30.

Bridge Type of 1964
Souvenir Sheet

Design: Elizabeth Bridge.

1964, Nov. 21   Photo.   Perf. 11
C250	A356	10fo silver & dp grn	3.75 3.50

No. C250 contains one 59x20mm stamp.
Exists imperf. Value $120.

Lt. Col. Alexei Leonov in Space — AP71

Design: 2fo, Col. Pavel Belyayev, Lt. Col. Alexei Leonov and Voskhod 2.

1965, Apr. 17   Photo.   Perf. 11½x12
C251	AP71	1fo violet & gray	.45 .20
C252	AP71	2fo rose claret & ocher	1.10 .65

Space flight of Voskhod 2 and of Lt. Col. Alexei Leonov, the first man floating in space.
Exists imperf. Value, set $20.

Mariner IV (USA) — AP72

New achievements in space research: 30f, San Marco satellite, Italy. 40f, Molniya satellite, USSR. 60f, Moon rocket, 1965, USSR. 1fo, Shapir rocket, France. 2.50fo, Zond III satellite, USSR. 3fo, Syncom III satellite, US. 10fo, Rocket sending off satellites, horiz.

1965, Dec. 31   Photo.   Perf. 11
C253	AP72	20f ultra, blk & org yel	.20 .20
C254	AP72	30f brn, vio & yel	.20 .20
C255	AP72	40f vio, brn & pink	.20 .20
C256	AP72	60f lt pur, blk & org yel	.20 .20
C257	AP72	1fo red lil, blk & buff	.30 .25
C258	AP72	2.50fo rose cl, blk & gray	.60 .35
C259	AP72	3fo bl grn, blk & bis	.75 .60
		Nos. C253-C259 (7)	2.45 2.00

Souvenir Sheet

1965, Dec. 20
C260	AP72	10fo brt bl, yel & dk ol	3.50 3.00

Exist imperf. Value: Nos. C253-C259 $20; No. C260 $30.

Sport Type of Regular Issue
Souvenir Sheet

10fo, Women hurdlers and Ferihegy airport.

1966, Sept. 4   Photo.   Perf. 12x11½
C261	A384	10fo brt bl, brn & red	4.00 3.75

Exists imperf. Value $30.

Plane over Helsinki — AP73

Plane over Cities Served by Hungarian Airlines: 50f, Athens. 1fo, Beirut. 1.10fo, Frankfort on the Main. 1.20fo, Cairo. 1.50fo, Copenhagen. 2fo, London. 2.50fo, Moscow. 3fo, Paris. 4fo, Prague. 5fo, Rome. 10fo, Damascus. 20fo, Budapest.

1966-67   Photo.   Perf. 12x11½
C262	AP73	20f brown org	.20 .20
C263	AP73	50f brown	.20 .20
C264	AP73	1fo blue	.20 .20
C265	AP73	1.10fo black	.20 .20
C266	AP73	1.20fo orange	.20 .20
C267	AP73	1.50fo blue grn	.25 .20
C268	AP73	2fo brt blue	.30 .20
C269	AP73	2.50fo brt red	.30 .20
C270	AP73	3fo yel grn	.40 .20
C271	AP73	4fo brown red	1.10 1.00
C272	AP73	5fo brt pur	.55 .20
C273	AP73	10fo violet bl ('67)	.75 .20
C274	AP73	20fo gray ol ('67)	1.10 .35
		Nos. C262-C274 (13)	5.75 3.55

Exist imperf. Value, set $90.
See No. C276.

Souvenir Sheet

Icarus Falling — AP73a

1968, May 11   Photo.   Perf. 11
C275	AP73a	10fo multicolored	2.75 2.50

In memory of the astronauts Edward H. White, US, Vladimir M. Komarov and Yuri A. Gagarin, USSR.
Exists imperf. Value $25.

Type of 1966-67 without "Legiposta"
Inscription

Design: 2.60fo, Malev Airlines jet over St. Stephen's Cathedral, Vienna.

1968, July 4   Photo.   Perf. 12x11½
C276	AP73	2.60fo violet	.50 .20

50th anniv. of regular airmail service between Budapest and Vienna.
Exists imperf. Value $15.

Women Swimmers and Aztec Calendar Stone — AP74

Aztec Calendar Stone, Olympic Rings and: 60f, Soccer. 80f, Wrestling. 1fo, Canoeing. 1.40fo, Gymnast on rings. 3fo, Fencing. 4fo, Javelin.

1968, Aug. 21   Photo.   Perf. 12
C277	AP74	20f brt bl & multi	.20 .20
C278	AP74	60f green & multi	.20 .20
C279	AP74	80f car rose & multi	.20 .20
C280	AP74	1fo grnsh bl & multi	.20 .20
C281	AP74	1.40fo violet & multi	.20 .20
C282	AP74	3fo brt lilac & multi	.65 .35
C283	AP74	4fo green & multi	1.00 .55
		Nos. C277-C283,CB31 (8)	3.00 2.25

Issued to publicize the 19th Olympic Games, Mexico City, Oct. 12-27.
Exist imperf. Value, set (8) $30.

Souvenir Sheet

Apollo 8 Trip Around the Moon — AP75

1969, Feb.   Photo.   Perf. 12½
C284	AP75	10fo multi	3.50 3.50

Man's 1st flight around the moon, Dec. 21-27, 1968.
Exists imperf. Value $30.

Soyuz 4 and 5, and Men in Space AP76

Design: No. C286, Soyuz 4 and 5.

1969, Mar. 21 Photo. Perf. 12x11½
C285 AP76 2fo multi .35 .35
C286 AP76 2fo dk bl, lt bl & red .35 .35
  a. Strip, # C285-C286 + label .85

First team flights of Russian spacecraft Soyuz 4 and 5, Jan. 16, 1969.
Exist imperf. Value, strip $10.

Journey to the Moon, by Jules Verne — AP77

Designs: 60f, Tsiolkovski's space station. 1fo, Luna 1. 1.50fo, Ranger 7. 2fo, Luna 9 landing on moon. 2.50fo, Apollo 8 in orbit around moon. 3fo, Soyuz 4 and 5 docking in space. 4fo, Lunar landing module landing on moon. 10fo, Apollo 11 astronauts on moon and lunar landing module.

1969 Photo. Perf. 12x11½
C287 AP77 40f multi .20 .20
C288 AP77 60f multi .20 .20
C289 AP77 1fo multi .20 .20
C290 AP77 1.50fo multi .20 .20
C291 AP77 2fo multi .20 .20
C292 AP77 2.50fo multi .25 .20
C293 AP77 3fo multi .50 .20
C294 AP77 4fo multi .75 .40
  Nos. C287-C294 (8) 2.50 1.80

Souvenir Sheet
Perf. 11
C295 AP77 10fo multi 5.00 5.00

Moon landing issue. See note after Algeria No. 427.
No. C295 contains one 74x49mm stamp.
Issued: #C287-C294, Nov. 1; #C295, Aug. 15.
Exist imperf. Value: Nos. C287-C294 $20; No. C295 $35.

Daimler, 1886 — AP78

Automobiles: 60f, Peugeot, 1894. 1fo, Benz, 1901. 1.50fo, Cudell mail truck, 1902. 2fo, Rolls Royce, 1908. 2.50fo, Model T Ford, 1908. 3fo, Vermorel, 1912. 4fo, Csonka mail car, 1912.

1970, Mar. Photo. Perf. 12
C296 AP78 40f ocher & multi .20 .20
C297 AP78 60f multi .20 .20
C298 AP78 1fo red & multi .20 .20
C299 AP78 1.50fo bl & multi .20 .20
C300 AP78 2fo multi .25 .20
C301 AP78 2.50fo vio & multi .30 .20
C302 AP78 3fo multi .40 .30
C303 AP78 4fo multi .70 .50
  Nos. C296-C303 (8) 2.45 2.00

Exist imperf. Value, set $20.

American Astronauts on Moon — AP79

No. C305, Soyuz 6, 7 and 8 in space.

1970, Mar. 20 Photo. Perf. 11
C304 AP79 3fo blue & multi .75 .75
C305 AP79 3fo car rose & multi .75 .75

Landing of Apollo 12 on the moon, Nov. 14, 1969, and group flight of Russian spacecraft Soyuz 6, 7 & 8, Oct. 11-13, 1969.
Nos. C304-C305 issued in sheets of 4. Size: 112½x78mm.
Exist imperf. Value: set $20; sheets of 4 $80.

"Rain at Foot of Fujiyama," by Hokusai, and Pavilion — AP80

3fo, Sun Tower, Peace Bell and globe.

1970, Apr. 30 Photo. Perf. 12½
C306 AP80 2fo multi .75 .75
C307 AP80 3fo multi .75 .75

Issued to publicize EXPO '70 International Exhibition, Osaka, Japan, Mar. 15-Sept. 13.
Exist imperf. Value, set $12.

Miniature Sheets

Phases of Apollo 13 Moon Flight — AP81

Vignettes of No. C308: Apollo 13 over moon; return to earth; capsule with parachutes; capsule floating, aircraft carrier and helicopter.
Vignettes of No. C309: Soyuz 9 on way to launching pad; launching of Soyuz 9 capsule in orbit; cosmonauts Andrian Nikolayev and Vitaly Sevastyanov.
Vignettes of No. C310: Luna 16 approaching moon; module on moon; landing; nose cone on ground.
Vignettes of No. C311: Lunokhod 1 on moon; trajectories of Luna 17 around earth and moon.

1970-71 Litho. Perf. 11½
C308 AP81 Sheet of 4 2.25 2.25
Photo.
C309 AP81 Sheet of 4 2.25 2.25
C310 AP81 Sheet of 4 ('71) 2.25 2.25
C311 AP81 Sheet of 4 ('71) 2.25 2.25

Nos. C308-C311 were valid for postage only as full sheets. Each contains four 2.50fo vignettes.
No. C308 for the aborted moon flight and safe return of Apollo 13, 4/11-17/70.
No. C309 for the 424-hour flight of Soyuz 9, 6/1-9.
No. C310 for Luna 16, the unmanned, automated moon mission, 9/12-24/70.
No. C311 for Luna 17, unmanned, automated moon mission, 11/10-17/70.
Exist imperf. Value, set $80.
Issued: #C308, 6/10; #C309, 9/4; #C310, 1/15; #C311 3/8.

American Astronauts on Moon — AP82

1971, Mar. 31 Perf. 12½
C312 AP82 10fo multi 2.50 2.50

Apollo 14 moon landing, 1/31-2/9/71.
Exist imperf. Value $25.
See Nos. C315, C326-C328.

Hunting Type of Regular Issue Souvenir Sheet

Design: 10fo, Red deer group.

1971, Aug. 27 Photo. Perf. 11
C313 A460 10fo multi 3.00 2.50

No. C313 contains one 70x45mm stamp.
Exists imperf. Value $50.

Astronauts Volkov, Dobrovolsky and Patsayev — AP83

Souvenir Sheet

1971, Oct. 4 Photo. Perf. 12½
C314 AP83 10fo multi 2.25 2.25

In memory of the Russian astronauts Vladislav N. Volkov, Lt. Col. Georgi T. Dobrovolsky and Victor I. Patsayev, who died during the Soyuz 11 space mission, June 6-30, 1971.
Exists imperf. Value $20.

Apollo 14 Type of 1971 Souvenir Sheet

10fo, American Lunar Rover on moon.

1972, Jan. 20 Photo. Perf. 12½
C315 AP82 10fo multi 3.00 3.00

Apollo 15 moon mission, 7/26-8/7/71.
Exists imperf. Value $20.

Soccer and Hungarian Flag — AP84

Various Scenes from Soccer and Natl. Flags of: 60f, Romania. 80f, DDR. 1fo, Great Britain. 1.20fo, Yugoslavia. 2fo, USSR. 4fo, Italy. 5fo, Belgium.

1972, Apr. 29
C316 AP84 40f gold & multi .20 .20
C317 AP84 60f gold & multi .20 .20
C318 AP84 80f gold & multi .20 .20
C319 AP84 1fo gold & multi .20 .20
C320 AP84 1.20fo gold & multi .20 .20
C321 AP84 2fo gold & multi .30 .20
C322 AP84 4fo gold & multi .75 .40
C323 AP84 5fo gold & multi 1.10 .70
  a. Sheet of 8, #C316-C323 3.75 3.75
  Nos. C316-C323 (8) 3.15 2.30

European Soccer Championships for the Henri Delaunay Cup.
Exist imperf. Value: set $55; sheet $55.
Nos. C316-C321 were later issued individually in sheets of 20 and in partly changed colors.

Souvenir Sheet

Olympic Rings and Globe — AP85

1972, June 10 Photo. Perf. 12½
C324 AP85 10fo multi 6.00 5.75

20th Olympic Games, Munich, 8/26-9/11.
Exists imperf. Value $95.

Olympic Type of Regular Issue Souvenir Sheet

Design: Equestrian and Olympic Rings.

1972, July 15 Photo. Perf. 12½
C325 A484 10fo multi 2.50 2.50

20th Olympic Games, Munich, Aug. 26-Sept. 11. #C325 contains one 43x43mm stamp.
Exists imperf. Value $25.

Apollo 14 Type of 1971 Souvenir Sheets

Design: 10fo, Astronaut in space, Apollo 16 capsule and badge.

1972, Oct. 10 Photo. Perf. 12½
C326 AP82 10fo blue & multi 2.75 2.75

Apollo 16 US moon mission, 4/15-27/72.
Exists imperf. Value $30.

1973, Jan. 15

Design: Astronaut exploring moon, vert.

C327 AP82 10fo blue & multi 3.00 3.00

Apollo 17 US moon mission, Dec. 7-19, 1972. No. C327 contains one vertical stamp.
Exists imperf. Value $30.

1973, Mar. 12 Photo. Perf. 12½
C328 AP82 10fo Venus 8 3.00 3.00

Venus 8 USSR space mission, Mar. 27-July 22, 1972.
Exist imperf. Value $17.50.

Equestrian (Pentathlon), Olympic Rings and Medal — AP86

Designs (Olympic Rings and Medals): 60f, Weight lifting. 1fo, Canoeing. 1.20fo, Swimming, women's. 1.80fo, Boxing. 4fo, Wrestling. 6fo, Fencing. 10fo, Allegorical figure lighting flame, vert.

1973, Mar. 31
C329 AP86 40f multi .20 .20
C330 AP86 60f multi .20 .20
C331 AP86 1fo blue & multi .20 .20
C332 AP86 1.20fo multi .20 .20
C333 AP86 1.80fo multi .30 .20
C334 AP86 4fo multi .65 .30
C335 AP86 6fo multi 1.00 .50
  Nos. C329-C335 (7) 2.75 1.80

Souvenir Sheet
Perf. 11
C336 AP86 10fo blue & multi 3.75 3.75

Hungarian medalists at 20th Olympic Games. #C336 contains one 44x71mm stamp.
Exist imperf. Value: Nos. C329-C335 $20; No. C336 $80.

Wrens — AP87

1973, Apr. 16   Litho.   Perf. 12
C337	AP87	40f shown	.20	.20
C338	AP87	60f Rock thrush	.20	.20
C339	AP87	80f Robins	.20	.20
C340	AP87	1fo Firecrests	.20	.20
C341	AP87	1.20fo Linnets	.25	.20
C342	AP87	2fo Blue titmice	.35	.20
C343	AP87	4fo White-spotted blue throat	.75	.25
C344	AP87	5fo Gray wagtails	1.10	.55
		Nos. C337-C344 (8)	3.25	2.00

Exist imperf. Value $25.

Exhibition Type of Regular Issue
Souvenir Sheet

10fo, Bavaria #1 with mill wheel cancellation; Munich City Hall, TV Tower and Olympic tent.

1973, May 11   Litho.   Perf. 11
| C345 | A506 | 10fo multi | 2.75 | 2.75 |

No. C345 contains one 83x45mm stamp.
Exists imperf. Value $30.

Souvenir Sheet

Skylab over Earth — AP88

1973, Oct. 16   Photo.   Perf. 12½
| C346 | AP88 | 10fo dk bl, lt bl & yel | 2.75 | 2.75 |

First US manned space station.
Exists imperf. Value $20.

Space Type of Regular Issue

Designs: 6fo, Mars "canals" and Giovanni V. Schiaparelli. 10fo, Mars 7 spacecraft.

1974, Mar. 11   Photo.   Perf. 12½
C347	A522	6fo gold & multi	.75	.50
		Souvenir Sheet		
C348	A522	10fo gold & multi	2.75	2.50

Exist imperf. Value, souvenir sheet $22.

UPU Type of 1974

Designs: a, Mail coach. b, Old mail automobile. c, Jet. d, Apollo 15.

1974, May 22   Litho.   Perf. 12
C349	A526	6fo UPU emblem and TU-154 jet	.75	.60
		Souvenir Sheet		
C350		Sheet of 4	2.75	2.75
a.-d.	A526	2.50fo, any single	.40	.40

No. C350 has bister UPU emblem in center where 4 stamps meet.
Exist imperf. Value, souvenir sheet $50.

Army Day Type of 1974

Designs: 2fo, Ground-to-air missiles, vert. 3fo, Parachutist, helicopter, supersonic jets.

1974, Sept. 28   Litho.   Perf. 12
| C351 | A537 | 2fo gold, emer & blk | .25 | .20 |
| C352 | A537 | 3fo gold, blue & blk | .45 | .20 |

Exist imperf.

Carrier Pigeon, Elizabeth Bridge, Mt. Gellert — AP89

1975, Feb. 7   Litho.   Perf. 12
| C353 | AP89 | 3fo multi | 1.25 | 1.25 |

Carrier Pigeons' Olympics, Budapest, Feb. 7-9. No. C353 printed checkerwise with black and violet coupon showing Pigeon Olympics emblem.
Exists imperf. Value $12.

Sputnik 2, Apollo-Soyuz Emblem AP90

Spacecraft and Apollo-Soyuz Emblem: 60f, Mercury-Atlas 5. 80f, Lunokhod I on moon. 1.20fo, Lunar rover, Apollo 15 mission. 2fo, Soyuz take-off, Baikonur. 4fo, Apollo take-off, Cape Kennedy. 6fo, Apollo-Soyuz link-up. 10fo, Apollo, Soyuz, American and Russian flags over earth, horiz.

1975, July 7   Photo.   Perf. 12x11½
C354	AP90	40f silver & multi	.20	.20
C355	AP90	60f silver & multi	.20	.20
C356	AP90	80f silver & multi	.20	.20
C357	AP90	1.20fo silver & multi	.20	.20
C358	AP90	2fo silver & multi	.25	.20
C359	AP90	4fo silver & multi	.45	.30
C360	AP90	6fo silver & multi	.75	.45
		Nos. C354-C360 (7)	2.25	1.75
		Souvenir Sheet		
		Perf. 12½		
C361	AP90	10fo blue & multi	3.25	3.00

Apollo Soyuz space test project (Russo-American cooperation), launching July 15; link-up July 17. No. C361 contains one 59x38mm stamp.
Exist imperf. Value: Nos. C354-C360 $25; No. C361 $28.

Souvenir Sheet

Map of Europe and Cogwheels — AP91

1975, July 30   Litho.   Perf. 12½
| C362 | AP91 | 10fo multi | 4.50 | 3.75 |

European Security and Cooperation Conference, Helsinki, July 30-Aug. 1.
Exists imperf. Value $70.

Souvenir Sheet

Hungary Nos. 1585, 1382, 2239, 2280, C81 — AP92

1975, Sept. 9   Photo.   Perf. 12½
| C363 | AP92 | 10fo multi | 2.75 | 2.50 |

30 years of stamps.

Exists imperf. Value $25.
A similar souvenir sheet with blue margin, no denomination and no postal validity was released for the 25th anniversary of Filatelica Hungarica.

Souvenir Sheet

Paintings by Károly Lotz and János Halápi — AP93

1976, Mar. 19   Photo.   Perf. 12½
C364	AP93	Sheet of 2	3.25	2.50
a.		5fo Horooo in Storm	1.00	1.00
b.		5fo Morning at Tihany	1.00	1.00

Tourist publicity. #C364a and C364b are imperf. between.
Exists imperf. Value $40.

Souvenir Sheet

Montreal Olympic Stadium — AP94

1976, June 29   Litho.   Perf. 12½
| C365 | AP94 | 20fo red, gray & blk | 3.75 | 3.75 |

21st Olympic Games, Montreal, Canada, July 17-Aug. 1.
Exists imperf. Value $35.

US Mars Mission AP95

60f, Viking in space. 1fo, Viking on Mars. 2fo, Venus, rocket take-off. 3fo, Venyera 9 in space. 4fo, Venyera 10, separation in space. 5fo, Venyera on moon. 20fo, Viking 1 landing on Mars, vert.

1976, Nov. 11   Photo.   Perf. 11
C366	AP95	40f silver & multi	.20	.20
C367	AP95	60f silver & multi	.20	.20
C368	AP95	1fo silver & multi	.20	.20
C369	AP95	2fo silver & multi	.25	.20
C370	AP95	3fo silver & multi	.35	.20
C371	AP95	4fo silver & multi	.55	.30
C372	AP95	5fo silver & multi	.75	.40
		Nos. C366-C372 (7)	2.50	1.70
		Souvenir Sheet		
		Perf. 12½		
C373	AP95	20fo black & multi	3.00	2.75

US-USSR space missions. No. C373 contains one stamp (size: 41x64mm).
Exist imperf. Value: Nos. C366-C372 $20; No. C373 $25.

Hungary No. CB33 — AP96

1977, Apr.   Litho.   Perf. 11½x12
| C374 | AP96 | 3fo multi | 1.50 | 1.50 |

European stamp exhibitions. Issued in sheets of 3 stamps and 3 labels. Labels show exhibition emblems respectively: 125th anniversary of Brunswick stamps, Brunswick, May 5-8; Regiofil XII, Lugano, June 17-19; centenary of San Marino Stamps, Riccione, Aug. 27-29.
Exists imperf. Value: single $20; sheetlet $30.

Space Type 1977
Souvenir Sheet

Design: 20fo, Viking on Mars.

1977, Sept. 20   Litho.   Perf. 11½
| C375 | A603 | 20fo multi | 3.75 | 3.75 |

Exists imperf. Value $25.

Souvenir Sheet

"EUROPA," Map and Dove — AP97

1977, Oct. 3   Perf. 12½
| C376 | AP97 | 20fo multi | 5.25 | 4.75 |

European Security Conference, Belgrade, Oct.-Nov.
Exists imperf. Value $35.

TU-154, Malev over Europe AP98

Planes, Airlines, Maps: 1.20fo, DC-8, Swissair, Southeast Asia. 2fo, IL-62, CSA, North Africa. 2.40fo, A 300B Airbus, Lufthansa, Northwest Europe. 4fo, Boeing 747, Pan Am, North America. 5fo, TU-144, Aeroflot, Northern Europe. 10fo, Concorde, Air France, South America. 20fo, IL-86, Aeroflot, Northeast Asia.

1977, Oct. 26   Litho.   Perf. 11½x12
Size: 32x21mm
C377	AP98	60f orange & blk	.20	.20
C378	AP98	1.20to violet & blk	.35	.20
C379	AP98	2fo yellow & blk	.35	.20
C380	AP98	2.40fo bl grn & blk	.50	.20
C381	AP98	4fo ultra & blk	.50	.20
C382	AP98	5fo dp rose & blk	.70	.25
C383	AP98	10fo blue & blk	1.25	.40
		Perf. 12x11½		
		Size: 37½x29mm		
C384	AP98	20fo green & blk	1.40	.90
		Nos. C377-C384 (8)	5.25	2.55

Exist imperf. Value, set $40.

Montgolfier Brothers and Balloon, 1783 — AP99

Designs: 60f, David Schwarz and airship, 1850. 1fo, Alberto Santos-Dumont and airship flying around Eiffel Tower, 1901. 2fo, Konstantin E. Tsiolkovsky, airship and Kremlin, 1857.

3fo, Roald Amundsen, airship Norge, Polar bears and map, 1872. 4fo, Hugo Eckener, Graf Zeppelin over Mt. Fuji, 1930. 5fo, Count Ferdinand von Zeppelin, Graf Zeppelin over Chicago, 1932. 20fo, Graf Zeppelin over Budapest, 1931.

1977, Nov. 1   Photo.   Perf. 12x11½
C385 AP99 40f gold & multi .20 .20
C386 AP99 60f gold & multi .20 .20
C387 AP99 1fo gold & multi .20 .20
C388 AP99 2fo gold & multi .25 .20
C389 AP99 3fo gold & multi .40 .25
C390 AP99 4fo gold & multi .50 .30
C391 AP99 5fo gold & multi .75 .50
  Nos. C385-C391 (7) 2.50 1.85

Souvenir Sheet
Perf. 12½
C392 AP99 20fo silver & multi 3.25 3.00
  History of airships. No. C392 contains one 60x36mm stamp.
  Exist imperf. Value: Nos. C385-C391 $20; No. C392 $30.

Moon Station — AP100

Science Fiction Paintings by Pal Varga: 60f, Moon settlement. 1fo, Spaceship near Phobos. 2fo, Exploration of asteroids. 3fo, Spaceship in gravitational field of Mars. 4fo, Spaceship and rings of Saturn. 5fo, Spaceship landing on 3rd Jupiter moon.

1978, Mar. 10   Litho.   Perf. 11
C393 AP100 40f multi .20 .20
C394 AP100 60f multi .20 .20
C395 AP100 1fo multi .20 .20
C396 AP100 2fo multi .25 .20
C397 AP100 3fo multi .40 .25
C398 AP100 4fo multi .50 .30
C399 AP100 5fo multi .75 .40
  Nos. C393-C399 (7) 2.50 1.75
  Exist imperf. Value, set $20.

Louis Bleriot and La Manche AP101

60f, J. Alcock & R. W. Brown, Vickers Vimy, 1919. 1fo, A. C. Read, Navy Curtiss NC-4, 1919. 2fo, H. Köhl, G. Hünefeld, J. Fitzmaurice, Junkers W33, 1928. 3fo, A. Johnson, J. Mollison, Gipsy Moth, 1930. 4fo, G. Endresz, S. Magyar, Lockheed Sirius, 1931. 5fo, W. Gronau, Dornier WAL, 1932. 20fo, Wilbur & Orville Wright & their plane.

1978, May 10   Litho.   Perf. 12
C400 AP101 40f multi .20 .20
C401 AP101 60f multi .20 .20
C402 AP101 1fo multi .20 .20
C403 AP101 2fo multi .25 .20
C404 AP101 3fo multi .40 .25
C405 AP101 4fo multi .55 .30
C406 AP101 5fo multi .85 .40
  Nos. C400-C406 (7) 2.65 1.75

Souvenir Sheet
C407 AP101 20fo multi 3.00 2.75
  75th anniv. of 1st powered flight by Wright brothers. #C407 contains one 75x25mm stamp.
  Exist imperf. Value: Nos. C400-C406 $20; No. C407 $35.

Souvenir Sheet

Jules Verne and "Voyage from Earth to Moon" — AP102

1978, Aug. 21   Perf. 12½x11½
C408 AP102 20fo multi 3.00 2.75
  Jules Verne (1828-1905), French science fiction writer.
  Exists imperf. Value $35.

Vladimir Remek Postmarking Mail on Board Salyut 6 — AP103

1978, Sept. 1   Photo.   Perf. 11½x12
C409 AP103 3fo multi .75 .75
  PRAGA '78 International Philatelic Exhibition, Prague, Sept. 8-17. Issued in sheets of 3 stamps and 3 labels, showing PRAGA '78 emblem and Golden Tower, Prague. FISA emblems in margin.
  Exists imperf. Value: single $6; sheetlet $20.

Ski Jump — AP104

Lake Placid '80 Emblem and: 60f, 20fo, Figure skating, diff. 1fo, Downhill skiing. 2fo, Ice hockey. 4fo, Bobsledding. 6fo, Cross-country skiing.

1979, Dec. 15   Litho.   Perf. 12
C410 AP104 40f multi .20 .20
C411 AP104 60f multi .20 .20
C412 AP104 1fo multi .20 .20
C413 AP104 2fo multi .30 .20
C414 AP104 4fo multi .60 .30
C415 AP104 6fo multi 1.00 .55
  Nos. C410-C415 (6) 2.50 1.65

Souvenir Sheet
C416 AP104 20fo multi 2.75 2.75
  13th Winter Olympic Games, Lake Placid, NY, Feb. 12-24, 1980.
  Exist imperf. Value: Nos. C410-C415 $30; No. C416 $35.

Soviet and Hungarian Cosmonauts AP105

1980, May 27   Litho.   Perf. 11½x12
C417 AP105 5fo multi .60 .25
  Intercosmos cooperative space program.
  Exists imperf. Value $30.

Women's Handball, Moscow '80 Emblem, Olympic Rings — AP106

1980, June 16   Photo.   Perf. 11½x12
C418 AP106 40f shown .20 .20
C419 AP106 60f Double kayak .20 .20
C420 AP106 1fo Running .20 .20
C421 AP106 2fo Gymnast .25 .20
C422 AP106 3fo Equestrian .40 .25
C423 AP106 4fo Wrestling .55 .35
C424 AP106 5fo Water polo .65 .50
  Nos. C418-C424 (7) 2.45 1.90

Souvenir Sheet
C425 AP106 20fo Torch bearers 3.00 3.00
  22nd Summer Olympic Games, Moscow, July 19-Aug. 3.
  See No. C427.
  Exist imperf. Value: Nos. C418-C424 $30; No. C425 $25.

Souvenir Sheet

Cosmonauts Bertalan Farkes and Valery Kubasov, Salyut 6-Soyuz 35 and 36 — AP107

1980, July 12   Litho.   Perf. 12½
C426 AP107 20fo multi 3.25 3.00
  Intercosmos cooperative space program (USSR-Hungary).
  Exists imperf. Value $30.

Olympic Type of 1980
Souvenir Sheet
1980, Sept. 26   Litho.   Perf. 12½
C427 AP106 20fo Greek Frieze and gold medal 3.25 3.00
  Olympic Champions.
  Exists imperf. Value $30.

Kalman Kittenberger (1881-1958), Zoologist and Explorer — AP108

1981, Mar. 6   Photo.   Perf. 11½
C427A AP108 40f Cheetah .20 .20
C427B AP108 60f Lion .20 .20
C427C AP108 1fo Leopard .20 .20
C427D AP108 2fo Rhinoceros .35 .20
C427E AP108 3fo Antelope .55 .25
C427F AP108 4fo African elephant .65 .30
C427G AP108 5fo shown .85 .40
  Nos. C427A-C427G (7) 3.00 1.75
  Exist imperf. Value, set $25.

Graf Zeppelin over Tokyo, First Worldwide Flight, Aug. 7-Sept. 4, 1929 — AP109

Graf Zeppelin Flights (Zeppelin and): 2fo, Icebreaker Malygin, Polar flight, July 24-31, 1931. 3fo, Nine Arch Bridge, Hortobagy, Hungary, Mar. 28-30, 1931. 4fo, Holsten Tor, Lubeck, Baltic Sea, May 12-15, 1931. 5fo, Tower Bridge, England, Aug. 18-20, 1931. 6fo, Federal Palace, Chicago World's Fair, 50th crossing of Atlantic, Oct. 14-Nov. 2, 1933. 7fo, Lucerne, first flight across Switzerland, Sept. 26, 1929.

Perf. 12½x11½
1981, Mar. 16   Litho.
C428 AP109 1fo multi .20 .20
C429 AP109 2fo multi .25 .20
C430 AP109 3fo multi .40 .25
C431 AP109 4fo multi .55 .35
C432 AP109 5fo multi .65 .40
C433 AP109 6fo multi .75 .55
C434 AP109 7fo multi .85 .60
  Nos. C428-C434 (7) 3.65 2.55
  LURABA '81, First Aviation and Space Philatelic Exhibition, Lucerne, Switzerland, Mar. 20-29. No. C434 se-tenant with label showing exhibition emblem.
  Exist imperf. Value, set $20.

Illustrator Type of 1981
Designs: Illustrations by A. Lesznai.

1981, Dec. 29   Litho.   Perf. 11½x12
C435 A693 4fo At the End of the Village .55 .50
C436 A693 5fo Dance .70 .55
C437 A693 6fo Sunday .80 .60
  Nos. C435-C437 (3) 2.05 1.65
  Exist imperf.

Manned Flight Bicentenary AP110

Various hot air balloons.

1983, Apr. 5   Litho.   Perf. 12x11½
C438 AP110 1fo 1811 .20 .20
C439 AP110 1fo 1896 .20 .20
C440 AP110 2fo 1904 .25 .20
C441 AP110 2fo 1977 .25 .20
C442 AP110 4fo 1981 .50 .25
C443 AP110 4fo 1982 .50 .25
C444 AP110 5fo 1983 .70 .35
  Nos. C438-C444 (7) 2.60 1.65

Souvenir Sheet
Perf. 12½
C445 AP110 20fo 1983 2.75 2.75
  No. C445 contains one 39x49mm stamp.
  Exist imperf. Value: Nos. C438-C444 $20; No. C445 $25.

Audubon Type of 1985
1985, June 19   Litho.   Perf. 12
C446 A778 4fo Colaptes auratus .60 .35
C447 A778 6fo Richmondena cardinalis .85 .50
  Exist imperf.

Aircraft — AP111

1988, Aug. 31   Litho.   Perf. 11
C448	AP111	1fo Lloyd CII	.20	.20
C449	AP111	2fo Brandenburg CI	.30	.20
C450	AP111	4fo UFAG CI	.50	.35
C451	AP111	10fo Gerle 13	1.40	.90
C452	AP111	12fo WM 13	1.60	1.10
		Nos. C448-C452 (5)	4.00	2.75

Exist imperf. Value, set $32.50.

AIR POST SEMI-POSTAL STAMPS

> Catalogue values for unused stamps in this section are for Never Hinged items.

Roosevelt Type of Semipostal Stamps, 1947

F. D. Roosevelt, Plane and Place: 10f+10f, Casablanca. 20f+20f, Tehran. 50f+50f, Yalta (map). 70f+70f, Hyde Park.

Perf. 12x12½
1947, June 11   Photo.   Wmk. 210
Portrait in Sepia
CB1	SP115	10f + 10f red vio	4.25	5.25
CB1A	SP115	20f + 20f brn ol	4.25	5.25
CB1B	SP115	50f + 50f vio	4.25	5.25
CB1C	SP115	70f + 70f blk	4.25	5.25
		Nos. CB1-CB1C (4)	16.00	20.00

Exist imperf.

A souvenir sheet contains one each of Nos. CB1-CB1C with border inscriptions and decorations in gray. Size: 161x122mm. Value $125. Exists imperf. Value $225.
See note below Nos. B198A-B198D.

Souvenir Sheet

Chain Bridge, Budapest — SPAP1

Perf. 12x12½
1948, May 15   Photo.   Wmk. 283
CB1D	SPAP1	2fo + 18fo brn car	120.00	120.00

Exists imperf. Value $2,500.

Souvenir Sheet

Chain Bridge — SPAP2

1948, Oct. 16
CB2	SPAP2	3fo + 18fo dp grnsh bl	120.00	120.00

Exists imperf. Value $2,500.

Type of Air Post Stamps of 1948 Portraits at Right

Writers: 1f, William Shakespeare. 2f, Francois Voltaire. 4f, Johann Wolfgang von Goethe. 5f, Lord Byron. 6f, Victor Hugo. 8f, Edgar Allen Poe. 10f, Sandor Petőfi. 12f, Mark Twain. 30f, Count Leo Tolstoy. 40f, Maxim Gorky.

1948, Oct. 16   Photo.
CB3	AP22	1f dp ultra	.25	.20
CB4	AP22	2f rose carmine	.25	.20
CB5	AP22	4f dp yellow grn	.25	.20
CB6	AP22	5f dp rose lilac	.35	.35

CB7	AP22	6f deep blue	.35	.35
CB8	AP22	8f olive brn	.35	.35
CB9	AP22	10f red	.50	.45
CB10	AP22	12f deep violet	.50	.45
CB11	AP22	30f orange brn	1.75	1.50
CB12	AP22	40f sepia	2.25	1.75
		Nos. CB3-CB12 (10)	6.80	5.80

Sold at a 50 per cent increase over face, half of which aided reconstruction of the Chain Bridge and the other half the hospital for postal employees.
Exist imperf. Value, set $115.

1st Stamp Type Souvenir Sheets

Perf. 12½x12
1951, Sept. 12   Engr.   Unwmk.
CB13	A208	1fo + 1fo red	75.00	65.00
CB14	A208	2fo + 2fo blue	75.00	65.00

Exist imperf. Value, each $200.

Children Inspecting Stamp Album — SPAP3

2fo+2fo, Children at stamp exhibition.

Perf. 12x12½
1952, Oct. 12   Photo.   Wmk. 106
CB15	SPAP3	1fo + 1fo blue	9.00	9.00
CB16	SPAP3	2fo + 2fo brn red	9.00	9.00

Stamp week, Oct. 11-19, 1952.
Exist imperf. Value, set $100.

Globe and Mailbox SPAP4

Designs: 1fo+50f, Mobile post office. 2fo+1fo, Telegraph pole. 3fo+1.50fo, Radio. 5fo+2.50fo, Telephone. 10fo+5fo, Post horn.

1957, June 20   Perf. 12x12½, 12
Size: 32x21mm
CB17	SPAP4	60f + 30f bister brn	.55	.20
CB18	SPAP4	1fo + 50f lilac	.75	.35
CB19	SPAP4	2fo + 1fo org ver	1.00	.45
CB20	SPAP4	3fo + 1.50fo blue	1.50	.70
CB21	SPAP4	5fo + 2.50fo gray	2.25	1.75

Size: 46x31mm
CB22	SPAP4	10fo + 5fo pale grn	4.50	4.00
		Nos. CB17-CB22 (6)	10.55	7.45

The surtax was for the benefit of hospitals for postal and telegraph employees.
Exist imperf. Value, set $80.

Parachute of Fausztusz Verancsics, 1617 SPAP5

History of Hungarian Aviation: No. CB24, Balloon of David Schwarz, 1897. No. CB25, Monoplane of Ernő Horvath, 1911. No. CB26, PKZ-2 helicopter, 1918.

Engraved and Lithographed

1967, May 6   Perf. 10½
CB23	SPAP5	2fo + 1fo sep & yel	.50	.50
CB24	SPAP5	2fo + 1fo sep & lt bl	.50	.50
CB25	SPAP5	2fo + 1fo sep & lt grn	.50	.50
CB26	SPAP5	2fo + 1fo sep & pink	.50	.50
a.		Horiz. strip of 4, #CB23-CB26	2.75	2.75
b.		Souv. sheet of 4, #CB23-CB26	3.75	2.75

"AEROFILA 67" International Airmail Exhibition, Budapest, Sept. 3-10.

Exist imperf. Value: strip $20; souvenir sheet $40.

1967, Sept. 3

Aviation, 1967: No. CB27, Parachutist. No. CB28, Helicopter Mi-1. No. CB29, TU-154 jet. No. CB30, Space station Luna 12.
CB27	SPAP5	2fo + 1fo slate & lt grn	.50	.50
CB28	SPAP5	2fo + 1fo slate & buff	.50	.50
CB29	SPAP5	2fo + 1fo slate & yel	.50	.50
CB30	SPAP5	2fo + 1fo slate & pink	.50	.50
a.		Horiz. strip of 4, #CB27-CB30	2.75	2.75
b.		Souv. sheet of 4, #CB27-CB30	3.75	3.75

Issued to commemorate (in connection with AEROFILA 67) the 7th Congress of FISA (Fédération Internationale des Sociétés Aérophilatéliques) and the 40th Stamp Day.
Exist imperf. Value: strip $20; souvenir sheet $35.

Olympic Games Airmail Type

Design: 2fo+1fo, Equestrian.

1968, Aug. 21   Photo.   Perf. 12
CB31	AP74	2fo + 1fo multi	.35	.35

Exists imperf.

1st Hungarian Airmail Letter, 1918, Plane — SPAP6

Designs: No. CB33, Letter, 1931, and Zeppelin. No. CB34, Balloon post letter, 1967, and balloon. No. CB35, Letter, 1969, and helicopter.
#CB36a, #C1. b, #C7. c, #C305. d, #C312.

1974, Oct. 19   Litho.   Perf. 12
CB32	SPAP6	2fo + 1fo multi	.95	.95
CB33	SPAP6	2fo + 1fo multi	.95	.95
a.		Pair, #CB32-CB33	2.00	2.00
CB34	SPAP6	2fo + 1fo multi	.95	.95
CB35	SPAP6	2fo + 1fo multi	.95	.95
a.		Pair, #CB34-CB35	2.00	2.00
		Nos. CB32-CB35 (4)	3.80	3.80

Souvenir Sheet
CB36		Sheet of 4	3.50	3.50
a.		SPAP6 2fo+1fo any single	.50	.50

AEROPHILA, International Airmail Exhibition, Budapest, Oct. 19-27.
No. CB36 contains 4 35x25mm stamps.
Exist imperf. Value: set of 2 pairs $35; souvenir sheet $30.

SPECIAL DELIVERY STAMPS

Issue of the Monarchy

SD1   SD2

1916   Typo.   Wmk. 137   Perf. 15
E1	SD1	2f gray green & red	.20	.20

Exists imperf. Value $4.
For overprints and surcharges see Nos. 1NE1, 2NE1, 4N5, 5NE1, 6NE1, 7NE1, 8NE1, 10NE1, 11NE1, 11NJ7-J8.

Issues of the Republic

Special Delivery Stamp of 1916 Overprinted

1919
E2	SD1	2f gray green & red	.20	.75

Exists imperf. Value $4.

General Issue
1919
E3	SD2	2f gray green & red	.20	.50

Exists imperf. Value $5.

REGISTRATION STAMPS

> Catalogue values for unused stamps in this section are for Never Hinged items.

Nos. 625, 609 and 626 Overprinted in Carmine

a   b

"Ajl." or "Ajánlás" = Registered Letter.

1946   Wmk. 266   Perf. 15
F1	A118(a)	"Ajl.1." on 20f	.20	.20
a.		"Ajl.1."	50.00	
F2	A99(a)	"Ajl.2." on 12f	.20	.20
F3	A118(b)	"Ajánlás" on 24f	.20	.20
		Nos. F1-F3 (3)	.60	.60

POSTAGE DUE STAMPS

Issues of the Monarchy

    D1

Perf. 11½, 11¾x12
1903   Typo.   Wmk. 135
J1	D1	1f green & blk	.50	.50
J2	D1	2f green & blk	3.00	1.50
J3	D1	5f green & blk	15.00	6.50
J4	D1	6f green & blk	12.00	6.00
J5	D1	10f green & blk	80.00	3.00
J6	D1	12f grcon & blk	2.50	2.50
J7	D1	20f green & blk	20.00	1.50
J8	D1	50f green & blk	16.00	12.50
J9	D1	100f green & blk	1.00	1.00
		Nos. J1-J9 (9)	150.00	35.00

See Nos. J10-J26, J28-J43. For overprints and surcharges see Nos. J27, J44-J50, 1NJ1-1NJ5, 2NJ1-2NJ16, 4NJ2-4NJ3, 5NJ1-5NJ8, 6NJ1-6NJ9, 7NJ1-7NJ4, 9NJ1-9NJ3, 10NJ1-10NJ6, 11NJ1-J6.

1908-09   Wmk. 136   Perf. 15
J10	D1	1f green & black	.75	.50
J11	D1	2f green & black	1.00	.50
J12	D1	5f green & black	2.50	.75
J13	D1	6f green & black	1.50	.50
J14	D1	10f green & black	1.50	.50
J15	D1	12f green & black	1.25	.50
J16	D1	20f green & black	10.00	.50
c.		Center inverted	9,000.	9,000.
J17	D1	50f green & black	1.75	.75
		Nos. J10-J17 (8)	20.25	4.50

1905   Wmk. 136a   Perf. 11½x12
J12a	D1	5f green & black	175.00	70.00
J13a	D1	6f green & black	14.00	7.50
J14a	D1	10f green & black	175.00	5.00
J15a	D1	12f green & black	25.00	16.00
J17a	D1	50f green & black	6.00	2.50
J18	D1	100f green & black	5.00	

1906   *Perf. 15*

J11b	D1	2f green & black	3.50	3.50
J12b	D1	5f green & black	2.50	2.00
J13b	D1	6f green & black	2.50	2.00
J14b	D1	10f green & black	15.00	.60
J15b	D1	12f green & black	.75	.60
J16b	D1	20f green & black	25.00	.60
d.		Center inverted	9,000.	9,000.
J17b	D1	50f green & black	1.00	1.00
		Nos. J11b-J17b (7)	50.25	10.30

1914   **Wmk. 137 Horiz.**   *Perf. 15*

J19	D1	1f green & black	.35	.25
J20	D1	2f green & black	.25	.20
J21	D1	5f green & black	.40	.40
J22	D1	6f green & black	.80	.60
J23	D1	10f green & black	.90	.70
J24	D1	12f green & black	.40	.35
J25	D1	20f green & black	.35	.20
J26	D1	50f green & black	.70	.40
		Nos. J19-J26 (8)	4.15	3.10

1914   **Wmk. 137 Vert.**

J20a	D1	2f green & black	57.50	57.50
J21a	D1	5f green & black	4.50	4.50
J22a	D1	6f green & black	9.00	7.50
J25a	D1	20f green & black	2,250.	900.00
J26a	D1	50f green & black	2.50	2.50

During 1921-24, a number of Postage Due stamps were punched with three holes prior to sale. See note following No. 105 in the Regular Postage section.

No. J9 Surcharged in Red

1915   **Wmk. 135**

J27	D1	20f on 100f grn & blk	.50	1.50
a.		On No. J18, Wmk. 136a	15.00	37.50

1915-22   **Wmk. 137**

J28	D1	1f green & red	.20	.20
J29	D1	2f green & red	.20	.20
J30	D1	5f green & red	.35	.20
J31	D1	6f green & red	.20	.20
J32	D1	10f green & red	.20	.20
J33	D1	12f green & red	.20	.20
J34	D1	15f green & red	.30	.50
J35	D1	20f green & red	.20	.20
J36	D1	30f green & red	.20	.20
J37	D1	40f green & red ('20)	.20	.20
J38	D1	50f green & red ('20)	.20	.20
a.		Center inverted	60.00	
J39	D1	120f green & red ('20)	.20	.20
J40	D1	200f green & red ('20)	.20	.20
J41	D1	2k green & red ('22)	.40	.75
J42	D1	3k green & red ('22)	.20	.20
J43	D1	50k green & red ('22)	.20	.20
		Nos. J28-J43 (16)	3.65	4.05

Issues of the Republic

Postage Due Stamps of 1914-18 Overprinted in Black

1918-19

On Issue of 1914

J44	D1	50f green & black	3.00	5.50

On Stamps and Type of 1915-18

J45	D1	2f green & red	.20	.20
J46	D1	3f green & red	.20	.20
a.		"KOZTARSASAG" omitted	650.00	
J47	D1	10f green & red	.20	.20
J48	D1	15f green & red	.20	.20
J49	D1	40f green & red	.20	.20
a.		Inverted overprint	60.00	60.00
J50	D1	50f green & red	.20	.20
a.		Center and overprint inverted	75.00	75.00
		Nos. J44-J50 (7)	4.20	6.70

Issues of the Kingdom

D3

1919-20   *Typo.*

J65	D3	2f green & black	.20	.20
a.		Inverted center	2,000.	
J66	D3	3f green & black	.20	.20
J67	D3	20f green & black	.20	.20
J68	D3	40f green & black	.20	.20
J69	D3	50f green & black	.20	.20
		Nos. J65-J69 (5)	1.00	1.00

Postage Due Stamps of this type have been overprinted "Magyar Tancskztarsasag" but

have not been reported as having been issued without the additional overprint "heads of wheat."

For overprints see Nos. J70-J75.

New Overprint in Black over "Magyar Tanacskoztarsasag"

1920

J70	D3	2f green & black	.85	1.25
J71	D3	3f green & black	.85	1.25
J72	D3	10f green & black	1.40	2.25
J73	D3	20f green & black	.85	1.25
J74	D3	40f green & black	.85	1.25
J75	D3	50f green & black	.85	1.25
		Nos. J70-J75 (6)	5.65	8.50

Postage Issues Surcharged

1921-25

Red Surcharge

J76	A9	100f on 15f violet	.20	.20
J77	A9	500f on 15f violet	.20	.20
J78	A9	2½k on 10f red vio	.20	.25
J79	A9	3k on 15f violet	.20	.25
J80	A9	6k on 1½k violet	.20	1.50
J81	A9	9k on 40f ol grn	.20	.25
J82	A9	10k on 2½k green	.20	1.25
J83	A9	12k on 60f blk brn	.20	.25
J84	A9	15k on 1½k vio	.20	.25
J85	A9	20k on 2½k grn	.20	1.10
J86	A9	25k on 1½k vio	.20	.25
J87	A9	30k on 1½k vio	.20	.25
J88	A9	40k on 2½k grn	.20	1.25
J89	A9	50k on 1½k vio	.20	.25
J90	A9	100k on 4½k dl vio	.20	.20
J91	A9	200k on 4½k dl vio	.20	.20
J92	A9	300k on 4½k dl vio	.20	.20
J93	A9	500k on 2k grnsh bl	.60	.25
J94	A9	500k on 3k org brn	2.10	.30
J95	A9	1000k on 2k grnsh bl	1.20	.25
J96	A9	1000k on 3k org brn	1.75	.20
J97	A9	2000k on 2k grnsh bl	1.20	.40
J98	A9	2000k on 3k org brn	2.10	.35
J99	A9	5000k on 5k brown	.90	1.75
		Nos. J76-J99 (24)	13.25	11.60

Year of issue: 6k, 15k, 25k, 30k, 50k, 1922. 10k, 20k, 40k, 100k - No. J93, Nos. J95, J97, 1923. 5,000k, 1924. Nos. J94, J96, J98, 1925. Others, 1921.

D6

Perf. 14x14½, 15

1926   **Wmk. 133**   **Litho.**

J100	D6	1f rose red	.20	.20
J101	D6	2f rose red	.20	.20
J102	D6	3f rose red	.30	.60
J103	D6	4f rose red	.20	.20
J104	D6	5f rose red	1.75	2.50
J105	D6	8f rose red	.20	.20
J106	D6	10f rose red	1.25	.20
J107	D6	16f rose red	.30	.20
J108	D6	32f rose red	.50	.20
J109	D6	40f rose red	.60	.20
J110	D6	50f rose red	.70	.40
J111	D6	80f rose red	1.25	.65
		Nos. J100-J111 (12)	7.45	5.75

Exist imperf. Value, set $100.

See Nos. J117-J123. For surcharges see Nos. J124-J129.

Nos. C7-C11 Surcharged in Red or Green

1926   **Wmk. 137**   *Perf. 14*

J112	AP3	1f on 500k (R)	.20	.30
J113	AP3	2f on 1000k (G)	.20	.30
J114	AP3	3f on 2000k (R)	.20	.30

Wmk. 133

J115	AP3	5f on 5000k (G)	.65	1.50
J116	AP3	10f on 10000k (G)	.50	1.10
		Nos. J112-J116 (5)	1.75	3.50

Type of 1926 Issue

1928-32   **Wmk. 210**   *Perf. 15*

J117	D6	2f rose red	.20	.20
J118	D6	4f rose red ('32)	.20	.20
J119	D6	8f rose red	.25	.20
J120	D6	10f rose red	.25	.20
J121	D6	16f rose red	.35	.20
J122	D6	20f rose red	.60	.20
J123	D6	40f rose red	.50	.20
		Nos. J117-J123 (7)	2.35	1.40

Exist imperf. Value, set $50.

Postage Due Stamps of 1926 Surcharged in Black

1931-33   **Wmk. 133**

J124	D6	4f on 5f rose red	.20	.20
J125	D6	10f on 16f rose red	1.50	3.75
J126	D6	10f on 80f rose red ('33)	.30	.20
J127	D6	12f on 50f rose red ('33)	.35	.20
J128	D6	20f on 32f rose red	.35	.30
		Nos. J124-J128 (5)	2.70	4.65

Surcharged on No. J121

1931   **Wmk. 210**   *Perf. 15*

J129	D6	10f on 16f rose red	.85	1.25

Catalogue values for unused stamps in this section, from this point to the end of the section, are for Never Hinged items.

Figure of Value — D7

1934   **Photo.**   **Wmk. 210**

J130	D7	2f ultra	.20	.20
J131	D7	4f ultra	.20	.20
J132	D7	6f ultra	.20	.20
J133	D7	8f ultra	.20	.20
J134	D7	10f ultra	.25	.20
J135	D7	12f ultra	.25	.20
J136	D7	16f ultra	.25	.20
J137	D7	20f ultra	.40	.20
J138	D7	40f ultra	.60	.20
J139	D7	80f ultra	2.00	.50
		Nos. J130-J139 (10)	4.55	2.30

Exist imperf. Value, set $60.

Coat of Arms and Post Horn — D8

1941

J140	D8	2f brown red	.20	.20
J142	D8	4f brown red	.20	.20
J143	D8	6f brown red	.20	.20
J144	D8	8f brown red	.20	.20
J145	D8	10f brown red	.20	.20
J146	D8	12f brown red	.30	.20
J147	D8	16f brown red	.40	.20
J148	D8	20f brown red	.50	.20
J150	D8	40f brown red	.75	.25
		Nos. J140-J150 (9)	3.00	1.85

Exist imperf. Value, set $20.

1941-44   **Wmk. 266**

J151	D8	2f brown red	.20	.20
J152	D8	3f brown red	.20	.20
J153	D8	4f brown red	.20	.20
J154	D8	5f brown red	.20	.20
J155	D8	8f brown red	.20	.20
J156	D8	10f brown red	.20	.20
J157	D8	12f brown red	.20	.20
J158	D8	16f brown red	.25	.20
J159	D8	18f brown red ('44)	.25	.20
J160	D8	20f brown red	.20	.20

J161	D8	24f brown red	.25	.20
J162	D8	30f brown red ('44)	.20	.20
J163	D8	36f brown red ('44)	.20	.20
J164	D8	40f brown red	.20	.20
J165	D8	50f brown red	.20	.20
J166	D8	60f brown red ('44)	.30	.20
		Nos. J151-J166 (16)	3.40	3.20

Exist imperf. Value, set $25.
For surcharges see Nos. J167-J185.

Issues of the Republic

Types of Hungary Postage Due Stamps, 1941-44, Surcharged in Carmine

1945   **Wmk. 266**   **Photo.**   *Perf. 15*

Blue Surface-tinted Paper

J167	D8	10f on 2f brn red	.20	.20
J168	D8	10f on 3f brn red	.20	.20
J169	D8	20f on 4f brn red	.20	.20
J170	D8	20f on 6f brn red	9.50	9.50
J171	D8	20f on 8f brn red	.20	.20
J172	D8	40f on 12f brn red	.20	.20
J173	D8	40f on 16f brn red	.20	.20
J174	D8	40f on 18f brn red	.20	.20
J175	D8	60f on 24f brn red	.20	.20
J176	D8	80f on 30f brn red	.20	.20
J177	D8	90f on 36f brn red	.20	.20
J178	D8	1p on 10f brn red	.20	.20
J179	D8	1p on 40f brn red	.20	.20
J180	D8	2p on 30f brn red	.20	.20
J181	D8	2p on 50f brn red	.20	.20
J182	D8	2p on 60f brn red	.20	.20

Surcharged in Black, Thicker Type

J183	D8	10p on 3f brn red	.20	.20
J184	D8	12p on 8f brn red	.20	.20
J185	D8	20p on 24f brn red	.20	.20
		Nos. J167-J185 (19)	13.10	13.10

D9

1946-50   **Wmk. 210**   *Perf. 15*

Numerals in Deep Magenta

J186	D9	4f magenta	.50	.20
J187	D9	10f magenta	1.25	.20
J188	D9	20f magenta	.50	.20
J189	D9	30f magenta	.50	.20
J190	D9	40f magenta	.75	.20
J191	D9	50f mag ('50)	2.25	.50
J192	D9	60f magenta	1.50	.20
J193	D9	1.20fo magenta	2.25	.25
J194	D9	2fo magenta	3.75	.30
		Nos. J186-J194 (9)	13.25	2.25

1951   **Wmk. 106**

Numerals in Deep Magenta

J194A	D9	4f magenta	.20	.20
J194B	D9	10f magenta	.20	.20
J194C	D9	20f magenta	1.25	.20
j.		"fiellr"	35.00	7.50
J194D	D9	30f magenta	1.50	.20
J194E	D9	40f magenta	.50	.20
J194F	D9	50f magenta	1.00	.20
J194G	D9	60f magenta	.85	.20
J194H	D9	1.20fo magenta	3.50	.20
J194I	D9	2fo magenta	3.00	.20
		Nos. J194A-J194I (9)	12.00	1.80

Nos. J194A-J194I are found in both large format (about 18x22mm) and small (about 17x21mm).

D10

D11

1951   **Unwmk.**   **Typo.**   *Perf. 14½x15*

Paper with Vertical Lines in Green

Revenue Stamps with Blue Surcharge

J195	D10	8f dark brown	.20	.20
J196	D10	10f dark brown	.20	.20
J197	D10	12f dark brown	.40	.40
		Nos. J195-J197 (3)	.80	.80

1951 **Wmk. 106** **Photo.** *Perf. 14½*

J198	D11	4f brown	.20	.20
J199	D11	6f brown	.20	.20
J200	D11	8f brown	.20	.20
J201	D11	10f brown	.20	.20
J202	D11	14f brown	.35	.25
J203	D11	20f brown	.20	.20
J204	D11	30f brown	.20	.20
J205	D11	40f brown	.20	.20
J206	D11	50f brown	.25	.20
J207	D11	60f brown	.30	.20
J208	D11	1.20fo brown	.30	.20
J209	D11	2fo brown	.50	.30
		Nos. J198-J209 (12)	3.10	2.55

Exist imperf. Value, set $25.

D12   D13

Photo., Numeral Typo. in Black
1953
Numerals 3mm High

J210	D12	4f dull green	.20	.20
J211	D12	6f dull green	.20	.20
J212	D12	8f dull green	.20	.20
J213	D12	10f dull green	.20	.20
J214	D12	12f dull green	.20	.20
J215	D12	14f dull green	.20	.20
J216	D12	16f dull green	.20	.20
J217	D12	20f dull green	.20	.20
J218	D12	24f dull green	.20	.20
J219	D12	30f dull green	.20	.20
J220	D12	36f dull green	.20	.20
J221	D12	40f dull green	.20	.20
J222	D12	50f dull green	.20	.20
J223	D12	60f dull green	.20	.20
J224	D12	70f dull green	.25	.20
J225	D12	80f dull green	.30	.20

Numerals 4½mm High

J226	D12	1.20fo dull green	.40	.20
J227	D12	2fo dull green	.75	.20
a.		Small "2" (3mm high)	4.00	1.00
		Nos. J210-J227 (18)	4.50	3.60

1st Hungarian postage due stamp, 50th anniv.
Exist imperf. Value, set $30.

Photo., Numeral Typo. in Black on Nos. J228-J243
1958 **Wmk. 106** *Perf. 14½*
Size: 21x16½mm

J228	D13	4f red	.20	.20
J229	D13	6f red	.20	.20
J230	D13	8f red	.20	.20
J231	D13	10f red	.20	.20
J232	D13	12f red	.20	.20
J233	D13	14f red	.20	.20
J234	D13	16f red	.20	.20
J235	D13	20f red	.20	.20
J236	D13	24f red	.20	.20
J237	D13	30f red	.20	.20
J238	D13	36f red	.20	.20
J239	D13	40f red	.20	.20
J240	D13	50f red	.20	.20
J241	D13	60f red	.20	.20
J242	D13	70f red	.20	.20
J243	D13	80f red	.25	.20

Perf. 12
Size: 31x21mm

J244	D13	1.20fo dk red brn	.35	.20
J245	D13	2fo dk red brn	.50	.25
		Nos. J228-J245 (18)	4.10	3.65

Exist imperf. Value, set $15.

Photo., Numeral Typo. in Black on Nos. J246-J261
1965-69 **Unwmk.** *Perf. 11½*
Size: 21x16½mm

J246	D13	4f red	.20	.20
J247	D13	6f red	.20	.20
J248	D13	8f red	.20	.20
J249	D13	10f red	.20	.20
J250	D13	12f red	.20	.20
J251	D13	14f red	.20	.20
J252	D13	16f red	.20	.20
J253	D13	20f red	.20	.20
J254	D13	24f red	.20	.20
J255	D13	30f red	.20	.20
J256	D13	36f red	.20	.20
J257	D13	40f red	.20	.20
J258	D13	50f red	.20	.20
J259	D13	60f red	.20	.20
J260	D13	70f red	.20	.20
J261	D13	80f red	.20	.20

Perf. 11½x12
Size: 31x21mm

J262	D13	1fo dk red brn ('69)	.20	.20
J263	D13	1.20fo dk red brn	.25	.20
J264	D13	2fo dk red brn	.30	.20
J265	D13	4fo dk red brn ('69)	.50	.20
		Nos. J246-J265 (20)	4.45	4.00

Mail Plane and Truck — D14

Postal History — D15

Designs: 20f, Money order canceling machine. 40f, Scales in self-service P.O. 80f, Automat for registering parcels. 1fo, Keypunch operator. 1.20fo, Mail plane and truck. 2fo, Diesel mail train. 3fo, Mailman on motorcycle with sidecar. 4fo, Rural mail delivery. 8fo, Automatic letter sorting machine. 10fo, Postman riding motorcycle.

1973-85 **Photo.** *Perf. 11*
Size: 21x18mm

J266	D14	20f brown & ver	.20	.20
J267	D14	40f dl bl & ver	.20	.20
J268	D14	80f violet & ver	.20	.20
J269	D14	1fo ol grn & ver	.20	.20

Perf. 12x11½
Size: 28x22mm

J270	D14	1.20fo green & ver	.20	.20
J271	D14	2fo lilac & ver	.20	.20
J272	D14	3fo brt blue & ver	.25	.20
J273	D14	4fo org brn & ver	.35	.20
J274	D14	8fo deep mag & dark red	1.10	.30
J275	D14	10fo green & dark red	1.25	.35
		Nos. J266-J275 (10)	4.15	2.25

Issued: 20f-4fo, 12/1973; 8fo, 10fo, 12/16/85.

1987, Dec. 10 **Litho.** *Perf. 12*

Designs: Excerpt from 18th cent. letter, innovations in letter carrying.

J276	D15	1fo Foot messenger, 16th cent.	.20	.20
J277	D15	4fo Post rider, 17th cent.	.55	.30
J278	D15	6fo Horse-drawn mail coach, 18th cent.	.75	.45
J279	D15	8fo Railroad mail car, 19th cent.	1.00	.60
J280	D15	10fo Mail truck, 20th cent.	1.25	.65
J281	D15	20fo Airplane, 20th cent.	2.25	1.25
		Nos. J276-J281 (6)	6.00	3.45

OFFICIAL STAMPS

During 1921-24, a number of Official stamps were punched with three holes prior to sale. See note following No. 105 in the Regular Postage section.

O1

1921-23 **Wmk. 137** **Typo.** *Perf. 15*

O1	O1	10f brn vio & blk	.20	.20
O2	O1	20f ol brn & blk	.20	.20
a.		"HIVATALOS" inverted		10,000.
O3	O1	60f blk brn & blk	.20	.20
O4	O1	100f dl rose & blk	.20	.20
O5	O1	250f bl & blk	.20	.20
O6	O1	350f gray & blk	.25	.20
O7	O1	500f lt brn & blk	.25	.20
O8	O1	1000f lil brn & blk	.25	.20
O9	O1	5k brn ('23)	.20	.20

O10	O1	10k choc ('23)	.20	.20
O11	O1	15k gray blk ('23)	.20	.20
O12	O1	25k org ('23)	.20	.20
O13	O1	50k brn & red ('22)	.20	.20
O14	O1	100k bis & red ('22)	.20	.20
O15	O1	150k grn & red ('23)	.20	.20
O16	O1	300k dl red & red ('23)	.25	.20
O17	O1	350k vio & red ('23)	.30	.20
O18	O1	500k org & red ('22)	.30	.20
O19	O1	600k ol bis & red ('23)	.80	.60
O20	O1	1000k bl & red ('22)	1.20	.60
		Nos. O1-O20 (20)	6.00	4.40

Counterfeits of No. O2a exist.

Stamps of 1921 Surcharged in Red

1922

O21	O1	15k on 20f ol brn & blk	.20	.20
O22	O1	25k on 60f blk brn & blk	.20	.20

Stamps of 1921 Overprinted in Red

1923

O23	O1	350k gray & blk	.25	.20

With Additional Surcharge of New Value in Red

1923-24
Paper with Gray Moiré on Face

O24	O1	150k on 100f dl rose & blk	.30	.20
O25	O1	2000k on 250f bl & blk	1.50	.40
		Nos. O23-O25 (3)	2.05	.80

O26	O1	500k org & red ('23)	2.10	.25
O27	O1	1000k bl & red ('23)	2.10	.25
O28	O1	3000k vio & red ('24)	2.10	1.25
O29	O1	5000k bl & red ('24)	2.40	1.50
		Nos. O26-O29 (4)	8.70	3.25

1924 **Wmk. 133**

O30	O1	500k orange & red	1.40	1.00
O31	O1	1000k blue & red	1.40	1.00

NEWSPAPER STAMPS

Issues of the Monarchy

St. Stephen's Crown and Post Horn
N1   N2

1871-72 **Unwmk.** **Litho. (#P1), Typo. (#P2)** *Imperf.*

P1	N1	(1k) ver red	50.00	20.00
P2	N2	(1k) rose red ('72)	10.00	2.00
a.		(1k) vermilion	10.00	2.00
b.		Printed on both sides		

Reprints of No. P2 are watermarked. Value, $450.

Letter with Crown and Post Horn — N3   N5

1874

P3	N3	1k orange	3.75	.35

1881 **Wmk. "kr" in Oval (132)**

P4	N3	1k orange	1.25	.20
a.		1k lemon yellow	16.00	3.50
b.		Printed on both sides		

1898 **Wmk. 135**

P5	N3	1k orange	1.25	.20

See watermark note after No. 46.

1900 **Wmk. Crown in Circle (135)**

P6	N5	(2f) red orange	.75	.20

1905 **Wmk. Crown (136a)**

P7	N5	(2f) red orange	1.00	.20
a.		Wmk. 136 ('08)	1.00	.20

1914-22 **Wmk. Double Cross (137)**

P8	N5	(2f) orange	.20	.20
a.		Wmk. horiz.	4.50	3.75
P9	N5	(10f) deep blue ('20)	.20	.20
P10	N5	(20f) lilac ('22)	.20	.20
		Nos. P8-P10 (3)	.60	.60

For overprints and surcharges see Nos. 1NJ6-1NJ10, 1NP1, 2NP1, 5NP1, 6NP1, 8NP1, 10NP1, 11NP1.

NEWSPAPER TAX STAMPS

Issues of the Monarchy

NT1   NT2

NT3

Wmk. 91; Unwmk. from 1871

1868 **Typo.** *Imperf.*

PR1	NT1	1k blue	5.50	1.50
a.		Pair, one sideways		
PR2	NT2	2k brown	17.50	15.00
a.		2k red brown	275.00	47.50

1868

PR2B	NT3	1k blue	9,500.	6,000.

No. PR2B was issued for the Military Border District only. All used stamps are precanceled (newspaper text printed on the stamp). A similar 2k was not issued.

1889-90 **Wmk. "kr" in Oval (132)**

PR3	NT1	1k blue	2.00	.80
PR4	NT2	2k brown	5.50	4.00

1898 **Wmk. Crown in Oval (135)**

PR5	NT1	1k blue	7.50	5.50

These stamps did not pay postage, but represented a fiscal tax collected by the postal authorities on newspapers.
Nos. PR3 and PR5 have a tall "k" in "kr."

PARCEL POST STAMPS

Nos. 629, 613, 612, 615, 630, 667 and Type of 1943-45 Overprinted in Black or Carmine

a   b

"Cs." or "Csomag"=Parcel

1946		Wmk. 266		Perf. 15
Q1	A118	"Cs. 5-1." on 70f	.20	.20
Q2	A109	"Cs. 5-1." on 30f	22.50	20.00
Q3	A99	"Cs. 5-2." on 24f	.20	.20
Q4	A118	"Cs. 10-1." on 70f	.20	.20
Q5	A118	"Cs. 10-1." on 80f	27.50	26.00
Q6	A118	"Cs. 10-2." on 80f	.20	.20
Q7	A99	"Csomag 5kg." on 2p on 4f (C+Bk)	.20	.20
Q8	A118	"Csomag 10kg." on 30f copper red, bl	.20	.20
		Nos. Q1-Q8 (8)	51.20	47.20

No. Q8 was not issued without overprint.

> Catalogue values for unused stamps in this section, from this point to the end of the section, are for Never Hinged items.

No. 796 Surcharged with New Value in Red or Black

1954		Wmk. 210		
Q9	A144	1.70fo on 1.40fo	1.40	.20
Q10	A144	2fo on 1.40fo (Bk)	1.60	.30
Q11	A144	3fo on 1.40fo	2.00	.50
		Nos. Q9-Q11 (3)	5.00	1.00
		Set, hinged	1.80	

OCCUPATION STAMPS

Issued under French Occupation

ARAD ISSUE

The overprints on this issue have been extensively forged. Even the inexpensive values are difficult to find with genuine overprints. Values are for genuine overprints. Collectors should be aware that stamps sold "as is" are likely to be forgeries, and unexpertized collections should be assumed to consist of mostly forged stamps. Education plus working with knowledgeable dealers is mandatory in this collecting area. More valuable stamps should be expertized.

Stamps of Hungary Overprinted in Red or Blue

On Issue of 1916-18

1919		Wmk. 137		Perf. 15, 14
1N1	A9	2f brn org (R)	1.60	1.60
1N2	A9	3f red lil (R)	.75	.75
1N3	A9	5f green (R)	20.00	20.00
1N4	A9	6f grnsh bl (R)	1.90	1.90
a.		Inverted overprint	30.00	30.00
1N5	A9	10f rose red	4.00	4.00
1N6	A9	15f violet (R)	1.75	1.75
a.		Double overprint	50.00	50.00
1N7	A9	20f gray brn (R)	50.00	50.00
1N8	A9	35f brown (R)	65.00	65.00
1N9	A9	40f ol grn (R)	37.50	37.50
1N10	A10	50f red vio & lil	6.00	6.00
1N11	A10	75f brt bl & pale bl	2.00	2.00
1N12	A10	80f grn & pale grn	2.75	2.75
1N13	A10	1k red brn & cl	15.00	15.00
1N14	A10	2k ol brn & bis	3.00	3.00
a.		Inverted overprint	17.50	17.50
1N15	A10	3k dk vio & ind	17.50	17.50
1N16	A10	5k dk brn & lt brn	13.50	13.50
1N17	A10	10k vio brn & vio	70.00	70.00
		Nos. 1N1-1N17 (17)	312.25	312.25

With Additional Surcharge:

a   b

c   d

1N18	A9 (a)	45f on 2f brn org	8.00	8.00
1N19	A9 (b)	45f on 2f brn org	8.00	8.00
1N20	A9 (c)	50f on 3f red lil	8.00	8.00
1N21	A9 (d)	50f on 3f red lil	8.00	8.00
		Nos. 1N18-1N21 (4)	32.00	32.00

Overprinted On Issue of 1918

1N22	A11	10f scarlet (Bl)	60.00	60.00
1N23	A11	20f dk brn	.90	.90
1N24	A11	25f brt bl	2.40	2.40
a.		Inverted overprint	30.00	30.00
1N25	A12	40f ol grn	3.25	3.25
		Nos. 1N22-1N25 (4)	66.55	66.55

Ovptd. On Issue of 1918-19, Overprinted "Koztarsasag"

1N26	A9	2f brn org	2.00	2.00
a.		Inverted overprint	50.00	50.00
1N27	A9	4f slate gray	2.00	2.00
1N28	A9	5f green	.60	.60
1N29	A9	6f grnsh bl	12.00	12.00
a.		Inverted overprint	30.00	30.00
1N30	A9	10f rose red (Bl)	60.00	60.00
1N31	A9	20f gray brn	15.00	15.00
1N32	A11	25f brt bl	2.75	2.75
a.		Inverted overprint	30.00	30.00
1N33	A9	40f ol grn	2.00	2.00
1N34	A12	40f ol grn	60.00	60.00
a.		Inverted overprint	125.00	125.00
1N35	A12	50f lilac	8.00	8.00
1N36	A10	1k red brn & cl (Bl)	3.25	3.25
1N37	A10	3k dk vio & ind (Bl)	15.00	15.00
		Nos. 1N26-1N37 (12)	182.60	182.60

No. 1N36 With Additional Surcharge:

e

f

1N38	A10 (e)	10k on 1k	13.50	13.50
1N39	A10 (f)	10k on 1k	13.50	13.50

On Issue of 1919
Inscribed "MAGYAR POSTA"

1N40	A13	10f red (Bl)	6.50	6.50

SEMI-POSTAL STAMPS

Hungarian Semi-Postal Stamps of 1916-17 Overprinted "Occupation francaise" in Blue or Red

1919		Wmk. 137		Perf. 15
1NB1	SP3	10f + 2f rose red	65.00	65.00
1NB2	SP4	15f + 2f dl vio (R)	9.50	9.50
1NB3	SP5	40f + 2f brn car	12.50	12.50
		Nos. 1NB1-1NB3 (3)	87.00	87.00

SPECIAL DELIVERY STAMP

Hungarian Special Delivery Stamp of 1916 Overprinted "Occupation francaise"

1919		Wmk. 137		Perf. 15
1NE1	SD1	2f gray green & red	.60	.60

POSTAGE DUE STAMPS

Hungarian Postage Due Stamps of 1915 Overprinted "Occupation francaise"

1919		Wmk. 137		Perf. 15
1NJ1	D1	2f green & red	7.50	7.50
1NJ2	D1	10f green & red	4.00	4.00
1NJ3	D1	12f green & red	32.50	32.50
1NJ4	D1	15f green & red	42.50	42.50
1NJ5	D1	20f green & red	3.00	3.00

Hungarian Newspaper Stamp of 1914 Surcharged

1NJ6	N5	12f on 2f orange	8.00	8.00
1NJ7	N5	15f on 2f orange	8.00	8.00
1NJ8	N5	30f on 2f orange	8.00	8.00
a.		Double surcharge	50.00	50.00
1NJ9	N5	50f on 2f orange	8.00	8.00
1NJ10	N5	100f on 2f orange	8.00	8.00
		Nos. 1NJ1-1NJ10 (10)	129.50	129.50

NEWSPAPER STAMP

Hungarian Newspaper Stamp of 1914 Overprinted "Occupation francaise"

1919		Wmk. 137		Imperf.
1NP1	N5	(2f) orange	1.25	1.25

ISSUED UNDER ROMANIAN OCCUPATION

FIRST DEBRECEN ISSUE

The overprints on this issue have been extensively forged. Even the inexpensive values are difficult to find with genuine overprints. The more extensive note before No. 1N1 also applies to Nos. 2N1-2NP16.

Hungarian Stamps of 1913-19 Overprinted in Blue, Red or Black

1919		Wmk. 137		Perf. 15, 14½x14
		On Stamps of 1913		
2N1	A4	2f olive yellow	90.00	90.00
2N2	A4	3f orange	125.00	125.00
2N3	A4	6f olive grn (R)	50.00	50.00
		On Stamps of 1916		
2N4	A8	10f rose	75.00	75.00
2N5	A8	15f violet (Bk)	65.00	65.00
		On Stamps of 1916-18		
2N6	A9	2f brown org	1.50	1.50
2N7	A9	3f red lilac	.70	.70
2N8	A9	5f green	4.75	4.75
2N9	A9	6f grnsh bl (R)	1.60	1.60
2N10	A9	15f violet (Bk)	.80	.80
a.		Red overprint	75.00	75.00
2N11	A9	20f gray brn	125.00	125.00
2N12	A9	25f dull bl (Bk)	4.50	4.50
2N13	A9	35f brown	60.00	60.00
2N14	A9	40f olive grn	3.75	3.75
2N15	A10	50f red vio & lil	8.25	8.25
2N16	A10	75f brt bl & pale bl (Bk)	8.25	8.25
2N17	A10	80f grn & pale grn (R)	3.50	3.50
2N18	A10	1k red brn & cl	4.75	4.75
2N19	A10	2k ol brn & bis (Bk)	1.75	1.75
2N20	A10	3k dk vio & ind (R)	30.00	30.00
a.		Blue overprint	65.00	65.00
b.		Black overprint	250.00	250.00
2N21	A10	5k dk brn & lt brn (Bk)	27.50	27.50
2N22	A10	10k vio brn & vio	160.00	160.00

With New Value Added

2N23	A9	35f on 3f red lil	2.00	2.00
2N24	A9	45f on 2f brn org	2.00	2.00
2N25	A10	3k on 75f brt bl & pale bl (Bk)	4.00	4.00
2N26	A10	5k on 75f brt bl & pale bl (Bk)	3.75	3.75
2N27	A10	10k on 80f grn & pale grn	3.50	3.50

On Stamps of 1918

2N28	A11	10f scarlet	60.00	60.00
2N28A	A11	15f violet (R)	75.00	75.00
b.		Black overprint	125.00	125.00
2N29	A11	20f dk brown (R)	6.25	6.25
a.		Black overprint	30.00	30.00
b.		Blue overprint	75.00	75.00
2N30	A11	25f brt blue (R)	7.00	7.00
a.		Black overprint	75.00	75.00
2N31	A12	40f olive green	3.00	3.00
2N32	A12	50f lilac	50.00	50.00

On Stamps of 1918-19, Overprinted "Koztarsasag"

2N33	A9	2f brn org	3.00	3.00
2N34	A9	3f red lilac	65.00	65.00
2N35	A9	4f sl gray (R)	1.75	1.75
2N36	A9	5f green	.65	.65
2N37	A9	6f grnsh bl (R)	30.00	30.00
2N38	A9	10f rose red	37.50	37.50
2N39	A11	10f scarlet	25.00	25.00
2N40	A11	15f dp vio (Bk)	45.00	45.00
a.		Red overprint	125.00	125.00
2N41	A11	20f gray brn	3.25	3.25
2N42	A11	20f dk brn (Bk)	37.50	37.50
b.		Red overprint	50.00	50.00
2N43	A10	40f olive grn	1.75	1.75
2N44	A10	1k red brn & cl	2.75	2.75
2N45	A10	2k ol brn & bis (Bk)	60.00	60.00
a.		Blue overprint	125.00	125.00
2N46	A10	3k dk vio & ind (R)	9.75	9.75
a.		Blue overprint	60.00	60.00
b.		Black overprint	200.00	200.00
2N47	A10	5k dk & lt brn	225.00	225.00
2N48	A10	10k vio brn & vio	500.00	500.00
2N49	A11	25f brt bl (R)	3.25	3.25
a.		Black overprint	25.00	25.00
2N50	A12	40f olive grn	125.00	125.00
2N51	A12	50f lilac	2.25	2.25

On Stamps of 1919

2N52	A13	5f green	.50	.50
2N53	A13	6f grnsh bl (Bk)	22.50	22.50
2N54	A13	10f red	.20	.20
2N55	A13	20f dk brown	.20	.20
2N56	A13	25f dl bl (Bk)	1.25	1.25
2N56A	A13	40f olive green	125.00	125.00
2N57	A13	45f orange	15.00	15.00
2N57A	A14	95f dark blue & blue	125.00	125.00
2N57B	A14	1.20k dark green & green	125.00	125.00
2N57C	A14	1.40k yellow green	125.00	125.00

No. 2N58

2N58	A14	5k dk brn & brn	3,000.	3,000.

#2N58 is handstamped. Counterfeits exist. Expertization is required.

On No. 103A

2N59	A5a	10f violet brn (R)	50.00	50.00

On No. 208

2N60	A13	10f red	75.00	75.00
		Nos. 2N1-2N57,2N59-2N60 (61)	2,529.	2,529.

SEMI-POSTAL STAMPS

Hungary Nos. B36, B37 Overprinted like Regular Issues in Blue

1919		Wmk. 137		Perf. 14
2NB1	A4(c)	2f olive yellow	125.00	125.00
2NB1A	A4(c)	3f orange	125.00	125.00

Same Overprint in Blue or Black on
Hungary Nos. B53--B55

1919		Wmk. 137		Perf. 15
2NB1B	SP3	10f + 2f rose red	4.00	4.00
2NB2	SP4	15f + 2f dl vio (Bk)	17.00	17.00
2NB3	SP5	40f + 2f brown car	11.00	11.00
		Nos. 2NB1B-2NB3 (3)	32.00	32.00

Same Overprint on Hungary Nos.
B58-B60 (with "Köztarsasag")

1919				
2NB4	SP3	10f + 2f rose red	42.50	42.50
2NB5	SP4	15f + 2f dl vio (Bk)	75.00	75.00
2NB6	SP5	40f + 2f brown car	32.50	32.50
		Nos. 2NB4-2NB6 (3)	150.00	150.00

SPECIAL DELIVERY STAMP

Hungarian Special Delivery Stamp of
1916 Overprinted like Regular Issues

1919		Wmk. 137		Perf. 15
2NE1	SD1	2f gray grn & red (Bl)	3.00	3.00

POSTAGE DUE STAMPS

Hungarian Postage Due Stamps of
1914-19 Overprinted in Black like
Regular Issues

1919		Wmk. 137		Perf. 15
		On Stamp of 1914		
2NJ1	D1	50f grn & blk	125.00	125.00

On Stamps of 1915

2NJ2	D1	1f green & red	62.50	62.50
2NJ3	D1	2f green & red	2.00	2.00
2NJ4	D1	5f green & red	225.00	225.00
2NJ5	D1	6f green & red	125.00	125.00
2NJ6	D1	10f green & red	.80	.80
2NJ7	D1	12f green & red	125.00	125.00
2NJ8	D1	15f green & red	20.00	20.00
2NJ9	D1	20f green & red	4.50	4.50
2NJ10	D1	30f green & red	13.50	13.50

On Stamps of 1918-19, Overprinted
"Koztarsasag"

2NJ11	D1	2f green & red	25.00	25.00
2NJ12	D1	3f green & red	30.00	30.00
2NJ13	D1	10f green & red	30.00	30.00
2NJ14	D1	20f green & red	30.00	30.00
2NJ15	D1	40f green & red	30.00	30.00
2NJ16	D1	50f green & red	30.00	30.00
		Nos. 2NJ1-2NJ16 (16)	878.30	878.30
		Nos. 2NJ1-2NJ13,2NJ15-2NJ16 (15)		848.30

NEWSPAPER STAMP

Hungarian Newspaper Stamp of 1914
Overprinted like Regular Issues

1919		Wmk. 137		Imperf.
2NP1	N5	(2f) orange (Bl)	.55	.55
a.		Inverted overprint	50.00	50.00
b.		Double overprint	125.00	125.00

SECOND DEBRECEN ISSUE

Complete forgeries exist of this issue
and are often found in large multiples or
even complete sheets. Values are for
genuine stamps.

Mythical
"Turul" — OS5

Throwing
Lariat
OS6

Hungarian
Peasant
OS7

1920		Unwmk. Typo.		Perf. 11½
3N1	OS5	2f lt brown	2.25	2.25
3N2	OS5	3f red brown	2.25	2.25
3N3	OS5	4f gray	2.25	2.25
3N4	OS5	5f lt green	.50	.50
3N5	OS5	6f slate	2.25	2.25
3N6	OS5	10f scarlet	.50	.50
3N7	OS5	15f dk violet	3.00	3.00
3N8	OS5	20f dk brown	.60	.60
3N9	OS6	25f ultra	1.25	1.25
3N10	OS6	30f buff	.65	.65
3N11	OS6	35f claret	1.25	1.25
3N12	OS6	40f olive grn	.75	.75
3N13	OS6	45f salmon	1.00	1.00
3N14	OS6	50f pale vio	.75	.75
3N15	OS6	60f yellow grn	.90	.90
3N16	OS6	75f Prus blue	.75	.75
3N17	OS7	80f gray grn	.85	.85
3N18	OS7	1k brown red	3.00	3.00
3N19	OS7	2k chocolate	3.00	3.00
3N20	OS7	3k brown vio	2.25	2.25
3N21	OS7	5k bister brn	2.25	2.25
3N22	OS7	10k dull vio	2.25	2.25
		Nos. 3N1-3N22 (22)	34.50	34.50

Thick, Glazed Paper

3N23	OS5	2f lt brown	3.00	3.00
3N24	OS5	3f red brown	3.00	3.00
3N25	OS5	4f gray	3.00	3.00
3N26	OS5	5f lt green	3.00	3.00
3N27	OS5	6f slate	3.00	3.00
3N28	OS5	10f scarlet	.75	.75
3N29	OS5	15f dk vio	3.00	3.00
3N30	OS5	20f dk brown	1.00	1.00
3N31	OS7	80f gray grn	1.50	1.50
3N32	OS7	1k brown red	4.00	4.00
3N33	OS7	1.20k orange	8.00	8.00
3N34	OS7	2k chocolate	4.50	4.50
		Nos. 3N23-3N34 (12)	37.75	37.75

SEMI-POSTAL STAMPS

Carrying Wounded

1920		Unwmk. Typo.		Perf. 11½
3NB1	SP1	20f green	1.25	1.25
3NB2	SP1	50f gray brn	2.25	2.25
3NB3	SP1	1k blue green	2.25	2.25
3NB4	SP1	2k dk green	2.25	2.25
		Colored Paper		
3NB5	SP1	20f green, bl	3.00	3.00
3NB6	SP1	50f brn, rose	3.00	3.00
3NB7	SP1	1k dk grn, grn	3.00	3.00
		Nos. 3NB1-3NB7 (7)	17.00	17.00

POSTAGE DUE STAMPS

D1

1920		Typo.		Perf. 15
3NJ1	D1	5f blue green	1.50	1.50
3NJ2	D1	10f blue green	1.50	1.50
3NJ3	D1	20f blue green	.75	.75
3NJ4	D1	30f blue green	.75	.75
3NJ5	D1	40f blue green	1.25	1.25
		Nos. 3NJ1-3NJ5 (5)	5.75	5.75

TEMESVAR ISSUE

Issued under Romanian Occupation

Forgeries exist of the inverted and
color error surcharges.

Hungary Nos. 108, 155, 109, 111, E1
Surcharged

1919		Wmk. 137		Perf. 15
4N1	A9	30f on 2f brn org (Bl)	.40	.40
a.		Red surcharge	2.00	2.00
b.		Inverted surcharge (R)	25.00	25.00
4N2	A9	1k on 4f sl gray (R)	.30	.30
4N3	A9	150f on 3f red lil (Rk)	.20	.20
4N4	A9	150f on 5f grn (Bk)	.40	.40
4N5	SD1	3k on 2f gray grn & red (Bk)	2.00	2.00
a.		Blue surcharge	.80	.80
		Nos. 4N1-4N5 (5)	3.30	3.30

POSTAGE DUE STAMPS

D1   D2

1919		Wmk. 137		Perf. 15
4NJ1	D1	40f on 15f + 2f vio (Bk)	.50	.50
a.		Red surcharge	2.00	2.00
4NJ2	D2	60f on 2f grn & red (Bk)	2.50	2.50
a.		Red surcharge	8.00	8.00
4NJ3	D2	60f on 10f grn & red (Bk)	1.25	1.25
a.		Red surcharge	4.00	4.00
		Nos. 4NJ1-4NJ3 (3)	4.25	4.25

FIRST TRANSYLVANIA ISSUE

Issued under Romanian Occupation

The scarcer values of this issue have
been extensively forged. Genuine common values are more easily found.

Issued in Kolozsvar (Cluj)

Hungarian Stamps of
1916-18 Overprinted

1919		Wmk. 137		Perf. 15, 14
		On Stamp of 1916, White Numerals		
5N1	A8	15b violet	4.75	4.75
		On Stamps of 1916-18		
5N2	A9	2b brown org	.20	.25
5N3	A9	3b red lilac	.20	.25
5N4	A9	5b green	.20	.25
5N5	A9	6b grnsh blue	.40	.40
5N5A	A9	10b rose red	60.00	60.00
5N6	A9	15b violet	.20	.25
5N7	A9	25b dull blue	.20	.25
5N8	A9	35b brown	.20	.25
5N9	A9	40b olive grn	.50	.50
5N10	A10	50b red vio & lil	1.00	1.00

5N11	A10	75b brt bl & pale bl	.30	.30
5N12	A10	80b grn & pale grn	.20	.25
5N13	A10	1 l red brn & cl	.20	.25
5N14	A10	2 l ol brn & bis	.60	.60
5N15	A10	3 l dk vio & ind	3.50	3.50
5N16	A10	5 l dk brn & lt brn	2.50	2.50
5N17	A10	10 l vio brn & vio	3.00	3.00
		On Stamps of 1918		
5N18	A11	10b scarlet	40.00	40.00
5N19	A11	15b dp violet	20.00	20.00
5N20	A11	20b dk brown	.25	.25
a.		Gold overprint	75.00	75.00
b.		Silver overprint	75.00	75.00
5N21	A11	25b brt blue	.65	.65
5N22	A12	40b olive grn	.30	.30
		On No. 103A		
5N23	A5a	10b violet brn	.35	.35
		Nos. 5N1-5N23 (24)	139.70	140.10

SEMI-POSTAL STAMPS

Hungarian Semi-Postal Stamps of
1913-17 Overprinted like Regular
Issues
On Issue of 1913

1919		Wmk. 137		Perf. 14
5NB1	SP1	1 l on 1f slate	27.50	27.50
5NB2	SP1	1 l on 2f ol yel	70.00	70.00
5NB3	SP1	1 l on 3f org	37.50	37.50
5NB4	SP1	1 l on 5f emer	3.25	3.25
5NB5	SP1	1 l on 10f car	4.50	4.50
5NB6	SP1	1 l on 12f vio, yel	16.00	16.00
5NB7	SP1	1 l on 16f gray grn	6.25	6.25
5NB8	SP1	1 l on 25f ultra	60.00	60.00
5NB9	SP1	1 l on 35f red vio	10.00	10.00
5NB10	SP2	1 l on 1k dl red	60.00	60.00
		On Issue of 1916-17		
		Perf. 15		
5NB11	SP3	10b + 2b rose red	.20	.25
5NB12	SP4	15b + 2b dull vio	.20	.25
5NB13	SP5	40b + 2b brn car	.20	.25
		Nos. 5NB1-5NB13 (13)	295.60	295.75

SPECIAL DELIVERY STAMP

Hungarian Special Delivery Stamp of
1916 Overprinted like Regular Issues

1919		Wmk. 137		Perf. 15
5NE1	SD1	2b gray grn & red	.30	.30

POSTAGE DUE STAMPS

Hungarian Postage Due Stamps of
1914-18 Overprinted like Regular
Issues
On Stamp of 1914

1919		Wmk. 137		Perf. 15
5NJ1	D1	50b green & blk	13.00	13.00
		On Stamps of 1915		
5NJ2	D1	1b green & red	350.00	350.00
5NJ3	D1	2b green & red	.70	.70
5NJ4	D1	5b green & red	60.00	60.00
5NJ5	D1	10b green & red	.45	.45
5NJ6	D1	15b green & red	20.00	20.00
5NJ7	D1	20b green & red	.40	.40
5NJ8	D1	30b green & red	30.00	30.00
		Nos. 5NJ1-5NJ8 (8)	474.55	474.55

NEWSPAPER STAMP

Hungarian Newspaper Stamp of 1914
Overprinted like Regular Issues

1919		Wmk. 137		Imperf.
5NP1	N5	2b orange	3.75	3.75

SECOND TRANSYLVANIA ISSUE

The scarcer values of this issue have
been extensively forged. Genuine common values are more easily found.

Issued in Nagyvarad (Oradea)

Hungarian Stamps of
1916-19 Overprinted
Bani

1919   **Wmk. 137**   **Perf. 15, 14**

On Stamps of 1913-16

6N1	A4	2b olive yel	7.00	7.00
6N2	A4	3b orange	13.00	13.00
6N3	A4	6b olive grn	1.75	1.75
6N4	A4	16b gray grn	37.50	37.50
6N5	A4	50b lake, *bl*	1.75	1.75
6N6	A4	70b red brn & grn	26.00	26.00

On Stamp of 1916 (White Numerals)

6N6A	A8	15b violet	125.00	125.00

On Stamps of 1916-18

6N7	A9	2b brown org	.20	.25
6N8	A9	3b red lilac	.20	.25
6N9	A9	5b green	.30	.30
6N10	A9	6b grnsh blue	1.60	1.60
6N11	A9	10b rose red	2.10	2.10
6N12	A9	15b violet	.20	.25
6N13	A9	20b gray brn	20.00	20.00
6N14	A9	25b dull blue	.30	.30
6N15	A9	35b brown	.45	.45
6N16	A9	40b olive grn	.30	.30
6N17	A10	50b red vio & lil	.60	.60
6N18	A10	75b brt bl & pale bl	.20	.25
6N19	A10	80b grn & pale grn	.30	.30
6N20	A10	1 l red brn & cl	.75	.75
6N21	A10	2 l ol brn & bis	.20	.25
6N22	A10	3 l dk vio & ind	6.50	6.50
6N23	A10	5 l dk brn & lt brn	3.25	3.25
6N24	A10	10 l vio brn & vio	1.50	1.50

On Stamps of 1918

6N25	A11	10b scarlet	3.25	3.25
6N26	A11	20b dk brown	.20	.25
6N27	A11	25b brt blue	.75	.75
6N28	A12	40b olive grn	1.10	1.10

On Stamps of 1918-19, Overprinted "Koztarsasag"

6N29	A9	2b brown org	4.00	4.00
6N30	A9	3b red lilac	.20	.25
6N31	A9	4b slate gray	.20	.25
6N32	A9	5b green	.50	.50
6N33	A9	6b grnsh bl	3.00	3.00
6N34	A9	10b rose red	17.50	17.50
6N35	A9	20b gray brn	2.50	2.50
6N36	A9	40b olive grn	.50	.50
6N37	A10	1 l red brn & cl	.20	.25
6N38	A10	3 l dk vio & ind	.75	.75
6N39	A10	5 l dk brn & lt brn	4.50	4.50
6N40	A11	10b scarlet	75.00	75.00
6N41	A11	20b dk brown	4.50	4.50
6N42	A11	25b brt blue	1.25	1.25
6N43	A12	50b lilac	.20	.25

On Stamps of 1919 Inscribed "MAGYAR POSTA"

6N44	A13	5b yellow grn	.20	.25
6N45	A13	10b red	.20	.25
6N46	A13	20b dk brown	.40	.40
6N47	A13	25b dull blue	2.00	2.00
6N48	A13	40b olive grn	.65	.65
6N49	A14	5 l dk brn & brn	6.50	6.50

On No. 103A

6N50	A5a	10b violet brn	.85	.85
		Nos. 6N1-6N50 (51)	381.85	382.45

SEMI-POSTAL STAMPS

Hungarian Semi-Postal Stamps of
1913-17 Overprinted like Regular Issues
On Stamps of 1913

1919   **Wmk. 137**   **Perf. 14**

6NB1	SP1	1 l on 1f slate	2.25	2.25
6NB2	SP1	1 l on 2f olive yel	8.50	8.50
6NB3	SP1	1 l on 3f orange	2.75	2.75
6NB4	SP1	1 l on 5f emerald	.25	.25
6NB5	SP1	1 l on 6f olive grn	2.25	2.25
6NB6	SP1	1 l on 10f carmine	.30	.30
6NB7	SP1	1 l on 12f vio, *yel*	60.00	60.00
6NB8	SP1	1 l on 16f gray grn	2.50	2.50
6NB9	SP1	1 l on 20f brn	11.00	11.00
6NB10	SP1	1 l on 25f ultra	7.50	7.50
6NB11	SP1	1 l on 35f red vio	7.75	7.75

On Stamp of 1915

Wmk. 135   **Perf. 11½**

6NB12	A4	5b emerald	20.00	20.00

On Stamps of 1916-17

Wmk. 137   **Perf. 15**

6NB13	SP3	10b + 2b rose red	1.25	1.25
6NB14	SP4	15b + 2b dull vio	.45	.45
6NB15	SP5	40b + 2b brown car	.20	.25
		Nos. 6NB1-6NB15 (15)	126.95	127.00

SPECIAL DELIVERY STAMP

Hungarian Special Delivery Stamp of
1916 Overprinted like Regular Issues

1919   **Wmk. 137**   **Perf. 15**

6NE1	SD1	2b gray grn & red	.40	.40

POSTAGE DUE STAMPS

Hungarian Postage Due Stamps of
1915 Overprinted like Regular Issues

1919   **Wmk. 137**   **Perf. 15**

6NJ1	D1	1b green & red	30.00	30.00
6NJ2	D1	2b green & red	.20	.25
6NJ3	D1	5b green & red	9.75	9.75
6NJ4	D1	6b green & red	6.75	6.75
6NJ5	D1	10b green & red	.20	.25
6NJ6	D1	12b green & red	1.50	1.50
6NJ7	D1	15b green & red	1.50	1.50
6NJ8	D1	20b green & red	.20	.25
6NJ9	D1	30b green & red	1.60	1.60
		Nos. 6NJ1-6NJ9 (9)	51.70	51.85

On Hungary No. J27

Perf. 11½x12

Wmk. 135

6NJ10	D1	20b on 100b grn & blk	350.00	350.00

NEWSPAPER STAMP

Hungarian Newspaper Stamp of 1914
Overprinted like Regular Issues

1919   **Wmk. 137**   **Imperf.**

6NP1	N5	2b orange	.45	.45

FIRST BARANYA ISSUE

Issued under Serbian Occupation

The scarcer values of this issue have
been extensively forged. Genuine common
values are more easily found.

Hungarian Stamps of 1913-18
Overprinted in Black or Red:

On A4, A9,   On A10
A11, A12

1919   **Wmk. 137**   **Perf. 15**

On Issue of 1913-16

7N1	A4	6f olive grn (R)	.90	.90
7N2	A4	50f lake, *bl*	.20	.20
7N3	A4	60f grn, *salmon*	.75	.75
7N4	A4	70f red brn & grn (R)	2.00	2.00
7N5	A4	70f red brn & grn (Bk)	.25	.25
7N6	A4	80f dl vio (R)	3.25	3.25

On Issue of 1916-18

7N7	A9	2f brown org (Bk)	4.25	4.25
7N8	A9	2f brown org (R)	.20	.20
7N9	A9	3f red lilac (Bk)	.20	.20
7N10	A9	3f red lilac (R)	.80	.80
7N11	A9	5f green (Bk)	.80	.80
7N12	A9	5f green (R)	.20	.20
7N13	A9	6f grnsh bl (Bk)	1.75	1.75
7N14	A9	6f grnsh bl (R)	2.00	2.00
7N15	A9	15f violet	.35	.35
7N16	A9	20f gray brn	20.00	20.00
7N17	A9	25f dull blue	3.50	3.50
7N18	A9	35f brown	5.75	5.75
7N19	A9	40f olive grn	20.00	20.00
7N20	A10	50f red vio & lil	2.00	2.00
7N21	A10	75f brt bl & pale bl	.40	.40
7N22	A10	80f grn & pale grn	.65	.65
7N23	A10	1k red brn & cl	.55	.55
7N24	A10	2k ol brn & bis	.65	.65
7N25	A10	3k dk vio & ind	.65	.65
7N26	A10	5k dk brn & lt brn	1.25	1.25
7N27	A10	10k vio brn & vio	4.00	4.00

7N28	A9	45f on 2f brn org	.35	.35
7N29	A9	45f on 5f green	.20	.20
7N30	A9	45f on 15f violet	.20	.20

On Issue of 1918

7N31	A11	10f scarlet (Bk)	.20	.20
7N32	A11	20f dk brn (Bk)	.20	.20
7N34	A11	25f dp blue (Bk)	1.90	1.90
7N35	A11	25f dp blue (R)	1.10	1.10
7N36	A12	40f olive grn (Bk)	4.50	4.50
7N37	A12	40f olive grn (R)	30.00	30.00

On Issue of 1918-19 (Koztarsasag)

7N38	A9	2f brown org (Bk)	3.50	3.50
7N39	A12	40f ol grn (Bk)	125.00	125.00
7N40	A12	40f olive grn (R)	20.00	20.00

With New Value Added

7N41	A9	45f on 2f brn org (Bk)	2.00	2.00
7N42	A9	45f on 2f brn org (R)	.45	.45

The overprints were set in groups of 25. In
each group two stamps have the figures "1" of
"1919" with serifs.

SEMI-POSTAL STAMPS

Hungarian Semi-Postal Stamps
Overprinted Regular Issue First Type
On Stamp of 1915

1919   **Wmk. 137**   **Perf. 15**

7NB1	A4	50f + 2f lake, *bl*	16.00	16.00

On Stamps of 1916

7NB2	SP3	10f + 2f rose red	.30	.30
7NB3	SP4	15f + 2f dull vio	.40	.40
		Nos. 7NB1-7NB3 (3)	16.70	16.70

SPECIAL DELIVERY STAMP

SD1

1919   **Wmk. 137**   **Perf. 15**

7NE1	SD1	105f on 2f gray grn & red	1.25	1.25

POSTAGE DUE STAMPS

Overprinted or
Surcharged on
Hungary Nos. J29,
J32, J35

1919   **Wmk. 137**   **Perf. 15**

7NJ1	D1	2f green & red	3.75	3.75
7NJ2	D1	10f green & red	1.25	1.25
7NJ3	D1	20f green & red	1.60	1.60

With New Value Added

7NJ4	D1	40f on 2f grn & red	1.50	1.50
		Nos. 7NJ1-7NJ4 (4)	8.10	8.10

SECOND BARANYA ISSUE

The scarcer values of this issue have
been extensively forged. Genuine common
values are more easily found.

Hungarian Stamps of
1916-19 Surcharged in
Black and Red

1919   **On Stamps of 1916-18**

8N1	A9	20f on 2f brn org	4.25	4.25
8N2	A9	50f on 5f green	2.00	2.00
8N3	A9	150f on 15f violet	2.00	2.00
8N4	A10	200f on 75f brt bl & pale bl	.75	.75

On Stamp of 1918-19, Overprinted "Koztarsasag"

8N5	A11	150f on 15f dp vio	.50	.50

On Stamps of 1919

8N6	A13	20f on 2f brn org	.35	.35
8N7	A13	30f on 6f grnsh bl	.70	.70
8N8	A13	50f on 5f yel grn	.20	.20
8N9	A13	100f on 25f dull bl	.25	.25
8N10	A13	100f on 40f ol grn	.25	.25
8N11	A13	100f on 45f orange	1.10	1.10
8N12	A13	150f on 20f dk brn	1.40	1.40

On No. 103A

8N13	A5a	10f on 10f vio brn	.75	.75
		Nos. 8N1-8N13 (13)	14.50	14.50

SPECIAL DELIVERY STAMP

Hungarian Special Delivery Stamp of
1916 Surcharged like Regular Issues

1919   **Wmk. 137**   **Perf. 15**

8NE1	SD1	10f on 2f gray grn & red	.65	.65

NEWSPAPER STAMP

Hungarian Newspaper Stamp of 1914
Surcharged like Regular Issues

1919   **Wmk. 137**   **Imperf.**

8NP1	N5	10f on 2f orange	.80	.80

TEMESVAR ISSUES

Issued under Serbian Occupation

Forgeries exist of the inverted and
color error surcharges.

Hungarian Stamps of 1916-18
Surcharged in Black, Blue or Brown:

a   b

1919

9N1	A9(a)	10f on 2f brn org (Bl)	.20	.25
a.		Black surcharge	15.00	15.00
9N2	A9(b)	30f on 2f brn org	.20	.25
a.		Inverted surcharge	75.00	75.00
9N3	A11(b)	50f on 20f dk brn (Bl)	.20	.25
a.		Inverted surcharge		
9N4	A9(b)	1k 50f on 15f vio	.30	.30
a.		Brown surcharge	.75	.75
b.		Double surcharge (Bk)	50.00	50.00
		Nos. 9N1-9N4 (4)	.90	1.05

SEMI-POSTAL STAMP

Hungarian Semi-Postal
Stamp of 1916
Surcharged in Blue

1919 — Wmk. 137 — Perf. 15

9NB1 SP3 45f on 10f + 2f rose red .20 .25

POSTAGE DUE STAMPS

Hungarian Postage Due Stamps of 1915 Surcharged

1919 — Wmk. 137 — Perf. 15

9NJ1	D1	40f on 2f grn & red	.80	.80
9NJ2	D1	60f on 2f grn & red	.80	.80
9NJ3	D1	100f on 2f grn & red	.80	.80
		Nos. 9NJ1-9NJ3 (3)	2.40	2.40

BANAT, BACSKA ISSUE

Issued under Serbian Occupation

Postal authorities at Temesvar applied these overprints. The stamps were available for postage, but were chiefly used to pay postal employees' salaries.

The overprints on this issue have been extensively forged. Even the inexpensive values are difficult to find with genuine overprints. The more extensive note before 1N1 also applies to Nos. 10N1-10NP1.

Hungarian Stamps of 1913-19 Overprinted in Black or Red:

a   b

1919

Type "a" on Stamp of 1913

10N1	A4	50f lake, blue	4.00	4.00

Type "a" on Stamps of 1916-18

10N2	A9	2f brown org	4.00	4.00
10N3	A9	3f red lilac	4.00	4.00
10N4	A9	5f green	4.00	4.00
10N5	A9	6f grnsh blue	4.00	4.00
10N6	A9	15f violet	4.00	4.00
10N7	A9	35f brown	35.00	35.00

Type "b"

10N8	A10	50f red vio & lil (R)	30.00	30.00
10N9	A10	75f brt bl & pale bl	4.00	4.00
10N10	A10	80f grn & pale grn	4.00	4.00
a.		Red overprint	37.50	37.50
10N11	A10	1k red brn & cl	4.00	4.00
10N12	A10	2k ol brn & bis	4.00	4.00
a.		Red overprint	37.50	37.50
10N14	A10	3k dk vio & ind	65.00	65.00
10N15	A10	5k dk brn & lt brn	4.00	4.00
10N16	A10	10k vio brn & vio	4.00	4.00

Type "a" on Stamps of 1918

10N17	A11	10f scarlet	4.00	4.00
10N18	A11	20f dk brown	4.00	4.00
10N19	A11	25f brt blue	4.00	4.00
10N20	A12	40f olive grn	4.00	4.00
10N21	A12	50f lilac	4.00	4.00

Type "a" on Stamps of 1919 Inscribed "Magyar Posta"

10N22	A13	10f red	30.00	30.00
10N23	A13	20f dk brown	30.00	30.00
10N24	A13	25f dull blue	37.50	37.50

Type "a" on Stamps of 1918-19 Overprinted "Koztarsasag"

10N25	A9	4f slate gray	3.50	3.50
10N26	A9	4f sl gray (R)	42.50	42.50
10N27	A9	5f green	4.00	4.00
10N28	A9	6f grnsh blue	4.00	4.00
10N29	A9	10f rose red	30.00	30.00
10N30	A11	15f dp violet	30.00	30.00
10N31	A9	20f gray brn	30.00	30.00
10N32	A11	25f brt blue	30.00	30.00
10N33	A9	40f olive grn	3.50	3.50
10N34	A9	40f ol grn (R)	32.50	32.50

Type "b"

10N35	A10	1k red brn & cl	4.00	4.00
10N36	A10	2k ol brn & bis	30.00	30.00
10N37	A10	3k dk vio & ind	30.00	30.00
10N38	A10	5k dk brn & lt brn	30.00	30.00
10N39	A10	10k vio brn & vio	30.00	30.00

Type "a" on Temesvár Issue

10N40	A9	10f on 2f brn org (Bl & Bk)	4.00	4.00
10N41	A9	1k50f on 15f vio	4.00	4.00

10N42	A5a	50f on 10f vio brn	4.00	4.00
a.		Red overprint	75.00	75.00
		Nos. 10N1-10N42 (41)	641.50	641.50

SEMI-POSTAL STAMPS

Semi-Postal Stamps of 1916-17 Overprinted Type "a" in Black

1919

10NB1	SP3	10f + 2f rose red	4.00	4.00
10NB2	SP4	15f + 2f dull vio	4.00	4.00
10NB3	SP5	40f + 2f brn car	4.00	4.00

Same Overprint on Temesvar Issue

10NB4	SP3	45f on 10f + 2f rose red (Bl & Bk)	4.00	4.00
		Nos. 10NB1-10NB4 (4)	16.00	16.00

SPECIAL DELIVERY STAMP

Hungary No. E1 Surcharged in Black

1919

10NE1	SD1	30f on 2f gray grn & red	4.00	4.00
a.		Red overprint	75.00	75.00

POSTAGE DUE STAMPS

Postage Due Stamps of 1914-15 Overprinted Type "a" in Black

1919

10NJ1	D1	2f green & red	4.00	4.00
10NJ2	D1	10f green & red	4.00	4.00
10NJ3	D1	15f green & red	32.50	32.50
10NJ4	D1	20f green & red	4.00	4.00
10NJ5	D1	30f green & red	30.00	30.00
10NJ6	D1	50f green & blk	30.00	30.00
		Nos. 10NJ1-10NJ6 (6)	104.50	104.50

NEWSPAPER STAMP

Stamp of 1914 Overprinted Type "a" in Black

1919

10NP1	N5	(2f) orange	4.00	4.00

SZEGED ISSUE

The "Hungarian National Government, Szeged, 1919," as the overprint reads, was an anti-Bolshevist government which opposed the Soviet Republic then in control at Budapest.

The overprints on this issue have been extensively forged. Even the inexpensive stamps are difficult to find with genuine overprints. The more extensive note before No. 1N1 also applies to Szeged Nos. 11N1-11NP1.

Hungary Stamps of 1916-19 Overprinted in Green, Red and Blue

On Stamps of 1916-18

1919 — Perf. 15, 14

11N1	A9	2f brn org (G)	2.25	2.25
11N2	A9	3f red lilac (G)	.75	.75
11N3	A9	5f green	2.75	2.75
11N4	A9	6f grnsh blue	32.50	32.50
11N5	A9	15f violet	3.50	3.50
11N6	A10	50f red vio & lil	19.00	19.00
11N7	A10	75f brt bl & pale bl	4.25	4.25
11N8	A10	80f grn & pale grn	18.00	18.00
11N9	A10	1k red brn & cl		
			2.25	2.25
11N10	A10	2k ol brn & bis	4.75	4.75
11N11	A10	3k dk vio & ind	7.25	7.25
11N12	A10	5k dk brn & lt brn	60.00	60.00
11N13	A10	10k vio brn & vio	60.00	60.00

With New Value Added

11N14	A9	45f on 3f red lil (R & G)	.80	.80
11N15	A10	10k on 1k red brn & cl (Bl & G)	8.00	8.00

On Stamps of 1918

11N16	A11	10f scarlet (G)	2.50	2.50
11N17	A11	20f dk brown	.60	.60
11N18	A11	25f brt blue	22.50	22.50
11N19	A12	40f olive grn	11.00	11.00

On Stamps of 1918-19 Overprinted "Koztarsasag"

11N20	A9	3f red lil (G)	42.50	42.50
11N21	A9	4f slate gray	11.00	11.00
11N22	A9	5f green	25.00	25.00
11N23	A9	6f grnsh blue	15.00	15.00
11N24	A9	10f rose red (G)	32.50	32.50
11N25	A11	10f scarlet)	30.00	30.00
11N26	A11	15f dp violet	10.00	10.00
11N27	A9	20f gray brown	50.00	50.00
11N28	A11	20f dk brown	65.00	65.00
11N29	A11	25f brt blue	20.00	20.00
11N30	A9	40f olive	2.25	2.25
11N31	A12	50f lilac	1.75	1.75
11N32	A10	3k dk vio & ind	37.50	37.50

With New Value Added

11N33	A9	20f on 2f brn org (R & G)	.80	.80

On Stamps of 1919 Inscribed "Magyar Posta"

11N34	A13	20f dk brown	60.00	60.00
11N35	A13	25f dull blue	1.75	1.75
		Nos. 11N1-11N35 (35)	667.70	667.70

SEMI-POSTAL STAMPS

Szeged Overprint on Semi-Postal Stamps of 1916-17 in Green or Red

1919

11NB1	SP3	10f + 2f rose red (G)	.85	.85
11NB2	SP4	15f + 2f dl vio (R)	3.75	3.75
11NB3	SP5	40f + 2f brn car (G)	10.00	10.00

With Additional Overprint "Koztarsasag"

11NB4	SP5	40f + 2f brn car (Bk & G)	15.00	15.00
		Nos. 11NB1-11NB4 (4)	29.60	29.60

SPECIAL DELIVERY STAMP

Szeged Overprint on Special Delivery Stamp of 1916 in Red

1919

11NE1	SD1	2f gray grn & red	11.00	11.00

POSTAGE DUE STAMPS

Szeged Overprint on Stamps of 1915-18 in Red

1919

11NJ1	D1	2f green & red	3.00	3.00
11NJ2	D1	6f green & red	9.75	9.75
11NJ3	D1	10f green & red	3.75	3.75
11NJ4	D1	12f green & red	4.75	4.75
11NJ5	D1	20f green & red	6.00	6.00
11NJ6	D1	30f green & red	9.00	9.00

Red Surcharge

11NJ7	SD1	50f on 2f gray grn & red	2.75	2.75
11NJ8	SD1	100f on 2f gray grn & red	2.75	2.75
		Nos. 11NJ1-11NJ8 (8)	41.75	41.75

NEWSPAPER STAMP

Szeged Overprint on Stamp of 1914 in Green

1919 — Wmk. 137 — Imperf.

11NP1	N5	(2f) orange	.85	.85

ICELAND
'ĭs-lənd

LOCATION — Island in the North Atlantic Ocean, east of Greenland
GOVT. — Republic
AREA — 39,758 sq. mi.
POP. — 272,069 (1997)
CAPITAL — Reykjavik

Iceland became a republic on June 17, 1944. Formerly this country was united with Denmark under the government of King Christian X who, as a ruling sovereign of both countries, was assigned the dual title of king of each. Although the two countries were temporarily united in certain affairs beyond the king's person, both were acknowledged as sovereign states.

96 Skillings = 1 Rigsdaler
100 Aurar (singular "Eyrir") = 1 Krona (1876)

Catalogue values for unused stamps in this country are for Never Hinged items, beginning with Scott 246 in the regular postage section, Scott B7 in the semipostal section and Scott C21 in the air post section.

Watermarks

Wmk. 112 — Crown

Wmk. 113 — Crown

Wmk. 47 — Multiple Rosette

Wmk. 114 — Multiple Crosses

Values for unused stamps are for examples with original gum as defined in the catalogue introduction. Very fine examples of Nos. 1-33A and O1-O12 will have centering with perforations clear of the framelines but with design noticeably off center, and Nos. 1-7 and O1-O3 additionally will have some irregular or shorter perforations. Well centered stamps are quite scarce and will command higher prices.

A1

Perf. 14x13½

		1873	Typo.	Wmk. 112	
1	A1	2s ultra		1,250.	3,000.
a.		Imperf.		700.	
2	A1	4s dark carmine		225.	1,250.
a.		Imperf.		700.	—
3	A1	8s brown		375.	1,400.
a.		Imperf.		400.	
4	A1	16s yellow		1,800.	3,000.
a.		Imperf.		450.	

Perf. 12½

5	A1	3s gray		550.	1,750.
a.		Imperf.		825.	
6	A1	4s carmine		1,600.	2,500.
7	A1	16s yellow		150.	700.

False and favor cancellations are often found on Nos. 1-7. Values are considerably less than those shown.

A2

		1876			
8	A2	5a blue		450.00	775.00

Perf. 14x13½

9	A2	5a blue		500.00	825.00
a.		Imperf.		2,250.	
10	A2	6a gray		160.00	35.00
11	A2	10a carmine		250.00	8.50
a.		Imperf.		650.00	750.00
12	A2	16a brown		125.00	62.50
13	A2	20a dark violet		40.00	550.00
14	A2	40a green		110.00	250.00

Fake and favor cancellations are often found on No. 13, and value is considerably less than that shown.

Small "3" — A3

Large "3" — A3a

		1882-98			
15	A3	3a orange		70.00	30.00
16	A2	5a green		57.50	15.00
17	A2	20a blue		350.00	60.00
a.		20a ultramarine		800.00	325.00
18	A2	40a red violet		57.50	47.50
a.		Perf. 13 ('98)		5,750.	
19	A2	50a bl & car ('92)		100.00	110.00
20	A2	100a brn & vio ('92)		95.00	160.00
		Nos. 15-20 (6)		730.00	422.50

See note after No. 68.

		1896-1901		**Perf. 13**	
21	A3	3a orange ('97)		110.00	14.00
22	A3a	3a yellow ('01)		7.50	25.00
23	A2	4a rose & gray ('99)		21.00	25.00
24	A2	5a green		4.50	3.25
25	A2	6a gray ('97)		20.00	21.00
26	A2	10a carmine ('97)		10.00	3.25
27	A2	16a brown		80.00	110.00
28	A2	20a dull blue ('98)		50.00	42.50
a.		20a dull ultramarine		500.00	47.50
29	A2	25a yel brown & blue ('00)		25.00	37.50
30	A2	50a bl & car ('98)		450.00	700.00

See note after No. 68.
For surcharges see Nos. 31-33A, 45-68.

Black and Red Surcharge

Surcharged 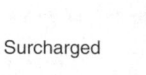 **þrír 3**

		1897		**Perf. 13**	
31	A2	3a on 5a green		800.00	600.00
a.		Perf. 14x13½		26,500.	4,750.
b.		Inverted surcharge		1,500.	1,250.
c.		As "a," inverted surcharge		7,500.	

Surcharged

32	A2	3a on 5a green		650.00	525.00
a.		Inverted surcharge		1,300.	1,000.
b.		Perf. 14x13½		12,500.	2,750.
c.		In vert. pair with #31		1,650.	1,300.
d.		As "b," in vert. pair with #31a		—	

All 5 known unused examples of #32b lack gum.

Black Surcharge

Surcharged **þrír**

33	A2	3a on 5a green		1,100.	900.
b.		Inverted surcharge		1,750.	1,500.

Surcharged **þrír**

33A	A2	3a on 5a green		850.00	650.00
c.		Inverted surcharge		1,500.	1,250.

Excellent counterfeits are known.

King Christian IX — A4

		1902-04	Wmk. 113	**Perf. 13**	
34	A4	3a orange		7.00	4.50
35	A4	4a gray & rose		4.50	1.60
36	A4	5a yel green		40.00	1.40
37	A4	6a gray brown		24.00	13.00
38	A4	10a car rose		7.00	1.40
39	A4	16a chocolate		10.00	13.00
40	A4	20a deep blue		3.50	5.50
a.		Inscribed "PJONUSTA"		75.00	110.00
41	A4	25a brn & grn		5.00	8.25
42	A4	40a violet		5.50	7.75
43	A4	50a gray & bl blk		7.00	29.00
44	A4	1k sl bl & yel brn		8.25	13.00
44A	A4	2k olive brn & brt blue ('04)		32.50	87.50
44B	A4	5k org brn & slate blue ('04)		175.00	275.00
		Nos. 34-44B (13)		329.25	460.90

For surcharge see No. 142.

Stamps of 1882-1901 Overprinted

		1902-03	Wmk. 112	**Perf. 13**	

Red Overprint

45	A2	5a green		1.10	9.50
a.		Inverted overprint		50.00	77.50
b.		"I" before Gildi omitted		175.00	
c.		'03-'03		300.00	
d.		02'-'03		300.00	
e.		Pair, one without overprint		100.00	
46	A2	6a gray		1.00	9.00
a.		Double overprint		60.00	
b.		Inverted overprint		47.50	
c.		'03-'03		350.00	
d.		02'-'03		350.00	
e.		Pair, one with invtd. ovpt.		250.00	
f.		Pair, one without overprint		140.00	
g.		As "f," inverted		200.00	
47	A2	20a dull blue		1.00	12.00
a.		Inverted overprint		35.00	55.00
b.		"I" before Gildi omitted		95.00	
c.		02'-'03		300.00	
48	A2	25a yel brn & bl		1.00	17.50
a.		Inverted overprint		47.50	60.00
b.		'03-'03		300.00	
c.		02'-'03		300.00	
d.		Double overprint		125.00	

Black Overprint

49	A3	3a orange		210.00	550.00
b.		Inverted overprint		350.00	675.00
c.		"I" before Gildi omitted		450.00	
d.		'03-'03		450.00	
e.		02'-'03		450.00	
50	A3a	3a yellow		1.40	2.40
a.		Double overprint		325.00	
b.		Inverted overprint		50.00	70.00
c.		"I" before Gildi omitted		300.00	
d.		02'-'03		375.00	
51	A2	4a rose & gray		45.00	67.50
a.		Double overprint		200.00	
b.		Inverted overprint		110.00	
c.		Dbl. ovpt., one invtd.		275.00	
d.		"I" before Gildi omitted		250.00	
e.		'03-'03		400.00	
f.		02'-'03		400.00	
g.		Pair, one with invtd. ovpt.		275.00	
52	A2	5a green		400.00	675.00
a.		Inverted overprint		450.00	
b.		Pair, one without overprint		550.00	
c.		As "b," inverted		700.00	
53	A2	6a gray		700.00	1,100.
a.		Inverted overprint		800.00	
b.		Pair, one without overprint		800.00	
c.		Double overprint		875.00	
54	A2	10a carmine		1.40	11.50
a.		Inverted overprint		50.00	77.50
b.		Pair, one without overprint		90.00	
55	A2	16a brown		30.00	52.50
a.		Inverted overprint		140.00	
b.		"I" before Gildi omitted		250.00	
c.		'03-'03		400.00	
d.		02'-'03		400.00	
56	A2	20a dull blue		12,000.	
a.		Inverted overprint		12,500.	
57	A2	25 yel brn & bl		12,750.	
a.		Inverted overprint		13,500.	
58	A2	40a red vio		1.25	50.00
a.		Inverted overprint		50.00	
59	A2	50a bl & car		3.75	77.50
a.		Double overprint		250.00	
b.		02'-'03		350.00	
c.		'03-'03		350.00	

Perf. 14x13½
Red Overprint

60	A2	5a green		2,250.	—
a.		'03-'03			
b.		02'-'03			
61	A2	6a gray		2,250.	—
a.		'03-'03			
62	A2	20a blue		5,750.	—
b.		02'-'03		10,000.	

Black Overprint

63	A3	3a orange		1,500.	2,100.
a.		Inverted overprint		1,650.	
b.		02'-'03		2,000.	
c.		'03-'03		2,000.	
64	A2	10a carmine		9,000.	
65	A2	16a brown		1,650.	2,000.
a.		Inverted overprint		1,750.	
b.		02'-'03		2,000.	
d.		'03-'03		2,000.	
65C	A2	20a dull blue		7,750.	—
a.		Inverted overprint		10,000.	
66	A2	40a red vio		25.00	110.00
a.		Inverted overprint		450.00	
b.		'03-'03		350.00	
c.		02'-'03		350.00	
67	A2	50a bl & car		45.00	140.00
a.		Inverted overprint		200.00	
b.		'03-'03		400.00	
c.		02'-'03		400.00	
d.		As "c," inverted			
68	A2	100a brn & vio		55.00	90.00
a.		Inverted overprint		160.00	
b.		02'-'03		300.00	
c.		'03-'03		300.00	

"I GILDI" means "valid."
In 1904 Nos. 20, 22-30, 45-59 (except 49, 52, 53, 56 and 57) and No. 68 were reprinted

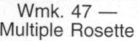

for the Postal Union. The reprints are perforated 13 and have watermark type 113. Value $75 each. Without overprint, $125 each.

Kings Christian IX and Frederik VIII — A5

Typo., Center Engr.

1907-08		Wmk. 113	Perf. 13	
71	A5	1e yel grn & red	1.90	1.40
72	A5	3a yel brn & ocher	4.50	1.75
73	A5	4a gray & red	2.50	2.10
74	A5	5a green	92.50	1.40
75	A5	6a gray & gray brn	57.50	4.00
76	A5	10a scarlet	160.00	1.60
77	A5	15a red & green	8.25	1.50
78	A5	16a brown	9.50	47.50
79	A5	20a blue	8.75	6.75
80	A5	25a bis brn & grn	7.00	14.00
81	A5	40a claret & vio	6.75	17.00
82	A5	50a gray & vio	7.75	17.00
83	A5	1k blue & brn	30.00	77.50
84	A5	4a dk brn & dk grn	40.00	90.00
85	A5	5k brn & slate	225.00	425.00
		Nos. 71-85 (15)	661.90	708.50

See Nos. 99-107.
For surcharges and overprints see Nos. 130-138, 143, C2, O69.

Jon Sigurdsson A6

Frederik VIII A7

1911		Typo. and Embossed		
86	A6	1e olive green	3.00	2.75
87	A6	3a light brown	5.75	17.50
88	A6	4a ultramarine	2.25	2.25
89	A6	6a gray	14.50	30.00
90	A6	15a violet	17.50	2.25
91	A6	25a orange	32.50	57.50
		Nos. 86-91 (6)	75.50	112.25

Sigurdsson (1811-79), statesman and author.
For surcharge see No. 149.

1912, Feb. 17				
92	A7	5a green	37.50	14.00
93	A7	10a red	37.50	14.00
94	A7	20a pale blue	52.50	20.00
95	A7	50a claret	10.50	40.00
96	A7	1k yellow	32.50	80.00
97	A7	2k rose	30.00	80.00
98	A7	5k brown	175.00	250.00
		Nos. 92-98 (7)	375.50	498.00

For surcharges and overprints see Nos. 140-141, O50-O51.

Type of 1907-08
Typo., Center Engr.

1915-18		Wmk. 114	Perf. 14x14½	
99	A5	1e yel grn & red	9.50	20.00
100	A5	3a bister brn	4.75	3.25
101	A5	4a gray & red	4.75	10.50
102	A5	5a green	110.00	1.50
103	A5	6a gray & gray brn	22.50	150.00
104	A5	10a scarlet	4.25	1.40
107	A5	20a blue	250.00	26.00
		Nos. 99-107 (7)	405.75	212.65

Revenue cancellations consisting of "TOLLUR" boxed in frame are found on stamps used to pay the tax on parcel post packages entering Iceland.

Christian X — A8

1920-22			Typo.	
108	A8	1e yel grn & red	1.00	1.25
109	A8	3a bister brn	9.00	18.50
110	A8	4a gray & red	5.25	2.75
111	A8	5a green	2.50	2.25
112	A8	5a ol green ('22)	5.25	1.75
113	A8	6a dark gray	15.00	9.50
114	A8	8a dark brown	9.00	2.50
115	A8	10a red	2.75	12.50
116	A8	10a green ('21)	3.75	2.00

117	A8	15a violet	45.00	1.60
118	A8	20a deep blue	3.00	19.00
119	A8	20a choc ('22)	65.00	1.75
120	A8	25a brown & grn	19.00	2.00
121	A8	25a red ('21)	19.00	62.50
		Revenue cancellation		4.25
122	A8	30a red & green	57.50	3.75
		Revenue cancellation		8.75
123	A8	40a claret	50.00	3.25
		Revenue cancellation		9.50
124	A8	40a dk bl ('21)	87.50	15.00
		Revenue cancellation		11.00
125	A8	50a dk gray & cl	200.00	14.00
		Revenue cancellation		13.50
126	A8	1k dp bl & dk brn	110.00	2.00
		Revenue cancellation		1.75
127	A8	2k ol brn & myr green	275.00	37.50
		Revenue cancellation		3.50
128	A8	5k brn & ind	62.50	20.00
		Revenue cancellation		3.50
		Nos. 108-128 (21)	1,047.	235.35

See Nos. 176-187, 202.
For surcharges and overprints see Nos.139, 150, C1, C9-C14, O52, O70-O71.

A9   A10   A11

1921-25		Wmk. 113	Perf. 13	
130	A9	5a on 16a brown	4.75	34.00
131	A11	5a on 16a brown	2.75	9.75
132	A10	20a on 25a brn & green	10.00	10.00
a.		Double surcharge	600.00	
133	A11	20a on 25a bis brn & green	5.25	9.25
134	A9	20a on 40a violet	10.00	25.00
135	A11	20a on 40a cl & vio	13.50	27.50
137	A9	30a on 50a gray & bl blk ('25)	40.00	40.00
		Revenue cancellation		17.50
138	A9	50a on 5k org brn & sl bl ('25)	72.50	62.50
		Revenue cancellation		35.00
		Nos. 130-138 (8)	158.75	218.00

No. 111 Surcharged

1922		Wmk. 114	Perf. 14x14½	
139	A8	10a on 5a green	9.00	4.00

Nos. 95-96, 44A, 85 Surcharged

1924-30		Wmk. 113	Perf. 13	
140	A7	10k on 50a ('25)	325.00	475.00
		Revenue cancellation		40.00
141	A7	10k on 1k	400.00	750.00
		Revenue cancellation		75.00
142	A4	10k on 2k ('29)	80.00	35.00
		Revenue cancellation		8.75
143	A5	10k on 5k ('30)	500.00	600.00
		Revenue cancellation		35.00

Landing the Mail — A12

Designs: 7a, 50a, Landing the mail. 10a, 35a, View of Reykjavik. 20a, Museum building.

Perf. 14x15

1925, Sept. 12		Typo.	Wmk. 114	
144	A12	7a yel green	45.00	8.50
145	A12	10a dp bl & brn	45.00	.90
146	A12	20a vermilion	45.00	.90
147	A12	35a deep blue	75.00	10.00
148	A12	50a yel grn & brn	75.00	2.00
		Nos. 144-148 (5)	285.00	22.30

No. 91 Surcharged

1925		Wmk. 113	Perf. 13	
149	A6	2k on 25a orange	175.00	190.00
		Revenue cancellation		20.00

No. 124 Surcharged in Red

1926				
150	A8	1k on 40a dark blue	175.00	42.50
		Revenue cancellation		25.00

Parliament Building A15

Designs: 5a, Viking ship in storm. 7a, Parliament meeting place, 1690. 10a, Viking funeral. 15a, Vikings naming land. 20a, The dash for Thing. 25a, Gathering wood. 30a, Thingvalla Lake. 35a, Iceland woman in national costume. 40a, Iceland flag. 50a, First Althing, 930 A.D. 1k, Map of Iceland. 2k, Winter-bound home. 5k, Woman spinning. 10k, Viking Sacrifice to Thor.

Perf. 12½x12

1930, Jan. 1		Litho.	Unwmk.	
152	A15	3a dull vio & gray vio	4.50	12.00
153	A15	5a dk bl & sl grn	4.50	12.00
154	A15	7a grn & gray grn	4.50	12.00
155	A15	10a dk vio & lilac	11.00	25.00
156	A15	15a dp ultra & bl gray	3.25	13.50
157	A15	20a rose red & sal	52.50	110.00
a.		Double impression	400.00	
158	A15	25a dk brn & lt brown	8.75	17.50
159	A15	30a dk grn & sl grn	7.50	17.00
160	A15	35a ultra & bl gray	8.00	16.50
161	A15	40a dk ultra, red & slate grn	7.25	17.00
162	A15	50a red brn & cinnamon	72.50	195.00
163	A15	1k ol grn & gray green	72.50	195.00
164	A15	2k turq bl & gray green	100.00	240.00
165	A15	5k org & yellow	57.50	190.00
166	A15	10k mag & dl rose	57.50	190.00
		Nos. 152-166 (15)	471.75	1,262.

Millenary of the "Althing," the Icelandic Parliament, oldest in the world.
Imperfs were privately printed.
For overprints see Nos. O53-O67.

Gullfoss (Golden Falls) — A30

1931-32		Unwmk.	Engr.	Perf. 14	
170	A30	5a gray		15.00	1.10
171	A30	20a red		12.50	.25
172	A30	35a ultramarine		25.00	16.00
		Revenue cancellation			1.90
173	A30	60a red lil ('32)		15.00	1.25
174	A30	65a red brn ('32)		2.50	1.25
175	A30	75a grnsh bl ('32)		100.00	35.00
		Revenue cancellation			5.00
		Nos. 170-175 (6)		170.00	54.85

Issued: 5a-35a, Dec. 15; 60a-75a, May 30.

Type of 1920 Christian X Issue Redrawn
Perf. 14x14½

1931-33		Typo.	Wmk. 114	
176	A8	1e yel grn & red	1.00	1.75
177	A8	3a bister brown	16.00	16.50
		Revenue cancellation		8.00
178	A8	4a gray & red	2.50	2.50
179	A8	6a dark gray	2.00	4.25
180	A8	7a yel grn ('33)	.65	1.75
181	A8	10a chocolate	140.00	1.10
182	A8	25a brn & green	19.00	4.25
		Revenue cancellation		3.25
183	A8	30a red & green	30.00	6.50
		Revenue cancellation		7.75
184	A8	40a claret	260.00	24.00
		Revenue cancellation		12.00
185	A8	1k dk bl & lt brn	47.50	8.00
		Revenue cancellation		3.25
186	A8	2k choc & dk grn	275.00	90.00
		Revenue cancellation		19.00
187	A8	10k yel grn & blk	325.00	225.00
		Nos. 176-187 (12)	1,118.	385.60

On the redrawn stamps the horizontal lines of the portrait and the oval are closer together than on the 1920 stamps by many fine vertical lines.
See No. 202.

Dynjandi Falls — A31

Mount Hekla — A32

Perf. 12½

1935, June 28		Engr.	Unwmk.	
193	A31	10a blue	24.00	.20
		Never hinged	75.00	
194	A32	1k greenish gray	45.00	.25
		Never hinged	140.00	

Matthias
Jochumsson — A33

1935, Nov. 11
195	A33	3a gray green	.75	*4.50*
196	A33	5a gray	15.00	*1.50*
197	A33	7a yel green	22.50	*2.50*
198	A33	35a blue	.65	*1.50*
		Nos. 195-198 (4)	38.90	*10.00*
		Set, never hinged	110.00	

Birth cent. of Matthias Jochumsson, poet.
For surcharges see Nos. 212, 236.

King Christian X — A34

1937, May 14   *Perf. 13x12½*
199	A34	10a green	2.50	*27.50*
200	A34	30a brown	2.50	*12.00*
201	A34	40a claret	2.50	*12.00*
		Nos. 199-201 (3)	7.50	*51.50*
		Set, never hinged	15.00	

Reign of Christian X, 25th anniv.

Christian X Type of 1931-33
1937   Unwmk.   Typo.   Perf. 11½
202	A8	1e yel grn & red	.80	*2.25*
		Never hinged	2.00	

Geyser
A35   A36

1938-47   Engr.   Perf. 14
203	A35	15a dp rose vio	6.50	*13.00*
a.		Imperf., pair	700.00	
		Never hinged	900.00	
204	A35	20a rose red	26.00	*.30*
205	A35	35a ultra	.80	*1.10*
206	A36	40a dk brn ('39)	15.50	*32.50*
207	A36	45a brt ultra ('40)	.90	*1.10*
208	A36	50a dk slate grn	24.00	*1.10*
208A	A36	60a brt ultra ('43)	6.50	*1.25*
c.		Perf. 11½ ('47)	3.50	*11.50*
		Never hinged (#208Ac)	7.00	
208B	A36	1k indigo ('45)	2.25	*.50*
d.		Perf. 11½ ('47)	3.25	*11.50*
		Never hinged (#208Bd)	7.50	
		Nos. 203-208B (8)	82.45	*50.85*
		Set, never hinged	175.00	

University
of Iceland
A37

1938, Dec. 1   *Perf. 13½*
209	A37	25a dark grn	8.50	*18.00*
210	A37	30a brown	8.50	*18.00*
211	A37	40a brt red vio	8.50	*18.00*
		Nos. 209-211 (3)	25.50	*54.00*
		Set, never hinged	40.00	

20th anniversary of independence.

No. 198 Surcharged with New Value
1939, Mar. 17   *Perf. 12½*
212	A33	5a on 35a blue	.90	*1.75*
		Never hinged	2.00	
a.		Double surcharge	275.00	
		Never hinged	450.00	

Trylon and   Leif Ericsson's
Perisphere   Ship and Route
A38   to America
                           A39

Statue of Thorfinn
Karlsefni — A40

1939   Engr.   Perf. 14
213	A38	20a crimson	4.00	*7.75*
214	A39	35a bright ultra	4.50	*9.75*
215	A40	45a bright green	4.75	*13.00*
216	A40	2k dark gray	62.50	*160.00*
		Nos. 213-216 (4)	75.75	*190.50*
		Set, never hinged	120.00	

New York World's Fair.
For overprints see Nos. 232-235.

Codfish — A41   Herring — A42

Flag of Iceland — A43

1939-45   Engr.   Perf. 14, 14x13½
217	A41	1e Prussian blue	.55	*5.00*
a.		Perf. 14x13½	2.00	*5.50*
218	A42	3a dark violet	.55	*1.25*
a.		Perf. 14x13½	2.75	*10.00*
219	A41	5a dark brown	.55	*.50*
c.		Perf. 14x13½	2.75	*1.40*
220	A42	7a dark green	7.00	*12.00*
221	A42	10a green ('40)	45.00	*1.75*
b.		Perf. 14x13½	77.50	*4.50*
		Never hinged	210.00	
222	A42	10a slate gray ('45)	.40	*.25*
223	A42	12a dk grn ('43)	.50	*1.00*
224	A41	25a brt red ('40)	32.50	*.70*
b.		Perf. 14x13½	65.00	*3.00*
		Never hinged (#224b)	210.00	
225	A41	25a hn brn ('45)	.45	*.45*
226	A42	35a carmine ('43)	.60	*.75*
227	A41	50a dk bl grn ('43)	.80	*.40*

Typo.
228	A43	10a car & ultra	2.50	*1.60*
		Nos. 217-228 (12)	91.40	*25.65*
		Set, never hinged	220.00	

Statue of Thorfinn
Karlsefni — A44

1939-45   Engr.   Perf. 14
229	A44	2k dark gray	3.50	*.50*
230	A44	5k dk brn ('43)	27.50	*.65*
231	A44	10k brn yel ('45)	15.00	*2.10*
		Nos. 229-231 (3)	46.00	*3.25*
		Set, never hinged	100.00	

1947
                              Perf. 11½
229a	A44	2k	9.25	*1.90*
230a	A44	5k	35.00	*2.50*
231a	A44	10k	15.00	*55.00*
		Nos. 229a-231a (3)	59.25	*59.40*
		Set, never hinged	175.00	

New York World's Fair Issue of 1939
Overprinted "1940" in Black
1940, May 11   *Perf. 14*
232	A38	20a crimson	10.00	*32.50*
233	A39	35a bright ultra	10.00	*32.50*
234	A40	45a bright green	10.00	*32.50*
235	A40	2k dark gray	125.00	*500.00*
		Nos. 232-235 (4)	155.00	*597.50*
		Set, never hinged	275.00	

No. 195 Surcharged in Red
1941, Mar. 6   *Perf. 12½*
236	A33	25a on 3a gray green	.85	*1.75*
		Never hinged	1.75	

Statue of Snorri   Jon Sigurdsson
Sturluson   A46
A45

1941, Nov. 17   Engr.   Perf. 14
237	A45	25a rose red	1.50	*2.75*
238	A45	50a deep ultra	2.10	*6.25*
239	A45	1k dk olive grn	2.10	*6.25*
		Nos. 237-239 (3)	5.70	*15.25*
		Set, never hinged	10.00	

Snorri Sturluson, writer and historian, 700th
death anniv.

Republic
1944, June 17   *Perf. 14x13½*
240	A46	10a gray black	.45	*1.00*
241	A46	25a dk red brn	.55	*1.00*
242	A46	50a slate grn	.55	*1.00*
243	A46	1k blue black	.95	*1.00*
244	A46	5k henna	3.00	*13.00*
245	A46	10k golden brn	47.50	*110.00*
		Nos. 240-245 (6)	53.00	*127.00*
		Set, never hinged	110.00	

Founding of Republic of Iceland, June 17,
1944.

> Catalogue values for unused
> stamps in this section, from this
> point to the end of the section, are
> for Never Hinged items.

A47

A48

Eruption of Hekla Volcano: 35a, 60a, Close
view of Hekla.

Unwmk.
1948, Dec. 3   Engr.   Perf. 14
246	A47	12a dark vio brn	.25	*.65*
247	A48	25a green	2.00	*.25*
248	A47	35a carmine rose	.55	*.40*
249	A47	50a brown	2.75	*.25*
250	A47	60a bright ultra	9.75	*5.50*
251	A48	1k orange brown	14.00	*.25*
252	A48	10k violet black	70.00	*.55*
		Nos. 246-252 (7)	99.30	*7.85*
		Set, hinged	47.50	

For surcharge see No. 283.

Pack Train
and UPU
Monument,
Bern — A49

UPU, 75th Anniv.: 35a, Reykjavik. 60a,
Map. 2k, Thingvellir Road.
1949, Oct. 9
253	A49	25a dark green	.40	*.65*
254	A49	35a deep carmine	.40	*.65*
255	A49	60a blue	.65	*1.40*
256	A49	2k orange red	1.60	*1.50*
		Nos. 253-256 (4)	3.05	*4.20*

Trawler — A50   Jon
                         Arason — A51

Designs: 20a, 75a, 1k, Tractor plowing. 60a,
5k, Flock of sheep. 5a, 90a, 2k, Vestman-
naeyjar harbor.

1950-54   *Perf. 13*
257	A50	5a dk brn ('54)	.20	*.20*
258	A50	10a gray	.50	*.50*
259	A50	20a brown	.50	*.50*
260	A50	25a car ('54)	.20	*.20*
261	A50	60a green	20.00	*25.00*
262	A50	75a red org ('52)	.55	*.20*
263	A50	90a carmine	.65	*.55*
264	A50	1k chocolate	7.50	*.20*
265	A50	1.25k red vio ('52)	25.00	*.45*
266	A50	1.50k deep ultra	18.00	*.70*
267	A50	2k purple	32.50	*.35*
268	A50	5k dark grn	45.00	*1.50*
		Nos. 257-268 (12)	150.60	*30.35*
		Set, hinged		

For surcharges see Nos. B12-B13.

1950, Nov. 7   *Perf. 14*
269	A51	1.80k carmine	4.00	*4.50*
270	A51	3.30k green	2.50	*4.00*

Bishop Jon Arason, 400th anniv. of death.

Mail Delivery,
1776 — A52

Design: 3k, Airmail, 1951.

1951, May 13
271	A52	2k deep ultra	3.25	*3.25*
272	A52	3k dark purple	4.50	*4.50*

175th anniv. of Iceland's postal service.

Parliament
Building — A53

1952, Apr. 1   *Perf. 13x12½*
273	A53	25k gray black	210.00	*20.00*
		Hinged	90.00	

Sveinn   Reykjabok
Björnsson   A55
A54

1952, Sept. 1   *Perf. 13½*
274	A54	1.25k deep blue	3.25	*.20*
275	A54	2.20k deep green	.75	*5.25*
276	A54	5k indigo	11.00	*1.90*
277	A54	10k brown red	47.50	*32.50*
		Nos. 274-277 (4)	62.50	*39.85*

Sveinn Björnsson, 1st President of Iceland.

1953, Oct. 1   *Perf. 13½x13*
Designs: 70a, Lettering manuscript. 1k, Corner of 15th century manuscript, "Stjorn."

1.75k, Reykjabok. 10k, Corner from law manuscript.

278	A55	10a black	.20	.20
279	A55	70a green	.30	.30
280	A55	1k carmine	.40	.20
281	A55	1.75k blue	32.50	1.90
282	A55	10k orange brn	14.50	1.50
		Nos. 278-282 (5)	47.90	4.10

No. 248 Surcharged With New Value and Bars in Black

1954, Mar. 31 **Perf. 14**

283	A47	5a on 35a car rose	.35	.35
a.		Bars omitted	90.00	
b.		Inverted surcharge	250.00	

Hannes Hafstein A56

Icelandic Wrestling A57

Portraits: 2.45k, in oval. 5k, fullface.

1954, June 1 **Engr.** **Perf. 13**

284	A56	1.25k deep blue	5.00	.70
285	A56	2.45k dark green	25.00	35.00
286	A56	5k carmine	27.50	3.25
		Nos. 284-286 (3)	57.50	38.95

Appointment of the first native minister to Denmark, 50th anniv.

1955, Aug. 9 **Unwmk.** **Perf. 14**

287	A57	75a shown	.20	.20
288	A57	1.25k Diving	.65	.30

See Nos. 300-301.

Skoga Falls — A58

Ellidaar Power Plant — A59

Waterfalls: 60a, Goda. 2kr, Detti. 5kr, Gull. Electric Power Plants: 1.50kr, Sogs. 2.45kr, Andakilsar. 3kr, Laxar.

Perf. 11½, 13½x14 (A59)

1956, Apr. 4 **Unwmk.**

289	A58	15a vio blue	.20	.20
290	A59	50a dull green	.30	.20
291	A59	60a brown	4.00	5.25
292	A59	1.50k violet	35.00	.20
293	A59	2k sepia	2.00	.65
294	A59	2.45k gray black	7.75	12.00
295	A59	3k dark blue	6.50	1.25
296	A58	5k dark green	15.00	2.25
		Nos. 289-296 (8)	70.75	22.00

Telegraph-Telephone Emblem and Map — A60

1956, Sept. 29 **Engr.** **Perf. 13**

297	A60	2.30k ultramarine	.35	1.10

Telegraph and Telephone service in Iceland, 50th anniv.

Northern Countries Issue

Whooper Swans — A60a

1956, Oct. 30 **Perf. 12½**

298	A60a	1.50k rose red	.70	1.25
299	A60a	1.75k ultra	10.50	12.50

To emphasize the bonds among Denmark, Finland, Iceland, Norway and Sweden.

Sports Type of 1955

1.50k, Icelandic wrestling. 1.75k, Diving.

1957, Apr. 1 **Engr.** **Perf. 14**

300	A57	1.50k carmine	1.40	.25
301	A57	1.75k ultramarine	.75	.25

Type of 1952 Air Post Stamps Plane Omitted

Glaciers: 2k, Snaefellsjokull. 3k, Eiriksjokull. 10k, Oraefajokull.

1957, May 8 **Perf. 13½x14**

302	AP16	2k green	5.25	.30
303	AP16	3k dark blue	5.75	.30
304	AP16	10k reddish brn	7.75	.45
		Nos. 302-304 (3)	18.75	1.05

Bessastadir, President's Residence A61

1957, Aug. 1 **Engr.** **Unwmk.**

305	A61	25k gray blk	25.00	5.25

Evergreen and Volcanoes A62

Jonas Hallgrimsson A63

1957, Sept. 4 **Perf. 13½x13**

306	A62	35a shown	.25	.20
307	A62	70a Birch	.25	.20

Issued to publicize a reforestation program.

1957, Nov 16

308	A63	5k grn & blk	1.90	.65

150th birth anniv. of Jonas Hallgrimsson, poet.

Willow Herb — A64

Icelandic Pony — A65

1958, July 8 **Litho.** **Unwmk.**

309	A64	1k shown	.20	.50
310	A64	2.50k Wild pansy	.50	.50

1958, Sept. 27 **Engr.**

311	A65	10a gray black	.25	.20
312	A65	2.25k brown	.70	.35

See No. 324.

Flag — A66

Old Icelandic Government Building — A67

Perf. 13½x14

1958, Dec. 1 **Litho.** **Unwmk.**
Size: 17½x21mm

313	A66	3.50k brt ultra & red	2.50	.70

Size: 23x26½mm

314	A66	50k brt ultra & red	8.00	8.00

40th anniversary of Icelandic flag.

1958, Dec. 9 **Photo.** **Perf. 11½**

315	A67	2k deep green	.55	.20
316	A67	4k deep brown	.65	.40

See Nos. 333-334.

Jon Thorkelsson Teaching — A68

1959, May 5 **Engr.** **Perf. 13½**

317	A68	2k green	.45	.55
318	A68	3k dull purple	.65	.75

Death bicentenary of Jon Thorkelsson, headmaster of Skaholt.

Sockeye Salmon A69

Eider Ducks — A70

Design: 25k, Gyrfalcon.

1959-60 **Engr.** **Perf. 14**

319	A69	25a dark blue	.20	.20
320	A70	90a chestnut & blk	.30	.20
321	A70	2k olive grn & blk	.65	.20
322	A69	5k gray green	11.00	1.10

Litho. **Perf. 11½**

323	A70	25k dl pur, gray & yel	17.50	14.00
		Nos. 319-323 (5)	29.65	15.70

Issued: 25k, Mar. 1, 1960; others, Nov. 25.

Pony Type of 1958

1960, Apr. 7 **Engr.** **Perf. 13½x13**

324	A65	1k dark carmine	.65	.50

"The Outlaw" by Einar Jonsson A71

Wild Geranium A72

1960, Apr. 7 **Perf. 14**

325	A71	2.50k reddish brn	.30	.30
326	A71	4.50k ultramarine	.85	.85

World Refugee Year, 7/1/59-6/30/60.

Common Design Types pictured following the introduction.

Europa Issue, 1960
Common Design Type

1960, Sept. 18 **Photo.** **Perf. 11½**
Size: 32½x22mm

327	CD3	3k grn & lt grn	.50	.50
328	CD3	5.50k dk bl & lt bl	.80	.80

1960-62 **Photo.** **Perf. 11½**

Flowers: 50a, Bellflower. 2.50k, Dandelion. 3.50k, Buttercup.

329	A72	50a gray grn, grn & violet ('62)	.20	.20
330	A72	1.20k sep, vio & grn	.20	.20
331	A72	2.50k brn, yel & grn	.20	.20
332	A72	3.50k dl bl, yel & green ('62)	.65	.20
		Nos. 329-332 (4)	1.25	.80

See Nos. 363-366, 393-394.

Building Type of 1958

1961, Apr. 11 **Unwmk.** **Perf. 11½**

333	A67	1.50k deep blue	.30	.20
334	A67	3k dark carmine	.30	.20

Jon
Sigurdsson
A73

Reykjavik
A74

Typographed and Embossed

	1961, June 17		**Perf. 12½x14**	
335	A73	50a crimson	.20	.20
336	A73	3k dark blue	1.75	1.25
337	A73	5k deep plum	.60	.55
		Nos. 335-337 (3)	2.55	2.00

Jon Sigurdsson (1811-1879), statesman and scholar.

	1961, Aug. 18	Photo.	**Perf. 11½**	
338	A74 2.50k blue & grn		.65	.30
339	A74 4.50k lilac & vio bl		1.00	.50

Municipal charter of Reykjavik, 175th anniv.

Europa Issue, 1961
Common Design Type
1961, Sept. 18
Size: 32x22½mm

340	CD4 5.50k multicolored	.45	.45
341	CD4 6k multicolored	.45	.45

Benedikt
Sveinsson — A75

University of
Iceland — A76

Design: 1.40k, Björn M. Olsen.

	1961, Oct. 6	Photo.	**Perf. 11½**	
342	A75	1k red brown	.20	.20
343	A75 1.40k ultramarine		.20	.20
344	A76	10k green	1.50	.60
a.	Souv. sheet of 3, #342-344, imperf.		1.00	1.60
		Nos. 342-344 (3)	1.90	1.00

50th anniv. of the University of Iceland; Benedikt Sveinsson (1827-1899), statesman; and Björn M. Olsen (1850-1919), first rector.

Production
Institute — A77

New Buildings: 4k, Fishing Research Institute. 6k, Farm Bureau.

	1962, July 6	Unwmk.	**Perf. 11½**	
345	A77 2.50k ultramarine		.40	.25
346	A77	4k dull green	.55	.25
347	A77	6k brown	.65	.30
		Nos. 345-347 (3)	1.60	.80

Europa Issue, 1962
Common Design Type
1962, Sept. 17
Size: 32½x22½mm

			Perf. 11½	
348	CD5 5.50k yel, lt grn & brn		.20	.20
349	CD5 6.50k lt grn, grn & brn		.60	.60

Map Showing
Submarine
Telephone
Cable — A78

1962, Nov. 20
Granite Paper

350	A78 5k multicolored		1.10	.65
351	A78 7k grn, lt bl & red		.65	.50

Inauguration of the submarine telephone cable from Newfoundland, via Greenland and Iceland to Scotland.

Sigurdur
Gudmundsson,
Self-portrait
A79

Herring Boat
A80

5.50k, Knight slaying dragon, Romanesque door from Valthjofsstad Church, ca. 1200 A.D.

	1963, Feb. 20	Photo.	**Perf. 11½**	
352	A79	4k bis brn & choc	.65	.50
353	A79 5.50k gray ol & brn		.50	.50

National Museum of Iceland, cent., and its first curator, Sigurdur Gudmundsson.

1963, Mar. 21

354	A80	5k multicolored	.90	.30
355	A80 7.50k multicolored		.25	.20

FAO "Freedom from Hunger" campaign.

View of
Akureyri
A81

1963, July 2	Unwmk.	**Perf. 11½**	
356	A81 3k gray green	.25	.50

Europa Issue, 1963
Common Design Type
1963, Sept. 16
Size: 32½x23mm

357	CD6 6k org brn & yel	.75	.75
358	CD6 7k blue & yellow	.75	.75

M.S.
Gullfoss
A82

1964, Jan. 17	Photo.	**Perf. 11½**	
359	A82 10k ultra, blk & gray	2.25	1.60
a.	Accent on 2nd "E" omitted	40.00	50.00

Iceland Steamship Company, 50th anniv.

Scout Emblem
and "Be
Prepared"
A83

Icelandic Coat of
Arms
A84

1964, Apr. 24

360	A83 3.50k multicolored	.65	.50
361	A83 4.50k multicolored	.65	.50

Issued to honor the Boy Scouts.

1964, June 17		**Perf. 11½**	
362	A84 25k multicolored	3.00	2.75

20th anniversary, Republic of Iceland.

Flower Type of 1960-62

Flowers: 50a, Eight-petal dryas. 1k, Crowfoot (Ranunculus glacialis). 1.50k, Buck bean. 2k, Clover (trifolium repens).

1964, July 15
Flowers in Natural Colors

363	A72	50a vio bl & lt vio bl	.30	.20
364	A72	1k gray & dk gray	.30	.20
365	A72 1.50k brn & pale brn	.30	.20
366	A72	2k ol & pale olive	.30	.20
		Nos. 363-366 (4)	1.20	.80

Europa Issue, 1964
Common Design Type
1964, Sept. 14 **Photo.** **Perf. 11½**
Granite Paper
Size: 22½x33mm

367	CD7 4.50k golden brn, yel & Prus grn	.75	.65
368	CD7	9k bl, yel & dk brn	1.25	1.00

Jumper — A85

1964, Oct. 20	Unwmk.	**Perf. 11½**	
369	A85 10k lt grn & blk	1.25	1.00

18th Olympic Games, Tokyo, Oct. 10-25.

ITU
Emblem
A86

1965, May 17	Photo.	**Perf. 11½**	
370	A86 4.50k green	.90	.60
371	A86 7.50k bright ultra	.20	.20

ITU, centenary.

Surtsey
Island, April
1964 — A87

1.50k, Underwater volcanic eruption, Nov. 1963, vert. 3.50k, Surtsey, Sept. 1964.

1965, June 23	Unwmk.	**Perf. 11½**	
372	A87 1.50k bl, bis & blk	.75	.75
373	A87	2k multicolored	.75	.75
374	A87 3.50k bl, blk & red	.90	.75
		Nos. 372-374 (3)	2.40	2.25

Emergence of a new volcanic island off the southern coast of Iceland.

Europa Issue, 1965
Common Design Type
1965, Sept. 27 **Photo.** **Perf. 11½**
Size: 33x22½mm

375	CD8 5k tan, brn & brt grn	1.50	1.00
376	CD8 8k brt grn, brn & yel green	1.00	.75

Einar
Benediktsson
A88

Engr. & Litho.
1965, Nov. 16 **Perf. 14**

377	A88 10k brt blue & brn	4.00	5.00

Einar Benediktsson, poet (1864-1940).

White-tailed Sea
Eagle — A89

National
Costume — A90

1965-66	Photo.	**Perf. 11½**	
378	A89	50k multicolored	13.00	13.00
379	A90 100k multicolored	10.00	9.00

Issued: #378, 4/26/66; #379, 12/3/65.

West
Iceland — A91

1966, Aug. 4	Photo.	**Perf. 11½**	
380	A91 2.50k shown	.35	.35
381	A91	4k North Iceland	.55	.35
382	A91	5k East Iceland	.90	.35
383	A91 6.50k South Iceland	.70	.35
		Nos. 380-383 (4)	2.50	1.40

Europa Issue, 1966
Common Design Type
1966, Sept. 26 **Photo.** **Perf. 11½**
Size: 22½x33mm

384	CD9 7k grnsh bl, lt bl & red	2.50	1.90
385	CD9 8k brn, buff & red	2.50	1.90

Literary
Society
Emblem
A92

1966, Nov. 18	Engr.	**Perf. 11½**	
386	A92	4k ultramarine	.35	.30
387	A92 10k vermilion	.80	.60

Icelandic Literary Society, 150th anniv.

Common
Loon — A93

1967, Mar. 16	Photo.	**Perf. 11½**	
388	A93 20k multicolored	6.50	6.50

Europa Issue, 1967
Common Design Type
1967, May 2 **Photo.** **Perf. 11½**
Size: 22½x33mm

389	CD10 7k yel, brn & dk bl	1.50	1.00
390	CD10 8k emer, gray & dk bl	1.50	1.00

Old and New
Maps of
Iceland and
North
America
A94

1967, June 8	Photo.	**Perf. 11½**	
391	A94 10k blk, tan & lt bl	.35	.30

EXPO '67 Intl. Exhibition, Montreal, Apr. 28-Oct. 27, 1967. The old map, drawn about 1590 by Sigurdur Stefansson, is at the Royal Library, Copenhagen.

Symbols of Trade, Fishing, Husbandry and Industry — A95

1967, Sept. 14   Photo.   Perf. 11½
392 A95 5k dk bl, yel & emerald   .35   .25
Icelandic Chamber of Commerce, 50th anniv.

Flower Type of 1960-62

Flowers: 50a, Saxifraga oppositifolia. 2.50k, Orchis maculata.

1968, Jan. 17   Photo.   Perf. 11½
Flowers in Natural Colors
393 A72 50a green & dk brn   .25   .20
394 A72 2.50k dk brn, yel & grn   .35   .35

Europa Issue, 1968
Common Design Type
1968, Apr. 29   Photo.   Perf. 11½
Size: 33½x23mm
395 CD11 9.50k dl yel, car rose & blk   1.75   1.50
396 CD11 10k brt yel grn, blk & org   1.25   1.00

Right-hand Driving — A96

1968, May 21   Photo.   Perf. 11½
397 A96 4k yellow & brn   .35   .20
398 A96 5k lt reddish brn   .35   .20
Introduction of right-hand driving in Iceland, May 26, 1968.

Fridrik Fridriksson, by Sigurjón Olafsson — A97

1968, Sept. 5   Photo.   Perf. 11½
399 A97 10k sky bl & dk gray   .45   .55
Rev. Fridrik Fridriksson (1868-1961), founder of the YMCA in Reykjavik and writer.

Reading Room, National Library A98

Prime Minister Jon Magnusson (1859-1926) A99

1968, Oct. 30   Photo.   Perf. 11½
Granite Paper
400 A98 5k yellow & brn   .25   .20
401 A98 20k lt bl & dp ultra   1.25   1.25
Natl. Library, Reykjavik, sesquicentennial.

1968, Dec. 12
Granite Paper
402 A99 4k carmine lake   .35   .25
403 A99 50k dark brown   4.00   4.25
50th anniversary of independence.

Nordic Cooperation Issue

Five Ancient Ships — A99a

1969, Feb. 28   Engr.   Perf. 12½
404 A99a 6.50k vermilion   .55   .50
405 A99a 10k bright blue   .65   .60

50th anniv. of the Nordic Society and centenary of postal cooperation among the northern countries. The design is taken from a coin found at the site of Birka, an ancient Swedish town. See also Denmark Nos. 454-455, Finland No. 481, Norway Nos. 523-524, and Sweden Nos. 808-810.

Europa Issue, 1969
Common Design Type
1969, Apr. 28   Photo.   Perf. 11½
Size: 32½x23mm
406 CD12 13k pink & multi   3.75   2.00
407 CD12 14.50k yel & multi   .45   .40

Flag of Iceland and Rising Sun — A100

1969, June 17   Photo.   Perf. 11½
408 A100 25k gray, gold, vio bl & red   .90   .55
409 A100 100k lt bl, gold, vio bl & red   6.50   6.50
25th anniversary, Republic of Iceland.

Boeing 727 A101

1969, Sept. 3   Photo.   Perf. 11½
410 A101 9.50k dk bl & sky bl   .55   .55
411 A101 12k dk bl & ultra   .55   .55
Design: 12k, Rolls Royce 400.
50th anniversary of Icelandic aviation.

Snaefellsjökull Mountain A102

1970, Jan. 6   Photo.   Perf. 11½
412 A102 1k shown   .20   .20
413 A102 4k Laxfoss   .35   .35
414 A102 5k Hattver, vert.   .40   .35
415 A102 20k Fjardargill, vert.   2.00   .75
    Nos. 412-415 (4)   2.95   1.65

First Meeting of Icelandic Supreme Court A103

1970, Feb. 16   Photo.   Perf. 11½
416 A103 6.50k multicolored   .30   .25
Icelandic Supreme Court, 50th anniv.

Column from "Skarosbók," 1363 (Law Book) — A104

Icelandic Manuscripts: 15k, Preface to "Flateyjarbók" (History of Norwegian Kings), 1387-1394. 30k, Initial from "Flateyjarbók" showing Harald Fairhair cutting fetters of Dofri.

1970, Mar. 20   Photo.   Perf. 11½
417 A104 5k multicolored   .25   .25
418 A104 15k multicolored   .65   .65
419 A104 30k multicolored   1.25   1.25
    Nos. 417-419 (3)   2.15   2.15

Europa Issue, 1970
Common Design Type
1970, May 4   Photo.   Perf. 11½
Size: 32x22mm
420 CD13 9k brn & yellow   2.50   1.50
421 CD13 25k brt grn & bister   3.50   2.50

Nurse — A105

Grimur Thomsen — A106

The Rest, by Thorarinn B. Thorlaksson A107

1970, June 19   Photo.   Perf. 11½
422 A105 7k ultra & lt bl   .35   .20
423 A106 10k ind & lt grnsh bl   .35   .45
424 A107 50k gold & multi   2.00   1.50
    Nos. 422-424 (3)   2.70   2.15

50th anniv. (in 1969) of the Icelandic Nursing Association (No. 422); 150th birth anniv. of Grimur Thomsen (1820-1896), poet (No. 423); Intl. Arts Festival, Reykjavik, June 1970 (No. 424).

Saxifraga Oppositifolia A108

Lakagigar A109

1970, Aug. 25   Photo.   Perf. 11½
425 A108 3k multicolored   .30   .30
426 A109 15k multicolored   .90   .80
European Nature Conservation Year.

UN Emblem and Map of Iceland A110

1970, Oct. 23   Photo.   Perf. 11½
427 A110 12k multicolored   .55   .65
25th anniversary of United Nations.

"Flight," by Asgrimur Jonsson A111

1971, Mar. 26   Photo.   Perf. 11½
428 A111 10k multicolored   .90   .90
Joint northern campaign for the benefit of refugees.

Europa Issue, 1971
Common Design Type
1971, May 3   Photo.   Perf. 11½
Size: 33x22mm
429 CD14 7k rose cl, yel & blk   2.50   1.75
430 CD14 15k ultra, yel & blk   3.00   2.00

Postal Checking Service Emblem A112

1971, June 22   Photo.   Perf. 11½
431 A112 5k vio bl & lt blue   .20   .25
432 A112 7k dk grn & yel grn   .30   .25
Introduction of Postal Checking Service, Apr. 30, 1971.

Tryggvi Gunnarsson A113

Haddock Freezing Plant A114

Design: 30k, Patriotic Society emblem.

1971, Aug. 19   Photo.   Perf. 11½
433 A113 30k lt bl & vio blk   1.50   1.00
434 A113 100k gray & vio blk   6.50   6.50
Icelandic Patriotic Society, cent.; Tryggvi Gunnarsson (1835-1917), founder and president.

1971, Nov. 18
Fish Industry: 7k, Cod fishing. 20k, Shrimp canning plant.
435 A114 5k multicolored   .20   .20
436 A114 7k multicolored   .20   .20
437 A114 20k green & multi   1.10   .55
    Nos. 435-437 (3)   1.50   .95

Herdubreid Mountain — A115

Engr. & Litho.
1972, Mar. 9   Perf. 14
438 A115 250k blue & multi   .70   .30

Europa Issue 1972
Common Design Type
1972, May 2   Photo.   Perf. 11½
Size: 22x32mm
439 CD15 9k lt vio & multi   1.50   .90
440 CD15 13k yel grn & multi   2.75   1.75

"United Municipalities" — A116

1972, June 14   Photo.   Perf. 11½
441 A116 16k multicolored   .25   .20
Legislation for local government, cent.

Chessboard, World Map, Rook — A117

1972, July 2   Litho.   Perf. 13
442 A117 15k lt ol & multi   .45   .35
World Chess Championship, Reykjavik, July-Sept. 1972.

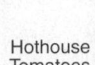

Hothouse Tomatoes A118

Designs: 12k, Steam valve and natural steam. 40k, Hothouse roses.

1972, Aug. 23   Photo.   Perf. 11½
443 A118 8k Prus bl & multi   .20   .20
444 A118 12k green & multi   .20   .20
445 A118 40k dk pur & multi   1.50   1.10
      Nos. 443-445 (3)   1.90   1.50
Hothouse gardening in Iceland, using natural steam and hot springs.

Iceland and the Continental Shelf — A119

1972, Sept. 27   Litho.   Perf. 13
446 A119 9k blue & multi   .25   .25
To publicize Iceland's offshore fishing rights.

Europa Issue 1973
Common Design Type
1973, Apr. 30   Photo.   Perf. 11½
Size: 32½x22mm
447 CD16 13k vio & multi   6.00   3.25
448 CD16 25k olive & multi   1.00   .80

Iceland No. 1 and Messenger — A120

Designs (First Issue of Iceland and): 15k, No. 5 and pony train. 20k, No. 2 and mailboat "Esja". 40k, No. 3 and mail truck. 80k, No. 4 and Beech-18 mail plane.

Litho. & Engr.
1973, May 23   Perf. 13x13½
449 A120 10k dl bl, blk & ultra   .30   .30
450 A120 15k grn, blk & gray   .20   .20
451 A120 20k maroon, blk & car   .20   .20
452 A120 40k vio, blk & brn   .20   .20
453 A120 80k olive, blk & yel   1.50   1.00
      Nos. 449-453 (5)   2.40   1.90
Centenary of Iceland's first postage stamps.

Nordic Cooperation Issue

Nordic House, Reykjavik A120a

1973, June 26   Engr.   Perf. 12½
454 A120a 9k multicolored   .50   .20
455 A120a 10k multicolored   1.50   1.25
A century of postal cooperation among Denmark, Finland, Iceland, Norway and Sweden, and in connection with the Nordic Postal Conference, Reykjavik.

Ásgeir Ásgeirsson, (1894-1972),President of Iceland 1952-1968 — A121

1973, Aug. 1   Engr.   Perf. 13x13½
456 A121 13k carmine   .45   .35
457 A121 15k blue   .20   .35

Islandia 73 Emblem A122

20k, Islandia 73 emblem; diff. arrangement.

1973, Aug. 31   Photo.   Perf. 11½
458 A122 17k gray & multi   .45   .45
459 A122 20k brn, ocher & yel   .35   .35
Islandia 73 Philatelic Exhibition, Reykjavik, Aug. 31-Sept. 9.

Man and WMO Emblem A123   The Settlement, Tapestry by Vigdis Kristjansdottir A124

1973, Nov. 14   Photo.   Perf. 12½
460 A123 50k silver & multi   .80   .65
Intl. meteorological cooperation, cent.

1974   Photo.   Perf. 11½
Designs: 13k, Establishment of Althing, painting by Johannes Johannesson, horiz. 15k, Gudbrandur Thorlakkson, Bishop ofHolar 1571-1627. 17k, Age of Sturlungar (Fighting Vikings), drawing by Thorvaldur Skulason. 20k, Stained glass window honoring Hallgrimur Petursson (1614-74), hymn writer. 25k, Illumination from Book of Flatey, 14th century. 30k, Conversion to Christianity (altarpiece, Skalholt), mosaic by Nina Tryggvadottir. 40k, Wood carving (family and plants), 18th century. 60k, Curing the Catch, cement bas-relief. 70k, Age of Writing (Saemundur Riding Seal), sculpture by Asmundur Sveinsson. 100k, Virgin and Child with Angels, embroidered antependium, Stafafell Church, 14th century.

461 A124 10k multicolored   .20   .20
462 A124 13k multicolored   .20   .20
463 A124 15k multicolored   .20   .20
464 A124 17k multicolored   .35   .20
465 A124 20k multicolored   .35   .20
466 A124 25k multicolored   .20   .20
467 A124 30k multicolored   .90   .70
468 A124 40k multicolored   1.25   .90
469 A124 60k multicolored   1.25   1.25

---

470 A124 70k multicolored   1.25   1.25
471 A124 100k multicolored   1.60   .75
      Nos. 461-471 (11)   7.75   6.05
1100th anniv. of settlement of Iceland.
Issued: 10k, 13k, 30k, 70k, 3/12; 17k, 25k, 100k, 6/11; 15k, 20k, 40k, 60k, 7/16.

Horseback Rider, Wood, 17th Century — A125

Europa: 20k, "Through the Sound Barrier," contemporary bronze by Asmundur Sveinsson.

1974, Apr. 29   Photo.   Perf. 11½
472 A125 13k brn red & multi   .70   .40
473 A125 20k gray & multi   1.60   1.00

Clerk Selling Stamps, UPU Emblem A126

Design: 20k, Mailman delivering mail.

1974, Oct. 9   Photo.   Perf. 11½
474 A126 17k ocher & multi   .35   .35
475 A126 20k olive & multi   .35   .35
Centenary of Universal Postal Union.

Volcanic Eruption, Heimaey, Jan. 23, 1973 — A127

Design: 25k, Volcanic eruption, night view.

1975, Jan. 23   Photo.   Perf. 11½
476 A127 20k multicolored   .65   .45
477 A127 25k multicolored   .35   .35

Europa Issue 1975

Bird, by Thorvaldur Skulason A128

Sun Queen, by Johannes S. Kjarval — A129

1975, May 12   Photo.   Perf. 11½
478 A128 18k multicolored   .50   .40
479 A129 23k gold & multi   1.50   1.00

Stephan G. Stephansson A130

1975, Aug. 1   Engr.   Perf. 13
480 A130 27k green & brn   .55   .35
Stephan G. Stephansson (1853-1927), Icelandic poet and settler in North America; centenary of Icelandic emigration to North America.

Petursson, by Hjalti Thorsteinsson A131   Einar Jonsson, Self-portrait A132

23k, Arni Magnusson, by Hjalti Thorsteinsson. 30k, Jon Eiriksson, sculpture by Olafur Olafsson.

1975, Sept. 18   Engr.   Perf. 13
481 A131 18k slate green & indigo   .20   .20
482 A131 23k Prussian blue   .20   .20
483 A131 30k deep magenta   .20   .20
484 A132 50k indigo   .50   .20
      Nos. 481-484 (4)   1.10   .80
Famous Icelanders: Hallgrimur Petursson (1614-1674), minister and religious poet; Arni Magnusson (1663-1730), historian, registrar and manuscript collector; Jon Eiriksson (1728-1787), professor of law and cabinet member; Einar Jonsson (1874-1954), sculptor, painter and writer.

Red Cross A133

1975, Oct. 15   Photo.   Perf. 11½x12
485 A133 23k multicolored   .45   .20
Icelandic Red Cross, 50th anniversary.

Abstract Painting, by Nina Tryggvadottir A134

1975, Oct. 15   Perf. 12x12½
486 A134 100k multicolored   1.40   .65
International Women's Year 1975.

Thorvaldsen Statue, by Thorvaldsen A135

Saplings Growing in Bare Landscape A136

1975, Nov. 19   Photo.   Perf. 11½
487 A135 27k lt vio & multi   .80   .45
Centenary of Thorvaldsen Society, a charity honoring Bertel Thorvaldsen (1768-1844), sculptor.

1975, Nov. 19   Perf. 12x11½
488 A136 35k multicolored   .60   .45
Reforestation.

Lang Glacier, by Asgrimur Jonsson A137

1976, Mar. 18   Photo.   Perf. 11½
489 A137 150k gold & multi   2.00 1.50
Asgrimur Jonsson (1876-1958), painter.

Wooden Bowl — A138

Europa: 45k, Spinning wheel, vert.

1976, May 3   Photo.   Perf. 11½
490 A138 35k ver & multi   1.40 1.00
491 A138 45k blue & multi   1.40 1.40

No. 9 with First Day Cancel — A139

Decree Establishing Postal Service — A140

1976, Sept. 22   Photo.   Perf. 11½
Granite Paper
492 A139 30k bis, blk & gray bl   .35   .20
Centenary of aurar stamps.

1976, Sept. 22   Engr.   Perf. 13
45k, Conclusion of Decree with signatures.
493 A140 35k dark brown   .45   .35
494 A140 45k dark blue   .45   .35
Iceland's Postal Service, bicentenary.

Federation Emblem, People — A141

1976, Dec. 2   Photo.   Perf. 12½
Granite Paper
495 A141 100k multicolored   1.25   .75
Icelandic Federation of Labor, 60th anniv.

Five Water Lilies — A142

Ofaerufoss, Eldgja — A143

Photo. & Engr.
1977, Feb. 2   Perf. 12½
496 A142 35k brt grn & multi   .90   .65
497 A142 45k ultra & multi   .90   .65
Nordic countries cooperation for protection of the environment and 25th Session of Nordic Council, Helsinki, Feb. 19.

1977, May 2   Photo.   Perf. 12
Europa: 85k, Kirkjufell Mountain, seen from Grundarfjord.
498 A143 45k multicolored   3.00 1.00
499 A143 85k multicolored   2.00   .45

Harlequin Duck — A144

1977, June 14   Photo.   Perf. 11½
500 A144 40k multicolored   .55   .35
Wetlands conservation, European campaign.

Society Emblem — A145

1977, June 14
501 A145 60k vio bl & ultra   .75   .65
Federation of Icelandic Cooperative Societies, 75th anniversary.

Hot Springs, Therapeutic Bath, Emblem A146

1977, Nov. 16   Photo.   Perf. 11½
502 A146 90k multicolored   .65   .55
World Rheumatism Year.

Stone Marker — A147

1977, Dec. 12   Engr.   Perf. 11½
503 A147 45k dark blue   .90   .65
Touring Club of Iceland, 50th anniversary.

Thorvaldur Thoroddsen, (1855-1921), Geologist, Scientist and Writer — A148

Design: 60k, Briet Bjarnhedinsdottir (1856-1940), Founder of Icelandic Women's Association and Reykjavik city councillor.

1977, Dec. 12   Engr.   Perf. 11½
504 A148 50k brn & slate grn   .20   .20
505 A148 60k grn & vio brn   .70   .60

Bailiff's Residence, Videy Island, 1752 — A149

Europa: 120k, Husavik Church, 1906.

1978, May 2   Photo.   Perf. 11½
506 A149 80k multicolored   2.25   .75
507 A149 120k multi, vert.   3.00 1.00

Alexander Johannesson, Junkers Planes — A150

100k, Fokker Friendship plane over mountains.

1978, June 21   Photo.   Perf. 12½
508 A150 60k multicolored   .55   .30
509 A150 100k multicolored   .55   .40
50th anniv. of domestic flights in Iceland.

Skeioara River Bridge A151

1978, Aug. 17   Photo.   Perf. 11½
510 A151 70k multicolored   .30   .30

Lava Near Mt. Hekla, by Jon Stefansson — A152

1978, Nov. 16   Photo.   Perf. 12
511 A152 1000k multicolored   5.00 4.25
Jon Stefansson (1881-1962), Icelandic painter.

Ship to Shore Rescue A153

1978, Dec. 1   Engr.   Perf. 13
512 A153 60k black   .30   .30
National Life Saving Assoc., 50th anniv.

Halldor Hermannsson (1878-1958), Historian, Librarian — A154

1978, Dec. 1
513 A154 150k indigo   .60   .50

Lighthouse A155

Telephone, c. 1900 A156

1978, Dec. 1   Photo.   Perf. 11½
514 A155 90k multicolored   .60   .50
Centenary of Icelandic lighthouses.

1979, Apr. 30   Photo.   Perf. 11½
Europa: 190k, Post horn and satchel.
515 A156 110k multicolored   3.75   .75
516 A156 190k multicolored   6.50 1.00

Jon Sigurdsson and Ingibjorg Einarsdottir A157

1979, Nov. 1   Engr.   Perf. 13x12½
517 A157 150k black   .60   .60
Jon Sigurdsson (1811-1879), Icelandic statesman and leader in independence movement.

Excerpt from Olafs Saga Helga — A158

1979, Nov. 1   Photo.   Perf. 11½
518 A158 200k multicolored   .80   .55
Snorri Sturluson (1178-1241), Icelandic historian and writer.

Children with Flowers ICY Emblem — A159

1979, Nov. 12
519 A159 140k multicolored   .80   .55
International Year of the Child.

A160

A161

Icelandic Arms, before 1904 and 1904-1919.

1979, Nov. 12
520 A160 500k multicolored   1.50 1.00

Home rule, 75th anniversary.

1979   **Engr.**   *Perf. 13*

Designs: 80k, Ingibjorg H. Bjarnason (1867-1941). 100k, Bjarni Thorsteinsson (1861-1938), composer. 120k, Petur Gudjohnsen (1812-77), organist. 130k, Sveinbjorn Sveinbjornson (1847-1927), composer. 170k, Torfhildur Holm (1845-1918), poet.

521	A161	80k rose violet	.20	.20
522	A161	100k black	.20	.20
523	A161	120k rose carmine	.20	.20
524	A161	130k sepia	.45	.45
525	A161	170k carmine rose	.55	.40
		Nos. 521-525 (5)	1.60	1.45

Issued: 80k, 170k, Aug. 3; others, Dec. 12.

Canis Familiaris — A162

Design: 90k, Alopex lagopus.

1980, Jan. 24
526	A162	10k black	.25	.20
527	A162	90k sepia	.25	.20

See Nos. 534-536, 543-545, 552, 553, 556-558, 610-612.

Jon Sveinsson Nonni (1857-1944), Writer — A163

Europa: 250k, Gunnar Gunnarsson (1889-1975), writer.

1980, Apr. 28   **Photo.**   *Perf. 11½*
Granite Paper
528	A163	140k dl rose & blk	1.00	.50
529	A163	250k tan & blk	1.25	.75

Mountain Ash Branch and Berries — A164

1980, July 8   **Photo.**   *Perf. 12½*
530 A164 120k multicolored   .35 .35

Year of the Tree.

Laugardalur Sports Complex, Reykjavik A165

1980, July 8   **Engr.**   *Perf. 13x12½*
531 A165 300k slate green   .70 .55

1980 Olympic Games.

Carved and Painted Cabinet Door, 18th Cent. — A166   Radio Receiver, 1930 — A168

Nordic Cooperation: 180k, Embroidered cushion, 19th cent.

1980, Sept. 9   **Photo.**   *Perf. 11½*
Granite Paper
532	A166	150k multicolored	.65	.50
533	A166	180k multicolored	.75	.60

Animal Type of 1980
1980, Oct. 16   **Engr.**   *Perf. 13*

Designs: 160k, Sebastes marinus. 170k, Fratercula arctica. 190k, Phoca vitulina.

534	A162	160k rose violet	.90	.20
535	A162	170k black	1.00	.60
536	A162	190k dark brown	.20	.35
		Nos. 534-536 (3)	2.10	1.15

1980, Nov. 20   **Photo.**   *Perf. 12½*
Granite Paper
537 A168 400k multicolored   1.10 .50

State Broadcasting Service, 50th anniv.

University Hospital, 50th Anniversary A169

1980, Nov. 20   *Perf. 11½*
538 A169 200k multicolored   .45 .45

A170

Design: 170a, Magnus Stephensen (1762-1833), Chief Justice. 190a, Finnur Magnusson (1781-1847), Privy Archives keeper.

1981, Feb. 24   **Engr.**   *Perf. 13*
539	A170	170a bright ultra	.55	.35
540	A170	190a olive green	.55	.35

Europa Issue 1981

Europa — A171

1981, May 4   **Photo.**   *Perf. 11½*
Granite Paper
541	A171	180a Luftur the Sorcerer	2.00	1.00
542	A171	220a Sea witch	2.00	1.00

Animal Type of 1980
1981, Aug. 20   **Engr.**   *Perf. 13*

Designs: 50a, Troglodytes troglodytes. 100a, Pluvialis apricaria. 200a, Corvus corax.

543	A162	50a brown	.25	.20
544	A162	100a blue	.25	.20
545	A162	200a black	.25	.20
		Nos. 543-545 (3)	.75	.60

Intl. Year of the Disabled — A173

1981, Sept. 29   **Photo.**   *Perf. 11½*
546 A173 200a multicolored   .30 .20

Skyggnir Earth Satellite Station, First Anniv. — A174

1981, Sept. 29   **Photo.**   *Perf. 11½*
547 A174 500a multicolored   1.40 .70

Hauling the Line, by Gunnlaugur Scheving (1904-1972) A175

1981, Oct. 21   **Photo.**   *Perf. 11½*
548 A175 5000a multi   7.00 3.75

Christian Missionary Work in Iceland Millennium A176

1981, Nov. 24   **Engr.**   *Perf. 13*
549 A176 200a dark violet   .55 .55

Christmas A177

1981, Nov. 24   **Photo.**   *Perf. 12½*
Granite Paper
550	A177	200a Leaf bread	1.00	.65
551	A177	250a Leaf bread, diff.	1.00	.55

Animal Type of 1980
1982, Mar. 23   **Engr.**   *Perf. 13*

Designs: 20a, Buccinum undatum, vert. 600a, Chlamys islandica.

552	A162	20a copper brn	.25	.25
553	A162	600a vio brown	1.00	.50

Europa Issue 1982

First Norse Settlement, 874 — A179

1982, May 3   **Photo.**   *Perf. 11½*
Granite Paper
554	A179	350a shown	7.50	1.25
555	A179	450a Discovery of North America, 1000	7.50	1.25

Animal Type of 1980
1982, June 3   **Engr.**   *Perf. 13*

Designs: 300a, Ovis aries, vert. 400a, Bos taurus, vert. 500a, Felis catus, vert.

556	A162	300a brown	.90	.50
557	A162	400a lake	.65	.35
558	A162	500a gray	.20	.20
		Nos. 556-558 (3)	1.75	1.05

Kaupfelag Thingeyinga Cooperative Society Centenary — A181

1982, June 3
559 A181 1000a black & red   1.10 .65

Man Riding Iceland Pony — A182

1982, July 1   **Photo.**   *Perf. 11½*
Granite Paper
560 A182 700a multicolored   .80 .35

Centenary of School of Agriculture, Holar A183

1982, July 1
Granite Paper
561 A183 1500a multi   1.25 1.10

Mount Herdubreid, by Isleifur Konradsson (1889-1972) A184

1982, Sept. 8   **Photo.**   *Perf. 11½*
Granite Paper
562 A184 800a multicolored   .75 .65

UN World Assembly on Aging, 7/26-8/6.

Borbjorg Sveinsdottir (1828-1903) — A185

1982, Sept. 8   **Engr.**   *Perf. 13*
563 A185 900a red brown   .70 .55

Borbjorg Sveinsdottir (1828-1903), midwife and Univ. founder.

Souvenir Sheet

NORDIA '84 — A186

Photo. & Engr.
1982, Oct. 7   *Perf. 13½*
564   Sheet of 2   7.00 7.00
   a. A186 400a Reynistaour Monastery seal   3.50 3.50
   b. A186 800a Bingeyrar   3.50 3.50

NORDIA '84 Intl. Stamp Exhibition, Reykjavik, July 3-8, 1984. Sold for 18k. See No. 581.

Christmas
A187

Score from The Night was Such a Splendid One.

1982, Nov. 16   Photo.   Perf. 11½
Granite Paper
565 A187 3k Birds   .90 .55
566 A187 3.50k Bells   1.00 .55

Caltha
Palustris — A188

1983, Feb. 10   Photo.
Granite Paper
567 A188 7.50k shown   .55 .55
568 A188 8k Lychnis alpina   .90 .55
569 A188 10k Potentilla palus-
             tris   1.40 .55
570 A188 20k Myosotis
             scorpioides   2.50 .85
         Nos. 567-570 (4)   5.35 2.50
See #586-587, 593-594, 602-605, 663-664.

Nordic
Cooperation
A189

1983, Mar. 24
Granite Paper
571 A189 4.50k Mt. Sulur   1.20 .75
572 A189 5k Urrida Falls   1.20 .75

Europa Issue, 1983

Thermal Energy
Projects — A190

1983, May 5
Granite Paper
573 A190 5k shown   4.50 2.00
574 A190 5.50k multi, diff.   25.00 2.50

Fishing
Industry
A191

1983, June 8   Engr.   Perf. 13x12½
575 A191 11k Fishing boats   .40 .40
576 A191 13k Fishermen   1.60 .80

Bicentenary of
Skaftareldar
Volcanic
Eruption
A192

1983, June 8   Photo.   Perf. 11½
Granite Paper
577 A192 15k Volcano, by Finnur
             Jonsson   .85 .75

Skiing — A193

1983, Sept. 8   Photo.   Perf. 11½
578 A193 12k shown   .85 .65
579 A193 14k Running   1.00 .75

World Communications Year — A194

1983, Sept. 8   Perf. 12½
580 A194 30k multi   2.75 1.40

NORDIA '84 Type of 1982
Souvenir Sheet

Bishops' Seals: 8k, Magnus Eyjolfsson of Skalholt, 1477-90. 12k, Ogmundur Palsson of Skalhot, 1521-40.

Photo. & Engr.
1983, Oct. 6   Perf. 13½
581 Sheet of 2   9.25 9.25
  a. A186 8k violet blue & black   4.50 4.50
  b. A186 12k pale green & black   4.50 4.50
         Sold for 30k.

Christmas   Pres. Kristjan
A195   Eldjarn (1916-82)
                     A196

1983, Nov. 10   Photo.   Perf. 11½
Granite Paper
582 A195 6k Virgin and Child   .90 .55
583 A195 6.50k Angel   .90 .55

1983, Dec. 6
584 A196 6.50k brn carmine   1.10 .80
585 A196 7k dark blue   .45 .25

Flower Type of 1983

1984, Mar. 1   Photo.   Perf. 11½
Granite Paper
586 A188 6k Rosa pimpinellifolia 1.10 .55
587 A188 25k Potentilla anserium 1.40 .55

Europa 1959-
84
A197

1984, May 3
588 A197 6.50k grnsh bl & blk   2.75 .75
589 A197 7.50k rose & black   1.50 .75

A198

Souvenir Sheet

Design: Abraham Ortelius' map of Northern Europe, 1570.

Photo. & Engr.
1984, June 6   Perf. 14x13½
590 A198 40k multi   18.00 18.00
NORDIA '84 Intl. Stamp Exhibition, Reykjavik, July 3-8. Sold for 60k.

A199

1984, June 17   Photo.   Perf. 11½
Granite Paper
591 A199 50k Flags   6.50 4.00
40th Anniv. of Republic.

Good Templars Headquarters,
Akureyri — A200

1984, July 18   Engr.   Perf. 13
592 A200 10k green   .70 .50
Order of the Good Templars, centenary in Iceland, temperance org.

Flower Type of 1983

1984, Sept. 11   Photo.   Perf. 11½
Granite Paper
593 A188 6.50k Loiseleuria
             procumbens   .55 .30
594 A188 7.50k Arctostaphylos
             uva-ursi   .55 .30

Christmas   Gudbrand's Bible,
A201   400th Anniv.
                     A202

1984, Nov. 29   Photo.
595 A201 600a Madonna and
             Child   .65 .30
596 A201 650a Angel, Christmas
             rose   .65 .45

1984, Nov. 29   Engr.   Perf. 12½x13
597 A202 6.50k Text   .55 .30
598 A202 7.50k Illustration   .35 .45
First Icelandic Bible.

Confederation of   Bjorn Bjarnarson
Employers, 50th   (1853-1918)
Anniv.   A204
A203

1984, Nov. 9   Photo.   Perf. 12x12½
Granite Paper
599 A203 30k Building blocks   2.00 2.00

1984, Nov. 9   Photo.   Perf. 11½
Granite Paper
600 A204 12k shown   .65 .65
601 A204 40k New gallery build-
             ing, horiz.   2.25 1.75
       Natl. Gallery centenary.

Flower Type of 1983

1985, Mar. 20   Photo.   Perf. 11½
Granite Paper
602 A188 8k Rubus saxatilis   .90 .35
603 A188 9k Veronica fruticans   .90 .35
604 A188 16k Lathyrus japonicus   2.50 .65
605 A188 17k Draba alpina   .70 .60
         Nos. 602-605 (4)   5.00 1.95

Music Year Emblem,
Woman Playing the
Langspil — A205

Europa: 7.50k, Man playing the Icelandic violin.

1985, May 3   Photo.   Perf. 11½
Granite Paper
606 A205 6.50k multicolored   3.50 .75
607 A205 7.50k multicolored   3.50 .95

Natl. Horticulture   Intl. Youth
Soc.,   Year — A207
Cent. — A206

1985, June 20   Photo.   Perf. 12
608 A206 20k Sorbus intermedia   1.10 .70

1985, June 20   Photo.   Perf. 11½
609 A207 25k Icelandic girl   1.25 .95

Animal Type of 1980

1985, Sept. 10   Engr.   Perf. 13
Designs: 700a, Todarodes sagittatus. 800a, Hyas araneus. 900a, Tealia felina.
610 A162 700a brn carmine   .20 .30
611 A162 800a dk brown   .35 .20
612 A162 900a carmine   1.10 .45
         Nos. 610-612 (3)   1.65 .95

Hannes Stephensen (1799-1856),
Cleric, Politician, Translator — A209

Famous men: 30k, Jon Gudmudsson (1807-1875), editor, politician.

1985, Sept. 10   Engr.
613 A209 13k dp magenta   .65 .55
614 A209 30k deep violet   1.50 .75

Yearning to
Fly, by
Johannes S.
Kjarval (1885-
1972),
Reykjavik Natl.
Museum
A210

1985, Oct. 15   Photo.   Perf. 12x11½
615 A210 100k multi   6.50 5.25

ÍSLAND 800
A211

ÍSLAND 600 Birds — A212

Abstract ice crystal paintings, by Snorri Sveinn Fridriksson (b. 1934).

1985, Nov. 14   Photo.   Perf. 11½
616 A211 8k Crucifix .80 .35
617 A211 9k Pine Trees .80 .35
Christmas.

1986, Mar. 19   Photo.   Perf. 11½
Granite Paper
618 A212 6k Motacilla alba .20 .20
619 A212 10k Anas acuta 1.75 .65
620 A212 12k Falco columbarius 1.10 .45
621 A212 15k Alca torda .70 .45
Nos. 618-621 (4) 3.75 1.95

See Nos. 642-645, 665-666, 671-672, 686-687, 721, 725.

Europa Issue 1986

Natl. Parks — A213

1986, May 5
622 A213 10k Skaftafell 13.50 1.10
623 A213 12k Jokulsargljufur 5.00 1.40

Nordic Cooperation Issue A214

Sister towns.

1986, May 27   Perf. 11½
624 A214 10k Stykkisholmur 1.10 .75
625 A214 12k Seydisfjordur 1.10 .75

Natl. Bank, Cent. A215

1986, July 1   Engr.   Perf. 14
626 A215 13k Headquarters, Reykjavik 1.10 .80
627 A215 250k Banknote reverse, 1928 11.00 10.00

Reykjavik Bicent. A216

1986, Aug. 18   Engr.   Perf. 13½x14
628 A216 10k City seal, 1815 .85 .40
629 A216 12k View from bank, illustration, 1856 .85 .40

630 A216 13k Laugardalur hot water brook .85 .75
631 A216 40k City Theater 2.25 1.75
Nos. 628-631 (4) 4.80 3.30

Introduction of the Telephone in Iceland, 80th Anniv. — A217

1986, Sept. 29   Photo.   Perf. 11½
Granite Paper
632 A217 10k Morse receiver, 1906 .55 .40
633 A217 20k Handset, microchip, 1986 1.25 .70

Souvenir Sheet

Hvita River Crossing, Loa, 1836, by Auguste Mayer — A218

Photo. & Engr.
1986, Oct. 9   Perf. 14
634 A218 20k bluish black 6.25 6.25
Stamp Day. Sold for 30k to benefit philatelic organizations. See Nos. 646, 667.

Christmas — A219

Paintings by Bjoerg Thorsteinsdottir: 10k, Christmas at Peace. 12k, Christmas Night.

1986, Nov. 13   Photo.   Perf. 12
635 A219 10k multicolored 1.00 .30
636 A219 12k multicolored .45 .30

Olafsvik Trading Station, 300th Anniv. A220

1987, Mar. 26   Engr.   Perf. 14x13½
637 A220 50k Merchantman Svanur, 1777 2.50 1.25

Keflavik Intl. Airport Terminal Inauguration — A221

1987, Apr. 14   Photo.   Perf. 12x11½
638 A221 100k multi 5.00 1.75

Europa Issue 1987

Stained Glass Windows by Leifur Breidfjoerd, Fossvogur Cemetery Chapel A222

1987, May 4   Photo.   Perf. 12x11½
639 A222 12k Christ carrying the cross 2.00 .75
640 A222 15k Soldiers, peace dove 2.00 .80

Rasmus Christian Rask (1787-1832), Danish Linguist — A223

1987, June 10   Engr.   Perf. 13½
641 A223 20k black 1.10 .80
Preservation of the Icelandic language.

Bird Type of 1986
1987, Sept. 16   Photo.   Perf. 11½
Granite Paper
642 A212 13k Asio flammeus 1.25 .50
643 A212 40k Turdus iliacus 2.25 .70
644 A212 70k Haematopus ostralegus 3.25 1.10
645 A212 90k Anas platyrhynchos 5.25 1.50
Nos. 642-645 (4) 12.00 3.80

Stamp Day Type of 1986
Souvenir Sheet
1987, Oct. 9   Engr.   Perf. 13½x14
Trading Station of Djupivogur in 1836, by Auguste Mayer.
646 A218 30k black 6.50 6.50
Stamp Day. Sold for 45k to benefit the Stamp and Postal History Fund.

Dental Protection — A226

1987, Oct. 9   Photo.   Perf. 11½x12
Granite Paper
647 A226 12k multi .55 .30

Vulture — A227

Perf. 13 on 3 sides
1987, Oct. 9   Engr.
Guardian Spirits of the North, East, South and West.

Booklet Stamps
648 A227 13k shown .75 .50
649 A227 13k Dragon .75 .50
650 A227 13k Bull .75 .50
651 A227 13k Giant .75 .50
a. Block of 4, #648-651 3.00 3.00
b. Bklt. pane of 12, 3 #651a 9.00 —

Legend of Heimskringla, the story of the Norse kings. Haraldur Gormsson, king of Denmark, deterred from invading Iceland after hearing of the guardian spirits.
See Nos. 656-659, 677, 688-695.

Christmas — A228

1987, Oct. 21   Photo.   Perf. 11½x12
652 A228 13k Fir branch .65 .20
653 A228 17k Candle flame .65 .45

Steinn Steinarr (1908-1958) A229

Poets: 21k, David Stefansson (1895-1964).

1988, Feb. 25   Photo.   Perf. 12
654 A229 16k multi .75 .35
655 A229 21k multi .90 .65

Guardian Spirit Type of 1987
Perf. 13 on 3 sides
1988, May 2   Engr.
Booklet Stamps
656 A227 16k Vulture .80 .55
657 A227 16k Dragon .80 .55
658 A227 16k Bull .80 .55
659 A227 16k Giant .80 .55
a. Block of 4, #656-659 3.25 3.25
b. Bklt. pane of 12, 3 #659a 9.75 —

Europa Issue, 1988

Modern Communication — A230

1988, May 2   Photo.   Perf. 12x11½
660 A230 16k Data transmission system 1.25 .60
661 A230 21k Facsimile machine 5.00 2.00

1988 Summer Olympics, Seoul A231

1988, June 9   Photo.   Perf. 12
Granite Paper
662 A231 18k Handball .80 .70

Flower Type of 1983
1988, June 9   Perf. 11½
Granite Paper
663 A188 10k Vicia cracca .55 .30
664 A188 50k Thymus praecox 3.00 .65

Bird Type of 1986
1988, Sept. 21   Photo.   Perf. 11½
Granite Paper
665 A212 5k Limosa limosa .50 .20
666 A212 30k Clangula hyemalis 1.90 .65

Stamp Day Type of 1986
Souvenir Sheet
1988, Oct. 9   Engr.   Perf. 14
Nupsstadur Farm, Fljotshverfi, 1836, by Auguste Mayer.
667 A218 40k black 5.25 5.25
Stamp Day. Sold for 60k to benefit the Stamp and Postal History Fund.

WHO, 40th Anniv. — A234

1988, Nov. 3 Photo. Perf. 11½x12
Granite Paper
668 A234 19k multicolored .80 .40

Christmas A235

1988, Nov. 3 Perf. 11½
Granite Paper
669 A235 19k Fisherman at sea 1.00 .30
670 A235 24k Ship, buoy 1.25 1.25

Bird Type of 1986

1989, Feb. 2 Photo.
671 A212 19k Phalaropus lobatus 1.50 .40
672 A212 100k Plectrophenax nivalis 6.00 1.60

Women's Folk Costumes — A236

1989, Apr. 20 Photo. Perf. 11½x12
Granite Paper
673 A236 21k Peysufot 1.75 .40
674 A236 26k Upphlutur 1.75 .65

Nordic cooperation.

Europa 1989 A237

Children's games.

1989, May 30 Photo. Perf. 11½
Granite Paper
675 A237 21k Sailing toy boats 7.00 1.25
676 A237 26k Hoop, stick pony 7.00 1.25

Guardian Spirit Type of 1987

1989, June 27 Engr. Perf. 13
677 A227 500k Dragon 19.00 8.50

Landscapes A238

1989, Sept. 20 Photo. Perf. 11½
Granite Paper
678 A238 35k Mt. Skeggi, Arnarfjord 1.40 .55
679 A238 45k Thermal spring, Namaskard 1.75 .55

See Nos. 713-714, 728, 737.

Agricultural College at Hvanneyri, Cent. A239

1989, Sept. 20 Engr. Perf. 14
680 A239 50k multi 2.00 1.25

Souvenir Sheet

NORDIA '91 — A240

Detail of *A Chart and Description of Northern Routes and Wonders to Be Found in the Nordic Countries,* 1539, by Olaus Magnus (1490-1557).

1989, Oct. 9 Perf. 12½
681 A240 Sheet of 3 11.00 11.00
a.-c. 30k any single 3.50 3.50

Stamp Day. Sold for 130k to benefit the exhibition.
See Nos. 715, 740.

Natural History Soc., Cent. A241

Flowers or fish and: 21k, Stefan Stefansson (1863-1921), botanist and founder. 26k, Bjarni Saemundsson (1867-1940), chairman.

1989, Nov. 9 Photo. Perf. 11½
Granite Paper
682 A241 21k multi .85 .85
683 A241 26k multi 1.00 .75

Christmas — A242

Paintings like stained-glass windows by Johannes Johannesson (b. 1921): 21k, Madonna and Child. 26k, Three Wise Men.

1989, Nov. 9
Granite Paper
684 A242 21k multi 1.25 .35
685 A242 26k multi 1.25 1.10

Bird Type of 1986

1990, Feb. 15
Granite Paper
686 A212 21k *Anas penelope* 1.60 .70
687 A212 80k *Anser brachyrhynchus* 4.00 1.60

Guardian Spirit Type of 1987
Perf. 13 on 3 Sides
1990, Feb. 15 Engr.
688 A227 5k Vulture .25 .25
689 A227 5k Dragon .25 .25
690 A227 5k Bull .25 .25
691 A227 5k Giant .25 .25
a. Block of 4, #688-691 1.00 1.00
692 A227 21k Vulture .75 .75
693 A227 21k Dragon .75 .75
694 A227 21k Bull .75 .75
695 A227 21k Giant .75 .75
a. Block of 4, #692-695 3.00 3.00
b. Block of 8, #688-695 5.25 5.25
c. Bklt. pane, 2 each #691a, 695a 9.00 9.00

Famous Women — A243

No. 696, Gudrun Larusdottir (1880-1938), author and politician, by Halldor Petursson. No. 697, Ragnhildur Petursdottir (1880-1961), educator, by Asgrimur Jonsson.

1990, Mar. 22 Litho. Perf. 13½x14
696 A243 21k multicolored .90 .75
697 A243 21k multicolored .90 .75

Europa 1990 A244

Old and new post offices in Reykjavik and letter scales.

1990, May 7 Photo. Perf. 12x11½
Granite Paper
698 A244 21k 1915 5.00 .90
699 A244 40k 1989 5.00 2.00

Sports — A245

1990-94 Litho. Perf. 13x14½
700 A245 21k Archery 1.00 .45
701 A245 21k Soccer 1.00 .45
706 A245 26k Golf 1.00 .65
707 A245 26k Icelandic wrestling 1.00 .65
Perf. 13½x14½
Photo.
708 A245 30k Volleyball 1.25 .60
709 A245 30k Skiing 1.25 .60
710 A245 30k Running 1.25 .60
711 A245 30k Team handball 1.25 .60
Litho.
Perf. 14x14½
711A A245 30k Swimming 1.10 .45
711B A245 30k Weight lifting 1.10 .45
Nos. 700-711B (10) 11.20 5.50

Issued: #700-701, 6/28; #706-707, 8/14/91; #708-709, 2/20/92; #710-711, 3/10/93; #711A-711B, 2/25/94.

European Tourism Year — A246

1990, Sept. 6 Litho. Perf. 13½
712 A246 30k multicolored 1.10 .70

Landscape Type of 1989

1990, Sept. 6 Photo. Perf.
713 A238 25k Hvitserkur 1.25 .65
714 A238 200k Lomagnupur 7.75 2.25

NORDIA '91 Map Type of 1989
Souvenir Sheet

Detail of 1539 Map by Olaus Magnus: a, Dania. b, Gothia. c, Gotlandia.
Perf. 12x12½
1990, Oct. 9 Lith & Engr.
715 A240 Sheet of 3 12.50 12.50
a.-c. 40k any single 4.00 4.00

Stamp Day. Sold for 170k to benefit the exhibition.

Christmas A247

1990, Nov. 8 Perf. 13½x13
716 A247 25k shown 1.50 .45
717 A247 30k Carolers 1.50 .55

Bird Type of 1986
1991, Feb. 7 Photo. Perf. 11½
Granite Paper
721 A212 25k Podiceps auritus 1.25 .45
722 A212 100k Sula bassana 6.50 1.00

Landscape Type of 1989
1991, Mar. 7 Photo. Perf. 11½
Granite Paper
728 A238 10k Vestrahorn .55 .30
737 A238 300k Kverkfjoll 11.00 2.75

Europa A248

1991, Apr. 29 Litho. Perf. 14
738 A248 26k Weather map 11.00 1.00
739 A248 47k Solar panels 5.50 2.00

NORDIA '91 Map Type of 1989
Souvenir Sheet

Detail of 1539 Map by Olaus Magnus: a, Iceland's west coast. b, Islandia. c, Mare Glacial.

Litho. & Engr.
1991, May 23 Perf. 12½
740 A240 Sheet of 3 15.00 15.00
a.-c. 50k any single 4.75 4.75

Sold for 215k to benefit the exhibition.

Jokulsarlon Lagoon A249

Design: 31k, Strokkur hot spring.

1991, May 23 Litho. Perf. 15x14
741 A249 26k multicolored 2.00 .45
742 A249 31k multicolored 2.00 .55

Ragnar Jonsson (1904-1984), Patron of the Arts — A250

70k, Pall Isolfsson (1893-1974), musician, vert.

1991, Aug. 14 Litho. Perf. 14
743 A250 60k multicolored 2.00 1.00
744 A250 70k multicolored 2.50 1.25

Ships A251

Designs: a, Soloven, schooner, 1840. b, Arcturus, steamer with sails, 1858. c, Gullfoss, steamer, 1915. d, Esja II, diesel ship, 1939.

1991, Oct. 9　Litho.　Perf. 14
745　　Block or strip of 4　　20.00　20.00
　a.-d.　A251 30k any single　　3.50　1.75
　e.　A251 Bklt. pane, 2 #745　25.00

Issued in sheet of 8. No. 745e is distinguished from sheet of 8 by rouletted selvage at left.
See Nos. 803-806.

College of Navigation, Reykjavik, Cent. A252

1991, Oct. 9　　Perf. 13½
746　A252　50k multicolored　　1.75　1.25

Christmas — A253

Paintings by Eirikur Smith (b. 1925): 30k, Christmas star. 35k, Star over winter landscape.

1991, Nov. 7　Litho.　Perf. 13½
747　A253　30k multicolored　　1.10　.50
748　A253　35k multicolored　　1.10　1.50

Europa A254

Map and: No. 749, Viking longboat of Leif Eriksson. No. 750, Sailing ship of Columbus.

1992, Apr. 6　Litho.　Perf. 13½x14
749　A254　55k multicolored　　5.00　2.25
750　A254　55k multicolored　　5.00　2.25

Souvenir Sheet
751　A254　Sheet of 2,　　13.50　8.00
　　　#749-750

First landing in the Americas by Leif Erikson (#749). Discovery of America by Christopher Columbus, 500th anniv. (#750).
Stamps on #751 printed in continuous design. #749-751 have borders.

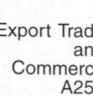

Export Trade and Commerce A255

Designs: 35k, Fishing boat, fish.

1992, June 16　Litho.　Perf. 13½
752　A255　30k multicolored　　1.40　.75
753　A255　35k multicolored　　1.40　.75

Bridges A256

1992, Oct. 9　Litho.　Perf. 13½
754　A256　5k Fnjoska, 1908　　.20　.20
755　A256　250k Olfusa, 1891　　9.50　5.50

See Nos. 766-767.

Mail Trucks A257

#756, Mail transport car RE 231, 1933. #757, Ford bus, 1946. #758, Ford TT, 1920-26. #759, Citroen snowmobile, 1929.

1992, Oct. 9　　Perf. 14
756　A257　30k multicolored　　2.40　.90
757　A257　30k multicolored　　2.40　.90
758　A257　30k multicolored　　2.40　.90
759　A257　30k multicolored　　2.40　.90
　a.　Block or strip of 4, #756-759　9.75　9.75
　b.　Bklt. pane, 2 ea #756-759　30.00

Issued in sheets of 8. No. 759b has rouletted selvage at left.
See Nos. 820-823.

Christmas — A258

Paintings by Bragi Asgeirsson.

1992, Nov. 9　Litho.　Perf. 13½x13
760　A258　30k shown　　1.50　.35
761　A258　35k Sun over mountains　　1.50　.65

Falco Rusticolus — A259

1992, Dec. 3　Photo.　Perf. 11½
Granite Paper
762　A259　5k Adult, two young　　2.30　.55
763　A259　10k Adult feeding　　2.90　.90
764　A259　20k Adult, head up　　2.90　1.00
765　A259　35k Adult　　2.90　1.60
　　　Nos. 762-765 (4)　　11.00　4.05

Bridges Type of 1992

1993, Mar. 10　Litho.　Perf. 13½x13
766　A256　90k Hvita, 1928　　2.75　1.60
767　A256　150k Jokulsa a Fjollum, 1947　　5.00　2.25

Nordica '93 — A260

Designs: 30k, The Blue Lagoon therapeutic bathing area, hot water plant, Svartsengi. 35k, Perlan hot water storage tanks, restaurant.

1993, Apr. 26　Litho.　Perf. 13½x13
768　A260　30k multicolored　　1.25　.65
769　A260　35k multicolored　　1.60　1.25

Sculptures — A261

Europa: 35k, Sailing, by Jon Gunnar Arnason. 55k, Hatching of the Jet, by Magnus Tomasson.

1993, Apr. 26　　Perf. 13x13½
770　A261　35k multicolored　　2.00　1.25
771　A261　55k multicolored　　3.25　2.50

Souvenir Sheet

Italian Group Flight, 60th Anniv. — A262

1993, Oct. 9　Litho.　Perf. 13½
772　A262　Sheet of 3, #a.-c.　　8.00　8.00
　a.　10k #C12　　.65　.65
　b.　50k #C13　　2.50　2.50
　c.　100k #C14　　4.50　4.50

No. 772 sold for 200k.

Seaplanes — A263

1993, Oct. 9　　Perf. 14
773　A263　30k Junkers F-13 (D463)　　2.50　1.00
774　A263　30k Waco YKS-7 (TF-ORN)　　2.50　1.00
775　A263　30k Grumman G-21A/JRF-5 (RVK)　　2.50　1.00
776　A263　30k PBY-5 Catalina (TF-ISP)　　2.50　1.00
　a.　Block or strip of 4, #773-776　10.00　10.00
　b.　Bklt. pane, 2 ea #773-776　22.50

No. 776b is distinguished from sheet of 8 by rouletted selvage at left.
Issued in sheet of 8.
See Nos. 838-841.

Christmas A264

1993, Nov. 8　Litho.　Perf. 12½
777　A264　30k Adoration of the Magi　　1.25　.45
778　A264　35k Virgin and Child　　1.25　1.25

Intl. Year of the Family A265

1994, Feb. 25　Litho.　Perf. 13½x13
779　A265　40k multicolored　　1.25　1.25

Voyages of St. Brendan (484-577) A266

Europa: 35k, St. Brendan, Irish monks sailing past volcano. 55k, St. Brendan on island with sheep, monks in boat.

1994, Apr. 18　Litho.　Perf. 14½x14
780　A266　35k multicolored　　2.50　1.10
　　　Booklet, 10 #780　　25.00

781　A266　55k multicolored　　2.75　1.40
　a.　Miniature sheet of 2, #780-781　5.75　4.25

See Ireland Nos. 923-924; Faroe Islands Nos. 264-265.

Icelandic Art and Culture A267

1994, May 25　Litho.　Perf. 13½x13
782　A267　30k Music　　1.00　.40
783　A267　30k Crafts　　1.00　.70
784　A267　30k Film making　　1.00　.70
785　A267　30k Ballet, modern dance　　1.00　.70
786　A267　30k Theatre　　1.00　.70
　　　Nos. 782-786 (5)　　5.00　3.20

Independence, 50th anniv.

Gisli Sveinsson (1880-1959), Politician — A268

1994, June 14　　Perf. 14
787　A268　30k multicolored　　1.10　1.00
Proclamation of new constitution, 50th anniv.

Souvenir Sheet

Republic of Iceland, 50th Anniv. — A269

Presidents of Iceland: a, Sveinn Bjornsson (1881-1952). b, Asgeir Asgeirsson (1894-1972). c, Kristjan Eldjarn (1916-82). d, Vigdis Finnbogadottir (b. 1930).

1994, June 17　Photo.　Perf. 11½
Granite Paper
788　A269　Sheet of 4, #a.-d.　　7.00　7.00
　a.-d.　50k any single　　1.75　1.75

Souvenir Sheet

Stamp Day — A270

Designs: a, Boy, girl with stamp album. b, Nos. 672, 713, portions of other Icelandic stamps. c, Girl, elderly man looking at globe.

1994, Oct. 7　Litho.　Perf. 13½
789　A270　Sheet of 3　　9.50　9.50
　a.　30k multicolored　　2.50　2.50
　b.　35k multicolored　　2.50　2.50
　c.　100k multicolored　　4.00　3.50

No. 789 sold for 200k for the benefit of the Stamp and Postal History Fund.

Christmas A271

1994, Nov. 9   Litho.   Perf. 14½
790 A271 30k Woman, stars   1.00 .30
791 A271 35k Man, stars   1.25 .70

ICAO, 50th Anniv. A272

1994, Nov. 9   Perf. 13½x14
792 A272 100k multicolored   4.00 2.25

A273   A274

1995, Mar. 14   Litho.   Perf. 13
793 A273 35k multicolored   1.25 .80

Salvation Army in Iceland, cent.

1995, Mar. 14
794 A274 90k multicolored   4.50 2.00

Town of Seydisfjordur, cent.

1995 Men's Team Handball World Championships, Iceland — A275

Federation emblem, handball and: No. 795, Geyser, landscape. No. 796, Silhouette of building, landscape. No. 797, Volcano, lake. No. 798, Inlet, sunlight on water.

1995, Mar. 14   Litho.   Perf. 14
795 A275 35k multicolored   1.75 1.10
796 A275 35k multicolored   1.75 1.10
797 A275 35k multicolored   1.75 1.10
798 A275 35k multicolored   1.75 1.10
a.   Block or strip of 4, #795-798   7.25 7.00
b.   Booklet pane, 2 #798a   17.50
      Complete booklet, #798b   17.50

Nos. 795-798 issued in sheets of 8 containing 2 each. No. 798b is separated from booklet by rouletted selvage at left, and sold for 480k in the complete booklet.

Norden 1995 — A276

Designs: 30k, Turf farmhouses, church. 35k, Volcano, Fjallsjokull glacier.

1995, May 5   Litho.   Perf. 13½x13
799 A276 30k multicolored   1.00 .55
      Booklet, 10 #799   10.00
800 A276 35k multicolored   1.40 .90

Spell-Broken, by Einar Jonsson (1874-1954) — A277

1995, May 5   Perf. 13x13½
801 A277 35k brown & multi   1.10 1.00
      Booklet, 10 #801   12.60
802 A277 55k blue & multi   2.00 1.75
      Booklet, 10 #802   20.00

Europa.

Ship Type of 1991

1995, June 30   Litho.   Perf. 14
803 A251 30k SS Laura   1.20 .90
804 A251 30k MS Dronning
            Alexandrine   1.20 .90
805 A251 30k MS Laxfoss   1.20 .90
806 A251 30k MS Godafoss III   1.20 .90
a.   Block or strip of 4, #803-806   5.00 4.50
b.   Bklt. pane, 2 ea #803-806   10.00
      Prestige booklet, #806b   16.00

No. 806b is distinguished from sheet of 8 by rouletted selvage at left.
Issued in sheets of 8.
Prestige booklet sold for 400k.

Luxembourg-Reykjavik, Iceland Air Route, 40th Anniv. — A278

1995, Sept. 18   Litho.   Perf. 13½
807 A278 35k multicolored   1.75 1.25

See Luxembourg No. 936.

Birds A279

1995, Sept. 18   Perf. 13½
808 A279 25k Acanthis flammea   .80 .65
809 A279 250k Gallinago gallinago   8.50 6.00

Souvenir Sheet

Nordia '96, Reykjavik — A280

Design: Hraunfossar Waterfalls, Hvita River.

1995, Oct. 9   Perf. 13½x14
810 A280 Sheet of 2, #a.-b.   11.00 11.00
a.   10k multicolored   3.25 3.25
b.   150k multicolored   7.00 7.00

See No. 830.

Christmas A281

1995, Nov. 8   Litho.   Perf. 13½
811 A281 30k Snowman, woman   1.00 .75
812 A281 35k Three trees   1.10 .90

UN, 50th Anniv. — A282

1995, Nov. 8   Perf. 13x13½
813 A282 100k multicolored   3.25 2.50

Water Birds A283

Designs: 20k, Phalacrocorax carbo. 40k, Bucephala islandica.

1996, Feb. 7   Litho.   Perf. 13½
814 A283 20k multicolored   .95 .55
815 A283 40k multicolored   2.00 1.00

See Nos. 834-835.

Paintings A284

100k, Seamen in a Boat, by Gunnlaugur Scheving (1904-72). 200k, At the Washing Springs, by Kristín Jónsdóttir (1888-1959).

1996, Feb. 7
816 A284 100k multicolored   5.25 4.50
817 A284 200k multicolored   6.50 5.25

Famous Women A285

Europa: 35k, Halldóra Bjarnadóttir (1873-1981), educator. 55k, Olafía Jóhannsdóttir (1863-1924), representative of women's rights, temperance affairs.

1996, Apr. 18   Litho.   Perf. 14½
818 A285 35k multicolored   1.50 1.00
      Booklet, 10 #818   15.00
819 A285 55k multicolored   1.75 1.25
      Booklet, 10 #819   17.50

Postal Vehicle Type of 1992

Designs: No. 820, 1931 Buick. No. 821, 1933 Studebaker, Reykjavik Municipal Bus Service. No. 822, 1937 Ford, Iceland Motor Coach Service. No. 823, 1946 REO, Post and Telecommunications.

1996, May 13   Litho.   Perf. 14
820 A257 35k multicolored   1.25 .85
821 A257 35k multicolored   1.25 .85
822 A257 35k multicolored   1.25 .85
823 A257 35k multicolored   1.25 .85
a.   Block or strip of 4, #820-823   5.00 5.00
b.   Bklt. pane, 2 ea #820-823   10.00 10.00
      Souvenir booklet, #823b   12.00

No. 823a issued in sheets of 8 stamps. No. 823b has rouletted selvage at left.

1996 Summer Olympic Games, Atlanta A286

1996, June 25   Litho.   Perf. 12½
824 A286 5k Running   .20 .20
825 A286 25k Javelin   .75 .40
826 A286 45k Long jump   1.40 1.10
827 A286 65k Shot put   2.10 1.50
      Nos. 824-827 (4)   4.45 3.20

Order of the Sisters of St. Joseph in Iceland, Cent. — A287

1996, Sept. 17   Litho.   Perf. 14½x13
828 A287 65k multicolored   2.00 2.00

Reykjavik School, 150th Anniv. A288

1996, Sept. 17   Perf. 12½x13
829 A288 150k multicolored   4.75 3.75

Nordia '96 Type of 1995

Design: Godafoss Waterfalls, Skjalfandafljot River.

1996, Oct. 9   Litho.   Perf. 13½x14
830 A280 Sheet of 3, #a.-c.   11.50 11.50
a.   45k multicolored   3.75 3.75
b.   65k multicolored   3.75 3.75
c.   90k multicolored   3.75 3.75

Reykjavik Cathedral, Bicent. — A289

1996, Nov. 5   Perf. 14
831 A289 45k multicolored   1.60 1.10

Christmas — A290

Artifacts from Natl. Museum of Iceland: 35k, Figurine of Madonna and Child carved from walrus tusk. 45k, Pax showing Nativity.

1996, Nov. 5   Perf. 13½
832 A290 35k multicolored   1.25 .75
a.   Booklet pane of 10   12.50
      Booklet, #832a   13.00
833 A290 45k multicolored   1.50 1.25

Bird Type of 1996

10k, Mergus serrator. 500k, Anas crecca.

1997, Apr. 2   Litho.   Perf. 13½
834 A283 10k multicolored   .35 .20
835 A283 500k multicolored   15.00 13.50

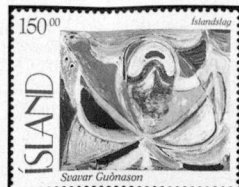

Paintings A291

150k, Song of Iceland, by Svavar Guthnason. 200k, The Harbor, by Thorvaldur Skúlason.

1997, Mar. 6   Litho.   Perf. 14
836 A291 150k multicolored   5.25 4.50
837 A291 200k multicolored   6.50 5.25

Airplane Type of 1993

#838, De Havilland DH-89A (TF-ISM). #839, Stinson SR 8B Reliant (TF-RVB). #840, Douglas DC-3 (TF-ISH). #841, De Havilland DHC-6 Twin Otter (TF-REG).

1997, Apr. 15   Litho.   Perf. 14
838 A263 35k multicolored   1.20   .90
839 A263 35k multicolored   1.20   .90
840 A263 35k multicolored   1.20   .90
841 A263 35k multicolored   1.20   .90
  a.   Block or strip of 4, #838-841   5.00 5.00
  b.   Booklet pane, 2 each #838-841   10.00
       Booklet, #841b   10.00

Issued in sheet of 8.
No. 841b has rouletted selvage at left.

European Games
A292

1997, May 13   Litho.   Perf. 14½
842 A292 35k Hurdles   1.10   .90
843 A292 45k Sailing   1.40 1.10

Europa
A293

Stories and legends by Asgrimur Jonsson: 45k, Couple on galloping horse. 65k, Old woman reaching for children.

1997, May 13   Perf. 13½
844 A293 45k multicolored   2.00 1.50
     Complete booklet of 10   20.00
845 A293 65k multicolored   2.50 1.75
     Complete booklet of 10   25.00

Union of Graphic Workers, Cent. — A294

1997, Sept. 3   Litho.   Perf. 13½
846 A294 90k multicolored   3.25 2.75

Reykjavik Theater, Cent. — A295

1997, Sept. 3   Perf. 13½x14
847 A295 100k multicolored   3.25 2.75

Stamp Day — A296

Icelandic row boats: a, Gideon, eight-oared lugger, 1836. b, Breidafjördur double-ended transport, 1904. c, Engey, six-oared craft, 1912.

1997, Oct. 9   Litho.   Perf. 15
848 A296 Sheet of 3   11.00 11.00
  a.   35k multicolored   2.40   2.40
  b.   100k multicolored   4.50   4.50
  c.   65k multicolored   3.50   3.50

Christmas
A297

1997, Nov. 5   Litho.   Perf. 13½x13
849 A297 35k Magi   1.00   .70
  a.   Booklet pane of 10   10.00
       Booklet, #849a   10.00
850 A297 45k Nativity   1.40   .90

Rural Postman
A298

Litho. & Engr.
1997, Nov. 5   Perf. 13½
851 A298 50k multicolored   1.50 1.25

1998 Winter Olympic Games, Nagano
A299

1998, Jan. 22   Litho.   Perf. 13½
852 A299 35k Downhill skier   1.00 1.00
853 A299 45k Cross country skier 1.40 1.25

Nordic Stamps
A300

1998, Mar. 5   Litho.   Perf. 13½x13
854 A300 35k Sailboats   1.00 1.00
855 A300 45k Power boats   1.40 1.00

Fish — A301

1998, Apr. 16
856 A301   5k Cyclopterus lumpus   .20   .20
857 A301 10k Gadus morhua   .30   .20
858 A301 60k Raja batis   1.75 1.40
859 A301 300k Anarhicus lupus   8.75 7.50
  a.   Min. sheet of 4, #856-859   11.00 11.00
       Nos. 856-859 (4)   11.00 9.30

Intl. Year of the Ocean (#859a).
See Nos. 871-872, 915-916, 928-929.

National Holidays and Festivals
A302

Independence Day, June 17th: 45k, Children standing at attention, flag. 65k, Monument, parade.

1998, May 12   Litho.   Perf. 14½
860 A302 45k multicolored   1.75 1.00
     Complete booklet, 10 #860   17.50
861 A302 65k multicolored   2.25 1.50
     Complete booklet, 10 #861   22.50

Europa.

Minerals — A303

1998, Sept. 3   Litho.   Perf. 13½
862 A303 35k Stilbite   1.20   .90
863 A303 45k Scolecite   1.40 1.10

See Nos. 885-886.

Leprosy Hospital, Laugarnes
A304

1998, Sept. 3   Perf. 13½x14
864 A304 70k multicolored   2.00 1.60

First Icelandic Postage Stamp, 125th Anniv. — A305

1998, Oct. 9   Litho.   Perf. 13½
865 A305 35k multicolored   1.20   .80

Agricultural Tools — A306

1998, Oct. 9   Perf. 15
866 A306 Sheet of 3   7.50 7.50
  a.   35k Turf scythe   1.75 1.75
  b.   65k Hay mower   2.50 2.50
  c.   100k Manure mincer   3.25 3.25

Stamp Day.

Christmas, Children's Drawings — A307

35k, Black cat, homes, mountains. 45k, Angels, Christmas tree, moon and stars.

1998, Nov. 5   Litho.   Perf. 13x13½
867 A307 35k multicolored   1.10   .90
  a.   Booklet pane of 10   11.00
       Complete booklet, #867a   11.00
868 A307 45k multicolored   1.25 1.10

Universal Declaration of Human Rights, 50th Anniv. — A308

1998, Nov. 5   Perf. 14½
869 A308 50k multicolored   1.50 1.50

Jón Leifs (1899-1968), Composer — A309

1999, Jan. 22   Litho.   Perf. 14½
870 A309 35k multicolored   2.40 1.60

Fish Type of 1998

35k, Pleuronectes platessa. 55k, Clupea harengus.

1999, Jan. 22   Perf. 14½x15
871 A301 35k multicolored   1.25   .90
872 A301 55k multicolored   1.60 1.60

Marine Mammals — A311

Designs: 35k, Orcinus orca. 45k, Physeter macrocephalus. 65k, Balaenoptera musculus. 85k, Phocoena phocoena.

1999, Mar. 4   Litho.   Perf. 14½
873 A311 35k multicolored   1.00   .90
874 A311 45k multicolored   1.25 1.10
875 A311 65k multicolored   1.90 1.90
876 A311 85k multicolored   2.40 2.40
  a.   Sheet of 4, #873-876   6.50 6.50
       Nos. 873-876 (4)   6.55 6.30

See Nos. 911-914, 945-948. For surcharge see No. 944.

Locomotive
A312

Perf. 13 on 2 or 3 Sides
1999, Apr. 15
Booklet Stamps
877 A312 25k green & multi   7.00 7.00
878 A312 50k brown & multi   2.50 2.50
  a.   Booklet pane, 1 #877, 3 #878 14.50
       Complete booklet, #878a   14.50
879 A312 75k Ship   3.50 3.50
  a.   Booklet pane of 4   14.00
       Complete booklet, #879a   14.00
       Nos. 877-879 (3)   13.00 13.00

See Nos. 908-909.

Council of Europe, 50th Anniv. — A313

1999, Apr.15   Perf. 13x13½
880 A313 35k multicolored   1.20   .90

Mushrooms
A314

35k, Suillus grevillei. 75k, Agaricus campestris.

1999, May 20   Litho.   Perf. 14½
881 A314 35k multicolored   1.10 1.10
882 A314 75k multicolored   2.25 2.25

See Nos. 898-899, 957-958, 1021-1022, 1087-1088.

National Parks — A315

1999, May 20   *Perf. 13¼*
883	A315	50k Skutustadagigar	2.00	1.50
a.		Booklet pane of 10	20.00	
		Complete booklet, #883a	21.00	
884	A315	75k Vid Arnarstapa	2.50	2.00
a.		Booklet pane of 10	25.00	
		Complete booklet, #884a	26.00	

Europa.

Minerals Type of 1998

1999, Sept. 9   **Litho.**   *Perf. 14¾*
885	A303	40k Calcite	1.25	1.25
886	A303	50k Heulandite	1.75	1.75

Nature Conservation A316

1999, Sept. 9   **Litho.**   *Perf. 14¼*
887	A316	35k "Hreinar"	1.40	1.40
888	A316	35k "Markviss"	1.40	1.40
889	A316	35k "Hreint"	1.40	1.40
890	A316	35k "Endurheimt"	1.40	1.40
891	A316	35k "Eflum"	1.40	1.40
a.		Strip of 5, #887-891	7.00	7.00

Reykjavik, European Cultural City for 2000 A317

35k, Facescape, by Erro. 50k, Book, violin, palette, masks, camera, computer.

1999, Oct. 7   **Litho.**   *Perf. 13¼*
892	A317	35k multi	1.50	1.50
893	A317	50k multi	2.00	2.00

Souvenir Sheet

View of Skagafhordur, by Carl Emil Baagoe — A318

1999, Oct. 7   *Perf. 13¼x13*
894	A318	200k olive & black	8.50	8.50

Stamp Day. #894 sold for 250k.

Children's Art — A319

1999, Nov. 4   **Litho.**   *Perf. 13*
895	A319	35k multi	1.00	1.00

Christmas — A320

No. 896, Elf: a, With walking stick. b, Jumping over rock. c, Waving. d, Licking spoon. e, With hand in cauldron. f, With cup. g, At door. h, With ladle and barrel. i, With sausages. j, At window.
No. 897, Elf: a, Looking up. b, With ham. c, With candles.

1999, Nov. 4
896		Strip of 10	15.00	15.00
a.-j.		A320 35k any single	1.50	1.50
k.		Booklet pane, #896a-896j	15.00	
		Complete booklet, #896k	15.00	
897		Strip of 3	5.25	5.25
a.-c.		A320 50k any single	1.75	1.75

See Nos. 924-926.

Mushroom Type of 1999

Designs: 40k, Cantharellus cibarius. 50k, Coprinus comatus.

2000, Feb. 4   **Litho.**   *Perf. 13*
898	A314	40k multi	1.25	1.25
a.		Booklet pane of 10	12.50	
		Complete booklet, #898a	12.50	
899	A314	50k multi	1.75	1.75

A321

Christianity in Iceland, 1000th Anniv. — A322

2000, Feb. 4   *Perf. 13¼x13¾*
900	A321	40k multi	1.25	1.25

Souvenir Sheet
Perf. 13¼x13
901	A322	40k multi	1.25	1.25

See Vatican City #1151.

Discovery of Vinland, 1000th Anniv. A323

Designs: 40k, Viking with shield, globe. 50k, Viking ship sailing. 75k, Viking ship at shore. 90k, Viking without shield, globe.

Litho. & Engr.

2000, Mar. 16   *Perf. 12½x13*
902	A323	40k multi	1.40	1.40
903	A323	50k multi	1.60	1.60
904	A323	75k multi	2.25	2.25
905	A323	90k multi	2.75	2.75
a.		Souvenir sheet, #902-905	8.00	8.00
		Nos. 902-905 (4)	8.00	8.00

Millennium A324

Designs: 40k, Head, quill pen. 50k, Man, genealogical chart, circuit board.

2000, Apr. 27   **Litho.**   *Perf. 13x13¼*
906	A324	40k multi	1.25	1.25
907	A324	50k multi	1.50	1.50

Locomotive Type of 1999
Perf. 13 on 2 or 3 sides
2000, Apr. 27   **Litho.**
Booklet Stamps
908	A312	50k Steam roller	1.50	1.50
a.		Booklet pane of 4	6.00	
909	A312	75k Fire pumper	2.25	2.25
a.		Booklet pane of 4	9.00	
		Booklet, #909a	9.00	

Europa, 2000
Common Design Type

2000, May 18   **Litho.**   *Perf. 13¼x13*
910	CD17	50k multi	2.00	2.00
a.		Booklet pane of 10	20.00	
		Booklet, #910a	21.00	

Marine Mammals Type of 1999

Designs: 5k, Hyperoodon ampullatus. 40k, Lagenorhynchus acutus. 50k, Megaptera novaeangliae. 75k, Balaenoptera acutorostrata.

2000, May 18   *Perf. 14½*
911	A311	5k multi	.20	.20
912	A311	40k multi	1.10	1.10
913	A311	50k multi	1.40	1.40
914	A311	75k multi	2.00	2.00
		Nos. 911-914 (4)	4.70	4.70

Fish Type of 1998

Designs: 10k, Melanogrammus aeglefinus. 250k, Mallotus villosus.

2000, Sept. 14   **Litho.**   *Perf. 13*
915-916	A301	Set of 2	9.00	9.00

Flowers — A325

Designs: 40k, Viola x wittrockiana. 50k, Petunia x hybrida.

2000, Sept. 14   *Perf. 13*
917-918	A325	Set of 2	3.50	2.50

See Nos. 931-932, 968-969, 982-983, 1005-1006.

Butterflies A326

Designs: 40k, Chloroclysta citrata. 50k, Cerapteryx graminis.

2000, Oct. 9   *Perf. 14x14½*
919-920	A326	Set of 2	3.50	2.50

Souvenir Sheet

Stamp Day — A327

Litho. & Engr.

2000, Oct. 9   *Perf. 13¼*
921	A327	200k multi	9.00	9.00

No. 921 sold for 250k.

Ancient Architecture — A328

Various buildings. Denominations: 45k, 75k.

2000, Nov. 9   **Litho.**   *Perf. 14*
922-923	A328	Set of 2	4.75	3.50

Christmas Type of 1999

Designs: 40k, Elf grasping walking stick. 50k, Female elf carrying bag.

2000, Nov. 9   *Perf. 13*
924	A320	40k multi	1.25	1.00
a.		Perf. 12¾x13¼	1.50	1.00
b.		Booklet pane, 4 #924a	6.00	
c.		Booklet pane, 6 #924a	9.00	
		Booklet, #924b, 924c	15.00	
925	A320	50k multi	1.50	1.25

Souvenir Sheet
926		Sheet of 2	2.75	2.25
a.		A320 40k As #924, 25x38mm	1.25	.95
b.		A320 50k As #925, 25x38mm	1.50	1.25

Coast Guard, 75th Anniv. A329

2001, Jan. 18   **Litho.**   *Perf. 13*
927	A329	(40k) multi	1.50	1.50
a.		Booklet pane of 10	15.00	
		Booklet, #927a	15.00	

Fish Type of 1998

Designs: 55k, Reinhardtius hippoglossoides. 80k, Pollachius virens.

2001, Jan. 18
928-929	A301	Set of 2	4.00	4.00

UN High Commissioner for Refugees, 50th Anniv. — A330

2001, Mar. 8   *Perf. 13¼x13*
930	A330	50k multi	1.50	1.25

Flower Type of 2000

Designs: 55k, Calendula officinalis. 65k, Dorotheanthus bellidiformis.

2001, Mar. 8   *Perf. 13*
931-932	A325	Set of 2	3.75	3.25

Icelandic Sheepdog A331

Dog's coat: 40k, Brown. 80k, Black.

2001, Apr. 18   *Perf. 14¼*
933-934	A331	Set of 2	4.25	3.25

Airplanes A332

Designs: 55k: TF-OGN (biplane). 80k, Klemm TF-SUX (monoplane).

Perf. 13½x12¾ on 2 or 3 Sides
2001, Apr. 18
Booklet Stamps
935	A332 55k multi	1.60	1.40
a.	Booklet pane of 4	6.50	
	Booklet, #935a	6.50	
936	A332 80k multi	2.50	2.25
a.	Booklet pane of 4	10.00	
	Booklet, #936a	10.00	

Europa
A333

Designs: 55k, Head, waterfall. 80k, Hand, wave.

2001, May 17   **Perf. 13**
937	A333 55k multi	1.75	1.50
a.	Booklet pane of 10	17.50	
	Booklet, #937a	19.00	
938	A333 80k multi	2.75	2.00
a.	Booklet pane of 10	27.50	
	Booklet, #938a	29.00	

Horses
A334

Designs: 40k, Fet. 50k, Tölt. 55k, Brokk. 60k, Skeidh. 80k, Stökk.

2001, May 17   **Perf. 13x13¼**
939-943	A334 Set of 5	9.75	9.75

No. 873 Surcharged in Red

2001, July 10 Litho.   Perf. 14½
944	A311 (53k) on 35k multi	1.75	1.75

Marine Mammals Type of 1999
Designs: 5k, Lagenorhynchus albirostris. 40k, Balaenoptera physalus. 80k, Balaenoptera borealis. 100k, Globicephala melas.

2001, Sept. 6 Litho.   Perf. 14½
945	A311 5k multi	.30	.30
946	A311 40k multi	1.25	1.25
947	A311 80k multi	2.50	2.50
948	A311 100k multi	3.25	3.25
	Nos. 945-948 (4)	7.30	7.30

Islands
A335

Designs: 40k, Grimsey. 55k, Papey.

2001, Oct. 9 Litho.   Perf. 13¼x13
949-950	A335 Set of 2	3.00	2.50

See Nos. 975-976, 1001-1002, 1033-1034, 1158-1159.

Souvenir Sheet

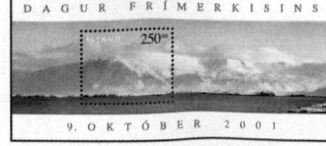

Esja Mountain — A336

2001, Oct. 9   **Perf. 13¼**
951	A336 250k multi	9.00	9.00

Stamp Day.

Birds — A337

Designs: 42k, Oenanthe oenanthe. 250k, Charadrius hiaticula.

2001, Nov. 8   **Perf. 13¼x13**
952-953	A337 Set of 2	10.00	10.00

Christmas
A338

Churches: (42k), Brautarholt. 55k, Vidhmyri.

2001, Nov. 8
954	A338 (42k) multi	1.25	1.25
a.	Booklet pane of 6	7.50	—
	Booklet, #954a, 4 #954	12.50	
955	A338 55k multi	1.60	1.40

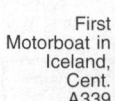

First Motorboat in Iceland, Cent.
A339

2002, Jan. 17 Litho.   Perf. 13x13½
956	A339 60k multi	1.90	1.90

Mushroom Type of 1999
Designs: (40k), Leccinum scabrum. 85k, Hydnum repandum.

2002, Jan. 17   Perf. 13¼x12¾
957-958	A314 Set of 2	3.75	3.75
	Booklet, 10 #957	12.50	

No. 957 is inscribed "Bref 20g."

Intl. Year of Mountains
A340

2002, Mar. 7 Litho.   Perf. 13
959	A340 (42k) multi	1.50	1.50

Halldór Laxness (1902-98), 1955 Nobel Literature Laureate
A341

2002, Mar. 7 Litho.   Perf. 13x13¼
960	A341 100k multi	3.50	3.50
a.	Souvenir sheet of 1	3.75	3.75

Examples of No. 960a with Nobel Prize medal in margin printed in gold foil and embossed sold for 1700k. Value, $125.

Lighthouses — A342

Perf. 12¾x13¼ on 2 or 3 Sides
2002, Apr. 18
Booklet Stamps
961	A342 60k Grótta	1.75	1.60
a.	Booklet pane of 4	7.00	
	Booklet, #961a	7.00	
962	A342 85k Kögur	2.50	2.25
a.	Booklet pane of 4	10.00	
	Booklet, #962a	10.00	

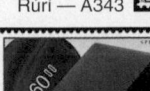

Fyssa, by Rúrí — A343

Spenna, by Hafsteinn Austmann
A344

2002, Apr. 18 Litho.   Perf. 14½x14¾
963	A343 (42k) multi	1.25	1.10
964	A344 60k multi	1.75	1.50

Nordic Council, 50th anniv. (No. 963).

Sesselja Sigmundsdóttir (1902-74), Advocate for Mentally Handicapped
A345

2002, May 9
965	A345 45k multi	1.40	1.10

Europa
A346

Designs: 60k, Acrobats, juggling clown. 85k, Head on stick, lion jumping through ring of fire.

2002, May 9   **Perf. 13**
966	A346 60k multi	1.75	1.25
a.	Booklet pane of 10	17.50	
	Booklet, #966a	19.00	
967	A346 85k multi	2.50	1.50
a.	Booklet pane of 10	25.00	
	Booklet, #967a	26.00	

Flowers Type of 2000
Designs: 10k, Lobelia erinus. 200k, Centaurea cyanus.

2002, Sept. 5 Litho.   Perf. 14¾x14½
968-969	A325 Set of 2	7.50	7.50

Fish of Lake Thingvallavatn — A347

Designs: (45k), Salvelinus alpinus (Murta). (55k), Salmo trutta, vert. 60k, Salvelinus alpinus (Sílableikja). 90k, Salvelinus alpinus (Kuthungableikja). 200k, Salvelinus alpinus (Dvergbleikja).

Perf. 13¼x12¾, 12¾x13¼ (#971)
2002, Sept. 5
970	A347 (45k) multi	1.50	1.50
a.	Perf. 13¼x12½x13¼x13	1.50	1.50
971	A347 (55k) multi	2.50	2.50
a.	Perf. 13¼x12½:13¼x13:12½	2.50	2.50
972	A347 60k multi	2.00	2.00
a.	Perf. 13¼x13	2.00	2.00
973	A347 90k multi	2.75	2.75
a.	Perf. 13¼x13	2.75	2.75
974	A347 200k multi	6.00	6.00
a.	Perf. 13¼x13	6.00	6.00
b.	Booklet pane, #970a-974a	27.50	
	Complete booklet, #974b	27.50	
	Nos. 970-974 (5)	14.75	14.75

Nos. 970-974 were issued both in sheet format, perf 13¼x12¾ or 12¾x13¼ (#971), and in booklet pane format (#970a-974a), with small differences in the gauge of the stamps' perforations.

Islands Type of 2001
Designs: 45k, Vigur. 55k, Flatey.

2002, Oct. 9   **Perf. 14**
975-976	A335 Set of 2	3.00	2.75

Souvenir Sheet

Sudurgata, Reykjavik — A348

2002, Oct. 9 Perf. 14½x14¾
977	A348 250k multi	9.75	9.75

Stamp Day.

Birds   Christmas
A349   A350

Designs: 50k, Tringa totanus. 85k, Phalaropus fulicarius.

2002, Nov. 7   **Perf. 13¼x13**
978-979	A349 Set of 2	4.50	4.50

See Nos. 997-998, 1029-1030, 1059-1060.

2002, Nov. 7   **Perf. 13**
Designs: 45k, Gifts and ornaments. 60k, Gifts.
980	A350 45k multi	1.40	1.40
a.	Booklet pane of 10	14.00	
	Booklet, #980a	14.00	
981	A350 60k multi	1.90	1.75

Flower Type of 2000
Designs: 45k, Phlox drummondii. 60k, Gazania x hybrida.

2003, Jan. 16   **Perf. 13**
982	A325 45k multi	1.40	1.40
a.	Booklet pane of 10	14.00	
	Booklet, #982a	14.00	
983	A325 60k multi	1.90	1.75

Icelandic Police Force, Bicent. — A351

Designs: 45k, Police officers, 2003. 55k, Policeman, 1803.

2003, Jan. 16
984-985	A351 Set of 2	3.25	3.25

Icelandic Cattle
A352

Designs: 45k, Bull. 85k, Cow.

2003, Mar. 13 Litho.   Perf. 13x13¼
986-987	A352 Set of 2	4.25	4.25

Souvenir Sheet

Nordia 2003 Philatelic Exhibition, Reykjavik — A353

Litho. & Engr.

2003, Mar. 13   *Perf. 14*
988 A353 250k multi   10.00 10.00

No. 988 sold for 300k.

Free Church, Reykjavik, Cent. — A354

2003, Apr. 23   **Litho.**   *Perf. 13*
989 A354 200k multi   7.00 7.00

Ferries A355

No. 990: a, Saefari. b, Saevar.
No. 991: a, Herjólfur. b, Baldur.

Perf. 13 on 2 or 3 Sides
2003, Apr. 23
Booklet Stamps
990   Pair   2.75 2.75
  a.-b.   A355 45k Either single   1.35 1.35
  c.   Booklet pane, 2 #990   5.50 —
   Complete booklet, #990c   5.50
991   Pair   3.75 3.75
  a.-b.   A355 60k Either single   1.75 1.75
  c.   Booklet pane, 2 #991   7.50 —
   Complete booklet, #991c   7.50

Icelandic Chickens — A356

2003, May 22   *Perf. 13¼*
992 A356 45k multi   1.50 1.50

Europa — A357

Poster art.

2003, May 22   *Perf. 13½*
993 A357 60k red & multi   1.75 *1.25*
  a.   Booklet pane of 10, perf. 13½ on 3 sides   17.50 —
   Complete booklet, #993a   19.00
994 A357 85k red & multi   2.50 *1.75*
  a.   Booklet pane of 10, perf. 13½ on 3 sides   25.00 —
   Complete booklet, #994a   26.00

Friendship A358

2003, Sept. 4   *Perf. 14¼x14½*
995 A358 45k multi   1.40 1.40

First Census, 300th Anniv. — A359

2003, Sept. 4   *Perf. 13*
996 A359 60k multi   2.10 2.10

Bird Type of 2002

Designs: 70k, Anthus pratensis. 250k, Numenius phaeopus.

2003, Sept. 4   *Perf. 13¼x13*
997-998 A349 Set of 2   11.00 11.00

Rangifer Tarandus A360

2003, Oct. 9   **Litho.**   *Perf. 13*
999 A360 45k multi   1.50 1.50

Souvenir Sheet

Quonset Hut — A361

2003, Oct. 9
1000 A361 250k multi   9.00 9.00

Stamp Day.

Islands Type of 2001

Designs: 85k, Heimaey. 200k, Hrísey.

2003, Nov. 6   *Perf. 13¼x13*
1001-1002 A335 Set of 2   9.50 9.50

Christmas — A362

Designs: 45k, Girl placing ornament on Christmas tree. 60k, Boy lighting candle.

2003, Nov. 6   *Perf. 14¼*
1003-1004 A362 Set of 2   3.25 3.25
  a.   Booklet pane of 10, #1003   14.00
   Booklet, #1003a   14.00

Flowers Type of 2000

Designs: 50k, Tagetes patula. 55k, Begonia x tuberhybrida.

2004, Jan. 15   **Litho.**   *Perf. 13*
1005-1006 A325 Set of 2   3.50 3.50

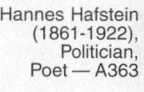

Hannes Hafstein (1861-1922), Politician, Poet — A363

2004, Jan. 15   *Perf. 13¼x13½*
1007 A363 150k multi   5.00 5.00
  a.   Souvenir sheet of 1   5.00 5.00

Icelandic home rule, cent.

Trawler "Coot," Cent. A364

2004, Mar. 11   **Litho.**   *Perf. 13¼*
1008 A364 50k multi   1.50 1.50

Geothermal Energy — A365

Designs: 50k, Snorralaug hot water pool. 55k, Valve on geodesic dome, steam cloud, vert. (29x47mm). 60k, Steam pipes. 90k, Turbine. 250k, Map of Iceland showing geothermal zones, vert. (29x47mm).

Perf. 13x13¼, 13¼ (55k, 250k)
2004, Mar. 11
1009 A365 50k multi   1.50 1.50
  a.   Perf. 13¼   4.00 4.00
1010 A365 55k multi   1.75 1.75
1011 A365 60k multi   2.00 2.00
  a.   Perf. 13¼   5.00 5.00
1012 A365 90k multi   2.75 2.75
  a.   Perf. 13¼   7.00 7.00
1013 A365 250k multi   7.50 7.50
  a.   Booklet pane, #1009a, 1010, 1011a, 1012a, 1013   25.00 —
   Complete booklet, #1013a   25.00
   Nos. 1009-1013 (5)   15.50 15.50

Complete booklet sold for 750k.
Nos. 1009a, 1011a and 1012a only come from the booklet pane No. 1013a.

Souvenir Sheet

Norse Mythology — A366

No. 1014: a, God Odin and bird. b, Odin's horse, Sleipnir, and bird.

2004, Mar. 26   *Perf. 13*
1014 A366 Sheet of 2   3.75 3.75
  a.   50k multi   1.75 1.75
  b.   60k multi   2.00 2.00

Automobiles A367

No. 1015: a, 1956 Ford Fairlane Victoria. b, 1954 Pobeta.
No. 1016: a, 1955 Chevrolet Bel Air. b, 1952 Volkswagen.

Perf. 13 on 2 or 3 Sides
2004, Apr. 15
Booklet Stamps
1015   Pair   6.50 6.50
  a.-b.   A367 60k Either single   3.25 3.25
  c.   Booklet pane, 2 #1015c   13.00
   Complete booklet, #1015c   13.00
1016   Pair   9.50 9.50
  a.-b.   A367 85k Either single   4.75 4.75
  c.   Booklet pane, 2 #1016   19.00
   Complete booklet, #1016c   19.00

Herring Industry, Cent. — A368

2004, May 19   *Perf. 13¼*
1017 A368 65k multi   2.00 2.00

Hringurin Women's Society, Cent. A369

2004, May 19   *Perf. 13x13¼*
1018 A369 100k violet blue   3.25 3.25

Europa A370

2004, May 19   *Perf. 13*
1019 A370 65k Cyclists   2.00 2.00
  a.   Booklet pane of 10   20.00
   Complete booklet, #1019a   20.00
1020 A370 90k Cars in snow   2.75 2.75
  a.   Booklet pane of 10   27.50 —
   Complete booklet, #1020a   27.50

Mushrooms Type of 1999

Designs: 50k, Amanita vaginata. 60k, Camarophyllus pratensis.

2004, Sept. 2   **Litho.**   *Perf. 13*
1021-1022 A314 Set of 2   4.25 4.25

Reykdal Power Station, Cent. — A371

2004, Sept. 2   *Perf. 13¼*
1023 A371 50k multi   1.50 1.50

First Automobile in Iceland, Cent. A372

2004, Sept. 2
1024 A372 100k multi   3.25 3.25

French Hospital, Fáskrúthsfirthi, Cent. — A373

Litho. & Engr.
2004, Oct. 8 **Perf. 13¾**
1025 A373 60k multi 1.90 1.90

Souvenir Sheet

Brúarhlöth — A374

2004, Oct. 8 **Litho.** **Perf. 13**
1026 A374 250k multi 8.00 8.00
Stamp Day.

Insects A375

Designs: 50k, Nebria gyllenhali. 70k, Bombus lucorum.

2004, Oct. 8
1027-1028 A375 Set of 2 4.00 4.00
See Nos. 1043-1044, 1089-1090, 1121-1122, 1161-1161.

Bird Type of 2002
Designs: 55k, Calidris maritima. 75k, Calidris alpina.

2004, Nov. 4 **Litho.** **Perf. 13¼x13**
1029-1030 A349 Set of 2 4.00 4.00

Christmas — A376

Designs: 45k, Ptarmigan in snow. 65k, Heindeer in snow.

2004, Nov. 4
1031-1032 A376 Set of 2 3.50 3.50
1031a Booklet pane of 10 #1031 14.00
Complete booklet, #1031a 14.00

Islands Type of 2001
Designs: 5k, Vithey. 90k, Flatey.

2005, Jan. 13 **Litho.** **Perf. 14**
1033-1034 A335 Set of 2 3.25 3.25

Organized Forestation, Cent. A377

2005, Jan. 13
1035 A377 45k multi 1.50 1.50
See No. 1155.

Souvenir Sheet

National Museum Artifacts — A378

No. 1036: a, Brooch, 11th cent. b, Statue of Thor, 10th cent.

Litho. & Embossed
2005, Jan. 13 **Perf. 13½x13**
1036 A378 Sheet of 2 + central label 8.50 8.50
a. 100k multi 3.50 3.50
b. 150k multi 5.00 5.00

Mice A379

Designs: 45k, Apodemus sylvaticus. 125k, Mus musculus.

Perf. 13½x12¾
2005, Mar. 10 **Litho.**
1037-1038 A379 Set of 2 6.00 6.00

Flowers — A380

Designs: No. 1039, 50k, Roses. No. 1040, 50k, African daisies. No. 1041, 50k, Red calla lilies. 70k, Tulip.

2005, Mar. 10 **Perf. 13¼**
1039-1042 A380 Set of 4 8.50 8.50
1042a Booklet pane, 2 each #1039-1042 17.00 —

Nos. 1039-1042 each printed in sheets of 10, with each stamp in the sheet having a different background swirl pattern. Stamps of the same kind in the booklet pane have the same swirl pattern, which is the same as one found on the sheet.

Insects Type of 2004
Designs: 50k, Araneus diadematus (spider). 70k, Musca domestica.

2005, Apr. 14 **Perf. 13¼x13**
1043-1044 A375 Set of 2 4.50 4.50

Fishing Boats A381

No. 1045: a, Vörthur ThH4. b, Karl VE47.
No. 1046: a, Saedís IS67. b, Guthbjörg NK74.

Perf. 13 on 2 or 3 Sides
2005, Apr. 14
Booklet Stamps
1045 Pair 4.50 4.50
a.-b. A381 70k Either single 2.25 2.25
c. Booklet pane, 2 #1045 9.00
Complete booklet, #1045c 9.00

1046 Pair 6.00 6.00
a.-b. A381 95k Either single 3.00 3.00
c. Booklet pane, 2 #1045 12.00
Complete booklet, #1045c 12.00

Bridges, Cent. A382

Designs: 50k, Sogith Bridge. 95k, Lagarfljót Bridge. 165k, Jökulsá Bridge.

2005, May 26 **Litho.** **Perf. 13¼x13½**
1047-1049 A382 Set of 3 12.00 12.00

Europa A383

Fork, knife and: 70k, Fish dish, gutted fish, waterfall. 90k, Meat dish, hanging meat, flowers.

2005, May 26 **Perf. 13½**
1050 A383 70k multi 2.10 2.10
a. Booklet pane of 10 21.00
Complete booklet, #1050a 21.00
1051 A383 90k multi 2.75 2.75
a. Booklet pane of 10 27.50
Complete booklet, #1050a 27.50

Salmon Fishermen and Fishing Flies — A384

Designs; 50k, Fisherman on Laxái Kjós River, Raud Frances fly. 60k, Fishermen in boat on Laxá í Athaldal River, Laxá Bla fly, vert.

Perf. 13¾x13½, 13½x13¾
2005, Sept. 1 **Litho.**
1052-1053 A384 Set of 2 3.75 3.75

Berries — A385

Designs: 65k, Vaccinium uliginosum. 90k, Fragaria vesca.

2005, Sept. 1 **Perf. 14**
1054 A385 65k multi 2.10 2.10
a. Tete-beche pair 4.25 4.25
1055 A385 90k multi 3.00 3.00
a. Tete-beche pair 6.00 6.00
See Nos. 1082-1083, 1116-1117.

Motorcycles — A386

2005, Oct. 7 **Perf. 13¼x13½**
1056 A386 50k multi 1.75 1.75
First motorcycle in Iceland, cent.

Commercial College of Iceland, Cent. A387

2005, Oct. 7 **Perf. 13½x14¼**
1057 A387 70k multi 2.25 2.25

Souvenir Sheet

Aerial View of Reykjavik Rooftops — A388

2005, Oct. 7 **Perf. 13¼**
1058 A388 200k multi 7.00 7.00
Stamp Day.

Birds Type of 2002
Designs: 60k, Anser anser. 105k, Sturnus vulgaris.

2005, Nov. 3 **Perf. 14**
1059-1060 A349 Set of 2 5.50 5.50

Christmas — A389

2005, Nov. 3 **Perf. 13½**
1061 A389 50k Apple 1.75 1.75
a. White border at top or bottom, perf. 13½ on 2 or 3 sides 1.75 1.75
b. Booklet pane of 10 #1061a 17.50
Complete booklet, #1061b 17.50
1062 A389 70k Christmas tree 2.40 2.40
No. 1061 is impregnated with an apple and cinnamon scent; No. 1062 with a pine scent.

National Flower Dryas Octopetala — A390

2006, Feb. 2 **Litho.** **Perf. 13¾**
1063 A390 50k multi 1.60 1.60

Rock and Roll Music, 50th Anniv. — A391

2006, Feb. 2
1064 A391 60k multi 1.90 1.90

Arrival in Iceland of Refugees of Hungarian Uprising, 50th Anniv. A392

2006, Feb. 2 **Perf. 13½x13¾**
1065 A392 70k multi 2.25 2.25

Souvenir Sheet

Europa Stamps, 50th Anniv. — A393

No. 1066: a, #407. b, #395.

2006, Feb. 2   *Perf. 14¼x14*
1066 A393 150k Sheet of 2, #a-b   9.50 9.50

Motion Pictures in Iceland, Cent. — A394

Designs: 50k, Early theater, projector and program. 95k, Projector reel, actor and actress. 160k, Actor in mask, clapboard, bag of popcorn, cameraman on location.

Perf. 13¾x13½
2006, Mar. 29   Litho.
1067-1069 A394 Set of 3   9.00 9.00

Souvenir Sheet

Mythical Beings of Nordic Folklore — A395

2006, Mar. 29   *Perf. 13¼x13*
1070 A395 95k multi   3.25 3.25

General Purpose Vehicles A396

No. 1071: a, 1951 Land Rover. b, 1946 Willys.
No. 1072: a, 1965 Austin Gypsy. b, 1955 GAZ-69.

Perf. 13 on 2 or 3 Sides
2006, Mar. 29
Booklet Stamps
1071   Pair   4.00 4.00
a.-b.   A396 70k Either single   2.00 2.00
c.   Booklet pane, 2 #1071   8.00
   Complete booklet, #1071c   8.00
1072   Pair   5.00 5.00
a.-b.   A396 90k Either single   2.50 2.50
c.   Booklet pane, 2 #1072   10.00
   Complete booklet, #1072c   10.00

A397

Europa A398

2006, May 18   *Perf. 13¼x13¾*
1073 A397 75k blk & red   2.40 2.40
Perf. 13¾x13¼
1074 A398 95k blue & blk   3.25 3.25
Booklet Stamps
Self-Adhesive
Serpentine Die Cut 11¾x12¼
1075 A397 75k blk & red   2.40 2.40
a.   Booklet pane of 10   24.00
Serpentine Die Cut 12¼x11¾
1076 A398 95k blue & blk   3.25 3.25
a.   Booklet pane of 10   32.50

Waterfalls — A399

Designs: 55k, Faxi. 65k, Oxaráfoss, vert. (29x47mm). 75k, Glymur, vert. (29x47mm). 95k, Hjálparfoss. 220k, Skeifárfoss.

2006, May 18   *Perf. 13¼*
1077-1081 A399   Set of 5   14.50 14.50
1081a   Booklet pane #1077-1081, perf. 13½   21.00 —
   Complete booklet, #1081a   21.00

Booklet containing No. 1081a sold for 750k.

Berries Type of 2005

Designs: 75k, Empetrum nigrum. 130k, Rubus saxatilis.

2006, Sept. 21   *Perf. 13¼x13¾*
1082 A385   75k multi   2.25 2.25
a.   Tete-beche pair   5.00 5.00
1083 A385 130k multi   3.75 3.75
a.   Tete-beche pair   8.00 8.00

Iceland's First Olympic Medal, 50th Anniv. — A400

Litho. & Embossed
2006, Sept. 21   *Perf. 13¼*
1084 A400 55k multi   1.60 1.60

First Telephone Service in Iceland, Cent. — A401

2006, Sept. 21   Litho.   *Perf. 14*
1085 A401 65k multi   2.00 2.00

Souvenir Sheet

Icelandic Wrestling Tournament, Cent. — A402

Litho. & Embossed
2006, Sept. 21   *Perf. 13¼x14*
1086 A402 200k multi   6.50 6.50
Stamp Day.

Mushrooms Type of 1999

Designs: 70k, Xerocomus subtomentosus. 95k, Kuehneromyces mutabilis.

2006, Nov. 2   Litho.   *Perf. 13¾x13¼*
1087-1088 A314   Set of 2   5.00 5.00

Insects Type of 2004

Designs: 65k, Dolichovespula norwegica. 110k, Coccinella undecimpunctata.

2006, Nov. 2   Litho.   *Perf. 13¾x14¼*
1089-1090 A375   Set of 2   5.25 5.25

Christmas — A403

Designs: Nos. 1091, 1093, Angel, denomination at LL. 75k, Heart. No. 1094, Angel, denomination at LR.

2006, Nov. 2   *Perf. 13½x13¾*
1091 A403 55k multi   1.60 1.60
1092 A403 75k multi   2.25 2.25
Self-Adhesive
Booklet Stamps
Serpentine Die Cut 9½x9¾
1093 A403 55k multi   1.75 1.75
1094 A403 55k multi   1.75 1.75
a.   Booklet pane, 5 each #1093-1094   20.00 —
  Nos. 1091-1094 (4)   7.35 7.35

Women's Rights in Iceland, Cent. — A404

Perf. 13½x13¼
2007, Feb. 15   Litho.
1095 A404 60k multi   1.90 1.90

Fishing Trawler Jón Forseti, Cent. A405

2007, Feb. 15   *Perf. 13¾x13½*
1096 A405 65k multi   2.00 2.00

Geothermal Energy A406

2007, Feb. 15   *Perf. 14*
1097 A406 75k multi   2.25 2.25
West Nordic Council, 10th anniv.

Souvenir Sheet

Intl. Polar Year — A407

2007, Feb. 15   *Perf. 14x13½*
1098 A407   Sheet of 2   5.25 5.25
a.   75k Volcano   2.25 2.25
b.   95k Ice cap mapping equipment   3.00 3.00

Youth Organization of Iceland, Cent. — A408

2007, Apr. 20   *Perf. 14*
1099 A408 70k multi   2.25 2.25

National Archives, 125th Anniv. — A409

2007, Apr. 20   *Perf. 12½*
1100 A409 80k multi   2.50 2.50
a.   Tete-beche pair, with tabs   6.00 6.00

Organized Forestry in Iceland, Cent. — A410

Various tree branches with frame color of: 10k, Olive green. 60k, Rose carmine.

2007, Apr. 20   *Perf. 14*
1101-1102 A410   Set of 2   2.25 2.25
1101a   Perf. 13½x14   .25 .25
1102a   Perf. 13½x14   1.50 1.50

Issued: 1101a, 1102a, 11/6/08.

Cargo Boats A411

No. 1103: a, Hamrafell. b, Tröllafoss.
No. 1104: a, Langjökull. b, Akranes.

Perf. 13 on 2 or 3 Sides
2007, Apr. 20
Booklet Stamps
1103   Pair   5.00 5.00
a.-b.   A411 80k Either single   2.50 2.50
c.   Booklet pane, 2 #1103   10.00
   Complete booklet, #1103c   10.00
1104   Pair   6.50 6.50
a.-b.   A411 105k Either single   3.25 3.25
c.   Booklet pane, 2 #1104   13.00
   Complete booklet, #1104c   13.00

Glaciers
A412

Designs: 5k, Breithamerkurjökull. 60k, Eystri Hagafellsjökull and Langjökull, vert. 80k, Mulajökull and Hofsjökull. 110k, Snaefellsjökull. 300k, Hvannadalshnúkur and Oraefajökull (70x30mm).

2007, May 24   **Perf. 14x13¼**
1105-1109 A412   Set of 5   18.00   18.00
1109a   Booklet pane, #1105-1109   25.00
    Complete booklet, #1109a   25.00
    No. 1109a sold for 750k.

Europa — A413

Designs: 80k, Scouting fleur-de-lis. 105k, Scouting clover emblem.

2007, May 24   **Perf. 13¼**
1110 A413   80k multi   2.60   2.60
1111 A413   105k multi   3.50   3.50

Booklet Stamps
Self-Adhesive
Die Cut
1112 A413   80k multi   2.60   2.60
a.   Booklet pane of 10   26.00
1113 A413   105k multi   3.50   3.50
a.   Booklet pane of 10   35.00
    Nos. 1110-1113 (4)   12.20   12.20

Scouting, cent.

Soil Conservation Service, Cent. — A414

Perf. 13⅜x14¼
2007, May 24   **Photo.**
1114 A414   (60k) multi   2.00   2.00

Self-Adhesive
Serpentine Die Cut 12
1115 A414   (60k) multi   2.00   2.00
    No. 1114 was printed in a sheet of 10, No. 1115 was printed in a folded sheet of 50.

Berries Type of 2005
Designs: 120k, Vaccinium myrtillus. 145k, Cornus suecica.

2007, Sept. 20   **Litho.**   **Perf. 14**
1116 A385   120k multi   4.00   4.00
a.   Tete-beche pair   8.50   8.50
1117 A385   145k multi   4.75   4.75
a.   Tete-beche pair   10.00   10.00

New Bible Translation — A415

Litho. With Foil Application
2007, Sept. 20   **Perf. 13½**
1118 A415   60k multi   2.00   2.00

Souvenir Sheet

Royal Visit, Cent. — A416

Litho. & Engr.
2007, Sept. 20   **Perf. 13x13¼**
1119 A416   250k multi   8.25   8.25

Jökulsá Canyon and Selfoss Waterfall — A417

No. 1120: a, Jökulsá Canyon (45x29mm). b, Selfoss Waterfall (30x29mm)

2007, Oct. 1   **Litho.**   **Perf. 13¼x13¾**
1120 A417   Horiz. pair   6.25   6.25
a.   80k multi   2.75   2.75
b.   105k multi   3.50   3.50

Insects Type of 2004
Designs: 70k, Prionocera turcica. 190k, Euceraphis punctipennis.

2007, Nov. 8   **Litho.**   **Perf. 14**
1121-1122 A375   Set of 2   8.75   8.75

Jónas Hallgrímsson (1807-45), Poet — A418

2007, Nov. 8   **Engr.**   **Perf. 12¾x13**
1123 A418   65k brown   2.25   2.25

Kleppur Psychiatric Hospital, Cent. — A419

2007, Nov. 8   **Litho.**   **Perf. 13¼**
1124 A419   80k multi   2.60   2.60

Christmas A420

Various cut patterns in Icelandic leaf bread: 60k, 80k.

2007, Nov. 8   *Serpentine Die Cut*
Self-Adhesive
1125 A420   60k red & multi   2.00   2.00
a.   Booklet pane of 10   20.00
1126 A420   80k grn & multi   2.60   2.60

Teachers' College of Iceland, Cent. — A421

2008, Feb. 14   **Litho.**   **Perf. 14x13¼**
1127 A421   85k multi   2.60   2.60

Kisses — A422

Lines from poem by Erla Thorsteindottir and people kissing with photograph colors in: No. 1128, 65k, Blue. No. 1129, 65k, Sepia. 75k, Green. 85k, Red violet.

2008, Feb. 14
1128-1131 A422   Set of 4   9.00   9.00

Agricultural Tools — A423

No. 1132: a, Ferguson tractor. b, International Harvester TD6 bulldozer.
No. 1133: a, Horse-drawn plow. b, Lanz turfkiller.

2008, Mar. 27   **Litho.**   **Perf. 13¼**
Booklet Stamps
1132   Pair   5.00   5.00
a.-b.   A423 85k Either single   2.50   2.50
c.   Booklet pane, 2 #1132   10.00
    Complete booklet, #1132c   10.00
1133   Pair   6.00   6.00
a.-b.   A423 110k Either single   3.00   3.00
c.   Booklet pane, 2 #1133   12.00
    Complete booklet, #1133c   12.00

Embroidery — A424

Designs: 65k, Refilsaumur. 85k, Augnsaumur. 110k, Krosssaumur.

2008, Mar. 27   **Perf. 14**
1134-1136 A424   Set of 3   8.00   8.00

Souvenir Sheet

Snaefellsnes — A425

2008, Mar. 27   **Perf. 14x13¼**
1137 A425   120k multi   3.50   3.50

Personalized Stamp — A426

Serpentine Die Cut 10 Syncopated
2008, May 8   **Litho.**
1138 A426   (75k) multi   2.25   2.25
    The vignette of the stamp shown above is the generic image for the issue, which was available at face value. Other images with the stamp frame shown are personalized stamps which sold for 3120k for a sheet of 24 stamps.

Geothermal Space Heating, Cent. — A427

2008, May 8   **Perf. 14x13½**
1139 A427   75k multi   2.25   2.25

Hafnarfjördhur, Cent. — A428

2008, May 8   **Perf. 13x12½**
1140 A428   80k multi   2.25   2.25

Icelandic Industrial Design A429

Designs: 65k, Proprio Foot prosthetic foot. 120k, Marel OptiCut volumetric portioning and meat cutting machine. 155k, Wish fly fishing reel. 200k, Gavia submarine.

2008, May 8   **Perf. 12½x13**
1141-1144 A429   Set of 4   15.00   15.00
1141a   Tete beche pair   4.00   4.00
1142a   Tete beche pair   7.00   7.00
1143a   Tete beche pair   9.00   9.00

Europa — A430

Letter folded into: 85k, Boat. 110k, Airplane.

2008, May 8   **Perf. 14**
1145 A430   85k multi   2.25   2.25
1146 A430   110k multi   2.75   2.75

Booklet Stamps
Self-Adhesive
Serpentine Die Cut 9½x10

1147	A430	85k multi	2.25 2.25
a.		Booklet pane of 10	22.50
1148	A430	110k multi	2.75 2.75
a.		Booklet pane of 10	27.50

Knight and Final Position of 1958 Chess Match Between Fridhrik Olafsson and Bobby Fischer — A431

2008, Sept. 18   Litho.   Perf. 13¼
1149 A431 80k multi   2.10 2.10

First Cod War, 50th Anniv. A432

2008, Sept. 18   Perf. 13¼x13
1150 A432 90k multi   2.10 2.10

Aegagropila Linnaei — A433

2008, Sept. 18   Perf. 13¼x13¾
1151 A433 140k multi   3.25 3.25

Souvenir Sheet

Intl. Year of Planet Earth — A434

2008, Sept. 18
1152 A434 215k multi   5.00 5.00

Stamp Day.

Peace Tower, Videy — A435

2008, Oct. 9   Litho.   Perf. 13¼
1153 A435 120k multi + label 2.75 2.75

Parts of the design were printed with a glow-in-the-dark ink.

Forestry Type of 2005 Redrawn and

Forestry in Vaglaskógur, Cent. — A436

2008, Nov. 6   Litho.   Perf. 13½x14
1154	A436	400k multi	8.00 8.00
1155		Booklet pane of 4, #1101a, 1102a, 1154, 1155a	17.50 17.50
a.		A377 45k multi, denomination as "45" only	3.00 3.00
		Complete booklet, #1155	18.00 18.00

No. 1155 sold for 800k.

Christmas A437

Winning designs in children's stamp art contest: 70k, Christmas goblin Stiff-legs, by Heidhar Jökull Hafsteinsson. 90k, Christmas Cat, by Konrádh Kárason Thormar.

Serpentine Die Cut 12½
2008, Nov. 6
Self-Adhesive
1156	A437	70k multi	1.75 1.75
a.		Booket pane of 10	17.50
1157	A437	90k multi	2.00 2.00

Vertical pairs in booklet pane are tete-beche.

Islands Type of 2001

Designs: 75k, Hjörsey. 90k, Málmey.

2009, Jan. 29   Litho.   Perf. 14
1158-1159 A335 Set of 2   3.75 3.75

Insects Type of 2004

Designs: 80k, Psychodidae. 120k, Gnaphosidae (spider).

2009, Jan. 29
1160-1161 A375 Set of 2   4.50 4.50

Souvenir Sheet

Intl. Polar Year — A438

No. 1162 — Map of ice cover of: a, 100k, North Pole, Northern Greenland. b, 130k, Iceland, Eastern Greenland.

Litho. & Photo.
2009, Jan. 29   Perf. 13x13½
1162 A438 Sheet of 2, #a-b   5.25 5.25

Parts of the design were printed with a thermographic ink that disappeared when warmed.

Civil Aviation in Iceland, 90th Anniv. A439

No. 1163: a, Avro 504K. b, Waco ZKS-7.
No. 1164: a, Boeing 757. b, Fokker 50.

Perf. 14¼ Horiz.
2009, Mar. 19   Litho.
Booklet Stamps
1163		Vert. pair	3.25 3.25
a.-b.	A439	90k Either single	1.60 1.60
c.		Booklet pane, 2 #1163	6.50 —
		Complete booklet, #1163c	6.50
1164		Vert. pair	4.25 4.25
a.-b.	A439	120k Either single	2.10 2.10
c.		Booklet pane, 2 #1164	8.50 —
		Complete booklet, #1164c	8.50

Miniature Sheet

Legendary Creatures from Folktales — A440

No. 1165: a, Hrosshvalur. b, Skoffín. c, Múshveli. d, Raudhkembingur. e, Selamódhir. f, Ofuguggi. g, Saeneyti. h, Skeljaskrímsli. i, Urdharköt tur. j, Fjörulalli.

2009, Mar. 19   Perf. 13¼
1165 A440 80k Sheet of 10, #a-j   20.00 20.00

Reykjavik Water Works, Cent. — A441

2009, May 7   Litho.   Perf. 12½
1166 A441 10k multi   .20 .20

Iceland Youth Organization National Tournaments, Cent. — A442

2009, May 7   Perf. 13¼
1167 A442 105k multi   2.50 2.50

Skrúdhur Garden, Cent. — A443

2009, May 7   Perf. 12½
1168 A443 140k multi   3.00 3.00

Europa — A444

Designs: 105k, Sun and shadows at different times. 140k, Observatory.

2009, May 7   Perf. 13¼
1169	A444	105k multi	1.75 1.75
1170	A444	140k multi	2.25 2.25

Booklet Stamps
Self-Adhesive
Serpentine Die Cut 9¾x10
1171	A444	105k multi	1.75 1.75
a.		Booklet pane of 10	17.50
1172	A444	140k multi	2.25 2.25
a.		Booklet pane of 10	22.50

Intl. Year of Astronomy.

Souvenir Sheet

Nordia 2009 Philatelic Exhibition, Hafnarfjördhur — A445

2009, May 7   Perf. 13
1173 A445 190k multi   4.00 4.00

Icelandic Sheep A446

Shepherds and sheep in: 95k, Open pasture. 160k, Pen, vert.

Perf. 12½x13, 13x12½
2009, Sept. 16
1174-1175 A446 Set of 2   5.00 5.00

Skaftafell, Vatnajökull National Park — A447

No. 1176 — Denomination at: a, UL (45x30mm). b, UR (30x30mm).

2009, Sept. 16   Perf. 13½x14
1176 A447 120k Horiz. pair, #a-b 5.00 5.00

Souvenir Sheet

National Center for Cultural Heritage, Cent. — A448

2009, Sept. 16   Perf. 13
1177 A448 150k multi   3.00 3.00

Stamp Day.

Birds — A449

Designs: 110k, Uria lomvia. 130k, Larus hyperboreus.

2009, Nov. 5 **Perf. 13x13¼**
1178-1179 A449 Set of 2 4.50 4.50

Thingvellir Church, 150th Anniv. — A450

2009, Nov. 5
1180 A450 190k multi 4.00 4.00

Christmas A451

Stained-glass windows: (70k), The Sermon on the Mount, by Gudmundur Einarsson. 120k, Holy Mother of God, by Finnur Jónsson.

2009, Nov. 5 **Die Cut Perf. 13½**
Self-Adhesive
1181 A451 (70k) multi 2.00 2.00
a. Booklet pane of 10 20.00
1182 A451 120k multi 2.75 2.75

Seals A452

Designs: 5k, Phoca vitulina. 220k, Phoca groenlandica.

2010, Jan. 28 Litho. Perf. 13¼x13¾
1183-1184 A452 Set of 2 3.50 3.50

Home Furnishings — A453

Designs: 75k, Hanger tree, designed by Katrin Ólina Pétursdóttir and Michael Young. 140k, Tango chair, designed by Sigurdhur Gústafsson. 155k, MGO 180 dining room table, designed by Gudhrún M. Olafsdóttir and Oddgeir Thórdharson, horiz. 165k, Dimon sofa, designed by Erla Sólveig Oskarsdóttir.

Perf. 13¼x12½, 12½x13¼
2010, Jan. 28
1185-1188 A453 Set of 4 8.50 8.50
1185a Tete-beche pair 2.40 2.40
1186a Tete-beche pair 4.50 4.50
1187a Tete-beche pair 5.00 5.00
1188a Tete-beche pair 5.25 5.25

Wood and Bone Carvings A454

Designs: 10k, Door of Valthjófsstadhir. Nos. 1190, 1192, (75k), Judge's drinking horn. 200k, Play in Leaves, sculpture by Sigrídhur Jóna Kristjánsdóttir.

2010, Mar. 18 Perf. 14x13¼, 13¼x14
1189-1191 A454 Set of 3 5.00 5.00
Self-Adhesive
Serpentine Die Cut 12
Size: 32x27mm
1192 A454 (75k) multi 1.25 1.25

Fishing Trawlers — A455

No. 1193: a, Bjarni Riddari GK 1. b, Ingólfur Arnarson RE 201.
No. 1194: a, Sólborg IS 260. b, Hardhbakur EA 3.

2010, Mar. 18 **Perf. 14 Horiz.**
Booklet Stamps
1193 Vert. pair 2.50 2.50
a.-b. A455 75k Either single 1.25 1.25
c. Booklet pane, 2 #1193 5.00
Complete booklet, #1193c 5.00
1194 Vert. pair 5.25 5.25
a.-b. A455 165k Either single 2.60 2.60
c. Booklet pane, 2 #1194 10.50
Complete booklet, #1194c 10.50

Souvenir Sheet

Life by the Sea — A456

No. 1195: a, Man rolling herring barrel. b, Women filling herring barrels, fish.

2010, Mar. 18 **Perf. 13¼x14**
1195 A456 75k Sheet of 2, #a-b 2.50 2.50

Europa A457

Illustrations from children's books: 165k, The Fate of the Gods, by Ingunn Asdísardóttir and Kristin Ragna Gunnarsdóttir. 220k, Good Evening, by Aslaug Jónsdóttir.

2010, May 6 Litho. **Perf. 13¾x14**
1196 A457 165k multi 2.60 2.60
1197 A457 220d multi 3.50 3.50
Booklet Stamps
Self-Adhesive
Die Cut Perf. 13¼
1198 A457 165k multi 2.60 2.60
a. Booklet pane of 10 26.00
1199 A457 220d multi 3.50 3.50
a. Booklet pane of 10 35.00

Garden Parks — A458

Designs: 90k, Jónsgardhur, Isafjödhur. 130k, Hellisgerdhi, Hafnarfjödhur. 285k, Skalla-grímsgardhur, Borgarnes, horiz.

Perf. 13¼x13¾, 13¾x13¼
2010, May 6
1200-1202 A458 Set of 3 7.75 7.75

A460

Personalized Stamps — A461

Serpentine Die Cut 10 Syncopated
2010, May 6
Self-Adhesive
1203 A460 (165k) silver & blue 2.60 2.60
1204 A461 (220k) bronze & brn 3.50 3.50

The vignettes shown above of Nos. 1203-1204 are generic images. The vignette portion of the stamp could be personalized.

Souvenir Sheet

Iceland Pavilion, Expo 2010, Shanghai — A462

2010, May 6 Perf. 13x12½x12¾x13
1205 A462 130k multi 2.00 2.00

A463

A464

2010 Eruption of Eyjafjallajökull Volcano — A465

Litho. & Silk-screened
2010, July 22 **Perf. 13¼**
1206 A463 (75k) multi 1.25 1.25
1207 A464 (165k) multi 2.75 2.75
1208 A465 (220k) multi 3.75 3.75
Nos. 1206-1208 (3) 7.75 7.75

Volcanic ash from the eruption was added to the ink used in the silk-screened parts of Nos. 1206 1200.

Vífilsstadhir Sanatorium, Cent. — A466

Perf. 13½x13¼
2010, Sept. 16 **Litho.**
1209 A466 (90k) multi 1.50 1.50

2010 Youth Olympics, Singapore A467

2010, Sept. 16 **Perf. 13x12½**
1210 A467 165k multi 2.75 2.75

Gas Lighting In Reykjavik, 150th Anniv. — A468

2010, Sept. 16 **Perf. 13**
1211 A468 450k multi 7.75 7.75

Souvenir Sheet

Intl. Year of Biodiversity — A469

No. 1212: a, Hawk, wolf, rodent. b, Fish, duck.

2010, Sept. 16 **Perf. 13¼**
1212 A469 90k Sheet of 2, #a-b 3.00 3.00

Visir Newspaper,
Cent. — A470

2010, Nov. 4   Litho.   Perf. 13
1213 A470 140k drab & blk   2.60 2.60

Foss, by Isleifur Konrádhsson — A471

Skeggjadhur
Madhur og
Blómaflúr, by
Sölvi Helgason
A472

Breidhfirskur
Víkingur, by
Sigurlaug
Jónasdóttir
A473

Fiskar, by Karl
Einarsson
Dunganon
A474

2010, Nov. 4
1214 A471 (75k) multi   1.40 1.40
1215 A472 (90k) multi   1.75 1.75
1216 A473 (165k) multi   3.00 3.00
1217 A474 (220k) multi   4.00 4.00
    Nos. 1214-1217 (4)   10.15 10.15
A booklet containing single stamps of Nos.
1214-1217 in mounts sold for 1,550k.

Wreath and
Dove — A475

Wreath and Two
Doves — A476

2010, Nov. 4   Die Cut Perf. 13¾
               Self-Adhesive
1218 A475 (75k) multi   1.40 1.40
   a.   Booklet pane of 10   14.00
1219 A476 (165k) multi   3.00 3.00

Halichoerus Grypus — A477

Phoca
Hispida
A478

2011, Jan. 27   Litho.   Perf. 13⅛x13¾
1220 A477 (90k) multi   1.60 1.60
1221 A478 (220k) multi   3.75 3.75

Branta
Leucopsis
A479

Melanitta
Nigra
A480

Anser
Albifrons
A481

Anas
Strepera
A482

2011, Jan. 27
1222 A479 (75k) multi   1.25 1.25
1223 A480 (75k) multi   1.25 1.25
1224 A481 (165k) multi   3.00 3.00
1225 A482 (165k) multi   3.00 3.00
    Nos. 1222-1225 (4)   8.50 8.50
Worldwide Fund for Nature (WWF).

SEMI-POSTAL STAMPS

Shipwreck
and Rescue
by
Breeches
Buoy
SP1

Children
Gathering
Rock
Plants
SP2

Old
Fisherman
at Shore
SP3

Unwmk.
1933, Apr. 28   Engr.   Perf. 14
B1 SP1 10a + 10a red brown   2.00 6.50
B2 SP2 20a + 20a org red   2.00 6.50
B3 SP1 35a + 25a ultra   2.00 6.50
B4 SP3 50a + 25a blue grn   2.00 6.50
    Nos. B1-B4 (4)   8.00 26.00
    Set, never hinged   15.00
Receipts from the surtax were devoted to a
special fund for use in various charitable
works especially those indicated on the
stamps: "Slysavarnir" (Rescue work),
"Barnahaeli" (Asylum for scrofulous children),
"Ellhaeli" (Asylum for the Aged).

Souvenir Sheets

King Christian X — SP4

1937, May 15   Typo.
B5 SP4 Sheet of 3   50.00 325.00
         Never hinged   85.00
   a.   15a violet   11.00   60.00
   b.   25a red   11.00   60.00
   c.   50a blue   11.00   60.00
Reign of Christian X, 25th anniv. Sheet sold
for 2kr.

SP5

Designs: 30a, 40a, Ericsson statue, Reykjavik. 60a, Iceland's position on globe.

1938, Oct. 9   Photo.   Perf. 12
B6 SP5 Sheet of 3   6.00   32.50
         Never hinged   10.00
   a.   30a scarlet   1.40   13.00
   b.   40a purple   1.40   13.00
   c.   60a deep green   1.40   13.00
Leif Ericsson Day, Oct. 9, 1938.

**Catalogue values for unused
stamps in this section, from this
point to the end of the section, are
for Never Hinged items.**

III Child — SP6

Red Cross
Nurse and
Patient — SP7

Nurse Covering
Patient — SP8

Elderly
Couple — SP9

Rescue at
Sea — SP10

Unwmk.
1949, June 8   Engr.   Perf. 14
B7   SP6 10a + 10a olive grn   .70 1.40
B8   SP7 35a + 15a carmine   .95 1.40
B9   SP8 50a + 25a choc   .95 1.40
B10 SP9 60a + 25a brt ultra   .95 1.40
B11 SP10 75a + 25a slate gray   .95 1.40
    Nos. B7-B11 (5)   4.50 7.00
The surtax was for charitable purposes.

Nos. 262 and 265
Surcharged in
Black

1953, Feb. 12   Unwmk.   Perf. 13
B12 A50 75a + 25a red org   3.25 5.50
B13 A50 1.25k + 25a red vio   4.50 5.50
The surtax was for flood relief in the
Netherlands.

St.
Thorlacus — SP11

Cathedral at
Skalholt
SP12

1.75k+1.25k, Bishop Jon Thorkelsson
Vidalin.

1956, Jan. 23   Perf. 11½
B14 SP11 75a + 25a car   .25   .30
B15 SP12 1.25k + 75a dk brn   .25   .65
B16 SP11 1.75k + 1.25k black   1.00 2.00
    Nos. B14-B16 (3)   1.50 2.95
Bishopric of Skalholt, 900th anniv.
The surtax was for the rebuilding of
Skalholt, former cultural center of Iceland.

Ambulance
SP13

1963, Nov. 15   Photo.   Unwmk.
B17 SP13 3k + 50a multi   .50 1.50
B18 SP13 3.50k + 50a multi   .50 1.50
Centenary of International Red Cross.

Rock Ptarmigan
in Summer
SP14

Design: #B20, Rock ptarmigan in winter.

1965, Jan. 27   Photo.   Perf. 12½
Granite Paper
B19 SP14 3.50k + 50a multi   .90 2.50
B20 SP14 4.50k + 50a multi   .90 2.50

Ringed
Plover's
Nest — SP15

Design: 5k+50a, Rock ptarmigan's nest.

1967, Nov. 22   Photo.   Perf. 11½
B21 SP15 4k + 50a multi   .90 2.00
B22 SP15 5k + 50a multi   .90 2.00

Arctic Terns — SP16

1972, Nov. 22   Litho.   Perf. 13
B23 SP16 7k + 1k multi   .65 1.25
B24 SP16 9k + 1k multi   .65 1.25

AIR POST STAMPS

No. 115 Overprinted

Perf. 14x14½
1928, May 31   Wmk. 114
C1 A8 10a red   1.10 14.00
      Never hinged   2.00

Same Overprint on No. 82

1929, June 29   Wmk. 113   Perf. 13
C2 A5 50a gray & violet   70.00 140.00
      Never hinged   200.00

Gyrfalcon
AP1

Perf. 12½x12
1930, Jan. 1   Litho.   Unwmk.
C3 AP1 10a dp ultra & gray
             blue   25.00 72.50
      Never hinged   50.00

Imperfs were privately printed.
For overprint see No. CO1.

Snaefellsjokull, Extinct Volcano — AP2

Parliament Millenary: 20a, Fishing boat.
35a, Iceland pony. 50a, Gullfoss (Golden
Falls). 1k, Ingolfour Arnarson Statue.

Wmk. 47
1930, June 1   Typo.   Perf. 14
C4 AP2 15a org brn & dl bl   30.00 60.00
C5 AP2 20a bis brn & sl bl   30.00 60.00
C6 AP2 35a olive grn & brn   60.00 125.00
C7 AP2 50a dp grn & dp bl   60.00 125.00
C8 AP2 1k olive grn & dk
             red   60.00 125.00
      Nos. C4-C8 (5)   240.00 495.00
      Set, never hinged   500.00

Regular Issue of 1920
Overprinted

Perf. 14x14½
1931, May 25   Wmk. 114
C9 A8 30a red & green   50.00 175.00
C10 A8 1k dp bl & dk brn   17.50 175.00
C11 A8 2k ol brn & myr
             grn   75.00 175.00
      Nos. C9-C11 (3)   142.50 525.00
      Set, never hinged   275.00

Nos. 185, 128 and 187
Overprinted in Red

1933, June 16
C12 A8 1k dk bl & lt brn   200.   675.
      Never hinged   450.
C13 A8 5k brn & indigo   650.   1,600.
      Never hinged   1,550.
C14 A8 10k yel grn & blk   1,400.   3,000.
      Never hinged   3,400.

Excellent counterfeit overprints exist.
Visit of the Italian Flying Armada en route
from Rome to Chicago; also for the payment of
the charges on postal matter sent from Iceland
to the US via the Italian seaplanes.

Plane over
Thingvalla
Lake — AP7

10a-20a, Plane over Thingvalla Lake. 25a-
50a, Plane and Aurora Borealis. 1k-2k, Map of
Iceland.

Perf. 12½x14
1934, Sept. 1   Engr.   Unwmk.
C15 AP7 10a blue   2.30 4.00
C16 AP7 20a emerald   5.00 9.00
   a.   Perf. 14   32.50 22.50
      Never hinged   110.00
C17 AP7 25a dark violet,
             perf. 14   13.00 20.00
      Revenue cancellation   50.00
   a.   Perf. 12½x14   32.50 40.00
      Never hinged   110.00
C18 AP7 50a red vio, perf. 14   4.00 9.00
      Revenue cancellation   25.00
C19 AP7 1k dark brown   22.50 40.00
C20 AP7 2k red orange   11.50 15.00
      Nos. C15-C20 (6)   58.30 97.00
      Set, never hinged   110.00

Catalogue values for unused
stamps in this section, from this
point to the end of the section, are
for Never Hinged items.

Thingvellir, Old
Site of the
Parliament
AP10

Isafjörthur
AP11

Eyjafjörthur
AP12

Mt.
Strandatindur
AP13

Mt. Thyrill
AP14

Aerial View of
Reykjavik
AP15

1947, Aug. 18   Perf. 14
C21 AP10 15a red orange   1.00 1.75
C22 AP11 30a gray black   1.00 1.75
C23 AP12 75a brown red   1.00 1.40
C24 AP13 1k indigo   1.00 1.40
C25 AP14 2k chocolate   1.75 2.75
C26 AP15 3k dark green   1.75 2.75
      Nos. C21-C26 (6)   7.50 11.80

Snaefellsjokull
AP16

Views: 2.50k,   Eiriksjokull.   3.30k,
Oraefajokull.

1952, May 2   Unwmk.   Perf. 13½x14
C27 AP16 1.80k slate blue   21.00 16.00
C28 AP16 2.50k green   37.50 1.40
C29 AP16 3.30k deep ultra   8.50 10.50
      Nos. C27-C29 (3)   67.00 27.90

See Nos. 302-304.

Vickers
Viscount
and Plane of
1919
AP17

4.05k, Skymaster and plane of 1919.

1959, Sept. 3   Engr.   Perf. 13½
C30 AP17 3.50k steel blue   1.00 .90
C31 AP17 4.05k green   .90 1.25

40th anniv. of air transportation in Iceland.

AIR POST OFFICIAL STAMPS

No. C3
Overprinted
In Red

1930, Jan. 1   Unwmk.   Perf. 12½x12
CO1 AP1 10a dp ultra & gray
             blue   22.50 140.00

Imperfs were privately printed.

OFFICIAL STAMPS

For Nos. O1-O12, see note on condition before No. 1.

    O1

    O2

O3

Perf. 14x13½
1873   Typo.   Wmk. 112
O1 O1 4s green   9,000. 9,000.
   a.   Imperf.   150.
O2 O1 8s red lilac   600. 750.
   a.   Imperf.   700.

Perf. 12½
O3 O1 4s green   100. 450.

The imperforate varieties lack gum.
No. O1 values are for stamps with perfs just
touching the design on at least one side.
Fake and favor cancellations are often found
on Nos. O1-O37. Values are considerably less
than those shown.

1876-95   Perf. 14x13½
O4 O2 3a yellow   45.00 70.00
O5 O2 5a brown   10.50 19.00
   a.   Imperf.   375.00
O6 O2 10a blue   77.50 17.50
   a.   10a ultramarine   500.00 85.00
O7 O2 16a carmine   30.00 60.00
O8 O2 20a yellow green   30.00 52.50
O9 O2 50a rose lilac ('95)   90.00 100.00
      Nos. O4-O9 (6)   283.00 319.00

1898-1902   Perf. 13
O10 O2 3a yellow   15.00 40.00
O11 O2 4a gray ('01)   40.00 50.00
O12 O2 10a ultra ('02)   72.50 125.00
      Nos. O10-O12 (3)   127.50 215.00

A 5a brown, perf. 13, Wmk. 112, exists. It
was not regularly issued.
See note after No. O30.
For overprints see Nos. O20-O30.

1902   Wmk. 113   Perf. 13
O13 O3 3a buff & black   4.75 3.25
O14 O3 4a dp grn & blk   4.75 2.75
O15 O3 5a org brn & blk   3.75 4.75
O16 O3 10a ultra & black   4.25 4.75
O17 O3 16a carmine & blk   3.75 17.00
O18 O3 20a green & blk   19.00 8.75
O19 O3 50a violet & blk   8.00 13.00
      Nos. O13-O19 (7)   48.25 54.25

Stamps of 1876-1901
Overprinted in Black

1902-03   Wmk. 112   Perf. 13
O20 O2 3a yellow   1.10 2.75
   a.   "I" before Gildi omitted   110.00
   b.   Inverted overprint   35.00 50.00
   c.   As "a," invtd.   250.00
   d.   Pair, one with invtd. ovpt.   110.00
   e.   '03-'03   300.00
   f.   02'-'03   300.00
O21 O2 4a gray   1.10 2.75
   a.   "I" before Gildi omitted   125.00
   b.   Inverted overprint   45.00 65.00
   e.   '03-'03   300.00
   f.   02'-'03   300.00
   g.   Pair, one without ovpt.   110.00
   h.   Pair, one with invtd. ovpt.   125.00
   i.   "L" only of "I GILDI" invert-
             ed   200.00
O22 O2 5a brown   1.00 2.75
O23 O2 10a ultramarine   1.00 2.75
   a.   "I" before Gildi omitted   35.00
   b.   Inverted overprint   45.00 65.00
   c.   '03-'03   300.00
   d.   02'-'03   300.00
   e.   "L" only of "I GILDI"   27.50
   f.   As "e," inverted   140.00
   g.   "IL" only of "I GILDI"   65.00
O24 O2 20a yel green   1.00 27.50
      Nos. O20-O24 (5)   5.20 38.50

Perf. 14x13½
O25 O2 3a yellow   350.00 1,500.
   a.   "02'-'03   700.00
   b.   '03-'03   700.00

O26	O2	5a brown	9.00	100.00
a.		Inverted overprint	82.50	
b.		'03-'03	250.00	
c.		02'-'03	250.00	
d.		"L" only of "I GILDI" inverted	—	
O27	O2	10a blue	475.00	900.00
a.		"I" before Gildi omitted	825.00	
b.		Inverted overprint	650.00	950.00
c.		'03-'03	900.00	
d.		02'-'03	900.00	
O28	O2	16a carmine	20.00	80.00
a.		"I" before Gildi omitted	250.00	
b.		Double overprint	125.00	
c.		Dbl. ovpt., one inverted	400.00	
d.		Inverted overprint	175.00	250.00
e.		'03-'03	375.00	
O29	O2	20a yel green	26.00	100.00
a.		Inverted overprint	125.00	175.00
b.		'03	325.00	
c.		02'-'03	325.00	
O30	O2	50a red lilac	7.00	70.00
a.		"I" before Gildi omitted	50.00	
b.		Inverted overprint	—	
		Nos. O25-O30 (6)	887.00	2,810.

Nos. O10-O12, O20-O24, O28 and O30 were reprinted in 1904. They have the watermark of 1902 (type 113) and are perf. 13. Value $70 each. Without overprint $90 each.

Christian IX, Frederik VIII — O4   Christian X — O5

Engraved Center

1907-08		**Wmk. 113**	**Perf. 13**	
O31	O4	3a yellow & gray	7.50	8.75
O32	O4	4a green & gray	4.00	9.25
O33	O4	5a brn org & gray	11.50	4.50
O34	O4	10a deep bl & gray	2.50	3.50
O35	O4	15a lt blue & gray	5.00	9.25
O36	O4	16a carmine & gray	5.00	32.50
O37	O4	20a yel grn & gray	15.00	6.00
O38	O4	50a violet & gray	8.00	11.50
		Nos. O31-O38 (8)	58.50	85.25
1918		**Wmk. 114**	**Perf. 14x14½**	
O39	O4	15a lt bl & gray	15.00	40.00
1920-30			**Typo.**	
O40	O5	3a yellow & gray	5.00	4.00
O41	O5	4a dp grn & gray	1.25	3.75
O42	O5	5a orange & gray	1.25	1.25
O43	O5	10a dk bl & gray	16.50	1.50
O44	O5	15a lt blue & gray	.75	1.25
O45	O5	20a yel grn & gray	50.00	4.50
O46	O5	50a violet & gray	45.00	2.25
O47	O5	1k car & gray	45.00	3.00
O48	O5	2k bl & blk ('30)	8.00	21.00
O49	O5	5k brn & blk ('30)	40.00	57.50
		Nos. O40-O49 (10)	212.75	100.00

See No. O68.

Nos. 97 and 98 Overprinted

1922, May		**Wmk. 113**	**Perf. 13**	
O50	A7	2k rose, larger letters, no period	32.50	65.00
a.		Smaller letters, with period	100.00	70.00
O51	A7	5k brown	250.00	290.00

No. 115 Surcharged

1923		**Wmk. 114**	**Perf. 14x14½**	
O52	A8	20a on 10a red	32.50	2.50

Parliament Millenary Issue

#152-166 Overprinted in Red or Blue

1930, Jan. 1		**Unwmk.**	**Perf. 12½x12**	
O53	A15	3a (R)	16.00	47.50
O54	A15	5a (R)	16.00	47.50
O55	A15	7a (R)	16.00	47.50
O56	A15	10a (Bl)	16.00	47.50
O57	A15	15a (R)	16.00	47.50
O58	A15	20a (Bl)	16.00	47.50
O59	A15	25a (Bl)	16.00	47.50
O60	A15	30a (R)	16.00	47.50
O61	A15	35a (R)	16.00	47.50
O62	A15	40a (Bl)	16.00	47.50
O63	A15	50a (Bl)	150.00	400.00
O64	A15	1k (R)	150.00	400.00
O65	A15	2k (R)	200.00	425.00
O66	A15	5k (Bl)	200.00	425.00
O67	A15	10k (Bl)	150.00	400.00
		Nos. O53-O67 (15)	1,010.	2,525.

Type of 1920 Issue Redrawn

1931		**Wmk. 114**	**Typo.**	
O68	O5	20a yel grn & gray	40.00	3.50

For differences in redrawing see note after No. 187.

No. 82 Overprinted in Black

Overprint 15mm long

1936, Dec. 7		**Wmk. 113**	**Perf. 13**	
O69	A5	50a gray & vio	25.00	30.00

Same Overprint on Nos. 180 and 115

Perf. 14x14½
Wmk. 114

O70	A8	7a yellow green	3.25	32.50
O71	A8	10a red	12.50	2.25
		Nos. O69-O71 (3)	40.75	64.75

IFNI

'if-nē

LOCATION — An enclave in southern Morocco on the Atlantic coast
GOVT. — Spanish possession
AREA — 580 sq. mi.
POP. — 51,517 (est. 1964)
CAPITAL — Sidi Ifni

Ifni was ceded to Spain by Morocco in 1860, but the Spanish did not occupy it until 1934. Sidi Ifni was also the administrative capital for Spanish West Africa. Spain turned Ifni back to Morocco June 30, 1969.

100 Centimos = 1 Peseta

Catalogue values for unused stamps in this country are for Never Hinged items, beginning with Scott 28 in the regular postage section, Scott B1 in the semipostal section, and Scott C38 in the airpost section.

Stamps of Spain, 1936-40, Overprinted in Red or Blue

1941-42		**Unwmk.**	**Imperf.**	
1	A159	1c green	8.50	6.00
		Perf. 10 to 11		
2	A160	2c org brn (Bl)	8.50	6.00
3	A161	5c gray brown	1.25	1.10
5	A161	10c dk car (Bl)	5.00	2.25
a.		Red overprint	17.50	8.25
6	A161	15c lt green	1.25	1.10
7	A166	20c brt violet	1.25	1.10
8	A166	25c deep claret	1.25	1.10
9	A166	30c blue	1.25	1.10
10	A166	40c Prus green	1.75	1.10
11	A166	50c indigo	9.25	2.00
12	A166	70c blue	9.25	5.00
13	A166	1p gray black	9.25	5.00
14	A166	2p dull brown	140.00	120.00

15	A166	4p dl rose (Bl)	600.00	210.00
16	A166	10p light brn	1,450.	600.00
		Nos. 1-16 (15)	2,247.	962.85
		Set, never hinged	3,000.	

Counterfeit overprints exist.

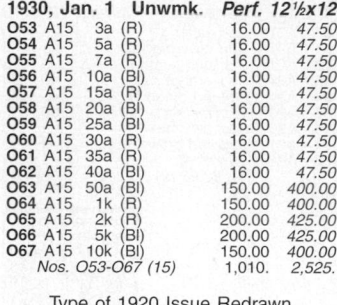

Nomads — A1   Alcazaba Fortress — A3

Designs: 2c, 20c, 45c, 3p, Marksman.

1943		**Litho.**	**Perf. 12½**	
17	A1	1c brn & lil rose	.30	.25
18	A1	2c yel grn & sl lil	.30	.25
19	A3	5c magenta & vio	.30	.25
20	A1	15c sl grn & grn	.30	.25
21	A1	20c vio & red brn	.30	.25
22	A1	40c rose vio & vio	.35	.30
23	A1	45c brn vio & red	.40	.35
24	A3	75c indigo & bl	.40	.35
25	A1	1p red & brown	2.00	1.75
26	A1	3p bl vio & sl grn	2.50	2.25
27	A3	10p blk brn & blk	28.50	26.00
		Nos. 17-27,E1 (12)	37.90	33.85
		Set, never hinged	65.00	

Nos. 17-27 exist imperforate. Value, set $125.

Catalogue values for unused stamps in this section, from this point to the end of the section, are for Never Hinged items.

1947, Feb.			**Perf. 10**	
28	A1	50c Nomad family	13.50	.75

Stamps of Spain, 1939-48, Overprinted in Carmine

1948, Aug. 2		**Perf. 9½x10½, 11, 13**		
29	A161	5c gray brown (#664)	5.50	.75
30	A194	15c gray green	6.25	.75
31	A167	90c dark green (#714a)	24.00	4.25
32	A166	1p gray black	.70	.30
		Nos. 29-32 (4)	36.45	6.05

See Nos. 36 and 45.

Spain Nos. 769 and 770 Overprinted in Violet Blue or Carmine

1949, Oct. 9			**Perf. 12½x13**	
33	A202	50c red brown (VB)	3.00	1.00
34	A202	75c violet blue (C)	3.00	1.00
		Nos. 33-34,C40 (3)	9.50	3.25

75th anniv. of the UPU.

Stamps of Spain, 1938-48, Overprinted in Blue or Carmine like Nos. 29-32

Perf. 13, 13½, 12½x13, 9½x10½

1949			**Unwmk.**	
35	A160	2c orange brn (Bl)	.30	.25
36	A161	5c gray brown (#664a)	.30	.25
37	A161	10c dk carmine (Bl)	.30	.25
38	A161	15c dk green (II)	.30	.25
39	A166	25c brown violet	.30	.25
40	A166	30c blue	.40	.25
41	A195	40c red brown	.40	.25
42	A195	45c car rose (Bl)	.75	.30
43	A195	50c indigo	.80	.30
44	A195	75c dk vio bl	1.00	.45
45	A167	90c dark green (#714)	1.00	.60
47	A167	1.35p purple	8.25	4.50

48	A166	2p dl brn	6.50	2.75
49	A166	4p dl rose (Bl)	22.00	8.00
50	A166	10p lt brn	52.50	24.00
		Nos. 35-50 (15)	95.10	42.65

Gen. Francisco Franco and Desert Scene — A4

Perf. 12½x13

1951, July 18		**Photo.**	**Unwmk.**	
51	A4	50c dp org	.45	.25
52	A4	1p chocolate	3.00	1.25
53	A4	5p bl grn	32.50	12.00
		Nos. 51-53 (3)	35.95	13.50

Visit of Gen. Francisco Franco, 1950.

View of Granada and Globe — A5

1952, Dec. 10			**Perf. 13x12½**	
54	A5	5c red org	.35	.20
55	A5	35c dk ol grn	.40	.25
56	A5	60c brown	.40	.30
		Nos. 54-56 (3)	1.15	.75

400th anniversary of the death of Leo Africanus (c. 1485-c. 1554), Arab traveler and scholar, author of "Descrittione dell' Africa."

Musician — A6

Design: 60c, Two musicians.

1953, June 1			**Perf. 12½x13**	
57	A6	15c olive gray	.30	.20
58	A6	60c brown	.35	.30
		Nos. 57-58,B13-B14 (4)	1.30	1.00

Issued to promote child welfare.

Fish and Branched Sponges A7

15c, Fish and jellyfish.

1953, Nov. 23				
59	A7	15c dark green	.30	.20
60	A7	60c brown	.45	.30
		Nos. 59-60,B15-B16 (4)	1.40	1.05

Colonial Stamp Day, Nov. 23, 1953.

Sea Gull — A8

Cactus — A9

25c, 60c, 2p, 5p, Salsola vermiculata.

1954, Apr. 22   *Perf. 12½x13, 13x12½*

61	A8	5c red org	.25	.20
62	A9	10c olive	.25	.20
63	A9	25c brn car	.25	.20
64	A8	35c olive gray	.25	.20
65	A9	40c rose lilac	.25	.20
66	A9	60c dk brn	.25	.25
67	A8	1p brown	7.25	.70
68	A9	1.25p car rose	.30	.25
69	A9	2p darp blue	.35	.25
70	A9	4.50p olive grn	.45	.40
71	A9	5p olive blk	37.50	10.50
		Nos. 61-71 (11)	47.35	13.35

Mother and Child
A10   A11

1954, June 1   *Perf. 13x12½*

72	A10	15c dk gray grn	.30	.20
73	A11	60c dk brn	.35	.30
		Nos. 72-73,B17-B18 (4)	1.30	1.00

Lobster
A12

Design: 60c, Hammerhead shark.

1954, Nov. 23   *Perf. 12½x13*

74	A12	15c olive green	.35	.25
75	A12	60c rose brown	.45	.35
		Nos. 74-75,B19-B20 (4)	1.45	1.15

Issued to publicize Colonial Stamp Day.

Farmer
Plowing
and Statue
of "Justice"
A13

1955, June 1   Photo.   Unwmk.

76	A13	50c gray olive	.35	.30
		Nos. 76,B21-B22 (3)	1.00	.80

Squirrel
A14

1955, Nov. 23

77	A14	70c yellow green	.35	.30
		Nos. 77,B23-B24 (3)	1.00	.85

Issued to publicize Colonial Stamp Day.

Senecio
Antheuphorbium
A15

Design: 50c, Limoniastrum Ifniensis.

1956, June 1   *Perf. 13x12½*

78	A15	20c bluish green	.35	.20
79	A15	50c brown	.40	.35
		Nos. 78-79,B25-B26 (4)	1.40	1.05

Arms of
Sidi Ifni
and
Shepherd
A16

1956, Nov. 23   *Perf. 12½x13*

80	A16	70c light green		.35 .25

Issued for Colonial Stamp Day.

Rock Doves — A17

1957, June 1   Photo.   *Perf. 13x12½*

81	A17	70c yel grn & brn	.40	.35
		Nos. 81,B29-B30 (3)	1.05	.90

See No. 86.

Jackal
A18

Design: 70c, Jackal's head, vert.

Perf. 12½x13, 13x12½

1957, Nov. 23

82	A18	20c emerald & lt grn	.35	.25
83	A18	70c green & brown	.45	.35
		Nos. 82-83,B31-B32 (4)	1.45	1.15

Issued for the Day of the Stamp, 1957.
See Nos. 87, B41.

Basketball   Red-legged
Players   Partridges
A19   A20

Design: 70c, Cyclists.

1958, June 1   *Perf. 13x12½*

84	A19	20c bluish green	.30	.25
85	A19	70c olive green	.45	.35
		Nos. 84-85,B36-B37 (4)	1.40	1.10

Types of 1957 inscribed "Pro-Infancia
1959"

Designs: 20c, Goat. 70c, Ewe and lamb.

1959, June 1   *Perf. 13x12½, 12½x13*

86	A17	20c dull green	.30	.25
87	A18	70c yellow green	.40	.35
		Nos. 86-87,B41-B42 (4)	1.35	1.10

Issued to promote child welfare.

1960, June 10   *Perf. 13x12½*

88	A20	35c shown	.30	.25
89	A20	80c Camels	.40	.35
		Nos. 88-89,B46-B47 (4)	1.35	1.10

White
Stork
A21

Birds: 50c, 1.50p, 5p, European gold-
finches. 75c, 2p, 10p, Skylarks, vert.

1960   Unwmk.   *Perf. 12½x13*

90	A21	25c violet	.25	.25
91	A21	50c olive black	.25	.25
92	A21	75c dull purple	.30	.25
93	A21	1p orange ver	.40	.25
94	A21	1.50p brt grnsh bl	.45	.30
95	A21	2p red lilac	.50	.35
96	A21	3p dark blue	.85	.40
97	A21	5p red brown	1.40	.65
98	A21	10p olive	5.25	1.75
		Nos. 90-98 (9)	9.65	4.45

Map of Ifni — A22

General
Franco
A23

Design: 70c, Government palace.

Perf. 13x12½, 12½x13

1961, Oct. 1   Photo.

99	A22	25c gray violet	.25	.20
100	A23	50c olive brown	.30	.20
101	A23	70c brt green	.35	.30
102	A23	1p red orange	.40	.35
		Nos. 99-102 (4)	1.30	1.05

25th anniv. of the nomination of Gen. Francisco Franco as Head of State.

Admiral Jofre   Mailman — A25
Tenoria — A24

Design: 50c, Cesareo Fernandez-Duro
(1830-1908), writer.

1962, July 10   *Perf. 13x12½*

103	A24	25c dull violet	.25	.20
104	A24	50c deep blue grn	.30	.20
105	A24	1p orange brown	.35	.35
		Nos. 103-105 (3)	.90	.75

1962, Nov. 23   Unwmk.

Stamp Day: 35c, Hands, letter and winged
wheel.

106	A25	15c dark blue	.25	.20
107	A25	35c lilac rose	.35	.30
108	A25	1p rose brown	.40	.35
		Nos. 106-108 (3)	1.00	.85

Golden Tower,   Butterflies
Seville   A27
A26

1963, Jan. 29   Photo.

109	A26	50c green	.30	.20
110	A26	1p brown orange	.40	.35

Issued for flood relief in Seville.

1963, July 6   *Perf. 13x12½*

Design: 50c, Butterfly and flower.

111	A27	25c deep blue	.30	.25
112	A27	50c light green	.35	.30
113	A27	1p carmine rose	.45	.40
		Nos. 111-113 (3)	1.10	.95

Issued for child welfare.

Child with
Flowers
and Arms
A28

1963, July 12   *Perf. 12½x13*

114	A28	50c gray olive	.30	.20
115	A28	1p reddish brown	.40	.35

Issued for Barcelona flood relief.

Beetle   Mountain
(Steraspis   Gazelle
Speciosa)   A30
A29

Stamp Day: 50c, Grasshopper.

1964, Mar. 6   *Perf. 13x12½*

116	A29	25c violet blue	.25	.25
117	A29	50c olive green	.35	.30
118	A29	1p red brown	.45	.30
		Nos. 116-118 (3)	1.05	.85

1964, June 1   Photo.

Design: 50c, Head of roebuck.

119	A30	25c brt violet	.25	.25
120	A30	50c slate blk	.35	.25
121	A30	1p orange red	.40	.35
		Nos. 119-121 (3)	1.00	.85

Issued for child welfare.

Bicycle
Race
A31

Stamp Day: 1p, Motorcycle race.

1964, Nov. 23   *Perf. 12½x13*

122	A31	50c brown	.30	.25
123	A31	1p orange ver	.35	.30
124	A31	1.50p Prus green	.40	.35
		Nos. 122-124 (3)	1.05	.90

Man — A32   Two Boys in
                  School — A33

Cable
Cars, Sidi
Ifni — A34

Perf. 13x12½, 12½x13

1965, Mar. 1 Photo. Unwmk.
125 A32 50c dark green .30 .20
126 A33 1p orange ver .35 .30
127 A34 1.50p dark blue .40 .35
Nos. 125-127 (3) 1.05 .85
25 years of peace after the Spanish Civil War.

Eugaster Fernandezi A35

Insect: 1p, Halter halteratus.

1965, June 1 Photo. Unwmk.
128 A35 50c purple .30 .20
129 A35 1p rose red .35 .30
130 A35 1.50p violet blue .40 .35
Nos. 128-130 (3) 1.05 .85
Issued for child welfare.

Eagle — A36

Arms of Sidi Ifni — A37

Perf. 13x12½, 12½x13

1965, Nov. 23 Photo.
131 A36 50c dk red brown .25 .25
132 A37 1p orange ver .35 .30
133 A36 1.50p grnsh blue .40 .35
Nos. 131-133 (3) 1.00 .90
Issued for Stamp Day 1965.

Jetliner over Sidi Ifni — A38

Design: 2.50p, Two 1934 biplanes, horiz.

Perf. 13x12½, 12½x13

1966, June 1 Photo. Unwmk.
134 A38 1p orange brn .30 .30
135 A38 1.50p brt blue .50 .40
136 A38 2.50p dull violet 2.25 2.00
Nos. 134-136 (3) 3.05 2.70
Issued for child welfare.

Syntomis Alicia — A39

1966, Nov. 23 Photo. Perf. 13
40c, 4p, Danais chrysippus (butterfly).
137 A39 10c green & red .40 .25
138 A39 40c dk brn & gldn brn .45 .30
139 A39 1.50p violet & yel .55 .35
140 A39 4p dk pur & brt bl .65 .40
Nos. 137-140 (4) 2.05 1.30
Issued for Stamp Day, 1966.

Coconut Palms — A40

Designs: 40c, 4p, Cactus.

1967, June 1 Photo. Perf. 13
141 A40 10c dp grn & brn .25 .20
142 A40 40c Prus grn & ocher .25 .20
143 A40 1.50p bl grn & sepia .35 .30
144 A40 4p sepia & ocher .45 .35
Nos. 141-144 (4) 1.30 1.05
Issued for child welfare.

Sidi Ifni Harbor A41

1967, Sept. 28 Photo. Perf. 12½x13
145 A41 1.50p grn & red brn .35 .20
Modernization of harbor installations.

Needlefish (Skipper) — A42

Fish: 1.50p, John Dory, vert. 3.50p, Gurnard (Trigla lucerna).

1967, Nov. 23 Photo. Perf. 13
146 A42 1p blue & green .30 .25
147 A42 1.50p vio blk & yel .35 .25
148 A42 3.50p brt bl & scar .45 .35
Nos. 146-148 (3) 1.10 .85
Issued for Stamp Day 1967.

Zodiac Issue

Pisces — A43

Signs of the Zodiac: 1.50p, Capricorn. 2.50p, Sagittarius.

1968, Apr. 25 Photo. Perf. 13
149 A43 1p brt mag, lt yel .30 .25
150 A43 1.50p brown, pink .35 .30
151 A43 2.50p dk vio, yel .45 .35
Nos. 149-151 (3) 1.10 .90
Issued for child welfare.

Mailing a Letter A44

Designs: 1.50p, Carrier pigeon carrying letter. 2.50p, Stamp under magnifying glass.

1968, Nov. 23 Photo. Perf. 12½x13
152 A44 1p org yel & sl grn .25 .20
153 A44 1.50p brt bl & vio blk .35 .30
154 A44 2.50p emer & vio blk .45 .35
Nos. 152-154 (3) 1.05 .85
Issued for Stamp Day.

SEMI-POSTAL STAMPS

Catalogue values for unused stamps in this section are for Never Hinged items.

Gen. Francisco Franco — SP1

Fennec — SP2

Perf. 13x12½

1950, Oct. 19 Unwmk.
B1 SP1 50c + 10c sepia .70 .55
B2 SP1 1p + 25c blue 18.00 7.00
B3 SP1 6.50p + 1.65c dl grn 7.50 3.25
Nos. B1-B3 (3) 26.20 10.80
The surtax was for child welfare.

1951, Nov. 30
B4 SP2 5c + 5c brown .30 .25
B5 SP2 10c + 5c red org .35 .25
B6 SP2 60c + 15c olive brn .55 .30
Nos. B4-B6 (3) 1.20 .80
Colonial Stamp Day, Nov. 23, 1951.

Mother and Child — SP3

Common Shag — SP4

1952, June 1
B7 SP3 5c + 5c brn .30 .20
B8 SP3 50c + 10c brn blk .40 .30
B9 SP3 2p + 30c dp bl 2.25 .85
Nos. B7-B9 (3) 2.95 1.35
The surtax was for child welfare.

1952, Nov. 23
B10 SP4 5c + 5c brn .30 .25
B11 SP4 10c + 5c brn car .30 .25
B12 SP4 60c + 15c dk grn .50 .35
Nos. B10-B12 (3) 1.10 .85
Colonial Stamp Day, Nov. 23, 1952.

Musician Type of Regular Issue

1953, June 1 Perf. 12½x13
B13 A6 5c + 5c as No. 57 .30 .20
B14 A6 10c + 5c as No. 58 .35 .30
The surtax was for child welfare.

Fish Type of Regular Issue

1953, Nov. 23
B15 A7 5c + 5c as No. 59 .30 .25
B16 A7 10c + 5c as No. 60 .35 .30
Colonial Stamp Day, Nov. 23, 1953.

Type of Regular Issue

1954, June 1 Perf. 13x12½
B17 A10 5c + 5c org .30 .20
B18 A11 10c + 5c rose vio .35 .30
The surtax was for child welfare.

Type of Regular Issue

1954, Nov. 23 Perf. 12½x13
B19 A12 5c + 5c as No. 74 .30 .25
B20 A12 10c + 5c as No. 75 .35 .30

"Dama de Elche" Protecting Caravan SP5

1955, June 1 Photo. Unwmk.
B21 A13 10c + 5c rose lilac .30 .20
B22 SP5 25c + 10c violet .35 .30
The surtax was to help Ifni people.

Squirrel Type of Regular Issue

Design: 15c+5c, Squirrel holding nut.

1955, Nov. 23
B23 A14 5c + 5c red brown .30 .25
B24 A14 15c + 5c olive bister .35 .30

Type of Regular Issue

1956, June 1 Perf. 13x12½
B25 A15 5c + 5c as No. 78 .30 .20
B26 A15 15c + 5c as No. 79 .35 .30
The tax was for child welfare.

Dorcas Gazelles and Arms of Spain — SP6

Design: 15c+5c, Arms of Sidi Ifni, boat and woman with drum.

1956, Nov. 23
B27 SP6 5c + 5c dark brown .30 .25
B28 SP6 15c + 5c golden brn .35 .30
Issued for Colonial Stamp Day.

Dove Type of Regular Issue

1957, June 1 Photo. Perf. 13x12½
B29 A17 5c + 5c as No. 81 .30 .25
B30 A17 15c + 5c Stock doves .35 .30
The surtax was for child welfare.

Type of Regular Issue

Perf. 12½x13, 13x12½
1957, Nov. 23 Photo. Unwmk.
B31 A18 10c + 5c as No. 82 .30 .25
B32 A18 15c + 5c as No. 83 .35 .30

Swallows and Arms of Valencia and Sidi Ifni — SP7

1958, Mar. 6 Perf. 12½x13
B33 SP7 10c + 5c org brn .30 .20
B34 SP7 15c + 10c bister .35 .25
B35 SP7 50c + 10c brn olive .40 .30
Nos. B33-B35 (3) 1.05 .75
The surtax was to aid the victims of the Valencia flood, Oct. 1957.

Sport Type of Regular Issue, 1958

1958, June 1 Photo. Perf. 13x12½
B36 A19 10c + 5c as No. 84 .30 .20
B37 A19 15c + 5c as No. 85 .35 .30
The surtax was for child welfare.

Guitarfish — SP8

Sailboats SP9

Stamp Day: 10c+5c, Spotted dogfish.

Perf. 13x12½, 12½x13

1958, Nov. 23
B38 SP9 10c + 5c brn red   .30 .20
B39 SP8 25c + 10c dull vio   .35 .25
B40 SP9 50c + 10c olive   .40 .30
Nos. B38-B40 (3)   1.05 .75

Donkey and Man — SP10   Soccer — SP11

Type of 1957 and SP10

Design: 10c+5c, Ewe and lamb.

Perf. 12½x13, 13x12½

1959, June 1   Photo.   Unwmk.
B41 A18 10c + 5c lt red brn   .30 .20
B42 SP10 15c + 5c golden brn   .35 .30

The surtax was for child welfare.

1959, Nov. 23   *Perf. 13x12½*

Designs: 20c+5c, Soccer players. 50c+20c, Javelin thrower.

B43 SP11 10c + 5c fawn   .30 .25
B44 SP11 20c + 5c slate green   .35 .30
B45 SP11 50c + 20c olive gray   .40 .35
Nos. B43-B45 (3)   1.05 .90

Issued for the day of the Stamp, 1959. See Nos. B52-B54.

Type of Regular Issue, 1960

1960, June 10   *Perf. 13x12½*
B46 A20 10c + 5c as No. 89   .30 .20
B47 A20 15c + 5c Wild boars   .35 .30

The surtax was for child welfare.

Santa Maria del Mar — SP12

Stamp Day: 20c+5c, 50c+20c, New school building, horiz.

Perf. 13x12½, 12½x13

1960, Dec. 29   Photo.
B48 SP12 10c + 5c org brn   .30 .20
B49 SP12 20c + 5c dk sl grn   .30 .20
B50 SP12 30c + 10c red brn   .35 .30
B51 SP12 50c + 20c sepia   .35 .30
Nos. B48-B51 (4)   1.30 1.00

Type of 1959 inscribed: "Pro-Infancia 1961"

Designs: 10c+5c, 80c+20c, Pole vaulting, horiz. 25c+10c, Soccer player.

Perf. 12½x13, 13x12½

1961, June 21   Unwmk.
B52 SP11 10c + 5c rose brn   .30 .20
B53 SP11 25c + 10c gray vio   .35 .25
B54 SP11 80c + 20c dk green   .40 .30
Nos. B52-B54 (3)   1.05 .75

The surtax was for child welfare.

Camel Rider and Truck SP13

Stamp Day: 25c+10c, 1p+10c, Ship in Sidi Ifni harbor.

1961, Nov. 23   *Perf. 12½x13*
B55 SP13 10c + 5c rose brn   .30 .20
B56 SP13 25c + 10c dk pur   .30 .20
B57 SP13 30c + 10c dk red brn   .35 .30
B58 SP13 1p + 10c red org   .35 .35
Nos. B55-B58 (4)   1.30 1.05

AIR POST STAMPS

Stamps formerly listed as Nos. C1-C29 were privately overprinted. These include 1936 stamps of Spain overprinted "VIA AEREA" and plane, and 1939 stamps of Spain, type AP30, overprinted "IFNI" or "Territorio de Ifni."

Oasis AP1   The Sanctuary AP2

1943   Unwmk.   Litho.   *Perf. 12½*
C30 AP2 5c cer & vio brn   .35 .25
C31 AP1 25c yel grn & ol grn   .35 .25
C32 AP2 50c ind & turq grn   .45 .35
C33 AP1 1p pur & grnsh bl   .50 .35
C34 AP2 1.40p gray grn & bl   .55 .35
C35 AP1 2p mag & org brn   1.50 1.25
C36 AP2 5p brn & pur   2.25 1.75
C37 AP1 6p brt bl & gray grn   35.00 30.00
Nos. C30-C37 (8)   40.95 34.55
Set, never hinged   70.00

Nos. C30-C37 exist imperforate. Value, set $115.

Catalogue values for unused stamps in this section, from this point to the end of the section, are for Never Hinged items.

Type of Spain, 1939-47, Overprinted in Carmine

1947, Nov. 29
C38 AP30 5c dull yellow   2.75 .85
C39 AP30 10c dk bl green   2.75 .85

Spain No. C126 Overprinted in Carmine like Nos. 33-34

1949, Oct. 9   *Perf. 12½x13*
C40 A202 4p dk olive grn   3.50 1.25

75th anniv. of the UPU.

Spain, Nos. C110 and C112 to C116, Overprinted in Blue or Carmine like Nos. 29-32

1949   *Perf. 10*
C41 AP30 25c redsh brn (Bl)   .65 .20
C42 AP30 50c brown   .75 .20
C43 AP30 1p chalky blue   .85 .25
C44 AP30 2p lt gray grn   5.00 .85
C45 AP30 4p gray blue   13.00 4.50
C46 AP30 10p brt purple   17.50 8.75
Nos. C41-C46 (6)   37.75 14.75

Lope Sancho de Valenzuela and Sheik — AP3   Woman Holding Dove — AP4

1950, Nov. 23   Photo.   *Perf. 13x12½*
C47 AP3 5p brown black   3.25 .85

Stamp Day, Nov. 23, 1950.

1951, Apr. 22   Engr.   *Perf. 10*
C48 AP4 5p red   24.00 8.25

500th anniversary of the birth of Queen Isabella I of Spain.
The majority of this issue are poorly centered. Values are for very fine examples.

Ferdinand the Catholic — AP5

1952, July 18   Photo.   *Perf. 13x12½*

C49 AP5 5p brown   32.00 8.25

500th anniv. of the birth of Ferdinand the Catholic of Spain.

Plane and Mountain Gazelle — AP6

1953, Apr. 1
C50 AP6 60c light grn   .25 .20
C51 AP6 1.20p brn car   .35 .25
C52 AP6 1.60p lt brown   .45 .25
C53 AP6 2p deep blue   2.10 .30
C54 AP6 4p grnsh blk   1.25 .30
C55 AP6 10p brt red vio   7.25 1.60
Nos. C50-C55 (6)   11.65 2.90

SPECIAL DELIVERY STAMPS

Type A3 inscribed "URGENTE"

1943   *Perf. 12½*
E1 A3 25c slate green & car   2.25 1.60

Spain, No. E20, Overprinted in Blue like Nos. 29-32

1949   Unwmk.   *Perf. 10*
E2 SD10 25c carmine   .35 .25

INDIA

ˈin-dē-ə

LOCATION — Southern, central Asia
GOVT. — Republic
AREA — 1,266,732 sq. mi.
POP. — 1,000,848,550 (1999 est.)
CAPITAL — New Delhi

On August 15, 1947, India was divided into two self-governing dominions: Pakistan and India. India became a republic in 1950.

The stamps of pre-partition India fall into three groups:

1) Issues inscribed simply "East India" (to 1881) and "India" (from 1882), for use mainly in British India proper, but available and valid throughout the country;

2) Issues as above and overprinted with one of the names of the six "Convention" states (Chamba, Faridkot, Gwalior, Jind, Nabha and Patiala) which had a postal convention with British India, for use in these states.

3) Issues of the feudatory states, over which the British India government exercised little internal control, valid only within the states issuing them.

12 Pies = 1 Anna
16 Annas = 1 Rupee
100 Naye Paise = 1 Rupee (1957)
100 Paise = 1 Rupee (1964)

Catalogue values for unused stamps in this country are for Never Hinged items, beginning with Scott 168 in the regular postage section, Scott C7 in the air post section, Scott M44 in the military section, Scott O113 in the official section, Scott RA1 in the postal tax section, Scott 51 in Hyderabad regular issues, Scott O54 in Hyderabad officials, Scott 49 in Jaipur regular issues, Scott O30 in Jaipur officials, Scott 39 in Soruth regular issues and Scott O19 in Soruth official

All of the values are for Never Hinged for all of the items in the sections for the International Commission in Indo-China, Jasdan, Rajasthan, and Travancore-Cochin.

Watermarks

Wmk. 36 — Crown and INDIA

Wmk. 37 — Coat of Arms in Sheet. (Reduced illustration. Watermark covers a large section of the sheet.)

Wmk. 38 — Elephant's Head   Wmk. 39 — Star

Wmk. 40

Wmk. 41 — Small Umbrella

Wmk. 42 — Urdu Characters

Wmk. 43 — Shell

Wmk. 196 — Multiple Stars

Wmk. 211 — Urdu Characters

Wmk. 294 — Letters and Ornaments in Sheet (size reduced)

Wmk. 324 — Asoka Pillar, Multiple

Wmk. 360 — Star and GOVT INDIA

SCINDE DISTRICT POST

A1

1852, July 1   Embossed   Imperf.

A1	A1	½a white	6,000.	1,500.
A2	A1	½a blue	15,000.	6,500.
A3	A1	½a red		14,000.

Obsolete October, 1854.
Nos. A1-A3 were issued without gum. No. A3 is embossed on red wafer. It is usually found with cracks and these examples are worth somewhat less than the values given, depending on the degree of cracking.

GENERAL ISSUES

Unused stamps of India are valued with original gum as defined in the catalogue introduction except for Nos. 1-7 which are valued without gum.

East India Company

A1

A2

A3

A4

A5

Queen Victoria
Litho.; Typo. (#5)

1854   Wmk. 37   Imperf.

1	A1	½a red	1,200.	
2	A2	½a blue	85.00	30.00
a.		½a deep blue	95.00	35.00
b.		Printed on both sides		11,000.
4	A3	1a red	100.00	47.50
a.		1a scarlet	175.00	52.50
5	A4	2a green	120.00	32.50
a.		Half used as 1a on cover		200,000.
6	A5	4a red & blue	4,500.	500.00
a.		4a deep red & blue	4,500.	575.00
		Cut to shape		42.50
c.		Head inverted		100,000.
		As "c," cut to shape		37,500.
e.		Double impression of head		6,250.

No. 1 was not placed in use.
Nos. 2, 4, 5 and 6 are known with unofficial perforation.
There are 3 dies of No. 2, and 2 dies of No. 4, showing slight differences.
There are 4 dies of the head and 2 dies of the frame of No. 6.
No. 5 is known with the watermark having the words "One Anna" in place of the lions and shield, with Urdu and Bengali characters. Values: $625 unused; $450 used.
Beware of forgeries.

A6

1855

| 7 | A6 | 1a red | 1,300. | 175.00 |

No. 7 was printed from a lithographic transfer made from the original die retouched. The lines of the bust at the lower left are nearly straight and meet in a point.
Beware of forgeries.

Nos. 9-35 are normally found with very heavy cancelations, and values are for stamps so canceled. Lightly canceled stamps are seldom seen. The same holds true for Nos. O1-O26.

Diadem includes Maltese Crosses — A7

1855-64   Unwmk.   Typo.   Perf. 14
Blue Glazed Paper

9	A7	4a black	725.00	22.50
a.		Imperf., pair	5,500.	5,500.
b.		Half used as 2a on cover		12,000.
10	A7	8a rose	650.00	19.00
a.		Imperf., pair	3,000.	
b.		Half used as 4a on cover		80,000.

See #11-18, 20, 22-25, 31. For overprints see #O1-O5, O7-O9, O16-O19, O22-O24.

1855-64   White Paper

11	A7	½a blue	95.00	4.50
a.		Imperf., pair	475.00	1,750.
12	A7	1a brown	80.00	3.00
a.		Imperf., pair	800.00	2,200.
b.		Vert. pair, imperf between		
c.		Half used as ½a on cover		85,000.
13	A7	2a dull rose	750.00	37.50
a.		Imperf., pair	2,500.	2,000.
14	A7	2a yellow green	725.00	825.00
a.		Imperf., pair	2,000.	
15	A7	2a buff	450.00	37.50
a.		2a orange	700.00	45.00
b.		Imperf., pair	1,750.	3,250.

16	A7	4a black	450.00	10.00
a.		Imperf., pair	2,750.	2,750.
b.		Diagonal half used as 2a on cover		35,000.
17	A7	4a green ('64)	1,750.	45.00
18	A7	8a rose	600.00	27.50
a.		Half used as 4a on cover		80,000.

No. 14 was not regularly issued. See note after No. 25.

Many stamps of types A7-A90 are overprinted "Service" or "On H. M. S." For these, see listings of Official stamps.

Crown Colony

Queen Victoria — A8

1860-64   Unwmk.   Perf. 14

19	A8	8p lilac	55.00	6.00
a.		Diagonal half used as 4p on cover		85,000.
b.		Imperf., pair	4,000.	5,000.
19C	A8	8p lilac, bluish	275.00	100.00

See #21. For overprint see #O6 and footnote after #O4.

1865-67   Wmk. 38

20	A7	½a blue	19.00	1.25
a.		Imperf., pair		1,600.
21	A8	8p lilac	10.00	12.00
22	A7	1a brown	9.00	1.50
23	A7	2a brownish orange	27.50	2.00
a.		2a yellow	175.00	7.00
b.		Imperf., pair		4,250.
24	A7	4a green	575.00	27.50
25	A7	8a rose	2,000.	85.00

No. 21 was variously surcharged locally, "NINE" or "NINE PIE," to indicate that it was being sold for 9 pies (the soldier's letter rate had been raised from 8 to 9 pies). These surcharges were made without government authorization.
Stamps of types A7 and A9 overprinted with crown and surcharged with new values were for use in Straits Settlements.

A9

A10

Diadem: Rows of pearls & diamonds — A11

FOUR ANNAS
Type I — Slanting line at corner of mouth extends downward only. Shading about mouth and chin. Pointed chin.
Type II — Line at corner of mouth extends both up and down. Upper lip and chin are defined by a colored line. Rounded chin.

1866-68

26	A9	4a green, type I	95.00	4.25
26B	A9	4a blue grn, type II	30.00	3.50
27	A10	6a8p slate	70.00	27.50
a.		Imperf., pair	3,000.	
28	A11	8a rose ('68)	45.00	7.00
		Nos. 26-28 (4)	240.00	42.25

Type A11 is a redrawing of type A7. Type A7 has Maltese crosses in the diadem, while type A11 has shaded lozenges.

For overprints see #O10, O20-O21, O25-O26.

For designs A9-A85 overprinted CHAMBA, FARIDKOT, GWALIOR, JIND (JHIND, JEEND), NABHA, PATI-ALA (PUTTIALLA), see the various Convention States.

A12

SIX ANNAS

Type I — "POSTAGE" 3½mm high
Type II — "POSTAGE" 2½mm high

Blue Glazed Paper

Green Overprint

Perf. 14 Vert.

1866, June 28				**Wmk. 36**
29	A12	6a violet, type I	1,000.	140.00
a.		Inverted overprint		*14,000.*
30	A12	6a violet, type II	1,850.	175.00

Nos. 29 and 30 were made from revenue stamps with the labels at top and bottom cut off. Most and sometimes all of the watermark was removed with the labels.

These stamps are often found with cracked surface or scuffs. Such examples sell for somewhat less.

A13

A14

A15

A16

1873-76		**Wmk. 38**	**Perf. 14**	
31	A7	½a blue, redrawn	7.50	1.00
32	A13	9p lilac ('74)	19.00	19.00
33	A14	6a bister ('76)	8.50	2.50
34	A15	12a red brown ('76)	12.00	27.50
35	A16	1r slate ('74)	65.00	30.00
		Nos. 31-35 (5)	112.00	80.00

In the redrawn ½ anna the lines of the mouth are more deeply cut, making the lips appear fuller and more open, and the nostril is defined by a curved line.

Victorian and Edwardian stamps overprinted "Postal Service" and new denominations were customs fee due stamps, not postage stamps.

Empire

A17

A18

A19

A20

A21

A22

A23

A24

A25

A26

A27

1882-87			**Wmk. 39**	
36	A17	½a green	4.50	.20
a.		Double impression	750.00	*1,000.*
37	A18	9p rose	1.10	*2.25*
38	A19	1a maroon	5.25	.35
a.		1a violet brown	5.25	.35
39	A20	1a6p bister brown	1.10	*1.40*
40	A21	2a ultra	4.00	.35
a.		Double impression	1,050.	*1,400.*
41	A22	3a brown org	9.50	1.75
a.		3a orange	14.00	6.25
42	A23	4a olive green	15.00	1.60
43	A24	4a6p green	30.00	5.50
44	A25	8a red violet	27.50	2.25
a.		8a rose lilac	25.00	2.25
45	A26	12a violet, *red*	8.00	3.50
46	A27	1r gray	27.50	6.00
		Nos. 36-46 (11)	133.45	25.15

A 6a die essay was prepared, but no stamps were printed.

A postal counterfeit exists of No. 46. Examples are scarce.

No. 40a used value is for copy with postal cancellation.

See Nos. 56-58. For surcharges see Nos. 47, 53 and British East Africa No. 59. For overprints see Nos. M2-M4, M6-M9, Gwalior Nos. O1-O5.

Beginning with the 1882-87 issue, higher denomination stamps exist used for telegrams. The telegraph cancellation has concentric circles. These sell for 10-15% of the postally used values.

No. 43 Surcharged

2½ As.

1891, Jan. 1

47	A24	2½a on 4a6p green	4.00	.65

A28

A29

1892

48	A28	2a6p green	3.25	.45
49	A29	1r aniline car & grn	17.50	2.25

See No. 59. For overprints see Nos. M5, M10 and Gwalior No. O6.

Queen Victoria

A30   A31

1895, Sept. 1

50	A30	2r brown & rose	42.50	12.50
51	A30	3r green & brown	37.50	11.00
52	A30	5r violet & ultra	47.50	30.00
		Nos. 50-52 (3)	127.50	53.50

Used high values such as Nos. 50-52, 71-76, 95-98, 124-125, as well as similar high value official issues are for postally used examples. Stamps bearing telegraph or revenue cancellations sell for much lower prices. Most telegraph cancellations on issues of Edward VII and George V can be recognized by the appearance of "T," "TEL" or "GTO" or if they contain the concentric circles of a target.

No. 36 Surcharged

1/4

1898

53	A17	¼a on ½a green	.20	*.55*
a.		Double surcharge	250.00	
b.		Double impression of stamp	260.00	

For #61, 81 with this overprint see #77, 105.

1899

54	A31	3p carmine rose	.45	.20

For overprint see No. M1, Gwalior No. O11.

1900

55	A31	3p gray	.80	*1.40*
56	A17	½a light green	1.75	.50
57	A19	1a carmine rose	2.50	.20
58	A21	2a violet	4.50	2.50
59	A28	2a6p ultramarine	3.75	4.25
		Nos. 55-59 (5)	13.30	8.85

For overprints see Nos. M11, Gwalior O7-O10.

Edward VII — A32

A33

A34

A35

A36

A37

A38

A39

A40

A41

A42

A43

1902-09

60	A32	3p gray	1.10	.20
61	A33	½a green	1.75	.20
a.		Booklet pane of 6 ('04)	32.50	
62	A34	1a carmine rose	1.60	.20
a.		Booklet pane of 6 ('04)	92.50	
63	A35	2a violet	4.25	.45
64	A36	2a6p ultra	5.00	.65
65	A37	3a brown org	5.00	.65
66	A38	4a olive green	3.25	.65
67	A39	6a bister	12.50	4.75
68	A40	8a red violet	8.75	1.10
69	A41	12a violet, *red*	9.50	2.25
70	A42	1r car rose & grn	6.75	.75
71	A43	2r brown & rose	47.50	4.50
72	A43	3r green & brn ('04)	30.00	20.00
73	A43	5r violet & ultra ('04)	72.50	40.00
74	A43	10r carmine rose & green ('09)	125.00	30.00
75	A43	15r olive gray & ultra ('09)	175.00	45.00
76	A43	25r ultra & org brown	925.00	925.00
		Telegraph cancel		300.00
		Nos. 60-75 (16)	509.45	151.35

For overprints and surcharge see #M12-M20, O33, O37-O44, O47-O51, O67-O69, O73, Gwalior O12-O18.

No. 61 Surcharged Like No. 53

1905

77	A33	¼a on ½a green	.60	.20
a.		Inverted surcharge		925.00

A44

A45

1906

78	A44	½a green	3.25	.20
a.		Booklet pane of 4	17.50	
79	A45	1a carmine rose	1.90	.20
a.		Booklet pane of 4	25.00	

For overprints see #O45-O46, Gwalior Nos. O19-O20.

A46

A47

A48

A49

A50

A51

A52

A53

A54   A55

George V — A56

1911-23   Wmk. 39

80	A46	3p gray	1.50	.20
a.		Booklet pane of 4	25.00	
81	A47	½a green	2.25	.20
a.		Double impression	175.00	
b.		Booklet pane of 4	21.00	
82	A48	1a carmine rose	2.75	.20
a.		Printed on both sides		
b.		Booklet pane of 4	35.00	
83	A48	1a dk brown ('22)	.85	.20
a.		Booklet pane of 4	42.50	
84	A49	2a dull violet	3.50	.40
a.		Booklet pane of 4	42.50	
85	A50	2a6p ultramarine	2.90	3.25
86	A51	3a brown org	4.25	.20
87	A51	3a ultra ('23)	13.00	.65
88	A52	4a olive green	8.00	.55
89	A53	6a yel bister	4.25	1.50
90	A53	6a bister ('15)	4.25	1.10
91	A54	8a red violet	6.25	1.25
92	A55	12a claret	6.50	2.40
93	A56	1r grn & red brn	19.00	1.75
94	A56	2r brn & car rose	22.50	1.90
95	A56	5r vio & ultra	55.00	7.00
96	A56	10r car rose & grn	82.50	13.00
97	A56	15r ol grn & ultra	115.00	26.00
98	A56	25r ultra & brn org	190.00	37.50
		Nos. 80-98 (19)	544.25	99.25

See #106-108, 110-111, 113-125. For surcharges and overprints see #104-105, M23-M25, M27, M29-M37, M39-M43, O52-O66, O70-O71, O74, O78-O81, O85, O87-O92, Gwalior O28-O29.

Nos. 93-98 also were used to pay for radio licenses, and stamps so used include "WIRELESS" in the cancel. Used values so canceled are worth 10-15% of the values shown, which are for postally used examples.

A57

1913-26

99	A57	2a6p ultramarine	2.90	.25
100	A57	2a6p brown org ('26)	6.00	6.00

See #112. For overprints see #M28, M38.

"One and Half" — A58

"One and a Half" — A59

1919

101	A58	1½a chocolate	3.75	.45
a.		Booklet pane of 4	35.00	

For overprint and surcharge see Nos. M26, O75.

1921-26

102	A59	1½a chocolate	3.50	4.75
103	A59	1½a rose ('26)	3.25	.35

See No. 109. For surcharge see #O76.

Type of 1911-26 Surcharged

1921

104	A48	9p on 1a rose	.90	.35
a.		Surcharged "NINE-NINE"	80.00	150.00
b.		Surcharged "PIES-PIES"	80.00	150.00
c.		Double surcharge	175.00	210.00
e.		Booklet pane of 4	27.50	

Forgeries exist of Nos. 104a-104c.

No. 81 Surcharged Like No. 53

1922

105	A47	¼a on ½a green	.60	.40
a.		Inverted surcharge	10.00	
b.		Pair, one without surcharge	240.00	

Types of 1911-26 Issues

1926-36   Wmk. 196

106	A46	3p slate	.35	.20
107	A47	½a green	1.40	.20
108	A48	1a dark brown	.55	.20
a.		Tete beche pair	1.50	11.00
b.		Booklet pane of 4	16.00	
109	A59	1½a car rose ('29)	3.50	.20
110	A49	2a dull violet	2.00	.20
a.		Booklet pane of 4	32.50	
111	A49	2a ver ('34)	4.00	.55
a.		Small die ('36)	5.00	.35
112	A57	2a6p buff	2.50	.20
113	A51	3a ultramarine	11.50	1.25
114	A51	3a blue ('30)	10.00	.20
115	A51	3a car rose ('32)	9.75	.20
116	A52	4a olive green	1.60	.20
117	A53	6a bister ('35)	9.50	2.00
118	A54	8a red violet	4.25	.20
119	A55	12a claret	5.25	.35
120	A56	1r green & brown	5.50	.50
121	A56	2r brn org & car rose	15.00	.85
122	A56	5r dk vio & ultra	30.00	1.40
123	A56	10r carmine & grn	62.50	3.50
124	A56	15r ol grn & ultra	28.00	32.50
125	A56	25r blue & ocher	115.00	40.00
		Nos. 106-125 (20)	322.15	84.90

No. 111 measures 19x22½mm, while the small die, No. 111a, measures 18½x22mm.
For overprints see Gwalior #O30-O39, O44-O45.

A60

A61

1926-32   Typo.

126	A60	2a dull violet	.55	.20
a.		Tete beche pair	10.00	37.50
b.		2a rose violet	.45	.20
c.		Booklet pane of 4	19.00	
127	A60	2a vermilion ('32)	11.00	7.00
128	A61	4a olive green	6.25	.20
		Nos. 126-128 (3)	17.80	7.40

For overprints see #O82-O83, O86, Gwalior O33-O34.

Fortress of Purana Qila — A62

George V Flanked by Dominion Columns A67

½a, War Memorial Arch. 1a, Council Building. 2a, Viceroy's House. 3a, Parliament Building.

Wmk. 196 Sideways

1931, Feb. 9   Litho.   Perf. 13½x14

129	A62	¼a brown & ol grn	3.00	4.50
130	A62	½a green & violet	1.75	.60
131	A62	1a choc & red vio	1.75	.30
132	A62	2a blue & green	2.25	1.50
133	A62	3a car & choc	5.25	3.00
134	A67	1r violet & green	13.50	30.00
		Nos. 129-134 (6)	27.50	39.90
		Set, never hinged	66.00	

Change of the seat of Government from Calcutta to New Delhi.

A68

A69

A70

Wmk. 196

1932, Apr. 22   Litho.   Perf. 14

135	A68	9p dark green	1.90	.20
136	A69	1a3p violet	.95	.20
137	A70	3a6p deep blue	4.75	.20
		Nos. 135-137 (3)	7.60	.60

No. 135 exists both litho. and typo.
For overprints see Nos. O94, O96, O104 and Gwalior #O41 and O43.

A71

A72

1934   Typo.

138	A71	½a green	5.75	.20
139	A72	1a dark brown	4.00	.20

For overprints see Nos. O93, O95 and Gwalior #O40 and O42.

Silver Jubilee Issue

Gateway of India, Bombay A73

Designs: 9p, Victoria Memorial, Calcutta. 1a, Rameswaram Temple, Madras. 1¼a, Jain Temple, Calcutta. 2½a, Taj Mahal, Agra. 3½a, Golden Temple, Amritsar. 8a, Pagoda, Mandalay.

Wmk. 196 Sideways

1935   Litho.   Perf. 13½x14

142	A73	½a lt green & black	1.50	.55
143	A73	9p dull green & blk	1.50	.55
144	A73	1a brown & black	2.25	.55
145	A73	1¼a violet & black	1.00	.55
146	A73	2½a brown org & blk	3.25	1.10
147	A73	3½a blue & black	6.50	2.50
148	A73	8a rose lilac & blk	7.25	.60
		Nos. 142-148 (7)	23.25	11.80
		Set, never hinged	32.00	

25th anniv. of the reign of George V.

A80

A82

King George VI

Dak Runner A81

Mail transport: 2a6p, Dak bullock cart. 3a, Dak tonga. 3a6p, Dak camel. 4a, Mail train. 6a, Mail steamer. 8a, Mail truck. 12a, 14a, Mail plane.

Perf. 13½x14 or 14x13½

1937-40   Typo.   Wmk. 196

150	A80	3p slate	.40	.20
151	A80	½a brown	1.10	.20
152	A80	9p green	3.00	.30
153	A80	1a carmine	.35	.20
a.		Tete beche pair	3.50	2.10
b.		Booklet pane of 4	5.25	
154	A81	2a scarlet	2.10	.35
155	A81	2a6p purple	.65	.30
156	A81	3a yellow green	3.75	.35
157	A81	3a6p ultramarine	2.50	.60
158	A81	4a dark brown	10.00	.30
159	A81	6a peacock blue	10.00	.95
160	A81	8a blue violet	6.00	.60
161	A81	12a car lake	13.00	1.25
161A	A81	14a rose vio ('40)	15.00	1.50
162	A82	1r brown & slate	.90	.20
163	A82	2r dk brn & dk violet	3.25	.40
164	A82	5r dp ultra & dk green	14.00	.70
165	A82	10r rose car & dk violet	14.00	1.10
166	A82	15r dk green & dk brown	70.00	90.00
167	A82	25r dk vio & blue violet	100.00	24.00
		Nos. 150-167 (19)	270.00	123.50
		Set, never hinged	580.00	

The King's portrait is larger on No. 161A than on other stamps of type A81.
For overprints see Nos. O97-O103, Gwalior Nos. O48-O51.

> **Catalogue values for unused stamps in this section, from this point to the end of the section, are for Never Hinged items.**

A83

A84

A85

Perf. 13½x14

1941-43   Typo.   Wmk. 196

168	A83	3p slate ('42)	1.00	.20
169	A83	½a rose vio ('42)	3.50	.20
170	A83	9p light green	3.50	.20
171	A83	1a car rose ('43)	3.50	.20
172	A84	1a3p bister	3.50	.20
172A	A84	1½a dark pur ('42)	4.00	.20
173	A84	2a scarlet	5.00	.20
174	A84	3a violet	10.00	.20
175	A84	3½a ultramarine	3.50	.65
176	A85	4a chocolate	2.50	.20
177	A85	6a peacock blue	11.50	.20
178	A85	8a blue violet	3.50	.20
179	A85	12a carmine lake	10.50	1.10
		Nos. 168-179 (13)	67.00	4.40

Early printings of the 1½a and 3a were lithographed.
For surcharge see No. 199.

For stamps with this overprint, or a smaller type, see Oman (Muscat).

Symbols of
Victory
A86

1946, Jan. 2　　Litho.　　Perf. 13

195	A86	9p green	.80	1.10
196	A86	1½a dull purple	.45	.40
197	A86	3½a ultramarine	1.00	1.00
198	A86	12a brown lake	2.50	1.10
		Nos. 195-198 (4)	4.75	3.60

Victory of the Allied Nations in WWII.

**No. 172 Surcharged With New Value
and Bars**

1946, Aug. 8　　　　　Perf. 13½x14

199	A84	3p on 1a3p bister	.35	.25

Dominion of India

Asoka Pillar — A87

National
Flag
A88

Four-Motor
Plane
A89

Perf. 14x13½, 13½x14

1947　　　Litho.　　　Wmk. 196

200	A87	1½a greenish gray	1.50	.45
201	A88	3½a multicolored	4.50	4.75
202	A89	12a ultramarine	6.00	4.75
		Nos. 200-202 (3)	12.00	9.95

Elevation to dominion status, Aug. 15, 1947.

Mahatma
Gandhi — A90

Design: 10r, Gandhi profile.

Perf. 11½

1948, Aug. 15　　Unwmk.　　Photo.

Size: 22x32½mm

203	A90	1½a brown	8.25	1.25
204	A90	3½a violet	18.00	5.00
205	A90	12a dark gray green	21.00	3.00

Size: 22x37mm

206	A90	10r rose brn & brn	210.00	95.00
		Nos. 203-206 (4)	257.25	104.25

Mohandas K. Gandhi, 1869-1948.
For overprints see #O112A-O112D.

Ajanta
Panel — A91

Konarak
Horse — A92

Bodhisattva
A93

Tomb of Muhammad
Adil Shah, Bijapur
A95

Sanchi Stupa
A94

Victory Tower,
Chittorgarh
A96

Red Fort,
Delhi
A97

Satrunjaya
Temple,
Palitana
A98

9p, Trimurti. 2a, Nataraja. 3½a, Bodh Gaya Temple. 4a, Bhuvanesvara. 8a, Kandarya Mahadeva Temple. 12a, Golden Temple, Amritsar. 5r, Taj Mahal. 10r, Qutb Minar.

Perf. 13½x14, 14x13½

1949, Aug. 15　　Typo.　　Wmk. 196

207	A91	3p gray violet	.30	.20
208	A92	6p red brown	.35	.20
209	A93	9p green	.60	.20
210	A93	1a turquoise	.85	.20
211	A93	2a carmine	1.25	.20
212	A94	3a red orange	3.00	.20
213	A94	3½a ultramarine	2.50	5.00
214	A94	4a brown lake	6.00	.35
215	A95	6a purple	2.75	.90
216	A95	8a blue green	2.25	.20
217	A95	12a blue	3.00	.35

Litho.

218	A96	1r dk green & pur	22.50	.20
219	A97	2r pur & rose red	20.00	.50
220	A97	5r brn car & dk grn	45.00	2.00
221	A96	10r dp bl & brn car	80.00	12.00

Perf. 13½x13

222	A98	15r dp car & dk brn	32.50	35.00
		Nos. 207-222 (16)	222.85	57.70

See #231, 235-236. For overprints see #M44-M46, M48-M55 and Intl. Commission in Indo-china issues for Cambodia, #1, 3-5, Laos #1, 3-5 and Vietnam #1, 3-5.

Symbols of
UPU and
Asoka
Pillar — A99

1949, Oct.　　Litho.　　Perf. 13½x13

223	A99	9p dull green	2.75	1.75
224	A99	2a carmine rose	2.75	1.75
225	A99	3½a ultramarine	4.00	3.00
226	A99	12a red brown	5.00	4.00
		Nos. 223-226 (4)	14.50	10.50

75th anniv. of the formation of the UPU.

Republic of India

Rejoicing
Crowds
A100

Designs: 3½a, Quill pen, vert. 4a, Plow and wheat. 12a, Charkha and cloth.

Perf. 13½x13

1950, Jan. 26　　　　　Wmk. 196

227	A100	2a carmine	2.75	.75
228	A100	3½a ultramarine	4.00	6.25
229	A100	4a purple	4.00	1.50
230	A100	12a claret	9.00	4.75
		Nos. 227-230 (4)	19.75	13.25

Type of 1949 Redrawn

Bodhisattva — A101

1950, July 15　　Typo.　　Perf. 13½x14

231	A101	1a turquoise	4.00	.30

For overprints see No. M47, Intl. Commission in Indo-china issues for Cambodia, No. 2, Laos, No. 2, and Vietnam, No. 2.

Extinct
Stegodon
Ganesa
A102

1951, Jan. 13　　　　　Perf. 13

232	A102	2a deep carmine & black	6.00	1.25

Geological Survey of India, cent.

Torch and
Map — A103

Kabir — A104

1951, Mar. 4　　　　　　Typo.

233	A103	2a red vio & red org	3.50	.90
234	A103	12a dark brown & ultra	12.00	2.25

First Asian Games, New Delhi.

Temple Type of 1949

2½a, Bodh Gaya Temple. 4a, Bhuvanesvara.

Perf. 13½x14

1951, Apr. 30　　　　　Wmk. 196

235	A94	2½a brown lake	6.00	3.50
236	A94	4a ultramarine	12.00	.40

1952, Oct. 1　　Photo.　　Perf. 14x13½

1a, Tulsidas, poet & saint. 2a, Meera, Rajput princess. 4a, Surdas, blind poet and saint. 4½a, Ghalib, Urdu poet. 12a, Rabindranath Tagore.

237	A104	9p emerald	1.40	.75
238	A104	1a crimson	1.40	.30
239	A104	2a red orange	5.50	.30
240	A104	4a ultramarine	8.50	1.00
241	A104	4½a red violet	1.75	1.75
242	A104	12a brown	12.50	1.50
		Nos. 237-242 (6)	31.05	5.60

First
Locomotive
and
Streamliner
A105

1953, Apr. 16　　　　Perf. 14½x14

243	A105	2a black	3.00	.50

Centenary of India's railroads.

Mt. Everest
A106

1953, Oct. 2

244	A106	2a violet	2.25	.35
245	A106	14a brown	6.50	1.50

Conquest of Mt. Everest, May 29, 1953.

Telegraph
Poles of
1851 and
1951
A107

1953, Nov. 1

246	A107	2a blue green	.75	.35
247	A107	12a blue	6.25	.85

Centenary of the telegraph in India.

Mail
Transport,
1854
A108

Designs: 2a and 14a, Pigeon and plane. 4a, Mail transport, 1954.

1954, Oct. 1

248	A108	1a rose lilac	.55	.30
249	A108	2a rose pink	.55	.30
250	A108	4a yellow brown	5.00	1.25
251	A108	14a blue	3.00	.40
		Nos. 248-251 (4)	9.10	2.25

Centenary of India's postage stamps.

UN Emblem
and Lotus
Blossom
A109

1954, Oct. 24

252	A109	2a Prussian green	.70	.45

United Nations Day.

Forest
Research
Institute,
Dehra Dun
A110

1954, Dec. 11

253	A110	2a ultramarine	.55	.30

4th World Forestry Cong., Dehra Dun.

Tractor
A111

Charkha
Operator
A112

Symbols of Malaria Control A113

Designs: 6p, Power looms. 9p, Bullock irrigation pump. 1a, Damodar Valley dam. 3a, Naga woman at hand loom. 4a, Bullock team. 8a, Chittaranjan Locomotive Works. 10a, Plane over Marine Drive, Bombay. 12a, Hindustan aircraft factory. 14a, Plane over Kashmir valley. 1r, Telephone factory worker. 1r2a, Plane over Cape Comorin. 1r8a, Plane over Kanchenjunga Mountains. 2r, Rare earth factory. 5r, Sindri fertilizer factory. 10r, Steel mill.

Perf. 14x14½, 14½x14

1955, Jan. 26   **Photo.**
254	A111	3p rose lilac	.40	.20
255	A111	6p deep violet	.40	.20
256	A111	9p orange brown	.55	.20
257	A111	1a dp blue green	.55	.20
258	A112	2a blue	.40	.20
259	A112	3a blue green	.60	.20
260	A111	4a rose red	.60	.20
261	A113	6a yellow brown	1.75	.20
262	A111	8a deep blue	8.75	.20
263	A113	10a aquamarine	4.50	2.75
264	A111	12a violet blue	4.00	.20
265	A113	14a emerald	6.50	.40
266	A111	1r greenish black	5.00	.20
267	A113	1r2a gray	2.75	5.75
268	A113	1r8a claret	10.00	6.00
269	A111	2r carmine rose	5.25	.20
270	A111	5r brown	17.00	.40
271	A111	10r orange	18.00	3.75
		Nos. 254-271 (18)	87.00	21.45

See Nos. 316-319.

Bodhi Tree — A114

Ornament and Bodhi Tree A115

1956, May 24   **Wmk. 196**   **Perf. 13**
272	A114	2a brown	1.75	.30
273	A115	14a brick red	7.00	4.00

2500th anniv. of the birth of Buddha.

Bal Gangadhar Tilak — A116

Map of India — A117

1956, July 23   **Wmk. 196**   **Photo.**
274	A116	2a orange brown	.55	.55

Birth cent. of Bal Gangadhar Tilak, independence leader.

1957-58   **Perf. 14x14½**
275	A117	1np blue green	.20	.20
276	A117	2np light brown	.20	.20
277	A117	3np brown	.20	.20
278	A117	5np emerald	4.00	.20
279	A117	6np gray	.60	.20
280	A117	8np brt green ('58)	6.50	.50
281	A117	10np dark green	4.50	.20
282	A117	13np brt carmine	1.10	.20
283	A117	15np violet ('58)	4.00	.20
284	A117	20np bright blue	1.25	.20
285	A117	25np ultramarine	.95	.20
286	A117	50np orange	3.50	.20

287	A117	75np plum	2.00	.20
288	A117	90np red lilac ('58)	6.00	2.50
		Nos. 275-288 (14)	35.00	5.40

Denominations of the 8np, 15np and 90np are inscribed nP.
See #302-315. For overprints see #M60 and Intl. Commission in Indo-China issues for Cambodia, #6-10, Laos, #6-10, and Vietnam, #6-10.

Laxmibai, Rani of Jhansi A118

Banyan Sapling, Arch and Flames — A119

Perf. 14½x14, 13

1957, Aug. 15   **Wmk. 196**
289	A118	15np brown	.50	.50
290	A119	90np bright red violet	3.75	1.40

Centenary of the struggle for independence (Indian Mutiny).

Henri Dunant A120

1957, Oct. 28   **Perf. 13½x13**
291	A120	15np car rose & black	.40	.40

19th Intl. Red Cross Conf., New Delhi.

Boy Eating Banana A121

Bankura Horse — A122

Children's Day: 15np, Girl writing on tablet.

1957, Nov. 14   **Perf. 13½**
292	A121	8np rose lilac	.35	.35
293	A121	15np aquamarine	.35	.35
294	A122	90np lt orange brown	.70	.35
		Nos. 292-294 (3)	1.40	1.05

Madras University A123

University Centenaries: No. 296, Calcutta. No. 297, Bombay, vert.

1957, Dec. 31   **Photo.**
Size: 29½x25mm
295	A123	10np light brown	.60	.50
296	A123	10np gray	.30	.50

Size: 21½x38mm
297	A123	10np violet	.30	.50
		Nos. 295-297 (3)	1.20	1.50

J. N. Tata and Steel Works, Jamshedpur — A124

1958, Mar. 1   **Perf. 14½x14**
298	A124	15np red orange	.40	.40

50th anniv. of Indian steel industry.

Dr. Dhondo Keshav Karve — A125

1958, Apr. 18   **Perf. 14x13½**
299	A125	15np orange brown	.40	.40

Cent. of the birth of Karve, educator and pioneer of women's education.

Wapiti and Hunter Planes A126

1958, Apr. 30   **Perf. 14½x14**
300	A126	15np bright blue	2.50	.35
301	A126	90np ultramarine	2.75	2.50

25th anniv. of the Indian Air Force.

Map Type of 1957-58 and Industrial Type of 1955

1r, Telephone factory worker. 2r, Rare earth factory. 5r, Sindri fertilizer factory. 10r, Steel mill.

Perf. 14x14½

1958-63   **Photo.**   **Wmk. 324**
302	A117	1np blue grn ('60)	1.40	.20
a.		Imperf., pair	240.00	
303	A117	2np light brown	.25	.20
304	A117	3np brown	.25	.20
305	A117	5np emerald	.25	.20
306	A117	6np gray ('63)	.25	4.00
307	A117	8np bright green	.25	.20
308	A117	10np dark green	.25	.20
309	A117	13np bright car ('63)	1.40	4.75
310	A117	15np violet ('59)	.80	.20
311	A117	20np bright blue	.50	.20
312	A117	25np ultramarine	.50	.20
313	A117	50np orange ('59)	.50	.20
314	A117	75np plum ('59)	.90	.20
315	A117	90np red lilac ('60)	8.00	.20
316	A111	1r dk grn ('59)	5.75	.20
317	A111	2r lilac rose ('59)	8.00	.20
318	A111	5r brown ('59)	14.00	.20
319	A111	10r orange ('59)	32.50	5.50
		Nos. 302-319 (18)	75.75	17.25

For overprints see Nos. M56-M59, M61, Intl. Commission in Indo-china issues for Cambodia, No. 12, Laos, Nos. 12-16, and Vietnam Nos. 11-16.

Bipin Chandra Pal — A128

Nurse and Child — A129

1958, Nov. 7   **Perf. 13½**
320	A128	15np dull green	.50	.50

Birth cent. of Pal, early leader of India's freedom movement.

1958, Nov. 30

Portrait: Sir Jagadis Chandra Bose.
321	A128	15np brt greenish blue	.50	.50

Bose, physicist, plant physiologist, birth cent.

1958, Nov. 14   **Wmk. 324**
322	A129	15np violet	.50	.50

Children's Day, Nov. 14.

Exhibition Gate A130

1958, Dec. 30   **Perf. 14½x14**
323	A130	15np claret	.50	.50

India 1958 Exhibition at Kanpur.

Sir Jamsetjee Jejeebhoy — A131

1959, Apr. 13   **Perf. 13½**
324	A131	15np brown	.50	.50

Cent. of the death of Jejeebhoy, philosopher and philanthropist.

"Triumph of Labor," by D. P. Roy Chowdhary A132

1959, June 15   **Perf. 14½x14**
325	A132	15np dull green	.50	.50

40th anniv. of the ILO.

Children Arriving at Institution — A133

Perf. 14x14½

1959, Nov. 14   **Photo.**   **Wmk. 324**
326	A133	15np dull green	.50	.50
a.		Imperf., pair	750.00	

Children's Day, Nov. 14.

Farmer Plowing with Bullocks A134

1959, Dec. 30 *Perf. 13*
327 A134 15np gray .50 .40
World Agriculture Fair, New Delhi.

Thiruvalluvar Holding Stylus and Palmyra Leaf — A135

1960, Feb. 15 *Perf. 14*
328 A135 15np rose lilac .50 .50
Honoring the ancient and saintly Tamil poet, Thiruvalluvar.

Scene from Meghduta — A136

Scene from Sakuntala A137

1960, June 22 *Perf. 13*
329 A136 15np gray 1.00 .40
330 A137 1.03r brown & bister 3.50 2.50
Honoring Kalidasa, 5th cent. poet and dramatist.
For surcharge see No. 371.

Subramania Bharati — A138

Dr. M. Visvesvaraya A139

1960, Sept. 11 Photo. *Perf. 14x13½*
331 A138 15np bright blue .50 .50
Honoring the poet and statesman Subramania Bharati (1882-1921).

1960, Sept. 15 *Perf. 13x13½*
332 A139 15np car rose & brown .50 .50
Birth cent. of Visvesvaraya, engineer and statesman.

Children Playing and Studying A140

1960, Nov. 14 *Perf. 13½x13*
333 A140 15np green .50 .50
Children's Day, Nov. 14.

Children and UN Emblem A141

1960, Dec. 11 *Wmk. 324*
334 A141 15np olive gray & org brn .50 .50
UNICEF Day.

Tyagaraja, Indian Musician — A142

1961, Jan. 6 Photo. *Perf. 14*
335 A142 15np bright blue .50 .50
114th anniv. of Tyagaraja's death.

First Airmail Postmark — A143

Boeing 707 Jetliner — A144

Design: 1r, Humber-Sommer biplane.

Perf. 14, 13x13½
1961, Feb. 18 *Wmk. 324*
336 A143 5np olive bister 2.25 .40
337 A144 15np gray & green 2.25 .40
338 A144 1r gray & claret 7.00 3.00
Nos. 336-338 (3) 11.50 3.80
50th anniv. of the world's 1st airmail. The flight was from Allahabad to Naini, Feb. 18, 1911.

Chatrapati Sivaji Maharaj (1627-1680) A145

1961, Apr. 17 *Perf. 13x13½*
339 A145 15np gray green & brown 1.40 .65
Leader of the Marahattas in the fight against the Moguls.

Motilal Nehru — A146

Rabindranath Tagore — A147

1961, May 6 *Perf. 14x13½*
340 A146 15np orange & ol gray .50 .40
Cent. of the birth of Motilal Nehru, leader in India's fight for freedom.

1961, May 7 *Perf. 13*
341 A147 15np blue grn & org 1.40 .60
Cent. of the birth of Tagore, poet.

Radio Masts and All India Radio Emblem A148

1961, June 8 Photo. *Wmk. 324*
342 A148 15np ultramarine .50 .50
25th anniv. of All India Radio.

Prafulla Chandra Ray — A149

Vishnu Narayan Bhatkhande A150

1961, Aug. 2 *Perf. 14x13½*
343 A149 15np gray .50 .50
Cent. of the birth of Ray, scientist.

1961, Sept. 1 *Perf. 13*
344 A150 15np olive gray .50 .50
Bhatkhande (1860-1936), musician.

Boy Making Pottery — A151

Gate at Fair — A152

1961, Nov. 14 *Perf. 13½*
345 A151 15np brown .50 .50
Children's Day, Nov. 14.

1961, Nov. 14 *Perf. 14x14½*
346 A152 15np blue & carmine .50 .50
Indian Industries Fair at New Delhi.

Forest and Himalayas — A153

1961, Nov. 21 *Perf. 13*
347 A153 15np brown & green .80 .45
Cent. of the introduction of scientific forestry in India.

Yaksha, God of Fertility — A154

Kalibangan Seal — A155

1961, Dec. 14 Photo. *Perf. 14*
348 A154 15np orange brown .50 .40
349 A155 90np orange brn & olive 1.10 .40
Cent. of the Archaeological Survey of India.

Madan Mohan Malaviya — A156

Nunmati Refinery, Gauhati — A157

1961, Dec. 25   *Perf. 14x13½*
350 A156 15np slate   .50   .50

Cent. of the birth of Malaviya, Pres. of the Indian Natl. Cong. and Vice Chancellor of Benares University.

1962, Jan. 1   **Photo.**   *Perf. 13*
351 A157 15np blue   .70   .40

1st Indian oil refinery at Gauhati.

Bhikaiji Cama — A158

1962, Jan. 26   *Perf. 14*
352 A158 15np rose lilac   .50   .50

Cent. of the birth of Madame Cama, a leader in India's fight for independence.

Village Council, Banyan Tree, Parliament and Map — A159

1962, Jan. 26   *Perf. 13*
353 A159 15np red lilac   .50   .50

Panchayati Raj, the system of government by village council.

Dayananda Sarasvati — A160

1962, Mar. 4   *Perf. 14*
354 A160 15np brown orange   .50   .50

135th anniv. of the birth of Sarasvati, reformer of the Vedic religion and founder of the Arya Samaj educational institutions.

Ganesh Shankar Vidyarthi — A161

1962, Mar. 25
355 A161 15np reddish brown   .50   .50

Vidyarthi (1890-1931), reformer of community life.

Malaria Eradication Emblem — A162

Dr. Rajendra Prasad — A163

1962, Apr. 7   *Perf. 13*
356 A162 15np dk car rose & yel   .50   .50

WHO drive to eradicate malaria.

1962, May 13   *Perf. 13*
357 A163 15np bright red lilac   .50   .40

Prasad, President of India (1950-62).

High Court, Calcutta A164

1962   **Photo.**   *Perf. 13½x14*
358 A164 15np green   .90   .35
359 A164 15np Madras   .90   .35
360 A164 15np Bombay   .90   .35
Nos. 358-360 (3)   2.70   1.05

Indian High Courts, cent. Issued: No. 358, July 1; No. 359, Aug. 8; No. 360, Aug. 14.

Ramabai Ranade — A165

Indian Rhinoceros A166

1962, Aug. 15   *Perf. 14*
361 A165 15np brown orange   .50   .50

Ramabai Ranade (1862-1924), woman social reformer.

1962-63   **Wmk. 324**   *Perf. 14*
10np, Gaur. No. 363, Lesser panda, vert. 30np, Elephant, vert. 50np, Tiger. 1r, Lion.

Size: 30x26mm
361A A166 10np yel org & blk
       ('63)   1.25   *1.75*
362 A166 15np Prus blue &
       brn   .75   .30

Perf. 13x13½, 13½x13
Size: 25x36mm, 36x25mm
363 A166 15np green & red
       brown ('63)   2.50   .70
364 A166 30np bister & slate
       ('63)   5.75   1.25
365 A166 50np dp grn, ocher
       & brown ('63)   4.50   .90
366 A166 1r brt bl & pale
       brown ('63)   4.25   .65
Nos. 361A-366 (6)   19.00   5.55

Child Reaching for Flag A167

1962, Nov. 14   *Perf. 13*
367 A167 15np lt bluish grn & ver   .50   .50

Children's Day.

Eye within Lotus Blossom A168

1962, Dec. 3   **Photo.**
368 A168 15np olive gray   .50   .40

16th Intl. Cong. of Ophthalmology, New Delhi, Dec. 1962.

Srinivasa Ramanujan A169

Swami Vivekananda — A170

1962, Dec. 22   *Perf. 13½x14*
369 A169 15np olive gray   1.10   .55

75th anniv. of the birth of Ramanujan (1887-1920), mathematician.

1963, Jan. 17   *Perf. 14x14½*
370 A170 15np olive & orange
       brn   .50   .50

Cent. of the birth of Vivekananda (1863-1902), philosopher.

No. 330 Surcharged with New Value and Two Bars

1963, Feb. 2   *Perf. 13*
371 A137 1r on 1.03r brown &
       bis   1.50   .45

Hands Reaching for "FAO" Emblem — A171

Henri Dunant and Centenary Emblem — A172

1963, Mar. 21   **Photo.**
372 A171 15np chalky blue   3.00   .70

UNFAO Freedom from Hunger campaign.

1963, May 8   *Perf. 13*
373 A172 15np gray & red   5.75   .60

Centenary of the International Red Cross.

Field Artillery and Helicopter A173

Design: 1r, Soldier guarding frontier and plane dropping supplies.

1963, Aug. 15   *Perf. 13½x14*
374 A173 15np dull green   1.00   .30
375 A173 1r red brown   1.60   1.25

Honoring the Armed Forces and the 16th anniv. of independence.

Dadabhoy Naoroji — A174

1963, Sept. 4   *Perf. 13*
376 A174 15np gray green   .50   .50

Honoring Dadabhoy Naoroji (1825-1917), mathematician and statesman.

Annie Besant — A175

School Lunch — A176

1963, Oct. 1   **Photo.**   *Perf. 14*
377 A175 15np blue green   .50   .50

Besant (1847-1933), an English woman devoted to the cause of India's freedom, theosophist and writer. Stamp gives birth date as 1837.

1963, Nov. 14   **Wmk. 324**   *Perf. 14*
378 A176 15np olive bister   .50   .50

Children's Day.

Eleanor Roosevelt at Spinning Wheel A177

1963, Dec. 10   *Perf. 13*
379 A177 15np rose violet   .50   .50

Honoring Eleanor Roosevelt on the 15th anniv. of the Universal Declaration of Human Rights.

Gopabandhu Das (1877-1928) A178

1964, Jan. 4   *Perf. 13*
380 A178 15np dull purple   .50   .50

Gopabandhu Das, social reformer.

1964, Jan. 4   **Photo.**
381 A179 15np dull violet blue   .50   .50

26th Intl. Cong. of Orientalists, New Delhi, Jan. 4-14.

Lakshmi, Goddess of Wealth — A179

Purandaradasa Holding Veena and Chipala — A180

1964, Jan. 14
382 A180 15np golden brown   .50   .50

400th anniv. of the death of Purandaradasa (1484-1564), musician.

Subhas Chandra Bose and INA Emblem A181

Design: 55np, Bose addressing troops.

1964, Jan. 23   *Perf. 13*
383 A181 15np olive   1.10   .45
384 A181 55np red & black   1.10   .85

67th anniv. of the birth of Bose, organizer of the Indian Natl. Army.

Sarojini Naidu (1879-1949) A182

Kasturba Gandhi A183

1964, Feb. 13   *Perf. 14x13½*
385 A182 15np dull lilac & slate grn   .50   .50

Mrs. Sarojini Naidu, poet, politician, governor of United Provinces.

1964, Feb. 22   **Photo.**   **Wmk. 324**
386 A183 15np brown orange   .50   .50

20th anniv. of the death of Kasturba Gandhi (1869-1944), wife of Mahatma Gandhi.

Dr. Waldemar M. Haffkine (1860-1930) A184

1964, Mar. 16   *Perf. 13*
387 A184 15np violet brown, *buff*   .50   .50

Haffkine, bacteriologist, who as director of Haffkine Institute introduced inoculations against cholera and plague.

Jawaharlal Nehru (1889-1964) and People A185

1964, June 12   **Unwmk.**   *Perf. 13*
388 A185 15p grayish blue   .50   .50

Prime Minister Jawaharlal Nehru.

Asutosh Mookerjee and High Court, Calcutta A186

1964, June 29   **Wmk. 324**
389 A186 15p olive green & brn   .50   .50

Cent. of the birth of Asutosh Mookerjee (1864-1924), educator, lawyer and judge.

Sri Aurobindo Ghose (1872-1950), Writer and Philosopher A187

1964, Aug. 15   **Photo.**
390 A187 15p violet brown   .50   .50

Raja Rammohun Roy — A188

1964, Sept. 27   *Perf. 13*
391 A188 15p reddish brown   .50   .50

Roy (1772-1833), Hindu religious reformer.

Globe, Lotus, and Calipers — A189

1964, Nov. 9   **Unwmk.**   **Photo.**
392 A189 15p carmine rose   .50   .50

6th gen. assembly of the Intl. Organization for Standardization.

Nehru Medal and Rose — A190

1964, Nov. 14   *Perf. 13½*
393 A190 15p blue gray   .50   .50

Children's Day. For overprints, see Nos. M62, Intl. Commission in Indo-china issues for Laos and Vietnam, No. 1.

St. Thomas Statue, Ortona, Italy — A191

Globe and Pickax — A192

1964, Dec. 2   **Unwmk.**   *Perf. 13½*
394 A191 15p rose violet   .50   .50

Visit of Pope Paul VI, Nov. 30-Dec. 2.

1964, Dec. 14   **Wmk. 324**
395 A192 15p bright green   .80   .65

22nd Intl. Geological Cong., New Delhi.

Jamsetji N. Tata A193

1965, Jan. 7   **Unwmk.**   *Perf. 13*
396 A193 15p dk brown & orange   .50   .25

125th anniv. of the birth of Tata (1839-1904), founder of India's steel industry.

Lala Lajpatrai (1865-1928), a Leader in India's Fight for Independence A194

1965, Jan. 28   **Photo.**   *Perf. 13*
397 A194 15p brown   .50   .50

ICC Emblem and Globe A195

1965, Feb. 8   **Litho.**
398 A195 15p dull green & car   .50   .50

20th cong. of the Intl. Chamber of Commerce, New Delhi.

Freighter Jalausha at Visakhapatnam — A196

Perf. 14½x14
1965, Apr. 5   **Photo.**   **Wmk. 324**
399 A196 15p ultramarine   .90   .90

National Maritime Day.

Death Centenary of Abraham Lincoln — A197

1965, Apr. 15   *Perf. 13*
400 A197 15p yellow & dk brown   .60   .60

ITU Emblem, Old and New Communication Equipment — A198

1965, May 17   **Photo.**   *Perf. 14½x14*
401 A198 15p rose violet   2.50   .75

Cent. of the ITU.

Torch and Rose — A199

1965, May 27   **Wmk. 324**   *Perf. 13*
402 A199 15p carmine & blue   .40   .40

1st anniv. of the death of Jawaharlal Nehru.

ICY Emblem A200

1965, June 26   **Photo.**   **Unwmk.**
403 A200 15p bister & dk green   2.75   1.25

International Cooperation Year.

Indians Raising Flag on Everest — A201

1965, Aug. 15 **Unwmk.** **Perf. 13**
404 A201 15p plum .75 .60
Success of the Indian Mt. Everest Expedition, May 20, 1965.

Elephant from Konarak Temple, Orissa A202

Tea Picking A203

Woman Writing Letter, Chandella Carving, 11th Century — A204

Trombay Atomic Center A205

Designs: 2p, Vase (bidri ware). 3p, Brass lamp. 4p, Coffee berries. 5p, Family (family planning). 8p, Axis deer (chital). 10p, Electric locomotive, 1961. 20p, Gnat plane. 30p, Male and female figurines. 40p, General Post Office, Calcutta, 1868. 50p, Mangoes. 60p, Somnath Temple. 70p, Stone chariot, Hampi, Mysore. 2r, Dal Lake, Kashmir. 5r, Bhakra Dam, Punjab.

Perf. 14½x14, 14x14½
1965-68 **Photo.** **Wmk. 324**
405 A202 2p redsh brown
  ('67) .20 .55
406 A202 3p olive bis ('67) .40 2.40
407 A203 4p orange brn ('68) .20 2.10
408 A202 5p cerise ('67) .20 .20
409 A202 6p gray ('66) .20 3.25
410 A202 8p red brown ('67) .40 4.00
411 A203 10p brt blue ('66) .60 .20
412 A203 15p dk yel green 3.50 .20
413 A202 20p plum ('67) 8.00 .20
414 A202 30p brown ('67) .20 .20
415 A202 40p brown vio ('68) .20 .20
416 A202 50p green ('67) .35 .20
417 A202 60p dark gray ('67) .45 .20
418 A203 70p violet ('67) .20 .20
419 A204 1r deep claret &
  red brown ('66) .95 .20
420 A205 2r vio & brt bl ('67) 3.25 .20
421 A205 5r brn & vio ('67) 3.50 1.60
422 A205 10r green & gray 24.00 1.10
  Nos. 405-422 (18) 47.55 17.20

See Nos. 623, 666-670, 678, 680, 684-685. For overprints see Nos. RA1-RA2, Intl. Commission in Indo-china issues for Laos and Vietnam, Nos. 2-9.

1975-76 **Wmk. 360** **Perf. 14½x14**
422A A202 2p redsh brown 1.50 2.25
423 A202 5p cerise 1.75 .20
Unwmk.
423A A202 5p cerise ('76) 1.50 .20

A206

A207

1965, Sept. 10 **Unwmk.** **Perf. 13**
424 A206 15p dark green &
  brown .50 .50
Govind Ballabh Pant (1887-1961), Home Minister of India.

1965, Oct. 31 **Perf. 14**
425 A207 15p gray .50 .50
Vallabhbhai Patel (1875-1950), Deputy Prime Minister of India.

Chittaranjan Das (1870-1925) A208

Vidyapati, 15th Cent. Poet A209

1965, Nov. 5 **Photo.** **Perf. 13**
426 A208 15p brown .50 .50
Das, freedom fighter, pres. of Indian Natl. Cong., mayor of Calcutta.

1965, Nov. 17 **Perf. 14x14½**
427 A209 15p brown .50 .50

Tomb of Akbar the Great, Sikandra A210

1966, Jan. 24 **Perf. 14**
428 A210 15p dark gray .50 .50
Pacific Area Travel Assoc. Conf., New Delhi.

Soldier, Planes and Warships A211

1966, Jan. 26
429 A211 15p bright violet 2.00 .65
Honoring the Indian armed forces.

Lal Bahadur Shastri A212

Kambar A213

1966, Jan. 26 **Perf. 13**
430 A212 15p gray 1.00 .60
Prime Minister Shastri (1904-66).

1966, Apr. 9 **Perf. 14x14½**
431 A213 15p green .50 .50
Kambar, 9th century Tamil poet.

B. R. Ambedkar A214

Kunwar Singh A215

1966, Apr. 14 **Unwmk.** **Perf. 14**
432 A214 15p violet brown .50 .50
10th anniv. of the death of Dr. Bhimrao R. Ambedkar (1891-1956), lawyer and leader in social reform.

1966, Apr. 23 **Photo.**
433 A215 15p orange brown .50 .50
Kunwar Singh (1777-1858), hero of 1857 War of Independence (1857 Mutiny).

Gopal Krishna Gokhale A216

1966, May 9 **Unwmk.** **Perf. 13**
434 A216 15p violet brown & yel .50 .50
Cent. of the birth of Gokhale (1866-1915), professor of history and political economy and leader of the opposition party.

A. M. P. Dvivedi (1864-1938) A217

1966, May 15 **Perf. 14**
435 A217 15p olive gray .50 .50
Acharya Mahavir Prasad Dvivedi, Hindi writer.

Ranjit Singh (1780-1839) — A218

1966, June 28 **Unwmk.** **Perf. 14**
436 A218 15p plum .50 .50
Maharaja Ranjit Singh, ruler of Punjab.

Homi Bhabha and Atomic Reactor A219

1966, Aug. 4 **Perf. 14½x14**
437 A219 15p brown violet 1.00 1.00
Dr. Homi Bhabha (1909-1966), scientist.

Rama Tirtha A220

1966, Nov. 11 **Unwmk.** **Perf. 13**
438 A220 15p greenish blue .50 .50
60th anniv. of the death of Swami Rama Tirtha (1873-1906).

A221

A222

1966, Nov. 11 **Photo.** **Perf. 13½**
439 A221 15p dark violet blue .50 .50
Abdul Kalam Azad (1888-1958), president of the All-India Congress.

1966, Nov. 14 **Perf. 13**
440 A222 15p Child and dove 1.25 .70
Children's Day.

Allahabad High Court, Cent. A223

1966, Nov. 25 **Perf. 14½x14**
441 A223 15p violet brown .50 .50

Family A224

1966, Dec. 12 **Perf. 13½x13**
442 A224 15p brown .50 .50
Intl. Conf. for Marriage Guidance, New Delhi, and Family Planning Week.

Hockey
A225

1966, Dec. 31   Unwmk.   Perf. 13
443 A225 15p bright blue   1.75 1.75
Victory of the Indian hockey team at the 5th
Asian Games, Bangkok, Dec. 19.

Grain Harvest
A226

1967, Jan. 11   Perf. 13½
444 A226 15p yellow green   .75 .90
1st anniv. of the death of Prime Minister Lal
Bahadur Shastri, who advocated self-sufficiency in food production.

Voters — A227

1967, Jan. 13   Photo.
445 A227 15p light red brown   .50 .50
General elections, Feb. 1967.

Guru Dwara Shrine,
Patna — A228

1967, Jan. 17   Perf. 14
446 A228 15p violet   .90 .70
300th anniv. of the birth of Gobind Singh
(1666-1708), religious leader.

Taj Mahal
A229

1967, Mar. 19   Perf. 14½x14
447 A229 15p brown & orange   .60 .60
International Tourist Year.

Nandalal Bose and
Garuda — A230

1967, Apr. 16   Perf. 13½
448 A230 15p brown   .50 .50
Nandalal Bose (1882-1966), painter.

Survey of
India
Emblem
A231

1967, May 1   Unwmk.   Perf. 13
449 A231 15p lilac   1.10 .80
Bicentenary of Survey of India.

Basaveswara,
12th Cent.
Statesman and
Philosopher, at
Work — A232

1967, May 11   Perf. 13½x14
450 A232 15p deep orange   .50 .50

Narsinha
Mehta — A233

Maharana
Pratap — A234

1967, May 30   Perf. 13½
451 A233 15p gray brown   .50 .50
Narsina Mehta, 15th cent. musician.

1967, June 11   Perf. 14x14½
452 A234 15p reddish brown   .50 .50
Pratap (1540-1597), Mewar ruler.

Narayana Guru
A235

Dr. Sarvepalli
Radhakrishnan
A236

1967, Aug. 21   Photo.   Perf. 14
453 A235 15p brown   .60 .60
Narayana Guru (1855-1928), religious
reformer.

1967, Sept. 5   Unwmk.   Perf. 13
454 A236 15p dull claret   1.00 .40
Radhakrishnan, Pres. of India 1962-67.

Martyrs'
Memorial,
Patna
A237

1967, Oct. 1   Photo.   Perf. 14½x14
455 A237 15p dark carmine   .50 .50
25th anniv. of the "Quit India" revolt led by
Gandhi.

Map Showing
Indo-European
Telegraph
A238

1967, Nov. 9   Photo.   Perf. 13½
456 A238 15p blue & black   1.25 .80
Cent. of the laying of the Indo-European telegraph line.

Wrestlers
A239

1967, Nov. 12
457 A239 15p ocher & plum   1.00 .55
World Wrestling Championships, New Delhi,
Nov. 1967.

Nehru and Naga
Tribesmen — A240

Rashbehari
Basu — A241

1967, Dec. 4   Photo.   Perf. 13
458 A240 15p ultramarine   .50 .50

1967, Dec. 26   Perf. 13½
459 A241 15p dull purple   .50 .50
Basu (1886-1945), Bengali leader.

Bugle,
Scout
Emblem
and Scout
Sign
A242

1967, Dec. 27   Perf. 14½x14
460 A242 15p orange brown   2.00 .60
Boy Scout Movement, 60th anniv.

People
Encircling
the Globe
and Human
Rights
Flame
A243

1968, Jan. 1   Perf. 13
461 A243 15p dark green   1.00 .75
Intl. Human Rights Year.

Conference
Emblem and
Gopuram
Temple — A244

1968, Jan. 3   Photo.   Unwmk.
462 A244 15p purple   1.00 .55
2nd Intl. Conf. on Tamil Studies, Madras.

UN
Emblem,
Plane and
Ship
A245

1968, Feb. 1   Perf. 14½x14
463 A245 15p greenish blue   1.25 .55
UN Conference on Trade and Development,
New Delhi, Feb. 1968.

Symbolic Bow
and Quill
Pen — A246

1968, Feb. 20   Perf. 13½x14
464 A246 15p ocher & sepia   .50 .50
Cent. of the newspaper Amrit Bazar Patrika,
Calcutta.

Maxim Gorky (1868-
1936), Russian
Writer — A247

1968, Mar. 28   Photo.   Perf. 14
465 A247 15p brown violet   .50 .50

Exhibition
Emblem — A248

Symbolic Mail
Box — A249

1968, Mar. 31   Perf. 13
466 A248 15p dark blue & org   .60 .30
First Triennial Exhibition, New Delhi.

1968, July 1   Unwmk.   Perf. 13
467 A249 20p vermilion & blue   .80 .45
Opening of 100,000th Indian post office.

Wheat and
Indian
Agricultural
Research
Institute
A250

1968, July 15   Photo.   Perf. 13
468 A250 20p brt grn & brn org   .60 .35
India's 1968 bumper wheat crop.

Gaganendranath Tagore (1867-1938), Self-portrait A251

1968, Sept. 17   Unwmk.   *Perf. 13*
469 A251 20p ocher & deep clar   1.00   .55

Lakshminath Bezbaruah (1868-1938), Writer — A252

1968, Oct. 5   Photo.   *Perf. 13½*
470 A252 20p sepia   .50   .40

19th Olympic Games, Mexico City A253

1968, Oct. 12   *Perf. 14½x14*
471 A253 20p blue gray & red brn   .40   .40
472 A253 1r olive gray & dk brn   1.00   .40

Bhagat Singh (1907-1931), Revolutionary — A254

1968, Oct. 19   Photo.   *Perf. 13½x13*
473 A254 20p orange brown   1.00   .80

Bose Reading Proclamation A255

Sister Nivedita A256

1968, Oct. 21   *Perf. 14x14½*
474 A255 20p dark blue   .80   .60
25th anniv. of the establishment of the Azad Hind (Free India) government by Subhas Chandra Bose (1897-1945), independence leader.

1968, Oct. 27
475 A256 20p blue green   .60   .50
Sister Nivedita (Margaret Noble, 1867-1911), Irish-born friend of India.

Marie Curie and Patient Receiving Radiation A257

1968, Nov. 6   *Perf. 14½x14*
476 A257 20p purple   2.50   .70
Marie Sklodowska Curie (1867-1934), discoverer of radium and polonium.

World Map — A258

Interior of Cochin Synagogue A259

1968, Dec. 1   *Perf. 13*
477 A258 20p blue   .60   .45
21st Intl. Geographical Congress.

Perf. 13x13½
1968, Dec. 15   Photo.   Unwmk.
478 A259 20p vio bl & car rose   1.75   .75
400th anniv. of Cochin Synagogue.

Frigate Nilgiri A260

1968, Dec. 15   *Perf. 13½x13*
479 A260 20p dull violet blue   3.50   .60
Navy Day. The Nilgiri, launched Oct. 23, 1968, was the 1st Indian warship.

Redbilled Blue Magpie A261

Birds: 50p, Brown-fronted pied woodpecker. 1r, Slaty-headed scimitar babbler, vert. 2r, Yellow-backed sunbirds.

1968, Dec. 31   *Perf. 14½x14, 14x14½*
480 A261 20p pink & multi   1.50   .70
481 A261 50p multicolored   2.00   2.25
482 A261 1r multicolored   3.50   1.40
483 A261 2r multicolored   3.00   2.00
Nos. 480-483 (4)   10.00   6.35

Chatterjee (1838-94) A262

Dr. Bhagavan Das A263

1969, Jan. 1   *Perf. 13½*
484 A262 20p ultramarine   .50   .50
Bankim Chandra Chatterjee, writer.

1969, Jan. 12   Photo.   *Perf. 13½*
485 A263 20p red brown   .50   .50
Das (1869-1958), philosopher.

Martin Luther King, Jr. (1929-1968), American Civil Rights Leader — A264

1969, Jan. 25
486 A264 20p olive gray   .90   .35

Mirza Ghalib A265

1969, Feb. 17   *Perf. 14½x14*
487 A265 20p dk gray & salmon   .50   .50
Mirza Ghalib (Asad Ullah Beg Khan 1797-1869), poet who modernized the Urdu language.

Osmania University, Hyderabad, 50th Avviv. A266

1969, Mar. 15   Photo.   *Perf. 14½x14*
488 A266 20p green   .50   .50

Rafi Ahmed Kidwai A267

1969, Apr. 1   *Perf. 13*
489 A267 20p grayish blue   1.75   .60
Minister of communications and food, introduced around-the-clock airmail service.

ILO Emblems A268

1969, Apr. 11   *Perf. 14½x14*
490 A268 20p orange brown   .50   .50
50th anniv. of the ILO.

Memorial Monument and Hands Strewing Flowers — A269

1969, Apr. 13   *Perf. 13½*
491 A269 20p rose carmine   .50   .50
50th anniv. of Jallianwala Bagh, Amritsar, massacre.

Nageswara Rao (1867-1938), Journalist and Congressman A270

1969, May 1   Photo.   *Perf. 13½x14*
492 A270 20p brown   .50   .50

Ardaseer Cursetjee Wadia and Ships A271

1969, May 27   Photo.   *Perf. 14½x14*
493 A271 20p blue green   1.00   .75
Wadia (1808-1877), shipbuilder.

Serampore College, 150th Anniv. — A272

1969, June 7   Photo.   *Perf. 13½*
494 A272 20p violet brown   .50   .50

Dr. Zakir Husain (1897-1969), President of India 1967-1969 A273

1969, June 11   *Perf. 13*
495 A273 20p olive gray   .50   .50

Laxmanrao Kirloskar and Plow A274

1969, June 20
496 A274 20p gray   .50   .50
Kirloskar (1869-1956), industrialist and social reformer, introduced the iron plow to India.

Mahatma Gandhi (1869-1948) A275

Gandhi on the Dandi March A276

20p, Gandhi and his wife Kasturba, horiz. 5r, Gandhi with spinning wheel, horiz.

1969, Oct. 2   Photo.   Unwmk.
Size: 29x25mm
Perf. 13½
497 A275 20p sepia   1.00   .80
Size: 28x38mm
Perf. 13
498 A275 75p ol gray, sal & brn   2.40   .30
Size: 20x38mm
Perf. 14x14½
499 A276 1r bright blue   2.40   2.00
Size: 35½x25½mm
Perf. 13
500 A275 5r orange & sepia   8.00   7.00
Nos. 497-500 (4)   13.80   10.10

Freighter and IMCO Emblem A277

1969, Oct. 14 *Perf. 13*
501 A277 20p ultramarine 3.50 .70
10th anniv. of the Intergovernmental Maritime Consultative Organization.

Globe and Parliament, New Delhi A278

1969, Oct. 30 Photo. *Perf. 14½x14*
502 A278 20p bright blue .50 .50
57th Interparliamentary Conf., New Delhi.

Astronaut on Moon — A279

Nanak Mausoleum, Talwandi, Punjab — A280

1969, Nov. 19 *Perf. 14x14½*
503 A279 20p olive brown 1.00 .60
See note after US No. C76.

1969, Nov. 23 Photo. *Perf. 13½*
504 A280 20p gray violet .50 .50
500th anniv. of the birth of the Guru Nanak, Sikh leader.

Tiger and Globe A281

1969, Nov. 24 *Perf. 14½x14*
505 A281 20p olive grn & red brn 1.10 .65
Intl. Union for the Conservation of Nature and Natural Resources.

T. L. Vaswani A282

Thakkar Bapa A283

1969, Nov. 25 *Perf. 14x14½*
506 A282 20p dark gray .50 .50
T. L. Vaswani (1879-1966), writer and orator.

1969, Nov. 29 *Perf. 13½*
507 A283 20p dark brown .50 .50
Thakkar Bapa (1869-1951), statesman who worked to help the untouchables.

Globe and Telecommunications Symbols — A284

1970, Jan. 21 *Perf. 13*
508 A284 20p Prussian blue .50 .25
12th Plenary Assembly of the Intl. Radio Consultative Committee.

C. N. Annadurai (1909-1969), Journalist — A285

1970, Feb. 2
509 A285 20p dk blue & magenta .50 .50

1970, Feb. 19 Photo. *Perf. 13x13½*
510 A286 20p dark carmine .50 .50
Kishore (1836-1895), publisher.

Munshi Newal Kishore and Printing Plant — A286

Cent. of Nalanda College A287

1970, Mar. 27 Photo. *Perf. 14½x14*
511 A287 20p light red brown .80 .45

Swami Shraddhanand (1856-1926), Patriot — A288

1970, Mar. 30 *Perf. 13½*
512 A288 20p orange brown 1.00 .50

Lenin A289

1970, Apr. 22 Photo. *Perf. 13*
513 A289 20p multicolored .80 .30

UPU Headquarters, Bern — A290

1970, May 20
514 A290 20p black & green .50 .50
New UPU Headquarters in Bern.

Sher Shah Suri — A291

1970, May 22 Photo. *Perf. 13*
515 A291 20p blue green .50 .50
Suri, 15th cent. ruler of Delhi and postal service reformer.

Vir D. Savarkar and Prison at Port Blair, Andamans A292

1970, May 28
516 A292 20p orange brown 1.00 1.00
V. D. Savarkar (1883-1966), patriot.

"UN" and UN Emblem — A293

1970, June 26 Photo. *Perf. 13*
517 A293 20p blue .60 .35
25th anniv. of the UN.

Harvest, Crane, Factory and Emblem A294

1970, Aug. 18 *Perf. 14½x14*
518 A294 20p violet .50 .40
Asian Productivity Year.

Dr. Maria Montessori and Education Symbol A295

1970, Aug. 31 *Perf. 13½x13*
519 A295 20p dull claret .60 .50
Intl. Education Year and Maria Montessori (1870-1952), Italian educator and physician.

Jatindra Nath Mukherjee A296

1970, Sept. 9 *Perf. 14½x14*
520 A296 20p dark red brown 1.75 .60
Mukherjee (1879-1915), revolutionary leader.

Srinivasa Sastri (1869-1946) A297

Iswar Chandra Vidyasagar A298

1970, Sept. 22 Photo. *Perf. 13*
521 A297 20p dk brown & ocher .60 .50
V. S. Srinivasa Sastri, statesman.

1970, Sept. 26
522 A298 20p rose lilac & brown .75 .65
Vidyasagar (1820-91), educator and writer.

Maharishi Valmiki (born c. 1400 B.C.), Poet A299

1970, Oct. 14 Photo. *Perf. 13*
523 A299 20p plum .80 .40

Calcutta Harbor A300

1970, Oct. 17
524 A300 20p blue 2.25 1.00
Cent. of Calcutta Port Commissioners.

Jamia Millia Islamia University, 50th Anniv. A301

1970, Oct. 29 *Perf. 14½x14*
525 A301 20p yellow green 1.10 .90

Jamnalal Bajai (1889-1942), Patriot — A302

1970, Nov. 4 Wmk. 324 *Perf. 13*
526 A302 20p sepia .50 .40

Nurse and Patient — A303

Ludwig van Beethoven A305

Sant Namdeo (1270-1350), Holy Man — A304

1970, Nov. 5
527 A303 20p Prus. blue & red 1.25 .65
50th anniv. of the Indian Red Cross Soc.

1970, Nov. 9 Photo.
528 A304 20p orange .50 .50

1970, Dec. 16 Unwmk. Perf. 13
529 A305 20p dk brn & org 3.75 .90

Children with Stamp Album A306

Design: 1r, Hands holding magnifying glass over Gandhi stamp.

1970, Dec. 23 Photo. Perf. 13
530 A306 20p dull green & lt brn .75 .35
531 A306 1r ocher & brown 5.00 1.25
INPEX 1970, Indian Natl. Phil. Exhib., New Delhi, Dec. 23, 1970-Jan. 6, 1971.

Girl Guide and Sign — A307

Hands Shielding Flame — A308

1970, Dec. 27
532 A307 20p dark brown violet 1.00 .40
Girl Guides, 60th anniv.

1971, Jan. 11
533 A308 20p bis brn & dp clar .50 .40
Centenary of Indian Life Insurance.

Kashi Vidyapith, 50th Anniv. A309

1971, Feb. 10 Perf. 14½x14
534 A309 20p black brown .50 .40
Kashi Vidyapith University, Benares.

Charles Freer Andrews (1871-1940), British Publicist, Friend of Gandhi — A310

1971, Feb. 12 Perf. 13x13½
535 A310 20p orange brown .60 .45

Ravidas, 15th Cent. Poet and Holy Man A311

1971, Feb. Perf. 13
536 A311 20p rose carmine 1.10 .60

Acharya Narendra Deo (1889-1956), Educator, Patriot, Statesman A312

1971, Feb. 18 Photo. Perf. 13
537 A312 20p olive bister .50 .50

Cent. of Indian Census A313

1971, Mar. 10
538 A313 20p ultra & sepia .50 .40

Ramana Maharshi (1879-1950), Holy Man — A314

1971, Apr. 14 Photo. Perf. 13½x14
539 A314 20p ol gray & orange .60 .50

Raja Ravi Varma (1848-1906) and His Painting, Damayanti and the Swan — A315

1971, Apr. 29 Perf. 13x13½
540 A315 20p deep yellow green .80 .65

Dadasaheb Phalke, Movie Camera A316

1971, Apr. 30 Perf. 13½x13
541 A316 20p violet brown 1.25 .60
Dadasaheb Phalke (1870-1944), motion picture pioneer.

Abhisarika, by Abanindranath Tagore A317

Swami Virjanand A318

1971, Aug. 7 Unwmk. Perf. 14x14½
542 A317 20p dark brn & ocher .60 .50
Tagore (1871-1951), painter.

1971, Sept. 14 Perf. 14x13½
543 A318 20p orange brown .60 .50
Virjanand (1778-1868), scholar and sage.

Scuptures and Stairway, Persepolis Palace A319

1971, Oct. 12 Perf. 13
544 A319 20p sepia 1.25 .70
2500th anniv. of the founding of the Persian empire by Cyrus the Great.

World Thrift Day A320

1971, Oct. 31 Perf. 14½x14
545 A320 20p dark violet blue .50 .40

Bodhisatva Padampani, from Ajanta Cave — A321

Girls at Work, by Geeta Gupta — A322

1971, Nov. 4 Perf. 13
546 A321 20p brown 3.00 .90
25th anniv. of UNESCO.

1971, Nov. 14 Perf. 14x14½
547 A322 20p salmon pink .50 .50
Chidren's Day.

C. V. Raman A323

1971, Nov. 21 Perf. 13
548 A323 20p brown & dp org 1.00 .55
Sir Chandrasekhara Venkata Raman (1888-1970), physicist, Nobel Prize winner.

Rabindranath Tagore, Visva-Bharati Building — A324

1971, Dec. 24 Perf. 14½x14
549 A324 20p blk brn & org brn 1.00 .80
50th anniv. of Visva-Bharati, center for Eastern cultural studies.

Indian Cricket Victories A325

1971, Dec. 24
550 A325 20p green 4.50 1.10

Intelsat 3 over Map of Eastern Hemisphere A326

1972, Feb. 26 Photo. Perf. 13½
551 A326 20p dark purple .50 .40
Arvi Satellite Earth Station.

Plumb Line and Symbols — A327

Signal Panel and Route Diagram — A328

1972, May 29   Photo.   Perf. 13
552 A327 20p bluish gray & black   .50 .50
India's Bureau of Standards, 25th anniv.

1972, June 30
553 A328 20p black & multi   2.50 1.25
Intl. Railroad Union (UIC), 50th anniv.

Hockey, Olympic Rings A329

20th Olympic Games, Munich, Aug. 26-Sept. 11: 1.45r, "1972," Olympic rings, symbols for running, wrestling, shooting and hockey.

1972, Aug. 10   Photo.   Perf. 13
554 A329 20p dull violet   3.50 .35
555 A329 1.45r bl grn & dk red   4.00 3.00

Marchers with Flag, Parliament A330

1972, Aug. 15
556 A330 20p blue & multi   1.25 1.00
25th anniv. of Independence.

Armed Forces' Emblems — A331

Symbol of Aurobindo and Sun — A332

1972, Aug. 15
557 A331 20p blue & multi   .75 .55
Honoring India's defense forces.

1972, Aug. 15   Perf. 14x13½
558 A332 20p yellow & blue   .50 .50
Sri Aurobindo Ghose (1872-1950).

V.O. Chidambaram Pillai and Ship — A333

Perf. 13½x13
1972, Sept. 5   Unwmk.
559 A333 20p bl & dk red brn   1.50 .65
V.O. Chidambaram Pillai (1872-1936), founder of steamship company, trade union leader, resistance fighter.

Vemana, 17th-18th Cent. Poet — A334

Bertrand Russell — A335

1972, Oct. 16   Wmk. 324   Perf. 14
560 A334 20p black   .50 .50

1972, Oct. 16   Unwmk.
561 A335 1.45r black   6.25 4.00
British philosopher and pacifist (1872-1970).

Bhai Vir Singh — A336

T. Prakasam — A337

1972, Oct. 16   Perf. 13½
562 A336 20p dull purple   1.10 .45
Bhai Vir Singh (1872-1957), poet and scholar.

1972, Oct. 16
563 A337 20p yellow brown   .50 .40
T. Prakasam (1872-1957), national leader and lawyer.

Hand of Buddha, 9th Century Sculpture — A338

20p, Stylized Hand of Buddha as Fair emblem.

1972, Nov. 3   Wmk. 324   Perf. 13
564 A338 20p orange & black   .40 .40
565 A338 1.45r orange, blk & ind   1.00 2.40
3rd Asian Intl. Trade Fair, ASIA 72, New Delhi.

Vikram Ambalal Sarabhai, Rohini Rocket and Dove A339

1972, Dec. 30   Unwmk.
566 A339 20p slate grn & brn   .60 .60
1st anniv. of the death of Dr. Vikram Ambalal Sarabhai (1919-1971), chairman of Natl. Committee for Space Research.

Flag of USSR and Spasski Tower A340

1972, Dec. 30   Perf. 13
567 A340 20p red & yellow   .60 .60
50th anniv. of the Soviet Union.

INDIPEX 73 Emblem — A341

Wheel of Asoka, Naga (Serpent) — A342

India Gate, Gnat Planes, India's Colors A343

1973, Jan. 8   Photo.   Perf. 13
568 A341 1.45r black, pink & gold   .80 1.40
Intl. Phil. Exhib., New Delhi, 11/14-23/73. See Nos. 597-599.

1973, Jan. 26   Perf. 13
569 A342 20p orange & multi   .35 .35
Perf. 14½x14
570 A343 1.45r violet & multi   2.50 2.50
Republic Day, 25th year of Independence.

Ramakrishna Paramahamsa (1836-86) — A344

Army Postal Service Corps Emblem — A345

1973, Feb. 18   Photo.   Perf. 13
571 A344 20p yellow brown   .60 .50
Hindu spiritual leader; Ramakrishna Mission founded by his followers.

1973, Mar. 1
572 A345 20p violet blue & red   .60 .60
1st anniv. of establishment of Army Postal Service Corps.

Flower, Flag, Map — A346

Kumaran Asan — A347

1973, Apr. 10   Unwmk.   Perf. 13
573 A346 20p blue & multi   .60 .60
1st anniv. of Bangladesh independence.

1973, Apr. 12
574 A347 20p brown   .50 .50
Kumaran Asan (1873-1924), Kerala social reformer and writer.

Flame and Flag of India — A348

1973, Apr. 13
575 A348 20p deep blue & multi   .50 .50
In honor of the martyrs of the massacre of Jallianwala Bagh, Apr. 13, 1919.

B. R. Ambedkar and Parliament Building A349

1973, Apr. 14   Perf. 14½x14
576 A349 20p olive & plum   .50 .50
Bhimrao R. Ambedkar (1891-1956), lawyer, reformer of Hindu law and one of the writers of India's Constitution.

Radha-Kishangarh, by Nihal Chand,
1778 — A350

Indian Miniatures: 50p, Dancing Couple,
late 17th century. 1r, Lovers on a Camel, by
Nasir-ud-Din, c. 1605. 2r, Chained Elephant,
by Zain-al-Abidin, 16th century.

1973, May 5   Photo.   Perf. 13½x13
577 A350 20p gold & multi   .55   .60
578 A350 50p lilac & multi   1.25   2.25
579 A350 1r ocher & multi   1.60   1.75
580 A350 2r gold & multi   2.25   3.75
       Nos. 577-580 (4)   5.65   8.35

Himalayas
A351

1973, May 15   Perf. 13½x13
581 A351 20p blue   .80   .65
  15th anniv. of Indian Mountaineering
Foundation.

Air India
Jet — A352

1973, June 8   Photo.   Perf. 13
582 A352 1.45r multicolored   7.00   5.50
  Air India, 25 years of intl. service.

Stone Cross on
St. Thomas's
Mount,
Madras — A353

Michael
Madhusudan
Dutt — A354

1973, July 3
583 A353 20p gray ol & blue gray .50   .50
  1900th anniv. of the death of St. Thomas.

1973, July 21   Photo.   Perf. 13
584 A354 20p ocher & olive   1.60   .80
  Dutt (1824-1873), writer and poet.

Vishnu Dingambar Paluskar (1872-
1931), Musician — A355

1973, July 21
585 A355 30p red brown   2.00   2.00

Dr. Armauer
G. Hansen,
Microscope,
Petri Dish
with Bacilli
A356

1973, July 21
586 A356 50p deep brown   2.40   2.00
  Cent. of the discovery by Hansen of the
Hansen bacillus, the cause of leprosy.

Nicolaus
Copernicus,
Heliocentric
System
A357

1973, July 21
587 A357 1r vio blue & red brown 2.40 2.00
  500th anniv. of the birth of Nicolaus Copernicus (1473-1543), Polish astronomer.

Allan Octavian
Hume (1829-1912)
A358

1973, July 31
588 A358 20p gray   .50   .50
  Hume, British civil servant and friend of
India, on the 25th anniv. of independence.

Nehru and
Gandhi
A359

1973, Aug. 15   Photo.   Perf. 13
589 A359 20p blue vio & red
            brown   .50   .50
  25th anniv. of India's independence.

Romesh Chunder
Dutt — A360

Ranjit
Sinhji — A361

Vithalbhai Patel
(1873-1933),
National
Leader — A362

1973, Sept. 27   Photo.   Perf. 13
590 A360 20p brown   .50   .50
591 A361 30p dark green   6.50   6.50
592 A362 50p brown   .50   .50
       Nos. 590-592 (3)   7.50   7.50

  Birth anniv.: Dutt (1848-1909), economist
and pres. of Natl. Cong. in 1890; Sinhji, Maharaja of Nawanagar (1872-1933), cricketer.

President's Body
Guard — A363

1973, Sept. 30
593 A363 20p multicolored   2.25   1.50
  Bicentenary of President's Body Guard.

INTERPOL
Emblem — A364

1973, Oct. 9   Photo.   Perf. 13
594 A364 20p brown   .70   .70
  50th anniv. of Intl. Criminal Police Org.

Syed
Ahmad
Khan,
Aligarh
University
A365

1973, Oct. 17
595 A365 20p olive gray   .50   1.00
  Khan (1817-1898), founder of Aligarh Muslim Univ.

Child's
Drawing
A366

1973, Nov. 14   Photo.   Perf. 13
596 A366 20p multicolored   .50   .50
  Children's Day.

Elephant with Howdah, and No.
200 — A367

1973, Nov. 14
597 A367 20p Emblem   .30   .30
598 A367 1r shown   1.60   1.25
599 A367 2r Peacock, vert.   2.00   2.00
  a. Souvenir sheet of 4   9.00   9.00
       Nos. 597-599 (3)   3.90   3.55

  Intl. Phil. Exhib., INDIPEX 73, New Delhi,
Nov. 14-23. No. 599a contains 4 imperf.
stamps similar to Nos. 568, 597-599. The
imperf. stamps from No. 599a were not valid
individually.

NCC
Emblem — A368

Rajagopalachari
A369

1973, Nov. 25
600 A368 20p multicolored   .50   .40
  National Cadet Corps, 25th anniv.

1973, Dec. 25
601 A369 20p gray olive   .50   .50
  Chakravarti Rajagopalachari (1878-1972),
statesman, governor general (1948-50).

Sun Mask — A370

Narasimha
Mask — A371

Designs: Masks.

1974, Apr. 15   Photo.   Perf. 13
602 A370 20p shown   .40   .40
603 A370 50p Moon   .60   .50
604 A371 1r shown   1.10   .80
605 A371 2r Ravana, horiz.   1.40   1.75
  a. Souvenir sheet of 4, #602-605 5.00 5.00
       Nos. 602-605 (4)   3.50   3.45

300th Anniv. of the Coronation of Chatrapati Sivaji Maharaj (1627-1680), Military Leader of the Maharattas and Enlightened Ruler — A372

1974, June 2 Photo. *Perf. 13*
606 A372 25p gold & multi 1.25 .90

Maithili Sharan Gupta — A373

Utkal Gourab Madhusudan Das — A374

Kandukuri Veeresalingam A375

Tipu Sultan — A376

No. 608, Jainarain Vyas. 1r, Max Mueller.

1974 Photo. *Perf. 13*
607 A373 25p red brown .30 .35
608 A373 25p brown .30 .35
609 A374 25p olive gray .30 .35
610 A375 25p red brown .45 .50
611 A376 50p violet brown .95 1.25
612 A376 1r brown 1.10 1.25
Nos. 607-612 (6) 3.40 4.05

Gupta (1886-1964), poet and patriot; Vyas (1899-1963), writer and member of parliament; Das (1848-1934), writer and patriot. Veeresalingam (1848-1919), reformer; Sultan (1750-99), military leader and reformer; Mueller (1823-1900), German scholar of Sanskrit and Indian culture.
Issued: #607-609, 7/3; #610-612, 7/15.

Kamala Nehru — A377

1974, Aug 1 Photo. *Perf. 14½x14*
613 A377 25p multicolored 1.25 1.10
Kamala Nehru (1899-1936), champion of India's freedom, mother of Indira Gandhi.

WPY Emblem — A378

V. V. Giri — A379

1974, Aug. 14 Unwmk. *Perf. 13½*
614 A378 25p buff & plum .50 .40

1974, Aug. 24 *Perf. 13x13½*
615 A379 25p green & multi .50 .50
Vaharagiri Venkata Giri, pres. of India, 1969-74.

Type of 1965-68 and

Tiger — A380

Veena A381

Design: 25p, Axis deer (chital).

1974 Wmk. 324 *Perf. 14½x14*
622 A380 15p dk brn (white "15") 4.50 .75
623 A202 25p brown 1.25 1.00
624 A381 1r black & brown 3.25 .25
Nos. 622-624 (3) 9.00 2.00

Issue dates: 25p, Aug. 20; 15p, 1r, Oct. 1.
See Nos. 671-682.

Madhubani Folk Design, UPU Emblem A384

Designs: 25p, UPU emblem. 2r, Arrows circling globe, UPU emblem, vert.

1974, Oct. 3 Unwmk. *Perf. 13*
634 A384 25p brt blue & gray .85 .30
635 A384 1r olive & multi 1.25 .85
636 A384 2r ocher & multi 2.00 1.90
a. Souvenir sheet of 3, #634-636 10.00 10.00
Nos. 634-636 (3) 4.10 3.05
Cent. of UPU.

A385

1974, Oct. 9 Photo. *Perf. 13½*
637 25p Flute player .60 .50
638 25p Vidyadhara with garland .60 .50
a. A385 Pair, #637-638 2.00 2.00
Cent. of Mathura Museum.

Nicholas Konstantin Roerich, by Henry Dropsy A387

1974, Oct. 9 *Perf. 13*
639 A387 1r dark gray & yellow 1.00 .80
Roerich (1874-1947), Russian painter and sponsor of Roerich Peace Pact.

Pavapuri Temple, Bihar A388

1974, Nov. 13 Photo. *Perf. 13*
640 A388 25p slate .80 .25
2500th anniv. of attainment of Nirvana by Bhagwan Mahavira, leader and preacher of Jainism.

Dancers and Musician (Child's Drawing) A389

1974, Nov. 14 *Perf. 14½x14*
641 A389 25p multicolored .80 .55
UNICEF in India.

Cat (Child's Drawing) — A390

1974, Nov. 14 *Perf. 13*
642 A390 25p multicolored 1.00 .50
Children's Day.

Territorial Army Emblem — A391

1974, Nov. 16 *Perf. 13*
643 A391 25p green, yel & black 1.10 .60
Territorial Army, 25th anniv.

Cows, from Handpainted Rajasthan Cloth — A392

1974, Dec. 2 *Perf. 14*
644 A392 25p ocher & maroon .60 .35
19th Intl. Dairy Cong., New Delhi, Dec. 2-6.

Symbol of Retardates and Child A393

1974, Dec. 8 Photo. *Perf. 13½x13*
645 A393 25p black & vermilion .90 .65
Help the Retardates!

Guglielmo Marconi — A394

1974, Dec. 12 *Perf. 13x13½*
646 A394 2r slate 4.50 3.00
Marconi (1874-1937), Italian electrical engineer and inventor.

St. Francis Xavier's Tomb and Statue A395

1974, Dec. 24 *Perf. 13½x13*
647 A395 25p multicolored .50 .50
Showing of the body of St. Francis Xavier, Apostle to the Indies.

Saraswati, Goddess of Language and Learning, Inscription in Hindi — A396

1975, Jan. 10 Photo. *Perf. 14x14½*
648 A396 25p dark red & gray .70 .60
World Hindi Convention, Nagpur, Jan. 10-14. See No. 654.

Parliament House A397

1975, Jan. 26 *Perf. 13*
649 A397 25p black, blue & silver 1.25 .95
Republic of India, 25th anniv.

Table Tennis Paddle and Ball — A398

1975, Feb. 6 *Perf. 13½x13*
650 A398 25p black, red & olive 1.50 .55
33rd World Table Tennis Championship, Calcutta.

Woman's Hands Releasing Doves A399

1975, Feb. 16
651 A399 25p yellow & multi 1.10 .55
International Women's Year.

Bicentenary of Army Ordnance Corps — A400

1975, Apr. 8 Photo. *Perf. 13x13½*
652 A400 25p black & vermilion 2.25 1.10

Flame A401

1975, Apr. 11 *Perf. 13½x13*
653 A401 25p orange & black .60 .50
Cent. of the founding of Arya Samaj, a movement dedicated to enlightenment and progress and to a revival of Vedic Law and Aryan culture.

Saraswati Type of 1975
25p, Saraswati and inscription in Telugu.

1975, Apr. 12 *Perf. 14x14½*
654 A396 25p dp green & dk gray .80 .45
World Telugu Conf., Hyderabad, Apr. 12-18.

Aryabhata Satellite A402

1975, Apr. 20 *Perf. 13½x13*
655 A402 25p multicolored 1.25 .85
Launching of 1st Indian satellite, Apr. 19, 1975.

Bluewinged Pitta A403

Birds: 50p, Black-headed oriole. 1r, Western tragopan, vert. 2r, Himalayan monal pheasant, vert.

1975, Apr. 28 Perf. 13½x13, 13x13½
656 A403 25p multicolored .95 .30
657 A403 50p multicolored 2.25 2.25
658 A403 1r multicolored 3.25 3.25
659 A403 2r multicolored 4.50 4.50
Nos. 656-659 (4) 10.95 10.30

Quotation from Ram Charit Manas A404

1975, May 24 Photo. *Perf. 13½x13*
660 A404 25p red, orange & black 1.00 .25
Ram Charit Manas, Hindi poem by Goswami Tulsidas (1532-1623).

Women and YWCA Emblem — A405

1975, June 20 Photo. *Perf. 13x13½*
661 A405 25p gray & multi .60 .50
YWCA of India, cent.

Creation of Adam, by Michelangelo — A406

Design: Nos. 664-665, Creation of sun, moon and stars, by Michelangelo.

1975, June 28 *Perf. 14x13½*
662 50p multicolored .65 .50
663 50p multicolored 1.25 1.00
a. A406 Pair #662-663 2.75 2.75
664 50p multicolored 1.25 1.00
665 50p multicolored 1.25 1.00
b. A406 Pair #664-665 2.75 2.75
Michelangelo Buonarroti (1475-1564), Italian sculptor, painter and architect.

Types of 1965-1974 Without Currency Designation and

Flying Crane — A408

Jawaharlal Nehru — A409

Mahatma Gandhi — A410

Himalayas A411

Designs: 2p, Bidri vase. 5p, Family. 10p, Electric locomotive. 15p, Tiger. 20p, Wooden toy horse. 30p, Male and female figurines. 60p, Somnath Temple. 1r, Veena. 5r, Bhakra Dam, Punjab. 10r, Trombay Atomic Center.

Perf. 14½x14, 14x14½, 14 (#674-676), 11½x12 (#681)
Wmk. 324; 360 (# 666A, 667, 668, 670)
1975-88 **Photo.**

Three types of 25p Nehru:
Type I: Size at top, 25mm. Character before NEHRU has 2 lower points.
Type II: Smaller portrait. Size at top, 23mm. Character has 3 points.
Type III: Portrait as in type I. Size at top, 25½mm. Character has 3 points.

666 A202 2(p) redsh brn, wmk. 324('76) 1.25 2.25
666A A202 2(p) redsh brn, wmk. 360('76) 1.25 2.25
667 A202 2(p) redsh brn, wmk. 360, litho ('79) 1.25 2.25
668 A202 5(p) cerise ('76) .75 .20
669 A203 10(p) brt blue ('76) .75 .20
670 A203 10(p) brt blue ('79) 4.00 .60
671 A380 15(p) dk brn (brown "15") 2.00 .20
672 A408 20(p) green .40 .20
673 A409 25(p) vio, I ('76) 10.00 .75
674 A409 25(p) vio, II ('76) 6.50 .75
675 A409 25(p) vio, III ('76) 5.00 .75
676 A410 25(p) red brn ('76) (23x29mm) 1.25 .30
677 A410 25(p) red brn ('78) (17x20mm) 8.00 2.25
678 A202 30(p) brown ('79) 4.00 .50
679 A408 50(p) violet blue 6.50 .30
680 A202 60(p) dk gray ('76) 2.00 1.00
681 A410 60(p) black ('88) 1.10 .25
682 A381 1(r) brown & blk 4.25 .25
683 A411 2(r) violet & brn 17.00 .50
684 A205 5(r) brn & vio ('76) 2.50 .90
685 A205 10(r) dl grn & sl ('76) 2.25 1.10
Nos. 666-685 (21) 82.00 17.75

No. 667 has a background of fine horizontal lines.
See #841-842, 844-845, 846A-846B, 916.
Size of No. 681, 17x20mm.

Irrigation Commission Emblem — A412

"Educational Television" A413

1975, July 28 Photo. *Perf. 14*
686 A412 25p multicolored .80 .30
9th Intl. Cong. on Irrigation and Drainage, Moscow, and 25th anniv. of the Intl. Commission on Irrigation and Drainage.

1975, Aug. 1 *Perf. 13x13½*
687 A413 25p multicolored .80 .45
Inauguration of the Satellite Instructional Television Experiment (SITE).

Arunagirinathar A414

1975, Aug. 14 Photo. *Perf. 13½*
688 A414 50p rose lilac 2.50 1.25
600th birth anniv. of Arunagirinathar, Advaita philosopher, saint and author of Tiruppugazh, a collection of songs.

A415

1975, Aug. 26 Photo. *Perf. 13½*
689 A415 25p rose & black .80 .55
Namibia Day. See note after UN No. 241.

A416

1975, Sept. 4
690 A416 25p slate green .50 .50
Mir Anees (1803-1874), Urdu poet.

Chhatri at Maheshwar A417

1975, Sept. 4 *Perf. 13x13½*
691 A417 25p red brown .50 .50
Queen Ahilyabai Holkar (1725-1795); building shown was place of last rites.

Bharata Natyam Dance — A418

1975, Oct. 20 Photo. *Perf. 13x13½*
Designs: Indian traditional dances.
692 A418 25p shown .95 .65
693 A418 50p Orissi 1.40 .70
694 A418 75p Kathak 1.90 .90
695 A418 1r Kathakali 2.25 1.10
696 A418 1.50r Kuchipudi 2.75 1.60
697 A418 2r Manipuri 2.75 1.60
Nos. 692-697 (6) 12.00 6.55

Krishna
Menon — A419

Ameer
Khusrau — A420

Poem by
Bahadur
Shah Zafar
A421

Design: No. 699, Sardar Vallabhbhai Patel.

1975   **Perf. 13x13½, 13½x13**
698 A419 25p olive   1.40   .70
699 A419 25p slate   .50   .50
700 A420 50p yellow & brown   1.60   .80
701 A421 1r black, brn & buff   2.00   1.00
       Nos. 698-701 (4)   5.50   3.00

Men of India: V. K. Krishna Menon (1896-1974), founder of India League and member of Parliament; Patel (1875-1950), statesman who unified India, birth cent.; Khusrau (1253-1325), poet; Zafar (1775-1862), last Mogul emperor and poet.
Issue dates: #699, Oct. 31; others Oct. 24.

Parliament
Annex,
New Delhi
A422

1975, Oct. 28   **Perf. 14½x14**
702 A422 2r gray olive   3.25   2.00

21st Commonwealth Parliamentary Conf., New Delhi, Oct. 28-Nov. 4.

Karmavir Nabin
Chandra Bardoloi
(1875-1936),
Writer and Gandhi
Associate — A423

1975, Nov. 3   Photo.   Perf. 13
703 A423 25p reddish brown   .50   .35

Cow, Child's
Painting
A424

1975, Nov. 14
704 A424 25p multicolored   1.00   .55

Children's Day.

Security
Press
Building
A425

1975, Dec. 13   Photo.   Perf. 13
705 A425 25p multicolored   .70   .35

India Security Press, 50th anniv.

Gurdwara Sisganj,
Chandni
Chawk — A426

Theosophical
Society
Emblem — A427

1975, Dec. 16
706 A426 25p multicolored   .80   .50

300th anniv. of martyrdom of Tegh Bahadur (1621-75), 9th Sikh Guru; building shown was place of beheading.

1975, Dec. 20
707 A427 25p multicolored   .70   .35

Centenary of Theosophical Society.

Meteorological
Instruments
A428

Indian Bishop
Mark,
1775 — A430

Early Mail
Cart
A429

1975, Dec. 24   Photo.   Perf. 13
708 A428 25p blue vio, blk & grn   1.00   .55

Indian Meteorological Dept., cent.

1975, Dec. 25
709 A429 25p brown & black   1.00   .40
710 A430 2r reddish brn & blk   3.25   1.75

INPEX 75, Indian Natl. Phil. Exhib., Calcutta, Dec. 25-31.

Lalit Narayan
Mishra — A431

Tiger — A432

1976, Jan. 3
711 A431 25p sepia   .60   .30

Mishra (1923-75), Minister of Railroads.

1976, Jan. 24
712 A432 25p multicolored   1.75   .90

Jim Corbett (1875-1955), conservationist.

Painted
Storks
A433

1976, Feb. 10   Photo.   Perf. 13
713 A433 25p sky blue & multi   1.75   .85

Keoladeo Ghana, Bharatpur Water Bird Sanctuary.

Tank
A434

1976, Mar. 4   Photo.   Perf. 13
714 A434 25p multicolored   2.75   .55

16th Light Cavalry, senior regiment of Armoured Corps, bicentenary.

Alexander Graham
Bell — A435

1976, Mar. 10   Photo.   Perf. 13x13½
715 A435 25p yellow & black   1.60   .90

Cent. of 1st telephone call by Bell, Mar. 10, 1876.

Muthuswami
Dikshitar — A436

1976, Mar. 18   **Perf. 14x13½**
716 A436 25p dull violet   1.00   .55

Dikshitar (1775-1835), musician, composer.

Eye and
Red Cross
A437

1976, Apr. 7   **Perf. 13½x13**
717 A437 25p dark brown & red   1.40   .55

World Health Day: "Foresight prevents blindness."

"Industries"
A438

Perf. 13x13½
1976, Apr. 30   **Unwmk.**
718 A438 25p multicolored   .40   .25

Industrial development and progress.

1 F/l type,
Ajmer,
1895
A439

Locomotives: 25p, WDM 2 Diesel Locomotive, 1963. 1r, 1 WP./1, 4-6-2 Pacific type, 1963. 2r, 1 GIP No. 1, 1853.

1976, May 15   **Perf. 15x14**
719 A439 25p multicolored   1.10   .25
720 A439 50p multicolored   1.75   .80
721 A439 1r multicolored   4.00   1.90
722 A439 2r multicolored   4.75   2.10
       Nos. 719-722 (4)   11.60   5.05

Kumaraswamy
Kamaraj (1903-1975),
Independence
Fighter — A440

1976, July 15   Photo.   Perf. 13x13½
723 A440 25p sepia   .50   .50

Target, Olympic
Rings — A441

Hockey — A442

1976, July 17   **Perf. 14**
724 A441 25p dk blue & carmine   .40   .30
725 A441 1r "Team handball"   1.60   .80

726 A442 1.50r black & brt pur
ple   2.75 1.60
727 A441 2.80r "Running"   2.75 2.75
Nos. 724-727 (4)   7.50 5.45

21st Olympic Games, Montreal, Canada, July 17-Aug. 1

Subhadra Kumari Chauhan — A443

Param Vir Chakra Medal — A444

1976, Aug. 6   Photo.   Perf. 13x13½
728 A443 25p grayish blue   .50 .50

Chauhan (1904-1948), Hindi poetess and member of Legislative Assembly.

1976, Aug. 15
729 A444 25p yellow & multi   .50 .50

Medal of Honor awarded for bravery to military men.

Women's University, Bombay A445

1976, Sept. 3   Photo.   Perf. 13½x14
730 A445 25p violet   .50 .30

Indian Women's Univ., 60th anniv.

Bharatendu Harishchandra A446

1976, Sept. 9   Perf. 13
731 A446 25p black brown   .50 .50

Harishchandra (1850-1885), writer, "Father of Modern Hindi."

Sarat Chandra Chatterji — A447

1976, Sept. 15   Unwmk.
732 A447 25p dull purple   .50 .50

Chatterji (1876-1938), writer.

Family Planning — A448

1976, Sept. 22   Photo.   Perf. 14x14½
733 A448 25p multicolored   .50 .50

Maharaja Agrasen, Coin and Brick Wall A449

1976, Sept. 24   Perf. 13½x13
734 A449 25p red brown   .50 .50

Maharaja Agrasen, legendary ruler of Agra.

India Blood Donation Day — A450

Wildlife Protection A451

1976, Oct. 1   Perf. 13x13½
735 A450 25p bister, car & black 1.40 .70

1976, Oct. 1   Perf. 14x14½, 14½x14
736 A451 25p Swamp deer   .70 .35
737 A451 50p Lion   1.90 .95
738 A451 1r Leopard, horiz.   2.75 1.25
739 A451 2r Caracal, horiz.   3.00 1.50
Nos. 736-739 (4)   8.35 4.05

Suryakant Tripathi "Nirala" (1896-1961), Hindi poet — A452

1976, Oct. 15   Perf. 13
740 A452 25p dark violet   .50 .50

Children's Day — A453

1976, Nov. 14   Unwmk.   Perf. 14
741 A453 25p Mongoose and
Woman   .60 .30

Hiralal Shastri — A454

Hari Singh Gour — A455

1976, Nov. 24   Perf. 13
742 A454 25p red brown   .50 .50

Hiralal Shastri (1899-1974), social worker and political leader.

1976, Nov. 26
743 A455 25p plum   .50 .50

Hari Singh Gour (1870-1949), University administrator, member Indian Legislative and Constituent Assemblies.

Airbus A456

1976, Dec. 1   Perf. 14½x14
744 A456 2r multicolored   4.00 2.10

Inauguration of Indian Airlines Airbus.

Hybrid Coconut Palm — A457

1976, Dec. 27   Photo.   Perf. 13x13½
745 A457 25p multicolored   .50 .40

75th anniv. of coconut research in India.

Vande Mataram, First Stanza A458

1976, Dec. 30   Perf. 13
746 A458 25p multicolored   .50 .40

Vande Mataram, national song of India, music by Bankim Chandra Chatterjee, 1896, words by Rabindranath Tagore, 1911.

Film and Globe A459

1977, Jan. 3
747 A459 2r multicolored   2.50 1.25

6th Intl. Film Festival, New Delhi, Jan. 3-16.

Earth's Crust with Fault, Seismograph A460

1977, Jan. 10
748 A460 2r dull purple   1.75 1.40

6th World Conference on Earthquake Engineering, New Delhi, Jan. 10-14.

Tarun Ram Phookun — A461

1977, Jan. 22   Photo.   Perf. 13x13½
749 A461 25p sepia   .50 .50

Phookun (1877-1939), lawyer, Assam political leader.

Paramahansa Yogananda A462

1977, Mar. 7   Photo.   Perf. 13½
750 A462 25p deep orange   1.50 .80

Yogananda (1893-1952), religious leader, founder of Self-realization Society in America.

Red Cross Conference Emblem — A463

Fakhruddin Ali Ahmed (1905-77) — A464

1977, Mar. 9
751 A463 2r multicolored   3.50 2.00

1st Asian Regional Red Cross Conference, New Delhi, Mar. 9-16.

1977, Mar. 22   Photo.   Perf. 13½x13
752 A464 25p multicolored   .60 .40

Ahmed, Pres. of India, 1974-77.

Asian-Oceanic Postal Union Emblem — A465

1977, Apr. 1   **Perf. 13**
753 A465 2r silver & multi   1.75 1.25
   Asian-Oceanic Postal Union, 15th anniv.

"Loyalty" and Morarjee A466

1977, Apr. 2   **Perf. 13½x13**
754 A466 25p blue   1.25 .70
   Narottam Morarjee (1877-1929), founder of Scindia Steam Ship Navigation Co.

Makhanlal Chaturvedi A467

1977, Apr. 4   **Perf. 13**
755 A467 25p orange brown   .50 .50
   Chaturvedi (1889-1968), Hindi writer.

Mahaprabhu Vallabhacharya A468

1977, Apr. 14
756 A468 1r olive brown   .50 .50
   Vallabhacharya (1479-1531), philosopher.

Federation Emblem A469

1977, Apr. 23   **Perf. 13½x13**
757 A469 25p ocher & purple   .50 .50
   Federation of Indian Chambers of Commerce, 50th anniv.

Protection of Environment A470

1977, June 5   **Photo.**   **Perf. 13**
758 A470 2r multicolored   .80 .55

Council of States Chamber A471

1977, June 21
759 A471 25p multicolored   .50 .50
   Council of States, Rajya Sabha (Parliament), 25th anniv.

Lotus A472

50p and 1r are vert.

1977, July 1   **Perf. 15x14, 14x15**
760 A472 25p shown   .50 .30
761 A472 50p Rhododendron   .85 .50
762 A472 1r Kadamba   1.10 .75
763 A472 2r Gloriosa lily   1.90 1.10
   Nos. 760-763 (4)   4.35 2.65

Berliner Gramaphone — A473

1977, July 20   **Perf. 13½x13**
764 A473 2r black & brown   1.50 .90
   Centenary of the phonograph.

Ananda Kentish Coomaraswamy (1877-1947) and Dancing Shiva — A474

1977, Aug. 22   **Photo.**   **Perf. 13x13½**
765 A474 25p multicolored   .60 .30
   Coomaraswamy, art historian and critic.

Ganga Ram (1851-1927) and Hospital, New Delhi — A475

1977, Sept. 4   **Perf. 14½x14**
766 A475 25p rose carmine   .50 .35
   Ram, social reformer and philanthropist.

Dr. Samuel Hahnemann and Cinchona — A476

19th Century Postman — A477

Lion and Palm Tree, East India Co. Essay — A478

1977, Oct. 6   **Photo.**   **Perf. 13**
767 A476 2r black & green   5.50 2.75
   32nd Intl. Homeopathic Cong., New Delhi.

1977, Oct. 12   **Perf. 13**
768 A477 25p multicolored   1.00 .50
     Perf. 13½
769 A478 2r mag & gray, *buff*   2.75 1.75
   INPEX '77 Phil. Exhib., Bangalore, 10/12-16.

Ram Manohar Lohia (1910-67), Founder of Congress Socialist Party, Sec. of Foreign Dept. — A479

1977, Oct. 12   **Perf. 13x13½**
770 A479 25p red brown   1.60 1.10

Red Scinde Dawks, 1852 A480

   Design: 3r, Foreign mail arriving at Ballard Pier, Bombay, 1927.

1977, Oct. 19   **Perf. 13½x13**
771 A480 1r orange & multi   2.50 1.10
772 A480 3r orange & multi   4.50 2.10
   ASIANA 77, First Asian International Philatelic Exhibition, Bangalore, Oct. 19-23.

Statue of Rani Channamma — A481

1977, Oct. 23
773 A481 25p gray green   2.25 1.10
   Rani Channamma of Kittue (1778-1829), who fought against British rule.

Mother and Child, Khajuraho Sculpture — A482

1977, Oct. 23   **Perf. 13x13½**
774 A482 2r gray & sepia   3.50 2.25
   15th Intl. Pediatrics Congress.

Sun and National Colors — A483

Stylized Grain — A484

1977, Nov. 8   **Photo.**   **Perf. 13**
775 A483 25p multicolored   .60 .35
   Union Public Service Commission, founded 1926.

1977, Nov. 13
776 A484 25p green   .60 .30
   AGRIEXPO '77, Intl. Agriculture Exhib.

Cats A485

   1r, Friends. Designs are from children's drawings.

1977, Nov. 14
777 A485 25p multicolored   .95 .45
778 A485 1r multicolored   3.50 2.25
   Children's Day.

Jotirao Phooley — A486

1977, Nov. 28   **Wmk. 324**
779 A486 25p gray olive   .50 .40
   Phooley (1827-1890), social reformer.

Senapati Bapat — A487

1977, Nov. 28
780 A487 25p brown orange   .50 .40
   Senapati Bapat (Pandurang Mahadev Bapat, 1880-1967), scholar and fighter for India's independence.

Diagram of Population Growth — A488

Perf. 13x13½
1977, Dec. 13 **Unwmk.**
781 A488 2r carmine & blue grn .80 .55
41st Session of Intl. Statistical Institute, New Delhi, Dec. 5-15.

Kamta Prasad (1875-1947) and Hindi Grammar A489

1977, Dec. 25 **Wmk. 324** **Perf. 14**
782 A489 25p sepia .50 .50
Prasad, compiler of Hindi Grammar.

Spasski Tower, Russian Flag — A490

1977, Dec. 30 **Unwmk.** **Perf. 13**
783 A490 1r multicolored .80 .55
60th anniv. of Russian October revolution.

Climber Crossing Crevasse — A491

Indian Flag near Summit A492

Perf. 13½x13, 13x13½
1978, Jan. 15 **Photo.**
784 A491 25p multicolored .30 .30
785 A492 1r multicolored .70 .55
Conquest of Kanchenjunga (Himalayas), by Indian team under Col. N. Kumar, May 31, 1977.

Tourists in Shikara on Dal Lake A493

1978, Jan. 23 **Perf. 13x13½**
786 A493 1r multicolored 3.50 1.75
27th Pacific Area Travel Assoc. Conf., New Delhi, Jan. 23-26.

Children in Library, Fair Emblem A494

1978, Feb. 11 **Photo.** **Perf. 13**
787 A494 1r rose brown & indigo .65 .40
3rd World Book Fair, New Delhi, Feb. 1978.

Mother of Pondicherry A495

1978, Feb. 21
788 A495 25p dark & light brown .50 .40
Mother of the Sri Aurobindo Ashram, Pondicherry (Mira Richard, 1878-1973, born in Paris).

Wheat, Globe and Genetic Helix — A496

1978, Feb. 23
789 A496 25p yellow & blue green .50 .40
5th Intl. Wheat Genetics Symposium.

Nanalal Dalpatram Kavi — A497

Wmk. 324
1978, Mar. 16 **Photo.** **Perf. 13**
790 A497 25p rose brown .50 .40
Kavi (1877-1946), Gujarati poet.

Surjya Sen (1894-1934), Patriot — A498

1978, Mar. 22
791 A498 25p ver, black & brown .50 .40

Two Vaishnavas (Vishnu Worshippers) by Jaminy Roy — A499

Modern Indian Paintings: 50p, The Mosque, by Sailoz Mookherjea. 1r, Woman's Head, by Rabindranath Tagore. 2r, Hill Women, by Amrita Sher Gil.

Perf. 13½x14
1978, Mar. 23 **Unwmk.**
792 A499 25p black & multi .30 .30
793 A499 50p black & multi .60 .60
794 A499 1r black & multi 1.10 1.10
795 A499 2r black & multi 1.25 1.25
Nos. 792-795 (4) 3.25 3.25

Rubens, Self-portrait A500

1978, Apr. 4 **Photo.** **Perf. 13½x13**
796 A500 2r multicolored 4.00 2.40

"The Little Tramp," Charlie Chaplin — A501

1978, Apr. 16 **Perf. 13**
797 A501 25p gold & indigo 2.75 1.25

Deendayal Upadhyaya (1916-68) — A502

1978, May 5 **Photo.** **Perf. 13**
798 A502 25p multicolored .50 .40
Upadhyaya, social and political reformer.

Syama Prasad Mookerjee (1901-1953) A503

"Airavat," 19th Century Wood Carving — A504

Kushan Gold Coin, 1st Century A505

1978, July 6 **Photo.** **Perf. 13**
799 A503 25p gray olive .50 .35
Dr. Mookerjee, educator, member of 1st natl. government.

1978, July 27
Designs: 50p, Wish-fulfilling tree, 2nd century B.C. 2r, Dagger and knife.
800 A504 25p multicolored .60 .60
801 A504 50p multicolored .80 .80
802 A505 1r multicolored 1.10 1.10
803 A505 2r multicolored 1.40 1.40
Nos. 800-803 (4) 3.90 3.90
Treasures from Indian museums.

Krishna and Arjuna on Battlefield, Quotation A506

1978, Aug. 25 **Unwmk.** **Perf. 13**
804 A506 25p orange red & gold .50 .40
Bhagavad Gita, part of Mahabharata Epic, the Divine Song of the Lord.

Bethune College for Women, Calcutta A507

1978, Sept. 4
805 A507 25p green & brown .50 .40

E. V. Ramasami A508

1978, Sept. 17
806 A508 25p black .50 .40
E. V. Ramasami (1879-1973), founder of Self-respect Movement, fighting caste system and social injustice.

Uday Shankar — A509

1978, Sept. 26
807 A509 25p buff & violet brown .50 .40
Uday Shankar (1900-77), dancer.

Leo Tolstoi — A510

Vallathol Narayana Menon — A511

1978, Oct. 2
808 A510 1r multicolored .75 .40
Tolstoi, novelist and philosopher.

1978, Oct. 15 Photo. Perf. 13
809 A511 25p multicolored .50 .50
Menon (1878-1958), poet.

"Two Friends" A512

1978, Nov. 14 Photo. Perf. 13
810 A512 25p multicolored .50 .40
Children's Day.

Worker at Lathe — A513

1978, Nov. 17 Perf. 13½
811 A513 25p green .50 .40
Small Industries Fair.

Skinner's Horse Soldiers — A514

Chakravarti Rajagopalachari A515

1978, Nov. 25 Perf. 13
812 A514 25p multicolored 1.50 .80
175th anniv. of Skinner's Horse Regiment.

1978, Dec. 10 Photo. Perf. 13
813 A515 25p maroon .50 .40
Chakravarti Rajagopalachari (1878-1972), first post-independence Governor General.

A516

A517

1978, Dec. 10
814 A516 25p olive green .50 .40
Mohammad Ali Jauhar (1878-1931), writer and patriot.

1978, Dec. 23 Perf. 13x14
815 A517 1r ocher & purple 1.25 .40
Wright Brothers, Flyer, 75th anniv. of 1st powered flight.

Ravenshaw College, Orissa, Centenary A518

1978, Dec. 24 Perf. 14
816 A518 25p green & maroon .50 .40

Franz Schubert (1797-1828), Austrian Composer — A519

1978, Dec. 25 Perf. 13
817 A519 1r multicolored 2.25 .90

Punjab Regiment, Uniforms and Crest A520

1979, Feb. 20 Photo. Unwmk.
818 A520 25p multicolored 2.50 1.00
Oldest Indian infantry unit.

Bhai Parmanand (1876-1947) A521

Gandhi and Child — A522

1979, Feb. 24
819 A521 25p violet blue .50 .40
Parmanand, writer and educator.

1979, Mar. 5 Photo. Perf. 13
Design: 1r, IYC emblem.
820 A522 25p dk brown & red .50 .30
821 A522 1r dp org & dk brn .75 .60

Albert Einstein (1879-1955), Theoretical Physicist — A523

1979, Mar. 14
822 A523 1r black 1.25 .65

Rajarshi Shahu Chhatrapati (1874-1922), Ruler of Kolhapur — A524

1979, May 1 Photo. Perf. 13x13½
823 A524 25p dull purple .50 .40

Lotus, India '80 Emblem A525

1979, July 2 Photo. Perf. 13
824 A525 30p deep orange & green .50 .40
India '80 Phil. Exhib., New Delhi, Jan. 25-Feb. 3, 1980.

Postal Cards, 1879 and 1979 — A526

Raja Mahendra Pratap (1886-1979), Patriot — A527

1979, July 2
825 A526 50p multicolored .50 .40

1979, Aug. 15 Photo. Perf. 13
826 A527 30p olive gray .50 .40

Jatindra Nath Das (1904-1929) A528

1979, Sept. 13
827 A528 30p dark brown .50 .40
Das, political martyr.

Early and Modern Light Bulbs — A529

1979, Oct. 21 Photo. Perf. 13
828 A529 1r rose magenta .80 .65
Centenary of invention of electric light.

Buddhist Text A530

1979, Oct. 23 Perf. 14½x14
829 A530 30p brown & bister .50 .40
National Archives.

Hirakud Dam A531

Perf. 13½x13
1979, Oct. 29 Wmk. 324
830 A531 30p brown red & dull grn .50 .40
13th Congress (Golden Jubilee) of the Intl. Commission on Large Dams, New Delhi, 10/29-11/2.

Boy and Alphabet Book A532

1979, Nov. 10   Photo.   Perf. 14½x14
831   A532   30p multicolored   .50   .40
Intl. Children's Book Fair, New Delhi, 11/10-19.

Fair Emblem — A533

1979, Nov. 10   Perf. 13
832   A533   1r black & orange   .50   .40
India Intl. Trade Fair, New Delhi, 11/10-12/9.

Dove, Agency Emblem A534

1979, Dec. 4   Perf. 13½x13
833   A534   1r multicolored   .60   .45
23rd Intl. Atomic Energy Agency Conf., New Delhi, Dec. 4-10.

Hindustan Pushpak Plane, Rohini-1 Glider A535

1979, Dec. 10   Perf. 13½x13
834   A535   30p multicolored   2.75   1.40

Gurdwara Baoli Shrine, Goindwal — A536

1979, Dec. 21   Perf. 13x13½
835   A536   30p multicolored   .50   .40
Guru Amardas (1469-1574), Sikh spiritual leader.

Types of 1975-79 and

Women in Rice Field A537

Family Planning A537a

Designs: 2p, Adult education. 5p, Fish. 15p, Agricultural technology. 20p, Child nutrition. No. 840, Poultry. No. 840B, Farm, wheat, farmer plowing. 1r, Hybrid cotton. 2r, Weaving. 5r, Rubber tapping.

Perf. 14x14½, 14½x14, 13 (#840B)
1979-85   Photo.   Wmk. 324
836   A537   2p violet   .80   .65
837   A537   5p blue   .80   .65
838   A537a   15p blue grn ('80)   .80   .65
839   A537a   20p henna brn ('81)   .80   .65
840   A537   25p brown   .80   .65
840B A537   25p brt green ('85)   .80   .65
841   A409   30p violet ('80)   3.00   .80
842   A410   30p red brown ('80)   2.00   .80
843   A537   30p yel green   .80   .65
844   A409   35p violet ('80)   2.00   .80
845   A410   35p red brown ('80)   1.40   .80
846   A537a   35p cerise ('80)   .80   .65
846A A409   50p violet ('83)   .80   .65
846B A410   50p red brown ('83)   2.00   .80

Size: 17x28mm
847   A537a   1r brown ('80)   .80   .65
848   A537a   2r rose violet ('80)   1.25   .65

Size: 20x37mm
849   A537a   5r multi ('80)   1.75   .80
Nos. 836-849 (17)   21.40   11.95

Size: #841-842, 844-845, 846A-846B, 17x20mm.
See Nos. 895-900A, 903-917.

1979-83   Perf. 13
837a   A537   5p   .25   .20
837b   A537   5p Litho. ('82)   .60   .30
838a   A537a   15p   .25   .20
839a   A537a   20p   .40   .20
840a   A537   25p brown   .40   .20
843a   A537   30p   .60   .30
844a   A409   35p   .90   .30
845a   A410   35p   .30   .20
04Cc   A537a   35p   .60   .20
846d   A409   50p   .60   .20
846e   A410   50p   .25   .20

Perf. 12½x13
847a   A537a   1r   .25   .20

Perf. 13x13½, 13½x13
848a   A537a   2r ('83)   .25   .20
849a   A537a   5r ('83)   .50   .35
Nos. 837a-849a (14)   6.15   3.15

People Holding Hands, UN Emblem — A538

1980, Jan. 21   Photo.   Perf. 13
851   A538   1r multicolored   .50   .40
UN Industrial Development Org. (INIDO), 3rd Gen. Conf., New Delhi, Jan. 21-Feb. 8.

Field Post Office, Cancels — A539

Money Order Centenary — A540

2-Anna Copper Coins, 1774 — A541

Rowland Hill, Birthplace, Kidderminster A542

Wmk. 360, Unwmkd. (1r)
1980, Jan. 25
852   A539   30p gray olive   .55   .40
853   A540   50p brown & citron   .85   .85
854   A541   1r bronze   1.10   1.00
855   A542   2r dark gray   1.10   1.00
Nos. 852-855 (4)   3.60   3.25
INDIA '80 Intl. Stamp Exhib., New Delhi, Jan. 25-Feb. 3.

India Institution of Engineers, 60th Anniversary A543

Uniforms, 1780 and 1980, Arms and Ribbon — A544

Perf. 13x13½
1980, Feb. 17   Unwmk.
856   A543   30p dark blue & gold   .50   .40

1980, Feb. 26
857   A544   30p multicolored   2.00   1.00
Madras Sappers bicentennial.

2nd Intl. Apiculture Conf., New Delhi A545

1980, Feb. 29   Perf. 13½
858   A545   1r multicolored   2.00   1.00

A546

A547

1980, Feb. 29   Wmk. 360
859   A546   30p bright blue   .60   .40
4th World Book Fair, New Delhi.

1980, Mar. 18   Perf. 13x13½
860   A547   30p blue gray   .50   .35
Welthy Fisher (b. 1879), educator, Literacy House, Lucknow.

Darul Uloom Islamic School, Deoband A548

1980, Mar. 21   Perf. 13½
861   A548   30p gray green   .50   .40

Keshub Chunder Sen — A549

Sivaji, Raigad Fort — A550

Perf. 13x13½
1980, Apr. 15   Photo.   Wmk. 360
862   A549   30p brown   .50   .40
Sen (1838-84), scholar, writer, journalist.

1980, Apr. 21   Unwmk.
863   A550   30p multicolored   .50   .40
Sivaji (1627-80), Indian patriot.

Narayan Malhar Joshi — A551

Ulloor S. Parameswara Iyer — A552

Perf. 13x13½
1980, June 5   **Wmk. 360**
864 A551 30p lilac rose   .80   .50
Joshi (1879-1955), trade union pioneer.

1980, June 6
865 A552 30p dull purple   .80   .50
Iyer (1877-1949), poet and scholar.

Syed Mohammad
Zamin Ali — A553

1980, June 25
866 A553 30p dk yellow green   .50   .40
Ali (1880-1955), linguist and educator.

Helen Keller
(1880-
1968) — A554

1980, June 27
867 A554 30p orange & black   1.60   .75
Keller, blind and deaf writer and lecturer.

High Jump,
Olympic
Rings
A555

Prem Chand
(1880-1936)
A556

1980, July 19   Photo.   Perf. 13½x14
868 A555   1r shown   1.00   .25
869 A555 2.80r Equestrian   2.50 1.50
22nd Summer Olympic Games, Moscow,
July 19-Aug. 3.

1980, July 31   **Perf. 13**
870 A556 30p red brown   .50   .40
Pen name of Nawab Rai, writer.

Mother
Teresa,
Nobel
Peace Prize
Medallion
A557

Perf. 13½x13
1980, Aug. 27   Photo.   Wmk. 360
871 A557 30p violet, *grayish*   2.50 1.25
Mother Teresa, founder of Missionaries of
Charity, 70th birthday.

Earl Mountbatten
of Burma — A558

Asian Table Tennis
Championship
A559

1980, Aug. 28   Perf. 13x13½
872 A558 2.80r multicolored   4.00 2.00
Mountbatten (1900-79), 1st governor gen. of
India.

1980, Sept.   Photo.   Perf. 13x13½
873 A559 30p magenta   .80   .55

Scottish Church College, Calcutta,
Sesquicentennial — A560

1980, Sept. 27   Photo.   Perf. 13½
874 A560 35p dull purple   .50   .40

Rajah Annamalai
Chettiar (1881-
1948), Banker,
Founder of
Annamalai
University — A561

1980, Sept. 30   Unwmk.   Perf. 14x15
875 A561 35p dull purple   .50   .40

Gandhi
A562

1980, Oct. 2   Perf. 15x14
876   35p Gandhi on Dandi
             March   .75   .50
877   35p Gandhi Defying Salt
             Law   .75   .50
  a. A562 Pair, #876-877   3.00 3.00

Jayaprakash
Narayan (1902-79),
Writer — A564

1980, Oct. 8   Wmk. 360   Perf. 14x15
878 A564 35p red brown   .80   .55

Intl. Symposium
on Bustards,
Jaipur — A565

1980, Nov. 1   Photo.   Perf. 13
879 A565 2.30r Great Indian bus-
               tards   2.25 1.75

Hegira
(Pilgrimage
Year)
A566

1980, Nov. 3   Perf. 13x13½
880 A566 35p multicolored   .50   .50

Children's
Day — A567

Perf. 13½x13
1980, Nov. 14   Unwmk.
881 A567 35p multicolored   1.50   .90

Dhyan   Miner, Molten
Chand — A568   Gold — A569

1980, Dec. 3   Wmk. 360   Perf. 14x15
882 A568 35p dark rose brown   1.50 1.00
Chand (1906-1979), field hockey player.

Perf. 13x13½
1980, Dec. 20   Unwmk.
883 A569 1r multicolored   2.75   .70
Kolar gold fields centenary.

Mukhtar Ahmad
Ansari (1880-1936),
Surgeon — A570

Perf. 14x15
1980, Dec. 25   Wmk. 360
884 A570 35p olive gray   .60   .30

Government Mint, Bombay,
Sesquicentennial — A571

Perf. 13½x13
1980, Dec. 27   Unwmk.
885 A571 35p multicolored   .25   .20

Regional Bridal   Mazharul Haque
Outfits — A572   (1866-1930),
                      Patriot — A573

1980, Dec. 30   Perf. 13x13½
886 A572 1r Kashmir   .75   .50
887 A572 1r Bengal   .75   .50
888 A572 1r Rajasthan   .75   .50
889 A572 1r Tamilnadu   .75   .50
  Nos. 886-889 (4)   3.00 2.00

1981, Jan. 2   Wmk. 360   Perf. 14x15
890 A573 35p violet   .50   .40

St. Stephen's College
Centenary — A574

1981, Feb. 1   Photo.   Perf. 14x14½
891 A574 35p dull red   .50   .40

Gommateshwara   Ganesh V.
Statue,   Mavalankar
Shravanabelgola   (1888-1956)
A575   A576

1981, Feb. 9   Unwmk.
892 A575 1r multicolored   .50   .40

1981, Feb. 27
893 A576 35p light red brown   .50   .40
Mavalankar, 1st speaker of parliament.

Type of 1979
Perf. 14½x14
1981-86   Photo.   Wmk. 324
Size: 19½x37½mm
895   A537 2.25r Cashew   .75   .50
  a.   Perf. 14x14½   .30   .20
  b.   Perf. 13   .25   .20
896   A537 2.80r Apples   1.00   .60
  a.   Perf. 14x14½   .40   .20
897   A537 3.25r Oranges ('83)   .60   .45
  a.   Perf. 13½x13 ('85)   .30   .20
  b.   Perf. 13   .30   .20
900   A537 10r Trees on hillside
                  ('84)   .75   .40
  b.   Perf. 13½x13½   1.25   .60
Perf. 13½x13
Size: 37½x19½mm
900A   A537 50r Windmill ('86)   2.00 1.25
  Nos. 895-900A (5)   5.10 3.20

Homage to Martyrs — A577

1981, Mar. 23   Unwmk.   *Perf. 14x15*
901 A577 35p multicolored   .50 .40

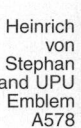

Heinrich von Stephan and UPU Emblem A578

1981, Apr. 8   *Perf. 15x14*
902 A578 1r red brown & brt blue .50 .40

Types of 1979 and

Telecommunications A578a

Natural Gas A578b

Perf. 14x14½, 14½x14, 13 (40p, 75p), 13x13½ (20r)
Wmk. 324, 360 (2p, 5p, 15p)
1981-90   Photo.
Size: 20x17mm, 17x20mm (1r)
903 A537   2p violet   .20 .20
904 A537   5p blue   .20 .20
905 A537   10p Irrigation   .20 .20
  a.   Perf. 13   .20 .20
906 A537a 15p blue green   .20 .20
912 A578a 40p dull red   .20 .20
914 A537   50p Dairy industry .20 .20
  a.   Perf. 13   .20 .20
915 A537a 75p vermilion   .20 .20
916 A410   1r orange brown   .20 .20
Size: 32x19mm
917 A578b 20r sepia & dark blue 1.00 .60
  Nos. 903-917 (9)   2.60 2.20

Issued: 10p, 50p, 1/25/82; 40p, 10/15/88; 20r, 11/30/88; 75p, 1990; 1r, 1/30/91; others, 3/25/81.

Intl. Year of the Disabled A579

Perf. 14½x14
1981, Apr. 20   Photo.   Unwmk.
919 A579 1r blue & black   .60 .40

Tribesman — A580

1981, May 30   *Perf. 14x14½*
920 A580 1r Khiamngan Naga   .70 .50
921 A580 1r Toda   .70 .50
922 A580 1r Bhil   .70 .50
923 A580 1r Dandami Maria   .70 .50
  Nos. 920-923 (4)   2.80 2.00

World Environment Day — A581

1981, June 15
924 A581 1r multicolored   .50 .40

Nilmoni Phukan (1880-1978), Writer — A582

1981, June 22
925 A582 35p red brown   .50 .40

Sanjay Gandhi (1946-1980), Politician — A583

1981, June 23   *Perf. 13x13½*
926 A583 35p multicolored   .90 .60

SLV-3 Take-off — A584

1981, July 18   Photo.   *Perf. 14x15*
927 A584 1r multicolored   .60 .40
Launching of India's 1st satellite, 1st anniv.

Mascot, Field Hockey A585

1981, July 28   *Perf. 13½x13*
928 A585 1r shown   1.60 .75
929 A585 1r Emblem   1.60 .75
9th Asian Games, New Delhi, 1982.

Flame of the Forest — A586

Designs: Flowering trees.

1981, Sept. 1   Photo.   *Perf. 13*
930 A586 35p shown   1.10 .35
931 A586 50p Crateva   .65 .45
932 A586 1r Golden shower   1.50 .75
933 A586 2r Bauhinia   2.25 1.50
  Nos. 930-933 (4)   5.50 3.05

World Food Day — A587

1981, Oct. 16   Photo.   *Perf. 14x14½*
934 A587 1r multicolored   .60 .45

Cyrestis Achates — A588

1981, Oct. 20   *Perf. 13*
935 A588 35p Stichophthalma camadeva, horiz. 1.50 .50
936 A588 50p Cethosia biblis, horiz.   2.50 1.50
937 A588 1r shown   3.25 1.00
938 A588 2r Treinopalpus imperialis   4.00 4.00
  Nos. 935-938 (4)   11.25 7.00

Bellary Raghava (1880-1946), Actor — A589

1981, Oct. 31   *Perf. 14½x14*
939 A589 35p olive gray   1.40 .60

40th Anniv. of Mahar Regiment — A590

Children's Day — A591

1981, Nov. 9   *Perf. 13*
940 A590 35p multicolored   1.75 .60

1981, Nov. 14   *Perf. 14x14½*
941 A591 35p multicolored   1.10 .45

Rajghat Stadium A591a

1981   *Perf. 13½x13*
942 A591a 1r shown   2.40 .45
943 A591a 1r Nehru Stadium   .35 .25
Asian games. Issued: #942, 11/19; #943, 12/30.

Kashi Prasad Jayaswal (1881-1937), Historian — A592

1981, Nov. 27   *Perf. 14x14½*
944 A592 35p chalky blue   .80 .35

Intl. Palestinian Solidarity Day A593

1981, Nov. 29   *Perf. 14½x14*
945 A593 1r multicolored   4.25 .70

Naval Ship Taragiri A594

1981, Dec. 4
946 A594 35p multicolored   5.00 2.25

Henry Heras (1888-1955), Historian — A595

1981, Dec. 14   Photo.   *Perf. 14½x14*
947 A595 35p rose violet   .60 .35

Indian Ocean Commonwealth Submarine Telephone Cable — A596

1981, Dec. 24   *Perf. 13½*
948 A596 1r multicolored   4.00 .55

5th World Field Hockey Championship, Bombay — A597

1981, Dec. 29   *Perf. 13½x13*
949 A597 1r multicolored   2.25 .60

Telephone Service Centenary — A598

Perf. 13x13½

1982, Jan. 28   **Unwmk.**
950 A598 2r multicolored   .75   .50

12th Intl.
Soil Science
Congress,
New Delhi,
Feb. 8-16
A599

1982, Feb. 8   **Perf. 13½x13**
951 A599 1r multicolored   .40   .25

Sir Jamsetjee
Jejeebhoy School
of Art,
Bombay — A600

1981, Mar. 2   **Photo.**   **Perf. 14x14½**
952 A600 35p multicolored   .40   .30

Three Musicians, by Pablo Picasso
(1881-1973) — A601

1982, Mar. 15   **Photo.**   **Perf. 14**
953 A601 2.85r multicolored   3.00   1.00

Deer, 5th Cent. Bas
Relief — A602

Radio
Telescope,
Ooty
A603

Festival of India, England: No. 955, Krishna,
9th cent. bronze sculpture.

1982, Mar. 23   **Perf. 14x15**
954 A602 2r multicolored   .90   .90
955 A602 3.05r multicolored   .60   .45
           Perf. 13
956 A603 3.05r multicolored   .60   .35
   Nos. 954-956 (3)   2.10   1.70

TB Bacillus
Centenary
A604

1982, Mar. 24   **Perf. 13**
957 A604 35p rose violet   3.50   1.60

Durgabai Deshmukh (1909-1981),
Social Worker — A605

1982, May 9   **Photo.**   **Perf. 14½x14**
958 A605 35p blue   .80   .35

Himalayan
Flowers — A606

1982, May 29   **Perf. 14x14½**
959 A606   35p Blue poppies   1.25   .60
960 A606   1r Showy inula   3.00   .60
961 A606   2r Cobra lily   3.50   2.50
962 A606   2.85r Brahma kamal   4.25   4.25
   Nos. 959-962 (4)   12.00   7.95

Ariana Passenger Payload
Experimental (APPLE) Satellite, First
Anniv. — A607

1982, June 19   **Perf. 13½x13**
963 A607 2r multicolored   1.00   .65

Bidhan Chandra Roy (1882-1962),
Physician and Politician — A608

1982, July 1   **Perf. 14½x14**
964 A608 50p orange brown   1.40   .95

Sagar
Samrat
Drilling
Rig — A609

1982, Aug. 14   **Photo.**   **Perf. 13**
985 A609 1r multicolored   3.00   1.25

Bindu (Cosmic   Kashmir
Spirit), by   Stag — A611
Raza — A610

Paintings; 3.05r, Between the Spider and
the Lamp, 1956, by M.F. Husain.

1982, Sept. 17   **Perf. 14x14½**
986 A610 2r multicolored   .90   .55
987 A610 3.05r multicolored   1.25   1.00

1982, Oct. 1   **Perf. 13x13½**
988 A611 2.85r multicolored   5.00   3.25

50th Anniv.
of Indian Air
Force
A612

1982, Oct. 8   **Perf. 13½x13**
989 A612 1r Wapiti, MiG 25   9.50   2.00

50th Anniv.
of Civil
Aviation
A613

1982, Oct. 15
990 A613 3.25r J.R.D. Tata and
his Puss Moth,
1932   8.50   3.00

Police
Memorial
Day — A614

1982, Oct. 21
991 A614 50p Beat patrol   1.10   .55

Post Office
Savings
Bank
Centenary
A615

1982, Oct. 23
992 A615 50p brown   .50   .40

9th Asian
Games
A616

1982   **Perf. 13½x14**
993   A616 1r Wrestling, by
         Janaki, 17th cent.   1.60   .70
993A A616 1r Archery   3.50   .60
   Issued: #993, Oct. 30; #993A, Nov. 6.

India-USSR Troposcatter
Communications Link — A617

1982, Nov. 2   **Perf. 13½x13**
994 A617 3.05r multicolored   .70   .50

Children's
Day — A618

1982, Nov. 14   **Perf. 14x15**
995 A618 50p multicolored   .60   .40

9th Asian
Games
A619

1982   **Perf. 13**
996   A619 50p Cycling   .25   .25
997   A619 2r Yachting   .40   .30
998   A619 2r Javelin   .45   .40
999   A619 2.85r Rowing   .65   .45
1000 A619 2.85r Discus   2.00   .45
1001 A619 3.25r Soccer   2.50   .65
   Nos. 996-1001 (6)   6.25   2.50
Issued: #997, 999, Nov. 25; others Nov. 19.

50th Anniv.
of Indian
Military
Academy,
Dehradun
A620

1982, Dec. 10   **Perf. 13½x13**
1002 A620 50p multicolored   .70   .50

Purushottamdas Tandon (1882-1962),
Politician — A621

1982, Dec. 15   **Perf. 13**
1003 A621 50p bister   .50   .40

Darjeeling
Himalayan
Railway
Centenary
A622

1982, Dec. 18   **Perf. 13½x13**
1004 A622 2.85r multicolored   10.00   7.50

Indian
Railway
Car — A623

Nos. 2 and
201 — A624

1982, Dec. 30   Photo.   *Perf. 13, 14*
1005 A623 50p multicolored   2.25 1.10
1006 A624 2r multicolored   3.75 3.00
INPEX '82 Stamp Exhibition.

First Anniv.
of Antarctic
Expedition
A625

1983, Jan. 9   Photo.   *Perf. 13½x13*
1007 A625 1r multicolored   7.50 3.50

Pres. Franklin D. Roosevelt (1882-
1945) — A626

1983, Jan. 30   *Perf. 13*
1008 A626 3.25r brown   .90 .75

Siberian
Cranes — A627

1983, Feb. 7   *Perf. 13x13½*
1009 A627 2.85r multicolored   5.00 3.25

180th Anniv.
of Jat
Regiment
A628

1983, Feb. 16   *Perf. 13½x13*
1010 A628 50p Soldiers, emblem 3.25 2.10

7th Non-
aligned
Summit
Conference
A629

1983, Mar. 7
1011 A629 1r Emblem   .35 .35
1012 A629 2r Jawaharlal Nehru   .45 .45

Commonwealth Day — A630

1983, Mar. 14   *Perf. 13*
1013 A630 1r Shore Temple,
    Mahabalipuram   .25 .30
1014 A630 2r Mountains,
    Gomukh   .45 .45

86th
Session of
Intl. Olympic
Committee,
New Delhi,
Mar. 21-28
A631

1983, Mar. 25   Litho.   *Perf. 13½x13*
1015 A631 1r Acropolis   .60 .40

A632   A633

St. Francis of Assisi (1182-1226), by Giovanni Collina.

1983, Apr. 4   Photo.   *Perf. 13*
1016 A632 1r brown   1.10 .55

1983, May 5   Photo.   *Perf. 13x12½*
1017 A633 1r brown   .70 .50

Karl Marx (1818-1883).

Charles Darwin (1809-1882) — A634

1983, May 18   *Perf. 12½x13*
1018 A634 2r multicolored   6.00 2.50

50th Anniv.
of Kanha
Natl. Park
A635

1983, May 30   *Perf. 13½x13*
1019 A635 1r Barasinga stag   4.25 1.25

World
Communications
Year — A636

1983, July 18   Photo.   *Perf. 13*
1020 A636 1r multicolored   .60 .30

Simon Bolivar (1783-1830) — A637

1983, July 24
1021 A637 2r multicolored   4.00 2.50

Quit India Resolution, Aug. 8,
1942 — A638

Meera Behn
(Madeleine Slade).
Disciple of Gandhi,
d. 1982 — A639

Design: No. 1024, Mahadev Desai (1892-
1942).

1983, Aug. 9   Photo.   *Perf. 14*
1022 A638 50p shown   1.40 1.10
    Perf. 13½x13
1023 A639 50p shown   1.40 1.10
1024 A639 50p org, green & brn 1.40 1.10
  a.   Pair, #1023-1024   2.75 2.75

See Nos. 1033, 1035, 1042, 1052-1057,
1077, 1093-1094, 1103, 1107, 1109, 1122,
1137-1139, 1144, 1147-1149, 1163, 1167,
1198, 1202-1205, 1229-1231, 1238, 1243,
1257, 1268-1271, 1277.

Ram Nath Chopra (1882-1973),
Pharma- cologist — A640

1983, Aug. 17   *Perf. 13*
1025 A640 50p brown   .80 .65

Indian Mountaineering Foundation,
25th Anniv. — A641

1983, Aug. 27   *Perf. 13½*
1026 A641 2r Nanda Devi,
    Himalayas   4.00 2.25

Bombay Natural
History
Soc. — A642

1983, Sept. 15   *Perf. 13x13½*
1027 A642 1r multicolored   6.00 1.60

Rock Garden,
Chandigarh
A643

1983, Sept. 23   *Perf. 13x13½*
1028 A643 1r multicolored   2.50 1.25

Wildlife
A644

1983, Oct. 1   *Perf. 13½x13*
1029 A644 1r Golden langur   3.50 .75
1030 A644 2r Lion-tailed ma-
    caque   5.25 3.75

World Tourism, 5th General
Assembly — A645

1983, Oct. 3   Photo.   *Perf. 14*
1031 A645 2r Ghats of Varanasi 1.00 .50

Krishna Kanta
Handique, Linguist,
Sanskritist,
Educator and
Scholar — A646

1983, Oct. 7   Litho.   *Perf. 13*
1032 A646 50p deep gray violet   .50 .35

Famous Indians Type of 1983

Design: Hemu Kalani, revolutionary patriot.

1983, Oct. 18   Photo.   *Perf. 13½x13*
1033 A639 50p org, grn & red
    brn   .50 .50

Children's
Day — A648

Painting: Festival, by Kashyap Premswala

1983, Nov. 14   Photo.   *Perf. 13*
1034 A648 50p multicolored   .60 .45

Famous Indians Type of 1983

Design: Acharya Vinoba Bhave (1895-
1982), freedom fighter.

1983, Nov. 15   Photo.   *Perf. 13½x13*
1035 A639 50p org, grn & dull
    brn   .50 .50

Manned Flight Bicent. — A650

Project Tiger — A651

1983, Nov. 21   Photo.   Perf. 13
1036 A650 1r 1st Indian Balloon   1.60   .55
1037 A650 2r Montgolfier Balloon   2.10   1.10

1983, Nov. 22   Photo.   Perf. 13
1038 A651 2r multicolored   6.00   4.25

Commonwealth Heads of Government Meeting, New Delhi — A652

Design: 2r, Goanese Couple, 19th century.

1983, Nov. 23   Photo.   Perf. 13
1039 A652 1r lt brnsh blue &
              multi   .70   .40
1040 A652 2r pink & multi   1.10   .50

Pratiksha — A653

1983, Dec. 5   Photo.   Perf. 13
1041 A653 1r multi   .40   .30
Nanda Lal Bose (1882-1966), artist.

Famous Indians Type of 1983
Design: Surendranath Banerjee, journalist.

1983, Dec. 28   Photo.   Perf. 13½x13
1042 A639 50p org, green & olive   .50   .50

7th Light Cavalry Bicent. A655

Deccan Horse Regiment, 194th Anniv. A656

1984, Jan. 7
1043 A655 1r Soldier, banner   6.00   2.25

1984, Jan. 9   Perf. 13x13½
1044 A656 1r multicolored   5.50   2.00

Asiatic Society Bicentenary — A657

Design: Society building, Calcutta; founder William Jones.

1984, Jan. 15   Perf. 13
1045 A657 1r brt green & dp lilac   .50   .35

Postal Life Insurance Centenary — A658

1984, Feb. 1   Photo.   Perf. 13x13½
1046 A658 1r Emblem   .50   .35

Presidential Review of Naval Fleet A659

1984, Feb. 3   Perf. 13½x13
1047 A659 1r Jet   2.50   1.50
1048 A659 1r Aircraft carrier   2.50   1.50
1049 A659 1r Submarine   2.50   1.50
1050 A659 1r Missile destroyer   2.50   1.50
  a.   Block of 4, #1047-1050   14.00 14.00

12th Intl. Leprosy Congress, New Delhi A660

1984, Feb. 10   Perf. 13x13½
1051 A660 1r Globe, emblem   .80   .60

Famous Indians Type of 1983
#1052, Vasudeo Balvant Phadke (d. 1884), freedom fighter. #1053, Baba Kanshi Ram. #1054, Begum Hazrat Mahal. #1055, Mangal Pandey. #1056, Nana Sahib. #1057, Tatya Tope.

1984   Perf. 13½x13
1052 A639 50p org, grn & dk ol   .55   .55
1053 A639 50p org, grn & brn   .55   .55
1054 A639 50p org, grn, red org
              & gray   1.25   .80
1055 A639 50p org, grn, brn &
              gray   1.25   .80
1056 A639 50p org, grn, vio &
              gray   1.25   .80
1057 A639 50p org, grn, dk ol &
              gray   1.25   .80
  Nos. 1052-1057 (6)   6.10   4.30
Issue dates: No. 1052, Feb. 23. No. 1053, Apr. 23. Nos. 1054-1057, May 10.

Indian-Russian Space Cooperation — A662

1984, Apr. 3   Photo.   Perf. 14
1058 A662 3r Spacecraft   1.50   .85

G. D. Birla (1894-1983), Industrialist — A663

Birla, Birla Institute of Technology, Pilani.

1984, June 11
1060 A663 50p sepia   .80   .45

1984 Summer Olympics — A664

Perf. 13x12½, 12½x13
1984, July 28   Photo.
1061 A664 50p Basketball   1.40   .65
1062 A664 1r   High jump   1.10   .35
1063 A664 2r   Gymnastics,
                 horiz.   1.50   .95
1064 A664 2.50r Weight lifting,
                 horiz.   1.75   1.50
  Nos. 1061-1064 (4)   5.75   3.45

Vellore Fort — A665

1984, Aug. 3   Perf. 13½x13, 13x13½
1065 A665 50p Gwalior, horiz.   1.00   .55
1066 A665 1r shown   1.50   .40
1067 A665 1.50r Simhagad   2.50   1.90
1068 A665 2r Jodhpur, horiz.   3.00   2.50
  Nos. 1065-1068 (4)   8.00   5.35

B.V. Paradkar, Editor — A665a

1984, Sept. 14   Photo.   Perf. 13x13½
1068A A665a 50p sepia   .80   .55

Dr. D.N. Wadia (1883-1969), Geologist — A665b

1984, Oct. 23   Perf. 13
1068B A665b 1r multicolored   2.50   .40

Indira Gandhi — A666

1984, Nov. 19   Photo.   Perf. 15x14
1069 A666 50p multicolored   4.00   4.00

Children's Day — A667

12th World Mining Congress — A668

1984, Nov. 14   Photo.   Perf. 13
1070 A667 50p Birds in trees   1.10   .70

1984, Nov. 20   Photo.   Perf. 13
1071 A668 1r Congress emblem   2.25   .45

Dr. Rajendra Prasad (1884-1963), 1st, Pres. — A669

1984, Dec. 3   Photo.   Perf. 13
1072 A669 50p multicolored   1.50   .90

Roses — A670

1984, Dec. 23   Litho.   Perf. 13
1073 A670 1.50r Mrinalini   4.00   2.25
1074 A670 2r Sugandha   4.25   2.50

Fergusson College Centenary A671

1985, Jan. 2   Photo.   Perf. 13x13½
1076 A671 100p multicolored   1.00   .50

Famous Indians Type of 1983

Design: Narhar Vishnu Gadgil (1896-1966), freedom fighter.

1985, Jan. 10 Photo. Perf. 13½x13
1077 A639 50p org, grn & brn   6.00 4.00

Artillery Regiment, 50th Anniv. A673

1985, Jan. 15 Perf. 13½x13
1078 A673 1r Gunner, howitzer   7.00 2.25

Indira Gandhi (1917-1984) — A674

1985, Jan. 31 Perf. 14
1079 A674 2r Addressing UN General Assembly   6.50 4.25
See Nos. 1098-1099.

Minicoy Lighthouse Cent. — A675

1985, Feb. 2 Perf. 13
1080 A675 1r multicolored   8.50 1.60

Bengal Medical College, 150th Anniv. A676

1985, Feb. 20 Perf. 13½x13
1081 A676 1r multicolored   4.50 .95

Madras Medical College, 150th Anniv. A677

1985, Mar. 8 Perf. 13½x13
1082 A677 1r multicolored   4.50 .95

Assam Rifles, North-East Sentinels, 150th Anniv. A679

1985, Mar. 29
1084 A679 1r multicolored   7.50 2.50

Potato Research, 50th Anniv. — A680

Baba Jassa Singh Ahluwalia, 1718-1783, Sikh Leader — A681

1985, Apr. 1 Perf. 13
1085 A680 50p brown & pale brown   2.75 1.60

1985, Apr. 4
1086 A681 50p rose violet   2.75 1.60

St. Xavier's College, 125th Anniv. A682

1985, Apr. 12
1087 A682 1r multicolored   2.50 .80

White-winged Wood Duck — A683

Bougainvillea A684

1985, May 18 Perf. 14
1088 A683 2r multicolored   11.50 5.50

1985, June 5 Perf. 13
1089 A684 50p multicolored   2.50 2.10
1090 A684 1r multicolored   3.00 1.75

Statue of Didarganj Yakshi, Indian Deity — A685

Yaudheya Tribal Republic Copper Coin, c. 200 B.C. — A686

1985
1091 A685 1r multicolored   4.00 2.10
1092 A686 2r multicolored   2.25 .50
Festival of India, festival in France and the US for cultural exchange.
Issue dates: 1r, June 7. 2r, June 13.

Famous Indians Type of 1983

Designs: No. 1093, Jairamdas Doulatram (1891-1979), journalist and politician. No. 1094, Nellie (1909-1973) & Jatindra Mohan (d. 1933) Sengupta, political activists, horiz.

1985 Perf. 13½x13
1093 A639 50p org, grn & dl red brn   .75 .50

Perf. 13x13½
1094 A639 50p org, green & fawn   .75 .50
Issued: #1093, July 21; #1094, July 22.

Swami Haridas (1478-1573), Philosopher A689

1985, Sept. 19 Photo. Perf. 13½x13
1095 A689 1r multicolored   2.50 1.50

Border Roads Org., 25th Anniv. — A690

1985, Oct. 10 Perf. 13x14
1096 A690 2r multicolored   4.00 2.75

Prime Minister Nehru at Podium A691

1985, Oct. 24 Perf. 13x13½
1097 A691 2r multicolored   1.75 1.10
UN, 40th anniv.

Indira Gandhi Memorial Type of 1985

1985 Perf. 14
1098 A674 2r Gandhi addressing crowd   4.50 4.50
1099 A674 3r Portrait   4.50 4.50
Issue dates: 2r, Oct. 31. 3r, Nov. 19.

Children's Day — A692

1985, Nov. 14 Perf. 13½x13
1100 A692 50p multicolored   1.40 .80

Halley's Comet — A693

1985, Nov. 19 Perf. 13x13½
1101 A693 1r multicolored   3.25 1.60
Intl. Astronomical Union, 19th General Assembly, New Delhi, Nov. 19-28.

St. Stephen's Hospital, Delhi, Cent. A694

1985, Nov. 25 Perf. 13
1102 A694 1r multicolored   1.25 .55

Famous Indians Type of 1983

Design: Kakasaheb Kalelkar (1885-1981), author.

1985, Dec. 2 Perf. 13½x13
1103 A639 50p org, grn & ol brn   .75 .50

Map of South Asia A696

Flags of India, Pakistan, Bangladesh, Nepal, Bhutan, Sri Lanka and the Maldive Islands — A697

1985, Dec. 8 Perf. 13½x13, 14
1104 A696 1r multicolored   2.50 .50
1105 A697 3r multicolored   4.00 3.50
South Asian Regional Cooperation, SARC.

Shyama Shastri (1762-1827), Composer — A698

1985, Dec. 21 Perf. 13½x13
1106 A698 1r multicolored   4.00 1.60

Famous Indians Type of 1983

Master Tara Singh (1885-1967), Sikh leader.

1985, Dec. 23 Perf. 13½x13
1107 A639 50p org, green & blue   .75 .50

Intl. Youth Year A700

1985, Dec. 24
1108 A700 2r multicolored   4.25 2.25

Famous Indians Type of 1983

Design: Ravishankar Maharaj (1884-1984), freedom fighter, politician.

1985, Dec. 24 Perf. 13½x13
1109 A639 50p org, green & slate   .75 .50

Handel and Bach — A702

1985, Dec. 27 *Perf. 13x13½*
1110 A702 5r multicolored 8.50 4.75

Congress Presidents, 1924-1985 A703

1985, Dec. 28 *Perf. 14*
1111 Block of 4 13.00 13.00
a.-d. A703 1r any single 2.50 2.25

Indian Natl. Congress, cent. Withdrawn on day of issue for a period of two weeks.

Naval Dockyard, Bombay, 250th Anniv. A704

1986, Jan. 11 Photo. *Perf. 13½*
1112 A704 2.50r multicolored 7.50 4.50

INPEX '86, Jaipur, Feb. 14-19 A705

Designs: 50p, Hawa Mahal Palace, Jaipur No. 3. 2r, Khar Desert mobile post office.

1986, Feb. 14 *Perf. 13½x13*
1113 A705 50p multicolored 2.50 .90
1114 A705 2r multicolored 3.75 2.10

Vikrant Aircraft Carrier, 25th Anniv. — A706

1986, Feb. 16 *Perf. 13x13½*
1115 A706 2r multicolored 11.50 8.00

Inaugural Airmail Flight, 75th Anniv. A707

1986, Feb. 18 *Perf. 13½x13, 13x13½*
1116 A707 50p Biplane 3.25 2.10
Size: 41x28mm
1117 A707 3r Jet 7.25 5.50

Sixth Triennale of the Arts, Lalit Kala Academy A708

Sri Chaitanya Mahaprabhu A709

1986, Feb. 22 *Perf. 13x13½*
1118 A708 1r multicolored 2.50 1.50

1986, Mar. 3 *Perf. 13*
1119 A709 2r multicolored 4.75 3.25

Mayo College, Ajmer, 111th Anniv. A710

1986, Apr. 12 *Perf. 13½x13*
1120 A710 1r multicolored 2.40 1.10

1986 World Cup Soccer Championships, Mexico — A711

1986, May 31 Photo. *Perf. 13*
1121 A711 5r multicolored 8.00 4.25

Famous Indians Type of 1983

Bhim Sen Sachar (1894-1978), freedom fighter.

1986, Aug. 14 Photo. *Perf. 13½x13*
1122 A639 50p org, green & sepia 8.25 4.50

Swami Sivananda (1887-1963), Religious Author — A713

1986, Sept. 8 Photo. *Perf. 13½x13*
1123 A713 2r multicolored 5.00 3.00

10th Asian Games — A714

1986, Sept. 16 *Perf. 13x13½*
1124 A714 1.50r Women's volleyball 4.50 2.50
1125 A714 3r Hurdling 4.75 3.50

Madras Post Office, Bicent. A715

1986, Oct. 9 Photo. *Perf. 13x13½*
1126 A715 5r black & brown orange 8.00 4.50

1st Battalion of Parachutists Regiment, 225th Anniv. — A716

Indian Police Force, 125th Anniv. — A717

1986, Oct. 17
1127 A716 3r multicolored 8.50 4.50

1986, Oct. 21 *Perf. 13½*

Uniforms, 1861-1986. No. 1129a has a continuous design.

1128 A717 1.50r multicolored 6.00 4.25
1129 A717 2r multicolored 6.00 4.25
a. Pair, #1129, 1128 14.00 14.00

Intl. Peace Year A718

1986, Oct. 24
1130 A718 5r sage grn, blue & rose 5.50 2.75

Children's Day — A719

1986, Nov. 14 Photo. *Perf. 13x13½*
1131 A719 50p multicolored 4.00 2.10

UN, 40th Anniv. A720

1986, Dec. 11 *Perf. 13½x13*
1132 A720 50p Growth monitoring 3.25 2.25
1133 A720 5r Immunization 6.50 5.00

Child Survival Campaign.

Miyan Tansen, 17th Cent. Dhrupad Singer, Playing the Surbahar — A721

1986, Dec. 12
1134 A721 1r multicolored 3.50 1.00

Corbett Natl. Park, 50th Anniv. A722

1986, Dec. 15
1135 A722 1r Elephant 6.50 1.75
1136 A722 2r Gavial 7.50 5.25

Famous Indians Type of 1983

Designs: No. 1137, Alluri Seetarama Raju (b. 1897), freedom fighter. No. 1138, Sagarmal Gopa (b. 1900), freedom fighter. No. 1139, Veer Surendra Sai (b. 1809), freedom fighter.

1986, Dec. *Perf. 13½x13*
1137 A639 50p red, green & sepia 2.00 1.00
1138 A639 50p red, green & sl blue 2.00 1.00
1139 A639 50p red, green & dp red brn 2.00 1.00
Nos. 1137-1139 (3) 6.00 3.00

Issued: #1137, 26th; #1138, 29th; #1139, 30th.

St. Martha's Hospital, Bangalore, Cent. A724

1986, Dec. 30 *Perf. 13½*
1140 A724 1r multicolored 4.00 2.25

Yacht Trishna A725

1987, Jan. 10
1141 A725 6.50r multicolored 8.00 4.25

1st Indian Army circumnavigation of the world, Sept. 28, 1985 to 1987.

Africa Fund — A726

1987, Jan. 25 Photo. *Perf. 14x14½*
1142 A726 6.50r black 8.25 4.50

ICC 29th Congress, New Delhi — A727

1987, Feb. 11 *Perf. 13½*
1143 A727 5r multicolored 6.00 3.00

Famous Indians Type of 1983

Design: Hakim Ajmal Khan (1864-1927), physician, politician.

1987, Feb. 13 *Perf. 13½x13*
1144 A639 60p org, grn & brn 2.75 .30

A729

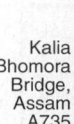

A SMALL FAMILY IS A HAPPY FAMILY

Family
Planning
A730

1987, Feb. 27   Perf. 13, 13x13½
1145 A729 35p dark red   .20   .20
1146 A730 60p green & dark red   .20   .20

Famous Indians Type of 1983

Designs: No. 1147, Lala Har Dayal (1884-
1939). No. 1148, Manabendra Nath Roy
(1887-1954). No. 1149, T. Ramaswamy
Chowdary (1887-1943).

1987   Photo.   Perf. 13½x13
1147 A639 60p org, green & pur-
             ple   .50   .25
1148 A639 60p org, green & red
             brn   .50   .25
1149 A639 60p org, grn & brt
             blue   .50   .25
      Nos. 1147-1149 (3)   1.50   .75

Issued: #1147, 3/18; #1148, 3/21; #1149,
4/25.

SER Emblem,
Blast
Furnaces — A732

Electric Train
Crossing
Bridge — A734

Steam
Locomotive
No.
691 — A733

1987, Mar. 28   Perf. 13x13½, 13½x13½
1150 A732   1r shown   .25   .25
1151 A733 1.50r shown   .65   .35
1152 A734   2r shown   1.10   .45
1153 A733   4r Steam locomo-
             tive, c. 1890   1.50   .75
      Nos. 1150-1153 (4)   3.50 1.80

Southeastern Railway, cent.

Kalia
Bhomora
Bridge,
Assam
A735

1987, Apr. 14   Perf. 13½
1154 A735 2r multicolored   .60   .30

Madras
Christian
College,
150th
Anniv.
A736

1987, Apr. 16   Perf. 13x13½
1155 A736 1.50r black & rose
             lake   .50   .40

A737   A738

1987, May 1   Perf. 13½
1156 A737 1r dull brown   .60   .30

Shree Shree Ma Anandamayee (1896-
1982), spiritualist.

1987, May 8   Perf. 14
1157 A738 2r multicolored   .70   .35

Rabindranath Tagore (1861-1941), 1913
Nobel Laureate for literature.

A739

A740

1987, May 10   Perf. 13½
1158 A739 1r multicolored   1.25   .50

Garhwal Rifles and Garhwal Scouts, cent.

1987, May 11
1159 A740 60p black brn & buff 1.10   .90

J. Krishnamurti (1895-1986), mystic.

7th
Battalion,
Mechanised
Infantry
Regiment,
Cent.
A741

1987, June 3   Perf. 13½x13
1160 A741 1r multicolored   .90   .45

INDIA '89,
New Delhi,
Jan. 20-29,
1989
A742

1987, June 15
1161 A742 50p Swan emblem   .25   .25
  a.   Bklt. pane of 4+inscribed mar-
        gin ('89)   .50
1162 A742   5r Hall of Nations,
             New Delhi   1.25   .45
  a.   Souv. sheet of 2, #1161-1162   3.50 3.50
  b.   Bklt. pane of 4+inscribed mar-
        gin ('89)   6.00 6.00

Inscribed 1986. No. 1162a sold for 8r.

Famous Indians Type of 1983
Kailas Nath Katju (1887-1968), Chief
Minister.

1987, June 17   Perf. 13½x13
1163 A639 60p org, grn & yel brn .35 .25

Sadyah-Snata,
Sanghol Sculpture,
c. 2000 B.C.
A744

1987, July 3
1164 A744 6.50r multicolored   1.75   .55

Festival of India in the USSR, July 3, 1987-
88.

Natl. Independence, 40th
Anniv. — A745

1987, Aug. 15 Photo. Perf. 13x13½
1165 A745 60p orange, brt blue
             & dk green   .50   .40

Sant Harchand
Singh Longowal
(1932-1985),
Social
Reformer — A746

1987, Aug. 20   Perf. 13½
1166 A746 1r multicolored   1.10   .40

Famous Indians Type of 1983
Design: S. Satyamurti (1887-1943), political
reformer, martyr.

1987, Aug. 22   Perf. 13½x13
1167 A639 60p org, green & brn .50   .25

Guru Ghasidas
(1756-1837),
Founder of the
Saman
Sect — A748

1987, Sept. 1
1168 A748 60p henna brown   .50   .40

Sri Sri Thakur
Anukul Chandra
(1888-1969),
Physician,
Guru — A749

1987, Sept. 2   Perf. 13½
1169 A749 1r multicolored   1.25   .60

University
of
Allahabad,
Cent.
A750

1987, Sept. 23   Perf. 13½x13
1170 A750 2r multicolored   .50   .30

Phoolwalon Ki
Sair — A751

Maharaja
Chhatrasal
A752

1987, Oct. 1   Perf. 13x13½
1171 A751 2r Pankha (embroi-
             dered apron)   .50   .30

Festival of thanksgiving for fulfilled prayers.

1987, Oct. 2   Perf. 14
1172 A752 60p henna brown   .50   .35

Chhatrasal (1649-1731), military commander during the war against the Moguls.

Intl. Year of
Shelter for
the
Homeless
A753

1987, Oct. 5   Perf. 13½x13
1173 A753 5r multicolored   .80   .40

Asia
Regional
Conference
of Rotary
Intl. — A754

1987, Oct. 14
1174 A754 60p shown   .20   .20
1175 A754 6.50r Polio immuniza-
             tion   1.10   .50

Service to
the Blind,
Cent.
A755

1987, Oct. 15
1176 A755 1r shown   .30   .30
1177 A755 2r Eye donation   .50   .35

World White Cane Day.

INDIA
'89 — A756

Designs: 60p, The Iron Pillar, Quwwat-ul-
Islam Mosque courtyard, 5th cent., Delhi.

1.50r, The India Gate, New Delhi, war memorial by Luytens, 1921. 5r, The Dewan-E-Khas, Hall of Private Audience, Red Fort, Delhi, c. 1648. 6.50r, Purana Qila, Old Fort, Delhi, c. 1540.

1987, Oct. 17
1178	A756	60p multicolored	.25	.25
a.		Bklt. pane of 4 + inscribed margin ('89)	.80	
1179	A756	1.50r multicolored	.50	.25
a.		Bklt. pane of 4 + inscribed margin ('89)	2.10	
1180	A756	5r multicolored	1.25	.45
a.		Bklt. pane of 4 + inscribed margin ('89)	5.25	
1181	A756	6.50r multicolored	2.00	.60
a.		Souv. sheet of 4, #1178-1811	4.00	4.00
b.		Bklt. pane of 4 + inscribed margin ('89)	7.75	
		Nos. 1178-1181 (4)	4.00	1.55

No. 1181a sold for 15r.

Tyagmurti Goswami Ganeshdutt (1889-1959), Educator, Social Activist — A757

1987, Nov. 2   **Perf. 13½**
1182	A757	60p terra cotta	.50	.40

Children's Day — A758

1987, Nov. 14
1183	A758	60p multicolored	.50	.30

Trees A759

1987, Nov. 19   **Photo.**   **Perf. 13½**
1184	A759	60p Chinar, vert.	.35	.30
1185	A759	1.50r Pipal	.40	.30
1186	A759	5r Sal, vert.	1.10	.65
1187	A759	6.50r Banyan	1.50	.90
		Nos. 1184-1187 (4)	3.35	2.15

Festival of the USSR in India — A760

Votive coin based on The Worker and the Peasant Woman, by Soviet sculptor Mukhina.

1987, Nov. 21   **Perf. 14**
1188	A760	5r multicolored	.80	.50

White Tiger — A761

Rameshwari Nehru (1886-1966), Human Rights and World Peace Activist — A762

1987, Nov. 29   **Photo.**   **Perf. 13½**
1189	A761	1r shown	.75	.25
1190	A761	5r Snow leopard, horiz.	2.25	.90

1987, Dec. 10
1191	A762	60p red brown	.50	.40

Execution of Veer Narayan Singh (1795-1857), Sikh Uprising Leader — A763

1987, Dec. 10
1192	A763	60p	.50	.40

Father Kuriakose Elias Chavara (1806-1871), Theologian Beatified by Pope John Paul II Feb. 8, 1986 — A764

1987, Dec. 20
1193	A764	60p dark brown olive	.50	.40

Dr. Rajah Sir M.A. Muthiah Chettiar (1905-1984), Politician, Pro-chancellor of Annamalai University — A765

1987, Dec. 21   **Perf. 13**
1194	A765	60p chalky blue black	.50	.40

Sri Harmandir Sahib (Gold Temple), Amritsar, 400th Anniv. — A766

1987, Dec. 26   **Perf. 13½**
1195	A766	60p multicolored	1.25	.70

Rukmini Devi (1904-1986), Dancer, Choreographer — A767

1987, Dec. 27
1196	A767	60p dark red	.60	.35

Dr. Hiralal (1867-1934), Historian — A768

1987, Dec. 31
1197	A768	60p dark blue	.50	.40

Famous Indians Type of 1983

Design: Pandit Hriday Nath Kunzru (1887-1978), human rights activist, statesman.

1987, Dec. 31   **Perf. 13½x13**
1198	A639	60p org, grn & red brn	.35	.25

75th Session of the Indian Science Congress Assoc. A770

1988, Jan. 1
1199	A770	4r multicolored	.90	.55

Solar Energy A771

13th Asia Pacific Dental Congress, New Delhi, Jan. 28-Feb.2 A772

Wmk. 324

1988, Jan. 1   **Photo.**   **Perf. 13**
1200	A771	5r dp orange & sepia	.80	.40

1988, Jan. 28   **Unwmk.**   **Perf. 13**
1201	A772	4r multicolored	1.00	.50

Famous Indians Type of 1983

Designs: No. 1202, Mohan Lal Sukhadia (1916-1982). No. 1203, Dr. S.K. Sinha (1887-1961). No. 1204, Chandra Shekhar Azad (1906-1931). No. 1205, Govind Ballabh Pant (1887-1961).

1988   **Perf. 13½x13**
1202	A639	60p org, grn & bluish blk	.75	.60
1203	A639	60p org, grn & org brn	.75	.60
1204	A639	60p org, grn & rose red	.75	.60
1205	A639	60p org, grn & purple	.75	.60
		Nos. 1202-1205 (4)	3.00	2.40

Issue dates: Nos. 1202, Feb. 2; No. 1203, Feb. 4; No. 1204, Feb. 27; No. 1205, Mar. 7.

U. Tirot Sing (1800-1833), Patriot — A774

1988, Feb. 3
1206	A774	60p dull brown	.50	.40

Kumaon Regiment 4th Battalion, Bicent. — A775

Balgandharva (1888-1967), Musician — A776

1988, Feb. 19   **Perf. 14**
1207	A775	1r Uniforms of 1788, 1947, 1988	.60	.30

1988, Feb. 22   **Perf. 13x13½**
1208	A776	60p brown	.50	.40

Mechanised Infantry Regiment A777

1988, Feb. 24   **Perf. 13½x13**
1209	A777	1r multicolored	.90	.45

A778

1988, Feb. 26   **Perf. 13**
1210	A778	60p bluish black	.50	.40

Sir B.N. Rau (1887-1953), constitutional advisor.

A779

1988, Mar. 14   **Photo.**   **Perf. 13x13½**
1211	A779	1r bright rose	.50	.40

Mohindra College, Patiala, founded in 1875 by Maharaja Mohinder Singh, is now part of Punjabi University.

Dr. D.V. Gundappa (1887-1975), Journalist, and Gikhala Institute of Public Affairs — A780

1988, Mar. 17   **Perf. 13½x13**
1212	A780	60p slate blue	.50	.40

Woman Warrior Riding into Battle — A781

1988, Mar. 20 *Perf. 13x13½*
1213 A781 60p bright rose .50 .40
Rani Avantibai (d. 1858), heroine of the 1857 independence war.

Malayala Manorama Newspaper, Cent. — A782

1988, Mar. 23
1214 A782 1r blue & black .50 .40
Malayala Manorama, published in Kottayam, is the largest circulated daily newspaper in India.

Maharshi Dadhichi, Vedic Period Saint Purported to Have Introduced Fire to Man — A783

1988, Mar. 26
1215 A783 60p deep orange .50 .40

Mohammad Iqbal (1877-1938), Poet — A784

1988, Apr. 21
1216 A784 60p carmine & gold .50 .40

Samarth Ramdas (1608-1682), Philosopher A785

1988, May 1 *Perf. 13*
1217 A785 60p dk yellow green .50 .40

Swati Tirunal Rama Varma (1813-1846), Carnatic Composer — A786

1988, May 2 *Perf. 13x13½*
1218 A786 60p brt violet .50 .40

1st War of Independence, the "Indian Mutiny of 1857" — A787

Painting: Rani Laxmi Bai transformed from a queen into a warrior fighting for justice, by M.F. Husain.

1988, May 9 Photo. *Perf. 13x13½*
1219 A787 60p multicolored .50 .40

Bhaurao Patil (b. 1887), Educator A788

1988, May 9 *Perf. 13½x13*
1220 A788 60p red brown .50 .40

Himalayan Peaks A789

1988, May 19
1221 A789 1.50r Broad Peak 1.40 .30
1222 A789 4r Godwin Austin 1.60 .40
1223 A789 5r Kanchenjunga 1.60 .55
1224 A789 6.50r Nandadevi 1.60 .70
Nos. 1221-1224 (4) 6.20 1.95

Care for the Elderly — A790

1988, May 24 *Perf. 13x13½*
1225 A790 60p multicolored .50 .40

Victoria Terminal, Bombay, Cent. A791

1988, May 30 *Perf. 13½x13*
1226 A791 1r multicolored .80 .30

Lawrence School, Lovedale, 130th Anniv. A792

1988, May 31 *Perf. 13*
1227 A792 1r dk green & red brown .70 .40

World Environment Day — A793

1988, June 5 *Perf. 14*
1228 A793 60p Khejri tree .50 .40

Famous Indians Type of 1983
#1229, Dr. Anugrah Narain Singh (1887-1957), statesman. #1230, Kuladhor Chaliha (1886-1963), political and social reformer. #1231, Shivprasad Gupta (1883-1944), freedom fighter.

1988 *Perf. 13½x13*
1229 A639 60p org, grn & rose vio .65 .40
1230 A639 60p org, grn & gray blk .65 .40
1231 A639 60p org, grn & dk vio .65 .40
Nos. 1229-1231 (3) 1.95 1.20
Issued: #1229, 6/18; #1230, 6/19; #1231, 6/28.

Rani Durgawati (d. 1564), Ruler of Gondwana — A795

1988, June 24
1232 A795 60p red .50 .40

A796

1988, July 28 Photo. *Perf. 13x13½*
1233 A796 60p red brown .50 .40
Acharya Shanti Dev (687-765), Sanskrit and Pali scholar.

A797

1988, Aug. 4
1234 A797 60p blue violet .50 .40
Yashwant Singh Parmar (1906-1981), administrator of Himachal Pradesh State.

Painting by M.F. Husain — A798

1988, Aug. 16 Photo. *Perf. 13x13½*
1235 60p India at upper left .60 .60
1236 60p India at lower left .60 .60
a. A798 Pair, #1235-1236 2.00 2.00
Natl. Independence 40th anniv.

Durgadas Rathore (1638-1718), Guardian of King Ajit Singh — A799

1988, Aug. 26 *Litho.*
1237 A799 60p dark red brown .50 .40

Famous Indians Type of 1983
Design: Sarat Chandra Bose (1889-1950), politician, lawyer, publisher.

1988, Sept. 6 Photo. *Perf. 13½x13*
1238 A639 60p org, grn & dk blue grn .50 .40

Gopinath Kaviraj (1887-1976), Scholar — A801

1988, Sept. 7 *Perf. 13x13½*
1239 A801 60p brown olive .50 .40

Hindi Language Day, Sept. 14 A802

Indian Olympic Assoc. Emblem A803

Glory of Sport, Independence 40th Anniv. — A804

1988, Sept. 14 Photo. *Perf. 13x13½*
1240 A802 60p ver & dk olive green .50 .40

Perf. 13½x13, 13x13½

1988, Sept. 17
1241 A803 60p deep claret   .80 .45
1242 A804 5r multicolored   4.50 1.60

Famous Indians Type of 1983
Baba Kharak (1867-1963), nationalist.

1988, Oct. 6   Perf. 13½x13
1243 A639 60p org, green & org
         brn   .50 .40

Jerdon's Courser — A806

1988, Oct. 7   Perf. 13½
1244 A806 1r multicolored   5.00 .65

The Times of India, Newspaper, 150th Anniv. — A807

1988, Nov. 3   Perf. 13½x14
1245 A807 1.50r black & gold   .50 .35

INDIA '89 — A808

Perf. 13½x13

1988, Oct. 9   Unwmk.   Photo.
1246 A808 4r Bangalore P.O.   .75 .30
  a.   Bklt. pane of 6+inscribed mar-
      gin ('89)   4.50
1247 A808 5r Bombay P.O.   1.50 .35
  a.   Bklt. pane of 6+inscribed mar-
      gin ('89)   9.00

Portrait of Azad by K.K. Hebbar — A809

1988, Nov. 11
1248 A809 60p multicolored   .50 .40
Maulana Abul Kalam Azad (1888-1958), minister of education, natl. resources and scientific research.

Jawaharlal Nehru — A810

Perf. 13x13½, 13½x13 (1r)

1988, Nov. 14
1249 A810 60p dk gray, dk or-
      ange & dk grn   .65 .35
1250 A810 1r Portrait, vert.   .75 .35

Birsa, Munda Leader A811

1988, Nov. 15   Perf. 13½x13
1251 A811 60p brown   .50 .40

Bhakra Dam, 25th Anniv. — A812

1988, Dec. 15   Perf. 14
1252 A812 60p carmine rose   .70 .70

INDIA '89 — A813

60p, Dead-letter cancellations, 1886. 6.50r, Traveling p.o. cancellation, 1864-69.

1988, Dec. 20   Perf. 13½x13
1253 A813   60p multicolored   .75 .40
  a.   Bklt. pane of 6+inscribed
      margin ('89)   5.00
1254 A813 6.50r multicolored   2.50 1.40
  a.   Bklt. pane of 6+inscribed
      margin ('89)   15.00

K.M. Munshi (1887-1971), Environmentalist, Statesmen — A814

1988, Dec. 30
1255 A814 60p dark olive green   .50 .40

Mannathu Padmanabhan (1878-1970), Social Reformer — A815

1989, Jan. 2   Perf. 13½x13
1256 A815 60p dull brown   .50 .40

Famous Indians Type of 1983
Hare Krushna Mahtab (1899-1987), author.

1989, Jan. 2   Perf. 13½x13
1257 A639 60p orange, grn &
      black   .60 .40

Lok Sabha Secretariat, 60th Anniv. A817

1989, Jan. 10   Perf. 13½x13
1258 A817 60p dark olive green   .50 .40

State Museum, Lucknow, 125th Anniv. — A818

1989, Jan. 11   Perf. 14
1259 A818 60p Goddess Durga,
      lion   .50 .40

INDIA '89 — A819

1989, Jan. 20   Perf. 13½x13
1260 A819   60p Youth collecting   .20 .20
  a.   Bklt. pane of 6 + inscribed
      margin   .60
1261 A819 1.50r Postal coach &
      p.o., 1842   .40 .20
  a.   Bklt. pane of 6 + inscribed
      margin   2.40
1262 A819   5r Travancore #2   1.00 .40
  a.   Bklt. pane of 6 + inscribed
      margin   6.00
1263 A819 6.50r Philatelic journal
      mastheads   1.50 .50
  a.   Bklt. pane of 6 + inscribed
      margin   9.00
    Nos. 1260-1263 (4)   3.10 1.30

St. John Bosco (1815-1888), Educator — A820

1989, Jan. 31   Perf. 13
1264 A820 60p carmine rose   .50 .40

3rd Cavalry, 148th Anniv. A821

1989, Feb. 8   Perf. 13½x13
1265 A821 60p multicolored   1.00 .55

Dargah Sharif Ajmer A822

1989, Feb. 13   Litho.   Perf. 13½x13
1266 A822 1r multicolored   .50 .40

President's Review of the Naval Fleet — A823

1989, Feb. 15   Perf. 14
1267 A823 6.50r multicolored   3.50 1.90

Famous Indians Type of 1983
#1268, Sheikh Mohammad Abdullah. #1269, Balasaheb Gangadhar Kher (1888-1957), politician. #1270, Saiffuddin Kitchlew (1000-1963), lawyer, diplomat. #1271, Rajkumari Amrit Kaur (d. 1964), minister of health and welfare.

1988-89   Photo.   Perf. 13½x13
1268 A639 60p org, grn & lil rose   .50 .40
1269 A639 60p org, grn & dk vio   .50 .40
1270 A639 60p org, grn & blk brn   .50 .40
1271 A639 60p org, grn & grnsh
      blk   .50 .40
    Nos. 1268-1271 (4)   2.00 1.60

Issue dates: No. 1268, Dec. 5; No. 1269, Mar. 8, 1989; Nos. 1270-1271, Apr. 13, 1989.

Freedom Fighters — A825

#1272, Baldev Ramji Mirdha (1889-1956). #1273, Rao Gopal Singh (1899-1939).

1989   Perf. 13x13½
1272 A825 60p slate   .50 .40
1273 A825 60p dark olive   .50 .40
Issue dates: #1272, Jan. 17; #1273, Mar. 30.

Freedom Fighters A826

Designs: No. 1274, Shaheed Laxman Nayak (1899-1943), protest leader. No. 1275, Bishu Ram Medhi (1888-1981), politician.

1989   Perf. 13½x13
1274 A826 60p org, sage grn &
      brn   .25 .20

Size: 24x37mm
1275 A826 60p org, sage grn &
      dp yel grn   .35 .20

Issued: #1274, Mar. 29; #1275, Apr. 24.
See #1292, 1299-1300, 1317, 1429, 1487.

Sydenham College, Bombay A827

1989, Apr. 19   Perf. 13½
1276 A827 60p black   .50 .40

Famous Indians Type of 1983
Design: Asaf Ali (1888-1953), patriot.

1989, May 11   Photo.   Perf. 13½x13
1277 A639 60p org, green & se-
      pia   .25 .20

N.S. Hardikar (1889-1975), Freedom Fighter — A829

1989, May 13   *Perf. 13x13½*
1278 A829 60p chestnut brown   .50   .40

Sankaracharya (b. 788), Philosopher — A830

1989, May 17   *Perf. 14x13½*
1279 A830 60p multicolored   .50   .40

Punjab University, Chandigarh A831

1989, May 19   *Perf. 13½x13*
1280 A831 1r blue green & brn   .50   .40

Film Industry, 75th Anniv. — A832

1989, May 30   **Photo.**   *Perf. 14*
1281 A832 60p dk olive bis & blk   .60   .45

Kirloskar Corporation, Cent. A833

1989, June 20   **Photo.**   *Perf. 13½x13*
1282 A833 1r multicolored   .50   .40

DAV Education Movement, Cent. A834

1989, June 27   **Photo.**   *Perf. 13½x13*
1283 A834 1r multicolored   .50   .40

Dakshin Gangotri Post Office in the Antarctic, 1988 A835

1989, July 11   *Perf. 14*
1284 A835 1r multicolored   2.50   .50

Allahabad Bank, 125th Anniv. A836

1989, July 19
1285 A836 60p multicolored   .50   .40

Central Reserve Police Force, 50th Anniv. A837

1989, July 27   *Perf. 13½x13*
1286 A837 60p golden brown   2.40   .80

Military Farms, Cent. A838

1989, Aug. 18
1287 A838 1r multicolored   1.20   4.50

Kemal Ataturk (1881-1938), 1st President of Turkey — A839

1989, Aug. 30   *Perf. 13½x13*
1288 A839 5r multicolored   2.40   .80

Sarvepalli Radhakrishnan, President of India, 1962-67 — A840

1989, Sept. 11   **Photo.**   *Perf. 13x13½*
1289 A840 60p black   .50   .40

P. Subbarayan (1889-1962), Lawyer, Political Reformer — A841

1989, Sept. 30   *Perf. 13x13½*
1290 A841 60p brown orange   .50   .40

Mohun Bagan Soccer Team, Cent. A842

1989, Sept. 23   **Photo.**   *Perf. 13½x13*
1291 A842 1r multicolored   2.40   1.00

Freedom Fighter Type of 1989
Shyamji Krishna Varma (1857-1930).

1989, Oct. 4   **Photo.**   *Perf. 13½x13*
1292 A826 60p org, sage grn &   dk red brn   .50   .40

Sayaji Rao Gaekwad III (1863-1939), Maharaja of the Former State of Baroda — A843

1989, Oct. 6   *Perf. 13x13½*
1293 A843 60p black   .50   .40

Use Pin Code A844

1989, Oct. 14   *Perf. 14*
1294 A844 60p multicolored   .65   .25

Namakkal Kavignar (1888-1972), Poet Laureate — A845

1989, Oct. 19   **Photo.**   *Perf. 13x13½*
1295 A845 60p black   .50   .40

18th Intl. Epilepsy Congress and 14th World Neurology Congress, New Delhi A846

1989, Oct. 21   *Perf. 13½x13*
1296 A846 6.50r multicolored   4.25   1.10

Ramabai and Sharada Sadan School A847

1989, Oct. 26
1297 A847 60p brown   .50   .30
Pandita Ramabai (1858-1920), women's rights activist, founder of mission to help destitute women and children.

Pigeon Post A848

1989, Nov. 3
1298 A848 1r brown orange   .90   .35

Freedom Fighter Type of 1989

#1299, Acharya Narendra Deo (1889-1956), democratic socialist movement founder. #1300, Acharya Kripalani (1888-1982), politician.

1989   *Perf. 13½x13*
1299 A826 60p org, sage grn &   brn   .50   .40
1300 A826 60p org, sage grn &   dp gray   .50   .40
Issue dates: #1299, Nov. 6; #1300, Nov. 11.

Jawaharlal Nehru, Birth Cent. — A849

1989, Nov. 14   *Perf. 14x15*
1301 A849 1r buff, dk red brn &   sepia   1.00   .30

8th Asian Track and Field Meet, Nov. 14-19, New Delhi — A850

1989, Nov. 19   *Perf. 14x14½*
1302 A850 1r black, org & dp grn   .80   .45

A851

1989, Nov. 20   *Perf. 13x13½*
1303 A851 60p deep brown   .60   .45
Gurunath Bewoor (b. 1888), 1st Indian appointed postmaster general.

A852

1989, Dec. 8   **Photo.**   *Perf. 13x13½*
1304 A852 60p black   .60   .45
Balkrishna Sharma Navin (1897-1960), litterateur, politician.

Bombay Art Soc., Cent. A853

1989, Dec. 15   *Perf. 13½x13*
1305 A853 1r multicolored   .60   .45

Likh
Florican — A854

Digboi Oil Field,
1889 — A855

1989, Dec. 20 *Perf. 13x13½*
1306 A854 2r multicolored 3.00 .95

1989, Dec. 29 *Perf. 14*
1307 A855 60p dark red brown .80 .45
Discovery of oil, Digboi, Assam, cent.

M.G.
Ramachandran
(1917-1987),
Actor, Chief
Minister — A856

1990, Jan. 17 *Perf. 13x13½*
1308 A856 60p dark red brown .80 .30

Extracting
Silt from
Sukhna
Lake,
Chandigarh
A857

1990, Jan. 29 *Perf. 13½x13*
1309 A857 1r multicolored .60 .45
Sukhna Shramda, society for the preservation of Sukhna Lake.

Presentation of Colors by Pres.
Venkataraman to the Bombay Sappers
(Corps of Engineers), Feb. 21 — A858

Perf. 15x14x14

1990, Feb. 21 Photo.
1310 A858 60p multicolored 1.75 1.25

Asian
Development
Bank — A859

1990, May 2 Photo. *Perf. 14*
1311 A859 2r Seashell 1.40 .45

Great
Britain No.
1,
Simulated
Cancel of
India,
Envelope
A860

1990, May 6 *Perf. 13x13½*
1312 A860 6r multicolored 2.25 .75
Penny Black, 150th anniv.

Residence
and Portrait
A861

1990, May 17 Photo. *Perf. 13½x13*
1313 A861 2r red brown & green .60 .40
Ho Chi Minh (1890-1969), Vietnamese Communist Party leader.

A862 A863

1990, May 29
1314 A862 1r orange brown .50 .45
Prime Minister Chaudhary Charan Singh (1902-1987).

1990, July 30 Photo. *Perf. 13x13½*
1315 A863 2r multicolored .80 .55
Indian peace keeping force in Sri Lanka.

Indian Council of
Agricultural
Research — A864

1990, July 31 *Perf. 14*
1316 A864 2r multicolored .60 .40

Freedom Fighter Type of 1989
Design: Khudiram Bose (1889-1908), vert.

1990, Aug. 11 Photo. *Perf. 13x13½*
Size: 26x35mm
1317 A826 1r orange, grn & red
brn .60 .45

Russian Child's Drawing of
India — A865

6.50r, Indian child's drawing of Red Square.

1990, Aug. 16 Photo. *Perf. 14*
1318 A865 1r multicolored 2.40 1.60
1319 A865 6.50r multicolored 2.40 1.60
a. Pair, #1318-1319 5.50 5.50
See Russia Nos. 5925-5926.

A866

A867

1990, Aug. 24 *Perf. 13*
1320 A866 1r lt red brown .60 .45
K. Kelappan (1889-1971), social revolutionary.

1990, Sept. 5 *Perf. 13x13½*
1321 A867 1r multicolored .90 .50
Care for young girls.

Intl. Literacy
Year
A868

1990, Sept. 8 *Perf. 13½x13*
1322 A868 1r blue, brn & tan .90 .50

A869

1990, Sept. 10 *Perf. 13x14*
1323 A869 4r blue grn & red 2.50 1.60
Safe drinking water.

1990, Sept. 28 Photo. *Perf. 13x13½*
1324 A870 60p rose lake .90 .50
Sunder Lal Sharma (1881-1940), social reformer.

A870

11th Asian
Games,
Beijing — A871

1990, Sept. 29
1325 A871 1r Kabbadi .80 .35
1326 A871 4r Sprinting 2.40 1.75
1327 A871 4r Cycling 2.40 1.75
1328 A871 6.50r Archery 3.00 2.25
Nos. 1325-1328 (4) 8.60 6.10

A.K. Gopalan
(1904-1977),
Political and Social
Reformer — A872

1990, Oct. 1
1329 A872 1r red brown .90 .50

5th Gurkha Rifles,
3rd and 5th
Battalions — A873

1990, Oct. 1
1330 A873 2r yel brown & dk vio 3.00 1.75

Suryamall Mishran
(1815-1868),
Poet — A874

1990, Oct. 19
1331 A874 2r brown & yel brown 1.00 .60

Children's
Day — A875

Perf. 13½x13
1990, Nov. 14 Photo. Unwmk.
1332 A875 1r multicolored 1.25 .60

Border
Security
Force, 25th
Anniv.
A876

1990, Nov. 30
1333 A876 5r multicolored 3.25 1.60

Greetings — A877

4r, Two elephants carrying riders, horiz.

Perf. 13x13½, 13½x13

1990, Dec. 17		Photo.
1334 A877 1r multicolored	.35	.30
1335 A877 4r multicolored	1.00	.50

Cities of India A878

1990, Dec. 24	Photo.	**Perf. 13½x13**
1336 A878	4r Bikaner	.80	.65
1337 A878	5r Hyderabad	1.25	.95
1338 A878	6.50r Cuttack	1.75	1.25
Nos. 1336-1338 (3)		3.80	2.85

Bhakta Kanakadas (1488-1578), Mystic — A879

1990, Dec. 26		**Perf. 14**
1339 A879 1r red orange	.90	.45

Dnyaneshwari, 700th Anniv. — A880

1990, Dec. 31		**Perf. 13½x13**
1340 A880 2r org red, red brown & blk	.60	.40

Calcutta, 300th Anniv. — A881

Unwmk.

1990, Dec. 28	Photo.	**Perf. 14**

Designs: 1r, Shaheed Minar. 6r, Sailing ships on Ganges River.

1341 A881 1r multicolored	.50	.30

Size: 44x35mm

1342 A881 6r multicolored	2.25	1.50

Pandit Mohan Malaviya, Banaras Hindu University A882

1991, Jan. 20		**Perf. 13½x13**
1343 A882 1r dk carmine rose	.60	.35

Banaras Hindu University, 75th Anniv.

Intl. Conference on Traffic Safety A883

1991, Jan. 30		**Perf. 13½x13**
1344 A883 6.50r blue, red & blk	1.25	.80

7th Art Triennial — A884

1991, Feb. 12	Photo.	**Perf. 13x13½**
1345 A884 6.50r multicolored	1.00	.60

Jagannath Sunkersett A885

1991, Feb. 15		
1346 A885 2r ultra & henna brn	.80	.50

Jagannath Sunkersett (1803-1865), educator, reformer.

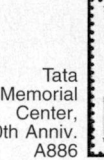

Tata Memorial Center, 50th Anniv. A886

1991, Feb. 28		**Perf. 13½x13**
1347 A886 2r brown & buff	.60	.35

River Dolphin A887

1991, Mar. 4		
1348 A887 4r shown	2.75	1.75
1349 A887 6.50r Sea cow	3.75	2.40

Fight Against Drugs — A888

World Peace — A889

1991, Mar. 5		**Perf. 13x13½**
1350 A888 5r dp violet & red	3.00	1.90

1991, Mar. 7	Photo.	**Perf. 13x13½**
1351 A889 6.50r black & tan	1.25	.75

Indian Remote Sensing Satellite 1A — A890

1991, Mar. 18		**Perf. 14**
1352 A890 6.50r blue, red brn & blk	1.00	.60

Babu Jagjivan Ram (1908-1976), Politician — A891

1991, Apr. 5	Photo.	**Perf. 13½**
1353 A891 1r yellow & brown	.60	.50

Dr. B.R. Ambedkar (1891-1956), Social Reformer — A892

1991, Apr. 14		**Perf. 13½x13**
1354 A892 1r red brown & blue	.60	.35

Tribal Dances A893

1991, Apr. 30	Photo.	**Perf. 13½x13**
1355 A893 2.50r Valar	.90	.50
1356 A893 4r Kayang	1.10	.60
1357 A893 5r Hozagiri	1.50	.70
1358 A893 6.50r Velakali	1.75	.85
Nos. 1355-1358 (4)		5.25	2.65

Ariyakudi Ramanuja Iyengar (1890-1967), Musician — A894

1991, May 18		
1359 A894 2r green & red brown	1.00	.60

Karpoori Thakur (1924-1988), Politician — A895

1991, May 30		**Perf. 13x13½**
1360 A895 1r red brown	.60	.50

Antarctic Treaty, 30th Anniv. A896

1991, June 23	Photo.	**Perf. 13½x13**
1361 A896 5r Penguins	3.50	2.10
1362 A896 6.50r Map, penguins	3.50	2.10
a. Pair, #1361-1362	7.50	7.50

No. 1362a printed in continuous design.

New Delhi, 60th Anniv. A897

Views of New Delhi architecture.

1991, June 25		
1363 A897 5r multicolored	3.00	1.60
1364 A897 6.50r multicolored	3.00	1.60
a. Pair, #1363-1364	6.00	6.00

No. 1364a printed in continuous design.

Sri Ram Sharma Acharya (1911-1990), Social Reformer — A898

1991, June 27		
1365 A898 1r red & blue green	.60	.50

K. Shankar Pillai (1902-1989), Cartoonist — A899

1991, July 31	Photo.	**Perf. 13½x13**
1366 A899 4r shown	1.75	1.25

Perf. 13x13½

1367 A899 6.50r The Big Show, vert.	2.50	1.90

Sriprakash (1890-1971), Politician — A900

1991, Aug. 3		**Perf. 13½x13**
1368 A900 2r yellow brown	.60	.40

Gopinath Bardoloi
(1890-1950),
Politician — A901

1991, Aug. 5   *Perf. 13x13½*
1369 A901 1r violet   .60   .50

Rajiv Gandhi (1944-1991), Prime
Minister — A902

1991, Aug. 20   *Perf. 13*
1370 A902 1r multicolored   1.50 1.00

Jain Muni Mishrimalji (1891-1984),
Philospher — A903

1991, Aug. 24 Photo.   *Perf. 13½*
1371 A903 1r brown   .60   .35

Mahadevi Verma (1907-1987), Writer
and Poet — A904

No. 1373: Jayshankar Prasad (1890-1937),
poet and dramatist.

1991, Sept. 16
1372 A904 2r black & blue   .35   .25
1373 A904 2r black & blue   .35   .25
  a.   Pair, #1372-1373   70   70

37th Commonwealth Parliamentary
Conference — A905

1991, Sept. 27 Photo. *Perf. 13½x13*
1374 A905 6.50r dk blue & brown .80   .60

Greetings — A906

Orchids — A907

1991, Sept. 30   *Perf. 13x13½*
1375 A906   1r Frog   .20   .20
1376 A906 6.50r Bird   .90   .45
  a.   Pair, #1375-1376   1.10 1.00

1991, Oct. 12
1377 A907   1r Cymbidium
               aloifolium   .40   .30
1378 A907 2.50r Paphiopedilum
               venustum   .75   .40
1379 A907   3r Aerides crispum   1.00   .50
1380 A907   4r Cymbidium bi-
               colour   1.50   .60
1381 A907   5r Vanda spathu-
               lata   1.75   .85
1382 A907 6.50r Cymbidium
               devonianum   2.25 1.25
       Nos. 1377-1382 (6)   7.65 3.90

2nd
Battalion,
Third
Gurkha
Rifles
A908

1991, Oct. 18   *Perf. 13½x13*
1383 A908 4r multicolored   3.50 2.00

Kamaladevi
Chattopadhyaya
(1903-1988),
Founder of All-
India Handicrafts
Board — A909

1991, Oct. 29   *Perf. 13x13½*
1384 A909   1r Horsemen   .70   .30
1385 A909 6.50r Puppet   1.90 1.10

Chithira Tirunal Bala Rama Varma
(1912-1991), Maharaja of
Travancore — A910

1991, Nov. 7 Photo.   *Perf. 13½x13*
1386 A910 2r violet   1.25   .90

Children's
Day — A911

1991, Nov. 14   *Perf. 13x13½*
1387 A911 1r multicolored   1.25   .50

18th Cavalry, Sesquicentennial (in
1992) — A912

1991, Nov. 14   *Perf. 13½x13*
1388 A912 6.50r multicolored   4.25 2.50

India
Tourism
Year
A913

1991, Nov. 15
1389 A913 6.50r multicolored   1.25   .95

Intl. Conference
on Youth
Tourism — A914

Wolfgang
Amadeus Mozart,
Death
Bicent. — A915

1991, Nov. 18 Photo.   *Perf. 13x13½*
1390 A914 6.50r multicolored   2.00 1.25

1991, Dec. 5
1391 A915 6.50r multicolored   3.25 1.90

SAARC
Year of
Shelter
A916

1991, Dec. 7   *Perf. 13½x13*
1392 A916 4r lake & bister   1.00   .75

Run for
Your Heart
A917

1991, Dec. 11
1393 A917 1r black, red & gray   .60   .50

Siddhartha With
An Injured
Bird — A918

1991, Dec. 28   *Perf. 13x13½*
1394 A918 2r multicolored   .60   .40

Asit Kumar Haldar (1890-1964), Painter

Yoga
Exercises
A919

1991, Dec. 30 Photo. *Perf. 13½x13*
1395 A919 2r Bhujangasana   .35   .30
1396 A919 5r Dhanurasana   .80   .35
1397 A919 6.50r Ustrasana   1.10   .50
1398 A919 10r Utthita
               trikonasana   1.90   .75
       Nos. 1395-1398 (4)   4.15 1.90

Intl. Assoc.
for Bridge
and
Structural
Engineering
A920

#1399, Hooghly River Bridge, Madurai Tem-
ple. #1400, Sanchi Stupa gates, Hall of
Nations.

1992, Mar. 1 Photo.   *Perf. 13½x13*
1399 A920 2r sal, brn & blue   1.40   .85
1400 A920 2r sal, brn & blue   1.40   .85
  a.   Pair, #1399-1400   2.75 2.75

Fifth Intl.
Conference on
Goats — A921

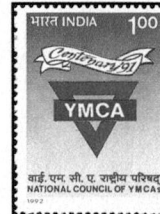

Natl. Council of
YMCAs, Cent. (in
1991) — A922

1992, Mar. 2   *Perf. 13x13½*
1401 A921 6r dk blue & brown   5.00 2.75

1992, Feb. 21
1402 A922 1r blue & vermilion   .60   .40

National
Archives
A923

1992, Apr. 20 Photo. *Perf. 13½x13*
1403 A923 6r multicolored   .80   .55

Krushna Chandra Gajapathi — A924

Vijay Singh Pathik, Writer — A925

1992, Apr. 2 **Perf. 13x13½**
1404 A924 1r violet .60 .40
1405 A925 1r red brown .60 .40

Adventure Sports A926

1992, Apr. 29 **Perf. 13½x13**
1406 A926 2r Hang gliding .45 .40
1407 A926 4r Wind surfing 1.25 .65
1408 A926 5r River rafting 1.75 1.10
1409 A926 11r Skiing 2.25 1.75
   Nos. 1406-1409 (4) 5.70 3.90

Henry Gidney (1873-1942), Physician and Politician — A927

1992, May 9 **Perf. 13½x13**
1410 A927 1r blue & black 1.10 .55

Telecommunication Training Center, Jabalpur, 50th Anniv. — A928

1992, May 30
1411 A928 1r lemon .60 .50

A929

A930

1992, July 31 **Perf. 13x13½**
1412 A929 1r black & brown .60 .50
Sardar Udham Singh (1899-1940), freedom fighter.

1992, Aug. 8
1413 A930 1r Discus .50 .25
1414 A930 6r Gymnastics 1.40 .85
1415 A930 8r Field hockey 3.25 1.90
1416 A930 11r Boxing 3.25 2.25
   Nos. 1413-1416 (4) 8.40 5.25
1992 Summer Olympics, Barcelona.

Quit India Movement, 50th Anniv. A931

Designs: 1r, Spinning wheel, inscription. 2r, Mahatma Gandhi, inscription.

1992, Aug. 9 **Perf. 13½x13**
1417 A931 1r pink, blk & pale pink 3.75 .65
1418 A931 2r gray, black & claret 4.75 3.75

60th Parachute Field Ambulance, 50th Anniv. A932

1992, Aug. 10
1419 A932 1r multicolored 2.75 .90

Indian Air Force, 60th Anniv. A933

1992, Oct. 8 Photo. **Perf. 13½x13**
1420 A933 1r shown 1.50 .85
1421 A933 10r Biplane, jet fighter 3.00 1.50
   a. Pair, #1420-1421 7.50 7.50

Phad Painting of Dev Narayan A934

1992, Sept. 2 Photo. **Perf. 13½x14**
1422 A934 5r multicolored 1.25 .95

Sisters of Jesus and Mary, 150th Anniv. — A935

1992, Nov. 13 Photo. **Perf. 13x13½**
1423 A935 1r gray & blue .60 .35

Children's Day A936

1992, Nov. 14 **Perf. 13½x13**
1424 A936 1r multicolored .60 .35

Shri Yogiji Maharaj, Religious Leader, Birth Cent. — A937

1992, Dec. 2 Photo. **Perf. 13x13½**
1425 A937 1r blue 2.75 1.50

Army Service Corps 1760-1992 A938

1992, Dec. 8 Photo. **Perf. 13½x13**
1426 A938 1r multicolored 3.50 .80

Stephen Smith (1891-1951), Rocket Mail Pioneer — A939

1992, Dec. 19 Photo. **Perf. 13½x13**
1427 A939 11r multicolored 1.75 1.10

State of Haryana, 25th Anniv. A940

1992, Dec. 20
1428 A940 2r green & orange .60 .60

Freedom Fighter Type of 1989
Design: Madan Lal Dhingra, vert.

1992, Dec. 28 **Perf. 13x13½**
1429 A826 1r org, grn & brn .60 .35

Dr. Shri Shiyali Ramamrita Ranganathan (1892-1972), Writer and Librarian — A941

1992, Aug. 30 Photo. **Perf. 13½x13**
1430 A941 1r blue 2.75 .65

Hanuman Prasad Poddar — A942

Pandit Ravishankar Shukla — A943

1992, Sept. 19 Photo. **Perf. 13x13½**
1431 A942 1r green .60 .30

1992, Dec. 31
1432 A943 1r rose lake .60 .30

Birds — A944

2r, Pandion haliaetus. 6r, Falco peregrinus. 8r, Gypaetus barbatus. 11r, Aquila chrysaetos.

1992, Dec. 30
1433 A944 2r multicolored 1.50 .85
1434 A944 6r multicolored 2.25 1.25
1435 A944 8r multicolored 2.50 1.40
1436 A944 11r multicolored 2.75 1.90
   Nos. 1433-1436 (4) 9.00 5.40

William Carey, Baptist Missionary to India, Bicent. of Appointment A945

1993, Jan. 9 Photo. **Perf. 13½x13**
1437 A945 6r multicolored 2.00 1.10

Fakir Mohan Senapati, Writer — A946

1993, Jan. 14 **Perf. 13x13½**
1438 A946 1r orange brown .75 .40

Council of Scientific and Industrial Research, 50th Anniv. — A947

1993, Feb. 28 **Perf. 13½x13**
1439 A947 1r violet brown 1.10 .45

Squadron No. 1, Indian Air Force, 60th Anniv. A948

1993, Apr. 1
1440 A948 1r shown   1.50 .35
1441 A948 1r Paratroopers, planes, artillery   1.50 .35

Parachute Field Regiment 9, 50th anniv. (#1441).

Rahul Sankrityayan (1893-1963), Politician — A949

1993, Apr. 9
1442 A949 1r multicolored   .75 .35

Mountain Locomotives A950

1993, Apr. 16   *Perf. 13½x13*
1443 A950 1r Neral Matheran   1.00 .30
1444 A950 6r DHR (Darjeeling)   2.00 1.00
1445 A950 8r Nilgiri Mountain Railway   2.25 1.25
1446 A950 11r Kalka-Simla   3.25 1.60
Nos. 1443-1446 (4)   8.50 4.15

89th Inter-Parliamentary Union Conference, New Delhi — A951

1993, Apr. 11   Photo.   Perf. 13x13½
1447 A951 1r indigo   .75 .35

Meerut College, Cent. (in 1992) — A952

1993, Apr. 25   *Perf. 14*
1448 A952 1r indigo & red brown   .75 .60

P.C. Mahalanobis (b. 1893), Statistician — A953

1993, June 29   *Perf. 13x13½*
1449 A953 1r olive yellow   .60 .35

Dadabhai Naoroji's Election to House of Commons, Cent. — A957

1993, Aug. 26   Photo.   Perf. 14
1453 A957 6r blue & red brown   1.00 .70

A958

A959

1993, Sept. 11   *Perf. 13x13½*
1454 A958 2r gray, red brn & org 1.00 .55
Swami Vivekananda, Chicago address, cent.

1993, Oct. 9   Photo.   Perf. 13x13½
Trees: 1r, Lagerstroemia speciosa. 6r, Cochlospermum religiosum. 8r, Erythrina variegata. 11r, Thespesia populnea.

1455 A959 1r multicolored   .40 .30
1456 A959 6r multicolored   1.00 .30
1457 A959 8r multicolored   1.50 .65
1458 A959 11r multicolored   2.25 .90
Nos. 1455-1458 (4)   5.15 2.15

Dr. Dwarkanath Kotnis A960

1993, Dec. 9   Photo.   Perf. 13½x13
1459 A960 1r black & gray   .80 .40

A961

A962

1993, Nov. 14   *Perf. 14*
1460 A961 1r multicolored   .60 .35
Children's Day.

1993, Nov. 8   *Perf. 13x13½*
1461 A962 2r multicolored   .60 .35
College of Military Engineering, Pune, 50th anniv.

A963

A964

Design: Dr. Dwarm Venkataswamy Naidu.

1993, Nov. 8
1462 A963 1r orange brown   .60 .35

1993, July 31
1463 A964 2r multicolored   .60 .35
Bombay Municipal Corporation Building, cent.

India Tea A965

1993, Dec. 11   *Perf. 13*
1464 A965 6r green & red   1.10 .75

Papal Seminary, Pune, Cent. A966

1993, Dec. 16   *Perf. 13½x13*
1465 A966 6r multicolored   1.25 .85

Natl. Integration A967

1993, Aug. 19
1466 A967 1r orange & green   .60 .30

Khan Abdul Ghaffar Khan A968

1993, Aug. 9
1467 A968 1r multicolored   .60 .30

Heart Care Festival A969

1993, Dec. 9
1468 A969 6.50r multicolored   1.40 .75

Inpex '93 — A970

1993
1469 A970 1r shown   .40 .40
1470 A970 2r Boats, beach   1.00 .40
Issued: 1r, Dec. 25; 2r, Dec. 27.

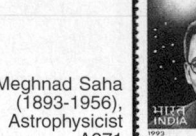

Meghnad Saha (1893-1956), Astrophysicist A971

1993, Dec. 23   Photo.   Perf. 13x13½
1471 A971 1r dark blue   .75 .45

Dinanath Mageshkar, Musician A972

1993, Dec. 29   *Perf. 13½x13*
1472 A972 1r orange brown   .60 .30

Nargis Dutt, Actress and Social Worker — A973

1993, Dec. 30   *Perf. 13*
1473 A973 1r orange brown   .60 .30

Indian Natl. Army, 50th Anniv. A974

1r, Netaji Subhash Bose inspecting soldiers.

1993, Dec. 31   *Perf. 13½x13*
1474 A974 1r multicolored   .80 .50

Satyendra Nath Bose (1894-1974), Mathematician and Physicist — A975

1994, Jan. 1
1475 A975 1r dark rose brown   .80 .45

Satyajit Ray (1921-92) A976

6r, Scene from film, Pather Panchali.

1994, Jan. 11   *Perf. 13*
1476 A976 6r multicolored   2.40 1.60
1477 A976 11r multicolored   2.75 1.60
   a.   Pair, #1476-1477   5.25 5.25

No. 1476 is 68x30mm. No. 1477a is a continuous design.

Dr. Sampurnanand — A977

1994, Jan. 10   **Photo.**   *Perf. 13½x13*
1478 A977 1r multicolored   .60 .60

Dr. Shanti Swarup Bhatnagar A978

1994, Feb. 21
1479 A978 1r dark blue   .70 .70

Eighth Triennale A979

1994, Mar. 14
1480 A979 6r multicolored   1.00 .50

Prajapita Brahma (1876-1969), Religious Leader — A980

1994, Mar. 7   **Photo.**   *Perf. 13½x13*
1481 A980 1r multicolored   .70 .70

Sanchi Stupa A981

Wmk. 324
1994, Apr. 4   **Photo.**   *Perf. 13*
1482 A981 5r blue green & brn   .60 .40

ILO, 75th Anniv. A982

1994, May 1   **Unwmk.**   *Perf. 13½x13*
1483 A982 6r multicolored   1.00 .70

United Planters Assoc. of Southern India, Cent. — A983

1994, Mar. 26   **Photo.**   *Perf. 13x13½*
1484 A983 2r multicolored   .70 .50

Rani Rashmoni (1793-1861), Philanthropist — A984

1994, Apr. 9   *Perf. 13½x13*
1485 A984 1r brown   .70 .55

Jallianwala Bagh Martyrdom, 75th Anniv. A985

1994, Apr. 13
1486 A985 1r red & black   .70 .70

Freedom Fighters Type of 1988

1r, Chandra Singh Garhwali (1891-1979).

1994, Apr. 23
1487 A826 1r org, sage grn & grn   .70 .70

IPTA A986

Small Families A987

1994, May 25   *Perf. 13*
1488 A986 2r multi   .70 .40

1994   *Perf. 13x12½*

1r, Family of 3 in front of house.
1489 A987 75p red brn & brn   .30 .30
1490 A987 1r green & rose   .30 .30

4th Battalion Madras Regiment, Bicent. — A988

1994, Aug. 12
1491 A988 6.50r multicolored   1.25 .85

Institute of Mental Health, Madras, Bicent. A989

1994, Sept. 23   **Photo.**   *Perf. 13½x13*
1492 A989 2r multicolored   .70 .40

Mahatma Gandhi (1869-1948) A990

Design: 11r, Flag colors, Gandhi walking and at spinning wheel.

1994, Oct. 2   *Perf. 13*
1493 A990 6r multicolored   2.25 1.50
1494 A990 11r multicolored   3.00 2.50
   a.   Pair, #1493-1494   5.50 5.50

No. 1494 is 68x30mm.

16th Intl. Cancer Congress — A991

1994, Oct. 30   **Photo.**   *Perf. 13½*
1495 A991 6r multicolored   1.25 .70

World Conference on Human Resource Development — A992

1994, Nov. 8   *Perf. 13½x13*
1496 A992 6r multicolored   1.00 .65

Intl. Year of the Family — A993

1994, Nov. 20   *Perf. 13x12½*
1497 A993 2r multicolored   .60 .35

Children's Day A994

1994, Nov. 14   *Perf. 13½x13*
1498 A994 1r multicolored   .60 .50

J.R.D. Tata (1904-93) — A995

1994, Nov. 29   *Perf. 14*
1499 A995 2r multicolored   .60 .40

Calcutta School for the Blind, Cent. A996

1994 Nov. 30   *Perf. 13½x13*
1500 A996 2r brown & carmine   .60 .35

Endangered Waterbirds — A996A

Designs: 1r, Andaman teal. 6r, Eastern white stork. 8r, Black-necked crane. 11r, Pink-headed duck.

1994, Nov. 23   *Perf. 13*
1501 A996A 1r multicolored   12.50 3.75
1502 A996A 6r multicolored   19.00 7.50
1503 A996A 8r multicolored   19.00 8.00
1504 A996A 11r multicolored   20.00 11.00
   a.   Block of 4, #1501-1504   75.00 75.00

This set was withdrawn shortly after issue, when it was discovered that it was printed with water soluble ink.

Begum Akhtar A996B

1994, Dec 2   *Perf. 13x13½*
1504B A996B 2r multicolored   15.00 10.00

No. 1504B was withdrawn shortly after issue, when it was discovered that it was printed with water soluble ink.

Remount Veterinary Corps, 215th Anniv. — A998

1994, Dec. 14   **Photo.**   *Perf. 13x13½*
1505 A998 6r multicolored   2.75 1.60

College of Engineering, Guindy, Madras, Bicent. — A999

1994, Dec. 19   *Perf. 14*
1506 A999 2r multicolored   .60   .35

Baroda Museum, Vadodara — A1000

Designs: 6r, Ancient artifact. 11r, Ancient artifact, man standing on pedestal.

1994, Dec. 20   *Perf. 14x13½*
1507   6r black & bister   4.50   2.25
1508   11r black & bister   4.50   2.25
   a. A1000 Pair, #1507-1508   9.50   9.50

Khuda Bakhsh Oriental Public Library A1001

1994, Nov. 21   **Photo.**   *Perf. 14*
1509 A1001 6r multicolored   8.50   1.60

A1002

A1003

1995, Jan. 9   **Photo.**   *Perf. 13x13½*
1510 A1002 1r Chhoturam   1.25   .30

1995, Jan. 7
1511 A1003 6r multicolored   .80   .55
India Natl. Science Academy, 30th Anniv.

St. Xavier's College, Bombay, 125th Anniv. A1005

1994, Dec. 4   **Photo.**   *Perf. 13½*
1513 A1005 2r multicolored   .35   .20

General Post Office, Bombay, Bicent. — A1006

Illustration reduced.

1994, Dec. 28   **Litho.**   *Perf. 13½*
1514 A1006 6r multicolored   9.00   3.00

Motion Pictures, Cent. A1007

Designs: 6r, Colored film, world map. 11r, Early camera, black & white film.

1995, Jan. 11   **Litho.**   *Perf. 13*
1515 A1007 6r multicolored   1.60   1.60
1516 A1007 11r multicolored   2.50   2.50
   a.   Pair, #1515-1516   4.25   4.25

Oil Conservation A1008

Rafi Ahmed Kidwai A1009

1995, Feb. 18   **Photo.**   *Perf. 13*
1517 A1008 1r red brown & black   .20   .20

1995, Feb. 18
1518 A1009 1r red brown   .60   .60

K. L. Saigal A1010

1995, Apr. 4   **Photo.**   *Perf. 13½x13*
1519 A1010 5r black & brown   1.75   1.00

A1011

1995, Jan. 5   **Photo.**   *Perf. 13*
1520 A1011 2r King Rajaraja Chola   6.25   1.10
8th Intl. Conference of Tamil Studies.

A1012

1995, Jan. 12   **Photo.**   *Perf. 13½x13*
1521 A1012 2r multicolored   .60   .40
SAARC Youth Year.

A1013

A1014

1995, Jan. 15
1522 A1013 2r multicolored   7.25   1.10
Prithvi Theater, 50th anniv.

1995, Jan. 15
Field Marshall K.M. Cariappa (1900-93).
1523 A1014 2r multicolored   .75   .45

A1015

A1017

1995, Jan. 18
1524 A1015 2r multicolored   .60   .40
Tex-Styles India '95, National Textile Fair, Bombay.

1995, June 6   **Photo.**   *Perf. 13*
UN, 50th Anniv.: 6r, Planting seedling, mother and child, child reading.
1526 A1017 1r multicolored   .20   .20
1527 A1017 6r multicolored   .65   .45

R.S. Ruikar — A1018

Bharti Bhavan Library, Allahabad A1019

1995, May 1   **Photo.**   *Perf. 13½*
1528 A1018 1r brown violet   .60   .60

1995, Aug. 30   *Perf. 14*
1529 A1019 6r multicolored   .75   .60

Asian Pacific Postal Training Center, Bangkok, 25th Anniv. A1020

1995, Sept. 4   **Litho.**   *Perf. 13½x13*
1530 A1020 10r multicolored   1.75   1.25

Headquarters Delhi Area — A1021

1995, Sept. 26   **Photo.**   *Perf. 13*
1531 A1021 2r multicolored   1.00   .55

Louis Pasteur (1822-95) A1022

1995, Sept. 28
1532 A1022 5r pale yel & black   3.00   1.50

La Martiniere College, Lucknow, 150th Anniv. A1023

1995, Oct. 1
1533 A1023 2r multicolored   .60   .40

Mahatma Gandhi (1869-1948) — A1024

1995, Oct. 2
1534   1r As young man   .85   .40
1535   2r As older man   .85   .40
   a. A1024 Pair, #1534-1535   1.75   1.75
   b. Souvenir sheet, #1535a   3.00   3.00
See South Africa Nos. 918-919.

FAO, 50th Anniv. A1025

1995, Oct. 16   *Perf. 13½*
1536 A1025 5r multicolored   1.60   1.00

A1026

1995, Oct. 30   **Perf. 13**
1537 A1026 1r carmine   .60 .50
        P.M. Thevar (1908-63), politician.

A1027

1995, Nov. 8   Photo.   Perf. 13x13½
1538 A1027 6r multicolored   3.25 1.90
        Wilhelm Roentgen (1845-1923), discovery
        of the X-Ray, cent.

JAT
Regiment,
Bicent.
A1028

1995, Nov. 20   **Perf. 13**
1539 A1028 5r multicolored   2.75 1.75

Radio Communication, Cent. — A1029

1995, May 17   Litho.   Perf. 13½x13
1540 A1029 5r multicolored   1.75 1.75

Dehli Development Authority — A1030

1995, May 23
1541 A1030 2r multicolored   .60 .60

Children's
Day — A1031

1995, Nov. 14   Photo.   Perf. 13x13½
1542 A1031 1r multicolored   .60 .50

Rajputana
Rifles,
175th
Anniv.
A1032

1995, Nov. 28   **Perf. 13½**
1543 A1032 5r multicolored   3.25 1.75

Communal
Harmony — A1033

1995, Nov. 19   Photo.   Perf. 13
1544 A1033 2r multicolored   2.75 1.40

Sant Tukdoji
Maharaj,
Patriot,
Social
Worker
A1034

1995, Dec. 10
1545 A1034 1r brown   .70 .55
        Dated 1993.

A1035   A1036

Design: Yellapragada Subbarow (1895-
1948), biochemist.

1995, Dec. 19
1546 A1035 1r yellow brown   .70 .55

1995, Dec. 25
        Giani Zail Singh (1916-94), Pres. of India.
1547 A1036 1r multicolored   .70 .55

Dome Barelvi's
Mausoleum,
Dargah — A1037

1995, Dec. 31   Litho.
1548 A1037 1r multicolored   .70 .55
        Ala Hazrat Barelvi (1856-1921), poet.

Cricket
Players — A1038

1996, Mar. 13   Photo.   Perf. 14
1549 A1038 2r Deodhar   1.00 .75
1550 A1038 2r Vijay Merchant 1.00 .75
1551 A1038 2r Vinoo Mankad   1.00 .75
1552 A1038 2r C.K. Nayudu   1.00 .75
        Nos. 1549-1552 (4)   4.00 3.00
                Dated 1995.

Homi Bhabha and Tata Institute of
Fundamental Research — A1039

1996, Feb. 9   Photo.   Perf. 13
1553 A1039 2r multicolored   .80 .50

Kasturba
Trust — A1040

Cardiac Surgery,
Cent. — A1041

1996, Feb. 22
1554 A1040 1r multicolored   .60 .35

1996, Feb. 25   Litho.
1555 A1041 5r multicolored   2.25 1.25

Miniature
Paintings
A1042

#1556, Two women picking berries from
trees. #1557, Woman, man embracing. #1558,
Women looking upward, men, animals. #1559,
Ceremony, black clouds.

1996, Mar. 13   **Perf. 13½**
1556 A1042 5r multicolored   1.75 1.00
1557 A1042 5r multicolored   1.75 1.00
1558 A1042 5r multicolored   1.75 1.00
1559 A1042 5r multicolored   1.75 1.00
        Nos. 1556-1559 (4)   7.00 4.00

Pt. Kunjilal
Dubey — A1043

1996, Mar. 18   Photo.   Perf. 13
1560 A1043 1r brown   .60 .50

Himalayan
Wildlife
A1044

#1561, Saussurea simpsoniana. #1562,
Capra falconeri. #1563, Ithaginis cruentus.
#1564, Meconopsis horridula.

1996, May 10   **Litho.**
1561 A1044 5r multicolored   2.25 1.75
1562 A1044 5r multicolored   2.25 1.75
1563 A1044 5r multicolored   2.25 1.75
1564 A1044 5r multicolored   2.25 1.75
  a.   Souv. sheet of 4, #1561-1564   9.00 9.00
        Nos. 1561-1564 (4)   9.00 7.00
No. 1564a sold for 30r. Stamps in No.
1564a do not have "1996."

Morarji
Desai — A1045

1996, Apr. 10   Photo.   Perf. 13x13½
1565 A1045 1r carmine   .60 .35

SKCG
College
A1047

1996, May 25   Photo.
1567 A1047 1r lt brn & dk brn   .80 .65

Muhammad Ismail
Sahib — A1048

1996 Summer
Olympic Games,
Atlanta — A1049

1996, June 5   **Perf. 13x13½**
1568 A1048 1r claret   .80 .80

1996, June 25
1569 A1049 5r Olympic stadium   .90 .55
1570 A1049 5r Torch   .90 .55

A1050

A1051

1996, July 19   *Perf. 13x13½*
1571 A1050 1r blue & black   .80   .80
Sister Alphonsa (1910-46).

1996, Aug. 2   *Litho.*   *Perf. 14*
1572 A1051 5r multicolored   2.25 1.40
VSNL, 125th anniv.

A1052   A1053

1r, Chembai Vaidyanatha Bhagavathar. 2r,
Ahilyabai Holkar.

1996   *Photo.*   *Perf. 13x13½*
1573 A1052 1r dk bl grn & brn   .80   .55
1574 A1052 2r rose brn & lt brn   .80   .65
Issued: 1r, 8/28; 2r, 8/25.

1996, Aug. 4   *Photo.*   *Perf. 13*
1575 A1053 1r Sir Pherozsha
Mehta   .80   .80

Poultry
Production
A1054

1996, Sept. 2
1576 A1054 5r Gallus gallus   4.00 3.00

Rani
Gaidinliu — A1055

1996, Sept. 12
1577 A1055 1r dark blue green   .80   .80

Barrister Nath
Pai — A1056

1996, Sept. 25
1578 A1056 1r blue   .80   .80

Indepex '97 World
Philatelic
Exhibition
A1057

1996, Oct. 5   *Litho.*   *Perf. 13x13½*
1579 A1057 2r lake & bister   .80   .50

Children's
Day
A1058

1996, Nov. 14   *Photo.*   *Perf. 13½x13*
1580 A1058 8r multicolored   2.25 1.25

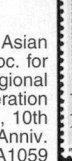

South Asian
Assoc. for
Regional
Cooperation
(SAARC), 10th
Anniv.
A1059

1996, Dec. 8   *Perf. 13*
1581 A1059 11r multicolored   2.40 1.60

Abai Konunbaev
(1845-1904),
Poet — A1060

2nd Intl. Crop
Science Congress
A1061

1996, Dec. 9   *Perf. 13x13½*
1582 A1060 5r red brown & lake   2.40 1.60
Dated 1995.

1996, Nov. 17   *Perf. 13*
1583 A1061 2r multicolored   1.10   .70

Sikh
Regiment,
150th
Anniv.
A1062

1996, Oct. 19
1584 A1062 5r multicolored   2.40 1.50

Natl. Rail Museum, 25th
Anniv. — A1063

1996, Oct. 7   *Litho.*   *Perf. 13½*
1585 A1063 5r multicolored   3.75 2.10

Jananayak
Debeswar Sarmah
(1896-1993),
Politician — A1064

1996, Oct. 10
1586 A1064 2r lt brn & red brn   .80   .50

Dr. Salim Ali, Birth Cent. — A1065

1996, Nov. 12   *Photo.*   *Perf. 13*
1587   8r Dr. Salim Ali   3.75 2.50
1588   11r Water fowl   3.75 2.50
   a. A1065 Pair, #1587-1588   9.00 9.00

Second
Battalion, The
Grenadiers,
Bicent.
A1066

1996, Dec. 4   *Perf. 14*
1589 A1066 5r multicolored   2.40 1.25

Vijay Divas
A1067

1996, Dec. 16
1590 A1067 2r multicolored   .35   .25

Vivekananda Rock Memorial,
Kanyakumari — A1068

Illustration reduced.

1996, Dec. 26   *Litho.*   *Perf. 13*
1591 A1068 5r multicolored   3.25 1.90

Use of
Anesthesia, 150th
Anniv. — A1069

1996, Dec. 27   *Perf. 13*
1592 A1069 5r multicolored   2.40 1.40

University
of
Roorkee,
150th
Anniv.
A1070

1997, Jan. 1   *Photo.*   *Perf. 13*
1593 A1070 8r multicolored   2.00 1.10

Vrindavan Lal
Verma,
Writer — A1071

1997, Jan. 9   *Photo.*   *Perf. 13x13½*
1594 A1071 2r red   .80   .50

Army Postal
Service
Corps.
(APS), 25th
Anniv.
A1072

1997, Jan. 22   *Perf. 13½x13*
1595 A1072 5r multicolored   2.75 1.90

Jose Marti (1853-
95), Cuban
Revolutionary
A1073

1997, Jan. 28   *Perf. 13x13½*
1596 A1073 11r multicolored   2.25 1.00

Inter-Parliamentary Specialized
Conference, New Dehli — A1074

1997, Feb. 15   *Photo.*   *Perf. 13*
1597 A1074 5r multicolored   .80   .40

A1075

1997, Mar. 4   Photo.   *Perf. 13*
1598 A1075 1r lt brn & dk brn   .80 .50
Shyam Lal Gupt (b. 1896), composer of song on natl. flag.

A1076

1997, Mar. 8   *Perf. 13x13½*
1599   5r Parijat Tree   1.25 .75
1600   6r Branch, flower   1.25 .75
  a.   A1076 Pair, #1599-1600   2.50 2.50

Rashtriya Indian Military College, Dehra Dun, 75th Anniv. A1077

1997, Mar. 13   *Perf. 13½*
1601 A1077 2r multicolored   1.60 .60

Netaji Subhas Chandra Bose (1897-1945), Nationalist Leader — A1078

1997, Jan. 23   *Perf. 13*
1602 A1078 1r dk brn & lt brn   .80 .45

A1079

1997, Feb. 25   Photo.   *Perf. 13x13½*
1603 A1079 8r St. Andrews Church   1.60 .95

Morarji Desai, Prime Minister, 1977-79 — A1080

1997, Feb. 28   Photo.   *Perf. 13*
1604 A1080 1r brown & buff   .80 .45

Saint Dnyaneshwar (1274-95), Poet — A1081

1997, Mar. 5   Photo.   *Perf. 13*
1605 A1081 5r multicolored   1.40 .65

Ram Manohar Lohia (1910-67), Politician — A1082

1997, Mar. 23   Litho.   *Perf. 13x13½*
1606 A1082 1r multicolored   .60 .40

CENTIPEX '97 — A1083

1997, Mar. 27
Philatelic Society of India, Cent.: No. 1608, #1, Front cover of "The Philatelic Journal of India," 1897.
1607   2r multicolored   1.25 1.00
1608   2r multicolored   1.25 1.00
  a.   Pair, #1607-1608   2.50 2.50

Jnanpith Award Winners — A1084

K.V. Puttappa, D.R. Bendre, Prof. V.K. Gokak, Dr. Masti V. Iyengar, writers.

1997, Mar. 28   Photo.   *Perf. 13*
1609 A1084 2r multi   .80 .50

Madhu Limaye (1922-95), Politician — A1085

1997, May 1
1610 A1085 2r green   .80 .50

A1086

A1087

1997, June 24 Photo. *Perf. 13x13½*
1611 A1086 2r Pandit Omkarnath Thakar   1.10 .65

1997, Aug. 6   Photo.   *Perf. 13*
1612 A1087 2r brown   1.75 1.25
Thirumathi Rukmini Lakshmipathi (1892-1951), reformer.

Independence, 50th Anniv. — A1088

Officers from Indian Natl. Army, Shah Nawaz Khan, G.S. Dhillon, P.K. Sahgal.

1997, Aug. 15
1613 A1088 2r multicolored   .40 .25

Newspaper Swantantra Bharat, 50th Anniv. A1089

1997, Aug. 15   *Perf. 13½x13*
1614 A1089 2r multicolored   .60 .40

A1090

A1091

1997, Aug. 20   *Perf. 13*
1615 A1090 2r black & gray   1.75 .75
Sir Ronald Ross (1857-1932), physician, medical researcher.

1997, Sept. 6
1616 A1091 5r red brown   2.10 1.00
Swami Bhaktivedanta (b. 1896), humanitarian.

A1092

A1093

1997, Sept. 14
1617 A1092 2r black & gray   .60 .40
Swami Brahmanand (1894-1984), social reformer.

1997, Aug. 8
1618 A1093 2r Sri Basaveswara   .60 .40

Maratha Parachute Regiment, Bicent. A1094

1997, Sept. 7   *Perf. 13½x13*
1619 A1094 2r multicolored   .90 .45

Hazari Prasad Dwivedi — A1095

Firaq Gorakhpuri A1096

1997, Dec. 13 Photo. *Perf. 13x13½*
1620 A1095 2r gray brown   .60 .40

1997, Aug. 28
1621 A1096 2r brown   .60 .40

Fossil Plants — A1097

Sir William Jones, 250th Birth Anniv. — A1098

No. 1622, Birbalsahnia divyadarshanii. No. 1623, Glossopteris. 6r, Pentoxylon. 10r, Williamsonia sewardiana.

1997, Sept. 11
1622	A1097	2r multicolored	.50	.35
1623	A1097	2r multicolored	.50	.35
1624	A1097	6r multicolored	1.50	.90
1625	A1097	10r multicolored	2.25	1.50
		Nos. 1622-1625 (4)	4.75	3.10

1997, Sept. 28
1626	A1098	4r multicolored	.70	.35

Lawrence School, Sanawar, 150th Anniv. A1099

1997, Oct. 4   *Perf. 13½x13*
1627	A1099	2r multicolored	.90	.55

Indepex '97 A1100

1997, June 6   Photo.   *Perf. 13½x13*
1628	A1100	2r Nalanda	.50	.40
1629	A1100	6r Bodhgaya	.80	.50
1630	A1100	10r Vaishali	1.25	.80
1631	A1100	11r Kushinagar	1.60	.80
a.		Block of 4, #1628-1631	4.50	4.50

66th General Assembly Session of Interpol, 1997 A1101

1997, Oct. 15   *Perf. 13½*
1632	A1101	4r multicolored	1.25	.80

V.K. Krishna Menon — A1102

1997, Oct. 6   *Perf. 13*
1633	A1102	2r brown carmine	1.00	.75

Indepex '97 World Philatelic Exhibition A1103

Rural Indian women.

1997, Oct. 15   Photo.   *Perf. 13x13½*
1634	A1103	2r Arunachal Pradesh	.50	.30
1635	A1103	6r Gujarat	.95	.50
1636	A1103	10r Ladakh	1.25	.70
1637	A1103	11r Kerala	1.50	.95
a.		Block of 4, #1634-1637	4.50	4.50

Scindia School, Cent. — A1104

Designs: No. 1638, Outdoor class. No. 1639, Founder, school building, aerial view.

1997, Oct. 20   *Perf. 14*
1638		5r multicolored	.70	.35
1639		5r multicolored	.70	.35
a.		A1104 Pair, #1638-1639	1.40	1.40

Medicinal Plants A1105

2r, Ocimum sanctum. 5r, Curcuma longa. 10r, Rauvolfia serpentina. 11r, Aloe barbadensis.

1997, Oct. 28
1640	A1105	2r multicolored	.60	.35
1641	A1105	5r multicolored	1.25	.60
1642	A1105	10r multicolored	1.60	1.10
1643	A1105	11r multicolored	1.90	1.10
a.		Block of 4, #1640-1643	5.50	4.50

A1106

A1107

1997, July 2   Litho.   *Perf. 13x13½*
1644	A1106	2r brown & sepia	.60	.40

Ram Sewak Yadav (1926-74), politician, social reformer.

1997, July 11
1645	A1107	2r multicolored	.60	.40

Sibnath Banerjee (1897-1982), politician, union leader.

Indian beaches: 2r, Gopalpur on Sea, Orissa. 6r, Kovalam Beach, Thiruvananthapuram. 10r, Anjuna Beach, Goa. 11r, Bogmalo Beach, Goa.

1997, Aug. 11   Photo.   *Perf. 13½x13*
1648	A1110	2r multicolored	.60	.30
1649	A1110	6r multicolored	.90	.55
1650	A1110	10r multicolored	1.60	.80
1651	A1110	11r multicolored	2.25	1.00
		Nos. 1648-1651 (4)	5.35	2.65

Sant Kavi Sunderdas (1596-1689) A1111

Kotamaraju Rama Rao — A1112

1997, Nov. 8   Photo.   *Perf. 13x13½*
1652	A1111	2r lt brn & dk brn	1.00	.50

1997, Nov. 9
1653	A1112	2r dk brn & yel brn	1.40	.70

Children's Day A1113

1997, Nov. 14   *Perf. 13½x13*
1654	A1113	2r Nehru with child	.70	.40

A1114

A1115

1997, Nov. 23   Photo.   *Perf. 13*
1655	A1114	4r multicolored	1.75	1.10

World Convention on Reverence for All Life.

1997, Dec. 15   Photo.   *Perf. 13x13½*
1656	A1115	2r dk brn & lt brn	.60	.40

Sardar Vallabhbhai Patel (1875-1950), politician.

Indepex '97 A1116

Designs: 2r, Post Office Heritage Building. 6r, Indian River Mail. 10r, Cancellations, Jal Cooper. 11r, Mail ship, SS Hindosthan.

1997, Dec, 15   Photo.   *Perf. 13½x13*
1657	A1116	2r multicolored	.60	.50
1657A	A1116	6r multicolored	1.25	.55
1657B	A1116	10r multicolored	1.60	1.10
1657C	A1116	11r multicolored	2.25	1.25
d.		Block of 4, #1657-1657C	5.75	4.75

Souvenir Sheet

Mother Teresa (1910-97) — A1117

Illustration reduced.

1997, Dec. 15   Litho.   *Perf. 13x13½*
1658	A1117	45r multicolored	6.00	6.00

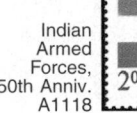

Indian Armed Forces, 50th Anniv. A1118

1997, Dec. 16   Photo.   *Perf. 13½x13*
1659	A1118	2r multicolored	.80	.40

Dr. B. Pattabhi Sitaramayya (1880-1959), Author, Politician — A1119

1997, Dec. 17   *Perf. 13x13½*
1660	A1119	2r dk brn & lt brn	1.10	.55

Fr. Jerome D'Souza (1897-1977) A1120

1997, Dec. 18   *Perf. 13½x13*
1661	A1120	2r red brown	.60	.40

Ashfaquallah Khan and Ram Prasad Bismil, Revolutionaries A1121

1997, Dec. 19   *Perf. 13*
1662	A1121	2r dk brn & brn	.60	.40

Cellular Jail Natl. Memorial, Port Blair A1122

1997, Dec. 30
1663 A1122 2r multicolored .60 .40

A1123

1998, Jan. 2
1664 A1123 2r red brown .40 .25
Nanak Singh (1897-1971), novelist.

A1124

1998, Jan. 9
1665 A1124 2r plum .40 .25
Nahar Singh, minor leader of Great Mutiny.

Rotary Intl., 1998 Council on Legislation, New Delhi A1125

1998, Jan. 12 **Perf. 13½X13**
1666 A1125 8r multicolored 1.25 1.00

A1126

A1127

#1667, Maharana Pratap (1540-97), ruler, warrior. #1668, Vishnu S. Khandekar (b. 1898), writer.

1998, Jan. 19 **Perf. 13x13½**
1667 A1126 2r violet brown .80 .50
1668 A1127 2r rose red & dull red .80 .50

A1128 A1129

1998, Jan. 25
1669 A1128 10r multicolored 2.25 1.50
Bharat Paryatan Diwas (India Tourism Day).

1998, Jan. 2 **Perf. 13½x13**
1670 A1129 4r multicolored 3.00 1.75
11th Gurkha Rifles, 50th anniv.

A1130

Mahatma Gandhi, 50th Anniv. of Death: 2r, Peasants' welfare. 6r, Social upliftment. 10r, Salt Satyagraha. 11r, Communal harmony.

1998, Jan. 30 **Photo.** **Perf. 14**
1671 A1130 2r multicolored .60 .45
1672 A1130 6r multicolored .90 .75
1673 A1130 10r multicolored 1.10 1.10
1674 A1130 11r multicolored 1.75 1.25
a. Block of 4, #1671-1674 4.75 4.25

A1131

1998, Mar. 8 **Photo.** **Perf. 13x13½**
1675 A1131 6r multicolored 1.25 .60
Universal Declaration of Human Rights, 50th anniv.

Savitribai Phule (1831-97), Educator, Women's Reformer A1132

1998, Mar. 10 **Perf. 13½x13**
1676 A1132 2r dk brn & lt brn .80 .50

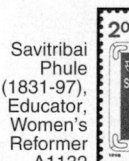

Jagdish Chandra Jain A1133

1998, Jan. 28 **Photo.** **Perf. 13x13½**
1677 A1133 2r red brown .80 .50

Syed Ahmad Khan (1817-98), Writer — A1134

Sardar A. Vedaratnam A1135

1998, Mar. 27
1678 A1134 2r brn & olive brn .80 .50

1998, Feb. 25
1679 A1135 2r violet black .80 .50

Global Environment Facility First Assembly Meeting — A1136

1998, Apr. 1 **Perf. 13**
1680 A1136 11r multicolored 1.75 1.10

A1137

A1138

1998, Apr. 16 **Photo.** **Perf. 14**
1681 A1137 6r carmine 1.10 .70
Defense Services Staff College.

1998, May 3 **Photo.** **Perf. 13**
Design: Pres. Zakir Husain (1897-1969).
1682 A1138 2r sepia .60 .40

A1139 A1140

Jnanpith Literary Award winners, year: Shri Bishnu Dey (1909-82), 1971; Shri Tarashankar Bandopadhyay (1898-1971), 1966; Smt. Ashapurna Devi (1909-95), 1976.

1998, June 5
1683 A1139 2r olive brown .60 .40

1998, June 8 **Photo.** **Perf. 13**
Designs: 5r, Parliament Clock Tower, London. 6r, Airplane, mascot, Gateway of India, Bombay.
1684 A1140 5r multicolored .75 .40
Size: 56x35mm
1685 A1140 6r multicolored 1.00 .50
a. Pair, #1684-1685 1.75 1.75
Air India's 1st intl. flight, 50th anniv.

A1141

A1142

Design: Salem C. Vijiaraghavachariar (1852-1944), freedom fighter.

1998, June 18
1686 A1141 2r red brown .60 .35

1998, May 1
1687 A1142 2r N.G. Goray .60 .35

Sri Ramana Maharshi A1143

1998, Apr. 14
1688 A1143 2r violet black .60 .40

Konkan Railway — A1143a

Illustration reduced.

1998, May 1 **Photo.** **Perf. 13**
1689 A1143a 8r multicolored 1.60 .95

A1144

A1145

Mohammed Abdurahiman Shahib.

1998, May 15
1690 A1144 2r red brown .60 .40

1998, May 21 **Photo.** **Perf. 14**
1691 A1145 2r brown & sepia .60 .40
Lokanayak Omeo Kumar Das, freedom fighter.

Revolutionaries — A1146

Design: Satyendra Chandra Bardhan, Vakkom Abdul Khader, Fouja Singh.

1998, May 25 *Perf. 13*
1692 A1146 2r brn & red brn .60 .40

Natl. Savings Organization, 50th Anniv. — A1147

Design: 6r, Hand dropping coin into bank.

1998, June 30
1693 A1147 5r multicolored .65 .30
1694 A1147 6r multicolored .80 .50
   a.   Pair, #1693-1694 1.50 1.25

Bhagwan Gopinathji, Spiritual Leader, Birth Cent. — A1148

1998, July 3 *Perf. 13½*
1695 A1148 3r brown & sepia .60 .40

Ardeshir (1868-1926) & Pirojsha (1882-1972) Godrej, Environmentalists — A1149

1998, July 11 *Perf. 13*
1696 A1149 3r green .60 .40

Aruna Asaf Ali, Revolutionay — A1150

1998, July 16
1697 A1150 3r brown .60 .40

Vidyasagar College, 125th Anniv. A1151

1998, July 29
1698 A1151 2r dark gray .60 .30

Shivpujan Sahai (1893-1963), Writer — A1152

1998, Aug. 9 *Photo. Perf. 13*
1699 A1152 2r brown .60 .30

Homage to Martyrs A1153

Designs: 3r, Minaret, silhouettes of soldiers standing in fort, flag of India. 8r, Symbols of industrial, scientific and technological developments.

1998, Aug. 15 *Perf. 14*
1700 A1153 3r multicolored .50 .30
1701 A1153 8r multicolored 1.10 .55
   a.   Pair, #1700-1701 1.60 1.40

Gostha Behari Paul (1896-1976), Soccer Player — A1154

1998, Aug. 20 *Perf. 13*
1702 A1154 3r sepia .60 .40

Youth Hostels Assoc. of India, 50th Anniv. — A1155

1998, Aug. 23 *Perf. 14*
1703 A1155 5r multicolored .80 .45

Brigade of the Guards, Fourth Battalion, Bicent. A1156

1998, Sept. 15 *Photo. Perf. 13½*
1704 A1156 6r multicolored 1.00 .55

Bhai Kanhaiyaji A1157

1998, Sept. 18 *Perf. 13*
1705 A1157 2r red .60 .30

20th Intl. Congress of Radiology A1158

1998, Sept. 18 *Perf. 13½x13*
1706 A1158 8r multicolored 1.75 .90

28th IBBY Congress A1159

1998, Sept. 20 *Perf. 13*
1707 A1159 11r multicolored 1.75 .85

Dr. Tristao Braganza Cunha — A1160

1998, Sept. 26
1708 A1160 3r dark brown .60 .40

Jananeta Hijam Irawat Singh — A1161

1998, Sept. 30
1709 A1161 3r brown .60 .40

Acharya Tulsi (1914-97) A1162

1998, Oct. 20 *Photo. Perf. 13½x13*
1710 A1162 3r brown & orange .60 .40

Indian Women in Aviation A1163

Pulse Polio Immunization A1164

1998, Oct. 15 *Perf. 13*
1711 A1163 8r blue 1.75 .85

1998, Sept. 21
1712 A1164 3r maroon .20 .20

2nd Battalion of the Rajput Regiment (Kalichindi), Bicent. — A1165

1998, Nov. 30
1713 A1165 3r multicolored .60 .30

David Sassoon Library & Reading Room, Mumbai — A1166

1998, Nov. 30
1714 A1166 3r lt blue & dk blue .60 .40

Army Postal Service Center, Kamptee, 50th Anniv. A1167

1998, Dec. 2
1715 A1167 3r multicolored 1.10 .55

Connemara Public Library, Chennai A1168

1998, Dec. 5 *Perf. 13½x13*
1716 A1168 3r bister & brown .60 .40

A1169

A1170

1998, Dec. 10 Litho. *Perf. 13½*
1717 A1169 3r multicolored 1.25 .60
Indian Pharmaceutical Cong. Assoc., 50th anniv.

1998, Dec. 12 Photo. *Perf. 13*
Design: Baba Raghv Das (1896-1958), reformer, freedom fighter.
1718 A1170 2r deep gray violet .60 .30

Indra Lal Roy (1898-1918), World War I Pilot — A1171

1998, Dec. 19
1719 A1171 3r multicolored .80 .40

Sant Gadge Baba (1876-1956), Religious Philosopher — A1172

1998, Dec. 20
1720 A1172 3r multicolored .60 .40

Traditional Musical Instruments A1173

Designs: 2r, Rudra veena (stringed instrument). 6r, Flute (wind insrument). 8r, Pakhawaj (percussion instrument). 10r, Sarod (stringed instrument).

1998, Dec. 29
1721 A1173 2r multicolored .35 .25
1722 A1173 6r multicolored .85 .55
1723 A1173 8r multicolored 1.10 .70
1724 A1173 10r multicolored 1.50 .90
Nos. 1721-1724 (4) 3.80 2.40

Children's Day A1174

1998, Nov. 14 Photo. *Perf. 13½*
1725 A1174 3r multicolored .60 .40

INS Delhi A1175

1998, Nov. 15
1726 A1175 3r multicolored 1.00 .60

President's Bodyguard A1176

1998, Nov. 16
1727 A1176 3r multicolored 1.25 .60

Shells A1177

Designs: No. 1728, Cypraea staphylaea. No. 1729, Cassis cornuta. No. 1730, Chicoreus brunneus. 11r, Lambis lambis.

1998, Dec. 30
1728 A1177 3r multicolored .65 .80
1729 A1177 3r multicolored .90 .80
1730 A1177 3r multicolored 1.60 .80
1731 A1177 11r multicolored 2.25 1.60
Nos. 1728-1731 (4) 5.40 4.00

Indian Police Service, 50th Anniv. A1178

1999, Jan. 13 Litho. *Perf. 13½x13¼*
1732 A1178 3r multicolored 1.10 .55

Defense Research & Development Organization — A1179

1999, Jan. 26 Photo. *Perf. 13*
1733 A1179 10r multicolored 2.00 1.00

Newpapers in Assam, 150th Anniv. — A1180

1999, Jan. 29 *Perf. 13x13½*
1734 A1180 3r multicolored 1.00 .70

Sanskrit College, Calcutta, 175th Anniv. A1181

1999, Feb. 25 *Perf. 13½x13*
1735 A1181 3r brown & yellow 1.00 .45

National Defense Academy, 50th Anniv. A1182

Perf. 13½x13¼
1999, Feb. 19 Litho.
1736 A1182 3r multicolored 1.00 .70

Hindu College, Delhi, Cent. A1183

1999, Feb. 17 Photo. *Perf. 13½x13*
1737 A1183 3r blue .60 .40

Biju Patnaik (1916-97), Politician A1184

1999, Mar. 5
1738 A1184 3r multicolored 1.00 .50

A1185 A1186

1999, Mar. 12 *Perf. 13*
1739 A1185 15r multicolored 1.75 1.00
Press Trust of India, 50th anniv.

1999, Mar. 6
1740 A1186 15r multicolored 1.75 1.00
Temple Complex of Khajuraho, 1000th anniv.

Dr. K.B. Hedgewar (1889-1940) A1187

1999, Mar. 18
1741 A1187 3r multicolored .60 .40

Bethune Collegiate School, 150th Anniv. A1188

1999 Photo. *Perf. 13*
1742 A1188 3r green .70 .50

Creation of the Khalsa, 300th Anniv. A1189

1999, Apr. 14
1743 A1189 3r multicolored 1.00 .55

Maritime Heritage A1190

1999, Apr. 5 Litho. *Perf. 13½x13¼*
1744 A1190 3r Boat from 2200 B.C. .70 .50
1745 A1190 3r Ship from 1700 .70 .50

Technology Day A1191

1999, May 11 Litho. *Perf. 13½x13¼*
1746 A1191 3r multicolored .70 .50

Mumbai Port Trust, 125th Anniv. A1192

1999, June 26 Photo. *Perf. 12¾x13*
1747 A1192 3r blue gray .70 .50

A1193 A1194

1999, June 30 Photo. *Perf. 13x12¾*
1748 A1193 3r multicolored .60 .40
Mizoram Accord.

1999, July 4 Photo. *Perf. 13¼*
1749 A1194 3r multicolored .60 .40
Gulzari Lal Nanda (b. 1899), interim Prime Minister.

Jijabai, Mother of Shivaji — A1195

1999, July 7 Photo. *Perf. 14x13½*
1750 A1195 3r claret .60 .40

P. S. Kumaraswamy Raja — A1196

1999, July 8 Photo. *Perf. 13¼*
1751 A1196 3r sky blue & brown .60 .40

Balai Chand Mukhopadhyay (1879-1979), Writer — A1197

1999, July 19 Photo. Perf. 13¼
1752 A1197 3r slate blue .60 .40

Sindh River Festival A1198

Perf. 13½x13¼
1999, July 28 Photo.
1753 A1198 3r multicolored .60 .40

Geneva Conventions, 50th Anniv. — A1199

1999, Aug. 12 Photo. Perf. 13¾
1754 A1199 15r black & red 2.25 1.60

Freedom Fighters A1200

#1755, Swami Ramanand Teerth. #1756, Vishwambhar Dayalu Tripathi. #1757, Swami Keshawanand. #1758, Sardar Ajit Singh.

Perf. 13½x13¼
1999, Aug. 15 Photo.
1755 A1200 3r multicolored .55 .40
1756 A1200 3r multicolored .55 .40
1757 A1200 3r multicolored .55 .40
1758 A1200 3r multicolored .55 .40
　Nos. 1755-1758 (4) 2.20 1.60

Kalki Krishnamurthy (1899-1954), Novelist — A1201

1999, Sept. 9 Photo. Perf. 13¾
1759 A1201 3r black .60 .50

Qazi Nazrul Islam (1899-1976), Poet — A1202

Rambriksh Benipuri, Writer A1203

Ramdhari Sinha "Dinkar," Poet A1204

Jhaverchand Kalidas Meghani (b. 1896), Poet — A1205

1999, Sept. 14 Photo. Perf. 13x13¼
1760 A1202 3r multicolored .60 .50
Perf. 13¼
1761 A1203 3r multicolored .60 .50
Perf. 13¼x13
1762 A1204 3r multicolored .60 .50
1763 A1205 3r multicolored .60 .50
　Nos. 1760-1763 (4) 2.40 2.00

Arati Gupta, First Asian Woman to Swim Across English Channel A1206

1999, Sept. 29 Photo. Perf. 13x13¼
1764 A1206 3r multi .60 .50

Worldwide Fund for Nature A1207

Asiatic lion: No. 1765, Male atop female. No. 1766, Two lions. No. 1767, Three lions. 15r, Two lions, diff.

1999, Oct. 4 Perf. 13¼x13
1765 A1207 3r multi 2.00 .60
1766 A1207 3r multi 2.00 .60
1767 A1207 3r multi 2.00 .60
1768 A1207 15r multi 3.50 1.75
　Nos. 1765-1768 (4) 9.50 3.55

UPU, 125th Anniv. A1208

#1769, Muria ritual object. #1770, Mask for Chhau dance. #1771, Rathva wall painting. 15r, Angami ornament.

1999, Oct. 9 Perf. 13¼x13, 13x13¼
1769 A1208 3r multi .70 .35
1770 A1208 3r multi .70 .35
1771 A1208 3r multi, vert. .70 .35
1772 A1208 15r multi, vert. 2.25 1.40
　Nos. 1769-1772 (4) 4.35 2.45

Dr. T. M. A. Pai (1898-1979) — A1209

Chhaganlal K. Parekh (1894-1968) — A1209a

A. B. Walawalkar, Draftsman for Konkar Railway — A1209b

A. D. Shroff — A1209c

1999, Oct. 9 Perf. 13x13¼
1773 A1209 3r yel & brn .60 .60
Perf. 12¾x13¼
1774 A1209a 3r org brn & ind .60 .60
Perf. 13¼
1775 A1209b 3r lilac & maroon .60 .60
1776 A1209c 3r bister & olive .60 .60
　Nos. 1773-1776 (4) 2.40 2.40

Veerapandia Kattabomman (1760-99), Freedom Fighter — A1210

1999, Oct. 16 Photo. Perf. 13x13¼
1777 A1210 3r olive green .60 .50

Musicians A1211

#1778, Ustad Allauddin Khan Saheb (1870-1972), sarod player. #1779, Musiri Subramania Iyer (1899-1975), music teacher.

1999, Oct. 19 Photo. Perf. 13¾
1778 A1211 3r multicolored .75 .60
1779 A1211 3r multicolored .75 .60

A1212

A1213

Perf. 13¼x13½
1999, Oct. 27 Photo.
1780 A1212 3r violet brown .70 .50
　Brigadier Rajinder Singh (1899-1947).

1999, Nov. 14 Photo. Perf. 14
1781 A1213 3r multi .60 .40
　Children's Day.

Sri Sathya Sai Water Supply Project A1214

Perf. 12¾x13¼
1999, Nov. 23 Photo.
1782 A1214 3r multi .90 .50

Supreme Court, 50th Anniv. A1215

Perf. 12¾x13¼
1999, Nov. 26 Photo.
1783 A1215 3r multi .60 .50

Dr. Punjabrao Deshmukh, Agriculture Minister A1215a

A. Vaidyanatha Iyer (d. 1955), Advocate of Untouchables — A1216

P. Kakkan, Politician A1217

Indulal Kanaiyalal Yagnik, Politician A1218

1999, Dec. 9 Perf. 13¼
1784 A1215a 3r brown & grn .35 .25
1785 A1216 3r orange brown .35 .25
1786 A1217 3r green & brn .35 .25
1787 A1218 3r tan & black .35 .25
　Nos. 1784-1787 (4) 1.40 1.00

Thermal Power, Cent. A1219

1999, Dec. 14 Photo. Perf. 13¼x13
1788 A1219 3r bister & brn .60 .50

Hindustan Times Newspaper, 75th Anniv. A1220

1999, Dec. 16   Photo.   Perf. 13¼
1789 A1220 15r multi   2.25 1.60

Family Planning Assoc. of India, 50th Anniv. — A1221

1999, Dec. 18   Perf. 14x13¾
1790 A1221 3r multi   .60   .50

Birth of Jesus Christ, 2000th Anniv. — A1222

1999, Dec. 25
1791 A1222 3r multi   1.00   .80

Tabo Monastery A1223

1999, Dec. 31   Perf. 12¾x13¼
1792 A1223 5r shown   .25   .25
1793 A1223 10r People   .45   .45
  a.   Pair, #1792-1793   .70   .70

First Sunrise of the Millennium A1224

2000, Jan. 1   Perf. 13¼x13
1794 A1224 3r multi   2.00 2.00

Agni II Missile A1225

2000, Jan. 1   Litho.   Perf. 13x13¼
1795 A1225 3r multi   .20   .20

Mahatma Gandhi — A1226

2000, Jan. 27   Perf. 14x13¾
1796 A1226 3r red & black   .60   .60
     Republic of India, 50th anniv.

Gallantry Award Winners A1227

Designs: No. 1797, Karam Singh, regimental crest. No. 1798, Abdul Hamid, jeep-mounted artillery gun. No. 1799, Albert Ekka, grenades, knife. No. 1800, N. J. S. Sekhon, airplane. No. 1801, M. N. Mulla, ship.

2000, Jan. 27   Perf. 13¼x13
1797 A1227 3r multi   .60   .60
1798 A1227 3r multi   .60   .60
1799 A1227 3r multi   .60   .60
1800 A1227 3r multi   .60   .60
1801 A1227 3r multi   .60   .60
  a.   Strip of 5, #1797-1801   2.50 2.50
     Republic of India, 50th anniv.

Millepex 2000 A1228

Endangered reptiles: No. 1802, Batagur terrapin. No. 1803, Olive ridley turtle.

2000, Jan. 29   Perf. 13¼
1802 A1228 3r multi   .50   .40
1803 A1228 3r multi   .50   .40
  a.   Pair, #1802-1803   2.00 1.75

Famous Men — A1229

Designs: No. 1804, Balwantrai Mehta. No. 1805, Arun Kumar Chanda. No. 1806, Dr. Harekrushna Mahatab, politician.

2000, Feb. 17   Litho.   Perf. 13x13¼
1804 A1229 3r multi   .60   .60
1805 A1229 3r multi   .60   .60
1806 A1229 3r multi   .60   .60
     Nos. 1804-1806 (3)   1.80 1.80

Patna Medical College, 75th Anniv. A1230

2000, Feb. 26   Perf. 13¼x13
1807 A1230 3r multi   .60   .60

Dr. Burgula Ramakrishna Rao, Politician — A1231

2000, Mar. 13   Perf. 13x13¾
1808 A1231 3r brn & ocher   .60   .60

Potti Sriramulu (1901-52), Advocate of Untouchables — A1232

2000, Mar. 16   Perf. 13¼x13
1809 A1232 3r red   .60   .60

Basawon Sinha (1909-89), Socialist Party Leader — A1233

2000, Mar. 23   Perf. 13x13¼
1810 A1233 3r multi   .60   .60

Indepex Asiana 2000 — A1234

2000, Mar. 31   Perf. 13x13¼
1811 A1234 3r Siroi lily   .50   .50
1812 A1234 3r Wild guava   .50   .50
1813 A1234 3r Sangai deer   .50   .50
1814 A1234 15r Slow loris   1.75 1.75
  a.   Souvenir sheet, #1811-1814   4.50 4.50
     Nos. 1811-1814 (4)   3.25 3.25
     See Nos. 1831-1834.

Arya Samaj, 125th Anniv. — A1235

Perf. 13x13¼
2000, Apr. 5   Litho.   Unwmk.
1815 A1235 3r multi   .80   .80

Indigenous Cattle Breeds A1236

Perf. 13¼x13
2000, Apr. 25   Litho.   Unwmk.
1816 A1236 3r Gir   .55   .45
1817 A1236 3r Kangayam   .55   .45
1818 A1236 3r Kankrej   .55   .45
1819 A1236 15r Hallikar   2.00 1.50
     Nos. 1816-1819 (4)   3.65 2.85

Blackbuck A1237   Patel A1237a

Smooth Indian Otter — A1238

Leopard Cat — A1239

Tiger A1240

Amaltaas — A1241

50p, Nilgiri tahr. 1r, Saras crane. 2r, Sardar Vallabhbhai Patel (1875-1950), Politician. 15r, Butterfly. 50r, Paradise flycatcher.

Perf. 12¾x13, 13x12¾
2000   Photo.   Wmk. 324
1820 A1237 25p olive brn   .30   .30
1821 A1237 50p yel brn   .30   .30
1822 A1237 1r blue   .30   .30
1823 A1237a 2r black   .30   .30
1824 A1238 3r gray vio   .30   .30
1825 A1239 5r multi   .30   .30
1826 A1240 10r multi   .70   .70
1827 A1240 15r multi   1.00 1.00
1828 A1241 20r multi   1.40 1.40
1829 A1241 50r multi   3.25 3.25
     Nos. 1820-1829 (10)   8.15 8.15

Issued: 25p, 50p, 1r, 3r, 7/20; 2r, 10/31; 5r, 10r, 4/30; 15r, 20r, 11/20; 50r, 10/30.

Railways in Doon Valley, Cent. — A1244

Perf. 13¼
2000, May 6   Litho.   Unwmk.
1830 A1244 15r multi   2.50 2.50

Indepex Asiana Type of 2000

Birds: #1831, Rosy pastor. #1832, Garganey teal. #1833, Forest wagtail. #1834, White stork.

2000, May 24   Perf. 13¼x13
1831 A1234 3r multi, horiz.   1.10 1.10
1832 A1234 3r multi, horiz.   1.10 1.10
1833 A1234 3r multi, horiz.   1.10 1.10
1834 A1234 3r multi, horiz.   1.10 1.10
  a.   Block of strip of 4, #1831-1834 4.50 4.50
  b.   Souvenir sheet, #1831-1834   6.00 6.00

Dr. Nandamuri Taraka Rama Rao (1923-96), Actor, Politician A1245

2000, May 28
1835 A1245 3r multi   .60   .60

Swami Sahajanand Saraswati (1889-1950), Freedom Fighter — A1246

2000, June 26 *Perf. 13x13¼*
1836 A1246 3r multi .60 .60

Christian Medical College and Hospital, Vellore, Cent. A1247

2000, Aug. 12 *Perf. 13¼x13*
1837 A1247 3r multi .60 .60

Social and Political Leaders — A1248

Designs: No. 1838, Radha Gobinda Baruah (1900-75), newspaper publisher. No. 1839, Vijaya Lakshmi Pandit (1900-90), President of UN General Assembly. No. 1840, Jaglal Choudhary (1895-1975), politician. No. 1841, R. Srinivasan (1859-1945), advocate of untouchables, newspaper founder.

2000, Aug. 15 *Perf. 13x13¼*
1838 A1248 3r multi .60 .60
1839 A1248 3r multi .60 .60
1840 A1248 3r multi .60 .60
1841 A1248 3r multi .60 .60
Nos. 1838-1841 (4) 2.40 2.40

Kodaikanal Intl. School, Cent. A1249

Perf. 13¼x13
2000, Aug. 26 Litho. Unwmk.
1842 A1249 15r multi 1.75 1.75

2000 Summer Olympics, Sydney A1250

Designs: 3r, Discus. 6r, Tennis. 10r, Field hockey. 15r, Weight lifting.

2000, Sept. 17 *Perf. 13x13¼*
1843-1846 A1250 Set of 4 5.50 5.50

India in Space A1251

#1847, Oceansat 1. #1848, Insat 3B in orbit.

No. 1849, vert.: a, Astronaut on planet, spacecraft. b, Earth, spacecraft.

Perf. 13¼x13, 13x13¼
2000, Sept. 29
1847-1848 A1251 3r Set of 2 1.50 1.50
1849 Pair 1.50 1.50
a.-b. A1251 3r Any single 1.00 1.00

Madhubani-Mithila Painting — A1252

#1850, 3 figures. #1851, 2 figures and bird. #1852, 2 figures and cow, vert.
No. 1853, vert.: a, Red fish, palanquin. b, Yellow fish, elephant.

2000, Oct. 15 *Perf. 13¼*
1850-1852 A1252 3r Set of 3 1.25 1.25
1853 Pair 2.10 2.10
a. A1252 5r multi .55 .55
b. A1252 10r multi 1.40 1.40

Raj Kumar Shukla (b. 1875), Farmer — A1253

2000, Oct. 16 Litho. *Perf. 13x13¼*
1854 A1253 3r multi 15.00 15.00

Pres. Shanker Dayal Sharma (1918-99) A1254

2000, Oct. 29 Litho.
1855 A1254 3r multicolored .60 .60

Children's Day — A1255

2000, Nov. 14
1856 A1255 3r multicolored .60 .60

Maharaja Bijli Pasi A1256

2000, Nov. 16 *Perf. 13¼x13*
1857 A1256 3r multicolored .60 .60

Gems and Jewelry — A1257

#1858, 3r, Ancient India. #1859, 3r, Sarpech. #1860, 3r. Taxila. #1861, 3r, Navratna. #1862, 3r, Temple. #1863, 3r, Bridal.

2000, Dec. 7 *Perf. 13¼*
1858-1863 A1257 Set of 6 6.50 6.50
a. Block of 0, #1050•1003 7.50 7.50
b. Souvenir sheet, #1858, 1860-1861, 1863 8.00 8.00
Issued: No. 1863b, 12/11. No. 1863b sold fo 15r.

Warship of Adm. Mohammed Kunjali Marakkar — A1258

2000, Dec. 17 *Perf. 13¼x13*
1864 A1258 3r multi 1.10 1.10

Ustad Hafiz Ali Khan (1888-1972), Musician — A1259

2000, Dec. 28
1865 A1259 3r multi .60 .60

Famous Men A1260

#1866, Gen. Zorawar Singh (1786-1841). #1867, Rajarshi Bhagyachandra (1740-98), King of Manipur, vert. #1868, Samrat Prithviraj Chauhan (1162-92), ruler of Delhi, vert. #1869, Raja Bhamashah (c. 1542-98), military leader, vert.

2000, Dec. 31 *Perf. 13¼x13, 13x13¼*
1866-1869 A1260 3r Set of 4 2.40 2.40

St. Aloysius College Chapel Paintings, Cent. A1261

Perf. 13¼
2001, Jan. 12 Litho. Unwmk.
1870 A1261 15r multi 2.40 2.40

Subhas Chandra Bose A1262

Dr. B. R. Ambedkar A1263

Perf. 12¾x13
2001 Photo. Wmk. 324
1871 A1262 1r brown .20 .20
1872 A1263 3r blue green .20 .20
Issued: 1r, 1/23; 3r, 4/14.

Famous Men — A1264

Designs: No. 1873, 3r, Sane Guruji (1899-1950), social reformer. No. 1874, 3r, N. G. Ranga (1900-95), politician. No. 1875, 3r, E. M. S. Namboodiripad (1909-98), Marxist leader. No. 1876, 3r, Giani Gurmukh Singh Musafir (1899-1976), politician.

Perf. 13x13¼
2001, Jan. Litho. Unwmk.
1873-1876 A1264 Set of 4 2.40 2.40
Issued: No. 1873, 1/25; others, 1/27.

Famous Men — A1265

Designs: No. 1877, 3r, Sheel Bhadra Yajee (1906-96), freedom fighter. No. 1878, 3r, Jubba Sahni (1906-44), revolt leader. No. 1879, 3r, Yogendra (1896-1966) and Baikunth (1907-34) Shukla, freedom fighters.

2001, Jan.
1877-1879 A1265 Set of 3 1.75 1.75
Issued: No. 1877, 1/28; others, 1/29.

Western Railways Building, Mumbai, Cent. (in 1999) A1266

2001, Feb. 6 *Perf. 13¼x13*
1880 A1266 15r multi 3.75 3.75
Dated 1999.

2001 Census — A1267

2001, Feb. 10 *Perf. 13x13¼*
1881 A1267 3r multi .60 .60

President's International Fleet Review — A1268

Designs: No. 1882, 3r, Pal. No. 1883, 3r, Galbat. No. 1884, 3r, Tarangini. 15r, Emblem.

2001, Feb. 18   Perf. 13¼x13
1882-1885 A1268   Set of 4   3.50 3.50

Geological Survey of India, 150th Anniv. A1269

2001, Mar. 4
1886 A1269 3r multi   .60 .60

4th Battalion of Maratha Light Infantry, Bicent. — A1270

2001, Mar. 6   Perf. 13x13¼
1887 A1270 3r multi   .60 .60

Bhagwan Mahavira, 2600th Anniv. of Birth — A1271

2001, Apr. 6
1888 A1271 3r multi   .60 .60

First Manned Space Flight, 40th Anniv. A1272

2001, Apr. 12   Perf. 13¼x13
1889 A1272 15r multi   3.25 3.25

Frederic Chopin (1810-49), Composer A1273

2001, May 4
1890 A1273 15r multi   3.25 3.25

Suraj Narain Singh (1908-73), Politician A1274

2001, May 31   Perf. 13x13¼
1891 A1274 3r multi   .60 .60

B. P. Mandal (1918-82), Politician — A1275

2001, June 1
1892 A1275 3r multi   .60 .60

Samanta Chandra Sekhar (1835-1904), Astronomer A1276

2001, June 11
1893 A1276 3r multi   .60 .60

Sant Ravidas, 15th Cent Religious Leader — A1277

2001, June 24
1894 A1277 3r multi   .60 .60

Famous Men — A1278

Designs: No. 1895, 4r, Krishna Nath Sarmah (1887-1947), social reformer. No. 1896, 4r, C. Sankaran Nair (1857-1934), President of Indian National Congress. No. 1897, 4r, Syama Prasad Mookerjee (1901-53), politician. No. 1898, 4r, U Kiang Nongbah (d. 1862), soldier.

2001, July 6   Litho.   Perf. 13x13¼
1895-1898 A1278   Set of 4   2.40 2.40

Chandragupta Maurya, Emperor, 3rd Cent. B.C. — A1279

2001, July 21   Litho.   Perf. 13¼
1899 A1279 4r multi   .60 .60

Jhalkari Bai — A1280

2001, July 22   Litho.   Perf. 13x13¼
1900 A1280 4r multi   .60 .60

Corals A1281

Designs: No. 1901, 4r, Acropora digitifera. No. 1902, 4r, Fungia horrida. 15r, Montipora acquituberculata. 45r, Acropora formosa.

2001, Aug. 2   Perf. 13¼
1901-1904 A1281   Set of 4   5.50 5.50

Dwarka Prasad Mishra (1901-88), Politician — A1282

2001, Aug. 5   Perf. 13x13¼
1905 A1282 4r multi   .60 .60

Chaudhary Brahm Parkash (1918-93), Government Minister — A1283

2001, Aug. 11
1906 A1283 4r multi   .80 .80

Ballia Revolution of August 1942 — A1284

2001, Aug. 19
1907 A1284 4r multi   .80 .80

Jagdev Prasad (1922-74), Socialist Politician — A1285

2001, Sept. 5
1908 A1285 4r multi   .80 .80

Rani Avantibai (d. 1858), Queen of Ramgarh — A1286

2001, Sept. 19
1909 A1286 4r multi   .80 .80

Painted Stork — A1287

Perf. 12¾x13
2001, Sept. 20   Photo.   Wmk. 324
1910 A1287 4r bister brown   .90 .90

Rao Tula Ram (1825-63), Chieftain — A1288

Perf. 13x13¼
2001, Sept. 23   Litho.   Unwmk.
1911 A1288 4r multi   .80 .80

Chaudhary Devi Lal (1914-2001), Deputy Prime Minister — A1289

2001, Sept. 25
1912 A1289 4r multi   .80 .80

Satis Chandra Samanta (1900-83), Politician — A1290

2001, Sept. 29
1913 A1290 4r multi   .80   .80

Sivaji Ganesan (1928-2001), Actor — A1291

2001, Oct. 1
1914 A1291 4r multi   .80   .80

Mahatma Gandhi, Man of the Millennium — A1292

No. 1915: a, Gandhi and followers, birds. b, Gandhi.
Type A Syncopation (1st stamp #1915): On the two longer sides, an oval hole equal in width to 3 holes is located in the center, with an equal number of normal round holes to either side.

Perf. 13x13¼ Syncopated Type A
2001, Oct. 2
1915 A1292 4r Horiz. pair, #a-b   2.50 2.50

Literary and Performing Arts Personalities A1293

Designs: No. 1916, 4r, Lachhu Maharaj (1901-78), choreographer. No. 1917, 4r, Master Mitrasen (1895-1946), playwright, theater founder. No. 1918, 4r, Bharathidasan (1891-1964), Tamil poet.

2001, Oct. 9   *Perf. 13¼x13*
1916-1918 A1293 Set of 3   2.40 2.40

Jayaprakash Narayan (1902-79), Socialist Politician A1294

2001, Oct. 11
1919 A1294 4r multi   .80   .80

Panchatantra Fables — A1295

No. 1920 — The Monkey and the Crocodile, 4r: a, Monkey in tree. b, Monkey on crocodile's back.

No. 1921 — The Lion and the Rabbit, 4r: a, Lion and rabbit. b, Lion and rabbit on bridge.
No. 1922 — The Crows and the Snake, 4r: a, Crows with necklace. b, Villagers pursuing snake.
No. 1923 — The Tortoise and the Geese, 4r: a, Tortoise in pond. b, Tortoise flying with geese.
Sizes: Nos. 1920a-1923a, 58x39mm; Nos. 1920b-1923b, 29x39mm. Illustration reduced.

2001, Oct. 17   *Perf. 13x13¼*
Horiz. Pairs, #a-b
1920-1923 A1295 Set of 4   6.00 6.00

Global Iodine Deficiency Disorders Day — A1296

2001, Oct. 21
1924 A1296 4r multi   .80   .80

Thangal Kunju Musaliar (1897-1966), Industrialist A1297

2001, Oct. 26
1925 A1297 4r multi   .80   .80

Children's Day — A1298

2001, Nov. 14 Litho.   *Perf. 13x13¼*
1926 A1298 4r multi   .80   .80

Dr. V. Shantaram (1901-90), Movie Producer A1299

Perf. 13¼x13 Syncopated
2001, Nov. 17
1927 A1299 4r multi   .80   .80

Sobha Singh (1901-86), Artist — A1300

2001, Nov. 29 Litho.   *Perf. 13x13¼*
1928 A1300 4r multi   .80   .80

Sun Temple, Konark — A1301

No. 1929: a, 4r, Carved wheel. b, 15r, Sun Temple.

Illustration reduced.

Perf. 13¼x13 Syncopated
2001, Dec. 1
1929 A1301 Horiz. pair, #a-b   4.50 4.50

Intl. Volunteers Year A1302

2001, Dec. 5 Litho.   *Perf. 13¼x13*
1930 A1302 4r multi   .80   .80

Raj Kapoor (1924-88), Film Actor, Director and Producer A1303

Perf. 13¼x13 Syncopated
2001, Dec. 14   Litho.
1931 A1303 4r multi   .80   .80

Greetings — A1304

Flowers and: 3r, Fireworks. 4r, Butterflies.

Perf. 13¼x13 Syncopated
2001, Dec. 18   Litho.
1932-1933 A1304 Set of 2   2.00 2.00

Digboi Refinery, Cent. A1305

2001, Dec. 18   *Perf. 13¼x13*
1934 A1305 4r multi   .80   .80

Vijaye Raje Scindia (1919-2001), Politician — A1306

Perf. 13¼x13 Syncopated
2001, Dec. 20
1935 A1306 4r multi   .80   .80

Temples A1307

Designs: No. 1936, 4r, Kedarnath. No. 1937, 4r, Tryambakeshwar. No. 1938, 4r, Aundha Nagnath. 15r, Rameswaram.

2001, Dec. 22   *Perf. 13¼x13*
1936-1939 A1307 Set of 4   3.50 3.50

Cancer Awareness Day — A1308

2001, Nov. 7   *Perf. 13x13¼*
1940 A1308 4r multi   .80   .80

Maharaja Ranjit Singh (1780-1839), Founder of Sikh Kingdom of the Punjab — A1309

2001, Nov. 9
1941 A1309 4r multi   .80   .80

Directorate General of Mine Safety, Cent. — A1310

Perf. 13x13¼ Syncopated
2002, Jan. 7   Litho.
1942 A1310 4r multi   1.00 1.00

May 2001 Ascent of Mt. Everest by Indian Army Mountaineers A1311

2002, Jan. 15   *Perf. 13x13¼*
1943 A1311 4r multi   2.50 2.50

Bauddha Mahotsav Festival A1312

Designs: No. 1944, 4r, Dhamek Stupa, Sarnath. No. 1945, 4r, Gridhakuta Hills, Rajgir. 8r, Mahaparinirvana Temple, Kushinagar. 15r, Mahabodhi Temple, Bodhgaya.

Perf. 13¼x13 Syncopated
2002, Jan. 21
1944-1947 A1312 Set of 4   4.00 4.00

Book Year A1313

2002, Jan. 28   *Perf. 13¼x13*
1948 A1313 4r multi   1.00 1.00

Swami Ramanand
A1314

2002, Feb. 4   *Perf. 13x13¼*
1949 A1314 4r multi   1.00 1.00

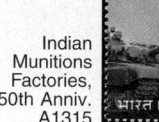

Indian Munitions Factories, 50th Anniv. A1315

Perf. 13¼ Syncopated
2002, Mar. 18   **Litho.**
1950 A1315 4r multi   1.00 1.00

Sido and Kanhu Murmu, 1855-57 Revolt Leaders A1316

2002, Apr. 6   *Perf. 13¼*
1951 A1316 4r multi   1.00 1.00

Indian Railways, 150th Anniv. — A1317

2002, Apr. 16   *Perf. 13¼x13*
1952 A1317 15r multi   5.00 5.00
   a.   Souvenir sheet of 1   5.00 5.00

India — Japan Diplomatic Relations, 50th Anniv. — A1318

No. 1953: a, Kathakali actor, India. b, Kabuki actor, Japan.

2002, Apr. 26   **Litho.**   *Perf. 13x13¼*
1953 A1318 15r Horiz. pair, #a-b   6.00 6.00
   c.   Souvenir sheet, #1953a-1953b   5.00 5.00

Parliament, 50th Anniv. A1319

Litho. & Embossed
2002, May 13   *Perf. 13¼*
1954 A1319 4r gold   1.00 1.00

Prabodhankar Thackeray (1885-1973), Writer — A1320

Perf. 13x13¼ Syncopated
2002, May 19   **Litho.**
1955 A1320 4r black   1.00 1.00

Cotton College, Guwahati A1321

2002, May 26   **Photo.**   *Perf. 13¼x13*
1956 A1321 4r grn & claret   1.00 1.00

P. L. Deshpande (1919-2000), Actor — A1322

2002, June 16   **Litho.**   *Perf. 13¼*
1957 A1322 4r multi   1.00 1.00

Brajlal Biyani (1896-1968), Politician and Writer — A1323

Perf. 13x13¼ Syncopated
2002, June 22
1958 A1323 4r multi   1.00 1.00

Writers — A1324

Designs: No. 1959, 5r, Babu Gulabrai (1888-1963). No. 1960, 5r, Pandit Suryanarayan Vyas (1902-76).

2002, June 22
1959-1960 A1324   Set of 2   2.00 2.00

Sree Thakur Satyananda (1902-69), Writer — A1325

2002, July 23   **Litho.**   *Perf. 13x13¼*
1961 A1325 5r multi   1.00 1.00

Anna Bhau Sathe (1920-69), Writer — A1326

Perf. 13x13¼ Syncopated
2002, Aug. 1   **Litho.**
1962 A1326 4r gray & black   1.00 1.00

Anand Rishiji Maharaj (1900-92), Humanitarian A1327

2002, Aug. 9   *Perf. 13¼*
1963 A1327 4r multi   1.00 1.00

Vithalrao Vikhe Patil (1901-80), Initiator of Cooperatives A1328

Perf. 13x13¼ Syncopated
2002, Aug. 10
1964 A1328 4r multi   1.00 1.00

Sant Tukaram (1608-50), Poet — A1329

2002, Aug. 10
1965 A1329 4r multi   1.00 1.00

Bhaurao Krishnaroao Gaikwad (1902-71), Politician — A1330

2002, Aug. 26
1966 A1330 4r multi   1.00 1.00

Social Reformers A1331

Designs: No. 1967, 5r, Ayyan Kali (1863-1941), advocate of rights for untouchables. No. 1968, 5r, Chandraprabha Saikiani (1901-72), women's rights advocate. No. 1969, 5r, Gora (1902-75), advocate of atheism.

Perf. 13¼x13 Syncopated
2002, Sept. 12
1967-1969 A1331   Set of 3   3.00 3.00

Ananda Nilayam Vimanam A1332

2002, Oct. 11   *Perf. 13¼x13*
1970 A1332 15r multi   4.00 4.00

Kanika Bandopadhyay (1924-2000), Singer — A1333

2002, Oct. 12   **Photo.**   *Perf. 13x13¼*
1971 A1333 5r multi   1.00 1.00

Arya Vaidya Sala Health Organization, Cent. — A1334

Perf. 13¼x13 Syncopated
2002, Oct. 12   **Litho.**
1972 A1334 5r multi   1.75 1.75

Bhagwan Baba (1896-1965), Religious Leader — A1335

Perf. 13x13¼ Syncopated
2002, Oct. 15
1973 A1335 5r multi   1.10 1.10

Bihar Chamber of Commerce, 75th Anniv. (in 2001) — A1336

2002, Oct. 28
1974 A1336 4r multi   1.75 1.75

UN Climate Change Convention A1337

Mangroves: No. 1975, 5r, Rhizophora mucronata. No. 1976, 5r, Nypa fruticans. No. 1977, 5r, Bruguiera gymnorrhiza. 15r, Sonneratia alba.

Perf. 13¼x13 Syncopated
2002, Oct. 30
1975-1978 A1337   Set of 4   5.00 5.00
1978a   Souvenir sheet, #1975-1978   7.50 7.50

Rose — A1338

Perf. 12¾x13
2002, Aug. 16   Photo.   Wmk. 324
1979 A1338 2r multi   .20 .20

Swami Pranavananda (1896-1941),
Religious Leader — A1339

Perf. 12¾x13¼
2002, Nov. 3   Litho.   Unwmk.
1980 A1339 5r multi   1.50 1.50

Nagpur, 300th Anniv. — A1340

2002, Nov. 11   Perf. 13x13¼
1981 A1340 5r multi   1.40 1.40

Children's
Day
A1341

2002, Nov. 14   Perf. 12¾x13¼
1982 A1341 5r multi   1.40 1.40

Crafts — A1342

No. 1983: a, Cane and bamboo containers.
b, Thewa. c, Patan's Patola. d, Dhokra.

2002, Nov. 15   Perf. 13¼
1983 A1342 5r Block of 4, #a-d   3.50 3.50
  e.   Souvenir sheet of 1 #1983   5.25 5.25

Santidev Ghose
(1910-99),
Dancer and
Musician
A1343

2002, Dec. 1
1984 A1343 5r multi   1.40 1.40

Formation of Tamralipta Jatiya Sarkar
(National Government of Tamluk), 60th
Anniv. — A1344

No. 1985: a, Ajoy Kumar Mukherjee (1901-
86). b, Matangini Hazra (d. 1942).
Illustration reduced.

2002, Dec. 17   Perf. 13¼x13
1985 A1344 5r Horiz. pair, #a-b   1.00 1.00

Anglo-Bengali Inter College,
Allahabad — A1345

Perf. 13¼x13 Syncopated
2002, Dec. 23
1986 A1345 5r multi   1.00 1.00

Gurukula Kangri
Vishwavidyalaya,
Hardwar — A1346

Perf. 13x13¼ Syncopated
2002, Dec. 24
1987 A1346 5r multi   1.00 1.00

Dhirubhai H.
Ambani (1932-
2002), Industrialist
A1347

2002, Dec. 28   Perf. 13¼
1988 A1347 5r multi   1.00 1.00

T. T.
Krishnamachari
(1899-1974),
Finance
Minister
A1348

2002, Dec. 31
1989 A1348 5r multi   1.00 1.00

Forts in Andhra Pradesh — A1349

Designs: No. 1990, 5r, Goloconda Fort. No.
1991, 5r, Palace, Chandragiri Fort.

2002, Dec. 31   Perf. 13¼x13
1990-1991 A1349 Set of 2   2.00 2.00

Aircraft
A1350

Designs: No. 1992, 5r, HT-2 airplane. No.
1993, 5r, Marut airplane. No. 1994, 5r, LCA
airplane. 15r, Dhruv helicopter.

2003, Feb. 5   Perf. 13¼
1992-1995 A1350 Set of 4   5.00 5.00
  1995a   Souvenir sheet, #1992-1995   5.25 5.25

Ghantasala
(1922-74),
Singer — A1351

2003, Feb. 11
1996 A1351 5r multi   1.00 1.00

S. L.
Kirloskar
(1903-94),
Industrialist
A1352

2003, Feb. 26
1997 A1352 5r multi   1.00 1.00

Kusumagraj
(V. V.
Shirwadkar)
(1912-99),
Poet
A1353

2003, Mar. 14
1998 A1353 5r multi   1.00 1.00

Sant Eknath (1533-
99) — A1354

2003, Mar. 23
1999 A1354 5r multi   1.00 1.00

Frank Anthony (b.
1908), Philantropist
A1355

2003, Mar. 28   Perf. 13x13¼
2000 A1355 5r multi   1.00 1.00

Kakaji Maharaj (1918-
86), Yogi — A1356

2003, Mar. 30   Perf. 13¼
2001 A1356 5r multi   1.00 1.00

Medicinal Plants — A1357

No. 2002: a, Commiphora wightii. b, Bacopa
monnieri. c, Withania somnifera. d, Emblica
officinalis.

2003, Apr. 7   Litho.   Perf. 13x13¼
2002 A1357 5r Block of 4, #a-d   4.00 4.00
  e.   Souvenir sheet, #2002a-2002d   4.50 4.50

Durga Das (1900-
74),
Journalist — A1358

2003, May 2   Photo.   Perf. 13x13¼
2003 A1358 5r multi   1.00 1.00

Singers — A1359

Designs: No. 2004, 5r, Kishore Kumar
(1929-87). No. 2005, 5r, Mukesh (1923-76).
No. 2006, 5r, Mohammed Rafi (1924-80). No.
2007, 5r, Hemant Kumar (1920-89).

Perf. 13x13¼ Syncopated
2003, May 15   Litho.
2004-2007 A1359 Set of 4   3.25 3.25
  2007a   Souvenir sheet, #2004-2007   4.50 4.50

Ascent of Mt.
Everest, 50th
Anniv. — A1360

Muktabai
(1279-99),
Poet
Saint — A1361

2003, May 29   Perf. 13x13¼
2008 A1360 15r multi   2.50 2.50
  a.   Souvenir sheet of 1   4.50 4.50

2003, May 30   Perf. 13¼x12½
2009 A1361 5r multi   1.00 1.00

Government Museum, Chennai — A1362

Designs: No. 2010, 5r, Sculpted medallion, Amravati, c. 150. No. 2011, 5r, Natesa, 12th cent. bronze sculpture. 15r, Museum Theater (58x28mm).

2003, June 19   **Perf. 13x13¼**
2010-2012 A1362 Set of 3   3.00 3.00
2012a   Souvenir sheet, #2010-2012   10.00 10.00

V. K. Rajwade (1863-1926), Historian — A1363

2003, June 23   **Photo.**
2013 A1363 5r multi   1.00 1.00

Bade Ghulam Ali Khan (1902-68), Singer — A1364

2003, June 30   **Litho.**
2014 A1364 5r multi   1.00 1.00

Temples — A1365

Designs: No.2015, Vishal Badri Temple, Badrinath. No.2016, Mallikarjunaswamy Temple, Srisailam. No.2017, Tripureswari Temple, Udaipur. No.2018, Jagannath Temple, Puri.

2003, Sept. 15   **Photo.**   **Perf. 13¼x13**
2015 A1365 5r multicolored   .85 .85
2016 A1365 5r multicolored   .85 .85
2017 A1365 5r multicolored   .85 .85
2018 A1365 5r multicolored   .85 .85
   a.   Horiz. strip of 4, #2015-2018   3.50 3.50

Janardan Swami — A1366

2003, Sept. 24   **Photo.**   **Perf. 13x13¼**
2019 A1366 5r brown   1.00 1.00

Intl. Autism Conference, Delhi A1367

2003, Sept. 30   **Litho.**   **Perf. 13¼x13**
2020 A1367 5r multi   .25 .25

Waterfalls A1368

Designs: No. 2021, 5r, Kempty Falls, No. 2022, 5r, Athirapalli Falls. No. 2023, 5r, Kakolat Falls. 15r, Jog Falls.

2003, Oct. 3   **Litho.**   **Perf. 13¼x13**
2021-2024 A1368 Set of 4   4.50 4.50
2024a   Souvenir sheet, #2021-2024   6.00 6.00

Jnanpith Award Winners for Literature A1369

No. 2025: a, G. Sankara Kurup (1901-78), poet. b, S. K. Pottekkatt (1913-82), novelist. c, Thakazhi Sivasankara Pillai (1912-99), novelist.

2003, Oct. 9   **Photo.**   **Perf. 13¼x13**
2025   Horiz. strip of 3   7.50 7.50
   a.-c.   A1369 5r Any single   1.00 1.00

Kota Shivarama Karanth (1902-97), Writer and Educator A1370

2003, Oct. 10   **Perf. 13x13¼**
2026 A1370 5r multi   1.00 1.00

Narendra Mohan (1934-2002), Journalist A1371

2003, Oct. 14   **Litho.**   **Perf. 13¼**
2027 A1371 5r brown   1.00 1.00

Govindrao Pansare (1913-46), Martyr A1372

2003, Oct. 21   **Photo.**   **Perf. 13¾x14**
2028 A1372 5r multi   1.00 1.00

Greetings — A1373

No. 2029: a, Birds. b, Fish and starfish. c, Squirrels. d, Butterflies and flowers.

2003, Oct. 30   **Litho.**   **Perf. 13¼x13**
2029   Horiz. strip of 4   4.50 4.50
   a.-b.   A1373 4r Either single   .95 .95
   c.-d.   A1373 5r Either single   1.25 1.25

First Telegraph Line in India, 150th Anniv. A1374

2003, Nov. 1   **Perf. 13¼**
2030 A1374 5r multi   1.00 1.00

Bengal Sappers, Bicent. A1375

2003, Nov. 7   **Photo.**   **Perf. 13¼x13**
2031 A1375 5r multi   1.00 1.00

Kalka-Shimla Railway, Cent. — A1376

2003, Nov. 9   **Litho.**
2032 A1376 5r multi   1.00 1.00

Snakes A1377

Designs: No. 2033, 5r, Python. No. 2034, 5r, Bamboo pit viper. No. 2035, 5r, King cobra. No. 2036, 5r, Gliding snake.

2003, Nov. 12
2033-2036 A1377   Set of 4   3.25 3.25
2036a   Souvenir sheet, #2033-2036   6.00 6.00

Children's Day A1378

2003, Nov. 14
2037 A1378 5r multi   1.00 1.00

2nd Guards Batttalion (1st Grenadiers Battalion), 225th Anniv. — A1379

2003, Nov. 22   **Photo.**   **Perf. 13**
2038 A1379 5r multi   1.00 1.00

Harivansh Rai Bachchan (1907-2003), Poet — A1380

2003, Nov. 27   **Litho.**   **Perf. 13¼x13¼**
2039 A1380 5r sepia & blk   1.00 1.00

French and Indian Artisan's Work — A1381

No. 2040: a, Illumination depicting rooster, France, 15th cent. b, Jewelry design, India, 19th cent.

2003, Nov. 29
2040 A1381 22r Horiz. pair, #a-b   5.00 5.00
   c.   Souvenir sheet, #2040   10.00 10.00

See France Nos. 2986-2987.

Yashpal (1903-76), Writer A1382

2003, Dec. 3   **Photo.**   **Perf. 13¼**
2041 A1382 5r multi   1.00 1.00

India — South Korea Diplomatic Relations, 30th Anniv. — A1383

No. 2042: a, Cheomsongdae Astronomical Observatory, Gyeongju, Korea. b, Jantar Mantar, Jaipur, India.

2003, Dec. 10   **Litho.**
2042 A1383 15r Pair, #a-b   5.00 5.00

See South Korea No. 2136.
A privately-produced booklet containing two strips of No. 2046 exists.

Rajya Sabha, 200th Session — A1384

2003, Dec. 11
2043 A1384 5r multi   1.00 1.00

Mukut Behari Lal Bhargava (b. 1903), Politician A1385

2003, Dec. 18   **Photo.**
2044 A1385 5r multi   1.00 1.00

Swami Swaroopanandji (1903-74),
Religious Leader — A1386

2003, Dec. 20   Litho.   Perf. 13¼x13
2045 A1386 5r multi   1.00 1.00

Sangeet
Natak
Akademi,
50th Anniv.
A1387

No. 2046: a, Musicians. b, Actors. c,
Dancers.

2003, Dec. 22
2046   Strip of 3, #a-c   4.75 4.75
a.-c. A1387 5r Any single   1.10 1.10
d.   Souvenir sheet, #2046   5.00 5.00

Folk Musicians
A1388

Designs: No. 2047, 5r, Allah Jilai Bai (1902-
92). No. 2048, 5r, Lalan Fakir (1774-1890).

2003, Dec. 29
2047-2048 A1388 Set of 2   2.00 2.00

Siddavanahalli
Nijalingappa
(1902-2000),
Politician
A1389

2003, Dec. 31   Perf. 13x13¼
2049 A1389 5r multi   1.00 1.00

Major Somnath
Sharma (1923-47),
Military
Hero — A1390

Perf. 13¼x12¾
2003, Dec. 31   Photo.
2050 A1390 5r multi   1.00 1.00

Chintaman D. Deshmukh (1896-1982),
Finance Minister — A1391

2004, Jan. 14   Litho.   Perf. 13¼x13
2051 A1391 5r multi   1.00 1.00

Nani A. Palkhivala
(1920-2002),
Jurist — A1392

2004, Jan. 16
2052 A1392 5r multi   1.00 1.00
A privately-produced booklet containing six
examples of No. 2052 exists.

Dr. Bhalchandra D.
Garware,
Businessman — A1393

2004, Feb. 6
2053 A1393 5r multi   1.00 1.00

Annamacharya,
Mystic
Saint — A1394

2004, Mar. 18   Photo.   Perf. 13¾
2054 A1394 5r multi   1.00 1.00

9th Battalion of Madras Regiment
(Travancore), 300th Anniv. — A1395

2004, Apr. 1   Litho.   Perf. 13¼x13
2055 A1395 5r multi   1.00 1.00

V. Lakshminarayana,
Violinist — A1396

2004, Apr. 14   Photo.
2056 A1396 5r multi   1.00 1.00

Indian Institute of
Social Welfare and
Business
Management, 51st
Anniv. — A1397

2004, Apr. 25   Litho.   Perf. 13x13¼
2057 A1397 5r multi   1.00 1.00

Baji Rao Peshwa,
General,
Statesman
A1398

2004, Apr. 25   Photo.
2058 A1398 5r multi   1.00 1.00

Circumnavigation of I.N.S.
Tarangini — A1399

2004, Apr. 25   Litho.   Perf. 13¼x13
2059 A1399 5r multi   1.00 1.00
a.   Souvenir sheet of 1   19.00 19.00

Siddhar Swamigal
(1904-64),
Spiritual
Leader — A1400

2004, May 15   Perf. 13x13¼
2060 A1400 5r multi   1.00 1.00

Indra Chandra
Shastri (1912-86),
Philosopher
A1401

2004, May 27   Photo.
2061 A1401 5r black & green   1.00 1.00

Woodstock
School,
Mussoorie,
150th
Anniv.
A1402

2004, June 2   Litho.   Perf. 12½x13¼
2062 A1402 5r multi   1.00 1.00

Jyotiprasad
Agarwalla (1903-
51), Musician,
Cinematographer
A1403

2004, June 17   Photo.   Perf. 13x13¼
2063 A1403 5r multi   1.00 1.00

P. N. Panicker
(1909-95),
Educator
A1404

2004, June 19
2064 A1404 5r multi   1.00 1.00

Great
Trigonometrical
Survey — A1405

Designs: No. 2065, 5r, Nain Singh (c. 1826-
1882), Himalayan explorer. No. 2066, 5r,
Radhanath Sikdan (1813-70), Surveyor who
calculated height of Mt. Everest. No. 2067, 5r,
Stylized map of India, triangles (38x28mm).

2004, June 27   Litho.   Perf. 13¼
2065-2067 A1405 Set of 3   2.50 2.50
2067a   Souvenir sheet, #2065-2067 8.00 8.00
A privately-produced booklet containing six
examples of No. 2067 exists.

Aacharya
Bhikshu, Founder
of Jain
Swetamber
Terapanth
Sect — A1406

2004, June 30   Photo.
2068 A1406 5r multi   .75   .75

2004 Summer Olympics,
Athens — A1407

No. 2069: a, 5r, Wrestling. b, 5r, Women's
long jump. c, 15r, Shooting. d, 15r, Field
hockey.
Illustration reduced.

Perf. 13¾x14¼
2004, Aug. 13   Photo.
2069 A1407 Block of 4, #a-d   2.75 2.75

Poets — A1408

No. 2070: a, Kabir (1440-1518), Indian poet.
b, Hafiz Shirazi (c. 1325-c. 1389), Persian
poet.

Illustration reduced.

2004, Aug. 16   *Perf. 13¼*
2070 A1408 15r Horiz. pair, #a-b   2.00   2.00
See Iran No. 2894.

Murasoli Maran (1934-2003),
Politician, Film Maker,
Journalist — A1409

2004, Aug. 17   *Perf. 12½x13¼*
2071 A1409 5r multi   1.00   1.00

Prime Minister Rajiv Gandhi (1944-91)
and Windmills — A1410

2004, Aug. 20   Litho.   *Perf. 13¼*
2072 A1410 5r multi   1.00   1.00
Rajiv Gandhi Renewable Energy Day.

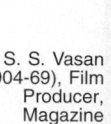

S. S. Vasan
(1904-69), Film
Producer,
Magazine
Publisher
A1411

2004, Aug. 28   Photo.   *Perf. 13x13¼*
2073 A1411 5r multi   1.00   1.00

Panini (c. 520 B.C.-c. 460 B.C.),
Grammarian — A1412

2004, Aug. 30   *Perf. 13¼x13*
2074 A1412 5r multi   .75   .75

K. Subrahmanyam (1904-71), Film
Director and Producer — A1413

2004, Sept. 10
2075 A1413 5r multi   1.00   1.00

M. C.
Chagla
(1900-81),
Judge,
Diplomat
A1414

2004, Oct. 1
2076 A1414 5r multi   .75   .75

Tirupur Kumaran
(1904-32),
Martyred
Protester — A1415

2004, Oct. 4   *Perf. 13x13¼*
2077 A1415 5r multi   .50   .50

India Post, 150th Anniv. — A1416

No. 2078: a, Boat, #2, coach, train on
bridge. b, Train on bridge, airplane, man with
spear, frame of #C1. c, Mail box, building,
#201. d, Computer, emblems for postal con-
sumer services.

2004, Oct. 4   *Perf. 14¼x13¾*
2078   Horiz. strip of 4   2.00   2.00
   a.-d.   A1416 5r Any single   .30   .30
   e.   Souvenir sheet, #2078, perf.
     13¼   10.00   10.00

Ashoka Chakra Winners — A1417

No. 2079: a, Neerja Bhanot (1963-86), air-
line purser killed in hijacking. b, Randhir
Prasad Verma (1952-91), slain policeman.
Illustration reduced.

2004, Oct. 8   *Perf. 13¼x13*
2079 A1417 5r Horiz. pair, #a-b   1.00   1.00

Guru Dutt
(1925-64),
Film Actor,
Director
A1418

2004, Oct. 10
2080 A1418 5r multi   1.00   1.00

Indian Soldiers in UN Peacekeeping
Forces — A1419

2004, Oct. 24   *Perf. 13¼*
2081 A1419 5r multi   .80   .80
   a.   Souvenir sheet of 1   12.00   12.00

Periya (1748-1801) and Chinna (1753-
1801) Marudhu, Rulers of Sivaganga,
Rebellion Leaders
A1420

2004, Oct. 24   *Perf. 13¾x14*
2082 A1420 5r multi   .80   .80
A privately-produced booklet containing six
examples of No. 2082 exists.

Greetings — A1421

No. 2083: a, Kites. b, Dolls.

2004, Oct. 25   *Perf. 13½x13*
2083 A1421 4r Horiz. pair, #a-b   .90   .90

Dr.
Svetoslav
Roerich
(1904-93),
Painter
A1422

2004, Oct. 27   *Perf. 13¼x13*
2084 A1422 5r multi   .80   .80

Tenneti
Viswanatham
(1895-1979),
Politician — A1423

2004, Nov. 10   Photo.   *Perf. 13x13¼*
2085 A1423 5r multi   .80   .80

Children's
Day — A1424

2004, Nov. 14
2086 A1424 5r multi   .75   .75

Walchand
Hirachand
(1882-1953),
Industrialist
A1425

2004, Nov. 23   *Perf. 13¾*
2087 A1425 5r multi   .75   .75

Dula Bhaya Kag
(1903-77),
Poet — A1426

2004, Nov. 25   *Perf. 13x13¼*
2088 A1426 5r multi   .75   .75

Aga Khan Award for
Architecture — A1427

No. 2089: a, Khas Mahal (blue panel). b,
Agra Fort (orange panel).
Illustration reduced.

2004, Nov. 28   *Perf. 14x13¾*
2089   Horiz. pair   2.50   2.50
   a.-b.   A1427 15r Either single   .95   .95
   c.   Souvenir sheet, #2089a,
     2089b, perf. 13¼   15.00   15.00

Bhagat Puran
Singh (1904-92),
Founder of Home
for Poor — A1428

2004, Dec. 10   Litho.   *Perf. 13x13¼*
2090 A1428 5r multi   .75   .75

Women's Insurrections of 1904 and
1939 — A1429

2004, Dec. 12   Photo.   *Perf. 13¼x13*
2091 A1429 5r multi   .75   .75

Energy Conservation Day — A1430

2004, Dec. 14
2092 A1430 5r multi   .75   .75

Completion of Taj Mahal, 350th
Anniv. — A1431

2004, Dec. 16   *Perf. 14x13¾*
2093 A1431 15r multi   1.25   1.25
   a.   Souvenir sheet of 1, perf.
     13¼   13.00   13.00
A privately produced booklet containing 3
#2093 exists.

Sahitya Academy, 50th Anniv. A1432

2004, Dec. 21 — Perf. 13¼x13
2094 A1432 5r multi　　　　　.75 .75

Bhaskara Sethupathy (1868-1903), Ramanathapuram Ruler — A1433

2004, Dec. 27 — Perf. 13x13¼
2095 A1433 5r multi　　　　　.75 .75

Dogs A1434

No. 2096: a, Himalayan sheepdog. b, Rampur hound. c, Mudhol hound. d, Rajapalayam.

2005, Jan. 9 — Perf. 13¼
2096　　Horiz. strip of 4　　4.00 4.00
a.-c.　A1434 5r Any single　　.40 .40
d.　　A1434 15r multi　　　.90 .90

Padampat Singhania (1905-79), Industrialist A1435

2005, Feb. 3
2097 A1435 5r multi　　　　　.75 .75

Rotary International, Cent. — A1436

2005, Feb. 23 — Perf. 13¼x13
2098 A1436 5r multi　　　　　.90 .90

Vice-President Krishan Kant (1927-2002) — A1437

2005, Feb. 27 Photo. — Perf. 13¼
2099 A1437 5r multi　　　　　.75 .75

Madhavrao Scindia (1945-2001), Government Minister — A1438

2005, Mar. 10
2100 A1438 5r multi　　　　　.75 .75

Flora and Fauna — A1439

No. 2101: a, Clouded leopard. b, Dillenia indica. c, Mishmi takin. d, Pitcher plant.

2005, Mar. 24 Photo. — Perf. 13¼
2101 A1439 5r Block of 4, #a-d　2.00 2.00
e.　　Souvenir sheet, #2101　11.00 11.00

Intl. Year of Physics A1440

— Perf. 12¾x13
2005, Mar. 31 — Wmk. 324
2102 A1440 5r multi　　　　1.00 1.00

Salt March to Dandi, 75th Anniv. — A1441

Mohandas Gandhi and: a, Marchers. b, Newspaper. c, Map of march. d, Text by Gandhi.
Illustration reduced.

— Perf. 13¼
2005, Apr. 5 Photo. — Unwmk.
2103 A1441 5r Block of 4, #a-d　2.00 2.00
e.　　Souvenir sheet, #2103　10.00 10.00

15th Punjab (Patiala) Battalion, 300th Anniv. A1442

2005, Apr. 13
2104 A1442 5r multi　　　　　.75 .75

Bandung Conference, 50th Anniv. — A1443

2005, Apr. 18
2105 A1443 15r multi　　　　1.00 1.00

Narayan Meghaji Lokhande (1848-1897), Labor Activist A1444

2005, May 3 — Perf. 13¾
2106 A1444 5r multi　　　　　.75 .75

Cooperative Movement in India, Cent. — A1445

2005, May 8 — Perf. 13¼
2107 A1445 5r multi　　　　　.75 .75

World Environment Day — A1446

2005, June 5
2108 A1446 5r multi　　　　1.25 1.25

Guru Granth Sahib A1447

2005, June 16 Photo. — Perf. 14x13¾
2109 A1447 10r multi　　　45.00 —
a.　　Souvenir sheet of 1　　90.00

Because of a lack of an agreement with Indian postal officials and Sikh religious representatives, local post offices were alerted that the issuance of Nos. 2109 and 2109a was to be postponed and the stamps were not to be placed on sale on June 16. Examples were sold at several locations that apparently did not receive the message.

Abdul Qaiyum Ansari (1905-73), Nationalist Leader A1448

2005, July 1 Photo. — Perf. 13¼
2110 A1448 5r brown　　　　.75 .75

Dheeran Chinnamalai (1765-1805), Freedom Fighter — A1449

2005, July 31
2111 A1449 5r multi　　　　　.75 .75

State Bank of India, Bicent. — A1450

Illustration reduced.

2005, Aug. 31
2112 A1450 15r multi　　　　1.00 1.00

Intl. Day of Peace — A1451

2005, Sept. 21 Photo. — Perf. 13x13¼
2113 A1451 5r multi　　　　　.75 .75

A. M. M. Murugappa Chettiar (1902-65), Industrialist A1452

2005, Oct. 1
2114 A1452 5r multi　　　　　.75 .75

Pratap Singh Kairon (1901-65), Government Minister — A1453

2005, Oct. 1 — Perf. 13¼x13
2115 A1453 5r multi　　　　　.75 .75

Dr. T. S. Soundram (1904-84), Founder of Gandhigram Development Program — A1454

2005, Oct. 2
2116 A1454 5r multi　　　　　.90 .90

Mailboxes
A1455

No. 2117: a, Victorian era box, horse-drawn carriage. b, Man inserting letter into Penfold box. c, Two cylindrical boxes. d, Two square letter boxes.

2005, Oct. 18   *Perf. 13x13¼*
2117   Horiz. strip of 4   3.50 3.50
   a.-d.   A1415 5r Any single   .75 .30
   e.   Souvenir sheet, #2117a-2117d, perf. 13¾   15.00 15.00

V. Kalyanasundarnar (1883-1953), Union Leader — A1456

2005, Oct. 21   *Perf. 13¼*
2118 A1456 5r multi   .75 .75

Ayothidhasa Pandithar (1845-1914), Social Reformer A1457

2005, Oct. 21
2119 A1457 5r multi   .75 .75

Kavimani Desiga Vinayagam Pillai (1876-1954), Poet — A1458

2005, Oct. 21   *Perf. 13¼x13*
2120 A1458 5r multi   .75 .75

Prabodh Chandra (1911-86), Writer — A1459

2005, Oct. 24   *Perf. 13x13¼*
2121 A1459 5r multi   .75 .75

Children's Day — A1460

2005, Nov. 14
2122 A1460 5r multi   .75 .75

Children's Film Society, 50th Anniv. A1461

2005, Nov. 14   *Perf. 13¾*
2123 A1461 5r multi   1.00 1.00

Progress, Harmony and Development Chamber of Commerce and Industry, Cent. — A1462

2005, Nov. 16
2124 A1462 5r multi   .75 .75

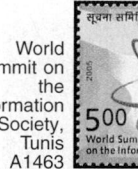

World Summit on the Information Society, Tunis A1463

2005, Nov. 17 Photo.   *Perf. 13¼x13*
2125 A1463 5r multi   .75 .75

Calcutta Police Commissionerate, 150th Anniv. — A1464

2005, Nov. 19   *Perf. 13¾*
2126 A1464 5r multi   .40 .40

Newborn Health — A1465

2005, Nov. 24   *Perf. 13¼*
2127 A1465 5r blue   .40 .40

Jawaharlal Darda, Politician A1466

2005, Dec. 2
2128 A1466 5r multi   .25 .25

Navy Ships Delhi, Kora and Udaygiri — A1467

2005, Dec. 4   *Perf. 13*
2129 A1467 5r multi   .40 .40

M. S. Subbulakshmi (1916-2004), Singer — A1468

2005, Dec. 18   *Perf. 13¼x13*
2130 A1468 5r multi   .40 .40

Integral Coach Factory, 50th Anniv. — A1469

2005, Dec. 19   *Perf. 13¾*
2131 A1469 5r multi   .70 .70

Jadavpur University, 50th Anniv. — A1470

2005, Dec. 21
2132 A1470 5r multi   .40 .40

16th Air Force Squadron, 55th Anniv. — A1471

2005, Dec. 27   *Perf. 14x13¾*
2133 A1471 5r multi   .40 .40

De Facto Transfer of Pondicherry, 50th Anniv. (in 2006) — A1472

2005, Dec. 30   *Perf. 13¼x13*
2134 A1472 5r multi   .35 .35

Pongal Festival A1473

2006, Jan. 12   *Perf. 13¾*
2135 A1473 5r multi   .70 .70

A. V. Meiyappan (1907-79), Film Producer and Director A1474

2006, Jan. 22   *Perf. 13¼*
2136 A1474 5r multi   .70 .70

N. M. R. Subbaraman, Politician, Cent. of Birth — A1475

2006, Jan. 29   **Photo.**
2137 A1475 5r multi   .35 .35
    Dated 2005.

Third Battalion of the Sikh Regiment, 150th Anniv. A1476

2006, Feb. 1   *Perf. 13¼x13*
2138 A1476 5r multi   .50 .50

President's Fleet Review, Visakhapatnam — A1477

No. 2139: a, Aircraft carrier and jet. b, Helicopter and two ships. c, Airplane and two ships. d, Two submarines. Illustration reduced.

2006, Feb. 12   *Perf. 13¾x13*
2139 A1477 5r Block of 4, #a-d   1.50 1.50

Thirumuruga Kirubananda Variyar (1906-93), Tamil Magazine Publisher A1478

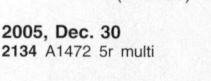

Devaneya Pavanar (1902-81), Tamil Writer — A1479

Dr. U. V. Swaminatha Iyer (1855-1942), Tamil Literature Researcher A1480

Tamilavel Umamaheswarar, Editor of Tamil Literary Magazine A1481

2006, Feb. 18   *Perf. 13¼*
2140 A1478 5r red brown .35 .35
2141 A1479 5r blue .35 .35
2142 A1480 5r brown .35 .35
2143 A1481 5r black .35 .35
Nos. 2140-2143 (4) 1.40 1.40

St. Bede's College, Shimla, 102nd Anniv. — A1482

2006, Feb. 24   *Perf. 13x13¼*
2144 A1482 5r multi .35 .35

Gemini Ganesan (1920-2005), Actor A1483

2006, Feb. 25   *Perf. 13¼x13*
2145 A1483 5r black .70 .70

Salesians of Don Bosco in India, Cent. — A1484

2006, Feb. 27   *Perf. 13x13¼*
2146 A1484 5r brown .40 .40

M. Singaravelar (1860-1946), Communist Politician A1485

2006, Mar. 2
2147 A1485 5r multi .35 .35

World Consumer Rights Day A1486

2006, Mar. 15   *Perf. 13¼x13*
2148 A1486 5r multi .40 .40

Indian Agricultural Research Institute, Delhi, Cent. A1487

2006, Mar. 30
2149 A1487 5r multi .40 .40

62nd Cavalry Armored Regiment, 50th Anniv. A1488

2006, Apr. 1
2150 A1488 5r multi .40 .40

Folk Dances — A1489

No. 2151 — Folk dances from: a, India. b, Cyprus. Illustration reduced.

2006, Apr. 12   *Perf. 13x13¾*
2151 A1489 15r Horiz. pair, #a-b 2.75 2.75
c.   Souvenir sheet, #2151, perf. 13¾x13¼   8.50 8.50

See Cyprus No. 1052.

Calcutta Girls' High School, 150th Anniv. A1490

2006, Apr. 21   *Perf. 13¾x13*
2152 A1490 5r multi .40 .40

Pannalal Barupal (1913-83), Politician A1491

2006, Apr. 28   *Perf. 13¼x13*
2153 A1491 5r multi .35 .35

Kurinji Flower A1492

2006, Apr. 29   *Perf. 13x13¾*
2154 A1492 15r multi 2.00 2.00
a.   Souvenir sheet of 1   9.00 9.00

Rainwater Harvesting A1493

2006, June 5   *Perf. 13¼x13*
2155 A1493 5r multi .70 .70

Sri Pratap College, Srinigar, Cent. — A1494

2006, June 15   *Perf. 13*
2156 A1494 5r multi .40 .40

Indraprastha Girls' School, New Delhi, 102nd Anniv. — A1495

2006, July 8   *Perf. 13¾x13*
2157 A1495 5r multi .40 .40

Voorhees College, Vellore, 111th Anniv. A1496

2006, July 10   *Perf. 13¼*
2158 A1496 5r multi .35 .35

Vellore Mutiny, Bicent. — A1497

2006, July 10   Litho.   *Perf. 13¼*
2159 A1497 5r multi .70 .70

High Court of Jammu and Kashmir — A1498

2006, July 29   *Perf. 13¾x13¼*   Photo.
2160 A1498 5r multi .40 .40

Pankaj Kumar Mullick (1904-78), Composer A1499

2006, Aug. 4   *Perf. 13¼x13*
2161 A1499 5r multi .50 .50

Oil and Natural Gas Corporation, Limited A1500

2006, Aug. 14
2162 A1500 5r multi .60 .60

M. P. Sivagnanam, Tamil Politician, Cent. of Birth — A1501

2006, Aug. 15   Litho.   *Perf. 13¼*
2163 A1501 5r multi .35 .35

University of Madras A1502

2006, Sept. 4   Photo.
2164 A1502 5r multi .40 .40

L. V. Prasad (1908-94), Film Actor and Director A1503

2006, Sept. 5
2165 A1503 5r multi .65 .65

Indian Merchants Chamber — A1504

2006, Sept. 7   *Perf. 13¼x13*
2166 A1504 5r multi .40 .40

Horse Sculptures — A1505

No. 2167: a, Horse and rider. b, Horse only. Illustration reduced.

2006, Sept. 11   *Perf. 13¼x13¾*
2167 A1505 15r Horiz. pair, #a-b 2.75 2.75
c.   Souvenir sheet, #2167   8.50 8.50

See Mongolia No. 2621.

Birds
A1506

No. 2168: a, Greater adjutant stork. b, Nilgiri laughing thrush. c, Manipur bush-quail. d, Lesser florican.

2006, Oct. 5   *Perf. 13*
2168   Vert. strip of 4   1.75   1.75
   a.-d.   A1506 5r Any single   .40   .40
   e.   Souvenir sheet, #2168a-2168d   7.00   7.00

Madhya Pradesh Chamber of Commerce and Industry, Cent. A1507

2006, Oct. 12   Photo.   *Perf. 13¼*
2169   A1507 5r multi   .40   .40

Bishwanath Roy (1906-84), Politician A1508

2007, Oct. 31   Litho.   *Perf. 13¼x13*
2170   A1508 5r multi   .30   .30

G. Varadaraj, Industrialist (1936-90) A1509

2006, Nov. 1
2171   A1509 5r multi   .30   .30

Lakes — A1510

No. 2172: a, Roop Kund. b, Chandra Tal, vert. c, Tsomo Riri. d, Sela. e, Tsangu.
Illustration reduced.

2006, Nov. 6   Photo.   *Perf. 13*
2172   A1510 5r Block of 5, #a-e   2.50   2.50

Lala Deen Dayal (1844-1905), Photographer A1511

2006, Nov. 11
2173   A1511 5r multi   .30   .30

Children's Day — A1512

No. 2174 — Various children's drawings: a, Denomination at LL. b, Denomination at UL.
Illustration reduced.

2006, Nov. 14   Litho.   *Perf. 13*
2174   A1512 5r Horiz. pair, #a-b   .60   .60

The Tribune, 125th Anniv. A1513

2006, Nov. 24   Photo.   *Perf. 14*
2175   A1513 5r multi   .40   .40

World AIDS Day — A1514

2006, Dec. 1   *Perf. 13x13¼*
2176   A1514 5r multi   .70   .70

Bartholomaeus Ziegenbalg (1682-1719), First Lutheran Missionary to India — A1515

2006, Dec. 8   *Perf. 13¼*
2177   A1515 5r multi   .40   .40

Army Field Post Offices, 150th Anniv. — A1516

No. 2178: a, Soldier, cancel, ship, map of Bushire-Bombay route. b, Soldier writing letter, camel. c, Soldier reading letter, sign. d, Soldier reading letter, helicopter.

2006, Dec. 10   Litho.   *Perf. 13x13¼*
2178   Horiz. strip of 4   1.60   1.60
   a.-d.   A1516 5r Any single   .40   .40

Sandalwood Carving A1517

2006, Dec. 18   Photo.   *Perf. 13¼x13*
2179   A1517 15r multi   2.00   2.00
   a.   Souvenir sheet of 1, perf. 13   8.50   8.50

Stamps are impregnated with a sandalwood scent.

Stop Child Labor — A1518

No. 2180: a, Girl on tightrope. b, Boy with hoe. c, Boy pouring tea. d, Boy with large basket.
Illustration reduced.

2006, Dec. 28   *Perf. 13¼x13*
2180   A1518 5r Block of 4, #a-d   1.40   1.40

Bimal Roy (1909-66), Film Director A1519

2007, Jan. 8   Litho.   *Perf. 13*
2181   A1519 5r multi   .40   .40

Tamil Nadu Cricket Association, 70th Anniv. — A1520

2007, Jan. 26   *Perf. 13x13¼*
2182   A1520 5r multi   .40   .40

Rose Varieties — A1521

No. 2183: a, 5r, Bhim. b, 5r, Neelam. c, 15r, Delhi Princess. d, 15r, Jawahar.

2007, Feb. 7   Photo.   *Perf. 13x13¼*
2183   A1521   Block of 4, #a-d   1.90   1.90
   e.   Souvenir sheet, #2183   5.00   5.00

Stamps are impregnated with a rose scent.

Manoharbhai Patel (1906-70), Politician A1522

2007, Feb. 9
2184   A1522 5r multi   .30   .30

Fairs — A1523

Designs: No. 2185, 5r, Sonepur Fair. No. 2186, 5r, Pushkar Fair. No. 2187, 5r, Goa Carnival. No. 2188, 5r, Baul Mela.

2007, Feb. 27   Litho.
2185-2188   A1523   Set of 4   1.00   1.00
   2188a   Souvenir sheet, #2185-2188   3.00   3.00

Women's Day — A1524

No. 2189: a, Two women. b, Woman, three birds. c, Two women and birds. d, Woman and birds.

2007, Mar. 8   Photo.   *Perf. 13x13¼*
2189   Horiz. strip of 4   1.90   1.90
   a.-b.   A1524 5r Either single   .25   .25
   c.-d.   A1524 15r Either single   .70   .70
   e.   Souvenir sheet, #2189   3.50   3.50

Raj Narain (1917-86), Politician A1525

2007, Mar. 23   Litho.   *Perf. 13¼*
2190   A1525 5r multi   .30   .30

Mehboob Khan (1907-64), Film Producer and Director — A1526

2007, Mar. 30
2191   A1526 5r multi   .40   .40

Dr. R. M. Alagappa Chettiar (1909-57), Industrialist and Philanthropist A1527

2007, Apr. 6   Photo.   *Perf. 13x13¼*
2192 A1527 5r multi   .30   .30

Mahaparinirvana of Buddha, 2550th Anniv. — A1533

2007, May 2   *Perf. 13¼*
2193 A1528 5r multi   .30   .30
2194 A1529 5r multi   .30   .30
2195 A1530 5r multi   .30   .30
2196 A1531 5r multi   .30   .30
2197 A1532 5r multi   .30   .30
2198 A1533 5r multi   .30   .30
    a.   Miniature sheet, #2193-2198   3.50 3.50
          Nos. 2193-2198 (6)   1.80 1.80

Natl. Parks — A1534

No. 2199: a, Bandhavgarh Natl. Park. b, Bandipur Natl. Park. c, Kaziranga Natl. Park. d, Mudumalai Natl. Park. e, Periyar Natl. Park.

2007, May 31
2199   Vert. strip of 5   1.50 1.50
    a.-e.   A1534 5r Any single   .30   .30

A1528

A1529

A1530

A1531

A1532

First War of Independence, 150th Anniv. — A1535

2007, Aug. 9   *Perf. 13¼x13*
2200 A1535   Vert. pair   1.50 1.50
    a.   5r Battle of Lucknow   .40   .40
    b.   15r Battle of Kanpur   1.10 1.10
    c.   Souvenir sheet, #2200a-2200b   2.50 2.50

Saint Vallalar (1823-74) A1536

Maraimalai Adigal (1876-1950), Tamil Scholar A1537

V. G. Suryanarayana Sastriar (1870-1903), Tamil Writer — A1538

2007, Aug. 18   Litho.   *Perf. 13x13¼*
2201 A1536 5r multi   .35   .35
2202 A1537 5r multi   .35   .35
2203 A1538 5r multi   .35   .35
          Nos. 2201-2203 (3)   1.05 1.05

Bridges A1539

No. 2204: a, Howrah Bridge. b, Mahatma Gandhi Bridge. c, Pamban Bridge. d, Vidyasagar Bridge.

2007, Aug. 17   Photo.
2204   Vert. strip or block of 4   1.40 1.40
    a.-d.   A1539 5r Any single   .35   .35
    e.   Souvenir sheet, #2204a-2204d   2.50 2.50

J. P. Naik (1907-81), Education Reformer — A1540

2007, Sept. 5   Litho.   *Perf. 13¼x13*
2205 A1540 5r multi   .30   .30

53rd Commonwealth Parliamentary Conference, New Delhi — A1541

2007, Sept. 23   Litho.   *Perf. 13¼*
2206 A1541 15r multi   .80   .80

Sachin Deb Burman (1906-75), Composer A1542

2007, Oct. 1   *Perf. 13¼x13*
2207 A1542 15r multi   .80   .80

Satyagraha (Non-Violent Resistance), Cent. A1543

No. 2208 — Mohandas Gandhi and: a, Train. b, House, newspaper article. c, Crowd, building. d, People marching.

2007, Oct. 2   Photo.   *Perf. 13¼x13*
2208   Horiz. strip of 4   1.00 1.00
    a.-d.   A1543 5r Any single   .25   .25
    e.   Souvenir sheet, #2208a-2208d   3.00 3.00

Indian Air Force, 75th Anniv. A1544

Designs: No. 2209, 5r, DHRUV helicopter. No. 2210, 5r, Westland Wapiti biplane. No. 2211, 5r, AWACS airplane (84x32mm). 15r, IL-78 (84x32mm).

2007, Oct. 8   Litho.   *Perf. 13¼x13*
2209-2212 A1544 Set of 4   1.60 1.60
    2212a Souvenir sheet, #2209-2212   4.00 4.00

Fourth Military World Games, Hyderabad A1545

No. 2213: a, Parachutist. b, Soccer player. c, Swimmer.

2007, Oct. 14   *Perf. 13¼x13*
2213   Vert. strip of 3   .80   .80
    a.-c.   A1545 5r Any single   .25   .25
    d.   Souvenir sheet, #2213, perf. 13 3.50 3.50

Maharashtra Police Academy — A1546

2007, Nov. 3   Photo.   *Perf. 13¼*
2214 A1546 5r multi   .50   .50

Children's Day A1547

Children's art: No. 2215, 5r, Children and stars. No. 2216, 5r, Fishermen and canoes at night.

2007, Nov. 14   Litho.   *Perf. 13¼x13*
2215-2216 A1547 Set of 2   .65   .65
    2216a Souvenir sheet, #2215-2216   2.00 2.00

Renewable Energy — A1548

Designs: No. 2217, 5r, Solar energy. No. 2218, 5r, Wind energy. No. 2219, 5r, Small hydroelectric power, vert. No. 2220, 5r, Biomass energy, vert.

2007, Nov. 22   Photo.   *Perf. 13*
2217-2220 A1548 Set of 4   1.25 1.25
    2220a Souvenir sheet, #2217-2220,
           perf. 13¾x13¼, 13¼x13¾   3.50 3.50
    2220b Miniature sheet, 6 each
           #2217-2218, 3 each #2219-
           2220   5.25 5.25

First Battalion of the Fourth Gorkha Rifles, 150th Anniv. A1549

2007, Nov. 27   Litho.   *Perf. 13¼*
2221 A1549 5r multi   .60 .60

Intl. Day of Disabled Persons — A1550

Photo. & Embossed
2007, Dec. 3   *Perf. 13*
2222 A1550 5r multi   .60 .60

Daly College, Indore, 125th Anniv. — A1551

2007, Dec. 8   Litho.   *Perf. 13¼*
2223 A1551 5r multi   .40 .40

Wilson College, Bombay, 175th Anniv. — A1552

2007, Dec. 11   Photo.   *Perf. 13*
2224 A1552 5r multi   .40 .40

Greetings A1553

No. 2225: a, Sun, wheat, path. b, Fish, lotus flower. c, Bird. d, Man, flower, butterfly, deer. e, Flowers, stars and text, "Happy New Year," (58x29mm).

2007, Dec. 15   Photo.   *Perf. 13*
2225   Horiz. strip of 5   1.50 1.50
a.-e. A1553 5r Any single   .30 .30

S. B. Chavan (1920-2004), Politician — A1554

2007, Dec. 17   Litho.   *Perf. 13¼x13*
2226 A1554 5r multi   .35 .35

Snows Basilica, 425th Anniv. — A1555

2007, Dec. 25   *Perf. 13*
2227 A1555 5r multi   .50 .50

Water Year — A1556

2007, Dec. 28
2228 A1556 5r multi   .40 .40

Ritwik Ghatak (1925-76), Film Director A1557

2007, Dec. 31   Photo.   *Perf. 13¼x13*
2229 A1557 5r brown & black   .40 .40

Butterflies Of Andaman and Nicobar Islands — A1558

No. 2230: a, Male Papilio mayo. b, Female Papilio mayo. c, Female Pachliopta rhodifer. d, Male Pachliopta rhodifer. Illustration reduced.

2008, Jan. 2   *Perf. 13*
2230 A1558 5r Block of 4, #a-d   1.25 1.25
e.   Souvenir sheet, #2230   3.00 3.00

Dr. Benjamin Peary Pal (1906-89), Rose Breeder and Plant Scientist A1559

2008, Jan. 5   Litho.
2231 A1559 5r multi   .40 .40

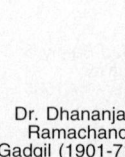

Dr. Dhananjaya Ramachandra Gadgil (1901-71), Economist A1560

2008, Feb. 8   Photo.
2232 A1560 5r multi   .40 .40

Damodaram Sanjeevaiah (1921-72), Politician — A1561

2008, Feb. 14   Litho.
2233 A1561 5r multi   .40 .40

Maharshi Bulusu Sambamurthy (1886-1958), Lawyer — A1562

2008, Mar. 4
2234 A1562 5r multi   .40 .40

Madhubala (1933-1969), Film Actress — A1563

2008, Mar. 18   Photo.   *Perf. 13*
2235 A1563 5r multi   .40 .40
a.   Souvenir sheet of 1, perf.
      13x13¾   1.75 1.75

Asrar Ul Haq (Majaaz) (1909-55), Urdu Poet A1564

2008, Mar. 28   Litho.   *Perf. 13*
2236 A1564 5r multi   .40 .40

Civil Service A1565

Photo. & Embossed
2008, Apr. 21
2237 A1565 5r multi   .40 .40

Tata Steel, Cent. — A1566

2008, Apr. 22   Litho.
2238 A1566 5r multi   .40 .40

Jasmine Flowers — A1567

2008, Apr. 26   Photo.
2239 A1567 5r shown   .30 .30
2240 A1567 15r Flowers, horiz.   .80 .80
a.   Souvenir sheet #2239-2240   3.00 3.00

Nos. 2239-2240, 2240a are impregnated with a jasmine scent.

Aga Khan Foundation, 30th Anniv. — A1568

No. 2241: a, 5r, Heritage restoration (46x39mm). b, 15r, Social commitment (70x39mm). Illustration reduced.

2008, May 17   Photo.   *Perf. 13*
2241 A1568   Horiz. pair, #a-b   1.10 1.10
c.   Souvenir sheet, #2241a-2241b 3.00 3.00

Shri Shirdi Sai Baba (1835-1918), Hindu Saint — A1569

2008, May 20
2242 A1569 5r multi   .40 .40

Rajesh Pilot (1945-2008), Politician A1570

2008, June 12   Litho.   *Perf. 13*
2243 A1570 5r multi   .25 .25

Henning Holck-Larsen (1907-2003), Engineer and Industrialist A1571

2008, June 12   Litho.   *Perf. 13¼x13*
2244 A1571 5r multi   .25 .25

Madhav Institute of Technology, Gwalior, 50th Anniv. — A1572

2008, June 30 Litho. **Perf. 13¼**
2245 A1572 5r multi .40 .40

Temples — A1573

No. 2246: a, Maha Bodhi Temple, India. b, White Horse Temple, China.

2008, July 11 Photo. **Perf. 13**
2246 A1573 15r Horiz. pair, #a-b 1.75 1.75
c. Souvenir sheet, #2246 4.00 4.00

See People's Republic of China Nos. 3678-3679.

Punjab Regiment 14th Battalion, 250th Anniv. — A1574

2008, July 21 Litho. **Perf. 13¼**
2247 A1574 5r multi .40 .40

Damodar Dharmananda Kosambi (1907-66), Mathematician — A1575

2008, July 31
2248 A1575 5r multi .40 .40

Aldabra Giant Tortoise A1576

Tortoise facing: 5r, Left. 15r, Forward.

2008, Aug. 2 Photo. **Perf. 13**
2249-2250 A1576 Set of 2 1.10 1.10

2008 Summer Olympics, Beijing — A1577

No. 2251 — 2008 Summer Olympics emblem and: a, 5r, Olympic torch and mascot. b, 5r, Boxing. c, 15r, Shooting. d, 15r, Archery. Illustration reduced.

2008, Aug. 8
2251 A1577 Block of 4, #a-d 2.10 2.10
e. Souvenir sheet, #2251a-2251d 3.50 3.50

Indian Coast Guard, 30th Anniv. — A1578

No. 2252: a, Airplane. b, Helicopter. c, Hovercraft (large wave at LL). d, Patrol boat (large wave at LR). Illustration reduced.

2008, Aug. 12 Litho. **Perf. 13¼**
2252 A1578 5r Block of 4, #a-d 1.10 1.10
e. Souvenir sheet, #2252a-2252d 3.00 3.00

Ustad Bismillah Khan (1916-2006), Musician — A1579

2008, Aug. 21
2253 A1579 5r multi .40 .40

Sir Pitti Theagarayar (1853-1925) — A1580

Dr. Taravat Mahadevan Nair (1868-1919) A1581

Dr. C. Natesan (1869-1937) A1582

2008, Sept. 17 **Perf. 13x13¼**
2254 A1580 5r multi .25 .25
Perf. 13¾ Syncopated
2255 A1581 5r multi .25 .25
2256 A1582 5r multi .25 .25
Nos. 2254-2256 (3) .75 .75

Founders of South Indian Welfare Association.

Festivals — A1583

Designs: No. 2257, 5r, Dussehra Festival, Calcutta (Kolkata). No. 2258, 5r, Dussehra Festival, Mysore. No. 2259, 5r, Deepavali Festival, vert.

2008, Oct. 7 Photo. **Perf. 13**
2257-2259 A1583 Set of 3 .65 .65
2259a Souvenir sheet, #2257-2259 3.00 3.00

3rd Commonwealth Youth Games, Pune — A1584

No. 2260: a, Tiger mascot. b, Wrestling. c, Badminton. d, Hurdling.

2008, Oct. 12 **Perf. 13x13¼**
2260 Horiz. strip of 4 .85 .85
a.-d. A1584 5r Any single .20 .20
e. Souvenir sheet, #2260a-2260d 3.00 3.00

Indian Post Office A1585

Perf. 13¾ Syncopated
2008, Oct. 13 Litho.
2261 A1585 5r multi .20 .20

Philately Day. A souvenir sheet of one sold for 15r.

Food Safety and Quality Year — A1586

2008, Oct. 16
2262 A1586 5r multi .20 .20

19th Commonwealth Games, Delhi — A1587

2008, Oct. 18 Photo. **Perf. 13¼x13**
2263 A1587 5r multi .20 .20

A souvenir sheet of one sold for 15r.

A1588

A1589

Children's Day — A1590

2008, Nov. 14 Litho. **Perf. 13¼**
2264 A1588 5r multi .20 .20
2265 A1589 5r multi .20 .20
2266 A1590 5r multi .20 .20
a. Souvenir sheet of 3, #2264-2266 2.75 2.75
Nos. 2264-2266 (3) .60 .60

Bomireddi N. Reddi (1908-77), Film Director A1591

2008, Nov. 16
2267 A1591 5r multi .20 .20

Canonization of Saint Alphonsa (1910-46) A1592

2008, Nov. 16 Photo. **Perf. 13x13¼**
2268 A1592 5r multi .20 .20

A souvenir sheet of one sold for 15r.

Standard Chartered Bank, 150th Anniv. A1593

2008, Nov. 17   Litho.   Perf. 13¼
2269 A1593 5r multi   .20 .20

Gas Authority of India Limited, 25th Anniv. A1594

2008, Nov. 19   Perf. 13
2270 A1594 5r multi   .20 .20

Joachim (1907-79) and Violet (1908-69) Alva, Politicians A1595

Perf. 13¾ Syncopated
2008, Nov. 20
2271 A1595 5r multi   .20 .20

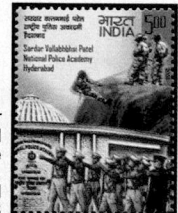

Sardar Vallabhbhai Patel Natl. Police Academy, Hyderabad A1596

Building and: 5r, Police cadets training and marching. 20r, Statue, policeman with sword.

2008, Nov. 27
2272-2273 A1596 Set of 2   1.00 1.00
2273a   Souvenir sheet, #2272-2273   3.50 3.50

St. Joseph's Boys' High School, Bangalore, 150th Anniv. A1597

2008, Nov. 28
2274 A1597 5r multi   .20 .20

Buddhadeva Bose (1908-74), Writer — A1598

2008, Nov. 30   Perf. 13
2275 A1598 5r multi   .20 .20

Prime Minister Jawaharlal Nehru (1889-1964) A1599

Mahatma Gandhi (1869-1948) A1601

Satyajit Ray (1921-92), Film Director A1603

Prime Minister Indira Gandhi (1917-84) A1605

C.V. Raman (1888-1970), 1930 Nobel Physics Laureate A1607

Mother Teresa (1910-97), 1979 Nobel Peace Laureate A1609

E.V. Ramasami (1879-1973), Politician A1600

Dr. Bhimrao R. Ambedkar (1891-1956), Politician A1602

Homi Jahangir Bhabha (1909-66), Nuclear Physicist A1604

Prime Minister Rajiv Gandhi (1944-91) A1606

J. R. D. Tata (1904-93), Industrialist A1608

Rukmini Devi Arundale (1904-86), Dancer A1610

Perf. 12¾x13¼
2008-09   Photo.   Wmk. 324
2276 A1599 25p rose lil & blk   .20 .20
2277 A1600 50p blue   .20 .20
2278 A1601 1r olive brown   .20 .20
2279 A1602 2r rose lilac   .20 .20
2280 A1603 3r vio brown   .20 .20
2281 A1604 4r brt blue   .20 .20
2282 A1605 5r gray grn & blk   .20 .20
2283 A1606 5r brown   .20 .20
2284 A1607 10r multi   .45 .45
2285 A1608 15r purple   .60 .60

2286 A1609 20r multi   .80 .80
2287 A1610 50r multi   2.10 2.10
    Nos. 2276-2287 (12)   5.55 5.55

Issued: 25p, Nos. 2282, 2283, 12/1; 1r, 2r, 3r, 4r, 15r, 20r, 3/1/09; 50p, 10r, 5/11/09. 50r, 5/11/09.

Discovery of Evershed Effect at Kodaikanal Solar Observatory, Cent. — A1611

Perf. 13¾ Syncopated
2008, Dec. 2   Litho.   Unwmk.
2288 A1611 5r multi   .20 .20

Map, Handshake, Indian Ship and Helicopter A1612

2008, Dec. 4
2289 A1612 5r multi   .20 .20

Navy Day.

Dr. Laxmi Mall Singhvi (1931-2007), Jurist — A1613

2008, Dec. 8
2290 A1613 5r multi   .20 .20

Christmas — A1614

No. 2291: a, 5r, Lambs. b, 20r, Madonna and Child.

2008, Dec. 8   Photo.   Perf. 13
2291 A1614 Horiz. pair, #a-b   1.10 1.10

Universal Declaration of Human Rights, 60th Anniv. A1615

2008, Dec. 10
2292 A1615 5r multi   .20 .20

Indian Institute of Science, Bangalore, Cent. — A1616

No. 2293: a, 5r, Building. b, 20r, Building and scientists. Illustration reduced.

2008, Dec. 14
2293 A1616 Horiz. pair, #a-b   1.10 1.10
    c.   Souvenir sheet, #2293a-2293b   3.50 3.50

Swami Ranganathananda (1908-2005), Hindu Monk — A1617

Perf. 13¾ Syncopated
2008, Dec. 15   Litho.
2294 A1617 5r multi   .20 .20

Field Marshal S. H. F. J. Manekshaw (1914-2008) A1618

2008, Dec. 16   Photo.   Perf. 13x13¼
2295 A1618 5r multi   .20 .20

Thazhuvia V. Ramasubbaiyer (1908-84), Founder of Dinamalar Newspaper A1619

Perf. 13¾ Syncopated
2008, Dec. 21   Litho.
2296 A1619 5r multi   .20 .20

Brahmos Cruise Missile, 10th Anniv. — A1620

Designs: 5r, Missile in flight, airplane. 20r, Missiles, airplane, ship, launch vehicle, horiz.

2008, Dec. 22   Photo.   Perf. 13
2297-2298 A1620 Set of 2   1.10 1.10
2298a   Souvenir sheet, #2297-2298   3.50 3.50

Udumalai Narayana Kavi (1899-1981), Lyricist — A1621

2008, Dec. 31   Perf. 13x13¼
2299 A1621 5r multi   .20 .20

Thillaiyadi Valliammai (1898-1914), Freedom Fighter — A1622

2008, Dec. 31   *Perf. 13*
2300 A1622 5r multi   .20   .20

Sheik Thambi Pavalar (1874-1950), Freedom Fighter — A1623

2008, Dec. 31
2301 A1623 5r multi   .20   .20

A. T. Paneerselvam, Politician A1624

2008, Dec. 31   *Perf. 13x13¼*
2302 A1624 5r multi   .20   .20

M. Bhakthavatsalam (1897-1987), Politician A1625

2008, Dec. 31   *Perf. 13*
2303 A1625 5r multi   .20   .20

Velu Nachchiyar, Tamil Queen A1626

2008, Dec. 31   *Litho.*
2304 A1626 5r multi   .20   .20

Louis Braille (1809-52), Educator of the Blind — A1627

Photo. & Embossed
2009, Jan. 4   *Perf. 13¼x13*
2305 A1627 5r multi   .20   .20

Vaikom Muhammad Basheer (1908-94), Writer — A1628

2009, Jan. 21   *Litho.*   *Perf. 13*
2306 A1628 5r multi   .20   .20

St. Paul's Church, Madras A1629

2009, Jan. 25 *Perf. 13¾ Syncopated*
2307 A1629 5r multi   .20   .20

Preservation of Heritage Monuments — A1630

No. 2308: a, Jaisalmer Fort, Jaisalmer. b, Mongyu Monastery, Laddakh. c, St. Anne Church, Goa. d, Qila Mubarak, Patiala.

2009, Jan. 28   *Photo.*   *Perf. 13*
2308 A1630 5r Block of 4, #a-d   .85   .85
   e.   Souvenir sheet, #2308a-2308d 2.75 2.75

Bishnu Prasad Rabha (1909-69), Writer, Singer A1631

Perf. 13¾ Syncopated
2009, Jan. 31   *Litho.*
2309 A1631 5r multi   .20   .20

Steel Authority of India, 50th Anniv. — A1632

2009, Mar. 3   *Photo.*   *Perf. 13*
2310 A1632 5r multi   .20   .20

Natl. Girl Child Day — A1633

2009, Feb. 5
2311 A1633 5r multi   .20   .20

Santaji Jagnade Maharaj (1624-88), Marathi Saint — A1634

Perf. 13¾ Syncopated
2009, Feb. 9   *Litho.*
2312 A1634 5r multi   .20   .20

Mahi Kavi Magh, 8th Cent. Poet — A1635

2009, Feb. 9   *Photo.*   *Perf. 13*
2313 A1635 5r multi   .20   .20

Postal Life Insurance, 125th Anniv. — A1636

Perf. 13¾ Syncopated
2009, Feb. 11   *Litho.*
2314 A1636 5r multi   .20   .20

Vallabh Suri (1870-1954), Jain Religious Leader — A1637

2009, Feb. 21
2315 A1637 5r multi   .20   .20

Harakh Chand Nahata (1936-99), Film Financer A1638

2009, Feb. 28
2316 A1638 5r multi   .20   .20

Medical Council of India, 75th Anniv. A1639

2009, Mar. 1   *Photo.*   *Perf. 13*
2317 A1639 5r multi   .20   .20

Pterospermum Acerifolium Tree and Flower — A1640

2009, Mar. 6   *Litho.*
2318 A1640 5r multi   .20   .20

Baburao Puleshwar Shedmake, 19th Cent. Freedom Fighter A1641

2009, Mar. 12
2319 A1641 5r multi   .20   .20

Dr. Krishna Kumar Birla (1918-2008), Industrialist — A1642

2009, Mar. 13
2320 A1642 5r multi   .20   .20

Spices — A1643

No. 2321: a, Black pepper. b, Cinnamon. c, Cardamom d, Cloves. e, Turmeric, coriander and chili peppers.

2009, Apr. 29   *Photo.*
2321   Strip of 5   1.60 1.60
   a.-d.   A1643 5r Any single   .20   .20
   e.   A1643 20r multi   .80   .80
   f.   Souvenir sheet of 5, #2321a-
           2321e   4.75 4.75

R. Sankar (1909-72), Politician A1644

Perf. 13¾ Syncopated
2009, Apr. 30   **Litho.**
2322 A1644 5r multi   .20   .20

Lifeline Express Hospital
Train — A1645

2009, May 12   **Perf. 13**
2323 A1645 5r multi   .25   .25

Madras Regiment,
250th
Anniv. — A1646

Perf. 13¾ Syncopated
2009, May 28   **Litho.**   **Unwmk.**
2324 A1646 5r multi   .25   .25

Rev. J.J.M.
Nichols Roy
(1883-1959),
Politician — A1647

2009, June 12   **Photo.**   **Perf. 13**
2325 A1647 5r multi   .25   .25

Sacred Heart Church, Pudducherry,
Cent. — A1648

Perf. 13¾ Syncopated
2009, June 19
2326 A1648 5r multi   .25   .25

Raza
Library,
Rampur
A1649

Ram, Laxman and
Jatayu From
Valmiki
Ramayana, by
Sumer
Chand — A1650

Madonna Holding
Book — A1651

Illustrated Page
from Diwan-i-Hafiz
of Akbar's
Collection
A1652

2009, June 19   **Litho.**
2327 A1649 5r multi   .25   .25
2328 A1650 5r multi   .25   .25
2329 A1651 5r multi   .25   .25
2330 A1652 5r multi   .25   .25
   a.   Souvenir sheet, #2327-2330   3.00   3.00
   Nos. 2327-2330 (4)   1.00   1.00

Indian Oil Corporation, 50th
Anniv. — A1653

2009, June 30   **Perf. 13**
2331 A1653 5r multi   .25   .25

Lal Bahadur Shastri Natl. Academy of
Administration, Mussoorie, 50th
Anniv. — A1654

2009, July 4   **Photo.**
2332 A1654 5r multi   .25   .25

Ramcharan
Agarwal
(1919-77),
Politician
A1655

Perf. 13¾ Syncopated
2009, July 25   **Litho.**
2333 A1655 5r multi   .25   .25

A1656

A1657

A1658

A1659

A1660

A1661

A1662

A1663

A1664

A1665

Scenes from Geetagovinda, Poem by
Jayadeva — A1666

2009, July 27   **Photo.**   **Perf. 13**
2334   Horiz. strip of 11   2.75   2.75
  a.   A1656 5r multi   .25   .25
  b.   A1657 5r multi   .25   .25
  c.   A1658 5r multi   .25   .25
  d.   A1659 5r multi   .25   .25
  e.   A1660 5r multi   .25   .25
  f.   A1661 5r multi   .25   .25
  g.   A1662 5r multi   .25   .25
  h.   A1663 5r multi   .25   .25
  i.   A1664 5r multi   .25   .25
  j.   A1665 5r multi   .25   .25
  k.   A1666 5r multi   .25   .25
  l.   Souvenir sheet, #2334a-2334k   5.00   5.00

St. Joseph's
College,
Bangalore
A1667

Perf. 13¾ Syncopated
2009, Aug. 1   **Litho.**
2335 A1667 5r multi   .25   .25

Maharishi
Patanjali,
Compiler of Yoga
Sutras — A1668

2009, Aug. 4   **Perf. 13**
2336 A1668 5r multi   .25   .25

Pingali Venkaiah (1876-1963),
Designer of Indian Flag — A1669

2009, Aug. 12   **Photo.**   **Perf. 13¼x13**
2337 A1669 5r multi   .25   .25

Railway Stations — A1670

Designs: No. 2338, 5r, Howrah Station, Cal-
cutta. No. 2339, 5r, Chennai Central Station.
No. 2340, 5r, Mumbai CST (Chhatrapati
Shivaji Terminus). No. 2341, 5r, Old Delhi
Station.

2009, Aug. 16   **Litho.**   **Perf. 13**
2338-2341 A1670   Set of 4   .85   .85
  2341a   Souvenir sheet, #2338-
      2341   3.25   3.25

Uttam Kumar (1926-80), Actor — A1671

Perf. 13¾ Syncopated
2009, Sept. 3   Litho.
2342 A1671 5r multi   .20 .20

Sacred Heart Matriculation Higher Secondary School, Chennai — A1672

2009, Sept. 9   Photo.   *Perf. 13*
2343 A1672 5r multi   .25 .25

Holy Cross Church, Mapranam A1673

Perf. 13¾ Syncopated
2009, Sept. 14   Litho.
2344 A1673 5r multi   .25 .25

Dushyant Kumar (1933-75), Writer A1674

2009, Sept. 27   *Perf. 13¼x13*
2345 A1674 5r multi   .25 .25

Mammals A1675

Designs: No. 2346, 5r, Red panda. No. 2347, 5r, Marbled cat, vert. No. 2348, 5r, Barbe's leaf monkey, vert.

Perf. 13¾ Syncopated
2009, Oct. 1   Litho.
2346-2348 A1675 Set of 3   .65 .65
2348a   Souvenir sheet, #2346-2348   2.50 2.50

Mahatma Gandhi — A1676

Wmk. 324
2009, Oct. 2   Photo.   *Perf. 13¼*
2349 A1676 25r multi   1.10 1.10

Bishop Cotton School, Shimla — A1677

Unwmk.
2009, Oct. 6   Litho.   *Perf. 13*
2350 A1677 5r multi   .25 .25

R.K. Narayan (1906-2001), Writer — A1678

Perf. 13¼
2009, Oct. 10   Litho.   **Unwmk.**
2351 A1678 5r multi   .25 .25

Dineshnandini Dalmia (1928-2007), Writer — A1679

Perf. 13¾ Syncopated
2009, Oct. 11   Litho.
2352 A1679 5r multi   .25 .25

India Post Airplane A1680

2009, Oct. 12   Litho.   *Perf. 13¼x13*
2353 A1680 5r multi   .25 .25

Temples — A1681

Designs: No. 2354, 5r, Dilwara Temple. No. 2355, 5r, Ranakpur Temple.

2009, Oct. 14   *Perf. 13*
2354-2355 A1681 Set of 2   .45 .45

Gulab Singh (1792-1857), First Maharaja of Jammu and Kashmir — A1682

Perf. 13¾ Syncopated
2009, Oct. 21   Litho.
2356 A1682 5r multi   .25 .25

Major General Dewan Misri Chand (1907-70), Pilot — A1683

2009, Oct. 22
2357 A1683 5r multi   .25 .25

Canonization of Jeanne Jugan — A1684

No. 2358: a, 5r, Little Sisters of the Poor Home for the Aged, Bangalore (40x32mm). b, 20r, St. Jeanne Jugan (1792-1879), Founder of Little Sisters of the Poor (29x32mm).

2009, Oct. 29   *Perf. 13*
2358 A1684   Horiz. pair, #a-b   1.10 1.10

Dr. Rajkumar (1929-2006), Actor — A1685

2009, Nov. 1
2359 A1685 5r multi   .25 .25

Dr. Mahendra Lal Sircar (1833-1904), Founder of Indian Association for the Cultivation of Science — A1686

2009, Nov. 2   *Perf. 13¾*
2360 A1686 5r multi   .25 .25

Apollo Hospitals A1687

2009, Nov. 2
2361 A1687 5r multi   .25 .25

Danmal Mathur, Scouting Leader — A1688

2009, Nov. 7   Photo.   *Perf. 13x13¼*
2362 A1688 5r multi   .25 .25

Virchand Raghavji Gandhi (1864-1901), Representative of Jains at 1893 World Parliament of Religions — A1689

2009, Nov. 8   Litho.   *Perf. 13*
2363 A1689 5r multi   .25 .25

Horse Breeds A1690

Designs: No. 2364, 5r, Kathiawan. No. 2365, 5r, Marwari. No. 2366, 5r, Zanskari. No. 2367, 5r, Manipuri.

2009, Nov. 9   *Perf. 13¾ Syncopated*
2364-2367 A1690   Set of 4   .90 .90
2367a   Souvenir sheet, #2364-2367   2.50 2.50

Rajabhau Khobragade (1925-84), Politician — A1691

2009, Nov. 11
2368 A1691 5r multi   .25 .25

Gaurishankar Dalmia (1910-88), Magazine Publisher A1692

2009, Nov. 12   *Perf. 13¼*
2369 A1692 5r multi   .25 .25

British Commonwealth, 60th Anniv. — A1693

2009, Nov. 13   *Perf. 13*
2370 A1693 5r multi   .25 .25

Children's Day A1694

Designs: No. 2371, 5r, Deer at pond. No. 2372, 5r, Tiger.

2009, Nov. 14   *Perf. 13¼*
2371-2372 A1694 Set of 2   .45 .45

Silent Valley National Park — A1695

2009, Nov. 15   **Perf. 13**
2373 A1695 5r multi   .25 .25
   a.   Souvenir sheet of 1   1.40 1.40

Marine Life — A1696

No. 2374: a, 5r, Gangetic dolphin. b, 20r, Butanding.

2009, Nov. 16
2374 A1696   Horiz. pair, #a-b   1.10 1.10
   c.   Souvenir sheet, #2374a-2374b   3.00 3.00

See Philippines No.

Ganpatrao Govindrao Jadhav (1908-87), Newspaper Publisher A1697

2009, Nov. 18   **Perf. 13¼**
2375 A1697 5r multi   .25 .25

Tamil Nadu Police, 150th Anniv. — A1698

2009, Nov. 30   **Perf. 13**
2376 A1698 5r multi   .25 .25

A1699

A1700

A1701

Greetings A1702

2009, Dec. 1
2377 A1699 5r multi   .25 .25
2378 A1700 5r multi   .25 .25
2379 A1701 5r brown   .25 .25
2380 A1702 5r multi   .25 .25
   a.   Souvenir sheet, #2377-2380   2.50 2.50
   Nos. 2377-2380 (4)   1.00 1.00

Convent of Jesus and Mary, Ambala Cantonment, Cent. — A1703

2009, Dec. 2
2381 A1703 5r multi   .25 .25

Second Lancers (Gardiner's Horse) Regiment A1704

2009, Dec. 2   **Perf. 13¼**
2382 A1704 5r multi   .25 .25

Traditional Textiles A1705

Designs: No. 2383, 5r, Kalamkari. No. 2384, 5r, Apa Tani weaves. No. 2385, 5r, Kanchipuram silk. No. 2386, 5r, Banaras silk.

2009, Dec. 10   **Perf. 13**
2383-2386 A1705   Set of 4   .90 .90
2386a   Souvenir sheet, #2383-2386   2.50 2.50

Henry Louis Vivian Derozio (1809-31), Poet — A1706

2009, Dec. 15   **Perf. 13x13¼**
2387 A1706 5r multi   .25 .25

Lal Pratap Singh, Prince of Kalakankar A1707

Perf. 13¾ Syncopated
2009, Dec. 17
2388 A1707 5r multi   .25 .25

Preservation of Polar Regions and Glaciers — A1708

Designs: No. 2389, 5r, Penguins. No. 2390, 5r, Polar bear.

2009, Dec. 19   **Perf. 13**
2389-2390 A1708   Set of 2   .45 .45
2390a   Souvenir sheet, #2389-2390   1.75 1.75

Indian Mathematical Society, Cent. — A1709

2009, Dec. 27   **Perf. 13¼**
2391 A1709 5r multi   .25 .25

Venkataramana Bhagavathar (1781-1874), Composer A1710

2009, Dec. 27   **Perf. 13¾**
2392 A1710 5r multi   .25 .25

Maharaja Surajmal (1707-63), Ruler of Bharatpur A1711

Perf. 13¾ Syncopated
2009, Dec. 29
2393 A1711 5r multi   .25 .25

20th Conference of Speakers and Presiding Officers of the Commonwealth, New Delhi — A1712

2010, Jan. 5   **Perf. 13¼**
2394 A1712 5r multi   .25 .25

Reserve Bank of India, 75th Anniv. — A1713

2010, Jan. 16   **Perf. 13**
2395 A1713 5r multi   .25 .25

Election Commission of India, 60th Anniv. — A1714

2010, Jan. 25   **Litho.**
2396 A1714 5r multi   .25 .25

Bible Society of India, Bicent. — A1715

2010, Feb. 21 Photo.   **Perf. 13x13¼**
2397 A1715 5r multi   .25 .25

P. C. Sorcar (1913-71), Magician A1716

2010, Feb. 23   **Litho.**
2398 A1716 5r multi   .25 .25

16th Punjab (2nd Patiala) Regiment A1717

2009, Mar. 19 Photo.   **Perf. 13¼x13**
2399 A1717 5r multi   .25 .25

Muthuramalinga Sethupathi (1760-1809), King of Ramanathapuram A1718

2010, Mar. 30   **Perf. 13x13¼**
2400 A1718 5r multi   .25 .25

Special Protection Group — A1719

2010, Mar. 30   **Litho.**   **Perf. 13**
2401 A1719 5r multi   .25 .25

Vallal Pachaiyappa (1754-94), Philantropist — A1720

2010, Mar. 31 Photo. *Perf. 13¼x13*
2402 A1720 5r multi .25 .25

Signs of the Zodiac A1721

Designs: No. 2403, 5r, Aries. No. 2404, 5r, Taurus. No. 2405, 5r, Gemini. No. 2406, 5r, Cancer, vert. No. 2407, 5r, Leo, vert. No. 2408, 5r, Virgo, vert. No. 2409, 5r, Libra. No. 2410, 5r, Scorpio. No. 2411, 5r, Sagittarius. No. 2412, 5r, Capricorn, vert. No. 2413, 5r, Aquarius, vert. No. 2414, 5r, Pisces, vert.

Perf. 13¼x13, 13x13¼
2010, Apr. 14 Litho.
2403-2414 A1721 Set of 12 2.75 2.75
2414a Souvenir sheet, #2403-2414, perf. 13 5.00 5.00

Chandra Shekhar (1927-2007), Prime Minister — A1722

2010, Apr. 17 Photo. *Perf. 13x13¼*
2415 A1722 5r multi .25 .25

Kanwar Ram Sahib (1885-1939), Religious Leader — A1723

2010, Apr. 26 Litho.
2416 A1723 5r multi .25 .25

Velu Thampi (1765-1809), Prime Minister of Travancore A1724

2010, May 6 *Perf. 13x13¼*
2417 A1724 5r multi .25 .25

Robert Caldwell (1814-91), Bishop and Linguist — A1725

2010, May 7 Photo.
2418 A1725 5r multi .25 .25

Dr. Guduru Venkata Chalam (1909-67), Agricultural Scientist — A1726

2010, May 8 Litho.
2419 A1726 5r multi .25 .25

Indian Post Offices — A1727

Post offices in: No. 2420, 5r, Lucknow. No. 2421, 5r, Cooch Behar. No. 2422, 5r, Nagpur. No. 2423, 5r, Udagamandalam. No. 2424, 5r, Delhi. No. 2425, 5r, Shimla.

2010, May 13 Litho. *Perf. 13*
2420-2425 A1727 Set of 6 1.40 1.40
2425a Souvenir sheet, #2420-2425 2.50 2.50

Indipex 2011 World Philatelic Exhibition, New Delhi.

C. V. Raman Pillai (1858-1922), Writer — A1728

2010, May 19 Photo. *Perf. 13x13¼*
2426 A1728 5r multi .25 .25

Intl. Year of Biodiversity A1729

Designs: 5r, Owl, sunflower, people in rice paddy. 20r, Birds, crab, water lilies.

Perf. 13¾ Syncopated
2010, June 5 Litho.
2427-2428 A1729 Set of 2 1.10 1.10
2428a Souvenir sheet, #2427-2428 3.00 3.00

Deshbandhu Gupta (1905-51), Politician and Journalist — A1730

2010, June 14
2429 A1730 5r multi .25 .25

2010 Commonwealth Games, Delhi — A1731

Map and: 5r, Tiger mascot holding torch. 20r, Hand holding torch, mascot running with torch.

2010, June 25 Photo. *Perf. 13*
2430-2431 A1731 Set of 2 1.10 1.10
2431a Souvenir sheet, #2430-2431 3.00 3.00

Kumaraguruparar Swamigal (1625-88), Poet — A1732

Perf. 13¾ Syncopated
2010, June 27 Litho.
2432 A1732 5r multi .25 .25

World Classical Tamil Conference, Kovai — A1733

2010, June 27 Photo. *Perf. 13x13¼*
2433 A1733 5r multi .25 .25

Indian Naval Air Squadron 300, 50th Anniv. — A1734

Perf. 13¾ Syncopated
2010, July 7 Litho.
2434 A1734 5r multi .25 .25

Birds A1735

Designs: No. 2435, 5r, Pigeons. No. 2436, 5r, Sparrows.

2010, July 9 Litho. *Perf. 13*
2435-2436 A1735 Set of 2 .45 .45
2436a Souvenir sheet of 2, #2435-2436 2.00 2.00

Rath Yatra Festival, Puri A1736

2010, July 12 Photo. *Perf. 13*
2437 A1736 5r multi .25 .25

Stadia for 2010 Commonwealth Games, Delhi — A1737

Designs: No. 2438, 5r, Jawaharlal Nehru Stadium. No. 2439, 5r, Talkatora Stadium.

2010, Aug. 1 Litho. *Perf. 13*
2438-2439 A1737 Set of 2 .45 .45
2439a Souvenir sheet, #2438-2439 2.00 2.00

Syed Mohammed Ali Shihab Thangal (1936-2009), Politician — A1738

Perf. 13¾ Syncopated
2010, Aug. 2 Litho.
2440 A1738 5r multi .25 .25

Vethathiri (1911-2006), Founder of World Community Service Center — A1739

2010, Aug. 14
2441 A1739 5r multi .25 .25

P. Jeevanandham (1907-63), Tamil Communist Leader — A1740

Perf. 13¾ Syncopated
2010, Aug. 21 Litho.
2442 A1740 5r multi .25 .25

Omanthur P. Ramaswamy Reddiar (1895-1970), Politician A1741

2010, Aug. 25
2443 A1741 5r multi .25 .25

G. K. Moopanar (1931-2001), Politician and Philanthropist A1742

2010, Aug. 30 Photo. Perf. 13x13¼
2444 A1742 5r multi .25 .25

Dr. Y. S. Rajasekhara Reddy (1949-2009), Politician A1743

2010, Sept. 2 Litho. Perf. 13¾x14
2445 A1743 5r multi .25 .25

Brihadeeswarar Temple, Thanjavur — A1744

Perf. 13¾ Syncopated
2010, Sept. 26
2446 A1744 5r multi .25 .25

Sports of 2010 Commonwealth Games, Delhi — A1745

Designs: No. 2447, 5r, Badminton. No. 2448, 5r, Archery. No. 2449, 5r, Field hockey. No. 2450, 5r, Track.

2010, Oct. 3 Perf. 13¾ Syncopated
2447-2450 A1745 Set of 4 .90 .90
2450a Souvenir sheet, #2447-2450 3.50 3.50

Feudatory States Stamps A1746

Designs: No. 2451, 5r, Indore #2, type A6, vignette of #1. No. 2452, 5r, Sirmoor #22, 2, 13. No. 2453, 5r, Bamra type A2, revenue stamp. No. 2454, 5r, Cochin #15, type A4.

2010, Oct. 6 Perf. 13¼x13
2451-2454 A1746 Set of 4 .90 .90
2454a Souvenir sheet, #2451-2454, perf. 13 3.50 3.50

Indipex 2011 World Philatelic Exhibition, New Delhi (No. 2454a).

Doon School, Dehradun, 75th Anniv. A1747

2010, Oct. 22 Perf. 13¾ Syncopated
2455 A1747 5r multi .25 .25

Sant Shadaram Sahib (1708-93), Religious Leader — A1748

2010, Oct. 25 Perf. 13x13¼
2456 A1748 5r multi .25 .25

Cathedral and John Connon School, Mumbai, 150th Anniv. A1749

2010, Oct. 27 Perf. 13¼x13
2457 A1749 5r multi .25 .25

Kranti Trivedi (1930-2009), Writer — A1750

2010, Oct. 29 Perf. 13x13¼
2458 A1750 5r multi .25 .25

K. A. P. Viswanatham (1899-1994), Medical Writer — A1751

2010, Nov. 10 Perf. 13¼x13
2459 A1751 5r multi .25 .25

Children's Day — A1752

Designs: No. 2460, 5r, Dolls depicting women carrying baskets on heads. No. 2461, 5r, Kite. No. 2462, 5r, Tops. No. 2463, 5r, Dolls depicting women in native costumes (28x38mm).

Perf. 13¼, 13x13¼ (#2463)
2010, Nov. 14
2460-2463 A1752 Set of 4 .90 .90
2463a Souvenir sheet, #2460-2463, perf. 13 3.00 3.00

Lakshmipat Singhania (1910-76), Industrialist A1753

Perf. 13¾ Syncopated
2010, Nov. 15
2464 A1753 5r multi .25 .25

Comptroller and Auditor General of India, 150th Anniv. — A1754

2010, Nov. 16 Photo. Perf. 13x13¼
2465 A1754 5r multi .25 .25

Performing Artists — A1757

Designs: No. 2468, 5r, Thanjavur Balasaraswathi (1918-84), dancer. No. 2469, 5r, T. N. Rajarathinam Pillai (1898-1956), musician. No. 2470, 5r, Veenai Dhanammai (1867-1938), musician, horiz.

Perf. 13¾ Syncopated
2010, Dec. 3 Litho.
2468-2470 A1757 Set of 3 .70 .70

Dances A1760

Designs: 5r, Jarabe Tapatío (Mexican Hat dance), Mexico. 20r, Kalbelia dance, India.

2010, Dec. 5 Litho. Perf. 13
2473-2474 A1760 Set of 2 1.10 1.10
See Mexico Nos.

AIR POST STAMPS

De Havilland Hercules over Lake AP1

Wmk. 196 Sideways
1929-30		Typo.		Perf. 14	
C1	AP1	2a dull green		1.00	.50
C2	AP1	3a deep blue		1.40	.90
C3	AP1	4a gray olive		4.00	1.90
a.		4a olive green ('30)		5.00	1.90
C4	AP1	6a bister		5.00	1.10
C5	AP1	8a red violet		5.75	5.75
C6	AP1	12a brown red		17.50	17.50
		Nos. C1-C6 (6)		34.65	27.65

Catalogue values for unused stamps in this section, from this point to the end of the section, are for Never Hinged items.

Dominion of India

Lockheed Constellation — AP2

Perf. 13½x14
1948, May 29 Litho. Wmk. 196
C7 AP2 12a ultra & slate blk 2.25 2.25
Bombay-London flight of June 8, 1948.

Republic of India

The Spirit of '76, by Archibald M. Willard — AP3

1976, May 29 Perf. 13x13½
C8 AP3 2.80r multicolored 4.00 4.00
American Bicentennial.

INDIA '80 Emblem, De Havilland Puss Moth AP4

1979, Oct. 15 Photo. Perf. 14½x14
C9	AP4	30p shown	.80	.30
C10	AP4	50p Chetak helicopter	1.00	.50
C11	AP4	1r Boeing 737	1.25	.90
C12	AP4	2r Boeing 747	1.60	1.10
		Nos. C9-C12 (4)	4.65	2.80

INDIA '80 Intl. Stamp Exhib., New Delhi, Jan. 25-Feb. 3, 1980.

MILITARY STAMPS

China Expeditionary Force

Regular Issues of India, 1882-99, Overprinted

1900		Wmk. 39		Perf. 14	
M1	A31	3p carmine rose		.70	2.10
M2	A17	½a dark green		1.25	.45
M3	A19	1a maroon		7.00	2.50
M4	A21	2a ultra		5.25	15.00
M5	A28	2a6p green		4.75	21.00
M6	A22	3a orange		4.75	27.50
M7	A23	4a olive green		4.75	13.00
M8	A25	8a red violet		4.75	30.00
M9	A26	12a violet, *red*		30.00	30.00
M10	A29	1r car rose & grn		37.50	37.50
a.		Double overprint			
		Nos. M1-M10 (10)		100.70	179.05

The 1a6p of this set was overprinted, but not issued. Value $250.

Overprinted on 1900 Issue of India
1904, Feb. 27
M11 A19 1a carmine rose 55.00 15.00

Overprinted on 1902-09 Issue of India
1904
M12	A32	3p gray	8.00	10.00
M13	A34	1a carmine rose	12.00	1.10
M14	A35	2a violet	22.50	3.75
M15	A36	2a6p ultra	5.25	8.00
M16	A37	3a brown org	5.75	6.50
M17	A38	4a olive green	13.50	19.00
M18	A40	8a red violet	13.00	12.00
M19	A41	12a violet, *red*	18.00	30.00
M20	A42	1r car rose & grn	20.00	45.00
		Nos. M12-M20 (9)	118.00	135.35

Overprinted on 1906 Issue of India
1909
M21 A44 ½a green   1.50 1.00
M22 A45 1a carmine rose   1.50 .40

Overprinted on 1911-19 Issues of India
1913-21
M23 A46 3p gray   8.00 35.00
M24 A47 ½a green   6.25 7.50
M25 A48 1a carmine
           rose   7.25 4.75
M26 A58 1½a chocolate   40.00 95.00
M27 A49 2a violet   27.50 80.00
M28 A57 2a6p ultra   20.00 30.00
M29 A51 3a brown
           org   40.00 240.00
M30 A52 4a olive
           green   37.50 210.00
M31 A54 8a red violet   40.00 400.00
M32 A55 12a claret   37.50 140.00
M33 A56 1r grn & red
           brn   110.00 375.00
  Nos. M23-M33 (11)   374.00 1,617.

Issue dates: No. M23, 1913; others, 1921.

Indian Expeditionary Force

Regular Issues of India,
1911-13, Overprinted

1914   Wmk. 39   Perf. 14
M34 A46 3p gray   .30 .55
  a.   Double overprint   70.00 55.00
M35 A47 ½a green   .80 .55
  a.   Double overprint   175.00 300.00
M36 A48 1a carmine rose   2.10 .55
M37 A49 2a violet   2.10 .55
M38 A57 2a6p ultra   2.50 4.00
M39 A51 3a brown org   1.75 2.75
M40 A52 4a olive green   1.75 2.75
M41 A54 8a red violet   2.10 4.25
M42 A55 12a claret   3.75 10.50
M43 A56 1r grn & red brn   4.50 7.25
  Nos. M34-M43 (10)   21.65 33.70

> Catalogue values for unused stamps in this section, from this point to the end of the section, are for Never Hinged items.

Korea Custodial Unit

Regular Issues of India
Overprinted in Black

Perf. 13½x14, 14x13½
1953   Wmk. 196
M44 A91 3p gray violet   .35 5.50
M45 A92 6p red brown   .35 5.50
M46 A91 9p green   .35 4.50
M47 A101 1a turquoise   .50 4.50
M48 A93 2a carmine   .80 4.50
M49 A94 2½a brown lake   1.50 4.75
M50 A94 3a red orange   1.75 5.50
M51 A94 4a ultra   2.10 4.75
M52 A95 6a purple   8.00 9.00
M53 A95 8a blue green   5.75 11.00
M54 A95 12a blue   7.75 17.00
M55 A96 1r dk grn & pur   12.50 17.00
  Nos. M44-M55 (12)   41.70 93.50

Hindi overprint reads "Indian Custodial Unit, Korea."

Indian UN Force in Congo
Nos. 302-303, 305, 307, 282 and 313
Overprinted: "U.N. FORCE (INDIA) CONGO"

Wmk. 324, 196 (13np)
1962, Jan. 15   Photo.   Perf. 14x14½
M56 A117 1np blue green   .90 .90
M57 A117 2np light brown   .90 .90
M58 A117 5np emerald   .90 .90
M59 A117 8np bright green   .90 .90
M60 A117 13np brt carmine   1.50 1.50
M61 A117 50np orange   2.75 2.75
  Nos. M56-M61 (6)   7.85 7.85

Indian UN Force in Gaza

No. 393 Overprinted in Carmine

1965, Jan. 15   Unwmk.   Perf. 13½
M62 A190 15p blue gray   4.00 8.00
  Overprint letters stand for "United Nations Emergency Force."

INTERNATIONAL COMMISSION IN INDO-CHINA

> Catalogue values for all unused stamps in this section are for Never Hinged items.

Cambodia

India Nos. 207, 231, 211, 216 and 217 Overprinted in Black

Perf. 13½x14
1954, Dec. 1   Wmk. 196
1 A91 3p gray violet   .50 .50
2 A101 1a turquoise   .60 .60
3 A93 2a carmine   1.00 1.00
4 A95 8a blue green   4.00 4.25
5 A95 12a blue   5.50 6.25
  Nos. 1-5 (5)   11.60 12.60

The overprint reads "International Commission Cambodia." Top line is 18mm on Nos. 4-5; 15½mm on Nos. 1-3, 6-12.

Same Overprint on India Nos. 276, 279, 282, 286 and 287
1957, Apr. 1   Perf. 14x14½
6 A117 2np light brown   .40 .40
7 A117 6np gray   .40 .40
8 A117 13np bright carmine   1.00 .70
9 A117 50np orange   4.75 2.50
10 A117 75np plum   5.25 4.75
  Nos. 6-10 (5)   11.80 8.75

Same Overprint on India No. 303
1962   Wmk. 324
12 A117 2np light brown   .65 .65

Laos

India Nos. 207, 231, 211, 216 and 217 Overprinted in Black

Perf. 13½x14
1954, Dec. 1   Wmk. 196
1 A91 3p gray violet   .50 .50
2 A101 1a turquoise   .60 .60
3 A93 2a carmine   1.00 1.00
4 A95 8a blue green   4.00 4.25
5 A95 12a blue   5.50 6.25
  Nos. 1-5 (5)   11.60 12.60

The overprint reads "International Commission Laos." Top line is 18mm on Nos. 4-5; 15½mm on Nos. 1-3, 6-16.

Same Overprint on India Nos. 276, 279, 282, 286 and 287
1957, Apr. 1   Perf. 14x14½
6 A117 2np light brown   .40 .40
7 A117 6np gray   .40 .40
8 A117 13np brt carmine   1.00 .70
9 A117 50np orange   4.75 2.50
10 A117 75np plum   5.25 4.75
  Nos. 6-10 (5)   11.80 8.75

Same Overprint on India Nos. 303-305, 313-314
1962-65   Wmk. 324
12 A117 2np light brown   2.50 3.00
13 A117 3np brown ('63)   .60 .60
14 A117 5np emerald ('63)   .60 .60
15 A117 50np orange ('65)   2.00 2.25
16 A117 75np plum ('65)   4.25 4.75
  Nos. 12-16 (5)   9.95 11.20

Laos and Viet Nam

No. 393 Overprinted in Carmine

1965, Jan. 15   Unwmk.   Perf. 13½
1 A190 15p blue gray   4.00 4.00
  Overprint letters stand for "International Control Commission."

Nos. 406-408, 411-412, 417 and 419-420 Overprinted in Carmine

Perf. 14½x14, 14x14½
1968, Oct. 2   Photo.   Wmk. 324
2 A202 2p reddish brown   .50 .50
3 A202 3p olive bister   .50 .50
4 A202 5p cerise   .50 .50
5 A203 10p bright blue   2.50 2.50
6 A203 15p green   .50 .50
7 A202 60p dark gray   1.10 1.10
8 A204 1r dp cl & red brn   1.75 2.25
9 A205 2r violet & brt blue   4.00 5.50
  Nos. 2-9 (8)   11.85 13.85

The arrangement of the lines of the overprint varies on each denomination.

Viet Nam

India Nos. 207, 231, 211, 216 and 217 Overprinted in Black

Perf. 13½x14
1954, Dec. 1   Wmk. 196
1 A91 3p gray violet   .50 .50
2 A101 1a turquoise   .60 .60
3 A93 2a carmine   1.00 1.00
4 A95 8a blue green   4.00 4.25
5 A95 12a blue   5.50 6.25
  Nos. 1-5 (5)   11.60 12.60

The overprint reads "International Commission Viet Nam." Top line of overprint is 18mm on Nos. 4-5; 15½mm on Nos. 1-3, 6-16.

Same Overprint on India Nos. 276, 279, 282, 286 and 287
1957, Apr. 1   Perf. 14x14½
6 A117 2np light brown   .40 .40
7 A117 6np gray   .40 .40
8 A117 13np bright carmine   1.00 .70
9 A117 50np orange   4.75 2.10
10 A117 75np plum   5.25 4.75
  Nos. 6-10 (5)   11.80 8.35

Same Overprint on India Nos. 302-305, 313-314
1961-65   Wmk. 324
11 A117 1np blue green   1.40 1.40
12 A117 2np light brown ('62)   2.75 2.75
13 A117 3np brown ('63)   1.00 1.00
14 A117 5np emerald ('63)   .65 .80
15 A117 50np orange ('65)   2.25 2.75
16 A117 75np plum ('65)   4.25 4.75
  Nos. 11-16 (6)   12.30 13.45

OFFICIAL STAMPS

Nos. O1-O26 are normally found with very heavy cancellations, and values are for stamps so canceled. Lightly canceled stamps are seldom seen.

Nos. 11-12, 18, 20-22, 23a, 24, 26 Overprinted in Black

1866, Aug. 1   Unwmk.   Perf. 14
O1 A7 ½a blue   1,100. 140.00
  a.   Inverted overprint
O3 A7 1a brown   140.00
O4 A7 8a rose   22.50 140.00
  The 8p lilac unwatermarked (No. 19) with "Service" overprint was not officially issued.

Wmk. 38
O5 A7 ½a blue   225.00 12.50
  a.   Inverted overprint
  b.   Without period   210.00
O6 A8 8p lilac   20.00 52.50
O7 A7 1a brown   190.00 15.00
  a.   Inverted overprint
O8 A7 2a yellow   175.00 85.00
  a.   Imperf.
  b.   Inverted overprint
O9 A7 4a green   200.00 80.00
  a.   Inverted overprint
O10 A9 4a green (I)   1,000. 250.00
  Reprints were made of #O5, O7, O10 (type II).

Revenue Stamps Surcharged or Overprinted

Queen Victoria — O1

Blue Glazed Paper
Black Surcharge
1866   Wmk. 36   Perf. 14 Vertically
O11 O1 2a violet   350.00 250.00
  The note after No. 30 will apply here also. No. O11 is often found with cracked surface or scuffs. Such examples sell for somewhat less.
  Reprints of No. O11 are surcharged in either black or green, and have the word "SERVICE" 16½x2½mm, instead of 16½x2¾mm and "TWO ANNAS" 18x3mm, instead of 20x3¼mm.

O2   O3

O4

1866

Green Overprint

O12	O2	2a violet	825.	325.
O13	O3	4a violet	4,500.	1,250.
O14	O4	8a violet	5,000.	5,000.

The note after No. 30 will apply here also. These stamps are often found with cracked surface or scuffs. Such examples sell for somewhat less.

Reprints of No. O12 have the overprint in sans-serif letters 2¼mm high, instead of Roman letters 2½mm high. On the reprints of No. O13 "SERVICE" measures 16½x2¼mm, instead of 20¼x3mm and "POSTAGE" 18x2¼mm, instead of 22x3mm.

On No. O14 "SERVICE" is 20½mm long, instead of 20mm and "POSTAGE" is 23mm long, instead of 22mm. All three overprints are in a darker green than on the original stamps.

 O5

Green Overprint

1866   **Wmk. 40**   **Perf. 15½x15**

Lilac Paper

O15	O5	½a violet	425.00	85.00
a.		Double overprint	3,000.	

Nos. 20, 31, 22-23, 23a, 26, 28 Overprinted in Black

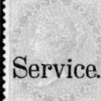

1866-73   **Wmk. 38**   **Perf. 14**

O16	A7	½a blue	30.00	.35
O17	A7	½a bl, re-engraved	140.00	67.50
a.		Double overprint		
O18	A7	1a brown	32.50	.40
O19	A7	2a orange	4.50	2.00
a.		2a yellow	20.00	2.25
O20	A9	4a green (I)	2.75	1.50
O21	A11	8a rose	3.00	1.50
		Nos. O16-O21 (6)	212.75	73.25

The 6a8p with this overprint was not issued. Value $25.

Nos. 31, 22-23, 26, 28 Overprinted in Black

1874-82

O22	A7	½a blue, re-engraved	8.00	.20
a.		Blue overprint	350.00	45.00
O23	A7	1a brown	12.50	.20
a.		Blue overprint	550.00	120.00
O24	A7	2a orange	40.00	17.50
O25	A9	4a green (I)	12.50	2.75
O26	A11	8a rose	4.25	4.00
		Nos. O22-O26 (5)	77.25	24.65

Same Overprint on Nos. 36, 38, 40, 42, 44, 49

1883-97   **Wmk. 39**

O27	A17	½a green	.40	.20
a.		Pair, one without overprint		
b.		Double overprint		1,150.
O28	A19	1a maroon	.35	.20
a.		Inverted overprint	350.00	475.00
b.		Double overprint		1,150.
c.		1a violet brown	2.25	.35
O29	A21	2a ultramarine	4.50	.50
O30	A23	4a olive green	15.00	.40
O31	A25	8a red violet	7.00	.40
O32	A29	1r car rose & grn	11.00	.40
		Nos. O27-O32 (6)	38.25	2.10

Same Overprint on No. 54

1899

O33	A31	3p carmine rose	.20	.20

Same Overprint on Nos. 56-58

1900

O34	A17	½a light green	1.25	.30
O35	A19	1a carmine rose	2.50	.20
a.		Double overprint		1,350.
b.		Inverted overprint		1,400.
O36	A21	2a violet	27.50	.50
		Nos. O34-O36 (3)	31.25	1.00

Same Overprint on Nos. 60-63, 66-68, 70

1902-09

O37	A32	3p gray	.85	.20
O38	A33	½a green	1.00	.20
O39	A34	1a carmine rose	.85	.20
O40	A35	2a violet	2.50	.20
O41	A38	4a olive green	4.25	.20
O42	A39	6a bister	2.25	.20
O43	A40	8a red lilac	5.25	.50
O44	A42	1r car rose & green ('05)	4.50	.20
		Nos. O37-O44 (8)	21.45	1.90

Same Overprint on Nos. 78-79

1906-07

O45	A44	½a green	1.00	.20
O46	A45	1a carmine rose	1.75	.20
a.		Pair, one without overprint		
b.		Overprint on back	—	

Same Overprint on Nos. 71, 73-76

1909

O47	A43	2r brown & rose	6.50	.90
O48	A43	5r violet & ultra	11.00	1.00
O49	A43	10r car rose & grn	21.00	8.50
a.		10r red & green	52.50	6.00
O50	A43	15r ol gray & ultra	52.50	30.00
O51	A43	25r ultra & org brn	130.00	50.00
		Nos. O47-O51 (5)	221.00	90.40

For surcharges see Nos. O67-O69.

Nos. 80-84, 88, 90-91 Overprinted in Black

1912-22

O52	A46	3p gray	.25	.20
O53	A47	½a green	.25	.20
a.		Double overprint	110.00	
O54	A48	1a carmine rose	.75	.20
a.		Double overprint	950.00	
O55	A48	1a dark brown	1.00	.20
a.		Imperf., pair ('22)	75.00	
O56	A49	2a violet	.50	.20
O57	A52	4a olive green	.75	.20
O58	A53	6a bister	1.25	1.75
O59	A54	8a red violet	1.75	.75

Nos. 93-98 Overprinted in Black

O60	A56	1r green & red brn	2.00	.80
O61	A56	2r yel brn & car rose	2.50	3.50
O62	A56	5r violet & ultra	10.50	13.50
O63	A56	10r car rose & grn	35.00	32.50
O64	A56	15r ol grn & ultra	80.00	95.00
O65	A56	25r ultra & brn org	180.00	150.00
		Nos. O52-O65 (14)	316.50	299.00

For surcharge see No. O69b.

O6   O7

Black Surcharge on No. O42

1921   **Black Surcharge**

O66	O6	9p on 1a rose	.75	.60

For overprint see Gwalior No. O28.

Nos. O49-O51 Surcharged

1925

O67	A43	1r on 15r ol gray & ultra	4.00	3.00
O68	A43	1r on 25r ultra & org brn	20.00	60.00
O69	A43	2r on 10r red & grn	3.50	3.50
a.		2r on 10r car rose & green	210.00	55.00
b.		Surcharge on #O63 (error)	800.00	

Nos. O64-O65 Surcharged

O70	A56	1r on 15r ol grn & ultra	19.00	65.00
a.		Inverted surcharge		
O71	A56	1r on 25r ultra & brn org	5.00	9.00
a.		Inverted surcharge	600.00	
		Nos. O67-O71 (5)	51.50	140.50

1926

O73	O7	1a on 6a bister	.40	.40

Nos. 83, 101, 102, 99 Surcharged

O74	A48	1a on 1a dk brn (error)	180.00	180.00
O75	A58	1a on 1½a choc	.20	.20
O76	A59	1a on 1½a choc	1.75	4.00
b.		Double surcharge	30.00	
O77	A57	1a on 2a6p ultra	.50	.50
		Nos. O73-O77 (5)	182.85	185.10

Nos. O74, O75 and O76 have short bars over the numerals in the upper corners.

Nos. 106-108, 111, 126-127, 112, 116, 128, 118-119 Overprinted

a

1926-35   **Wmk. 196**

O78	A46	3p slate ('29)	.20	.20
O79	A47	½a green ('31)	5.00	.40
O80	A48	1a dark brown	.20	.20
a.		Overprint as on No. O55	100.00	4.75
O81	A49	2a vermilion ('35)	1.00	1.00
a.		Small die	.85	.20
O82	A60	2a dull violet	.20	.20
O83	A60	2a vermilion ('32)	.90	2.00
O84	A57	2a6p buff ('32)	.25	.20
O85	A52	4a olive green ('35)	1.00	.20
O86	A61	4a olive green	.35	.20
O87	A53	6a bister ('35)	18.00	9.00
O88	A54	8a red violet	.50	.20
O89	A55	12a claret	.50	1.75

Nos. 120-121, 123 Overprinted

O90	A56	1r green & brn ('30)	2.25	.90
O91	A56	2r brn org & car rose ('30)	6.00	6.00
O92	A56	10r car & green ('31)	70.00	50.00
		Nos. O78-O92 (15)	106.35	72.45

#138, 135, 139, 136 Overprinted Type "a"

1932-35

O93	A17	½a green ('35)	.60	.20
O94	A68	9p dark green	.25	.20
O95	A72	1a dark brown ('35)	1.90	.20
O96	A69	1a3p violet	.25	.20
		Nos. O93-O96 (4)	3.00	.80

Nos. 151-153, 162-165 Overprinted Type "a"

1937-39   **Perf. 13½x14**

O97	A80	½a brown ('38)	18.00	.45
O98	A80	9p green	20.00	.60
O99	A80	1a carmine	3.75	.35

Type "b" Overprint

O100	A82	1r brown & slate ('38)	.55	.55
O101	A82	2r dk brown & dk vio ('38)	1.50	3.25
O102	A82	5r dp ultra & dk green ('38)	2.50	7.50
O103	A82	10r rose car & dark violet ('39)	15.00	6.75
		Nos. O97-O103 (7)	61.30	19.45

No. 136 Surcharged in Black

1939, May   **Wmk. 196**   **Perf. 14**

O104	A69	1a on 1a3p violet	17.00	3.00

King George VI — O8

1939-43   **Typo.**   **Perf. 13½x14**

O105	O8	3p slate	.40	.40
O106	O8	½a brown	8.00	.40
O106A	O8	½a dk rose vio ('43)	.40	.40
O107	O8	9p green	.40	.40
O108	O8	1a car rose	.40	.40
O108A	O8	1a3p bister ('41)	7.00	1.25
O108B	O8	1½a dull pur ('43)	.40	.40
O109	O8	2a scarlet	.40	.40
O110	O8	2½a purple	.40	.40
O111	O8	4a dark brown	.60	.40
O112	O8	8a blue violet	.60	.40
		Nos. O105-O112 (11)	18.80	5.25

For overprints see Gwalior Nos. O52-O61. Stamps overprinted "Postal Service" or "I. P. N." were not used as postage stamps.

Catalogue values for unused stamps in this section, from this point to the end of the section, are for Never Hinged items.

Nos. 203-206 (Gandhi Issue) Overprinted Type "a"

Perf. 11½

1948, Aug.   **Unwmk.**   **Photo.**

O112A	A90	1½a brown	65.00	45.00
O112B	A90	3½a green	1,300.	750.00
O112C	A90	12a dk gray green	4,000.	2,500.
O112D	A90	10r rose brn & brown	25,000.	

Overprint forgeries exist.

Capital of Asoka Pillar

O9   O10

1950   **Wmk. 196**   **Typo.**

Perf. 13½x14

O113	O9	3p violet blue	.40	.40
O114	O9	6p chocolate	.40	.40
O115	O9	9p green	.65	.40
O116	O9	1a turquoise	.95	.40
O117	O9	2a red	.40	.40
O118	O9	3a vermilion	4.75	2.75
O119	O9	4a brown car	7.00	.40
O120	O9	6a purple	5.75	.40
O121	O9	8a orange brn	2.75	.40

Litho.
Perf. 14x13½

O122	O10	1r dark purple	3.75	.40
O123	O10	2r brown red	1.50	.40
O124	O10	5r dark green	2.75	2.25
O125	O10	10r red brown	8.50	22.50

Nos. O113-O125 (13)   39.55   31.50

Issue dates: 1r-10r, Jan. 2, others, July 1.

1951, Oct. 1   **Typo.**

O126	O9	4a violet blue	.20	.20

Type of 1950 Redrawn;
Denomination in Naye Paise
Typo. or Litho.

1957-58   *Perf. 13½x14*

O127	O9	1np slate blue	.55	.55
O128	O9	2np blue violet	.55	.55
O129	O9	3np chocolate	.55	.55
O130	O9	5np yellow green	.55	.55
O131	O9	6np turquoise	.55	.55
O132	O9	13np red	.55	.55
O133	O9	15np dk purple ('58)	.55	.55
O134	O9	20np vermilion	.55	.55
O135	O9	25np violet blue	.55	.55
O136	O9	50np reddish brown	1.00	.55

Nos. O127-O136 (10)   5.95   5.50

Issue dates: 15np, June; others, Apr. 1.

Redrawn Type of 1957-58
Typo. or Litho.

1958-71   **Wmk. 324**   *Perf. 13½x14*

O137	O9	1np slate blue ('59)	.30	.30
O138	O9	2np blue violet ('59)	.30	.30
O139	O9	3np chocolate	.30	.30
O140	O9	5np yel green	.30	.30
O141	O9	6np turquoise ('59)	.30	.30
O142	O9	10np dk green ('63)	.30	.30
O142A	O9	13np red ('63)	.30	.30
O143	O9	15np dk purple	.30	.30
O144	O9	20np ver ('59)	.30	.30
O145	O9	25np vio blue ('59)	.30	.30
O146	O9	50np redsh brown ('59)	.30	.30

Litho.
Perf. 14

O147	O10	1r rose vio ('59)	.30	.30
O148	O10	2r rose red ('60)	.50	.40
a.		Watermark sideways ('69)	.50	.60
O149	O10	5r green ('59)	1.40	1.40
a.		Watermark sideways ('69)	.90	.30
O150	O10	10r rose lake ('59)	2.50	1.10
a.		Watermark sideways ('71)	3.75	3.75

Nos. O137-O150 (15)   8.00   6.40

Capital of Asoka Pillar
O11   O12

1967-76   **Photo.**   **Wmk. 360**
Without Gum

O151	O11	2p violet black	.85	.85
O152	O11	3p dk red brown	.85	.85
O153	O11	5p bright green	.85	.85
O154	O11	6p Prussian blue	3.25	3.25
O155	O11	10p slate green	.85	.85
O156	O11	15p purple	.85	.85
O157	O11	20p orange ver	.85	.85
O158	O11	25p deep car ('76)	26.00	11.00
O159	O11	30p violet blue	.85	.85
O160	O11	50p red brown	.85	.85

Nos. O151-O160 (10)   36.05   21.05

No. O153 Overprinted

1971, Nov. 15   **Wmk. 360**
Without Gum

O161	O11	5p green	.40	.40

No. O153 Overprinted "Refugee / Relief"

O162	O11	5p green	1.00	1.00

No. O162 was used in Maharashtra state.

1971, Dec. 1(?)
Without Gum

O163	O12	5p green	.20	.20

Nos. O161-O163 were obligatory on all official mail as a postal tax to benefit refugees from East Pakistan. The tax was paid out of

the various governmental departments' budgets.

Type of 1968

1967-74   **Wmk. 324**   *Perf. 14½x14*

O164	O11	2p violet	.80	1.00
O165	O11	5p brt green ('74)	.80	.20
O166	O11	10p slate green ('74)	1.25	.20
O167	O11	15p purple ('73)	1.60	.40
O168	O11	20p dp orange ('74)	5.25	5.00
O169	O11	30p ultramarine	3.50	1.00
O170	O11	50p red brown ('73)	2.75	2.00
O171	O11	1r dull purple	.55	.20

Nos. O164-O171 (8)   16.50   10.00

O13   O14

Without Currency Designation
Perf. 14½x14

1976-80   **Litho.**   **Wmk. 360**
Without Gum

O172	O13	2p violet black	.35	.35
O173	O13	5p bright green	.35	.35
O174	O13	10p slate green	.35	.35
O175	O13	15p purple	.35	.35
O176	O13	20p brown orange	.35	.35
O177	O13	25p carmine rose	.80	.80
O178	O13	30p blue ('79)	2.50	2.50
O179	O13	35p violet ('80)	.75	.35
O180	O13	50p red brown	3.50	1.75
O181	O13	1r dull purple ('80)	4.00	.90

Wmk. 324

O182	O13	1r dull purple	.90	.90

Perf. 14x13½

O183	O14	2r salmon rose	3.50	3.50
O184	O14	5r deep green	3.50	3.50
O185	O14	10r red brown	1.25	1.25

Nos. O172-O185 (14)   22.45   17.20

O15

Perf. 15x14

1981, Feb.   **Litho.**   **Wmk. 360**
Without Gum

O186	O15	2r orange vermilion	1.00	.60
O187	O15	5r dark green	3.00	1.40
O188	O15	10r dark red brown	6.00	3.00

Nos. O186-O188 (3)   10.00   5.00

Unwmk.

1981, Dec. 10   **Litho.**   *Imperf.*
Cream Paper

O189	O13	5p bright green	.90	1.25
O190	O13	10p slate green	1.00	1.25
O191	O13	15p purple	1.00	1.25
O192	O13	20p brown orange	1.00	1.25
O193	O13	25p carmine rose	2.25	2.75
O194	O13	35p violet	1.25	.90
O195	O13	50p brown	2.25	2.25
O196	O13	1r dull purple	2.50	2.25
O197	O13	2r salmon rose	2.50	5.25
O198	O15	5r deep green	2.75	7.25
O199	O15	10r red brown	3.75	9.75

Nos. O189-O199 (11)   21.15   35.40

Perf. 12½x13

1982, Nov. 22   **Photo.**   **Wmk. 360**
Without Gum

O200	O13	5p bright green	.80	1.10
O201	O13	10p slate green	1.00	1.25
O202	O13	15p purple	1.10	1.25
O203	O13	20p fawn	1.25	1.25
O204	O13	25p car rose	1.60	2.50
O205	O13	30p dark blue	1.60	2.50
O206	O13	35p violet	1.60	.70
O207	O13	50p light brown	2.50	2.50
O208	O13	1r dull purple	2.50	2.50
O209	O14	2r salmon rose	2.75	3.75
O210	O15	5r deep green	3.25	6.50
O211	O15	10r red brown	4.00	9.00

Nos. O200-O211 (12)   23.95   34.80

Perf. 12½x13

1984-99   **Photo.**   **Wmk. 324**
Without Gum

O212	O13	5p green	.20	.20
O213	O13	10p dark green	.20	.20
O214	O13	15p rose lake	.20	.20
O215	O13	20p fawn	.20	.20
O216	O13	25p deep carmine	.20	.20
O217	O13	30p blue	.20	.20
O218	O13	35p purple	.20	.20
O219	O13	40p violet	.20	.20
O220	O13	50p brown	.20	.20
O221	O13	60p brown	.20	.20
O222	O15	1r violet brown	.20	.20
O223	O15	2r orange ver	.40	.20
O223A	O15	3r orange	.20	.20
O224	O15	5r gray green	1.00	.50
O225	O15	10r red brown	2.00	1.00

Nos. O213-O225 (14)   5.60   3.90

Issued: 25p, 1986. 60p, 4/15/88; 40p, 10/15/88; 3r, 3/22/99; others, 4/16/84.
This is an expanding set. Numbers may change again.

POSTAL TAX STAMPS

Catalogue values for unused stamps in this section are for Never Hinged items.

No. 408 Overprinted

Perf. 14½x14

1971, Nov. 15   **Photo.**   **Wmk. 324**

RA1	A202	5p cerise	.20	.20

No. 408 Overprinted "Refugee/Relief"

RA2	A202	5p cerise	.20	.20

No. RA2 was used in Maharashtra. In order to make the obligatory tax stamps available immediately throughout India postmasters were authorized to overprint locally No. 408. This resulted in a great variety of mostly hand-stamped overprints of various types and sizes.

Refugees — PT1

Perf. 14x14½

1971, Dec. 1   **Photo.**   **Wmk. 324**

RA3	PT1	5p cerise	.20	.20

Nos. RA1-RA3 were obligatory on all mail. The tax was for refugees from East Pakistan. See Nos. O161-O163.

INDIA - CONVENTION STATES

CONVENTION STATES OF THE BRITISH EMPIRE IN INDIA
Stamps of British India overprinted for use in the States of Chamba, Faridkot, Gwalior, Jhind, Nabha and Patiala.
These stamps had franking power throughout all British India.

Forgeries
Numerous forgeries exist of the high valued Convention States stamps, unused and used. Most cancelled examples of those stamps whose value used is far greater than unused bear favor or counterfeit cancels. Such stamps are worth far less than the values below, which are for postally used examples. More valuable Indian States stamps should be expertized.

CHAMBA

ˈchəm-bə

LOCATION — A State of India located in the north Punjab, south of Kashmir.
AREA — 3,127 sq. mi.
POP. — 168,908 (1941)
CAPITAL — Chamba

The varieties with small letters in the overprint are not listed as the letters are merely broken and not from another font of type.

Indian Stamps
Overprinted in Black

1887-95   **Wmk. 39**   *Perf. 14*

1	A17	½a green	1.50	1.75
a.		"CHMABA"	600.00	950.00
c.		Double overprint	950.00	
2	A19	1a violet brown	3.75	3.75
a.		"CHMABA"	700.00	950.00
3	A20	1a6p bis brown ('95)	4.50	21.00
4	A21	2a ultramarine	2.00	3.25
a.		"CHMABA"	2,750.	4,000.
5	A28	2a6p green ('95)	52.50	150.00
6	A22	3a brn org	4.50	9.00
a.		3a orange	16.00	35.00
b.		Inverted overprint		
c.		"CHMABA"	7,500.	11,000.
7	A23	4a olive green	8.25	14.00
a.		"CHMABA"	2,400.	4,000.
8	A25	8a red violet	13.50	18.00
a.		"CHMABA"	6,000.	6,250.
9	A26	12a vio, red ('90)	10.50	24.00
a.		"CHMABA"	12,500.	
b.		1st "T" of "STATE" invtd.	12,500.	
10	A27	1r gray	72.50	225.00
a.		"CHMABA"	21,000.	
11	A29	1r car rose & grn ('95)	14.00	25.00
12	A30	2r brown & rose ('95)	150.00	600.00
13	A30	3r grn & brown ('95)	175.00	525.00
14	A30	5r vio & bl ('95)	190.00	825.00

Wmk. 38

15	A14	6a bister ('90)	8.25	32.50

Nos. 1-15 (15)   710.75   2,477.

1900   **Wmk. 39**

15B	A31	3p carmine rose	.90	1.40

1902-04

16	A31	3p gray ('04)	.90	3.25
a.		Inverted overprint	120.00	
17	A17	½a light green	1.00	2.50
18	A19	1a carmine rose	1.00	.60
19	A21	2a violet ('03)	16.00	52.50

Nos. 16-19 (4)   18.90   58.85

1903-05

20	A32	3p gray	.35	2.40
21	A33	½a green	1.20	.90
22	A34	1a carmine rose	2.40	1.40
23	A35	2a green	2.75	5.25
24	A37	3a brown org ('05)	7.00	9.00
25	A38	4a olive green ('04)	10.50	32.50
26	A39	6a bister ('05)	6.50	35.00
27	A40	8a red violet ('04)	9.00	35.00
28	A41	12a violet, red	12.00	47.50
29	A42	1r car rose & grn ('05)	11.00	35.00

Nos. 20-29 (10)   62.70   203.95

1907

30	A44	½a green	3.75	6.00
31	A45	1a carmine rose	3.75	6.00

1913-24

32	A46	3p gray	.60	1.90
33	A47	½a green	1.50	1.90
34	A48	1a carmine rose	15.00	17.50
35	A48	1a dark brown ('22)	5.25	8.25
36	A49	2a violet	6.00	17.50
37	A51	3a brown orange	7.00	13.00
38	A51	3a ultra ('24)	6.25	35.00
39	A52	4a olive green	6.00	8.25

40	A53	6a bister	6.50	11.00
41	A54	8a red violet	9.00	24.00
42	A55	12a claret	8.25	19.00
43	A56	1r green & red brown	27.50	47.50
		Nos. 32-43 (12)	98.85	204.80

India No. 104 Overprinted

1921

44	A48	9p on 1a rose	1.50	27.50

India Stamps of 1913-26 Overprinted

1922-27

45	A58	1½a chocolate	40.00	190.00
46	A59	1½a chocolate	3.75	9.50
47	A59	1½a rose	1.40	35.00
48	A57	2a6p ultramarine	.90	6.50
49	A57	2a6p brown orange	4.00	35.00
		Nos. 45-49 (5)	50.05	276.00

India Stamps of 1926 Overprinted

1927-28   Wmk. 196

50	A46	3p slate	.30	2.50
51	A47	½a green	.45	3.75
52	A48	1a dark brown	2.50	2.25
53	A60	2a dull violet	3.25	6.00
54	A51	3a ultramarine	1.90	32.50
55	A61	4a olive green	1.90	10.00
57	A54	8a red violet	2.40	17.50
58	A55	12a claret	2.40	24.00

Overprinted

59	A56	1r green & brown	17.50	45.00
		Nos. 50-55,57-59 (9)	32.60	143.50

India Stamps of 1926-35 Overprinted

1932-37

60	A71	½a green	1.60	16.00
61	A68	9p dark green	7.50	32.50
62	A72	1a dark brown	2.50	2.25
63	A69	1a3p violet	2.10	9.50
64	A59	1½a carmine rose	9.50	11.00
65	A49	2a vermilion	1.90	37.50
a.		Small die	175.00	210.00
66	A57	2a6p buff	5.00	30.00
67	A51	3a carmine rose	3.25	17.50
68	A52	4a olive green ('36)	8.25	25.00
69	A53	6a bister ('37)	45.00	250.00
		Nos. 60-69 (10)	86.60	431.25

Same Overprint on India Stamps of 1937

1938   Wmk. 196   Perf. 13½x14

70	A80	3p slate	14.00	32.50
71	A80	½a brown	2.00	21.00
72	A80	9p green	12.50	57.50
73	A80	1a carmine	2.50	5.50

Overprinted

74	A81	2a scarlet	10.00	24.00
75	A81	2a6p purple	11.00	47.50
76	A81	3a yellow green	11.50	42.50
77	A81	3a6p ultra	11.50	45.00
78	A81	4a dark brown	30.00	45.00
79	A81	6a peacock blue	32.50	100.00
80	A81	8a blue violet	30.00	97.50

81	A81	12a carmine lake	22.50	97.50

Overprinted

82	A82	1r brown & slate	45.00	110.00
83	A82	2r dk brn & dk vio	75.00	525.00
84	A82	5r dp ultra & dk green	120.00	700.00
85	A82	10r rose car & dk vio	190.00	1,100.
86	A82	15r dk grn & dk brown	200.00	1,500.
87	A82	25r dk vio & bl vio	290.00	1,600.
		Nos. 70-87 (18)	1,110.	6,150.
		Set, never hinged	1,300.	

India Nos. 151 and 153 Overprinted

1942

87B	A80	½a brown	62.50	67.50
		Never hinged	75.00	
88	A80	1a carmine	95.00	90.00
		Never hinged	110.00	

Same Ovpt. on India Stamps of 1941-42

1942-44

89	A83	3p slate	1.50	8.25
90	A83	½a rose violet ('43)	1.00	9.50
91	A83	9p lt green ('43)	1.40	30.00
92	A83	1a car rose ('43)	2.50	8.25
93	A84	1½a dk purple ('44)	3.00	21.00
94	A84	2a scarlet ('43)	11.00	24.00
95	A84	3a violet ('43)	26.00	72.50
96	A84	3½a ultra ('43)	14.00	67.50
97	A85	4a chocolate ('43)	19.00	75.00
98	A85	6a pck blue ('43)	21.00	62.50
99	A85	8a blue violet ('43)	22.50	75.00
100	A85	12a car lake ('43)	30.00	97.50
		Nos. 89-100 (12)	152.90	551.00
		Set, never hinged	200.00	

1943   Wmk. 196   Perf. 13½x14

101	A82	1r brown & slate	26.00	97.50
102	A82	2r dk brown & dk vio	30.00	400.00
103	A82	5r dp ultra & dk grn	55.00	450.00
104	A82	10r rose car & dk vio	85.00	700.00
105	A82	15r dk grn & dk brn	190.00	1,250.
106	A82	25r dk vio & bl vio	175.00	1,250.
		Nos. 101-106 (6)	561.00	4,147.
		Set, never hinged	850.00	

India No. 161A Overprinted

1947

107	A81	14a rose violet	17.50	4.50

OFFICIAL STAMPS

Indian Stamps Overprinted in Black

1887-98   Wmk. 39   Perf. 14

O1	A17	½a green	1.10	.20
a.		"CHMABA"	375.00	375.00
c.		"SERV CE"		
O2	A19	1a violet brown	3.75	2.25
a.		"CHMABA"	600.00	600.00
c.		"SERV CE"	5,250.	
d.		"SERVICE" double	3,000.	1,600.
O3	A21	2a ultra	4.50	3.00
a.		"CHMABA"	1,500.	3,250.
O4	A22	3a brown orange	3.75	19.00
a.		3a orange	4,500.	5,250.
b.		"CHMABA"		
O5	A23	4a olive green	5.50	12.00
a.		"CHMABA"	1,600.	3,250.
c.		"SERV CE"	6,000.	
O6	A25	8a red violet	5.50	4.50
a.		"CHMABA"	12,000.	12,000.
O7	A26	12a vio, red ('90)	15.00	72.50
a.		"CHMABA"	11,000.	
b.		1st "T" of "STATE" invtd.	10,000.	
O8	A27	1r gray ('90)	22.50	225.00
a.		"CHMABA"	7,500.	
O9	A29	1r car rose & grn ('98)	9.00	62.50

Wmk. 38

O10	A14	6a bister	7.50	22.50
		Nos. O1-O10 (10)	78.10	423.45

1902-04   Wmk. 39

O11	A31	3p gray ('04)	.90	1.20
O12	A17	½a light green	1.90	6.00
O13	A19	1a carmine rose	2.25	.90
O14	A21	2a violet ('03)	17.50	52.50
		Nos. O11-O14 (4)	22.55	60.60

1903-05

O15	A32	3p gray	.50	.20
O16	A33	½a green	.30	.20
O17	A34	1a carmine rose	1.90	.45
O18	A35	2a violet	1.90	2.25
O19	A38	4a olive green ('05)	5.25	30.00
O20	A40	8a red violet ('05)	12.50	30.00
O21	A42	1r car rose & grn ('05)	2.50	21.00
		Nos. O15-O21 (7)	24.85	84.10

1907

O22	A44	½a green	.60	1.10
a.		Inverted overprint	6,750.	8,250.
O23	A46	1a carmine rose	3.25	3.75

1913

O24	A49	2a violet	22.50	
O25	A52	4a olive green	20.00	

India No. 63 Overprinted

O26	A35	2a violet	60.00	

No. O26 was never placed in use.

India Stamps of 1911-29 Overprinted:

a   b

1913-25

O27	A46 (a)	3p gray	.30	.60
O28	A47 (a)	½a green	.30	.90
O29	A48 (a)	1a carmine rose	.30	.20
O30	A48 (a)	1a dk brown ('25)	6.50	1.00
O31	A49 (a)	2a violet ('14)	1.60	22.50
O32	A52 (a)	4a olive green	1.60	30.00
O33	A54 (a)	8a red violet	2.50	30.00
O34	A56 (b)	1r grn & red brn	8.25	47.50
		Nos. O27-O34 (8)	21.35	132.70

India No. O66 Overprinted

1921

O35	O6	9p on 1a rose	.20	12.50

India Stamps of 1926-35 Overprinted

1927-39   Wmk. 196

O36	A46	3p slate	.75	.60
O37	A47	½a green	.50	.20
O38	A68	9p dark green ('32)	6.00	16.00
O39	A48	1a dark brown	.30	.20
O40	A69	1a3p violet ('32)	9.00	1.50
O41	A60	2a dull violet	3.75	.90
O42	A61	4a olive green	2.25	4.00
O43	A54	8a red violet	12.00	16.00
O44	A55	12a claret	7.50	37.50

Overprinted

O45	A56	1r green & brown	22.50	72.50
O45A	A56	2r brn org & car rose ('39)	35.00	375.00
O45B	A56	5r dk vio & ultra ('39)	62.50	450.00
O45C	A56	10r car & grn ('39)	97.50	450.00
		Nos. O36-O45C (13)	259.55	1,424.

India Stamps of 1926-35 Overprinted

1935-36

O46	A71	½a green	8.25	.75
O47	A72	1a dark brown	8.00	.65
O48	A49	2a vermilion	8.25	1.90
a.		Small die	11.00	30.00
O49	A52	4a olive grn ('36)	12.00	11.00
		Nos. O46-O49 (4)	36.50	14.30

Same Overprint on India Stamps of 1937

1938   Perf. 13½x14

O50	A80	9p green	30.00	100.00
		Never hinged	37.50	
O51	A80	1a carmine	37.50	9.00
		Never hinged	45.00	

India Stamps of 1937 Overprinted

1940-41

O51A	A82	1r brn & sl ('41)	300.00	1,100.
O52	A82	2r dk brn & dk vio	52.50	600.00
O53	A82	5r dp ultra & dk grn	75.00	650.00
O54	A82	10r rose car & dk vio	105.00	1,200.
		Set, never hinged	625.00	

India Official Stamps of 1939-43 Overprinted

1941-46			**Wmk. 196**		
O55	O8	3p slate ('44)		.85	1.90
O56	O8	½a brown		37.50	5.50
O57	O8	½a dk rose vio ('44)		.85	5.50
O58	O8	9p green		8.75	17.50
O59	O8	1a carmine rose		1.25	4.50
O60	O8	1a3p bister ('46)		105.00	32.50
O61	O8	1½a dull pur ('46)		9.50	12.50
O62	O8	2a scarlet ('44)		9.50	12.50
O63	O8	2½a purple ('44)		5.50	35.00
O64	O8	4a dark brown ('44)		9.50	27.50
O65	O8	8a blue vio ('41)		21.00	100.00
		Nos. O55-O65 (11)		209.20	254.90
		Set, never hinged		250.00	

India Nos. 162-165 Overprinted

1944					
O66	A82	1r brown & slate		27.50	325.00
O67	A82	2r dk brn & dk vio		42.50	450.00
O68	A82	5r dp ultra & dk grn		80.00	650.00
O69	A82	10r rose car & dk vio		95.00	1,100.
		Nos. O66-O69 (4)		245.00	2,525.
		Set, never hinged		295.00	

FARIDKOT

fe-'rēd-ˌkōt

LOCATION — A State of India lying northeast of Nabha in the central Punjab.
AREA — 638 sq. mi.
POP. — 164,364
CAPITAL — Faridkot

Previous stamp issues are listed under Feudatory States. Stamps of Faridkot were superseded by those of India in 1901.

The varieties with small letters in the overprint are not listed as the letters are merely broken and not from another font.

India Stamps Overprinted in Black

1887-93		**Wmk. 39**		**Perf. 14**	
4	A17	½a green		3.75	2.50
a.		"ARIDKOT"			
b.		"FAR DKOT"		—	2,500.
5	A19	1a violet brown		2.25	3.75
6	A21	2a ultramarine		4.75	10.50
7	A22	3a orange		5.50	9.00
8	A23	4a olive green		12.50	27.50
a.		"ARIDKOT"		2,100.	
9	A25	8a red violet		22.50	67.50
a.		"ARIDKOT"		4,500.	
10	A27	1r gray		67.50	550.00
a.		"ARIDKOT"		5,250.	
11	A29	1r car rose & grn ('93)		60.00	175.00
		Wmk. 38			
12	A14	6a bister		3.00	27.50
a.		"ARIDKOT"		2,750.	
		Nos. 4-12 (9)		181.75	873.25

1900			**Wmk. Star. (39)**		
13	A31	3p car rose		2.25	67.50
14	A26	12a violet, red		67.50	625.00

OFFICIAL STAMPS

India Stamps Overprinted in Black

1886		**Wmk. 39**		**Perf. 14**	
O1	A17	½a green		.90	1.10
a.		"SERV CE"		3,750.	
b.		"FAR DKOT"		3,500.	
c.		"ESRVICE"		3,500.	
O2	A19	1a violet brown		1.50	3.00
a.		"SERV CE"		5,500.	
O3	A21	2a ultramarine		3.00	16.00
a.		"SERV CE"		5,500.	
O4	A22	3a orange		6.00	57.50
O5	A23	4a olive green		7.00	45.00
a.		"SERV CE"		4,750.	
O6	A25	8a red lilac		15.00	45.00
a.		"SERV CE"		4,500.	
O7	A27	1r gray		82.50	400.00
		Wmk. 38			
O8	A14	6a bister		37.50	42.50
a.		"ARIDKOT"		2,100.	
b.		"SERVIC"		4,500.	
		Nos. O1-O8 (8)		153.40	610.10

1896			**Wmk. 39**		
O9	A29	1r car rose & green		140.00	1,000.

Obsolete March 31, 1901.

GWALIOR

'gwäl-ē-ˌoˌәr

LOCATION — One of the Central Provinces of India
AREA — 26,008 sq. mi.
POP. — 4,006,159 (1941)
CAPITAL — Lashkar

The varieties with small letters in the overprint are not listed as the letters are merely broken and not from another font.

India Stamps Overprinted in Black

Lines Spaced 16-17mm

1885		**Wmk. 39**		**Perf. 14**	
1	A17	½a green		90.00	
2	A19	1a violet brown		97.50	
3	A20	1a6p bister brown		125.00	
4	A21	2a ultramarine		100.00	
5	A25	8a red lilac		110.00	
6	A27	1r gray		110.00	
		Wmk. 38			
7	A9	4a green		140.00	
8	A14	6a bister		140.00	
		Nos. 1-8 (8)		912.50	

The Hindi overprint measures 13½-14x2mm and 15-15½x2½mm.

The two sizes are found in the same sheet in the proportion of one of the smaller to three of the larger.

The ½a, 1a, 2a, also exist with lines 13mm apart and the short Hindi overprint.

Reprints of the ½a and 1a have the 13mm spacing, the short Hindi overprint and usually carry the overprint "Specimen."

India Stamps Overprinted

Red Overprint

1885			**Wmk. 39**		
9	A17	½a green		1.90	.25
10	A21	2a ultramarine		35.00	27.50
11	A27	1r gray		12.50	37.50
		Wmk. 38			
12	A9	4a green		42.50	24.00
		Nos. 9-12 (4)		91.90	89.25

Nos. 9-12 have been reprinted. They have the short Hindi overprint. Most stamps bear the word "Reprint." Those without it cannot be distinguished from the originals.

Black Overprint

1885-91			**Wmk. 39**		
13	A17	½a green		.75	.20
a.		"GWALICR"		125.00	150.00
b.		Double overprint			1,250.

14	A18	9p rose		47.50	82.50
15	A19	1a violet brown		3.00	.25
16	A20	1a6p bister brown		3.25	1.20
17	A21	2a ultramarine		4.00	.20
18	A22	3a orange		6.25	.20
19	A23	4a olive green		7.50	1.90
20	A25	8a red violet		7.50	1.90
21	A26	12a violet, red		5.00	1.00
22	A27	1r gray		6.50	3.75
		Wmk. 38			
23	A14	6a bister		5.25	12.50
		Nos. 13-23 (11)		96.50	105.60

The Hindi overprint measures 13½-14x2mm and 15-15½x2½mm as in the preceding issue.

1896			**Wmk. 39**		
24	A28	2a6p green		13.50	30.00
a.		"GWALICR"		1,000.	
25	A29	1r car rose & grn		9.50	8.25
a.		"GWALICR"		1,350.	2,100.
26	A30	2r bis brn & rose		8.25	4.50
27	A30	3r green & brown		11.00	5.25
28	A30	5r violet & blue		21.00	9.50
		Nos. 24-28 (5)		63.25	57.50

The Hindi inscription varies from 13 to 15½mm long.

1899					
29	A31	3p carmine rose		.75	.20
a.		Inverted overprint		1,650.	825.00

1901-04					
30	A31	3p gray ('04)		11.00	90.00
31	A17	½a light green		2.10	2.40
32	A19	1a carmine rose		1.90	.50
33	A21	2a violet		4.00	8.25
34	A28	2a6p ultra ('03)		2.25	9.50
		Nos. 30-34 (5)		21.25	110.65

1903-08					
35	A32	3p gray		2.10	.25
36	A33	½a green		2.25	.45
37	A34	1a carmine rose		.30	.20
38	A35	2a violet		3.00	1.50
39	A36	2a6p ultra ('05)		37.50	120.00
40	A37	3a brown org ('04)		3.00	.50
41	A38	4a olive green		3.75	.60
42	A39	6a bister ('06)		9.00	2.10
43	A40	8a red violet		7.50	2.40
44	A41	12a vio, red ('05)		4.50	30.00
45	A42	1r car rose & grn ('05)		4.50	2.50
46	A43	2r brown & rose		13.50	16.50
47	A43	3r grn & brn ('08)		42.50	75.00
48	A43	5r vio & bl ('08)		27.50	40.00
		Nos. 35-48 (14)		160.90	292.00

There are two settings of the overprint on Nos. 35, 37-46. In the first (1903), "GWALIOR" is 14mm long and lines are spaced 1¾mm. In the second (1908), "GWALIOR" is 13mm long and lines are 2¾mm apart. No. 36 exists only with first overprint, Nos. 47-48 only with second.

1907					
49	A44	½a green		.30	1.00
50	A45	1a carmine rose		2.25	.25

No. 49 exists with both settings of overprint. See note below No. 48.

1912-23					
51	A46	3p gray		.30	.20
52	A47	½a green		.30	.20
a.		Inverted overprint			600.00
53	A48	1a car rose		.35	.20
a.		Double overprint		37.50	
54	A48	1a dk brown ('23)		1.60	.20
55	A49	2a violet		1.20	.20
56	A51	3a brown orange		1.00	.20
57	A52	4a olive grn ('13)		.90	.90
58	A53	6a bister		1.90	2.10
59	A54	8a red vio ('13)		3.25	1.20
60	A55	12a claret ('14)		2.10	6.00
61	A56	1r green & red brn		13.50	.65
62	A56	2r brn & car rose		7.50	6.50
63	A56	5r violet & ultra		35.00	9.50
		Nos. 51-63 (13)		68.90	28.05

India No. 104 Overprinted

1921					
64	A48	9p on 1a rose		.20	.75
a.		Inverted overprint			

India Stamps of 1911-26 Overprinted

Hindi Overprint 15mm Long

1923-27					
66	A59	1½a choc ('25)		3.25	.75
67	A59	1½a rose ('27)		.30	.25
a.		Inverted overprint			
68	A57	2a6p ultra ('25)		3.25	2.50
69	A57	2a6p brown org ('27)		.50	.75
70	A51	3a ultra ('24)		3.75	.90
		Nos. 66-70 (5)		11.05	5.15

Similar Ovpt. on India Stamps of 1926-35

Hindi Overprint 13½mm Long

1928-32			**Wmk. 196**		
71	A46	3p slate ('32)		1.50	.20
72	A47	½a green ('30)		2.25	.20
73	A48	1a dark brown		1.25	.20
74	A60	2a dull violet		.80	.45
75	A51	3a ultramarine		1.50	.60
76	A61	4a olive green		1.90	1.50
77	A54	8a red violet		1.90	1.60
78	A55	12a claret		3.25	5.25

Overprinted

79	A56	1r green & brown		4.50	6.00
80	A56	2r brn org & car rose		8.00	6.50
81	A56	5r dk vio & ultra ('29)		27.50	37.50
82	A56	10r car & grn ('30)		97.50	62.50
83	A56	15r olive green & ultra ('30)		150.00	100.00
84	A56	25r bl & ocher ('30)		325.00	250.00
		Nos. 71-84 (14)		626.85	472.50

India Stamps of 1932-35 Overprinted in Black

Hindi Overprint 13½mm Long

1933-36					
85	A71	½a green ('36)		.75	.25
86	A68	9p dk green ('33)		4.50	.45
87	A72	1a dk brown ('36)		.30	.20
88	A69	1a3p violet ('36)		.75	.20
89	A49	2a vermilion ('36)		4.50	5.25
		Nos. 85-89 (5)		10.80	6.35

Same Ovpt. on India Stamps of 1937

1938-40			**Perf. 13½x14**		
90	A80	3p slate ('40)		12.00	.25
91	A80	½a brown		13.50	.20
92	A80	9p green ('40)		72.50	6.00
93	A80	1a carmine		12.50	.20
94	A81	3a yel green ('39)		42.50	7.50
95	A81	4a dark brown		67.50	.25
96	A81	6a pck blue ('39)		6.00	16.50
		Nos. 90-96 (7)		226.50	35.90
		Set, never hinged		225.00	

Same Overprinted on India Stamps of 1941-43

1942-49					
100	A83	3p slate ('44)		.55	.20
101	A83	½a rose vio ('46)		1.25	.20
102	A83	9p light green		.55	.20
103	A83	1a car rose ('44)		1.25	.20
104	A84	1½a dk purple ('44)		8.75	.25
105	A84	2a scarlet ('44)		1.90	.25
106	A84	3a violet ('44)		20.00	2.50
108	A85	4a choc ('44)		4.00	.25
109	A85	6a pck blue ('48)		17.50	40.00
110	A85	8a blue violet		4.75	4.00
111	A85	12a carmine lake		7.00	35.00

India Nos. 162-167 Overprinted

			Perf. 13½x14		
112	A82	1r brn & sl ('45)		15.00	2.50
113	A82	2r dk brn & dk vio ('49)		62.50	14.00
114	A82	5r dp ultra & dk grn ('49)		40.00	60.00
115	A82	10r rose car & dk vio ('49)		40.00	62.50

116 A82 15r dk grn & dk brn
('48) 110.00 *250.00*
117 A82 25r dk vio & blue
vio ('48) 110.00 *190.00*
Nos. 100-106,108-117 (17) 445.00 662.05
Set, never hinged 525.00

India Stamps of 1941-
43 Overprinted

1949
118 A83 3p slate 2.50 .75
119 A83 ½a rose violet 2.50 .75
120 A83 1a carmine rose 2.25 .90
121 A84 2a scarlet 32.50 3.25
122 A84 3a violet 80.00 45.00
123 A85 4a chocolate 9.25 5.00
124 A85 6a pck blue 67.50 97.50
125 A85 8a blue violet 140.00 82.50
126 A85 12a carmine lake 525.00 225.00
Nos. 118-126 (9) 861.50 460.65
Set, never hinged 1,050.

OFFICIAL STAMPS

India Stamps
Overprinted in Black

1895 Wmk. 39 Perf. 14
O1 A17 ½a green .75 .20
a. Double overprint 1,400.
O2 A19 1a maroon 18.00 2.10
O3 A21 2a ultramarine 5.00 .60
O4 A23 4a olive green 5.25 2.25
O5 A25 8a red violet 6.50 5.00
O6 A29 1r car rose & grn 12.50 4.50
Nos. O1-O6 (6) 48.00 14.65

Nos. O1 to O6 inclusive are known with the last two characters of the lower word transposed.

1901-04
O7 A31 3p gray ('04) 3.75 *5.25*
O8 A17 ½a light green 1.10 .20
O9 A19 1a carmine rose 9.00 .20
O10 A21 2a violet ('03) 2.50 2.25
Nos. O7-O10 (4) 16.35 7.90

1902
O11 A31 3p carmine rose 1.90 .35

1903-05
O12 A32 3p gray 1.00 .20
O13 A33 ½a green 4.50 .20
O14 A34 1a carmine rose 1.60 .20
O15 A35 2a violet 2.50 .45
O16 A38 4a olive grn ('05) 25.00 2.50
O17 A40 8a red violet 11.00 1.00
O18 A42 1r car rose & grn
('05) 4.00 3.00
Nos. O12-O18 (7) 49.60 7.55

1907
O19 A44 ½a green 2.50 .20
O20 A45 1a carmine rose 1.60 .20

Two spacings of the overprint lines, 10mm and 8mm, are found on Nos. O12-O20.

1913
O21 A46 3p gray .35 .20
O22 A47 ½a green .30 .20
O23 A48 1a carmine rose .45 .20
a. Double overprint 97.50
O24 A49 2a violet 2.25 .25
O25 A52 4a olive green .90 *2.25*
O26 A54 8a red violet 1.90 1.50
O27 A56 1r grn & red brn 40.00 35.00
Nos. O21-O27 (7) 46.15 39.60

India No. O66 Overprinted

1921
O28 O6 9p on 1a rose .20 *.45*

India No. 83
Overprinted

1923
O29 A481a dark brown 5.50 .20

Similar Ovpt. on India Stamps of 1926-35

1927-35 Wmk. 196
O30 A46 3p slate .30 .20
O31 A47 ½a green .30 .20
O32 A48 1a dark brown .30 .20
O33 A60 2a dull violet .30 .20
O34 A61 4a olive grn 1.00 .90
O35 A54 8a red violet .90 *1.60*

Overprinted

O36 A56 1r green & brown 1.50 *2.50*
O37 A56 2r brn org & car
rose ('32) 29.00 *30.00*
O38 A56 5r dk vio & ultra
('32) 35.00 *250.00*
O39 A56 10r car & grn ('32) 240.00 *650.00*
Nos. O30-O39 (10) 308.60 935.35

India Stamps of 1926-
35 Overprinted

1933-37 Perf. 13½x14, 14
O40 A71 ½a green ('36) .35 .25
O41 A68 9p dk green ('35) .30 .25
O42 A72 1a dk brown ('36) .30 .20
O43 A69 1a3p violet ('33) .75 .20
O44 A49 2a ver ('36) .30 *.60*
a. Small die ('36) 3.75 1.90
O45 A52 4a olive green ('37) .90 *1.10*
Nos. O40-O45 (6) 2.90 2.60

For surcharge see No. O62.

Same Overprint on India Stamps

1938 Perf. 13½x14
O46 A80 ½a brown 8.00 .45
Never hinged 9.50
O47 A80 1a carmine 2.00 .20
Never hinged 2.25

India Nos. 162-
165 Overprinted

1945-48 Wmk. 196 Perf. 13½x14
O48 A82 1r brown & slate 12.50 *32.50*
O49 A82 2r dk brn & dk
vio 22.50 *140.00*
O50 A82 5r dp ultra & dk
grn ('46) 37.50 *825.00*
O51 A82 10r rose car & dk
vio ('48) 100.00 *1,650.*
Nos. O48-O51 (4) 172.50 *2,647.*
Set, never hinged 200.00

India Official Stamps of
1939-43 Overprinted

1940-44 Wmk. 196 Perf. 13½x14
O52 O8 3p slate .65 .20
O53 O8 ½a brown 5.50 .35
O54 O8 ½a dk rose vio
('43) .75 .20
O55 O8 9p green ('43) .85 *1.00*
O56 O8 1a car rose ('41) 2.75 .20
O57 O8 1a3p bister ('42) 55.00 2.50
O58 O8 1½a dull purple
('43) 1.50 .45
O59 O8 2a scarlet ('41) 1.50 .45
O60 O8 4a dark brown
('44) 1.50 *5.00*
O61 O8 8a blue vio ('44) 6.00 *14.00*
Nos. O52-O61 (10) 76.00 24.35
Set, never hinged 95.00

Gwalior No. O43 with
Additional Surcharge in
Black

1942
O62 A69 1a on 1a3p violet 30.00 4.50
Never hinged 37.50

JIND

'jind

(Jhind)

LOCATION — A State of India in the north Punjab.
AREA — 1,299 sq. mi.
POP. — 361,812 (1941)
CAPITAL — Sangrur

Previous stamp issues are listed under Feudatory States.
The varieties with small letters are not listed as the letters are merely broken and not from another font.

India Stamps
Overprinted in Black

1885 Wmk. 39 Perf. 14
33 A17 ½a green 7.00 *8.25*
a. Overprint reading down 140.00 *160.00*
34 A19 1a violet
brown 62.50 *90.00*
a. Overprint reading down 1,400. *1,500.*
35 A21 2a ultra 29.00 *32.50*
a. Overprint reading down 1,000. *1,200.*
36 A25 8a red lilac 625.00
a. Overprint reading down 18,000.
37 A27 1r gray 700.00
a. Overprint reading down 21,000.
Wmk. 38
38 A9 4a green 97.50 *140.00*
Nos. 33-38 (6) 1,521. 270.75

On the reprints of Nos. 33 to 38 "Jhind" measures 8mm instead of 9mm and "State" 9mm instead of 9½mm.
Examples of "inverted overprints" exist of the ½a, 1a and 2a with the lines much less curved. These are thought to come from a trial printing.

India Stamps Overprinted in Red or
Black

1885 Wmk. 39
39 A17 ½a green (R) 210.00
40 A19 1a violet brown 210.00
41 A21 2a ultra (R) 210.00
42 A25 8a red lilac 290.00
43 A27 1r gray (R) 290.00
Wmk. 38
44 A9 4a green (R) 290.00
Nos. 39-44 (6) 1,500.

India Stamps Overprinted

1886 Wmk. 39
Red Overprint
45 A17 ½a green 52.50
a. "JEIND" 1,800.
46 A21 2a ultramarine 57.50
a. "JEIND" 1,800.

47 A27 1r gray 90.00
a. "JEIND" 2,750.
Wmk. 38
48 A9 4a green 90.00
Nos. 45-48 (4) 290.00

Nos. 46, 47 and 48 were not placed in use.

Black Overprint

1886-98 Wmk. 39
49 A17 ½a green ('88) 1.20 .20
a. Inverted overprint 300.00
50 A19 1a violet
brown 3.75 .25
a. "JEIND" 750.00
51 A20 1a6p bister brn
('97) 3.75 *5.50*
52 A21 2a ultra 3.75 .60
53 A22 3a orange 5.00 1.00
54 A23 4a olive green 6.00 3.25
55 A25 8a red violet 12.50 *30.00*
a. "JEIND" 2,400.
56 A26 12a vio, red
('97) 10.00 *37.50*
57 A27 1r gray ('91) 17.50 *82.50*
58 A29 1r car rose &
green
('98) 16.50 *90.00*
59 A30 2r brn & rose
('97) 525.00 *1,500.*
60 A30 3r grn & brn
('97) 750.00 *1,350.*
61 A30 5r vio & bl
('97) 750.00 *1,250.*
Wmk. 38
62 A14 6a bister 6.50 *21.00*
Nos. 49-62 (14) 2,111. *4,371.*

1900 Wmk. 39
63 A31 3p carmine rose 1.60 *2.50*

1902-04
64 A31 3p gray ('04) .60 *6.00*
65 A17 ½a light green 7.00 *10.00*
66 A19 1a carmine rose 1.90 *10.00*
Nos. 64-66 (3) 9.50 26.00

1903-09
67 A32 3p gray .35 .20
68 A33 ½a green 3.00 *2.50*
69 A34 1a car rose ('09) 3.25 *2.40*
70 A35 2a violet ('06) 5.00 *3.25*
70A A36 2a6p ultra ('09) 1.00 *10.00*
71 A37 3a brown orange 3.75 .60
a. Double overprint 175.00 *325.00*
72 A38 4a olive green 13.50 *14.00*
73 A39 6a bister ('05) 11.00 *32.50*
74 A40 8a red violet 4.50 *32.50*
75 A41 12a vio, red ('05) 5.00 *17.50*
76 A42 1r car rose &
grn ('05) 5.50 *32.50*
Nos. 67-76 (11) 55.85 147.95

1907
77 A44 ½a green .60 .25
78 A45 1a carmine rose 2.25 1.00

1913
80 A46 3p gray .30 *3.50*
81 A47 ½a green .30 *1.10*
82 A48 1a carmine rose .30 .65
83 A49 2a violet .30 *6.25*
84 A51 3a brown orange 2.25 *21.00*
85 A53 6a bister 12.50 *42.50*
Nos. 80-85 (6) 15.95 *75.00*

India Stamps of 1911-
26 Overprinted

1913-14
88 A46 3p gray 1.50 .20
89 A47 ½a green 3.75 .20
90 A48 1a carmine rose 2.40 .20
91 A49 2a violet 6.50 1.90
92 A51 3a brown orange .75 *6.00*
93 A52 4a olive green 3.00 *14.00*
94 A53 6a bister 6.00 *24.00*
95 A54 8a red violet 8.25 *24.00*
96 A55 12a claret 7.50 *30.00*
97 A56 1r grn & red brn 17.50 *35.00*
Nos. 88-97 (10) 57.15 *135.50*

India No. 104 Overprinted

1921
98 A48 9p on 1a rose 1.90 *22.50*

India Stamps of 1913-
19 Overprinted

1922
99	A58	1½a chocolate	5.00	9.00
100	A57	2a6p ultramarine	.75	7.00

Same Overprint on India Stamps of 1911-26

1924
101	A48	1a dark brown	9.00	4.50
102	A59	1½a chocolate	.75	2.25

Same Overprint on India No. 87

1925
103	A51	3a ultramarine	3.00	7.50

Same Overprint on India Stamps of 1911-26

1927
104	A59	1½a rose	.30	2.25
105	A57	2a6p brown orange	1.90	12.00
106	A56	2r yel brn & car rose	9.50	225.00
107	A56	5r violet & ultra	67.50	450.00
		Nos. 104-107 (4)	79.20	689.25

India Stamps of 1926-35 Overprinted

1927-32   **Wmk. 196**
108	A46	3p slate	.30	.20
109	A47	½a green	.30	.50
110	A68	9p dark green ('32)	3.25	.60
111	A48	1a dark brown	.30	.20
112	A69	1a3p violet ('32)	.35	.45
113	A59	1½a carmine rose	.90	5.50
114	A60	2a dull violet	5.00	.60
115	A57	2a6p buff	2.40	16.00
116	A51	3a ultramarine	9.50	27.50
117	A61	4a olive green	2.50	5.25
118	A54	8a red violet	9.00	3.25
119	A55	12a claret	12.00	32.50

Overprinted

120	A56	1r green & brown	7.50	9.00
121	A56	2r buff & car rose	62.50	225.00
122	A56	5r dk vio & ultra	19.00	62.50
123	A56	10r car rose & grn	22.50	27.50
124	A56	15r ol grn & blue	140.00	1,050.
125	A56	25r blue & ocher	225.00	1,250.
		Nos. 108-125 (18)	522.30	2,716.

India Stamps of 1926-35 Overprinted

1934-37
126	A71	½a green	.45	.35
127	A72	1a dark brown	3.00	.45
128	A49	2a vermilion	5.50	.90
129	A51	3a carmine rose	5.00	.60
130	A70	3a6p deep blue ('37)	3.75	30.00
131	A52	4a olive green	5.00	2.25
132	A53	6a bister ('37)	1.00	32.50
		Nos. 126-132 (7)	23.70	67.05

Same Overprint on India Stamps of 1937

1937-38   **Wmk. 196**   **Perf. 13½x14**
133	A80	3p slate ('38)	12.50	3.75
134	A80	½a brown ('38)	.95	7.50
135	A80	9p green	.95	6.00
136	A80	1a carmine	.95	.90
137	A81	2a scarlet ('38)	2.10	27.50
138	A81	2a6p purple ('38)	1.60	35.00
139	A81	3a yel grn ('38)	8.00	30.00
140	A81	3a6p ultra ('38)	5.00	35.00
141	A81	4a dk brown ('38)	12.00	27.50
142	A81	6a pck blue ('38)	7.50	42.50
143	A81	8a blue vio ('38)	6.25	35.00
144	A81	12a car lake ('38)	3.50	45.00

Overprinted

1938
145	A82	1r brown & slate	15.00	62.50
146	A82	2r dk brn & dk violet	19.00	190.00
147	A82	5r dp ultra & dk green	32.50	125.00
148	A82	10r rose car & dk violet	60.00	120.00
149	A82	15r dk grn & dk brown	125.00	1,200.
150	A82	25r dk vio & bl vio	690.00	1,400.
		Nos. 133-150 (18)	1,002.	3,393.
		Set, never hinged	1,200.	

India Stamps of 1937 Overprinted

1942-43   **Wmk. 196**   **Perf. 13½x14**
155	A80	3p slate	17.50	32.50
156	A80	½a brown	1.25	3.75
157	A80	9p green	16.00	30.00
158	A80	1a carmine	1.25	9.00
159	A82	1r brn & slate	11.00	40.00
160	A82	2r dk brn & dk violet	22.50	52.50
161	A82	5r dp ultra & dk green	50.00	140.00
162	A82	10r rose car & dk vio ('43)	75.00	140.00
163	A82	15r dk grn & dk brn ('43)	160.00	250.00
164	A82	25r dk vio & bl vio	75.00	525.00
		Nos. 155-164 (10)	429.50	1,222.
		Set, never hinged	510.00	

Same Overprint on India Stamps of 1941-43

165	A83	3p slate	.60	2.10
166	A83	½a rose vio ('43)	.60	3.25
167	A83	9p light green	.95	6.50
168	A83	1a car rose ('43)	1.25	2.25
169	A84	1a3p bister ('43)	1.25	7.50
170	A84	1½a dark purple	10.00	7.50
171	A84	2a scarlet	2.25	7.50
172	A84	3a violet ('43)	30.00	9.00
173	A84	3½a ultramarine	11.00	17.50
174	A85	4a chocolate	7.50	9.00
175	A85	6a peacock blue	8.00	25.00
176	A85	8a blue violet	5.25	22.50
177	A85	12a carmine lake	17.50	27.50
		Nos. 165-177 (13)	96.15	147.10
		Set, never hinged	115.00	

OFFICIAL STAMPS

India Stamps Overprinted in Black

1885   **Wmk. 39**   **Perf. 14**
O1	A17	½a green	3.00	.60
a.		"JHIND STATE" reading down	150.00	90.00
O2	A19	1a violet brown	1.00	.20
a.		"JHIND STATE" reading down	17.50	11.00
O3	A21	2a ultra	60.00	72.50
a.		"JHIND STATE" reading down	1,500.	1,750.
		Nos. O1-O3 (3)	64.00	73.30

The reprints may be distinguished by the same measurements as the reprints of the corresponding regular issue.

SERVICE

India Stamps Overprinted in Red or Black

JEEND STATE

1885
O4	A17	½a green (R)	150.00	
O5	A19	1a violet brown	125.00	
O6	A21	2a ultra (R)	140.00	
		Nos. O4-O6 (3)	415.00	

India Stamps Overprinted

1886

Red Overprint
O7	A17	½a green	42.50	
a.		"JEIND"	1,050.	
b.		"ERVICE"	6,000.	
O8	A21	2a ultramarine	47.50	
a.		"JEIND"	1,750.	
b.		"ERVICE"	3,750.	

No. O8 was not placed in use.

1886-96

Black Overprint
O9	A17	½a green ('88)	3.00	.25
O10	A19	1a violet brown	19.00	2.25
a.		"JEIND"	750.00	
b.		"ERVICE"		
O11	A21	2a ultramarine	5.00	1.50
O12	A23	4a olive green	5.25	3.00
O13	A25	8a red violet	8.25	12.50
O14	A29	1r car rose & grn ('96)	9.50	75.00
		Nos. O9-O14 (6)	50.00	94.50

1902
O15	A17	½a light green	3.75	.45

1903-06
O16	A32	3p gray	1.00	.20
O17	A33	½a green	5.25	.20
a.		"HIND"	4,500.	450.00
O18	A34	1a carmine rose	4.50	.20
a.		"HIND"	5,250.	400.00
O19	A35	2a violet	3.00	.20
O20	A38	4a olive green	2.50	.65
O21	A40	8a red violet	9.00	2.25
O22	A42	1r car rose & grn ('06)	3.75	3.25
		Nos. O16-O22 (7)	29.00	6.95

1907
O23	A44	½a green	1.50	.20
O24	A45	1a carmine rose	2.50	.20

Indian Stamps of 1911-26 Overprinted

a	b

1914-27
O25	A46(a)	3p gray	.30	.20
O26	A47(a)	½a green	.40	.20
O27	A48(a)	1a car rose	1.00	.20
O28	A49(a)	2a violet	.35	.45
O29	A52(a)	4a olive green	1.90	.25
O30	A54(a)	8a red violet	1.00	1.50
O31	A56(b)	1r grn & red brn	3.75	2.50
O32	A56(b)	2r yel brn & car rose ('27)	27.50	100.00
O33	A56(b)	5r vio & ultra ('27)	35.00	375.00
		Nos. O25-O33 (9)	71.20	480.30

India Nos. 83 and 89 Overprinted Type "a"

1924-27
O34	A48	1a dark brown	.90	.20
O35	A53	6a bister ('27)	2.50	3.25

India Stamps of 1926-35 Overprinted

c

1927-32
O36	A46	3p slate	.20	.20
O37	A47	½a green	.20	1.50
O38	A68	9p dark green ('32)	.90	.20

O39	A48	1a dark brown	.20	.20
O40	A69	1a3p violet ('32)	.60	.25
O41	A60	2a dull violet	.35	.20
O42	A61	4a olive green	.50	.35
O43	A54	8a red violet	.90	2.50
O44	A55	12a claret	3.25	27.50

Overprinted

d

O45	A56	1r green & brown	7.50	8.25
O46	A56	2r buff & car rose	75.00	62.50
O47	A56	5r dk vio & ultra	19.00	400.00
O48	A56	10r car rose & grn	57.50	225.00
		Nos. O36-O48 (13)	166.10	728.65

India Stamps of 1926-35 Overprinted Type "c"

1934-37
O49	A71	½a green	.30	.20
O50	A72	1a dark brown	.30	.20
O51	A49	2a vermilion	.45	.20
O52	A57	2a6p buff ('37)	1.90	30.00
O53	A52	4a olive green	9.00	.45
O54	A53	6a bister ('37)	5.50	25.00
		Nos. O49-O54 (6)	17.45	56.05

India Nos. 151-153 Overprinted Type "c"

1937-42   **Perf. 13½x14**
O55	A80	½a brown ('42)	80.00	.45
O56	A80	9p green	3.00	24.00
O57	A80	1a carmine	2.25	.45

India Nos. 162-165 Overprinted Type "d"

O58	A82	1r brn & sl ('40)	52.50	67.50
O59	A82	2r dk brn & dk vio ('40)	55.00	375.00
O60	A82	5r dp ultra & dk grn ('40)	120.00	600.00
O61	A82	10r rose car & dk vio ('40)	525.00	1,500.
		Nos. O55-O61 (7)	837.75	2,567.
		Set, never hinged	875.00	

India Official Stamps of 1939-43 Overprinted

1940-43
O62	O8	3p slate	.75	3.00
O63	O8	½a brown	2.50	1.90
O64	O8	½a dk rose vio ('43)	.75	.45
O65	O8	9p green	3.75	19.00
O66	O8	1a car rose	4.50	.20
O67	O8	1½a dull pur ('43)	11.00	2.40
O68	O8	2a scarlet	10.00	.45
O69	O8	2½a purple	6.25	14.00
O70	O8	4a dark brown	11.00	7.00
O71	O8	8a blue violet	11.00	12.00

India Nos. 162-165 Overprinted

1942   **Wmk. 196**   **Perf. 13½x14**
O72	A82	1r brn & slate	22.50	82.50
O73	A82	2r dk brn & dk violet	52.50	250.00
O74	A82	5r dp ultra & dk green	87.50	625.00
O75	A82	10r rose car & dk violet	175.00	825.00
		Nos. O62-O75 (14)	399.00	1,842.
		Set, never hinged	500.00	

NABHA

'näb-hə

LOCATION — A State of India in the eastern and southeastern Punjab
AREA — 966 sq. mi.
POP. — 340,044 (1941)
CAPITAL — Nabha

The varieties with small letters in the overprint are not listed as the letters are merely broken and not from another font.

Indian Stamps Overprinted in Black

1885   **Wmk. 39**   *Perf. 14*

1	A17	½a green	6.25	9.00
2	A19	1a violet brown	82.50	290.00
3	A21	2a ultramarine	37.50	97.50
4	A25	8a red lilac	475.00	
5	A27	1r gray	550.00	

Wmk. 38

6	A9	4a green	125.00	375.00

On the reprints "Nabha" and "State" each measure 9½mm. On the originals they measure 11 and 10mm respectively.

Indian Stamps Overprinted

Red Overprint

1885   **Wmk. 39**

7	A17	½a green	1.90	1.50
8	A21	2a ultramarine	3.75	3.25
9	A27	1r gray	190.00	450.00

Wmk. 38

10	A9	4a green	67.50	325.00

Black Overprint

1885-97   **Wmk. 39**

11	A17	½a green	.90	.20
12	A18	9p rose ('92)	.30	5.25
13	A19	1a violet brown	4.50	1.50
14	A20	1a6p bister brn	2.50	6.00
a.		"ABHA"	450.00	
15	A21	2a ultramarine	4.50	3.00
16	A22	3a orange	16.00	32.50
17	A23	4a olive green	9.00	5.00
18	A25	8a red lilac	6.00	5.25
19	A26	12a vio, red ('89)	7.00	8.25
20	A27	1r gray	22.50	90.00
21	A29	1r car rose & grn ('93)	21.00	10.50
a.		"N BHA"	210.00	—
22	A30	2r brn & rose ('97)	210.00	450.00
23	A30	3r grn & brn ('97)	210.00	550.00
24	A30	5r vio & blk ('97)	225.00	825.00

Wmk. 38

25	A14	6a bister ('89)	5.50	6.50
		Nos. 11-25 (15)	744.70	1,998.

Nos. 7, 8, 9, 10, 13, and 18 have been reprinted. They usually bear the overprint "Specimen."

1900   **Wmk. 39**

26	A31	3p carmine rose	.45	.20

1903-09

27	A32	3p gray	1.10	.20
28	A33	½a green	1.60	1.00
a.		"NABH"	1,650.	
29	A34	1a car rose	2.50	2.25
30	A35	2a violet	3.75	5.25
30A	A36	2a6p ultra	29.00	130.00
31	A37	3a brown orange	2.40	.60
32	A38	4a olive green	7.00	2.50
33	A39	6a bister	6.00	30.00
34	A40	8a red violet	15.00	40.00
35	A41	12a violet, red	6.50	40.00
36	A42	1r car rose & grn	14.00	27.50
		Nos. 27-36 (11)	88.85	279.30

1907

37	A44	½a green	2.25	1.90
38	A45	1a carmine rose	2.25	1.00

1913

40	A46	3p gray	.75	.75
41	A47	½a green	.75	.45
42	A48	1a carmine rose	1.60	.20
43	A49	2a violet	1.50	1.50

44	A51	3a brown orange	.75	.45
45	A52	4a olive green	1.00	3.00
46	A53	6a bister	1.90	9.50
47	A54	8a red violet	9.50	9.00
48	A55	12a claret	4.50	35.00
49	A56	1r green & red brn	15.00	11.00
		Nos. 40-49 (10)	37.25	70.85

1924

50	A48	1a dark brown	10.00	6.00

India Stamps of 1926-35 Overprinted

1927-32   **Wmk. 196**

51	A46	3p slate ('32)	2.50	.20
52	A47	½a green	1.50	.45
53	A48	1a dark brown	2.25	.20
54	A60	2a dull violet ('32)	3.75	.50
55	A57	2a6p buff ('32)	1.75	14.00
56	A51	3a blue ('30)	4.50	2.10
57	A61	4a olive green ('32)	6.75	3.75

Overprinted

58	A56	2r brown org & car rose ('32)	47.50	210.00
59	A56	5r dk violet & ultra ('32)	110.00	600.00
		Nos. 51-59 (9)	180.50	831.20

India Stamps of 1926-35 Overprinted

1936-37

63	A71	½a green	.75	.60
64	A68	9p dark green ('37)	3.00	1.60
65	A72	1a dark brown	.75	.45
66	A69	1a3p violet ('37)	3.50	11.00
67	A51	3a car rose ('37)	5.00	25.00
68	A52	4a olive green ('37)	7.50	7.50
		Nos. 63-68 (6)	20.50	46.15
		Set, never hinged	25.00	

Same Overprint in Black on 1937 Stamps of India

1938-39   *Perf. 13½x14*

69	A80	3p slate	11.00	2.25
70	A80	½a brown	8.75	2.50
71	A80	9p green	25.00	7.50
72	A80	1a carmine	3.75	1.50
73	A81	2a scarlet	1.50	12.00
74	A81	2a6p purple	1.50	17.50
75	A81	3a yel green	1.75	9.00
76	A81	3a6p ultramarine	2.00	37.50
77	A81	4a dark brown	9.50	10.50
78	A81	6a peacock blue	4.00	40.00
79	A81	8a blue violet	2.75	37.50
80	A81	12a car lake	3.00	37.50

Overprinted

81	A82	1r brown & slate	15.00	52.50
82	A82	2r dk brn & dk vio	37.50	175.00
83	A82	5r dp ultra & dk green	50.00	300.00
84	A82	10r rose car & dk vio ('39)	75.00	600.00
85	A82	15r dk grn & dk vio ('39)	240.00	1,250.
86	A82	25r dk vio & blue vio ('39)	175.00	1,250.
		Nos. 69-86 (18)	667.00	3,842.
		Set, never hinged	1,200.	

India Stamps of 1937 Overprinted in Black

1942   *Perf. 13½x14*

87	A80	3p slate	50.00	9.00
88	A80	½a brown	100.00	10.50
89	A80	9p green	14.00	24.00
90	A80	1a carmine	15.00	6.50
		Nos. 87-90 (4)	179.00	50.00
		Set, never hinged	210.00	

Same on India Nos. 168-179

1942-46   **Wmk. 196**

100	A83	3p slate	1.50	1.50
101	A83	½a rose vio ('43)	3.75	2.50
102	A83	9p lt green ('43)	3.00	2.50
103	A83	1a car rose ('46)	1.25	6.50
104	A84	1a3p bister ('44)	1.25	5.50
105	A84	1½a dark pur ('43)	3.00	4.50
106	A84	2a scarlet ('44)	1.40	6.50
107	A84	3a violet ('44)	8.00	8.00
108	A84	3½a ultramarine ('44)	21.00	100.00
109	A85	4a choc ('43)	2.25	1.50
110	A85	6a pck blue ('44)	17.50	82.50
111	A85	8a blue vio ('44)	16.00	62.50
112	A85	12a car lake ('44)	14.00	100.00
		Nos. 100-112 (13)	93.90	384.00
		Set, never hinged	110.00	

OFFICIAL STAMPS

Indian Stamps Overprinted in Black

1885   **Wmk. 39**   *Perf. 14*

O1	A17	½a green	7.50	2.25
O2	A19	1a violet brown	1.00	.30
O3	A21	2a ultra	125.00	250.00
		Nos. O1-O3 (3)	133.50	252.55

The reprints have the same measurements as the reprints of the regular issue of the same date.

Indian Stamps Overprinted

1885

Red Overprint

O4	A17	½a green	11.00	8.25
O5	A21	2a ultramarine	2.40	.80

1885-97

Black Overprint

O6	A17	½a green	.60	.20
a.		Period after "SERVICE"	190.00	3.25
O7	A19	1a violet brown	3.00	.35
a.		"NABHA STATE" double	2,750.	375.00
b.		Period after "SERVICE"	13.50	1.10
O8	A21	2a ultra	5.00	2.50
O9	A22	3a orange	37.50	140.00
O10	A23	4a olive green	5.25	2.25
O11	A25	8a red vio ('89)	4.00	2.25
O12	A26	12a vio, red ('89)	9.50	32.50
O13	A27	1r gray ('89)	62.50	525.00
O14	A29	1r car rose & grn ('97)	24.00	35.00

Wmk. 38

O15	A14	6a bister ('89)	32.50	52.50
		Nos. O6-O15 (10)	183.85	792.55

Nos. O4, O5, and O7 have been reprinted. They usually bear the overprint "Specimen."

1903-06   **Wmk. 39**

O16	A32	3p gray ('06)	3.75	25.00
O17	A33	½a green	1.20	.50
O18	A34	1a carmine rose	1.20	.20
O19	A35	2a violet	5.00	2.10
O20	A38	4a olive green	2.40	.75
O21	A40	8a red violet	2.50	2.25
O22	A42	1r car rose & grn	2.50	3.75
		Nos. O16-O22 (7)	18.55	34.55

1907

O23	A44	½a green	2.50	.75
O24	A45	1a carmine rose	1.00	.40

1913

O25	A52	4a olive green	17.50	100.00
O26	A56	1r grn & red brn	92.50	750.00

Indian Stamps of 1911-26 Overprinted:

     a   b

1913

O27	A46(a)	3p gray	1.60	15.00
O28	A47(a)	½a green	1.00	.20
O29	A48(a)	1a carmine rose	.90	.20
O30	A49(a)	2a violet	1.90	.20
O31	A52(a)	4a olive green	1.50	.90
O32	A54(a)	8a red violet	2.50	3.00
O33	A56(b)	1r grn & red brn	10.00	6.50
		Nos. O27-O33 (7)	19.40	26.00

India Stamps of 1926-35 Overprinted

Perf. 13½x14, 14

1932-45   **Wmk. 196**

O34	A46	3p slate	.30	.20
O35	A72	1a dark brown ('35)	.30	.20
O36	A52	4a olive green ('45)	35.00	3.75
O37	A54	8a red violet ('37)	1.50	4.00
		Nos. O34-O37 (4)	37.10	8.15

Same Overprint in Black on India Stamps of 1937

1938

O38	A80	9p green	6.00	6.00
		Never hinged	7.00	
O39	A80	1a carmine	22.50	1.60
		Never hinged	27.50	

Official Stamps of India 1939-43 Overprinted in Black

1942-44   *Perf. 13½x14*

O40	O8	3p slate	1.50	3.00
O41	O8	½a brown ('43)	1.40	.45
O42	O8	½a dk rose vio ('44)	5.50	2.25
O43	O8	9p green ('43)	1.50	.45
O44	O8	1a car rose ('43)	.75	.25
O45	O8	1½a dull purple ('43)	.85	.60
O46	O8	2a scarlet ('43)	2.75	2.25
O47	O8	4a dark brown ('43)	4.25	5.25
O48	O8	8a blue violet ('43)	6.75	30.00

India Nos. 162-164 Overprinted in Black

O49	A82	1r brown & slate	10.50	62.50
O50	A82	2r brn & dk vio	37.50	275.00
O51	A82	5r dp ultra & dk green	210.00	825.00
		Nos. O40-O51 (12)	283.25	1,207.
		Set, never hinged	350.00	

PATIALA

,pət-ē-'äl-ə

LOCATION — A State of India in the central Punjab

AREA — 5,942 sq. mi.
POP. — 1,936,259 (1941)
CAPITAL — Patiala

The varieties with small letters in the overprint are not listed as the letters are merely broken and not from another font.

Indian Stamps Overprinted in Red

1884		**Wmk. 39**		**Perf. 14**
1	A17	½a green	6.00	7.00
a.		Double ovpt., one horiz.	4,750.	1,200.
2	A19	1a violet brown	75.00	110.00
a.		Double overprint		
b.		Double ovpt., one in black	1,050.	
c.		Pair, one as "b," one without overprint		
3	A21	2a ultra	19.00	24.00
4	A25	8a red lilac	650.00	1,600.
a.		Double ovpt., one in black	190.00	650.00
c.		Overprint reversed		
d.		Pair like "a," one with overprint reversed		
5	A27	1r gray	225.00	950.00
		Wmk. 38		
6	A9	4a green	140.00	150.00
		Nos. 1-6 (6)	1,115.	2,841.

Indian Stamps Overprinted in Red

1885		**Wmk. 39**		
7	A17	½a green	3.25	.45
a.		"AUTTIALLA"	24.00	52.50
c.		"STATE" only		
8	A21	2a ultra	9.00	2.50
a.		"AUTTIALLA"	62.50	
9	A27	1r gray	24.00	125.00
a.		"AUTTIALLA"	650.00	
		Wmk. 38		
10	A9	4a green	6.00	6.25
a.		Double overprint, one in black	375.00	
b.		Pair, one as "a," one with black overprint		

Same, Overprinted in Black
Wmk. 39

11	A19	1a violet brown	.90	.45
a.		"AUTTIALLA"	100.00	
c.		Double overprint, one in red	17.50	140.00
d.		Pair, one as "c," one without overprint		
12	A25	8a red lilac	35.00	82.50
a.		"AUTTIALLA"	550.00	
		Nos. 7-12 (6)	78.15	217.15

Nos. 7-12 have been reprinted. Most of them bear the word "Reprint." The few stamps that escaped the overprint cannot be distinguished from the originals.

The error "AUTTIALLA" has been reprinted in entire sheets, in red on the ½, 2, 4a and 1r and in black on the ½, 1, 2, 4, 8a and 1r. "STATE" is 7¾mm long, instead of 8½mm. Most stamps are overprinted "Reprint."

Same, Overprinted in Black

1891-96				
13	A17	½a green	.75	.20
14	A18	9p rose	1.50	3.25
15	A19	1a violet brown	2.10	.45
a.		"STATE" only	300.00	625.00
16	A20	1a6p bister brown	2.10	3.00
17	A21	2a ultra	3.25	1.50
18	A22	3a orange	3.75	1.10
19	A23	4a olive grn ('96)	3.75	1.10
a.		"STATE" only	750.00	375.00
20	A25	8a red violet ('96)	5.50	24.00
21	A26	12a violet, red ('96)	3.75	24.00
22	A29	1r car rose & grn ('96)	6.50	82.50
23	A30	2r brn & rose ('95)	210.00	1,250.
24	A30	3r grn & brn ('95)	290.00	1,350.
25	A30	5r vio & bl ('95)	325.00	1,400.

		Wmk. 38		
26	A14	6a bister	3.75	22.50
		Nos. 13-26 (14)	861.70	4,163.
1899			**Wmk. 39**	
27	A31	3p carmine rose	.45	.20
a.		Pair, one without overprint	6,000.	
1902				
28	A17	½a light green	1.50	.90
29	A19	1a carmine rose	3.75	2.50
1903-06				
31	A32	3p gray	.60	.20
32	A33	½a green	1.60	.20
33	A34	1a carmine rose	2.10	.20
a.		Pair, one without overprint	1,500.	
34	A35	2a violet	2.40	1.00
35	A37	3a brown orange	2.40	.50
36	A38	4a olive green ('06)	4.00	2.25
37	A39	6a bister ('05)	5.00	15.00
38	A40	8a red violet ('06)	5.50	4.50
39	A41	12a vio, red ('06)	11.00	40.00
40	A42	1r car rose & grn ('05)	6.50	9.00
		Nos. 31-40 (10)	41.10	72.85
1908				
41	A44	½a green	.60	.35
42	A45	1a carmine rose	2.50	1.50
1912-14				
43	A46	3p gray	.35	.20
44	A47	½a green	1.00	.25
45	A48	1a carmine rose	2.40	.25
46	A49	2a violet	2.25	2.25
47	A51	3a brown orange	3.75	2.50
48	A52	4a olive green	5.25	5.25
49	A53	6a bister	3.00	6.50
50	A54	8a red violet	4.50	4.50
51	A55	12a claret	5.50	15.00
52	A56	1r green & red brn	14.00	22.50
		Nos. 43-52 (10)	42.00	59.20
1922-26				
53	A48	1a dk brown ('23)	4.00	.75
54	A58	1½a chocolate	.40	.85
55	A51	3a ultra ('26)	5.00	14.00
56	A56	2r yel brn & car rose ('26)	21.00	225.00
57	A56	5r vio & ultra ('26)	52.50	300.00
		Nos. 53-57 (5)	82.90	540.60

India Stamps of 1926-35 Overprinted

1928-34			**Wmk. 196**	
60	A46	3p slate	3.00	.20
61	A47	½a green	.35	.20
62	A68	9p dark green	3.25	1.50
63	A48	1a dark brown	1.10	.35
64	A69	1a3p violet	4.50	.20
65	A60	2a dull violet	2.50	.60
66	A57	2a6p buff	7.00	4.00
67	A51	3a blue	4.50	4.00
68	A61	4a olive green	7.50	3.00
69	A54	8a red violet	10.50	6.00

Overprinted

70	A56	1r green & brown	10.50	15.00
71	A56	2r buff & car rose	16.00	82.50
		Nos. 60-71 (12)	70.70	117.55

India Stamps of 1926-35 Overprinted Like Nos. 60-69

1935-37			**Perf. 14**	
75	A71	½a green ('37)	1.00	.45
76	A72	1a dk brown ('36)	1.40	.25
77	A49	2a ver ('36)	.50	2.25
78	A51	3a car rose ('37)	7.00	8.00
79	A52	4a olive green	2.25	3.50
		Nos. 75-79 (5)	12.15	14.45
		Set, never hinged	29.00	

Same Overprint in Black on Stamps of India, 1937

1937-38			**Perf. 13½x14**	
80	A80	3p slate ('38)	25.00	.50
81	A80	½a brown ('38)	10.00	.75
82	A80	9p green	6.25	1.50
83	A80	1a carmine	3.50	.25
84	A81	2a scarlet ('38)	1.90	14.00
85	A81	2a6p purple ('38)	7.00	30.00

86	A81	3a yel green ('38)	7.50	13.50
87	A81	3a6p ultra ('38)	8.00	37.50
88	A81	4a dark brown ('38)	29.00	25.00
89	A81	6a pck blue ('38)	30.00	90.00
90	A81	8a blue violet ('38)	32.50	62.50
91	A81	12a car lake ('38)	30.00	105.00

Overprinted Like Nos. 70-71

1938				
92	A82	1r brown & slate	35.00	62.50
93	A82	2r dk brn & dk vio	35.00	160.00
94	A82	5r dp ultra & dk green	47.50	375.00
95	A82	10r rose car & dk vio	62.50	600.00
96	A82	15r dk grn & dk brn	150.00	950.00
97	A82	25r dk vio & bl vio	175.00	950.00
		Nos. 80-97 (18)	695.65	3,478.
		Set, never hinged	850.00	

India Nos. 150-153 Overprinted in Black

1942-43			**Perf. 13½x14**	
98	A80	3p slate	13.50	4.00
99	A80	½a brown ('43)	8.00	3.25
100	A80	9p green ('43)	375.00	12.00
101	A80	1a carmine	30.00	3.75
		Nos. 98-101 (4)	426.50	23.00
		Set, never hinged	515.00	

India Stamps of 1941-43 with same Overprint in Black

1942-47			**Perf. 13½x14**	
102	A83	3p slate	5.00	.20
103	A83	½a rose violet ('43)	5.00	.20
104	A83	9p lt green ('43)	1.90	.20
a.		Pair, one without overprint	4,750.	
105	A83	1a car rose ('46)	1.25	.20
106	A84	1a3p bister ('43)	2.00	5.25
107	A84	1½a dk purple ('43)	16.00	5.50
108	A84	2a scarlet ('46)	11.00	.75
109	A84	3a violet ('46)	10.00	3.75
110	A84	3½a ultra ('46)	24.00	57.50
111	A85	4a choc ('46)	11.00	6.50
112	A85	6a pck blue ('46)	4.25	45.00
113	A85	8a blue vio ('46)	3.75	22.50
114	A85	12a car lake ('45)	30.00	125.00

No. 102 India No. 162 Overprinted in Black

115	A82	1r brown & slate ('47)	19.00	120.00
		Nos. 102-115 (14)	144.15	392.55
		Set, never hinged	170.00	

OFFICIAL STAMPS

Indian Stamps Overprinted in Black and Red

1884			**Wmk. 39**	**Perf. 14**
O1	A17	½a green	27.50	.60
O2	A19	1a vio brown	1.50	.20
a.		"SERVICE" double	3,000.	950.00
b.		"SERVICE" inverted		2,500.
c.		"PUTTIALLA STATE" dbl.		175.00
d.		"PUTTIALLA STATE" invtd.	3,000.	400.00
O3	A21	2a ultra	7,500.	175.00

Same, Overprinted in Red or Black:

     a   b

1885-90				
O4	A17(a)	½a green (R & Bk)	2.25	.35
a.		"AUTTIALLA"	80.00	25.00
d.		"SERVICE" double		1,050.
O5	A17(b)	½a green (Bk)	2.25	.20
O6	A19(a)	1a vio brn (Bk)	2.25	.20
a.		"AUTTIALLA"	1,050.	72.50
c.		"SERVICE" dble., one invtd.		900.00
d.		"SERVICE" inverted	3,000.	
O7	A21(b)	2a ultra (R)	1.10	.60
c.		"SERVICE" dbl., one invtd.	45.00	290.00
		Nos. O4-O7 (4)	7.85	1.35

There are reprints of Nos. O4, O6 and O7. That of No. O4 has "SERVICE" overprinted in red in large letters and that of No. O6 has the same overprint in black. The originals have the word in small black letters. The reprints of No. O7, except those overprinted "Reprint," cannot be distinguished from the originals. These three reprints also exist with the error "AUTTIALLA."

Same, Overprinted in Black

1891-1900				
O8	A17	½a green ('95)	.75	.20
b.		"SERVICE" inverted	90.00	
O9	A19	1a vio brown ('00)	9.00	.20
a.		"SERVICE" inverted	90.00	
O10	A21	2a ultramarine	5.00	3.25
a.		"SERVICE" inverted	90.00	300.00
O11	A22	3a orange	3.75	5.00
O12	A23	4a olive green	3.00	.45
O13	A25	8a red violet	5.25	2.50
O14	A26	12a violet, red	3.50	.80
O15	A27	1r gray	3.75	1.00
		Wmk. 38		
O16	A14	6a bister	2.40	.50
		Nos. O8-O16 (9)	36.40	13.90
1902			**Wmk. 39**	
O17	A19	1a carmine rose	1.40	.20
1903				
O18	A29	1r car rose & green	9.00	15.00
1903-09				
O19	A32	3p gray	.60	.20
O20	A33	½a green	1.50	.20
O21	A34	1a carmine rose	.90	.20
O22	A35	2a violet	1.20	.20
O23	A37	3a brown orange	6.00	5.25
O24	A38	4a olive green ('05)	4.00	.25
O25	A40	8a red violet	2.50	1.10
O26	A42	1r car rose & grn ('06)	3.00	1.20
		Nos. O19-O26 (8)	19.70	8.60
1907				
O27	A44	½a green	.75	.25
O28	A45	1a carmine rose	.90	.20

India Stamps of 1911-26 Overprinted:

     a   b

1913-26				
O29	A46(a)	3p gray	.30	.25
O30	A47(a)	½a green	.20	.20
O31	A48(a)	1a car rose	.20	.20
O32	A49(a)	2a violet	1.40	1.10
O33	A52(a)	4a olive green	.75	.50
O34	A54(a)	8a red violet	.80	1.00
O35	A56(b)	1r grn & red brn	2.10	2.10
O36	A56(b)	2r yel brn & car rose ('26)	27.50	75.00

O37 A56(b) 5r vio & ultra
('26)   17.50 *35.00*
Nos. O29-O37 (9)   50.75 *115.35*

Same Overprint on India Nos. 83 and 89

1925-26
O38 A48(a) 1a dark brown   11.00 1.50
O39 A53(a) 6a bister ('26)   2.50 3.75

India Stamps of 1926-35 Overprinted

1927-36   **Wmk. 196**
O40 A46 3p slate   .20   .20
O41 A47 ½a green   1.50   .80
O42 A48 1a dark brown   .20   .20
O43 A69 1a3p violet   .60   .20
O44 A60 2a dull violet   .25   .45
O45 A60 2a vermilion   .45   .50
O46 A57 2a6p buff   4.50   .50
O47 A61 4a olive green   .75   .45
O48 A54 8a red violet   1.90 1.00

Overprinted

O49 A56 1r green & brown   7.50 5.00
O50 A56 2r brn org & car rose
('36)   24.00 62.50
Nos. O40-O50 (11)   41.85 71.80

India Stamps of 1926-34 Overprinted

1935-36
O51 A71 ½a green ('36)   .20   .20
O52 A72 1a dark brown ('36)   .45   .45
O53 A49 2a vermilion   .30   .45
  a. Small die   21.00 7.50
O54 A52 4a olive green ('36) 3.50 2.50
Nos. O51-O54 (4)   4.45 3.60
Set, never hinged   5.00

Same Overprint on India #151-153
1938-39   **Perf. 13½x14**
O55 A80 ½a brown ('39)   .95   .30
O56 A80 9p green ('39)   16.00 95.00
O57 A80 1a carmine   .95   .60
Nos. O55-O57 (3)   17.90 95.90
Set, never hinged   22.00

India No. 136 Surcharged in Black

1939   **Perf. 14**
O58 A69 1a on 1a3p violet   15.00 5.25
  Never hinged   18.00
"SERVICE" measures 9¼mm.

No. 64 Surcharged in Black

1940
O59 A69 1a on 1a3p violet   12.50 5.00
  Never hinged   15.00
"SERVICE" measures 8½mm.

India Nos. 162-164 Overprinted

Perf. 13½x14
O60 A82 1r brown & slate   1.25 10.50
O61 A82 2r dk brn & dk vio   7.50   7.50
O62 A82 5r dp ultra & dk grn 21.00 95.00
Set, never hinged   36.00

India Official Stamps of 1939-43 Overprinted

1940-45
O63 O8 3p slate ('41)   2.25   .20
O64 O8 ½a brown   6.25   .20
O65 O8 ½a dk rose vio
('43)   1.25   .20
O66 O8 9p green   1.25   .20
O67 O8 1a carmine rose   4.00   .20
O68 O8 1a3p bister ('41)   1.50   .35
O69 O8 1½a dull purple ('45) 8.00 1.90
O70 O8 2a scarlet ('41)   12.50   .50
O71 O8 2½a purple ('41)   4.75 1.50
O72 O8 4a dk brown ('45)   2.25 3.75
O73 O8 8a blue violet ('45)   6.25 9.00

India Nos. 162-164 Overprinted in Black

O74 A82 1r brn & slate ('43) 6.25 16.00
O75 A82 2r dk brn & dk vio
('45)   16.00 95.00
O76 A82 5r dp ultra & dk
grn ('45)   26.00 125.00
Nos. O63-O76 (14)   98.50 254.55
Set, never hinged   145.00

INDIA - FEUDATORY STATES

FEUDATORY STATES
These stamps had franking power solely in the states in which they were issued, except for Cochin and Travancore which had a reciprocal postal agreement.

ALWAR

'əl-wər

LOCATION — A Feudatory State of India, lying southwest of Delhi in the Jaipur Residency.
AREA — 3,158 sq. mi.
POP. — 749,751.
CAPITAL — Alwar

Katar (Indian
Dagger) — A1

1877   Unwmk.   Litho.   Rouletted

1	A1	¼a ultramarine	7.00	1.60
a.		¼a blue	7.00	1.60
2	A1	1a brown	5.25	1.90
a.		1a yellow brown	16.00	8.25
b.		1a red brown	5.00	2.25

Redrawn

1899-1901   Pin-perf. 12

3	A1	¼a sl blue, wide margins	12.50	4.50
a.		Horiz. pair, imperf. between	600.00	750.00
b.		Vert. pair, imperf. between	1,200.	1,250.
4	A1	¼a yel grn, narrow margins ('01)	11.00	4.00
a.		Horiz. pair, imperf. between		950.00
b.		Imperf, pair	950.00	
c.		¼a emer, wide margins ('99)	600.00	
d.		¼a emer, narrow margins	5.25	4.75
e.		As "d," imperf, pair	550.00	
f.		As "d," vert. pair, imperf horiz.	500.00	
g.		As "d," horiz. pair, imperf vert.	450.00	525.00
h.		As "d," vert. pair, imperf horiz.	450.00	525.00

Nos. 3 and 4b are printed farther apart in the sheet.
On Nos. 3 and 4, the shading of the left border line is missing.
Nos. 1 to 4 occasionally show portions of the papermaker's watermark, W. T. & Co.
Alwar stamps became obsolete in 1902.

BAMRA

'bäm-rə

LOCATION — A Feudatory State in the Eastern States, Orissa States Agency, Bengal.
AREA — 1,988 sq. mi.
POP. — 151,259
CAPITAL — Deogarh

Stamps of Bamra were issued without gum.

A1   A2

1888   Unwmk.   Typeset   Imperf.

1	A1	¼a black, yellow	700.00	
a.		"g" inverted		7,000.
2	A1	½a black, rose	125.00	
a.		"g" inverted		2,400.
3	A1	1a black, blue	100.00	
a.		"g" inverted		2,100.

4	A1	2a black, green	140.00	550.00
a.		"postge"		2,400.
5	A1	4a black, yellow	120.00	550.00
a.		"postge"		2,250.
6	A1	8a black, rose	72.50	
a.		"postge"		1,900.
		Nos. 1-6 (6)	1,257.	

All values may be found with the scroll inverted, and with the long end of the scroll pointing to the right or left.
On No. 5 the last character on the 3rd line is a vertical line. On No. 1 it is not vertical. On No. 2 the last character on the 3rd line looks like a backwards "R" with a bent leg. On No. 6 it looks like an apostrophe.
Nos. 1 and 2 have been reprinted in blocks of 8 and Nos. 1-6 in blocks of 20. In the reprints the 4th character of the native inscription often has the curved upper line broken at the left, but in many instances comparison with photographic reproductions of the original settings is the only certain test.

1890

7	A2	¼a black, rose lilac	7.00	9.00
a.		"Quatrer"	32.50	57.50
b.		"e" of "Postage" inverted	32.50	57.50
c.		"Eeudatory"	32.50	57.50
8	A2	½a black, green	5.25	5.25
a.		"Eeudatory"	90.00	110.00
b.		"postage" with small "p"	5.25	5.25
9	A2	1a black, yellow	6.50	5.00
a.		"Eeudatory"	195.00	225.00
b.		"postage" with small "p"	6.50	5.00
c.		"annas"	300.00	325.00
10	A2	2a black, rose lilac	30.00	57.50
a.		"Eeudatory"	275.00	550.00
11	A2	4a black, bright rose	9.50	12.50
a.		"Eeudatory"	6,750.	
12	A2	8a black, rose lilac	40.00	100.00
a.		"BAMBA"	375.00	550.00
b.		"Foudatory" & "Postage"	375.00	550.00
c.		"postage" with small "p"	40.00	100.00
13	A2	1r black, rose lilac	100.00	160.00
a.		"BAMBA"	650.00	825.00
b.		"Eeudatory"	825.00	1,050.
c.		"postage" with small "p"	100.00	160.00
		Nos. 7-13 (7)	198.25	349.25

1893

14	A2	¼a black, rose	3.00	4.50
a.		"postage" with small "p"	3.00	4.50
15	A2	¼a black, magenta	3.00	4.00
a.		"postage" with small "p"	3.00	4.00
d.		"AMRA" of "BAMRA" inverted	100.00	100.00
e.		"M" and 2nd "A" of "BAMRA" inverted	140.00	140.00
f.		First "a" of "anna" inverted	72.50	82.50
16	A2	2a black, rose	21.00	12.00
a.		"postage" with small "p"	21.00	12.00
17	A2	4a black, rose	16.00	12.00
a.		"postage" with small "p"	16.00	12.00
b.		"BAMBA"	1,600.	1,800.
18	A2	8a black, rose	42.50	29.00
a.		"postage" with small "p"	42.50	29.00
19	A2	1r black, rose	35.00	35.00
a.		"postage" with small "p"	35.00	35.00
		Nos. 14-19 (6)	120.50	96.50

The central ornament varies in size and may be found in various positions.
Bamra stamps became obsolete Dec. 31, 1894.

BARWANI

bər-'wän-ē

LOCATION — A Feudatory State of Central India, in the Malwa Agency.
AREA — 1,178 sq. mi.
POP. — 141,110
CAPITAL — Barwani

The stamps of Barwani were all typographed and normally issued in booklets containing panes of four. Exceptions are noted (Nos. 14-15, 20-25). The majority were completely perforated, but some of the earlier printings were perforated only between the stamps, leaving one or two sides imperf. Nos. 1-25 were issued without gum. Many shades exist.

Rana Ranjit Singh
A1   A2

1921, April (?)   Unwmk.   Pin-Perf 7
Toned Medium Wove Paper
Clear Impression

1	A1	¼a dull Prus green	225.00	625.00
2	A1	½a dull blue	500.00	950.00

1921   Coarse Perf. 7 x Imperf.
White Thin Wove Paper
Blurred Impression

3	A1	¼a dull green	37.50	190.00
4	A1	½a pale blue	25.00	275.00

1921   Toned Laid Paper   Imperf.

5	A1	¼a light green	30.00	125.00
6	A1	½a light green	8.25	
a.		Perf. 11, top or bottom only		

1921   Coarse Perf. 7, 7 x Imperf.
Thick Wove Paper
Very Blurred Impression

7	A1	¼a dull blue	25.00	
8	A1	½a dull green	22.50	

In 1927 #7-8 were printed on thin hard paper.

1922   Perf. 7 x Imperf.
Thick Glazed Paper

9	A1	¼a dull ultra	160.00	

Rough Perf. 11 x Imperf.

10	A2	1a vermilion	3.75	30.00
11	A2	2a violet	3.25	37.50
a.		Double impression	450.00	
		Nos. 9-11 (3)	167.00	67.50

Shades of No. 11 include purple. No. 11 was also printed on thick dark toned paper.

1923-26   Perf.
Wove, Laid Paper

12	A1	¼a grayish ultra, perf. 8½	2.40	72.50
13	A1	¼a black, perf. 7 x imperf.	110.00	550.00
14	A1	¼a dull rose, perf. 11½-12	3.75	21.00
15	A1	¼a dk bl, perf. 11 ('26)	2.25	16.00
16	A1	½a grn, perf. 11 x imperf.	1.90	30.00
		Nos. 12-16 (5)	120.30	689.50

No. 12 was also printed on pale gray thin toned paper.
No. 14 was printed on horizontally laid paper in horizontal sheets of 12 containing three panes of 4.
No. 15 was printed on vertically laid paper in horizontal sheets of 8.

Rana Ranjit
Singh — A3

1927-28   Perf. 7
Thin Wove Paper

17	A3	4a dull orange	140.00	675.00

No. 17 was also printed in light brown on thick paper, pin-perf. 6, and in orange brown on thick paper, rough perf. 7.

1928   Coarse Perf. 7
Thick Glazed Paper

18	A1	¼a bright blue	16.00	
19	A1	½a bright yel green	37.50	

1928, Nov.   Rough Perf. 10½

20	A1	¼a deep ultra	9.50	
a.		Tête bêche pair	19.00	
21	A1	½a yellow green	7.00	
a.		Tête bêche pair	14.00	

1929-31   Perf. 11

22	A1	¼a blue	3.25	21.00
a.		¼a ultramarine	3.00	21.00

23	A1	½a emerald green	4.00	24.00
24	A2	1a car pink ('31)	24.00	67.50
25	A3	4a salmon	120.00	325.00
		Nos. 22-25 (4)	151.25	437.50

Nos. 20-25 were printed in sheets of 8 (4x2). No. 22 had five printings in various shades (bright to deep blue) in horizontal or vertical format.
No. 23 also printed in dark myrtle green.

Rana Devi Singh
A4   A5

1932-48   Perf. 11, 12
Glazed Paper

26	A4	¼a dark gray	3.75	35.00
27	A4	½a blue green	6.00	35.00
28	A4	1a brown	6.00	32.50
a.		1a chocolate, perf. 8½ ('48)	21.00	75.00
29	A4	2a deep red violet	5.50	62.50
a.		Perf. 12x11	12.50	
b.		2a red lilac		
30	A4	4a olive green	9.00	62.50
		Nos. 26-30 (5)	30.25	227.50

Types of 1921-27

1934-48   Perf. 11

31	A1	¼a slate gray	6.00	47.50
32	A1	½a green	6.50	60.00
33	A2	1a dark brown	16.00	29.00
a.		1a brown, perf. 8½ ('48)	15.00	75.00
34	A2	2a brt purple ('38)	125.00	490.00
35	A2	2a rose car ('46)	35.00	190.00
36	A3	4a olive green	20.00	67.50
		Nos. 31-36 (6)	208.50	884.00

In the nine printings of Nos. 26-36, several plate settings spaced the cliches from 2 to 9mm apart. Hence the stamps come in different overall sizes. Not all values were in each printing. Values are for the commonest varieties.
No. 36 was also printed in pale sage green.

1938

37	A5	1a dark brown	50.00	110.00
a.		Booklet pane of 4		

Stamps of type A5 in red are revenues. Barwani stamps became obsolete July 1, 1948.

BHOPAL

bō-'päl

LOCATION — A Feudatory State of Central India, in the Bhopal Agency.
AREA — 6,924 sq. mi.
POP. — 995,745
CAPITAL — Bhopal

Inscription in Urdu in an octagon embossed on Nos. 1-83, in a circle embossed on Nos. 84-90. On designs A1-A3, A7, A11-A12, A14-A15, A19-A21 the embossing makes up the central part of the design.
The embossing may be found inverted or sideways.

Expect irregular perfs on the perforated stamps, Nos. 19-77, due to a combination of imperfect perforating methods and the fragility of the papers.
Nos. 1-90 issued without gum.

A1   A2

Double Lined Frame

1876   Unwmk.   Litho.   Imperf.

1	A1	¼a black	950.00	700.00
a.		"EGAM"	2,750.	2,400.
b.		"BFGAM"	2,750.	2,400.
c.		"BEGAN"	1,500.	1,250.

2	A1	½a red	30.00	*72.50*
a.		"EGAM"	110.00	*250.00*
b.		"BFGAM"	110.00	*250.00*
c.		"BEGAN"	72.50	*160.00*

Single Lined Frame

1877

3	A2	¼a black		*9,000.*
4	A2	½a red	52.50	*110.00*
a.		"NWAB"	250.00	*490.00*

A3   A4

1878

5	A3	¼a black	12.00	*24.00*
a.		"J" diagonal, plate II	13.50	*27.50*

All stamps of type A3 are lettered "EEGAM" for "BEGAM."

1878

6	A4	½a pale red	10.50	*24.00*
a.		½a brown red	42.50	*67.50*
b.		"NWAB"	35.00	
c.		"JAHN"	57.50	
d.		"EECAM"	57.50	

A5   A6

1879-80

7	A5	¼a green	21.00	*40.00*
8	A5	½a red	27.50	*35.00*

Perf.

9	A5	¼a green	16.00	*27.50*
10	A5	½a red	160.00	
		Nos. 7-10 (4)	224.50	*102.50*

Nos. 7 and 9 have the value in parenthesis; Nos. 8 and 10 are without parenthesis.

1881   **Imperf.**

11	A6	¼a green	13.50	
a.		"NAWA"	42.50	
b.		"CHAH"	120.00	

Perf.

12	A6	¼a green	18.00	
a.		"NAWA"	67.50	
b.		"CHAH"	160.00	

A7

1881-89   **Imperf.**

13	A7	¼a black	9.00	*35.00*
a.		"NWAB"	22.50	
14	A7	½a red	7.50	*25.00*
a.		"NWAB"	18.00	
15	A7	1a brown	6.50	*29.00*
a.		"NWAB"	14.00	
16	A7	2a blue	5.00	*29.00*
a.		"NWAB"	9.50	
17	A7	4a yellow	30.00	*100.00*
a.		"NWAB"	82.50	
		Nos. 13-17 (5)	58.00	*218.00*

A8   A9

1884   **Perf.**

19	A8	¼a green	225.00	*275.00*
a.		"JAN"	225.00	*275.00*
b.		"BEGM"	450.00	*625.00*
c.		"NWAB"	950.00	
d.		"SHAHAN"	950.00	
f.		"JAHA"	450.00	
20	A9	¼a green	8.25	*27.50*

On type A9 there is a dash at the left of "JA" of "JAHAN" instead of a character like a comma as on types A5 and A6.

Imitations of No. 19 were printed about 1904 in black on wove paper and in red on laid paper, both imperf. and pin-perf.

A10

1884   **Laid Paper**   **Imperf.**

21	A10	¼a blue green	240.00	*275.00*
a.		"NWAB"	675.00	
b.		"NAWAJANAN"	675.00	
c.		"SAH"	675.00	
22	A10	½a black	3.25	*3.75*
a.		"NWAB"	15.00	*18.00*
b.		"NAWAJANAN"	15.00	*18.00*
c.		"SAH"	15.00	*18.00*

Perf.

23	A10	¼a blue green	1.50	*6.00*
a.		"NWAB"		*6.00*
b.		"NAWAJANAN"		*6.00*
c.		"SAH"		*6.00*
24	A10	½a black	1.40	*5.00*
a.		"NWAB"	5.50	*12.50*
b.		"NAWAJANAN"	5.50	*12.50*
c.		"SAH"	5.50	*12.50*
		Nos. 21-24 (4)	246.15	*289.75*

Type Redrawn

1886   **Wove Paper**   **Imperf.**

25	A10	¼a grayish green	.80	*5.00*
a.		¼a green	.80	*5.00*
b.		"NWAB"	4.50	*13.50*
c.		"NAWA"	3.00	*10.50*
d.		"NAWAA"	4.50	*13.50*
e.		"NAWABABEGAAM"	4.50	*13.50*
f.		"NWABA"	4.50	*13.50*
26	A10	½a red	1.00	*2.50*
a.		"SAH"	6.00	*9.50*
b.		"NAWABA"	4.50	*7.50*

Perf.

27	A10	¼a green	3.75	*6.00*
a.		"NWAB"	20.00	
b.		"NAWA"	12.00	
c.		"NAWAA"	20.00	
d.		"NAWABABEGAAM"	20.00	
e.		"NWABA"	20.00	
28	A10	½a red	1.20	*3.00*
a.		"SAH"	9.00	
b.		"NAWABA"	12.00	
		Nos. 25-28 (4)	6.75	*16.50*

On Nos. 25-28 the inscriptions are closer to the value than on Nos. 21-24.

A11

A12

1886   **Imperf.**

29	A11	½a red	4.00	*15.00*
a.		"BEGAM"	18.00	*47.50*
b.		"NWAB"	18.00	

Laid Paper

30	A12	4a yellow	18.00	*57.50*
a.		"EEGAM"	24.00	
b.		Wove paper	1,500.	
c.		As "a," wove paper	1,900.	

Perf.

31	A12	4a yellow	6.50	*30.00*
a.		"EEGAM"	9.50	*42.50*
		Nos. 29-31 (3)	28.50	

A13

A14

1889   **Wove Paper**   **Imperf.**

32	A13	¼a green	1.50	*3.00*
a.		"SAH"	6.50	*10.50*
b.		"NAWA"	6.50	*10.50*

33	A14	¼a black	3.25	*8.25*
a.		"EEGAN"	27.50	*47.50*

Perf.

34	A13	¼a green	3.00	*4.00*
a.		"SAH"	11.00	*13.50*
b.		"NAWA"	11.00	*13.50*
c.		Vert. pair, imperf between	325.00	
35	A14	¼a black	2.50	*8.25*
a.		"EEGAM"	22.50	*47.50*
b.		Horiz. pair, imperf. between	400.00	
		Nos. 32-35 (4)	10.25	*23.50*

Type A13 has smaller letters in the upper corners than Type A10.

A15   A16

1890   **Imperf.**

36	A15	¼a black	3.25	*3.00*
37	A15	1a brown	3.25	*7.00*
a.		"EEGAM"	21.00	*40.00*
b.		"BBGAM"	21.00	*40.00*
38	A7	2a greenish blue	3.00	*3.25*
a.		"BBEGAM"	12.50	*21.00*
b.		"NAWAH"	12.50	*21.00*
39	A7	4a yellow	3.75	*5.50*
40	A16	8a blue	100.00	*180.00*
a.		"HAH"	110.00	*190.00*
b.		"JABAN"	120.00	
		Nos. 36-40 (5)	113.25	*198.75*

An imperf. imitation of Nos. 36 and 41 was printed about 1904 in black on wove paper.

Perf.

41	A15	¼a black	4.50	*6.25*
a.		Pair, imperf. between	500.00	
42	A15	1a brown	6.50	*11.00*
a.		"EECAM"	37.50	*52.50*
b.		"BBGAM"	37.50	*52.50*
43	A7	2a greenish blue	3.75	*5.50*
a.		"BBEGAM"	14.00	*27.50*
b.		"NAWAH"	14.00	*27.50*
44	A7	4a yellow	4.50	*12.00*
45	A16	8a blue	100.00	*180.00*
a.		"HAH"	110.00	
b.		"JABAN"	120.00	
		Nos. 41-45 (5)	119.25	*214.75*

Nos. 40 and 45 have a frame line around each stamp.

Imperf

46	A12	½a red (BECAM)	3.00	*5.50*
47	A13	½a red (NWAB)	3.00	*2.25*
a.		Inverted "N"		
b.		"SAH"	9.00	

Perf.

48	A12	½a red (BECAM)	2.50	*7.00*
a.		Without embossing		
49	A13	½a red (NWAB)	1.20	*3.00*
a.		Inverted "N"		
b.		"SAH"	7.50	
		Nos. 46-49 (4)	9.70	*17.75*

1891-93   **Laid Paper**   **Imperf.**

50	A16	8a deep green	110.00	*225.00*
a.		"HAH"	125.00	
b.		"JABAN"	140.00	

Perf.

51	A16	8a deep green	110.00	*225.00*
a.		"HAH"	125.00	
b.		"JABAN"	140.00	

For overprint, see No. 83.

1894   **Redrawn**   **Imperf.**

53	A10	¼a green	2.25	*2.50*
a.		"NAWAH"	11.00	*12.00*
54	A11	½a brick red	3.25	*3.25*
55	A16	8a blue black	32.50	*32.50*
a.		Laid paper	300.00	*450.00*

Perf.

56	A10	¼a green	4.50	*3.25*
a.		"NAWAH"	19.00	*16.00*
57	A11	½a brick red	1.20	*3.00*
58	A16	8a blue black	45.00	*60.00*
		Nos. 53-58 (6)	88.70	*104.50*

The ¼a redrawn has letters in corners larger; value in very small characters.
The 8a redrawn has no frame to each stamp but a frame to the sheet.

1898   **Imperf.**

60	A16	8a black	62.50	*82.50*
b.		"E" of "BEGAM" inverted	140.00	*150.00*

A17

A18

A19

A20

A21

1895

        Laid Paper

61	A17	¼a green	2.25	*2.50*
62	A18	½a red	10.50	*5.00*
63	A19	¼a black	5.25	*4.50*
a.		"A" inserted in "NAW B"	12.50	*10.00*
64	A20	½a black	2.25	*2.50*
65	A21	½a red	3.25	*3.25*

        Perf.

66	A17	¼a green	4.50	*3.25*
67	A18	¼a red		*1,250.*
		Nos. 61-67 (7)	28.00	*1,271.*

On No. 63a, the second "A" in "NAWAB" has been inserted by hand and varies somewhat in size.

Imperf. imitations of No. 65 were printed about 1904 in deep red on laid paper and in black on wove paper.

Stamps of types A16 and A19-A21 with a circular embossed seal and perforated, were prepared but not issued.

A22

A23

1898   **Imperf.**

72	A22	¼a black	.75	*.75*
a.		"SHAN"	5.00	*5.00*
73	A22	¼a green	1.10	*1.20*
a.		"SHAN"	5.25	*5.25*
74	A23	¼a black	2.10	*2.10*
		Nos. 72-74 (3)	3.95	*4.05*

1899

75	A13	½a black ("NWAB")	6.50	*9.50*
b.		"NWASBAHJAHNJ"	32.50	*42.50*
d.		"SBAH"	15.00	*22.50*
e.		"SBAN"	32.50	*42.50*
f.		"NWIB"	32.50	*42.50*
g.		"BEIAM"	32.50	*42.50*

A24

Coat of
Arms — A25

1902

76	A24	¼a red	5.50	*9.00*
77	A24	½a black	6.00	*10.00*
a.		Printed on both sides	1,100.	
78	A24	1a brown	10.00	*25.00*
79	A24	2a blue	12.50	*22.50*
80	A24	4a orange	110.00	*160.00*
81	A24	8a violet	150.00	*290.00*
82	A24	1r rose	400.00	*600.00*
		Nos. 76-82 (7)	694.00	*1,116.*

No. 50 Overprinted in Red

1903

83	A16	8a deep green	210.00	225.00
a.		Inverted overprint	550.00	*600.00*

There are two types of the overprint which is the Arabic S, initial of the Begum.

Inscription in Circle
Embossed on Each Stamp

1903

Wove Paper

84	A24	¼a red	2.25	7.50
85	A24	½a black	1.90	7.50
86	A24	1a brown	4.50	11.00
87	A24	2a blue	10.00	37.50
88	A24	4a orange	27.50	75.00
89	A24	8a violet	82.50	190.00
90	A24	1r rose	125.00	290.00
	Nos. 84-90 (7)		253.65	618.50

Laid Paper

84a	A24	¼a red	1.50	12.00
85a	A24	½a black	1.50	12.50
86a	A24	1a brown	10.00	
87a	A24	2a blue	250.00	325.00
88a	A24	4a orange	500.00	500.00
89a	A24	8a violet	2,400.	
90a	A24	1r rose	1,900.	
	Nos. 84a-90a (7)		5,063.	849.50

The embossing in a circle, which was first used in 1903, has been applied to many early stamps and impressions from redrawn plates of early issues. So far as is now known, these should be classed as reprints.

1908   Engr.   Perf. 13½

99	A25	1a yellow green	5.50	6.75
a.		Printed on both sides	180.00	

OFFICIAL STAMPS

O1

Size: 20½x25mm

Overprinted

1908   Unwmk.   Engr.   Perf. 13½

O1	O1	½a yellow green	3.25	.20
a.		Pair, one without ovpt.	950.00	
b.		Inverted overprint	275.00	225.00
c.		Double ovpt., one invtd.	160.00	
O2	O1	1a carmine	6.25	.60
a.		Inverted overprint	180.00	150.00
O3	O1	2a blue	36.00	.20
O4	O1	4a red brown	21.00	.80
	Nos. O1-O4 (4)		66.50	1.80

Overprinted

O5	O1	½a yellow green	11.00	1.90
O6	O1	1a carmine	14.00	1.40
O7	O1	2a blue	6.00	.90
a.		Inverted overprint	37.50	
O8	O1	4a red brown	120.00	2.25
a.		Inverted overprint	30.00	100.00
	Nos. O5-O8 (4)		151.00	6.45

The difference in the two overprints is in the shape of the letters, most noticeable in the "R."

Type of 1908 Issue
Size: 25½x30½mm

Overprinted

1930-31   Litho.   Perf. 14

O9	O1	½a gray green ('31)	18.00	2.50
O10	O1	1a carmine	16.00	.20
O11	O1	2a blue	14.00	.65
O12	O1	4a brown	15.00	1.40
	Nos. O9-O12 (4)		63.00	4.75

½a, 2a, 4a are inscribed "POSTAGE" on the left side; 1a "POSTAGE AND REVENUE."

Similar to Type O1
Size: 21x25mm
"POSTAGE" at left
"BHOPAL STATE" at right

1932-33   Perf. 11½, 13, 13½, 14

O13	O1	¼a orange yellow	3.75	.75
a.		Pair, one without overprint	180.00	
b.		Perf. 13½	16.00	.45
c.		Perf. 14	18.00	.45

"BHOPAL GOVT." at right
Perf. 13½

O14	O1	½a yellow green	11.00	.20
a.		Perf 14 ('34)	24.00	.60
O15	O1	1a brown red	16.00	.20
O16	O1	2a blue	16.00	.65
O17	O1	4a brown	16.00	1.50
a.		Perf 14 ('34)	24.00	16.00
	Nos. O13-O17 (5)		62.75	3.30

No. O14, O16-O17 Surcharged in
Red, Violet, Black or Blue:

a

b

c

1935-36   Perf. 13½

O18	O1(a)	¼a on ½a (R)	47.50	21.00
a.		Inverted surcharge	300.00	125.00
O19	O1(b)	3p on ½a (R)	5.50	5.25
O20	O1(a)	¼a on 2a (R)	42.50	30.00
a.		Inverted surcharge	300.00	110.00
O21	O1(b)	3p on 2a (R)	6.75	6.75
a.		Inverted surcharge	120.00	60.00
O22	O1(a)	¼a on 4a (R)	1,500.	500.00
O23	O1(a)	¼a on 4a (Bk) ('36)	120.00	40.00
O24	O1(b)	3p on 4a (R)	210.00	100.00
O25	O1(b)	3p on 4a (Bk) ('36)	3.75	*5.00*
O26	O1(c)	1a on ½a (V)	7.50	2.25
a.		Inverted surcharge	100.00	67.50
O27	O1(c)	1a on 2a (R)	3.25	3.00
a.		Inverted surcharge	140.00	140.00
O28	O1(c)	1a on 2a (Bk) ('36)	1.00	*3.75*
O29	O1(c)	1a on 4a (Bl)	10.50	*7.50*
	Nos. O18-O29 (12)		1,958.	724.50

Nos. O18-O25 are arranged in composite sheets of 100. The 2 top horizontal rows of each value are surcharged "a" and the next 5 rows as "b." The next 3 rows as "b" but in a narrower setting.
Various errors of spelling or inverted letters are found on Nos. O18-O29.

Arms of Bhopal — O2

1935   Litho.

O30	O2	1a3p claret & blue	5.25	2.25

Inscribed: "Bhopal State Postage"
Ovptd. "SERVICE" 11mm long

1937   Perf. 12

O31	O2	1a6p dk claret & blue	3.75	1.50
a.		Overprint omitted	275.00	210.00
b.		Double overprint, one inverted	750.00	750.00
c.		Blue printing double		250.00
d.		Imperf, pair		275.00
e.		Pair, imperf between	300.00	*325.00*

See Nos. O42, O45.

Arms of
Bhopal — O3

Brown or Black Overprint

1936-38   Typo.

O32	O3	¼a orange (Br)	1.40	.90
a.		Inverted overprint	525.00	400.00
b.		Vert. pair, imperf between	250.00	
c.		Horiz. pair, imperf between		450.00
d.		Black overprint	12.50	1.10
e.		As "d," inverted ovpt.		600.00
f.		As "d," double ovpt.		450.00
O32B	O3	¼a yellow (Br) ('38)	5.25	2.25
O33	O3	1a carmine	1.90	.20
a.		Horiz. pair, imperf vert.		250.00
b.		Vert. pair, imperf between		490.00
c.		Horiz. pair, imperf between	200.00	225.00
d.		Block of 4, imperf between	625.00	625.00
	Nos. O32-O33 (3)		8.55	3.35

Moti
Mahal
O4

Overprinted "SERVICE"

1936   Perf. 11½

O34	O4	½a green & chocolate	.85	1.20
a.		Double impression of stamp	150.00	22.50
b.		Double overprint	350.00	250.00
c.		Vert. pair, imperf between		325.00
d.		Horiz. pair, imperf between		325.00

Moti
Masjid —
O5

4a, Taj Mahal and Be-Nazir Palaces.

Overprinted "SERVICE"

1937   Perf. 11½

O35	O5	2a dk blue & brown	2.50	1.40
a.		Inverted overprint	375.00	*550.00*
b.		Vert. pair, imperf between		525.00
c.		Horiz. pair, imperf between		375.00
O36	O5	4a bister brn & blue	4.50	.75
a.		Double overprint		240.00
b.		Center double		600.00
c.		Horiz. pair, imperf between		1,000.
d.		Overprint omitted		490.00

Types of 1937
Overprinted "SERVICE" in Black or Brown

Designs: 4a, Taj Mahal. 8a, Ahmadabad Palace. 1r, Rait-Ghat.

1938-44

O37	O4	½a dp green & brown	.90	.60
O38	O5	2a violet & dp grn	15.00	.45
O39	O5	4a red brn & brt bl	4.25	.80
a.		Frame double		450.00

O40	O5	8a red vio & blue	7.00	3.25
a.		"SERAICE"	550.00	*825.00*
b.		Overprint omitted		250.00
c.		Double overprint		240.00
d.		Vert. pair, imperf between		625.00
e.		"1" for "I" in "SERVICE"	550.00	*825.00*
O41	O5	1r bl & red vio (Br)	27.50	12.50
a.		Black overprint ('44)	21.00	6.50
b.		"SREVICE"	160.00	*375.00*
c.		Overprint omitted	1,100.	
d.		Vert. pair, imperf horiz.		2,250.
	Nos. O37-O41 (5)		54.65	17.60

#O39 measures 36½x22½mm, #O40 39x24mm, #O41 45½x27¾mm.

Type of 1935

1939   Perf. 12

O42	O2	1a6p dark claret	7.50	2.50
a.		Overprint omitted		625.00
b.		Double overprint		625.00
c.		Double overprint, one inverted		625.00
d.		Pair, imperf between	250.00	325.00

Tiger — O6

Design: 1a, Deer.

1940   Typo.   Perf. 11½

O43	O6	¼a ultramarine	6.00	2.50
O44	O6	1a red violet	35.00	4.50

Type of 1935
Inscribed: "Bhopal State Postage"

1941

O45	O2	1a3p emerald	2.50	3.25
a.		Pair, imperf between	550.00	*700.00*

Moti Palace — O7

Coat of Arms — O8

2a, Moti Mosque. 4a, Be-Nazir Palaces.

Perf. 11½, 12

1944-46		**Unwmk.**		**Typo.**	
O46	O8	3p ultramarine	1.25	1.25
O47	O7	½a light green	1.10	*1.50*
O48	O8	9p orange brn ('46)	12.00	5.00
a.		Imperf., pair		290.00
O49	O8	1a brt red vio ('45)	6.25	2.60
O50	O8	1½a deep plum	1.90	1.90
O51	O7	2a red violet ('45)	13.50	6.00
O52	O8	3a yellow ('46)	16.00	*21.00*
a.		Imperf., pair		290.00
O53	O7	4a brown ('45)	8.75	3.25
O54	O8	6a brt rose ('46)	24.00	*75.00*
a.		Imperf., pair		400.00
	Nos. O46-O54 (9)		84.75	117.50

For surcharges see Nos. O58-O59.

1946-47   Unwmk.   Perf. 11½

O55	O8	1a violet	11.00	4.75
O56	O7	2a violet ('47)	13.50	22.50
O57	O8	3a deep orange	125.00	*160.00*
a.		Imperf., pair	—	275.00
	Nos. O55-O57 (3)		149.50	187.25

No. O50 Surcharged "2 As." and Bars

1949   Perf. 12

O58	O8	2a on 1½a dp plum	3.00	*11.00*
c.		Imperf., pair	300.00	*450.00*

Same Surcharged "2 As." and Rosettes

1949   Imperf.

O59	O8	2a on 1½a dp plum	1,250.	1,500.
a.		Perf 12	1,350.	*1,600.*

Three or more types of "2" in surcharge. Bhopal stamps became obsolete in 1950.

BHOR

ˈbōˌər

LOCATION — A Feudatory State in the Kolhapur Residency and Deccan States Agency.
AREA — 910 sq. mi.
POP. — 141,546
CAPITAL — Bhor

A1

A2

Handstamped
1879   Unwmk.   Imperf.
Without Gum

1	A1	½a carmine	5.50	7.50
2	A2	1a carmine	8.25	12.00

Pant Sachiv
Shankarrao — A3

1901   Typo.
Without Gum

3	A3	½a red	24.00	60.00

BIJAWAR

bi-'jä-wər

LOCATION — A Feudatory State in the Bundelkhand Agency of Central India.
AREA — 973 sq. mi.
POP. — 115,852
CAPITAL — Bijawar

A1

Maharaja Sir
Sawant
Singh — A2

1935-36   Typo.   Unwmk.   Perf. 10½

1	A1	3p brown	11.00	8.25
a.		Imperf., pair	13.50	
b.		Rouletted 7 ('36)	9.00	9.00
2	A1	6p carmine	9.50	8.25
a.		Rouletted 7 ('36)	12.00	32.50
3	A1	9p purple	12.50	7.50
a.		Rouletted 7 ('36)	9.00	160.00
4	A1	1a dark blue	14.00	8.25
a.		Rouletted 7 ('36)	15.00	180.00
5	A1	2a slate green	13.50	12.00
a.		Rouletted 7 ('36)	19.00	190.00

1937   Perf. 9

6	A2	4a red orange	22.50	120.00
7	A2	6a yellow	22.50	120.00
8	A2	8a emerald	24.00	160.00
9	A2	12a turquoise blue	24.00	160.00

10	A2	1r purple	62.50	250.00
a.		"1Rs" instead of "1R"	75.00	500.00
		Nos. 1-10 (10)	216.00	849.75

Bijawar stamps became obsolete in 1939.

BUNDI

'bün-dē

LOCATION — A Feudatory State in the Rajputana Agency of India.
AREA — 2,220 sq. mi.
POP. — 216,722
CAPITAL — Bundi

Katar (Indian
Dagger) — A1

A2

A3

Laid Paper
1894   Unwmk.   Litho.   Imperf.
Without Gum
Gutters between Stamps

1	A1	½a slate	19,000.	3,250.

Redrawn; Blade Does Not Touch Oval
No Gutters between Stamps
Wove Paper

1A	A1	½a slate	67.50	72.50
b.		Value above, name below	400.00	525.00
c.		Top right ornament omitted	3,750.	4,000.

On No. 1A, the dagger is thinner and its point does not touch the oval inner frame.

1896
Laid Paper
Without Gum

2	A2	½a slate	9.00	14.00

1897-98   Without Gum

3	A3	1a red	18.00	27.50
4	A3	2a yellow green	21.00	40.00
5	A3	4a yellow green	100.00	140.00
6	A3	8a red	160.00	450.00
7	A3	1r yellow, blue	500.00	825.00
		Nos. 3-7 (5)	799.00	1,482.

A4

A5

Redrawn; Blade Wider and Diamond-shaped
1898-1900   Without Gum

8	A3	½a slate	7.00	7.00
9	A3	1a red	5.50	5.50
10	A3	2a emerald	19.00	25.00
a.		1st 2 characters of value omitted	3,000.	3,000.
11	A3	4a yel grn	42.50	100.00
12	A4	8a red	21.00	27.50
13	A5	1r yellow, blue	47.50	82.50
a.		Wove paper	24.00	40.00
		Nos. 8-13 (6)	142.50	247.50

On Nos. 9-10, the blade is wider and nearly diamond-shaped.

Point of Dagger to Left

14	A3	4a green	5.00	5.00

Maharao Rajah
with Symbols of
Spiritual and
Temporal
Power — A6

Rouletted 11 to 13 in Color
1915   Typo.
Without Gum
"Bundi" in 3 Characters (word at top right)

15	A6	¼a blue	2.90	6.25
a.		Laid paper	6.75	35.00
16	A6	½a black	4.00	9.00
17	A6	1a vermilion	5.50	18.00
a.		Laid paper	15.00	45.00
18	A6	2a emerald	11.00	35.00
19	A6	2½a yellow	11.00	40.00
20	A6	3a brown	12.50	67.50
21	A6	4a yel green	5.25	62.50
23	A6	6a ultramarine	21.00	160.00
a.		6a deep blue	11.00	180.00
24	A6	8a orange	11.00	160.00
25	A6	10a olive	24.00	150.00
26	A6	12a dark green	19.00	140.00
27	A6	1r violet	40.00	250.00
28	A6	2r car brn & blk	125.00	325.00
29	A6	3r blue & brown	200.00	450.00
30	A6	4r pale grn & red brown	400.00	550.00
31	A6	5r ver & pale grn	400.00	550.00
		Nos. 15-31 (16)	1,292.	2,973.

Minor differences in lettering in top and bottom panels may be divided into 8 types, but not all values come in each type. In one sub-type the top appears as one word. Nos. 30-31 have an ornamental frame around the design. For overprints see Nos. O1-O39.

1941   Perf. 11
"Bundi" in 4 Characters (word at top right)

32	A6	¼a light blue	2.25	62.50
33	A6	½a black	40.00	47.50
34	A6	1a carmine	15.00	75.00
35	A6	2a yellow green	20.00	110.00
		Nos. 32-35 (4)	77.25	295.00

The 4-character spelling of "Bundi" is found also on stamps rouletted in color: on ½a and 4a in small characters, and on ¼a, ½a, 1a, 4a, 4r and 5r in large characters like those on Nos. 32-35.
For overprints see Nos. O41-O48.

Arms of Bundi — A7

1941-45   Typo.   Perf. 11

36	A7	3p bright ultra	3.50	7.50
37	A7	6p indigo	5.25	12.50
38	A7	1a red orange	8.00	15.00
39	A7	2a fawn	10.50	27.50
a.		2a brown ('45)	19.00	30.00
40	A7	4a brt yel green	19.00	82.50
41	A7	8a dull green	25.00	300.00
42	A7	1r royal blue	52.50	450.00
		Nos. 36-42 (7)	123.75	895.00

The 1st printing of Nos. 36-42 was gummed. All later printings were without gum. **Values are for stamps without gum.**
For overprints see Nos. O49-O55.

A8

Maj. Maharao
Rajah Bahadur
Singh — A9

View of
Bundi — A10

1947   Perf. 11

43	A8	¼a deep green	2.75	57.50
44	A8	½a purple	2.50	47.50
45	A8	1a yellow green	2.50	47.50
46	A9	2a red	2.40	97.50
47	A9	4a deep orange	2.75	140.00
48	A10	8a violet blue	3.75	
49	A10	1r chocolate	19.00	
		Nos. 43-49 (7)	35.65	

For overprints see Rajasthan Nos. 1-14.

OFFICIAL STAMPS

Regular Issue of 1915 Handstamped in Black, Red or Green

a

Rouletted 11 to 13 in Color
1918   Unwmk.
Without Gum

O1	A6	¼a dark blue	1.90
O2	A6	½a black	1.10
O3	A6	1a vermilion	1.90
O4	A6	2a emerald	9.50
O5	A6	2½a yellow	6.00
O6	A6	3a brown	5.50
O7	A6	4a yel green	18.00
O8	A6	6a blue	22.50
O9	A6	8a orange	22.50
O10	A6	10a olive green	75.00
O11	A6	12a dark green	75.00
O12	A6	1r violet	90.00
O13	A6	2r car brn & blk	600.00
O14	A6	3r blue & brown	525.00
O15	A6	4r pale grn & red brn	450.00
O16	A6	5r ver & pale grn	490.00
		Nos. O1-O16 (16)	2,393.

All values come with black handstamp and most exist in red. The overprint is found in various positions, double, inverted, etc.
Several denominations exist in two or more types. See notes following Nos. 31 and 35.

Regular Issue of 1915 Handstamped in Black, Red or Green

b

1919   Without Gum

O17	A6	¼a dark blue	2.60
O18	A6	½a black	4.50
O19	A6	1a vermilion	16.00
O20	A6	2a emerald	29.00
O21	A6	2½a yellow	30.00
O22	A6	3a brown	35.00
O23	A6	4a yel green	120.00
O24	A6	6a blue	45.00
O25	A6	8a orange	52.50
O26	A6	10a olive green	140.00
O27	A6	12a dark green	120.00
O28	A6	1r violet	82.50
O29	A6	2r car brn & blk	275.00

O30	A6	3r blue & brown	325.00	
O31	A6	4r pale grn & red brn	450.00	
O32	A6	5r ver & pale grn	490.00	
		Nos. O17-O32 (16)	2,217.	

Note following No. O16 applies to this issue.

Regular Issue of 1915 Handstamped in Carmine or Black

c

1919 *Rouletted in Color*
Without Gum

O33	A6	¼a blue	11.00
O34	A6	½a black	18.00
O35	A6	1a vermilion	35.00
O36	A6	2a yel green	140.00
O37	A6	8a orange	450.00
O38	A6	10a olive	700.00
O39	A6	12a dark green	900.00
		Nos. O33-O39 (7)	2,254.

Nos. 33 and 35 Handstamped Type "a" in Black or Carmine

1941 *Perf. 11*

O41	A6	½a black	24.00
O42	A6	2a yellow green	825.00

Nos. 32 and 35 Handstamped Type "b" in Black or Carmine
1941

O43	A6	¼a light blue	90.00
O44	A6	2a yellow green	210.00

Nos. 32-35 Handstamped Type "c" in Black or Carmine
1941

O45	A6	¼a light blue	190.00
O46	A6	½a black	375.00
O47	A6	1a carmine	700.00
O48	A6	2a yellow green	625.00
		Nos. O45-O48 (4)	1,890.

Nos. 36 to 42 Overprinted in Black or Carmine

1941 *Perf. 11*

O49	A7	3p brt ultra (C)	7.50	24.00
O50	A7	6p indigo (C)	20.00	24.00
O51	A7	1a red orange	19.00	16.00
O52	A7	2a fawn	20.00	19.00
O53	A7	4a brt yel green	72.50	160.00
O54	A7	8a dull green	225.00	950.00
O55	A7	1r royal blue (C)	310.00	950.00
		Nos. O49-O55 (7)	674.00	2,143.

BUSSAHIR

ˈbus-ə-ˌhiˌəˌr

(Bashahr)

LOCATION — A Feudatory State in the Punjab Hill States Agency
AREA — 3,439 sq. mi.
POP. — 100,192
CAPITAL — Bashahr

Tiger
A1 A2

 A3   A4

 A5 A6

A7 A8

Overprinted "R S" in Violet, Rose, or Blue Green (RG)

Laid Paper

1895		**Unwmk.**	**Litho.**	*Imperf.*
1	A1	¼a pink (V)	3,750.	
2	A2	½a slate (R)	750.00	1,000.
3	A3	1a red (V)	300.00	
4	A4	2a yellow (V,R)	110.00	300.00
5	A5	4a violet (V,R)	190.00	
6	A6	8a brown (V,BG)	210.00	375.00
a.		Without overprint	400.00	
7	A7	12a green (R)	450.00	
8	A8	1r ultra (R)	190.00	
		Nos. 1-8 (8)	5,950.	

Perf. 7 to 14

9	A1	¼a pink (V,BG)	100.00	150.00
10	A2	½a slate (R)	35.00	210.00
11	A3	1a red (V)	35.00	140.00
a.		Pin-perf.	275.00	300.00
12	A4	2a yel (V,R,BG)	47.50	140.00
a.		Pin-perf. (V,R)	100.00	240.00
13	A5	4a vio (V,R,BG)	37.50	140.00
a.		Pin-perf. (R)	450.00	
14	A6	8a brown (V,BG)	35.00	160.00
15	A7	12a green (V,R)	120.00	200.00
a.		Pin-perf. (R)	650.00	825.00
b.		Without overprint	325.00	
16	A8	1r ultra (V,R)	65.00	180.00
a.		Pin-perf. (R)	700.00	
		Nos. 9-16 (8)	475.00	1,320.

"R. S." are the initials of Tika Raghunath Singh, son of the Raja.

 A9   A10

 A11   A12

 A13   A14

Overprinted "R S" Like Nos. 1-16 Wove Paper

1896		**Engr.**		*Pin-perf.*
17	A9	¼a dk gray vio (R)	—	1,500.
18	A10	½a blue gray (R)	1,200.	450.00

1900		**Litho.**		*Imperf.*
19	A9	¼a red (V,BG)	7.50	16.00
20	A9	¼a violet (V,R)	12.50	
21	A10	½a blue (V,R)	15.00	40.00
22	A11	1a olive (R)	27.50	65.00
23	A11	1a red (V,BG)	7.00	24.00
24	A12	2a yellow (V)	75.00	
a.		2a ocher (R)	75.00	
25	A13	2a yellow (V)	90.00	
26	A14	4a brn vio (V,R,BG)	82.50	180.00
		Nos. 19-26 (8)	317.00	

Pin-perf.

27	A9	¼a red (V,BG)	6.25	16.00
28	A9	¼a violet (R)	30.00	27.50
29	A10	½a blue (V,R)	90.00	140.00
30	A11	1a olive (V,R)	40.00	
31	A11	1a red (V)	—	300.00
32	A11	1a vermilion (BG)	11.00	22.50
33	A12	2a yellow (BG)	1,250.	1,300.
34	A13	2a yellow (V,R)	75.00	120.00
a.		2a ocher (V)	100.00	
35	A14	4a brn vio (V,R,BG)	120.00	
		Nos. 27-35 (9)	1,622.	

Obsolete March 31, 1901.

Stamps overprinted with the monogram above (RNS) or with the monogram "PS" were never issued for postal purposes. They are either reprints or remainders to which this overprint has been applied. Many other varieties have appeared since the stamps became obsolete. It is probable that all or nearly all of them are reprints.

CHARKHARI

chər-ˈkär-ē

LOCATION — A Feudatory State in the Bundelkhand Agency in Central India.
AREA — 880 sq. mi.
POP. — 120,351
CAPITAL — Maharajnagar

 A1

Thin White or Blue Wove Paper

1894		**Unwmk.**	**Typo.**	*Imperf.*
		Value in the Plural		
		Without Gum		
1	A1	1a green	2,750.	3,750.
2	A1	2a green	3,250.	
3	A1	4a green	2,100.	

1897
Value in the Singular
Without Gum

3A	A1	¼a rose	1,800.	1,100.
4	A1	¼a purple	5.50	5.50
5	A1	½a purple	3.75	4.50
6	A1	1a green	6.50	9.50
7	A1	2a green	11.00	12.50
8	A1	4a green	17.50	27.50
		Nos. 4-8 (5)	44.25	59.50

In a later printing, the numerals of Nos. 4-8 are smaller or of different shape.
Proofs are known on paper of various colors.

 A2   A3

Size: 19½x23mm

1909		**Litho.**		*Perf. 11*
9	A2	1p red brown	7.00	57.50
10	A2	1p pale blue	.90	.65
11	A2	½a scarlet	1.50	1.90
12	A2	1a light green	3.75	2.40
13	A2	2a ultra	4.50	5.25
14	A2	4a deep green	6.25	8.25
15	A2	8a brick red	11.00	30.00
16	A2	1r red brown	19.00	62.50
		Nos. 9-16 (8)	53.90	168.45

See #22-27, 39-43. For surcharges see #37-38A.

1912-17 **Handstamped** *Imperf.* **Without Gum**

21	A3	1p violet ('17)	10.50	7.50
c.		Double frameline	1,050.	125.00

The 1p black, type A3, is a proof.

A3a

Wove Paper
1922 **Handstamped** *Imperf.* **Without Gum**

21A	A3a	1a violet	120.00	125.00
b.		Perf. 11, laid paper	110.00	210.00

Type of 1909 Issue Redrawn
Size: 20x23½mm
1930-40 **Typo.** **Without Gum**

22	A2	1p dark blue	.90	21.00
23	A2	½a olive green	3.75	21.00
23A	A2	½a cop brown ('40)	9.00	37.50
24	A2	1a light green	3.75	24.00
25	A2	1a chocolate	19.00	40.00
25A	A2	1a dull red ('40)	190.00	100.00
26	A2	2a light blue	1.90	25.00
a.		Tête bêche pair	14.00	
27	A2	4a carmine	4.50	30.00
a.		Tête bêche pair	21.00	
		Nos. 22-27 (8)	232.80	298.50

Guesthouse of Raja at Charkhari Reservoir — A4

Imlia Palace — A5

Industrial School — A6

View of City — A7

Maharajnagar Fort, Charkhari City — A8

Guesthouse A9

Palace Gate — A10

Temples at Rampur — A11

Govordhan Temple — A12

1931   **Perf. 11, 11½, 12**
28	A4	½a dull green	3.25	.20
29	A5	1a black brown	2.40	.20
30	A6	2a purple	2.50	.20
31	A7	4a olive green	2.25	.20
32	A8	8a magenta	3.00	.20
33	A9	1r rose & green	4.00	.30
34	A10	2r brown & red	6.00	.35
35	A11	3r bl grn & choc	22.50	.60
36	A12	5r violet & blue	14.00	.75
		Nos. 28-36 (9)	59.90	3.00

Size range of A4-A12: 30-31x19½-24mm.
Many errors of perforation and printing exist.
Used values are for canceled to order stamps.

Nos. 15-16
Surcharged in Black

1940   **Perf. 11**
37	A2	½a on 8a brick red	52.50	200.00
a.		Surcharge inverted	450.00	600.00
b.		"1" of "½" inverted	400.00	
38	A2	1a on 1r red brown	175.00	625.00
b.		Surcharge inverted	490.00	
38A	A2	"1 ANNA" on 1r red brown	400.00	450.00

Type of 1930

1943   **Unwmk.**   **Typo.**   *Imperf.*
Size: 20x23½mm
39	A2	1p violet	32.50	240.00
a.		Tête bêche pair	82.50	
40	A2	1p apple green	90.00	325.00
41	A2	½a orange red	30.00	62.50
42	A2	½a black	90.00	290.00
43	A2	2a grayish green	140.00	290.00
a.		Tête bêche pair	180.00	
		Nos. 39-43 (5)	382.50	1,207.

COCHIN

kō-'chin

LOCATION — A Feudatory State in the Madras States Agency in Southern India.
AREA — 1,480 sq. mi.
POP. — 1,422,875 (1941)
CAPITAL — Ernakulam

See the United State of Travancore and Cochin.

6 Puttans = 5 Annas
12 Pies = 1 Anna
16 Annas = 1 Rupee

A1

A1a

State Seal

1892   **Unwmk.**   **Typo.**   *Perf. 12*
1	A1	½p yellow	3.75	4.50
a.		Imperf., pair		
b.		Laid paper	700.00	200.00
2	A1	1p red violet	4.50	4.00
a.		1p purple (error)	175.00	125.00
3	A1	2p purple	3.00	3.25
a.		Imperf.		
		Nos. 1-3 (3)	11.25	11.75

Nos. 1 to 3 sometimes have watermark large umbrella in the sheet.

Wmk. Coat of Arms and Inscription in Sheet

1896
4	A1a	1p violet	140.00	140.00

Wmk. 43
4A	A1a	1p violet	27.50	47.50

Originally intended for revenue use, Nos. 4-4A were later authorized for postal use. Beware of fraudulently removed fiscal markings.

1894   **Wmk. 41**
Thin Paper
5	A1	½p orange	3.75	2.25
a.		Imperf., pair		
6	A1	1p magenta	10.50	10.50
7	A1	2p purple	6.25	6.75
a.		Imperf., pair		
		Nos. 5-7 (3)	20.50	19.50

A2

A3

A4

A5

Thin Paper

1898
8	A2	3p ultra	2.10	1.60
a.		Double impression	950.00	
9	A3	½p gray green	2.50	2.25
a.		Pair, one sideways		3,750.
10	A4	1p rose	5.50	2.50
a.		Laid paper		2,400.
b.		Tete beche pair	5,250.	3,250.
c.		As "a," tete beche pair		12,000.
11	A5	2p purple	5.00	3.25
		Nos. 8-11 (4)	15.10	9.60

Thick Paper

1903
12	A2	3p ultra	1.80	.20
a.		Double impression		450.00
12A	A3	½p gray green	1.90	.60
e.		Double impression		450.00
f.		Pair, one sideways	1,250.	1,250.
12B	A4	1p rose	2.50	
g.		Tete beche pair		5,250.

12C	A5	2p purple	3.75	.75
h.		Double impression	1,250.	450.00
		Nos. 12-12C (4)	9.95	1.75

Beware of fake overprint surcharge varieties, such as double, inverted, etc. This applies also to early official varieties. Such varieties require expertization.

Type of 1898 Surcharged

1909
13	A2	2p on 3p red violet	.20	.75
a.		Inverted surcharge	150.00	150.00
b.		Pair, stamps tete beche	250.00	290.00
c.		Pair, stamps & surch. tete beche	300.00	375.00

The surcharge is also known in a thin "2" measuring 5½x7mm, with curving foot. Values: unused $1,200; used $600.

Sri Rama Varma I — A6

1911-13   **Engr.**   *Perf. 14*
14	A6	2p brown	.45	.20
a.		Imperf., pair		
15	A6	3p blue	2.25	.20
a.		Perf. 14x12½	40.00	3.00
16	A6	4p yel green	2.50	.20
17	A6	9p car rose	2.10	.20
18	A6	1a orange buff	4.50	.20
19	A6	1½a lilac	11.00	.65
20	A6	2a gray	11.00	.60
21	A6	3a vermilion	57.50	57.50
		Nos. 14-21 (8)	91.30	59.75

For surcharge and overprints see Nos. 34, O2-O9, O23-O24, O27.

Sri Rama Varma II
A7   A8

1918-23   **Engr.**   *Perf. 14*
23	A7	2p brown	12.00	.20
24	A7	4p green	1.50	.20
25	A7	6p red brown ('22)	3.75	.20
26	A7	8p black brown ('23)	2.50	.20
27	A7	9p carmine rose	30.00	.50
28	A7	10p deep blue	9.00	.20
29	A8	1a brown orange	27.50	4.50
30	A7	1½a red violet ('21)	5.50	.30
31	A7	2a gray	6.25	.20
32	A7	2¼a yel green ('22)	10.50	4.75
33	A7	3a vermilion	17.50	.50
		Nos. 23-33 (11)	126.00	11.75

The 2p and 1a are found in two types, the difference lying in the first of the three characters directly above the maharaja's head.
For surcharges and overprints see Nos. 36-40, 52-53, O10-O22, O25-O26, O28-O36, O71A.

No. 15 Surcharged

Type I — Numeral 8mm high. Curved foot. Top begins with a ball. (As illustrated.)
Type II — Numeral 9mm high. Curved foot. Top begins with a curved line.

Type III — Numeral 6mm high. Straight foot. "Two pies" 15mm wide.
Type IV — "2" as in type III. Capital "P" in "Pies." "Two Pies" 13mm wide.
Type V — Heavy gothic numeral. Capital "P" in "Pies."

1922-29
34	A6	2p on 3p blue (Type I)	.60	.45
a.		Type II	5.00	1.50
b.		Type III	10.50	.50
c.		Type IV	16.00	16.00
d.		Type V	110.00	200.00
e.		Double surcharge, I	500.00	500.00
f.		Double surcharge II	1,100.	

Types II and III exist with a capital "P" in "Pies." It occurs once in each sheet of the second and third settings. There are four settings.
Type V is the first stamp, fourth row, of the fourth setting.

No. 32 Surcharged

1928
36	A7	1a on 2¼a yel green	9.00	18.00
a.		Double surcharge		

Nos. 24, 26 and 28 Surcharged in Black

1932-33
38	A7	3p on 4p green	1.90	2.10
39	A7	3p on 8p black brown	3.25	4.00
40	A7	9p on 10p deep blue	2.25	5.00
		Nos. 38-40 (3)	7.40	11.10

Sri Rama Varma III
A9   A10

1933-38   **Engr.**   *Perf. 13x13½*
41	A9	2p brown ('36)	1.25	.75
42	A9	4p green	.90	.20
43	A9	6p red brown	1.00	.20
44	A10	1a brown org ('34)	1.25	.30
45	A9	1a8p rose red	4.50	9.50
46	A9	2a gray black ('38)	9.00	2.40
47	A9	2¼a yellow green	2.50	.45
48	A9	3a red org ('38)	8.25	2.40
49	A9	3a4p violet	2.50	2.10
50	A9	6a8p black brown	2.50	22.50
51	A9	10a deep blue	4.50	25.00
		Nos. 41-51 (11)	38.15	65.80

See Nos. 55-58. For overprints and surcharges see Nos. 54, 59-62, 73A-74, 76-77, 89, O37-O57, O70-O71, O72-O77A, O89.

Nos. 26 and 28 Surcharged in Red

1934   *Perf. 13½*
52	A7	6p on 8p black brown	1.10	.90
53	A7	6p on 10p dark blue	2.50	3.00

No. 44 Overprinted in Black

a

1939   **Engr.**
54   A10   1a brown orange   6.25   2.50

Types of 1933-38

1938-41		**Litho.**	**Perf. 11, 13**	
55	A9	2p dull brown	1.25	.60
56	A9	4p dull green	1.25	.50
		('41)		
57	A9	6p red brown	4.50	.20
c.		Perf. 13		4,750.
57A	A10	1a brown orange	95.00	140.00
58	A10	2¼a yellow green	7.50	.35
		Nos. 55-58 (5)	109.50	141.65

Type of 1934 Overprinted in Black
Type "a" or

b

1941-42		**Perf. 11 (#59), 13 (#60)**		
59	A10(a)	1a brown orange	425.00	2.50
a.		Perf. 13		525.00
60	A10(b)	1a brown org		.90
		('42)	16.00	
a.		Perf. 11	1.00	2.50

No. 45 Surcharged in Black

c

1943-44		**Engr.**	**Perf. 13x13½**	
61	A9	3p on 1a8p rose red		
		('44)	4.25	30.00
62	A9	1a3p on 1a8p rose red	1.25	.75

Maharaja Sri Kerala Varma
   A11   A12

1943		**Litho.**	**Wmk. 294**	**Perf. 11, 13**	
63	A11	2p dull gray brn,			
			wmk. 41	4.25	6.75
a.		Wmk. 294		37.50	5.50
64	A11	4p gray green		4.50	8.25
a.		Wmk. 41		1,100.	550.00
65	A11	6p red brown		4.75	.20
66	A11	9p ultramarine		55.00	1.90
67	A12	1a brown orange		29.00	80.00
a.		Wmk. 41		120.00	175.00
68	A11	2¼a lt ol green		32.50	3.75
		Nos. 63-68 (6)		130.00	100.85

For surcharges and overprints see Nos. 69-73, 75, 78, 78B, O58-O69.

No. 64 Surcharged Type "c"

1944				
69	A11	3p on 4p gray green	8.75	.20
a.		Wmk. 41	110.00	35.00

Nos. 64, 64a and 65 Surcharged in Black

d

1944-48		**Wmk. 294**		
70	A11	2p on 6p red brown	.95	6.00
71	A11	3p on 4p gray green	8.75	.20
72	A11	3p on 6p red brown	1.00	.20
73	A11	4p on 6p red brown	6.25	18.00
		Nos. 70-73 (4)	16.95	24.40

Nos. 57A, 67a
Surcharged in Black

1944		**Litho.**	**Wmk. 41**	
73A	A10	6p on 1a brown org	300.00	225.00
74	A10	9p on 1a brown org	450.00	60.00
75	A12	9p on 1a brown org	8.00	5.50
		Nos. 73A-75 (3)	758.00	290.50

No. 56 Surcharged Type "c" in Black

1944				
76	A9	3p on 4p dull green	8.75	6.00

Nos. 57A, 67a
Surcharged in Black

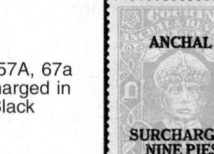

1944				
77	A10	9p on 1a brown orange	30.00	12.00
78	A12	9p on 1a brown orange	9.50	3.25

No. 67a Surcharged Type "c"

1944		**Wmk. 41**		
78B	A12	1a3p on 1a brn org		7,750.

Maharaja Ravi Varma
   A13   A15

1944-46		**Wmk. 294**	**Perf. 13**	
79	A13	9p ultra ('46)	20.00	27.50
a.		Perf. 11	20.00	6.00
80	A13	1a3p magenta	10.00	12.50
81	A13	1a9p ultra ('46)	12.00	24.00
		Nos. 79-81 (3)	42.00	64.00

For overprints and surcharges see Nos. O78-O80, Travancore 12, 14, O10.

1946-50		**Litho.**	**Perf. 13**	
82	A15	2p dull brown	3.25	.25
a.		Perf. 11	10.00	.90
b.		Perf. 11x13	450.00	210.00
83	A15	3p carmine rose	.60	.45
83A	A15	4p gray green		
		('50)	3,100.	120.00
84	A15	6p red brown		
		('47)	30.00	9.50
a.		Perf. 11	210.00	8.25
85	A15	9p ultramarine	1.90	.20
86	A15	1a dp orange		
		('47)	11.00	47.50
a.		Perf. 11	625.00	
87	A15	2a gray ('47)	150.00	12.50
a.		Perf. 11	190.00	10.00
88	A15	3a vermilion	100.00	2.25
		Nos. 82-83,84-88 (7)	296.75	72.65

For surcharges and overprints see Nos. 98-99, O81-O88, Travancore 8, 13, 15-15A, O11.

No. 45 Surcharged Type "d"

Perf. 13x13½

1947-48		**Wmk. 41**	**Engr.**	
89	A9	6p on 1a8p rose red	4.25	30.00

Maharaja Sri
Kerala Varma
II — A16

Die I   Die II

Two dies on 2p: Die I, back of headdress almost touches value tablet; Die II, back of headdress farther away from value tablet.

Die I   Die II

Two dies on 3a4p: Die I, white frame line around head is continuous, and two white lines beneath value inscriptions at bottom; Die II, white frame line around head broken by value tablets at the sides, and single white line beneath value inscriptions at bottom. Die II comes from the first two stamps of the bottom row of the sheet.

1948-49		**Wmk. 294**	**Perf. 11**	
90	A16	2p olive brown	2.25	.20
a.		Die II	190.00	3.25
91	A16	3p car ('49)	1.90	.20
92	A16	4p gray green	21.00	5.25
a.		Horiz. pair, imperf. vert.	350.00	500.00
93	A16	6p red brown	22.50	.35
94	A16	9p ultra ('49)	3.00	.75
95	A16	2a black	80.00	3.75
96	A16	3a ver ('49)	87.50	1.50
97	A16	3a4p violet ('49)	87.50	525.00
a.		Die II	275.00	
		Nos. 90-97 (8)	305.65	537.00

For overprints see Nos. O90-O97, Travancore 9-11, O8-O9.

No. 86 Surcharged Type "d" in Black

1949				
98	A15	6p on 1a dp orange	80.00	225.00
99	A15	9p on 1a dp orange	120.00	225.00

Dutch Palace
A17

Design: 2a, Chinese fishing net.

1949		**Unwmk.**	**Perf. 11**	
100	A17	2a gray	6.25	12.50
a.		Imperf. vert., horiz. pair	600.00	
101	A17	2¼a gray green	3.50	14.00
a.		Imperf. vert., horiz. pair	600.00	600.00

See Travancore-Cochin for succeeding issues.

OFFICIAL STAMPS

See note above No. 13.

Stamps and Type of 1911-14
Overprinted

h

1913-14		**Wmk. 41**	**Engr.**	**Perf. 14**	
O2	A6	4p yel green		13.50	.20
a.		Inverted overprint			450.00
O3	A6	9p car rose		160.00	.20
O4	A6	1½a red violet		72.50	.20
a.		Double overprint			1,000.
O5	A6	2a gray		19.00	.20
O6	A6	3a vermilion		82.50	.65
O7	A6	6a violet		90.00	3.00
O8	A6	12a blue		60.00	10.00
O9	A6	1½r deep green		52.50	110.00
		Nos. O2-O9 (8)		550.00	124.45

Stamps and Type of 1918-23
Overprinted

i

1918-34				
O10	A7	4p green	6.00	.20
a.		Double overprint	—	750.00
O11	A7	6p red brn ('22)	18.00	.20
a.		Double overprint		650.00
O12	A7	8p blk brn ('26)	16.00	.20
O13	A7	9p carmine rose	97.50	.20
O14	A7	10p dp blue ('23)	21.00	.20
O16	A7	1½a red vio ('21)	8.25	.20
a.		Double overprint		1,000.
O17	A7	2a gray	62.50	.45
O18	A7	2¼a yel grn ('22)	19.00	.20
b.		Double overprint		625.00
O19	A7	3a ver ('22)	27.50	.35
a.		Double overprint		650.00
O20	A7	6a violet ('22)	57.50	.75
O21	A7	12a blue ('29)	57.50	7.50
O22	A7	1½r dk green ('34)	37.50	175.00
		Nos. O10-O22 (12)	395.75	185.45

On Nos. O2-O22, width of overprint varies from 14¾mm to 16½mm.

No. 15 Overprinted in Red

j

1921				
O23	A6	3p blue	175.00	.20
a.		Overprint in black		1,750.

Nos. O3 and O13 Surcharged with
New Values

1923-29				
O24	A6	8p on 9p car rose	525.00	2.50
O25	A7	8p on 9p car rose	100.00	.20
a.		Double surcharge		400.00
O26	A7	10p on 9p car rose		
		('25)	120.00	1.50
a.		Double surcharge		450.00
O27	A6	10p on 9p car rose		
		('29)	1,750.	27.50
		Nos. O24-O27 (4)	2,495.	31.70

Regular Issue of 1918-23 Overprinted

k

1933-34				
O28	A7	4p green	32.50	2.50
O29	A7	6p red brown ('34)	21.00	.20
O30	A7	8p black brown	10.00	.20
O31	A7	10p deep blue	9.00	.20
O32	A7	2a gray ('34)	60.00	.20
O33	A7	3a vermilion	12.50	.30
O34	A7	6a dk violet ('34)	150.00	4.50
		Nos. O28-O34 (7)	295.00	8.25

Same with Additional Surcharge on Type of Regular Issue of 1918-23 in Red

O35	A7	6p on 8p black brown	3.75	.20
O36	A7	6p on 10p dk blue ('34)	6.00	.20

Regular Issue of 1933 Overprinted Type "k" in Black as in 1933-34

1933-35   *Perf. 13x13½*
O37	A9	4p green	6.25	.20
O38	A9	6p red brown	5.50	.20
O39	A10	1a brown orange	24.00	.20
O40	A9	1a8p rose red	2.25	.45
O41	A9	2a gray	27.50	.20
O42	A9	2¼a yellow green	9.00	.20
O43	A9	3a vermilion	67.50	.20
O44	A9	3a4p violet	2.25	.20
O45	A9	6a8p black brown	2.25	.30
O46	A9	10a deep blue	2.25	1.50
		Nos. O37-O46 (10)	148.75	3.65

Regular Stamps of 1934-38 Overprinted in Black

 m

1939-41   *Perf. 11, 13x13½*
O47	A10	1a brown orange	50.00	.90
O48	A9	2a gray black	27.50	3.00
O49	A9	3a red orange	13.50	3.75
		Nos. O47-O49 (3)	91.00	7.65

Similar Overprint on Types of 1933-36

Perf. 11, 13x13½

1939-41   **Litho.**   **Wmk. 294**
O50	A9	4p dull green ('41)	92.50	24.00

Wmk. 41
O51	A9	6p red brown ('41)	14.00	6.50
a.		Wmk. 294	25.00	1.50
O52	A10	1a brown orange	1.25	.20
a.		Wmk. 294	2.25	6.50
O53	A9	3a orange ('40)	3.75	2.50
b.		Wmk. 294	24.00	11.00
		Nos. O50-O53 (4)	111.50	33.20

O53A — Similar Overprint in Narrow Serifed Capitals on No. 57

Wmk. 41   *Perf. 11*
O53A	A9	6p red brown	1,050.	600.00

Type of 1933-36 Overprinted in Black

 o

Perf. 10½, 11, 13x13½
O54	A9	4p dull green ('41)	35.00	4.00
O55	A9	6p red brown ('41)	32.50	.60
O56	A9	2a gray black	25.00	1.50
		Nos. O54-O56 (3)	92.50	6.10

Type of 1934 Overprinted in Black

 p

1941   *Perf. 11*
O57	A10	1a brown orange	375.00	3.75

Stamps and Types of 1944 Overprinted in Black

 q

Perf. 11, 13x13½

1944-48   **Wmk. 294**
O58	A11	4p gray green	50.00	10.00
a.		Perf. 11	175.00	8.25
O59	A11	6p red brown	3.50	.20
O60	A11	2a gray black	8.75	1.50
O61	A11	2¼a dull yel green	5.25	1.60
a.		Additional ovpt. on back	160.00	
O62	A11	3a red orange	12.50	2.50
		Nos. O58-O62 (5)	80.00	15.80

Same Overprint with Additional Surcharge

O63	A11	3p on 4p gray green	4.25	.20
a.		Additional overprint on back	210.00	
O64	A12	3p on 1a brown org	32.50	11.00
O65	A11	9p on 6p red brown	16.00	5.25
O66	A12	1a3p on 1a brown org	16.00	4.00
		Nos. O63-O66 (4)	68.75	20.45

Same Overprint in Black on Types of 1944 Surcharged Type "c"
O67	A11	3p on 4p gray green	6.25	.60
O68	A11	9p on 6p red brown	5.50	.60
O69	A12	1a3p on 1a brown org	4.50	.20
		Nos. O67-O69 (3)	16.25	1.40

Nos. O52 and O16 Surcharged Type "d"

1944   **Wmk. 41**   *Perf. 11, 13x13½, 14*
O70	A10	3p on 1a brown org	2.75	5.00
O71	A10	9p on 1a brown org	325.00	82.50

Engr.
O71A	A7	9p on 1½a red vio	800.00	40.00

No. O52 Surcharged Type "c"
O72	A10	1a3p on 1a brn org	375.00	150.00

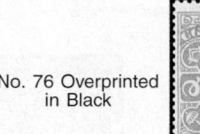

No. 76 Overprinted in Black

Perf. 13
O72A	A9	3p on 4p dull green	210.00	90.00

No. 45 Overprinted Type "k" and Surcharged Type "d"

1944-48   **Wmk. 41**   *Perf. 13x13½*
O73	A9	9p on 1a8p rose red	160.00	50.00
O74	A9	1a9p on 1a8p rose red	3.50	4.00

No. 45 Overprinted Type "k" and Surcharged Type "c"
O75	A9	3p on 1a8p rose red	7.00	4.50
O76	A9	1a9p on 1a8p rose red	1.90	.60

Type of 1939-41 Overprinted in Black

1946   **Wmk. 294**   *Perf. 11*
O77	A9	2a gray	92.50	1.20
O77A	A9	2¼a yellow green	2,000.	10.00

Same Overprint in Black on #79-81

1946   **Litho.**   *Perf. 13*
O78	A13	9p ultramarine	3.75	.20
O79	A13	1a3p magenta	2.00	.20
a.		Double overprint	25.00	18.00
O80	A13	1a9p ultramarine	.50	1.50
		Nos. O78-O80 (3)	6.25	1.90

Types and Stamps of 1946-48 Overprinted Type "h"

1946-48
O81	A15	3p car rose	1.50	.20
O82	A15	4p gray green	37.50	10.00
O83	A15	6p red brown	17.50	2.50
O84	A15	9p ultra	.95	.20
O85	A15	1a3p magenta	5.00	2.10
O86	A15	1a9p ultra	6.00	.60
O87	A15	2a gray black	19.00	4.50
O88	A15	2¼a olive green	29.00	7.50
		Nos. O81-O88 (8)	116.45	27.60

No. 56 Overprinted Type "q" and Surcharged Type "d"

1947   **Wmk. 41**   **Engr.**   *Perf. 13x13½*
O89	A9	3p on 4p dull green	32.50	11.00

Stamps and Type of 1948-49 Overprinted Type "o"

1948-49   **Wmk. 294**   **Litho.**   *Perf. 11*
O90	A16	3p carmine ('49)	1.50	.20
O91	A16	4p gray green	1.90	.60
O92	A16	6p red brown	3.50	.45
O93	A16	9p ultramarine	4.00	.20
O94	A16	2a black ('49)	3.50	.20
O95	A16	2¼a lt ol green ('49)	4.00	9.50
O96	A16	3a vermilion ('49)	1.40	1.50
O97	A16	3a4p deep pur ('49)	55.00	67.50
		Nos. O90-O97 (8)	74.80	80.15

See Travancore-Cochin for succeeding issues.

DHAR

'där

LOCATION — A Feudatory State in the Malwa Agency in Central India.
AREA — 1,800 sq. mi.
POP. — 243,521
CAPITAL — Dhar

 A1

Arms of Dhar — A2

The stamps of type A1 have an oval control mark handstamped in black.

Unwmk.

1897-1900   **Typeset**   *Imperf.*
Without Gum
1	A1	½p black, *red*	4.50	5.00
a.		Characters for "pice" transposed	100.00	
b.		Four characters in first word	4.00	6.00
c.		Without control mark	500.00	
2	A1	¼a black, *org red* ('00)	5.50	7.50
a.		Without control mark	375.00	
3	A1	½a black, *lil rose*	6.75	8.25
4	A1	1a black, *bl grn*	12.50	25.00
5	A1	2a black, *yel* ('00)	42.50	75.00
		Nos. 1-5 (5)	71.75	120.75

1898-1900   **Typo.**   *Perf. 11½*
6	A2	½a red	7.00	9.50
7	A2	½a rose ('00)	6.25	9.00
a.		Imperf., pair	60.00	
8	A2	1a maroon	6.25	12.00
9	A2	1a violet ('00)	6.25	22.50
10	A2	1a claret ('00)	6.25	12.00
11	A2	2a dark green ('00)	11.00	37.50
		Nos. 6-11 (6)	43.00	102.50

Obsolete Mar. 31, 1901.

DUNGARPUR

LOCATION — A princely state in Rajasthan, in northwestern India.
AREA — 1,447 sq. mi.
POP. — 100,103 (1901)
CAPITAL — Dungarpur

Arms of Dungarpur — A1

1933-1947   **Unwmk.**   **Litho.**   *Perf. 11*
1	A1	¼a bister yellow	2,000.	400.00
a.		¼a lemon yellow ('34)	2,500.	500.00
2	A1	¼a salmon ('35)	5,000.	1,000.
a.		¼a red brown ('36)	3,750.	750.00
b.		¼a orange red ('38)	6,250.	1,250.
3	A1	1a pale turquoise blue	1,500.	300.00
a.		1a turquoise blue	2,000.	400.00
4	A1	1a3p deep red violet ('35)	3,000.	600.00
5	A1	2a deep dull green ('47)	3,750.	750.00
6	A1	4a dull rose red	6,250.	1,250.
a.		4a rose red ('34)	7,000.	1,400.

A2

A3

A4

A5

A6

A7

A8

A9

A10

Maharawal Lakshman Singh

1934-38   Typo.   Perf. 12

7	A2 ¼a org buff ('36)	1,750.	200.00
8	A3 ½a vermilion, Die I	500.00	125.00
9	A4 1a blue		
a.	Perf 11½ ('38)	750.00	125.00
10	A5 4a gray brown	2,000.	650.00

There are three dies of the ½ anna: Die I measures 21x25½mm, and width of turban is 7½mm; Die II measures 20x20½mm; Die III measures 21x25½mm, and width of turban is 6½mm. There are 4 distinct cliches of Die III, printed in a block of 4, differing in the space between the top of the turban and the frame: Pos. 1 = 2mm; Pos. 2 = 2.5mm; Pos. 3 = 1mm; Pos. 4 = 1.5mm.

1940-41   Perf. 11, 11½ (#15)

11	A2 ¼a dull org('41)	1,500.	150.00
12	A3 ½a carmine, Die I	500.00	150.00
13	A4 1a blue	500.00	100.00
14	A6 2a bright green	2,500.	900.00
15	A5 4a gray brown	1,800.	450.00

1943   Pin-Perf 11½

16	A6 2a bright green	2,500.	900.00

1943-44   Perf. 10½

17	A2 ¼a dull org('44)	1,500.	150.00
18	A3 ½a vermilion, Die I ('44)	600.00	175.00
19	A7 ½a vermilion, Die II ('44)	600.00	175.00
a.	Horiz. pair, #18 + #19	1,300.	450.
b.	Vert. pair, imperf between		5,000.
20	A4 1a blue ('44)	500.00	100.00
21	A8 1a3p mauve	2,000.	450.00
22	A5 4a pale brown ('44)	2,400.	650.00

1945   Perf. 10

23	A2 ¼a orange	2,000.	150.00
24	A9 ½a vermilion, Die III ('44)	800.00	100.00
25	A4 1a blue	500.00	100.00
26	A8 1a3p bright mauve	2,000.	450.00
27	A10 1½a deep violet	2,000.	450.00
28	A5 4a brown	1,600.	450.00

The stamps of Dungarpur became obsolete in Sept. 1949.

DUTTIA

ˈdət-ē-ə,

(Datia)

LOCATION — A Feudatory State in the Bundelkhand Agency in Central India.
AREA — 912 sq. mi.
POP. — 158,834
CAPITAL — Datia

Ganesh, Elephant-headed God

A1   A2

All Duttia stamps have a circular control mark, about 23mm in diameter, handstamped in blue or black. All were issued without gum.

1893   Typeset   Unwmk.   Imperf.

1	A1 ¼a black, org red	6,250.	
2	A1 ½a blk, grysh grn	24,000.	
3	A2 1a black, red	4,750.	7,500.
4	A1 2a black, yellow	5,250.	
5	A1 4a black, rose	1,900.	

Type A2 with Frameline around God, Rosettes in Lower Corners

1896 (?)

5A	A2 ½ black, green	15,000.	
5C	A2 2a dk blue, lemon	3,750.	

A 1a in this revised type has been reported.

1897

6	A2 ½a black, green	100.00	675.00
7	A2 1a black	150.00	525.00
a.	Laid paper	32.50	
8	A2 2a black, yellow	42.50	500.00
9	A2 4a black, rose	40.00	325.00
	Nos. 6-9 (4)	332.50	2,025.

A3   A4

10	A3 ½a black, green	150.00	825.00
11	A3 1a black	290.00	
12	A3 2a black, yellow	175.00	825.00
13	A3 4a black, rose	175.00	825.00
	Nos. 10-13 (4)	790.00	2,475.

1899-1900
Rouletted in Colored Lines on 2 or 3 Sides

14	A4 ¼a red (shades)	5.00	32.50
b.	Tete beche pair	4,900.	
15	A4 ½a black, green	4.00	30.00
16	A4 1a black	4.50	30.00
17	A4 2a black, yellow	5.25	35.00
18	A4 4a black, rose red	5.00	32.50
a.	Tete beche pair		
	Nos. 14-18 (5)	23.75	160.00

1904   Imperf.

22	A4 ¼a carmine	5.50	47.50
23	A4 ½a black, green	27.50	
24	A4 1a black	21.00	75.00
	Nos. 22-24 (3)	54.00	122.50

1911   Perf. 13½

25	A4 ¼a carmine	9.50	75.00

1916   Imperf.

26	A4 ¼a dull blue	8.25	40.00
27	A4 ½a green	8.25	40.00
28	A4 1a violet	10.00	42.50
a.	Tete beche pair	35.00	
29	A4 2a brown	22.50	52.50
29A	A4 4a brick red	110.00	
	Nos. 26-29A (5)	159.00	175.00

1918

31	A4 ½a ultramarine	5.25	27.50
32	A4 1a rose	5.25	27.50
33	A4 2a violet	11.00	40.00

Perf. 12

34	A4 ¼a black	7.50	37.50
	Nos. 31-34 (4)	29.00	132.50

1920   Rouletted

35	A4 ¼a blue	4.00	21.00
36	A4 ½a rose	5.25	24.00

Perf. 7

37	A4 ½a dull red	24.00	62.50
	Nos. 35-37 (3)	33.25	107.50

Duttia stamps became obsolete in 1921.

FARIDKOT

fe-ˈrēd-ˌkōt

LOCATION — A Feudatory State in the Punjab Agency of India.
AREA — 638 sq. mi.
POP. — 164,364
CAPITAL — Faridkot

4 Folus or Paisas = 1 Anna

A1   A2

A3

Handstamped
1879-86   Unwmk.   Imperf.
Without Gum

1	A1 1f ultramarine	4.00	6.00
a.	Laid paper	21.00	24.00
b.	Tete beche pair	400.00	
2	A2 1p ultramarine	7.50	16.00
a.	Laid paper	125.00	150.00
3	A3 1p ultramarine	2.25	
a.	Tete beche pair	340.00	
	Nos. 1-3 (3)	13.75	22.00

Several other varieties exist, but it is believed that only the stamps listed here were issued for postal use. They became obsolete Dec. 31, 1886. See Faridkot under Convention States for issues of 1887-1900.

HYDERABAD (DECCAN)

ˈhīd-ə-ˌrə-ˌbad

LOCATION — Central India
AREA — 82,313 sq. mi.
POP. — 16,338,534 (1941)
CAPITAL — Hyderabad

This independent princely state was occupied and annexed by India in 1948.

> Catalogue values for unused stamps in this State are for Never Hinged items, beginning with Scott 51 in the regular postage section, and Scott O54 in the officials section.

Expect irregular perfs on the Nos. 1-14 and O1-O20 due to the nature of the paper.

A1   A2

1869-71   Engr.   Unwmk.   Perf. 11½

1	A1 ½a brown ('71)	6.00	6.50
2	A2 1a olive green	27.50	11.00
a.	Imperf. horiz., pair	900.00	175.00
3	A1 2a green ('71)	90.00	72.50
	Nos. 1-3 (3)	123.50	90.00

For overprints see Nos. O1-O3, O11-O13.
The reprints are perforated 12½.

A3   A4

Wove Paper
1871-1909   Perf. 12½

4	A3 ½a orange brown	4.00	.20
a.	½a red brown	4.00	.20
b.	½a magenta (error)	75.00	12.00
c.	Perf. 11½	27.50	30.00
d.	½a rose	4.00	.30
e.	½a bright vermilion	4.00	

5	A3 1a dark brown	1.90	.20
a.	Imperf., pair		550.00
b.	Horiz. pair, imperf. vert.		1,350.
c.	Vert. pair, imperf. horiz.		1,350.
d.	Perf. 11½	180.00	200.00
6	A3 1a black ('09)	3.50	.20
7	A3 2a green	5.50	.20
a.	2a olive green ('09)	5.50	.50
b.	Perf. 11½		1,900.
8	A3 3a yellow brown	4.50	2.25
a.	Perf. 11½	60.00	82.50
9	A3 4a slate	11.00	5.25
a.	Imperf. horiz., pair	1,350.	1,350.
b.	Perf. 11½	225.00	225.00
10	A3 4a deep green	8.25	5.00
a.	4a olive green	9.00	3.75
11	A3 8a bister brown	5.25	6.50
	Perf. 11½		
12	A3 12a blue	7.00	12.00
a.	Perf. 11½	500.00	
b.	12a slate green	7.50	7.50
	Nos. 4-12 (9)	50.90	31.80

For overprints see Nos. 13, O4-O10, O14-O20, O25-O26.

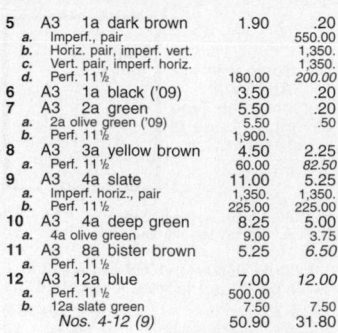

Surcharged

1900

13	A3 ¼a on ½a brt ver	.75	1.25
a.	Inverted surcharge	57.50	35.00

1900, Sept. 20

14	A4 ¼a blue	8.25	5.25

Seal of the Nizam
A5   A6
Engraved by A. G. Wyon
1905   Wmk. 42

17	A5 ¼a blue	3.75	.90
18	A5 ½a red	6.00	.35
19	A5 ½a orange	9.00	.50
	Nos. 17-19 (3)	18.75	1.75

For overprints see Nos. O21-O23.

Perf. 11, 11½, 12½, 13½ and Compound
1908-11

20	A5 ¼a gray	1.50	.20
21	A5 ½a green	7.00	.20
22	A5 1a carmine	5.25	.20
23	A5 2a lilac	2.40	.20
24	A5 3a brn orange ('09)	4.00	1.50
25	A5 4a olive green ('09)	4.50	1.90
26	A5 8a violet ('11)	1.90	1.20
27	A5 12a blue green ('11)	10.50	6.00
	Nos. 20-27 (8)	37.05	11.40

For overprints see Nos. O24, O27-O38.

Engr. by Bradbury, Wilkinson & Co.
1912

28	A5 ¼a brown violet	1.20	.20
29	A5 ½a deep green	2.50	.20
a.	Imperf., pair		550.00

The frame of type A5 differs slightly in each denomination.
Nos. 20-21 measure 19½x20½mm.
Nos. 28-29 measure 20x21½mm.
For overprints see Nos 37, O39-O40, O44.

1915-16

30	A6 ½a green	1.50	.20
31	A6 1a carmine rose	3.75	.20
32	A6 1a rose	2.50	.20
	Nos. 30-32 (3)	7.75	.60

Unless used, imperf. stamps of types A5 and A6 are from plate proof sheets.
See #58. For overprints see #38, O41-O43, O45.

A7

1927   Wmk. 211   Perf. 13½

36	A7 1r yellow	13.50	18.00

Stamps of 1912-16 Surcharged in Red

(4 pies)   (8 pies)

1930

37	A5	4p on ¼a brown violet	.45	.20
a.		Perf. 11		675.00
b.		Double surcharge		350.00
38	A6	8p on ½a green	.60	.20
a.		Perf. 11	400.00	210.00

For overprints see Nos. O44-O45.

Seal of Nizam — A8   Char Minar — A9

High Court of Justice A10

Reservoir for City of Hyderabad A11

Bidar College — A13

Entrance to Ajanta Caves A12   Victory Tower at Daulatabad A14

Wmk. 211

1931-48		Engr.	Perf. 13½	
39	A8	4p black	.45	.20
a.		Laid paper ('47)	3.75	8.25
39B	A8	6p car lake ('48)	15.00	12.50
40	A8	8p green	.75	.20
a.		8p yel grn, laid paper ('47)	4.50	6.75
b.		Imperf., pair	90.00	180.00
41	A9	1a dark brown	.75	.20
42	A10	2a dark violet	4.50	.20
a.		Imperf., pair	195.00	400.00
43	A11	4a ultramarine	2.40	1.00
a.		Imperf., pair	210.00	500.00
44	A12	8a deep orange	10.50	6.00
45	A13	12a scarlet	11.00	18.00
46	A14	1r yellow	7.50	7.00
		Nos. 39-46 (9)	52.85	45.30

On No. 39B, "POSTAGE" has been moved to ribbon at bottom of design.
Nos. 39a and 40a are printed from worn plates. The background of the design is unshaded.
See #59. For overprints see #O46-O53, O56.

Unani General Hospital A15

Osmania General Hospital A16

Osmania University A17

Osmania Jubilee Hall — A18

Perf. 13½x14

1937, Feb. 13		Litho.	Unwmk.	
47	A15	4p violet & black	.75	3.25
48	A16	8p brown & black	1.25	3.25
49	A17	1a dull orange & gray	1.75	2.10
50	A18	2a dull green & gray	2.25	6.75
		Nos. 47-50 (4)	6.00	15.35

The Nizam's Silver Jubilee.

> **Catalogue values for unused stamps in this section, from this point to the end of the section, are for Never Hinged items.**

Returning Soldier — A19

1946		**Typo.**	**Perf. 13½**	
51	A19	1a dark blue	.20	.20

Wmk. 211

| 52 | A19 | 1a blue | .20 | .20 |

Wmk. Nizam's Seal in Sheet
Laid Paper

| 53 | A19 | 1a dark blue | 1.00 | 1.20 |
| | | Nos. 51-53 (3) | 1.40 | 1.60 |

Victory of the Allied Nations in WW II.

Town Hall, Hyderabad A20

1947, Feb. 17		Litho.	Wove Paper	
54	A20	1a black	2.00	2.90

Inauguration of the Reformed Legislature, Feb. 17th, 1947.

Power House, Hyderabad A21

Designs: 3a, Kaktyai Arch, Warangal Fort. 6a, Golkunda Fort.

Perf. 13½x14

1947-49		Typo.	Wmk. 211	
55	A21	1a4p dark green	1.50	3.25
56	A21	3a blue	2.50	6.50
57	A21	6a olive brown	5.50	27.50
a.		6a red brown ('49)	25.00	47.50
b.		Imperf., pair	190.00	
		Nos. 55-57 (3)	9.50	37.25

Seal Type of 1915

1947		Engr.	Perf. 13½	
58	A6	½a rose lake	3.75	1.10

For overprint see No. O54.

Seal Type of 1931

1949		Litho.		
59	A8	2p brown	3.00	3.50

For overprint see No. O55.

OFFICIAL STAMPS

Regular Issues of
1869-71 Overprinted

1873		Unwmk.	Perf. 11½, 12½	

Red Overprint

O1	A1	½a brown	195.00	125.00
O2	A2	1a olive green	35.00	35.00
O3	A1	2a green	72.50	57.50
O4	A3	½a red brown	27.50	9.00
O5	A3	1a dark brown	195.00	125.00
O6	A3	2a green	72.50	57.50
O7	A3	3a yel brown	250.00	250.00
O8	A3	4a slate	120.00	72.50
O9	A3	8a bister	125.00	225.00
O10	A3	12a blue	195.00	240.00

Black Overprint

O11	A1	½a brown		52.50
O12	A2	1a olive green	4.50	3.75
O13	A1	2a green	7.50	9.00
O14	A3	½a red brown	16.00	5.25
O15	A3	1a dark brown		52.50
O16	A3	2a green	7.50	9.00
O17	A3	3a yel brown	62.50	52.50
O18	A3	4a slate	32.50	30.00
O19	A3	8a bister	75.00	62.50
O20	A3	12a blue	90.00	62.50

The above official stamps became obsolete in August, 1878. Since that date the "Official" overprint has been applied to the reprints and probably to original stamps. Two new varieties of the overprint have also appeared, both on the reprints and on the current stamps. These are overprinted in various colors, positions and combinations.

Same Ovpt. On Regular Issues of
1905-11

1908			Wmk. 42	
O21	A5	½a green	30.00	.20
O22	A5	1a carmine	97.50	.20
O23	A5	2a lilac	97.50	.20
		Nos. O21-O23 (3)	225.00	.60

Perf. 11, 11½, 12½, 13½ and
Compound

1909-11				
O24	A5	½a red	210.00	.20
O25	A3	1a black	140.00	.75
O26	A3	2a olive green	150.00	1.50
O27	A3	3a brown orange	11.00	5.00
O28	A5	4a olive green ('11)	45.00	1.90
O29	A5	8a violet ('11)	19.00	5.25
O30	A5	12a blue green ('11)	15.00	5.00
		Nos. O24-O30 (7)	590.00	19.60

Regular Issue of 1908-
11 Overprinted

1911-12				
O31	A5	¼a gray	6.75	1.10
O32	A5	½a green	5.25	.20
O33	A5	1a carmine	3.00	.20
O34	A5	2a lilac	2.50	1.90
O35	A5	3a brown orange	27.50	1.10
O36	A5	4a olive green	7.00	.20
O37	A5	8a violet	11.00	.30
O38	A5	12a blue green	36.00	3.75
		Nos. O31-O38 (8)	99.00	8.75

Same Overprint on Regular Issue of
1912

1912				
O39	A5	¼a brown violet	5.50	.20
a.		¼a gray violet	5.50	.20
O40	A5	½a deep green	5.25	.20

Same Ovpt. On Regular Issue of
1915-16

1917				
O41	A6	½a green	5.25	.20
O42	A6	1a carmine rose	7.00	.20
O43	A6	1a red	4.00	.20
		Nos. O41-O43 (3)	16.25	.60

Same Overprint on Nos. 37 and 38

1930				
O44	A5	4p on ¼a brown violet	3.25	.20
O45	A6	8p on ½a green	2.25	.20

Same Overprint on Regular Issue of
1931

1934-47		Wmk. 211	Perf. 13½	
O46	A8	4p black	4.00	.20
a.		Laid paper ('47)		7.50
b.		Imperf., pair	120.00	
O47	A8	8p green	1.90	.20
a.		8p yel grn, laid paper ('47)	10.00	7.50
b.		Inverted overprint		240.00
O48	A9	1a dark brown	3.00	.20
O49	A10	2a dark violet	11.00	.20
O50	A11	4a ultramarine	6.00	.35
O51	A12	8a deep orange	21.00	.90
O52	A13	12a scarlet	19.00	2.50
O53	A14	1r yellow	30.00	3.75
		Nos. O46-O53 (8)	95.90	8.30

> **Catalogue values for unused stamps in this section, from this point to the end of the section, are for Never Hinged items.**

Same Overprint on Nos. 58-59, 39B

1947-50			Perf. 13½	
O54	A6	½a rose lake	9.00	10.50
O55	A8	2p brown ('49)	9.00	15.00
O56	A8	6p car lake ('50)	11.00	35.00
		Nos. O54-O56 (3)	29.00	60.50

IDAR

ī′ē-dər

LOCATION — A Feudatory State in the Western India States Agency.
AREA — 1,669 sq. mi.
POP. — 262,660
CAPITAL — Himmatnagar

Stamps of Idar are in booklet panes of four. All stamps have one or two straight edges.

Maharaja Shri Himatsinhji
A1   A2

1939		Unwmk.	Typo.	Perf. 11	
1	A1	½a light green	21.00	37.50

1941			Same Redrawn	
2	A1	½a green	17.50	40.00

The panels containing denomination and name of state are shaded.

1944		Unwmk.	Perf. 12	
3	A2	½a green	4.00	110.00
4	A2	1a purple	4.00	100.00
a.		Imperf., pair	250.00	
5	A2	2a blue	4.50	150.00
6	A2	4a red	4.75	160.00
		Nos. 3-6 (4)	17.25	

INDORE

in-'dōₑr

(Holkar)

LOCATION — A Feudatory State in the Indore Agency in Central India.
AREA — 9,902 sq. mi.
POP. — 1,513,966
CAPITAL — Indore

Maharaja Tukoji Rao II — A1

A2

1886   Unwmk.   Litho.   Perf. 15

1	A1	½a lilac	5.50	3.25

1889   Handstamped   Imperf.

3	A2	¼a black, rose	5.25	5.50

No. 3 exists in two types.
The originals of this stamp are printed in water color. The reprints are in oil color and on paper of a deeper shade of rose.

Maharaja Shivaji Rao — A3

1889-92   Engr.   Perf. 15

4	A3	¼a orange	2.25	1.20
5	A3	½a brown violet	3.75	.20
6	A3	1a green	4.50	1.90
7	A3	2a vermilion	10.50	3.00
		Nos. 4-7 (4)	21.00	6.30

For overprint see No. 14.

Maharaja Tukoji Rao III
A4   A5

1904-08   Perf. 13½, 14

8	A4	¼a orange	.90	.20
9	A5	½a lake ('08)	13.50	.20
a.		Imperf., pair	35.00	
10	A5	1a green ('07)	3.75	.20
a.		Imperf., pair	175.00	
11	A5	2a brown ('05)	22.50	1.50
a.		Imperf., pair	120.00	
12	A5	3a violet	35.00	10.50
13	A5	4a ultramarine	7.50	2.10
		Nos. 8-13 (6)	83.15	14.70

For overprints see Nos. O1-O7.

No. 5 Surcharged

1905   Perf. 15

14	A3	¼a on ½a brown violet	9.00	30.00

Maharaja Yeshwant Rao II
A6   A7

1928-38   Engr.   Perf. 13½

15	A6	¼a orange	.90	.30
16	A6	½a claret	3.25	.20
17	A6	1a green	4.00	.20
18	A6	1¼a green ('33)	6.00	1.25
19	A6	2a dark brown	19.00	3.25
20	A6	2a Prus blue ('36)	19.00	3.25
a.		Imperf, pair	37.50	275.00
21	A6	3a dull violet	3.00	14.00
22	A6	3½a dull violet ('34)	10.50	15.00
a.		Imperf, pair	100.00	650.00
23	A6	4a ultramarine	10.50	7.50
24	A6	4a bister ('38)	52.50	2.50
a.		Imperf, pair	45.00	500.00
25	A6	8a gray	9.50	6.50
26	A6	8a red orange ('38)	40.00	35.00
27	A6	12a rose red ('34)	7.50	15.00

Perf. 14

28	A7	1r lt blue & black	12.50	22.50
29	A7	2r car lake & black	82.50	90.00
30	A7	5r org brn & black	140.00	140.00
		Nos. 15-30 (16)	420.65	356.45

Imperforates of types A6 and A7 were used with official sanction at Indore City during a stamp shortage in 1938. They were from sheets placed by the printers (Perkins, Bacon) on top of packets of 100 perforated sheets as identification.

Stamps of 1929-33 Surcharged in Black

1940   Perf. 13, 14

31	A7	¼a on 5r org brn & blk	19.00	2.50
a.		Dbl. surch., black over green	700.00	
32	A7	½a on 2r car lake & blk	32.50	5.00
33	A6	1a on 1¼a green	32.50	1.20
a.		Inverted surcharge	110.00	
		Nos. 31-33 (3)	84.00	8.70

Stamps with green surcharge only are proofs.

A8

1941-47   Typo.   Perf. 11

34	A8	¼a orange	2.50	.20
35	A8	½a rose lilac	4.75	.20
36	A8	1a dk olive green	12.50	.20
37	A8	1¼a yellow green	20.00	20.00
a.		Imperf., pair	275.00	
38	A8	2a turquoise blue	14.00	1.75
39	A8	4a bister ('47)	20.00	20.00

Size: 23x28¼mm

40	A8	2r car lake & blk ('47)	16.00	250.00
41	A8	5r brn org & blk	15.00	325.00
		Nos. 34-41 (8)	104.75	617.35

OFFICIAL STAMPS

Stamps and Type of 1904-08 Overprinted

1904-06   Perf. 13½, 14

O1	A5	½a lake	1.10	1.90
a.		Inverted overprint	35.00	62.50
b.		Double overprint	35.00	
c.		Imperf., pair	110.00	
O2	A5	1a green	.20	.20
O3	A5	2a brown ('05)	.45	.45

O4	A5	3a violet ('06)	2.50	5.50
a.		Imperf., pair	425.00	
O5	A5	4a ultra ('05)	7.50	2.25
		Nos. O1-O5 (5)	11.75	10.30

Same Overprint on No. 8

1907

O6	A4	¼a orange	1.10	1.90

No. 9 Overprinted

O7	A5	½a lake	.20	1.75

#O1, O7 differ mainly in the shape of the "R."

JAIPUR

ˈjī-ˌpu̇(ə)r

LOCATION — A Feudatory State in the Jaipur Residency of India.
AREA — 15,610 sq. mi.
POP. — 3,040,876
CAPITAL — Jaipur

> Catalogue values for unused stamps in this State are for Never Hinged items, beginning with Scott 49 in the regular postage section, and Scott O30 in the officials section.

A1   A1a

Chariot of Surya, Sun God
Pin-perf. 14x14½

1904   Typo.   Unwmk.

1	A1	½a ultramarine	290.00	275.00
a.		½a pale blue	210.00	275.00
b.		½a gray blue	3,250.	300.00
c.		As "b," imperf.	525.00	900.00
1D	A1a	½a blue	5.00	10.00
e.		½a ultramarine	5.50	10.00
f.		Imperf.	5.50	10.00
2	A1	1a dull red	8.25	21.00
a.		1a chestnut	8.25	21.00
3	A1	2a pale green	8.25	21.00
a.		2a emerald	9.00	
		Nos. 1-3 (4)	311.50	327.00

No. 1 has 36 varieties (on 2 plates), differing in minor details. Nos. 1b and 1c are from plate II. No. 1D has 24 varieties (one plate).

Chariot of Surya — A2

Perf. 12½x12 and 13½

1904-06   Engr.

4	A2	¼a olive green ('06)	1.25	1.60
5	A2	½a deep blue	2.75	.75
6	A2	1a carmine	3.75	6.75
7	A2	2a dark green	5.25	2.25
8	A2	4a red brown	11.00	3.25
9	A2	8a violet	6.00	4.00
10	A2	1r yellow	35.00	24.00
		Nos. 4-10 (7)	65.00	42.60

For overprints see Nos. 21-22.

A4

1911   Typo.   Imperf.
Without Gum

11	A3	¼a yellow green	3.75	5.00
a.		¼a olive green	3.75	5.00
b.		"¼" inverted	9.00	
12	A3	¼a olive yellow	.45	1.50
b.		¼a blue (error)		
13	A3	½a ultramarine	.45	1.50
a.		½a dull blue	4.00	4.00
b.		"½" for "¼"	7.00	
14	A3	1a carmine	.75	1.50
15	A3	2a deep green	3.00	9.50
a.		2a gray green	4.00	8.25
		Nos. 11-15 (5)	8.40	19.00

There are six types for each value and several settings of the ¼a and ½a in the 1911 issue.

Wmk. "Dorling & Co., London" in Sheet

1913-18   Perf. 11

16	A4	¼a olive bister	1.00	2.25
a.		Vert. pair, imperf. between	300.00	300.00
b.		Horiz. pair, imperf. between	—	240.00
17	A4	½a ultramarine	2.25	1.90
18	A4	1a carmine ('18)	8.25	8.25
a.		1a scarlet	6.00	5.50
b.		Vert. pair, imperf. btwn.	1,250.	1,250.
c.		Vert. pair, imperf. horiz.		1,250.
19	A4	2a green ('18)	6.00	7.50
20	A4	4a red brown	10.50	15.00
		Nos. 16-20 (5)	28.00	34.90

For overprints see Nos. O1-O6, O9-O10.

Stamps of 1904-06 Surcharged

1926   Unwmk.   Engr.   Perf. 13½

21	A2	3a on 8a violet	3.00	5.25
a.		Inverted surcharge	275.00	210.00
22	A2	3a on 1r yellow	4.00	9.50
a.		Inverted surcharge	825.00	275.00

Wmk. "Overland Bank" in Sheet

1928   Typo.   Perf. 12

17a	A4	½a ultramarine	4.75	6.00
18d	A4	1a rose red	40.00	25.00
18e	A4	1a scarlet	62.50	17.50
19a	A4	2a green	140.00	45.00
20a	A4	4a pale brown		
23	A4	1r red orange	600.00	825.00

Durbar Commemorative Issue

Chariot of Surya, Sun God — A5

Maharaja Man Singh II — A6

Elephant with Standard — A7

Sowar in Armor — A8

Blue Peafowl — A9

Royal Bullock Carriage — A10

Royal Elephant Carriage — A11

Albert Museum — A12

Sireh-Deorhi Gate — A13

Chandra Palace — A14

Amber Palace — A15

Rajas Jai Singh II and Man Singh II — A16

Perf. 13½x14, 14, 14x13½

1931, Mar. 14		**Typo.**	**Unwmk.**	
24	A5	¼a red brown & blk	4.50	4.00
25	A6	½a dull vio & blk	.75	.30
26	A7	1a blue & black	13.50	14.00
27	A8	2a ocher & black	13.50	14.00
28	A9	2½a rose & black	47.50	90.00
29	A10	3a dk green & blk	27.50	67.50
30	A11	4a dull grn & blk	27.50	82.50
31	A12	6a dk blue & blk	9.00	82.50
32	A13	8a brown & black	30.00	140.00
33	A14	1r olive & black	60.00	500.00
34	A15	2r lt green & blk	62.50	550.00
35	A16	5r violet & black	82.50	600.00
		Nos. 24-35 (12)	378.75	2,144.

Investiture of the Maharaja Man Singh II with full ruling powers.
Eighteen sets of this issue were overprinted in red "INVESTITURE—MARCH 14, 1931" for presentation to distinguished personages.
For surcharges see Nos. 47, 48, 58. For overprints see Nos. O12-O16, Rajasthan 16.

Man Singh II Type of 1931 and

Raja Man Singh II — A18

1932-46			**Perf. 14**	
36	A6	¼a red brn & blk	.75	.75
36A	A6	¾a brn orange & black ('43)	12.00	6.25
37	A18	1a blue & black	5.00	2.50
37A	A6	1a blue & black	14.00	6.75
38	A18	2a ocher & black	6.75	4.00
38A	A6	2a ocher & blk ('45)	19.00	7.50
39	A6	2½a dk car & blk	6.75	5.00
40	A6	3a green & black	6.00	1.00
41	A6	4a gray grn & blk	6.75	17.50
41A	A6	4a gray green & blk ('45)	72.50	2.40
42	A6	6a blue & black	9.00	45.00
43	A18	8a choc & black	9.00	22.50
43A	A6	8a choc & blk ('45)	42.50	190.00
44	A18	1r bis & gray blk	40.00	175.00
44A	A6	1r bis & gray blk ('46)	30.00	240.00
45	A18	2r yel grn & blk	140.00	700.00
		Nos. 36-45 (16)	420.00	1,426.

For overprints see Nos. O17-O30, Rajasthan Nos. 15, 17-25.

One Rupee

Stamps of 1931-32 Surcharged in Red or Black

1936		**Perf. 14x13½, 13½x14**		
46	A18	1r on 2r yel grn & blk (R)	15.00	160.00
47	A16	1r on 5r violet & blk	15.00	125.00

पाव आना

No. 25 Surcharged in Red

1938		**Perf. 14x13½**		
48	A6	¼aon ½a dull vio & blk	17.50	25.00

> **Catalogue values for unused stamps in this section, from this point to the end of the section, are for Never Hinged items.**

Amber Palace A19

Designs: ¼a, Palace gate. ¾a, Map of Jaipur. 1a, Observatory. 2a, Palace of the Winds. 3a, Arms of the Raja. 4a, Gate of Amber Fort. 8a, Chariot of the Sun. 1r, Raja Man Singh II.

1947-48		**Unwmk. Engr.**	**Perf. 14**	
49	A19	¼a dk green & red brn ('48)	2.25	7.50
50	A19	½a blue vio & dp grn	.75	6.75
51	A19	¾a dk car & blk ('48)	2.25	9.00
52	A19	1a dp ultra & choc	1.50	7.00
53	A19	2a car & blue vio	1.50	7.50
54	A19	3a dk gray & grn ('48)	2.50	9.50
55	A19	4a choc & dp ultra	1.50	7.50
56	A19	8a dk brown & red	1.50	9.00
57	A19	1r dk red vio & bl grn ('48)	4.00	67.50
		Nos. 49-57 (9)	17.75	131.25

25th anniv. of the enthronement of Raja Man Singh II.

No. 25 Surcharged in Carmine with New Value and Bars

1947				
58	A6	3p on ½a	25.00	40.00
a.		"3 PIE"	75.00	160.00
b.		Inverted surcharge	72.50	62.50
c.		Double surch., one inverted	110.00	82.50
d.		As "a," inverted surcharge	375.00	325.00

For overprint see No. O31.

OFFICIAL STAMPS

Regular Issue of 1913-22 Overprinted in Black or Red

1929		**Unwmk.**	**Perf. 12½x12, 11**	
O1	A4	¼a olive green	3.75	4.00
O2	A4	½a ultramarine	1.90	.30
a.		Inverted overprint		675.00
O3	A4	½a ultra (R)	4.00	.45
O4	A4	1a red	2.25	.45
O5	A4	2a green	2.25	.60
O6	A4	4a red brown	3.00	2.50
O7	A4	8a purple (R)	25.00	82.50
O8	A4	1r red orange	57.50	550.00
		Nos. O1-O8 (8)	99.65	640.80

The 8a and 1r not issued without overprint.
For overprint see No. O11.

Regular Issue of 1913-22 Overprinted in Black or Red

b

1931			**Perf. 11, 12½x12**	
O9	A4	½a ultra	575.00	.20
O10	A4	½a ultra (R)	300.00	.20
O10A	A4	8a purple	675.00	300.00
O10B	A4	1r red orange	700.00	400.00
		Nos. O9-O10B (4)	2,250.	700.40

आध आना

No. O5 Surcharged

1932				
O11	A4	½a on 2a green	225.00	3.00

Regular Issue of 1931 Overprinted in Red

1931-37		**Perf. 13½x14, 14**		
O12	A6	¼a red brn & blk ('36)	.60	.20
O13	A6	½a dull vio & blk	.45	.20
O14	A7	1a blue & black	400.00	4.50
O15	A8	2a ocher & blk ('36)	6.75	8.25
O16	A11	4a dl grn & blk ('37)	72.50	60.00

For overprint see No. O32.

Same on Regular Issue of 1932 in Red

1932-37		**Perf. 14**		
O17	A18	1a blue & black	6.75	.30
O18	A18	2a ocher & black	8.25	.30
O19	A18	4a gray grn & blk ('37)	550.00	16.00
O20	A18	8a choc & black	17.50	1.60
O21	A18	1r bister & gray blk	45.00	40.00
		Nos. O17-O21 (5)	627.50	58.20

No. 36 Overprinted Type "b" in Black

1939		**Perf. 14**		
O22	A6	¼a red brown & blk	140.00	110.00

Nos. 36A, 38A, 39, 41A, 43A, 44A and Type of 1931 Overprinted in Carmine

SERVICE

1941-46		**Unwmk.**	**Perf. 13½, 14**	
O23	A6	¾a brn org & blk ('43)	2.25	.75
O24	A6	1a blue & blk ('41)	6.75	.45
O25	A6	2a ocher & black	6.00	5.00
O26	A6	2½a dk car & blk ('46)	16.00	160.00
O27	A6	4a gray grn & blk ('46)	9.00	11.00
O28	A6	8a choc & black	6.00	12.50
O29	A6	1r bis & gray blk	60.00	
		Nos. O23-O28 (6)	46.00	189.70

> **Catalogue values for unused stamps in this section, from this point to the end of the section, are for Never Hinged items.**

No. O24 Surcharged with New Value and Bars in Carmine

1947		**Perf. 13½**		
O30	A6	9p on 1a blue & blk	5.50	5.50

No. 58 Overprinted in Red "SERVICE"

Perf. 14

O31	A6	3p on ½a	9.00	21.00
a.		Inverted surcharge	—	2,250.
b.		Double surch., one inverted	72.50	72.50
c.		"3 PIE"	400.00	450.00

No. O13 Surcharged "Three-quarter Anna" in Devanagari, similar to surcharge on No. 48, and Bars in Carmine

1949		**Perf. 14x13½**		
O32	A6	¾a on ½a dl vio & blk	27.50	30.00

For later issues see Rajasthan.

JAMMU AND KASHMIR

ˈjəm-ˌü and ˈkash-ˌmiəˌr

LOCATION — A Feudatory State in the Kashmir Residency in the extreme north of India.
AREA — 82,258 sq. mi.
POP. — 4,021,616 (1941)
CAPITAL — Srinagar

All stamps of Jammu and Kashmir were issued without gum.

½ Anna — A1

1 Anna — A2

4 Annas (¼
Rupee) — A3

Native Grayish Laid Paper
Handstamped
1866-67   Unwmk.   Imperf.
Printed in Water Colors

1	A1	½a gray black	375.00	150.00
		Cut to shape	75.00	30.00
2	A2	1a dull blue	900.00	180.00
a.		1a ultramarine	900.00	180.00
b.		1a royal blue	—	750.00
		Cut to shape	—	150.00
3	A2	1a gray black	2,400.	2,100.
		Cut to shape	475.00	425.00
4	A3	4a dull blue	4,500.	4,500.
a.		4a ultramarine	4,500.	4,500.
b.		4a indigo	4,500.	4,500.
		Cut to shape	900.00	900.00
5	A3	4a gray black	3,000.	
		Cut to shape	1,600.	—
		Nos. 1-5 (5)	11,175.	6,930.

It has now been proved by the leading authorities on Indian stamps that all stamps of ½ anna and 1 anna printed from the so-called Die A are forgeries and that no such die was ever in use.
See Nos. 24-59.

JAMMU

A part of the Feudatory State of Jammu & Kashmir, both being ruled by the same sovereign.

½ Anna — A4   1 Anna — A5

Printed in blocks of four, three types of the ½a and one of the 1a.

Native Grayish Laid Paper
Printed in Water Colors
1867-77   Unwmk.   Imperf.

6	A4	½a black	1,800.	625.00
7	A4	½a indigo	625.00	490.00
a.		½a deep ultramarine	490.00	290.00
b.		½a deep violet blue	325.00	160.00
8	A4	½a red	12.50	6.75
a.		½a orange red	375.00	120.00
b.		½a orange	195.00	225.00
9	A5	1a black	3,750.	2,600.
10	A5	1a indigo	1,350.	625.00
a.		1a deep ultramarine	1,200.	625.00
b.		1a deep violet blue	1,200.	625.00
11	A5	1a red	30.00	19.00
a.		1a orange red	1,250.	525.00
b.		1a orange	4,750.	2,750.

1876

12	A4	½a emerald	3,750.	1,900.
13	A4	½a bright blue	2,400.	550.00
14	A5	1a emerald	5,250.	3,000.
15	A5	1a bright blue	700.00	750.00

Native Grayish Laid Paper
1877   Printed in Oil Colors

16	A4	½a red	18.00	13.50
a.		½a brown red	—	67.50
17	A4	½a black	1,800.	
18	A5	1a red	57.50	40.00
a.		1a brown red	—	225.00
19	A5	1a black	3,750.	2,750.

The formerly listed ½a dark blue, ½a dark green, 1a dark blue and 1a dark green are believed to be reprints.

European White Laid Paper

20	A4	½a red	—	1,600.
a.		Thin laid bâtonné paper		2,750.
21	A5	1a red	—	
a.		Thin laid bâtonné paper	6,750.	

European White Wove Paper

22	A4	½a red		675.00
23	A5	1a red		

RE-ISSUES
For Jammu Only
Native Grayish Laid Paper
Printed in Water Colors
1869-76   Imperf.

24	A1	½a deep black	500.00	
25	A1	½a bright blue	550.00	675.00
26	A1	½a orange red	1,000.	1,100.
a.		½a orange to salmon	400.00	
b.		½a red	150.00	525.00
27	A1	½a emerald	175.00	450.00
28	A1	½a yellow	1,100.	1,400.
29	A2	1a deep black	500.00	
30	A2	1a bright blue	195.00	550.00
31	A2	1a orange red	1,000.	1,100.
b.		1a red	300.00	500.00
32	A2	1a emerald	195.00	450.00
33	A2	1a yellow	1,400.	
34	A3	4a deep black	450.00	—
35	A3	4a bright black	325.00	
a.		4a indigo	—	
36	A3	4a orange red	325.00	425.00
a.		4a orange		
b.		4a red	325.00	425.00
37	A3	4a emerald	450.00	1,000.
38	A3	4a yellow	900.00	

Native Grayish Laid Paper
1877   Printed in Oil Colors

39	A1	½a red	52.50	90.00
40	A1	½a black	57.50	97.50
41	A1	½a slate blue	240.00	400.00
42	A1	½a sage green	210.00	
43	A2	1a red	72.50	290.00
45	A2	1a slate blue	57.50	450.00
46	A2	1a sage green	225.00	
47	A3	4a red	475.00	825.00
50	A3	4a sage green	225.00	

European White Laid Paper

51	A1	½a red		1,800.
52	A1	½a black	47.50	97.50
53	A1	½a slate blue	82.50	450.00
54	A1	½a yellow	240.00	
56	A2	1a slate blue	90.00	600.00
57	A3	4a red	650.00	750.00
58	A3	4a sage green	2,250.	

European Brownish Wove Paper

59	A1	½a red		1,400.

It is probable that the issues of 1876, 1877 and the re-issues of the circular stamps were made to supply the demands of philatelists more than for postal needs. They were, however, available for postage.

There exist also reprints, printed in a variety of colors, on native and European thin wove paper. Collectors are warned against official imitations, which are very numerous. They are printed on several kinds of paper and in a great variety of colors.

A5a

Handstamped in Oil Color
1877, Nov.

60	A5a	(½a) red		1,900.

This provisional, made with a canceling device, was used only in Nov. 1877, at Jammu city.

KASHMIR

A part of the Feudatory State of Jammu & Kashmir, both being ruled by the same sovereign.

½ Anna — A6

Printed in Water Colors
Native Grayish Laid Paper
Printed from a Single Die
1866   Unwmk.   Imperf.

62	A6	½a black	5,250.	675.00

¼ Anna — A7   ½ Anna — A8

1 Anna   2 Annas
A9   A10

4 — A11   8 — A12
Annas   Annas

The ¼a, 1a and 2a are printed in strips of five varieties, the ½a in sheets of twenty varieties and the 4a and 8a from single dies.

1866-70

63	A7	¼a black	6.75	7.00
64	A8	½a black	2,250.	300.00
65	A8	½a ultra	7.50	2.50
a.		½a blue	13.50	0.75
66	A9	1a black	4,000.	750.00
67	A9	1a red orange	22.50	17.50
68	A9	1a Venetian red	27.50	19.00
69	A9	1a orange brown	22.50	17.50
70	A9	1a ultra	6,500.	2,500.
71	A10	2a olive yellow	30.00	32.50
72	A11	4a emerald	75.00	72.50
73	A12	8a red	75.00	72.50

All the stamps printed in oil colors are reprints.
As in Jammu, official imitations are numerous and are found in many colors and on various papers.

JAMMU & KASHMIR

    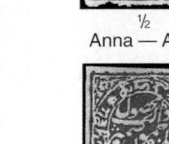

¼   ½
Anna — A13   Anna — A14

1   2
Anna — A15   Annas — A16

4   8
Annas — A17   Annas — A18

Laid Paper
Printed in Oil Colors
1878   Rough Perf. 10-14

74	A13	¼a red	21.00	25.00
75	A14	½a red		
a.		Wove paper		500.00
76	A14	½a slate blue	110.00	110.00
77	A15	1a red	1,900.	
78	A15	1a bright violet		

1878-80   Imperf.

79	A13	¼a red	35.00	30.00
80	A14	½a red	15.00	16.00
81	A14	½a slate	27.50	24.00
82	A15	1a red	14.00	17.50

83	A15	1a violet	40.00	42.50
a.		1a dull purple	67.50	62.50
84	A16	2a red	140.00	140.00
85	A16	2a bright violet	60.00	57.50
86	A16	2a dull ultra	175.00	175.00
87	A17	4a red	340.00	290.00

Thick Wove Paper

88	A14	½a red	47.50	90.00
89	A15	1a red	75.00	37.50
90	A16	2a red	32.50	40.00

Thin Toned Wove Paper
1879-80

91	A13	¼a red	5.50	6.75
92	A14	½a red	1.50	1.50
93	A15	1a red	3.75	5.25
94	A16	2a red	5.00	7.00
95	A17	4a red	16.00	16.00
96	A18	8a red	17.50	20.00
		Nos. 91-96 (6)	49.25	56.50

Thin Laid Bâtonné Paper
Printed in Water Color
1880

97	A13	¼a ultramarine	1,350.	900.00

Thin Toned Wove Paper
Printed in Oil Colors
1881

98	A13	¼a orange	17.50	24.00
99	A14	½a orange	35.00	25.00
100	A15	1a orange	37.50	21.00
101	A16	2a orange	27.50	21.00
102	A17	4a orange	67.50	82.50
103	A18	8a orange	110.00	120.00
		Nos. 98-103 (6)	295.00	293.50

⅛ Anna — A19

Thin White or Yellowish Wove Paper
1883-94

104	A19	⅛a yellow brown	2.25	3.00
a.		⅛a yellow	2.25	3.00
105	A13	¼a brown	1.90	1.50
a.		Double impression	1,800.	
106	A14	½a red	1.90	1.25
a.		½a rose	2.40	1.50
106B	A19	½a bright blue	82.50	
c.		½a dull blue	12.00	
107	A15	1a bronze green	1.50	1.50
108	A15	1a yel green	1.50	1.50
109	A15	1a blue green	3.00	
110	A15	1a bister	—	
111	A17	4a green	6.50	6.00
112	A17	4a olive green	6.00	7.00
113	A18	8a deep blue	19.00	22.50
114	A18	8a dark ultra	18.00	21.00
115	A18	8a gray violet	15.00	32.50

Printed in Water Color

116	A18	8a gray blue	225.00	225.00

Printed in Oil Colors
Yellow Pelure Paper

117	A16	2a red	4.00	1.90

Yellow Green Pelure Paper

118	A16	2a red	5.50	6.00

Deep Green Pelure Paper

119	A16	2a red	27.50	27.50

Coarse Green Pelure Paper

120	A16	2a red	4.00	1.90
		Nos. 104-120 (18)	425.05	360.05

Thin Creamy Laid Paper
1886-94

121	A19	⅛a yellow	90.00	100.00
122	A13	¼a brown	13.50	10.00
123	A14	½a vermilion	15.00	9.50
124	A14	½a rose red	—	110.00
125	A15	1a green	150.00	150.00
126	A17	4a green	—	

Printed in Water Color

127	A18	8a gray blue	160.00	150.00
		Nos. 121-127 (7)	428.50	529.50

Impressions of types A13 to A19 in colors other than the issued stamps are proofs. Forgeries to defraud the post exist, and some are common.

1/4 Anna

Stamps of the above type, printed in red or black, were never placed in use.

OFFICIAL STAMPS
Same Types as Regular Issues
White Laid Paper

1878 Unwmk. Rough Perf. 10-14

O1	A14	½a black		3,000.

Imperf

O3	A14	½a black	150.00	140.00
O4	A15	1a black	100.00	100.00
O5	A16	2a black	82.50	90.00
		Nos. O3-O5 (3)	332.50	330.00

Thin White or Yellowish Wove Paper

1880

O6	A13	¼a black	2.50	3.00
O7	A14	½a black	.20	1.10
O8	A15	1a black	3.00	1.50
O9	A16	2a black	.45	.65
O10	A17	4a black	1.90	2.50
O11	A18	8a black	3.75	1.60
		Nos. O6-O11 (6)	11.80	10.35

Thin Creamy Laid Paper

1890-91

O12	A13	¼a black	12.50	13.50
O13	A14	½a black	7.00	7.00
O14	A15	1a black	4.00	5.25
O15	A16	2a black	22.50	
O16	A17	4a black	82.50	97.50
O17	A18	8a black	42.50	75.00
		Nos. O12-O17 (6)	171.00	

Obsolete October 31, 1894.

JASDAN

LOCATION — A Feudatory State in the Kathiawar Agency in Western India.
AREA — 296 sq. mi.
POP. — 34,056 (1931)
CAPITAL — Jasdan

In 1948 Jasdan was incorporated in the United State of Saurashtra (see Soruth).

> **Catalogue values for all unused stamps in this state are for Never Hinged items.**

Sun — A1

Perf. 8½ to 10½

1942 Unwmk. Typo.

1	A1	1a green	30.00	240.00

Issued in booklet panes of 4 and 8.
The 1a carmine is a revenue stamp.
Jasdan's stamp became obsolete Feb. 15, 1948.

JHALAWAR

'jäl-ə-,wär

LOCATION — A Feudatory State in the Rajputana Agency of India.
AREA — 813 sq. mi.
POP. — 107,890
CAPITAL — Jhalrapatan

Apsaras, Hindu Nymph
A1   A2

Laid Paper
1887-90 Unwmk. Imperf.
Without Gum

1	A1	1p yellow green	7.00	22.50
2	A2	¼a green	1.90	3.75

Obsolete October 31, 1900.

JIND

'jind

(Jhind)

LOCATION — A State of India in the north Punjab.
AREA — 1,299 sq. mi.
POP. — 361,812 (1941)
CAPITAL — Sangrur

A1   A2

A3   A4

A5

1874 Unwmk. Litho. Imperf.
Thin White Wove Paper
Without Gum

1	A1	½a blue	10.00	6.25
2	A2	1a lilac	10.00	9.50
3	A3	2a yellow	1.50	6.75
4	A4	4a green	37.50	9.00
5	A5	8a dark violet	340.00	140.00
		Nos. 1-5 (5)	399.00	171.50

1875

Thick Blue Laid Paper
Without Gum

6	A1	½a blue	1.50	7.00
7	A2	1a red violet	4.00	16.00
8	A3	2a brown orange	6.50	22.50
9	A4	4a green	5.50	22.50
10	A5	8a purple	13.50	32.50
		Nos. 6-10 (5)	31.00	100.50

Nos. 3 and 6 were perforated 12 in 1885 for use as fiscal stamps.

A6   A7

A8   A9

A10   A11

1882-84 Without Gum Imperf.
Thin Yellowish Wove Paper

12	A6	¼a buff	.45	2.25
a.		Double impression	75.00	
13	A7	½a yellow	3.75	2.50
14	A8	1a brown	2.50	5.00
15	A9	2a blue	3.00	13.50
16	A10	4a green	2.25	1.50
17	A11	8a red	9.50	6.75
		Nos. 12-17 (6)	21.45	31.50

Perf. 12

18	A6	¼a buff	1.50	4.00
19	A7	½a yellow	240.00	240.00
20	A8	1a brown	3.75	8.25
21	A9	2a blue	5.50	15.00
22	A10	4a green	7.50	16.00
23	A11	8a red	18.00	
a.		Thick white paper	15.00	
		Nos. 18-23 (6)	276.25	283.25

Laid Paper
Imperf

24	A6	¼a buff	1.90	
25	A7	½a yellow	1.90	
26	A8	1a brown	1.90	3.75
27	A9	2a blue	27.50	30.00
28	A11	8a red	3.75	16.00
		Nos. 24-28 (5)	36.95	49.75

Perf. 12

29	A6	¼a buff	12.50	
30	A7	½a yellow	190.00	40.00
31	A8	1a brown	2.25	
32	A11	8a red	3.75	15.00
		Nos. 29-32 (4)	208.50	55.00

As postage stamps these issues became obsolete in July, 1885, but some possibly remained in use as revenue stamps.
For later issues see Jind under Convention States.

KISHANGARH

'kish-ən-,gär

LOCATION — A Feudatory State in the Jaipur Residency of India.
AREA — 858 sq. mi.
POP. — 85,744
CAPITAL — Kishangarh

Kishangarh was incorporated in Rajasthan in 1947-49.
Stamps were issued without gum except Nos. 27-35.

Coat of Arms — A1

1899-1900 Unwmk. Typo. Imperf.
Soft Porous Paper

1	A1	1a green	32.50	90.00
2	A1	1a blue ('00)	600.00	

Pin-perf

3	A1	1a green	110.00	

A2   A3

Coat of
Arms — A4

Maharaja
Sardul
Singh — A5

A6   A7

A8   A9

Coat of Arms—A9
A8

Thin Wove Paper

1899-1900 Handstamped Imperf.

4	A2	¼a rose pink	1.90	4.00
a.		¼a carmine	12.50	
5	A2	¼a green	825.00	1,200.
6	A3	½a light blue	1.90	2.50
7	A3	½a green	57.50	62.50
8	A3	½a carmine	3,750.	1,900.
9	A3	½a violet	240.00	490.00
10	A4	1a gray violet	1.60	1.50
a.		1a gray	7.50	7.50
11	A4	1a rose	110.00	300.00
11A	A5	2a orange	7.50	6.75
12	A6	4a chocolate	9.00	15.00
a.		4a chocolate	125.00	125.00
13	A7	1r dull green	35.00	52.50
13A	A7	1r light brown	30.00	37.50
14	A8	2r brown red	125.00	190.00
a.		Laid paper	100.00	
15	A9	5r violet	120.00	150.00
a.		Laid paper	120.00	

Pin-perf

16	A2	¼a magenta	7.50	10.00
a.		¼a rose	.35	.60
17	A2	¼a green	400.00	700.00
a.		Imperf. vertically, pair	1,900.	
18	A3	½a blue	1.50	.75
a.		½a dark blue	3.75	5.00
19	A3	½a green	27.50	40.00
a.		Imperf. vert., pair	275.00	
20	A4	1a gray violet	1.10	1.50
a.		1a gray	8.25	5.25
b.		1a red lilac	2.25	3.00
d.		As "b," laid paper	62.50	19.00
20E	A4	1a rose	125.00	375.00
21	A5	2a orange	6.00	7.50
21B	A6	4a pale red brown	5.25	9.00
c.		4a chocolate	3.50	9.00
22	A7	1r dull green	16.00	22.50
b.		Laid paper	140.00	
23	A8	2r brown red	52.50	82.50
b.		Laid paper	67.50	
24	A9	5r red violet	52.50	82.50
d.		Laid paper	110.00	

Nos. 4-24 exist tête bêche and sell for a slight premium.
For overprints see #O1-O11, Rajasthan #26-28, 30-32.

A9a   A9b

Soft Porous Paper

1901 Typo.

24A	A9a	½a rose	12.00	9.00
24B	A9b	1a dull violet	72.50	40.00

For overprint see No. O12.

      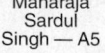

A10   A11

1903 Stout Hard Paper Imperf.

25	A10	½a pink	20.00	5.25
a.		Printed on both sides		2,100.

1904   **Thin Wove Paper**   *Pin-perf.*
25B   A11   8a gray   7.50   *11.00*
   c.   tête bêche pair   40.00

For overprints see #O13, O33, Rajasthan #29.

A11a   Maharaja Sardul Singh — A12

25D   A11a   1r green   27.50   27.50
For overprint see No. O13A.

1903   *Imperf.*
Stout Hard Paper
26   A12   2a yellow   4.50   9.00

For overprints see Nos. O14, O34.

Maharaja Madan Singh
A13   A14

1904-05   **Engr.**   **Perf. 12½, 13½**
27   A13   ¼a carmine   .65   *1.10*
28   A13   ½a chestnut   1.90   *.45*
29   A13   1a deep blue   3.75   *4.00*
30   A13   2a orange   22.50   *10.00*
31   A13   4a dark brown   22.50   *25.00*
32   A13   8a purple ('05)   19.00   *37.50*
33   A13   1r dark green   42.50   *67.50*
34   A13   2r lemon yellow   42.50   *250.00*
35   A13   5r purple brown   35.00   *300.00*
    Nos. 27-35 (9)   190.30   *695.55*

For overprints see Nos. O15-O22, O35-O38, Rajasthan Nos. 33-39.

1913   **Thin Wove Paper**
     Typo.   **Rouletted 9½**
37   A14   2 "ANNA" violet   8.25   *13.50*
   a.   tête bêche pair   18.00   *60.00*

See #40-50. For overprint see Rajasthan #43.

Maharaja Madan Singh
A15   A16
Thick, Chalk-surfaced Paper

1913   **Rouletted 6½, 12**
38   A15   ¼a pale blue   .45   *1.40*
   a.   "Kishangahr"   7.50   *10.00*
   b.   Imperf., pair   11.00
39   A16   2a purple   12.50   *27.50*
   a.   "Kishangahr"   75.00   *140.00*

For overprint see No. O23.

1913-16   **Rouletted 12, 14½**
40   A14   ¼a pale blue   .30   *.65*
41   A14   ½a green ('15)   .30   *1.50*
   a.   Printed on both sides   350.00
42   A14   1a carmine   1.90   *3.75*
43   A14   2 "ANNAS" purple   9.00   *12.00*
44   A14   4a ultramarine   9.00   *12.00*
45   A14   8a brown   10.00   *60.00*
46   A14   1r rose lilac   24.00   *190.00*
47   A14   2r dark green   150.00   *525.00*
48   A14   5r brown   60.00   *675.00*
    Nos. 40-48 (9)   264.50   *1,479.*

On Nos. 40-48 the halftone screen covers the entire design.
Nos. 41-48 have ornaments on both sides of value in top panel.
For overprints see Nos. O24-O30, O39-O43, Rajasthan Nos. 40-42, 44-48.

Type of 1913-16 Redrawn
1918   *Rouletted*
50   A14   1a rose red   2.25   *8.25*

The redrawn stamp is 24¾mm wide instead of 26mm. There is a white oval around the portrait with only traces of the red line. There is less shading outside the wreath.
For overprint see No. O44.

Maharaja Jagjanarajan Singh
A17   A18
Thick Glazed Paper

1928-29   **Pin-perf. 14½ to 16**
52   A17   ¼a light blue   1.90   *3.00*
53   A17   ½a lt yellow green   6.00   *3.50*
   a.   Imperf., pair   180.00   *180.00*
54   A18   1a carmine rose   1.10   *2.25*
55   A18   2a red violet   5.00   *12.50*
56   A17   4a yellow brown   2.50   *2.50*
57   A17   8a purple   8.25   *42.50*
58   A17   1r green   30.00   *95.00*
59   A17   2r lemon   42.50   *340.00*
60   A17   5r red brown   67.50   *400.00*
   a.   Imperf., pair   190.00
    Nos. 52-60 (9)   164.75   *901.25*

Thick Soft Unglazed Paper

1945-47
52a   A17   ¼a gray blue   6.25   *19.00*
   b.   ¼a greenish blue ('47)   4.00   *15.00*
53b   A17   ½a deep green   2.25   *4.00*
54a   A18   1a dull carmine   12.50   *6.50*
55a   A18   2a deep red violet   16.00   *19.00*
   b.   2a violet brown, imperf.   125.00   *30.00*
56a   A17   4a brown   35.00   *30.00*
57a   A17   8a violet   60.00   *240.00*
58a   A17   1r deep green   75.00   *250.00*
59a   A17   2r lemon
60b   A17   5r red brown   875.00   *1,100.*

For overprints see Rajasthan Nos. 49-58.
For later issues see Rajasthan.

OFFICIAL STAMPS
Used values are for CTO stamps.

Regular Issues of 1899-1916 Handstamped

Black Handstamp
On Issue of 1899-1900
1918   **Unwmk.**   *Imperf.*
O1   A2   ¼a carmine   12.00
O2   A4   1a gray violet   82.50   *8.25*
O3   A6   4a chocolate   —   *190.00*

         Pin-perf
O4   A2   ¼a carmine   3.25   *.90*
O4A   A2   ¼a green   —   *175.00*
O4B   A3   ½a blue   640.00   *67.50*
O6   A4   1a gray violet   67.50   *2.25*
O7   A5   2a orange   —   *225.00*
O8   A6   4a chocolate   100.00   *24.00*
O9   A7   1r dull green   250.00   *180.00*
O10   A8   2r brown red   —   *1,400.*
O11   A9   5r red violet   —   *3,000.*

See tete beche note after No. 24.

On Issue of 1901
O12   A9b   1a dull violet   75.00   *2.25*
On Issue of 1904
O13   A11   8a gray   140.00   *35.00*
O13A   A11a   1r green   —   *1,350.*
         Imperf.
O14   A12   2a yellow   125.00   *7.50*
On Issue of 1904-05
     Perf. 12½, 13
O15   A13   ¼a carmine   —   *450.00*
O16   A13   ½a chestnut   1.50   *.50*
O17   A13   1a deep blue   16.00   *6.00*
O18   A13   2a orange   —   *1,500.*
O19   A13   4a dark brown   90.00   *27.50*
O20   A13   8a purple   600.00   *375.00*
O21   A13   1r dark green   1,200.   *1,100.*
O22   A13   5r purple brn

On Issue of 1913
       Rouletted
O23   A15   ¼a pale blue   11.00
On Issue of 1913-16
O24   A14   ¼a pale blue   .90   *.75*
O25   A14   ½a green   1.50   *1.10*
O26   A14   1a carmine   24.00   *13.50*
O27   A14   2a purple   12.50   *6.00*
O28   A14   4a ultra   42.50   *22.50*
O29   A14   8a brown   190.00   *67.50*
O30   A14   1r rose lilac   525.00   *500.00*
O31   A14   2r dark green
O32   A14   5r brown   2,750.

Red Handstamp
On Issue of 1904
       Pin-perf
O33   A11   8a gray   —   *450.00*
       Imperf
O34   A12   2a yellow   675.00   *400.00*
On Issue of 1904-05
     Perf. 12½, 13
O35   A13   1a deep blue   35.00   *10.00*
O36   A13   4a dark brown   140.00   *62.50*
O37   A13   8a purple   —   *400.00*
O38   A13   1r dark green   —   *1,000.*
On Issue of 1913-16
       Rouletted
O39   A14   ¼a pale blue   3.00   *2.50*
O40   A14   ½a green   6.50   *2.40*
O41   A14   2a purple   210.00   *100.00*
O42   A14   4a ultra   —   *52.50*
O43   A14   8a brown   —   *140.00*
On Issue of 1918
Redrawn
O44   A14   1a rose red

The overprint on Nos. O1 to O44 is handstamped and, as usual with that style of overprint, is found inverted, double, etc. In this instance there is evidence that many of the varieties were deliberately made.

KOTAH

LOCATION — A Feudatory State in the Rajputana Agency of India.
AREA — 5714 sq. mi.
POP. — 526,827 (1880)
CAPITAL — Kotah City

All Kotah stamps are only known on cover, including the uncanceled stamps. Values are for covers bearing a single stamp.

A1

A2   A3

Handstamped
1883   **Unwmk.**   *Imperf.*
      Wove Paper
1   A1   2p green, *yellow*   20,000.   *8,500.*
   a.   Double impression
2   A2   2p black, *yellow*   *20,000.*
3   A3   2p indigo, *pink*   *20,000.*

A4

1886   **Wove Paper**
4   A4   1p green, *yellow*   —

The stamps of Kotah became obsolete in 1886.

LAS BELA

ləs ˈbāl-ə

LOCATION — A Feudatory State in the Baluchistan District.
AREA — 7,132 sq. mi.
POP. — 63,008
CAPITAL — Bela

A1

A2

1897-98   **Unwmk.**   **Typo.**   **Perf. 12**
1   A1   ½a black, *white*   45.00   25.00
2   A1   ½a black, *gray*   25.00   16.00
3   A1   ½a black, *blue* ('98)   30.00   16.00
    Nos. 1-3 (3)   100.00   57.00

1901
4   A2   1a black, *red orange*   35.00   *40.00*

1904   *Pin-perf*
5   A1   ½a black, *lt blue*   24.00   13.50
       Granite Paper
6   A1   ½a black, *greenish gray*   24.00   13.50

Las Bela stamps became obsolete in Mar. 1907.

MORVI

ˈmor-vē

LOCATION — A Feudatory State in the Kathiawar Agency, Western India.
AREA — 822 sq. mi.
POP. — 113,023
CAPITAL — Morvi

In 1948 Morvi was incorporated in the United State of Saurashtra (see Soruth).

Sir Lakhdhirji Waghji The Thakur Sahib of Morvi — A1

MORVI

1931   Unwmk.   Typo.   Perf. 12
Size: 21½x26½mm

1	A1	3p red	4.50	22.50
a.		3p deep blue (error)	6.50	35.00
2	A1	½a deep blue	40.00	67.50
3	A1	1a red brown	5.00	25.00
4	A1	2a yellow brown	6.00	60.00
		Nos. 1-4 (4)	55.50	175.00

Nos. 1-4 and 1a were printed in two blocks of four, with stamps 5½mm apart, and perforated on four sides. Nos. 1 and 2 were also printed in blocks of four, with stamps 10mm apart, and perforated on two or three sides.

A2

A3

1932   Size: 21x25½mm   Perf. 11

5	A2	3p rose	7.50	21.00
6	A2	6p gray green	12.00	25.00
7	A2	6p emerald	9.50	21.00
8	A2	1a ultramarine	6.50	21.00
9	A2	2a violet	16.00	60.00
		Nos. 5-9 (5)	51.50	148.00

1934-48   Perf. 14, Rough Perf. 11

10	A3	3p carmine rose	3.75	5.25
a.		3p red	2.50	6.50
11	A3	6p emerald	2.50	10.00
a.		6p green	10.00	25.00
12	A3	1a red brown	2.75	21.00
a.		1a brown	15.00	25.00
13	A3	2a violet	3.75	30.00
		Nos. 10-13 (4)	12.75	66.25

The 1934 London printing of Nos. 10-13 is perf. 14; the later Morvi Press printing is rough perf. 11.

Morvi stamps became obsolete Feb. 15, 1948.

NANDGAON

'nänˌdˌ-ˌgaun

LOCATION — A Feudatory State in the Chhattisgarh States Agency in Central India.
AREA — 871 sq. mi.
POP. — 182,380
CAPITAL — Rajnandgaon

A1

A2

White Paper
1892, Feb.   Unwmk.   Typo.   Imperf.
Without Gum

1	A1	½a blue	10.00	275.00
2	A1	2a rose	40.00	825.00

Some authorities claim that No. 2 was a revenue stamp.
For overprints see Nos. O1-O2.

1893   Without Gum

4	A2	½a green	19.00	140.00
5	A2	2a rose	19.00	140.00

For overprint see No. O5.

Same Redrawn
1894   Without Gum

6	A2	½a yellow green	37.50	140.00
7	A2	1a rose	82.50	175.00
a.		Laid paper	375.00	

The redrawn stamps have smaller value characters and wavy lines between the stamps.
For overprints see Nos. O3-O4.

OFFICIAL STAMPS

Regular Issues
Handstamped in
Violet

1893-94   Unwmk.   Imperf.
Without Gum

O1	A1	½a blue	550.00	
O2	A1	2a red	1,350.	
O3	A2	½a yellow green	9.50	17.50
O4	A2	1a rose	16.00	37.50
a.		Laid paper	16.00	125.00
O5	A2	2a rose	3.00	3.00

Some authorities believe that this handstamp was used as a control mark, rather than to indicate a stamp for official mail.
The 1 anna has been reprinted in brown and in blue.
Nandgaon stamps became obsolete in July, 1895.

NOWANUGGUR

ˌnau-ə-'nəg-ər

(Navanagar)

LOCATION — A Feudatory State in the Kathiawar Agency, Western India.
AREA — 3,791 sq. mi.
POP. — 402,192
CAPITAL — Navanagar

Stamps of Nowanuggur were superseded by those of India.

6 Dokra = 1 Anna
16 Annas = 1 Rupee

Kandjar (Indian
Dagger) — A1

A2

1877   Unwmk.   Typo.   Imperf.
Without Gum
Laid Paper

1	A1	1d dull blue	1.00	37.50
a.		1d ultramarine	1.00	37.50
b.		Tete beche pair	1,900.	

Perf. 12½

2	A1	1d slate	120.00	175.00
a.		Tete beche pair	2,400.	

No. 2 on wove paper is of private origin.

1877-88   Imperf.
Without Gum
Wove Paper

3	A2	1d black, red violet	5.25	16.00
a.		1d black, rose	5.25	
b.		Characters at beginning of 3rd line read "4102" instead of "418"		
4	A2	2d black, green	8.25	21.00
a.		2d black, blue green	12.50	
b.		"4102" instead of "418"		
5	A2	3d black, yellow	9.00	30.00
a.		3d black, orange yellow	19.00	
b.		"4102" instead of "418"		
c.		Laid paper	160.00	

---

d.		2d black, yellow (error in sheet of 3d)	600.00	
		Nos. 3-5 (3)	22.50	67.00

Nos. 3-5 range in width from 14 to 19mm.

Seal of the
State — A3

1893   Thick Paper   Imperf.
Without Gum

6	A3	1d black	450.00	

Perf. 12

7	A3	1d black	6.50	
8	A3	3d orange	7.50	

Imperf
Thin Paper

9	A3	1d black	350.00	
10	A3	2d dark green	450.00	
11	A3	3d orange	400.00	
		Nos. 9-11 (3)	1,200.	

Perf. 12

12	A3	1d black	2.50	9.00
13	A3	2d green	3.40	12.00
14	A3	3d orange	3.40	17.50
a.		Imperf. vert., pair		
		Nos. 12-14 (3)	9.30	38.50

Obsolete at end of 1895.

ORCHHA

'or-chə

(Orcha)

LOCATION — A Feudatory State in the Bundelkhand Agency in Central India.
AREA — 2,080 sq. mi.
POP. — 314,661
CAPITAL — Tikamgarh

Seal of Orchha — A1

1913-17   Unwmk.   Litho.   Imperf.
Without Gum

1	A1	¼a ultra ('15)	3.00	7.50
2	A1	½a emerald ('14)	.85	9.50
a.		Background of arms unshaded	52.50	150.00
3	A1	1a carmine ('14)	3.75	10.00
a.		Background of arms unshaded	30.00	275.00
4	A1	2a brown ('17)	6.75	35.00
5	A1	4a orange ('14)	12.00	57.50
		Nos. 1-5 (5)	26.35	119.50

Essays similar to Nos. 2-5 are in different colors.

A2

Maharaja Singh
Dev — A3

1939-40   Perf. 13½, 13½x14

6	A2	¼a chocolate	5.00	12.00
7	A2	½a yellow green	4.50	100.00
8	A2	¾a ultramarine	7.00	150.00
9	A2	1a rose red	4.50	30.00
10	A2	1¼a deep blue	5.50	150.00
11	A2	1½a lilac	6.00	190.00
12	A2	2a vermilion	4.50	120.00
13	A2	2½a turq green	7.50	340.00
14	A2	3a dull violet	8.00	180.00
15	A2	4a blue gray	9.00	42.50

16	A2	8a rose lilac	15.00	340.00
17	A3	1r sage green	26.00	750.00
18	A3	2r lt violet ('40)	60.00	1,000.
19	A3	5r yel org ('40)	200.00	2,750.
20	A3	10r blue	700.00	4,500.
		Nos. 6-20 (15)	1,062.	10,654.

POONCH

'pünch

LOCATION — A Feudatory State in the Kashmir Residency in India.
AREA — 1,627 sq. mi.
POP. — 287,000 (estimated)
CAPITAL — Poonch

Poonch was feudatory to Jammu and Kashmir. Cancellations of Jammu and Kashmir are found on Poonch stamps, which became obsolete in 1894. The stamps are all printed in watercolor and handstamped from single dies. They may be found on various papers, including wove, laid, wove batonne, laid batonne and ribbed, in various colors and tones. Nearly all Poonch stamps exist tete beche and impressed sideways. Issued without gum.

A1

White Paper
Handstamped
1876   Unwmk.   Imperf.
Size: 22x21mm

1	A1	6p red	18,000.	240.

1877
Size: 19x17mm

1A	A1	½a red	22,500.	7,500.

1879
Size: 21x19mm

1B	A1	½a red	—	7,500.

A2

A3

A4

A5

A6

1880-88

White Paper

2	A2	1p red ('84)	40.00	40.00
3	A3	½a red	4.00	5.25
4	A4	1a red	6.75	
5	A5	2a red	16.00	19.00
6	A6	4a red	25.00	

Yellow Paper

7	A2	1p red	5.50	5.50
8	A3	½a red	9.50	9.50
9	A4	1a red	82.50	
10	A5	2a red	15.00	17.50
11	A6	4a red	7.50	7.50

Blue Paper

12	A2	1p red	4.00	3.75
13	A4	1a red	600.00	625.00

Orange Paper

14	A2	1p red	5.50	5.50
15	A3	½a red	42.50	
16	A5	2a red	150.00	
17	A6	4a red	37.50	

Green Paper

18	A3	½a red	67.50	
19	A4	1a red	5.00	7.50
20	A5	2a red	67.50	
21	A6	4a red	100.00	

Lavender Paper

22	A2	1p red	75.00	82.50
23	A4	1a red	125.00	160.00
24	A5	2a red	5.00	5.50

OFFICIAL STAMPS
White Paper
Handstamped

1888   **Unwmk.**   *Imperf.*

O1	A2	1p black	4.00	4.50
O2	A3	½a black	4.50	6.00
O3	A4	1a black	4.00	4.50
O4	A5	2a black	7.50	7.50
O5	A6	4a black	12.00	16.00
		Nos. O1-O5 (5)	32.00	38.50

1890
Yellowish Paper

O6	A2	1p black	3.75	
O7	A3	½a black	4.50	5.25
O8	A4	1a black	22.50	21.00
O9	A5	2a black	9.50	9.50
O10	A6	4a black	15.00	
		Nos. O6-O10 (5)	55.25	35.75

Obsolete since 1894.

RAJASTHAN

'rä-jə-ˌstän

(Greater Rajasthan Union)

AREA — 128,424 sq. miles
POP. — 13,085,000

The Rajasthan Union was formed in 1947-49 by 14 Indian States, including the stamp-issuing States of Bundi, Dungarpur, Jaipur and Kishangarh.

> Catalogue values for all unused stamps in this state are for Never Hinged items.

Bundi Nos. 43 to 49 Overprinted

a

1948   **Unwmk.**   *Perf. 11*
Handstamped in Black

1	A8	¼a dp grn	8.25	50.00
a.		Pair, one without overprint	550.00	
2	A8	½a purple	8.25	50.00
a.		Pair, one without overprint	600.00	
3	A8	1a yel green	7.00	42.50
4	A9	2a red	21.00	125.00
5	A9	4a dp orange	72.50	450.00
6	A10	8a vio blue	13.50	80.00
		Nos. 1-6 (6)	130.50	797.50

Handstamped in Violet

1b	A8	¼a dp grn	9.00	55.00
2b	A8	½a purple	9.00	55.00
c.		Pair, one without overprint	550.00	
3a	A8	1a yel green	24.00	140.00
b.		Pair, one without overprint	550.00	
4a	A9	2a red	47.50	275.00
5a	A9	4a dp orange	47.50	275.00
6a	A10	8a vio blue	14.00	80.00
7	A10	1r chocolate	400.00	2,400.
		Nos. 1b-7 (7)	551.00	3,280.

Handstamped in Blue

1c	A8	¼a dp grn	52.50	300.00
2d	A8	½a purple	72.50	450.00
3c	A8	1a yel green	67.50	400.00
5b	A9	4a dp orange	190.00	1,100.
6b	A10	8a vio blue	120.00	725.00
7a	A10	1r chocolate	140.00	825.00
		Nos. 1c-7a (6)	642.50	3,800.

Typo. in Black

11	A9	2a red	15.00	100.00
a.		Inverted overprint	450.00	
12	A9	4a deep orange	6.00	100.00
a.		Double overprint	400.00	
13	A10	8a violet blue	27.50	
a.		Inverted overprint	950.00	
b.		Double overprint	600.00	
14	A10	1r chocolate	11.00	
		Nos. 11-14 (4)	59.50	

Stamps of Jaipur, 1931-47, Overprinted in Blue or Carmine

1949   **Center in Black**   *Perf. 14*

15	A6	¼a red brown (Bl)	12.00	32.50
16	A6	½a dull violet	9.50	35.00
17	A6	¾a brown org (Bl)	15.00	40.00
18	A6	1a blue	11.00	72.50
19	A6	2a ocher	12.50	100.00
20	A6	2½a rose (Bl)	13.50	45.00
21	A6	3a green	16.00	110.00
22	A6	4a gray green	14.00	125.00
23	A6	6a blue	14.00	180.00
24	A6	8a chocolate	24.00	250.00
25	A6	1r bister	35.00	375.00
		Nos. 15-25 (11)	176.50	1,365.

Kishangarh Stamps and Types of 1899-1904 Handstamped Type "a" in Rose

1949   *Pin-perf., Rouletted*

26	A3	½a blue (#18)	900.00	
27	A4	1a dull lilac (#20)	21.00	62.50
28	A6	4a pale red brown (#21B)	125.00	160.00
29	A11	8a gray (#25B)	160.00	275.00
30	A7	1r dull green (#22)	450.00	500.00
31	A8	2r brown red (#23)	550.00	
32	A9	5r red violet (#24)	525.00	525.00
		Nos. 26-32 (7)		2,731.

Kishangarh Nos. 28, 31-36 Handstamped Type "a" in Rose or Green

1949   **Engr.**   *Perf. 13½, 12½*

33	A13	½a chestnut (R)	300.00	
34	A13	4a dark brown (G)	375.00	
35	A13	4a dark brown (R)	20.00	
36	A13	8a purple (R)	16.00	
37	A13	1r dark green (R)	21.00	
38	A13	2r lemon yellow (R)	27.50	
39	A13	5r purple brown (R)	47.50	
		Nos. 33-39 (7)	507.00	

Kishangarh Nos. 40-42, 37, 43, 46-48 Handstamped Type "a" in Rose

1949   **Typo.**   *Rouletted*

40	A14	¼a pale blue	8.00	8.00
41	A14	½a green	675.00	375.00
42	A14	1a carmine	—	450.00
43	A14	2 "anna" violet	825.00	
44	A14	2 "annas" purple	4.50	12.50
45	A14	8a brown	7.50	
46	A14	1r rose lilac	15.00	
47	A14	2r dark green	15.00	
48	A14	5r brown	675.00	
		Nos. 40-48 (9)		2,225.

Kishangarh Stamps and Types of 1928-29 Handstamped Type "a" in Rose

1949   *Pin-perf*

49	A17	¼a greenish blue	75.00	75.00
50	A17	½a yel green	60.00	60.00
51	A18	1a car rose	110.00	110.00
52	A18	2a red violet	325.00	325.00
53	A17	4a yel brown	4.00	12.50
54	A17	8a purple	21.00	90.00
55	A17	1r deep green	10.00	
56	A17	2r lemon	140.00	
57	A17	5r red brown	75.00	
		Nos. 49-57 (9)	820.00	

Type of Kishangarh 1928-29, Handstamped Type "a" in Rose

1949   *Pin-perf*

58	A18	1a dark violet blue	140.00	

No. 58 exists imperf.
Rajasthan stamps became obsolete Apr. 1, 1950.

RAJPEEPLA

räj-'pē-plə

(Rajpipla)

LOCATION — A Feudatory State near Bombay in the Gujarat States Agency in India.
AREA — 1,517 sq. mi.
POP. — 206,086
CAPITAL — Nandod

4 Paisas = 1 Anna

Kandjar (Indian Daggers) — A1

A2   A3

1880   **Unwmk.**   **Litho.**   *Perf. 11, 12½*
Without Gum

1	A1	1pa ultramarine	5.25	57.50
2	A2	2a green	45.00	160.00
a.		Horiz. pair, imperf. btwn.	900.00	900.00
3	A3	4a red	24.00	100.00
		Nos. 1-3 (3)	74.25	317.50

The stamps of Rajpeepla have been obsolete since 1886.

SIRMOOR

sir-'mu̇ə̇r

(Sirmur)

LOCATION — A Feudatory State in the Punjab District of India.
AREA — 1,046 sq. mi.
POP. — 148,568
CAPITAL — Nahan

A1   Raja Sir Shamsher Prakash — A2

1879   **Unwmk.**   *Perf. 11½*
Wove Paper

1	A1	1p green	24.00	500.00
a.		Imperf., pair		

Laid Paper

2	A1	1p blue	6.75	250.00
a.		Imperf., pair		

1885-88   **Litho.**   *Perf. 14 and 14½.*

3	A2	3p brown	1.00	.60
4	A2	3p orange	2.50	.45
5	A2	6p green	6.50	6.00

6	A2	1a blue	4.00	5.50
7	A2	2a carmine	6.25	21.00
		Nos. 3-7 (5)	20.25	33.55

There are several printings, dies and minor variations of this issue.
For overprints see Nos. O1-O16.

A3   Elephant — A4

1893   *Perf. 11½*

9	A3	1p yellow green	1.60	1.60
a.		1pa dark blue green	1.10	1.10
10	A3	1p ultramarine	1.90	1.20
b.		Imperf., pair	110.00	

Nos. 9 and 10 are re-issues, which were available for postage.
The printed perforation, which is a part of the design, is in addition to the regular perforation.

1895-99   **Engr.**   *Perf. 14*

11	A4	3p orange	5.45	.45
12	A4	6p green	1.10	.45
a.		Vert. pair, imperf between	15,000.	
13	A4	1a dull blue	6.50	5.25
14	A4	2a dull red	5.25	2.25
15	A4	3a yellow green	35.00	67.50
16	A4	4a dark green	24.00	35.00
17	A4	8a deep blue	27.50	42.50
18	A4	1r vermilion	57.50	110.00
		Nos. 11-18 (8)	162.30	263.40

No. 12a is unique.

Sir Surendar Bikram Prakash — A5

1899

19	A5	3a yellow green	6.25	32.50
20	A5	4a dark green	8.25	35.00
21	A5	8a blue	11.00	30.00
22	A5	1r vermilion	18.00	75.00
		Nos. 19-22 (4)	43.50	172.50

OFFICIAL STAMPS

Regular Stamps Overprinted

Black Overprint

1890-91   **Unwmk.**   *Perf. 14, 14½*

O1	A2	3p orange	4.50	52.50
O2	A2	6p green	2.25	2.25
a.		Double overprint	275.00	
b.		Double ovpt., one in red	1,250.	
O3	A2	1a blue	600.00	700.00
O4	A2	2a carmine	27.50	100.00
		Nos. O1-O4 (4)	634.25	

1890-92

Red Overprint

O5	A2	6p green	42.50	3.50
O6	A2	1a blue	37.50	47.50

O7	A2	6p green	8.25	.75
b.		Inverted overprint	210.00	150.00
O8	A2	1a blue	27.50	6.25
a.		Inverted overprint	500.00	300.00
b.		Double overprint	500.00	

1892

Black Overprint

O9	A2 3p orange	.90	.75
a.	Inverted overprint	375.00	
O10	A2 6p green	12.00	3.25
O11	A2 1a blue	18.00	1.50
a.	Double overprint	600.00	
O12	A2 2a carmine	10.00	10.00
a.	Inverted overprint	1,350.	1,350.
	Nos. O9-O12 (4)	40.90	15.50

Black Overprint

O13	A2 3p orange	19.00	1.90
a.	Inverted overprint		
b.	Double overprint		1,000.
O14	A2 6p green	8.25	.90
O15	A2 1a blue	11.00	1.90
O16	A2 2a carmine	25.00	21.00
	Nos. O13-O16 (4)	63.25	25.70

There are several settings of some of these overprints, differing in the sizes and shapes of the letters, the presence or absence of the periods, etc.

The overprints on Nos. O1-O16 are press printed. In addition, nine varieties of handstamped overprints were applied in 1894-96. Most of the handstamps are very similar to the press printed overprints.

Obsolete Mar. 31, 1901.

SORUTH

(Sorath)
(Junagarh)
(Saurashtra)

LOCATION — A Feudatory State near Bombay in the Western India States Agency in India.
AREA — 3,337 sq. mi.
POP. — 670,719
CAPITAL — Junagarh

The United State of Saurashtra (area 31,885 sq. mi.; population 2,900,000) was formed in 1948 by 217 States, including the stamp-issuing States of Jasdan, Morvi, Nowanuggur and Wadhwan.

Nos. 1-27 were issued without gum.

> **Catalogue values for unused stamps in this State are for Never Hinged items, beginning with Scott 39 in the regular postage section, and Scott O19 in the officials section.**

Junagarh

A1   A2

Handstamped in Watercolor

1864   Unwmk.   Imperf.
Laid Paper

1	A1 (1a) black, bluish	950.00	125.00
a.	Wove paper		275.00
1B	A1 (1a) black, gray	950.00	125.00

Wove Paper

2	A1 (1a) black, cream		1,500.

1868   Typo.   Imperf.
Wove Paper

3	A2 1a black, yellowish	37,500.	
4	A2 1a red, green		16,000.
5	A2 1a red, blue		12,500.
6	A2 1a black, pink	825.00	110.00
7	A2 2a black, yellow		16,000.

Laid Paper

8	A2 1a black, blue	140.00	13.50
a.	Left character, 3rd line, omitted		

9	A2 1a red	32.50	37.50
a.	Left character, 3rd line, omitted		
10	A2 4a black	400.00	675.00
a.	Left character, 3rd line, omitted		

A 1a black on white laid paper exists in type A2. Value, used $9,500.

In 1890 official imitations of 1a and 4a stamps, type A2, were printed in sheets of 16 and 4. Original sheets have 20 stamps. Four of these imitations are perf. 12, six are imperf.

A3   A4

1877-86   Laid Paper   Imperf.

11	A3 1a green	1.50	.75
a.	Printed on both sides	750.00	825.00
12	A4 4a vermilion	4.00	2.50
a.	Printed on both sides	950.00	
13	A4 4a scarlet, bluish	5.50	5.00
	Nos. 11-13 (3)	11.00	8.25

Perf. 12

14	A3 1a green	.60	.20
a.	1a blue (error)	900.00	900.00
c.	Wove paper	5.25	2.25
d.	Imperf., pair	120.00	160.00
e.	As "a," wove paper	—	900.00
f.	As "c," vert. pair, imperf horiz.	240.00	
15	A3 1a green, bluish	5.25	6.75
a.	Vert. pair, imperf horiz.		525.00
b.	Horiz. pair, imperf vert.	210.00	—
16	A4 4a red	4.00	1.90
a.	4a carmino	6.50	5.25
c.	Wove paper	7.50	18.00
d.	As "c," imperf., pair	340.00	450.00
17	A4 4a scarlet, bluish	16.00	25.00
	Nos. 14-17 (4)	25.85	33.85

Nos. 14d and 16c Surcharged

1913-14   Perf. 12

18	A3 3p on 1a green	.20	.45
a.	Laid paper	110.00	45.00
b.	Inverted surcharge	52.50	30.00
c.	Imperf., pair	52.50	
19	A4 4a on 4a red	3.75	10.00
a.	Laid paper	11.00	82.50
b.	Imperf., pair	950.00	
c.	Double surcharge	1,000.	

A5   A6

1914   Perf. 12

20	A5 3p green	2.10	.50
a.	Imperf., pair	12.50	40.00
21	A6 1a rose carmine	2.25	3.25
a.	Imperf., pair	30.00	140.00
b.	Laid paper	375.00	160.00

Nawab Mahabat Khan III
A7   A8

1923-29   Wove Paper   Perf. 12

22	A7 3p violet	.50	.65
a.	Imperf, pair	450.00	
b.	Laid paper ('29)	7.50	6.50
c.	As "b," imperf, pair ('29)	5.25	52.50
d.	As "b," horiz. pair, imperf btwn.	4.50	37.50
23	A8 1a red	4.50	14.00
b.	Laid paper	4.50	14.00

Single examples of Nos. 23 and 23b cannot usually be distinguished.

Surcharged with New Value

27	A8 3p on 1a red	7.50	10.00

Two types of surcharge.

Junagarh City and The Girnar
A9

Gir Lion — A10

Nawab Mahabat Khan III — A11

Kathi Horse A12

1929   Perf. 14

30	A9 3p dk green & blk	1.50	.20
31	A10 ½a dk blue & blk	9.00	.20
32	A11 1a claret & blk	7.50	1.50
33	A12 2a org buff & blk	19.00	3.00
34	A9 3a car rose & blk	9.00	19.00
35	A10 4a dull vio & blk	19.00	42.50
36	A12 8a apple grn & blk	25.00	35.00
37	A11 1r dull blue & blk	21.00	45.00
	Nos. 30-37 (8)	111.00	146.40

For surcharges see Nos. 40-42, O20-O25.
For overprints see Nos. O1-O14.

Type of 1929
Inscribed "Postage and Revenue"
1937

38	A11 1a claret & black	15.00	1.50

For overprint see No. O15.

> **Catalogue values for unused stamps in this section, from this point to the end of the section, are for Never Hinged items.**

United State of Saurashtra

A13

Bhavnagar Court Fee Stamp
Overprinted in Black
"U.S.S. Revenue & Postage Saurashtra"

1949   Unwmk.   Typo.   Perf. 11

39	A13 1a deep claret	16.00	15.00
a.	"POSTAGE" omitted	525.00	375.00
b.	Double overprint	525.00	600.00

Nos. 30, 31 Surcharged in Black or Carmine "POSTAGE & REVENUE ONE ANNA"

1949-50   Perf. 14

40	A9 1a on 3p dk grn & blk (bl) ('50)	60.00	82.50
a.	"OSTAGE" omitted	750.00	900.00
41	A10 1a on ½a dk bl & blk (C)	14.00	7.50
a.	Double surcharge		825.00

For overprint see No. O19.

No. 33 Surcharged in Green "Postage & Revenue ONE ANNA"
1949

42	A12 1a on 2a org buff & blk	24.00	40.00
a.	"EVENUE" omitted		1,100.

For overprint see No. O26.

OFFICIAL STAMPS

Regular Issue of 1929 Overprinted in Red

a

1929   Unwmk.   Perf. 14

O1	A9 3p dk green & black	2.50	.20
O2	A10 ½a dk blue & black	6.00	.20
O3	A11 1a claret & black	6.00	.20
O4	A12 2a org buff & black	3.75	.90
O5	A9 3a car rose & black	1.10	.75
O6	A10 4a dull violet & blk	6.25	.65
O7	A12 8a apple green & blk	5.50	4.50
O8	A11 1r dull blue & blk	5.50	35.00
	Nos. O1-O8 (8)	36.60	42.40

For surcharges see Nos. O20-O24.

Regular Issue of 1929 Overprinted in Red

b

1933-49

O9	A9 3p dk grn & black ('49)	375.00	25.00
O10	A10 ½a dk bl & black ('49)	900.00	22.50
O11	A9 3a car rose & blk	32.50	27.50
O12	A10 4a dull vio & blk	42.50	24.00
O13	A12 8a apple grn & blk	42.50	27.50
O14	A11 1r dull blue & blk	52.50	140.00

The 3p is also known with ms. "SARKARI" overprint in carmine.
For surcharge see No. O25.

No. 38 Overprinted Type "a" in Red
1938

O15	A11 1a claret & black	21.00	2.25

> **Catalogue values for unused stamps in this section, from this point to the end of the section, are for Never Hinged items.**

United State of Saurashtra

No. 41 with Manuscript "Service" in Carmine
1949

O19	A10 1a on ½a dk bl & blk (C)		225.00

Used value for No. O19 is for an example used on piece, cancelled at Gadhda or Una between June and December, 1949.

No. 42 is also known with carmine ms. "Service" overprint in English or Gujarati.

Nos. O4-O8 and O14 Surcharged "ONE ANNA" in Blue or Black
1949

Surcharge 2¼mm high

O20	A12 1a on 2a (Bl)	21,000.	40.00
O21	A9 1a on 3a	5,250.	100.00
O22	A10 1a on 4a	600.00	100.00
O23	A11 1a on 8a	525.00	72.50

Surcharge 4mm High, Handstamped

O24	A11 1a on 1r (#O8)	3,250.	72.50
O25	A11 1a on 1r (#O14)	1,350.	75.00
	Nos. O20-O25 (6)	31,975.	460.00

No. 42 Overprinted Type "b" in Carmine
1949   Unwmk.   Perf. 14

O26	A12 1a on 2a	125.00	35.00

TONK

LOCATION — A Feudatory State in the Rajputana Agency of India.
AREA — 2509 sq. mi.
POP. — 307,528 (1900)
CAPITAL — Nimbahera

Three examples of Tonk No. 1 are known. All are on covers dated 1906.

A1

Handstamped with black octagonal control seal

1906   Unwmk.   Litho.   *Imperf.*
Wove Paper

1	A1	¼a yellow brown	—	

The stamps of Tonk became obsolete in 1907.

TRAVANCORE

'trav-ən-ˌkōˌəˌr

LOCATION — A Feudatory State in the Madras States Agency, on the extreme southwest coast of India.
AREA — 7,662 sq. mi.
POP. — 6,070,018 (1941)
CAPITAL — Trivandrum

16 Cash = 1 Chuckram
2 Chuckrams = 1 Anna

Conch Shell (State Seal)
A1   A2

1888   Unwmk.   Typo.   Perf. 12
Laid Paper

1	A1	1ch ultramarine	7.00	6.50
2	A1	2ch orange red	9.00	16.00
3	A1	4ch green	30.00	25.00
		Nos. 1-3 (3)	46.00	47.50

The frame and details of the central medallion differ slightly on each denomination of type A1.
Laid paper printings of Nos. 1-3, 5-7 in completely different colors are essays.

1889-99   Wmk. 43
Wove Paper

4	A1	½ch violet	.90	.35
a.		Vertical pair, imperf. between	450.00	450.00
5	A1	1ch ultramarine	2.25	.20
a.		Vertical pair, imperf. between		675.00
6	A1	2ch scarlet	4.50	.20
a.		Horiz. pair, imperf. between	550.00	550.00
b.		Vertical pair, imperf. between		250.00
7	A1	4ch dark green	5.00	1.00
		Nos. 4-7 (4)	12.65	1.75

Shades exist for each denomination.
For surcharges see #10-11. For type surcharged see #20. For overprints see #O1-O2, O4, O6, O18, O24-O25, O27B, O32-O33, O42.

1901-32

8	A2	¾ch black	4.50	2.10
9	A2	¾ch brt violet ('32)	.50	.20
a.		Horizontal pair, imperf. between		

For overprints see Nos. O26-O27, O44, O52.

No. 4 Surcharged

1906

10	A1	¼ch on ½ch violet	1.10	.45
a.		Inverted surcharge	90.00	52.50
11	A1	⅜ch on ½ch violet	.60	.50
a.		Pair, one without surcharge	—	
b.		Inverted surcharge		75.00
c.		Double surcharge		

A3   A4

1908-11

12	A3	4ca rose	.45	.20
13	A1	6ca red brown ('10)	.45	.20
a.		Printed on both sides	75.00	
14	A4	3ch purple ('11)	4.00	.30
		Nos. 12-14 (3)	4.90	.70

For surcharge & overprints see #19, O3, O5, O8, O13, O15, O20, O22, O30-O31, O53.

A5   A6

1916

15	A5	7ch red violet	3.50	.75
16	A6	14ch orange	4.00	3.75

For overprints see Nos. O11-O12, O34-O35.

A7   A8

1920-33

17	A7	1¼ch claret	.80	.80
18	A7	1½ch light red ('33)	4.00	.20

For surcharges see Nos. 27-28. For overprints see Nos. O7, O17, O28-O29, O38, O56.

No. 12 and Type of 1888 Surcharged

1921

19	A3	1ca on 4ca rose	.20	.20
a.		Inverted surcharge	37.50	16.00
20	A1	5ca on 1ch dull bl (R)	1.50	.20
a.		Inverted surcharge	19.00	12.50
b.		Double surcharge	100.00	67.50

1921-32

21	A8	5ca bister	1.20	.20
22	A8	5ca brown ('32)	4.00	.20
23	A8	10ca rose	.60	.20
		Nos. 21-23 (3)	5.80	.60

For surcharges & overprints see #29-30, O9-O10, O14, O16, O19, O21, O23, O36-O37.

Sri Padmanabha Shrine at Trivandrum
A9

State Chariot — A10

Maharaja Sir Bala Rama Varma — A11

1931, Nov. 6

24	A9	6ca emerald & black	2.40	2.40
25	A10	10ca ultra & black	1.90	1.00
26	A11	3ch violet & black	4.00	4.50
		Nos. 24-26 (3)	8.30	7.90

Investiture of Sir Bala Rama Varma with full ruling powers.

No. 17 Surcharged

1932, Jan. 14

27	A7	1ca on 1¼ch claret	.20	.75
a.		Inverted surcharge	6.50	10.00
b.		Double surcharge	47.50	47.50
28	A7	2ca on 1¼ch claret	.20	.20
a.		Inverted surcharge	6.50	10.00
b.		Double surcharge	42.50	
c.		Pair, one without surcharge	180.00	190.00

Type of 1932 and No. 23 Surcharged like Nos. 19-20

1932, Mar. 5

29	A8	1ca on 5ca vio brown	.20	.20
a.		Inverted surcharge	11.00	15.00
b.		Double surcharge		
c.		Pair, one without surcharge	180.00	
30	A8	2ca on 10ca rose	.20	.20
a.		Inverted surcharge	7.50	12.00
b.		Double surcharge	32.50	35.00

Untouchables Entering Temple and Maharaja — A12

Designs: Different temples and frames.

Perf. 11½, 12½

1937, Mar. 29   Litho.

32	A12	6ca carmine	3.75	1.90
33	A12	12ca ultramarine	5.25	.60
34	A12	1½ch light green	2.25	3.00
35	A12	3ch purple	6.50	3.50
		Nos. 32-35 (4)	17.75	9.00

Temple Entry Bill.

Lake Ashtamudi
A13

A14   A15

Sir Bala Rama Varma — A16

Sri Padmanabha Shrine — A17

View of Cape Comerin
A18

Pachipara Reservoir
A19

Perf. 11, 12, 12½ or Compound

1939, May 9   Litho.

36	A13	1ch yellow green	8.25	.20
37	A14	1½ch carmine	5.25	6.75
a.		Perf. 13½	27.50	100.00
38	A15	2ch orange	10.00	3.50
39	A16	3ch chocolate	9.50	.20
40	A17	4ch henna brown	12.50	.60
41	A18	7ch light blue	16.00	30.00
42	A19	14ch turq green	10.00	100.00
		Nos. 36-42 (7)	71.50	141.25

27th birthday of Maharaja Sir Bala Rama Varma.
For surcharges and overprints see Nos. 45, O45-O51, Travancore-Cochin 3-7, O3-O7.

Maharaja Sir Bala Rama Varma and Aruvikara Falls
A20

Maharaja and Marthanda Varma Bridge, Alwaye
A21

1941, Oct. 20   Typo.

43	A20	6ca violet black	11.00	.20
44	A21	¾ch dull brown	12.50	.30

29th birthday of the Maharaja, Oct. 20, 1941.
For overprints & surcharges see #46-47, 49, O54-O55, Travancore-Cochin 1, O1.

Stamps and Types of 1939-41 Surcharged in Black

Perf. 11, 12½

1943, Sept. 17   Wmk. 43

45	A14	2ca on 1½ch carmine	2.25	1.90
46	A21	4ca on ¾ch dull brown	6.00	.45
47	A20	8ca on 6ca red	7.00	.20
		Nos. 45-47 (3)	15.25	2.55

For overprints see Nos. O57-O59.

Maharaja Sir Bala
Rama Varma — A22

1946, Oct. 24   Typo.   Perf. 11, 12
48   A22 8ca rose red   1.90 3.00

For overprint see No. O60. For surcharges
see Travancore-Cochin Nos. 2, O2.

No. O54 Overprinted "SPECIAL"
Vertically in Orange

1946   Perf. 12½
49   A20 6ca violet black   9.50 4.50

OFFICIAL STAMPS

Nos. O1-O60 were issued without
gum.

Regular Issues of
1889-1911
Overprinted in Red or
Black

Perf. 12, 12½
1911, Aug. 16   Wmk. 43
O1   A1   1ch indigo (R)   1.10   .20
  a.   Inverted overprint   10.00 6.50
  b.   "nO" for "On"   120.00 120.00
  c.   Double overprint   100.00 75.00
O2   A1   2ch scarlet   .50   .20
  a.   Inverted overprint   12.00 12.00
O3   A4   3ch purple   .50   .20
  a.   Inverted overprint   15.00 15.00
  b.   Double overprint   120.00 100.00
O4   A1   4ch dark green   .80   .20
  a.   Inverted overprint   82.50 19.00
  b.   Double overprint   190.00 140.00
    Nos. O1-O4 (4)   2.90   .80

Same Ovpt. on Regular Issues of
1889-1920

1918-20
O5   A3   4ca rose   .20   .20
  a.   Imperf., pair   450.00 450.00
  b.   Inverted overprint   120.00
  c.   Double overprint   180.00 140.00
O6   A1   ½ch violet (R)   3.75   .35
  a.   Inverted overprint   19.00 5.25
O7   A7   1¼ch claret   .60   .20
  a.   Inverted overprint   14.00 12.00
  b.   Double overprint   67.50
    Nos. O5-O7 (3)   4.55   .75

Same Ovpt. on Regular Issues of
1909-21

1921
O8   A1   6ca red brown   .45   .20
  a.   Inverted overprint   200.00 180.00
O9   A8   10ca rose   1.00   .20
  a.   Inverted overprint   27.50
  b.   Double overprint   140.00 110.00

Same Overprint on Regular Issue of
1921

1922
O10 A8   5ca bister   1.40   .20
  a.   Inverted overprint   21.00 13.50

For surcharge see No. O39B.

Same Overprint on Regular Issue of
1916

1925
O11 A5   7ch plum   2.50   .45
O12 A6   14ch orange   3.25   .60

Same Overprint in Blue on Regular
Issues of 1889-1921
O13 A3   4ca rose   80.00 1.00
O14 A5   5ca bister   .90   .20
O15 A1   6ca red brown   19.00 2.50
O16 A8   10ca rose   120.00 32.50
O17 A7   1¼ch claret   —   120.00
O18 A1   4ch dark green   —   100.00

Some authorities question the authenticity
of No. O14.

1930

Black Overprint
O19 A8   5ca brown   .35   .90

Regular Issues of
1889-1932
Overprinted in Black
or Red

1930-34
O20 A3   4ca rose   18.00 60.00
O21 A8   5ca brown   35.00 14.00
  a.   Inverted overprint   100.00 100.00
O22 A1   6ca org brown   .20   .20
O23 A8   10ca rose   6.50 4.50
O24 A1   ½ch violet ('34)   .75   .20
O25 A1   ½ch purple (R)   .20   .20
O26 A2   ¾ch black (R)   .60   .45
O27 A2   ¾ch brt vio ('33)   .45   .20
O27B A1   1ch gray blue
          (R) ('33)   1.50   .35
O28 A7   1¼ch claret   2.10 2.40
O29 A7   1½ch dull red
          ('32)   .60   .20
O30 A4   3ch purple ('33)   1.90   .90
O31 A4   3ch purple (R)   1.20   .20
O32 A1   4ch deep green
          (R)   2.25   .20
O33 A1   4ch deep green   2.75 1.40
O34 A5   7ch maroon   1.90   .45
O35 A6   14ch orange ('31) 2.50   .60
    Nos. O20-O35 (17)   78.40 86.45

The overprint on Nos. O22, O26 and O28 is
smaller than the illustration. There are two
sizes of the overprint on No. O27.
For surcharges see Nos. O39, O40-O41.

Type of 1921-32 and
No. 17 Surcharged
and Overprinted

1932
O36 A8   6ca on 5ca dk
          brown   .20   .45
O36A A8   6ca on 5ca bister 2.50 3.00
O37 A8   12ca on 10a rose   .20   .20
  a.   New value inverted   9.00 11.00
O38 A7   1ch8ca on 1¼ch cl   .50   .30
    Nos. O36-O38 (4)   3.40 3.95

Nos. O21, O10, O23
and O28 Surcharged
in Black

O39 A8   6ca on 5ca dk
          brown   .30   .45
  a.   New value inverted   16.00 19.00
O39B A8   6ca on 5ca bis   .60   .20
O40 A8   12ca on 10ca
          rose   3.00 2.25
  a.   New value inverted   10.00 10.00
  b.   "On S S" inverted   24.00 27.50
  c.   Ovpt. & surch. inverted 60.00 62.50
O41 A7   1ch8ca on 1¼ch cl 4.50 1.90
  a.   New value inverted   150.00
    Nos. O39-O41 (4)   8.40 4.80

Regular Issue of
1889-94 Overprinted

1933
O42 A1   ½ch violet   1.75 1.25

Regular Issue of 1901
Overprinted in Red

1933
O44 A2   ¾ch black   .50   .20

Regular Issue of 1939 Overprinted in
Black

a

1939   Perf. 11, 12, 12½
O45 A13 1ch yellow green   10.00   .50
  a.   Inverted overprint   15.00 15.00
  b.   Double overprint   15.00 15.00
O46 A14 1½ch carmine   11.00 1.00
  a.   "SESVICE"   250.00
O47 A15 2ch orange   11.00 11.00
  a.   "SESVICE"   190.00 210.00
O48 A16 3ch chocolate   9.50   .30
  a.   "SESVICE"   150.00 30.00
O49 A17 4ch henna brown   22.50 7.50
O50 A18 7ch light blue   24.00 5.50
O51 A19 14ch turq green   30.00 8.25
    Nos. O45-O51 (7)   118.00 34.95

27th birthday of Maharaja Sir Bala Rama
Varma.

No. 9 Overprinted

b

1939   Wmk. 43   Perf. 12.
O52 A2   ¾ch violet   27.50   .30

No. 13 Overprinted Type "b"

1941
O53 A1   6ca red brown   1.20   .45

Nos. 43-44 Overprinted Type "a"

1941   Perf. 12½
O54 A20 6ca violet black   .90   .75
O55 A21 ¾ch dull brown   9.50   .20

29th birthday of the Maharaja, Oct. 20, 1941.
For overprint see No. 49.

No. 18 Overprinted Type "b"

1945   Perf. 12
O56 A7   1½ch light red   21.00 12.00

Nos. 45-48 Overprinted Type "a"

1945-49   Perf. 11, 12
O57 A14 2ca on 1½ch car   .90 1.50
O58 A21 4ca on ¾ch dull brn 6.00 .60
O59 A20 8ca on 6ca red   5.25   .45
O60 A22 8ca rose red ('49) 3.75 1.25
  a.   Double impression of stamp 47.50
    Nos. O57-O60 (4)   15.90 3.80

Travancore stamps became obsolete June
30, 1949.

TRAVANCORE-COCHIN

ˈtrav-ən-ˌkō͟ə͟r kō-ˈchin

LOCATION — Southern India
AREA — 9,155 sq. mi.
POP. — 7,492,000

The United State of Travancore-
Cochin was established July 1, 1949.

Catalogue values for all unused
stamps in this state are for Never
Hinged items.

Travancore Stamps of 1939-47
Surcharged in Red or Black

a

1949, July 1   Wmk. 43
1   A20 2p on 6ca vio blk
          (R)   .75   .30
2   A22 4p on 8ca rose red 2.25   .45
3   A13 ½a on 1ch yel grn 5.25   .45
  a.   Inverted surcharge   7.50
  b.   "NANA"   300.00 180.00
4   A15 1a on 2ch orange   1.10   .45
5   A17 2a on 4ch hn brn   5.00   .80
  a.   Inverted surcharge   450.00
6   A18 3a on 7ch lt blue 9.00 5.50
7   A19 6a on 14ch turq grn 27.50 45.00
    Nos. 1-7 (7)   50.85 52.95

For overprints see Nos. O1-O7, O12-O17.
For types overprinted see Nos. O18-O23.

Cochin Nos. 80, 91 and Types of
1944-46 Surcharged in Black or
Carmine

b

1949-50   Wmk. 294   Perf. 11, 13
8   A15 3p on 9p ultra   18.00 35.00
9   A16 3p on 9p ultra   4.00 3.00
10   A16 3p on 9p ultra (C) 8.25 4.00
11   A16 6p on 9p ultra (C) 2.50   .60
12   A13 6p on 1a3p mag ('50) 8.25 6.75
13   A15 6p on 1a3p magenta 24.00 22.50
14   A13 1a on 1a9p ultra (C) 3.50 2.10
15   A15 1a on 1a9p ultra (C) 5.25 3.50
    Nos. 8-15 (8)   73.75 77.45

The surcharge exists with line of Hindi characters varying from 16½ to 23mm wide.
For overprints see Nos. O10-O11, O24.

Cochin No. 86
Overprinted

1949
15A A15 1a deep orange   9.00 100.00

Conch   View of
Shell — A23   River — A24

Wmk. 196
1950, Oct.   Litho.   Perf. 14
16   A23 2p rose red   4.50 5.00
17   A24 4p ultramarine   5.50 24.00

Cochin No. 86 and
Type of 1948-50
Overprinted in
Black

1950, Apr. 1   Wmk. 294   Perf. 13, 11
18   A15 1a deep orange   11.00 100.00

No. 18 Surcharged
in Black

20	A15	6p on 1a deep orange	6.75	82.50
21	A15	9p on 1a deep orange	6.50	72.50

OFFICIAL STAMPS

Travancore Stamps of 1939-46
Surcharged Type "a" in Red or Black
and Overprinted

c

1949   **Wmk. 43**   **Perf. 11, 12, 12½**

O1	A20	2p on 6ca vio blk (R)	.90	.70
O2	A22	4p on 8ca rose red	5.50	.50
O3	A13	½a on 1ch yel grn	1.50	.35
O4	A15	1a on 2ch orange	24.00	11.00
O5	A17	2a on 4ch hn brn	3.50	.90
O6	A18	3a on 7ch lt blue	5.50	1.50
O7	A19	6a on 14ch turq grn	24.00	16.00
		Nos. O1-O7 (7)	64.90	30.95

Cochin Nos. O90-O91 Surcharged
Type "b" in Black

1950   **Wmk. 294**   **Perf. 11**

O8	A16	6p on 3p carmine	1.90	1.10
a.		Double surcharge		525.00
O9	A16	9p on 4p gray grn	1.60	1.60

No. O9 exists with Hindi characters varying
from 18 to 22mm wide.

Travancore-Cochin Nos. 14-15
Overprinted "ON C G S"
Perf. 13

O10	A13	1a on 1a9p ultra	.90	1.00
O11	A15	1a on 1a9p ultra	35.00	25.00

Nos. 2-7 Overprinted in Black

d

1949-51   **Wmk. 43**   **Perf. 11, 12½**

O12	A22	4p on 8ca rose red	.75	.30
O13	A13	½a on 1ch yel green	1.50	.30
a.		"AANA"	260.00	85.00
O14	A15	1a on 2ch orange	.60	.30
O15	A17	2a on 4ch hn brn	2.25	1.60
O16	A18	3a on 7ch lt blue	2.25	1.60
O17	A19	6a on 14ch turq grn	2.25	6.50
		Nos. O12-O17 (6)	9.60	10.60

Types of 1949 Overprinted Type "d"

1951   **Wmk. 294**

O18	A13	½a on 1ch yel green	.60	.60
O19	A15	1a on 2ch orange	.75	.60

Type of 1949 Overprinted Type "c"
Unwmk.

O20	A22	4p on 8ca rose red	1.40	1.10

No. O20 is not from an unwatermarked part
of sheet with wmk. 294 but is printed on paper
entirely without watermark.

Nos. 1, 3 and 5 Overprinted Type "c"
Wmk. 294

O21	A13	½a on 1ch yel green	1.10	.50
O22	A20	2p on 6ca violet black	.20	1.00
O23	A17	2a on 4ch henna brn	1.10	.75
		Nos. O21-O23 (3)	2.40	2.25

No. 9 Overprinted
in Black

1951

O24	A16	3p on 9p ultra	.90	1.20

WADHWAN

wə-'dwän

LOCATION — A Feudatory State in
  Kathiawar Agency, Western India.
AREA — 242 sq. mi.
POP. — 44,259
CAPITAL   Wadhwan

Coat of
Arms — A1

1888   **Litho.**   **Unwmk.**   **Pin-perf.**
Thin Paper

1	A1	½p black	160.00	

Perf. 12½

2	A1	½p black	30.00	100.00

1889   **Perf. 12 and 12½**
Thick Paper

3	A1	½p black	12.50	14.00
		Nos. 1-3 (3)	202.50	

INDO-CHINA

ˌin-ˌdō-ˈchī-nə

LOCATION — French possessions on the Cambodian Peninsula in southeastern Asia, bordering on the South China Sea and the Gulf of Siam
GOVT. — French Colony and Protectorate
AREA — 280,849 sq. mi.
POP. — 27,030,000 (estimated 1949)
CAPITAL — Hanoi

In 1949, Indo-China was divided into Cambodia, Laos and Viet Nam each issuing its own stamps.

100 Centimes = 1 Franc
100 Cents = 1 Piaster (1918)

Stamps of French Colonies Surcharged in Black or Red:

a   b

1889   Unwmk.   Perf. 14x13½

1	A9(a)	5c on 35c dp vio, *org*	14.00	12.00
a.		Date in smaller type	240.00	225.00
2	A9(b)	5c on 35c dp vio, *org* (R)	100.00	95.00
a.		Date in smaller type	200.00	200.00
b.		Inverted surcharge, #2	1,900.	1,900.
c.		Inverted surcharge, #2a	2,600.	2,600.

Issue dates: No. 1, Jan. 8; No. 2, Jan. 10.
"R" is the Colonial Governor, P. Richaud, "D" is the Saigon P.M. General P. Demars.

For other overprints on designs A3-A27a see various issues of French Offices in China.

Navigation & Commerce A3   France A4

Name of Colony in Blue or Carmine

1892-1900   Typo.   Perf. 14x13½

3	A3	1c blk, *lil bl*	1.25	1.25
4	A3	2c brn, *buff*	1.60	1.60
5	A3	4c claret, *lav*	1.60	1.60
6	A3	5c grn, *grnsh*	2.40	2.40
7	A3	5c yel grn ('00)	2.00	1.25
8	A3	10c blk, *lavender*	7.50	2.00
9	A3	10c red ('00)	3.50	2.00
10	A3	15c blue, quadrille paper	37.50	2.00
11	A3	15c gray ('00)	9.00	2.40
12	A3	20c red, *grn*	10.00	7.00
13	A3	25c blk, *rose*	19.00	3.75
a.		"INDO-CHINE" omitted	7,200.	7,200.
14	A3	25c blue ('00)	22.00	5.00
15	A3	30c brn, *bis*	26.00	7.50
16	A3	40c red, *straw*	26.00	13.50
17	A3	50c car, *rose*	42.00	16.00
18	A3	50c brn, *az* ('00)	29.00	9.50
19	A3	75c dp vio, *org*	23.00	17.00
a.		"INDO-CHINE" inverted	7,200.	7,200.
20	A3	1fr brnz grn, *straw*	55.00	36.00
a.		"INDO-CHINE" double	1,100.	1,300.
21	A3	5fr red lil, *lav* ('96)	125.00	110.00
		Nos. 3-21 (19)	443.35	241.75

Perf. 13½x14 stamps are counterfeits.
For surcharges and overprints see Nos. 22-23, Q2-Q4.

Nos. 11 and 14 Surcharged in Black

1903

| 22 | A3 | 5c on 15c gray | 2.00 | 1.25 |
| 23 | A3 | 15c on 25c blue | 2.50 | 1.60 |

Issue dates: No. 22, Dec. 4; No. 23, Aug. 8.

1904-06

24	A4	1c olive grn	.80	.80
25	A4	2c vio brn, *buff*	1.25	.80
26	A4	4c claret, *bluish*	.80	.80
27	A4	5c deep green	1.25	.50
28	A4	10c carmine	1.60	.75
29	A4	15c org brn, *bl*	1.60	1.00
30	A4	20c red, *grn*	3.50	1.60
31	A4	25c deep blue	14.00	1.60
32	A4	30c pale brn	6.00	3.00
33	A4	35c blk, *yel* ('06)	21.50	3.25
34	A4	40c blk, *bluish*	5.50	4.00
35	A4	50c bister brn	10.50	3.00
36	A4	75c red, *org*	45.00	29.00
37	A4	1fr pale grn	21.50	8.25
38	A4	2fr brn, *org*	52.50	40.00
39	A4	5fr dp vio, *lil*	220.00	180.00
40	A4	10fr org brn, *grn*	220.00	180.00
		Nos. 24-40 (17)	627.30	455.95

For surcharges see Nos. 59-64.

Annamite Girl — A5   Cambodian Girl — A6

Cambodian Woman — A7   Annamite Women — A8

Hmong Woman — A9   Laotian Woman — A10

Cambodian Woman — A11

1907   Perf. 14x13½

41	A5	1c ol brn & blk	.40	.40
42	A5	2c yel brn & blk	.40	.40
43	A5	4c blue & blk	1.25	1.25
44	A5	5c grn & blk	1.60	.80
45	A5	10c red & blk	1.60	.55
46	A5	15c vio & blk	1.40	1.25
47	A6	20c vio & blk	3.00	1.60
48	A6	25c bl & blk	7.25	1.25
49	A6	30c brn & blk	12.00	6.50
50	A6	35c ol grn & blk	2.75	2.25
51	A6	40c yel brn & blk	4.50	2.00
52	A6	45c org & blk	10.50	6.50
53	A6	50c car & blk	15.00	5.75

Perf. 13½x14

54	A7	75c ver & blk	12.00	7.75
55	A8	1fr car & blk	55.00	20.00
56	A9	2fr grn & blk	17.00	16.00
57	A10	5fr blue & blk	42.50	42.50
58	A11	10fr pur & blk	92.50	92.50
		Nos. 41-58 (18)	280.65	209.25

For surcharges see Nos. 65-93, B1-B7.

Stamps of 1904-06 Surcharged in Black or Carmine

1912, Nov.   Perf. 14x13½

59	A4	5c on 4c cl, *bluish*	6.00	6.00
60	A4	5c on 15c org brn, *bl* (C)	1.25	1.25
61	A4	5c on 30c pale brn	1.60	1.60
62	A4	10c on 40c blk, *bluish* (C)	1.60	1.60
63	A4	10c on 50c bis brn (C)	2.00	2.00
64	A4	10c on 75c red, *org*	5.25	5.25
		Nos. 59-64 (6)	17.70	17.70

Two spacings between the surcharged numerals are found on Nos. 59-64.

Nos. 41-58 Surcharged with New Values in Cents or Piasters in Black, Red or Blue

1919, Jan.

65	A5	⅖c on 1c	.80	.55
66	A5	⅘c on 2c	1.25	.90
67	A5	1⅗c on 4c (R)	2.00	.80
68	A5	2c on 5c	1.60	.30
a.		Inverted surcharge	135.00	
69	A5	4c on 10c (Bl)	1.60	.55
a.		Closed "4"	9.00	3.25
b.		Double surcharge	130.00	
70	A5	6c on 15c	6.50	1.25
a.		Inverted surcharge	130.00	
71	A6	8c on 20c	5.25	1.90
72	A6	10c on 25c	5.00	1.00
73	A6	12c on 30c	6.75	1.10
74	A6	14c on 35c	3.25	.75
a.		Closed "4"	12.00	5.75
75	A6	16c on 40c	6.50	2.00
76	A6	18c on 45c	8.00	2.75
77	A6	20c on 50c (Bl)	12.00	1.25
78	A7	30c on 75c (Bl)	16.00	2.75
79	A8	40c on 1fr (Bl)	24.00	2.75
80	A9	80c on 2fr (R)	27.50	8.50
a.		Double surcharge	350.00	275.00
81	A10	2pi on 5fr (R)	105.00	105.00
82	A11	4pi on 10fr (R)	150.00	150.00
		Nos. 65-82 (18)	383.00	284.10

Types of 1907 Issue Surcharged with New Values in Black or Red

Nos. 88-92   No. 93

1922

88	A5	1c on 5c ocher & blk	1.60	
89	A5	2c on 10c gray grn & blk	2.40	
90	A6	6c on 30c lt red & blk	2.75	
91	A6	10c on 50c lt bl & blk	2.75	
92	A6	11c on 55c vio & blk, *bluish*	2.90	
93	A6	12c on 60c lt bl & blk, *pnksh* (R)	2.75	
		Nos. 88-93 (6)	15.15	

Nos. 88-93 were sold officially in Paris but were never placed in use in the colony.

Nos. 88-93 exist without surcharge but were not regularly issued in that condition. Value, Nos. 88-89, each $190; Nos. 90-91, each $140; Nos. 92-93, each $100.

A12   A13

"CENTS" below Numerals

Two types of "CENTS" for the 4c, 5c, 10c-12c values: Type 1, thin font (April 1922); type 2, thicker font (Oct. 1922 and later printings). All other denominations are type 2. For more detailed listings, see the *Scott Classic Specialized Catalogue of Stamps and Covers*.

1922-23   Perf. 14x13½

94	A12	¹⁄₁₀c blk & sal ('23)	.25	.25
a.		Double impression of frame		
95	A12	⅛c blue & blk	.25	.25
96	A12	⅖c ol brn & blk	.25	.25
a.		Head and value doubled	260.00	260.00
97	A12	⅘c rose & blk, *lav*	.40	.35
98	A12	1c yel brn & blk	.25	.25
99	A12	2c gray grn & blk	.75	.55
100	A12	3c vio & blk	.35	.35
101	A12	4c org & blk, type 2	.35	.35
b.		Head and value doubled	175.00	175.00
102	A12	5c car & blk, type 2	.35	.35
b.		Head and value doubled	290.00	290.00
103	A13	6c dl red & blk	.50	.30
104	A13	7c grn & blk	.75	.65
105	A13	8c blk, *lav*	2.00	1.25
106	A13	9c ocher & blk, *grnsh*	1.50	.90
107	A13	10c bl & blk, type 2	.80	.75
108	A13	11c vio & blk, type 2	.75	.75
109	A13	12c brn & blk, type 2	.55	.55
b.		Head and value double (11c+12c)	450.00	450.00
110	A13	15c org & blk	1.00	.80
111	A13	20c bl & blk, *straw*	1.60	.80
112	A13	40c ver & blk, *bluish*	2.75	1.40
113	A13	1pi bl grn & blk, *grnsh*	5.00	5.25
114	A13	2pi vio brn & blk, *pnksh*	13.00	13.00
		Nos. 94-114 (21)	33.40	29.35

For overprints see Nos. O17-O32.

Plowing near Tower of Confucius A14   Bay of Along A15

Angkor Wat, Cambodia A16

Carving Wood A17

That Luang Temple, Laos A18

Founding of Saigon A19

1927, Sept. 26

115	A14	¹⁄₁₀c lt olive grn	.25	.25
116	A14	⅛c yellow	.25	.25
117	A14	⅖c light blue	.25	.25
118	A14	⅘c dp brn	.55	.55
119	A14	1c orange	.65	.30
120	A14	2c blue grn	1.10	.50

121	A14	3c indigo	.70	.30
122	A14	4c lil rose	1.60	1.25
123	A14	5c dp vio	.80	.30
a.		Booklet pane of 10	200.00	
124	A15	6c deep red	2.10	.80
a.		Booklet pane of 10	200.00	
125	A15	7c lt brn	1.50	.80
126	A15	8c gray green	2.10	1.00
127	A15	9c red vio	1.50	1.00
128	A15	10c light blue	2.00	1.25
129	A15	11c orange	2.00	1.25
130	A15	12c myrtle grn	1.50	1.00
131	A16	15c dl rose & ol brn	7.50	7.50
132	A16	20c vio & slate	4.00	2.40
133	A17	25c org brn & lil rose	8.00	6.50
134	A17	30c dp bl & ol gray	5.00	4.00
135	A18	40c ver & lt bl	7.50	3.25
136	A18	50c lt grn & slate	10.00	3.25
137	A19	1pi dk bl, blk & yel	22.00	9.50
a.		Yellow omitted	275.00	
138	A19	2pi red, dp bl & org	27.50	16.50
		Nos. 115-138 (24)	110.35	63.95

Common Design Types pictured following the introduction.

Colonial Exposition Issue
Common Design Types
Surcharged with New Values
1931, Apr. 13   Engr.   *Perf. 12½*
Name of Country in Black

140	CD71	4c on 50c violet	3.25	3.25
141	CD72	6c on 90c red org	3.25	3.25
142	CD73	10c on 1.50fr dl bl	4.00	4.00
		Nos. 140-142 (3)	10.50	10.50

Junk — A20   Tower at Ruins of Angkor Thom — A21

Planting Rice — A22

Apsaras, Celestial Dancer A23

1931-41   Photo.   *Perf. 13½x13*

143	A20	1/10c Prus blue	.25	.25
144	A20	1/5c lake	.25	.25
145	A20	2/5c org red	.25	.25
146	A20	1/2c red brn	.25	.25
147	A20	4/5c dk vio	.25	.25
148	A20	1c blk brn	.25	.25
149	A20	2c dk grn	.25	.25
150	A21	3c dp brn	.25	.25
151	A21	3c dk grn ('34)	5.75	1.60
152	A21	4c dk bl	1.25	.50
153	A21	4c dk grn ('38)	.80	.55
153A	A21	4c yel org ('40)	.40	.40
154	A21	5c dp vio	.30	.30
154A	A21	5c dp grn ('41)	.40	.40
155	A21	6c org red	.25	.25
a.		Bklt. pane 5 + 1 label	100.00	
156	A21	7c blk ('38)	.30	.30
157	A21	8c rose lake ('38)	.40	.40
157A	A21	9c blk, yel ('41)	.75	.75
158	A22	10c dark blue	.65	.50
158A	A22	10c ultra, *pink* ('41)	.55	.55
159	A22	15c dk brn	5.75	1.40
160	A22	15c dk bl ('33)	.25	.25
161	A22	18c blue ('38)	.75	.50
162	A22	20c rose	.30	.25
163	A22	21c olive grn	.30	.30
164	A22	22c dk grn ('38)	.55	.55
165	A22	25c dp vio	3.25	1.60
165A	A22	25c dk bl ('41)	.55	.55
166	A22	30c org brn ('32)	.55	.30

Perf. 13½

167	A23	50c dk brn	.75	.25
168	A23	60c dl vio ('32)	.90	.65
168A	A23	70c lt bl ('41)	.55	.55
169	A23	1pi yel grn	.90	.65
170	A23	2pi red	1.10	.75
		Nos. 143-170 (34)	30.20	17.05

Nos. 166, 167, 169 and 170 were issued without the letters "RF" in 1943, by the Vichy Government.
For surcharge & overprints see #214A, O1-O16.

Emperor Bao-Dai A24   King Sisowath Monivong A25

For Use in Annam
1936, Nov. 20   Engr.   *Perf. 13*

171	A24	1c brown	1.00	1.00
172	A24	2c green	1.00	1.00
173	A24	4c violet	1.00	1.00
174	A24	5c red brn	1.50	1.50
175	A24	10c lil rose	2.00	2.00
176	A24	15c ultra	2.75	2.75
177	A24	20c scarlet	2.75	2.75
178	A24	30c plum	3.50	3.50
179	A24	50c slate grn	3.50	3.50
180	A24	1pi rose vio	4.50	4.50
181	A24	2pi black	5.25	5.25
		Nos. 171-181 (11)	28.75	28.75

For Use in Cambodia

182	A25	1c brown	1.00	1.00
183	A25	2c green	1.00	1.00
184	A25	4c violet	1.10	1.10
185	A25	5c red brn	1.10	1.10
186	A25	10c lil rose	2.40	2.40
187	A25	15c ultra	3.25	3.25
188	A25	20c scarlet	2.75	2.75
189	A25	30c plum	3.25	3.25
190	A25	50c slate grn	3.25	3.25
191	A25	1pi rose vio	4.00	4.00
192	A25	2pi black	5.25	5.25
		Nos. 182-192 (11)	28.35	28.35

Paris International Exposition Issue
Common Design Types
1937, Apr. 15

193	CD74	2c dp vio	1.60	1.60
194	CD75	3c dk grn	1.10	1.10
195	CD76	4c car rose	1.10	1.10
196	CD77	6c dk brn	1.10	1.10
197	CD78	9c red	1.10	1.10
198	CD79	15c ultra	1.25	1.25
		Nos. 193-198 (6)	7.25	7.25

Colonial Arts Exhibition Issue
Souvenir Sheet
Common Design Type
1937, Apr. 15   *Imperf.*

199	CD79	30c dull violet	9.00	12.00

Governor-General Paul Doumer — A26

1938, June 8   Photo.   *Perf. 13½x13*

200	A26	5c rose car	1.00	.65
201	A26	6c brown	1.10	1.10
202	A26	18c brt bl	1.10	1.10
		Nos. 200-202,C18 (4)	3.95	3.10

Trans-Indo-Chinese Railway, 35th anniv.

New York World's Fair Issue
Common Design Type
1939, May 10   Engr.   *Perf. 12½x12*

203	CD82	13c car lake	.80	.80
204	CD82	23c ultra	1.25	1.25

Mot Cot Pagoda, Hanoi — A27

1939, June 12   *Perf. 13*

205	A27	6c blk brn	1.10	1.10
206	A27	9c vermilion	1.10	1.10
207	A27	23c ultra	1.10	1.10
208	A27	39c rose vio	1.50	1.50
		Nos. 205-208 (4)	4.80	4.80

Golden Gate International Exposition.

Angkor Wat and Marshal Pétain A27a

1941   Engr.   *Perf. 12½x12*

209	A27a	10c dk car	.80
209A	A27a	25c blue	.80

Nos. 209-209A were issued by the Vichy government in France, but were not placed on sale in Indo-China.
For overprints, see Nos. 262-263. For surcharges, see B21A-B21B.

Gum
#210-261 issued without gum.

Imperfs
Many issues between Nos. 209-263, B19A-B26 and C1-C28, plus some postage dues and official stamps, exist imperf.

King Norodom Sihanouk of Cambodia A28   Harnessed Elephant on Parade A29

Pin-perf. 12½
1941, Oct. 15   Unwmk.   Litho.

210	A28	1c red org	1.60	1.60
211	A28	6c violet	3.25	3.25
212	A28	25c dp ultra	21.00	21.00
		Nos. 210-212 (3)	25.85	25.85

Coronation of Norodom Sihanouk, King of Cambodia, October, 1941.

1942, Mar. 29

213	A29	3c reddish brown	2.00	1.60
214	A29	6c crimson	2.00	1.60

Fête of Nam-Giao in Annam.

No. 165 Surcharged in Black

1942   *Perf. 13*

214A	A22	10c on 25c dp vio	.50	.30

View of Saigon Fair — A30

1942, Dec. 20   *Perf. 13½*

215	A30	6c carmine rose	.80	.80

Saigon Fair of 1942.

Nam-Phuong, Empress of Annam — A31   Marshal Pétain — A32

1942, Sept. 1   *Pin-perf. 11½*

216	A31	6c carmine rose	1.25	.80

1942-44   *Perf. 12, 13½*

217	A32	1c blk brn	.35	.35
218	A32	3c olive brn ('43)	.35	.35
219	A32	6c rose red	.55	.55
220	A32	10c dull grn ('43)	1.20	1.20
221	A32	40c dk blue ('43)	1.60	1.60
222	A32	40c slate bl ('44)	.80	1.25
		Nos. 217-222 (6)	4.85	5.30

Bao-Dai, Emperor of Annam A33   Norodom Sihanouk, King of Cambodia A34

1942   *Perf. 13½*

223	A33	½c brown	1.25	*1.60*
224	A33	6c carmine rose	1.25	1.25

Issue dates: ½c, Nov. 1; 6c, Sept. 1.

1943   *Perf. 11½*

225	A34	1c brown	1.25	.80
226	A34	6c red	1.00	.55

Issue dates: 1c, Mar. 10; 6c, May 10.

Types of 1931-32 Without "RF"
1943   Photo.   *Perf. 13½x13*

226A	A22	30c orange brown	1.60
226B	A23	50c dark brown	1.60
226C	A23	1pi yellow green	2.75
226D	A23	2pi red	3.50
		Nos. 226A-226D (4)	9.45

Nos. 226A-226D were issued by the Vichy government in France, but were not placed on sale in Indo-China.

Sisavang-Vong, King of Laos — A35   Family, Country and Labor — A36

1943

227	A35	1c bister brown	.55	*1.25*
228	A35	6c carmine rose	1.25	.65

Issue dates: 1c, Mar. 10; 6c, June 1.

1943, Nov. 5   *Perf. 12*

229	A36	6c carmine rose	.65	.50

National revolution, 3rd anniversary.

Admiral Rigault de Genouilly A37

François
Chasseloup-Laubat
A38

Admiral
André A. P.
Courbet
A39

1943   *Perf. 11½, 12, 12x11½*
230 A37 6c carmine rose   .50 1.40
231 A38 6c carmine rose   .50 .35
232 A39 6c carmine rose   1.40 .25
    Nos. 230-232 (3)   2.40 2.00

  Issued: #230, 232, Sept. 1; #231, Oct. 5.
  A 5c dull brown, type A37, was not regularly issued without the Viet Nam overprint. Value, $10.
  A 3c light brown, type A39, was prepared but not issued. Value, $10.

Pigneau de
Behaine, Bishop
of Adran — A40

Alexandre
Yersin — A41

1943, June 10   *Perf. 12*
233 A40 20c dull red   1.50 1.75

1943-45   *Perf. 12x11½*
234 A41 6c carmine rose   1.50 1.50
235 A41 15c vio brn ('44)   .55 .55
236 A41 1pi yel grn ('45)   .75 .75
    Nos. 234-236 (3)   2.80 2.80

  Issued to honor Dr. Alexandre Yersin (1863-1943), the Swiss bacteriologist who introduced rubber culture into Indo-China.
  Issued: 6c, 10/5; 15c, 12/10; 1pi, 1/10.

Lt. M. J.
François
Garnier
A42

1943, Sept.   *Perf. 12*
237 A42 1c dull olive bister   .90 1.25

  A 15c brown violet was prepared but not issued. Value, $16.

Alexandre
de Rhodes
A43

1943-45   *Pin-perf., Perf. 12*
238 A43 15c dk vio brn ('45)   .40 .40
239 A43 30c org brn   .80 .80
  a. 30c yellow brown, perf. 13½   .80 .80

  Nos. 239, 239a carry the monogram "EF."
  Issue dates: 15c, Mar. 10; 30c, June 15.

Athlete
Giving
Olympic
Salute
A44

1944, July 10   *Perf. 12*
241 A44 10c dk vio brn & yel   2.40 2.40
242 A44 50c dl red   2.75 2.75

Adm.
Pierre de
La
Grandière
A45

1943-45
243 A45 1c dull brn   .25 1.25
244 A45 5c dark brn ('45)   .30 .30

  The upper left corner of No. 244 contains the denomination "5c" instead of "EF" monogram.
  Issue dates: 1c, Aug.; 5c, Jan. 10.

Auguste
Pavie
A46

1944   *Perf. 12*
245 A46 4c org yel   .50 .30
246 A46 10c dl grn   .30 .65

  Issue dates: 4c, Feb. 10; 10c, Jan. 5.
  A 20c dark red, type A46, was not regularly issued without the Viet Nam overprint. Value without overprint, $10.

Governor-General
Pierre
Pasquier — A47

1944
247 A47 5c brn vio   .65 .65
248 A47 10c dl grn   .30 1.25

  Issue dates: 5c, Nov. 1; 10c, Sept.

Joost Van Vollenhoven — A48

1944, Oct. 10
249 A48 1c olive brown   .35 .35
250 A48 10c green   .75 .90

Governor-General J. M. A. de
Lanessan — A49

1944
251 A49 1c dl gray brn   .65 .50
252 A49 15c dl rose vio   1.90 1.60

  Issued: 1c, Dec. 10; 15c, Oct. 16.

Governor-General
Paul Doumer — A50

1944
253 A50 2c red vio   .30 .30
254 A50 4c lt brn   .30 .30
255 A50 10c yel grn   .30 .30
    Nos. 253-255 (3)   .90 .90

  Issue dates: 2c, May 15; 4c, June 15; 10c, Jan. 5.

Admiral
Charner — A51

Doudart de
Lagrée — A52

1944
256 A51 10c green   .50 1.40
257 A51 20c brn red   .65 1.40
258 A51 1pi pale yel grn   1.00 1.00
    Nos. 256-258 (3)   2.15 3.80

  Issue dates: 10c, 20c, Aug. 10; 1pi, July.

1944-45
259 A52 1c dl gray brn ('45)   .25 .25
260 A52 15c dl rose vio   .50 .55
261 A52 40c brt bl   .65 1.00
    Nos. 259-261 (3)   1.40 1.80

  Issue dates: 1c, Jan. 10; 15c, 40c, Nov.

Nos. 209-209A Overprinted in Black

1946   **Unwmk.**   *Perf. 12½x12*
262 A27a 10c dk car   1.10 1.60
263 A27a 25c blue   2.75 3.25

SEMI-POSTAL STAMPS

No. 45 Surcharged

      Perf. 14x13½
1914, Oct. 28   **Unwmk.**
B1 A5 10c +5c red & blk   1.60 1.60

Nos. 44-46 Surcharged

1915-17
B2 A5 5c + 5c grn & blk   1.60 1.60
         ('17)
  a. Double surcharge   210.00 210.00
B3 A5 10c + 5c red & blk   2.40 2.00
B4 A5 15c + 5c vio & blk   2.40 2.00
         ('17)
  a. Triple surcharge   190.00
  b. Quadruple surcharge   190.00
    Nos. B2-B4 (3)   6.40 5.60

    Nos. B2-B4 Surcharged with New
       Values in Blue or Black
1918-19
B5 A5 4c on 5c + 5c (Bl)   4.00 4.00
  a. Closed "4"   220.00
B6 A5 6c on 10c + 5c   3.75 *4.00*
B7 A5 8c on 15c + 5c ('19)   13.00 13.00
  a. Double surcharge   220.00
    Nos. B5-B7 (3)   20.75 21.00

France Nos. B5-B10
Surcharged

1919 (?)
B8 SP5 10c on 15c + 10c   1.60 1.60
  a. "10 CENTS" double   525.00 525.00
B9 SP5 16c on 25c + 15c   4.00 4.00
B10 SP6 24c on 35c + 25c   6.50 6.50
  a. Double surcharge   800.00 800.00
  b. CENTS" double   875.00
B11 SP7 40c on 50c + 50c   12.50 12.50
B12 SP8 80c on 1fr + 1fr   27.50 27.50
B13 SP8 4pi on 5fr + 5fr   220.00 220.00
  a. PIASTRES" double   6,000. 5,400.
    Nos. B8-B13 (6)   272.10 272.10

Curie Issue
Common Design Type
Inscription and Date in Upper Margin
1938, Oct. 24   **Engr.**   *Perf. 13*
B14 CD80 18c + 5c brt ultra   11.00 11.00

French Revolution Issue
Common Design Type
Name and Value Typo. in Black
1939, July 5   **Photo.**
B15 CD83 6c + 2c green   12.00 12.00
B16 CD83 7c + 3c brown   12.00 12.00
B17 CD83 9c + 4c red org   12.00 12.00
B18 CD83 13c + 10c rose pink   12.00 12.00
B19 CD83 23c + 20c blue   12.00 12.00
    Nos. B15-B19 (5)   60.00 60.00

Common Design Type and

Tonkinese
Sharpshooter
SP1

Legionary
SP2

1941   **Photo.**   *Perf. 13½*
B19A SP1 10c + 10c red   1.60
B19B CD86 15c + 30c maroon   1.60
B19C SP2 25c + 10c blue   1.60
    Nos. B19A-B19C (3)   4.80

  Nos. B19A-B19C were issued by the Vichy government in France, but were not placed on sale in Indo-China.

Portal and Flags,
City University,
Hanoi — SP3

Coat of Arms
and
Sword — SP4

      Perf. 11½
1942, June 1   **Unwmk.**   **Litho.**
B20 SP3 6c + 2c car rose   1.25 1.25
B21 SP3 15c + 5c brn vio   1.25 1.25

Nos. 209-209A
Surcharged in Black or Red

1944		Engr.	Perf. 12½x12	
B21A		5c + 15c on 25c blue (R)	.95	
B21B		+ 25c on 10c dk car	1.00	

Colonial Development Fund.
Nos. B21A-B21B were issued by the Vichy government in France, but were not placed on sale in Indo-China.

No. B20
Surcharged in Black

1944, June 10				
B22	SP3	10c + 2c on 6c + 2c	.65	.65

1942, Aug. 1			Perf. 12	
B23	SP4	6c + 2c red & blue	.80	.80
B24	SP4	15c + 5c vio blk, red & bl	.80	.80

#B23 Surcharged in Black Like #B22

1944, Mar. 15				
B25	SP4	10c + 2c on 6c + 2c	.75	.75

Aviator Do-
Huu-Vi
SP5

1943, Aug. 1				
B26	SP5	6c + 2c car rose	.65	1.60

#B26 Surcharged in Black Like #B22

1944, Feb. 10				
B27	SP5	10c + 2c on 6c + 2c	.80	.80

Surcharge arranged to fit size of stamp.

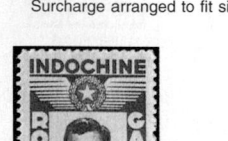

Aviator Roland
Garros — SP6

1943, Nov. 15				
B28	SP6	6c + 2c rose car	.80	.80

#B28 Surcharged in Black Like #B22

1944, Feb. 10				
B29	SP6	10c + 2c on 6c + 2c	.80	.80

Cathedral
of Orléans
SP7

1944, Dec. 20				
B30	SP7	15c + 60c brn vio	1.60	1.60
B31	SP7	40c + 1.10pi blue	1.60	2.75

Type of
France,
1945,
Surcharged
in Black

1945		Unwmk.	Engr.	Perf. 13	
B32	A152	50c + 50c on 2fr green	.65	.65
B33	A152	1pi + 1pi on 2fr hn brn	.65	.65
B34	A152	2pi + 2pi on 2fr Prus grn	1.00	1.00
		Nos. B32-B34 (3)	2.30	2.30

AIR POST STAMPS

Airplane
AP1

1933-41		Unwmk. Photo.	Perf. 13½	
C1	AP1	1c ol brn	.25	.25
C2	AP1	2c dk grn	.30	.25
C3	AP1	5c yel grn	.30	.25
C4	AP1	10c red brn	.65	.30
C5	AP1	11c rose car ('38)	.80	.30
C6	AP1	15c dp bl	.50	.25
C6A	AP1	16c brt pink ('41)	.35	.35
C7	AP1	20c grnsh gray	.50	.50
C8	AP1	30c org brn	.30	.25
C9	AP1	36c car rose	1.90	.35
C10	AP1	37c ol grn ('38)	.80	.30
C10A	AP1	39c dk ol grn ('41)	.35	.35
C11	AP1	60c dk vio	1.90	.35
C12	AP1	66c olive grn	.55	.25
C13	AP1	67c brt bl ('38)	1.20	1.00
C13A	AP1	69c brt ultra ('41)	.65	.65
C14	AP1	1pi black	.70	.25
C15	AP1	2pi yel org	1.00	.35
C16	AP1	5pi purple	1.90	.50
C17	AP1	10pi deep red	3.75	.90
		Nos. C1-C17 (20)	18.65	7.95

See Nos. C27-C28.
Issue dates: 11c, 37c, June 8; 67c, Oct. 5; 16c, 39c, 69c, Feb. 5; others, June 1, 1933.
See Nos. C18A-C18O, C27-C28.

Trans-Indo-Chinese Railway Type

1938, June 8				
C18	A26	37c red orange	.75	.25

Type of 1933-38 Without "RF"

1942-44			Perf. 13½	
C18A	AP1	5c yellow green	.25	
C18B	AP1	10c red brown	.25	
C18C	AP1	11c rose carmine	.30	
C18D	AP1	15c deep blue	.40	
C18E	AP1	20c greenish gray	.40	
C18F	AP1	36c carmine rose	.40	
C18G	AP1	37c olive green	.65	
C18H	AP1	60c dark violet	.65	
C18I	AP1	66c brown olive	.65	
C18J	AP1	67c bright blue	.80	
C18K	AP1	69c br ultramarine	.90	
C18L	AP1	1pi black	1.25	
C18M	AP1	2pi yellow orange	1.25	
C18N	AP1	5pi purple	1.75	
C18O	AP1	10pi deep red	3.50	
		Nos. C18A-C18O (15)	13.40	

Nos. C18A-C18O were issued by the Vichy government in France, but were not placed on sale in Indo-China.

Victory Issue
Common Design Type
Perf. 12½

1946, May 8		Unwmk.	Engr.	
C19	CD92	80c red org	1.00	.55

Chad to Rhine Issue
Common Design Types

1946, June 6				
C20	CD93	50c yel grn	.90	.90
C21	CD94	1pi violet	.90	.90
C22	CD95	1.50pi carmine	1.10	1.10
C23	CD96	2pi vio brn	1.10	1.10
C24	CD97	2.50pi dp bl	1.10	1.10
C25	CD98	5pi org red	1.30	1.30
		Nos. C20-C25 (6)	6.40	6.40

UPU Issue
Common Design Type

1949, July 4			Perf. 13	
C26	CD99	3pi dp bl, dk vio, grn & red		4.75 4.00

Plane Type of 1933-41

1949, June 13		Photo.	Perf. 13½	
C27	AP1	20pi dk bl grn	11.50	6.50
C28	AP1	30pi brown	13.00	6.50

AIR POST SEMI-POSTAL STAMP

French Revolution Issue
Common Design Type
Unwmk.

1939, July 5		Photo.	Perf. 13	
Name and Value Typo. in Orange				
CB1	CD83	39c + 40c brn blk	25.00	25.00

Poor Family — SPAP1

Orphans
SPAP2

Caring for Children — SPAP3

Perf. 13½x12½, 13 (#CB4)
Photo., Engr. (#CB4)

1942, June 22				
CB2	SPAP1	15c + 35c green	1.00	
CB3	SPAP2	20c + 60c brown	1.00	
CB4	SPAP3	30c + 90c car red	1.05	
		Nos. CB2-CB4 (3)	3.05	

Native children's welfare fund.
Nos. CB2-CB4 were issued by the Vichy government in France, but were not placed on sale in Indo-China.

Colonial Education Fund
Common Design Type
Perf. 12½x13½

1942, June 22			Engr.	
CB5	CD86a	12c + 18c blue & red	1.10	

No. CB5 was issued by the Vichy government in France, but was not placed on sale in Indo-China.

POSTAGE DUE STAMPS

French Colonies No. J21
Surcharged

1904, June 26		Unwmk.	Imperf.	
J1	D1	5c on 60c brn, buff	14.00	14.00

French Colonies Nos. J10-J11
Surcharged in Carmine

1905, July 22				
J2	D1	5c on 40c black	32.00	16.00
J3	D1	10c on 60c black	32.00	20.00
J4	D1	30c on 60c black	32.00	20.00
		Nos. J2-J4 (3)	96.00	56.00

Dragon from Steps of
Angkor Wat

		D1		D2	
1908		Typo.	Perf. 14x13½		
J5	D1	2c black	1.25	1.00	
J6	D1	4c dp bl	1.25	1.00	
J7	D1	5c bl grn	1.60	1.10	
J8	D1	10c carmine	2.90	1.10	
J9	D1	15c violet	3.50	2.50	
J10	D1	20c chocolate	1.75	1.40	
J11	D1	30c ol grn	1.75	1.40	
J12	D1	40c claret	8.25	6.50	
J13	D1	50c grnsh bl	7.00	1.60	
J14	D1	60c orange	11.00	9.50	
J15	D1	1fr gray	24.00	18.50	
J16	D1	2fr yel brn	24.00	18.50	
J17	D1	5fr red	40.00	37.50	
		Nos. J5-J17 (13)	128.25	101.60	

Surcharged with New Values in Cents
or Piasters

1919					
J18	D1	⅘c on 2c blk	1.60	1.25	
J19	D1	1⅘c on 4c dp bl	1.60	1.25	
J20	D1	2c on 5c bl grn	2.90	1.60	
J21	D1	4c on 10c car	4.00	1.25	
J22	D1	6c on 15c vio	9.00	2.75	
J23	D1	8c on 20c choc	6.50	2.40	
J24	D1	12c on 30c ol grn	9.25	2.40	
J25	D1	16c on 40c cl	9.25	2.00	
J26	D1	20c on 50c grnsh bl	12.00	6.50	
J27	D1	24c on 60c org	3.25	2.00	
a.		Closed "4"	20.00	16.00	
J28	D1	40c on 1fr gray	5.25	1.60	
a.		Closed "4"	20.00	16.00	
J29	D1	80c on 2fr yel brn	40.00	19.00	
J30	D1	2pi on 5fr red	57.50	40.00	
a.		Double surcharge	220.00	175.00	
b.		Triple surcharge	220.00	175.00	
		Nos. J18-J30 (13)	162.10	84.00	

"CENTS" below Numerals

1922, Oct.					
J31	D2	⅖c black	.25	.25	
J32	D2	⅘c red	.30	.30	
J33	D2	1c buff	.50	.40	
J34	D2	2c gray grn	.65	.50	
J35	D2	3c violet	.75	.75	
J36	D2	4c orange	.75	.40	
a.		"4 CENTS" omitted	675.00		
b.		"4 CENTS" double	105.00	105.00	
J37	D2	6c ol grn	1.60	.65	
J38	D2	8c blk, lav	1.25	.65	
J39	D2	10c dp bl	2.00	.65	
J40	D2	12c ocher, grnsh	1.60	1.10	
J41	D2	20c dp bl, straw	2.00	.90	
J42	D2	40c red, bluish	2.00	1.10	
J43	D2	1pi brn vio, pnksh	6.50	3.50	
		Nos. J31-J43 (13)	20.15	11.15	

Pagoda of
Mot Cot,
Hanoi — D3

Dragon of
Annam — D4

Perf. 14x13½, 13½x14

1927, Sept. 26					
J44	D3	⅖c vio brn & org	.25	.25	
J45	D3	⅘c vio & blk	.25	.25	
J46	D3	1c brn red & sl	.90	.90	
J47	D3	2c grn & brn ol	1.00	1.00	
J48	D3	3c red brn & bl	1.60	1.60	
J49	D3	4c ind & brn	1.60	1.60	
J50	D3	6c dp red & ver	2.00	1.60	
J51	D3	8c ol brn & vio	1.60	1.25	
J52	D4	10c dp bl	2.40	1.25	
J53	D4	12c olive	5.25	4.50	
J54	D4	20c rose	3.50	2.00	
J55	D4	40c bl grn	3.50	3.25	
J56	D4	1pi red org	17.50	17.50	
		Nos. J44-J56 (13)	41.35	36.95	

D5

Value Surcharged in Black or Blue

1931-41			Perf. 13		
J57	D5	⅕c red, org ('38)	.25	.25	
J58	D5	⅖c vio & blk	.25	.25	
J59	D5	⅘c red, org	.25	.25	
J60	D5	1c red, org	.25	.25	
J61	D5	2c red, org	.25	.25	

J62	D5	2.5c red, *org* ('40)	.25	.25
J63	D5	3c red, *org* ('38)	.40	.25
J64	D5	4c red, *org*	.30	.30
J65	D5	5c red, *org* ('38)	.40	.30
J66	D5	6c red, *org*	.30	.30
J67	D5	10c red, *org*	.30	.30
J68	D5	12c red, *org*	.50	.30
J69	D5	14c red, *org* ('38)	.50	.30
J70	D5	18c red, *org* ('41)	.50	.50
J71	D5	20c red, *org*	.50	.50
J72	D5	50c red, *org*	.75	.50
J72A	D5	1pi red, *org*	9.50	8.50
J73	D5	1pi red, *org* (Bl)	2.25	1.25
		Nos. J57-J73 (18)	17.70	14.80

D6   D7

Perf. 12, 13½ and Compound
1943-44   Litho.   Unwmk.

J74	D6	1c red, *org*	.25	.25
J75	D6	2c red, *org*	.25	.25
J76	D6	3c red, *org*	.30	.30
J77	D6	4c red, *org*	.30	.30
J78	D6	6c red, *org*	.40	.40
J79	D6	10c red, *org*	.40	.40
J80	D7	12c blue, *pnksh*	.50	.50
J81	D7	20c blue, *pnksh*	.50	.50
J82	D7	30c blue, *pnksh*	.50	.50
		Nos. J74-J82 (9)	3.40	3.40

Issued: 2c, 3c, 7/15/43; 6c-30c, 8/43; 1c, 4c, 6/10/44.

OFFICIAL STAMPS

Regular Issues of 1931-32 Overprinted in Blue or Red

Overprinted

Perf. 13, 13½
1933, Feb. 27   Unwmk.

O1	A20	1c black brown (Bl)	.80	.75
O2	A20	2c dark green (Bl)	.90	.50

Overprinted

O3	A21	3c deep brown (Bl)	1.25	.65
a.		Inverted overprint	150.00	
O4	A21	4c dark blue (R)	1.50	.90
a.		Inverted overprint	150.00	
O5	A21	5c deep violet (Bl)	2.40	.90
O6	A21	6c orange red (Bl)	2.40	1.25

Overprinted

O7	A22	10c dk blue (R)	1.25	.90
O8	A22	15c dk brown (Bl)	2.75	1.60
O9	A22	20c rose (Bl)	3.25	.75
O10	A22	21c olive grn (Bl)	2.75	1.50
O11	A22	25c dp violet (Bl)	1.60	.50
O12	A22	30c orange brn (Bl)	3.25	.80

Overprinted

O13	A23	50c dark brown (Bl)	11.50	3.50
O14	A23	60c dull violet (Bl)	2.75	2.40
O15	A23	1pi yellow green (Bl)	28.00	10.50
O16	A23	2pi red (Bl)	10.00	9.00
		Nos. O1-O16 (16)	76.35	36.40

Type of Regular Issue, 1922-23 Overprinted diagonally in Black or Red "SERVICE"

1934, Oct. 4   Perf. 14x13

O17	A13	1c olive green	1.00	.75
O18	A13	2c brown orange	1.00	.75
O19	A13	3c yellow green	1.25	.65

O20	A13	4c cerise	2.25	1.30
O21	A13	5c yellow	1.25	.75
O22	A13	6c orange red	5.25	5.00
O23	A13	10c gray grn (R)	3.00	2.25
O24	A13	15c ultra	2.10	1.50
O25	A13	20c gray black (R)	1.80	1.50
O26	A13	21c light violet	10.00	8.25
O27	A13	25c rose lake	11.50	10.00
O28	A13	30c lilac gray	1.50	1.30
O29	A13	50c brt violet	7.50	6.25
O30	A13	60c gray	14.00	10.50
O31	A13	1pi blue (R)	27.50	23.00
O32	A13	2pi deep red	45.00	32.50
		Nos. O17-O32 (16)	135.90	106.25

The value tablet has colorless numeral and letters on solid background.

PARCEL POST STAMPS

French Colonies No. 50 Overprinted

1891		**Unwmk.**	**Perf. 14x13½**	
Q1	A9	10c black, *lavender*	24.00	10.50

The overprint on No. Q1 was also handstamped in shiny ink. Value unused, $750.

Indo-China No. 8 Overprinted

1898				
Q2	A3	10c black, *lavender*	28.00	28.00

Nos. 8 and 9 Overprinted

1902				
Q3	A3	10c black, *lavender*	52.50	32.50
a.		Inverted overprint	110.00	48.00
Q4	A3	10c red	52.50	32.50
a.		Inverted overprint	80.00	48.00
b.		Double overprint	80.00	48.00

INDONESIA
ˌin-də-ˈnē-zhə

LOCATION — In the East Indies
GOVT. — Republic
AREA — 741,101 sq. mi.
POP. — 195,280,000 (1995 est.)
CAPITAL — Jakarta

Formerly Netherlands Indies, Indonesia achieved independence late in 1949 as the United States of Indonesia and became the Republic of Indonesia August 15, 1950. See Netherlands Indies for earlier issues.

100 Sen = 1 Rupiah

> **Catalogue values for all unused stamps in this country are for Never Hinged items.**

Watermarks

Wmk. 404

Wmk. 228

REVOLUTIONARY ISSUES

Following the surrender of Japan to the Allies in 1945, Indonesian nationalists declared independence and formed the Republic of Indonesia. On Sept. 27, the Djawan PTT (now PT Pos Indonesia) was established and assumed reponsibility for the postal system. Within days, civil war had broken out between the nationalists and the returning Dutch, who sought to reestablish control over their East Indies colony. During the hostilities, which continued until Dec. 1949, a Dutch blockade of the rebel strongholds in Java and Sumatra made regular communications between the two islands impossible, and the Djawan PTT was forced to organize separate postal services, using locally produced stamps, on Java and Sumatra.

JAVA ISSUES

Netherlands Indies Nos. 168, 200, 201 Overprinted "Repoeblik Indonesia" and 3 bars in Black or Red (R)

1945, Nov.   Perf. 11½

1L1	A17	1c lilac gray (R)	2.25	2.75
1L2	A17	2c plum	4.50	6.25
1L3	A17	3½c dark gray (R)	60.00	60.00
		Nos. 1L1-1L3 (3)	66.75	69.00

Forgeries of Nos. 1L1-1L3 exist.

Netherlands Indies Nos. 228-231 Overprinted "Repoeblik Indonesia" and 2 bars in Black or Red (R)

1945, Nov.   Perf. 12½

1L4	A23	2½c rose violet	1.75	2.75
1L5	A24	3c green (R)	1.75	2.75
1L6	A25	4c olive green (R)	1.90	3.00
1L7	A26	5c blue (R)	75.00	65.00
		Nos. 1L4-1L7 (4)	80.40	73.50

Forgeries of Nos. 1L4-1L7 exist.

Netherlands Indies Nos. N2, N3 Overprinted "Repoeblik Indonesia" and 2 bars in Black or Red (R)

1945, Nov.   Perf. 12½

1L8	OS2	3½s carmine	350.00	325.00
1L9	OS3	5s green (R)	22.50	20.00

Forgeries of Nos. 1L8-1L9 exist.

Netherlands Indies Nos. N5-N11 Overprinted "Repoeblik Indonesia" and 2 bars in Black or Red (R)

1945, Nov.   Perf. 12½

1L10	OS5	3½s rose red	40.00	40.00
1L11	OS6	5s yel green (R)	.65	1.40
1L12	OS7	10s dk blue (R)	.65	1.40
a.		Perf 12	1.75	2.25
1L13	OS8	20s gray olive (R)	.65	1.40

1L14	OS9	40s rose lilac (R)	.70	1.40
1L15	OS10	60s red orange	.90	1.20
1L16	OS11	80s fawn	20.00	20.00
Nos. 1L10-1L16 (7)			63.55	66.80

Forgeries of Nos. 1L10-1L16 exist.

Netherlands Indies Nos. 200, 201, 228-230, N38 Overprinted "Repoeblik Indonesia" and a thick Red or Brown (Br) bar

Perf. 12½, 12x12½ (#A18, A19)
1945, Nov.

1L17	A17	1s lilac gray	2.25	2.90
1L18	A17	1s lilac gray (Br)	10.00	12.00
1L19	OS21	2s carmine	1.40	2.25
1L20	A23	2½s rose violet	20.00	20.00
1L21	A24	3s green	3.50	3.50
1L22	A25	4s olive green	3.50	3.50
Nos. 1L17-1L22 (6)			40.65	44.15

Forgeries of Nos. 1L17-1L22 exist.

A large number of proofs, both perf and imperf, in original and in different colors, exist for Nos. 1L23-1L50. All are scarce.

Bull — A1

Bull & Flag — A2

Perf. 11½
1945, Dec. 1 Typo. Unwmk.
With Gum

1L23	A1	10s chocolate	7.00	7.00
a.		Imperf	95.00	150.00
1L24	A2	20s choc & carmine red	6.50	6.50

Issued to celebrate the first half-year of Indonesian independence.

Nos. 1L25-1L50 were issued without gum.

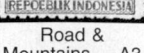

Road & Mountains — A3

Sentry — A4

Boat in Storm — A5

Wayang Puppet — A6

Kris & Flag — A7

Temple — A8

1946-47 Various perfs

1L25	A3	5s pale gray blue	.75	.95
1L26	A4	20s lt red brown	.75	.95
1L27	A5	30s carmine red	.80	1.00
1L28	A6	50s deep blue	17.50	16.00

1L29	A7	60s deep rose	6.50	300.00
1L30	A8	80s dp red vio ('47)	65.00	600.00
Nos. 1L25-1L30 (6)			91.30	918.90

Issued: 5s, 20s, 6/1/46. 30s, 50s, 7/1/46. 60s, 9/1/46. 80s, 7/1/47.

Buffalo Breaking Chains — A9

Bandung, March 1946 — A10

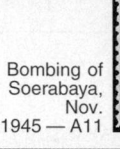

Bombing of Soerabaya, Nov. 1945 — A11

Anti-aircraft Crew — A12

Quai at Tandjong Priok — A13

Pilot — A14

Ambarawa A15

Wonokroma Dam, Soerabaya A16

Meeting, Jakarta — A17

Mounted Soldier — A18

1946-47 Various perfs

1L31	A9	3s dull carmine	.35	1.75
a.		Imperf	.20	.20
1L32	A10	5s gray blue	.60	.95
a.		Imperf	.35	.50
1L33	A11	10s blue black	11.50	6.25
a.		Imperf	11.50	11.50
1L34	A11	15s dark purple	.95	1.25
a.		Imperf	.95	.95

1L35	A12	30s green	2.40	5.75
a.		Imperf	1.75	2.40
1L36	A13	40s dk blue vio	.95	2.40
a.		Imperf	1.00	1.00
1L37	A9	50s violet black	1.75	2.90
a.		Imperf	1.20	1.20
1L38	A10	60s dp red vio	3.50	4.50
a.		Imperf	1.75	1.75
1L39	A14	80s br rose red	1.20	7.00
a.		Imperf		150.00
1L40	A15	100s dull brn red	1.75	3.50
a.		Imperf	1.20	1.20
1L41	A16	200s dull lilac	2.90	3.50
a.		Imperf	1.50	2.40
1L42	A17	500s car red	14.00	24.00
a.		Imperf	9.00	9.00
1L43	A18	1000s lt blue green	14.00	30.00
a.		Imperf	7.00	7.00
Nos. 1L31-1L43 (13)			55.85	93.75

First anniv. of independence.
Issued: 3s, 10s-200s, 8/17/46. 5s, 500s, 1000s, 2/1/47.

Worker & Ship — A19

1948, Aug. 17 Imperf.

1L44	A19	50s dull blue	3.50	4.50
a.		Perf 11		11.50
1L45	A19	100s dull scarlet	4.00	5.00
a.		Perf 11		11.50

Nos. 1L44 and 1L45 were printed on paper with papermaker's watermark. Nos. A45a and A46a were printed on unwatermarked paper.

Flag Over Waves — A20

1949, July 20 Imperf.

1L46	A20	100s car rose	5.25	6.75
a.		Perf 11	175.00	290.00
1L47	A20	150s car rose	7.50	17.00
a.		Perf 11	47.50	180.00

Return of the Indonesian government to Jakarta.
Nos. 1L46-1L47 were printed on paper bearing papermaker's watermark "MADE IN U.S.A." once in each sheet, and a few stamps within each sheet bear portions of the watermark.

Nos. 1L46a, 1L47a overprinted "Republik Indonesia Serikat 27 Des '49"

No. A49

1949, Dec. 27 Perf. 11

1L48	A20	100s car rose	17.00	
1L49	A20	150s car rose	19.00	

Return of the Indonesian government to Jakarta.

POSTAGE DUE STAMPS
Netherlands Indies Nos. J29, J32a overprinted "SEGEL, 25 sen, PORTO"

No. AJ1

1948 Perf. 12½

1LJ1	D5	25s on 7½c salmon	24.00	35.00
1LJ2	D5	25s on 15c salmon	12.50	30.00

MILITARY STAMP

M1

1949, Aug. Imperf.
Without Gum

1LM1	M1	15r ultramarine	6,750.	5,250.

No. 1LM1 was issued for provisional use at Surakarta, a Dutch stronghold in central Java, occupied by Indonesian forces in August, 1949.

SUMATRA ISSUES

Netherlands Indies Nos. 231, 201 Overprinted "Repoeblik Indonesia," New Value and Thick Bar

1946

2L1	A26	15s on 5c blue	.75	1.00
2L2	A17	40s on 2c plum	.40	1.00

Netherlands Indies Nos. 168//201 Overprinted "Repoeblik Indonesia," New Value and 5mm Thick Bar

1946

2L3	A17	20s on 3½c dk gray	24.00	24.00
2L4	A17	30s on 1c lilac gray	12.00	12.00
2L5	A17	40s on 2c plum	1.00	1.50
2L6	A17	60s on 2½c bister	175.00	175.00
2L7	A17	80s on 3c yel grn	12.50	12.50
Nos. 2L3-2L7 (5)			224.50	225.00

Netherlands Indies Nos. 234, 236 Overprinted "Repoeblik Indonesia," New Value and Two Bars

1946

2L8	A28	50s on 17½c orange	90.00	90.00
2L9	A28	1r on 10c red orange	15.00	15.00

Some examples of Nos. 2L8 and 2L9 bear handstamps previously applied by local authorities during and after the Japanese occupation. Such multiply-overprinted stamps command prices that may be more or less than the values shown, which are for examples without other overprints.

Nos. 2L10-2L84 were issued without gum.

Farmer & Oxen in Rice Paddy — A23

Sentry & Flag — A24

Airplane over City — A25

1946, May 17   **Perf. 11½x10**
2L10	A23	5s (+25s) yel grn	1.00	2.25
2L11	A24	15s (+35s) deep red	2.00	4.75
2L12	A25	40s (+60s) orange	1.00	2.25
		Nos. 2L10-2L12 (3)	4.00	9.25

Nos. 2L10-2L12 were sold at a premium over face value, not indicated on the stamps themselves, to benefit the Freedom Fund ("Fonds Kemerdekkan").

Pres. Soekarno — A26

1946, June 1   **Perf. 10¾**
2L13	A26	40s (+60s) red	1.50	3.00
2L14	A26	40s (+60s) deep red	12.00	12.00

Nos. 2L13-2L14 were sold at a premium over face value, not indicated on the stamps themselves, to benefit the Freedom Fund ("Fonds Kemerdekkan").

As Nos. 2L10-2L12, in different colors on thicker paper

1946, Aug. 17   **Perf. 11½x10**
2L15	A23	5s (+25s) turquoise	.75	2.40
2L16	A24	15s (+35s) purple	.75	2.40
2L17	A25	40s (+60s) deep red	6.25	7.00
2L18	A25	40s (+60s) bister	13.00	32.50
		Nos. 2L15-2L18 (4)	20.75	44.30

Nos. 2L15-2L18 were sold at a premium over face value, not indicated on the stamps themselves, to benefit the Freedom Fund ("Fonds Kemerdekkan").

Nos. 2L15-2L17, One- or two-bar overprint over "FONDS KEMERDEKAAN"

1946   **Perf. 11½x10¾**
2L19	A23	5s turquoise	100.00	175.00
2L20	A24	15s purple	100.00	175.00
2L21	A25	40s deep red	100.00	87.50
		Nos. 2L19-2L21 (3)	300.00	437.50

As Nos. 2L10-2L12, 2L15-18 without "FONDS KEMERDEKAAN" inscription

1946-47   **Perf. 11¾x10½**

First Issue
2L22	A23	2s red	.75	4.00
2L23	A23	3s green	1.20	7.00
2L24	A23	5s turquoise	.40	7.00
2L25	A24	15s purple	.40	2.40
2L26	A25	40s brown	.50	25.00
		Nos. 2L22-2L26 (5)	3.25	45.40

Second Issue
2L27	A23	2s chocolate	4.00	5.50
2L28	A23	3s orange	4.75	4.50
2L29	A24	15s green	4.75	5.00
2L30	A25	40s blue	24.00	40.00
		Nos. 2L27-2L30 (4)	37.50	55.00

Japanese Occupation of Sumatra Revenue Stamps Overprinted "prangko," "N.R.I." and new value

A27

1947, May 12   **Various Rough Perfs**
2L31	A27	50s light red	30.00	40.00
2L32	A27	1f light red	30.00	40.00
2L33	A27	2f light red	25.00	50.00
2L34	A27	2.50f light red	22.50	30.00
		Nos. 2L31-2L34 (4)	107.50	170.00

No. 2L13 Surcharged with New Values

1947, May 12
2L35	A26	50s on 40s red	7.75	7.75
2L36	A26	1f on 40s red	14.50	14.50
2L37	A26	1.50f on 40s red	9.00	9.00
2L38	A26	2.50f on 40s red	1.20	3.75
2L39	A26	3.50f on 40s red	1.75	4.00
2L40	A26	5f on 40s red	1.20	3.75
		Nos. 2L35-2L40 (6)	35.40	42.75

Nos. 2L24, 2L26 Surcharged, with Small Ornament covering Original Value

1947
2L41	A23	50s on 5s turq	9.50	9.50
2L42	A23	1f on 5s turq	8.25	8.25
2L43	A23	1.50f on 5s turq	9.75	9.75
2L44	A25	1r on 40s purple	.85	4.50
2L45	A23	2r on 5s turq	1.00	4.50
		Nos. 2L41-2L45 (5)	29.35	36.50

Types of 2L22-2L30, Surcharged in Black or Red (R), with Large Ornament covering Original Value

1947
2L46	A24	1s on 15s violet (R)	.80	3.00
2L47	A23	5s on 3s slate blue (R)	.75	3.00
2L48	A24	10s on 15s orange	.85	3.00
2L49	A25	50s on 3s br red	25.00	35.00
		Nos. 2L46-2L49 (4)	27.40	44.00

Nos. 2L48 and 2L49 were not issued without ovpt.

No. 2L15 Surcharged with New Values

1947
2L50	A25	30s on 40s dp red	1.00	2.50
2L51	A25	50s on 40s dp red	17.50	25.00
2L52	A25	1f on 40s dp red	3.50	2.50
2L53	A25	1.50f on 40s dp red	5.00	8.50
2L54	A25	2.50f on 40s dp red	.75	2.50
		Nos. 2L50-2L54 (5)	27.75	41.00

Nos. 2L23-2L26, Surcharged in Black or Red, with Rectangle covering Original Value, New Value 2.8mm High

1948
2L55	A23	.50f on 5s turq.	900.00	850.00
2L56	A24	.50f on 15s purple	900.00	850.00
2L57	A23	1f on 5s turq.	175.00	175.00
2L58	A24	1f on 15s purple	350.00	350.00
2L59	A25	1f on 40s brown	575.00	
2L60	A23	2.50f on 5s turq.	900.00	850.00
2L61	A24	2.50f on 15s purple	575.00	475.00
2L62	A24	5f on 15s purple	900.00	900.00
2L63	A25	5f on 40s brown	400.00	400.00
2L64	A23	50s on 5s turq.	1,000.	1,000.
2L65	A24	50s on 15s purple	400.00	400.00
		Nos. 2L55-2L65 (11)	7,075.	6,300.

New Currency
Values 3.2mm High

1949
2L66	A23	2.50r on 3s green	25.00	30.00
a.		Red overprint	25.00	30.00
2L67	A24	5r on 15s purple	10.00	30.00
a.		Red overprint	10.00	30.00
2L68	A23	10r on 3s green	110.00	110.00
a.		Red overprint	110.00	110.00
		Nos. 2L66-2L68 (3)	145.00	170.00

Emergency provisional issue for Aceh Province.

Nos. 2L15, 2L22, 2L23, 2L25 Surcharged in Black or Red, with Rectangle covering Original Value, New Value 4.5mm High

1949
2L69	A23	2r on 3s green	42.50	80.00
a.		Red overprint	42.50	80.00
2L70	A23	2.50r on 3s green	24.00	60.00
a.		Red overprint	24.00	60.00
2L71	A24	5r on 15s purple	10.00	16.00
a.		Red overprint	10.00	16.00
2L72	A23	10r on 3s green	18.00	40.00
a.		Red overprint	18.00	40.00
2L73	A23	20r on 2s red	300.00	600.00
a.		Red overprint	350.00	600.00
2L74	A24	50r on 15s purple	400.00	575.00
a.		Red overprint	400.00	575.00
2L75	A24	100r on 15s purple	150.00	150.00
a.		Red overprint	150.00	150.00
2L76	A25	200r on 40s brown	175.00	175.00
a.		Red overprint	175.00	175.00
		Nos. 2L69-2L76 (8)	1,119.	1,696.

Nos. 2L22, 2L25, 2L26 Surcharged in Black, with Rectangle covering Original Value, New Value 7.2mm High

1949
2L77	A24	10s on 15s purple	18.00	18.00
2L78	A24	20s on 15s purple	18.00	18.00
2L79	A24	30s on 15s purple	18.00	8.50
2L80	A23	1r on 2s red	60.00	125.00
2L81	A24	1.50f on 15s purple		500.00
2L82	A24	2.50f on 15s purple	22.50	50.00
2L83	A25	5r on 40s brown	290.00	210.00
		Nos. 2L77-2L83 (7)	426.50	929.50

Nos. 1L46-1L47 Surcharged with New Values

1949
2L84	A20	15r on 100s car rose	25.00	60.00
2L85	A20	15r on 150s car rose	27.50	70.00

AIR POST STAMPS
Nos. 66, 75 overprinted "POS UDARA" and New Values

1947
2LC1	A26	10r on 40s br red	3.00	4.50
2LC2	A26	20r on 5s turq	1.80	4.50

REPUBLIC OF INDONESIA

Nos. 1-119, C1-C61, CE1-CE4, CO1-CO16, E1-E1G, J1-J39 and O1-O24 were authorized by the Indonesia PTT and were produced in Vienna and Philadelphia. Because most were printed by the Austrian State Printing Office (Staatsdruckerei), they are usually described as the "Vienna" issues. The first issue was released in Dec. 1948, but supplies did not reach republican-held areas of Java and Sumatra until mid-Jan., 1949. Through 1949, small supplies of these issues were sent to some 20 post offices in Java and Sumatra, where they were used both for local mail and for mail to foreign destinations, which was carried through the Dutch blockade by overseas (largely Indian) air carriers.

Following independence, the Vienna issues continued to be valid for postage for several years. While most covers on the market are philatelic in nature, commercial covers dated 1949-53 exist.

The Vienna issues were produced and heavily marketed by a U.S. stamp dealer. Proofs, deluxe sheetlets of one, and various overprints exist for these issues, as well as several unissued sets.

Values for the Vienna Issues are for mint never hinged stamps. Hinged examples are generally offered at 50-75% of these values. Used stamps are scarce, though generally not rare, and pricing information on values for used stamps is not presently available.

Map, Indonesian Archipelago A28

Farmer — A29

Red Cross Airplane A30

Balinese Dancer — A31

Military Officer, Flag of Republic A32

Designs: 1s, Map of Indonesian Archipelago. 2s, Republican sentry and Toba Lake, Sumatra. 2½, Military review, Gen. Soedirmari. 3s, Farmer working field with pitchfork. 3½s, Sultan Sjahrir and Thomas Jefferson. 4s, Buffalo Canyon, Sumatra. 5s, Policemen on motorcycles, Sastroamidjojo. 7½s, Red Cross nurse with wounded soldier. 10s, Dr. Maramis, Minister of Finance, and Alexander Hamilton. 15s, Construction of Great Postal Road, Java. 17½s, Hadji Agoes Salim, philosopher, and Benjamin Franklin. 20s, Red Cross Boeing aircraft. 30s, Djanger dancer, Bali. 35s, Planting rice. 40s, Vice Pres. Mohammed Hatta and Abraham Lincoln. 50s, Mountain, Sumatra. 60s, Rice fields, Java. 80s, Boy holding pineapple. 1r, Pres. Soekarno and George Washington. 2r, Mosque, Medan, Sumatra. 2½r, Fish ponds, Tjipanas. 5r, Officer presenting flag. 10r, Vice Pres. Hatta. 25r, Pres. Soekarno.

Perf. 14x13¾, 13¼x14 (#6), 13½x14¼ (#12, 14-16, 19, 20), 14¼x13½ (#13, 17, 17, 21), 12½ (#22-24)
Photo., Engr. (#22-24)

				Unwmk.
1948, Dec. 15				
1	A28	1s dk turq grn & brn	.45	—
2	A28	2s dp brn & dp blue	.20	—
3	A28	2½s dk brn & org red	.35	—
4	A29	3s dk lil & dp red brn	.20	—
5	A28	3½s dk bl vio & br grn	.20	—
6	A29	4s dk bl vio & dp ol grn	.30	—
7	A28	5s turq & dull blue	.20	—
8	A28	7½s dp brn & dk lil	.35	—
9	A28	10s dp blue & brn rose	.50	—
10	A28	15s brown & dk grn	.60	—
11	A28	17½s ultra & org brn	.30	—
12	A30	20s Prus grn & dp bis brn	.45	—
13	A31	30s dk brn & dull vio	.30	—
14	A30	35s dk lilac & brn	.30	—
15	A30	40s dk brn & blue	.30	—
16	A30	50s dk brn & turq	.30	—
17	A31	60s dk brn & lt red brn	.50	—
18	A31	80s dk lilac & slate	.45	—
19	A30	1r br blue & pur brn	.35	—
20	A30	2r dk brn & dk grn	.55	—
21	A31	2½r dk lilac & blue	.65	—
22	A32	5r yel brn & black	3.50	—
23	A32	10r emerald & black	5.00	—
24	A32	25r rose red & blk	7.00	—
		Nos. 1-24 (24)	23.30	

See Nos. C1-C13.
For overprints, see Nos. 70-90, O1-O6.

A33

Designs: 10s, 25s, Map, ships. 15s, 60s, Dockworkers loading ship, vert. 1r, Ships. Illustration reduced.

1949, Aug. 17		**Photo.**	**Perf. 12½**	
25	A33	10s gray & green	.80	—
26	A33	15s gray & maroon	.80	—
27	A33	25s gray & blue	.80	—
28	A33	60s maroon & gray	3.00	—
29	A33	1r org & dull blue	8.00	—
		Nos. 25-29 (5)	13.40	

Failure of Dutch blockade.
See Nos. C14-C18.

Sentry — A34

Soekarno Decorating Soldier — A35

Planting Rice — A36

Boy Holding Pineapple — A37

Military Officer, Flag of Republic A38

Designs: 1s, Republican sentry and Toba Lake, Sumatra. 2s, Soekarno decorating soldier. 2½s, Woman weaving batik. 3s, Metalcraft worker. 3½s, Construction of Great Postal Road, Java. 4s, Farmer working field with pitchfork. 5s, Javanese Wajang Wong dancer. 7½s, Planting rice on the sawah. 10s, Red Cross nurse with wounded soldier. 15s, Buffalo Canyon, Sumatra. 17½s, Plowing with oxen. 20s, Planting rice. 30s, Mountain, Sumatra. 35s, Boy holding pineapple. 40s, Fish ponds, Tjipanas. 50s, Djanger dancer, Bali. 60s, Javanese Serimpi court dancer. 80s, Mosque, Medan, Sumatra. 1r, Overcoming illiteracy. 2r, Idol. 2½r, Map of Indonesian Archipelago. 5r, Officer presenting flag. 10r, Vice Pres. Mohammed Hatta. 25r, Pres. Soekarno.
Country name inscription has been changed from "Repoeblik" to "Republik," to make spelling more American and less Dutch. This spelling change also officially changed Pres. Soekarno's name to Sukarno.

Perf. 14x13¾, 13¾x14 (#31-33, 35, 36, 39), 13½x14¼ (#41, 42, 47, 50), 14¼x13½ (#43-46), 12½ (#51-53)
Photo., Engr. (#51-53)

1949, Aug. 17				
30	A34	1s dp brn & dp blue	.30	—
31	A35	2s dk red vio & dp grn	.40	—
32	A35	2½s dk brn & br scarlet	.35	—
33	A35	3s dp turq & org ver	.45	—
34	A34	3½s dp brn & dp grn	.40	—
35	A35	4s turq & dull blue	.50	—
36	A35	5s dull vio & dk yel brn	.35	—
37	A34	7½s dp brn & dk lil	.40	—
38	A34	10s dk brn & dp vio	.50	—
39	A35	15s dk vio & dp dull grn	.65	—
40	A34	17½s dk brn & red org	.55	—
41	A36	20s dull vio & dp brn	.25	—
42	A36	30s dp brn & dk blue vio	.45	—
43	A37	35s sl vio & blue	.25	—
44	A37	40s dull vio & dk yel brn	.45	—
45	A37	50s dk brn & Prus grn	.40	—
46	A37	60s br blue & dk yel brn	.55	—
47	A36	80s dull vio & dull bl	.50	—
48	A36	1r dp blue & dp choc	.50	—
49	A37	2r dp brn & org ver	.30	—
50	A36	2½r dp brn & br blue	1.00	—
51	A38	5r red vio & black	6.50	—
52	A38	10r green & black	4.25	—
53	A38	25r orange & black	6.50	—
		Nos. 30-53 (24)	26.75	

For overprints, see Nos. 89-109, O7-O12.

A39

A40

Designs: 10s, 25s, Map, ships. 15s, 60s, Dockworkers loading ship, vert. 1r, Ships. Illustrations reduced.

1948, Dec. 15		**Photo.**	**Perf. 14½**	
54	A39	10s gray & red	1.25	—
55	A39	15s gray & dp blue	1.25	—
56	A39	25s gray & red brn	1.10	—
57	A39	60s gray & maroon	2.00	—
58	A39	1r gray & maroon	4.50	—
		Nos. 54-58 (5)	10.10	

Souvenir Sheets

59	A40	10s, 15s, 25s, 60s	50.00	—
a.		Imperf	325.00	—
60	A40	10s, 30s, 50s, 1r, 2½r	25.00	—
a.		Imperf	150.00	—
b.	A39	2½r gray & maroon		—
c.		As "b," imperf		—
61	A40	1r, 4½r	40.00	—
a.		Imperf	50.00	—
b.	A39	4½r maroon		—
c.		As "b," imperf		—

Failure of Dutch blockade, second issue.
The stamps contained in No. 60 and the 4½r stamp contained in No. 61 are air post stamps and are inscribed "POS UDARA."
See Nos. C32-C36.
For overprints, see Nos. 112-119.

Map, UPU Emblem & *Banteng* (Nationalist Symbol) — A41

Wmk. 404

1949, Dec. 1		**Photo.**	**Perf. 14**	
62	A41	10s multicolored	.55	—
a.		Imperf	.60	
63	A41	20s multicolored	.55	—
a.		Imperf	.60	
64	A41	50s multicolored	.60	—
a.		Imperf	.70	
65	A41	1r multicolored	.60	—
a.		Imperf	.75	
b.		Souvenir Sheet of 4, #62-65	22.50	
c.		As "b," imperf	25.00	
		Nos. 62-65 (4)	2.30	

Unwatermarked

66	A41	10s multicolored	.45	—
a.		Imperf	.45	
67	A41	20s multicolored	.45	—
a.		Imperf	.45	
68	A41	50s multicolored	.45	—
a.		Imperf	.45	
69	A41	1r multicolored	.45	—
a.		Imperf	.45	
		Nos. 66-69 (4)	1.80	

Nos. 64, 65, 68 and 69 are air post stamps and are inscribed "POS UDARA."
Souvenir sheets of 4, as No. 65c, without watermark, are proofs.
Most varieties of Nos. 1-69 exist overprinted "RIS," "RIS Merdeka" and "RIS Djakarta." These were not issued in Indonesia.

Liberation of Jakarta

Nos. 1-61 overprinted "Merdeka Djojakarta 6 Djuli 1949"

Nos. 1-21 Overprinted

1949, Dec. 7				
70	A28	1s dk turq grn & brn	.25	—
71	A28	2s dp brn & dp blue	.90	—
72	A28	2½s dk brn & org red	.25	—
73	A29	3s dk lil & dp red brn	.45	—
74	A28	3½s dk bl vio & br grn	.25	—
75	A29	4s dk bl vio & dp ol grn	.55	—
76	A28	5s turq & dull blue	.25	—
77	A28	7½s dp brn & dk lil	.45	—
78	A28	10s dp blue & brn rose	.25	—
79	A28	15s brown & dk grn	1.25	—
80	A28	17½s ultra & org brn	2.00	—
81	A30	20s Prus grn & dp bis brn	1.00	—
82	A31	30s dk brn & dull vio	3.50	—

83	A30	35s dk lilac & brn	5.75	—
84	A30	40s dk brn & blue	.85	—
85	A30	50s dk brn & turq	4.50	—
86	A31	60s dk brn & lt red brn	6.75	—
87	A31	80s dk lilac & slate	1.75	—
88	A30	1r br blue & pur brn	3.50	—
89	A30	2r dk brn & dk grn	1.00	—
90	A31	2½r dk lilac & blue	7.50	—

Nos. 70-90 (21) 42.95

Nos. 30-50 overprinted

93ovpt

91	A34	1s dp brn & dp blue	.20	—
92	A35	2s dk red vio & dp grn	1.25	—
93	A35	2½s dk brn & br scarlet	.20	—
94	A35	3s dp turq & org ver	.20	—
95	A34	3½s dp brn & dp grn	.20	—
96	A35	4s turq & dull blue	.25	—
97	A35	5s dull vio & dk yel brn	.50	—
98	A34	7½s dp brn & dk lil	.60	—
99	A34	10s dk brn & dp vio	.75	—
100	A35	15s dk vio & dp dull grn	1.25	—
101	A34	17½s dk brn & red org	1.25	—
102	A36	20s dull vio & dp brn	3.25	—
103	A36	30s dk brn & dk blue vio	2.75	—
104	A37	35s sl vio & blue	2.75	—
105	A37	40s dull vio & dk yel brn	2.75	—
106	A37	50s dk brn & Prus brn	5.00	—
107	A37	60s br blue & dk yel brn	5.00	—
108	A36	80s dull vio & dull bl	5.00	—
109	A36	1r dp blue & dp choc	2.75	—
110	A37	2r dp brn & org ver	2.75	—
111	A36	2½r dp brn & br blue	6.00	—

Nos. 91-111 (21) 44.65

Nos. 54-61 overprinted

112	A39	10s gray & red	.40	—
113	A39	15s gray & dp blue	.40	—
114	A39	25s gray & red brn	1.40	—
115	A39	60s gray & maroon	1.40	—
116	A39	1r gray & maroon	2.75	—

Nos. 112-116 (5) 6.35

Souvenir Sheets

117	A40	10s, 15s, 25s, 60s	650.00	—
a.		Imperf	1,750.	—
118	A40	30s, 50s, 1r, 2½r	50.00	—
a.		Imperf	100.00	—
b.	A39	2½r gray & maroon	—	—
c.		As "b," imperf	—	—
119	A40	1r, 4½r	35.00	—
a.		Imperf	50.00	—
b.	A39	4½r maroon	—	—
c.		As "b," imperf	—	—

The stamps contained in No. 118 and the 4½r stamp contained in No. 119 are air post stamps and are inscribed "POS UDARA."

United States of Indonesia

Mountain, Palms and Flag of Republic — A49

Perf. 12½x12

1950, Jan. 17   Photo.   Unwmk.
Size: 20½x26mm

333	A49	15s red	1.40	.30

Exists imperf, without gum. Value $70.

1950, June   Perf. 11½
Size: 18x23mm

334	A49	15s red	6.25	2.00

Exists imperf, without gum. Value $50.

Netherlands Indies
Nos. 307-315
Overprinted in Black

1950   Perf. 11½, 12½

335	A42	1s gray	1.00	.80
336	A42	2s claret	1.40	3.50
a.		Perf 11½	1.75	2.25
337	A42	2½s olive brown	1.00	.80
a.		Perf 12½	1.40	.70
338	A42	3s rose pink	1.00	.65
a.		Perf 12½	1.00	.55
339	A42	4s green	1.00	.80
a.		Perf 12½	1.75	1.00
340	A42	5s blue	1.00	.80
341	A42	7½s dark green	1.00	.80
342	A42	10s violet	1.00	.75
a.		Perf 12½	1.75	1.75
343	A42	12½s bright red	1.25	.80

Netherlands Indies Nos. 317-330
Overprinted in Black

Perf. 11½, 12½

345	A43	20s gray black	30.00	35.00
346	A43	25s ultra	1.00	.80
a.		Perf 12½	1.75	.80
347	A44	30s bright red	10.00	22.50
a.		Perf 12½	52.50	72.50
348	A44	40s gray green	1.00	.50
a.		Perf 12½	1.00	.50
349	A45	45s claret	2.10	1.25
350	A45	50s orange brown	1.75	1.10
351	A45	60s brown	8.75	13.50
a.		Perf 12½	—	37.50
352	A45	80s scarlet	4.00	1.25
a.		Perf 12½	3.75	1.25

Perf. 11½, 20s, 45s, 50s. Others, both perfs.

Overprint 12mm High
Perf. 12½

353	A46	1r purple	2.75	.75
354	A46	2r olive green	450.00	160.00
355	A46	3r red violet	150.00	72.50
356	A46	5r dark brown	65.00	24.00
357	A46	10r gray	110.00	45.00
358	A46	25r orange brown	30.00	17.50

Nos. 335-358 (23) 876.00 405.35
Set, hinged 325.00

For overprints see Riau Archipelago #17-22.

Republic of Indonesia

Arms of the Republic A50

Doves in Flight A51

Perf. 12½x12

1950, Aug. 17   Photo.   Unwmk.

359	A50	15s red	2.00	.50
360	A50	25s dull green	3.00	2.00
361	A50	1r sepia	10.00	2.50

Nos. 359-361 (3) 15.00 5.00

5th anniv. of Indonesia's proclamation of independence.

1951, Oct. 24   Engr.   Perf. 12

362	A51	7½s blue green	5.00	1.00
363	A51	10s violet	1.25	.45
364	A51	20s red	2.50	1.00
365	A51	30s carmine rose	3.25	1.25

366	A51	35s ultra	3.25	1.25
367	A51	1r sepia	27.50	4.00

Nos. 362-367 (6) 42.75 8.95

6th anniv. of the UN and the 1st anniv. of the Republic of Indonesia as a member.

A52

Post Office — A53

Mythological Hero — A54

Pres. Sukarno — A55

1951-53   Photo.   Perf. 12½

368	A52	1s gray	.45	.90
369	A52	2s plum	.45	.80
370	A52	2½s brown	6.50	.50
371	A52	5s car rose	.45	.20
372	A52	7½s green	.45	.50
373	A52	10s blue	1.25	.20
a.		Perf 11½	8.75	8.75
374	A52	15s purple	.90	.40
375	A52	20s rose red	.50	.40
376	A52	25s deep green	.50	.20
377	A53	30s red orange	.20	.20
378	A53	35s purple	.80	.20
379	A53	40s dull green	.20	.40
380	A53	45s deep claret	.20	.20
381	A53	50s brown	5.75	.20
382	A54	60s dark brown	.20	.20
383	A54	70s gray	.20	.20
384	A54	75s ultra	.20	.20
385	A54	80s claret	.20	.20
386	A54	90s gray green	.20	.20

Nos. 368-386 (19) 19.60 6.30

Perf. 12½x12

387	A55	1r purple	.30	.20
388	A55	1.25r dp orange	2.10	.20
389	A55	1.50r brown	.30	.20
390	A55	2r green	.30	.20
391	A55	2.50r rose brown	.30	.90
392	A55	3r blue	.30	.20
392A	A55	4r apple green	.30	.20
393	A55	5r brown	.30	.20
394	A55	6r rose lilac	.30	.20
395	A55	10r slate	.30	.20
396	A55	15r yellow	.30	.20
397	A55	20r sepia	.30	.20
398	A55	25r scarlet	.80	.20
399	A55	40r yellow green	1.00	2.75
400	A55	50r violet	1.40	.75

Nos. 387-400 (15) 8.60 6.10

Nos. 368-376, 387, 390, 392, 393, 395, 398 were issued in 1951; Nos. 377-386, 388-389, 391, 392A, 394, 396-397, 399-400 in 1953.

Values are for the later Djakarta printings which have thicker numerals and a darker over-all impression. Earlier printings by Joh. Enschede and Sons, Haarlem, Netherlands, sell for more.

For surcharge see No. B68. For overprints see Riau Archipelago Nos. 1-16, 32-40.

Melati Flowers — A56

Crowd Releasing Doves — A57

1953, Dec. 22   Perf. 12½

401	A56	50s blue green	12.00	.70

25th anniv. of the formation of the Indonesian Women's Congress.

1955, Apr. 18   Perf. 13x12½

402	A57	15s gray	.75	.75
403	A57	35s brown	.90	.75
404	A57	50s deep magenta	2.40	.75
405	A57	75s blue green	1.50	.75

Nos. 402-405 (4) 5.55 3.00

Asian-African Conf., Bandung, April 18-24.

Proclamation of Independence A58

1955, Aug. 17   Photo.   Perf. 12½

406	A58	15s green	.75	1.00
407	A58	35s ultra	1.25	1.00
408	A58	50s brown	8.00	.90
409	A58	75s magenta	1.25	.60

Nos. 406-409 (4) 11.25 3.50

Ten years of independence.

Voters — A59

1955, Sept. 29   Perf. 12
Without gum

410	A59	15s rose violet	.60	.60
411	A59	35s green	.60	.80
412	A59	50s carmine rose	2.10	1.00
413	A59	75s lt ultra	.85	.45

Nos. 410-413 (4) 4.15 2.85

First free elections in Indonesia.

Mas Soeharto Postmaster General A60

Helmet, Wreath and Monument A61

1955, Sept. 27   Perf. 12½

414	A60	15s brown	1.25	.35
415	A60	35s dark carmine	1.25	.35
416	A60	50s ultra	5.50	4.00
417	A60	75s dull green	1.25	.35

Nos. 414-417 (4) 9.25 5.05

Issued to mark 10 years of Indonesia's Postal, Telegraph and Telephone system.

1955, Nov. 10

418	A61	25s bluish green	1.25	.60
419	A61	50s ultra	1.50	.70
420	A61	1r dk car rose	11.00	.40

Nos. 418-420 (3) 13.75 1.70

Issued in honor of the soldiers killed in the war of liberation from the Netherlands.

Torch, Book and Map A62

Lesser Malay Chevrotain A63

1956, May 26   Photo.

421	A62	25s ultra	1.40	.50
422	A62	50s carmine rose	7.00	1.25
423	A62	1r dark green	2.00	1.25

Nos. 421-423 (3) 10.40 3.00

Asia-Africa Student Conf., Bandung, May, 1956.

1956   Unwmk.   Perf. 12½x13½

Animals: 5s, 10s, Lesser Malay chevrotain. 20s, 25s, Otter. 35s, Malayan pangolin. 50s, Banteng. 75s, Asiatic two-horned rhinoceros.

424	A63	5s deep ultra	.25	.20
425	A63	10s yellow brown	.25	.20
426	A63	15s rose violet	.40	.20
427	A63	20s dull green	.40	.20
428	A63	25s deep claret	.40	.20
429	A63	35s brt violet blue	.40	.20
430	A63	50s brown	.75	.20
431	A63	75s dark brown	.40	.20

Nos. 424-431 (8) 3.25 1.60

See Nos. 450-456. For overprints see Riau Archipelago Nos. 23-31.

Dancing Girl and Gate — A64

Telegraph Key — A65

1956, Oct. 7   Perf. 12½x12
432 A64 15s slate green   1.25 .65
433 A64 35s brown violet   1.25 .65
434 A64 50s blue black   2.50 2.00
435 A64 75s deep claret   3.00 1.00
   Nos. 432-435 (4)   8.00 4.30

Founding of the city of Jogjakarta, 200th anniv.

1957, May 10   Unwmk.
436 A65 10s lt crimson   2.40 .60
437 A65 15s brt blue   .55 .45
438 A65 25s gray   .50 .20
439 A65 50s brown red   .65 .30
440 A65 75s lt blue green   .80 .20
   Nos. 436-440 (5)   4.90 1.75

Indonesian telegraph system centenary.

Thrift Symbolism A66

Douglas DC-3 A67

Design: 15s, 1r, People and hands holding wreath of rice and cotton.

1957, July 12   Photo.   Perf. 12½
441 A66 10s blue   .50 .45
442 A66 15s rose carmine   .65 .45
443 A66 50s green   1.25 .95
444 A66 1r brt violet   1.25 .50
   Nos. 441-444 (4)   3.65 2.35

Cooperation Day, July 12.

1958, Apr. 9   Perf. 12½x12

Aircraft: 15s, Helicopter. 30s, Miles Magister. 50s, Two-motor plane of Indonesian Airways. 75s, De Havilland Vampire.

445 A67 10s reddish brown   .45 .20
446 A67 15s blue   .45 .20
447 A67 35s orange   .45 .25
448 A67 50s bright green   .45 .40
449 A67 75s gray   .45 .55
   Nos. 445-449 (5)   2.25 1.60

Issued for National Aviation Day, April 9.

Animal Type of 1956

Animals: 30s, Otter. 40s, 45s, Malayan pangolin. 60s, 70s, Banteng. 80s, 90s, Asiatic two-horned rhinoceros.

1958   Photo.   Perf. 12½x13½
450 A63 30s orange   .25 .20
451 A63 40s brt yellow grn   .30 .20
452 A63 45s rose lilac   1.40 .20
453 A63 60s dark blue   .45 .20
454 A63 70s orange ver   2.00 .30
455 A63 80s red   .60 .20
456 A63 90s yellow green   .60 .20
   Nos. 450-456 (7)   5.60 1.50

Thomas Cup A68

1958, Aug. 15   Perf. 13½x13
457 A68 25s rose carmine   .20 .20
458 A68 50s orange   .20 .20
459 A68 1r brown   .30 .20
   Nos. 457-459 (3)   .75 .60

Indonesia's victory in the 1958 Thomas Cup World Badminton Championship.

Satellite Circling Globe — A69

1958, Oct. 15   Litho.   Perf. 12½x12
460 A69 10s dk grn, pink & lt bl   1.10 .60
461 A69 15s vio, gray & pale bluish grn   .30 .20
462 A69 35s brown, blue & pink   .30 .20
463 A69 50s bl, redsh brn & gray   .30 .20
464 A69 75s black, vio & buff   .30 .20
   Nos. 460-464 (5)   2.30 1.40

International Geophysical Year, 1957-58.

Bicyclist and Map A70

1958, Nov. 15   Photo.   Perf. 13½x13
465 A70 25s bright blue   .45 .30
466 A70 50s brown carmine   .80 .30
467 A70 1r gray   .45 .30
   Nos. 465-467 (3)   1.70 .90

Bicycle Tour of Java, Aug. 15-30.

Man Looking into Light A71

Wild Boar (Babirusa) A72

Designs: 15s, Hands and flame. 35s, Woman holding candle. 50s, Family hailing torch. 75s, Torch and "10."

1958, Dec. 10   Perf. 12½x12
468 A71 10s gray brown   .20 .20
469 A71 15s dull red brn   .20 .20
470 A71 35s ultra   .25 .20
471 A71 50s pale brown   .25 .20
472 A71 75s lt blue grn   .30 .20
   Nos. 468-472 (5)   1.20 1.00

10th anniv. of the signing of the Universal Declaration of Human Rights.

1959, June 1   Photo.   Perf. 12

Animals: 15s, Anoa (smallest buffalo). 20s, Orangutan. 50s, Javan rhinoceros. 75s, Komodo dragon (lizard). 1r, Malayan tapir.

473 A72 10s olive bis & sepia   .20 .20
474 A72 15s org brn & sepia   .25 .25
475 A72 20s lt ol grn & sepia   .30 .30
476 A72 50s bister brn & sepia   .60 .45
477 A72 75s dp rose & sepia   .80 .20
478 A72 1r blue grn & blk   1.00 .20
   Nos. 473-478 (6)   3.15 1.60

Issued to publicize wildlife preservation.

A73

Factories — A74

1959, Aug. 17   Litho.   Perf. 12
479 A73 20s blue & red   .20 .20
480 A73 50s rose red & blk   .20 .20
481 A73 75s brown & red   .20 .20
482 A73 1.50r lt green & blk   .40 .40
   Nos. 479-482 (4)   1.00 1.00

Introduction of the constitution of 1945 embodying "guided democracy."

1959, Oct. 26   Photo.   Perf. 12

Designs: 20s, 75s, Cogwheel and train. 1.15r, Means of transportation.

483 A74 15s brt green & blk   .20 .20
484 A74 20s dull org & blk   .20 .20
485 A74 50s red & black   .20 .20
486 A74 75s brt grnsh bl & blk   .20 .20
487 A74 1.15r magenta & blk   .20 .20
   Nos. 483-487 (5)   1.00 1.00

11th Colombo Plan Conference, Jakarta.

Mother & Child, WRY Emblem — A75

15s, 75s, Destroyed town & fleeing family. 20s, 1.15r, World Refugee Year emblem.

1960, Apr. 7   Unwmk.   Perf. 12½x12
488 A75 10s claret & blk   .20 .20
489 A75 15s bister & blk   .20 .20
490 A75 20s org brn & blk   .20 .20
491 A75 50s green & blk   .20 .20
492 A75 75s dk blue & blk   .25 .20
493 A75 1.15r scarlet & blk   .25 1.10
   Nos. 488-493 (6)   1.30 2.10

World Refugee Year, 7/1/59-6/3/60.

Tea Plantation — A76

5s, Oil palms. 10s, Sugar cane and railroad. 15s, Coffee. 20s, Tobacco. 50s, Coconut palms. 75s, Rubber plantation. 1.15r, Rice.

1960   Perf. 12x12½
494 A76 5s gray   .20 .20
495 A76 10s red brown   .20 .20
496 A76 15s plum   .20 .20
497 A76 20s ocher   .20 .20
498 A76 25s brt blue grn   .20 .20
499 A76 50s deep blue   .20 .20
500 A76 75s scarlet   .20 .20
501 A76 1.15r plum   .20 .20
   Nos. 494-501 (8)   1.60 1.60

For surcharges see Nos. B132-B134.

Anopheles Mosquito — A77

1960, Nov. 12   Photo.   Perf. 12x12½
502 A77 25s carmine rose   .20 .20
503 A77 50s orange brown   .20 .20
504 A77 75s brt green   .20 .20
505 A77 3r orange   .30 .30
   Nos. 502-505 (4)   .90 .90

World Health Day, Nov. 12, 1960, and to promote malaria control.

Pres. Sukarno with Hoe — A78

1961, Feb. 15   Perf. 12½x12
506 A78 75s gray   .70 .20

Planned National Development.

Dayak Dancer of Borneo A79

Designs: 10s, Ambonese boat. 15s, Tangkubanperahu crater. 20s, Bull races. 50s, Toradja houses. 75s, Balinese temple. 1r, Lake Toba. 1.50r, Balinese dancer and musicians. 2r, Buffalo hole, view. 3r, Borobudur Temple, Java.

1961   Perf. 13½x13
507 A79 10s rose lilac   .65 .50
508 A79 15s gray   .65 .50
509 A79 20s orange   .65 .50
510 A79 25s orange ver   .65 .50
511 A79 50s carmine rose   .65 .50
512 A79 75s red brown   .65 .50
513 A79 1r brt green   1.25 .50
514 A79 1.50r bister brn   1.25 .50
515 A79 2r grnsh blue   1.60 .50
516 A79 3r gray   1.75 .50
   Set of 4 souvenir sheets   24.00 22.50
   Nos. 507-516 (10)   9.75 5.00

Issued for tourist publicity.
The four souvenir sheets among them contain one each of Nos. 507-516 imperf., with two or three stamps to a sheet and English marginal inscriptions: "Visit Indonesia" and "Visit the Orient Year." Size: 139x105mm or 105x139mm.

Sports Hall and Thomas Cup A80

Perf. 13½x12½
1961, June 1   Photo.
517 A80 75s pale violet & blue   .20 .20
518 A80 1r citron & dk grn   .20 .20
519 A80 3r salmon pink & dk bl   .30 .20
   Nos. 517-519 (3)   .70 .60

1961 Thomas Cup World Badminton Championship.

New Buildings and Workers A81

1961, July 6   Unwmk.
520 A81 75s violet & grnsh bl   .20 .20
521 A81 1.50r emerald & buff   .20 .20
522 A81 3r dk red & salmon   .40 .20
   Nos. 520-522 (3)   .80 .60

16th anniversary of independence.

Sultan Hasanuddin — A82

Portraits: 20s, Abdul Muis. 30s, Surjopranoto. 40s, Tengku Tjhik Di Tiro. 50s, Teuku Umar. 60s, K. H. Samanhudi. 75s, Captain Pattimura. 1r, Raden Adjeng Kartini. 1.25r, K. H. Achmad Dahlan. 1.50r, Tuanku Imam Bondjol. 2r, Si Singamangaradja XII. 2.50r, Mohammad Husni Thamrin. 3r, Ki Hadjar Dewantoro. 4r, Djenderal Sudirman. 4.50r, Dr. G. S. S. J. Ratulangie. 5r, Pangeran Diponegoro. 6r, Dr. Setyabudi. 7.50r, H. O. S. Tjokroaminoto. 10r, K. H. Agus Salim. 15r, Dr. Soetomo.

Perf. 13½x12½
1961-62   Unwmk.   Photo.
Black Inscriptions; Portraits in Sepia
523 A82 20s olive   .20 .30
524 A82 25s gray olive   .20 .30
525 A82 30s brt lilac   .20 .30
526 A82 40s brown orange   .50 .30
527 A82 50s bluish green   .50 .30
528 A82 60s green ('62)   .50 .30
529 A82 75s lt red brown   .50 .30
530 A82 1r lt blue   .85 .30
531 A82 1.25r lt ol grn ('62)   .55 .30

532	A82	1.50r emerald	.85	.30
533	A82	2r org red ('62)	.55	.30
534	A82	2.50r rose claret	.85	.30
535	A82	3r gray blue	.70	.30
536	A82	4r olive green	.90	.30
537	A82	4.50r red lilac ('62)	.55	.30
538	A82	5r brick red	1.10	.30
539	A82	6r bister ('62)	.55	.30
540	A82	7.50r violet bl ('62)	.80	.30
541	A82	10r green ('62)	1.25	.30
542	A82	15r dp org ('62)	1.10	.30
		Nos. 523-542 (20)	12.90	6.00

National heroes. The 25s, 75s, 1.50r, 5r issued on 8/17, Independence Day; 40s, 50s, 4r on 10/5, Army Day; 20s, 30s, 1r, 2.50r, 3r on 11/10, Republic Day; 60s, 2r, 7.50r, 15r on 10/5/62; 1.25r, 4.50r, 6r, 10r on 11/10/62.

Symbols of Census A83

1961, Sept. 15   *Perf. 13½x12½*
543	A83	75s rose violet	.60	.20

First census in Indonesia.

Djataju — A84

Scenes from Ramayana Ballet: 40s, Hanuman. 1r, Dasamuka. 1.50r, Kidang Kentiana. 3r, Dewi Sinta. 5r, Rama.

Perf. 12x12½
1962, Jan. 15   Unwmk.
544	A84	30s ocher & red brn	.40	.45
545	A84	40s rose lilac & vio	.40	.45
546	A84	1r green & claret	.65	.45
547	A84	1.50r sal pink & dk grn	.75	.45
548	A84	3r pale grn & dp bl	2.00	.45
549	A84	5r brn org & dk brn	1.75	.45
		Nos. 544-549 (6)	5.95	2.70

Asian Games Emblem — A85

Main Stadium — A86

Designs: 10s, Basketball. 15s, Main Stadium, Jakarta. 20s, Weight lifter. 25s, Hotel Indonesia. 30s, Cloverleaf intersection. 40s, Discus thrower. 50s, Woman diver. 60s, Soccer. 70s, Press House. 75s, Boxers. 1r, Volleyball. 1.25r, 2r, 3r, 5r, Asian Games emblem. 1.50r, Badminton. 1.75r, Wrestlers. 2.50r, Woman rifle shooter. 4.50r, Hockey. 6r, Water polo. 7.50r, Tennis. 10r, Table tennis. 15r, Bicyclist. 20r, Welcome Monument.

1962   Photo.   *Perf. 12½*
550	A85	10s green & yel	.20	.20
551	A86	15s grnsh blk & bis	.20	.20
552	A85	20s red lil & lt grn	.30	.25
553	A86	25s car & lt grn	.25	.25
554	A86	30s bl grn & yel	.35	.20
555	A85	40s ultra & pale bl	.35	.20

556	A85	50s choc & gray	.35	.30
557	A85	60s lil rose & vio gray	.35	.30
558	A85	70s dk brn & rose	.35	.30
559	A85	75s choc & org	.35	.30
560	A85	1r purple & lt bl	.35	.30
561	A85	1.25r dk bl & rose car	.35	.40
562	A85	1.50r red org & lil	1.25	.40
563	A85	1.75r dk car & rose	.80	.40
564	A85	2r brn & yel grn	.55	.40
565	A85	2.50r dp bl & lt grn	.70	.40
566	A85	3r black & dk red	.70	.40
567	A85	4.50r dk grn & red	.70	.40
568	A85	5r gray grn & lem	.70	.40
569	A85	6r brn red & dp yel	.75	.40
570	A85	7.50r red brn & sal	.75	.25
571	A85	10r dk blue & blue	1.00	.55
572	A85	15r dl vio & pale vio	1.25	1.10
573	A85	20r dk grn & ol bis	2.40	1.25
		Nos. 550-573 (24)	15.30	9.45

4th Asian Games, Jakarta.

Malaria Eradication Emblem — A87

1962, Apr. 7   *Perf. 12½x12*
574	A87	40s dull bl & vio bl	.20	.20
575	A87	1.50r yel org & brn	.20	.20
576	A87	3r green & indigo	.20	.20
577	A87	6r lilac & blk	.25	.20
		Nos. 574-577 (4)	.85	.80

WHO drive to eradicate malaria. The 1.50r and 6r have Indonesian inscription on top.

Atom Diagram — A88

1962, Sept. 24 Photo.   *Perf. 12x12½*
578	A88	1.50r dk blue & yel	.20	.20
579	A88	4.50r brick red & yel	.25	.30
580	A88	6r green & yel	.40	.30
		Nos. 578-580 (3)	.85	.80

Development through science.

Pacific Travel Association Emblem — A89

Mechanized Plow — A90

1.50r, Prambanan Temple and Mount Merapi. 6r, Balinese Meru (Buildings), Pura Taman Ajun.

1963, Mar. 14   Unwmk.
581	A89	1r grn & indigo	.20	.20
582	A89	1.50r olive & indigo	.20	.20
583	A89	3r ocher & indigo	.40	.20
584	A89	6r dp org & indigo	.40	.20
		Nos. 581-584 (4)	1.20	.80

12th conf. of the Pacific Area Travel Assoc., Bandung.

1963, Mar. 21   *Perf. 12½x12, 12x12½*

1r, 3r, Hand holding rice stalks, vert.
585	A90	1r blue & yel	.20	.20
586	A90	1.50r brt grn & indigo	.20	.20
587	A90	3r rose car & org	.20	.20
588	A90	6r orange & blk	.25	.20
		Nos. 585-588 (4)	.85	.80

FAO "Freedom from Hunger" campaign. English inscription on 3r and 6r.

Long-Armed Lobster — A91

Fish: 1.50r, Little tuna. 3r, River roman. 6r, Chinese pompano.

1963, Apr. 6   *Perf. 12½x12*
589	A91	1r ver, blk & yel	.45	.20
590	A91	1.50r ultra, blk & yel	.45	.20
591	A91	3r Prus bl, bis & car	.95	.40
592	A91	6r ol grn, blk & ocher	.95	.65
		Nos. 589-592 (4)	2.80	1.45

Pen and Conference Emblem — A92

Designs: 1.50r, Pen, Emblem and map of Africa and Southeast Asia. 3r, Globe, pen and broken chain, vert. 6r, Globe, hand holding pen and broken chain, vert.

Perf. 12½x12, 12x12½
1963, Apr. 24 Photo.   Unwmk.
593	A92	1r lt bl & dp org	.25	.20
594	A92	1.50r pale vio & mar	.25	.20
595	A92	3r olive, bl & blk	.40	.20
596	A92	6r brick red & blk	.55	.25
		Nos. 593-596 (4)	1.45	.85

Asian-African Journalists' Conference.

"Indonesia's Flag from Sabang to Merauke" — A93

4.50r, Parachutist landing in New Guinea. 6r, Bird of paradise & map of New Guinea.

1963, May 1   *Perf. 12½x12*
597	A93	1.50r org brn, blk & red	.20	.20
598	A93	4.50r multicolored	.20	.20
599	A93	6r multicolored	.95	.65
		Nos. 597-599 (3)	1.35	1.05

Issued to mark the acquisition of Netherlands New Guinea (West Irian).

Centenary Emblem — A94

Design: 1.50r, 6r, Red Cross.

1963, May 8   *Perf. 12*
600	A94	1r brt grn & red	.25	.20
601	A94	1.50r lt bl & red	.25	.20
602	A94	3r gray & red	.25	.20
603	A94	6r yel bis & red	.25	.20
		Nos. 600-603 (4)	1.00	.80

Centenary of the International Red Cross.

Bank of Indonesia, Djalan A95   Daneswara, God of Prosperity A96

1963, July 5   Photo.   *Perf. 12*
604	A95	1.75r lt bl & pur	.20	.20
605	A96	4r citron & sl grn	.20	.20
606	A95	6r lt green & brn	.20	.20
607	A96	12r org & dk red brn	.25	.20
		Nos. 604-607 (4)	.85	.80

Issued for National Banking Day.

Standard Bearers — A97

Designs: 1.75r, "Pendet" dance. 4r, GANEFO building, Senajan, Jakarta. 6r, Archery. 10r, Badminton. 12r, Javelin. 25r, Sailing. 50r, Torch.

1963, Nov. 10   Unwmk.   *Perf. 12½*
608	A97	1.25r gray vio & dk brn	.20	.20
609	A97	1.75r org & ol grn	.20	.20
610	A97	4r emer & dk brn	.20	.20
611	A97	6r rose brn & blk	.25	.20
612	A97	10r lt ol grn & dk brn	.25	.20
613	A97	12r rose car & grnsh blk	.30	.20
614	A97	25r blue & dk blue	.40	.40
615	A97	50r red & black	.45	.45
		Nos. 608-615 (8)	2.25	2.05

1st Games of the New Emerging Forces, GANEFO, Jakarta, Nov. 10-22.

Pres. Sukarno — A98

1964   Photo.   *Perf. 12½x12*
616	A98	6r brown & dk bl	.20	.20
617	A98	12r bister & plum	.20	.20
618	A98	20r blue & org	.20	.20
619	A98	30r red org & bl	.20	.20
620	A98	40r green & brn	.20	.20
621	A98	50r red & dp grn	.20	.20
622	A98	75r vio & red org	.20	.20
623	A98	100r sil & red brn	.20	.20
624	A98	250r dk blue & sil	.25	.20
625	A98	500r red & gold	.30	.30
		Nos. 616-625 (10)	2.15	2.10

See Nos. B165-B179. For surcharges see Nos. 661, 663-667.

Trailer Truck — A99

Designs: 1r, Oxcart. 1.75r, Freighter. 2r, Lockheed Electra plane. 2.50r, Buginese sailboat, vert. 4r, Mailman with bicycle. 5r, Dakota plane. 7.50r, Teletype operator. 10r, Diesel train. 15r, Passenger ship. 25r, Convair Coronado Plane. 35r, Telephone switchboard operator.

1964   *Perf. 12x12½, 12½x12*
626	A99	1r dull claret	.20	.20
627	A99	1.25r red brown	.20	.20
628	A99	1.75r Prus blue	.20	.20
629	A99	2r red orange	.20	.20
630	A99	2.50r brt blue	.20	.20
631	A99	4r bluish grn	.20	.20
632	A99	5r olive bister	.20	.20
633	A99	7.50r brt green	.20	.20
634	A99	10r orange	.20	.20

635	A99	15r dark blue	.20	.20
636	A99	25r violet blue	.30	.20
637	A99	35r red brown	.30	.20

Nos. 626-637 (12) 2.60 2.40

For surcharges see Nos. 659-660, 662.

Ramses II — A100

Design: 6r, 18r, Kiosk of Trajan, Philae.

1964, Mar. 8 **Perf. 12½x12**

638	A100	4r ol bis & ol grn	.30	.20
639	A100	6r grnsh bl & ol grn	.30	.20
640	A100	12r rose & ol grn	.35	.20
641	A100	18r emer & ol grn	.45	.20

Nos. 638-641 (4) 1.40 .80

UNESCO world campaign to save historic monuments in Nubia.

Stamps of Netherlands Indies and Indonesia — A101

1964, Apr. 1 **Perf. 12½**

642	A101	10r gold, dk bl & red org	1.00	.40

Centenary of postage stamps in Indonesia.

Indonesian Pavilion — A102

1964, May 16 **Perf. 12½x12**

643	A102	25r sil, blk, red & dk bl	.45	.45
644	A102	50r gold, Prus bl, red & grn	1.25	.45

New York World's Fair, 1964-65.

Thomas Cup — A103

1964, Aug. 15 **Perf. 12½x13½**

645	A103	25r brt grn, gold & red	.25	.30
646	A103	50r ultra, gold & red	.30	.30
647	A103	75r purple, gold & red	.80	.95

Nos. 645-647 (3) 1.35 1.55

Thomas Cup Badminton World Championship, 1964.

Cruisers and Map of West Irian — A104

30r, Submarine. 40r, Torpedo boat.

Perf. 12½x12
1964, Oct. 5 **Photo.** **Unwmk.**

648	A104	20r yellow & brn	.30	.20
649	A104	30r rose & blk	.40	.20
650	A104	40r brt grn & ultra	.70	.95

Nos. 648-650 (3) 1.40 1.35

Issued to honor the Indonesian Navy.

Map of Africa and Asia and Mosque — A105

15r, 50r, Mosque and clasped hands.

1965, Mar. 6 **Photo.** **Perf. 12½**

651	A105	10r lt blue & pur	.30	.20
652	A105	15r org & red brn	.30	.20
653	A105	25r brt grn & brn	.45	.20
654	A105	50r brn red & blk	.45	.70

Nos. 651-654 (4) 1.50 1.30

Afro-Asian Islamic Conf., Bandung, Mar. 1965.

Hand Holding Scroll — A106

Design: 25r, 75r, Conference emblem (globe, cotton and grain).

1965, Apr. 18 **Unwmk.** **Perf. 12½**

655	A106	15r silver & dp car	.25	.20
656	A106	25r aqua, gold & red	.25	.20
657	A106	50r gold & dp ultra	.40	.20
658	A106	75r pale vio, gold & red	.55	.80

Nos. 655-658 (4) 1.45 1.40

10th anniv. of the First Afro-Asian Conf.

Nos. 618-623 and Nos. 634-636 Surcharged in Revalued Currency in Orange or Black

1965, Dec. **Perf. 12x12½, 12½x12**

659	A99	10s on 10r (B)	.25	.20
660	A99	15s on 15r	.25	.20
661	A98	20s on 20r	.20	.20
662	A99	25s on 25r (B)	.25	.20
663	A98	30s on 30r	.20	.20
664	A98	40s on 40r	.20	.20
665	A98	50s on 50r	.20	.20
666	A98	75s on 75r	.20	2.00
667	A98	100s on 100r	.30	.20

Nos. 659-667 (9) 2.05 3.60

The surcharge on Nos. 659-660 and No. 662 is in two lines and larger.

Pres. Sukarno — A107

1966-67 **Photo.** **Perf. 12½x12**

668	A107	1s sep & Prus grn	.20	.20
669	A107	3s sep & lt ol grn	.20	.20
670	A107	5s sep & dp car	.20	.20
671	A107	8s sep & Prus grn	.20	.20
672	A107	10s sep & vio bl	.20	.20
673	A107	15s sep & blk	.20	.20
674	A107	20s sep & dp green	.20	.20
675	A107	25s sep & dk red brn	.20	.20
676	A107	30s sep & dp bl	.20	.20
677	A107	40s sep & red brn	.20	.20
678	A107	50s sep & brt vio	.20	.20
679	A107	80s sep & org	.20	.20
680	A107	1r sep & emer	.20	.20
681	A107	1.25r sep & dk gray ol	.20	.20
682	A107	1.50r sep & emer	.20	.20
683	A107	2r sep & mag	.20	.20
684	A107	2.50r sep & gray	.20	.20
685	A107	5r sep & ocher	.25	.30
686	A107	10r sep & ol grn	.25	.20
686A	A107	12r grn & org ('67)	.30	.20
686B	A107	25r grn & brt pur ('67)	.25	.30

Nos. 668-686B (21) 4.45 4.40

The 12r is inscribed "1967" instead of "1966."

Dockyard Workers — A108   Gen. Ahmad Yani — A109

Designs: 40s, Lighthouse. 50s, Fishermen. 1r, Maritime emblem (wheel and eagle). 1.50r, Sailboat. 2r, Loading dock. 2.50r, Diver emerging from water. 3r, Liner at pier.

1966 **Photo.** **Perf. 12x12½**

687	A108	20s lt ultra & grn	.20	.20
688	A108	40s pink & dk bl	.20	.20
689	A108	50s green & brn	.20	.20
690	A108	1r salmon, bl & yel	.20	.20
691	A108	1.50r dull lil & dl grn	.20	.20
692	A108	2r gray & dp org	.20	.20
693	A108	2.50r rose lil & dk red	.25	.20
694	A108	3r brt green & blk	.25	.20
a.		Souvenir sheet	10.50	13.50

Nos. 687-694 (8) 1.70 1.60

Maritime Day. Issued: #687-690, Sept. 23; #691-694, Oct. 23.

No. 694a contains one imperf. stamp similar to No. 694.

1966, Nov. 10

Heroes of the Revolution: #696, Lt. Gen. R. Suprapto. #697, Lt. General Harjono. #698, Lt. Gen. S. Parman. #699, Maj. Gen. D. I. Pandjaitan. #700, Maj. Gen. Sutojo Siswomihardjo. #701, Brig. General Katamso. #702, Colonel Soegijono. #703, Capt. Pierre Andreas Tendean. #704, Adj. Insp. Karel Satsuit Tubun.

Deep Blue Frame

695	A109	5r org brn	.30	.30
696	A109	5r brt grn	.30	.30
697	A109	5r gray brn	.30	.30
698	A109	5r olive	.30	.30
699	A109	5r gray	.30	.30
700	A109	5r brt purple	.30	.30
701	A109	5r red lilac	.30	.30
702	A109	5r slate green	.30	.30
703	A109	5r dull rose lil	.30	.30
704	A109	5r orange	.30	.30

Nos. 695-704 (10) 3.00 3.00

Issued to honor military men killed during the Communist uprising, October, 1965.

Tjlempung, Java — A110

Musical Instruments and Maps: 1r, Sasando, Timor. 1.25r, Foi doa, Flores. 1.50r, Kultjapi, Sumatra. 2r, Arababu, Sangihe and Talaud Islands. 2.50r, Drums, West New

---

Guinea. 3r, Katjapi, Celebes. 4r, Hape, Borneo. 5r, Gangsa, Bali. 6r, Serunai, Sumatra. 8r, Rebab, Java. 10r, Trompet, West New Guinea. 12r, Totobuang, Moluccas. 15r, Drums, Nias. 20r, Kulintang, Celebes. 25r, Keledi, Borneo.

1967 **Unwmk.** **Photo.** **Perf. 12½x12**

705	A110	50s red & gray	.40	.40
706	A110	1r brn & dp org	.40	.40
707	A110	1.25r mar & ultra	.40	.40
708	A110	1.50r grn & lt vio	.40	.40
709	A110	2r vio bl & yel bis	.40	.40
710	A110	2.50r ol grn & dl red	.40	.40
711	A110	3r brt grn & dl cl	.40	.40
712	A110	4r vio bl & org	.65	.40
713	A110	5r dull red & bl	.65	.40
714	A110	6r blk & brt pink	.45	.45
715	A110	8r red brn & brt grn	.45	.45
716	A110	10r lilac & red	.45	.40
717	A110	12r ol grn & lil	.70	.65
718	A110	15r vio & lt ol grn	.65	.40
719	A110	20r gray & sepia	.65	.40
720	A110	25r black & green	.90	.40

Nos. 705-720 (16) 8.35 6.75

Issued: 1.25r, 10r, 12r, 15r, 20r, 25r, Mar. 1; others Feb. 1.

For surcharges see Nos. J118-J137.

Aviator and MiG-21 — A111

1967, Apr. 9 **Perf. 12½**

Aviation Day: 4r, Traffic control tower and 990A Convair jetliner. 5r, Hercules transport plane.

721	A111	2.50r multicolored	.50	.30
722	A111	4r multicolored	.50	.30
723	A111	5r multicolored	.80	.30

Nos. 721-723 (3) 1.80 .90

Thomas Cup with Victory Dates — A112

Design: 12r, Thomas Cup and globe.

1967, May 31 **Perf. 12x12½**

724	A112	5r multicolored	.25	.20
725	A112	12r multicolored	.50	.20

Issued to commemorate the Thomas Cup Badminton World Championship of 1967.

Balinese Girl in Front of Temple Gate — A113

1967, July 1 **Photo.** **Perf. 12½**

726	A113	12r multicolored	1.25	1.00
a.		Souv. sheet of 1, imperf.	4.50	5.50

Intl. Tourist Year, 1967. See No. 739.

Heroes of the Revolution Monument, Lubang Buaja — A114

Designs: 5r, Full view of monument, horiz. 7.50r, Shrine at monument.

Perf. 12x12½, 12½x12

1967, Aug. 17   Photo.
727 A114   2.50r pale grn & dk brn   .25   .20
728 A114   5r brt rose lil & pale
              brn   .50   .30
729 A114   7.50r pink & Prus grn   .50   .30
       Nos. 727-729 (3)   1.25   .80

Issued to publicize the "Heroes of the Revolution" Monument in Lubang Buaja.

Forest Fire, by Raden Saleh A115

50r, Fight to Death, by Raden Saleh.

1967, Oct. 30   Photo.   Perf. 12½
730 A115   25r org & gray grn   .30   .50
  a.   Souvenir sheet of 1   5.50 7.00
731 A115   50r vio brn & org   .60   .45

Indonesian painter Raden Saleh (1813-80).

Human Rights Flame — A116

1968, Jan. 1   Photo.   Perf. 12½
732 A116   5r grn, lt vio bl & red   .30   .20
733 A116   12r grn, ol bis & red   .35   .25

International Human Rights Year 1968.

Armed Forces College Emblem — A117

1968, Jan. 29   Litho.   Perf. 12½
734 A117   10r lt blue, yel & brn   .55   .30

Integration of the Armed Forces College.

WHO Emblem and "20" — A118

20th anniv. of WHO: 20r, WHO emblem.

1968, Apr. 7   Photo.   Perf. 12½
735 A118   2r dp yel, pale yel &
              dk brn   .30   .30
736 A118   20r emerald & blk   .40   .30

Trains of 1867 and 1967 and Railroad's Emblem — A119

1968, May 15   Photo.   Perf. 12½x12
737 A119   20r multicolored   .70   .30
738 A119   30r multicolored 1.00 1.00

Indonesian railroad centenary (in 1967).

Tourist Type of 1967

Tourist Publicity: 30r, Butterfly dancer from West Java.

1968, July 1   Perf. 12½
739 A113   30r gray & multi   1.40 1.60
  a.   Souv. sheet of 1 + label 5.50 7.50

Bosscha Observatory and Andromeda Nebula — A120

30r, Observatory, globe and sky, vert.

1968, Sept. 20   Photo.   Perf. 12½x12
740 A120   15r ultra & yellow   .50   .30
741 A120   30r violet & orange .75   .30

Bosscha Observatory, 40th anniversary.

Weight Lifting — A121

Designs: 7.50r+7.50r, Sailing, horiz. 12r, Basketball. 30r, Dove, Olympic flame and emblem, horiz.

1968, Oct. 12   Perf. 12½
742 A121   5r ocher, blk & grn   .25   .20
743 A121   Pair   .55   .55
  a.   7.50r Left half   .25   .20
  b.   7.50r Right half   .25   .20
  c.   Souvenir sheet   5.50 8.00
744 A121   12r blue & multi   .30   .40
745 A121   30r blue grn & multi .80   .25
       Nos. 742-745 (4)   1.90 1.40

19th Olympic Games, Mexico City, Oct. 12-27. No. 743 is perforated vertically in the center, dividing it into two separate stamps, each inscribed "Republic Indonesia" and "7.50r." There is no gutter along the center perforation; and the design is continous over the two stamps.
No. 743c contains one No. 743 with track design surrounding the stamps.

Eugenia Aquea Burm. f. — A122

Fruits: 15r, Papaya. 30r, Durian, vert.

Perf. 12½x12, 12x12½
1968, Dec. 20   Photo.
746 A122   7.50r multicolored   .40   .35
747 A122   15r multicolored   .55   .45
  a.   Souvenir sheet of 1   4.25 6.00

748 A122   30r multicolored   .85   .85
  a.   Souvenir sheet of 1   4.25 6.00
       Nos. 746-748 (3)   1.80 1.65

Issued for the 11th Social Day.

Globe, ILO and UN Emblems A123

Designs: 7.50r, 25r, ILO and UN emblems.

1969, Feb. 1   Photo.   Perf. 12½
749 A123   5r yel grn & scar   .20   .20
750 A123   7.50r org & dk grn   .20   .20
751 A123   15r lilac & org   .25   .20
752 A123   25r bl grn & dull red   .40   .25
       Nos. 749-752 (4)   1.05   .85

50th anniv. of the ILO.

R. Dewi Sartika   Red Crosses
A124   A125

#754, Tjoet Nja Din. #755, Tjoet Nja Meuthia. #756, General Gatot Subroto. #757, Sutan Sjahrir. #758, Dr. F. L. Tobing. #753-755 show portraits of women.

1969, Mar. 1   Photo.   Perf. 12½x12
753 A124   15r green & pur   .30   .20
754 A124   15r red lilac & grn   .30   .20
755 A124   15r dk blue & ver   .30   .20
756 A124   15r lilac & dk blue   .30   .20
757 A124   15r lemon & red   .30   .20
758 A124   15r pale brn & blue   .30   .20
       Nos. 753-758 (6)   1.80 1.20

Heroes of Indonesian independence.

1969, May 5   Photo.   Perf. 12

20r, Red Cross surrounded by arms.

759 A125   15r green & dp red   .45   .20
760 A125   20r org yel & red   .50   .40

50th anniversary of the League of Red Cross Societies.

"Family Planning Leads to National Development and Prosperity" — A126

Design: 10r, Family, birds and factories.

1969, June 2   Photo.   Perf. 12½
761 A126   10r blue grn & org   .30   .20
762 A126   20r gray & magenta   .50   .30

Planned Parenthood Conference of Southeast Asia and Oceania, Bandung, June 1-7.

Map of Bali and Mask A127

Designs: 15r, Map of Bali and woman carrying basket with offerings on head. 30r, Map of Bali and cremation ceremony.

1969, July 1   Litho.   Perf. 12½x12
763 A127   12r gray & multi   .55   .55
764 A127   15r lilac & multi   1.00 1.00
765 A127   30r multicolored   1.00   .65
  a.   Souvenir sheet of 1   4.75 6.00
       Nos. 763-765 (3)   2.55 2.20

Issued for tourist publicity.

Agriculture A128

Designs: 5r, Religious coexistence (roofs of mosques and churches). 10r, Social welfare (house and family). 12r, Import-export (cargo and ship). 15r, Clothing industry (cloth and spindles). 20r, Education (school children). 25r, Research (laboratory). 30r, Health care (people and syringe). 40r, Fishing (fish and net). 50r, Statistics (charts).

1969   Photo.   Perf. 12x12½
766 A128   5r yel grn & bl   .25   .20
767 A128   7.50r rose brn & yel .25   .20
768 A128   10r slate & red   .50   .20
769 A128   12r blue & dp org   1.40   .65
770 A128   15r slate grn & org .50   .20
771 A128   20r purple & yel   .50   .20
772 A128   25r orange & blk   .50   .20
773 A128   30r car rose & gray .60   .20
774 A128   40r green & org   .80   .20
775 A128   50r sepia & org   .90   .20
       Nos. 766-775 (10)   6.00 2.45

Five-year Development Plan.
See No. 968a.

Radar, Djatiluhur Station — A129

30r, Communications satellite and earth.

1969, Sept. 29   Perf. 12½
776 A129   15r multicolored   .45   .20
777 A129   30r multicolored   .70   .55

Vickers Vimy and Borobudur Temple A130

100r, Vickers Vimy and map of Indonesia.

1969, Nov. 1   Perf. 13½x12½
778 A130   75r dp org & dull pur   .60   .60
779 A130   100r yellow & green   .80   .60

50th anniv. of the 1st flight from England to Australia (via Java).

EXPO '70, Indonesian Pavilion — A131

Designs: 15r, Garuda, symbol of Indonesian EXPO '70 committee. 30r, like 5r.

1970, Feb. 15   Photo.   Perf. 12x12½
780 A131   5r brown, yel & grn   .50   .30
781 A131   15r dk bl, yel grn & red .80   .40
782 A131   30r red, yel & dk bl   1.40   .65
       Nos. 780-782 (3)   2.70 1.35

Issued to publicize EXPO '70 International Exposition, Osaka, Japan, Mar. 15-Sept. 13.

Upraised Hands, Bars and Scales of Justice — A132

1970, Mar. 15 Photo. Perf. 12½

| 783 | A132 | 10r red orange & pur | .65 | .40 |
| 784 | A132 | 15r brt green & pur | .80 | .40 |

Rule of law and justice in Indonesia.

UPU Monument, Bern — A133

Dancers — A134

Design: 30r, UPU Headquarters, Bern.

1970, May 20 Photo. Perf. 12x12½

| 785 | A133 | 15r emer & copper red | .75 | .40 |
| 786 | A133 | 30r ocher & blue | 1.25 | .95 |

Inauguration of the new UPU Headquarters in Bern, Switzerland.

1970, July 1 Photo. Perf. 12

787	A134	20r Timor dancers	1.00	.60
788	A134	45r Bali dancers	2.25	.95
a.		Souvenir sheet of 1	7.75	10.00

Tourist publicity. No. 788a sold for 60r.

Asian Productivity Year — A135

Independence Proclamation Monument — A136

1970, Aug. 1 Photo. Perf. 12

| 789 | A135 | 5r emerald, org & red | .45 | .25 |
| 790 | A135 | 30r violet, org & red | 1.25 | .75 |

1970, Aug. 17

| 791 | A136 | 40r lt ultra & magenta | 13.50 | 6.00 |

The 25th anniversary of independence.

Post and Telecommunications Emblems — A137

Postal Worker and Telephone Dial — A138

Perf. 12x12½, 12½x12

1970, Sept. 27 Photo.

| 792 | A137 | 10r green, ocher & yel | 4.75 | 1.00 |
| 793 | A138 | 25r pink, blk & yel | 8.00 | .80 |

25th anniversary of the postal service.

UN Emblem A139

Education Year and UNESCO Emblems A140

1970, Oct. 10 Photo. Perf. 12½

| 794 | A139 | 40r pur, red & yel grn | 13.50 | 6.00 |

25th anniversary of the United Nations.

1970, Nov. 16 Photo. Perf. 12½

Design: 50r, similar to 25r, but without oval background.

| 795 | A140 | 25r yel, dk red & brn | 10.50 | 3.75 |
| 796 | A140 | 50r lt blue, blk & red | 15.00 | 6.00 |

International Education Year.

Batik Worker — A141

50r, Woman with bamboo musical instrument (angklung). 75r, Menangkabau house & family in traditional costumes.

1971, May 26 Litho. Perf. 12½

797	A141	20r multi	3.00	1.50
798	A141	50r multi, vert.	5.00	4.00
a.		Souvenir sheet of 1	50.00	65.00
799	A141	75r multi	9.50	6.00
		Nos. 797-799 (3)	17.50	11.50

"Visit Asian lands." No. 798a sold for 70r.

Fatahillah Park, Djakarta — A142

30f, City Hall. 65r, Lenong Theater performance. 80r, Ismail Marzuki Cultural Center.

1971, June 19 Photo. Perf. 12½

800	A142	15r yel grn, brn & bl	2.75	1.25
801	A142	65r org brn, dk brn & lt grn	5.50	4.75
802	A142	80r olive, bl & mag	9.50	4.00
		Nos. 800-802 (3)	17.75	10.00

Souvenir Sheet

| 803 | A142 | 30r bl, yel & lil rose | 25.00 | 27.50 |

444th anniv. of Djakarta. #803 sold for 60r.

Rama and Sita — A143

Design: 100r, Rama with bow.

1971, Aug. 31

| 804 | A143 | 30r yellow, grn & blk | 2.40 | .95 |
| 805 | A143 | 100r blue, red & blk | 4.50 | 2.00 |

International Ramayana Festival.

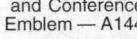

Carrier Pigeon and Conference Emblem — A144

1971, Sept. 20

| 806 | A144 | 50r ocher & dp brown | 1.90 | 1.10 |

5th Asian Regional Postal Conference.

Globes and UPU Monument, Berne — A145

1971, Oct. 4 Photo. Perf. 13½x13

| 807 | A145 | 40r blue & dull vio | 2.00 | 1.10 |

Universal Postal Union Day.

Boy Writing, UNICEF Emblem — A146

40r, Boy with sheaf of rice, emblem.

1971, Dec. 11 Perf. 12½

| 808 | A146 | 20r orange & multi | 2.50 | .65 |
| 809 | A146 | 40r blue & multi | 4.00 | 1.25 |

25th anniv. UNICEF.

Lined Tang A147

Fish: 30r, Moorish goddess. 40r, Imperial angelfish.

1971, Dec. 27 Litho. Perf. 12½

810	A147	15r lilac & multi	4.75	1.40
811	A147	30r dull grn & multi	11.00	3.50
812	A147	40r blue & multi	13.00	5.25
		Nos. 810-812 (3)	28.75	10.15

See #834-836, 859-861, 926-928, 959-961.

UN Emblem A148

Radio Tower A149

Design: 100r, Road and dam.

1972, Mar. 28 Photo. Perf. 12½

813	A148	40r lt grnsh bl & bl	3.00	1.10
814	A149	75r dk car, yel & grnsh bl	3.50	1.10
815	A148	100r green, yel & blk	6.00	2.40
		Nos. 813-815 (3)	12.50	4.60

UN Economic Commission for Asia and the Far East (ECAFE), 25th anniv.

"Your Heart is your Health" — A150

Woman Weaver, Factories — A151

1972, Apr. 7

| 816 | A150 | 50r multicolored | 2.00 | .85 |

World Health Day.

1972, Apr. 22

| 817 | A151 | 35r orange, yel & pur | 2.00 | .85 |

Textile Technology Institute, 50th anniv.

Book Readers A152

1972, May 15 Perf. 13½x12½

| 818 | A152 | 75r blue & multi | 3.00 | 1.40 |

International Book Year 1972.

Weather Satellite — A153

1972, July 20 Photo. Perf. 12½

819	A153	35r shown	2.50	.70
820	A153	50r Astronaut on moon	3.50	3.50
821	A153	60r Indonesian rocket Kartika 1	6.00	1.25
		Nos. 819-821 (3)	12.00	5.45

Space achievements.

Hotel Indonesia — A154

1972, Aug. 5

| 822 | A154 | 50r grn, lt bl & car | 2.60 | 1.25 |

Hotel Indonesia, 10th anniversary.

Silat (Self Defense) A155

Family, Houses of Worship A156

Olympic Emblems and: 35r, Running. 50r, Diving. 75r, Badminton. 100r, Olympic Stadium.

1972, Aug. 26 Photo.

823	A155	20r lt blue & multi	1.50	.25
824	A155	35r multicolored	1.50	.40
825	A155	50r yel grn & multi	2.75	.70
826	A155	75r multicolored	3.00	1.75
827	A155	100r multicolored	4.75	2.75
		Nos. 823-827 (5)	13.50	5.85

20th Olympic Games, Munich, 8/26-9/11.

1972, Sept. 27   *Perf. 12½x13½*

Family planning: 75r, Healthy family. 80r, Working family (national prosperity).

828	A156	30r lemon & multi	1.75	.70
829	A156	75r lilac & multi	3.25	2.50
830	A156	80r multicolored	5.50	3.25
		Nos. 828-830 (3)	10.50	6.45

Moluccas Dancer
A157

Thomas Cup, Shuttlecock
A158

60r, Man, woman and Toradja house, Celebes. 100fr, West Irian house, horiz.

Perf. 12½x13½, 13½x12½

1972, Oct. 28   Photo.

831	A157	30r olive pink & brn	1.90	.70
832	A157	60r multicolored	4.25	3.00
833	A157	100r lt bl, brn & dl yel	6.25	3.00
		Nos. 831-833 (3)	12.40	6.70

Fish Type of 1971

Fish: 30r, Butterflyfish. 50r, Regal angelfish. 100r, Spotted triggerfish.

1972, Dec. 4   Litho.   *Perf. 12½*

834	A147	30r blue & multi	6.00	2.00
835	A147	50r blue & multi	10.50	2.75
836	A147	100r blue & multi	13.50	5.00
		Nos. 834-836 (3)	30.00	9.75

1973, Jan. 2   Litho.   *Perf. 12½*

Thomas Cup, Shuttlecock and: 75r, National monument & Istora Sports Hall. 80r, Indonesian flag & badminton player.

837	A158	30r emerald & brt bl	1.00	.30
838	A158	75r dull grn & dk car	2.00	.55
839	A158	80r gold & red	2.75	1.10
		Nos. 837-839 (3)	5.75	1.95

Thomas Cup Badminton World Championship 1973.

WMO Emblem, Anemometer, Wayang Figure — A159

Perf. 13½x12½

1973, Feb. 15   Litho.

840	A159	80r blue, grn & claret	2.00	.85

Cent. of intl. meteorological cooperation.

"Health Begins at Home" — A160

1973, Apr. 7   Photo.   *Perf. 12½*

841	A160	80r dk grn, org & ultra	2.00	.85

25th anniv. of WHO.

Ceremonial Mask, Java — A161

842	A161	30r shown	4.50	1.00
843	A161	60r Mask, Kalimantan	8.00	4.00
844	A161	100r Mask, Bali	12.50	2.00
		Nos. 842-844 (3)	25.00	7.00

1973, June 1   Photo.   *Perf. 12½*

Tourist publicity.

Hand Putting Coin into Bank — A162

1973, July 2   Photo.   *Perf. 12½*

30r, Symbolic coin bank and hand, horiz.

845	A162	25r yellow, lt brn & blk	1.10	.55
846	A162	30r green, yel & gold	1.60	.55

National savings movement.

Chess — A163

INTERPOL Emblem and Policemen — A164

8th National Sports Week: 60r, Karate. 75r, Hurdling, horiz.

1973, Aug. 4   Photo.   *Perf. 12½*

847	A163	30r red, yellow & blk	2.00	1.25
848	A163	60r black, ocher & lt grn	2.50	1.25
849	A163	75r black, lt bl & rose	4.00	1.00
		Nos. 847-849 (3)	8.50	3.50

1973, Sept. 3

Design: 50r, INTERPOL emblem and guard statue from Sewu Prambanan Temple, vert.

850	A164	30r yellow, grn & blk	1.40	.40
851	A164	50r yellow, brn & blk	2.00	.70

50th anniv. of Intl. Police Organization.

Batik Worker and Parang Rusak Pattern A165

Batik designs: 80r, Man and Pagi Sore pattern. 100r, Man and Merak Ngigel pattern.

1973, Oct. 9   Photo.   *Perf. 12½*

852	A165	60r multicolored	2.75	2.00
853	A165	80r multicolored	4.75	2.25
854	A165	100r multicolored	8.00	4.00
		Nos. 852-854 (3)	15.50	8.25

Farmer, Grain, UN and FAO Emblems — A166

1973, Oct. 24   Photo.   *Perf. 12½*

855	A166	30r lilac & multi	2.50	.70

World Food Program, 10th anniversary.

Houses of Worship — A167

Family planning: 30r, Classroom. 60r, Family and home.

1973, Nov. 10

856	A167	20r dk bl, lt bl & ver	.90	.45
857	A167	30r ocher, blk & yel	1.40	.70
858	A167	60r lt grn, yel & blk	3.75	.60
		Nos. 856-858 (3)	6.05	1.75

Fish Type of 1971

Fish: 40r, Acanthurus leucosternon. 65r, Chaetodon trifasciatus. 100r, Pomacanthus annularis.

1973, Dec. 10   Litho.   *Perf. 12½*

859	A147	40r multicolored	3.00	1.10
860	A147	65r multicolored	7.75	2.00
861	A147	100r multicolored	11.00	3.25
		Nos. 859-861 (3)	21.75	6.35

Adm. Sudarso and Battle of Arafuru — A168

1974, Jan. 15

862	A168	40r brt blue & multi	2.50	.85

12th Navy Day.

Bengkulu Costume A169

Designs: Regional Costumes.

1974, Mar. 28   Litho.   *Perf. 12½*

863	A169	5r shown	14.00	1.10
864	A169	7.50r Kalimantan, Timor	8.00	1.10
865	A169	10r Kalimantan, Tengah	4.75	.80
866	A169	15r Jambi	1.25	.80
867	A169	20r Sulawesi, Tenggara	1.25	.80
868	A169	25r Nusatenggara, Timor	1.40	.80
869	A169	27.50r Maluku	1.40	2.50
870	A169	30r Lampung	1.40	1.50
871	A169	35r Sumatra, Barat	1.40	.80
872	A169	40r Aceh	1.40	.80
873	A169	45r Nusatenggara, Barat	3.50	.80
874	A169	50r Riouw	2.75	2.00
875	A169	55r Kalimantan, Barat	2.75	.80
876	A169	60r Sulawesi, Utara	2.75	.80
877	A169	65r Sulawesi, Tengah	2.75	.80
878	A169	70r Sumatra, Selatan	2.75	.80
879	A169	75r Java, Barat	2.75	.80
880	A169	80r Sumatra, Utara	2.75	.80
881	A169	90r Yogyakarta	2.75	5.00
882	A169	95r Kalimantan, Selatan	2.75	.80
883	A169	100r Java, Timor	2.75	1.60
884	A169	120r Irian, Java	7.00	1.10
885	A169	130r Java, Tengah	7.00	.80
886	A169	135r Sulawesi, Selatan	6.25	.80
887	A169	150r Bali	6.25	.80
888	A169	160r Djakarta	6.25	1.60
		Nos. 863-888 (26)	100.00	31.10

Baladewa A170

Designs (Figures from Shadow Plays): 80r, Kresna. 100r, Bima.

1974, June 1   Photo.   *Perf. 12½*

889	A170	40r lt violet & multi	3.25	1.40
890	A170	80r salmon & multi	5.75	2.75
891	A170	100r rose	7.00	2.75
		Nos. 889-891 (3)	16.00	6.90

Pres. Suharto A171

Family and WPY Emblem A172

1974-76   Photo.   *Perf. 12½*
Portrait in Dark Brown

901	A171	40r lt green & blk	.80	.20
903	A171	50r ultra & blk	1.90	.20
906	A171	65r brt pink & blk	1.10	.65
908	A171	75r yellow & blk	1.90	.20
912	A171	100r buff & blk	1.90	.20
913	A171	150r citron & blk	2.75	.30
914	A171	200r green & blue	5.25	.40
915	A171	300r brn org & car	3.00	.55
916	A171	400r green & yellow	6.00	.75
917	A171	500r lilac & car	8.00	1.00
		Nos. 901-917 (10)	32.60	4.45

#914-917 have wavy lines in background. Issued: #901-913, 8/17/74; #914-917, 8/17/76.

1974, Aug. 19

918	A172	65r ultra, gray & ocher	1.60	.55

World Population Year 1974.

"Welfare" A173

"Development" A174

"Religion" A175

1974, Sept. 9

919	A173	25r green & multi	.80	.45
920	A174	40r yellow grn & multi	1.60	.45
921	A175	65r dk vio brn & multi	2.40	.45
		Nos. 919-921 (3)	4.80	1.35

Family planning.

Mailmen with Bicycles, UPU Emblem — A176

UPU cent.: 40r, Horse-drawn mail cart. 65r, Mailman on horseback. 100r, Sailing ship, 18th century.

1974, Oct. 9
922	A176	20r dk green & multi	2.50	.45
923	A176	40r dull blue & multi	2.50	.70
924	A176	65r black brn & yel	2.50	.70
925	A176	100r maroon & multi	2.50	1.90
		Nos. 922-925 (4)	10.00	3.75

Fish Type of 1971

Fish: 40fr, Zebrasoma veliferum. 80r, Euxiphipops navarchus. 100r, Synchiropus splendidus.

1974, Oct. 30   Photo.   Perf. 12½
926	A147	40r blue & multi	4.00	.45
927	A147	80r blue & multi	6.00	1.90
928	A147	100r blue & multi	6.00	2.40
		Nos. 926-928 (3)	16.00	4.75

Drill Team Searching for Oil — A177

Designs (Pertamina Emblem and): 75r, Oil refinery. 95r, Pertamina telecommunications and computer center. 100r, Gasoline truck and station. 120r, Plane over storage tanks. 130r, Pipes and tanker. 150r, Petro-chemical storage tanks. 200r, Off-shore drilling platform. 95r, 100r, 120r, 130r, vertical.

1974, Dec. 10   Perf. 13½
929	A177	40r black & multi	.55	.45
930	A177	75r black & multi	.55	.45
931	A177	95r black & multi	.70	.45
932	A177	100r black & multi	.70	.45
933	A177	120r black & multi	.85	.45
934	A177	130r black & multi	.90	.45
935	A177	150r black & multi	1.10	.45
936	A177	200r black & multi	1.50	.45
		Nos. 929-936 (8)	6.85	3.60

Pertamina State Oil Enterprise, 17th anniv.

Spittoon, Sumatra A178

Artistic Metalware: 75r, Condiment dish, Sumatra. 100r, Condiment dish, Kalimantan.

1975, Feb. 24   Photo.   Perf. 12½
937	A178	50r red & black	1.90	1.40
938	A178	75r green & black	2.25	1.40
939	A178	100r brt blue & multi	3.75	1.40
		Nos. 937-939 (3)	7.90	4.20

Blood Donors' Emblem A179   Globe, Standard Meter and Kilogram A180

1975, Apr. 7
940	A179	40r yellow, red & grn	1.40	.70

"Give blood, save lives."

1975, May 20
941	A180	65r blue, red & yel	2.50	.70

Cent. of Intl. Meter Convention, Paris, 1875.

Farmer, Teacher, Mother, Policewoman and Nurse — A181

IWY Emblem — A182

1975, June 26   Photo.   Perf. 12½
942	A181	40r multicolored	1.50	.70
943	A182	100r multicolored	2.25	.70

International Women's Year 1975.

Dendrobium Pakarena A183

Stupas and Damaged Temple — A184

Orchids: 70r, Aeridachnis bogor. 85r, Vanda genta.

1975, July 21
944	A183	40r multicolored	4.00	1.25
945	A183	70r multicolored	6.00	2.40
946	A183	85r multicolored	10.00	3.50
		Nos. 944-946 (3)	20.00	7.15

See Nos. 1010-1012, 1036-1038.

1975, Aug. 10   Perf. 12½
Designs (UNESCO Emblem and): 40r, Buddha statues, stupas and damaged wall. 65r, Stupas and damaged wall, horiz. 100r, Buddha statue and stupas, horiz.

947	A184	25r yellow, brn & org	2.60	.80
948	A184	40r black, grn & yel	4.25	1.00
949	A184	65r lemon, cl & grn	8.50	4.25

950	A184	100r bister, brn & sl bl	12.50	4.25
		Nos. 947-950 (4)	27.85	10.30

UNESCO campaign to save Borobudur Temple, Java.

Banjarmasin Battle — A185

Battle Scenes: 40r, Batua, 9/8/46. 75r, Margarana, 11/20/46. 100r, Palembang, 1/1/47.

1975, Aug. 17
951	A185	25r yellow & blk	.65	.45
952	A185	40r org ver & red	.95	.45
953	A185	75r vermilion & blk	1.75	1.25
954	A185	100r orange & blk	2.75	.90
		Nos. 951-954 (4)	6.10	3.05

Indonesian independence, 30th anniversary.

"Education" A186   Heroes' Monument, Surabaya A187

Family plannings: 25r, "Religion." 40r, "Prosperity."

1975, Oct. 20   Photo.   Perf. 12½
955	A186	20r blue, salmon & blk	1.00	.25
956	A186	25r emerald, sal & blk	1.25	.40
957	A186	40r dp org, blue & blk	1.50	.55
		Nos. 955-957 (3)	3.75	1.20

1975, Nov. 10
958	A187	100r maroon & green	3.00	.60

War of independence, 30th anniversary.

Fish Type of 1971

Fish: 40r, Coris angulata. 75r, Chaetodon ephhippium. 150r, Platax pinnatus, vert.

1975, Dec. 15   Litho.   Perf. 12½
959	A147	40r multicolored	2.25	.45
960	A147	75r multicolored	4.25	1.40
961	A147	150r multicolored	8.50	2.75
		Nos. 959-961 (3)	15.00	4.60

Thomas Cup — A188

40r, Uber Cup. 100r, Thomas & Uber Cups.

1976, Jan. 31   Photo.   Perf. 12½
962	A188	20r blue & multi	.75	.35
963	A188	40r multicolored	1.00	.60
964	A188	100r green & multi	2.50	.60
		Nos. 962-964 (3)	4.25	1.55

Indonesia, Badminton World Champions.

Refugees on Truck and New Village — A189

Designs: 50r, Neglected and restored village streets. 100r, Derelict and rebuilt houses.

1976, Feb. 28   Photo.   Perf. 12½
965	A189	30r yellow & multi	.80	.25
966	A189	50r blue & multi	1.25	.45
967	A189	100r ocher & multi	2.25	.50
		Nos. 965-967 (3)	4.30	1.20

World Human Settlements Day.

Telephones, 1876 and 1976 — A190

1976, Mar. 10   Photo.   Perf. 12½
968	A190	100r yel, org & brn	1.60	.55
a.		Bklt. pane of 8, 4 #968, 4 #775 + 2 labels ('78)	7.75	

Centenary of first telephone call by Alexander Graham Bell, Mar. 10, 1876. Stamps from #968a have straight edges.

Eye and WHO Emblem — A191

Design: 40r, Blind man, eye and World Health Organization emblem.

1976, Apr. 7   Photo.   Perf. 12½
969	A191	20r yel, lt grn & blk	.75	.35
970	A191	40r yel, blue & blk	.95	.50

Foresight prevents blindness.

Montreal Stadium — A192

1976, May 17
971	A192	100r ultra	1.60	.65

21st Olympic Games, Montreal, Canada, July 17-Aug. 1.

Lake Tondano, Celebes — A193

Tourist publicity: 40r, Lake Kelimutu, Flores. 75r, Lake Maninjau, Sumatra.

1976, June 1
972	A193	35r lt green & blk	.90	.45
973	A193	40r gray, rose & lt grn	1.10	.45
974	A193	75r blue & sl grn	2.00	.55
a.		Bklt. pane of 8 (7 #974, #998, 2 labels) ('78)	7.75	
		Nos. 972-974 (3)	4.00	1.45

Stamps from #974a have straight edges.

Radar Station — A194

Designs: 50r, Master control radar station. 100r, Apalata satellite.

1976, July 8   **Photo.**   **Perf. 12½**
975 A194   20r multicolored   .65   .40
976 A194   50r green & blk   1.25   .40
977 A194   100r multicolored   2.25   .75
   a.   Bklt. pane of 9 (4 #977, 5
     #987, label) ('78)   13.50
     Nos. 975-977 (3)   4.15   1.55

Inauguration of domestic satellite system. Stamps from #977a have straight edges.

Arachnis Flos-aeris — A195

Orchids: 40r, Vanda putri serang. 100r, Coelogyne pandurata.

1976, Sept. 7
978 A195   25r multicolored   1.60   1.10
   a.   Souvenir sheet of 1   57.50   72.50
979 A195   40r multicolored   2.00   1.10
980 A195   100r multicolored   6.00   2.40
     Nos. 978-980 (3)   9.60   4.60

Tree and Mountain — A196

1976, Oct. 4
981 A196   20r green, blue & brn   1.10   .40
16th National Reforestation Week.

Dagger and Sheath from Timor — A197

Historic Daggers and Sheaths: 40r, from Borneo. 100r, from Aceh.

1976, Nov. 1   **Perf. 12½**
982 A197   25r multicolored   1.25   .45
983 A197   40r multicolored   2.00   .85
   a.   Souvenir sheet of 1, imperf   22.50   22.50
984 A197   100r green & multi   4.00   2.25
     Nos. 982-984 (3)   7.25   3.55

No. 983a exists perf. Value $15.

Open Book   Children
A198   Reading
         A199

1976, Dec. 8   **Photo.**   **Perf. 12½**
985 A198   20r multicolored   .80   .30
986 A199   40r multicolored   1.50   .45

Better books for children.

UNICEF   Ballot Box
Emblem   A201
A200

1976, Dec. 11
987 A200   40r multicolored   1.75   .50
UNICEF, 30th anniv.
See No. 977a.

1977, Jan. 5   **Photo.**   **Perf. 12½**
1977 elections: 75r, Ballot box, grain and factory. 100r, Coat of arms.
988 A201   40r multicolored   2.25   .30
989 A201   75r multicolored   2.50   .45
990 A201   100r multicolored   4.00   1.40
     Nos. 988-990 (3)   8.75   2.15

Camp and Flags Scout Emblems, A202

Designs: 30r, Tent, emblems and trees. 40r, Boy and Girl Scout flags and emblems.

1977, Feb. 28
991 A202   25r multicolored   1.60   .55
992 A202   30r multicolored   1.75   .55
993 A202   40r multicolored   2.00   1.25
     Nos. 991-993 (3)   5.35   2.35

11th National Scout Jamboree.

Letter with   Anniversary
"AOPU" — A203   Emblem,
         Djakarta
         Arms — A204

Design: 100r, Stylized bird and letter.

1977, Apr. 1   **Photo.**   **Perf. 12½**
994 A203   65r multicolored   1.00   .40
995 A203   100r multicolored   1.50   .55

Asian-Oceanic Postal Union, 15th convention.

1977, May 23   **Photo.**   **Perf. 12½**
Designs: Anniversary emblem and arms of Djakarta in different arrangements.
996 A204   20r orange & blue   .75   .45
997 A204   40r emerald & blue   1.00   .50
998 A204   100r slate & blue   2.00   .85
   a.   Souvenir sheet of 1   10.00   10.00
     Nos. 996-998 (3)   3.75   1.80

450th anniversary of Djakarta. No. 998a also issued imperf. Value $27.50.

Rose — A205   Various Sports
         Emblems — A206

1977, May 26   **Photo.**   **Perf. 12½**
999   A205   100r shown   2.00   .60
   a.   Souvenir sheet   12.00   12.00

1000   A205   100r Envelope   2.00   .60
   a.   Souvenir sheet of 4   12.00   12.00
   b.   Pair, Nos. 999-1000   4.00   3.00

Amphilex 77 Phil. Exhib., Amsterdam, May 26-June 5. No. 999a contains one stamp similar to No. 999 with blue background. No. 1000a contains 2 each of Nos. 999-1000. Nos. 999a, 1000a exist imperf. Values: No. 999a, $27.50; No. 1000a, $32.50. See No. 1013a.

1977, June 22
9th Natl. Sports Week: 50r, 100r, Different sports emblems.
1001 A206   40r silver & multi   2.25   1.75
1002 A206   50r silver & multi   3.25   1.75
1003 A206   100r gold & multi   8.00   4.00
     Nos. 1001-1003 (3)   13.50   7.50

Contest Trophy   Emblem
A207   A208

1977, July 20
1004 A207   40r green & multi   2.00   .55
1005 A208   100r yellow & multi   3.75   1.00

10th Natl. Koran Reading Contest, 7/20-27.

Map of ASEAN Countries, Satellite — A209

35r, Map of ASEAN countries. 50r, Flags of founding members: Indonesia, Malaysia, Philippines, Singapore & Thailand; ship, plane & train.

1977, Aug. 8
1006 A209   25r multicolored   1.50   .20
1007 A209   35r multicolored   1.90   .70
1008 A209   50r multicolored   2.50   .85
     Nos. 1006-1008 (3)   5.90   1.75

Association of South East Asian Nations (ASEAN), 10th anniversary.

Uniform, Jakarta Regiment A210

1977, Aug. 19
1009 A210   25r green, gold & brn   .75   .30

Indonesia-Pakistan Economic and Cultural Organization, 1968-1977.

Orchid Type of 1975

Orchids: 25r, Taeniophyllum. 40r, Phalaenopsis violacea. 100r, Dendrobium spectabile.

1977, Oct. 28   **Photo.**   **Perf. 12½**
1010 A183   25r orange & multi   1.75   .85
1011 A183   40r blue & multi   2.75   1.75
1012 A183   100r yel grn & multi   5.75   2.75
   a.   Souvenir sheet of 1, imperf   12.00   12.00
     Nos. 1010-1012 (3)   10.25   5.35

No. 1012a contains one stamp similar to No. 1012 with blue background. No. 1012a exists perf. Value $14.

Child and Mosquito A211

1977, Nov. 7   **Perf. 12½**
1013 A211   40r brt grn, red & blk   .75   .35
   a.   Bklt. pane of 9+label (4 #999,
     5 #1013) ('78)   7.75

Natl. health campaign to eradicate malaria. Stamps from #1013a have straight edges. Issue date: No. 1013a, Sept. 27, 1978.

Proboscis Monkey — A212

Designs: 40r, Indian elephant. 100r, Tiger.

1977, Dec. 22
1014 A212   20r multicolored   1.60   .70
1015 A212   40r multicolored   2.25   1.25
1016 A212   100r multicolored   6.00   3.00
   a.   Souvenir sheet of 1   10.00   10.00
     Nos. 1014-1016 (3)   9.85   4.95

Wildlife protection. No. 1016a exists imperf. Value $13.

Conference   Mother and
Emblem   Child
A213   A214

1978, Mar. 27   **Photo.**   **Perf. 12½**
1017 A213   100r lt blue & ultra   1.50   .65

United Nations Conference on Technical Cooperation among Developing Countries.

1978, Apr. 7   **Photo.**   **Perf. 12½**
75r, Mother and child, symbolic design.
1018 A214   40r lt green & blue   .90   .35
1019 A214   75r orange red & brn   1.40   .65

Promotion of breast feeding.

Dome of The Rock, Jerusalem — A215

1978, May 15   **Photo.**   **Perf. 12½**
1020 A215   100r multicolored   2.75   .60

Palestinian fighters and their families.

Argentina '78   Head and "Blood
Emblem   Circulation"
A216   A217

1978, June 1
1021 A216   40r multicolored   .70   .30
1022 A216   100r multicolored   1.50   .70

11th World Cup Soccer Championships, Argentina, June 1-25.

1978, June 17   **Photo.**   **Perf. 12½**
1023 A217   100r black, blue & red   1.25   .55

World Health Day and drive against hypertension.

Leather Puppets — A218

Art from Wayang Museum, Djakarta: 75r, Wooden puppets. 100r, Actors with puppet masks.

1978, July 22   Litho.   Perf. 12½
1024 A218 40r multicolored   2.40   .70
1025 A218 75r multicolored   3.50   1.40
1026 A218 100r multicolored   5.25   2.40
　Nos. 1024-1026 (3)   11.15   4.50

Congress Emblem A219

IAAY Emblem A220

1978, Aug. 1
1027 A219 100r slate   1.25   .45

27th Congress of World Confederation of Organizations of Teachers (WCOTP), Djakarta, June 26-Aug. 2.

1978, Aug. 16   Photo.   Perf. 12½
1028 A220 100r org & dk blue   1.50   .45

International Anti-Apartheid Year.

Congress Emblem A221

Youth Pledge Emblem A222

Design: 100r, People and trees.

1978, Oct. 16   Photo.   Perf. 12½
1029 A221 40r emerald & blue   .60   .35
1030 A221 100r emerald & blk   1.10   .75

8th World Forestry Congress, Djakarta.

1978, Oct. 28
1031 A222 40r dk brown & red   .85   .50
1032 A222 100r salmon, brn & red   1.40   .75

50th anniv. of Youth Pledge. See #1044b.

Wildlife Protection — A223

1978, Nov. 1
1033 A223 40r Porcupine ant-eater   1.60   .50
1034 A223 75r Deer   2.75   1.40
　a.　Souv. sheet of 5, #1034, 4 #1035 + label   14.00   14.00
1035 A223 100r Clouded tiger   4.50   1.60
　a.　Souvenir sheet of 1   4.75   4.75
　Nos. 1033-1035 (3)   8.85   3.50

Stamps in No. 1034a are in changed colors. Souvenir sheets inscribed for Essen 2nd Intl. Stamp Fair.

Orchid Type of 1975

Orchids: 40r, Phalaenopsis sri rejeki. 75r, Dendrobium macrophilium. 100r, Cymbidium fynlaysonianum.

1978, Dec. 22   Photo.   Perf. 12½
1036 A183 40r multicolored   1.50   .50
1037 A183 75r multicolored   2.25   .85
1038 A183 100r multicolored   3.75   1.10
　a.　Souvenir sheet of 1   5.50   6.75
　Nos. 1036-1038 (3)   7.50   2.45

Douglas DC-3, 1949, over Volcano — A224

Designs: 75r, Douglas DC-9 over village. 100r, Douglas DC-10 over temple.

1979, Jan. 26   Photo.   Perf. 12½
1039 A224 40r multicolored   1.00   .40
1040 A224 75r multicolored   1.25   .40
1041 A224 100r multicolored   2.10   1.10
　Nos. 1039-1041 (3)   4.35   1.90

Garuda Indonesian Airways, 30th anniv.

A225

40r, Thomas Cup and badminton player.

1979, Feb. 24   Photo.   Perf. 12½
1042 A225 40r Thomas Cup & player   .50   .55
1043 A225 100r Player hitting ball   1.10   .85
1044 A225 100r Player facing left   1.40   .85
　a.　Pair, #1043-1044   2.50
　b.　Blkt. pane, 3 each #1042, 1043-1044 + label   8.00
　Nos. 1042-1044 (3)   3.00   2.25

11th Thomas Cup, Djakarta, May 24-June 2. #1044a forms a continuous design. Stamps from #1044b have straight edges.

Paphiopedilum Lowii — A227

Orchids: 100r, 300r, Vanda limbata. 125r, Phalaenopsis gigantea. 250r, as 60r.

1979, Mar. 22   Photo.   Perf. 12½
1045 A227 60r multi   1.40   .40
1046 A227 100r multi   2.00   .60
1047 A227 125r multi   2.75   1.00
　a.　Souvenir sheet of 1   7.50   7.50
　b.　Souv. sheet of 2 (250r, 300r)   10.00   10.00
　Nos. 1045-1047 (3)   6.15   2.00

No. 1047b, issued for Asian Phil. Exhib., Dortmund, West Germany, May 24-27. Sold for 650r.

Family and Houses — A228

Third Five-year Plan: 60r, Pylon and fields. 100r, School and clinic. 125r, Factories and trucks. 150r, Motorized mail delivery.

1979-82
1047C A228 12.50r Plane, food ('80)   .50   .20
1047D A228 17.50r Bridge ('82)   .60   .20
1048 A228 35r green & olive   .60   .20
1049 A228 60r blue & olive   .35   .20
1050 A228 100r blue & dk brn   .60   .20
1051 A228 125r red brn & ol   .85   .25
1052 A228 150r carmine & yel   .90   .45
　Nos. 1047C-1052 (7)   4.00   1.70
　See No. 1058a.

R. A. Kartini and Girls' School A229

1979, Apr. 21   Photo.   Perf. 12½
1053 A229 100r Kartini   1.00   .40
1054 A229 100r School   1.00   .40
　a.　Pair, #1053-1054   2.00   2.00

Mrs. R. A. Kartini, educator, birth centenary.

Bureau of Education, UNESCO Emblems — A231

1979, May 25   Photo.   Perf. 12½
1055 A231 150r multicolored   1.75   .45

50th anniversary of the statutes of the International Bureau of Education.

Self Defense A232

Cooperation Emblem A233

Designs: 125r, Games' emblem. 150r, Senayan Main Stadium.

1979, June 21   Photo.   Perf. 12½
1056 A232 60r multicolored   .60   .30
1057 A232 125r multicolored   1.10   .45
1058 A232 150r multicolored   1.50   .70
　a.　Bklt. pane of 6+4 labels (#1052, 5 #1058)   7.75
　Nos. 1056-1058 (3)   3.20   1.45

10th So. East Asia Games, Djakarta, Sept. 21-30. Stamps from #1058a have straight edges. Issue date: No. 1058a, Sept. 27.

1979, July 12   Photo.   Perf. 12½
1059 A233 150r multicolored   1.25   .40

32nd Indonesian Cooperative Day.

A234

Designs: 60r, IYC and natl. IYC emblems. 150r, IYC emblem.

1979, Aug. 4   Photo.   Perf. 12½
1060 A234 60r emerald & blk   .55   .20
1061 A234 150r blue & blk   1.00   .45

International Year of the Child.

A235

1979, Sept. 20   Photo.   Perf. 12½
1062 A235 150r TELECOM 79   1.25   .55

3rd World Telecommunications Exhibition, Geneva, Sept. 20-26.

Fight Drug Abuse — A236

1979, Oct. 17   Photo.   Perf. 12½
1063 A236 150r deep rose & blk   1.25   .55

Dolphin — A237

Wildlife Protection: 125r, Freshwater dolphin. 150r, Leatherback turtle.

1979, Nov. 24   Photo.   Perf. 12½
1064 A237 60r multi   1.50   .75
1065 A237 125r multi   3.00   .85
1066 A237 150r multi   5.50   1.25
　Nos. 1064-1066 (3)   10.00   2.85

Souvenir Sheet
1066A A237 200r like #1066   8.00   8.00

Ship Made of Cloves — A238

Spice Race, Jakarta-Amsterdam (Sailing Ships): 60r, Penisi, vert. 150r, Madurese boat, vert.

1980, Mar. 12   Photo.   Perf. 12½
1067 A238 60r bright blue   .50   .20
1068 A238 125r red brown   1.00   .45
1069 A238 150r red lilac   1.50   .45
　Nos. 1067-1069 (3)   3.00   1.10

1980

Souvenir Sheets
1069A A238 300r like #1068   5.50   2.10
1069B A238 500r like #1067   7.50   2.75

Issue dates: 300r, Mar. 12. 500r, May 6. 500r for London 1980 Intl. Stamp Exhib.

Rubber Raft in Rapids A239

Perf. 13½x13, 13x13½
1980, Mar. 21   Photo.
1070 A239 60r shown   .40   .20
1071 A239 125r Mountain climbing, vert.   1.10   .55
1072 A239 150r Hang gliding, vert.   1.50   .85
　Nos. 1070-1072 (3)   3.00   1.60

Souvenir Sheet
1072A A239 300r like #1070   5.00   5.00

A240

A241

1980, Apr. 15   *Perf. 12½*
1073 A240 150r multicolored   1.25   .45

Anti-smoking Campaign.

1980, Apr. 21   **Photo.**   *Perf. 12½*
1074 A241 125r Flowers In vase   1.10   .45
1075 A241 150r Bouquet   1.60   .70

2nd Flower Festival, Jakarta, Apr. 19-21.
See No. 1080a-1080b.

A242

A243

1980, Apr. 24   *Perf. 13x13½*

Conference building.
1076 A242 150r gold & lil rose   1.40   .45

Souvenir Sheet
1076A A242 300r multicolored   4.00   5.25

1st Asian-African Conf., 25th anniv.

1980, May 2   *Perf. 12½*

Designs: 60r, Male figure. 125r, Elephant
stone. 150r, Taman Bali Stone Sarcophagus,
2000 B.C.

1077 A243 60r multicolored   .65   .30
1078 A243 125r multicolored   1.25   .55
1079 A243 150r multicolored   1.75   .70
    Nos. 1077-1079 (3)   3.65   1.55

Flower and Sculpture Types of 1980
Souvenir Sheet
1980   **Photo.**   *Perf. 12½*
1080   Sheet of 8   18.00   18.00
  a. A241 100r like #1074   1.10   1.10
  b. A241 100r like #1075   1.10   1.10
  c. A243 200r like #1077   2.00   2.00
  d. A243 200r like #1079   2.00   2.00

London 1980 Intl. Stamp Exhib., May 6-14.
No. 1080 contains 2 stamps of each design
(4x2).

Draftsman in   Discus Thrower
Wheelchair   A245
A244

1980, May 18   **Photo.**   *Perf. 12½*
1081 A244 100r multicolored   1.00   .30

Disabled Veterans Corp, 30th anniversary.

1980, May 18
1082 A245 75r dp orange & sep   1.10   .30

Olympics for the Disabled, Arnhem, Netherlands, June 21-July 5.

Pres. Suharto — A246

A246a

A246b

Perf. 13½x12½, 12½
1980-83   **Photo.**
1083 A246 12.50r lt grn & grn   .50   .25
1084 A246 50r lt grn & bl   .50   .30
1084A A246 55r red rose &
        red lil   .50   .20
1085 A246 75r lem & gldn
        brn   .75   .20
1086 A246 100r brt pink & bl   1.25   .40
  a.   Bklt pane of 8 + 2 labels (6
      #1086, 2 #1088, Inscribed
      1981)   8.00
1087 A246a 110r dull org &
        dp red lil   .50   .20
1088 A246 200r dull org &
        brn   1.25   1.25
1088A A246a 250r dull org &
        brn   2.25   .50
1089 A246a 275r lt ap grn &
        dk grn   1.25   .40
1090 A246 300r rose lil &
        gold   3.25   .60
1091 A246 400r multicolored   3.50   .80

Engr.
Perf. 12½x13
1092 A246b 500r dk red brown   3.75   1.00
    Nos. 1083-1092 (12)   19.25   5.90

Issued: 12.50r, 50r, 75r, 100r, 200r, 6/8;
300r, 400r, 8/8/81; 250r, 9/82; 500r, 3/11/83;
55r, 7/83; 110r, 275r, 9/27/83.
See Nos. 1257-1261, 1265, 1268. For
surcharge see No. 1527.

Map of
Indonesia,
People — A247

1980, July 17   *Perf. 12½*
1093 A247 75r blue & pink   .45   .20
1094 A247 200r blue & dull yel   1.50   .40

1980 population census.

Ship Laying
Cable — A248

1980, Aug. 8   **Photo.**   *Perf. 12½*
1095 A248 75r multicolored   .45   .20
1096 A248 200r multicolored   1.50   .45

Singapore-Indonesia submarine cable
opening.

50s Stamp of
1946 — A249

100r, 15s Battle of Surabaya stamp, 1946,
horiz. 200r, 15s Independence Fund stamp,
1946.

1980, Aug. 17
1097 A249 75r dk brn & dp org   .60   .40
1098 A249 100r gold & purple   1.25   .50
1099 A249 200r multicolored   1.90   .80
    Nos. 1097-1099 (3)   3.75   1.70

Independence, 35th anniversary.

Asian Oceanic   OPEC Anniv.
Postal Training   Emblem — A251
School — A250

1980, Sept. 10   **Photo.**   *Perf. 12½*
1100 A250 200r multicolored   1.60   .40

1980, Sept. 14
1101 A251 200r multicolored   1.60   .40

Organization of Petroleum Exporting Countries, 20th anniversary.

Armed Forces, 35th
Anniversary — A252

1980, Oct. 5   **Photo.**   *Perf. 13½x13*
1102 A252 75r shown   .80   .50
1103 A252 200r Service men and
        emblem   1.40   .75

Vulturine   One Day
Parrot — A253   Beauty
               Orchid — A254

Designs: Parrots.

1980, Nov. 25   **Photo.**   *Perf. 13x12½*
1104 A253 75r shown   1.90   .70
1105 A253 100r Yellow-
        backed lory   3.00   1.40
1106 A253 200r Red lory   6.00   2.00
    Nos. 1104-1106 (3)   10.90   4.10

Souvenir Sheet
Perf. 12½
1106A   Sheet of 3   25.00   25.00
  b. A253 250r like #1105   4.50   4.50
  c. A253 350r like #1104   7.00   7.00
  d. A253 400r like #1106   8.00   8.00

1980, Dec. 10   *Perf. 13x13½*

Designs: Orchids.

1107 A254 75r *shown*   1.25   .35
1108 A254 100r *Dendrobium dis-
        color*   2.25   1.00
1109 A254 200r *Dendrobium la-
        sianthera*   4.00   .85
    Nos. 1107-1109 (3)   7.50   2.20

Souvenir Sheet
1980   *Perf. 13x13½*
1110   Sheet of 2   19.00   15.00
  a. A254 250r like #1109   8.00   5.00
  b. A254 350r like #1108   10.50   7.00

Heinrich von Stephan (1831-1897),
UPU Founder — A255

1981, Jan. 7   *Perf. 13½x12½*
1111 A255 200r brt bl & dk bl   1.60   .80

6th Asian
Pacific
Scout
Jamboree
A256

1981   *Perf. 13½x12½, 12½x13½*
1112 A256 75r Emblems   .65   .50
1113 A256 100r Scouts, vert.   1.00   .50
1114 A256 200r Emblems, diff.   1.60   .90
    Nos. 1112-1114 (3)   3.25   1.90

Souvenir Sheet
1115 A256 150r like #1113   5.50   .60

Issued: #1112-1114, 2/22; #1115, 8/14.

4th Asian-Oceanian   Blood Donor
Postal Union   Campaign
Congress   A258
A257

1981, Mar. 18   *Perf. 12½*
1116 A257 200r multicolored   1.90   .40

1981, Apr. 22
1117 A258 75r Girl holding
        blood drop   .50   .20
1118 A258 100r Hands holding
        blood drop   .90   .40
1119 A258 200r Hands, blood,
        diff.   1.60   .70
    Nos. 1117-1119 (3)   3.00   1.30

Intl. Family Planning
Conference — A259

1981, Apr. 26
1120 A259 200r multicolored   1.50   .60

Natl. Education Day — A260

Traditional Bali Paintings: Nos. 1121-1122,
Song of Sritanjung. No. 1123, Birth of the
Eagle.

1981, May 2
1121   100r multicolored   1.10   .20
1122   200r multicolored   2.10   .40
  a. A260 Pair #1121-1122   3.20   .60

Souvenir Sheet
1123   Sheet of 2   12.00   12.00
  a. A260 400r multicolored   3.50   3.50
  b. A261 600r multicolored   6.00   6.00

No. 1123 has margin showing WIPA '81
emblem. No. 1123 exists with marginal inscription "Indonesien grusst WIPA." Value, $17.50.

A262

A263

1981, May 9
1124 A262 200r multicolored   1.75   .45
ASEAN Building Jakarta, opening.

1981, May 22
1125 A263 200r multicolored   3.00   .45
Uber Cup '81 Badminton Championship, Tokyo.

World Environment Day — A264

Bas-reliefs, Candhi Merut Buddhist Temple, Central Java: 75r, Tree of Life. 200r, Reclining Buddha.

1981, June 5
1126 A264 75r multicolored   .65   .20
1127 A264 200r multicolored   1.50   .40

12th Koran Reading Competition, June 7-14 — A265

1981, June 7   *Perf. 13½x12½*
1128 A265 200r multicolored   1.25   .45

Intl. Year of the Disabled A266

1981, July 31   *Perf. 12½*
1129 A266 75r Blind man   .60   .20
1130 A266 200r Speech, hearing disabilities   1.40   .45

Soekarno-Hatta Independence Monument, Jakarta — A267

1981, Aug. 17
1131 A267 200r multicolored   1.75   .40

Natl. Sports Week, Sept. 19-30 — A268   World Food Day — A268a

---

1981, Sept. 19
1132 A268 75r Skydiving   .50   .20
1133 A268 100r Skin diving, horiz.   .90   .70
1134 A268 200r Equestrian   1.60   .55
    Nos. 1132-1134 (3)   3.00   1.45

The horse on No. 1134 is brown black, See Nos. 1374-1375 for souvenir sheets containing No. 1134 in different colors.

1981, Oct. 16
1135 A268a 200r multicolored   3.00   .70

Provincial Arms — A269

Natl. Arms A270

1981-83
1136 A269 100r Aceh   2.00   .75
1137 A269 100r Bali   2.00   .75
1138 A269 100r Bengkulu   2.00   .75
1139 A269 100r Jakarta   2.50   1.50
1140 A269 100r West Irian   5.00   .85
1141 A269 100r West Java   2.00   .65
1142 A269 100r Jambi   2.00   .65
1143 A269 100r Central Java   2.00   .65
1144 A269 100r East Java   2.00   .65
1145 A269 100r South Kalimantan   2.00   .65
1146 A269 100r East Kalimantan   2.00   .65
1147 A269 100r West Kalimantan   2.00   .65
1148 A269 100r Lampung   2.00   .65
1149 A269 100r Central Kalimantan   2.00   .65
1150 A269 100r Moluccas   2.00   .65
1151 A269 100r West Nusa Tenggara   2.00   .65
1152 A269 100r East Nusa Tenggara   2.00   .65
1153 A269 100r Southeast Celebes   2.00   .65
1154 A269 100r Central Celebes   2.00   .65
1155 A269 100r West Sumatra   2.00   .65
1156 A269 100r North Celebes   2.00   .65
1157 A269 100r North Sumatra   2.00   .65
1158 A269 100r South Sumatra   2.00   .65
1159 A269 100r Riau   2.00   .65
1160 A269 100r South Sulawesi   2.00   .65
1161 A269 100r Yogyakarta   2.00   .65
1161A A269 100r Timor   1.00   .60
1162 A270 250r shown   5.75   1.75
    Nos. 1136-1162 (28)   62.25   20.60

Issued: Nos. 1136-1140, 1981; Nos. 1141-1161, 1162, 1982; No. 1161A, 1983.

Pink-crested Cockatoo — A271

1981, Dec. 10
1163 A271 75r shown   2.50   .80
1164 A271 100r Sulphur-crested cockatoo   3.25   .80
1165 A271 200r King cockatoo   6.75   2.75
    Nos. 1163-1165 (3)   12.50   4.35

Souvenir Sheet
1166   Sheet of 2   21.00   21.00
  a.   A271 150r like #1164   4.75   4.75
  b.   A271 350r like #1165   15.00   15.00

Bumiputra Mutual Life Insurance Co., 70th Anniv. — A272

1982, Feb. 12
1167 A272 75r Family   .50   .20
1168 A272 100r Family, diff.   .85   .40
1169 A272 200r Hands holding symbols   1.40   .65
    Nos. 1167-1169 (3)   2.75   1.25

Search and Rescue Institute, 10th Anniv. — A273   General Election — A274

1982, Feb. 28   *Perf. 12½x13½*
1170 A273 250r multicolored   1.90   .50

1982, Mar. 1   *Perf. 12½*
1171 A274 75r Ballot, houses   .50   .20
1172 A274 100r Farm   .85   .30
1173 A274 200r Arms   1.40   .70
    Nos. 1171-1173 (3)   2.75   1.20

2nd UN Conference on Exploration and Peaceful Uses of Outer Space, Vienna, Aug. 9-21 — A275

1982, Apr. 19   *Perf. 13x13½*
1174 A275 150r Couple   1.10   .40
1175 A275 250r Emblem   2.50   .65

12th Thomas Badminton Cup, London, May — A276

1982, May 19
1176 A276 250r multicolored   2.00   .50
  a.   Souvenir sheet of 2   8.00

No. 1176a also exists overprinted "INDONESIE SALUE PHILEXFRANCE" in red or black. Value, each $60.

1982 World Cup — A277

1982, June 14
1177 A277 250r multi   2.50   .50
  a.   Souvenir sheet of 2   10.00
  b.-c.   Souvenir sheets of 2, each   *150.00 80.00*

No. 1177b overprinted "ITALIA WORLD CHAMPION" in black; No. 1177c overprinted same in red. Fake overprints exist.

60th Anniv. of Taman Siswa Educational System — A278

1982, July 3
1178 A278 250r multicolored   1.25   .50

15th Anniv. of Assoc. of South East Asian Nations (ASEAN) — A279

1982, Aug. 8   *Photo.*   *Perf. 12½*
1179 A279 150r Members' flags   2.50   .45

Balinese Starling A280   Red Birds of Paradise A281

1982, Oct. 11   *Photo.*   *Perf. 13x13½*
1180 A280 100r shown   2.50   .40
1181 A280 250r King birds of paradise   4.75   .55

Souvenir Sheet
1181A A280 500r like 100r   15.00   15.00

3rd World Natl. Park Cong., Denpasar Bali.

1982, Dec. 20   *Perf. 12½x13½*
1182 A281 100r Lawe's six-wired parotia   2.75   .40
1183 A281 150r Twelve-wired birds of paradise   4.50   .80
1184 A281 250r shown   6.25   1.25
    Nos. 1182-1184 (3)   13.50   2.45

Souvenir Sheet
    Perf. 12½x13½
1184A   Sheet of 2   25.00   25.00
  b.   A281 200r like 100r   7.75   7.75
  c.   A281 300r like 250r   12.50   12.50

Scouting Year A282

1983, Feb. 22   *Photo.*   *Perf. 13½x13*
1185 A282 250r multi   2.25   .50

Restoration of Borobudur Temple — A283

1983, Feb. 23   *Perf. 12½*
1186 A283 100r Scaffolding, crane, vert.   1.75   .45
1187 A283 150r Buddha statue, stupas, vert.   2.75   .45
1188 A283 250r Statue, temple   6.00   2.75
    Nos. 1186-1188 (3)   10.50   3.65

Souvenir Sheet
1189 A283 500r Temple   19.00   19.00

Gas Plant — A284

World Communications Year — A285

1983, May 16   Photo.   Perf. 12½
1190 A284 275r multi   1.75   .40

7th Intl. Liquefied Natural Gas Conference and Exhibition, Jakarta, May 16-19.

1983, May 17   Perf. 12½x13½
1191 A285 75r Dove, ships   .55   .20
1192 A285 110r Satellite   .70   .25
1193 A285 175r Dish antenna, jet   1.10   .40
1194 A285 275r Airmail envelope,
                globe   1.40   .65
     Nos. 1191-1194 (4)   3.75 1.50

See Nos. 1215-1216.

13th Natl. Koran Reading Competition, Padang, May 23-31 — A286

1983, May 23   Perf. 13½x13
1195 A286 275r multi   1.75   .55

Total Solar Eclipse, June 11 — A287

1983, June 11   Perf. 12½
1196 A287 110r Map, eclipse   1.10   .25
1197 A287 275r Map   2.25   .40

Souvenir Sheet
1198 A287 500r like 275r   17.00 17.00

Launch of Palapa B Satellite — A288

Agricultural Census — A289

1983, June 18   Perf. 12½x13½
1199 A288 275r multi   1.75   .55

1983, July 1   Photo.   Perf. 12½
1200 A289 110r Produce   .80   .20
1201 A289 275r Farmer   1.60   .25

15th Anniv. of Indonesia-Pakistan Economic and Cultural Cooperation Org. — A290

Weavings.
1983, Aug. 19
1202 A290 275r Indonesian,
                Lombok   2.00   .85
1203 A290 275r Pakistani, Balu-
                chistan   2.00   .85

Krakatoa Eruption Centenary A291

1983, Aug. 26
1204 A291 110r Volcano   1.00   .30
1205 A291 275r Map   2.00   .45

CN-235, Light Air Transport — A292

1983, Sept. 10   Photo.   Perf. 12½
1206 A292 275r multi   1.60   .55

Tropical Fish — A293

1983, Oct. 17   Photo.   Perf. 12½
1207 A293 110r Puntius te-
                trazona   2.50   .65
1208 A293 175r Rasbora
                einthoveni   3.50   .65
1209 A293 275r Toxotes jacu-
                lator   7.00 2.00
     Nos. 1207-1209 (3)   13.00 3.30

Canderawasih Birds — A294

1983, Nov. 30   Photo.   Perf. 12½
1210 A294 110r Diphyllodes
                respublica   1.60   .20
1211 A294 175r Epimachus
                fastuosus   2.25   .20
1212 A294 275r Drepanornis
                albertisi   4.25   .20
1213 A294 500r as #1212   6.75   .40
     a. Souvenir sheet of 1   24.00 24.00
     Nos. 1210-1213 (4)   14.85 1.00

Inalienable Rights of the Palestinian People A295

1983, Dec. 20   Perf. 13½x13
1214 A295 275r multi   1.75   .30

WCY Type of 1983
Souvenir Sheets
1983   Photo.   Perf. 12½x13½
1215 A285 400r like No. 1192   11.00 8.00
1216 A285 500r like No. 1194   11.00 7.00

Telecom '83 exhib., Geneva, Oct. 26-Nov. 1 (400r). Philatelic Museum opening, Jakarta (500r). Issued: 400r, Oct. 26; 500r, Sept. 29.

Fight Against Polio — A296

4th Five-Year Development Plan — A297

1984, Feb. 17   Photo.   Perf. 12½
1217 A296 110r Emblem   .65   .20
1218 A296 275r Stylized person   1.50   .30

1984, Apr. 1   Photo.   Perf. 12½
1219 A297 55r Fertilizer industry   .25   .20
1220 A297 75r Aviation   .35   .20
1221 A297 110r Shipping   .50   .25
1222 A297 275r Communications   1.25   .60
     Nos. 1219-1222 (4)   2.35 1.25

Forestry Resources A298

1984, May 17   Photo.   Perf. 12½
1223 A298 75r Forest, paper
                mill   .65   .20
1224 A298 110r Seedling   1.10   .20
1225 A298 175r Tree cutting   1.50   .40
1226 A298 275r Logs   2.75   .55
     a. Souv. sheet of 2, #1225-
         1226   20.00 12.00
     Nos. 1223-1226 (4)   6.00 1.35

17th Annual Meeting of ASEAN Foreign Ministers — A299

1984, July 9   Photo.   Perf. 12½
1227 A299 275r Flags   2.75   .55

1984 Summer Olympics A300

Horse Dancers, Central Java — A301

1984, July 28   Photo.   Perf. 12½
1228 A300 75r Pole vault   .75   .20
1229 A300 110r Archery   .75   .20
1230 A300 175r Boxing   1.25   .20
1231 A300 250r Shooting   2.25   .45
1232 A300 275r Weight lifting   2.50   .45
1233 A300 325r Swimming   2.50   .30
     Nos. 1228-1233 (6)   10.00 1.80

1984, Aug. 17   Perf. 12½x13½
Processions.
1234 A301 75r shown   .75   .20
1235 A301 110r Reyog Po-
                norogo, East
                Java   1.25   .25

1236 A301 275r Lion Dance,
                West Java   2.50   .60
1237 A301 325r Barong of Bali   3.50   .60
     Nos. 1234-1237 (4)   8.00 1.65

Natl. Sports Day A302

1984, Sept. 9   Photo.   Perf. 13½x13
1238 A302 110r Thomas Cup vic-
                tory   .75   .30
1239 A302 275r Gymnastics   2.00   .45

Postcode System Inauguration A303

1984, Sept. 27   Photo.   Perf. 12½
1240 A303 110r multi   .55   .30
1241 A303 275r multi   1.25   .70

Birds of Irian Jaya — A304

Oath of the Youth — A305

1984, Oct. 15   Perf. 12½x13½
1242 A304 75r Chlamydera
                lauterbachi   1.60   .20
1243 A304 110r Sericulus au-
                reus   2.50   .20
1244 A304 275r Astrapia nigra   6.00   .25
1245 A304 325r Lophorhina
                superba   6.50   .30
     a. Souv. sheet of 2, #1242,
         1245   29.00 29.00
     Nos. 1242-1245 (4)   16.60   .95

No. 1245a for PHILAKOREA '84.

1984, Oct. 28   Perf. 12½
1246 A305 275r Emblem   1.60   .70

ICAO, 40th Anniversary — A306

1984, Dec. 7 Photo. Perf. 13½x12½
1247 A306 275r Airplane, Em-
                blem   2.25   .70

Indonesia Netherlands Marine Exped., 1984-85 — A307

75th Intl. Women's Day — A308

Survey ship Snellius II and: 50r, Marine geological and geophysical exploration. 100r, Mapping ocean currents. 275r, Studying marine flora and fauna.

1985, Feb. 27 Photo. Perf. 13x13½
1248 A307 50r multi .50 .20
1249 A307 100r multi 1.00 .20
1250 A307 275r multi 3.00 .40
Nos. 1248-1250 (3) 4.50 .80

1985, Mar. 8
1251 A308 100r Emblem 2.25 .65
1252 A308 275r Silhouettes, emblem 5.75 2.50

Five Year Plan
A309

1985, Apr. 1 Perf. 13½x13
1254 A309 75r Mecca pilgrimage program .40 .20
1255 A309 140r Compulsory education .75 .45
1256 A309 350r Cement industry,
Padang works 1.90 1.00
Nos. 1254-1256 (3) 3.05 1.65

Suharto Type of 1980-83 and

A310

A310a

A310b   A310c

Perf. 13½x12½, 12½ (A310, A310a, A310b, A310c)

1983-93 Photo.
1257 A246 10r pale grn &
dk grn 1.60 .20
1258 A246 25r pale org &
dk cop red .45 .20
1259 A246 50r beige & dk
brn .45 .20
1260 A246 55r sal rose &
rose .45 .20
1261 A246 100r lt blue
green &
ultra .45 .20
1262 A310 140r rose & dp
brn .85 .20
1263 A310c 150r yel grn &
multi .75 .20
1264 A310b 200r pink, bl &
red .75 .20
1265 A246 300r lt dull grn,
bl grn &
gold 2.00 .20
1266 A310c 300r multicolored 1.75 .20
1267 A310 350r red & brt lil 2.40 .35
1268 A246 400r blue grn, int
blue &
gold 2.50 .30
1268A A310b 700r pale grn,
rose lil &
grn 2.75 .35
1268B A310c 700r red & multi 4.00 1.10
1269 A310a 1000r multi 6.50 .75
Nos. 1257-1269 (15) 27.65 4.85

Issued: 10r, 25r, 3/11; 140r, 350r, 4/10/85; 50r, 100r, #1265, 12/24/86; 55r, 400r, 12/87; 200r, 12/89; 700r, 3/90; 1000r, 8/17/88; 150r, #1266, 1268B, 8/17/93.
For surcharge see No. 1527.

Asia-Africa Conference, 30th
Anniv. — A311

1985, Apr. 24 Perf. 12½
1270 A311 350r Emblem, inscription 2.50 .45

Intl. Youth
Year — A312

UN Decade for
Women — A313

1985, July 12 Perf. 12½x13½
1271 A312 75r Three youths,
globe 1.00 .20
1272 A312 140r Youths supporting globe 2.00 .20

1985, July 26
1273 A313 55r Profiles of women, emblem .55 .25
1274 A313 140r Globe, emblem 1.25 .25

Indonesian Trade
Fair — A314

1985, Aug. 1
1275 A314 140r Hydro-electric
plant 1.00 .20
1276 A314 350r Farmer, industrial plant 2.50 .40
Republic of Indonesia, 40th anniv.

11th Natl.
Sports
Week,
Jakarta,
Sept. 9-20
A315

Perf. 13½x12½, 12½x13½
1985, Sept. 9 Photo.
1277 A315 55r Sky diving .40 .20
1278 A315 100r Combat sports .75 .20
1279 A315 140r High jump 1.00 .25
1280 A315 350r Wind surfing,
vert. 2.50 .45
Nos. 1277-1280 (4) 4.65 1.10

Org. of Petroleum
Exporting Countries,
OPEC, 25th
Anniv. — A316

1985, Sept. 14 Perf. 12½
1281 A316 140r multi 1.50 .30

Natl. Oil
Industry,
Cent.
A317

1985, Oct. 8 Perf. 13½x13
1282 A317 140r Oil tankers .80 .30
1283 A317 250r Refinery 1.40 .45
1284 A317 350r Offshore oil rig 2.00 .90
Nos. 1282-1284 (3) 4.20 1.65

UN, 40th
Anniv. — A318

Design: 140r, Doves, 40, emblem. 300r,
Bombs transformed into plants.

1985, Oct. 24 Perf. 12½
1285 A318 140r multicolored .85 .20
1286 A318 300r multicolored 1.60 .45

Wildlife
A318a

1985, Dec. 27 Photo. Perf. 14½x13
1286A A318a 75r Rhinoceros
sondaicus 1.25 .30
1286B A318a 150r Anoa depressicornis 2.50 .45
1286C A318a 300r Varanus
komodoensis 5.00 .70
Nos. 1286A-1286C (3) 8.75 1.45

1986 Industrial Census — A319

1986, Feb. 8 Photo. Perf. 12½
1287 A319 Pair 1.75 1.25
a. 175r Census emblem .85 .30
b. 175r Symbols of industry .85 .30

UN Child
Survival
Campaign
A320

1986, Mar. 15 Photo. Perf. 12½
1288 A320 75r Breastfeeding .80 .25
1289 A320 140r Immunization 1.40 .30
UNICEF, 40th anniv.

4th 5-year
Development
Plan — A321

14th Thomas
Cup, 13th Uber
Cup,
Jakarta — A322

1986, Apr. 1 Photo. Perf. 12½
1290 A321 140r Construction .30 .30
1291 A321 500r Agriculture 1.25 .40

1986, Apr. 22
1292 A322 55r Cup, racket .90 .25
1293 A322 150r Cups, horiz. 2.00 .25

EXPO '86,
Vancouver — A323

1986, May 2 Perf. 12½x14½
1294 A323 75r Pinisi junk .65 .25
1295 A323 150r Kentongan, satellite 1.25 .30
1296 A323 300r Pavilion emblem 2.25 .40
Nos. 1294-1296 (3) 4.15 .95

Natl. Scout Jamboree, JAMNAS '86,
Cibubur Jakarta East
A324

Perf. 13½x12½, 12½x13½
1986, June 21 Photo.
1297 A324 100r Saluting flag 1.25 .25
1298 A324 140r Cookout 1.75 .30
1299 A324 210r Map-reading,
vert. 2.50 .40
Nos. 1297-1299 (3) 5.50 .95

Air Show
'86,
Jakarta,
June 22-
July 1
A325

1986, June 23 Perf. 13½x12½
1300 A325 350r multi 2.25 .40

Folk Dances — A326

1986, July 30 Photo. Perf. 12½
1301 A326 140r Legong Kraton 1.25 .25
1302 A326 350r Barong 3.25 .45
1303 A326 500r Kecak 4.50 .60
Nos. 1301-1303 (3) 9.00 1.30

19th Congress of
Intl. Society of Sugar
Cane Technologists,
Jakarta — A327

1986, Aug. 5 Perf. 12½x13½
1304 A327 150r Planting 1.00 .25
1305 A327 300r Sugar 1.75 .40

Sea-Me-We Submarine Cable
Inauguration — A328

1986, Sept. 8   *Perf. 12½*
1306 A328 140r shown   .75   .25
1307 A328 350r Map, diff.   2.25   .45
    Southeast Asia, Middle East, Western Europe Submarine Cable.

Intl. Peace Year — A329

1987 General Election — A330

1986, Dec. 17   Photo.   *Perf. 12½*
1308 A329 350r shown   1.25   .30
1309 A329 500r Dove circling Earth   2.50   .35

1987, Jan. 19
    75r, Tourism, party emblems, industry. 350r, Emblems, natl. eagle, ballot box.
1310 A330   75r multi   .35   .20
1311 A330 140r multi   .70   .20
1312 A330 350r multi   1.60   .40
    Nos. 1310-1312 (3)   2.65   .80

A331   A332

1987, Mar. 21   Photo.   *Perf. 12½*
1313 A331 350r Satellite, horiz.   1.00   .40
1314 A331 500r shown   2.25   .35
    Launch of Palapa B-2P, Cape Canaveral.

1987, Apr. 1
1315 A332 140r Boy carving figurines, horiz.   .40   .20
1316 A332 350r shown   1.00   .35
    4th 5-Year Development Plan.

Folk Costumes — A333

1987, May 25   *Perf. 13x13½*
1317 A333 140r Kalimantan Timur   4.25   .40
1318 A333 350r Daerah Aceh   10.00   4.75
1319 A333 400r Timor Timur   11.50   1.10
    Nos. 1317-1319 (3)   25.75   6.25
    See Nos. 1358-1363, 1412-1417, 1448-1453, 1464-1469.

14th Southeast Asia Games, Jakarta, Sept. 9-20   Anniv. Emblems
A334   A335

1987, June 10   *Perf. 12½*
1320 A334 140r Weight lifting   .70   .20
1321 A334 250r Swimming   1.40   .30
1322 A334 350r Running   1.90   .45
    Nos. 1320-1322 (3)   4.00   .95

1987, June 20
1323 A335   75r multi, horiz.   1.50   .20
1324 A335 100r shown   2.00   .20
    City of Jakarta, 460th anniv.; Jakarta Fair, 20th anniv.

Children's Day — A336   ASEAN Headquarters, Jakarta — A337

1987, July 23
1325 A336 100r Education, horiz.   .60   .20
1326 A336 250r Universal immunization   1.40   .25

1987, Aug. 8
1327 A337 350r multi   1.75   .45
    ASEAN, 20th anniv.

Assoc. of Physicians Specializing in Internal Diseases, 30th Anniv. — A338

1987, Aug. 23   Photo.
1328 A338 300r Stylized man, caduceus   1.40   .25

Sand Craters, Mt. Bromo, Timur A339

1987, Oct. 20   *Perf. 13½x12½*
1329 A339 140r shown   .75   .20
1330 A339 350r Bratan (Bedugul) Lake, Bali   2.50   .65
1331 A339 500r Sea gardens, Bunaken Is.   3.50   .45
    Nos. 1329-1331 (3)   6.75   1.30
    Tourism. See Nos. 1367-1370A, 1408-1410, 1420-1422.

Role of Women in the Fight for Independence A340

1987, Nov. 10   *Perf. 12½*
1332 A340   75r Veteran   .65   .20
1333 A340 100r Soldiers, barbed wire (Laskar Wanita)   .85   .20

Fish — A341

1987, Dec. 30
1334 A341 150r Osphronemus goramy   1.50   .65
1335 A341 200r Cyprinus carpio   2.00   .30
1336 A341 500r Clarias batrachus   5.00   .55
    Nos. 1334-1336 (3)   8.50   1.50

Natl. Veteran's League, 31st Anniv. — A342

1988, Jan. 2
1337 A342 250r blue grn & org   1.25   .25

Occupational Health and Safety for Greater Efficiency and Productivity — A343

1988, Jan. 12   *Perf. 13½x12½*
1338 A343 350r Worker using safety equipment   1.75   .45
    See No. 1419.

Natl. Craft Council, 8th Anniv. — A344

1988, Mar. 3   Photo.   *Perf. 12½*
1339 A344 120r ultra & dark brn   .65   .20
1340 A344 350r lt blue & dark brn   1.60   .45
1341 A344 500r yel grn & dark brn   2.25   .40
    Nos. 1339-1341 (3)   4.50   1.05
    Crafts: 120r, Carved wood snake and frog. 350r, Cane rocking chair. 500r, Ornate carved bamboo containers and fan.

Pelita IV (Five-Year Development Plan) — A345

1988, Apr. 1
1342 A345 140r Oil rig, refinery   .30   .20
1343 A345 400r Crayfish, trawler   .95   .30

World Expo '88, Brisbane, Australia A346   Intl. Red Cross and Red Crescent Organizations, 125th Annivs. A347

    Designs: 200r, Two children, Borobudur Temple in silhouette. 300r, Boy wearing armor and headdress. 350r, Girl, boy and a Tongkonan house, Toraja, South Sulawesi.

1988, Apr. 30   Photo.   *Perf. 12½*
1344 A346 200r multi   .90   .20
1345 A346 300r multi   1.40   .25
1346 A346 350r multi   1.90   .35
   a.   Souv. sheet of 3, #1344-1346   15.00   12.00
    Nos. 1344-1346 (3)   4.20   .80
    No. 1346a exists imperf. Value: $40 unused, $30 used.

1988, May 8
1347 A347 350r black & red   1.60   .30

Orchids — A348

1988, May 17   *Perf. 13x13½*
1348 A348 400r Dendrobium none   2.00   .45
1349 A348 500r Dendrobium abang   2.50   .35

1988 Summer Olympics, Seoul — A349   Intl. Council of Women, Cent. — A350

1988, June 15   Photo.   *Perf. 12½*
1350 A349   75r Running   .50   .20
1351 A349 100r Weight lifting   .55   .20
1352 A349 200r Archery   1.10   .20
1353 A349 300r Table tennis   1.60   .20
1354 A349 400r Swimming   2.25   .30
   a.   Souv. sheet of 3 + label, #1351-1352, 1354, imperf   22.50   16.00
1355 A349 500r Tennis   2.75   .35
   a.   Souv. sheet of 3 + label, #1350, 1353, 1355, imperf   22.50   16.00
    Nos. 1350-1355 (6)   8.75   1.45
    Sheets exist perf. Value, each $30.

1988, June 26
1356 A350 140r brt blue & blk   1.00   .20

7th Natl. Farmers' Week — A351

1988, July 9
1357 A351 350r lake & bister   1.75   .55

    Folk Costumes Type of 1987
    Traditional wedding attire from: 55r, West Sumatra. 75p, Jambi. 100r, Bengkulu. 120r, Lampung. 200r, Moluccas. 250r, East Nusa.

1988, July 15   *Perf. 12½x14½*
1358 A333   55r multicolored   .55   .20
         Perf. 12½x13½
1359 A333   75r multicolored   .80   .20
1360 A333 100r multicolored   1.00   .20
1361 A333 120r multicolored   1.25   .20
         Perf. 12½x14½
1362 A333 200r multicolored   1.90   .20
1363 A333 250r multicolored   2.50   1.00
    Nos. 1358-1363 (6)   8.00   2.00

A352   A353

1988, Sept. 29   Photo.   *Perf. 12½*
1364 A352 500r multicolored   2.00   .30
    13th Congress of the Non-Aligned News Agencies Pool, Jakarta, Sept. 29-Oct. 1.

1988, Oct. 9
1365 A353 140r multi   1.10   .20
    Intl. Letter Writing Week.

Transportion and Communications Decade for Asia and the Pacific (1985-1995) A354

1988, Oct. 24
1366 A354 350r blk & lt blue   2.25   .55

Tourism Type of 1987

Architecture: 250r, Al Mashun Mosque, Medan. 300r, Pagaruyung Palace, Batusangkar. 500r, 1000r, Keong Emas Taman Theater, Jakarta.

1988-89   Photo.   Perf. 13½x13
1367 A339 250r multi   1.25   .40
1368 A339 300r multi   1.50   .30
1369 A339 500r multi   2.50   .35
  Nos. 1367-1369 (3)   5.25 1.05

Souvenir Sheets
Imperf
1370 A339 1000r multi   15.00 10.00

Perf. 14½x13
1370A   Sheet of 2   21.00 15.00
  b. A339 1500r like No. 1367   7.25 1.60
  c. A339 2500r like No. 1368 11.50 2.75

No. 1370 exists perf 14½x12½. Value $10.
Issue dates: No. 1370A, Nov. 1989; others, Nov. 25, 1988. World Stamp Expo '89, Washington, DC.

Butterflies   Flora
A356   A357

1988, Dec. 20   Perf. 12½x13½
1371 A356 400r *Papilio gigon*   2.25   .45
1372 A356 500r *Graphium androcles*   3.00   .65

Souvenir Sheet
Imperf
1373 A356 1000r like 500r   12.00 8.00

No. 1373 exists perf. 12½x14½. Value $26.

Equestrian Type of 1981
Souvenir Sheets

1988   Imperf.
1374   Sheet of 4   12.50 5.00
  a. A268 200r blk, dark red & grn   .50   .20
1375   Sheet of 1 + label, dk bl, dark red & deep org   12.50 5.00

FILACEPT '88, The Hague, Oct. 18-23, 1988. Nos. 1374-1375 exist perf. 12½. Value, each $18.

1989, Jan. 7   Photo.   Perf. 13½x13
1376 A357 200r *Rafflesia*   .90   .40
1377 A357 1000r *Amorphophallus titanum*   4.50   .70

Souvenir Sheet
Perf. 13½x14½
1378 A357 1000r like No. 1377, value in blk   35.00 27.50

Garuda Indonesia Airlines, 40th Anniv. — A358

1989, Jan. 26   Perf. 12½
1379 A358 350r bl grn & brt bl   2.00   .65

World Wildlife Fund — A359

Orangutans, *Pongo pygmaeus*.

1989, Mar. 6   Photo.   Perf. 12½
1380 A359 75r Adult and young   4.00   .85
1381 A359 100r Adult hanging in tree   4.00   .45
  a. Souv. sheet of 2, #1380-1381   72.50 72.50
1382 A359 140r Adult, young in tree   4.00   .55
1383 A359 500r Adult's head   11.00 3.00
  a. Souv. sheet of 2, #1382-1383   72.50 72.50
  Nos. 1380-1383 (4)   23.00 4.85

Use of Postage Stamps in Indonesia, 125th Anniv. — A360

1989, Apr. 1
1384 A360 1000r grn, rose lilac & deep blue   2.75   .40

5th Five-year Development Plan — A361

Industries.

1989, Apr. 1
1385 A361 55r Fertilizer   .25   .20
1386 A361 150r Cilegon Iron and Steel Mill   .35   .20
1387 A361 350r Petroleum   .90   .25
  Nos. 1385-1387 (3)   1.50   .65

See Nos. 1427-1428, 1461-1462, 1488-1489, 1530-1532.

Natl. Education Day — A362

Ki Hadjar Dewantara (b. 1889), founder of Taman Siswa school and: 140r, Graduate. 300r, Pencil, globe and books.

1989, May 2
1388 A362 140r ver, lake & brt rose lil   .60   .20
1389 A362 300r vio & pale grn   1.40   .30

Terbuka University (140r) and freedom from illiteracy (300r).

Asia-Pacific   Sudirman Cup,
Telecommunity, 10th   Flag — A364
Anniv. — A363

1989, July 1   Photo.   Perf. 12½
1390 A363 350r green & vio   1.60   .85

1989, July 3
1391 A364 100r scar, gold & dark red brn   1.90   .20

Sudirman Cup world badminton mixed team championships, Jakarta, May 24-28.

Natl. Children's   CIRDAP, 10th
Day — A365   Anniv. — A366

1989, July 23
1392 A365 100r Literacy   .60   .20
1393 A365 250r Physical fitness   1.40   .30

1989, July 29
1394 A366 140r blue & dark red brn   1.10   .20

Center on Integrated Rural Development for Asia and the Pacific.

A367   A368

Paleoanthropological Discoveries in Indonesia: Fossils of *Homo erectus* and *Homo sapiens* men.

1989, Aug. 31
1395 A367 100r Sangiran 17   .90   .20
1396 A367 150r Perning 1   1.25   .20
1397 A367 200r Sangiran 10   1.75   .40
1398 A367 250r Wajak 1   2.10   .30
1399 A367 300r Sambungmacan   3.00   .45
1400 A367 350r Ngandong 7   3.00   .30
  Nos. 1395-1400 (6)   12.00 1.85

  Nos. 1398-1400 vert.

1989, Sept. 4
1401 A368 350r deep blue & yel grn   1.50   .35

Interparliamentary Union, Cent.

12th Natl. Sports Week — A369

1989, Sept. 18
1402 A369 75r Tae kwando   .45   .20
1403 A369 100r Tennis   .55   .20
1404 A369 140r Judo   .80   .20
1405 A369 350r Volleyball   2.00   .70
1406 A369 500r Boxing   2.75   .35
1407 A369 1000r Archery   5.00   .70
  Nos. 1402-1407 (6)   11.55 2.35

Tourism Type of 1987

Structures in Miniature Park: 120r, Taman Burung. 350r, Natl. Philatelic Museum. 500r, Istana Anak-Anak, vert.

Perf. 13½x12½, 12½x13½
1989, Oct. 9
1408 A339 120r multicolored   .65   .20
1409 A339 350r multicolored   1.75   .60
1410 A339 500r multicolored   2.50   .50
  Nos. 1408-1410 (3)   4.90 1.30

Film Festival — A370

1989, Nov. 11   Photo.   Perf. 12½
1411 A370 150r yel bister & blk   1.50   .20

Folk Costumes Type of 1987

Traditional wedding attire from: 50r, North Sumatra. 75r, South Sumatra. 100r, Jakarta. 140r, North Sulawesi. 350r, Mid Sulawesi. 500r, South Sulawesi. 1500r, North Sulawesi.

1989, Dec. 11   Perf. 13x13½
1412 A333 50r multicolored   .30   .20
1413 A333 75r multicolored   .40   .20
1414 A333 100r multicolored   .50   .20
1415 A333 140r multicolored   .70   .20
1416 A333 350r multicolored   2.25   .90
1417 A333 500r multicolored   3.00   .50
  Nos. 1412-1417 (6)   7.15 2.20

Souvenir Sheet
Imperf
1418 A333 1500r multicolored   10.50 8.00

No. 1418 exists perf. 12½x13½. Value $13.

Health and Safety Type of 1988

1990, Jan. 12   Perf. 13x12½
Size: 29x21mm
1419 A343 200r Lineman, power lines   1.25   .20

Tourism Type of 1987

Architecture: 200r, Fort Marlborough, Bengkulu. 400r, 1000r, National Museum, Jakarta. 500r, 1500r, Mosque of Baiturrahman, Banda Aceh.

1990, Feb. 1   Perf. 13½x13
1420 A339 200r multicolored   .75   .20
1421 A339 400r multicolored   1.60   .20
1422 A339 500r multicolored   2.00   .30
  Nos. 1420-1422 (3)   4.35   .70

Souvenir Sheet
1423   Sheet of 2   12.00 8.00
  a. A339 1000r multicolored   4.75   .50
  b. A339 1500r multicolored   7.25   .75

Flora
A371

1990, Mar. 1
1424 A371 75r Mammilaria fragilis   .20   .20
1425 A371 1000r Gmelina ellipitca   3.00 1.00

Souvenir Sheet
1426 A371 1500r like #1425   15.00 9.50

5th Five-year Development Plan Type of 1989

1990, Apr. 1   Perf. 12½
1427 A361 200r Road construction   .35   .20
1428 A361 1000r Lighthouse, ship   1.90 1.10

Visit Indonesia Year, 1991 A372

Perf. 13½x12½, 12½x13½
1990, May 1
1429 A372 100r shown   .35   .20
1430 A372 500r Steps, ruin   1.90   .40

Souvenir Sheet
Perf. 14½x12½
1430A A372 5000r like #1429   21.00 14.00

No. 1430A, Stamp World London '90.

A373

A374

1990, May 18 **Perf. 12½**
1431 A373 1000r gray grn & brn
org   2.25 .90
Disabled Veterans Corps, 40th anniv.

1990, June 8 **Perf. 12½**
1432 A374 75r shown   .45 .20
1433 A374 150r multi, diff. .90 .20
1434 A374 400r multi, diff. 2.25 .40
    Nos. 1432-1434 (3)   3.60 .80

Souvenir Sheet
1435 A374 1500r multi   12.00 8.50
World Cup Soccer Championships, Italy.

Family Planning
in Indonesia,
20th
Anniv. — A375

1990, June 29
1436 A375 60r brown & red   .85 .20

Natl.
Census — A376

1990, July 1
1437 A376 90r yel grn & dk grn 1.10 .20

Natl. Children's
Day — A377

1990, July 23
1438 A377 500r multicolored   1.60 .40

Souvenir Sheet

Traditional Lampung Wedding
Costumes — A378

Perf. 12½x14½
1990, June 10 **Photo.**
1439 A378 2000r multicolored 9.50 6.00
Natl. Philatelic Exhibition, Stamp World
London '90 and New Zealand '90.

Independence, 45th
Anniv. — A379

1990, Aug. 17 **Perf. 12½x13½**
1440 A379 200r Soldier raising
flag   .70 .20
1441 A379 500r Skyscraper,
highway   1.60 .45

Souvenir Sheet
1442 A379 1000r like #1441   9.50 6.00

Indonesia-Pakistan Economic &
Cultural Cooperation
Organization — A380

Designs: 400r, Woman dancing in traditional
costume, vert.

Perf. 13½x12½, 12½x13½
1990, Aug. 19 **Litho.**
1443 A380 75r multicolored   .55 .20
1444 A380 400r multicolored 1.75 .55

Asian Pacific
Postal Training
Center, 20th
Anniv. — A381

1990, Sept. 10 **Photo.** **Perf. 12½**
1445 A381 500r vio bl, bl & ultra 1.40 .45

A382

A383

1990, Sept. 14
1446 A382 200r gray, blk & org 1.25 .20
Organization of Petroleum Exporting Countries (OPEC), 30th anniv.

1990, Oct. 24
1447 A383 1000r multicolored   2.75 .85
Environmental Protection Laws, 40th anniv.

Folk Costumes Type of 1987
Traditional wedding attire from: 75r, West
Java. 100r, Central Java. 150r, Yogyakarta.
200r, East Java. 400r, Bali. 500r, West Nusa
Tenggara.

1990, Nov. 1 **Perf. 13x13½**
1448 A333 75r multicolored   .35 .20
1449 A333 100r multicolored .45 .20
1450 A333 150r multicolored .70 .20
1451 A333 200r multicolored .90 .20
1452 A333 400r multicolored 1.75 .40
1453 A333 500r multicolored 2.10 .55
    Nos. 1448-1453 (6)   6.25 1.75

A385

A386

Visit Indonesia Year 1991: Women in traditional costumes.

1991, Jan. 1 **Photo.** **Perf. 12½x13½**
1454 A385 200r multicolored .60 .20
1455 A385 500r multicolored 1.75 .60
1456 A385 1000r multicolored 3.00 .45
    Nos. 1454-1456 (3)   5.35 1.25

Souvenir Sheet
1456A A385 1500r As No.
                 1454   17.00 12.00

1991, Feb. 4 **Perf. 12½**
1457 A386 200r yel, grn & bl grn 1.40 .20
16th natl. Koran reading competition,
Jogjakarta.

Palace of
Sultan
Ternate,
the
Moluccas
A387

Design: 1000r, 2500r, Bari House, Palembang, South Sumatra.

1991, Mar. 1 **Perf. 13½x12½**
1458 A387 500r multicolored 1.10 .30
1459 A387 1000r multicolored 2.25 .55

Souvenir Sheet
1460 A387 2500r multicolored 9.50 6.00

5th Five Year Development Plan Type
of 1989

1991, Apr. 1 **Perf. 12½**
1461 A361 75r Steel mill, vert. .35 .20
1462 A361 200r Computers   .80 .20

Danger of
Smoking — A388

1991, May 31 **Photo.** **Perf. 12½**
1463 A388 90r multicolored   1.40 .20

Folk Costumes Type of 1987
Traditional wedding attire from: 100r, West
Kalimantan. 200r, Mid Kalimantan. 300r,
South Kalimantan. 400r, Southeast Sulawesi.
500r, Riau. 1000r, Irian Jaya.

1991, June 15 **Perf. 13x13½**
1464 A333 100r multicolored .30 .20
1465 A333 200r multicolored .60 .20
1466 A333 300r multicolored .90 .20
1467 A333 400r multicolored 1.40 .25
1468 A333 500r multicolored 1.75 .30
1469 A333 1000r multicolored 3.25 .65
    Nos. 1464-1469 (6)   8.20 1.80

Natl. Scouting
Jamboree,
Cibubur
A389

Monument
A390

1991, June 15 **Perf. 12½**
1470 A389 200r multicolored 1.50 .20

1991, July 6
1471 A390 200r multicolored 1.50 .20

Natl. Farmers'
Week — A391
Indonesian Chemical
Society, 4th Natl.
Congress — A392

1991, July 15
1472 A391 500r brt bl, yel & grn 1.90 .25

1991, July 28
1473 A392 400r grn, ver & dull
grn   1.90 .25
Chemindo '91.

A393

A394

1991, Aug. 24 **Photo.** **Perf. 12½**
1474 A393 300r blk, red & gray 1.75 .35
5th Junior Men's and 4th Women's Asian
Weightlifting Championships.

1991, Aug. 30
1475 A394 500r lilac & sky blue 1.90 .45
World Cup Parachuting Championships.

A395

A396

1991, Sept. 17
1476 A395 200r multicolored 1.60 .20
Indonesian Red Cross, 46th aAnniv.

1991, Oct. 6
1477 A396 300r yellow & blue 1.60 .35
Intl. Amateur Radio Union, 8th regional
conf., Bandung.

Istiqlal
(Independence)
Festival,
Jakarta — A397

1991, Oct. 15
1478 A397 200r gray, blk & ver 1.60 .20

Intl. Conference on the Great Apes — A398

Pongo pygmaeus: 200r, Sitting in tree. 500r, Walking. 1000r, 2500r, Sitting on ground.

1991, Dec. 18   Perf. 12½x13½
1479	A398	200r multicolored	.75	.20
1480	A398	500r multicolored	1.75	.55
1481	A398	1000r multicolored	3.50	1.00
		Nos. 1479-1481 (3)	6.00	1.75

Souvenir Sheet
1481A	A398	2500r multicolored	11.00	8.00

Intl. Convention on Quality Control Circles, Bali — A399

1991, Oct. 22   Perf. 12½
1482	A399	500r multicolored	2.00	.50

Automation of the Post Office — A400

200r, P.O. 500r, Mail sorting equipment.

1992, Jan. 9   Photo.   Perf. 13½x13
1483	A400	200r multicolored	.40	.20
1484	A400	500r multicolored	.95	.30

National Elections A401

1992, Feb. 10   Perf. 12½
1485	A401	75r shown	.20	.20
1486	A401	100r Ballot boxes, globe	.20	.20
1487	A401	500r Hands dropping ballots in ballot boxes	1.25	.35
		Nos. 1485-1487 (3)	1.65	.75

5th Five-year Development Plan Type of 1989

1992, Apr. 1   Photo.   Perf. 12½
1488	A361	150r Construction worker	.30	.20
1489	A361	300r Aviation technology	.65	.20

Visit Asia Year, 1992 A402

1992, Mar. 1   Perf. 13½x13
1490	A402	300r Lembah Baliem, Irian Jaya	.75	.20
1491	A402	500r Tanah Lot, Bali	1.25	.40
1492	A402	1000r Lombah Anai, Sumatra Barat	2.75	.60
		Nos. 1490-1492 (3)	4.75	1.20

Souvenir Sheet
1493	A402	3000r like #1491	10.00	8.00

Birds — A403

1992, July 1   Photo.   Perf. 12½x13½
1494	A403	100r Garrulax leucolophus	.25	.20
1495	A403	200r Dinopium javanense	.50	.20
1496	A403	400r Buceros rhinoceros	1.00	.45
1497	A403	500r Alisterus amboinensis	1.50	.55
		Nos. 1494-1497 (4)	3.25	1.40

Souvenir Sheet
1498	A403	3000r like #1494	11.00	8.00

Children's Day — A404

75r, Street scene. 100r, Children with balloons. 200r, Boating scene. 500r, Girl feeding bird.

1992, July 23   Perf. 12½
1499	A404	75r multicolored	.20	.20
1500	A404	100r multicolored	.30	.20
1501	A404	200r multicolored	.65	.20
1502	A404	500r multicolored	1.50	.75
		Nos. 1499-1502 (4)	2.65	1.35

1992 Summer Olympics, Barcelona — A405

Designs: No. 1508a, 2000r, like #1504. b, 3000r, like #1507.

1992, June 1   Perf. 12½x13½
1503	A405	75r Weight lifting	.20	.20
1504	A405	200r Badminton	.40	.20
1505	A405	300r Symbols of events	.65	.20
1506	A405	500r Women's tennis	1.10	.35
1507	A405	1000r Archery	2.10	.65
		Nos. 1503-1507 (5)	4.45	1.60

Souvenir Sheet
1508	A405	Sheet of 2, #a.-b.	13.00	9.00

ASEAN, 25th Anniv. A406

1992, Aug. 8   Perf. 13½x12½
1509	A406	200r shown	.55	.20
1510	A406	500r Flags, map	1.25	.40
1511	A406	1000r Flags on poles	2.50	.65
		Nos. 1509-1511 (3)	4.30	1.25

Flowers A407

Designs: 200r, Phalaenopsis ambilis. 500r, Rafflesia arnoldii. 1000r, 2000r, Jasminum sambae.

1992, Jan. 20   Perf. 13½x12½   Photo.
1512	A407	200r multicolored	.50	.20
1513	A407	500r multicolored	1.25	.40
1514	A407	1000r multicolored	2.25	.65
		Nos. 1512-1514 (3)	4.00	1.25

Souvenir Sheet
Perf. 13½x13
1515	A407	2000r multicolored	10.00	8.00

A408

A409

Perf. 12½x13½

1992, Sept. 6   Photo.
1516	A408	200r shown	.55	.20
1517	A408	500r Flags, emblem	1.25	.45

10th Non-Aligned Summit, Jakarta.

1992, Nov. 29   Photo.   Perf. 12½
1518	A409	200r green & blue	1.10	.30

Intl. Planned Parenthood Federation, 40th anniv.

A410   A411

Perf. 12½x13½

1992, Aug. 16   Photo.
1519	A410	200r Globe, satellite	.45	.20
1520	A410	500r Palapa satellite	1.10	.40
1521	A410	1000r Old, new telephones	2.10	.65
		Nos. 1519-1521 (3)	3.65	1.25

Satellite Communications in Indonesia, 16th anniv.

1992, Oct. 1   Perf. 12½x13½

Traditional Dances: 200r, 3000r, Tari Ngremo, Timor. 500r, Tari Gending Sriwijaya, Sumatra.

1522	A411	200r multicolored	.65	.20
1523	A411	500r multicolored	1.40	1.40

Souvenir Sheet
1524	A411	3000r like #1522	9.00	6.00

No. 1523 was withdrawn from sale on 10/5.
See Nos. 1564-1567, 1596-1600, 1628-1632, 1688-1692, 1747-1751, 1815-1820.

Antara News Agency, 55th Anniv. — A412

1992, Dec. 13   Photo.   Perf. 12½
1525	A412	500r blue & black	1.40	.20

Natl. Afforestation Campaign — A413

Perf. 13½x12½

1992, Dec. 24   Photo.
1526	A413	500r multicolored	1.40	.30

No. 1260 Surcharged

1993, Feb. 1   Photo.   Perf. 13½x12½
1527	A246	50r on 55r #1260	.75	.20

1993 General Session of the People's Consultative Assembly — A414

1993, Mar. 1   Photo.   Perf. 13½x12½
1528	A414	300r Building exterior	.50	.20
1529	A414	700r Building interior	1.25	.55

5th Five Year Development Plan Type of 1989

300r, Soldier's silhouettes over city. 700r, Immunizing children. 1000r, Runners.

1993, Apr. 1   Perf. 12½
1530	A361	300r multicolored	.40	.30
1531	A361	700r multicolored	.85	.75
1532	A361	1000r multicolored	1.25	1.00
		Nos. 1530-1532 (3)	2.50	2.05

Ornithoptera Goliath — A415

1993, Apr. 20   Photo.   Perf. 12½
1533	A415	1000r multicolored	2.25	.95

For overprint see No. 1540.

Surabaja, 700th Anniv. A416

Designs: 300r, Siege of Yamato Hotel. 700r, World Habitat Award, Surabaya skyline. 1000r, Candi Bajang Ratu, natl. monument.

Perf. 13½x12½

1993, May 29   Photo.
1534	A416	300r multicolored	.50	.40
1535	A416	700r multicolored	1.10	.80
1536	A416	1000r multicolored	1.75	1.25
		Nos. 1534-1536 (3)	3.35	2.45

For overprints see Nos. 1538-1539, 1541.

Nos. 1533-1536 Ovptd. in Red

Indopex '93 — A417

1993　**Perfs. as Before**
1538 A416 300r on #1534 .50 .20
1539 A416 700r on #1535 1.40 .40
1540 A415 1000r on #1533 2.25 .80
1541 A416 1000r on #1536 2.00 .60
　Nos. 1538-1541 (4) 6.15 2.00
Souvenir Sheet
Perf. 13½x12½
1542 A417 3500r multicolored 6.00 4.50

Location of overprint varies. Issued: No. 1540, Apr. 20; others, May 29.

Environmental Protection — A418

Flowers: Nos. 1543a, 1545a, Jasminum sambac. No. 1543b, Phalaenopsis amabilis. No. 1543c, Rafflesia arnoldi.
Wildlife: Nos. 1544a, 1545b, Varanus komodoensis. No. 1544b, Scleropages formasus. No. 1544c, Spizaetus bartelsi.

Perf. 12½x13½
1993, June 5　**Photo.**
1543 A418 300r Tripytych, #a.-c. 2.50 .85
1544 A418 700r Tripytych, #a.-c. 5.75 1.90
Souvenir Sheet of 2
1545 A418 1500r #a.-b. 8.25 5.00

1st World Community Development Camp — A419

Designs: 300r, Boy scouts working on road. 700r, Pres. Suharto shaking hands with scout.

Perf. 13½x12½
1993, July 27　**Photo.**
1546 A419 300r multicolored .50 .20
1547 A419 700r multicolored 1.25 .45

Papilio Blumei — A420　　Armed Forces Day — A421

Perf. 12½x13½
1993, Aug. 24　**Photo.**
1548 A420 700r multicolored 1.50 .60
Souvenir Sheets
1549 A420 3000r multicolored 8.00 6.00
1550 A420 3000r multicolored 8.00 6.00

Inscription at top of No. 1549 is like that on No. 1548. No. 1550 contains a stamp inscribed "1993," a se-tenant label and Bangkok '93 Philatelic Exhibition inscription in sheet margin.

1993, Oct. 5　**Perf. 12½**
1551 A421 300r Soedirman .55 .20
1552 A421 300r Oerip
　　　 Soemohardjo .55 .20
　a.　 Pair, #1551-1552 1.10 .45

Tourism — A422　　13th Natl. Sports Week — A423

300r, 3000r, Waterfall. 700r, Cave formations. 1000r, Dormant volcanic crater, horiz.

Perf. 12½x13½, 13½x12½
1993, Oct. 4
1553 A422 300r multicolored .45 .40
1554 A422 700r multicolored .95 .85
1555 A422 1000r multicolored 1.60 1.25
　Nos. 1553-1555 (3) 3.00 2.50
Souvenir Sheet
1556 A422 3000r multicolored 5.50 4.00

1993, Sept. 9　**Perf. 12½x13½**
1557 A423 150r Swimming .25 .20
1558 A423 300r Cycling .50 .30
1559 A423 700r Mascot 1.10 .70
1560 A423 1000r High jump 1.60 1.00
　Nos. 1557-1560 (4) 3.45 2.20
Souvenir Sheet
1561 A423 3500r like No. 1560 7.00 4.50

Flora and Fauna — A424

Designs: a, Michelia champaca. b, Cananga odorata. c, Copsychus pyrropygus. d, Gracula religiosa robusta.

1993, Nov. 5　**Photo.**　**Perf. 12½x13½**
1562 A424 300r Block of 4, #a.-d. 5.00 3.50

Migratory Farm Workers — A425

1993, Dec. 4　**Perf. 12½**
1563 A425 700r Field workers 1.00 .70

Traditional Dance Type of 1992

Dance and region: 300r, Gending Sriwijaya, South Sumatra. 700r, Tempayan, West Kalimantan. 1000r, 3500r, Tifa, Irian Jaya.

1993, Dec. 22　**Perf. 12½x13½**
1564 A411 300r multicolored .75 .20
1565 A411 700r multicolored 1.40 .40
1566 A411 1000r multicolored 2.00 .55
　Nos. 1564-1566 (3) 4.15 1.15
Souvenir Sheet
1567 A411 3500r multicolored 6.00 4.50

Intl. Year of the Family A426

1994, Mar. 1　**Photo.**　**Perf. 13½x12½**
1568 A426 300r multicolored .75 .20

Indonesian Postage Stamps, 130th Anniv. — A427

Design: 700r, Netherlands Indies #B7, #N7, Indonesia #B214.

1994, Apr. 1　**Perf. 12½**
1569 A427 700r multicolored 1.25 .55
Souvenir Sheet
Imperf
1569A A427 3500r like #1569 7.00 4.00
　　PHILAKOREA '94 (#1569A).

6th Five Year Development Plan — A428

Buddhist dieties and: 100r, Professional women. 700r, Education. 2000r, Medical care for children.

1994, Apr. 1　**Perf. 12½**
1570 A428 100r multicolored .30 .20
1571 A428 700r multicolored 1.25 .70
1572 A428 2000r multicolored 4.00 2.00
　Nos. 1570-1572 (3) 5.55 2.90

Tropical Fish A429

Designs: 300r, Telmatherina ladigesi. 700r, 3500r, Melanotaenia boesemani.

1994, Apr. 20　**Photo.**　**Perf. 13**
1573 A429 300r multicolored .80 .20
1574 A429 700r multicolored 1.60 .70
Souvenir Sheet
1575 A429 3500r multicolored 7.00 4.00

No. 1575 has continuous design.

Intl. Federation of Red Cross & Red Crescent Societies, 75th Anniv. — A429a

1994, May 5　**Perf. 12½x13**
1575A A429a 300r multicolored .90 .20

Second Asian and Pacific Ministerial Conference on Women, Jakarta — A430

1994, June 13　**Perf. 13½x12½**
1576 A430 700r multicolored 1.40 .45

1994 World Cup Soccer Championships, US: 150r, Player dribbling ball, vert. 300r, Mascot chasing ball, vert. 700r, 1994 Tournament emblem. 1000r, Ball in net. 3500r, Soccer ball in net.

1994, June 17　**Perf. 12½x13½**
1577 A431 150r multicolored .25 .20
1578 A431 300r multicolored .60 .20
Perf. 13½x12½
1579 A431 700r multicolored 1.40 .50
1580 A431 1000r multicolored 1.90 .65
　Nos. 1577-1580 (4) 4.15 1.55
Souvenir Sheet
1581 A431 3500r multicolored 6.50 4.00

Thomas & Uber Cups — A432

Designs: a, Uber Cup. b, Thomas Cup.

1994, June 22　**Perf. 12½**
1582 A432 300r Pair, #a.-b. 1.25 .55
Souvenir Sheet of 2
1583 A432 1750r #a.-b. 6.00 3.50

A433　　　　　　A434

Perf. 12½x13½
1994, July 27　**Photo.**
1584 A433 700r multicolored 1.25 .50
Human Rights Day.

Perf. 13]x13½
1994, Aug. 19　**Photo.**
1585 A434 300r Brown pottery
　　　 vase .75 .25
1586 A434 700r Blue & white
　　　 vase 1.75 .65

Indonesia-Pakistan Economic & Cultural Cooperation Organization.
See Pakistan Nos. 822-823.

Bogoriense Zoological Museum, Cent. — A435

700r, Skeleton of Javan rhinoceros. 1000r, 3500r, Skeleton of blue whale.

1994, Aug. 20　**Perf. 13½x13**
1587 A435 700r multicolored 1.50 .55
Size: 80x22mm
1588 A435 1000r multicolored 3.00 1.20
Souvenir Sheet
Perf. 13x13½
1588A A435 3500r multicolored 7.50 4.75

12th Asian Games, Hiroshima 1994 A436

1994, Oct. 2   Litho.   Perf. 13½x13
1589 A436 300r Mascots   .70 .25
1590 A436 700r Hurdlers   1.50 .70

Bakosurtanal, 25th Anniv. — A437

1994, Oct. 17   Litho.   Perf. 13½x13
1591 A437 700r multicolored   1.50 .50

Flora & Fauna — A438

Designs: a, Morus macroura. b, Oncosperma tigillaria. c, Eucalyptus urophylla. d, Phalaenopsis amabilis. e, Pometia pinnata. f, Argusianus argus. g, Loriculus pusillus. h, Philemon buceroides. i, Alisterus amboinensis. j, Seleucidis melanoleuca.
3500r, Philemon buceroides, diff.

1994, Nov. 5   Photo.   Perf. 12½x13½
1592 A438 150r Block or strip
          of 10, #a.-j.   10.00 5.00
Souvenir Sheet
1593 A438 3500r multicolored   8.00 4.00
  a.   With added inscription in blue 12.00

Inscription in sheet margin of No. 1593a contains emblem and "PRIMERA '95." Issued: No. 1593a, 8/21/95.
See Nos. 1622, 1680-1682, 1737-1738, 1812-1814.

Asian-Pacific Economic Cooperation Summit (APEC '94) — A439

Design: 700r, Presidential retreat, Bogor.

1994, Nov. 15   Perf. 13½X13
1594 A439 700r multicolored   1.50 .50

For overprint see No. 1616A.

ICAO, 50th Anniv. A440

1994, Dec. 7
1595 A440 700r multicolored   1.75 .50

Traditional Dance Type of 1992

Dance, region: 150r, Mengaup, Jambi. 300r, Mask, West Java. 700r, Anging Mamiri, South Sulawesi. 1000r, Pisok, North Sulawesi. 2000r, Bidu, East Nusa Tenggara. 3500r, Mask dance, West Java.

1994, Dec. 27   Perf. 12½x13½
1596 A411 150r multicolored   .25 .20
1597 A411 300r multicolored   .60 .20
1598 A411 700r multicolored 1.40 .50
1599 A411 1000r multicolored 1.90 .70

1600 A411 2000r multicolored   4.00 1.50
  a.   Bklt. pane, 2 ea #1596-1600 19.00
        Complete booklet, #1600a   19.00
      Nos. 1596-1600 (5)   8.15 3.10
Souvenir Sheet
1601 A411 3500r multicolored   7.00 5.75

World Tourism Organization, 20th Anniv. — A441

Designs: 300r, Yogyakarta Palace. 700r, Floating market. 1000r, Pasola Sumba ritual.

1995, Jan. 2   Perf. 13½x12½
1602 A441 300r multicolored   .50 .25
1603 A441 700r multicolored 1.25 .65
1604 A441 1000r multicolored 1.40 .85
      Nos. 1602-1604 (3)   3.15 1.75

Indonesian Children, First Lady & Pres. Suharto A442

Perf. 13½x12½
1995, Mar. 11   Photo.
1605 A442 700r multicolored   1.50 .65

6th Five Year Development Plan — A443

Designs: 300r, Letter from King of Klunglung, 18th-19th cent. 700r, Carrier pigeon mascot of natl. letter writing campaign.

1995, Apr. 1   Photo.   Perf. 12½
1606 A443 300r multicolored   .60 .25
1607 A443 700r multicolored 1.40 .70

4th Intl. Bamboo Conference — A444

Designs: 300r, Schizostachyum brachycladum. 700r, Dendrocalamus asper.

Perf. 12½x13½
1995, June 19   Photo.
1608 A444 300r multicolored   .60 .25
1609 A444 700r multicolored 1.40 .70

First Flight of N250 Turboprop Commuter Airplane A445

1995, Aug. 10   Perf. 13½x12½
1610 A445 700r multicolored   1.40 .65

Independence, 50th Anniv. — A446

1995, Aug. 17
1611 A446 300r Anniv. emblem   .55 .25

1612 A446 700r Boy, natl. flag 1.50 .70
Souvenir Sheet
1612A A446 2500r like No. 1612 6.00 4.00

JAKARTA '95, 8th Asian Intl. Philatelic Exhibition A447

Scenes in Jakarta: 300r, Kota Intan Drawbridge. 700r, Fatahillah Historical Museum.

1995, Aug. 19
1613 A447 300r multicolored   .60 .25
1614 A447 700r multicolored 1.40 .70

No. 1613 exists in 7 souvenir sheets of 1, each with different color margins. Sold at the 2nd International Stamp Exhibition in Jakarta. Value, set of 7 sheets $125.

Sail Indonesia '95 A448

1995, Aug. 19
1615 A448 700r multicolored   1.25 .60
Souvenir Sheet
1616 A448 2500r multicolored   6.50 4.00

No. 1594 Overprinted "PRIMERA '95" in Blue
1995, Aug. 21   Photo.   Perf. 13½x13
1616A A439 700r on #1594   3.00 3.00

Istiqlal (Independence) Festival II 1995, Jakarta — A449

1995, Sept. 23   Perf. 12½x13½
1617 A449 700r multicolored   1.25 .60

Takeover of Post, Telegraph, & Telephone Headquarters, 50th Anniv. — A450

1995, Sept. 27   Perf. 13½x12½
1618 A450 700r multicolored   1.25 .60

FAO, 50th Anniv. — A451   UN, 50th Anniv. — A452

1995, Oct. 16   Perf. 12½x13½
1619 A451 700r multicolored   1.25 .60

1995, Oct. 24   Perf. 12½

UN emblem, "50," and: 300r, Flags of nations. 700r, Rainbow over earth.

1620 A452 300r multicolored   .60 .25
1621 A452 700r multicolored 1.40 .70

Flora and Fauna Type of 1994

Designs: a, Cyrtostachys renda. b, Panthera tigris sumatrae. c, Bouea macrophylla. d, Rhinoceros sondaicus. e, Santalum album. f, Varanus komodoensis. g, Diospyros celebica. h, Macrocephalon maleo. i, Nephleium ramboutan-ake. j, Polyplectron schleiermacheri.
2500r, Panthera tigris sumatrae.

1995, Nov. 5   Photo.   Perf. 12½x13½
1622 A438 150r Block of 10,
          #a.-j.   7.50 3.25
Souvenir Sheet
1623 A438 2500r multicolored 13.00 8.00

1995 Aga Khan Award for Architecture — A453

Designs: 300r, Masjid Agung, Kraton Yogyakarta. 700r, Kraton Surakarta.

1995, Nov. 23   Perf. 13½x13
1624 A453 300r multicolored   .60 .25
1625 A453 700r multicolored 1.40 .70

Sir Rowland Hill (1795-1879) — A454

300r, Hill, letter carriers on motorcycles. 700r, Hill, Indonesian postal service logo.

1995, Dec. 3   Perf. 13½x12½
1626 A454 300r multicolored   .60 .25
1627 A454 700r multicolored 1.40 .70

Traditional Dance Type of 1992

Dance and region: 150r, Nguri, West Nusa Tenggara. 300r, Muli Betanggai, Lampung. 700r, Mutiara, Maluku. 1000r, Gantar, East Kalimantan. 2500r, Tari Nguri, Nusa Tenggara Barrat.

1995, Dec. 27   Perf. 12½x13½
1628 A411 150r multicolored   .25 .25
1629 A411 300r multicolored   .60 .25
1630 A411 700r multicolored 1.40 .60
1631 A411 1000r multicolored 1.90 .80
      Nos. 1628-1631 (4)   4.15 1.90
Souvenir Sheet
1632 A411 2500r multicolored   4.50 3.00

1996 Economic Census — A455

Design: 300r, Economic sectors, vert.

1996, Jan. 2   Perf. 12½
1633 A455 300r multicolored   .60 .25
1634 A455 700r multicolored 1.40 .70

Greetings Stamps — A456

Various flowers.

1996, Feb. 1   Photo.   Perf. 12½
1635 A456 150r multicolored   .25 .20
1636 A456 300r multicolored   .50 .25
1637 A456 700r multicolored 1.25 .55
      Nos. 1635-1637 (3)   2.00 1.00

See Nos. 1657-1659.

PWI Journalists' Assoc., 50th Anniv. — A457

Designs: 300r, RM Soemanang Soeriowinoto. 700r, Djamaluddin Adinegoro.

1996, Feb. 9
1638	A457	300r multicolored	.45	.25
1639	A457	700r multicolored	1.25	.55

Australian Spotted Cuscus — A458

Design: Nos. 1640, 1642a, shown. Nos. 1641, 1642b, Indonesian bear cuscus.

1996, Mar. 22   Photo.   Perf. 13x13½
1640	A458	300r multicolored	.60	.40
1641	A458	300r multicolored	.60	.40
a.		Pair, Nos. 1640-1641	1.25	1.25
b.		Sheet of 5 #1641a	35.00	17.50

Souvenir Sheet
1642	A458	1250r Sheet of 2, #a.-b.	4.50	2.50
c.		#1642 with added inscription, ovpt.	10.00	2.75

No. 1642c has black CHINA '96 exhibition emblem in upper right corner. The bottom sheet margin contains gold overprint: "CHINA '96 - 9th Asian International Philatelic Exhibition" in both Chinese and English.
No. 1641b exists folded and affixed to a booklet cover. Value, $15.
See Australia Nos. 1489-1490.

A459

Launching of Palapa C Satellite — A460

1996, Jan. 31   Perf. 13
1643	A459	300r multicolored	.65	.25

Perf. 12½
1644	A460	700r multicolored	1.60	.60

Indonesia '96, World Junior Philatelic Exhibition A461

Designs: 300r, No. 1647a, Building. 700r, No. 1647b, Decorated sun umbrellas.

1996, Mar. 21   Perf. 13½x13
1645	A461	300r multicolored	.45	.25
1646	A461	700r multicolored	1.25	.55

Souvenir Sheet of 2
1647	A461	1250r #a.-b.	6.50	3.25

No. 1647 exists imperf with different color margins. A souvenir sheet containing No. 1645-1646 and progressive color proofs of No. 1646 exists.

Education Day A462

Children's drawings: 150r, Teachers, students with outstretched arms. 300r, Children carrying books to school. 700r, Classroom instruction.

1996, May 2   Photo.   Perf. 13½x13
1648	A462	150r multicolored	.25	.25
1649	A462	300r multicolored	.50	.50
1650	A462	700r multicolored	1.40	1.00
		Nos. 1648-1650 (3)	2.15	1.75

Natl. Youth Kirab A463

1996, June 8
1651	A463	300r shown	.60	.25
1652	A463	700r Holding flag, emblem	1.40	.70

1996 Summer Olympics, Atlanta A464

1996, May 15
1653	A464	300r Archery	.50	.30
1654	A464	700r Weight lifting	1.25	.60
1655	A464	1000r Badminton	1.60	1.00
		Nos. 1653-1655 (3)	3.35	1.90

Souvenir Sheet
1656	A464	2500r like #1653	4.50	2.50

No. 1656 is a continuous design.

Greetings Type of 1996

1996, Apr. 15   Photo.   Perf. 12½
1657	A456	150r Roses	.25	.20
1658	A456	300r Orchids	.50	.25
1659	A456	700r Chrysanthemums	1.40	.55
		Nos. 1657-1659 (3)	2.15	1.00

Maritime and Aviation Year — A465

300r, N-2130 aircraft, control tower at Soekarno-Hatta Airport. 700r, Inter-island passenger ship.

1996, June 22
1660	A465	300r multicolored	.50	.25
1661	A465	700r multicolored	1.25	.90

1996 Natl. Scout Jamboree A466

Designs: a, Climbing rope. b, Sliding down rope. c, Girls at bottom of ropes. d, Girls assembling wood and rope ladder. e, Riding unicycle, eagle emblem, boys building scaffolding. f, Girls building scaffolding, campground. g, Two boys with project. h, Woman seated at control center.
No. 1662I, like #1662a-1662d. No. 1662J, like #1662e-1662h.

1996, June 26
1662	A466	150r Block of 8, #a.-h.	3.75	1.75

Souvenir Sheets
1662I	A466	1250d multicolored	4.25	2.25
1662J	A466	1250d multicolored	4.25	2.25

Istanbul '96 (#1662I-1662J). Nos. 1662I-1662J each contain one 64x48mm stamp. Nos. 1662a-1662d, 1663e-1662h are continuous designs.

Bank BNI, 50th Anniv. A467

1996, July 5
1663	A467	300r shown	.45	.25
1664	A467	700r Sailing ship	1.25	.55

UNICEF, 50th Anniv. A468

1996, July 23   Perf. 13½x13
1665	A468	300r Child reading	.45	.30
1666	A468	700r Two children	1.10	.60
1667	A468	1000r Three children	1.50	.90
		Nos. 1665-1667 (3)	3.05	1.80

Ibu Tien Suharto (1923-96) First Lady — A469

1996, Aug. 5   Perf. 12½x13½
1668	A469	700r multicolored	1.25	.55

Souvenir Sheet
1669	A469	2500r like #1668	4.00	2.00

No. 1669 is a continuous design.

14th Natl. Sports Week, Jakarta A470

Perf. 13½x12½
1996, Sept. 2   Photo.
1670	A470	300r Softball	.50	.30
1671	A470	700r Field hockey	1.25	.60
1672	A470	1000r Basketball	1.60	.90
		Nos. 1670-1672 (3)	3.35	1.80

World Wildlife Fund A471

Rhinoceros sondaicus: a, #1674a, Adult. b, Adult with young. Dicerorhinus sumatrensis: c, Up close. d, #1674b, Adult.

1996, Oct. 2   Photo.   Perf. 13½x13
1673	A471	300r Block of 4, #a.-d.	2.75	1.75
e.		Souvenir sheet, 2 #1673	7.25	4.00
f.		As "e," ovptd. in sheet margin	5.75	3.75

Overprint in margin of No. 1673f reads: "Bursa Filateli SEA Games XIX / Jakarta, 11-19 Oktober 1997" in gold.
1674	A471	1500r Sheet of 2, #a.-b.	6.75	4.00

Greetings Stamps — A472

Bouquets of various flowers.

1996, Oct. 15   Photo.   Perf. 12½
Background Colors
1675	A472	150r yellow & blue	.25	.20
1676	A472	300r yellow & green	.50	.25
1677	A472	700r pink & blue	1.25	.55
		Nos. 1675-1677 (3)	2.00	1.00

Financial Day, 50th Anniv. A473

1996, Oct. 30   Perf. 13½x12½
1678	A473	700r multicolored	2.00	.55

Flora & Fauna Type of 1994

Fauna: No. 1680: a, Aceros cassidix. b, Orcaella brevirostris. c, Oriolus chinensis. d, Helarctos malayanus. e, Leucopsar rothschildi.
Flora: f, Borassus flabellifer. g, Coelogyne pandurata. h, Michelia alba. i, Amorphophallus titanum. j, Dysoxylum densiflorum.
No. 1681, Like #1680e. No. 1682, Like #1680g.

1996, Nov. 5   Litho.   Perf. 12½x13½
1680	A438	300r Block or strip of 10, #a.-j.	6.50	3.25
a.-j.		Any single	.65	.30

Souvenir Sheets
1681	A438	1250r multicolored	3.75	2.00
1682	A438	1250r multicolored	3.75	2.00

Souvenir Sheet

Aceros Cassidix — A474

Perf. 12½x13½
1996, Dec. 14   Photo.
1683	A474	2000r multicolored	22.50	22.50

ASEANPEX '96.

Scenes from Timor A475

Designs: 300r, Deep sea diving. 700r, Sailing ships entering harbor, 18th cent.

1996-97   Perf. 13½x12½
1684	A475	300r multicolored	.60	.30
1685	A475	700r multicolored	1.75	.60

Souvenir Sheet
1685A	A475	2000d like #1685	5.50	2.75

Hong Kong '97 (#1685A).
Issued: #1686-1687, 12/18/96; #1685A, 2/12/97.

Foster
Parents
A476

150r, Children at playground, vert. 300r,
Children, adult's hand holding picture of girl.

Perf. 12½x13½, 13½x12½

1996, Dec. 20
1686	A476	150r multicolored	.30	.20
1687	A476	300r multicolored	.60	.25

Traditional Dance Type of 1992

Dance, region: 150r, Tari Baksa Kembang,
Kalimantan Selatan. 300r, 2000r, Tari
Ngarojeng, Jakarta. 700r, Tari Rampai, Aceh.
1000r, Tari Boituka, Timor.

1996, Dec. 27   **Perf. 12½x13½**
1688	A411	150r multicolored	.50	.20
1689	A411	300r multicolored	.50	.25
1690	A411	700r multicolored	1.10	.55
1691	A411	1000r multicolored	1.75	.80
		Nos. 1688-1691 (4)	3.85	1.80

Souvenir Sheet
1692	A411	2000r multicolored	4.00	2.00

Telecommunications Year — A477

Designs: 300r, Satellite dish, men at computers, map. 700r, Telephone keypad, woman
using telephone, satellite in earth orbit.

1997, Jan. 1   **Perf. 13½x12½**
1693	A477	300r multicolored	.50	.25
1694	A477	700r multicolored	1.40	.70

Greetings
Stamps — A478

Designs: No. 1695, Heart, ribbon. No. 1696,
Children, "Happy Birthday."

1997, Jan. 15   **Perf. 12½**
1695	A478	600r multicolored	.95	.45
1696	A478	600r multicolored	.95	.45

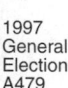

1997
General
Election
A479

Ballot box and: 300r, Means of transportation.
700r, Indonesian Archipelago, House of Representatives Building. 1000r, Map, symbols of
development.

1997, Feb. 3   **Perf. 13½x13**
1697	A479	300r multicolored	.45	.30
1698	A479	700r multicolored	1.40	.60
1699	A479	1000r multicolored	1.75	.90
		Nos. 1697-1699 (3)	3.60	1.80

Birth of Indonesia's 200-millionth
Citizen — A480

Perf. 13½x12½

1997, Mar. 24   **Litho.**
1700	A480	700r Pres. Suharto, baby	1.25	.55

A481

A482

Indonesian Philatelists Assoc., 75th Anniv.:
300r, Youth examining stamps, #1672. 700r,
Magnifying glass, #1660, #1592h, #1580.

1997, Mar. 29   **Perf. 12½x13½**
1701	A481	300r multicolored	.60	.30
1702	A481	700r multicolored	1.50	.75

1997, Apr. 30   Litho.   Perf. 13x13½

Indonesian Artists: 300r, Wage Rudolf
Soepratman (1903-38), composer, violinist.
700r, Usmar Ismail (1921-71), film pioneer,
director. 1000r, Affandi (1907-90), painter.

1703	A482	300r multicolored	.50	.30
1704	A482	700r multicolored	1.25	.60
1705	A482	1000r multicolored	1.75	.90
b.		Sheet, 3 each #1703-1705 + label	15.00	7.00
		Nos. 1703-1705 (3)	3.50	1.80

Souvenir Sheet
1705A	A482	2000r like #1705	3.00	1.50

Indonesia
2000
A483

Gemstones: 300r, Picture jasper. 700r,
Chrysocolla. 1000r, Geode. 2000r, Banded
agate.

1997, May 20   Litho.   Perf. 13½x13
1706	A483	300r multicolored	.55	.30
1707	A483	700r multicolored	1.40	.60
1708	A483	1000r multicolored	2.00	.90
a.		Sheet, 3 each #1706-1708 + label	10.00	4.75
b.		As "a," control No. in margin	17.50	8.75
		Nos. 1706-1708 (3)	3.95	1.80

Souvenir Sheet
1709	A483	2000r multicolored	3.00	.85
a.		Control No. in margin	4.75	2.50

Nos. 1708b, 1709a promote INDONESIA
2000, Jakarta, Aug. 15-21, 2000. Nos. 1708a-
1709 and 1708b-1709a were issued in presentation packs with certificate of authenticity.
See Nos. 1764-1767A, 1848-1851, 1851A,
1888-1891.

A484

1997, May 31   Photo.   Perf. 12½
1710	A484	1000r multicolored	1.75	.80

World Day to Stop Smoking.

World Environment
Day — A485

1997, June 5   Litho.   Perf. 13x13½

Various marine life of the coral reefs.
1711	A485	150r multicolored	.45	.20
1712	A485	300r multicolored	.55	.25
1713	A485	700r multicolored	1.25	.55
		Nos. 1711-1713 (3)	2.25	1.00

Souvenir Sheet
1714	A485	2000r multicolored	5.50	2.50

ASEAN,
30th
Anniv.
A486

300r, Hands reaching out to each other.
700r, Rice stalks arranged to form number 30,
globe.

1997, Aug. 8   Litho.   Perf. 13½x13
1715	A486	300r multicolored	.45	.25
1716	A486	700r multicolored	1.25	.60

19th Southeast
Asia Games,
Jakarta — A487

#1717, Logo, "Hanoman" mascot. #1718,
Runner carrying torch, flags of participating
nations, logo. #1719, Runner, track, discus
thrower. #1720, Hurdler, runners.

1997, Sept. 9   Litho.   Perf. 12½
1717	A487	300r multicolored	.45	.25
1718	A487	300r multicolored	.45	.25
a.		Pair, #1717-1718	.90	.50
1719	A487	700r multicolored	1.25	.50
1720	A487	700r multicolored	1.25	.50
a.		Pair, #1719-1720	2.50	1.00
b.		Bklt. pane, 2 ea #1717-1720	7.00	
		Complete booklet, 1 #1720b	7.00	
		Nos. 1717-1720 (4)	3.40	1.50

Transportation — A488

1997, Sept. 17
1721	A488	300r Buses, ox cart	.45	.25
1722	A488	300r Trains	.45	.25
a.		Pair, #1721-1722	.90	.50
1723	A488	700r Ships	1.25	.50
1724	A488	700r Airplanes	1.25	.50
a.		Pair, #1723-1724	2.50	1.00
		Nos. 1721-1724 (4)	3.40	1.50

Souvenir Sheet

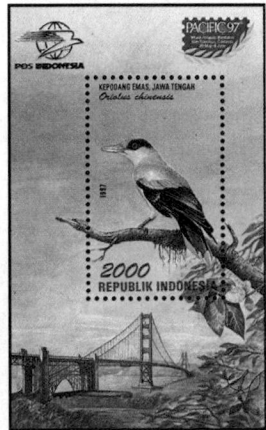

Oriolus Chinensis — A489

1997, May 29   Perf. 12½x13½
1725	A489	2000r multicolored	6.50	3.25
		PACIFIC 97.		

Nusantara
Royal
Palace
Festival
A490

Royal carriages: 300r, Singa Baraong
wooden carriage, 1549, with carving of mythical animal. 700r, Paksi Naga Liman carriage,
phoenix-like bird.

1997, July 1   Litho.   Perf. 13½x12½
1726	A490	300r multicolored	.45	.25
1727	A490	700r multicolored	1.25	.50

18th Natl. Koran Reading
Contest — A491

Designs: 300r, Decorated roof peaks, windows. 700r, Al-Ikhsaniah Mosque.

1997, July 9   **Perf. 12½**
1728	A491	300r multicolored	.45	.25
1729	A491	700r multicolored	1.25	.50

Indonesian Membership in UPU, 50th
Anniv. — A492

Emblem of UPU and: 300r, Mas Soeharto.
700r, Heinrich von Stephan.

1997, Sept. 27   Litho.   Perf. 13½x13
1730	A492	300r multicolored	.45	.25
1731	A492	700r multicolored	1.25	.50

1997-98 General Session of People's
Consultative Assembly — A493

1997, Oct. 1   **Perf. 12½**
1732	A493	700r multicolored	1.10	.50

Indonesian
Armed
Forces
Day
A494

Designs: a, ABRI Village Program. b, Jales-
veva Jayamahe Monument. c, Blue Falcon
Flight Demonstration Team. d, Police Fast
Reaction Unit.

1997, Oct. 5   **Perf. 13½x12½**
1733	A494	300r Block of 4, #a.-d.	2.00	1.00

Flora and Fauna Type of 1994

Fauna: No. 1737: a, Chitala lopis. b, Haliastur indus. c, Rhinoplax vigil. d, Cervus
timornsis. e, Bubalus depressicornis.
Flora: f, Lansium domesticum. g, Salacca
zalacca. h, Shorea stenoptera. i, Diospyros
macrophylla. j, Diplocaulobium utile.
#1738: a, Shorea stenoptera. b, Haliastur
indus.

1997, Nov. 5   **Perf. 12½x13½**
1737	A438	300r Block of 10	5.00	2.50
a.-j.		Any single	.50	.25

Souvenir Sheet
1738	A438	1250r Sheet of 2, #a.- b.	4.00	2.00

A495

Indonesian
Cooperatives
Day — A496

Designs: No. 1739, Cooperatives Monument, Tasikmalaya. No. 1740, Cooperatives Monument, Jakarta. No. 1741, Adult taking child's hand. No. 1742, Globe, movement towards globalization. No. 1743, Dr. Mohammad Hatta, Pres. Suharto.

1997, July 12 Litho. Perf. 12½x13½
1739 A495 150r multicolored .40 .20
1740 A495 150r multicolored .40 .20
a. Pair, #1739-1740 .80 .40
1741 A495 300r multicolored .50 .25
1742 A495 300r multicolored .50 .25
a. Pair, #1741-1742 1.00 .50
Perf. 12½
1743 A496 700r multicolored 1.40 .60
Nos. 1739-1743 (5) 3.20 1.50

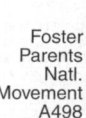

ASCOPE '97 (Asian Council on Petroleum) A497

a, LNG tanker. b. Petroleum trucks. c, Drilling rig, pumping wells. d, Refinery.

1997, Nov. 24 Perf. 13½x12½
1744 A497 300r Block of 4, #a.-d. 1.75 .90

Foster Parents Natl. Movement A498

1997, Dec. 20 Photo.
1745 A498 700r multicolored .80 .40

Family Welfare Movement, 25th Anniv. A499

1997, Dec. 27 Litho.
1746 A499 700r multicolored .80 .45

Traditional Dance Type of 1992

Dance, region: 150r, Mopuputi Cengke (clove picking), Central Sulawesi. 300r, Mandau Talawang Nyai Balau, Central Kalimantan. 600r, 200r, Gambyong, Central Java. 700r, Cawan (bowl,) North Sumatra. 1000r, Legong Keraton, Bali.

1997, Dec. 27
1747 A411 150r multicolored .35 .20
1748 A411 300r multicolored .35 .25
1749 A411 600r multicolored .70 .40
1750 A411 700r multicolored .85 .45
1751 A411 1000r multicolored 1.25 .60
Nos. 1747-1751 (5) 3.50 1.90
Souvenir Sheet
Perf. 12½x13½
1752 A411 2000r multicolored 3.25 1.60
No. 1752 is a continuous design.

Souvenir Sheet

Sulawesi Selatan — A500

1997, Oct. 11 Litho. Perf. 13½x12½
1753 A500 2000r multicolored 3.50 1.75
Makasser '97 National Philatelic Exhibition.

Year of Art and Culture 1998 — A501

Designs: 300r, Erau Festival, East Kalimantan. 700r, Tabot Festival, Bengkulu.

1998, Jan. 1 Litho. Perf. 12½
1754 A501 300r multicolored .35 .20
1755 A501 700r multicolored .90 .25

Indonesian Folktales A502

Folktale, region — No. 1759; a-e, Malin Kundang, West Sumatra. f-j: Sangkuriang, West Java. k-o, Roro Jonggrang, Central Java. p-t: Tengger, East Java. Each horizontal strip of 5 has continuous design. 2500r, Kasodo Ceremony, Tenegger, East Java.

1998, Feb. 2 Perf. 13½x12½
1759 Sheet of 20 7.50 4.00
a.-t. A502 300r Any single .35 .20
Souvenir Sheet
1760 A502 2500r like #1759e 2.75 1.50
See Nos. 1828-1829, 1886-1887, 1929-1930.

Presidential Palaces — A503

Designs: a, Jakarta. b, Bogor. c, Cipanas. d, Yogyakarta. e, Tampak Siring.

1998, Apr. 1
1761 A503 300r Strip of 5, #a.-e. 1.25 .65

World Health Organization, 50th Anniv. — A504

Designs: 300r, Pregnant woman, man, vert. 700r, Woman holding baby.

1998, Apr. 7 Litho. Perf. 12½
1762 A504 300r multicolored .30 .20
1763 A504 700r multicolored .75 .40

Indonesia 2000 Type of 1997

Gemstones: 300r, Chrysopal. 700r, Tektite. 1000r, Amethyst. #1767, Petrified wood. #1767A, opal.

1998, May 20 Perf. 13½x12½
1764 A483 300r multicolored .40 .20
1765 A483 700r multicolored .40 .20
1766 A483 1000r multicolored .40 .30
a. Sheet, 3 each #1764-1766 + label 5.00 2.50
Nos. 1764-1766 (3) 1.20 .70
Souvenir Sheets
1767 A483 2500r multicolored 2.00 1.00
Perf. 13½x14
1767A A483 2500r multicolored 6.00 3.50
b. Sheet, 2 each, #1764-1766, 1 each #1767, 1767A 18.00 16.00

Nos. 1767A, 1767Ab were issued in presentation packs with control numbers printed in margin and certificate of authenticity. No. 1767A sold for 10,000r. No. 1767Ab sold for 25,000r.

1998 World Cup Soccer Championships, France — A505

Young boys playing soccer in Indonesia: 300r, Outside school, boy on bicycle. 700r, In neighborhood lot. 1000r, 2500r, In rural area.

1998, June 1
1768 A505 300r multicolored .30 .20
1769 A505 700r multicolored .70 .35
1770 A505 1000r multicolored 1.00 .45
Nos. 1768-1770 (3) 2.00 1.00
Souvenir Sheet
1771 A505 2500r multicolored 2.50 2.50

World Environment Day — A506

Trees along river bank, denomination at: No. 1772, lower right. No. 1773, lower left.

1998, June 5
1772 A506 700r multicolored .70 .35
1773 A506 700r multicolored .70 .35
a. Pair, #1772-1773 1.40 .70

Souvenir Sheet

Juvalux '98, World Philatelic Exhibition, Luxembourg — A507

1998, June 18 Perf. 12½x13½
1774 A507 5000r Felis viverrina 6.00 3.00

World Day to Fight Drug Abuse and Illicit Drug Trafficking — A508

Cartoons depicting how to say no to drugs.

1998, June 26
1775 A508 700r red & multi .70 .35
1776 A508 700r yellow & multi .70 .35
a. Pair, #1775-1776 1.40 .70
b. Tete beche pair, #1775-1776 1.40 .70

Tourism — A509

Temples, shrines in Bali: Nos. 1777, 1779, Pura Besakih. No. 1778, Pura Taman Ayun.

1998, July 1 Perf. 12½
1777 A509 700r multicolored .70 .35
1778 A509 700r shown .70 .35
a. Pair, #1777-1778 1.40 .70
Souvenir Sheet
Perf. 13½x13
1779 A509 2500r multicolored 3.75 1.75
No. 1777 is 64x24mm. No. 1779 contains one 41x25mm stamp.

Souvenir Sheet

Panthera Tigris — A510

1998, July 23 Litho. Perf. 13½x12½
1780 A510 5000r multicolored 4.00 2.00
Singpex '98.

Trains A511

Train going right: a, Cattle, freight cars. b, Freight, box cars. c, Passenger cars. d, Passenger car, tender. e, Locomotive 850.
Train going left: f, Locomotive D52. g, Coal tender. h, Car with 2 doors. i, Dining car with large windows. j, Car with two windows.
2500r, Locomotive.

1998, Aug. 10
1781 A511 300r Block of 10, #a.-j. 4.50 2.25
Souvenir Sheet
1782 A511 2500r multicolored 2.25 1.10
No. 1781 issued in sheets of 20 stamps consisting of two tete-beche blocks of 10. No. 1782 contains one 41x25mm stamp.

Pres. H.B.J. Habibie — A512

1998, Aug. 17 — Perf. 12½x13½

1783	A512	300r pink & multi	.45	.25
1784	A512	700r blue & multi	.45	.25
1785	A512	4500r green & multi	2.25	1.10
1786	A512	5000r yellow & multi	2.50	1.25
		Nos. 1783-1786 (4)	5.65	2.85

13th Asian Games A513

1998, Sept. 9 — Perf. 13½x12½

1787	A513	300r Fencing	.40	.20
1788	A513	700r Taekwondo	.40	.20
1789	A513	4000r Wushu	2.00	.85
a.		Sovenir sheet, #1787-1789	3.00	1.50
		Nos. 1787-1789 (3)	2.80	1.25

Intl. Year of the Ocean A514

1998, Sept. 26 — Litho. — Perf. 13½x12½

1790	A514	700r multicolored	1.10	.25

Souvenir Sheets

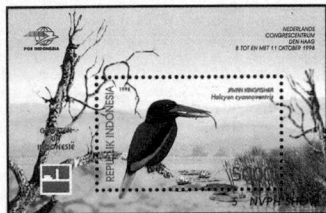

5th NVPH (Netherlands Philatelic Congress) Exhibition, The Hague — A514a

Birds: 5000r, Halcyon cyannoventris. 35,000r, Vannelus macropterus, vert.

1998, Oct. 8 — Litho. — Perf. 13½x12½

1790A	A514a	5000r multi	4.00	4.00
1790B	A514a	35,000r multi	15.00	15.00

A515   A516

1998, Oct. 9 — Perf. 12½x13½

1791	A515	700r #922	.60	.20
1792	A515	700r #414	.60	.20
a.		Pair, #1791-1792	1.25	.30

World Stamp Day.

Litho. (#1793-1799, 1805)

1998 — Perf. 12½

Ducks and Geese: 250r, #1805, Aythya australis. 500r, Anas superciliosa. 700r, Anas gibberifrons. 1000r, Nettapus coromandelianus. 1500r, Nettapus pulchelus. 2500r, Dendrocygna javanica. 3500r, Dendrocygna arcuata. 4000r, Anseranas semipalmata. #1801, Dendrocygna guttata. 10,000r, Anas waigiuensis. 15,000r, Tadorna radjah. 20,000r, Cairina scutulata.

1793	A516	250r multi	.50	.20
1794	A516	500r multi	.50	.20
1795	A516	700r multi	.50	.20
1796	A516	1000r multi	.60	.30
1797	A516	1500r multi	.90	.40
1798	A516	2500r multi	1.50	.65
1799	A516	3500r multi	1.90	.85

Litho. With Hologram
Perf. 13½x12½
Size: 42x25mm

1800	A516	4000r horiz.	1.50	.90
1801	A516	5000r horiz.	2.00	1.25
1802	A516	10,000r horiz.	4.00	2.25
1803	A516	15,000r horiz.	6.25	3.25
1804	A516	20,000r horiz.	7.50	4.25
a.		Sheet of 5, #1800-1804, + 4 labels	25.00	12.50
		Nos. 1793-1804 (12)	27.65	14.70

Souvenir Sheet
Perf. 12½

1805	A516	5000r lt blue sky	3.25	3.25

Soaking in water may affect the hologram on #1800-1804.
Issued: #1793-1799, 1805, 12/1; others 10/19.
See Nos. 1918-1919.

Souvenir Sheet

Italia '98 — A516a

1998, Oct. 23 — Perf. 12½x13½

1805A	A516a	5000r Jakarta Cathedral	3.25	3.25

National Flag — A517

Mountains and: #1806, Flagpole at right. #1807, Flagpole at left.

1998, Oct. 28 — Litho. — Perf. 12½x13½

1806	A517	700r multicolored	.60	.20
1807	A517	700r multicolored	.60	.20
a.		Pair, #1806-1807	1.25	.40

Reform Movement A518

No. 1809, Dove, national flag. No. 1810, Students, Parliament Building.

1998, Oct. 28 — Perf. 13½x12½

1808	A518	700r shown	.60	.20
1809	A518	700r multicolored	.60	.20
a.		Pair, #1808-1809	1.25	.40

Size: 83x25mm

1810	A518	1000r multicolored	.65	.30

Flora and Fauna Type of 1994

Flora — #1812: a, Stelechocarpus burahol. b, Polianthes tuberosa. c, Mirabilis jalapa. d, Mangifera casturi. e, Ficus minahassae.
Fauna — f, Geopelia striata. g, Gallus varius. h, Elephas maximus. i, Nasalis larvatus. j, Tarsius spectrum.
No. 1813, like #1812b. No. 1814, like #1812i.

1998, Nov. 5 — Perf. 12½x13½

1812	A438	500r Block of 10	4.00	2.00
a.-j.		Any single	.40	.20

Souvenir Sheets

1813	A438	2500r multicolored	2.00	2.00
1814	A438	2500r multicolored	2.00	2.00

Traditional Dance Type of 1992

Dance, region: 300r, Oreng-oreng Gae, Southeast Sulawesi. 500r, Tribute dance, Bengkulu. 700r, Fan dance, Riau. 1000r, Srimpi, Yogyakarta. 2000r, 5000r, Tribute dance, West Sumatra.

1998, Dec. 27

1815	A411	300r multicolored	.45	.20
1816	A411	500r multicolored	.45	.20
1817	A411	700r multicolored	.45	.20
1818	A411	1000r multicolored	.55	.25
1819	A411	2000r multicolored	1.25	.40
		Nos. 1815-1819 (5)	3.15	1.25

Souvenir Sheet

1820	A411	5000r multicolored	3.00	1.40

Creation and Engineering Year — A519

Designs: 500r, Hydroelectric turbine, power lines. 700r, Plumbing fixture, water pipes.

1999, Jan. 1 — Litho. — Perf. 12½

1821	A519	500r multicolored	.40	.20
1822	A519	700r multicolored	.50	.20

7th Far East & South Pacific Games for Disabled A520   Garuda Indonesia Airways, 50th Anniv. A521

1999, Jan. 10 — Perf. 12½x13½

1823	A520	500r Throwing shotput	.40	.20
1824	A520	500r Medals, wheelchair	.40	.20
a.		Pair, #1823-1824	.80	.25

1999, Jan. 26 — Perf. 13x13½

1825	A521	500r Logo	.50	.20
1826	A521	700r Aircraft maintenance	.50	.20
1827	A521	2000r Pilot, attendant	1.10	.50
		Nos. 1825-1827 (3)	2.10	.90

Indonesian Folktales Type of 1998

Folktale, region — #1828: a-e, Danau Toba, North Sumatra. f-j, Banjarmasin, South Kalimantan. k-o, Buleleng, Bali. p-t, Woiram, Irian Jaya.
5000r, like #1828e.

1999, Feb. 15 — Perf. 13½x12½

1828		Sheet of 20	8.00	4.00
a.-e.	A502	500r Strip of 5	2.00	1.00
f.-j.	A502	500r Strip of 5	2.00	1.00
k.-o.	A502	500r Strip of 5	2.00	1.00
p.-t.	A502	500r Strip of 5	2.00	1.00

Souvenir Sheet

1829	A502	5000r multicolored	3.00	1.50

Nos. 1829 is a continuous design.

Souvenir Sheet

Surabaya '99, Natl. Philatelic Exhibition — A522

1999, Mar. 4 — Litho. — Perf. 13½x12½

1830	A522	5000r Apples	3.50	1.75
a.		Ovptd. in sheet margin	6.00	3.00

No. 1830a Overprinted in Gold in Sheet Margin with "APPI SHOW '99 / SURABAYA, 10-18 JULI 1999" and Emblem. Issued, 7/10.

Souvenir Sheet

Australia '99, World Stamp Expo — A523

1999, Mar. 19 — Perf. 12½x13½

1831	A523	5000r Tarsius spectrum	3.50	3.50
a.		Ovptd. in sheet margin	6.00	6.00

No. 1831a Overprinted in Gold in Sheet Margin with "The 13th / Thaipex / China / Stamp Exhibition / Bangkok '99 / 4 -15. 8. 99" and Emblem. Issued, 8/15.

Mushrooms — A524

No. 1832: a, Mutinus bambusinus. b, Ascosparassis heinricherii. c, Mycena sp.
No. 1833: a, Microporus xanthopus. b, Gloeophyllum imponens. c, Termitomyces eurrhizus.
No. 1834: a, Aseroe rubra. b, Calostoma orirubra. c, Boedijnopeziza insititia.
5000r, Termitomyces eurrhizus.

1999, Apr. 1 — Perf. 12½

1832	A524	500r Triptych, #a.-c.	1.40	.70
1833	A524	700r Triptych, #a.-c.	1.90	.90
1834	A524	1000r Triptych, #a.-c.	2.50	1.25
d.		Souvenir sheet of 3, #1832-1834	6.00	3.00

Souvenir Sheet

1835	A524	5000r multicolored	3.50	1.75

Booklet Stamps
Size:32x24mm

1836	A524	500r Like #1832a	.80	.25
1837	A524	500r Like #1832b	.80	.25
1838	A524	500r Like #1832c	.80	.25
a.		Booklet pane, 3 each #1836-1838, + label	7.50	
		Complete booklet, #1838a	7.50	
		Nos. 1836-1838 (3)	2.40	.75

No. 1835 contains one 25x41mm stamp. Numbers have been reserved for additional values in this set.

Public Health Care Insurance A525

1999, Apr. 7 — *Perf. 13½x12½*
1845	A525	700r multicolored	.70	.20

Souvenir Sheet

IBRA '99, Intl. Philatelic Exhibition, Nuremberg — A526

1999, Apr. 27 — *Perf. 12½x13½*
1846	A526	5000r Dendrobium abang betawi	3.50	3.50

Y2K Millennium Bug — A527

Designs: a, "Bug." b, Circuit, android.

1999, May 2 — *Perf. 13½x12½*
1847	A527	500r Pair, #a.-b.	1.10	.20

Indonesia 2000 Type of 1997

1999, May 20 — Litho. — *Perf. 13½x12¾*
1848	A483	500r Chrysoprase	.40	.20
1849	A483	1000r Smoky quartz	.60	.30
1850	A483	2000r Opal blue	1.25	.65
a.		Sheet, 3 ea #1848-1850 + label	9.50	9.50
		Nos. 1848-1850 (3)	2.25	1.15

Souvenir Sheet
1851	A483	4000r Silicified coral	7.50	7.50
1851A	A483	4000r Javan jade	15.00	15.00
b.		Sheet, #1851-1851A, 2 ea #1849-1850, 4 #1848	25.00	25.00

Nos. 1851A, 1851Ab were issued in presentation packs with certificate of authenticity. Control numbers and silver overprint "1 Tahun/ Lagi / 1 Year / to Go" printed in margin. No. 1851A sold for 10,000r; No. 1851Ab for 30,000r.

Environmental Care — A528

Winning designs of 1999 Ecophila Stamp Design Contest: 500r, Girl wrapped in blanket, people walking through water. 1000r, 3000r, Boy swimming with duck, plant, cherry. 2000r, Elderly woman drinking water from pitcher, outdoor scene.

1999, June 5
1852	A528	500r multicolored	.40	.20
1853	A528	1000r multicolored	.60	.45
1854	A528	2000r multicolored	1.25	.80
		Nos. 1852-1854 (3)	2.25	1.45

Souvenir Sheet
1855	A528	3000r multicolored	2.50	1.10

1999 General Election — A529

Designs: a, "48," Banner, people standing in line to vote. b, People waiting turn to enter election booth, map.

1999, June 4
1856	A529	1000r Pair, #a.-b.	1.60	.75

Souvenir Sheet

PhilexFrance '99 — A530

1999, July 2 — Litho. — *Perf. 12¾x13½*
1858	A530	5000r multi	4.00	4.00

Red Cross / Red Crescent Millennium Year Campaign — A531

Photo. & Litho.
1999, Aug. 12 — *Perf. 12½*
1859	A531	1000r multicolored	.80	.40

National Heroes — A532

No. 1860: a, Dr. W. Z. Johannes (1895-1924). b, Martha Christina Tijahahu (1800-18), freedom fighter. c, Frans Kaisiepo (1921-79), politician. d, Maria Walanda Maramis (1872-1924), educator.

Litho. & Engr.
1999, Aug. 17 — *Perf. 12½*
1860		Strip of 4	1.75	.80
a.-d.		A532 500r any single	.40	.20
e.		Booklet pane of 4, #1860a	2.00	
f.		Booklet pane of 4, #1860b	2.00	
g.		Booklet pane of 4, #1860c	2.00	
h.		Booklet pane of 4, #1860d	2.00	
		Complete bklt., #1860e-1860h	8.00	

Complete booklet sold for 10,000r.

Souvenir Sheet

China 1999 World Philatelic Exhibition — A533

Perf. 13½x12¾
1999, Aug. 21 — Litho.
1861	A533	5000r multi	5.00	2.50

Gadjah Mada University, 50th Anniv. — A534

1999, Sept. 19 — *Perf. 12½*
1862	A534	500r shown	.50	.25
1863	A534	1000r Building, diff.	.60	.30

Intl. Year of Older Persons A535

1999, Oct. 1 — *Perf. 13½x12¾*
1864	A535	500r multi	.60	.30

UPU, 125th Anniv. — A536

1999, Oct. 9 — *Perf. 12½*
1865	A536	500r Postman on horse	.40	.20
1866	A536	500r Postman on motorcycle	.40	.20
a.		Pair, #1865-1866 + label	.80	.20
1866B		Pair + 2 labels	6.00	3.00
c.		A536 1000r Like #1865, 30x32mm	3.00	1.50
d.		A536 1000r Like #1866, 30x32mm	3.00	1.50

No. 1866B issued in sheets of 5 pairs. As the labels could be personalized, sheets were available only through special orders with Indonesia Post and sold for 20,000r.

Batik Designs — A537

1999, Oct. 1
1867	A537	500r Cirebon	.45	.20
1868	A537	500r Madura	.45	.20
1869	A537	500r Jambi	.45	.20
1870	A537	500r Yogyakarta	.45	.20
		Nos. 1867-1870 (4)	1.80	.80

Domesticated Animals — A538

1999, Nov. 5 — *Perf. 13½x12¾*
1871	A538	500r Dogs	.60	.20
1872	A538	500r Chickens	.60	.20
a.		Pair, #1871-1872	1.25	.40
1873	A538	500r Cat	.60	.20
1874	A538	500r Rabbits	.60	.20
a.		Pair, #1873-1874	1.25	.40
1875	A538	1000r Pigeon	.80	.40
1876	A538	1000r Geese	.80	.40
a.		Pair, #1875-1876	1.60	.80
b.		Sheet of 6, #1871-1876	5.00	2.50
		Nos. 1871-1876 (6)	4.00	1.60

Souvenir Sheet
1877	A538	4000r Like #1874	3.75	1.75

Millennium — A539

Designs: No. 1878, 1000r, No. 1880, 20,000r, 1999 agenda book. No. 1879, 1000r, No. 1881, 20,000r, Clock, child.

Litho. & Photo.
1999-2000 — *Perf. 13½x12¾*
1878-1879	A539	Set of 2	1.00	.50
a.		Sheet of 20 + 20 labels	22.50	22.50

Souvenir Sheets
1880-1881	A539	Set of 2	20.00	8.00

Labels on No. 1879a could be personalized. The sheet sold for 38,000r.

Issued: Nos. 1878, 1880, 12/31/99; Nos. 1879, 1879a, 1881, 1/1/00.

Visit Indonesia Decade — A540

Designs: 500r, Satellite, fish. 1000r, Hydroponic agriculture.

2000, Jan. 1 — *Perf. 12¾x13½*
1882-1883	A540	Set of 2	1.40	.65

University of Indonesia, 50th Anniv. — A541

Designs: 500r, Salemba campus. 1000r, University building, Depok.

2000, Feb. 2 — *Perf. 12½*
1884-1885	A541	Set of 2	1.40	.65

Indonesian Folktales Type of 1998

Folktale, region — #1886: a-e, Tapak Tuan, Aceh. f-j, Batu Ballah, West Kalimantan. k-o, Sawerigading, South Sulawesi. p-t, 7 Putri kahyangan, Moluccas.
5000r, Like #1886e

2000, Feb. 5 — Perf. 13½x12¾

1886	Sheet of 20	10.00	5.00
a.-e.	500r Strip of 5	2.50	1.25
f.-j.	500r Strip of 5	2.50	1.25
k.-o.	500r Strip of 5	2.50	1.25
p.-t.	500r Strip of 5	2.50	1.25

Souvenir Sheet

1887	A502 5000r multi	4.00	2.00

Indonesia 2000 Type of 1997

Designs: 500r, Prehnite. 1000r, Chalcedony. 2000r, Volcanic obsidian.

2000, Mar. 1

1888-1890	A483 Set of 3	3.00	1.50
1890a	Souvenir sheet, 3 each #1888-1890 + label	7.00	3.50

Souvenir Sheet

1891	A483 5000r Jasperized limestone	4.00	2.00
a.	Sheet, #1891, 14 #1888, 2 #1889, 3 #1890 + 20 labels	20.00	—

No. 1891a sold for 41,000r with labels personalized.

Comic Strip Characters — A542

Designs: No. 1892, 500r, I Brewok, by Gungun. No. 1893, 500r, Pak Tuntung, by Basuki. No. 1894, Pak Bei, by Masdi Sunardi. No. 1895, 500r, Mang Ohle, by Didin D. Basuni. No. 1896, 500r, Panji Koming, by Dwi Koendoro.

Perf. 12¾x13½

2000, Mar. 13 — Photo.

1892-1896	A542 Set of 5	2.25	1.10
1896a	Souvenir sheet, 3 each #1892-1896 + label	7.50	3.50

World Meteorological Organization, 50th Anniv. — A543

Litho. & Photo.

2000, Mar. 23 — Perf. 12½

1897	A543 500r multi	1.00	.50

Souvenir Sheet

Bangkok 2000 Stamp Exhibition — A544

2000, Mar. 23 — Perf. 13½x12¾

1898	A544 5000r multi	5.00	2.25

15th Natl. Sports Week A545

Designs: 500r, Cycling. 1000r, Canoeing. 2000r, High jump.

2000, Apr. 1

1899-1901	A545 Set of 3	3.50	1.60

Souvenir Sheet

The Stamp Show 2000, London — A546

2000, May 22

1902	A546 5000r multi	5.00	2.50

Environmental Care — A547

Designs; 500r, Birds in nest. 1000r, Monkeys. 2000r, Fish.

2000, June 5

1903-1905	A547 Set of 3	3.50	1.75

Souvenir Sheet

1906	A547 4000r Like #1904	4.00	2.00

2000 Summer Olympics, Sydney — A548

No. 1907, 500r: a, Boxing. b, Judo.
No. 1908, 1000r: a, Badminton. b, Weight lifting.
No. 1909, 2000r: a, Swimming. b, Running.

2000, July 1 — Pairs, #a-b

1907-1909	A548 Set of 3	6.00	3.00

Souvenir Sheet

1910	A548 5000r Like #1908b	5.00	2.25

Worldwide Fund for Nature (WWF) — A549

Komodo dragon: No. 1911, 500r, No. 1915a, 2500r, With tongue extended. No. 1912, 500r, On log. No. 1913, 500r, Pair walking. No. 1914, 500r, No. 1915b, 2500r, Pair fighting.

2000, Aug. 13

1911-1914	A549 Set of 4	3.00	2.00
a.	Souvenir sheet, 2 each #1911-1914	10.00	7.50

Souvenir Sheet

1915	A549 2500r Sheet of 2, #a-b	6.50	4.00

Souvenir Sheet

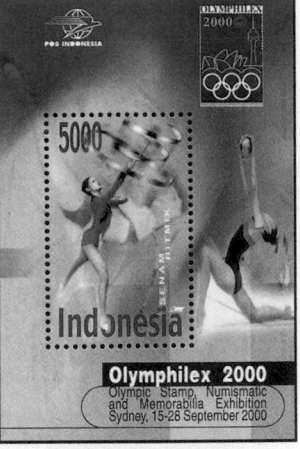

Olymphilex 2000 Stamp Exhibition — A550

2000, Sept. 15 — Perf. 12¾x13½

1916	A550 5000r multi	4.50	2.25

A551

No. 1917: a, Pres. Abdurrahman Wahid. b, Vice Pres. Megawati Soekarnoputri
Illustration reduced.

Photo. & Engr.

2000, Sept. 27 — Perf. 12½

1917	A551 1000r Pair, #a-b	2.00	1.00

Ducks and Geese Type of 1998

2000, Sept. 27 — Photo. — Perf. 12½

1918	A516 800r Like #1798	1.25	1.00
1919	A516 900r Like #1793	1.25	1.00

Traditional Costumes A552

Provinces and regions: a, Aceh. b, Jambi. c, Banten. d, Yogyakarta. e, Central Kalimantan (Kalimantan Tengah). f, Southeast Sulawesi (Sulawesi Tenggara). g, East Nusa Tenggara (Nusa Tenggara Timur). h, North Sumatra (Sumatera Utara). i, Bengkulu. j, Jakarta. k, East Java (Jawa Timur). l, East Kalimantan (Kalimantan Timur). m, South Sulawesi (Sulawesi Selatan). n, Maluku. o, West Sumatra (Sumatera Barat). p, South Sumatra (Sumatera Selatan). q, West Java (Jawa Barat). r, West Kalimantan (Kalimantan Barat). s, North Sulawesi (Sulawesi Utara). t, Bali. u, North Maluku (Maluku Utara). v, Riau. w, Lampung. x, Central Java (Jawa Tengah). y, South Kalimantan (Kalimantan Selatan). z, Central Sulawesi (Sulawesi Tengah). aa, West Nusa Tenggara (Nusa Tenggara Barat). ab, Irian Jaya.

Litho. & Photo.

2000, Oct. 28 — Perf. 12½

1920	Sheet of 28 + 7 labels	25.00	15.00
a.-ab.	A552 900r Any single	.70	.50

Artists and Entertainers — A553

No. 1921, horiz.: a, Bing Slamet (1927-74), singer, comedian. b, S. Sudjono (1913-86), painter. c, I Ketut Maria (1897-1968), dancer. d, Chairil Anwar (1922-49), poet. e, Ibu Sud (1908-93), musician.

2000, Nov. 1 — Perf. 13½x12¾

1921	Horiz. strip of 5	4.00	2.00
a.-e.	A553 900r Any single	.80	.40

Souvenir Sheet

1922	A553 4000r Chairil Anwar	4.00	2.00

Indonesia Post in the 21st Century — A554

Designs: 800r, Philately, vert. 900r, Business communications, vert. 1000r, Business financial services, vert. 4000r, Business logistics, vert.

Litho. & Photo.

2000, Dec. 20 — Perf. 12½

1923	A554 800r multi	.60	.30
1924	A554 900r multi	.60	.40
1925	A554 1000r multi	1.00	.50
1926	A554 4000r multi	3.50	1.75
	Nos. 1923-1926 (4)	5.70	2.95

Solar System — A555

No. 1927: a, Sun. b, Mercury. c, Venus. d, Earth. e, Mars. f, Jupiter. g, Saturn. h, Uranus. i, Neptune. j, Pluto.
Illustration reduced.

2001, Jan. 1 — Litho. — Perf. 13½x12¾

1927	Block of 10 + 5 labels	7.50	
a.-j.	A555 900r Any single	.75	.30
k.	Sheet of 10 + 5 labels	10.00	
l.	Sheet of 20 + 20 labels	25.00	25.00

Souvenir Sheet

1928	A555 5000r Sun	4.00	2.00

Labels on No. 1927l could be personalized. The sheet sold for 36,000r.

Indonesian Folktales Type of 1998

Folktale, region — No. 1929: a-e, Batang Tuaka, Riau. f-j, Si Pitung, Jakarta. k-o, Terusan Nusa, Central Kalimantan. p-t, Ile Mauraja, East Nusa Tenggara.
5000r, Like No. 1929h.

Litho. & Photo.

2001, Feb. 2		Perf. 13½x12¾
1929	Sheet of 20	16.00 8.00
a.-e.	A502 900r Strip of 5	4.00 2.00
f.-j.	A502 900r Strip of 5	4.00 2.00
k.-o.	A502 900r Strip of 5	4.00 2.00
p.-t.	A502 900r Strip of 5	4.00 2.00

Souvenir Sheet

1930	A502 5000r multi	2.75 1.25

Masks — A556

No. 1931, 500r — Arsa Wijaya, Bali: a, Denomination at L. b, Denomination at R.
No. 1932, 800r — Asmat, Irian Jaya: a, Denomination at L. b, Denomination at R.
No. 1933, 800r — Cirebon, West Java: a, Denomination at L. b, Denomination at R.
No. 1934, 900r — Hudoq, East Kalimantan: a, Denomination at L. b, Denomination at R.
No. 1935, 900r — Wayang Wong, Yogyakarta: a, Denomination at L. b, Denomination at R.
5000r, l like No. 1934b.

2001, Mar. 2		Perf. 12¾x13½

Pairs, #a-b

1931-1935	A556 Set of 5	6.00 2.25
c.	Sheet, #1931-1935 +2 labels	6.00

Souvenir Sheet

1936	A556 5000r multi	4.00 2.00
a.	Ovptd. in margin in silver	6.00 3.00

Issued: No. 1936a, 10/16/01. No. 1936 overprinted with "HAFNIA '01 / World Philatelic Exhibition / Copenhagen / 16-21 October 2001," show emblem and new price of 7500r.

Traditional Communication Instruments — A557

No. 1937: a, Beduk. b, Bendé. c, Kentongan. d, Nafiri.

2001, Mar. 10		Perf. 12½
1937	Vert. strip of 4	3.00 1.50
a.-d.	A557 900r Any single	.75 .35
e.	Sheet, 2 each #1937a-1937d	8.00 4.00

Greetings — A558

Various flowers. Denominations: 800, 900, 1000, 1500, 2000, 4000, 5000, 10000r

Litho. & Typo.

2001, Apr. 21		Perf. 12½
1938-1945	A558 Set of 8	17.50 8.75

A558a

Greetings — A558b

Illustration A558a reduced.

	Perf. 13½x12¾
2001, Apr. 21	**Litho. & Typo.**
1945A A558a 900r multi + label	4.00 4.00

	Perf. 12½
1945B A558b 900r multi + label	4.00 4.00

No. 1945A was issued in sheets of 20 + 20 labels that could be personalized. The sheet sold for 36,000r. No. 1945B was issued in sheets of 10 + 10 labels that could be personalized. The sheet sold for 20,000r.

Environmental Care — A559

Children and: 800r, Fish. 900r, 5000r, Deer. 1000r, Sea turtle.

Litho. & Photo.

2001, June 5		Perf. 13½x12¾
1946	A559 800r multi	1.25 .40
a.	Tete-beche pair	2.50 2.50
1947	A559 900r multi	1.25 .40
a.	Tete-beche pair	2.50 2.50
1948	A559 1000r multi	1.25 .40
a.	Tete-beche pair	2.50 2.50
	Nos. 1946-1948 (3)	3.75 1.20

Souvenir Sheet

1949	A559 3000r multi	4.00 3.00

No. 1949 exists imperf. Value $5.

Pres. Sukarno (1901-70) — A560

Various portraits: 500, 800, 900, 1000. 5000r, Sukarno at microphone.

2001, June 6		Perf. 12½
1950-1953	A560 Set of 4	2.50 1.25
a.	Sheet, 2 each #1950-1953	6.50 3.25

Souvenir Sheet

Perf. 13½x12¾

1954	A560 5000r multi	4.00 2.00

No. 1954 contains one 41x25mm stamp

National Police — A561

Police and: a, Children. b, Helicopter. Illustration reduced.

2001, July 1 Photo.		Perf. 13½x12¾
1955	A561 1000r Horiz. pair, #a-b	2.50 1.10

National Scouting Jamboree — A562

Scouts: a, Raising flag. b, Pitching tent. Illustration reduced.

2001, July 3		
1956	A562 1000r Horiz. pair, #a-b	3.00 1.25

Children's Games A563

Designs: 800r, Kaki Siapa. 900r, Egrang Bambu. 1000r, Dakon. 2000r, Kuda Pelepah Pisang.

Litho. & Photo.

2001, July 23		Perf. 13½x12¾
1957-1960	A563 Set of 4	3.75 1.75
a.	Sheet, 2 each #1957-1960	9.00 4.50

Souvenir Sheet

Phila Nippon '01, Japan — A564

2001, Aug. 1		Photo.
1961	A564 10,000r multi	8.00 4.00

Dr. R. Soeharso Orthopedic Hospital, Surakarta, 50th Anniv. A565

Litho. & Photo.

2001, Aug. 28		Perf. 13½x12¾
1962	A565 1000r multi	1.25 .40

Traditional Transportation — A566

Designs: No. 1963, 1000r, Rowboat. No. 1964, 1000r, Trishaw. No. 1965, Horse-drawn carriage.

2001, Sept. 17		
1963-1965	A566 Set of 3	3.50 1.00
a.	Sheet, 3 each #1963-1965 +label	9.00 9.00

Post Offices A567

Buildings in: 800r, Makassar. 900r, Bandung. 1000r, Balikpapan. 2000r, Padang.

2001, Sept. 27		
1966-1969	A567 Set of 4	3.50 1.60

Gemstones — A568

Designs: 800r, Rose quartz. 900r, Brecciated jasper. 1000r, Malachite. 5000r, Diamond.

2001, Oct. 1		
1970-1972	A568 Set of 3	2.50 1.10
a.	Sheet, 3 each #1970-1972 + label	10.00 6.75

Souvenir Sheet

1973	A568 5000r multi	4.00 2.00

Year of Dialogue Among Civilizations — A569

2001, Oct. 9 Litho.		Perf. 12¾x13½
1974	A569 1000r multi	1.60 .40

Beetles — A570

Designs: 800r, Agestrata dehaan. 900r, Mormolyce phyllodes. No. 1977, 1000r, Batocera rosenbergi. No. 1978, 1000r, Chrysochroa buqueti. 2000r, 5000r, Chalcosoma caucasus.

2001, Nov. 5		Litho. & Photo.
1975-1979	A570 Set of 5	4.50 2.25
a.	Booklet pane, #1975-1979 + label	6.00 —
	Booklet, 2 #1979a	12.00

Souvenir Sheet

1980	A570 5000r multi	4.00 2.00

Folktales — A571

No. 1981, 1000r — Pulau Kembara, South Sumatra: a, Four people, lanterns. b, Two men, woman, boat. c, Man and woman standing in boat. d, Man and woman in water. e, Boat, snake, fish.
No. 1982, 1000r — Nyi Koro Kidul, Yogyakarta: a, Woman at tight pointing. b, Woman at foreground with hand at mouth. c, Two men with hats at right. d, Woman in sea. e, Sea and island.
No. 1983, 1000r — Aji Tatin, East Kalimantan: a, Bird in tree, woman, man with hand outstretched. b, Woman, bird boat. c, Sinking boat. d, Woman and tree. e, Bird in tree.
No. 1984, 1000r — Danau Tondano, North Sulawesi: a, Woman with long hair in foreground. b, Man holding spear. c, Man at left with arm to head. d, Man and woman embracing. e, Sea and island.
5000r, Like No. 1981e.
Illustration reduced.

Litho. & Photo.

2002, Feb. 2		Perf. 13½x12¾

Blocks of 5, #a-e

1981-1984	A571 Set of 4	8.00 4.00

Souvenir Sheet

1985	A571 5000r multi	4.00 2.00

Nos. 1981-1984 are printed in sheets of four blocks of five. Stamp "e" is always adjacent to the LL stamp in the block of the remaining four stamps, and is found tete beche to both stamps "a" and "e" from adjacent blocks of five.

2002 World Cup Soccer Championships, Japan and Korea — A572

Celebrations: 1000r, Player lifting shirt over face. 1500r, Four players with fists raised, horiz. 2000r, 5000r, Player with arms outstretched.

Perf. 12¾x13½, 13½x12¾

2002, Apr. 1　　　　　　**Litho. & Photo.**
1986-1988　A572　Set of 3　　3.75　1.60

Souvenir Sheet

1989　A572　5000r multi　　　4.00　2.00

Indonesian Cancer Foundation, 25th Anniv. — A573

2002, Apr. 17　　　*Perf. 12¾x13½*
1990　A573　1000r multi　　　1.50　.60
　a.　　Tete-beche pair　　　4.50　2.25

Telecommunications — A574

No. 1991: a, Woman using telephone (2/4). b, Man using cellular phone (1/4). c, Satellite above Earth (4/4). d, Satellite, world map, computer, satellite dish (3/4).

2002, May 17
1991　A574　1000r Block of 4,
　　　　　#a-d　　　　3.50　1.75
　e.　Sheet, 2 each #1991a-
　　　1991d　　　　7.00　3.50
　f.　Booklet pane, 4 #1991a　3.50
　g.　Booklet pane, 4 #1991b　3.50
　h.　Booklet pane, 4 #1991c　3.50
　i.　Booklet pane, 4 #1991d　3.50
　　　Booklet, #1991f-1991i　14.00

Marine Life — A575

No. 1992, 1000r: a, Charonia tritonis. b, Symphyllia radians.
No. 1993, 1500r: a, Cromileptes altivelis. b, Acanthaster planci.
No. 1994, 2000r, horiz.: a, Paracanthurus hepatus. b, Tridacna gigas.
5000r, Acanthaster planci.

2002, June 5
Horiz. Pairs, #a-b
1992-1994　A575　Set of 3　　7.00　3.50
　c.　Sheet, #1992, 1993, 1994a,
　　　1994b　　　　　7.00　3.50

Souvenir Sheet

1995　A575　5000r multi　　　4.00　2.00

Aceh Province — A576

Designs: 1500r, Student, Aceh dance, map of Aceh. 3500r, Masjid Raya Banda Aceh, map of Indonesia.

2002, June 15　　　　　*Perf. 12½*
1996-1997　A576　Set of 2　　4.00　2.00

Natl. Family Day A577

2002, June 29　　　**Litho. & Typo.**
1998　A577　1000r multi　　　1.50　.60

Perf. 13½x12¾

33rd Intl. Physics Olympiad, Bali — A578

No. 1999: a, Eclipse (1/2). b, Spectrum colors and Balinese symbols (2/2).

2002, July 14　　　*Perf. 12¾x13½*
1999　A578　1000r Horiz. pair,
　　　　　#a-b　　　　2.00　1.00

Kites A579

No. 2000: a, Popotengan (bird-shaped) (1/5). b, Barong (dragon head) (2/5). c, Fighting (3/5). d, Bebean (4/5). e, Modern (box and wing) (5/5).
5000r, Popotengan.

Litho. & Photo.
2002, July 15　　　*Perf. 13½x12¾*
2000　Horiz. strip of 5　　　4.00　2.00
　a.-e.　A579 1000r Any single　.80　.30

Souvenir Sheet

2001　A579　5000r multi　　　4.00　2.00

Fruit — A580

Designs: 300r, Morinda citrifolia. 500r, Mangifera indica. 1500r, Averrhoa carambola. 3000r, Durio zibethinus.

2002, Aug. 1　Photo.　*Perf. 13½x12¾*
2002　A580　300r multi　　　.60　.25
2003　A580　500r multi　　　.60　.30
2004　A580　1500r multi　　　1.60　.80
2005　A580　3000r multi　　　2.40　1.10
　　　Nos. 2002-2005 (4)　　5.20　2.45

Souvenir Sheet

Philakorea 2002 World Stamp Exhibition, Seoul — A581

2002, Aug. 2　Litho.　*Perf. 12¾x13½*
2006　A581　7000r multi　　　5.00　2.50

Mohammad Hatta (1902-80), Prime Minister — A582

No. 2007, 1000r: a, Denomination at left. b, Denomination at right.
No. 2008, 1500r: a, Denomination at left. b, Denomination at right.
5000r, Hatta standing.

Litho. & Photo.
2002, Aug. 12　　　　　*Perf. 12½*
Pairs, #a-b
2007-2008　A582　Set of 2　　4.00　2.00
　c.　Sheet, 2 each #2007-2008 + 2 la-
　　　bels　　　　　9.00　4.50

Souvenir Sheet
Perf. 12¾x13½

2009　A582　5000r multi　　　4.00　2.25

No. 2009 contains one 25x41mm stamp.

President and Vice-President — A583

No. 2010, 1500r: a, Pres. Megawati Soekarnoputri. b, Vice-president Hamzah Haz.
Illustration reduced.

Photo. with Foil Application
2002, Aug. 17　　　　　*Perf. 12½*
2010　A583　Horiz. pair, #a-b, +
　　　　　central label　　4.50　4.50

Souvenir Sheet

Amphilex 2002 Intl. Stamp Exhibition, Amsterdam — A584

Perf. 13½x12¾
2002, Aug. 30　　　　　**Photo.**
2011　A584　7000r multi　　　7.00　3.50

Souvenir Sheet

Panfila 2002 Philatelic Exhibition, Yogyakarta — A585

2002, Sept. 19　　　*Perf. 12¾x13½*
2012　A585　6000r multi　　　5.00　2.50

Paintings — A586

No. 2013, 1000r: a, Seko, Guerrilla Vanguard, by S. Sudjojono. b, Cat, by Popo Iskandar.
No. 2014, 1500r, vert.: a, Catching Lice, by Hendra Gunawan. b, Gatut Kaca with Prigiwa and Prigiwati, by R. Basuki Abdullah.

Litho. & Photo.
2002, Sept. 27　　　　　*Perf. 12½*
Pairs, #a-b
2013-2014　A586　Set of 2　　5.00　2.50
　c.　Sheet, 2 each #2013-2014　9.00　4.50

Souvenir Sheet

España 2002 Youth Philatelic Exhibition, Salamanca — A587

2002, Oct. 4　Photo.　*Perf. 13½x12¾*
2015　A587　7000r multi　　　5.00　2.50

Flora and Fauna A588

No. 2016, 1000r: a, Trimeresurus hageni. b, Rafflesia micropylora.
No. 2017, 1500r: a, Panthera pardus. b, Terminalia catappa.
No. 2018, 2000r: a, Papilionanthe hookeriana. b, Varanus salvator.
3500r, Panthera pardus.

Litho. & Photo.
2002, Nov. 5   *Perf. 12¾x13½*
Horiz. Pairs, #a-b
2016-2018   A588   Set of 3   7.00   3.50
Souvenir Sheet
2019   A588   3500r multi   4.00   2.00
No. 2019 exists imperf. Value $5.

Antara,
Indonesian News
Agency — A589

Litho. & Typo.
2002, Dec. 13   *Perf. 12½*
2020   A589   1500r multi   2.00   1.00

Happy
Birthday — A590

No. 2021: a, Food platter. b, Birthday cake.

2003   **Photo.**   *Perf. 12½*
2021   Strip of 2 stamps and 2
    alternating labels   3.50   1.75
 a.-b.   A590 1500r Any single   1.75   .85
 c.   Sheet of 5 #2021   15.00   15.00

No. 2021 was printed in sheets containing 10 strips with labels that could be personalized. The sheet sold for 45,000r. The labels on No. 2021c could also be personalized, and that sheet sold for 30,000r.

Folklore — A591

No. 2022 — Scenes from Danau Ranau, Lampung (#a.-e.), Kongga Owose, Southeast Sulawesi (#f.-j.), Putri Gading Cempaka, Bengkulu (#k.-o.), Putri Mandalika Nyale, West Nusa Tenggara (#p.-t.) and stamp numbers: a, 01/20. b, 02/20. c, 03/20. d, 04/20. e, 05/20. f, 06/20. g, 07/20. h, 08/20. i, 09/20. j, 10/20. k, 11/20. l, 12/20. m, 13/20. n, 14/20. o, 15/20. p, 16/20. q, 17/20. r, 18/20. s, 19/20. t, 20/20.
5000r, Like #2022e.

Litho. & Photo.
2003, Feb. 2   *Perf. 13½x12¾*
2022   A591   1500r Sheet of 20,
    #a-t   15.00   7.00
Souvenir Sheet
2023   A591   5000r multi   3.00   2.00

22nd South
East Asia
Games, Hanoi, Viet
Nam
A592

Designs: 1000r, Billiards. 1500r, Rowing. 2500r, Rhythmic gymnastics.

Litho. & Photo.
2003, May 12   *Perf. 14*
2024-2026   A592   Set of 3   4.00   2.00
Values are for stamps with surrounding selvage.

Volcanoes — A593

Designs: 500r, Kerinci. No. 2028, 1000r, Krakatoa. No. 2029, 1000r, Merapi. No. 2030, 1000r, Tambora. 2000r, Ruang.
Illustration reduced.

2003, June 5   *Perf. 12½*
2027-2031   A593   Set of 5   4.00   2.00
 2031a   Sheet, 2 each #2027-2031 +
    2 labels   9.00   4.50

Astronomy — A594

No. 2032: a, Andromeda Galaxy (1/5). b, Earth and Mars (2/5). c, Moon (3/5).
No. 2033: a, External view of observatory (4/5). b, Zeiss telescope (5/5).
5000r, Like No. 2033a.

2003, June 7   *Perf. 12½*
2032   Strip of 3   2.00   1.00
 a.-c.   A594 1000r Any single   .65   .40
2033   Pair   2.00   1.00
 a.-b.   A594 1500r Either single   1.00   .40
 c.   Sheet, 2 each #2032a-2032c,
    2033a-2033b   7.00   3.50
Souvenir Sheet
Perf. 13½x12¾
2034   A594   5000r multi   4.00   2.50

Stamps in No. 2033c are tete-beche. No. 2034 contains one 41x25mm stamp.

Bank Indonesia, 50th Anniv. — A595

Designs: 1000r, Tower and flowers. 1500r, People at graduation ceremony, books.
Illustration reduced.

Perf. 13½x13¼ Syncopated
2003, July 1
2035-2036   A595   Set of 2   3.00   1.50

Sri Sultan Hamengku Buwono IX and
Lord Robert Baden-Powell — A596

Illustration reduced.

Perf. 13½x12¾
2003, Aug. 14   **Photo.**
2037   A596   1500r multi   3.00   1.50

Independence Day Games — A597

No. 2038, 1000r: a, Panjat Pinang (1/4). b, Pukul Bantal (2/4).
No. 2039, 1500r, horiz.: a, Balap Kelom (3/4). b, Balap Karung (4/4).

Perf. 12¾x13½, 13½x12¾
2003, Aug. 17   **Litho. & Photo.**
Pairs, #a-b
2038-2039   A597   Set of 2   3.50   1.75
 2039c   Sheet, 2 each #2038a-2038b,
    2039a-2039b   8.00   3.75

Souvenir Sheet

Paintings of Srihadi
Soedarsono — A598

No. 2040: a, Pendet, Dinamika Remaja. b, Borobudur-Purnama dalam Keheningan.

2003   *Perf. 13½ Syncopated*
2040   A598   3000r Sheet of 2,
    #a-b   6.00   6.00
 c.   Sheet with margin design in
    cyan only   6.00   6.00
 d.   As "c," with magenta added
    to margin design   6.00   6.00
 e.   As "d," with yellow added to
    margin design   6.00   6.00
 f.   As "e," with black added to
    margin design, but lacking
    artist's face and signature   6.00   6.00
 g.   Sheet, 2 each #2040a-
    2040b   11.00   11.00

Emmitan-Philex 2003, Surabaya (#2040, 2040c, 2040d, 2040e, 2040f), 10th ASEAN Postal Business Meeting (#2040g).
Issued: No. 2040, 9/4; No. 2040c, 8/29; No. 2040d, 8/30; No. 2040e, 8/31; No. 2040f, 9/1; No. 2040g, 9/3. No. 2040 exists imperf, issued 9/2. Value, $6.

Tourism — A599

No. 2041, 1000r: a, Jou Uci Sabea, North Maluku (1/4). b, Mome'ati, Gorontalo (2/4).
No. 2042, 1500r: a, Muang Jong, Bangka Belitung (3/4). b, Seba Baduy, Banten (4/4).
5000r, Like No. 2042a.

2003, Sept. 27   *Perf. 12½*
Vert. Pairs, #a-b
2041-2042   A599   Set of 2   3.00   1.50
Souvenir Sheet
2043   A599   5000r multi   5.00   2.50

Souvenir Sheet

Bangkok 2003 World Philatelic
Exhibition — A600

2003, Oct. 4   *Perf. 13½x12¾*
2044   A600   8000r multi   3.00   1.75

Handshake — A601

Fish and Water Lily — A602

Birds — A603

Handshake and Flag — A604

Flower — A605

Illustrations reduced.

2003, Oct. 27   **Litho.**   *Perf. 12½*
2045   A601   1000r multi + label   1.50   1.50
2046   A602   1500r multi + label   1.75   1.75
2047   A603   1500r multi + label   1.75   1.75
2048   A604   1500r multi + label   1.75   1.75
2049   A605   1500r multi + label   1.75   1.75
   Nos. 2045-2049 (5)   8.50   8.50

Nos. 2045-2049 were each issued in sheets of 20 stamps + 20 labels that could be personalized. Sheets of No. 2045 sold for 35,000r, while sheets of Nos. 2046-2049 each sold for 45,000r.

Indonesian Youth
Pledge, 75th
Anniv. — A606

2003, Oct. 28   **Litho.**   *Perf. 12¾x13¼*
2050   A606   1500r Nos. 1031-
    1032, 1246   2.00   1.00

Flowers and Insects — A607

No. 2051: a, Paphiopedilum mastersianum (9/12). b, Platylomia flavida (8/12). c, Osmoxylon palmatum (7/12). d, Apis dorsata (12/12).

e, Freycinetia pseudoinsignis (11/12). f, Sia ferox (10/12). g, Aularches miliaris (3/12). h, Butea monosperma (2/12). i, Orthetrum testaceum (1/12). j, Anaphalis javanica (6/12). k, Hierodula vitrea (5/12). l, Saraca declinata (4/12).

No. 2052: a, Like #2051j. b, Like #2051i.

Litho. & Photo.

2003, Nov. 5   *Perf. 12½*
2051 A607 1500r Block of 12,
     #a-l   15.00 7.50
m.   Booklet pane, #2051a, 2051c,
     2051e, 2051h, 2051j, 2051l   7.50 —
n.   Booklet pane, #2051b, 2051d,
     2051f, 2051g, 2051i, 2051k   7.50 —
     Complete booklet, #2051m,
     2051n   15.00

Souvenir Sheet

2052 A607 3000r Sheet of 2,
     #a-b, + label   4.50 2.25

Famous Men — A608

No. 2053: a, Prof. Roosseno (1908-96) (3/4). b, Prof. Sutami (1928-80) (4/4). c, Nurtanio Pringgoadisuryo (1923-66) (1/4). d, Martinus Putuhena (1901-82) (2/4).

Litho. & Engr.

2003, Nov. 10   *Perf. 13¼x13*
2053   Strip of 4   4.50 2.25
a.-d.   A608 2000r Any single   1.10 .55

Flowers — A609

No. 2054: a, Styrax benzoin (1/30). b, Kopsia fruticosa (2/30). c, Impatiens tujuhensis (3/30). d, Hoya diversifolia (4/30). e, Etlingera elatior (5/30). f, Dillenia suffruticosa (6/30). g, Papilionanthe hookerianum (7/30). h, Medinilla speciosa (8/30). i, Costus speciosus (9/30). j, Melastoma sylvaticum (10/30). k, Nelumbo nucifera (11/30). l, Begonia robusta (12/30). m, Anaphalis longifolia (13/30). n, Pisonia grandis (14/30). o, Ixora javanica (15/30). p, Plumeria acuminata (16/30). q, Cassia fistula (17/30). r, Calotropis gigantea (18/30). s, Dimorphorchis lowii (19/30). t, Aeschynanthus radicans (20/30). u, Sonneratia caseolaris (21/30). v, Rhododendron orbiculatum (22/30). w, Passiflora edulis (23/30). x, Pterospermum celebicum (24/30). y, Quisqualis indica (25/30). z, Spathiphyllum commutatum (26/30). aa, Lilium longiflorum (27/30). ab, Clitoria ternatea (28/30). ac, Pecteilis susannae (29/30). ad, Grammatophyllum speciosum (30/30).

Litho. & Photo.

2004, Jan. 5   *Perf. 12½*
2054   Sheet of 30   22.50 11.00
a.-ad.   A609 1500r Any single   .75 .30

Folktales — A610

No. 2055 — Scenes from Putri Selaras Pinang Masak, Jambi (#a.-e.), Tanjung Lesung, Banten (#f.-j.), Patung Palindo, Central Sulawesi (#k.-o.), Danau Tolire, North Maluku (#p.-t.) and stamp number: a, 01/20. b, 02/20. c, 03/20. d, 04/20. e, 05/20. f, 06/20. g, 07/20. h, 08/20. i, 09/20. j, 10/20. k, 11/20. l, 12/20. m, 13/20. n, 14/20. o, 15/20. p, 16/20. q, 17/20. r, 18/20. s, 19/20. t, 20/20.
6000r, Like # 2055j.

Litho. & Photo.

2004, Feb. 20   *Perf. 13½x12¾*
2055 A610 1500r Sheet of 20,
     #a-t   15.00 7.00

Souvenir Sheet

2056 A610 6000r multi   4.50 2.50

Museums — A611

No. 2057: a, Sri Baduga Museum, Bandung (3/4). b, Bahari Museum, Jakarta (1/4). c, Telecommunications Museum, Jakarta (4/4). d, Geology Museum, Bandung (2/4).

2004, Feb. 29   *Perf. 13¼x12¾*
2057   Vert. strip of 4   3.50 1.75
a.-d.   A611 1500r Any single   .85 .40

General Elections — A612

No. 2058: a, Man and woman pointing at people holding flags (1/2). b, Man and woman casting ballots (2/2).

2004, Apr. 5   **Litho.**   *Perf. 12¾x13¼*
2058 A612 1500r Horiz. pair,
     #a-b   2.25 1.10

Famous Women — A613

No. 2059: a, Gedong Bagoes Oka (1921-2002), social worker, religious leader (2/4). b, Ani Idrus (1918-99), journalist (1/4). c, Nyonya Meneer (1895-1978), founder of herbal medicine factory (3/4). d, Sandiah (Ibu Kasur) (1926-2002), composer of children's songs, television personality (4/4).

Perf. 13¼x13½ Syncopated
2004, Apr. 21   **Litho. & Engr.**
2059   Horiz. strip of 4   5.00 2.50
a.-d.   A613 2500r Any single   1.25 .60

2004 Summer Olympics, Athens A614

No. 2060: a, Swimming (1/3). b, Women's high jump (2/3). c, Hurdling (3/3).

Litho. & Photo.

2004, May 5   *Perf. 14*
2060   Horiz. strip of 3   4.50 2.25
a.-c.   A614 2500r Any single   1.50 .75

Environmental Protection — A615

Designs: Nos. 2061a, 2062a, Bird, killer whale (1/2). Nos. 2061b, 2062b, Shark, turtle (2/2).

2004, June 5   *Perf. 13¼x12¾*
2061 A615 1500r Vert. pair,
     #a-b   2.25 1.10

Souvenir Sheet

2062 A615 2500r Sheet of 2,
     #a-b   4.50 2.50

Indonesian Cuisine — A616

No. 2063: a, Gajebo, West Sumatra (1/4). b, Sambal Udang Terung Pipit, West Kalimantan (3/4). c, Kare Rajungan, East Java (2/4). d, Tinotuan, North Sulawesi (4/4).
Illustration reduced.

2004, July 6   **Litho.**   *Perf. 13¼x12¾*
2063 A616 1500r Block of 4, #a-d   4.00 2.00

Presidential Limousines — A617

No. 2064: a, 1939 Buick with REP-1 license plate (1/2). b, 1942 DeSoto with REP-2 license plate (2/2).

2004, Aug. 17
2064 A617 2500r Vert. pair, #a-b   4.00 2.00
c.   Souvenir sheet #2064a-2064b   4.00 2.00

16th National Games — A618

No. 2065: a, Volleyball (1/2). b, Sepak takraw (2/2).
Illustration reduced.

Litho. & Photo.

2004, Sept. 2   *Perf. 14*
2065 A618 1500r Pair, #a-b   3.00 1.50

Flowers and Insects Type of 2003

No. 2066: a, Gryllotalpa hirsuta (4/6). b, Alstonia scholaris (5/6). c, Scolopendra subspinipes (6/6). d, Cinnamomun sintok (3/6). e, Heterometrus cyaneus (2/6). f, Parkia roxburghii (1/6).
No. 2067: a, Like #2066e. b, Like #2066f.

2004, Nov. 5   *Perf. 12½*
2066 A607 1500r Block of 6, #a-f   6.00 3.25

Souvenir Sheet

2067 A607 3000r Sheet of 2, #a-b, + label   5.00 2.50

National Teacher's Day — A619

No. 2068: a, Teacher, students with microscope and book (1/2). b, Teacher students with pen and book (2/2).

2004, Nov. 25   *Perf. 12¾x13¼*
2068 A619 1500r Horiz. pair, #a-b   3.00 1.50

Souvenir Sheet

National Philatelic Exhibition, Surabaya — A620

No. 2069 — Paintings by Sunaryo: a, Setagen Rhythm. b, Sebelum Pentas. c, Bercinta.

2004, Dec. 16   **Litho.**   *Perf. 12½*
2069 A620 5000r Sheet of 3, #a-c   8.00 3.50
d.   Souvenir sheet of 1, #2069a   3.00 2.00
e.   Souvenir sheet of 1, #2069b   3.00 2.00
f.   Souvenir sheet of 1, #2069c   3.00 2.00
g.   Souvenir sheet of 1, #2069a, imperf.   3.00 2.00
h.   Souvenir sheet of 1, #2069b, imperf.   3.00 2.00
i.   Souvenir sheet of 1, #2069c, imperf.   3.00 2.00

Folktales — A621

No. 2070 — Scenes from Lahilote, Gorontalo (#a.-e.), Kolam Putri, Riau Islands (#f.-j.), Batu Balai, Bangka Belitung (#k.-o.), Bulan & Sagu di Ibuanari, Papua (#p.-t.) and stamp number: a, 1/20. b, 2/20. c, 3/20. d, 4/20. e, 5/20. f, 6/20. g, 7/20. h, 8/20. i, 9/20. j, 10/20. k, 11/20. l, 12/20. m, 13/20. n, 14/20. o, 15/20. p, 16/20. q, 17/20. r, 18/20. s, 19/20. t, 20/20.
6000r, Like #2070j.

2005, Feb. 2   **Litho.**   *Perf. 13½x12¾*
2070 A621 1500r Sheet of 20,
     #a-t   14.00 7.00

Souvenir Sheet

2071 A621 6000r multi   4.00 2.00

Asian-African Summit, 50th
Anniv. — A622

No. 2072: a, Dove and "50." b, Dove, world
map and people.

Perf. 13½x13¼ Syncopated

2005, Apr. 18	Litho. & Photo.
2072	Horiz. pair + central label	3.00	1.50
a.-b.	A622 2500r Either single	1.50	.75
c.	Souvenir sheet, #2072b	1.50	.75

Mangrove Forest Protection — A623

No. 2073 — Mangroves and: a, Bird. b, Fish.

2005, June 5	Litho.	Perf. 12¾x13¼
2073	A623 1500r Horiz. pair, #a-b	2.00	1.00
c.	Souvenir sheet, #2073	2.00	1.00

Voyages of Admiral Zheng He, 600th Anniv. A624

Litho. & Photo.

2005, June 28	Perf. 13½x12¾
2074	A624 2500r multi	2.00	1.00
a.	Souvenir sheet of 1	3.00	1.00

Traditional Food A625

No. 2075: a, Sayur Tauco (North Sumatra)
(1/4). b, Soto Banjar (South Kalimantan) (3/4).
c, Nasi Timbel (West Java) (2/4). d, Langga
Roko (South Sulawesi) (4/4).

2005, July 6	Litho.
2075	Vert. strip of 4	2.75	1.40
a.-d.	A625 1500r Any single	.70	.30

Energy Conservation A626

Designs: 1500r, Bus, electric plug (1/3).
2000r, Electric plugs and outlet (2/3). 2500r,
Automobile (3/3).

2005, Aug. 17	Perf. 12½
2076-2078 A626	Set of 3	2.75	1.40

Indonesian Leaders A627

Designs: Nos. 2079a, 2080a, Pres. Susilo
Banbang Yudhoyono. Nos. 2079b, 2080b,
Vice-president Muhammad Jusuf Kalla.

2005, Aug. 17	Litho.
2079	Horiz. pair with central label	1.50	.75
a.-b.	A627 1500r Either single	.75	.25

Litho. With Foil Application

2080	Horiz. pair with central label	3.00	1.50
a.-b.	A627 2500r Either single	1.50	.75
c.	Souvenir sheet, #2080a, 2080b	3.00	1.50

Borobudur Ship Expedition — A628

No. 2081: a, Ship, head of Buddha (2/2). b,
Carving of ship (1/2).
Illustration reduced.

2005, Sept. 17		
2081 A628 1500r Pair, #a-b	3.00	1.50
c.	As "a," with "2/2" removed	2.00	1.00
d.	As "b," with "1/2" removed	2.00	1.00
e.	Souvenir sheet, #2081c, 2081d + central label	4.00	2.00

Souvenir Sheet

National Philatelic Exhibition,
Cilegon — A629

No. 2082 — Paintings by Sudjana Kerton: a,
Nyawer. b, Makan Siang. c, Wayang Golek. d,
Tanah Air Indonesia.

2005, Sept. 23		Perf. 12½
2082 A629	Sheet of 4	8.00	4.00
a.-c.	5000r Any single	2.00	1.00
d.	8000r multi	3.00	1.50
e.	Souvenir sheet, #2082a, imperf.	1.75	.85
f.	Souvenir sheet, #2082b, imperf.	1.75	.85
g.	Souvenir sheet, #2082c, imperf.	1.75	.85
h.	Souvenir sheet, #2082d, imperf.	3.00	1.50

Sea Mammals and Plants — A630

No. 2083: a, Neophocaena phocaenoides
(1/4). b, Dugong dugon (2/4). c, Gelidium
latifolium (3/4). d, Halimeda opuntia (4/4).
Illustration reduced.

2005, Nov. 5		Perf. 12½
2083 A630 1500r Block of 4, #a-d	3.00	1.50
e.	As "a," with "1/4" removed	2.00	1.00
f.	As "b," with "3/4" removed	2.00	1.00
g.	Souvenir sheet, #2083e, 2083f + central label	2.00	1.00

Folktales — A631

No. 2084: a, Bawang Merah & Bawang
Putih (1/4). b, Keong Emas (2/4). c, Si Kancil
(3/4). d, Timun Emas (4/4).

2006, Feb. 6	Litho.	Perf. 12¾x13½
2084	Block or strip of 4	3.25	1.60
a.-d.	A631 1500r Any single	.80	.40
e.	Souvenir sheet, #2084a-2084d, imperf.	5.00	2.50

Miniature Sheets

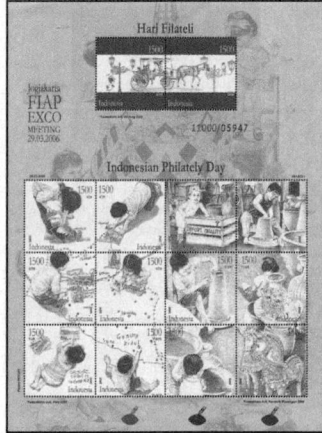

Philately Day — A632

No. 2085, 1500r — Illustrations in brown: a,
Family in coach (1/28). b, Horse pulling coach
(2/28). c, Girl, standing, with three photographs (3/28). d, Boy with one photograph
(4/28). e, Boy with three photographs (5/28). f,
Girl, wearing sandals, holding photograph
(6/28). g, Barefoot girl touching photograph
(7/28). h, Boy drawing map (8/28). i, Boy and
crate (9/28). j, Boy at potter's wheel, finished
pottery (10/28). k, Boy at potter's wheel
(11/28). l, Girl pointing (12/28). m, Boy touching pottery (13/28). n, Caparisoned pottery
horses (14/28).

No. 2086, 1500r — Illustrations in color: a,
Like #2085a (15/28). b, Like #2085b (16/28).
c, Like #2085c (17/28). d, Like #2085d (18/28).
e, Like #2085e (19/28). f, Like #2085f (20/28).
g, Like #2085g (21/28). h, Like #2085h
(22/28). i, Like #2085i (23/28). j, Like #2085j
(24/28). k, Like #2085k (25/28). l, Like #2085l
(26/28). m, Like #2085m (27/28). n, Like
#2085n (28/28).

2006, Mar. 29	Litho.	Perf. 14
Sheets of 14, #a-n		
2085-2086 A632	Set of 2	16.00	8.25

2006 World Cup Soccer
Championships, Germany — A633

No. 2087: a, World Cup emblem, goal, soccer ball (1/4). b, World Cup emblem, soccer
ball (2/4). c, World Cup trophy at right, soccer
ball at bottom (3/4). d, World Cup trophy at left,
soccer ball at right (4/4).
Illustration reduced.

**Die Cut, With Perf. 14 Selvage
Between Stamps**

2006, May 6		
Self-Adhesive		
2087 A633 2500r Block of 4, #a-d	5.50	2.75
e.	Booklet pane, #2087a-2087d, die cut, imperf. selvage between stamps	6.00	
	Complete booklet, #2087e	7.00	

Individual stamps have various die cut soccer players in center. Values are for unused
stamps with surrounding selvage. Used
stamps may or may not have the die cut soccer players.

Environmental Care — A634

No. 2088: a, Village, flowers, butterfly (1/2).
b, Girl (2/2).

2006, June 5	Litho.	Perf. 13¼x12¾
2088 A634 1500r Pair, #a-b	2.00	.90
c.	Souvenir sheet, #2088a-2088b	2.00	.90

Local Foods A635

No. 2089: a, Pempek (South Sumatra, 1/4).
b, Gudeg (Yogyakarta, 2/4). c, Ayam Betutu
(Bali, 3/4). d, Aunu Senebre (Papua, 4/4).

2006, July 6		
2089	Block or strip of 4	2.50	1.25
a.-d.	A635 1500r Any single	.60	.30

National Scout Jamboree — A636

No. 2090: a, Kak Mashudi and scouts
around campfire (1/2). b, Jigsaw puzzle of
scouts (2/2).
Illustration reduced.

Litho. & Photo.

2006, July 16		Perf. 12½
2090 A636 1500r Pair, #a-b	2.00	1.00

Sultans
A637

No. 2091d Overprinted in Red Foil

No. 2091: a, Sultan Ma'moen Al Rasyid
Perkasa Alamsyah Sultan Deli IX (1873-1924)
(1/4). b, Sultan Agung Sultan Mataram III
(1613-45) (2/4). c, Sultan Adji Mohamad
Parikesit Sultan Kutai Kertanegara XX (1920-
60) (3/4). d, Sultan Hasanuddin Sultan Gowa
XVI (1653-69) (4/4).

Litho., Litho. with Foil Application (#2091e)

Perf. 13½ Syncopated

2006, Aug. 17
2091		Block or strip of 4	3.00 1.50
a.-d.		A637 1500r Any single	.75 .35
e.		As "d," overprinted in red foil	3.00 1.50
f.		Block or strip of 4, #2091a-2091c, 2091e	8.00 4.00

Puppets — A638

No. 2092: a, Indonesian puppet (1/2). b, Slovakian marionette (2/2).

Litho. & Photo.

2006, Sept. 27 — **Perf. 13x13¼**
2092	A638	2500r Horiz. pair, #a-b	2.00 1.00
c.		Souvenir sheet, #2092	2.00 1.00

See Slovakia Nos. 506-507.

Miniature Sheet

Eid ul-Fitr — A639

No. 2093: a, Man sitting with crossed legs in prayer (1/8). b, Drummer (5/8). c, Older woman hugging young woman (2/8). d, Woman and man with hands in prayer (6/8). e, Mosque (3/8). f, People getting on bus (7/8). g, Geometric design (4/8). h, People and horse cart (8/8).

Nos. 2093lj-2093lq: As Nos. 2039a-2093h, but with Prisma emblem in lower corner of stamp and persoanlized photo above arc.

2006, Oct. 3 — **Litho.** — **Perf. 12½**
2093	A639	1500r Sheet of 8, #a-h	4.00 2.00
2093l	A639	1500r Sheet of 8, #j-q	5.25 5.25

No. 2093l sold for 20,000r.

Flora and Fauna — A640

No. 2094: a, Licuala arbuscula (3/4). b, Livistona mamberamoensis (4/4). c, Melipotes carolae (1/4). d, Amblyornis flavifrons (2/4). Illustration reduced.

2006, Nov. 5 — **Perf. 12½**
2094	A640	1500r Block of 4, #a-d	3.00 1.50
e.		As "a," with "3/4" removed	2.00 1.00
f.		As "d," with "2/4" removed	2.00 1.00
g.		Souvenir sheet, #2094e-2094f + label	4.00 2.00

Souvenir Sheet

Bandung '06 Natl. Philatelic Exhibition — A641

No. 2095: a, Panthera pardus (1/2). b, Bouea macrophylla (2/2).

Perf. 13½x12¾

2006, Nov. 30 — **Litho.**
2095	A641	2500r Sheet of 2, #a-b	4.00 2.00
c.		Like #2095, with margin illustration in blue and black	2.00 1.00
d.		Like #2095, with margin illustration in red and black	2.00 1.00
e.		Like #2095, with margin illustration in yellow and black	2.00 1.00
f.		Like #2095, with margin illustration in black	2.00 1.00

On No. 2095, the code number at lower left of sheet ends with "5," that of Nos. 2095c-2095f end in "1" to "4" respectively. Margin illustrations show progressive color printing.

Containers — A642

No. 2096: a, Container from Bali (2/2). b, Lidded basket from East Kalimantan (1/2). Illustration reduced.

2006, Dec. 23 — **Perf. 13½x12¾**
2096	A642	1500r Horiz. pair, #a-b	1.50 .75

New Year 2007 (Year of the Pig) A643

No. 2097: a, Chinese zodiac animals and lanterns (1/2). b, Chinese zodiac animals, people and temple (2/2).

No. 2098: a, Rat (1/13). b, Ox (2/13). c, Tiger (3/13). d, Rabbit (4/13). e, Dragon (5/13). f, Snake (6/13). g, Horse (7/13). h, Goat (8/13). i, Monkey (9/13). j, Rooster (10/13). k, Dog (11/13). l, Pig (12/13). m, Like #2097b (96x64mm, 13/13).

No. 2099, Like #2097b.

Litho., Litho. With Foil Application (#2098m, 2099)

2007, Feb. 1 — **Perf. 12½**
2097		Pair	1.10 .70
a.-b.		A643 1500r Either single	.55 .30
2098		Sheet of 13	10.00 10.00
a.-l.		A643 2000r Any single	.60 .30
m.		A643 6000r multi	2.00 1.00

Souvenir Sheet
2099	A643	6000r multi	2.00 1.00

Dances — A644

No. 2100: a, Lion dance (1/2). b, Dragon dance (2/2).

Perf. 13¼x13½ Syncopated

2007, Apr. 13 — **Litho.**
2100	A644	2500r Pair, #a-b	1.60 .80
c.		Souvenir sheet, #2100a-2100b	2.50 1.25

See People's Republic of China Nos. 3581-3582.

Reading and Writing A645

No. 2101: a, Boy writing in book, mother reading (2/2). b, Boy looking at girl writing in book (1/2).

2007, May 2 — **Litho.** — **Perf. 13½x12¾**
2101	A645	1500r Pair, #a-b	1.10 .55

A646

Environmental Care — A647

Nos. 2102, 2104: a, Iceberg, top of polar bear's head (1/4). b, Crying polar bear (2/4).

No. 2103: a, Forest fire (3/4). b, Burnt forest (4/4).

2007, June 5
2102	A646	1500r Vert. pair, #a-b	1.10 .55
2103	A647	1500r Vert. pair, #a-b	1.10 .55

Souvenir Sheet
2104	A646	2500r Sheet of 2, #a-b	1.75 .85

Nos. 2102 and 2103 were each printed in sheets containing 10 pairs with the bottom stamp in the pair tete-beche with the same stamp.

Campaign Against Drug Abuse — A648

No. 2105: a, Guitarist, Indonesian inscription (1/2). b, Basketball player, English inscription (2/2).

2007, June 26 — **Perf. 12¾x13½**
2105	A648	1500r Pair, #a-b	1.75 .85

Traditional Foods — A649

No. 2106: a, Roti Cane and Kari Kambing (Aceh, 1/4). b, Gecok (West Nusa Tenggara, 3/4). c, Soto Kudus (Central Java, 2/4). d, Ikan Air Garam (Maluku, 4/4).

2007, July 6 — **Perf. 13½x12¾**
2106		Strip of 4	2.50 1.25
a.-d.		A649 1500r Any single	.60 .30

A650

A651

A652

Greetings With Hands — A653

Illustrations reduced.

2007, June 3 — **Litho.** — **Perf. 12½**
2107	A650	1500r multi + label	2.00 2.00
2108	A651	1500r multi + label	2.00 2.00
a.		Pair, #2107-2108, + 2 labels	4.00 4.00
2109	A652	1500r multi + label	2.00 2.00
2110	A653	1500r multi + label	2.00 2.00
a.		Pair, #2109-2110, + 2 labels	4.00 4.00
		Nos. 2107-2110 (4)	8.00 8.00

Nos. 2107-2108 and 2109-2110 were each printed in sheets of 20 stamps + 20 labels, containing ten of each stamp. Sheets sold for 45,000r. Labels could be personalized. A sheet of 20 No. 2107 + 20 non-personalizable labels, issued in 2008, also sold for 45,000r.

Fireworks — A654

Guitar and G Clef A655

Paint Brushes — A656

Film and Reel A657

Perf. 12½x12½x12½x4

2007, July 21 Litho.
2111	A654	1500r multi + label	2.00	2.00
2112	A655	1500r multi + label	2.00	2.00
2113	A656	1500r multi + label	2.00	2.00
2114	A657	1500r multi + label	2.00	2.00
	Nos. 2111-2114 (4)		8.00	8.00

Nos. 2111-2114 were each printed in sheets of 8 stamps + 8 labels that sold for 15,000r face. No. 2111 also was printed in four different sheets of 12 stamps + 12 labels that each sold for 30,000r. Labels could not be personalized.

Scouting, Cent. — A658

No. 2115, 2500r: a, Centenary emblem, full color background (1/4). b, Scout, full color (2/4).
No. 2116, 1500r: a, Centenary emblem, blue background (3/4). b, Scout in blue (4/4).

2007, Aug. 1 **Perf. 13½ Syncopated**
2115	A658	Horiz. pair, #a-b	2.25	1.10

Booklet Stamps
2116	A658	Horiz. pair, #a-b	1.10	.55
c.		Booklet pane, 5 #2116	5.50	—
		Complete booklet, #2116c	5.50	

Nepenthes Mirabilis — A659

Nepenthes Ampullaria — A660

2007, Aug. 3 **Perf. 13½x12¾**
2117	A659	1500r multi	.60	.30

Perf. 12¾x13½
2118	A660	1500r multi	.60	.30

Souvenir Sheet
Perf. 13½x12¾
2119		Sheet of 2	2.50	1.25
a.		A659 2500r multi	1.25	.60
b.		A660 2500r multi	1.25	.60

Bangkok 2007 Intl. Stamp Exhibition.

Association of South East Asian Nations (ASEAN), 40th Anniv. A661

Designs: 1500r, Fatahillah Museum, Jakarta.
No. 2121: a, Secretariat Building, Bandar Seri Begawan, Brunei (1/10). b, National Museum of Cambodia (2/10). c, Fatahillah Museum, Jakarta (3/10). d, Typical house, Laos (4/10). e, Malayan Railway Headquarters Building, Kuala Lumpur, Malaysia (5/10). f, Yangon Post Office, Myanmar (6/10). g, Malacañang Palace, Philippines (7/10). h, National Museum of Singapore (8/10). i, Vimanmek Mansion, Bangkok, Thailand (9/10). j, Presidential Palace, Hanoi, Viet Nam (10/10).

2007, Aug. 8 **Perf. 13½ Syncopated**
2120	A661	1500r multi	1.00	.50
2121		Sheet of 10	9.00	4.50
a.-j.		A661 2500r Any single	.90	.45

See Brunei No. 607, Burma No. 370, Cambodia No. 2339, Laos Nos. 1717-1718, Malaysia No. 1170, Philippines Nos. 3103-3105, Singapore No. 1265, Thailand No. 2315, and Viet Nam Nos. 3302-3311.

Lighthouses — A662

No. 2122: a, Semarang Lighthouse (1/2). b, Cikoneng Lighthouse (2/2).

2007, Aug. 17 **Perf. 12¾x13½**
2122	A662	1500r Horiz. pair, #a-		
		b	1.25	.60

Padjadjaran University, 50th Anniv. — A663

No. 2123: a, Tiger and ram (1/4). b, Men and dancers (2/4). c, Building (3/4). d, Symbols and globe (4/4).

2007, Sept. 5 **Perf. 13½x12¾**
2123		Horiz. strip of 4 + central label	4.00	2.00
a.-d.		A663 1500r Any single	1.00	.50

Butterflies — A664

No. 2124: a, Delias kristianiae (1/4). b, Ornithoptera aesacus (2/4). c, Ornithoptera croesus (3/4). d, Troides hypolitus (4/4).
No. 2125: a, Like #2124a. b, Like #2124c.

2007, Nov. 5 **Perf. 12½**
2124		Block of 4	2.25	1.10
a.-d.		A664 1500r Any single	.35	.30

Souvenir Sheet
2125		Sheet of 2 + central label	2.00	1.00
a.-b.		A664 2500r Either single	1.00	.50

No. 2125 Surcharged in Gold

2007, Nov. 21 **Litho.** **Perf. 12½**
2126		Sheet of 2 + central label	6.00	3.00
a.-b.		A664 5000r on 2500r Either single	3.00	1.50

No. 2126 also is overprinted in gold in margin and label with emblem and text for Bandungfilex 2007 and Jakarta 2008 Intl. Stamp Exhibition.

24th South East Asian Games, Nakhon Ratchasima, Thailand — A665

No. 2127: a, Bowling (1/4). b, Indoor soccer (2/4). c, Kempo (3/4). d, Hammer throw (4/4).

2007, Dec. 6 **Perf. 14**
2127		Horiz. strip of 4	4.00	2.00
a.-d.		A665 2500r Any single	1.00	.50

Djuanda Declaration, 50th Anniv. — A666

No. 2128: a, Map of Indonesia, children (1/3). b, Prime Minister Djuanda Kartawidjaja, eagle, and procession (2/3). c, Djuanda Kartawidjaja and map of Indonesia (3/3).

2007, Dec. 13 **Perf. 13½x12¾**
2128		Vert. strip of 3	2.50	1.25
a.-c.		A666 1500r Any single	.80	.40

Miniature Sheet

Jakarta 2008 Intl. Stamp Exhibition — A667

No. 2129: a, Prasasti Tugu (2/7). b, Arca Dewa Visnu (statue of Vishnu) (3/7). c, Prasasti Padrao (4/7). d, Peta Nusantara Zaman Portugis (5/7). e, Naskah Perjanjian Sunda Kelapa (6/7). f, Kapal Bangsa Portugis (7/7). g, Bendera Singa Ali and Fatahillah

(1/7). Nos. 2129a-2129f are 41x25mm; No. 2129g, 83x25mm.

2008, Jan. 20 **Litho.** **Perf. 13½x12¾**
2129	A667	Sheet of 7	5.50	2.75
a.-f.		2500r Any single	.55	.25
g.		10,000r multi	2.10	1.10

A668

New Year 2008 (Year of the Rat) — A669

No. 2130: a, Rat facing right (1/3). b, Rat facing left (2/3). c, Rat on hind legs (3/3).

2008, Jan. 26 **Perf. 13½x12¾**
2130		Vert. strip of 3 + label	1.60	.80
a.-c.		A668 2000r Any single	.50	.25

Souvenir Sheet
Perf. 12½
2131	A669	5000r black & gray	2.25	1.10

Souvenir Sheet

Flora and Fauna — A670

No. 2132: a, Casuarius casuarius (1/2). b, Crinum asiaticum (2/2).

2008, Mar. 7 **Perf. 12¾x13½**
2132	A670	5000r Sheet of 2, #a-		
		b	3.00	1.50

Jakarta 2008 Intl. Stamp Exhibition, Taipei 2008 Intl. Stamp Exhibition, Stamp Passion '08 Stamp Exhibition, Netherlands.

2008 Summer Olympics, Beijing — A671

No. 2133: a, Sailboarding (1/4). b, Soccer (2/4). c, Badminton (3/4). d, Weight lifting (4/4).
Illustration reduced.

2008, Mar. 18 **Perf. 14**
2133	A671	2500r Block of 4, #a-		
		d	3.00	1.50

Miniature Sheet

Jakarta 2008 Intl. Stamp
Exhibition — A672

No. 2134: a, Istana Pemerintahan Batavia (2/7). b, Gedung Keuangan (3/7). c, Penyerangan Batavia oleh Sultan Agung, denomination at LR (4/7). d, Penyerangan Batavia oleh Sultan Agung, denomination at LL (5/7). e, Perubahan Batavia Menjadi Jakarta (6/7). f, Penyerahan Kekuasaan Indonesia (7/7). g, Penangkapan Pangeran Jayawikarta oleh Pasukan Banten (1/7). Nos. 2134a-2134f are 41x25mm; No. 2134g, 83x25mm.

Perf. 13½x12¾

2008, Mar. 29			Litho.
2134	A672	Sheet of 7	5.50	2.75
a.-f.		2500r Any single	.55	.25
g.		10,000r multi	2.10	1.10

Diplomatic Relations Between
Indonesia and Japan, 50th
Anniv. — A673

No. 2135, 2500r: a, Kelimutu Volcano, Indonesia (1/10). b, Mt. Fuji, Japan (2/10).
No. 2136, 2500r: a, Borobudur, Indonesia (3/10). b, Toji Temple, Japan (4/10).
No. 2137, 2500r: a, Rafflesia arnoldi (5/10). b, Cherry blossoms (6/10).
No. 2138, 2500r: a, Angklung (7/10). b, Gaku biwa (8/10).
No. 2139, 2500r, horiz: a, Scleropages formosus (9/10). b, Nishiki-goi (10/10).
Illustration reduced.

2008, Apr. 15			*Perf. 12½*
	Horiz. Pairs, #a-b		
2135-2139	A673	Set of 5	6.50	3.25
2139c		Miniature sheet, #2135-2139	6.50	3.25

Nos. 2135-2139 were each printed in sheets of 4 pairs. See Japan No. 3018.

Special
Needs
Education
A674

No. 2140: a, Boy in wheelchair waving flags (1/3). b, Man in racing wheelchair (2/3). c, Handicapped children playing anklungs (3/3).

	Litho. & Embossed		
2008, May 2		*Perf. 13½x12¾*	
2140		Strip of 3	1.60	.80
a.-c.	A674	1500r Any single	.50	.25

National Awakening, Cent. — A675

No. 2141: a, People with fists raised, flag. b, Flag, people, satellite.

2008, May 20	Litho.	*Perf. 12¾x13½*		
2141	A675	1500r Horiz. pair, #a-b	.80	.40

Environmental Care — A676

Nos. 2142 and 2143: a, Cyclists, motor vehicles (1/2). b, Seedling, forest (2/2). Stamps from No. 2143 lack stamp numbers.

2008, June 5		*Perf. 13½x12¾*		
2142	A676	1500r Pair, #a-b	.80	.40
	Souvenir Sheet			
2143	A676	2500r Sheet of 2, #a-b	1.25	1.25

Miniature Sheet

Jakarta 2008 Intl. Stamp
Exhibition — A677

No. 2144: a, Jakarta Philatelic Center (Kantor Filateli Jakarta) (2/7). b, National Museum (3/7). c, Dunia Fantasi (4/7). d, Taman Mini Indonesia (5/7). e, Wisana Seni dan Budaya (6/7). f, Wisata Bihari (7/7). g, Warna Warni Jakarta (1/7). Nos. 2144a-2144f are 41x25mm; No. 2144g, 83x25mm.

2008, June 22			*Perf. 13½x12¾*
2144	A677	Sheet of 7	5.50	2.75
a.-f.		2500r Any single	.55	.25
g.		10,000r multi	2.10	1.10

17th National Games — A678

No. 2145: a, Mountain biking (1/4). b, Bodybuilding (2/4). c, Steeplechase (3/4). d, Palaran Main Stadium, Samarinda (4/4). Illustration reduced.

2008, July 5			*Perf. 14*
2145	A678	1500r Block of 4, #a-d	2.00	1.00

Traditional Foods Type of 2007

No. 2146: a, Nasi Lemak (Riau, 1/4). b, Sate Bandeng (Banten, 2/4). c, Ayem Cincane (East Kalimantan, 3/4). d, Kaledo (Central Sulawesi, 4/4).

2008, July 6			*Perf. 13½x12¾*
2146		Block of 4	1.60	.80
a.-d.	A649	1500r Any single	.40	.20

Printed in sheets containing four of each stamp + four labels.

Provincial Arms and
Architecture — A679

Arms of: Nos. 2147, 1500r, 2158a, 2500r, Bali (1/33). Nos. 2148, 1500r, 2158b, 2500r, Gorontalo (2/33). Nos. 2149, 1500r, 2158c, 2500r, Jawa Barat (West Java) (3/33). Nos. 2150, 1500r, 2158d, 2500r, Jawa Tengah (Central Java) (4/33). Nos. 2151, 1500r, 2158e, 2500r, Kalimantan Barat (West Kalimantan) (5/33). Nos. 2152, 1500r, 2158f, 2500r, Maluku (Moluccas) (6/33). Nos. 2153, 1500r, 2158g, 2500r, Aceh (7/33). Nos. 2154, 1500r, 2158h, 2500r, Papua (8/33). Nos. 2155, 1500r, 2158i, 2500r, Riau (9/33). Nos. 2156, 1500r, 2158j, 2500r, Sulawesi Barat (West Sulawesi) (10/33). Nos. 2157, 1500r, 2158k, 2500r, Sumatera Barat (West Sumatra) (11/33).

2008, Aug. 17			*Perf. 12½*
2147-2157	A679	Set of 11	5.50	2.75
2158		Sheet of 11 + label	7.50	4.00
a.-k.	A679	2500r Any single	.65	.30

Nos. 2147-2157 each were printed in sheets of 10.
See Nos. 2200-2211.

Great
Post
Road of
Java
A680

No. 2159: a, Lighthouse, map of western part of road (1/4). b, Building, map of central part of road (2/4). c, Lighthouse, map of eastern part of road (3/4). d, Letter from Governor General Herman Daendels (4/4).
10,000r, Map of entire road.

2008, Sept. 27			*Perf. 13½x12¾*
2159		Horiz. strip of 4	3.00	1.50
a.-d.	A680	2500r Any single	.75	.35
	Souvenir Sheet			
2160	A680	10,000r multi	3.50	1.75

No. 2160 contains one 125x25mm stamp.

Souvenir Sheets

A681

A682

A683

A684

A685

Jakarta 2008 Intl. Stamp
Exhibition — A686

2008			*Perf. 13½x12¾*
2161	A681	5000r multi	1.40	.70
2162	A682	5000r multi	1.40	.70
2163	A683	5000r multi	1.40	.70
2164	A684	5000r multi	1.40	.70

2165 A685 5000r multi 1.40 .70
2166 A686 5000r multi 1.40 .70
Nos. 2161-2166 (6) 8.40 4.20

Issued: No. 2161, 10/23; No. 2162, 10/24; No. 2163, 10/25; No. 2164, 10/26; No. 2165, 10/27; No. 2166, 10/28.

Miniature Sheet

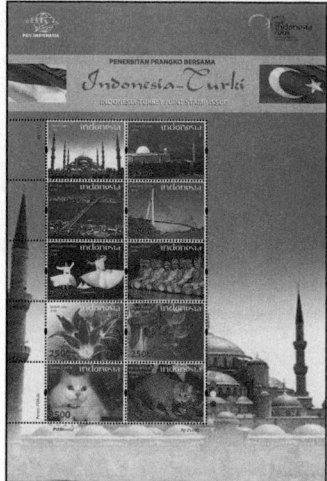

Friendship Between Indonesia and Turkey — A687

No. 2167: a, Blue Mosque, Turkey (1/10). b, Istiqlal Mosque, Indonesia (2/10). c, Bosporus Bridge, Turkey (3/10). d, Barelang Bridge, Indonesia (4/10). e, Whirling dervishes (5/10). f, Saman dance (6/10). g, Turkish tulip (7/10). h, Flame of Irian (8/10). i, Turkish Van cat (9/10). j, Flat-headed cat (10/10).

2008, Oct. 24 **Perf. 13½ Syncopated**
2167 A687 2500r Sheet of 10,
#a-j 7.50 3.75

Miniature Sheet

Flora and Fauna of the Provinces — A688

No. 2168: a, Leucopsar rothschildi, Dysoxylum densiflorum, Bali (1/11). b, Liza dussumieri, Vitex cofassus, Gorontalo (2/11). c, Panthera pardus, Bouea macrophylla, Jawa Barat (West Java) (3/11). d, Oriolus chinensis, Michelia alba, Jawa Tengah (Central Java) (4/11). e, Rhinoplax vigil, Shorea stenoptera, Kalimantan Barat (West Kalimantan) (5/11). f, Alisterus amboinensis, Dendrobium phalaenopsis, Maluku (Moluccas) (6/11). g, Copsychus pyrropygus, Michelia champaca, Aceh (7/11). h, Seleucidis melanoleuca, Pometia pinnata, Papua (8/11). i, Loriculus galgulus, Oncosperma tigillarium, Riau (9/11). j, Aramidopsis plateni, Elmerrillia ovalis, Sulawesi Barat (West Sulawesi) (10/11). k, Argusianus argus, Morus macroura, Sumatera Barat (West Sumatra) (11/11).

2008, Nov. 5 **Perf. 13½x12¾**
2168 A688 2500r Sheet of 11,
#a-k, + label 8.00 4.00
See Nos. 2217, 2249-2252.

Cut Nyak Dhien (1848-1908), Leader of Aceh Resistance to Dutch Rule — A689

No. 2169: a, House (1/2). b, Cut Nyak Dhien (2/2).

2008, Nov. 5
2169 A689 1500r Horiz. pair, #a-
b 1.00 .50

Islands A690

No. 2170: a, Damar Island (1/4). b, Sebatik Island (2/4). c, Batubawaikang Island (3/4). d, Bras Island (4/4).

2008, Dec. 3
2170 Block or strip of 4 2.00 1.00
a.-d. A690 1500r multi .50 .25
e. Miniature sheet, 4 each #2170a-2170d 8.00 4.00

New Year 2009 (Year of the Ox) A691

Designs: Nos. 2171, 2174a, 2000r, Head of ox (1/3). Nos. 2172, 2174b, 2000r, Ox looking left (2/3). Nos. 2173, 2174c, 2000r, Ox in water (3/3). 10,000r, Ox, diff.

2009, Jan. 10 **Litho.**
2171-2173 A691 Set of 3 1.75 .85
Litho. & Embossed With Foil Application (Chinese Character in Gold)
2174 A691 2000r Vert. strip of 3, #a-c 2.00 1.00
Souvenir Sheet
2175 A691 10,000r multi 2.75 1.40

Nos. 2171-2173 were printed in a sheet of 24 stamps containing 8 of each stamp. No. 2174 was printed in a sheet containing 2 strips.

Bandung Institute of Technology, 50th Anniv. — A692

No. 2176: a, Building, colored triangles (1/4). b, Emblems, crowd of dignitaries (2/4). c, "89 Tahun," text (3/4). d, Emblem dated "1920" (4/4).

2009, Mar. 2 **Litho.**
2176 Horiz. strip of 4 + central label 1.75 .85
a.-d. A692 1500r Any single .45 .20

A693

A694

A695

General Elections — A696

2009, Mar. 5 **Perf. 13x13¼**
2177 Strip of 4 1.60 .80
a. A693 1500r multi .40 .20
b. A694 1500r multi .40 .20
c. A695 1500r multi .40 .20
d. A696 1500r multi .40 .20

Souvenir Sheet

Preservation of Polar Regions and Glaciers — A697

No. 2178 — Snowflake emblem and: a, Iceberg, top of polar bear's head. b, Crying polar bear.

2009, Mar. 18 **Perf. 13½x12¾**
2178 A697 2500r Sheet of 2, #a-
b 2.00 1.00
Compare with No. 2104.

Souvenir Sheet

China 2009 World Stamp Exhibition, Luoyang — A698

2009, Apr. 10
2179 A698 10,000r multi 2.75 1.40

Intl. Year of Astronomy A699

Nos. 2180 and 2181: a, Galileo's telescope (1/3). b, Intl. Year of Astronomy emblem (2/3). c, Galileo Galilei (1564-1642) (3/3).

2009, May 2 **Litho.** **Perf. 13x13¼**
2180 Horiz. strip of 3 2.50 1.25
a.-c. A699 2500r Any single .80 .25
Souvenir Sheet
Litho. With Hologram
2181 Sheet of 3 5.00 2.50
a.-c. A699 5000r Any single 1.60 .80

World Ocean Conference, Manado — A700

No. 2182: a, Blue-ringed angelfish (1/4). b, Anemone shrimp and sea anemone (2/4). c, Goldback anthias (3/4). d, Coral reef (4/4). 5000r, Sea turtle.
Illustration reduced.

2009, May 11 **Perf. 13½x12¾**
2182 A700 2500r Block or strip of 4, #a-d 3.00 1.50
Souvenir Sheet
2183 A700 5000r multi 1.75 .85

World Environment Day — A701

No. 2184: a, Boy holding plant, parched earth (3/3). b, Factories, people in bubble (2/3). c, Smokestacks, tree, boy near forest (1/3). 5000r, Like 2184c.

2009, June 5
2184 Strip of 3 1.50 .75
a.-c. A701 1500r Any single .50 .25
Souvenir Sheet
2185 A701 5000r multi 1.50 .75

Opening of Suramadu Bridge — A702

No. 2186: a, City, statue, end of bridge (1/3). b, Bridge towers (2/3). c, End of bridge, boat, farmer with oxen (3/3). 10,000r, Entire bridge, city, sculpture, boat, farmer with oxen.

2009, June 10
2186 Horiz. strip of 3 1.50 .75
a.-c. A702 1500r Any single .50 .25
Souvenir Sheet
2187 A702 10,000r multi 3.00 1.50
No. 2187 contains one 126x25mm stamp.

Traditional Foods A703

No. 2188: a, Ihutilinanga (Gorontalo, 1/6). b, Gulai Balak (Lampung, 2/6). c, Sate Tambulinas (Southeast Sulawesi, 3/6). d, Sambal Goreng Papai (Central Kalimantan, 4/6). e, Nasi Uduk (Jakarta, 5/6). f, Ikan Bobara Kuah Asam (West Papua, 6/6).

2009, July 6
2188 Block of 6 3.00 1.50
a.-f. A703 1500r Any single .50 .25

BirdLife International — A704

No. 2189, 2500r: a, Ciconia stormi, with first "0" in denomination below bird (6/6). b, Aceros corrugatus, with first "0" in denomination touching central line of leaf (1/6).

No. 2190, 2500r, horiz.: a, Harpactes kasumba, with "A" of "Indonesia" barely touching bird's tail (41x25mm, 2/6). b, Actenoides concretus, with entire center of "D" in "Indonesia" over tree branch (41x25mm, 3/6).

No. 2191, 2500r, horiz.: a, Cairina scutulata, with farthest extent of white water ripple line running through "5" in denomination (41x25mm, 4/6). b, Argusianus argus, with white water ripple line touching "2" and "5" in denomination (41x25mm, 5/6).

No. 2192, 2500r: a, Like #2189a, with first "0" in denomination touching bird. b, Like #2189b, with first "0" in denomination above central line of leaf. c, Like #2190a, with "A" of "Indonesia" half on bird's tail, and without "2/6." d, Like #2190b, with center of "D" of "Indonesia" partly on tree branch. e, Like #2191a, with farthest extent of white water ripple line to left of "5" in denomination. f, Like #2191b, with white water ripple line below "2" and "5" in denomination.

2009, July 15   **Perf. 13½x12¾**
Horiz. Pairs, #a-b
"Burung" in Blue
2189-2191 A704   Set of 3   5.00   2.50
Souvenir Sheet
"Burung" in Black
2192 A704 2500r Sheet of 6, #a-f 5.00 2.50
     For overprint see No. 2212.

Children's Day — A705

No. 2193 — Children: a, Jumping rope (1/4). b, Flying kites (2/4). c, Playing hide-and-seek (3/4). d, Riding bicycles (4/4).
    Illustration reduced.

2009, July 23
2193 A705 1500r Block of 4, #a-d 2.00 1.50

Souvenir Sheet

Philakorea 2009 Intl. Philatelic Exhibition, Seoul — A706

2009, July 30   **Perf. 14**
2194 A706   10,000r multi   3.00 1.50

A707

A708

A709

A710

A711

Personalizable Stamps — A711

2009   **Litho.**   **Perf. 12½x4x12½x12½**
2195 A707 1500r multi + label   2.00 2.00
2196 A708 1500r multi + label   2.00 2.00
2197 A709 1500r multi + label   2.00 2.00
2198 A710 1500r multi + label   2.00 2.00
2199 A711 1500r multi + label   2.00 2.00
   Nos. 2195-2199 (5)   10.00 10.00

Nos. 2195-2199 each were printed in sheets of 8 stamps + 8 labels that could be personalized. Each sheet sold for 20,000r.

Provincial Arms Type of 2008

Arms of: Nos. 2200, 1500r, 2211a, 2500r, Banten (12/33). Nos. 2201, 1500r, 2211b, 2500r, Jawa Timur (East Java) (13/33). Nos. 2202, 1500r, 2211c, 2500r, Kalimantan Tengah (Central Kalimantan) (14/33). Nos. 2203, 1500r, 2211d, 2500r, Kalimantan Timur (East Kalimantan) (15/33). Nos. 2204, 1500r, 2211e, 2500r, Kepulauan Riau (Riau Archipelago) (16/33). Nos. 2205, 1500r, 2211f, 2500r, Lampung (17/33). Nos. 2206, 1500r, 2211g, 2500r, Nusa Tenggara Timur (East Nusa Tenggara) (18/33). Nos. 2207, 1500r, 2211h, 2500r, Papua Barat (West Papua) (19/33). Nos. 2208, 1500r, 2211i, 2500r, Sulawesi Tengah (Central Sulawesi) (20/33). Nos. 2209, 1500r, 2211j, 2500r, Sulawesi Tenggara (Southeast Sulawesi) (21/33). Nos. 2210, 1500r, 2211k, 2500r, Sumatera Selatan (South Sumatra) (22/33).

2009, Aug. 17   **Litho.**   **Perf. 12½**
2200-2210 A679   Set of 11   5.50 2.75
2211   Sheet of 11 + label   8.00 4.00
   a.-k.   A679 2500r Any single   .75 .35

No. 2192 Overprinted in Gold With JIPEX 2009 Emblem

Methods and Perfs As Before
2009, Oct. 28
2212 A704 2500r Sheet of 6, #a-f 5.50 2.25

Tourist Sites in Indonesia and Singapore — A712

Designs: 1500r, Sentosa, Singapore (4/4). 2500r, Taman Mini Indonesia Indah (Beautiful Indonesia Miniature Park), Indonesia (3/4). 4000r, Merlion, Singapore (2/4). 7500r, Singaraja Statue, Indonesia (1/4).

2009, Oct. 28 Litho.   **Perf. 13½x12¾**
2213-2216 A712   Set of 4   5.50 2.75
2216a   Miniature sheet, 2 each
      #2213-2216   10.00 5.00

See Singapore Nos. 1402-1405.

Flora and Fauna of the Provinces Type of 2008
Miniature Sheet

No. 2217: a, Rhinoceros sondaicus, Vatica bantenensis, Banten (1/11). b, Gallus varius x Gallus gallus, Polyanthes tuberosa, Jawa Timur (East Java) (2/11). c, Polyplectron schleirmacheri, Nephelium ramboutan-ake, Kalimantan Tengah (Central Kalimantan) (3/11). d, Orcaella brevirostris, Coelogyne pandurata, Kalimantan Timur (East Kalimantan) (4/11). e, Lutjanus sanguineus, Piper betle, Kepulauan Riau (Riau Archipelago) (5/11). f, Elephas maximus sumatranus, Magnolia candolili, Lampung (6/11). g, Varanus komodoensis, Santalum album, Nusa Tenggara Timur (East Nusa Tenggara) (7/11). h, Paradisaea rubra, Pandanus conoideus, Papua Barat (West Papua) (8/11). i, Macrocephalon maleo, Diospyros celebica, Sulawesi Tengah (Central Sulawesi) (9/11). j, Bubalus depressicornis, Diplocaulobium utile, Sulawesi Tenggara (Southeast Sulawesi) (10/11). k, Notopterus chitala, Lansium domesticum, Sumatera Selatan (South Sumatra) (11/11).

2009, Nov. 5
2217 A688 2500r Sheet of 11,
       #a-k, + label   9.00 4.50

Buildings in Indonesia and Iran — A713

Designs: 1500r, Soltanieh Dome, Iran (2/2). 3000r, Al-Markaz Mosque, Indonesia (1/2).

2009, Dec. 18   **Perf. 13x13¼**
2218 A713 1500r multi   .70 .35
2219 A713 3000r multi   1.40 .70
   a.   Miniature sheet of 12, 6 each
      #2218-2219   9.00 4.50

See Iran No. 3013.

New Year 2010 (Year of the Tiger) A714

Tiger: No. 2220, 1500r, Head (1/3). No. 2221, 1500r, Walking (2/3). No. 2222, 1500r, Running (3/3).
    5000r, Tiger, sky.

2010, Feb. 6 Litho.   **Perf. 13½x12¾**
2220-2222 A714   Set of 3   1.00 .50
2222a   Souvenir sheet of 6, 2
      each #2220-2222   2.00 1.00
Souvenir Sheet
2223 A714 5000r multi   1.10 .55

UNESCO Intangible Cultural Heritage A720

Designs: 1000r, Batik in Campuran design (4/6). 1500r, Hanoman puppet, vert. (3/6). 2000r, Arjuna puppet, vert. (1/6). 2500r, Kresna puppet, vert. (2/6). 3000r, Kris, vert. (6/6). No. 2234, 5000r, Batik in Kembangan design (5/6).

No. 2235, 5000r, Hanoman puppet, diff., vert. No. 2236, 5000r, Kris, diff., vert.

Perf. 13½x12¾, 12¾x13½
2010, Mar. 29   **Litho.**
2229-2234 A720   Set of 6   3.50 1.75
Souvenir Sheets
2235-2236 A720   Set of 2   2.25 1.10

Nos. 2235-2236 exist imperforate.

2010 World Cup Soccer Championships, South Africa — A721

No. 2237: a, Soccer player (1/4). b, Mascot (2/4). c, Emblem (3/4). d, Goalie making save (4/4).

2010, May 1   **Perf. 12¾x13½**
2237 A721 1500r Block or horiz.
      strip of 4, #a-d 1.40 .70
   e.   Booklet pane of 4, #2237a-
      2237d   1.40 —
     Complete booklet, #2237e   1.40

A722

Environmental Care — A723

Designs: No. 2238, Hands holding seedling (3/3).
No. 2239: a, Bird, sheep, palm tree, child (1/3). b, Earth and hands (2/3).
    5000r, Like #2238.

Perf. 12¾x13½, 13½x12¾
2010, June 5
2238 A722 1500r multi   .35 .20

2239 A723 1500r Vert. pair, #a-b .65 .30

Souvenir Sheet

2240 A722 5000r multi 1.10 .55

Muhammadiyah Islamic Organization, Cent. — A724

No. 2241: a, Building (1/3). b, Kyai Haji Ahmad Dahlan (1868-1923), founder (2/3). c, Student, graduate, building (3/3).

2010, July 3 **Perf. 12½**
2241 Strip of 3 1.10 .55
  a.-c. A724 1500r Any single .35 .20
  d. Souvenir sheet of 6, 2 each #2241a-2241c 2.25 1.10

Traditional Foods A725

No. 2242: a, Sup Lobster Kelapa Muda, West Sulawesi (1/7). b, Gulai Iga Kemba'ang, Bengkulu (2/7). c, Ayam Cincane, East Kalimantan (3/7). d, Sate Udang Pentuk Asam Manis, Jambi (4/7). e, Lempah Kuning, Bangka Belitung (5/7). f, Asam Padeh Baung, Riau (6/7). g, Lapis Palaro, North Moluccas (7/7).

2010, July 6 **Perf. 13½x12¾**
2242 Block of 7 + label 2.50 1.25
  a.-g. A725 1500r Any single .35 .20

Elected Leaders A726

No. 2243 — Flag and: a, Pres. Susilo Bambang Yudhoyono (1/2). b, Vice-president Boediono (2/2).

2010, Aug. 17 **Perf. 14**
2243 Pair 1.10 .55
  a.-b. A726 2500r Either single .55 .25
  c. Souvenir sheet of 2, #2243a-2243b 1.10 .55

2010 Youth Olympic Games, Singapore — A727

No. 2244 — Badminton player with denomination at: a, LR. b, LL.

2010, July 15 Litho. Perf. 13½x12¾
2244 A727 1500r Pair, #a-b .70 .35

Bandung, 200th Anniv. — A728

No. 2245: a, Soccer player. b, R. Dewi Sartika (1884-1947), advocate for women's education.

No. 2246: a, Pasupati Bridge. b, City street. 5000r, Pasupati Bridge.

2010, Sept. 25 **Perf. 12¾x13½**
2245 A728 1000r Pair, #a-b .45 .20
2246 A728 1500r Pair, #a-b .70 .35

Souvenir Sheet

2247 A728 5000r multi 1.25 .60

Worldwide Fund for Nature (WWF) — A729

No. 2248 — Sea turtles: a, Lepidochelys olivacea (1/4). b, Chelonia mydas (2/4). c, Dermochelys coriacea (3/4). d, Eretmochelys imbricata (4/4).

2010, Oct. 24 **Perf. 13½x12¾**
2248 Strip or block of 4 1.40 .70
  a.-d. A729 1500r Any single .35 .20

Flora and Fauna of the Provinces Type of 2008

No. 2249: a, Haliastur indus, Salacca zalacca, Jakarta (5/11). b, Geopelia striata, Stelechocarpus burahol, Yogyakarta (6/11).
No. 2250: a, Gracula religiosa robusta, Cananga odorata, Sumatera Utara (North Sumatra) (1/11). b, Panthera tigris sumatrae, Cyrtostachys renda, Jambi (2/11). c, Helarctos malayanus, Amorphophallus titanum, Bengkulu (3/11). d, Tarsius bancanus saltator, Palaquium rostratum, Bangka Belitung (4/11).
2000r, Cervus timorensis, Diospyros macrophylla, Nusa Tenggara Barat (West Nusa Tenggara) (11/11).
No. 2252: a, Nasalis larvatus, Mangifera casturi, Kalimantan Selatan (South Kalimantan) (7/11). b, Aceros cassadix, Borassus flabellifer, Sulawesi Selatan (South Sulawesi) (8/11). c, Tarsius spectrum, Ficus minahassae, Sulawesi Utara (North Sulawesi) (9/11). d, Semiopthera wallacii, Syzygium aromaticum, Maluku Utara (North Moluccas (10/11).

2010, Nov. 5 **Litho.**
2249 A688 1000r Pair, #a-b .45 .20
2250 A688 1500r Strip or block of 4, #a-d 1.40 .70
2251 A688 2000r multi .45 .20
2252 A688 2500r Strip or block of 4, #a-d 2.25 1.10
  e. Souvenir sheet, #2249a-2249b, 2250a-2250d, 2251, 2252a-2252d, + label 4.75 2.25
  Nos. 2249-2252 (4) 4.55 2.20

SEMI-POSTAL STAMPS

Symbols of Olympic Games SP43

Wings and Flame SP44

Perf. 12½x12
1951, Jan. 2 Photo. Unwmk.
B58 SP43 5s + 3s gray grn .20 .20
B59 SP43 10s + 5s dk vio bl .20 .20
B60 SP43 20s + 5s org red .20 .20
B61 SP43 30s + 10s dk brn .65 .25
B62 SP43 35s + 10s ultra 3.00 2.10
  Nos. B58-B62 (5) 4.25 2.95

Issued to publicize the Asiatic Olympic Games of 1951 at New Delhi, India.

1951, Oct. 15
B63 SP44 5s + 3s olive green .30 .30
B64 SP44 10s + 5s dull blue .30 .30
B65 SP44 20s + 5s red .35 .30
B66 SP44 30s + 10s brown .45 .30
B67 SP44 35s + 10s ultra .80 1.10
  Nos. B63-B67 (5) 2.20 2.30

2nd Natl. Games, Djakarta, 10/21-28/51.

No. 378 Surcharged in Black

1953, May 8 **Perf. 12½**
B68 A53 35s + 10s purple .40 .20

The surcharge reads "Natural Disaster." Surtax was for emergency relief following volcanic eruption and floods.

Merapi Erupting SP45

Young Musicians SP46

1954, Apr. 15 Litho. Perf. 12½x12
B69 SP45 15s + 10s bl grn 1.25 1.75
B70 SP45 35s + 15s pur 1.25 1.40
B71 SP45 50s + 25s red 1.25 1.40
B72 SP45 75s + 25s vio bl 1.25 1.40
B73 SP45 1r + 25s car 1.25 1.40
B74 SP45 2r + 50s blk brn 3.25 1.40
B75 SP45 3r + 1r gray grn 12.00 8.75
B76 SP45 5r + 2.50r org brn 14.00 12.00
  Nos. B69-B76 (8) 35.50 29.50

The surtax was for victims of the Merapi volcano eruption.

1954, Dec. 22 Photo. Perf. 12½

15s+10s, Parasol dance. 35s+15s, Girls playing dakon. 50s+15s, Boy on stilts. 75s+25s, Bamboo flute players. 1r+25s, Javanese dancer.

B77 SP46 10s + 10s dk pur .20 .70
B78 SP46 15s + 10s dk grn .20 .80
B79 SP46 35s + 15s car rose .20 .80
B80 SP46 50s + 15s rose brn .45 .80
B81 SP46 75s + 25s ultra .40 3.00
B82 SP46 1r + 25s red org .70 5.00
  Nos. B77-B82 (6) 2.15 11.10

The surtax was for child welfare.

Scout Emblem SP47

Scout Signaling SP48

Designs: 50s+25s, Campfire. 75s+25s, Scout feeding fawn. 1r+50s, Scout saluting.

1955, June 27 Unwmk. Perf. 12½
B83 SP47 15s + 10s bl grn .40 .50
B84 SP48 35s + 15s ultra .40 .50
B85 SP48 50s + 25s scar .40 .50
B86 SP48 75s + 25s brn .40 .50
B87 SP48 1r + 50s vio .40 .50
  Nos. B83-B87 (5) 2.00 2.50

First National Boy Scout Jamboree.

Blind Weaver SP49

Red Cross and Heart SP50

35s+15s, Basket weaver. 50s+25s, Boy studying map. 75s+50s, Woman reading Braille.

1956, Jan. 4
B88 SP49 15s + 10s dp grn .20 .70
B89 SP49 35s + 15s yel brn .30 .70
B90 SP49 50s + 25s rose car 2.25 1.50
B91 SP49 75s + 50s ultra 1.25 .70
  Nos. B88-B91 (4) 4.00 3.60

The surtax was for the benefit of the blind.

1956, July 26 **Litho.**
Designs: 35s+15s, 50s+15s, Transfusion bottle. 75s+25s, 1r+25s, Outstretched hands.

Cross in Red
B92 SP50 10s + 10s ultra .20 .20
B93 SP50 15s + 10s carmine .20 .20
B94 SP50 35s + 15s lt brn .20 .20
B95 SP50 50s + 15s bl grn .45 .20
B96 SP50 75s + 25s orange .45 .30
B97 SP50 1r + 25s brt pur .45 .45
  Nos. B92-B97 (6) 1.95 1.55

Surtax for the Indonesian Red Cross.

Invalids Doing Batik Work — SP51

Designs: 15s+10s, Amputee painting. 35s+15s, Lathe operator. 50s+15s, Crippled child learning to walk. 75s+25s, Treating amputee. 1r+25s, Painting with artificial hand.

1957, Mar. 26 Photo. Perf. 12½
B98 SP51 10s + 10s dp blue .20 .20
B99 SP51 15s + 10s brown .30 .20
B100 SP51 35s + 15s red .30 .20
B101 SP51 50s + 15s dp vio .30 .30
B102 SP51 75s + 25s green .45 .40
B103 SP51 1r + 25s dk car rose .45 .65
  Nos. B98-B103 (6) 2.00 1.95

The surtax was for rehabilitation of invalids.

Kembodja Flower SP52

Designs: 15s+10s, Michelia. 35s+15s, Sunflower. 50s+15s, Jasmine. 75s+50s, Orchid.

1957, Dec. 23 **Perf. 13½x12½**
Flowers in Natural Colors
B104 SP52 10s + 10s blue 2.00 1.25
B105 SP52 15s + 10s dp yel grn 1.40 1.25
B106 SP52 35s + 15s dk red brn .70 .95
B107 SP52 50s + 15s ol & dk brn .50 .80
B108 SP52 75s + 60s rose brn .55 .80
  Nos. B104-B108 (5) 5.15 5.05

Children SP53

Indonesian Scout Emblem SP54

15s+10s, 50s+25s, 1r+50s, Girl and boy.

1958, July 1 Photo. Perf. 12½x12
B109 SP53 15s + 10s blue .20 .20
B110 SP53 15s + 10s rose brn .20 .20
B111 SP53 35s + 15s gray green .20 .20
B112 SP53 50s + 25s gray olive .20 .20
B113 SP53 75s + 50s brn car .20 .20
B114 SP53 1r + 50s brown .25 .20
  Nos. B109-B114 (6) 1.25 1.20

The surtax was for orphans.

1959, July 17 Photo. Unwmk.
Design: 15s + 10s, 50s + 25s, 1r + 50s, Scout emblem and compass.

Emblem in Red
B115 SP54 10s + 5s bister .20 .20
B116 SP54 15s + 10s bluish grn .25 .20
B117 SP54 20s + 10s lilac gray .25 .30
B118 SP54 50s + 25s olive .30 .50
B119 SP54 75s + 35s yel brn .30 .50
B120 SP54 1r + 25s dark gray .30 .50
  Nos. B115-B120 (6) 1.60 2.20

10th World Scout Jamboree, Makiling National Park near Manila, July 17-26.

Palm-leaf Ribs, Gong and 5 Rings SP55

Young Couple Holding Sharpened Bamboo Weapon SP56

Design: 20s+10s, 75s+35s, Bamboo musical instrument and 5-ring emblem.

1960, Feb. 14   **Perf. 12½x12**

B121	SP55	15s + 5s bis & dk brn		
B122	SP55	20s + 10s grn & blk	.20	.30
B123	SP55	50s + 25s bl & pur	.20	.30
B124	SP55	75s + 35s ol & dk grn	.20	.30
B125	SP56	1.15r + 5s car & blk	.20	.30
		Nos. B121-B125 (5)	1.15	1.50

All-Indonesian Youth Cong., Bandung, 2/14-21/60.

Social Emblem SP57

Pineapple SP58

Designs: 15s+15s, Rice, lotus and cotton. 20s+20s, Lotus blossom and tree. 50s+25s, Girl and boy. 75s+25s, Watering of plant in man's hand. 3r+50s, Woman nursing infant.

            Perf. 12½x12
1960, Dec. 20   **Photo.**   **Unwmk.**
Inscribed: "Hari Sosial Ke III"

B126	SP57	10s + 10s ocher & blk	.20	.20
B127	SP57	15s + 15s dp cl & blk	.20	.20
B128	SP57	20s + 20s bl & blk	.20	.20
B129	SP57	50s + 25s bis brn & blk	.20	.30
B130	SP57	75s + 25s emer & blk	.20	.30
B131	SP57	3r + 50s red & blk	.30	.30
		Nos. B126-B131 (6)	1.30	1.50

3rd Social Day, Dec. 20.

Type of 1960 Surcharges: "BENTJANA ALAM 1961"

1961, Feb. 17   **Perf. 12x12½**

B132	A76	15s + 10s plum	.20	.20
B133	A76	20s + 15s ocher	.20	.20
B134	A76	75s + 25s scarlet	.20	.20
		Nos. B132-B134 (3)	.60	.60

The surtax was for flood relief.

1961, Dec. 20   **Perf. 12½x13½**

4th Social Day: 75s+25s, Mangosteen. 3r+1r, Rambutan.

B135	SP58	20s + 10s bl, yel & red	.40	.50
B136	SP58	75s + 25s gray, grn & dp claret	.65	.50
B137	SP58	3r + 1r grn, yel & red	1.25	1.40
		Nos. B135-B137 (3)	2.30	2.40

Istiqlal Mosque, Djakarta — SP59

40s+20s, 3r+1r, Different view of mosque.

1962, Feb. 22   **Perf. 12½x12**

B138	SP59	30s + 20s Prus grn & yel	.20	.30
B139	SP59	40s + 20s dk red & yel	.20	.30
B140	SP59	1.50r + 50s brn & yel	.50	.30
B141	SP59	3r + 1r grn & yel	.55	.30
		Nos. B138-B141 (4)	1.45	1.20

Issued for the benefit of the new Istiqlal Mosque.

National Monument, Djakarta — SP60

1.50r+50s, 6r+1.50r, Aerial view of monument.

1962, May 20   **Photo.**   **Perf. 12x12½**

B142	SP60	1r + 50s org brn & blk	.20	.20
B143	SP60	1.50r + 50s ol grn & ultra	.20	.20
B144	SP60	3r + 1r lil rose & dk grn	.30	.20
B145	SP60	6r + 1.50r vio bl & red	.45	.20
		Nos. B142-B145 (4)	1.15	.80

Vanda Tricolor SP61

Orchids: 1.50r+50s, Phalaenopsis amabilis, vert. 3r+1r, Dendrobium phalaenopsis, vert. 6r+1.50r, Paphiopedilum praestans.

    Perf. 13½x12½, 12½x13½
1962, Dec. 20   **Unwmk.**
Orchids in Natural Colors

B146	SP61	1r + 50s ultra & yel	.40	.20
B147	SP61	1.50r + 50s grnsh bl & ver	.40	.20
B148	SP61	3r + 1r dp bl & ocher	.40	.20
B149	SP61	6r + 1.50r org & dl vio	.40	.20
		Nos. B146-B149 (4)	1.60	.80

Issued for the 5th Social Day.

West Irian Monument, Djakarta — SP62

1963, Feb. 15   **Perf. 12½x13½**

B150	SP62	1r + 50s rose red & blk	.25	.20
B151	SP62	1.50r + 50s mag & dk brn	.25	.20
B152	SP62	3r + 1r bl & dk brn	.25	.20
B153	SP62	6r + 1.50r grn & brn	.25	.20
		Nos. B150-B153 (4)	1.00	.80

The surtax was for the construction of the West Irian Monument in Djakarta.

Erupting Volcano SP63

1963, June 29   **Photo.**   **Perf. 13½x13**

B154	SP63	4r + 2r rose red	.25	.20
B155	SP63	6r + 3r grnsh bl	.25	.20

The surtax was for victims of national natural disasters.

Papilio Blumei, Celebes — SP64

Butterflies: 4r+1r, Charaxes dehaani, Java. 6r+1.50r, Graphium, West Irian. 12r+3r, Troides amphrysus, Sumatra.

1963, Dec. 20   **Perf. 12x12½**

B156	SP64	1.75r + 50s multi	.35	.20
B157	SP64	4r + 1r multi	.35	.20
B158	SP64	6r + 1.50r multi	.35	.20
B159	SP64	12r + 3r multi	.70	.40
		Nos. B156-B159 (4)	1.75	1.00

Issued for the 6th Social Day.

Malaysian Fantails — SP65

Birds: 6r+1.50r, Zebra doves. 12r+3r, Black drongos. 20r+5r, Black-naped orioles. 30r+7.50r, Javanese sparrows.

       Perf. 12½x13½
1965, Jan. 25   **Photo.**   **Unwmk.**

B160	SP65	4r + 1r dl yel, lil & blk	.50	.25
B161	SP65	6r + 1.50 grn, blk & pink	.50	.25
B162	SP65	12r + 3r ol & blk	.50	.30
B163	SP65	20r + 5r gray, yel & red	.50	.40
B164	SP65	30r + 7.50r car rose, sl bl & blk	.75	.40
		Nos. B160-B164 (5)	2.75	1.60

Issued for the 7th Social Day.

Type of Regular Issue, 1964, Inscribed Vertically "Conefo"

1965   **Perf. 12½x12**

B165	A98	1r + 1r org red & brn	.20	.20
B166	A98	1.25r + 1.25r org red & brn	.20	.20
B167	A98	1.75r + 1.75r org, red & brn blk	.20	.20
B168	A98	2r + 2r org red & sl grn	.20	.20
B169	A98	2.50r + 2.50r org red & red brn	.20	.20
B170	A98	4r + 3.50r org red & dp bl	.20	.20
B171	A98	6r + 4r org red & emer	.20	.20
B172	A98	10r + 5r org red & yel grn	.20	.20
B173	A98	12r + 5.50r org red & org	.20	.20
B174	A98	15r + 7.50r org red & bl grn	.20	.20
B175	A98	20r + 10r org red & dk gray	.20	.20
B176	A98	25r + 10r org red & pur	.20	.20
B177	A98	40r + 15r ver & plum	.20	.20
B178	A98	50r + 15r org red & dp vio	.20	.20
B179	A98	100r + 25r org red & dk ol gray	.20	.20
		Nos. B165-B179 (15)	3.00	3.00

Conference of New Emerging Forces.

Makara Mask and Magic Rays — SP66

1965, July 17   **Perf. 12**

B180	SP66	20r + 10r red & dk bl	.35	.20
B181	SP66	30r + 15r bl & dk red	.35	.20

Issued to publicize the fight against cancer.

Papilio Blumei,

Family and Produce SP67

State Principles: 20r+10r, Humanitarianism; clasped hands, globe, flags and chain. 25r+10r, Nationalism; map of Indonesia and tree. 40r+15r, Democracy; conference and bull's head. 50r+15r, Belief in God; houses of worship and star.

1965, Aug. 17   **Photo.**   **Perf. 12½**

B182	SP67	10r + 5r fawn, yel & blk	.40	.25
B183	SP67	20r + 10r dp yel, red & blk	.30	.25
B184	SP67	25r + 10r rose red, red, grn & blk	.30	.25
B185	SP67	40r + 15r bl, red & blk	.45	.25
B186	SP67	50r + 15r lil, yel & blk	.45	.25
		Nos. B182-B186 (5)	1.90	1.25

Samudra Beach Hotel and Pres. Sukarno — SP68

Designs: 25r+10r, 80r+20r, Ambarrukmo Palace Hotel and Pres. Sukarno.

1965, Dec. 1   **Photo.**   **Perf. 12½**

B187	SP68	10r + 5r dk bl & lt bl grn	.25	.30
B188	SP68	25r + 10r vio blk & yel grn	.30	.30
B189	SP68	40r + 15r dk brn & vio bl	.40	.40
B190	SP68	80r + 20r dk pur & org	.60	.40
		Nos. B187-B190 (4)	1.55	1.40

Issued for tourist publicity.

Gloriosa — SP69

40r+15r, Magaguabush. 80r+20r, Balsam. 100r+25r, Crape myrtle.

1965, Dec. 20   **Photo.**   **Perf. 12**
Flowers in Natural Colors

B191	SP69	30r + 10r deep blue	.70	.95
B192	SP69	40r + 15r deep blue	.70	.95
B193	SP69	80r + 20r deep blue	.70	.95
B194	SP69	100r + 25r deep blue	.70	.95
		Nos. B191-B194 (4)	2.80	3.80

Dated "1966"

10s+5s, Senna. 20s+5s, Crested barleria. 30s+10s, Scarlet ixora. 40s+10s, Rose of China (hibiscus).

1966, Feb. 10
Flowers in Natural Colors

B195	SP69	10s + 5s Prus bl	.55	.95
B196	SP69	20s + 5s grn	.55	.95
B197	SP69	30s + 10s grn	.55	.95
B198	SP69	40s + 10s Prus bl	.55	.95
		Nos. B195-B198 (4)	2.20	3.80

Nos. B191-B198 issued for the 8th Social Day, Dec. 20, 1965. An imperf. souvenir sheet contains one No. B198. Size: 58x78mm. Value, $7.

Type of 1965 Inscribed: "BENTJANA / ALAM / NASIONAL 1966"

15s+5s, Gloriosa. 25s+5s, Magaguabush. 30s+10s, Balsam. 80s+20s, Crape myrtle.

1966, May 2
Flowers in Natural Colors

B199	SP69	15s + 5s blue	.40	.65
B200	SP69	25s + 5s dk bl	.40	.65
B201	SP69	30s + 10s dk bl	.45	.65
B202	SP69	80s + 20s lt bl	1.00	.65
		Nos. B199-B202 (4)	2.25	2.60

The surtax was for victims of national natural disasters.

Reticulated Python — SP70

Reptiles: 3r+50s, Bloodsucker. 4r+75s. Saltwater crocodile. 6r+1r, Hawksbill turtle (incorrectly inscribed *chelonia mydas,* "green turtle").

1966, Dec. 20   Photo.   *Perf. 12½x12*

B203	SP70	2r + 25s multi	.30	.30
B204	SP70	3r + 50s multi	.30	.30
B205	SP70	4r + 75s multi	.55	.30
B206	SP70	6r + 1r multi	.65	.30
		Nos. B203-B206 (4)	1.80	1.20

Flooded Village SP71

Buddha & Stupa, Borobudur Temple SP72

2.50r+25s, Landslide. 4r+40s, Fire destroying village. 5r+50s, Erupting volcano.

1967, Dec. 20   Photo.   *Perf. 12½*

B207	SP71	1.25r + 10s dl vio bl & yel	.30	.40
B208	SP71	2.50r + 25s dl vio bl & yel	.30	.40
B209	SP71	4r + 40s dp org & blk	.30	.40
B210	SP71	5r + 50s dp org & blk	.50	.40
a.		Souv. sheet of 2, #B209-B210	30.00	45.00
		Nos. B207-B210 (4)	1.40	1.60

Surtax for victims of natl. natural disasters.

1968, Mar. 1   Photo.   *Perf. 12½*

Designs: No. B211, Musicians. No. B212, Sudhana and Princess Manohara. No. B213, Procession with elephant and horses.

B211	SP72	2.50r + 25s brt grn & gray ol	.55	.30
B212	SP72	2.50r + 25s brt grn & gray ol	.55	.30
B213	SP72	2.50r + 25s brt grn & gray ol	.55	.30
a.		Souv. sheet of 3, #B211-B213	30.00	40.00
b.		Strip of 3, #B211-B213	1.75	1.75

B214	SP72	7.50r + 75s org & gray ol	.55	.30
		Nos. B211-B214 (4)	2.20	1.20

The surtax was to help save Borobudur Temple in Central Java, c. 800 A.D.
No. B213b has continuous design showing a frieze from Borobudur.

Scout with Pickax — SP73

Designs: 10r+1r, Bugler. 30r+3r, Scouts singing around campfire, horiz.

1968, June 1   Photo.   *Perf. 12½*
Size: 28½x44½mm

B215	SP73	5r + 50 dp org & brn	.50	.50
B216	SP73	10r + 1r brn & gray ol	.60	.75

Size: 68x28½mm

B217	SP73	30r + 3r ol gray & grn	1.00	.65
		Nos. B215-B217 (3)	2.10	1.90

Surtax for Wirakarya Scout Camp.

Woman with Flower SP74

1969, Apr. 21   *Perf. 13½x12½*

B218	SP74	20r + 2r emer, red & yel	.75	.40

Emancipation of Indonesian women.

Noble Voluta — SP75

Sea shells: 7.50r+50s, Common hairy triton. 10r+1r, Spider conch. 15r+1.50r, Murex ternispina.

1969, Dec. 20   Photo.   *Perf. 12½*

B219	SP75	5r + 50s multi	.40	.55
B220	SP75	7.50r + 50s multi	.45	.55
B221	SP75	10r + 1r multi	.75	.80
B222	SP75	15r + 1.50r multi	.65	.80
		Nos. B219-B222 (4)	2.25	2.70

Issued for the 12th Social Day, Dec. 20.

Chrysocoris Javanus SP76

Insects: 15r+1.50r, Dragonfly. 20r+2r, Carpenter bee.

1970, Dec. 21   Photo.   *Perf. 12½*

B223	SP76	7.50r + 50c multi	6.00	1.60
B224	SP76	15r + 1.50r multi	15.00	8.00
B225	SP76	20r + 2r multi	19.00	5.50
		Nos. B223-B225 (3)	40.00	15.10

The 13th Social Day, Dec. 20.

Fight Against Cancer — SP77

Patient receiving radiation treatment, Jakarta Hospital.

1983, July 1   Photo.   *Perf. 12½*

B226	SP77	55r + 20r multi	.80	.50
B227	SP77	75r + 25r multi	1.40	.50

Children's Day SP78

Children's Drawings. Surtax was for Children's Palace building fund.

1984, June 17   Photo.   *Perf. 13½x13*

B228	SP78	75r + 25r multi	.95	.20
B229	SP78	110r + 25r multi	1.25	.25
B230	SP78	175r + 25r multi	1.75	.40
B231	SP78	275r + 25r multi	3.00	.50
a.		Souv. sheet of 2, #B230-B231	30.00	30.00
b.		Souv. sheet of 4 + 2 labels	25.00	25.00
		Nos. B228-B231 (4)	6.95	1.35

AUSIPEX '84. No. B231b for FILACENTO '84, Netherlands, Sept. 6-9

SP79   SP80

1987, May 12   Photo.   *Perf. 12½*

B232	SP79	350r +25r dark ultra & yel	2.25	.60

Yayasan Cancer Medical Assoc., 10th anniv.

1991, June 1   Photo.   *Perf. 12½*

B233	SP80	200r +25r multi	1.25	.30

Natl. Fed. for Welfare of Mentally Handicapped, 24th anniv.

Yayasan Cancer Medical Assoc., 15th Anniv. — SP81

1992, May 12   Photo.   *Perf. 12½*

B234	SP81	200r +25r brown & mag	.50	.20
B235	SP81	500r +50r blue & mag	1.00	.35

Natl. Kidney Foundation — SP82

1994, Apr. 30   Photo.   *Perf. 13½x12½*

B236	SP82	300r +30r multi	1.00	.30

Rehibilitation Intl., 10th Asia & Pacific Regional Conference — SP83

Design: 700r+100r, Painting, Mother's Love, by disabled artist Patricia Saerang.

1995, Sept. 12   *Perf. 13½x12½*   **Photo.**

B238	SP83	700r + 100r multi	1.60	.85

March 1, 1949, Day of Total Attack SP84

Designs: No. B239, Natl. flag, tanks, map. No. B240, Soldiers fighting, soldiers standing at attention, natl. flag.

1996, Mar. 1   Photo.   *Perf. 13½x12½*

B239	SP84	700r + 100r multi	1.60	.80
B240	SP84	700r + 100r multi	1.60	.80
a.		Pair, #B239-B240	3.25	1.60

World AIDS Day SP85

1997, Dec. 1   Photo.   *Perf. 13½x12½*

B241	SP85	700r + 100r multi	1.25	.65

PETA (Pembela Tanah Air) Volunteer Army — SP86

1998, Nov. 10   *Perf. 12½x13½*   **Litho.**

B242	SP86	700r Statue, museum	.80	.20

National Disaster Fund — SP87

2005, May 20   Litho.   *Perf. 12½*

B243	SP87	1500r +300r multi + label	1.25	1.25

Surtax for victims of Dec. 26, 2004 tsunami.

AIR POST STAMPS

Airplane, Marshal Surydarma AP1

Airplane Over
Buffalo
Canyon
AP2

Designs: 10s, Airplane, Air Chief Marshal Suryadi Surydarma. 20s, Sentry and aircraft, Lake Toba, Sumatra. 30s, Pilots. 40c, Indian Red Cross plane, Sumatra. 50s, Red Cross plane. 75s, Airplane over Buffalo Canyon. 1r, Crew studying flight plan. 1½r, Aircraft over Tjipanas Fish Ponds, Java. 4½r, DC-3 over rice fields. 7½r, DC-4 over Indonesian Archipelago.

Nos. C10, C12 and C13 are overprinted ("POS UDARA" and Airplane) on Nos. 22-24.

Perf. 14½, 12½ (#C10, C12, C13)

		1948, Dec. 15	Photo.
C1	AP1	10s dk lilac & brn	.35
C2	AP1	20s Pruss grn & org red	.40 —
C3	AP1	30s dp blue & dull lil	.45 —
C4	AP1	40s red brn & blue emerald	.25 —
C5	AP1	50s dp vio & dull bl	.25 —
C6	AP2	75s dp brn & org brn	.75 —
C7	AP2	1r dp choc & purple brown	.90 —
C8	AP2	1½r dk viol & dp yel brown	2.25 —
C9	AP2	4½r Pruss grn & dull purple	2.25 —
C10	A32	5r yel brn & black	7.50 —
C11	AP1	7½r brn & slate vio	3.75 —
C12	A32	10r emerald & black	9.00 —
C13	A32	25r rose red & black	12.00 —
		Nos. C1-C13 (13)	40.10

AP3

Designs: 30s, 1r, Map, ships. 50s, Harbor scene, vert. 2½r, 4½r, Ships.
Illustration reduced.

		1949, Aug. 17 Photo.	Perf. 12½
C14	AP3	30s blue & orange	1.75 —
C15	AP3	50s green & orange	3.00 —
C16	AP3	1r brn & green	1.90 —
C17	AP3	2½r blk & dull grn	6.00 —
C18	AP3	4½r blue & rose red	15.00 —
		Nos. C14-C18 (5)	27.65

Failure of Dutch blockade.

Airplane, Indonesian
Archipelago — AP4

Hot Spring,
Java — AP5

Designs: 10s, DC-4 over Indonesian Archipelago. 20s, Aircraft mechanics working on plane. 30s, Servicing plane on runway. 40c, Pilots. 50s, Briefing pilots. 75s, Sentry and aircraft, Lake Toba, Sumatra. 1r, Plane, mountain in Sumatra. 1½r, DC-3 over rice fields. 4½r, Airplane over Buffalo Canyon. 7½r, Aircraft over Tjipanas Fish Ponds, Java.

Nos. C28, C30 and C31 are overprinted ("POS UDARA" and Airplane) on Nos. 51-53.

Perf. 14½, 12½ (#C10, C12, C13)

		1949, Aug. 17	Photo.
C19	AP4	10s pur & lt blue	.50
C20	AP5	20s brn & sl blue	1.00 —
C21	AP4	30s red brn & bl grn	2.00 —
C22	AP4	40s dk brn & pur	1.50 —
C23	AP4	50s dp bl grn & red brn	2.25 —
C24	AP4	75s bl grn & brn	.95 —
C25	AP4	1r pur & dk grn	1.25 —
C26	AP4	1½r blk bl & org	3.00 —
C27	AP5	4½r pur & chestnut	3.50 —
C28	A38	5r red vio & black	3.50 —
C29	AP5	7½r dk grn & vio brn	3.50 —
C30	A38	10r grn & black	6.00 —
C31	A38	25r red & black	14.00 —
		Nos. C19-C31 (13)	42.95

AP6

Designs: 50s, Map, airplanes, horiz. 30s, 1r, Harbor scene. 2½r, Airplane on runway, horiz. 4½r, Airplane landing, horiz.

		1949 Photo.	Perf. 14½
C32	AP6	30s multicolored	1.75 —
C33	AP6	50s multicolored	2.00 —
C34	AP6	1r multicolored	1.25 —
C35	A39	2½r multicolored	2.00 —
C36	A39	4½r multicolored	3.50 —
		Nos. C32-C36 (5)	10.50

Liberation of Jakarta

Nos. C1//C31 overprinted "Merdeka Djojakarta 6 Djuli 1949"

Nos. C1-C9, C11, C12 Overprinted

		1949, Dec. 7	
C37	AP1	10s dk lilac & brn	.25 —
C38	AP1	20s Pruss grn & org red	.25 —
C39	AP1	30s dp blue & dull lil	.25 —
C40	AP1	40s red brn & blue emerald	12.00 —
C41	AP1	50s dp vio & dull bl	.55 —
C42	AP2	75s dp brn & org brn	.55 —
C43	AP2	1r dp choc & purple brown	1.25 —
C44	AP2	1½r dk viol & dp yel brown	1.40 —
C45	AP2	4½r Pruss grn & dull purple	2.00 —
C46	AP1	7½r brn & slate vio	12.50 —
		Nos. C37-C46 (10)	31.00

Nos. C19-C27, C29 Overprinted

		1949, Dec. 7	
C47	AP4	10s pur & lt blue	.25 —
C48	AP5	20s brn & sl blue	1.25 —
C49	AP4	30s red brn & bl grn	.30 —

C50	AP4	40s dk brn & pur	1.10 —
C51	AP4	50s dp bl grn & red brn	.30 —
C52	AP4	75s bl grn & brn	.30 —
C53	AP4	1r pur & dk grn	1.50 —
C54	AP4	1½r blk bl & org	2.00 —
C55	AP5	4½r pur & chestnut	2.50 —
C56	AP5	7½r dk grn & vio brn	2.75 —
		Nos. C47-C56 (10)	12.25

Nos. C32-C36 Overprinted

C57	AP6	30s multicolored	5.00 —
C58	AP6	50s multicolored	3.00 —
C59	AP6	1r multicolored	3.00 —
C60	A39	2½r multicolored	4.50 —
C61	A39	4½r multicolored	6.50 —
		Nos. C57-C61 (5)	22.00

AIR POST SPECIAL DELIVERY STAMPS

Aircraft
Over
Beach
APSD1

Perf. 14½

		1948, Dec. 15 Photo.	Unwmk.
CE1	APSD1	40s dk brn & blue emerald	1.00 —

Type APSD1, inscribed "REPUBLIK"

		1948, Dec. 15	Perf. 13½x14
CE2	APSD1	40s brn & blue emer	.75 —

No. CE1, Overprinted "Merdeka Djojakarta 6 Djuli 1949"

		1949, Dec. 7	
CE3	APSD1	40s brn & blue emer	.75 —

No. CE2, Overprinted "Merdeka Djojakarta 6 Djuli 1949"

		1949, Dec. 7	
CE4	APSD1	40s brn & blue emer	7.00 —

AIR POST OFFICIAL STAMPS

RESMI

Nos. C1//C7 Overprinted "RESMI"

		1948, Dec. 15	
CO1	AP1	10s dk lilac & brown	1.25 —
CO2	AP1	30s dp blue & dull lil	2.00 —
CO3	AP1	50s dp vio & dull blue	2.25 —
CO4	AP2	1r dp choc & purle brown	5.00 —
		Nos. CO1-CO4 (4)	10.50

RESMI

Nos. C19//C25 Overprinted "RESMI"

		1949, Aug. 17	
CO5	AP4	10s pur & lt blue	3.50 —
CO6	AP4	30s red brn & bl grn	2.00 —
CO7	AP4	50s dp bl grn & red brn	4.50 —
CO8	AP4	1r pur & dk grn	3.25 —
		Nos. CO5-CO8 (4)	13.25

Nos. CO1-CO4 Overprinted "Merdeka Djojakarta 6 Djuli 1949"

		1949, Dec. 7	
CO9	AP1	10s dk lilac & brown	2.50 —
CO10	AP1	30s dp blue & dull lil	5.00 —
CO11	AP1	50s dp vio & dull bl	2.50 —
CO12	AP2	1r dp choc & purle brown	2.00 —
		Nos. CO9-CO12 (4)	12.00

RESMI

Nos. CO5-CO8 Overprinted "Merdeka Djojakarta 6 Djuli 1949"

		1949, Dec. 7	
CO13	AP4	10s pur & lt blue	2.00 —
CO14	AP4	30s red brn & bl grn	6.00 —
CO15	AP4	50s dp bl grn & red brn	1.25 —
CO16	AP4	1r pur & dk grn	3.50 —
		Nos. CO13-CO16 (4)	12.75

SPECIAL DELIVERY STAMPS

Train & Minangkabau House — SD1

Perf. 13½x14¼

		1948, Dec. 15 Unwmk.	Photo.
E1	SD1	10s dp bluish grn & chestnut	.20 —
E1A	SD1	15s ches & steel bl	.45 —

Type SD1, Inscribed "REPUBLIK"

		1949, Aug. 17	
E1B	SD1	10s red brn & dp blue	.50 —
E1C	SD1	15s turq & dk yel brn	.35 —

Nos. E1-E1A Overprinted "Merdeka Djojakarta 6 Djuli 1949"

		1949, Dec. 7	
E1D	SD1	10s dp bluish grn & chestnut	.30 —
E1E	SD1	15s ches & steel bl	.75 —

Nos. E1B-E1C Overprinted "Merdeka Djojakarta 6 Djuli 1949"

		1949, Dec. 7	
E1F	SD1	10s red brn & dp blue	.30 —
E1G	SD1	15s urq & dk yel brn	.60 —

Garuda
SD2

Perf. 13½x12½

1967		**Unwmk.**	**Photo.**
E1H	SD2	10r lt ultra & dl pur	.50 .20
E2	SD2	15r org & dl pur	1.10 .50
		Nos. E1-E2 (10)	5.05 .70

Inscribed "1968"

1968			
E3	SD2	10r lt ultra & dl pur	.60 .20
E4	SD2	15r org & dl pur	.80 .30
E5	SD2	20r yel & dl pur	.90 .30
E6	SD2	30r brt grn & dl pur	1.25 .60
E7	SD2	40r lil & dl pur	1.75 .30
		Nos. E3-E7 (5)	5.30 1.70

Same Inscribed "1969"

1969			
E8	SD2	20r yel & dl pur	.50 .20
E9	SD2	30r brt grn & dl pur	.75 .20
E10	SD2	40r lil & dl pur	.85 .25
		Nos. E8-E10 (3)	2.10 .65

POSTAGE DUE STAMPS

D1

Perf. 13¾x14, 14½ (#J8-J13)

1948			**Unwmk.**
J1	D1	1s blue & brn	.30 —
J2	D1	2½s dk brn & dk pur	.45 —
J3	D1	3½s pur & lt grn	.20 —
J4	D1	5s dk grn & brn	.40 —
J5	D1	7½s dk brn & dk grn	.50 —
J6	D1	10s dk pur & brn	.45 —
J7	D1	20s brn & org yel	1.25 —
J8	D1	25s dk pur & brn	1.50 —
J9	D1	30s blue & car red	1.25 —
J10	D1	40s blue & org yel	1.50 —
J11	D1	50s lt brn & pur	2.00 —
J12	D1	75s dk bl & dk grn	3.50 —
J13	D1	1r brn & green	4.00 —
		Nos. J1-J13 (13)	17.30

As Type D1, inscribed "REPUBLIK"
Perf. 13¾x14, 14½ (#J8-J13)

1949, Aug. 17			**Unwmk.**
J14	D1	1s dk blue & brn	35.00 —
J15	D1	2½s brn & pur	35.00 —
J16	D1	3½s pur & grn	35.00 —
J17	D1	5s dk grn & brn	35.00 —
J18	D1	7½s dk brn & dk grn	35.00 —
J19	D1	10s pur & brn	35.00 —
J20	D1	20s dk brn & yel	35.00 —
J21	D1	25s vio & dk pur	35.00 —
J22	D1	30s blue & red	35.00 —
J23	D1	40s blue & yel	35.00 —
J24	D1	50s brn & pur	35.00 —
J25	D1	75s dk bl & dk grn	35.00 —
J26	D1	1r dk brn & green	35.00 —
		Nos. J14-J26 (13)	455.00

Nos. J1-J13 Overprinted "Merdeka Djojakarta 6 Djuli 1949"

1949, Dec. 7			
J27	D1	1s blue & brn	1.25 —
J28	D1	2½s dk brn & dk pur	.65 —
J29	D1	3½s pur & lt grn	.75 —
J30	D1	5s dk grn & brn	.75 —
J31	D1	7½s dk brn & dk grn	1.25 —
J32	D1	10s dk pur & brn	.35 —
J33	D1	20s brn & org yel	9.00 —
J34	D1	25s dk pur & dk brn	4.50 —

J35	D1	30s blue & car red	12.50 —
J36	D1	40s blue & org yel	15.00 —
J37	D1	50s lt brn & pur	7.50 —
J38	D1	75s dk bl & dk grn	22.50 —
J39	D1	1r brn & green	15.00 —
		Nos. J27-J39 (13)	91.00

Netherlands Indies Nos. J57 to J59 Surcharged in Black

1950		**Wmk. 228**	**Perf. 14½x14**
J60	D7	2½s on 50c yellow	1.50 .50
J61	D7	5s on 100c apple grn	3.50 1.25
J62	D7	10s on 75c aqua	8.00 1.75
		Nos. J60-J62 (3)	13.00 3.50

D8   "1966" — D9

Wmk. 228

1951-52		**Litho.**	**Perf. 12½**
J63	D8	2½s vermilion	.20 .50
J64	D8	5s vermilion	.20 .20
J65	D8	10s vermilion	.20 .20
J66	D8	20s blue ('52)	.20 .20
J67	D8	25s olive bister ('52)	.85 .50
J68	D8	50s vermilion	9.00 2.00
J69	D8	1r citron	3.00 3.00
		Nos. J63-J69 (7)	13.65 6.60

1953-55			**Unwmk.**
J70	D8	15s lt magenta ('55)	1.00 .25
J71	D8	30s red brown	1.25 .30
J72	D8	40s green	1.25 .30
		Nos. J70-J72 (3)	3.50 .85

1958-61			**Perf. 13½x12½**
J73	D8	10s orange	.30 .55
J74	D8	15s orange ('59)	.30 .55
J74A	D8	20s orange ('61)	1.00 .55
J75	D8	25s orange	.30 .55
J76	D8	30s orange ('60)	.30 .55
J77	D8	50s orange	3.00 .55
J78	D8	100s orange ('60)	1.50 .55
		Nos. J73-J78 (7)	6.70 3.85

1962-65			**Perf. 13½x12½**
J79	D8	50s light bluish green	.20 .20
J80	D8	100s bister	.20 .20
J81	D8	250s blue	.20 .20
J82	D8	500s dull yellow	.20 .20
J83	D8	750s pale lilac	.25 .20
J84	D8	1000s salmon	.50 .25
J85	D8	50r red ('65)	.20 .20
J86	D8	100r maroon ('65)	.45 .25
		Nos. J79-J86 (8)	2.20 1.70

1966-67		**Unwmk.**	**Photo.**
J91	D9	5s dl grn & dl yel	.35 .25
J92	D9	10s red & lt bl	.35 .25
J93	D9	20s dk bl & pink	.35 .25
J94	D9	30s brn & rose	.35 .25
J95	D9	40s plum & bis	.35 .25
J96	D9	50s ol grn & pale lil	.35 .25
J97	D9	100s dk red & yel grn	.60 .25
J98	D9	200s brt grn & pink ('67)	.45 .25
J99	D9	500s yel & lt bl ('67)	.60 .25
J100	D9	1000s rose lil & yel ('67)	1.00 .25
		Nos. J91-J100 (10)	4.75 2.55

Dated "1967"

1967			
J101	D9	50s ol grn & pale lil	.30 .40
J102	D9	100s dk red & yel grn	.40 .40
J103	D9	200s brt grn & pink	.50 .40
J104	D9	500s yel & lt bl	.25 .40
J105	D9	1000s rose lil & yel	1.40 .40
J106	D9	15r org & gray	1.40 .60
J107	D9	25r lil & citron	2.25 1.00
		Nos. J101-J107 (7)	6.50 3.60

Similar stamps inscribed "Bajar" or "Bayar", year date and "Sumbangan Ongkos Tjetak" or ". . . Cetak" are revenues.

Dated "1973"
Inscribed "BAYAR PORTO"

1973			
J108	D9	25r lilac & citron	2.00 .30

Dated "1974"
Inscribed "BAYAR PORTO"

1974			
J109	D9	65r olive grn & bister	1.90 1.00
J110	D9	125r lil & pale pink	8.00 4.00

Dated "1975"
Inscribed "BAYAR PORTO"

1975	**Photo.**		**Perf. 13½x12½**
J111	D9	25r lilac & citron	2.25 1.00

"1976" — D10

1976			
J112	D10	125r lil & pale pur	3.75 1.25

Dated "1977"

1977			
J113	D10	100r dp vio & pale pink	.75 .50
J114	D10	200r brt bl & lt lil	1.00 .85
J115	D10	300r choc & lt sal	1.50 1.25
J116	D10	400r brt grn & tan	2.25 2.00
J117	D10	500r red & tan	2.75 2.50
		Nos. J113-J117 (5)	8.25 7.10

See Nos. J138, J139, J142.

Nos. 706, 709, 712-713, 716, 718 Surcharged in Red

1978	**Photo.**		**Perf. 12½x12**
J118	A110	25r on 1r	.30 .30
J119	A110	50r on 2r	.55 .55
J120	A110	100r on 4r	1.75 1.75
J121	A110	200r on 5r	3.25 3.25
J122	A110	300r on 10r	4.25 4.25
J123	A110	400r on 15r	6.00 6.00
		Nos. J118-J123 (6)	16.10 16.10

Surcharged in Black

J124	A110	25r on 1r	.30 .30
J125	A110	50r on 2r	.60 .60
J126	A110	100r on 4r	1.75 1.75
J127	A110	200r on 5r	4.25 4.25
J128	A110	300r on 10r	5.25 5.25
J129	A110	400r on 15r	7.00 7.00
		Nos. J124-J129 (6)	19.15 19.15

Nos. 710, 717 Surcharged

1978	**Photo.**		**Perf. 12½x12**
J130	A110	40r on 2.50r	1.10 1.10
J131	A110	40r on 12r	1.10 1.10
J132	A110	65r on 2.50r	1.50 1.50
J133	A110	65r on 12r	1.50 1.50
J134	A110	125r on 2.50r	3.00 3.00
J135	A110	125r on 12r	3.00 3.00
J136	A110	150r on 2.50r	4.00 4.00
J137	A110	150r on 12r	2.50 2.50
		Nos. J130-J137 (8)	17.70 17.70

Type of 1976 Dated "1979"

1979			**Perf. 13½x12½**
J138	D10	25r lilac & citron	1.00 .20

Type of 1976 and

D11

Perf. 13½x12½, 13½x13 (#J144-J148, J150-J153), 14½x13 (#J154-J156A)

1980-90			**Photo.**

Dated "1980"

J139	D10	25r dk lil & beige	.20 .20
J140	D11	50r multi	.60 .50
J141	D11	75r rose lake & rose	1.00 .90
J142	D10	125r rose lil & lt pink	1.50 1.00
		Nos. J139-J142 (4)	3.30 2.60

Dated "1981"

J144	D11	25r brt vio & pale yel grn	.30 .30
J145	D11	50r sl grn & lt vio	.60 .60
J146	D11	75r rose vio & pink	1.10 1.10
J147	D11	125r pur & yel grn	1.75 1.75
		Nos. J144-J147 (4)	3.75 3.75

Dated "1982"

J148	D11	125r dp rose lil & pink	4.00 .50

Dated "1983"

J149	D11	125r dp rose & lil pink	.60 .40
J150	D11	200r dp vio & lt bl	1.25 .55
J151	D11	300r dk grn & cit	1.50 .80
J152	D11	400r ol grn & brn ol	2.00 1.00
J153	D11	500r sepia & beige	2.50 1.25
		Nos. J149-J153 (5)	7.85 4.00

Dated "1984"

J154	D11	25r brt vio & pale yel grn	1.25 .35
J155	D11	50r sl grn & lt vio	1.25 .90
J156	D11	125r rose lil & lt pink	3.50 .35
J156A	D11	500r sepia & beige	15.00 2.50
		Nos. J154-J156A (4)	21.00 4.10

Dated "1988"

J157	D11	1000r dp vio & gray	1.40 .75
J158	D11	2000r red & dp rose lil	2.75 1.25
J159	D11	3000r brn & dl org	4.50 2.00
J160	D11	5000r grn & bl grn	8.75 2.50
		Nos. J157-J160 (4)	17.40 6.50

Dated "1990"

J161	D11	2000r emer & brt yel	4.75 2.50
J162	D11	3000r dk bl grn & rose lil	7.00 3.50
J163	D11	4000r brn vio & brt yel grn	12.50 6.50
		Nos. J161-J163 (3)	24.25 12.50

OFFICIAL STAMPS

Nos. 2//16 Overprinted "RESMI"

1948, Dec. 15			
O1	A28	2s dp brn & dp blue	.20 —
O2	A28	5s turq & dull blue	.50 —
O3	A28	10s dp blue & brn rose	.45 —
O4	A28	15s brown & dk grn	.20 —
O5	A31	30s dk brn & dull vio	1.50 —
O6	A30	50s dk brn & turq	.60 —
		Nos. O1-O6 (6)	3.45

Nos. 31//45 Overprinted "RESMI"

1949, Aug. 17			
O7	A35	2s dk red vio & dp grn	.30 —
O8	A35	5s turq & dull blue	.30 —
O9	A34	10s dk brn & dp vio	1.00 —
O10	A35	15s dk vio & dp dull grn	1.50 —
O11	A36	30s dp brn & dk blue vio	.75 —
O12	A37	50s dk brn & Prus grn	2.00 —
		Nos. O7-O12 (6)	5.85

Nos. O1-O6
Overprinted "Merdeka Djojakarta 6 Djuli 1949"

1948, Dec. 15

O13	A28	2s dp brn & dp blue	.75	—
O14	A28	5s turq & dull blue	1.60	—
O15	A28	10s dp blue & brn rose	1.60	—
O16	A28	15s brown & dk grn	1.60	—
O17	A31	30s dk brn & dull vio	3.00	—
O18	A30	50s dk brn & turq	3.00	—
		Nos. O13-O18 (6)	11.55	

Nos. O7-O12
Overprinted "Merdeka Djojakarta 6 Djuli 1949"

1948, Dec. 15

O19	A28	2s dp brn & dp blue	1.00	—
O20	A28	5s turq & dull blue	.45	—
O21	A28	10s dp blue & brn rose	.45	—
O22	A28	15s brown & dk grn	1.00	—
O23	A31	30s dk brn & dull vio	2.50	—
O24	A30	50s dk brn & turq	3.00	—
		Nos. O19-O24 (6)	8.40	

RIAU ARCHIPELAGO

(Riouw Archipelago)
100 Sen = 1 Rupiah
(1 rupiah = 1 Malayan dollar)

Indonesia Nos. 371-386 Overprinted in Black

a   b

Overprint "a"

1954   Unwmk.   Perf. 12½

1	A52	5s car rose	67.50	57.50
2	A52	7½s green	1.50	1.50
3	A52	10s blue	80.00	80.00
4	A52	15s purple	3.00	3.00
5	A52	20s rose red	3.00	3.00
6	A52	25s dp green	150.00	42.50

Overprint "b"

7	A53	30s red orange	6.00	6.00
8	A53	35s purple	1.50	1.50
9	A53	40s dull green	1.50	1.50
10	A53	45s dp claret	1.50	1.50
11	A53	50s brown	525.00	100.00
12	A54	60s dk brown	1.50	1.50
13	A54	70s gray	2.75	2.75
14	A54	75s ultra	12.00	3.25
15	A54	80s claret	2.40	3.50
16	A54	90s gray green	2.40	3.50

Netherlands Indies Nos. 325-330 Overprinted Type "a" in Black

Perf. 12½x12½

17	A46	1r purple	15.00	5.25
18	A46	2r olive grn	3.25	6.00
19	A46	3r red violet	5.25	6.00
20	A46	5r dk brown	5.25	6.00
21	A46	10r gray	6.75	10.00
22	A46	25r orange brn	6.75	10.00
		Nos. 1-22 (22)	903.80	355.75

Mint values are for stamps with somewhat tropicalized gum (stained brown and cracked). Stamps with clean, clear gum sell for about twice as much.

Indonesia Nos. 424-428, 450 and 430 Overprinted Type "b" or

1957-64   Photo.   Perf. 12½x13½

23	A63(b)	5s dp ultra	.90	.90
24	A63	10s yellow brn	13.00	10.00
25	A63(b)	10s yellow brn	.90	.90

26	A63(b)	15s rose vio ('64)	.90	.90
27	A63(b)	20s dull grn ('60)	.90	.90
27A	A63	25s dp claret	40.00	40.00
28	A63(b)	25s dp claret	.90	.90
29	A63(b)	30s orange	.90	.90
30	A63	50s brown	13.00	10.00
31	A63(b)	50s brown	.90	.90

The "b" overprint measures 12mm in this set.

Sukarno Type of Indonesia Overprinted Type "a"

1960   Perf. 12½x12

32	A55	1.25r dp orange	4.50	6.75
33	A55	1.50r brown	4.50	6.75
34	A55	2.50r rose brown	6.75	10.00
35	A55	4r apple green	1.25	.50
36	A55	6r rose lilac	1.25	.50
37	A55	15r yellow	1.25	.50
38	A55	20r sepia	1.25	.50
39	A55	40r yellow grn	1.25	.50
40	A55	50r violet	2.40	.50
		Nos. 23-40 (19)	96.70	92.80

Nos. 20, 35-37, 39-40 are valued CTO with Bandung cancels. Postally used sell for much more.

WEST IRIAN

'west ,ir-ē-'än

(Irian Barat)
(West New Guinea)

LOCATION — Western half of New Guinea, southwest Pacific Ocean
GOVT. — Province of Indonesia
AREA — 162,927 sq. mi.
POP. — 923,440 (1973)
CAPITAL — Djajapura (formerly Hollandia)

The former Netherlands New Guinea became a territory under the administration of the United Nations Temporary Executive Authority on Oct. 1, 1962.
The territory came under Indonesian administration on May 1, 1963.

100 Sen = 1 Rupiah
(1 rupiah = 1 former Netherlands New Guinea gulden)

> Catalogue values for all unused stamps in this country are for Never Hinged items.

Netherlands New Guinea Stamps of 1950-60 Overprinted

Type 2 Overprint
Perf. 12½x12, 12½x13½

1962-63   Photo.   Unwmk.

1a	A4	1c vermilion & yel	.20	.20
2a	A4	2c deep orange	.25	.20
3a	A4	5c choc & yel	.25	.20
4a	A5	7c org red, bl & brn vio	.25	.20
5a	A4	10c aqua & red brn	.25	.20
6a	A5	12c grn, bl & brn vio	.25	.20
7a	A4	15c dp yel & red brn	.50	.25
8a	A5	17c brn vio & bl	.60	.35
9a	A4	20c lt bl grn & red brn	.60	.35
10a	A6	25c red	.35	.30
11a	A6	30c deep blue	.80	.35
12a	A6	40c deep orange	.80	.35
13a	A6	45c dark olive	1.40	.75
14a	A6	55c slate blue	1.25	.55
15a	A6	80c dl gray brn	5.75	5.75
16a	A6	85c dk vio brn	3.00	3.00
17a	A6	1g plum	3.50	1.90

Engr.

18a	A3	2g reddish brn	12.00	15.00
19a	A3	5g green	6.75	5.00
		Nos. 1a-19a (19)	38.75	35.10

The overprint exists in four types:

1) Size 17½mm. Applied locally and sold in 1962 in West New Guinea. Top of "N" is slightly lower than the "U," and the base of the "T" is straight, or nearly so. This set sells for about $20 more than Nos. 1a-19a.
2) Size 17½mm. Applied in the Netherlands and sold in 1963 by the UN in New York. Top of the "N" is slightly higher than the "U," and the base of the "T" is concave. This is the set listed above.
3) Size 14mm. Exists on eight values. Set value, $200.
4) Size 19mm. Exists on 1c and 10c. Set value, $160.

Types 3 and 4 were applied in West New Guinea and it is doubtful whether they were regularly issued.
See the *U.S. Specialized Catalogue* for complete listings and values of the UNTEA overprints.

Indonesia Nos. 454, 456, 494-501, 387, 390, 392 and 393 Surcharged or Overprinted: "IRIAN BARAT"

Perf. 12½x13½

1963, May 1   Photo.   Unwmk.

20	A63	1s on 70s org ver	.20	.20
21	A63	2s on 90s yel grn	.20	.20

Perf. 12x12½

22	A76	5s gray	.20	.20
23	A76	6s on 20s ocher	.20	.20
24	A76	7s on 50s dp bl	.20	.20
25	A76	10s red brn	.20	.20
26	A76	15s plum	.20	.20
27	A76	25s brt bl grn	.20	.20
28	A76	30s on 75s scar	.20	.25
29	A76	40s on 1.15r plum	.20	.30

Perf. 12½x12

30	A55	1r purple	.45	.55
31	A55	2r green	.80	.90
32	A55	3r dk bl	1.40	1.50
33	A55	5r brown	2.25	3.00
		Nos. 20-33 (14)	6.90	8.10

"Indonesia's Flag from Sabang to Merauke" — A1

20s, 50s, Parachutist landing in New Guinea. 60s, 75s, Bird of paradise and map of New Guinea.

1963, May 1

34	A1	12s org brn, blk & red	.20	.30
35	A1	17s org brn, blk & red	.20	.40
36	A1	20s multi	.30	.60
37	A1	50s multi	.30	1.00
38	A1	60s multi	.70	1.10
39	A1	75s multi	.90	1.20
		Nos. 34-39 (6)	2.60	5.40

Liberation of West New Guinea.

Maniltoa Gemmipara — A2

15s, Dendrobium lancifolium (orchid). 30s, Gardenia gjellerupii. 40s, Maniltoa flower. 50s, Phalanger. 75s, Cassowary. 1r, Kangaroo. 3r, Crowned pigeons.

1968, Aug. 17   Photo.   Perf. 12½x12

40	A2	5s dl grn & vio blk	.55	.75
41	A2	15s emer & dk pur	.80	1.50
42	A2	30s org & dp grn	1.75	2.40
43	A2	40s lemon & brt pur	1.75	2.50
44	A2	50s rose car & blk	2.40	3.50
45	A2	75s dl bl & blk	2.75	4.75
46	A2	1r brn org & blk	4.50	7.25
47	A2	3r apple grn & blk	7.00	9.50
		Nos. 40-47 (8)	21.50	32.15

Man, Map of Indonesia and Torches — A3

1968, Aug. 17

48	A3	10s ultra & gold	3.25	2.00
49	A3	25s crimson & gold	5.00	3.00

Issued to publicize the pledge of the people of West Irian to remain unified and integrated with the Republic of Indonesia.

Carving, Mother and Child — A4   Black-capped Lory — A5

West Irian Wood Carvings: 6s, Shield with 3 human figures. 7s, Child atop filigree carving. 10s, Drum. 25s, Seated man. 30s, Drum (3-tiered base). 50s, Carved bamboo. 75s, Man-shaped ornament. 1r, Shield. 2r, Seated man (hands raised).

1970   Photo.   Perf. 12½x12

50	A4	5s multi	.40	.55
51	A4	6s multi	.40	.55
52	A4	7s multi	.55	1.50
53	A4	10s multi	.55	1.50
54	A4	25s multi	.55	.55
55	A4	30s multi	.65	.80
56	A4	50s multi	.70	.80
57	A4	75s multi	.80	.95
58	A4	1r multi	.90	1.25
59	A4	2r multi	1.25	1.40
		Nos. 50-59 (10)	6.75	9.85

Issued: #50-54, 4/30; #55-59, 4/15.

1970, Oct. 26   Photo.   Perf. 12x12½

60	A5	5r shown	1.75	4.00
61	A5	10r Bird of paradise	1.60	6.00

POSTAGE DUE STAMPS
Type of Indonesia Overprinted: "IRIAN BARAT"

Perf. 13½x12½

1963, May 1   Litho.   Unwmk.

J1	D8	1s light brown	.20	.45
J2	D8	5s light gray olive	.20	.50
J3	D8	10s light blue	.20	.50
J4	D8	25s gray	.25	.90
J5	D8	40s salmon	.45	1.40
J6	D8	100s bister	1.00	2.50
		Nos. J1-J6 (6)	2.30	6.25

Type of Indonesia Dated "1968" and Overprinted: "IRIAN BARAT"

1968   Photo.   Perf. 13½x12½

J7	D9	1s blue & lt grn	.20	.55
J8	D9	5s red & pink	.20	.65
J9	D9	10s red & gray	.20	.65
J10	D9	25s grn & yel	.25	1.00
J11	D9	40s vio brn & pale grn	.55	1.60
J12	D9	100s org & bister	1.10	3.25
		Nos. J7-J12 (6)	2.50	7.70

INHAMBANE

ˌin-yəm-ˈban-ə

LOCATION — East Africa
GOVT. — A district of Mozambique,
former Portuguese colony
AREA — 21,000 sq. mi. (approx.)
POP. — 248,000 (approx.)
CAPITAL — Inhambane

1000 Reis = 1 Milreis
100 Centavos = 1 Escudo (1913)

Stamps of
Mozambique
Overprinted

On 1886 Issue

1895, July 1   Unwmk.   Perf. 12½
Without Gum

1	A2	5r black	37.50	30.00
2	A2	10r green	35.00	25.00
a.		Perf. 13½	80.00	75.00
3	A2	20r rose	60.00	30.00
4	A2	25r lilac	500.00	250.00
5	A2	40r chocolate	55.00	40.00
6	A2	50r blue	55.00	32.50
a.		Perf. 13½	50.00	50.00
7	A2	100r yellow brown	750.00	400.00
8	A2	200r gray violet	50.00	40.00
9	A2	300r orange	50.00	40.00
		Nos. 1-9 (9)	1,592.	887.50

On 1894 Issue
Perf. 11½

10	A3	50r lt blue	42.50	35.00
a.		Perf. 12½	55.00	42.50
11	A3	75r rose	55.00	40.00
12	A3	80r yellow green	45.00	37.50
13	A3	100r brown, buff	140.00	60.00
14	A3	150r carmine, rose	50.00	45.00
		Nos. 10-14 (5)	332.50	217.50

700th anniv. of the birth of St. Anthony of
Padua.
The status of Nos. 4 and 7 is questionable.
No. 3 is always discolored.
Forged overprints exist. Genuine overprints
are 21mm high.

King Carlos — A1

1903, Jan. 1   Typo.   Perf. 11½
Name and Value in Black except
500r

15	A1	2½r gray	.30	.30
16	A1	5r orange	.30	.30
17	A1	10r lt green	.60	.40
18	A1	15r gray green	1.00	.75
19	A1	20r gray violet	.85	.55
20	A1	25r carmine	.70	.55
21	A1	50r brown	1.75	1.25
22	A1	65r dull blue	20.00	15.00
23	A1	75r lilac	2.00	1.40
24	A1	100r dk blue, blue	2.75	1.25
25	A1	115r org brn, pink	5.00	5.00
26	A1	130r brown, straw	5.00	5.00
27	A1	200r red vio, pink	5.00	4.25
28	A1	400r dull bl, straw	8.25	7.50
29	A1	500r blk & red, bl	18.00	12.00
30	A1	700r gray blk, straw	20.00	13.00
		Nos. 15-30 (16)	91.50	68.50

For surcharge & overprints see #31-47, 88-
101.

No. 22 Surcharged in
Black

1905

31	A1	50r on 65r dull blue	2.75	2.00

Nos. 15-21, 23-30
Overprinted in
Carmine or Green

1911

32	A1	2½r gray	.20	.20
33	A1	5r orange	.20	.20
34	A1	10r lt green	.20	.20
35	A1	15r gray green	.30	.30
36	A1	20r gray violet	.30	.30
37	A1	25r carmine (G)	.70	.50
38	A1	50r brown	.50	.50
39	A1	75r lilac	.50	.50
40	A1	100r dk blue, bl	.50	.50
41	A1	115r org brn, pink	1.00	.95
42	A1	130r brown, straw	1.00	.95
43	A1	200r red vio, pink	1.00	.95
44	A1	400r dull bl, straw	1.25	1.00
45	A1	500r blk & red, bl	1.50	1.00
46	A1	700r gray blk, straw	1.75	1.50
		Nos. 32-46 (15)	10.90	9.55

No. 31 Overprinted in
Red

1914

47	A1	50r on 65r dull blue	1.75	1.25
a.		"Republica" inverted	25.00	25.00

Vasco da Gama Issue of Various
Portuguese Colonies

Common
Design Types
CD20-CD27
Surcharged

1913

On Stamps of Macao

48	CD20	¼c on ½a bl grn	1.25	1.25
49	CD21	½c on 1a red	1.25	1.25
50	CD22	1c on 2a red vio	1.25	1.25
a.		Inverted surcharge	35.00	35.00
51	CD23	2½c on 4a yel grn	1.25	1.25
52	CD24	5c on 8a dk bl	1.25	1.25
53	CD25	7½c on 12a vio brn	2.25	2.25
54	CD26	10c on 16a bis brn	1.75	1.75
55	CD27	15c on 24a bis	1.75	1.75
		Nos. 48-55 (8)	12.00	12.00

On Stamps of Portuguese Africa

56	CD20	¼c on 2½r bl grn	1.00	1.00
57	CD21	½c on 5r red	1.00	1.00
58	CD22	1c on 10r red vio	1.00	1.00
59	CD23	2½c on 25r yel grn	1.00	1.00
60	CD24	5c on 50r dk bl	1.00	1.00
61	CD25	7½c on 75r vio brn	2.00	2.00
62	CD26	10c on 100r bis brn	1.50	1.50
63	CD27	15c on 150r bis	1.50	1.50
		Nos. 56-63 (8)	10.00	10.00

On Stamps of Timor

64	CD20	¼c on ½a bl grn	1.25	1.25
a.		Inverted surcharge	35.00	35.00
65	CD21	½c on 1a red	1.25	1.25
66	CD22	1c on 2a red vio	1.25	1.25
67	CD23	2½c on 4a yel grn	1.25	1.25
68	CD24	5c on 8a dk bl	1.25	1.25
69	CD25	7½c on 12a vio brn	2.50	2.50
70	CD26	10c on 16a bis brn	1.75	1.75
71	CD27	15c on 24a bis	1.75	1.75
		Nos. 64-71 (8)	12.25	12.25
		Nos. 48-71 (24)	34.25	34.25

Ceres — A2

1914   Typo.   Perf. 15x14
Name and Value in Black

72	A2	¼c olive brown	.50	.50
73	A2	½c black	.50	.50
a.		Imperf.		
74	A2	1c blue green	.50	.50
75	A2	1½c lilac brown	.50	.50
76	A2	2c carmine	.50	.50
77	A2	2½c lt violet	.35	.35
78	A2	5c deep blue	.80	.80
79	A2	7½c yellow brown	1.25	1.25

80	A2	8c slate	1.25	1.25
81	A2	10c orange brown	1.10	1.10
82	A2	15c plum	2.00	1.60
83	A2	20c yellow green	2.00	1.60
84	A2	30c brown, grn	3.00	2.50
85	A2	40c brown, pink	3.00	3.00
86	A2	50c orange, sal	5.00	5.00
87	A2	1e green, blue	6.00	6.00
		Nos. 72-87 (16)	28.25	26.95

No. 31 Overprinted in
Carmine

1915   Perf. 11½

88	A1	50c on 65r dull blue	9.00	6.00

Nos. 15-21, 23-30
Overprinted Locally

1917

89	A1	2½r gray	25.00	25.00
90	A1	5r orange	25.00	25.00
91	A1	15r gray green	2.50	2.50
92	A1	20r gray violet	2.00	2.00
93	A1	50r brown	2.00	2.00
94	A1	75r lilac	2.00	2.00
95	A1	100r blue, blue	3.00	2.50
96	A1	115r org brn, pink	3.00	3.00
97	A1	130r brn, straw	3.00	2.50
98	A1	200r red vio, pink	3.00	2.50
99	A1	400r dull bl, straw	6.00	3.00
100	A1	500r blk & red, bl	5.00	3.00
101	A1	700r gray blk, straw	14.00	8.00
		Nos. 89-101 (13)	95.50	82.50

The stamps of Inhambane have been superseded by those of Mozambique.

ININI

ē-ni-ˈnē

LOCATION — In northeastern South
America, adjoining French Guiana
GOVT. — Territory of French Guiana
AREA — 30,301 sq. mi.
POP. — 5,024 (1946)
CAPITAL — St. Elie

Inini was separated from French Guiana in 1930 and reunited with it in when
the colony became an integral part of
the Republic, acquiring the same status
as the departments of Metropolitan
France, under a law effective Jan. 1,
1947.

100 Centimes = 1 Franc

> Used values are for canceled-to-
> order stamps.

Stamps of French Guiana, 1929-40,
Overprinted in Black, Red or Blue:

Nos. 1-9

Nos. 27-40

1932-40   Unwmk.   Perf. 13½x14

1	A16	1c gray lil & grnsh bl	.40	.55
2	A16	2c dk red & bl grn	.40	.55
3	A16	3c gray lil & grnsh bl ('40)	.55	.70
4	A16	4c ol brn & red vio ('38)	.55	.80
5	A16	5c Prus bl & red org	.55	.80
6	A16	10c magenta & brn	.40	.55
7	A16	15c yel brn & red org	.40	.55
8	A16	20c dk bl & ol grn	.40	.55
9	A16	25c dk red & dk brn	.90	1.25
		Perf. 14x13½		
10	A17	30c dl grn & lt grn	1.90	2.40
11	A17	30c grn & brn ('40)	.55	.90
12	A17	35c Prus grn & ol ('38)	1.10	1.40
13	A17	40c org brn & ol gray	.80	1.20
14	A17	45c ol grn & lt grn ('40)	1.30	1.50
15	A17	50c dk bl & ol gray	.70	1.05
16	A17	55c vio bl & car ('38)	4.75	6.50
17	A17	60c sal & grn ('40)	.70	1.05
18	A17	65c sal & grn ('38)	1.75	2.25
19	A17	70c ind & sl bl ('40)	.80	1.10
20	A17	75c ind & sl bl (Bl)	2.75	3.50
21	A17	80c blk & vio bl (R)	1.00	1.25
22	A17	90c dk red & ver	1.75	2.25
23	A17	90c red vio & brn ('39)	.80	1.40
24	A17	1fr lt vio & brn	16.00	22.50
25	A17	1fr car & lt brn ('38)	1.50	1.75
26	A17	1fr blk & vio bl ('40)	1.00	1.40
27	A18	1.25fr brn blk & grn ('33)	1.25	1.60
28	A18	1.25fr rose & lt red ('39)	1.00	1.40
29	A18	1.40fr ol brn & red vio ('40)	1.00	1.40
30	A18	1.50fr dk bl & lt bl	1.05	1.50
31	A18	1.60fr ol brn & bl grn ('40)	1.00	1.40
32	A18	1.75fr brn, red & blk brn ('33)	18.00	22.50
33	A18	1.75fr vio bl ('38)	1.60	2.40
34	A18	2fr dk grn & rose red	1.25	1.75
35	A18	2.25fr vio bl ('39)	1.05	1.40
36	A18	2.50fr cop red & brn ('40)	1.00	1.40
37	A18	3fr brn red & red vio	1.25	1.75
38	A18	5fr dl vio & yel grn	1.25	1.75
39	A18	10fr ol gray & dp ultra (R)	1.50	2.10
40	A18	20fr indigo & ver	1.50	2.10
		Nos. 1-40 (40)	77.40	104.15

Without "RF," see Nos. 46-49.

Common Design Types
pictured following the introduction.

Colonial Arts Exhibition Issue
Souvenir Sheet
Common Design Type

1937   Imperf.

41	CD75	3fr red brown	17.50	22.50

New York World's Fair Issue
Common Design Type

1939, May 10   Engr.   Perf. 12½x12

42	CD82	1.25fr car lake	3.75	4.50
43	CD82	2.25fr ultra	3.75	4.50

French Guiana Nos. 170A-170B
Overprinted "ININI" in Green or Red

1941   Engr.   Perf. 12½x12

44	A21a	1fr deep lilac	1.00	
45	A21a	2.50fr blue (R)	1.00	

Nos. 44-45 were issued by the Vichy government in France, but were not placed on
sale in Inini.
For surcharges, see Nos. B9-B10.

Types of 1932-40 Without "RF"
Methods and Perfs as Before
1942

46	A16	20c dk bl & ol grn	1.20
47	A17	1fr black & ultra	1.10
48	A18	10fr ol gr & dp ultra (R)	1.40
49	A18	20fr indigo & ver	2.40
		Nos. 46-49 (4)	6.10

Nos. 46-49 were issued by the Vichy government in France, but were not placed on sale in Inini.

SEMI-POSTAL STAMPS

French Revolution Common Design Type
Photo.; Name & Value Typo. in Black

1939, July 5		**Unwmk.**	**Perf. 13**	
B1	CD83	45c + 25c green	14.50	17.50
B2	CD83	70c + 30c brown	14.50	17.50
B3	CD83	90c + 35c red org	14.50	17.50
B4	CD83	1.25fr + 1fr rose pink	14.50	17.50
B5	CD83	2.25fr + 2fr blue	14.50	17.50
		Nos. B1-B5 (5)	72.50	87.50

"Defense" Common Design Type and French Guiana Nos. B9 and B11 Overprinted "ININI" in Blue or Red

1941		**Photo.**	**Perf. 13½**
B6	SP1	1fr + 1fr red (B)	1.75
B7	CD86	1.50fr + 3fr maroon	1.75
B8	SP2	2.50fr + 1fr blue (R)	1.75
		Nos. B6-B8 (3)	5.25

Nos. B6-B8 were issued by the Vichy government in France, but were not placed on sale in Inini.

Nos. 44-45
Surcharged in Black or Red

1944		**Engr.**	**Perf. 12½x12**
B9		50c + 1.50fr on 2.50fr deep blue (R)	1.00
B10		+ 2.50fr on 1fr dp lilac	1.00

Colonial Development Fund.
Nos. B9-B10 were issued by the Vichy government in France, but were not placed on sale in Inini.

AIR POST SEMI-POSTAL STAMPS

Nurse with Mother & Child — SPAP1

Unwmk.

1942, June 22		**Engr.**	**Perf. 13**
CB1	SPAP1	1.50fr + 50c green	1.10
CB2	SPAP1	2fr + 6fr brn & red	1.10

Native children's welfare fund.
Nos. CB1-CB2 were issued by the Vichy government in France, but were not placed on sale in Inini.

Colonial Education Fund
Common Design Type

1942, June 22

CB3	CD86a	1.20fr + 1.80fr blue & red	1.10

No. CB3 was issued by the Vichy government in France, but was not placed on sale in Inini.

POSTAGE DUE STAMPS

Postage Due Stamps of French Guiana, 1929, Overprinted in Black

1932, Apr. 7		**Unwmk.**	**Perf. 13½x14**	
J1	D3	5c indigo & Prus bl	.25	.40
J2	D3	10c bis brn & Prus grn	.65	1.00
J3	D3	20c grn & rose red	.65	1.00
J4	D3	30c ol brn & rose red	.65	1.00
J5	D3	50c vio & ol brn	1.00	1.50
J6	D3	60c brn red & ol brn	1.10	1.50

Overprinted in Black or Red

J7	D4	1fr dp bl & org brn	1.10	1.50
J8	D4	2fr brn red & bluish grn	1.40	2.00
J9	D4	3fr vio & blk (R)	7.00	9.50
J10	D4	3fr vio & blk	3.00	3.75
		Nos. J1-J10 (10)	16.80	23.15

IONIAN ISLANDS

ī-'ō-nē-ən 'ī-lənds

LOCATION — Seven Islands, of which six-Corfu, Paxos, Lefkas (Santa Maura), Cephalonia, Ithaca and Zante-are in the Ionian Sea west of Greece, and a seventh-Cerigo (Kithyra)-is in the Mediterranean south of Greece.
GOVT. — Integral part of Kingdom of Greece
AREA — 752 sq. miles
POP. — 231,510 (1938)

These islands were acquired by Great Britain in 1815 but in 1864 were ceded to Greece on request of the inhabitants.
In 1941 the islands were occupied by Italian forces. The Italians withdrew in 1943 and German forces continued the occupation, using current Greek stamps without overprinting, except for Zante.
For stamps of the Italian occupation of Corfu, see Corfu.

10 Oboli	=	1 Penny
12 Pence	=	1 Shilling
100 Lepta	=	1 Drachma
100 Centesimi	=	1 Lira

Watermarks

Wmk. 138 — "2"   Wmk. 139 — "1"

ISSUES OF THE BRITISH PROTECTORATE

Queen Victoria — A1

1859		**Unwmk.**	**Engr.**	**Imperf.**	
1	A1	(½p) orange		110.00	600.00
		Wmk. 138			
2	A1	(1p) blue		27.50	225.00
		Wmk. 139			
3	A1	(2p) lake		22.50	225.00
		Nos. 1-3 (3)		160.00	1,050.

Forged cancellations are plentiful.

ISSUED UNDER ITALIAN OCCUPATION

Values of stamps overprinted by letterpress in pairs are for unsevered pairs. Single stamps, unused, sell for one third the price of a pair; used, one half the price of a pair.
Handstamped overprints were also applied to pairs, with "isola" instead of "isole."

Issue for Cephalonia and Ithaca
Stamps of Greece, 1937-38, Overprinted in Pairs Vertically, Reading Down, or Horizontally (H) in Black

Perf. 12½x12, 13½x12, 12x13½

1941		**Wmk. 252, Unwmk.**		
N1	A69	5 l brn red & bl	40.00	40.00
N2	A70	10 l bl & red brn (#413) (H)	40.00	40.00
a.		On No. 397	160.00	160.00
N3	A71	20 l blk & grn (H)	40.00	40.00
a.		Overprint inverted	250.00	
N4	A72	40 l green & blk	40.00	40.00
N5	A73	50 l brown & blk	40.00	40.00
N6	A74	80 l ind & yel brn (H)	55.00	55.00
a.		Overprint inverted	325.00	250.00
N7	A67	1d green (H)	250.00	160.00
N8	A84	1.50d green (H)	175.00	95.00
a.		Overprint inverted	275.00	200.00
N9	A75	2d ultra	40.00	40.00
N10	A76	5d red	140.00	52.50
N11	A77	6d olive brown	140.00	52.50
N12	A78	7d dark brown	140.00	52.50
N13	A67	8d dp blue (H)	225.00	110.00
N14	A79	10d red brn	140.00	52.50
N15	A80	15d green	240.00	95.00
N16	A81	25d dk blue (H)	275.00	130.00
a.		Overprint inverted	525.00	
N17	A84	30d org brn (H)	1,200.	675.00
a.		Overprint inverted	1,300.	800.00
		Nos. N1-N17 (17)	3,220.	1,770.

A variety with wrong font "C" in "Cephalonia" is found in several positions in each sheet of all denominations except those overprinted on single stamps. It sells for about three times the price of a normal pair.
Several other minor spelling errors in the overprint occur on several denominations in one of the printings.
Forgeries exist of many of the higher valued stamps and minor varieties of Nos. N1-N17, NC1-NC11 and NRA1-NRA5.

ISSUED UNDER ITALIAN OCCUPATION
(continued)

Overprint Reading Up

N1a	A69	5 l	40.00	40.00
N4a	A72	40 l	40.00	40.00
N5a	A73	50 l	40.00	40.00
N9a	A75	2d	55.00	52.50
N10a	A76	5d	140.00	52.50
N11a	A77	6d	140.00	52.50
N12a	A78	7d	140.00	55.00
N14a	A79	10d	140.00	55.00
N15a	A80	15d	240.00	95.00
		Nos. N1a-N15a (9)	975.00	480.00

General Issue

Stamps of Italy, 1929, Overprinted in Red or Black

1941		**Wmk. 140**	**Perf. 14**	
N18	A90	5c olive brn (R)	.65	2.40
N19	A92	10c dk brown (R)	.65	2.40
N20	A91	20c rose red	.65	2.40
N21	A94	25c deep green	.65	2.40
N22	A95	30c olive brn (R)	.65	2.40
a.		"SOLE" for "ISOLE"	65.00	
N23	A95	50c purple (R)	.65	2.40
N24	A94	75c rose red	.65	2.40
N25	A94	1.25 l dp blue (R)	.65	2.40
		Nos. N18-N25 (8)	5.20	19.20

The stamps overprinted "Isole Jonie" were issued for all the Ionian Islands except Cerigo which used regular postage stamps of Greece.

ISSUED UNDER GERMAN OCCUPATION

Zante Issue

Nos. N21 and N23 with Additional Handstamped Overprint in Black

1943		**Wmk. 140**	**Perf. 14**	
N26	A94	25c deep green	20.00	45.00
a.		Carmine overprint	30.00	75.00
N27	A95	50c purple	20.00	45.00
a.		Carmine overprint	30.00	75.00

No. N19 with this overprint is a proof. Value, black $70; carmine $375.
Nos. N26-N27 were in use 8 days, then were succeeded by stamps of Greece.
Forgeries of Nos. N26-N27, NC13 and their cancellations are plentiful.

Greek stamps with Italian overprints for the islands of Cerigo (Kithyra), Paxos and Lefkas (Santa Maura) are fraudulent.

OCCUPATION AIR POST STAMPS

Issued under Italian Occupation

Issue for Cephalonia and Ithaca
Stamps of Greece Overprinted in Pairs Vertically, Reading Down, or Horizontally (H) in Black Like Nos. N1-N17

Perf. 13x12½, 12½x13

1941			**Unwmk.**	
		On Greece Nos. C22, C23, C25 and C27 to C30		
		Grayish Paper		
NC1	AP16	1d dp red	120.00	95.00
NC1A	AP17	2d dl bl	55.00	47.50
NC2	AP19	7d bl vio (H)	120.00	190.00
NC3	AP21	25d rose (H)	450.00	350.00
a.		Overprint inverted	800.00	450.00
NC4	AP22	30d dk grn	725.00	450.00
a.		Overprint reading up	725.00	450.00
b.		Horizontal overprint on single stamp	—	
c.		As "b," inverted	—	
NC5	AP23	50d vio (H)	3,600.	2,500.
NC6	AP24	100d brown	1,900.	1,900.
a.		Overprint reading up	1,600.	1,200.

No. NC1A is known only with overprint reading up.

On Greece Nos. C31-C34
Reengraved; White Paper

NC7	AP16	1d red	120.00	95.00
NC8	AP17	2d gray bl	40.00	25.00
a.		Overprint reading up	40.00	25.00
b.		Horiz. ovpt. on pair	800.00	425.00
c.		Horizontal overprint on single stamp		
NC9	AP18	5d vio (H)	95.00	72.50
a.		Overprint inverted	800.00	425.00
b.		Vert. ovpt. on single stamp, up or down	800.00	450.00
NC10	AP19	7d dp ultra (H)	275.00	200.00
a.		Overprint inverted	800.00	300.00

Overprinted Horizontally on No. C36
Rouletted 13½

NC11	D3	50 l vio brn	1,200.	900.00
a.		Pair, one without ovpt.	2,000.	
b.		On No. C36a	—	

See footnote following No. N17.

General Issue
Italy No. C13 Overprinted in Red Like Nos. N18-N25

1941		Wmk. 140	Perf. 14
NC12	AP3	50c olive brown	.80	3.25
a.		"SOLE" for "ISOLE"	65.00	

Used in all the Ionian Islands except Cerigo which used air post stamps of Greece.
No. NC12 with additional overprint "BOLLO" is a revenue stamp.

Issued under German Occupation
ZANTE ISSUE
No. NC12 with Additional Handstamped Overprint in Black Like Nos. N26-N27

1943		Wmk. 140	Perf. 14
NC13	AP3	50c olive brown	25.00	50.00
a.		"SOLE" for "ISOLE"	300.00	
b.		Carmine overprint	135.00	260.00

See note after No. N27.

OCCUPATION POSTAGE DUE STAMPS

General Issue
Postage Due Stamps of Italy, 1934, Overprinted in Black Like Nos. N18-N25

1941		Wmk. 140	Perf. 14
NJ1	D6	10c blue	3.25	6.50
NJ2	D6	20c rose red	3.25	6.50
NJ3	D6	30c red orange	3.25	6.50
NJ4	D7	1 l red orange	3.25	6.50
		Nos. NJ1-NJ4 (4)	13.00	26.00

See footnote after No. N25.

OCCUPATION POSTAL TAX STAMPS

Issued under Italian Occupation

Issue for Cephalonia and Ithaca
Greece No. RA56 with Additional Overprint on Horizontal Pair in Black Like Nos. N1-N17

Serrate Roulette 13½

1941			Unwmk.
NRA1	D3	10 l car (Bl+Bk)	24.00	24.00
a.		Blue overprint double	95.00	95.00
b.		Inverted overprint	275.00	275.00

Same Overprint Reading Down on Vertical Pairs of Nos. RA61-RA63

Perf. 13½x12

NRA2	PT7	10 l brt rose, pale rose	32.50	24.00
a.		Overprint on horiz. pair	100.00	40.00
b.		Horizontal overprint on single stamp	950.00	
c.		Overprint reading up	15.00	12.50
NRA3	PT7	50 l gray grn, pale grn	32.50	24.00
a.		Overprint reading up	32.50	24.00
b.		Ovpt. on horiz. pair	24.00	24.00
c.		Horizontal overprint on single stamp	300.00	
NRA4	PT7	1d dl bl, lt bl	65.00	45.00
a.		Overprint reading up	65.00	45.00

Same Overprint Reading Down on Vertical Pair of No. RA65

NRA5	PT7	50 l gray grn, pale grn	800.00	650.00
a.		Overprint reading up	800.00	650.00

Nos. NRA5 and NRA5a were not placed in use on any compulsory day.
See footnote following No. N17.

IRAN

i-'ràn

(Persia)

LOCATION — Western Asia, bordering on the Persian Gulf and the Gulf of Oman
GOVT. — Islamic republic
AREA — 636,000 sq. mi.
POP. — 65,179,752 (1999 est.)
CAPITAL — Tehran

20 Shahis (or Chahis) = 1 Kran
10 Krans = 1 Toman
100 Centimes = 1 Franc = 1 Kran (1881)
100 Dinars = 1 Rial (1933)
100 Rials = 1 Pahlavi
100 Rials = 1 Toman

Catalogue values for unused stamps in this country are for Never Hinged items, beginning with Scott 1054 in the regular postage section, Scott B36 in the semi-postal section, Scott C83 in the airpost section, Scott O72 in the officials section, Scott Q36 in the parcel post section, and Scott RA4 in the postal tax section.

Values of early stamps vary according to condition. Quotations for Nos. 1-20, 33-40 are for fine copies. Very fine to superb specimens sell at much higher prices, and inferior or poor copies sell at reduced prices, depending on the condition of the individual specimen.
Cracked gum on unused stamps does not detract from the value.

Beware of forgeries and/or reprints of most Iran stamps between the years 1870-1925. Scott values are for genuine stamps. Collectors should be aware that forgeries of many issues outnumber genuine examples by factors of 10 or 20 to one. Failing specialized knowledge on the part of the collector, these stamps should be examined or authenticated by acknowledged experts before purchase.

Watermarks

Wmk. 161 — Lion

Wmk. 306 — Arms of Iran

Wmk. 316 — Persian Inscription

Wmk. 349 — Persian Inscription and Crown in Circle

Illustration of Wmk. 349 shown sideways. Circles in Wmk. 349 are 95mm apart.

Wmk. 353 — Persian Inscription and Coat of Arms in Circle

Wmk. 381 — "Islamic Republic of Iran" in Persian (Partial Illustration)

Many issues have handstamped surcharges. As usual with such surcharges there are numerous inverted, double and similar varieties.

Coat of Arms
A1   A2

Design A2 has value numeral below lion.

1870	Unwmk.	Typo.	Imperf.
1	A1 1s dull violet		200.00
2	A1 2s green		125.00
3	A1 4s greenish blue		125.00
4	A1 8s red		125.00
	Nos. 1-4 (4)		575.00

Values for used examples of Nos. 1-4 are omitted, since this issue was only pen canceled. After 1875, postmarked remainders were sold to collectors. Values same as unused.
Printed in blocks of 4. Many shades exist. Forgeries exist.

Printed on Both Sides

1a	A1	1s	1,300.
2a	A1	2s	900.
3a	A1	4s	2,000.
4a	A1	8s	1,200.

Vertically Rouletted 10½ on 1 or 2 Sides

1875		Thick Wove Paper	
11	A2 1s black	150.00	50.00
a.	Imperf., pair	400.00	400.00
12	A2 2s blue	125.00	50.00
a.	Tête bêche pair	10,000.	
b.	Imperf., pair	575.00	575.00
13	A2 4s vermilion	250.00	75.00
a.	Imperf., pair	625.00	625.00
b.	4s bright red, thin paper, imperf.	525.00	525.00
14	A2 8s yellow green	100.00	60.00
a.	Tête bêche pair	12,500.	7,500.
b.	Imperf., pair	200.00	250.00
	Nos. 11-14 (4)	625.00	235.00

Four varieties of each.

Nos. 11-14 were printed in horizontal strips of 4 with 3-10mm spacing between stamps. The strips were then cut very close all around (generally touching or cutting the outer frame-lines). Then they were hand-rouletted between the stamps. Values are for stamps with rouletting on both sides and margins clear at top and bottom. Stamps showing the rouletting on only one side sell for considerably less.
Nos. 11 to 14 also exist pin-perforated and percé en scie.
No. 13b has spacing of 2-3mm.
See Nos. 15-20, 33-40.

Medium to Thin White or Grayish Paper

1876			Imperf.
14A	A2 1s black	200.00	300.00
15	A2 1s gray black	37.50	75.00
a.	Printed on both sides	1,000.	
b.	Laid paper	500.00	
16	A2 2s gray blue	550.00	700.00
a.	Printed on both sides	1,600.	
17	A2 2s black	600.00	
a.	Tête bêche pair	5,750.	
18	A2 4s vermilion	250.00	75.00
a.	Printed on both sides	800.00	450.00
19	A2 1k rose	750.00	50.00
a.	Printed on both sides		350.00
b.	Laid paper	2,500.	250.00
c.	1k yellow (error)	9,500.	5,500.
d.	Tête bêche pair		25,000.
20	A2 4k yellow	1,500.	125.00
a.	Printed on both sides		1,000.
b.	Laid paper	2,000.	225.00
c.	Tête bêche pair		18,000.

Nos. 15-16, 18-20 were printed in blocks of 4, and Nos. 14A and 17 in vertical strips of 4, with spacing of 2mm or less.
Nos. 14A and 17 are on medium to thick grayish wove paper. Forgeries exist.
Official reprints of the 1s and 4s are on thick coarse white paper without gum. Value, each $350.

Unofficial Reprints:
1875 and 1876 issues.
The reprints of the 1s and 1k stamps are readily told; the pearls of the circle are heavier, the borders of the circles containing the Persian numeral of value are wider and the figure "1" below the lion is always Roman.
The reprints of the 2s have the outer line of the frame at the left and at the bottom broken and on some specimens entirely missing.
A distinguishing mark by which to tell the 4s and 4k stamps is the frame, the outer line of which is of the same thickness as the inner line, while on the originals the inner line is very thin and the outer line thick; another feature of most of the reprints is a gash in the lower part of the circle below the figure "4."
In the reprints of the 8s stamps the small scroll nearest to the circles with Persian numerals at the bottom of the stamp touches the frame below it; the inner and outer lines of the frame are of equal thickness, while in the originals the outer line is much heavier than the inner one.
All reprints are found canceled to order.

Nasser-eddin Shah Qajar — A3

Perf. 10½, 11, 12, 13, and Compounds

1876			Litho.
27	A3 1s lilac & blk	30.00	6.00
28	A3 2s green & blk	35.00	7.50
29	A3 5s rose & blk	30.00	4.00
30	A3 10s blue & blk	45.00	8.00
	Nos. 27-30 (4)	140.00	25.50

Bisects of the 5s and 1s, the latter used with 2s stamps, were used to make up the 2½ shahis postcard rate. Bisects of the 10s were used in the absence of 5s stamps to make up the letter rate.

The 10s was bisected and surcharged "5 Shahi" or "5 Shahy" for local use in Azerbaijan province and Khoy in 1877.

"Imperfs" of the 5s are envelope cutouts.

Forgeries and official reprints exist.

Very fine examples will have perforations cutting the background net on one side. Genuine stamps withs perfs clear of net on all four sides are very scarce.

1878   Typo.   Imperf.
33	A2	1k car rose	400.00	90.00
34	A2	1k red, *yellow*	*2,500.*	100.00
a.		Tête bêche pair		6,000.
35	A2	4k ultramarine	275.00	100.00
a.		Printed on both sides		4,000.
36	A2	5k violet	900.00	250.00
37	A2	5k gold	*5,000.*	450.00
38	A2	5k red bronze	*10,000.*	1,750.
39	A2	5k vio bronze	*35,000.*	2,750.
40	A2	1t bronze, *bl*	*65,000.*	6,000.

Four varieties of each except for 4k which has 3.

Nos. 33 and 34 are printed from redrawn clichés. They have wide colorless circles around the corner numerals.

Nasser-eddin Shah
Qajar — A6

Sun — A7

Perf. 10½, 12, 13, and Compounds
1879   Litho.
41	A6	1k brown & blk	450.00	7.00
a.		Imperf., pair		—
b.		Inverted center		4,500.
42	A6	5k blue & blk	400.00	5.00
a.		Imperf., pair		500.00
b.		Inverted center		1,750.
c.		Inverted center, imperf		1,500.

1880
43	A6	1s red & black	50.00	15.00
b.		Pair, imperf between		3,000.
44	A6	2s yellow & blk	85.00	10.00
45	A6	5s green & blk	350.00	2.00
46	A6	10s violet & blk	625.00	25.00
		Nos. 43-46 (4)	1,110.	52.00

Forgeries and official reprints exist.

The 2, 5 and 10sh of this issue and the 1 and 5kr of the 1879 issue have been reprinted from a new die which resembles the 5 shahi envelope. The aigrette is shorter than on the original stamps and touches the circle above it.

Imperf., Pair
43a	A6	1s		1,500.
44a	A6	2s		2,000.
46a	A6	10s	—	600.00

1881   Litho.   Perf. 12, 13, 12x13
47	A7	5c dull violet	50.00	25.00
48	A7	10c rose	50.00	25.00
49	A7	25c green	6,500.00	100.00
		Nos. 47-49 (3)	6,600.00	150.00

1882   Engr., Border Litho.
50	A7	5c blue vio & vio	50.00	60.00
51	A7	10c dp pink & rose	50.00	60.00
52	A7	25c deep grn & grn	800.00	20.00
		Nos. 50-52 (3)	900.00	140.00

Very fine examples of Nos. 50-52 will have perforations cutting the outer colored border but clear of the inner framelines.

Counterfeits of Nos. 50-52, 53, 53a are plentiful and have been used to create forgeries of Nos. 66, 66a, 70 and 70a. They usually have a strong, complete inner frameline at right. On genuine stamps that line is weak or missing.

A8

Shah Nasr-ed-Din
A9   A10

A11

Type I

Type II (error)

Type I: Three dots at right end of scroll.
Type II: Two dots at right end of scroll.

1882-84   Engr.
53	A8	5s green, type I	50.00	1.50
a.		5s green, type II	100.00	10.00
54	A9	10s buff, org & blk	75.00	10.00
55	A10	50c buff, org & blk	500.00	55.00
56	A10	50c gray & blk ('84)	125.00	65.00
57	A10	1fr blue & black	150.00	10.00
58	A10	5fr rose red & blk	125.00	10.00
59	A11	10fr buff, red & blk	150.00	30.00
		Nos. 53-59 (7)	1,175.	181.50

Crude forgeries of Nos. 58-59 exist. Halves of the 10s, 50c and 1fr surcharged with Farsi characters in red or black are frauds. The 50c and 1fr surcharged with a large "5" surrounded by rays are also frauds.

No. 59 used is valued for c-t-o.

For overprints and surcharges see #66-72.

Very fine examples of Nos. 53-59 will have perforations cutting the outer colored border but clear of the inner framelines.

A12   A13

Perf. 12-12½, 13
1885, March-May   Litho.
59A	A12	5c blue	1,000.	50.00
a.		5c violet blue	1,000.	75.00
b.		5c ultramarine	1,000.	75.00
c.		5c dp reddish lilac	1,500.	250.00
d.		As "a," imperf	5,000.	

No. 59A was issued because of an urgent need for 5c stamps, pending the arrival of No. 62 in July. No. 59A has 88 sunrays instead of the 124 sunrays on the typographed stamp, No. 62.

1885-86   Typo.
60	A12	1c green	20.00	1.50
61	A12	2c rose	20.00	1.50
62	A12	5c dull blue	150.00	.75
63	A13	10c brown	20.00	1.50
64	A13	1k slate	60.00	2.00
65	A13	5k dull vio ('86)	700.00	35.00
		Nos. 60-65 (6)	970.00	42.25

Nos. 53, 54, 56 and 58 Surcharged in Black:

a   b

c   d

e   f

1885
66	(a)	6c on 5s grn, type I	125.00	30.00
a.		6c on 5s green, type II	200.00	100.00
67	(b)	12c on 50c gray & blk	125.00	30.00
68	(c)	18c on 10s buff, org & black	125.00	30.00
69	(d)	1t on 5fr rose red & black	125.00	30.00
		Nos. 66-69 (4)	500.00	120.00

1887
70	(e)	3c on 5s grn, type I	125.00	30.00
a.		3c on 5s green, type II	200.00	100.00
71	(a)	6c on 10s buff, org & blk	125.00	30.00
72	(f)	8c on 50c gray & blk	125.00	30.00
		Nos. 70-72 (3)	375.00	90.00

The word "OFFICIEL" indicated that the surcharged stamps were officially authorized.

Surcharges on the same basic stamps of values other than those listed are believed to be bogus.

Counterfeits of Nos. 66-72 abound.

Very fine examples of Nos. 66-72 will have perforations cutting the outer colored border but clear of the inner framelines.

Beware of forgeries and/or reprints of most Iran stamps between the years 1870-1925. Scott values are for genuine stamps. Collectors should be aware that forgeries of many issues outnumber genuine examples by factors of 10 or 20 to one. Failing specialized knowledge on the part of the collector, these stamps should be examined or authenticated by acknowledged experts before purchase.

A14   A15

1889   Typo.   Perf. 11, 13½, 11x13½
73	A14	1c pale rose	2.50	.75
74	A14	2c pale blue	2.50	.75
75	A14	5c lilac	1.50	.50
76	A14	7c brown	7.50	1.50
77	A15	10c black	2.50	.75
78	A15	1k red orange	4.50	.75
79	A15	2k rose	40.00	6.00
80	A15	5k green	25.00	6.00
		Nos. 73-80 (8)	86.00	17.00

All values exist imperforate.

Canceled to order stamps of No. 76 abound. For surcharges see Nos. 622-625.

Nos. 73-80 with average centering, faded colors and/or toned paper sell for much less.

A16   A17

1891   Perf. 10½, 11½
81	A16	1c black	2.50	1.00
82	A16	2c brown	2.50	1.00
83	A16	5c deep blue	2.50	.20
84	A16	7c gray	350.00	12.00
85	A16	10c rose	2.50	.50
86	A16	14c orange	2.50	1.50
87	A17	1k green	30.00	2.00
88	A17	2k orange	700.00	25.00
89	A17	5k ocher yellow	8.00	30.00
		Nos. 81-89 (9)	1,100.	73.20

For surcharges see Nos. 626-629.

A18   Nasser-eddin Shah
Qajar — A19

1894   Perf. 12½
90	A18	1c lilac	1.00	.20
91	A18	2c blue green	1.00	.20
92	A18	5c ultramarine	1.00	.20
93	A18	8c brown	1.00	.20

Perf. 11½x11
94	A19	10c orange	1.25	.75
95	A19	16c rose	25.00	50.00
96	A19	1k red & yellow	3.00	.75
97	A19	2k brn org & pale bl	4.00	1.00
98	A19	5k violet & silver	5.00	1.50
99	A19	10k red & gold	15.00	10.00
100	A19	50k green & gold	50.00	10.00
		Nos. 90-100 (11)	107.25	74.80

Canceled to order stamps sell for one-third of listed values.

Reprints exist. They are hard to distinguish from the originals. Value, set $15.

See Nos. 104-112, 136-144. For overprints see Nos. 120-128, 152-167, 173-181. For surcharges see Nos. 101-103, 168, 206, 211.

Nos. 93, 98 With Violet or Magenta Surcharge

a   b

1897   **Perf. 12½, 11½x11**

101	A18(a)	5c on 8c brown (V)	25.00	4.00
102	A19(b)	1k on 5k vio & sil (V)	35.00	16.00
103	A19(b)	2k on 5k vio & sil (M)	50.00	30.00
		Nos. 101-103 (3)	110.00	50.00

Forgeries exist.

Lion Type of 1894 and

Mozaffar-eddin Shah Qajar — A22

1898   **Typo.**   **Perf. 12½**

104	A18	1c gray	5.00	.35
105	A18	2c pale brown	5.00	.35
106	A18	3c dull violet	10.00	3.00
107	A18	4c vermilion	10.00	3.00
108	A18	5c yellow	5.00	.25
109	A18	8c orange	20.00	7.00
110	A18	10c light blue	5.00	.50
111	A18	12c rose	15.00	1.00
112	A18	16c green	20.00	7.00
113	A22	1k ultramarine	10.00	1.00
114	A22	2k pink	10.00	2.00
115	A22	3k yellow	10.00	3.00
116	A22	4k gray	10.00	5.00
117	A22	5k emerald	10.00	6.00
118	A22	10k orange	30.00	15.00
119	A22	10k bright vio	50.00	25.00
		Nos. 104-119 (16)	225.00	79.45

Unauthorized reprints of Nos. 104-119 were made from original clichés. Paper shows a vertical mesh. These abound unused and canceled to order. Value unused, hinged, $20.

See Nos. 145-151. For overprints see Nos. 129-135, 182-188. For surcharges see Nos. 169, 171, 207, 209, 215.

Reprints have been used to make counterfeits of Nos. 120-135, 152-167.

Stamps of 1898 Handstamped in Violet:

a   b

c   d

---

e   f

g   h

1899

120	(a)	1c gray	5.00	5.00
121	(b)	2c pale brown	5.00	8.00
122	(b)	3c dull violet	12.00	15.00
123	(c)	4c vermilion	18.00	30.00
124	(c)	5c yellow	10.00	3.00
125	(d)	8c orange	15.00	40.00
126	(d)	10c light blue	6.50	8.00
a.		Type "b" handstamp	350.00	350.00
127	(d)	12c rose	15.00	8.00
128	(d)	16c green	25.00	30.00
129	(e)	1k ultramarine	25.00	10.00
130	(f)	2k pink	30.00	25.00
131	(f)	3k yellow	80.00	200.00
132	(g)	4k gray	100.00	200.00
133	(g)	5k emerald	30.00	40.00
134	(h)	10k orange	60.00	60.00
135	(h)	50k brt violet	120.00	150.00
		Nos. 120-135 (16)	556.50	832.00

The handstamped control marks on Nos. 120-135 exist sideways, inverted and double. Counterfeits are plentiful.

Types of 1894-98

1899   **Typo.**   **Perf. 12½**

136	A18	1c gray, *green*	7.50	.75
137	A18	2c brown, *green*	7.50	.75
138	A18	3c violet, *green*	20.00	5.00
139	A18	4c red, *green*	12.00	5.00
140	A18	5c yellow, *green*	5.00	.30
141	A18	8c orange, *green*	15.00	5.00
142	A18	10c pale blue, *grn*	5.00	.50
143	A18	12c lake, *green*	15.00	1.25
144	A18	16c green, *green*	25.00	5.00
145	A22	1k red	30.00	1.25
146	A22	2k deep green	35.00	8.50
147	A22	3k lilac brown	35.00	17.00
148	A22	4k orange red	35.00	17.00
149	A22	5k gray brown	40.00	17.00
150	A22	10k deep blue	400.00	100.00
151	A22	50k brown	75.00	30.00
		Nos. 136-151 (16)	762.00	214.30

Canceled to order stamps abound.

Unauthorized reprints of Nos. 136-151 were made from original clichés. Paper is chalky and has white gum. The design can be seen through the back of the reprints. Value unused, hinged, set, $30.

For surcharges and overprints see Nos. 171, 173-188, 206-207, 209, 211, 215.

Nos. 104-111 Handstamped in Violet

(Struck once on every two stamps.)

1900

152	A18	1c gray	50.00	20.00
153	A18	2c pale brown	60.00	25.00
154	A18	3c dull violet	100.00	50.00
155	A18	4c vermilion	100.00	50.00
156	A18	5c yellow	25.00	10.00
158	A18	10c light blue	*1,000.*	*1,000.*
159	A18	12c rose	100.00	50.00
		Nos. 152-159 (7)	1,435.	1,205.

Values are for single authenticated stamps. Pairs sell for much more.

This control mark, in genuine state, was not applied to the 8c orange (Nos. 109, 125).

Same Overprint Handstamped on Nos. 120-127 in Violet

(Struck once on each block of 4.)

160	A18	1c gray		50.00
163	A18	4c vermilion	300.00	140.00
164	A18	5c yellow	50.00	20.00

166	A18	10c light blue		500.00
a.		Type "b" handstamp	400.00	200.00
167	A18	12c rose	150.00	50.00
		Nos. 160-167 (5)	550.00	760.00

Values are for single authenticated stamps. Blocks are rare and worth much more.

Counterfeits exist of Nos. 152-167.

No. 93 Surcharged in Violet

1900

168	A18	5c on 8c brown	50.00	2.50

No. 145 Surcharged in Violet

1901

169	A22	12c on 1k red	100.00	100.00
a.		Blue surcharge	125.00	125.00

Counterfeits exist.
Some specialists state that No. 169 with black surcharge was made for collectors.

A23

1902   **Violet Surcharge**

171	A23	5k on 50k brown	200.00	80.00
a.		Blue surcharge	200.00	90.00

Counterfeits exist. See No. 207.

Nos. 136-151 Overprinted in Black

1902

173	A18	1c gray, *green*	50.00	20.00
174	A18	2c brown, *green*	50.00	20.00
175	A18	3c violet, *green*	125.00	50.00
176	A18	4c red, *green*	175.00	200.00
177	A18	5c yellow, *green*	20.00	5.00
178	A18	8c orange, *green*	175.00	200.00
179	A18	10c pale blue, *grn*	50.00	15.00
180	A18	12c lake, *green*	125.00	50.00
181	A18	16c green, *green*	300.00	200.00
182	A22	1k red	100.00	45.00
183	A22	2k deep green	250.00	100.00
188	A22	50k brown	300.00	125.00

Overprinted on No. 168

206	A18	5c on 8c brown	200.00	100.00

Overprinted on Nos. 171 and 171a

207	A23	5k on 50k brown	200.00	100.00
a.		On #171a	250.00	100.00

Overprinted on Nos. 169 and 169a

209	A22	12c on 1k red	100.00	50.00
a.		On #169a	100.00	50.00

Counterfeits of the overprint of Nos. 173-183, 188, 206-207, 209 are plentiful. Practically all examples with overprint sideways, inverted, double and double with one inverted are frauds.

Nos. 142 Surcharged in Violet

1902

211	A18	5c on 10c pale bl, *grn*	60.00	20.00

Surcharges in different colors were made for collectors.

Initials of Victor Castaigne, Postmaster of Meshed — A24

1902   **Typo.**   **Imperf.**

222	A24	1c black	1,500.	*450.00*
a.		Inverted frame	—	*3,000.*
b.		Inverted center	—	*3,000.*
223	A24	2c black	1,250.	*450.00*
a.		Inverted frame	—	—
b.		"2" in right upper corner	3,000.	*1,750.*
c.		Frame printed on both sides	—	*1,750.*
224	A24	3c black	3,250.	*1,750.*
225	A24	5c violet	750.00	*200.00*
a.		"5" in right upper corner	—	—
b.		Frame printed on both sides	2,250.	*1,000.*
c.		Inverted center	—	—
226	A24	5c black	900.00	*350.00*
a.		Persian "5" in lower left corner	—	—
b.		Inverted center	—	—
227	A24	12c dull blue	4,000.	*1,500.*
a.		Inverted frame	—	—
b.		Inverted center	—	—
228	A24	1k rose	30,000.	*3,500.*

Used values for Nos. 222-228 canceled to order are about ⅓ to ½ the values shown, which are for postally used stamps.

The design of No. 228 differs slightly from the illustration.

Nos. 222-228 are printed in three operations. Inverted centers have frames and numerals upright. Inverted frames have centers and numerals upright.

Pin-perforated

234	A24	12c dull blue	4,000.	*1,500.*

The post office at Meshed having exhausted its stock of stamps, the postmaster issued the above series provisionally. The center of the design is the seal of the postmaster who also wrote his initials upon the upper part, using violet ink for the 1k and red for the others.

Unauthorized reprints, including pinperforated examples of Nos. 222-226, and forgeries exist.

Expert knowledge or certificates of authenticity are required.

A25

TWO TYPES:
Type I — "CHAHI" or "KRANS" are in capital letters.
Type II — Only "C" of "Chahi" or "K" of "Krans" is a capital.

The 3c and 5c sometimes have a tall narrow figure in the upper left corner. The 5c is also found with the cross at the upper left broken or missing. These varieties are known with many of the overprints.

Stamps of Design A25 have a faint fancy background in the color of the stamp. All issued stamps have handstamped controls as listed.

Handstamp Overprinted in Black

1902 Typeset — Imperf.

Type I

235	A25	1c gray & buff	300.00	150.00
236	A25	2c brown & buff	300.00	150.00
237	A25	3c green & buff	300.00	150.00
238	A25	5c red & buff	200.00	100.00
239	A25	12c ultra & buff	500.00	150.00
		Nos. 235-239 (5)	1,600.	700.00

Counterfeits abound. Type II stamps with this overprint are forgeries.

The 3c with violet overprint is believed not to have been regularly issued.

Handstamp Overprinted in Rose

1902 Type I

247	A25	1c gray & buff	25.00	2.00
248	A25	2c brown & buff	25.00	2.00
249	A25	3c dp grn & buff	25.00	2.00
250	A25	5c red & buff	25.00	.75
251	A25	10c ol yel & buff	50.00	3.00
252	A25	12c ultra & buff	75.00	5.00
253	A25	1k violet & bl	60.00	6.00
254	A25	2k ol grn & bl	100.00	12.50
256	A25	10k dk bl & bl	150.00	30.00
257	A25	50k red & blue	1,500.	600.00
		Nos. 247-257 (10)	2,035.	663.25

A 5k exists but its' status is doubtful.

Nos. 247-257 and the 12c on brown paper and on blue paper with blue quadrille lines are known without overprint but are not believed to have been regularly issued in this condition.

The 1c to 10k, A25 type I, with violet overprint are believed not to have been regularly issued. Five denominations also exist with overprint in blue, black or green.

Type II

280	A25	1c gray & yellow	150.00	150.00
281	A25	2c brown & yel	150.00	150.00
282	A25	3c dk green & yel	1,000.	750.00
a.		"Persans"		
283	A25	5c red & yellow	50.00	15.00
284	A25	10c ol yel & yel	100.00	15.00
285	A25	12c blue & yel	125.00	25.00
290	A25	50k org red & bl	1,250.	600.00

The 3c, inscribed "Persans," is not believed to have been regularly issued.

The same overprint in violet was applied to nine denominations of the Type II stamps, but these, too, are believed not to have been regularly issued. The overprint also exists in blue, black and green.

Reprints, counterfeits, counterfeit overprints, with or without cancellations, are plentiful for Nos. 247-257, 280-290.

Five stamps of type A25, type II, in high denominations (10, 20, 25, 50 and 100 tomans), with "Postes 1319" lion overprint in blue, were used only on money orders, not for postage. They are usually numbered on the back in red, blue or black.

Beware of forgeries and/or reprints of most Iran stamps between the years 1870-1925. Scott values are for genuine stamps. Collectors should be aware that forgeries of many issues outnumber genuine examples by factors of 10 or 20 to one. Failing specialized knowledge on the part of the collector, these stamps should be examined or authenticated by acknowledged experts before purchase.

Handstamp Surcharged in Black

1902 Type I

| 308 | A25 | 5k on 5k ocher & bl | 200.00 | 50.00 |

Counterfeits of No. 308 abound.

This surcharge in rose, violet, blue or green is considered bogus.

This surcharge on 50k orange red and blue, and on 5k ocher and blue, type II, is considered bogus.

Handstamp Overprinted Diagonally in Black

1902

Type I

| 315 | A25 | 2c brown & buff | 200.00 | 100.00 |
| a. | | Rose overprint | 500.00 | 500.00 |

Type II

| 316 | A25 | 2c brown & yel | — | — |
| a. | | Rose overprint | — | — |

"P. L." stands for "Poste Locale."
Counterfeits of Nos. 315-316 exist.
Some specialists believe that Type II stamps were not used officially for this overprint.

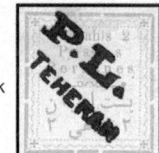

Handstamp Overprinted in Black or Rose

1902 Type II

| 317 | A25 | 2c brn & yellow | 200.00 | 100.00 |
| 318 | A25 | 2c brown & yel (R) | 500.00 | 500.00 |

Counterfeits of Nos. 317-318 exist.

Overprinted in Blue

1903

Type I

| 321 | A25 | 1k violet & blue | 100.00 | 100.00 |

Type II

336	A25	1c gray & yellow	60.00	60.00
337	A25	2c brown & yellow	60.00	60.00
338	A25	5c red & yellow	40.00	40.00
339	A25	10c olive yel & yel	75.00	75.00
340	A25	12c blue & yellow	75.00	75.00
		Nos. 321-340 (6)	410.00	410.00

The overprint also exists in violet and black, but it is doubtful whether such items were regularly issued.

Forgeries of Nos. 321, 336-340 abound. Genuine unused examples are seldom found.

| Arms of Persia — A26 | Mozaffar-eddin Shah Qajar — A27 |

1902 (Dec.)-1904 Typo. Perf. 12½

351	A26	1c violet	2.00	.20
352	A26	2c gray	2.00	.20
353	A26	3c green	2.00	.20
354	A26	5c rose	2.00	.20
355	A26	10c yellow brn	3.00	1.50
356	A26	12c blue	4.00	.50

Engr.
Perf. 11½x11

357	A27	1k violet	12.00	.50
358	A27	2k ultramarine	20.00	1.25
359	A27	5k orange brn	30.00	2.00
360	A27	10k rose red	30.00	4.00
361	A27	20k orange ('04)	35.00	5.00
362	A27	30k green ('04)	60.00	12.50
363	A27	50k green	400.00	100.00
		Nos. 351-363 (13)	602.00	128.05

Nos. 351-363 used are valued canceled to order.

No. 355 exists with blue diagonal surcharge "1 CHAHI"; its status is questioned.

A government decree in November, 1903, required that all picture postcards be censored by the Central Post Office, which would apply a control mark on each card to show that the 2c tax for this service had been paid. No. 352

---

was overprinted "Controle" in several styles, for this purpose. Value: unused $100; used, from $25.

See Nos. 428-433. For surcharges and overprints see #364-420, 446-447, 464-469, O8-O28, P1.

No. 353 Surcharged in Violet or Blue

1903

| 364 | A26 | 1c on 3c green (V) | 50.00 | 20.00 |
| 365 | A26 | 2c on 3c green (Bl) | 50.00 | 20.00 |

A 2c surcharge on No. 354 exists, but its status is dubious.

No. 360 Surcharged in Blue

366	A27	12c on 10k rose red	75.00	40.00
a.		Black surcharge	150.00	70.00
b.		Violet surcharge	150.00	70.00
		Nos. 364-366 (3)	175.00	80.00

Nos. 366, 366a and 366b used are valued canceled to order.

No. 363 Surcharged in Blue or Black

1903

368	A27	2t on 50k grn (Bl)	200.00	60.00
a.		Rose surcharge	225.00	100.00
b.		Black surcharge	225.00	100.00
370	A27	3t on 50k grn (Bk)	200.00	60.00
a.		Violet surcharge	225.00	60.00
b.		Rose surcharge	250.00	125.00

No. 363 Surcharged in Blue or Black

1904

| 372 | A27 | 2t on 50k grn (Bl) | 200.00 | 60.00 |
| 375 | A27 | 3t on 50k grn (Bk) | 200.00 | 60.00 |

The 2t on 50k also exists with surcharge in rose, violet, black and magenta; the 3t on 50k in rose, violet and blue. Values about the same unused; about 50 percent higher used.

No. 352 Overprinted in Violet

1904 Perf. 12½

393	A26	2c gray	85.00	25.00
a.		Black overprint	100.00	30.00
b.		Rose overprint	90.00	25.00

This overprint also exists in blue, violet blue, maroon and gray, but these were not regularly issued.

Stamps of 1903 Surcharged in Black:

a

b

---

c

1904

400	A26(a)	3c on 5c rose	40.00	.75
401	A26(b)	6c on 10c brown	50.00	.75
402	A27(c)	9c on 1k violet	50.00	3.50
		Nos. 400-402 (3)	140.00	5.00

Stamps of 1903 Surcharged in Black, Magenta or Violet:

1905-06

404	A26	1c on 3c green ('06)	50.00	20.00
405	A27	1c on 1k violet	35.00	15.00
406	A27	2c on 5k orange brn	40.00	25.00
407	A26	1c on 3c grn (M) ('06)	15.00	5.00
408	A27	1c on 1k violet (M)	20.00	10.00
409	A27	2c on 5k org brn (V)	30.00	15.00
		Nos. 404-409 (6)	190.00	90.00

Nos. 355 and 358 Surcharged in Violet

1906

| 419 | A26 | 1c on 10c brown | 150.00 | — |
| 420 | A27 | 2c on 2k ultra | 250.00 | — |

Forgeries of Nos. 419-420 are common. Forgeries of No. 420, especially, are hard to distinguish since the original handstamp was used. Genuine used stamps may, in some cases, be identified by the cancellation.

A28

Typeset; "Provisoire" Overprint Handstamped in Black

1906 Imperf.

422	A28	1c violet	15.00	1.00
a.		Irregular pin perf. or perf. 10½	50.00	17.50
423	A28	2c gray	30.00	10.00
424	A28	3c green	15.00	1.00
425	A28	6c red	15.00	.75
426	A28	10c brown	70.00	75.00
427	A28	13c blue	45.00	10.00
		Nos. 422-427 (6)	190.00	97.75

Stamps of type A28 have a faint background pattern of tiny squares within squares, an ornamental frame and open rectangles for the value corners.

The 3c and 6c also exist perforated.

Nos. 422-427 are known without overprint but were probably not issued in that condition. Nearly all values are known with overprint inverted and double.

Forgeries are plentiful.

Lion Type of 1903 and

Mohammed-Ali Shah Qajar
A29   A30

		1907-09	**Typo.**	**Perf. 12½**
428	A26	1c vio, *blue*	5.00	.25
429	A26	2c gray, *blue*	5.00	.25
430	A26	3c green, *blue*	5.00	.25
431	A26	6c rose, *blue*	5.00	.25
432	A26	9c org, *blue*	5.00	.30
433	A26	10c brown, *blue*	6.00	1.00

Engr.

Perf. 11, 11½

434	A29	13c dark blue	5.00	2.00
435	A29	1k red	7.00	1.50
436	A29	26c red brown	7.00	2.00
437	A29	2k deep grn	20.00	1.50
438	A29	3k pale blue	20.00	1.00
439	A29	4k brt yellow	400.00	10.00
440	A29	4k bister	20.00	3.00
441	A29	5k dark brown	20.00	3.00
442	A29	10k pink	25.00	3.00
443	A29	20k gray black	25.00	10.00
444	A29	30k dark violet	25.00	15.00
445	A30	50k gold, ver &		
		brown ('09)	125.00	25.00
		Nos. 428-445 (18)	730.00	79.30

Frame of No. 445 lithographed. Nos. 434-444 were issued in 1908.

Remainders canceled to order abound. Used values for Nos. 437-445 are for c-t-os.

Nos. 428-429
Overprinted in Black

		1909	**Perf. 12½**
446	A26	1c violet, *blue*	80.00 30.00
447	A26	2c gray, *blue*	80.00 30.00

Counterfeits of Nos. 446-447 exist.

Coat of Arms — A31

		1909	**Typo.**	**Perf. 12½x12**
448	A31	1c org & maroon	.50	.35
449	A31	2c vio & maroon	.50	.35
450	A31	3c yel grn & mar	.50	.35
451	A31	6c red & maroon	.50	.25
452	A31	9c gray & maroon	.50	.35
453	A31	10c red vio & mar	.50	.35
454	A31	13c dk blue & mar	.50	2.00
455	A31	1k sil, vio & bis		
		brown	1.00	2.00
456	A31	26c dk grn & mar	1.00	3.00
457	A31	2k sil, dk grn &		
		bis brown	1.00	2.00
458	A31	3k sil, gray & bis		
		brown	1.00	3.50
459	A31	4k sil, by & bis		
		brn	1.00	3.50
460	A31	5k gold, brn & bis		
		brown	2.50	3.50
461	A31	10k gold, org & bis		
		brown	5.00	10.00
462	A31	20k gold, ol grn &		
		bister brn	7.00	20.00
463	A31	30k gold, car & bis		
		brown	12.00	20.00
		Nos. 448-463 (16)	35.00	71.50

Unauthorized reprints of Nos. 448-463 abound. Originals have clean, bright colors, centers stand out clearly, and paper is much thinner. Nos. 460-463 originals have gleaming gold margins; reprint margins appear as blackish yellow. Centers of reprints of Nos. 448-454, 456 are brown.

Values above are for unused reprints and for authenticated used stamps. Original unused stamps sell for much higher prices.

For surcharges & overprints see #516-519, 541-549, 582-585, 588-594, 597, 601-606, 707-722, C1-C16, O31-O40.

Nos. 428-444, Imperf., Surcharged in Red or Black:

		1910	**Blue Paper**	**Imperf.**
464	A26	1c on 1c violet	200.00	140.00
465	A26	1c on 2c green	200.00	140.00
466	A26	1c on 3c green	200.00	140.00
467	A26	1c on 6c rose		
		(Bk)	200.00	140.00
468	A26	1c on 9c orange	200.00	140.00
469	A26	1c on 10c brown	200.00	140.00

White Paper

470	A29	2c on 13c dp bl	200.00	140.00
471	A29	2c on 26c red		
		brown (Bk)	200.00	140.00
472	A29	2c on 1k red		
		(Bk)	200.00	140.00
473	A29	2c on 2k dp grn	200.00	140.00
474	A29	2c on 3k pale bl	200.00	140.00
475	A29	2c on 4k brt yel	200.00	140.00
476	A29	2c on 4k bister	200.00	140.00
477	A29	2c on 5k dk brn	200.00	140.00
478	A29	2c on 10k pink		
		(Bk)	200.00	140.00
479	A29	2c on 20k gray		
		blk	200.00	140.00
480	A29	2c on 30k dk vio	200.00	140.00
		Nos. 464-480 (17)	3,400.	2,380.

Nos. 464-480 were prepared for use on newspapers, but nearly the entire printing was sold to stamp dealers. The issue is generally considered speculative. Counterfeit surcharges exist on trimmed stamps.

Used values are for c-t-o.

Ahmad Shah
Qajar — A32

Perf. 11½, 11½x11, 11½x12
Engr. center, Typo. frame

1911-13

481	A32	1c green & org	.50	.20
482	A32	2c red & sepia	.50	.20
483	A32	3c gray brn & grn	.50	.20
a.		3c bister brown & green	.50	1.00
484	A32	5c brn & car ('13)	.50	.75
485	A32	6c gray & car	.50	.20
486	A32	6c grn & red brown		
		('13)	.50	.20
487	A32	9c yel brn & vio	.75	.20
488	A32	10c red & org brn	.75	.20
489	A32	12c grn & ultra ('13)	.50	.50
490	A32	13c violet & ultra	1.00	2.00
491	A32	1k ultra & car	1.00	.50
492	A32	24c vio & grn ('13)	1.00	1.00
493	A32	26c ultra & green	1.00	5.00
494	A32	2k grn & red vio	2.00	1.00
495	A32	3k violet & blk	2.00	1.50
496	A32	4k ultramarine &		
		gray ('13)	2.00	20.00
497	A32	5k red & ultra	3.00	2.00
498	A32	10k ol bis & cl	5.00	3.00
499	A32	20k vio brn & bis	6.00	4.00
500	A32	30k red & green	7.00	5.00
		Nos. 481-500 (20)	36.00	47.65

Values for Nos. 481-500 unused are for reprints, which cannot be distinguished from the late printings of the stamps. These are perf 11½ (11½x12 for the 4k) with the distance between the inner lines of the inscription tablets at top and bottom of the portrait being 19mm. Unused stamps with other perfs or a shorter vignette sell for much higher prices.

The reprints include inverted centers for some denominations. Values, each $30-$50.

For surcharges and overprints see Nos. 501-515, 520-540, 586-587, 595, 598, 600, 607-609, 630-634, 646-666.

Stamps of 1911
Overprinted in Black

1911

501	A32	1c grn & orange	45.00	6.00
502	A32	2c red & sepia	45.00	6.00
503	A32	3c gray brn &		
		grn	45.00	6.00
504	A32	6c gray & car-		
		mine	45.00	6.00
505	A32	9c yel brn & vio	45.00	6.00
506	A32	10c red & org brn	75.00	6.00
507	A32	13c vio & ultra	100.00	8.00
508	A32	1k ultra & car	150.00	10.00
509	A32	26c ultra & green	150.00	12.00
510	A32	2k grn & red vio	200.00	15.00
511	A32	3k vio & black	250.00	15.00
512	A32	5k red & ultra	300.00	20.00
513	A32	10k ol bis & claret	1,000.	40.00
514	A32	20k vio brn & bis	1,000.	50.00
515	A32	30k red & green	1,000.	50.00
		Nos. 501-515 (15)	4,450.	256.00

The "Officiel" overprint does not signify that the stamps were intended for use on official correspondence but that they were issued by authority. It was applied to the stocks in Tabriz and all post offices in the Tabriz region after a large quantity of stamps had been stolen during the Russian occupation of Tabriz.

The "Officiel" overprint has been counterfeited.

Stamps of 1909-11
Overprinted in Black

On #449-451, 454

1911, Oct.

516	A31	2c vio & maroon	300.00	150.00
517	A31	3c yel grn & mar	300.00	150.00
518	A31	6c red & maroon	300.00	150.00
519	A31	13c dk blue & mar	300.00	150.00

On #482-483, 485, 490

520	A32	2c red & sepia	400.00	200.00
521	A32	3c gray brn & grn	400.00	200.00
522	A32	6c gray & car	400.00	200.00
523	A32	13c violet & ultra	400.00	200.00

Stamps were sold at a 10% discount to stagecoach station keepers on the Tehran-Recht route. To prevent speculation, these stamps were overprinted "Stagecoach Stations" in French and Farsi.

Forgeries exist, usually overprinted on reprints of the 1909 issue and used examples of the 1911 issue. Values are for authenticated stamps.

In 1912 this overprint, reading 'Sultan Mohammad Ali Shah Kajar,' was handstamped on outgoing mail in the Persian Kurdistan region occupied by the forces of the former Shah Mohammad Ali. It was applied after the stamps were on cover and is found on 8 of the Shah Ahmed stamps of 1911 (1c, 2c, 3c, 6c, 9c, 13c, 1k and 26c). Some specialists add the 10c. Forgeries are abundant.

Nos. 490 and 493 Surcharged:

a   b

1914

535	A32(a)	1c on 13c	25.00	2.00
536	A32(b)	3c on 26c	25.00	4.00

In 1914 a set of 19 stamps was prepared as a coronation issue. The 10 lower values each carry a different portrait; the 9 higher values show buildings and scenes. The same set printed with black centers was overprinted in red "SERVICE." The stamps were never placed in use, but were sold to stamp dealers in 1923.

Nos. 484 and 489 Surcharged in Black or Violet:

c   d

1915

537	A32(c)	1c on 5c	20.00	2.00
538	A32(c)	2c on 5c (V)	20.00	2.00
539	A32(c)	2c on 5c	175.00	40.00
540	A32(d)	6c on 12c	30.00	2.00
		Nos. 537-540 (4)	245.00	46.00

Nos. 455, 454 Surcharged:

e   f

		1915	**Perf. 12½x12**
541	A31(e)	5c on 1k multi	50.00	5.00
542	A31(f)	12c on 13c multi	75.00	7.00

Counterfeit surcharges on reprints abound.

Nos. 448-453, 455
Overprinted

1915

543	A31	1c org & maroon	50.00	5.00
544	A31	2c vio & maroon	50.00	5.00
545	A31	3c grn & maroon	60.00	5.00
546	A31	6c red & maroon	60.00	5.00
547	A31	9c gray & maroon	100.00	7.00
548	A31	10c red vio & mar	150.00	10.00
549	A31	1k sil, vio & bis		
		brn	200.00	10.00
		Nos. 543-549 (7)	670.00	47.00

This overprint ("1333") also exists on the 2k, 10k, 20k and 30k, but they were not issued.

Counterfeit overprints, usually on reprints, abound.

Beware of forgeries and/or reprints of most Iran stamps between the years 1870-1925. Scott values are for genuine stamps. Collectors should be aware that forgeries of many issues outnumber genuine examples by factors of 10 or 20 to one. Failing specialized knowledge on the part of the collector, these stamps should be examined or authenticated by acknowledged experts before purchase.

Imperial
Crown — A33

King Darius,
Farohar
overhead — A34

Ruins of
Persepolis — A35

Perf. 11½ or Compound 11x11½
Engr., Typo.

1915, Mar.			Wmk. 161
560	A33	1c car & indigo	.20	2.00
561	A33	2c bl & carmine	.20	2.00
562	A33	3c dark green	.20	2.00
a.		Inverted center	—	
564	A33	5c red	.20	2.50
565	A33	6c olive grn & car	.20	2.00
a.		Inverted center	—	
566	A33	9c yel brn & vio	.20	2.00
567	A33	10c bl grn & yel brn	.20	2.00
568	A33	12c ultramarine	.20	2.00
569	A34	1k sil, yel brn & gray	.65	5.00
570	A33	24c yel brn & dk brn	.25	5.00
571	A34	2k silver, bl & rose	.65	5.00
572	A34	3k sil, vio & brn	.65	5.00
573	A34	5k sil, brn & green	.65	7.00
574	A35	1t gold, pur & blk	.65	10.00
575	A35	2t gold, grn & brn	1.00	10.00
576	A35	3t gold, cl & red brn	1.00	10.00
577	A35	5t gold, blue & ind	1.00	10.00
		Nos. 560-577 (17)	8.10	83.50

Coronation of Shah Ahmed.
Nos. 560-568, 570 are engraved. Nos. 569, 571-573 are engraved except for silver margins. Nos. 574-577 have centers engraved, frames typographed.
The 3c and 6c with inverted centers are considered genuine errors. Unauthorized reprints exist of these varieties and of other denominations with inverted centers. **Values unused for Nos. 560-577 are for reprints.**
For surcharges and overprints see Nos. 610-616, 635-646, O41-O57, Q19-Q35.

Nos. 455, 461-463
Overprinted

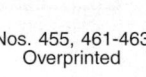

1915 Unwmk. Typo.		Perf. 12½x12
582	A31	1k sil, vio & bis brn	2.00	20.00
583	A31	10k multicolored	5.00	30.00
584	A31	20k multicolored	10.00	100.00
585	A31	30k multicolored	12.00	60.00
		Nos. 582-585 (4)	29.00	210.00

Genuine unused examples are rare. Most unused stamps offered in the marketplace are reprints, and the unused values above are for reprints. Used values for authenticated stamps.
Forgeries abound of Nos. 582-585.

No. 491 Surcharged

1917		Perf. 11½
586	A32	12c on 1k multi	3,000.	3,500.
587	A32	24c on 1k multi	1,500.	1,750.

Issued during the Turkish occupation of Kermanshah. Forgeries exist.

Values for unused stamps are for reprints. Unused examples of the original stamps are rare, and most stamps offered in the marketplace are reprints.

No. 448 Overprinted "1335" in Persian
Numerals

1917		Perf. 12½x12
588	A31	1c org & maroon	350.00	250.00

Overprint on No. 588 is similar to date in "k" and "l" surcharges. Forgeries exist.

Nos. 449, 452-453, 456 Surcharged:

k   l

1917			
589	A31(k)	1c on 2c	30.00	3.00
590	A31(k)	1c on 9c	40.00	4.00
591	A31(k)	1c on 10c	30.00	3.00
592	A31(l)	3c on 9c	40.00	4.00
593	A31(l)	3c on 10c	30.00	3.00
594	A31(l)	3c on 26c	40.00	5.00

Same Surcharge on No. 488

595	A32(k)	1c on 10c	75.00	1.50
596	A32(l)	3c on 10c	75.00	1.50

Nos. 454 & 491 Surcharged Type "e"

597	A31	5c on 13c	40.00	5.00
598	A32	5c on 1k	40.00	2.00

Counterfeit surcharges on "canceled" reprints of Nos. 449, 452-454, 456 abound.

No. 489 Surcharged

600	A32	6c on 12c grn & ultra	100.00	15.00

No. 457 Overprinted

1918			
601	A31	2k multi	100.00	20.00

Nos. 459-460 Surcharged:

1918			
602	A31	24c on 4k multi	75.00	15.00
603	A31	10k on 5k multi	125.00	20.00

The surcharges of Nos. 602-603 have been counterfeited.

Nos. 457-463
Overprinted

1918			
603A	A34	2k multicolored	3.00	65.00
604	A31	3k multicolored	3.00	15.00
604A	A31	4k multicolored	5.00	150.00
604B	A31	5k multicolored	5.00	75.00
605	A31	10k multicolored	8.00	50.00
605A	A31	20k multicolored	20.00	200.00
606	A31	30k multicolored	15.00	100.00
		Nos. 603A-606 (7)	59.00	655.00

Genuine unused examples are rare. Most unused stamps offered in the marketplace are reprints, and the unused values above are for reprints. Used values for for authenticated stamps.
Forgeries abound of Nos. 603A-606.

Nos. 489, 488 and 491 Surcharged:

m   n

607	A32(m)	3c on 12c	75.00	1.50
608	A32(n)	6c on 10c	75.00	1.50
609	A32(m)	6c on 1k	75.00	1.50
		Nos. 607-609 (3)	225.00	4.50

Genuine unused examples are rare. Most unused stamps offered in the marketplace are reprints, and the unused values above are for reprints.

Nos. 571-577
Overprinted in
Black or Red

1918		Wmk. 161
610	A34	2k sil, blue & rose	10.00	10.00
611	A34	3k sil, vio & brn (R)	10.00	10.00
612	A34	5k sil, brn & grn (R)	10.00	10.00
613	A35	1t gold, pur & black (R)	15.00	15.00
614	A35	2t gold, grn & brn	15.00	15.00
615	A35	3t gold, cl & red brn	15.00	15.00
616	A35	5t gold, bl & ind (R)	15.00	20.00
		Nos. 610-616 (7)	90.00	95.00

The overprint commemorates the end of World War I. Counterfeits of this overprint are plentiful.

A36

Color Litho., Black Typo.

1919		Unwmk.	Perf. 11½
617	A36	1c yel & black	20.00	1.00
618	A36	3c green & black	20.00	1.00
619	A36	5c rose & black	45.00	3.00
620	A36	6c vio & black	35.00	1.00
621	A36	12c blue & black	100.00	10.00
		Nos. 617-621 (5)	220.00	16.00

Nos. 617-621 exist imperf., in colors other than the originals, with centers inverted and double impressions. Some specialists call them fraudulent, others call them reprints.
This issue has been extensively counterfeited, and most examples in the marketplace are forgeries.
Counterfeits having double line over "POSTES" abound.

Nos. 75, 85-86
Surcharged in Various
Colors

1919		Perf. 10½, 11, 11½, 13½
622	A14	2k on 5c lilac (Bk)	7.50	7.50
623	A14	3k on 5c lilac (Br)	7.50	7.50
624	A14	4k on 5c lilac (G)	7.50	7.50
625	A14	5k on 5c lilac (V)	7.50	7.50

626	A16	10k on 10c rose (Bl)	20.00	20.00
627	A16	20k on 10c rose (G)	20.00	20.00
628	A16	30k on 10c rose (Br)	20.00	20.00
629	A16	50k on 14c org (V)	20.00	20.00
		Nos. 622-629 (8)	110.00	110.00

Nos. 622-629 exist with inverted and double surcharge. Some specialists consider these fraudulent.

Nos. 486, 489
Handstamp
Surcharged

1921		Perf. 11½, 11½x11
630	A32	10c on 6c	75.00	15.00
631	A32	1k on 12c	75.00	15.00

Counterfeits exist.

No. 489
Surcharged

632	A32	6c on 12c	400.00	20.00

Nos. 486, 489 Surcharged in Violet:

1921			
633	A32	10c on 6c	150.00	50.00
a.		Surcharge handstamped in black	350.00	350.00
634	A32	1k on 12c	150.00	50.00
a.		Surcharge handstamped in black	350.00	350.00

Counterfeits exist.

Coronation Issue of
1915 Overprinted

1921, May Wmk. 161		Perf. 11, 11½
635	A33	3c dark grn	15.00
a.		Center and overprint inverted	—
636	A33	5c red	15.00
637	A33	6c olive grn & car	15.00
638	A33	10c bl grn & yel brn	15.00
639	A33	12c ultramarine	15.00
640	A34	1k sil, yel brn & gray	20.00
641	A34	2k sil, blue & rose	20.00
642	A34	5k sil, brn & green	20.00
643	A35	2t gold, grn & brn	25.00
644	A35	3t gold, cl & red brn	30.00
645	A35	5t gold, blue & ind	30.00
		Nos. 635-645 (11)	220.00

Counterfeits of this Feb. 21, 1921, overprint are plentiful. Inverted overprints exist on all values; some specialists consider them fraudulent.

Stamps of 1911-13
Overprinted

1922   Unwmk.   Perf. 11½, 11½x11

646	A32	1c grn & orange	10.00	.20
a.		Inverted overprint	200.00	
647	A32	2c red & sepia	10.00	.20
648	A32	3c brn & green	15.00	.20
a.		3c bister brown & green	10.00	.20
649	A32	5c brown & car	85.00	25.00
650	A32	6c grn & red brn	10.00	.20
651	A32	9c yel brn & vio	10.00	.20
652	A32	10c red & org brn	10.00	.20
a.		Double ovpt., one inverted	300.00	
653	A32	12c green & ultra	15.00	.50
a.		Double overprint	300.00	
654	A32	1k ultra & car	20.00	1.00
655	A32	24c vio & green	20.00	1.00
656	A32	2k grn & red vio	60.00	1.00
657	A32	3k vio & black	60.00	1.50
658	A32	4k ultra & gray	100.00	45.00
659	A32	5k red & ultra	100.00	2.00
660	A32	10k ol bis & cl	650.00	5.00
661	A32	20k vio brn & bis	550.00	7.00
662	A32	30k red & green	750.00	10.00
		Nos. 646-662 (17)	2,525.	100.20

The status of inverted overprints on 5c and 12c is dubious. Unlisted inverts on other denominations are generally considered fraudulent. Counterfeits of this overprint exist.

Nos. 653, 655
Surcharged

1922

663	A32	3c on 12c	75.00	1.00
664	A32	6c on 24c	110.00	2.00

Nos. 661-662 Surcharged:

1923

665	A32	10c on 20k	120.00	10.00
666	A32	1k on 30k	145.00	15.00

Ahmed Shah
Qajar — A37

Perf. 11½, 11x11½, 11½x11

1924-25   Engr.

667	A37	1c orange	2.50	.20
668	A37	2c magenta	2.50	.20
a.		Imperf. btwn., pair		2,000.
669	A37	3c orange brown	2.50	.20
670	A37	6c black brown	2.50	.20
671	A37	9c dark green	2.00	5.00
672	A37	10c dark violet	2.00	.30
673	A37	12c red	2.00	.30
674	A37	1k dark blue	2.00	.35
675	A37	2k indigo & red	2.00	5.00
a.		Center inverted	12,500.	4,000.
676	A37	3k dk vio & red brown	17.00	2.00
677	A37	5k red & brown	20.00	30.00
678	A37	10k choc & lilac	25.00	25.00
679	A37	20k dk grn & brn	30.00	30.00
680	A37	30k org & blk brn	40.00	40.00
		Nos. 667-680 (14)	152.00	138.75

For overprints see Nos. 703-706.

A38

SIX CHAHIS

Type I   Type II

Dated 1924

Color Litho., Black Typo.

1924   Perf. 11

681	A38	1c yel brn & blk	20.00	1.00
682	A38	2c gray & blk	20.00	1.00
683	A38	3c dp rose & blk	20.00	1.00
684	A38	6c orange & blk (I)	30.00	1.50
a.		6c orange & blk (II)	35.00	2.00
		Nos. 681-684 (4)	90.00	4.50

The 1c was surcharged "Chahis" by error. Later the "s" was blocked out in black.
Counterfeits having double line over "POSTES" are plentiful.

Dated 1925

1925

686	A38	2c yel grn & blk	10.00	1.00
687	A38	3c red & blk	10.00	1.00
689	A38	6c chalky bl & blk	10.00	1.00
690	A38	9c lt brn & blk	30.00	2.00
691	A38	10c gray & blk	55.00	5.00
694	A38	1k emer & blk	65.00	10.00
695	A38	2k lilac & blk	150.00	40.00
		Nos. 686-695 (7)	330.00	60.00

Counterfeits having double line over "POSTES" are plentiful.

A39

Gold Overprint on Treasury
Department Stamps

1925

697	A39	1c red	7.00	6.00
698	A39	2c yellow	7.00	6.00
699	A39	3c yellow green	7.00	6.00
700	A39	5c dark gray	30.00	30.00
701	A39	10c deep orange	15.00	10.00
702	A39	1k ultramarine	15.00	15.00
		Nos. 697-702 (6)	81.00	73.00

Deposition of Ahmad Shah Qajar and establishment of provisional government of Reza Shah Pahlavi.

#697-702 have same center (Persian lion in sunburst) with 6 different frames. Overprint reads: "Post / Provisional Government / of Pahlavi / 9th Abanmah / 1304 / 1925."

Nos. 667-670
Overprinted

1926   Perf. 11½, 11x11½, 11½x11

703	A37	1c orange	5.00	3.00
704	A37	2c magenta	5.00	5.00
705	A37	3c orange brown	5.00	3.00
706	A37	6c black brown	100.00	85.00
		Nos. 703-706 (4)	115.00	96.00

Overprinted to commemorate the Pahlavi dynasty, dated 16 December 1925. Counterfeits exist.

Nos. 448-463
Overprinted

1926   Perf. 11½, 12½x12

707	A31	1c org & maroon	10.00	.25
a.		Inverted overprint	1,250.	
708	A31	2c vio & maroon	10.00	.25
709	A31	3c yel grn & mar	10.00	.25
a.		Inverted overprint	1,000.	
710	A31	6c red & maroon	10.00	.25
711	A31	9c gray & maroon	10.00	.25
712	A31	10c red vio & mar	10.00	.35
713	A31	13c dk bl & mar	20.00	.35
714	A31	1k multi	35.00	.35
715	A31	26c dk grn & mar	20.00	.35
716	A31	2k multi	40.00	1.00
717	A31	3k multi	100.00	2.00
718	A31	4k sil, bl & bis brn	500.00	35.00
719	A31	5k multi	150.00	10.00
720	A31	10k multi	500.00	15.00
721	A31	20k multi	600.00	15.00
722	A31	30k multi	600.00	20.00
		Nos. 707-722 (16)	2,625.	100.65

Overprinted to commemorate the Pahlavi government in 1926.

Values for Nos. 707-722 are for stamps perf. 11½, on thick paper. Stamps perf. 12½x12 on thin paper are worth substantially more.

Forgeries exist perf. 12½x12, with either machine overprints or handstamps. Most of these fakes can be identified by the absence of the top serif of the "1" in "1926."

A40   Reza Shah
Pahlavi — A41

1926-29   Typo.   Perf. 11

723	A40	1c yellow green	6.00	.20
724	A40	2c gray violet	6.00	.20
725	A40	3c emerald	6.00	.20
727	A40	6c magenta	6.00	.25
728	A40	9c rose	12.00	.50
729	A40	10c bister brown	30.00	5.00
730	A40	12c deep orange	30.00	3.00
731	A40	15c pale ultra	35.00	2.00
733	A41	1k dull bl ('27)	60.00	15.00
734	A41	2k brt vio ('29)	180.00	75.00
		Nos. 723-734 (10)	371.00	101.35

1928   Redrawn

740	A40	1c yellow green	30.00	.25
741	A40	2c gray violet	30.00	.25
742	A40	3c emerald	30.00	.25
743	A40	6c rose	30.00	.25
		Nos. 740-743 (4)	120.00	1.25

On the redrawn stamps much of the shading of the face, throat, collar, etc., has been removed.

The letters of "Postes Persanes" and those in the circle at upper right are smaller. The redrawn stamps measure 20¼x25¾mm instead of 19¾x25¼mm.

A42

Reza Shah
Pahlavi — A43

Perf. 11½, 12, 12½, Compound

1929   Photo.

744	A42	1c yel grn & cer	3.50	.25
745	A42	2c scar & brt blue	3.50	.25
746	A42	3c mag & myr grn	3.50	.25
747	A42	6c yel brn & ol grn	3.50	.25
748	A42	9c Prus bl & ver	5.00	.25
749	A42	10c bl grn & choc	6.00	.25
750	A42	12c gray blk & pur	8.00	.30
751	A42	15c citron & ultra	10.00	.30
752	A42	1k dull bl & blk	15.00	.50
753	A42	24c ol grn & red brn	12.00	.50

Engr.
Perf. 11½

754	A42	2k brn org & dk vio	125.00	3.00
755	A42	3k dark grn & dp rose	150.00	5.00
756	A42	5k red brn & dp green	75.00	5.00
757	A42	1t ultra & dp rose	75.00	10.00
758	A42	2t carmine & blk	100.00	20.00

Engr. and Typo.

759	A43	3t gold & dp vio	175.00	35.00
		Nos. 744-759 (16)	770.00	81.10

For overprints see Nos. 810-817.

Reza Shah
Pahlavi — A44

1931-32   Litho.   Perf. 11

760	A44	1c ol brn & ultra	6.00	.20
761	A44	2c red brn & blk	6.00	.20
762	A44	3c lilac rose & ol	6.00	.20
763	A44	6c red org & vio	6.00	.20
764	A44	9c ultra & red org	12.00	.40
765	A44	10c ver & gray	30.00	1.00
766	A44	11c bl & dull red	35.00	30.00
767	A44	12c turq blue & lil rose	45.00	.70
768	A44	16c black & red	50.00	1.75
769	A44	1k car & turq bl	85.00	1.75
770	A44	27c dk gray & dl bl	90.00	1.75
		Nos. 760-770 (11)	371.00	38.15

For overprints see Nos. 818-826.

A45   Reza Shah
Pahlavi — A46

1933-34

771	A45	5d olive brown	3.00	.25
772	A45	10d blue	3.00	.25
773	A45	15d gray	3.00	.25
774	A45	30d emerald	3.00	.25
775	A45	45d turq blue	3.00	.50
776	A45	50d magenta	4.00	.50
777	A45	60d green	5.00	.50
778	A45	75d brown	8.00	1.50
779	A45	90d red	10.00	2.50
780	A46	1r dk rose & blk	25.00	2.00
781	A46	1.20r gray blk & rose	30.00	2.00
782	A46	1.50 citron & bl	35.00	2.00
783	A46	2r lt bl & choc	45.00	2.00
784	A46	3r mag & green	60.00	4.00
785	A46	5r dk brn & red org	225.00	50.00
		Nos. 771-785 (15)	462.00	68.50

For overprints see Nos. 795-809.

"Justice"   "Education"
A47   A49

Ruins of Persepolis A48

Tehran Airport A50

Sanatorium at Sakhtessar — A51

Cement Factory, Chah-Abdul-Azim — A52

Gunboat "Palang" A53

Railway Bridge over Karun River A54

Post Office and Customs Building, Tehran A55

1935, Feb. 21   Photo.   Perf. 12½

786	A47	5d red brn & grn	1.00	.75
787	A48	10d red org & gray black	1.00	.75
788	A49	15d mag & Prus bl	1.50	.75
789	A50	30d black & green	1.50	.75
790	A51	45d ol grn & red brn	2.00	.75
791	A52	75d grn & dark brn	6.00	1.25
792	A53	90d blue & car rose	20.00	5.00
793	A54	1r red brn & pur	60.00	30.00
794	A55	1½r violet & ultra	25.00	10.00
		Nos. 786-794 (9)	118.00	50.00

Reign of Riza Shah Pahlavi, 10th anniv.

Stamps of 1933-34 Overprinted in Black

1935   Perf. 11

795	A45	5d olive brown	3.00	.50
796	A45	10d blue	3.00	.50
797	A45	15d gray	3.00	.50
798	A45	30d emerald	3.00	.50
799	A45	45d turq blue	10.00	3.00
800	A45	50d magenta	6.00	.50
801	A45	60d green	6.00	.50
802	A45	75d brown	10.00	10.00
803	A45	90d red	35.00	40.00

804	A46	1r dk rose & blk	100.00	150.00
805	A46	1.20r gray black & rose	15.00	2.00
806	A46	1.50r citron & bl	15.00	2.00
807	A46	2r lt bl & choc	40.00	2.00
808	A46	3r mag & green	75.00	10.00
809	A46	5r dk brn & red org	300.00	300.00
		Nos. 705-800 (15)	624.00	522.00

Same Overprint on Stamps of 1929

1935   Perf. 12, 12x12½

810	A42	1c yel green & cer	500.00	600.00
811	A42	2c scar & brt blue	300.00	400.00
812	A42	3c mag & myr grn	200.00	200.00
813	A42	6c yel brn & ol grn	140.00	150.00
814	A42	9c Prus bl & ver	85.00	80.00

Perf. 11½

815	A42	1t ultra & dp rose	42.50	30.00
816	A42	2t carmine & blk	50.00	40.00
817	A43	3t gold & dp vio	70.00	50.00
		Nos. 810-817 (8)	1,387.	1,550.

No. 817 is overprinted vertically. Forged overprints exist.

Same Ovpt. on Stamps of 1931-32

1935   Perf. 11

818	A44	1c ol brn & ul-tra	400.00	400.00
819	A44	2c red brn & blk	150.00	150.00
820	A44	3c lilac rose & ol	100.00	125.00
821	A44	6c red org & vio	200.00	200.00
822	A44	9c ultra & red org	200.00	225.00
823	A44	11c blue & dull red	12.50	3.50
824	A44	12c turq bl & lil rose	500.00	600.00
825	A44	16c black & red	15.00	5.00
826	A44	27c dk gray & dull bl	19.00	5.00
		Nos. 818-826 (9)	1,596.	1,713.

Forged overprints exist.

Reza Shah Pahlavi — A56

1935   Photo.   Perf. 11
Size: 19x27mm

827	A56	5d violet	2.00	.20
828	A56	10d lilac rose	2.00	.20
829	A56	15d turquoise bl	2.00	.20
830	A56	30d emerald	2.00	.20
831	A56	45d orange	2.00	.20
832	A56	50d dull lt brn	2.75	.30
833	A56	60d ultramarine	4.00	.65
834	A56	75d red orange	10.00	.75
835	A56	90d rose	12.50	.75

Size: 21½x31mm

836	A56	1r dull lilac	25.00	.50
837	A56	1.50r blue	40.00	2.00
838	A56	2r dk olive grn	40.00	.75
839	A56	3r dark brown	45.00	2.00
840	A56	5r slate black	250.00	15.00
		Nos. 827-840 (14)	445.25	23.70

Reza Shah Pahlavi
A57   A58

1936-37   Litho.   Perf. 11
Size: 20x27mm

841	A57	5d bright vio	2.00	.20
842	A57	10d magenta	2.00	.20
843	A57	15d bright ultra	2.00	.20
844	A57	30d yellow green	2.00	.20
845	A57	45d vermilion	3.00	.20
846	A57	50d black brn ('37)	3.00	.20
847	A57	60d brown orange	3.00	.20
848	A57	75d rose lake	3.00	.25
849	A57	90d rose red	5.00	.35

Size: 23x31mm

850	A57	1r turq green	15.00	.25
851	A57	1.50r deep blue	15.00	.35
852	A57	2r bright blue	20.00	.35
853	A57	3r violet brown	25.00	.80
854	A57	5r slate green	40.00	1.00
855	A57	10r dark brown & ultra ('37)	225.00	20.00
		Nos. 841-855 (15)	365.00	25.00

1938-39   Perf. 11
Size: 20x27mm

856	A58	5d light violet	2.00	.20
857	A58	10d magenta	2.00	.20
858	A58	15d violet blue	2.00	.20
859	A58	30d bright green	2.00	.20
860	A58	45d vermilion	3.00	.20
861	A58	50d black brown	3.00	.20
862	A58	60d brown orange	3.00	.20
863	A58	75d rose lake	3.00	.20
864	A58	90d rose red	5.00	.25

Size: 22½x30mm

865	A58	1r turq green	10.00	.25
866	A58	1.50r deep blue	15.00	.30
867	A58	2r lt blue ('39)	20.00	.30
868	A58	3r violet brown	30.00	.70
869	A58	5r gray grn ('39)	50.00	1.25
870	A58	10r dark brown & ultra ('39)	175.00	7.50
		Nos. 856-870 (15)	325.00	12.15

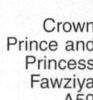

Reza Shah Pahlavi — A58a

1939, Mar. 15   Perf. 13

870A	A58a	5d gray blue	3.00	3.00
870B	A58a	10d brown	3.00	3.00
870C	A58a	30d green	3.00	3.00
870D	A58a	60d dark brown	3.00	3.00
870E	A58a	90d red	5.00	5.00
870F	A58a	1.50r blue	15.00	10.00
870G	A58a	5r lilac	35.00	30.00
870H	A58a	10r carmine	50.00	50.00
		Nos. 870A-870H (8)	117.00	107.00

60th birthday of Riza Shah Pahlavi. Printed in sheets of 4, perf. 13 and imperf. The 1r violet and 2r orange were not available to the public. Value of sheets (including 1r and 2r), perf. 13 $950, imperf. $1,500. Value, perf. 13 unused $35 each.

Crown Prince and Princess Fawziya A59

1939, Apr. 25   Photo.   Perf. 11½

871	A59	5d red brown	.50	.50
872	A59	10d bright violet	.50	.50
873	A59	30d emerald	1.50	.50
874	A59	90d red	12.00	2.00
875	A59	1.50r bright blue	20.00	4.00
		Nos. 871-875 (5)	34.50	7.50

Wedding of Crown Prince Mohammad Pahlavi to Princess Fawziya of Egypt.

Bridge over Karun River A60

Veresk Bridge, North Iran — A61

Granary, Ahwaz A62

Train and Bridge A63

Museum, Side View
A64   A67

Ministry of Justice A65

School Building A66

Mohammad Reza Shah Pahlavi
A68   A69

1942-46   Unwmk.   Litho.   Perf. 11

876	A60	5d violet	3.00	.20
877	A60	5d red org ('44)	1.00	.20
878	A61	10d magenta	3.00	.20
879	A61	10d pck grn ('44)	1.00	.20
880	A62	20d lt red violet	4.00	.25
881	A62	20d mag ('44)	2.00	.25
882	A63	25d rose carmine	30.00	5.00
883	A63	25d violet ('44)	7.50	.50
884	A64	35d emerald	2.00	.30
885	A65	50d ultramarine	3.50	.30
886	A65	50d emerald ('44)	2.00	.20
887	A66	70d dull vio brn	2.00	.35
888	A67	75d rose lake	15.00	.35
889	A67	75d rose car ('46)	15.00	.35
890	A68	1r carmine	15.00	.25
891	A68	1r maroon ('45)	15.00	.25
892	A68	1.50r red	15.00	.25
893	A68	2r light blue	35.00	.25
894	A68	2r sage grn ('44)	35.00	.30
895	A68	2.50r dark blue	20.00	.30
896	A68	3r peacock grn	100.00	1.00
897	A68	3r brt vio ('44)	45.00	.35
898	A68	5r sage green	250.00	10.00
899	A68	5r lt blue ('44)	35.00	.50
900	A69	10r brn org & blk	60.00	3.00
901	A69	10r dk org brn & black ('44)	35.00	1.00
902	A69	20r choc & vio	800.00	50.00
903	A69	20r orange & black ('44)	130.00	4.00
904	A69	30r gray blk & emerald	1,250.	50.00
905	A69	30r emer & black ('44)	50.00	5.00
906	A69	50r dl bl & brn red	250.00	25.00
907	A69	50r brt vio & black ('45)	75.00	10.00
908	A69	100r rose red & blk ('45)	500.00	50.00
909	A69	200r bl & blk ('45)	400.00	50.00
		Nos. 876-909 (34)	4,206.	270.05

Sixteen denominations of this issue were handstamped at Tabriz in 1945-46 in Persian characters: 'Azerbaijan National Government, Dec. 12, 1945.' A rebel group did this overprinting while the Russian army held that area.

Flag of Iran A70

Designs: 50d, Docks at Bandar Shapur. 1.50r, Motor convoy. 2.50r, Gorge and railway viaduct. 5r, Map and Mohammad Reza Shah Pahlavi.

Inscribed: "En souvenir des efforts de l'Iran pour la Victoire"

Engr. & Litho.

1949, Apr. 28			**Perf. 12½**	
910	A70	25d multicolored	5.00	3.00

Engr.

911	A70	50d purple	5.00	3.00
a.		Imperf.	400.00	
912	A70	1.50r carmine rose	12.50	3.00
913	A70	2.50r deep blue	17.50	4.00
a.		Imperf.	500.00	
914	A70	5r green	45.00	5.00
a.		Imperf.	750.00	
		Nos. 910-914 (5)	85.00	18.00

Iran's contribution toward the victory of the Allied Nations in World War II.

Bridge over Zaindeh River A71

National Bank A72

Former Ministry of P.T.T. — A73

Mohammad Reza Shah Pahlavi — A74

5d-20r, Various views and buildings.

1949-50		**Unwmk. Litho.**	**Perf. 10½**	
915	A71	5d rose & dk grn	1.50	.20
916	A71	10d ultra & brown	1.50	.20
917	A71	20d vio & ultra	1.50	.25
918	A71	25d blk brn & dp blue	1.50	.20
919	A71	50d grn & ultra	1.50	.20
920	A71	75d dk brn & red	2.50	.25
921	A72	1r vio & green	2.50	.20
922	A72	1.50r dk grn & ver	3.00	.20
923	A72	2r dp car & blk brn	6.00	.25
924	A72	2.50r chlky bl & bl	6.00	.25
925	A72	3r vio bl & red orange	6.00	.20
926	A72	5r dp car & vio	10.00	.20
927	A73	10r car & blue green ('50)	35.00	.50
a.		Inverted center	2,750.	
928	A73	20r brown black & red ('50)	350.00	20.00
929	A74	30r choc & deep blue ('50)	100.00	15.00
930	A74	50r red & deep blue ('50)	100.00	15.00
		Nos. 915-930 (16)	628.50	53.10

Globes and Pigeons A75

Symbols of UPU — A76

1950, Mar. 16			**Photo.**	
931	A75	50d brn carmine	30.00	25.00
932	A76	2.50r deep blue	35.00	32.50

UPU, 75th anniv. (in 1949).

Riza Shah Pahlavi and his Tomb — A77

1950, May 8

933	A77	50d brown	18.00	10.00
934	A77	2r sepia	30.00	15.00

Re-burial of Riza Shah Pahlavi, May 12, 1950.

Mohammad Reza Shah Pahlavi, 31st Birthday — A78

Various portraits.

1950, Oct. 26		**Engr.**	**Perf. 12½**	
		Center in Black		
935	A78	25d carmine	10.00	2.00
936	A78	50d orange	10.00	2.00
937	A78	75d brown	30.00	12.00
938	A78	1r green	25.00	10.00
939	A78	2.50r deep blue	25.00	10.00
940	A78	5r brown lake	40.00	10.00
		Nos. 935-940 (6)	140.00	46.00

Shah and Queen Soraya A79

A80

1951, Feb. 12		**Litho.**	**Perf. 10½**	
941	A79	5d rose violet	2.50	1.00
942	A79	25d orange red	3.50	1.00
943	A79	50d emerald	6.00	2.00
944	A80	1r brown	10.00	2.00

945	A80	1.50r carmine	15.00	2.00
946	A80	2.50r blue	25.00	2.50
		Nos. 941-946 (6)	62.00	10.50

Wedding of Mohammad Reza Shah Pahlavi to Soraya Esfandiari.

Farabi — A81

1951, Feb. 20				
947	A81	50d red	12.50	1.50
948	A81	2.50r blue	17.50	2.50

Death millenary of Farabi, Persian philosopher.

Mohammad Reza Shah Pahlavi

A82　　　　　　　　A83

1951-52		**Unwmk. Photo.**	**Perf. 10½**	
950	A82	5d brown orange	.50	.20
951	A82	10d violet	.50	.20
952	A82	20d choc ('52)	1.50	.35
953	A82	25d blue ('52)	1.50	.20
954	A82	50d green	1.50	.20
955	A82	75d rose	1.50	.30
956	A83	1r gray green	1.50	.20
957	A83	1.50r cerise	1.50	.45
958	A83	2r chocolate	5.00	.20
959	A83	2.50r deep blue	5.00	.25
960	A83	3r red orange	6.00	.20
961	A83	5r dark green	12.00	.20
962	A83	10r olive ('52)	35.00	.50
963	A83	20r org brn ('52)	20.00	3.00
964	A83	30r vio bl ('52)	15.00	2.00
965	A83	50r blk brn ('52)	45.00	7.50
		Nos. 950-965 (16)	153.00	15.95

See Nos. 975-977.

Oil Well and Mosque — A84

Oil Well, Mosque and Monument A85

1953, Feb. 20			**Litho.**	
966	A84	50d green & yel	2.00	.50
967	A85	1r lil rose & yel	2.00	.50
968	A84	2.50r blue & yellow	3.00	1.00
969	A85	5r blk brn & yel	6.00	2.50
		Nos. 966-969 (4)	13.00	4.50

Discovery of oil at Qum.

Abadan Oil Refinery A86

Super Fractionators — A87

Designs: 1r, Storage tanks. 5r, Pipe lines. 10r, Abadan refinery.

1953, Mar. 20			**Photo.**	
970	A86	50d blue green	2.00	.50
971	A86	1r rose	3.00	.50
972	A87	2.50r bright ultra	4.00	1.50
973	A86	5r red orange	6.00	1.50
974	A86	10r dark violet	12.00	2.00
		Nos. 970-974 (5)	27.00	6.00

Nationalization of oil industry, 2nd anniv.

Shah Types of 1951-52

1953-54		**Photo.**	**Perf. 10½**	
975	A82	50d dark gray grn	20.00	.35
976	A83	1r dk blue green	2.50	.20
977	A83	1.50r cerise ('54)	2.50	.20
		Nos. 975-977 (3)	25.00	.75

The background has been highlighted on the 1r and 1.50r.

Gymnast — A88

Archery A89

Designs: 3r, Climbing Mt. Demavend. 5r, Ancient polo. 10r, Lion hunting.

1953, Oct. 26				
978	A88	1r deep green	5.00	3.00
979	A89	2.50fr brt grnsh bl	17.50	5.00
980	A89	3r gray	22.50	6.00
981	A88	5r bister	20.00	12.00
982	A88	10r rose lilac	65.00	20.00
		Nos. 978-982 (5)	130.00	46.00

Mother with Children and UN Emblem A90

1953, Oct. 24				
983	A90	1r bl grn & dk grn	2.00	.30
984	A90	2.50r lt bl & indigo	3.00	.70

United Nations Day, Oct. 24.

Herring A91

Refrigeration Compressor — A92

Processing Equipment, National Fisheries — A93

Designs: 2.50r, Sardines. 10r, Sturgeon.

1954, Jan. 31
985	A91	1r multi	5.00	3.00
986	A91	2.50r multi	35.00	15.00
987	A92	3r vermilion	15.00	7.00
988	A93	5r deep bl grn	15.00	10.00
989	A91	10r multi	55.00	25.00
		Nos. 985-989 (5)	125.00	60.00

Nationalization of fishing industry.

Broken Shackles — A94

Mother Feeding Baby — A95

3r, Torch flag. 5r, Citizen holding flag of Iran.

1954, Aug. 19   **Litho.**
990	A94	2r multicolored	7.00	3.00
991	A94	3r multicolored	12.00	5.00
992	A94	5r multicolored	16.00	7.00
		Nos. 990-992 (3)	35.00	15.00

Return of the royalist government, 1st anniv.

1954, Oct. 24   **Photo.**
993	A95	2r red lil & org	2.50	.75
994	A95	3r vio bl & org	3.50	1.25

Issued to honor the United Nations.

Woodsman Felling Tree — A96

Designs: 2.50r, Laborer carrying firewood. 5r, Worker operating saw. 10r, Wooden galley.

1954, Dec. 11
995	A96	1r brn & grnsh black	30.00	20.00
996	A96	2.50r grnsh blk & bl	35.00	30.00
997	A96	5r lil & dk brn	60.00	40.00
998	A96	10r bl & claret	80.00	50.00
		Nos. 995-998 (4)	205.00	140.00

4th World Forestry Congress, Dehra Dun, India, 1954.

Mohammad Reza Shah Pahlavi
A97   A98

1954-55   **Unwmk.**
999	A97	5d yellow brn	1.00	.25
1000	A97	10d violet	1.00	.25
1001	A97	25d scarlet	1.00	.20
1002	A97	50d black brn	1.00	.20

1003	A98	1r blue green	1.00	.20
1004	A98	1.50r cerise	1.00	.25
1005	A98	2r ocher	2.50	.25
1006	A98	2.50r blue	3.00	.20
1007	A98	3r olive	7.50	.25
1008	A98	5r dk sl grn	7.50	1.50
1009	A98	10r lilac rose	25.00	1.50
1010	A98	20r indigo	40.00	8.00
1011	A98	30r dp yel brn	175.00	12.50
1012	A98	50r dp orange	40.00	15.00
1013	A98	100r light vio	400.00	75.00
1014	A98	200r yellow	150.00	35.00
		Nos. 999-1014 (16)	856.50	150.55

See Nos. 1023-1036.

Regional Costume — A99

Regional Costumes: 1r, 2r, Men's costumes. 2.50r, 3r, 5r, Women's costumes.

1955, June 26   **Photo.**   **Perf. 11**
1015	A99	1r bluish gray & multi	10.00	3.00
1016	A99	2r dl rose & multi	10.00	4.00
1017	A99	2.50r buff & multi	30.00	5.00
1018	A99	3r rose lil & multi	15.00	6.00
1019	A99	5r gray brn & multi	30.00	10.00
		Nos. 1015-1019 (5)	95.00	28.00

Parliament Gate — A100

Designs: 3r, Statue of Liberty, vert. 5r, Old Gate of Parliament.

1955, Aug. 6   **Wmk. 306**   **Perf. 11**
1020	A100	2r red vio & grn	5.00	2.00
1021	A100	3r dk bl & aqua	12.00	3.00
1022	A100	5r Prus grn & red org	15.00	7.00
		Nos. 1020-1022 (3)	32.00	12.00

50th anniversary of constitution.

Shah Types of 1954-55

1955-56   **Wmk. 306**   **Perf. 11**
1023	A97	5d violet ('56)	5.00	1.50
1024	A97	10d carmine ('56)	1.00	.20
1025	A97	25d brown	1.00	.20
1026	A97	50d dk carmine	1.00	.20
1027	A98	1r dark bl grn	1.00	.20
1028	A98	1.50r red brn ('56)	50.00	3.00
1029	A98	2r ol grn ('56)	25.00	.25
1030	A98	2.50r blue ('56)	5.00	.30
1031	A98	3r bister	7.00	.20
1032	A98	5r red lilac	10.00	.20
1033	A98	10r brt grnsh bl	12.00	.35
1034	A98	20r slate green	30.00	4.00
1035	A98	30r red org ('56)	150.00	25.00
1036	A98	50r red brn ('56)	125.00	30.00
		Nos. 1023-1036 (14)	423.00	65.60

UN Emblem and Globes A101

1955, Oct. 24   **Perf. 11x12½**
1039	A101	1r dp car & org	1.50	.75
1040	A101	2.50r dk bl & grnsh blue	2.00	1.50

UN, 10th anniv.Nations, Oct. 24, 1955.

Wrestlers A102

1955, Oct. 26   **Wmk. 306**   **Perf. 11**
1041	A102	2.50r multi	15.00	7.50

Victory in intl. wrestling competitions.

Garden, Namazi Hospital A103   *Immortal Guardsman* A105

Nemazi Hospital, Shiraz A104

5r, Gate of the Koran. 10r, Ha'fez of Shiraz.

1956, Mar. 21   **Perf. 11x12½**
1042	A103	50d multi	5.00	2.00
1043	A104	1r multi	6.00	2.50
1044	A105	2.50r multi	9.00	7.00
1045	A104	5r multi	15.00	6.00
1046	A105	10r multi	25.00	10.00
		Nos. 1042-1046 (5)	60.00	27.50

Opening of Namazi Hospital, Shiraz.

Arms of Iran and Olympic Rings — A106

Tomb at Maragheh A107

1956, May 15   **Wmk. 306**
1047	A106	5r rose lilac	40.00	30.00

National Olympic Committee, 10th anniv.

1956, May 26   **Photo.**   **Perf. 11x12½**
2.50r, Astrolabe. 5r, Nasr-ud-Din of Tus.
1048	A107	1r orange	5.00	2.50
1049	A107	2.50r deep ultra	7.50	3.50
1050	A107	5r sepia & pur	12.50	4.00
		Nos. 1048-1050 (3)	25.00	10.00

700th death anniv. of Nasr-up-Din of Tus, mathematician and astronomer.

WHO Emblem — A108

Perf. 11x12½

1956, Sept. 19   **Wmk. 306**
1051	A108	6r cerise	4.00	1.50

6th Regional Congress of the WHO.

Scout Bugler and Camp A109

5r, Scout badge and Shah in scout uniform.

1956, Aug. 5   **Perf. 12½x11**
1052	A109	2.50r ultra & blue	15.00	9.00
1053	A109	5r lil & red lil	20.00	12.00

National Boy Scout Jamboree.

> **Catalogue values for unused stamps in this section, from this point to the end of the section, are for Never Hinged items.**

Former Telegraph Office, Tehran A110

6r, Telegraph lines & ancient monument.

1956, Oct. 26
1054	A110	2.50r brt bl & grn, bluish	12.00	5.00
1055	A110	6r rose car & lil	13.00	7.50

Centenary of Persian telegraph system.

UN Emblem and People of the World A111

Design: 2.50r, UN Emblem and scales.

1956, Oct. 24
1056	A111	1r bluish green	1.50	.40
1057	A111	2.50r blue & green	3.00	.60

United Nations Day, Oct. 24.

Shah and Pres. Iskander Mirza of Pakistan A112

1956, Oct. 31
1058	A112	1r multicolored	10.00	2.50

Visit of Pres. General Iskander Mirza of Pakistan to Tehran, Oct. 31-Nov. 10.

Mohammad Reza Shah Pahlavi
A113   A114

Perf. 13½x11

1956-57		**Wmk. 306**	**Photo.**	
1058A	A113	5d brt car & red	.50	1.00
1058B	A113	10d vio bl & dl vio	.50	1.00
1059	A113	25d dk brn & brn	.75	.35
1059A	A113	50d brn & ol brn	.75	.20
b.		Inverted center	3,750.	
1060	A113	1r brn & brt grn	.75	.20
1061	A113	1.50r brt lil & brown	1.00	.20
1062	A113	2r red vio & red	1.00	.20
1063	A113	2.50r ultra & blue	1.50	.20
1064	A113	3r brn & dk ol bis	1.50	.20
1065	A113	5r ver & mar	2.00	.20
1066	A114	6r dk vio & brn lil	7.00	.25
1067	A114	10r lt blue & grn	15.00	.20
1068	A114	20r green & blue	30.00	3.00
1069	A114	30r rose red & org	35.00	5.00
1070	A114	50r dk grn & ol grn	35.00	5.00
1071	A114	100r lilac & cer	350.00	27.50
1072	A114	200r dp plum & vio bl	210.00	15.00
		Nos. 1058A-1072 (17)	692.25	59.70

Issued: 1.50r, 2r, 3r, 5r, 6r, 1956; others, 1957.
See Nos. 1082-1098.

Lord Baden-Powell
A115

Train and Map
A117

1957, Feb. 22   Perf. 12½
1073 A115 10r dk grn & brn   12.50 7.00
Birth cent. of Robert Baden-Powell, founder of the Boy Scout movement.

Railroad Tracks — A116

1957, May 2   Perf. 11x12½, 12½x11
Design: 10r, Train and mosque.
1074 A116 2.50r grnsh blk, bl & ocher 15.00 2.00
1075 A117 5r multi   20.00 7.00
1076 A116 10r blk, yel & bl   35.00 11.00
      Nos. 1074-1076 (3)   70.00 20.00

Opening of the Tehran Meshed-Railway.

Pres. Giovanni Gronchi of Italy and Shah — A118

Design: 6r, Ruins of Persepolis and Colosseum in Rome and flags.

Wmk. 316
1957, Sept. 7   Photo.   Perf. 11
1077 A118 2r slate bl, grn & red   5.00 2.00
1078 A118 6r slate bl, grn & red 10.00 3.00
Visit of Pres. Giovanni Gronchi of Italy to Iran, Sept. 7.

Queen Soraya and Hospital A119

1957, Sept. 29   Wmk. 316   Perf. 11
1079 A119 2r lt bl & grn   10.00 3.00
Sixth Medical Congress, Ramsar.

Globes Showing Location of Iran — A120

1957, Oct. 22   Litho.   Perf. 12½x11
1080 A120 10r blk, lt bl, yel & red   10.00 3.00
Intl. Cartographic Conference, Tehran.

Shah and King Faisal II — A121

1957, Oct. 18   Photo.
1081 A121 2r slate bl, grn & red 10.00 3.00
Visit of King Faisal of Iraq, Oct. 19.

Shah Types of 1956-57

1957-58		**Wmk. 316**	**Perf. 11**	
1082	A114	5d violet & pur	.50	2.00
1083	A114	10d claret & rose car	.50	2.00
1084	A114	25d rose car & brick red	.50	.35
1085	A114	50d grn & olive grn	.60	.20
1086	A114	1r dark green	.90	.20
1087	A114	1.50r claret & red lil	1.00	.25
1088	A114	2r bl & grnsh blue	2.00	.20
1089	A114	2.50r dk bl & blue	2.00	.25
1090	A114	3r rose car & ver	2.00	.20
1091	A114	5r violet blue	2.00	.20
1092	A113	6r bright blue	3.00	.20
1093	A113	10r deep green	6.00	.30
1094	A113	20r grn & olive grn	30.00	.45
1095	A113	30r vio bl & dk brn	35.00	10.00
1096	A113	50r dk brn & lt brn	40.00	12.00
1097	A113	100r rose lil & car rose	150.00	30.00

1098	A113	200r vio & yel brn	125.00	35.00
		Nos. 1082-1098 (17)	401.00	93.80

Issued: 1.50r, 2r, 3r, 1957; others, 1958.

Weight Lifter — A122

Modern and Old Houses, Radio Transmitter A123

1957, Nov. 8   Perf. 11x14½
1099 A122 10r bl, grn & red   10.00 4.00
Iran's victories in weight lifting.

1958, Feb. 22   Litho.
1100 A123 10r brn, ocher & bl 10.00 4.00
30th anniversary of radio in Iran.

Oil Derrick and Symbolic Flame — A124

Train on Viaduct — A125

Wmk. 316
1958, Mar. 10   Photo.   Perf. 11
1101 A124 2r gray & multi   10.00 2.00
1102 A124 10r multicolored   15.00 3.00
Drilling of Iran's 1st oil well, 50th anniv.

1958, Apr. 24   Wmk. 306   Perf. 11
Design: 8r, Train and map.
1103 A125 6r dull purple   25.00 7.50
1104 A125 8r green   35.00 12.50
Opening of Tehran-Tabriz railway line.

Exposition Emblem A126

1958, Apr. 17   Perf. 12½x11
1105 A126 2.50r bl & light bl   1.25 .30
1106 A126 6r car & salmon   2.25 .50
World's Fair, Brussels, Apr. 17-Oct. 19.

Mohammad Reza Shah Pahlavi — A127   UN Emblem and Map of Iran — A128

1958-59		**Wmk. 316 Photo.**	**Perf. 11**	
1107	A127	5d blue violet	.75	.25
1108	A127	10d lt vermilion	.75	.25
1109	A127	25d crimson	.75	.25
1110	A127	50d brt blue	.75	.25
1111	A127	1r dark green	1.50	.20
1113	A127	2r dark brown	10.00	.25
1115	A127	3r dk red brown	17.50	.20
1117	A127	6r bright blue	8.00	.45
1118	A127	8r magenta	8.00	.35
1120	A127	14r blue violet	15.00	1.75
1121	A127	20r green	25.00	.45
a.		Wmk. 306	30.00	15.00
1122	A127	30r brt car rose	20.00	3.00
1123	A127	50r rose violet	60.00	10.00
1124	A127	100r red orange	30.00	6.00
1125	A127	200r slate green	75.00	12.00
		Nos. 1107-1125 (15)	273.00	35.65

See Nos. 1138-1151, 1173-1179.

1958, Oct. 24
1126 A128 6r bright blue   1.50 1.00
1127 A128 10r dk violet & grn   2.50 1.25
Issued for United Nations Day, Oct. 24.

Globe and Hands A129

1958, Dec. 10
1128 A129 6r dk red brn & brn   1.50 .50
1129 A129 8r dk grn & gray grn   2.50 .75
Universal Declaration of Human Rights, 10th anniv.

Rudaki — A130

Wrestlers, Flag and Globe — A131

Flag A130a

Design: 5r, Rudaki, different pose.

1958, Dec. 24   Photo.   Wmk. 306
1130 A130 2.50r bluish black   10.00 2.00
1131 A130 5r violet   15.00 3.00
1132 A130 10r dark brown   25.00 4.00
      Nos. 1130-1132 (3)   50.00 9.00

1100th birth anniv. of Rudaki, blind Persian poet.

Design: Red Lion & Sun flag (Iranian Red Cross Organization).

Perf. 14½x11

1959, May 8   **Wmk. 316**
1132A A130a 1r multicolored   3.00   1.00
1132B A130a 6r multicolored   5.00   1.50
Centenary of the Red Cross.

1959   **Litho.**   **Perf. 11x12½**
1133 A131 6r multicolored   25.00   10.00
World Wrestling Championships, Tehran.

Globe, UN Building and Hand Holding Torch of Freedom A132

1959, Oct. 24   **Photo.**   **Perf. 11**
1134 A132 6r gray brn, red & bister   2.00   .60
Issued for United Nations Day, Oct. 24.

Shah and Pres. Ayub Khan of Pakistan — A133

1959, Nov. 9   **Litho.**   **Perf. 11x16**
1135 A133 6r multicolored   10.00   3.00
Visit of Pres. Khan to Iran.

ILO Emblem — A134

1959, Nov. 12   **Perf. 16**
1136 A134 1r blue   1.50   .40
1137 A134 5r brown   2.00   .60
ILO, 40th anniversary.

Shah Type of 1958-59

1959-63 Wmk. 316 Photo. Perf. 11
1138   A127   5d red brn ('60)   .50   .30
1139   A127   10d Prus grn ('60)   .50   .30
   a.   10d Prussian blue ('63)   .75   .50
1140   A127   25d orange   1.50   .20
   a.   Perf. 12x11½   75.00   20.00
1141   A127   50d scarlet   1.50   .25
1142   A127   1r deep violet   1.50   .20
1142A A127   2r brown   10.00   .20
1143   A127   3r olive   4.00   .20
1143A A127   6r cobalt blue   7.50   .20
1144   A127   8r brown olive   2.00   .20
1145   A127   10r ol blk ('60)   2.00   .20
1146   A127   14r yel green   2.50   .25
   a.   14r emerald green   4.00   .50
1147   A127   20r sl grn ('60)   7.00   .35
1148   A127   30r choc ('60)   10.00   2.00
1149   A127   50r dp blue ('60)   10.00   2.00
1150   A127   100r green ('60)   135.00   12.50
1151   A127   200r cer ('60)   250.00   17.50
   Nos. 1138-1151 (16)   445.50   36.85

Pahlavi Foundation Bridge, Karun River — A135

Design: 5r, Bridge, different view.

1960, Feb. 29   **Litho.**   **Perf. 16x11**
1152 A135 1r dk brn & brt bl   2.00   .20
1153 A135 5r blue & emerald   3.00   .70
Opening of Pahlavi Foundation Bridge at Khorramshahr on the Karun River.

Uprooted Oak Emblem A136

Design: 6r, Arched frame.

1960, Apr. 7   **Perf. 11**
1154 A136 1r brt ultra   .70   .30
1155 A136 6r gray olive   .80   .35
World Refugee Year, 7/1/59-6/30/60.

Mosquito — A137

Man with Spray Gun — A138

Design: 3r, Mosquito on water.

1960, Apr. 7   **Wmk. 316**
1156 A137 1r blk & red, yel   2.00   1.00
1157 A138 2r lt bl, ultra & blk   3.00   1.00
1158 A137 3r blk & red, yel grn   5.00   1.50
   Nos. 1156-1158 (3)   10.00   3.50
Issued to publicize malaria control.

Polo Player — A139

Design: 6r, Persian archer.

1960, June 9   **Litho.**   **Wmk. 316**
1159 A139 1r deep claret   3.00   .50
1160 A139 6r dk blue & lt blue   5.00   1.00
17th Olympic Games, Rome, 8/25-9/11.

Shah and King Hussein of Jordan — A140

1960, July 6   **Perf. 11**
1161 A140 6r multicolored   10.00   3.00
Visit of King Hussein of Jordan to Tehran.

Iranian Scout Emblem in Flower — A141

Tents and Pillars of Persepolis A142

1960, July 18
1162 A141 1r green   1.00   .50
1163 A142 6r brn, brt bl & buff   2.00   .75
3rd National Boy Scout Jamboree.

Shah and Queen Farah — A143

1960, Sept. 9   **Litho.**   **Perf. 11**
1164 A143 1r green   5.00   1.50
1165 A143 5r blue   10.00   2.00
Marriage of Shah Mohammad Reza Shah Pahlavi and Farah Diba.

UN Emblem and Globe — A144

1960, Oct. 24   **Wmk. 316**
1166 A144 6r bl, blk & lt brn   2.00   .50
15th anniversary of the United Nations.

Shah and Queen Elizabeth II A145

1961, Mar. 2   **Litho.**   **Perf. 11**
1167 A145 1r lt red brown   3.00   .45
1168 A145 6r bright ultra   5.00   .90
Visit of Queen Elizabeth II to Tehran, Feb. 1961.

Girl Playing Arganoon — A146

Safiaddin Amavi — A147

1961, Apr. 10   **Wmk. 316**   **Perf. 11**
1169 A146 1r dk brown & buff   2.00   .50
1170 A147 6r greenish gray   3.00   .75
International Congress of Music, Tehran.

Shah Type of 1958-59 Redrawn

1961-62   **Litho.**   **Perf. 11**
1173 A127 25d orange   3.50   .50
1174 A127 50d scarlet   3.50   .40
1175 A127 1r deep violet   6.00   .20
1176 A127 2r chocolate   7.00   .20
1177 A127 3r olive brown   10.00   .50
1178 A127 6r brt blue ('62)   50.00   3.50
1179 A127 8r brown ol ('62)   20.00   2.25
   Nos. 1173-1179 (7)   100.00   7.55

On Nos. 1173-1179 (lithographed), a single white line separates the lower panel from the shah's portrait. On Nos. 1107-1125, 1138-1151 (photogravure), two lines, one in color and one in white, separate panel from portrait. Other minor differences exist.

Shah and Queen Farah Holding Crown Prince — A148

1961, June 2   **Litho.**
1186 A148 1r bright pink   5.00   2.50
1187 A148 6r light blue   10.00   5.00
Birth of Crown Prince Reza Kourosh Pahlavi, Oct. 31, 1960.

Swallows and UN Emblem — A149

Planting Tree — A150

1961, Oct. 24 — Perf. 11
1188 A149 2r blue & car rose 1.50 .25
1189 A149 6r blue & violet 2.00 .35
Issued for United Nations Day, Oct. 24.

1962, Jan. 11
1190 A150 2r ol grn, citron & dk
bl 1.50 .25
1191 A150 6r ultra, grn & pale bl 2.00 .35
Tree Planting Day.

Worker and Symbols of Labor and Agriculture A151

Map, Family and Cogwheel A152

1962, Mar. 15 — Litho.
1192 A151 2r bl grn, brn & blk 1.50 .25
1193 A151 6r lt ultra, brn & blk 2.00 .35
Issued for Workers' Day.

1962, Mar. 20 — Perf. 11
1194 A152 2r black, yel & lil 2.00 .30
1195 A152 6r black, bl & ultra 2.50 .65
Social Insurance Week.

Sugar Refinery, Khuzistan — A153

1962, Apr. 14 — Wmk. 316
1196 A153 2r dk & lt blue & grn 2.00 .35
1197 A153 6r ultra, buff & blue 2.50 .65
Opening of sugar refinery in Khuzistan.

Karaj Dam — A154

1962, May 15
1198 A154 2r dk brn & gray grn 1.50 .25
1199 A154 6r vio bl & lt blue 2.00 .50
Inauguration of Karaj Dam, renamed Amir Kabir Dam.

Sefid Rud Dam A155

1962, May 19 — Litho.
1200 A155 2r dk grn, lt bl & buff 2.00 .35
1201 A155 6r red brn, sl grn & lt
blue 2.50 .65
Inauguration of Sefid Rud Dam.

"UNESCO" and UN Emblem — A156

1962, June 2 — Wmk. 316 — Perf. 11
1202 A156 2r black, emer & red 1.50 .30
1203 A156 6r blue, emer & red 2.50 .50
15th anniv. of UNESCO.

Malaria Eradication Emblem and Sprayer A157

2r, Emblem & arrow piercing mosquito, horiz. 10r, Emblem & globe, horiz. Sizes: 2r, 10r, 40x25mm; 6r, 29½x34½mm.

1962, June 20
1204 A157 2r black & bluish grn 2.00 .35
1205 A157 6r pink & vio blue 2.50 .50
1206 A157 10r lt blue & ultra 3.00 .75
Nos. 1204-1206 (3) 7.50 1.60
WHO drive to eradicate malaria.

Oil Field and UN Emblem A158

1962, Sept. 1 — Photo.
1207 A158 6r grnsh blue & brn 3.00 .50
1208 A158 14r gray & sepia 5.00 1.50
2nd Petroleum Symposium of ECAFE (UN Economic Commission for Asia and the Far East).

Mohammad Reza Shah Pahlavi — A159

Palace of Darius, Persepolis A160

Perf. 11, 10½x11, 11x10½
1962		Photo.		Wmk. 316
1209	A159	5d	green	1.00 .25
1210	A159	10d	chestnut	1.00 .50
1211	A159	25d	dark blue	1.00 .35
1212	A159	50d	Prus green	1.00 .20
1213	A159	1r	orange	3.00 .20
1214	A159	2r	violet blue	2.00 .20
1215	A159	5r	dark brown	3.00 .20
1216	A160	6r	blue	12.00 2.50
1217	A160	8r	yellow grn	5.00 1.00
1218	A160	10r	grnsh blue	8.00 .20
1219	A160	11r	slate green	4.50 .65
1220	A160	14r	purple	10.00 .65
1221	A160	20r	red brown	11.00 1.50
1222	A160	50r	vermilion	15.00 1.50
	Nos. 1209-1222 (14)			77.50 10.20

See Nos. 1331-1344.
No. 1219 perf. 10½x11 is valued unused $9. Otherwise, all perf. varieties have the same values.

Hippocrates and Avicenna — A161

1962, Oct. 7 — Litho.
1226 A161 2r brown, buff & ultra 3.00 .35
1227 A161 6r grn, pale grn & ultra 3.50 .60
Near and Middle East Medical Congress.

Hands Laying Bricks A162

Design: 6r, Houses and UN emblem, vert.

1962, Oct. 24
1228 A162 6r dk blue & ultra 3.00 .35
1229 A162 14r dk blue & emer 3.50 .60
Issued for United Nations Day, Oct. 24.

Crown Prince Receiving Flowers — A163

1962, Oct. 31
1230 A163 6r blue gray 6.00 1.00
1231 A163 14r dull green 12.00 1.90
Children's Day, Oct. 31; 2nd birthday of Crown Prince Riza.

Map of Iran and Persian Gulf — A164

Hilton Hotel, Tehran — A165

1962, Dec. 12 — Wmk. 316 — Perf. 11
1232 A164 6r dk & lt bl, vio bl &
rose 3.00 .35
1233 A164 14r dk & lt bl, pink &
rose 3.50 .60
The Persian Gulf Seminar.

1963, Jan. 21 — Photo.
1234 A165 6r deep blue 4.00 .45
1235 A165 14r dark red brown 6.00 .60
Opening of the Royal Tehran Hilton Hotel.

Mohammad Riza Shah Dam A166

1963, Mar. 14 — Litho.
Center Multicolored
1236 A166 6r violet blue 4.00 .40
1237 A166 14r dark brown 7.00 .75
Mohammad Riza Shah Dam inauguration (later Dez Dam).

Worker with Pickax — A167

Stylized Bird over Globe — A168

1963, Mar. 15
1238 A167 2r cream & black 1.50 .20
1239 A167 6r lt blue & blk 2.50 .30
Issued for Labor Day.

1963, Mar. 21 — Perf. 11
Designs: 6r, Stylized globe and "FAO." 14r, Globe in space and wheat emblem.
1240 A168 2r ultra, lt bl & bis 2.00 .20
1241 A168 6r lt ultra, ocher &
blk 3.00 .30
1242 A168 14r slate bl & ocher 4.00 .85
Nos. 1240-1242 (3) 9.00 1.35
FAO "Freedom from Hunger" campaign.

Shah and List of Bills — A169

1963, Mar. 21 — Wmk. 316
1243 A169 6r green & lt blue 7.00 2.00
1244 A169 14r green & dull yel 10.00 3.00
Signing of six socioeconomic bills by Shah, 1st anniv.

Shah and King of Denmark — A170

1963, May 3   **Litho.**   *Perf. 11*
1245   A170   6r indigo & dk ultra   5.00   .55
1246   A170   14r dk brn & red brn   7.00   1.00
Visit of King Frederik IX of Denmark.

Flags, Shah Mosque, Isfahan, and Taj Mahal, Agra A171

1963, May 19
1247   A171   6r blue, yel grn & red   5.00   .55
1248   A171   14r multicolored   7.00   1.00
Visit of Dr. Sarvepalli Radhakrishnan, president of India.

Chahnaz Dam — A172

Cent. Emblem with Red Lion and Sun — A173

1963, June 8   **Wmk. 316**   *Perf. 11*
1249   A172   6r ultra, bl & grn   3.50   .45
1250   A172   14r dk grn, bl & buff   5.00   .75
Inauguration of Chahnaz Dam (later Hamadan Dam).

1963, June 10
1251   A173   6r blue, gray & red   5.00   .65
1252   A173   14r buff, gray & red   7.00   .90
Centenary of International Red Cross.

Shah and Queen Juliana A174

     Perf. 11x10½
1963, Oct. 3   **Wmk. 349**
1253   A174   6r ultra & blue   5.00   .50
1254   A174   14r sl grn & dull grn   7.00   .75
Visit of Queen Juliana of the Netherlands.

Literacy Corps Emblem and Soldier Teaching Village Class — A175

1963, Oct. 15   **Litho.**   *Perf. 10½*
1255   A175   6r multicolored   7.00   1.00
1256   A175   14r multicolored   8.00   1.00
Issued to publicize the Literacy Corps.

Gen. Charles de Gaulle and View of Persepolis — A176

1963, Oct. 16
1257   A176   6r ultra & blue   5.00   1.00
1258   A176   14r brn & pale brn   7.00   1.00
Visit of General de Gaulle of France.

Fertilizer Plant, Oil Company Emblem and Map — A177

Design: 14r, Factory and Iranian Oil Company emblem, horiz.

     Perf. 10½x11, 11x10½
1963, Oct. 18   **Wmk. 316**
1259   A177   6r black, yel & red   6.00   .50
1260   A177   14r black, bl & yel   8.00   1.50
Opening of Shiraz Chemical Factory.

Pres. Heinrich Lübke of Germany and Mosque in Tehran A178

1963, Oct. 23   **Wmk. 349**   *Perf. 10½*
1261   A178   6r ultra & dk blue   5.00   .65
1262   A178   14r gray & brown   7.00   1.60
Visit of Pres. Lubke of Germany.

UN Emblem and Iranian Flag A179

1963, Oct. 24
1263   A179   8r multicolored   5.00   .50
Issued for United Nations Day.

UN Emblem and Jets A180

1963, Oct. 24
1264   A180   6r multicolored   6.00   1.00
Iranian jet fighters with UN Force in the Congo.

Crown Prince Rzza — A181

1963, Oct. 31
1265   A181   2r brown   3.00   .25
1266   A181   6r blue   6.00   .50
Children's Day; Crown Prince Riza's 3rd birthday.

Pres. Brezhnev of USSR — A182

1963, Nov. 16   **Wmk. 349**   *Perf. 10½*
1267   A182   6r dk brn, yel & bl   5.00   .35
1268   A182   11r dk brn, yel & red   8.00   .75
Visit of Pres. Leonid I. Brezhnev.

Atatürk's Mausoleum, Ankara — A183

1963, Nov. 28   **Litho.**
1269   A183   4r shown   4.50   .30
1270   A183   5r Kemal Ataturk   5.50   .30
25th death anniv. of Kemal Atatürk, president of Turkey.

Scales and Globe — A184

1963, Dec. 10
1271   A184   6r brt yel grn, blk & ultra   3.00   .35
1272   A184   14r org brn, blk & buff   5.00   .45
Universal Declaration of Human Rights, 15th anniv.

Mother and Child — A185

1963, Dec. 16
1273   A185   2r multicolored   3.00   .25
1274   A185   4r multicolored   5.00   .50
Issued for Mother's Day.

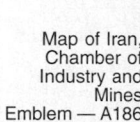

Map of Iran, Chamber of Industry and Mines Emblem — A186

1963, Dec. 17   **Litho.**
1275   A186   8r bl grn, buff & dk bl   5.00   .40
Chamber of Industry and Mines.

Factories and Hand Holding Bill — A187

Designs: 4r, Factories and bills on scale. 6r, Man on globe carrying torch of education. 8r, Tractor, map and yardstick. 10r, Forest. 12r, Gate of Parliament and heads of man and woman.

1964, Jan. 26   **Wmk. 349**   *Perf. 10½*
1276   A187   2r multicolored   4.00   .75
1277   A187   4r brown & gray   5.00   .75
1278   A187   6r multicolored   6.00   .75
1279   A187   8r multicolored   7.00   1.00
1280   A187   10r multicolored   8.00   1.25
1281   A187   12r red org & brn   10.00   1.50
   Nos. 1276-1281 (6)   40.00   6.00
2nd anniv. of six socioeconomic bills: 2r, Shareholding for factory workers. 4r, Sale of shares in government factories. 6r, Creation of Army of Education. 8r, Land reforms. 10r, Nationalization of forests. 12r, Reforms in parliamentary elections.

"ECAFE" and UN Emblem A188

1964, Mar. 2   **Wmk. 349**
1282   A188   14r brt green & blk   4.00   .45
20th session of ECAFE (Economic Commission for Asia and the Far East), Mar. 2-17.

Flowering Branch — A189

1964, Mar. 5   *Perf. 10½*
1283   A189   50d emerald, blk & org   .60   .25
1284   A189   1r brt blue, blk & org   .90   .25
Novrooz, Iranian New Year, Mar. 21.

Anemometer A190

Mosque and Arches, Isfahan — A191

1964, Mar. 23   **Litho.**
1285   A190   6r brt blue & vio bl   3.50   .25
4th World Meteorological Day.

1964, Apr. 7   *Perf. 10½*
11r, Griffon & winged bull, Persepolis.
1286   A191   6r lilac, grn & blk   4.00   .40
1287   A191   11r orange, brn & blk   6.00   .55
Issued for tourist publicity.

Rudaki and Harp — A192

1964, May 16   Photo.   Wmk. 349
1288 A192 6r blue   3.50   .45
1289 A192 8r red brown   6.00   .55

Opening of an institute for the blind. The inscription translates: "Wisdom is better than eye and sight."

Sculpture, Persepolis A193

Designs: 4r, Achaemenian horse-drawn mail cart, map of Iran, horiz. 6r, Vessel with sculptured animals. 10r, Head of King Shapur, sculpture.

1964, June 5   Wmk. 349   Litho.
1290 A193 2r gray & blue   6.00   1.75
1291 A193 4r vio bl, lt bl & bl   10.00   2.00
1292 A193 6r brown & yellow   12.00   2.50
1293 A193 10r yel & ol grn   15.00   3.00
    Nos. 1290-1293 (4)   43.00   9.75

Opening of the "7000 Years of Persian Art" exhibition in Washington, D.C.

Shah and Emperor Haile Selassie A194

1964, Sept. 14   Wmk. 349   Perf. 10½
1294 A194 6r ultra & lt blue   5.00   .60

Visit of Emperor Haile Selassie of Ethiopia.

Tooth and Dentists' Assoc. Emblem A195

"2 I.D.A." A196

1964, Sept. 14   Litho.
1295 A195 2r blue, red & dk blue   3.00   .30
1296 A196 4r ultra, bl & pale brn   4.00   .35

Iranian Dentists' Association, 2nd congress.

Research Institute, Microscope, Wheat and Locust — A197

Beetle under Magnifying Glass — A198

1964, Sept. 23   Wmk. 349   Perf. 10½
1297 A197 2r red, orange & brn   5.00   .40
1298 A198 6r blue, brn & indigo   6.00   .60

Fight against plant diseases and damages.

Mithras (Mehr) on Ancient Seal — A199

Eleanor Roosevelt (1884-1962) A200

1964, Oct. 8   Litho.
    Size: 26x34mm
1299 A199 8r org & brn org   4.00   1.00

Mehragan celebration. See No. 1406.

1964, Oct. 11
1300 A200 10r vio bl & rose vio   6.00   .75

Clasped Hands and UN Emblem — A201

Symbolic Airplane and UN Emblem — A202

1964, Oct. 24   Wmk. 349   Perf. 10½
1301 A201 6r ultra, yel, red & blk   3.00   .30
1302 A202 14r org, ultra & red   4.00   .50

Issued for United Nations Day.

Persian Gymnast — A203

Polo Player A204

1964, Oct. 26
1303 A203 4r tan, sep & Prus bl   3.00   .35
1304 A204 6r red & black   4.00   .40

18th Olympic Games, Tokyo, Oct. 10-25.

Crown Prince Riza — A205

1964, Oct. 31   Litho.
1305 A205 1r dull green & brn   2.00   .30
1306 A205 2r deep rose & ultra   3.50   .50
1307 A205 6r ultra & red   5.00   .65
    Nos. 1305-1307 (3)   10.50   1.45

Children's Day; Crown Prince Riza's 4th birthday.

UN Emblem, Flame and Smokestack — A206

1964, Nov. 16   Wmk. 349   Perf. 10½
1308 A206 6r black, lt bl & car   2.00   .35
1309 A206 8r black, emer & car   3.50   .40

Petro-Chemical Conference and Gas Seminar, Nov.-Dec. 1964.

Shah and King Baudouin — A207

1964, Nov. 17
1310 A207 6r black, org & yel   2.00   .35
1311 A207 8r black, org & emer   4.00   .75

Visit of King Baudouin of Belgium.

Rhazes A208

1964, Dec. 27   Wmk. 349   Perf. 10½
1312 A208 2r multicolored   3.00   .35
1313 A208 6r multicolored   5.00   .60

1100th birth anniv. of Rhazes (abu-Bakr Mohammad Zakariya Razi), Persian physician.

Shah and King Olav V A209

1965, Jan. 7   Litho.
1314 A209 2r dk brown & lilac   3.00   .35
1315 A209 4r brown & green   4.00   .75

Visit of King Olav V of Norway.

Map of Iran and Six-pointed Star — A210

1965, Jan. 26   Wmk. 349   Perf. 10½
1316 A210 2r black, brt bl & org   2.50   .20

Shah's six socioeconomic bills, 3rd anniv.

Woman and UN Emblem — A211   Green Wheat and Tulip — A212

1965, Mar. 1   Wmk. 349   Perf. 10½
1317 A211 6r black & blue   1.50   .20
1318 A211 8r ultra & red   2.50   .20

18th session of the UN commission on the status of women.

1965, Mar. 6
1319 A212 50d multicolored   .50   .20
1320 A212 1r multicolored   .70   .20

Novrooz, Iranian New Year, Mar. 21.

Pres. Habib Bourguiba and Minarets of Tunis Mosque — A213

1965, Mar. 14   Litho.   Perf. 10½
1321 A213 4r multicolored   2.25   .35

Visit of Pres. Habib Bourguiba of Tunisia.

Map of Iran and Trade Mark of Iranian Oil Co. A214

1965, Mar. 20   **Litho.**
1322 A214 6r multicolored   3.50 .25
1323 A214 14r multicolored   4.50 .55

Oil industry nationalization, 14th anniv.

ITU Emblem, Old and New Communication Equipment — A215

1965, May 17   **Wmk. 349**   **Perf. 10½**
1324 A215 14r dp car rose & gray   2.00 .60

ITU, centenary.

ICY Emblem A216

1965, June 22   **Litho.**   **Perf. 10½**
1325 A216 10r sl grn & gray bl   3.00 .60

International Cooperation Year, 1965.

Iran Airways Emblem A217

1965, July 17   **Wmk. 349**   **Perf. 10½**
1326 A217 14r multicolored   3.50 .75

Tenth anniversary of Iran Airways.

Hands Holding Book A218

Map and Flags of Turkey, Iran and Pakistan A219

1965, July 21   **Litho.**
1327 A218 2r dk brn, org brn & buff   1.50 .25
1328 A219 4r multicolored   2.00 .25

Signing of the Regional Cooperation for Development Pact by Turkey, Iran and Pakistan, 1st anniv.

Iranian Scout Emblem and Ornament A220

1965, July 23
1329 A220 2r multicolored   2.00 .20
    a.   Vert. pair, imperf. horiz.   75.00

Middle East Rover Moot (senior Boy Scout assembly).

Majlis Gate A221

1965, Aug. 5   **Wmk. 349**   **Perf. 10½**
1330 A221 2r lilac rose & brn   1.00 .20

60th anniversary of Iranian constitution.

Types of Regular Issue, 1962
Wmk. 349

1964-65   **Photo.**   **Perf. 10½**
1331 A159 5d dk sl grn ('65)   .35 .30
    a.   Wmk. 353   .35 .30
1332 A159 10d chestnut   .35 .30
1333 A159 25d dk blue ('65)   .50 .25
1334 A159 50d Prus green   .75 .20
1335 A159 1r orange   .75 .20
1336 A159 2r violet blue   .50 .20
1337 A159 5r dark brown   3.00 .50
1338 A160 6r blue ('65)   11.00 1.00
1339 A160 8r yel grn ('65)   3.50 .25
1340 A160 10r grnsh bl ('65)   3.00 .25
1341 A160 11r sl grn ('65)   10.00 1.50
1342 A160 14r purple ('65)   7.00 1.40
1343 A160 20r red brn ('65)   6.00 2.00
1344 A160 50r org ver ('65)   7.50 2.00
    Nos. 1331-1344 (14)   54.20 10.35

Perf. 11x10½
1331b A159 5d Wmk. 353   4.00 1.00
1332a A159 10d   .55 .50
1333a A159 25d   .80 .25
1334a A159 50d   3.00 2.00
1335a A159 1r   3.00 2.00
1337a A159 5r   6.00 .50
    Nos. 1331b-1337a (6)   17.35 6.25

Dental Congress Emblem — A222

1965, Sept. 7   **Litho.**   **Perf. 10½**
1345 A222 6r gray, ultra, & car   1.00 .25

Iranian Dentists' Association, 3rd congress.

Classroom and Literacy Corps Emblem A223

Alphabets on Globe — A224

1965, Sept. 8
1346 A223 2r multi   .60 .25
1347 A224 5r multi   .75 .30
    Size: 30x30mm
1348 A223 6r multi   1.25 .40
    Size: 35x23mm
1349 A223 8r dk bl, car emer & buff   1.50 .45

Designs: 6r, UNESCO emblem and open book (diamond shape). 8r, UNESCO emblem and inscription, horiz. 14r, Mohammad Reza Shah Pahlavi and inscription in six languages.

    Size: 34x46mm
1350 A223 14r cit, dk bl & brn   3.00 .75
    Nos. 1346-1350 (5)   7.10 2.15

World Congress Against Illiteracy, Tehran, Sept. 8-19.

Mohammad Reza Pahlavi — A225

1965, Sept. 16   **Litho.**   **Perf. 10½**
1351 A225 1r crim, rose red & gray   2.00 .50
1352 A225 2r dk red, rose red & yel   3.00 .75

Reign of Shah, 25th anniv.

Emblem of Persian Medical Society A226

1965, Sept. 21   **Wmk. 349**
1353 A226 5r ultra, dp ultra & gold   .75 .25

14th Medical Congress, Ramsar.

Pres. Jonas of Austria A227

1965, Sept. 30
1354 A227 6r bl, brt bl & gray   2.00 .25

Visit of President Franz Jonas of Austria.

Mithras (Mehr) on Ancient Seal — A228

1965, Oct. 8   **Litho.**   **Wmk. 353**
1355 A228 4r brt grn, gold, brn & blk   2.50 .20

Mehragan celebration during month of Mehr, Sept. 23-Oct. 22. Persian inscription of watermark vertical on No. 1355.

UN Emblem — A229

1965, Oct. 24   **Wmk. 353**   **Perf. 10½**
1356 A229 5r bl, grn & rose car   1.00 .20

20th anniversary of the United Nations.

Symbolic Arches A230

1965, Oct. 26
1357 A230 3r vio bl, blk, yel & red   1.00 .20

Exhibition of Iranian Commodities.

Crown Prince Reza A231

1965, Oct. 31
1358 A231 2r brown & yellow   1.50 .45

Children's Day; Crown Prince Reza's 5th birthday.

Weight Lifters — A232

1965, Nov. 1
1359 A232 10r brt bl, vio & brt pink   1.25 .20

World Weight Lifting Championships, Tehran.

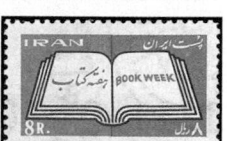

Open Book A233

1965, Dec. 1   **Wmk. 353**   **Perf. 10½**
1360 A233 8r bl, brt pink & blk   1.00 .20

Issued for Book Week.

Shah and King Faisal A234

1965, Dec. 8   **Litho.**
1361 A234 4r olive bister & brn   3.50 .50

Visit of King Faisal of Saudi Arabia.

Scales and Olive Branch A235

1965, Dec. 12
1362 A235 14r multicolored   .90 .20

Human Rights Day (Dec. 10).

Tractor, "Land Reform" A236

Symbols of Reform Bills: 2r, Trees, nationalization of forests. 3r, Factory and gear wheel, sale of shares in government factories. 4r, Wheels, shareholding for factory workers. 5r, Parliament gate, women's suffrage. 6r, Children before blackboard, Army of Education. 7r, Caduceus, Army of Hygiene. 8r, Scales, creation of rural courts. 9r, Two girders, creation of Army of Progress.

1966, Jan. 26　Wmk. 353　Perf. 10½
1363	A236	1r orange & brown	.40	.20
1364	A236	2r dl grn & green	.50	.25
1365	A236	3r silver & gray	.60	.40
1366	A236	4r light & dk vio	.70	.50
1367	A236	5r rose & brown	.90	.55
1368	A236	6r olive & brown	1.25	.65
1369	A236	7r bl & vio blue	1.50	.75
1370	A236	8r ultra & dp ultra	1.75	.85
1371	A236	9r brn org & dk brn	2.00	.90
		Nos. 1363-1371 (9)	9.60	5.05

Parliamentary approval of the Shah's reform plan.

Shah — A237

Ruins of Persepolis A238

**　　　　　Wmk. 353**
1966-71　　Photo.　　Perf. 10½
1372	A237	5d green	.30	.25
1373	A237	10d chestnut	.30	.25
1374	A237	25d dark blue	.30	.25
1375	A237	50d Prussian green	.50	.25
a.		50d blue green ('71)	.50	.30
1376	A237	1r orange	.50	.20
1377	A237	2r violet	.50	.20
1377A	A237	4r cl brn ('68)	6.00	1.00
1378	A237	5r dark brn	1.00	.25
1379	A238	6r deep blue	1.50	.25
1380	A238	8r yellow grn	1.50	.25
a.		8r dull green ('71)	1.00	.25
1381	A238	10r Prus bl	1.50	.20
1382	A238	11r slate grn	1.50	.20
1383	A238	14r purple	2.00	.25
1384	A238	20r brown	17.00	.50
1385	A238	50r cop red	7.50	1.50
1386	A238	100r brt blue	17.00	2.50
1387	A238	200r chnt brn	12.50	4.50
		Nos. 1372-1387 (17)	71.40	12.80

Set, except 4r, issued Feb. 22, 1966.

Student Nurse Taking Oath A239

Narcissus A240

1966, Feb. 24　　　　　　Litho.
1388	A239	5r brt pink & mag	2.00	.50
1389	A239	5r lt bl & brt bl	2.00	.50
a.		Se-tenant pair, #1388-1389	5.00	3.00

Nurses' Day. Nos. 1388-1389 printed in sheets of 50 arranged checkerwise.

1966, Mar. 7
1390	A240	50d ultra, yel & emer	.60	.25
1391	A240	1r lilac, yel & emer	.75	.30

Novrooz, Iranian New Year, Mar. 21.

Oil Derricks in Persian Gulf — A241

1966, Mar. 20　　　　　　Perf. 10½
1392	A241	14r blk, brt bl & brt rose lil	2.50	.50

Formation of six offshore oil companies.

Radio Tower — A242

2r, Radar, horiz. 6r, Emblem & waves. 8r, Compass rose & waves. 10r, Tower & waves.

1966, Apr. 27　　Litho.　　Wmk. 349
1393	A242	2r dark grn	.40	.35
1394	A242	4r ultra & dp org	.50	.35
1395	A242	6r gray ol & plum	.60	.40
1396	A242	8r brt bl & dk bl	.65	.50
1397	A242	10r brn & bister	.80	.55
		Nos. 1393-1397 (5)	2.95	2.15

Inauguration of the radio telecommunication system of the Central Treaty Organization of the Middle East (CENTO).

WHO Headquarters, Geneva — A243

1966, May 3　　　　　　Wmk. 353
1398	A243	10r brt bl, yel & blk	.90	.30

Opening of the WHO Headquarters, Geneva.

World Map — A244

1966, May 14　　　　　　Litho.
1399	A244	6r bl & multi	.70	.30
1400	A244	8r multicolored	.85	.30

Intl. Council of Women, 18th Conf., Tehran, May 1966.

Globe, Map of Iran and Ruins of Persepolis — A245

1966, Sept. 5　Wmk. 353　Perf. 10½
1401	A245	14r multicolored	1.40	.50

International Iranology Congress, Tehran.

Emblem of Iranian Medical Society A246

1966, Sept. 21
1402	A246	4r ultra, grnsh bl & bis	.75	.30

15th Medical Congress, held at Ramsar.

Gate of Parliament, Mt. Demavend and Congress Emblem — A247

8r, Senate building, Mt. Demavend & emblem.

1966, Oct. 2　Wmk. 353　Perf. 10½
1403	A247	6r brick red, ultra & dk grn	.65	.30
1404	A247	8r lt lil, ultra & dk grn	.85	.30

55th Interparliamentary Union Conf., Tehran.

Visit of President Cevdet Sunay of Turkey — A248

1966, Oct. 2　　　　　　Litho.
1405	A248	6r vio & dk brn	.75	.20

Mithras Type of 1964

1966, Oct. 8
**　　　　Size: 30x40mm**
1406	A199	6r olive bister & brn	.75	.30

Mehragan celebration.

Farmers — A249

1966, Oct. 13
1407	A249	5r olive bister & brn	3.00	1.00

Establishment of rural courts of justice.

UN Emblem — A250

1966, Oct. 24　Wmk. 353　Perf. 10½
1408	A250	6r brn org & blk	.60	.30

21st anniversary of United Nations.

Crown Prince Reza — A251

1966, Oct. 31　　　　　　Litho.
1409	A251	1r ultramarine	1.25	.75
1410	A251	2r violet	1.75	.75
a.		Pair, #1409-1410	3.50	2.50

Children's Day; Crown Prince Reza's 6th birthday.

Symbolic Woman's Face — A252

1966, Nov. 6
1411	A252	5r gold, blk & ultra	.60	.20

Founding of the Iranian Women's Org.

Film Strip and Song Bird A253

1966, Nov. 6
1412	A253	4r blk, red lil & vio	.75	.25

First Iranian children's film festival.

"Census Count" — A254

1966, Nov. 11
1413 A254 6r dk brn & gray .60 .20
National census.

Book Cover — A255

1966, Nov. 15
1414 A255 8r tan, brn & ultra .60 .20
Issued to publicize Book Week.

Reza Shah Pahlavi A256

Design: 2r, Reza Shah Pahlavi without kepi.

1966, Nov. 16 **Litho.**
1415 A256 1r slate blue 3.25 1.00
1416 A256 1r brown 3.25 1.00
  a. Pair, #1415-1416 7.75 3.00
1417 A256 2r gray green 3.50 1.00
1418 A256 2r violet blue 3.50 1.00
  a. Pair, #1417-1418 8.00 3.00
  Nos. 1415-1418 (4) 13.50 4.00
Reza Shah Pahlavi (1877-1944), founder of modern Iran.

EROPA Emblem and Map of Persia A257

1966, Dec. 4 **Wmk. 353** **Perf. 10½**
1419 A257 8r dk brn & emerald 1.10 .25
4th General Assembly of the Org. of Public Administrators, EROPA.

Shah Giving Deeds to Farmers A258

1967, Jan. 9 **Wmk. 353** **Perf. 10½**
1420 A258 6r ol bis, yel & brn 2.25 .25
Approval of land reform laws, 5th anniv.

Shah and 9-Star Crescent — A259

Design: 2r, Torch and 9-star crescent.

1967, Jan. 26 **Wmk. 353** **Litho.**
1421 A259 2r multicolored 2.00 .50
1422 A259 6r multicolored 2.75 .50
5th anniv. of Shah's reforms, the "White Revolution."

Ancient Sculpture of Bull — A260

Designs: 5r, Sculptured mythical animals. 8r, Pillar from Persepolis.

1967, Feb. 25 **Wmk. 353** **Perf. 10½**
1423 A260 3r dk brn & ocher 1.25 .35
1424 A260 5r Prus grn, brn & ocher 1.50 .45
1425 A260 8r vio, blk & sil 2.00 .65
  Nos. 1423-1425 (3) 4.75 1.45
Issued to publicize Museum Week.

Planting Tree — A261

1967, Mar. 6
1426 A261 8r brn org & grn .60 .20
Tree Planting Day.

Goldfish — A262

1967, Mar. 11
Size: 26x20mm
1427 A262 1r shown .40 .20
Size: 35x27mm
1428 A262 8r Swallows 1.50 .30
Issued for Novrooz, Iranian New Year.

Microscope, Animals and Emblem — A263

1967, Mar. 11 **Perf. 10½**
1429 A263 5r blk, gray & mag .60 .20
Second Iranian Veterinary Congress.

Pres. Arif of Iraq, Mosque — A264

1967, Mar. 14 **Litho.** **Wmk. 353**
1430 A264 6r brt bl & grn .60 .30
Visit of Pres. Abdul Salam Mohammad Arif.

Fireworks A265

1967, Mar. 17
1431 A265 5r vio bl & multi 3.00 .50
Issued for United Nations Stamp Day.

Map of Iran and Oil Company Emblem — A266

1967, Mar. 20
1432 A266 6r multicolored 2.10 .45
Nationalization of Iranian Oil Industry.

Fencers A267

1967, Mar. 23
1433 A267 5r vio & bister 1.50 .60
Intl. Youth Fencing Championships, Tehran.

Shah and King of Thailand A268

1967, Apr. 23 **Wmk. 353** **Perf. 10½**
1434 A268 6r brn org & dk brn 1.90 .45
Visit of King Bhumibol Adulyadej.

Old and Young Couples A269

1967, Apr. 24 **Litho.**
1435 A269 5r ol bis & vio bl .60 .20
15th anniversary of Social Insurance.

Skier and Iranian Olympic Emblem A270

Designs: 6r, Assyrian soldiers, Olympic rings and tablet inscribed "I.O.C." 8r, Wrestlers and Iranian Olympic emblem.

1967, May 5
1436 A270 3r brown & black .90 .25
1437 A270 6r multicolored 1.10 .45
1438 A270 8r ultra & brown 1.40 .75
  Nos. 1436-1438 (3) 3.40 1.45
65th Intl. Olympic Cong., Tehran, May 2-11.

Lions International — A271

1967, May 11
Size: 41½x30½mm
1439 A271 3r shown 1.00 .50
Size: 36x42mm
1440 A271 7r Emblem, vert. 1.50 .75
50th anniversary of Lions International.

Visit of Pres. Chivu Stoica of Romania — A272

1967, May 13
1441 A272 6r orange & dk bl .60 .20

International Tourist Year Emblem — A273

1967, June 6 **Wmk. 353** **Perf. 10½**
1442 A273 3r brick red & ultra .60 .20

Iranian Pavilion and Ornament A274

1967, June 7 **Litho.**
1443 A274 4r dk brn, red & gold .60 .20
1444 A274 10r red, dk brn & gold 1.00 .30
EXPO '67, Montreal, Apr. 28-Oct. 27.

Stamp of
1870,
No. 1
A275

1967, July 23   Wmk. 353   Perf. 10½
1445 A275 6r multri .60 .30
1446 A275 8r multi .90 .30
Centenary of first Persian postage stamp.

World Map and
School
Children — A276

1967, Sept. 8   Litho.   Wmk. 353
1447 A276 3r ultra & brt & brt bl .50 .25
1448 A276 5r brown & yellow .75 .35
World campaign against illiteracy.

Globe and
Oriental
Musician — A277

1967, Sept. 10   Perf. 10½
1449 A277 14r brn org & dk brn .90 .50
Intl. Conf. on Music Education in Oriental
Countries, Sept. 1967.

Child's Hand
Holding
Adult's — A278

1967, Sept. 14   Litho.   Wmk. 353
1450 A278 8r dk brn & yel 7.50 3.00
Introduction of Children's Villages in Iran.
(Modelled after Austrian SOS Villages for
homeless children).

Winged Wild
Goat — A279

1967, Sept. 19
1451 A279 8r dk brn & lemon .85 .25
Festival of Arts, Persepolis.

UN
Emblem
A280

1967, Oct. 17
1452 A280 6r olive bister & vio bl .40 .20
Issued for United Nations Day.

Shah and
Empress
Farah — A281

1967, Oct. 26   Wmk. 353   Perf. 10½
Various Frames
1453 A281 2r sil, bl & brn 1.25 .40
1454 A281 10r sil, bl & vio 1.50 .60
1455 A281 14r lt bl, bl, gold & vio 3.00 1.50
 Nos. 1453-1455 (3) 5.75 2.50
Coronation of Shah Mohammad Reza Pahlavi and Empress Farah, Oct. 26, 1967.
Nos. 1453-1455 exist in imperf between
pairs, with top sheet margin, and in imperf
between blocks of 4, ungummed. Fake imperf
between pairs, lacking the top sheet margin,
have been manufactured by fraudulently perforating imperf-between blocks.

1967, Oct. 31   Litho.
Design: Crown Prince Reza.
1456 A281 2r silver & violet 1.00 .35
1457 A281 8r sil & red brown 1.50 .45
Children's Day; Crown Prince Reza's 7th
birthday.

Visit of Pres. Georgi
Traikov of
Bulgaria — A283

1967, Nov. 20
1458 A283 10r lilac & dk brn .50 .20

Persian
Boy
Scout
Emblem
A284

1967, Dec. 3   Wmk. 353   Perf. 10½
1459 A284 8r olive & red brn 1.75 .50
Cooperation Week of the Iranian Boy
Scouts, Dec. 5-12.

Hands
Holding
Chain
Link
A285

1967, Dec. 6   Litho.
1460 A285 6r multicolored .60 .20
Issued to publicize Cooperation Year.

Visit of Sheik
Sabah of
Kuwait — A286

1968, Jan. 10   Wmk. 353   Perf. 10½
1461 A286 10r lt bl & slate grn .70 .20

List of Shah's 12 Reform Laws
4 — A287

1968, Jan. 27   Litho.   Wmk. 353
1462 A287 2r sl grn, brn & sal .35 .30
1463 A287 8r vio, dk grn & lt
 grn 1.75 .35
1464 A287 14r brn, pink & lt lil 2.25 .50
 Nos. 1462-1464 (3) 4.35 1.15
"White Revolution of King and People."

Almond
Blossoms
A288

Haji Firooz
(New Year
Singer)
A289

Design: 2r, Tulips.

1968, Mar. 12   Wmk. 353   Perf. 10½
1465 A288 1r multi .50 .25
1466 A288 2r bluish gray & multi .50 .25
1467 A288 2r brt rose lil & multi .50 .25
1468 A289 6r multi 1.50 .45
 Nos. 1465-1468 (4) 3.00 1.20
Issued for Novrooz, Iranian New Year.

Oil Worker and
Derrick
A290

1968, Mar. 20   Litho.
1469 A290 14r grn, blk & org yel 1.75 .50
Oil industry nationalization, 17th anniv.

WHO Emblem
A291

1968, Apr. 7   Wmk. 353   Perf. 10½
1470 A291 14r brn, bl & org .90 .30
WHO, 20th anniversary.

Marlik Chariot,
Ancient
Sculpture
A292

1968, Apr. 13
1471 A292 8r blue, brn & buff .60 .20
Fifth World Congress of Persian Archaeology and Art, Tehran.

Shah
and
King
Hassan
II
A293

1968, Apr. 16
1472 A293 6r bright vio & buff 1.25 .25
Visit of King Hassan II of Morocco.

Human Rights
Flame — A294

Soccer
Player — A295

Design: 14r, Frameline inscription reads,
"International Conference on Human Rights
Tehran 1968"; "Iran" at left.

1968, May 5   Wmk. 353   Perf. 10½
1473 A294 8r red & dk grn .50 .25
1474 A294 14r vio bl & bl 1.00 .30
Intl. Human Rights Year. The 8r commemorates the Iranian Human Rights Committee;
the 14r, the Intl. Conference on Human Rights,
Tehran, 1968.

1968, May 10   Litho.
1475 A295 8r multicolored .50 .30
1476 A295 10r multicolored .85 .30
Asian Soccer Cup Finals, Tehran.

Tehran Oil
Refinery
A296

1968, May 21   Wmk. 353   Perf. 10½
1477 A296 14r brt bl & multi 1.50 .35
Opening of the Tehran Oil Refinery.

Queen Farah as Girl Guide — A297

1968, June 24   Litho.   Perf. 10½
1478 A297 4r brt rose lil & bl green   2.25   .75
1479 A297 6r car & brn   2.75   1.00
Great Camp of Iranian Girl Guides.

Anopheles Mosquito, Congress Emblem — A298

Winged Figure with Banner, and Globe — A299

1968, Sept. 7   Wmk. 353   Perf. 10½
1480 A298 6r brt pur & blk   .75   .35
1481 A298 14r dk grn & mag   1.25   .40
8th Intl. Congress on Tropical Medicine and Malaria, Tehran, Sept. 7-15.

1968, Sept. 8   Litho.
1482 A299 6r lt vio, bis & bl   .60   .25
1483 A299 14r dl yel, sl grn & brn   .90   .30
World campaign against illiteracy.

Oramental Horse and Flower — A300

1968, Sept. 11
1484 A300 14r sl grn, org & yel grn   1.00   .20
2nd Festival of Arts, Shiraz-Persepolis.

INTERPOL Emblem and Globe — A301

1968, Oct. 6   Wmk. 353   Perf. 10½
1485 A301 10r dk brn & bl   .90   .20
37th General Assembly of the Intl. Police Org. (INTERPOL) in Tehran.

Police Emblem on Iran Map in Flag Colors — A302

Peace Dove and UN Emblem — A303

1968, Oct. 7   Litho.
1486 A302 14r multicolored   1.40   .30
Issued for Police Day.

1968, Oct. 24
1487 A303 14r bl & vio bl   1.25   .25
Issued for United Nations Day.

Empress Farah — A304

Designs: 8r, Mohammad Reza Shah Pahlavi. 10fr, Shah, Empress and Crown Prince.

1968, Oct. 26
1488 A304 6r multi   7.50   3.75
1489 A304 8r multi   8.50   5.50
1490 A304 10r multi   11.00   6.75
Nos. 1488-1490 (3)   27.00   16.00
Coronation of Mohammad Reza Shah Pahlavi and Empress Farah, 1st anniv.

Shah's Crown and Bull's Head Capital — A305

UNICEF Emblem and Child's Drawing — A306

1968, Oct. 30
1491 A305 14r ultra, gold, sil & red   .85   .20
Festival of Arts and Culture.

1968, Oct. 31   Litho.
Children's Drawings and UNICEF Emblem: 3r, Boat on lake, house and trees, horiz. 5r, Flowers, horiz.
1492 A306 2r dk brn & multi   .35   .25
1493 A306 3r dk grn & multi   .50   .30
1494 A306 5r multicolored   .70   .40
Nos. 1492-1494 (3)   1.55   .95
Issued for Children's Day.

Labor Union Emblem A307

Factory and Insurance Company Emblem A308

Designs: 8r, Members of Army of Hygiene, and Insurance Company emblem. 10r, Map of Persia, Insurance Company emblem, car, train, ship and plane.

1968, Nov. 6   Wmk. 353   Perf. 10½
1495 A307 4r sil & vio bl   .50   .35
1496 A308 5r multicolored   .65   .35
1497 A308 8r ultra, gray & yel   .85   .35
1498 A308 10r multicolored   .95   .40
Nos. 1495-1498 (4)   2.95   1.45
Issued to publicize Insurance Day.

Human Rights Flame, Man and Woman — A309

1968, Dec. 10   Litho.   Perf. 10½
1499 A309 8r lt bl, vio bl & car   .65   .20
International Human Rights Year.

Symbols of Shah's Reform Plan — A310

Design: Each stamp shows symbols of 3 of the Shah's reforms. No. 1503a shows the 12 symbols in a circle with a medallion in the center picturing 3 heads and a torch.

1969, Jan. 26   Wmk. 353   Perf. 10½
1500 2r ocher, grn & lil   1.75   .50
1501 4r lil, ocher & grn   2.00   .60
1502 6r lil, ocher & grn   2.25   .75
1503 8r lil, ocher & grn   3.00   1.10
a. A310 Block of 4, #1500-1503   10.00   4.50
Nos. 1500-1503 (4)   9.00   2.95
Declaration of the Shah's Reform Plan.

Shah and Crowd A311

1969, Feb. 1   Litho.
1504 A311 6r red, bl & brn   2.50   .35
10,000th day of the reign of the Shah.

European Goldfinch A312

2r, Ring-necked pheasant. 8r, Roses.

1969, Mar. 6   Wmk. 353   Perf. 10½
1505 A312 1r multicolored   .35   .20
1506 A312 2r multicolored   .50   .20
1507 A312 8r multicolored   1.25   .20
Nos. 1505-1507 (3)   2.10   .60
Issued for Novrooz, Iranian New Year.

"Woman Lawyer" Holding Scales of Justice — A313

Workers, ILO and UN Emblems — A314

1969, Apr. 8   Litho.   Perf. 10½
1508 A313 6r blk & brt bl   .60   .20
15th General Assembly of Women Lawyers, Tehran, Apr. 8-14.

1969, Apr. 30   Wmk. 353   Perf. 10½
1509 A314 10r bl & vio bl   .75   .20
ILO, 50th anniversary.

Freestyle Wrestlers and Aryamehr Cup — A315

1969, May 6   Litho.
1510 A315 10r lilac & multi   2.50   .75
Intl. Freestyle Wrestling Championships, 3rd round.

Birds and Flower
A316

1969, June 10 Wmk. 353 Perf. 10½
1511 A316 10r vio bl & multi .85 .20
Issued to publicize Handicrafts Day.

Boy Scout Symbols
A317

1969, July 9 Wmk. 353 Perf. 10½
1512 A317 6r lt bl & multi 1.40 .30
Philia 1969, an outdoor training course for Boy Scout patrol leaders.

Lady Serving Wine, Safavi Miniature, Iran — A318

#1514, Lady on Balcony, Mogul miniature, Pakistan. #1515, Sultan Suleiman Receiving Sheik Abdul Latif, 16th cent. miniature, Turkey.

1969, July 21 Litho.
1513 A318 25r multi 3.00 1.00
1514 A318 25r multi 3.00 1.00
1515 A318 25r multi 3.00 1.00
     Nos. 1513-1515 (3) 9.00 3.00
Signing of the Regional Cooperation for Development Pact by Turkey, Iran and Pakistan, 5th anniv.

Neil A. Armstrong and Col. Edwin E. Aldrin on Moon — A319

1969, July 26
1516 A319 24r bister, bl & brn 9.00 3.50
     See note after Algeria No. 427.

Quotation from Shah's Declaration on Education and Art — A320

1969, Aug. 6 Wmk. 353 Perf. 10½
1517 A320 10r car, cream & emer .85 .20
Anniv. of educational and art reforms.

Offshore Oil Rig in Persian Gulf — A321

1969, Sept. 1 Litho.
1518 A321 8r multicolored 1.50 .35
Marine drillings by the Iran-Italia Oil Co., 10th anniv.

Dancers Forming Flower — A322

Crossed-out Fingerprint, Moon and Rocket — A323

1969, Sept. 6 Wmk. 353 Perf. 10½
1519 A322 6r multicolored .50 .25
1520 A322 8r multicolored .75 .25
3rd Festival of Arts, Shiraz and Persepolis, Aug. 30-Sept. 9.

1969, Sept. 8 Litho.
1521 A323 4r multicolored .50 .20
World campaign against illiteracy.

Persepolis, Simulated Stamp with UPU Emblem, and Shah — A324

1969, Sept. 28
1522 A324 10r lt bl & multi 3.50 1.00
1523 A324 14r multicolored 4.00 1.50
16th Congress of the UPU, Tokyo.

Fair Emblem — A325

14r, like 8r, inscribed "ASIA 69." 20r, Fair emblem, world map and "ASIA 69," horiz.

1969, Oct. 5 Wmk. 353 Perf. 10½
1524 A325 8r rose & multi .65 .30
1525 A325 14r blue & multi .75 .30
1526 A325 20r tan & multi 1.40 .40
     Nos. 1524-1526 (3) 2.80 1.00
2nd Asian Trade Fair, Tehran.

Justice — A326

1969, Oct. 13 Litho.
1527 A326 8r bl grn & dk brn .70 .20
Rural Courts of Justice Day.

UN Emblem A327

1969, Oct. 24
1528 A327 2r lt bl & dp bl .50 .20
25th anniversary of the United Nations.

Emblem and Column Capital, Persepolis — A328

1969, Oct. 28
1529 A328 2r deep blue & multi .70 .25
2nd Festival of Arts and Culture. See Nos. 1577, 1681, 1735.

Child's Drawing and UNICEF Emblem A329

Children's Drawings and UNICEF Emblem: 1r, Boy and birds, vert. 5r, Dinner.

**1969, Oct. 31 Wmk. 353 Perf. 10½
Size: 28x40mm, 40x28mm**
1530 A329 1r lt blue & multi .35 .20
1531 A329 2r lt grn & multi .45 .20
1532 A329 5r lt lil & multi .75 .25
     Nos. 1530-1532 (3) 1.55 .65
Children's Week. See Nos. 1578-1580.

Globe Emblem A330

1969, Nov. 6
1533 A330 8r dk brn & bl .65 .20
Meeting of the Natl. Society of Parents and Educators, Tehran.

Satellite Communications Station — A331

1969, Nov. 19 Litho.
1534 A331 6r blk brn & bis 1.10 .30
1st Iranian Satellite Communications Earth Station, Hamadan.

Mahatma Gandhi (1869-1948) A332

1969, Dec. 29 Wmk. 353 Perf. 10½
1535 A332 14r gray & dk rose brn 9.00 3.00

Globe, Flags and Emblems A333

Design: 6r, Globe and Red Cross, Red Lion and Sun, and Red Crescent Emblems.

1969, Dec. 31
1536 A333 2r red & multi 1.10 .35
1537 A333 6r red & multi 1.60 .45
League of Red Cross Societies, 50th anniv.

Symbols of Reform Laws and Shah A334

1970, Jan. 26 Litho. Wmk. 353
1538 A334 1r bister & multi 1.40 .40
1539 A334 2r multicolored 1.60 .60
Declaration of the Shah's Reform Plan.

Pansies A335

New Year's Table A336

1970, Mar. 6   Wmk. 353   Perf. 10½
1540 A335 1r multicolored .40 .20
1541 A336 8r multicolored 2.10 .30

Issued for the Iranian New Year.

Chemical Plant, Kharg Island, and Iranian Oil Company Emblem — A337

Designs (Iranian Oil Company Emblem and): 2r, Shah's portrait and quotation. 4r, Laying of gas pipe line and tractor. 8r, Tankers at pier of Kharg Island, vert. 10r, Tehran refinery.

1970, Mar. 20   Wmk. 353   Perf. 10½
1542 A337 2r gray & multi 1.60 .50
1543 A337 4r multicolored 1.90 .75
1544 A337 6r lt bl & multi 2.10 .95
1545 A337 8r multicolored 2.60 1.00
1546 A337 10r multicolored 3.25 1.25
    Nos. 1542-1546 (5) 11.45 4.45

Nationalization of the oil industry, 20th anniv.

EXPO '70
Emblem — A338

Radar, Satellite and Congress Emblem — A339

1970, Mar. 27   Litho.
1547 A338 4r brt rose lil & vio bl .50 .20
1548 A338 10r lt bl & pur .85 .20

EXPO '70, Osaka, Japan, Mar. 15-Sept. 13.

1970, Apr. 20   Wmk. 353   Perf. 10½
1549 A339 14r multicolored 1.40 .35

Asia-Australia Telecommunications Congress, Tehran.

UPU Headquarters, Bern — A340

1970, May 10
1550 A340 2r gray, brn & lil rose .60 .25
1551 A340 4r lil, brn & lil rose .85 .25

Inauguration of the new UPU Headquarters, Bern.

Asia Productivity Year Emblem — A341

1970, May 19   Wmk. 353   Perf. 10½
1552 A341 8r gray & multi .65 .20

Asian Productivity Year, 1970.

Bird Bringing Baby A342

1970, June 15   Litho.
1553 A342 8r brn & dk blue .75 .25

Iranian School for Midwives, 50th anniv.

Tomb of Cyrus the Great, Meshed-Morghab in Fars — A343

Designs: 8r, Pillars of Apadana Palace, Persepolis, vert. 10r, Bas-relief from a Mede tomb, Iraq. 14r, Achaemenian officers, bas-relief, Persepolis.

1970, June 21   Photo.   Perf. 13
1554 A343 6r gray, red & vio 2.00 .25
1555 A343 8r pale rose, blk & bl grn 2.25 .50
1556 A343 10r yel, red & brn 2.50 .65
1557 A343 14r bl, blk & red brn 2.75 1.00
    Nos. 1554-1557 (4) 9.50 2.40

2500th anniversary of the founding of the Persian Empire by Cyrus the Great.
See #1561-1571, 1589-1596, 1605-1612.

Seeyo-Se-Pol Bridge, Isfahan — A344

#1559, Saiful Malook Lake, Pakistan, vert. #1560, View of Fethiye, Turkey, vert.

Wmk. 353
1970, July 21   Litho.   Perf. 10½
1558 A344 2r multicolored 1.10 .30
1559 A344 2r multicolored 1.10 .30
1560 A344 2r multicolored 1.10 .30
    Nos. 1558-1560 (3) 3.30 .90

Signing of the Regional Cooperation for Development Pact by Iran, Turkey and Pakistan, 6th anniv.

Queen Buran, Dirhem Coin A345

Wine Goblet with Lion's Head — A346

Designs: No. 1562, Achaemenian eagle amulet. No. 1563, Mithridates I, dirhem coin. No. 1564, Sassanidae art (arch, coin, jugs). No. 1566, Shapur I, dirhem coin. No. 1567, Achaemenian courier. No. 1568, Winged deer. No. 1569, Ardashir I, dirhem coin. No. 1570, Seal of Darius I (chariot, palms, lion). 14r, Achaemenian tapestry.

1970   Wmk. 353   Photo.   Perf. 13
1561 A346 1r gold & multi 1.50 .50
1562 A346 2r gold & multi 1.60 .40
1563 A345 2r gold & multi 1.75 .50
1564 A346 2r lilac & multi 2.00 .50
1565 A345 6r lilac & multi 1.90 .40
1566 A346 6r lilac & multi 2.50 .60
1567 A345 8r lilac & multi 2.50 .60
1568 A346 8r lilac & multi 2.50 .50
1569 A345 8r lilac & multi 2.50 .75
1570 A345 8r lilac & multi 2.50 .75
1571 A345 14r lt bl & multi 3.00 1.10
    Nos. 1561-1571 (11) 24.25 6.60

2500th anniversary of the founding of the Persian Empire by Cyrus the Great.
Issued: 1r, #1563, 1566, 1569, 8/22; #1562, 1565, 1568, 14r, 8/6; others, 9/22.

Candle and Globe — A347

Persian Decoration A348

1970, Sept. 8   Litho.   Perf. 10½
1572 A347 1r lt bl & multi .30 .20
1573 A347 2r pale sal & multi .40 .20

Issued to publicize World Literacy Day.

1970, Sept. 14
1574 A348 6r multi .50 .20

Isfahan Intl. Cong. of Architects, Sept. 1970.

Emblem — A349

UN Emblem, Dove and Scales — A350

1970, Sept. 28   Perf. 10½
1575 A349 2r lt bl & pur .40 .20

Congress of Election Committees of Persian States and Tehran.

1970, Oct. 24   Litho.   Wmk. 353
1576 A350 2r lt bl, mag & dk bl .40 .20

Issued for United Nations Day.

Festival Type of 1969
1970, Oct. 28   Perf. 10½
1577 A328 2r org & multi .50 .20

3rd Festival of Arts and Culture.

UNICEF Type of 1969
Children's Drawings and UNICEF Emblem: 50d, Herdsman and goats. 1r, Family picnic. 2r, Mosque.

1970, Oct. 31
Size: 43½x31mm
1578 A329 50d black & multi .30 .20
1579 A329 1r black & multi .35 .20
1580 A329 2r black & multi .50 .20
    Nos. 1578-1580 (3) 1.15 .60

Issued for Children's Week.

Mohammad Reza Shah Pahlavi A351

1971, Jan. 26   Wmk. 353   Perf. 10½
1581 A351 2r lt bl & multi 3.50 1.00

Publicizing the "White Revolution of King and People" and the 12 reform laws.

Sheldrake — A352

2r, Ruddy shelduck. 8r, Flamingo, vert.

1971, Jan. 30   Litho.
1582 A352 1r multicolored 1.75 .50
1583 A352 2r multicolored 2.00 .75
1584 A352 8r multicolored 3.25 1.00
    Nos. 1582-1584 (3) 7.00 2.25

Intl. Wetland and Waterfowl Conf., Ramsar.

Reza Shah Pahlavi — A353

1971, Feb. 22   Wmk. 353   Perf. 10½
1585 A353 6r multicolored   6.50   2.75

50th anniversary of the Pahlavi dynasty's accession to power.

Rooster A354

2r, Barn swallow and nest. 6r, Hoopoe.

1971, Mar. 6   Photo.   Perf. 13½x13
1586 A354 1r multicolored   1.40   .45
1587 A354 2r multicolored   1.90   .75
1588 A354 6r multicolored   3.25   1.00
    Nos. 1586-1588 (3)   6.55   2.20

Novrooz, Iranian New Year.

Shapur II Hunting — A355

Bull's Head, Persepolis A356

1r, Harpist, mosaic. #1591, Investiture of Ardashir I, bas-relief. 5r Winged lion ornament. 6r, Persian archer, bas-relief. 8r, Royal audience, bas-relief. 10r, Bronze head of Parthian prince.

1971   Litho.   Perf. 10½
1589 A356 1r multicolored   1.60   .45
1590 A355 2r blk & brn org   2.00   .45
1591 A355 2r lil, gldn brn & blk   2.00   .45
1592 A356 4r pur & multi   2.00   .45
1593 A356 5r multicolored   2.25   .55
1594 A356 6r multicolored   2.25   .55
1595 A356 8r lt bl & multi   3.00   .80
1596 A356 10r dp bis, blk & slate   3.00   .90
    Nos. 1589-1596 (8)   18.10   4.60

2500th anniversary of the founding of the Persian Empire by Cyrus the Great.
Issued: 4r, 5r, 6r, 8r, 5/15; others, 6/15.

Prisoners Leaving Jail — A357

1971, May 20   Litho.   Wmk. 353
1597 A357 6r multicolored   2.00   .20
1598 A357 8r multicolored   3.25   .20

Rehabilitation of Prisoners Week.

Religious School, Chaharbagh, Ispahan A358

#1600, Mosque of Selim, Edirne, Turkey. #1601, Badshahi Mosque, Lahore, Pakistan, horiz.

1971, July 21   Litho.   Perf. 10½
1599 A358 2r multicolored   .55   .25
1600 A358 2r multicolored   .55   .25
1601 A358 2r multicolored   .55   .25
    Nos. 1599-1601 (3)   1.65   .75

7th anniversary of Regional Cooperation among Iran, Pakistan and Turkey.

"Fifth Festival of Arts" — A359

1971, Aug. 26   Litho. & Typo.
1602 A359 2r lt & dk grn, red & gold   .90   .30

5th Festival of Arts, Shiraz-Persepolis.

"Fight Against Illiteracy" — A360

1971, Sept. 8   Litho.
1603 A360 2r grn & multi   .65   .30

International Literacy Day, Sept. 8.

Kings Abdullah and Hussein II of Jordan A361

1971, Sept. 11
1604 A361 2r yel grn, blk & red   .75   .35

Hashemite Kingdom of Jordan, 50th anniv.

Shahyad Aryamehr Monument — A362

Designs: 1r, Aryamehr steel mill, near Isfahan. 3r, Senate Building, Tehran. 11r, Shah Abbas Kabir Dam, Zayandeh River.

1971, Sept. 22
1605 A362 1r blue & multi   1.75   .50
1606 A362 2r multicolored   2.00   .50
1607 A362 3r brt pink & multi   2.00   .50
1608 A362 11r org & multi   2.75   1.00
    Nos. 1605-1608 (4)   8.50   2.50

2500th anniversary of the founding of the Persian empire by Cyrus the Great.

Mohammad Reza Shah Pahlavi — A363

Designs: 2r, Riza Shah Pahlavi. 5r, Stone tablet with proclamation of Cyrus the Great, horiz. 10r, Crown of present empire (erroneously inscribed *Le Couronne*).

1971, Oct. 12
1609 A363 1r gold & multi   4.50   2.50
1610 A363 2r gold & multi   4.50   2.50
1611 A363 5r gold & multi   5.50   3.00
1612 A363 10r gold & multi   6.50   3.00
    Nos. 1609-1612 (4)   21.00   11.00

2500th anniversary of the founding of the Persian empire by Cyrus the Great.

Ghatour Railroad Bridge — A364

1971, Oct. 7
1613 A364 2r multicolored   2.25   .85

Iran-Turkey railroad.

Racial Equality Emblem A365

Mohammad Riza Pahlavi — A366

1971, Oct. 24
1614 A365 2r lt blue & multi   .25   .20

Intl. Year Against Racial Discrimination.

Perf. 13½x13
1971, Oct. 26   Photo.   Wmk. 353
Size: 20½x28mm
1615 A366 5d lilac   .20   .20
1616 A366 10d henna brown   .20   .20
1617 A366 50d brt bl grn   .25   .20
1618 A366 1r dp yel grn   .30   .20
1619 A366 2r brown   .30   .20

Size: 27x36½mm
1620 A366 6r slate green   1.10   .20
1621 A366 8r violet blue   1.60   1.10
1622 A366 10r red lilac   1.40   .30
1623 A366 11r blue green   5.00   1.10
1624 A366 14r brt blue   8.50   .50
1625 A366 20r car rose   8.00   .65
1626 A366 50r yellow bis   6.75   1.25
    Nos. 1615-1626 (12)   33.60   6.10

See Nos. 1650-1661B, 1768-1772.

Child's Drawing and Emblem — A367

Designs: No. 1631, Ruins of Persepolis, vert. No. 1632, Warrior, mosaic, vert.

1971, Oct. 31   Litho.   Perf. 10½
1630 A367 2r multicolored   .50   .25
1631 A367 2r multicolored   .50   .25
1632 A367 2r multicolored   .50   .25
    Nos. 1630-1632 (3)   1.50   .75

Children's Week.

UNESCO Emblem and "25" A368

1971, Nov. 4
1633 A368 6r ultra & rose claret   .60   .20

25th anniversary of UNESCO.

Domestic Animals and Emblem A369

1971, Nov. 22
1634 A369 2r gray, blk & car   .50   .30

4th Iranian Veterinarians' Congress.

ILO Emblem, Cog Wheels and Globe A370

1971, Dec. 4
1635 A370 2r black, org & bl   .50   .20

7th ILO Conference for the Asian Region.

UNICEF Emblem, Bird Feeding Young A371

1971, Dec. 16   Perf. 13x13½
1636 A371 2r lt bl, mag & blk   .60   .30

25th anniversary of UNICEF.

Mohammad Reza Shah Pahlavi A372

1972, Jan. 26   Wmk. 353   Perf. 10½
1637   A372   2r lt green & multi   4.50   2.25
  a.   20r Souvenir sheet   16.00   11.50

"White Revolution of King and People" and the 12 reform laws. No. 1637a contains one stamp with simulated perforations.

Pintailed Sandgrouse — A373

#1639, Rock ptarmigan. 2r, Yellow-billed waxbill and red-cheeked cordon-bleu.

1972, Mar. 6   Litho.   Perf. 13x13½
1638   A373   1r lt green & multi   1.10   .50
1639   A373   1r lt blue & multi   1.10   .50
1640   A373   2r yellow & multi   2.25   .60
    Nos. 1638-1640 (3)   4.45   1.60

Iranian New Year.

"Your Heart is your Health" — A374

Film Strip and Winged Antelope A375

1972, Apr. 4   Perf. 10½
1641   A374   10r lemon & multi   2.00   .30

World Health Day; Iranian Society of Cardiology.

1972, Apr. 16   Litho. & Engr.
8r, Film strips and winged antelope.
1642   A375   6r ultra & gold   1.00   .30
1643   A375   8r yellow & multi   1.75   .35

Tehran International Film Festival.

Rose and Bud — A376

1972, May 5   Litho.
1644   A376   1r shown   .40   .30
1645   A376   2r Yellow roses   .70   .35
1646   A376   5r Red rose   .85   .40
    Nos. 1644-1646 (3)   1.95   1.05

See Nos. 1711-1713.

Persian Woman, by Behzad A377

Paintings: No. 1648, Fisherman, by Cevat Dereli (Turkey). No. 1649, Young Man, by Abdur Rehman Chughtai (Pakistan).

1972, July 21   Wmk. 353
1647   A377   5r gray & multi   1.40   .30
1648   A377   5r gray & multi   1.40   .30
1649   A377   5r gray & multi   1.40   .30
    Nos. 1647-1649 (3)   4.20   .90

Regional Cooperation for Development Pact among Iran, Turkey and Pakistan, 8th anniv.

Shah Type of 1971

1972-73   Photo.   Perf. 13½x13
Bister Frame & Crown
Size: 20½x28mm
1650   A366   5d lilac   .20   .20
1651   A366   10d henna brown   .20   .20
1652   A366   50d brt blue grn   .25   .20
1653   A366   1r dp yel grn   .30   .20
  a.   Brn frame & crown ('73)   .55   .20
1654   A366   2r brown   .50   .20

Size: 27x36½mm
1655   A366   6r slate grn   .75   .20
1656   A366   8r violet blue   .75   .20
1657   A366   10r red lilac   1.00   .20
1658   A366   11r blue green   1.40   .80
1659   A366   14r dull blue   5.50   .60
1660   A366   20r car rose   8.50   .50
1661   A366   50r grnsh blue   3.75   1.00
1661A   A366   100r violet ('73)   5.00   2.00
1661B   A366   200r slate ('73)   11.00   3.50
    Nos. 1650-1661B (14)   39.10   10.00

Festival Emblem A378

1972, Aug. 31   Litho.   Perf. 10½
1662   A378   6r emerald, red & blk   1.10   .20
1663   A378   8r brt mag, blk & grn   1.60   .25

6th Festival of Arts, Shiraz-Persepolis, Aug. 31-Sept. 8.

Pens and Emblem A379

"10" and Emblems A380

1972, Sept. 8
1664   A379   1r lt blue & multi   .25   .20
1665   A379   2r yellow & multi   .40   .20

World Literacy Day, Sept. 8.

1972, Sept. 18
1666   A380   1r lilac & multi   .25   .20
1667   A380   2r dull yel & multi   .45   .25

10th Congress of Iranian Dentists' Assoc., Sept. 18-22.

Asian Broadcasting Union Emblem — A381

No. 450 on Cover — A382

1972, Oct. 1
1668   A381   6r lt green & multi   .75   .20
1669   A381   8r gray & multi   1.50   .20

9th General Assembly of Asian Broadcasting Union, Tehran, Oct. 1972.

1972, Oct. 9
1670   A382   10r lt blue & multi   2.25   .25

International Stamp Day.

Chess and Olympic Rings — A383

Olympic Rings and: 2r, Hunter. 3r, Archer. 5r, Equestrians. 6r, Polo. 8r, Wrestling.

1972, Oct. 17
1671   A383   1r brown & multi   3.00   1.50
1672   A383   2r blue & multi   2.50   .50
1673   A383   3r lilac & multi   2.50   .50
1674   A383   5r bl grn & multi   3.00   .75
1675   A383   6r red & multi   4.00   .75
1676   A383   8r yel grn & multi   6.00   1.00
  a.   Souv. sheet of 6, #1671-1676, imperf.   25.00   15.00
    Nos. 1671-1676 (6)   21.00   5.00

20th Olympic Games, Munich, 8/26-9/11.

Communications Symbol, UN Emblem — A384

Children and Flowers — A385

1972, Oct. 24
1677   A384   10r multicolored   2.00   .20

United Nations Day.

1972, Oct. 31   Litho.   Wmk. 353
Children's Drawings and Emblem: No. 1679, Puppet show. 6r, Boys cutting wood, horiz.
1678   A385   2r gray & multi   .35   .20
1679   A385   2r bister & multi   .70   .20
1680   A385   6r pink & multi   1.40   .20
    Nos. 1678-1680 (3)   2.45   .60

Children's Week.

Festival Type of 1969

Design: 10r, Crown, emblems and column capital, Persepolis.

1972, Nov. 11
1681   A328   10r dp blue & multi   6.00   1.00

10th anniv. of White Revolution; Festival of Culture and Art.

Family Planning Emblem A386

1972, Dec. 5
1682   A386   1r blue & multi   .30   .20
1683   A386   2r brt pink & multi   .40   .20

To promote family planning.

Iranian Scout Organization, 20th anniv. — A387

1972, Dec. 9
1684   A387   2r multicolored   .50   .20

Ancient Seal A388

Designs: Various ancient seals.

1973, Jan. 5   Perf. 10½
1685   A388   1r blue, red & brn   .60   .20
1686   A388   1r yellow & multi   .60   .20
1687   A388   1r pink & multi   .60   .20
1688   A388   2r lt brick red & multi   .60   .20
1689   A388   2r dull org & multi   .60   .20
1690   A388   2r olive & multi   .60   .20
    Nos. 1685-1690 (6)   3.60   1.20

Development of writing.

Books and
Book Year
Emblem
A389

Design: 6r, Illuminated page, 10th century,
from Shahnameh, by Firdousi.

1973, Jan. 10
1691 A389 2r black & multi .75 .20
1692 A389 6r yellow & multi 1.10 .20
International Book Year.

"12
Improvements by
the King" — A390

Designs: 2r, 10r, 12 circles symbolizing 12
improvements. 6r, like 1r.

1973, Jan. 26 **Litho.**
Size: 29x43mm
1693 A390 1r gold, ultra, red &
yel .30 .20
1694 A390 2r sil, plum, ol & yel .35 .20
Size: 65x84mm
1695 A390 6r gold, ultra, red &
yel 2.50 1.50
Nos. 1693-1695 (3) 3.15 1.90
Souvenir Sheet
Imperf
1696 A390 10r sil, plum, ol & yel 4.25 2.50
Introduction of the King's socioeconomic
reforms, 10th anniv.

Blue
Surgeonfish
A391

Fish: No. 1698, Gilthead. No. 1699, Banded
sergeant major. No. 1700, Porkfish. No. 1701,
Black-spot snapper.

1973, Mar. 6 **Wmk. 353** *Perf. 10½*
1697 A391 1r multicolored .75 .30
1698 A391 1r multicolored .75 .30
1699 A391 2r multicolored 1.25 .45
1700 A391 2r multicolored 1.25 .45
1701 A391 2r multicolored 1.25 .45
Nos. 1697-1701 (5) 5.25 1.95
Iranian New Year.

WHO
Emblem
A392

1973, Apr. 7 **Litho.** **Wmk. 353**
1702 A392 10r brn, grn & red 1.25 .20
25th anniversary of the WHO.

Soccer — A393

Tracks and
Globe — A394

1973, Apr. 13
1703 A393 14r orange & multi 1.40 .25
15th Asian Youth Football (soccer)
Tournament.

1973, May 10 **Wmk. 353** *Perf. 10½*
1704 A394 10r dk grn, lil & vio bl 2.00 .60
13th International Railroad Conference.

Clay Tablet
with Aryan
Script — A395

Designs: Clay tablets with various scripts.

1973, June 5 *Perf. 10½*
1705 A395 1r shown .50 .20
1706 A395 1r Kharoshthi .50 .20
1707 A395 1r Achaemenian .50 .20
1708 A395 2r Parthian (Mianeh) .90 .20
1709 A395 2r Parthian (Arsacide) .90 .20
1710 A395 2r Gachtak (Dabireh) .90 .20
Nos. 1705-1710 (6) 4.20 1.20
Development of writing.

Flower Type of 1972
1973, June 20
1711 A376 1r Orchid .20 .20
1712 A376 2r Hyacinth .55 .20
1713 A376 6r Columbine 1.25 .20
Nos. 1711-1713 (3) 2.00 .60

Regional
Cooperation for
Development
Pact Among
Iran, Turkey and
Pakistan, 9th
Anniv. — A396

Designs: No. 1714, Head from mausoleum
of King Antiochus I (69-34 B.C.), Turkey. No.
1715, Statue, Shahdad Kerman, Persia, 4000
B.C. No. 1716, Street, Mohenjo-Daro,
Pakistan.

1973, July 21
1714 A396 2r brown & multi .35 .20
1715 A396 2r green & multi .35 .20
1716 A396 2r blue & multi .35 .20
a. Strip of 3, #1714-1716 1.25 .75

Shah, Oil
Pump,
Refinery and
Tanker
A397

1973, Aug. 4
1717 A397 5r blue & black 2.50 .75
Nationalization of oil industry.

Soldiers and
Rising
Sun — A398

1973, Aug. 19 **Litho.** **Wmk. 353**
1718 A398 2r ultra & multi .45 .20
20th anniversary of return of monarchy.

Gymnasts and
Globe — A399

1973, Aug. 23 *Perf. 10½*
1719 A399 2r olive & multi .30 .20
1720 A399 2r violet bl & multi .30 .20
7th Intl. Congress of Physical Education and
Sports for Girls and Women, Tehran, Aug. 19-
25.

Shahyad Monument (later Azadi
Monument), Rainbow and WMO
Emblem — A400

1973, Sept. 4
1721 A400 5r multicolored .75 .20
Intl. meteorological cooperation, centenary.

Festival
Emblem — A401

Wrestlers
A402

1973, Aug. 31
1722 A401 1r silver & multi .30 .20
1723 A401 5r gold & multi .50 .20
7th Festival of Arts, Shiraz-Persepolis.

1973, Sept. 6 **Litho.** **Wmk. 353**
1724 A402 6r lt green & multi 1.50 .50
World Wrestling Championships, Tehran,
Sept. 6-14.

"Literacy as
Light" — A403

1973, Sept. 8
1725 A403 2r multicolored .30 .20
World Literacy Day, Sept. 8.

Audio-Visual
Equipment
A404

1973, Sept. 11
1726 A404 10r yellow & multi 1.00 .35
Tehran Intl. Audio-Visual Exhib., Sept. 11-24.

Warrior
Taming
Winged
Bull
A405

1973, Sept. 16
1727 A405 8r blue gray & multi .75 .20
Intl. Council of Military Sports, 25th anniv.

Abu Rayhan Biruni
(973-1048),
Philosopher and
Mathematician
A406

1973, Sept. 16
1728 A406 10r brown & black 1.50 .50

Soccer Cup — A407

1973, Oct. 2   Wmk. 353   Perf. 10½
1729 A407 2r lilac, blk & buff   .35   .20
Soccer Games for the Crown Prince's Cup.

INTERPOL Emblem — A408

1973, Oct. 7
1730 A408 2r multicolored   .35   .20
50th anniversary of INTERPOL.

Symbolic Arches and Globe A409

1973, Oct. 8
1731 A409 10r orange & multi   .55   .25
World Federation for Mental Health, 25th anniv.

UPU Emblem, Letter, Post Horn — A410

1973, Oct. 9
1732 A410 6r blue & orange   .50   .20
World Post Day, Oct. 9.

Honeycomb A411

1973, Oct. 24
1733 A411 2r lt brown & multi   .30   .20
1734 A411 2r gray olive & multi   .30   .20
UN Volunteer Program, 5th anniv.

Festival Type of 1969
2r, Crown & column capital, Persepolis.
1973, Oct. 26
1735 A328 2r yellow & multi   .40   .20
Festival of Culture and Art.

Turkish Bosporus Bridge, Flag A412

8r, Kemal Ataturk & Reza Shah Pahlavi.

1973, Oct. 29   Litho.   Perf. 10½
1736 A412 2r multicolored   .75   .20
1737 A412 8r multicolored   1.25   .25
50th anniversary of the Turkish Republic.

Mother and Child, Emblem — A413

Children's Drawings and Emblem: No. 1739, Wagon, horiz. No. 1740, House and garden with birds.
1973, Oct. 31
1738 A413 2r multicolored   .30   .20
1739 A413 2r multicolored   .30   .20
1740 A413 2r multicolored   .30   .20
Nos. 1738-1740 (3)   .90   .00
Children's Week.

Cow, Wheat and FAO Emblem A414

1973, Nov. 4
1741 A414 10r multicolored   1.00   .20
10th anniversary of World Food Program.

Proclamation of Cyrus the Great; Red Cross, Lion and Crescent Emblems A415

1973, Nov. 8
1742 A415 6r lt blue & multi   .75   .20
22nd Intl. Red Cross Conf., Tehran, 1972.

"Film Festival" — A416

1973, Nov. 26   Wmk. 353   Perf. 10½
1743 A416 2r black & multi   .35   .20
2nd International Tehran Film Festival.

Globe and Travelers — A417

1973, Nov. 26   Litho.
1744 A417 10r orange & multi   .60   .20
12th annual Congress of Intl. Assoc. of Tour Managers.

Human Rights Flame A418

Score and Emblem — A419

1973, Dec. 10
1745 A418 8r lt blue & multi   .75   .20
Universal Declaration of Human Rights, 25th anniv.

1973, Dec. 21
Design: No. 1747, Score and emblem, diff.
1746 A419 10r yel grn, red & blk   .75   .25
1747 A419 10r lt bl, ultra & red   .75   .25
Dedicated to the art of music.

Forestry, Printing, Education — A420

Designs (Symbols of Reforms): No. 1749, Land reform, sales of shares, women's suffrage. No. 1750, Army of progress, irrigation, women's education. No. 1751, Hygiene, rural courts, housing.

1974, Jan. 26   Litho.   Perf. 10½
1748   1r lt blue & multi   .20   .20
1749   1r lt blue & multi   .20   .20
1750   2r lt blue & multi   .25   .20
1751   2r lt blue & multi   .25   .20
  a. A420   Block of 4, #1748-1751   2.25   1.50
Imperf
Size: 76½x102mm
1752 A420 20r multicolored   5.00   3.00
"White Revolution of King and People" and 12 reform laws.

Pir Amooz Ketabaty Script — A421

Various Scripts: No. 1754, Mo Eghely Ketabaty. No. 1755, Din Dabireh, Avesta script. No. 1756, Pir Amooz, Naskh style. No. 1757, Pir Amooz, decorative style. No. 1758, Decorative and architectural style.

1974, Feb. 14   Wmk. 353   Perf. 10½
1753 A421 1r silver, ocher & multi   .75   .30
1754 A421 1r gold, gray & multi   .75   .30
1755 A421 1r silver, yel & multi   .75   .30
1756 A421 2r gold, gray & multi   .75   .30
1757 A421 2r gold, slate & multi   .75   .30
1758 A421 2r gold, claret & multi   .75   .30
  Nos. 1753-1758 (6)   4.50   1.80
Development of writing.

Fowl, Syringe and Emblem A422

1974, Feb. 23
1759 A422 6r red brown & multi   .60   .20
5th Iranian Veterinary Congress.

Monarch Butterfly A423

Designs: Various butterflies.

1974, Mar. 6   Litho.   Perf. 10½
1760 A423 1r rose lilac & multi   1.00   .35
1761 A423 1r brt rose & multi   1.00   .35
1762 A423 2r lt blue & multi   1.50   .45
1763 A423 2r green & multi   1.50   .45
1764 A423 2r bister & multi   1.50   .45
  Nos. 1760-1764 (5)   6.50   2.05
Novrooz, Iranian New Year.

Jalaludin Mevlana (1207-1273), Poet — A424

1974, Mar. 12   Perf. 13
1765 A424 2r pale violet & multi   .50   .25

Shah Type of 1971
1974   Photo.   Perf. 13½x13
Size: 20½x28mm
1768 A366 50d orange & bl   .45   .20
1769 A366 1r emerald & bl   .50   .20
1770 A366 2r red & blue   .80   .20
Size: 27x36½mm
1771 A366 10r lt green & bl   7.00   .20
1772 A366 20r lilac & bl   4.25   .20
  Nos. 1768-1772 (5)   13.00   1.00

Palace of the Forty Columns,
Hippocrates, Avicenna — A425

1974, Apr. 11   Litho.   Perf. 10½
1773 A425 10r multicolored   .75   .20
9th Medical Congress of the Near and Middle East, Isfahan.

Onager — A426

Athlete and Games
Emblem — A427

1974, Apr. 13
1774 A426 1r shown   .50   .20
1775 A426 2r Great bustard   .75   .20
1776 A426 6r Fawn and deer   1.50   .35
1777 A426 8r Caucasian black
            grouse   2.25   .40
  a.   Strip of 4, #1774-1777   6.00 3.00
      Nos. 1774-1777 (4)   5.00 1.15
Intl. Council for Game and Wildlife
Preservation.

1974, Apr. 30
1778 A427 1r shown   .55   .20
1779 A427 1r Table tennis   .55   .20
1780 A427 2r Boxing   1.00   .20
1781 A427 2r Hurdles   1.00   .20
1782 A427 6r Weight lifting   1.60   .20
1783 A427 8r Basketball   2.50   .20
      Nos. 1778-1783 (6)   7.20 1.20
7th Asian Games, Tehran; first issue.

Lion of Venice — A428

Painting: 8r, Audience with the Doge of
Venice.

1974, May 5
1784 A428 6r multicolored   .55   .25
1785 A428 8r multicolored   1.00   .35
Safeguarding Venice.

Links and
Grain — A429

1974, May 13   Litho.   Perf. 10½
1786 A429 2r multicolored   .30   .20
Cooperation Day.

Military
Plane,
1924
A430

1974, June 1
1787 A430 10r shown   2.00   .40
1788 A430 10r Jet, 1974   2.00   .40
50th anniversary of Iranian Air Force.

Swimmer and
Games Emblem
A431

Bicyclists and
Games Emblem
A432

1974, July 1   Wmk. 353   Perf. 10½
1789 A431 1r shown   .65   .20
1790 A431 1r Tennis, men's
            doubles   .65   .20
1791 A431 2r Wrestling   .80   .20
1792 A431 2r Hockey   .80   .20
1793 A431 4r Volleyball   1.25   .40
1794 A431 10r Tennis, women's
            singles   2.50   .50
      Nos. 1789-1794 (6)   6.65 1.70
7th Asian Games, Tehran; second issue.

1974, Aug. 1
1795 A432 2r shown   .90   .20
1796 A432 2r Soccer   .90   .20
1797 A432 2r Fencing   .90   .20
1798 A432 2r Small-bore rifle
            shooting   .90   .20
      Nos. 1795-1798 (4)   3.60   .80
7th Asian Games, Tehran; third issue.

Ghaskai
Costume — A433

Gold Winged
Lion
Cup — A434

Regional Costumes: No. 1800, Kurdistan,
Kermanshah District. No. 1801, Kurdistan,
Sanandaj District. No. 1802, Mazandaran. No.
1803, Bakhtiari. No. 1804, Torkaman.

1974, July 6
1799 A433 2r lt ultra & multi   1.40   .75
1800 A433 2r buff & multi   1.40   .75
1801 A433 2r green & multi   1.40   .75
1802 A433 2r lt blue & multi   1.40   .75
1803 A433 2r gray & multi   1.40   .75
1804 A433 2r dull grn & multi   1.40   .75
  a.   Block of 6, #1799-1804   8.50 4.50

1974, July 13
1805 A434 2r dull green & multi   .30   .20
Iranian Soccer Cup.

Tabriz Rug, Late
16th
Century — A435

King Carrying Vases,
Bas-relief — A436

Designs: No. 1807, Anatolian rug, 15th century. No. 1808, Kashan rug, Lahore.

1974, July 21
1806 A435 2r brown & multi   .45   .20
1807 A435 2r blue & multi   .45   .20
1808 A435 2r red & multi   .45   .20
  a.   Strip of 3, #1806-1808   1.40   .30
Regional Cooperation for Development Pact
among Iran, Turkey and Pakistan, 10th anniv.

1974, Aug. 15   Litho.   Perf. 10½
1809 A436 2r black & multi   .30   .20
8th Iranian Arts Festival, Shiraz-Persepolis.

Aryamehr Stadium, Tehran — A437

#1811, Games' emblem and inscription.
#1812, Aerial view of games' site.

1974
1810 A437 6r multicolored   1.00   .20
Souvenir Sheets
1811 A437 10r multicolored   3.00 1.50
1812 A437 10r multicolored   3.00 1.50
7th Asian Games, Tehran; fourth and fifth
issues. Nos. 1811-1812 contain one imperf
51x38mm stamp each.
Issued: #1811-1812, 9/1; #1810, 9/16.

"Welfare" — A438

"Education"
A439

1974, Sept. 11
1813 A438 2r orange & multi   .30   .20
1814 A439 2r blue & multi   .30   .20
Welfare and free education.

Map of
Hasanlu, 1000-
800
B.C. — A440

1974, Sept. 24
1815 A440 8r multicolored   .70   .20
2nd Intl. Congress of Architecture, Shiraz-
Persepolis, Sept. 1974.

Achaemenian Mail Cart and UPU
Emblem — A441

Design: 14r, UPU emblem and letters.

1974, Oct. 9   Wmk. 353   Perf. 10½
1816 A441 6r orange, grn & blk   1.00   .40
1817 A441 14r multicolored   1.50   .50
Centenary of Universal Postal Union.

Road Through Farahabad
Park — A442

1974, Oct. 16
1818 A442 1r shown   .30   .20
1819 A442 2r Recreation Bldg.   .35   .20
Inauguration of Farahabad Park, Tehran.

Farahnaz Dam
and Mohammad
Reza Shah
Pahlavi — A443

Designs: 5d, Kharg Island petro-chemical
plant. 10d, Ghatour Railroad Bridge. 1r,
Tehran oil refinery. 2r, Satellite communication
station, Hamadan, and Mt. Alvand. 6r, Aryamehr steel mill, Isfahan. 8r, University of

Tabriz. 10r, Shah Abbas Kabir Dam. 14r, Rudagi (later Vahdat) Music Hall. 20r, Shayad Monument. 50r, Aryamehr Stadium.

1974-75   Photo.   Perf. 13x13½
Size: 28x21mm
Frame & Shah in Brown

1820	A443	5d slate green	.30	.20
1821	A443	10d orange	.30	.20
1822	A443	50d blue green	.30	.20
1823	A443	1r ultra	.30	.20
1824	A443	2r deep lilac	.30	.20

Size: 36x26½mm
Frame & Shah in Dark Blue

1825	A443	6r brown	.50	.30
1826	A443	8r grnsh blue	.50	.40
1827	A443	10r deep lilac	.80	.30
a.		Value in Farsi omitted	30.00	30.00
1828	A443	14r deep green	17.00	.60
1829	A443	20r magenta	3.50	.50
1830	A443	50r violet	4.50	1.40
		Nos. 1820-1830 (11)	28.30	4.50

Issued: 50d, 1r, 2r, 10/16/74; 14r, 11/1974; others 3/6/75.
See Nos. 1831-1841. For overprints see Nos. 2008, 2010.

1975-77
Size: 28x21mm
Frame & Shah in Green

1831	A443	5d orange ('77)	.30	.20
1832	A443	10d rose mag ('77)	.30	.20
1833	A443	50d lilac	.30	.20
1834	A443	1r dark blue	.30	.20
1835	A443	2r brown	.30	.20

Size: 36x26½mm
Frame & Shah in Brown

1836	A443	6r vio bl ('76)	.40	.35
1837	A443	8r deep org ('77)	2.00	.30
1838	A443	10r dp yel grn ('76)	1.75	.30
1839	A443	14r lilac	8.00	.20
1840	A443	20r brt green ('76)	3.50	.40
1841	A443	50r dp blue ('76)	3.00	.90
		Nos. 1831-1841 (11)	20.15	3.35

Festival Emblem, Crown and Column Capital, Persepolis — A444

1974, Oct. 26   Litho.   Perf. 10½
1842 A444 2r multicolored   .40   .20
Festival of Culture and Art.

Destroyer "Palang" and Flag — A445

1974, Nov. 5
1843 A445 10r multicolored   1.50   .35
Navy Day.

Girl at Spinning Wheel A446

Designs: Children's drawings.

1974, Nov. 7   Perf. 10½
1844 A446 2r shown   .35   .20
1845 A446 2r Scarecrow, vert.   .35   .20
1846 A446 2r Picnic   .35   .20
    Nos. 1844-1846 (3)   1.05   .60
Children's Week.

Winged Ibex — A447

1974, Nov. 25   Litho.   Wmk. 353
1847 A447 2r vio, org & blk   .35   .20
Third Tehran International Film Festival.

WPY Emblem A448

1974, Dec. 1
1848 A448 8r orange & multi   .60   .20
World Population Year.

Gold Bee A449

Design: 8r, Gold crown, gift of French people to Empress Farah. Bee pin was gift of the Italian people.

1974, Dec. 20
1849 A449 6r multicolored   .70   .30
1850 A449 8r multicolored   .90   .35
14th wedding anniv. of Shah and Empress Farah.

Angel with Banner — A450

1975, Jan. 7   Litho.   Perf. 10½
1851 A450 2r org & vio bl   .30   .20
International Women's Year.

Symbols of Agriculture, Industry and the Arts — A451

1975, Jan. 26   Wmk. 353
1852 A451 2r multicolored   .30   .20
"White Revolution of King and People."

Tourism Year 75 Emblem — A452

1975, Feb. 17
1853 A452 6r multicolored   .30   .20
South Asia Tourism Year.

"Farabi" in Shape of Musical Instrument or Alembic — A453

1975, Mar. 1
1854 A453 2r brn red & multi   .30   .20
Abu-Nasr al-Farabi (870?-950), physician, musician and philosopher, 1100th birth anniversary.

Ornament, Rug Pattern — A454

1975, Mar. 6
1855 A454 1r shown   .25   .20
1856 A454 1r Blossoms and
           cypress trees   .25   .20
1857 A454 1r Shah Abbasi flower .25   .20
a.   Strip of 3, #1855-1857   1.00   .60
Novrooz, Iranian New Year. Nos. 1855-1857 printed in sheets of 45 stamps + 5 labels.

Nasser Khosrov, Poet, Birth Millenary — A455

Formula — A456

1975, Mar. 11
1858 A455 2r blk, gold & red   .30   .20

1975, May 5   Litho.   Perf. 10½
1859 A456 2r buff & multi   .40   .20
5th Biennial Symposium of Iranian Biochemical Society.

Charioteer, Bas-relief, Persepolis — A457

Design: 2r, Heads of Persian warriors, bas-relief from Persepolis, vert.

1975, May 5
1860 A457 2r lt brn & multi   2.00   .75
1861 A457 10r blue & multi   4.00   1.25
Rotary International, 70th anniversary.

Signal Fire, Persian Castle A458

Design: 8r, Communications satellite.

1975, May 17
1862 A458 6r multicolored   .75   .45
1863 A458 8r lil & multi   .85   .55
7th World Telecommunications Day.

Cooperation Day — A459

1975, May 13
1864 A459 2r multicolored   .30   .20

Jet, Shayad Monument, Statue of Liberty — A460

1975, May 29   Litho.   Wmk. 353
1865 A460 10r org & multi   1.00   .50
Iran Air's 1st flight to New York, May 1975.

Emblem — A461

1975, June 5
1866 A461 6r blue & multi   .45   .20
World Environment Day.

Dam
A462

1975, June 10
1867 A462 10r multicolored   .70 .20
9th Intl. Congress on Irrigation & Drainage.

Resurgence Party
Emblem — A463

Girl Scout
Symbols
A464

1975, July 1   Wmk. 353   Perf. 10½
1868 A463 2r multicolored   .30 .20
Organization of Resurgence Party.

1975, July 16
1869 A464 2r multicolored   .50 .25
2nd Natl Girl Scout Camp, Tehran, July 1976.

Festival of
Tus — A465

1975, July 17
1870 A465 2r gray, lil & vio   .30 .20
Festival of Tus in honor of Firdausi (940-1020), Persian poet born near Tus in Khorasan.

Ceramic
Plate,
Iran
A466

#1872, Camel leather vase, Pakistan, vert.
#1873, Porcelain vase, Turkey, vert.

1975, July 21
1871 A466 2r bister & multi   .35 .20
1872 A466 2r bister & multi   .35 .20
1873 A466 2r bister & multi   .35 .20
    Nos. 1871-1873 (3)   1.05 .60
Regional Cooperation for Development Pact among Iran, Pakistan and Turkey.

Majlis
Gate
A467

1975, Aug. 5   Litho.   Perf. 10½
1874 A467 10r multi   .75 .20
Iranian Constitution, 70th anniversary.

Column with
Stylized
Branches — A468

1975, Aug. 21   Litho.   Wmk. 353
1875 A468 8r red & multi   .60 .20
9th Iranian Arts Festival, Shiraz-Persepolis.

Flags over
Globe — A469

1975, Sept. 8
1876 A469 2r vio bl & multi   .30 .20
Intl. Literacy Symposium, Persepolis.

Stylized
Globe — A470

World Map and Envelope — A471

1975, Sept. 13
1877 A470 2r vio & multi   .30 .20
3rd Tehran International Trade Fair.

1975, Oct. 9   Litho.   Perf. 10½
1878 A471 14r ultra & multi   1.00 .20
World Post Day, Oct. 9.

Crown, Column
Capital,
Persepolis — A472

1975, Oct. 26   Litho.   Wmk. 353
1879 A472 2r ultra & multi   .35 .20
Festival of Culture and Art. See No. 1954.

Face and
Film — A473

1975, Nov. 2
1880 A473 6r multicolored   .65 .20
Tehran Intl. Festival of Children's Films.

"Mother's
Face" — A474

Girl — A475

Design: No. 1882, 2r, "Our House," horiz.
All designs after children's drawings.

1975, Nov. 5
1881 A474 2r multicolored   .35 .20
1882 A475 2r multicolored   .35 .20
1883 A475 2r multicolored   .35 .20
    Nos. 1881-1883 (3)   1.05 .60
Children's Week.

"Film" — A476

1975, Dec. 4   Wmk. 353   Perf. 10½
1884 A476 8r multicolored   .60 .20
4th Tehran International Film Festival.

Symbols of
Reforms — A477

People — A478

1976, Jan. 26   Litho.   Perf. 10½
1885 A477 2r shown   .35 .20
1886 A478 2r shown   .35 .20
1887 A477 2r Five reform symbols   .35 .20
    Nos. 1885-1887 (3)   1.05 .60
"White Revolution of King and People."

Motorcycle
Policeman
A479

Police Helicopter — A480

1976, Feb. 16
1888 A479 2r multicolored   1.25 .75
1889 A480 6r multicolored   2.00 1.00
Highway Police Day.

Soccer
Cup — A481

Candlestick
A482

1976, Feb. 24   Litho.   Wmk. 353
1890 A481 2r org & multi   .30 .20
3rd Intl. Youth Soccer Cup, Shiraz and Ahvaz.

1976, Mar. 6
Designs: No. 1892, Incense burner. No. 1893, Rose water container.

1891 A482 1r olive & multi   .30 .20
1892 A482 1r claret & multi   .30 .20
1893 A482 1r Prus bl & multi   .30 .20
  a.   Strip of 3, #1891-1893   1.00 .60
Novrooz, Iranian New Year.

Telephones, 1876 and 1976 — A483

Eye Within Square — A484

1976, Mar. 10
1894 A483 10r multicolored   .75 .20
Centenary of first telephone call by Alexander Graham Bell, Mar. 10, 1876.

1976, Apr. 29   Litho.   Perf. 10½
1895 A484 6r blk & multi   2.00 .20
  a.   Perf. 12½   9.50 7.50
World Health Day: "Foresight prevents blindness."

Nurse with Infant A485

Young Man Holding Old Man's Hand — A486

1976, May 10
1896 A485 2r shown   .50 .20
1897 A485 2r Engineering apprentices   .50 .20
1898 A486 2r shown   .50 .20
  Nos. 1896-1898 (3)   1.50 .60
Royal Org. of Social Services, 30th anniv.

Map of Iran, Men Linking Hands — A487

Waves and Ear Phones — A488

1976, May 13   Wmk. 353
1899 A487 2r yel & multi   .30 .20
Iranian Cooperatives, 10th anniversary.

1976, May 17
1900 A488 14r gray & multi   .75 .20
World Telecommunications Day.

Emblem, Woman with Flag, Man with Gun — A489

1976, June 6
1901 A489 2r bister & multi   .35 .20
To publicize the power of stability.

Map of Iran, Columns of Persepolis, Nasser Khosrow — A490

1976, July 6   Litho.   Perf. 10½
1902 A490 6r yel & multi   .50 .20
Tourist publicity.

Reza Shah Pahlavi — A491

1976, July 21   Litho.   Wmk. 353
6r, Mohammad Ali Jinnah. 8r, Kemal Ataturk.

1903 A491 2r gray & multi   .50 .20
1904 A491 6r gray & multi   .60 .20
1905 A491 8r gray & multi   .75 .25
  Nos. 1903-1905 (3)   1.85 .65
Regional Cooperation for Development Pact among Iran, Turkey and Pakistan, 12th anniversary.

Torch, Montreal and Iranian Olympic Emblems A492

1976, Aug. 1
1906 A492 14r multicolored   1.00 .25
21st Olympic Games, Montreal, Canada, July 17-Aug. 1.

Reza Shah Pahlavi in Coronation Robe — A493

Festival Emblem — A494

Designs: 2r, Reza Shah and Mohammad Reza Shah Pahlavi, horiz. 14r, 20r, Mohammad Reza Shah Pahlavi in coronation robe and crown.

1976, Aug. 19   Wmk. 353   Perf. 10½
1907 A493 2r lilac & multi   1.00 .50
1908 A493 6r blue & multi   2.00 .75
1909 A493 14r grn & multi   3.00 1.00
  Nos. 1907-1909 (3)   6.00 2.25

Souvenir Sheet
1976, Oct. 8   Imperf.
1910 A493 20r multi   10.00 6.00
50th anniv. of Pahlavi dynasty; 35th anniv. of reign of Mohammad Reza Shah Pahlavi. No. 1910 contains one stamp 43x62mm.

1976, Aug. 29   Litho.   Perf. 10½
1911 A494 10r multicolored   .65 .20
10th Iranian Arts Festival, Shiraz-Persepolis.

Iranian Scout Emblem — A495

1976, Oct. 2   Litho.   Perf. 10½
1912 A495 2r lt bl & multi   .30 .20
10th Asia Pacific Conference, Tehran 1976.

Cancer Radiation Treatment — A496

1976, Oct. 6
1913 A496 2r black & multi   .30 .20
Fight against cancer.

Target, Police Woman Receiving Decoration A497

1976, Oct. 7
1914 A497 2r lt bl & multi   .30 .20
Police Day.

UPU Emblem, No. 1907 on Cover A498

1976, Oct. 9
1915 A498 10r multicolored   1.00 .20
International Post Day.

Crown Prince Riza with Cup — A499

1976, Oct. 10
1916 A499 6r multicolored   .50 .20
Natl. Soc. of Village Culture Houses, anniv.

Riza Shah and Mohammad Reza Shah Pahlavi, Railroad A500

1976, Oct. 15
1917 A500 8r black & multi   4.00 1.50
Railroad Day.

Emblem & Column Capital, Persepolis — A501

Census Emblem — A502

1976, Oct. 26
1918 A501 14r blue & multi   1.00 .30
Festival of Culture and Art.

1976, Oct. 30
1919 A502 2r gray & multi   .30 .20
Natl. Population & Housing Census, 1976.

Flowers and Birds — A503

Mohammad Ali Jinnah — A504

Designs: No. 1921, Flowers and bird. No. 1922, Flowers and butterfly. Designs are from covers of children's books.

1976, Oct. 31   *Perf. 10½*
1920	A503	2r multicolored	.35	.20
1921	A503	2r multicolored	.35	.20
1922	A503	2r multicolored	.35	.20
		Nos. 1920-1922 (3)	1.05	.60

Children's Week.

1976, Dec. 25   Litho.   Wmk. 353
1923	A504	10r multicolored	.60	.20

Jinnah (1876-1948), 1st Governor General of Pakistan.

Development and Agriculture Corps — A505

17-Point Reform Law: 5d, Land reform. 10d, Nationalization of forests. 50d, Sale of shares of state-owned industries. 1r, Profit sharing for factory workers. 2r, Parliament Gate, Woman suffrage. 3r, Education Corps formation. 5r, Health Corps. 8r, Establishment of village courts. 10r, Nationalization of water resources. 12r, Reconstruction program, urban and rural. 14r, Administrative and educational reorganization. 20r, Sale of factory shares. 30r, Commodity pricing. 50r, Free education. 100r, Child care. 200r, Care of the aged (social security).

1977, Jan. 26   Photo.   *Perf. 13x13½*
Frame and Shah's Head in Gold
Size: 28x21mm
1924	A505	5d rose & green	.20	.20
1925	A505	10d lt grn & brn	.20	.20
1926	A505	50d yel & vio bl	.20	.20
1927	A505	1r lil & vio bl	.20	.20
1928	A505	2r org & green	.20	.20
1929	A505	3r lt bl & red	.20	.20
1930	A505	5r bl grn & mag	.40	.20

Size: 37x27mm
1931	A505	6r brn, mar & black	.55	.20
1932	A505	8r ultra, mar & blk	.55	.20
1933	A505	10r lt grn, bl & black	1.50	.20
1934	A505	12r vio, mar & black	1.10	.20
1935	A505	14r org, red & blk	1.60	.75
1936	A505	20r gray, ocher & black	3.25	.50
1937	A505	30r bl, grn & blk	3.25	.65
1938	A505	50r yel, brn & blk	5.50	.60
1939	A505	100r multi	5.00	1.25
1940	A505	200r multi	11.00	2.50
		Nos. 1924-1940 (17)	35.10	8.45

"White Revolution of King and People" reform laws.

Man in Guilan Costume — A506

Electronic Tree — A507

2r, Woman in Guilan costume (Northern Iran).

1977, Mar. 6   Wmk. 353   *Perf. 13*
1941	A506	1r multicolored	.30	.20
1942	A506	2r multicolored	.35	.20

Novrooz, Iranian New Year.

1977, May 17   Photo.   *Perf. 13*
1943	A507	20r multicolored	1.25	.35

World Telecommunications Day.

Reza Shah Dam A508

1977, May 31   *Perf. 13x13½*
1944	A508	5r multicolored	.40	.20

Inauguration of Reza Shah Dam.

Olympic Rings A509

1977, June 23   Litho.   *Perf. 10½*
1945	A509	14r multicolored	.90	.20

Olympic Day.

Terra-cotta Jug, Iran A510

#1947, Terra-cotta bullock cart, Pakistan. #1948, Terra-cotta pot with human face, Turkey.

Perf. 13x13½
1977, July 21   Photo.   Wmk. 353
1946	A510	5r violet & multi	.40	.20
1947	A510	5r emer & multi	.40	.20
1948	A510	5r green & multi	.40	.20
		Nos. 1946-1948 (3)	1.20	.60

Regional Cooperation for Development Pact among Iran, Turkey and Pakistan, 13th anniv.

Flowers with Scout Emblems, Map of Asia — A511

1977, Aug. 5   Litho.   *Perf. 13*
1949	A511	10r multicolored	1.00	.25

2nd Asia-Pacific Jamboree, Nishapur.

Map of Eastern Hemisphere with Iran — A512

Tree of Learning, Symbolic Letters — A513

1977, Sept. 20   Photo.   Wmk. 353
1950	A512	3r multicolored	.35	.20

9th Asian Electronics Conference, Tehran.

1977, Oct. 8   Wmk. 353   *Perf. 13*
1951	A513	10r multicolored	.60	.20

Honoring the teachers.

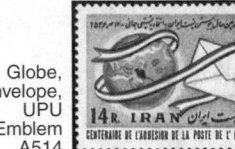

Globe, Envelope, UPU Emblem A514

1977, Oct. 9   Photo.
1952	A514	14r multicolored	1.00	.20

Iran's admission to the UPU, cent.

Folk Art — A515

1977, Oct. 16
1953	A515	5r multicolored	.40	.20

Festival of Folk Art.

Festival Type of 1975

Design: 20r, similar to 1975 issue, but with small crown within star.

1977, Oct. 26   *Perf. 10½*
1954	A472	20r bis, grn, car & blk	1.25	.20

Festival of Culture and Art.

Joust — A516

Emblem — A517

#1956, Rapunzel. #1957, Little princess with attendants.

1977, Oct. 31   Photo.
1955	A516	3r multicolored	.30	.20
1956	A516	3r multicolored	.30	.20
1957	A516	3r multicolored	.30	.20
a.		Strip of 3, #1955-1957	1.25	.60

Children's Week.

1977, Nov. 7   Wmk. 353   *Perf. 13*
1958	A517	5r multicolored	.40	.20

First Regional Seminar on the Education and Welfare of the Deaf.

Mohammad Iqbal A518

African Sculpture A519

1977, Nov. 9   Litho.   *Perf. 10½*
1959	A518	5r multicolored	.45	.20

Iqbal (1877-1938) of Pakistan, poet and philosopher.

1977, Dec. 14
1960	A519	20r multicolored	3.25	.55

African art.

Shah Mosque, Isfahan — A520

Designs: 1r, Ruins, Persepolis. 2r, Khajou Bridge, Isfahan. 5r, Imam Riza Shrine, Meshed. 9r, Warrior frieze, Persepolis. 10r, Djameh Mosque, Isfahan. 20r, King on throne, bas-relief. 25r, Sheik Lotfollah Mosque. 30r, Ruins, Persepolis, diff. view. 50r, Ali Ghapou Palace, Isfahan. 100r, Bas-relief, Tagh Bastan. 200r, Horseman and prisoners, bas-relief, Naqsh Rostam.

1978-79   Photo.   *Perf. 13x13½*
"Iran" and Head in Gold
Size: 28x21mm
1961	A520	1r deep brn	.30	.25
1962	A520	2r emerald	.30	.25
1963	A520	3r magenta	.50	.25
1964	A520	5r Prus blue	.70	.25

Size: 36x27mm
1965	A520	9r sepia ('79)	1.75	.75
1966	A520	10r brt bl ('79)	5.75	.85
1967	A520	20r rose	1.75	.55
1968	A520	25r ultra ('79)	25.00	9.75
1969	A520	30r magenta	2.75	.55
1970	A520	50r deep yel grn ('79)	4.50	3.50
1971	A520	100r dk bl ('79)	14.00	9.75
1972	A520	200r vio bl ('79)	19.00	19.00
		Nos. 1961-1972 (12)	76.30	45.70

For overprints see Nos. 2009, 2011-2018.

Persian Rug — A521

Designs: Persian rugs.

1978, Feb. 11   Litho.   *Perf. 10½*
1973	A521	3r sil & multi	.35	.25
1974	A521	5r sil & multi	.45	.25
1975	A521	10r sil & multi	.75	.35
		Nos. 1973-1975 (3)	1.55	.85

Opening of Carpet Museum.

Mazanderan Man — A522

Design: 5r, Mazanderan woman.

1978, Mar. 6   *Perf. 13*
1976 A522 3r yel & multi   .35 .20
1977 A522 5r lt bl & multi   .55 .20

Novrooz, Iranian New Year.

Mohammad Reza Shah Pahlavi — A523

1978, Jan. 26
1978 A523 20r multicolored   4.00 1.25

Shah's White Revolution, 15th anniv.

Reza Shah Pahlavi and Crown Prince Inspecting Girls' School — A524

Designs (Reza Shah Pahlavi and Crown Prince Mohammad Reza Shah Pahlavi): 5r, Inauguration of Trans-Iranian railroad. 10r, At stairs of Palace, Persepolis. 14r, Shah handing Crown Prince (later Shah) officer's diploma at Tehran Officers' Academy.

1978, Mar. 15
1979 A524 3r multicolored   .50 .25
1980 A524 5r multicolored   .75 .35
1981 A524 10r multicolored   1.25 .40
1982 A524 14r multicolored   1.75 .70
   Nos. 1979-1982 (4)   4.25 1.70

Reza Shah Pahlavi (1877-1944), founder of Pahlavi dynasty.

Communications Satellite over Map of Iran — A525

1978, Apr. 19   Litho.   *Perf. 10½*
1983 A525 20r multicolored   1.25 .30

ITU, 7th meeting, Tehran; 10th anniv. of Iran's membership.

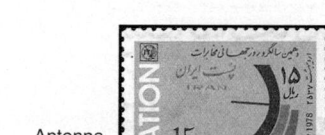

Antenna, ITU Emblem A526

1978, May 17   Litho.   *Perf. 10½*
1984 A526 15r multicolored   .90 .30

10th World Telecommunications Day.

Welfare Legion Emblem — A527

1978, June 13   Photo.   *Perf. 13x13½*
1985 A527 10r multicolored   .60 .30

Universal Welfare Legion, 10th anniversary.

Pink Roses, Iran — A528

Designs: 10r, Yellow rose, Turkey. 15r, Red roses, Pakistan.

      Perf. 13½x13
1978, July 21   Wmk. 353
1986 A528 5r multicolored   .60 .25
1987 A528 10r multicolored   .90 .25
1988 A528 15r multicolored   1.00 .40
   Nos. 1986-1988 (3)   2.50 .90

Regional Cooperation for Development Pact among Iran, Turkey and Pakistan, 14th anniversary.

Rhazes, Pharmaceutical Tools — A529

1978, Aug. 26   Wmk. 353   *Perf. 13*
1989 A529 5r multicolored   .60 .25

Pharmacists' Day. Rhazes (850-923), chief physician of Great Hospital in Baghdad.

Girl Scouts, Aryamehr Arch A530

1978, Sept. 2   *Perf. 10½*
1990 A530 5r multicolored   1.00 .35

23rd World Girl Scouts Conference, Tehran, Sept. 1978.

Reza Shah Pahlavi A531

Design: 5r, Mohammad Reza Shah Pahlavi.

1978, Sept. 11   Litho.   *Perf. 10½*
1991 A531 3r multicolored   1.50 .40
1992 A531 5r multicolored   1.75 .50

Bank Melli Iran, 50th anniversary.

Girl and Bird A532

1978, Oct. 31   Photo.   *Perf. 13*
1993 A532 3r multicolored   .75 .30

Children's Week.

Envelope, Map of Iran, UPU Emblem A533

1978, Nov. 22   *Perf. 13x13½*
1994 A533 14r gold & multi   1.50 .40

World Post Day, Oct. 22.

Communications Symbols and Classroom — A534

1978, Nov. 22   *Perf. 10½*
1995 A534 10r multicolored   1.25 .40

Faculty of Communications, 50th anniv.

Human Rights Flame A535

1978, Dec. 17   Photo.   *Perf. 13*
1996 A535 20r bl, blk & gold   3.50 .50

Universal Declaration of Human Rights, 30th anniv.

Kurdistani Man — A536

Design: 5r, Kurdistani woman.

1979, Mar. 17
1997 A536 3r multicolored   .90 .25
1998 A536 5r multicolored   1.25 .25

Rose — A537

1979, Mar. 17
1999 A537 2r multicolored   .25 .20

Novrooz, Iranian New Year.
See No. 2310i.

Islamic Republic

Demonstrators — A538

Islamic revolution: 3r, Demonstrators. 5r, Hands holding rose, gun and torch breaking

through newspaper. 20r, Hands breaking prison bars, and dove, vert.

1979, Apr. 20   *Perf. 10½*
2000 A538 3r multicolored   2.00 .35
2001 A538 5r multicolored   1.40 .35
2002 A538 10r multicolored   1.40 .65
2003 A538 20r multicolored   3.00 .75
   Nos. 2000-2003 (4)   7.80 2.10

Nos. 1837-1838, 1966, 1970 and Type A520 Overprinted

Designs: 15r, Warriors on horseback, bas-relief, Naqsh-Rostam. 19r, Chehel Sotoon Palace, Isfahan.

1979   Wmk. 353   *Perf. 13x13½*
2008 A443 8r org & brown   3.00 1.00
2009 A520 9r gold & dp brn   1.50 1.50
2010 A443 10r dp yel grn   50.00 10.00
2011 A520 10r gold & brt bl   1.75 1.00
2012 A520 15r gold & red lil   1.75 1.00
2013 A520 19r gold & slate grn   1.75 1.00
2016 A520 50r gold & dp yel grn   5.00 2.00
2017 A520 100r gold & vio bl   10.00 4.00
2018 A520 200r gold & vio bl   12.50 8.50
   Nos. 2008-2018 (9)   87.25 30.00

Overprint means Islamic revolution. Forgeries of No. 2010 exist.

Symbolic Tulip — A539

1979, June 5   Photo.   *Perf. 13*
2019 A539 5r multicolored   1.50 .40

Potters, by Kamalel Molk A540

No. 2021, at the Well, by Allah Baksh, Pakistan. No. 2022, Threshing, by Namik Ismail, Turkey.

1979, July 21   Litho.   *Perf. 10½*
2020 A540 5r multicolored   3.75 .35
2021 A540 5r multicolored   2.75 .35
2022 A540 5r multicolored   2.75 .35
   Nos. 2020-2022 (3)   9.25 1.05

Regional Cooperation for Development Pact among Iran, Turkey and Pakistan, 15th anniv.

"TELECOM 79" — A541

1979, Sept. 20   *Perf. 10½*
2023 A541 20r multicolored   12.50 .30

3rd World Telecommunications Exhibition, Geneva, Sept. 20-26.

Greeting the Sunrise — A542

Persian Rug Design — A543

Children's Drawings and IYC Emblem: 2r, Tulip over wounded man. 2r, Children with banners.

1979, Sept. 23
2024	A542	2r multicolored	2.00	.50
2025	A542	3r multicolored	2.00	.50
2026	A542	5r multicolored	3.50	.50
		Nos. 2024-2026 (3)	7.50	1.50

International Year of the Child.

1979-80   Photo.   Perf. 13½x13
2027	A543	50d brn & pale sal	.20	.20
2028	A543	1r dark & lt bl	.20	.20
2029	A543	2r red & yellow	.20	.20
2030	A543	3r dk bl & lt lil	.20	.20
2031	A543	5r slate grn & lt grn	.20	.20
2032	A543	10r blk & salmon pink ('80)	.30	.20
2033	A543	20r brn & gray ('80)	.55	.20

Size: 27x37½mm
2034	A543	50r dp violet & gray ('80)	1.40	.50
2035	A543	100r blk & slate grn ('80)	5.00	1.40
2036	A543	200r dk bl & cr ('80)	5.50	2.75
		Nos. 2027-2036 (10)	13.75	6.05

Globe in Envelope — A544

1979, Oct. 9   Litho.   Perf. 10½
2041	A544	10r multicolored	3.00	.40

World Post Day.

Ghyath-al-din Kashani, Astrolabe A545

1979, Dec. 5   Litho.   Perf. 10½
2042	A545	5r ocher & blk	1.50	.40

Kashani, mathematician, 550th death anniv.

Ka'aba, Flame and Mosque A546

Hegira (Pilgrimage Year): 5r, Koran open over globe, vert. 10r, Salman Farsi (follower of Mohammad), map of Iran.

1980, Jan. 19
2043	A546	3r multicolored	.20	.20
2044	A546	5r multicolored	.25	.20
2045	A546	10r multicolored	.55	.25
		Nos. 2043-2045 (3)	1.00	.65

Reissued in May-June, 1980, with shiny gum and watermark position changed.

People, Map and Flag of Iran — A547

Islamic Revolution, 1st Anniversary: 3r, Blood dripping on broken sword. 5r, Window open on sun of Islam, people.

1980, Feb. 11
2046	A547	1r multicolored	.20	.20
2047	A547	3r multicolored	.35	.25
2048	A547	5r multicolored	.65	.30
		Nos. 2046-2048 (3)	1.20	.75

For similar stamps measuring 24x36mm see Nos. 2310a, 2310b, 2310d.

Dehkhoda, Dictionary Editor, Birth Cent. — A548

1980, Feb. 26
2049	A548	10r multicolored	.30	.20

East Azerbaijani Woman A549

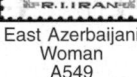
Mohammad Mossadegh A550

Novrooz (Iranian New Year): 5r, East Azerbaijani man.

1980, Mar. 5
2050	A549	3r multicolored	.20	.20
2051	A549	5r multicolored	.25	.20

1980, Mar. 19   Photo.   Perf. 13x13½
2052	A550	20r multi	.60	.20

Oil industry nationalization, 29th anniv.; Mohammad Mossadegh, prime minister who initiated nationalization, birth cent.

Professor Morteza Motahhari, 1st Death Anniversary — A551

1980, May 1   Litho.   Perf. 10½
2053	A551	10r black & red	.50	.20

World Telecommunications Day — A552

1980, May 17   Photo.   Perf. 13x13½
2054	A552	20r multicolored	.50	.20

Interior of Mosque A553

1980, June 11   Litho.   Perf. 10½
2055	A553	50d shown	.20	.20
2056	A553	1r Demonstration	.20	.20
2057	A553	3r Avicenna, al-Biruni, Farabi	.40	.20
2058	A553	5r Hegira emblem	.30	.20
		Nos. 2055-2058 (4)	1.10	.80

Hegira, 1400th anniv.

Ali Sharyati, Educator A554

1980, June 15   Photo.   Perf. 13x13½
2059	A554	5r multicolored	.30	.20

Holy Ka'aba and Hand Waving Banner — A555

1980, June 28
2060	A555	5r multicolored	.30	.20

Hazrat Mehdi, 12th Imam's birth anniv.

A556

OPEC Emblem — A557

1980, Sept. 10   Perf. 13½x13
2061	A556	5r multicolored	.30	.20

Ayatollah Seyed Mahmood Talegani, death anniv. Compare with design A829.

1980, Sept. 15
2062	A557	5r shown	.30	.20
2063	A557	10r Men holding OPEC emblem	.60	.20

20th anniversary of OPEC.

"Let Us Liberate Jerusalem" A558

Tulip and Fayziyye Seminary, Qum A559

1980, Oct. 9   Perf. 13x13½
2064	A558	5r multicolored	.25	.20
2065	A558	20r multicolored	.85	.20

1981, Feb. 11   Perf. 13
2066	A559	3r shown	.20	.20
2067	A559	5r Blood spilling on tulip	.20	.20
2068	A559	20r Tulip, Republic emblem	.50	.20
		Nos. 2066-2068 (3)	.90	.60

Islamic Revolution, 2nd anniversary.
See Nos. 2310c, 2310e, 2310j, watermark 381 (3r, unserifed "R" in denomination. 5r, bright yellow background; 20r, light blue background behind flower.)

Lorestani Man — A560

Telecommunications Day — A561

Novrooz (Iranian New Year): 10r, Lorestani woman.

1981, Mar. 11
2069	A560	5r multicolored	.20	.20
2070	A560	10r multicolored	.30	.20

Perf. 13½x13
1981, May 17   Photo.   Wmk. 353
2071	A561	5r dk grn & org	.20	.20

Ayatollah Kashani Birth Centenary — A562

Adult Education A563

Perf. 13x13½
1981, July 21   Wmk. 381
2072	A562	15r dk grn & dl pur	.40	.20

Perf. 13x13½, 13½x13 (5r, 10r, 200r)
1981, Aug.

50d, Citizens bearing arms. 2r, Irrigation. 3r, Friday prayer service. 5r, Paasdaar emblem and members. 10r, Koran text. 20r, Hejaab (women's veil). 50r, Industrial development. 100r, Religious ceremony, Mecca. 200r, Mosque interior. 5r, 10r, 200r vert.

2073	A563	50d blk & dp bister	.20	.20
2074	A563	1r dl pur & grn	.20	.20
2075	A563	2r brn & grnsh bl	.20	.20

Size: 38x28mm, 28x38mm
2076	A563	3r brt yel grn & black	.20	.20
2077	A563	5r dk bl & brn org	.20	.20

2078	A563	10r dk bl & grnsh blue	.25	.20
2079	A563	20r red & black	.60	.20
2080	A563	50r lilac & black	1.40	.30
2081	A563	100r org brn & blk	3.00	.60
2082	A563	200r blk & bl grn	5.75	1.25
		Nos. 2073-2082 (10)	12.00	3.55

Islamic Iranian Army A564

1981, Sept. 21   Photo.   Perf. 13
2087 A564 5r multicolored   .65   .30

World Post Day and 12th UPU Day — A565

Perf. 13x13½
1981, Oct. 9   Wmk. 381
2088 A565 20r black & blue   .85   .45

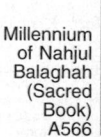

Millennium of Nahjul Balaghah (Sacred Book) A566

1981, Oct. 17   Perf. 13
2089 A566 25r multicolored   .60   .20

Martyrs' Memorial — A567

1981, Nov. 9   Photo.   Perf. 13
2090 A567 3r June 28, 1981 victims   .20   .20
2091 A567 5r Pres. Rajai, Prime Minister Bahonar   .20   .20
2092 A567 10r Gen. Chamran   .25   .20
    Nos. 2090-2092 (3)   .65   .60

Ayatollah M. H. Tabatabaee, Scholar — A568

1981, Dec. 25   Photo.   Perf. 13
2093 A568 5r multicolored   .20   .20

Literacy Campaign A569

Islamic Revolution, 3rd Anniv. — A570

1982, Jan. 20   Photo.   Perf. 13x13½
2094 A569 5r blue & gold   .20   .20

1982, Feb. 11   Wmk. 381   Perf. 13
2095 A570 5r Map   .20   .20
2096 A570 10r Tulip   .25   .20
2097 A570 20r Globe   .50   .20
    a.   Strip of 3, #2095-2097   .90   .40

See Nos. 2310f, 2310g, 2310k (5r, orange background, Arabian "5" 6mm above black panel. 10r, dark green background, gray dove with thick black lines around it. 20r, pink background, bright blue globe, faint latitude and longitude lines.)

Unity Week — A571   Khuzestan Man — A573

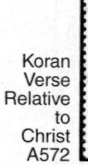

Koran Verse Relative to Christ A572

1982, Feb. 20   Photo.   Perf. 13
2098 A571 25r multicolored   1.00   .20

1982, Mar. 11   Photo.   Wmk. 381
2099 A572 20r multicolored   .50   .20

1982, Mar. 13
2100 A573 3r shown   .20   .20
2101 A573 5r Khuzestan woman   .20   .20
    a.   Pair, #2100-2101   .20   .20

Novrooz (New Year).

3rd Anniv. of Islamic Revolution A574

1982, Apr. 1
2102 A574 30r multicolored   .90   .25

Seyed Mohammad Bagher Sadr — A575

1982, Apr. 8   Photo.   Perf. 13½x13
2103 A575 50r multicolored   1.00   .40

Martyrs of Altar (Ayatollahs Madani and Dastgeyb) — A576

1982, Apr. 21   Perf. 13
2104 A576 50r multicolored   1.00   .40

A577   A578

1982, May 1   Photo.   Perf. 13½x13
2105 A577 100r multi   2.25   .80
Intl. Workers' Solidarity Day.

1982, May 17   Perf. 13x13½
2106 A578 100r multi   2.25   .80
14th World Telecommunications Day.

Mab'as Day (Mohammad's Appointment as Prophet) — A579

1963 Islamic Rising, 19th Anniv. — A580

1982, May 21   Perf. 13½x13
2107 A579 32r multicolored   .90   .30

1982, June 5   Wmk. 381   Perf. 13
2108 A580 28r multicolored   .60   .30

Lt. Islambuli, Assassin of Anwar Sadat — A581   1st Death Anniv. of Ayatollah Beheshti — A582

1982, June 17
2109 A581 2r multicolored   .40   .20

1982, June 28
2110 A582 10r multicolored   .40   .20
    a.   Missing dot in Arabic numeral   1.00   1.00

Iran-Iraq War A583

1982, July 7   Perf. 13x13½
2111 A583 5r multicolored   .20   .20

Universal Jerusalem Day A584

1982, July 15   Perf. 13
2112 A584 1r Dome of the Rock   .20   .20

Pilgrimage to Mecca — A585

13th World UPU Day — A586

1982, Sept. 28
2113 A585 10r multicolored   .30   .20

1982, Oct. 9   Perf. 13½x13
2114 A586 30r multicolored   .75   .25

4th Anniv. of Islamic Revolution — A587

1983, Feb. 11   Photo.   Perf. 13
2115 A587 30r multicolored   .75   .25

See No. 2310n for stamp with orange or orange red crowd and thick sharp lettering in black panels.

4th Anniv. of Islamic Republic — A588

1983, Apr. 1   Photo.   Perf. 13
2116 A588 10r multicolored   .30   .20

Teachers'
Day — A589

World Com-
munications
Year — A590

Perf. 13½x13

1983, May 1 **Wmk. 381**
2117 A589 5r multicolored .25 .20

1983, May 17
2118 A590 20r multicolored .60 .20

First Session of Islamic Consultative
Assembly — A591

1983, May 28 **Perf. 13**
2119 A591 5r multicolored .20 .20

20th Anniv. of
Islamic
Movement — A592

1983, June 5 **Photo.** **Perf. 13**
2120 A592 10r multicolored .30 .20

Iraqi MiG
Bombing
Now Rooz
Oil Well
A593

1983, June 11 **Perf. 13x13½**
2121 A593 5r multicolored .50 .20
Ecology week.

Ayatollah Mohammad
Sadooghi — A594

1983, July 2 **Photo.** **Perf. 13½**
2122 A594 20r blk & dl red .60 .20

Universal Day of
Jerusalem — A595

Government Week — A596

1983, July 8
2123 A595 5r Dome of the Rock .20 .20

1983, Aug. 30 **Wmk. 381** **Perf. 13**
2124 A596 3r multicolored .20 .20
Death of Pres. Rajai and Prime Minister
Bahonar, 2nd anniv.

Iran-Iraq War, 3rd
Anniv. — A597

1983, Sept. 28 **Photo.** **Perf. 13**
2125 A597 5r rose red & blk .20 .20

Ayatollah Ashrafi
Esphahani,
Martyr of
Altar — A598

Mirza Kuchik
Khan — A599

1983, Oct. 15 **Photo.** **Perf. 13**
2126 A598 5r multicolored .20 .20

1983-84 **Photo.** **Perf. 13**
Religious and Political Figures: 1r, Sheikh
Mohammad Khiabani. 3r, Seyd Majtaba
Navab Safavi. 5r, Seyd Jamal-ed-Din
Assadabadi. 10r, Seyd Hassan Modaress.
20r, Sheikh Fazel Assad Nouri. 30r, Mirza
Mohammad Hossein Naiyni. 50r, Sheikh
Mohammad Hossein Kashef. 100r, Seyd Has-
san Shirazi. 200r, Mirza Reza Kermani.

2128	A599	1r black & pink	.20	.20
2129	A599	2r org & black	.20	.20
2130	A599	3r brt bl & blk	.20	.20
2131	A599	5r rose red & blk	.20	.20
2132	A599	10r yel grn & blk	.30	.20
2133	A599	20r lilac & blk	.60	.20
2134	A599	30r gldn brn & blk	.90	.30
2135	A599	50r blk & lt bl	1.50	.50
2136	A599	100r blk & org	3.00	1.00
2137	A599	200r blk & bluish grn	6.00	2.00
		Nos. 2128-2137 (10)	13.10	5.00

Issue dates: 1r, 50r-200r, Feb. 1984.
Others, Oct. 23, 1983.

UPU Day
A600

1983, Oct. 9 **Photo.** **Wmk. 381**
2138 A600 10r multi .25 .20

Takeover of the US
Embassy, 4th
Anniv. — A601

1983, Nov. 4 **Photo.** **Perf. 13**
2139 A601 28r multicolored .50 .50

UN Day
A602

1983, Oct. 24 **Perf. 13½**
2140 A602 32r multicolored .90 .25
Protest of veto by US, Russia, People's
Rep. of China, France and Great Britain.

Intl. Medical
Seminar,
Tehran — A603

1983, Nov. 20
2141 A603 3r Avicenna .20 .20

People's Forces Preparation
Day — A604

1983, Nov. 26 **Perf. 13**
2142 A604 20r multicolored .60 .20

Conference on Crimes of Iraqi Pres.
Saddam Hussein — A605

1983, Nov. 28 **Perf. 13½x13**
2143 A605 5r multicolored .20 .20

Mohammad Mofatteh — A606

1983, Dec. 18 **Photo.** **Perf. 13**
2144 A606 10r multicolored .30 .20

Birth Anniversary of
the Prophet
Mohammad
A607

1983, Dec. 22 **Photo.** **Perf. 13**
2145 A607 5r multicolored .45 .20
Approximately 700,000 examples of No.
2145 were issued before a spelling error was
discovered, and the remainder of the issue
was then withdrawn from sale.

5th Anniv. of
Islamic
Revolution — A608

1984, Feb. 11 **Photo.** **Perf. 13x13½**
2146 A608 10r multicolored .75 .20
See No. 2310h for stamp with splotchy colors in blue background and denomination,
flag colors and darker, thicker black lines
around tulips. Background and denominations
on No. 2146 have a screened appearance.

Nurses'
Day
A609

1984, Feb. 24 **Perf. 13**
2147 A609 20r Attending wounded
soldiers .45 .20

Invalids'
Day — A610

Local
Flowers — A611

1984, Feb. 29
2148 A610 5r Man in wheelchair .20 .20

1984, Mar. 10 **Perf. 13½x13**
2149 A611 3r Lotus gebelia .20 .20
2150 A611 5r Tulipa chrysantha .20 .20
2151 A611 10r Glycyrrhiza glabra .25 .20
2152 A611 20r Matthiola alyssifolia .45 .20
Novrooz (New Year).

Islamic Republic,
5th
Anniv. — A612

Sheik Ragheb
Harb, Lebanese
Religious
Leader — A614

World
Health Day
A613

1984, Apr. 1   Photo.   Perf. 13
2153 A612 5r Flag, globe, map   .20   .20

1984, Apr. 7
2154 A613 10r Children   .30   .20

1984, Apr. 18
2155 A614 5r multicolored   .20   .20

World Red Cross
Day — A615

16th World Telecom-
munications
Day — A616

1984, May 8   Photo.   Perf. 13½x13
2156 A615 5r multicolored   .20   .20

1984, May 17
2157 A616 20r multicolored   .45   .20

Martyrdom of
Seyyed
Ghotb — A617

1984, May 28   Perf. 13
2158 A617 10r multicolored   .30   .20

Struggle Against
Discrimination — A618

1984, Mar. 21   Photo.   Perf. 13
2159 A618 5r Malcolm X   1.00   .20

Conquest
of Mecca
Anniv.
A619

1984, June 20
2160 A619 5r Holy Ka'aba, idol
destruction   .20   .20

Universal Day of
Jerusalem
A620

Id Al-fitr Feast
A621

1984, June 29
2161 A620 5r Map, Koran   .20   .20
2162 A621 10r Moon, praying
crowd, mosque   .25   .20
a.   Pair, #2161-2162   .40   .20

Tchogha Zanbil Excavation,
Susa — A622

Cultural Heritage Preservation: b,
Emamzadeh Hossein Shrine, Kazvin. c,
Emam Mosque, Isfahan. d, Ark Fortress,
Tabriz. e, Mausoleum of Daniel Nabi, Susa.

1984, Aug. 20   Perf. 13½
2163   Strip of 5   .75   .25
a.-e.   A622 5r, any single   .20   .20

"Eid Ul-
Adha"
A623

Perf. 13x13½
1984, Sept. 6   Photo.   Wmk. 381
2164 A623 10r Holy Ka'aba   .30   .20
Feast of Sacrifices (end of pilgrimage to
Mecca).

10th Tehran Intl.
Trade
Fair — A624

Iraq-Iran War, 4th
Anniv. — A625

1984, Sept. 11
2165 A624 10r multicolored   .30   .20

1984, Sept. 22   Photo.   Perf. 13x13½
2166 A625 5r Flower, bullets   .20   .20

UPU Day
A626

1984, Oct. 9   Perf. 13½
2167 A626 20r Dove, UPU emblems   .50   .20

Haj
Seyyed
Mostafa
Khomeini
Memorial
A627

1984, Oct. 23
2168 A627 5r multicolored   .20   .20

Ghazi Tabatabaie
Memorial — A628

Mohammad's
Birthday, Unity
Week — A630

Intl. Saadi
Congress
A629

1984, Nov. 1   Perf. 13x13½
2169 A628 5r Portrait   .20   .20

1984, Nov. 25   Perf. 13½
2170 A629 10r Portrait, mausoleum, emblem   .50   .20
Saadi (c. 1213-1292), Persian poet.

1984, Dec. 6   Photo.   Perf. 13x13½
2171 A630 5r Koran, mosque   .25   .20

Islamic
Revolution, 6th
Anniv. — A631

Arbor
Day — A632

1985, Feb. 11   Perf. 13x13½
2172 A631 40r multicolored   .90   .40
See No. 2310o for stamp with bright pink
denomination and dove tail.

1985, Mar. 6   Perf. 13
2173 A632 3r Sapling, deciduous
trees   .20   .20
2174 A632 5r Maturing trees   .20   .20
a.   Pair, #2173-2174   .30   .20

Local
Flowers — A633

1985, Mar. 9   Perf. 13½x13
2175 A633 5r Fritillaria imperialis   .20   .20
2176 A633 5r Ranunculus fi-
carioides   .20   .20
2177 A633 5r Crocus sativus   .20   .20
2178 A633 5r Primula heter-
ochroma stapf   .20   .20
a.   Block of 4, #2175-2178   .50   .30
Novrooz (New Year).

Women's
Day — A634

Republic of Iran,
6th
Anniv. — A635

1985, Mar. 13   Perf. 13x13½
2179 A634 10r Procession of women   .30   .20
Birth anniv. of Mohammad's daughter,
Fatima.

1985, Apr. 1
2180 A635 20r Tulip, ballot box   .45   .20

Mab'as
Festival
A636

1985, Apr. 18
2181 A636 10r Holy Koran   .30   .20
Religious festival celebrating the recognition
of Mohammad as the true prophet.

Day of the
Oppressed
A637

World Telecom-
munications Day
A638

1985, May 6
2182 A637 5r Koran, flag, globe   .20   .20
Birthday of the 12th Imam.

1985, May 17   Perf. 13½x13
2183 A638 20r ITU emblem   .45   .20

Liberation of Khorramshahr, 1st
Anniv. — A639

1985, May 24
2184 A639 5r Soldier, bridge   .20   .20

Fist, Theological
Seminary,
Qum — A640

Day of Jerusalem
A642

World
Handicrafts
Day
A641

1985, June 5   *Perf. 13x13½*
2185 A640 10r multicolored   .50 .20
1963 Uprising, 22nd Anniv.

1985, June 10   *Perf. 13½*
2186 A641 20r Plates, flasks   .45 .20

1985, June 14
2187 A642 5r multicolored   .20 .20

Id Al-fitr
Feast — A643

Founding of the
Islamic
Propagation
Org. — A644

1985, June 20   *Perf. 13x13½*
2188 A643 5r multicolored   .20 .20

1985, June 22
2189 A644 5r tan & emerald   .20 .20

Ayatollah
Sheikh
Abdolhossein
Amini — A645

1985, July 3   Photo.   *Perf. 13*
2190 A645 5r multicolored   .25 .20

Pilgrimage to
Mecca — A646

Goharshad Mosque
Uprising, 50th
Anniv. — A648

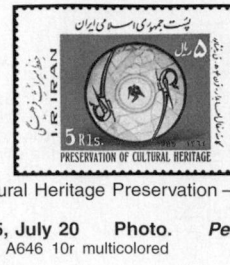

Cultural Heritage Preservation — A647

1985, July 20   Photo.   *Perf. 13½*
2191 A646 10r multicolored   .30 .20

1985, Aug. 20
Ceramic plates from Nishabur: a, Swords. b,
Farsi script. c, Peacock. d, Four leaves.
2192   Block of 4   .60 .20
   a.-d. A647 5r, any single   .20 .20

1985, Aug. 21   *Perf. 13x13½*
2193 A648 10r multicolored   .20 .20

Week of
Government
A649

Bleeding Tulips
A650

Designs: a, Industry and communications.
b, Industry and agriculture. c, Health care, red
crescent. d, Education.

1985, Aug. 30   Photo.   *Perf. 13x13½*
2194   Block of 4   .60 .20
   a.-d. A649 5r, any single   .20 .20

1985, Sept. 8
2195 A650 10r multicolored   .30 .20
17th Shahrivar, Bloody Friday memorial.

OPEC, 25th
Anniv. — A651

Design: No. 2196b, OPEC emblem and 25.

1985, Sept. 14   *Perf. 13½*
2196   Pair   .50 .20
   a.-b. A651 5r, any single   .25 .20

Iran-Iraq War, 5th
Anniv. — A652

Designs: a, Dead militiaman. b, Mosque
and Ashura in Persian. c, Rockets descending
on doves. d, Palm grove, rifle shot exploding
rocket.

1985, Sept. 22
2197   Block of 4   .60 .20
   a.-d. A652 5r any single   .20 .20
Ashura mourning.

Ash-Sharif Ar-
Radi — A653

1985, Sept. 26   Photo.   *Perf. 13x13½*
2198 A653 20r brt bl, lt bl & gold   .60 .20
Ash-Sharif Ar-Radi, writer, death millennium.

UPU Day
A654

1985, Oct. 9   *Perf. 13½*
2199 A654 20r multicolored   .60 .20

World
Standards
Day
A655

1985, Oct. 14
2200 A655 20r Natl. Standards Office emblem   .60 .20

Agricultural Training
and Development
Year — A656

Takeover of US
Embassy, 6th
Anniv. — A657

1985, Oct. 19   *Perf. 13x13½*
2201 A656 5r Hand, wheat   .20 .20

1985, Nov. 4   *Perf. 13*
2202 A657 40r multicolored   .60 .40

Moslem Unity
Week
A658

High Council of
the Cultural
Revolution
A659

1985, Nov. 25   *Perf. 13x13½*
2203 A658 10r Holy Ka'aba   .30 .20
Birth of prophet Mohammad, 1015th anniv.

1985, Dec. 10
2204 A659 5r Roses   .20 .20

Intl. Youth
Year — A660

Designs: a, Education. b, Defense. c, Construction. d, Sports.

1985, Dec. 18   Photo.   *Perf. 13x13½*
2205   Block of 4   .60 .20
   a.-d. A660 5r, any single   .20 .20

Ezzeddin al-
Qassam, 50th
Death
Anniv. — A661

1985, Dec. 20   *Perf. 13½*
2206 A661 20r sil, sep & hn brn   .60 .20

Map, Fists,
Bayonets
A662

1985, Dec. 25   *Wmk. 381*
2207 A662 40r multi   1.25 .40
Occupation of Afghanistan and Moslem
resistance, 6th anniv.

Mirza Taqi
Khan Amir
Kabir (d.
1851) — A663

1986, Jan. 8   Litho.   *Perf. 13*
2208 A663 5r multicolored   1.25 .20

Students Destroying Statue of the Shah, Tulips — A664

Women's Day — A666

Islamic Republic of Iran, 7th Anniv. — A670

1986, Apr. 1   *Perf. 13*
2215 A670 10r Flag, map   .30   .20

Mab'as Festival A671

1986, Apr. 7
2216 A671 40r multicolored   .60   .20

World Telecommunications Day — A676

1986, May 17   *Perf. 13½x13*
2221 A676 20r blk, sil & ultra   .60   .20

Universal Day of the Child — A677

1986, June 1   *Perf. 13*
2222 A677 15r Child's war drawing   .45   .20
2223 A677 15r Hosein Fahmide,
        Iran-Iraq war hero   .45   .20
   a.   Pair, #2222-2223   .90   .30

Intl. Day for Solidarity with Black So. Africans — A682

Ayatollah Beheshti — A683

1986, June 26
2228 A682 10r multicolored   .30   .20

1986, June 28   *Perf. 13x13½*
2229 A683 10r multicolored   .30   .20

Death of Beheshti and Islamic Party workers, Tehran headquarters bombing, 5th anniv.

Sulayman Khater, 40th Death Anniv. — A665

1986, Feb. 11   Photo.   *Perf. 13½*
2209 A664 20r multicolored   .60   .20

Iranian Revolution, 7th anniv.
See No. 2310l for 24x36mm stamp with yellow Arabic script.

1986, Feb. 15   *Perf. 13*
2210 A665 10r multicolored   .30   .20

1986, Mar. 3   *Perf. 13½*
2211 A666 10r multicolored   .30   .20

Birth anniv. of Mohammad's daughter, Fatima.

Army Day — A672

Day of the Oppressed — A673

1986, Apr. 18   *Perf. 13½*
2217 A672 5r multicolored   .20   .20

1986, Apr. 25   *Perf. 13x13½*
2218 A673 10r blk, gold & dk red   .20   .20

1963 Uprising, 23rd Anniv. — A678

1986, June 5   *Perf. 13x13½*
2224 A678 10r Qum Theological
      Seminary   .30   .20

Ayatollah Mohammad Taqi Shirazi, Map of Iraq — A684

Shrine of Imam Reza — A685

1986, June 30   Photo.   *Wmk. 381*
2230 A684 20r multicolored   .60   .20

Iraqi Moslem uprising against the British.

1986, July 19   *Perf. 13½*
2231 A685 10r multicolored   .30   .20

Flowers — A667

a, Papaver orientale. b, Anemone coronaria.
c, Papaver bracteatum. d, Anemone biflora.

1986, Mar. 11   Photo.   *Perf. 13½*
2212   Block of 4   .60   .20
   a.   A667 5r any single   .20   .20

Novrooz (New Year).

Helicopter Crash — A674   Teacher's Day — A675

1986, Apr. 25   *Wmk. 381*
2219 A674 40r multicolored   1.25   .40

US air landing at Tabass Air Base, 6th anniv.

1986, May 2   Photo.   *Perf. 13x13½*
2220 A675 5r multicolored   .20   .20

Day of Jerusalem — A679

1986, June 6
2225 A679 10r multicolored   .30   .20

Id Al-Fitr Feast A680

1986, June 9   *Perf. 13*
2226 A680 10r Moslems praying   .75   .20

Eid Ul-Adha, Feast of Sacrifice — A686   Eid Ul-Ghadir Feast — A688

Cultural Heritage Preservation — A687

1986, Aug. 17   *Perf. 13x13½*
2232 A686 10r multicolored   .30   .20

2000th Day of Sacred Defense A668   Intl. Day Against Racial Discrimination A669

1986, Mar. 14   Photo.   *Perf. 13x13½*
2213 A668 5r scarlet & grn   .20   .20

1986, Mar. 21
2214 A669 5r multicolored   .20   .20

World Handicrafts Day A681

a, Baluchi cross-hatched rug. b, Craftsman.
c, Qalamkar flower rug. d, Copper repoussé vase.

1986, June 10   *Perf. 13½*
2227   Block of 4   1.25   .40
   a.-d.   A681 10r, any single   .30   .20

1986, Aug. 20

Designs: No. 2233, Bam Fortress. No. 2234, Kabud (Blue) Mosque, Tabriz. No. 2235, Mausoleum of Sohel Ben Ali at Astenah, Arak. No. 2236, Soltanieh Mosque, Zendjan Province.

2233	A687	5r Hilltop	.25	.20
2234	A687	5r shown	.25	.20
2235	A687	5r Intact roof	.25	.20
2236	A687	5r Damaged roof	.25	.20
		Nos. 2233-2236 (4)	1.00	.80

1986, Aug. 25

2237	A688	20r multicolored	.60	.20

Population and Housing Census — A689

Iran-Iraq War, 6th Year — A690

1986, Sept. 9   *Perf. 13½x13*

2238	A689	20r multicolored	.40	.20

1986, Sept. 22   *Perf. 13*

2239	A690	10r Battleship Paykan	.30	.20
2240	A690	10r Susangerd	.30	.20
2241	A690	10r Khorramshahr	.30	.20
2242	A690	10r Howeizeh	.30	.20
2243	A690	10r Siege of Abadan	.30	.20
		Nos. 2239-2243 (5)	1.50	1.00

10th Asian Games, Seoul A691

1986, Oct. 2   Photo.   Wmk. 381

2244	A691	15r Wrestling	.40	.20
2245	A691	15r Rifle shooting	.40	.20

World Post Day A692

1986, Oct. 9

2246	A692	20r multicolored	.60	.20

UNESCO, 40th Anniv. — A693

1986, Nov. 4   Photo.   *Perf. 13x13½*

2247	A693	45r blk, sky bl & brt rose	1.25	.45

Ayatollah Tabatabaie (d. 1981) — A694

1986, Nov. 15   Photo.   *Perf. 13½x13*

2248	A694	10r multicolored	.30	.20

Unity Week — A695

1986, Nov. 20

2249	A695	10r multicolored	.30	.20

Birth anniv. of Mohammad.

People's Militia — A696

1986, Nov. 26   *Perf. 13*

2250	A696	5r multicolored	.20	.20

Mobilization of the Oppressed Week.

Afghan Resistance Movement, 7th Anniv. — A697

1986, Dec. 27

2251	A697	40r multicolored	1.25	.40

Nurses' Day — A698

1987, Jan. 12   Photo.   *Perf. 13*

2252	A698	20r multicolored	.60	.20

Hazrat Zainab birth anniv.

Fifth Islamic Theology Conference, Tehran — A699

Wmk. 381

1987, Jan. 29   Photo.   *Perf. 13*

2253	A699	20r multicolored	.60	.20

Islamic Revolution, 8th Anniv. — A700

1987, Feb. 11

2254	A700	20r multicolored	.60	.20

See No. 2310m for 24x36mm stamp.

Islamic Revolutionary Committees, 8th Anniv. — A701

1987, Feb. 12

2255	A701	10r brt bl, scar & yel	.30	.20

Women's Day — A702

1987, Feb. 19

2256	A702	10r multicolored	.30	.20

Birthday of Fatima, daughter of Mohammad.

Iran Air, 25th Anniv. A703

1987, Feb. 24

2257	A703	30r multicolored	.90	.30

Ayatollah Mirza Mohammad Hossein Naeini, 50th Death Anniv. — A704

1987, Mar. 6   Photo.   *Perf. 13*

2258	A704	10r multicolored	.30	.20

New Year — A705

Mab'as Festival A706

Flowers: a, Iris persica. b, Rosa damascena. c, Iris paradoxa. d, Tulipa clusiana.

1987, Mar. 11   *Perf. 13½x13*

2259		Block of 4	2.00	.50
a.-d.	A705	5r, any single	.50	.20

See Nos. 2313, 2361, 2411, 2443.

1987, Mar. 28   *Perf. 13*

2260	A706	45r gold, dk grn & grn	1.40	.45

Universal Day of the Oppressed A707

1987, Apr. 14

2261	A707	20r multicolored	.60	.20

Savior Mahdi's birthday.

Memorial to Lebanese Hizbollah Martyrs — A708

1987, Apr. 5

2262	A708	10r grn, gray & brt car	.30	.20

Revolutionary Guards Day A709

1987, Apr. 2
2263 A709 5r multi .20 .20
Imam Hossein's birthday.

8th Anniv. of Islamic Republic A710

1987, Apr. 1
2264 A710 20r multicolored .60 .20

World Health Day — A711

Child survival through immunization: 3r, Intravenous. 5r, Oral.

1987, Apr. 7 **Perf. 13x13½**
2265 A711 3r multicolored .20 .20
2266 A711 5r multicolored .30 .20
a. Pair, #2265-2266 .50 .25

Int'l. Labor Day — A712

1987, May 1 **Photo.** **Perf. 13**
2267 A712 5r multicolored .20 .20

Teachers' Day — A713

1987, May 2 **Wmk. 381**
2268 A713 5r Ayatollah Mottahari .20 .20

A714

1987, May 17 **Perf. 13½x13**
2269 A714 20r multicolored .70 .20
World Telecommunications Day.

A715

1987, May 18 **Perf. 13**
2270 A715 20r Sassanian silver gilt vase .60 .20
2271 A715 20r Bisque pot, Rey, 12th cent. .60 .20
Intl. Museum Day.

Universal Day of Jerusalem A716

1963 Uprising, 24th Anniv. A718

World Crafts Day A717

1987, May 22 **Perf. 13½x13**
2272 A716 20r multicolored .60 .20

1987, June 10 **Perf. 13x13½**
a, Blown glass tea service. b, Stained glass window. c, Ceramic plate. d, Potter.

2273 Block of 4 .75 .20
a.-d. A717 5r any single .20 .20

1987, June 5 **Photo.** **Perf. 13½**
2274 A718 20r multicolored .60 .20

Tax Reform Week — A719

1987, July 10 **Perf. 13**
2275 A719 10r black, sil & gold .30 .20

Welfare Week — A720

1987, July 17
2276 A720 15r multicolored .45 .20

Eid Ul-adha, Feast of Sacrifice — A721

1987, Aug. 6
2277 A721 12r sil, blk & Prus grn .45 .20

Eid Ul-Ghadir Festival A722

Banking Week — A723

1987, Aug. 14
2278 A722 18r black, green & gold .55 .20

1987, Aug. 17 **Perf. 13½x13**
2279 A723 15r red brn, gold & pale grnsh bl .45 .20

1st Cultural and Artistic Congress of Iranian Calligraphers A724

1987, Aug. 21 **Photo.** **Perf. 13x13½**
2280 A724 20r multicolored .60 .20

Memorial to Iranian Pilgrims Killed in Mecca — A725

1987, Aug. 26 **Wmk. 381** **Perf. 13**
2281 A725 8r multicolored .30 .20

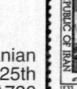

Assoc. of Iranian Dentists, 25th Anniv. — A726

Intl. Peace Day — A727

1987, Aug. 27 **Photo.** **Perf. 13½x13**
2282 A726 10r multicolored .30 .20

1987, Sept. 1 **Perf. 13**
2283 A727 20r gold & lt ultra .60 .20

Iran-Iraq War, 7th Anniv. — A728

Police Day — A729

1987, Sept. 22 **Perf. 13½x13**
2284 A728 25r shown .75 .25
2285 A728 25r Soldier, battle scene .75 .25
a. Pair, #2284-2285

1987, Sept. 28
2286 A729 10r multicolored .30 .20

Intl. Social Security Week, Oct. 4-10 — A730

World Post Day — A731

1987, Oct. 4 **Wmk. 381**
2287 A730 15r blk, gold & brt blue .45 .20

1987, Oct. 9 **Perf. 13x13½**
UPU emblem and: No. 2288, M. Ghandi, minister of the Post and Telecommunications Bureau. No. 2289, Globe, dove.

2288 A731 15r multicolored .45 .20
2289 A731 15r multicolored .45 .20

Importation Prohibited
Importation of stamps was prohibited effective Oct. 29, 1987.

A732

A733

Wmk. 381

1987, Nov. 4   **Photo.**   *Perf. 13*
2290 A732 40r multicolored   1.25   .20
     Takeover of US Embassy, 8th anniv.

1987, Nov. 5
2291 A733 20r multicolored   .90   .20
     1st Intl. Tehran Book Fair.

Mohammad's
Birthday, Unity
Week — A734

1987, Nov. 10
2292 A734 25r multicolored   .60   .20

Ayatollah
Modarres
Martyrdom,
50th
Anniv. — A735

1987, Dec. 1
2293 A735 10r brn & bister   .40   .20

Agricultural Training and Extension
Week — A736

1987, Dec. 6
2294 A736 10r multicolored   .50   .20

Afghan Resistance, 8th Anniv. — A737

1987, Dec. 27
2295 A737 40r multicolored   1.25   .40

Main Mosques
A738

1987-92   *Perf. 13x13½, 13½x13*
     Silver Background
2295A A738   1r Shoushtar   .20   .20
2296   A738   2r Ouroumieh   .20   .20
2296A A738   3r Kerman   .20   .20
2297   A738   5r Kazvin   .30   .30
2298   A738   10r Varamin   .50   .30
   a.   Unwatermarked ('91)   1.25   1.25
2299   A738   20r Saveh   .75   .75
   a.   Unwatermarked ('91)   .85   .85
2300   A738   30r Natanz, vert.   1.40   1.40
2301   A738   40r Shiraz   1.75   1.75
   a.   Unwatermarked ('92)   1.40   1.40
2302   A738   50r Isfahan, vert.   1.25   1.25
   a.   Unwatermarked ('91)   1.10   1.10
2303   A738   100r Hamadan   2.00   2.00
   a.   Unwatermarked ('91)   1.90   1.90
2304   A738   200r Dezfoul, vert.   3.50   3.50
   a.   Unwatermarked ('91)   3.00   3.00
2305   A738   500r Yazd, vert.   13.00   10.00
   a.   Unwatermarked ('91)   10.00   8.00
     Nos. 2295A-2305 (12)   25.05   21.85
     Nos. 2298a-2305a (7)   18.00   18.00

     Issued: 10r, 12/1; 5r, 12/30; 500r, 1/10/88;
20r, 1/14/88; 2r, 1/24/88; 50r, 1/24/89; 100r,
10/21/89; 200r, 10/28/89; 30r, 40r, 3/17/90; 1r,
3r, 3/92.
     For surcharges see #2750-2751.
     Watermarks on this issue can be difficult to
discern. The paper of the unwatermarked
stamps show fluoresence under long wave
ultraviolet light.

Qum Uprising, 10th
Anniversary — A739

1988, Jan. 9   *Perf. 13*
2306 A739 20r multicolored   .50   .20

Bombing of Schools
by Iraq — A740

1988, Feb. 1   *Perf. 13x13½*
2307 A740 10r multicolored   .80   .20

Gholamreza Takhti, World Wrestling
Champion — A741

1988, Feb. 4   *Perf. 13½*
2308 A741 15r multicolored   .50   .50

Women's
Day — A742

1988, Feb. 9   *Perf. 13*
2309 A742 20r multicolored   .40   .20
     Birth anniv. of Mohammad's daughter,
Fatima.

Souvenir Sheet
Types of 1979-88 and

Islamic Revolution,
9th Anniv. — A743

1988, Feb. 11   **Wmk. 381**   *Perf. 13*
2310   Sheet of 16   7.00
   a.   A547 1r like #2046
   b.   A547 3r like #2047
   c.   A559 3r like #2066
   d.   A547 5r like #2048
   e.   A559 5r like #2067
   f.   A547 5r like #2095
   g.   A570 10r like #2096
   h.   A608 10r like #2146
   i.   A537 18r like #1999
   j.   A559 20r like #2068
   k.   A570 20r like #2097
   l.   A664 20r like #2209
   m.   A700 20r like #2254
   n.   A587 30r like #2115
   o.   A631 40r like #2172
   p.   A743 40r not shown

     Nos. 2310a, 2310b, 2310d, 2310l, 2310m
are smaller than the original issues. See original issues for distinguishing features on other
stamps.
     Exists imperf. Value $14.

Tabriz Uprising, 10th Anniv. — A744

1988, Feb. 18   *Perf. 13*
2311 A744 25r multicolored   .50   .40

Arbor
Day — A745

1988, Mar. 5
2312 A745 15r multicolored   .70   .20

New Year Festival Type of 1987

     Flowers: a, Anthemis hyalina. b, Malva
silvestria. c, Viola odorata. d, Echium
amaenum.

1988, Mar. 10   *Perf. 13½x13*
2313   Block of 4
   a.-d.   A705 10r any single   2.00   2.00

Islamic
Republic, 9th
Anniv. — A746

1988, Apr. 1   *Perf. 13*
2314 A746 20r multicolored   .40   .20

Universal Day
of the
Oppressed
A747

1988, Apr. 3
2314A A747 20r multicolored   .30   .20
     Savior Mahdi's Birthday.

Cultural Heritage — A748

1988, Apr. 18
2315 A748 10r Mosque   .50   .40
2316 A748 10r Courtyard   .50   .40
   a.   Pair, #2315-2316   1.50   1.00
2317 A748 10r Minarets, vert.   .50   .40
2318 A748 10r Corridor, vert.   .50   .40
   a.   Pair, #2317-2318   1.50   1.00

Chemical
Bombardment
of Halabja,
Iraq — A749

1988, Apr. 26
2319 A749 20r multicolored   .90   .40

A750

Palestinian
Uprising
A750b

1988, May 13
2320 Strip of 5   2.50 1.75
   a. A750 10r multi
   b. A750a 10r multi
   c. A750b 10r multi
   d. A750b 10r multi, diff.
   e. A750b 10r Rock in hand, rioters

A750a

World Telecommunications
Day — A751

1988, May 17   *Perf. 13x13½*
2321 A751 20r green & blue   .80   .30

Intl. Museum
Day — A752

Designs: a, Ceramic vase, 1982. b, Bastan
Museum, entranceway. c, Tabriz silk rug, 14th
cent. d, Gold ring, 7th cent. B.C.

1988, May 18   *Perf. 13*
2322 Block of 4   1.50 1.50
   a.-d. A752 10r any single   .30   .20

Mining
Day — A753

1988, May 22   **Photo.**   **Wmk. 381**
2323 A753 20r multicolored   1.25   .50

Intl. Day of the
Child — A754

1988, June 1
2324 A754 10r multicolored   .50   .30

June 5th
Uprising, 25th
Anniv. — A755

1988, June 5
2325 A755 10r multicolored   .40   .40

World
Crafts Day
A756

1988, June 10   *Perf. 13x13½*
2326 A756 10r Straw basket   .30   .20
2327 A756 10r Weaver   .30   .20
   a. Pair, #2326-2327   .80   .60
2328 A756 10r Tapestry, vert.   .30   .20
2329 A756 10r Miniature, vert.   .30   .20
   a. Pair, #2328-2329   .80   .60

Child Health
Campaign
A757

1988, July 6   *Perf. 13*
2330 A757 20r blk, blue & green   .40   .20

Tax Reform
Week — A758

1988, July 10
2331 A758 20r multicolored   .40   .20

A759

1988, July 15   *Perf. 13½x13*
2332 A759 20r Allameh Balkhi   .40   .20

A760

1988, July 21   *Perf. 13*
2333 A760 10r Holy Ka'aba,
         dove, stars   .25   .20
2334 A760 10r shown   .25   .20
Massacre of Muslim Pilgrims at Mecca.
Nos. 2333-2334 were printed together in
one sheet, with alternating placement.

Destruction of
Iranian
Airliner — A761

1988, Aug. 11
2335 A761 45r multicolored   1.25 1.00

A762

1988, Aug. 13
2336 A762 20r Seyyed Ali
         Andarzgou   .50   .25

A763

1988, Sept. 1   *Perf. 13½x13*
2337 A763 20r multicolored   .50   .25
   Islamic Banking Week.

Divine Day of
17 Shahrivar,
10th
Anniv. — A764

1988, Sept. 8
2338 A764 25r multicolored   .70   .25

1988 Summer
Olympics,
Seoul — A765

Designs: a, Weightlifting. b, Pommel horse.
c, Judo. d, Soccer. e, Wrestling.

1988, Sept. 10
2339 Strip of 5   2.00 1.50
   a.-e. A765 10r any single   .35   .20

A766   A767

1988, Sept. 17   *Perf. 13½x13*
2340 A766 30r blk, grn & yel   .60   .20
   Agricultural census.

1988, Sept. 22   *Perf. 13x13½*
2341 A767 20r multicolored   .50   .25
   Iran-Iraq War, 8th anniv.

World
Post
Day
A768

1988, Oct. 9   *Perf. 13*
2342 A768 20r blk, ultra & grn   .80   .30

Parents and
Teachers
Cooperation
Week — A769

1988, Oct. 16
2343 A769 20r multicolored   .70   .25

Mohammad's Birthday, Unity Week — A770

1988, Oct. 29
2344 A770 10r multicolored .50 .30

A771

1988, Nov. 4
2345 A771 45r multicolored 1.10 .50

Takeover of US embassy, 9th anniv.

A772

1988, Nov. 6 Perf. 13½x13
2346 A772 10r multicolored .80 .30

Insurance Day.

Intl. Congress on the Writings of Hafiz — A773

Illustration reduced.

1988, Nov. 19 Perf. 13x13½
2347 A773 20r blue, gold & pink .50 .30

Agricultural Training and Extension Week — A774

1988, Dec. 6 Perf. 13
2348 A774 15r multicolored .60 .30

Scientists, Artists and Writers A775

1988, Dec. 18 Perf. 13x13½
2349 A775 10r Parvin E'Tessami .35 .35
2350 A775 10r Jalal Al-Ahmad .35 .35
2351 A775 10r Muhammad Mo'in .35 .35
 a. Pair, #2350-2351 .80 .35

2352 A775 10r Qaem Maqam
  Farahani .35 .35
2353 A775 10r Kamal Al-Molk .35 .35
 a. Pair, #2352-2353 .80 .75
  See Nos. 2398-2402.

Afghan Resistance, 9th Anniv. — A776

1988, Dec. 27 Perf. 13
2354 A776 40r multicolored .45 .40

Transportation and Communication Decade — A777

Perf. 13x13½

1989, Jan. 16 Wmk. 381
2355 A777 20r Satellite, envelopes, microwave
  dish .70 .70
2356 A777 20r Cargo planes .70 .70
 a. Pair, #2355-2356 1.90 1.75
2357 A777 20r Train, trucks .70 .70
2358 A777 20r Ships .70 .70
 a. Pair, #2357-2358 1.90 1.75

Prophethood of Mohammad A778

1989, Mar. 6 Perf. 13
2359 A778 20r multicolored .50 .40

Mab'as festival.

Arbor Day — A779

1989, Mar. 6
2360 A779 20r multicolored .70 .40

New Year Festival Type of 1987

Flowers: a, Cephalanthera kurdica. b, Dactylorhiza romana. c, Comperia comperiana. d, Orchis mascula.

1989, Mar. 11 Perf. 13½x13
2361 Block of 4 1.25 1.25
 a.-d. A705 10r any single .25 .20

A780

A781

1989, Mar. 23
2362 A780 20r shown .60 .60
2363 A780 30r Meteorological
  devices, ship .60 .60
 a. Pair, #2362-2363 1.50 1.25

World Meteorology Day.

1989, Apr. 1 Perf. 13
2364 A781 20r multicolored .40 .40

Islamic Republic, 10th anniv.

Reconstruction of Abadan Refinery A782

1989, Apr. 1
2365 A782 20r multicolored .70 .30

Ayatollah Morteza Motahhari, 10th Death Anniv. — A783

1989, May 2
2366 A783 20r multi .40 .30

Teachers' Day.

A784

10th ANNIVERSARY OF THE UNIVERSAL GHODS DAY

A785

1989, May 5
2367 A784 30r multicolored .75 .30

Universal Day of Jerusalem.

1989, May 17 Perf. 13½x13
2368 A785 20r multicolored .70 .30

World Telecommunications Day.

A786

1989, May 18 Perf. 13x13½
2369 A786 20r Jar .50 .50
2370 A786 20r Bottle .50 .50
 a. Pair, #2369-2370 1.25 1.10

Intl. Museum Day: Gurgan pottery, 6th cent.

A787

1989, June 4 Perf. 13
2371 A787 20r multicolored .40 .25

Nomads' Day.

World Crafts Day A788

1989, July 5 Perf. 13x13½
2372 A788 20r Engraver .40 .40
2373 A788 20r Copper vase .40 .40
 a. Pair, #2372-2373 1.10 1.00
2374 A788 20r Copper plate,
  vert. .40 .40
2375 A788 20r Copper wall hanging, vert. .40 .40
 a. Pair, #2374-2375 1.10 1.00

Ayatollah Khomeini (1900-89) A789

1989, July 6 Perf. 13
2376 A789 20r multicolored .50 .30

Pasteur and Avicenna
A790

1989, July 7
2377 A790 30r multicolored .... .70 .70
2378 A790 50r multicolored 1.00 1.00
a. Pair, #2377-2378 .... 1.75 1.75

PHILEXFRANCE.

Asia-Pacific Telecommunity, 10th Anniv. — A791

1989, July 25
2379 A791 30r blk, org brn & bl .80 .40

Mehdi Araghi, 10th Death Anniv. — A792

1989, Aug. 30
2380 A792 20r brn org & org brn .40 .20

M.H. Shahryar, Poet — A793

1989, Sept. 17
2381 A793 20r multicolored .... .50 .20

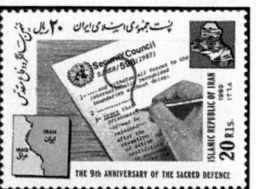

Iran-Iraq War, 9th Anniv. — A794

1989, Sept. 22
2382 A794 20r UN Security
Council res. 598 .60 .60

Ayatollah Khomeini — A795

Designs: 1r, Khomeini's birthplace, flower. 2r, Portrait as youth. 3r, Giving speech. 5r,

---

Map, rifles, exile. 10r, Khomeini returns to Iran, Feb. 1, 1979. 20r, Khomeini seated before microphone. 30r, Khomeini with grandson. 40r, Other mullahs. 50r, Khomeini gesturing with hands. 70r, On balcony before crowd. 100r, Slogan. 200r, Empty lectern. 500r, Mausoleum. 1000r, Sun rays.

1989-92 Litho. Unwmk. Perf. 13½
2382A A795 1r green & multi .25 .20
2382B A795 2r green & multi .20 .20
2383 A795 3r green & multi .25 .20
2384 A795 5r brt vio & multi .25 .20
2385 A795 10r brt bl & multi .35 .20
2386 A795 20r blue & multi .30 .25
2387 A795 30r pink & multi .35 .25
2388 A795 40r red & multi .35 .30
2389 A795 50r gray & multi .40 .30
2390 A795 70r brt grn & multi .55 .35
2391 A795 100r ultra & multi .75 .45
2392 A795 200r red brn & multi 1.50 .75
2393 A795 500r black & multi 3.50 1.75
2393A A795 1000r multi 7.50 3.50
Nos. 2382A-2393A (14) 16.50 8.90

Issued: 1r, 1/3/91; 3r, 3/16/90; 5r, 12/13; 10r, 10/22; 20r, 30r, 50r, 9/23/90; 40r, 2/9/90; 100, 200r, 9/26/90; 70r, 500r, 6/4/91; 2r, 1000r, 3/16/92.

World Post Day
A796

Wmk. 381
1989, Oct. 9 Photo. Perf. 13
2394 A796 20r multicolored .85 .50

Mohammad's Birthday, Unity Week — A797

1989, Oct. 18
2395 A797 10r multi .80 .50

Takeover of US Embassy, 10th Anniv. — A798

1989, Nov. 4 Perf. 13½x13
2396 A798 40r multicolored .40 .30

Bassij of the Oppressed (Militia), 10th Anniv. — A799

1989, Nov. 27 Perf. 13
2397 A799 10r multicolored .40 .30

Scientists, Artists and Writers Type of 1988

1989, Dec. 18 Perf. 13x13½
2398 A775 10r Mehdi Elahi Ghomshei .30 .30
2399 A775 10r Dr. Abdulazim Gharib .30 .30
2400 A775 10r Seyyed Hossein Mirkhani .30 .30
a. Pair, #2399-2400 .80 .75
2401 A775 10r Ayatollah Seyyed Hossein Boroujerdi .30 .30
2402 A775 10r Ayatollah Sheikh Abdulkarim Haeri .30 .30
a. Pair, #2401-2402 .80 .75

Intl. Literacy Year — A800

Wmk. 381
1990, Jan. 1 Photo. Perf. 13½
2403 A800 20r multicolored .70 .40

Cultural Heritage A801

Designs: No. 2404, Drinking vessel, 1980. No. 2405, Footed vase, 1979.

1990, Jan. 21 Perf. 13
2404 A801 20r blk & deep org .50 .30
2405 A801 20r blk & yel grn .50 .30
a. Pair, #2404-2405 1.25 1.00

New Identification Card System — A802

1990, Feb. 9
2406 A802 10r multicolored .25 .20

Islamic Revolution, 11th Anniv. — A803

1990, Feb. 11
2407 A803 50r multicolored 1.00 .40

Intl. Koran Recitation Competition A804

1990, Feb. 23
2408 A804 10r blk, bl & grn .70 .40

A805

A806

1990, Mar. 2 Perf. 13½x13
2409 A805 10r multicolored .70 .40

Invalids of Islamic Revolution.

1990, Mar. 6 Perf. 13
2410 A806 20r multicolored .40 .30

Arbor Day.

New Year Festival Type of 1987

Flowers: a, Coronilla varia. b, Astragalus cornu-caprae. c, Astragalus obtusifolius. d, Astragalus straussii.

1990, Mar. 11 Perf. 13½x13
2411 Block of 4 1.00 .80
a.-d. A705 10r any single .25 .20

Islamic Republic, 11th Anniv. — A807

1990, Apr. 1 Perf. 13
2412 A807 30r multicolored .70 .60

World Health Day — A808

1990, Apr. 7
2413 A808 40r multicolored .90 .50

A809

1990, June 4 Unwmk. Perf. 11x10½
2414 A809 50r multicolored .70 .50

Ayatollah Khomeini, 1st death anniv.

A810

1990, Dec. 15 Litho. Perf. 10½
2415 A810 100r multicolored 2.00 .60

Jerusalem Day.

A811

A812

1990, Oct. 20 Perf. 13
2416 A811 20r Turkoman jewelry .40 .40
2417 A811 50r Gilded steel bird 1.00 1.00
  a. Pair, #2416-2417 1.90 1.75

World Crafts Day.

1990, Nov. 17 Perf. 10½
2418 A812 20r multicolored .60 .30

Intl. Day of the Child.

Aid to Earthquake Victims — A813

1990, Nov. 19 Perf. 13x13½
2419 A813 100r multicolored .45 .30

Return and Tribute to Former Prisoners of Iran-Iraq War — A814

1990, Nov. 21 Perf. 13
2420 A814 250r multicolored 3.00 .50

Ferdowsi Intl. Congress — A815

Illustration reduced.

1990, Dec. 22 Litho. Imperf.
        Size: 60x75mm

2421	A815	100r	Portrait	3.00 4.00
2422	A815	100r	Statue	3.00 4.00
2423	A815	100r	Monument	3.00 4.00
2424	A815	100r	Slogan, diamond cartouche	3.00 4.00
2425	A815	100r	Rectangular slogan	3.00 4.00
2426	A815	100r	Slogan, diff.	3.00 4.00
2427	A815	200r	Two riders embracing	5.00 6.00
2428	A815	200r	Archer, birds	5.00 6.00
2429	A815	200r	Six men	5.00 6.00
2430	A815	200r	White elephant	5.00 6.00
2431	A815	200r	Warrior, genie, horse	5.00 6.00
2432	A815	200r	Hunting scene	5.00 6.00
2433	A815	200r	Riding through fire	5.00 6.00
2434	A815	200r	Four slogan tablets	5.00 6.00
2435	A815	200r	Man with feet shackled	5.00 6.00
2436	A815	200r	Palace scene	5.00 6.00
		Nos. 2421-2436 (16)		68.00 84.00

Conference on epic poem "Book of Kings" by Ferdowsi.
In 1991 some imperf between blocks of 4 were released. Value, set $250.

"Victory Over Iraq" — A816

1991, Feb. 25 Perf. 13
2437 A816 100r multicolored 1.25 .50

Intl. Museum Day — A817

Designs: No. 2438, Gold jug with Kufric inscription, 10th cent. A.D. No. 2439, Silver-inlaid brass basin, 14th cent. A.D.

1991, Feb. 25
2438 A817 50r multicolored 1.10 .50
2439 A817 50r multicolored 1.10 .50
  a. Pair, #2438-2439 2.25 1.50

A818

A819

1991, Mar. 12 Perf. 10½
2440 A818 50r multicolored 1.00 .50

World Telecommunications Day.

1991, Feb. 25 Perf. 13
2441 A819 200r org brn & blk 3.00 2.00

Opening of Postal Museum.

Islamic Revolution, 12th Anniv. — A820

1991, Feb. 11 Photo. Perf. 13
2442 A820 100r multicolored 2.50 1.00

New Year Festival Type of 1987

Designs: No. 2443a, Iris spuria. b, Iris lycotis. c, Iris demawendica. d, Iris meda.

1991, Mar. 11 Perf. 13½x13
2443 A705 20r Block of 4, #a.-d. 2.00 1.50

Saleh Hosseini, 10th Death Anniv. — A821

1991, Mar. 19 Perf. 13½x13
2444 A821 30r red & black .90 .50

Mab'as Festival A822

1991, Mar. 19 Perf. 13x13½
2445 A822 100r multicolored 1.50 .50

Universal Day of the Oppressed A823

1991, Mar. 25 Perf. 13
2446 A823 50r multicolored 1.00 .50

Savior Mahdi's Birthday.

Revolutionaries, 25th Death Anniv. — A824

1990, June 16
2447 A824 50r maroon & red org .80 .50
Dated 1990.

Islamic Republic, 12th Anniv. — A825

Unwmk.
1991, Apr. 1   Photo.   Perf. 13
2448 A825 20r blk, slate, grn & red .60 .50

World Health Day — A826

1991, Apr. 7   Perf. 13½x13
2449 A826 100r multicolored 1.50 .50

Day of Jerusalem A827

1991, Apr. 12   Perf. 13
2450 A827 100r bl, blk & brn 1.60 .75

A828   A829

1991, Apr. 12   Litho.   Perf. 10½
2451 A828 50r multicolored .80 .50
Women's Day. Birth anniv. of Mohammad's daughter, Fatima.

Perf. 13½x13
1991, Apr. 28   Photo.   Unwmk.
2452 A829 200r bl grn & blk 4.00 .50
Ayatollah Borujerdi, 30th death anniv.

Teachers' Day — A830

Illustration reduced.

1991, May 2   Perf. 13x13½
2453 A830 50r multicolored 1.10 .50

Decade for Natural Disaster Reduction A831

1991, May 11   Litho.   Perf. 10½
2454 A831 100r multicolored 1.75 .50

World Telecommunications Day — A832

Perf. 13½x13
1991, May 17   Photo.   Unwmk.
2455 A832 100r multicolored 1.50 .50

Intl. Museum Day — A833

Flags — A834

Ewers, Kashan, 13th cent.: 20r, With spout. 40r, Baluster.

1991, May 18   Perf. 13
2456 A833 20r multicolored .50 .50
2457 A833 40r multicolored 1.00 .50
a.   Pair, #2456-2457 2.00 1.10

1991, May 24   Perf. 13x13½
2458 A834 30r multicolored .85 .50
Liberation of Khorramshahr, 7th anniv.

Abol-Hassan Ali-ebne-Mosa Reza, Birth Anniv. — A835

Views of shrine, Meshed.

1991, May 26   Perf. 13
2459   10r Mausoleum .25 .25
2460   30r Gravestone .75 .50
a.   A835 Pair, #2459-2460 1.25 1.10

First Intl. Conf. on Seismology and Earthquake Engineering A836

1991, May 27   Perf. 13½x13
2461 A836 100r multicolored 2.00 .50

World Child Day — A837

1991, June 1   Photo.   Perf. 13½
2462 A837 50r multicolored 1.00 .50

Holy Shrine at Karbola, Iraq Destroyed by Invasion — A838

Unwmk.
1991, June 3   Photo.   Perf. 13
2463 A838 70r multicolored 1.10 .50

Ayatollah Khomeini, 2nd Death Anniv. — A839

1991, June 4
2464 A839 100r multicolored 2.50 .75

World Handicrafts Day — A840

Designs: No. 2465, Engraved brass wares. No. 2466, Gilded samovar set.

1991, June 10   Perf. 13½x13
2465 A840 40r multicolored 1.00 .50
2466 A840 40r multicolored 1.00 .50
a.   Pair #2465-2466 2.50 1.25

Intl. Congress on Poet Nezami — A841

1991, June 22   Perf. 13
2467 A841 50r multicolored 1.10 .50

A842

A843

1991, July 15   Photo.   Perf. 13
2468 A842 50r multicolored .80 .50
Ali Ibn Abi Talib, 1330th death anniv.

Unwmk.
1991, July 29   Photo.   Perf. 13
2469 A843 50r multicolored 1.00 .50
Blood Transfusion Week.

Return of Prisoners of War, First Anniv. — A844

Illustration reduced.

1991, Aug. 27   Perf. 13x13½
2470 A844 100r multicolored 1.75 .50

Ayatollah Marashi, Death
Anniv. — A845

Illustration reduced.

1991, Aug. 29   *Perf. 13½x13*
2471   A845   30r multicolored   1.25   .50

Ayatollah-ol-Ozma Seyyed Abdol-
Hossein Lary, Revolutionary — A846

Design includes 1909 stamp issued by Lary.

1991, Sept. 9   *Perf. 13x13½*
2472   A846   30r multicolored   .70   .50

Start of Iran-Iraq
War, 11th
Anniv. — A847

1991, Sept. 22   *Perf. 13½x13*
2473   A847   20r multicolored   .50   .50

Mosque,
Kaaba, Unity
Week — A848

1991, Sept. 22   *Perf. 13*
2474   A848   30r multicolored   .70   .50

World
Tourism
Day
A849

1991, Sept. 27   Photo.   *Perf. 13½*
2475   A849   200r multicolored   4.50   1.00

Dr. Mohammad
Gharib,
Pediatrician
A849a

1991, Sept. 29   Photo.   *Perf. 13*
2475A   A849a   100r bl & blk   1.50   .50
Official first day covers are dated 1/19/1991.

World Post
Day
A850

Unwmk.
1991, Oct. 9   Photo.   *Perf. 13*
2476   A850   70r #2071 on cover   1.00   .50

Khaju-ye Kermani Intl.
Congress — A851

1991, Oct. 15
2477   A851   30r multicolored   1.00   .50

A852

A853

1991, Oct. 16
2478   A852   80r multicolored   .90   .50
World Food Day.

1991, Oct. 19   *Perf. 13½x13*
2479   A853   40r bl vio & gold   .70   .50
Intl. Conference Supporting Palestinians.

Illustrators of
Children's
Books, 1st
Asian Biennial
A854

1991, Oct. 25   *Perf. 13*
2480   A854   100r Hoopoe   1.75   .50
"Children" misspelled.

World Standards
Day — A855

1991, Oct. 14   *Perf. 13½*
2481   A855   100r multicolored   2.00   .50

1st Seminar on
Adolescent and
Children's
Literature
A856

1991, Nov. 3   *Perf. 13*
2482   A856   20r multicolored   .70   .50

Roshid Intl.
Educational
Film Festival
A857

1991, Nov. 6
2483   A857   50r multicolored   1.20   .75

7th Ministerial
Meeting of the
Group of
77 — A858

1991, Nov. 16
2484   A858   30r vio & bl grn   .70   .50

Bassij of the Oppressed (Militia), 12th
Anniv. — A859

1991, Nov. 25
2485   A859   30r multicolored   .65   .50

Ayatollah Aref
Hosseini — A860

1991, Dec. 18   *Perf. 13½*
2486   A860   50r multicolored   1.10   .50

Sadek
Ghanji
A861

1991, Dec. 20
2487   A861   50r multicolored   1.10   .50

Agricultural
Training and
Extension
Week — A862

1991, Dec. 22   *Perf. 13*
2488   A862   70r multicolored   1.25   .50

World Telecommunications
Day — A863

#2489: a, 20r, Telegraph key. b, 20r, Phone
lines. c, 20r, Early telephones. d, 40r, Satellite
dishes. e, 40r, Telecommunications satellite.

1992, May 17   Photo.   *Perf. 13*
2489   A863   Strip of 5, #a.-e.   3.50   1.50

New Year — A863a

Flora of Iran: Nos. 2490a, 2490d, 20r. Nos.
2490b, 2490c, 40r.

1992, Apr. 18   *Perf. 13½x13*
2490   A863a   Block of 4, #a.-d. 3.00   1.50

Mosque of
Jerusalem
A864

1992, Mar. 27   *Perf. 13x13½*
2491   A864   200r multicolored   2.50   1.25

Day of Jerusalem and honoring A. Mousavi,
the Shiva leader of Lebanon, with Sheikh
Ragheb Harb in background.

IRAN

1119

Reunification of Yemen — A865

1992, May 22   *Perf. 13½x13*
2492 A865 50r multicolored .90 .50

World Child Day A866

1992, June 1   *Perf. 13x13½*
2493 A866 50r multicolored .90 .50

Intl. Conference of Surveying and Mapping A867

1992, May 25   *Perf. 13*
2494 A867 40r multicolored .70 .50

21st FAO Regional Conference A868

1992, May 17   *Perf. 13x13½*
2495 A868 40r blk, bl & grn .50 .35

South and West Asia Postal Union — A869

Mosques: No. 2496, Imam's Mosque, Isfahan. No. 2497, Lahore Mosque, Pakistan. No. 2498, St. Sophia Mosque, Turkey.

1992, Mar. 27   *Perf. 13½x13*
2496 A869 50r multicolored .90 .50
2497 A869 50r multicolored .90 .50
2498 A869 50r multicolored .90 .50

Economic Cooperation Organization Summit — A870

Design: 20r, Flags, emblem, vert.

1992   *Perf. 13½x13, 13x13½*
2499 A870 20r multicolored .75 .50
2500 A870 200r multicolored 4.50 1.00

Issued: 20r, Apr. 25; 200r, Feb. 17.

Natural Resources A871

1992, Apr. 15   Litho.   *Perf. 13½x13*
2501 A871 100r multicolored 2.00 1.00

Islamic Republic, 13th Anniv. — A872

1992, Apr. 1   *Perf. 13½x13*
2502 A872 50r multicolored .70 .50

Establishment of Postal Airline — A873

1992, Apr. 1   *Perf. 13x13½*
2503 A873 60r multicolored 1.25 .50

Islamic Revolution, 13th Anniv. — A874

Unwmk.
1992, Feb. 11   Photo.   *Perf. 13*
2504 30r multicolored 1.00 .50
2505 50r multicolored 1.25 .50
   a. A874 Pair, #2504-2505 2.50 1.25

A875

A876

1992, Mar. 23   Photo.   *Perf. 13½x13*
2506 A875 100r multicolored 1.10 .50
World Meteorological Day.

1991-92   *Perf. 13x13½*
Famous Men: No. 2507, Mohammad Bagher Madjlessi. No. 2508, Hadi Sabzevari, wearing turban. No. 2509, Omman Samani, wearing fez. No. 2510, Chapter of praise from Koran (Arabic script), by Ostad Mir Emad.
2507 A876 50r shown .70 .50
2508 A876 50r brown & multi .70 .50
2509 A876 50r multicolored .70 .50
2510 A876 50r multicolored .70 .50

Issued: #2510, 12/18/91; others, 5/17/92. First day covers of #2507-2509 may be dated 12/18/91.

Intl. Museum Day A877

#2511, Gray ceramic ware, 1st millennium B.C. #2512, Painted ceramic bowl.

1992, May 18
2511 A877 40r multicolored .90 .50
2512 A877 40r multicolored .90 .50

Ayatollah Khomeini, 3rd Anniv. of Death — A878

1992, June 4   *Perf. 13*
2513 A878 100r multicolored 1.40 .50

Intl. Conference on Engineering Applications of Mechanics A879

1992, June 9   *Perf. 13½x13*
2514 A879 50r multicolored .80 .50

A880

1992, June 13   *Perf. 13x13½*
2515 A880 20r multicolored .60 .40
In memory of clergy-lady Amini.

Sixth Conference of Nonaligned News Agencies — A881

1992, June 15
2516 A881 100r multicolored 1.10 .50

A882

1992, June 23   *Perf. 13x13½*
2517 A882 100r grn, blk & gold 1.25 .50
Meeting of Ministers of Industry and Technology.

A883

1992, June 26   *Perf. 13½x13*
2518 A883 100r multicolored 1.75 .60
World Anti-narcotics Day.

Holy Ka'aba — A884

Prayer Calligraphy A885

Designs: No. 2520, Ayatollah Khomeini in prayer. No. 2521, Khomeini holding prayer beads. No. 2522, Khomeini unwrapping turban. Nos. 2523-2524, Islamic prayers.

1992   Photo.   *Perf. 13½x13*
2519 A884 50r multicolored .70 .50
2520 A884 50r multicolored .70 .50
2521 A884 50r multicolored .70 .50
2522 A884 50r multicolored .70 .50
   Perf. 13x13½
2523 A885 50r dk green & lt green .70 .50
2524 A885 50r dk blue & lt blue .70 .50

Issue dates: July 27, Aug. 24.

Iran Shipping Line, 25th Anniv. A886

1992, Aug. 24   Photo.   *Perf. 13½x13*
2525 A886 200r multicolored 2.00 1.00

A887

A888

1992, Sept. 15   *Perf. 13½x13*
2526 A887 40r multicolored   .60 .45
Mohammad's Birthday, Unity Week.

Perf. 13½x13, 13x13½
1992, Sept. 22
Iranian Defense Forces: 20r, Soldiers on patrol. 40r, Soldier seated at water's edge, horiz.
2527 A888 20r multicolored   .50 .40
2528 A888 40r multicolored   .50 .40

Intl. Congress on the History of Islamic Medicine — A889

1992, Sept. 23   **Litho.**   *Perf. 13*
2529 A889 20r Avicenna, child   .60 .50
2530 A889 40r Physician's instruments   .90 .50
  a.   Pair, #2529-2530   1.75 1.10

Mobarake Steel Plant — A890

1992, Sept. 26   **Photo.**   *Perf. 13x13½*
2531   20r Inside plant   .40 .50
2532   70r Outside plant   .70 .50
  a.   A890 Pair, #2531-2532   1.40 1.25

Intl. Tourism Day A891

1992, Sept. 27   *Perf. 13x13½*
2533 A891 20r Mazandaran   .45 .35
2534 A891 20r Isfahan   .45 .35
2535 A891 30r Bushehr (Bushire)   .65 .50
2536 A891 30r Hormozgan   .65 .50

Intl. Trade Fair — A892

1992, Oct. 2   *Perf. 13½x13*
2537 A892 200r multicolored   2.25 1.00

World Post Day A893

1992, Oct. 9   *Perf. 13x13½*
2538 A893 30r Early post office   .80 .50

World Food Day A894

1992, Oct. 16   *Perf. 13*
2539 A894 100r blk, bl & yel   1.10 .50

Intl. Youth Photo Festival — A895

1992, Nov. 1   **Photo.**   *Perf. 13½x13*
2540 A895 40r multicolored   1.00 .50

A896

a, Seizure of US embassy, 12th anniv. b, Student's day (Eagles flying over dead doves). c, Khomeini's exile (Eagles, dove).

1992, Nov. 4   *Perf. 13*
2541 A896 100r Strip of 3, #a.-c.   4.50 1.50

Fighting in Bosnia and Herzegovina A897

Islamic Development Bank — A898

1992, Nov. 4   *Perf. 13½x13*
2542 A897 40r multicolored   .90 .50

1992, Nov. 10   **Litho.**   *Perf. 13½x13*
2543 A898 20r multicolored   .50 .40

Iran-Azerbaijan Telecommunications — A899

1992, Nov. 21   **Photo.**   *Perf. 13x13½*
2544 A899 40r multicolored   .90 .50

Azad (Open) University, 10th Anniv. — A900

1992, Nov. 23   *Perf. 13½x13*
2545 A900 200r dark grn & emer   1.75 .50

Week of the Basij (Militia) A901

1992, Nov. 26   *Perf. 13x13½*
2546 A901 40r multicolored   .60 .50

Seyed Mohammad Hosseyn Shahrian, Poet — A902

1992, Dec. 1
2547 A902 80r multicolored   .70 .50

Women's Day — A903

1992, Dec. 15
2548 A903 70r multicolored   .70 .50
Birth anniv. of Fatima.

Famous Iranians — A904

Scientists and writers: No. 2551a, Ayatollah Mirza Abolhassan Shar'rani (in turban). b, Prof. Mahmoud Hessabi, U=o formula. c,

Mohiyt Tabatabaiy, books on shelves. d, Mehrdad Avesta, calligraphy.

1992, Dec. 18
2549 A904 20r Block of 4, #a.-d.   2.00 1.00

Natl. Iranian Oil Drilling Co. A905

1992, Dec. 22
2550 A905 100r shown   1.50 .50
2551 A905 100r Ocean drilling platform   1.50 .50

A906   A907

1992, Dec. 28   *Perf. 13½x13*
2552 A906 80r multicolored   .70 .50
Promotion of literacy.

1993-95   **Photo.**   *Perf. 13½x13*
2553 A907   20r Narcissus
2554 A907   30r Iris
2555 A907   35r Tulips
2556 A907   40r Tuberose
2557 A907   50r White jasmine
2558 A907   60r Guelder rose
2559 A907   70r Pansies
2560 A907   75r Snapdragons
2561 A907   100r Lily
2562 A907   120r Petunia
2563 A907   150r Hyacinth
2564 A907   200r Damascus rose
2565 A907   500r Morning glory
2566 A907   1000r Corn rose
   Nos. 2553-2566 (14)   15.00 8.00

The 60r exists with inverted flowers. Value $9.

Issued: 20r, 1/12/93; 40r, 2/22/93; 100r, 4/21/93; 200r, 4/29/93; 500r, 6/27/93; 1000r, 7/19/93; 30r, 60r, 10/93; 50r, 8/93; 120r, 5/94; 35r, 75r, 3/95; 70r, 150r, 5/95.
For surcharges see Nos. 2759-2760, 2792-2794.

Prophethood of Mohammad — A908

1993, Jan. 21   **Photo.**   *Perf. 13x13½*
2567 A908 200r multicolored   1.75 .50
Mab'as Festival.

Day of the Disabled — A909

Designs: 40r, Player wearing medal, team members with hands raised.

1993, Jan. 27
2568   20r multicolored   .50 .50
2569   40r multicolored   .50 .50
  a.   A909 Pair, #2568-2569   1.25 1.10

Cultural Heritage
Preservation
A910

Planning
Day — A911

1993, Jan. 31 *Perf. 13½x13*
2570 A910 40r Mosque, exterior 1.00 .50
2571 A910 40r Mosque, interior 1.00 .50
a. Pair, #2570-2571 2.50 1.75

1993, Jan. 31 *Perf. 13*
2572 A911 100r multicolored 2.00 .50

Universal
Day of the
Oppressed
A912

1993, Feb. 8 *Litho.* *Perf. 13*
2573 A912 60r multicolored .80 .50
Savior Mahdi's Birthday.

Islamic
Revolution,
14th Anniv.
A913

a, Iranian flag. b, Flag, soldiers. c, Soldiers, shellbursts. d, Oil derricks, storage tanks, people harvesting. e, Crowd, car, Ayatollah Khomeini.

1993, Feb. 11 *Photo.* *Perf. 13x13½*
2574 A913 20r Strip of 5, #a.-e. 5.00 3.00

A914

1st Islamic Women's Games: a, Volleyball. b, Basketball. c, Medal. d, Swimming. e, Running.

1993, Feb. 13 *Perf. 13*
2575 A914 40r Strip of 5, #a.-e. 6.00 3.00

A915

1993, Feb. 16 *Perf. 13½*
2576 A915 40r Morteza Ansari .80 .50

Arbor Day
A916

1993, Mar. 6
2577 A916 70r multicolored 1.10 .50

New
Year
A917

a, 20r, Butterfly, tulip. b, 20r, Butterfly, lily. c, 40r, Butterfly, flowers. d, 40r, Butterfly, 3 roses.

1993, Mar. 11 *Perf. 13½x13*
2578 A917 Block of 4, #a.-d. 5.00 2.00

World Jerusalem
Day — A918

End of Ramadan
A919

1993, Mar. 14 *Perf. 13½x13*
2579 A918 20r multicolored .90 .50

1993, Mar. 26 *Perf. 13½x13*
2580 A919 100r multicolored 3.00 1.00

Islamic
Republic,
14th Anniv.
A920

1993, Apr. 1 *Perf. 13x13½*
2581 A920 40r Natl. anthem .90 .50

Intl. Congress on the Millennium of
Sheik Mofeed — A921

1993, Apr. 17 *Perf. 13*
2582 A921 80r multicolored 1.10 .50

A922

1993, Apr. 21 *Perf. 13½x13*
2583 A922 100r multicolored 1.10 .50
13th Conference of Asian and Pacific Labor Ministers.

1993, May 17 *Perf. 13½x13*
2585 A924 50r multicolored 1.20 .50
Intl. Congress for Advancement of Science and Technology in Islamic World.

A924

A925

A928

1993, May 1
2586 A925 40r multicolored 1.00 .50
Intl. Museum Day.

1993, June 1 *Photo.* *Perf. 13½x13*
2589 A928 50r multicolored 1.00 .50
Intl. Child Day.

Ayatollah
Khomeini, 4th
Death
Anniv. — A929

1993, June 4 *Perf. 13*
2590 A929 20r multicolored .70 .50

World
Crafts Day
A930

World Population
Day — A931

1993, June 10 *Perf. 13½x13*
2591 A930 70r multicolored 1.50 .60

1993, July 11 *Perf. 13*
2592 A931 30r multicolored .90 .50

1st Cultural-Athletic Olympiad of Iran
University Students — A932

Various sports.

1993, July 22 *Perf. 13x13½*
Background Colors
2593 A932 20r blue 1.00 .35
2594 A932 40r henna brown 2.50 .75
2595 A932 40r ocher 2.50 .75

Intl. Festival of Films for Children and
Young Adults, Isfahan — A935

1993, Sept. 11 *Photo.* *Perf. 13*
2598 A935 60r multicolored 1.25 .50

World Post
Day — A937

1993, Oct. 9 *Photo.* *Perf. 13*
2600 A937 60r multicolored 1.25 .50

A939

World of water with fish and: a, Birds. b, Girl. c, Angel with trumpet. d, Trees.

1993, Nov. 5 *Photo.* *Perf. 13½x13*
2602 A939 30r Block of 4, #a.-d. 3.50 2.00
Illustrators of Children's Books, Intl. Biennial.

A940

1993, Nov. 16   Photo.   Perf. 13
2603 A940 30r multicolored   .80   .50

Khaje Nassireddin Tussy, scientist and astronomer.

Week of the Bassij (Militia) A941

Designs: No. 2604, Woman tying bandana around militiman's head. No. 2605, Militiaman facing line of tanks.

1993, Dec. 1   Perf. 13x13½
2604 A941 50r multicolored   1.00   .50
2605 A941 50r multicolored   1.00   .50

Death of Grand Ayatollah Mohammad Reza Golpaigani A942

1993, Dec. 20   Perf. 13
2606 A942 300r multicolored   4.00 2.00

Support for Bosnia and Herzegovina A943

#2607, Children playing hopscotch. #2608, Soldier, minaret. #2609, Woman, mosque.

1993, Dec. 27
2607 A943 40r multicolored   1.00   .50
2608 A943 40r multicolored   1.00   .50
2609 A943 40r multicolored   1.00   .50
  a. Strip of 3, #2607-2609   4.00 2.00

Day of Invalids — A944

1994, Jan. 18
2610 A944 80r multicolored   .90   .50

Agriculture Week — A945

1994, Jan. 23
2611 A945 60r multicolored   .80   .50

Conf. on Islamic Law — A946

1994, Feb. 20
2612 A946 60r multicolored   1.00   .50

Islamic Revolution, 15th Anniv. — A947

Designs: a, Town, farm, telephone lines. b, Flag, Ayatollah Khomeini, revolutionaries. c, Fisherman, bridge. d, Women working.

1994, Feb. 11
2613 A947 40r Block of 4, #a.-d.   3.50 2.25

Youth Welfare A948

1994, Mar. 1
2614 A948 30r multicolored   .90   .50

A949

A951

A950

1994, Mar. 28   Photo.   Perf. 13½x13
2615 A949 30r multicolored   .90   .50

25th Iranian Mathematics Conference, Shareef Industrial University.

1994, Mar. 11   Perf. 13
2616 A950 50r multicolored   .90   .50

World Jerusalem Day.

1994, Mar. 16   Perf. 13x13½, 13½x13
2617 A951 40r Partridges, horiz.   3.50 1.25
2618 A951 40r Heron   3.50 1.25
2619 A951 40r Bustard   3.50 1.25
2620 A951 40r Pheasants, horiz.   3.50 1.25

New year.

Islamic Republic, 15th Anniv. — A952

1994, Apr. 1   Photo.   Perf. 13
2621 A952 40r multicolored   .90   .50

A953

1994, Apr. 7
2622 A953 100r multicolored   1.50   .50

Intl. congress of Dentist's Assoc. and World Health Day.

Re-els Ali Delvary, 80th Anniv. of Death A954

1994, Apr. 9   Perf. 13x13½
2623 A954 50r multicolored   1.00   .50

Intl. Year of the Family — A955

1994, May 10   Photo.   Perf. 13½x13
2624 A955 50r multicolored   .75   .50

World Telecommunications Day — A956

1994, May 17   Perf. 13x13½
2625 A956 50r multicolored   6.50 2.00

A957

A958

1994, May 18   Perf. 13
2626 A957 40r Marlik gold cup   .90   .50

World Museum Day.

1994, May 21

Cultural Preservation: 40r, Enameled pot with Kufic inscription, 13th cent.
2627 A958 40r multicolored   .80   .25

Ayatollah Khomeini, 5th Death Anniv. — A959

1994, June 4
2628 A959 30r multicolored   .50   .20

Ayatollah Motahari, 15th Anniv. of Death — A961

1994, June 10
2630 A961 30r multicolored   .60   .20

World Crafts
Day — A962

1994, June 10   Photo.   *Perf. 13*
2631 A962 60r Weaver   2.50 1.00
2632 A962 60r Glass pitcher   2.50 1.00

Islamic
University
Students'
Solidarity
Games — A963

1994, July 18
2633 A963 60r multicolored   .90 .40

Mohammad's
Birthday, Unity
Week — A964

1994, Aug. 26
2634 A964 30r multicolored   .80 .40

Seyed
Mortaza
Avini,
Sacred
Defense
Week
A965

1994, Sept. 22   *Perf. 13x13½*
2635 A965 70r multicolored   .80 .50

World Post
Day
A966

1994, Oct. 9
2636 A966 50r multicolored   .75 .50

Women's
Day — A967

A968

1994, Nov. 24   *Perf. 13*
2637 A967 70r multicolored   .90 .50
  Birth anniv. of Fatima.

1994, Nov. 26
2638 A968 30r multicolored   .45 .20
  Week of the Bassij (Militia).

Book
Week — A969

1994, Dec. 10
2639 A969 40r multicolored   .60 .50

Support for
Moslems of
Bosnia &
Herzegovina
A970

1994, Dec. 27
2640 A970 80r Moslem family   1.25 .50
2641 A970 80r Map, arms,
                  homes   1.25 .50

Grand Ayatollah
Araky — A971

1995, Jan. 5
2642 A971 100r multicolored   1.25 .50

Universal Day
of the
Oppressed
A972

1995, Jan. 17
2643 A972 50r multicolored   .75 .50
  Savior Mahdi's birthday.

Major General
Mehdi Zin-el-
Din
A973

Major General
Mehdi
Bakeri — A974

Major General
Hasan Bagheri
A975

  Martyred commanders: #2647, Major General Hosein Kherazi.

1995, Feb. 2
2644 A973 50r multicolored   .55 .20
2645 A974 50r multicolored   .55 .20
2646 A975 50r multicolored   .55 .20
2647 A975 50r multi, diff.   .55 .20

A976

A977

1995, Feb. 11
2648 A976 100r multicolored   1.50 .50
  Islamic Revolution, 16th anniv.

1995, Feb. 24
2649 A977 100r multicolored   2.25 .75
  World Jerusalem Day.

Arbor
Day — A978

New
Year — A979

1995, Mar. 6
2650 A978 50r multicolored   .70

1995, Mar. 16   *Perf. 13½x13*
2651 A979 50r shown   1.50 .55
2652 A979 50r Pansies   1.50 .55
2653 A979 50r Hyacinths   1.50 .55
2654 A979 50r Tulips, fish bowl   1.50 .55

Opening of Bafq-Bandar Abbas
Railway Line — A980

1995, Mar. 17
2655 A980 100r multicolored   1.75 1.00

Islamic
Republic of
Iran, 16th
Anniv. — A981

1995, Apr. 1   Photo.   *Perf. 13*
2656 A981 100r multicolored   1.10 .50

Second Press
Fesitval
A982

1995, Apr. 26
2657 A982 100r multicolored   .90 .50

Ayatollah
Ahmad
Khomeini
A983

1995, Apr. 27
2658 A983 50r multicolored   .70   .50

Day of
Invalids — A984

1995, June 1
2659 A984 80r Arabic script   .80   .50

Ayatollah Ali Vaziri — A985

1995, May 4
2660 A985 100r multicolored   .80   .50

World Telecommunications
Day — A986

1995, May 17
2661 A986 100r multicolored   1.10   .50

Ayatollah
Khomeini, 6th
Death
Anniv. — A987

1995, June 4
2662 A987 100r multicolored   1.25   .50

UN, 50th Anniv. — A988

a, Infant, hand holding vaccination (WHO).
b, Child laughing (UNICEF). c, Shafts of grain,
world map (FAO). d, Woman reading
(UNESCO).

1995, June 10   **Perf. 13x13½**
2663 A988 100r Block of 4, #a.-d. 3.50 2.25

Iqbal Ashtiany,
Writer — A989

1995, Aug. 14   **Perf. 13**
2664 A989 100r multicolored   1.10   .50

Government Week — A990

1995, Aug. 28   **Perf. 13x13½**
2665 A990 100r Workers, dam   1.10   .50
   Construction of the Karun dam and hydo-
electric power station.

Sacred Defense
Week — A991

1995, Sept. 22   **Perf. 13**
2666 A991 100r Gun, Koran   1.25   .50

World Post
Day — A992

1995, Oct. 9   **Perf. 13½x13**
2667 A992 100r Globe, enve-
                  lopes   1.25   .50

M.J.
Tondgooyan,
Oil Minister
A993

1995, Dec. 20   **Perf. 13**
2668 A993 100r multicolored   1.10   .50

Prophet
Mohammad
A994

1995, Dec. 20
2669 A994 100r Arabic calligra-
                  phy   1.25   .50

Fathi
Shaghaghi,
Islamic Jihad
Secretary
General
A995

1995, Dec. 31
2670 A995 100r multicolored   1.25   .50

Islamic Revolution,
17th Anniv. — A996

1996, Feb. 11
2671 A996 100r multicolored   1.40   .60

World Jerusalem
Day — A997

1996, Feb. 17
2672 A997 100r Dome of the
                  Rock   1.25   .60

Birds
A998

1996, Mar. 15
2673 A998 100r shown   2.00   .75
2674 A998 100r Crested head   2.00   .75
2675 A998 100r blue & multi   2.00   .75
2676 A998 100r yel, grn & multi   2.00   .75
        New year.

Air Force Maj.
Gen. Abbas
Babai — A999

Major Ali Akbar
Shiroody
A1000

Maj. Gen.
Mahammed
Ebrahim
Hemmat
A1001

Maj. Gen.
Mohammad
Broujerdi
A1002

1996, Mar. 18
2677 A999   100r multicolored   2.25 1.00
2678 A1000 100r multicolored   2.25 1.00
2679 A1001 100r multicolored   2.25 1.00
2680 A1002 100r multicolored   2.25 1.00
   See Nos. 2700-2707 for similar stamps
dated 1997.

Islamic
Republic of
Iran, 17th
Anniv. — A1003

1996, Mar. 31   **Photo.**   **Perf. 13**
2681 A1003 200r multicolored   2.25 1.00

Intl. Book Fair,
Tehran
A1004

1996, May 8
2682 A1004 85r multicolored   1.25   .50
   For surcharge see No. 2759A.

Mashhad-Sarakhs-Tajan Intl.
Railway — A1005

1996, May 13
2683 A1005 200r multicolored 2.00 1.00
Turkmenistan intl. railway link,

Prisoners of
War — A1006

1996, May 29
2684 A1006 200r multicolored 2.25 1.00
Captives and Missing Day.

Ayatollah
Khomeini, 7th
Death
Anniv. — A1007

1996, June 3
2685 A1007 200r multicolored 2.00 1.00

World Crafts
Day — A1008

1996, June 24 Photo. Perf. 13
2686 A1008 200r multicolored 2.00 1.00

Third PTT
Ministerial
Conference,
Tehran
A1009

1996, July 8
2687 A1009 200f multicolored 1.60 .50

Prophet
Mohammad's
Birthday, Unity
Week — A1010

Designs: a, Zouqeblateyne Mosque. b,
Tomb of Imam Hossein (red flag on top of
dome). c, Mohammad's Mosque (dome without flag). d, Tomb of Imam Riza (green flag on
top of dome). e, Qaba Mosque (four minarets).

1996, Aug. 3
2688 A1010 200r Strip of 5, #a.-
e. 12.50 3.00

Government
Week — A1011

Flag colors and: a, Tehran Subway. b, Iron
works, Isfahan. c, Merchant fleet. d, Oil refinery, Bandar-e-Imam (clouds in sky). e, Satellite dish, Boumehen.

1996, Aug. 23
2689 A1011 200r Strip of 5, #a.-
e. 13.00 3.50

Ayatollah
Moqddas
Ardebily
A1012

1996, Sept. 12 Photo. Perf. 13
2690 A1012 200r multicolored 1.60 .75

Sacred Defense Week — A1013

1996, Sept. 21
2691 A1013 200r multicolored 1.60 .60

World Standards Day — A1014

1996, Oct. 13
2692 A1014 200r multicolored 1.60 .50

World Food
Day — A1015

1996, Oct. 16
2693 A1015 200r multicolored 1.60 .60

Natl. Census
A1016

1996, Oct. 22
2694 A1016 200r multicolored 1.50 .65

2nd World University Wrestling
Championships, Tehran — A1017

1996, Dec. 10
2695 A1017 500r multicolored 5.00 2.00

Islamic Revolution,
18th
Anniv. — A1018

a, Ayatollah Khomeini holding man to his
chest. b, Martyrs. c, Khomeini waving. d,
Khomeini, leaders, airplane. e, Soldiers wearing helmets.

1997, Feb. 10
2696 A1018 200r Strip of 5, #a.-
e. 16.00 7.50

Arbor
Day — A1019

1997, Mar. 5
2697 A1019 200r multicolored 2.00 .80

Islamic
Republic, 18th
Anniv. — A1020

1997, Apr. 1
2698 A1020 200r multicolored 1.60 .60

8th Intl.
Conference on
Rainwater
Catchment
Systems
A1021

1997, Apr. 21
2699 A1021 200r multicolored 1.50 .60

Sheikh
Fazlollah
Mahallati
A1022

Brig. Gen.
Abbas Karimi
A1023

Brig. Gen.
Alireza
Movahed
Danesh
A1024

Sheikh
Abdollah
Mishmi
A1025

Brig. Gen.
Naser Kazemi
A1026

Gen.
Mohammad
Reza Vasture
A1027

Maj. Gen.
Yousef
Kolahdooz
A1028

Brig. Gen.
Yadollah Kalhor
A1029

1997, May 4
2700 A1022 100r multicolored 1.25 .50
2701 A1023 100r multicolored 1.25 .50
2702 A1024 100r multicolored 1.25 .50
2703 A1025 100r multicolored 1.25 .50
2704 A1026 100r multicolored 1.25 .50
2705 A1027 100r multicolored 1.25 .50
2706 A1028 100r multicolored 1.25 .50
2707 A1029 100r multicolored 1.25 .50

Martyred commanders. See Nos. 2677-2680 for similar stamps.

Post, Telecommunications — A1030

1997, May 22
2708 A1030 200r multicolored 1.75 .50

Ayatollah
Khomeini, 8th
Death
Anniv. — A1031

1997, June 4
2709 A1031 200r multicolored 1.60 .50

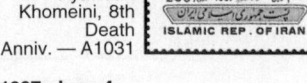

Montreal
Protocol on
Substances
that Deplete
Ozone Layer,
10th
Anniv. — A1032

1997, Sept. 16 Photo. Perf. 13
2710 A1032 200r multicolored 1.50 .50

Tehran
Subway — A1033

Designs: 50r, Grain elevator. 65r, Medals, Students' Science Olympiad. 70r, Mobarake Steel Plant. 100r, Telecommunications. 130r, Port facilities. 150r, Bandar Abbas Oil Refinery. 200r, Rajai Dam. 350r, Rajai power station. 400r, Front of Foreign Affairs office. 500r, Child receiving oral polio vaccine. 650r, Printing house for Koran. 1000r, Imam Khomeini Intl. Airport. 2000r, Prayer place and tomb of Ayatollah Khomeini, Teheran.

1997 Photo. Perf. 13½x13
2711 A1033 40r multicolored
2712 A1033 50r multicolored
2713 A1033 65r multicolored
2714 A1033 70r multicolored
2715 A1033 100r multicolored
2716 A1033 130r multicolored
2717 A1033 150r multicolored
2718 A1033 200r multicolored
2719 A1033 350r multicolored
2720 A1033 400r multicolored
2721 A1033 500r multicolored
2722 A1033 650r multicolored
2723 A1033 1000r multicolored
2724 A1033 2000r multicolored
Nos. 2711-2724 (14) 30.00 18.50
Issued: 2000r, 10/22; others, Sept.

Sacred Defense
Week — A1034

1997, Sept. 28 Photo. Perf. 13
2725 A1034 200r multicolored 1.50 .50

Poets — A1035

#2726, Maitre Eqbal Lahouri. #2727, Molana Djalaleddin Mohammad Molavi.

1997, Oct. 15
2726 A1035 200r green & multi 1.50 .50
2727 A1035 200r salmon & multi 1.50 .50

World Post
Day — A1036

1997, Oct. 15
2728 A1036 200r multicolored 1.50 .50

Naim Frasheri (1846-1900), Albanian
Moslem Poet — A1037

1997, Nov. 5
2729 A1037 200r multicolored 1.50 .50

Eighth Islamic
Summit
A1038

Various ornate designs, Islamic texts: a, Seven ornaments. b, Ornament at bottom. c, Ornament at right. d, Ornament at upper left. e, Ornament above crescent.

1997, Dec. 9
2730 A1038 300r Strip of 5, #a.-
e. 20.00 7.50

2nd Islamic
Countries
Women's
Sports Games,
Tehran
A1039

1997, Dec. 12
2731 A1039 200r multicolored 1.50 .50

Islamic
Revolution,
19th Anniv. — A1040

a, Natl. flags. b, Harvesting grain, factory. c, Soldiers carrying flags. d, Crowd cheering, picture of Ayatollah Khomeini. e, Ayatollah Khomeini.

1998, Feb. 11
2732 A1040 200r Strip of 5, #a.-
e. 12.50 5.00

World
Jerusalem
Day — A1041

1998, Feb. 17
2733 A1041 250r multicolored 3.00 1.25

New
Year — A1042

1998, Mar. 5
2734 A1042 200r Still life 1.60 .60

Arbor
Day
A1043

1998, Mar. 11
2735 A1043 200r multicolored 1.60 .90

Islamic Republic, 19th Anniv. — A1044

1998, Apr. 1 Photo. Perf. 13
2736 A1044 250r multicolored 4.00 1.50

A1045

A1046

1998, May 17 *Perf. 13½x13*
2737 A1045 200r multicolored 2.25 1.00
World Telecommunications Day.

1998, May 23 Photo. *Perf. 13*
2738 A1046 200r multicolored 2.25 1.00
Election day.

War Martyrs

A1047

A1048

A1049

A1050

1998, May 24 Photo. *Perf. 13*
2739 A1047 100r multicolored 2.50 .90
2740 A1048 100r multicolored 2.50 .90
2741 A1049 100r multicolored 2.50 .90
2742 A1050 100r multicolored 2.50 .90

Shahriyar,
Poet — A1051

1998, May 27
2743 A1051 200r multicolored 2.25 1.00

Ayatollah
Khomeini, 9th
Death
Anniv. — A1052

1998, June 4 *Perf. 13*
2744 A1052 200r multicolored 2.50 1.25

2nd Congress
of the South
West Asia
Postal Union,
Tehran
A1053

1998, June 8
2745 A1053 250r multicolored 1.75 1.00

1998 World Cup Soccer
Championships, France — A1054

1998, June 10
2746 A1054 500r multicolored 3.50 1.00

A1055

A1056

1998, June 10
2747 A1055 200r multicolored 2.25 1.25
World Handicrafts Day.

1998, Sept. 4
2748 A1056 250r Union Day 2.50 1.50

1000th Friday
of Public Prayer
A1057

1998, Oct. 30 Litho. *Perf. 13*
2749 A1057 250r multicolored 2.50 1.50

Nos. 2295A & 2296A Surcharged in
Black or Green

1998, Nov. 11 *Perf. 13x13½*
2750 A738 200r on 1r Shoustar 5.50 3.00
2751 A738 200r on 3r Kerman
(G) 5.50 3.00

Intl. Year of the
Ocean
A1058

1998, Nov. 14 *Perf. 13*
2752 A1058 250r multicolored 3.00 1.75

Sacred Defense Week — A1059

1998, Nov. 23
2753 A1059 250r multicolored 2.50 1.00

World
Post
Day
A1060

1998, Dec. 2
2754 A1060 200r multicolored 2.00 .75

1998 World Wrestling Championships,
Tehran — A1061

1998, Dec. 8
2755 A1061 250r multicolored 5.00 2.75

Children and
Cancer
A1062

1998, Dec. 13
2756 A1062 250r multicolored 2.00 .75

Cultural
Development
A1063

1998, Dec. 16 Photo. *Perf. 13*
2757 A1063 250r multicolored 2.25 1.00

Islamic
Revolution,
20th
Anniv. — A1064

1999, Feb. 11 Photo. *Perf. 13*
2758 A1064 250r multicolored 2.00 .75

#2554, 2682, 2555 Surcharged in
Black or Red

#2759, 2760

#2759A

1999, Feb.   Photo.   Perf. 13, 13½x13
2759 A907 200r on 35r
                (#2555)   10.00   —
2759A A1004 250r on 85r (R,
                #2682)   20.00   —
2760 A907 900r on 30r
                (#2554)   10.00   —

Establishment of Islamic Republic,
20th Anniv. — A1065

1999, Apr. 1   Photo.   Perf. 13
2761 A1065 250r multicolored   2.00 1.00

Ghadir Khom
Religious
Feast — A1066

1999, Apr. 5   Photo.   Perf. 13
2762 A1066 250r multicolored   2.00 1.00

Ayatollah Khomeini's Charity
Account — A1067

1999, Apr. 10   Photo.   Perf. 13
2763 A1067 250r Houses   2.25 1.00
2764 A1067 250r Village, palm
                trees   2.25 1.00

Army
Day
A1068

1999, Apr. 18
2765 A1068 250r multicolored   2.50 1.25

Mullah
Sadra — A1069

1999, May 22
2766 A1069 250r multicolored   2.00 1.00

Ayatollah
Khomeini, 10th
Anniv. of
Death — A1070

1999, May 25
2767 A1070 250r multicolored   4.00 2.00

Islamic Parliament, 20th
Anniv. — A1071

1999, May 28   Photo.   Perf. 13
2768 A1071 250r multicolored   2.00 1.00

Islamic Inter-parliamentary
Conference — A1072

1999, June 15   Photo.   Perf. 13
2769 A1072 250r multicolored   2.00 1.25

Unity
Week
A1073

1999, July 1   Photo.   Perf. 13
2770 A1073 250r multicolored   2.00 1.25

Handicrafts
Day — A1074

1999, July 25   Photo.   Perf. 13
2771 A1074 250r multicolored   3.00 1.25

Total Solar
Eclipse, Aug.
11 — A1075

Designs: a, Moon over right portion of sun.
b, Baily's beads at top. c, Totality. d, Baily's
beads at right. e, Moon over left portion of sun.

1999, Feb. 11   Photo.   Perf. 13
2772 A1075 250r Strip of 5,
                #a.-e.   25.00 20.00

Birds — A1076

1999-2002   Photo.   Perf. 13x13½
2776 A1076 100r Hoopoe   .50
2778 A1076 150r Kingfisher   .50
2779 A1076 200r Robin   .50
2780 A1076 250r Lark   .50
2781 A1076 300r Red-backed
                shrike   .50
2782 A1076 350r Eurasian
                roller   .50
2782A A1076 400r Blue tit   .50
2783 A1076 500r Eurasian
                bee-eater   .50
2784 A1076 1000r Redwing   1.00
2785 A1076 2000r Twite   1.00
2786 A1076 3000r White throat 1.00
2786A A1076 4500r Turtle dove   1.00

  Numbers have been reserved for additional
values in this set.
  Issued: 150r, 8/6; 250r, 8/4; 100r, 6/17/00;
300r, 5/31/00; 500r, 8/30/00; 1000r, 10/30/00;
2000r, 1/13/01; 3000r, 1/23/01. 200r, 4/24/02;
400r, 5/18/02; 4500r, 7/16/02; 350r, 4/17/01.

UPU,
125th
Anniv.
A1077

1999, Oct. 2   Photo.   Perf. 13
2787 A1077 250r multicolored   2.25 1.00

Children's
Day — A1078

a, Iranian girl. b, Latin American boy. c,
Eskimo boy. d, African girl. e, Russian boy. f,
French girl. g, Chinese girl. h, Asian Indian
girl. i, American Indian girl. j, Arabian boy.

1999, Oct. 8
2788 A1078 150r Strip of 10,
                #a.-j.   20.00 15.00
  Order of stamps in strip varies.

Intl. Exhibition
of Children's
Book
Illustrators
A1079

  Background colors: a, Blue. b, Yellow. c,
Red. d, Green.

1999, Nov. 15
2789 A1079 250r Block of 4,
                #a.-d.   17.50 10.00

Ayatollah
Mohammad
Taghi
Jafari — A1080

1999, Nov. 16
2790 A1080 250r multicolored   2.00 1.00

Islamic
Revolution, 21st
Anniv. — A1081

2000, Feb. 11   Photo.   Perf. 13
2791 A1081 300r multi   2.25 1.25

**Nos. 2558, 2560, 2562 Surcharged
Like No. 2759**

Methods and Perfs. as Before
2000, Feb.
2792 A907 250r on 60r   3.25 3.25
2793 A907 250r on 75r   3.25 3.25
2794 A907 250r on 120r   3.25 3.25

  The 60r stamp with the inverted flowers footnoted after No. 2566 is known with the 250r
surcharge. Value $25.

New
Year — A1082

2000, Mar. 13   Photo.   Perf. 13
2795 A1082 300r multi   2.75 1.50

Science & Technology University, 70th Anniv. — A1083

2000, July 9 **Photo.** *Perf. 13*
2796 A1083 300r multi 8.00 5.00

Dated 1999.

Dr. Mohammad Mofatteh (1928-79), Martyr — A1084

2000, July 22
2797 A1084 300r multi 2.00

A1085

A1086

A1087

A1088

A1089

A1090

A1091

Martyrs A1092

2000
2798 A1085 150r multi 2.00 .50
2799 A1086 150r multi 2.00 .50
2800 A1087 150r multi 2.00 .50
2801 A1088 150r multi 2.00 .50
2802 A1089 150r multi 1.25 .50
2803 A1090 150r multi 1.25 .50
2804 A1091 150r multi 1.25 .50
2805 A1092 150r multi 1.25 .50
    Nos. 2798-2805 (8) 13.00 4.00

Issued: Nos. 2798-2801, 8/6/00; Nos. 2802-2805, 7/30/01.

National Archives Day — A1093

2000, May 5 **Photo.** *Perf. 13*
2806 A1093 300r multi 2.25 1.50

University Jihad Movement A1094

2000, Aug. 6
2807 A1094 300r multi 2.00 1.25

8th Asia-Pacific Postal Union Congress, Tehran — A1095

2000, Sept. 12
2808 A1095 300r multi 2.00 1.25

World Space Week A1096

Satellite and: No. 2809, 500r, Dish at R. No. 2810, 500r, Dish at L.

2000, Oct. 4
2809-2810 A1096 Set of 2 6.00 4.00

World Breastfeeding Week A1097

2000, Oct.
2811 A1097 300r multi 2.00 1.25

Ghadir Khom Festival A1098

2001, Mar. 14
2812 A1098 500r multi 2.25 1.25

Year of H. H. Ali — A1099

2001, Mar. 14
2813 A1099 500r multi 2.25 1.00

New Year — A1100

Birds: No. 2814, 300r, shown. No. 2815, 300r, Bird, diff., vert.

2001, Mar. 18 *Perf. 13x13½, 13½x13*
2814-2815 A1100 Set of 2 6.50 3.00

Palestinian Intifada — A1100a

2001, Apr. 24 **Photo.** *Perf. 13*
2815A A1100a 350r multi 7.00 5.00

Belgica 2001 Intl Stamp Exhibition, Brussels — A1101

Designs: No. 2816, 350r, Chaffinch (shown). No. 2817, 350r, Waxwing. No. 2818, 350r, National Garden, vert.

2001, June 9 *Perf. 13*
2816-2818 A1101 Set of 3 12.00 8.00

Phila Nippon '01, Japan A1102

Emblem and: No. 2819, 250r, Mount Fuji, Japan. No. 2820, 250r, Mount Damavand, Iran.

2001, Aug. 1 **Photo.** *Perf. 13*
2819-2820 A1102 Set of 2 4.00 2.50

World Tourism Day — A1103

2001, Sept. 22
2821 A1103 500r multi 2.00 1.25

Police Week — A1104

No. 2822: a, Helicopters, parachutists, police cars, motorcycle police. b, Parachutists, officer saluting flag, motorcycle police, naval patrol.
Illustration reduced.

2001, Sept. 29 *Perf. 13x13½*
2822 A1104 250r Horiz. pair,
#a-b 2.75 2.00

Year of Dialogue Among Civilizations A1105

Designs: No. 2823, 250r, Shown. No. 2824, 250r, Cubist and Oriental art, horiz.

2001, Oct. 9 *Perf. 13*
2823-2824 A1105 Set of 2 4.50 2.50

Third Moslem Women's Games, Tehran — A1106

2001, Oct. 24
2825 A1106 250r multi 2.00 1.25

Spring of the Holy Koran — A1107

2001, Nov. 26
2826 A1107 500r multi 2.50 1.50

Honeybee — A1108

2001, Dec. 3
2827 A1108 500r multi 2.75 1.75

UN High Commissioner for Refugees, 50th Anniv. — A1109

2001, Dec. 10
2828 A1109 500r multi 2.00 1.00

Transportation Day — A1110

No. 2829: a, Truck on road. b, Truck on bridge, truck on road, gate.
Illustration reduced.

2001, Dec. 17 *Perf. 13x13½*
2829 A1110 350r Horiz. pair,
#a-b 5.00 3.00

Navy Day A1111

No. 2830, 500r: a, Ship heading right. b, Ship heading left.
No. 2831, 500r: a, Helicopter, hovercraft. b, Submarine.

2001, Nov. 28 Photo. *Perf. 13*
Vert. Pairs, #a-b
2830-2831 A1111 Set of 2 8.50 8.50

Tehran Subway A1112

No. 2832: a, Train headed right. b, Train headed left.

2001, Dec. 13
2832 A1112 500r Vert. pair, #a-b 4.00 3.00

Iranian-made Automobiles — A1113

Designs: No. 2833, 500r, shown. No. 2834, 500r, Automobile, vert.

2002, Jan. 15
2833-2834 A1113 Set of 2 4.00 2.50

Arbor Day — A1114

2002, Mar. 6
2835 A1114 500r multi 1.75 1.25

A1115

New Year's Day — A1116

No. 2836: a, Bird with yellow breast. b, Parrot.
No. 2837: a, Stork facing left. b, Hoopoe facing right.
Illustration reduced.

2002, Mar. 16
2836 A1115 500r Horiz. pair,
#a-b 3.75 3.00
2837 A1116 500r Horiz. pair,
#a-b 3.75 3.00

Imam Hossein — A1117

Illustration reduced.

2002, July 8 Photo. *Imperf.*
2838 A1117 400r multi 1.50 1.50

Butterflies — A1118

No. 2839: a, Danaus sita. b, Polygonia c-album. c, Precis orithya. d, Vanessa cardui. e, Papilio maacki.

2002, July 29 *Perf. 13*
2839 Horiz. strip of 5 6.50 6.50
a.-e. A1118 400r Any single 1.10 .90

A1119

PhilaKorea 2002 World Stamp Exhibition, Seoul — A1120

No. 2840 — Flowers: a, Hyoscyamus muticus. b, Frittillaria. c, Calotropis procera. d, Ranuculus.
No. 2841 — Horse breeds: a, Caspian. b, Kurd. c, Turkoman. d, Arab.
Illustrations reduced.

2002, Aug. 2
2840 A1119 400r Block of 4, #a-
d, + 2 labels 6.00 6.00
2841 A1120 400r Block of 4, #a-
d, + 2 labels 6.00 6.00

Ayatollah Khomeini (1900-89) A1121

2002, Aug. 20
2842 A1121 400r multi 2.00 1.00

Jerusalem Day — A1122

2002, Nov. 29
2843 A1122 400r multi 2.00 1.00

Iran — Brazil Diplomatic Relations, Cent. — A1123

No. 2844: a, Iranian ceramics. b, Brazilian ceramics.

2002, Dec. 15
2844   Horiz. pair + label   5.00   5.00
a.-b.   A1123 400r Either single   2.00   1.00
     See Brazil Nos. 2868-2869.

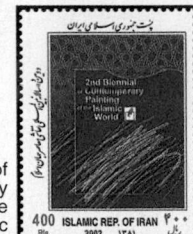

2nd Biennial of
Contemporary
Painting of the
Islamic
World — A1124

2002, Dec. 25
2845   A1124 400r multi   2.00   1.00

Esco Production Line, 30th
Anniv. — A1125

Illustration reduced.

2003, Jan. 13   *Perf. 13x13½*
2846   A1125 400r multi   2.50   1.50

Air
Force
Day
A1126

   Various aircraft: 300r, 400r, 500r, 600r,
700r.

2003, Feb. 8   Photo.   *Perf. 13*
2847-2851 A1126   Set of 5   7.50   7.50

New
Year
2003
A1127

   Mammals: No. 2852, 1000r, Goitered
gazelle without horns. No. 2853, 1000r,
Goitered gazelle with horns. No. 2854, 1000r,
Red deer. No. 2855, 1000r, Urial.

2003, Mar. 15
2852-2855 A1127   Set of 4   9.00   9.00

Iranian and
Chinese
Buildings
A1128

   No. 2856: a, Mosque, Isfahan. b, Bell Tower,
Xian, People's Republic of China.

2003, Apr. 15   *Perf. 13x13½*
2856   Horiz. pair + label   6.00   6.00
a.-b.   A1128 400r Either single   1.50   1.25
     See China (People's Republic) Nos. 3271-
3272.

Book, Children
and
Family — A1129

2003, May 4   Photo.   *Perf. 13*
2857   A1129 500r multi   1.75   1.25

Butterflies
A1130

2003-05   Photo.   *Perf. 13x13½*
2858   A1130 100r Zygaena sp.   .25   —
2859   A1130 200r Issoria
       lathonia   .40   —
2859A A1130 250r Utethesia
       pulchella   .50   —
2860   A1130 300r Argynnis
       paphia   .60   —
   a.   Longer "Rls." + label ('04)   1.50
2862   A1130 500r Polygonia
       egea   1.00   —
2863   A1130 600r Papilio
       machaon   1.25   —
   a.   Longer "Rls." + label ('04)   2.50
2864   A1130 650r Colias
       aurorina
       ('04)   1.25   —
2866   A1130 1000r Inachis io
       ('04)   1.40   —
2867   A1130 2000r Papilio
       demoleus
       ('03)   4.00   —
2867A A1130 2100r Papilio
       domoleus
       ('05)   2.25   —
2868   A1130 3000r Euphydryas
       aurinia ('04) 3.75   —
2868A A1130 4400r Danaus me-
       lanippus   4.25   —
2869   A1130 5500r Colias
       aurorina   5.50   —

   Issued: 100r, 7/14; 200r, 5/12; 300r, 5/14;
500r, 8/25; 600r, 6/10; 250r, 12/17; 1000r,
1/6/04; Nos. 2860a, 2863a, 1/21/04; 1000r,
2/22/04; 3000r, 3/10/04, 650r, 2004. 2100r,
4/18/05; 4400r, 3/15/05; 5500r, 4/13/05.
   The period in "Rls." is under the second
zero on Nos. 2860a and 2863a. It is under the
first zero on Nos. 2860 and 2863.

Social Security
Organization,
50th
Anniv. — A1131

2003, Aug. 16   Photo.   *Perf. 13*
2870   A1131 600r multi   1.75   1.00

Government Martyrs — A1132

Illustration reduced.

2003, Aug. 24
2871   A1132 600r multi + label   2.00   2.00

Government
Week — A1133

2003, Aug. 25
2872   A1133 600r multi   1.50   1.00

Caspian
Sea
Fauna
A1134

   No. 2873: a, Caspian seal. b, Beluga.

2003, Sept. 9
2873   Horiz. pair + label   7.50   7.50
a.-b.   A1134 600r Either single   1.50   1.50
   c.   Souvenir sheet, 2 each #2873a-
       2873b   9.50   9.50

     See Russia No. 6795.

World
Post
Day
A1135

   No. 2874: a, Computer, UPU emblem, satellite. b, Post office loading dock, mail box, airplanes. c, Postal clerk at desk, truck. d, Post
rider, ruins and statues.

2003, Oct. 9
2874   Horiz. strip of 4   8.00   8.00
a.-d.   A1135 600r Any single   1.00   .75

Shared
Functions of
the Police and
Post
Office — A1136

2003, Oct. 5   Photo.   *Perf. 13*
2875   A1136 500r multi   1.00   .75

Worldwide Fund for Nature
(WWF) — A1137

   No. 2876 — Cheetah: a, Cub. b, Two adults
lying in grass. c, Two adults standing. d, Head
of adult.

2003, Nov. 18
2876   A1137 500r Block of 4,
       #a-d   4.75   4.75

Eid ul-Fitr
A1138

2003, Nov. 26
2877   A1138 600r multi   1.75   1.25

Miniature Sheet

Bam Earthquake, Dec. 26,
2003 — A1139

   No. 2878: a, Landmarks in Bam before
earthquake. b, Earthquake devastation. c,
Doctors treating injured people. d, Rescue
personnel, map of world.

2004, Feb. 4
2878   A1139 500r Sheet of 4,
       #a-d   3.25   3.25

Islamic
Revolution,
25th Anniv.
A1140

2004, Feb. 11
2879   A1140 600r multi   1.00   1.00

Hossein Rezazadeh,
Weightlifter — A1141

Illustration reduced.

2004, Feb. 15
2880   A1141 1200r multi   2.00   2.00

     Dated 2003.

ISO 9001-2000
Certification
A1142

2004, Feb. 29
2881   A1142 600r multi   1.00   1.00

Freshwater Fish — A1143

Designs: Nos. 2882, 2888a, 100r, Carassius auratus. Nos. 2883, 2888b, 200r, Carassius auratus, diff. Nos. 2884, 2888c, 300r, Poecilia reticlate. Nos. 2885, 2888d, 400r, Betta splendens. Nos. 2886, 2888e, 500r, Carassius auratus, diff. Nos. 2887, 2888f, 600r, Carassius auratus, diff.

2004, Mar. 6
Stamps With White Frames
2882-2887 A1143 Set of 6   4.00 4.00
Miniature Sheet
Stamps Without White Frames
2888 A1143 Sheet of 6, #a-f   5.00 5.00

FIFA (Fédération Internationale de Football Association), Cent. — A1144

Illustration reduced.

2004, May 21   **Perf. 13**
2889 A1144 600r multi   1.00 1.00

Miniature Sheet

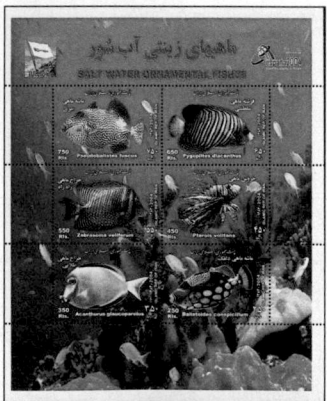

Saltwater Fish — A1145

No. 2890: a, 250r, Balistoides conspicillum. b, 350r, Acanthurus glaucopareius. c, 450r, Pterois volitans. d, 550r, Zebrasoma veliferum. e, 650r, Pygoplites diacanthus. f, 750r, Pseudobalistes fuscus.

2004, May 22   **Perf. 13**
2890 A1145 Sheet of 6, #a-f 4.25 4.25
España 2004 Intl. Philatelic Exhibition, Riccione Philatelic Exhibition.

Reporter's Day — A1147

2004, Aug. 7
2892 A1147 650r multi   .80 .80

2004 Summer Olympics, Athens — A1148

No. 2893: a, Taekwondo. b, Weight lifting. c, Wrestling. d, Judo.
Illustration reduced.

2004, Aug. 12
2893 A1148 650r Block of 4, #a-d   3.50 3.50

Poets — A1149

No. 2894: a, Kabir (1440-1518), Indian poet. b, Hafiz Shirazi (c. 1325-c. 1389), Persian poet.
Illustration reduced.

2004, Aug. 16   **Perf. 13**
2894 A1149 600r Horiz. pair,
            #a-b   1.50 1.50
See India No. 2070.

International Avicenna Congress — A1150

No. 2895: a, Memorial. b, Avicenna (980-1037), scientist, philosopher.
Illustration reduced.

2004, Aug. 22
2895 A1150 650r Horiz. pair,
            #a-b   1.60 1.60

Miniature Sheet

Primates — A1151

No. 2896: a, Chacma baboons. b, Chimpanzee. c, Chimpanzees. d, Mandrill.

2004, Aug. 28
2896 A1151 500r Sheet of 4,
            #a-d   5.00 5.00
World Stamp Championship 2004, Singapore.

Miniature Sheet

Cats — A1152

No. 2897: a, Gray cat, no tail visible. b, Gray cat, tail at right. c, Brown and white cat. d, White cat. e, Gray cat on rock. f, Gray cat, tail at left.

2004, Aug. 31
2897 A1152 500r Sheet of 6,
            #a-f   6.00 6.00

12th Paralympic Games, Athens — A1153

2004, Sept. 17
2898 A1153 650r multi   .80 .50

Iran - Iraq War, 24th Anniv. — A1154

2004, Sept. 21
2899 A1154 650r multi   .80 .50

Tehran University, 70th Anniv. — A1155

2004, Oct. 22
2900 A1155 650r multi   .80 .50

Poets — A1156

No. 2901: a, Dr. Jalal-eddin Ashtiani (wearing turban). b, Mahmoud Farschian (with hand on chin). c, Dr. Jafar Shahidi (looking right). d, Dr. Hosain Mirshamsi (looking left).
Illustration reduced.

2004, Nov. 9   Photo.   Perf. 13
2901 A1156 500r Block of 4, #a-d 2.50 2.00

Mountains — A1157

No. 2902: a, Damavand Mountain, Iran. b, Bolivar Peak, Venezuela.
Illustration reduced.

2004, Nov. 28   Photo.   Perf. 13
2902 A1157 650r Horiz. pair,
            #a-b   1.50 1.00

First Intl. Biennale of Islamic Poster Art — A1158

No. 2903: a, Hand. b, Dove in nest. c, Slingshot. d, Crescent.

2004, Nov. 29
2903 A1158 500r Block of 4, #a-d   2.50 2.00

Imam Reza's Birthday — A1159

No. 2904: a, Corner of mosque. b, Dome. c, Facade. d, Archway.

Illustration reduced.

2004, Dec. 24 Photo. Perf. 13x13¼
2904 A1159 500r Block of 4, #a-d 2.50 2.00

Ali Daei,
Soccer Player
A1160

2005, Feb. 2 Photo. Perf. 13
2905 A1160 650r multi .75 .50

Iran Film Museum — A1161

No. 2906: a, Scene from *Where is the Friend's Home?* b, Scene from *The Children of Heaven.* c, Museum building. d, Scene from *The Cow.*
Illustration reduced.

2005, Feb. 10
2906 A1161 500r Block of 4, #a-d 2.00 1.00

Airplanes — A1162

No. 2907: a, AN-140. b, IR-140.
Illustration reduced.

2005, Mar. 6 Perf. 13x13½
2907 Horiz. pair with central
label 2.00 1.00
a.-b. A1162 850r Either single
See Ukraine No. 568.

Souvenir Sheet

Expo 2005, Aichi, Japan — A1163

No. 2908: a, Persepolis. b, Yazd air ventilation towers. c, Iranian flag, typical Iranian desert architecture. d, Clay tablet with inscriptions.

2005, Mar. 24 Perf. 13
2908 A1163 650r Sheet of 4, #a-d 2.50 2.00

Tehran University of Medical Sciences, 70th Anniv. — A1164

2005, May 2
2909 A1164 650r multi .75 .50

Police Week — A1165

2005, Oct. 29
2910 A1165 650r multi .75 .50

Mevlana Jalal ad-Din ar-Rumi (1207-73), Islamic Philosopher A1166

2005, Dec. 3
2911 A1166 650r multi 1.50 1.00
See Afghanistan Nos. 1449-1451, Syria No. 1574, Turkey No. 2971.

Gardens — A1167

No. 2912: a, Gardens of Royal Palace of La Granja de San Ildefonso, Segovia, Spain. b, Bagh-e-Shahzadeh, Kerman, Iran.
Illustration reduced.

2005, Dec. 17
2912 A1167 650r Horiz. pair, #a-b 1.50 1.00
See Spain No. 3374.

Self-Sufficiency in Wheat Production A1168

2006, Jan. 4
2913 A1168 650r multi .75 .50

Souvenir Sheet

Maps of the Persian Gulf — A1169

No. 2914: a, German map, 16th cent. b, Egyptian Ministry of Culture map, 1966. c, Saudi Arabian map, 1952. d, Map by Scoteri Motthaei, 18th cent.

2006, June 7
2914 A1169 650r Sheet of 4, #a-d 5.00 2.50

2006 World Cup Soccer Championships, Germany — A1170

Illustration reduced.

2006, June 10
2915 A1170 650r multi .90 .50

Abbas Shafi — A1171

Alama Mohammed Reza Hakimi A1172

Mohamed Hossein Gandji A1173

Alama Mohammed Hassan Amoli — A1174

2006, Sept. 18 Litho. Perf. 13
2916 Block of 4 1.00 .75
a. A1171 650r multi 1.00 .75
b. A1172 650r multi 1.00 .75
c. A1173 650r multi 1.00 .75
d. A1174 650r multi 1.00 .75
Dated 2005.

Third Meeting of Economic Cooperation Organization Postal Authorities, Tehran — A1175

Illustration reduced.

2006, Sept. 20
2917 A1175 650r multi 2.00 1.00
Compare with Pakistan No. 1101.

Basij, 27th Anniv. A1176

2006, Nov. 26
2918 A1176 650r multi 2.00 1.00

Souvenir Sheet

Isfahan, 2006 Islamic Cultural Capital — A1177

No. 2919: a, Chehel Sotun Palace. b, Emam Mosque. c, Aliqapu Palace. d, Khajo Bridge.

2006, Dec. 30
2919 A1177 650r Sheet of 4, #a-d 5.00 2.50

A1177a A1177b

Iran Post Emblem
Hologram on Foil

2006, Dec. | | **Die Cut**
Self-Adhesive

2919E	A1177a	4400r silver	3.50	3.50
2919F	A1177b	5500r silver	4.50	4.50

Martyrs — A1178

No. 2920: a, Man and flags. b, Ten men.

2007, Jan. 7
2920 A1178 650r Horiz. pair, #a-
b   2.00 1.00
Dated 2006.

Souvenir Sheet

Iranian Constitution, Cent. — A1179

No. 2921: a, Man, gate. b, Parliament. c, Three men, gate. d, Two men, gate.

2006, May 8   **Litho.**   **Perf. 13**
2921 A1179 650r Sheet of 4, #a-
d   5.00 3.00

Souvenir Sheet

Seventh General Assembly of
Association of Asian Parliaments for
Peace, Tehran — A1180

No. 2922: a, Emblem of Association of Asian Parliaments for Peace. b, Dove, colors of Iranian flag. c, Gate and flags. d, Emblem of Islamic Consultative Assembly.

2006, Nov. 14
2922 A1180 650r Sheet of 4, #a-
d   5.00 2.50

Peaceful Nuclear Energy — A1181

Illustration reduced.

2007, Feb. 11
2923 A1181 650r multi   2.00 1.00

Iranian-built
Engine
A1182

2007, Feb. 26
2924 A1182 650r multi   1.50 .60

Shrine of
Fatima,
Qom — A1183

2007, Mar. 18
2925 A1183 650r multi   1.50 .50

New Year — A1184

No. 2926: a, Flowers, man with drum. b, Trumpeters, fishbowl, Koran, apples, grass. Illustration reduced.

2007, Mar. 19
2926 A1184 650r Horiz. pair, #a-
b   2.00 1.00

Map of Persian
Gulf — A1185

2007   **Litho.**   **Perf. 13x13½**
Side Panel Color

2927	A1185	200r brown	1.00	.50
2928	A1185	300r yellow	1.00	.50
a.		Taller Arabic "Rls." + label	—	
2929	A1185	650r orange	1.00	.50
a.		Wider "650" + label	—	
2930	A1185	2100r blue	4.00	2.00
2931	A1185	4400r blue	8.00	3.00

Issued: 200r, 9/9; 300r, 5/23; 4400r, 7/25. 650r, 10/30; 2100r, 11/24; No. 2929a, 1/27/09. See Nos. 2943-2945, 2956-2960.

Chemical Weapons Convention, 10th
Anniv. — A1186

2007, June 29   **Perf. 13**
2932 A1186 650r multi   1.50 .50

38th Intl. Physics Olympiad,
Isfahan — A1187

2007, July 3
2933 A1187 650r multi   1.50 .50

K. K. Sarughy
A1188

2007, Aug. 22
2934 A1188 650r multi   1.50 .50

Imam Moussa
Sadr, Shiite
Leader Who
Disappeared in
1978 — A1189

2007, Aug. 31
2935 A1189 650r multi   1.50 .50

Worldwide Fund for Nature
(WWF) — A1190

No. 2936 — Grus leucogranus: a, Pair, one with head raised, other with head lowered. b, Pair, facing each other. c, Pair, both standing on one leg. d, Running with wings extended. Illustration reduced.

2007, Sept. 9
2936 A1190 650r Block of 4, #a-d 4.00 2.50

Miniature Sheet

Great Messenger Year — A1191

No. 2937 — Arabic text and: a, Arch. b, Arabic text in diamond. c, Roman Colosseum. d, Pyramids.

2007, Jan. 6   **Litho.**   **Perf. 13**
2937 A1191 650r Sheet of 4, #a-
d   5.00 2.50

Communications and Public Relations
Day — A1192

2007, May 17
2938 A1192 650r multi   1.50 .50

Miniature Sheet

Return of Prisoners of War — A1193

No. 2939 — Flowers and: a, Geese. b, Iranian man, hand symbol. c, Prisoners of war on bus. d, People on motorcycles greeting prisoners of war.

2007, Aug. 17
2939 A1193 650r Sheet of 4, #a-
d   5.00 2.50

Jamkaran
Mosque
A1194

2007, Aug. 29
2940 A1194 650r multi   1.50 .50

World Post
Day — A1195

2007, Sept. 10
2941 A1195 650r multi   2.00 1.00

Mevlana Jalal
ad-Din ar-Rumi
(1207-73),
Islamic
Philosopher
A1196

2007, Oct. 28
2942 A1196 650r multi   2.00 1.00

Map of Persian Gulf Type of 2007

2008   *Perf. 13x13½*

Side Panel Color

2943	A1185	1000r green	2.00	1.00
2944	A1185	2000r lilac	4.00	2.00
2945	A1185	5500r red	10.00	4.00

Issued: 1000r, 1/16; 2000r, 2/5; 5500r, 1/5.

Information Technology Infrastructure Development A1197

2008, Jan. 16   *Perf. 13*
2946 A1197 650r multi   2.00   .75

Navvab Safavi (1924-55), Founder of Islamic Fedayeen A1198

2008, Jan. 17
2947 A1198 650r multi   1.50   .75

Falsafi, Preacher, 100th Anniv. of Birth — A1199

2008, Feb. 27
2948 A1199 650r multi   1.50   .75

Death of Emad Moghnie, Hezbollah Leader — A1200

Illustration reduced.

2008, Mar. 10
2949 A1200 650r multi   2.00   1.00

New Year A1201

2008, Mar. 15
2950 A1201 650r multi   1.50   .75

Abdulazim Shrine — A1202

Illustration reduced.

2008, Apr. 11   *Perf. 13x13½*
2951 A1202 650r multi   1.50   .75

Children and Youth Water Festival A1203

2008, Apr. 21   *Perf. 13*
2952 A1203 650r multi   1.50   .75

Islamic City Councils, 10th Anniv. A1204

2008, Apr. 28
2953 A1204 650r multi   1.50   .75

Thiqat al-Islam Kulayni, Islamic Legal Scholar, 1100th Anniv. of Death — A1205

2008, May 8
2954 A1205 650r multi   1.50   .75

Buildings in Morocco and Iran — A1206

No. 2955: a, Kasbah, Oudayas, Morocco. b, Falak-Ol-Aflak Castle, Iran.
Illustration reduced.

2008, May 12   Litho.   *Perf. 13*
2955 A1206 650r Horiz. pair, #a-
    b, + label   2.50   1.50

See Morocco No. 1061.

Map of Persian Gulf Type of 2007

2008-09   Litho.   *Perf. 13x13½*

Side Panel Color

2956	A1185	100r blue	.50	.50
2957	A1185	250r pale orange	.50	.50
2958	A1185	400r red	.50	.50
2959	A1185	500r dark green	.50	.50
2960	A1185	3000r pink		
		Nos. 2956-2960 (5)	2.00	2.00

Issued: 100r, 9/8; 250r, 10/20; 400r, 9/13; 500r, 5/28; 3000r, 2/15/09.

Handicrafts Day — A1207

No. 2961: a, Engraved copper cup. b, Mina vase.
Illustration reduced.

2008, June 10   Litho.   *Perf. 13*
2961 A1207 650r Horiz. pair, #a-
    b   2.50   1.50

Miniature Sheet

Trenchless Trench Makers — A1207a

No. 2962 — Men and: a, Construction equipment with extendable arm. b, Bulldozer under roof. c, Utility vehicle. d, Ship on truck's flat-bed trailer.

2008, June 16   Litho.   *Perf. 13*
2962 A1207a 650r Sheet of 4,
    #a-d   .60   .60

Javid-al-Asar Haj Ahmed Motevasselian, Diplomat A1208

2008, July 3
2963 A1208 650r multi   1.50   .75

Mountains in Kyrgyzstan and Iran — A1209

No. 2964: a, Khan-Tengri, Kyrgyzstan. b, Sabalan Peak, Iran.
Illustration reduced.

2008, Aug. 15   650r Horiz. pair, #a-
    b, + central la-
    bel   2.50   1.50
2964 A1209

See Kyrgyzstan No. 313.

Ancient Jewelry From Iran and Kazakhstan — A1210

No. 2965: a, Gold medal depicting lions, 7th cent. B.C., Iran. b, Buckle depicting snow leopard and mountains, 4th-5th cent. B.C., Kazakhstan.
Illustration reduced.

2008, Sept. 7
2965 A1210 650r Horiz. pair, #a-
    b   2.50   1.50

See Kazakhstan No. 578.

Iran Post Corporation, 20th Anniv. — A1211

Illustration reduced.

2008, Oct. 8   *Perf. 13x13½*
2966 A1211 1200r multi   2.00   1.00

Consumer Rights Day — A1212

2008, Feb. 28   *Perf. 13*
2967 A1212 650r multi

Ayatollah Sheikh Hashem Ghazvini A1213

2008, May 5
2968 A1213 650r multi

Bank Melli Iran, 80th Anniv. A1214

2008, Sept. 10
2969 A1214 650r multi

World
Jerusalem
Day — A1215

2008, Sept. 26
2970 A1215 650r multi

Statue of
Sheikh
Abulhassan
Kharaghani
A1216

2008, Nov. 6
2971 A1216 650r multi

Commander M.
R. Pourkian
and
Tank — A1217

2008, Nov. 13
2972 A1217 650r multi

28-Year
Achievements
of Security
Services
A1218

2008, Nov. 19
2973 A1218 650r multi

Zabol Burnt City Archaeological
Site — A1219

2008, Dec. 21
2974 A1219 650r multi

National Day of
Exports
A1220

2008, Oct. 21   **Perf. 13**
2975 A1220 650r multi

Musical Instruments — A1221

No. 2976: a, Gijak of Badahshon. b,
Khorasan local dotaar.
Illustration reduced.

2008, Dec. 15
2976 A1221 650r Horiz. pair, #a-b

See Tajikistan No. 340.

Support for Gaza
Palestinians — A1222

2009, Jan. 27
2977 A1222 1200r multi

Ayatollah Khomeini (1900-
89) — A1223

2009, Feb. 10
2978 A1223 650r multi

Islamic Revolution, 30th anniv.

Abbas, Karimi, Reza Cheraghi, and
Mohammad Hemat — A1224

Illustration reduced.

2009, Mar. 3
2979 A1224 650r multi

Safir Omid, First Iranian
Satellite — A1225

No. 2980: a, Iranian flag, rocket on launch
pad, emblem. b, Satellite, Earth.
Illustration reduced.

2009, Mar. 7
2980 A1225 1300r Horiz. pair,
#a-b

10th Economic Cooperation
Organization Summit, Tehran — A1226

2009, Mar. 11
2981 A1226 1300r multi

New
Year
2009
A1227

2009, Mar. 25
2982 A1227 1300r multi

Nurse's
Day — A1228

2009, Apr. 28
2983 A1228 1300r multi

Fish — A1229

Designs: 100r, Chaetodon mesoleucos.
200r, Holacanthus ciliaris. 250r, Euxiphipops

xanthomelapon. 300r, Pomacanthus
maculosus. 500r, Centropyge bicolor. 1000r,
Chaetodontoplus septentrionalis. 2000r,
Chaetodon larvatus. 3100r, Chaetodon semilarvatus. 4000r, Pomacanthus chrysurus.
5000r, Pomacanthus navarchus. 6400r, Paracanthurus hepatus. 7500r, Premnas
biaculeatus.

2009-10   Litho.   Perf. 13x13½
2984	A1229	100r multi	.20	.20
2985	A1229	200r multi	.20	.20
2986	A1229	250r multi	.20	.20
2987	A1229	300r multi	.20	.20
2990	A1229	500r multi	.20	.20
2993	A1229	1000r multi	.20	.20
2994	A1229	2000r multi	.40	.40
2995	A1229	3100r multi	.65	.65
2996	A1229	4000r multi	.80	.80
2997	A1229	5000r multi	1.00	1.00
2998	A1229	6400r multi	1.40	1.40
2999	A1229	7500r multi	1.50	1.50
		Nos. 2984-2999 (12)	6.95	6.95

Issued: 100r, 9/25/10; 200r, 10/26; 250r,
4/7/10; 300r, 4/12/10; 500r, 12/21; 1000r,
6/22; 2000r, 8/1/10; 3100r, 1/19/10; 4000r,
7/18/10; 5000r, 6/15/10; 6400r, 11/10; 7500r,
10/12.

Epic of
Presence
A1230

2009, June 12   Litho.   Perf. 13
3000 A1230 1300r multi   .30   .30

Mother's
Day — A1231

2009, June 14
3001 A1231 1100r multi   .25   .25

Birds — A1232

No. 3002: a, White-tailed eagle. b, Osprey.

2009, June 24
3002 A1232 2000r Horiz. pair,
#a-b   .80   .80

See Portugal Nos. 3155-3156.

Left Part of Stamp

Center Part of Stamp

Birds (Right Part of Stamp) — A1233

2009, July 11   **Perf. 13x13½**
3003 A1233 1500r multi   .30   .30

The illustration of No. 3003 is shown above broken into the three sections shown on the stamp. See Cuba No. 4835.

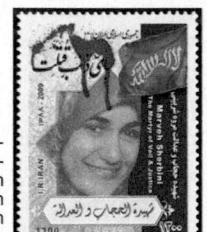

Marwa El-Sherbini (1977-2009), Woman Murdered in German Courtroom A1234

2009, July 19   **Perf. 13**
3004 A1234 1300r multi   .30   .30

Islamic Human Rights and Human Dignity Day A1235

2009, Aug. 5
3005 A1235 1200r multi   .25   .25

Rural Information and Communication Technologies in Iran — A1236

2009, Aug. 11
3006 A1236 1000r multi   .20   .20

Miniature Sheet

Conservation of Marine Turtles — A1237

No. 3007: a, 650r, Eretmochelys imbricata. b, 1000r, Eretmochelys imbricata, diff. c, 1500r, Chelonia mydas. d, 1850r, Chelonia mydas, diff.

2009, Aug. 26
3007 A1237   Sheet of 4, #a-d   1.00 1.00

A1238

No. 3008: a, World Post Day. b, World Child Day.

2009, Oct. 9
3008 A1238 1200r Horiz. pair,
     #a-b   .50   .50

17th Book Week — A1239

2009, Nov. 14
3009 A1239 1200r multi   .25   .25

Rob'e Rashidi University Endowment Document — A1240

2009, Dec. 1   **Litho.**
3010 A1240 1200r multi   .25   .25

Universal Declaration of Human Rights, 60th Anniv. — A1241

2009, Dec. 13
3011 A1241 1200r multi   .25   .25

Ayatollah Mohammad Mofatteh (1928-79) A1242

2009, Dec. 18   **Perf. 13¾x14¼**
3012 A1242 1200r multi   .25   .25

Buildings in Indonesia and Iran — A1243

No. 3013: a, Soltanieh Dome, Iran. b, Al-Markaz Mosque, Indonesia.

2009, Dec. 23   **Perf. 13**
3013 A1243 2000r Horiz. pair,
     #a-b, + central label   .80   .80

See Indonesia Nos. 2218-2219.

Intl. Year of Astronomy — A1244

No. 3014: a, 1000r, Artificial plan of Maragheh Observatory. b, 1200r, Al-Tafhim, by Abu Ryehan Biruni. c, 1300r, Armillary sphere. d, 1500r, Taqi al-Din and astronomers, 16th cent.

2010, Feb. 24   **Perf. 13¾x14¼**
3014 A1244   Block of 4, #a-d   1.00 1.00

Mullah Sadra (c. 1571-1641) A1245

2010, May 18
3015 A1245 1300r multi   .25   .25

Khaje Abdullah Ansari (1006-88), Religious Commentator — A1246

2010, July 25   **Perf. 13¾**
3016 A1246 2000r multi   .40   .40

See Afghanistan No. , Tajikistan No.

Destroyer Jamaran — A1247

2010, Sept. 1   **Perf. 14¼x13¾**
3017 A1247 2000r multi   .40   .40

Martyred Engineers of the Sacred Defense A1248

2010, oct. 20   **Perf. 13¾x14¼**
3018 A1248 2000r multi   .40   .40

Shah-e-Cheragh Holy Shrine, Shiraz — A1249

No, 3019: a, 1200r, Mosque dome and minaret. b, 1300r, Shrine.

2010, Nov. 14   **Perf. 13¾**
3019 A1249   Horiz. pair, #a-b   .50   .50

SEMI-POSTAL STAMPS

Lion and Bull, Persepolis SP1

Persian Soldier, Persepolis — SP2

Palace of Darius the Great — SP3

Tomb of Cyrus the Great, Pasargadae SP4

King Darius on his Throne — SP5

Perf. 13x13½, 13½x13

1948, Jan. 30   Engr.   Unwmk.

B1	SP1	50d + 25d emer	2.00	2.00
B2	SP2	1r + 50d red	2.00	2.00
B3	SP3	2½r + 1¼r blue	2.00	2.00
B4	SP4	5r + 2½r pur	3.00	3.00
B5	SP5	10r + 5r vio brn	3.00	3.00
			12.00	12.00

The surtax was for reconstruction of the tomb of Avicenna (980-1037), Persian physician and philosopher, at Hamadan.

Ardashir II — SP6

Shapur I and Valerian SP7

Designs: 1r+50d, King Narses, Naqsh-i-Rustam. 5r+2½r, Taq-i-Kisra, Ctesiphon. 10r+5r, Ardashir I and Ahura Mazda.

1949, June 11

B6	SP6	50d + 25d green	1.75	2.00
B7	SP6	1r + 50d ver	1.75	2.00
B8	SP7	2½r + 1½r blue	1.75	2.00
B9	SP7	5r + 2½r magenta	3.00	3.25
B10	SP7	10r + 5r grnsh gray	3.00	3.25
		Nos. B6-B10 (5)	11.25	12.50

The surtax was for reconstruction of Avicenna's tomb at Hamadan.

Gunbad-i-Ali — SP8

Alaviyan, Hamadan SP9

Seldjukide Coin — SP10

Designs: 1r+½r, Masjid-i-Jami, Isfahan. 5r+2½r, Masjid-i-Jami, Ardistan.

1949, Dec. 22

B11	SP8	50d + 25d bl grn	1.50	1.50
B12	SP8	1r + ½r dk brn	1.50	1.50
B13	SP9	2½r + 1¼r blue	1.50	1.50
B14	SP9	5r + 2½r red	2.50	2.50
B15	SP10	10r + 5r olive gray	2.75	3.00
		Nos. B11-B15 (5)	9.75	10.00

The surtax was for reconstruction of Avicenna's tomb at Hamadan.

Koran, Crescent and Flag — SP11

1950, Oct. 2   Litho.   Perf. 11

B16	SP11	1.50r + 1r multi	32.50	20.00

Economic Conference of the Islamic States.

Tomb of Baba Afzal at Kashan SP12

Gorgan Vase — SP13

Designs: 2½r+1¼r, Tower of Ghazan. 5r+2½r, Masjid-i Gawhar. 10r+5r, Mihrab of the Mosque at Rezaieh.

Perf. 13x13½, 13½x13

1950, Aug. 23   Engr.

B17	SP12	50d + 25d dk grn	1.50	1.50
B18	SP13	1r + ½r blue	1.50	1.50
B19	SP13	2½r + 1¼r choc	1.50	1.50
B20	SP12	5r + 2½r red	2.50	2.50
B21	SP12	10r + 5r gray	2.75	3.00
		Nos. B17-B21 (5)	9.75	10.00

The surtax was for reconstruction of Avicenna's tomb at Hamadan.

Mohammad Reza Shah Pahlavi and Map — SP14

Monument to Fallen Liberators of Azerbaijan SP15

Designs: 1r+50d, Marching troops. 1.50r+75d, Running advance with flag. 2.50r+1.25r, Mohammad Reza ShahPahlavi. 3r+1.50r, Parade of victors.

1950, Dec. 12   Litho.

B22	SP14	10d + 5d blk brn	10.00	5.00
B23	SP15	50d + 25d blk brn	12.00	5.00
B24	SP15	1r + 50d brown lake	18.00	7.00
B25	SP14	1.50r + 75d org ver	20.00	10.00
B26	SP14	2.50r + 1.25r blue	25.00	17.50
B27	SP15	3r + 1.50r ultra	27.50	16.00
		Nos. B22-B27 (6)	112.50	60.50

Liberation of Azerbaijan Province from communists, 4th anniv.

The surtax was for families of Persian soldiers who died in the struggle.

Koran Gate at Shiraz SP16

Saadi — SP17

Design: 50d+50d, Tomb of Saadi, Shiraz.

Perf. 11x10½, 10½x11

1952, Apr. 30   Photo.   Unwmk.

B28	SP16	25d + 25d dl bl grn	3.75	2.50
B29	SP16	50d + 50d brn ol	4.25	2.50
B30	SP17	1.50r + 50d vio bl	25.00	7.50
		Nos. B28-B30 (3)	33.00	12.50

770th birthday of Saadi, Persian poet. The surtax was to help complete Saadi's tomb at Shiraz.

Three stamps of same denominations and colors, with values enclosed in tablets, were prepared but not officially issued.

View of Hamadan SP18

Avicenna — SP19

Designs: 2½r+1¼r, Gonbad Qabus (tower of tomb). 5r+2½r, Old tomb of Avicenna. 10r+5r, New tomb.

Perf. 13x13½, 13½x13

1954, Apr. 21   Engr.   Unwmk.

B31	SP18	50d + 25d dp grn	1.50	1.50
B32	SP19	1r + ½r vio brn	1.50	1.50
B33	SP19	2½r + 1¼r blue	1.50	1.50
B34	SP18	5r + 2½r ver	2.50	2.50
B35	SP18	10r + 5r ol gray	3.50	3.50
		Nos. B31-B35 (5)	10.50	10.50

The surtax was for reconstruction of Avicenna's tomb at Hamadan.

> **Catalogue values for unused stamps in this section, from this point to the end of the section, are for Never Hinged items.**

Mother with Children and Ruins — SP20

Wmk. 316

1963, Feb. 4   Litho.   Perf. 10½

B36	SP20	14r + 6r dk bl grn & lt brn	3.00	1.00

The surtax was for the benefit of survivors of the Kazvin earthquake.

For overprints see Nos. C86-C88.

AIR POST STAMPS

Type of 1909 Overprinted

1927   Unwmk.   Typo.   Perf. 11½

C1	A31	1c org & maroon	3.50	1.25
C2	A31	2c vio & maroon	3.50	1.25
C3	A31	3c grn & maroon	3.50	1.25
C4	A31	6c red & maroon	3.50	1.25
C5	A31	9c gray & maroon	5.00	1.25
C6	A31	10c red vio & mar	7.00	1.25
C7	A31	13c dk bl & mar	8.00	2.75
C8	A31	1k sil, vio & bis brown	8.00	2.75
C9	A31	26c dk grn & mar	8.00	2.75
C10	A31	2k sil, dk grn & bis brown	15.00	3.50
C11	A31	3k sil, gray & bis brown	25.00	7.00
C12	A31	4k sil, bl & bis brown	40.00	17.50
C13	A31	5k gold, brn & bis brown	40.00	12.50
C14	A31	10k gold, org & bis brown	250.00	275.00
C15	A31	20k gold, ol grn & bis brn	250.00	275.00
C16	A31	30k gold, car & bis brown	250.00	275.00
		Nos. C1-C16 (16)	920.00	881.25

Counterfeit overprints are plentiful. They are found on Nos. 448-463, perf. 12½x12 instead of 11½.

Exist without overprint. Value, set $4,000.

AP1

AP2

AP3

AP4

AP5

Airplane, Value and "Poste aérièn" Surcharged on Revenue Stamps

1928   Perf. 11

C17	AP1	3k yellow brn	125.00	40.00
C18	AP2	5k dark brown	30.00	15.00
C19	AP3	1t gray vio	30.00	15.00
C20	AP4	2t olive bister	30.00	15.00
C21	AP5	3t deep green	35.00	20.00
		Nos. C17-C21 (5)	250.00	105.00

AP6

AP7

"Poste aerienne"

1928-29
C22	AP6	1c emerald	1.25	.50
a.		1c yellow green	1.25	.50
b.		Double overprint	35.00	
C23	AP6	2c light blue	1.25	.20
C24	AP6	3c bright rose	1.25	.20
C25	AP6	5c olive brn	1.25	.20
a.		"5" omitted	750.00	850.00
b.		Horiz. pair, imperf. btwn.	300.00	
C26	AP6	10c dark green	1.25	.20
a.		"10" omitted	40.00	
b.		"1" inverted	75.00	
C27	AP7	1k dull vio	3.00	1.00
a.		"1" inverted	75.00	
C28	AP7	2k orange	7.50	2.50
a.		"S" for "s" in "Krs"	150.00	
		Nos. C22-C28 (7)	16.75	4.80

Counterfeits exist.

Revenue Stamps Similar to Nos. C17 to C21, Overprinted like Nos. C22 to C28: "Poste aerienne"

1929
C29	AP1	3k yellow brn	100.00	25.00
C30	AP2	5k dark brn	20.00	10.00
C31	AP3	10k violet	25.00	15.00
C32	AP4	20k olive grn	30.00	15.00
C33	AP5	30k deep grn	40.00	20.00
		Nos. C29-C33 (5)	215.00	85.00

Riza Shah Pahlavi and Eagle — AP8

1930, July 6   Photo.   *Perf. 12½x11½*
C34	AP8	1c ol bis & brt bl	.50	.50
C35	AP8	2c blue & gray blk	.50	.50
C36	AP8	3c ol grn & dk vio	.50	.50
C37	AP8	4c dk vio & pck bl	.50	.50
C38	AP8	5c lt grn & mag	.50	.50
C39	AP8	6c mag & bl grn	.50	.50
C40	AP8	8c dk gray & dp violet	.50	.50
C41	AP8	10c dp ultra & ver	.50	.50
C42	AP8	12c slate & org	.50	.50
C43	AP8	15c brn & ol green	.50	.50
C44	AP8	1k Prus bl & scar	5.00	2.50

Engr.
C45	AP8	2k black & ultra	5.00	2.50
C46	AP8	3k dk brn & gray green	6.50	3.00
C47	AP8	5k dp red & gray black	6.50	4.00
C48	AP8	1t orange & vio	25.00	8.00
C49	AP8	2t dk grn & red brown	25.00	10.00
C50	AP8	3t brn vio & sl bl	175.00	50.00
		Nos. C34-C50 (17)	253.00	85.00

Same Overprinted in Black

1935   Photo.
			Photo.	
C51	AP8	1c ol bis & brt bl	.50	.50
C52	AP8	2c blue & gray blk	.50	.50
C53	AP8	3c ol grn & dk vio	.50	.50
C54	AP8	4c dk vio & pck bl	.50	.50
C55	AP8	5c lt grn & mag	.50	.50
C56	AP8	6c mag & bl grn	.50	.50
C57	AP8	8c dk gray & dp violet	.50	.50
C58	AP8	10c dp ultra & ver	.50	.50
C59	AP8	12c slate & org	.50	.50
C60	AP8	15c org brn & ol green	.50	.50
C61	AP8	1k Prus bl & scar	35.00	35.00

Engr.
C62	AP8	2k blk & ultra	30.00	30.00
C63	AP8	3k dk brn & gray green	25.00	15.00
C64	AP8	5k dp red & gray black	10.00	10.00
C65	AP8	1t orange & vio	225.00	175.00
C66	AP8	2t dk grn & red brown	35.00	25.00
C67	AP8	3t brn vio & sl bl	50.00	30.00
		Nos. C51-C67 (17)	415.00	325.00

Plane Over Mt. Demavend AP9

Plane above Mosque AP10

Unwmk.

1953, Jan. 21   Photo.   *Perf. 11*
C68	AP9	50d bl green	1.50	.20
C69	AP10	1r car rose	1.50	.20
C70	AP10	2r dark blue	1.50	.20
C71	AP10	3r dark brn	1.50	.20
C72	AP10	5r purple	3.50	.20
C73	AP10	10r org ver	4.00	.30
C74	AP10	20r vio blue	5.00	.50
C75	AP10	30r olive	10.00	7.00
C76	AP10	50r brown	20.00	4.00
C77	AP10	100r black brn	70.00	15.00
C78	AP10	200r dk bl grn	50.00	20.00
		Nos. C68-C78 (11)	168.50	47.80

AP11

Golden Dome Mosque and Oil Well AP12

1953, May 4   Litho.   *Perf. 10½*
Mosque in Deep Yellow
C79	AP11	3r violet	15.00	10.00
C80	AP12	5r chocolate	20.00	15.00
C81	AP11	10r bl green	55.00	30.00
C82	AP12	20r red vio	110.00	50.00
		Nos. C79-C82 (4)	200.00	105.00

Discovery of oil at Qum.

> Catalogue values for unused stamps in this section, from this point to the end of the section, are for Never Hinged items.

Globe and UN Emblem AP13

Perf. 10½x12½
1957, Oct. 24   Photo.   Wmk. 316
C83	AP13	10r brt red lil & rose	3.00	.90
C84	AP13	20r dl vio & rose vio	6.00	1.25

United Nations Day, Oct. 24, 1957.

UNESCO Emblem AP14

Wmk. 353
1966, June 20   Litho.   *Perf. 10½*
C85	AP14	14r multi	1.10	.30

20th anniversary of UNESCO.

No. B36 Surcharged in Maroon, Brown or Red

1969, Dec. 4   Wmk. 316   *Perf. 10½*
C86	SP20	4r on 14r + 6r (M)	3.00	.95
C87	SP20	10r on 14r + 6r (B)	3.25	.95
C88	SP20	14r on 14r + 6r (R)	3.50	.95
		Nos. C86-C88 (3)	9.75	2.85

1st England-Australia flight, via Iran, made by Capt. Ross Smith and Lt. Keith Smith, 50th anniv.

IATA Emblem and Persepolis AP15

Perf. 13x13½
1970, Oct. 27   Photo.   Wmk. 353
C89	AP15	14r multi	6.50	.80

26th meeting of the Intl. Air Transport Assoc. (IATA), Tehran.

"UIT" AP16

1972, May 17   Litho.   *Perf. 10½*
C90	AP16	14r multicolored	3.25	.75

4th World Telecommunications Day.

Shah and Jet AP17

1974, June 1   Photo.   *Perf. 13*
C91	AP17	4r org & black	.75	.25
C92	AP17	10r blue & black	2.00	.25
C93	AP17	12r dull yel & blk	2.00	.40
C94	AP17	14r lt green & blk	2.25	.40
C95	AP17	20r red lilac & blk	3.00	.65
C96	AP17	50r dull bl & blk	7.50	1.60
		Nos. C91-C96 (6)	17.50	3.55

Crown Prince at Controls of Light Aircraft — AP18

1974, Oct. 31   Litho.   *Perf. 10½*
C97	AP18	14r gold & multi	1.75	.65

Crown Prince Reza's 14th birthday.

> **Importation Prohibited**
> Importation of stamps was prohibited effective Oct. 29, 1987.

Islamic Revolution, 10th Anniv. — AP19

1989, Feb. 11   *Perf. 13x13½*
C98	AP19	40r red vio, blk & gold	.75	.50
C99	AP19	50r bl vio, blk & gold	.75	.50
a.		Pair, #C98-C99	1.75	1.50

Ayatollah Khomeini — AP20

1989, July 11   *Perf. 13*
C100	AP20	70r multicolored	1.00	.50

OFFICIAL STAMPS

Four bicolored stamps of this design (1s, 2s, 5s, 10s), with centers embossed, exist, but were never issued or used in Iran. Value $40. They are known imperforate and in many trial colors.

Shah Muzaffar-ed-Din O1

No. 145 Surcharged in Black

1902   *Perf. 12½*
O5	O1	5c on 1k red	30.00	30.00
O6	O1	10c on 1k red	30.00	30.00
O7	O1	12c on 1k red	40.00	40.00
		Nos. O5-O7 (3)	100.00	100.00

Nos. 351-363
Overprinted in Black

1903-06

O8	A26	1c violet	5.00	.75
O9	A26	2c gray	5.00	.75
O10	A26	3c green	5.00	.75
O11	A26	5c rose	5.00	.75
O12	A26	10c yel brown	8.00	.75
O13	A26	12c blue	12.00	.75

Perf. 11½x11

O14	A27	1k violet	14.00	7.50
O15	A27	2k ultra	22.50	9.00
a.		Violet overprint	50.00	
O16	A27	5k org brown	37.50	17.50
O17	A27	10k rose red	40.00	19.00
a.		Violet overprint		50.00
O18	A27	20k orange ('06)	175.00	40.00
O19	A27	30k green ('06)	225.00	75.00
O20	A27	50k green	250.00	100.00
		Nos. O8-O20 (13)	804.00	272.50

Overprinted on Nos. 368, 370a

O21	A27	2t on 50k grn (Bl)	175.00	75.00
O22	A27	3t on 50k grn (V)	175.00	75.00

Overprinted on Nos. 372, 375, New
Value Surcharged in Blue or Black

1905

O23	A27	2t on 50k grn (Bl)	175.00	75.00
O28	A27	3t on 50k grn (Bk)	175.00	75.00

The 2t on 50k also exists with surcharge in
black and magenta; the 3t on 50k in violet and
magenta. Values about the same.

Regular Issue of
1909 Overprinted

There is a space between the word "Service" and the Persian characters.

1911　　　　　　　**Perf. 12½x12**

O31	A31	1c org & maroon	10.00	7.50
O32	A31	2c vio & maroon	10.00	7.50
O33	A31	3c yel grn & mar	10.00	7.50
O34	A31	6c red & maroon	10.00	7.50
O35	A31	9c gray & maroon	20.00	13.00
O36	A31	10c multicolored	20.00	13.00
O38	A31	1k multicolored	47.50	40.00
O40	A31	2k multicolored	125.00	80.00
		Nos. O31-O40 (8)	252.50	176.00

The 13c, 26c and 3k to 30k denominations
were not regularly issued with this overprint.
Dangerous counterfeits exist, usually on
reprints.

Regular Issue of
1915 Overprinted

1915　　**Wmk. 161**　　**Perf. 11, 11½**

O41	A33	1c car & indigo	2.50	2.50
O42	A33	2c bl & carmine	2.50	2.50
O43	A33	3c dark green	2.50	2.50
O44	A33	5c red	2.50	2.50
O45	A33	6c ol grn & car	2.50	2.50
O46	A33	9c yel brn & vio	2.50	2.50
O47	A33	10c multicolored	2.50	2.50
O48	A33	12c ultramarine	3.00	3.00
O49	A34	1k multicolored	7.00	7.00
O50	A34	24c multicolored	3.50	3.50
O51	A34	2k sil, bl & rose	7.00	7.00
O52	A34	3k sil, vio & brn	7.00	7.00
O53	A34	5k multicolored	7.50	7.50
O54	A35	1t gold, pur & blk	10.00	10.00
O55	A35	2t gold, grn & brn	10.00	10.00
O56	A35	3t multicolored	12.50	12.50
O57	A35	5t gold, bl & ind	15.00	15.00
		Nos. O41-O57 (17)	100.00	100.00

Coronation of Shah Ahmed.
*Reprints have dull rather than shiny over-
print. Value, set, $17.50.*

Coat of Arms
O2　　　　O3

1941　**Unwmk.**　**Litho.**　**Perf. 11**
For Internal Postage

O58	O2	5d violet	5.00	.20
O59	O2	10d magenta	5.00	.20
O60	O2	25d carmine	5.00	.20
O61	O2	50d brown black	5.00	.20
O62	O2	75d claret	7.50	.45

Size: 22½x30mm

O63	O2	1r peacock grn	10.00	.45
O64	O2	1½r deep blue	12.00	1.50
O65	O2	2r light blue	15.00	1.50
O66	O2	3r vio brown	17.50	1.50
O67	O2	5r gray green	35.00	2.00
O68	O2	10r dk brn & bl	350.00	5.00
O69	O2	20r chlky bl & brt pink	450.00	20.00
O70	O2	30r vio & brt grn	600.00	150.00
O71	O2	50r turq grn & dk brown	1,200.	250.00
		Nos. O58-O71 (14)	2,717.	433.20

> **Catalogue values for unused stamps in this section, from this point to the end of the section, are for Never Hinged items.**

Perf. 13½x13

1974, Feb. 25　**Photo.**　**Wmk. 353**
Size: 20x28mm

O72	O3	5d vio & lilac	.30	.25
O73	O3	10d mag & grnsh bl	.30	.25
O74	O3	50d org & lt green	.30	.25
O75	O3	1r green & gold	.40	.20
O76	O3	2r emerald & org	.70	.20

Perf. 13
Size: 23x37mm

O77	O3	6r slate grn & org	.75	.20
O78	O3	8r ultra & yellow	1.00	.20
O79	O3	10r dk bl & lilac	4.25	.25
O80	O3	11r pur & light bl	1.75	.25
O81	O3	14r red & lt ultra	1.75	.60
O82	O3	20r vio blue & org	3.50	.50
O83	O3	50r dk brn & brt grn	9.00	1.75
		Nos. O72-O83 (12)	24.00	4.85

1977-79　**Wmk. 353**　**Perf. 13½x13**
Size: 20x28mm

O87	O3	1r black & lt grn	.35	.20
O88	O3	2r brown & gray	.40	.20
O89	O3	3r ultra & orange	.50	.20
O90	O3	5r green & rose	.65	.20

Perf. 13
Size: 23x37mm

O91	O3	6r dk bl & lt bl ('78)	.75	.45
O92	O3	8r red & bl grn ('78)	.80	.50
O93	O3	10r dk grn & yel grn	.80	.25
O94	O3	11r dk blue & brt yellow ('79)	1.75	.50
O95	O3	14r dl grn & gray	1.75	.50
O96	O3	15r bl & rose lil ('78)	3.25	1.00
O97	O3	20r purple & yel	3.25	.40
O98	O3	30r brn & ocher ('78)	3.75	1.25
O99	O3	50r blk & gold ('78)	10.00	1.25
		Nos. O87-O99 (13)	28.00	6.90

NEWSPAPER STAMP

No. 429 Overprinted

1909　**Typo.**　**Unwmk.**　**Perf. 12½**

P1	A26	2c gray, *blue*	60.00	30.00

PARCEL POST STAMPS

Regular issues of 1907-08 (types
A26, A29) with the handstamp above in
blue, black or green are of questionable
status as issued stamps. The handstamp probably is a cancellation.

No. 436 Overprinted
in Black

1909　**Engr.**　**Perf. 11½**

Q18	A29	26cred brown	20.00	15.00

The overprint is printed.

Regular Issue of
1915 Overprinted in
Black

1915　　**Wmk. 161**　　**Perf. 11, 11½**

Q19	A33	1c car & indigo	2.50	2.50
Q20	A33	2c bl & carmine	2.50	2.50
Q21	A33	3c dark green	2.50	2.50
Q22	A33	5c red	2.50	2.50
Q23	A33	6c ol green & car	2.50	2.50
Q24	A33	9c yel brn & vio	2.50	2.50
Q25	A33	10c bl grn & yel brn	2.50	2.50
Q26	A33	12c ultramarine	3.00	3.00
Q27	A34	1k multicolored	7.00	7.00
Q28	A34	24c multicolored	3.50	3.50
Q29	A34	2k multicolored	7.00	7.00
Q30	A34	3k multicolored	7.00	7.00
Q31	A34	5k multicolored	7.50	7.50
Q32	A35	1t multicolored	10.00	10.00
Q33	A35	2t gold, grn & brn	10.00	10.00
Q34	A35	3t multicolored	12.50	12.50
Q35	A35	5t multicolored	15.00	15.00
		Nos. Q19-Q35 (17)	100.00	100.00

Coronation of Shah Ahmed.
*Reprints have dull rather than shiny over-
print. Value, set, $16.*

> **Catalogue values for unused stamps in this section, from this point to the end of the section, are for Never Hinged items.**

Post Horn — PP1

Black frame and "IRAN" (reversed) are
printed on back of Nos. Q36-Q65, to show
through when stamp is attached to parcel.

1958　**Wmk. 306**　**Typo.**　**Perf. 12½**

Q36	PP1	50d olive bis	.75	.25
Q37	PP1	1r carmine	1.00	.25
Q38	PP1	2r blue	1.00	.25
a.		Imperf., pair	100.00	
Q39	PP1	3r green	1.00	.25
Q40	PP1	5r purple	1.00	.25
Q41	PP1	10r orange brn	3.75	.25
Q42	PP1	20r dp orange	10.00	.35
Q43	PP1	30r lilac	12.50	1.60
Q44	PP1	50r dk carmine	19.00	2.50
Q45	PP1	100r yellow	40.00	5.00
Q46	PP1	200r light grn	60.00	9.00
		Nos. Q36-Q46 (11)	150.00	19.95

1961-66　　　　　　　**Wmk. 316**

Q51	PP1	5r purple ('66)	12.50	5.00
Q52	PP1	10r org brn ('62)	12.50	5.00
Q53	PP1	20r orange	17.50	7.00
Q54	PP1	30r red lil ('63)	17.50	8.00
Q55	PP1	50r dk car ('63)	25.00	10.00
Q56	PP1	100r yellow ('64)	65.00	30.00
Q57	PP1	200r emer ('64)	80.00	30.00
		Nos. Q51-Q57 (7)	230.00	95.00

1967-74　　　　　　　**Wmk. 353**
Shiny Gum

Q58	PP1	2r blue ('74)	5.00	—
Q59	PP1	5r dk pur ('69)	5.00	—
Q60	PP1	10r orange brn	5.00	—
Q61	PP1	20r orange ('69)	10.00	—
Q62	PP1	30r red lilac	12.00	—
Q63	PP1	50r red brn ('68)	15.00	—
Q64	PP1	100r yellow	50.00	—
Q65	PP1	200r emerald ('69)	80.00	—
		Nos. Q58-Q65 (8)	182.00	

1977　　　　　　　　　**Wmk. 353**
White Dry Gum

Q58a	PP1	2r blue	1.00	.20
Q59a	PP1	5r dk pur	1.00	.20
Q60a	PP1	10r orange brn	1.00	.20
Q61a	PP1	20r orange	1.50	.20
Q62a	PP1	30r pink	2.00	.25
Q63a	PP1	50r red brn	2.50	.50
Q64a	PP1	100r yellow	3.50	1.00
Q65a	PP1	200r emerald	6.00	3.00
		Nos. Q58a-Q65a (8)	18.50	5.55

Perf. 13½x13, 10½ (#100r)

1981　**Typo.**　**Wmk. 353**
**Without Black Frame and IRAN on
Back**

Q67	PP1	50r orange brown	25.00	25.00
Q68	PP1	100r yellow	125.00	100.00
a.		100r dull orange		
Q69	PP1	200r green	25.00	25.00

Nos. Q67, Q69 printed from new dies.
Numerals are larger and higher in the value
tablet on No. Q67. Numerals read down from
upper left to lower right in value tablet on No.
Q69.

POSTAL TAX STAMPS

Iranian Red
Cross Lion
and Sun
Emblem
PT1

1950　**Unwmk.**　**Litho.**　**Perf. 11**

RA1	PT1	50d grn & car rose	10.00	.90
RA2	PT1	2r vio & lil rose	4.00	1.50

1955　　　　　　　　　**Wmk. 306**

RA3	PT1	50d emer & car rose	75.00	5.00

> **Catalogue values for unused stamps in this section, from this point to the end of the section, are for Never Hinged items.**

1957-58　　　　　　　**Wmk. 316**

RA4	PT1	50d emer & rose lil	4.00	.90
RA5	PT1	2r vio & car rose ('58)	2.50	1.00

1965　**Wmk. 349**　**Perf. 10½**

RA6	PT1	50d emer & car rose	2.00	.50
RA7	PT1	2r vio & lil rose	2.50	.65

1965-66　　　　　　　**Wmk. 353**

RA8	PT1	50d emer & car rose (I)	1.00	.20
a.		Type II	3.00	.20
RA9	PT1	2r vio & car rose ('66)	3.00	.35

No. RA8 was printed in two types: I. Without diagonal line before Persian "50." II. With
line.

1976, Sept.-78 Photo.　**Perf. 13x13½**

RA10	PT1	50d emerald & red	2.50	.30
RA11	PT1	2r slate & red ('78)	2.50	2.50

Nos. RA10-RA11 are redrawn and have vertical watermark.

Nos. RA1-RA11 were obligatory on all mail.
50d stamps were for registered mail, 2r
stamps for parcel post. The tax was for
hospitals.
The 2.25r and 2.50r of type PT1 were used
only on telegrams.

IRAQ

i-räk

LOCATION — In western Asia, bounded on the north by Syria and Turkey, on the east by Iran, on the south by Saudi Arabia and Kuwait, and on the west by Jordan
GOVT. — Republic
AREA — 167,925 sq. mi.
POP. — 22,427,150 (1999 est.)
CAPITAL — Baghdad

Iraq, formerly Mesopotamia, a province of Turkey, was mandated to Great Britain in 1920. The mandate was terminated in 1932. For earlier issues, see Mesopotamia.

16 Annas = 1 Rupee
1000 Fils = 1 Dinar (1932)

Catalogue values for unused stamps in this country are for Never Hinged items, beginning with Scott 79 in the regular postage section, Scott C1 in the air post section, Scott CO1 in the air post official section, Scott O90 in the officials section, Scott RA1 in the postal tax section, and Scott RAC1 in the air post postal tax section.

Issues under British Mandate

Sunni Mosque — A1

Gufas on the Tigris — A2

Assyrian Winged Bull — A4

Ctesiphon Arch — A5

Motif of Assyrian Origin — A3

Colors of the Dulaim Camel Corps — A6

Golden Shiah Mosque of Kadhimain — A7

Conventionalized Date Palm or "Tree of Life" — A8

1923-25   Engr.   Wmk. 4   Perf. 12

1	A1	½a olive grn	1.00	.25
2	A2	1a brown	1.75	.25
3	A3	1½a car lake	.95	.25
4	A4	2a brown org	.95	.25
5	A5	3a dp blue	2.00	.25
6	A6	4a dull vio	3.50	.35
7	A7	6a blue grn	2.75	.35
8	A6	8a olive bis	4.00	.75
9	A8	1r grn & brn	6.00	.90
10	A1	2r black	21.00	8.50
11	A1	2r bister ('25)	57.50	4.00
12	A6	5r orange	52.50	17.50
13	A7	10r carmine	67.50	25.00
		Nos. 1-13 (13)	221.40	58.60

For overprints see Nos. O1-O24, O42, O47, O51-O53.

King Faisal I — A9

1927

14	A9	1r red brown	13.50	2.00

See No. 27. For overprint and surcharges see Nos. 43, O25, O54.

King Faisal I
A10   A11

1931

15	A10	½a green	1.00	.30
16	A10	1a chestnut	1.00	.30
17	A10	1½a carmine	1.50	.45
18	A10	2a orange	1.25	.20
19	A10	3a light blue	1.50	.20
20	A10	4a pur brown	2.00	1.75
21	A10	6a Prus blue	2.50	.80
22	A10	8a dark green	3.00	2.00
23	A11	1r dark brown	5.50	1.75
24	A11	2r yel brown	7.75	5.00
25	A11	5r dp orange	27.50	35.00
26	A11	10r red	82.50	85.00
27	A9	25r violet	700.00	800.00
		Nos. 15-27 (13)	837.00	932.75

See Nos. 44-60. For overprints see Nos. O26-O41, O43-O46, O48-O50, O54-O71.

Issues of the Kingdom
Nos. 6, 15-27 Surcharged in "Fils" or "Dinars" in Red, Black or Green:

a

b

c   d

1932, Apr. 1

28	A10(a)	2f on ½a (R)	.50	.20
29	A10(a)	3f on ½a	.50	.20
a.		Double surcharge	160.00	
b.		Inverted surcharge	160.00	
30	A10(a)	4f on 1a (G)	1.75	.35
31	A10(a)	5f on 1a	.65	.20
a.		Double surcharge	275.00	
b.		Inverted Arabic "5"	35.00	40.00
32	A10(a)	8f on 1½a	.75	.50
a.		Inverted surcharge	160.00	
33	A10(a)	10f on 2a	.80	.20
34	A10(a)	15f on 3a	1.75	1.50
35	A10(a)	20f on 4a	2.75	1.50
36	A6(b)	25f on 4a	4.50	3.75
a.		"Fils" for "Filo"	350.00	425.00
b.		Inverted Arabic "5"	425.00	550.00
37	A10(a)	30f on 6a	3.25	.75
38	A10(a)	40f on 8a	4.25	2.75
39	A11(c)	75f on 1r	4.00	2.75
40	A11(c)	100f on 2r	10.00	4.75
41	A11(c)	200f on 5r	22.50	24.00
42	A11(d)	½d on 10r	125.00	95.00
a.		Bar in "½" omitted	800.00	925.00
43	A9(d)	1d on 25r	250.00	200.00
		Nos. 28-43 (16)	432.95	338.40

King Faisal I
A12   A13

A14

Values in "Fils" and "Dinars"

1932, May 9   Engr.

44	A12	2f ultra	.50	.20
45	A12	3f green	.50	.20
46	A12	4f vio brown	.50	.20
47	A12	5f gray green	.60	.20
48	A12	8f deep red	.80	.20
49	A12	10f yellow	1.00	.20
50	A12	15f deep blue	1.50	.20
51	A12	20f orange	1.75	.55
52	A12	25f rose lilac	1.75	.55
53	A12	30f olive grn	3.00	.20
54	A12	40f dark violet	2.25	1.00
55	A13	50f deep brown	2.25	.30
56	A13	75f lt ultra	3.75	2.00
57	A13	100f deep green	5.50	1.25
58	A13	200f dark red	25.00	7.00
59	A14	½d gray blue	90.00	40.00
60	A14	1d claret	175.00	100.00
		Nos. 44-60 (17)	315.65	154.25

For overprints see Nos. O55-O71.

A15   A16

King Ghazi — A17

1934-38   Unwmk.

61	A15	1f purple ('38)	.75	.25
62	A15	2f ultra	.45	.25
63	A15	3f green	.45	.25
64	A15	4f pur brown	.45	.25
65	A15	5f gray green	.45	.25
66	A15	8f deep red	.75	.25
67	A15	10f yellow	.95	.25
68	A15	15f deep blue	.95	.25
69	A15	20f orange	.95	.25
70	A15	25f brown vio	1.75	.35
71	A15	30f olive grn	1.50	.25
72	A15	40f dark vio	1.75	.25
73	A16	50f deep brown	3.50	.45
74	A16	75f ultra	4.00	.40
75	A16	100f deep green	5.00	.50
76	A16	200f dark red	7.50	3.00

77	A17	½d gray blue	27.50	20.00
78	A17	1d claret	85.00	30.00
		Nos. 61-78 (18)	143.65	57.25

For overprints see Nos. 226, O72-O89.

Catalogue values for unused stamps in this section, from this point to the end of the section, are for Never Hinged items.

Sitt Zubaidah Mosque — A18   Mausoleum of King Faisal I — A19

Lion of Babylon — A20   Malwiye of Samarra (Spiral Tower) — A21

Oil Wells — A22   Mosque of the Golden Dome, Samarra — A23

Perf. 14, 13½, 12½, 12x13½, 13½x12, 14x13½

1941-42   Engr.

79	A18	1f dark violet ('42)	.40	.20
80	A18	2f chocolate ('42)	.40	.20
81	A19	3f brt green ('42)	.40	.20
82	A19	4f purple ('42)	.40	.20
83	A19	5f dk car rose ('42)	.40	.20
84	A20	8f carmine	.70	.25
85	A20	8f ocher ('42)	.55	.20
86	A20	10f ocher	16.00	3.25
87	A20	10f carmine ('42)	1.25	.20
88	A20	15f dull blue	2.10	.20
89	A20	15f black ('42)	2.50	.20
90	A20	20f black	4.25	.60
91	A20	20f dull blue ('42)	1.00	.20
92	A21	25f dark violet	.45	.30
93	A21	30f deep orange	.45	.30
94	A21	40f brn orange	1.75	.50
95	A21	40f chestnut ('42)	1.75	.50
96	A21	50f ultra	3.00	.60
97	A21	75f rose violet	2.50	.50
98	A22	100f olive green ('42)	3.00	1.00
99	A22	200f dp orange ('42)	10.00	1.00
100	A23	½d lt bl, perf. 12x13½ ('42)	35.00	5.50
a.		Perf. 14	40.00	9.00
101	A23	1d grnsh bl ('42)	55.00	11.00
		Nos. 79-101 (23)	143.25	27.35

Nos. 92-95 measure 17¾x21½mm. Nos. 96-97 measure 21x24mm.
For overprints see #O90-O114, O165, RA5.

King Faisal II
A24   A25

Photo.; Frame Litho.

1942   Perf. 13 x 13½

102	A24	1f violet & brown	.50	.50
103	A24	2f dk blue & brown	.50	.50
104	A24	3f lt green & brown	.50	.50
105	A24	4f dull brown & brn	.50	.50
106	A24	5f sage green & brn	.50	.50
107	A24	6f red orange & brn	.50	.50

108	A24	10f dl rose red & lt brn	.50	.50
109	A24	12f yel green & brown	.50	.50
		Nos. 102-109 (8)	4.00	4.00

For overprints see Nos. O115-O122.

Perf. 11½x12
1948, Jan. 15   Engr.   Unwmk.
Size: 17¾x20½mm

110	A25	1f slate	.60	.20
111	A25	2f sepia	.35	.20
112	A25	3f emerald	.35	.20
113	A25	4f purple	.35	.20
114	A25	5f rose lake	.35	.20
115	A25	6f plum	2.00	.80
116	A25	8f ocher	4.50	.75
117	A25	10f rose red	.45	.20
118	A25	12f dark olive	.45	.20
119	A25	15f black	8.00	2.00
120	A25	20f blue	1.00	.20
121	A25	25f rose violet	1.10	.20
122	A25	30f red orange	1.10	.20
123	A25	40f orange brn	2.25	.75

Perf. 12x11½
Size: 22x27½mm

124	A25	60f deep blue	1.50	.70
125	A25	75f lilac rose	1.50	.70
126	A25	100f olive green	7.00	1.50
127	A25	200f deep orange	5.75	1.50
128	A25	½d blue	15.00	5.00
129	A25	1d green	50.00	17.50
		Nos. 110-129 (20)	103.60	32.65

Sheets of 6 exist, perforated and imperforate, containing Nos. 112, 117, 120 and 125-127, with arms and Arabic inscription in blue green in upper and lower margins. Value perf or imperf, unused $100 each, used $160 each. See Nos. 133-138. For overprints see Nos. 188-194, O123-O142, O166-O177, O257, O258, O272-O282, RA1-RA4, RA6.

Post Rider and King Ghazi — A26

Designs: 40f, Equestrian statue & Faisal I. 50f, UPU symbols & Faisal II.

1949, Nov. 1   Perf. 13x13½

130	A26	20f blue	2.50	2.00
131	A26	40f red orange	3.50	2.00
132	A26	50f purple	10.00	7.00
		Nos. 130-132 (3)	16.00	11.00

75th anniv. of the UPU.

Type of 1948
1950-51   Unwmk.   Perf. 11½x12
Size: 17¾x20½mm

133	A25	3f rose lake	8.00	2.00
134	A25	5f emerald	8.50	4.00
135	A25	14f dk olive ('50)	2.10	.75
136	A25	16f rose red	2.00	.75
137	A25	28f blue	2.10	.45

Perf. 12x11½
Size: 22x27½mm

138	A25	50f deep blue ('50)	6.50	1.50
		Nos. 133-138 (6)	29.20	9.45

For overprints see Nos. 160, O143-O148, O258, O273, O275-O276.

King Faisal II
A27   A28

1953, May 2   Engr.   Perf. 12

139	A27	3f deep rose car	1.25	1.25
140	A27	14f olive	2.50	1.25
141	A27	28f blue	7.00	1.75
b.		Souv. sheet of 3, #139-141	110.00	200.00
		Nos. 139-141 (3)	10.75	4.25

Coronation of King Faisal II, May 2, 1953.

1954-57
Size: 18x20½mm

141A	A28	1f blue ('56)	.65	.20
142	A28	2f chocolate	.25	.20
143	A28	3f rose lake	.25	.20
144	A28	4f violet	.25	.20
145	A28	5f emerald	.30	.20
146	A28	6f plum	.30	.20

147	A28	8f ocher	.30	.20
148	A28	10f blue	.30	.20
149	A28	15f black	1.75	1.25
149A	A28	16f brt rose ('57)	2.75	2.25
150	A28	20f olive	1.25	.30
151	A28	25f rose vio ('55)	1.25	.20
152	A28	30f ver ('55)	1.25	.20
153	A28	40f orange brn	1.50	.45

Size: 22x27½mm

154	A28	50f blue	2.00	.70
155	A28	75f pink	3.00	.75
156	A28	100f olive green	6.00	.80
157	A28	200f orange	10.00	1.75
		Nos. 141A-157 (18)	33.35	10.25

For overprints see Nos. 158-159, 195-209, 674, 676, 678, O148A-O161A, O178-O191, O259-O260, O263, O266, O268, O270, O283-O291.

No. 143, 148 and 137
Overprinted in Black

1955, Apr. 6   Perf. 11½x12

158	A28	3f rose lake	1.10	.45
159	A28	10f blue	1.25	.45
160	A25	28f blue	2.10	1.00
		Nos. 158-160 (3)	4.45	1.90

Abrogation of Anglo-Iraq treaty of 1930.

King Faisal II — A29

1955, Nov. 26   Perf. 13½x13

161	A29	3f rose lake	.90	.40
162	A29	10f light ultra	1.60	.60
163	A29	28f blue	2.25	1.50
		Nos. 161-163 (3)	4.75	2.50

6th Arab Engineers' Conf., Baghdad, 1955.
For surcharge see No. 227.

Faisal II and
Globe — A30

1956, Mar. 3   Perf. 13x13½

164	A30	3f rose lake	1.25	.60
165	A30	10f light ultra	1.60	.60
166	A30	28f blue	2.25	1.25
		Nos. 164-166 (3)	5.10	2.45

Arab Postal Conf., Baghdad, Mar. 3.
For overprint see #173. For surcharge see #251.

Mechanical
Loom
A31

Designs: 3f, Dam. 5f, Modern city development. 10f, Pipeline. 40f, Tigris Bridge.

1957, Apr. 8   Photo.   Perf. 11½
Granite Paper

167	A31	1f Prus bl & org yel	.50	.20
168	A31	3f multicolored	.50	.20
169	A31	5f multicolored	.60	.20
170	A31	10f lt bl, ocher & red	1.00	.20
171	A31	40f lt bl, blk & ocher	2.00	.70
		Nos. 167-171 (5)	4.60	1.50

Development Week, 1957. See #185-187.

Fair Emblem — A32

1957, June 1   Unwmk.
Granite Paper

172	A32	10f brown & buff	1.00	1.00

Agricultural and Industrial Exhibition, Baghdad, June 1.

No. 166
Overprinted in
Red

1957, Nov. 14   Perf. 13x13½

173	A30	28f blue	5.00	2.25
a.		Double overprint	250.00	275.00

Iraqi Red Crescent Soc., 25th anniv.

King Faisal II — A33

Perf. 11½x12
1957-58   Unwmk.   Engr.

174	A33	1f blue	.40	.40
175	A33	2f chocolate	.40	.40
176	A33	3f dark car ('57)	.40	.40
177	A33	4f dull violet	.40	.40
177A	A33	5f emerald	1.00	1.00
178	A33	6f plum	1.00	1.00
179	A33	8f ocher	2.00	1.25
180	A33	10f blue	2.00	1.25
		Nos. 174-180 (8)	7.60	6.10

Higher denominations exist without Republic overprint. They were probably not regularly issued.
See note below No. 225.
For overprints see Nos. 210-225, 675, O162-O164, O192-O199, O269, O292-O294. For types overprinted see #677, 679, O261, O264, O267, O271, O295.

Tanks — A34

King Faisal II — A35

Army Day, Jan. 6: 10f, Marching soldiers. 20f, Artillery and planes.

1958, Jan. 6   Perf. 13x13½

181	A34	8f green & black	1.00	.85
182	A34	10f brown & black	1.25	1.10
183	A34	20f blue & red brown	1.25	1.10
184	A35	30f car & purple	2.00	1.50
		Nos. 181-184 (4)	5.50	4.55

Type of 1957

3f, Sugar beet, bag & refining machinery, vert. 5f, Farm. 10f, Dervendi Khan dam.

1958, Apr. 26   Photo.   Perf. 11½
Granite Paper

185	A31	3f gray vio, grn & lt gray	.60	.35
186	A31	5f multicolored	.90	.55
187	A31	10f multicolored	2.25	1.10
		Nos. 185-187 (3)	3.75	2.00

Development Week, 1958.

Republic

Stamps of 1948-51
Overprinted

Perf. 11½x12, 12x11½
1958   Engr.   Unwmk.
Size: 17¾x20½mm

188	A25	12f dark olive	.80	.25
189	A25	14f olive	1.00	.25
190	A25	16f rose red	15.00	4.50
191	A25	28f blue	1.25	.65

Size: 22x27½mm

192	A25	60f deep blue	4.00	.75
193	A25	½d blue	25.00	6.00
194	A25	1d green	50.00	22.00
		Nos. 188-194 (7)	97.05	34.40

Other denominations of type A25 exist with this overprint, but these were probably not regularly issued.

Same Overprint on Stamps of 1954-57
Size: 18x20½mm

195	A28	1f blue	.85	.30
196	A28	2f chocolate	.85	.30
196A	A28	4f violet	.85	.30
196B	A28	5f emerald	.85	.30
197	A28	6f plum	.85	.30
198	A28	8f ocher	.85	.30
199	A28	10f blue	1.00	.30
200	A28	15f black	1.25	.30
201	A28	16f bright rose	3.25	.50
202	A28	20f olive	1.50	.65
203	A28	25f rose violet	1.00	.65
204	A28	30f vermilion	1.75	.50
205	A28	40f orange brn	1.75	.35

Size: 22½x27½mm

206	A28	50f blue	8.00	4.00
207	A28	75f pink	6.50	1.50
208	A28	100f olive green	7.00	4.00
209	A28	200f orange	20.00	7.50
		Nos. 195-209 (17)	58.10	21.90

The lines of this overprint are found transposed on Nos. 195, 196 and 199.

Same Overprint on Stamps and Type of 1957-58
Size: 18x20mm

210	A33	1f blue	3.50	.75
211	A33	2f chocolate	.75	.30
212	A33	3f dark carmine	.75	.30
213	A33	4f dull violet	.80	.30
214	A33	5f emerald	.75	.30
215	A33	6f plum	.75	.30
216	A33	8f ocher	.75	.50
217	A33	10f blue	.75	.30
218	A33	20f olive	.75	.30
219	A33	25f rose violet	1.60	.80
220	A33	30f vermilion	1.75	.30
221	A33	40f orange brn	4.50	1.60

Size: 22x27½mm

222	A33	50f rose violet	3.50	.75
223	A33	75f olive	3.50	1.50
224	A33	100f orange	4.50	1.50
225	A33	200f blue	12.50	2.50
		Nos. 210-225 (16)	41.40	12.30

#218-225 were not issued without overprint.
The lines of this overprint are found transposed on Nos. 210 and 214.
Many errors of overprint exist of #188-226.
For overprint see No. O198.

Same Overprint on No. 78
Perf. 12

226	A17	1d claret	37.50	35.00

No. 163 Surcharged in Red

1958, Nov. 26   **Perf. 13x13½**
227 A29 10f on 28f blue   2.00   1.00

Arab Lawyers' Conf., Baghdad, Nov. 26.

Soldier and Flag — A36

1959, Jan. 6   **Photo.**   **Perf. 11½**
228 A36 3f bright blue   .40   .20
229 A36 10f olive green   .75   .35
230 A36 40f purple   1.40   .70
    Nos. 228-230 (3)   2.55   1.25

Issued for Army Day, Jan. 6.

Orange Tree — A37

Emblem of Republic — A38

1959, Mar. 21   **Unwmk.**   **Perf. 11½**
231 A37 10f green, dk grn & org   .90   .25

Issued for Arbor Day.

1959-60   **Litho. & Photo.**   **Perf. 11½**
Granite Paper
Emblem in Gold, Red and Blue;
Blue Inscriptions
232 A38 1f gray   .25   .20
233 A38 2f salmon   .25   .20
234 A38 3f pale violet   .25   .20
235 A38 4f bright yel   .25   .20
236 A38 5f light blue   .25   .20
237 A38 10f bright pink   .25   .20
238 A38 15f light green   .75   .20
239 A38 20f bister brn   .75   .20
240 A38 30f light gray   .75   .20
241 A38 40f orange yel   1.40   .35
242 A38 50f yel green   5.50   .90
243 A38 75f pale grn ('60)   2.25   .45
244 A38 100f orange ('60)   4.00   .90
245 A38 200f lilac ('60)   6.50   1.00
246 A38 500f bister ('60)   10.00   3.50
247 A38 1d brt grn ('60)   22.00   9.00
    Nos. 232-247 (16)   55.40   17.90

See Nos. 305A-305B. For overprints see Nos. 252, 293-295, O200-O221.

Worker and Buildings — A39

Victorious Fighters — A40

Perf. 12½x13, 13x12½
1959, July 14   **Photo.**
248 A39 10f ocher & blue   .60   .55
249 A40 30f ocher & emerald   1.10   .70

1st anniv. of the Revolution of July 14 (1958), which overthrew the kingdom.

Harvest — A41

1959, July 14   **Perf. 11½**
250 A41 10f lt grn & dk grn   .65   .20

No. 166 Surcharged in Dark Red

1959, June 1   **Engr.**   **Perf. 13x13½**
251 A30 10f on 28f blue   1.75   .75

Issued for Children's Day, 1959.

No. 237 Overprinted

Litho. and Photo.
1959, Oct. 23   **Perf. 11½**
252 A38 10f multicolored   1.10   .55

Health and Sanitation Week.

Abdul Karim Kassem and Army Band — A42

Abdul Karim Kassem and: 16f, Field maneuvers, horiz. 30f, Antiaircraft. 40f, Troops at attention, flag and bugler. 60f, Fighters and flag, horiz.

1960, Jan. 6   **Photo.**   **Perf. 11½**
253 A42 10f blue, grn & mar   .80   .55
254 A42 16f brt blue & red   1.25   .70
255 A42 30f ol grn, yel & brn   1.25   .70
256 A42 40f deep vio & buff   1.90   .90
257 A42 60f dk brown & buff   2.50   1.00
    Nos. 253-257 (5)   7.70   3.85

Issued for Army Day, Jan. 6.

Prime Minister Abdul Karim Kassem — A43

Maroof el Rasafi — A44

1960, Feb. 1   **Engr.**   **Perf. 12½**
258 A43 10f lilac   .90   .45
259 A43 30f emerald   1.50   .65

Issued to honor Prime Minister Kassem on his recovery from an assassination attempt.

1960, May 10   **Photo.**   **Perf. 13½x13**
260 A44 10f maroon & blk   4.00   1.40
   a.   Inverted overprint   150.00   150.00
   b.   Without overprint ('66)   11.00   11.00

No. 260b was released for postal use in 1966.

Symbol of the Republic — A45

Unknown Soldier's Tomb and Kassem with Freedom Torch — A46

1960, July 14   **Perf. 11½**
261 A45 6f ol grn, red & gold   .90   .55
262 A46 10f green, blue & red   .95   .55
263 A46 16f vio, blue & red   1.00   .80
264 A45 18f ultra, red & gold   1.00   .80
265 A45 30f brown, red & gold   1.50   1.00
266 A46 60f dk brn, bl & red   2.50   1.50
    Nos. 261-266 (6)   7.85   5.20

2nd anniv. of the July 14, 1958 revolution.

Gen. Kassem and Marching Troops — A47

Gen. Kassem and Arch — A48

1961, Jan. 6   **Perf. 11½**
Granite Paper
267 A47 3f gray ol, emer, yel & gold   .65   .20
268 A47 6f pur, emer, yel & gold   .70   .20
269 A47 10f sl, emer, yel & gold   .85   .20
270 A48 20f bl grn, blk & buff   1.00   .25
271 A48 30f bis brn, blk & buff   1.10   .35
272 A48 40f ultra, black & buff   1.50   .65
    Nos. 267-272 (6)   5.80   1.85

Issued for Army Day, Jan. 6.

Gen. Kassem and Children — A49

1961, June 1   **Photo.**   **Unwmk.**
Granite Paper
273 A49 3f yellow & brown   .80   .45
274 A49 6f blue & brown   1.10   .45
275 A49 10f pink & brown   1.50   .45
276 A49 30f yellow & brown   1.75   .45
277 A49 50f lt grn & brown   2.75   .70
    Nos. 273-277 (5)   7.90   2.50

Issued for World Children's Day.

Gen. Kassem and Flag — A50

5f, 30f, 40f, Gen. Kassem saluting and flags.

1961, July 14   **Perf. 11½**
Granite Paper
278 A50 1f multicolored   .50   .20
279 A50 3f multicolored   .50   .20
280 A50 5f multicolored   .50   .20
281 A50 6f multicolored   .50   .20
282 A50 10f multicolored   .50   .20
283 A50 30f multicolored   .75   .50
284 A50 40f multicolored   1.00   .55
285 A50 50f multicolored   1.75   1.00
286 A50 100f multicolored   4.50   1.75
    Nos. 278-286 (9)   10.50   4.85

3rd anniv. of the July 14, 1958 revolution.

Gen. Kassem and Flag — A51

Gen. Kassem and Symbol of Republic — A52

Perf. 11½
1962, Jan. 6   **Unwmk.**   **Photo.**
Granite Paper
287 A51 1f multicolored   .65   .20
288 A51 3f multicolored   .65   .20
289 A51 6f multicolored   .75   .20
290 A52 10f blk, lilac & gold   1.00   .20
291 A52 30f black, org & gold   1.25   .30
292 A52 50f blk, pale grn & gold   2.00   .50
    Nos. 287-292 (6)   6.30   1.60

Issued for Army Day, Jan. 6.

Nos. 234, 237 and 240 Overprinted

Litho. & Photo.
1962, May 29   **Perf. 11½**
293 A38 3f multicolored   .50   .20
294 A38 10f multicolored   .50   .20
295 A38 30f multicolored   1.25   .30
    Nos. 293-295 (3)   2.25   .75

Fifth Islamic Congress.

Hands Across Map of Arabia and North Africa — A53

1962, July 14   **Photo.**
296 A53 1f brn, org, grn & gold   .65   .20
297 A53 3f brn, yel grn, grn & gold   .65   .20
298 A53 6f blk, lt brn, grn & gold   .75   .20
299 A53 10f brn, lil, grn & gold   1.00   .20
300 A53 30f brn, rose, grn & gold   1.25   .30
301 A53 50f brn, gray, grn & gold   2.00   .45
    Nos. 296-301 (6)   6.30   1.55

Revolution of July 14, 1958, 4th anniv.

al-Kindi — A54

Emblem of Republic — A54a

Designs: 3f, Horsemen with standards and trumpets. 10f, Old map of Baghdad and Tigris. 40f, Gen. Kassem, modern building and flag.

Perf. 14x13½

1962, Dec. 1   Litho.   Unwmk.
302	A54	3f multicolored	.65	.20
303	A54	6f multicolored	.65	.20
304	A54	10f multicolored	.75	.35
305	A54	40f multicolored	2.00	1.00
		Nos. 302-305 (4)	4.05	1.75

9th century Arab philosopher al-Kindi; millenary of the Round City of Baghdad.

1962, Dec. 20   Perf. 13½x14
305A	A54a	14f brt green & blk	2.25	.50
305B	A54a	35f ver & black	2.75	.75

Nos. 305A-305B were originally sold affixed to air letter sheets, obliterating the portrait of King Faisal II. They were issued in sheets for general use in 1966.
For overprints see Nos. RA15-RA16.

Tanks on Parade and Gen. Kassem — A55

Malaria Eradication Emblem — A56

1963, Jan. 6   Photo.   Perf. 11½
306	A55	3f black & yellow	.60	.20
307	A55	5f brown & plum	.65	.20
308	A55	6f blk & lt green	.75	.20
309	A55	10f blk & lt blue	.80	.20
310	A55	10f black & pink	.85	.20
311	A55	20f black & ultra	1.00	.20
312	A55	40f blk & rose lilac	1.25	.25
313	A55	50f brn & brt ultra	1.75	.40
		Nos. 306-313 (8)	7.65	1.85

Issued for Army Day, Jan. 6.

1962, Dec. 31   Perf. 14
Republic Emblem in Red, Blue & Gold
314	A56	3f yel grn, blk & dk grn	.50	.20
315	A56	10f org, blk & dark blue	.75	.20
316	A56	40f lilac, black & blue	1.00	.30
		Nos. 314-316 (3)	2.25	.70

WHO drive to eradicate malaria.

Gufas on the Tigris — A57

Shepherd and Sheep A58

Designs: 2f, 500f, Spiral tower, Samarra. 4f, 15f, Ram's head harp, Ur. 5f, 75f, Map and Republic emblem. 10f, 50f, Lion of Babylon. 20f, 40f, Baghdad University. 30f, 200f, Kadhimain mosque. 100f, 1d, Winged bull, Khorsabad.

Engr.; Engr. and Photo. (bicolored)
1963, Feb. 16   Unwmk.   Perf. 12x11
317	A57	1f green	.65	.20
318	A57	2f purple	.65	.20
319	A57	3f black	.65	.20
320	A57	4f black & yel	.65	.20
321	A57	5f lilac & lt grn	.70	.20
322	A57	10f rose red	1.00	.20
323	A57	15f brn & buff	1.50	.20
324	A57	20f violet blue	1.60	.20
325	A57	30f orange	1.00	.35
326	A57	40f brt green	1.75	.20
327	A57	50f dark brown	7.50	.65
328	A57	75f blk & lt grn	3.75	.45
329	A57	100f brt lilac	4.00	.20
330	A57	200f brown	7.50	.55
331	A57	500f blue	10.00	2.25
332	A57	1d deep claret	13.50	4.50
		Nos. 317-332 (16)	56.40	10.75

For overprints see Nos. O314-O317, RA7-RA12.

1963, Mar. 21   Litho.   Perf. 13½x14

10f, Man holding sheaf. 20f, Date palm grove.
333	A58	3f emerald & gray	.40	.20
334	A58	10f dp brn & lil rose	.65	.20
335	A58	20f dk bl & red brn	1.10	.35
a.		Souv. sheet of 3, #333-335	5.75	
		Nos. 333-335 (3)	2.15	.75

FAO "Freedom from Hunger" campaign. No. 335a sold for 50f.
No. 335a was overprinted in 1970 in black to commemorate the UN 25th anniv. Denominations on the 3 stamps were obliterated, leaving "Price 50 Fils" in the margin. Value $7.50.

Cent. Emblem — A59

Rifle, Helmet and Flag — A60

Design: 30f, Iraqi Red Crescent Society Headquarters, horiz.

Perf. 11x11½, 11½x11
1963, Dec. 30   Photo.
336	A59	3f violet & red	.40	.30
337	A59	10f gray & red	.60	.30
338	A59	30f blue & red	1.25	.65
		Nos. 336-338 (3)	2.25	1.25

Centenary of International Red Cross.

1964, Jan. 6   Unwmk.   Perf. 11½
Granite Paper
339	A60	3f brn, blue & emer	.40	.30
340	A60	10f brn, pink & emer	.60	.30
341	A60	30f brown, yel & emer	1.25	.70
		Nos. 339-341 (3)	2.25	1.30

Issued for Army Day, Jan. 6.

Flag and Soldiers Storming Government Palace — A61

1964, Feb. 8   Perf. 11½
Granite Paper
342	A61	10f pur, red, grn & blk	.65	.30
343	A61	30f red brn, red, grn & blk	1.10	.65
a.		Souv. sheet of 2, imperf	6.25	2.75
b.		Souv. sheet of 2 (4th anniv.) ('67)	7.25	2.75

Revolution of Ramadan 14, 1st anniv. #343a contains stamps similar to #342-343 in changed colors (10f olive, red, green & black; 30f ultra, red, green & black). Sold for 50f.
No. 343b consists of various block-outs and overprints on No. 343a. It commemorates the 4th anniv. of the Revolution of Ramadan 14. Sold for 70f. Issued Feb. 8, 1967.

Hammurabi and a God from Stele in Louvre — A62

Design: 10f, UN emblem and scales.

1964, June 10   Litho.   Perf. 13½
344	A62	6f lilac & pale grn	.60	.50
345	A62	10f org & vio blue	1.10	.50
346	A62	30f blue & pale grn	1.80	.75
		Nos. 344-346 (3)	3.50	1.75

15th anniv. (in 1963) of the Universal Declaration of Human Rights.

"Industrialization of Iraq" — A63

Soldier Planting New Flag — A64

1964, July 14   Perf. 11
347	A63	3f gray, org & black	.40	.30
348	A64	10f rose red, blk & emer	.40	.30
349	A64	20f rose red, blk & emer	.65	.30
350	A63	30f gray, org & black	1.25	.60
		Nos. 347-350 (4)	2.65	1.50

6th anniv. of the July 14, 1958 revolution.

Star and Fighters A65

1964, Nov. 18   Photo.   Perf. 11½
351	A65	5f sepia & orange	.40	.30
352	A65	10f lt bl & orange	1.25	.30
353	A65	50f vio & red orange	1.25	.60
		Nos. 351-353 (3)	2.90	1.20

Revolution of Nov. 18, 1963, 1st anniv.

Musician with Lute — A66

Perf. 13x13½
1964, Nov. 28   Litho.   Unwmk.
354	A66	3f bister & multi	1.00	.30
355	A66	10f dl grn & multi	1.00	.30
356	A66	30f dl rose & multi	1.50	.90
		Nos. 354-356 (3)	3.50	1.50

International Arab Music Conference.

Map of Arab Countries and Emblem A67

1964, Dec. 13   Perf. 12½x14
357	A67	10f lt grn & rose lilac	1.00	.30

9th Arab Engineers' Conference, Baghdad.

Arab Postal Union Emblem — A67a

Soldier, Flag and Rising Sun — A68

1964, Dec. 21   Photo.   Perf. 11
358	A67a	3f sal pink & blue	.40	.20
359	A67a	10f brt red lil & brn	.50	.20
360	A67a	30f orange & blue	1.40	.50
		Nos. 358-360 (3)	2.30	.90

10th anniv. of Permanent Office of APU
For overprint see No. 707.

Perf. 14x12½
1965, Jan. 6   Litho.   Unwmk.
361	A68	5f dull green & multi	.40	.20
362	A68	15f henna brn & multi	.40	.30
363	A68	30f black brn & multi	1.40	.65
		Nos. 361-363 (3)	2.20	1.15

Issued for Army Day, Jan. 6.
An imperf. souvenir sheet carries a revised No. 363 with "30 FILS" omitted, and a portrait of Pres. Abdul Salam Arif. Violet inscriptions including "PRICE 60 FILS." Value $10.

Symbols of Agriculture and Industry A69

1965, Jan. 8   Perf. 12½x14
364	A69	10f ultra, brn & blk	.60	.30

Arab Labor Ministers' Conference.

Tanker A70

1965, Jan. 30   Perf. 14
365	A70	10f multicolored	1.00	.45

Inauguration (in 1962) of the deep sea terminal for oil tankers.

Soldier with Flag and Rifle — A71

Tree Week — A72

1965, Feb. 8   Litho.   Perf. 13½
366 A71 10f multicolored   .75   .20
Revolution of Ramadan 14, 2nd anniv.

1965, Mar. 6   Unwmk.   Perf. 13
367 A72 6f multicolored   .40   .30
368 A72 20f multicolored   1.25   .30

Federation Emblem — A73

Dagger in Map of Palestine — A74

1965, Mar. 24   Unwmk.   Perf. 14
369 A73 3f lt bl, vio bl & gold   .40   .30
370 A73 10f gray, black & gold   .40   .30
371 A73 30f rose, car & gold   1.00   .75
     Nos. 369-371 (3)   1.80 1.35
Arab Federation of Insurance.

1965, Apr. 9   Litho.   Perf. 14x12½
372 A74 10f gray & black   3.50   .35
373 A74 20f lt brn & dk blue   6.50   .55
Deir Yassin massacre, Apr. 9, 1948.
See Jordan No. 499 and Kuwait Nos. 281-282.

Smallpox Attacking People — A75

1965, Apr. 30   Litho.   Perf. 14
374 A75 3f multicolored   .60   .30
375 A75 10f multicolored   .75   .30
376 A75 20f multicolored   1.75   .80
     Nos. 374-376 (3)   3.10 1.40
WHO's fight against smallpox. Exist imperf. Value $6.25.

ITU Emblem, Old and New Telecommunication Equipment — A76

1965, May 17   Perf. 14, Imperf.
377 A76 10f multicolored   .75   .20
378 A76 20f multicolored   2.00   .55
 a.   Souv. sheet of 2, #377-378   20.00 15.00
ITU, centenary. No. 378a sold for 40f and exists imperf. Value same.

Map of Arab Countries and Banner — A77

1965, May 26   Litho.   Perf. 14x12½
379 A77 10f multicolored   .50   .20
Anniversary of the treaty with the UAR.

Library Aflame and Lamp A78

1965, June   Photo.   Perf. 11
380 A78 5f black, grn & red   .50   .30
381 A78 10f blk, green & red   .75   .30
Burning of the Library of Algiers, 6/7/62.

Revolutionist with Torch, Cannon and Flames — A79

1965, June 30   Litho.   Perf. 13
382 A79 5f multicolored   .40   .20
383 A79 10f multicolored   .45   .20
45th anniversary, Revolution of 1920.

Mosque — A80

1965, July 12   Photo.   Perf. 12
384 A80 10f multicolored   .90   .60
Prophet Mohammed's birthday. A souvenir sheet contains one imperf. stamp similar to No. 384. Sold for 50f. Value $8.

Factories and Grain — A81

Arab Fair Emblem — A82

1965, July 14   Litho.   Perf. 13
385 A81 10f multicolored   .55   .55
7th anniv. of the July 14, 1958 Revolution.

1965, Oct. 22   Unwmk.   Perf. 13
386 A82 10f multicolored   .55   .20
Second Arab Fair, Baghdad.

Pres. Abdul Salam Mohammed Arif — A83

1965, Nov. 18   Photo.   Perf. 11½
Granite Paper
387 A83 5f org, buff & dk blue   .65   .20
388 A83 10f lt ultra, gray & dk brn   .90   .20
389 A83 50f lil, pale pink & sl blk   2.50   .90
     Nos. 387-389 (3)   4.05 1.30
Revolution of Nov. 18, 1963, 2nd anniv.

Census Chart and Adding Machine — A84

1965, Nov. 29   Litho.   Perf. 13
390 A84 3f gray & plum   .50   .20
391 A84 5f brown red & brn   .60   .20
392 A84 15f olive bis & dl bl   1.50   .60
     Nos. 390-392 (3)   2.60 1.00
Issued to publicize the 1965 census.

Date Palms — A85

Soldiers' Monument A86

1965, Dec. 27   Litho.   Perf. 13½x14
393 A85 3f olive bis & multi   .40   .20
394 A85 10f car rose & multi   .90   .20
395 A85 15f blue & multi   2.40   .90
     Nos. 393-395 (3)   3.70 1.30
2nd FAO Intl. Dates Conference, Baghdad, Dec. 1965.
For surcharges see Nos. 694-695.

1966, Jan. 6   Photo.   Perf. 12
396 A86 2f car rose & multi   .45   .20
397 A86 5f multicolored   .45   .20
398 A86 40f yel grn & multi   1.75   .75
     Nos. 396-390 (3)   2.65 1.15
Issued for Army Day.

Eagle and Flag of Iraq — A87

Perf. 12½
1966, Feb. 8   Photo.   Unwmk.
399 A87 5f dl bl & multi   .40   .25
400 A87 10f orange & multi   .75   .25
3rd anniv. of the Revolution of Ramadan 14, which overthrew the Kassem government.

Arab League Emblem — A88

Soccer Players — A89

1966, Mar. 22   Perf. 11x11½
401 A88 5f org, brn & brt grn   .50   .20
402 A88 15f ol, rose lil & ultra   .50   .20
Arab Publicity Week.

1966, Apr. 1   Perf. 12
5f, Player and goal post. 15f, As 2f. 50f, Legs of player, ball and emblem, horiz.
403 A89 2f multicolored   .75   .20
404 A89 5f multicolored   .50   .20
405 A89 15f multicolored   1.50   .45
     Nos. 403-405 (3)   2.75   .85
Miniature Sheet
Imperf
406 A89 50f vio & multi   7.50 10.50
3rd Arab Soccer Cup, Baghdad, Apr. 1-10.
For overprint, see No. O296.

Steam Shovel Within Cogwheel A90

1966, May 1   Litho.   Perf. 13½

407	A90	15f multicolored	.40 .20
408	A90	25f red, blk, & sil	.50 .20

Issued for Labor Day, May 1, 1966.

Queen Nefertari — A91

Facade of Abu Simbel A92

Perf. 12½x13, 13½

1966, May 20   Litho.

409	A91	5f olive, yel & blk	.40 .20
410	A91	15f blue, yel & brn	.40 .20
411	A92	40f bis brn, red & blk	2.00 1.50
		Nos. 409-411 (3)	2.80 1.90

UNESCO world campaign to save historic monuments in Nubia.

President Arif and Flag — A93

1966, July 14   Photo.   Perf. 11½

412	A93	5f multicolored	.40 .25
413	A93	15f multicolored	.50 .25
414	A93	50f multicolored	1.75 1.00
		Nos. 412-414 (3)	2.65 1.50

8th anniv. of the July 14, 1958 revolution.

A94

1966, July 22   Litho.   Perf. 12
Multicolored Vignette

415	A94	5f lt olive green	.40 .20
416	A94	15f lt greenish blue	.40 .20
417	A94	30f lt yellow green	1.00 .75
		Nos. 415-417 (3)	1.80 1.15

Mohammed's 1,396th birthday.

Iraqi Museum, Baghdad A95

Designs: 50f, Golden headdress, Ur. 80f, Carved Sumerian head, vert.

1966, Nov. 9   Litho.   Perf. 14

418	A95	15f multicolored	.50 .20
419	A95	50f lt bl, blk, gold & pink	1.50 .80
420	A95	80f crim, blk, bl & gold	3.25 1.00
		Nos. 418-420 (3)	5.25 2.00

Opening of New Iraqi Museum, Baghdad.

UNESCO Emblem — A96

Iraqi Citizens — A97

1966, Dec.   Perf. 13½

421	A96	5f blue, black & tan	.40 .20
422	A96	15f brt org brn, blk & gray	.40 .30

20th anniv. of UNESCO.

1966, Nov. 18   Perf. 13½x13

423	A97	15f multicolored	.60 .50
424	A97	25f multicolored	1.10 1.10

3rd anniv. of the Revolution of 11/18/63.

Rocket Launchers and Soldier A98

1967, Jan. 6   Photo.   Perf. 11½

425	A98	15f citron, dk brn & dp bis	.45 .20
426	A98	20f brt lil, dk brn & dp bis	.60 .25

Issued for Army Day, Jan. 6.

Oil Derrick, Pipeline, Emblem — A99

15f, 50f, Refinery and emblem, horiz.

1967, Mar. 6   Litho.   Perf. 14

427	A99	5f ol grn, pale yel & blk	.40 .20
428	A99	15f multicolored	.40 .20
429	A99	40f vio, yel & blk	.80 .70
430	A99	50f multicolored	1.75 1.00
		Nos. 427-430 (4)	3.35 2.10

6th Arab Petroleum Cong., Baghdad, Mar. 1967.

New Year's Emblem and Spider's Web A100

1967, Apr. 11   Litho.   Perf. 13½

431	A100	5f multicolored	.40 .20
432	A100	15f multicolored	.40 .20

Issued for the Hajeer Year (New Year).

Worker Holding Cogwheel and Map of Arab Countries — A101

1967, May 1   Perf. 12½x13

433	A101	10f gray & multi	.40 .20
434	A101	15f lt ultra & multi	.40 .20

Issued for Labor Day.

A102

1967, June 20   Litho.   Perf. 14

435	A102	5f multicolored	.40 .25
436	A102	15f blue & multi	.50 .25

Mohammed's 1,397th birthday.

Flag, Hands with Clubs — A103

1967, July 7   Litho.   Perf. 13x13½

437	A103	5f multicolored	.40 .20
438	A103	15f multicolored	.50 .20

47th anniversary of Revolution of 1920.

Um Qasr Harbor A104

10f, 15f, Freighter loading in Um Qasr harbor.

1967, July 14   Litho.   Perf. 14x13½

439	A104	5f multicolored	.40 .20
440	A104	10f multicolored	.60 .30
441	A104	15f multicolored	1.10 .30
442	A104	40f multicolored	2.00 1.00
		Nos. 439-442 (4)	4.10 1.80

9th anniv. of the July 14, 1958 revolution and the inauguration of the port of Um Qasr.

Iraqi Man — A105   President Arif — A106

Iraqi Costumes: 5f, 15f, 25f, Women's costumes. 10f, 20f, 30f, Men's costumes.

1967, Nov. 10   Litho.   Perf. 13

443	A105	2f pale brn & multi	.40 .25
444	A105	5f ver & multi	.40 .25
445	A105	10f multicolored	.70 .25
446	A105	15f ultra & multi	.95 .50
447	A105	20f lilac & multi	1.25 .50
448	A105	25f lemon & multi	1.25 .60
449	A105	30f fawn & multi	1.50 .60
		Nos. 443-449,C19-C21 (10)	16.45 6.85

For overprints see Nos. 597-599, O228-O231, RA17.

Perf. 11x11½, 11½x11
1967, Nov. 18

15f, Pres. Arif and map of Iraq, horiz.

450	A106	5f bl, vio blk & yel	.40 .25
451	A106	15f rose & multi	.75 .40

4th anniversary of Nov. 18th revolution.

Ziggurat of Ur — A107

Designs: 5f, Gate with Nimrod statues. 10f, Gate, Babylon. 15f, Minaret of Mosul, vert. 25f, Arch and ruins of Ctesiphon.

1967, Dec. 1   Litho.   Perf. 13

452	A107	2f orange & multi	.40 .25
453	A107	5f lilac & multi	.40 .25
454	A107	10f orange & multi	.40 .25
455	A107	15f rose red & multi	.60 .25
456	A107	25f vio bl & multi	.80 .25
		Nos. 452-456,C22-C26 (10)	54.10 24.35

International Tourist Year.
For overprints see Nos. 593, 680, O225-O227, O308, RA18.

Iraqi Girl Scout Emblem and Sign — A108

5f, Girl Scouts at campfire & Girl Scout emblem. 10f, Boy Scout emblem & Boy Scout sign. 15f, Boy Scouts pitching tent & Boy Scout sign.

1967, Dec. 15

457	A108	2f orange & multi	1.40 .40
458	A108	5f blue & multi	1.60 .40
459	A108	10f green & multi	1.75 .65
460	A108	15f blue & multi	1.75 .40
a.		Souv. sheet of 4	12.00 9.00
		Nos. 457-460 (4)	6.50 2.25

Issued to honor the Scout movement.
No. 460a contains 4 stamps similar to Nos. 457-460 with simulated perforations. Sold for 50f.
For overprint see No. RA19.

Soldiers on Maneuvers A109

1968, Jan. 6   Photo.   Perf. 11½

461	A109	5f lt bl, brn & brt grn	.40 .20
462	A109	15f lt bl, ind & olive	.65 .25

Issued for Army Day 1968.

White-cheeked Bulbul — A110

Birds: 10f, Hoopoe. 15f, Eurasian jay. 25f, Peregrine falcon. 30f, White stork. 40f, Black partridge. 50f, Marbled teal.

1968, Jan.   Litho.   Perf. 14

463	A110	5f org & black	.70 .25
464	A110	10f blue, blk & brn	.90 .25
465	A110	15f pink & multi	1.40 .50
466	A110	25f dl org & multi	2.00 .50
467	A110	30f emer, blk & brn	2.50 .50
468	A110	40f rose lil & multi	3.25 .75
469	A110	50f multicolored	4.75 1.25
		Nos. 463-469 (7)	15.50 3.75

For overprint, see No. O311.

Fighting
Soldiers
A111

1968, Feb. 8   *Perf. 11½*
470 A111 15f blk, org & brt bl   3.50   .90
Revolution of Ramadan 14, 5th anniv.

Factories, Tractor and Grain — A112

1968, May 1   **Litho.**   *Perf. 13*
471 A112 15f lt bl & multi   .40   .25
472 A112 25f multicolored   .60   .25
Issued for Labor Day.

Soccer
A113

5f, 25f, Goalkeeper holding ball, vert.

1968, June 14   *Perf. 13½*
473 A113 2f multicolored   .40   .25
474 A113 5f multicolored   .40   .25
475 A113 15f multicolored   .50   .25
476 A113 25f multicolored   2.25   .75
   a.   Souv. sheet, 70f, imperf.   9.00 10.00
     Nos. 473-476 (4)   3.55 1.50
23rd C.I.S.M. (Conseil Internationale du
Sports Militaire) Soccer Championships.
No. 476a shows badge of Military Soccer
League.

Soldier, Flag,
Chain and
Rising
Sun — A114

1968, July 14   **Photo.**   *Perf. 13½x14*
478 A114 15f multicolored   .50   .20
10th anniv. of the July 14, 1958 revolution.

World Health Organization
Emblem — A115

5f, 10f, Staff of Aesculapius over emblem,
vert.

1968, Nov. 29   **Litho.**   *Perf. 13½*
479 A115 5f multicolored   .40   .20
480 A115 10f multicolored   .40   .20
481 A115 15f blue, red & black   .50   .20
482 A115 25f yel grn, red & blk   .75   .30
     Nos. 479-482 (4)   2.05   .90
WHO, 20th anniv. Exist imperf. Value $5.
For overprints, see Nos. O222-O224.

Human Rights
Flame — A116
       Mother and
       Children — A117

1968, Dec. 22   **Litho.**   *Perf. 13½*
483 A116 10f lt bl, yel & car   .40   .25
484 A116 25f lt yel grn, yel & car   .50   .25
   a.   Souv. sheet, 100f, imperf.   5.00 5.00
International Human Rights Year.
For overprint, see No. O232.

1968, Dec. 31   **Litho.**   *Perf. 13½*
485 A117 15f multi   .50   .25
486 A117 25f bl & multi   1.25   .35
   a.   Souv. sheet, 100f, imperf   8.00 5.25
UNICEF. For overprints see Nos. 624-625,
O234-O235.

Tanks
A118

1969, Jan. 6   **Photo.**
487 A118 25f vio, car & brn   3.50 2.00
Issued for Army Day, Jan. 6.
For overprint, see No. O244.

Harvester
A119

1969, Feb.   **Photo.**   *Perf. 13½*
488 A119 15f yel brn & multi   .50   .25
6th anniv. of the Revolution of Ramadan 14.

Mosque
A119a

1969, Mar. 19   **Photo.**   *Perf. 13x13½*
488A A119a 15f multicolored   .50   .50
Issued for Hajeer (pilgrimage) Year.

Emblem
A120

1969, Apr. 12   **Litho.**   *Perf. 12½x12*
489 A120 10f yel grn & multi   .60   .30
490 A120 15f orange & multi   1.00   .30
1st conference of the Arab Veterinary Union,
Baghdad, Apr. 1969.

Barbus
Grypus
A121

Fish: 3f, Barbus puntius sharpeyi. 10f,
Pampus argenteus. 100f, Barbus esocinus.

1969, May 9   *Perf. 14*
491 A121 2f multicolored   1.75   .45
492 A121 3f multicolored   1.90   .45
493 A121 10f multicolored   2.00   .45
494 A121 100f multicolored   6.00 3.75
     Nos. 491-494 (4)   11.65 5.10
For overprints, see Nos. O312-313.

Holy Kaaba,
Mecca
A122

1969, May 28   **Photo.**   *Perf. 12*
495 A122 15f blue & multi   .65   .25
Mohammed's 1,399th birthday.

ILO Emblem
A123

1969, June 6   **Litho.**   *Perf. 13x12½*
496 A123 5f lt vio, yel & blk   .25   .20
497 A123 15f grnsh gray, yel &
     black   .25   .20
498 A123 50f rose, yel & blk   1.25   .80
   a.   Souv. sheet, 100f, imperf.   6.00 7.00
     Nos. 496-498 (3)   1.75 1.20
ILO, 50th anniv.
For overprint, see No. O297.

Weight
Lifting — A124

Design: 5f, 35f, High jump.

1969, June 20   *Perf. 13½x13*
500 A124 3f org yel & multi   .55   .25
501 A124 5f blue & multi   .55   .25
502 A124 10f rose pink & multi   .65   .30
503 A124 35f yellow & multi   1.25 1.00
   a.   Souv. sheet of 4, #500-503,
      imperf.   12.00 12.00
     Nos. 500-503 (4)   3.00 1.80
19th Olympic Games, Mexico City, Oct. 12-
27, 1968. No. 503a sold for 100f.

Coat of Arms,
Symbols of
Industry — A125

1969, July 14   **Photo.**   *Perf. 13*
504 A125 10f brn org & multi   .40   .25
505 A125 15f multicolored   .60   .25
11th anniv. of the July 14, 1958 revolution.

Street
Fighting
A126

Pres. Ahmed
Hassan al-
Bakr — A127
       Wheat and Fair
       Emblem — A128

Design: 20f, Baghdad International Airport.

1969, July 17   *Perf. 13½*
506 A126 10f yel & multi   .50   .30
507 A126 15f blue & multi   .50   .30
508 A126 20f blue & multi   1.60   .45
509 A127 200f gold & multi   20.00 9.00
     Nos. 506-509 (4)   22.60 10.05
Coup of July 17, 1968, 1st anniv. #508 also
for the inauguration of Baghdad Intl. Airport.
No. 509 exists imperf. Value $27.50.

1969, Oct. 1   **Photo.**   *Perf. 13½*
510 A128 10f brt grn, gold & dl
     red   .65   .25
511 A128 15f ultra, gold & red   .80   .35
6th International Fair, Baghdad.
For overprints see Nos. 567A-567B.

Motor Ship
Al-Waleed
A129

Designs: 15f, Floating crane Antara. 30f,
Pilot ship Al-Rasheed. 35f, Suction dredge
Hillah. 50f, Survey ship Al-Fao.

1969, Oct. 8   **Litho.**   *Perf. 12½*
512 A129 15f black & multi   .50   .25
513 A129 20f black & multi   .70   .45
514 A129 30f black & multi   1.10   .55
515 A129 35f black & multi   1.75 1.00
516 A129 50f black & multi   5.25 2.25
     Nos. 512-516 (5)   9.30 4.50
50th anniversary of Basrah Harbor.

Radio Tower and
Map of Palestine
A130
     "Search for
     Knowledge"
     A131

1969, Nov. 9   **Litho.**   *Perf. 12½x13*
517 A130 15f multicolored   3.50   .35
518 A130 50f multicolored   6.50   .80
10th anniversary of Iraqi News Agency.
For overprints see Nos. 698-699.

1969, Nov. 21   **Photo.**   *Perf. 13*
519 A131 15f blue & multi   .35   .20
520 A131 20f green & multi   .50   .30
Campaign against illiteracy.

Front Page of
First Baghdad
Newspaper
A132

1969, Dec. 26   **Litho.**   *Perf. 13½*
521 A132 15f yel, org & black   .70   .30
    Centenary of the Iraqi press.
For overprint see No. 552.

Soldier, Map of Iraq and
Plane — A133

1970, Jan. 6   **Photo.**   *Perf. 13*
522 A133 15f lt vio & multi   .70   .30
523 A133 20f yellow & multi   1.40   .65
    Issued for Army Day 1970.

Soldier, Farmer
and Worker
Shoring up Wall
in Iraqi
Colors — A134

Poppies — A135

1970, Feb. 8   **Photo.**   *Perf. 13*
524 A134 10f multicolored   .20   .20
525 A134 15f brick red & multi   .40   .20
7th anniv. of the Revolution of Ramadan 14.

1970, June 12   **Litho.**   *Perf. 13*
   Flowers: 3f, Poet's narcissus. 5f, Tulip. 10f,
50f, Carnations. 15f, Rose.

526 A135   2f emer & multi   .40   .20
527 A135   3f blue & multi   .40   .20
528 A135   5f multicolored   .40   .20
529 A135 10f lt grn & multi   .60   .35
530 A135 15f pale sal & multi   1.10   .55
531 A135 50f lt grn & multi   3.25   1.25
    Nos. 526-531 (6)   6.15   2.75

   The overprinted sets Nos. 532-543 were
released before Nos. 526-531.
   For overprints see Nos. 621-623, RA20. For
surcharge see No. 726.

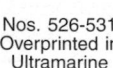

Nos. 526-531
Overprinted in
Ultramarine

1970, Mar. 21
532 A135   2f emer & multi   .60   .50
533 A135   3f lt bl & multi   .60   .50
534 A135   5f multicolored   .60   .50
535 A135 10f lt grn & multi   .60   .50
536 A135 15f pale sal & multi   1.20   .80
537 A135 50f lt grn & multi   3.50   1.25
    Nos. 532-537 (6)   7.10   4.05
    Issued for Novrooz (New Year).

Nos. 526-531
Overprinted in Black

1970, Apr. 18
538 A135   2f emer & multi   .50   .50
539 A135   3f lt bl & multi   .50   .50
540 A135   5f multicolored   .50   .50
541 A135 10f lt grn & multi   .50   .50
542 A135 15f pale sal & multi   1.40   .90
543 A135 50f lt grn & multi   3.00   1.10
    Nos. 538-543 (6)   6.40   4.00
    Issued for the Spring Festival, Mosul.

Map of Arab Countries,
Slogans — A136

   50f, 150f, People, flag, sun and map of
Palestine.

1970, Apr. 7   *Perf. 13x12½*
544 A136 15f gold & multi   .40   .25
545 A136 35f sil & multi   .60   .55
546 A136 50f red & multi   2.00   .70
   a.   Souv. sheet, 150f, imperf.   11.00   11.00
    Nos. 544-546 (3)   3.00   1.50
    23rd anniversary of Al-Baath Party.

Workers and Cogwheel — A137

1970, May 1
547 A137 10f silver & multi   .40   .25
548 A137 15f silver & multi   .50   .35
549 A137 35f silver & multi   1.50   .75
    Nos. 547-549 (3)   2.40   1.35
    Issued for Labor Day.

Kaaba,
Mecca,
and
Koran
A138

1970, May 17   **Photo.**   *Perf. 13*
550 A138 15f brt bl & multi   .40   .20
551 A138 20f orange & multi   .40   .25
    Mohammed's 1,400th birthday.

No. 521 Overprinted "1970" and
Arabic Inscription in Prussian Blue
1970, June 15   **Litho.**   *Perf. 13½*
552 A132 15f yel, org & black   .55   .55
    Day of Iraqi press.

Revolutionists and Guns — A139

Designs: 35f, Revolutionist and rising sun.

1970, June 30   **Litho.**   *Perf. 13*
553 A139 10f blk & apple grn   .25   .20
554 A139 15f black & gold   .40   .20
555 A139 35f blk & red org   .90   .45
   a.   Souv. sheet, 100f, imperf.   5.50   5.50
    Nos. 553-555 (3)   1.55   .85
    50th anniversary, Revolution of 1920.

Broken Chain
and New
Dawn — A140

1970, July 14   *Perf. 13x13½*
557 A140 15f multicolored   .35   .20
558 A140 20f multicolored   .50   .20
   12th anniv. of the July 14, 1958 revolution.

Map of Arab Countries and
Hands — A141

1970, July 17   *Perf. 13*
559 A141 15f gold & multi   .30   .20
560 A141 25f gold & multi   .55   .25
   2nd anniversary of coup of July 17, 1968.

Pomegranates
A142

1970, Aug. 21   *Perf. 14*
561 A142   3f shown   .40   .20
562 A142   5f Grapefruit   .40   .20
563 A142 10f Grapes   .40   .20
564 A142 15f Oranges   1.10   .35
565 A142 35f Dates   3.50   1.90
    Nos. 561-565 (5)   5.80   2.85

   The Latin inscriptions on the 5f and 10f have
been erroneously transposed.
   For overprints & surcharge see #613-615,
725, O240-O245.

Kaaba, Mecca, Moon over Mountain
and Spider Web — A143

1970, Sept. 4   **Photo.**   *Perf. 13*
566 A143 15f multicolored   .40   .20
567 A143 25f multicolored   .55   .25
    Issued for Hajeer (Pilgrimage) Year.

Nos. 510-511
Overprinted in Red

1970, Sept.   **Photo.**   *Perf. 13½*
567A A128 10f multi   3.50   2.00
567B A128 15f multi   3.50   2.00
    7th International Fair, Baghdad.

Intl.
Education
Year
Emblem
A144

1970, Nov. 13   **Photo.**   *Perf. 13*
568 A144   5f yel green & multi   .35   .20
569 A144 15f brick red & multi   .50   .25

Flag and
Map of
Arab
League
Countries
A145

1970   *Perf. 11*
570 A145 15f olive & multi   .40   .20
571 A145 35f gray & multi   .50   .40
    25th anniversary of the Arab League.

Baghdad
Hospital
and
Emblem
A146

1970, Dec. 7   **Litho.**   *Perf. 12*
572 A146 15f yellow & multi   .40   .20
573 A146 40f lt green & multi   1.10   .60
    Iraqi Medical Society, 50th anniv.

Sugar
Beet — A147

   15f, Sugar factory, horiz. 30f, like 5f.

         Perf. 13x13½, 13½x13
1970, Dec. 25   **Photo.**
574 A147   5f ocher, grn & blk   .30   .20
575 A147 15f black & multi   .50   .20
576 A147 30f org ver, grn & blk   1.50   .75
    Nos. 574-576 (3)   2.30   1.15
    Publicity for Mosul sugar factory.

OPEC
Emblem
A148

1970, Dec. 30   **Litho.**   *Perf. 13x13½*
577 A148 10f rose claret, bis & bl   .75   .40
578 A148 40f emer, bis & blue   3.25   1.25
    OPEC, 10th anniversary.

Soldiers — A149

Soldiers, Maps of Arab Countries and Israel — A150

Perf. 13½x14, 11½x12½
1971, Jan. 6
579 A149 15f multicolored .55 .25
580 A150 40f red org & multi 3.25 1.00
a. Souv. sheet of 2, #579-580, imperf. 10.00 10.00

Army Day, 50th anniversary. No. 580a sold for 100f.

Marchers and Map of Arab Countries — A151

1971, Feb. 8 Litho. Perf. 11½x12½
581 A151 15f yellow & multi .45 .25
582 A151 40f pink & multi 1.25 .50

Revolution of Ramadan 14, 8th anniversary.

Spider Web, Pilgrims A152

1971, Feb. 26 Photo. Perf. 13
583 A152 10f pink & multi .25 .20
584 A152 15f buff & multi .45 .25

Hajeer (New) Year.

President al-Bakr A153

1971, Mar. 11 Litho. Perf. 14
585 A153 15f orange & multi .70 .40
586 A153 100f emer & multi 3.25 1.50

First anniversary of Mar. 11th Manifesto.

Marshland A154

Tourist Publicity: 10f, Stork flying over Baghdad. 15f, "Summer Resorts." 100f, Return of Sindbad the Sailor.

1971, Mar. 15 Perf. 13
587 A154 5f multicolored .45 .25
588 A154 10f lt grn & multi .80 .25
589 A154 15f pink & multi 1.00 .50
590 A154 100f multicolored 5.25 3.00
Nos. 587-590 (4) 7.50 4.00

Blacksmith Taming Serpent — A155

1971, Mar. 21 Perf. 11½x12
591 A155 15f multicolored .85 .35
592 A155 25f yel & multi 1.75 .70

Novrooz Festival.

No. 455 Overprinted

1971, Mar. 23 Litho. Perf. 13
593 A107 15f rose red & multi 3.25 1.25

World Meteorological Day. See No. C39.

Workers, Soldier, Map of Arab Countries — A156

1971, Apr. 7
594 A156 15f yel & multi .80 .45
595 A156 35f multicolored 1.60 .75
596 A156 250f multicolored 12.00 12.00
Nos. 594-596 (3) 14.40 13.20

24th anniv. of the Al Baath Party. No. 596 has circular perforation around vignette set within a white square of paper, perforated on 4 sides. The design of No. 596 is similar to Nos. 594-595, but with denomination within the circle and no inscriptions in margin.

Nos. 443-444, 448 Overprinted

1971, Apr. 14
597 A105 2f pale brn & multi .50 .25
598 A105 5f ver & multi .70 .25
599 A105 25f lemon & multi 2.25 1.00
Nos. 597-599 (3) 3.45 1.50

Mosul Festival.

Worker, Farm Woman with Torch A157

1971, May 1 Litho. Perf. 13
600 A157 15f ocher & multi .35 .25
601 A157 40f olive & multi 1.25 .30

Labor Day.

Muslim Praying in Mecca A158

1971, May 7
602 A158 15f yellow & multi .55 .25
603 A158 100f pink & multi 2.75 1.25

Mohammed's 1,401st birthday.

People, Fists, Map of Iraq A159

1971, July 14 Photo. Perf. 14
604 A159 25f green & multi .55 .25
605 A159 50f lt bl & multi 1.75 .60

13th anniv. of the July 14, 1958 revolution.

Surveyor, Preacher, Rising Sun A160

1971, July 17 Perf. 13
606 A160 25f multicolored .60 .30
607 A160 70f orange & multi 1.90 .75

3rd anniversary of July 17, 1968, coup.

Rafidain Bank Emblem A161

1971, Sept. 24 Photo. Perf. 13½
Diameter: 27mm
608 A161 10f multicolored .55 .55
609 A161 15f multicolored .90 .90
610 A161 25f multicolored 1.75 1.75
Diameter: 32mm
611 A161 65f multicolored 8.50 6.50
612 A161 250f multicolored 22.50 21.00
Nos. 608-612 (5) 34.20 30.70

30th anniversary of Rafidain Bank. Nos. 608-612 have circular perforation around design within a white square of paper, perforated on 4 sides.

Nos. 561, 564-565 Overprinted

1971, Oct. 15 Litho. Perf. 14
613 A142 3f bl grn & multi 2.75 2.75
614 A142 15f red & multi 2.75 2.75
615 A142 35f orange & multi 2.75 2.75
Nos. 613-615 (3) 8.25 8.25

Agricultural census, Oct. 15, 1971.

Soccer A162

Designs: 25f, Track and field. 35f, Table tennis. 75f, Gymnastics. 95f, Volleyball and basketball.

1971, Nov. 17 Litho. Perf. 13½
616 A162 15f green & multi .30 .30
617 A162 25f pink & multi .80 .40
618 A162 35f lt bl & multi 1.00 .90
619 A162 70f lt grn & multi 4.25 1.50
620 A162 95f yel grn & multi 7.50 2.50
a. Souvenir sheet of 5 24.00 24.00
Nos. 616-620 (5) 13.85 5.60

4th Pan-Arab Schoolboys Sports Games, Baghdad. No. 620a contains 5 stamps similar to Nos. 616-620 with simulated perforations. Sold for 200f.

Nos. 527-528, 530 Overprinted and Surcharged

1971, Nov. 23 Litho. Perf. 13
621 A135 15f multicolored 1.75 .40
622 A135 25f on 5f multi 2.50 1.25
623 A135 70f on 3f multi 9.50 3.00
Nos. 621-623 (3) 13.75 4.65

Students' Day. The 15f has only first 3 lines of Arabic overprint.

Nos. 485-486 Overprinted

1971, Dec. 11 Litho. Perf. 13½
624 A117 15f multicolored 2.75 1.00
625 A117 25f blue & multi 7.25 3.25

25th anniv. of UNICEF.

Children Crossing Street — A162a

1971, Dec. 17 Litho. Perf. 13x12½
625A A162a 15f yel & multi 2.50 .80
625B A162a 25f brt rose & multi 4.50 2.50

2nd Traffic Week. For overprints see #668-669.

Arab Postal Union Emblem A163

1971, Dec. 24   Photo.   Perf. 11½
626 A163 25f emer, yel & brn .45 .25
627 A163 70f vio bl, yel & red 1.75 .65

25th anniv. of the Conf. of Sofar, Lebanon, establishing Arab Postal Union.

Racial Equality Emblem — A164

1971, Dec. 31   Perf. 13½x14
628 A164 25f brt grn & multi .25 .20
629 A164 70f orange & multi 1.00 .90

Intl. Year Against Racial Discrimination.

Soldiers with Flag and Torch — A165

Workers A166

1972, Jan. 6   Photo.   Perf. 14x13½
630 A165 25f blue & multi 1.20 .65
631 A165 70f brt grn & multi 4.00 2.50

Army Day, Jan. 6.

1972, Feb. 8
632 A166 25f brt grn & multi 2.50 .60
633 A166 95f lilac & multi 4.50 2.50

Revolution of Ramadan 14, 9th anniv.

Mosque, Minaret, Crescent and Caravan A167

1972, Feb. 26   Litho.   Perf. 12½x13
634 A167 25f bl grn & multi .35 .20
635 A167 35f purple & multi .70 .40

Hegira (Pilgrimage) Year.

Peace Symbols and "11" — A168

1972, Mar. 11   Photo.   Perf. 11x12½
636 A168 25f lt blue & blk 1.50 .30
637 A168 70f brt lilac & blk 4.25 1.25

2nd anniversary of Mar. 11 Manifesto.

Mountain Range and Flowers — A169

1972, Mar. 21   Perf. 11½x11
638 A169 25f vio blue & multi 1.25 .25
639 A169 70f vio blue & multi 4.25 1.50

Novrooz, New Year Festival.

Party Emblem A170

Symbolic Design — A171

Perf. 14 (A170), 13 (A171)
1972   Litho.
640 A170 10f brn org & multi .35 .20
641 A171 25f bister & multi .80 .40
642 A170 35f brn org & multi .90 .50
643 A171 70f red & multi 2.75 2.10
Nos. 640-643 (4) 4.80 3.20

Iraqi Arab Baath Socialist Party, 25th anniv. Issued: 25f, 70f, Mar. 23; 10f, 35f, Apr. 7.

Emblem, Map, Weather Balloons and Chart — A172

Cogwheel and Ship — A173

1972, Mar. 23   Photo.   Perf. 14x13½
644 A172 25f multicolored 1.90 .50
645 A172 35f yel & multi 3.25 1.50

12th World Meteorological Day.

1972, Mar. 25   Perf. 11x11½
646 A173 25f ocher & multi .50 .25
647 A173 35f pink & multi 1.00 .40

Arab Chamber of Commerce.

Derrick and Flame A174

Quill Pens, Map of Arab Countries A175

1972, Apr. 7   Perf. 13x13½
648 A174 25f multicolored 1.40 .30
649 A174 35f multicolored 1.90 1.00

Opening of North Rumaila (INOC, North Iraq Oil Fields).

1972, Apr. 17   Photo.   Perf. 11x11½
650 A175 25f orange & multi .55 .20
651 A175 35f blue & multi 1.75 1.00

3rd Congress of Arab Journalists.

Women's Federation Emblem A176

1972, Apr. 22   Litho.   Perf. 13½
652 A176 25f green & multi .55 .30
653 A176 35f lilac & multi 1.75 1.20

Iraqi Women's Federation, 4th anniversary.

Hand Holding Globe-shaped Wrench — A177

1972, May 1   Photo.   Perf. 11½
654 A177 25f yel grn & multi .45 .20
655 A177 35f orange & multi .80 .40

Labor Day.

Kaaba, Mecca, and Crescent — A178

1972, May 26
656 A178 25f green & multi .55 .20
657 A178 35f purple & multi 1.75 1.10

Mohammed's 1,402nd birthday.

Soldier, Civilian and Guns — A179

1972, July 14   Photo.   Perf. 13½x14
658 A179 35f multicolored .90 .40
659 A179 70f lilac & multi 3.00 1.20

14th anniv. of July 14, 1958, revolution.

Dome of the Rock, Arab Countries' Map, Fists A180

1972, July 17   Perf. 13
660 A180 25f citron & multi 1.20 .70
661 A180 95f blue & multi 3.25 3.00

4th anniv. of July 17, 1968 coup.

Congress Emblem, Scout Saluting Iraqi Flag — A182

1972, Aug. 12   Photo.   Perf. 13½x14
664 A182 20f multicolored 2.25 1.00
665 A182 25f lilac & multi 3.25 1.10

10th Arab Boy Scouts Jamboree and Conference, Mosul, Aug. 10-19.

1972, Aug. 24

Congress emblem and Girl Guide in camp.

666 A182 10f yellow & multi 1.50 .65
667 A182 45f multicolored 4.75 1.40

4th Arab Guides Camp & Conf., Mosul, Aug. 24-30.

No. 625A Overprinted and Surcharged, No. 625B Overprinted with New Date:

1972, Oct. 4   Photo.   Perf. 13x12½
668 A162a 25f brt rose & multi 6.75 3.00
669 A162a 70f on 15f multi 8.50 7.00

Third Traffic Week.

Central
Bank of
Iraq
A183

1972, Nov. 16   Photo.   Perf. 13
670 A183 25f lt blue & multi   .80   .40
671 A183 70f lt green & multi   2.25   .90

25th anniversary, Central Bank of Iraq.

UIC
Emblem
A184

1972, Dec. 29
672 A184 25f dp rose & multi   1.75   .70
673 A184 45f brt vio & multi   5.00 3.00

50th anniv., Intl. Railroad Union (UIC).

Nos. 148-149, 151, 180 and Type of
1957-58 Overprinted with 3 Bars

1973, Jan. 29   Engr.   Perf. 11½x12
674 A28 10f blue   3.50 1.25
675 A33 10f blue   3.50 1.25
676 A28 15f black   3.50 1.25
677 A33 15f black   3.50 1.25
678 A28 25f rose violet   3.50 1.25
679 A33 25f rose violet   3.50 1.25
    Nos. 674-679 (6)   21.00 7.50

The size and position of the bottom bar of
overprint differs; the bar can be same size as 2
top bars, short and centered or moved to the
right.

No. 455
Overprinted

1973, Mar. 25   Litho.   Perf. 13
680 A107 15f rose red & multi   10.00 4.00

Intl. History Cong. See Nos. C52-C53.

Workers
and Oil
Wells
A185

Ram's-head
Harp — A186

1973, June 1   Litho.   Perf. 13
681 A185 25f yel & multi   2.00   .90
682 A185 70f rose & multi   9.50 3.00

1st anniv. of nationalization of oil industry.
For overprint, see No. O298.

1973, June   Litho.   Perf. 13x12½
Designs: 25f, 35f, 45f, Minaret, Mosul, 50f,
70f, 95f, Statue of goddess. 10f, 20f, like 5f.
683 A186 5f orange & blk   .25   .20
684 A186 10f bister & blk   .25   .20
685 A186 20f brt rose & blk   .25   .20
686 A186 25f ultra & blk   .20   .20
687 A186 35f emer & blk   .50   .30
688 A186 45f blue & black   .55   .30
689 A186 50f olive & yel   .80   .30
690 A186 70f violet & yel   1.00   .50
691 A186 95f brown & yel   1.90   .75
    Nos. 683-691 (9)   5.70 3.00

For overprints see Nos. O299-O307, RA21.

People with
Flags,
Grain
A187

1973, July 14
692 A187 25f multicolored   .70   .30
693 A187 35f multicolored   1.40   .40

July Festivals.

Nos. 393 and
395 Surcharged

1973   Litho.   Perf. 13½x14
694 A85 25f on 3f multi   4.00 2.25
695 A85 70f on 15f multi   10.00 5.00

Festival of Date Trees.

INTERPOL Headquarters — A188

1973, Sept. 20   Litho.   Perf. 12
696 A188 25f multicolored   1.00   .60
697 A188 70f brt bl & multi   5.50 3.75

50th anniv. of Intl. Criminal Police Org.

Nos. 517-518
Overprinted in
Silver

1973, Sept. 29   Litho.   Perf. 12½x13
698 A130 15f multicolored   6.50 2.50
699 A130 50f multicolored   12.00 3.50

Meeting of Intl. Org. of Journalists' Executive Committee, Sept. 26-29.

Flags and Fair
Emblem — A189

WMO
Emblem — A190

1973, Oct. 10   Photo.   Perf. 11
700 A189 10f brt grn & dk brn   .45   .25
701 A189 20f ocher & multi   .80   .30
702 A189 65f blue & multi   1.75   .90
    Nos. 700-702 (3)   3.00 1.45

10th International Baghdad Fair, Oct. 1-21.

1973, Nov. 15   Litho.   Perf. 12
703 A190 25f org, blk & green   .70   .20
704 A190 35f brt rose, blk & grn 2.25 1.00

Intl. meteorological cooperation, cent.

Flags of
Arab
League
and Iraq,
Maghreb
Emblem
A191

1973, Dec. 1   Photo.   Perf. 14
705 A191 20f dl org & multi   .40   .20
706 A191 35f blue & multi   1.40   .90

11th session of Civil Aviation Council of
Arab States, Baghdad, Dec. 1973.

No. 360 Overprinted

1973, Dec. 12   Photo.   Perf. 11
707 A67a 30f orange & blue   5.00 2.75

6th Executive Council Meeting of APU.

Human Rights
Flame — A192

1973, Dec. 25   Perf. 11½
708 A192 25f multicolored   .25   .25
709 A192 70f ultra & multi   .90   .50

Universal Declaration of Human Rights,
25th anniv.

Military
College
Crest
and
Cadets
A193

1974, Jan. 6   Perf. 12x11½
710 A193 25f ocher & multi   .45   .25
711 A193 35f ultra & multi   1.60 1.00

50th anniversary of the Military College.

UPU and Arab
Postal Union
Emblems
A194

1974, May 28   Photo.   Perf. 11½x12
712 A194 25f gold & multi   .90   .25
713 A194 35f gold & multi   .90   .40
714 A194 70f gold & multi   1.60   .90
    Nos. 712-714 (3)   3.40 1.55

Centenary of the Universal Postal Union.

Symbols of Ancient Mesopotamia and
Oil Industry — A195

1974, June 1   Litho.   Perf. 12½
715 A195 10f blue & multi   .40   .20
716 A195 25f ocher & multi   .85   .25
717 A195 70f rose & multi   2.75 1.00
    Nos. 715-717 (3)   4.00 2.45

Nationalization of the oil industry, 2nd anniv.

Festival
A196

1974, July 17   Perf. 11½x12
718 A196 20f lilac & multi   .35   .20
719 A196 35f dull org & multi   1.00   .50

July Festivals.

National
Front
Emblem
and
People
A197

1974, July 17   Perf. 12x11½
720 A197 25f blue & multi   .65   .25
721 A197 70f brt grn & multi   1.50   .75

1st anniv. of Progressive National Front.

Cement Plant
and Brick
Wall — A198

1974, Oct. 19   Perf. 11½x12
722 A198 20f gray bl & multi   .45   .25
723 A198 25f red & multi   .65   .30
724 A198 70f emerald & multi   1.40 1.00
    Nos. 722-724 (3)   2.50 1.55

25th anniversary of Iraqi Cement Plant.

Nos. 561 and 527 Surcharged

a

b

1975, Jan. 9   Litho.   Perf. 13, 14
725 A142 (a) 10f on 3f multi   3.50 2.50
726 A135 (b) 25f on 3f multi   11.00 7.25

Globe and WPY
Emblem
A199

1975, Jan. 30   Perf. 11½x12
727 A199 25f dull bl & blk   .60   .20
728 A199 35f brt pink & ind   1.25   .65
729 A199 70f yel grn & vio   3.50 1.40
     Nos. 727-729 (3)   5.35 2.25

World Population Year 1974.

Festival Symbols — A200

1975, July 17   Litho.   Perf. 12x11½
730 A200   5f lt brn & multi   .25   .20
731 A200 10f lt brn & multi   .25   .20
732 A200 35f lt brn & multi   1.75   .75
     Nos. 730-732 (3)   2.25 1.15

Festivals, July 1975.

Map of
Arab
Countries
A201

1975, Aug. 5   Photo.   Perf. 13
733 A201 25f rose & multi   .50   .20
734 A201 35f multicolored   .90   .60
735 A201 45f multicolored   1.00   .65
     Nos. 733-735 (3)   2.40 1.45

Arab Working Org., 10th anniv.

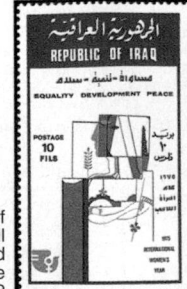

Symbols of
Women, Oil
Industry and
Agriculture
A202

1975, Aug. 15   Perf. 14
736 A202 10f lilac & multi   .50   .30
737 A202 35f multicolored   1.00   .85
738 A202 70f bl & multi   4.25 1.50
   a. Souv. sheet, 100f, imperf. 10.00 10.00
     Nos. 736-738 (3)   5.75 2.65

International Women's Year.

Euphrates Dam and
Causeway — A203

1975, Sept. 5   Litho.   Perf. 12x11½
739 A203   3f orange & multi   .20   .20
740 A203 25f purple & multi   .70   .25
741 A203 70f rose red & multi   2.75 1.25
     Nos. 739-741 (3)   3.65 1.70

Intl. Commission on Irrigation and Drainage,
25th anniv.

National
Insurance
Co. Seal
A204

1975, Oct. 11   Photo.   Perf. 13
742 A204 20f brt bl & multi   .80   .25
743 A204 25f crim & multi   1.00   .40
   a. Souv. sheet, 100f, imperf.   7.00 8.50

Natl. Insurance Co., Baghdad, 25th anniv.

Musician
Entertaining
King — A205

1975, Nov. 21   Perf. 14
744 A205 25f silver & multi   .65   .25
745 A205 45f gold & multi   1.50   .90

Baghdad Intl. Music Conf., Nov. 1975.

Telecommunications Center — A206

1975, Dec. 22   Litho.   Perf. 12½
746 A206   5f lil rose & multi   .20   .20
747 A206 10f blue & multi   .30   .20
748 A206 60f green & multi   1.90 1.20
     Nos. 746-748 (3)   2.40 1.60

Inauguration of Telecommunications Center
Building during July 1975 Festival.

Diesel Locomotive — A207

Conference Emblem and: 30f, Diesel passenger locomotive #511. 35f, 0-3-0 steam tank
locomotive with passenger train. 50f, 2-3-0
German steam locomotive, c. 1914.

1975, Dec. 22   Photo.   Perf. 14
749 A207 25f tan & multi   5.50 1.00
750 A207 30f tan & multi   8.50 2.00
751 A207 35f yel grn & multi   11.00 3.50
752 A207 50f yel grn & multi   16.00 9.50
     Nos. 749-752 (4)   41.00 16.00

15th Taurus Railway Conference, Baghdad.

A208

A209

Design: Soldier on guard.

1976, Jan. 6   Perf. 13
753 A208   5f silver & multi   .20   .20
754 A208 25f silver & multi   .55   .20
755 A208 50f gold & multi   1.60   .60
     Nos. 753-755 (3)   2.35 1.00

55th Army Day.

1976, Jan. 8   Photo.   Perf. 13½x13

Fingerprint crossed out, Arab world.

756 A209   5f violet & multi   .25   .25
757 A209 15f blue & multi   .45   .25
758 A209 35f green & multi   1.60 1.00
     Nos. 756-758 (3)   2.30 1.50

Statue of
Goddess — A210

20f-30f, Two female figures forming column.
35f-75f, Head of bearded man.

1976, Jan. 1   Litho.   Perf. 13x12½
759 A210   5f lilac & multi   .20   .20
760 A210 10f rose & multi   .20   .20
761 A210 15f yellow & multi   .30   .20
762 A210 20f bister & multi   .30   .25
763 A210 25f lt grn & multi   .45   .25
764 A210 30f blue & multi   .70   .25
765 A210 35f lil rose & multi   .80   .30
766 A210 50f citron & multi   1.20   .30
767 A210 75f violet & multi   1.75   .70
     Nos. 759-767 (9)   5.90 2.65

Iraq Earth
Station
A211

1976, Feb. 8   Perf. 13x13½
768 A211 10f silver & multi   .40   .25
769 A211 25f silver & multi   1.25   .45
770 A211 75f gold & multi   4.50 2.00
     Nos. 768-770 (3)   6.15 2.70

Revolution of Ramadan 14, 13th anniv.

Telephones
1876 and
1976 — A212

Map of Maghreb,
ICATU
Emblem — A213

1976, Mar. 17   Litho.   Perf. 12x12½
771 A212 35f multicolored   1.25   .45
772 A212 50f multicolored   2.50   .70
773 A212 75f multicolored   4.00 1.00
     Nos. 771-773 (3)   7.75 2.15

Centenary of first telephone call by Alexander Graham Bell, Mar. 10, 1876.

1976, Mar. 24   Photo.   Perf. 13½
774 A213   5f green & multi   .35   .20
775 A213 10f green & multi   .35   .20
     Nos. 774-775,C54 (3)   5.20 2.40

20th Intl. Conf. of Arab Trade Unions.

Map of Iraq, Family,
Torch and
Wreath — A214

1976, Apr. 1   Perf. 12½
776 A214   5f multicolored   .20   .20
777 A214 15f lilac & multi   .45   .20
778 A214 35f multicolored   2.25   .90
     Nos. 776-778 (3)   2.90 1.30

Police Day.

Pipeline, Map of
Iraq — A215

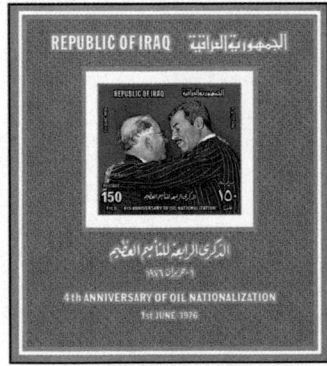

Pres. A. H. al-Bakr Embracing Vice
Pres. Saddam Hussein — A216

1976, June 1   Photo.   Perf. 13
779 A215 25f multicolored   1.50   .20
780 A215 75f multicolored   4.50 2.00

Souvenir Sheet
Imperf
781 A216 150f multicolored   32.50 32.50

4th anniversary of oil nationalization.

"Festival" — A217

1976, July 17   *Perf. 14*
782 A217 15f orange & multi   .35   .25
783 A217 35f orange & multi   1.00   .70
Festivals, July 1976.

Archbishop
Capucci,
Map of
Palestine
A218

1976, Aug. 18   Litho.   *Perf. 12*
784 A218 25f multicolored   .70   .25
785 A218 35f multicolored   1.00   .40
786 A218 75f multicolored   2.75   1.25
    Nos. 784-786 (3)   4.45   1.90
Detention of Archbishop Hilarion Capucci in
Israel, Aug. 18, 1974.

Common
Kingfisher — A219

"15" — A220

10f, Turtle dove. 15f, Pin-tailed sandgrouse.
25f, Blue rock thrush. 50f, Purple and gray
herons.

1976, Sept. 15   Litho.   *Perf. 13½x14*
787 A219   5f multicolored   2.75   .85
788 A219 10f multicolored   2.75   .85
789 A219 15f multicolored   3.75   .85
790 A219 25f multicolored   7.25   1.10
791 A219 50f multicolored   11.00   1.50
    Nos. 787-791 (5)   27.50   5.15

1976, Nov. 23   Photo.   *Perf. 13½*
792 A220 30f multicolored   .75   .25
793 A220 70f multicolored   2.50   .75
15th anniv. of National Students Union.

Oil Tanker and
Emblems
A221

25f, 50f, Pier, refinery, pipeline.

1976, Dec. 25   *Perf. 12½x12*
794 A221 10f multicolored   .70   .25
795 A221 15f multicolored   .90   .40
796 A221 25f multicolored   2.10   .75
797 A221 50f multicolored   3.00   1.25
    Nos. 794-797 (4)   6.70   2.65
1st Iraqi oil tanker (10f, 15f) and Nationalization of Basrah Petroleum Co. Ltd., 1st anniv.
(25f, 50f).

Happy
Children — A222

Ornament
A223

UNESCO Emblem and: 25f, Children with
flowers and butterflies. 75f, Children planting
flowers around flagpole.

1976, Dec. 25   *Perf. 12x12½*
798 A222 10f multicolored   .25   .20
799 A222 25f multicolored   2.00   .40
800 A222 75f multicolored   3.50   1.10
    Nos. 798-800 (3)   5.75   1.70
30th anniv. of UNESCO, and Books for Children Campaign.

1977, Mar. 2   Photo.   *Perf. 13½*
801 A223 25f gold & multi   .70   .25
802 A223 35f gold & multi   1.00   .30
Birthday of Mohammed (570-632).

Peace
Dove — A224

Dahlia — A225

1977, Mar. 11   *Perf. 14x13½*
803 A224 25f lt bl & multi   .35   .20
804 A224 30f buff & multi   .65   .30
Peace Day.

1977, Mar. 21   Litho.   *Perf. 12½*
Flowers: 10f, Sweet peas. 35f, Chrysanthemums. 50f, Verbena.
805 A225   5f multicolored   .25   .20
806 A225 10f multicolored   .45   .20
807 A225 35f multicolored   1.10   .30
808 A225 50f multicolored   2.25   .65
    Nos. 805-808 (4)   4.05   1.35
Spring Festivals, Baghdad.

Emblem
with
Doves
A226

Designs: 75f, Emblem with flame. 100f,
Dove with olive branch.

1977, Apr. 7   Photo.   *Perf. 13*
809 A226 25f yel & multi   .60   .20
810 A226 75f yel & multi   2.25   1.00
    Souvenir Sheet
    Imperf
811 A226 100f multicolored   6.00   6.00
Al Baath Party, 30th anniversary. No. 811
contains one 49x35mm stamp.

APU
Emblem,
Members'
Flags
A227

1977, Apr. 12   Litho.   *Perf. 14*
812 A227 25f orange & multi   .35   .20
813 A227 35f gray & multi   .70   .40
25th anniversary of Arab Postal Union.

Cogwheel, Globe
and "1" — A228

1977, May 1   Litho.   *Perf. 14½x14*
814 A228 10f multicolored   .20   .20
815 A228 30f multicolored   .55   .20
816 A228 35f multicolored   .70   .60
    Nos. 814-816 (3)   1.45   1.00
Labor Day.

Weight
Lifting
A229

75f, Weight lifter, standing up. 100f, Symbolic weight lifter with Iraqi flag, laurel wreath.

1977, May 8   Photo.   *Perf. 14*
817 A229 25f multicolored   .90   .60
818 A229 75f multicolored   2.50   1.10
    Souvenir Sheet
    Imperf
819 A229 100f multicolored   8.50   8.50
8th Asian Weight Lifting Championship,
Baghdad, May 1977. No. 819 contains one
42x52mm stamp.

Arabian
Garden
A230

Grain and
Dove — A231

Arab Tourist Year: 10f, View of town with
minarets, horiz. 30f, Landscape with bridge
and waterfall. 50f, Hosts welcoming tourists,
and drum, horiz.

    Perf. 11½x12, 12x11½
1977, June 15   Litho.
820 A230   5f multicolored   .25   .25
821 A230 10f multicolored   .25   .25
822 A230 30f multicolored   .95   .25
823 A230 50f multicolored   2.75   1.75
    Nos. 820-823 (4)   4.20   2.50

1977, July 17   Photo.   *Perf. 14*
824 A231 25f multicolored   .55   .20
825 A231 30f multicolored   .70   .30
Festivals, July 1977.

Map of Arab
Countries
A232

1977, Sept. 9   Photo.   *Perf. 13½x14*
826 A232 30f multicolored   .80   .45
827 A232 70f multicolored   2.40   .90
UN Conference on Desertification, Nairobi,
Kenya, Aug. 29-Sept. 9.

Census
Emblem — A233

Festival
Emblem — A234

1977, Oct. 17   Litho.   *Perf. 14x14½*
828 A233 20f ultra & multi   .30   .20
829 A233 30f brown & multi   .70   .25
830 A233 70f gray & multi   1.40   .80
    Nos. 828-830 (3)   2.40   1.25
Population Census Day, Oct. 17.

1977, Nov. 1   Photo.   *Perf. 14*
831 A234 25f silver & multi   .30   .20
832 A234 50f gold & multi   .65   .40
Al Mutanabby Festival, Nov. 1977.

A235   A236

Jumblatt, caricatures of Britain, US, Israel.

1977, Nov. 16   Photo.   *Perf. 14*
833 A235 20f multicolored   .40   .25
834 A235 30f multicolored   .55   .25
835 A235 70f multicolored   1.25   .60
    Nos. 833-835 (3)   2.20   1.10
Kemal Junblatt, Druse leader, killed in Lebanese war.

1977, Dec. 12   Photo.   *Perf. 14*
836 A236 30f gold & multi   .40   .20
837 A236 35f silver & multi   .50   .25
Hegira (Pilgrimage) Year.

Young People
and
Flags — A237

Coins and Coin
Bank — A238

1978, Apr. 7   **Photo.**   *Perf. 11½x11*
838	A237	10f multicolored	.20	.20
839	A237	15f multicolored	.25	.20
840	A237	35f multicolored	.55	.35
		Nos. 838-840 (3)	1.00	.75

Youth Day.

1978, Apr. 15
841	A238	15f multicolored	.30	.20
842	A238	25f multicolored	.50	.20
843	A238	35f multicolored	1.00	.40
		Nos. 841-843 (3)	1.80	.80

6th anniversary of postal savings law.

Microwave
Transmission
and Receiving
A239

Emblems and Flags
of
Participants — A240

1978, May 17   **Photo.**   *Perf. 14*
844	A239	25f org & multi	.40	.20
845	A239	35f lilac & multi	.40	.20
846	A239	75f emer & multi	1.00	.60
		Nos. 844-846 (3)	1.80	1.00

10th World Telecommunications Day and
1st anniversary of commissioning of national
microwave network.

       Perf. 12½x11½
1978, June 19   **Litho.**
847	A240	25f multicolored	.55	.20
848	A240	35f multicolored	.85	.50

Conference of Postal Ministers of Arabian
Gulf Countries, Baghdad (Saudi Arabia,
United Arab Emirates, Qatar, Bahrain, Kuwait,
Oman, People's Republic of Yemen).

Ancient
Coin — A241

Designs: Ancient Iraqi coins. 75f vertical.

     Perf. 11½x12½
1978, June 25   **Photo.**
849	A241	1f citron & multi	.20	.20
850	A241	2f blue & multi	.20	.20
851	A241	3f salmon & multi	.20	.20
852	A241	4f salmon & multi	.20	.20
853	A241	75f bl grn & multi	2.40	2.40
		Nos. 849-853 (5)	3.20	3.20

Festival
Emblem — A242

Festival Poster — A243

1978, July 17   *Perf. 13½x13*
854	A242	25f multicolored	.35	.20
855	A242	35f multicolored	.55	.25

Souvenir Sheet
Perf. 13x13½
856	A243	100f multicolored	6.50	6.50

Festivals, July 1978.

WHO
Emblem,
Nurse,
Hospital,
Sick Child
A244

1978, Aug. 18   **Photo.**   *Perf. 14*
857	A244	25f multicolored	.25	.20
858	A244	35f multicolored	.65	.25
859	A244	75f multicolored	1.75	.95
		Nos. 857-859 (3)	2.65	1.40

Eradication of smallpox.

Maritime
Union
Emblem
A245

1978, Aug. 30   **Photo.**   *Perf. 11½x12*
860	A245	25f multicolored	.55	.30
861	A245	75f multicolored	1.40	.55

1st World Maritime Day.

Workers
A246

1978, Sept. 12   *Perf. 14*
862	A246	10f multicolored	.25	.20
863	A246	25f multicolored	.55	.20
864	A246	35f multicolored	1.00	.65
		Nos. 862-864 (3)	1.80	1.05

10th anniv. of People's Work Groups.

Fair Emblem with
Atom
Symbol — A247

Map of Iraq,
Ruler and
Globe — A248

1978, Oct. 1
865	A247	25f multicolored	.25	.20
866	A247	35f multicolored	.30	.20
867	A247	75f multicolored	1.40	.85
		Nos. 865-867 (3)	1.95	1.25

15th International Fair, Baghdad, Oct. 1-15.

1978, Oct. 14
868	A248	25f multicolored	.25	.20
869	A248	35f multicolored	.30	.20
870	A248	75f multicolored	1.40	.85
		Nos. 868-870 (3)	1.95	1.25

World Standards Day.

Altharthar-Euphrates Dam — A249

1978   **Photo.**   *Perf. 11½*
871	A249	5f multicolored	.20	.20
872	A249	10f multicolored	.20	.20
873	A249	15f multicolored	.20	.20
874	A249	25f multicolored	.30	.20
875	A249	35f multicolored	.40	.20
876	A249	50f multicolored	.65	.30
		Nos. 871-876 (6)	1.95	1.30

Arab Summit
Conference
A250

Surgeons'
Conference
Emblem — A251

1978, Nov. 2   **Photo.**   *Perf. 14*
890	A250	25f multicolored	.25	.20
891	A250	35f multicolored	.45	.25
892	A250	75f multicolored	1.10	.85
		Nos. 890-892 (3)	1.80	1.30

9th Arab Summit Conference, Baghdad,
Nov. 2-5.

1978, Nov. 8   **Litho.**   *Perf. 12x11½*
893	A251	25f multicolored	.35	.20
894	A251	75f multicolored	1.00	.65

4th Cong. of the Assoc. of Thoracic & Cardiovascular Surgeons of Asia, Baghdad, Nov.
6-10.

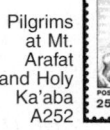

Pilgrims
at Mt.
Arafat
and Holy
Ka'aba
A252

1978, Nov. 9   **Photo.**   *Perf. 14*
895	A252	25f multicolored	.35	.20
896	A252	35f multicolored	.55	.25

Pilgrimage to Mecca.

Atom
Symbol,
Map of
South
America,
Africa,
Arabia
A253

Hands Holding
Emblem — A254

1978, Nov. 11   *Perf. 13½*
897	A253	25f multicolored	.25	.20
898	A253	50f multicolored	.55	.25
899	A253	75f multicolored	.90	.55
		Nos. 897-899 (3)	1.70	1.00

Technical Cooperation Among Developing
Countries Conf., Buenos Aires, Argentina,
Sept. 1978.

Globe and Flame
Emblem — A255

1978, Nov. 30   **Litho.**   *Perf. 13½x13*
900	A254	25f multicolored	.40	.25
901	A254	50f multicolored	.70	.30
902	A254	75f multicolored	2.00	.65
		Nos. 900-902 (3)	3.10	1.20

Anti-Apartheid Year.

1978, Dec. 20   *Perf. 14*
903	A255	50f multicolored	.50	.20
904	A255	75f multicolored	1.50	1.00

Declaration of Human Rights, 30th anniv.

Candle and
Emblem — A256

Book, Pencil and
Flame — A257

1979, Jan. 9   **Photo.**   *Perf. 14*
905	A256	10f multicolored	.35	.25
906	A256	25f multicolored	.35	.25
907	A256	35f multicolored	.65	.25
		Nos. 905-907 (3)	1.35	.75

Police Day.

1979, Feb. 15   **Photo.**   *Perf. 14*
908	A257	15f multicolored	.25	.20
909	A257	25f multicolored	.35	.20
910	A257	35f multicolored	.90	.25
		Nos. 908-910 (3)	1.50	.65

Application of Compulsory Education Law,
anniversary.

Pupils, School
and Teacher
A258

1979, Mar. 1   *Perf. 13*
911 A258 10f multicolored   .20   .20
912 A258 15f multicolored   .20   .20
913 A258 50f multicolored   .80   .50
   Nos. 911-913 (3)   1.20   .90
Teacher's Day.

Pupils, Flag, Pencil — A259

1979, Mar. 10   *Perf. 13½x13*
914 A259 15f multicolored   .25   .25
915 A259 25f multicolored   .45   .25
916 A259 35f multicolored   .70   .25
   Nos. 914-916 (3)   1.40   .75
National Comprehensive Compulsory Literacy Campaign.

Book, World Map, Arab Achievements A260

1979, Mar. 22   *Perf. 13*
917 A260 35f multicolored   .50   .20
918 A260 75f multicolored   1.50   .65
Achievements of the Arabs.

Girl Playing Flute — A261

1979, Apr. 15   *Litho.*   *Perf. 13½*
919 A261 15f multicolored   .35   .20
920 A261 25f multicolored   .55   .20
921 A261 35f multicolored   1.00   .45
   Nos. 919-921 (3)   1.90   .85
Mosul Spring Festival.

Iraqi Flag, Globe, UPU Emblem A262

1979, Apr. 22   *Photo.*   *Perf. 13x13½*
922 A262 25f multicolored   .60   .25
923 A262 50f multicolored   .60   .25
924 A262 75f multicolored   1.50   .65
   Nos. 922-924 (3)   2.70   1.15
50th anniv. of Iraq's admission to the UPU.

Soccer Tournament Emblem A263

1979, May 4   *Photo.*   *Perf. 13*
925 A263 10f multicolored   .20   .20
926 A263 15f multicolored   .30   .20
927 A263 50f multicolored   1.00   .50
   Nos. 925-927 (3)   1.50   .90
5th Arabian Gulf Soccer Championship.

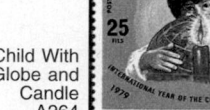

Child With Globe and Candle A264

Design: 100f, IYC emblem, boy and girl reaching for UN emblem, vert.

1979, June 1   *Photo.*   *Perf. 13x13½*
928 A264 25f multicolored   .70   .30
929 A264 75f multicolored   1.75   1.00

Souvenir Sheet

930 A264 100f multicolored   30.00   27.50
International Year of the Child.
No. 930 contains one 30x42mm stamp.

Leaf and Flower — A265

1979, July 17   *Litho.*   *Perf. 12½*
931 A265 15f multicolored   .20   .20
932 A265 25f multicolored   .35   .20
933 A265 35f multicolored   .35   .20
   Nos. 931-933 (3)   .90   .60
July festivals.

Students Holding Globe, UNESCO Emblem A266

1979, July 25
934 A266 25f multicolored   .50   .25
935 A266 40f multicolored   .90   .45
936 A266 100f multicolored   2.00   .90
   Nos. 934-936 (3)   3.40   1.60
Intl. Bureau of Education, Geneva, 50th anniv.

S. al Hosari, Philosopher A267

Designs: No. 938, Mustapha Jawad, historian. No. 939, Jawad Selim, sculptor.

1979, Oct. 15   *Litho.*   *Perf. 12½*
937 A267 25f multicolored   .45   .25
938 A267 25f multicolored   .45   .25
939 A267 25f multicolored   .45   .25
   Nos. 937-939 (3)   1.35   .75

Pilgrimage to Mecca A268

1979, Oct. 25   *Litho.*   *Perf. 12½*
940 A268 25f multicolored   .45   .25
941 A268 50f multicolored   .80   .35

Iraqi News Agency, 20th Anniversary A269

1979, Nov. 9   *Photo.*   *Perf. 11½*
942 A269 25f multicolored   .45   .20
943 A269 50f multicolored   1.00   .25
944 A269 75f multicolored   1.25   .40
   Nos. 942-944 (3)   2.70   .85

Telecom 79 — A270

1979, Nov. 20   *Litho.*   *Perf. 11½*
945 A270 25f multicolored   .45   .20
946 A270 50f multicolored   .70   .30
947 A270 75f multicolored   1.25   .65
   Nos. 945-947 (3)   2.40   1.15
3rd World Telecommunications Exhibition, Geneva, Sept. 20-26.

International Palestinian Solidarity Day — A271

1979, Nov. 29   *Photo.*   *Perf. 11½x12*
948 A271 25f multicolored   1.25   .25
949 A271 50f multicolored   2.25   .45
950 A271 75f multicolored   3.50   .85
   Nos. 948-950 (3)   7.00   1.55

A272   A273

Designs: 25f, 75f, Ahmad Hassan Al-Bakr. 35f, 100f, Pres. Saddam Hussein.

1979, Dec. 1   *Photo.*   *Perf. 13x13½*
951 A272 25f multicolored   .35   .25
952 A272 35f multicolored   .50   .25
953 A272 75f multicolored   1.00   .40
954 A272 100f multicolored   4.00   2.25
   Nos. 951-954 (4)   5.85   3.15

1979, Dec. 10   *Perf. 14*

Vanguard Emblem and: 10f, Boy and violin. 15f, Children, map of Iraq. 25f, Youths. 35f, Vanguard emblem alone.

955 A273 10f multicolored   .25   .25
956 A273 15f multicolored   .25   .25
957 A273 25f multicolored   .40   .25
958 A273 35f multicolored   .50   .25
   Nos. 955-958 (4)   1.40   1.00

World Meteorological Day — A274

World Health Day — A275

1980, Mar. 23   *Photo.*   *Perf. 14*
959 A274 15f multicolored   .20   .20
960 A274 25f multicolored   .30   .20
961 A274 35f multicolored   .70   .25
   Nos. 959-961 (3)   1.20   .65

1980, Apr. 7   *Photo.*   *Perf. 14*
962 A275 25f multicolored   .35   .25
963 A275 35f multicolored   .50   .25
964 A275 75f multicolored   1.90   .50
   Nos. 962-964 (3)   2.75   1.00

Festivals Emblem — A276

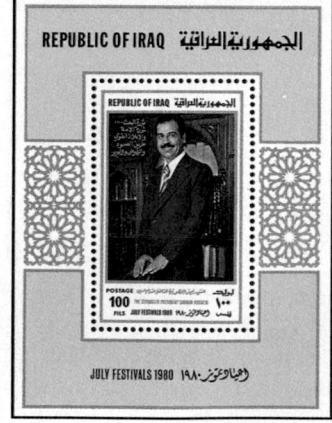

Pres. Hussein — A277

1980, July 17   *Photo.*   *Perf. 13½x13*
965 A276 25f multicolored   .35   .30
966 A276 35f multicolored   .45   .30

Souvenir Sheet
Perf. 13½

967 A277 100f multicolored   8.00   8.00
July Festivals.

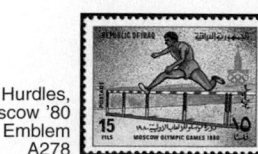

Hurdles, Moscow '80 Emblem A278

1980, July 30   *Photo.*   *Perf. 14*
968 A278 15f shown   .25   .25
969 A278 20f Weight lifting, vert.   .45   .35

970	A278	30f Boxing	.85	.40
971	A278	35f Soccer, vert.	1.75	.75
		Nos. 968-971 (4)	3.30	1.75

Souvenir Sheet

972	A278	100f Wrestling	10.50	10.50

22nd Summer Olympic Games, Moscow, July 19-Aug. 3.

Fruits — A279

1980, Aug. 15

973	A279	5f Blackberries	.25	.20
974	A279	15f Apricots	.50	.20
975	A279	20f Pears	.70	.20
976	A279	25f Apples	.85	.20
977	A279	35f Plums	1.10	.35
		Nos. 973-977 (5)	3.40	1.15

World Tourism Conference, Manila, Sept. 27 — A279a

1980, Aug. 30   Litho.   Perf. 12½

978	A279a	25f multicolored	.35	.20
979	A279a	50f multicolored	.85	.25
980	A279a	100f multicolored	1.75	.85
		Nos. 978-980 (3)	2.95	1.30

Postal Union Emblem, Posthorn, Map of Arab States — A280

1980, Sept. 8   Perf. 12

981	A280	10f multicolored	.25	.25
982	A280	30f multicolored	.35	.25
983	A280	35f multicolored	.70	.25
		Nos. 981-983 (3)	1.30	.75

Arab Postal Union, 11th Congress, Baghdad.

20th Anniversary of OPEC — A281

1980, Sept. 30

984	A281	30f multicolored	1.00	.25
985	A281	75f multicolored	1.60	.75

Papilio Machaon A282

1980, Oct. 20   Photo.   Perf. 13½x14

987	A282	10f shown	2.00	.35
988	A282	15f Danaus chrysip- pus	2.25	.65

989	A282	20f Vanessa atalanta	3.25	.80
990	A282	30f Colias croceus	5.25	1.25
		Nos. 987-990 (4)	12.75	3.05

Hegira, 1,500th Anniv. A283

1980, Nov. 9   Litho.   Perf. 11½x12

991	A283	15f multicolored	.25	.20
992	A283	25f multicolored	.60	.20
993	A283	35f multicolored	.70	.30
		Nos. 991-993 (3)	1.55	.70

International Palestinian Solidarity Day — A284

1980, Nov. 29

994	A284	25f multicolored	1.00	.20
995	A284	35f multicolored	1.25	.25
996	A284	75f multicolored	2.50	.75
		Nos. 994-996 (3)	4.75	1.20

Army Day — A285

February Revolution, 18th Anniversary A286

1981, Jan. 6   Photo.   Perf. 14x13½

997	A285	5f multicolored	.30	.20
998	A285	30f multicolored	.55	.20
999	A285	75f multicolored	1.60	.70
		Nos. 997-999 (3)	2.45	1.10

1981, Feb. 8   Perf. 12

1000	A286	15f multicolored	.25	.20
1001	A286	30f multicolored	.45	.20
1002	A286	35f multicolored	.70	.25
		Nos. 1000-1002 (3)	1.40	.65

Map of Arab Countries A287

1981, Mar. 22   Litho.   Perf. 12½

1003	A287	5f multicolored	.20	.20
1004	A287	25f multicolored	.50	.20
1005	A287	35f multicolored	.70	.25
		Nos. 1003-1005 (3)	1.40	.65

Battle of Qadisiya — A288

1981, Apr. 7   Photo.   Perf. 13½x13

1006	A288	30f multicolored	.45	.20
1007	A288	35f multicolored	.60	.20
1008	A288	75f multicolored	1.10	.50
		Nos. 1006-1008 (3)	2.15	.90

Souvenir Sheet

1009	A288	100f multicolored	6.50	6.50

No. 1009 contains one horiz. stamp.

Helicopters and Tank A289

1981, June 1   Photo.

1010	A289	5f shown	.20	.20
1011	A289	10f Plane	.35	.20
1012	A289	15f Rocket	.50	.20
		Nos. 1010-1012,C66 (4)	5.05	3.10

Air Force, 50th anniv.

Natl. Assembly Election, First Anniv. — A290

1981, June 20   Perf. 12½

1013	A290	30f multicolored	.45	.20
1014	A290	35f multicolored	.60	.20
1015	A290	45f multicolored	.95	.35
		Nos. 1013-1015 (3)	2.00	.75

July Festivals A291

1981, July 17   Photo.

1016	A291	15f multicolored	.25	.20
1017	A291	25f multicolored	.40	.20
1018	A291	35f multicolored	.70	.20
		Nos. 1016-1018 (3)	1.35	.60

Pottery Maker — A292

Designs: Popular industries.

1981, Aug. 15   Perf. 14

1019	A292	5f Straw weaver	.20	.20
1020	A292	30f Metal worker	.55	.20
1021	A292	35f shown	.75	.20
1022	A292	50f Rug maker, horiz.	1.00	.35
		Nos. 1019-1022 (4)	2.50	.95

Islamic Pilgrimage — A293

1981, Oct. 7   Photo.   Perf. 12x11½

1023	A293	25f multicolored	.55	.20
1024	A293	45f multicolored	1.00	.30
1025	A293	50f multicolored	1.00	.30
		Nos. 1023-1025 (3)	2.55	.80

World Food Day A294

1981, Oct. 16   Photo.   Perf. 14

1026	A294	30f multicolored	.55	.20
1027	A294	45f multicolored	1.00	.40
1028	A294	75f multicolored	1.50	.75
		Nos. 1026-1028 (3)	3.05	1.35

Intl. Year of the Disabled — A295

1981, Nov. 15

1029	A295	30f multicolored	.45	.20
1030	A295	45f multicolored	.75	.30
1031	A295	75f multicolored	1.10	.60
		Nos. 1029-1031 (3)	2.30	1.10

5th Anniv. of United Arab Shipping Co. A296

1981, Dec. 2   Perf. 13x13½

1032	A296	50f multicolored	1.40	.60
1033	A296	120f multicolored	4.00	1.75

Saddam Hussein Gymnasium A297

1981, Sept. 26   Litho.   Perf. 12x12½

1034	A297	45f shown	.70	.25
1035	A297	50f Palace of Con- ferences	.70	.30
1036	A297	120f like #1035	2.10	1.25
1037	A297	150f like #1034	2.75	1.50
		Nos. 1034-1037 (4)	6.25	3.30

For surcharges see Nos. 1097-1099.

35th Anniv. of Al Baath Party — A298

Mosul Spring Festival — A299

1982, Apr. 7   Photo.   Perf. 13½x13

1038	A298	25f Pres. Hussein, flowers	.45	.20
1039	A298	30f "7 7 7"	.45	.20
1040	A298	45f like 25f	.75	.40
1041	A298	50f like 30f	.75	.40
		Nos. 1038-1041 (4)	2.40	1.20

Souvenir Sheet
Imperf
1042 A298 150f multicolored　5.75 5.75

1982, Apr. 15　Litho.　Perf. 11½x12
1043 A299 25f Birds　1.10 .20
1044 A299 30f Girl　.70 .20
1045 A299 45f like 25f　1.10 .50
1046 A299 50f like 30f　1.10 .40
　Nos. 1043 1046 (4)　4.00 1.30

Intl. Workers' Day A300

1982, May 1　Perf. 12½
1047 A300 25f multicolored　.45 .20
1048 A300 45f multicolored　.70 .20
1049 A300 50f multicolored　.75 .40
　Nos. 1047-1049 (3)　1.90 .90

14th World Telecommunications Day — A301

1982, May 17　Photo.　Perf. 13x13½
1050 A301 5f multicolored　.20 .20
1051 A301 45f multicolored　.70 .35
1052 A301 100f multicolored　1.60 .90
　Nos. 1050-1052 (3)　2.50 1.45

10th Anniv. of Oil Nationalization A302

1982, June 1　Litho.　Perf. 12½
1053 A302 5f Oil gusher　.25 .20
1054 A302 25f like 5f　.60 .20
1055 A302 45f Statue　1.25 .25
1056 A302 50f like 45f　1.50 .35
　Nos. 1053-1056 (4)　3.60 1.00

Martyrs' Day — A303

Women's Day — A304

1981, Dec. 1　Photo.　Perf. 14
1057 A303 45f multicolored　.45 .35
1058 A303 50f multicolored　.55 .45
1059 A303 120f multicolored　1.50 1.00
Nos. 1057-1059,O339A-O339C (6) 8.50 3.80

1982, Mar. 4　Litho.　Perf. 12½x13
1060 A304 25f multicolored　.55 .20
1061 A304 45f multicolored　.90 .30
1062 A304 50f multicolored　.90 .50
　Nos. 1060-1062 (3)　2.35 1.10

A305

A305a

1982, Apr. 12　Perf. 12½
1063 A305 25f multicolored　.55 .20
1064 A305 45f multicolored　.90 .30
1065 A305 50f multicolored　.90 .30
　Nos. 1063-1065 (3)　2.35 .80
Arab Postal Union, 30th anniv.

1982, June 7　Photo.　Perf. 14
1065A A305a 30f Nuclear power
　　emblem, lion　.60 .30
1065B A305a 45f shown　1.00 .35
1065C A305a 50f like 30f　1.10 .50
1065D A305a 120f like 45f　2.40 1.50
　Nos. 1065A-1065D (4)　5.10 2.65
First anniv. of attack on nuclear power reactor.

July Festivals — A306

1982, July 17　Photo.　Perf. 14½x14
1066 A306 25f multicolored　.40 .20
1067 A306 45f multicolored　.60 .25
1068 A306 50f multicolored　.65 .30
　Nos. 1066-1068 (3)　1.65 .75

Lacerta Viridis A307

1982, Aug. 20　Litho.　Perf. 12½
1069 A307 25f shown　2.25 .75
1070 A307 30f Vipera aspis　2.25 .75
1071 A307 45f Lacerta virdis,
　　diff.　3.00 1.10
1072 A307 50f Natrix tessellata　3.50 1.50
　Nos. 1069-1072 (4)　11.00 4.10

7th Non-aligned Countries Conference, Baghdad, Sept. — A308

#1073, Tito. #1074, Nehru. #1075, Nasser. #1076, Kwame Nkrumah. #1077, Hussein.

1982, Sept. 6　Photo.　Perf. 13x13½
1073 A308 50f multicolored　.85 .40
1074 A308 50f multicolored　.85 .40
1075 A308 50f multicolored　.85 .40
1076 A308 50f multicolored　.85 .40
1077 A308 100f multicolored　1.90 .55
　Nos. 1073-1077 (5)　5.30 2.15

TB Bacillus Centenary A309

1982, Oct. 1　Perf. 14x14½
1078 A309 20f multicolored　.65 .20
1079 A309 50f multicolored　1.10 .30
1080 A309 100f multicolored　2.10 .85
　Nos. 1078-1080 (3)　3.85 1.35

1982 World Cup — A310

Designs: Various soccer players. 150f horiz.

1982, July 1　Litho.　Perf. 11½x12
1081 A310 5f multicolored　.50 .25
1082 A310 45f multicolored　1.00 .45
1083 A310 50f multicolored　1.10 .50
1084 A310 100f multicolored　2.00 1.00
　Nos. 1081-1084 (4)　4.60 2.20

Souvenir Sheet
Perf. 12½
1085 A310 150f multicolored　3.50 3.50

13th UPU Day A311

1982, Oct. 9　Perf. 12x11½
1086 A311 5f multicolored　.20 .20
1087 A311 45f multicolored　.70 .30
1088 A311 100f multicolored　1.60 .85
　Nos. 1086-1088 (3)　2.50 1.35

Musical Instruments A312

1982, Nov. 15　Perf. 12½x13
1089 A312 5f Drums　.25 .20
1090 A312 10f Zither　.25 .20
1091 A312 35f Stringed instru-
　　ment　.85 .35
1092 A312 100f Lute　2.75 .95
　Nos. 1089-1092 (4)　4.10 1.70

Birth Anniv. of Mohammed — A313

Mecca Mosque views.

1982, Dec. 27　Litho.　Perf. 12x11½
1093 A313 25f multicolored　.25 .20
1094 A313 30f multicolored　.40 .25
1095 A313 45f multicolored　.55 .25
1096 A313 50f multicolored　.70 .35
　Nos. 1093-1096 (4)　1.90 1.05

Nos. 1034-1036 Surcharged

1983, May 15　Litho.　Perf. 12x12½
1097 A297 60f on 50f multi　1.25 .50
1098 A297 70f on 45f multi　1.75 .60
1099 A297 160f on 120f multi　4.50 2.00
　Nos. 1097-1099 (3)　7.50 3.10

July Festivals A314

1983, July 17　Litho.　Perf. 14½x14
1100 A314 30f multicolored　.45 .20
1101 A314 60f multicolored　1.00 .35
1102 A314 70f multicolored　1.40 .45
　Nos. 1100-1102 (3)　2.85 1.00

Local Flowers — A315

1983, June 15　Photo.　Perf. 15x14
Border Color
1103 A315 10f shown, light blue　.25 .20
1104 A315 20f Flowers, diff.,
　　pale yellow　.45 .20
1105 A315 30f like 10f, yellow　.55 .20
1106 A315 40f like 20f, gray　.95 .40
1107 A315 50f like 10f, pale
　　green　1.10 .50
1108 A315 100f like 20f, pink　2.25 1.00
　a.　Bklt. pane of 6, #1103-1108　9.75
　Nos. 1103-1108 (6)　5.55 2.50

Nos. 1103-1108 issued in booklets only.
For surcharges see Nos. 1501-1506.

A316

Battle of Thi Qar — A317

1983, Oct. 30　Photo.　Perf. 12½x13
1109 A316 20f silver & multi　.25 .20
1110 A317 50f silver & multi　.75 .30
1111 A316 60f gold & multi　1.00 .35
1112 A317 70f gold & multi　1.10 .40
　Nos. 1109-1112 (4)　3.10 1.25

World Communications Year — A318

25f, 70f show emblem and hexagons.

1983, Oct. 20   Photo.   Perf. 11½x12

1113	A318	5f brt yel grn & multi	.20	.20
1114	A318	25f rose lil & multi	.30	.20
1115	A318	60f brt org yel & multi	.90	.35
1116	A318	70f brt bl vio & multi	1.10	.40
		Nos. 1113-1116 (4)	2.50	1.15

Souvenir Sheet

1117	A318	200f apple grn & multi	4.25	4.25

Baghdad Intl. Fair — A319

Symbolic "9" — A320

1983, Nov. 1   Photo.   Perf. 12½

1118	A319	60f multicolored	.75	.40
1119	A319	70f multicolored	.95	.50
1120	A319	160f multicolored	2.10	1.25
		Nos. 1118-1120 (3)	3.80	2.15

1983, Nov. 10   Photo.   Perf. 14

9th Natl. Congress of Arab Baath Socialist Party: 30f, 70f, Symbols of development. 60f, 100f, Torch, eagle, globe, open book.

1121	A320	30f multicolored	.35	.20
1122	A320	70f multicolored	.75	.40
1123	A320	70f multicolored	.95	.50
1124	A320	100f multicolored	1.40	.70
		Nos. 1121-1124 (4)	3.45	1.80

Festival Crowd — A321

Various Paintings.

1983, Nov. 20   Litho.   Perf. 12½

1125	A321	60f shown	1.50	.60
1126	A321	60f Men hauling boat, vert.	1.50	.60
1127	A321	60f Decorations	1.50	.60
1128	A321	70f Village	2.00	.85
1129	A321	70f Crowd	2.00	.85
		Nos. 1125-1129 (5)	8.50	3.50

Sabra and Shattela Palestinian Refugee Camp Massacre A322

Various Victims.

1983, Nov. 29   Perf. 11½x12

1130	A322	10f multicolored	.25	.20
1131	A322	60f multicolored	1.00	.40
1132	A322	70f multicolored	1.25	.50
1133	A322	160f multicolored	2.75	1.25
		Nos. 1130-1133 (4)	5.25	2.35

Pres. Hussein, Map — A323

1983   Photo.   Perf. 13½x13

1134	A323	60f multicolored	.75	.30
1135	A323	70f multicolored	1.00	.50
1136	A323	250f multicolored	3.50	2.00
		Nos. 1134-1136 (3)	5.25	2.80

Hussein as head of Al Baath Party, 4th anniv.

Modern Building — A324

Various buildings.

1983, Dec. 31   Litho.   Perf. 14

1137	A324	60f multicolored	.70	.40
1138	A324	70f multicolored	.90	.50
1139	A324	160f multicolored	2.25	1.10
1140	A324	200f multicolored	2.75	1.40
		Nos. 1137-1140,O340-O341 (6)	8.50	4.55

Medical Congress Emblem A325

1984, Mar. 10   Perf. 13x12½

1141	A325	60f multicolored	.80	.40
1142	A325	70f multicolored	1.00	.50
1143	A325	200f multicolored	3.00	1.40
		Nos. 1141-1143 (3)	4.80	2.30

25th Intl. Congress of Military Medicine and Pharmacy, Baghdad, Mar. 10-15.

Pres. Hussein's Birthday — A326

Various portraits of Hussein.

1984, Apr. 28   Litho.   Perf. 12½x13

1144	A326	60f multicolored	.65	.30
1145	A326	70f multicolored	.70	.40
1146	A326	160f multicolored	2.10	1.25
1147	A326	200f multicolored	2.50	1.60
		Nos. 1144-1147 (4)	5.95	3.55

Souvenir Sheet

Imperf

1148	A326	250f multicolored	5.00	5.00

Gold ink on Nos. 1144-1147 and dark green ink in "margin" of No. 1148 was applied by a thermographic process, producing a raised effect. No. 1148 has perf. 12½x13 label picturing Pres. Hussein.

1984 Summer Olympics, Los Angeles — A327

1984, Aug. 12   Litho.   Perf. 12x11½

1149	A327	50f Boxing	.70	.50
1150	A327	60f Weight lifting	.90	.50
1151	A327	70f like 50f	1.10	.60

1152	A327	100f like 60f	1.60	.90

Size: 80x60mm

Imperf

1153	A327	200f Soccer	5.00	5.00
		Nos. 1149-1153 (5)	9.30	7.50

Nos. 1153 contains one 32x41mm perf. 12½ label within the stamp.

A328

A329

50f, 70f, Pres. Hussein, flaming horses heads, map. 60f, 100f, Abstract of woman, sapling, rifle. 200f, Shield, heraldic eagle.

1984, Sept. 22   Perf. 11½x12

1154	A328	50f multicolored	.55	.30
1155	A328	60f multicolored	.70	.40
1156	A328	70f multicolored	.85	.50
1157	A328	100f multicolored	1.25	.65

Size: 80x60mm

Imperf

1158	A328	200f multicolored	3.50	3.50
		Nos. 1154-1158 (5)	6.85	5.35

Battle of Qadisiya. No. 1158 contains one 32x41mm perf. 12½ label within the stamp.

1984, Dec. 1   Perf. 13½

Martyrs' Day: 50f, 70f, Natl. flag as flame. 60f, 100f, Woman holding rifle, medal.

1159	A329	50f multicolored	.45	.35
1160	A329	60f multicolored	.65	.35
1161	A329	70f multicolored	.75	.40
1162	A329	100f multicolored	1.00	.65
		Nos. 1159-1162 (4)	2.85	1.75

Pres. Hussein's Visit to Al-Mustansiriyah University, 5th Anniv. — A330

1985, Apr. 2   Photo.   Perf. 12x11½

1163	A330	60f dk bl gray & dk pink	.55	.35
1164	A330	70f myr grn & dk pink	.65	.40
1165	A330	250f blk & dk pink	2.50	1.40
		Nos. 1163-1165 (3)	3.70	2.15

Iraqi Air Force, 54th Anniv. — A331

Pres. Hussein, 48th Birthday — A332

10f, 160f, Pres. Hussein, fighter planes, pilot's wings. 60f, 70f, 200f, Planes, flag, "54," horiz.

Perf. 13x12½, 13½ (60f, 70f)

1985, Apr. 22   Litho.

1166	A331	10f multicolored	.30	.20
1167	A331	60f multicolored	1.50	.75
1168	A331	70f multicolored	1.60	.75
1169	A331	160f multicolored	4.00	2.00
		Nos. 1166-1169 (4)	7.40	3.70

Souvenir Sheet

Perf. 12½

1170	A331	200f multicolored	6.75	6.75

1985, Apr. 28   Perf. 13½

30f, 70f, Pres. Hussein, sunflower. 60f, 100f, Pres., candle & flowers. 200f, Flowers & text.

1171	A332	30f multicolored	.35	.20
1172	A332	60f multicolored	.65	.30
1173	A332	70f multicolored	.75	.40
1174	A332	100f multicolored	1.10	.60
		Nos. 1171-1174 (4)	2.85	1.50

Souvenir Sheet

Perf. 13x12½

1175	A332	200f multicolored	3.75	3.75

Posts and Telecommunications Development Program — A333

Designs: 20f, 60f, Graph, woman in modern office. 50f, 70f, Satellite dish and graphs.

1985, June 30   Perf. 12½

1176	A333	20f multicolored	.35	.20
1177	A333	50f multicolored	.70	.30
1178	A333	60f multicolored	.70	.30
1179	A333	70f multicolored	.95	.50
		Nos. 1176-1179 (4)	2.70	1.30

Battle of Qadisiya A334

Designs: 10f, 60f, Shown. 20f, 70f, Pres. Hussein, Al-Baath Party emblem. 200f, Dove, natl. flag as shield, soldier.

1985, Sept. 4   Perf. 11½x12

1180	A334	10f multicolored	.20	.20
1181	A334	20f multicolored	.25	.20
1182	A334	60f multicolored	.90	.40
1183	A334	70f multicolored	1.10	.65
		Nos. 1180-1183 (4)	2.45	1.45

Souvenir Sheet

Perf. 12x12½

1184	A334	200f multicolored	3.25	3.25

No. 1184 contains one stamp 30x45mm.

Solar Energy Research Center A335

1985, Sept. 19   *Perf. 13½*
1185	A335	10f multicolored	.20	.20
1186	A335	50f multicolored	.95	.40
1187	A335	100f multicolored	1.90	.95
		Nos. 1185-1187 (3)	3.05	1.55

UN Child Survival
Campaign
A336

Al Sharif, Poet,
Death Millennium
A337

Designs: 10f, 50f, Stop Polio Campaign.
15f, 100f, Girl, infant.

1985, Oct. 10
1188	A336	10f multicolored	.20	.20
1189	A336	15f multicolored	.20	.20
1190	A336	50f multicolored	.75	.30
1191	A336	100f multicolored	1.50	.85
		Nos. 1188-1191 (4)	2.65	1.55

1985, Oct. 20
1192	A337	10f multicolored	.25	.20
1193	A337	50f multicolored	.55	.30
1194	A337	100f multicolored	1.25	.80
		Nos. 1192-1194 (3)	2.05	1.30

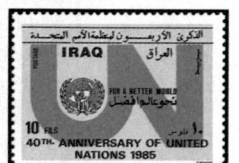

UN, 40th
Anniv.
A338

1985, Oct. 24
1195	A338	10f multicolored	.20	.20
1196	A338	40f multicolored	.55	.20
1197	A338	100f multicolored	1.40	.75
		Nos. 1195-1197 (3)	2.15	1.15

Death of Iraqi
Prisoners of War
in Iran — A339

30f, 100f, Knife, Geneva Convention declaration, red crescent, red cross. 70f, 200f,
POWs, gun shell, natl. flag, cherub & dove.

1985, Nov. 10   *Perf. 14*
1198	A339	30f multicolored	.35	.20
1199	A339	70f multicolored	.75	.40
1200	A339	100f multicolored	1.10	.65
1201	A339	200f multicolored	2.50	1.25

Size: 110x80mm
Imperf
| 1202 | A339 | 250f multicolored | 5.00 | 5.00 |
| | | Nos. 1198-1202 (5) | 9.70 | 7.50 |

No. 1202 contains 2 perf. 14 labels similar
to 100f and 200f designs within the stamp.

Intl.
Palestinian
Solidarity
Day
A341

1985, Nov. 29   Litho.   *Perf. 13½*
1207	A341	10f multicolored	.25	.20
1208	A341	50f multicolored	.95	.40
1209	A341	100f multicolored	2.10	.95
		Nos. 1207-1209 (3)	3.30	1.55

Martyrs'
Day — A342

1985, Dec. 1   *Perf. 11½x12*
1210	A342	10f multicolored	.20	.20
1211	A342	40f multicolored	.45	.20
1212	A342	100f multicolored	1.40	.75
		Nos. 1210-1212 (3)	2.05	1.15

Intl. Youth
Year — A343

1985, Dec. 12   Litho.   *Perf. 11½x12*

IYY emblem and: 40f, 100f, Soldier holding
flag. 50f, 200f, Youths, flag. 250f, Flag, cogwheel, rifle muzzle, symbols of industry.

1213	A343	40f multicolored	.45	.20
1214	A343	50f multicolored	.65	.30
1215	A343	100f multicolored	1.40	.75
1216	A343	200f multicolored	2.75	2.00
		Nos. 1213-1216 (4)	5.25	3.25

Souvenir Sheet
Perf. 12x12½
| 1217 | A343 | 250f multicolored | 5.00 | 5.00 |

No. 1217 contains one stamp 30x45mm.
Exists imperf.

Army Day
A344

Pres. Hussein, "6" and: 10f, 50f, Soldier,
flowers, vert. 40f, 100f, Flag, cogwheel, rockets. 200f, Al-Baath Party emblem, rifle,
waves.

1986, Jan. 6   *Perf. 11½x12, 12x11½*
1218	A344	10f multicolored	.20	.20
1219	A344	40f multicolored	.65	.20
1220	A344	50f multicolored	.85	.30
1221	A344	100f multicolored	1.75	.95
		Nos. 1218-1221 (4)	3.45	1.65

Miniature Sheet
Perf. 12½x11½
| 1222 | A344 | 200f multicolored | 5.00 | 5.00 |

No. 1222 contains one stamp 52x37mm.

Women's
Day
A345

Designs: 30f, 100f, Women in traditional
and modern occupations, vert. 50f, 150f,
Emblem, green flag, battle scene, grapes.

Perf. 11½x12, 12x11½
1986, Mar. 8   Litho.
1223	A345	30f multicolored	.45	.20
1224	A345	50f multicolored	.65	.30
1225	A345	100f multicolored	1.40	.75
1226	A345	150f multicolored	2.25	1.00
		Nos. 1223-1226 (4)	4.75	2.25

Pres. Hussein,
49th Birthday
A346

Designs: 30f, 100f, Children greeting Pres.
50f, 150f, Portrait. 250f, Portrait, flag, flowers.

1986, Apr. 28   Litho.   *Perf. 11½x12*
1227	A346	30f multicolored	.45	.20
1228	A346	50f multicolored	.75	.25
1229	A346	100f multicolored	1.50	.45
1230	A346	150f multicolored	2.10	.65

Size: 80x60mm
Imperf
| 1231 | A346 | 250f multicolored | 5.00 | 5.00 |
| | | Nos. 1227-1231 (5) | 9.80 | 6.55 |

Oil
Nationalization
Day,
June 1 — A347

Labor
Day — A348

Designs: 10f, 100f, Symbols of industry,
horiz. 40f, 150f, Oil well, pipeline to refinery.

Perf. 12x11½, 11½x12
1986, July 25   Litho.
1232	A347	10f multicolored	.20	.20
1233	A347	40f multicolored	.55	.20
1234	A347	100f multicolored	1.50	.75
1235	A347	150f multicolored	2.10	1.25
		Nos. 1232-1235 (4)	4.35	2.40

1986, July 28   *Perf. 11½x12*

Designs: 10f, 100f, Laborer, cog wheel.
40f, 150f, May Day emblem.

1236	A348	10f multicolored	.25	.20
1237	A348	40f multicolored	.75	.20
1238	A348	100f multicolored	1.40	.65
1239	A348	150f multicolored	2.10	.95
		Nos. 1236-1239 (4)	4.50	2.00

Iraqi Air
Force,
55th
Anniv.
A349

Designs: 30f, 100f, Fighter plane, pilot's
wings, vert. flag. 50f, 150f, Fighter planes.
250f, Medal, aircraft in flight.

1986, July 28   *Perf. 12x11½*
1240	A349	30f multicolored	.70	.20
1241	A349	50f multicolored	1.40	.30
1242	A349	100f multicolored	2.75	1.40
1243	A349	150f multicolored	4.25	1.90

Size: 81x61mm
Imperf
| 1244 | A349 | 250f multicolored | 5.00 | 5.00 |
| | | Nos. 1240-1244 (5) | 14.10 | 8.80 |

No. 1244 also exists perf.

July Festivals
A350

Pres. Hussein and: 20f, 100f, Flag. 30f,
150f, "17." 250f, Inscription, portrait inside
medal of honor.

1986, July 29   *Perf. 11½x12*
1245	A350	20f multicolored	.30	.20
1246	A350	30f multicolored	.40	.20
1247	A350	100f multicolored	1.50	.75
1248	A350	150f multicolored	2.25	1.25

Size: 81x61mm
Imperf
| 1249 | A350 | 250f multicolored | 4.00 | 4.00 |
| | | Nos. 1245-1249 (5) | 8.45 | 6.40 |

1st Qadisiya
Battle — A351

Designs: 20f, 70f, Warrior, shield, vert. 60f,
100f, Pres. Hussein, star, battle scene.

Perf. 13x13½, 13½x13
1986, Sept. 4   Litho.
1250	A351	20f multicolored	.35	.20
1251	A351	60f multicolored	.80	.40
1252	A351	70f multicolored	.95	.50
1253	A351	100f multicolored	1.60	.65
		Nos. 1250-1253 (4)	3.70	1.75

Battle between the Arabs and Persian
Empire.

Hussein's Battle of Qadisiya — A352

30f, 100f, Pres. Hussein, soldiers saluting
peace, vert. 40f, 150f, Pres., armed forces.
250f, Pres., soldiers, flags, military scenes.

Perf. 11½x12½, 12½x11½
1986, Sept. 4
1254	A352	30f multicolored	.90	.20
1255	A352	40f multicolored	1.25	.20
1256	A352	100f multicolored	2.50	.50
1257	A352	150f multicolored	4.25	.70

Size: 80x60mm
Imperf
| 1258 | A352 | 250f multicolored | 4.75 | 4.75 |
| | | Nos. 1254-1258 (5) | 13.65 | 6.35 |

Intl. Peace
Year — A353

1986, Nov. 15 Litho.   Perf. 11½x12
1259	A353	50f Dove, flag, G clef	.65 .25
1260	A353	100f Globe, dove, rifle	1.10 .60
1261	A353	150f like 50f	1.75 1.00
1262	A353	250f like 100f	2.50 1.40

Size: 80x69mm
Imperf
1263	A353	200f Emblem, flag, map, fist	2.75 2.75
		Nos. 1259-1263 (5)	8.75 6.00

Pres. Hussein
A354   A355

1986   Perf. 12½x12
1264	A354	30f multicolored	.70 .20
1265	A355	50f multicolored	.70 .20
1266	A354	50f multicolored	.90 .25
1267	A355	50f multicolored	.90 .25
1268	A354	100f multicolored	1.90 .65
1269	A355	100f multicolored	1.90 .65
1270	A354	150f multicolored	2.40 .85
1271	A355	150f multicolored	2.60 .85
1272	A354	250f multicolored	4.75 1.40
1273	A355	350f multicolored	6.25 1.90
		Nos. 1264-1273 (10)	23.00 7.20

For overprints & surcharges see #1347-1348, 1455, 1480-1481, 1484, 1499-1500, 1518-1519.

Army
Day — A356

1987, Jan. 6   Litho.   Perf. 12x12½
1274	A356	20f shown	.25 .20
1275	A356	40f Hussein, armed forces	.35 .30
1276	A356	90f like 20f	.95 .90
1277	A356	100f like 40f	1.00 1.00
		Nos. 1274-1277 (4)	2.55 2.40

United Arab Shipping Co., 10th Anniv. (in 1986) A357

1987, Apr. 3   Litho.   Perf. 12½
1278	A357	50f Cargo ship	.55 .25
1279	A357	100f Container ship Chaleb Ibn Al Waleeb	1.10 .60
1280	A357	150f like 50f	1.75 .85
1281	A357	250f like 100f	3.00 1.40

Size: 102x91mm
Imperf
1282	A357	200f Loading cargo aboard the Waleeb	3.75 3.75
		Nos. 1278-1282 (5)	10.15 6.85

Arab Baath Socialist Party, 40th Anniv. — A358

1987, Apr. 7   Litho.   Perf. 12x12½
1283	A358	20f shown	.25 .20
1284	A358	40f Hussein, "7," map	.35 .30
1285	A358	90f like 20f	.95 .90
1286	A358	100f like 40f	1.00 1.00
		Nos. 1283-1286 (4)	2.55 2.40

Pres. Hussein's 50th Birthday A359

1987, Apr. 28   Perf. 12½x12
1287	A359	20f shown	.25 .20
1288	A359	40f Portrait	.35 .30
1289	A359	90f like 20f	.95 .90
1290	A359	100f like 40f	1.10 1.00
		Nos. 1287-1290 (4)	2.65 2.40

July Festivals — A360

UNICEF, 40th Anniv. — A361

1987, July 17   Perf. 12½x12, 12x12½
1291	A360	20f Hussein, star, flag, horiz.	.25 .20
1292	A360	40f shown	.35 .30
1293	A360	90f like 20f, horiz.	.95 .90
1294	A360	100f like 40f	1.00 1.00
		Nos. 1291-1294 (4)	2.55 2.40

1987, Oct. 4   Perf. 12x12½, 12½x12
1295	A361	20f shown	.25 .20
1296	A361	40f "40," horiz.	.35 .30
1297	A361	90f like 20f	.95 .90
1298	A361	100f like 40f, horiz.	1.00 1.00
		Nos. 1295-1298 (4)	2.55 2.40

Census Day A362

1987, Nov. 1   Perf. 12x11½
1299	A362	20f shown	.25 .20
1300	A362	30f Graph, Arabs, diff.	.35 .20
1301	A362	50f like 30f	.55 .35
1302	A362	500f like 20f	5.25 4.00
		Nos. 1299-1302 (4)	6.40 4.75

Army Day A363

Perf. 11½x12, 12x11½
1988, Jan. 6   Litho.
1303	A363	20f "6," Hussein, troops, vert.	.25 .20
1304	A363	30f shown	.25 .20

1305	A363	50f like 20f, vert.	.55 .20
1306	A363	150f like 30f	1.60 .60
		Nos. 1303-1306 (4)	2.65 1.20

Art Day — A364

A365

1988, Jan. 8   Litho.   Perf. 11½x12
1307	A364	20f shown	.35 .20
1308	A364	30f Hussein, rainbow, gun barrel, music	.50 .30
1309	A364	50f like 20f	.70 .35
1310	A364	100f like 30f	1.25 .40

Size: 60x80mm
Imperf
1311	A364	150f Notes, instruments, floral ornament	2.50 2.50
		Nos. 1307-1311 (5)	5.30 3.75

1988, Feb. 8   Perf. 11½x12, 12x11½
1312	A365	20f "8," troops, Hussein, horiz.	.35 .20
1313	A365	30f "8," Hussein, eagle	.45 .20
1314	A365	50f like 20f, horiz.	.65 .35
1315	A365	150f like 30f	2.10 .65
		Nos. 1312-1315 (4)	3.55 1.40

Popular Army, 18th anniv. (20f, 50f); Feb. 8th Revolution, 25th anniv. (30f, 150f).

Al-Baath Arab Socialist Party, 50th Anniv. — A366

President Hussein's 41st Birthday — A367

1988, Apr. 7   Perf. 12x12½, 12½x12
1316	A366	20f Flag, grain, convention, horiz.	.35 .20
1317	A366	30f shown	.45 .30
1318	A366	50f like 20f, horiz.	.65 .30
1319	A366	150f like 30f	2.10 .60
		Nos. 1316-1319 (4)	3.55 1.40

1988, Apr. 28   Perf. 12x12½
1320	A367	20f shown	.40 .30
1321	A367	30f Hussein, 3 hands, flowers	.50 .40
1322	A367	50f like 50f	.75 .40
1323	A367	100f like 50f	1.50 .60

Size: 90x99mm
Imperf
1324	A367	150f Sun, Hussein, heart, flowers	4.25 4.25
		Nos. 1320-1324 (5)	7.40 5.95

World Health Organization, 40th Anniv. — A368

Regional Marine Environment Day, Apr. 4 — A369

1988, June 1   Perf. 12½x12, 12x12½
1325	A368	20f WHO anniv. emblem, horiz.	.35 .20
1326	A368	40f shown	.45 .30
1327	A368	90f like 20f, horiz.	1.25 .40
1328	A368	100f like 40f	1.40 .40
		Nos. 1325-1328 (4)	3.45 1.30

1988, Apr. 24   Perf. 12x12½, 12½x12
1329	A369	20f shown	.45 .20
1330	A369	40f Flag in map, fish, horiz.	.45 .30
1331	A369	90f like 20f	1.25 .40
1332	A369	100f like 40f, horiz.	1.25 .40
		Nos. 1329-1332 (4)	3.40 1.30

Shuhada School Victims Memorial A370

A371

1988, June 1   Perf. 11½x12, 12x11½
1333	A370	20f shown	.35 .20
1334	A370	40f Girl caught in explosion, horiz.	.45 .30
1335	A370	90f like 20f	1.25 .40
1336	A370	100f like 40f, horiz.	1.40 .40
		Nos. 1333-1336 (4)	3.45 1.30

Souvenir Sheet
Perf. 12½
1337	A371	150f red, blk & brt grn	2.10 2.10

Pilgrimage to Mecca — A372

1988, July 24   Litho.   Perf. 13½
1338	A372	90f multicolored	1.25 .40
1339	A372	100f multicolored	1.50 .60
1340	A372	150f multicolored	2.25 .70
		Nos. 1338-1340 (3)	5.00 1.70

Basra,
1350th
Anniv.
A373

1988, Oct. 22 *Perf. 12x11½*
1341 A373 100f multicolored 1.40 .00

Natl. Flag, Grip
on
Lightning — A374

Pres. Hussein, Natl. Flag — A375

1988, July 17 *Perf. 12x12½*
1342 A374 50f shown .75 .40
1343 A374 90f Map, Hussein,
　desert 1.40 .50
1344 A374 100f like 50f 1.50 .50
1345 A374 150f like 90f 2.00 .60

Size: 90x70mm

Imperf
1346 A375 250f shown 6.00 4.50
　Nos. 1342-1346 (5) 11.65 6.50

July Festivals and 9th anniv. of Pres. Hussein's assumption of office.

Nos. 1272-1273
Overprinted

Imperf

1988, Aug. 7 Litho. *Perf. 12½x12*
1347 A354 250f multicolored 6.00 2.00
1348 A354 350f multicolored 8.50 4.00

Victory.

Navy Day — A376

1988, Aug. 12 *Perf. 12x12½*
1349 A376 50f shown 1.10 .40
1350 A376 90f Map, boats 2.00 .60
1351 A376 100f like 50f 2.25 .85
1352 A376 150f like 90f 3.50 1.00

Size: 91x70mm

Imperf
1353 A376 250f Emblem, Pres.
　Hussein decorating officers 9.00 9.00
　Nos. 1349-1353 (5) 17.85 11.85

1988 Summer
Olympics,
Seoul — A377

1988, Sept. 19 *Perf. 12x12½*
1354 A377 100f Boxing, character trademark 2.25 .80
1355 A377 150f Flag, emblems 3.50 1.10

Size: 101x91mm

Imperf
1356 A377 500f Emblem,
　trademark,
　Hussein, trophy 17.00 17.00
　Nos. 1354-1356 (3) 22.75 18.90

Liberation of Fao — A378

1988, Sept. 1 *Perf. 12x11½*
1357 A378 100f multicolored 2.00 .60
1358 A378 150f multicolored 3.00 .95

Size: 60x80mm

Imperf
1359 A378 500f Hussein, text 16.50 16.50
　Nos. 1357-1359 (3) 21.50 18.05

Mosul
A379

Baghdad
A380

Ancient cities.

1988, Oct. 22 *Perf. 12x11½, 11½x12*
1360 A379 50f Fortress .95 .20
1361 A380 150f Astrolabe, modern architecture 3.00 .95

Al-Hussein
Missile — A381

1988, Sept. 10 *Perf. 11½x12*
1362 A381 100f multicolored 1.40 .50
1363 A381 150f multicolored 2.25 .70

Size: 80x60mm

Imperf
1364 A381 500f Hussein, map,
　missile 10.00 10.00
　Nos. 1362-1364 (3) 13.65 11.20

2nd Intl.
Festival,
Babylon
A382

1988, Sept. 30 *Perf. 11½x12*
1365 A382 100f multicolored 1.40 .60
1366 A382 150f multicolored 2.00 .70

Size: 60x80mm

Imperf
1367 A382 500f Medallions 8.50 8.50
　Nos. 1365-1367 (3) 11.90 9.80

Victorious
Iraq
A383

1988, Aug. 8 Litho. *Perf. 12x11½*
1368 A383 50f multicolored 6.00 6.00
1369 A383 100f multicolored 10.00 10.00
1370 A383 150f multicolored 14.50 14.50
　Nos. 1368-1370 (3) 30.50 30.50

Birthday of
Mohammed
A384

1988, Oct. 23 Litho. *Perf. 11½x12*
1371 A384 100f multicolored 1.50 .60
1372 A384 150f multicolored 2.00 .90
1373 A384 1d multicolored 14.00 5.25
　Nos. 1371-1373 (3) 17.50 6.75

Martyrs'
Day
A385

1988, Dec. 1 Litho. *Perf. 13½*
1374 A385 100f multicolored 1.00 .40
1375 A385 150f multicolored 1.90 .75
1376 A385 500f multicolored 6.50 2.00
　Nos. 1374-1376 (3) 9.40 3.15

Police
Day
A386

1989, Jan. 9 Litho. *Perf. 12x11½*
1377 A386 50f multicolored .60 .40
1378 A386 100f multicolored 1.40 .45
1379 A386 150f multicolored 2.00 .90
　Nos. 1377-1379 (3) 4.00 1.75

Postal Savings
Bank — A387

a

1988 **Litho.** *Perf. 11½x12*
1380 A387 50f shown 1.60 .80

Size: 23½x25mm

Perf. 13½x13
1381 A387(a) 100f multi 6.25 3.00
1382 A387(a) 150f multi 6.75 3.25
　Nos. 1380-1382 (3) 14.60 7.05

#1381-1382 have a line of Arabic at the top.
#1381-1382 without overprint are postal savings stamps.
For surcharges see #1507-1510, 1512-1514.

Arab Cooperation Council — A388

1989, Feb. 12 Litho. *Perf. 12x11½*
1383 A388 100f shown 1.40 .40
1384 A388 150f Statesmen, diff. 2.00 .70

52nd
Birthday
of Pres.
Hussein
A392

1989, Apr. 28 Litho. *Perf. 12x11½*
1392 A392 100f multicolored 1.25 .50
1393 A392 150f multicolored 1.75 .50

Size: 60x81mm

Imperf
1394 A392 250f Hussein, diff. 6.00 6.00
　Nos. 1392-1394 (3) 9.00 7.00

Fao Liberation, 1st Anniv. — A393

1989, Apr. 18 *Perf. 12x11½*
1395 A393 100f multi 1.25 .50
1396 A393 150f multi 2.00 .50

Size: 60x81mm

Imperf
1397 A393 250f Calendar 3.00 3.00
　Nos. 1395-1397 (3) 6.25 4.00

Gen. Adnan
Khairalla — A394

Reconstruction of
Basra — A395

1989, May 6   Litho.   Perf. 13½
1398 A394 50f gold & multi   .80   .30
1399 A394 100f copper & multi   1.60   .40
1400 A394 150f silver & multi   2.40   .75
   Nos. 1398-1400 (3)   4.80   1.45

Gen. Adnan Khairalla (1940-1989), deputy
commander-in-chief of the armed forces and
minister of defense.

1989, June 14
1401 A395 100f multi   1.60   .40
1402 A395 150f multi   2.40   .75

Reconstruction of   Women — A397
Fao — A396

1989, June 25
1403 A396 100f multi   1.60   .40
1404 A396 150f multi   2.40   .75

1989, June 25   Litho.   Perf. 11½x12
1405 A397 100f yel & multi   1.25   .35
1406 A397 150f brt pink &
             multi   1.40   .55
1407 A397 1d brt blue &
             multi   12.00   3.75
1408 A397 5d white & multi   50.00 16.00
   Nos. 1405-1408 (4)   64.65 20.65

For surcharges see Nos. 1485-1486, 1511,
1522.

July
Festivals — A398

1989, July 17   Litho.   Perf. 12x12½
1409 A398 50f multicolored   .65   .30
1410 A398 100f multicolored   1.25   .40
1411 A398 150f multicolored   2.10   .65
   Nos. 1409-1411 (3)   4.00   1.35

Election of Pres. Hussein, 10th anniv.

Family
A399

1989, July 19   Perf. 13½
1412 A399 50f multicolored   1.00   .45
1413 A399 100f multicolored   1.75   .75
1414 A399 150f multicolored   4.75   1.25
   Nos. 1412-1414 (3)   7.50   2.45

A400

Victory Day — A401

1989, Aug. 8   Perf. 12x12½
1415 A400 100f multicolored   1.25   .40
1416 A400 150f multicolored   2.10   .65

Size: 71x91mm

Imperf
1417 A401 250f multicolored   4.25   4.25
   Nos. 1415-1417 (3)   7.60   5.30

Interparliamentary Union,
Cent. — A402

1989, Sept. 15   Perf. 12½x12
1418 A402 25f multicolored   .35   .20
1419 A402 100f multicolored   1.25   .40
1420 A402 150f multicolored   2.10   .65
   Nos. 1418-1420 (3)   3.70   1.25

Ancient Cities
A403

1989, Oct. 15   Perf. 11½x12½
1421 A403 100f Dhi Qar-ur   1.75   .55
1422 A403 100f Erbil   1.75   .55
1423 A403 100f An Najaf   1.75   .55
   Nos. 1421-1423 (3)   5.25   1.65

5th Session of the Arab Ministers of
Transport Council, Baghdad, Oct. 21
A404

Designs: 100f, Land, air and sea transport,
diff. 150f, Modes of transport, flags, vert.

1989, Oct. 21   Perf. 12x11½, 11½x12
1424 A404 50f shown   1.25   .55
1425 A404 100f multicolored 2.60   .75
1426 A404 150f multicolored 4.00   1.10
   Nos. 1424-1426 (3)   7.85   2.40

Iraqi News
Agency,
30th Anniv.
A405

1989, Nov. 9   Perf. 13½
1427 A405 50f multicolored   .55   .30
1428 A405 100f multicolored   1.10   .40
1429 A405 150f multicolored   1.75   .65
   Nos. 1427-1429 (3)   3.40   1.35

Declaration of
Palestinian State,
1st
Anniv. — A406

1989, Nov. 15   Perf. 12x12½
1430 A406 25f shown   .25   .20
1431 A406 50f Palestinian upris-
             ing   .65   .30
1432 A406 100f like 25f   1.25   .40
1433 A406 150f like 50f   2.10   .60
   Nos. 1430-1433 (4)   4.25   1.50

Flowers — A407

1989, Nov. 20   Perf. 13½x13
1434 A407 25f Viola sp.   .35   .35
1435 A407 50f Antirrhinum
             majus   .75   .35
1436 A407 100f Hibiscus trionum   1.50   .45
1437 A407 150f Mesembryanthe-
             mum sparkles   2.40   .45
   Nos. 1434-1437 (4)   5.00   1.60

Miniature Sheet
Perf. 12½x11½
1438   Sheet of 4   9.25   9.25
   a.   A407 25f like No. 1434   2.10   2.10
   b.   A407 50f like No. 1435   2.10   2.10
   c.   A407 100f like No. 1436   2.10   2.10
   d.   A407 150f like No. 1437   2.10   2.10

No. 1438 has a continuous design. No.
1438 sold for 500f.
For overprints and surcharges see Nos.
1450-1451, 1456, 1516, 1524.

A408

A409

1989, Oct. 25   Litho.   Perf. 13½
1439 A408 100f multicolored   1.40   .40
1440 A408 150f multicolored   2.10   .65

Reconstruction of Fao.

1989, Dec. 4   Litho.   Perf. 13½
1441 A409 50f multicolored   .65   .30
1442 A409 100f multicolored   1.25   .40
1443 A409 150f multicolored   1.75   .65
   Nos. 1441-1443 (3)   3.65   1.35

Martyrs' Day.

Iraqi Red
Crescent
Soc. — A410

1989, Dec. 10   Litho.   Perf. 13½
1444 A410 100f multicolored   .70   .35
1445 A410 150f multicolored   2.00   .80
1446 A410 500f multicolored   6.75   2.50
   Nos. 1444-1446 (3)   9.45   3.65

Arab Cooperation Council, 1st
Anniv. — A411

1990, Feb. 16   Litho.   Perf. 13x13½
1447 A411 50f yellow & multi   1.00   .50
1448 A411 100f orange & multi 2.75   .90

Size: 80x62mm

Imperf
1449 A411 250f blue & multi   7.50   7.50
   Nos. 1447-1449 (3)   11.25   8.90

For surcharge see No. 1523.

Nos. 1435, 1437
Ovptd.

1990, May 28   Litho.   Perf. 13½x13
1450 A407 50f multicolored   1.10   .85
1451 A407 150f multicolored   3.75   2.50

Arab League Summit Conf., Baghdad.

End of Iran-Iraq
War, 2nd
Anniv. — A412

1990, Aug. 30   Litho.   Perf. 13½x13
1452 A412 50f purple & multi   .75
1453 A412 100f blue & multi   1.50

Imperf
Size: 59x81mm
1454 A412 250f Saddam Hussein, dove   5.00

For surcharge see No. 1525.

The surcharged issues of 1992-97 have been extensively forged. Collectors are urged to purchase these stamps with certificates of authenticity or from expert sellers who can attest to their authenticity

No. 1269 Surcharged

1992(?)   **Litho.**   **Perf. 12½x12**
1455 A355 1d on 100f #1269   8.50

No. 1434 Surcharged

Type I

Type II

1993, Aug. 1   **Litho.**   **Perf. 13½x13**
1456 A407 10d on 25f Type I   30.00
    a.   Type II   40.00

No. RA23 Surcharged

1992   **Photo.**   **Perf. 14**
1457 PT3 100f on 5f multi   3.00

Reconstruction of Iraq — A413

Designs: 250f, Satellite dish. 500f, Bridges. 750f, Power plant, horiz. 1d, Factory.

1993, Sept.   **Photo.**   **Perf. 14**
1459 A413 250f red & multi   .85
1460 A413 500f blue & multi   1.50
1461 A413 750f yellow & multi   2.25
1462 A413   1d multicolored   3.00
    Nos. 1459-1462 (4)   7.60

Stamps of this issue may be poorly centered or have perforations running through the design.
For surcharge see No. 1526.

Peace Ship
A414

1993   **Photo.**   **Perf. 14**
1463 A414 2d red & multi   2.50
1464 A414 5d green & multi   6.50

No. RA23 Surcharged

b   c

d   e

f   g

h   i

j   k

l   m

n   o

---

p   q

r

s

t

1994, Feb. 5   **Photo.**   **Perf. 14**
1465 PT3(b) 500f on 5f multi, ovpt. 17mm wide   15.00
    a.   Overprint 14½mm wide   40.00
1466 PT3(c)   1d on 5f multi   2.00
1467 PT3(d)   1d on 5f multi   3.50
    a.   PT3(e) 1d on 5f multi   6.00
    b.   PT3(f) 1d on 5f multi   3.00
    c.   PT3(g) 1d on 5f multi   3.00
1468 PT3(h)   2d on 5f multi   7.00
1469 PT3(i)   2d on 5f multi   3.50
1470 PT3(j)   3d on 5f multi   2.00
1471 PT3(k)   3d on 5f multi   2.00
1472 PT3(l)   5d on 5f multi   3.00
    a.   PT3(m) 5d on 5f multi   2.00
    b.   PT3(n) 5d on 5f multi   4.50
1473 PT3(o)   5d on 5f multi   4.25
1474 PT3(p)   10d on 5f multi   4.25
1475 PT3(q)   25d on 5f multi   8.50
    a.   PT3(r) 25d on 5f multi   14.00
1476 PT3(s)   25d on 10d on 5f   5.00
1477 PT3(t)   50d on 5f multi   28.00

No. 1273 Surcharged

u   v

1994, Apr. 28   **Litho.**   **Perf. 12½x12**
1480 A354(u) 5d on 350f #1273   7.00
1481 A354(v) 5d on 350f #1273   7.00
    a.   Pair, #1480-1481   22.50

Alqa'id Two-Deck Bridge
A415

1994, July 17   **Perf. 14**
1482 A415 1d pink & multi   3.50
1483 A415 3d blue & multi   3.50
    a.   Pair, #1482-1483   8.50

No. 1273 Surcharged

1994, Aug. 8   **Perf. 12½x12**
1484 A354 5d on 350f #1273   4.75

No. 1406 Surcharged

w

x

1995, Jan. 2   **Perf. 11½x12**
1485 A397(w) 5d on 150f #1406   5.00
1486 A397(x) 5d on 150f #1406   5.00
    a.   Pair   20.00

Baghdad Clock — A416   Saddam Tower — A417

1995, Feb. 28   **Perf. 11**
1487 A416 7d blue & black   2.50

Size: 76x98mm
Imperf
1488 A416 25d multicolored   14.00

1995, Mar. 12   **Perf. 14**
1489 A417 2d multicolored   1.00
1490 A417 5d multicolored   3.25
    a.   Vert. pair, #1489-1490   4.50

Honoring Dead From Battle of Um Almariq (Mother of All Battles) — A418

1995   **Imperf.**
1491 A418 100d multicolored   14.00

Saddam Hussein, 58th Birthday — A419

Design: No. 1492, Saddam seated, flowers & flag behind him, vert.

1995, Apr. 28   **Imperf.**
1492	A419	25d multicolored		16.00
1493	A419	25d multicolored		16.00

Saddam River Canal Project A420

1995, July 17   **Perf. 11**
1494	A420	4d olive yellow & blue		4.00
1495	A420	4d red & blue		4.00

Size: 97x57mm
Imperf
1496	A420	25d multicolored, denom. in black		13.50
a.		Denomination in red		13.50

Embargo of Iraq — A421

1995, Aug. 6   **Perf. 11**
1497	A421	10d blue green & rose lilac		3.00

Size: 77x100mm
Imperf
1498	A421	25d multicolored		14.00

No. 1273 Surcharged

y

z

1995, Oct. 15   Litho.   Perf. 12½x12
1499	A354(y)	25d on 350f #1273		3.00
1500	A354(z)	25d on 350f #1273		3.00
a.		Pair		20.00

Nos. 1103-1108 Surcharged

aa   ab

1995(?)   Photo.   Perf. 15x14
1501	A315(aa)	25d on 10f #1103		2.00
1502	A315(ab)	25d on 20f #1104		2.00
1503	A315(aa)	25d on 30f #1105		2.00
1504	A315(ab)	25d on 40f #1106		8.00
1505	A315(aa)	25d on 50f #1107		8.00
1506	A315(ab)	25d on 100f #1108		8.00
a.		Bklt. pane of 6, #1501-1506		32.00

No. 1380, Postal Savings Stamps Similar to Type A387 Surcharged in Red or Black

ac   ad

ae

1995(?)   Litho.   Perf. 11½x12
Size: 23½x25mm
1507	A387(ac)	25d on 100f multi		2.00
1508	A387(ac)	25d on 100f blue & multi		2.00
1509	A387(ad)	50d on 250f yel & multi (R)		4.00
1510	A387(ae)	50d on 50f #1380		4.00

The 250f postal savings stamp was also overprinted in denominations of 500f, 2500f and 5000f. These were not issued and were demonitized Feb. 1, 1996. They were subsequently surcharged with new values and with a bar obliterating the original overprint. See Nos. 1512-1514.

No. 1406 Surcharged

1995(?)
1511	A397	100d on 150f multi		5.00

Postal Savings Stamps Similar to Type A387 Surcharged in Red

af

ag

---

ah

1996   Litho.   Perf. 11½x12
Size: 23½x25mm
On 250f Yellow & Multi
1512	A387(af)	25d on 500f		6.00
1513	A387(ag)	25d on 5000d		5.00
1514	A387(ah)	50d on 2500d		10.00
		Nos. 1512-1514 (3)		21.00

A421a

A421b

Children, Bank — A421c

1996   Litho.   Perf. 13½
1514A	A421a	25d on 10f grn & multi		35.00
1514B	A421b	25d on 25f bl & multi		2.00
1514C	A421c	50d on 10f grn & multi		110.00

Children, Bank — A422

1996   Litho.   Perf. 13½
1515	A422	50d on 50f multi		3.00

No. 1515 without surcharge is a postal savings stamp.

No. 1435 Surcharged

1996   Perf. 13½x13
1516	A407	100d on 50f multi		6.50

No. O341 Surcharged

1996   Perf. 14
1517	A324	100d on 70f #O341		5.00

No. 1273 Surcharged

ak   al

1996   Litho.   Perf. 12½x12
1517A	A354(ak)	25d on 350f		1.25
1519A	A354(al)	1000d on 350f		42.50

No. 1273 Surcharged in Blue or Black

ai   aj

1996   Perf. 12½x12
1518	A354(ai)	250d on 350f		7.50
		(Bl)		
1519	A354(aj)	350d on 350f		18.00

No. O345 Surcharged

1996   Litho.   Perf. 13½
1519B	A329	100d on 60f		5.00

Battle of Um Al Maarik — A423

1997, Feb. 13   Photo.   Perf. 11
1520	A423	25d blk, red & green		1.00
1521	A423	100d blue, red & grn		5.00
a.		Arabic word at right center reversed		20.00

No. 1406 Surcharged

1997, Apr. 22   Litho.   Perf. 11½x12
1522	A397	25d on 150f #1406		4.25

Post Day.

No. 1448 Surcharged

1997   **Perf. 13x13½**
1523 A411 25d on 100f #1448   2.00
    Baath Party, 50th anniv.

No. 1450 Surcharged like No. 1516
1997   **Litho.**   **Perf. 13½**
1524 A407 100d on 50f multi   45.00

No. 1452 Surcharged

1997   **Perf. 13½x13**
1525 A412 100d on 50f multi   8.00

No. 1459 Surcharged

1997   **Perf. 14**
1526 A413 25d on 250f multi   1.25

A424

A425

Referendum Day: 250d, Saddam Hussein, map of Arab nations.

1997   **Perf. 14**
1527 A424 25d shown   1.50
1527A A424 100d multicolored   6.00
    Imperf
    Size: 91x77mm
1528 A424 250d multicolored   10.00

1997, Dec. 19   **Perf. 14**
    Saddam Hussein and: 25d, 100d, #1531, Water irrigating trees, grain. #1532, Water pipeline, flowers, grain.
    Self-Adhesive (#1530)
1529 A425 25d multicolored   1.00
1530 A425 100d multicolored   3.00

    Imperf
    Size: 68x81mm
1531 A425 250d multicolored   6.00
    Size: 64x82mm
1532 A425 250d multicolored   6.00
    Wafa'a Alqa'id project.

Saladin (1169-1250), Founder of Ayyubid Dynasty, Saddam Hussein — A426

1998, Feb.   **Litho.**   **Perf. 14**
    Self-Adhesive
1533 A426 25d multicolored   1.00
1534 A426 100d multicolored   3.00
    Size: 79x67mm
    Imperf
1535 A426 250d multicolored   18.00
    Nos. 1533-1534 exist imperf. No. 1535 has water-activated gum.

New Year — A427

1998, Mar. 21   *Imperf.*
1536 A427 250d Zinnias   9.00
1537 A427 250d Irises   9.00

1998 World Cup Soccer Championship, France — A428

1998, June   *Imperf.*
1538 A428 250d shown   7.00
    Size: 63x76mm
1539 A428 250d Two players, vert.   6.00

Souvenir Sheet

Arab Police & Security Leaders Conf., 25th Anniv. — A429

1998, July 12   **Litho.**   *Imperf.*
1540 A429 250d multicolored   6.00

A430

"Zad" Day (Arabic Alphabet) — A431

1998, Oct. 25   **Perf. 14**
1541 A430 25d multicolored   .50
1542 A431 100d multicolored   2.00

Flowers — A432

Designs: 25d, Chamomilla recutita. 50d, Helianthus annuus. 1000d, Carduus nutans.

1998, Oct. 27
1543 A432 25d multicolored   .40
1544 A432 50d brown leaves   .75
1545 A432 50d green leaves   .75
1546 A432 1000d multicolored   8.50
    Self-Adhesive
1547 A432 25d like #1543   7.50
    No. 1547 is printed on glossy paper.

A433

Martyr's Day — A434

1998, Dec. 1
1548 A433 25d multicolored   .50
1549 A434 100d multicolored   1.75
    Nos. 1548-1549 exist imperf.

Martyr's Day — A434a

1998, Dec. 1   **Litho.**
    Imperf
1550 A434a 250d multicolored   4.50

Anthocharis Euphome — A435

1998, Dec. 20
1551 A435 100d Precis orithya   3.00
1552 A435 150d shown   4.50
    Exist imperf. Value, set $15.

Intl. Conference on Tower of Babel and Ziggurat of Borsippa — A436

1999, Jan. 23   **Litho.**   **Perf. 14**
1553 A436 25d multicolored   1.00
1554 A436 50d multicolored   2.00
    Imperf
    Size: 71x89mm
1555 A436 250d multicolored   9.00

Great Dam — A437

Saddam Hussein, 62nd Birthday — A439

Saddam Theater — A438

1999, Apr. 28   *Perf. 14*
1556 A437 25d Dam   1.00
1557 A437 100d Dam, Saddam
     Hussein   2.50

Imperf
Size: 70x92mm

1558 A437 250d Like #1557   9.00

1999, May 7   *Perf. 14*
1559 A438 25d Saddam Hussein,
     emblem   1.00
1560 A438 100d Al-Saddamiyah
     City   2.00

Imperf
Size: 92x70mm

1561 A438 250d Clock tower   9.00

1999, May 17   *Perf. 14*
1562 A439   25d multicolored   .25
1563 A439   50d multicolored   .50
1564 A439   150d multicolored   1.75
1565 A439   500d multicolored   6.00
1566 A439   1000d multicolored   14.00
1567 A439   5000d multi, horiz.   55.00
    Nos. 1562-1567 (6)   77.50

1998 World Cup,
France — A440

Honey
Bees — A441

1999, July 17
1568 A440 25d Two players   1.75
1569 A440 100d Goalie save, horiz.   4.00

1999, Sept. 18
1570 A441 25d brown & multi   2.00
1571 A441 50d black & multi   3.00

Al Fat'h
Day
A442

Saddam Hussein and: 25d, Eagle, flowers.
50d, People. 250d, Eagle, flag.

1999, Dec. 12   *Litho.*   *Perf. 14*
1572-1573 A442   Set of 2   2.00
Imperf
Size: 93x71mm

1574 A442 250d multi   6.75

A443

A444

A445

Jerusalem
Day
A446

2000, Feb.   *Perf. 14*
1575 A443 25d multi   .50
1576 A444 50d multi   .75
1577 A445 100d multi   1.50
1578 A446 150d multi   2.75
    Nos. 1575-1578 (4)   5.50

Imperf
Size: 93x71mm

1579 A446 250d multi   6.75

A447

Saddam
Hussein's
Birthday
A448

2000, May 17   *Perf. 14*
1580 A447 25d multi   .50
1581 A448 50d multi   .75

Imperf
Size: 92x71mm

1582 A448 500d Saddam Hus-
     sein, stars   9.00

Sculpture
A449

Text "July Festivals 2000": a, At right. b, At
left. c, At bottom center on two lines. d, At
lower left. e, At bottom center on 3 lines.

2000, July 12   *Perf. 14*
1583   Horiz. strip of 5   2.00
  a.-e. A449 25d Any single   .35
    Exists imperf. Value, strip $10.

Victory
Day — A450

Designs: 25d, 250d, Saddam Hussein. 50d,
Saddam Hussein, flag.

2000, Aug. 8   *Perf. 14*
1584-1585 A450   Set of 2   2.50
Imperf
Size: 71x91mm

1586 A450 250d multi   4.50

Birds
A451

Designs: 25d, Anas platyrhynchos. 50d,
Passer domesticus. 150d, Porphyrio
poliocephalus.

2000, Aug. 28   *Perf. 14*
1587-1589 A451   Set of 3   5.00
Imperf
Size: 93x71mm

1590 A451 500d Carduelis
     carduelis   10.00

Prophet
Mohammad's
Birthday — A452

Designs: 25d, Green background. 50d, Tan
background.

2000, Oct. 11   *Perf. 14*
1591-1592 A452   Set of 2   2.00

A453

Referendum Day — A454

2000, Oct. 15   *Perf. 14*
1593 A453 25d multi   .35
1594 A454 50d multi   .75

Imperf
Size: 93x72mm

1595 A453 250d Saddam Hus-
     sein, crowd   4.50

Baytol Hikma,
1200th
Anniv. — A455

2001, Jan.   *Perf. 14*
1596-1597 A455   Set of 2   1.50
1597a   Pair   4.50

A456

A457

Writing, 5th
Millennium
A458

2001, Mar.   *Litho.*   *Perf. 14*
1598 A456   25d multi   .30
1599 A457   50d multi   .55
1600 A456   75d multi   .80
1601 A457   100d multi   1.10
1602 A458   150d multi   1.75
1603 A458   250d multi   2.75
    Nos. 1598-1603 (6)   7.25

Bombing of
Al Amiriya
Shelter,
10th Anniv.
A459

Designs: 25d, 150d, Mother, injured child,
rescue workers. 50d, Doves, wreath, picture
frames, vert.

2001, Mar.   *Perf. 14*
1604-1605 A459   Set of 2   1.50
Imperf
Size: 91x71mm
Without Gum

1606 A459 150d multi   4.00

Al Baath
Party, 54th
Anniv.
A460

Designs: 25d, People, torch. 50d, Presidents Hassan al-Bakr, Saddam Hussein.
100d, Map of Middle East.

2001, Apr. 7   *Perf. 14*
1607-1609 A460   Set of 3   2.00

Saddam Hussein's 64th Birthday A461

Saddam Hussein: 25d, Seated, with flowers, vert. 50d, Seated. 100d, Seated, with people. 250d, Standing, with crowd.

2001, Apr. 28   *Perf. 14*
1610-1612 A461   Set of 3   *1.50*
Imperf
Size: 89x69mm
Without Gum
1613 A461 250d multi   4.50

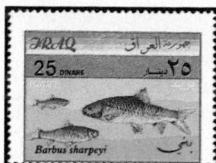

Fish A462

Designs: 25d, Barbus sharpeyi. 50d, Barbus esocinus. 100d, Barbus xanthopterus. 150d, Pampus argenteus.

2001, Aug. 4   *Perf. 14*
1614-1617 A462   Set of 4   5.00

Battle of Um Al Maarik, 10th Anniv. — A463

Frame color: 25d, Red. 100d, Black.

2001, Aug.
1618-1619 A463   Set of 2   *1.25*

Mammals A464

Designs: 100d, Gazella subgutturosa. 250d, Lepus europaeus. 500d, Camelus dromedarius. 1000d, Various mammals.

2001, Aug.   *Perf. 14*
1620-1622 A464   Set of 3   7.50
Imperf
Size: 92x70mm
Without Gum
1623 A464 1000d multi   9.00

Nationalization of Oil Industries, 29th Anniv. — A465

Designs: 25d, Oil rig, workers, soldier, Iraqi flag. 50d, Oil rig, refinery, pipeline.

2001, Sept. 15   Litho.   *Perf. 14*
1624-1625 A465   Set of 2   *1.00*

Support for Palestinians A466

Designs: No. 1626, 25d, Saddam Hussein, map of Israel and Iraq. No. 1627, 25d, Dome of the Rock, Palestinian flag, gunman, vert. 50d, Dome of the Rock, Palestinian flag, gunman with arms raised, vert.
No. 1629, 250d, Dome of the Rock, Israeli tank and Palestinian rock-thrower. No. 1630, 250d, Dome of the Rock, doves, Palestinian flag and Mohammad J. Durra and father.

2001, Sept. 20
1626-1628 A466   Set of 3   *1.25*
Imperf
Size: 88x67mm
Without Gum
1629-1630 A466   Set of 2   5.00

2001 Youth Soccer World Cup A467

Designs: 25d, Players, map of world. 50d, Map of Asia, player, trophy, vert.

2001, Oct. 7   *Perf. 14*
1631-1632 A467   Set of 2   *1.00*

Iraqi Claim of Depleted Uranium US Bombs Dropped on Iraqi Citizens — A468

Falling bombs and: No. 1633, 25d, Woman and children. No. 1634, 25d, No. 1636, 250d, Disfigured people. 50d, People, Iraqi flag, horiz.

2001, Nov.
1633-1635 A468   Set of 3   4.00
Imperf
Size: 70x91mm
Without Gum
1636 A468 250d multi   7.00

Army Day — A469

Designs: 25d, Iraqi flag, soldiers, airplanes, ship and tank. No. 1638, 50d, No. 1640, 250d, Monument, vert. 100d, Soldier, Iraqi flag, tank, vert.

2002, Jan. 6   *Perf. 14*
1637-1639 A469   Set of 3   3.50
Imperf
Size: 73x91mm
Without Gum
1640 A469 250d multi   3.50

Liberation of Fao — A470

Saddam Hussein and : 25d, Mosque. 100d, Soldier, map of Iraq, horiz.

2002, Apr. 17   *Perf. 14*
1641-1642 A470   Set of 2   *1.50*

February 8 Revolution, 39th Anniv. — A470a

February 8 Revolution, 39th Anniv. — A470b

2002, Feb. 8   Litho.   *Perf. 14*
1642A A470a 50d multi   8.00 —
1642B A470b 100d multi   12.00 —

Jerusalem Day — A471

Frame color: 25d, Blue. 50d, Yellow. 100d, Pink.

2002, Apr.
1643-1645 A471   Set of 3   2.00

Hegira, Year 1423 A472

Designs: 25d, Mosques, Holy Kaaba. 50d, Minaret and mosque, vert. 75d, Bird, spider web.

2002, Apr.
1646-1648 A472   Set of 3   *1.75*

Bombardment of Al Amirya Shelter, 11th Anniv. — A473

Frame color: 25d, Black. 50d, Red.

2002, Apr.
1649-1650 A473   Set of 2   *1.00*

War Against Iraq, 11th Anniv. — A474

2002, Apr.
1651 A474 100d multi   *1.75*

Flowers — A475

Designs: 25d, Roses. 50d, Roses, diff. 150d, Poppies, carnations. 250d, Roses, diff.

2002, Apr.   *Perf. 14*
1652-1654 A475   Set of 3   3.50
Imperf
Size: 73x91mm
Without Gum
1655 A475 250d multi   5.00

Saddam Hussein's 65th Birthday — A476

Color of vignette frame and country name: 25d, Red. 50d, Purple. 75d, Green. 100d, Dark blue.
No. 1660, 250d, Saddam Huseein, hearts and flowers. No. 1661, 250d, Saddam Hussoin with headdress.

2002, Apr. 28   *Perf. 14*
1656-1659 A476   Set of 4   *2.75*
Imperf
Size: 74x91mm
Without Gum
1660-1661 A476   Set of 2   6.00

Palestinian Unity — A477

2002   Litho.   *Perf. 14*
1662 A477 5000d multi   35.00

Mosques — A478

Designs: 25d, Sheikh Maroof Mosque. 50d, Al-Mouiz Mosque. 75d, Um Al Marik Mosque.

2002
1663-1665 A478   Set of 3   2.00

Post Day — A479

Air mail envelope and: 50d, Stamp with dove. 100d, Airplane, ship, train, map of world. 250d, Globe and dove.

2002
1666-1667 A479   Set of 2   2.00

Imperf
Size: 70x91mm
Without Gum
1668   A479   250d multi   4.50

2002 World Cup Soccer Championships, Japan and Korea — A480

World Cup, various players and background color of: 50d, Blue. 100d, Yellow. 150d, Red violet.
250d, Purple.

2002   **Perf. 14**
1669-1671   A480   Set of 3   3.00
Imperf
Size: 70x92mm
Without Gum
1672   A480   250d multi   4.00

Ancient Ships A481

Various ships: 150d, 250d, 500d.

2002   **Perf. 14**
1673-1675   A481   Set of 3   9.00

Victory Day — A482

Frame color: 25d, Blue. 50d, Pink. 150d, Eagle, vert.

2002   **Perf. 14**
1676-1677   A482   Set of 2   1.75
Imperf
Size: 71x90mm
Without Gum
1678   A482   150d multi   4.00

A483

A484

A485

A486

Poets — A487

Illustration A487 reduced.

2002   **Litho.**   **Perf. 14**
1679   A483   25d multi   .35
1680   A484   50d multi   .50
1681   A485   75d multi   1.00
1682   A486   100d multi   1.25
      Nos. 1679-1682 (4)   3.10
Imperf
Size: 70x92mm
Without Gum
1683   A487   150d multi   4.00

A488

A489

A490

Baghdad Day — A491

Illustration A491 reduced.

2002   **Perf. 14**
1684   A488   25d multi   .35
1685   A489   50d multi   .50
1686   A490   75d multi   1.00
      Nos. 1684-1686 (3)   1.85
Imperf
Size: 91x70mm
Without Gum
1687   A491   250d multi   5.00

Referendum Day — A492

Designs: 100d, 250d, Saddam Hussein, people, hands, heart and flowers. 150d, Fist, ballot box.

2002   **Perf. 14**
1688-1689   A492   Set of 2   2.50
Imperf
Size: 71x92mm
Without Gum
1690   A492   250d multi   2.75

Mammals A493

Designs: 25d, Oryx leucoryx. 50d, Acionyx jubatus, vert. 75d, 250d, Panthera leo persica, vert. 100d, Castor fiber. 150d, Equus hemionus hemippus.

2002   **Perf. 14**
1691-1695   A493   Set of 5   7.00
Imperf
Size: 70x93mm
Without Gum
1696   A493   250d multi   8.00

Saddam University A494

Background colors: 50d, Brown. 100d, Blue.

2002   **Perf. 14**
1697-1698   A494   Set of 2   2.00

Iraqi Coalition Provisional Authority postal officials have declared as illegal 13 Iraqi stamps of the Saddam Hussein regime with various overprints and surcharges that read "Iraq / In Coalition / Occupation."

Issues of the Coalition Provisional Authority

Transportation — A495

Designs: 50d, Raft. 100d, Horse-drawn carriage. 250d, Horse-drawn rail car. 500d, Boat. 5000d, Camel caravan.

2004, Jan. 15   **Litho.**   **Perf. 14**
1699-1703   A495   Set of 5   9.75   9.75
        Dated 2003.

New Year — A496

2006, Mar. 16   **Litho.**   **Perf. 13**
1704   A496   250d multi   1.00   1.00

A497

June 30, 2004 Installation of Iraqi Interim Government A498

2006, Sept. 7   **Litho.**   **Perf. 14½**
1705   A497   100d multi   .35   .35
1706   A498   250d multi   .90   .90

Iraq Civilization A499

Designs: 100d, Mannequin with headdress. 150d, Golden bull. 200d, Stone carving. 250d, Paintings of horses on walls.

2006, Sept. 11   **Litho.**   **Perf. 14½**
1707-1709   A499   Set of 3   1.75   1.75
Imperf
Size: 80x61mm
1710   A499   250d multi   2.00   2.00

2004 Summer Olympics,
Athens — A500

Designs: 100d, Soccer players. 150d,
Runners.
500d, Various athletes.

2006, Sept. 24   **Perf. 14¼**
1711-1712 A500   Set of 2   1.50 1.50
        Imperf
    Size: 100x70mm
1713 A500 500d multi   2.75 2.75

Paintings — A501

Unnamed paintings by: 100d, Akram
Shukri. 150d, Hafidh Al Duroubi. 200d,
Faiq Hassan. 250d, Atheer M. G.

2006, Oct. 9   **Perf. 14¼**
1714-1716 A501   Set of 3   2.00 2.00
        Imperf
    Size: 88x70mm
1717 A501 250d multi   2.25 2.25

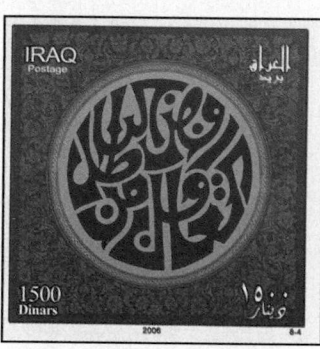

The items shown above were prepared in 2006 but not issued.

Flowers — A502

Designs: 250d, Anemone. 750d, Viola mam-
mola. 1000d, Atropa belladonna.

2007   **Litho.**   ***Die Cut***
    Self-Adhesive
1718-1720 A502   Set of 3   3.50 3.50
1720a   Souvenir sheet, #1718-1720   3.75 3.75
   Issued: Nos. 1718-1720, 4/11; No. 1720a,
5/7.

Street Vendor
—A502a

Two Women —
A502b

2007, Apr. 23 Litho.   **Perf. 13½x13¼**
1720B A502a 100d multi   .30 .30
1720C A502b 250d multi   .75 .75

Singers and
Cat — A503

2007, Apr. 23   **Perf. 13½x13¼**
1721 A503 5000d multi   15.00 15.00
    Dated 2006.

Butterflies
A504

Designs: 100d, Papilio demodocus. 250d,
Precis orithua. 500d, Coitas croceus.
1000d, Papilio demodocus, diff.

2007, Apr. 23   **Perf. 13½x13¼**
1722-1724 A504   Set of 3   2.50 2.50
    Size: 80x61mm
        Imperf
1725 A504 1000d multi   2.75 2.75

Artisans — A505

Designs: 250d, Rug maker. 350d, Blanket
maker. 500d, Basket maker.

2007, May 22   **Litho.**   ***Die Cut***
    Self-Adhesive
1726-1728 A505   Set of 3   3.50 3.50
1728a   Miniature sheet, #1726-1728   4.00

Folklore — A506

2007, June 7   ***Imperf.***
1729 A506 1000d multi   2.75 2.75
    Dated 2006.

Rafidain Bank,
65th Anniv. (in
2006) — A507

Background colors: 100d, Light blue. 150d,
Orange red. 250d, Brown. 500d, Lilac.

2007, July 10   **Perf. 14**
1730-1733 A507   Set of 4   2.75 2.75
    Dated 2006.

Birds
A508

Designs: 150d, Anser anser. 250d, Merops
superciliosus. 500d, Pterocles alchata.
1500d, Ducks in flight.

2007, Sept.   **Perf. 14**
1734-1736 A508   Set of 3   2.25 2.25
        Imperf
    Size: 80x80mm
1737 A508 1500d multi   3.75 3.75

A509

Musicians
and Actors
A510

Designs: 250d, Mohammad al-Qubanchi,
singer. 500d, Haqi al-Shibly, actor, horiz.
750d, Nazem al-Ghazaly, singer, horiz. 1000d,
Munir Bashir, musician.

2007, Oct. 1   ***Die Cut***
    Self-Adhesive
1738 A509 250d multi   1.25 1.25
1739 A509 500d multi   2.25 2.25
1740 A509 750d multi   3.25 3.25
1741 A510 1000d multi   4.50 4.50
a.   Miniature sheet, #1738-1741   12.00
   Nos. 1738-1741 (4)   11.25 11.25

A511

A512

National Reconciliation — A513

2008, Oct. 27 Litho.   **Perf. 12¾x13¼**
1742 A511 250d multi   .75 .75
       Perf. 13
1743 A512 500d multi   1.50 1.50
1744 A513 750d multi   2.25 2.25
   Nos. 1742-1744 (3)   4.50 4.50

Diplomatic Relations Between Iraq and
People's Republic of China, 50th
Anniv. — A514

2008, Oct. 28   **Perf. 12**
1745 A514 500d multi   1.75 1.75

   A three-dimensional souvenir sheet of one
500d stamp without white borders was
presented as a gift to Chinese and Iraqi
officials.

Wasit Poetry Festival — A515

2008, Nov. 24   **Perf. 13¼x13**
1746 A515 5000d multi   12.00 12.00

Collective Cemeteries — A516

Rose and: 250d, Corpses and mourners. 500d, Skeletal remains.

2008, Dec. 14
1747-1748 A516 Set of 2 2.10 2.10

Campaign to Regain Stolen Antiquities A517

Buildings and various antiquities: 250d, 500d, 750d.

2009, Mar. 17 *Perf. 13x13¼*
1749-1751 A517 Set of 3 3.75 3.75

Environmental Protection — A518

2009, Mar. 29
1752 A518 1000d multi 3.00 3.00

Campaign to Restore Marshes A519

2009, Apr. 22
1753 A519 10,000d multi 32.50 32.50

Intl. Children's Day — A520

Children's art: No. 1754, 50d, Shown. No. 1755, 50d, Two women wearing traditional clothing. No. 1756, 50d, Three men, palm trees. No. 1757, 50d, Woman hugging daughter. No. 1758, 50d, Three women.
500d, Woman holding baby, horiz.

2009, June 1 Litho. *Perf. 13¼x13*
1754-1758 A520 Set of 5 2.50 2.50
Imperf
Size:80x60mm
1759 A520 500d multi 3.00 3.00

2009 FIFA Confederations Cup Soccer Tournament — A521

Emblem and: 100d, Goalie. 250d, Player dribbling ball. 500d, Player kicking ball. 750d, Emblem only.

2009, June 13 *Perf. 13x13¼*
1760-1762 A521 Set of 3 2.50 2.50
Imperf
Size: 80x80mm
1763 A521 750d multi 2.00 2.00

Iraqi Tourism Week (in 2008) — A522

No. 1764, 250d — "Iraqi Tourism Week" in white, with denomination at: a, Right (5-1). b, Left (5-2).
No. 1765, 250d — "Iraqi Tourism Week" in black, with denomination at: a, Right (5-3). b, Left (5-4).
500d, Horsemen (5-5).

2009, July 14 *Perf. 13¼x13*
Horiz. Pairs, #a-b
1764-1765 A522 Set of 2 3.00 3.00
Imperf
Size: 90x60mm
1766 A522 500d multi 1.50 1.50
Dated 2009.

Jerusalem, Capital of Arab Culture — A523

2009, Aug. 2 *Perf. 13¼x13*
1767 A523 250d org brn & multi .80 .80
Imperf
Size: 60x80mm
1768 A523 750d ol grn & multi 2.10 2.10

Emmanuel Baba Dawud (1934-2009), Soccer Player and Coach — A524

Dawud and: 250d, Pink frame. 500d, Green frame.

2009, Dec. 30 Litho. *Perf. 13x13¼*
1769-1770 A524 Set of 2 1.75 1.75

Iraqi Republic Railways — A525

Designs: 250d, Steam locomotive. 500d, Diesel locomotive. 750d, Steam locomotive, diff.
1000d, Diesel locomotive, building.

2010, Jan. 25 Litho. *Perf. 13¼x13*
1772-1774 A525 Set of 3 3.75 3.75
Size: 80x80mm
Imperf
1775 A525 1000d multi 2.50 2.50

Elections — A526

Color of stylized people: 250d, Purple. 500d, Green. 1000d, Red.

2010, Mar. 7 *Perf. 13¼x13*
1776-1778 A526 Set of 3 4.25 4.25

Arabian Brotherhood Scouts Day — A527

Designs: No. 1779, 250d, Bugler. No. 1780, 250d, Girls in field. No. 1781, 250d, Boys saluting flag. No. 1782, 250d, Girls standing at attention.
1000d, Scouts carrying flags.

2010, Mar. 23 *Perf. 13x13¼*
1779-1782 A527 Set of 4 2.50 2.50
Size: 80x60mm
Imperf
1783 A527 1000d multi 2.50 2.50

Iraqi Post Day — A528

Designs: 250d, Envelope in mail slot. 500d, Dove, envelope, clay tablet.

2010, Apr. 27 *Perf. 13¼x13*
1784-1785 A528 Set of 2 1.90 1.90

A529

Prehistoric Animals — A530

No. 1786 — Various prehistoric animals with stamps numbered: a, 10-1. b, 10-2. c, 10-3. d, 10-4. e, 10-5. f, 10-6. g, 10-7. h, 10-8.
No. 1787, 500d, 10-9. No. 1788, 500d, 10-10.

2010, June 28 *Perf. 13¼x13*
1786 Block of 8 7.25 7.25
a.-h. A529 250d Any single .90 .90
Imperf
1787-1788 A530 Set of 2 2.50 2.50

2010 World Cup Soccer Championships, South Africa — A531

Emblem and various soccer players with frame in: 250d, Maroon. 500d, Brown. 750d, Purple. No. 1792, 1000d, Red.
No. 1793, Emblem and two soccer players.

2010, July 13 *Perf. 13¼x13*
1789-1792 A531 Set of 4 6.25 6.25
Size: 125x70mm
Imperf
1793 A531 1000d multi 2.50 2.50

Koran — A532

2010, Aug. 11 Litho. *Perf. 13¼x13*
1794 A532 250d multi .65 .65
Size:90x70mm
Imperf
1795 A532 500d multi 1.25 1.25

Intl. Youth Year — A533

"2010," Arabic text and : No. 1796, 250d, Youths, candle, olive branch. No. 1797, 250d, Young woman and man, leaves.

2010, Sept. 8 *Perf. 13¼x13*
1796-1797 A533 Set of 2 1.25 1.25

Organization of Petroleum Exporting Countries, 50th Anniv. — A534

Sites in Iraq, OPEC 50th anniversary emblem and: 250d, Map of Iraq. 500d, World map.

2010, Sept. 14 *Perf. 13x13¼*
1798-1799 A534 Set of 2 1.90 1.90

Kirkuk, City of Iraqi Culture — A535

2010, Oct. 4   Litho.   Perf. 13¼x13
1800 A535 1000d multi   2.50 2.50

Convention on the Rights of the Child, 20th Anniv. — A536

Stylized faces in oval and: 500d, Child holding adult's hand. 750d, Child solving math problem on blackboard. 1000d, Children on carousel.

2010, Nov.
1801-1803 A536 Set of 3   5.50 5.50

AIR POST STAMPS

Catalogue values for unused stamps in this section are for Never Hinged items.

Basra Airport — AP1

Diyala Railway Bridge — AP2

Vickers Viking over: 4f, 20f, Kut Dam. 5f, 35f, Faisal II Bridge.

Perf. 11½, 11½x12

1949, Feb. 1		**Engr.**	**Unwmk.**
C1	AP1	3f blue green	.75 .25
C2	AP1	4f red violet	.75 .25
C3	AP1	5f red brown	.80 .25
C4	AP1	10f carmine	5.00 1.50
C5	AP1	20f blue	3.25 .65
C6	AP1	35f red orange	3.50 .65
C7	AP2	50f olive	4.50 1.10
C8	AP2	100f violet	9.00 2.25
		Nos. C1-C8 (8)	27.55 6.90

Sheets exist, perf. and imperf., containing one each of Nos. C1-C8, with arms and Arabic inscription in blue green in upper and lower margin. Value (2 sheets), each $80.

Republic

ICY Emblem — AP3

1965, Aug. 13   Litho.   Perf. 13½
C9   AP3 5f brn org & black   .75 .25
C10 AP3 10f citron & dk brn   1.25 .25
C11 AP3 30f ultra & black   3.00 1.10
     Nos. C9-C11 (3)   5.00 1.60

International Cooperation Year.

Trident 1E Jet Plane AP4

1965, Dec. 1   Photo.   Perf. 11½
Granite Paper
C12 AP4 5f multicolored   .65 .55
C13 AP4 10f multicolored   .65 .55
C14 AP4 40f multicolored   5.50 4.75
     Nos. C12-C14 (3)   6.80 5.85

Introduction by Iraqi Airways of Trident 1E jet planes.

Arab International Tourist Union Emblem — AP5

Travelers on Magic Carpet AP6

1966, Dec. 3   Litho.   Perf. 13½, 14
C15 AP5 2f multicolored   .80 .30
C16 AP6 5f yellow & multi   1.25 .30
C17 AP5 15f blue & multi   1.40 .50
C18 AP6 50f multicolored   2.50 .80
     Nos. C15-C18 (4)   5.95 1.90

Meeting of the Arab Intl. Tourist Union, Baghdad.
For overprint see No. RAC1.

Costume Type of Regular Issue

Iraqi Costumes: 40f, Woman's head. 50f, Woman's costume. 80f, Man's costume.

1967, Nov. 10   Litho.   Perf. 13
C19 A105 40f multicolored   2.00 .90
C20 A105 50f blue & multi   3.00 1.25
C21 A105 80f green & multi   5.00 1.75
     Nos. C19-C21 (3)   7.00 2.80

For overprints, see CO1-CO3.

International Tourist Year Type of Regular Issue

Designs: 50f, Female statue, Temples of Hatra. 80f, Spiral Tower (Malwiye of Samarra). 100f, Adam's Tree. 200f, Aladdin's Cave. 500f, Golden Shiah Mosque of Kadhimain. 50f, 80f, 100f and 200f are vert.

1967, Dec. 1   Litho.
C22 A107 50f multicolored   3.50 .40
C23 A107 80f multicolored   3.75 .65
C24 A107 100f multicolored   3.75 .40
C25 A107 200f ver & multi   8.00 3.25
C26 A107 500f brn & multi   32.50 18.00
     Nos. C22-C26 (5)   51.50 23.10

For overprints see Nos. C39, C52, C53, CO4.

Arabian AP7

Animals: 2f, Striped hyena. 3f, Leopard. 5f, Mountain gazelle. 200f, Arabian stallion.

1969, Sept. 1   Litho.   Perf. 14
C27 AP7 2f multicolored   .60 .25
C28 AP7 3f multicolored   .60 .25
C29 AP7 5f multicolored   .60 .25
C30 AP7 10f multicolored   .85 .30
C31 AP7 200f multicolored   12.50 6.00
     Nos. C27-C31 (5)   15.15 7.05

For overprints, see Nos. CO5-CO7.

Ross Smith's Vickers Vimy AP8

1969, Dec. 4   Litho.   Perf. 14
C32 AP8 15f dk bl & multi   3.00 1.20
C33 AP8 35f multicolored   4.50 2.75
a.   Souv. sheet of 2, #C32-C33, imperf.   15.00 13.00

50th anniv. of the first England to Australia flight of Capt. Ross Smith and Lt. Keith Smith. No. C33a sold for 100f.

View Across Euphrates — AP9

Iraqi Banknotes and Pres. Hassan al-Bakr AP10

1970, Oct. 30   Litho.   Perf. 13
C34 AP9 10f brt bl & multi   2.00 .50
C35 AP9 15f multicolored   3.00 1.10
C36 AP10 1d multicolored   65.00 24.00
     Nos. C34-C36 (3)   70.00 25.60

National Development Plan.
For overprints see Nos. C42-C43.

Telecommunications Emblem — AP11

1970, Dec. 15   Litho.   Perf. 14x13½
C37 AP11 15f gray & multi   .65 .20
C38 AP11 25f lt bl & multi   .90 .50

10th Conf. of Arab Telecommunications Union.

No. C23 Overprinted

1971, Apr. 23   Perf. 13
C39 A107 80f multicolored   9.00 5.50

World Meteorological Day.

Iraqi Philatelic Society Emblem — AP12

1972, Feb. 25   Litho.   Perf. 13
C40 AP12 25f multicolored   1.25 .95
C41 AP12 70f pink & multi   4.00 2.40

Iraqi Philatelic Society, 20th anniversary.

Nos. C34-C35 Overprinted

1972, Feb. 25
C42 AP9 10f brt bl & multi   2.50 2.40
C43 AP9 15f multicolored   2.50 2.40

9th Cong. of Natl. Union of Iraqi Students.

Soccer and C.I.S.M. Emblem AP13

20f, 35f, Players, soccer ball, C.I.S.M. emblem. 100f, Winged lion, Olympic & C.I.S.M. emblems.

1972, June 9   Litho.   Perf. 13½
C46 AP13 10f lt bl & multi   .75 .30
C47 AP13 20f dp bl & multi   1.75 .30
C48 AP13 25f green & multi   1.75 .30
C49 AP13 35f brt bl & multi   4.75 .80
a.   Souv. sheet, 100f, imperf.   22.50 22.50
     Nos. C46-C49 (4)   9.00 1.70

25th Military Soccer Championships (C.I.S.M.), Baghdad, June 9-19.

Statue of Athlete — AP14

Design: 70f, Mesopotamian archer on horseback, ancient and modern athletes.

1972, Nov. 15   Photo.   Perf. 14x13½
C50 AP14 25f multicolored   1.50 .65
C51 AP14 70f multicolored   3.75 2.10

Cong. of Asian and World Body Building Championships, Baghdad, Nov. 15-23, 1972.

Nos. C23, C26 Overprinted

1973, Mar. 25　Litho.　Perf. 13

C52	A107	80f multi	21.00	7.25
C53	A107	500f multi	75.00	75.00

International History Congress.

ICATU Type of 1976

1976, Mar. 24　Photo.　Perf. 13½

C54	A213	75f blue & multi	4.50	2.00

Symbolic Eye
AP15

Basketball
AP16

1976, June 20　Photo.　Perf. 14

C55	AP15	25f ultra & dk brn	.40	.20
C56	AP15	35f brt grn & dk brn	.60	.20
C57	AP15	50f orange & multi	1.25	.60
		Nos. C55-C57 (3)	2.25	1.00

World Health Day: Foresight prevents
blindness.

1976, July 30　Litho.　Perf. 12x12½

Montreal Olympic Games Emblem and: 35f,
Volleyball. 50f, Wrestling. 75f, Boxing. 100f,
Target shooting, horiz.

C58	AP16	25f yel & multi	.75	.20
C59	AP16	35f blue & multi	1.00	.50
C60	AP16	50f ver & multi	1.25	.95
C61	AP16	75f yel grn & multi	2.25	1.25
		Nos. C58-C61 (4)	5.25	2.90

Souvenir Sheet

Imperf

C62	AP16	100f grn & multi	7.00	7.00

21st Olympic Games, Montreal, Canada,
July 17-Aug. 1.

13th World Telecommunications
Day — AP17

1981, May 17　Photo.　Perf. 12½

C63	AP17	25f multicolored	.50	.20
C64	AP17	50f multicolored	1.00	.40
C65	AP17	75f multicolored	1.75	.85
		Nos. C63-C65 (3)	3.25	1.45

Air Force Type of 1981

1981, June 1　Photo.　Perf. 14x13½

C66	A289	120f Planes, vert.	4.00	2.50

AIR POST OFFICIAL STAMP

Catalogue values for all unused
stamps in this section are for
Never Hinged items.

Nos. C19-C22
Overprinted

1971　Litho.　Perf. 13

CO1	A105	40f multicolored	4.75	1.40
CO2	A105	50f multicolored	6.00	1.40
CO3	A105	80f multicolored	5.50	1.40

"Official" Reading Down

CO4	A107	50f multicolored	5.25	3.25
		Nos. CO1-CO4 (4)	21.50	7.45

**Nos. C27-C28, C30 Overprinted or
Surcharged**

1971　　　　　　　　Perf. 14

CO5	AP7	10f multicolored	7.50	5.00
CO6	AP7	15f on 3f multi	7.50	5.00
CO7	AP7	25f on 2f multi	7.50	5.00
		Nos. CO5-CO7 (3)	22.50	15.00

No bar and surcharge on No. CO5.

OFFICIAL STAMPS

British Mandate
Regular Issue of 1923 Overprinted:

k　　　　　　　　l

1923　　Wmk. 4　　Perf. 12

O1	A1(k)	½a olive grn	1.10	.50
O2	A2(k)	1a brown	1.25	.20
O3	A3(l)	1½a car lake	3.00	.75
O4	A4(k)	2a brown org	2.00	.30
O5	A5(k)	3a deep blue	3.75	.75
O6	A6(l)	4a dull violet	4.00	.50
O7	A7(k)	6a blue green	5.75	1.40
O8	A6(l)	8a olive bister	6.25	1.30
O9	A8(l)	1r green & brn	7.00	1.40
O10	A1(k)	2r black (R)	21.00	9.00
O11	A6(l)	5r orange	62.50	27.50
O12	A7(k)	10r carmine	90.00	60.00
		Nos. O1-O12 (12)	207.60	103.60

Regular Issue of 1923-25 Overprinted:

m

n

1924-25

O13	A1(m)	½a olive green	1.50	.30
O14	A2(m)	1a brown	1.25	.30
O15	A3(n)	1½a car lake	1.25	.30
O16	A4(m)	2a brown org	2.00	.30
O17	A5(n)	3a deep blue	2.50	.30
O18	A6(n)	4a dull violet	5.50	.30
O19	A6(n)	6a blue green	2.50	.30
O20	A6(n)	8a olive bister	5.50	.40
O21	A8(n)	1r green & brn	12.00	1.00
O22	A1(m)	2r bister ('25)	40.00	4.50
O23	A6(n)	5r orange	65.00	50.00
O24	A7(m)	10r brown red	90.00	52.50
		Nos. O13-O24 (12)	229.00	110.50

For overprint see Nos. O42, O47, O51-O53.

No. 14 Overprinted Type "n"

1927

O25	A9	1r red brown	9.00	2.00

Regular Issue of 1931 Overprinted
Vertically

o

1931

O26	A10	½a green	.25	3.00
O27	A10	1a chestnut	.25	.20
O28	A10	1½a carmine	8.00	16.00
O29	A10	2a orange	.75	.20
O30	A10	3a light blue	1.40	.70
O31	A10	4a purple brown	1.50	.90
O32	A10	6a Pruss blue	5.25	12.50
O33	A10	8a dark green	5.25	12.50

Overprinted Horizontally

p

O34	A11	1r dark brown	10.00	12.50
O35	A11	2r yellow brown	21.00	45.00
O36	A11	5r deep orange	50.00	85.00
O37	A11	10r red	90.00	140.00
		Nos. O26-O37 (12)	193.65	328.50

Overprinted Vertically Reading Up

O38	A9(p)	25r violet	900.00	1,200.

For overprints see Nos. O39-O41, O43-
O46, O48-O50, O54.

Kingdom

Nos. O15, O19, O22-O24, O26-O31,
O33-O35, O38 Surcharged with New
Values in Fils and Dinars, like Nos.
28-43

1932, Apr. 1

O39	A10	3f on ½a	4.00	4.00
O40	A10	4f on 1a (G)	2.75	.20
O41	A10	5f on 1a	2.75	.20
a.		Inverted Arabic "5"	52.50	35.00
O42	A3	8f on 1½a	6.25	.60
O43	A10	10f on 2a	3.50	.20
O44	A10	15f on 3a	4.75	2.75
O45	A10	20f on 4a	4.75	2.75
O46	A10	25f on 4a	5.00	2.25
O47	A7	30f on 6a	5.25	2.00
O48	A10	40f on 8a	4.50	4.00
a.		"Flis" for "Fils"	300.00	450.00
O49	A11	50f on 1r	6.25	4.00
O50	A11	75f on 1r	7.00	7.00
O51	A1	100f on 2r	20.00	4.00
O52	A6	200f on 5r	26.00	26.00
O53	A7	½d on 10r	75.00	100.00
a.		Bar in "½" omitted	850.00	975.00
O54	A9	1d on 25r	140.00	210.00
		Nos. O39-O54 (16)	317.75	369.95

Regular Issue of 1932 Overprinted
Vertically like Nos. O26-O33

1932, May 9

O55	A12	2f ultramarine	1.00	.20
O56	A12	3f green	1.00	.20
O57	A12	4f violet brn	1.25	.20
O58	A12	5f gray	1.25	.20
O59	A12	8f deep red	1.25	.20
O60	A12	10f yellow	2.25	.20
O61	A12	15f deep blue	2.75	.20
O62	A12	20f orange	2.75	.20
O63	A12	25f rose lilac	2.75	.40
O64	A12	30f olive grn	4.00	.40
O65	A12	40f dark violet	5.75	.40

**Overprinted Horizontally Like Nos.
O34 to O37**

O66	A13	50f deep brown	3.75	.50
O67	A13	75f lt ultra	2.75	1.00
O68	A13	100f deep green	12.50	1.50
O69	A13	200f dark red	22.50	8.75

Overprinted Vertically like No. O38

O70	A14	½d gray blue	15.00	22.50
O71	A14	1d claret	70.00	100.00
		Nos. O55-O71 (17)	152.50	137.05

Regular Issue of 1934-38 Overprinted
Type "o" Vertically Reading up in Black

1934-38　　　　　　Unwmk.

O72	A15	1f purple ('38)	1.10	.50
O73	A15	2f ultramarine	1.10	.20
O74	A15	3f green	.65	.20
O75	A15	4f purple brn	1.10	.20
O76	A15	5f gray green	1.00	.20
O77	A15	8f deep red	4.50	.20
O78	A15	10f yellow	.45	.20
O79	A15	15f deep blue	10.00	1.50
O80	A15	20f orange	1.00	.20
O81	A15	25f brown violet	20.00	6.25
O82	A15	30f olive green	4.50	.20
O83	A15	40f dark violet	5.75	.40

Overprinted Type "p"

O84	A16	50f deep brown	1.00	.65
O85	A16	75f ultramarine	6.75	.90
O86	A16	100f deep green	1.75	1.00
O87	A16	200f dark red	4.50	2.75

**Overprinted Type "p" Vertically
Reading Up**

O88	A17	½d gray blue	11.00	18.00
O89	A17	1d claret	45.00	55.00
		Nos. O72-O89 (18)	121.15	88.55

Catalogue values for unused
stamps in this section, from this
point to the end of the section, are
for Never Hinged items.

Stamps of 1941-42 Overprinted in
Black or Red:

r　　　　　　　　s

**Perf. 11½x13½, 13 to 14 and
Compound**

1941-42

O90	A18(r)	1f dk vio ('42)	.50	.20
O91	A18(r)	2f choc ('42)	.50	.20
O92	A19(r)	3f brt grn ('42)	.50	.20
O93	A19(r)	4f pur (R) ('42)	.50	.20
O94	A19(r)	5f dk car rose ('42)	.50	.20
O95	A20(s)	8f carmine	1.75	.20
O96	A20(s)	8f ocher	.50	.20
O97	A20(s)	10f ocher	12.75	.85
O98	A20(s)	10f car ('42)	1.40	.20
O99	A20(s)	15f dull blue	12.75	1.50
O100	A20(s)	15f blk (R) ('42)	2.25	.65
O101	A20(s)	20f black (R)	3.75	.65
O102	A20(s)	20f dl bl ('42)	1.25	.20
O103	A21(s)	25f dark vio	1.75	.65
O104	A21(r)	25f dk vio ('42)	2.00	.65
O105	A21(s)	30f dp or- ange	1.75	.65
O106	A21(r)	30f dk org ('42)	1.75	.65
O107	A21(s)	40f brown org	1.10	.25
O108	A21(r)	40f chnt ('42)	1.75	.65
O109	A21(r)	50f ultra	3.25	.25
O110	A21(r)	75f rose vio	2.00	.85
O111	A22(s)	100f ol grn ('42)	4.50	.65
O112	A22(s)	200f dp org ('42)	6.00	1.75
O113	A23(r)	½d blue ('42)	20.00	20.00
O114	A23(r)	1d grnsh bl ('42)	32.50	29.00
		Nos. O90-O114 (25)	117.25	61.45

The space between the English and Arabic
on overprints "r" and "s" varies with the size of
the stamps.

For overprints see Nos. O165, RA5.

Stamps of 1942
Overprinted in Black

1942　Unwmk.　Perf. 13x13½

O115	A24	1f violet & brown	.65	.65
O116	A24	2f dark blue & brn	.65	.65
O117	A24	3f lt green & brn	.65	.65
O118	A24	4f lt brown & brn	.65	.65
O119	A24	5f sage green & brn	.85	.85
O120	A24	6f red orange & brn	.85	.85
O121	A24	10f dl rose red & brn	1.10	1.10
O122	A24	12f yel green & brn	1.50	1.50
		Nos. O115-O122 (8)	6.90	6.90

Stamps of 1948
Overprinted in Black

1948, Jan. 15   *Perf. 11½x12*
Size: 17¾x20½mm

O123	A25	1f slate	.20	.35
O124	A25	2f sepia	.20	.45
O125	A25	3f emerald	.20	.45
O126	A25	4f purple	.20	.35
O127	A25	5f rose lake	.20	.25
O128	A25	6f plum	.20	.45
O129	A25	8f ocher	.20	.45
O130	A25	10f rose red	.20	.35
O131	A25	12f dark olive	.20	.35
O132	A25	15f black	4.00	6.75
O133	A25	20f blue	.25	.20
O134	A25	25f rose violet	.25	.20
O135	A25	30f red orange	.25	.25
O136	A25	40f orange brn	.55	.45

Perf. 12x11½
Size: 22x27½mm

O137	A25	60f deep blue	.80	.25
O138	A25	75f lilac rose	1.40	.40
O139	A25	100f olive grn	1.40	1.00
O140	A25	200f dp orange	2.25	1.00
O141	A25	½d blue	19.00	16.00
O142	A25	1d green	27.50	35.00
	Nos. O123-O142 (20)		59.45	64.95

For overprints see Nos. O166-O177, O257, O272, O274, O277, O282, RA1, RA3, RA4.

Same Overprint on Nos. 133-138

1949-51   *Perf. 11½x12*
Size: 17¾x20½mm

O143	A25	3f rose lake ('51)	3.25	1.00
O144	A25	5f emerald ('51)	3.50	1.00
O145	A25	14f dk olive ('50)	1.75	.35
O146	A25	16f rose red ('51)	3.25	.35
O147	A25	28f blue ('51)	1.00	.35

Perf. 12x11½
Size: 22x27½mm

O148	A25	50f deep blue	1.25	.50
	Nos. O143-O148 (6)		14.00	3.55

For overprints see #O258, O273, O275, O276.

Same Overprint in Black on Stamps and Type of 1954-57

1955-59   *Perf. 11½x12*

O148A	A28	1f blue ('56)	.20	.20
O149	A28	2f chocolate	.20	.20
O150	A28	3f rose lake	.20	.20
O151	A28	4f violet	.25	.20
O152	A28	5f emerald	.25	.20
O153	A28	6f plum ('56)	.25	.20
O154	A28	8f ocher ('56)	.25	.20
O155	A28	10f blue	.25	.20
O155A	A28	16f brt rose ('57)	22.50	22.50
O156	A28	20f olive	.45	.25
O157	A28	25f rose violet	2.25	1.00
O158	A28	30f vermilion	1.00	.20
O159	A28	40f orange brn	.45	.20

Size: 22½x27½mm

O160	A28	50f blue	2.25	.75
O161	A28	60f pale purple	14.00	5.75
O161A	A28	100f ol grn ('59)	32.50	16.00
	Nos. O148A-O161A (16)		77.25	48.25

Dates of issue for Nos. O155A and O161A are suppositional.

For overprints see Nos. O178-O191, O259-O260, O283-O291.

Same Ovpt. on Stamps of 1957-58

1961

O162	A33	1f blue	4.25	1.75
O162A	A33	2f chocolate	5.00	3.75
O162B	A33	3f dk carmine	6.50	2.75
O162C	A33	4f dull violet	7.75	1.75
O162D	A33	5f emerald	4.25	1.75
O163	A33	6f plum	4.25	2.75
O164	A33	10f blue	4.25	1.40
	Nos. O162-O164 (7)		36.25	15.90

For overprints see #O192-O199, O292-O293.

Republic

Official Stamps of
1942-51 with
Additional Overprint

Perf. 13½x14
1958-59   Engr.   Unwmk.

O165	A22	200f dp orange	10.00	5.75

Perf. 11½x12, 12x11½

O166	A25	12f dk olive	1.00	.75
O167	A25	14f olive	1.10	.95
O168	A25	15f black	.95	.50
O169	A25	16f rose red	3.75	2.10
O170	A25	25f rose vio	3.50	2.00
O171	A25	28f blue	2.00	1.60
O172	A25	40f orange brn	1.25	.95
O173	A25	60f deep blue	5.00	2.50
O174	A25	75f lilac rose	2.25	1.90
O175	A25	200f dp orange	2.75	2.40
O176	A25	½d blue	17.00	6.25
O177	A25	1d green	27.50	12.50
	Nos. O166-O177 (12)		68.05	34.40

Other denominations of types A22 and A25 exist with this overprint, but these were probably not regularly issued.

Same Ovpt. on Nos. O148A-O161A

O178	A28	1f blue	.60	.20
O179	A28	2f chocolate	.60	.20
O180	A28	3f rose lake	.60	.20
O181	A28	4f violet	.60	.20
O181A	A28	5f emerald	.65	.40
O182	A28	6f plum	.60	.20
O183	A28	8f ocher	.55	.20
O183A	A28	10f blue	.80	.25
O184	A28	16f bright rose	7.50	7.00
O185	A28	20f olive	.65	.20
O186	A28	25f rose violet	.65	.20
O187	A28	30f vermilion	.70	.40
O188	A28	40f orange brn	1.00	.40
O189	A28	50f blue	1.00	.50
O190	A28	60f pale purple	1.00	.60
O191	A28	100f olive grn	2.10	.60
	Nos. O178-O191 (16)		19.60	11.75

Same Ovpts. on #O162-O164, 216

O192	A33	1f blue	.20	.20
O193	A33	2f chocolate	.20	.20
O194	A33	3f dark carmine	.45	.20
O195	A33	4f dull violet	.20	.20
O196	A33	5f emerald	.20	.20
O197	A33	6f plum	.20	.20
O198	A33	8f ocher	.65	.20
O199	A33	10f blue	.70	.20
	Nos. O192-O199 (8)		2.80	1.60

Nos. 232-233, 235-237, 242
Overprinted

Litho. & Photo.
1961, Apr. 1   Unwmk.   *Perf. 11½*

O200	A38	1f multi	.40	.30
O201	A38	2f multi	.40	.30
O202	A38	4f multi	.40	.30
O203	A38	5f multi	.50	.30
O204	A38	10f multi	.80	.60
O205	A38	50f multi	13.50	10.50
	Nos. O200-O205 (6)		16.00	12.30

Nos. 232-247
Overprinted

1961
Emblem in Gold, Red and Blue; Blue Inscriptions

O206	A38	1f gray	.40	.30
O207	A38	2f salmon	.40	.30
O208	A38	3f pale violet	.40	.30
O209	A38	4f bright yel	.40	.30
O210	A38	5f light blue	.40	.30
O211	A38	10f bright pink	.40	.30
O212	A38	15f lt green	.40	.30
O213	A38	20f bister brn	.40	.30
O214	A38	30f light gray	.50	.30
O215	A38	40f orange yel	.50	.30
O216	A38	50f yel green	.60	.30
O217	A38	75f pale green	.80	.40
O218	A38	100f orange	.90	.65
O219	A38	200f lilac	3.25	1.40
O220	A38	500f bister	11.50	5.50
O221	A38	1d brt green	22.50	11.50
	Nos. O206-O221 (16)		43.75	22.75

Nos. 480-482 Overprinted

1971   Litho.   *Perf. 13½*

O222	A115	10f multicolored	.80	1.50
O223	A115	15f blue & multi	8.00	1.50
O224	A115	25f multicolored	8.00	3.00
	Nos. O222-O224 (3)		16.80	6.00

Overprint lines are spaced 16mm on No. O222, 32½mm on Nos. O223-O224.

Same Overprint on Nos. 453, 455-456

1971   *Perf. 13*

O225	A107	5f lilac & multi	6.00	.30
O226	A107	15f rose red & multi	6.00	.50
O227	A107	25f vio bl & multi	8.50	1.50
	Nos. O225-O227 (3)		20.50	2.30

Overprint horizontal on Nos. O225 and O227; vertical, reading down on No. O226. Distance between English and Arabic words: 8mm.

Nos. 446, 448-449
Overprinted

1971   Litho.   *Perf. 13*

O228	A105	15f multicolored	1.50	.65
O229	A105	15f multi, wide ovpt. setting	62.50	7.50
a.		Narrow setting		47.50
O230	A105	25f multicolored	10.50	3.00
O231	A105	30f multicolored	10.50	3.00
	Nos. O228-O231 (4)		85.00	14.15

No. O229 overprinted "Official" horizontally. Two overprint settings on O229: wide, 6.5mm between English and Arab inscriptions; narrow, 2mm between inscriptions.

Same Overprint on Nos. 483-486

1972   *Perf. 13½*

O232	A116	10f multicolored	5.00	.50
O233	A116	25f multicolored	5.00	1.00

1972

O234	A117	15f multicolored	5.00	.50
O235	A117	25f multicolored	5.00	1.00

Same Overprint, "Official" Reading Down on Nos. 562-565

1972

O240	A142	5f multicolored	5.00	3.75
O241	A142	10f multicolored	5.00	3.75
O242	A142	15f multicolored	5.00	3.75
O243	A142	35f multicolored	5.00	3.75
	Nos. O240-O243 (4)		20.00	15.00

Latin inscription on Nos. O240-O241 obliterated with heavy bar.

No. 487 Overprinted "Official" like No. CO5

1972   Photo.   *Perf. 13½*

O244	A118	25f multicolored	10.50	3.00

#O134, O148 Ovptd. with 3 Bars
Perf. 11½x12, 12x11½

1973, Jan. 29   Engr.

O257	A25	25f rose violet	6.00	1.50
O258	A25	50f deep blue	6.00	5.50

Same on Nos. O157 and O160

O259	A28	25f rose violet	6.00	1.50
O260	A28	50f blue	6.00	1.50

Type of 1957
Overprinted

Size: 22x27½mm

O261	A33	50f rose violet	6.00	1.50
	Nos. O257-O261 (5)		30.00	11.50

See note after No. 679. No. O261 not issued without overprints.

King Faisal Issues
Overprinted

Two sizes of overprint: Arabic 6½mm or 9mm.

1973

O263	A28	15f black (#149)	4.00	3.75
O264	A33	15f black	4.00	1.00
O265	A25	25f rose vio (#121)	15.00	6.00
O266	A28	25f rose vio (#151)	4.00	1.00
O267	A33	15f black	4.00	1.00

Same Overprint on Nos. 674-677

O268	A33	10f blue	3.75	3.75
O269	A33	10f blue	52.50	60.00
O270	A33	15f black	67.50	75.00
O271	A33	15f black	2.50	2.00
	Nos. O263-O271 (9)		157.25	153.50

Official Stamps of 1948-51 Overprinted

Overprint design faces left or right.

1973

O272	A25	12f (#O131)	1.75	.30
O273	A25	14f (#O145)	1.75	.50
O274	A25	15f (#O132)	1.75	.50
O275	A25	16f (#O146)	3.25	.85
O276	A25	28f (#O147)	6.75	1.10
O277	A25	30f (#O135)	6.75	.95
O278	A25	40f (#O136)	6.75	1.40
O279	A25	60f (#O137)	6.75	5.25
O280	A25	100f (#O139)	22.50	8.50
O281	A25	½d (#O141)	57.50	22.50
O282	A25	1d (#O142)	110.00	110.00
	Nos. O272-O282 (11)		225.50	151.85

Same Overprint on Official Stamps of 1955-59

O283	A28	3f (#O150)	1.75	.60
O284	A28	6f (#O153)	1.75	.60
O285	A28	8f (#O154)	1.75	.60
O286	A28	16f (#O155A)	15.00	15.00
O287	A28	20f (#O156)	1.75	.60
O288	A28	30f (#O158)	1.75	.95
O289	A28	40f (#O159)	1.75	1.60
O290	A28	60f (#O161)	8.75	2.00
O291	A28	100f (#O161A)	27.50	8.00
	Nos. O283-O291 (9)		61.75	29.95

Same Overprint on 1957-58 Issues

O292	A33	3f dk car (#O162B)	5.00	1.25
O293	A33	6f plum (#O163)	5.00	1.25
O294	A33	8f ocher (#179)	5.00	1.25
O295	A33	30f red orange	5.00	5.00
	Nos. O292-O295 (4)		20.00	5.00

The overprint on Nos. O294-O295 includes the "On State Service" overprint; No. O295 was not issued without overprints. The overprint leaf design faces left or right and varies in size.

Nos. 403, 497, 681
Overprinted

Perf. 12½, 13x12½, 13½
1974 (?)   Photo., Litho.

O296	A89	2f multicolored	5.00	
O297	A123	15f multicolored	6.00	.50
O298	A185	25f multicolored	3.75	1.00
	Nos. O296-O298 (3)		14.75	

Size of "Official" on Nos. O297-O298 9mm.

Nos. 683-691
Overprinted

1974		Litho.	Perf. 13x12½	
O299	A186	5f orange & blk	.30	.30
O300	A186	10f bister & blk	.30	.30
O301	A186	20f brt rose & blk	.65	.30
O302	A186	25f ultra & blk	1.25	1.25
O303	A186	35f emerald & blk	1.25	.50
O304	A186	45f blue & black	1.25	.60
O305	A186	50f olive & yel	1.75	.65
O306	A186	70f violet & yel	1.75	.95
O307	A186	95f brown & yel	2.50	1.10
	Nos. O299-O307 (9)		11.00	5.95

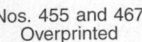

Nos. 455 and 467
Overprinted

1975		Litho.	Perf. 13, 14	
O308	A107	15f multicolored	3.50	3.50
O311	A110	30f multicolored	6.25	4.25

Space between Arabic and English lines of overprint is 4mm on No. O308, 13mm on No. O311.

Nos. 491-493 Overprinted or
Surcharged like Nos. CO5-CO7

1975			Perf. 14	
O312	A121	10f multicolored	6.50	4.00
O312A	A121	15f on 3f multi	6.50	4.00
O313	A121	25f on 2f multi	6.50	4.00
	Nos. O312-O313 (3)		19.50	12.00

Nos. 322-325
Overprinted

		Engr.; Engr. & Photo.		
1975			Perf. 12x11	
O314	A57	10f rose red	8.00	.60
O315	A57	15f brown & buff	8.00	.75
O316	A57	20f violet blue	8.00	.75
O317	A57	30f orange	15.00	.80
	Nos. O314-O317 (4)		39.00	2.90

Arms of
Iraq — O1

Altharthar -
Euphrates
Canal — O2

1975		Photo.	Perf. 14	
O318	O1	5f multicolored	.30	.30
O319	O1	10f blue & multi	.30	.30
O320	O1	15f yel & multi	.40	.40
O321	O1	20f ultra & multi	.65	.65
O322	O1	25f org & multi	.90	.90
O323	O1	30f rose & multi	1.00	1.00
O324	O1	50f multicolored	1.75	1.75
O325	O1	100f multicolored	3.25	3.25
	Nos. O318-O325 (8)		8.55	8.55

Nos. 787-791 Overprinted "OFFICIAL"
in English and Arabic

1976, Sept. 15		Litho.	Perf. 13½x14	
O327	A219	5f multicolored	1.25	.75
O328	A219	10f multicolored	1.25	.95
O329	A219	15f multicolored	1.40	.95
O330	A219	25f multicolored	3.75	1.25
O331	A219	50f multicolored	6.25	2.25
	Nos. O327-O331 (5)		13.90	6.15

1978		Photo.	Perf. 11½	
O332	O2	5f multicolored	.30	.30
O333	O2	10f multicolored	.30	.30
O334	O2	15f multicolored	.45	.30
O335	O2	25f multicolored	.90	.30
	Nos. O332-O335 (4)		1.95	1.20

Baghdad
University
Entrance — O3

1981, Oct. 21		Litho.	Perf. 12x12½	
O336	O3	45f multicolored	.65	.40
O337	O3	50f multicolored	.70	.50

Nos. O336-O337 Surcharged

1983, May 15		Litho.	Perf. 12x12½	
O338	O3	60f on 45f multi	2.50	.50
O339	O3	70f on 50f multi	3.00	.75

Martyrs Type of 1981

1981		Photo.	Perf. 14	
O339A	A303	45f silver border	1.25	.40
O339B	A303	50f gold border	1.25	.50
O339C	A303	120f metallic bl border	3.50	1.10
	Nos. O339A-O339C (3)		6.00	2.00

Building Type of 1983

1982, Dec. 31		Litho.	Perf. 14	
O340	A324	60f multicolored	.90	.50
O341	A324	70f multicolored	1.00	.65

For surcharge see No. 1517.

Martyr Type of 1984

1984, Dec. 1			Perf. 13½	
O342	A329	20f multicolored	.30	.30
O343	A329	30f multicolored	.30	.30
O344	A329	50f multicolored	.55	.40
O345	A329	60f multicolored	.70	.40
	Nos. O342-O345 (4)		1.85	1.40

No. RA22 Overprinted

1985 (?)		Litho.	Perf. 13x12½	
O346	PT2	5f bister, blk & yel	3.25	1.00

POSTAL TAX STAMPS

Catalogue values for unused stamps in this section are for Never Hinged items.

Nos. O125 and 115
Surcharged in Carmine
or Black

1949		Unwmk.	Perf. 11½x12	
RA1	A25	2f on 3f emer (C)	25.00	15.00
RA2	A25	2f on 6f plum	32.50	14.00

Similar Overprint in Carmine or Black
on Nos. O124, O127 and O94
Middle Arabic Line Omitted
Perf. 11½x12

RA3	A25	2f sepia (C)	20.00	9.00
RA4	A25	5f rose lake	40.00	20.00
		Perf. 12x13½, 14		
RA5	A19	5f dark car rose	20.00	10.50

Larger overprint on #RA5, 20½mm wide.
Value $22.50.

No. 115 Surcharged in
Black

Perf. 11½x12

RA6	A25	5f on 6f plum	45.00	17.00

The tax on Nos. RA1-RA6 was to aid the war in Palestine.

Nos. 317, 322-326 Surcharged

		Engr.; Engr. & Photo.		
1963			Perf. 12x11	
RA7	A57	5f on 1f green	3.75	4.50
RA8	A57	5f on 10f rose red	3.75	4.50
RA9	A57	5f on 15f brn & buff	3.75	4.50
RA10	A57	5f on 20f vio blue	3.75	4.50
RA11	A57	5f on 30f orange	3.75	4.50
RA12	A57	5f on 40f brt green	3.75	4.50
	Nos. RA7-RA12 (6)		22.50	27.00

Surtax was for the Defense Fund.

PT1   b

1967, Aug.		Photo.	Perf. 13½	
RA13	PT1	5f brown	.45	.20

Surtax was for flood victims.

Same Overprinted "b"

1967, Nov.				
RA14	PT1	5f brown	.45	.45

Surtax was for Defense Fund.

Nos. 305A-305B with Surcharge
Similar to Nos. RA7-RA12

1972		Litho.	Perf. 13½x14	
RA15	A54a	5f on 14f	7.00	7.00
RA16	A54a	5f on 35f	7.00	7.00

Surtax was for the Defense Fund. The 2 disks obliterating old denominations are on one line at the bottom. Size of Arabic inscription: 17x12mm.

No. 452 with Surcharge Similar to
Nos. RA7-RA12, and Nos. 443, 457
and 526 Surcharged:

1973		Litho.	Perf. 13	
RA17	A105	5f on 2f multi	8.50	8.50
RA18	A107	5f on 2f multi	8.50	8.50
RA19	A108	5f on 2f multi	8.50	8.50
RA20	A135	5f on 2f multi	8.50	8.50
	Nos. RA17-RA20 (4)		34.00	34.00

Surtax was for the Defense Fund. Surcharges on Nos. RA17-RA20 are adjusted to fit shape of stamps and to obliterate old denominations.

No 683 Overprinted

1974		Litho.	Perf. 13x12½	
RA21	A186	5f orange & blk	6.00	4.00

Soldier
PT2

Dome of the
Rock, Jerusalem
PT3

1974				
RA22	PT2	5f bister, blk & yel	2.50	3.00

Surtax of Nos. RA21-RA22 was for the Defense Fund.
For overprint see No. O346.

1977		Photo.	Perf. 14	
RA23	PT3	5f multicolored	2.75	1.50

Surtax was for families of Palestinians.
For surcharges see Nos. 1457, 1465-1477.

AIR POST POSTAL TAX STAMPS

Catalogue values for unused stamps in this section are for Never Hinged items.

#C15 Surcharged Like #RA17-RA20

1973		Litho.	Perf. 13½	
RAC1	AP5	5f on 2f multi	8.50	8.50

Surtax was for the Defense Fund.

1943, Nov. 13 Typo. Wmk. 262
126 A17 ½p deep green 1.00 1.50
127 A17 2½p dk red brown 2.50 1.25

Centenary of discovery of the mathematical formula of Quaternions by William Rowan Hamilton.

Brother Michael O'Clery — A18

1944, June 30 Perf. 14x15
128 A18 ½p emerald .35 .35
a. Booklet pane of 6 25.00
129 A18 1sh reddish brown 1.75 1.75

300th anniv. of the death of Michael O'Clery, Irish historian.

Edmund Rice — A19

Sower — A20

1944, Aug. 29 Perf. 15x14
130 A19 2½p slate 2.10 1.40

Death centenary of Edmund Ignatius Rice, founder of the Christian Brothers of Ireland.

1945, Sept. 15
131 A20 2½p ultramarine 2.00 .25
132 A20 6p red violet 13.00 8.75

Commemorates the work of the Young Irelanders and the death centenary of Thomas Davis, Sept. 16, 1845.

Plowman A21

1946, Sept. 16 Typo.
133 A21 2½p red 2.00 .25
134 A21 3p dark blue 7.50 6.75

Birth centenary of Charles Stewart Parnell and Michael Davitt, leaders in the struggle for Irish political independence.

Theobald Wolfe Tone A22

Perf. 15x14
1948, Nov. 19 Wmk. 262
135 A22 2½p deep plum 3.00 .25
136 A22 3p deep violet 11.00 9.50

Insurrection of 1798, 150th anniversary.

Types of 1922-23
1949
137 A1 8p bright red 3.00 1.50
138 A4 11p carmine rose 3.00 1.50

Leinster House, Dublin A23

1949, Nov. 21
139 A23 2½p red brown 2.50 .75
140 A23 3p violet blue 11.50 7.75

International recognition of the Republic, Easter Monday, 1949.

James Clarence Mangan A24

Statue of St. Peter A25

1949, Dec. 5
141 A24 1p dark green 4.75 1.40

Mangan (1803-1849), poet.

Wmk. 262
1950, Sept. 11 Engr. Perf. 12½
142 A25 2½p violet 2.00 .50
143 A25 3p blue 14.00 15.00
144 A25 9p brown 14.00 17.00
Nos. 142-144 (3) 30.00 32.50

Holy Year, 1950.

Thomas Moore — A26

Irish Harp — A27

1952, Nov. 10 Perf. 13
145 A26 2½p deep plum .25 .25
146 A26 3½p dk olive green 4.75 4.75

Death centenary of Thomas Moore (1779-1852), poet.

1953, Feb. 9 Typo. Perf. 14x15
147 A27 2½p bright green 2.50 .25
148 A27 1sh4p bright blue 35.00 32.50

Ireland's National festival "An Tostal."

Robert Emmet — A28

Madonna by della Robbia — A29

1953, Sept. 21 Engr. Perf. 12½x13
149 A28 3p deep green 5.00 .35
150 A28 1sh3p carmine rose 70.00 26.00

150th anniv. of the execution of Robert Emmet (1778-1803), Irish nationalist.

1954, May 24 Perf. 15
151 A29 3p blue 1.50 .25
152 A29 5p deep green 11.00 7.75

Marian Year, 1953-54.

John Henry Cardinal Newman A30

Statue of John Barry A31

1954, July 19 Typo. Perf. 15x14
153 A30 2p rose lilac 3.75 .25
154 A30 1sh3p blue 24.00 9.00

Opening of the Catholic University of Ireland, centenary.

1956, Sept. 16 Engr. Perf. 15
155 A31 3p dull purple 1.25 .25
156 A31 1sh3p blue 18.00 12.00

John Barry (1745-1803), "Father of the American Navy," on the occasion of the unveiling of a statue in Wexford, Ireland, his birthplace.

Redmond A32

O'Crohan A33

Perf. 14x15
1957, June 11 Wmk. 262
157 A32 3p dark blue 2.50 .25
158 A32 1sh3p rose lake 22.50 17.50

Birth cent. of John Edward Redmond (1856-1918), Irish political leader.

1957, July 1
159 A33 2p dull purple 2.50 .25
160 A33 5p violet 9.50 8.00

Birth cent. of Thomas O'Crohan (Tomas O'Criomhthain) (1856-1937), fisherman and author.

Brown A34

Father Luke Wadding A35

1957, Sept. 23 Typo. Perf. 15x14
161 A34 3p blue 5.00 .75
162 A34 1sh3p carmine rose 60.00 30.00

Adm. William (Guillermo) Brown (1777-1857), founder of the Argentine Navy.

1957, Nov. 25 Engr. Perf. 15
163 A35 3p dark blue 2.50 .70
164 A35 1sh3p deep claret 27.50 12.50

Luke Wadding (1588-1657), Irish Franciscan friar and historian.

Clarke A36

Aikenhead A37

1958, July 28 Wmk. 262
165 A36 3p deep green 1.40 .25
166 A36 1sh3p red brown 24.00 13.50

Thomas J. Clarke (1858-1916), patriot.

1958, Oct. 20 Perf. 15x14
167 A37 3p blue 2.00 .25
168 A37 1sh3p carmine 26.00 15.00

Mother Mary Aikenhead (1787-1858), founder of the Irish Sisters of Charity.

Constitution Type of 1937
1958, Dec. 29 Typo. Wmk. 262
169 A12 3p brown 1.10 .25
170 A12 5p bright green 8.00 6.50

21st anniv. of the constitution.

Arthur Guinness — A38

1959, July 20 Engr. Perf. 15
171 A38 3p rose lake 3.50 .25
172 A38 1sh3p dark blue 26.00 10.00

Bicentenary of Guinness Brewery.

Flight of the Holy Family A39

1960, June 20 Perf. 15
173 A39 3p rose violet .35 .25
174 A39 1sh3p sepia 1.40 2.50

World Refugee Year, 7/1/59-6/30/60.

Europa Issue

Symbolic Wheel CD3

1960, Sept. 19 Engr. Perf. 15
175 CD3 6p orange brown 30.00 2.00
176 CD3 1sh3p violet 70.00 12.00

No. 176 has fugitive ink.

De Havilland Dragon, Boeing 707 Jet and Dublin Airport A41

1961, June 26 Perf. 15
177 A41 6p dull blue 2.75 2.50
178 A41 1sh3p green 7.00 4.50

25th anniv. of the founding of Aer Lingus, Irish International Airlines.

St. Patrick — A42

1961, Sept. 25 Perf. 14½
179 A42 3p blue .80 .25
180 A42 8p pale purple 2.25 6.00
181 A42 1sh3p green 2.50 1.60
Nos. 179-181 (3) 5.55 7.85

1,500th anniv. of St. Patrick's death.

John O'Donovan and Eugene O'Curry A43

1962, Mar. 26 Perf. 15
182 A43 3p crimson .55 .25
183 A43 1sh3p purple 6.50 5.50

Death centenaries of John O'Donovan (1806-1861) and Eugene O'Curry (1794-1862), Gaelic scholars and translators.

Europa Issue

19 Leaves
on Young
Tree
CD5

1962, Sept. 17   Engr.   Wmk. 262

184	CD5	6p pink & dark red	.85	.60
185	CD5	1sh3p bluish grn & dk blue grn	2.00	1.25

Wheat
Emblem
and Globe
A45

1963, Mar. 21   Wmk. 262

186	A45	4p violet	.70	.25
187	A45	1sh3p red	4.25	4.25

FAO "Freedom from Hunger" campaign.

Europa Issue

Stylized
Links,
Symbolizing
Unity
CD6

1963, Sept. 16   Perf. 15

188	CD6	6p rose carmine	1.75	1.25
189	CD6	1sh3p dark blue	3.50	2.00

Centenary
Emblem
A47

1963, Dec. 2   Photo.   Perf. 14½x14

190	A47	4p gray & red	.60	.25
191	A47	1sh3p brt green, gray & red	1.60	2.75

Centenary of the International Red Cross.

Wolfe Tone
A48

1964, Apr. 13   Engr.   Perf. 15

192	A48	4p black	1.00	.25
193	A48	1sh3p dark blue	7.00	7.50

Birth bicentenary of Theobald Wolfe Tone (1763-1798), Irish revolutionist.

Irish
Pavilion
A49

1964, July 20   Photo.   Perf. 14½x14

194	A49	5p multicolored	1.50	.25
a.		Brown omitted	5,500.	
195	A49	1sh5p multicolored	7.50	7.50

New York World's Fair, 1964-65.

Europa Issue

CEPT Daisy (22
Petals) — CD7

Perf. 14x14½

1964, Sept. 14   Litho.   Wmk. 262

196	CD7	8p dull grn & ultra	4.50	1.25
197	CD7	1sh5p red brown & org	20.00	3.00

ITU Emblem, Globe and
Communication Waves — A51

1965, May 17   Photo.   Perf. 14½x14

198	A51	3p dp blue & emerald	1.00	.25
199	A51	8p black & emerald	5.00	5.75

ITU, cent.

William Butler
Yeats — A52

1965, June 14   Perf. 15

200	A52	5p orange brn & blk	.75	.30
201	A52	1sh5p gray green, brn & black	7.25	5.75

Birth centenary of William Butler Yeats (1865-1939), poet and dramatist.

ICY
Emblem
A53

1965, Aug. 16   Photo.   Perf. 15

202	A53	3p brt blue & vio bl	1.50	.70
203	A53	10p redsh brn & dk brn	6.50	7.25

International Cooperation Year.

Europa Issue

Leaves and
Fruit — CD8

1965, Sept. 27   Perf. 15

204	CD8	8p brick red & blk	7.50	.60
205	CD8	1sh5p lt blue & claret	18.50	2.75

James
Connolly
A55

Designs: No. 207, Thomas J. Clarke. No. 208, Patrick Henry Pearse. No. 209, Symbolic of lives lost in fight for independence, and of Ireland marching into freedom. No. 210, Eamonn Ceannt. No. 211, Sean MacDiarmada. No. 212, Thomas MacDonagh. No. 213, Joseph Plunkett.

1966, Apr. 12   Wmk. 262   Perf. 15

206	A55	3p blue & black	1.60	.55
207	A55	3p olive green	1.60	.55
a.		Pair, #206-207	4.50	2.25
208	A55	5p olive & black	2.00	.55
209	A55	5p brt grn, blk & orange	2.00	.55
a.		Pair, #208-209	5.00	2.50
210	A55	7p dull org & blk	2.00	4.00
211	A55	7p blue grn & blk	2.00	4.00
a.		Pair, #210-211	5.75	12.00
212	A55	1sh5p grnsh bl & blk	2.00	3.50
213	A55	1sh5p emerald & blk	2.00	3.50
a.		Pair, #212-213	8.00	8.00
		Nos. 206-213 (8)	15.20	17.20

50th anniv. of the Easter Week Rebellion, and to honor the signers of the Proclamation of the Irish Republic.

Roger
Casement
A56

Symbolic
Sailboat
CD9

1966, Aug. 3   Perf. 15

214	A56	5p black	.40	.40
215	A56	1sh dark red brown	2.40	1.75

50th death anniv. of Roger Casement (1864-1916), British consular agent and Irish rebel who was executed for treason.

Europa Issue

1966, Sept. 26   Photo.   Perf. 15

216	CD9	7p orange & green	2.25	.40
217	CD9	1sh5p gray & green	5.75	1.60

Ballintubber
Abbey
A58

1966, Nov. 8   Perf. 15

218	A58	5p red brown	.60	.60
219	A58	1sh black	1.50	1.50

750th anniversary of Ballintubber Abbey.

Cross and Sword Types of 1922

1966-67   Photo.   Perf. 15
Size: 17x20½mm

225	A4	3p blue ('67)	1.75	1.50
226	A1	5p brt vio, type II ('68)	2.00	1.50
a.		Booklet pane of 6, No. 226b	62.50	
b.		Type I ('66)	10.00	10.00

Type I has irregularly spaced lines in shading behind sword.

Europa Issue

Cogwheels — CD10

1967, May 2

232	CD10	7p green & gold	3.00	.80
233	CD10	1sh5p dk red & gold	6.75	1.75

Maple
Leaves
A60

1967, Aug. 28   Photo.

234	A60	5p multicolored	.40	.40
235	A60	1sh5p multicolored	1.50	1.50

Centenary of the Canadian Confederation.

Rock of
Cashel
A61

1967, Sept. 25   Wmk. 262   Perf. 15

236	A61	7p sepia	.40	.40
237	A61	10p Prussian blue	1.50	1.50

International Tourist Year.

One Cent
Fenian
Fantasy — A62

Swift's Bust
and St.
Patrick's
Cathedral,
Dublin — A63

Design: 1sh, 24c Fenian fantasy.

1967, Oct. 23   Photo.   Perf. 15

238	A62	5p lt green & slate grn	.80	.40
239	A62	1sh pale pink & gray	1.90	1.50

Fenian Rising, centenary. The Fenian fantasy was created by S. Allan Taylor.

1967, Nov. 30   Perf. 15

Design: 1sh5p, Gulliver, Lilliputian army.

240	A63	3p gray & sepia	.40	.40
241	A63	1sh5p lt blue & sepia	1.50	1.50

Birth tercentenary of Jonathan Swift (1667-1745), author of Gulliver's Travels.

Europa Issue

Golden Key
with CEPT
Emblem
CD11

1968, Apr. 29   Photo.   Wmk. 262

242	CD11	7p multicolored	1.60	1.10
243	CD11	1sh5p multicolored	4.50	2.00

St. Mary's
Cathedral,
Limerick
A65

1968, Aug. 26   Engr.   Perf. 15

244	A65	5p dull blue	.40	.75
245	A65	10p olive	1.50	3.00

800th anniv. of the founding of St. Mary's Cathedral by Donal Mor O'Brien, last King of Munster.

Countess
Markievicz
A66

1968, Sept. 23   Photo.   Wmk. 262

246	A66	3p black	.80	.40
247	A66	1sh5p dark blue	1.90	1.50

Birth centenary of Countess Constance Markievicz (1868-1927), champion of Irish Independence and first Minister of Labor.

James
Connolly — A67

1968, Sept. 23   Perf. 15

248	A67	6p brown, dk brn & blk	1.20	1.00
249	A67	1sh dull grn, grn & blk	1.75	1.00

Birth centenary of James Connolly (1868-1916), founder of the Irish Socialist Party, editor of "Workers' Republic" and Commander of the Irish Citizen Army.

Dog from Ancient Brooch, County Kilkenny — A68

Winged Ox from Lichfield Gospel Book A69

Designs: ½p, 1p, 2p, 3p, 4p, 5p, 6p, Dog. 7p, 8p, 9p, 10p, 1sh, 1sh9p, Stag from ancient bowl, Kent. 2sh6p, 5sh, Winged ox. 10sh, Eagle, from ancient manuscript.

1968-70   Photo.   Wmk. 262   Perf. 15

250	A68	½p orange	.30	.50
251	A68	1p yellow green	.30	.50
252	A68	2p ocher	.30	.50
253	A68	3p bright blue	.30	.50
254	A68	4p dark red	.45	.50
255	A68	5p deep green	.50	1.25
256	A68	6p brown	.45	.50
a.		Booklet pane of 6 ('70)	35.00	
257	A68	7p yel & brown	1.10	3.25
258	A68	8p red org & blk	1.10	3.00
259	A68	9p ol grn & dk bl	1.10	1.50
260	A68	10p violet & dk brn	1.25	3.00
261	A68	1sh dk red brn & brown	1.00	2.25
262	A68	1sh9p grnsh bl & dk brown	1.00	3.00
263	A69	2sh6p red org, bl, ol & dull yel	5.75	3.00
264	A69	5sh ol, gray, bis & yel	6.75	1.40
265	A69	10sh dk red brn, yel & dp org	14.00	2.50
		Nos. 250-265 (16)	35.65	27.15

Issued: 2p, 8p, 2sh6p, 10sh, 10/14/68; 6p, 9p, 1sh9p, 5sh, 2/24/69; 4p, 5p, 10p, 1sh, 3/31/69; ½p, 1p, 3p, 7p, 6/9/69.
See Nos. 290-304, 343-359, 395-402, 466-475.

Coil Stamps

1970   Perf. 14x15

251a	A68	1p yellow green	2.25	4.25
252a	A68	2p ocher	2.25	4.25
253a	A68	3p bright blue	2.25	4.25
		Nos. 251a-253a (3)	6.75	12.75

Human Rights Flame — A70

1968, Nov. 4   Wmk. 262   Perf. 15

266	A70	5p black, ocher & gold	.70	.70
267	A70	7p crim, ocher & gold	1.25	1.25

International Human Rights Year.

First Meeting of Irish Parliament A71

1969, Jan. 21   Perf. 15x14½

268	A71	6p dark slate green	.70	.70
269	A71	9p dark blue gray	1.25	1.25

50th anniv. of the first meeting of the Dail Eireann at the Mansion House, Dublin, Jan. 21, 1919.

"EUROPA" and "CEPT" CD12

1969, Apr. 28   Photo.   Perf. 15

270	CD12	9p ultra, gray & ocher	3.00	.75
271	CD12	1sh9p car, gray & gold	5.00	1.25

Europa and CEPT, 10th anniv.

ILO Emblem — A73

1969, July 14   Perf. 15

272	A73	6p gray & black	.50	.50
273	A73	9p yellow & black	1.50	1.50

ILO, 50th anniv.

Last Supper and Crucifixion, by Evie Hone A74

Perf. 15x14½

1969, Sept. 1   Photo.   Wmk. 262

274	A74	1sh multicolored	2.00	4.00

The design is after a stained-glass window by Evie Hone (1894-1955) in the Eton College Chapel.

Mahatma Gandhi A75

1969, Oct. 2   Perf. 15

275	A75	6p dk yel grn & blk	.75	.75
276	A75	1sh9p yel, grn & black	2.25	2.25

Mohandas K. Gandhi (1869-1948), leader in India's fight for independence.

Stylized Bird, Tree and Shamrock A76

1970, Feb. 23   Perf. 15

277	A76	6p olive bister & black	.40	.65
278	A76	9p violet & black	1.60	2.10

Nature Conservation Year.

Europa Issue

Interwoven Threads CD13

1970, May 4   Photo.   Perf. 15

279	CD13	6p purple & silver	3.00	.30
280	CD13	9p yel brn & silver	4.50	1.25
281	CD13	1sh9p dk gray & sil	7.00	1.75
		Nos. 279-281 (3)	14.50	3.30

Sailing Boats, by Peter Monamy (1670-1749) A78

1970, July 13   Perf. 15

282	A78	4p gold & multi	1.40	1.40

250th anniv. of the Royal Cork Yacht Club.

Madonna of Eire, by Mainie Jellett (1896-1943) A79

Tomás MacCurtain A80

1970, Sept. 1   Photo.   Perf. 15

283	A79	1sh violet blue & multi	2.00	2.00

1970, Oct. 26   Perf. 15

Nos. 285, 287, Terence MacSwiney.

284	A80	9p violet & black	1.90	1.40
285	A80	9p violet & black	1.90	1.40
a.		Pair, #284-285	6.50	6.75
286	A80	2sh9p brt blue & blk	5.00	4.00
287	A80	2sh9p brt blue & blk	5.00	4.00
a.		Pair, #286-287	13.50	18.00

50th anniv. of the deaths of Tomás Mac-Curtain (1884-1920) and Terence MacSwiney (1879-1920), lord mayors of Cork, who died during the Irish war of independence.

Kevin Barry A81

1970, Nov. 2

288	A81	6p olive green	.75	.40
289	A81	1sh2p violet blue	2.00	1.60

50th anniv. of the death of Kevin Barry (1902-1920), who was hanged during the Irish war of independence.

Decimal Currency Issue
Types of 1968-69 (Numerals only)

Designs: ½p, 1p, 1½p, 2p, 2½p, 3p, 3½p, 4p, No. 298A, Dog. 5p, 6p, 7p, 7½p, 9p, Stag. 10p, 12p, 20p, Winged ox. 50p, Eagle.

Two types of 10p:
I — Ox outlined in lilac
II — Outlined in brown

1971-75   Wmk. 262   Photo.   Perf. 15

290	A68	½p yellow green	.30	.25
a.		Booklet pane of 6	40.00	
291	A68	1p bright blue	1.25	.60
a.		Booklet pane of 6	5.75	
c.		Bklt. pane of 5 + label ('74)	1.75	
292	A68	1½p brown red	.35	.35
293	A68	2p dark green	.50	.50
b.		Booklet pane of 5 + label ('75)	1.75	
294	A68	2½p sepia	.60	.60
a.		Booklet pane of 6	15.00	
295	A68	3p yel orange	.50	.50
296	A68	3½p deep orange	.60	.60
297	A68	4p violet	.40	.40
298	A68	5p ap grn & brn	1.75	1.25
298A	A68	5p apple grn ('74)	2.75	1.25
c.		Booklet pane of 6 ('74)	12.00	
d.		Bklt. pane of 5 + label ('74)	2.50	
299	A68	6p blue gray & dk brown	1.75	1.10
299A	A68	7p ol green & ind ('74)	4.75	4.75
300	A68	7½p rose vio & dk brown	.80	1.10
301	A68	9p bl grn & blk	2.50	1.25
302	A68	10p lil & multi (I)	21.00	1.25
b.		Type II	27.50	9.00
302A	A69	12p multi ('74)	1.50	1.75
303	A69	20p slate & multi	5.00	1.25
304	A69	50p rose brn & multi	14.50	1.75
		Nos. 290-304 (18)	60.80	20.50

Booklet panes have watermark sideways.

Issued: No. 298A, 7p, 12p, 1/29/74; others, 2/15/71.
See Nos. 343-359, 395-402, 466-475.

Coil Stamps

1971-74   Perf. 14x15

291b	A68	1p bright blue	.90	.50
292a	A68	1½p brown red	.25	.50
293a	A68	2p dark green ('72)	.30	.40
294b	A68	2½p sepia	.30	.75
c.		Strip of 3 (1p, 1½p, 2½p)	2.50	1.50
297a	A68	4p violet ('72)	1.25	1.00
b.		Strip of 4 (1½p, 2p, 2½p, 4p) ('72)	2.50	2.00
298b	A68	5p apple green ('74)	1.25	1.00
e.		Strip of 4 (2x1½p, 2p, 5p) ('74)	2.50	2.00

Europa Issue, 1971 — CD14

Common Design Type

1971, May 3   Wmk. 262   Perf. 15

305	CD14	4p apple green & blk	1.50	.20
306	CD14	6p blue & black	4.00	1.25

John M. Synge — A82

An Island Man, by Jack B. Yeats — A83

1971, July 19   Photo.   Perf. 15

307	A82	4p gray, black & gold	.30	.30
308	A82	10p org, black & gold	1.25	1.25

Birth cent. of John Millington Synge (1871-1909), poet and dramatist.

1971, Aug. 30   Perf. 15

309	A83	6p multicolored	1.10	1.10

Jack Butler Yeats (1871-1957), painter.

Racial Equality Emblem A84

Madonna, by John Hughes, Loughrea Cathedral A85

Perf. 14x14½

1971, Oct. 18   Litho.   Unwmk.

310	A84	4p red	.20	.20
311	A84	10p black	.80	.80

Intl. Year Against Racial Discrimination.

1971, Nov. 15   Photo.   Perf. 15

312	A85	2½p dp bl grn, gold & slate	.25	.25
313	A85	6p ultra, gold & slate	1.25	1.25

Christmas.

"Your Heart is your Health" A86

1972, Apr. 7   Photo.   Wmk. 262

314	A86	2½p gold & brown	.35	.35
315	A86	12p silver & black	3.75	3.25

World Health Day.

Europa Issue

Sparkles, Symbolic of Communications — CD15

1972, May 1 *Perf. 15*
316 CD15 4p red, black & sil   4.50 .50
317 CD15 6p blue, black & sil   12.50 4.00

Dove Soaring Past Rising Moon — A88

1972, June 1 *Photo.*
318 A88 4p gray blue, org & dk bl   .40 .25
319 A88 6p olive, yel & dk green   1.10 .75

The patriot dead of 1922-23.

Black Lake, by Gerard Dillon A89

1972, July 10 *Perf. 15*
320 A89 3p indigo & multi   .75 .75

Rider from Clonmacnoise Slab and Olympic Rings — A90

1972, Aug. 28 *Photo. Wmk. 262*
321 A90 3p yellow, black & gold   .40 .40
322 A90 6p salmon, black & gold   1.10 1.10

20th Olympic Games, Munich, Aug. 26-Sept. 11, and 50th anniversary of the Olympic Council of Ireland.

Madonna and Child — A91   Ireland No. 68 — A92

1972, Oct. 16 *Unwmk. Perf. 15*
323 A91 2½p dk green & multi   .40 .25
324 A91 4p tan & multi   .85 .35
325 A91 12p multicolored   2.50 1.10
   Nos. 323-325 (3)   3.75 1.70

Christmas. The design is after a miniature in the Book of Kells, 9th century.

1972, Dec. 6 *Photo.*
326 A92 6p blue gray & dp grn   1.00 1.50
   a.   Souvenir sheet of 4   13.50 16.00

50th anniv. of 1st Irish postage stamp.

Recurrent Celtic Head Motif — A93

1973, Jan. 1 *Unwmk.*
327 A93 6p orange & multi   .50 .60
328 A93 12p green & multi   2.25 2.10

Ireland's entry into the European Community.

Europa Issue

Post Horn of Arrows CD16

1973, Apr. 30
329 CD16 4p bright ultra   1.50 .20
330 CD16 6p black   5.00 1.75

"Berlin Blues I," by William Scott A95

Perf. 15x14½
1973, Aug. 9 *Photo. Unwmk.*
331 A95 5p lt blue, blue & dk brn   .70 .55

Weather Map of Northwest Europe — A96

1973, Sept. 4 *Perf. 14½x15*
332 A96 3½p ultra & multi   .50 .25
333 A96 12p lilac & multi   2.50 1.60

Intl. meteorological cooperation, cent.

Tractor Plowing and Birds A97

1973, Oct. 5 *Perf. 15x14½*
334 A97 5p emerald & multi   .35 .35
335 A97 7p emerald & multi   1.90 1.10

World Plowing Championships, Wellington Bridge, County Wexford, Oct. 1-7.

Flight into Egypt, by Jan de Cock — A98

1973, Nov. 1 *Perf. 15*
336 A98 3½p black & multi   .25 .20
337 A98 12p gold & multi   2.00 1.40

Christmas.

Rescue, by Bernard Gribble A99

Design: Ballycotton lifeboat rescuing crew of Daunt Rock Lightship, 1936.

1974, Mar. 28 *Photo. Wmk. 262*
338 A99 5p multicolored   .70 .55

Sesquicentennial of the founding of the Royal National Lifeboat Institution.

Edmund Burke, by John Henry Foley — A100

Oliver Goldsmith, by John Henry Foley — A101

Europa Issue
Perf. 14½x15
1974, Apr. 29 *Unwmk.*
339 A100 5p lt ultra & black   2.00 .20
340 A100 7p lt green & black   11.00 1.25

1974, June 24 *Photo.*
341 A101 3½p brt citron & blk   .30 .25
342 A101 12p emerald & black   3.50 2.00

Oliver Goldsmith (1728-1774), writer.

Types of 1968-69

½p, 1p, 2p, 3p, 3½p, 5p, Nos. 350, 352, Dog. Nos. 349, 351, 8p, 9p, Stag. 10p, 15p, 20p, Winged ox. 50p, £1, Eagle.
Two types of 50p: I, fine screen. II, coarse screen.

			Perf. 15	
1974-78		**Unwmk.**		
343	A68	½p yel green ('78)	.25	.25
344	A68	1p brt blue ('75)	.25	.25
345	A68	2p dark green ('76)	.25	.25
346	A68	3p ocher ('75)	.25	.25
347	A68	3½p deep orange	4.75	4.75
348	A68	5p apple green	.60	.25
349	A68	6p bl gray & dk brn	2.25	2.50
350	A68	6p blue gray ('75)	.50	.45
351	A68	7p lt ol grn & indigo	3.25	3.25
352	A68	7p olive green ('75)	.70	.70
a.		Bklt. pane of 5 + label ('77)	14.00	16.00
353	A68	8p brown & dk brn ('75)	1.40	1.25
354	A68	9p lt bl grn & black ('75)	2.10	.70
355	A69	10p lil & multi ('75)	3.25	1.00
356	A69	15p multi ('75)	2.50	1.40
357	A69	20p slate & multi	1.60	.40
358	A69	50p rose brown & multi, type I ('74)	2.00	.70
a.		Type II ('83)	3.25	3.25
359	A69	£1 multi ('75)	4.75	1.75
		Nos. 343-359 (17)	30.65	20.10

Coil Stamps

			Perf. 14x15	
1977, Mar. 21				
344b	A68	1p bright blue	.75	.85
345b	A68	2p dark green	.50	.60
348b	A68	5p apple green	1.25	1.50
c.		Strip of 4 (1p, 2x2p, 5p)	2.50	2.75

Kitchen Table, by Norah McGuinness A102

1974, Aug. 19 *Photo. Perf. 14x15*
360 A102 5p multicolored   1.00 1.00

Rugby A103

1974, Sept. 2 *Engr. Perf. 15x14*
361 A103 3½p slate green   1.00 1.00
   a.   3½p deep slate green   12.00 12.00
362 A103 12p multicolored   4.00 4.00

Centenary of Irish Rugby Union. No. 361a was printed from a reengraved plate with more deeply engraved lines. The original printing (No. 361) was considered to be of unsatisfactory quality.

UPU "Postmark" A104

Virgin and Child, by Bellini — A105

1974, Oct. 9 *Photo. Perf. 14½x15*
363 A104 5p emerald & black   .40 .30
364 A104 7p ultra & black   1.10 1.10

Centenary of Universal Postal Union.

1974, Nov. 14
365 A105 5p multicolored   .75 .30
366 A105 15p multicolored   2.50 2.75

Christmas.

"Peace" — A106

1975, Mar. 25 *Photo. Perf. 14½x15*
367 A106 8p dp rose lil & ultra   .50 .30
368 A106 15p ultra & emerald   2.50 2.25

International Women's Year.

Europa Issue

Castletown Hunt (detail), by Robert Healy A107

1975, Apr. 28 Photo. Perf. 15x14½
369 A107 7p black   4.00 .25
370 A107 9p green   9.50 2.00

Chipping from the Fringe A108

1975, June 26 Photo. Perf. 15x14½
371 A108 6p shown   .75 .30
372 A108 9p Putting   3.25 1.60

9th European Amateur Golf Team Championships, Killarney.

Bird of Prey, by Oisín Kelly A109

1975, July 28
373 A109 15p ocher   .90 1.10

Nano Nagle and Pupils, Engraving by Charles Turner — A110

Clock Tower, St. Ann's Church, Shandon — A111

1975, Sept. 1 Photo. Perf. 14½x15
374 A110 5p light blue & black   .25 .25
375 A110 7p buff & black   1.10 1.10

Presentation Order of Nuns, bicentenary.

1975, Oct. 6 Photo. Perf. 12½
Designs: 7p, 9p, Holycross Abbey.
376 A111 5p multicolored   .35 .25
377 A111 6p ultra & multi   .60 1.25
378 A111 7p sapphire   .85 .35
379 A111 9p multicolored   1.25 1.25
    Nos. 376-379 (4)   3.05 3.10

European Architectural Heritage Year.

St. Oliver Plunkett, by Imogen Stuart — A112

Madonna and Child, by Fra Filippo Lippi — A113

1975, Oct. 13 Engr. Perf. 14x14½
380 A112 7p black   .35 .25
381 A112 15p dull red   1.40 1.60

Canonization of Oliver Plunkett (1625-1681), Primate of Ireland.

1975, Nov. 13 Photo. Perf. 15
382 A113 5p multicolored   .40 .30
383 A113 7p multicolored   1.00 .30
384 A113 10p gold & multi   2.00 1.25
    Nos. 382-384 (3)   3.40 1.85

Christmas.

James Larkin — A114

Bell Making First Call — A115

1976 Jan. 21 Photo. Perf. 14½x15
385 A114 7p gray & slate grn   .25 .25
386 A114 11p ocher & brown   1.50 1.25

James Larkin (1876-1947), trade union leader.

1976, Mar. 10 Photo. Perf. 14½x15
387 A115 9p multicolored   .35 .35
388 A115 15p multicolored   1.90 1.40

Centenary of first telephone call by Alexander Graham Bell, March 10, 1876.

13 Stars and Stripes A116

Designs: 8p, 50 stars, and stripes. 9p, 15p, Benjamin Franklin on Albany essay of 1847.

1976, May 17 Litho. Perf. 15x14
389 A116 7p ultra, sil & red   .35 .20
  a. Silver (inscription) omitted 2,000. 1,200.
390 A116 8p ultra, sil & red   .55 .80
  a. Silver (inscription) omitted 2,000. 1,200.
391 A116 9p bl, sil & ocher   1.00 .40
  a. Silver (inscription) omitted 2,000. 1,200.
392 A116 15p red, sil & bl   1.10 .80
  a. Silver (inscription) omitted 950.00 1,200.
  b. Souvenir sheet of 4, #389-392 10.00 12.00
    Nos. 389-392 (4)   3.00 2.20

American Bicentennial. No. 392b exists with silver omitted.

Irish Delft Spirit Barrel — A117

Europa: 11p, Bowl, Irish Delft. Designs show mark of Henry Delamain's Factory, Dublin, both pieces c. 1756.

1976, July 1 Photo. Perf. 15x14½
393 A117 9p gray & magenta   2.50 .25
394 A117 11p gray & blue   5.00 1.00

Types of 1968
Designs: 8p, 9p, 9½p, No. 399, Dog. No. 398, 11p, 12p, Stag. 17p, Winged ox.

1976-79 Photo. Unwmk. Perf. 15
395 A68 8p brown   .50 .25
396 A68 9p blue green   .60 .25
397 A68 9½p red ('79)   .75 .25
398 A68 10p lilac & black   2.25 .60
399 A68 10p purple ('77)   .60 .25
400 A68 11p carmine & black   1.10 .60
401 A68 12p emer & black ('77) 1.25 .25
402 A69 17p ol, bl & ocher ('77) 2.00 .90
    Nos. 395-402 (8)   9.05 3.35

The Lobster Pots, by Paul Henry A118

1976, Aug. 30 Photo. Perf. 15
405 A118 15p gold & multi   1.40 1.00

Paul Henry (1876-1958), birth centenary.

Radio Waves A119

Radio Tower and Waves, Globe — A120

Perf. 14½x14, 14x14½
1976, Oct. 5   Litho.
406 A119 9p brt blue & black   .25 .25
407 A120 11p black & multi   1.40 1.60

Irish broadcasting, 50th anniversary.

Nativity, by Lorenzo Monaco A121

1976, Nov. 11   Perf. 15x14½
408 A121 7p multicolored   .30 .25
409 A121 9p multicolored   .60 .30
410 A121 15p multicolored   1.25 1.00
    Nos. 408-410 (3)   2.15 1.55

Christmas.

Irish Manuscript, 16th Century A122

Stone from Newgrange Burial Mound A123

1977, May 9 Photo. Perf. 15x14½
411 A122 8p multicolored   .35 .35
412 A123 10p multicolored   .75 .70

Centenaries of National Library (8p) and National Museum (10p).

Europa Issue

View of Ballynahinch A124

Lugalla Lake — A125

1977, June 27 Litho. Perf. 14x14½
413 A124 10p multicolored   3.50 .25
414 A125 12p multicolored   12.50 1.40

Head, by Louis le Brocquy, 1973 — A126

1977, Aug. 8   Perf. 14x14½
415 A126 17p multicolored   1.25 1.25

Girl Guide and Tents A127

Design: 17p, Boy Scout and tents.

1977, Aug. 22 Photo. Perf. 15x14½
416 A127 8p multicolored   .50 .25
417 A127 17p multicolored   1.25 1.25

European Scout and Guide Conference, Ireland, and 50th anniversary of Catholic Boy Scouts of Ireland.

The Shanachie, by Jack B. Yeats — A128

Eriugena
A129

Perf. 14x14½, 14½x14
1977, Sept. 12 **Litho.**
418 A128 10p black .45 .35
419 A129 12p black 1.25 1.40

Folklore of Ireland Society, 50th anniv. and 1100th death anniv. of Johannes Scottus Eriugena, philospher, poet and mystic.

"Electricity," Mural by Robert Ballagh — A130

Bulls, from Contemporary Coin — A131

Greyhound
A132

Litho. (10p, 17p); Photo. (12p)
Perf. 14½x14; 15x14½ (12p)
1977, Oct. 10
420 A130 10p multicolored .30 .20
421 A131 12p multicolored .60 .60
422 A132 17p multicolored 1.00 .80
Nos. 420-422 (3) 1.90 1.60

50th anniversaries of: Electricity Supply Board (10p); Agricultural Credit Act (12p); introduction of greyhound racing (17p).

Holy Family, by Giorgione — A133

Bremen, Junkers Monoplane A134

1977, Nov. 3 **Photo.** **Perf. 14½x15**
423 A133 8p multicolored .35 .20
424 A133 10p multicolored .60 .60
425 A133 17p multicolored 1.00 1.00
Nos. 423-425 (3) 1.95 1.80

Christmas.

1978, Apr. 13 **Litho.** **Perf. 14**
426 A134 10p ultra & black .40 .40
427 A134 17p lt brown & black 1.00 1.00

50th anniversary of first East-West transatlantic flight from Baldonnel, County Dublin, to Greenly Island, Gulf of St. Lawrence.

Spring Gentian — A135

Wild flowers: 10p, Strawberry tree. 11p, Large-flowered butterwort. 17p, St. Daboec's heath.

1978, June 12 **Litho.** **Perf. 14x14½**
428 A135 8p multicolored .30 .30
429 A135 10p multicolored .60 .60
430 A135 11p multicolored .80 1.10
431 A135 17p multicolored 1.00 1.40
Nos. 428-431 (4) 2.70 3.40

Catherine McAuley — A136

William Orpen, Self-portrait A138

Vaccination, lithograph by Manigaud — A137

1978, Sept. 18 **Litho.** **Perf. 14**
432 A136 10p multicolored .35 .25
433 A137 11p multicolored .60 .60
434 A138 17p multicolored 1.25 .95
Nos. 432-434 (3) 2.20 1.80

Catherine McAuley (1778-1841), founder of Sisters of Mercy (10p); eradication of smallpox (11p); William Orpen (1878-1931), painter (17p).

Offshore Oil Well — A139

Woodcock on Farthing A140

Virgin and Child, by Guercino — A141

1978, Oct. 18 **Litho.** **Perf. 14**
435 A139 10p multicolored .55 .35

First natural gas coming in off the Irish Coast at Kinsale.

1978, Oct. 26 **Photo.** **Perf. 15x14½**
Coins: 10p, Salmon on florin. 11p, Hen and chicks on penny. 17p, Horse on half crown.
436 A140 8p multicolored .45 .20
437 A140 10p multicolored .55 .25
438 A140 11p multicolored .65 .60
439 A140 17p multicolored 1.10 1.00
Nos. 436-439 (4) 2.75 2.05

Irish currency, 50th anniversary.

1978, Nov. 16 **Photo.** **Perf. 14½x15**
440 A141 8p multicolored .35 .25
441 A141 10p multicolored .45 .30
442 A141 17p multicolored .85 .75
Nos. 440-442 (3) 1.65 1.30

Christmas.

Conolly Folly, Castletown A142

Europa: 11p, Belvedere on Tower Hill at Dromoland.

1978, Dec. 6 **Perf. 15x14½**
443 A142 10p brown 3.00 .25
444 A142 11p dull green 9.00 1.00

Cross-country Runners — A143

1979, Aug. 20 **Litho.** **Perf. 14½x14**
445 A143 8p multicolored .35 .35

7th World Cross-country Championships, Greenpark Racecourse, Limerick, March 25.

Rowland Hill, Bronze Statue — A144

"European Communities" (7 Languages) A145

1979, Aug. 20 **Perf. 14x14½**
446 A144 17p multicolored .70 .70

Sir Rowland Hill (1795-1879), originator of penny postage.

1979, Aug. 20 **Photo.** **Perf. 14½x15**
447 A145 10p lt greenish gray .45 .45
448 A145 11p rose lilac .50 .50

European Parliament, first direct elections, June 7-10.

Wren A146

Birds: 10p, Great crested grebe. 11p, Greenland white-fronted geese. 17p, Peregrine falcon.

1979, Aug. 30 **Litho.** **Perf. 14½x14**
449 A146 8p multicolored .40 .25
450 A146 10p multicolored .60 .60
451 A146 11p multicolored .70 .70
452 A146 17p multicolored 1.25 1.25
Nos. 449-452 (4) 2.95 2.80

A Happy Flower A147

Children's Drawings: 11p, "Me and my skipping rope," vert. 17p, "Swans on a lake."

Perf. 14½x14, 14x14½
1979, Sept. 13 **Litho.**
453 A147 10p multicolored .40 .30
454 A147 11p multicolored 1.00 .45
455 A147 17p multicolored 1.40 .60
Nos. 453-455 (3) 2.80 1.35

International Year of the Child.

Pope John Paul II A148

1979, Sept. 29 **Litho.** **Perf. 14½x14**
456 A148 12p multicolored .60 .45

Visit of Pope John Paul II to Ireland.

Hospitaller Brother Teaching Child A149

1979, Oct. 4
457 A149 9½p rose & black .55 .35

Hospitaller Order of St. John of God, centenary in Ireland.

Windmill and Sun — A150

1979, Oct. 4 **Photo.** **Perf. 14½x15**
458 A150 11p multicolored .55 .45

Energy conservation.

"Seated Figure," by F.E. McWilliam A151

1979, Oct. 4   Litho.   Perf. 14½x14
459 A151 20p multicolored   1.25 .75

Patrick Pearse A152

1979, Nov. 10   Photo.   Perf. 15x14½
460 A152 12p multicolored   .55 .35
Patrick Henry Pearse (1879-1916), Irish writer and leader of Easter Rebellion.

Mother and Child, Panel, Domnach Argid Shrine — A153

1979, Nov. 15   Photo.   Perf. 14½x15
461 A153 9½p multicolored   .55 .25
462 A153 20p multicolored   1.10 .85
Christmas.

Europa Issue

Bianconi Long Car, 1836 A154

Laying Transatlantic Cable, Steamer William Cory, 1866 — A155

1979, Dec. 6   Litho.   Perf. 15x14
463 A154 12p multicolored   1.50 .40
464 A155 13p multicolored   9.50 .85

Type of 1968
Designs: 13p, 16p, Stag; others, Dog.

1980-82   Photo.   Perf. 15
466 A68 12p green   .70 .70
467 A68 13p red brown & dk brn   1.40 .30
468 A68 15p ultra   1.25 .50
469 A68 16p olive green & blk   1.40 .50

Litho.
Perf. 14x15
470 A68 18p dull red brn ('81)   1.25 .60
471 A68 19p dull blue ('81)   1.40 .55
472 A68 22p gray blue ('81)   1.25 .20
473 A68 24p brown olive ('81)   1.75 .40
474 A68 26p bluish green ('82)   1.75 .65
475 A68 29p dp rose lilac ('82)   2.00 .80
    Nos. 466-475 (10)   14.15 5.20

Issued: 12p, 13p, 3/26/80; 15p, 16p, 7/10/80; 18p, 19p, 4/27/81; 22p, 9/1/81; 24p, 10/29/81; 26p, 29p, 4/1/82.

St. Jean Baptiste de la Salle — A156

1980, Mar. 19   Litho.   Perf. 14x15
477 A156 12p multicolored   .55 .35
The Brothers of the Christian School (founded by St. Jean Baptiste), centenary in Ireland.

Europa Issue

George Bernard Shaw, by Alick Ritchie A157

Oscar Wilde, by Toulouse-Lautrec A158

1980, May 7   Litho.   Perf. 14x15
478 A157 12p multicolored   3.50 .30
479 A158 13p multicolored   3.50 .65

Irish Ermine — A159

Bodhran Drum and Whistle Players — A160

1980, July 30   Litho.   Perf. 14x15
480 A159 12p shown   .35 .30
481 A159 15p Irish hare   .60 .35
482 A159 16p Fox   .60 .45
483 A159 25p Red deer   1.25 1.25
    a.   Miniature sheet of 4, #480-483   3.50 4.75
    Nos. 480-483 (4)   2.80 2.35

1980, Sept. 25   Photo.   Perf. 14x15
484 A160 12p shown   .55 .25
485 A160 15p Piper, Uilleann pipes   .75 .60
486 A160 25p Irish jig   1.00 .85
    Nos. 484-486 (3)   2.30 1.70

Sean O'Casey (1880-1964), Playwright A161

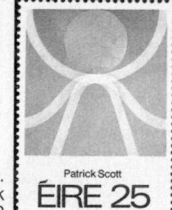

Gold Painting No. 57, by Patrick Scott — A162

1980, Oct. 23   Litho.   Perf. 14x14½
487 A161 12p multicolored   .55 .40

1980, Oct. 23   Perf. 14x15
488 A162 25p multicolored   1.10 .80

A163

A164

1980, Dec. 4   Photo.   Perf. 15x14½
489 A163 12p multicolored   .40 .25
490 A163 15p multicolored   .75 .40
491 A163 25p multicolored   1.25 .70
    Nos. 489-491 (3)   2.40 1.35
Christmas.

1981, Mar. 12   Litho.   Perf. 14x14½
Scientists and Inventions: 12p, Robert Boyle (1627-1691), and Air Pump, 1659. 15p, Harry Ferguson (1884-1960), hydraulic tractor, 1936. 16p, Charles Parsons (1854-1931), Parsons' turbine, 1884. 25p, John Holland (1841-1914), Holland submarine, 1878.

492 A164 12p multicolored   .35 .25
493 A164 15p multicolored   .55 .30
494 A164 16p multicolored   .65 .40
495 A164 25p multicolored   1.40 .80
    Nos. 492-495 (4)   2.95 1.75

The Cock and the Pot, Rubbing, 1841 — A165

Europa: 19p, The Scales of Judgment, rubbing, 1827.

1981, May 4   Litho.   Perf. 14½x15
496 A165 18p multicolored   4.00 .30
497 A165 19p multicolored   7.00 .50

Hiking A166

Perf. 14x15, 15x14
1981, June 24   Litho.
498 A166 15p Bicycling, vert.   .50 .25
499 A166 18p shown   .75 .45
500 A166 19p Mountain climbing   1.00 .75

501 A166 30p Rock climbing, vert.   1.75 .90
    Nos. 498-501 (4)   4.00 2.35
Youth Hostel Assn., 50th anniv.

Jeremiah O'Donovan Rossa (1831-1915), Journalist — A167

Railway Embankment, by William John Leech (1881-1968) — A168

Perf. 14½x15, 15x14½
1981, Aug. 31
502 A167 15p multicolored   .45 .55
503 A168 30p multicolored   1.40 1.40

James Hoban (1762-1831), White House Architect — A169

1981, Sept. 29   Perf. 15x14
504 A169 18p multicolored   1.00 .70
Same design used for US Nos. 1935-1936.

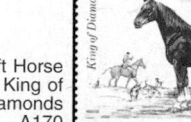

Draft Horse King of Diamonds A170

Famous Horses: No. 505, Show-jumper Boomerang. No. 506, Steeplechaser Arkle. 24p, Flat racer Ballymoss. 36p, Connemara pony Coosheen Finn.

1981, Oct. 23   Litho.   Perf. 15x14
505 A170 18p multicolored   1.10 .55
506 A170 18p multicolored   1.10 .55
    a.   Pair, #505-506   2.50 2.50
507 A170 22p multicolored   1.40 .85
508 A170 24p multicolored   1.10 1.40
509 A170 36p multicolored   2.25 2.25
    Nos. 505-509 (5)   6.95 5.60

Nativity, by Federico Barocci — A171

A172

1981, Nov. 19　Litho.　*Perf. 14x15*
510　A171　18p multicolored　　　.60　.25
511　A171　22p multicolored　　　.80　.35
512　A171　36p multicolored　　1.60　.70
　　　Nos. 510-512 (3)　　　3.00　1.30
Christmas 1981.

1981, Dec. 10　Litho.　*Perf. 14x14½*
513　A172　18p multicolored　　　.80　.55
Land Law Act centenary.

250th
Anniv. of
Royal
Dublin
Society
A173

1981, Dec. 10　　*Perf. 14½x14*
514　A173　22p multicolored　　1.10　.60

50th Anniv.
of Killarney
Natl. Park
A174

1982, Feb. 26　Litho.　*Perf. 14½x14*
515　A174　18p Upper Lake　　1.10　.35
516　A174　36p Eagle's Nest　　1.90　1.25

The
Stigmatization of
St. Francis, by
Sassetta — A175

Francis Makemie, Old Presbyterian
Church, Ramelton — A176

1982, Apr. 2　　*Perf. 14x15, 15x14*
517　A175　22p multicolored　　　.95　.50
518　A176　24p brown　　　　　1.40　.90
800th birth anniv. of St. Francis of Assisi;
300th anniv. of Francis Makemie's ordination
(father of American Presbyterianism).

Europa Issue

Great Famine of
1845-50 — A177

Conversion of Ireland to Christianity
(St. Patrick and his Followers, by
Vincenzo Valdre)
A178

1982, May 4
519　A177　26p tan & brown　　11.00　.75
520　A178　29p multicolored　　15.00　4.00

Padraic
O'Connaire
(1882-1928),
Writer — A179

Designs: 26p, James Joyce (1882-1941),
writer and poet, by Brancusi. 29p, John Field
(1782-1837), Composer and pianist, Nocturne
score. 44p, Charles Joseph Kickham (1828-
1882), journalist and writer. 29p, 44p by Colin
Harrison.

1982, June 16　Litho.　*Perf. 14x15*
521　A179　22p blue & black　　　.70　.40
522　A179　26p black & brown　1.10　.85
523　A179　29p black & blue　　1.60　1.60
524　A179　44p gray green & black　2.50　2.50
　　　Nos. 521-524 (4)　　　5.90　5.35

Porbeagle
Shark
A180

1982, July 29　　*Perf. 15x14*
525　A180　22p shown　　　　　.85　.55
526　A180　22p Oyster　　　　　.85　.55
527　A180　26p Salmon　　　　1.40　.55
528　A180　29p Dublin Bay prawn　1.75　1.75
　　　Nos. 525-528 (4)　　　4.85　3.40

Currach
A181

1982, Sept. 21　　*Perf. 15x14, 14x15*
529　A181　22p shown　　　　　.90　.45
530　A181　22p Galway hooker,
　　　　　　vert.　　　　　　.90　.45
531　A181　26p Asgard II training
　　　　　　ship　　　　　　1.40　.75
532　A181　29p Howth 17-footer,
　　　　　　vert.　　　　　1.90　1.90
　　　Nos. 529-532 (4)　　　5.10　3.55

The Irish
House of
Commons,
by Francis
Wheatley
A182

1982, Oct. 14　Litho.　*Perf. 14½x14*
533　A182　22p multicolored　　　.70　.45
Bicentenary of Grattan's Parliament.

A183

A183a

Eamon de Valera (1882-1975), President,
by Robert Ballagh.

1982, Oct. 14　　*Perf. 14x14½*
534　A183　26p multicolored　　1.00　1.00

1982, Nov. 11　Litho.　*Perf. 14½x15*
Madonna and Child, by Andrea della Robbia
(1435-1525)
535　A183a　22p lt violet & multi　.75　.50
536　A183a　26p gray & multi　　.95　.65
Christmas.

A184

A185

Killarney Cathedral,
1855 — A186

Designs: 1p-5p, Central Pavilion, Dublin
Botanical Gardens. 6p, 7p, 10p, 12p, Dr.
Steeven's Hospital, Dublin. 15p, 20p, 22p,
Aughnanure Castle, Oughterard, 16th cent.
23p, 26p, Cormac's Chapel, 1134. 29p, 30p,
St. Mac Dara's Church. 50p, Casino, Marino.
£1, Cahir Castle, 15th century. £5 Central Bus
Station, Dublin, 1953.
50p, £1, £5 horiz.

1982-90　Litho.　*Perf. 14x15, 15x14*
537　A184　1p dull blue　　　　.30　.20
538　A184　2p gray green　　　.30　.20
539　A184　3p black　　　　　.30　.20
540　A184　4p rose lake　　　　.30　.20
　　a.　Perf. 13½ on 3 or 4 sides　1.50　.20
541　A184　5p brown　　　　　.75　.50
542　A184　6p dull blue　　　　.75　.50
543　A184　7p gray green　　　1.40　.75
544　A184　10p black　　　　　1.40　.75
545　A184　12p rose lake　　　1.40　.75
546　A185　15p gray green　　1.90　.90
547　A185　20p rose lake　　　1.90　.90
548　A185　22p dull blue　　　1.90　.90
　　a.　Bklt. pane of 7+label (3 4p, 4
　　　　22p) ('88)　　　　　9.00
549　A185　23p gray green　　2.50　1.50
550　A185　26p black　　　　　3.00　1.50
　　a.　Bklt. pane, 2 ea 2p, 22p, 26p　10.50
　　b.　Bklt. pane, 4 ea 2p, 22p, 26p　21.00
　　c.　Bklt. pane, 3 4p, 5 22p, 4 26p
　　　　('88)　　　　　　32.50
　　d.　Perf. 13½ on 3 sides　　4.50　2.00
551　A184　29p gray green　　3.50　2.00
552　A184　30p black　　　　　2.25　1.00
　　a.　Perf. 13½ on 3 or 4 sides　3.75　1.00

Perf. 14x15, 15x14
553　A186　44p gray & black　　3.50　2.00
554　A186　50p gray & dull blue　3.50　1.25
555　A186　£1 gray & brown　1.20　4.00
556　A186　£5 gray & rose lake　30.00　15.00
　　　Nos. 537-556 (20)　　72.85　35.00

Stamps from No. 550c imprinted "Booklet
Stamp" in green on reverse side. No. 550c
sold for £2.
Issued: 4p, 6p-7p, 20p, 23p, 30p, 50p,
3/16/83; 1p-3p, 5p, 10p-15p, 7/6/83; Nos.
540a, 550d, 552a, 5/3/90; others, 12/15/82.
See Nos. 638-645, 803a, 804b.

Dublin Chamber
of Commerce
Bicentenary
A187

Bank of Ireland Bicentenary — A188

1983, Feb. 23　　Litho.
557　A187　22p Ouzel Galley gob-
　　　　　let　　　　　　.70　.65
558　A188　26p Bank　　　　1.10　.85

Padraig
Siochfhradha
(1883-1964),
Writer — A189

Boys' Brigade
Centenary
A190

1983, Apr. 7　Litho.　*Perf. 14x14½*
559　A189　26p multicolored　　1.00　.45
560　A190　29p multicolored　　1.60　1.25

Europa
A191

Design: 26p, Newgrange Winter Solstice,
Neolithic Pattern Drawing by Louis le Brocquy.
29p, Quaternion formula, by William Rowan
Hamilton (1805-1865).

1983, May 4　Litho.　*Perf. 14½x14*
561　A191　26p black & gold　　7.00　.65
562　A191　29p multicolored　　19.00　6.00

Kerry Blue
Terrier
A192

Drawings of dogs by Wendy Walsh.

1983, June 23
563　A192　22p shown　　　　　.90　.90
564　A192　26p Irish wolfhound　1.10　1.10
565　A192　26p Irish water
　　　　　　spaniel　　　　1.10　1.10
566　A192　29p Irish terrier　　1.25　1.25
567　A192　44p Irish setters　　2.00　2.00
　　a.　Miniature sheet of 5, #563-
　　　　567　　　　　　11.50　11.50
　　　Nos. 563-567 (5)　　　6.35　6.35

Sean
Mac Diarmada
(1883-1916),
Nationalist
A193

Society for the Prevention of Cruelty to Animals A194

Society of St. Vincent de Paul Sesquicentennial A195

Industrial Credit Co., 50th Anniv. A196

US Pres. Andrew Jackson (1767-1845) A197

Perf. 14x14½, 14½x14

1983, Aug. 11
568	A193	22p multicolored	1.00	.85
569	A194	22p multicolored	1.00	.85
570	A195	26p multicolored	1.25	1.10
571	A196	26p multicolored	1.25	1.10
572	A197	44p gray	2.75	2.25
		Nos. 568-572 (5)	7.25	6.15

WCY — A198

Handicrafts A199

1983, Sept. 15   Litho.   Perf. 14x15
573	A198	22p Mailman	1.25	1.00
574	A198	29p Dish antenna	1.50	1.25

1983, Oct. 13   Litho.   Perf. 14x15
575	A199	22p Weaving	1.00	.45
576	A199	26p Basketweaving	1.25	.75
577	A199	29p Irish crochet	1.60	1.00
578	A199	44p Harpmaking	3.25	1.75
		Nos. 575-578 (4)	7.10	3.95

La Natividad by Rogier van der Weyden — A200

1983, Nov. 30   Litho.   Perf. 14x14½
579	A200	22p multicolored	.80	.35
580	A200	26p multicolored	1.60	1.25

Christmas.

Irish Railways Sesquicentenary — A201

Locomotives: 23p, Princess, Dublin and Kingstown Railway. 26p, Macha, Great Southern Railways. 29p, Kestrel, Great Northern Railway. 44p, Link-Hoffman railcar, Coras Iompair Eireann.

1984, Jan. 30   Perf. 14½x14
581	A201	23p multicolored	1.40	1.40
582	A201	26p multicolored	.85	.85
503	A201	29p multicolored	1.60	1.60
584	A201	44p multicolored	2.75	2.75
a.		Souvenir sheet of 4, #581-584	9.00	9.75
		Nos. 581-584 (4)	6.60	6.60

Private Overprints
Nos. 584a, 684a, 708a, 708b, 803a, 804a, 811a, 826a, 847a, 855a, 876b, and others, exist with privately applied show overprints.

Local Trees A202

1984, Mar. 1   Litho.   Perf. 15x14
585	A202	22p Irish whitebeam	.90	.75
586	A202	26p Irish yew	1.10	.95
587	A202	29p Irish willow	1.75	1.40
588	A202	44p Birch	2.50	2.50
		Nos. 585-588 (4)	6.25	5.60

St. Vincent's Hospital, Dublin, Sesquicentenary — A203

Royal College of Surgeons in Ireland Bicentenary — A204

1984, Apr. 12   Litho.
589	A203	26p multicolored	1.25	.95
590	A204	44p multicolored	2.25	1.90

2nd European Parliament Election A205

1984, May 10   Litho.   Perf. 15x14
591	A205	26p multicolored	2.75	2.25

Europa (1959-84) A206

1984, May 10
592	A206	26p multicolored	7.00	3.00
593	A206	29p multicolored	15.00	3.75

John McCormack (1884-1945), Singer — A207

1984, June 6   Litho.   Perf. 14x14½
594	A207	22p multicolored	2.25	2.25

See US No. 2090.

1984 Summer Olympics A208

1984, June 21   Litho.   Perf. 14½x14
595	A208	22p Hammer throw	1.00	.75
596	A208	26p Hurdles	1.40	1.10
597	A208	29p Running	1.60	1.50
		Nos. 595-597 (3)	4.00	3.35

Gaelic Athletic Assoc. Centenary A209

1984, Aug. 23   Litho.   Perf. 14x15
598	A209	22p Hurlers	1.25	1.25
599	A209	26p Soccer, vert.	2.00	2.00

Mayoral City of Galway, 500th Anniv. — A210

St. Brendan (484-577) A211

1984, Sept. 18   Perf. 14x15, 15x14
600	A210	26p Medal	1.00	1.00
601	A211	44p Portrait, manuscript	2.25	2.25

Post Office Bicentenary — A212

1984, Oct. 19   Perf. 15x14
602	A212	26p Handing sealed letter	2.00	2.00

A213

Virgin And Child by Sassoferrato A214

Perf. 14½x14, 14x14½

1984, Nov. 26   Litho.
603	A213	17p multicolored	.65	.65
604	A214	22p multicolored	1.10	1.10
605	A214	26p multicolored	1.90	1.90
		Nos. 603-605 (3)	3.65	3.65

Christmas.

Love A215

A216

1985, Jan. 31   Litho.   Perf. 15x14
606	A215	22p Heart-shaped balloon	1.00	1.00
607	A216	26p Bouquet of hearts	2.25	2.25

Dunsink Observatory, 200th Anniv. — A217

Cork City Charter, 800th Anniv. A218

Royal Irish Academy, 200th Anniv. — A219

1st Manned Flight in Ireland, 200th Anniv. — A220

1985, Mar. 14 Litho.
608	A217	22p black	.90	.90
609	A218	26p multicolored	1.25	1.25
610	A219	37p multicolored	1.90	1.90
611	A220	44p multicolored	2.25	2.25
		Nos. 608-611 (4)	6.30	6.30

Butterflies A221

1985, Apr. 11 Litho. Perf. 14x15
612	A221	22p Common blue	1.75	1.50
613	A221	26p Red admiral	1.90	1.75
614	A221	28p Brimstone	2.10	1.75
615	A221	44p Marsh fritillary	3.00	2.75
		Nos. 612-615 (4)	8.75	7.75

Europa A222

26p, Charles Villiers Stanford (1852-1924), composer. 37p, Turlough O'Carolan (1670-1738), Composer.

1985, May 16 Litho. Perf. 15x14
616	A222	26p multicolored	3.75	.75
617	A222	37p multicolored	9.50	6.50

European Music Year — A223

Composers: No. 618, Giuseppe Domenico Scarlatti (1685-1757). No. 619, George Frideric Handel (1685-1759). No. 620, Johann Sebastian Bach (1685-1750).

1985, May 16 Litho. Perf. 14x15
618	A223	22p multicolored	1.75	2.10
619	A223	22p multicolored	1.75	2.10
a.		Pair, #618-619	4.00	4.50
620	A223	26p multicolored	1.75	2.10
		Nos. 618-620 (3)	5.25	6.30

Irish UN Defense Forces in the Congo, 1960 A224

Thomas Ashe (1885-1917), Patriot and Educator — A225

Bishop George Berkeley (1685-1753), Philosopher and Educator — A226

Perf. 15x14, 14x15
1985, June 20 Litho.
621	A224	22p multicolored	1.10	.75
622	A225	26p multicolored	1.25	1.25
623	A226	44p multicolored	2.10	2.10
		Nos. 621-623 (3)	4.45	4.10

Irish forces as part of the UN Defense Forces, 25th anniv. (22p).

Intl. Youth Year — A227

1985, Aug. 1 Litho.
624	A227	22p multi, horiz.	1.25	1.25
625	A227	26p multicolored	1.50	1.50

Architecture Type of 1982

Designs: 24p, 39p, Cormac's Chapel. 28p, 32p, 37p, St. Mac Dara's Church. 46p, Cahir Castle. £1, Killarney Cathedral. £2, Casino, Marino. 46p, £2, horiz.

Perf. 15x14, 14x15 (A184, No. 644)
1985-88 Litho.
638	A185	24p brown	1.40	.70
639	A184	28p rose lake	1.75	.40
a.		Bklt. pane, 4 2p, 2 24p, 1 4p, 5 28p ('88)	8.00	
c.		Bklt. pane, 2 2p, 3 4p, 3 24p, 4 28p ('88)	8.50	
640	A184	32p brown	2.00	1.00
641	A184	37p dull blue	3.50	3.50
642	A185	39p rose lake	3.50	2.40
643	A186	46p gray & gray grn	3.75	2.75
644	A186	£1 gray & dull bl	7.00	2.00
645	A186	£2 gray & gray grn	16.00	6.25
		Nos. 638-645 (8)	38.90	19.00

Issued: 24p, 28p, 37p, £1, June 27, 1985; 32p, 39p, 46p, May 1, 1986; £2, July 26, 1988.

Industrial Innovations A228

Institution of Engineers, 150th Anniv. A229

1985, Oct. 3 Litho. Perf. 15x14
646	A228	22p Computer technology	.90	.65
647	A228	26p Peat production	1.25	1.25
648	A229	44p The Key Man, by Sean Keating	2.25	1.75
		Nos. 646-648 (3)	4.40	3.65

Candle, Holly — A230

Virgin and Child in a Landscape, by Adrian van Ijsenbrandt A231

Christmas: No. 651, The Holy Family, by Murillo. 26p, Adoration of the Shepherds, by Louis Le Nain, horiz.

Perf. 14x15, 15x14
1985, Nov. 26 Litho.
649	A230	22p shown	1.50	1.00
650	A231	22p shown	1.50	1.00
651	A231	22p multicolored	1.50	1.00
a.		Pair, #650-651	3.00	3.00
652	A231	26p multicolored	2.10	2.10
		Nos. 649-652 (4)	6.60	5.10

No. 649 was issued in discount sheets of 16 that sold for £3. Value $16.

Love — A232

1986, Jan. 30 Perf. 14x15
653	A232	22p shown	1.40	.80
654	A232	26p Heart-shaped mailbox	1.60	1.50

Ferns — A233

Europa — A234

Aer Lingus, 50th Anniv. A235

1986, Mar. 20 Litho. Perf. 14½x15
655	A233	24p Hart's tongue	.90	.35
656	A233	28p Rusty-back	1.25	.90
657	A233	46p Killarney	2.10	2.10
		Nos. 655-657 (3)	4.25	3.35

1986, May 1 Perf. 14x15, 15x14
658	A234	28p Industry and nature	10.00	1.25
659	A234	39p Hedgerows, horiz.	35.00	6.00

1986, May 27 Perf. 15x14
660	A235	28p Jet, 1986	2.10	1.50
661	A235	46p The Eagle, 1936	3.25	3.00

Inland Waterways A236

1986, May 27 Perf. 15x14, 14x15
662	A236	24p Robertstown Grand Canal	1.50	.90
663	A236	28p Fishing, County Mayo, vert.	1.90	1.50
664	A236	30p Yachting, River Shannon	2.25	2.25
		Nos. 662-664 (3)	5.65	4.65

British & Irish Steam Packet Co., 150th Anniv. A237

1986, July 10 Perf. 15x14
665	A237	24p Steamer Severn, 1836	1.50	1.00
666	A237	28p M.V. Leinster, 1986	2.00	1.75

Lighthouses A238

1986, July 10 Perf. 14½x15
667	A238	24p Kish, helicopter	1.90	1.60
668	A238	30p Fastnet	3.00	2.25

Dublin Council of Trade Unions, Cent. — A239

Arthur Griffith (1871-1922), Statesman
A240

Women in Society, Construction Surveyor — A241

A242

Intl. Peace Year A242a

Perf. 14½x15, 14x15 (#670, 672), 15x14½, 15x14

1986, Aug. 21
669	A239	24p multicolored	.95	.75
670	A240	28p multicolored	1.25	.80
671	A241	28p multicolored	1.25	.80
672	A242	30p multi, vert.	1.40	1.00
673	A242a	46p shown	2.00	1.60
	Nos. 669-673 (5)		6.85	4.95

See Nos. 699, 711, 749, 807, 836.

William Mulready (1786-1863), Letter Sheet Designer — A243

Carriages by Charles Bianconi (1786-1875) — A244

Perf. 15x14, 14x15

1986, Oct. 2   Litho.
674	A243	24p multicolored	.90	.70
675	A244	28p multi, vert.	1.50	1.25
676	A244	39p shown	2.10	1.75
	Nos. 674-676 (3)		4.50	3.70

Adoration of the Shepherds, by Francesco Pascucci
A245

Adoration of the Magi, by Frans Francken III (1542-1616) A246

1986, Nov. 20   **Perf. 15x14, 14½x15**
677	A245	21p multicolored	1.00	.75
678	A246	28p multicolored	1.50	1.25

Christmas. No. 677 was issued in discount sheets of 12 that sold for £2.50. Vaue $30.

Love A247

Perf. 15x14, 14x15

1987, Jan. 27   Litho.
679	A247	24p Flowers, butterfly	1.25	.95
680	A247	28p Postman, vert.	1.75	1.25

Trolleys A248

1987, Mar. 4   Litho.   **Perf. 15x14**
681	A248	24p Cork Electric	1.10	.70
682	A248	28p Dublin Standard	1.40	.85
683	A248	30p Howth (G.N.R.)	1.60	1.25
684	A248	46p Galway Horse	2.40	2.10
a.	Miniature sheet of 4, #681-684		7.50	7.50
	Nos. 681-684 (4)		6.50	4.90

See note following No. 584.

Waterford Chamber of Commerce, 200th Anniv.
A249

Muintir Na Tire, 50th Anniv.
A250

Trinity College Botanical Gardens, Dublin, 300th Anniv. — A251

Medical Missionaries of Mary, 50th Anniv. — A252

Anniversaries and events: 24p, Three ships, Chamber crest. 28p, Canon Hayes (1887-1957), founder, and symbols of Muintir Na Tire

activities. 30p, College crest, Calceolaria burbidgei. 39p, Intl. Missionary Training Hospital, Drogheda, and Mother Mary Martin.

Perf. 15x14, 14x15

1987, Apr. 9   Litho.
685	A249	24p vio bl, blk & dk grn	1.00	1.00
686	A250	28p multicolored	1.25	1.25
687	A251	30p multicolored	1.40	1.40
688	A252	39p multicolored	1.75	1.75
	Nos. 685-688 (4)		5.40	5.40

Europa A253

Modern architecture, art: 28p, Borda na Mona headquarters, Dublin, and The Turf Cutter, by sculptor John Behan. 39p, St. Mary's Church and ruins of Romanesque monastery at Cong.

1987, May 14   **Perf. 15x14**
689	A253	28p multicolored	6.00	2.00
690	A253	39p multicolored	9.00	5.00

Cattle A254

1987, July 2   **Perf. 15x14**
691	A254	24p Kerry	1.25	.60
692	A254	28p Friesian	1.60	1.60
693	A254	30p Hereford	1.60	1.60
694	A254	39p Shorthorn	2.25	2.25
	Nos. 691-694 (4)		6.70	6.05

Festivals A255

1987, Aug. 27   **Perf. 14x15**
695	A255	24p Fleadh Nua, Ennis	1.00	1.00
696	A255	28p Festival Queen, Tralee	1.40	1.40
697	A255	30p Wexford opera festival	1.75	1.75
698	A255	46p Ballinasloe horse fair	2.75	2.75
	Nos. 695-698 (4)		6.90	6.90

Nos. 695-696 vert.

Statesmen Type of 1986 and

Ewer and Chalice, Company Crest A256

Harp in Shield, Preamble Excerpt A257

Woman Leading Board Meeting — A258

Design: No. 699, Cathal Brugha, vert.

Perf. 14x15, 15x14

1987, Oct. 1   Litho.
699	A240	24p black	1.10	1.10
700	A256	24p multicolored	1.10	1.10
701	A257	28p multicolored	1.25	1.25
702	A258	46p multicolored	2.10	2.10
	Nos. 699-702 (4)		5.55	5.55

Company of Goldsmiths of Dublin, 350th anniv. (No. 700); Irish Constitution, 50th anniv. (28p); Women in Society, (46p).

A259

Christmas A260

21p, 12 Days of Christmas (1st 3 days). 24p, Embroidery (detail), Waterford Vestments, 15th cent. 28p, Neapolitan creche (detail), 1850.

Perf. 15x14, 14x15

1987, Nov. 17   Litho.
703	A259	21p multicolored	.85	.40
704	A260	24p multicolored	1.10	.85
705	A260	28p multicolored	1.40	1.10
	Nos. 703-705 (3)		3.35	2.35

No. 703 issued in discount sheets of 14 + center label; sheet sold for £2.90. Value $22.50.

Love A261

Perf. 15x14½, 14½x15

1988, Jan. 27   Litho.
706	A261	24p shown	1.75	1.75
707	A261	28p Pillar box, vert.	1.90	1.90

Dublin Millennium A262

1988, Mar. 1   **Perf. 15x14**
708	A262	28p multicolored	3.00	2.25
a.	Booklet pane of 4, Gaelic		12.00	
b.	Booklet pane of 4, English		12.00	

Nos. 708a, 708b consist of two vert. pairs separated by a history in Gaelic or English. See note following No. 584.

A263

Impact of the Irish Abroad A264

Designs: No. 709, Robert O'Hara Burke (1820-1861), by Sir Sidney Nolan; 19th cent. map of Australia with Burke & Wills expedition route. 46p, Mural (detail) of the Eureka Stockade by Nolan.

1988, Mar. 1
709 A263 24p multicolored 2.00 2.00
710 A264 46p multicolored 3.00 3.00

Statesmen Type of 1986 and

1988 Summer Olympics, Seoul A265

Order of Malta Ambulance Corps, 50th Anniv. A266

Barry Fitzgerald (1888-1961), Actor — A267

Designs: 24p, William T. Cosgrave (1880-1965), president of the United Ireland and Fine Gael party. No. 713, Cycling.

Perf. 14x15, 15x14
1988, Apr. 7 **Litho.**
711 A240 24p black 1.25 1.25
712 A265 28p multicolored 1.60 1.60
713 A265 28p multicolored 1.60 1.60
  a. Pair, #712-713 3.25 3.25
714 A266 30p multicolored 2.00 2.00
715 A267 50p multicolored 2.40 2.40
  Nos. 711-715 (5) 8.85 8.85

Nos. 712-713 printed in sheets of 5 each plus two labels. Value, $16.50.

Sirius Sailing from Passage West, County Cork A268

1988, May 12 **Litho.** **Perf. 15x14**
716 A268 24p multicolored 2.00 2.00

1st scheduled transatlantic crossing by steamship, sesquicentennial.

Europa A269

28p, Air traffic controllers and A320 Airbus. 39p, Europe on globe, letters.

1988, May 12 **Litho.** **Perf. 15x14**
717 A269 28p multicolored 4.00 1.00
718 A269 39p multicolored 7.00 3.00

Maia and Mercury Flying Boats in Foynes Harbor A269a

1988, May 12 **Litho.** **Perf. 15x14**
719 A269a 46p multicolored 3.50 3.50

1st east-west transatlantic crossing by seaplane, 50th anniv.

Conservation of Flora — A270

1988, June 21 **Litho.** **Perf. 14x15**
720 A270 24p Otanthus maritimus 1.40 1.40
721 A270 28p Saxifraga hartii 1.75 1.75
722 A270 46p Astragalus danicus 2.75 2.75
  Nos. 720-722 (3) 5.90 5.90

Irish Security Forces A271

1988, Aug. 23 **Litho.** **Perf. 15x14**
723 A271 28p Garda Siochana (police) 3.00 2.00
724 A271 28p Army 3.00 2.00
725 A271 28p Navy, air corps 3.00 2.00
726 A271 28p FCA, Slua Muiri 3.00 2.00
  a. Strip of 4, #723-726 12.00 12.00

Institute of Chartered Accountants, Cent. — A272

Defeat of the Spanish Armada, 400th Anniv. A273

Perf. 14x15, 15x14
1988, Oct. 6 **Litho.**
727 A272 24p multicolored 2.00 2.00
728 A273 46p Duquesa Santa Ana off Donegal Coast 3.50 3.50

John F. Kennedy, Portrait by James Wyeth A274

1988, Nov. 24 **Litho.** **Perf. 15x14**
729 A274 28p multicolored 4.00 3.00

A275

Christmas A276

1988, Nov. 24 **Perf. 14x15**
730 A275 21p St. Kevin's Church, Glendalough .70 .40
731 A276 24p Adoration of the Magi .90 .60
732 A276 28p Flight into Egypt 1.50 1.50
733 A276 46p Holy Family 2.25 2.25
  Nos. 730-733 (4) 5.35 4.75

No. 730 issued only in discount sheets of 14. Sheet sold for £2.90. Value $20.

Love A277

The Sonnet, by William Mulready (1786-1863) A278

Perf. 15x14, 14x15
1989, Jan. 24 **Litho.**
734 A277 24p multicolored 1.40 1.40
735 A278 28p multicolored 1.75 1.75

Mulready, designer of Rowland Hill's first stamped envelope.

Classic Automobiles — A279

1989, Apr. 11 **Litho.** **Perf. 15x14**
736 A279 24p Silver Stream 1.10 1.10
737 A279 28p Benz Comfortable 1.50 1.50
  a. Booklet pane, 2 each 24p, 28p 5.25
738 A279 39p Thomond Car 1.90 1.90
739 A279 46p Chambers Car 2.25 2.25
  a. Booklet pane of 4, #736-739 7.75
  Nos. 736-739 (4) 6.75 6.75

Parks and Gardens A280

1989, Apr. 11
740 A280 24p Garinish Is. 1.00 1.00
741 A280 28p Glenveagh 1.40 1.40
742 A280 32p Connemara Natl. Park 1.75 1.75

---

743 A280 50p St. Stephen's Green 2.75 2.75
  Nos. 740-743 (4) 6.90 6.90

Europa A281

1989, May 11
744 A281 28p Ring-a-ring-a-rosie 1.00 .90
745 A281 39p Hopscotch 1.75 1.50

Irish Red Cross Soc., 50th Anniv. — A282

1989, May 11 **Perf. 14x15**
746 A282 24p multicolored 1.50 1.50

European Parliament 3rd Elections — A283

1989, May 11
747 A283 28p Stars from flag 1.50 1.50

Sts. Kilian, Colman and Totnan (d. 689), Martyred Missionaries, and Shamrock — A284

1989, June 15 **Litho.** **Perf. 13½**
748 A284 28p multicolored 2.00 2.00
  a. Booklet pane of 4, English 7.00
  b. Booklet pane of 4, Gaelic 7.00
  c. Booklet pane of 4, German 7.00
  d. Booklet pane of 4, Latin 7.00

See Federal Republic of Germany No. 1580.

Statesmen Type of 1986 and

RIAI Emblem — A285

Dublin-Cork Coach, 1789 — A286

Singer, Scene from La Boheme A287

Nehru — A288

Design: 24p, Sean Thomas O'Kelly (1883-1966), 2nd president.

Perf. 14x15, 15x14

1989, July 25   Litho.
749	A240	24p black	1.40	1.40
750	A285	28p multicolored	1.40	1.40
751	A286	28p multicolored	1.40	1.40
752	A287	30p multicolored	1.60	1.60
753	A288	46p red brown	2.50	2.50
		Nos. 749-753 (5)	8.30	8.30

Royal Institute of Architects, 150th anniv.; Mail coach in Ireland, bicent.; Margaret Burke Sheridan (1889-1958), soprano; Jawaharlal Nehru, 1st prime minister of independent India.

Flags and *Sail Ireland Yacht Rounding Cape Horn*, by Des Fallon A289

1989, Aug. 31   Litho.   Perf. 15x14
754	A289	28p multicolored	1.75	1.40

Whitbread round of the World Yacht Race 1989-90.

Wildlife: Game Birds — A290

1989, Oct. 5   Litho.   Perf. 13½
755	A290	24p *Lagopus lagopus*	1.40	.55
756	A290	28p *Vanellus vanellus*	1.50	1.50
757	A290	39p *Scolopax rusticola*	2.10	2.10
758	A290	46p *Phasianus colchicus*	2.75	2.75
a.		Miniature sheet of 4, #755-758	11.00	11.00
		Nos. 755-758 (4)	7.75	6.90

Children and Creche — A291

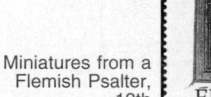

Miniatures from a Flemish Psalter, 13th Cent. — A292

1989, Nov. 14   Litho.   Perf. 14x15
759	A291	21p multicolored	1.00	1.00
760	A292	24p Annunciation	1.00	1.00
761	A292	28p Nativity	1.40	1.40
762	A292	46p Adoration of the Magi	2.10	2.10
		Nos. 759-762 (4)	5.50	5.50

No. 759 issued only in discount sheets of 14. Sheet sold for £2.90. Value $15.

Ireland's Presidency of the European Communities — A293

European Tourism Year A294

1990, Jan. 9   Litho.   Perf. 15x14
763	A293	30p multicolored	1.40	1.40
764	A294	50p multicolored	2.75	2.75

Love Issue — A295

Love Issue — A296

1990, Jan. 30   Litho.   Perf. 14x15
765	A295	26p shown	1.75	1.75
766	A296	30p "Love!"	1.75	1.75

Enamel Latchet Brooch — A297

Ardagh Chalice A298

Art treasures of Ireland: 1p, 2p, Silver Kite Brooch, vert. 4p, 5p, Dunamase Food Vessel, vert. 10p, Derrinboy Armlets. 20p, Gold Dress Fastener. 26p, 28p, Lismore Crosier, vert. 32p, Broighter Collar. 34p, 37p, 38p, 40p, Gleninsheen Collar, vert. 41p, 44p, 45p, Silver thistle brooch, vert. 50p, 52p, Broighter boat,

---

vert. £2, Tara Brooch. £5, St. Patrick's Bell Shrine, vert.

1990-95   Litho.   Perf. 15x14, 14x15
767	A297	1p blue & blk	.30	.30
768	A297	2p orange & blk	.30	.30
770	A297	4p violet & blk	.40	.40
a.		Perf. 13x13½	.40	.40
b.		Photo.	.40	.40
771	A297	5p green & blk	.50	.50
774	A297	10p orange & blk	.85	.85
777	A297	20p yel & blk (I)	1.25	1.25
778	A297	26p violet & blk	2.10	.85
a.		Perf. 13½ on 3 or 4 sides	3.50	3.50
779	A297	28p org & blk (I)	2.10	.90
a.		Bklt. pane, 3 #770, 4 #779 + label	4.25	
b.		Photo.	2.75	2.75
780	A297	30p brt blue & blk	2.10	1.00
a.		Perf. 13½	3.50	3.50
b.		Bklt. pane, 3 #540a, 1 #550d, 2 #778a, 2 #780a	7.75	
c.		Bklt. pane, #768, 3 #770, #778, 2 #780 + label	5.50	
781	A297	32p green & blk	2.10	1.00
a.		Bklt. pane, 2 #770b, #779b, 2 #781d	4.50	
b.		Perf. 13½x13	1.75	1.75
c.		Bklt. pane, #770a, 3 #781b	5.25	
d.		Photo.	1.40	1.40
e.		Booklet pane, 1 #770, 3 #781	5.25	
782	A297	34p yellow & blk	2.75	2.00
783	A297	37p green & blk	3.50	2.50
784	A297	38p purple & blk	3.50	2.50
785	A297	40p blue & black	2.75	2.50
786	A297	41p orange & blk	2.75	2.50
787	A297	44p yellow & blk	3.50	2.50
788	A297	45p violet & black	3.50	2.50
789	A297	50p yellow & blk	2.75	2.00
790	A297	52p blue & blk (I)	3.50	2.75
791	A298	£1 yellow & blk (III)	6.00	3.00
792	A298	£2 green & blk (III)	10.00	6.00
793	A298	£5 blue & blk (III)	26.00	14.00

Self-Adhesive
Die cut perf 11
Size: 27x21mm
794	A297	32p like #781	2.75	1.25
a.		Die cut perf. 11½	4.25	1.25
b.		Die cut perf. 9½x9	2.75	1.25
		Nos. 767-794 (23)	85.25	53.35

Issued: 26p, 30p, 32p, 41p, 50p, £1, 3/8; #780b, 5/3; 1p, 2p, 4p, 10p, 34p, £2, 7/26; #780c, 11/15; 5p, 20p, £5, 1/26/91; #781a, 5/14/91; 28p, 37p, 38p, 44p, 52p, 4/3/91; #779a, 10/17/91; #794, 10/31/91; 40p, 45p, 5/14/92; #770a, 781b, 9/24/93; #781e, 11/16/95; No. 794b, 6/8/95.

#777, 779, 790, Type I - Course Dot Structure

#777a, 779c, 790a, Type II - Fine Dot Structure

#791-793, Type III

#791a-793a, Type IV

Perf. 14x15, 15x14
1995, Nov. 15   Litho.
777a	A297	20p Type II	3.75	3.75
779c	A297	28p Type II	3.75	3.75
790a	A297	52p Type II	5.50	5.50
791a	A298	£1 Type IV	6.50	6.50
792a	A298	£2 Type IV	13.50	13.50
793a	A298	£5 Type IV	32.50	32.50
		Nos. 777a-793a (6)	65.50	65.50

A299

A300

1990, Mar. 22   Litho.   Perf. 14x15
Booklet Stamps
795	A299	26p Gift boxes	4.25	4.25
796	A299	26p Nosegay	4.25	4.25
797	A299	30p Horseshoe	4.25	4.25
798	A299	30p Balloons	4.25	4.25
a.		Bklt. pane of 4, #795-798 English labels	17.00	
b.		As "a," 4 English, 4 Gaelic labels	17.00	

Greetings. Available only in discount booklets containing #798a, 798b. Bklts. sold for £1.98.

1990, Apr. 5   Litho.   Perf. 14x15
799	A300	30p Tackle	2.75	2.75
800	A300	30p Heading the ball	2.75	2.75
a.		Pair, #799-800	6.00	6.00

1990 World Cup Soccer Championships, Italy.
Printed in sheets of 4 No. 800a plus label. Value, $25.

Williamite Wars, 300th Anniv. — A301

1990, Apr. 5   Litho.   Perf. 13½
801	A301	30p Siege of Limerick	2.25	2.25
802	A301	30p Battle of the Boyne	2.25	2.25
a.		Pair, #801-802	5.00	5.00

Penny Black, 150th Anniv. A302

1990, May 3   Litho.   Perf. 15x14
803	A302	30p #780	1.75	1.25
a.		Bklt. pane, #803, 2 each #552a, 780a	11.00	
804	A302	50p #68, 255, 550, 780	2.50	2.50
a.		Bklt. pane, 2 ea #803-804	13.00	
b.		Bklt. pane of 4, #552a, 780a, 803-804	11.00	
		Complete bklt., #803a, 804a, 804b, 780b	35.00	

See note following No. 584.

Europa 1990 — A303

Post offices.

1990, May 3   Perf. 14x15
805	A303	30p GPO, Dublin	1.50	1.25
806	A303	41p Westport P.O., County Mayo	1.75	1.50

Printed in sheets of 10+2 labels. Value $35.

Statesman Type of 1986
1990, June 21   Litho.   Perf. 14x15
807	A240	30p Michael Collins	6.00	4.00

Irish Missionaries — A304

Design: 50p, Working at water pump.

1990, June 21   **Perf. 15x14**
808 A304 26p multicolored   1.25 1.25
809 A304 50p multicolored   2.50 2.50

Garden
Flowers — A305

1990, Aug. 30   Litho.   Perf. 14x15
810 A305 26p Narcissus   1.00 1.00
811 A305 30p Rosa x hibernica   1.25 1.25
  a.   Bklt. pane, 2 each #810-811   10.00
812 A305 41p Primula   1.90 1.90
813 A305 50p Erica erigena   2.10 2.10
  a.   Booklet pane of 4, #810-813   11.00
        Nos. 810-813 (4)   6.25 6.25

See note following No. 584.

Theater
A306

Designs: No. 814, Playboy of the Western
World. No. 815, Juno and the Paycock. No.
816, The Field. No. 817, Waiting for Godot.

1990, Oct. 18   Litho.   Perf. 13½
814 A306 30p multicolored   2.25 2.25
815 A306 30p multicolored   2.25 2.25
816 A306 30p multicolored   2.25 2.25
817 A306 30p multicolored   2.25 2.25
  a.   Block or strip of 4, #814-817   9.00 9.00

A307

Christmas
A308

1990, Nov. 15   Litho.   Perf. 14x15
818 A307 26p Child praying   1.00 1.00
819 A307 26p Nativity scene   1.00 1.00
820 A308 30p Madonna and
            Child   1.25 1.25
821 A308 50p Adoration of the
            Magi   2.00 2.00
        Nos. 818-821 (4)   5.25 5.25

No. 818 sold only in discount sheets of 12
for £2.86. Value $17.50.

Love — A309

Irish
Cycles — A310

1991, Jan. 29   Litho.   Perf. 14x15
822 A309 26p shown   1.40 1.40
823 A309 30p Boy, girl kissing   1.75 1.75

1991, Mar. 5
824 A310 26p Starley rover   1.25 1.25
825 A310 30p Child's horse tricy-
            cle   1.50 1.50
826 A310 50p Penny farthing   2.40 2.40
  a.   Souvenir sheet of 3, #824-826   8.75 8.75
        Nos. 824-826 (3)   5.15 5.15

See note following No. 584.

1916
Rising,
75th Anniv.
A311

Design: Statue of Cuchulainn by Oliver
Sheppard, 1916 Proclamation.

1991, Apr. 3   Litho.   Perf. 15x14
827 A311 32p multicolored   6.00 5.00

Dublin,
European
City of
Culture
A312

Designs: 28p, La Traviata, performed by
Dublin Grand Opera Society. 32p, Dublin City
Hall. 44p, St. Patrick's Cathedral, 800th anniv.
52p, Custom House, 200th anniv.

1991, Apr. 11   Perf. 15x14
828 A312 28p multicolored   1.10 1.10
829 A312 32p multicolored   1.40 1.40
830 A312 44p multicolored   1.90 1.90
  a.   Booklet pane of 3, #828-830   6.75

Size: 41x25mm
Perf. 13½
831 A312 52p multicolored   2.25 2.25
  a.   Booklet pane of 4, #828-831   8.75
        Complete booklet, #830a, 831a   16.00
        Nos. 828-831 (4)   6.65 6.65

50th anniv. of Dublin Grand Opera Soc. (No.
828).

Europa
A313

1991, May 14   Litho.   Perf. 15x14
832 A313 32p Giotto probe   1.00   .75
833 A313 44p Hubble telescope   1.75 1.75

Williamite
Wars,
300th
Anniv.
A314

1991, May 14
834 A314 28p Siege of Athlone   2.50 2.50
835 A314 28p Treaty of Limerick   2.50 2.50
  a.   Pair, #834-835   5.00 5.00

Statesman Type of 1986 and

Charles Stewart
Parnell (1846-
1891),
Politician — A315

Society of
United
Irishmen,
Bicent.
A316

28p, John A. Costello (1891-1976),
politician.

Perf. 14x15, 15x14
1991, July 2   Litho.
836 A240 28p black   1.40 1.40
837 A315 32p multicolored   1.50 1.50
838 A316 52p multicolored   2.50 2.50
        Nos. 836-838 (3)   5.40 5.40

A317

Perf. 15x14, 14x15
1991, Sept. 3   Litho.
839 A317 28p Golfer putting,
            horiz.   2.00 2.00
840 A317 32p shown   3.00 3.00

Walker Cup Competition, Portmarnock Golf
Club (No. 839).

Irish
Sheep — A318

1991, Sept. 3   Perf. 14x15, 15x14
841 A318 32p Wicklow Cheviot   1.40 1.40
842 A318 38p Donegal Blackface   2.10 2.10
843 A318 52p Galway, horiz.   2.75 2.75
        Nos. 841-843 (3)   6.25 6.25

Fishing
Fleet
A319

1991, Oct. 17   Litho.   Perf. 15x14
844 A319 28p Boatyard   .90   .90
845 A319 32p Inshore trawler   1.25 1.25
  a.   Bklt. pane of 5, #845, 2 each
        #768, 783   6.75
  b.   Bklt. pane, 2 each #844, 845   8.00
846 A319 44p Inshore potter   2.25 2.25
847 A319 52p Factory ship   3.00 3.00
  a.   Booklet pane of 4, #844-847   11.00
        Nos. 844-847 (4)   7.40 7.40

See note following No. 584.

A320

Christmas
A321

1991, Nov. 14   Litho.   Perf. 14x15
848 A320 28p Wise men, star   1.00 1.00
849 A321 28p Annunciation   1.10 1.10
850 A321 32p Nativity   1.25 1.25
851 A321 52p Adoration of the
            Magi   3.00 3.00
        Nos. 848-851 (4)   6.35 6.35

No. 848 issued only in discount sheets of
13+2 labels which sold for £3.36. Value
$17.50.

Love
A322

Design: 32p, Rainbow over meadow, love
etched in stone, vert.

Perf. 15x14, 14x15
1992, Jan. 28   Litho.
852 A322 28p shown   1.25 1.25
853 A322 32p multicolored   1.90 1.90

1992
Summer
Olympics,
Barcelona
A323

1992, Feb. 25   Litho.   Perf. 15x14
854 A323 32p Boxing   1.60 1.60
855 A323 44p Sailing   1.90 1.90
  a.   Sheet of 4, 2 each #854-855   8.75 9.25

See note following No. 584.

Healthy
Lifestyle — A324

1992, Feb. 25   Perf. 14x15
856 A324 28p multicolored   2.25 2.25

Galway Chamber of Commerce and Industry, Bicent. A325

1992, Apr. 2   **Litho.**   **Perf. 15x14**
857 A325 28p multicolored   1.25 1.25

Intl. Maritime Heritage Year A326

Perf. 15x14, 14x15
1992, Apr. 2   **Litho.**
858 A326 32p Mari Cog   1.50 1.50
859 A326 52p Ovoca, vert.   2.00 2.00

Greetings — A327

1992, Apr. 2   **Perf. 14x15**
860 A327 28p Coastline   3.50 3.50
861 A327 28p Mountain   3.50 3.50
862 A327 32p Flowers   3.50 3.50
863 A327 32p Pond   3.50 3.50
  a.   Bklt. pane of 4, #860-863, 8
     English labels   14.00
  b.   Bklt. pane of 4, #860-863, 4
     English labels + 4 Gaelic
     labels   14.00
     Nos. 860-863 (4)   14.00 14.00

No. 863a contains Nos. 860-863 in order. No. 863b contains Nos. 862, 863, 860 and 861 in order.

Discovery of America, 500th Anniv. A328

Europa: 44p, Landing in New World.

1992, May 14   **Litho.**   **Perf. 15x14**
864 A328 32p multicolored   1.25 1.00
865 A328 44p multicolored   1.50 1.25

Irish in the Americas — A329

Design: No. 867, The White House, bridge, railroad workers, musicians, workers.

1992, May 14   **Perf. 13½**
866 A329 52p multicolored   2.50 2.50
867 A329 52p multicolored   2.50 2.50
  a.   Pair, #866-867   5.00 5.00

Pine Marten A330

1992, July 9   **Litho.**   **Perf. 15x14**
868 A330 28p shown   1.60 1.60
869 A330 32p In tree   1.90 1.90
870 A330 44p With young   2.75 2.75
871 A330 52p Holding bird   3.50 3.50
     Nos. 868-871 (4)   9.75 9.75

World Wildlife Fund.

Trinity College, Dublin, 400th Anniv. — A331

1992, Sept. 2   **Litho.**   **Perf. 13½**
872 A331 32p Library   1.40 1.40
873 A331 52p Main entrance   2.25 2.25

Views of Dublin by James Malton, Bicent. A332

1992, Sept. 2   **Perf. 15x14**
874 A332 28p Rotunda, Assem-
     bly rooms   1.25 1.25
875 A332 44p Charlemont House   1.90 1.90

Single European Market A333

1992, Oct. 15   **Litho.**   **Perf. 15x14**
876 A333 32p multicolored   2.00 2.00
  a.   Bklt. pane of 3   6.50
  b.   Bklt. pane of 4   8.50

No. 876b comes with stamps in three formats: four singles, two pairs, and block of four. See note following No. 584.

Food and Farming — A334

1992, Oct. 15   **Perf. 14x15**
877 A334 32p Fresh food   2.50 2.50
878 A334 32p Cattle   2.50 2.50
879 A334 32p Combine har-
     vesting grain   2.50 2.50
880 A334 32p Growing vegeta-
     bles   2.50 2.50
  a.   Strip of 4, #877-880   10.00 10.00

A335

Christmas A336

Designs: No. 881, Rural churchyard. No. 882, The Annunciation, manuscript illustration, Chester Beatty Library, Dublin. 32p, Adoration of the Shepherds, by Jocopo da Empoli. 52p, Adoration of the Magi, by Johann Rottenhammer.

1992, Nov. 19
881 A335 28p multicolored   1.10 1.10
882 A336 28p multicolored   1.25 1.25
883 A336 32p multicolored   1.25 1.25
884 A336 52p multicolored   2.25 2.25
     Nos. 881-884 (4)   5.85 5.85

No. 881 issued only in discount sheets of 13+2 labels which sold for £3.36. Value $17.50.

Love A337

Design: 28p, Queen of Hearts, vert.

Perf. 14x15, 15x14
1993, Jan. 26   **Litho.**
885 A337 28p multicolored   1.25 1.25
886 A337 32p multicolored   1.60 1.60

Irish Impressionist Paintings — A338

Designs: 28p, Evening at Tangier, by Sir John Lavery. 32p, The Goose Girl, by William J. Leech. 44p, La Jeune Bretonne, by Roderic O'Conor, vert. 52p, Lustre Jug, by Walter Osborne, vert.

1993, Mar. 4   **Perf. 13**
887 A338 28p multicolored   1.40 1.40
888 A338 32p multicolored   1.75 1.75
  a.   Booklet pane of 2, #887-888   4.25
889 A338 44p multicolored   2.00 2.00
890 A338 52p multicolored   2.75 2.75
  a.   Booklet pane of 2, #889-890   5.50
  b.   Booklet pane of 4, #887-890   8.50
     Nos. 887-890 (4)   7.90 7.90

No. 890b exists in two formats with different margin inscriptions.

Orchids — A339

1993, Apr. 20   **Litho.**   **Perf. 14x15**
891 A339 28p Bee orchid   1.10 1.10
892 A339 32p O'Kelly's orchid   1.40 1.40
893 A339 38p Dark red hel-
     leborine   2.50 2.50

894 A339 52p Irish lady's
     tresses   2.75 2.75
  a.   Souvenir sheet of 4, #891-
     894   9.75 9.75
  b.   As "a," with blue inscription   15.00 15.00
     Nos. 891-894 (4)   7.75 7.75

No. 894b has a larger top margin than No. 894a. Added Inscription includes text and flags of Ireland and Thailand.

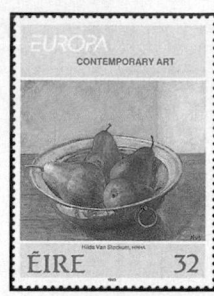

Contemporary Paintings — A340

Europa: 32p, Pears in a Copper Pan, by Hilda van Stockum. 44p, Arrieta Orzola, by Tony O'Malley.

1993, May 18   **Litho.**   **Perf. 13x13½**
895 A340 32p multicolored   1.25 1.25
896 A340 44p multicolored   1.75 1.75

Issued in sheets of 10 + 2 labels.

Gaelic League, Cent. A341

Design: 52p, Illuminated manuscript presented to founder Douglas Hyde, vert.

Perf. 15x14, 14x15
1993, July 8   **Litho.**
897 A341 32p multicolored   1.50 1.50
898 A341 52p multicolored   2.50 2.50

Irish Amateur Swimming Assoc., Cent. A342

Designs: No. 899, Swimmer diving into water. No. 900, Woman swimming.

1993, July 8   **Perf. 15x14**
899 A342 32p multicolored   2.00 2.00
900 A342 32p multicolored   2.00 2.00
  a.   Pair, #899-900   4.00 4.00

Royal Hospital Donnybrook, 250th Anniv. — A343

Ceide Fields, County Mayo A345

Carlow College,
Bicent. — A344

Edward Bunting
(1773-1843),
Composer — A346

Perf. 15x14, 14x15, 13½ (52p)

1993, Sept. 2   **Litho.**
901	A343	28p multicolored	1.25	1.25
902	A344	32p multicolored	1.40	1.40
903	A345	44p multicolored	2.00	2.00
904	A346	52p multicolored	2.50	2.50
		Nos. 901-904 (4)	7.15	7.15

Irish Buses
A347

Designs: 28p, Great Northern Railways Gardner. 32p, CIE Leyland Titan. No. 907, Horse-drawn omnibus. No. 908, Char-a-banc.

1993, Oct. 12   **Litho.**   **Perf. 15x14**
905	A347	28p multicolored	1.25	1.25
906	A347	32p multicolored	1.25	1.25
a.		Booklet pane, 2 each #905-906	6.50	
907	A347	52p multicolored	2.50	2.50
908	A347	52p multicolored	2.50	2.50
a.		Pair, #907-908	5.00	5.00
b.		Booklet pane of 4, #905-908	7.50	
		Nos. 905-908 (4)	7.50	7.50

A348

Christmas
A349

Designs: 32p, Mary placing infant Jesus in manger. 52p, Adoration of the shepherds.

Perf. 14x15, 15x14

1993, Nov. 16   **Litho.**
909	A348	28p multicolored	1.10	1.10
910	A349	28p multicolored	1.10	1.10
911	A349	32p multicolored	1.25	1.25
912	A349	52p multicolored	2.50	2.50
		Nos. 909-912 (4)	5.95	5.95

No. 909 issued only in discount sheets of 13+2 labels which sold for £3.36. Value $15.

Love
A350

32p, Man, woman in shape of heart, vert.

Perf. 15x14, 14x15

1994, Jan. 27   **Litho.**
913	A350	28p multicolored	1.10	1.10
914	A350	32p multicolored	1.60	1.60

Greetings
Stamps — A351

1994, Jan. 27   **Perf. 14x15**
915	A351	32p Face in sun	3.75	3.75
916	A351	32p Face in flower	3.75	3.75
917	A351	32p Face in heart	3.75	3.75
a.		Souv. sheet of 3, #915-917	11.50	11.50
918	A351	32p Face in rose	3.75	3.75
a.		Booklet pane of 4, #915-918, 4 English + 4 Gaelic labels	15.00	
b.		As "a," 8 English labels	15.00	
		Nos. 915-918 (4)	15.00	15.00

New Year 1994 (Year of the Dog), Hong Kong '94 (No. 917a).
No. 918a contains Nos. 915-918 in order. No. 918b contains Nos. 917, 918, 915, 916 in order.

Macra na
Feirme,
50th Anniv.
A352

The Taking
of Christ,
by
Caravaggio
A353

Irish Co-operative Organization
Society, Cent. — A354

Irish
Congress
of Trade
Unions,
Cent.
A355

1994, Mar. 2   **Litho.**   **Perf. 15x14**
919	A352	28p blue & gold	1.00	1.00
920	A353	32p multicolored	1.25	1.25
921	A354	38p multicolored	1.60	1.60
922	A355	52p blue, blk & lt blue	1.90	1.90
		Nos. 919-922 (4)	5.75	5.75

Voyages of
St.
Brendan
(484-577)
A356

Europa: 32p, St. Brendan, Irish monks sailing past volcano. 44p, St. Brendan on island with sheep, monks in boat.

1994, Apr. 18   **Litho.**   **Perf. 15x14**
923	A356	32p multicolored	1.25	1.25
924	A356	44p multicolored	1.75	1.75
a.		Miniature sheet of 2, #923-924	3.00	3.00

See Faroe Islands Nos. 264-265; Iceland Nos. 780-781.

Parliamentary Anniversaries — A357

#925, 1st meeting of the Dail, 1919. #926, 4th direct elections to European Parliament.

1994, Apr. 27
925	A357	32p multicolored	1.60	1.60
926	A357	32p multicolored	1.60	1.60
a.		Booklet pane, 1 each #925-926	3.75	
b.		Booklet pane, 2 each #925-926	7.50	
		Complete booklet, #926a, 926b	11.50	

1994 World Cup
Soccer
Championships,
US — A358

Players from: No. 927, Argentina in striped shirt, Ireland in green. No. 928, Ireland, Germany.

1994, May 31   **Perf. 14x15**
927	A358	32p multicolored	2.50	2.50
928	A358	32p multicolored	2.50	2.50
a.		Pair, #927-928	5.00	5.00

Printed in sheets of 4 No. 928a plus label. Value, $20.

Women's
Hockey
A359

32p, 1994 Women's Hockey World Cup, Dublin. 52p, Irish Ladies' Hockey Union, cent.

1994, May 31   **Perf. 13x13½**
929	A359	32p multicolored	1.75	1.75
930	A359	52p multicolored	2.00	2.00

Moths
A360

1994, July 12   **Litho.**   **Perf. 14½x14**
931	A360	28p Garden tiger	1.40	1.40
932	A360	32p Burren green	1.50	1.50
933	A360	38p Emperor	1.90	1.90
934	A360	52p Elephant hawkmoth	2.40	2.40
a.		Souvenir sheet of 4, #931-934	9.00	9.00
b.		As "a," overprinted	12.00	12.00
		Nos. 931-934 (4)	7.20	7.20

Size: 34x23mm
Self-Adhesive
Die Cut Perf. 11½
935	A360	32p like #932	4.50	4.50
936	A360	32p like #931	4.50	4.50
937	A360	32p like #934	4.50	4.50
938	A360	32p like #933	4.50	4.50
a.		Strip of 4, #935-938	18.00	18.00

Overprint on No. 934b shows PHILAKOREA '94 exhibition emblem and Chinese inscription.

A361

A362

A363

Anniversaries and Events — A364

28p, Medieval view of Drogheda. No. 940, Edmund Ignatius Rice (1762-1844), philantropist. No. 941, Edmund Burke (1729-97), political commentator. No. 942, Eamonn Andrews (1922-87), broadcaster. No. 943, Vickers Vimy aircraft.

1994, Sept. 6   **Litho.**   **Perf. 13½**
939	A361	28p multicolored	1.25	1.25

Perf. 14x14½
940	A362	32p multicolored	1.40	1.40

Perf. 14x13½
941	A363	32p multicolored	1.40	1.40
942	A363	52p multicolored	2.25	2.25

Perf. 15x14
943	A364	52p multicolored	2.25	2.25
		Nos. 939-943 (5)	8.55	8.55

Drogheda, 800th anniv. (No. 939). First Newfoundland-Ireland transatlantic flight, 75th anniv. (No. 943).

Nobel
Prize
Winners
A365

No. 944, George Bernard Shaw (1856-1950), dramatist, essayist. No. 945, Samuel Beckett (1906-89), playwright. 32p, Sean McBride (1904-88), statesman. 52p, William Butler Yeats (1865-1939), poet.

1994, Oct. 18   **Litho.**   **Perf. 15x14**
944	A365	28p multicolored	1.10	1.10
945	A365	28p multicolored	1.10	1.10
a.		Pair, #944-945	2.25	2.25
946	A365	32p multicolored	1.25	1.25
a.		Booklet pane of 3, #944-946	3.25	
b.		Bklt. pane, #944-945, 2 #946	4.50	
947	A365	52p multicolored	1.75	1.75
a.		Booklet pane, 1 #946, 2 #947	5.00	
b.		Booklet pane of 4, #944-947	5.50	
		Complete bklt., #946a-946b, 947a-947b	22.50	
		Nos. 944-947 (4)	5.20	5.20

A366

Christmas
A367

#948, Stained glass nativity scene. #949, Annunciation, detail, 11th cent. ivory plaque. 32p, Flight Into Egypt, 15th cent. wood carving. 52p, Nativity, detail, 11th cent. ivory plaque.

1994, Nov. 17   Litho.   Perf. 14x15

948	A366	28p multicolored	1.25 1.25
949	A367	28p multicolored	1.40 1.40
950	A367	32p multicolored	1.50 1.50
951	A367	52p multicolored	2.50 2.50
		Nos. 948-951 (4)	6.65 6.65

No. 948 issued only in discount sheets of 13 plus 2 labels which sold for £3.36. Value $16.50.

Greetings
Stamps — A368

1995, Jan. 24   Litho.   Perf. 14x15

952	A368	32p Tree of hearts	3.00 3.00

Booklet Stamps

953	A368	32p Teddy bear, balloon	3.00 3.00
954	A368	32p Clown juggling hearts	3.00 3.00
955	A368	32p Bouquet of flowers	3.00 3.00
a.		Booklet pane, #952-955 + 4 English, 4 Gaelic labels	12.00
b.		As "a," 8 English labels Complete booklet, #955a-955b	12.00 24.00
c.		Souvenir sheet, #952, 954-955 + 3 English, 3 Gaelic labels	10.00 10.00

New Year 1995 (Year of the Boar) (No. 955c).

No. 955a contains Nos. 953-954, 952, 955 in order. No. 955b contains Nos. 952, 955, 953-954 in order.

Narrow Gauge Railways A369

1995, Feb. 28   Litho.   Perf. 15x14

956	A369	28p West Clare	1.10 1.10
957	A369	32p Co. Donegal	1.40 1.40
958	A369	38p Cork & Muskerry	1.60 1.60
959	A369	52p Cavan & Leitrim	2.25 2.25
a.		Souvenir sheet of 4, #956-959	9.00 9.00
		Nos. 956-959 (4)	6.35 6.35

No. 959a exists with Singapore '95 overprint in sheet margin. Value $10.

Peace & Freedom A370

Europa: Nos. 960, 962, Stylized dove, reconstructed city. 44p, No. 963, Stylized dove, map of Europe.

1995, Apr. 6   Litho.   Perf. 15x14

960	A370	32p multicolored	1.00 1.00
961	A370	44p multicolored	1.75 1.75

Size: 34½x23mm
Self-Adhesive Coil Stamps
Die Cut Perf. 11½

962	A370	32p multicolored	4.00 4.00
963	A370	32p multicolored	4.00 4.00

Nos. 962-963 are coil stamps, printed in horizontal rolls of 100, with 50 of each design alternating.

1995 Rugby World Cup A371

1995, Apr. 6   Perf. 14

964	A371	32p shown	1.40 1.40
965	A371	52p Player being tackled	2.00 2.00

Souvenir Sheet

966	A371	£1 like #964	8.00 9.00

No. 966 has a continuous design.

A372   A373

32p, Irish soldiers, Cross of Fontenoy.

1995, May 15   Photo.   Perf. 11½

967	A372	32p multicolored	1.40 1.40

Battle of Fontenoy, 250th Anniv. See Belgium No. 1583.

1995, May 15   Litho.   Perf. 14x15

Military uniforms: 28p, Irish Brigade, French Army, 1745. No. 969, Tercio Irlanda, Army of Flanders, 1605. No. 970, Royal Dublin Fusiliers, 1914. 38p, St. Patrick's Battalion, Papal Army, 1860. 52p, The Fighting 69th, Army of Potomac, 1861.

968	A373	28p multicolored	1.25 1.25
969	A373	32p multicolored	1.40 1.40
a.		Bklt. pane, 2 ea #968-969	5.00
970	A373	32p multicolored	1.40 1.40
971	A373	38p multicolored	1.75 1.75
a.		Bklt. pane of 3, #968-969, #971	4.50
972	A373	52p multicolored	3.00 3.00
a.		Bklt. pane of 3, #968-969, 972	4.00
b.		Bklt. pane of 4, #968-969, 971-972	4.75
		Complete booklet, #969a, 971a, 972a, 972b	22.50
		Nos. 968-972 (5)	8.80 8.80

Radio, Cent. A374

Designs: No. 973, Guglielmo Marconi, transmitting equipment. No. 974, Radio channel dial.

1995, June 8   Litho.   Perf. 13½

973	A374	32p multicolored	12.50 12.50
974	A374	32p multicolored	12.50 12.50
a.		Pair, #973-974	25.00 25.00

See Germany No. 1900, Italy Nos. 2038-2039, San Marino No. 1336-1337, Vatican City No. 978-979.

A375

A376

A377

Anniversaries & Events A378

Designs: 28p, Dr. Bartholomew Mosse, Rotunda Hospital. No. 976, Piper, laurel wreath over map of Europe. No. 977, St. Patrick's College. 52p, Geological map of Ireland.

1995, July 27   Litho.   Perf. 14½x14

975	A375	28p multicolored	1.25 1.25
976	A376	32p multicolored	1.40 1.40

Perf. 14½

977	A377	32p multicolored	1.40 1.40

Perf. 13½

978	A378	52p multicolored	2.25 2.25
		Nos. 975-978 (4)	6.30 6.30

Rotunda Hospital, 250th anniv. (No. 975). End of World War II, 50th anniv. (No. 976). St. Patrick's College, Maynooth, bicent. No. 977). Geological survey of Ireland, 150th anniv. (No. 978).

Reptiles & Amphibians — A379

1995, Sept. 1   Litho.   Perf. 15x14

979	A379	32p Natterjack toad	1.25 1.25
980	A379	32p Common lizard	1.25 1.25
981	A379	32p Smooth newt	1.25 1.25
982	A379	32p Common frog	1.25 1.25
a.		Strip of 4, #979-982	12.50 12.50

Die Cut Perf. 9¼
Size: 34½x22½mm
Self-Adhesive

982B	A379	32p like No. 979	4.50 4.50
982C	A379	32p like No. 980	4.50 4.50
982D	A379	32p like No. 981	4.50 4.50
982E	A379	32p like No. 982	4.50 4.50
f.		Strip of 4, Nos. 982B-982E	18.00 18.00

Natl. Botanic Gardens, Bicent. — A380

Designs: 32p, Crinum moorei. 38p, Sarracenia x moorei. 44p, Solanum crispum "glasnevin".

1995, Oct. 9   Litho.   Perf. 14x15

983	A380	32p multicolored	1.25 1.25
984	A380	38p multicolored	1.40 1.40
985	A380	44p multicolored	1.75 1.75
a.		Booklet pane of 3, #983-985	6.50
b.		Bklt. pane of 4, #984-985, 2 #983	7.75
		Complete booklet, #985a-985b	13.50
		Nos. 983-985 (3)	4.40 4.40

UN, 50th Anniv. A381

1995, Oct. 19   Perf. 13x13½

986	A381	32p shown	1.50 1.50
987	A381	52p UN, "50" emblem	2.50 2.50

A382

Christmas A383

Designs: No. 988, Adoration of the Magi. No. 989, Adoration of the Shepherds. 32p, Adoration of the Magi. 52p, Nativity.

1995, Nov. 16   Litho.   Perf. 14½x14

988	A382	28p multicolored	1.25 1.25
989	A383	28p multicolored	1.25 1.25
990	A383	32p multicolored	1.60 1.60
991	A383	52p multicolored	2.25 2.25
		Nos. 988-991 (4)	6.35 6.35

No. 988 issued only in discount sheets of 13+2 labels, which sold for £3.36. Value $15.

Greetings/Love Stamps — A384

Television cartoon characters from "Zog, Zig and Zag:" No. 992, With hearts. No. 993, Waving hands. No. 994, In car, wearing space helmets. No. 995, Holding out hands, wearing hats.

1996, Jan. 23   Litho.   Perf. 14x15

992	A384	32p multicolored	3.75 3.75

Booklet Stamps

993	A384	32p multicolored	3.75 3.75
994	A384	32p multicolored	3.75 3.75
995	A384	32p multicolored	3.75 3.75
a.		Booklet pane, Nos. 992-995, 5 English, 3 Gaelic labels	13.50
b.		As "a," 7 English, 1 Gaelic label Complete booklet, #995a-995b	13.50 30.00

c. Souvenir sheet, Nos. 992, 994-995 + 4 English, 2 Gaelic labels, 1 large label with Chinese inscription   10.00 10.00

No. 995a contains Nos. 993-995, 992 in order. No. 995b contains Nos. 995, 992-994 in order.

New Year 1996 (Year of the Rat) (No. 995c).

A385

1996 Summer/Paralympic Games, Atlanta — A386

1996, Feb. 1
996	A385	28p show	1.50	1.50
997	A386	32p Discus	1.50	1.50
998	A386	32p Canoeing	1.50	1.50
999	A386	32p Running	1.50	1.50
a.		Strip of 3, Nos. 997-999	6.00	6.00

No. 999a printed in sheets of 9 stamps. Value $18.

L'Imaginaire Irlandais — A387

1996, Mar. 12   **Litho.**   ***Perf. 15x14***
1000	A387	32p multicolored	3.00	3.00

Irish Horse Racing A388

1996, Mar. 12   **Litho.**   ***Perf. 15x14***
1001	A388	28p Fairyhouse	1.25	1.25
1002	A388	32p Punchestown	1.40	1.40
1003	A388	32p The Curragh	1.40	1.40
a.		Pair, #1002-1003	2.75	2.75
b.		Booklet pane, 2 #1001, 1 each #1002-1003	5.50	
c.		Souv. sheet, #1002-1003	22.50	22.50
1004	A388	38p Galway	1.75	1.75
a.		Booklet pane, 2 #1002, 1 #1004	5.25	
1005	A388	52p Leopardstown	2.25	2.25
a.		Bklt. pane, #1005, 2 #1003	5.25	
b.		Bklt. pane, 1 ea #1002-1005	6.75	
		Complete bklt., Nos. 1003b, 1004a, 1005a, 1005b	23.00	
		Nos. 1001-1005 (5)	*8.05*	*8.05*

No. 1003c for China '96.

UNESCO World Heritage Site A389

UNICEF, 50th Anniv. A390

Designs: 28p, Passage tombs, Bru na Bóinne National Monument, Boyne Valley. 32p, Children.

1996, Apr. 2   **Litho.**   ***Perf. 14***
1006	A389	28p sepia & black	1.50	1.50
1007	A390	32p multicolored	2.00	2.00

Europa A391

32p, Louie Bennett (1870-1956), Suffragette, trade unionist. 44p, Lady Augusta Gregory (1852-1932), playwright, co-founder of Abbey Theatre.

1996, Apr. 2   ***Perf. 15x14***
1008	A391	32p violet	*1.00*	*1.00*
1009	A391	44p green	*1.50*	*1.50*

Die Cut 9¼
Self-Adhesive Coil Stamps
1009A	A391	32p like #1008	5.00	5.00
1009B	A391	32p like #1009	5.00	5.00

Nos. 962-963 are coil stamps, printed in horizontal rolls with each value alternating.

Irish Winners of Tourist Trophy Motorcycle Races — A392

32p, Stanley Woods. 44p, Artie Bell. No. 1012, Alec Bennett. 52p, No. 1014, Robert & Joey Dunlop.

1996, May 30   ***Perf. 14***
1010	A392	32p multicolored	1.25	1.25
1011	A392	44p multicolored	1.90	1.90
1012	A392	50p multicolored	2.50	2.50
1013	A392	52p multicolored	2.50	2.50
		Nos. 1010-1013 (4)	*8.15*	*8.15*

Souvenir Sheet
1014	A392	50p multicolored	4.50	4.50

See Isle of Man Nos. 701-705.

Michael Davitt (1846-1906), Nationalist Leader — A393

1996, July 4   **Litho.**   ***Perf. 13½x13***
1015	A393	28p multicolored	1.40	1.40

Ireland's Presidency of the European Union A394

1996, July 4   ***Perf. 13x13½***
1016	A394	32p multicolored	1.50	1.50

Thomas A. McLaughlin (1896-1971), Designer of Ardnacrusha Hydro-electric Power Station — A395

1996, July 4
1017	A395	38p multicolored	1.90	1.90

Bord na Móna (Irish Peat Corp.), 50th Anniv. A396

1996, July 4
1018	A396	52p multicolored	2.40	2.40

Irish Naval Service, 50th Anniv. A397

Designs: 32p, Coastal patrol vessel. 44p, Corvette. 52p, Motor torpedo boat, vert.

1996, July 18   ***Perf. 15x14***
1019	A397	32p multicolored	1.50	1.50
a.		Booklet pane, 3 #1019	5.50	
1020	A397	44p multicolored	2.25	2.25
1021	A397	52p multicolored	3.00	3.00
a.		Booklet pane of 3, #1019-1021	10.50	
		Complete booklet, #1019a, 1021a	16.00	
		Nos. 1019-1021 (3)	*6.75*	*6.75*

People with Disabilities A398

1996, Sept. 3   **Litho.**   ***Perf. 14x15***
1022	A398	28p Man in wheelchair	1.40	1.40
1023	A398	28p Blind woman, child	1.40	1.40
a.		Pair, #1022-1023	3.00	3.00

Freshwater Ducks A399

Designs: 32p, Anas crecca. 38p, Anas clypeata. 44p, Anas penelope. 52p, Anas platyrhynchos.

1996, Sept. 24   ***Perf. 15x14***
1024	A399	32p multicolored	1.40	1.40
1025	A399	38p multicolored	1.75	1.75
1026	A399	44p multicolored	2.10	2.10
1027	A399	52p multicolored	2.75	2.75
a.		Souvenir sheet, #1024-1027	9.75	9.75
		Nos. 1024-1027 (4)	*8.00*	*8.00*

No. 1027a is a continuous design.

Motion Pictures, Cent. A400

1996, Oct. 17   **Litho.**   ***Perf. 13½***
1028	A400	32p Man of Aran	2.00	2.00
1029	A400	32p My Left Foot	2.00	2.00
1030	A400	32p The Commitments	2.00	2.00
1031	A400	32p The Field	2.00	2.00
a.		Strip of 4, #1028-1031	8.00	8.00

A401

Christmas A402

No. 1032, Stained glass scene of Holy Family. No. 1033, Adoration of the Magi. 32p, The Annunciation. 52p, Shepherds receive news of Christ's birth.

1996, Nov. 19   ***Perf. 14***
1032	A401	28p multicolored	1.40	1.40
1033	A402	28p multicolored	1.40	1.40
1034	A402	32p multicolored	1.50	1.50
1035	A402	52p multicolored	2.75	2.75
		Nos. 1032-1035 (4)	*7.05*	*7.05*

No. 1032 sold only in discount sheets of 15 for £3.92. Value $21.

Spideog Robin — A403

Greenland White-fronted Goose — A404

Perf. 15x14, 14x15
1997, Jan. 16   **Litho.**
1036	A403	28p Blue tit. horiz.	2.00	2.00
1037	A403	32p shown	2.50	2.50
b.		Perf. 14	2.50	2.50
1038	A403	44p Puffin	3.50	3.50
1039	A403	52p Barn owl	4.00	4.00
1040	A404	£1 shown	6.50	6.50

Booklet Stamp
Size: 18x21mm, 21x18mm
1040A	A403	32p Like #1037	3.00	3.00
b.		Booklet pane, 3 #1040A, 1 #770	14.00	
		Complete booklet, #1040b	14.00	

Size: 20x23mm
Perf. 14x15
1040C	A403	32p Like #1037, "Eire" 8½mm wide ('99)	3.00	3.00
d.		Bklt. pane of 5 + 5 labels	15.00	
		Complete booklet	15.00	
		Nos. 1036-1040C (7)	*24.50*	*24.50*

On Nos. 1037,1037b "Eire" is 9mm wide, and size of design is 21x24mm.
See Nos. 1053-1054, 1067, 1076-1081A, 1094, 1105-1115C, 1314-1319B, 1340-1343. Compare with Nos. 1353-1373.
Issued: No. 1040C, 6/30/99.

Greetings
Stamps — A405

Designs: No. 1041, Doves on tree limb. No. 1042, Cow jumping over moon. No. 1043, Pig going to market. No. 1044, Rooster on fence.

1997, Jan. 28   Litho.   Perf. 14x15
1041 A405 32p multicolored   3.00 3.00

Booklet Stamps
1042 A405 32p multicolored   3.00 3.00
1043 A405 32p multicolored   3.00 3.00
1044 A405 32p multicolored   3.00 3.00
  a.   Booklet pane, #1041-1044,
    5 English, 3 Gaelic labels   12.00
  b.   As "a," #1041-1044, 7 En-
    glish, 1 Gaelic label   12.00
    Complete booklet, #1044a,
    1044b   24.00
  c.   Souvenir sheet, 1042-1044,
    3 English, 3 Gaelic labels
    + 1 large label with "Year
    of the Ox," Hong Kong '97   10.00 10.00

No. 1044a contains Nos. 1042, 1041, 1043-1044 in order. No. 1044b contains Nos. 1043-1044, 1041-1042 in order.

Irish State,
75th Anniv.
A406

Designs: No. 1045, Dáil, national flag, constitution. No. 1046, Defense forces, badges, UN flag. No. 1047, Four Courts, scales of justice. No. 1048, Garda badge, Garda Síochána.

1997, Feb. 18   Perf. 15x14
1045 A406 32p multicolored   1.75 1.75
1046 A406 32p multicolored   1.75 1.75
  a.   Pair, #1045-1046   3.50 3.50
1047 A406 52p multicolored   2.50 2.50
1048 A406 52p multicolored   2.50 2.50
  a.   Pair, #1047-1048   5.00 5.00

See Nos. 1055-1058, 1082-1084, 1095-1096.

Marine
Mammals
A407

Designs: 28p, Halichoerus grypus, vert. 32p, Tursiops truncatus, vert. 44p, Phocaena phocaena. 52p, Orcinus orca.

Perf. 14x15, 15x14
1997, Mar. 6   Litho.
1049 A407 28p multicolored   1.10 1.10
1050 A407 32p multicolored   1.25 1.25
1051 A407 44p multicolored   1.75 1.75
1052 A407 52p multicolored   2.25 2.25
  a.   Souvenir sheet, #1049-1052   8.50 8.50
    Nos. 1049-1052 (4)   6.35 6.35

Bird Type of 1997
Die Cut Perf. 9x9½

1997, Mar. 6   Litho.
Self-Adhesive Coil Stamps
1053 A403 32p Peregrine
    falcon   7.50 7.50
1054 A403 32p like #1037   7.50 7.50
  a.   Pair, #1053-1054   17.50

Die Cut Perf. 11x11¼
1054B A403 32p Like #1053   20.00 20.00
1054C A403 32p Like #1054   20.00 20.00
  d.   Pair, #1054B-1054C   40.00
    Nos. 1053-1054C (4)   55.00 55.00

Issued: Nos. 1053-1054, 3/6/97; Nos. 1054B-1054C, 4/97.

Irish State, 75th Anniv. Type of 1997
No. 1055, Singer, violinist, bodhran player. No. 1056, Athlete, soccer and hurling players. No. 1057, Irish currency, blueprint, food processing plant. No. 1058, Abbey Theatre

emblem, books, palette, paintbrushes, Séamus Heaney manuscript.

1997, Apr. 3   Perf. 15x14
1055 A406 32p multicolored   1.50 1.50
1056 A406 32p multicolored   1.50 1.50
  a.   Pair, #1055-1056   3.00 3.00
1057 A406 52p multicolored   2.50 2.50
1058 A406 52p multicolored   2.50 2.50
  a.   Pair, #1057-1058   5.00 5.00

Irish
Coinage,
Millennium
A408

1997, Apr. 3   Perf. 15x14
1059 A408 32p First Irish coin   4.00 4.00

Stories and
Legends
A409

Europa: 32p, "The Children of Lir" flying as swans. 44p, "Oisin & Niamh" on horse.

1997, May 14   Litho.   Perf. 14
1060 A409 32p multicolored   1.00 1.00
1061 A409 44p multicolored   1.50 1.50

Die Cut Perf. 9x9½
Self-Adhesive Coil Stamps
1062 A409 32p like #1060   2.50 2.50
1063 A409 44p like #1061   2.50 2.50
  a.   Pair, #1062-1063   5.00

The Great
Famine,
150th
Anniv.
A410

Designs: 28p, Passengers waiting to board emigrant ship. 32p, Family group attending dying child. 52p, Irish Society of Friends soup kitchen.

1997, May 14   Litho.   Perf. 15x14
1064 A410 28p multicolored   1.40 1.40
1065 A410 32p multicolored   1.50 1.50
1066 A410 52p multicolored   2.50 2.50
    Nos. 1064-1066 (3)   5.40 5.40

Bird Type of 1997
Souvenir Sheet
1997, May 29   Perf. 14
1067 A404 £2 Pintail, horiz.   16.00 16.00

PACIFIC 97.
No. 1067 shows the duck's head in brown. See No. 1111 for stamp with duck's head in black.

Kate O'Brien
(1897-1974),
Novelist — A411

1997, July 1   Litho.   Perf. 14
1068 A411 28p multicolored   1.25 1.25

St. Columba
(521-97), Irish
Patron
Saint — A412

1997, July 1   Perf. 14x15
1069 A412 28p multicolored   1.25 1.25

A413

A414

Designs: 32p, Daniel O'Connell (1775-1847), politician. 52p, John Wesley (1703-91), founder of Methodism, first visit to Ireland, 250th anniv.

1997, July 1   Perf. 14x14½
1070 A413 32p multicolored   1.60 1.60
1071 A414 52p multicolored   2.25 2.25

Lighthouses — A415

Designs: No. 1072, Baily. No. 1073, Tarbert. 38p, Hook Head, vert. 50p, Fastnet.

1997, July 1   Perf. 15x14, 14x15
1072 A415 32p multicolored   1.75 1.75
1073 A415 32p multicolored   1.75 1.75
  a.   Pair, #1072-1073   3.50 3.50
  b.   Bklt. pane, #1073, 2 #1072   4.50
  c.   Bklt. pane, 2 ea #1072-1073   6.00
1074 A415 38p multicolored   1.75 1.75
1075 A415 50p multicolored   2.40 1.60
  a.   Booklet pane, #1074-1075   4.50
  b.   Bklt. pane of 4, #1073a,
    1074-1075   7.50
    Complete booklet, #1073b,
    1073c, 1075a, 1075b   24.00

Bird Types of 1997
Perf. 14x15, 15x14
1997, Aug. 27   Litho.
1076 A403   1p Magpie   .75   .75
1077 A403   2p Gannet   .75   .75
1078 A403   4p Corncrake   .75   .75
1079 A403 10p Kingfisher   1.00 1.00
1080 A403 20p Lapwing   1.75 1.75
1081 A404   £5 Shelduck   25.00 19.00

Booklet Stamp
Size: 18x21mm
1081A A403   4p Like #1078   4.00 4.00
    Nos. 1076-1081A (7)   34.00 27.25

Irish State, 75th Anniv. Type of 1997
28p, Quill, page from Annals of Four Masters, No. 128. 32p, Stained glass window, No. 82. 52p, Aer Lingus airplane, letter, No. C7.

1997, Aug. 27   Perf. 15x14
1082 A406 28p multicolored   1.10 1.10
1083 A406 32p multicolored   1.25 1.25
1084 A406 52p multicolored   2.25 2.25
    Nos. 1082-1084 (3)   4.60 4.60

St. Patrick's
Battalion, 150th
Anniv. — A416

1997, Sept. 12 Litho. Perf. 14x13½
1085 A416 32p multicolored   2.75 2.75
    See Mexico No. 2049.

Bram
Stoker's
"Dracula"
A417

Scenes of Dracula: 28p, Being transformed into a bat, vert. 32p, With potential victim, vert. 38p, Emerging from coffin. 52p, With wolf.

1997, Oct. 1   Perf. 14x15, 15x14
1086 A417 28p multicolored   1.60 1.60
1087 A417 32p multicolored   2.00 2.00
  a.   Souvenir sheet of 1   5.50 5.50
1088 A417 38p multicolored   2.50 2.50
1089 A417 52p multicolored   3.00 3.00
  a.   Souv. sheet of 4, #1086-
    1089   11.50 11.50
    Nos. 1086-1089 (4)   9.10 9.10

Stamps from Nos. 1087a, 1089a have souvenir sheet background framing vignette.

A418

Christmas — A419

Nos. 1090-1092: Different images of Holy Family in stained glass. No. 1093, Christmas tree.

1997, Nov. 18   Litho.   Perf. 14x15
1090 A418 28p multicolored   1.10 1.10
1091 A418 32p multicolored   1.40 1.40
1092 A418 52p multicolored   2.00 2.00
    Nos. 1090-1092 (3)   4.50 4.50

Self-Adhesive
Serpentine Die Cut 9x9½
1093 A419 28p multicolored   1.25 1.25
  a.   Booklet pane, 20 #1093   25.00

By its nature, No. 1093a is a complete booklet. The peelable paper backing serves as a booklet cover.
No. 1093 sold only in discount booklets for £5.32.

Bird Type of 1997
Perf. 15x14 (on 3 Sides)
1997, Dec. 6   Litho.
Booklet Stamp
1094 A403 32p like #1053   3.00 3.00
  a.   Bklt. pane, #1081A, 3 #1094   12.50
    Complete booklet, #1094a   13.50

Irish State, 75th Anniv. Type of 1997
No. 1095, General Post Office, No. 68.
No. 1096: a, like No. 1048. b, like No. 1047. c, like No. 1057. d, like No. 1058. e, like No. 1082. f, like No. 1084.

1997, Dec. 6   Litho.   Perf. 15x14
1095 A406 32p multicolored   3.00 3.00

Sheet of 12

1096	A406	32p #a.-f. + #1045-1046, 1055-1056, 1083, 1095	22.50	22.50

Greetings Stamps — A420

Love is: No. 1097, "...from my heart." No. 1098, "...a birthday wish." No. 1099, "...thinking of you." No. 1100, "...keeping in touch."

1998, Jan. 26   Litho.   Perf. 14x15

1097	A420	32p multicolored	3.00	3.00
1098	A420	32p multicolored	3.00	3.00
1099	A420	32p multicolored	3.00	3.00
1100	A420	32p multicolored	3.00	3.00
a.		Bkt. pane, #1097-1100 + 8 labels	12.00	
		Complete booklet, 2 #1100a	24.00	
b.		Souv. sheet, #1098-1100 + 7 labels	12.00	12.00

No. 1100a exists with stamps in two different orders. No. 1100b has 1 English, 4 Chinese, 1 Gaelic labels + 1 large label with "Year of the Tiger," in English and Chinese. Same value.

See Nos. 1120-1123.

Aviation Pioneers A421

28p, Lady Mary Heath (Sophie Catherine Pierce), 1st solo flight, Capetown-Croydon via Cairo, 1928. 32p, Col. James Fitzmaurice, navigator on "Bremen," 1st east-west Atlantic flight, 1928. 44p, Capt. J.P. (Paddy) Saul, navigator aboard Southern Cross, Dublin-Newfoundland, 1930. 52p, Capt. Charles Blair, 1st non-stop commercial flight Foynes-NYC, 1942.

1998, Feb. 24   Perf. 15x14

1101	A421	28p multicolored	1.25	1.25
1102	A421	32p multicolored	1.60	1.60
a.		Bklt. pane, 2 ea #1101-1102	4.50	
1103	A421	44p multicolored	1.90	1.90
a.		Bklt. pane, #1103, 2 #1102	4.50	
1104	A421	52p multicolored	2.25	2.25
a.		Bklt. pane, #1102, 2 #1104	5.25	
b.		Bklt. pane, 4 #1101-1104	5.75	
		Complete booklet, 2 #1102a, 1103a, 1104a, 1104b	26.00	
		Nos. 1101-1104 (4)	7.00	7.00

Bird Types of 1997

No. 1111A: b, Like No. 1107. c, Like No. 1080. d, Like No. 1077. e, Like No. 1078. f, Like No. 1076. g, Like No. 1106B, "Eire" 8½mm wide. h, Like No. 1079. i, Like No. 1053. j, Like No. 1039. k, Like No. 1037. l, Like No. 1109. m, Like No. 1106, "Eire" 8½mm wide. n, Wren. o, Pied wagtail. p, Like No. 1038.

1998-99   Litho.   Perf. 15x14, 14x15

1105	A403	5p Woodpigeon, horiz.	.90	.75
1106	A403	30p Blackbird	1.50	1.10
d.		Perf. 14	1.90	1.10
1106B	A403	30p Goldcrest, bklt. stamp	1.90	1.90
c.		Booklet pane, 5 each #1106, 1106B	18.00	
		Complete booklet, #1106Bc	18.00	
1107	A403	35p Stonechat	1.90	1.90
a.		Perf. 14	2.25	2.25
1108	A403	40p Ringed plover, horiz.	2.25	2.25
a.		Perf. 14	2.75	2.75
1109	A403	45p Song thrush	3.50	3.50
a.		Perf. 14	3.75	3.75
1110	A403	50p Sparrowhawk, horiz.	3.75	3.75
a.		Perf. 14	4.25	4.25
1111	A404	£2 Pintail	9.00	9.00

Sheet of 15

1111A	A403	30p #b.-p.	25.00	25.00

See note under #1067.

Booklet Stamps

Size: 18x21mm, 21x18mm

1112	A403	5p Like #1105	1.50	1.50
1113	A403	30p Like #1106	1.90	1.90
a.		Booklet pane, 2 #1112, 3 #1113	9.00	
		Complete booklet, #1113a	9.00	
1113B	A403	30p like #1106B	1.10	1.10
c.		Bkt. pane, 2 #1112, 3 #1113B + label	4.50	
		Complete booklet, #1113c	4.50	

Size: 20x23mm

1113D	A403	45p Like #1109, "Eire" 8½mm wide	3.00	3.00
e.		Booklet pane of 4 + 4 labels	12.00	
		Complete booklet	12.00	

Size: 21x24mm
Perf. 10¾x13 on 3 sides

1113F	A403	30p Like #1106, "Eire" 8½mm wide	2.00	2.00
i.		Like #1113F, perf. 14¼x14¾ on 3 sides ('99)	2.00	2.00
1113G	A403	30p Like #1106B, "Eire" 8½mm wide	2.00	2.00
h.		Booklet pane, 5 each #1113F-1113G	20.00	—
		Booklet #1113Gh	20.00	
j.		Like #1113G, perf. 14¼x14¾ on 3 sides ('99)	2.00	2.00
k.		Pair, #1113F-1113G	4.00	4.00

Die Cut Perf. 9x9½
Self-Adhesive

1114	A403	30p like #1106	7.00	7.00
1115	A403	30p like #1106B	7.00	7.00
a.		Pair, #1114-1115	14.00	14.00

Litho.
Die Cut Perf. 11x11¼
Self-Adhesive Coil Stamps

1115B	A403	30p Like #1114	7.00	7.00
1115C	A403	45p Like #1115	7.00	7.00
d.		Pair, #1115B-1115C	14.00	14.00

Issued: No. 1115B-1115C, 5/98; No. 1106B, 1113B, 9/4/98; No. 1111A, 2/16/99; No. 1113D, 6/30/99; No. 1113F, 1113G, 5/3/01.

Equestrian Sports A422

30p, Show jumping. 32p, Three-day event. 40p, Gymkhana. 45p, Dressage, vert.

1998, Apr. 2

1116	A422	30p multicolored	1.40	1.25
1117	A422	32p multicolored	1.50	1.25
1118	A422	40p multicolored	2.00	2.00
1119	A422	45p multicolored	2.25	2.25
a.		Souvenir sheet, #1116-1119	7.50	7.50
		Nos. 1116-1119 (4)	7.15	6.75

Greetings Type of 1998

1998, May 6   Litho.   Perf. 14x15
Booklet Stamps

1120	A420	30p like #1098	2.25	2.25
1121	A420	30p like #1099	2.25	2.25
1122	A420	30p like #1100	2.25	2.25
1123	A420	30p like #1097	2.25	2.25
a.		Bklt. pane, #1120-1123 + 8 labels	9.00	9.00
		Complete booklet, 2 #1123a	18.00	

No. 1123a exists with stamps in different order. Complete booklet contains two different panes.

Festivals A423

Europa: 30p, Crinniú na mBáid, Kinvara (sailboats). 40p, Puck Fair, Killorglin.

1998, May 6   Perf. 15x14

1124	A423	30p multicolored	1.25	1.25
1125	A423	40p multicolored	1.75	1.75

Serpentine Die Cut Perf 9x9½
Self-Adhesive

1126	A423	30p like #1124	2.25	2.25
1127	A423	30p like #1125	2.25	2.25
a.		Pair, #1126-1127	4.50	4.50
		Nos. 1124-1127 (4)	7.50	7.50

1798 Rebellion, Bicent. A424

Battle scene and: No. 1128, "Liberty." No. 1129, Pikeman. No. 1130, French soldier. No. 1131, Wolfe Tone. No. 1132, Henry Joy McCracken.

1998, May 6

1128	A424	30p multicolored	1.40	1.40
1129	A424	30p multicolored	1.40	1.40
1130	A424	30p multicolored	1.40	1.40
a.		Strip of 3, #1128-1130	4.25	4.25
1131	A424	45p multicolored	2.10	2.10
1132	A424	45p multicolored	2.10	2.10
a.		Pair, #1131-1132	4.25	4.25

Tour de France Bicycle Race A425

No. 1133, 4 cyclists. No. 1134, 2 cyclists, 1 wearing dark glasses. No. 1135, 2 cyclists, 1 wearing hat. No. 1136, Leading rider in yellow jersey.

1998, June 2   Litho.   Perf. 15x14

1133	A425	30p multicolored	1.75	1.75
1134	A425	30p multicolored	1.75	1.75
1135	A425	30p multicolored	1.75	1.75
1136	A425	30p multicolored	1.75	1.75
a.		Strip of 4, #1133-1136	7.75	7.75

Democracy Stamps A426

Designs: 30p, Local government (Ireland Act), cent. 32p, Entrance into European Union, 25th anniv. 35p, Women's vote in local elections, cent. 45c, Republic of Ireland Act, 50th anniv.

1998, June 2

1137	A426	30p multicolored	1.25	1.25
1138	A426	32p multicolored	1.25	1.25
1139	A426	35p multicolored	1.50	1.50
1140	A426	45p multicolored	1.90	1.90
		Nos. 1137-1140 (4)	5.90	5.90

1998 Tall Ships Race — A427

Perf. 14x15, 15x14

1998, July 20   Litho.

1141	A427	30p Asgard II	1.00	1.00
a.		Perf. 15	1.40	1.40
1142	A427	30p Eagle	1.40	1.40
a.		Pair, #1141-1142	2.50	2.50
b.		Perf. 15	3.50	3.50
c.		Bklt. pane, #1142b, 2 #1141a	3.25	
1143	A427	45p Boa Esperanza, horiz.	1.75	1.75
a.		Perf. 15	2.00	2.00
1144	A427	£1 T.S. Royalist, horiz.	4.25	4.25
a.		Perf. 15	7.00	7.00
b.		Bklt. pane of 3, #1142b, 1143a, 1144a	12.50	

		Complete booklet, #1142c, 1144b	16.00	
		Nos. 1141-1144 (4)	8.40	8.40

Souvenir Sheet

1145	A427	£2 like #1143	8.00	8.00

Die Cut Perf. 9x9½, 9½x9
Self-Adhesive

1145A	A427	30p like #1143	3.75	3.75
1145B	A427	30p like #1141	3.75	3.75
1145C	A427	30p like #1142	3.75	3.75
1145D	A427	30p like #1144	3.75	3.75
e.		Strip of 4, #1145A-1145D	16.00	16.00

Portugal '98 (#1145).
Issued: £2, 9/4; others, 7/20.

Postboxes — A428

1998, Sept. 3

No. 1146, Ashworth, 1856. No. 1147, Wallbox, 1922. No. 1148, Double Pillarbox, 1899. No. 1149, Penfold, 1866.

1146	A428	30p multicolored	1.75	1.75
1147	A428	30p multicolored	1.75	1.75
1148	A428	30p multicolored	1.75	1.75
1149	A428	30p multicolored	1.75	1.75
a.		Strip of 4, #1146-1149	7.00	7.00

Mary Immaculate College, Limerick, Cent. — A429

Newton School, Waterford, Bicent. — A430

1998, Sept. 3   Perf. 15x14, 14x15

1150	A429	30p multicolored	1.00	1.00
1151	A430	40p multicolored	1.50	1.50

Universal Declaration of Human Rights, 50th Anniv. A431

1998, Sept. 3   Perf. 15x14

1152	A431	45p multicolored	1.50	1.50

Endangered Animals — A432

No. 1153, Cheetah. No. 1154, Scimitarhorned oryx. 40p, Golden lion tamarin. 45p, Tiger.

1998, Oct. 8   Litho.   Perf. 14

1153	A432	30p multi	1.50	1.50
1154	A432	30p multi	1.50	1.50
a.		Pair, #1153-1154	3.00	3.00

2001, Jan. 24 Litho. *Perf. 14¼x14¾*
1279 A460 30p multi 2.50 2.50

Souvenir Sheet
1280 Sheet of 3 10.00 10.00
a.-c. A460 30p Any single 3.25 3.25

Booklet Stamps
Size: 25x30mm
Self-Adhesive
Serpentine Die Cut 12
1281 A460 30p multi 1.90 1.90
1282 A460 30p multi 1.90 1.90
1283 A460 30p multi 1.90 1.90
1284 A460 30p multi 1.90 1.90
1285 A460 30p multi 1.90 1.90
a. Booklet, 2 each #1281-1285 + 10 labels 19.00
Nos. 1281-1285 (5) 9.50 9.50

New Year 2001 (Year of the Snake), No. 1280.

Broadcasting in Ireland — A461

Designs: 30p, Camera, audience, man. 32p, Microphone, announcers. 45p, People listening to radio. 50p, Television.

2001, Feb. 27 *Perf. 14¾x14¼*
1286 A461 30p multi 1.00 1.00
1287 A461 32p multi 1.40 1.40
1288 A461 45p multi 2.10 2.10
1289 A461 50p multi 2.50 2.50
Nos. 1286-1289 (4) 7.00 7.00

Literary Anniversaries A462

Designs: 30p, Marsh's Library, first public library in Ireland, 300th anniv. 32p, Book of Common Prayer, first book printed in Ireland, 450th anniv.

2001, Mar. 14 *Perf. 14¼x14¾*
1290 A462 30p multi 2.00 2.00
1291 A462 32p multi 3.00 3.00

Comhaltas Ceoltóirí Eirann, 50th Anniv. — A463

Musician with: No. 1292, Bagpipes. No. 1293, Tambourine. No. 1294, Flute, horiz. No. 1295, Violin, horiz.

Perf. 14¼x14¾, 14¾x14¼
2001, Mar. 14
1292 A463 30p multi 1.50 1.50
1293 A463 30p multi 1.50 1.50
a. Pair, #1292-1293 3.00 3.00
1294 A463 45p multi 2.10 2.10
1295 A463 45p multi 2.10 2.10
a. Pair, #1294-1295 4.25 4.25
Nos. 1292-1295 (4) 7.20 7.20

Race Cars A464

Designs: Nos. 1296, 1300, 1301, Jordan Grand Prix Formula 1. Nos. 1297, 1304, Hillman Imp, Tulip Rally. Nos. 1298, 1303, Mini Cooper S, Monte Carlo Rally. Nos. 1299, 1302, Mercedes SSK, Irish Grand Prix.

2001, Apr. 26 *Perf. 13¾x14¼*
1296 A464 30p multi .95 .95
1297 A464 32p multi 1.25 1.25
1298 A464 45p multi 2.00 2.00
1299 A464 £1 multi 4.25 4.25
Nos. 1296-1299 (4) 8.45 8.45

Souvenir Sheet
1300 A464 £2 multi 11.50 11.50
a. With Belgica show emblem in margin 14.00 14.00

Booklet Stamps
Size: 36x24mm
Self-Adhesive
Serpentine Die Cut 11¾
1301 A464 30p multi 5.00 5.00
1302 A464 30p multi 5.00 5.00
1303 A464 30p multi 5.00 5.00
1304 A464 30p multi 5.00 5.00
a. Booklet, 4 #1301, 2 each #1302-1304 50.00
Nos. 1301-1304 (4) 20.00 20.00

Issued: No. 1300a, 6/9/01.

Irish Heritage in Australia A465

2001, May 3 *Perf. 14¾x14¼*
1305 A465 30p Ned Kelly 1.50 1.50
1306 A465 30p Peter Lalor 1.50 1.50
a. Pair, #1305-1306 3.00 3.00
1307 A465 45p Settlers 2.00 2.00
1308 A465 45p Emigrants 2.00 2.00
a. Pair, #1307-1308 4.00 4.00
Nos. 1305-1308 (4) 7.00 7.00

Souvenir Sheet
1309 A465 £1 Like #1305 5.25 5.25

Europa A466

2001, May 16 Litho. *Perf. 14¾x14¼*
1310 A466 30p Wading .75 .75
1311 A466 32p Fishing 1.25 1.25

Coil Stamps
Self-Adhesive
Die Cut Perf. 9¼x9½
1312 A466 30p Wading 2.00 2.00
1313 A466 30p Fishing 2.00 2.00
a. Strip, #1312-1313 4.00

Bird Types of 1997 With Added Euro Denominations
Designs: Nos. 1314, 1319A, Blackbird. 1319B, Goldcrest. 32p, Robin. 35p, Puffin. 40p, Wren. 45p, Song thrush. £1, Greenland white-fronted goose.

Perf. 14¼x14¾
2001, June 11 *Litho.*
1314 A403 30p multi 2.10 2.10
1315 A403 32p multi 3.00 3.00
1316 A403 35p multi 3.50 3.50
1317 A403 40p multi 4.25 4.25
1318 A403 45p multi 5.25 5.25

Perf. 14¾x14¼
1319 A404 £1 multi 7.75 7.75
Nos. 1314-1319 (6) 25.85 25.85

Self-Adhesive
Coil Stamps
Size: 21x26mm
1319A A403 30p multi 4.50 4.50
1319B A403 30p multi 4.50 4.50
c. Pair, #1319A-1319B 9.00

Battle of Kinsale, 400th Anniv. A467

Designs: No. 1320, Soldiers on horseback. No. 1321, Soldiers in stream. 32p, Soldiers and ramparts. 45p, View of Kinsale.

2001, July 10 *Perf. 13½*
1320 A467 30p multi 1.10 1.10
1321 A467 30p multi 1.10 1.10
a. Pair, #1320-1321 2.25 2.25
1322 A467 32p multi 2.00 2.00
1323 A467 45p multi 2.25 2.25
Nos. 1320-1323 (4) 6.45 6.45

Hall of Fame Athletes A468

Designs: Nos. 1324, 1328, Padraic Carney, soccer player. Nos. 1325, 1329, Frank Cummins, hurler. Nos. 1326, 1330, Jack O'Shea, soccer player. Nos. 1327, 1331, Nicky Rackard, hurler.

2001, Sept. 5 Litho. *Perf. 14¾x14*
1324 A468 30p multi 1.50 1.50
1325 A468 30p multi 1.50 1.50
1326 A468 30p multi 1.50 1.50
1327 A468 30p multi 1.50 1.50
a. Horiz. strip, #1324-1327 6.00 6.00

Booklet Stamps
Size: 33x22mm
Self-Adhesive
Serpentine Die Cut 11x11½
1328 A468 30p multi 2.50 2.50
1329 A468 30p multi 2.50 2.50
1330 A468 30p multi 2.50 2.50
1331 A468 30p multi 2.50 2.50
a. Booklet, 2 each #1328, 1331, 3 each #1329-1330 25.00
Nos. 1324-1331 (8) 16.00 16.00

Sailboats — A469

Designs: No. 1332, Ruffian 23. No. 1333, Howth 17. No. 1334, 1720 Sportsboat. No. 1335, The Glen. No. 1336, Ruffian 23. No. 1337, Howth 17. No. 1338, The Glen. No. 1339, 1720 Sportsboat.

2001, Sept. 5 *Perf. 14x14¾*
1332 A469 30p multi 1.50 1.50
1333 A469 32p multi 1.50 1.50
1334 A469 45p multi 2.25 2.25
1335 A469 45p multi 2.25 2.25
a. Horiz. pair, #1334-1335 4.50 4.50
Nos. 1332-1335 (4) 7.50 7.50

Coil Stamps
Self-Adhesive
Serpentine Die Cut 9½x9¼
1336 A469 30p multi 3.00 3.00
1337 A469 30p multi 3.00 3.00
1338 A469 30p multi 3.00 3.00
1339 A469 30p multi 3.00 3.00
a. Strip of 4, #1336-1339 12.00

Bird Type of 1997
Serpentine Die Cut 11¼
2001, Oct. 9 *Litho.*
Booklet Stamps
Self-Adhesive
1340 A403 N Blackbird 2.25 2.25
1341 A403 N Goldcrest 2.25 2.25
a. Booklet, 5 each #1340-1341 22.50 22.50
1342 A403 E Robin 2.50 2.50
a. Booklet of 10 + 10 etiquettes 25.00

1343 A403 W Song thrush 4.00 4.00
a. Booklet of 10 + 10 etiquettes 40.00
Nos. 1340-1343 (4) 11.00 11.00

Fish A470

Designs: 30p, Perch. No. 1345, Arctic char. No. 1346, Pike. 45p, Common bream.

2001, Oct. 9 *Perf. 14¾x14*
1344 A470 30p multi 1.25 1.25
1345 A470 32p multi 1.75 1.75
1346 A470 32p multi 1.75 1.75
a. Horiz. pair, #1345-1346 3.50 3.50
1347 A470 45p multi 2.50 2.50
a. Booklet pane, #1344-1347 6.25 —
b. Booklet pane, #1345, 1346, 2 #1347 8.75 —
c. Booklet pane, 2 each #1344, 1347 7.50 —
Booklet, #1347b, 1347c, 2 #1347a 29.00

No. 1347a exists with stamps in different order. The booklet contains the two different panes.

Governmental Support of Arts, 50th Anniv. — A471

2001, Nov. 5 *Perf. 14x14¾*
1348 A471 50p multi 3.50 3.50

Christmas — A472

Designs: No. 1349, Nativity. 32p, Annunciation. 45p, Presentation in the Temple. No. 1352, Madonna and Child.

2001, Nov. 5 *Perf. 14x14¾*
1349 A472 30p multi 1.00 1.00
1350 A472 32p multi 1.40 1.40
1351 A472 45p multi 2.50 2.50

Booklet Stamp
Size: 21x27mm
Self-Adhesive
Serpentine Die Cut 11x11¼
1352 A472 30p multi 1.50 1.50
a. Booklet of 24 35.00
Nos. 1349-1352 (4) 6.40 6.40

No. 1352a sold for £6.60.

100 Cents = 1 Euro (€)

A473

Birds (With Euro Denominations Only) — A474

Designs: 1c, Magpie. 2c, Gannet. 3c, Blue tit, horiz. 4c, Corncrake. 5c, Wood pigeon, horiz. Nos. 1358, 1370, 10c, Kingfisher. 20c,

Lapwing. Nos. 1360, 1371, 1372, 38c, Blackbird. No. 1373, 38c, Goldcrest. 41c, Chaffinch. 44c, Robin. 50c, Gray heron, horiz. 51c, Roseate tern, horiz. 57c, Curlew. €1, Barnacle goose. €2, Greenland white-fronted goose, vert. €5, Pintail. €10, Shelduck, vert.

Perf. 14x14¾, 14¾x14

2002, Jan. 1			Litho.	
1353	A473	1c multi	.25	.25
1354	A473	2c multi	.25	.25
1355	A473	3c multi	.25	.25
1356	A473	4c multi	.25	.25
1357	A473	5c multi	.25	.25
1358	A473	10c multi	.40	.30
1359	A473	20c multi	.75	.65
1360	A473	38c multi	1.40	1.25
1361	A473	41c multi	1.60	1.40
1362	A473	44c multi	1.75	1.60
1363	A473	50c multi	1.90	1.75
1364	A473	51c multi	1.90	1.75
1365	A473	57c multi	2.25	1.90
1366	A474	€1 multi	3.75	3.50
1367	A474	€2 multi	7.50	7.00
1368	A474	€5 multi	19.00	17.50
1369	A474	€10 multi	37.50	35.00

Booklet Stamps
Size: 18x20mm

Perf. 14¾x14¼ on 3 Sides

1370	A473	10c multi	1.25	1.25
1371	A473	38c multi	2.75	2.75
a.		Booklet pane, #1370, 5 #1371	14.00	—
		Booklet, #1371a	14.00	

Coil Stamps
Size: 21x26mm
Self-Adhesive

Serpentine Die Cut 11x11¼

1372	A473	38c multi	5.75	5.75
1373	A473	38c multi	5.75	5.75
a.		Pair, #1372-1373	14.00	14.00
		Nos. 1353-1373 (21)	96.45	90.35

See Nos. 1392-1398, 1421-1423, 1433-1434, 1447-1449, 1492-1495, 1511-1515, 1523-1526.

Introduction of the Euro
A475

Designs: 38c, 1 euro coin introduced in 2002. 41c, 50p coin used from 1971-2001. 57c, 1p coin used from 1928-71.

2002, Jan. 1		Litho.	Perf. 14¾x14¼	
1374	A475	38c multi	1.50	1.50
1375	A475	41c multi	1.75	1.75
1376	A475	57c multi	2.40	2.40
		Nos. 1374-1376 (3)	5.65	5.65

Toys — A476

Designs: Nos. 1377, 1379, Teddy bear. Nos. 1378a, 1381, Rocking horse. Nos. 1378b, 1382, Wooden locomotive. Nos. 1378c, 1380, Doll. No. 1383, Blocks.

2002, Jan. 22			Perf. 14¼x14¾	
1377	A476	38c multi	2.75	2.75

Souvenir Sheet
Perf. 14¼x14¾ on 3 or 4 Sides

1378		Sheet of 3	9.00	9.00
a.-c.	A476	38c Any single	3.00	3.00

Booklet Stamps
Self-Adhesive
Size: 21x27mm

Serpentine Die Cut 11¼

1379	A476	38c multi	2.50	2.50
1380	A476	38c multi	2.50	2.50
1381	A476	38c multi	2.50	2.50
1382	A476	38c multi	2.50	2.50
1383	A476	38c multi	2.50	2.50
a.		Booklet of 10, 2 each #1379-1383, + 10 labels	25.00	
		Nos. 1379-1383 (5)	12.50	12.50

New Year 2002 (Year of the Horse), No. 1378.

Steeplechasing in Ireland, 250th Anniv. — A477

2002, Mar. 12			Perf. 14¾x14¼	
1384	A477	38c Arkle	1.75	1.75
1385	A477	38c L'Escargot	1.75	1.75
1386	A477	38c Dawn Run	1.75	1.75
1387	A477	38c Istabraq	1.75	1.75
a.		Horiz. strip of 4, #1384-1387	7.00	7.00

Scouting
A478

Designs: No. 1388, Scout with peg and mallet. No. 1389, Scouts and leader around camp fire. No. 1390, Scouts on hike. No. 1391, Scouts kayaking.

2002, Mar. 12				
1388	A478	41c multi	1.50	1.50
1389	A478	41c multi	1.50	1.50
a.		Horiz. pair, #1388-1389	3.00	3.00
1390	A478	57c multi	2.25	2.25
1391	A478	57c multi	2.25	2.25
a.		Horiz. pair, #1390-1391	4.50	4.50
		Nos. 1388-1391 (4)	7.50	7.50

Bird Type of 2002

Designs: No. 1395, Chaffinch. No. 1396, Goldcrest. 44c, Robin. 47c, Kestrel, horiz. 55c, Oystercatcher. 57c, Song thrush. 60c, Jay, horiz.

2002		Litho.	Perf. 14¾x14	
1392	A473	47c multi	4.25	4.25
1393	A473	55c multi	4.75	4.75
1394	A473	60c multi	6.00	6.00

Self-Adhesive
Serpentine Die Cut 11x11¼
Size: 21x26mm

1395	A473	41c multi	3.75	3.75
1396	A473	41c multi	3.75	3.75
a.		Coil pair, #1395-1396	7.50	
b.		Booklet of 10, 5 each #1395-1396	37.50	

Booklet Stamps

1397	A473	44c multi	2.50	2.50
a.		Booklet of 10	25.00	
1398	A473	57c multi	2.75	2.75
a.		Booklet of 10	27.50	
		Nos. 1392-1398 (7)	27.75	27.75

Issued: Nos. 1395-1398, 4/2. Nos. 1392-1394, 6/17.
Compare Nos. 1395-1396 with Nos. 1433-1434.

Europa
A480

Mammals
A479

Designs: 41c, Meles meles. 50c, €5, Lutra lutra. 57c, Sciurus vulgaris, vert. €1, Erinaceus europaeus, vert.

Perf. 14¾x14¼, 14¼x14¾

2002, Apr. 23			Litho.	
1399	A479	41c multi	1.50	1.50
1400	A479	50c multi	1.75	1.75
1401	A479	57c multi	2.10	2.10
1402	A479	€1 multi	3.50	3.50
		Nos. 1399-1402 (4)	8.85	8.85

Souvenir Sheet

1403	A479	€5 multi	21.00	21.00

Designs: Nos. 1404, 1406, Clown. Nos. 1405, 1407, Equestrian act.

2002, May 14		Litho.	Perf. 14¾x14	
1404	A480	41c multi	1.25	1.25
1405	A480	44c multi	1.40	1.40

Coil Stamps
Size: 34x23mm
Self-Adhesive
Die Cut Perf. 9¼x9½

1406	A480	41c multi	1.25	1.25
1407	A480	41c multi	1.25	1.25
a.		Horiz. pair, #1406-1407	2.50	2.50
		Nos. 1404-1407 (4)	5.15	5.15

Soccer Stars
A481

Designs: Nos. 1408, 1415, Packie Bonner. Nos. 1409, 1412, Roy Keane, vert. Nos. 1410, 1413, Paul McGrath, vert. Nos. 1411, 1414, David O'Leary, vert.

2002, May 14		Perf. 14¾x14, 14x14¾		
1408	A481	41c multi	1.75	1.75
1409	A481	41c multi	1.75	1.75
1410	A481	41c multi	1.75	1.75
1411	A481	41c multi	1.75	1.75
a.		Vert. strip of 3, #1409-1411	7.00	7.00

Booklet Stamps
Sizes: 23x34, 34x23mm
Self-Adhesive
Serpentine Die Cut 11½x11¾, 11¾x11½

1412	A481	41c multi	3.00	3.00
1413	A481	41c multi	3.00	3.00
1414	A481	41c multi	3.00	3.00
1415	A481	41c multi	3.00	3.00
a.		Booklet, 3 #1412-1413, 2 #1414-1415	30.00	

Canonization of St. Pio of Pietrelcina (1887-1968)
A482

2002, June 17		Litho.	Perf. 14x14¾	
1416	A482	41c multi	3.50	3.50

Brian Ború, 1000th Anniv of High Kingship
A483

Designs: 41c, Leading troops into battle. 44c, Commanding ships. 57c, On throne. €1, Decreeing Armagh as the primacy of the Irish church.

2002, July 9			Perf. 14¾x14	
1417	A483	41c multi	1.25	1.25
1418	A483	44c multi	1.50	1.50
1419	A483	57c multi	1.75	1.75
1420	A483	€1 multi	3.00	3.00
		Nos. 1417-1420 (4)	7.50	7.50

Bird Type of 2002

Designs: No. 1421, Goldcrest. No. 1422, 36c, Wren. No. 1423, Chaffinch.

Perf. 14x14¾ on 3 Sides

2002, Aug. 6			Litho.	

Booklet Stamps

1421	A473	41c multi	2.25	2.25
a.		Booklet pane of 10, 5 each #1361, 1421	22.50	—
		Booklet, #1421a	22.50	

Size: 18x21mm
Perf. 14¾x14¼ on 3 Sides

1422	A473	36c multi	2.25	2.25
1423	A473	41c multi	2.75	2.75
a.		Booklet pane of 5, #1422, 4 #1423 + label	21.00	—
		Booklet, #1423a	21.00	

Paintings in National Gallery
A484

Designs: No. 1424, Before the Start, by Jack B. Yeats. No. 1425, The Conjuror, by Nathaniel Hone. No. 1426, The Colosseum and Arch of Constantine, Rome, by Giovanni Paolo Panini. No. 1427, The Gleaners, by Jules Breton.

2002, Aug. 29			Perf. 14¾x14	
1424	A484	41c multi	1.90	1.90
a.		Booklet pane of 4	7.75	—
1425	A484	41c multi	1.90	1.90
a.		Booklet pane of 4	7.75	—
1426	A484	41c multi	1.90	1.90
a.		Booklet pane of 4	7.75	—
1427	A484	41c multi	1.90	1.90
a.		Horiz. strip, #1424-1427	7.75	7.75
b.		Booklet pane of 4	7.75	—
		Booklet, #1424a, 1425a, 1426a, 1427b	32.50	

See Nos. 1496-1499, 1572-1575.

Archbishop Thomas Croke (1823-1902)
A485

2002, Sept. 17			Perf. 14x14¾	
1428	A485	44c multi	2.75	2.75

Hall of Fame Athletes Type of 2001

Designs: No. 1429, Peter McDermott, soccer player. No. 1430, Jimmy Smyth, hurler. No. 1431, Matt Connor, soccer player. No. 1432, Seanie Duggan, hurler.

2002, Sept. 17			Perf. 14¾x14	
1429	A468	41c multi	1.75	1.75
1430	A468	41c multi	1.75	1.75
1431	A468	41c multi	1.75	1.75
1432	A468	41c multi	1.75	1.75
a.		Horiz. strip, #1429-1432	7.00	7.00

Bird Type of 2002 Redrawn

Designs: No. 1433, Chaffinch. No. 1434, Goldcrest

Serpentine Die Cut 11x11¼

2002, Oct. 17			Photo.	

Coil Stamps
Self-Adhesive

1433	A473	41c multi	5.00	5.00
1434	A473	41c multi	5.00	5.00
a.		Coil pair, #1433-1434	10.00	

Text appears grayer on Nos. 1433-1434 than on Nos. 1395-1396. On No. 1433, the second "h" of "Chaffinch" touches the branch, while it does not touch on No. 1395. On No. 1434, the points of the pine needles at the bottom of the stamp are shown, while they are cut off on No. 1396.

Irish Rock Musicians
A486

Designs: Nos. 1435, 1439, U2. Nos. 1436, 1440, Phil Lynott. Nos. 1437, 1441, Van Morrison. Nos. 1438, 1442, Rory Gallagher.

2002, Oct. 17		Litho.	Perf. 13¼x12¾	
1435	A486	41c multi	1.50	1.50
1436	A486	41c multi	1.50	1.50
a.		Horiz. pair, #1435-1436	3.00	3.00
1437	A486	57c multi	2.25	2.25
1438	A486	57c multi	2.25	2.25
a.		Horiz. pair, #1437-1438	4.50	4.50
		Nos. 1435-1438 (4)	7.50	7.50

Souvenir Sheets
Perf. 12¾x13¼

1439	A486	€2 multi	12.00	12.00
1440	A486	€2 multi	12.00	12.00
1441	A486	€2 multi	12.00	12.00
1442	A486	€2 multi	12.00	12.00

Christmas — A487

Scenes from *Les Très Riches Heures du Duc de Berry*: No. 1443, Adoration of the Magi. 44c, The Annunciation. 57c, Angels Announcing Birth to Shepherds. No. 1446, Adoration of the Shepherds.

2002, Nov. 7   Litho.   Perf. 14¼x14¾

1443	A487	41c multi	1.25	1.25
1444	A487	44c multi	1.40	1.40
1445	A487	57c multi	1.90	1.90

Booklet Stamp
Self-Adhesive
Size: 21x27mm
Serpentine Die Cut 11x11¼

1446	A487	41c multi	2.00	2.00
a.		Booklet pane of 24	47.50	
		Nos. 1443-1446 (4)	6.55	6.55

No. 1446a sold for €9.43.

Bird Type of 2002

Designs: 50c, Puffin. 75c, Ringed plover, horiz.. 95c, Sparrowhawk, horiz.

2003, Jan. 6   Litho.   Perf. 14¾x14

1447	A473	75c multi	2.50	2.50
1448	A473	95c multi	3.50	3.50

Booklet Stamp
Self-Adhesive
Size: 21x27mm
Serpentine Die Cut 11x11¼

1449	A473	50c multi	2.00	2.00
a.		Booklet pane of 10 + 10 etiquettes	20.00	

Baby Animals — A488

Designs: Nos. 1450, 1452, Puppies. Nos. 1451a, 1454, Goats. Nos. 1451b, 1453, Chicks. Nos. 1451c, 1455, Kittens. No. 1456, Rabbits.

2003, Jan. 28   Perf. 14x14¾

1450	A488	41c multi	2.75	2.75

Souvenir Sheet
Perf. 14x14¾ on 3 or 4 Sides

1451		Sheet of 3	9.50	9.50
a.-c.		A488 50c Any single	3.00	3.00

Booklet Stamps
Size: 22x28mm
Self-Adhesive
Serpentine Die Cut 11x11¼

1452	A488	41c multi	2.25	2.25
1453	A488	41c multi	2.25	2.25
1454	A488	41c multi	2.25	2.25
1455	A488	41c multi	2.25	2.25
1456	A488	41c multi	2.25	2.25
a.		Booklet pane of 10, 2 each #1452-1456 + 10 labels	22.50	
		Nos. 1452-1456 (5)	11.25	11.25

New Year 2003 (Year of the Goat), No. 1451.

St. Patrick's Day — A489

Designs: Nos. 1457, 1460, St. Patrick. Nos. 1458, 1461, St. Patrick's Day Parade, Dublin. Nos. 1459, 1462, St. Patrick's Day Parade, New York.

2003, Feb. 28   Perf. 14x14¾

1457	A489	41c multi	1.25	1.25
a.		Booklet pane of 4	5.00	
1458	A489	50c multi	1.50	1.50
a.		Booklet pane of 4	6.00	
1459	A489	57c multi	1.75	1.75
a.		Booklet pane of 4	7.00	
b.		Booklet pane of 3, #1457-1459	4.50	
		Complete booklet, #1457a, 1458a, 1459a, 1459b	22.50	
		Nos. 1457-1459 (3)	4.50	4.50

Booklet Stamps
Self-Adhesive
Size: 22x32mm
Serpentine Die Cut 11¼

1460	A489	41c multi	3.50	3.50
a.		Booklet pane of 10	35.00	
1461	A489	50c multi	4.25	4.25
a.		Booklet pane of 10	42.50	
1462	A489	57c multi	4.75	4.75
a.		Booklet pane of 10	47.50	
		Nos. 1460-1462 (3)	12.50	12.50

Beetles A490

Designs: 41c, €2, Seven-spotted ladybug. 50c, Great diving beetle. 57c, Leaf beetle. €1, Green tiger beetle.

2003, Apr. 1   Perf. 13¾x14

1463	A490	41c multi	1.25	1.25
1464	A490	50c multi	1.50	1.50
1465	A490	57c multi	1.75	1.75
1466	A490	€1 multi	3.00	3.00
		Nos. 1463-1466 (4)	7.50	7.50

Souvenir Sheet

1467	A490	€2 multi	9.00	9.00

European Year of People With Disabilities A491

2003, May 9   Perf. 14¾x14

1468	A491	41c multi	2.50	2.50

Europa — A492

Posters by Paul Henry: 41c, Dingle Peninsula (Ireland for Holidays). 57c, Connemara (Ireland This Year).

2003, May 9   Perf. 14x14¾

1469	A492	41c multi	1.25	1.25
1470	A492	57c multi	1.75	1.75

11th Special Olympics World Summer Games A493

Designs: 41c, Competitors waving. 50c, Swimmer. 57c, Sprinter. €1, Shot put.

2003, May 20   Perf. 13¾x14

1471	A493	41c multi	1.25	1.25
1472	A493	50c multi	1.50	1.50
1473	A493	57c multi	1.75	1.75
1474	A493	€1 multi	3.00	3.00
		Nos. 1471-1474 (4)	7.50	7.50

Ford Motor Company, Cent. A494

2003, June 30   Litho.   Perf. 14¼x14

1475	A494	41c multi	2.75	2.75

Gordon Bennett Race in Ireland, Cent. A495

Race map and 1903 automobiles: Nos. 1476, 1483, Napier. Nos. 1477, 1482, Mercedes. Nos. 1478, 1481, Mors. Nos. 1479, 1480, Winton.

2003, June 30   Perf. 14¼x14

1476	A495	41c multi	1.75	1.75
1477	A495	41c multi	1.75	1.75
1478	A495	41c multi	1.75	1.75
1479	A495	41c multi	1.75	1.75
a.		Horiz. strip of 4, #1476-1479	7.00	7.00

Coil Stamps
Size: 33x22mm
Self-Adhesive
Serpentine Die Cut 11¼

1480	A495	41c multi	3.25	3.25
1481	A495	41c multi	3.25	3.25
1482	A495	41c multi	3.25	3.25
1483	A495	41c multi	3.25	3.25
a.		Strip of 4, #1480-1483	13.00	

Rebellion of 1803, Bicent. A496

Designs: 41c, Robert Emmet (1778-1803), rebellion leader. 50c, Thomas Russell (1767-1803), rebellion leader. 57c, Anne Devlin (1780-1851), assistant to Emmet.

2003, July 29   Litho.   Perf. 14¾x14

1484	A496	41c multi	1.50	1.50
1485	A496	50c multi	1.75	1.75
1486	A496	57c multi	2.25	2.25
		Nos. 1484-1486 (3)	5.50	5.50

Powered Flight, Cent. A497

Designs: 41c, First Irish-built monoplane, built by Harry Ferguson, 1909. 50c, John Alcock & Arthur Brown's non-stop transatlantic flight, 1919. No. 1489, Lillian Bland, first female aircraft designer, 1910. Nos. 1490, 1491, Wright Flyer.

2003, July 29

1487	A497	41c multi	1.50	1.50
1488	A497	50c multi	1.75	1.75
1489	A497	57c multi	2.00	2.00
1490	A497	57c multi	2.00	2.00
a.		Horiz. pair, #1489-1490	4.00	4.00

Souvenir Sheet

1491	A497	€5 multi	21.00	21.00

Bird Type of 2002

Designs: 7c, Stonechat. 48c, No. 1494, Peregrine falcon. No. 1495, Pied wagtail.

2003, Aug. 25   Litho.   Perf. 14x14¾

1492	A473	7c multi	.40	.40
1493	A473	48c multi	3.00	3.00

Self-Adhesive
Serpentine Die Cut 11x11¼

1494	A473	N multi	2.00	2.00
1495	A473	N multi	2.00	2.00
a.		Coil pair, #1494-1495	4.00	
b.		Booklet pane, 5 each #1494-1495	20.00	

Nos. 1494-1495 each sold for 48c on day of issue.

National Gallery Paintings Type of 2002

Designs: No. 1496, Self-portrait as Timanthes, by James Barry. No. 1497, Man Writing a Letter, by Gabriel Metsu. No. 1498, Woman Reading a Letter, by Metsu. No. 1499, Woman Seen From the Back, by Antoine Watteau.

2003, Sept. 9   Perf. 14x14¾

1496	A484	48c multi	1.75	1.75
a.		Booklet pane of 4	7.00	—
1497	A484	48c multi	1.75	1.75
1498	A484	48c multi	1.75	1.75
a.		Booklet pane, 2 each #1497-1498	7.00	
1499	A484	48c multi	1.75	1.75
a.		Horiz. strip, #1496-1499	7.00	7.00
b.		Booklet pane of 4	7.00	—
		Complete booklet, #1496a, 1499b, 2 #1498a	28.00	

Frank O'Connor (1903-66), Writer — A498

2003, Sept. 16   Litho.   Perf. 14x14¼

1500	A498	50c multi	2.75	2.75

Ernest Thomas Sinton Walton (1903-95), 1951 Nobel Laureate in Physics — A499

2003, Sept. 16

1501	A499	57c multi	3.50	3.50

Mariners A500

Designs: Nos. 1502, 1507, Argentine Admiral William (Guillermo) Brown (1777-1857). Nos. 1503, 1506, 1510, American Commodore John Barry (1745-1803). Nos. 1504, 1508, Captain Robert Halpin (1836-94). Nos. 1505, 1509, Captain Richard Roberts (1803-41).

Perf. 14¼x14 (#1502-1505, 1510)
2003, Sept. 30

1502	A500	48c multi	1.75	1.75
1503	A500	48c multi	1.75	1.75
a.		Horiz. pair, #1502-1503	3.50	3.50
1504	A500	57c multi	2.00	2.00
1505	A500	57c multi	2.00	2.00
a.		Horiz. pair, #1504-1505	4.00	4.00

Coil Stamps
Self-Adhesive (#1506-1509)
Size: 33x22mm (#1506-1509)
Serpentine Die Cut 11x11¼ (#1506-1509)

1506	A500 48c multi	3.25	3.25
1507	A500 48c multi	3.25	3.25
1508	A500 48c multi	3.25	3.25
1509	A500 48c multi	3.25	3.25
a.	Horiz. strip, #1506-1509	13.00	13.00
	Nos. 1502-1509 (8)	20.50	20.50

Souvenir Sheet
1510	A500 €5 multi	21.00	21.00

Bird Type of 2002
Designs: 4c, Corncrake. Nos. 1511, 1515, Pied wagtail. Nos. 1513, 1514, Peregrine falcon.

Perf. 14x14¾ on 3 Sides

2003, Sept. 30   Litho.
Booklet Stamps (#1511-1513)
1511	A473 48c multi	2.00	2.00
a.	Booklet pane, 5 each #1493, 1511	20.00	—
	Complete booklet, #1511a	20.00	

Size: 18x20mm
Perf. 15x14 on 3 Sides
1512	A473 4c multi	.30	.30
1513	A473 48c multi	2.50	2.50
a.	Booklet pane, 2 #1512, 4 #1513	10.50	
	Complete booklet, #1513a	10.50	
	Nos. 1511-1513 (3)	4.80	4.80

Self-Adhesive
Size: 20x25mm
Serpentine Die Cut 11x11¼
1514	A473 48c multi	2.00	2.00
1515	A473 48c multi	2.00	2.00
a.	Coil pair, #1514-1515	4.00	
b.	Booklet pane, 5 each #1514-1515	20.00	

Examples of Nos. 1514-1515 from booklets are on a heavy, opaque paper, while those from coils are on a thinner, semi-transparent paper.

Election of Pope John Paul II, 25th Anniv. — A501

Pope John Paul II: 48c, In Ireland, 1979. 50c, At Vatican. 57c, At United Nations.

2003, Oct. 16   *Perf. 14x14¾*
1516	A501 48c multi	2.25	2.25
1517	A501 50c multi	2.25	2.25
1518	A501 57c multi	2.50	2.50
	Nos. 1516-1518 (3)	7.00	7.00

Christmas A502

Designs: No. 1519, Flight into Egypt. 50c, Angel. 57c, Three Kings. No. 1522, Nativity.

2003, Nov. 10   *Perf. 13¼*
1519	A502 48c multi	1.50	1.50

Size: 37x27mm
Perf. 14¾x14
1520	A502 50c multi	1.50	1.50
1521	A502 57c multi	1.75	1.75
	Nos. 1519-1521 (3)	4.75	4.75

Booklet Stamp
Self-Adhesive
Size: 26x21mm
Serpentine Die Cut 11¼
1522	A502 48c multi	2.50	2.50
a.	Booklet pane of 24	36.00	

No. 1522a sold for €11.04.

Bird Type of 2002
Designs: Nos. 1523, 1525, Puffin. Nos. 1524, 1526, Song thrush.

2004, Jan. 5   Litho.   *Perf. 14x14¾*
1523	A473 60c multi	2.50	2.50
1524	A473 65c multi	2.50	2.50

Booklet Stamps
Self-Adhesive
Size: 21x26mm
Serpentine Die Cut 11x11¼
1525	A473 60c multi	2.50	2.50
a.	Booklet pane of 10	25.00	
1526	A473 65c multi	2.75	2.75
a.	Booklet pane of 10	27.50	

Irish Presidency of the European Union — A503

2004, Jan. 15   *Perf. 14x14¾*
1527	A503 48c multi	2.50	2.50

Love — A504

Designs: Nos. 1528, 1529a, 1530, Chimpanzees. Nos. 1529b, 1531, Panda. Nos. 1529c, 1532, Koala. No. 1533, Hippopotamus.

2004, Jan. 30   *Perf. 14x14¾*
1528	A504 48c multi	2.75	2.75

Souvenir Sheet
Perf. 14x14¾ on 3 or 4 Sides
1529	Sheet of 3	9.00	9.00
a.-c.	A504 60c Any single	3.00	3.00

Booklet Stamps
Self-Adhesive
Size: 21x26mm
Serpentine Die Cut 11x11¼
1530	A504 48c multi	2.50	2.50
1531	A504 48c multi	2.50	2.50
1532	A504 48c multi	2.50	2.50
1533	A504 48c multi	2.50	2.50
a.	Booklet pane, 3 each #1530-1531, 2 each #1532-1533 + 10 labels	25.00	
	Nos. 1530-1533 (4)	10.00	10.00

New Year 2004 (Year of the Monkey), No. 1529.

Abbey Theater, Dublin, Cent. — A505

2004, Feb. 27   *Perf. 14x14¾*
1534	A505 48c multi	2.50	2.50

St. Patrick's Day — A506

2004, Feb. 27
1535	A506 65c multi	2.75	2.75

Antarctic Expedition of Ernest Shackleton, 90th Anniv. A507

Designs: No. 1536, Ship's stern, expedition members, dogs. No. 1537, Ship's bow, expedition members, dogs. Nos. 1538, 1540a, Man emerging from tent. Nos. 1539, 1540b, Tents, expedition members.

2004, Mar. 19   *Perf. 13½*
1536	A507 48c multi	1.50	1.50
1537	A507 48c multi	1.50	1.50
a.	Horiz. pair, #1536-1537	3.00	3.00
b.	Booklet pane, 2 #1537a	6.00	—
1538	A507 65c multi	2.00	2.00
1539	A507 65c multi	2.00	2.00
a.	Horiz. pair, #1538-1539	4.00	4.00
b.	Booklet pane, 2 #1539a	8.00	—
c.	Booklet pane, #1537a, 1539a, 1539b, 2 #1539c	7.00	—
	Complete booklet, #1537b, 1539b, 2 #1539c	28.00	
	Nos. 1536-1539 (4)	7.00	7.00

Souvenir Sheet
Perf. 13½ on 2 or 3 Sides
1540	Sheet of 2	7.00	7.00
a.-b	A507 €1 Either single	3.50	3.50

No. 1539c exists with two different margins, both of which are in complete booklet.

FIFA (Fédération Internationale de Football Association), Cent. A508

2004, Mar. 31   *Perf. 13½x13*
1541	A508 60c multi	2.75	2.75

Expansion of the European Union A509

2004, May 1   Litho.   *Perf. 14¾x14*
1542	A509 65c multi	6.25	6.25

Europa — A510

Designs: 48c, Ross Castle. 65c, Cliffs of Moher.

2004, May 11   *Perf. 14x13¾*
1543	A510 48c multi	1.50	1.50
1544	A510 65c multi	2.00	2.00

Ducks A511

Designs: 48c, Tufted duck. 60c, Red-breasted merganser. 65c, Gadwall. €1, Garganey.

2004, May 11   *Perf. 13x13¼*
1545	A511 48c multi	1.50	1.50
1546	A511 60c multi	1.90	1.90
1547	A511 65c multi	2.00	2.00
1548	A511 €1 multi	3.00	3.00
a.	Souvenir sheet, #1545-1548	8.75	8.75
	Nos. 1545-1548 (4)	8.40	8.40

Intl. Year of the Family, 10th Anniv. — A512

2004, May 15   Litho.   *Perf. 13¼x13*
1549	A512 65c multi	2.75	2.75

Winning Artwork in Texaco Children's Art Competition A513

Designs: 48c, Untitled work (Frog), by Daire Lee. 60c, Marmalade Cat, by Cian Colman. 65c, Ralleshin Dipditch, by Daire O'Rourke. €1, Fish on a Dish, by Ailish Fitzpatrick, horiz.

2004, May 19   *Perf. 14x14¾*
1550	A513 48c multi	1.50	1.50
1551	A513 60c multi	1.90	1.90
1552	A513 65c multi	2.00	2.00

Perf. 14¾x14
1553	A513 €1 multi	3.00	3.00
	Nos. 1550-1553 (4)	8.40	8.40

Publication of *Ulysses,* by James Joyce, Cent. — A514

Designs: 48c, Caricature of Joyce, by Tullio Percoli. 65c, Photograph of Joyce.

2004, June 16   Litho.   *Perf. 13¼*
1554	A514 48c multi	1.50	1.50
1555	A514 65c multi	2.00	2.00

Irish College, Paris, France — A515

2004, June 26   *Perf. 14x14¾*
1556   A515   65c multi   2.50   2.50

Inauguration of LUAS Tram System, Dublin A516

2004, June 30   *Perf. 13¼*
1557   A516   48c Environment   2.10   2.10
1558   A516   48c Accessibility   2.10   2.10
    a.   Horiz. pair, #1557-1558   4.25   4.25

2004 Summer Olympics, Athens A517

Olympic flame, rings and: 48c, Javelin thrower. 60c, Myron's Discobolus.

2004, July 22   *Perf. 13¾x14*
1559   A517   48c multi   1.60   1.60
1560   A517   60c multi   2.10   2.10

Camogie, Cent. A518

Camogie players and: No. 1561, Camogie Association emblem. No. 1562, Cup.

2004, July 22   *Perf. 14¾x14*
1561   A518   48c multi   1.75   1.75
1562   A518   48c multi   1.75   1.75
    a.   Horiz. pair, #1561-1562   3.50   3.50

Flowers — A519

Designs: 4c, Common dog-violet. 5c, Dandelion. Nos. 1565, 1571, Primrose. Nos. 1569A, 1570, Daisy. 60c, Hawthorn. 65c, Bluebell. €2, Lords-and-ladies. €5, Dog-rose, horiz.

Perf. 14x14¾, 14¾x14
2004, Sept. 9   *Litho.*
1563   A519   4c multi   .20   .20
1564   A519   5c multi   .20   .20
1565   A519   48c multi   1.50   1.50
1566   A519   60c multi   1.90   1.90
1567   A519   65c multi   2.00   2.00
      Size: 23x44mm
1568   A519   €2 multi   6.00   6.00
      Size: 44x23mm
1569   A519   €5 multi   15.00   15.00
    Nos. 1563-1569 (7)   26.80   26.80
     Booklet Stamp
   Perf. 14x14¾ on 3 Sides
1569A   A519   48c multi   1.50   1.50
    b.   Booklet pane 5 each
        #1565, 1569A   15.00   —
        Complete booklet,
        #1569Ab   15.00

      Self-Adhesive
     Size: 20x25mm
   Serpentine Die Cut 11x11¼
1570   A519   48c multi   1.50   1.50
1571   A519   48c multi   1.50   1.50
    a.   Vert. coil pair, #1570-1571   3.00   3.00
    b.   Booklet pane, 5 each
        #1570-1571   15.00

No. 1571 is on the left side of No. 1571b. See Nos. 1606-1610, 1650-1655, 1708-1713, 1723-1729, 1770-1773, 1814, 1852.

National Gallery Paintings Type of 2002

Designs: No. 1572, The House Builders, by Walter Osborne. No. 1573, Kitchen Maid with the Supper at Emmaus, by Diego Velázquez. No. 1574, The Lamentation Over the Dead Christ, by Nicolas Poussin. No. 1575, The Taking of Christ, by Caravaggio.

2004, Sept. 16   *Perf. 14¾x14*
1572   A484   48c multi   1.90   1.90
    a.   Booklet pane of 4   7.50
1573   A484   48c multi   1.90   1.90
    a.   Booklet pane of 4   7.50
1574   A484   48c multi   1.90   1.90
    a.   Booklet pane of 4   7.50
1575   A484   48c multi   1.90   1.90
    a.   Horiz. strip of 4, #1572-1575   7.50   7.50
    b.   Booklet pane of 4   7.50
        Complete booklet, #1572a,
        1573a, 1574a, 1575b   30.00

Complete booklet sold for €8.

Nobel Prize Winners for Literature — A520

Designs: No. 1576, William Butler Yeats (1865-1939), 1923 winner. No. 1577, George Bernard Shaw (1856-1950), 1925 winner. No. 1578, Samuel Beckett (1906-89), 1969 winner. No. 1579, Seamus Heaney (b. 1939), 1995 winner.

     Perf. 12½x13½
2004, Oct. 1   *Litho. & Engr.*
1576   A520   N multi   1.50   1.50
1577   A520   N multi   1.50   1.50
1578   A520   N multi   1.50   1.50
1579   A520   N multi   1.50   1.50
    b.   Booklet pane of 4, #1576-1579   6.00   —
        Complete booklet, #1579b   6.00

Nos. 1576-1579 each sold for 48c on day of issue. See Sweden No. 2492.

Patrick Kavanagh (1904-67), Poet A521

2004, Oct. 21   *Litho.*   *Perf. 13x13¼*
1580   A521   48c green & black   1.50   1.50

Quakerism in Ireland, 350th Anniv. A522

2004, Oct. 21
1581   A522   60c multi   1.90   1.90

Christmas A523

Designs: 48c, Holy Family. 60c, Flight into Egypt. 65c, Adoration of the Magi.

2004, Nov. 10   *Litho.*   *Perf. 14x14¾*
1582   A523   48c multi   1.50   1.50
1583   A523   60c multi   1.90   1.90
1584   A523   65c multi   2.00   2.00
    Nos. 1582-1584 (3)   5.40   5.40
     Booklet Stamp
     Self-Adhesive
   Serpentine Die Cut 11x11¼
     Size: 21x27mm
1585   A523   48c multi   1.50   1.50
    a.   Booklet pane of 24   36.00

No. 1585a sold for €11.04.

Love A524

Birds: Nos. 1586, 1587b, 1590, Parrots. Nos. 1587a, 1588, Rooster. Nos. 1587c, 1591, Owl. No. 1589, Storks.

2005, Jan. 28   *Perf. 14¾x14*
1586   A524   48c multi   4.25   4.25
1587   Sheet of 3   7.50   7.50
    a.-c.   A524 60c Any single   2.50   2.50
     Booklet Stamps
     Self-Adhesive
   Serpentine Die Cut 11¼x11
     Size: 27x21mm
1588   A524   48c multi   1.75   1.75
1589   A524   48c multi   1.75   1.75
1590   A524   48c multi   1.75   1.75
1591   A524   48c multi   1.75   1.75
    a.   Booklet pane, 3 each #1588,
        1590, 2 each #1589, 1591
        + 10 labels   17.50

New Year 2005 (Year of the Rooster).

St. Patrick's Day — A525

2005, Feb. 17   *Litho.*   *Perf. 14x14¾*
1592   A525   65c multi   2.75   2.75

Works of Women Artists A526

Designs: No. 1593, Landscape, Co. Wicklow, by Evie Hone (1894-1955). No. 1594, Seabird and Landmarks, by Nano Reid (1905-81). No. 1595, Threshing, by Mildred Anne Butler (1858-1941), vert. No. 1596, Three Graces, by Gabriel Hayes (1909-78), vert.

2005, Feb. 24   *Perf. 14¾x14, 14x14¾*
1593   A526   48c multi   1.50   1.50
1594   A526   48c multi   1.50   1.50
    a.   Horiz. pair, #1593-1594   3.00   3.00
1595   A526   65c multi   2.00   2.00
1596   A526   65c multi   2.00   2.00
    a.   Horiz. pair, #1595-1596   4.00   4.00

Cork, 2005 European Cultural Capital A527

Intl. Year of Physics — A528

Designs: 48c, William Rowan Hamilton (1805-65), mathematician and astronomer. 60c, UNESCO Headquarters, Paris. 65c, Albert Einstein (1879-1955), physicist.

2005, Mar. 14
1599   A528   48c multi   1.50   1.50
1600   A528   60c multi   1.90   1.90
1601   A528   65c multi   2.00   2.00
    Nos. 1599-1601 (3)   5.40   5.40

Dublin-Belfast Railway, 150th Anniv. — A529

Designs: No. 1602, Modern train. No. 1603, Steam locomotive at Connolly Station, Dublin. 60c, Steam locomotive on Boyne Valley Viaduct. 65c, Modern train at station platform.

2005, Apr. 5   *Litho.*   *Perf. 14¾x14*
1602   A529   48c multi   1.50   1.50
    a.   Booklet pane of 4   6.00
1603   A529   48c multi   1.50   1.50
    a.   Booklet pane of 4   6.00
    b.   Horiz. pair, #1602-1603   3.00   3.00
1604   A529   60c multi   1.90   1.90
    a.   Booklet pane of 4   7.75
1605   A529   65c multi   2.00   2.00
    a.   Booklet pane of 4   8.00
        Complete booklet, #1602a,
        1603a, 1604a, 1605a   27.75
    b.   Souvenir sheet, #1602-1605   8.50   8.50
    Nos. 1602-1605 (4)   6.90   6.90

Complete booklet sold for €9.

Flowers Type of 2004

Designs: 1c, Bloody crane's-bill. 2c, Irish orchid. 7c, Fly orchid. 10c, Mountain avens. €10, Spring gentian, horiz.

2005, Apr. 12   *Perf. 14x14¾*
1606   A519   1c multi   .20   .20
1607   A519   2c multi   .20   .20
1608   A519   7c multi   .20   .20
1609   A519   10c multi   .30   .30
      Size: 44x23mm
1610   A519   €10 multi   30.00   30.00
    Nos. 1606-1610 (5)   30.90   30.90

Biosphere Reserves in Ireland and Canada — A530

Designs: 48c, Deer, Killarney National Park, Ireland. 65c, Saskatoon berries, Waterton Lakes National Park, Canada.

2005, Apr. 22   *Perf. 13¼x13*
1611   A530   48c multi   1.50   1.50
1612   A530   65c multi   2.00   2.00
    a.   Souvenir sheet, #1611-1612   5.00   5.00

See Canada Nos. 2105-2106.

Europa A531

2005, Mar. 7   *Litho.*   *Perf. 13¼*
1597   A527   48c shown   2.10   2.10
1598   A527   48c Buildings, bridge   2.10   2.10
    a.   Horiz. pair, #1597-1598   4.25   4.25

2005, May 9 Litho. Perf. 14¼x14
1613 A531 48c Irish stew 1.50 1.50
1614 A531 65c Oysters 2.00 2.00

Worldwide Fund for Nature (WWF) A532

Butterflies: 48c, Small copper. 60c, Green hairstreak. 65c, €5, Painted lady. €1, Pearl-bordered fritillary.

2005, May 24 Perf. 13¼
1615 A532 48c multi 1.50 1.50
1616 A532 60c multi 1.90 1.90
1617 A532 65c multi 2.00 2.00
1618 A532 €1 multi 3.00 3.00
Nos. 1615-1618 (4) 8.40 8.40
Souvenir Sheet
1619 A532 €5 multi 17.50 17.50

Tall Ships A533

2005, July 4 Litho. Perf. 13½
1620 A533 48c Dunbrody 1.50 1.50
1621 A533 60c Tenacious 1.90 1.90
1622 A533 65c Eagle 2.00 2.00
Nos. 1620-1622 (3) 5.40 5.40

Round Towers — A534

2005, July 27 Litho. Perf. 13¼
1623 A534 48c Glendalough 1.50 1.50
1624 A534 48c Ardmore 1.50 1.50
1625 A534 48c Clones 1.50 1.50
1626 A534 48c Kilmacduagh 1.50 1.50
a. Horiz. strip of 4, #1623-1626 6.00 6.00

Apimondia 2005 Apriarists Congress, Dublin — A535

2005, Aug. 19 Perf. 13½x13
1627 A535 65c multi 2.25 2.25

2006 Ryder Cup Golf Tournament, K Club, Straffan — A536

Designs: No. 1628, Golfers Darren Clark, Paul McGinley, and Pádraig Harrington. No. 1629, Golfers Eamonn Darcy, Christy

O'Connor, Jr., and Philip Walton. 60c, Golfers Harry Bradshaw, Ronan Rafferty, and Christy O'Connor, Sr. 65c, K Club.

2005, Sept. 27 Litho. Perf. 14¾x14
1628 A536 48c multi 1.50 1.50
a. Booklet pane of 4 6.00 —
1629 A536 48c multi 1.50 1.50
a. Pair, #1628-1629 3.00 3.00
b. Booklet pane of 4 6.00 —
1630 A536 60c multi 2.00 2.00
a. Booklet pane of 4 8.00 —
b. Booklet pane, 2 each #1628-1630 ('06) 10.00 —
1631 A536 65c multi 2.00 2.00
a. Booklet pane of 4 8.00 —
b. Booklet pane, 2 #1631 ('06) 4.00 —
Complete booklet, #1628a, 1629a, 1630a, 1631a 28.00 —
Nos. 1628-1631 (4) 7.00 7.00
Nos. 1630b, 1631b issued 9/14/06.

Pres. Erskine Childers (1905-74) A537

2005, Oct. 10 Perf. 14x14¾
1632 A537 48c multi 3.50 3.50

Ireland in the United Nations A538

Designs: No. 1633, Irish Defense Force member assisting man in East Timor. No. 1634, Medical worker aiding child in East Timor. 60c, F. H. Boland, Ireland's signer of United Nations Charter. 65c, Irish Defense Force member in classroom in Lebanon.

2005, Oct. 14 Perf. 14¾x14
1633 A538 48c multi 1.50 1.50
1634 A538 48c multi 1.50 1.50
a. Horiz. pair, #1633-1634 3.00 3.00
1635 A538 60c multi 1.90 1.90
1636 A538 65c multi 2.00 2.00
Nos. 1633-1636 (4) 6.90 6.90

Arthur Griffith's Policy Establishing Sinn Féin, Cent. — A539

2005, Nov. 10 Perf. 13½
1637 A539 48c multi 2.00 2.00

Christmas A540

Designs: 48c, Nativity. 60c, Choir of angels. 65c, Choir of angels, diff.

2005, Nov. 10 Perf. 14x14¾
1638 A540 48c multi 1.50 1.50
1639 A540 60c multi 1.90 1.90
1640 A540 65c multi 2.00 2.00
Nos. 1638-1640 (3) 5.40 5.40
Booklet Stamp
Self-Adhesive
Size: 21x27mm
Serpentine Die Cut 11x11¼
1641 A540 48c multi 1.50 1.50
a. Booklet pane of 26 35.00 35.00
No. 1641a sold for €12.

Patrick Gallagher and Templecrone Cooperative Store — A541

2006, Jan. 16 Litho. Perf. 14¾x14
1642 A541 48c sepia 1.75 1.75
Templecrone Cooperative Agricultural Society, cent.

New Year 2006 (Year of the Dog) A542

Designs: Nos. 1643, 1644b, 1647, Dog, man and woman. Nos. 1644a, 1645, Two dogs, man. Nos. 1644c, 1646, Dog on leash, woman. No. 1648, Dog biting sneaker.

2006, Jan. 16 Perf. 14¾x14
1643 A542 48c multi 1.75 1.75
Souvenir Sheet
1644 Sheet of 3 7.50 7.50
a.-c. A542 65c Any single 2.50 2.50
Booklet Stamps
Self-Adhesive
Size: 26x21mm
Serpentine Die Cut 11¼x11
1645 A542 48c multi 1.75 1.75
1646 A542 48c multi 1.75 1.75
1647 A542 48c multi 1.75 1.75
1648 A542 48c multi 1.75 1.75
a. Booklet pane, 3 each #1645-1646, 2 each #1647-1648, + 10 labels 17.50
Nos. 1645-1648 (4) 7.00 7.00

St. Patrick Lights the Paschal Fire at Slane, by Sean Keating A543

2006, Feb. 16 Perf. 14¾x14
1649 A543 65c multi 2.50 2.50
St. Patrick's Day.

Flowers Type of 2004

Designs: 12c, Autumn gorse. 25c, Common knapweed. 75c, Navelwort. 90c, Viper's bugloss. €1, Foxglove.

2006, Feb. 20 Perf. 14x14¾
1650 A519 12c multi .40 .40
1651 A519 25c multi .75 .75
1652 A519 75c multi 2.25 2.25
1653 A519 90c multi 2.75 2.75
Size: 23x44mm
1654 A519 €1 multi 3.00 3.00
Nos. 1650-1654 (5) 9.15 9.15
Booklet Stamp
Self-Adhesive
Size: 21x27mm
Serpentine Die Cut 11x11¼
1655 A519 75c multi 2.25 2.25
a. Booklet pane of 10 22.50

Trees A544

2006, Mar. 7 Perf. 13¼
1656 A544 48c Sessile oak 1.50 1.50
1657 A544 60c Yew 1.90 1.90
1658 A544 75c Ash 2.25 2.25
1659 A544 €1 Strawberry tree 3.00 3.00
a. Souvenir sheet, #1656-1659 9.00 9.00
b. As "a," with Washington 2006 World Philatelic Exhibition emblem in margin 10.00 10.00
Nos. 1656-1659 (4) 8.65 8.65
No. 1659b issued in June. No. 1659b sold for €3.

St. Hubert, Stained Glass Window by Harry Clarke (1889-1931) A545

2006, Mar. 21 Perf. 13¼
1660 A545 48c multi 1.75 1.75

Easter Rebellion, 90th Anniv. — A546

2006, Apr. 12 Perf. 13½
1661 A546 48c multi 1.75 1.75

Adoption of European Union Flag, 20th Anniv. A547

2006, May 9 Perf. 14¼x14
1662 A547 48c multi 1.75 1.75

Europa — A548

Winning art in children's stamp design contest: 48c, People holding Irish and European Union flags, by Katie McMillan. 75c, Flowers with flags, by Sarah Naughter.

2006, May 9 Perf. 14x14¼
1663 A548 48c multi 2.00 2.00
1664 A548 75c multi 2.75 2.75

University Church, Dublin, 150th Anniv. — A549

2006, May 25 Litho. Perf. 14x14¾
1665 A549 48c multi 1.75 1.75

Department of the Gaeltacht, 50th Anniv. — A550

2006, June 6   **Perf. 13¼**
1666 A550 48c multi   1.75 1.75

TG4 Television Channel, 10th Anniv. A551

2006, June 6
1667 A551 48c multi   1.75 1.75

Celtic Scholars — A552

Designs: No. 1668, Máirtín O Cadhain (1906-70), writer. No. 1669, Johann Caspar Zeuss (1806-56), philologist.

2006, June 6   **Perf. 14x14¾**
1668 A552 48c multi   1.75 1.75
1669 A552 48c multi   1.75 1.75
   a.   Pair, #1668-1669   3.50 3.50

Rosslare-Fishguard Ferry Service, Cent. — A553

Designs: No. 1670, Steam ferry. No. 1671, Modern ferry.

2006, June 20   **Perf. 14¾x14**
1670 A553 48c multi   1.75 1.75
1671 A553 48c multi   1.75 1.75
   a.   Pair, #1670-1671   3.50 3.50
   b.   Souvenir sheet, #1670-1671   4.25 4.25

Battle of the Somme, 90th Anniv. A554

2006, June 26   **Perf. 13½x13¾**
1672 A554 75c multi   2.50 2.50

Guide Dog — A555

Litho. & Embossed
2006, July 7   **Perf. 13¼x13**
1673 A555 48c multi   1.75 1.75

A556

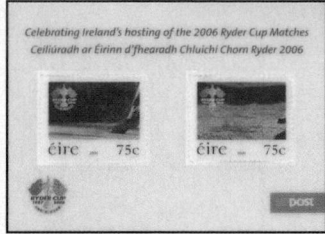

2006 Ryder Cup Golf Tournament, K Club, Straffan — A557

Golf ball: Nos. 1674, 1678, On tee. Nos. 1675, 1679, In rough. Nos. 1676, 1680, In sand trap. Nos. 1677, 1681, Near green. No. 1682: a, Tee shot. b, Sand trap shot.

2006   **Litho.**   **Perf. 14x14¾**
1674 A556 48c multi   1.50 1.50
1675 A556 48c multi   1.50 1.50
1676 A556 48c multi   1.50 1.50
1677 A556 48c multi   1.50 1.50
   a.   Horiz. strip, #1674-1677   6.00 6.00
   b.   Souvenir sheet #1674-1677   6.50 6.50
   c.   Booklet pane, 2 each #1674-1677   12.00 —
   d.   Booklet pane, #1674-1677   6.00 —

Coil Stamps
Self-Adhesive
Size: 21x27mm

Serpentine Die Cut 11x11¼

1678 A556 48c multi   1.50 1.50
1679 A556 48c multi   1.50 1.50
1680 A556 48c multi   1.50 1.50
1681 A556 48c multi   1.50 1.50
   a.   Vert. strip, #1678-1681   6.00

Souvenir Sheet
Self-Adhesive
Litho. With Three-Dimensional Plastic Affixed

Serpentine Die Cut 9¼

1682 A557   Sheet of 2   6.50
   a.-b.   75c Either single   3.25 3.25
   Complete booklet, #1630b, 1631b, 1677c, 1677d, and unbound #1682   40.00

Issued: Nos. 1674-1678, 7/25; No. 1682, 9/14. Complete booklet sold for €12. No. 1677b has Ryder Cup emblem in margin while No. 1677d does not.

Winning of Olympic 1500-Meter Running Gold Medal by Ronnie Delany, 50th Anniv. — A558

Perf. 13¾x13½
2006, Aug. 16   **Litho.**
1683 A558 48c multi   1.75 1.75

Michael Cusack (1847-1906), Sports Journalist A559

2006, Aug. 23   **Perf. 14x14¾**
1684 A559 48c multi   1.75 1.75

Michael Davitt (1846-1906), Founder of National Land League — A560

2006, Sept. 5
1685 A560 48c multi   1.75 1.75

National Concert Hall, Dublin, 25th Anniv. — A561

2006, Sept. 8
1686 A561 48c multi   1.75 1.75

Inland Waterways — A562

Designs: No. 1687, Barrow River at Graiguenamanagh. No. 1688, Belturbet Marina, Erne River. No. 1689, Grand Canal at Cornalaur. No. 1690, Meelick Pier, Shannon River.

2006, Oct. 20 Litho.   **Perf. 13½x13¾**
1687 A562 75c multi   2.25 2.25
   a.   Booklet pane of 4   9.00
1688 A562 75c multi   2.25 2.25
   a.   Booklet pane of 4   9.00
1689 A562 75c multi   2.25 2.25
   a.   Booklet pane of 4   9.00
1690 A562 75c multi   2.25 2.25
   a.   Booklet pane of 4   9.00 —
   Complete booklet, #1687a-1690a   36.00

Traditional Irish Music Groups — A563

Designs: No. 1691, The Chieftains. No. 1692, The Dubliners. No. 1693, The Clancy Brothers and Tommy Makem. No. 1694, Altan.

2006, Nov. 7 Litho.   **Perf. 13½x13¾**
1691 A563 48c multi   1.75 1.75
   a.   Booklet pane of 4   7.00
1692 A563 48c multi   1.75 1.75
   a.   Booklet pane of 4   7.00
1693 A563 75c multi   2.50 2.50
   a.   Booklet pane of 4   10.00
1694 A563 75c multi   2.50 2.50
   a.   Booklet pane of 4   10.00 —
     Complete booklet, #1691a, 1692a, 1693a, 1694a   34.00
   c.   Souvenir sheet, #1691-1694   7.00 7.00
   c.   As "b," with Belgica '06 emblem added in margin   7.00 7.00
   d.   As "b," with MonacoPhil 2006 emblem added in margin   7.00 7.00

Complete booklet sold for €10. No. 1694c issued 11/16; No. 1694d, 12/1.

Christmas
A564   A565

Designs: No. 1695, Madonna and Child. 75c, Shepherd and lamb. No. 1697, Nativity.

2006, Nov. 9   **Perf. 14x14¾**
1695 A564 48c multi   1.50 1.50
1696 A564 75c multi   2.25 2.25

Booklet Stamp
Self-Adhesive
Serpentine Die Cut 11x11¼
1697 A565 48c multi   1.50 1.50
   a.   Booklet pane of 26   39.00
   Nos. 1695-1697 (3)   5.25 5.25

No. 1697a sold for €12.

Father Luke Wadding (1588-1657) A566

Irish Franciscan College, Louvain, 400th Anniv. — A567

2007, Jan. 24 Litho.   **Perf. 14x14¾**
1698 A566 75c multi   2.25 2.25
1699 A567 75c multi   2.25 2.25

Hands With Wedding Rings A568   Greetings A569

Designs: No. 1701, Stamp with hat, heart balloon. No. 1702, Birthday cake.

Serpentine Die Cut 11¼
2007, Jan. 26
Booklet Stamps
Self-Adhesive

1700 A568 N multi   1.50 1.50
   a.   Booklet pane of 10   15.00
1701 A569 N multi   1.50 1.50
1702 A569 N multi   1.50 1.50
   a.   Booklet pane of 10, 5 each #1701-1702   15.00
   Nos. 1700-1702 (3)   4.50 4.50

Nos. 1700-1702 each sold for 48c on day of issue.

New Year 2007 (Year of the Pig) A570

2007, Feb. 9   Litho.   Perf. 14¾x14
1703 A570 75c grn & multi   2.00 2.00

Souvenir Sheet
1704   Sheet of 3, #1704a, 2
            #1703   7.50 7.50
  a. A570 75c red & multi   2.50 2.50

St. Patrick's
Day — A571

2007, Feb. 9   Perf. 13½
1705 A571 75c multi   2.00 2.00

Flight of the
Earls, 400th
Anniv. — A572

Designs: No. 1706, Hugh O'Neill, Earl of Tyrone, and ship at right. No. 1707, Rory O'Donnell, Earl of Tyrconnell, and rowboat at left.

2007, Feb. 23   Perf. 14x14¾
1706 A572 48c multi   1.50 1.50
1707 A572 48c multi   1.50 1.50
  a. Horiz. pair, #1706-1707   3.00 3.00
  b. Souvenir sheet, #1707a   3.00 3.00

Flowers Type of 2004
Designs: 3c, Yellow flag. 55c, No. 1712, Large-flowered butterwort. 78c, Black bog-rush. 95c, Purple loosestrife. No. 1713, Blue-eyed grass.

2007, Mar. 1   Litho.   Perf. 14x14¾
1708 A519 3c multi   .20 .20
1709 A519 55c multi   1.50 1.50
1710 A519 78c multi   2.10 2.10
1711 A519 95c multi   2.50 2.50
        Nos. 1708-1711 (4)   6.30 6.30

Self-Adhesive
Size: 21x26mm
Serpentine Die Cut 11x11¼
1712 A519 N multi   1.50 1.50
1713 A519 N multi   1.50 1.50
  a. Booklet pane, 5 each #1712-
        1713   15.00
  b. Vert. coil pair, #1712-1713   3.00

Nos. 1712-1713 each sold for 55c on day of issue.

Castles
A573

Designs: No. 1714, Trim Castle. No. 1715, Dunluce Castle. No. 1716, Lismore Castle. No. 1717, Portumna Castle.

2007, Mar. 9   Perf. 14¾x14
1714 A573 55c multi   1.50 1.50
1715 A573 55c multi   1.50 1.50
1716 A573 55c multi   1.50 1.50
1717 A573 55c multi   1.50 1.50
  b. Souvenir sheet, #1714-1717   6.00 6.00

Treaty of Rome,
50th
Anniv. — A574

2007, Mar. 28   Perf. 14x14¾
1718 A574 55c multi   1.50 1.50

Planets — A575

Earth and: No. 1719, Jupiter. No. 1720, Neptune. No. 1721, Saturn. No. 1722, Uranus.

2007, Apr. 20   Litho.   Perf. 13¼
1719 A575 55c multi   1.50 1.50
1720 A575 55c multi   1.50 1.50
  a. Horiz. pair, #1719-1720   3.00 3.00
1721 A575 78c multi   2.25 2.25
1722 A575 78c multi   2.25 2.25
  a. Horiz. pair, #1721-1722   4.50 4.50
  b. Souvenir sheet, #1719-1722   7.50 7.50
  c. Booklet pane, #1719-1722   7.50 —
        Complete booklet, 4 #1722c   30.00
        Nos. 1719-1722 (4)   7.50 7.50

No. 1722c has stamps with straight edges at right. Complete booklet contains four examples of No. 1722c with different margins.

Flower Type of 2004
Designs: 5c, Dandelion. 25c, Common knapweed. 55c, Large-flowered butterwort. 78c, Black bog-rush.

Die Cut Perf. 12¾
2007, Apr. 20   Litho.
Coil Stamp
Self-Adhesive (#1723, 1728-1729)
Size: 21x26mm
1723 A519 55c multi   1.50 1.50

Booklet Stamps
Size: 17x20mm
Perf. 14¾x14 on 3 Sides
1724 A519 5c multi   .20 .20
1725 A519 25c multi   .70 .70
1726 A519 55c multi   1.50 1.50
  a. Booklet pane of 6, #1725, 2
        #1724, 3 #1726   5.75 —
        Complete booklet, #1726a   5.75

Size: 20x23mm
Perf. 14x14¾ on 3 Sides
1727 A519 55c multi   1.50 1.50
  a. Booklet pane of 10   15.00
        Complete booklet, #1727a   15.00

Size: 21x26mm
Serpentine Die Cut 11x11¼
1728 A519 55c multi   1.50 1.50
  a. Booklet pane of 10   15.00
1729 A519 78c multi   2.25 2.25
  a. Booklet pane of 10   22.50
        Nos. 1723-1729 (7)   9.15 9.15

Europa
A576

2007, May 9   Perf. 14¼x14
1730 A576 55c Female Scout   1.50 1.50
1731 A576 78c Male Scout   2.10 2.10
        Scouting, cent.

Canonization
of St.
Charles of
Mount Argus
(1821-93)
A577

2007, June 5   Perf. 13¼
1732 A577 55c multi   1.50 1.50

Institute of Public Administration, 50th
Anniv. — A578

2007, June 13
1733 A578 55c multi   1.50 1.50

RTE
Performing
Groups
A579

Designs: Nos. 1734, 1742, National Symphony Orchestra (Ceolfhoireann Shiansach Náisiúnta). Nos. 1735, 1740, Concert Orchestra (Ceolfhoireann Cheolchoirme). Nos. 1736, 1743, Vanbrugh Quartet (Ceathairéad Vanbrugh). Nos. 1737, 1741, Philharmonic Choir (Cór Fiolarmónach). Nos. 1738, 1739, Children's Choir (Cór na nOg).

2007, June 19   Perf. 13¼x13½
1734 A579 55c multi   1.50 1.50
1735 A579 55c multi   1.50 1.50
1736 A579 55c multi   1.50 1.50
  a. Booklet pane, 2 each
        #1734-1736   9.00 —
1737 A579 55c multi   1.50 1.50
1738 A579 55c multi   1.50 1.50
  a. Horiz. strip of 5, #1734-
        1738   7.50 7.50
  b. Booklet pane, 2 each
        #1737-1738   6.00 —
        Complete booklet, 2 each
        #1736a, 1738b   30.00

Booklet Stamps
Self-Adhesive
Serpentine Die Cut 11¼x11½
1739 A579 55c multi   1.50 1.50
1740 A579 55c multi   1.50 1.50
1741 A579 55c multi   1.50 1.50
1742 A579 55c multi   1.50 1.50
1743 A579 55c multi   1.50 1.50
  a. Booklet pane of 10, 2 each
        #1739-1743   15.00
        Nos. 1734-1743 (10)   15.00 15.00

Revival of
Honorable Society
of King's Inns,
400th
Anniv. — A580

2007, July 10   Perf. 13¼
1744 A580 55c multi   1.50 1.50

Registry of
Deeds Act,
300th
Anniv.
A581

2007, July 10   Perf. 14¾x14
1745 A581 78c multi   2.25 2.25

National
Anthem,
Cent.
A582

2007, July 17   Litho.   Perf. 13½
1746 A582 55c multi   1.50 1.50

Weddings Type of 2007
Serpentine Die Cut 11¼
2007, July 25
Booklet Stamp
Self-Adhesive
1747 A568 55c multi   1.50 1.50
  a. Booklet pane of 10   15.00

Viking Ship
Skuldelev
2 — A583

Designs: 55c, Ship. €3, Ship on water.

2007, Aug. 7   Litho.   Perf. 14¾x14
1748 A583 55c multi   1.50 1.50

Souvenir Sheet
1749 A583 €3 multi   8.25 8.25

2007 Rugby
World Cup,
France — A584

Designs: 55c, Player carrying ball. 78c, Player catching ball.

2007, Aug. 20   Perf. 13¼
1750 A584 55c multi   1.50 1.50
  a. Souvenir sheet of 1   1.50 1.50
1751 A584 78c multi   2.25 2.25
  a. Souvenir sheet of 1   2.25 2.25

Cat Caricatures
by Martyn
Turner — A585

Designs: Nos. 1752, 1756a, Fat Cat. Nos. 1753, 1756b, Celtic Tigress. Nos. 1754, 1756c, Cool Cats. Nos. 1755, 1756d, Kilkenny Cat.

2007, Sept. 6   Perf. 14x14¾
1752 A585 55c multi   1.50 1.50
1753 A585 55c multi   1.50 1.50
  a. Horiz. pair, #1752-1753   3.00 3.00

1754 A585 78c multi 2.25 2.25
1755 A585 78c multi 2.25 2.25
a. Horiz. pair, #1754-1755 4.50 4.50

Souvenir Sheet
Perf. 13¼

1756 Sheet of 4 7.50 7.50
a.-b. A585 55c Either single,
16x16mm 1.50 1.50
c.-d. A585 78c Either single,
16x16mm 2.25 2.25

Excavations of San Clemente Basilica,
Rome, 150th Anniv. — A586

2007, Sept. 12 **Perf. 14¾x14**
1757 A586 55c multi 1.60 1.60

James Fintan
Lalor (1807-49),
Political
Writer — A587

2007, Sept. 18 **Perf. 14x14¾**
1758 A587 55c multi 1.60 1.60

Natural History Museum, Dublin, 150th
Anniv. — A588

2007, Oct. 25 **Litho.** **Perf. 13¼**
1759 A588 55c multi 1.60 1.60

Christmas
A589

Designs: No. 1760, Presentation in the Temple. No. 1761, Three Magi. No. 1762, Adoration of the Shepherds.

2007, Nov. 8 **Perf. 14¾x14**
1760 A589 55c multi 1.60 1.60
1761 A589 78c multi 2.40 2.40

Self-Adhesive
Booklet Stamp
Size: 21x27mm
Serpentine Die Cut 11x11¼
1762 A589 55c multi 1.60 1.60
a. Booklet pane of 26 42.50

No. 1762a sold for €13.75.

Charles Wesley
(1707-88), Hymn
Writer — A590

2007, Nov. 15 **Perf. 14x14¾**
1763 A590 78c multi 2.40 2.40

Bride and
Groom
A591

Serpentine Die Cut 11¼
2008, Jan. 16 **Litho.**
Booklet Stamp
Self-Adhesive
1764 A591 55c multi 1.60 1.60
a. Booklet pane of 10 16.00

Greetings — A592

Serpentine Die Cut 11¼
2008, Jan. 16
Booklet Stamps
Self-Adhesive
1765 A592 55c Frog 1.60 1.60
1766 A592 55c Elephant 1.60 1.60
a. Booklet pane of 10, 5 each
#1765-1766 16.00

New Year
2008 (Year
of the Rat)
A593

2008, Jan. 23 **Perf. 14¾x14**
1767 A593 78c multi 2.40 2.40
a. Souvenir sheet of 3 7.25 7.25

Liam Whelan (1935-58), Soccer Player
Killed in Airplane Crash — A594

2008, Feb. 4 **Perf. 13½x13¾**
1768 A594 55c multi 1.75 1.75

St. Patrick's
Day — A595

2008, Feb. 11 **Perf. 13¼x13**
1769 A595 78c multi 2.40 2.40

Flower Type of 2004
Designs: 20c, Thrift. 50c, Biting stonecrop.
82c, Sea aster.

2008, Mar. 3 **Litho.** **Perf. 14x14¾**
Size: 20x23mm
1770 A519 20c multi .65 .65
1771 A519 50c multi 1.60 1.60
1772 A519 82c multi 2.50 2.50
a. Booklet pane of 10 25.00
Complete booklet, #1772a 25.00
Nos. 1770-1772 (3) 4.75 4.75

Booklet Stamp
Self-Adhesive
Size: 21x25mm
Serpentine Die Cut 11x11¼
1773 A519 82c multi 2.50 2.50
a. Booklet pane of 10 25.00

European Year of Intercultural
Dialogue — A596

2008, Mar. 7 **Perf. 13¼**
1774 A596 55c multi 1.75 1.75

Hugh Lane, by
Antonio
Mancini — A597

2008, Mar. 28 **Litho.** **Perf. 13½**
1775 A597 55c multi 1.75 1.75
Dublin City Gallery, cent. (founded by Lane).

Paintings by
Paul Henry
(1876-1958)
A598

Designs: No. 1776, A Connemara Village
(left half, "Paul Henry" in blue). No. 1777, A
Connemara Village (right half, "Paul Henry" in
white). No. 1778, West of Ireland Landscape
(left half, "Paul Henry" in gray at left). No.
1779, West of Ireland Landscape (right half,
"Paul Henry" in gray at right).

2008, Apr. 17 **Perf. 13¼**
1776 A598 55c multi 1.75 1.75
1777 A598 55c multi 1.75 1.75
1778 A598 55c multi 1.75 1.75
1779 A598 55c multi 1.75 1.75
a. Horiz. strip of 4, #1776-1779 7.00 7.00
b. Booklet pane of 4, #1776-
1779 7.00 —
Complete booklet, 4 #1779b 28.00

No. 1779b has example of No. 1779 with
straight edge at right. The four examples of
No. 1779b in the complete booklet have different margins. The complete booklet sold for
€9.

Credit
Union
Movement,
50th Anniv.
A599

2008, Apr. 23 **Perf. 14¾x14**
1780 A599 55c multi 1.75 1.75

Intl. Year
of Planet
Earth
A600

Plasticine sculptures of Earth created by
children: No. 1781, Africa and Europe, by
Mohammed Rahman. No. 1782, South and
North America, by Conor Reid.

2008, Apr. 28 **Die Cut Perf.**
Self-Adhesive
1781 A600 55c red & multi 1.75 1.75
1782 A600 55c blue & multi 1.75 1.75
a. Horiz. pair, #1781-1782, on
backing paper without back
printing 3.50
b. Booklet pane of 10, 5 each
#1781-1782 17.50

Institute of
Creative
Advertising
and Design,
50th Anniv.
A601

2008, May 23 **Perf. 13¼**
1783 A601 55c multi 1.75 1.75

R. M. S.
Leinster,
90th Anniv.
of Sinking
A602

2008, May 30 **Perf. 14¾x14**
1784 A602 55c multi 1.75 1.75

Europa — A603

Designs: 55c, Boy writing letter. 82c, Girl
writing letter.

2008, June 9 **Perf. 14x14¾**
1785 A603 55c multi 1.75 1.75
1786 A603 82c multi 2.50 2.50

Tidy Towns
Competition, 50th
Anniv. — A604

2008, June 19
1787 A604 55c multi 1.75 1.75

Participation of Irish Defense Forces in
UN Missions, 50th Anniv. — A605

2008, June 26 **Perf. 14¾x14**
1788 A605 55c multi 1.75 1.75

Movies Filmed in Ireland — A606

Designs: No. 1789, Kings. No. 1790, Cré na Cille. No. 1791, The Wind that Shakes the Barley. No. 1792, Garage.

2008, July 8	**Litho.**	**Perf. 14¾x14**	
1789	A606	55c multi	1.75	1.75
1790	A606	55c multi	1.75	1.75
1791	A606	82c multi	2.60	2.60
1792	A606	82c multi	2.60	2.60
a.	Booklet pane of 4, #1789-1792	9.25	—
	Complete booklet, 4 #1792a	37.50	
b.	Souvenir sheet of 4, #1789-1792	8.75	8.75
	Nos. 1789-1792 (4)	8.70	8.70

No. 1792b has a printed margin. The complete booklet, which sold for €12, contains 4 examples of No. 1792a, each with a different order of stamps and without a printed margin.

2008 Summer Olympics, Beijing A607

Designs: 52c, Rowing. 82c, Shot put.

2008, July 15			
1793	A607	55c multi	1.75	1.75
1794	A607	82c multi	2.60	2.60

Souvenir Sheet
Stamps Inscribed "Olympex 2008"

1795	Sheet of 2	4.50	4.50
a.	A607 55c multi	1.75	1.75
b.	A607 82c multi	2.60	2.60

Mushrooms A608

Designs: No. 1796, Parasol. No. 1797, Orange birch bolete. 82c, Pink waxcap. 95c, Scarlet elfcup.

2008, Aug. 1	**Litho.**	**Perf. 14x14¾**	
1796	A608	55c multi	1.75	1.75
1797	A608	55c multi	1.75	1.75
a.	Horiz. pair, #1796-1797	3.50	3.50
1798	A608	82c multi	2.60	2.60
	Nos. 1796-1798 (3)	6.10	6.10

Souvenir Sheet

1799	A608	95c multi	3.00	3.00

First Transatlantic Cable Message From Europe to US, 150th Anniv. — A609

2008, Aug. 15		**Perf. 13¼**	
1800	A609	82c multi	2.40	2.40

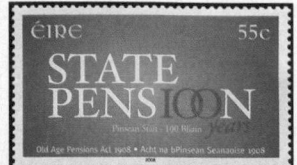

Old Age Pensions Act, Cent. — A610

2008, Sept. 19	**Litho.**	**Perf. 13¼**	
1801	A610	55c multi	1.50	1.50

National University of Ireland, Cent. — A611

2008, Sept. 19		**Perf. 13½**	
1802	A611	55c multi	1.50	1.50

Patrick Pearse (1879-1916), Patriot, and Founder of St. Enda's School — A612

Pearse and school buildings: No. 1803, Cullenswood House. No. 1804, The Hermitage.

2008, Sept. 25		**Perf. 14¾x14¼**	
1803	A612	55c multi	1.50	1.50
1804	A612	55c multi	1.50	1.50

Irish Bands A613

2008, Oct. 10	**Litho.**	**Perf. 13½**	
1805	A613	55c Planxty	1.50	1.50
1806	A613	55c De Danann	1.50	1.50
1807	A613	82c Tulla Ceili Band	2.25	2.25
1808	A613	82c Bothy Band	2.25	2.25
a.	Souvenir sheet, #1805-1808	7.50	7.50
	Nos. 1805-1808 (4)	7.50	7.50

Dancers — A614

2008, Nov. 7	**Litho.**	**Perf. 13½**	
1809	A614	55c Irish dancer	1.40	1.40

Souvenir Sheet

1810	Sheet of 2, #1809, 1810a	3.50	3.50
a.	A614 82c Flamenco dancer	2.10	2.10

See Spain No. 3609.

A615

Christmas — A616

Creche figures: No. 1811, Flight into Egypt. 82c, Annunciation. No. 1813, Infant Jesus.

2008, Nov. 7		**Perf. 14¾x14**	
1811	A615	55c multi	1.40	1.40
1812	A615	82c multi	2.10	2.10

Booklet Stamp
Self-Adhesive
Serpentine Die Cut 11x11¼

1813	A616	55c multi	1.40	1.40
a.	Booklet pane of 26	37.50	

No. 1813a sold for €13.75.

Flowers Type of 2004

Design: N, Yellow horned poppy.

Serpentine Die Cut 14

2008, Dec. 5		**Litho.**	

Booklet Stamp
Self-Adhesive
Size: 17x21mm

1814	A519	N multi	1.40	1.40
a.	Booklet pane of 10	14.00	

No. 1814 sold for 55c on day of issue.

Louis Braille (1809–1852)

Eye — A617

Litho. & Embossed

2009, Jan. 23		**Perf. 14¼**	
1815	A617	55c black	1.50	1.50

Louis Braille (1809-52), educator of the blind.

Love A618

Die Cut Perf. 13¼

2009, Jan. 23		**Litho.**	

Self-Adhesive

1816	A618	55c multi	1.50	1.50
a.	Vert. pair on backing paper without back printing	3.00	
b.	Booklet pane of 10	15.00	

All pairs from booklet pane are on backing paper with printing.

New Year 2009 (Year of the Ox) A619

2009, Jan. 23		**Perf. 14¾x14**	
1817	A619	82c multi	2.25	2.25
a.	Souvenir sheet of 3	6.75	6.75

St. Patrick Climbs Croagh Patrick, by Margaret Clarke — A620

2009, Feb. 19		**Perf. 14x14¾**	
1818	A620	82c multi	2.10	2.10

St. Patrick's Day.

Greetings — A621

Designs: No. 1819, Man lifting girl with letter to mailbox slot. No. 1820, Woman with letter, dog.

2009, Mar. 6		*Die Cut Perf. 12¾x13¼*	

Self-Adhesive

1819	A621	55c multi	1.40	1.40
1820	A621	55c multi	1.40	1.40
a.	Horiz. pair, #1819-1820, on backing paper withour back printing	2.80	
b.	Booklet pane of 10, 5 each #1819-1820, + 10 stickers	14.00	

All pairs from booklet pane are on backing paper with printing.

Charles Darwin (1809-82), Naturalist — A622

2009, Mar. 20		**Perf. 13½**	
1821	A622	82c multi	2.25	2.25

Scene from "The Playboy of the Western World" — A623

2009, Mar. 24		**Perf. 14x14¾**	
1822	A623	55c multi	1.50	1.50

John Millington Synge (1871-1909), writer.

Irish Times Newspaper, Cent. — A624

2009, Mar. 27   *Perf. 13¼*
1823   A624   55c multi   1.50   1.50

A625   A626

A627   A628

A629   A630

A631   A632

An Post, 25th Anniv.
A633   A634

Serpentine Die Cut 11x11¼
2009, Apr. 3   *Litho.*
Coil Stamps
Self-Adhesive
Size: 25x30mm
1824   A625   55c multi   1.50   1.50
1825   A626   55c multi   1.50   1.50
1826   A627   55c multi   1.50   1.50
1827   A628   55c multi   1.50   1.50
1828   A629   55c multi   1.50   1.50
   a.   Vert. strip of 5, #1824-1828   7.50
1829   A630   55c multi   1.50   1.50
1830   A631   55c multi   1.50   1.50
1831   A632   55c multi   1.50   1.50
1832   A633   55c multi   1.50   1.50
1833   A634   55c multi   1.50   1.50
   a.   Vert. strip of 5, #1829-1833   7.50
   b.   Vert. strip of 10, #1824-
       1833   15.00
     Nos. 1824-1833 (10)   15.00   15.00
Serpentine Die Cut 14
1834   Booklet pane of 10   15.00
   a.   A625 55c multi, 20x24mm   1.50   1.50
   b.   A626 55c multi, 20x24mm   1.50   1.50
   c.   A627 55c multi, 20x24mm   1.50   1.50
   d.   A628 55c multi, 20x24mm   1.50   1.50
   e.   A629 55c multi, 20x24mm   1.50   1.50
   f.   A630 55c multi, 20x24mm   1.50   1.50
   g.   A631 55c multi, 20x24mm   1.50   1.50

   h.   A632 55c multi, 20x24mm   1.50   1.50
   i.   A633 55c multi, 20x24mm   1.50   1.50
   j.   A634 55c multi, 20x24mm   1.50   1.50

No. 1833b was only available in a full roll of 100 stamps. The philatelic bureau sold Nos. 1828a and 1833a as a convenience to collectors rather than No. 1833b.

Paintings by Francis Bacon (1909-92) — A635

Designs: 55c, Self-portrait. 82c, Artist's Studio.

2009, Apr. 24   *Perf. 13½*
1835   A635   55c multi   1.50   1.50
Souvenir Sheet
1836   A635   82c multi   2.25   2.25

James Larkin (1875-1947), Union Organizer — A636

2009, Apr. 30   *Perf. 13¼*
1837   A636   55c multi   1.50   1.50
Irish Transport and General Workers' Union, cent.

Volvo Ocean Race Stopover in Galway A637

Designs: 55c, Green Dragon yacht. €3, Green Dragon and another yacht, vert.

2009, May 8   *Perf. 13¾x14*
1838   A637   55c multi   1.60   1.60
Souvenir Sheet
1839   A637   €3 multi   8.50   8.50
No. 1839 contains one 27x48mm stamp.

European Conference of Postal and Telecommunications Administrations, 50th Anniv. — A638

2009, May 15   *Perf. 13¼*
1840   A638   82c multi   2.40   2.40

Europa
A639

Designs: 55c, Crab Nebula. 82c, Jets from a brown dwarf.

2009, May 15
1841   A639   55c multi   1.60   1.60
1842   A639   82c multi   2.40   2.40

Intl. Year of Astronomy.

European Dog Show, Dublin — A640

2009, May 21   *Die Cut Perf. 13x13¼*
Self-Adhesive
1843   A640   55c multi   1.60   1.60
   a.   Horiz. pair on backing paper
       without back printing   3.25
   b.   Booklet pane of 10 #1843   16.00

City Status of Kilkenny, 400th Anniv. — A641

2009, June 16   *Perf. 13½*
1844   A641   55c multi   1.60   1.60

Anthony Trollope (1815-82), Writer — A642

2009, June 26   *Perf. 14x14¾*
1845   A642   82c multi   2.40   2.40

Birrell Land Act, Cent. — A643

2009, July 15   *Perf. 13¼*
1846   A643   82c multi   2.40   2.40

Composers — A644

Designs: No. 1847, Wolfgang Amadeus Mozart (1756-91). No. 1848, George Frideric Handel (1685-1759). No. 1849, Joseph Haydn (1732-1809). No. 1850, Frédéric Chopin (1810-49).

2009, Aug. 14   *Perf. 13¼x13*
1847   A644   55c multi   1.60   1.60
1848   A644   55c multi   1.60   1.60
   a.   Horiz. pair, #1847-1848   3.25   3.25
1849   A644   82c multi   2.40   2.40
1850   A644   82c multi   2.40   2.40
   a.   Horiz. pair, #1849-1850   5.00   5.00
   b.   Souvenir sheet of 4, #1847-
       1850   8.25   8.25

   c.   Booklet pane of 4, #1847-
       1850   8.50   —
       Complete booklet, 4 #1850c   34.00
     Nos. 1847-1850 (4)   8.00   8.00

On No. 1847, stamps are at upper left with No. 1847 having straight edges at top and left, No. 1848 having straight edge at top and No. 1849 having straight edge at left. On No. 1850c, stamps are at right with Nos. 1848 and 1850 having straight edges at right. Complete booklet sold for €12 and contains four examples of No. 1850c, each with different margins.

Arthur Guinness (1725-1803), Founder of Guinness Brewery — A645

2009, Aug. 28   *Perf. 14x14¾*
1851   A645   82c multi   2.40   2.40
Guinness Brewery, 250th anniv.

Flower Type of 2004
Design: 82c, Sea aster.

2009, Aug. 7   *Serpentine Die Cut 14*
Booklet Stamp
Self-Adhesive
Size: 17x20mm
1852   A519   82c multi   2.40   2.40
   a.   Booklet pane of 10   24.00
Compare No. 1852 with No. 1773.

Plantation of Ulster, 400th Anniv. A646

Designs: No. 1853, English text. No. 1854, Gaelic text.

2009, Sept. 4   *Perf. 14¾x14*
1853   A646   55c multi   1.60   1.60
1854   A646   55c multi   1.60   1.60
   a.   Horiz. pair, #1853-1854   3.20   3.20

Playwrights — A647

Designs: No. 1855, Brian Friel. No. 1856, Tom Murphy. No. 1857, Frank McGuinness.

2009, Sept. 18
1855   A647   55c multi   1.60   1.60
1856   A647   55c multi   1.60   1.60
1857   A647   55c multi   1.60   1.60
     Nos. 1855-1857 (3)   4.80   4.80

Dragonflies
A648

Designs: No. 1858, Large red damselfly. No. 1859, Irish bluet. 82c, Four-spotted chaser, horiz.
95c, Banded demoiselle, horiz.

2009, Oct. 16   Litho.   Perf. 14x14¾

1858	A648	55c multi	1.75	1.75
1859	A648	55c multi	1.75	1.75
a.		Horiz. pair, #1858-1859	3.50	3.50

Perf. 14¾x14

1860	A648	82c multi	2.50	2.50
		Nos. 1858-1860 (3)	6.00	6.00

Souvenir Sheet
Perf. 13¼

1861	A648	95c multi	3.00	3.00

No. 1861 contains one 60x25mm stamp.

Illustrations From Gospel Book, Monastery of Gamaghiel, Armenia — A649

Virgin and Child, by Simon Bening — A650

Christmas: No. 1862, Nativity. 82c, Annunciation.

2009, Nov. 6   Perf. 14¾x14

1862	A649	55c multi	1.75	1.75
1863	A649	82c multi	2.50	2.50

Booklet Stamp
Self-Adhesive
Serpentine Die Cut 11x11¼

1864	A650	55c multi	1.75	1.75
a.		Booklet pane of 26	46.00	

No. 1864a sold for €13.75.

Flowers Type of 2004

Design: Large-flowered butterwort.

Serpentine Die Cut 14
2009, Oct. 16   Litho.
Booklet Stamp
Self-Adhesive
Size:17x21mm

1865	A519	55c multi	1.75	1.75
a.		Booklet pane of 10	17.50	

Compare with No. 1728.

Douglas Hyde (1860-1949), First President of Ireland — A651

2010, Jan. 21   Litho.   Perf. 14x14¾

1866	A651	55c multi	1.60	1.60

Lovebirds A652

2010, Jan. 21   Die Cut Perf. 13¼
Self-Adhesive

1867	A652	55c multi	1.60	1.60
a.		Vert. pair on backing paper without back printing	3.20	
b.		Booklet pane of 10	16.00	

Greetings A653

Designs: No. 1868, Girl astronaut in spaceship, birthday cake. No. 1869, Boy astronaut, heart.

Die Cut Perf. 13¼x12¾
2010, Jan. 28
Self-Adhesive

1868	A653	55c multi	1.60	1.60
1869	A653	55c multi	1.60	1.60
a.		Vert. pair, #1868-1869, on backing paper without back printing	3.20	
b.		Booklet pane of 10, 5 each #1868-1869	16.00	

New Year 2010 (Year of the Tiger) A654

2010, Feb. 11   Perf. 13¼

1870	A654	82c multi	2.25	2.25
a.		Souvenir sheet of 3	6.75	6.75

St. Patrick's Day — A655

2010, Feb. 18   Perf. 14x14¾

1871	A655	82c multi	2.25	2.25

President's Award, 25th Anniv. A656

2010, Mar. 11   Litho.   Perf. 13¼

1872	A656	55c multi	1.50	1.50

Irish Countrywoman's Association, Cent. — A657

2010, Mar. 25

1873	A657	55c multi	1.50	1.50

Crosses — A658

Designs: No. 1874, Monasterboice Cross, County Louth. No. 1875, Carndonagh Cross, County Donegal. No. 1876, Drumcliffe Cross, County Sligo. No. 1877, Ahenny Cross, County Tipperary.

2010, Apr. 8

1874	A658	55c black	1.50	1.50
1875	A658	55c black	1.50	1.50
1876	A658	55c black	1.50	1.50
1877	A658	55c black	1.50	1.50
a.		Horiz. strip of 4, #1874-1877	6.00	6.00
		Nos. 1874-1877 (4)	6.00	6.00

Europa — A659

Scenes from children's books: 55c, The Happy Prince, by Oscar Wilde. 82c, Gulliver's Travels, by Jonathan Swift.

2010, May 6

1878	A659	55c multi	1.40	1.40
1879	A659	82c multi	2.10	2.10

Máirtín O Direáin (1910-88), Poet A660

2010, May 27   Perf. 14¾x14

1880	A660	55c multi	1.40	1.40

Paintings by Roderic O'Conor (1860-1940) — A661

Designs: No. 1881, The Breton Girl (shown). No. 1882, Self-portrait.

2010, May 27   Perf. 13¼

1881	A661	55c multi	1.40	1.40
1882	A661	55c multi	1.40	1.40

Humanitarians — A662

Designs: No. 1883, Mother Teresa (1910-97), 1979 Nobel Laureate for Peace. No. 1884, Henry Dunant (1828-1910), founder of the Red Cross, 1901 Nobel Laureate for Peace.

2010, June 17

1883	A662	55c multi	1.40	1.40
1884	A662	55c multi	1.40	1.40
a.		Horiz. pair, #1883-1884	2.80	2.80

Fashion Designers A663

Work of Irish designers: No. 1885, Paul Costelloe. No. 1886, Louise Kennedy. No. 1887, Lainey Keogh. No. 1888, John Rocha. No. 1889, Philip Treacy. No. 1890, Orla Kiely.

Litho. & Embossed
2010, July 15   Perf. 13¼

1885	A663	55c multi	1.50	1.50
a.		Booklet pane of 3	4.50	—
1886	A663	55c multi	1.50	1.50
a.		Booklet pane of 3	4.50	—
1887	A663	55c multi	1.50	1.50
a.		Horiz. strip of 3, #1885-1887	4.50	4.50
b.		Booklet pane of 3	4.50	—
1888	A663	82c multi	2.25	2.25
a.		Booklet pane of 3	6.75	—
1889	A663	82c multi	2.25	2.25
a.		Booklet pane of 3	6.75	—
1890	A663	82c multi	2.25	2.25
a.		Horiz. strip of 3, #1888-1890	6.75	6.75
b.		Booklet pane of 3	6.75	—
		Complete booklet, #1885a, 1886a, 1887b, 1888a, 1889a, 1890b	34.00	
		Nos. 1885-1890 (6)	11.25	11.25

Complete booklet sold for €13.

Birds — A664

2010, July 29   Litho.   Perf. 13¼

1891	A664	55c Buzzard	1.50	1.50
1892	A664	55c Golden eagle	1.50	1.50
a.		Horiz. pair, #1891-1892	3.00	3.00
1893	A664	82c Peregrine falcon	2.25	2.25
1894	A664	95c Merlin	2.50	2.50
a.		Souvenir sheet, #1891-1894	7.75	7.75
		Nos. 1891-1894 (4)	7.75	7.75

Romeo and Juliet (Vignette of Sweden No. 1141) — A665

Litho. & Engr.
2010, Aug. 26   Perf. 12¾

1895	A665	55c multi	1.40	1.40

Stamp engraving work of Czeslaw Slania. See Sweden No. 2642.

Irish Wheelchair Association, 50th Anniv. — A666

2010, Sept. 8   Litho.   Perf. 14¾x14

1896	A666	55c multi	1.40	1.40

Showbands — A667

Designs: No. 1897, The Miami Showband.
No. 1898, The Drifters Showband. No. 1899,
The Royal Showband. No. 1900, The
Freshmen.

2010, Sept. 23			Perf. 13½	
1897	A667	55c multi	1.50	1.50
1898	A667	55c multi	1.50	1.50
1899	A667	82c multi	2.25	2.25
1900	A667	82c multi	2.25	2.25
a.	Souvenir sheet of 4, #1897-1900		7.50	7.50
b.	Booklet pane of 4, #1897-1900		8.25	—
	Complete booklet, 4 #1900b		33.00	
	Nos. 1897-1900 (4)		7.50	7.50

On No. 1900a, stamps are not near the
edge of the sheet and stamps have perforations on all four sides. On No. 1900b, Nos.
1898 and 1900 are at the right side of the
sheet and have a straight edge at right. The
complete booklet sold for €12 and contains
four examples of No. 1900b, each with different margins.

Ireland Automobile Association,
Cent. — A668

2010, Oct. 14			Perf. 14¾x14	
1901	A668	55c multi	1.60	1.60

Irishmen Involved
With Chilean
Independence
A669

Designs: No. 1902, Commander General
John Mackenna (1771-1814). No. 1903,
Supreme Director Bernardo O'Higgins (1778-
1842).

2010, Oct. 28			Perf. 13¼	
1902	A669	82c multi	2.40	2.40
1903	A669	82c multi	2.40	2.40
a.	Horiz. pair, #1902-1903		4.80	4.80

See Chile Nos.

A670

Christmas
A671

Stained-glass windows from churches in
Roscommon: No. 1904, Holy Family. 82c,
Joseph and Mary.

2010, Nov. 4			Perf. 13½	
1904	A670	55c multi	1.60	1.60

1905	A670	82c multi	2.40	2.40

Self-Adhesive
Serpentine Die Cut 11¼x11

1906	A671	55c multi	1.60	1.60
a.	Vert. pair on backing paper without printing on back		3.25	
b.	Booklet pane of 26 #1906		42.00	

No. 1906b sold for €13.75 and all stamps
have printing on the back of the backing paper.

Bride and
Groom — A672

2011, Jan. 20			Die Cut Perf. 13¼	

Self-Adhesive

1907	A672	55c multi	1.50	1.50
a.	Horiz. pair on backing paper without printing on back		3.00	
b.	Booklet pane of 10		15.00	

Tulips — A673

Balloons — A674

2011, Jan. 27		Die Cut Perf. 13¼x13	

Self-Adhesive

1908	A673	55c multi	1.50	1.50
1909	A674	55c multi	1.50	1.50
a.	Vert. pair, #1908-1909 on backing paper without print-ing on back		3.00	
b.	Booklet pane of 10, 5 each #1908-1909, + 10 stickers		15.00	

American
Chamber of
Commerce,
Ireland, 50th
Anniv. — A675

2011, Feb. 3			Perf. 14x14¾	
1910	A675	55c multi	1.50	1.50

AIR POST STAMPS

Catalogue values for unused
stamps in this section are for
Never Hinged items.

Angel over
Rock of
Cashel
AP1

Designs: 1p, 1sh3p, 1sh5p, Rock of Cashel.
3p, 8p, Lough Derg. 6p, Croagh Patrick. 1sh,
Glendalough.

			Perf. 15x14		
1948-65		**Wmk. 262**	**Engr.**		
C1	AP1	1p dk brown ('49)		9.00	9.00
C2	AP1	3p blue		15.00	13.00
C3	AP1	6p rose lilac		1.50	1.25
C4	AP1	8p red brown ('54)		6.00	4.75
C5	AP1	1sh green ('49)		3.00	1.60
C6	AP1	1sh3p ver ('54)		7.50	1.60

			Perf. 15		
C7	AP1	1sh5p dark blue ('65)		6.00	1.25
	Nos. C1-C7 (7)			48.00	32.45

POSTAGE DUE STAMPS

D1

1925		Typo.	Wmk. 44	Perf. 14x15	
J1	D1	½p emerald		27.50	42.50
		Never hinged		140.00	
J2	D1	1p carmine		17.00	12.50
		Never hinged		60.00	
J3	D1	2p dark green		32.50	15.00
		Never hinged		125.00	
J4	D1	6p plum		10.50	14.00
		Never hinged		45.00	
	Nos. J1-J4 (4)			87.50	84.00

Catalogue values for unused
stamps in this section, from this
point to the end of the section, are
for Never Hinged items.

1940-70			Wmk. 262	
J5	D1	½p emerald ('43)	27.50	22.50
J6	D1	1p brt carmine ('41)	1.10	.50
J7	D1	1½p vermilion ('52)	2.25	5.00
J8	D1	2p dark green	1.25	.55
J9	D1	3p blue ('52)	2.25	2.00
J10	D1	5p royal purple ('43)	3.50	7.50
J11	D1	6p plum ('60)	4.00	1.75
J12	D1	8p orange ('62)	7.50	7.50
J13	D1	10p red lilac ('65)	8.50	7.00
J14	D1	1sh lt yel grn ('69)	25.00	9.00
	Nos. J5-J14 (10)		82.85	63.30

1971, Feb. 15		Typo.	Wmk. 262	
J15	D1	1p sepia	2.50	3.50
J16	D1	1½p bright green	2.50	3.50
J17	D1	3p gray green	2.50	3.50
J18	D1	4p orange	2.50	3.50
J19	D1	5p bright blue	2.50	3.50
J20	D1	7p yellow	2.50	3.50
J21	D1	8p scarlet	2.50	3.50
	Nos. J15-J21 (7)		17.50	24.50

1978			Unwmk.	
J25	D1	3p gray green	3.50	3.50
J26	D1	4p orange	5.00	10.50
J27	D1	5p bright blue	3.50	3.50
	Nos. J25-J27 (3)		12.00	17.50

Celtic
Knot — D2

D3

1980-85		Photo.	Perf. 15	
J28	D2	1p brt yel green	.75	1.25
J29	D2	2p ultramarine	.75	1.25
J30	D2	4p dark green	.75	1.25
J31	D2	6p yel orange	.75	1.25
J32	D2	8p violet blue	1.00	2.00
J33	D2	18p green	1.60	2.00
J33A	D2	20p org brown ('85)	3.50	6.50
J34	D2	24p emerald	2.25	1.90
J35	D2	30p violet blue ('85)	7.00	9.00
J36	D2	50p rose pink ('85)	4.00	4.00
	Nos. J28-J36 (10)		22.35	30.40

Issue dates: 1p, 2p, 4p, 6p, 8p, 18p, 24p,
June 11; 20p, 30p, 50p, Aug. 22.

1988, Oct. 6		Litho.	Perf. 14x15	
J37	D3	1p blk, dp yel & brt red	.80	1.25
J38	D3	2p blk, vio brn & brt red	.80	1.25
J39	D3	3p blk, dull vio & brt red	.80	1.25
J40	D3	4p blk, vio & brt red	.80	1.25
J41	D3	5p blk, vio bl & brt red	.80	1.25
J42	D3	17p blk, brt ol grn & brt red	1.60	2.40
J43	D3	20p blk, bluish gray & brt red	2.10	2.75
J44	D3	24p blk, bl grn & brt red	2.40	3.25
J45	D3	30p blk & brt red	2.40	3.25
J46	D3	50p blk, gray & brt red	3.25	4.25
J47	D3	£1 blk, dk ol brn & brt red	6.75	8.25
	Nos. J37-J47 (11)		22.50	30.40

ISRAEL

'iz-rē-əl

LOCATION — Western Asia, bordering
on the Mediterranean Sea
GOVT. — Republic
AREA — 8,017 sq. mi.
POP. — 5,749,760 (1999 est.)
CAPITAL — Jerusalem

When the British mandate of Palestine ended in May 1948, the Jewish
state of Israel was proclaimed by the
Jewish National Council in Palestine.

1000 Mils = 1 Pound
1000 Prutot = 1 Pound (1949)
100 Agorot = 1 Pound (1960)
100 Agorot = 1 Shekel (1980)

Catalogue values for all unused
stamps in this country are for
Never Hinged items.

Tabs

Stamps of Israel are printed in
sheets with tabs (labels) usually
attached below the bottom row,
sometimes at the sides.

Tabs of the following numbers
are in two parts, perforated
between: 9, 15, 23-37, 44, 46-47,
50, 55, 62-65, 70-72, 74-77, 86-91,
94-99, 104-118, 123-126, 133-136B,
138-141, 143-151, 160-161, 165-
167, 178-179, 182, 187-189, 203,
211-213, 222-223, 228-237, 243-
244, 246-250, 256-258, 269-270,
272-273, 275, 294-295, 312, 337-
339, 341-344, 346-347, 353-354, C1-
C13, C22-C30. Both parts must be
present to qualify for with tab
value. Stamps with only one part
sell for about one-quarter to one-
third of full tab prices.

Watermarks

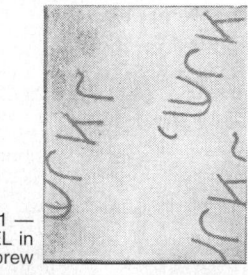

Wmk. 301 —
ISRAEL in
Hebrew

Wmk. 302 — Multiple Stag

Ancient Judean Coins
A1   A2

Designs: Nos. 1-6, Various coins.

		Perf. 10, 11 and Compound		
1948, May 16		**Typo.**	**Unwmk.**	
1	A1	3m orange	.30	.20
2	A1	5m yellow grn	.30	.20
3	A1	10m red violet	.50	.20
4	A1	15m red	.75	.25

5	A1	20m bright ultra	2.50	.35
6	A1	50m orange brown	9.50	1.00
		Nos. 1-6 (6)	13.85	2.20
		Nos. 1-6 (6) with tabs	275.00	
		Set, with tabs, hinged	110.00	

Size: 34½x22mm

7	A2	250m dark sl grn	35.00	11.00
8	A2	500m red brn, *cr*	150.00	55.00

Size: 36½x24mm

9	A2	1000m blk bl, *pale bl*	225.00	110.00
		Nos. 7-9 (3)	410.00	176.00
		Nos. 7-9 with tabs	7,500.	
		Set, hinged	190.00	

Nos. 1-9 exist imperf.
See design A6. For overprints see #J1-J5.

Rouletted

1a	A1	3m	.50	.20
2b	A1	5m	.65	.25
3b	A1	10m	11.00	.90
		Nos. 1a-3b (3)	12.15	1.35
		Set, with tabs	265.00	
		Set with tabs, hinged	125.00	

Flying Scroll — A3

1948, Sept. 26   Litho.   Perf. 11½

10	A3	3m brn red & ultra	.40	.20
11	A3	5m dl grn & ultra	.40	.20
12	A3	10m dp car & ultra	.40	.20
13	A3	20m dp ultra & ultra	1.50	.85
14	A3	65m brown & red	12.00	3.75
		Nos. 10-14 (5)	14.70	5.20
		With tabs	250.00	
		With tabs, hinged	110.00	

Jewish New Year, 5709.

Flag of Israel — A4

1949, Mar. 31

15	A4	20m bright blue	.50	.25
		With tab	50.00	

Appointment of the government by the Knesset.

Souvenir Sheet

A5

1949, May 1   Imperf.

16	A5	Sheet of 4	90.00	27.50
a.		10m dark carmine rose	17.50	4.00

1st anniv. of Israeli postage stamps.
The sheet was sold at "TABUL," First National Stamp Exhibition, in Tel Aviv, May 1-6, 1949. Tickets, costing 100 mils, covered the entrance fee and one sheet.

Bronze Half-Shekel of 67 A.D. — A6

1949-50   Unwmk.   Perf. 11½, 14

17	A6	3p gray black	.25	.20
18	A6	5p purple	.20	.20
19	A6	10p green	.20	.20
20	A6	15p deep rose	.25	.20
21	A6	30p dark blue	.30	.20
22	A6	50p brown	1.25	.20
23	A7	100p Prus grn	.40	.20
		With tab	20.00	
24	A8	250p org brn & gray	1.25	.65
		With tab	37.50	
25	A9	500p dp org & brown	7.50	5.50
		With tab	240.00	
		Nos. 17-25 (9)	11.60	7.55
		Nos. 17-22 with tabs (6)	75.00	
		Tete beche pairs, Nos. 18-21	80.00	80.00

Each of Nos. 17-22 portrays a different coin.
25th anniv. of the Hebrew University in Jerusalem (No. 23).
Issued: 250p, 2/16; 3p-50p, 12/18; 100p, 5/9/50; 500p, 12/26/50.
See Nos. 38-43, 56-61, 80-83, and design A1. For overprints see Nos. O1-O4.

Well at Petah Tikva — A10

1949, Aug. 10   Perf. 11

27	A10	40p dk grn & brn	8.50	.30
		With tab	90.00	

70th anniv. of Petah Tikva.

Arms and Service Insignia A11

1949, Sept. 20   Perf. 11½

28	A11	5p Air Force	.35	.25
29	A11	10p Navy	.95	.40
30	A11	35p Army	4.25	2.75
		Nos. 28-30 (3)	5.55	3.40
		With tabs	675.00	

Jewish New Year, 5710.

Running Stag — A12

1950, Mar. 26

31	A12	40p purple	.55	.30
a.		Booklet pane of 4	3.75	
32	A12	80p rose red	.70	.35
a.		Booklet pane of 4	7.50	
		Complete booklet, 1 ea. #31a, 32a	27.50	
b.		Nos. 31 and 32 tête bêche	45.00	25.00
		With tabs	72.50	

75th anniv. (in 1949) of the UPU.

Struggle for Free Immigration A13

Approach to Jerusalem A8 Arrival of Immigrants A14

1950, Apr. 23

33	A13	20p dull brown	2.50	1.50
34	A14	40p dull green	5.25	3.50
		With tabs	575.00	

Independence Day, Apr. 22, 1950.

Fruit and Star of David — A15

1950, Aug. 31   Litho.   Perf. 14

35	A15	5p vio blue & org	.20	.20
36	A15	15p red brn & grn	.35	.20
		With tabs	47.50	

Jewish New Year, 5711.

Runner and Track A16

1950, Oct. 1

37	A16	80p olive & sl blk	1.60	.60
		With tab	70.00	

3rd Maccabiah, Ramat Gan, Sept. 27, 1950.

Coin Type of 1949 Redrawn

Designs: Various coins.

1950

38	A6	3p gray black	.20	.20
39	A6	5p purple	.20	.20
a.		Tête bêche pair	3.00	3.00
40	A6	10p green	.20	.20
a.		Tête bêche pair	1.25	1.00
41	A6	15p deep rose	.20	.20
a.		Tête bêche pair	2.00	1.75
42	A6	30p dark blue	.20	.20
a.		Tête bêche pair	4.00	4.00
43	A6	50p brown	.20	.20
		Nos. 38-43 (6)	1.20	1.20
		With tab	2.90	

Inscription at left measures 11mm on Nos. 38-43; 9mm on Nos. 17-22.

Detail from Tablet, "Founding of Tel Aviv" A17

1951, Mar. 22

44	A17	40p dark brown	.30	.20
		With tab	20.00	

40th anniversary of Tel Aviv.

Young Man Holding Outline Map of Israel — A18

1951, Apr. 30   Litho.

45	A18	80p red brown	.20	.20
		With tab	3.75	

Issued to promote the sale of Independence Bonds.

Metsudat Yesha A19

Hakastel
A20

1951, May 9   **Unwmk.**
46   A19   15p red brown   .30   .20
47   A20   40p deep blue   .60   .20
    With tabs   45.00

Proclamation of State of Israel, 3rd anniv.

Tractor and
Wheat — A21   Tree — A22

Hebrew
University,
Jerusalem
A7Plower and
National Fund
Stamp of 1902
A23

1951, June 24   **Perf. 14**
48   A21   15p red brown   .20   .20
49   A22   25p Prussian green   .20   .20
50   A23   80p dull blue   .35   .20
    Nos. 48-50 (3)   .75   .60
    With tabs   90.00

Jewish National Fund, 50th anniversary.

Theodor Zeev   Carrier
Herzl — A24   Pigeons — A25

1951, Aug. 14
51   A24   80p gray green   .20   .20
    With tab   4.00

23rd Zionist Congress, Jerusalem.

1951, Sept. 16
Designs: 15p, Girl holding dove and fruit.
40p, Scrolls of the law.
52   A25   5p blue   .20   .20
53   A25   15p cerise   .20   .20
54   A25   40p rose violet   .20   .20
    Nos. 52-54 (3)   .60   .60
    With tabs   3.25

Jewish New Year, 5712.

Menorah and
Emblems of
Twelve
Tribes — A26

1952, Feb. 27
55   A26   1000p dk bl & gray   16.00   7.00
    With tab   250.00

Redrawn Coin Type of 1950
Designs: Various coins.

1952, Mar. 30
56   A6   20p orange   .20   .20
    a.   Tête bêche pair   2.50   2.50
57   A6   35p olive green   .20   .20
58   A6   40p orange brown   .20   .20

59   A6   45p red violet   .20   .20
    a.   Tête bêche pair   4.50   4.50
60   A6   60p carmine   .20   .20
61   A6   85p aquamarine   .20   .20
    Nos. 56-61 (6)   1.20   1.20
    With tabs   12.00

Thistle and
Yad
Mordecai
Battlefield
A27

Battlefields: 60p, Cornflower and Deganya.
110p, Anemone and Safed.

1952, Apr. 29
62   A27   30p lil rose & vio brn   .20   .20
63   A27   60p ultra & gray blk   .20   .20
64   A27   110p crimson & gray   .35   .25
    Nos. 62-64 (3)   .75   .65
    With tabs   20.00

Proclamation of State of Israel, 4th anniv.

Manhattan
Skyline and
American
Zionists'
House
A28

1952, May 13
65   A28   220p dark blue & gray   .35   .20
    With tab   11.00

Opening of American Zionists' House, Tel
Aviv.

Figs — A29

    Unwmk.
1952, Sept. 3   **Litho.**   **Perf. 14**
66   A29   15p shown   .30   .20
67   A29   40p Lily   .30   .20
68   A29   110p Dove   .30   .20
69   A29   220p Nut cluster   .50   .20
    Nos. 66-69 (4)   1.40   .80
    With tabs   26.00

Jewish New Year, 5713.

Pres. Chaim Weizmann (1874-1952)
and Presidential Standard — A30

1952, Dec. 9
70   A30   30p slate   .20   .20
71   A30   110p black   .25   .20
    With tabs   9.00

Weizmann, president of Israel 1948-52.

Numeral Incorporating Agricultural
Scenes — A31

1952, Dec. 31
72   A31   110p brown, buff &
         emer   .40   .20
    With tab   8.50

70th anniversary of B.I.L.U. (Bet Yaakov
Lechu Venelcha) immigration.

Five Anemones and
State
Emblem — A32

1953, Apr. 19
73   A32   110p grnsh bl, bl blk &
         red   .20   .20
    With tab   4.25

5th anniversary of State of Israel.

Rabbi Moshe   Holy Ark,
ben Maimon   Jerusalem
(Maimonides)   A34
A33

1953, Aug. 3   **Wmk. 301**   **Perf. 14x13**
74   A33   110p brown   .35   .35
    With tab   8.25

7th International Congress of History of Science, Jerusalem, Aug. 4-11.

1953, Aug. 11
Holy Arks: 45p, Petah Tikva. 200p, Safed.
75   A34   20p sapphire   .20   .20
76   A34   45p brown red   .20   .20
77   A34   200p purple   .20   .20
    Nos. 75-77 (3)   .60   .60
    With tabs   9.75

Jewish New Year, 5714.

Combined Ball-   Desert Rose
Globe   A36
A35

    Unwmk.
1953, Sept. 20   **Litho.**   **Perf. 14**
78   A35   110p blue & dark brn   .20   .20
    With tab   4.25

4th Maccabiah, Sept. 20-29, 1953.

1953, Sept. 22
79   A36   200p multicolored   .20   .20
    With tab   4.50

Conquest of the Desert Exhib., 9/22-10/14.

Redrawn Type of 1950
Designs: Various coins.

1954, Jan. 5
80   A6   80p olive bister   .20   .20
81   A6   95p blue green   .20   .20
82   A6   100p fawn   .20   .20
83   A6   125p violet blue   .20   .20
    Nos. 80-83 (4)   .80   .80
    With tabs   3.00

Marigold and Ruins
at Yehiam — A37

350p, Narcissus and bridge at Gesher.

1954, May 5   **Litho.**
84   A37   60p dk bl, mag & ol
         gray   .20   .20
85   A37   350p dk brn, grn & yel   .20   .20
    With tabs   2.25

Memorial Day and 6th anniversary of proclamation of State of Israel.

Theodor Zeev Herzl (1860-1904),
Founder of Zionist Movement — A38

1954, July 21   **Wmk. 302**
86   A38   160p dk bl, dk brn & cr   .20   .20
    With tab   .85

Bearers
with Grape
Cluster
A39

1954, Sept. 8   **Perf. 13x14**
87   A39   25p dark brown   .20   .20
    With tab   .20

Jewish New Year, 5715.

19th
Century
Mail Coach
and
Jerusalem
Post Office
A40

200p, Mail truck & present G.P.O.,
Jerusalem.

1954, Oct. 13   **Perf. 14**
88   A40   60p blue, blk & yel   .20   .20
89   A40   200p dk grn, blk & red   .20   .20
    With tabs   3.00

TABIM, National Stamp Exhibition, Jerusalem, Oct. 13-18.

Baron Edmond de Rothschild (1845-
1934) and Grape Cluster — A41

1954, Nov. 23   **Perf. 13x14**
90   A41   300p dark blue green   .20   .20
    With tab   .85

Lighted Oil
Lamp
A42

1955, Jan. 13   **Perf. 13x14**
91   A42   250p dark blue   .20   .20
    With tab   .75

Teachers' Association, 50th anniversary.

Parachutist and Barbed Wire — A43

1955, Mar. 31　Litho.　Perf. 14
92　A43　120p dk Prus green　.20　.20
　　With tab　　　　　　　.45

Jewish volunteers from Palestine who served in British army in World War II.

Lighted Menorah A44

1955, Apr. 26
93　A44　150p dk grn, blk & org　.20　.20
　　With tab　　　　　　　.35

Proclamation of State of Israel, 7th anniv.

Immigration by Ship — A45

Designs: 10p, Immigration by plane. 25p, Agricultural training. 30p, Gardening. 60p, Vocational training. 750p, Scientific education.

1955, May 10　Unwmk.　Perf. 14
94　A45　5p brt blue & black　.20　.20
95　A45　10p red & black　　　.20　.20
96　A45　25p deep grn & black　.20　.20
97　A45　30p orange & black　.20　.20
98　A45　60p lilac rose & blk　.20　.20
99　A45　750p olive bis & blk　.25　.20
　　Nos. 94-99 (6)　　　　1.25　1.20
　　With tabs　　　　　　1.75

Israel's Youth Immigration Institution, 20th anniv.

Musicians with Tambourine and Cymbals — A46

Musician with: 60p, Ram's Horn. 120p, Loud Trumpet. 250p, Harp.

1955, Aug. 25　Photo.　Wmk. 302
100　A46　25p dark green & org　.20　.20
Unwmk.
101　A46　60p dk gray & orange　.20　.20
102　A46　120p dark blue & yel　.20　.20
103　A46　250p red brn & org　.20　.20
　　#100-103, with tabs　　　.50

Jewish New Year, 5716.
See Nos. 121-123.

Ambulance A47

1955, Nov. 1　Wmk. 301　Perf. 14
104　A47　160p grn, red & blk　.20　.20
　　With tab　　　　　　　.30

Magen David Adom (Israeli Red Cross), 25th anniv.

Mandrake, Reuben — A48

1955-57　Wmk. 302　Perf. 13x14
　　Twelve Tribes: 20p, Gates of Sechem, Simeon. 30p, Ephod, Levi. 40p, Lion, Judah. 50p, Scales, Dan. 60p, Stag, Naphtali. 80p, Tents, Gad. 100p, Tree, Asher. 120p, Sun and stars, Issachar. 180p, Ship, Zebulon. 200p, Sheaf of wheat, Joseph. 250p, Wolf, Benjamin.

105　A48　10p bright green　　　.20　.20
106　A48　20p red lilac ('56)　　.20　.20
107　A48　30p bright ultra　　　.20　.20
108　A48　40p brown ('56)　　　.20　.20
109　A48　50p grnsh bl ('56)　　.20　.20
110　A48　60p lemon　　　　　　.20　.20
111　A48　80p deep vio ('56)　　.20　.20
112　A48　100p vermilion　　　　.20　.20
113　A48　120p olive ('56)　　　.20　.20
114　A48　180p lil rose ('56)　　.20　.20
115　A48　200p green ('56)　　　.20　.20
116　A48　250p gray ('56)　　　.20　.20
　　#105-116, with tabs　　　2.00

See Nos. 133-136B.

Albert Einstein (1879-1955) and Equation of his Relativity Theory — A49

1956, Jan. 3　Perf. 13x14
117　A49　350p brown　　　　　.20　.20
　　With tab　　　　　　　.60

Technion, Haifa A50

1956, Jan. 3　Wmk. 302
118　A50　350p lt ol grn & blk　.20　.20
　　With tab　　　　　　　.20

Israel Institute of Technology, 30th anniv.

"Eight Years of Israel" — A51　　Jaffa Oranges — A52

1956, Apr. 12　Litho.　Perf. 14
119　A51　150p multicolored　　.20　.20
　　With tab　　　　　　　.20

Proclamation of State of Israel, 8th anniv.

1956, May 20　Wmk. 302　Perf. 14
120　A52　300p bl grn & orange　.20　.20

4th Intl. Congress of Mediterranean Citrus Growers.

New Year Type of 1955

Musician with: 30p, Lyre. 50p, Cymbals. 150p, Double oboe, horiz.

1956, Aug. 14　Photo.　Perf. 14x13
121　A46　30p brown & brt blue　.20　.20

Perf. 14
122　A46　50p purple & orange　.20　.20
123　A46　150p dk bl grn & org　.20　.20
　　#121-123, with tabs　　　.25

Jewish New Year, 5717.

Haganah Insignia A54

1957, Jan. 1　Perf. 13x14
124　A54　20p + 80p brt grn　　.20　.20
125　A54　50p + 150p car rose　.20　.20
126　A54　50p + 350p ultra　　.20　.20
　　#124-126, with tabs　　　.25

Defense issue. Divided denomination used to show increased postal rate.

Bezalel Museum and Antique Lamp A55

1957, Apr. 29　Litho.　Perf. 14
127　A55　400p multicolored　　.20　.20
　　With tab　　　　　　　.20

Bezalel Natl. Museum, Jerusalem, 50th anniv.

Jet Plane and "9" — A56　　Horse and Seal — A57

1957, Apr. 29
128　A56　250p deep bl & blk　.20　.20
　　With tab　　　　　　　.20

Proclamation of State of Israel, 9th anniv.

1957, Sept. 4　Wmk. 302　Perf. 14
　Ancient Seals: 160p, Lion. 300p, Gazelle.
129　A57　50p ocher & blk, lt bl　.20　.20

Perf. 14x13
Photo.　　　　　　Unwmk.
130　A57　160p grn & blk, bis brn　.20　.20
131　A57　300p dp car & blk, pink　.20　.20
　　#130-131, with tabs　　　.25

Jewish New Year, 5718.

**TABIL
Souvenir Sheet**

Bet Alpha Synagogue Mosaic — A58

1957, Sept. 17　Litho.　Roulette 13
132　A58　Sheet of 4　　　　.30　.30
　a.　　100p multicolored　　.20　.20
　b.　　200p multicolored　　.20　.20
　c.　　300p multicolored　　.20　.20
　d.　　400p multicolored　　.20　.20

1st Intl. stamp exhib. in Israel, Tel Aviv, 9/17-23.

Tribes Type of 1955-57
Perf. 13x14
1957-59　Unwmk.　Photo.
133　A48　10p brt grn ('58)　　.20　.20
133A　A48　20p red lilac　　　　.20　.20
133C　A48　40p brown ('59)　　.55　.45
134　A48　50p greenish blue　　.20　.20
135　A48　60p lemon　　　　　　.20　.20
136　A48　100p vermilion　　　　.20　.20
136B　A48　120p olive ('58)　　.20　.20
　　Nos. 133-136B (7)　　　1.75　1.65
　　With tabs　　　　　　42.50

Hammer Thrower — A59

1958, Jan. 20　Perf. 14x13
137　A59　500p bister & car　　.20　.20
　　With tab　　　　　　　.25

Maccabiah Games, 25th anniversary.

Ancient Ship — A60

Ships: 20p, Three-master used for "illegal immigration." 30p, Cargo ship "Shomron." 1000p, Passenger ship "Zion."

Wmk. 302
1958, Jan. 27　Litho.　Perf. 14
Size: 36½x22½mm
138　A60　10p ocher, red & blk　.20　.20
Perf. 13x14
Photo.
139　A60　20p brt grn, blk & brn　.20　.20
140　A60　30p red, blk & grnsh
　　　　　　bl　　　　　　　.20　.20
Size: 56½x22½mm
141　A60　1000p brt bl, blk & grn　.20　.20
　　#138-141, with tabs　　　.35

Issued to honor Israel's merchant fleet.

Menorah and Olive Branch — A61

1958, Apr. 21　Litho.　Perf. 14
142　A61　400p gold, blk & grn　.20　.20
　　With tab　　　　　　　.20

Memorial Day and 10th anniversary of proclamation of State of Israel.

Dancing Youths Forming "10" — A62

1958, July 2
143　A62　200p dk org & dk grn　.20　.20
　　With tab　　　　　　　.20

First World Conference of Jewish Youth, Jerusalem, July 28-Aug. 1.

Convention Center, Jerusalem A63

1958, July 2
144 A63 400p vio & org, *yellow* .20 .20
With tab .20

10th Anniversary of Independence Exhibition, Jerusalem, June 5-Aug. 21.

Wheat — A64

1958, Aug. 27   Photo.   Perf. 14x13
145 A64 50p shown .20 .20
146 A64 60p Barley .20 .20
147 A64 160p Grapes .20 .20
148 A64 300p Figs .20 .20
#145-148, with tabs .30

Jewish New Year, 5719.

"Love Thy Neighbor . . ." — A65

1958, Dec. 10   Litho.   Perf. 14
149 A65 750p yel, gray & grn .20 .20
With tab .90

Universal Declaration of Human Rights, 10th anniversary.

Designing and Printing Stamps A66

Radio and Telephone — A67

120p, Mobile post office. 500p, Teletype.

1959, Feb. 25   Wmk. 302   Perf. 14
150 A66 60p olive, blk & red .20 .20
151 A66 120p olive, blk & red .20 .20
152 A67 120p olive, blk & red .20 .20
153 A67 500p olive, blk & red .20 .20
#150-153, with tabs .45

Decade of postal activities in Israel.

Shalom Aleichem A68

Cyclamen A69

Portraits: No. 155, Chaim Nachman Bialik. No. 156, Eliezer Ben-Yehuda.

1959   Unwmk.   Photo.   Perf. 14x13
154 A68 250p yel grn & red brn .20 .20
155 A68 250p ocher & ol gray .20 .20
#154-155, with tabs .35

Perf. 14
156 A68 250p bl & vio bl .20 .20
With tab .40

Birth cent. of Aleichem (Solomon Rabinowitz), Yiddish writer (No. 154); 25th death anniv. of Bialik, Hebrew poet (No. 155); birth cent. of Ben-Yehuda, father of modern Hebrew (No. 156).
Issued: #154, 3/30; #155, 7/22; #156, 11/25.

1959, May 11   Wmk. 302   Perf. 14
Flowers: 60p, Anemone. 300p, Narcissus.

Flowers in Natural Colors
157 A69 60p deep green .20 .20
158 A69 120p deep plum .20 .20
159 A69 300p blue .20 .20
#157-159, with tabs .35

Memorial Day and 11th anniversary of proclamation of State of Israel.

Buildings, Tel Aviv — A70

1959, May 4
160 A70 120p multicolored .20 .20
With tab .20

50th anniversary of Tel Aviv.

Bristol Britannia and Windsock A71

1959, July 22
161 A71 500p multicolored .20 .20
With tab .30

Civil Aviation in Israel, 10th anniversary.

Pomegranates A72

Perf. 14x13
1959, Sept. 9   Photo.   Unwmk.
162 A72 60p shown .20 .20
163 A72 200p Olives .20 .20
164 A72 350p Dates .20 .20
Nos. 162-164 (3) .60 .60
With tabs 1.50

Jewish New Year, 5720.

Merhavya A73

Settlements: 120p, Yesud Ha-Maala. 180p, Deganya.

1959, Nov. 25   Photo.   Perf. 13x14
165 A73 60p citron & dk grn .20 .20
166 A73 120p red brn & ocher .20 .20
167 A73 180p blue & dk grn .20 .20
Nos. 165-167 (3) .60 .60
With tabs 1.90

Settlements of Merhavya and Deganya, 50th anniv.; Yesud Ha-Maala, 75th anniv.

Judean Coin (66-70 A.D.) — A74

1960   Unwmk.   Perf. 13x14
Denominations in Black
168 A74 1a brn, *pinkish* .20 .20
 a. On surface colored paper .20 .20
    As "a," with tab .75
 b. Black overprint omitted
169 A74 3a brt red, *pinkish* .20 .20
170 A74 5a gray, *pinkish* .20 .20
171 A74 6a brt grn, *lt bl* .20 .20
171A A74 7a gray, *bluish* .20 .20
172 A74 8a mag, *lt blue* .20 .20
173 A74 12a grnsh bl, *lt bl* .20 .20
 b. Black overprint omitted
174 A74 18a orange .20 .20
175 A74 25a blue .20 .20
176 A74 30a carmine .20 .20
177 A74 50a bright lilac .20 .20
#168-177, with tabs 2.00

Issue dates: 7a, July 6; others, Jan. 6.

Operation "Magic Carpet" A75

Design: 50a, Resettled family in front of house, grapes and figs.

1960, Apr. 7   Unwmk.   Perf. 13x14
178 A75 25a red brown .20 .20
179 A75 50a green .20 .20
#178-179, with tabs .35

World Refugee Year, July 1, 1959-June 30, 1960.

Sand Lily — A76

Design: 32a, Evening primrose.

1960, Apr. 27   Litho.   Perf. 14
180 A76 12a multicolored .20 .20
181 A76 32a brn, yel & grn .20 .20
#180-181, with tabs .55

Memorial Day; proclamation of State of Israel, 12th anniv. See #204-206, 238-240.

Atom Diagram and Atomic Reactor A77

1960, July 6   Wmk. 302   Perf. 14
182 A77 50a blue, red & blk .20 .20
With tab .60

Installation of Israel's first atomic reactor.

Theodor Herzl and Rhine at Basel — A78

King Saul — A79

1960, Aug. 31   Litho.   Perf. 14
183 A78 25a gray brown .20 .20
With tab .40

1960, Aug. 31   Wmk. 302
Designs: 25a, King David. 40a, King Solomon.

Kings in Multicolor
184 A79 7a emerald .20 .20

Unwmk.
185 A79 25a brown .20 .20
186 A79 40a blue .25 .20
Nos. 185-186 (2) .45 .40
With tabs 1.25

Jewish New Year, 5721. See Nos. 208-210.

Jewish Postal Courier, Prague, 18th Century A80

Perf. 13x14
1960, Oct. 9   Photo.   Unwmk.
187 A80 25a olive blk, *gray* .25 .20
With tab 2.50
 a. Souvenir sheet 13.00 8.00

TAVIV Natl. Stamp Exhib., Tel Aviv, Oct. 9-19.
No. 187a sold only at Exhibition for 50a.

Henrietta Szold and Hadassah Medical Center A81

1960, Dec. 14   Perf. 13x14
188 A81 25a turq bl & vio gray .20 .20
With tab .30

Birth cent. of Henrietta Szold, founder of Hadassah, American Jewish women's organization.

Shields of Jerusalem and First Zionist Congress A82

1960, Dec. 14   Unwmk.   Perf. 14
189 A82 50a vio bl & turq blue .20 .20
With tab 1.10

25th Zionist Congress, Jerusalem, 1960.

Ram — A83

Signs of Zodiac — A84

1961, Feb. 27   Photo.   Perf. 13x14
190 A83 1a Ram .20 .20
191 A83 2a Bull .20 .20
192 A83 6a Twins .20 .20
193 A83 7a Crab .20 .20
194 A83 8a Lion .20 .20
 a. Booklet pane of 6 ('65) .45
195 A83 10a Virgin .20 .20
196 A83 12a Scales .20 .20
 a. Booklet pane of 6 ('65) .45
197 A83 18a Scorion .20 .20
198 A83 20a Archer .20 .20
199 A83 25a Goat .20 .20
200 A83 32a Water bearer .20 .20
201 A83 50a Fishes .20 .20

Perf. 14
Litho.
202 A84 £1 dk bl, gold & lt bl .25 .20
Nos. 190-202 (13) 2.65 2.60
With tabs 5.25

Booklet pane sheets (Nos. 194a, 196a) of 36 (9x4) contain 6 panes of 6, with gutters dividing the sheet in four sections. Each sheet yields 4 tete beche pairs and 4 tete beche gutter pairs, or strips. See Nos. 215-217.

Vertical strips of 6 of the 1a, 10a and No. 216 (5a) are from larger sheets from which coils were produced. Regular sheets of 50 are arranged 10x5.

Javelin Thrower and "7" — A85

1961, Apr. 18   Litho.   Perf. 14
203 A85 25a multicolored   .20   .20
     With tab   .45

7th Intl. Congress of the Hapoel Sports Org., Ramat Gan, May 1961.

Flower Type of 1960

7a, Myrtle. 12a, Sea onion. 32a, Oleander.

1961, Apr. 18   Unwmk.
Flowers in Natural Colors
204 A76 7a green   .20   .20
205 A76 12a rose carmine   .20   .20
206 A76 32a brt greenish bl   .20   .20
     Nos. 204-206 (3)   .60   .60
     With tabs   1.00

Memorial Day; proclamation of State of Israel, 13th anniv.

Scaffold Around "10" and Sapling — A86

1961, June 14   Photo.   Perf. 14
207 A86 50a Prussian blue   .20   .20
     With tab   .55

Israel bond issue 10th anniv.

Type of 1960

Designs: 7a, Samson. 25a, Judas Maccabaeus. 40a, Bar Cocheba.

1961, Aug. 21   Litho.   Perf. 14
Multicolored Designs
208 A79 7a red orange   .20   .20
209 A79 25a gray   .20   .20
210 A79 40a lilac   .20   .20
     Nos. 208-210 (3)   .60   .60
     With tabs   1.25

Jewish New Year, 5722.

Bet Hamidrash Synagogue, Medzibozh A87

1961, Aug. 21   Photo.   Perf. 13x14
211 A87 25a dk brn & yel   .20   .20
     With tab   .40

Bicentenary of death of Rabbi Israel Baal-Shem-Tov, founder of Hasidism.

Pine Cone A88

Design: 30a, Symbolic trees.

1961, Dec. 26   Unwmk.   Perf. 13x14
212 A88 25a green, yel & blk   .20   .20
213 A88 30a org, green & ind   .20   .20
     #212-213, with tabs   2.00

Achievements of afforestation program.

Cello, Harp, French Horn and Kettle Drum — A89

1961, Dec. 26   Litho.   Perf. 14
214 A89 50a multicolored   .25   .25
     With tab   2.00

Israel Philharmonic Orchestra, 25th anniv.

Zodiac Type of 1961 Surcharged with New Value

1962, Mar. 18   Photo.   Perf. 13x14
215 A83 3a on 1a lt lilac   .20   .20
 a. Without overprint   80.00
216 A83 5a on 7a gray   .20   .20
217 A83 30a on 32a emerald   .20   .20
 a. Without overprint   32.50
     #215-217, with tabs   .25

See note after No. 202.

Anopheles Maculipennis and Chart Showing Decline of Malaria in Israel — A90

View of Rosh Pinna — A91

1962, Apr. 30   Perf. 14x13
218 A90 25a ocher, red & blk   .20   .20
     With tab   .50

WHO drive to eradicate malaria.

1962, Apr. 30   Unwmk.
219 A91 20a yel, green & brn   .20   .20
     With tab   .50

Rosh Pinna agricultural settlement, 80th anniv.

Flame ("Hear, O Israel . . .") A92

Yellow Star of David and Six Candles A93

1962, Apr. 30   Photo.
220 A92 12a black, org & red   .20   .20
Perf. 14
221 A93 55a multicolored   .20   .20
     #220-221, with tabs   1.40

Heroes and Martyrs Day, in memory of the 6,000,000 Jewish victims of Nazi persecution.

Vautour Fighter-Bomber — A94

Design: 30a, Fighter-Bombers in formation.

1962, Apr. 30   Perf. 13x14
222 A94 12a blue   .20   .20
223 A94 30a olive green   .20   .20
     #222-223, with tabs   1.75

Memorial Day; proclamation of the state of Israel, 14th anniv.

Symbolic Flags — A95

Wolf and Lamb, Isaiah 11:6 — A96

1962, June 5   Perf. 14
224 A95 55a multicolored   .20   .20
     With tab   1.00

Near East Intl. Fair, Tel Aviv, June 5-July 5.

1962, Sept. 5

Designs: 28a, Leopard and kid, Isaiah 11:6. 43a, Child and asp, Isaiah 11:8.

225 A96 8a buff, red & black   .20   .20
226 A96 28a buff, lilac & black   .20   .20
227 A96 43a buff, org & black   .20   .20
     Nos. 225-227 (3)   .60   .60
     With tabs   3.00

Jewish New Year, 5723.

Boeing 707 — A97

1962, Nov. 7   Perf. 13x14
228 A97 55a bl, dk bl & rose lil   .30   .20
     With tab   1.25
 a. Souvenir sheet   2.25   1.75

El Al Airlines; El Al Philatelic Exhibition, Tel Aviv, Nov. 7-14. Issued in sheets of 15.

No. 228a contains one stamp in greenish blue, dark blue & rose lilac with greenish blue color continuing into margin design (No. 228 has white perforations). Sold for £1 for one day at philatelic counters in Jerusalem, Haifa and Tel Aviv and for one week at the El Al Exhibition.

Cogwheel Symbols of UJA Activities A98

1962, Dec. 26   Unwmk.   Perf. 13x14
229 A98 20a org red, sil & bl   .20   .20
     With tab   .50

25th anniv. of the United Jewish Appeal (United States) and its support of immigration, settlement, agriculture and care of the aged and sick.

Janusz Korczak A99

1962, Dec. 26   Photo.
230 A99 30a olive grn & blk   .20   .20
     With tab   .45

Dr. Janusz Korczak (Henryk Goldszmit, 1879-1942), physician, teacher and writer, killed in Treblinka concentration camp.

Orange butterflyfish A100

Red Sea fish: 3a, Pennant Coral Fish. 8a, Lionfish. 12a, Zebra-striped angelfish.

1962, Dec. 26   Litho.   Perf. 14
Fish in Natural Colors
231 A100 3a green   .20   .20
232 A100 6a purple   .20   .20
233 A100 8a brown   .20   .20
234 A100 12a dark blue   .20   .20
     #231-234, with tabs   .60

See Nos. 246-249.

Stockade at Dawn A101

Design: 30a, Completed stockade at night.

1963, Mar. 21   Unwmk.   Perf. 14
235 A101 12a yel brn, blk & yel   .20   .20
236 A101 30a dp plum, blk & lt bl   .20   .20
     #235-236, with tabs   .85

25th anniv. of the "Stockade and Tower" villages.

Hand Offering Food to Bird A102

1963, Mar. 21   Photo.   Perf. 13x14
237 A102 55a gray & black   .25   .25
     With tab   .80
 a. Booklet pane of 4   32.50

FAO "Freedom from Hunger" campaign.

Issued in sheets of 15 (5x3) with 5 tabs. The booklet pane sheet of 16 (4x4) is divided into 2 panes of 8 (4x2) by horizontal gutter. The 4 stamps at left in each pane are inverted in relation to the 4 at right, making 4 horizontal tete beche pairs down the center of the sheet.

Flower Type of 1960

8a, White lily. 30a, Hollyhock. 37a, Tulips.

1963, Apr. 25   Litho.   Perf. 14
Flowers in Natural Colors
238 A76 8a slate   .20   .20
239 A76 30a yellow green   .20   .20
240 A76 37a sepia   .20   .20
     Nos. 238-240 (3)   .60   .60
     With tabs   3.00

Memorial Day; proclamation of the State of Israel, 15th anniv.

Typesetter, 19th Century — A103

1963, June 19   Photo.   Perf. 14x13
241 A103 12a tan & vio brn   .50   .40
     With tab   1.60
 a. Sheet of 16   45.00 65.00

Hebrew press in Palestine, cent. The background of the sheet shows page of 1st issue of "Halbanon" newspaper, giving each stamp a different background.

"The Sun Beat upon the Head of Jonah" — A104

Hoe Clearing Thistles — A105

Designs: 30a, "There was a mighty tempest in the sea." 55a, "Jonah was in the belly of the fish." 30a, 55a horiz.

1963, Aug. 21   Perf. 14x13, 13x14
242 A104 8a org, lil & blk   .20 .20
243 A104 30a multicolored   .20 .20
244 A104 55a multicolored   .20 .20
  Nos. 242-244 (3)   .60 .60
  With tabs   2.75

Jewish New Year, 5724.

1963, Aug. 21   Perf. 14
245 A105 37a multicolored   .20 .20
  With tab   .90

80 years of agricultural settlements in Israel; "Year of the Pioneers."

Fish Type of 1962

Red Sea Fish: 2a, Undulate triggerfish. 6a, Radiate turkeyfish. 8a, Bigeye. 12a, Imperial angelfish.

1963, Dec. 16   Litho.   Perf. 14
Fish in Natural Colors
246 A100 2a violet blue   .20 .20
247 A100 6a green   .20 .20
248 A100 8a orange   .20 .20
249 A100 12a olive green   .20 .20
  Nos. 246-249 (4)   .80 .80
  With tabs   .90

S.S. Shalom, Sailing Vessel and Ancient Map of Coast Line — A106

1963, Dec. 16   Photo.   Perf. 13x14
250 A106 £1 ultra, brt grn & lil .85 .45
  With tab   8.00

Maiden voyage of S.S. Shalom.

"Old Age and Survivors Insurance" A107

Pres. Izhak Ben-Zvi (1884-1963) A108

Designs (Insurance): 25a, Maternity. 37a, Large family. 50a, Workers' compensation.

1964, Feb. 24   Litho.   Perf. 14
251 A107 12a multicolored   .20 .20
252 A107 25a multicolored   .20 .20
253 A107 37a multicolored   .20 .20
254 A107 50a multicolored   .30 .30
  Nos. 251-254 (4)   .90 .90
  With tabs   7.75

Natl. Insurance Institute 10th anniv.

1964, Apr. 13   Photo.   Perf. 14x13
255 A108 12a dark brown   .20 .20
  With tab   .20

Terrestrial Spectroscopy — A109

Designs: 35a, Macromolecules of the living cell. 70a, Electronic computer.

1964, Apr. 13   Perf. 14
256 A109 8a multicolored   .20 .20
257 A109 35a multicolored   .20 .20
258 A109 70a multicolored   .20 .20
  Nos. 256-258 (3)   .60 .60
  With tabs   3.50

Proclamation of the State of Israel, 16th anniv.; Israel's contribution to science.

Basketball Players A110

Serpent of Aesculapius and Menorah A111

8a, Runner. 12a, Discus thrower. 50a, Soccer.

1964, June 24   Perf. 14x13
259 A110 8a brt brick red & dk brown   .20 .20
260 A110 12a rose lil & dk brn   .20 .20
261 A110 30a bl, car & dk brn   .20 .20
262 A110 50a yel grn, org red & dk brown   .20 .20
  Nos. 259-262 (4)   .80 .80
  With tabs   .90

Israel's participation in the 18th Olympic Games, Tokyo, Oct. 10-25.

1964, Aug. 5   Unwmk.
263 A111 £1 ol bis & slate grn .40 .30
  With tab   .75

6th World Congress of the Israel Medical Association, Haifa, Aug. 3-13.

Ancient Glass Vase — A112

Different glass vessels, 1st-3rd centuries.

1964, Aug. 5   Litho.
264 A112 8a vio, brn & org   .20 .20
265 A112 35a ol, grn & bl grn   .20 .20
266 A112 70a brt car rose, blue & violet blue .20 .20
  Nos. 264-266 (3)   .60 .60
  With tabs   .85

Jewish New Year, 5725.

Steamer Bringing Immigrants A113

Eleanor Roosevelt (1884-1962) A114

1964, Nov. 2   Litho.   Perf. 14
267 A113 25a slate bl, bl grn & blk   .20 .20
  With tab   .35

30th anniv. of the blockade runners bringing immigrants to Israel.

1964, Nov. 2   Photo.   Perf. 14x13
268 A114 70a dull purple   .20 .20
  With tab   .45

Chess Board, Knight and Emblem of Chess Olympics — A115

1964, Nov. 2   Perf. 13x14
269 A115 12a shown   .20 .20
270 A115 70a Rook   .35 .30
  With tabs   1.90

16th Chess Olympics, Tel Aviv, Nov. 1964.

"Africa-Israel Friendship" — A116

1964, Nov. 30   Photo.   Perf. 14x13
271 A116 57a ol, blk, gold & red brown   .35 .20
  With tab   2.00
  a. Souvenir sheet   1.40 1.40

TABAI, Natl. Stamp Exhibition, dedicated to African-Israel friendship, Haifa, Nov. 30-Dec. 6. No. 271a contains one imperf. stamp. Sold for £1.

View of Masada from West A117

Designs: 36a, Northern Palace, lower terrace. £1, View of Northern Palace, vert.

1965, Feb. 3   Photo.   Perf. 13x14
272 A117 25a dull green   .20 .20
273 A117 36a bright blue   .20 .20
274 A117 £1 dark red brn   .20 .20
  Nos. 272-274 (3)   .60 .60
  With tabs   1.75

Ruins of Masada, the last stronghold in the war against the Romans, 66-73 A.D.

Book Fair Emblem A118

1965, Mar. 24   Photo.   Perf. 13x14
275 A118 70a gray ol, brt bl & blk   .20 .20
  With tab   .30

2nd Intl. Book Fair, Jerusalem, April.

Arms of Ashdod — A119

1965-66   Perf. 13x14
Town Emblems: 1a, Lydda (Lod). 2a, Qiryat Shemona. 5a, Petah Tikva. 6a, Nazareth. 8a, Beersheba. 10a Bet Shean. 12a, Tiberias. 20a, Elat. 25a, Acre (Akko). 35a, Dimona. 37a,

Zefat. 50a, Rishon Leziyyon. 70a, Jerusalem. £1, Tel Aviv-Jaffa. £3, Haifa.

Size: 17x22½mm
276 A119 1a brown   .20 .20
277 A119 2a lilac rose   .20 .20
278 A119 5a gray   .20 .20
279 A119 6a violet   .20 .20
280 A119 8a orange   .20 .20
  a. Booklet pane of 6   .45
281 A119 10a emerald   .20 .20
282 A119 12a dark purple   .20 .20
  a. Booklet pane of 6   .50
283 A119 15a green   .20 .20
284 A119 20a rose red   .20 .20
285 A119 25a ultramarine   .20 .20
286 A119 35a magenta   .20 .20
287 A119 37a olive   .20 .20
288 A119 50a greenish bl   .20 .20

Perf. 14x13
Size: 22x27mm
289 A119 70a dark brown   .20 .20
290 A119 £1 dark green   .25 .20
291 A119 £3 dk carmine rose   .55 .20
  Nos. 276-291 (16)   3.60 3.20
  With tabs   10.00

Issued: #283-286, 3/24/65; #290, 11/24/65; #291, 3/14/66; others, 2/2/66.
The uncut booklet pane sheets of 36 are divided into 4 panes (2 of 6 stamps, 2 of 12) by horizontal and vertical gutters. alf of the stamps in the 2 panes of 12 are inverted, causing 4 horizontal tête bêche pairs and 4 horizontal tête bêche gutter pairs.
Vertical strips of 6 of the 1a, 5a and 10a are from larger sheets, released Jan. 10, 1967, from which coils were produced. Regular sheets of 50 are arranged 10x5.
No. 290 also comes tagged (1975).
See Nos. 334-336, 386-393.

Hands Reaching for Hope, and Star of David — A120

"Irrigation of the Desert" — A121

1965, Apr. 27   Unwmk.   Perf. 14x13
292 A120 25a gray, black & yel .20 .20
  With tab   .40

Liberation of Nazi concentration camps, 20th anniv.

1965, Apr. 27   Photo.
293 A121 37a olive bister & blue .20 .20
  With tab   .20

Memorial Day; proclamation of the state of Israel, 17th anniv.

Telegraph Pole and Syncom Satellite A122

1965, July 21   Unwmk.   Perf. 13x14
294 A122 70a vio, blk & grnsh bl .20 .20
  With tab   .45

ITU, centenary.

Symbol of Cooperation and UN Emblem A123

1965, July 21   Litho.   Perf. 14
295 A123 36a gray, dp claret, bl, red & bis   .20 .20
  With tab   .30

International Cooperation Year.

Dead Sea
Extraction Plant
A124

"Let There
be Light . . ."
A125

1965, July 21
296 A124 12a Crane .20 .20
297 A124 50a shown .20 .20
#296-297, with tabs .70

Dead Sea chemical industry.

1965, Sept. 7 Photo. Perf. 13x14
Genesis 1, The Creation: 8a, Firmament
and Waters. 12a, Dry land and vegetation.
25a, Heavenly lights. 35a, Fish and fowl. 70a,
Man.
298 A125 6a dk pur, lil & gold .20 .20
299 A125 8a brt grn, dk bl & gold .20 .20
300 A125 12a red brn, blk & gold .20 .20
301 A125 25a dk pur, pink & gold .20 .20
302 A125 35a lt & dk bl & gold .20 .20
303 A125 70a dp cl, car & gold .35 .25
Nos. 298-303 (6) 1.35 1.25
With tabs 1.50

Jewish New Year, 5726. Sheets of 20 (10x2).

Charaxes Jasius
A126

Flags over
Rooftops
A127

Butterflies & Moths: 6a, Papilio alexanor
maccabaeus. 8a, Daphnis nerii. 12a, Zegris
eupheme uarda.

1965, Dec. 15 Litho. Perf. 14
Butterflies in Natural Colors
304 A126 2a lt olive green .20 .20
305 A126 6a lilac .20 .20
306 A126 8a ocher .20 .20
307 A126 12a blue .20 .20
#304-307, with tabs .60

1966, Apr. 20 Litho. Perf. 14
Designs: 30a, Fireworks over Tel Aviv. 80a,
Warships and Super Mirage jets, Haifa.
308 A127 12a multi .20 .20
309 A127 30a multi .20 .20
310 A127 80a multi .20 .20
#308-310, with tabs .45

Proclamation of state of Israel, 18th anniv.

Memorial, Upper
Galilee — A128

1966, Apr. 20 Photo. Perf. 14x13
311 A128 40a olive gray .20 .20
With tab .20

Issued for Memorial Day.

Knesset Building, Jerusalem — A129

1966, June 22 Photo. Perf. 13x14
312 A129 £1 deep blue .25 .20
With tab .50

Inauguration of the Knesset Building (Parliament). Sheets of 12.

Road Sign and
Motorcyclist
A130

Spice Box
A131

Road Signs and: 5a, Bicyclist. 10a, Pedestrian. 12a, Child playing ball. 15a, Automobile.

1966, June 22 Perf. 14
313 A130 2a sl, red brn & lil rose .20 .20
314 A130 5a ol bis, sl & lil rose .20 .20
315 A130 10a vio, lt bl & lil rose .20 .20
316 A130 12a bl, grn & lil rose .20 .20
317 A130 15a grn, red & lil rose .20 .20
#313-317, with tabs .25

Issued to publicize traffic safety.

1966, Aug. 24 Photo. Perf. 13x14
Ritual Art Objects: 15a, Candlesticks. 35a,
Kiddush cup. 40a, Torah pointer. 80a, Hanging
lamp.
318 A131 12a sil, gold, blk & bl .20 .20
319 A131 15a sil, gold, blk & lil .20 .20
320 A131 35a sil, gold, blk & em- er .20 .20
321 A131 40a sil, gold, blk & vio bl .20 .20
322 A131 80a sil, gold, blk & red .20 .20
#318-322, with tabs .75

Jewish New Year, 5727.

Bronze Panther, Avdat, 1st Century,
B.C. — A132

30a, Stone menorah, Tiberias, 2nd Cent.
40a, Phoenician ivory sphinx, 9th cent., B.C.
55a, Gold earring (calf's head), Ashdod, 6th-
4th cents. B.C. 80a, Miniature gold capital,
Persia, 5th cent., B.C. £1.15, Gold drinking
horn (ram's head), Persia, 5th cent., B.C., vert.

1966, Oct. 26 Litho. Perf. 14
323 A132 15a dp bl & yel brn .20 .20
324 A132 30a vio brn & bister .25 .20
325 A132 40a sepia & lt bis .30 .20
326 A132 55a Prus grn, dp yel & brown .35 .20
327 A132 80a lake, dp yel & brown .55 .25

Perf. 13x14
328 A132 £1.15 vio, gold & brn 1.25 .70
Nos. 323-328 (6) 2.90 1.75
With tabs 6.00

Israel Museum, Jerusalem. Sheets of 12.

Coach and
Mailman of
Austrian
Levant — A133

Microscope and
Cells — A134

Designs: 15a, Turkish mailman and caravan.
40a, Palestinian mailman and locomotive. £1,
Israeli mailman and jet liner.

1966, Dec. 14 Photo. Perf. 14
329 A133 12a ocher & green .20 .20
330 A133 15a lt grn, brn & dp car .20 .20
331 A133 40a brt rose & dk blue .20 .20
332 A133 £1 grnsh bl & brown .20 .20
Nos. 329-332 (4) .80 .80
With tabs .80

Issued for Stamp Day.

1966, Dec. 14 Perf. 14x13
333 A134 15a red & dark slate grn .20 .20
With tab .20

Campaign against cancer.

Arms Type of 1965-66

Town Emblems: 40a, Mizpe Ramon. 55a,
Ashkelon. 80a, Rosh Pinna.

1967, Feb. 8 Unwmk. Perf. 13x14
334 A119 40a dark olive .20 .20
335 A119 55a dk carmine rose .20 .20
336 A119 80a red brown .20 .20
Nos. 334-336 (3) .60 .60
With tab 1.75

Port of
Acre
A135

Ancient Ports: 40a, Caesarea. 80a, Jaffa.

1967, Mar. 22 Photo. Perf. 13x14
337 A135 15a dark brown .20 .20
338 A135 40a dark blue grn .20 .20
339 A135 80a deep blue .20 .20
Nos. 337-339 (3) .60 .60
With tabs 1.00

Page of Shulhan
Aruk and
Crowns — A136

1967, Mar. 22 Perf. 13½x13
340 A136 40a dk & lt bl, gray & gold .20 .20
With tab .25

400th anniv. of the publication (in 1565) of
the Shulhan Aruk, a compendium of Jewish
religious and civil law, by Joseph Karo (1488-
1575).

War of Independence
Memorial — A137

1967, May 10 Unwmk. Perf. 13x14
341 A137 55a lt bl, indigo & sil .20 .20
With tab .40

Issued for Memorial Day, 1967.

Auster
Plane over
Convoy on
Jerusalem
Road
A138

Military Aircraft: 30a, Mystère IV jet fighter
over Dead Sea area. 80a, Mirage jet fighters
over Masada.

1967, May 10 Photo.
342 A138 15a lt ol grn & dk bl grn .20 .20
343 A138 30a ocher & dark brn .20 .20
344 A138 80a grnsh bl & vio bl .20 .20
Nos. 342-344 (3) .60 .60
With tabs .80

Issued for Independence Day, 1967.

Israeli
Ships in
Straits of
Tiran
A139

15a, Star of David, sword & olive branch,
vert. 80a, Wailing (Western) Wall, Jerusalem.

1967, Aug. 16 Perf. 14x13, 13x14
345 A139 15a dk red, blk & yel .20 .20
346 A139 40a Prussian green .20 .20
347 A139 80a deep violet .20 .20
#345-347, with tabs .25

Victory of the Israeli forces, June, 1967.

Torah, Scroll of the
Law — A140

Various ancient, decorated Scrolls of the
Law.

1967, Sept. 13 Perf. 13x14
348 A140 12a gold & multi .20 .20
349 A140 15a silver & multi .20 .20
350 A140 35a gold & multi .20 .20
351 A140 40a silver & multi .20 .20
352 A140 80a gold & multi .20 .20
#348-352, with tabs .70

Jewish New Year, 5728. Sheets of 20 (10x2).

Chaim
Weizmann
A141

Design: 40a, Lord Balfour.

1967, Nov. 2 Photo. Perf. 13x14
353 A141 15a dark green .20 .20
354 A141 40a brown .20 .20
#353-354, with tabs .25

50th anniv. of the Balfour Declaration, which
established the right to a Jewish natl. home in
Palestine. Issued in sheets of 15.

Emblem and
Doll — A142

Nubian
Ibex — A143

Inscriptions: 30a, Hebrew. 40a, French.

1967, Nov. 2 **Litho.** *Perf. 14*
355 A142 30a yellow & multi .20 .20
356 A142 40a brt bl & multi .20 .20
357 A142 80a brt grn & multi .20 .20
  #355-357, with tabs .45

Intl. Tourist Year. Issued in sheets of 15.

1967, Dec. 27 **Litho.** *Perf. 13*
18a, Caracal lynx. 60a, Dorcas gazelles.

Animal in Ocher & Brown
358 A143 12a dull purple .20 .20
359 A143 18a bright green .20 .20
360 A143 60a bright blue .20 .20
  #358-360, with tabs .40

Flags Forming Soccer Ball — A144

1968, Mar. 11 **Photo.** *Perf. 13*
361 A144 80a ocher & multi .20 .20
  With tab .25

Pre-Olympic soccer tournament.

Welcoming Immigrants A145

Resistance Fighter A146

Design: 80a, Happy farm family.

1968, Apr. 24 **Litho.** *Perf. 14*
362 A145 15a lt green & multi .20 .20
363 A145 80a cream & multi .20 .20
  #362-363, with tabs .25

Issued for Independence Day, 1968.

1968, Apr. 24 **Photo.** *Perf. 14x13*
364 A146 60a brown olive .20 .20
  With tab .20

Warsaw Ghetto Uprising, 25th anniv. Design from Warsaw Ghetto Memorial.

Sword and Laurel A147

Rifles and Helmet A148

1968, Apr. 24 **Litho.** *Perf. 14*
365 A147 40a gold & multi .20 .20
366 A148 55a black & multi .20 .20
  #365-366, with tabs .30

Zahal defense army, Independence Day (No. 365); Memorial Day (No. 366).

Candle and Prison Window A149

Prime Minister Moshe Sharett (1894-1965) A150

1968, June 5 **Photo.** *Perf. 14x13*
367 A149 80a blk, gray & sepia .20 .20
  With tab .20

Issued to honor those who died for freedom.

1968, June 5 **Unwmk.**
368 A150 £1 deep brown .20 .20
  With tab .20

27th Zionist Congress.

Knot Forming Star of David — A151

Dome of the Rock and Absalom's Tomb — A152

1968, Aug. 21 **Litho.** *Perf. 13*
369 A151 30a multi .20 .20
  With tab .20

50 years of Jewish Scouting. Sheets of 15.

1968, Aug. 21 **Photo.** *Perf. 14x13*
Views of Jerusalem: 15a, Church of the Resurrection. 35a, Tower of David and City Wall. 40a, Yemin Moshe District and Mount of Olives. 60a, Israel Museum and "Shrine of the Book."

370 A152 12a gold & multi .20 .20
371 A152 15a gold & multi .20 .20
372 A152 35a gold & multi .20 .20
373 A152 40a gold & multi .20 .20
374 A152 60a gold & multi .20 .20
  #370-374, with tabs .50

Jewish New Year, 5729. Sheets of 15.

Detail from Lions' Gate, Jerusalem (St. Stephen's Gate) A153

1968, Oct. 8 **Unwmk.** *Perf. 13x14*
375 A153 £1 brown org .20 .20
  With tab .20
  a. Souvenir sheet .35 .30

TABIRA Natl. Philatelic Exhibition. No. 375a contains one imperf. stamp. Sold only at exhibition for £1.50. No. 375 Issued in sheets of 15.

Abraham Mapu A154

Wheelchair Basketball A155

1968, Oct. 8 **Photo.** *Perf. 14x13*
376 A154 30a dark olive grn .20 .20

Mapu (1808-1867), novelist and historian.

1968, Nov. 6 **Photo.** *Perf. 14x13*
377 A155 40a green & yel grn .20 .20
  With tab .20

17th Stoke-Mandeville Games for the Para-lyzed, Nov. 4-13. Sheets of 15.

Port of Elat — A156

Ports of Israel: 60a, Ashdod. £1, Haifa.

1969, Feb. 19 **Unwmk.** *Perf. 13x14*
378 A156 30a deep magenta .20 .20
379 A156 60a brown .20 .20
380 A156 £1 dull green .20 .20
  Nos. 378-380 (3) .60 .60
  With tabs 2.00

Tank A157

1969, Apr. 16 **Photo.** *Perf. 13x14*
381 A157 15a shown .20 .20
382 A157 80a Destroyer .20 .20
  #381-382, with tabs .40

Issued for Independence Day 1969.

Israel's Flag at Half-mast — A158

1969, Apr. 16
383 A158 55a vio, gold & bl .20 .20
  With tab .25

Issued for Memorial Day.

Worker and ILO Emblem A159

1969, Apr. 16
384 A159 80a dark blue grn .20 .20
  With tab .25

ILO, 50th anniversary.

Hand Holding Torch A160

Arms of Hadera A161

1969, July 9 **Photo.** *Perf. 14x13*
385 A160 60a gold & multi .20 .20
  With tab .60

Issued to publicize the 8th Maccabiah.

1969-73 *Perf. 13x14*
Town Emblems: 3a, Hertseliya. 5a, Holon. 15a, Bat Yam. 18a, Ramla. 20a, Kefar Sava. 25a, Giv'atayim. 30a, Rehovot. 40a, Netanya. 50a, Bene Beraq. 60a, Nahariyya. 80a, Ramat Gan.

386 A161 2a green .20 .20
387 A161 3a deep magenta .20 .20
388 A161 5a orange .20 .20
389 A161 15a bright rose .20 .20
  c. Bklt. pane of 6 (2 #389 + 4 #389A) ('71) .65
389A A161 18a ultra ('70) .20 .20
  d. Bklt. pane of 6 ('71) .70
  e. Bklt. pane of 6 (1 #281 + 5 #389A) ('73) .65
389B A161 20a brown ('70) .20 .20
  f. Bklt. pane of 5 + label ('73) .90
390 A161 25a dark blue .20 .20
390A A161 30a brt pink ('70) .20 .20
391 A161 40a purple .20 .20
392 A161 50a greenish bl .20 .20
392A A161 60a olive ('70) .20 .20
393 A161 80a dark green .20 .20
  Nos. 386-393 (12) 2.40 2.40
  With tabs 3.75

Nos. 389c and 389d were also sold in uncut sheets of 36, No. 389e in uncut sheet of 18. See note after No. 291 about similar sheets.

Noah Building the Ark — A162

The Story of the Flood: 15a, Animals board-ing the Ark. 35a, The Ark during the flood. 40a, Noah sending out the dove. 60a, Noah and the rainbow.

1969, Aug. 13 **Unwmk.** *Perf. 14*
394 A162 12a multicolored .20 .20
395 A162 15a multicolored .20 .20
396 A162 35a multicolored .20 .20
397 A162 40a multicolored .20 .20
398 A162 60a multicolored .20 .20
  #394-398, with tabs .70

Jewish New Year, 5730. Sheets of 15.

King David by Marc Chagall A163

1969, Sept. 24 **Photo.** *Perf. 14*
399 A163 £3 multicolored .65 .55
  With tab 1.25

Atom Diagram and Test Tube — A164

1969, Nov. 3 *Perf. 14x13*
400 A164 £1.15 vio bl & multi .70 .45
  With tab 2.25

Weizmann Institute of Science, 25th anniv.

Joseph Trumpeldor A165

Dum Palms, Emeq Ha-Arava A166

1970, Jan. 21   Photo.   Perf. 14x13
401 A165 £1 dark purple   .25   .20
   With tab   .60

50th anniv. of the defense of Tel Hay under the leadership of Joseph Trumpeldor.

1970, Jan. 21

Views: 3a, Tahana Waterfall. 5a, Nahal Baraq Canyon, Negev. 6a, Cedars in Judean Hills. 30a, Soreq Cave, Judean Hills.

402 A166 2a olive   .20   .20
403 A166 3a deep blue   .20   .20
404 A166 5a orange red   .20   .20
405 A166 6a slate green   .20   .20
406 A166 30a brt purple   .20   .20
   #402-406, with tabs   .35

Issued to publicize nature reserves.

Magic Carpet Shaped as Airplane A167

Prime Minister Levi Eshkol (1895-1969) A168

1970, Jan. 21   Litho.   Perf. 13
407 A167 30a multicolored   .20   .20
   With tab   .20

20th anniv. of "Operation Magic Carpet" which airlifted the Yemeni Jews to Israel.

1970, Mar. 11   Litho.   Perf. 14
408 A168 15a bl & multi   .20   .20
   With tab   .20

Mania Shochat — A169

Camel and Train — A170

Portrait: 80a, Ze'ev Jabotinsky (1880-1940), writer and Zionist leader.

1970, Mar. 11   Photo.   Perf. 14x13
409 A169 40a dp plum & buff   .20   .20
410 A169 80a green & cream   .20   .20
   #409-410, with tabs   1.10

Ha-Shomer (Watchmen defense organization), 60th anniv. (No. 409); defense of Jerusalem, 50th anniv. (No. 410)

1970, Mar. 11   Litho.   Perf. 13
411 A170 80a orange & multi   .40   .25
   With tab   .75

Opening of Dimona-Oron Railroad.

Scene from "The Dibbuk" — A171

1970, Mar. 11   Photo.   Perf. 14x13
412 A171 £1 multicolored   .20   .20
   With tab   .60

Habimah Natl. Theater, 50th anniv.

Memorial Flame A172

Orchis Laxiflorus A173

1970, May 6   Photo.   Perf. 13x14
413 A172 55a vio, pink & blk   .20   .20
   With tab   .25

Issued for Memorial Day, 1970.

1970, May 6   Litho.   Perf. 14

Flowers: 15a, Iris mariae. 80a, Lupinus pilosus.

414 A173 12a pale gray, plum &
          grn   .20   .20
415 A173 15a multicolored   .20   .20
416 A173 80a pale bl & multi   .30   .30
   Nos. 414-416 (3)   .70   .70
   With tabs   .95

Issued for Independence Day, 1970.

Charles Netter — A174

420 Class Yachts — A175

80a, Agricultural College (Mikwe Israel) & garden.

1970, May 6   Photo.   Perf. 14x13
417 A174 40a lt grn, dk brn &
          gold   .20   .20
418 A174 80a gold & multi   .20   .20
   With tabs   1.25

Centenary of first agricultural college in Israel; its founder, Charles Netter.

1970, July 8   Photo.   Perf. 14x13

Designs: Various 420 Class yachts.

419 A175 15a grnsh bl, blk & sil .20 .20
420 A175 30a ol, red, blk & sil   .20 .20
421 A175 80a ultra, blk & silver .25 .60
   Nos. 419-421 (3)   .65   .60
   With tabs   1.10

World "420" Class Sailing Championships.

Hebrew Letters Shaped Like Ship and Buildings A176

1970, July 8   Perf. 13x14
422 A176 40a gold & multi   .20   .20
   With tab

Keren Hayesod, a Zionist Fund to maintain schools and hospitals in Palestine, 50th anniv.

Arava Plane A177

1970, July 8
423 A177 £1 brt blue, blk & sil .20 .20
   With tab   .35

First Israeli designed and built aircraft.

Bird (Exiles) and Sun (Israel) A178

1970, Sept. 7   Litho.   Perf. 14
424 A178 80a yel & multi   .20   .20
   With tab   .25

"Operation Ezra and Nehemiah," the exodus of Iraqi Jews.

Old Synagogue, Cracow — A179

Historic Synagogues: 15a, Great Synagogue, Tunis. 35a, Portuguese Synagogue, Amsterdam. 40a, Great Synagogue, Moscow. 60a, Shearith Israel Synagogue, New York.

Perf. 14, 13 (15a)
1970, Sept. 7   Photo.
425 A179 12a gold & multi   .20   .20
426 A179 15a gold & multi   .20   .20
427 A179 35a gold & multi   .20   .20
428 A179 40a gold & multi   .20   .20
429 A179 60a gold & multi   .20   .20
   #425-429, with tabs   .40

Jewish New Year, 5731.

Tel Aviv Post Office, 1920 — A180

1970, Oct. 18   Photo.   Perf. 14
430 A180 £1 multicolored   .20   .20
   With tab   .25
  a. Souvenir sheet   1.50 1.50

TABIT Natl. Stamp Exhibition, Tel Aviv, Oct. 18-29. No. 430a contains an imperf. stamp similar to No. 430. Sold for £1.50.

Mother and Child A181

1970, Oct. 18   Perf. 13x14
431 A181 80a dp grn, yel & gray .20 .20
   With tab   .45

WIZO, Women's Intl. Zionist Org., 50th anniv.

Paris Quai, by Camille Pissarro — A182

Paintings from Tel Aviv Museum: 85a, The Jewish Wedding, by Josef Israels. £2, Flowers in a Vase, by Fernand Leger.

1970, Dec. 22   Litho.   Perf. 14
432 A182 85a black & multi   .20   .20
433 A182 £1 black & multi   .20   .20
434 A182 £2 black & multi   .50   .30
   Nos. 432-434 (3)   .90   .70
   With tabs   1.75

Hammer and Menorah Emblem — A183

Persian Fallow Deer — A184

1970, Dec. 22
435 A183 35a gold & multi   .20   .20
   With tab   .20

General Federation of Labor in Israel (Histadrut), 50th anniversary.

1971, Feb. 16   Litho.   Perf. 13

Animals of the Bible: 3a, Asiatic wild ass. 5a, White oryx. 78a, Cheetah.

436 A184 2a multicolored   .20   .20
437 A184 3a multicolored   .20   .20
438 A184 5a multicolored   .20   .20
439 A184 78a multicolored   .20   .20
   #436-439, with tabs   .45

"Samson and Dalila," Israel National Opera — A185

Theater Art in Israel: No. 441, Inn of the Ghosts, Cameri Theater. No. 442, A Psalm of David, Inbal Dance Theater.

1971, Feb. 16   Perf. 14x13
440 A185 50a bister & multi   .20   .20
441 A185 50a lt grn & multi   .20   .20
442 A185 50a blue & multi   .20   .20
   Nos. 440-442 (3)   .60   .60
   With tabs   .60

Basketball A186

Defense Forces Emblem A187

No. 444, Runner. No. 445, Athlete on rings.

1971, Apr. 13 — Litho. — Perf. 14

443	A186	50a green & multi	.20	.20
444	A186	50a ocher & multi	.20	.20
445	A186	50a lt vio & multi	.20	.20
		#443-445, with tabs		.50

9th Hapoel Games.

1971, Apr. 13 — Photo. — Perf. 14x13

446	A187	78a multicolored	.20	.20
		With tab		.25

Memorial Day, 1971, and the war dead.

Jaffa Gate, Jerusalem — A188

Gates of Jerusalem: 18c, New Gate. 35c, Damascus Gate. 85c, Herod's Gate.

1971, Apr. 13 — Size: 41x41mm — Perf. 14

447	A188	15a gold & multi	.20	.20
448	A188	18a gold & multi	.20	.20
449	A188	35a gold & multi	.25	.25
450	A188	85a gold & multi	.60	.40
a.		Souvenir sheet of 4	3.50	3.50
		Nos. 447-450 (4)	1.25	1.00
		With tabs		2.00

Independence Day, 1971. No. 450a contains 4 stamps similar to Nos. 447-450, but smaller (27x27mm). Sold at the Jerusalem Exhibition for £2.

See Nos. 488-491.

"He Wrote . . . Words of the Covenant" A189

"You shall rejoice in your feast" A190

85a, "First Fruits . . ." Exodus 23:19. £1.50, ". . . Feast of Weeks" Exodus 34:22. The quotation on 50a is from Exodus 34:28. The quotations are in English on the tabs.

1971, May 25 — Photo. — Perf. 14x13

451	A189	50a yellow & multi	.20	.20
452	A189	85a yellow & multi	.25	.20
453	A189	£1.50 yellow & multi	.45	.30
		Nos. 451-453 (3)	.90	.70
		With tabs		1.75

For the Feast of Weeks (Shabuoth).

1971, Aug. 24 — Photo. — Perf. 14x13

Designs: 18a, "You shall dwell in booths for seven days . . ." Leviticus 23:42. 20a, "That I made the people of Israel dwell in booths . . ." Lev. 23:43. 40a, ". . . when you have gathered in the produce of the land" Lev. 23:39. 65a, ". . . then I will give you your rains in their season" Lev. 26:4. The quotation on 15a is from Deuteronomy 16:14. The quotations are in English on tabs.

454	A190	15a yellow & multi	.20	.20
455	A190	18a yellow & multi	.20	.20
456	A190	20a yellow & multi	.20	.20
457	A190	40a yellow & multi	.20	.20
458	A190	65a yellow & multi	.20	.20
		#454-458, with tabs		.75

For the Feast of Tabernacles (Sukkoth).

Sun Shining on Fields A191

1971, Aug. 24 — Perf. 14

459	A191	40a gold & multi	.20	.20
		With tab		.20

1st cooperative settlement in Israel, at Emeq (Valley of Israel), 50th anniv.

Retort and Grain — A192

1971, Oct. 25 — Litho. — Perf. 14

460	A192	£1 green & multi	.20	.20
		With tab		.25

50th anniversary of Volcani Institute of Agricultural Research.

Tagging

Starting in 1975, vertical luminescent bands were overprinted on various regular and commemorative stamps.

In the 1971-75 regular series, values issued both untagged and tagged are: 20a, 25a, 30a, 35a, 45a, 50a, 65a, £1.10, £1.30, £2 and £3. Also No. 290 was re-issued with tagging in 1975.

Regular issues from 1975 onward, including the £1.70, are tagged unless otherwise noted.

Tagged commemoratives include Nos. 562-563 and all from Nos. 567-569 onward unless otherwise noted.

Negev — A193

1971-75 — Photo. — Perf. 13x14

Landscapes: 3a, Judean desert. 5a, Gan Ha-Shelosha. 18a, Kinneret. 20a, Tel Dan. 22a, Fishermen, Yafo. 25a, Arava. 30a, En Avedat. 35a, Brekhat Ram, Golan Heights. 45a, Grazing sheep, Mt. Hermon. 50a, Rosh Pinna. 55a, Beach and park, Netanya. 65a, Plain of Zebulun. 70a, Shore, Engedi. 80a, Beach at Elat. 88a, Boats in Akko harbor. 95a, Hamifratz Hane'elam. £1.10, Aqueduct near Akko. £1.30, Zefat. £1.70, Upper Nazareth. £2, Coral Island. £3, Haifa.

461	A193	3a deep blue	.20	.20
462	A193	5a green	.20	.20
463	A193	15a deep org	.20	.20
464	A193	18a bright mag	.65	.20
464A	A193	20a dark green	.20	.20
465	A193	22a brt blue	1.00	.25
465A	A193	25a orange red	.20	.20
466	A193	30a brt rose	.20	.20
466A	A193	35a plum	.20	.20
467	A193	45a dull vio blue	.20	.20
468	A193	50a green	.20	.20
469	A193	55a olive	.20	.20
469A	A193	65a black	.20	.20
470	A193	70a deep car	.20	.20
470A	A193	80a deep ultra	.20	.20
471	A193	88a greenish blue	1.00	.20
472	A193	95a org ver	.80	.20
472A	A193	£1.10 olive	.20	.20
472B	A193	£1.30 deep blue	.20	.20
472C	A193	£1.70 dark brown	.40	.20
473	A193	£2 brown	.40	.20
474	A193	£3 deep violet	.55	.20
		Nos. 461-474 (22)	7.80	4.45
		With tabs	12.00	

Issued: 15a, 18a, 50a, 88a, 10/25; 22a, 55a, 70a, 1/4/72; 3a, 5a, 30a, £3, 11/7/72; 45a, 95a, 2, 1/16/73; 20a, 65a, 10/23/73; 35a, £1.10, 12/20/73; 25a, 80a, £1.30, 11/5/74; £1.70, 6/17/75.
See No. 592.

The Scribe, Sculpture by Boris Schatz A195

Works by Israeli Artists: 55a, Young Girl (Sarah), by Abel Pann. 70a, Zefat (landscape), by Menahem Shemi, horiz. 85a, Old Jerusalem, by Jacob Steinhardt. £1, Resurrection (abstract), by Aharon Kahana.

Perf. 13x14 (40a, 85a), 14

1972, Mar. 7

479	A195	40a black & tan	.20	.20
480	A195	55a red brn & multi	.20	.20
481	A195	70a lt grn & multi	.20	.20
482	A195	85a blk & yellow	.25	.20
483	A195	£1 blk & multi	.30	.25
		Nos. 479-483 (5)	1.15	1.05
		With tabs	1.40	

Exodus — A196

Passover: 45a, Baking unleavened bread. 95a, Seder.

1972, Mar. 7 — Litho. — Perf. 13

484	A196	18a buff & multi	.20	.20
485	A196	45a buff & multi	.20	.20
486	A196	95a buff & multi	.30	.20
		Nos. 484-486 (3)	.70	.60
		With tabs	1.25	

"Let My People Go" — A197

1972, Mar. 7 — Perf. 14

487	A197	55a blk, bl & yel grn	.45	.30
		With tab	3.00	

No. 487 inscribed in Hebrew, Arabic, Russian and English.

Gate Type of 1971

Gates of Jerusalem: 15a, Lions' Gate. 18a, Golden Gate. 45a, Dung Gate. 55a, Zion Gate.

"Get Wisdom" Proverbs 4:7 — A194

Abstract Designs: 18a, Mathematical and scientific formula. 20a, Tools and engineering symbols. 40a, Abbreviations of various college degrees.

1972, Jan. 4 — Litho. — Perf. 14

475	A194	15a brt grn & multi	.20	.20
476	A194	18a multicolored	.20	.20
477	A194	20a multicolored	.20	.20
478	A194	40a red, blk & gold	.20	.20
		#475-478, with tabs		.30

1972, Apr. 17 — Photo. — Perf. 14 — Size: 40x40mm

488	A188	15a gold & multi	.20	.20
489	A188	18a gold & multi	.20	.20
490	A188	45a gold & multi	.25	.25
491	A188	55a gold & multi	.35	.35
a.		Souvenir sheet of 4	2.60	2.60
		Nos. 488-491 (4)	1.00	1.00
		With tabs	2.25	

Independence Day. #491a contains 4 27x27mm stamps similar to #488-491. Sold for £2.

Jethro's Tomb — A198

1972, Apr. 17 — Litho. — Perf. 13

492	A198	55a multicolored	.20	.20
		With tab		.25

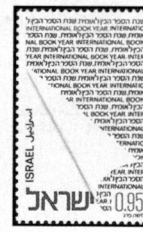

Memorial Day — A199

1972, Apr. 17 — Perf. 14

493	A199	55a Flowers	.20	.20
		With tab		.25

Hebrew Words Emerging from Opened Ghetto — A200

1972, June 6 — Perf. 13

494	A200	70a blue & multi	.45	.35
		With tab	2.00	

Rabbi Isaac ben Solomon Ashkenazi Luria ("Ari") (1534-72), Palestinian cabalist.

International Book Year — A201

1972, June 6 — Perf. 14x13

495	A201	95a Printed page	.25	.20
		With tab		.35

Satellite Earth Station, Satellite and Rainbow — A202

1972, June 6 — Perf. 13

496	A202	£1 tan & multi	.20	.20
		With tab		.30

Opening of satellite earth station in Israel.

17th Cent. Ark,
Ancona — A203

Menorah and
"25" — A204

Holy Arks from: 45a, Padua, 1729. 70a, Parma, 17th century. 95a, Reggio Emilia, 1756. Arks moved to Israel from Italian synagogues.

1972, Aug. 8   Photo.   Perf. 14x13
497 A203 15a deep brn & yel   .20   .20
498 A203 45a dp grn, yel grn &
            gold   .20   .20
499 A203 70a brn red, yel & bl   .20   .20
500 A203 95a magenta & gold   .20   .20
      Nos. 497-500 (4)   .80   .80
      With tabs   1.50

Jewish New Year, 5733.

1972, Aug. 8
501 A204 £1 silver, bl & mag   .20   .20
      With tab   .25

25th anniversary of the State of Israel.

Brass
Menorah,
Morocco,
18th-19th
Century
A205

Menorahs: 25a, Brass, Poland, 18th century. 70a, Silver, Germany, 17th century.

1972, Nov. 7   Litho.   Perf. 14x13
502 A205 12a emer, blk & bl grn   .20   .20
503 A205 25a lil rose, blk & org   .20   .20
504 A205 70a blue, blk & vio   .20   .20
      #502-504, with tabs   .55

Hanukkah (Festival of Lights), 1972.

Child's
Drawing — A206

Pendant — A207

Designs: Children's drawings.

1973, Jan. 16   Litho.   Perf. 14
      Sizes: 22½x37mm (2a, 55a);
             17x48mm (3a)
505 A206 2a blk & multi   .20   .20
506 A206 3a multicolored   .20   .20
507 A206 55a multicolored   .20   .20
      #505-507, with tabs   .30

Youth Wing of Israel Museum, Jerusalem (2a, 3a) and Youth Workshops, Tel Aviv Museum (55a).

1973, Jan. 16   Photo.   Perf. 14x13
508 A207 18a silver & multi   .20   .20
      With tab   .20

Immigration of North African Jews.

Levi, by
Marc
Chagall
A208

Tribes of Israel: #510, Simeon. #511, Reuben. #512, Issachar. #513, Zebulun. #514, Judah. #515, Dan. #516, Gad. #517, Asher. #518, Naphtali. #519, Joseph. No.520, Benjamin.

1973   Litho.   Perf. 14
509 A208 £1 multicolored   .40   .40
510 A208 £1 gray grn & multi   .40   .40
511 A208 £1 olive & multi   .40   .40
512 A208 £1 gray bl & multi   .40   .40
513 A208 £1 lemon & multi   .40   .40
514 A208 £1 gray & multi   .40   .40
515 A208 £1 bl grn & multi   .40   .40
516 A208 £1 gray & multi   .40   .40
517 A208 £1 yel grn & multi   .40   .40
518 A208 £1 sepia & multi   .40   .40
519 A208 £1 olive & multi   .40   .40
520 A208 £1 tan & multi   .40   .40
      Nos. 509-520 (12)   4.80 4.80
      With tabs   8.50

Designs from stained glass windows by Marc Chagall, Hadassah-Hebrew University Medical Center Synagogue, Jerusalem. Issued: #509-514, 3/26; #515-520, 8/21.

Israel's Declaration of
Independence — A209

1973, May 3   Photo.   Perf. 14
521 A209 £1 ocher & multi   .20   .20
      With tab   .25
a.   Souvenir sheet   .65   .75

25 years of Independence. No. 521a sold for £1.50.

Star of
David and
Runners
A210

1973, May 3   Litho.
522 A210 £1.10 multicolored   .20   .20
      With tab   .25

9th Maccabiah.

Prison-cloth
Hand — A211

1973, May 3   Photo.
523 A211 55a blue black   .20   .20
      With tab   .20

Heroes and martyrs of the Holocaust, 1933-1945.

Flame
A212

1973, May 3   Litho.
524 A212 65a multicolored   .20   .20
      With tab   .25

Memorial Day.

Prophets
A213

1973, Aug. 21   Photo.   Perf. 13x14
525 A213 18a Isaiah   .20   .20
526 A213 65a Jeremiah   .20   .20
527 A213 £1.10 Ezekiel   .20   .20
      #525-527, with tabs   .25

Jewish New Year, 5734.

Torch of Learning,
Cogwheel — A214

1973, Oct. 23   Perf. 14x13
528 A214 £1.25 slate & multi   .20   .20
      With tab   .25

50th anniversary of the Technion, Israel Institute of Technology.

Rescue Boat and
Danish
Flag — A215

1973, Oct. 23   Perf. 13x14
529 A215 £5 bister, red & blk   .40   .30
      With tab   .50

30th anniversary of the rescue by the Danes of the Jews in Denmark.

Spectators at
Stamp
Show — A216

Design: £1, Spectators, different design.

1973, Dec. 20   Litho.   Perf. 13
530 A216 20a brown & multi   .20   .20
531 A216 £1 brown & multi   .20   .20
      #530-531, with tabs   .20

JERUSALEM '73 Philatelic Exhibition, Mar. 25-Apr. 2, 1974.

Souvenir Sheets

Israel No. 7 — A217

Designs: £2, No. 8. £3, No. 9.

1974, Mar. 25   Photo.   Perf. 14x13
532 A217 £1 silver & dk slate
            grn   .20   .20
533 A217 £2 silver & red brn   .20   .20
534 A217 £3 silver & blk blue   .20   .20
      Nos. 532-534 (3)   .60   .60

Jerusalem '73 Philatelic Exhibition, Mar. 25-Apr. 2, 1974 (postponed from Dec. 1973), 25th anniv. of State of Israel. Each sheet was sold with a 50 per cent surcharge.

Soldier with
Prayer Shawl
A218

Quill and Inkwell
with Hebrew
Letters
A219

1974, Apr. 23   Perf. 13x14
535 A218 £1 blk & light bl   .20   .20
      With tab   .20

Memorial Day.

1974, Apr. 23   Perf. 14x13
536 A219 £2 gold & black   .20   .20
      With tab   .25

50th anniversary of Hebrew Writers Assn.

Lady in
Blue, by
Moshe
Kisling
A220

Designs: £2, Mother and Child, Sculpture by Chana Orloff. £3, Girl in Blue, by Chaim Soutine.

1974, June 11   Litho.   Perf. 14
537 A220 £1.25 multicolored   .20   .20
538 A220 £2 multicolored   .20   .20
539 A220 £3 multicolored   .30   .30
      #537-539, with tabs   1.00

Art works from Tel Aviv, En Harod and Jerusalem Museums.

Wrench
A221

1974, June 11
540 A221 25a multicolored   .20   .20
      With tab   .20

50th anniv. of Working Youth Movement.

Istanbuli Synagogue,
Jerusalem — A222

Designs: Interiors of restored synagogues
in Jerusalem's Old City.

1974, Aug. 6 **Photo.** *Perf. 13x14*
541 A222 25a shown .20 .20
542 A222 70a Emtzai Syna-
gogue .20 .20
543 A222 £1 Rabbi Yohanan
Synagogue .20 .20
#541-543, with tabs .25

Jewish New Year, 5735.

Lady Davis Technical Center "AMAL,"
Tel Aviv — A223

60a, Elias Sourasky Library, Tel Aviv University. £1.45, Mivtahim Rest Home, Zikhron
Yaaqov.

1974, Aug. 6 *Perf. 13½x14*
544 A223 25a violet black .20 .20
545 A223 60a dark blue .20 .20
546 A223 £1.45 maroon .20 .20
#544-546, with tabs .25

Modern Israeli architecture.

David Ben-Gurion — A224

1974, Nov. 5 *Perf. 14*
547 A224 25a brown .20 .20
548 A224 £1.30 slate green .20 .20
#547-549, with tabs .25

David Ben-Gurion (1886-1973), first Prime
Minister and Minister of Defense of Israel.

Arrows on   Dove Delivering
Globe — A225   Letter — A226

1974, Nov. 5 **Litho.** *Perf. 14*
549 A225 25a black & multi .20 .20
Photo.
550 A226 £1.30 gold & multi .20 .20
#549-550, with tabs .25

Centenary of Universal Postal Union.

Hebrew University, Mount Scopus,
Jerusalem — A227

1975, Jan. 14 **Litho.** *Perf. 13*
551 A227 £2.50 multicolored .20 .20
With tab .25

Hebrew University, 50th anniv.

Girl Carrying   Welder — A229
Plant — A228

Arbor Day: 35a, Bird singing in tree. £2,
Boy carrying potted plant.

1975, Jan. 14 *Perf. 14*
552 A228 1a multicolored .20 .20
553 A228 35a multicolored .20 .20
554 A228 £2 multicolored .20 .20
#552-554, with tabs .25

1975, Jan. 14 **Photo.** *Perf. 14x13*
80a, Tractor driver. £1.20, Electrical
lineman.
555 A229 30a multicolored .20 .20
556 A229 80a multicolored .20 .20
557 A229 £1.20 ultra & multi .20 .20
#555-557, with tabs .25

Occupational safety and publicity for the
Institute for Safety and Hygiene.

Hebrew University Synagogue,
Jerusalem — A230

Modern Israeli architecture: £1.30, Yad
Mordecai Museum. £1.70, Bat Yam City Hall.

Perf. 14, 13½x14 (#559)
1975, Mar. 4 **Photo.**
558 A230 80a brown .20 .20
559 A230 £1.30 slate green .20 .20
560 A230 £1.70 brown olive .20 .20
#558-560, with tabs .40

US President Harry
S Truman (1884-
1972) — A231

1975, Mar. 4 **Engr.** *Perf. 14*
561 A231 £5 dark brown .35 .20
With tab .40

Eternal Flame   Memorial
over Soldier's   Tablet — A233
Grave — A232

1975, Apr. 10 **Photo.** *Perf. 14x13*
562 A232 £1.45 black & multi .20 .20
With tab .25

Memorial Day.

1975, Apr. 10
563 A233 £1.45 blk, red & gray .20 .20
With tab .25

In memory of soldiers missing in action.

Hurdling
A234

1975, Apr. 10 *Perf. 13x14*
564 A234 25a shown .20 .20
565 A234 £1.70 Bicycling .20 .20
566 A234 £3 Volleyball .20 .20
#564-566, with tabs .40

10th Hapoel Games; 50th anniv. of Hapoel
Org.

Yom
Kippur, by
Maurycy
Gottlieb
A235

Paintings of religious holidays: £1.00
Hanukkah, by Mortiz D. Oppenheim. 1.40, The
Purim Players, by Jankel Adler, horiz.

1975, June 17 **Litho.** *Perf. 14*
567 A235 £1 multicolored .20 .20
568 A235 £1.40 multicolored .20 .20
569 A235 £4 multicolored .20 .20
#567-569, with tabs .50

Old Couple
A236

1975, June 17 **Photo.** *Perf. 13x14*
570 A236 £1.85 multicolored .20 .20
With tab .25

International Gerontological Association,
10th triennial conference, Jerusalem.

Pres. Zalman
Shazar (1889-
1974) — A237

1975, Aug. 5 **Photo.** *Perf. 14x13*
571 A237 35a silver & blk .20 .20
With tab .20

Pioneer Women,
50th
Anniv. — A238

1975, Aug. 5 *Perf. 14½*
572 A238 £5 Emblem .30 .20
With tab .35

Judges of Israel — A239

1975, Aug. 5 *Perf. 13x14*
573 A239 35a Gideon .20 .20
574 A239 £1 Deborah .20 .20
575 A239 £1.40 Jephthah .20 .20
#573-575, with tabs .35

Jewish New Year, 5736.

Hebrew University, Mt.
Scopus — A240

1975, Oct. 14 **Photo.** *Perf. 14x13*
576 A240 £4 multicolored .20 .20
With tab .25

Return of Hadassah to Mt. Scopus,
Jerusalem.

Collared
Pratincoles
A241

Protected Birds: £1.70, Spur-winged plover.
£2, Black-winged stilts.

1975, Oct. 14 **Litho.** *Perf. 13*
577 A241 £1.10 pink & multi .20 .20
578 A241 £1.70 lemon & multi .20 .20
579 A241 £2 multicolored .20 .20
#577-579, with tabs .40

Butterfly and
Factory (Air
Pollution) — A242

Designs: 80a, Fish and tanker (water pollution). £1.70, Ear and jet (noise pollution).

1975, Dec. 9 **Photo.** *Perf. 14*
580 A242 50a car & multi .20 .20
581 A242 80a green & multi .20 .20
582 A242 £1.70 orange & multi .20 .20
With tabs .45

Environmental protection.

Star of David — A243

1975-80   Perf. 13x14

583	A243	75a vio bl & car	.20	.20
584	A243	£1.80 violet bl & gray	.20	.20
585	A243	£1.85 vio bl & lt brn	.20	.20
586	A243	£2.45 vio bl & brt green	.20	.20
587	A243	£2.70 vio bl & purple	.20	.20
588	A243	£4.30 ultra & red	.20	.20
589	A243	£5.40 vio bl & ol	.30	.20
590	A243	£8 vio bl & bl	.40	.20
		Nos. 583-590 (8)	1.90	1.60
		With tabs		2.75

Issued: £1.85, 12/9; £2.45, 6/22/76; 75a, 12/77; £5.40, 5/23/78; £1.80, £8, 5/22/79; £2.70, 12/25/79; £4.30, 5/26/80.

Landscape Type of 1971-75

Design: £10, View of Elat and harbor.

1976, Aug. 17   Photo.   Perf. 14x14½

592	A193	£10 Prussian blue	.85	.20
		With tab		1.00

No. 592 issued both tagged and untagged.

"In the days of Ahasuerus." — A247

Designs (from Book of Esther): 80a, "He set the royal crown on her head." £1.60, "Thus shall it be done to the man whom the king delights to honor."

1976, Feb. 17   Photo.   Perf. 14

593	A247	40a multicolored	.20	.20
594	A247	80a multicolored	.20	.20
595	A247	£1.60 multicolored	.20	.20
a.		Souv. sheet of 3, #593-595, perf 13x14	.35	.35
		#593-595, with tabs		.30

Purim Festival. No. 595a sold for £4.

Border Settlement, Barbed Wire — A248

1976, Feb. 17

596	A248	£1.50 olive & multi	.20	.20
		With tab		.25

Border settlements, part of Jewish colonization of Holy Land.

Symbolic Key — A249

1976, Feb. 17

597	A249	£1.85 multicolored	.20	.20
		With tab		.25

Bezalel Academy of Arts and Design, Jerusalem, 70th anniv.

"200" US Flag A250

1976, Apr. 25   Photo.   Perf. 13x14

598	A250	£4 gold & multi	.25	.20
		With tab		.30

American Bicentennial.

Dancers of Meron, by Reuven Rubin A251

1976, Apr. 25   Litho.   Perf. 14

599	A251	£1.30 multicolored	.20	.20
		With tab		.25

Lag Ba-Omer festival.

8th Brigade Monument, Ben-Gurion Airport — A252

1976, Apr. 25   Photo.   Perf. 14x13

600	A252	£1.85 multicolored	.20	.20
		With tab		.25

Memorial Day.

Souvenir Sheet

Tourism, Sport and Industry — A253

1976, Apr. 25

601	A253	Sheet of 3	.60	.50
a.		£1 multicolored	.20	.20
b.		£2 multicolored	.20	.20
c.		£4 multicolored	.35	.25

No. 601 sold for £10.

High Jump A254

1976, June 22   Perf. 13x14

602	A254	£1.60 shown	.20	.20
603	A254	£2.40 Diving	.20	.20
604	A254	£4.40 Gymnastics	.30	.25
		#602-604, with tabs		.65

21st Olympic Games, Montreal, Canada, July 17-Aug. 1.

Tents and Suns — A255

1976, June 22   Perf. 14

605	A255	£1.50 green & multi	.20	.20
		With tab		.25

Israel Camping Union.

"Truth" A256

Pawn A257

Design: £1.50, "Judgment" (scales). £1.90, "Peace" (dove and olive branch).

1976, Aug. 17   Photo.   Perf. 14x13   Tagged

606	A256	45a gold & multi	.20	.20
607	A256	£1.50 gold & multi	.20	.20
608	A256	£1.90 gold & multi	.20	.20
		#606-608, with tabs		.30

Festivals 5737.

1976, Oct. 19   Litho.   Perf. 14

609	A257	£1.30 shown	.20	.20
610	A257	£1.60 Rook	.20	.20
		#609-610, with tabs		.35

22nd Men's and 7th Women's Chess Olympiad, Haifa, Oct. 24-Nov. 11.

Byzantine Building, 6th Century A258

70a, City wall, 7th cent. B.C. £2.40, Robinson's Arch. £2.80, Steps to Gate of Hulda. Both from area leading to 2nd Temple, 1st cent. B.C. £5, Wall, Omayyad Palace, 8th cent. A.D.

1976   Litho.   Perf. 14

611	A258	70a multicolored	.20	.20
612	A258	£1.30 multicolored	.20	.20
613	A258	£2.40 multicolored	.20	.20
614	A258	£2.80 multicolored	.35	.20
615	A258	£5 multicolored	.45	.40
		Nos. 611-615 (5)	1.40	1.20
		With tabs		1.75

Excavations in Old Jerusalem.

Issued: #612-614, 10/19; #611, 615, 12/23.

Clearing the Land, 1890 A259

Designs: 10a, Building harbor wall. 60a, Road building, vert. £1.40, Plower and horse-drawn plow. £1.80, Planting trees.

1976, Dec. 23   Photo.   Perf. 13

616	A259	5a brown & gold	.20	.20
617	A259	10a purple & gold	.20	.20
618	A259	60a gold & car	.20	.20
619	A259	£1.40 gold & blue	.20	.20
620	A259	£1.80 green & gold	.20	.20
		#616-620, with tabs		.40

Work of the pioneers.

"Let's Pull up Grandfather's Carrot" — A260

1977, Feb. 15   Litho.   Perf. 14

621	A260	£2.60 multicolored	.25	.20
		With tab		.30

Voluntary service.

Doves, Jew and Arab Shaking Hands A261

£1.40, Arab & Jew holding hands, and flowers. £2.70, Peace dove, Arab and Jew dancing. Illustrations for the book "My Shalom-My Peace."

1977, Feb. 15

622	A261	50a multicolored	.20	.20
623	A261	£1.40 multicolored	.20	.20
624	A261	£2.70 multicolored	.25	.25
		622-#624, with tabs		.55

Children's drawings for peace.

"By the Rivers of Babylon . . ." — A262

Drawings by Efraim Moshe Lilien: £1.80, Abraham, vert. £2.10, "May our eyes behold thee when thou returnest to Zion in compassion."

**   Perf. 14x13, 13x14**

625	A262	£1.70 gray, brn & blk	.20	.20
626	A262	£1.80 yel, blk & brn	.20	.20
627	A262	£2.10 lt grn & dk grn	.25	.20
		Nos. 625-627 (3)	.65	.60
		With tabs		.75

Souvenirs for 5th Zionist Congress, 1902.

Trumpet A263

Embroidered Sabbath Cloth A264

1977, Apr. 19   Litho.   Perf. 14

628	A263	£1.50 shown	.20	.20
629	A263	£2 Lyre	.20	.20
630	A263	£5 Cymbals	.25	.20
		#628-630, with tabs		.55

Ancient musical instruments, Haifa Music Museum and Amli Library.

1977, Apr. 19   Perf. 13x14

631	A264	£3 buff & multi	.25	.20
		With tab		.30

Importance of Sabbath observation in Jewish life.

Parachutists' Memorial, Bilu-Gedera, Tel Aviv — A265

1977, Apr. 19   *Perf. 13x14*
632 A265 £3.30 gray, blk & grn   .30   .25
   With tab   .40

Memorial Day.

10th
Maccabiah — A266

1977, June 23   **Photo.**   *Perf. 14x13*
633 A266 £1 Fencing   .20   .20
634 A266 £2.50 Shot put   .20   .20
635 A266 £3.50 Judo   .25   .20
   Nos. 633-635 (3)   .65   .60
   With tabs   .70

ZOA Convention
Emblem — A267

1977, June 23   *Perf. 14*
636 A267 £4 silver & multi   .30   .20
   With tab   .40

Convention of Zionist Organization of
America (ZOA), Jerusalem, June 1977.

Petah Tikva Centenary — A268

1977, June 23   **Photo.**   *Perf. 14x13*
637 A268 £1.50 multicolored   .20   .20
   With tab   .20

Matriarchs of the
Bible — A269

1977, Aug. 16   **Photo.**   *Perf. 14*
638 A269 70a Sarah   .20   .20
639 A269 £1.50 Rebekah   .20   .20
640 A269 £2 Rachel   .20   .20
641 A269 £3 Leah   .20   .20
   #638-641, with tabs   .75

Jewish New Year, 5738.

Frontier   Illuminated
Guards — A270   Page — A271

1977, Aug. 16   **Litho.**   *Perf. 14*
642 A270 £1 shown   .20   .20
643 A270 £1 Police   .20   .20
644 A270 £1 Civil Guard   .20   .20
   #642-644, with tabs   .35

Israel Police Force, established Mar. 26,
1948.

1977, July 21   **Photo.**   *Perf. 14x13*
645 A271 £4 multicolored   .20   .20
   With tab   .25

4th cent. of Hebrew printing at Safad.

Farm Growing   Koffler
from Steel   Accelerator
Helmet   A273
A272

1977, Oct. 18   **Litho.**   *Perf. 14*
646 A272 £3.50 multicolored   .20   .20
   With tab   .25

Fighting Pioneer Youth (NAHAL), established 1949.

1977, Oct. 18   **Photo.**   *Perf. 14x13*
647 A273 £8 black & blue   .60   .40

Inauguration of Koffler accelerator at
Weizmann Institute of Science, Rehovot.
Untagged.

Caesarea — A274

Scenes: £1, Arava on the Dead Sea. £20,
Rosh Pinna.

1977-78   *Perf. 13½x14*
    Size: 27x22mm
649 A274 10a violet blue   .20   .20
664 A274 £1 olive bister   .20   .20
    Perf. 14½x14
    Size: 27½x26½mm
672 A274 £20 org & dk grn ('78)   .80   .20
   #649-672, with tabs   1.50

The 10a is untagged. The £1, £20 issued
tagged and untagged.
Issued: 10a, £1, 10/18/77; £20, 7/4/78.

First Holy
Land
Locomotive
A276

Locomotives: £1.50, Jezreel Valley train.
£2, British Mandate period. £2.50, Israel
Railways.

1977, Dec. 13   **Photo.**   *Perf. 13x14*
674 A276 65a multicolored   .20   .20
675 A276 £1.50 multicolored   .20   .20
676 A276 £2 multicolored   .20   .20
677 A276 £2.50 multicolored   .25   .25
   a. Souvenir sheet of 4, #674-677   1.50   1.25
   #674-677, with tabs   .90

Railways in the Holy Land. #677a sold for
£10.

Cypraea
Isabella — A277

Designs: Red Sea shells.

1977, Dec. 13   **Litho.**   *Perf. 14*
678 A277 £2 shown   .20   .20
679 A277 £2 Lioconcha castren-
     sis   .20   .20
680 A277 £2 Gloripallium palli-
     um   .20   .20
681 A277 £2 Malea pomum   .20   .20
   #678-681, with tabs   .50

Street in
Jerusalem,
by Haim
Glicksberg
(1904-1970)
A278

Paintings: £3.80, Thistles, by Leopold
Krakauer (1890-1954). £4.40, An Alley in
Zefat, by Mordekhai Levanon (1901-1968).

1978, Feb. 14
682 A278 £3 multicolored   .20   .20
683 A278 £3.80 multicolored   .20   .20
684 A278 £4.40 multicolored   .25   .25
   Nos. 682-684 (3)   .65   .65
   With tabs   .65

Marriage Contract, Netherlands,
1648 — A279

Marriage Contracts (Ketubah): £3.90,
Morocco, 1897. £6, Jerusalem, 1846.

1978, Feb. 14
685 A279 75a multicolored   .20   .20
686 A279 £3.90 multicolored   .20   .20
687 A279 £6 multicolored   .30   .20
   #685-687, with tabs   .65

Eliyahu
Golomb — A280

Designs: Portraits.

1978, Apr. 23   **Photo.**   *Perf. 14x13*
688 A280 £2 shown   .20   .20
689 A280 £2 Dr. Moshe Sneh   .20   .20
690 A280 £2 David Raziel   .20   .20
691 A280 £2 Yitzhak Sadeh   .20   .20
692 A280 £2 Abraham Stern   .20   .20
   #688-692, with tabs   .60

Heroes of underground movement. Nos.
688-692 issued in sheets of 15.
See Nos. 695-696, 699-700, 705-706, 712-
714, 740-742.

Souvenir Sheet

Jerusalem, Mosaic, from Madaba
Map — A281

1978, Apr. 23   **Litho.**   *Perf. 14*
693 A281 Sheet of 4   1.40   1.40
   a. £1 multicolored   .20   .20
   b. £2 multicolored   .25   .20
   c. £3 multicolored   .40   .35
   d. £4 multicolored   .50   .45

Tabir '78 National Stamp Exhibition, Jerusalem, Apr. 23. No. 693 sold for £15.

Flowers
A282

Design: Flowers, after children's paintings
on Memorial Wall in Yad-Lebanim Museum,
Petah Tikva. Each stamp shows different
flowers.

1978, Apr. 23   *Perf. 14*
694   Sheet of 15   1.40   1.25
   a.-o. A282 £1.50 single stamp   .20   .20

Memorial Day.

Heroes Type

Designs: No. 695, Theodor Herzl. No. 696,
Chaim Weizmann.

1978, July 5   **Photo.**   *Perf. 14x13*
695 A280 £2 gray & gray ol   .20   .20
696 A280 £2 buff & vio bl   .20   .20
   #695-696, with tabs   .25

Herzl, founder of Zionism; Weizmann, 1st
President of Israel.

Hatiqwa, 1st   YMCA Building,
Verse   Jerusalem
A285   A286

1978, July 4   *Perf. 13x14*
697 A285 £8.40 multicolored   .45   .35
   With tab   .50

Centenary of Israeli National Anthem,
Hatiqwa, by poet Naftali Herz Imber.

1978, July 4   **Litho.**   *Perf. 13*
698 A286 £5.40 multicolored   .25   .20
   With tab   .35

Centenary of YMCA in Jerusalem.

Heroes Type

Designs: No. 699, Rabbi Kook (1865-1935).
No. 700, Rabbi Ouziel (1880-1963).

1978, Aug. 22   **Photo.**   *Perf. 14x13*
699 A280 £2 pale gray & slate
     grn   .20   .20
700 A280 £2 pale gray & dk pur   .20   .20
   #699-700, with tabs   .25

Patriarchs
A288

1978, Aug. 22   *Perf. 14*
701 A288 £1.10 Abraham & Isaac .20   .20
702 A288 £5.20 Isaac   .25   .25
703 A288 £6.60 Jacob   .30   .30
   #701-703, with tabs   .70

Festivals 5739.

Families
and
Houses
A289

1978, Aug. 22   *Perf. 13x14*
704 A289 £5.10 multicolored   .30   .20
   With tab   .35

Social welfare.

Heroes Type

Designs: No. 705, David Ben-Gurion. No. 706, Ze'ev Jabotinsky.

1978, Oct. 31   Photo.   Perf. 14x13
705 A280 £2 buff & vio brn   .20   .20
706 A280 £2 gray & indigo   .20   .20
#705-706, with tabs   .25

30 years of independence. Ben-Gurion, first Prime Minister, and Ze'ev Vladimir Jabotinsky (1880-1940), leader of World Union of Zionist Revisionists.

Star of David and Growing Tree — A291

1978, Oct. 31   Litho.   Perf. 14
707 A291 £8.40 multicolored   .45   .35
With tab   .50

United Jewish Appeal, established 1939 in US to help Israel.

Old and New Hospital Buildings A292

1978, Oct. 31
708 A292 £5.40 multicolored   .25   .20
With tab   .30

Opening of new Shaare Zedek Medical Center, Jerusalem.

Silver and Enamel Vase, India — A293

Iris Lortetii — A295

£3, Elephant with howdah, Persia, 13th cent. £4, Mosque lamp, glass and enamel, Syria, 14th cent.

1978, Oct. 31
709 A293 £2.40 multicolored   .20   .20
710 A293 £3 multicolored   .20   .20
711 A293 £4 multicolored   .20   .20
Nos. 709-711 (3)   .60   .60
With tabs   .65

Leo Arie Mayer Memorial Museum for Islamic Art, Jerusalem.

Heroes Type

#712, Menachem Ussishkin (1863-1941). #713, Berl Katzenelson (1878-1944). #714, Max Nordau (1849-1923).

1978, Dec. 26   Photo.   Perf. 14x13
712 A280 £2 citron & sl grn   .20   .20
713 A280 £2 gray & vio blue   .20   .20
714 A280 £2 buff & black   .20   .20
#712-714, with tabs   .45

30th anniversary of independence.

1978, Dec. 26   Litho.   Perf. 14

Protected Wild Flowers: £5.40, Iris haynei. £8.40, Iris nazarena.

715 A295 £1.10 multicolored   .20   .20
716 A295 £5.40 multicolored   .30   .25
717 A295 £8.40 multicolored   .45   .35
Nos. 715-717 (3)   .95   .80
With tabs   .95

Agricultural Mechanization A296

Symbolic Designs: £2.40, Seawater desalination. £4.30, Electronics. £5, Chemical fertilizers.

1979, Feb. 13   Litho.   Perf. 13
718 A296 £1.10 multicolored   .20   .20
719 A296 £2.40 multicolored   .20   .20
720 A296 £4.30 multicolored   .20   .20
721 A296 £5 multicolored   .20   .20
#718-721, with tabs   .70

Technological Achievements.

"Hope from Darkness" A297

1979, Feb. 13
722 A297 £5.40 multicolored   .30   .25
                                            .35

Salute to "the Righteous among Nations," an award to those who helped during Nazi period.

Jewish Brigade Flag — A298

1979, Feb. 13   Photo.   Perf. 14
723 A298 £5.10 blue, yel & blk   .25   .25
With tab   .30

Jewish Brigade served with British Armed Forces during WWII.

Paper (Prayer for Peace) in Crevice of Western Wall — A299

1979, Mar. 26   Photo.   Perf. 14x13
724 A299 £10 multicolored   .35   .25
With tab   .40
a.   Souv. sheet of 1, imperf.   .40   .45

Signing of peace treaty between Israel and Egypt, Mar. 26.

11th Hapoel Games — A300

1979, Apr. 23   Litho.   Perf. 13
725 A300 £1.50 Weightlifting   .20   .20
726 A300 £6 Tennis   .30   .20
727 A300 £11 Gymnastics   .50   .40
Nos. 725-727 (3)   1.00   .80
With tabs   1.00

"50" and Rotary Emblem — A301

1979, Apr. 23   Photo.   Perf. 14x13
728 A301 £7 multicolored   .35   .25
With tab   .40

Rotary Intl. in Israel, 50th anniv.

Navy Memorial, Ashdod A302

1979, Apr. 23
729 A302 £5.10 multicolored   .25   .20
With tab   .30

Memorial Day.

Rabbi Yehoshua ben Hananya A303

Flag Colors as Search Light A304

Craftsmen-Sages: £8.50, Rabbi Meir Baal Ha-Ness, scribe. £13, Rabbi Johanan, sandal maker.

1979, Sept. 4   Photo.   Perf. 14x13
730 A303 £1.80 multicolored   .20   .20
731 A303 £8.50 multicolored   .20   .20
732 A303 £13 multicolored   .35   .30
Nos. 730-732 (3)   .75   .70
With tabs   .75

Jewish New Year 5740.

1979, Sept. 4
733 A304 £10 multicolored   .25   .20
With tab   .30

Jewish Agency, 50th anniversary.

Hot Springs, Tiberias A305

Boy Riding Rainbow A306

Design: £12, Dead Sea health resorts.

1979, Sept. 4   Litho.   Perf. 14
734 A305 £8 multicolored   .20   .20
735 A305 £12 multicolored   .30   .20
#734-735, with tabs   .55

1979, Nov. 13   Photo.   Perf. 13x14
736 A306 £8.50 multicolored   .20   .20
With tab   .25

International Year of the Child.

Jerusalem — A307

Children's Drawings of Jerusalem: £4, People of different nationalities, horiz. £5, Praying at the Western Wall, horiz.

1979, Nov. 13   Perf. 14
737 A307 £1.80 multicolored   .20   .20
738 A307 £4 multicolored   .20   .20
739 A307 £5 multicolored   .20   .20
#737-739, with tabs   .30

Heroes Type

Designs: £7, Arthur Ruppin (1876-1943). £9, Joseph Trumpeldor (1880-1920). £13, Aaron Aaronsohn (1876-1919).

1979, Nov. 13   Photo.   Perf. 14x13
740 A280 £7 gray & magenta   .20   .20
741 A280 £9 pale grn & Prus
             bl   .25   .25
742 A280 £13 pale yel & dk ol   .35   .35
Nos. 740-742 (3)   .80   .80
With tabs   1.10

Sorek Cave — A308

1980, Jan. 15   Litho.   Perf. 13x14
743 A308 £50 multicolored   1.00   .50
With tab   1.25

Star of David in Cogwheel A309

Scolymus Maculatus A310

1980, Jan. 15   Perf. 14
744 A309 £13 multicolored   .40   .40
With tab   .45

Organization for Rehabilitation through Training (ORT), centenary.

1980, Jan. 15

Thistles: £5.50, Echinops viscosus. £8.50, Cynara syriaca.

745 A310 50a multicolored   .20   .20
746 A310 £5.50 multicolored   .20   .20
747 A310 £8.50 multicolored   .25   .20
#745-747, with tabs   .50

Men and Drop of Blood — A311

Mobile Intensive Care Unit — A312

1980, Apr. 15 Photo. Perf. 14x13
748 A311 £2.70 multicolored .20 .20
749 A312 £13 multicolored .30 .30
a. Souv. sheet, 2 each #748-749 1.00 1.00
#748-749, with tabs .45

Magen David Adom (Red Star of David), 50th anniv.

Road of Courage Monument A313

Sabbath Lamp, Netherlands, 18th Century A314

1980, Apr. 15 Litho. Perf. 14
750 A313 £12 multicolored .30 .25
With tab .35

Memorial Day.

1980, Aug. 5 Photo. Perf. 13x14
Sabbath Lamps: £20, Germany, 18th century. £30, Morocco, 19th century.
751 A314 £4.30 multicolored .20 .20
752 A314 £20 multicolored .30 .30
753 A314 £30 multicolored .50 .50
Nos. 751-753 (3) 1.00 1.00
With tabo 1.10

Yizhak Gruenbaum A315

Renewal of Jewish Settlement in Gush Etzion A316

1980, Aug. 5 Perf. 14x13
754 A315 £32 sepia .80 .70
With tab .85

Yizhak Gruenbaum (1879-1970), first minister of the interior.

1980, Aug. 5
755 A316 £19 multicolored .35 .30
With tab .40

View of Haifa and Mt. Carmel, 17th Century — A317

1980, Sept. 28 Litho. Perf. 14x13
756 A317 Sheet of 2 2.00 2.25
a. 2s multicolored .75 .85
b. 3s multicolored 1.00 1.10

Haifa 80 National Stamp Exhibition, Haifa, Sept. 28-Oct. 7.

  A318

1980-81 Photo. Perf. 13x14
757 A318 5a brt yel grn & green .20 .20
758 A318 10a red & brt mag .20 .20
759 A318 20a grnsh bl & dk blue .20 .20
760 A318 30a lil & dp vio .20 .20
761 A318 50a red org & red brown .20 .20
762 A318 60a brt yel grn & dk brown .20 .20
762A A318 70a Prus bl & black .20 .20
763 A318 1s brt mag & dk green .20 .20
764 A318 2s dk bl grn & brn red .25 .20
765 A318 2.80s brown & grn .30 .20
766 A318 3.20s gray & red .35 .20
767 A318 4.20s ultra & dk pur .40 .20
768 A318 5s green & blk .55 .20
769 A318 10s brn org & brn 1.25 .20
#757-769, with tabs 5.00

Issued: 70a, 5/5/81; others, 12/16/80.
See Nos. 784-786, 807-808.

Prime Minister Golda Meir (1898-1978) — A319

1981, Feb. 10 Photo. Perf. 14x13
770 A319 2.60s rose violet .40 .40
With tab .45

View of Jerusalem, by Mordechai Ardon — A320

1981, Feb. 10 Litho. Perf. 14
Paintings of Jerusalem by: 50a, Anna Ticho. 1.50s, Joseph Zaritsky, vert.
771 A320 50a multicolored .20 .20
772 A320 1.50s multicolored .25 .20
773 A320 2.50s multicolored .40 .35
Nos. 771-773 (3) .85 .75
With tabs .95

Hand Putting Coin in Light Bulb — A321

1981, Mar. 17 Photo. Perf. 14
774 A321 2.60s shown .25 .25
775 A321 4.20s Hand squeezing solar energy .40 .35
#774-775, with tabs .80

Shmuel Yosef Agnon (1880-1970), Writer — A322

Wind Surfing — A323

Designs: 2.80s, Moses Montefiore (1784-1885), first knighted English Jew. 3.20s, Abba Hillel Silver (1893-1963), statesman.

Perf. 14x13, 14 (3.20s)
1981, Mar. 17
776 A322 2s dk blue & blk .25 .25
777 A322 2.80s dk bl grn & blk .30 .30
778 A322 3.20s deep bis & blk .35 .30
Nos. 776-778 (3) .90 .85
1.00

1981, May 5 Perf. 14x13
779 A323 80a shown .20 .20
780 A323 4s Basketball .55 .55
781 A323 6s High jump .75 .75
Nos. 779-781 (3) 1.50 1.50
With tabs 1.50

11th Maccabiah Games, July 8-16.

Biq'at Hayarden Memorial A324

Jewish Family Heritage A325

1981, May 5 Perf. 13x14
782 A324 1s red & black .20 .20
With tab .25

1981, May 5 Litho. Perf. 14
783 A325 3s multicolored .40 .35
With tab .45

Type of 1980
1981, Aug. 25 Photo. Perf. 13x14
784 A318 90a dp vio & brn org .20 .20
785 A318 3s red & dk blue .45 .30
786 A318 4s dk brn vio & dp lil rose .50 .35
Nos. 784-786 (3) 1.15 .85
With tabs 1.25

The Burning Bush A326

Roses A327

Festivals 5742 (Book of Exodus): 1s "Let my people go . . ." 3s, Crossing of the Red Sea. 4s, Moses with Tablets.

1981, Aug. 25
787 A326 70a multicolored .20 .20
788 A326 1s multicolored .20 .20
789 A326 3s multicolored .35 .35
790 A326 4s multicolored .45 .40
Nos. 787-790 (4) 1.20 1.15
With tabs 1.25

1981, Oct. 22 Litho. Perf. 14
791 A327 90a Rosa damascena .20 .20
792 A327 3.50s Rosa phoenicia .40 .35
793 A327 4.50s Rosa hybrida .50 .45
Nos. 791-793 (3) 1.10 1.00
With tabs 1.50

Ha-Shiv'a Interchange, Morasha-Ashod Highway — A328

1981, Oct. 22 Photo. Perf. 14x13
794 A328 8s multicolored .70 .65
With tab .75

Elat Stone A329

Arbutus Andrachne A330

1981, Dec. 29 Litho. Perf. 14
795 A329 2.50s shown .25 .25
796 A329 5.50s Star sapphire .55 .55
797 A329 7s Emerald .70 .70
Nos. 795-797 (3) 1.50 1.50
With tabs 2.25

1981, Dec. 29
798 A330 3s shown .30 .30
799 A330 3s Cercis siliquastrum .30 .30
800 A330 3s Quercus ithaburensis .30 .30
a. Vert. or horiz. strip of 3, #798-800 1.00 1.00
#800a, horiz. strip of 3 with tabs 1.25

Sheets of 9.

Road Safety — A331

1982, Mar. 2 Photo. Perf. 14x13
801 A331 7s multicolored .70 .70
With tab 1.00
a. Souvenir sheet 1.25 1.25

No. 801a sold for 10s.

Joseph Gedalyah Klausner (1874-1958), Historian and Philosopher A331a

7s, Perez Bernstein (1890-1971), writer and editor. 8s, Rabbi Arys Levin (1885-1969).

1982, Mar. 2
802 A331a 7s multi .50 .50
803 A331a 8s multi .55 .55
804 A331a 9s cream & dk bl .65 .65
Nos. 802-804 (3) 1.70 1.70
With tabs 1.90

Type of 1980 and

Produce — A332

1982-83   Photo.   Perf. 13 x 14

805	A332	40a Prus bl & grn	.20 .20
806	A332	80a lt bl & pur	.20 .20
807	A318	1.10s ol & red	.20 .20
808	A318	1.20s bl & red	.20 .20
809	A332	1.40s ol grn & red	.20 .20
810	A332	6s red vio & brn org	.25 .20
811	A332	7s brn org & ol	.20 .20
812	A332	8s brt grn & red brn	.25 .20
813	A332	9s ol & brn	.25 .20
814	A332	15s ver & brt grn	.40 .20
		Nos. 805-814 (10)	2.30 2.00
		With tabs	5.00

Issued: 1.10s, 2/11; 1.20s, 3/16; 1.40s, 6/22/82; 40a, 80a, 6s, 1/11/83; 7s-15s, 10/11/83.
See Nos. 876-879.

Tel Aviv Landscape, by Aryeh Lubin (d. 1980) — A333

Landscapes by: 8s, Sionah Tagger, vert. 15s, Israel Paldi (1892-1979).

1982, Apr. 22   Litho.   Perf. 14

815	A333	7s multicolored	.50 .50
816	A333	8s multicolored	.50 .50
817	A333	15s multicolored	1.00 1.00
		Nos. 815-817 (3)	2.00 2.00
		With tabs	3.00

Gedudei Nouar Youth Corps A334

Armour Memorial, En Zetim A335

1982, Apr. 22   Photo.   Perf. 14x13

818	A334	5s multicolored	.40 .35
		With tab	.55

1982, Apr. 22   Litho.   Perf. 14

819	A335	1.50s multicolored	.20 .20
		With tab	.20

Memorial Day.

Joshua Addressing Crowd — A336

Festivals 5743 (Book of Joshua): 5.50s, Crossing River Jordan. 7.50s, Blowing down walls of Jericho. 9.50s, Battle with five kings of Amorites.

1982, Aug. 10   Perf. 14

820	A336	1.50s multicolored	.20 .20
821	A336	5.50s multicolored	.30 .30
822	A336	7.50s multicolored	.45 .45
823	A336	9.50s multicolored	.55 .55
		Nos. 820-823 (4)	1.50 1.50
		With tabs	1.50

Hadassah, 70th Anniv. — A337

1982, Aug. 10   Litho.

824	A337	12s multicolored	.85 .70
		With tab	1.25

Rosh Pinna Settlement Centenary A338

1982   Photo.   Perf. 13x14

825	A338	2.50s shown	.20 .20
826	A338	3.50s Rishon Leziyyon	.20 .20
827	A338	6s Zikhron Yaaqov	.35 .30
828	A338	9s Mazkeret Batya	.65 .60
		Nos. 825-828 (4)	1.40 1.30
		With tabs	1.50

Issued: 2.50s, 3.50s, Aug. 10; others, Oct. 5.
See Nos. 849-850.

Olive Branch A339

Emblem of Council for a Beautiful Israel A340

1982, Sept. 12

829	A339	multicolored	.20 .20
		With tab	.40
a.		Booklet pane of 8 + 8 ('84)	3.00

Sold at various values.

1982, Oct. 5   Litho.   Perf. 14

830	A340	17s multicolored	.90 .75
		With tab	1.00
a.		Souv. sheet of 1, imperf.	2.25 2.25

No. 830a was for Beer Sheva '82 National Stamp Exhibition. Sold for 25s.

Eliahu Bet Tzuri — A341

Independence Martyrs: b, Hannah Szenes. c, Shlomo Ben Yosef. d, Yosef Lishanski. e, Naaman Belkind. f, Eliezer Kashani. g, Yechiel Dresner. h, Dov Gruner. i, Mordechai Alkachi. j, Eliahu Hakim. k, Meir Nakar. l, Avshalom Havlv. m, Yaakov Weiss. n, Moir Feinstein. o, Moshe Barazani. p, Eli Cohen. q, Samuel Azaar. r, Moshe Marzouk. s, Shalom Salih. t, Yosef Basri.

1982, Dec.   Perf. 14x13½

831		Sheet of 20	5.50 5.50
a.-t.	A341	3s multicolored	.20 .20

Anti-Smoking Campaign A342

1983, Feb. 15   Litho.   Perf. 13

832	A342	7s Candy in ash tray	.35 .25
		With tab	.50

Beekeeping A343

1983, Feb. 15   Photo.   Perf. 13x14

833	A343	30s multi	1.60 1.50
		With tab	1.75

A343a

1983, Feb. 15   Litho.   Perf. 14

834	A343a	8s Golan	.30 .30
835	A343a	15s Galil	.65 .55
836	A343a	20s Yehuda and Shomeron	.95 .70
		Nos. 834-836 (3)	1.90 1.55
		With tabs	3.00

Memorial Day (Apr. 17) — A344

1983, Apr. 12   Perf. 13

837	A344	3s Division of Steel Memorial, Besor Region	.20 .20
		With tab	.20

Independence Day — A345

1983, Apr. 12   Perf. 14

838	A345	25s multicolored	1.25 1.00
		With tab	1.40
a.		Souvenir sheet, imperf.	2.50 2.25

No. 838a sold for 35s.

12th Hapoel Games — A346

1983, Apr. 12   Perf. 14x13

839	A346	6s multicolored	.25 .25
		With tab	.35

50th Anniv. of Israel Military Industries — A347

1983, Apr. 12

840	A347	12s multicolored	.55 .55
		With tab	.60

Souvenir Sheet

WWII Uprising Leaders — A348

Designs: a, Yosef Glazman (1908-1943), Founder of United Partisans Org. b, Text.1 c, Mordechai Anilewicz (1919-1943), leader of Warsaw Ghetto revolt. No. 841 sold for 45s.

1983, June 7   Perf. 14

841	A348	Sheet of 3	2.75 2.75
a.		10s multicolored	.75 .60
b.		10s multicolored	.75 .60
c.		10s multicolored	.75 .60

Raoul Wallenberg (1912-1945), Swedish Diplomat — A349

1983, June 7   Perf. 14x13

842	A349	14s multicolored	.65 .45
		With tab	1.00

The Last Way, by Yosef Kuzkovski — A350

1983, June 7   Perf. 14

843	A350	35s multicolored	1.10 1.10
		With tab	1.25

Ohel Moed Synagogue, Tel Aviv A351

1983, Aug. 23

844	A351	3s shown	.20 .20
845	A351	12s Yeshurun Society, Jerusalem	.35 .35
846	A351	16s Ohel Aharon, Haifa	.50 .50
847	A351	20s Eliyahu Khakascni, Beer Sheva	.60 .60
		Nos. 844-847 (4)	1.65 1.65
		With tabs	1.90

View of Afula, Jezreel Valley — A352

1983, Aug. 23

848	A352	15s multicolored	.65 .55
		With tab	.80

Settlement Type of 1982

1983, Aug. 23

849	A338	11s Yesud Ha-Maala	.45 .40
850	A338	13s Nes Ziyyona	.50 .45
		#849-850, with tabs	1.25

Souvenir Sheet

Tel Aviv Seashore Promenade — A353

1983, Sept. 25   *Perf. 14x13*
851 A353 Sheet of 2   8.00 8.00
   a.   30s multicolored   2.50 2.25
   b.   50s multicolored   4.00 3.75

Tel Aviv '83, 13th Natl. Stamp Show, Sept.
Sold for 120s.

KFIR-C2 Tactical Fighter — A354

1983, Dec. 13   Photo.   *Perf. 14*
852 A354   8s shown   .20 .20
853 A354 18s Reshef class mis-
         sile boat   .25 .25
854 A354 30s Merkava-MK1 bat-
         tle tank   .45 .45
   Nos. 852-854 (3)   .90 .90
   With tabs   .90

Rabbi Meir Bar-Ilan
(1880-1949),
Founder of Mizrachi
Movement — A355

1983, Dec. 13   Photo.   *Perf. 14x13*
855 A355 9s multicolored   .20 .20
   With tab   .20

Jewish
Immigration
from
Germany,
50th Anniv.
A356

1983, Dec. 13   Photo.   *Perf. 13x14*
856 A356 14s multicolored   .40 .35
   With tab   .45

Michael Halperin
(1860-1919),
Zionist — A357

Uri Zvi Grinberg
(1896-1981),
Poet — A358

15s, Yigal Allon (1918-1980), military commander, founder of Israel Labor Party.

1984, Mar. 15   Photo.   *Perf. 14x13*
857 A357   7s multicolored   .20 .20
        Litho.
        Perf. 14
858 A357 15s multicolored   .25 .25
        Perf. 13
859 A358 16s multicolored   .30 .30
   Nos. 857-859 (3)   .75 .75
   With tabs   1.00

Hevel Ha-Besor
Settlement — A359

1984, Mar. 15   *Perf. 14*
860 A359 12s shown   .20 .20
861 A359 17s Arava   .30 .25
862 A359 40s Gaza Strip   .75 .50
   Nos. 860-862 (3)   1.25 .95
   With tabs   1.50

Monument
of
Alexander
Zaid, by
David Polus
A360

Monuments: No. 864, Tel Hay Defenders
(seated lion), by Abraham Melnikov (1892-
1960). No. 865, Dov Gruner, by Chana Orloff
(1888-1968).

1984, Mar. 15   *Perf. 13x14*
863 A360 15s multicolored   .35 .25
864 A360 15s multicolored   .35 .25
865 A360 15s multicolored   .35 .25
   Nos. 863-865 (3)   1.05 .75
   With tabs   1.35

Memorial
Day — A361

Natl. Labor Fed.,
50th
Anniv. — A362

Design: Oliphant House (Druse military
memorial), Dalyat Al Karmil.

1984, Apr. 26   Photo.   *Perf. 14x13*
866 A361 10s multicolored   .20 .20
   With tab   .20

1984, Apr. 26
867 A362 35s multicolored   .35 .25
   With tab   .40

Produce Type of 1982-83

1984   Photo.   *Perf. 13x14*
876 A332 30s vio brn & red   .35 .25
877 A332 50s dp bis & rose
         mag   .65 .40
878 A332 100s gray & green   1.25 .80
879 A332 500s dp org & bl blk   1.10 .90
   Nos. 876-879 (4)   3.35 2.35
   With tabs   7.00

Issued: 500s, 11/27; others 4/26.

Leon Pinsker
(1821-91),
A363

Gen. Charles O.
Wingate (1903-
44)
A364

1984, July 3   *Perf. 14x13*
880 A363 20s Hovevei Zion
         founder   .20 .20
881 A364 20s British soldier   .20 .20
   #880-881, with tabs   .50

Hearts,
Stars — A365

1984, July 3
882 A365 30s multicolored   .25 .25
   With tab   .30

70th anniv. of American Jewish Joint Distribution Committee (philanthropic org. created
during World War I).

1984 Summer
Olympics
A366

1984, July 3   Litho.   *Perf. 14*
883 A366 80s Dove   .70 .70
   With tab   .90

Souvenir Sheet
Perf. 14x13

884 A366 240s like 80s   5.00 4.25

No. 884 contains one 23x32mm stamp.
Sold for 350s.

Biblical
Women
A367

David Wolffsohn
(1856-1914),
Jewish Colonial
Trust Founder
A368

1984, Sept. 4   Photo.   *Perf. 13x14*
885 A367 15s Hannah   .20 .20
886 A367 70s Ruth   .35 .35
887 A367 100s Huldah   .60 .60
   Nos. 885-887 (3)   1.15 1.15
   With tabs   1.25

1984, Sept. 4   *Perf. 14x14½*
888 A368 150s multicolored   .90 .60
   With tab   1.25

Nahalal
Settlement
(Founded
1921)
A369

1984, Sept. 4   *Perf. 14*
889 A369 80s multicolored   .50 .45
               .60

World Food
Day, Oct.
16 — A370

1984, Nov. 27   Litho.
891 A370 200s Bread, wheat   1.00 .65
   With tab   1.10

Rabbi Isaac
Herzog (1888-
1959),
Statesman,
Scholar — A371

1984, Nov. 27   Photo.   *Perf. 14½*
892 A371 400s multicolored   1.60 1.40
   With tab   1.75

A372

Perf. 14, 13 (30s)

1984, Nov. 27   Litho.

Children's Book Illustrations (Authors and
their books): 20s, Apartment to Let, by Leah
Goldberg (1911-70). 30s, Why is the Zebra
Wearing Pajamas, by Omer Hillel (b. 1926)
(30x30mm). 50s, Across the Sea, by Haim
Nahman Bialik (1873-1934).

893 A372 20s multicolored   .20 .20
894 A372 30s multicolored   .20 .20
895 A372 50s multicolored   .30 .20
   Nos. 893-895 (3)   .70 .60
   With tabs   .80

Birds of Prey — A373

1985, Feb. 5   Litho.   *Perf. 14*
896 A373 100s Lappet faced
         vulture   .35 .35
897 A373 200s Bonelli's eagle   .60 .60
898 A373 300s Sooty falcon   .80 .80
899 A373 500s Griffon vulture   1.50 1.50
   Nos. 896-899 (4)   3.25 3.25
   With tabs   6.00

Souvenir Sheet

899A   Sheet of 4   8.00 5.00
   b.   A373 100s like #896   .50 .40
   c.   A373 200s like #897   .90 .80
   d.   A373 300s like #898   1.25 1.10
   e.   A373 500s like #899   1.75 1.60

No. 899A sold for 1650s. Nos. 899Ab-
899Ad do not have inscriptions below the
design.

Aviation in
the Holy
Land
A374

1985, Apr. 2   Litho.   *Perf. 14*
900 A374   50s Bleriot XI, 1913   .20 .20
901 A374 150s Scipio-Short S-17
         Kent, 1931   .50 .40
902 A374 250s Tiger Moth DH-
         82, 1934   .80 .70
903 A374 300s Scion-Short S-16,
         1937   .85 1.00
   Nos. 900-903 (4)   2.35 2.30
   With tabs   2.75

Natl. Assoc. of Nurses — A375

1985, Apr. 2 Litho. **Perf. 14**
904 A375 400s multicolored 1.00 .95
With tab 1.50

Golani Brigade Memorial and Museum — A376

1985, Apr. 2 Photo. **Perf. 14x13**
905 A376 50s multicolored .25 .20
With tab .45

Zivia (1914-1978) and Yitzhak (1915-1981) Zuckerman, Resistance Heroes, Warsaw Ghetto — A377

1985, Apr. 2 Photo. **Perf. 13x14**
906 A377 200s multicolored .65 .50
With tab .80

Souvenir Sheets

Dome of the Rock A378

16th Cent. Bas-relief, Ottoman Period A379

Adam, Eve and the Serpent (detail) — A380

#907b, The Western Wall. #907c, Church of the Holy Sepulchre. #908b, Hand, 18th cent. bas-relief, Jewish Quarter. #908c, Rosette carving, 12th-13th cent. Crusader capital. #909, Frontispiece and detail, Schocken Bible, South Germany, ca. 1290.

1985, May 14 Litho. **Perf. 13x14**
907 Sheet of 3 3.00 3.00
a.-c. A378 200s any single .80 .75
Sold for 900s.

Perf. 14x13
908 Sheet of 3 4.00 4.00
a.-c. A379 350s any single 1.25 1.10
Sold for 1500s.

Perf. 14
909 A380 800s multi 3.75 3.75
Nos. 907-909 (3) 10.75 10.75
Sold for 1200s.

The Israeli postal administration authorized the Intl. Philatelic Federation (FIP) to overprint a limited number of these souvenir sheets for sale exclusively at ISRAPHIL '85 to raise funds. The FIP overprints have control numbers and are inscribed "Under the Patronage of the Philatelic Federation" in the sheet margin. The sheets remained valid for postage but were not sold by the post office. Value for set of sheets $45.

12th Maccabiah Games A381

1985 Festivals A382

1985, July 16 Litho. **Perf. 14**
910 A381 400s Basketball .75 .75
911 A381 500s Tennis .90 .90
912 A381 600s Windsurfing 1.10 1.10
Nos. 910-912 (3) 2.75 2.75
With tabs 4.00

1985, July 16 Litho. **Perf. 14**
Tabernacle utensils: 100sh, Ark of the Covenant. 150sh, Acacia showbread table. 200sh, Menora. 300sh, Incense altar.
913 A382 100s multi .20 .20
914 A382 150s multi .30 .30
915 A382 200s multi .35 .35
916 A382 300s multi .55 .55
Nos. 913-916 (4) 1.40 1.40
With tabs 2.25

A383

A384

1985, July 16 Litho. **Perf. 14**
917 A383 150s Emblem, badges .40 .25
With tab .55
Intl. Youth Year.

1985, Nov. 5 Litho. **Perf. 14**
918 A384 200s multi .80 .25
With tab .95
Leon Yehuda Recanati (1890-1945), financier and philanthropist.

Meir Dizengoff (1861-1936), Founder and Mayor of Tel Aviv — A385

1985, Nov. 5
919 A385 500s multi 1.00 .65
With tab 1.25

Gedera Settlement, Cent. A386

1985, Nov. 5 Photo. **Perf. 13x14**
920 A386 600s multi 1.10 .80
With tab 1.40

The Kibbutz — A387

1985, Nov. 5 Litho. **Perf. 14**
921 A387 900s multi 1.25 1.10
With tab 1.50

Theodor Herzl A388

Capital, Second Temple, Jerusalem A389

Designs: 1s, Corinthian, A.D. 1st cent. 3s, Ionic, 1st cent. B.C.

1986, Jan. 1 Photo. **Perf. 13x14**
922 A388 1a red & ultra .20 .20
923 A388 2a green & ultra .20 .20
924 A388 3a brown & ultra .20 .20
925 A388 5a blue & ultra .20 .20
926 A388 10a org & ultra .20 .20
927 A388 20a pink & ultra .20 .20
928 A388 30a lemon & ultra .25 .25
929 A388 50a pur & ultra .45 .40
930 A389 1s multi 1.00 .95
931 A389 3s multi 2.75 2.75
Nos. 922-931 (10) 5.65 5.55
With tabs 6.25

1s and 3s designs with 1000a and 1500a values were not issued.
See Nos. 1014-1020, 1699.

Red Sea Coral A390

1986, Mar. 4 Litho. **Perf. 14**
932 A390 30a Balanophyllia .35 .35
933 A390 40a Goniopora .50 .50
934 A390 50a Dendronephthya .65 .65
Nos. 932-934 (3) 1.50 1.50
With tabs 3.00

Arthur Rubinstein (1887-1982), Pianist — A391

1986, Mar. 4 Photo. **Perf. 13x14**
935 A391 60a Picasso portraits .90 .80
With tab 1.25

Broadcasting from Jerusalem, 50th Anniv. — A392

1986, Mar. 4 Litho. **Perf. 14**
936 A392 70a Map and microphone, 1936 .90 .90
1.10

Negev Brigade Memorial, Beer Sheva — A393

1986, May 4 Litho. **Perf. 13**
937 A393 20a multicolored .30 .30
With tab .40
Memorial Day.

Al Jazzar Mosque, Akko — A394

1986, May 4 Photo. **Perf. 14x13**
938 A394 30a multicolored .40 .40
With tab .50
Id Al-Fitr Feast.

Institutes of Higher Learning in the US — A395

Designs: No. 939, 942a, Hebrew Union College, Jewish Institute of Religion, 1875, Cincinnati. No. 940, 942b, Yeshiva University, 1886, NYC. No. 941, 942c, Jewish Theological Seminary of America, 1886, NYC.

1986, May 4 Litho. **Perf. 14**
939 A395 50a multicolored .60 .60
940 A395 50a multicolored .60 .60
941 A395 50a multicolored .60 .60
Nos. 939-941 (3) 1.80 1.80
With tabs 2.75

Souvenir Sheet
942 Sheet of 3 + label 4.00 4.00
a.-c. A395 75a any single 1.25 1.25
AMERIPEX '86. Size of Nos. 942a-942c: 36x23mm. No. 942 sold for 3s.

Ben Gurion Airport, 50th Anniv. A396

1986, July 22 **Perf. 14x13**
943 A396 90a Terminal from aircraft 1.25 1.25
With tab 1.50

"No to Racism" in Graffiti — A397

1986, July 22 **Perf. 14**
944 A397 60a multicolored .90 .80
With tab 1.10

Druze Feast of Prophet Nabi Sabalan — A398

1986, July 22   **Photo.**   *Perf. 14*
945   A398   40a Tomb, Hurfeish   .50   .50
     With tab   .60

Joseph Sprinzak (1885-1959), 1st Speaker of Knesset — A399

1986, July 22   **Litho.**   *Perf. 13*
946   A399   80a multicolored   1.00   1.00
     With tab   1.10

Worms Illuminated Mahzor, 13th Cent. — A400

1986, Sept. 23   **Litho.**   *Perf. 13x14*
947   A400   20a Gates of Heaven   .25   .25
948   A400   40a Sheqalim, prayer   .50   .50
949   A400   90a Rose flower prayer introduction   1.10   1.10
     Nos. 947-949 (3)   1.85   1.85
     With tabs   2.25

David Ben-Gurion (1886-1973) — A401

1986, Oct. 19   **Litho.**   *Perf. 14x13*
950   A401   1s multicolored   1.25   1.25
     With tab   1.40

Souvenir Sheet

Map of the Holyland, by Gerard de Jode, 1578 — A402

1986, Oct. 19   *Perf. 14½*
951   A402   2s multicolored   4.00   3.50
     NATANYA '86 Stamp Exhibition; Organized philately in Natanya, 50th anniv. Sold for 3s.

Israel Meteorological Service, 50th Anniv. — A403

1986, Dec. 18   **Litho.**   *Perf. 13*
952   A403   50a multicolored   .70   .70
     With tab   1.25

Basilica of the Annunciation, Nazareth — A404

1986, Dec. 18   **Litho.**   *Perf. 14*
953   A404   70a multicolored   .90   .90
     With tab   1.60

Israel Philharmonic Orchestra, 50th Anniv. — A405

1986, Dec. 18
954   A405   1.50s Bronislaw Huberman, violinist   2.25   2.00
955   A405   1.50s Arturo Toscanini, conductor   2.25   2.00
  a.   Pair, #954-955   4.50   4.00
     With tabs   6.75

Owls — A406

1987, Feb. 24   **Litho.**   *Perf. 14x13*
956   A406   30a Bubo bubo   .55   .55
957   A406   40a Otus brucei   .70   .70
958   A406   50a Tyto alba   .90   .90
959   A406   80a Strix butleri   1.50   1.50
     Nos. 956-959 (4)   3.65   3.65
     With tab   8.00

Souvenir Sheet
960   Sheet of 4   10.00   10.00
  a.   A406   30a like #956   1.40   1.40
  b.   A406   40a like #957   1.75   1.75
  c.   A406   50a like #958   2.25   2.25
  d.   A406   80a like #959   3.50   3.50

     Sold for 3s. Nos. 960a-960d do not have inscriptions below the design.

Ammunition Hill Memorial, Jerusalem — A407

1987, Apr. 16   **Litho.**   *Perf. 14*
961   A407   30a multicolored   .40   .40
     With tab   .65

     Memorial Day.

13th Hapoel Games — A408

1987, Apr. 16
962   A408   90a multicolored   1.10   1.10
     With tab   1.60

Souvenir Sheet

HAIFA '87 Stamp Exhibition — A409

1987, Apr. 16   *Perf. 14x13*
963   A409   2.70s No. C8   6.00   6.00
     Sold for 4s.

Amateur Radio Operators — A410

1987, June 14   **Litho.**   *Perf. 14*
964   A410   2.50s multi   3.75   3.75
     With tab   4.50

World Dog Show, June 23-27 — A411

1987, June 14
965   A411   40a Saluki   .90   .70
966   A411   50a Sloughi   1.10   .90
967   A411   2s Canaan   5.00   4.00
     Nos. 965-967 (3)   7.00   5.60
     With tabs   9.00

Clean Environment — A412

1987, June 14   *Perf. 13*
968   A412   40a multicolored   .75   .45
     With tab   .85

Rabbi Moshe Avigdor Amiel (1883-1945), Founder of Yeshivas — A413

1987, Sept. 10   **Litho.**   *Perf. 14*
969   A413   1.40s multi   1.40   1.40
     With tab   1.50

Synagogue Models, Nahum Goldmann Museum, Tel Aviv — A414

Kupat Holim Health Insurance Institute, 75th Anniv. — A415

1987, Sept. 10   *Perf. 13x14*
970   A414   30a Altneuschul, Prague, 13th cent.   .40   .40
971   A414   50a Aleppo, Syria, 9th cent.   .60   .60
972   A414   60a Florence, Italy, 19th cent.   .75   .75
     Nos. 970-972 (3)   1.75   1.75
     With tabs   1.90
     See Nos. 996-998.

1987, Sept. 10   *Perf. 14*
973   A415   1.50s multi   1.50   1.50
     With tab   1.75

Pinhas Rosen (1887-1978), First Minister of Justice — A416

1987, Nov. 24   **Litho.**   *Perf. 13*
974   A416   80a multicolored   .90   .90
     With tab   1.25

A417

1987, Nov. 24   *Perf. 14*
     Exploration of the Holy Land, 19th cent.: 30a, Thomas Howard Molyneux (1847) and Christopher Costigan (1835). 50a, William Francis Lynch (1848). 60a, John MacGregor (1868-1869).
975   A417   30a multi   .45   .45
976   A417   50a multi   .70   .70
977   A417   60a multi   .85   .55
     Nos. 975-977 (3)   2.00   1.70
     With tabs   2.50

Souvenir Sheet
978   Sheet of 3   4.00   4.00
  a.   A417   40a like #975   .85   .85
  b.   A417   50a like #976   1.25   1.25
  c.   A417   80a like #977   1.75   1.75

     No. 978 sold for 2.50s.

A418   A419

1988, Jan. 26
979   A418   10a Computer technology   .20   .20
980   A418   80a Genetic engineering   .95   .95

981 A418 1.40s Medical engi-
neering   1.60 1.60
Nos. 979-981 (3)   2.75 2.75
With tabs
Industrialization of Israel, cent.

1988, Jan. 26
982 A419 40a multicolored   .50   .50
With tab   .60
Water conservation.

Australia Bicentennial — A420

1988, Jan. 26   *Perf. 14*
983 A420 1s multi   1.25 1.25
With tab   1.50

Sunflower — A421

1988, Mar. 9   Photo.   Perf. 13x14
984 A421 (30a) dk yel grn & yel .25 .25
With tab   .35

A422

Design: Anne Frank (1929-45), Amsterdam
house where she hid.

1988, Apr. 19   *Litho.*
985 A422 60a multicolored   .50   .50
With tab   .60

Independence 40
Stamp Exhibition,
Jerusalem
A423

1988, Apr. 19
Design: Modern Jerusalem.
986 A423 1s shown   .90   .90
With tab   1.00
Souvenir Sheet
987 A423 2s detail from 1s 3.50 3.50
No. 987 sold for 3s.

Memorial
Day
A424

1988, Apr. 19   *Perf. 14x13*
988 A424 40a multicolored   .35   .35
With tab   .45
a. Souvenir sheet of 1   .75   .75
Natl. independence, 40th anniv. No. 988a
contains one stamp like No. 988 but without
copyright inscription LR. Sold for 60a.

Souvenir Sheet

Israel's 40th
Anniv.
Exhibition, Tel
Aviv — A425

Stamps on stamps: a, No. 245. b, No. 297.
c, No. 120. d, No. 96. e, Like No. 794. f, No.
252. g, No. 333. h, No. 478.

1988, June 9   Litho.   Perf. 14
989   Sheet of 8 + label   2.75 2.75
a.-h.   A425 20a any single   .30   .30
Sold for 2.40s. Center label pictures Israel
40 emblem.

B'nai B'rith in
Jerusalem,
Cent. — A426

1988, June 27   *Perf. 14*
990 A426 70a multicolored   .70   .70
With tab   .75

Nature
Reserves in
the Negev
A427

1988, June 27
991 A427 40a Ein Zin   .50   .40
992 A427 60a She'Zaf   .70   .60
993 A427 70a Ramon   .90   .75
Nos. 991-993 (3)   2.10 1.75
With tabs   2.40
See Nos. 1052-1054, 1154-1156.

Agents
Executed
During
World War
II — A428

Portraits: 40a, Havivah Reik (1914-1944).
1.65s, Enzo Hayyim Sereni (1905-1944).

1988, Sept. 1   *Litho.*
994 A428 40a multicolored   .35   .35
995 A428 1.65s multicolored 1.40 1.40
#994-995, with tabs   1.90

Synagogue Models Type of 1987
Models in the Nahum Goldmann Museum,
Tel Aviv: 35a, Kai-Feng Fu Synagogue, 12th
cent., China. 60a, Zabludow Synagogue, 17th
cent., Poland. 70a, Touro Synagogue, 1763,
Newport, Rhode Island, designed by Peter
Harrison.

1988, Sept. 1   *Perf. 13x14*
996 A414 35a multicolored   .30   .30
997 A414 60a multicolored   .55   .55
998 A414 70a multicolored   .65   .65
Nos. 996-998 (3)   1.50 1.50
With tabs   1.60

A429

1988, Nov. 9   *Perf. 14*
999 A429 80a multicolored   .85   .85
With tab   1.00
Kristallnacht, Nazi pogrom in Germany, 50th
anniv.

Moshe Dayan
(1915-1981),
Foreign Minister,
Minister of
Defense — A430

1988, Nov. 9   *Perf. 13*
1000 A430 40a multicolored   .40   .40
With tab   .50

Jewish
Legion,
70th Anniv.
A431

1988, Nov. 9   *Perf. 14*
1001 A431 2s yel brn, sepia & 1.60 1.60
lem
With tab   1.75

Agricultural Achievements — A433

50a, Avocado (fruit-growing). 60a, Lilium
longiflorum (horticulture). 90a, Irrigation.

1988, Dec. 22   *Perf. 14*
1004 A433 50a multicolored   .45   .45
1005 A433 60a multicolored   .55   .55
1006 A433 90a multicolored   .85   .85
Nos. 1004-1006 (3)   1.85 1.85
With tabs   2.00

Natl.
Tourism — A434

1989, Mar. 12   Litho.   Perf. 13
1007 A434   40a Red Sea   .45   .35
1008 A434   60a Dead Sea   .60   .50
1009 A434   70a Mediterranean
Sea   .75   .55
1010 A434 1.70s Sea of Galilee 1.75 1.40
Nos. 1007-1010 (4)   3.55 2.80
With tabs   3.75

Rabbi Judah Leib
Maimon (1875-
1962) — A435

1989, Mar. 12   *Perf. 14*
1011 A435 1.70s multi   1.75 1.25
With tab   2.00

Rashi, Rabbi Solomon Ben Isaac (b.
1039), Talmudic Commentator — A436

1989, Mar. 12
1012 A436 4s buff & black   4.25 3.00
With tab   4.50

Memorial   UNICEF — A438
Day — A437

Fallen Airmen's Memorial at Har Tayassim.

1989, Apr. 30   Litho.   Perf. 14
1013 A437 50a multi   .50   .45
With tab   .60

Archaeology Type of 1986
Gates of Huldah, Temple Compound, Mt.
Moriah: 40a, Rosettes and rhomboids, frieze
and columns, facade of the eastern gate, 1st
cent. B.C. 60a, Corinthian capital, 6th cent.
70a, Bas-relief from the Palace of Umayade
Caliphs, 8th cent. 80a, Corinthian capital from
the Church of Ascension on the Mount of
Olives, 12-13th cent. 90a, Star of David, limestone relief, northern wall, near the new gate,
Suleiman's Wall. 2s, Mamluk relief, 14th century. 10s, Carved frieze from a sepulcher
entrance, end of the Second Temple Period.

1988-90   *Litho.   Perf. 14*
1014 A389 40a multi   .35   .30
1015 A389 60a multi   .50   .40
1016 A389 70a multi   .55   .40
1017 A389 80a multi   .65   .45
1018 A389 90a multi   .65   .45
1019 A389 2s multi   1.40 .95
1020 A389 10s multi   8.75 5.75
Nos. 1014-1020 (7)   12.85 8.70
With tabs   14.00
Issued: 40a, 60a, 12/22/88; 70a, 80a,
6/11/89; 10s, 4/30/89; 90a, 10/17/89; 2s,
6/12/90.

1989, Apr. 30   *Perf. 14*
1022 A438 90a multicolored   .80   .65
With tab   .90

Moshe Smoira
(1888-1961), 1st
Pres. of Israeli
Supreme
Court — A439

1989, June 11   *Perf. 14*
1023 A439 90a deep blue   .80   .65
With tab   .90

13th
Maccabiah
Games,
July 3-13
A440

1989, June 11   *Perf. 13x14*
1024 A440 80a multi   .80   .65
With tab   .90

Ducks — A441

Designs: a, Garganey. b, Mallard. c, Teal. d,
Shelduck.

1989, July 18   Litho.   Perf. 14
1025   Strip of 4   5.75 5.75
With tabs   9.00

a.-d. A441 80a any single   1.25 .85

Souvenir Sheet
1025E   Sheet of 4   7.00 7.00
   f.   A441 80a like No. 1025d   1.60 1.60
   g.   A441 80a like No. 1025b   1.60 1.60
   h.   A441 80a like No. 1025a   1.60 1.60
   i.   A441 80a like No. 1025c   1.60 1.60

World Stamp Expo '89. No. 1025E contains four 29x33mm stamps. Sold for 5s.

Graphic Design Industry — A442

1989, July 18
1026 A442 1s multi   1.00 .75
   With tab   1.10

Souvenir Sheet

French Revolution, Bicent. — A443

1989, July 7
1027 A443 3.50s multi   8.50 8.50
Sold for 5s.

Hebrew Language Council, Cent. — A444

1989, Sept. 3   Litho.   *Perf. 13x14*
1028 A444 1s multi   .95 .70
   With tab   1.10

Rabbi Yehuda Hai Alkalai (1798-1878), Zionist — A445

1989, Sept. 3   *Perf. 14*
1029 A445 2.50s multi   5.00 1.75
   With tab   6.50

Mizrah Festival A446

Paper cutouts: 50a, Menorah and lions, by Gadoliahu Neminsky, Holbenisk, Ukraine, 1921. 70a, Menorah and hands, Morocco, 19th-20th cent. 80a, "Misrah," hunting scene and deer, Germany, 1818.

1989, Sept. 3   *Perf. 14x13*
1030 A446 50a multi   .45 .35
1031 A446 70a multi   .65 .50
1032 A446 80a multi   .75 .55
   Nos. 1030-1032 (3)   1.85 1.40
   With tabs   2.00

Tevel '89 Youth Stamp Exhibition, Oct. 15-21 A447

1989, Oct. 12   Photo.   *Perf. 13x14*
1033 A447 50a multi   .45 .30
   With tab   .60

1st Israeli Stamp Day — A448

1989, Oct. 17   Litho.   *Perf. 14*
1034 A448 1s multi   .85 .75
   With tab   .95

Special Occasions A449

1989, Nov. 17   Photo.   *Perf. 13½x14*
1035 A449 (50a) Good luck   .45 .35
1036 A449 (50a) With love   .45 .35
   a.   Booklet pane of 10   5.00
1037 A449 (50a) See you again   .45 .35
   a.   Booklet pane of 10 + 2 labels   5.75
   b.   Sheet of 20 + 5 labels   11.50
   Nos. 1035-1037 (3)   1.35 1.05
   With tabs   1.75

Nos. 1036a, 1037a contain 5 tete-beche pairs, No. 1037b contains 10 tete-beche pairs. #1037a-1037b had value of 80a when released.
Issued: No. 1036a, Aug. 7, 1990. Nos. 1037a-1037b, June 22, 1993.
See Nos. 1059-1061, 1073-1075.

A450

Design: Tapestry and Rebab, a Stringed Instrument, from the Museum of Bedouin Culture.

1990, Feb. 13   Litho.   *Perf. 13*
1038 A450 1.50s multicolored   1.25 .95
   With tab   1.50

The Circassians in Israel — A451

1990, Feb. 13   Photo.   *Perf. 14x13*
Designs: Circassian folk dancers.
1039 A451 1.50s multicolored   1.25 .95
   With tab   1.50

Rehovot City, Cent. A452

1990, Feb. 13   *Perf. 14*
1040 A452 2s multicolored   1.90 1.40
   With tab   2.25

Souvenir Sheet

Isaiah's Vision of Eternal Peace, by Mordecai Ardon — A453

Series of 3 stained-glass windows, The Hall of Eternal Jewishness and Humanism, Hebrew University Library, Jerusalem: a, "Roads to Jerusalem" (inscription at L). b, Isaiah's prophecy of broken guns beaten into ploughshares (inscription at R).

1990, Apr. 17   Litho.   *Perf. 14*
1041   Sheet of 2   7.00 7.00
   a.-b.   A453 1.50s any single   3.00 3.00

Stamp World London '90. Sold for 4.50s. Also exists imperf. Value $85.

Architecture — A454

Design: 75a, School, Doganya Kibbutz, 1930. 1.10s, Dining hall, Kibbutz Tel Yosef by Leopold Krakauer, 1933. 1.20s, Engel House by Ze'ev Rechter, 1933. 1.40s, Home of Dr. Chaim Weizmann, Rehovot by Erich Mendelsohn, 1936. 1.60s, Jewish Agency for Palestine, Jerusalem, by Yohanan Ratner, 1932.

1990-92   Photo.   *Perf. 14x13½*
1044 A454   75a black, pale grn & buff   .60 .55
1045 A454   1.10s blk, yel & grn   .95 .95
1046 A454   1.20s blk, bl & yel   1.10 1.10
1047 A454   1.40s blk, lt lil & buff   1.25 1.25
1048 A454   1.60s multicolored   1.10 1.10
   a.   Dotted rose lilac background   1.10 1.10
   Nos. 1044-1048 (5)   5.00 4.95
   With tabs   5.25

No. 1051 has a solid bluish lilac background.
Issued: 75a, 4/17; 1.10s, 1.20s, 12/12; 1.40s, 4/9/91; 1.60s, 4/26/92; #1048a, 7/14/96.

Nature Reserves Type of 1988
1990, Apr. 17   Litho.   *Perf. 14*
1052 A427 60a Gamla, Yehudiyya   .55 .45
1053 A427 80a Huleh   .75 .55
1054 A427 90a Mt. Meron   .90 .65
   Nos. 1052-1054 (3)   2.20 1.65
   With tabs   2.50

Memorial Day A456

1990, Apr. 17   Photo.   *Perf. 13x14*
1055 A456 60a Artillery Corps Memorial   .60 .45
   With tab   .80

Intl. Folklore Festival, Haifa — A457

1990, June 12   Litho.   *Perf. 14*
1056   1.90s Denom at UL   2.50 2.50
1057   1.90s Denom at UR   2.50 2.50
   a.   A457 Pair, #1056-1057   5.00 5.00
   With tabs   6.00

Hagana, 70th Anniv. — A459

1990, June 12
1058 A459 1.50s multicolored   1.40 1.40
   With tab   1.50

Special Occasions Type of 1989
1990, June 12   *Perf. 13½x14*
1059 A449 55a Good luck   .50 .35
1060 A449 80a See you again   .75 .50
1061 A449 1s With love   .95 .60
   Nos. 1059-1061 (3)   2.20 1.45
   With tabs   2.50

Spice Boxes — A460

55a, Austro-Hungarian spice box, 19th cent. 80a, Italian, 19th cent. 1s, German, 18th cent.

1990, Sept. 4   Litho.   *Perf. 13x14*
1062 A460 55a sil, gray & blk   .40 .40
1063 A460 80a sil, gray & blk   .60 .60
1064 A460 1s multicolored   .75 .75
   a.   Bklt. pane of 6 (3 #1062, 2 #1063, #1064)   7.50 7.50
   Nos. 1062-1064 (3)   1.75 1.75
   With tabs   1.90

A461

1990, Sept. 4   *Perf. 13*
1065 A461 1.10s Aliya absorption   .85 .85
   With tab   .90

Electronic Mail — A462

1990, Sept. 4   *Perf. 14x13*
1066 A462 1.20s black & grn   .90 .90
   With tab   1.00

Souvenir Sheet

Beersheba '90 Stamp
Exhibition — A463

1990, Sept. 4   **Perf. 13x14**
1067 A463 3s multicolored   5.50 5.50
     Sold for 4s.

Computer
Games — A464

1990, Dec. 12   **Litho.**   **Perf. 13x14**
1068 A464 60a Basketball   .45 .45
1069 A464 60a Chess   .45 .45
1070 A464 60a Auto racing   .45 .45
   Nos. 1068-1070 (3)   1.35 1.35
   With tabs   1.50

Ze'ev Jabotinsky
(1880-1940),
Zionist
Leader — A465

1990, Dec. 12   **Litho.**   **Perf. 13x14**
1071 A465 1.90s multicolored   1.40 1.40
   With tab   1.50

Philately
Day — A466

1990, Dec. 12   **Perf. 14**
1072 A466 1.20s P.O., Yafo, #5   .90 .90
   With tab   1.00

Special Occasions Type of 1989
1991, Feb. 19   **Photo.**   **Perf. 13½x14**
1073 A449 (60a) Happy birthday   .45 .35
1074 A449 (60a) Keep in touch   .45 .35
   a. Booklet pane of 10 + 2 labels   5.75
   b. Sheet of 20 + 5 labels   11.50
1075 A449 (60a) Greetings   .45 .35
   Nos. 1073-1075 (3)   1.35 1.05
   With tabs   1.50

No. 1074a contains 5 tete-beche pairs. No.
1074b contains 10 tete-beche pairs.
Nos. 1074a-1074b had value of 85a when
released.
Issued: Nos. 1074a-1074b, 4/18/94.

Famous
Women
A467

Designs: No. 1076, Sarah Aaronsohn
(1890-1917), World War I heroine. No. 1077,
Rahel Bluwstein (1890-1931), poet. No. 1078,
Lea Goldberg (1911-1970), poet.

1991, Feb. 19   **Perf. 14**
1076 A467 1.30s multicolored   1.10 1.10
1077 A467 1.30s multicolored   1.10 1.10
1078 A467 1.30s multicolored   1.10 1.10
   Nos. 1076-1078 (3)   3.30 3.30
   With tabs   3.50

See Nos. 1096-1097, 1102-1103.

Hadera,
Cent. — A468

1991, Feb. 19   **Perf. 13**
1079 A468 2.50s multicolored   2.00 2.00
   With tab   2.25

Intelligence
Services
Memorial,
G'lilot
A469

1991, Apr. 9   **Litho.**   **Perf. 14**
1080 A469 65a multicolored   .60 .60
   With tab   .70

14th
Hapoel
Games
A470

1991, Apr. 9
1081 A470 60a multicolored   .55 .50
1082 A470 90a multicolored   .75 .70
1083 A470 1.10s multicolored   .95 .90
   Nos. 1081-1083 (3)   2.25 2.10
   With tabs   2.50

Electrification
A471

Designs: 70a, First power station, Tel Aviv,
1923. 90a, Yarden Power Station, Naharayim,
1932. 1.20s, Rutenberg Power Station,
Ashqelon, 1991.

1991, June 11   **Litho.**   **Perf. 13**
1084 A471 70a multicolored   .65 .60
1085 A471 90a multicolored   .80 .75
1086 A471 1.20s multicolored   1.10 1.00
   Nos. 1084-1086 (3)   2.55 2.35
   With tabs   2.75

Rabbi Shimon
Hakham (1843-
1910)
A472

1991, June 11
1087 A472 2.10s multicolored   1.90 1.50
   With tab   2.00

Souvenir Sheet

Postal and Philatelic Museum, Tel
Aviv — A473

Israel #5, Palestine #70, Turkey #133.

1991, June 11   **Perf. 14x13**
1088 A473 3.40s multicolored   7.00 7.00

No. 1088 sold for 5s. Exists imperf. Value
$90.

A474

Jewish Festivals: 65a, Man blowing ram's
horn, Rosh Hashanah. 1s, Father blessing
children, Yom Kippur. 1.20s, Family seated at
harvest table, Sukkoth.

1991, Aug. 27   **Litho.**   **Perf. 14**
1089 A474 65a multicolored   .50 .50
1090 A474 1s multicolored   .75 .75
1091 A474 1.20s multicolored   .90 .90
   Nos. 1089-1091 (3)   2.15 2.15
   With tabs   2.50

Jewish Chronicle,
150th
Anniv. — A475

1991, Aug. 27
1092 A475 1.50s multicolored   1.10 1.10
   With tab   1.25

Baron Maurice De Hirsch (1831-1896),
Founder of Jewish Colonization
Assoc. — A476

1991, Aug. 27   **Perf. 14**
1093 A476 1.60s multicolored   1.25 1.25
   With tab   1.40

Souvenir Sheet

Haifa, by Gustav Bauernfeind — A477

1991, Aug. 27   **Perf. 14x13**
1094 A477 3s multicolored   6.25 5.00

Haifa '91, Israeli-Polish Philatelic Exhibition.
Sold for 4s.

Philately
Day — A478

1991, Dec. 2   **Litho.**   **Perf. 13**
1095 A478 70a #2 on piece   .50 .50
   With tab   .60

Famous Women Type of 1991
Designs: 1s, Rahel Yanait Ben-Zvi (1886-
1979), politician. 1.10s, Dona Gracia (Nasi,
1510?-1569), philanthropist.

1991, Dec. 2   **Litho.**   **Perf. 14**
1096 A467 1s multicolored   .70 .70
1097 A467 1.10s multicolored   .75 .75
   #1096-1097, with tabs   1.60

1992 Summer
Olympics,
Barcelona — A479

1991, Dec. 2
1098 A479 1.10s multicolored   .85 .85
   With tab   1.40

Lehi — A480   Etzel — A481

1991, Dec. 2   **Perf. 14**
1099 A480 1.50s multicolored   1.00 1.00
   With tab   1.25

1991, Dec. 2
1100 A481 1.50s blk & red   1.00 1.00
   With tab   1.25

Wolfgang
Amadeus Mozart,
Death
Bicent. — A482

1991, Dec. 2   **Perf. 13**
1101 A482 2s multicolored   2.75 1.75
   With tab   3.25
   a. Booklet pane of 4   11.00

One pair in No. 1101a is tete beche.

Famous Women Type of 1991
80a, Hanna Rovina (1889-1980), actress.
1.30s, Rivka Guber (1902-81), educator.

1992, Feb. 18   **Litho.**   **Perf. 14**
1102 A467 80a multicolored   .50 .50
1103 A467 1.30s multicolored   .90 .90
   #1102-1103, with tabs   1.50

Sea of Galilee   Anemone
A483   A483a

1992, Feb. 18

1104	A483	85a Trees	1.50	.70
1105	A483	85a Sailboat	1.50	.70
1106	A483	85a Fish	1.50	.70
a.		Strip of 3, #1104-1106	4.50	2.10
		With tabs	5.00	

1992, Feb. 18 — Photo. — Perf. 13x14

1107	A483a	(75a) multi	.50	.45
		With tab	.60	

PALMAH, 50th Anniv. A484

The Samaritans A485

1992, Feb. 18 — Litho. — Perf. 14

1108	A484	1.50s multicolored	1.00	1.00
		With tab	1.25	

1992, Feb. 18

1109	A485	2.60s multicolored	1.75	1.75
		With tab	2.25	

Rabbi Hayyim Joseph Joseph David Azulai (1724-1806) A486

Rabbi Joseph Hayyim Ben Elijah (1834-1909) A487

1992, Apr. 26 — Perf. 13

1110	A486	85a multicolored	.60	.60

Perf. 14

1111	A487	1.20s multicolored	.80	.80
		#1110-1111, with tabs	1.75	

Discovery of America, 500th Anniv. A488

1992, Apr. 26 — Perf. 14

1112	A488	1.60s multicolored	1.25	1.25
		With tab	1.40	

Memorial Day — A488a

1992, Apr. 26 — Litho. — Perf. 13

1113	A488a	85a multicolored	.55	.55
		With tab	.60	

Souvenir Sheet

Expulsion of Jews from Spain, 500th Anniv. A489

Designs: No. 1114a, 80a, Map of Palestine. b, 1.10s, Map of Italy, Sicily, Greece and central Mediterranean. c, 1.40s, Map of Spain and Portugal.

1992, Apr. 26 — Perf. 14

1114	A489	Sheet of 3, #a.-c.	3.75	3.75

Jaffa-Jerusalem Railway, Cent. — A490

Different train and four scenes on each stamp showing railroad equipment and memorabilia.

1992

1115	A490	85a multicolored	.65	.60
1116	A490	1s multicolored	.80	.75
1117	A490	1.30s multicolored	1.00	.95
1118	A490	1.60s multicolored	1.25	1.10
		#1115-1118, with tabs	4.00	
a.		Bklt. pane of 4, #1115-1118	4.00	

Souvenir Sheet

1118B		Sheet of 4 + 4 labels	4.75	4.75
c.		A490 50a like #1118	1.00	1.00
d.		A490 50a like #1117	1.00	1.00
e.		A490 50a like #1115	1.00	1.00
f.		A490 50a like #1116	1.00	1.00

Nos. 1115 and 1118, 1116 and 1117 are tete beche in No. 1118a. Nos. 1118c and 1118f, 1118d and 1118e are tete beche in No. 1118B.

Issued: #1118B, Sept. 17; others June 16.

Rabbi Hayyim Benatar (1696-1743) A491

Rabbi Shalom Sharabi (1720-1777) A492

1992, June 16 — Perf. 13

1119	A491	1.30s multicolored	.90	.90
1120	A492	3s multicolored	2.00	2.00
		#1119-1120, with tabs	3.25	

Jewish Natl. & University Library, Jerusalem, Cent. — A493

85a, Parables, 1491. 1s, Italian manuscript, 15th cent. 1.20s, Bible translation by Martin Buber.

1992, Sept. 17 — Litho. — Perf. 13x14

1121	A493	85a multicolored	.55	.55
1122	A493	1s multicolored	.65	.65
1123	A493	1.20s multicolored	.80	.80
		Nos. 1121-1123 (3)	2.00	2.00
		With tabs	2.25	

Supreme Court A494

1992, Sept. 17 — Perf. 14

1124	A494	3.60s multicolored	2.10	2.10
		With tab	2.25	

Wild Animals A495

#1125, Panthera pardus saxicolor. #1126, Elephas maximus. #1127, Pan troglodytes. #1128, Panthera leo persica.

1992, Sept. 17

1125	A495	50a multicolored	.50	.50
1126	A495	50a multicolored	.50	.50
1127	A495	50a multicolored	.50	.50
1128	A495	50a multicolored	.50	.50
a.		Strip of 4, #1125-1128	2.25	2.25
		With tabs	2.50	

European Unification A496

1992, Dec. 8 — Litho. — Perf. 13

1129	A496	1.50s multicolored	.90	.90
		With tab	1.00	

Stamp Day.

First Hebrew Film, 75th Anniv. — A497

Films: 80a, Liberation of the Jews, 1918. 2.70s, Oded, the Vagabond, 1932, first Hebrew feature film. 3.50s, The Promised Land, 1935, first Hebrew talkie.

1992, Dec. 8

1130	A497	80a multicolored	.60	.60
1131	A497	2.70s multicolored	1.90	1.90
1132	A497	3.50s multicolored	2.50	2.50
		Nos. 1130-1132 (3)	5.00	5.00
		With tabs	5.25	

Birds — A498

1992-98 — Photo. — Perf. 13x14

1133	A498	10a Wallcreeper	.20	.20
1134	A498	20a Tristram's grackle	.20	.20
1135	A498	30a White wagtail	.20	.20
1137	A498	50a Palestine sunbird	.30	.20
1141	A498	85a Sinai rosefinch	.45	.30
1142	A498	90a Swallow	.60	.60
1142A	A498	1s Trumpeter finch	.65	.65
b.		Violet background	.65	.65
1143	A498	1.30s Graceful warbler	.70	.45
1144	A498	1.50s Black-eared wheatear	.85	.55
1146	A498	1.70s Common bulbul	.85	.55
		Nos. 1133-1146 (10)	5.00	3.90
		With tabs	5.25	

No. 1142A has a gray background.

Souvenir Sheet

Designs: a, like #1133. b, like #1137. c, like #1135. d, like #1134. e, like #1141. f, like #1144. g, like #1146. h, like #1142A. i, like #1143. j, like #1142.

Litho. — Perf. 14

1152		Sheet of 10	6.00	6.00
a.-j.		A498 30a Any single	.50	.50

Nos. 1152a-1152j, issued for China '96, 9th Asian Intl. Philatelic Exhibition, have color variations and a gray border.

Issued: 10a, 20a, 30a, 90a, 12/8; 1.30s, 1.70s, 12/9/93; 50a, 1.50s, 2/16/93; 85a, 2/8/94; 1s, 6/7/95; #1152, 4/17/96; #1142Ab, 11/22/98.

This is an expanding set. Numbers may change.

Menachem Begin (1913-92), Prime Minister 1977-83 — A499

1993, Feb. 16 — Litho. — Perf. 13

1153	A499	80a multicolored	.45	.45
		With tab	.50	

Nature Reserves Type of 1988

1993, Feb. 16 — Perf. 14

1154	A427	1.20s Hof Dor	.70	.70
1155	A427	1.50s Nahal Ammud	.90	.90
1156	A427	1.70s Nahal Ayun	.95	.95
		Nos. 1154-1156 (3)	2.55	2.55
		With tabs	2.75	

Baha'i World Center, Haifa — A500

1993, Feb. 16 — Perf. 13

1157	A500	3.50s multicolored	3.25	2.25
		With tab	5.25	

Medical Corps Memorial — A501

1993, Apr. 18 — Litho. — Perf. 13

1158	A501	80a multicolored	.45	.45
		With tab	.55	

Scientific Concepts A502

Warsaw Ghetto Uprising, 50th Anniv. A503

1993, Apr. 18 — Perf. 14

1159	A502	80a Principle of lift	.50	.50
1160	A502	80a Waves	.50	.50
1161	A502	80a Color mixing	.50	.50
1162	A502	80a Eye's memory	.50	.50
a.		Strip of 4, #1159-1162	2.00	2.00
		With tabs	2.25	

1993, Apr. 18 — Perf. 14

1163	A503	1.20s gray, black & yel	.80	.80
		With tab	.85	

See Poland No. 3151.

Independence, 45th Anniv. — A504

1993, Apr. 18 — Perf. 14

1164	A504	3.60s multicolored	2.25	2.25
		With tab	2.50	

Giulio Racah (1909-1965),
Physicist — A505

1.20s, Aharon Katchalsky-Katzir (1913-72),
chemist.

1993, June 29   Photo.   Perf. 13x14
1165 A505 80a magenta, bister
            & blue   .45 .45
1166 A505 1.20s magenta, bister
            & blue   .65 .65
     #1165-1166, with tabs   1.25

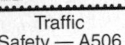

Traffic Safety — A506

Fight Against Drugs — A507

Children's drawings: 80a, Family crossing
street. 1.20s, Traffic signs. 1.50s, Traffic director with hand as face.

1993, June 29   Litho.   Perf. 14
1167 A506 80a multicolored   .50 .50
1168 A506 1.20s multicolored   .80 .80
1169 A506 1.50s multicolored   .95 .95
     Nos. 1167-1169 (3)   2.25 2.25
     With tabs   2.50

1993, June 29   Perf. 14
1170 A507 2.80s multicolored   1.75 1.75
     With tab   1.90

14th Maccabiah Games A508

1993, June 29   Perf. 14
1171 A508 3.60s multicolored   2.25 2.25
     With tab   2.50

Respect for the Elderly A509

Festivals A510

1993, Aug. 22   Litho.   Perf. 14
1172 A509 80a multicolored   .50 .50
     With tab   .55

1993, Aug. 22   Perf. 14
1173 A510 80a Wheat   .55 .55
1174 A510 1.20s Grapes   .75 .75
1175 A510 1.50s Olives   .95 .95
     Nos. 1173-1175 (3)   2.25 2.25
     With tabs   2.50

Environmental Protection — A511

1993, Aug. 22
1176 A511 1.20s multicolored   .80 .80
     With tab   .85

B'nai B'rith, 150th Anniv. — A512

1993, Aug. 22   Perf. 13
1177 A512 1.50s multicolored   .90 .90
     With tab   1.00

Souvenir Sheet

Telafila '93, Israel-Romania Philatelic
Exhibition — A513

3.60s, Immigrant Ship, by Marcel Janco.

1993, Aug. 21   Litho.   Perf. 14x13
1178 A513 3.60s multicolored   2.50 2.50

Hebrew Magazines for Children, Cent. A514

1993, Dec. 9   Litho.   Perf. 14
1179 A514 1.50s multicolored   .90 .90
     With tab   1.00

Philately Day.

Hanukkah A515

Hanukkah lamp with candles lit and: 90a, Oil
lamp, Talmudic Period. 1.30s, Hanukkah
Lamp, Eretz Israel carved stone, 20th cent. 2s,
Lighting the Hanukkah Lamp, Rothschild Mis-
cellany illuminated manuscript, c. 1470.
#1183, Moroccan lamp, Mazagan. #1184:
Folding Hanukkah Lamp, Lodz Ghetto, 1944.
2.10s, Coin of the Bar-Kokhba War. 1.80s,
Cubic copper savivon (dreidel). 2.15s, Hanuk-
kah lamp "Mattathias the Hasmonean," by
Boris Schatz.

1993-99
1180 A515 90a multicolored   .55 .55
1181 A515 1.30s multicolored   .80 .80
1182 A515 2s multicolored   1.25 1.25
1183 A515 1.50s multicolored   .90 .90
1184 A515 1.50s multicolored   1.00 1.00
1185 A515 2.10s multicolored   1.25 1.25
1186 A515 1.80s multicolored   1.00 1.00
1187 A515 2.15s multicolored   1.10 1.10
     Nos. 1180-1187 (8)   7.85 7.85
     With tabs   8.75

The numbering of this set reflects the lighting of the candles on the Menorah.
     Issued: 90a, 1.30s, 2s, 12/9/93; #1183,
11/27/94; #1184, 12/14/95; #1185-1186,
12/23/97; 2.15s, 1/5/99.
     This is an expanding set. Numbers have
been reserved for additional values.

Beetles A516

#1189, Graphopterus serrator. #1190, Poto-
sia cuprea. #1191, Coccinella
septempunctata. #1192, Chlorophorus varius.

1994, Feb. 8   Litho.   Perf. 14
1189 A516 85a multicolored   .45 .40
1190 A516 85a multicolored   .45 .40
1191 A516 85a multicolored   .45 .40
1192 A516 85a multicolored   .45 .40
  a. Bklt. pane, 2 each #1189-1192 4.25
     Nos. 1189-1192 (4)   1.80 1.60
     With tabs   1.90

Health — A517

1994, Feb. 8   Perf. 13
1193 A517 85a Exercise   .55 .40
1194 A517 1.30s Don't smoke   .75 .60
1195 A517 1.60s Eat sensibly   .95 .75
     Nos. 1193-1195 (3)   2.25 1.75
     With tabs   2.50

Mordecai Haffkine (1860-1930),
Developer of Cholera Vaccine — A518

1994, Feb. 8   Perf. 14
1196 A518 3.85s multicolored   2.25 1.75
     With tab   2.50

Intl. Style Architecture in Tel Aviv, 1930-39 A519

#1197, Citrus House, by Karl Rubin, 1936-
38. #1198, Assuta Hospital, by Yosef Neufeld,
1934-35. #1199, Cooperative Workers' Housing, by Arieh Sharon, 1934-36.

1994, Apr. 5   Perf. 14
1197 A519 85a multicolored   .50 .50
1198 A519 85a multicolored   .50 .50
1199 A519 85a multicolored   .50 .50
     Nos. 1197-1199 (3)   1.50 1.50
     With tabs   1.60

Memorial Day — A520

85a, Monument to fallen soldiers of Communications, Electronics & Computer Corps,
Yehud.

1994, Apr. 5   Litho.   Perf. 14
1200 A520 85a multicolored   .50 .50
     With tab   .55

Prevent Violence — A521

1994, Apr. 5   Perf. 13
1201 A521 3.85s black & red   2.10 2.10
     With tab   2.25

Saul Adler (1895-1966),
Scientist — A522

1994, Apr. 5   Perf. 14
1202 A522 4.50s multicolored   2.60 2.60
     With tab   2.75

Hot Air Ballooning A523

#1203, Filling balloon. #1204, Balloons in
flight. #1205, Marking target.

1994, June 21   Litho.   Perf. 14
1203 A523 85a multicolored   .50 .50
1204 A523 85a multicolored   .50 .50
1205 A523 85a multicolored   .50 .50
     Nos. 1203-1205 (3)   1.50 1.50
     With tabs   1.60

Tarbut Elementary Schools, 75th Anniv. A524

1994, June 21
1206 A524 1.30s multicolored   .80 .80
     With tab   .90

Antoine de St. Exupery (1900-44) A525

1994, June 21
1207 A525 5s multicolored   3.00 3.00
     With tab   3.25

Intl. Olympic Committee, Cent. — A526

Peace — A527

1994, June 21
1208 A526 2.25s multicolored   1.40 1.40
     With tab   1.50

1994, Aug. 23   Litho.   Perf. 14
1209 A527 90a multicolored   .55 .55
     With tab   .60

Peace Between Arabs and Israelis.

Children's Drawings of Bible Stories A528

Designs: 85a, Adam and Eve. 1.30s,
Jacob's Dream. 1.60s, Moses in the Bul-
rushes. 4s, Parting of the Red Sea.

1994, Aug. 23
1210	A528	85a multicolored	.50	.50
1211	A528	1.30s multicolored	.80	.80
1212	A528	1.60s multicolored	.95	.95
		Nos. 1210-1212 (3)	2.25	2.25
			2.50	

Souvenir Sheet
Perf. 13x14

1213	A528	4s multicolored	2.75	2.75

No. 1213 contains one 40x51mm stamp.

Immigration to Israel — A529

1994, Aug. 23   **Perf. 13**
1214	A529	Third Aliya	.80	.80
1215	A529	1.70s Fourth Aliya	.95	.95
		#1214-1215, with tabs	1.90	

Israel-Jordan Peace Treaty — A530

1994, Oct. 26   Litho.   Perf. 14
1216	A530	3.50s multicolored	2.00	2.00
		With tab	2.25	

Public Transportation — A531

Designs: 90a, Ford Model T's, 1920's. 1.40s, White Super buses, 1940's. 1.70s, Leyland Royal Tiger buses, 1960's.

1994, Nov. 27
1217	A531	90a multicolored	.55	.55
1218	A531	1.40s multicolored	.90	.90
1219	A531	1.70s multicolored	1.00	1.00
		Nos. 1217-1219 (3)	2.45	2.45
		With tabs	2.75	

Computerization of Post Offices — A532

1994, Nov. 27
1220	A532	3s multicolored	1.90	1.90
		With tab	2.00	

Dreyfus Affair, Cent. A533

1994, Nov. 27
1221	A533	4.10s multicolored	2.50	2.50
		With tab	2.75	

Outdoor Sculpture A534

Designs: 90a, Serpentine, by Itzhak Danziger (1916-77), Yarkon Park, Tel Aviv. 1.40s, Stabile, by Alexander Calder (1898-1976), Mount Herzl, Jerusalem. 1.70s, Gate to the Hall of Remembrance, by David Palombo (1920-66), Yad Vashem, Jerusalem.

1995, Feb. 7   Litho.   Perf. 14x13
1222	A534	90a multicolored	.55	.55
1223	A534	1.40s multicolored	.90	.90
1224	A534	1.70s multicolored	1.00	1.00
		Nos. 1222-1224 (3)	2.45	2.45
		With tabs	2.75	

Jewish Composers A535

Title of work, composer: No. 1225, Schelomo, by Ernest Bloch (1880-1959). No. 1226, Symphony No. 1 - Jeremiah, by Leonard Bernstein (1918-90).

1995, Feb. 7
1225	A535	4.10s multicolored	2.50	2.50
1226	A535	4.10s multicolored	2.50	2.50
		#1225-1226, with tabs	5.50	

See Nos. 1231-1232, 1274-1275.

Ordnance Corps Monument, Netanya — A536

1995, Apr. 25   Litho.   Perf. 13
1227	A536	1s multicolored	.65	.65
		With tab	.70	

End of World War II, Liberation of Concentration Camps, 50th Anniv. — A537

1995, Apr. 25   Perf. 14x13
1228	A537	1s multicolored	.65	.65
		With tab	.70	

Souvenir Sheet
1229	A537	2.50s like #1228	1.60	1.60

No. 1229 contains one 51x40mm stamp.

UN, 50th Anniv. A538

1995, Apr. 25   Perf. 14
1230	A538	1.50s multicolored	.90	.90
		With tab	1.00	

Composer Type of 1995

#1231, Arnold Schoenberg (1874-1951). #1232, Darius Milhaud (1892-1974).

1995, Apr. 25
1231	A535	2.40s multicolored	1.50	1.50
1232	A535	2.40s multicolored	1.50	1.50
		#1231-1232, with tabs	3.25	

Souvenir Sheet

Jewish Volunteers to British Army in World War II — A539

1995, Apr. 25
1233	A539	2.50s multicolored	1.75	1.75
		With tab	2.00	

15th Hapoel Games, Ramat Gan A540

1995, June 7   Litho.   Perf. 14
1234	A540	1s Kayak	.65	.65
		With tab	.70	

Kites — A541

Designs: No. 1235, Hexagonal "Tiara" kite, bird-shaped kite, rhombic Eddy kite. No. 1236, Drawing of kite glider, "Cody War Kite," box kite. No. 1237, Rhombic aerobatic kites, aerobatic "Delta" kite, drawing by Otto Lilienthal.

1995, June 7
1235		1s multicolored	.65	.65
1236		1s multicolored	.65	.65
1237		1s multicolored	.65	.65
a.	A541	Strip of 3, #1235-1237	2.00	2.00
		With tabs	2.25	

Children's Books A542

Designs: 1s, Stars in a Bucket, by Anda Amir-Pinkerfeld. 1.50s, Hurry, Run, Dwarfs, by Miriam Yallan-Stekelis. 1.80s, Daddy's Big Umbrella, by Levin Kipnis.

1995, June 7
1238	A542	1s multicolored	.65	.65
1239	A542	1.50s multicolored	1.00	1.00
1240	A542	1.80s multicolored	1.25	1.25
		Nos. 1238-1240 (3)	2.90	2.90
		With tabs	3.25	

Zim Israel Navigation Co. Ltd., 50th Anniv. A543

1995, June 7
1241	A543	4.40s multicolored	3.00	3.00
		With tab	3.25	

Festivals A544

Designs: 1s, Elijah's Chair for circumcision, linen cloth. 1.50s, Tallit bag, usually a Bar-Mitzvah gift. 1.80s, Marriage Stone for breaking glass at wedding, cloth.

1995, Sept. 4   Litho.   Perf. 14
1242	A544	1s multicolored	.65	.65
1243	A544	1.50s multicolored	1.00	1.00
1244	A544	1.80s multicolored	1.25	1.25
		Nos. 1242-1244 (3)	2.90	2.90
		With tabs	3.25	

Jerusalem, 3000th Anniv. A545

Designs: 1s, 6th Cent. mosaic pavement, Gaza Synagogue. 1.50s, 19th Cent. illustration of city from map of Eretz Israel, by Rabbi Pinie of Safed. 1.80s, Aerial photograph of Knesset, Supreme Court.

1995, Sept. 4
1245	A545	1s multicolored	.65	.65
1246	A545	1.50s multicolored	1.00	1.00
1247	A545	1.80s multicolored	1.25	1.25
		Nos. 1245-1247 (3)	2.90	2.90
		With tabs	3.25	

Veterinary Services, 75th Anniv. A546

1995, Sept. 4
1248	A546	4.40s multicolored	3.00	3.00
			3.25	

Yitzhak Rabin (1922-95), Prime Minister A547

1995, Dec. 5
1249	A547	5s multicolored	3.25	3.25
		With tab	3.50	

Fire Fighting and Rescue Service, 70th Anniv. A548

Designs: No. 1250, Fighting fire. No. 1251, Rescue vehicle, fireman beside car.

1995, Dec. 14
1250	A548	1s multicolored	.65	.65
1251	A548	1s multicolored	.65	.65
		#1250-1251, with tabs	1.50	

Model Planes A549

1995, Dec. 14
1252	A549	1.80s multicolored	1.25	1.25
		With tab	1.40	

Philately Day.

Motion Pictures, Cent. A550

Silhouettes of people in theater viewing: 4.40s, Marx Brothers, Simone Signoret, Peter Sellers, Danny Kaye, Al Jolson.

1995, Dec. 14
1253	A550	4.40s multicolored	3.00	3.00
		With tab	3.25	

Souvenir Sheet

Jerusalem, City of David, 3000th Anniv. A551

Designs: a, Mosaic pavement of King David playing harp, Gaza Synagogue, 6th cent. CE. b, Map of Eretz Israel drawn by Rabbi Pinie, 19th cent. c, Present day aerial view of Knesset and Supreme Court.

1995, Dec. 16

1254		Sheet of 3	2.75	2.75
a.	A551	1s multicolored	.60	.60
b.	A551	1.50s multicolored	.90	.90
c.	A551	1.80s multicolored	1.25	1.25

Sports — A552

1996-98 Photo. Perf. 13x14

1256	A552	1.05s Mountain cycling	.65	.65
1257	A552	1.10s Horseback riding	.65	.65
a.		Booklet pane of 20	13.00	
		Complete booklet, #1257a	13.00	
1258	A552	1.80s Water skiing	1.00	1.00
1259	A552	1.90s Paragliding	1.25	1.25
1260	A552	2s Women's volleyball	1.25	1.25
1261	A552	2.20s Whitewater rafting	1.25	1.25
1262	A552	3s Beach bat & ball	1.75	1.75
1263	A552	5s Archery	3.00	3.00
1264	A552	10s Rappelling	5.75	5.75
		Nos. 1256-1264 (9)	16.55	16.55
		With tabs	18.50	

Issued: 1.05s, 1.90s, 2s, 2/20/96; 1.10s, 5s, 2/13/97; 10s, 7/8/97; 3s, 9/23/97; 1258, 1261, 2/17/98.

Souvenir Sheet

Synagogue, Dura-Europos, Syria, 3rd Century A.D. — A553

Murals from synagogue walls: a, Temple, walls of Jerusalem. b, Torah Ark niche. c, Anointing of David as king by Prophet Samuel.

1996, Feb. 20 Litho. Perf. 14x13

1266	A553	Sheet of 3	2.75	2.75
a.		1.05s multicolored	.60	.60
b.		1.60s multicolored	.90	.90
c.		1.90s multicolored	1.25	1.25

Jerusalem, 3000th anniv.

Israel Cattle Breeders' Assoc., 70th Anniv. A554

1996, Feb. 20 Perf. 14

1267	A554	4.65s multicolored	3.00	3.00
		With tab	3.25	

Hebrew Writers' Assoc., 75th Anniv. — A555

No. 1269: a, M.J. Berdyczewski. b, Yehuda Burla. c, Devorah Baron. d, Haim Hazaz. e, J.L. Gordon. f, Joseph Hayyim Brenner. g, Abraham Shlonsky. h, Yaakov Shabtai. i, I.L. Peretz. j, Nathan Alterman. k, Saul Tchernichowsky. l, Amir Gilboa. m, Yokheved Bat-Miriam. n, Mendele Mokher Sefarim.

1996, Apr. 17 Litho. Perf. 14

1269		Pane of 14	3.50	3.50
a.-n.	A555	40a Any single	.25	.25

Manufacturers Assoc. of Israel, 75th Anniv. — A556

1996, Apr. 17

1271	A556	1.05s multicolored	.65	.65
		With tab	.75	

Monument to the Fallen Israel Police A557

1996, Apr. 17

1272	A557	1.05s multicolored	.65	.65
		With tab	.75	

Settlement of Metulla, Cent. — A558

1996, Apr. 17

1273	A558	1.90s multicolored	1.25	1.25
		With tab	1.40	

Composer Type of 1995

Designs: No. 1274, Felix Mendelssohn (1809-47). No. 1275, Gustav Mahler (1860-1911).

1996 Litho. Perf. 14

1274	A535	4.65s multicolored	3.00	3.00
1275	A535	4.65s multicolored	3.00	3.00
		#1274-1275, with tabs	6.50	

Issued: #1275, 4/17/96; #1274, 6/25/96.

A559   A560

1996, June 25

1276	A559	1.05s multicolored	.65	.65
		With tab	.75	

Eleven Jewish settlements in Negev Desert, 50th Anniv.

1996, June 25

1277	A560	1.05s Fencing	.65	.65
1278	A560	1.60s Pole vault	1.00	1.00
1279	A560	1.90s Wrestling	1.25	1.25
a.		Booklet pane of 6, 1 #1277, 2 #1278, 3 #1279	6.50	
		Complete booklet, #1279a	6.50	
		Nos. 1277-1279 (3)	2.90	2.90
		With tabs	3.25	

1996 Summer Olympics, Atlanta.

Fruit A561

1.05s, Orange, "sweety", kumquat, lemon. 1.60s, Avocado, persimmon, date, mango, grapes. 1.90s, Carambola, lychee, papaya.

1996, June 25

1280	A561	1.05s multicolored	.65	.65
1281	A561	1.60s multicolored	1.00	1.00
1282	A561	1.90s multicolored	1.25	1.25
		Nos. 1280-1282 (3)	2.90	2.90
		With tabs	3.25	

Public Works Department, 75th Anniv. — A562

1996, Sept. 3 Litho. Perf. 14

1283	A562	1.05s multicolored	.65	.65
		With tab	.75	

Festivals A563

Stylized designs: 1.05s, Bowl of honey, two lighted candles, Rosh Hashanah. 1.60s, Sukka booth, Sukkot. 1.90s, Inside of synagogue during Torah reading, Simchat Torah.

1996, Sept. 3

1284	A563	1.05s multicolored	.65	.65
1285	A563	1.60s multicolored	1.00	1.00
1286	A563	1.90s multicolored	1.25	1.25
		Nos. 1284-1286 (3)	2.90	2.90
		With tabs	3.25	

1st Zionist Congress, Cent. — A564

Designs: 4.65s, Tapestry of Theodore Herzl, David's Tower, shining sun. 5s, Casino building, Basel, site of first congress.

1996, Sept. 3

1287	A564	4.65s multicolored	3.00	3.00
		With tab	3.25	

Souvenir Sheet

1288	A564	5s multicolored	3.00	3.00

No. 1288 contains one 40x51mm stamp.

Hanukkah A565

Serpentine Die Cut 11

1996, Oct. 22 Photo.

1289	A565	2.50s multicolored	1.50	1.50
		With tab	1.60	

See US No. 3118.

Ha-Shilo'ah, Cent., edited by Ahad Ha'am (1856-1927) — A566

1996, Dec. 5 Litho. Perf. 14

1290	A566	1.15s multicolored	.70	.70
		With tab	.80	

Coexistence: Man and Animals — A567

1996, Dec. 5

1291	A567	1.10s Birds, aircraft	.65	.65
1292	A567	1.75s Pets	1.10	1.10
1293	A567	2s Dolphins	1.25	1.25
		Nos. 1291-1293 (3)	3.00	3.00
		With tabs	3.25	

Space Research in Israel A568

1996, Dec. 5

1294	A568	2.05s multicolored	1.25	1.25
		With tab	1.40	

Philately Day.

UOAD (Umbrella Organization of Associations for the Disabled) — A569

1996, Dec. 5

1295	A569	5s multicolored	3.00	3.00
		With tab	3.25	

Souvenir Sheet

Inventors — A570

Designs: a, 1.50s, Alexander Graham Bell (1847-1922). b, 2s, Thomas Alva Edison (1847-1931).

1997, Feb. 13 Litho. Perf. 13

1296	A570	Sheet of 2, #a.-b.	2.25	2.25

Hong Kong '97.

Ethnic Costumes A571

1.10s, Ethiopia. 1.70s, Kurdistan. 2s, Salonica.

1997, Feb. 13 Perf. 14

1297	A571	1.10s multicolored	.65	.65
1298	A571	1.70s multicolored	1.00	1.00
1299	A571	2s multicolored	1.25	1.25
		Nos. 1297-1299 (3)	2.90	2.90
		With tabs	3.25	

Miguel de Cervantes (1547-1616), Writer — A572

1997, Feb. 13
1300 A572 3s multicolored 1.75 1.75
With tab 2.00

Mounument to the Fallen Soldiers of
the Logistics Corps
A573

1997, Apr. 30   Litho.   Perf. 14
1301 A573 1.10s multicolored .65 .65
With tab .70

A574   A575

Jewish monuments in Prague: No. 1302,
Tombstone of Rabbi Judah Loew MaHaRal.
No. 1303, Altneuschul Synagogue.

1997, Apr. 30
1302 A574 1.70s blue & multi 1.00 1.00
1303 A574 1.70s red & multi 1.00 1.00
a. Sheet, 4 each, #1302-1303 8.00 8.00
    #1302-1303, with tabs 2.25

Stamps in No. 1303a do not have tabs.
See Czech Republic Nos. 3009-3010.

1997, Apr. 30

Design: "The Vilna Gaon," Rabbi Elijah Ben
Solomon Zalman (1720-97).

1304 A575 2s multicolored 1.25 1.25
With tab 1.40

Organized
Clandestine
Immigration (1934-
48) — A576

1997, Apr. 30
1305 A576 5s multicolored 3.00 3.00
With tab 3.25

Souvenir Sheet

Discovery of the Cairo Geniza, Cent.,
Discovery of Dead Sea Scrolls, 50th
Anniv. — A577

Designs: a, 2s, Ben Ezra Synagogue, Cairo.
b, 3s, Cliffs, Dead Sea, Prof. Sukenik examining scrolls.

1997, May 29   Litho.   Perf. 13
1306 A577 Sheet of 2, #a.-b. 3.00 3.00

Pacific '97.

Hello First
Grade
A578

1997, July 8   Litho.   Perf. 14
1307 A578 1.10s multicolored .65 .65
With tab .70

Road
Safety — A579

#1308, "Keep in Lane," car sinking into lake,
fish. #1309, "Keep Your Distance," car with
bird on front grille. #1310, "Don't Drink and
Drive," man holding drink, car balanced on
edge of cliff.

1997, July 8   Perf. 13
1308 A579 1.10s multicolored .65 .65
1309 A579 1.10s multicolored .65 .65
1310 A579 1.10s multicolored .65 .65
    Nos. 1308-1310 (3) 1.95 1.95
    With tabs 2.25

15th
Maccabiah
Games
A580

1997, July 8   Perf. 14
1311 A580 5s Ice skating 3.00 3.00
With tab 3.25

Festival
Stamps — A581

The Visiting Patriarchs, Sukkot: 1.10s, Abraham. 1.70s, Isaac. 2s, Jacob.

1997, Sept. 23   Litho.   Perf. 14
1312 A581 1.10s multicolored .60 .60
1313 A581 1.70s multicolored .95 .95
1314 A581 2s multicolored 1.10 1.10
a. Booklet pane, 1 #1312, 2
    #1313, 3 of #1314 5.75
    Complete booklet, #1314a 5.75
    Nos. 1312-1314 (3) 2.65 2.65
    With tabs 3.00

Compare with Nos. 1375-1378.

Music and Dance
in Israel — A582

Designs: 1.10s, Zimriya, World assembly of
choirs. 2s, Karmiel Dance Festival. 3s, Festival
of Klezmers (musical instruments).

1997, Sept. 23   Perf. 13
1315 A582 1.10s multicolored .60 .60
1316 A582 2s multicolored 1.10 1.10
1317 A582 3s multicolored 1.75 1.75
    Nos. 1315-1317 (3) 3.45 3.45
    With tabs 3.75

UN Resolution on
Creation of
Jewish State,
50th
Anniv. — A583

1997, Sept. 23   Perf. 13x14
1318 A583 5s multicolored 2.75 2.75
With tab 3.00

Souvenir Sheet

Pushkin's "Eugene Onegin," Translated
by Abraham Shlonsky — A584

1997, Nov. 19   Perf. 14x13
1319 A584 5s multicolored 2.75 2.75

See Russia No. 6418.

State of Israel, 50th
Anniv. in 1998 — A585

1997, Dec. 23   Perf. 14
1320 A585 (1.10s) multicolored .60 .60
    With tab .65
a. Size: 17x22mm .60 .60
    With tab .65
b. Booklet pane, 20 #1320a 12.00
    Complete booklet, #1320b 12.00
c. As "a," perf. 13x14, photo. .60 .60
    With tab .65

No. 1320b consists of two blocks of 10
stamps, tete-beche in relationship to each
other. No. 1320 is 18x23mm. No. 1320a has
brighter blue stripes in flag.
    Issued: #1320a, 2/17/98; #1320c, 5/3/98.

"MACHAL,"
Overseas
Volunteers
A586

Designs: 1.80s, "GACHAL," recruitment in
the Diaspora.

1997, Dec. 23
1321 A586 1.15s multicolored .65 .65
1322 A586 1.80s multicolored 1.00 1.00
    #1321-1322, with tabs 1.75

Chabad's
Children of
Chernobyl
A587

1997, Dec. 23
1323 A587 2.10s multicolored 1.10 1.10
With tab 1.25

A588   A589

1997, Dec. 23
1324 A588 2.50s Julia Set Fractal 1.40 1.40
With tab 1.50

Philately Day.

1998, Feb. 17   Litho.   Perf. 14x13

Three battle fronts during war: Nos. 1325,
1328a (1.50s), Northern Front, photograph of
people, Zefat, 1948. Nos. 1326, 1328b
(2.50s), Central Front, drawing over photograph of vehicles coming down mountain, outskirts of Jerusalem, 1948. Nos. 1327, 1328c

(3s), Southern Front, raising Israeli flag, Elat,
1949.

1325 A589 1.15s multicolored .65 .65
1326 A589 1.15s multicolored .65 .65
1327 A589 1.15s multicolored .65 .65
    Nos. 1325-1327 (3) 1.95 1.95
    With tabs 2.25

Souvenir Sheet
1328 A589 Sheet of 3, #a.-c. 3.90 3.90

War of Independence, 1947-49. No. 1328b
is 51x40mm.

Chaim
Herzog
(1918-97),
President
of Israel
A590

1998, Feb. 17   Perf. 14
1329 A590 5.35s multicolored 3.00 3.00
With tab 3.25

A591   A592

Jewish Contributions to Modern World Culture: a, Franz Kafka (1883-1924), writer. b,
George Gershwin. c, Lev Davidovich Landau
(1908-68), physicist. d, Albert Einstein. e,
Leon Blum (1872-1950), statesman. f, Elizabeth Rachel Felix (1821-58), actress.

1998, Apr. 27   Litho.   Perf. 14
1330   Sheet of 6 + 6 labels 3.00 3.00
a.-f. A591 90a Any single .50 .50

See No. 1362.

1998, Apr. 27
1331 A592 1.15s multicolored .60 .60
With tab .65

Memorial Day.

A593   A594

1998, Apr. 27
1332 A593 1.15s multicolored .60 .60
With tab .65

Declaration of the Establishment of the
State of Israel, 50th anniv.

1998, Apr. 27
1333 A594 5.35s multicolored 3.00 3.00
With tab 3.25

Israel Defense Forces, 50th anniv.

Holocaust Memorial Day — A595

Non-Jews who risked their lives to save
Jews during Holocaust: Giorgio Perlasca, Aristides de Sousa Mendes, Carl Lutz, Sempo
Sugihara, Selahattin Ulkumen.

1998, Apr. 27   Perf. 13
1334 A595 6s multicolored 3.25 3.25
With tab 3.50

Children's
Pets — A596

Israel '98: a, Cat. b, Dog. c, Bird. d, Gold-fish. e, Hamster. f, Rabbit.

1998, May 13
1335　　Sheet of 6　　　　　　2.00　2.00
　a.-f.　A596 60a Any single　　.35　.35

No. 1335 contains diagonal perforations so that lower left corner of each stamp can be removed leaving denominated portion in shape of a pentagon.

Postal and
Philatelic
Museum
A597

Illustrations by Kariel Gardosh featuring cartoon character, "Srulik:" a, At post office counter. b, Looking at stamp with magnifying glass. c, Putting mail into post box.

1998, May 13　　　　　*Perf. 14*
1336　　Sheet of 3　　　　　3.75　3.75
　a.　A597 1.50s multicolored　.80　.80
　b.　A597 2.50s multicolored　1.25　1.25
　c.　A597 3s multicolored　　1.60　1.60

Aircraft Used in War of Independence,
1948 — A598

1998, May 3　　*Litho.*　　*Perf. 14*
1337　A598　2.20s Dragon Rapide　1.25　1.25
1338　A598　2.20s Spitfire　　　1.25　1.25
1339　A598　2.20s B-17 Flying For-
　　　　　　　tress　　　　　1.25　1.25
　a.　Strip of 3, #1337-1339　3.75　3.75
　　　With tabs　　　　　　4.00　4.00

Israel '98.
No. 1339a was issued in sheets containing 2 strips printed tete beche separated by strip of three labels.
A limited-edition booklet exists. It contained the following panes: 1 #1305, 1 #1318, 1 #1320, 1 #1320b, 1 each #1321-1322, 1 each #1325-1327, 1 #1332, 1 #1333, 1 #1339a. Value, $85.

Souvenir Sheet

Mosaic of a Young Woman,
Zippori — A599

1998, May 13
1340　A599　5s multicolored　　3.25　3.25

Israel '98. Sold for 6s

Souvenir Sheet

King Solomon's Temple — A600

a, Drawing of the temple. b, Inscribed ivory pomegranate.

1998, May 13
1341　A600　Sheet of 2　　　4.00　4.00
　a.　2s multicolored　　　1.60　1.60
　b.　3s multicolored　　　2.40　2.40

Israel '98. Sold for 7s

Israel
Jubilee
Exhibition
A601

1998, Aug. 3　*Litho.*　*Perf. 14x13*
1342　A601　5.35s multicolored　2.50　2.50
　　　With tab　　　　　　　2.75

Child's
Drawing
"Living in a
World of
Mutual
Respect"
A602

1998, Sept. 8　　　　　*Perf. 14*
1343　A602　1.15s multicolored　.55　.55
　　　With tab　　　　　　　　.60

Holy Cities
A603

1998, Sept. 8
1344　A603　1.80s Hebron　　.85　.85
1345　A603　2.20s Jerusalem　1.00　1.00
　　　#1344-1345, with tabs　2.10

1999
1346　A603　1.15s Zefat　　　.60　.60
1347　A603　5.35s Tiberias　2.75　2.75
　　　#1346-1347, with tabs　3.75

Festival
Stamps
A604

Holy ark curtains: 1.15s, Peacocks on both sides of menorah, text, Star of David. 1.80s, Menorah, text, two lions. 2.20s, Text surrounded by ornate floral pattern.

1998, Sept. 8
1348　A604　1.15s multicolored　.55　.55
1349　A604　1.80s multicolored　.85　.85
1350　A604　2.20s multicolored　1.00　1.00
　　　Nos. 1348-1350 (3)　　2.40　2.40
　　　With tabs　　　　　　　2.75

Natl. Flag　　　Hyacinth
A605　　　　　A606

1998, Dec. 17　*Litho.*　*Die Cut*
Self-Adhesive
1351　A605　1.15s dk bl & bl　　.55　.55
1352　A605　2.15s dk bl & grn　1.00　1.00
1353　A605　3.25s dk bl & rose red　1.60　1.60
1354　A605　5.35s dk bl & yel org　2.75　2.75
　　　Nos. 1351-1354 (4)　　5.90　5.90

1999, Feb. 1　*Photo.*　*Perf. 15*
1355　A606　(1.15s) multicolored　.60　.60
　　　With tab　　　　　　　　.65

See Nos. 1492A, 1539D-1540.

Knesset,
50th Anniv.
A607

1999, Feb. 1　*Litho.*　*Perf. 14*
1356　A607　1.80s multicolored　.90　.90
　　　With tab　　　　　　　1.00

Manuscript of Rabbi
Shalem Shabazi
(1619-80),
Poet — A608

1999, Feb. 1
1357　A608　2.20s multicolored　1.10　1.10
　　　With tab　　　　　　　1.25

Jewish
Colonial
Trust, Cent.
A609

Drawings from one pound sterling share.

1999, Feb. 16
1358　A609　1.80s multicolored　.90　.90
　　　With tab　　　　　　　1.00

Ethnic
Costumes
A610

Designs: 2.15s, Yemenite Jewry, Yemen. 3.25s, Bene Israel Community, India.

1999, Feb. 16
1359　A610　2.15s multicolored　1.10　1.10
1360　A610　3.25s multicolored　1.60　1.60
　　　#1359-1360, with tabs　3.00

See Nos. 1373-1374.

Souvenir Sheet

Ancient Boat from Sea of
Galilee — A611

a, 3s, Reconstructed boat. b, 5s, Ancient boat.

1999, Mar. 19　*Litho.*　*Perf. 13*
1361　A611　Sheet of 2, #a.-b.　4.00　4.00

Australia '99, World Stamp Expo.

**Jewish Contributions to Modern
World Culture Type of 1998**

Designs: a, Emile Durkheim (1858-1917), social scientist. b, Paul Ehrlich (1854-1915), medical researcher. c, Rosa Luxemburg (1870-1919), politician. d, Norbert Wiener (1894-1964), mathematician, developer of computer science. e, Sigmund Freud (1856-1939), psychologist, founder of psychoanalysis. f, Martin Buber (1878-1965), religious philosopher.

1999, Apr. 18　*Litho.*　*Perf. 14*
1362　　Sheet of 6 + 6 labels　2.75　2.75
　a.-f.　A591 90a Any single　.45　.45

Monument
for Fallen
Bedouin
Soldiers
A612

1999, Apr. 18
1363　A612　1.20s multicolored　.60　.60
　　　With tab　　　　　　　　.65

Israel's
Admission
to UN, 50th
Anniv.
A613

1999, Apr. 18
1364　A613　2.30s multicolored　1.10　1.10
　　　With tab　　　　　　　1.25

Simcha Holtzberg (1924-94),
Holocaust Survivor, "Father of
Wounded Soldiers"
A614

1999, Apr. 18
1365　A614　2.50s multicolored　1.25　1.25
　　　With tab　　　　　　　1.40

Painting, "My Favorite Room," by
James Ensor (1860-1949) — A614a

1999, May 16　*Photo.*　*Perf. 11½*
1365A　A614a 2.30s multi　1.10　1.10
　　　With tab　　　　　　1.25

See Belgium No. 1738.

"Lovely
Butterfly,"
Children's
Television
Show
A615

Puppets: No. 1366, Ouza, the goose. No. 1367, Nooly, the chick & Shabi, the snail. No. 1368, Batz, the tortoise, and Pingi, the penguin.

1999, June 22　*Litho.*　*Perf. 14*
1366　A615　1.20s multicolored　.60　.60
1367　A615　1.20s multicolored　.60　.60
1368　A615　1.20s multicolored　.60　.60
　a.　Strip of 3 #1366-1368　1.80　1.80
　　　With tabs　　　　　　2.00

Pilgrimage to the Holy Land
A616

1999, June 22
1369	A616	3s Nazareth	1.50	1.50
1370	A616	3s River Jordan	1.50	1.50
1371	A616	3s Jerusalem	1.50	1.50
	Nos. 1369-1371 (3)		4.50	4.50
	With tabs		5.00	

Rabbi Or Sharga (?-1794) — A617

Illustration from Musa-Nameh manuscript, by Shahin, depicting battle of Isreal over Amalek.

1999, June 22
1372	A617	5.60s multicolored	2.75	2.75
	With tab		3.00	

Ethnic Costumes Type of 1999

Designs: 2.30s, Jewish woman in traditional Moroccan costume. 3.40s, Jewish man in traditional costume of Bukhara.

1999, Sept. 1   Litho.   Perf. 14
1373	A610	2.30s multicolored	1.10	1.10
1374	A610	3.40s multicolored	1.60	1.60
	#1373-1374, with tab		3.00	

"Ushpizin," Guests in the Sukkah, Festival of Sukkoth — A619

1999, Sept. 1
1375	A619	1.20s Joseph	.60	.60
1376	A619	1.90s Moses	.90	.90
1377	A619	2.30s Aaron	1.10	1.10
1378	A619	5.60s David	2.75	2.75
a.	Bklt. pane, #1376-1378, 3 #1375		6.75	6.75
	Complete booklet, #1378a		6.75	
	Nos. 1375-1378 (4)		5.35	5.35
	With tabs		6.00	

Stamp Day
A620

1999, Sept. 1
1379	A620	5.35s multicolored	2.50	2.50
	With tab		2.75	

Ceramic Urns, Museum of Jewish Culture, Bratislava, Slovakia — A621

Designs: No. 1380, Urn from 1776 showing man on sick bed, denomination at UL. No. 1381, Urn from 1734 showing funeral procession, denomination at UR.

1999, Nov. 23   Litho.   Perf. 14
1380	A621	1.90s multi	.95	.95
1381	A621	1.90s multi	.95	.95
	#1380-1381, with tabs		2.10	

See Slovakia Nos. 344-345.

Kiryat Shemona, 50th Anniv. A622

1999, Dec. 7
1382	A622	1.20s multicolored	.60	.60
	With tab		.65	

Proclamation of Jerusalem as Israel's Capital, 50th Anniv. — A623

1999, Dec. 7   Perf. 13x14
1383	A623	3.40s multicolored	1.60	1.60
	With tab		1.75	

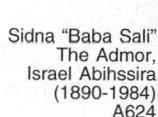

Sidna "Baba Sali" The Admor, Israel Abihssira (1890-1984) A624

1999, Dec. 7   Perf. 13
1384	A624	4.40s multi	2.25	2.25
	With tab		2.50	

Millennium A625

Designs: 1.40s, Joggers in park. 1.90s, Researcher with flask. 2.30s, Man at computer. 2.80s, Astronaut in space.

2000, Jan. 1
1385	A625	1.40s multi	.70	.70
1386	A625	1.90s multi	.95	.95
1387	A625	2.30s multi	1.10	1.10
1388	A625	2.80s multi	1.40	1.40
	Nos. 1385-1388 (4)		4.15	4.15
	With tabs		4.75	

Stampin' the Future Children's Stamp Design Contest Winners A626

Various children's drawings.

2000, Jan. 1   Perf. 13x13½
Background Colors
1389	A626	1.20s blue	.60	.60
1390	A626	1.90s yel org	.95	.95
1391	A626	2.30s red	1.10	1.10
1392	A626	3.40s green	1.60	1.60
	Nos. 1389-1392 (4)		4.25	4.25
	With tabs		4.75	

Fairy Tales of Hans Christian Andersen (1805-75) A627

1.20s, The Little Mermaid. 1.90s, The Emperor's New Clothes. 2.30s, The Ugly Duckling.

2000, Feb. 15   Litho.   Perf. 13x14
1393	A627	1.20s multi	.60	.60
1394	A627	1.90s multi	.95	.95
1395	A627	2.30s multi	1.10	1.10
	Nos. 1393-1395 (3)		2.65	2.65
	With tabs		3.00	

Pilgrimage to the Holy Land A628

Churches: 1.40s, All Apostles, Capernaum. 1.90s, St. Andrew's, Jerusalem. 2.30s, Church of the Visitation, Ein Kerem.

2000, Feb. 15   Perf. 14x13
1396	A628	1.40s multi	.70	.70
1397	A628	1.90s multi	.95	.95
1398	A628	2.30s multi	1.10	1.10
	Nos. 1396-1398 (3)		2.75	2.75
	With tabs		3.00	

King Hussein of Jordan (1935-99) A629

Shuni Historic Site A630

2000, Feb. 15   Litho.   Perf. 14
1399	A629	4.40s multi	2.25	2.25
	With tab		2.50	

Perf. 14 Syncopated
2000, Feb. 15   Photo.
1400	A630	2.30s multi	1.10	1.10
	With tab		1.25	

See #1409, 1427-1428, 1442, 1478, 1492, 1601.

A631   A632

Worldwide Fund for Nature: Various depictions of Blanford's fox.

2000, May 3   Litho.   Perf. 14
Denomination Color
1401	A631	1.20s red violet	.80	.80
1402	A631	1.20s green	.80	.80
1403	A631	1.20s blue	.80	.80
1404	A631	1.20s yellow	.80	.80
a.	Strip, #1401-1404 + central label		4.00	4.00
	With tabs		4.75	

See Nos. 1435-1438.

2000, May 3
1405	A632	1.20s multi	.60	.60
	With tab		.65	

Memorial Day.

Intl. Communications Day — A633

2000, May 3   Perf. 13
1406	A633	2.30s multi	1.10	1.10
			1.25	

Land of Three Religions A634

2000, May 3
1407	A634	3.40s multi	1.60	1.60
	With tab		1.75	

Johann Sebastian Bach (1685-1750) A635

2000, May 3
1408	A635	5.60s multi	2.75	2.75
	With tab		3.00	

Historic Site Type of 2000
Perf. 14 Syncopated
2000, July 25   Photo.
1409	A630	1.20s Juara	.60	.60
	With tab		.70	
a.	Perf. 14¾x15 Syncopated		.60	.60
	With tab		.70	

The line containing the country name in English and Arabic is 10mm long on No. 1409, 11 mm long on No. 1409a.
Issued: #1409a, 2001.

2000 Summer Olympics, Sydney — A636

2000, July 25   Litho.   Perf. 13
1410	A636	2.80s multi	1.40	1.40
	With tab		1.50	

A637   A638

2000, July 25   Perf. 14
1411	A637	4.40s multi	2.25	2.25
	With tab		2.50	

King Hassan II of Morocco (1929-99).

2000, June 25   *Perf. 13½x13*

Israeli food.

1412	A638	1.40s Couscous	.70	.70
1413	A638	1.90s Gefilte fish	.95	.95
1414	A638	2.30s Falafel	1.10	1.10
a.		Booklet pane, #1412, 2 #1413, 3 #1414	6.00	
		Booklet, #1414a	6.00	
		Nos. 1412-1414 (3)	2.75	2.75
		With tabs	3.00	

Dental Health A639

2000, Sept. 19   *Litho.*   *Perf. 14*

1415	A639	2.20s multi	1.10	1.10
		With tab	1.25	

Dohany Synagogue, Budapest A640

2000, Sept. 19   *Perf. 13x14*

1416	A640	5.60s multi	2.75	2.75
		With tab	3.00	

See Hungary No. 3710.

Jewish New Year Cards — A641

Designs: 1.20s, Boy giving girl a gift. 1.90s, Girl holding Zionist flag. 2.30s, Man giving flowers and greetings to woman.

2000, Sept. 19   *Perf. 14*

1417	A641	1.20s multi	.60	.60
1418	A641	1.90s multi	.95	.95
1419	A641	2.30s multi	1.10	1.10
		Nos. 1417-1419 (3)	2.65	2.65
		With tabs	3.00	

See Nos. 1455-1457.

Aleppo Codex — A642

2000, Dec. 5   *Perf. 13*

1420	A642	4.40s multi	2.10	2.10
		With tab	2.40	

Dinosaurs A643

Designs: No. 1421, Struthiomimuses on beach. No. 1422, Struthiomimuses in forest. No. 1423, Struthiomimus on hill.

2000, Dec. 5   *Litho.*   *Perf. 13*

1421	A643	2.20s multi	1.10	1.10
1422	A643	2.20s multi	1.10	1.10
1423	A643	2.20s multi	1.10	1.10
a.		Strip of 3, #1421-1423	3.30	3.30
		With tabs	3.50	

Science Fiction A644

Designs: 2.80s, Robot. 3.40s, Time travel. 5.60s, Space flight.

2000, Dec. 5   *Perf. 14*

1424	A644	2.80s multi	1.40	1.40
1425	A644	3.40s multi	1.75	1.75
1426	A644	5.60s multi	2.75	2.75
		Nos. 1424-1426 (3)	5.90	5.90
		With tabs	6.50	

Historic Sites Type of 2000
Perf. 14 Syncopated

2000-2001   **Photo.**

1427	A630	2.20s Mitzpe Revivim	1.10	1.10
		With tab	1.25	
1428	A630	3.40s Ilaniyya	1.75	1.75
		With tab	1.90	

Issued: 2.20s, 12/5; 3.40s, 2/13/01.

Settlements, Cent. — A645

2001, Feb. 13   *Litho.*   *Perf. 14*

1429	A645	2.50s Yavne'el	1.25	1.25
1430	A645	4.70s Menahamia	2.25	2.25
1431	A645	5.90s Kefar Tavor	3.00	3.00
		Nos. 1429-1431 (3)	6.50	6.50
		With tabs	7.25	

Hebrew Letters Aleph and Beth — A646

No. 1432: a, Aleph. b, Beth. c, Gimel. d, Daleth. e, He. f, Waw. g, Zayin. h, Heth. i, Teth. j, Yod. k, Kaph. l, Lamed. m, Mem. n, Nun. o, Samekh. p, Ayin. q, Pe. r, Sadhe. s, Qoph. t, Resh. u, Sin. v, Taw.
No. 1433 — End-of-word letters: a, Kaph. b, Mem. c, Nun. d, Pe. e, Sadhe.

2001, Feb. 13   **Photo.**   *Perf. 15*

1432		Sheet of 22	1.10	1.10
a.-v.	A646	10a Any single	.20	.20

Litho.
Perf. 14

1433		Horiz. strip of 5	.25	.25
a.-e.	A646	10a Any single	.20	.20
1434	A646	1s shown	.50	.50
		With tab	.55	

No. 1433 issued in sheets of two tete-beche strips. The horizontal strips of stamps in No. 1432 are printed tete-beche.

Worldwide Fund for Nature Type of 2000 Without WWF Emblem

Designs: 1.20s, Lesser kestrel. 1.70s, Kuhl's pipistrelle. 2.10s, Roe deer. 2.50s, Greek tortoise.

2001, Mar. 18   *Litho.*   *Perf. 14*

1435	A631	1.20s multi	.65	.65
1436	A631	1.70s multi	.85	.85
1437	A631	2.10s multi	1.10	1.10
1438	A631	2.50s multi	1.40	1.40
a.		Booklet pane, 2 each #1435-1438	8.00	
		Nos. 1435-1438 (4)	4.00	4.00
		With tabs	4.25	

Flowers — A647

No. 1439: a, Prairie gentian (purple). b, Barberton daisy (yellow) c, Star of Bethlehem (orange). d, Calla lily (white).

2001, Mar. 18

1439		Horiz. strip of 4 + 6 labels	2.40	2.40
a.-d.	A647	1.20s Any single	.60	.60

No. 1439 was printed in sheets of four strips. The second and fourth strips in the sheet have the stamps in reverse order. Sheets sold at the Jerusalem 2001 Stamp Exhibition could have their labels personalized by the purchaser.
See No. 1463.

Souvenir Sheet

Jerusalem 2001 Stamp Exhibition — A648

2001, Mar. 18

1440	A648	10s multi	5.00	5.00

Monument to Fallen Nahal Soldiers — A649

2001, Apr. 18   *Litho.*   *Perf. 13*

1441	A649	1.20s multi	.55	.55
		With tab	.60	

Memorial Day.

Historic Sites Type of 2000
Perf. 14 Syncopated

2001, May 23   **Photo.**

1442	A630	2s Sha'ar HaGay Inn	.95	.95
		With tab	1.10	

Shrine of the Báb Terraces, Haifa — A650

2001, May 23   *Perf. 13x13¼*

1443	A650	3s multi	1.40	1.40
		With tab	1.60	

Karaite Jews — A651

2001, May 23   *Litho.*   *Perf. 14*

1444	A651	5.60s multi	2.75	2.75
		With tab	3.00	

Souvenir Sheet

Belgica 2001 Intl. Stamp Exhibition, Brussels — A652

Cut diamonds: a, 1.40s, Marquise. b, 1.70s, Round. c, 4.70s, Square.

2001, May 23   *Perf. 14¾x14½*

1445	A652	Sheet of 3	4.75	4.75
a.		1.40s multi	.85	.85
b.		1.70s multi	1.00	1.00
c.		4.70s multi	2.75	2.75

No. 1445 sold for 10s.

Youth Movements — A653

2001, July 17   *Perf. 14*

1446	A653	5.60s multi	2.75	2.75
		With tab	3.00	

Bezalel School of Art Ceramic Facade Tiles — A654

Landscapes of: 1.20s, Hebron. 1.40s, Jaffa. 1.90s, Haifa. 2.30s, Tiberias.

2001, July 17   *Perf. 13x14*

1447	A654	1.20s multi	.55	.55
1448	A654	1.40s multi	.65	.65
1449	A654	1.90s multi	.90	.90
1450	A654	2.30s multi	1.10	1.10
		Nos. 1447-1450 (4)	3.20	3.20
		With tabs	3.50	

Souvenir Sheet

Phila Nippon '01, Japan — A655

Children's stamp design contest winners: a, 1.20s, Balloons. b, 1.40s, Cat. c, 2.50s, Veterinarian with dog. d, 4.70s, Dolphins.

2001, July 17 — Perf. 14¾

1451	A655	Sheet of 4	4.75	4.75
a.		1.20s multi	.55	.55
b.		1.40s multi	.70	.70
c.		2.50s multi	1.25	1.25
d.		4.70s multi	2.25	2.25

No. 1451 sold for 10s.

Shota Rustaveli (c. 1172-c. 1216), Georgian Poet — A656

2001, Sept. 3 — Litho. — Perf. 13x14
1452	A656	3.40s multi	1.60	1.60
		With tab		1.75

Yehuda Amichai (1924-2000), Poet — A657

2001, Sept. 3
1453	A657	5.60s multi	2.60	2.60
				2.75

Jewish National Fund, Cent. A658

2001, Sept. 3 — Perf. 14
1454	A658	5.60s multi	2.60	2.60
		With tab		2.75

Jewish New Year Cards Type of 2000
Designs: 1.20s, Soldier, dove with olive branch. 1.90s, Two women. 2.30s, Boy with flowers.

2001, Sept. 3
1455	A641	1.20s multi	.55	.55
1456	A641	1.90s multi	.90	.90
1457	A641	2.30s multi	1.10	1.10
		Nos. 1455-1457 (3)	2.55	2.55
		With tabs		2.75

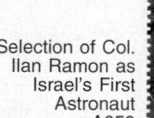

Selection of Col. Ilan Ramon as Israel's First Astronaut A659

2001, Dec. 11 — Litho. — Perf. 13
1458	A659	1.20s multi	.55	.55
		With tab		.65

Akim Association for the Rehabilitation of the Mentally Handicapped, 50th Anniv. — A660

2001, Dec. 11 — Perf. 13x14
1459	A660	2.20s multi	1.00	1.00
		With tab		1.10

Heinrich Heine (1797-1856), Poet — A661

2001, Dec. 11
1460	A661	4.40s multi	2.10	2.10
			2.40	

Institute for the Blind, Jerusalem, Cent. A662

Litho. & Embossed
2001, Dec. 11 — Perf. 14¾
1461	A662	5.60s multi	2.60	2.60
		With tab	3.00	

Coastal Conservation A663

2001, Dec. 11 — Litho. — Perf. 13
1462	A663	10s multi	4.75	4.75
		With tab	5.25	

Flower Type of 2001
2002, Feb. 24 — Litho. — Perf. 14
1463	A647	1.20s Yellow lily	.55	.55
		With tab	.60	

No. 1463 has small picture of flower at left, while No. 1439b has small picture of flower at right.

Languages A664

2002, Feb. 24 — Perf. 13x14
1464	A664	2.10s Yiddish	.90	.90
1465	A664	2.10s Ladino	.90	.90
		With tabs	2.00	

Mushrooms A665

Designs: 1.90s, Agaricus campester. 2.20s, Amanita muscaria. 2.80s, Suillus granulatus.

2002, Feb. 24
1466	A665	1.90s multi	.80	.80
1467	A665	2.20s multi	.95	.95
1468	A665	2.80s multi	1.25	1.25
		Nos. 1466-1468 (3)	3.00	3.00
		With tabs	3.50	

Months of the Year — A666

Designs: a, Tishrei (shofar, pomegranates). b, Heshvan (dried leaves). c, Kislev (dreidel, Hanukkah candles). d, Tevet (orange, flowers). e, Shevat (seedling, flowers, seeds). f, Adar (party hat, noisemaker, hamentashen). g, Nisan (cup, matzoh, flowers). h, Iyyar (bow and arrows, seeds). i, Sivan (wheat, sickle). j, Tammuz (flower, shells). k, Av (bride, groom, grapes). l, Elul, (cotton, dates, prayer book).

2002, Feb. 24 — Photo. — Perf. 14x14¼
1469	A666	Sheet of 12	6.25	6.25
a.-l.		1.20s Any single	.50	.50

Self-Adhesive
Serpentine Die Cut 16
1470	A666	Booklet of 12	6.25	
a.-l.		1.20s Any single	.50	.50

Monument to Fallen Military Police A667

2002, Apr. 10 — Litho. — Perf. 14
1471	A667	1.20s multi	.50	.50
		With tab	.60	

Hakhel Le Yisrael — A668

2002, Apr. 10 — Perf. 13x14
1472	A668	4.70s multi	2.00	2.00
		With tab	2.25	

Israel Foundation for Handicapped Children, 50th Anniv. — A669

2002, Apr. 10
1473	A669	5.90s multi	2.50	2.50
		With tab	2.75	

Historians — A670

Designs: No. 1474, Heinrich Graetz (1817-91). No. 1475, Simon Dubnow (1860-1941). No. 1476, Benzion Dinur (1884-1973). No. 1477, Yitzhak Baer (1888-1980).

2002, Apr. 10 — Perf. 14
1474	A670	2.20s multi	.90	.90
1475	A670	2.20s multi	.90	.90
1476	A670	2.20s multi	.90	.90
1477	A670	2.20s multi	.90	.90
		Nos. 1474-1477 (4)	3.60	3.60
		With tabs	4.00	

See Nos. 1553-1555.

Historic Sites Type of 2000
Perf. 14 Syncopated
2002, June 18 — Photo.
1478	A630	3.30s Hatsar Kinneret	1.40	1.40
		With tab	1.60	

Cable Cars — A671

2002, June 18 — Litho. — Perf. 14
1479	A671	2.20s Haifa	.95	.95
1480	A671	2.20s Massada	.95	.95
1481	A671	2.20s Menara	.95	.95
1482	A671	2.20s Rosh Haniqra	.95	.95
		Nos. 1479-1482 (4)	3.80	3.80
		With tabs	4.25	

Souvenir Sheet

Geology — A672

2002, June 18
1483	A672	Sheet of 3	5.00	5.00
a.		2.20s Fish fossil	1.10	1.10
b.		3.40s Copper minerals	1.75	1.75
c.		4.40s Ammonite	2.10	2.10

No. 1483 sold for 12s.

Rechavam Ze'evy (1926-2001), Assassinated Tourism Minister A673

Baruch Spinoza (1632-77), Philosopher A674

2002, Aug. 27 — Litho. — Perf. 14
1484	A673	1.20s multi	.50	.50
		With tab	.60	

2002, Aug. 27 — Perf. 13x14
1485	A674	5.90s multi	2.50	2.50
		With tab	2.75	2.75

Wine — A675

Designs: 1.20s, Clippers, bunch of grapes. 1.90s, Corkscrew, cork. 2.30s, Wine glass, bottle.

2002, Aug. 27 — Perf. 14
1486	A675	1.20s multi	.50	.50
1487	A675	1.90s multi	.80	.80
1488	A675	2.30s multi	1.00	1.00
		Nos. 1486-1488 (3)	2.30	2.30
		With tabs	2.60	

Birds of the Jordan Valley A676

2002, Aug. 27 **Perf. 14½x14**
1489 A676 2.20s Golden eagle .95 .95
1490 A676 2.20s Black stork .95 .95
1491 A676 2.20s Common crane .95 .95
Nos. 1489-1491 (3) 2.85 2.85
With tabs 3.25

Historic Sites Type of 2000
Perf. 14 Syncopated
2002, Aug. 27 **Photo.**
1492 A630 4.60s Kadoorie School 2.00 2.00
With tab 2.25

Hyacinth Type of 1999
Perf. 14 Syncopated
2002, Oct. 21 **Photo.**
1492A A606 (1.20s) multi .55 .55
With tab .60

Political Journalists A677

Designs: 1.20s, Abba Ahimeir (1897-1962). 3.30s, Israel Eldad (1910-96). 4.70s, Moshe Beilinson (1890-1936). 5.90s, Rabbi Binyamin (1880-1957).

2002, Nov. 26 **Litho.** **Perf. 14**
1493 A677 1.20s multi .50 .50
1494 A677 3.30s multi 1.40 1.40
1495 A677 4.70s multi 2.00 2.00
1496 A677 5.90s multi 2.50 2.50
Nos. 1493-1496 (4) 6.40 6.40
With tabs 7.25

Toys A678   Menorah A679

2002, Nov. 26
1497 A678 2.20s Five Stones .95 .95
1498 A678 2.20s Marbles .95 .95
1499 A678 2.20s Spinning top .95 .95
1500 A678 2.20s Yo-yo .95 .95
Nos. 1497-1500 (4) 3.80 3.80
With tabs 4.25

2002-03 **Photo.** **Perf. 15x14¾**
1501 A679 20a red .20 .20
1502 A679 30a gray olive .20 .20
1503 A679 40a gray green .20 .20
1504 A679 50a gray brown .20 .20
1505 A679 1s purple .40 .40
1506 A679 1.30s blue .50 .50
Nos. 1501-1506 (6) 1.70 1.70
With tabs 1.90

Issued: 30a, 1s, 11/26/02; 20a, 40a, 50a, 1.30s, 2/11/03. See Nos. 1758-1760.

Yeshivot Hahesder, 50th Anniv. (in 2004) A680

2003, Feb. 11 **Litho.** **Perf. 14**
1507 A680 1.20s multi .50 .50
With tab .60

11 September 2001, by Michael Gross — A681

2003, Feb. 11 **Perf. 13x14**
1508 A681 2.30s multi .95 .95
With tab 1.10

Monument for the Victims of Hostile Acts, Jerusalem A682

2003, Feb. 11 **Perf. 14x13**
1509 A682 4.70s multi 1.90 1.90
With tab 2.25

Powered Flight, Cent. A683

Designs: 2.30s, Wright Flyer in flight. 3.30s, Engine, propellor, Wright brothers. 5.90s, Orville Wright piloting Wright Flyer.

2003, Feb. 11 **Perf. 14**
1510 A683 2.30s multi .95 .95
1511 A683 3.30s multi 1.40 1.40
1512 A683 5.90s multi 2.40 2.40
Nos. 1510-1512 (3) 4.75 4.75
With tabs 5.25

Memorial Day — A684

2003, Apr. 27 **Litho.** **Perf. 14**
1513 A684 1.20s multi .55 .55
With tab .65

Holocaust Memorial Day — A685

2003, Apr. 27 **Perf. 13**
1514 A685 2.20s multi 1.00 1.00
With tab 1.10

Yemeni Jewish Immigration A686

2003, Apr. 27 **Perf. 14**
1515 A686 3.30s multi 1.50 1.50
With tab 1.60

Israeli Aircraft Industries, 50th Anniv. A687

2003, Apr. 27
1516 A687 3.30s multi 1.50 1.50
With tab 1.60

Independence, 55th Anniv. — A688

2002, Apr. 27
1517 A688 5.90s multi 2.75 2.75
With tab 3.00

Famous Men — A689

Designs: 1.90s, Ya'akov Meridor (1913-95), government minister. 2.20s, Ya'akov Dori (1899-1973), first chief of staff of the Israel Defense Forces. 2.80s, Sheikh Ameen Tarif (1898-1993), President of Druse Religious Court.

2003, Apr. 27 **Perf. 13**
1518 A689 1.90s multi .85 .85
1519 A689 2.20s multi 1.00 1.00
1520 A689 2.80s multi 1.25 1.25
Nos. 1518-1520 (3) 3.10 3.10
With tabs 3.50

Greetings — A690

Designs: No. 1521, Open box, Hebrew letters. No. 1522, Bride and groom. No. 1523, Heart as flower. No. 1524, Hot air balloon, flowers. No. 1525, Flowers and ladybug. No. 1526, Boy and teddy bear.

2003 **Perf. 14**
1521 A690 (1.20s) multi .55 .55
  a. Sheet of 12 + 12 labels 9.50 9.50
1522 A690 (1.20s) multi .55 .55
  a. Sheet of 12 + 12 labels 9.50 9.50
1523 A690 (1.20s) multi .55 .55
  a. Sheet of 12 + 12 labels 9.50 9.50
Nos. 1521-1523 (3) 1.65 1.65
With tabs 1.90
1524 A690 (1.20s) multi .55 .55
  a. Sheet of 12 + 12 labels 9.50 9.50
1525 A690 (1.20s) multi .55 .55
  a. Sheet of 12 + 12 labels 9.50 9.50
1526 A690 (1.20s) multi .55 .55
  a. Sheet of 12 + 12 labels 9.50 9.50
Nos. 1524-1526 (3) 1.65 1.65
With tabs 1.90

Issued: Nos. 1521-1523, 4/27; Nos. 1524-1526, 6/24; Nos. 1521a-1523a, 1524a-1526a, 10/19. Nos. 1521a-1526a each sold for 21.20s. Labels could be personalized.
Self-adhesive examples of Nos. 1521, 1523, 1524-1526 come from sheets issued in 1999 that sold for much more than face value.

Village Centenaries A691

2003, June 24 **Litho.** **Perf. 14**
1527 A691 3.30s Atlit 1.50 1.50
1528 A691 3.30s Givat-Ada 1.50 1.50
1529 A691 3.30s Kfar-Saba 1.50 1.50
Nos. 1527-1529 (3) 4.50 4.50
With tabs 5.00

Evolution of the Israeli Flag A692

Designs: 1.90s, Flag of the Prague Jewish community, 15th cent. 2.30s, Ness Ziona flag, 1891. 4.70s, Theodor Herzl's "Der Judenstaat" flag design, 1896. 5.90s, Israeli flag, 1948.

2003, June 24
1530 A692 1.90s multi .90 .90
1531 A692 2.30s multi 1.10 1.10
1532 A692 4.70s multi 2.10 2.10
1533 A692 5.90s multi 2.75 2.75
Nos. 1530-1533 (4) 6.85 6.85
With tabs 7.50

Yad Vashem, 50th Anniv. — A693

Stars of David and: No. 1534, List of Jewish forced laborers. No. 1535, Teddy bear, page of testimony.

2003, Sept. 9 **Litho.** **Perf. 14**
1534 A693 2.20s multi 1.00 1.00
1535 A693 2.20s multi 1.00 1.00
  a. Pair, #1534-1535 2.00 2.00
    Pair with tabs 2.25
  b. Miniature sheet, 3 #1535a 6.00 6.00

No. 1535b issued 2004.

Olive Oil — A694

Designs: 1.30s, Olives. 1.90s, Olive press. 2.30s, Jars of oil.

2003, Sept. 9
1536 A694 1.30s multi .55 .55
1537 A694 1.90s multi .85 .85
1538 A694 2.30s multi 1.00 1.00
  a. Booklet pane, #1536, 2 #1537, 3 #1538 5.25 —
    Complete booklet, #1538a 5.25
Nos. 1536-1538 (3) 2.40 2.40
With tabs 2.75

Souvenir Sheet

Armenian Ceramics in Jerusalem — A695

No. 1539: a, Deer, by Karakashian-Balian Studio, 1930s-1940s. b, Bird, by Stepan Karakashian, 1980s. c, Tree of Life, by Marie Balian, 1990s.

2003, Sept. 9 **Perf.**
1539 A695 Sheet of 3 6.50 6.50
  a. 2.30s multi 1.40 1.40
  b. 3.30s multi 2.10 2.10
  c. 4.70s multi 3.00 3.00

No. 1539 contains three 31mm diameter stamps and sold for 15s.

Hyacinth Type of 1999
2003 **Photo.** **Perf. 15 Syncopated**
1539D A606 (1.20s) multi .60 .60

Booklet Stamp
Self-Adhesive
Serpentine Die Cut 13½x14
1540 A606 (1.30s) multi .60 .60
  a. Booklet pane of 20 12.00

Issued: 1.20s, 10/8; 1.30s, 12/4.

Immigrants to Israel — A696

Designs: 2.10s, Leibowitch family, clerical house, Zikhron Ya'acov. 6.20s, Second Aliya immigrants, Rothschild Ave., Tel Aviv.

2003, Dec. 9   **Litho.**   **Perf. 13**
1541 A696 2.10s multi   .95 .95
1542 A696 6.20s multi   3.00 3.00
   With tabs   4.50

Famous Men — A697

Designs: 3.30s, Aharon David Gordon (1856-1922), laborer. 4.90s, Emile Habiby (1921-96), journalist, politician. 6.20s, Yehoshua Hankin (1865-1945), land developer.

2003, Dec. 9   **Perf. 14**
1543 A697 3.30s multi   1.50 1.50
1544 A697 4.90s multi   2.25 2.25
1545 A697 6.20s multi   3.00 3.00
   Nos. 1543-1545 (3)   6.75 6.75
   With tabs   7.50

Children on Wheels — A698

No. 1546: a, Boy on bicycle. b, Girl on roller blades. c, Girl on scooter. d, Boy on skateboard.

2003, Dec. 9   **Perf. 13¾**
1546   Horiz. strip of 4   2.40 2.40
a.-d.   A698 1.30s Any single   .60 .60
   Strip with tabs   2.75

Philately Day.

Red Sea Fish A699

Designs: No. 1547, Amphiprion bicinctus. No. 1548, Pseudanthias squamipinnis. No. 1549, Pseudochromis fridmani. No. 1550, Chaetodon paucifasciatus.

2004, Jan. 30   **Litho.**   **Perf. 14**
1547 A699 1.30s multi   .60 .60
1548 A699 1.30s multi   .60 .60
1549 A699 1.30s multi   .60 .60
1550 A699 1.30s multi   .60 .60
a.   Souvenir sheet, #1547-1550   3.50 3.50
   Nos. 1547-1550 (4)   2.40 2.40
   With tabs   2.75

2004 Hong Kong Stamp Expo (#1550a). No. 1550a sold for 7.50s.

Menachem Begin Heritage Center, Jerusalem A700

2004, Feb. 24   **Perf. 13**
1551 A700 2.50s multi   1.10 1.10
   With tab   1.25

Col. Ilan Ramon (1954-2003), First Israeli Astronaut A701

2004, Feb. 24
1552 A701 2.60s multi   1.25 1.25
   With tab   1.40

Historians Type of 2002

Designs: 2.40s, Emanuel Ringelblum (1900-44). 3.70s, Jacob Talmon (1916-80). 6.20s, Jacob Herzog (1921-72).

2004, Feb. 24   **Perf. 14**
1553 A670 2.40s multi   1.10 1.10
1554 A670 3.70s multi   1.60 1.60
1555 A670 6.20s multi, Type I   2.75 2.75
a.   Type II   —
   Nos. 1553-1555 (3)   5.45 5.45
   With tabs   6.00

Type II has thicker shadows behind the Hebrew characters and numerals, with the shadow at the top of the "6" with a projection, the shadow is visible below, to the right, and above the horizontal line of the "2," and a shadow all around the "0." The background and face are greener, and the width of the color band at the bottom is wider.

Type I has thin shadows behind the Hebrew characters and numerals, with the shadow at the top of the "6" without a projection, the shadow visible below and to the right only of the horizontal line of the "2," and a partial shadow around the "0." The background and face have a lighter shade. The width of the color band at the bottom is narrower.

Memorial Day A702

2004, Apr. 20   **Litho.**   **Perf. 14**
1556 A702 1.30s multi   .60 .60
   With tab   .65

FIFA (Fédération Internationale de Football Association), Cent. — A703

2004, May 3   **Perf. 13**
1557 A703 2.10s multi   .95 .95
   With tab   1.10

Printed in sheets of 12 + 4 central labels.

UEFA (European Football Union), 50th Anniv. — A704

2004, May 3   **Perf. 14**
1558 A704 6.20s multi   2.75 2.75
   With tab   3.00

Ottoman Clock Towers — A705

2004, May 3   **Perf. 13x14**
1559 A705 1.30s Acre   .60 .60
1560 A705 1.30s Safed   .60 .60
1561 A705 1.30s Jaffa   .60 .60

1562 A705 1.30s Jerusalem   .60 .60
1563 A705 1.30s Haifa   .60 .60
   Nos. 1559-1563 (5)   3.00 3.00
   With tabs   3.25

Booklet Stamps

1563A A705 3.10s Safed   1.40 1.40
f.   Booklet pane of 1   1.40 —
1563B A705 3.70s Acre   1.60 1.60
g.   Booklet pane of 1   1.60 —
1563C A705 5.20s Haifa   2.25 2.25
h.   Booklet pane of 1   2.25 —
1563D A705 5.50s Jerusalem   2.40 2.40
i.   Booklet pane of 1   2.40 —
1563E A705 7s Jaffa   3.00 3.00
j.   Booklet pane of 1   3.40 —
k.   Booklet pane, #1563A-
   1563E   11.00 —
   Complete booklet,
   #1563Af, 1563Bg,
   1563Ch, 1563Di,
   1563Ej, 1563Ek   22.00
   Nos. 1563A-1563E (5)   10.65 10.65

A706

Great Synagogue of Rome — A707

2004, May 20   **Litho.**   **Perf. 13x14**
1564 A706 2.10s multi   .95 .95
1565 A707 2.10s multi   .95 .95
   With tabs   2.25

See Italy Nos. 2607-2608.

Theodor Herzl (1860-1904), Zionist Leader — A708

2004, July 6   **Perf. 13**
1566 A708 2.50s multi   1.10 1.10
   With tab   1.25

See Austria No. 1960, Hungary No. 3903.

National Insurance Institute, 50th Anniv. — A709

2004, July 6
1567 A709 7s multi   3.25 3.25
   With tab   3.75

2004 Summer Olympics, Athens A710

Medals won by Israeli athletes in previous Olympics: 1.50s, 1992 Silver medal, Judo. 2.40s, 1996 Bronze medal, Men's Mistral (windsurfing). 6.90s, 2000 Bronze medal, Kayaking.

2004, July 6   **Perf. 14**
1568 A710 1.50s multi   .65 .65
1569 A710 2.40s multi   1.10 1.10
1570 A710 6.90s multi   3.25 3.25
   Nos. 1568-1570 (3)   5.00 5.00
   With tabs   5.50

Founding of Herzliya Hebrew High School, Tel Aviv, Cent. (in 2005) — A711

2004, Aug. 31   **Litho.**   **Perf. 13x14**
1571 A711 2.20s multi   1.00 1.00
   With tab   1.10

Ben-Gurion Heritage Institute — A712

2004, Aug. 31   **Perf. 13**
1572 A712 2.50s multi   1.10 1.10
   With tab   1.25

Adventure Stories — A713

Designs: 2.20s, Eight on the Trail of One, by Yemima Avidar-Tchernovitz (parachutist). 2.50s, The "Hasamba" Series, by Igal Mossinsohn (children, donkey). 2.60s, Our Gang, by Pucho (four people).

2004, Aug. 31
1573 A713 2.20s multi   1.00 1.00
1574 A713 2.50s multi   1.10 1.10
1575 A713 2.60s multi   1.25 1.25
   Nos. 1573-1575 (3)   3.35 3.35
   With tabs   3.75

Festivals A714

Bread making: 1.50s, Wheat ears, sickle. 2.40s, Mill, wooden fork. 2.70s, Oven, bread shovel.

2004, Aug. 31   **Perf. 14x13**
1576 A714 1.50s multi   .65 .65
1577 A714 2.40s multi   1.10 1.10
1578 A714 2.70s multi   1.25 1.25
   Nos. 1576-1578 (3)   3.00 3.00
   With tabs   3.25

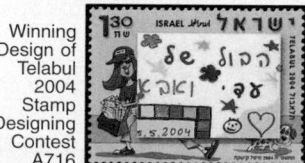

Opening of Third Terminal at Ben-Gurion Airport A715

2004, Nov. 2   **Litho.**   **Perf. 14x13**
1579 A715 2.70s multi   1.25 1.25
   With tab   1.40

Winning Design of Telabul 2004 Stamp Designing Contest A716

2004, Dec. 14
1580 A716 1.30s multi   .60 .60
   With tab   .70

Bank of Israel, 50th Anniv. A717

2004, Dec. 14
1581 A717 6.20s multi 3.00 3.00
With tab 3.25

Philately Day A718

Designs: 2.10s, Mailbox of Austrian Postal Services, Jerusalem Post Office. 2.20s, Mailbox of British Mandate era, Lilienblum St. Post Office, Tel Aviv. 3.30s, Modern mailbox, Main Post Office, Tel Aviv.

2004, Dec. 14
1582 A718 2.10s multi ..... .95 .95
1583 A718 2.20s multi 1.00 1.00
1584 A718 3.30s multi 1.60 1.60
Nos. 1582-1584 (3) 3.55 3.55
With tabs 4.00

Ancient Water Systems A719

Designs: 2.10s, Hazor water tunnel and ivory cosmetics spoon. 2.20s, Megiddo water system and seal. 3.30s, Caesarea Aqueduct, coin from Caesarea. 6.20s, Hezekiah's tunnel, pool of Siloam, Jerusalem, and imprinted piece of clay.

2005, Feb. 22 Litho. Perf. 14x13
1585 A719 2.10s multi ..... .95 .95
1586 A719 2.20s multi 1.00 1.00
1587 A719 3.30s multi 1.50 1.50
1588 A719 6.20s multi 3.00 3.00
Nos. 1585-1588 (4) 6.45 6.45
With tabs 7.25

Animals in the Bible A720

Designs: Nos. 1589, 1593a, Ostrich. Nos. 1590, 1593b, Brown bear. Nos. 1591, 1593c, Wolf. Nos. 1592, 1592d, Nile crocodile.

2005, Feb. 22 Perf. 14x13
1589 A720 1.30s yel & multi ..... .60 .60
1590 A720 1.30s blue & multi ..... .60 .60
1591 A720 2.20s org & multi 1.00 1.00
1592 A720 2.20s pink & multi 1.00 1.00
Nos. 1589-1592 (4) 3.20 3.20
With tabs 3.50

Souvenir Sheet
Perf. 14
1593 Sheet of 4 ..... 5.50 5.50
a. A720 1.30s yel & multi ..... .85 .85
b. A720 2.10s blue & multi 1.40 1.40
c. A720 2.30s org & multi 1.50 1.50
d. A720 2.80s pink & multi 1.75 1.75

No. 1593 sold for 12s and contains four 40x25mm stamps.

Memorial Day A721

2005, May 3 Litho. Perf. 14x13½
1594 A721 1.50s multi ..... .70 .70
With tab ..... .80

Reserve Force A722

2005, May 3
1595 A722 2.20s multi 1.00 1.00
With tab 1.10

Bar-Ilan University, 50th Anniv. A723

2005, May 3
1596 A723 2.20s multi 1.00 1.00
With tab 1.10

End of World War II, 60th Anniv. — A724

No. 1597: a, Jewish partisan and underground fighters. b, Jewish soldiers in Allied forces.

2005, May 3
1597 A724   Horiz. pair 3.00 3.00
a.-b. 3.30s Either single 1.50 1.50
With tab 3.25

Schools — A725

Designs: 2.10s, Hebrew kindergarden, Rishon Le-Zion. 6.20s, Lemel Elementary School, Jerusalem.

2005, May 3 Perf. 13½x14
1598 A725 2.10s multi 1.00 1.00
1599 A725 6.20s multi 3.00 3.00
With tabs 4.50 4.50

Pope John Paul II (1920-2005) A726

2005, May 18 Litho. Perf. 13¾x14
1600 A726 3.30s multi 1.50 1.50
With tab 1.75

Historic Sites Type of 2000
Serpentine Die Cut 11¼x11
2005, June 7 Litho.
Booklet Stamp
Self-Adhesive
1601 A630 2.20s Mitzpe Revivim 1.00 1.00
a. Booklet pane of 12 ..... 12.00

2005 Maccabiah Games — A727

2005, July 11 Perf. 13¾x14
1602 A727 3.30s multi 1.50 1.50
With tab 1.75

Gagea Commutate — A728

Perf. 14 Syncopated
2005, July 26 Photo.
1603 A728 (1.30s) multi ..... .60 .60
With tab ..... .70

See Nos. 1618, 1656D.

Maimonides (1138-1204), Rabbi, Philosopher A729

2005, July 26 Litho. Perf. 13¾x14
1604 A729 8.20s multi 3.75 3.75
With tab 4.25

Paintings — A730

Designs: 2.20s, Agrippas Street, by Arie Aroch. 4.90s, Tablets of the Covenant, by Moshe Castel. 6.20s, The Rift in Time, No. 7, by Moshe Kupferman.

2005, July 26 Perf. 13¾x14
1605 A730 2.20s multi 1.00 1.00
1606 A730 4.90s multi 2.25 2.25
1607 A730 6.20s multi 2.75 2.75
Nos. 1605-1607 (3) 6.00 6.00
With tabs 6.75

Prime Minister Yitzhak Rabin (1922-95) and Yitzhak Rabin Center, Tel Aviv — A731

2005, Sept. 27 Litho. Perf. 13
1608 A731 2.20s multi ..... .95 .95
With tab 1.10

Albert Einstein (1879-1955), Physicist — A732

2005, Sept. 27
1609 A732 3.30s multi 1.50 1.50
With tab 1.60

Intl. Year of Physics.

See No. 1620.

Priestly Blessing at Western Wall — A733

2005, Sept. 27 Perf. 13½x14
1610 A733 6.20s multi 2.75 2.75
With tab 3.00

Medicine in Israel A734

2005, Sept. 27 Perf. 14x13½
1611 A734 1.40s Geriatrics ..... .65 .65
1612 A734 2.20s Pediatrics ..... .95 .95
1613 A734 2.20s Rehabilitation ..... .95 .95
1614 A734 6.20s Mental Health 2.75 2.75
Nos. 1611-1614 (4) 5.30 5.30
With tabs 6.00

Orders of the Mishnah A735

2005, Sept. 27
1615 A735 1.30s Zeraim ..... .60 .60
1616 A735 2.10s Moed ..... .90 .90
1617 A735 2.30s Nashim 1.00 1.00
Nos. 1615-1617 (3) 2.50 2.50
With tabs 2.75

See Nos. 1653-1655.

Gagea Commutate Type of 2005
Serpentine Die Cut 13½x14
2005, Nov. 3 Photo.
1618 A728 (1.30s) multi ..... .60 .60
a. Booklet pane of 20 ..... 12.00

Diplomatic Relations With Germany, 40th Anniv. — A736

2005, Nov. 3 Litho. Perf. 13
1619 A736 2.10s multi ..... .90 .90
With tab 1.00

See Germany No. 2359.

Einstein Type of 2005
Souvenir Sheet
2005, Dec. 27
1620 A732 8.20s multi 5.25 5.25

Philately Day, Jerusalem 2006 National Stamp Exhibition. No. 1620 sold for 12s.

Children's Rights — A737

Inscriptions: No. 1621, Childhood is happiness. No. 1622, Indifference hurts. No. 1623, A warm home.

2005, Dec. 27 — **Perf. 13½x14**
1621	A737	1.30s multi	.60	.60
1622	A737	1.30s multi	.60	.60
1623	A737	1.30s multi	.60	.60
	Nos. 1621-1623 (3)		1.80	1.80
	With tabs		2.00	

Theater Personalities A738

Designs: No. 1624, Joseph Millo (1916-97), director. No. 1625, Moshe Halevy (1895-1974), director. No. 1626, Shai K. Ophir (1928-87), actor. No. 1627, Nissim Aloni (1926-88), playwright.

2005, Dec. 27
1624	A738	2.20s multi	.95	.95
1625	A738	2.20s multi	.95	.95
1626	A738	6.20s multi	2.75	2.75
1627	A738	6.20s multi	2.75	2.75
	Nos. 1624-1627 (4)		7.40	7.40
	With tabs		8.25	

Manufacturers Association of Israel, 85th Anniv. — A739

2005, Dec. 29   Litho.   Perf. 13¾x14
1628	A739	1.50s multi	.65	.65
	With tab		.75	

Emblem of Israel Post A740

2006   Perf. 14x13¾
1629	A740	1.50s multi	.65	.65
	With tab		.75	

Souvenir Sheet
Imperf
1630	A740	5.90s multi	3.50	3.50

Issued: 1.50s, 2/28; 5.90s, 5/8. Jerusalem 2006 National Stamp Exhibition (#1630). No. 1630 sold for 7.50s. Embossed and numbered examples of No. 1630 were given as gifts and were not available for sale.

Headquarters of Chabad Lubavitch Hasidism, Brooklyn, NY — A741

2006, Feb. 28   Perf. 14x13¾
1631	A741	2.50s multi	1.10	1.10
	With tab		1.25	

Pres. Ezer Weizman (1924-2005) A742

2005, Feb. 28   Perf. 13¾x14
1632	A742	7.40s multi	3.25	3.25
	With tab		3.50	

Children's Art A743

Contest-winning art by Jewish children in US: Nos. 1633, 1637a, Desert Bloom, by Yael Bildner. Nos. 1634, 1637c, Harmony, by Michela T. Janower. Nos. 1635, 1637d, Together in Israel, by Jessica Deutsch. Nos. 1636, 1637b, Colors of Israel, by Marissa Galin.

2006   Perf. 14x13¾
1633	A743	1.50s multi	.65	.65
1634	A743	2.40s multi	1.00	1.00
1635	A743	3.60s multi	1.60	1.60
1636	A743	7.40s multi	3.25	3.25
	Nos. 1633-1636 (4)		6.50	6.50
	With tabs		7.25	

Souvenir Sheet
Perf. 14
1637		Sheet of 4	6.75	6.75
a.	A743	2.20s multi	1.10	1.10
b.	A743	2.40s multi	1.25	1.25
c.	A743	3.60s multi	1.75	1.75
d.	A743	5.10s multi	2.60	2.60

Issued: Nos. 1633-1636, 2/28; No. 1637, 5/28. Washington 2006 World Philatelic Exhibition (#1637). No. 1637 sold for 15s and contains four 40x35mm stamps.

Yad Lashiron Armored Corps Memorial, Latrun A744

2006, Apr. 11   Perf. 14x13¾
1638	A744	1.50s multi	.70	.70
	With tab		.80	

Memorial Day.

Tel Aviv University, 50th Anniv. A745

2006, May 8
1639	A745	3.60s multi	1.60	1.60
	With tab		1.75	

Tulips — A746

2006, May 8   Perf. 14x14¼
1640	A746	1.50s shown	.70	.70
a.		Sheet of 12 + 12 labels	12.50	12.50

1641	A746	1.50s Columbines	.70	.70
	With tabs		1.60	
a.		Sheet of 12 + 12 labels	12.50	12.50

Nos. 1640a and 1641a each sold for 27s. Labels could be personalized. Compare with type A647.

Souvenir Sheet

Jerusalem 2006 National Stamp Exhibition — A747

2006, May 8   Perf. 14
1642	A747	10s multi	6.75	6.75

The Solar System — A748

Designs: Nos. 1643a, 1644d, Sun, Mercury and Venus. Nos. 1643b, 1644c, Earth, Moon and Mars. Nos. 1643c, 1644e, Neptune, Pluto, and moons. Nos. 1643d, 1644b, Jupiter, moons and asteroids. Nos. 1643e, 1644f, Saturn, moon, Sun and asteroids. Nos. 1643f, 1644a, Uranus, moons, asteroids, part of Saturn.

2006, May 8   Perf. 13
1643	A748	Sheet of 6	6.75	6.75
a.-f.		2.50s Any single	1.10	1.10

Self-Adhesive
Serpentine Die Cut 11
1644	A748	Booklet pane of 6	6.75	
a.-f.		2.50s Any single	1.10	1.10

Jerusalem 2006 National Stamp Exhibition. The six individual stamps, when separated, could be rearranged to produce a Star of David over the planets.

Religious Zionist Education, Cent. — A749

2006, July 25   Perf. 13¾x14
1645	A749	3.60s multi	1.60	1.60
	With tab		1.75	

Rabbis of Jerusalem A750

Rabbis: 1.50s, Jacob Saul Eliachar (1817-1906). 2.20s, Samuel Salant (1816-1909). 2.40s, Jacob Meir (1856-1939).

2006, July 25
1646	A750	1.50s multi	.70	.70
1647	A750	2.20s multi	1.00	1.00
1648	A750	2.40s multi	1.10	1.10
	Nos. 1646-1648 (3)		2.80	2.80
	With tabs		3.00	

Silver Khamsas A751

Khamsa from: 1.50s, Morocco, 1920. 2.50s, Tunisia, 1930. 7.40s, Iran, 1925.

2006, July 26
1649	A751	1.50s multi	.70	.70
1650	A751	2.50s multi	1.10	1.10
1651	A751	7.40s multi	3.50	3.50
	Nos. 1649-1651 (3)		5.30	5.30
	With tabs		5.75	

Abba Eban (1915-2002), Foreign Minister — A752

2006, Sept. 12   Perf. 14x13¾
1652	A752	7.30s multi	3.50	3.50
	With tab		4.00	

Orders of the Mishnah Type of 2005
2006, Sept. 12
1653	A735	1.50s Nezikin	.70	.70
1654	A735	2.20s Kodashim	1.00	1.00
1655	A735	2.40s Tohorot	1.10	1.10
	Nos. 1653-1655 (3)		2.80	2.80
	With tabs		3.00	

Bezalel Academy of Arts and Design, Cent. — A753

2006, Sept. 12   Perf. 13
1656		Horiz. strip of 3	3.50	3.50
a.	A753	2.50s green	1.10	1.10
b.	A753	2.50s blue	1.10	1.10
c.	A753	2.50s orange	1.10	1.10
	Strip with tabs		4.00	

Gagea Commutate Type of 2005
Redrawn With Two Leaves at Right
2006, Sept. 20   Litho.   Perf. 14
1656D	A728	(1.50s) multi	.70	.70

Medicinal Herbs and Spices — A754

Designs: 1.50s, Coriandrum sativum. 2.50s, Micromeria fructicosa. 3.30s, Mentha piperita.

2006, Dec. 17   **Litho.**   **Perf. 14¼x14**
1657	A754 1.50s multi	.70	.70
1658	A754 2.50s multi	1.25	1.25
1659	A754 3.30s multi	1.60	1.60
	Nos. 1657-1659 (3)	3.55	3.55
	With tabs	4.00	

See Nos. 1700-1701, 1747.

Creation of
Esperanto
Language,
120th
Anniv.
A755

2006, Dec. 17   **Perf. 14x13¾**
1660	A755 3.30s multi	1.60	1.60
	With tab	1.75	

Israeli Fashions
A756

Women's fashions from: 1.50s, 1882-1948. 2.50s, 1948-73. 3.30s, 1973-90. 7.30s, 1990-2005.

2006, Dec. 17   **Perf. 13**
1661	A756 1.50s multi	.70	.70
1662	A756 2.50s multi	1.25	1.25
1663	A756 3.30s multi	1.60	1.60
1664	A756 7.30s multi	3.50	3.50
	Nos. 1661-1664 (4)	7.05	7.05
	With tabs	7.75	

Crusader
Sites in
Israel
A757

2006, Dec. 17   **Litho.**   **Perf. 14x13¾**
1665	A757 2.50s Atlit	1.25	1.25
1666	A757 2.50s Caesarea	1.25	1.25
1667	A757 2.50s Montfort	1.25	1.25
1668	A757 2.50s Belvoir	1.25	1.25
	Nos. 1665-1668 (4)	5.00	5.00
	With tabs	5.50	

Development — A758

Development of the: 2.50s, Negev. 3.30s, Galilee.

2007, Feb. 20   **Litho.**   **Perf. 14x13¾**
1669	A758 2.50s multi	1.25	1.25
1670	A758 3.30s multi	1.60	1.60
	With tab	3.25	

Sports and
Physical
Education
A759

Inscriptions: 2.90s, Physical education in schools. 3s, Wingate Institute. 7.30s, Sport for all.

2007, Feb. 20
1671	A759 2.90s multi	1.40	1.40
1672	A759 3s multi	1.50	1.50
1673	A759 7.30s multi	3.50	3.50
	Nos. 1671-1673 (3)	6.40	6.40
	With tabs	7.25	

Educational
Television
A760

Designs: Nos. 1674a, 1675, Ma Pit'om (green panel). Nos. 1674b, 1676, Krovim Krovim (blue panel). Nos. 1674c, 1677, No Secrets (orange panel).

2007, Feb. 20   **Perf. 13¾x14**
1674	Strip of 3	3.75	3.75
a.-c.	A760 2.50s Any single	1.25	1.25
	Strip with tabs	4.25	

Booklet Stamps
Self-Adhesive
Serpentine Die Cut 10¾x11
1675	A760 2.50s multi	1.25	1.25
1676	A760 2.50s multi	1.25	1.25
1677	A760 2.50s multi	1.25	1.25
a.	Booklet pane, 2 each #1675-1677	7.50	

Memorial
Day
A761

2007, Apr. 17   **Litho.**   **Perf. 14x13¾**
1678	A761 1.50s multi	.75	.75
	With tab	.85	

Scouting,
Cent.
A762

2007, Apr. 17
1679	A762 2.50s multi	1.25	1.25
	With tab	1.40	

Regional Development Towns — A763

Towns in: 2.50s, Northern region. 3.30s, Central region. 7.30s, Southern region.

2007, Apr. 17
1680	A763 2.50s multi	1.25	1.25
1681	A763 3.30s multi	1.75	1.75
1682	A763 7.30s multi	3.75	3.75
	Nos. 1680-1682 (3)	6.75	6.75
	With tabs	7.50	

Souvenir Sheet

Neve-Tzedek Neighborhood of Tel
Aviv, 120th Anniv. — A764

2007, Apr. 17   **Perf. 13¾x14**
1683	A764 Sheet of 3	7.50	7.50
a.	2.20s Founders	1.50	1.50
b.	3.30s Neve-Tzedek	2.25	2.25
c.	5.80s Intellectuals	3.75	3.75

No. 1683 sold for 15s.

Reunification of
Jerusalem, 40th
Anniv. — A765

2007, May 16
1684	A765 1.50s multi	.75	.75
	With tab	.85	

Volunteer
Organizations
A766

2007, June 20   **Perf. 13**
1685	A766 1.50s multi	.75	.75
	With tab	.85	

Israel Prison
Service — A767

2007, June 20   **Perf. 13¾x14**
1686	A767 2.50s multi	1.25	1.25
	With tab	1.40	

Dance — A768

No. 1687: a, Ballet. b, Ethnic dance. c, Israeli folk dance. d, Modern dance.

2007, June 20
1687	Horiz. strip of 4	4.25	4.25
a.-d.	A768 2.20s Any single	1.00	1.00
	Strip with tabs	4.75	

UNESCO
World
Heritage
Sites
A769

Designs: 3.30s, Akko (Acre). 5s, 10s, Tel Aviv. 5.80s, Masada.

2007   **Perf. 14x13¾**
1688	A769 3.30s multi	1.60	1.60
1689	A769 5s multi	2.40	2.40
1690	A769 5.80s multi	2.75	2.75
	Nos. 1688-1690 (3)	6.75	6.75
	With tabs	7.50	

Souvenir Sheet
1691	A769 10s multi	7.25	7.25

Issued: 3.30s, 5s, 5.80s, 6/20; 10s, 8/27. Tel Aviv, cent. (#1691). No. 1691 sold for 15s.

Beach — A770

2007, Aug. 27   **Perf. 14**
1692	A770 (1.50s) multi	.75	.75
	With tab	.85	
a.	Miniature sheet of 12 + 12 labels	13.50	13.50

No. 1692a sold for 27s. Labels could be personalized. Self-adhesive examples of No. 1692 come from sheets issued in 1999 that sold for much more than face value.

Hashomer
A771

2007, Aug. 27   **Perf. 14x13¾**
1693	A771 3.30s multi	1.60	1.60
	With tab	1.75	

Israel Reserve
Forces — A772

2007, Aug. 27   **Perf. 13¾x14**
1694	A772 7.30s multi	3.75	3.75
	With tab	4.25	

Chalom Messas
(1909-2003),
Chief Rabbi of
Morocco and
Jerusalem
A773

2007, Aug. 27
1695	A773 7.30s multi	3.75	3.75
	With tab	4.25	

Women of the
Bible — A774

2007, Aug. 27
1696	A774 1.50s Jael	.75	.75
1697	A774 2.20s Esther	1.10	1.10
1698	A774 2.40s Miriam	1.25	1.25
	Nos. 1696-1698 (3)	3.10	3.10
	With tabs	3.50	

Theodor Herzl Type of 1986
Serpentine Die Cut 13½x13¾
2007, Nov. 1   **Litho.**
Self-Adhesive
1699	A388 5a blue & ultra	.20	.20

Medicinal Herbs and Spices Type of 2006

Designs: 1.55s, Laurus nobilis. 2.25s, Coridothymus capitatus.

2007, Nov. 5   *Perf. 14*
1700 A754 1.55s multi   .80   .80
1701 A754 2.25s multi   1.25   1.25
    With tabs   2.25

Rabbi Itzhak Kaduri (1902-2006) A775

2007, Dec. 5   *Perf. 13½x14*
1702 A775 8.15s multi   4.25   4.25
    With tab   4.75

Tel Aviv Movie Theaters A776

Designs: 4.50s, Eden Cinema. 4.60s, Mograbi Cinema.

2007, Dec. 5   *Perf. 14x13½*
1703 A776 4.50s multi   2.40   2.40
1704 A776 4.60s multi   2.40   2.40
    With tabs   5.25

Family Love — A777

Designs: 1.55s, Boy giving flower to mother. 2.25s, Girl with baby brother. 3.55s. Father and son.

2007, Dec. 5   *Perf. 13½x14*
1705 A777 1.55s multi   .80   .80
1706 A777 2.25s multi   1.25   1.25
1707 A777 3.55s multi   1.90   1.90
    Nos. 1705-1707 (3)   3.95   3.95
    With tabs   4.50

Hula Nature Reserve A778

Designs: Nos. 1708a, 1710, Pelicans, Caspian terrapins, iris (denomination in yellow). Nos. 1708b, 1709, Water buffalos, marbled duck, reed warbler, wildcat, wild raspberry (denomination in red violet). Nos. 1708c, 1711, Otter, catfish, cranes, willow herb (denomination in orange).

2007, Dec. 5   *Perf. 14x13½*
1708   Strip of 3   3.75   3.75
   a.-c.   A778 2.25s Any single   1.25   1.25
    Strip with tabs   4.25

Booklet Stamps
Self-Adhesive
Serpentine Die Cut 11x10¼
1709 A778 2.25s multi   1.25   1.25
1710 A778 2.25s multi   1.25   1.25
1711 A778 2.25s multi   1.25   1.25
   a.   Booklet pane, 2 each #1709-1711   7.50
    Nos. 1709-1711 (3)   3.75   3.75

Miniature Sheet

Noah's Ark — A779

No. 1712: a, Dove and olive branch. b, Noah and family, animals, leaving ark. c, Camels, giraffes, zebra, elephants, whale. d, Peafowl, bears, tiger. e, Lions, wolf. f, Wolf, leopards, goats, kangaroos.

2007, Dec. 5   *Perf. 14*
1712 A779   Sheet of 6   8.50   8.50
   a.-f.   2.25s Any single   1.40   1.40
World Stamp Championship Israel 2008. No. 1712 sold for 16s.

Israel Rokach (1896-1959), Mayor of Tel Aviv — A780

2008, Jan. 27   *Litho.*   *Perf. 14x13¾*
1713 A780 2.25s multi   1.25   1.25
    With tab   1.40

Tel Aviv Land Lottery, Cent. (in 2009) — A781

2008, Jan. 27   *Perf. 13*
1714 A781 4.50s multi   2.50   2.50
    With tab   2.75

Intl. Holocaust Remembrance Day — A782

2008, Jan. 27   *Perf. 14*
1715 A782 4.60s multi   2.60   2.60
    With tab   3.00

See United Nations No.948, United Nations Offices in Geneva No.479, United Nations Offices in Vienna No. 412.

Mekorot, National Water System, 70th Anniv. — A783

2008, Jan. 27   *Perf. 13¾x14*
1716 A783 5.80s multi   3.25   3.25
    With tab   3.75

Akiva Aryeh Weiss (1868-1947), Tel Aviv Builder and Developer — A784

2008, Jan. 27   *Perf. 14x13¾*
1717 A784 8.15s multi   4.75   4.75
    With tab   5.25

UNESCO World Heritage Sites A785

Designs: 2.25s, Biblical Tels. 3.40s, Incense Route.

2008, Jan. 27
1718 A785 2.25s multi   1.25   1.25
1719 A785 3.40s multi   1.90   1.90
    With tab   3.50

Israeli Boy and Flag — A786

2008, Apr. 28   *Litho.*   *Perf. 14*
1720 A786 (1.55s) multi   .90   .90
    With tab   1.00

Booklet Stamp
Self-Adhesive
Serpentine Die Cut 13½x14
1721 A786 (1.55s) multi   .90   .90
   a.   Booklet pane of 20   18.00

Flowers — A787

2008, Apr. 28   *Perf. 14*
1722 A787 (1.55s) White roses   .90   .90
1723 A787 (1.55s) Cyclamen persicum   .90   .90
    With tabs   2.00

Self-adhesive examples of Nos. 1722-1723 come from sheets issued in 1999 that sold for much more than face value.

Independence, 60th Anniv. — A788

2008, Apr. 28   *Perf. 14x13¾*
1724 A788 1.55s multi   .90   .90
    With tab   1.00

Memorial Day — A789

2008, Apr. 28   *Perf. 13¾x14*
1725 A789 1.55s multi   .90   .90
    With tab   1.00

Israel Export Institute, 50th Anniv. A790

2008, Apr. 28   *Perf. 14x13¾*
1726 A790 2.80s multi   1.60   1.60
    With tab   1.75

Souvenir Sheet

Hatikva (National Anthem), 120th Anniv. — A791

2008, Apr. 28   *Perf. 13¾*
1727 A791 10s multi   8.75   8.75
No. 1727 sold for 15s.

Miniature Sheet

Independence Day Posters — A792

No. 1728 — Poster from: a, 1981 (green panel). b, 1991 (brown panel). c, 2006 (blue panel). d, 1971 (purple panel). e, 1965 (dark red panel). f, 1952 (orange panel).

2008, Apr. 28   *Perf. 13¾x14*
1728 A792   Sheet of 6   8.00   8.00
   a.-f.   2.25s Any single   1.25   1.25

Children's Art — A793

Designs: No. 1729, I Love Israel (numbers, symbols, Hebrew and Roman letters), by Etai Epstein. No. 1730, Israel is My Home (Hebrew letters, house and map of Israel), by Yuval Sulema and Eden Vilker. No. 1731, Israel's 60th, (girl, telescope, cat, butterflies, flowers and "60"), by Daniel Hazan.

2008, May 14   *Litho.*   *Perf. 13½x14*
1729 A793 2.25s multi   1.40   1.40
1730 A793 2.25s multi   1.40   1.40
1731 A793 2.25s multi   1.40   1.40
    Nos. 1729-1731 (3)   4.20   4.20
    With tabs   4.75

Souvenir Sheet

Jerusalem of Gold — A794

Litho. & Embossed With Foil Application

2008, May 14		Perf. 14½x14¼
1732 A794 18s multi	13.50	13.50

No. 1732 sold for 22.50s.

Souvenir Sheet

Tel Aviv, Cent. (in 2009) — A795

No. 1733 — Sketches of Tel Aviv life by Nahum Gutman: a, The First Concert. b, The First Lamp Post. c, Dr. Hisin.

2008, May 14	Litho.	Perf. 14x13¾
1733 A795 Sheet of 3	11.00	11.00
a. 3.50s multi	2.75	2.75
b. 4.50s multi	3.75	3.75
c. 5.50s multi	4.50	4.50

2008 World Stamp Championships, Israel. No. 1733 sold for 18s.

Gush Katif, 1970-2005 Gaza Strip Settlement A796

2008, July 14	Litho.	Perf. 14x13
1734 A796 1.55s multi	.90	.90
With tab	1.00	

Promenades — A797

Designs: 4.50s, Tabgha Promenade (on Sea of Galilee), Capernaum. 4.60s, Armon Hanatziv Promenade, Jerusalem. 8.15s, Rishonim Promenade, Netanya.

2008, July 14		
1735 A797 4.50s multi	2.60	2.60
1736 A797 4.60s multi	2.75	2.75
1737 A797 8.15s multi	4.75	4.75
Nos. 1735-1737 (3)	10.10	10.10
With tabs	11.00	

2008 Summer Olympics, Beijing A798

2008, July 14		
1738 A798 1.55s Swimming	.90	.90
1739 A798 1.55s Gymnastics	.90	.90
1740 A798 2.25s Sailing	1.40	1.40
1741 A798 2.25s Tennis	1.40	1.40
Nos. 1738-1741 (4)	4.60	4.60
With tabs	5.00	

Rabbis A799

Designs: 2.30s, Rabbi Samuel Mohilewer (1824-98). 8.50s, Rabbi Zvi Hirsch Kalischer (1795-1874).

2008, Sept. 17		Perf. 12½x13
1742 A799 2.30s multi	1.40	1.40
1743 A799 8.50s multi	5.00	5.00
With tabs	7.00	

Torah Crowns A800

Torah crown from: 1.60s, Aden, late 19th cent. No. 1737, Turkey, 19th cent. No. 1738, Poland, 1729.

2008, Sept. 17		Perf. 14x13
1744 A800 1.60s multi	.95	.95
1745 A800 3.80s multi	2.25	2.25
1746 A800 3.80s multi	2.25	2.25
Nos. 1744-1746 (3)	5.45	5.45
With tabs	6.00	

Herbs and Spices Type of 2006 and

Salvia Fruticosa — A801

Design: 1.60s, Artemisia arborescens.

2008-09		Perf. 13
1747 A754 1.60s multi	.95	.95
1748 A801 (2.90s) multi	1.75	1.75
With tabs	3.00	

Self-Adhesive
Booklet Stamps
Serpentine Die Cut 11x10¾

1749 A801 (2.90s) multi	1.75	1.75
a. Booklet pane of 10 + 10 etiquettes	17.50	

With Different Arabic Inscription and Dash Before "24"

1749B A801 (2.90s) multi	1.50	1.50
c. Booklet pane of 10 + 10 etiquettes	15.00	

Issued: Nos. 1747-1749, 9/17/08. No. 1749B, 1/25/09.

Landmarks of France and Israel — A802

Airplane, stamped first flight cover and: 1.60s, Haifa waterfront, Israel. 3.80s, Eiffel Tower, Paris.

2008, Nov. 6	Litho.	Perf. 14
1750 A802 1.60s multi	.85	.85
1751 A802 3.80s multi	2.00	2.00
With tabs	3.25	

First flight between France and Israel, 60th anniv. See France Nos. 3533-3534.

2008 Census A803

2008, Dec. 17		Perf. 14x13
1752 A803 1.60s multi	.85	.85
With tab	.95	

Israeli Defense Forces Radio A804

2008, Dec. 17		Perf. 14x13¾
1753 A804 2.30s multi	1.25	1.25
With tab	1.40	

Taglit-Birthright Israel — A805

2008, Dec. 17		Perf. 14x13
1754 A805 5.60s multi	3.00	3.00
With tab	3.25	

Ancient Letters A806

Designs: 1.60s, Bar Kokhba letters, A.D. 134. 2.30s, Lachish letters, 589 B.C. 8.50s, Letter from Ugarit, 1230 B.C.

2008, Dec. 17		
1755 A806 1.60s multi	.85	.85
1756 A806 2.30s multi	1.25	1.25
1757 A806 8.50s multi	4.50	4.50
Nos. 1755-1757 (3)	6.60	6.60
With tabs	7.25	

Menorah Type of 2002-03

2009	Serpentine Die Cut 13½x13¾	
	Self-Adhesive	
1758 A679 30a gray olive	.20	.20
1758A A679 40a gray green	.25	.25
1759 A679 50a gray brown	.25	.25
1760 A679 1s purple	.50	.50
Nos. 1758-1760 (3)	.95	.95

Issued: 30a, 50a, 1s, 2/17; 40a, 9/8.

Tel Aviv, Cent. A807

People and: 1.60s, Boardwalk and beaches. 2.30s, Buildings with different architectural styles. 3.80s, Parks.

2009		Perf. 14x13¾
1761 A807 1.60s multi	.80	.80
1762 A807 2.30s multi	1.10	1.10
1763 A807 3.80s multi	1.90	1.90
Nos. 1761-1763 (3)	3.80	3.80
With tabs	4.25	

Extreme Sports A808

2009, Feb. 17		
1764 A808 4.40s Mountain biking	2.10	2.10
1765 A808 5.40s Skydiving	2.60	2.60
1766 A808 5.60s Surfing	2.75	2.75
Nos. 1764-1766 (3)	7.45	7.45
With tabs	8.25	

Fruit — A809

No. 1767: a, Grapes. b, Lemons. c, Avocados. d, Oranges. e, Pomegranates.

2009, Feb. 17		Perf. 14
1767 Vert. strip of 5	4.00	4.00
a.-e. A809 (1.60s) Any single	.80	.80
Strip with tabs	4.50	

See Nos. 1792-1796.

Memorial Day A810

2009, Apr. 22		Perf. 14x13¾
1768 A810 1.60s multi	.75	.75
With tab	.85	

Intl. Year of Astronomy A811

Designs: 2.30s, Gersonides using Jacob's staff. 3.80s, Gravitational lensing. 8.50s, Laser Interferometer Space Antenna.

2009, Apr. 22		
1769 A811 2.30s multi	1.10	1.10
1770 A811 3.80s multi	1.90	1.90
1771 A811 8.50s multi	4.00	4.00
Nos. 1769-1771 (3)	7.00	7.00
With tabs	7.75	

Souvenir Sheet

Berek Joselewicz, A Jewish Fighter for Polish Freedom's Last Battle, Kock, by Juliusz Kossak — A812

2009, Apr. 22		Perf. 14
1772 A812 6.10s multi	3.00	3.00

See Poland No. 3935.

Miniature Sheet

Israeli Musicians — A813

No. 1773: a, Zohar Argov (1955-87). b, Sasha Argov (1914-95). c, Meir Ariel (1942-99). d, Yossi Banai (1932-2006). e, Naomi Shemer (1930-2004). f, Shoshana Damari (1923-2006). g, Yair Rosenblum (1944-96). h,

Moshe Wilensky (1910-97). i, Ehud Manor (1941-2005). j, Arik Lavie (1927-2004). k, Uzi Hitman (1952-2004). l, Ofra Haza (1957-2000).

2009, Apr. 22   **Perf. 13**
1773 A813   Sheet of 12 + 4 labels   9.00   9.00
   a.-l.   1.60s Any single   .75   .75

Love — A814

2009, June 30   **Perf. 14**
1774 A814 (1.60s) multi   .85   .85
   With tab   .95

Dead Sea — A815

2009, June 30   **Perf. 13¾x14**
1775 A815   2.30s multi   1.25   1.25
   With tab   1.40

18th Maccabiah Games — A816

2009, June 30
1776 A816   5.60s multi   3.00   3.00
   With tab   3.25

Intl. Harp Contest, 50th Anniv. — A817

2009, June 30
1777 A817   8.50s multi   4.50   4.50
   With tab   5.00

Environmental Quality — A818

No. 1778: a, Geothermal energy (Earth as teakettle, 31x31mm). b, Global warming (Earth melting in frying pan, 62x31mm). c, Solar energy (house with solar panels on Earth, 31x31mm).

2009, June 30   **Perf. 13**
1778   Horiz. strip of 3   3.75   3.75
   a.-c.   A818 2.30s Any single   1.25   1.25
    Strip with tabs   4.25

Leumit Health Fund, 75th Anniv. A819

2009, Sept. 8   **Perf. 14x13¾**
1779 A819   8.80s multi   4.75   4.75
   With tab   5.25

Honey A820

Honeycomb and: 1.60s, Bee on flower. 4.60s, Honeycomb on plate. 6.70s, Honey dripping on apple slice.

2009, Sept. 8
1780 A820   1.60s multi   .85   .85
1781 A820   4.60s multi   2.50   2.50
1782 A820   6.70s multi   3.75   3.75
    Nos. 1780-1782 (3)   7.10   7.10
    With tabs   8.00

Virtual Communications — A821

Designs: 2.40s, Instant messaging software. 5.30s, USB flash drive. 6.50s, Voice over Internet protocol.

2009, Sept. 8
1783 A821   2.40s multi   1.25   1.25
1784 A821   5.30s multi   3.00   3.00
1785 A821   6.50s multi   3.50   3.50
    Nos. 1783-1785 (3)   7.75   7.75
    With tabs   8.50

Animal Assisted Therapy A822

Designs: Nos. 1786, 1789, Woman and dog. Nos. 1787, 1790, Girl and horse. Nos. 1788, 1791, Girl and dolphin.

2009, Sept. 8   **Perf. 14x13¾**
1786 A822   2.40s multi   1.25   1.25
1787 A822   2.40s multi   1.25   1.25
1788 A822   2.40s multi   1.25   1.25
    Nos. 1786-1788 (3)   3.75   3.75
    With tabs   4.25

Booklet Stamps
Self-Adhesive
Serpentine Die Cut 11x10¼
1789 A822   2.40s multi   1.25   1.25
1790 A822   2.40s multi   1.25   1.25
1791 A822   2.40s multi   1.25   1.25
   a.   Booklet pane of 6, 2 each
     #1789-1791   7.50
    Nos. 1789-1791 (3)   3.75   3.75

Fruit Type of 2009
Serpentine Die Cut 14¼x13
2009, Nov. 26   **Litho.**
Booklet Stamps
Self-Adhesive
1792 A809   (1.60s) Lemons   .85   .85
1793 A809   (1.60s) Grapes   .85   .85
1794 A809   (1.60s) Pomegranates   .85   .85
1795 A809   (1.60s) Oranges   .85   .85
1796 A809   (1.60s) Avocados   .85   .85
   a.   Booklet pane of 20, 4 each
     #1792-1796   17.00
    Nos. 1792-1796 (5)   4.25   4.25

Yiddish Theater, Iasi, Romania A823

2009, Nov. 26   **Litho.**   **Perf. 14**
1797 A823   4.60s multi   2.50   2.50
   With tab   2.75
    See Romania No. 5142.

Lighthouses — A824

Lighthouses at: 4.60s, Jaffa. 6.70s, Tel Aviv. 8.80s, Ashdod.

2009, Nov. 26   **Perf. 14x13¾**
1798 A824   4.60s multi   2.50   2.50
1799 A824   6.70s multi   3.75   3.75
1800 A824   8.80s multi   4.75   4.75
    Nos. 1798-1800 (3)   11.00   11.00
    With tabs   12.00

Maritime Archaeology — A825

Diver and: No. 1801, Earthenware jugs. No. 1802, Figurines. 3.60s, Weapons. 5s, Anchors.

2009, Nov. 26
1801 A825   2.40s multi   1.25   1.25
1802 A825   2.40s multi   1.25   1.25
1803 A825   3.60s multi   1.90   1.90
1804 A825   5s multi   2.75   2.75
    Nos. 1801-1804 (4)   7.15   7.15
    With tabs   8.00

Arava Valley Settlements, 50th Anniv. — A826

2010, Jan. 27   **Litho.**   **Perf. 14x13¾**
1805 A826   1.60s multi   .85   .85
   With tab   .95

Lions Club of Israel, 50th Anniv. A827

2010, Jan. 27
1806 A827   4.60s multi   2.50   2.50
   With tab   2.75

Intl. Holocaust Remembrance Day — A828

2010, Jan. 27   **Perf. 14**
1807 A828   6.70s multi   3.75   3.75
   With tab   4.25

Alliance Israelite Universelle, 150th Anniv. — A829

2010, Jan. 27   **Perf. 14x13¾**
1808 A829   8.80s multi   4.75   4.75
   With tab   5.25

Birds — A830

No. 1809: a, Carduelis carduelis. b, Upupa epops. c, Prinia gracilis.

2010, Jan. 27   **Perf. 13¾x14**
1809   Strip of 3, #a-c   4.00   4.00
   a.-c.   A830 2.40s Any single   1.25   1.25
    Strip with tabs   4.50

Memorial Day — A831

2010, Apr. 14   **Litho.**   **Perf. 13¾x14**
1810 A831   1.60s multi   .85   .85
   With tab   .95

Tribute to World Trade Center Victims, by Eliezer Weishoff, Jerusalem A832

2010, Apr. 14
1811 A832   2.40s multi   1.40   1.40
   With tab   1.60   1.60

Friendship Between Israel and Canada, 60th Anniv. A833

2010, Apr. 14   **Perf. 14x13¾**
1812 A833   4.60s multi   2.50   2.50
   With tab   2.75
    See Canada No. 2379.

Israeli Innovations A834

Designs: No. 1813, Drip irrigation dripper and farm field. No. 1814, Computer chip and computer. No. 1815, Gastrointestinal camera and intestines.

2010, Apr. 14   **Perf. 14x13¼**
1813   A834   2.40s multi   1.40   1.40
1814   A834   2.40s multi   1.40   1.40
1815   A834   2.40s multi   1.40   1.40
    Nos. 1813-1815 (3)   4.20   4.20
    With tabs   4.75

Expo 2010, Shanghai.

Souvenir Sheet

Children's Books — A835

No. 1816: a, Alice's Adventures in Wonderland, by Lewis Carroll. b, Peter Pan, by Sir James M. Barrie. c, Gulliver's Travels, by Jonathan Swift.

2010, Apr. 14   **Perf. 14¾x14**
1816   A835   Sheet of 3   7.50   7.50
a.-c.   4.60s Any single   2.50   2.50

London 2010 International Stamp Exhibition.

Souvenir Sheet

Theodor Herzl (1860-1904), Zionist Leader — A836

No. 1817: a, Herzl leaning on railing, settlers. b, Settlers at settlement. c, Boy waving Israeli flag, adults, city skyline.

2010, Apr. 14
1817   A836   Sheet of 3   8.25   8.25
a.   3.70s multi   2.00   2.00
b.   4.60s multi   2.50   2.50
c.   6.70s multi   3.75   3.75

Kibbutzim, Cent. A837

2010, June 14   **Litho.**   **Perf. 14x13½**
1818   A837   2.50s multi   1.40   1.40
    With tab   1.60

Rabbi Nachman of Breslev (1772-1810), Philosopher — A838

2010, June 14   **Perf. 13½x14**
1819   A838   3.70s multi   1.90   1.90
    With tab   2.10

Simon Wiesenthal (1908-2005), Hunter of Nazi War Criminals — A839

2010, June 14   **Perf. 12½**
1820   A839   5s multi   2.60   2.60
    With tab   3.00

The Star of David is made up of tiny holes made by a laser. See Austria No. 2264.

World 420 Sailing Championships, Haifa — A840

2010, June 14   **Perf. 14x15**
1821   A840   9s multi   4.75   4.75
    With tab   5.25

Story Gardens, Holon A841

Sculptures based on children's stories: No. 1822, Where is Pluto? (Dog). No. 1823, Shmuel the Hedgehog. No. 1824, Soul Bird.

2010, June 14   **Perf. 14x13½**
1822   A841   2.50s multi   1.40   1.40
1823   A841   2.50s multi   1.40   1.40
1824   A841   2.50s multi   1.40   1.40
    Nos. 1822-1824 (3)   4.20   4.20
    With tabs   4.75

Musical Instruments A842

No. 1825: a, Zoma and oboe. b, Rebab and violin. c, Darbouka and drum. d, Qanun and piano. e, Oud and guitar.

2010, June 14   **Perf. 13½x14**
1825   Horiz. strip of 5   4.50   4.50
a.-e.   A842   1.70s Any single   .90   .90
    Strip with tabs   5.00

Tzevet (Israel Defense Forces Veterans Association), 50th Anniv. — A843

2010, Aug. 25   **Litho.**   **Perf. 13¼x13**
1826   A843   2.50s multi   1.40   1.40
    With tab   1.60

Settlements Outside of Jerusalem's Old City Walls, 150th Anniv. — A844

2010, Aug. 25   **Perf. 13¼**
1827   A844   3.70s multi   2.00   2.00
    With tab   2.25

Urban Renaissance — A845

2010, Aug. 25   **Perf. 13x13¼**
1828   A845   8.90s multi   4.75   4.75
    With tab   5.25

Shofars — A846

Shofar blower and shofar made of: 1.70s, Ram's horn. 4.20s, Kudu horn. 6.10s, Ram's horn, diff.

2010, Aug. 25   **Perf. 13¼x13**
1829   A846   1.70s multi   .90   .90
1830   A846   4.20s multi   2.25   2.25
1831   A846   6.10s multi   3.25   3.25
    Nos. 1829-1831 (3)   6.40   6.40
    With tabs   7.00

Greetings
A847   A848

2010, Aug. 25   **Perf. 13¾x14**
1832   A847   (1.70s) multi   .90   .90
    With tab   1.00
a.   Sheet of 12 + 12 labels   15.00   15.00
1833   A848   (1.70s) multi   .90   .90
    With tab   1.00
a.   Sheet of 12 +12 labels   15.00   15.00

Booklet Stamps
Self-Adhesive
Serpentine Die Cut 12½x12¾

1834   A847   (1.70s) multi   .90   .90
1835   A848   (1.70s) multi   .90   .90
a.   Booklet pane of 12, 6 each
      #1834-1835   11.00

Nos. 1832a and 1833a each sold for 28s. Labels could be personalized.

Miniature Sheet

Animals and Their Young — A849

No. 1836: a, Chicks. b, Hen. c, Kitten with ball of yarn. d, Cat. e, Rabbit kit, flower, carrot. f, Rabbit.

2010, Aug. 25   **Perf. 13x13¼**
1836   A849   Sheet of 6 + 3 labels   5.50   5.50
a.-f.   1.70s Any single   .90   .90

Garden of Gethsemane, Jerusalem — A850

2010, Nov. 15   **Litho.**   **Perf. 13x13¼**
1837   A850   4.20s multi   2.40   2.40
    With tab   2.75

Printed in sheets of 4. See Vatican City No.

Flag of Israel — A851

2010, Nov. 21   **Perf. 13¾x14**
1838   A851   (1.70s) multi   .95   .95
    With tab   1.10

Movie Theaters A852

Designs: 4.20s, Armon Cinema, Haifa. 9s, Zion Cinema, Jerusalem.

2010, Nov. 21   *Perf. 13x13¼*
1839	A852	4.20s multi	2.40	2.40
1840	A852	9s multi	5.00	5.00
		With tabs	8.25	

Bible Stories — A853

Designs: No. 1841, Adam and Eve. No. 1842, Samson and the Lion. No. 1843, Jonah and the Fish.
6s, Moses parting the Red Sea, vert.

2010, Nov. 21   *Perf. 14½x14¼*
1841	A853	1.70s multi	.95	.95
1842	A853	1.70s multi	.95	.95
1843	A853	1.70s multi	.95	.95
		Nos. 1841-1843 (3)	2.85	2.85
		With tabs	3.25	

Souvenir Sheet
Perf. 13½x13
1844	A853	6s multi	3.50	3.50

Jerusalem 2010 Intl. Philatelic Exhibition (No. 1844). No. 1844 contains one 30x40mm stamp.

AIR POST STAMPS

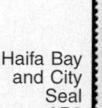

Doves Pecking at
Grapes — AP1

Marisa
Eagle — AP2

Designs: 30p, Beth Shearim eagle. 40p, Mosaic bird. 50p, Stylized dove. 250p, Mosaic dove and olive branch.

Perf. 11½
1950, June 25   **Unwmk.**   **Litho.**
C1	AP1	5p brt grnsh bl	.60	.20
C2	AP1	30p gray	.30	.20
C3	AP1	40p dark green	.30	.20
C4	AP1	50p henna brown	.30	.20
C5	AP2	100p rose car	11.00	11.00
C6	AP2	250p dk gray bl	1.50	.50
		Nos. C1-C6 (6)	14.00	12.30
		With tabs	275.00	

Haifa Bay
and City
Seal
AP3

120p, Haifa, Mt. Carmel and city seal.

1952, Apr. 13   *Perf. 14*
Seal in Gray
C7	AP3	100p ultramarine	.30	.20
C8	AP3	120p purple	.20	.20
		#C7-C8, with tabs	15.00	

Stamps were available only on purchase of a ticket to the National Stamp Exhibition, Haifa. Price, including ticket, 340p.

Olive
Tree — AP4

Tanur Cascade
AP5

Coast at Tel
Aviv-Jaffa
AP6

70p, En Gev, Sea of Galilee. 100p, Road to Jerusalem. 150p, Lion Rock. 350p, Bay of Elat, Red Sea. 750p, Lake Hule. 3000p, Tomb of Rabbi Meir Baal Haness, Tiberias.

1953-56   **Litho.**
C9	AP4	10p olive grn	.20	.20
C10	AP4	70p violet	.20	.20
C11	AP4	100p green	.20	.20
C12	AP4	150p orange brn	.20	.20
C13	AP4	350p car rose	.20	.20
C14	AP5	500p dull & dk bl	.20	.20
C15	AP6	750p brown	.20	.20
C16	AP6	1000p deep bl grn	4.50	.75
		With tab	95.00	
C17	AP6	3000p claret	.20	.20
		Nos. C9-C17 (9)	6.10	2.35
		Nos. C9-C15, C17 with tabs	5.00	

Issued: 1000p, 3/16/53; 10p, 100p, 500p, 3/2/54; 70p, 150p, 350p, 4/6/54; 750p, 8/21/56; 3000p, 11/13/56.

Old Town,
Zefat — AP7

Houbara
Bustard — AP9

Port of Elat ('Aqaba) — AP8

Designs: 20a, Ashkelon, Afridar Center. 25a, Acre, tower and boats. 30a, Haifa, view from Mt. Carmel. 35a, Capernaum, ancient synagogue, horiz. 40a, Jethro's tomb, horiz. 50a, Jerusalem, horiz. 65a, Tiberias, tower and lake, horiz. £1, Jaffa, horiz.

1960-61   **Photo.**   *Perf. 13x14, 14x13*
C18	AP7	15a light lil & blk	.20	.20
C19	AP7	20a brt yel grn & blk	.20	.20
C20	AP7	25a orange & blk ('61)	.20	.20
C21	AP7	30a grnsh bl & blk ('61)	.20	.20
C22	AP7	35a yel grn & blk ('61)	.20	.20
C23	AP7	40a lt vio & blk ('61)	.20	.20
C24	AP7	50a olive & blk ('61)	.20	.20
C25	AP7	65a lt ultra & black	.20	.20
C26	AP7	£1 pink & blk ('61)	.40	.30
		Nos. C18-C26 (9)	2.00	1.90
		With tabs	11.00	

Issued: #C18, C19, C25, 2/24/60; #C20-C22, 6/14/61; #C23, C24, C26, 10/26/61.

Wmk. 302
1962, Feb. 21   **Litho.**   *Perf. 14*
C27	AP8	£3 multicolored	1.60	1.00
		With tab	9.00	

Perf. 13x14, 14x13
1963   **Unwmk.**   **Photo.**

Birds: 5a, Sinai rose finch, horiz. 20a, White-breasted kingfisher, horiz. 28a, Mourning wheatear, horiz. 30a, Blue-cheeked bee eater. 40a, Graceful prinia. 45a, Palestine sunbird. 70a, Scops owl. £1, Purple heron. £3, White-tailed Sea eagle.
C28	AP9	5a dp vio & multi	.20	.20
C29	AP9	20a red & multi	.20	.20
C30	AP9	28a emerald & multi	.20	.20
C31	AP9	30a orange & multi	.20	.20
C32	AP9	40a multicolored	.20	.20
C33	AP9	45a yellow & multi	.20	.20

C34	AP9	55a multicolored	.20	.20
C35	AP9	70a black & multi	.20	.20
C36	AP9	£1 multicolored	.35	.35
C37	AP9	£3 ultra & multi	.85	.70
		Nos. C28-C37 (10)	2.80	2.65
		With tabs	5.75	

Issue dates: #C28-C30, Apr. 15; #C31-C33, June 19; #C34-C36, Feb. 13; #C37, Oct. 23.

Diamond
and Boeing
707
AP10

Boeing 707 and: 10a, Textiles. 30a, Symbolic stamps. 40a, Vase, jewelry. 50a, Chick, egg. 55a, Melon, avocado, strawberries. 60a, Gladioli. 80a, Electronic equipment, chart. £1, Heavy oxygen isotopes (chemical apparatus). £1.50, Women's fashions.

1968   **Photo.**   *Perf. 13x14*
C38	AP10	10a ultra & multi	.20	.20
C39	AP10	30a gray & multi	.20	.20
C40	AP10	40a multicolored	.20	.20
C41	AP10	50a multicolored	.20	.20
C42	AP10	55a multicolored	.20	.20
C43	AP10	60a sl grn, lt grn & red	.20	.20
C44	AP10	80a yel, brn & lt bl	.20	.20
C45	AP10	£1 dark bl & org	.20	.20
C46	AP10	£1.50 multicolored	.25	.20
C47	AP10	£3 pur & lt bl	.30	.25
		Nos. C38-C47 (10)	2.15	2.05
		With tabs		

Israeli exports. Sheets of 15 (5x3).
Issued: #C38-C41, 3/11; #C47, 2/7; #C42-C43, C45, 11/6; #C44, C46, 12/23.

POSTAGE DUE STAMPS

Types of Regular Issue
Overprinted in Black

Various coins, as on postage denominations.

Unwmk.
1948, May 28   **Typo.**   *Perf. 11*
Yellow Paper
J1	A1	3m orange	3.00	1.25
J2	A1	5m yellow green	4.00	1.75
J3	A1	10m red violet	7.00	4.00
J4	A1	20m ultramarine	13.00	8.00
J5	A1	50m orange brown	52.50	47.50
		Nos. J1-J5 (5)	79.50	62.50
		With tabs (blank)	2,750.	

The 3m, 20m and 50m are known with overprint omitted.
Nos. J1-J5 exist imperf.

D1   Running
Stag — D2

1949, Dec. 18   **Litho.**   *Perf. 11½*
J6	D1	2p orange	.20	.20
J7	D1	5p purple	.20	.20
J8	D1	10p yellow green	.20	.20
J9	D1	20p vermilion	.20	.20
J10	D1	30p violet blue	.25	.20
J11	D1	50p orange brown	.45	.25
		Nos. J6-J11 (6)	1.50	1.25
		With tabs (blank)	125.00	

1952, Nov. 30   **Unwmk.**   *Perf. 14*
J12	D2	5p orange brown	.20	.20
J13	D2	10p Prussian blue	.20	.20
J14	D2	20p magenta	.20	.20
J15	D2	30p gray black	.20	.20
J16	D2	40p green	.20	.20
J17	D2	50p brown	.20	.20
J18	D2	60p purple	.20	.20

J19	D2	100p red	.20	.20
J20	D2	250p blue	.20	.20
		Nos. J12-J20 (9)	1.80	1.80
		With tabs (blank)	5.00	

OFFICIAL STAMPS

Redrawn Type of 1950
Overprinted in Black

1951, Feb. 1   **Unwmk.**   *Perf. 14*
O1	A6	5p bright red violet	.20	.20
O2	A6	15p vermilion	.20	.20
O3	A6	30p ultramarine	.20	.20
O4	A6	40p orange brown	.20	.20
		Nos. O1-O4 (4)	.80	.80
		With tabs	20.00	

ITALIAN COLONIES

ə-'tal-yən 'kä-lə-nēz

General Issues for all Colonies

100 Centesimi = 1 Lira

Used values in italics are for postaly used stamps. Cancelled-to-order copies sell for about the same as unused, hinged stamps.

Watermark

Wmk. 140

Type of Italy, Dante Alighieri Society Issue, in New Colors and Overprinted in Red or Black

1932, July 11	**Wmk. 140**		**Perf. 14**	
1	A126	10c gray blk	1.20	3.25
2	A126	15c olive brn	1.20	3.25
3	A126	20c slate grn	1.20	2.00
4	A126	25c dk grn	1.20	2.00
5	A126	30c red brn (Bk)	1.20	2.00
6	A126	50c bl blk	1.20	1.20
7	A126	75c car rose (Bk)	2.00	4.75
8	A126	1.25 l dk bl	2.00	8.00
9	A126	1.75 l violet	2.00	12.00
10	A126	2.75 l org (Bk)	2.00	22.50
11	A126	5 l + 2 l ol grn	2.00	25.00
12	A126	10 l + 2.50 l dp bl	2.00	40.00
		Nos. 1-12,C1-C6 (18)	37.00	233.95

Types of Italy, Garibaldi Issue, in New Colors and Inscribed: "POSTE COLONIALI ITALIANE"

1932, July 1				**Photo.**
13	A138	10c green	4.00	14.00
14	A138	20c car rose	4.00	8.00
15	A138	25c green	4.00	8.00
16	A138	30c green	4.00	14.00
17	A138	50c car rose	4.00	8.00
18	A141	75c car rose	4.00	16.00
19	A141	1.25 l deep blue	4.00	16.00
20	A141	1.75 l + 25c dp bl	7.25	22.50
21	A144	2.55 l + 50c ol brn	7.25	37.50
22	A145	5 l + 1 l dp bl	7.25	47.50
		Nos. 13-22,C8-C12 (15)	79.50	313.50

See Nos. CE1-CE2.

Plowing with Oxen — A1

Pack Camel — A2

Lioness — A3

1933, Mar. 27		**Wmk. 140**		
23	A1	10c ol brn	14.50	20.00
24	A2	20c dl vio	14.50	20.00
25	A3	25c green	14.50	20.00
26	A1	50c purple	14.50	20.00
27	A2	75c carmine	14.50	22.50
28	A3	1.25 l blue	14.50	22.50
29	A1	2.75 l red orange	22.50	40.00
30	A2	5 l + 2 l gray grn	32.50	87.50
31	A3	10 l + 2.50 l org brn	32.50	130.00
		Nos. 23-31,C13-C19 (16)	350.00	787.50

Annexation of Eritrea by Italy, 50th anniv.

Agricultural Implements A4

Arab and Camel — A5

"Eager with New Life" — A7

"The Negev" by Reuven Rubin A9 Steam Roller A6

1933		**Photo.**		**Perf. 14**
32	A4	5c orange	9.50	13.00
33	A5	25c green	9.50	13.00
34	A6	50c purple	9.50	11.00
35	A5	75c carmine	9.50	22.50
36	A6	1.25 l deep blue	9.50	22.50
37	A6	1.75 l rose red	9.50	22.50
38	A4	2.75 l dark blue	9.50	32.50
39	A6	5 l brnsh blk	17.50	45.00
40	A6	10 l bluish blk	17.50	55.00
41	A7	25 l gray black	22.50	87.50
		Nos. 32-41,C20-C27 (18)	243.50	645.00

10th anniversary of Fascism. Each denomination bears a different inscription.
Issue dates: 25 l, Dec. 26; others, Oct. 5.

Mercury and Fasces — A8

Soccer Kickoff — A10

Scoring a Goal — A9

1934, Apr. 18				
42	A8	20c red orange	1.75	6.50
43	A8	30c slate green	1.75	6.50
44	A8	50c indigo	1.75	6.50
45	A8	1.25 l blue	1.75	14.50
		Nos. 42-45 (4)	7.00	34.00

15th annual Trade Fair, Milan.

1934, June 5				
46	A9	10c olive green	27.50	45.00
47	A9	50c purple	55.00	30.00
48	A9	1.25 l blue	55.00	110.00
49	A10	5 l brown	80.00	350.00
50	A10	10 l gray blue	80.00	350.00
		Nos. 46-50,C29-C35 (12)	592.00	1,725.

2nd World Soccer Championship.

SEMI-POSTAL STAMPS

Many issues of Italy and Italian Colonies include one or more semi-postal denominations. To avoid splitting sets, these issues are generally listed as regular postage, airmail, etc., unless all values carry a surtax.

AIR POST STAMPS

Italian Air Post Stamps for Dante Alighieri Society Issue in New Colors and Overprinted in Red or Black Like #1-12

1932, July 11		**Wmk. 140**		**Perf. 14**
C1	AP10	50c gray blk (R)	2.40	8.00
C2	AP11	1 l indigo (R)	2.40	8.00
C3	AP11	3 l gray (R)	3.25	12.00
C4	AP11	5 l ol brn (R)	3.25	17.50
C5	AP10	7.70 l + 2 l car rose	3.25	22.50
C6	AP11	10 l + 2.50 l org	3.25	40.00
		Nos. C1-C6 (6)	17.80	108.00

Leonardo da Vinci — AP1

1932, Sept. 7		**Photo.**		**Perf. 14½**
C7	AP1	100 l dp grn & brn	13.50	120.00

Types of Italian Air Post Stamps, Garibaldi Issue, in New Colors and Inscribed: "POSTE AEREA COLONIALE ITALIANA"

1932, July 1				
C8	AP13	50c car rose	4.00	16.00
C9	AP14	80c green	4.00	16.00
C10	AP13	1 l + 25c ol brn	7.25	25.00
C11	AP13	2 l + 50c ol brn	7.25	25.00
C12	AP14	5 l + 1 l ol brn	7.25	40.00
		Nos. C8-C12 (5)	28.25	122.00

Eagle AP2

Savoia Marchetti 55 — AP3

Savoia Marchetti 55 Over Map of Eritrea AP4

1933				**Perf. 14**
C13	AP2	50c org brn	13.00	20.00
C14	AP2	1 l blk vio	13.00	20.00
C15	AP3	3 l carmine	26.00	40.00
C16	AP3	5 l olive brn	26.00	40.00

C17	AP2	7.70 l + 2 l slate	32.50	95.00
C18	AP3	10 l + 2.50 l dp bl	32.50	95.00
C19	AP4	50 l dk vio	32.50	95.00
		Nos. C13-C19 (7)	154.50	387.50

50th anniv. of Italian Government of Eritrea. Issue dates: 50 l, June 1; others, Mar. 27.

Macchi-Costoldi Seaplane — AP5

Savoia S73 — AP6

Winding Propeller AP7

"More Efficient Machinery" AP8

1933-34				
C20	AP5	50c org brn	12.00	19.00
C21	AP6	75c red vio	12.00	19.00
C22	AP5	1 l bis brn	12.00	19.00
C23	AP6	3 l olive gray	12.00	38.00
C24	AP5	10 l dp vio	12.00	38.00
C25	AP6	12 l bl grn	12.00	55.00
C26	AP7	20 l gray blk	17.50	67.50
C27	AP8	50 l blue ('34)	30.00	65.00
		Nos. C20-C27 (8)	109.50	300.00

Tenth anniversary of Fascism.
Issue dates: 50 1, Dec. 26; others, Oct. 5.

Natives Hailing Dornier Wal — AP9

1934, Apr. 24				
C28	AP9	25 l brown olive	25.00	200.00

Issued in honor of Luigi Amadeo, Duke of the Abruzzi (1873-1933).

Airplane over Stadium AP10

Goalkeeper Leaping — AP11

Seaplane and Soccer Ball AP12

1934, June

C29	AP10	50c yel brn		16.00	45.00
C30	AP10	75c dp vio		16.00	45.00
C31	AP11	5 l brn blk		55.00	110.00
C32	AP11	10 l red org		55.00	110.00
C33	AP10	15 l car rose		55.00	110.00
C34	AP11	25 l green		55.00	260.00
C35	AP12	50 l bl grn		55.00	260.00
		Nos. C29-C35 (7)		307.00	940.00

World Soccer Championship Games, Rome. Issued: 50 l, June 21; others, June 5.

AIR POST SPECIAL DELIVERY STAMPS

Garibaldi Type of Italy
Wmk. 140

1932, Oct. 6   Photo.   Perf. 14

CE1	APSD1	2.25 l + 1 l dk vio & sl	8.75	25.00
CE2	APSD1	4.50 l + 1.50 l dk brn & grn	8.75	40.00

ITALIAN EAST AFRICA

ə-'tal-yən 'ēst 'a-fri-kə

LOCATION — In eastern Africa, bordering on the Red Sea and Indian Ocean
GOVT. — Italian Colony
AREA — 665,977 sq. mi. (estimated)
POP. — 12,100,000 (estimated)
CAPITAL — Asmara

This colony was formed in 1936 and included Ethiopia and the former colonies of Eritrea and Italian Somaliland. For previous issues see listings under these headings.

100 Centesimi = 1 Lira

Used values in italics are for postally used stamps. Cancelled-to-order copies sell for about the same as unused, hinged stamps.

Grant's Gazelle — A1

Eagle and Lion — A2

Victor Emmanuel III — A3

Fascist Legionary — A5

Statue of the Nile — A4

Desert Road — A6

Wmk. 140

1938, Feb. 7   Photo.   Perf. 14

1	A1	2c red orange	1.25	1.10
2	A2	5c brown	1.25	.20
3	A3	7½c dk violet	1.75	4.00
4	A4	10c olive brown	2.40	.20
5	A5	15c slate green	1.25	.40
6	A3	20c crimson	1.25	.20
7	A6	25c green	2.40	.20
8	A1	30c olive brown	1.75	.80
9	A2	35c sapphire	2.50	9.50
10	A3	50c purple	1.25	.20

Engr.

11	A5	75c carmine lake	2.50	.40
12	A6	1 l olive green	1.75	.20
13	A3	1.25 l deep blue	2.50	.40
14	A4	1.75 l orange	17.00	.20
15	A2	2 l cerise	2.50	.40
16	A6	2.55 l dark brown	16.00	28.00
17	A1	3.70 l purple	52.50	55.00
18	A5	5 l purple	14.50	4.25
19	A2	10 l henna brown	20.00	17.50
20	A4	20 l dull green	32.50	28.00
		Nos. 1-20,C1-C11,CE1-CE2 (33)	386.05	278.20

Augustus Caesar (Octavianus) A7

Goddess Abundantia A8

1938, Apr. 25   Photo.   Perf. 14

21	A7	5c bister brn	.85	2.00
22	A8	10c copper red	.85	1.25
23	A7	25c deep green	1.60	1.25
24	A8	50c purple	1.60	.85
25	A7	75c crimson	1.60	3.00
26	A8	1.25 l deep blue	1.60	8.50
		Nos. 21-26,C12-C13 (8)	9.70	24.85

Bimillenary of the birth of Augustus Caesar (Octavianus), first Roman emperor.

Rome-Berlin Axis.
Four stamps of type AP8, without "Posta Aerea," were prepared in 1941, but not issued. Value, each $2,400.

Native Boat — A9

Native Soldier — A10

Statue Suggesting Italy's Conquest of Ethiopia — A11

1940, May 11   Wmk. 140

27	A9	5c olive brown	.85	1.20
28	A10	10c red orange	.85	1.20
29	A11	25c green	2.00	2.00
30	A9	50c purple	2.00	1.20
31	A10	75c rose red	2.00	6.50
32	A11	1.25 l dark blue	2.00	4.75
33	A10	2 l + 75c carmine	2.00	22.50
		Nos. 27-33,C14-C17 (11)	20.50	53.85

Issued in connection with the first Triennial Overseas Exposition held at Naples.

Hitler and Mussolini ("Two Peoples, One War") A12

1941, June 19

34	A12	5c ocher		2.50
35	A12	10c chestnut		2.50
36	A12	20c black		4.50
37	A12	25c turquoise grn		4.50
38	A12	50c rose lilac		4.50
39	A12	75c rose car		4.50
40	A12	1.25 l brt ultra		4.50
		Nos. 34-40,C18-C19 (9)		147.00

SEMI-POSTAL STAMPS

Many issues of Italy and Italian Colonies include one or more semi-postal denominations. To avoid splitting sets, these issues are generally listed as regular postage, airmail, etc., unless all values carry a surtax.

AIR POST STAMPS

Plane Flying over Mountains AP1

Mussolini Carved in Stone Cliff — AP2

Airplane over Lake Tsana AP3

Bateleur Eagle — AP4

Eagle Attacking Serpent — AP5

Wmk. Crowns (140)

1938, Feb. 7   Photo.   Perf. 14

C1	AP1	25c slate green	3.25	4.75
C2	AP2	50c olive brown	72.50	.20
C3	AP3	60c red orange	3.25	12.00
C4	AP1	75c orange brn	4.00	2.50
C5	AP4	1 l slate blue	1.25	.20

Engr.

C6	AP2	1.50 l violet	1.75	.40
C7	AP3	2 l slate blue	1.75	1.75
C8	AP1	3 l carmine lake	2.50	6.75
C9	AP4	5 l red brown	65.00	30.00
C10	AP2	10 l violet brn	12.00	13.00
C11	AP1	25 l slate blue	24.00	30.00
		Nos. C1-C11 (11)	173.75	95.55

1938, Apr. 25   Photo.

C12	AP5	50c bister brown	.80	2.75
C13	AP5	1 l purple	.80	5.25

Bimillenary of the birth of Augustus Caesar (Octavianus), first Roman emperor.

Triennial Overseas Exposition Type

#C14, C16, Tractor. #C15, C17, Plane over city.

1940, May 11

C14	A10	50c olive gray	2.00	7.25
C15	A9	1 l purple	2.00	7.25
C16	A10	2 l + 75c gray blue	2.40	—

C17	A9	5 l + 2.50 l red brn	2.40	—
		Nos. C14-C17 (4)	7.20	13.00

Hitler and Mussolini ("Two Peoples, One War") AP8

AP9

1941, Apr. 24

C18	AP8	1 l slate blue		110.00
C19	AP9	1 l slate blue		9.50

Rome-Berlin Axis.

AIR POST SPECIAL DELIVERY STAMPS

Plow and Airplane — APSD1

Wmk. 140

1938, Feb. 7   Engr.   Perf. 14

CE1	APSD1	2 l slate blue	8.00	9.50
CE2	APSD1	2.50 l dark brown	8.00	16.00

SPECIAL DELIVERY STAMPS

Victor Emmanuel III — SD1

Wmk. 140

1938, Apr. 16   Engr.   Perf. 14

E1	SD1	1.25 l dark green	9.50	8.00
E2	SD1	2.50 l dark carmine	11.00	32.00

POSTAGE DUE STAMPS

Italy, Nos. J28 to J40, Overprinted in Black

1941   Wmk. 140   Perf. 14

J1	D6	5c brown	1.60
J2	D6	10c blue	1.60
J3	D6	20c rose red	3.25
J4	D6	25c green	3.25
J5	D6	30c red orange	6.75
J6	D6	40c black brown	6.75
J7	D6	50c violet	6.75
J8	D6	60c slate black	10.00
J9	D7	1 l red orange	20.00
J10	D7	2 l green	20.00
J11	D7	5 l violet	32.50
J12	D7	10 l blue	20.00
J13	D7	20 l carmine rose	20.00
		Nos. J1-J13 (13)	152.45

In 1943 a set of 11 "Segnatasse" stamps, picturing a horse and rider and inscribed "A. O. I.," was prepared but not issued. Value, $16.

ITALIAN STATES

ə-'tal-yən 'stāts

Watermarks

Wmk. 157 —
Large Letter "A"

Wmk. 184 —
Interlaced Wavy
Lines

Wmk. 184 has double lined letters diagonally across the sheet reading: "II R R POSTE TOSCANE."

Wmk. 185 — Crowns in the sheet

The watermark consists of twelve crowns, arranged in four rows of three, with horizontal and vertical lines between them. Only parts of the watermark appear on each stamp. (Reduced illustration.)

Wmk. 186 —
Fleurs-de-Lis in
Sheet

MODENA

LOCATION — In northern Italy
GOVT. — Duchy
AREA — 1,003 sq. mi.
POP. — 448,000 (approx.)
CAPITAL — Modena

In 1852, when the first postage stamps were issued, Modena was under the rule of Duke Francis V of the House of Este-Lorraine. In June, 1859, he was overthrown and the Duchy was annexed to the Kingdom of Sardinia which on March 17, 1861, became the Kingdom of Italy.

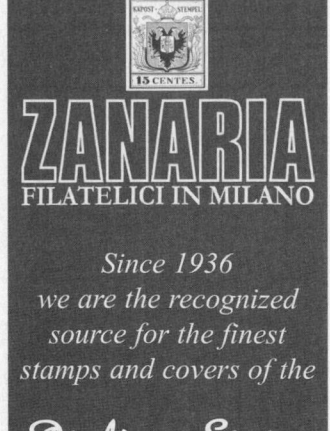
100 Centesimi = 1 Lira

Values of Modena stamps vary tremendously according to condition. Values are for very fine examples, and values for unused stamps are for examples with original gum as defined in the catalogue introduction. Extremely fine or superb examples sell at much higher prices, and fine or poor examples sell at greatly reduced prices. In addition, very fine unused examples without gum sell for about 20% of the values shown.

Coat of Arms
A1   A2

1852-57   **Unwmk.**   **Typo.**   *Imperf.*
Without Period After Figures of Value

1	A1	5c blk, *green*	2,300.	140.00
2	A1	10c blk, *rose*	575.00	90.00
a.		"EENT. 10"	7,250.	2,500.
b.		"1" of "10" inverted	7,250.	2,500.
c.		"CNET"	1,450.	1,800.
d.		No period after "CENT"	2,175.	875.00
3	A1	15c blk, *yellow*	57.50	35.00
a.		"CETN 15."	7,250.	1,100.
b.		No period after "CENT"	290.00	575.00
4	A1	25c blk, *buff*	72.50	42.50
a.		No period after "CENT"	650.00	1,100.
b.		"ENT.25" omitted	1,000.	—
c.		25c black, *green* (error)	2,900.	2,000.
d.		"N" of "CENT" omitted	725.00	1,800.
5	A1	40c blk, *blue*	440.00	125.00
a.		40c black, *pale blue*	14,500.	1,350.
b.		No period after "CENT"	1,800.	1,800.
c.		As "a," no period after "CENT"	—	—

Full margins = 1mm.
There are dividing lines between stamps.

Unused examples of No. 5a lack gum.
Used examples of No. 4c have a green administrative cancellation.
See Nos. PR3-PR4.

With Period After Figures of Value

6	A1	5c blk, *green*	35.00	47.50
a.		5c black, *olive green* ('55)	440.00	140.00
b.		"ENT"	—	2,500.
c.		"CNET"	4,250.	3,600.
d.		As "a," "CNET"	2,200.	2,200.
e.		"E" of "CENT" sideways	—	5,750.
f.		As "a," "CEN1"	2,500.	2,500.
g.		As "a," no period after "5"	650.00	575.00
h.		Double impression, no gum	1,200.	—
i.		As "a," double impression	1,200.	—
j.		Pair, #6a, 6g	1,200.	2,350.
7	A1	10c blk, *rose* ('57)	440.00	325.00
a.		"CENE"	1,450.	1,800.
b.		"CNET"	650.00	900.00
c.		"CE6T"	1,450.	1,800.
d.		"N" of "CENT" sideways	10,000.	4,350.
e.		Double impression	1,500.	4,400.
f.		Raised period after "10"	1,450.	1,800.
8	A1	40c blk, *blue* ('54)	50.00	125.00
a.		"CNET"	290.00	900.00
b.		"CENE"	650.00	1,800.
c.		"CE6T"	650.00	1,800.
d.		"49"	290.00	900.00
e.		"4C"	650.00	1,800.
f.		"CEN.T"	32,500.	—
g.		Space between "T" and period	290.00	925.00
h.		Pair, one with no period after value	725.00	2,500.

Wmk. 157

9	A1	1 l black ('53)	57.50	2,150.
a.		With period after "LIRA"	160.00	4,000.
b.		No period after "1"	150.00	3,250.

Full margins = 1mm.
There are dividing lines between stamps.

Provisional Government

1859   **Unwmk.**

10	A2	5c green	1,450.	700.00
a.		5c emerald	1,525.	800.00
b.		5c dark green	1,525.	800.00
11	A2	15c brown	2,350.	4,000.
a.		15c gray brown	325.00	
b.		15c black brown	2,600.	5,000.
c.		No period after "15"	2,900.	4,750.
d.		Period before "CENT"	4,000.	6,500.
e.		Double impression (#11a)	1,450.	
12	A2	20c lilac	65.00	1,200.
a.		20c violet	4,000.	160.00
b.		20c blue violet	2,200.	160.00
c.		As #12, no period after "20"	100.00	1,450.
d.		As #12, "ECNT"	250.00	3,100.
e.		As #12, "N" inverted	200.00	2,200.
f.		Double impression (#12b)	—	5,750.
13	A2	40c carmine	190.00	1,275.
a.		40c brown rose	190.00	1,275.
b.		No period after "40"	360.00	2,275.
c.		Period before "CENT"	360.00	2,275.
d.		Inverted "5" before the "C", no gum	32,500.	44,000.
14	A2	80c buff	190.00	19,000.
a.		80c brown orange	190.00	19,000.
b.		"CENT 8"	360.00	—
c.		"CENT 0"	1,200.	—
d.		No period after "80"	360.00	—
e.		"N" inverted	360.00	—

Full margins = 1mm.
There are dividing lines between stamps.

The reprints of the 1859 issue have the word "CENT" and the figures of value in different type from the originals. There is no frame line at the bottom of the small square in the lower right corner.

NEWSPAPER TAX STAMPS

NT1   NT2

Type I

Type II

1853   **Unwmk.**   **Typo.**   *Imperf.*

PR1	NT1	9c blk, *violet* (I)	—	3,100.
PR2	NT1	9c blk, *violet* (II)	725.00	80.00
a.		No period after "9"	1,100.	275.00

Full margins = 1mm.
There are dividing lines between stamps.

All known unused examples of #PR1 lack gum.

1855-57

PR3	A1	9c blk, *violet*	3.65	
a.		No period after "9"	7.25	
b.		No period after "CENT"	11.00	
PR4	A1	10c blk, *gray vio* ('57)	72.50	250.00
a.		"CEN1"	360.00	1,450.

Full margins = 1mm.
There are dividing lines between stamps.

No. PR3 was never placed in use.

1859

PR5	NT2	10c black	1,150.	2,200.
a.		Double impression	16,500.	20,000.
b.		Vert. guidelines between stamps	1,150.	

Full margins = 1½mm.
No. PR5 has horizontal guide lines between stamps. No. PR5b is a second printing, which was not issued.

These stamps did not pay postage, but were a fiscal tax collected by the postal authorities on newspapers arriving from foreign countries.
The stamps of Modena were superseded by those of Sardinia in February, 1860.

PARMA

LOCATION — Comprising the present provinces of Parma and Piacenza in northern Italy.
GOVT. — Independent Duchy
AREA — 2,750 sq. mi. (1860)
POP. — 500,000 (1860)
CAPITAL — Parma

Parma was annexed to Sardinia in 1860.

100 Centesimi = 1 Lira

Values of Parma stamps vary tremendously according to condition. Values are for very fine examples, and values for unused stamps are for examples with original gum as defined in the catalogue introduction except for No. 8 which is known only without gum. Extremely fine or superb copies sell at much higher prices, and fine or poor stamps sell at greatly reduced prices. In addition, very fine unused stamps without gum sell for about 20% of the values shown.

Crown and Fleur-de-lis
A1   A2

1852   **Unwmk.**   **Typo.**   *Imperf.*

1	A1	5c blk, *yellow*	125.00	140.00
2	A1	10c blk, *white*	125.00	140.00
3	A1	15c blk, *pink*	3,600.	72.50
a.		Tête bêche pair, horiz.	—	100,000.
b.		Double impression	—	4,250.
4	A1	25c blk, *violet*	14,500.	215.00
5	A1	40c blk, *blue*	2,900.	400.00
a.		40c black, *pale blue*	—	525.00

Full margins = ½mm.

1854-55

6	A1	5c org yel	8,600.	875.00
a.		5c lemon yellow	11,500.	1,100.
b.		Double impression	—	18,000.
7	A1	15c red	10,000.	215.00
8	A1	25c red brn ('55)	7,500.	425.00
a.		Double impression	—	36,000.

Full margins = ½mm.

No. 8 unused is without gum.

1857-59

9	A2	15c red ('59)	360.00	360.00
10	A2	25c red brown	575.00	215.00
11	A2	40c bl, wide "0" ('58)	80.00	500.00
a.		Narrow "0" in "40"	85.00	550.00

Full margins = 1mm.

Provisional Government

A3

1859

12	A3	5c yel grn	650.00	23,000.
a.		5c blue green	2,900.	4,250.
13	A3	10c brown	1,325.	650.00
a.		10c deep brown	1,325.	650.00
b.		"1" of "10" inverted	2,700.	5,400.
c.		Thick "0" in "10"	2,700.	5,500.
14	A3	20c pale blue	1,325.	200.00
a.		20c deep blue	1,325.	240.00
b.		Thick "0" in "20"	1,550.	250.00
15	A3	40c red	725.00	8,750.
a.		40c brown red	23,000.	12,500.
b.		Thick "0" in "40," (#15)	825.00	10,500.
c.		Thick "0" in "40," (#15a)	25,000.	14,500.
16	A3	80c olive yellow	8,000.	230,000.
a.		80c orange yellow	11,000.	—
b.		80c bister	8,600.	
c.		80c orange bister	9,750.	

Full margins = 1¼mm.

Nos. 12-16 exist in two other varieties: with spelling "CFNTESIMI" and with small "A" in "STATI." These are valued about 50 per cent more than normal stamps.
See Nos. PR1-PR2.

NEWSPAPER TAX STAMPS

Type of 1859

1853-57   Unwmk.   Typo.   Imperf.
Normal Paper ('53)

PR1	A3	6c black, deep rose	2,300.	325.00
PR2	A3	9c black, blue	1,275.	15,500.

Full margins = 1¼mm.

Thin, Semitransparent Paper ('57)

PR1a	A3	6c black, rose ('57)	140.00
PR2a	A3	9c black, blue	72.50

These stamps belong to the same class as the Newspaper Tax Stamps of Modena, Austria, etc.
Note following #16 also applies to #PR1-PR2.
Nos. PR1a-PR2a were not issued.
The stamps of Parma were superseded by those of Sardinia in 1860.

ROMAGNA

LOCATION — Comprised the present Italian provinces of Forli, Ravenna, Ferrara and Bologna.
GOVT. — One of the Roman States
AREA — 5,626 sq. mi.
POP. — 1,341,091 (1853)
CAPITAL — Ravenna

Postage stamps were issued when a provisional government was formed pending the unification of Italy. In 1860 Romagna was annexed to Sardinia and since 1862 the postage stamps of Italy have been used.

100 Bajocchi = 1 Scudo

Values of Romagna stamps vary tremendously according to condition. Values are for very fine examples, and values for unused stamps are for examples with original gum as defined in the catalogue introduction. Extremely fine or superb stamps sell at much higher prices, and fine or poor stamps sell at greatly reduced prices. In addition, very fine unused stamps without gum sell for about 20% of the values shown.

A1

1859   Unwmk.   Typo.   Imperf.

1	A1	½b blk, straw	35.00	325.00
a.		Half used as ¼b on cover		14,750.
2	A1	1b blk, drab	35.00	160.00
3	A1	2b blk, buff	50.00	175.00
a.		Half used as 1b on cover		6,400.
4	A1	3b blk, dk grn	57.50	350.00
5	A1	4b blk, fawn	650.00	160.00
a.		Half used as 2b on cover		32,500.
6	A1	5b blk, gray vio	72.50	400.00
7	A1	6b blk, yel grn	475.00	8,000.
a.		Half used as 3b on cover		145,000.
8	A1	8b blk, rose	225.00	1,800.
a.		Half used as 4b on cover		145,000.
9	A1	20b blk, gray grn	225.00	2,500.

Full margins = 1mm.
There are dividing lines between stamps.

Forged cancellations are plentiful.
Bisects used Oct. 12, 1859 to Mar. 1, 1860.

These stamps have been reprinted several times. The reprints usually resemble the originals in the color of the paper but there are impressions on incorrect colors and also in colors on white paper. They often show broken letters and other injuries. The Y shaped ornaments between the small circles in the corners are broken and blurred and the dots outside the circles are often missing or joined to the circles.
The stamps of Romagna were superseded by those of Sardinia in February, 1860.

ROMAN STATES

LOCATION — Comprised most of the central Italian Peninsula, bounded by the former Kingdom of Lombardy-Venetia and Modena on the north, Tuscany on the west, and the Kingdom of Naples on the southeast.
GOVT. — Under the direct government of the See of Rome.
AREA — 16,000 sq. mi.
POP. — 3,124,758 (1853)
CAPITAL — Rome

Upon the formation of the Kingdom of Italy, the area of the Roman States was greatly reduced and in 1870 they disappeared from the political map of Europe. Postage stamps of Italy have been used since that time.

100 Bajocchi = 1 Scudo
100 Centesimi = 1 Lira (1867)

Values of Roman States stamps vary tremendously according to condition. Values are for very fine examples, and values for unused stamps are for examples with original gum as defined in the catalogue introduction. Extremely fine or superb stamps sell at much higher prices, and fine or poor stamps sell at greatly reduced prices. In addition, very fine unused stamps without gum sell for about 20% of the values shown.

Papal Arms
A1   A2

A3   A4

A5   A6

1852   Unwmk.   Typo.   Imperf.

1	A1	½b black, dull violet	57.50	125.00
a.		½b black, gray blue	725.00	95.00
b.		½b black, gray lilac	725.00	325.00
c.		½b black, gray	725.00	92.50
d.		½b black, reddish violet	3,600.	1,800.
e.		½b black, dark violet	275.00	275.00
f.		Tête bêche pair		32,500.
h.		As "a," half used as ¼b on wrapper, pen canceled		65,000.
i.		As #1, double impression	—	5,750.
j.		Impression on both sides	—	13,000.
2	A2	1b black, gray green	290.00	11.00
a.		1b black, blue green	850.00	57.50
b.		As "a," half used as ½b on cover		550.00
c.		Grayish oily ink	1,075.	40.00
d.		Double impression		6,000.
e.		Impression on both sides	—	13,000.
3	A3	2b black, greenish white	14.00	72.50
a.		2b black, yellow green	215.00	15.00
b.		As #3, half used as 1b on cover		6,500.
c.		As "a," half used as 1b on cover		475.00
d.		Grayish oily ink	1,075.	40.00
e.		No period after "BAJ"	150.00	42.50
f.		As "a" and "e"	425.00	27.50
g.		Double impression		5,500.
4	A4	3b black, brown	175.00	65.00
a.		3b black, light brown	5,250.	125.00
b.		3b black, yellow brown	2,500.	50.00
c.		3b black, yellow buff	2,500.	50.00
d.		3b black, chrome yellow	42.50	200.00
e.		One-third used as 1b on circular		3,600.
f.		Two-thirds used as 2b on circular		11,500.
g.		Grayish oily ink	5,250.	215.00
h.		Impression on both sides	—	13,000.
i.		Double impression		6,000.
j.		Half used as 1½b on cover		14,250.
5	A5	4b black, lemon	250.00	85.00
a.		4b black, yellow	250.00	85.00
b.		4b black, rose brown	10,000.	125.00
c.		4b black, gray brown	7,750.	87.50
d.		Half used as 2b on cover		2,700.
e.		One-quarter used as 1b on cover		25,000.
f.		Impression on both sides	—	13,000.
g.		Ribbed paper	300.00	75.00
h.		Grayish oily ink	16,000.	350.00
i.		As "a," half used as 2b on cover		4,250.
j.		As "a," one-quarter used as 1b on cover		23,500.
6	A6	5b black, rose	250.00	16.00
a.		5b black, pale rose	260.00	18.00
c.		Impression on both sides		13,000.
d.		Double impression		6,000.
e.		Grayish oily ink	1,500.	47.50
f.		Half used as 2½b on cover		72,500.
7	A7	6b black, greenish gray	1,000.	85.00
a.		6b black, gray	1,600.	92.50
b.		6b black, grayish lilac	1,400.	225.00
c.		Grayish oily ink	4,250.	250.00
d.		Double impression		6,000.
e.		Half used as 3b on cover		5,750.
f.		One-third used as 2b on cover		21,500.
8	A8	7b black, blue	1,425.	80.00
a.		Half used as 3½b on cover		36,000.
b.		Double impression	—	5,500.
c.		Grayish oily ink	4,300.	160.00

A7   A8

A9   A10

A11

9	A9	8b black	650.00	47.50
a.		Half used as 4b on cover		9,500.
b.		Quarter used as 2b on cover		90,000.
c.		Double impression	—	250.00
d.		Grayish oily ink	2,650.	250.00
10	A10	50b dull blue	16,000.	1,800.
a.		50b blue (worn impression)	23,000.	2,900.
11	A11	1sc rose	4,000.	3,600.

Full margins: Nos. 1-2, 4-5, 10-11 = ½mm; Nos. 3, 6-8 = ¾mm; No. 9 = 1¼mm. There are double dividing lines between stamps on Nos. 1-2, 4-5, 9.

Counterfeits exist of Nos. 10-11. Fraudulent cancellations are found on No. 11.

A12   A13

A14   A15

A16   A17

A18

1867   Imperf.
Glazed Paper

12	A12	2c black, green	115.00	275.00
a.		No period after "Cent"	140.00	290.00
13	A13	3c black, gray	1,275.	7,750.
a.		3c black, lilac gray	3,200.	2,500.
14	A14	5c black, light blue	175.00	250.00
a.		No period after "5"	350.00	500.00
15	A15	10c black, vermilion	1,575.	92.50
a.		Double impression		7,250.
16	A16	20c black, copper red (unglazed)	200.00	115.00
a.		No period after "20"	650.00	325.00
b.		No period after "CENT"	650.00	315.00
17	A17	40c black, yellow	225.00	215.00
a.		No period after "40"	290.00	275.00
18	A18	80c black, lilac rose	200.00	525.00
a.		No period after "80"	350.00	850.00

Full margins: No. 12 = 2mm; Nos. 13, 17 = 1¼mm; Nos. 14, 18 = 1½mm at sides, 1mm at top and bottom; No. 15 = 2½mm at sides, 1mm at top and bottom; No. 16 = 1½mm at sides, ¼mm at top and bottom.
There are double dividing lines between stamps.

Imperforate stamps on unglazed paper, or in colors other than listed, are unfinished remainders of the 1868 issue.
Fraudulent cancellations are found on Nos. 13, 14, 17, 18.

1868   Glazed Paper   Perf. 13

19	A12	2c black, green	10.50	72.50
a.		No period after "CENT"	12.50	90.00
20	A13	3c black, gray	47.50	3,200.
a.		3c black, lilac gray	9,000.	20,000.
21	A14	5c black, light blue	29.00	57.50
a.		No period after "5"	32.50	72.50
b.		No period after "Cent"	110.00	290.00
c.		5c black, lt bl (unglazed imperf., without gum)	90.00	—

22	A15	10c black, *orange ver*	3.50	12.50
a.		10c black, *vermilion*	72.50	14.00
b.		10c black, *ver* (unglazed)	1.00	—
c.		10c black, *ver* (unglazed, imperf., without gum)	1.00	—
23	A16	20c black, *deep crimson*	5.75	26.50
a.		20c black, *magenta*	7.25	42.50
b.		20c black, *magenta* (unglazed)	350.00	35.00
c.		20c black, *magenta* (imperf., without gum)	2.90	—
d.		20c black, *copper red* (unglazed)	1,800.	50.00
e.		20c black, *deep crimson* (imperf., without gum)	2.90	—
f.		No period after "20" (copper red)	2,500.	350.00
g.		No period after "20" (mag)	29.00	215.00
h.		No period after "20" (deep crimson)	29.00	215.00
i.		No period after "CENT" (copper red)	2,500.	350.00
j.		No period after "CENT" (magenta)	29.00	215.00
k.		No period after "CENT" (deep crimson)	29.00	215.00
24	A17	40c black, *greenish yellow*	10.00	140.00
a.		40c black, *yellow*	250.00	90.00
b.		40c black, *orange yellow*	110.00	900.00
c.		No period after "40"	14.50	115.00
25	A18	80c black, *rose lilac*	250.00	360.00
a.		80c black, *bright rose*	5,750.	45,000.
b.		80c black, *rose* (unglazed)	57.50	—
c.		No period after "80" (rose lilac)	110.00	500.00
d.		80c black, *pale rose lilac* (unglazed)	85.00	—
e.		80c black, *pale rose*	50.00	350.00
f.		As "e," no period after "80"	65.00	600.00
g.		As "a," no period after "80"	6,750.	—
h.		As "e," double impression		
		Nos. 19-25 (7)	356.25	3,869.

All values except the 3c are known imperforate vertically or horizontally, and in vertical and horizontal pairs, imperf between. See the *Scott Specialized Catalogue of Stamps and Covers* for detailed listings.

Double impressions are known of the 5c, 10c, 20c (all three colors), 40c and 80c.

Fraudulent cancellations are found on Nos. 20, 24 and 25.

The stamps of the 1867 and 1868 issues have been privately reprinted; many of these reprints are well executed and it is difficult to distinguish them from the originals. Most reprints show more or less pronounced defects of the design. On the originals the horizontal lines between stamps are unbroken, while on most of the reprints these lines are broken. Most of the perforated reprints gauge 11½.

Roman States stamps were replaced by those of Italy in 1870.

SARDINIA

LOCATION — An island in the Mediterranean Sea off the west coast of Italy and a large area in northwestern Italy, including the cities of Genoa, Turin and Nice.

GOVT. — Kingdom

As a result of war and revolution, most of the former independent Italian States were joined to the Kingdom of Sardinia in 1859 and 1860. On March 17, 1861, the name was changed to the Kingdom of Italy.

100 Centesimi = 1 Lira

Values of Sardinia stamps vary tremendously according to condition. Values are for very fine examples, and values for unused stamps are for examples with original gum as defined in the catalogue introduction. Extremely fine or superb stamps sell at much higher prices, and fine or poor stamps sell at greatly reduced prices. In addition, very fine unused stamps without gum sell for about 20-30% of the values shown.

King Victor Emmanuel II
A1   A2

A3   A4

1851		**Unwmk.**	**Litho.**	**Imperf.**
1	A1	5c gray black	10,000.	2,150.
a.		5c black	10,000.	2,150.
2	A1	20c blue	8,250.	215.00
a.		20c deep blue	8,250.	215.00
b.		20c pale blue	8,250.	360.00
3	A1	40c rose	17,250.	4,250.
a.		40c violet rose	17,250.	7,250.

Full margins = ½mm.

Vignette & Inscriptions Embossed
1853

4	A2	5c *blue green*	16,000.	1,325.
a.		Double embossing		3,250.
5	A2	20c *dull blue*	17,250.	175.00
a.		Double embossing		1,400.
6	A2	40c *pale rose*	10,750.	1,100.
b.		Double embossing		2,500.

Full margins = ¾mm.

Lithographed Frame in Color, Colorless Embossed Vignette
1854

7	A3	5c yellow green	32,500.	650.00
a.		Double embossing		1,450.
b.		5c grayish green		3,250.
8	A3	20c blue	18,000.	140.00
a.		Double embossing		550.00
b.		20c indigo		900.00
9	A3	40c rose	100,000.	3,250.
a.		Double embossing		5,750.
b.		40c brown rose		215.00

Full margins = ¾mm.

Nos. 7b, 8b and 9b, differing in shade from the original stamps, were prepared but not issued.

Typographed Frame in Color, Colorless Embossed Vignette
1855-63   Unwmk.   Imperf.

Stamps of this issue vary greatly in color, paper and sharpness of embossing as between the early (1855-59) printings and the later (1860-63) ones. Year dates after each color name indicate whether the stamp falls into the Early or Late printing group.

As a rule, early printings are on smooth thick paper with sharp embossing, while later printings are usually on paper varying from thick to thin and of inferior quality with embossing less distinct and printing blurred. The outer frame shows a distinct design on the early printings, while this design is more or less blurred or even a solid line on the later printings.

10	A4	5c green ('62-63)	5.75	14.50
a.		5c yellow green ('62-63)	35.00	21.00
b.		5c olive green ('60-61)	425.00	275.00
c.		5c yellow green ('55-59)	1,000.	200.00
d.		5c myrtle green ('57)	5,000.	500.00
e.		5c emerald ('55-57)	3,600.	425.00
f.		Head inverted	—	3,250.
g.		Double head, one inverted	—	3,250.
11	A4	10c bister ('63)	5.75	21.00
a.		10c ocher ('62)	105.00	21.00
b.		10c olive bister ('62)	175.00	27.50
c.		10c olive green ('61)	250.00	37.50
d.		10c reddish brown ('61)	1,250.	140.00
e.		10c gray brown ('61)	175.00	50.00
f.		10c olive gray ('60-61)	350.00	72.50
g.		10c gray ('60)	1,275.	225.00
h.		10c grayish brown ('59)	125.00	215.00
i.		10c violet brown ('59)	650.00	275.00
j.		10c dark brown ('58)	775.00	400.00
k.		Head inverted		4,000.
l.		Double head, one inverted	—	4,000.
m.		Pair, one without embossing	2,500.	—
n.		Half used as 5c on cover (15c rate)		100,000.
12	A4	20c indigo ('62)	115.00	50.00
a.		20c blue ('61)	215.00	21.00
b.		20c light blue ('60-61)	215.00	21.00
c.		20c Prussian bl ('59-60)	725.00	35.00
d.		20c indigo ('57-58)	540.00	50.00
e.		20c sky blue ('55-56)	5,000.	215.00
f.		20c cobalt ('55)	2,850.	125.00
g.		Head inverted		1,425.
h.		Double head, one inverted	2,850.	

i.		Pair, one without embossing	1,425.	—
j.		Half used as 10c on cover		125,000.
13	A4	40c red ('63)	22.50	50.00
a.		40c rose ('61-62)	180.00	72.50
b.		40c carmine ('60)	725.00	425.00
c.		40c light red ('57)	3,250.	140.00
d.		40c vermilion ('55-57)	5,000.	425.00
e.		Head inverted		5,500.
f.		Double head, one inverted	—	5,500.
g.		Pair, one without embossing	2,150.	—
h.		Half used as 20c on cover		72,500.
14	A4	80c orange yellow ('62)	27.50	500.00
a.		80c yellow ('60-61)	32.50	400.00
b.		80c yellow ocher ('59)	900.00	725.00
c.		80c ocher ('58)	225.00	575.00
d.		80c brown orange ('58)	225.00	575.00
e.		Head inverted		20,000.
f.		Half used as 40c on cover		72,500.
15	A4	3 l bronze, thin paper ('61)	500.00	3,250.
		Nos. 10-15 (6)	676.50	3,885.

Full margins = 1mm.

Forgeries of the inverted and double head varieties have been made by applying a faked head embossing to printer's waste without head. These forgeries are plentiful.

Fraudulent cancellations are found on #13-15.

The 5c, 20c and 40c have been reprinted; the embossing of the reprints is not as sharp as that of the originals, the colors are dull and blurred.

NEWSPAPER STAMPS

N1

Typographed and Embossed
1861   Unwmk.   Imperf.

P1	N1	1c black	8.00	14.00
a.		Numeral "2"	725.00	2,500.
b.		Figure of value inverted	2,150.	34,000.
c.		Double impression		
P2	N1	2c black	160.00	115.00
a.		Numeral "1"	11,000.	32,500.
b.		Figure of value inverted	2,150.	34,000.

Full margins = 1mm.

Forgeries of the varieties of the embossed numerals have been made from printer's waste without numerals.

See Italy No. P1 for 2c buff.

The stamps of Sardinia were superseded in 1862 by those of Italy, which were identical with the 1855 issue of Sardinia, but perforated. Until 1863, imperforate and perforated stamps were issued simultaneously.

TUSCANY

LOCATION — In the north central part of the Apennine Peninsula.

GOVT. — Grand Duchy

AREA — 8,890 sq. mi.

POP. — 2,892,000 (approx.)

CAPITAL — Florence

Tuscany was annexed to Sardinia in 1860.

60 Quattrini = 20 Soldi = 12 Crazie = 1 Lira

100 Centesimi = 1 Lira (1860)

Values of Tuscany stamps vary tremendously according to condition. Values are for very fine examples, and values for unused stamps are for examples with original gum as defined in the catalogue introduction. Extremely fine or superb stamps sell at much higher prices, and fine or poor stamps sell at greatly reduced prices.

> Dangerous counterfeits exist of #1-PR1c.

Lion of Tuscany — A1

1851-52 Typo. Wmk. 185 Imperf.
Blue, Grayish Blue or Gray Paper

1	A1	1q black ('52)	17,500.	2,500.
2	A1	1s ocher, *grayish*	22,000.	2,750.
a.		1s orange, *grayish*	25,000.	2,750.
b.		1s yellow, *bluish*	27,500.	3,000.
3	A1	2s scarlet	72,500.	10,000.
4	A1	1cr carmine	12,000.	175.00
a.		1cr brown carmine	15,000.	175.00
5	A1	2cr blue	7,250.	190.00
a.		2cr greenish blue	7,750.	200.00
6	A1	4cr green	12,000.	250.00
a.		4cr bluish green	12,000.	250.00
7	A1	6cr slate blue	13,250.	375.00
a.		6cr blue	12,000.	400.00
b.		6cr indigo	12,000.	400.00
8	A1	9cr gray lilac	27,500.	375.00
a.		9cr deep violet	27,500.	400.00
9	A1	60cr red ('52)	120,000.	33,000.

Full margins = ¼mm.

The first paper was blue, later paper more and more grayish. Stamps on distinctly blue paper sell about 20 percent higher, except Nos. 3 and 9 which were issued on blue paper only. Examples without watermark are proofs.

Reprints of Nos. 3 and 9 have re-engraved value labels, color is too brown and impressions blurred and heavy. Paper same as originals.

No. 14a

1857-59   Wmk. 184
White Paper

10	A1	1q black	2,400.	1,325.
11	A1	1s yellow	66,000.	7,750.
12	A1	1cr carmine	16,500.	825.00
13	A1	2cr blue	5,000.	190.00
14	A1	4cr green	12,000.	250.00
a.		Inverted value tablet		1,100,000.
15	A1	6cr deep blue	15,500.	375.00
16	A1	9cr gray lilac ('59)	60,000.	7,750.

Full margins = ¼mm.

Provisional Government

Coat of Arms — A2

1860

17	A2	1c brn lilac	4,250.	1,400.
a.		1c red lilac	5,500.	1,550.
b.		1c gray lilac	4,250.	1,400.
18	A2	5c green	17,500.	325.00
a.		5c olive green	20,000.	350.00
b.		5c yellow green	24,000.	500.00
19	A2	10c deep brown	5,000.	82.50
a.		10c gray brown	6,000.	82.50
b.		10c purple brown	5,000.	82.50
20	A2	20c blue	15,000.	250.00
a.		20c deep blue	15,000.	300.00
b.		20c gray blue	16,500.	300.00
21	A2	40c rose	22,000.	425.00
a.		40c carmine	22,000.	425.00
b.		Half used as 20c on cover		300,000.
22	A2	80c pale red brn	42,500.	2,000.
a.		80c brown orange	42,500.	2,000.
23	A2	3 l ocher	300,000.	135,000.

Full margins = ¼mm.

NEWSPAPER TAX STAMPS

NT1

1854 Unwmk. Typo. Imperf.
Yellowish Pelure Paper

PR1	NT1	2s black		120.00
a.		Tête bêche pair		1,100.
b.		As "a," one stamp on back		1,100.
c.		Double impression		825.00

Full margins = 10mm.

This stamp represented a fiscal tax on newspapers coming from foreign countries. It was not canceled when used.

The stamps of Tuscany were superseded by those of Sardinia in 1861.

TWO SICILIES

LOCATION — Formerly comprised the island of Sicily and the lower half of the Apennine Peninsula.
GOVT. — Independent Kingdom
CAPITAL — Naples

The Kingdom was annexed to Sardinia in 1860.

200 Tornesi = 100 Grana = 1 Ducat

Values of Two Sicilies stamps vary tremendously according to condition. Values are for very fine examples, and values for unused stamps are for examples with original gum as defined in the catalogue introduction. Extremely fine or superb copies sell at much higher prices, and fine or poor copies sell at greatly reduced prices. In addition, very fine unused stamps without gum sell for about 20%-30% of the values shown.

Naples

Coat of Arms
A1   A2

A3   A4

A5   A6

A7

1858 Engr. Wmk. 186 Imperf.

1	A1	½g pale lake	2,000.	360.00
a.		½g rose lake	2,000.	360.00
b.		½g lake	2,600.	550.00
c.		½g carmine lake	3,250.	800.00
d.		Half used as ¼g on newspaper		215,000.
2	A2	1g pale lake	1,000.	50.00
a.		1g rose lake	575.00	50.00
b.		1g brown lake	1,450.	110.00
c.		1g carmine lake	900.00	87.50
d.		Printed on both sides		2,000.
e.		Printed on both sides, one inverted		900.00
3	A3	2g pale lake	400.00	16.00
a.		2g rose lake	400.00	16.00
b.		2g lake	650.00	29.00
c.		2g carmine lake	900.00	25.00
d.		Impression of 1g on reverse		1,800.
e.		Double impression		11,000.
f.		Printed on both sides		2,000.
4	A4	5g brown lake	3,100.	60.00
a.		5g rose lake	2,600.	60.00
b.		5g carmine lake	4,000.	65.00
d.		Printed on both sides		5,000.
e.		5g rose carmine	5,500.	175.00

---

f.		5g bright carmine	6,000.	215.00
g.		5g dark carmine	7,000.	325.00
5	A5	10g rose lake	5,750.	215.00
a.		10g lake	6,200.	290.00
b.		10g carmine lake	6,100.	290.00
c.		Printed on both sides		16,000.
d.		Double impression		18,000.
6	A6	20g rose lake	5,100.	650.00
a.		20g lake	5,100.	725.00
b.		Double impression	72,500.	
c.		20g pale rose	7,250.	1,500.
d.		20g pale car rose	8,500.	1,750.
7	A7	50g rose lake	11,500.	2,900.
a.		50g lake	11,500.	2,900.

Nos. 1-2, 4-7 have been reprinted in bright rose and Nos. 1, 7 in dull brown. The reprints are on thick unwatermarked paper. Value $8 each.

Provisional Government

A8   A9

1860

8	A8	½t deep blue	180,000.	11,500.
9	A9	½t blue	44,000.	3,800.
a.		½t deep blue	44,000.	3,800.

Full margins = 1¼mm at sides, 2mm at top and bottom.

100 varieties of each.

No. 8 was made from the plate of No. 1, which was altered by changing the "G" to "T."

No. 9 was made from the same plate after a second alteration erasing the coat of arms and inserting the Cross of Savoy. Dangerous counterfeits exist of Nos. 8-9.

Sicily

Ferdinand II — A10

1859 Unwmk. Engr. Imperf.
Soft Porous Paper, Brownish Gum
(Naples consignment)

10g	A10	½g orange	575.00	4,000.
c.		Printed on both sides	—	40,000.
11	A10	1g dark brown	17,500.	700.00
12h	A10	1g pale olive green (III)	200.00	180.00
c.		Double impression	4,400.	4,400.
13g	A10	2g blue	180.00	120.00
b.		Printed on both sides		26,000.
14	A10	5g deep rose	725.00	600.00
15	A10	5g vermilion	600.00	1,600.
16	A10	10g dark blue	800.00	375.00
17	A10	20g dk gray vio	800.00	625.00
18	A10	50g dk brn red	800.00	4,750.

Full margins = 1mm.

There were three plates each for the 1g and 2g, two each for the ½g and 5g and one plate each for the other values.

Nos. 10a, 10b, 11, 11a, 14, 14a, 14b and 15 are printed from Plate I on which the stamps are 2 to 2½mm apart. On almost all stamps from Plate I, the S and T of POSTA touch.

Nos. 12a, and 15a are from Plate II and No. 12 is from Plate III. On both Plates II and III stamps are spaced 1½mm apart. Most stamps from Plate II have a white line about 1mm long below the beard.

Nos. 10-18 are on soft, porous paper with brownish gum, while Nos. 10, 12 and 13 exist also on hard white paper, with white gum. Color shades exist, some on both types of paper. For detailed listings, see the *Scott Classic Specialized Catalogue of Stamps and Covers.*

The ½g blue is stated to be a proof of which two examples are known used on cover.

Fraudulent cancellations are known on Nos. 10, 15, 15a and 18.

Neapolitan Provinces

King Victor
Emmanuel II — A11

Lithographed, Center Embossed

1861 Unwmk. Imperf.

19	A11	½t green	18.00	225.00
a.		½t yellow green	500.00	290.00
b.		½t emerald	5,750.	900.00
c.		½t black (error)	47,500.	57,500.
d.		Head inverted (green)	240.00	
e.		Head inverted (yel grn)		11,500.
f.		Printed on both sides		29,000.
20	A11	½g bister	175.00	225.00
a.		½g brown	175.00	250.00
b.		½g gray brown	215.00	225.00
c.		Head inverted	1,800.	
21	A11	1g black	350.00	32.50
a.		Head inverted		1,800.
22	A11	2g blue	115.00	12.50
a.		2g deep blue	115.00	12.50
b.		Head inverted	400.00	900.00
c.		2g black (error)		60,000.
23	A11	5g car rose	215.00	125.00
a.		5g vermilion	215.00	175.00
b.		5g lilac rose	250.00	290.00
c.		Head inverted	1,100.	8,000.
e.		Printed on both sides		18,000.
25	A11	10g orange	110.00	275.00
a.		10g ocher	1,300.	725.00
b.		10g bister	125.00	275.00
26	A11	20g yellow	500.00	2,500.
a.		Head inverted		36,000.
27	A11	50g gray	35.00	9,000.
a.		50g slate	42.50	9,000.
b.		50g slate blue	50.00	11,500.
		Nos. 19-27 (8)	1,518.	12,395.

Full margins = 1mm.

Counterfeits of the inverted head varieties of this issue are plentiful. See note on forgeries after Sardinia No. 15.

Fraudulent cancellations are found on Nos. 19-20, 23-27.

Stamps similar to those of Sardinia 1855-61, type A4 but with inscriptions in larger, clearer lettering, were prepared in 1861 for the Neapolitan Provinces. They were not officially issued although a few are known postally used. Denominations: 5c, 10c, 20c, 40c and 80c.

Stamps of Two Sicilies were replaced by those of Italy in 1862.

ITALY

ˈi-tᵊl-ē

LOCATION — Southern Europe
GOVT. — Republic
AREA — 119,764 sq. mi.
POP. — 56,735,130 (1999 est.)
CAPITAL — Rome

Formerly a kingdom, Italy became a republic in June 1946

100 Centesimi = 1 Lira
100 Cents = 1 Euro (2002)

Catalogue values for unused stamps in this country are for Never Hinged items, beginning with Scott 691 in the regular postage section, Scott B47 in the semipostal section, Scott C129 in the airpost section, Scott D21 in the pneumatic post section, Scott E32 in the special delivery section, Scott EY11 in the authorized delivery section, Scott J83 in the postage due section, Scott Q77 in the parcel post section, Scott QY5 in the parcel post authorized delivery section, Scott 1N1 in the A.M.G. section, Scott 1LN1 in the Venezia Giulia section, 1LNC1 in the occupation air post section, 1LNE1 in the occupation special delivery section, and all of the items in the Italian Social Republic area.

Watermarks

Wmk. 87 — Honeycomb

Wmk. 140 — Crown

Wmk. 277 — Winged Wheel

Wmk. 303 — Multiple Stars

Values of Italy stamps vary tremendously according to condition. Quotations are for very fine examples, and values for unused stamps are for examples with original gum as defined in the catalogue introduction. Extremely fine or superb copies sell at much higher prices, and fine or poor copies sell at greatly reduced prices. In addition, unused examples without gum are discounted severely.

Very fine examples of Nos. 17-21, 24-75, J2-J27, O1-O8 and Q1-Q6 will have perforations barely clear of the frameline or design due to the narrow spacing of the stamps on the plates.

King Victor Emmanuel II
A4   A5

Typographed; Head Embossed

1862		Unwmk.		Perf. 11½x12
17	A4	10c bister	9,500.	360.00
g.		Vert. half used as 5c on cover		160,000.
19	A4	20c dark blue	24.00	40.00
f.		Vert. half used as 10c on cover		210,000.
20	A4	40c red	325.00	200.00
21	A4	80c orange	65.00	2,400.

The outer frame shows a distinct design on the early printings, while this design is more or less blurred, or even a solid line, on the later printings.

Numerous shades of Nos. 17-21 exist. Some are very expensive. For listings, see the *Scott Classic Catalogue.*

The 20c and 40c exist perf. 11½. These are remainders of Sardinia with forged perforations.

Counterfeit cancellations are often found on No. 21.

Lithographed; Head Embossed

1863				Imperf.
22	A4	15c blue	80.00	55.00
a.		Head inverted		92,000.
b.		Double head	160.00	87.50
c.		Head omitted	800.00	55,000.
j.		Triple head	480.00	560.00

See note after Sardinia No. 15.
No. 22c is valued with original gum only.

Two types of No. 23:

Type I — First "C" in bottom line nearly closed.
Type II — "C" open. Line broken below "Q."

1863				Litho.
23	A5	15c blue, Type II	8.00	14.50
a.		Type I	400.00	27.50
b.		No gum		47.50
c.		As "a," double impression		5,250.
f.		As "a," printed on both sides		24,000.

One example of No. 23f is known used, cancelled "Milano, 25-VII-1863." Unused examples always lack gum and are from printer's waste. They are of little value.

A6   A7

A8   A13

1863-77		Typo.	Wmk. 140	Perf. 14
24	A6	1c gray green	8.00	4.00
a.		Imperf., pair		12,000.
25	A7	2c org brn ('65)	32.50	2.75
a.		Imperf., pair	150.00	200.00
26	A8	5c slate grn	2,400.	4.50
27	A8	10c buff	4,000.	5.50
a.		10c orange brown	4,000.	5.50
28	A8	10c blue ('77)	7,500.	6.50
29	A8	15c blue	3,000.	4.00
a.		Imperf., single		5,500.
30	A8	30c brown	12.00	12.00
a.		Imperf., single		—
31	A8	40c carmine	8,750.	8.00
a.		40c rose	8,750.	8.00
32	A8	60c lilac	12.00	19.00
33	A13	2 l vermilion	32.50	125.00

Nos. 26 to 32 have the head of type A8 but with different corner designs for each value.

Early printings of Nos. 24-27, 29-33 were made in London by De La Rue, later printings in Turin. Used examples can be determined by cancellation date. Unused singles cannot be distinguished.

For overprints see Italian Offices Abroad Nos. 1-5, 8-11.

No. 29 Surcharged in Brown

1865

Type I — Dots flanking stars in oval, and dot in eight check-mark ornaments in corners.
Type II — Dots in oval, none in corners.
Type III — No dots.

34	A8	20c on 15c bl (I)	750.00	4.75
a.		Type II	10,500.	20.00
b.		Type III	2,100.	8.00
c.		Inverted surcharge (I)		80,000.

A15

1867-77				Typo.
35	A15	20c blue	800.00	1.60
36	A15	20c orange ('77)	5,500.	4.00

For overprints see Italian Offices Abroad #9-10.

Official Stamps Surcharged in Blue

1877

37	O1	2c on 2c lake	200.00	32.50
38	O1	2c on 5c lake	240.00	40.00
39	O1	2c on 20c lake	875.00	4.75
40	O1	2c on 30c lake	800.00	16.00
41	O1	2c on 1 l lake	650.00	4.75
42	O1	2c on 2 l lake	650.00	12.00
43	O1	2c on 5 l lake	875.00	16.00
44	O1	2c on 10 l lake	650.00	20.00
		Nos. 37-44 (8)	4,940.	146.00

Inverted Surcharge

37a	O1	2c on 2c		2,000.
38a	O1	2c on 5c		1,600.
39a	O1	2c on 20c	47,500.	1,000.
40a	O1	2c on 30c		1,600.
41a	O1	2c on 1 l	55,000.	1,400.
42a	O1	2c on 2 l	55,000.	1,600.
43a	O1	2c on 5 l		1,600.
44a	O1	2c on 10 l		1,600.

King Humbert I — A17

1879		Typo.		Perf. 14
45	A17	5c blue green	9.50	1.60
46	A17	10c claret	475.00	1.75
47	A17	20c orange	450.00	1.60
48	A17	25c blue	800.00	9.50
49	A17	30c brown	175.00	2,800.
50	A17	50c violet	24.00	27.50
51	A17	2 l vermilion	65.00	400.00

Nos. 45-51 have the head of type A17 with different corner designs for each value.
Beware of forged cancellations on No. 49, on or off cover.
For surcharges and overprints see Nos. 64-66, Italian Offices Abroad 12-17.

Arms of Savoy — A24   Humbert I — A25

A26

A28   A29

1889

52	A24	5c dark green	875.00	3.25
53	A25	40c brown	14.50	20.00
54	A26	45c gray green	2,600.	9.50
55	A27	60c violet	19.00	47.50
56	A28	1 l brown & yel	19.00	24.00
a.		1 l brown & orange	21.00	30.00
57	A29	5 l grn & claret	30.00	1,200.

Forged cancellations exist on #51, 57.

Parcel Post Stamps of 1884-86 Surcharged in Black

1890

58	PP1	2c on 10c ol gray	6.00	8.00
a.		Inverted surcharge	550.00	3,600.
59	PP1	2c on 20c blue	6.00	8.00
60	PP1	2c on 50c claret	65.00	47.50
a.		Inverted surcharge		52,500.
61	PP1	2c on 75c blue grn	6.00	8.00
62	PP1	2c on 1.25 l org	55.00	40.00
a.		Inverted surcharge	95,000.	47,500.
63	PP1	2c on 1.75 l brn	24.00	60.00
		Nos. 58-63 (6)	162.00	171.50

Stamps of 1879
Surcharged

1890-91

64	A17	2c on 5c bl grn ('91)	22.50	55.00
a.		"2" with thin tail	140.00	325.00
65	A17	20c on 30c brown	475.00	12.00
66	A17	20c on 50c violet	550.00	47.50
		Nos. 64-66 (3)	1,047.	114.50

Arms of
Savoy — A33

Humbert
I — A34

 A35   A36

 A37   A38

1891-96   Typo.

67	A33	5c green	550.00	2.40
68	A34	10c claret ('96)	9.50	2.40
69	A35	20c orange ('95)	9.50	2.40
70	A36	25c blue	9.50	10.00
71	A37	45c ol grn ('95)	9.50	10.00
72	A38	5 l blue & rose	95.00	240.00

Arms of
Savoy — A39   A40

A41

1896-97

73	A39	1c brown	11.00	8.00
a.		Half used as ½c on cover		1,600.
74	A40	2c orange brown	11.00	2.00
75	A41	5c green ('97)	40.00	2.00
		Nos. 73-75 (3)	62.00	12.00

A42

Coat of Arms
A43   A44

Victor Emmanuel III
A45   A46

1901-26

76	A42	1c brown	1.60	.40
a.		Imperf, single	450.00	725.00
77	A43	2c org brn	1.60	.40
a.		Double impression	125.00	225.00
b.		Imperf, single	125.00	175.00
78	A44	5c blue grn	87.50	.60
a.		Imperf, single	2,000.	
79	A45	10c claret	120.00	1.25
a.		Imperf, single	—	10,500.
80	A45	20c orange	24.00	1.25
81	A45	25c ultra	275.00	4.00
a.		25c dp blue	275.00	4.00
82	A46	25c grn & pale grn ('26)	1.60	.35
83	A45	40c brown	800.00	9.50
84	A45	45c olive grn	12.50	.40
a.		Imperf, single	160.00	225.00
85	A45	50c violet	950.00	17.50
86	A46	75c dk red & rose ('26)	4.75	.35
87	A46	1 l brown & grn	4.75	.40
a.		Imperf, single	80.00	120.00
b.		Floral design (green) omitted	160.00	
c.		Double impression of vignette (brown)	80.00	110.00
88	A46	1.25 l bl & ultra ('26)	12.50	.35
89	A46	2 l dk grn & org ('23)	24.00	8.00
90	A46	2.50 l dk grn & org ('26)	65.00	8.00
91	A46	5 l blue & rose	32.50	7.25
		Nos. 76-91 (16)	2,417.	60.00

Nos. 83, 85, unused, are valued in fine condition.
The borders of Nos. 79-81, 83-85, 87, 89 and 91 differ slightly for each denomination.
On Nos. 82, 86, 88 and 90, the value is expressed as "Cent. 25," etc.
See No. 87b in set following No. 174G.
For surcharges and overprints see Nos. 148-149, 152, 158, 174F-174G, B16; Austria N20-N21, N27, N30, N52-N53, N58, N60, N64-N65, N71, N74; Dalmatia 1, 6-7.

Overprints & Surcharges
See Offices in China, Crete, Africa, Turkish Empire (Albania to Valona) and Aegean Islands for types A36-A58 overprinted or surcharged.

No. 80 Surcharged in
Black

C. 15

1905

92	A45	15c on 20c org	80.00	2.00
a.		Double surcharge		5,000.

A47

No.   No.   No.
93   111   123

1906   Unwmk.   Engr.   *Perf. 12*

93	A47	15c slate	80.00	1.00
a.		Vert. pair, imperf horiz.	200.00	200.00
b.		Horiz. pair, imperf vert.	200.00	200.00
c.		Booklet pane of 6	3,750.	
		Complete bklt., 4 #93c	15,000.	

A48   A49

1906-19   Wmk. 140   Typo.   *Perf. 14*

94	A48	5c green	1.60	.35
a.		Imperf, single	40.00	40.00
b.		Printed on both sides	250.00	
95	A48	10c claret	3.25	.35
a.		Imperf, single	40.00	40.00
b.		Printed on both sides	250.00	
96	A48	15c slate ('19)	3.25	.40
a.		Imperf, single	140.00	225.00
		Nos. 94-96 (3)	8.10	1.10

The frame of #95 differs in several details.
See Nos. 96b-96d following No. 174G.
For overprints and surcharge see Nos. 142A-142B, 150, 174A, B5, B9-B10; Austria N22-N23, N31, N54-N55, N61-N62, N66-N67; Dalmatia 2-5.

1908-27

97	A49	20c brn org ('25)	1.60	1.00
98	A49	20c green ('25)	.40	.20
99	A49	20c lil brn ('26)	3.20	.35
100	A49	25c blue	2.40	.35
a.		Imperf., pair	72.50	72.50
b.		Printed on both sides	225.00	360.00
101	A49	25c lt grn ('27)	6.50	16.00
102	A49	30c org brn ('22)	3.20	.80
a.		Imperf, single	250.00	—
103	A49	30c gray ('25)	4.75	.20
104	A49	40c brown	4.00	.35
a.		Imperf., pair	95.00	95.00
105	A49	50c violet	1.60	.35
a.		Imperf., pair	87.50	87.50
106	A49	55c dl vio ('20)	19.00	27.50
107	A49	60c car ('17)	2.40	.40
108	A49	60c blue ('23)	9.50	80.00
109	A49	60c brn org ('26)	12.50	.60
110	A49	85c red brn ('20)	24.00	22.50
		Nos. 97-110 (14)	95.05	150.60

The upper panels of Nos. 104 and 105 are in solid color with white letters. A body of water has been added to the background.
See Nos. 100c-105j following No. 174G.
For overprints & surcharges see #142C-142D,147, 151, 153-157, 174B-174E, B7-B8, B12-B15A; Austria N24-N26, N28-N29, N32, N56-N57, N59, N63, N68-N70, N72-N73.

A50   A51

Redrawn
Perf. 13x13½, 13½x14

1909-17   Typo.   Unwmk.

111	A50	15c slate black	300.00	2.40
112	A50	20c brown org ('16)	65.00	4.75

No. 111 is similar to No. 93, but the design has been redrawn and the stamp is 23mm high instead of 25mm. There is a star at each side of the coat collar, but one is not distinct. See illustrations next to A47.
For overprints see Nos. B6, B11.

Wmk. 140   *Perf. 14*

113	A50	20c brn org ('17)	8.00	3.00
a.		Imperf., pair	32.50	40.00

Stamps overprinted "Prestito Nazionale, 1917," or later dates, are Thrift or Postal Savings Stamps.

1910, Nov. 1

114	A51	10 l gray grn & red	80.00	35.00
a.		Red inverted		5,500.

For surcharge see Dalmatia No. 8.

Giuseppe Garibaldi
A52   A53

Perf. 14x13½

1910, Apr. 15   Unwmk.

115	A52	5c green	32.50	27.50
116	A52	15c claret	55.00	55.00

50th anniversary of freedom of Sicily.

1910, Dec. 1

117	A53	5c claret	140.00	140.00
118	A53	15c green	250.00	200.00

50th anniversary of the plebiscite of the southern Italian provinces in 1860.

Used values in italics are for postally used stamps. CTO's sell for about the same as unused, hinged stamps.

Symbols of   Symbol of
Rome and   Valor — A55
Turin — A54

Genius of
Italy — A56

Glory of
Rome — A57

1911, May 1   Engr.   Perf. 14x13½

119	A54	2c brown	3.25	6.50
a.		Vert. pair, imperf horiz.	95.00	95.00
b.		Horiz. pair, imperf vert.	95.00	95.00
120	A55	5c deep green	45.00	40.00
121	A56	10c carmine	32.50	60.00
a.		Vert. pair, imperf horiz.	—	—
b.		Horiz. pair, imperf vert.	200.00	200.00
122	A57	15c slate	42.50	80.00
		Nos. 119-122 (4)	123.25	186.50

50th anniv. of the union of Italian States to
form the Kingdom of Italy.
Nos. 115 to 122 were sold at a premium
over their face value.
For surcharges see Nos. 126-128.

Victor
Emmanuel III
A58

Campanile,
Venice
A59

1911, Oct.   Re-engraved   Perf. 13½

123	A58	15c slate	32.50	1.25
a.		Imperf., single	95.00	125.00
b.		Printed on both sides	400.00	525.00
c.		Bklt. pane of 6	1,500.	
		Cplt. bklt., 4 #123c	6,000.	

The re-engraved stamp is 24mm high. The
stars at each side of the coat collar show
plainly and the "C" of "Cent" is nearer the
frame than in No. 93. See illustrations next to
A47.
For surcharge see No. 129.

1912, Apr. 25   Perf. 14x13½

124	A59	5c indigo	9.50	14.50
125	A59	15c dk brn	52.50	67.50

Re-erection of the Campanile at Venice.

Nos. 120-121
Surcharged in Black

1913, Mar. 1

126	A55	2c on 5c dp grn	2.40	6.75
127	A56	2c on 10c car	2.40	6.75

No. 122 Surcharged
in Violet

128	A57	2c on 15c slate	2.40	6.75
		Nos. 126-128 (3)	7.20	20.25
		Set, never hinged	18.00	

No. 123 Surcharged

1916

129	A58	20c on 15c slate	17.50	1.25
		Never hinged	45.00	
a.		Bklt. pane of 6	750.00	
		Cplt. bklt., 4 #129a	3,000.	
b.		Inverted surcharge	350.00	350.00
c.		Double surcharge	225.00	225.00
e.		Vert. pair, one without surcharge	1,300.	
g.		Imperf, single	160.00	200.00

Old Seal of
Republic of
Trieste
A60

Allegory of
Dante's Divine
Comedy
A61

Italy Holding
Laurels for
Dante — A62

Dante
Alighieri — A63

Wmk. 140

1921, June 5   Litho.   Perf. 14

130	A60	15c blk & rose	7.25	55.00
a.		Horiz. pair, imperf btwn.	950.00	
131	A60	25c bl & rose	7.25	55.00
132	A60	40c brn & rose	7.25	55.00
		Nos. 130-132 (3)	21.75	165.00
		Set, never hinged	48.00	

Reunion of Venezia Giulia with Italy.

1921, Sept. 28   Typo.

133	A61	15c vio brn	7.25	35.00
a.		Imperf, single	40.00	40.00
134	A62	25c gray grn	7.25	35.00
a.		Imperf, single	40.00	40.00
135	A63	40c brown	7.25	35.00
a.		Imperf, single	40.00	40.00
		Nos. 133-135 (3)	21.75	105.00
		Set, never hinged	48.00	

600th anniversary of the death of Dante.
A 15c gray was not issued. Value: hinged
$160, never hinged $400, used $550.
Nos. 133-135 exist in part perforate pairs.

"Victory" — A64

1921, Nov. 1   Engr.   Perf. 14

136	A64	5c olive green	1.60	2.00
b.		Imperf, single	250.00	275.00
137	A64	10c red	2.40	2.40
c.		Imperf, single	250.00	525.00
138	A64	15c slate green	4.00	9.50
139	A64	25c ultra	2.40	6.50
c.		Imperf, single	190.00	190.00
d.		As "c," double impression	650.00	
		Nos. 136-139 (4)	10.40	20.40
		Set, never hinged	19.00	

3rd anniv. of the victory on the Piave.
For surcharges see Nos. 171-174.

Flame of
Patriotism
Tempering
Sword of
Justice — A65

Giuseppe
Mazzini — A66

Mazzini's
Tomb
A67

1922, Sept. 20   Typo.   Perf. 14

140	A65	25c maroon	13.00	35.00
141	A66	40c vio brn	25.00	45.00
142	A67	80c dk bl	13.00	55.00
		Nos. 140-142 (3)	51.00	135.00
		Set, never hinged	127.50	

Mazzini (1805-1872), patriot and writer.

Nos. 95, 96, 100 and
104 Overprinted in
Black

1922, June 4   Wmk. 140   Perf. 14

142A	A48	10c claret	475.00	475.00
142B	A48	15c slate	250.00	250.00
142C	A49	25c blue	250.00	250.00
142D	A49	40c brown	400.00	400.00
		Nos. 142A-142D (4)	1,375.	1,375.
		Set, never hinged	3,300.	

9th Italian Philatelic Congress, Trieste.
Counterfeits exist.

Christ Preaching The Gospel — A68

Portrait at upper right and badge at lower
right differ on each value. Portrait at upper left
is of Pope Gregory XV. Others: 20c, St. Theresa. 30c, St. Dominic. 50c, St. Francis of
Assisi. 1 l, St. Francis Xavier.

1923, June 11

143	A68	20c ol grn & brn org	6.50	175.00
a.		Imperf, single	475.00	650.00
b.		Vert. pair, imperf btwn.	1,000.	1,450.
144	A68	30c claret & brn org	6.50	175.00
a.		Imperf, single	475.00	650.00
c.		Horiz. pair, imperf btwn.	1,000.	1,450.
145	A68	50c vio & brn org	6.50	175.00
a.		Imperf, single	475.00	650.00
c.		Horiz. pair, imperf btwn.	1,200.	1,600.
d.		Vert. pair, imperf btwn.	1,000.	1,450.
146	A68	1 l bl & brn org	6.50	175.00
a.		Imperf, single	475.00	650.00
c.		Horiz. pair, imperf btwn.	1,000.	1,450.
d.		Vert. pair, imperf btwn.	1,000.	1,450.
		Nos. 143-146 (4)	26.00	700.00
		Set, never hinged	64.00	

Forged cancellations exist on Nos. 143-146.

300th anniv. of the Propagation of the Faith.
Practically the entire issue was delivered to
speculators.

a

b

c

d

e

1923-25

147	A49(a)	7½c on 85c	.40	1.25
a.		Double surcharge	—	1,600.
148	A42(b)	10c on 1c	.40	.35
a.		Inverted surcharge	24.00	40.00
149	A43(b)	10c on 2c	.40	.35
a.		Inverted surcharge	60.00	95.00
150	A48(c)	10c on 15c	.40	.35
a.		Vert. pair, one without surcharge	875.00	
151	A49(a)	20c on 25c	.40	.35
152	A45(d)	25c on 45c	1.60	16.00
a.		Vert. pair, one without surcharge	875.00	
153	A49(a)	25c on 60c	3.25	1.00
a.		Vert. pair, one without surcharge	725.00	—
154	A49(a)	30c on 50c	.40	.35
155	A49(a)	30c on 55c	1.60	.35
156	A49(a)	50c on 40c	6.50	.40
a.		Inverted surcharge	240.00	360.00
b.		Double surcharge	130.00	150.00
157	A49(a)	50c on 55c	22.50	12.00
a.		Inverted surcharge	1,100.	2,200.
158	A51(e)	1.75 l on 10 l	16.00	32.50
a.		Vert. pair, one without surcharge	1,250.	
		Nos. 147-158 (12)	53.85	65.25
		Set, never hinged	133.00	

Years of issue: Nos. 148-149, 156-157,
1923; Nos. 147, 152-153, 1924; others, 1925.

Emblem of the
New
Government
A69

Wreath of
Victory, Eagle
and Fasces
A70

Symbolical
of Fascism
and
Italy — A71

Unwmk.

1923, Oct. 24   Engr.   Perf. 14

159	A69	10c dark green	4.75	11.00
a.		Imperf, single	800.00	950.00
160	A69	30c dark violet	4.75	11.00
161	A69	50c brown carmine	9.50	20.00

Wmk. 140   Typo.

162	A70	1 l blue	16.00	20.00
163	A70	2 l brown	19.00	24.00
164	A71	5 l blk & bl	32.50	65.00
a.		Imperf, single	325.00	—
		Nos. 159-164 (6)	86.50	151.00
		Set, never hinged	225.50	

Anniv. of the March of the Fascisti on Rome.

Fishing Scene A72

Designs: 15c, Mt. Resegone. 30c, Fugitives bidding farewell to native mountains. 50c, Part of Lake Como. 1 l, Manzoni's home, Milan. 5 l, Alessandro Manzoni. The first four designs show scenes from Manzoni's work "I Promessi Sposi."

1923, Dec. 29　　　　**Perf. 14**

165	A72	10c brn red & blk	24.00	200.00
166	A72	15c bl grn & blk	24.00	200.00
167	A72	30c blk & slate	24.00	200.00
a.		Imperf, single	3,000.	
		Imperf, pair	—	
168	A72	50c org brn & blk	24.00	200.00
169	A72	1 l blue & blk	160.00	800.00
a.		Imperf, single, no gum	160.00	875.00
170	A72	5 l vio & blk	800.00	4,400.
a.		Imperf, pair	950.00	
		Nos. 165-170 (6)	1,056.	6,000.
		Set, never hinged	2,640.	

50th anniv. of the death of Alessandro Manzoni.

Nos. 136-139 Surcharged

1924, Feb.

171	A64	1 l on 5c ol grn	25.00	250.00
172	A64	1 l on 10c red	16.00	250.00
173	A64	1 l on 15c slate grn	25.00	250.00
174	A64	1 l on 25c ultra	16.00	250.00
		Nos. 171-174 (4)	82.00	1,000.
		Set, never hinged	200.00	

Surcharge forgeries exist.

Perf. 14x13½

171a	A64	1 l on 5c	35.00	300.00
172a	A64	1 l on 10c	20.00	300.00
173a	A64	1 l on 15c	35.00	300.00
174h	A64	1 l on 25c	20.00	300.00
		Nos. 171a-174h (4)	110.00	1,200.
		Set, never hinged	220.00	

Nos. 95, 102, 105, 108, 110, 87 and 89 Overprinted in Black or Red

1924, Feb. 16

174A	A48	10c claret	2.40	47.50
174B	A49	30c org brn	2.40	47.50
174C	A49	50c violet	2.40	47.50
174D	A49	60c bl (R)	14.50	140.00
174E	A49	85c choc (R)	6.50	140.00
174F	A46	1 l brn & grn	47.50	450.00
174G	A46	2 l dk grn & org	35.00	450.00
		Nos. 174A-174G (7)	110.70	1,322.
		Set, never hinged	275.00	

These stamps were sold on an Italian warship which made a cruise to South American ports in 1924.

Overprint forgeries exist of #174D-174G.

Stamps of 1901-22 with Advertising Labels Attached

Perf. 14 all around, Imperf. between

1924-25

96b	A48	15c + Bitter Campari	4.00	24.00
96c	A48	15c + Cordial Campari	4.00	20.00
96d	A48	15c + Columbia	65.00	52.50
100c	A49	25c + Abrador	125.00	125.00
100d	A49	25c + Coen	240.00	65.00
100e	A49	25c + Piperno	1,600.	1,000.
100f	A49	25c + Reinach	125.00	87.50
100g	A49	25c + Tagliacozzo	950.00	1,000.
102b	A49	30c + Columbia	32.50	40.00
105b	A49	50c + Coen	1,600.	87.50
105c	A49	50c + Columbia	24.00	16.00
105d	A49	50c + De Montel	4.00	16.00
105e	A49	50c + Piperno	2,200.	325.00
105f	A49	50c + Reinach	240.00	65.00
105g	A49	50c + Siero Casali	24.00	47.50
105h	A49	50c + Singer	4.00	9.50
105i	A49	50c + Tagliacozzo	2,400.	650.00
105j	A49	50c + Tantal	400.00	200.00
87d	A46	1 l + Columbia	950.00	950.00
		Nos. 96b-87d (19)	10,991.	4,780.
		Set, never hinged	22,700.	

No. 113 with Columbia label and No. E3 with Cioccolato Perugina label were prepared but not issued. Values: Columbia, unused $55, never hinged $140; Cioccolato, unused $20, never hinged $47.50.

King Victor Emmanuel III — A78

1925-26　Engr.　Unwmk.　Perf. 11

175	A78	60c brn car	1.60	.80
a.		Perf. 13½	8.00	2.40
b.		Imperf., pair	275.00	
176	A78	1 l dk bl	1.60	.80
a.		Perf. 13½	16.00	11.00
b.		Imperf., pair	275.00	

Perf. 13½

177	A78	1.25 l dk bl ('26)	4.75	2.40
a.		Perf. 11	110.00	120.00
b.		Imperf., pair	600.00	
		Nos. 175-177 (3)	7.95	4.00
		Set, never hinged	20.00	

25th year of the reign of Victor Emmanuel III.

Nos. 175 to 177 exist with sideways watermark of fragments of letters or a crown, which are normally on the sheet margin.

St. Francis and His Vision A79

Monastery of St. Damien A80

Assisi Monastery A81

St. Francis' Death A82

St. Francis — A83

1926, Jan. 30　Wmk. 140　Perf. 14

178	A79	20c gray grn	.80	1.00
a.		Imperf single	950.00	950.00
179	A80	40c dk vio	.80	1.00
180	A81	60c red brn	.80	1.00
a.		Imperf single	475.00	475.00

Unwmk.　Perf. 11

181	A83	30c slate blk	.80	1.00
a.		Perf. 13½	12.00	20.00
		Never hinged	30.00	
182	A82	1.25 l dark blue	4.00	1.00
a.		Perf. 13½	475.00	40.00
		Never hinged	1,200.	

Perf. 13½

183	A83	5 l + 2.50 l dk brn	11.00	120.00
		Nos. 178-183 (6)	18.20	125.00
		Set, never hinged	45.00	

700th anniv. of the death of St. Francis of Assisi.

Alessandro Volta — A84

1927　Wmk. 140　Typo.　Perf. 14

188	A84	20c dk car	3.25	1.25
189	A84	50c grnsh blk	3.25	.80
190	A84	60c chocolate	4.75	4.75
191	A84	1.25 l ultra	16.00	8.00
		Nos. 188-191 (4)	27.25	14.80
		Set, never hinged	68.00	

Cent. of the death of Alessandro Volta.

The 20c in purple is Cyrenaica No. 25 with overprint omitted. Values: $4,000 unused; $6,000 never hinged.

A85　　　　A86

1927-29　Size: 17½x22mm　Perf. 14

192	A85	50c brn & slate	3.25	.40
a.		Imperf, pair		

Unwmk.
Engr.　Perf. 11
Size: 19x23mm

193	A85	1.75 l dp brn	4.00	.35
a.		Perf. 13½ ('29)	35,000.	3,250.
		Never hinged	55,000.	
b.		Perf. 11x13½ ('29)	—	2,250.
c.		Perf. 13½x11 ('29)	—	2,250.
d.		Imperf, single	2,750.	
194	A85	1.85 l black	3.25	.70
195	A85	2.55 l brn car	4.00	9.50
196	A85	2.65 l dp vio	6.50	80.00
a.		Imperf, single	2,100.	
		Nos. 192-196 (5)	21.00	90.95
		Set, never hinged	45.00	

1928-29　Wmk. 140　Typo.　Perf. 14

197	A86	7½c lt brown	3.25	12.00
198	A86	15c brown org ('29)	3.25	.35
199	A86	35c gray blk ('29)	8.75	14.50
200	A86	50c dull violet	19.00	.35
a.		Imperf single	250.00	
		Nos. 197-200 (4)	34.25	27.20
		Set, never hinged	85.50	

Emmanuel Philibert, Duke of Savoy — A87

Statue of Philibert, Turin — A88

Philibert and Italian Soldier of 1918 — A89

1928　Perf. 11, 14

201	A87	20c red brn & ultra	9.50	16.00
a.		Perf. 13½	240.00	240.00
202	A87	25c dp red & bl grn	9.50	16.00
a.		Perf. 13½	47.50	52.50
203	A87	30c bl grn & red brn	16.00	32.00
a.		Center inverted	57,500.	7,600.
b.		Perf. 13½	35.00	35.00
204	A89	50c org brn & bl	4.00	1.25
205	A89	75c dp red	4.75	4.00
206	A88	1.25 l bl & blk	4.75	4.00
207	A89	1.75 l bl grn	32.50	40.00
208	A87	5 l vio & bl grn	29.00	110.00
209	A89	10 l blk & pink	35.00	225.00
210	A88	20 l vio & blk	70.00	725.00
		Nos. 201-210 (10)	215.00	1,173.
		Set, never hinged	535.00	

400th anniv. of the birth of Emmanuel Philibert, Duke of Savoy; 10th anniv. of the victory of 1918; Turin Exhibition.

She-wolf Suckling Romulus and Remus
A90　　　　A95a

Julius Caesar A91　　　　Augustus Caesar A92

"Italia" — A93

A94　　　　A95

1929-42　Wmk. 140　Photo.　Perf. 14

213	A90	5c olive brn	.20	.20
214	A91	7½c deep vio	1.60	.20
215	A92	10c dark brown	.20	.20
216	A93	15c slate grn	.20	.20
217	A91	20c rose red	.20	.20
218	A94	25c dp green	.20	.20
219	A95	30c olive brn	.20	.20
a.		Imperf., pair	1,100.	
220	A93	35c dp blue	.20	.20
221	A95	50c purple	.20	.20
a.		Imperf., pair	725.00	875.00
222	A94	75c rose red	.20	.20
222A	A91	1 l dk pur ('42)	.20	.20
223	A94	1.25 l dp blue	.20	.20
224	A92	1.75 l red org	.20	.20
225	A93	2 l car lake	.20	.20
226	A95a	2.55 l slate grn	.20	.80
226A	A95a	3.70 l pur ('30)	.20	.80
227	A95a	5 l rose red	.20	.20
228	A93	10 l purple	4.00	4.00
229	A91	20 l lt green	4.75	12.00
230	A92	25 l bluish sl	11.00	35.00
231	A94	50 l dp violet	13.00	40.00
		Nos. 213-231 (21)	37.55	95.60
		Set, never hinged	94.00	

Stamps of the 1929-42 issue overprinted "G.N.R." are 1943 local issues of the Guardia Nazionale Republicana.

See Nos. 427-438, 441-459.

For surcharge and overprints see Nos. 460, M1-M13, 1N10-1N13, 1LN1-1LN1A, 1LN10; Italian Social Republic 1-5A; Yugoslavia-Ljubljana N36-N54.

Courtyard of Monte Cassino A96

Monks Laying Cornerstone — A98

St. Benedict of
Nursia — A100

Designs: 25c, Fresco, "Death of St. Benedict." 75c+15c, 5 l+1 l, Monte Cassino Abbey.

1929, Aug. 1		**Photo.**	**Wmk. 140**	
232	A96	20c red orange	1.60	1.60
233	A96	25c dk green	1.60	1.60
234	A98	50c + 10c ol brn	4.00	30.00
235	A98	75c + 15c crim	4.75	40.00
236	A96	1.25 l + 25c saph	6.50	45.00
237	A98	5 l + 1 l dk vio	9.50	100.00
		Unwmk.		
		Engr.		
238	A100	10 l + 2 l slate grn	14.50	260.00
		Nos. 232-238 (7)	42.45	478.20
		Set, never hinged	105.00	

14th cent. of the founding of the Abbey of
Monte Cassino by St. Benedict in 529 A.D.
The premium on some of the stamps was
given to the committee for the celebration of
the centenary.

Prince
Humbert
and
Princess
Marie José
A101

1930, Jan. 8		**Photo.**	**Wmk. 140**	
239	A101	20c orange red	.80	.60
240	A101	50c + 10c ol brn	2.40	4.00
241	A101	1.25 l + 25c dp bl	5.50	13.00
		Nos. 239-241 (3)	8.70	17.60
		Set, never hinged	22.00	

Marriage of Prince Humbert of Savoy with
Princess Marie José of Belgium.

The surtax on Nos. 240 and 241 was for the
benefit of the Italian Red Cross Society.

The 20c in green is Cyrenaica No. 35 with
overprint omitted. Values: $35,000 unused;
$52,500 never hinged.

Ferrucci
Leading His
Army
A102

Fabrizio
Maramaldo
Killing
Ferrucci
A103

Francesco
Ferrucci — A104

1930, July 10				
242	A102	20c rose red	.80	.80
243	A103	25c deep green	1.40	.80
244	A103	50c purple	.80	.40
245	A103	1.25 l deep blue	11.00	4.75

246	A104	5 l + 2 l org red	22.50	140.00
		Nos. 242-246 (5)	36.50	146.75
		Set, never hinged	90.00	
		Nos. 242-246,C20-C22 (8)	60.50	314.75
		Set, never hinged	150.00	

4th cent. of the death of Francesco Ferrucci,
Tuscan warrior.

Overprints
See Aegean Islands for types
A103-A145 Overprinted.

Helenus
and
Aeneas
A106

Designs: 20c, Anchises and Aeneas watch
passing of Roman Legions. 25c, Aeneas
feasting in shade of Albunea. 30c, Ceres and
her children with fruits of Earth. 50c, Harvesters at work. 75c, Woman at loom, children and
calf. 1.25 l, Anchises and his sailors in sight of
Italy. 5 l+1.50 l, Shepherd piping by fireside.
10 l+2.50 l, Aeneas leading his army.

1930, Oct. 21		**Photo.**	**Perf. 14**	
248	A106	15c olive brn	2.40	2.40
249	A106	20c orange	2.40	1.60
250	A106	25c green	3.20	1.60
251	A106	30c dull vio	9.50	4.00
252	A106	50c violet	16.00	.80
253	A106	75c rose red	4.00	12.00
254	A106	1.25 l blue	4.00	12.00
		Unwmk.		**Engr.**
255	A106	5 l +1.50 l red brn	60.00	400.00
256	A106	10 l +2.50 l gray grn	60.00	550.00
		Nos. 248-256 (9)	161.50	984.40
		Set, never hinged	405.00	
		Nos. 248-256,C23-C26 (13)	332.00	2,019.
		Set, never hinged	835.00	

Bimillenary of the birth of Virgil. Surtax on
Nos. 255-256 was for the National Institute
Figli del Littorio.

Arms of Italy (Fascist
Emblems Support
House of Savoy
Arms) — A115

1930, Dec. 16		**Photo.**	**Wmk. 140**	
257	A115	2c deep orange	1.60	.20
		Never hinged	4.00	

St. Anthony
being
Installed as
a
Franciscan
A116

Olivares
Hermitage,
Portugal
A118

St. Anthony
Freeing
Prisoners
A120

St.
Anthony's
Death
A121

St. Anthony
Succoring the
Poor — A122

Designs: 25c, St. Anthony preaching to the
fishes. 50c, Basilica of St. Anthony, Padua.

		Wmk. 140		
1931, Mar. 9		**Photo.**	**Perf. 14**	
258	A116	20c dull violet	4.00	1.25
259	A116	25c gray green	2.40	1.25
260	A118	30c brown	6.50	2.40
261	A118	50c violet	2.00	.80
262	A120	1.25 l blue	20.00	9.50
		Unwmk.		**Engr.**
263	A121	75c brown red	9.50	16.00
a.		Perf. 12	100.00	300.00
		Never hinged	240.00	
264	A122	5 l + 2.50 l ol grn	40.00	250.00
		Nos. 258-264 (7)	84.40	281.20
		Set, never hinged	210.00	

7th centenary of the death of Saint Anthony
of Padua.

Tower of
Meloria — A123

Training
Ship
"Amerigo
Vespucci"
A124

Cruiser
"Trento"
A125

1931, Nov. 29		**Photo.**	**Wmk. 140**	
265	A123	20c rose red	8.75	2.00
266	A124	50c purple	8.75	1.60
267	A125	1.25 l dk bl	24.00	4.75
		Nos. 265-267 (3)	41.50	8.35
		Set, never hinged	165.00	

Royal Naval Academy at Leghorn (Livorno),
50th anniv.

Giovanni
Boccaccio
A126

Designs: 15c, Niccolo Machiavelli. 20c,
Paolo Sarpi. 25c, Count Vittorio Alfieri. 30c,
Ugo Foscolo. 50c, Count Giacomo Leopardi.
75c, Giosue Carducci. 1.25 l, Carlo Giuseppe
Botta. 1.75 l, Torquato Tasso. 2.75 l, Francesco Petrarca. 5 l+2 l, Ludovico Ariosto.
10 l+2.50 l, Dante Alighieri.

1932, Mar. 14			**Perf. 14**	
268	A126	10c olive brn	3.25	1.60
269	A126	15c slate green	3.25	2.00
270	A126	20c rose red	3.25	1.60
271	A126	25c dp green	3.25	1.25
272	A126	30c olive brn	4.00	1.60
273	A126	50c violet	2.40	.80
274	A126	75c car rose	16.00	8.00
275	A126	1.25 l dp blue	4.75	4.00
276	A126	1.75 l orange	12.00	8.00
277	A126	2.75 l gray	24.00	40.00
278	A126	5 l + 2 l car rose	29.00	225.00

279	A126	10 l + 2.50 l ol grn	35.00	350.00
		Nos. 268-279 (12)	140.15	643.85
		Set, never hinged	350.00	
		Nos. 268-279,C28-C33,C34 (19)	239.15	1,952.
		Set, never hinged	600.00	

Dante Alighieri Society, a natl. literary association founded to promote development of the
Italian language and culture. The surtax was
added to the Society funds to help in its work.

View of
Caprera
A138

Garibaldi
Carrying
His Dying
Wife
A141

Garibaldi
Memorial
A144

Giuseppe
Garibaldi
A145

Designs: 20c, 30c, Garibaldi meeting Victor
Emmanuel II. 25c, 50c, Garibaldi at Battle of
Calatafimi. 1.25 l, Garibaldi's tomb. 1.75
l+25c, Rock of Quarto.

1932, Apr. 6				
280	A138	10c gray blk	2.40	1.60
281	A138	20c olive brn	2.40	1.25
282	A138	25c dull grn	3.25	1.60
283	A138	30c orange	3.25	2.40
284	A138	50c violet	1.60	.40
285	A141	75c rose red	16.00	9.50
286	A141	1.25 l dp blue	32.50	4.00
287	A141	1.75 l + 25c bl gray	40.00	87.50
288	A144	2.55 l + 50c red brn	32.50	125.00
289	A145	5 l + 1 l cop red	32.50	130.00
		Nos. 280-289 (10)	166.40	363.25
		Set, never hinged	410.00	
		Nos. 280-289,C35-C39,CE1-CE2 (17)	242.40	619.25
		Set, never hinged	600.00	

50th anniv. of the death of Giuseppe Garibaldi, patriot.

Plowing
with Oxen
and Tractor
A146

10c, Soldier guarding mountain pass. 15c,
Marine, battleship & seaplane. 20c, Head of
Fascist youth. 25c, Hands of workers & tools.
30c, Flags, Bible & altar. 35c, "New roads for
the new Legions." 50c, Mussolini statue,
Bologna. 60c, Hands with spades. 75c, Exca-
vating ruins. 1 l, Steamers & galleons. 1.25 l,
Italian flag, map & points of compass. 1.75 l,
Flag, athlete & stadium. 2.55 l, Mother & child.
2.75 l, Emblems of drama, music, art & sport.
5 l+2.50 l, Roman emperor.

1932, Oct. 27			**Photo.**	
290	A146	5c dk brown	2.40	1.25
291	A146	10c dk brown	2.40	.80
292	A146	15c dk gray grn	2.40	1.25
293	A146	20c car rose	2.40	.60
294	A146	25c dp green	2.40	.40
295	A146	30c dk brown	3.25	2.40
296	A146	35c dk blue	8.00	9.50
297	A146	50c purple	1.60	.40
298	A146	60c orange brn	12.00	8.00
299	A146	75c car rose	4.00	4.00
300	A146	1 l black vio	16.00	6.50
301	A146	1.25 l dp blue	4.00	1.60
302	A146	1.75 l orange	24.00	2.00
303	A146	2.55 l dk gray	29.00	40.00
304	A146	2.75 l slate grn	29.00	40.00

305	A146	5 l + 2.50 l	
		car rose	40.00 300.00

Nos. 290-305 (16) 182.85 418.70
Set, never hinged 455.00
Nos. 290-305,C40-C41,E16-
E17 (20) 200.75 608.45
Set, never hinged 520.00

10th anniv. of the Fascist government and the March on Rome.

Statue of Athlete — A162

Cross in Halo, St. Peter's Dome — A163

1933, Aug. 16   **Perf. 14**

306	A162	10c dk brown	.80	.80
307	A162	20c rose red	.80	.80
308	A162	50c purple	.80	.40
309	A162	1.25 l blue	4.75	6.50

Nos. 306-309 (4) 7.15 8.50
Set, never hinged 18.00

Intl. University Games at Turin, Sept., 1933.

1933, Oct. 23

Designs: 25c, 50c, Angel with cross. 1.25 l, as 20c. 2.55 l, + 2.50 l, Cross with doves.

310	A163	20c rose red	4.75	1.25
311	A163	25c green	12.00	1.60
312	A163	50c purple	4.75	.40
313	A163	1.25 l dp blue	12.00	4.75
314	A163	2.55 l + 2.50 l blk	8.00	175.00

Nos. 310-314 (5) 41.50 183.00
Set, never hinged 105.00
Nos. 310-314,CB1-CB2 (7) 47.90 209.00
Set, never hinged 121.00

Issued at the solicitation of the Order of the Holy Sepulchre of Jerusalem to mark the Holy Year.

Anchor of the "Emanuele Filiberto" A166

Antonio Pacinotti A172

Designs: 20c, Anchor. 50c, Gabriele d'Annunzio. 1.25 l, St. Vito's Tower. 1.75 l, Symbolizing Fiume's annexation. 2.55 l+2 l, Victor Emmanuel III arriving aboard "Brindisi." 2.75 l+2.50 l, Galley, gondola and battleship.

1934, Mar. 12

315	A166	10c dk brown	8.00	4.00
316	A166	20c rose red	1.60	1.60
317	A166	50c purple	1.60	1.60
318	A166	1.25 l blue	1.60	6.50
319	A166	1.75 l + 1 l indigo	1.60	35.00
320	A166	2.55 l + 2 l dull vio	1.60	55.00
321	A166	2.75 l + 2.50 l ol	1.60	55.00

Nos. 315-321 (7) 17.60 158.70
Set, never hinged 44.00
Nos. 315-321,C56-C61,CE5-
CE7 (16) 29.95 312.10
Set, never hinged 66.50

10th anniversary of annexation of Fiume.

1934, May 23

322	A172	50c purple	.80	.40
323	A172	1.25 l sapphire	1.25	2.75

Set, never hinged 5.00

75th anniv. of invention of the dynamo by Antonio Pacinotti (1841-1912), scientist.

Guarding the Goal — A173

Players — A175

Soccer Players — A174

1934, May 23

324	A173	20c red orange	6.50	8.00
325	A174	25c green	6.50	2.40
326	A174	50c purple	6.50	1.25
327	A174	1.25 l blue	16.00	16.00
328	A175	5 l + 2.50 l brn	95.00	550.00

Nos. 324-328 (5) 130.50 577.65
Set, never hinged 330.00
Nos. 324-328,C62-C65 (9) 264.00 1,465.
Set, never hinged 625.00

2nd World Soccer Championship.
For overprints see Aegean Islands Nos. 31-35.

Luigi Galvani — A176

1934, Aug. 16

329	A176	30c brown, buff	1.00	.80
330	A176	75c carmine, rose	1.40	3.25

Set, never hinged 6.00

Intl. Congress of Electro-Radio-Biology.

Carabinieri Emblem — A177

Cutting Barbed Wire A178

Designs: 20c, Sardinian Grenadier and soldier throwing grenade. 25c, Alpine Infantry. 30c, Military courage. 75c, Artillery. 1.25 l, Acclaiming the Service. 1.75 l+1 l, Cavalry. 2.55 l+2 l, Sapping Detail. 2.75 l+2 l, First aid.

1934, Sept. 6   **Photo.**   **Wmk. 140**

331	A177	10c dk brown	2.40	2.40
332	A178	15c olive grn	2.40	4.00
333	A178	20c rose red	2.40	1.60
334	A177	25c green	4.00	1.60
335	A178	30c dk brown	4.00	8.00
336	A178	50c purple	2.40	.80
337	A178	75c car rose	40.00	12.00
338	A178	1.25 l dk blue	40.00	8.00
339	A177	1.75 l + 1 l red org	17.50	52.50
340	A178	2.55 l + 2 l dp cl	17.50	67.50
341	A178	2.75 l + 2 l vio	21.00	72.50

Nos. 331-341 (11) 153.60 230.90
Set, never hinged 385.00
Nos. 331-341,C66-C72 (18) 202.10 379.90
Set, never hinged 505.00

Centenary of Military Medal of Valor.
For overprints see Aegean Islands Nos. 36-46.

Man Holding Fasces A187

Standard Bearer, Bayonet Attack A188

Design: 30c, Eagle and soldier.

1935, Apr. 23   **Perf. 14**

342	A187	20c rose red	.80	.80
343	A187	30c dk brown	6.50	8.00
344	A188	50c purple	.80	.40

Nos. 342-344 (3) 8.10 9.20
Set, never hinged 20.00

Issued in honor of the University Contests.

Fascist Flight Symbolism A190

Leonardo da Vinci — A191

1935, Oct. 1

345	A190	20c rose red	20.00	2.00
346	A190	30c brown	35.00	6.50
347	A191	50c purple	72.50	1.25
348	A191	1.25 l dk blue	80.00	7.25

Nos. 345-348 (4) 207.50 17.00
Set, never hinged 830.00

International Aeronautical Salon, Milan.

Vincenzo Bellini — A192

Bellini's Villa — A194

Bellini's Piano A193

1935, Oct. 15

349	A192	20c rose red	16.00	4.00
350	A192	30c brown	24.00	12.00
351	A192	50c violet	24.00	1.60
352	A192	1.25 l dk blue	40.00	16.00
353	A193	1.75 l + 1 l red org	35.00	240.00
354	A194	2.75 l + 2 l ol blk	65.00	260.00

Nos. 349-354 (6) 204.00 533.60
Set, never hinged 510.00
Nos. 349-354,C79-C83 (11) 287.00 1,021.
Set, never hinged 710.00

Bellini (1801-35), operatic composer.

Map of Italian Industries A195

Designs: 20c, 1.25 l, Map of Italian Industries. 30c, 50c, Cogwheel and plow.

1936, Mar. 23

355	A195	20c red	.80	.40
356	A195	30c brown	.80	1.25
357	A195	50c purple	.80	.35
358	A195	1.25 l blue	4.75	3.25

Nos. 355-358 (4) 7.15 5.25
Set, never hinged 18.00

The 17th Milan Trade Fair.

Flock of Sheep A197

Ajax Defying the Lightning A199

Bust of Horace A200

Designs: 20c, 1.25 l+1 l, Countryside in Spring. 75c, Capitol. 1.75 l+1 l, Pan piping. 2.55 l+1 l, Dying warrior.

Wmk. Crowns (140)
1936, July 1   **Photo.**   **Perf. 14**

359	A197	10c dp green	6.50	1.25
360	A197	20c rose red	4.75	.80
361	A199	30c olive brn	6.50	2.25
362	A200	50c purple	6.50	.40
363	A197	75c rose red	16.00	9.50
364	A197	1.25 l + 1 l dk bl	27.50	130.00
365	A199	1.75 l + 1 l car rose	32.50	240.00
366	A197	2.55 l + 1 l sl blk	40.00	275.00

Nos. 359-366 (8) 140.25 659.20
Set, never hinged 350.00
Nos. 359-366,C84-C88 (13) 202.00 1,153.
Set, never hinged 500.00

2000th anniv. of the birth of Quintus Horatius Flaccus (Horace), Roman poet.

Child Holding Wheat — A204

Child Giving Salute — A205

Child and Fasces — A206

"Il Bambino" by della Robbia — A207

1937, June 28

367	A204	10c yellow brn	3.25	1.60
368	A205	20c car rose	3.25	1.25
369	A204	25c green	3.25	2.00
370	A206	30c dk brown	4.75	4.00
371	A205	50c purple	3.25	.40
372	A207	75c rose red	16.00	17.50
373	A205	1.25 l dk blue	20.00	17.50
374	A206	1.75 l + 75c org	40.00	175.00
375	A207	2.75 l + 1.25 l dk bl grn	32.50	200.00

376	A205	5 l + 3 l bl		
		gray	40.00	275.00
	Nos. 367-376 (10)		166.25	694.25
	Set, never hinged		415.00	
	Nos. 367-376,C89-C94 (16)		262.25	1,377.
	Set, never hinged		655.00	

Summer Exhibition for Child Welfare. The surtax on Nos. 374-376 was used to support summer camps for children.

Rostral Column — A208

15c, Army Trophies. 20c, Augustus Caesar (Octavianus) offering sacrifice. 25c, Cross Roman Standards. 30c, Julius Caesar and Julian Star. 50c, Augustus receiving acclaim. 75c, Augustus Caesar. 1.25 l, Symbolizing maritime glory of Rome. 1.75 l+1 l, Sacrificial Altar. 2.55 l+2 l, Capitol.

1937, Sept. 23

377	A208	10c myrtle grn	3.25	.80
378	A208	15c olive grn	3.25	1.25
379	A208	20c red	3.25	.60
380	A208	25c green	3.25	.60
381	A208	30c olive bis	4.00	.60
382	A208	50c purple	3.25	.35
383	A208	75c scarlet	3.25	4.75
384	A208	1.25 l dk blue	8.00	5.50
385	A208	1.75 l + 1 l plum	40.00	160.00
386	A208	2.55 l + 2 l sl blk	52.50	225.00
	Nos. 377-386 (10)		124.00	399.65
	Set, never hinged		300.00	
	Nos. 377-386,C95-C99 (15)		259.00	812.65
	Set, never hinged		625.00	

Bimillenary of the birth of Emperor Augustus Caesar (Octavianus) on the occasion of the exhibition opened in Rome by Mussolini, Sept. 22, 1937.

For overprints see Aegean Islands #47-56.

Gasparo Luigi Pacifico Spontini A218

Antonius Stradivarius A219

Count Giacomo Leopardi A220

Giovanni Battista Pergolesi A221

Giotto di Bondone — A222

1937, Oct. 25

387	A218	10c dk brown	1.60	.80
388	A219	20c rose red	1.60	.80
389	A220	25c dk green	1.60	.80
390	A221	30c dk brown	1.60	1.60
391	A220	50c purple	1.60	.80
392	A221	75c crimson	2.25	4.75
393	A222	1.25 l dp blue	3.25	4.75

394	A218	1.75 l dp orange	3.25	4.75
395	A219	2.55 l + 2 l gray grn	16.00	200.00
396	A222	2.75 l + 2 l red brn	16.00	240.00
	Nos. 387-396 (10)		48.75	459.05
	Set, never hinged		125.00	

Centennials of Spontini, Stradivarius, Leopardi, Pergolesi and Giotto.
For overprints see Aegean Islands #57-58.

Guglielmo Marconi A223

Augustus Caesar (Octavianus) A224

1938, Jan. 24

397	A223	20c rose pink	3.25	.80
398	A223	50c purple	.80	.35
399	A223	1.25 l blue	3.25	5.50
	Nos. 397-399 (3)		7.30	6.65
	Set, never hinged		18.00	

Guglielmo Marconi (1874-1937), electrical engineer, inventor of wireless telegraphy.

1938, Oct. 28

10c, Romulus Plowing. 25c, Dante. 30c, Columbus. 50c, Leonardo da Vinci. 75c, Victor Emmanuel II and Garibaldi. 1.25 l, Tomb of Unknown Soldier, Rome. 1.75 l, Blackshirts' March on Rome, 1922. 2.75 l, Map of Italian East Africa and Iron Crown of Monza. 5 l, Victor Emmanuel III.

400	A224	10c brown	2.40	.80
401	A224	20c car rose	2.40	.80
402	A224	25c dk green	2.40	.80
403	A224	30c olive brn	2.40	2.00
404	A224	50c lt violet	2.40	.80
405	A224	75c rose red	3.25	3.25
406	A224	1.25 l dp blue	6.50	3.25
407	A224	1.75 l vio blk	8.00	4.00
408	A224	2.75 l slate grn	26.00	47.50
409	A224	5 l lt red brn	32.50	52.50
	Nos. 400-409 (10)		88.25	115.70
	Set, never hinged		220.00	
	Nos. 400-409,C100-C105 (16)		142.25	286.20
	Set, never hinged		350.00	

Proclamation of the Empire.

Wood-burning Engine and Streamlined Electric Engine — A234

1939, Dec. 15　Photo.　Perf. 14

410	A234	20c rose red	.80	.60
411	A234	50c brt violet	1.60	.80
412	A234	1.25 l dp blue	4.00	4.00
	Nos. 410-412 (3)		6.40	5.40
	Set, never hinged		16.00	

Centenary of Italian railroads.

Adolf Hitler and Benito Mussolini A235

Hitler and Mussolini A236

1941　　　　　Wmk. 140

413	A235	10c dp brown	2.40	2.40
414	A235	20c red orange	2.40	2.40
415	A235	25c dp green	8.00	2.40
416	A236	50c violet	6.50	2.00
417	A236	75c rose red	8.00	6.50
418	A236	1.25 l deep blue	9.50	9.50
	Nos. 413-418 (6)		36.80	25.20
	Set, never hinged		80.00	

Rome-Berlin Axis.
Stamps of type A236 in the denominations and colors of Nos. 413-415 were prepared but

not issued. They were sold for charitable purposes in 1948. Value $35 each.

Galileo Teaching Mathematics at Padua — A237

Designs: 25c, Galileo presenting telescope to Doge of Venice. 50c, Galileo Galilei (1564-1642). 1.25 l, Galileo studying at Arcetri.

1942, Sept. 28

419	A237	10c dk org & lake	.80	.60
420	A237	25c gray grn & grn	.80	.60
421	A237	50c brn vio & vio	.80	.60
	a. Frame missing		800.00	
422	A237	1.25 l Prus bl & ultra	.80	2.75
	Nos. 419-422 (4)		3.20	4.55
	Set, never hinged		6.00	

Statue of Rossini — A241

Gioacchino Rossini — A242

1942, Nov. 23　　　　　Photo.

423	A241	25c deep green	.80	.80
424	A241	30c brown	.80	.80
425	A242	50c violet	.80	.80
426	A242	1 l blue	.80	2.00
	Nos. 423-426 (4)		3.20	4.40
	Set, never hinged		6.00	

Gioacchino Antonio Rossini (1792-1868), operatic composer.

"Victory for the Axis" A243

"Discipline is the Weapon of Victory" A244

"Everything and Everyone for Victory" A245

"Arms and Hearts Must Be Stretched Out Towards the Goal" A246

Perf. 14 all around, Imperf. between

1942　　Photo.　Wmk. 140

427	A243	25c deep green	.40	1.25
428	A244	25c deep green	.40	1.25
429	A245	25c deep green	.40	1.25
430	A246	25c deep green	.40	1.25
431	A243	30c olive brown	.40	4.00
432	A244	30c olive brown	.40	4.00
433	A245	30c olive brown	.40	4.00
434	A246	30c olive brown	.40	4.00
435	A243	50c purple	.40	1.25
436	A244	50c purple	.40	1.25
437	A245	50c purple	.40	1.25
438	A246	50c purple	.40	1.25
	Nos. 427-438 (12)		4.80	26.00
	Set, never hinged		12.00	

Issued in honor of the Italian Army.
The left halves of #431-438 are type A95.
For overprints see Italian Social Republic #6-17.

She-Wolf Suckling Romulus and Remus — A247

Perf. 10½x11½, 11x11½, 11½, 14

1944, Jan.　Litho.　Wmk. 87
Without Gum

439	A247	50c rose vio & bis rose	2.40	4.00

Unwmk.

440	A247	50c rose vio & pale rose	.40	1.60

Nos. 439-440 exist imperf., part perf.

Types of 1929

1945, May　Unwmk.　Perf. 14

441	A93	15c slate green	.20	.20
442	A93	35c deep blue	.20	.40
443	A91	1 l deep violet	.50	.20
	Nos. 441-443 (3)		.90	.80
	Set, never hinged		2.00	

Types of 1929 Redrawn
Fasces Removed

Victor Emmanuel III A248

Julius Caesar A249

Augustus Caesar A250

"Italia" A251

A252

1944-45　Wmk. 140　Photo.　Perf. 14

444	A248	30c dk brown	.20	.20
445	A248	50c purple	2.75	4.00
446	A248	60c slate grn ('45)	.20	1.25
447	A249	1 l dp violet ('45)	.20	.20
	Nos. 444-447 (4)		3.35	5.65
	Set, never hinged		7.25	

1945　　Unwmk.　Perf. 14

448	A250	10c dk brown	.20	1.60
448A	A249	20c rose red	.20	.20
449	A251	50c dk violet	.20	.20
450	A248	60c slate grn	.20	.20
451	A251	60c red org	.20	.20
452	A249	1 l dp violet	.20	.20
452A	A249	1 l dp vio, redrawn	.20	.20
452B	A251	2 l dp car	1.60	1.25
452C	A251	10 l purple	4.75	7.25
	Nos. 448-452C (9)		7.75	11.30
	Set, never hinged		19.00	

1945   **Wmk. 277**

453	A249	20c rose red	.20	.80
454	A248	60c slate grn	.20	.80
455	A249	1 l dp violet	.20	.20
456	A251	1.20 l dk brown	.20	.80
457	A251	2 l dk red	.20	.80
458	A252	5 l dk red	.20	.80
459	A251	10 l purple	5.50	8.00
		Nos. 453-459 (7)	6.70	11.60
		Set, never hinged	17.00	

Nos. 452A and 457 are redrawings of types A249 and A251. In the redrawn 1 l, the "L" of "LIRE" extends under the "IRE" and the letters of "POSTE ITALIANE" are larger. In the original the "L" extends only under the "I."

In the redrawn 2 l, the "2" is smaller and thinner, and the design is less distinct.

For overprints see Nos. 1LN2-1LN8.

No. 224 Surcharged in Black

1945, Mar.   **Wmk. 140**

460	A92	2.50 l on 1.75 l red org	.20	.50
		Never hinged	.20	
a.		Six bars at left	1.50	1.50

Loggia dei Mercanti, Bologna A253   Basilica of San Lorenzo, Rome A254

Stamps of Italian Social Republic Surcharged in Black

1945, May 2   **Photo.**   **Perf. 14**

461	A253	1.20 l on 20c crim	.20	.25
462	A254	2 l on 25c green	.20	.25
a.		2½ mm between "2" and "LIRE"	1.50	1.50
		Set, never hinged	.80	

Breaking Chain A255   United Family and Scales A256

Planting Tree — A257   Tying Tree — A258

Torch A259   "Italia" and Sprouting Oak Stump A260

1945-47   **Wmk. 277**   **Photo.**   **Perf. 14**

463	A255	10c rose brown	.20	.20
464	A256	20c dk brown	.20	.20
464A	A259	25c brt bl grn ('46)	.20	.20
465	A257	40c slate	.20	.20
465A	A259	50c dp vio ('46)	.20	.20
466	A258	60c dk green	.20	.40
467	A255	80c car rose	.20	.20
468	A257	1 l dk green	.20	.20
469	A259	1.20 l chestnut	.20	1.25
470	A259	2 l dk claret brn	.20	.40
471	A259	3 l red	.20	.20
471A	A259	4 l red org ('46)	.25	.20

472	A256	5 l deep blue	.30	.20
472A	A259	6 l dp vio ('47)	6.50	.20
473	A255	10 l slate	.80	.20
473A	A257	15 l dp bl ('46)	8.00	.20
474	A259	20 l dk red vio	2.50	.20
475	A260	25 l dk grn	24.00	.20
476	A260	50 l dk vio brn	8.00	.20
		Nos. 463-476 (19)	52.55	5.25
		Set, never hinged	200.00	

See Nos. 486-488.
For overprints see Nos. 1LN11-1LN12, 1LN14-1N19, Trieste 1-13, 15-17, 30-32, 58-68, 82-83.

United Family and Scales A261

1946   **Engr.**   **Perf. 14**

477	A261	100 l car lake	175.00	2.00
		Never hinged	450.00	
a.		Perf. 14x13½	190.00	2.50
		Never hinged	475.00	

For overprints see #1LN13, Trieste 14, 69.

Cathedral of St. Andrea, Amalfi — A262   Church of St. Michael, Lucca — A263

"Peace" from Fresco at Siena A264   Signoria Palace, Florence A265

View of Cathedral Domes, Pisa A266

Republic of Genoa A267

"Venice Crowned by Glory," by Paolo Veronese A268

Oath of Pontida A269

1946, Oct. 30

478	A262	1 l brown	.20	.20
479	A263	2 l dk blue	.20	.20
480	A264	3 l dk bl grn	.20	.20
481	A265	4 l dp org	.20	.20
482	A266	5 l dp violet	.20	.20
483	A267	10 l car rose	.20	.20

484	A268	15 l dp ultra	.65	.65
485	A269	20 l red brown	.20	.20
		Nos. 478-485 (8)	2.05	2.05
		Set, never hinged	3.25	

Proclamation of the Republic.

Types of 1945

1947-48   **Wmk. 277**   **Photo.**   **Perf. 14**

486	A255	8 l dk green ('48)	2.50	.20
487	A256	10 l red orange	29.00	.20
488	A259	30 l dk blue ('48)	175.00	.25
		Nos. 486-488 (3)	206.50	.65
		Set, never hinged	515.00	

St. Catherine Giving Mantle to Beggar — A270

5 l, St. Catherine carrying cross. 10 l, St. Catherine, arms outstretched. 30 l, St. Catherine & scribe.

1948, Mar. 1   **Photo.**

489	A270	3 l yel grn & gray grn	.20	.20
490	A270	5 l vio & bl	.30	.35
491	A270	10 l red brn & vio	1.60	4.00
492	A270	30 l bis & gray brn	11.00	27.50
		Nos. 489-492 (4)	13.10	32.05
		Set, never hinged	32.50	
		Nos. 489-492,C127-C128 (6)	86.60	97.05
		Set, never hinged	182.50	

600th annlv. of the birth of St. Catherine of Siena, Patroness of Italy.

"Constitutional Government" — A271

1948, Apr. 12

493	A271	10 l rose vio	.80	1.00
494	A271	30 l blue	1.75	3.00
		Set, never hinged	6.50	

Proclamation of the constitution of 1/1/48.

Uprising at Palermo, Jan. 12, 1848 A272

Designs (Revolutionary scenes): 4 l, Rebellion at Padua. 5 l, Proclamation of statute, Turin. 6 l, "Five Days of Milan." 8 l, Daniele Manin proclaiming the Republic of Venice. 10 l, Defense of Vicenza. 12 l, Battle of Curtatone. 15 l, Battle of Gioto. 20 l, Insurrection at Bologna. 30 l, "Ten Days of Brescia." 50 l, Garibaldi in Rome fighting. 100 l, Death of Goffredo Mameli.

1948, May 3

495	A272	3 l dk brown	.50	1.25
496	A272	4 l red violet	.50	1.25
497	A272	5 l dp blue	3.25	1.25
498	A272	6 l dp yel grn	1.60	1.25
499	A272	8 l brown	1.60	1.25
500	A272	10 l orange red	1.25	1.25
501	A272	12 l dk gray grn	3.75	3.25
502	A272	15 l gray blk	9.00	2.00
503	A272	20 l car rose	21.00	14.50
504	A272	30 l brt ultra	4.50	2.00
505	A272	50 l violet	45.00	5.50
506	A272	100 l blue blk	82.50	27.50
		Nos. 495-506 (12)	174.45	62.25
		Set, never hinged	430.00	
		Nos. 495-506,E26 (13)	249.45	82.25
		Set, never hinged	580.00	

Centenary of the Risorgimento, uprisings of 1848-49 which led to Italian unification.
For overprints see Trieste Nos. 18-29, E5.

Alpine Soldier and Bassano Bridge A273

1948, Oct. 1   **Wmk. 277**   **Perf. 14**

507	A273	15 l dark green	1.60	2.40
		Never hinged	3.25	

Bridge of Bassano, re-opening, Oct. 3, 1948.
For overprint see Trieste No. 33.

Gaetano Donizetti — A274

1948, Oct. 23   **Photo.**

508	A274	15 l dark brown	1.25	2.25
		Never hinged	2.50	

Death cent. of Gaetano Donizetti, composer.
For overprint see Trieste No. 34.

Fair Buildings A275

1949, Apr. 12

509	A275	20 l dark brown	3.25	4.00
		Never hinged	9.50	

27th Milan Trade Fair, April 1949.
For overprint see Trieste No. 35.

Standard of Doges of Venice — A276

15 l, Clock strikers, Lion Tower and Campanile of St. Mark's. 20 l, Lion standard and Venetian galley. 50 l, Lion tower and gulls.

1949, Apr. 12
Buff Background

510	A276	5 l red brown	.20	.20
511	A276	15 l dk green	2.40	2.40
512	A276	20 l dp red brn	4.75	.20
513	A276	50 l dk blue	26.00	2.40
		Nos. 510-513 (4)	33.35	5.20
		Set, never hinged	85.00	

Biennial Art Exhibition of Venice, 50th anniv.
For overprints see Trieste Nos. 36-39.

"Transportation" and Globes — A277

1949, May 2   **Wmk. 277**   **Perf. 14**

514	A277	50 l brt ultra	27.50	9.50
		Never hinged	60.00	

75th anniv. of the UPU.
For overprint see Trieste No. 40.

Workman and Ship — A278

1949, May 30　　　　　**Photo.**
515 A278 5 l dk green　　　4.75　*8.00*
516 A278 15 l violet　　　12.00　*24.00*
517 A278 20 l brown　　　22.50　24.00
　Nos. 515-517 (3)　　　39.25　*56.00*
　Set, never hinged　　　100.00

European Recovery Program.
For overprints see Trieste Nos. 42-44.

The
Vascello,
Rome
A279

1949, May 18
518 A279 100 l brown　　140.00　125.00
　Never hinged　　　　　275.00

Centenary of Roman Republic.
For overprint see Trieste No. 41.

Giuseppe
Mazzini — A280

Vittorio
Alfieri — A281

1949, June 1
519 A280 20 l gray　　　4.00　4.75
　Never hinged　　　　　12.00

Erection of a monument to Giuseppe Mazzini (1805-72), Italian patriot and revolutionary.
For overprint see Trieste No. 45.

1949, June 4　　　　　**Photo.**
520 A281 20 l brown　　　3.25　3.50
　Never hinged　　　　　9.50

200th anniv. of the birth of Vittorio Alfieri, tragic dramatist.
For overprint see Trieste No. 46.

Basilica of
St. Just,
Trieste
A282

1949, June 8
521 A282 20 l brown red　　9.50　*20.00*
　Never hinged　　　　　14.50

Trieste election, June 12, 1949.
For overprint see Trieste No. 47.

Staff of Aesculapius,
Globe — A283

1949, June 13　Wmk. 277　Perf. 14
522 A283 20 l violet　　　16.00　16.00
　Never hinged　　　　　40.00

2nd World Health Cong., Rome, 1949.
For overprint see Trieste No. 49.

Lorenzo de
Medici
A284

Andrea Palladio
A285

1949, Aug. 4
523 A284 20 l violet blue　　4.00　4.00
　　　　　　　　　　　12.00

Birth of Lorenzo de Medici, 500th anniv.
For overprint see Trieste No. 50.

1949, Aug. 4
524 A285 20 l violet　　　6.50　*9.50*
　　　　　　　　　　　16.00

Andrea Palladio (1518-1580), architect.
For overprint see Trieste No. 51.

Tartan and
Fair
Buildings
A286

1949, Aug. 16
525 A286 20 l red　　　　2.75　*3.25*
　Never hinged　　　　　8.00

133th Levant Fair, Bari, September, 1949.
For overprint see Trieste No. 52.

Voltaic
Pile — A287

Alessandro
Volta — A288

1949, Sept. 14　　Engr.　　Perf. 14
526 A287 20 l rose car　　3.25　2.00
　a.　Perf. 13x14　　　13.00　10.00
527 A288 50 l deep blue　37.50　37.50
　a.　Perf. 13x14　　　160.00　67.50
　Set, never hinged　　　105.00

Invention of the Voltaic Pile, 150th anniv.
For overprints see Trieste Nos. 53-54.

Holy Trinity
Bridge — A289

1949, Sept. 19　　　　**Photo.**
528 A289 20 l deep green　4.00　3.50
　Never hinged　　　　　9.50

Issued to publicize plans to reconstruct Holy Trinity Bridge, Florence.
For overprint see Trieste No. 55.

Gaius Valerius
Catullus
A290

Domenico
Cimarosa
A291

1949, Sept. 19　Wmk. 277　Perf. 14
529 A290 20 l brt blue　　4.75　3.50
　Never hinged　　　　　12.00

2000th anniversary of the death of Gaius Valerius Catullus, Lyric poet.
For overprint see Trieste No. 56.

1949, Dec. 28
530 A291 20 l violet blk　　4.00　3.25
　Never hinged　　　　　11.50

Bicentenary of the birth of Domenico Cimarosa, composer.
For overprint see Trieste No. 57.

Milan Fair
Scene
A292

1950, Apr. 12　　　　　**Photo.**
531 A292 20 l brown　　　2.40　3.25
　Never hinged　　　　　4.75

The 28th Milan Trade Fair.
For overprint see Trieste No. 70.

Flags and
Italian
Automobile
A293

1950, Apr. 29
532 A293 20 l vio gray　　4.50　2.75
　　　　　　　　　　　12.00

32nd Intl. Auto Show, Turin, May 4-14, 1950.
For overprint see Trieste No. 71.

Pitti Palace,
Florence
A294

"Perseus" by
Cellini — A295

Composite of
Italian Cathedrals
and
Churches — A296

1950, May 22
533 A294 20 l olive grn　　3.25　3.25
534 A295 55 l blue　　　30.00　17.50
　Set, never hinged　　　85.00

5th General Conf. of UNESCO.
For overprints see Trieste Nos. 72-73.

1950, May 29
535 A296 20 l violet　　　6.50　.80
536 A296 55 l blue　　　32.50　3.25
　Set, never hinged　　　100.00

Holy Year, 1950.
For overprints see Trieste Nos. 74-75.

Gaudenzio
Ferrari
A297

Radio Mast
and Tower of
Florence
A298

1950, July 1　Wmk. 277　Perf. 14
537 A297 20 l gray grn　　8.00　3.50
　Never hinged　　　　　20.00

Issued to honor Gaudenzio Ferrari.
For overprint see Trieste No. 76.

1950, July 15　　　　　**Photo.**
538 A298 20 l purple　　　9.50　10.00
539 A298 55 l blue　　　75.00　*160.00*
　Set, never hinged　　　240.00

Intl. Shortwave Radio Conf., Florence, 1950.
For overprints Trieste see Nos. 77-78.

Ludovico A.
Muratori
A299

Guido d'Arezzo
A300

1950, July 22
540 A299 20 l brown　　　2.40　2.75
　Never hinged　　　　　7.25

200th anniv. of the death of Ludovico A. Muratori, writer.
For overprint see Trieste No. 79.

1950, July 29
541 A300 20 l dark green　8.00　3.25
　　　　　　　　　　　24.00

900th anniv. of the death of Guido d'Arezzo, music teacher and composer.
For overprint see Trieste No. 80.

Tartan and
Fair
Buildings
A301

1950, Aug. 21
542 A301 20 l chestnut brown　4.00　2.75
　Never hinged　　　　　12.00

Levant Fair, Bari, September, 1950.
For overprint see Trieste No. 81.

G. Marzotto
and A.
Rossi — A302

Tobacco
Plant — A303

1950, Sept. 11
543 A302 20 l indigo　　　2.40　2.00
　Never hinged　　　　　4.75

Pioneers of the Italian wool industry.
For overprint see Trieste No. 84.

1950, Sept. 11
Designs: 20 l, Mature plant, different background. 55 l, Girl holding tobacco plant.

544 A303 5 l dp claret & grn　1.60　*4.00*
545 A303 20 l brown & grn　　2.50　1.25
546 A303 55 l dp ultra & brn　35.00　32.50
　Nos. 544-546 (3)　　　39.10　37.75
　Set, never hinged　　　100.00

Issued to publicize the European Tobacco Conference, Rome, 1950.
For overprints see Trieste Nos. 85-87.

Arms of the
Academy of
Fine
Arts — A304

Augusto
Righi — A305

1950, Sept. 16
547 A304 20 l ol brn & red brn 2.75 2.75
Never hinged 6.50
200th anniv. of the founding of the Academy of Fine Arts, Venice.
For overprint see Trieste No. 88.

1950, Sept. 16
548 A305 20 l cream & gray blk 2.75 2.75
Never hinged 6.50
Centenary of the birth of Augusto Righi, physicist.
For overprint see Trieste No. 89.

Blacksmith, Aosta Valley — A306

1851 Stamp of Tuscany — A307

Designs: 1 l, Auto mechanic. 2 l, Mason. 5 l, Potter. 6 l, Lace-making. 10 l, Weaving. 12 l, Sailor steering boat. 15 l, Shipbuilding. 20 l, Fisherman. 25 l, Sorting oranges. 30 l, Woman carrying grapes. 35 l, Olive picking. 40 l, Wine cart. 50 l, Shepherd and flock. 55 l, Plowing. 60 l, Grain cart. 65 l, Girl worker in hemp field. 100 l, Husking corn. 200 l, Woodcutter.

1950, Oct. 20 Wmk. 277 Perf. 14
549	A306	50c vio blue	.20	.20
550	A306	1 l dk bl vio	.20	.20
551	A306	2 l sepia	.20	.20
552	A306	5 l dk gray	.20	.20
553	A306	6 l chocolate	.20	.20
554	A306	10 l dp green	3.75	.20
555	A306	12 l dp blue grn	1.90	.20
556	A306	15 l dk gray bl	1.25	.20
557	A306	20 l blue vio	9.50	.20
558	A306	25 l brn org	1.60	.20
559	A306	30 l magenta	1.25	.20
560	A306	35 l crimson	8.00	1.25
561	A306	40 l brown	.30	.20
562	A306	50 l violet	11.50	.20
563	A306	55 l dp blue	.65	.20
564	A306	60 l red	2.25	.20
565	A306	65 l dk grn	.65	.20

Perf. 13x14, 14x13 Engr.
566	A306	100 l brn org	32.50	.20
a.		Perf. 13	32.50	.20
b.		Perf. 14	35.00	.20
567	A306	200 l ol brn	9.50	3.25
a.		Perf. 14	9.50	3.25
		Nos. 549-567 (19)	85.60	7.90
		Set, never hinged	210.00	

See Nos. 668-673A. For overprints see Trieste Nos. 90-108, 122-124, 178-180.

1951, Mar. 27 Photo. Perf. 14
Design: 55 l, Tuscany 6cr.
568	A307	20 l red vio & red	1.60	1.10
569	A307	55 l ultra & blue	19.00	40.00
		Set, never hinged	52.50	

Centenary of Tuscany's first stamps.
For overprints see Trieste Nos. 109-110.

Italian Automobile A308

1951, Apr. 2
570 A308 20 l dk green 5.50 3.50
Never hinged 16.00
33rd Intl. Automobile Exhib., Turin, Apr. 4-15, 1951.
For overprint see Trieste No. 111.

Altar of Peace, Medea A309

1951, Apr. 11
571 A309 20 l blue vio 3.25 3.25
Never hinged 11.00
Consecration of the Altar of Peace at Redipuglia Cemetery, Medea.
For overprint see Trieste No. 112.

Helicopter over Leonardo da Vinci Heliport — A310

P. T. T. Building, Milan Fair — A311

1951, Apr. 12 Photo.
572	A310	20 l brown	9.50	2.00
573	A311	55 l dp blue	32.50	70.00
		Set, never hinged	105.00	

29th Milan Trade Fair.
For overprints see Trieste Nos. 113-114.

Symbols of the International Gymnastic Festival A312

Statue of Diana, Spindle and Turin Tower A313

Wmk. 277
1951, May 18 Photo. Perf. 14
Fleur-de-lis in Red
574	A312	5 l dk brown	20.00	600.00
575	A312	10 l Prus green	20.00	600.00
576	A312	15 l vio blue	20.00	600.00
		Nos. 574-576 (3)	60.00	1,800.
		Set, never hinged	100.00	

International Gymnastic Festival and Meet, Florence, 1951.
Fake cancellations exist on Nos. 574-576.
For overprints see Trieste Nos. 115-117.

1951, Apr. 26
577 A313 20 l purple 10.00 4.50
Never hinged 30.00
Tenth International Exhibition of Textile Art and Fashion, Turin, May 2-16.
For overprint see Trieste No. 118.

Landing of Columbus A314

1951, May 5
578 A314 20 l Prus green 5.00 4.00
Never hinged 22.50
500th anniversary of birth of Columbus.
For overprint see Trieste No. 119.

Reconstructed Abbey of Montecassino — A315

Design: 55 l, Montecassino Ruins.

1951, June 18
579 A315 20 l violet 4.00 2.00
580 A315 55 l brt blue 40.00 55.00
Set, never hinged 90.00
Issued to commemorate the reconstruction of the Abbey of Montecassino.
For overprints see Trieste Nos. 120-121.

Pietro Vannucci (Il Perugino) A316

Stylized Vase A317

Cartouche of Amenhotep III and Pitcher A318

1951, July 23
581 A316 20 l brn & red brn 2.75 4.00
Never hinged 5.00
500th anniversary (in 1950) of the birth of Pietro Vannucci, painter.
For overprint see Trieste No. 125.

1951, July 23
582 A317 20 l grnsh gray & blk 6.00 4.00
583 A318 55 l vio bl & pale sal 22.50 52.50
Set, never hinged 60.00
Triennial Art Exhibition, Milan, 1951.
For overprints see Trieste Nos. 126-127.

Cyclist — A319

1951, Aug. 23
584 A319 25 l gray black 5.50 5.50
Never hinged 12.00
World Bicycle Championship Races, Milan, Aug.-Sept. 1951.
For overprint see Trieste No. 128.

Tartan and Globes A320

1951, Sept. 8 Photo.
585 A320 25 l deep blue 3.25 3.25
Never hinged 12.00
15th Levant Fair, Bari, September 1951.
For overprint see Trieste No. 129.

"La Figlia di Jorio" by Michetti A321

1951, Sept. 15 Wmk. 277 Perf. 14
586 A321 20 l dk brown 3.25 3.25
Never hinged 9.00
Centenary of the birth of Francesco Paolo Michetti, painter.
For overprint see Trieste No. 130.

Sardinia Stamps of 1851 A322

1951, Oct. 5
587	A322	10 l shown	1.25	3.25
588	A322	25 l 20c stamp	1.60	1.60
589	A322	60 l 40c stamp	8.00	15.00
		Nos. 587-589 (3)	10.85	19.85
		Set, never hinged	26.00	

Centenary of Sardinia's 1st postage stamp.
For overprints see Trieste Nos. 131-133.

Mercury — A323

Roman Census A324

1951, Oct. 31
590	A323	10 l green	1.00	2.00
591	A324	25 l vio gray	3.00	2.00
		Set, never hinged	8.50	

3rd Industrial and the 9th General Italian Census.
For overprints see Trieste Nos. 134-135.

Winter Scene — A325

Trees A326

1951, Nov. 21
592	A325	10 l ol & dl grn	1.25	4.50
593	A326	25 l dull grn	3.50	1.25
		Set, never hinged	10.00	

Issued to publicize the Festival of Trees.
For overprints see Trieste Nos. 136-137.

Giuseppe Verdi A327

Portraits of Verdi, various backgrounds.

1951, Nov. 19 Engr.
594	A327	10 l vio brn & dk grn	2.40	4.00
595	A327	25 l red brn & dk brn	6.00	1.60
596	A327	60 l dp grn & indigo	24.00	20.00
		Nos. 594-596 (3)	32.40	25.60
		Set, never hinged	65.00	

50th anniversary of the death of Giuseppe Verdi, composer.
For overprints see Trieste Nos. 138-140.

Vincenzo Bellini — A328

Wmk. 277
1952, Jan. 28   Photo.   Perf. 14
597 A328 25 l gray & gray blk   2.00 1.60
                                           6.00

150th anniversary of the birth of Vincenzo Bellini, composer.
For overprint see Trieste No. 141.

Palace of Caserta and Statuary A329

1952, Feb. 1
598 A329 25 l dl grn & ol bis   1.60 1.25
       Never hinged   5.00

Issued to honor Luigi Vanvitelli, architect.
For overprint see Trieste No. 142.

Statues of Athlete and River God Tiber — A330

1952, Mar. 22
599 A330 25 l brn & sl blk   1.00 1.10
       Never hinged   2.00

Issued on the occasion of the first International Exhibition of Sports Stamps.
For overprint see Trieste No. 143.

Milan Fair Buildings A331

1952, Apr. 12   Engr.
600 A331 60 l ultra   27.50 24.00
       Never hinged   55.00

30th Milan Trade Fair.
For overprint see Trieste No. 144.

Leonardo da Vinci — A332   Virgin of the Rocks — A332a

1952   Wmk. 277   Photo.   Perf. 14
601 A332 25 l deep orange   .20 .20

Unwmk.
Engr.   Perf. 13
601A A332a 60 l ultra   2.40 9.25

Wmk. 277
601B A332 80 l brn car   12.00 .40
  c.   Perf. 14x13   10.00 .40
       Set, never hinged   40.00

Leonardo da Vinci, 500th birth anniv.
For overprints see Trieste #145, 163-164.

First Stamps and Cathedral Bell Towers of Modena and Parma A333

1952, May 29   Perf. 14
602 A333 25 l blk & red brn   1.00 1.25
603 A333 60 l blk & ultra   4.00 15.00
       Set, never hinged   12.00

Cent. of the 1st postage stamps of Modena and Parma.
For overprints see Trieste Nos. 146-147.

Globe and Torch — A334

Lion of St. Mark — A335

1952, June 7
604 A334 25 l bright blue   1.00 1.25
       Never hinged   2.75

Issued to honor the Overseas Fair at Naples and Italian labor throughout the world.
For overprint see Trieste No. 148.

1952, June 14
605 A335 25 l black & yellow   1.25 1.25
                                           3.00

26th Biennial Art Exhibition, Venice.
For overprint see Trieste No. 149.

"P" and Basilica of St. Anthony A336

Flag and Basilica of St. Just A337

1952, June 19
606 A336 25 l bl gray, red & dk
             bl   2.00 1.60
       Never hinged   6.00

30th International Sample Fair of Padua.
For overprint see Trieste No. 150.

1952, June 28
607 A337 25 l dp grn, dk brn &
             red   1.40 1.40
       Never hinged   3.25

4th International Sample Fair of Trieste.
For overprint see Trieste No. 151.

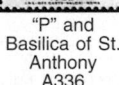

Fair Entrance and Tartan A338

1952, Sept. 6   Wmk. 277   Perf. 14
608 A338 25 l dark green   1.00 1.25
       Never hinged   2.25

16th Levant Fair, Bari, Sept. 1952.
For overprint see Trieste No. 152.

Girolamo Savonarola A339

1952, Sept. 20
609 A339 25 l purple   1.60 1.00
       Never hinged   4.50

500th anniversary of the birth of Girolamo Savonarola.
For overprint see Trieste No. 153.

1952, Oct. 4
610 A340 25 l gray   .60 .60
       Never hinged   1.25

Issued to publicize the National Exhibition of the Alpine troops, Oct. 4, 1952.
For overprint see Trieste No. 154.

Colosseum and Plane A341

1952, Sept. 29
611 A341 60 l vio bl & dk bl   9.00 12.00
       Never hinged   16.00

Issued to publicize the first International Civil Aviation Conference, Rome, Sept. 1952.
For overprint see Trieste No. 155.

Guglielmo Cardinal Massaia and Map A342

1952, Nov. 21   Engr.   Perf. 13
612 A342 25 l brn & dk brn   1.25 1.75
       Never hinged   1.75

Centenary of the establishment of the first Catholic mission in Ethiopia.
For overprint see Trieste No. 156.

Symbols of Army, Navy and Air Force A343

Sailor, Soldier and Aviator A344

Design: 60 l, Boat, plane and tank.

1952, Nov. 3   Photo.   Perf. 14
613 A343 10 l dk green   .20 .20
614 A344 25 l blk & dk brn   .40 .20
615 A344 60 l black & blue   3.50 7.00
       Nos. 613-615 (3)   4.10 7.40
       Set, never hinged   9.50

Armed Forces Day, Nov. 4, 1952.
For overprints see Trieste Nos. 157-159.

Antonio Mancini — A345

Vincenzo Gemito — A346

1952, Dec. 6
616 A345 25 l dark green   .60 1.00
617 A346 25 l brown   .60 1.00
       Set, never hinged   2.50

Birth centenaries of Antonio Mancini, painter, and Vincenzo Gemito, sculptor.
For overprints see Trieste Nos. 160-161.

Martyrs, Jailer and Artist Boldini A347

1952, Dec. 31
618 A347 25 l gray blk & dk blue   .80 .80
                                           3.00

Centenary of the deaths of the five Martyrs of Belfiore.
For overprint see Trieste No. 162.

Antonello da Messina — A349

1953, Feb. 21   Photo.   Perf. 14
621 A349 25 l car lake   .85 .85
       Never hinged   2.75

Messina Exhibition of the paintings of Antonello and his 15th cent. contemporaries.
For overprint see Trieste No. 165.

Racing Cars A350

1953, Apr. 24
622 A350 25 l violet   .85 .85
       Never hinged   1.25

20th 1,000-mile auto race.
For overprint see Trieste No. 166.

Decoration "Knights of Labor" Bee and Honeycomb A351

Arcangelo Corelli A352

1953, Apr. 30
623 A351 25 l violet   .60 .80
       Never hinged   1.25

For overprint see Trieste No. 167.

1953, May 30
624 A352 25 l dark brown   .60 .80
       Never hinged   1.25

300th anniv. of the birth of Arcangelo Corelli, composer.
For overprint see Trieste No. 168.

St. Clare of Assisi and Convent of St. Damien A353

"Italia" after Syracusean Coin A354

1953, June 27
625 A353 25 l brown & dull red .40 *.50*
Never hinged .85

St. Clare of Assisi, 700th death anniv.
For overprint see Trieste No. 169.

1953-54   **Wmk. 277**   **Perf. 14**
Size: 17x21mm
626 A354 5 l gray .20 .20
627 A354 10 l org ver .20 .20
628 A354 12 l dull green .20 .20
628A A354 13 l brt lil rose
('54) .20 .20
629 A354 20 l brown 1.90 .20
630 A354 25 l purple 2.50 .20
631 A354 35 l rose car .30 .20
632 A354 60 l blue 16.00 7.25
633 A354 80 l orange brn 32.50 .80
Nos. 626-633 (9) 54.00 9.45
Set, never hinged 150.00

See Nos. 661-662, 673B-689, 785-788, 998A-998W, 1288-1290. For overprints see Trieste Nos. 170-177.

Mountain Peaks — A355

Tyche, Goddess of Fortune — A356

1953, July 11
634 A355 25 l blue green .60 .60
Never hinged 1.75

Festival of the Mountain.
For overprint see Trieste No. 181.

1953, July 16
635 A356 25 l dark brown .50 .20
636 A356 60 l deep blue 2.50 *3.50*
Set, never hinged 7.25

Intl. Exposition of Agriculture, Rome, 1953.
For overprints see Trieste Nos. 182-183.

Continents Joined by Rainbow A357

1953, Aug. 6
637 A357 25 l org & Prus bl 2.75 .20
638 A357 60 l lil rose & dk vio
bl 6.00 1.40
Set, never hinged 18.00

Signing of the North Atlantic Treaty, 4th anniv.
For overprints see Trieste Nos. 184-185.

Luca Signorelli A358

Agostino Bassi A359

1953, Aug. 13
639 A358 25 l dk brn & dull grn .40 .40
Never hinged 1.10

Issued to publicize the opening of an exhibition of the works of Luca Signorelli, painter.
For overprint see Trieste No. 186.

1953, Sept. 5
640 A359 25 l dk gray & brown .35 .35

6th International Microbiology Congress, Rome, Sept. 6-12, 1953.
For overprint see Trieste No. 187.

Siena — A360

Rapallo A361

Views: 20 l, Seaside at Gardone. 25 l, Mountain, Cortina d'Ampezzo. 35 l, Roman ruins, Taormina. 60 l, Rocks and sea, Capri.

1953, Dec. 31   **Perf. 14**
641 A360 10 l dk brn & red brn .20 .20
642 A361 12 l lt blue & gray .20 .20
643 A361 20 l brn org & dk brn .25 .20
644 A360 25 l dk grn & pale bl .60 .20
645 A361 35 l cream & brn .65 .40
646 A361 60 l bl grn & ind 1.60 1.75
Nos. 641-646 (6) 3.50 2.95
Set, never hinged 10.00

For overprints see Trieste Nos. 188-193, 204-205.

Lateran Palace, Rome — A362

Television Screen and Aerial — A363

1954, Feb. 11
647 A362 25 l dk brown & choc .30 .20
648 A362 60 l blue & ultra 1.60 *3.00*
Set, never hinged 5.00

Signing of the Lateran Pacts, 25th anniv.
For overprints see Trieste Nos. 194-195.

1954, Feb. 25
649 A363 25 l purple .65 .20
650 A363 60 l dp blue grn 2.75 *4.50*
Set, never hinged 9.00

Introduction of regular natl. television service.
For overprints see Trieste Nos. 196-197.

"Italia" and Quotation from Constitution A364

1954, Mar. 20
651 A364 25 l purple .70 .20
Never hinged 2.00

Propaganda for the payment of taxes.
For overprint see Trieste No. 198.

Vertical Flight Trophy — A365

Eagle Perched on Ruins — A366

1954, Apr. 24
652 A365 25 l gray black .40 *.70*
Never hinged .90

Issued to publicize the experimental transportation of mail by helicopter, April 1954.
For overprint see Trieste No. 199.

1954, June 1
653 A366 25 l gray, org brn & blk .20 *.35*
Never hinged .40

10th anniv. of Italy's resistance movement.
For overprint see Trieste No. 200.

Alfredo Catalani, Composer, Birth Centenary — A367

1954, June 19   **Perf. 14**
654 A367 25 l dk grnsh gray .20 *.30*
Never hinged .40

For overprint see Trieste No. 201.

Marco Polo, Lion of St. Mark and Dragon A368

1954, July 8   **Engr.**   **Perf. 14**
655 A368 25 l red brown .25 .20

Perf. 13
656 A368 60 l gray green 1.75 *5.50*
a. Perf. 13x12 6.00 6.00
Set, never hinged 5.25

700th anniv. of the birth of Marco Polo.
For overprints see Trieste Nos. 202-203.

Automobile and Cyclist A369

1954, Sept. 6   **Photo.**   **Perf. 14**
657 A369 25 l dp green & red .30 .30
Never hinged .60

Italian Touring Club, 60th anniv.
For overprint see Trieste No. 206.

St. Michael Overpowering the Devil — A370

1954, Oct. 9
658 A370 25 l rose red .25 .20
659 A370 60 l blue .85 1.10
Set, never hinged 1.90

23rd general assembly of the International Criminal Police, Rome 1954.
For overprints see Trieste Nos. 207-208.

Pinocchio and Group of Children — A371

1954, Oct. 26
660 A371 25 l rose red .40 .30
Never hinged .80

Carlo Lorenzini, creator of Pinocchio.

Italia Type of 1953-54
1954, Dec. 28   **Engr.**   **Perf. 13**
Size: 22½x27½mm
661 A354 100 l brown 55.00 .30
662 A354 200 l dp blue 5.00 .50
Set, never hinged 190.00

Madonna, Perugino A372

Amerigo Vespucci and Map A373

60 l, Madonna of the Pieta, Michelangelo.

1954, Dec. 31   **Photo.**   **Perf. 14**
663 A372 25 l brown & bister .25 .20
664 A372 60 l black & cream 1.10 *2.75*
Set, never hinged 3.00

Issued to mark the end of the Marian Year.

1954, Dec. 31   **Engr.**   **Perf. 13**
665 A373 25 l dp plum .25 .20
a. Perf. 13x14 5.75 .80
666 A373 60 l blue blk 1.25 *2.75*
a. Perf. 13x14 1.25 *2.75*
Set, never hinged 3.50

500th anniv. of the birth of Amerigo Vespucci, explorer, 1454-1512.

Silvio Pellico (1789-1854), Dramatist — A374

Wmk. 277
1955, Jan. 24   **Photo.**   **Perf. 14**
667 A374 25 l brt blue & vio .30 .20
Never hinged .40

Italy at Work Type of 1950

1955-57			Wmk. 303	
668	A306	50c vio bl	.20	.20
669	A306	1 l dk bl vio	.20	.20
670	A306	2 l sepia	.20	.20
671	A306	15 l dk gray bl	.65	.25
672	A306	30 l magenta	27.50	.50
673	A306	50 l violet	12.00	.25
673A	A306	65 l dk grn ('57)	14.00	45.00
		Nos. 668-673A (7)	54.75	46.60
		Set, never hinged	140.00	

Italia Type of 1953-54 and

St. George, by
Donatello — A374a

1955-58		Wmk. 303 Photo.	Perf. 14	
		Size: 17x21mm		
673B	A354	1 l gray ('58)	.20	.20
674	A354	5 l slate	.20	.20
675	A354	6 l ocher ('57)	.20	.20
676	A354	10 l org ver	.20	.20
677	A354	12 l dull green	.20	.20
678	A354	13 l brt lil rose	.20	.20
679	A354	15 l gray vio ('56)	.20	.20
680	A354	20 l brown	.20	.20
681	A354	25 l purple	.20	.20
682	A354	35 l rose car	.20	.20
683	A354	50 l olive ('58)	.25	.20
685	A354	60 l blue	.20	.20
686	A354	80 l brown org	.20	.20
687	A354	90 l lt red brn ('58)	.20	.20

		Engr.	Perf. 13½	
		Size: 22½x28mm		
688	A354	100 l brn ('56)	4.50	.20
a.		Perf. 13½x12	4.50	.20
b.		Perf. 13½x14	1,300.	24.00
689	A354	200 l gray bl ('57)	3.75	.20
690	A374a	500 l grn ('57)	1.25	.20
b.		Perf. 14x13½	.65	.20
690A	A374a	1000 l rose car ('57)	2.25	.60
c.		Perf. 14x13½	1.25	.20
		Nos. 673B-690A (18)	14.60	4.00
		Set, never hinged	45.00	

Nos. 690-690A were printed on ordinary and fluorescent paper.
See Nos. 785-788. See Nos. 998A-998W for small-size set.

> **Catalogue values for unused stamps in this section, from this point to the end of the section, are for Never Hinged items.**

"Italia"
A375

Oil Derrick and
Old Roman
Aqueduct
A376

1955, Mar. 15   Photo.   Perf. 14
691   A375   25 l rose vio   2.00   .20

Issued as propaganda for the payment of taxes.

1955, June 6
60 l, Marble columns and oil field on globe.
692   A376   25 l olive green   .40   .20
693   A376   60 l henna brown   1.40   1.50

4th World Petroleum Cong., Rome, June 6-15, 1955.

Antonio Rosmini, Philosopher, Death Centenary — A377

1955, July 1   Wmk. 303   Perf. 14
694   A377   25 l sepia   1.00   .20

Girolamo
Fracastoro
and
Stadium at
Verona
A378

1955, Sept. 1
695   A378   25 l gray blk & brn   .70   .20

Intl. Medical Congress, Verona, Sept. 1-4.

Basilica of
St. Francis,
Assisi
A379

1955, Oct. 4
696   A379   25 l black & cream   .40   .20

Issued in honor of St. Francis and for the 7th centenary (in 1953) of the Basilica in Assisi.

Young Man at
Drawing
Board — A380

1955, Oct. 15
697   A380   25 l Prus green   .40   .20

Centenary of technical education in Italy.

Harvester — A381

FAO Headquarters, Rome — A382

1955, Nov. 3
698   A381   25 l rose red & brn   .30   .25
699   A382   60 l blk & brt pur   1.60   1.25

Intl. Institute of Agriculture, 50th anniv. and FAO, successor to the Institute, 10th anniv.

A383   A384

1955, Nov. 10
700   A383   25 l rose brown   1.10   .20

70th anniversary of the birth of Giacomo Matteotti, Italian socialist leader.

1955, Nov. 19
701   A384   25 l dark green   .35   .20

Death of Battista Grassi, zoologist, 30th anniv.

"St. Stephen
Giving
Alms" — A385

"St. Lorenzo
Giving
Alms"
A386

1955, Nov. 26
702   A385   10 l black & cream   .20   .20
703   A386   25 l ultra & cream   .40   .20

Death of Fra Angelico, painter, 500th anniv.

Giovanni
Pascoli
A387

1955, Dec. 31
704   A387   25 l gray black   .30   .20

Centenary of the birth of Giovanni Pascoli, poet.

Ski Jump
"Italia"
A388

Stadiums at Cortina: 12 l, Skiing. 25 l, Ice skating. 60 l, Ice racing, Lake Misurina.

1956, Jan. 26   Photo.
705   A388   10 l blue grn & org   .20   .20
706   A388   12 l yellow & blk   .20   .20
707   A388   25 l vio blk & org brn .35   .20
708   A388   60 l sapphire & org   2.25   2.50
        Nos. 705-708 (4)   3.00   3.10

VII Winter Olympic Games at Cortina d'Ampezzo, Jan. 26-Feb. 5, 1956.

Mail Coach
and Tunnel
Exit
A389

1956, May 19   Wmk. 303   Perf. 14
709   A389   25 l dk blue grn   6.00   .80

50th anniv. of the Simplon Tunnel.

Arms of
Republic
and
Symbols of
Industry
A390

1956, June 2
710   A390   10 l gray & slate bl   .30   .20
711   A390   25 l pink & rose red   .45   .20
712   A390   60 l lt bl & brt bl   4.75   5.50
713   A390   80 l orange & brn   7.00   .20
        Nos. 710-713 (4)   12.50   6.10

Tenth anniversary of the Republic.

Amedeo
Avogadro
A391

1956, Sept. 8
714   A391   25 l black vio   .25   .20

Centenary of the death of Amedeo Avogadro, physicist.

Europa Issue

"Rebuilding
Europe" — A392

1956, Sept. 15
715   A392   25 l dark green   1.50   .20
716   A392   60 l blue   10.00   1.00

Issued to symbolize the cooperation among the six countries comprising the Coal and Steel Community.

Globe and
Satellites
A393

1956, Sept. 22
717   A393   25 l intense blue   .25   .20

7th Intl. Astronautical Cong., Rome, Sept. 17-22.

Globe — A394

1956, Dec. 29   Litho.   Unwmk.
718   A394   25 l red & bl grn, pink   .30   .20
719   A394   60 l bl grn & red, pale bl grn   .40   .20

Italy's admission to the United Nations. The design, viewed through red and green glasses, becomes three-dimensional.

Postal
Savings
Bank and
Notes
A395

1956, Dec. 31   Photo.   Wmk. 303
720   A395   25 l sl bl & dp ultra   .25   .20

80th anniversary of Postal Savings.

Ovid
A396

Antonio Canova
A397

Paulina
Borghese
as Venus
A398

1957, June 10   *Perf. 14*
721 A396 25 l ol grn & blk   .30   .20
2000th anniversary of the birth of the poet Ovid (Publius Ovidius Naso).

1957, July 15   *Engr.*
60 l, Sculpture: Hercules and Lichas.
722 A397 25 l brown   .20   .20
723 A397 60 l gray   .25   .60
724 A398 80 l vio blue   .25   .20
    Nos. 722-724 (3)   .70 1.00
Birth of Antonio Canova, sculptor, 200th anniv.

Traffic Light
A399

"United Europe"
A400

Wmk. 303
1957, Aug. 7   *Photo.*   *Perf. 14*
725 A399 25 l green, blk & red   .35   .20
Campaign for careful driving.

1957, Sept. 16   *Litho.*   *Perf. 14*
Flags in Original Colors
726 A400 25 l light blue   .75   .20
            Perf. 13
727 A400 60 l violet blue   5.50   .60
United Europe for peace and prosperity.

Giosue
Carducci
A401

Filippino Lippi
A402

1957, Oct. 14   *Engr.*   *Perf. 14*
728 A401 25 l brown   .30   .20
Death of the poet Giosue Carducci, 50th anniv.

1957, Nov. 25   *Wmk. 303*   *Perf. 14*
729 A402 25 l reddish brown   .30   .20
Birth of Filippino Lippi, painter, 500th anniv.

2000th Anniv. of the Death of Marcus Tullius Cicero, Roman Statesman and Writer — A403

1957, Nov. 30   *Photo.*
730 A403 25 l brown red   .25   .20

St. Domenico Savio and Students of Various Races A404

1957, Dec. 14
731 A404 15 l brt lil & blk   .25   .20
Cent. of the death of St. Domenico Savio.

St. Francis of Paola
A405

Giuseppe Garibaldi
A406

1957, Dec. 21   *Engr.*
732 A405 25 l black   .25   .20
450th anniv. of the death of St. Francis of Paola, patron saint of seafaring men.

1957, Dec. 14   *Perf. 14x13, 13x14*
Design: 110 l, Garibaldi monument, horiz.
733 A406   15 l slate green   .25   .20
734 A406 110 l dull purple   .35   .20
150th anniv. of the birth of Giuseppe Garibaldi.

Peasant, Dams and Map of Sardinia
A407

1958, Feb. 1   *Engr.*   *Perf. 14*
738 A407 25 l bluish grn   .25   .20
Completion of the Flumendosa-Mulargia irrigation system.

Immaculate Conception Statue, Rome, and Lourdes Basilica — A408

1958, Apr. 16   *Wmk. 303*   *Perf. 14*
739 A408 15 l rose claret   .25   .20
740 A408 60 l blue   .25   .20
Apparition of the Virgin Mary at Lourdes, cent.

Book and Symbols of Labor Industry and Agriculture
A409

Designs: 60 l, "Tree of Freedom," vert. 110 l, Montecitorio Palace.

1958, May 9   *Photo.*   *Perf. 14*
741 A409   25 l bl grn & ocher   .25   .20
742 A409   60 l blk brn & bl   .25   .20
743 A409 110 l ol bis & blk brn   .25   .20
    Nos. 741-743 (3)   .75   .60
10th anniversary of the constitution.

Brussels Fair Emblem
A410

Prologue from Pagliacci
A411

1958, June 12
744 A410 60 l blue & yellow   .25   .20
Intl. and Universal Exposition at Brussels.

1958, July 10
745 A411 25 l dk bl & dk red   .25   .20
Birth of Ruggiero Leoncavallo, composer, cent.

Scene from La Bohème
A412

1958, July 10   *Engr.*   *Unwmk.*
746 A412 25 l dark blue   .25   .20
Birth of Giacomo Puccini, composer, cent.

Giovanni Fattori, Self-portrait
A413

"Ave Maria on the Lake" by Giovanni Segantini
A414

1958, Aug. 7   *Wmk. 303*   *Perf. 13x14*
747 A413 110 l redsh brown   .40   .30
Death of Giovanni Fattori, painter, 50th anniv.

1958, Aug. 7   *Perf. 14*
748 A414 110 l slate, *buff*   .40   .30
Birth of Giovanni Segantini, painter, cent.

Map of Brazil, Plane and Arch of Titus
A415

1958, Aug. 23   *Photo.*   *Perf. 14*
749 A415 175 l Prus green   .80 1.25
Italo-Brazilian friendship on the occasion of Pres. Giovanni Gronchi's visit to Brazil.

Common Design Types pictured following the introduction.

Europa Issue, 1958
Common Design Type
1958, Sept. 13
Size: 20½x35½mm
750 CD1 25 l red & blue   .60   .20
751 CD1 60 l blue & red   1.25   .35
Issued to show the European Postal Union at the service of European integration.

½g Stamp of Naples
A416

Evangelista Torricelli
A417

Design: 60 l, 1g Stamp of Naples.

Perf. 14x13½, 13½

1958, Oct. 4   *Engr.*   *Unwmk.*
752 A416 25 l brown red   .20   .20
753 A416 60 l blk & red brn   .20   .20
Centenary of the stamps of Naples.

1958, Oct. 20   *Wmk. 303*   *Perf. 14*
754 A417 25 l rose claret   .65   .20
350th anniv. of the birth of Evangelista Torricelli, mathematician and physicist.

"The Triumph of Caesar," Montegna
A418

Persian Style Bas-relief, Sorrento
A419

25 l, Coats of Arms of Trieste, Rome & Trento, horiz. 60 l, War memorial bell of Rovereto.

1958, Nov. 3   *Engr.*   *Perf. 14x13½*
755 A418 15 l green   .20   .20
756 A418 25 l gray   .20   .20
757 A418 60 l rose claret   .20   .20
    Nos. 755-757 (3)   .60   .60
40th anniv. of Italy's victory in World War I.

1958, Nov. 27   *Photo.*
758 A419 25 l sepia, *bluish*   .25   .20
759 A419 60 l vio bl, *bluish*   .45   .60
Visit of the Shah of Iran to Italy.

Eleonora Duse — A420

Dancers and Antenna — A421

Unwmk.
1958, Dec. 11   *Engr.*   *Perf. 14*
760 A420 25 l brt ultra   .25   .20
Cent. of the birth of Eleonora Duse, actress.

1958, Dec. 29   Photo.   Wmk. 303

Design: 60 l, Piano, dove and antenna.

761	A421	25 l red, bl & blk	.20 .20
762	A421	60 l ultra & blk	.20 .20

10th anniv. of the Prix Italia (International Radio and Television Competitions).

Stamp of Sicily — A422

Design: 60 l, Stamp of Sicily, 5g.

Perf. 14x13½

1959, Jan. 2   Engr.   Unwmk.

763	A422	25 l Prus green	.20 .20
764	A422	60 l dp orange	.20 .20

Centenary of the stamps of Sicily.

Dome of St. Peter's and Tower of Lateran Palace A423

Wmk. 303

1959, Feb. 11   Photo.   Perf. 14

765 A423 25 l ultra .25 .20

30th anniversary of the Lateran Pacts.

Map of North Atlantic and NATO Emblem A424

1959, Apr. 4

766	A424	25 l dk bl & ocher	.20 .20
767	A424	60 l dk bl & green	.20 .20

10th anniv. of NATO.

Arms of Paris and Rome A425

1959, Apr. 9

768	A425	15 l blue & red	.20 .20
769	A425	25 l blue & red	.20 .20

Cultural ties between Rome and Paris.

"A Gentle Peace Has Come" — A426

Statue of Lord Byron — A427

1959, Apr. 13   Engr.   Unwmk.

770 A426 25 l olive green .20 .20

International War Veterans Association convention, Rome.

1959, Apr. 21

771 A427 15 l black .20 .20

Unveiling in Rome of a statue of Lord Byron by Bertel Thorvaldson, Danish sculptor.

Camillo Prampolini — A428

1959, Apr. 27   Unwmk.   Perf. 14

772 A428 15 l car rose 3.50 .40

Camillo Prampolini, socialist leader and reformer, birth centenary.

Fountain of Dioscuri and Olympic Rings — A429

Baths of Carcalla A430

Designs: 25 l, Capitoline tower. 60 l, Arch of Constantine. 110 l, Ruins of Basilica of Massentius.

1959, June 23   Photo.   Wmk. 303
Designs in Dark Sepia

773	A429	15 l red orange	.20 .20
774	A429	25 l blue	.20 .20
775	A430	35 l bister	.20 .20
776	A430	60 l rose lilac	.25 .30
777	A430	110 l yellow	.30 .20
		Nos. 773-777 (5)	1.15 1.10

1960 Olympic Games in Rome.

Victor Emanuel II, Garibaldi, Cavour, Mazzini A431

Battle of San Fermo A432

25 l, "After the Battle of Magenta" by Fattori and Red Cross, vert. 60 l, Battle of Palestro. 110 l, "Battle of Magenta" by Induno, vert.

Engr., Cross Photo. on 25 l

1959, June 27   Unwmk.

778	A431	15 l gray	.20 .20
779	A431	25 l brn & red	.20 .20
780	A432	35 l dk violet	.20 .20
781	A432	60 l ultra	.20 .20
782	A432	110 l magenta	.20 .20
		Nos. 778-782 (5)	1.00 1.00

Cent. of the war of independence. No. 779 for the centenary of the Red Cross idea.

Labor Monument, Geneva A433

Stamp of Romagna A434

1959, July 20   Perf. 14x13, 14

783	A433	25 l violet	.20 .20
784	A433	60 l brown	.30 .20

40th anniv. of the ILO.

Italia Type of 1953-54
Photo.; Engr. (100 l, 200 l)
1959-66   Wmk. 303   Perf. 14
Size: 17x21mm

785	A354	30 l bis brn ('60)	.25 .20
786	A354	40 l lil rose ('60)	1.25 .20
786A	A354	70 l Prus grn ('60)	.35 .20
787	A354	100 l brown	.65 .20
787A	A354	130 l gray & dl red ('66)	.25 .20
788	A354	200 l dp blue	.65 .20
		Nos. 785-788 (6)	3.40 1.20

1959, Sept. 1   Photo.

Design: 60 l, Stamp of Romagna, 20b.

789	A434	25 l pale brn & blk	.20 .20
790	A434	60 l gray grn & blk	.20 .20

Centenary of the stamps of Romagna.

Europa Issue, 1959
Common Design Type

1959, Sept. 19
Size: 22x27½mm

791	CD2	25 l olive green	.40 .20
792	CD2	60 l blue	.40 .20

Stamp of 1953 with Facsimile Cancellation A435

Aeneas Fleeing with Father and Son, by Raphael A436

1959, Dec. 20   Wmk. 303   Perf. 14

793 A435 15 l gray, rose car & blk .20 .20

Italy's first Stamp Day, Dec. 20, 1959.

1960, Apr. 7   Engr.   Unwmk.

794	A436	25 l lake	.20 .20
795	A436	60 l gray violet	.20 .20

World Refugee Year, 7/1/59-6/30/60. Design is detail from "The Fire in the Borgo."

Garibaldi's Proclamation to the Sicilians — A437

King Victor Emmanuel and Garibaldi Meeting at Teano — A438

60 l, Volunteers embarking, Quarto, Genoa.

Wmk. 303

1960, May 5   Photo.   Perf. 14

796 A437 15 l brown .20 .20

Perf. 13x14, 14x13
Engr.   Unwmk.

797	A438	25 l rose claret	.20 .20
798	A437	60 l ultramarine	.20 .20

Cent. of the liberation of Southern Italy (Kingdom of the Two Sicilies) by Garibaldi.

Emblem of 17th Olympic Games — A439

Olympic Stadium A440

Statues: 15 l, Roman Consul on way to the games. 35 l, Myron's Discobolus. 110 l, Seated boxer. 200 l, Apoxyomenos by Lysippus.
Stadia: 25 l, Velodrome. 60 l, Sports palace. 150 l, Small sports palace.

Photogravure, Engraved
Perf. 14x13½, 13½x14
1960   Wmk. 303, Unwmk.

799	A439	5 l yellow brn	.20 .20
800	A440	10 l dp org & dk bl	.20 .20
801	A440	15 l ultra	.20 .20
802	A440	25 l lt vio & brn	.20 .20
803	A439	35 l rose cl	.20 .20
804	A440	60 l bluish grn & brn	.20 .20
805	A439	110 l plum	.20 .20
806	A439	150 l blue & brn	1.60 2.75
807	A439	200 l green	.80 .20
		Nos. 799-807 (9)	3.80 4.35

17th Olympic Games, Rome, 8/25-9/11. The photo. denominations (5-10, 25, 60, 150 l) are wmkd.; the engraved (15, 35, 110, 200 l) are unwmkd.

Bottego Statue, Parma A441

Michelangelo da Caravaggio A442

1960   Unwmk.   Engr.   Perf. 14

808 A441 30 l brown .20 .20

Birth cent. of Vittorio Bottego, explorer.

Europa Issue, 1960
Common Design Type

1960   Photo.   Wmk. 303
Size: 37x27mm

809	CD3	30 l dk grn & bis brn	.30 .20
810	CD3	70 l dk bl & salmon	.40 .25

1960   Unwmk. Engr.   Perf. 13x13½

811 A442 25 l orange brn .20 .20

350th anniv. of the death of Michelangelo da Caravaggio (Merisi), painter.

Mail Coach and Post Horn A443

1960   Wmk. 303   Photo.   Perf. 14

812 A443 15 l blk brn & org brn .20 .20

Issued for Stamp Day, Dec. 20.

Slave, by Michelangelo — A444

Designs from Sistine Chapel by Michelangelo: 5 l, 10 l, 115 l, 150 l, Heads of various "slaves." 15 l, Joel. 20 l, Libyan Sybil. 25 l, Isaiah. 30 l, Eritrean Sybil. 40 l, Daniel. 50 l, Delphic Sybil. 55 l, Cumaean Sybil. 70 l, Zachariah. 85 l, Jonah. 90 l, Jeremiah. 100 l, Ezekiel. 200 l, Self-portrait. 500 l, Adam. 1000 l, Eve.

Wmk. 303

1961, Mar. 6	Photo.	Perf. 14

Size: 17x21mm

813	A444	1 l gray	.20	.20
814	A444	5 l brown org	.20	.20
815	A444	10 l red org	.20	.20
816	A444	15 l brt lil	.20	.20
817	A444	20 l Prus grn	.20	.20
818	A444	25 l brown	.30	.20
819	A444	30 l purple	.20	.20
820	A444	40 l rose red	.20	.20
821	A444	50 l olive	.45	
822	A444	55 l red brn	.20	.20
823	A444	70 l blue	.20	.20
824	A444	85 l slate grn	.20	.20
825	A444	90 l lil rose	.40	.20
826	A444	100 l vio gray	.75	.20
827	A444	115 l ultra	.25	.20

Engr.

828	A444	150 l chocolate	1.10	.20
829	A444	200 l dark blue	1.75	.20
a.		Perf. 13½	1.75	.20

Perf. 13½
Size: 22x27mm

830	A444	500 l blue grn	3.50	.20
831	A444	1000 l brown red	3.25	.50
		Nos. 813-831 (19)	13.75	4.10

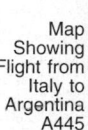

Map Showing Flight from Italy to Argentina A445

185 l, Italy to Uruguay. 205 l, Italy to Peru.

1961, Apr.	Photo.	Perf. 14

832	A445	170 l ultra	4.50	4.50
833	A445	185 l dull green	4.50	4.50
834	A445	205 l violet blk	9.00	9.00
a.		205 l rose lilac	1,650.	
		Nos. 832-834 (3)	18.00	18.00

Visit of Pres. Gronchi to South America, 4/61.

Nos. 832-833 and 834a were issued Apr. 4, to become valid on Apr. 6. The map of Peru on No. 834a was drawn incorrectly and the stamp was therefore withdrawn on Apr. 4. A corrected design in new color (No. 834) was issued Apr. 6. Forgeries of No. 834a exist.

Statue of Pliny, Como Cathedral A446

Ippolito Nievo (1831-61), Writer A447

1961, May 27

835	A446	30 l brown	.20	.20

1900th anniversary of the birth of Pliny the Younger, Roman consul and writer.

1961, June 8	Wmk. 303	Perf. 14

836	A447	30 l multi	.20	.20

St. Paul Aboard Ship A448

1961, June 28

837	A448	30 l multi	.20	.20
838	A448	70 l multi	.30	.30

1,900th anniversary of St. Paul's arrival in Rome. The design is after a miniature from the Bible of Borso D'Este.

Cavalli Gun and Gaeta Fortress A449

Cent. of Italian unity: 30 l, Carignano palace, Turin. 40 l, Montecitorio palace, Rome. 70 l, Palazzo Vecchio, Florence. 115 l, Villa Madama, Rome. 300 l, Steel construction, Italia '61 Exhibition, Turin.

1961, Aug. 12		Photo.

839	A449	15 l dk bl & redsh brn	.20	.20
840	A449	30 l dk bl & red brn	.20	.20
841	A449	40 l bl & brn	.35	.20
842	A449	70 l brn & pink	.50	.20
843	A449	115 l org brn & dk bl	1.75	.20
844	A449	300 l brt grn & red	5.00	4.00
		Nos. 839-844 (6)	8.00	5.00

Europa Issue, 1961
Common Design Type

1961, Sept. 18	Wmk. 303	Perf. 14

Size: 36½x21mm

845	CD4	30 l carmine	.25	.20
846	CD4	70 l yel grn	.30	.25

Giandomenico Romagnosi — A450

Perf. 13½

1961, Nov. 28	Unwmk.	Engr.

847	A450	30 l green	.20	.20

Bicentenary of the birth of Giandomenico Romagnosi, jurist and philosopher.

Design from 1820 Sardinia Letter Sheet A451

1961, Dec. 3	Photo.	Perf. 14

848	A451	15 l lil rose & blk	.20	.20

Issued for Stamp Day 1961.

Family Scene "I am the Lamp that Glows so Gently . . ." A452

1962, Apr. 6	Wmk. 303	Perf. 14

849	A452	30 l red	.20	.20
850	A452	70 l blue	.25	.30

Death of Giovanni Pascoli, poet, 50th anniv.

Pacinotti's Dynamo A453

1962, June 12

851	A453	30 l rose & blk	.20	.20
852	A453	70 l ultra & blk	.25	.30

Antonio Pacinotti (1841-1912), physicist and inventor of the ring winding dynamo.

St. Catherine of Siena, by Andrea Vanni — A454

Lion of St. Mark — A455

70 l, St. Catherine, 15th century woodcut.

1962, June 26		Photo.

Engraved and Photogravure

853	A454	30 l black	.20	.20
854	A454	70 l red & blk	.25	.40

500th anniversary of the canonization of St. Catherine of Siena, Patroness of Italy.

1962, Aug. 25		Photo.

Design: 30 l, Stylized camera eye.

855	A455	30 l bl & blk	.20	.20
856	A455	70 l red org & blk	.20	.20

Intl. Film Festival in Venice, 30th anniv.

Motorcyclist and Bicyclist A456

70 l, Group of cyclists. 300 l, Bicyclist.

1962, Aug. 30

857	A456	30 l grn & blk	.20	.20
858	A456	70 l bl & blk	.20	.20
859	A456	300 l dp org & blk	4.00	2.50
		Nos. 857-859 (3)	4.40	2.90

World Bicycle Championship Races.

Europa Issue, 1962
Common Design Type

1962, Sept. 17
Size: 37x21mm

860	CD5	30 l carmine	.45	.20
861	CD5	70 l blue	.90	.30

Swiss and Italian Flags, Eugenio and Angela Lina Balzan Medal A457

1962, Oct. 25	Wmk. 303	Perf. 14

862	A457	70 l rose red, grn & brn	.30	.20

1st distribution of the Balzan Prize by the Intl. Balzan Foundation for Italian-Swiss Cooperation.

Malaria Eradication Emblem — A458

Stamps of 1862 and 1961 — A459

1962, Oct. 31		Photo.

863	A458	30 l light violet	.20	.20
864	A458	70 l light blue	.25	.25

WHO drive to eradicate malaria.

1962, Dec. 2

865	A459	15 l pur, buff & bister	.20	.20

Stamp Day and cent. of Italian postage stamps.

A460   A461

Holy Spirit Descending on Apostles.

1962, Dec. 8

866	A460	30 l org & dk bl grn, buff	.20	.20
867	A460	70 l dk bl grn & org, buff	.20	.20

21st Ecumenical Council of the Roman Catholic Church, Vatican II. The design is an illumination from the Codex Syriacus.

1962, Dec. 10	Engr.	Unwmk.

Statue of Count Camillo Bensi di Cavour.

868	A461	30 l dk grn	.20	.20

Centenary of Court of Accounts.

Count Giovanni Pico della Mirandola A462

Gabriele D'Annunzio A463

Wmk. 303

1963, Feb. 25	Photo.	Perf. 14

869	A462	30 l gray blk	.20	.20

Mirandola (1463-94), Renaissance scholar.

1963, Mar. 12	Engr.	Unwmk.

870	A463	30 l dk grn	.20	.20

Issued to commemorate the centenary of the birth of Gabriele d'Annunzio, author and soldier.

Sower — A464

Design: 70 l, Harvester tying sheaf, sculpture from Maggiore Fountain, Perugia.

1963, Mar. 21	Photo.	Wmk. 303

871	A464	30 l rose car & brn	.20	.20
872	A464	70 l bl & brn	.30	.30

FAO "Freedom from Hunger" campaign.

Mt. Viso, Alpine Club Emblem, Ax and Rope — A465

Map of Italy and "INA" Initials — A466

1963, Mar. 30   Wmk. 303   *Perf. 14*
873   A465   115 l   dk brn & brt bl   .20   .20

Italian Alpine Club founding, cent.

1963, Apr. 4
874   A466   30 l   grn & blk   .20   .20

50th anniv. of the Natl. Insurance Institute.

Globe and Stamp A467

1963, May 7   Photo.   *Perf. 14*
875   A467   70 l   bl & grn   .20   .20

1st Intl. Postal Conf., Paris, 1863.

Crosses and Centenary Emblem on Globe — A468

1963, June 8   Wmk. 303   *Perf. 14*
876   A468   30 l   dk gray & red   .20   .20
877   A468   70 l   dl bl & red   .25   .25

International Red Cross founding, cent.

Roman Column, Globe and Highways A469

1963, Aug. 21   Wmk. 303   *Perf. 14*
878   A469   15 l   gray ol & dk bl   .20   .20
879   A469   70 l   dl bl & brn   .20   .20

UN Tourist Conf., Rome, Aug. 21-Sept. 5.

Europa Issue, 1963
Common Design Type
1963, Sept. 16
Size: 27½x23mm
880   CD6   30 l   rose & brn   .30   .20
881   CD6   70 l   brn & grn   .35   .25

Bay of Naples, Vesuvius and Sailboats A470

Athlete on Greek Vase A471

1963, Sept. 21   Wmk. 303   *Perf. 14*
882   A470   15 l   bl & org   .20   .20
883   A471   70 l   dk grn & org brn   .20   .20

4th Mediterranean Games, Naples, Sept. 21-29.

Giuseppe Gioachino Belli (1791-1863), Poet — A472

Stamps Forming Flower — A473

1963, Nov. 14   Wmk. 303   *Perf. 14*
884   A472   30 l   red brn   .20   .20

1963, Dec. 1
885   A473   15 l   bl & car   .20   .20

Issued for Stamp Day.

Pietro Mascagni and Old Costanzi Theater, Rome — A474

#886, Giuseppe Verdi & La Scala, Milan.

1963   Photo.
886   A474   30 l   gray grn & yel brn   .20   .20
887   A474   30 l   yel brn & gray grn   .20   .20

Verdi (1813-1901), and Mascagni (1863-1945), composers. Issued: #886, Oct. 10; #887, Dec. 7.

Galileo Galilei A475

Nicodemus by Michelangelo A476

1964, Feb. 15   Wmk. 303   *Perf. 14*
888   A475   30 l   org brn   .20   .20
889   A475   70 l   black   .20   .20

Galilei (1564-1642), astronomer & physicist.

1964, Feb. 18   Photo.
890   A476   30 l   brown   .20   .20

Michelangelo Buonarroti (1475-1564), artist. Head of Nicodemus (self-portrait?) from the Pieta, Florence Cathedral. See No. C137.

Carabinieri A477

70 l, Charge of Pastrengo, 1848, by De Albertis.

1964, June 5   Wmk. 303   *Perf. 14*
891   A477   30 l   vio bl & red   .20   .20
892   A477   70 l   brown   .20   .20

150th anniv. of the Carabinieri (police corps).

Giambattista Bodoni — A478

Perf. 14x13
1964, July 30   Engr.   Unwmk.
893   A478   30 l   carmine   .20   .20
    a.   Perf. 13   .20   .20

Death of Giambattista Bodoni (1740-1813), printer & type designer (Bodoni type), 150th anniv.

Europa Issue, 1964
Common Design Type
**   Wmk. 303**
1964, Sept. 14   Photo.   *Perf. 14*
**   Size: 21x37mm**
894   CD7   30 l   brt rose lilac   .25   .20
895   CD7   70 l   blue green   .30   .25

Walled City — A479

Left Arch of Victor Emmanuel Monument, Rome — A480

1964, Oct. 15   Photo.   *Perf. 14*
896   A479   30 l   emer & dk brn   .20   .20
897   A479   70 l   bl & dk brn   .20   .20

             Unwmk.   Engr.
898   A479   500 l   red   1.00   .50
    Nos. 896-898 (3)   1.40   .90

7th Congress of European Towns. The buildings in design are: Big Ben, London; Campodoglio, Rome; Town Hall, Bruges; Römer, Frankfurt; Town Hall, Paris; Belfry, Zurich; Gate, Kampen (Holland).

1964, Nov. 4   Photo.   Wmk. 303
899   A480   30 l   dk red brn   .20   .20
900   A480   70 l   blue   .20   .20

Pilgrimage to Rome of veterans living abroad.

Giovanni da Verrazano and Verrazano-Narrows Bridge, New York Bay — A481

1964, Nov. 21   Wmk. 303   *Perf. 14*
901   A481   30 l   blk & brn   .20   .20

Opening of the Verrazano-Narrows Bridge connecting Staten Island and Brooklyn, NY, and to honor Giovanni da Verrazano (1485-1528), discoverer of New York Bay. See No. C138.

Italian Sports Stamps, 1934-63 — A482

1964, Dec. 6   Photo.   *Perf. 14*
902   A482   15 l   gldn brn & dk brn   .20   .20

Issued for Stamp Day.

Italian Soldiers in Concentration Camp — A483

Victims Trapped by Swastika A484

15 l, Italian soldier, sailor and airman fighting for the Allies. 70 l, Guerrilla fighters in the mountains. 115 l, Marchers with Italian flag. 130 l, Ruins of city and torn Italian flag.

1965, Apr. 24   Photo.   Wmk. 303
903   A483   10 l   black   .20   .20
904   A483   15 l   grn & rose car   .20   .20
905   A484   30 l   plum   .20   .20
906   A483   70 l   deep blue   .20   .20
907   A484   115 l   rose car   .20   .20
908   A484   130 l   grn, sepia & red   .20   .20
    Nos. 903-908 (6)   1.20   1.20

Italian resistance movement during World War II, 20th anniv.

Antonio Meucci, Guglielmo Marconi and ITU Emblem A485

1965, May 17   *Perf. 14*
909   A485   70 l   red & dk grn   .20   .20

Cent. of the ITU.

Sailboats of Flying Dutchman Class A486

Designs: 70 l, Sailboats of 5.5-meter class, vert. 500 l, Sailboats, Lightning class.

1965, May 31   Photo.   Wmk. 303
910   A486   30 l   blk & dl rose   .20   .20
911   A486   70 l   blk & ultra   .20   .20
912   A486   500 l   blk & gray bl   .40   .30
    Nos. 910-912 (3)   .80   .70

Issued to publicize the World Yachting Championships, Naples and Alassio.

Mont Blanc and Tunnel A487

1965, June 16   Wmk. 303   *Perf. 14*
913   A487   30 l   black   .20   .20

Opening of the Mont Blanc Tunnel connecting Entrayes, Italy, and Le Polerins, France.

Alessandro Tassoni and Scene from "Seccia Rapita" — A488

Unwmk.
1965, Sept. 20   Photo.   _Perf. 14_
914 A488 40 l blk & multi   .20 .20
Tassoni (1565-1635), poet. Design is from
1744 engraving by Bartolomeo Soliani.

Europa Issue, 1965
Common Design Type
1965, Sept. 27   Wmk. 303
Size: 36½x27mm
915 CD8 40 l ocher & ol grn   .20 .20
916 CD8 90 l ultra & ol grn   .25 .20

Dante, 15th Century Bust — A489

Designs (from old Manuscripts): 40 l, Dante
in Hell. 90 l, Dante in Purgatory led by Angel
of Chastity. 130 l, Dante in Paradise interro-
gated by St. Peter on faith, horiz.

Perf. 13½x14, 14x13½
1965, Oct. 21   Photo.   Unwmk.
917 A489 40 l multi   .20 .20
918 A489 90 l multi   .20 .20
919 A489 130 l multi   .20 .20
Wmk. 303   _Perf. 14_
920 A489 500 l slate grn   .40 .30
    Nos. 917-920 (4)   1.00 .90
Dante Alighieri (1265-1321), poet.

House under Construction — A490

1965, Oct. 31   Wmk. 303   _Perf. 14_
921 A490 40 l buff, blk & org brn .20 .20
Issued for Savings Day.

Jet Plane, Moon and Airletter Border A491

Design: 40 l, Control tower and plane.

1965, Nov. 3
922 A491 40 l dk Prus bl & red   .20 .20
Unwmk.
923 A491 90 l red, grn, dp bl &
              buff   .20 .20
Night air postal network.

Map of Italy with Milan-Rome Highway — A492

Two-Man Bobsled — A493

1965, Dec. 5   Photo.   _Perf. 13x14_
924 A492 20 l bl, blk, ocher &
              gray   .20 .20
Issued for Stamp Day.

1966, Jan. 24   Wmk. 303   _Perf. 14_
Design: 90 l, Four-man bobsled.
925 A493 40 l dl bl, gray & red   .20 .20
926 A493 90 l vio & bl   .20 .20
Intl. Bobsled Championships, Cortina
d'Ampezzo.

Woman Skater — A494   Benedetto Croce — A495

Winter University Games: 40 l, Skier holding torch, horiz. 500 l, Ice hockey.

1966, Feb. 5   Photo.
927 A494 40 l blk & red   .20 .20
928 A494 90 l vio & red   .20 .20
929 A494 500 l brn & red   .40 .30
    Nos. 927-929 (3)   .80 .70

1966, Feb. 25   Wmk. 303   _Perf. 14_
930 A495 40 l brown   .20 .20
Benedetto Croce (1866-1952), philosopher,
statesman and historian.

Arms of Venice and Other Cities in Venezia — A496

1966, Mar. 22   Photo.   Unwmk.
932 A496 40 l gray & multi   .20 .20
Centenary of Venezia's union with Italy.

Battle of Bezzecca — A497

1966, July 21   Wmk. 303   _Perf. 14_
933 A497 90 l ol grn   .20 .20
Centenary of the unification of Italy and of
the Battle of Bezzecca.

Umbrella Pine — A498

Carnations62 A499

25 l, Apples. 50 l, Florentine iris. 55 l,
Cypresses. 90 l, Daisies. 170 l, Olive tree. 180
l, Juniper.

1966-68   Unwmk.   _Perf. 13½x14_
934   A498 20 l multi   .20 .20
934A A498 25 l multi ('67)   .20 .20
935   A498 40 l multi   .20 .20
935A A498 50 l multi ('67)   .20 .20
935B A498 55 l multi ('68)   .20 .20
936   A499 90 l multi   .20 .20
937   A498 170 l multi   .25 .20
937A A498 180 l multi ('68)   .25 .20
    Nos. 934-937A (8)   1.70 1.60

Tourist Attractions A500

"I" in Flag Colors — A501

1966, May 28   Wmk. 303   _Perf. 14_
938 A500 20 l yel, org & blk   .20 .20
Issued for tourist publicity and in connection
with the National Conference on Tourism,
Rome.

Perf. 13½x14
1966, June 2   Photo.   Unwmk.
939 A501 40 l multi   .20 .20
940 A501 90 l multi   .20 .20
20th anniversary of the Republic of Italy.

Singing Angels, by Donatello — A502

Madonna, by Giotto — A503

Perf. 13½x14
1966, Sept. 24   Photo.   Unwmk.
941 A502 40 l multi   .20 .20
Donatello (1386-1466), sculptor.

Europa Issue, 1966
Common Design Type
1966, Sept. 26   Wmk. 303   _Perf. 14_
Size: 22x38mm
942 CD9 40 l brt pur   .20 .20
943 CD9 90 l brt bl   .25 .20

Perf. 13½x14
1966, Oct. 20   Photo.   Unwmk.
944 A503 40 l multi   .20 .20
700th anniversary of the birth of Giotto di
Bondone (1266?-1337), Florentine painter.

Italian Patriots A504

1966, Nov. 3   Wmk. 303   _Perf. 14_
945 A504 40 l gray & dl grn   .20 .20
50th anniv. of the execution by Austrians of
4 Italian patriots: Fabio Filzi, Cesare Battisti,
Damiano Chiesa and Nazario Sauro.

Postrider — A505

Perf. 14x13½
1966, Dec. 4   Photo.   Unwmk.
946 A505 20 l multi   .20 .20
Issued for Stamp Day.

Globe and Compass Rose A506

1967, Mar. 20   Photo.   Wmk. 303
947 A506 40 l dull blue   .20 .20
Centenary of Italian Geographical Society.

Arturo Toscanini (1867-1957), Conductor — A507

1967, Mar. 25   _Perf. 14_
948 A507 40 l dp vio & cream   .20 .20

Seat of
Parliament
on
Capitoline
Hill, Rome
A508

1967, Mar. 25   *Perf. 14*
949 A508 40 l sepia   .20   .20
950 A508 90 l rose lil & blk   .20   .20

10th anniv. of the Treaty of Rome, establishing the European Common Market.

Europa Issue, 1967
Common Design Type
1967, Apr. 10   Wmk. 303   *Perf. 14*
Size: 22x28mm
951 CD10 40 l plum & pink   .20   .20
952 CD10 90 l ultra & pale gray   *.35   .25*

Alpine Ibex,
Grand Paradiso
Park — A509

National Parks: 40 l, Brown bear, Abruzzi
Apennines, horiz. 90 l, Red deer, Stelvio Pass,
Ortler Mountains, horiz. 170 l, Oak and deer,
Circeo.

Perf. 13½x14, 14x13½
1967, Apr. 22   Photo.
953 A509   20 l multi   .20   .20
954 A509   40 l multi   .20   .20
955 A509   90 l multi   .20   .20
956 A509 170 l multi   .30   .30
    Nos. 953-956 (4)   .90   .90

Claudio
Monteverdi
and
Characters
from
"Orfeo"
A510

1967, May 15   *Perf. 14*
957 A510 40 l bis brn & brn   .20   .20
Monteverdi (1567-1643), composer.

Bicyclists
and
Mountains
A511

50th Bicycle Tour of Italy: 90 l. Three bicyclists on the road. 500 l, Group of bicyclists.

Perf. 14x13½
1967, May 15   Photo.   Unwmk.
958 A511   40 l multi   .20   .20
959 A511   90 l brt bl & multi   .20   .20
960 A511 500 l yel grn & multi   .95   .45
    Nos. 958-960 (3)   1.35   .85

Luigi
Pirandello
and Stage
A512

1967, June 28   *Perf. 14x13*
961 A512 40 l blk & multi   .20   .20
Pirandello (1867-1936), novelist & dramatist.

Stylized
Mask
A513

1967, June 30   Wmk. 303   *Perf. 14*
962 A513 20 l grn & blk   .20   .20
963 A513 40 l car rose & blk   .20   .20

10th "Festival of Two Worlds," Spoleto.

Postal Card
with Postal
Zone
Number
A514

Design: 40 l, 50 l, Letter addressed with
postal zone number.

Wmk. 303, Unwmkd, (20 l, 40 l)
1967-68
964 A514 20 l multi   .20   .20
965 A514 25 l multi ('68)   .20   .20
966 A514 40 l multi   .20   .20
967 A514 50 l multi ('68)   .20   .20
    Nos. 964-967 (4)   .80   .80

Introduction of postal zone numbers, 7/1/67.

Pomilio PC-
1 Biplane
and 1917
Airmail
Postmark
A515

1967, July 18   Photo.   Wmk. 303
968 A515 40 l blk & lt bl   .20   .20
1st airmail stamp, Italy #C1, 50th anniv.

St. Ivo Church,
Rome — A516

Umberto
Giordano and
"Improvisation"
from Opera
Andrea
Chenier — A517

1967, Aug. 2   Unwmk.   *Perf. 14*
969 A516 90 l multi   .20   .20
Francesco Borromini (1599-1667), architect.

1967, Aug. 28   Wmk. 303
970 A517 20 l blk & org brn   .20   .20
Umberto Giordano (1867-1948), composer.

Oath of Pontida,
by Adolfo
Cao — A518

ITY
Emblem — A519

1967, Sept. 2
971 A518 20 l dk brn   .20   .20
800th anniv. of the Oath of Pontida, which
united the Lombard League against Emperor
Frederick I.

Perf. 13½x14
1967, Oct. 23   Photo.   Unwmk.
972 A519 20 l blk, cit & brt bl   .20   .20
973 A519 50 l blk, org & brt bl   .20   .20

Issued for International Tourist Year, 1967.

Lions
Emblem — A520

Soldier at the
Piave — A521

1967, Oct. 30   *Perf. 14x13½*
974 A520 50 l multi   .20   .20
50th anniversary of Lions International.

1967, Nov. 9   *Perf. 13x14*
975 A521 50 l multi   .20   .20
50th anniversary of Battle of the Piave.

Enrico Fermi at
Los Alamos and
Model of 1st
Atomic
Reactor — A522

"Day and Night"
and Pigeon
Carrying Italy No.
924 — A523

Wmk. 303
1967, Dec. 2   Photo.   *Perf. 14*
976 A522 50 l org brn & blk   .20   .20
25th anniv. of the 1st atomic chain reaction
under Enrico Fermi (1901-54), Chicago, IL.

1967, Dec. 3   Unwmk.   *Perf. 13½x14*
977 A523 25 l multi   .20   .20
Issued for Stamp Day, 1967.

Scouts at
Campfire — A524

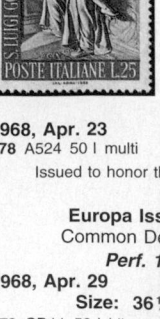

St. Aloysius
Gonzaga, by
Pierre
Legros — A525

1968, Apr. 23   *Perf. 13x14*
978 A524 50 l multi   .20   .20
Issued to honor the Boy Scouts.

Europa Issue, 1968
Common Design Type
Perf. 14x13
1968, Apr. 29   Wmk. 303
Size: 36½x26mm
979 CD11 50 l blk, rose & sl grn   .20   .20
980 CD11 90 l blk, bl & brn   .25   .20

Perf. 13½x14
1968, May 28   Photo.   Wmk. 303
981 A525 25 l red brn & dl vio   .20   .20
Aloysius Gonzaga (1568-1591), Jesuit
priest who ministered to victims of the plague.

Arrigo Boito and
Mephistopheles — A526

1968, June 10   Unwmk.   *Perf. 14*
982 A526 50 l multi   .20   .20
Boito (1842-1918), composer and librettist.

Francesco Baracca and "Planes," by
Giacomo Balla
A527

1968, June 19
983 A527 25 l multi   .20   .20
Major Francesco Baracca (1888-1918),
World War I aviator.

Giambattista
Vico — A528

Bicycle Wheel and
Velodrome,
Rome — A529

Designs: No. 985, Tommaso Campanella.
No. 986, Gioacchino Rossini.

Perf. 14x13½
1968   Engr.   Wmk. 303
984 A528 50 l ultra   .20   .20
985 A528 50 l black   .20   .20
   a.   Perf. 13½   .90   .20
986 A528 50 l car rose   .20   .20
    Nos. 984-986 (3)   .60   .60

Vico (1668-1744), philosopher; Campanella
(1568-1639), Dominican monk, philosopher
poet and teacher; Rossini (1792-1868),
composer. Issued: #984, 6/24; #985, 9/5; #986, 10/25.

Perf. 13x14
1968, Aug. 26 Photo. Unwmk.
90 l, Bicycle and Sforza Castle, Imola.

| 987 | A529 | 25 l slate, rose & brown | .20 | .20 |
| 988 | A529 | 90 l slate, blue & ver | .20 | .20 |

Bicycling World Championships: 25 l for the track championships at the Velodrome in Rome; 90 l, the road championships at Imola.

"The Small St. Mark's Place," by Canaletto — A531

1968, Sept. 30 Unwmk. Perf. 14
| 989 | A531 | 50 l pink & multi | .20 | .20 |

Canaletto (Antonio Canale, 1697-1768), Venetian painter.

"Mobilization" — A533

Symbolic Designs: 25 l, Trench war. 40 l, The Navy. 50 l, The Air Force. 90 l, The Battle of Vittorio Veneto. 180 l, The Unknown Soldier.

1968, Nov. 2 Photo. Unwmk.
990	A533	20 l brn & multi	.20	.20
991	A533	25 l bl & multi	.20	.20
992	A533	40 l multi	.20	.20
993	A533	50 l multi	.20	.20
994	A533	90 l grn & multi	.20	.20
995	A533	180 l bl & multi	.30	.30
		Nos. 990-995 (6)	1.30	1.30

50th anniv. of the Allies' Victory in WW I.

Emblem — A534

1968, Nov. 20 Perf. 14x13½
| 996 | A534 | 50 l blk, bl grn & red | .20 | .20 |

50th anniv. of the Postal Checking Service.

Parabolic Antenna, Fucino A535

1968, Nov. 25 Photo. Perf. 14
| 997 | A535 | 50 l multi | .20 | .20 |

Issued to publicize the expansion of the space communications center at Fucino.

Development of Postal Service — A536

1968, Dec. 1 Wmk. 303
| 998 | A536 | 25 l car & yel | .20 | .20 |

Issued for the 10th Stamp Day.

Fluorescent Paper was introduced in 1968 for regular and special delivery issues. These stamps are about 1mm. smaller each way than the non-fluorescent ones they replaced, except Nos. 690-690A which remained the same size.

Commemorative or nonregular stamps issued only on fluorescent paper are Nos. 935B, 937A, 965, 967 and from 981 onward unless otherwise noted.

Italia Type of 1953-54
Small Size: 16x19½-20mm
Photo.; Engr. (100, 150, 200-400 l)

1968-76		Wmk. 303	Perf. 14	
998A	A354	1 l dk gray	.20	.20
998B	A354	5 l slate	.20	.20
998C	A354	6 l ocher	.20	.20
998D	A354	10 l org ver	.20	.20
998E	A354	15 l gray vio	.20	.20
998F	A354	20 l brown	.20	.20
998G	A354	25 l purple	.20	.20
998H	A354	30 l bis brn	.20	.20
998I	A354	40 l lil rose	.20	.20
998J	A354	50 l olive	.20	.20
998K	A354	55 l vio ('69)	.20	.20
998L	A354	60 l blue	.20	.20
998M	A354	70 l Prus grn	.20	.20
998N	A354	80 l brn org	.20	.20
998O	A354	90 l lt red brn	.20	.20
998P	A354	100 l redsh brn	.20	.20
998Q	A354	125 l ocher & lil red	.20	.20
998R	A354	130 l gray & dl red	.20	.20
998S	A354	150 l vio ('76)	.25	.20
998T	A354	180 l gray & vio brn ('71)	.30	.20
998U	A354	200 l slate blue	.35	.20
998V	A354	300 l Prus grn ('72)	.50	.20
998W	A354	400 l dull red ('76)	.65	.20
		Nos. 998A-998W (23)	5.65	4.60

Memorial Medal — A537

Unwmk.
1969, Apr. 22 Photo. Perf. 14
| 999 | A537 | 50 l pink & blk | .20 | .20 |

Centenary of the State Audit Bureau.

Europa Issue, 1969
Common Design Type
1969, Apr. 28 Perf. 14x13
Size: 35½x25½mm

| 1000 | CD12 | 50 l mag & multi | .25 | .20 |
| 1001 | CD12 | 90 l bl & multi | .45 | .20 |

Niccolo Machiavelli A538

ILO Emblem A539

1969, May 3 Perf. 14x13½
| 1002 | A538 | 50 l blue & multi | .20 | .20 |

Niccolo Machiavelli (1469-1527), statesman and political philosopher.

Wmk. 303
1969, June 7 Photo. Perf. 14
| 1003 | A539 | 50 l grn & blk | .20 | .20 |
| 1004 | A539 | 90 l car & blk | .20 | .20 |

50th anniv. of the ILO.

Federation Emblem, Tower of Superga Basilica and Matterhorn A540

1969, June 26 Unwmk. Perf. 14
| 1005 | A540 | 50 l gold, bl & car | .20 | .20 |

Federation of Italian Philatelic Societies, 50th anniv.

Sondrio-Tirano Stagecoach, 1903 — A541

1969, Dec. 7 Engr. Wmk. 303
| 1006 | A541 | 25 l violet blue | .20 | .20 |

Issued for the 11th Stamp Day.

Downhill Skier — A542

90 l, Sassolungo & Sella Group, Dolomite Alps.

Perf. 13x14
1970, Feb. 6 Unwmk. Photo.
| 1007 | A542 | 50 l blue & multi | .20 | .20 |
| 1008 | A542 | 90 l blue & multi | .20 | .20 |

World Alpine Ski Championships, Val Gardena, Bolzano Province, Feb. 6-15.

Galatea, by Raphael A543

Painting: 50 l, Madonna with the Goldfinch (detail), by Raphael, 1483-1520.

1970, Apr. 6 Photo. Perf. 14x13
| 1009 | A543 | 20 l multi | .20 | .20 |
| 1010 | A543 | 50 l multi | .20 | .20 |

Symbol of Flight, Colors of Italy and Japan A544

1970, May 2 Unwmk. Perf. 14
| 1011 | A544 | 50 l multi | .20 | .20 |
| 1012 | A544 | 90 l multi | .20 | .20 |

50th anniv. of Arturo Ferrarin's flight from Rome to Tokyo, Feb. 14-May 31, 1920.

Europa Issue, 1970
Common Design Type
1970, May 4 Wmk. 303
Size: 36x20mm

| 1013 | CD13 | 50 l red & org | .25 | .20 |
| 1014 | CD13 | 90 l bl grn & org | .40 | .20 |

Gattamelata, Bust by Donatello — A545

1970, May 30 Engr. Perf. 14x13
| 1015 | A545 | 50 l slate green | .20 | .20 |

Erasmo de' Narni, called Il Gattamelata (1370-1443), condottiere.

Runner A546

Unwmk.
1970, Aug. 26 Photo. Perf. 14
| 1016 | A546 | 20 l shown | .20 | .20 |
| 1017 | A546 | 180 l Swimmer | .30 | .20 |

1970 World University Games, Turin, 8/26-9/6.

Dr. Maria Montessori and Children A547

1970, Aug. 31 Perf. 14x13
| 1018 | A547 | 50 l multi | .20 | .20 |

Montessori (1870-1952), educator & physician.

Map of Italy and Quotation of Count Camillo Cavour — A548

1970, Sept. 19 Unwmk. Perf. 14
| 1019 | A548 | 50 l multi | .20 | .20 |

Union of the Roman States with Italy, cent.

Loggia of St. Mark's Campanile, Venice A549

Perf. 14x13½
1970, Sept. 26   Engr.   Wmk. 303
1020 A549 50 l red brown .20 .20

Iacopo Tatti "Il Sansovino" (1486-1570), architect.

Garibaldi at Battle of Dijon A550

1970, Oct. 15   Photo.   Perf. 14
1021 A550 20 l gray & dk bl .20 .20
1022 A550 50 l brt rose lil & dk bl .20 .20

Cent. of Garibaldi's participation in the Franco-Prussian War during Battle of Dijon.

Tree and UN Emblem — A551

1970, Oct. 24   Unwmk.   Perf. 13x14
1023 A551 25 l blk, sep & grn .20 .20
1024 A551 90 l blk, brt bl & yel grn .20 .20

25th anniversary of the United Nations.

Rotary Emblem A552

1970, Nov. 12   Wmk. 303   Perf. 14
1025 A552 25 l bluish vio & org .20 .20
1026 A552 90 l bluish vio & org .20 .20

Rotary International, 65th anniversary.

Telephone Dial and Trunk Lines A553

1970, Nov. 24
1027 A553 25 l yel grn & dk red .20 .20
1028 A553 90 l ultra & dk red .20 .20

Issued to publicize the completion of the automatic trunk telephone dialing system.

"Man Damaging Nature" — A554

Virgin and Child, by Fra Filippo Lippi — A556

Mail Train A555

1970, Nov. 28   Wmk. 303   Perf. 14
1029 A554 20 l car lake & grn .20 .20
1030 A554 25 l dk bl & emer .20 .20

For European Nature Conservation Year.

1970, Dec. 6   Engr.
1031 A555 25 l black .20 .20

For the 12th Stamp Day.

1970, Dec. 12   Photo.   Unwmk.
1032 A556 25 l multi .20 .20

Christmas 1970. See No. C139.

Saverio Mercadante (1795-1870), Composer — A557

1970, Dec. 17   Wmk. 303
1033 A557 25 l vio & gray .20 .20

Mercury, by Benvenuto Cellini — A558

Bramante's Temple, St. Peter in Montorio — A559

1971, Mar. 20   Photo.   Perf. 14
1034 A558 50 l Prussian blue .20 .20

Benvenuto Cellini (1500-1571), sculptor.

Photogravure and Engraved
1971, Apr. 8   Perf. 13x14
1035 A559 50 l ocher & blk .20 .20

Honoring Bramante (Donato di Angelo di Antonio, 1444-1514), architect.

Adenauer, Schuman, De Gasperi A560

Perf. 14x13½
1971, Apr. 28   Photo.   Wmk. 303
1036 A560 50 l blk & lt grnsh bl .20 .20
1037 A560 90 l blk & lil rose .20 .20

European Coal & Steel Community, 20th anniv.

Europa Issue, 1971
Common Design Type
1971, May 3   Perf. 14
1038 CD14 50 l ver & dk red .25 .20
1039 CD14 90 l brt rose lil & dk lil .40 .20

Giuseppe Mazzini, Italian Flag — A561

Perf. 14x13½
1971, June 12   Unwmk.
1040 A561 50 l multi .20 .20
1041 A561 90 l multi .20 .20

25th anniversary of the Italian Republic.

Kayak Passing Between Poles A562

Design: 90 l, Kayak in free descent.

1971, June 16   Photo.   Perf. 14
1042 A562 25 l multi .20 .20
1043 A562 90 l multi .20 .20

Canoe Slalom World Championships, Merano.

Skiing, Basketball, Volleyball — A563

50 l, Gymnastics, cycling, track and swimming.

Perf. 13½x14
1971, June 26   Photo.   Unwmk.
1044 A563 20 l emer, ocher & blk .20 .20
1045 A563 50 l dl bl, org & blk .20 .20

Youth Games.

Plane Circling Globe and "A" — A564

Designs: 50 l, Ornamental "A." 150 l, Tail of B747 in shape of "A."

1971, Sept. 16   Perf. 14x13½
1046 A564 50 l multi .20 .20
1047 A564 90 l multi .20 .20
1048 A564 150 l multi .25 .20
Nos. 1046-1048 (3) .65 .60

ALITALIA, Italian airlines founding, 25th anniv.

Grazia Deledda (1871-1936), Novelist — A565

Photogravure and Engraved
Perf. 13½x14
1971, Sept. 28   Wmk. 303
1049 A565 50 l blk & salmon .20 .20

Child in Barrel Made of Banknote — A566

Perf. 13x14
1971, Oct. 27   Photo.   Unwmk.
1050 A566 25 l blk & multi .20 .20
1051 A566 50 l multi .20 .20

Publicity for postal savings bank.

UNICEF Emblem and Children A567

90 l, Children hailing UNICEF emblem.

1971, Nov. 26   Perf. 14x13
1052 A567 25 l pink & multi .20 .20
1053 A567 90 l multi .20 .20

25th anniv. of UNICEF.

Packet Tirrenia and Postal Ensign A568

1971, Dec. 5   Wmk. 303   Perf. 14
1054 A568 25 l slate green .20 .20

Stamp Day.

Nativity A569

Christmas: 90 l, Adoration of the Kings. Both designs are from miniatures in Evangelistary of Matilda in Nonantola Abbey, 12th-13th centuries.

Perf. 14x13
1971, Dec. 10   Photo.   Unwmk.
1055 A569 25 l gray & multi .20 .20
1056 A569 90 l gray & multi .20 .20

Giovanni Verga and Sicilian Cart A570

1972, Jan. 27
1057 A570 25 l org & multi .20 .20
1058 A570 50 l multi .20 .20

Verga (1840-1922), writer & playwright.

Giuseppe Mazzini (1805-1872), Patriot and Writer — A571

Wmk. 303
1972, Mar. 10   Engr.   Perf. 13
1059 A571 25 l blk & Prus grn .20 .20
1060 A571 90 l black .20 .20
1061 A571 150 l blk & rose red .25 .20
Nos. 1059-1061 (3) .65 .60

Flags, Milan Fair A572

Designs: 50 l, 90 l, Different abstract views.

Perf. 14x13½

1972, Apr. 14   Photo.   Unwmk.
1062 A572 25 l emer & blk   .20 .20
1063 A572 50 l dp org & blk   .20 .20
1064 A572 90 l bl & blk   .20 .20
    Nos. 1062-1064 (3)   .60 .60

50th anniversary of the Milan Sample Fair.

Europa Issue 1972
Common Design Type

1972, May 2   Perf. 13x14
    Size: 26x36mm
1065 CD15 50 l multi   .25 .20
1066 CD15 90 l multi   .40 .20

Alpine Soldier and Pack Mule A573

50 l, Mountains, Alpinist's hat, pick & laurel. 90 l, Alpine soldier & mountains.

1972, May 10   Perf. 14x13
1067 A573 25 l ol & multi   .20 .20
1068 A573 50 l bl & multi   .20 .20
1069 A573 90 l grn & multi   .20 .20
    Nos. 1067-1069 (3)   .60 .60

Centenary of the Alpine Corps.

Brenta Mountains, Society Emblem A574

Emblem and: 50 l, Mountain climber & Brenta Mountains. 180 l, Sunset over Mt. Crozzon.

Perf. 14x13
1972, Sept. 2   Photo.   Unwmk.
1070 A574 25 l multi   .20 .20
1071 A574 50 l multi   .20 .20
1072 A574 180 l multi   .30 .20
    Nos. 1070-1072 (3)   .70 .60

Tridentine Alpinist Society centenary.

Conference Emblem, Seating Diagram A575

1972, Sept. 21
1073 A575 50 l multi   .20 .20
1074 A575 90 l multi   .20 .20

60th Conference of the Inter-Parliamentary Union, Montecitorio Hall, Rome.

St. Peter Damian, by Giovanni di Paoli, c. 1445 A576

1972, Sept. 21   Photo.
1075 A576 50 l multi   .20 .20

St. Peter Damian (1007-72), church reformer, cardinal, papal legate.

The Three Graces, by Antonio Canova (1757-1822), Sculptor — A577

1972, Oct. 13   Engr.   Wmk. 303
1076 A577 50 l black   .20 .20

Page from Divine Comedy, Foligno Edition A578

Designs (Illuminated First Pages): 90 l, Mantua edition, vert. 180 l, Jesina edition.

Perf. 14x13½, 13½x14
1972, Nov. 23   Photo.   Unwmk.
1077 A578 50 l ocher & multi   .20 .20
1078 A578 90 l multi   .20 .20
1079 A578 180 l multi   .30 .20
    Nos. 1077-1079 (3)   .70 .60

500th anniversary of three illuminated editions of Dante's Divine Comedy.

Angel — A579

Christmas: 25 l, Christ Child in cradle, horiz. 150 l, Angel. All designs from 18th century Neapolitan crèche.

Perf. 13x14, 14x13
1972, Dec. 6   Photo.
1080 A579 20 l multi   .20 .20
1081 A579 25 l multi   .20 .20
1082 A579 150 l multi   .25 .20
    Nos. 1080-1082 (3)   .65 .60

Passenger and Mail Autobus A580

1972, Dec. 16   Engr.   Wmk. 303
1083 A580 25 l magenta   .20 .20

Stamp Day.

Leòn Battista Alberti — A581   Lorenzo Perosi — A582

1972, Dec. 16   Perf. 14
1084 A581 50 l ultra & ocher   .20 .20

Leòn Battista Alberti (1404-1472), architect, painter, organist and writer.

1972, Dec. 20   Photo.   Unwmk.
1085 A582 50 l dk vio brn & org   .20 .20
1086 A582 90 l blk & yel grn   .20 .20

Lorenzo Perosi (1872-1956), priest & composer.

Luigi Orione and Boys — A583   Ship Exploring Ocean Floor — A584

1972, Dec. 30
1087 A583 50 l lt bl & dk bl   .20 .20
1088 A583 90 l ocher & slate grn   .20 .20

Orione (1872-1940), founder of CARITAS; Catholic Welfare Organization.

1973, Feb. 15   Photo.   Perf. 13x14
1089 A584 50 l multi   .20 .20

Cent. of the Naval Hydrographic Institute.

Palace Staircase, Caserta A585

1973, Mar. 1   Engr.   Perf. 14x13½
1090 A585 25 l gray olive   .20 .20

Luigi Vanvitelli (1700-1773), architect.

Schiavoni Shore — A586

The Tetrarchs, 4th Century Sculpture — A587

50 l, "Triumph of Venice," by Vittore Carpaccio. 90 l, Bronze horses from St. Mark's. 300 l, St. Mark's Square covered by flood.

1973   Photo.   Perf. 14
1091 A586 20 l ultra & multi   .20 .20
1092 A587 25 l ultra & multi   .20 .20
1093 A586 50 l ultra & multi   .20 .20
1094 A587 90 l ultra & multi   .20 .20
1095 A586 300 l ultra & multi   .50 .30
    Nos. 1091-1095 (5)   1.30 1.10

Save Venice campaign. Issued: #1091, 3/5; others 4/10.

Verona Fair Emblem — A588

Title Page for Book about Rosa — A589

1973, Mar. 10   Perf. 13x14
1096 A588 50 l multi   .20 .20

75th International Fair, Verona.

1973, Mar. 15   Perf. 14
1097 A589 25 l org & blk   .20 .20

Salvator Rosa (1615-1673), painter & poet.

G-91 Jet Fighters A590

Designs: 25 l, Formation of S-55 seaplanes. 50 l, G-91Y fighters. 90 l, Fiat CR-32's flying figure 8. 180 l, Camprini-Caproni jet, 1940.

1973, Mar. 28   Perf. 14x13½
1098 A590 20 l multi   .20 .20
1099 A590 25 l multi   .20 .20
1100 A590 50 l multi   .20 .20
1101 A590 90 l multi   .20 .20
1102 A590 180 l multi   .30 .20
    Nos. 1098-1102,C140 (6)   1.40 1.20

50th anniversary of military aviation.

Soccer Field and Ball A591

Design: 90 l, Soccer players and goal.

1973, May 19   Photo.   Perf. 14x13½
1103 A591 25 l ol, blk & lt grn   .20 .20
1104 A591 90 l grn & multi   .60 .20

75th anniv. of Italian Soccer Federation.

Alessandro Manzoni, by Francisco Hayez — A592   Villa Rotunda, by Andrea Palladio (1508-80), Architect. — A593

1973, May 22   Engr.
1105 A592 25 l blk & brn   .20 .20

Manzoni (1785-1873), novelist and poet.

1973, May 30   Photo.   Unwmk.
    Perf. 13x14
1106 A593 90 l blk, yel & lem   .20 .20

Spiral and Cogwheels A594

1973, June 20 *Perf. 14x13*
1107 A594 50 l gold & multi .20 .20
50th anniversary of the State Supply Office.

Europa Issue 1973
Common Design Type
1973, June 30 Litho. *Perf. 14*
Size: 36x20mm
1108 CD16 50 l lil, gold & yel .25 .20
1109 CD16 90 l lt bl grn, gold & yel .40 .25

Palazzo Farnese, Caprarola, by Vignola A599

1973, Sept. 21 Engr. *Perf. 14x13½*
1115 A599 90 l choc & yel .20 .20
Giacomo da Vignola (real name, Giacomo Barocchio), 1507-1573, architect.

Photogravure and Engraved
1973, Nov. 10 *Perf. 13½x14*
1128 A603 25 l blk & multi .20 .20
1129 A603 25 l blk & multi .20 .20
1130 A603 25 l blk & multi .60 .60
Nos. 1128-1130 (3)
See Nos. 1166-1168, 1201-1203, 1251-1253, 1277-1279, 1341-1343, 1379-1381.

Christ Crowning King Roger — A609

Norman art in Sicily: 50 l, King William II offering model of church to the Virgin, mosaic from Monreale Cathedral. The design of 20 l, is from a mosaic in Martorana Church, Palermo.

Lithographed and Engraved
1974, Mar. 4 *Perf. 13½x14*
1138 A609 20 l ind & buff .20 .20
1139 A609 50 l red & lt grn .20 .20

Catcher and Diamond A595

Design: 90 l, Diamond and batter.

1973, July 21 Photo. *Perf. 14x13½*
1110 A595 25 l multi .20 .20
1111 A595 90 l multi .20 .20
International Baseball Cup.

Angels, by Agostino di Duccio — A604

Sculptures by Agostino di Duccio: 25 l, Virgin and Child. 150 l, Angels with flute and trumpet.

1973, Nov. 26
1131 A604 20 l yel grn & blk .20 .20
1132 A604 25 l lt bl & blk .20 .20
1133 A604 150 l yel & blk .25 .20
Nos. 1131-1133 (3) .65 .60
Christmas 1973.

Luigi Einaudi (1874-1961), Pres. of Italy — A610

1974, Mar. 23 Engr. *Perf. 14x13½*
1140 A610 50 l green .20 .20

Guglielmo Marconi (1874-1937), Italian Inventor and Physicist — A611

Design: 90 l, Marconi and world map.

1974, Apr. 24 Photo. *Perf. 14x13½*
1141 A611 50 l bl grn & gray .20 .20
1142 A611 90 l vio & multi .20 .20

St. John the Baptist, by Caravaggio A600

Lithographed & Engraved
1973, Sept. 28 *Perf. 14*
1116 A600 25 l blk & dl yel .20 .20
400th anniversary of the birth of Michelangelo da Caravaggio (1573-1610?), painter.

Viareggio by Night — A596

1973, Aug. 10 Photo. *Perf. 13x14*
1112 A596 25 l blk & multi .20 .20
Viareggio Carnival.

Assassination of Giovanni Minzoni — A597

1973, Aug. 23 *Perf. 14x13*
1113 A597 50 l multi .20 .20
Minzoni (1885-1923), priest & social worker.

Gaetano Salvemini (1873-1957), Historian, Anti-Fascist — A598

1973, Sept. 8 *Perf. 14x13½*
1114 A598 50 l pink & multi .20 .20

Tower of Pisa — A601

1973, Oct. 8 Photo.
1117 A601 50 l multi .20 .20
8th century of Leaning Tower of Pisa.

Sandro Botticelli — A602

1973-74 Photo. *Perf. 14x13½*
1118 A602 50 l shown .20 .20
1119 A602 50 l Giambattista Piranesi .20 .20
1120 A602 50 l Paolo Veronese .20 .20
1121 A602 50 l Andrea del Verrocchio .20 .20
1122 A602 50 l Giovanni Battista Tiepolo .20 .20
1123 A602 50 l Francesco Borromini .20 .20
1124 A602 50 l Rosalba Carriera .20 .20
1125 A602 50 l Giovanni Bellini .20 .20
1126 A602 50 l Andrea Mantegna .20 .20
1127 A602 50 l Raphael .20 .20
Nos. 1118-1127 (10) 2.00 2.00
Famous artists.
Issued: #1118-1122, 11/5; #1123-1127, 5/25/74.
See #1204-1209, 1243-1247, 1266-1270.

Trevi Fountain, Rome — A603

Designs: No. 1129, Immacolatella Fountain, Naples. No. 1130, Pretoria Fountain, Palermo.

Map of Italy, Rotary Emblems — A605

1973, Nov. 28 Photo.
1134 A605 50 l red, grn & dk bl .20 .20
50th anniv. of Rotary International of Italy.

Caravelle A606

Wmk. 303
1973, Dec. 2 Engr. *Perf. 14*
1135 A606 25 l Prussian blue .20 .20
15th Stamp Day.

Gold Medal of Valor, 50th Anniv. — A607

Perf. 13½x14
1973, Dec. 10 Photo. Unwmk.
1136 A607 50 l gold & multi .20 .20

Enrico Caruso (1873-1921), Operatic Tenor — A608

1973, Dec. 15 Engr.
Design: 50 l, Caruso as Duke in Rigoletto.
1137 A608 50 l magenta .20 .20

David, by Giovanni L. Bernini — A612

Europa: 90 l, David, by Michelangelo.

1974, Apr. 29 Photo. *Perf. 13½x14*
1143 A612 50 l sal, ultra & gray .50 .20
1144 A612 90 l grn, ultra & buff .50 .20

Customs Frontier Guards, 1774, 1795, 1817 A613

Uniforms of Customs Service: 50 l, Lombardy Venetia, 1848, Sardinia, 1815, Tebro Battalion, 1849. 90 l, Customs Guards, 1866, 1880 and Naval Marshal, 1892. 180 l, Helicopter pilot, Naval and Alpine Guards, 1974. All bordered with Italian flag colors.

1974, June 21 Photo. *Perf. 14*
1145 A613 40 l multi .20 .20
1146 A613 50 l multi .20 .20
1147 A613 90 l multi .20 .20
1148 A613 180 l multi .30 .20
Nos. 1145-1148 (4) .90 .80
Customs Frontier Guards bicentenary.

Sprinter A614

1974, June 28 Photo. Perf. 14x13
1149 A614 40 l shown .20 .20
1150 A614 50 l Pole vault .20 .20
European Athletic Championships, Rome.

Sharpshooter — A615

Design: 50 l, Bersaglieri emblem.

1974, June 27
1151 A615 40 l multi .20 .20
1152 A615 50 l grn & multi .20 .20
Bersaglieri Veterans Association, 50th anniv.

View of Portofino — A616

1974, July 10 Perf. 14
1153 A616 40 l shown .20 .20
1154 A616 40 l View of Gradara .20 .20
Tourist publicity.
See Nos. 1190-1192, 1221-1223, 1261-1265, 1314-1316, 1357-1360, 1402-1405, 1466-1469, 1520-1523, 1563A-1563D, 1599-1602, 1630-1633, 1708-1711, 1737-1740, 1776-1779, 1803-1806, 1830-1833, 1901-1904.

Petrarch (1304-74), Poet — A617

50 l, Petrarch at his desk (from medieval manuscript).

Lithographed and Engraved
1974, July 19 Perf. 13½x14
1155 A617 40 l ocher & multi .20 .20
1156 A617 50 l ocher, yel & bl .20 .20

Niccolo Tommaseo (1802-1874), Writer, Venetian Education Minister — A618

Tommaseo Statue, by Ettore Ximenes, Shibenik.

1974, July 19
1157 A618 50 l grn & pink .20 .20

Giacomo Puccini (1858-1924), Composer A619

1974, Aug. 16 Photo.
1158 A619 40 l multi .20 .20

Lodovico Ariosto (1474-1533), Poet — A620

1974, Sept. 9 Engr. Perf. 14x13½
1159 A620 50 l King Roland, woodcut .20 .20
The design is from a contemporary illustration of Ariosto's poem "Orlando Furioso."

Quotation from Menippean Satire by Varro A621

1974, Sept. 21
1160 A621 50 l ocher & dk red .20 .20
Marcus Terentius Varro (116-27 BC), Roman scholar and writer.

"October," 15th Century Mural A622

1974, Sept. 28 Photo. Perf. 14
1161 A622 50 l multi .20 .20
14th International Wine Congress, Trento.

"UPU" and Emblem A623

Design: 90 l, Letters, "UPU" and emblem.

1974, Oct. 19 Perf. 14
1162 A623 50 l multi .20 .20
1163 A623 90 l multi .20 .20
Centenary of Universal Postal Union.

St. Thomas Aquinas, by Francesco Traini — A624

1974, Oct. 25 Perf. 13x14
1164 A624 50 l multi .20 .20
St. Thomas Aquinas (1225-1274), scholastic philosopher, 700th death anniversary.

Bas-relief from Ara Pacis — A625

1974, Oct. 26
1165 A625 50 l multi .20 .20
Centenary of the Ordini Forensi (Bar Association).

Fountain Type of 1973

Designs: No. 1166, Oceanus Fountain, Florence. No. 1167, Neptune Fountain, Bologna. No. 1168, Fontana Maggiore, Perugia.

Photogravure and Engraved
1974, Nov. 9 Perf. 13x14
1166 A603 40 l blk & multi .20 .20
1167 A603 40 l blk & multi .20 .20
1168 A603 40 l blk & multi .20 .20
Nos. 1166-1168 (3) .60 .60

St. Francis Adoring Christ Child, Anonymous — A626

Photogravure and Engraved
1974, Nov. 26 Perf. 14x13½
1169 A626 40 l multi .20 .20
Christmas 1974.

Masked Dancers — A627

1974, Dec. 1 Photo. Perf. 13½x14
1170 A627 40 l Pulcinella .20 .20
1171 A627 50 l shown .20 .20
1172 A627 90 l Pantaloon .20 .20
Nos. 1170-1172 (3) .60 .60
16th Stamp Day 1974.

God Admonishing Adam, by Jacopo della Quercia — A628

Courtyard, Uffizi Gallery, Florence, by Giorgio Vasari A629

1974, Dec. 20 Engr. Perf. 14
1173 A628 90 l dk vio bl .20 .20
Lithographed and Engraved
1174 A629 90 l multi .20 .20
Italian artists: Jacopo della Quercia (1374-c. 1438), sculptor, and Giorgio Vasari (1511-1574), architect, painter and writer.

Angel with Tablet — A630

Angel with Cross — A632

Angels' Bridge, Rome — A631

Holy Year 1975: 50 l, Angel holding column. 150 l, Angel holding Crown of Thorns. The angels are statues by Giovanni Bernini on the Angels' Bridge (San Angelo).

1975, Mar. 25 Photo. Perf. 14
1175 A630 40 l multi .20 .20
1176 A630 50 l bl & multi .20 .20
1177 A631 90 l bl & multi .20 .20
1178 A630 150 l vio & multi .25 .20
1179 A632 180 l multi .30 .20
Nos. 1175-1179 (5) 1.15 1.00

Pitti Madonna, by Michelangelo A633

Works of Michelangelo: 50 l, Niche in Vatican Palace. 90 l, The Flood, detail from Sistine Chapel.

1975, Apr. 18   Engr.   Perf. 13½x14
1180 A633 40 l dl grn   .20   .20
1181 A633 50 l sepia   .20   .20
1182 A633 90 l red brn   .20   .20
    Nos. 1180-1182 (3)   .60   .60
Michelangelo Buonarroti (1475-1564), sculptor, painter and architect.

Flagellation of Jesus, by Caravaggio
A634

Europa: 150 l, Apparition of Angel to Hagar and Ishmael, by Tiepolo (detail).

1975, Apr. 29   Photo.   Perf. 13x14
1183 A634 100 l multi   .30   .25
1184 A634 150 l multi   .30   .25

Four Days of Naples, by Marino Mazzacurati
A635

Resistance Fighters of Cuneo, by Umberto Mastroianni
A636

Design: 100 l, Martyrs of Ardeatine Caves, by Francesco Coccia.

1975, Apr. 23
1185 A635 70 l multi   .20   .20
1186 A636 100 l ol & multi   .20   .20
1187 A636 150 l multi   .25   .20
    Nos. 1185-1187 (3)   .65   .60
Resistance movement victory, 30th anniv.

Globe and IWY Emblem
A637

1975, May   Perf. 14x13½
1188 A637 70 l multi   .20   .20
International Women's Year 1975.

Satellite, San Rita Launching Platform — A638

1975, May 28   Perf. 13½x14
1189 A638 70 l multi   .20   .20
San Marco satellite project.

Tourist Type of 1974
Paintings: No. 1190, View of Isola Bella. No. 1191, Baths of Montecatini. No. 1192, View of Cefalù.

1975, June 16   Photo.   Perf. 14
1190 A616 150 l grn & multi   .25   .20
1191 A616 150 l bl grn & multi   .25   .20
1192 A616 150 l red brn & multi   .25   .20
    Nos. 1190-1192 (3)   .75   .60

Artist and Model, Armando Spadini
A640

Painting: No. 1194, Flora, by Guido Reni.

1975, June 20   Engr.   Perf. 14
1193 A640 90 l blk & multi   .20   .20
1194 A640 90 l multi   .20   .20
50th death anniv. of Armando Spadini and 400th birth anniv. of Guido Reni.

Giovanni Pierluigi da Palestrina (1525-94), Composer of Sacred Music — A641

1975, June 27   Engr.   Perf. 13½x14
1195 A641 100 l magenta & tan   .20   .20

Emmigrants and Ship
A642

1975, June 30   Photo.   Perf. 14x13½
1196 A642 70 l multi   .20   .20
Italian emigration centenary.

Emblem of United Legal Groups
A643

and   Perf. 14x13½
1975, July 25   Photo.   Engr.
1197 A643 100 l yel, grn & red   .20   .20
Unification of Italian legal organizations, cent.

Locomotive Wheels
A644

1975, Sept. 15   Photo.   Perf. 14x13½
1198 A644 70 l multi   .20   .20
Intl. Railroad Union, 21st cong., Bologna.

Salvo D'Acquisto, by Vittorio Pisano
A645

1975, Sept. 23
1199 A645 100 l multi   .20   .20
D'Acquisto died in 1943 saving 22 people.

Stylized Syracusean Italia — A646

1975, Sept. 26   Photo.   Perf. 13½x14
1200 A646 100 l org & multi   .20   .20
Cent. of unification of the State Archives.

Fountain Type of 1973
Designs: No. 1201, Rosello Fountain, Sassari. No. 1202, Fountain of the 99 Faucets, Aquila. No. 1203, Piazza Fontana, Milan.

Photogravure and Engraved
1975, Oct. 30   Perf. 13x14
1201 A603 70 l blk & multi   .20   .20
1202 A603 70 l blk & multi   .20   .20
1203 A603 70 l blk & multi   .20   .20
    Nos. 1201-1203 (3)   .60   .60

Botticelli Type of 1973-74
1975, Nov. 14   Photo.   Perf. 14x13½
1204 A602 100 l Alessandro Scarlatti   .20   .20
1205 A602 100 l Antonio Vivaldi   .20   .20
1206 A602 100 l Gaspare Spontini   .20   .15
1207 A602 100 l F. B. Busoni   .20   .20
1208 A602 100 l Francesco Cilea   .20   .20
1209 A602 100 l Franco Alfano   .20   .20
    Nos. 1204-1209 (6)   1.20   1.15
    Famous musicians.

Annunciation to the Shepherds
A648

Christmas: 100 l, Nativity. 150 l, Annunciation to the Kings. Designs from painted wood panels, portal of Alatri Cathedral, 14th century.

Lithographed and Engraved
1975, Nov. 25   Perf. 13½x14
1210 A648 70 l grn & multi   .20   .20
1211 A648 100 l ultra & multi   .20   .20
1212 A648 150 l brn & multi   .20   .20
    Nos. 1210-1212 (3)   .60   .60

"The Magic Orchard" — A649

Children's Drawings: 70 l, Children on Horseback, horiz. 150 l, Village and procession, horiz.

Perf. 14x13½, 13½x14
1975, Dec. 7   Photo.
1213 A649 70 l multi   .20   .20
1214 A649 100 l multi   .20   .20
1215 A649 150 l multi   .25   .20
    Nos. 1213-1215 (3)   .65   .60
17th Stamp Day.

Boccaccio, by Andrea del Castagno — A650

Design: 150 l, Frontispiece for "Fiammetta," 15th century woodcut.

Engraved and Lithographed
1975, Dec. 22   Perf. 13½x14
1216 A650 100 l yel grn & blk   .20   .20
1217 A650 150 l buff & multi   .25   .20
Giovanni Boccaccio (1313-1375), writer.

State Advocate's Office, Rome — A651

1976, Jan. 30   Photo.   Perf. 13½x14
1218 A651 150 l multi   .25   .20
State Advocate's Office, centenary.

ITALIA 76 Emblem — A652

Design: 180 l, Milan Fair pavilion.

1976, Mar. 27   Photo.   Perf. 13½x14
1219 A652 150 l blk, red & grn   .35   .20
1220 A652 180 l blk, red, grn & bl   .45   .20
ITALIA 76 International Philatelic Exhibition, Milan, Oct. 14-24.

Tourist Type of 1974
Tourist publicity: #1221, Fenis Castle. #1222, View of Ischia. #1223, Itria Valley.

1976, May 21   Photo.   Perf. 14
1221 A616 150 l grn & multi   .25   .20
1222 A616 150 l plum & multi   .25   .20
1223 A616 150 l yel & multi   .25   .20
    Nos. 1221-1223 (3)   .75   .60

Majolica Plate, Deruta — A653

Europa: 180 l, Ceramic vase in shape of woman's head, Caltagirone.

1976, May 22   Perf. 13½x14
1224 A653 150 l multi   .25   .20
1225 A653 180 l brn & multi   .30   .20

Italian Flags — A654

Italian Presidents A655

1976, June 1
1226 A654 100 l multi .20 .20
1227 A655 150 l multi .25 .20

30th anniversary of Italian Republic.

Fortitude, by Giacomo Serpotta, 1656-1732 A656

Paintings: No. 1229, Woman at Table, by Umberto Boccioni, 1882-1916. No. 1230, The Gunner's Letter, by F. T. Marinetti, 1876-1944.

1976, July 26   Engr.   Perf. 14
1228 A656 150 l blue .25 .20

Lithographed and Engraved
1229 A656 150 l multi .25 .20
1230 A656 150 l blk & red .25 .20
    Nos. 1228-1230 (3) .75 .60

Italian art.

Paintings by Vittore Carpaccio (1460-1526), Venetian Painter — A657

Designs: No. 1231, St. George. No. 1232, Dragon, after painting in Church of St. George Schiavoni, Venice.

1976, July 30   Engr.   Perf. 14x13½
1231 A657 150 l rose lake .25 .20
1232 A657 150 l rose lake .25 .20
    a.   Pair, #1231-1232 + label .50 .20

Flora, by Titian A658

1976, Sept. 15   Engr.   Perf. 14
1233 A658 150 l carmine .25 .20

Titian (1477-1576), Venetian painter.

St. Francis, 13th Century Fresco — A659

1976, Oct. 2   Engr.   Perf. 14
1234 A659 150 l brown .25 .20

St. Francis of Assisi, 750th death anniv.

Cart, from Trajan's Column A660

100 l, Emblem of Kingdom of Sardinia. 150 l, Marble mask, 19th cent. 200 l, Hand canceler, 19th cent. 400 l, Automatic letter sorting machine.

1976, Oct. 14   Photo.   Perf. 14x13½
1235 A660 70 l multi .20 .20
1236 A660 100 l multi .20 .20
1237 A660 150 l multi .25 .20
1238 A660 200 l multi .30 .20
1239 A660 400 l multi .65 .20
    Nos. 1235-1239 (5) 1.60 1.00

ITALIA 76 International Philatelic Exhibition, Milan, Oct. 14-24.

Girl and Animals — A661

Designs (Children' Drawings): 100 l, Trees, rabbit and flowers. 150 l, Boy healing tree.

1976, Oct. 17   Perf. 13½x14
1240 A661 40 l multi .20 .20
1241 A661 100 l multi .20 .20
1242 A661 150 l multi .25 .20
    Nos. 1240-1242 (3) .65 .60

18th Stamp Day and nature protection.

Botticelli Type of 1973-74
1976, Nov. 22   Photo.   Perf. 14x13½
1243 A602 170 l Lorenzo Ghiberti .25 .20
1244 A602 170 l Domenico Ghir-
            landaio .25 .20
1245 A602 170 l Sassoferrato .25 .20
1246 A602 170 l Carlo Dolci .25 .20
1247 A602 170 l Giovanni Piaz-
            zetta .25 .20
    Nos. 1243-1247 (5) 1.25 1.00

Famous painters.

The Visit, by Silvestro Lega A662

1976, Dec. 7   Photo.   Perf. 14x13½
1248 A662 170 l multi .25 .20

Silvestro Lega (1826-1895), painter.

Adoration of the Kings, by Bartolo di Fredi — A663

Christmas: 120 l, Nativity, by Taddeo Gaddi.

1976, Dec. 11   Perf. 13½x14
1249 A663 70 l multi .20 .20
1250 A663 120 l multi .20 .20

Fountain Type of 1973
Designs: No. 1251, Antique Fountain, Gallipoli. No. 1252, Madonna Fountain, Verona. No. 1253, Silvio Cosini Fountain, Palazzo Doria, Genoa.

Lithographed and Engraved
1976, Dec. 21   Perf. 13½x14
1251 A603 170 l blk & multi .25 .20
1252 A603 170 l blk & multi .25 .20
1253 A603 170 l blk & multi .25 .20
    Nos. 1251-1253 (3) .75 .60

Snakes Forming Net A664

Design: 170 l, Drug addict and poppy.

1977, Feb. 28   Photo.   Perf. 14x13½
1254 A664 120 l multi .20 .20
1255 A664 170 l multi .25 .20

Fight against drug abuse.

Micca Setting Fire A665

1977, Mar. 5
1256 A665 170 l multi .25 .20

Pietro Micca (1677-1706), patriot who set fire to the powder magazine of Turin Citadel.

Globe with Cross in Center — A666

Design: 120 l, People of the World united as brothers by St. John Bosco.

1977, Mar. 29   Photo.   Perf. 13x13½
1257 A666 70 l multi .20 .20
1258 A666 120 l multi .20 .20

Honoring the Salesian missionaries.

Italian Constitution, Article 53 — A667

1977, Apr. 14   Photo.   Perf. 14
1259 A667 120 l bis, brn & blk .20 .20
1260 A667 170 l lt grn, grn & blk .25 .20

"Pay your taxes."

Tourist Type of 1974
Europa (Europa Emblem and): 170 l, Taormina. 200 l, Castle del Monte.

1977, May 2
1261 A616 170 l multi .65 .20
1262 A616 200 l multi .85 .25

Tourist Type of 1974
Paintings: No. 1263, Canossa Castle. No. 1264, Fermo. No. 1265, Castellana Caves.

1977, May 30   Photo.   Perf. 14
1263 A616 170 l brn & multi .25 .20
1264 A616 170 l vio & multi .25 .20
1265 A616 170 l gray & multi .25 .20
    Nos. 1263-1265 (3) .75 .60

Botticelli Type of 1973-74
1977, June 27   Perf. 14x13½
1266 A602 70 l Filippo Brunelles-
            chi .20 .20
1267 A602 70 l Pietro Aretino .20 .20
1268 A602 70 l Carlo Goldoni .20 .20
1269 A602 70 l Luigi Cherubinl .20 .20
1270 A602 70 l Eduardo Bassini .20 .20
    Nos. 1266-1270 (5) 1.00 1.00

Famous artists, writers and scientists.

Justice, by Andrea Delitio A669

Painting: No. 1272, Winter, by Giuseppe Arcimboldi, 1527-c.1593.

Engraved and Lithographed
1977, Sept. 5   Perf. 14
1271 A669 170 l multi .25 .20
1272 A669 170 l multi .25 .20

Corvette Caracciolo — A670

Italian Ships: No. 1274, Hydrofoil gunboat Sparviero. No. 1275, Paddle steamer Ferdinando Primo. No. 1276, Passenger liner Saturnia.

Photogravure and Engraved
1977, Sept. 23   Perf. 14x13½
1273 170 l multi .25 .20
1274 170 l multi .25 .20
1275 170 l multi .25 .20
1276 170 l multi .25 .20
    a.   A670 Block or strip of 4, #1273-
            1276 + 2 labels 1.00 .50

See #1323-1326, 1382-1385, 1435-1438.

Fountain Type of 1973
Designs: No. 1277, Pacassi Fountain, Gorizia. No. 1278, Fraterna Fountain, Isernia. No. 1279, Palm Fountain, Palmi.

Lithographed and Engraved
1977, Oct. 18   Perf. 13x14
1277 A603 120 l blk & multi .20 .20
1278 A603 120 l blk & multi .20 .20
1279 A603 120 l blk & multi .20 .20
    Nos. 1277-1279 (3) .60 .60

Volleyball — A671

Designs (Children's Drawings): No. 1281, Butterflies and net. No. 1282, Flying kites.

1977, Oct. 23   Photo.   Perf. 13x14
1280 A671 120 l multi .... .20 .20
1281 A671 120 l multi .... .20 .20
1282 A671 120 l multi .... .20 .20
  a. Block of 3, #1280-1282 + label ..... .50 .30

19th Stamp Day.

Symbolic
Blood
Donation
A672

Design: 70 l, Blood donation symbolized.

1977, Oct. 26   Perf. 14x13½
1283 A672 70 l multi .... .20 .20
1284 A672 120 l multi .... .30 .20

Blood donors.

Quintino Sella
and Italy No.
24 — A673

1977, Oct. 23   Perf. 13½x14
1285 A673 170 l olive & blk brn .... .30 .20
Quintino Sella (1827-1884), statesman, engineer, mineralogist, birth sesquicentenary.

Italia Type of 1953-54 and

Italia — A674

1977-87   Wmk. 303   Perf. 14
Size: 16x20mm
Photo.
1288 A354 120 l dk bl & emer .... .20 .20
Photo. & Engr.
1289 A354 170 l grn & ocher .... .25 .20
Litho. & Engr.
1290 A354 350 l red, ocher & pur .55 .20
Perf. 14x13½
		Engr.		**Unwmk.**
1291	A674	1500 l multi	2.40	.20
1292	A674	2000 l multi	3.25	.20
1293	A674	3000 l multi	5.00	.20
1294	A674	4000 l multi	6.50	.20
1295	A674	5000 l multi	8.25	.65
1296	A674	10,000 l multi	16.00	.20
1297	A674	20,000 l multi	32.50	17.00
		Nos. 1288-1297 (10)	74.90	21.45

Issued: 120 l, 170 l, 350l, 11/22/77; 5,000 l, 12/4/78; 4,000 l, 2/12/79; 3,000 l, 3/12/79; 2,000 l, 4/12/79; 1,500 l, 5/14/79; 10,000 l, 6/27/83; 20,000 l, 1/5/87.

Dina Galli (1877-
1951),
Actress — A675

Perf. 13½x14
1977, Dec. 2   Photo.   Unwmk.
1309 A675 170 l multi .... .25 .20

Adoration of the Shepherds, by Pietro
Testa — A676

Christmas: 120 l, Adoration of the Shepherds, by Gian Jacopo Caraglio.

Lithographed and Engraved
1977, Dec. 13   Perf. 14
1310 A676 70 l blk & ol .... .20 .20
1311 A676 120 l blk & bl grn .... .20 .20

La Scala Opera
House, Milan,
Bicent. — A677

Designs: 170 l, Facade. 200 l, Auditorium.

1978, Mar. 15   Litho.   Perf. 13½x14
1312 A677 170 l multi .... .25 .20
1313 A677 200 l multi .... .30 .20

Tourist Type of 1974
Paintings: 70 l, Gubbio. 200 l, Udine. 600 l, Paestum.

1978, Mar. 30   Photo.   Perf. 14
1314 A616 70 l multi .... .20 .20
1315 A616 200 l multi .... .30 .20
1316 A616 600 l multi .... 1.00 .55
   Nos. 1314-1316 (3) .... 1.50 .95

Giant
Grouper
A678

Designs (outline of "Amerigo Vespucci" in background): No. 1318, Leatherback turtle. No. 1319, Mediterranean monk seal. No. 1320, Audouin's gull.

1978, Apr. 3   Perf. 14x13
1317 A678 170 l multi .... .45 .20
1318 A678 170 l multi .... .45 .20
1319 A678 170 l multi .... .45 .20
1320 A678 170 l multi .... .45 .20
  a. Strip of 4, #1317-1320 + label 1.90 1.00

Endangered species in Mediterranean.

Castel Nuovo, Angevin Fortifications,
Naples — A679

Europa: 200 l, Pantheon, Rome.

1978, Apr. 29   Litho.   Perf. 14x13½
1321 A679 170 l multi .... .45 .25
1322 A679 200 l multi .... .55 .25

Ship Type of 1977
Designs: No. 1323, Cruiser Benedetto Brin. No. 1324, Frigate Lupo. No. 1325, Ligurian brigantine Fortuna. No. 1326, Container ship Africa.

1978, May 8   Litho. & Engr.
1323   170 l multi .... .55 .20
1324   170 l multi .... .55 .20
1325   170 l multi .... .55 .20
1326   170 l multi .... .55 .20
  a. A670 Block of 4, #1323-1326 +
    2 labels .... 2.25 .75

Matilde
Serao — A680

Designs: Portraits of famous Italians.

1978, May 10   Engr.   Perf. 14x13½
1327 A680 170 l shown .... .25 .20
1328 A680 170 l Vittorino da Fel-
    tre .... .25 .20
1329 A680 170 l Victor Emmanu-
    el II .... .25 .20
1330 A680 170 l Pope Pius IX .... .25 .20
1331 A680 170 l Marcello Malpi-
    ghi .... .25 .20
1332 A680 170 l Antonio Meucci .... .25 .20
  a. Block of 6, #1327-1332 ...... 1.50 .75

Constitution, 30th
Anniv. — A681

1978, June 2   Litho.   Perf. 13½x14
1333 A681 170 l multi .... .25 .20

Telegraph Wires
and
Lens — A682

1978, June 30   Photo.
1334 A682 120 l lt bl & gray .... .20 .20
Photographic information.

The Lovers, by Tranquillo Cremona
(1837-1878) — A683

Design: 520 l, The Cook (woman with goose), by Bernardo Strozzi (1581-1644).

Engraved and Lithographed
1978, July 12   Perf. 14
1335 A683 170 l multi .... .55 .20
1336 A683 520 l multi .... 2.25 .75

Holy Shroud of Turin, by Giovanni
Testa, 1578 — A684

1978, Sept. 8   Photo.   Perf. 14
1337 A684 220 l yel, red & blk .... .35 .20
400th anniversary of the transfer of the Holy Shroud from Savoy to Turin.

Volleyball — A685

Design: 120 l, Volleyball, diff.

1978, Sept. 20
1338 A685 80 l multi .... .45 .20
1339 A685 120 l multi .... .45 .20
Men's Volleyball World Championship.

Mother and Child,
by
Masaccio — A686

1978, Oct. 18   Engr.   Perf. 13½x14
1340 A686 170 l indigo .... .25 .20
Masaccio (real name Tommaso Guidi; 1401-28), painter.

Fountain Type of 1973
Designs: No 1341, Neptune Fountain, Trent. No. 1342, Fortuna Fountain, Fano. No. 1343, Cavallina Fountain, Genzano di Lucania.

1978, Oct. 25   Litho. & Engr.
1341 A603 120 l blk & multi .... .20 .20
1342 A603 120 l blk & multi .... .20 .20
1343 A603 120 l blk & multi .... .20 .20
   Nos. 1341-1343 (3) .... .60 .60

Virgin and Child,
by
Giorgione — A687

Adoration of the Kings, by
Giorgione — A688

1978, Nov. 8   Engr.   Perf. 13x14
1344 A687 80 l dark red .... .20 .20

Photo.   Perf. 14x13½
1345 A688 120 l multi .... .20 .20
Christmas 1978.

Flags as Flowers — A689

Designs: No. 1347, European flags. No. 1348, "People hailing Europe."

1978, Nov. 26   Photo.   Perf. 13x14
1346 A689 120 l multi .20 .20
1347 A689 120 l multi .20 .20
1348 A689 120 l multi .20 .20
Nos. 1346-1348 (3) .60 .60

20th Stamp Day on theme "United Europe."

State Printing Office, Stamps A690

Design: 220 l, Printing press and stamps.

1979, Jan. 6   Photo.   Perf. 14x13½
1349 A690 170 l multi .25 .20
1350 A690 220 l multi .35 .20

1st stamps printed by State Printing Office, 50 anniv.

St. Francis Washing Lepers, 13th Century Painting A691

1979, Jan. 22
1351 A691 80 l multi .20 .20

Leprosy relief.

Bicyclist Carrying Bike — A692

1979, Jan. 27   Perf. 13½x14
1352 A692 170 l multi .25 .20
1353 A692 220 l multi .35 .20

World Crosscountry Bicycle Championships.

Virgin Mary, by Antonello da Messina A693

Painting: 520 l, Haystack, by Ardengo Soffici (1879-1964).

1979, Feb. 15   Engr.   Perf. 14
1354 A693 170 l multi .30 .20
1355 A693 520 l multi .85 .50

Albert Einstein (1879-1955), Theoretical Physicist and His Equation. — A694

Lithographed and Engraved
1979, Mar. 14   Perf. 13x14
1356 A694 120 l multi .20 .20

Tourist Type of 1974

Paintings: 70 l, Asiago. 90 l, Castelsardo. 170 l, Orvieto. 220 l, Scilla.

1979, Mar. 30   Photo.   Perf. 14
1357 A616 70 l grn & multi .20 .20
1358 A616 90 l car & multi .20 .20
1359 A616 170 l ultra & multi .25 .20
1360 A616 220 l gray & multi .35 .20
Nos. 1357-1360 (4) 1.00 .80

Famous Italians — A695

No. 1361, Carlo Maderno (1556-1629), architect. No. 1362, Lazzaro Spallanzani (1729-1799), physiologist. No. 1363, Ugo Foscolo (1778-1827), writer. No. 1364 Massimo Bontempelli (1878-1960), journalist. No. 1365, Francesco Severi (1879-1961), mathematician.

1979, Apr. 23   Engr.   Perf. 14x13½
1361 A695 170 l multi .25 .20
1362 A695 170 l multi .25 .20
1363 A695 170 l multi .25 .20
1364 A695 170 l multi .25 .20
1365 A695 170 l multi .25 .20
Nos. 1361-1365 (5) 1.25 1.00

Telegraph A696

Europa: 220 l, Carrier pigeons.

1979, Apr. 30   Photo.   Perf. 14
1366 A696 170 l multi .65 .20
1367 A696 220 l multi .65 .30

Flags and "E" — A697

1979, May 5   Perf. 14x13½
1368 A697 170 l multi .25 .20
1369 A697 220 l multi .35 .20

European Parliament, first direct elections, June 7-10.

Exhibition Emblem, Dome of Milan A698

1979, June 22   Photo.   Perf. 14
1370 A698 170 l multi .25 .20
1371 A698 220 l multi .35 .20

3rd World Machine Tool Exhib., Milan, Oct. 10-18.

Aeneas and Rotary Emblem — A699

1979, June 9   Perf. 13½x14
1372 A699 220 l multi .35 .20

70th World Rotary Cong., Rome, June 1979.

Basket — A700

1979, June 13   Perf. 14
1373 A700 80 l shown .20 .20
1374 A700 120 l Basketball players .30 .20

21st European Basketball Championship, June 9-20.

A701

Patient & Physician, 16th cent. woodcut.

1979, June 16   Photo. & Engr.
1375 A701 120 l multi .20 .20

Digestive Ailments Study Week.

A702

Lithographed and Engraved
1979, July 9   Perf. 13x14

Design: Ottorino Respighi (1879-1936), composer, Roman landscape.
1376 A702 120 l multi .20 .20

Woman Making Phone Call A703

200 l, Woman with old-fashioned phone.

1979, Sept. 20   Photo.   Perf. 14
1377 A703 170 l red & gray .25 .20
1378 A703 220 l grn & slate .35 .20

3rd World Telecommunications Exhibition, Geneva, Sept. 20-26.

Fountain Type of 1973

Designs: No. 1379, Great Fountain, Viterbo. No. 1380, Hot Springs, Acqui Terme. No. 1381, Pomegranate Fountain, Issogne Castle.

Lithographed and Engraved
1979, Sept. 22   Perf. 13x14
1379 A603 120 l multi .30 .20
1380 A603 120 l multi .30 .20
1381 A603 120 l multi .30 .20
Nos. 1379-1381 (3) .90 .60

Ship Type of 1977

Designs: No. 1382, Cruiser Enrico Dandolo. No. 1383, Submarine Carlo Fecia. No. 1384, Freighter Cosmos. No. 1385, Ferry Deledda.

1979, Oct. 12   Perf. 14x13½
1382 170 l multi .30 .20
1383 170 l multi .30 .20
1384 170 l multi .30 .20
1385 170 l multi .30 .20
a. A670 Block of 4, #1382-1385 + 2 labels 1.60 .75

Penny Black, Rowland Hill A704

1979, Oct. 25   Photo.
1386 A704 220 l multi .35 .20

Minstrels and Church A705

1979, Nov. 7   Photo.   Perf. 14x13½
1387 A705 120 l multi .20 .20

Christmas 1979.

Black and White Boys Holding Hands A706

Children's Drawings: 120 l, Children of various races under umbrella map, vert. 150 l, Children and red balloons.

Perf. 14x13½, 13½x14
1979, Nov. 25   Photo.
1388 A706 70 l multi .20 .20
1389 A706 120 l multi .20 .20
1390 A706 150 l multi .25 .20
Nos. 1388-1390 (3) .65 .60

21st Stamp Day.

Solar Energy Panels A707

Energy Conservation: 170 l, Sun & pylon.

1980, Feb. 25   Photo.   Perf. 14x13½
1391 A707 120 l multi .20 .20
1392 A707 170 l multi .25 .20

St. Benedict of
Nursia, 1500th
Birth
Anniv. — A708

1980, Mar. 21   Engr.   Perf. 13½x14
1393 A708 220 l dark blue   .35   .20

Royal Palace,
Naples — A709

Lithographed and Engraved
1980, Apr. 16   Perf. 13½x14
1394 A709 220 l multi   .35   .20
20th International Philatelic Exhibition,
Europa '80, Naples, Apr. 26-May 4.

Antonio
Pigafetta,
Caravel
A710

Europa: 220 l, Antonio Lo Surdo (1880-
1949) geophysicist.

1980, Apr. 28   Litho.   Perf. 14x13½
1395 A710 170 l multi   .40   .20
1396 A710 220 l multi   .70   .30

St. Catherine,
Reliquary
Bust — A711

1980, Apr. 29   Photo.
1397 A711 170 l multi   .25   .20
St. Catherine of Siena (1347-1380).

Italian Red
Cross
A712

1980, May 15   Photo.   Perf. 14x13½
1398 A712 70 l multi   .20   .20
1399 A712 80 l multi   .20   .20

Temples of Philae, Egypt — A713

1980, May 20
1400   Pair + label   .70   .20
  a. A713 220 l shown   .35   .20
  b. A713 220 l Temple of Philae, diff. .35   .20
Italian civil engineering achievements (Temples of Philae saved from ruin by Italian
engineers).

Soccer
Player
A714

1980, June 11
1401 A714 80 l multi   1.75   .75
European Soccer Championships, Milan,
Turin, Rome, Naples, June 9-22.

Tourist Type of 1974
Paintings: 80 l, Erice. 150 l, Villa Rufolo,
Ravello. 200 l, Roseto degli Abruzzi. 670 l,
Public Baths, Salsomaggiore Terme.

1980, June 28   Perf. 14
1402 A616 80 l multi   .20   .20
1403 A616 150 l multi   .30   .20
1404 A616 200 l multi   .35   .20
1405 A616 670 l multi   1.10   .60
     Nos. 1402-1405 (4)   1.95 1.20

Cosimo I with his Artists, by Giorgio
Vasari, and Armillary sphere — A715

1980, July 2   Perf. 13½x14
1406 A715   Pair + label   .50   .50
  a. 170 l Cosimo I   .25   .20
  b. 170 l Armillary sphere   .25   .20
The Medici in Europe of the 16th Century
Exhibition, Florence.

Fonte
Avellana
Monastery
Millennium
A716

1980, Sept. 3   Engr.   Perf. 14x13½
1407 A716 200 l grn & brn   .30   .20

St. Angelo Castle,
Rome — A717

Designs: Castles.

**Photo. (#1408-1417), Litho. and
Engr. (#1418-1422, 1425, 1427-1428),
Engr. (#1423-1424, 1426, 1429-1434)**
Perf. 14x13½
1980, Sept. 22   Wmk. 303
1408   5 l shown   .20   .20
1409   10 l Sforzesco, Milan   .20   .20
1410   20 l Del Monte, Andria   .20   .20
1411   40 l Ursino, Catania   .20   .20
1412   50 l Rocca di Calascio   .20   .20
1413   60 l Norman Tower, St.
              Mauro Fort   .20   .20
1414   90 l Isola Capo Riz-
              zuto   .20   .20
1415   100 l Aragonese, Ischia   .20   .20
1416   120 l Estense, Ferrara   .20   .20
1417   150 l Miramare, Trieste   .25   .20
1418   170 l Ostia, Rome   .25   .20
1419   180 l   .25 1.00
1420   200 l Cerro al Volturno,
              Isernia   .30   .20
1421   250 l Rocca di
              Mondavio   .40   .20
1422   300 l Svevo, Bari   .50   .20

1423   350 l Mussomeli, Calta-
              nissetta   .55   .20
1424   400 l Imperatore-Prato,
              Florence   .65   .20
1425   450 l Bosa, Nuoro   .70   .20
1426   500 l Rovereto, Trento   .80   .20
1427   600 l Scaligero,
              Sirmione   1.00   .20
1428   700 l Ivrea, Turin   1.10   .20
1429   800 l Rocca Maggiore,
              Assisi   1.25   .20
1430   900 l St. Pierre, Aosta   1.50   .20
1431   1000 l Montagnana, Pad-
              ua   1.60   .20
     Nos. 1408-1431 (24)   12.90 5.60

Coil Stamps
Perf. 14 Vert.
Size: 16x21mm
1432   30 l St. Severna, Rome   .20   .20
1433   120 l Lombardia, Enna   .25   .20
  a. Pair, Nos. 1432-1433   .40
1434   170 l Serralunga d'Alba,
              Cuneo   .30   .20
  a. Pair, Nos. 1432, 1434   .75   .75
     Nos. 1432-1434 (3)   .75   .60

No. 1412 exists dated "1980."
See #1475-1484, 1657-1666, 1862-1866.

Ship Type of 1977
#1435, Corvette Gabbiano. #1436, Torpedo
boat Audace. #1437, Sailing ship Italia. #1438,
Floating dock Castoro Sei.

Lithographed and Engraved
1980, Oct. 11   Perf. 14x13½
1435   200 l multi   1.25   .20
1436   200 l multi   1.25   .20
1437   200 l multi   1.25   .20
1438   200 l multi   1.25   .20
  a. A670 Block of 4, #1435-1438 +
           2 labels   7.00 1.00

Philip Mazzei
(1730-1816),
Political Writer in
US — A718

1980, Oct. 18   Photo.   Perf. 13½x14
1439 A718 320 l multi   .50   .20

Villa Foscari Malcontenta,
Venezia — A719

Villas: 150 l, Barbaro Maser, Treviso. 170 l,
Godi Valmarana, Vicenza.

Lithographed and Engraved
1980, Oct. 31   Perf. 14x13½
1440 A719 80 l multi   .40   .20
1441 A719 150 l multi   .40   .20
1442 A719 170 l multi   .40   .20
     Nos. 1440-1442 (3)   1.20   .60

See Nos. 1493-1495, 1528-1530, 1565-
1568, 1606-1609, 1646-1649, 1691-1695.

St. Barbara, by Palma the Elder
(1480-1528) — A720

Design: No. 1444, Apollo and Daphne, by
Gian Lorenzo Bernini (1598-1680).

1980, Nov. 20   Perf. 14
1443 A720 520 l multi   .85   .55
1444 A720 520 l multi   .85   .55

Nativity Sculpture by Federico
Brandini, 16th Cent. — A721

1980, Nov. 22   Engr.
1445 A721 120 l brn org & blk   .20   .20
Christmas 1980.

View of
Verona
A722

22nd Stamp Day: Views of Verona drawings
by school children.

1980, Nov. 30   Photo.   Perf. 14x13½
1446 A722 70 l multi   .20   .20
1447 A722 120 l multi   .20   .20
1448 A722 170 l multi   .25   .20
     Nos. 1446-1448 (3)   .65   .60

Daniele Comboni (1831-1881), Savior
of the Africans — A723

1981, Mar. 14   Engr.
1449 A723 80 l multi   .20   .20

Alcide de Gasperi
(1881-1954),
Statesman
A724

1981, Apr. 3   Perf. 13½x14
1450 A724 200 l olive green   .30   .20

International Year
of the
Disabled — A725

1981, Apr. 11   Photo.
1451 A725 300 l multi   .50   .20

A726

1981, Apr. 27   Photo.   Perf. 13½x14
1452 A726 200 l Roses   .30 .20
1453 A726 200 l Anemones   .30 .20
1454 A726 200 l Oleanders   .30 .20
      Nos. 1452-1454 (3)   .90 .60

See Nos. 1510-1512, 1555-1557.

Europa — A727

Designs: No. 1455, Chess game with human pieces, Marostica. No. 1456, Horse race, Siena.

1981, May 4
1455 A727 300 l shown   1.00 .40
1456 A727 300 l multicolored   1.00 .40

St. Rita Offering Thorn — A728

1981, May 22
1457 A728 600 l multi   1.00 .60

St. Rita of Cascia, 600th birth anniversary.

Ciro Menotti (1798-1831), Patriot — A729

1981, May 26   Engr.   Perf. 14x13½
1458 A729 80 l brn & blk   .20 .20

G-222 Aeritalia Transport Plane — A730

1981, June 1   Photo.
1459   200 l shown   .30 .20
1460   200 l MB-339 Aermacchi
                  jet   .30 .20
1461   200 l A-109 Agusta heli-
                  copter   .30 .20
1462   200 l P-68 Partenavia
                  transport plane   .30 .20
  a. A730 Block of 4, #1459-1462 + 2
             labels   1.35 .65

See Nos. 1505-1508, 1550-1553.

Hydro-geological Research — A731

1981, June 8   Perf. 13½x14
1463 A731 80 l multi   .20 .20

Sao Simao Dam and Power Station, Brazil — A732

Civil Engineering Works Abroad: No. 1465, High Island Reservoir, Hong Kong.

1981, June 26   Engr.   Perf. 14x13½
1464 A732 300 l dark blue   .50 .20
1465 A732 300 l red   .50 .20
  a.   Pair, #1464-1465 + label 1.00 .35

See Nos. 1516-1517, 1538-1539.

Tourist Type of 1974
1981, July 4   Photo.   Perf. 14
1466 A616   80 l View of Matera   .20 .20
1467 A616 150 l Lake Garda   .20 .20
1468 A616 300 l St. Teresa di
                   Gallura beach   .60 .20
1469 A616 900 l Tarquinia   1.75 .40
      Nos. 1466-1469 (4)   2.75 1.00

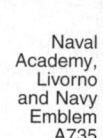

Naval Academy, Livorno and Navy Emblem A735

Naval Academy of Livorno Centenary: 150 l, View. 200 l, Cadet with sextant, training ship Amerigo Vespucci.

1981, July 24   Perf. 14x13½
1472 A735   80 l multi   .20 .20
1473 A735 150 l multi   .25 .20
1474 A735 300 l multi   .30 .20
      Nos. 1472-1474 (3)   .75 .60

Castle Type of 1980
Perf. 14x13½
1981-84   Photo.   Wmk. 303
1475 A717   30 l Aquila   .20 .20
1476 A717   70 l Aragonese, Reg-
                   gio Calabria   .20 .20
1477 A717   80 l Sabbionara, Avio .20 .20
Perf. 13½
1478 A717 550 l Rocca
                   Sinibalda   .90 .20
1479 A717 1400 l Caldoresco,
                   Vasto   2.25 .65
      Nos. 1475-1479 (5)   3.75 1.45

Issue dates: Nos. 1475-1477, Aug. 20, 1981; Nos. 1478-1479, Feb. 14, 1984.

Coil Stamps
1981-88   Engr.   Perf. 14 Vert.
Size: 16x21mm
1480 A717   50 l Scilla   .20 .20
1481 A717 200 l Angionia,
                   Lucera   2.75 2.00
1482 A717 300 l Norman Castle,
                   Melfi   .60 .20
1483 A717 400 l Venafro   .65 .20
1484 A717 450 l Piobbico Pesaro .75 .20
  a.   Pair, #1480, 1484   .95 .40
      Nos. 1480-1484 (5)   4.95 2.80

Issued: #1481-1482, 9/30; #1483, 6/25/83; #1480, 1484, 7/25/85; #1484a, 3/1/88.

Palazzo Spada, Rome (Council Seat) A736

1981, Aug. 31   Engr.   Unwmk.
1485 A736 200 l multi   .30 .20

State Council sesquicentennial.

World Cup Races — A737

1981, Sept. 4   Photo.   Perf. 13½x14
1486 A737 300 l multi   .50 .20

Harbor View, by Carlo Carra (1881-1966) — A738

#1488, Castle, by Guiseppe Ugonia (1881-1944).

Lithographed and Engraved
1981, Sept. 7   Perf. 14
1487 A738 200 l multi   .30 .20
1488 A738 200 l multi   .30 .20
   See #1532-1533, 1638-1639, 1697-1698, 1732.

Riace Bronze, 4th Cent. B.C. — A739

1981, Sept. 9   Photo.   Perf. 13½x14
1489   200 l Statue   .30 .20
1490   200 l Statue, diff.   .30 .20
  a. A739 Pair, #1489-1490   .65 .30

Greek statues found in 1972 in sea near Reggio di Calabria.

Virgil, Mosaic, Treviri A740

1981, Sept. 19   Perf. 14
1491 A740 600 l multi   1.00 .60

Virgil's death bimillennium.

Food and Wine, by Gregorio Sciltian A741

1981, Oct. 16   Litho.   Perf. 14
1492 A741 150 l multi   .30 .20

World Food Day.

Villa Type of 1980
Lithographed and Engraved
1981, Oct. 17   Perf. 14x13½
1493 A719 100 l Villa Campolieto,
                   Ercolano   .20 .20
1494 A719 200 l Cimbrone, Ravel-
                   lo   .30 .20
1495 A719 300 l Pignatelli, Naples .50 .20
      Nos. 1493-1495 (3)   1.00 .60

Adoration of the Magi, by Giovanni de Campione d'Italia (Christmas 1981) — A743

1981, Nov. 21   Engr.   Perf. 14
1496 A743 200 l multi   .35 .20

Pope John XXIII (1881-1963) A744

1981, Nov. 25   Photo.   Perf. 13½x14
1497 A744 200 l multi   .30 .20

Stamp Day — A745

Photogravure, Photogravure and Engraved (200 l)
Perf. 14x13½, 13½x14
1981, Nov. 29
1498 A745 120 l Letters, horiz. .20 .20
1499 A745 200 l Angel, letter
                   chest   .35 .20
1500 A745 300 l Letter seal   .55 .20
      Nos. 1498-1500 (3)   1.10 .60

St. Francis of Assisi, 800th Birth Anniv. — A746

Design: St. Francis Receiving the Stigmata, by Pietro Cavaro.

1982, Jan. 6   *Perf. 13½x14*
1501   A746   300 l   dk bl & brn   .50   .20

Niccolo Paganini (1782-1840), Composer, Violinist — A748

1982, Feb. 19   **Photo.**   *Perf. 13½x14*
1503   A748   900 l   multi   1.50   .85

Anti-smoking Campaign — A749

1982, Mar. 2   **Photo.**   *Perf. 14x13½*
1504   A749   300 l   multi   .50   .20

Aircraft Type of 1981

1982, Mar. 27   **Litho.**   *Perf. 14x13½*
1505   300 l   Aeritalia MRCA   .50   .20
1506   300 l   SIAI 260 Turbo   .50   .20
1507   300 l   Piaggio 166-dl3 Turbo   .50   .20
1508   300 l   Nardi NH-500   .50   .20
   a.   A730   Block of 4, #1505-1508 + 2 labels   4.25

Sicilian Vespers, 700th Anniv. — A750

1982, Mar. 31   **Engr.**   *Perf. 13½x14*
1509   A750   120 l   multi   .20   .20

Flower Type of 1981

1982, Apr. 10   **Photo.**
1510   A726   300 l   Cyclamens   .55   .20
1511   A726   300 l   Camellias   .55   .20
1512   A726   300 l   Carnations   .55   .20
   Nos. 1510-1512 (3)   1.65   .60

Europa — A751

Photogravure and Engraved

1982, May 3   *Perf. 13½x14*
1513   A751   200 l   Coronation of Charlemagne, 799   .85   .45
1514   A751   450 l   Treaty of Rome signatures, 1957   1.00   .55

Engineering Type of 1981

1982, May 29   **Photo.**   *Perf. 14x13½*
1516   A732   450 l   Microwaves across Red Sea   .75   .20
1517   A732   450 l   Automatic letter sorting   .75   .20
   a.   Pair, #1516-1517 + label   1.50   .65

Giuseppe Garibaldi (1807-82) A753

1982, June 2   *Perf. 13½x14*
1518   A753   200 l   multi   .65   .20

Game of the Bridge, Pisa — A754

1982, June 5
1519   A754   200 l   multi   .35   .20
   See Nos. 1562, 1603, 1628-1629, 1655, 1717, 1749, 1775, 1807.

Tourist Type of 1974

1982, June 28   *Perf. 14*
1520   A616   200 l   Frasassi Caves   .40   .20
1521   A616   200 l   Paganella Valley   .40   .20
1522   A616   450 l   Temple of Agrigento   .75   .20
1523   A616   450 l   Rodi Garganico Beach   .75   .20
   Nos. 1520-1523 (4)   2.30   .80

World Junior Canoeing Championship — A755

1982, Aug. 4   **Photo.**   *Perf. 14*
1524   A755   200 l   multi   .40   .20

Duke Federico da Montefeltro (1422-1482) — A756

Photogravure and Engraved

1982, Sept. 10   *Perf. 14x13½*
1525   A756   200 l   Urbino Palace, Gubbio Council House   .30   .20

Italy's Victory in 1982 World Cup A757

1982, Sept. 12   **Photo.**   *Perf. 14*
1526   A757   1000 l   World Cup   1.75   .75

69th Inter-Parliamentary Conference, Rome — A758

1982, Sept. 14   *Perf. 14x13½*
1527   A758   450 l   multi   .75   .20

Villa Type of 1980

Designs: 150 l, Temple of Aesculapius, Villa Borghese, Rome. 250 l, Villa D'Este, Tivoli, Rome. 350 l, Villa Lante, Bagnaia, Viterbo.

Photogravure and Engraved

1982, Oct. 1   *Perf. 14x13½*
1528   A719   150 l   multi   .25   .20
1529   A719   250 l   multi   .40   .20
1530   A719   350 l   multi   1.75   .20
   Nos. 1528-1530 (3)   2.40   .60

Thurn and Taxis Family Postal Service — A759

1982, Oct. 23   **Engr.**   *Perf. 13½x14*
1531   A759   300 l   Franz von Taxis (1450-1517)   .50   .20

Art Type of 1981

Paintings: No. 1532, The Fortune Teller by G.B. Piazzetta (1682-1754). No. 1533, Antonietta Negroni Prati Morosini as a Little Girl by Francesco Hayez (1791-1882).

Lithographed and Engraved

1982, Nov. 3   *Perf. 14*
1532   A738   300 l   multi   .60   .20
1533   A738   300 l   multi   .60   .20

24th Stamp Day A761

Children's Drawings.

1982, Nov. 28   **Photo.**   *Perf. 14x13½*
1534   A761   150 l   multi   .25   .20
1535   A761   250 l   multi   .40   .20
1536   A761   350 l   multi   .55   .20
   Nos. 1534-1536 (3)   1.20   .60

Cancer Research — A762

1983, Jan. 14   **Photo.**   *Perf. 13½x14*
1537   A762   400 l   multi   .65   .20

Engineering Type of 1981

1983, Jan. 20   *Perf. 13½*
1538   A732   400 l   Globe, factories   .65   .20
1539   A732   400 l   Automated assembly line   .65   .20
   a.   Pair, #1538-1539   1.40   .65

Crusca Academy, 400th Anniv. — A763

1983, Jan. 25   **Engr.**   *Perf. 14x13½*
1540   A763   400 l   Emblem   .65   .20

World Biathlon Championship — A764

1983, Feb. 5   **Photo.**   *Perf. 14*
1541   A764   200 l   multi   .30   .20

Gabriele Rossetti (1783-1854), Writer — A765

1983, Feb. 28   **Engr.**   *Perf. 14x13½*
1542   A765   300 l   dk brn & dk bl   .50   .20

Francesco Guicciardini (1483-1540), Historian — A766

1983, Mar. 5   **Engr.**   *Perf. 13½x14*
1543   A766   450 l   sepia   .75   .20

Umberto Saba (1883-1957), Poet — A767

1983, Mar. 9   **Photo.**   *Perf. 14x13½*
1544   A767   600 l   multi   1.00   .20

Pope Pius XII (1876-1958) A768

1983, Mar. 21   **Engr.**   *Perf. 13½x14*
1545   A768   1400 l   dark blue   2.25   .40

Holy Year — A769

1983, Mar. 25   Photo.   *Perf. 14*
1546	A769	250 l	St. Paul's Basilica	.40	.20
1547	A769	300 l	St. Maria Maggiore Church	.50	.20
1548	A769	400 l	San Giovanni Church	.65	.20
1549	A769	500 l	St. Peter's Church	1.10	.20
		Nos. 1546-1549 (4)		2.65	.80

Aircraft Type of 1981
1983, Mar. 28   Litho.   *Perf. 14x13½*
1550		400 l	Caproni C22J glider	.65	.20
1551		400 l	Aeritalia Macchi jet fighter	.65	.20
1552		400 l	SIAI-211 jet trainer	.65	.20
1553		400 l	A-129 Agusta helicopter	.65	.20
a.		A730 Block or strip of 4, #1550-1553 + 2 labels		4.00	

Intl. Workers' Day (May 1) — A770

1983, Apr. 29   Engr.   *Perf. 14x13½*
| 1554 | A770 | 1200 l | blue | 2.00 | .50 |

Flower Type of 1981
1983, Apr. 30   Photo.   *Perf. 13½x14*
1555	A726	200 l	Mimosa	.60	.20
1556	A726	200 l	Rhododendron	1.00	.20
1557	A726	200 l	Gladiolus	1.00	.20
		Nos. 1555-1557 (3)		2.60	.60

Europa 1983 A771

Litho. & Engr.
1983, May 2   *Perf. 14x13½*
| 1558 | A771 | 400 l | Galileo, telescope, 160l | 4.00 | 1.00 |
| 1559 | A771 | 500 l | Archimedes and his screw | 4.00 | .40 |

Ernesto T. Moneta (1833-1918), Nobel Peace Prize Winner, 1907 — A772

1983, May 5   Engr.   *Perf. 14x13½*
| 1560 | A772 | 500 l | multi | .80 | .20 |

Monument, Globe, Computer Screen A773

20th Natl. Eucharistic Congress A775

1983, May 9   Photo.   *Perf. 13½x14*
| 1561 | A773 | 500 l | multi | .80 | .20 |

3rd Intl. Congress of Jurisdicial Information.

Folk Celebration Type of 1982
#1562, La Corsa Dei Ceri Procession, Gubbio.

1983, May 13   *Perf. 13½*
| 1562 | A754 | 300 l | multi | .55 | .20 |

1983, May 14   *Perf. 14*
| 1563 | A775 | 300 l | multi | .50 | .20 |

Tourist Type of 1974
1983, July 30   Photo.   *Perf. 14*
1563A	A616	250 l	Alghero	.40	.20
1563B	A616	300 l	Bardonecchia	.80	.25
1563C	A616	400 l	Riccione	1.40	.35
1563D	A616	500 l	Taranto	2.00	.40
		Nos. 1563A-1563D (4)		4.60	1.20

Girolamo Frescobaldi (1583-1643), Composer A776

1983, Sept. 14   Engr.   *Perf. 13½x14*
| 1564 | A776 | 400 l | brn & grn | .65 | .30 |

Villa Type of 1980
Designs: 250 l, Fidelia, Spello. 300 l, Imperiale, Pesaro. 400 l, Michetti Convent, Francavilla al Mare. 500 l, Riccia.

Photogravure and Engraved
1983, Oct. 10   *Perf. 14x13½*
1565	A719	250 l	multi	.75	.20
1566	A719	300 l	multi	.60	.20
1567	A719	400 l	multi	1.25	.25
1568	A719	500 l	multi	1.40	.35
		Nos. 1565-1568 (4)		4.00	1.00

Francesco de Sanctis (1817-1883), Writer — A777

1983, Oct. 28   Photo.
| 1569 | A777 | 300 l | multi | .50 | .20 |

Christmas 1983 — A778

Raphael Paintings: 250 l, Madonna of the Chair. 400 l, Sistine Madonna. 500 l, Madonna of the Candelabra.

1983, Nov. 10   *Perf. 13½x14*
1570	A778	250 l	multi	.40	.20
1571	A778	400 l	multi	.65	.25
1572	A778	500 l	multi	1.40	.30
		Nos. 1570-1572 (3)		2.45	.75

25th Stamp Day, World Communications Year — A779

Children's Drawings. 200 l, 400 l horiz.

Perf. 14x13½, 13½x14
1983, Nov. 27
1573	A779	200 l	Letters holding hands	.30	.20
1574	A779	300 l	Spaceman	.60	.20
1575	A779	400 l	Flag train, globe	1.00	.25
		Nos. 1573-1575 (3)		1.90	.65

Road Safety A780

Perf. 13½x14, 14x13½
1984, Jan. 20   Photo.
| 1576 | A780 | 300 l | Bent road sign, vert. | .50 | .20 |
| 1577 | A780 | 400 l | Accident | .65 | .35 |

Promenade in Bois de Boulogne, by Giuseppe de Nittis (1846-1884) — A781

Design: 400 l, Portrait of Paul Guillaume, 1916, by Amedeo Modigliani (1884-1920).

Lithographed and Engraved
1984, Jan. 25   *Perf. 14*
| 1578 | A781 | 300 l | multi | .60 | .20 |
| 1579 | A781 | 400 l | multi | .65 | .30 |

Galaxy-Same Tractor — A782

Italian-made vehicles.

1984, Mar. 10   Photo.   *Perf. 14x13½*
1580	A782	450 l	shown	.70	.40
1581	A782	450 l	Alfa-33 car	.70	.40
1582	A782	450 l	Maserati Biturbo car	.70	.40
1583	A782	450 l	Iveco 190-38 truck	.70	.40
a.		Block of 4, #1580-1583 + 2 labels		6.00	1.90

See Nos. 1620-1623, 1681-1684.

A783

1984, Apr. 10
1584	A783	300 l	Mosaic, furnace	.50	.20
1585	A783	300 l	Glass Blower	.50	.20
a.		Pair, #1584-1585 + label		1.25	.55

2nd European Parliament Elections — A784

1984, Apr. 16
| 1586 | A784 | 400 l | Parliament Strasbourg | .55 | .25 |

Forest Preservation — A785

1984, Apr. 24   Photo.   *Perf. 14x13½*
1587	A785	450 l	Helicopter fire patrol	.70	.40
1588	A785	450 l	Hedgehog, squirrel, badger	.70	.40
1589	A785	450 l	Riverside waste dump	.70	.40
1590	A785	450 l	Plant life, animals	.70	.40
a.		Block of 4, #1587-1590		9.50	1.90

Italia '85 A786

1984, Apr. 26   *Perf. 14*
| 1591 | A786 | 450 l | Ministry of Posts, Rome | .80 | .30 |
| 1592 | A786 | 550 l | Via Appia Antiqua, Rome | 1.00 | .35 |

Rome Pacts, 40th Anniv. A787

Trade Unionists: Giuseppe di Vittorio, Bruno Buozzi, Achille Grandi.

1984, Apr. 30   *Perf. 14x13½*
| 1593 | A787 | 450 l | multi | .70 | .30 |

Europa (1959-84) A788

1984, May 5
| 1594 | A788 | 450 l | multi | 5.00 | .90 |
| 1595 | A788 | 550 l | multi | 8.50 | 3.25 |

Intl. Telecommunications Symposium, Florence, May — A789

1984, May 7   *Perf. 14*
| 1596 | A789 | 550 l | multi | .90 | .35 |

Italian Derby Centenary A790

Lithographed and Engraved
1984, May 12   *Perf. 14x13½*
| 1597 | A790 | 250 l | Racing | 1.40 | .20 |
| 1598 | A790 | 400 l | Racing, diff. | 1.75 | .25 |

Tourist Type of 1974

1984, May 19   Photo.   Perf. 14

1599	A616	350 l	Campione d'Italia	.80	.25
1600	A616	400 l	Chianciano Terme baths	.80	.25
1601	A616	450 l	Padula	1.60	.30
1602	A616	550 l	Greek ampitheater, Syracuse	1.60	.35
	Nos. 1599-1602 (4)			4.80	1.15

Folk Celebration Type of 1982

Design: La Macchina Di Santa Rosa.

1984, Sept. 3   Photo.   Perf. 13½x14

1603	A754	400 l	multi	.70	.25

Peasant Farming A792

1984, Oct. 1   Photo.   Perf. 14x13½

1604	A792	250 l	Grain harvester, thresher	.40	.20
1605	A792	350 l	Cart, hand press	.55	.20

Villa Type of 1980

Designs: 250 l, Villa Caristo, Stignano. 350 l, Villa Doria Pamphili, Genoa. 400 l, Villa Reale, Stupinigi. 450 l, Villa Mellone, Lecce.

Lithographed and Engraved

1984, Oct. 6   Perf. 14x13½

1606	A719	250 l	multi	.75	.20
1607	A719	350 l	multi	.75	.20
1608	A719	400 l	multi	1.50	.25
1609	A719	450 l	multi	1.50	.25
	Nos. 1606-1609 (4)			4.50	.90

Italia '85 — A793

1984, Nov. 9   Perf. 13½x14

1610	A793	550 l	Etruscan bronze statue	.90	.30
1611	A793	550 l	Italia '85 emblem	.90	.30
1612	A793	550 l	Etruscan silver mirror	.90	.30
a.	Strip of 3, #1610-1612			4.00	1.50

Journalistic Information A794

1985, Jan. 15   Photo.   Perf. 13½x14

1613	A794	350 l	Globe, paper tape, microwave dish	.55	.20

Modern Problems — A795

1985, Jan. 23   Photo.   Perf. 13½x14

1614	A795	250 l	Aging	.40	.20

A796

Italia '85. No. 1615, The Hunt, by Raphael (1483-1520). No. 1616, Emblem. No. 1617, Detail from fresco by Baldassare Peruzzi (1481-1536) in Bishop's Palace, Ostia Antica.

Photo. and Engr., Photo. (#1616)

1985, Feb. 13   Perf. 13½x14

1615	A796	600 l	multi	1.00	.30
1616	A796	600 l	multi	1.00	.30
1617	A796	600 l	multi	1.00	.30
a.	Strip of 3, #1615-1617			5.00	1.50

Faience Tiles, Plate, Flask and Covered Bowl — A797

Italian ceramics: No. 1619, Tile mural, gladiators in combat.

1985, Mar. 2   Photo.   Perf. 14x13½

1618	A797	600 l	multi	1.00	.30
1619	A797	600 l	multi	1.00	.30
a.	Pair, #1618-1619 + label			3.25	.75

Italian Vehicle Type of 1984

1985, Mar. 21

1620	A782	450 l	Lancia Thema	.75	.25
1621	A782	450 l	Fiat Abarth	.75	.25
1622	A782	450 l	Fiat Uno	.75	.25
1623	A782	450 l	Lamborghini	.75	.25
a.	Block of 4, #1620-1623 + 2 labels			15.00	1.50

A799

Italia '85: No. 1624, Church of St. Mary of Peace, Rome, by Pietro de Cortona (1596-1669). No. 1625, Exhibition emblem. No. 1626, Church of St. Agnes, Rome, fountain and obelisk.

Photo. and Engr., Photo. (#1625)

1985, Mar. 30   Perf. 13½x14

1624	A799	250 l	multi	.40	.20
1625	A799	250 l	multi	.40	.20
1626	A799	250 l	multi	.40	.20
a.	Strip of 3, #1624-1626			1.50	.50

Pope Sixtus V, (1520-1590), 400th Anniv. of Papacy — A800

Sixtus V, dome of St. Peter's Basilica, Rome.

1985, Apr. 24   Litho. and Engr.

1627	A800	1500 l	multi	2.40	1.25

Folk Celebration Type of 1982

Folktales: No. 1628, The March of the Turks, Potenza. No. 1629, San Marino Republican Regatta, Amalfi.

1985, May 29   Photo.

1628	A754	250 l	multi	.70	.20
1629	A754	350 l	multi	1.10	.20

Tourist Type of 1974

Scenic views: 350 l, Bormio town center. 400 l, Mt. Vesuvius from Castellamare di Stabia. 500 l, Stromboli Volcano from the sea. 600 l, Beach, old town at Termoli.

1985, June 1   Perf. 14

1630	A616	350 l	multi	.55	.20
1631	A616	400 l	multi	.80	.25
1632	A616	450 l	multi	1.00	.30
1633	A616	600 l	multi	2.25	.35
	Nos. 1630-1633 (4)			4.60	1.10

Nature Conservation A803

1985, June 5   Perf. 13½x14

1634	A803	500 l	European beaver	.80	.30
1635	A803	500 l	Primula	.80	.30
1636	A803	500 l	Nebrodi pine	.80	.30
1637	A803	500 l	Italian sandpiper	.80	.30
a.	Block of 4, #1634-1637			13.00	1.50

Art Type of 1981

Designs: No. 1638, Madonna bu Il Sassoferrato, G.B. Salvi, 1609-1685. No. 1639, Pride of the Work by Mario Sironi, 1885-1961.

Lithographed and Engraved

1985, June 15   Perf. 14

1638	A738	350 l	multi	.80	.20
1639	A738	400 l	multi	1.10	.25

Europa — A805

Tenors and Composers: 500 l, Aureliano Pertile (1885-1969) and Giovanni Martinelli (1885-1962). 600 l, Johann Sebastian Bach (1685-1750) and Vincenzo Bellini (1801-1835).

1985, June 20   Photo.   Perf. 13½x14

1640	A805	500 l	multi	4.50	.60
1641	A805	600 l	multi	8.00	1.10

San Salvatore Abbey, Monte Amiata, 950th Anniv. A806

Lithographed and Engraved

1985, Aug. 1   Perf. 14x13½

1642	A806	450 l	multi	.75	.30

World Cycling Championships — A807

1985, Aug. 21   Photo.

1643	A807	400 l	multi	1.10	.25

7th Intl. Congress for Crime Prevention, Milan, Aug. 26-Sept. 6 — A808

1985, Aug. 26

1644	A808	600 l	multi	1.00	.35

Intl. Youth Year A809

1985, Sept. 3

1645	A809	600 l	multi	1.00	.35

Villa Type of 1980

Designs: 300 l, Nitti, Maratea. 400 l, Aldrovandi Mazzacorati, Bologna. 500 l, Santa Maria, Pula. 600 l, De Mersi, Villazzano.

Lithographed and Engraved

1985, Oct. 1   Perf. 14x13½

1646	A719	300 l	multi	.90	.20
1647	A719	400 l	multi	1.10	.25
1648	A719	500 l	multi	1.75	.30
1649	A719	600 l	multi	2.25	.35
	Nos. 1646-1649 (4)			6.00	1.10

Natl. and Papal Arms, Treaty Document A810

1985, Oct. 15   Photo.

1650	A810	400 l	multi	.75	.25

Ratification of new Concordat with the Vatican.

Souvenir Sheets

Parma #10, View of Parma A812

Switzerland #3L1 A813

Sardinia #1, Great Britain #1 — A814

No. 1651: b, Two Sicilies #3, Naples. c, Two Sicilies #10, Palermo. d, Modena #3, Modena. e, Roman States #8, Rome. f, Tuscany #5, Florence. g, Sardinia #15, Turin. h, Romagna #7, Bologna. i, Lombardy-Venetia #4, Milan. No. 1652b, Japan #1. c, US #2. d, Western Australia #1. e, Mauritius #4. Illustration A814 reduced.

Lithographed and Engraved

1985, Oct. 25   **Perf. 14**
1651   Sheet of 9   6.00 2.75
   a.-i.   A812 300 l, any single   .50 .20

          Perf. 14x13½
1652   Sheet of 5 + label   5.50 1.90
   a.-e.   A813 500 l, any single   .80 .30

          Imperf
1653   A814 4000 l multi   6.50 3.25

Italia '85, Rome, Oct. 25-Nov. 3.

Long-distance Skiing — A815

1986, Jan. 25   **Photo.**   **Perf. 14x13½**
1654   A815 450 l multi   .75 .30

Folk Celebration Type of 1982

Design: Procession of St. Agnes, Le Candelore Folk Festival, Catania.

1986, Feb. 3   **Perf. 13½x14**
1655   A754 450 l multi   .75 .30

Amilcare Ponchielli (1834-1886),
Composer — A816

Photogravure and Engraved

1986, Mar. 8   **Perf. 14x13½**
1656   A816 2000 l Scene from La
          Giaconda   3.25 1.75

Castle Type of 1980

Designs: 380 l, Vignola, Modena. 650 l, Montecchio Castle, Castiglion Fiorentino. 750 l, Rocca di Urbisaglia.

          Perf. 14x13½
1986-90   **Photo.**   **Wmk. 303**
1657   A717 380 l multi ('87)   .60 .30
1658   A717 650 l multi   1.10 .30

          Engr.
1659   A717 750 l multi ('90)   1.25 .75
   Nos. 1657-1659 (3)   2.95 1.35

   Issue date: 750 l, Sept. 20.

Coil Stamps
          Perf. 14 Vert.
1988-91   **Engr.**   **Wmk. 303**
          Size: 16x21mm
1661   A717 100 l St. Severa   .20 .20
1662   A717 500 l Norman Cas-
          tle, Melfi   .80 .40
1663   A717 600 l Scaligero,
          Sirmione   1.10 .55
1664   A717 650 l Serralunga
          D'Alba   1.10 .50
1665   A717 750 l Venafro   1.25 .60
1666   A717 800 l Rocca Mag-
          giore, Assisi   1.50 .75
   Nos. 1661-1666 (6)   5.95 3.00

Issued: 600 l, 800 l, 2/20/91; others, 3/1/88.

Giovanni Battista
Pergolesi (1710-
1736),
Musician — A817

          Perf. 13½x14
1986, Mar. 15   **Photo.**   **Unwmk.**
1667   A817 2000 l multi   3.25 1.25

The Bay, Acitrezza — A818

1986, Mar. 24   **Perf. 14**
1668   A818 350 l shown   .65 .25
1669   A818 450 l Piazetta, Capri   .90 .30
1670   A818 550 l Kursaal, Merano   1.00 .35
1671   A818 650 l Lighthouse, San
          Benedetto del
          Tronto   1.25 .45
   Nos. 1668-1671 (4)   3.80 1.35

Europa
1986 — A819

Trees in special shapes: a, Heart (life). b, Star (poetry). c, Butterfly (color). d, Sun (energy).

1986, Apr. 28   **Photo.**   **Perf. 13x14**
1672   Block of 4   12.00 12.00
   a.-d.   A819 650 l, any single   1.10 .45

25th Intl. Opthalmological Congress,
Rome, May 4-10 — A820

1986, May 3   **Photo.**   **Perf. 14**
1673   A820 550 l multi   .90 .40

Police in Uniform — A821

1986, May 10
1674   A821 550 l multi   1.60 .40
1675   A821 650 l multi   1.90 .45

European Police Conference, Chianciano Terme, May 10-12. Nos. 1674-1675 printed se-tenant with labels picturing male or female police.

Battle of
Bezzecca,
120th
Anniv.
A822

1986, May 31   **Perf. 14x13½**
1676   A822 550 l multi   .90 .35

Memorial Day for Independence
Martyrs — A823

1986, May 31   **Perf. 14**
1677   A823 2000 l multi   3.25 1.40

Bersaglieri Corps
of Mountain
Troops, 150th
Anniv. — A824

1986, June 1   **Perf. 13½x14**
1678   A824 450 l multi   .75 .30

Telecommunications — A825

1986, June 16   **Perf. 14x13½**
1679   A825 350 l multi   .55 .25

Sacro Monte di Varallo
Monastery — A826

1986, June 28   **Engr.**   **Perf. 14**
1680   A826 2000 l Prus bl & sage
          grn   3.00 1.40

Italian Vehicle Type of 1984
1986, July 4   **Photo.**   **Perf. 14x13½**
1681   A782 450 l Alfa Romeo
          AR8 Turbo   .75 .30
1682   A782 450 l Innocenti 650
          SE   .75 .30
1683   A782 450 l Ferrari Testaros-
          sa   .75 .30
1684   A782 450 l Fiatallis FR 10B   .75 .30

Ladies' Fashions — A827

Breda Heavy Industry — A828

Olivetti Computer Technology — A829

1986, July 14
1685   A827 450 l shown   .75 .30
1686   A827 450 l Men's fashions   .75 .30
   a.   Pair, #1685-1686 + label   3.50 .75
1687   A828 650 l shown   3.00 .45
1688   A829 650 l shown   3.00 .45
   Nos. 1685-1688 (4)   7.50 1.50

Alitalia,
Italian
Airlines,
40th Anniv.
A830

1986, Sept. 16   **Photo.**   **Perf. 14x13½**
1689   A830 550 l Anniv. emblem   1.00 .40
1690   A830 650 l Jet, runway lights   1.25 .50

Villa Type of 1980
1986, Oct. 1   **Photo. & Engr.**
1691   A719 350 l Necker, Trieste   .65 .25
1692   A719 350 l Borromeo, Cas-
          sano D'Adda   .65 .25
1693   A719 450 l Palagonia,
          Bagheria   .85 .35
1694   A719 550 l Medicea, Poggio
          a Caiano   1.00 .40
1695   A719 650 l Castello
          d'Issogne, Is-
          sogne   1.25 .50
   Nos. 1691-1695 (5)   4.40 1.75

Christmas — A831

Madonna and Child, bronze sculpture by Donatello, Basilica del Santo, Padua.

1986, Oct. 10   **Engr.**   **Perf. 14**
1696   A831 450 l brown olive   .75 .35

Art Type of 1981

Designs: 450 l, Seated Woman Holding a Book, drawing by Andrea del Sarto, Uffizi, Florence, vert. 550 l, Daphne at Pavarola, painting by Felice Casorati, Museum of Modern Art, Turin, vert.

1986, Oct. 11   **Litho. & Engr.**
1697   A738 450 l blk & pale org   1.75 .35
1698   A738 550 l multi   2.25 .40

Memorial, Globe,
Plane — A832

Plane, Cross,
Men — A833

1986, Nov. 11   Photo.   *Perf. 13½x14*
1699 A832 550 l multi   .90   .45
1700 A833 650 l multi   1.10   .55

Intl. Peace Year, memorial to Italian airmen who died at Kindu, Zaire, while on a peace mission.

Stamp Day
A834

1986, Nov. 29   *Perf. 14x13½*
1701 A834 550 l Die of Sardinia
                    No. 2   1.50   .45

Francesco Matraire, printer of first Sardinian stamps.

A835

Industries — A836

**   *Perf. 14½x13½***
1987, Feb. 27   Photo.
1702 A835 700 l Marzotto Textile,
                    1836   1.10   .55
1703 A836 700 l Italgas Energy
                    Corp., 1837   1.10   .55

Environmental Protection — A837

Designs: a, Volturno River. b, Garda Lake. c, Trasimeno Lake. d, Tirso River.

1987, Mar. 6   Litho.   *Perf. 14x13½*
1704   Block of 4   8.00 2.00
a.-d. A837 500 l, any single   .80   .40

Antonio Gramsci
(1891-1937), Author
and Artist — A838

1987, Apr. 27   Litho.   *Perf. 14x13½*
1705 A838 600 l scar & gray black 1.00   .50

Europa
1987
A839

Modern architecture: 600 l, Church of Sun Motorway, Florence, designed by Michelucci. 700 l, Railway station, Rome, designed by Nervi.

1987, May 4   Photo.
1706 A839 600 l multi   *2.50 .60*
1707 A839 700 l multi   *3.25 .60*

Tourist Type of 1974

1987, May 9   *Perf. 14*
1708 A616 380 l Verbania Pal-
                    lanza   .75   .30
1709 A616 400 l Palmi   .80   .35
1710 A616 500 l Vasto   1.00   .40
1711 A616 600 l Villacidro   1.25   .50
        Nos. 1708-1711 (4)   3.80 1.55

Naples Soccer
Club, Nat'l.
Champions
A840

1987, May 18   Litho.   *Perf. 13½x14*
1712 A840 500 l multi   1.90   .40

The Absinthe
Drinkers, by
Degas — A841

1987, May 29
1713 A841 380 l multi   .80   .30

Fight against alcoholism.

St. Alfonso M. de Liguori (1696-1787)
and Gulf of Naples — A842

1987, Aug. 1   *Perf. 14x13½*
1714 A842 400 l multi   .65   .30

Events
A843

Emblems and natl. landmarks: No. 1715, OLYMPHILEX '87, Intl. Olympic Committee Building, Foro Italico, Rome. No. 1716, World Athletics Championships, Olympic Stadium, Rome.

1987, Aug. 29   Photo.   *Perf. 14x14½*
1715 A843 700 l multi   1.10   .55
1716 A843 700 l multi   1.10   .55

Folk Celebration Type of 1982
Design: Quintana Joust, Foligno.

**   *Perf. 13½x14½***
1987, Sept. 12   Photo.
1717 A754 380 l multi   .70   .30

Piazzas
A844

380 l, Piazza del Popolo, Ascoli Piceno. 500 l, Piazza Giuseppe Verdi, Palermo. 600 l, Piazza San Carlo, Turin. 700 l, Piazza dei Signori, Verona.

**   Litho. & Engr.**
1987, Oct. 10   *Perf. 14x13½*
1718 A844 380 l multi   .75   .30
1719 A844 500 l multi   1.00   .40
1720 A844 600 l multi   1.25   .50
1721 A844 700 l multi   1.40   .55
        Nos. 1718-1721 (4)   4.40 1.75

See Nos. 1747-1748, 1765-1766.

Christmas
A845

Paintings by Giotto: 500 l, Adoration in the Manger, Basilica of St. Francis, Assisi. 600 l, The Epiphany, Scrovegni Chapel, Padua.

1987, Oct. 15   Photo.   *Perf. 13½x14*
1722 A845 500 l multi   .90   .40
1723 A845 600 l multi   1.10   .50

Battle of
Mentana,
120th
Anniv.
A846

**   Litho. & Engr.**
1987, Nov. 3   *Perf. 14x13½*
1724 A846 380 l multi   .70   .35

Il Pantocrator (Christ), Mosaic,
Monreale Cathedral — A847

Coat of Arms and San Carlo Theater,
Naples, from an 18th Cent.
Engraving — A848

1987, Nov. 4   *Perf. 14*
1725 A847 500 l multi   1.50   .45
1726 A848 500 l multi   1.50   .45

Artistic heritage. See Nos. 1768-1769.

Nunziatella
Military
School,
200th
Anniv.
A849

1987, Nov. 14   *Perf. 14x13½*
1727 A849 600 l multi   1.00   .50

Stamp
Day — A850

Philatelist Marco DeMarchi (d. 1936) holding magnifying glass and stamp album, Milan Cathedral.

1987, Nov. 20   Photo.   *Perf. 13½x14*
1728 A850 500 l multi   1.60   .45

Homo
Aeserniensis
(Flint
Knapper) — A851

**   Photo. & Engr.**
1988, Feb. 6   *Perf. 13½x14*
1729 A851 500 l multi   .80   .40

Remains of Isernia Man, c. 736,000 years-old, discovered near Isernia.

E. Quirino
Visconti
School,
Rome
A852

**   Litho. & Engr.**
1988, Mar. 1   Unwmk.   *Perf. 14x13½*
1730 A852 500 l multi   .80   .40

See Nos. 1764, 1824, 1842.

St. John Bosco
(1815-1888),
Educator — A853

1988, Apr. 2   Photo.   *Perf. 13½x14*
1731 A853 500 l multi   .80   .40

Art Type of 1981

Painting: *The Archaeologists,* by Giorgio de Chirico (1888-1978).

1988, Apr. 7   Engr.   *Perf. 14*
1732 A738 650 l multi, vert.   1.90   .55

1st Printed
Hebrew
Bible, 500th
Anniv.
A854

Soncino Bible excerpt, 15th cent.

1988, Apr. 22   Photo.   *Perf. 14x13½*
1733 A854 550 l multi   .90   .45

Epilepsy Foundation A855

Design: St. Valentine, electroencephalograph readout, epileptic in seizure and medieval crest.

1988, Apr. 23
1734 A855 500 l multi .80 .40

Europa 1988 A856

Transport and communication: 650 l, ETR 450 locomotive. 750 l, Electronic mail, map of Italy.

1988, May 2
1735 A856 650 l multi 1.75 .60
1736 A856 750 l multi 2.25 .85

Tourist Type of 1974

Scenic views: 400 l, Castiglione della Pescaia. 500 l, Lignano Sabbiadoro. 650 l, Noto. 750 l, Vieste.

1988, May 7   Photo.   Perf. 14
1737 A616 400 l multi .65 .30
1738 A616 500 l multi .80 .40
1739 A616 650 l multi 1.10 .55
1740 A616 750 l multi 1.25 .60
  Nos. 1737-1740 (4) 3.80 1.85

A858

1988, May 16
1741 A858 500 l Golf .80 .40

1990 World Cup Soccer Championships — A859

1988, May 16   Litho.   Perf. 14x13½
1742 A859 3150 l blk, grn & dark red 5.25 3.25

1988 Natl. Soccer Championships, Milan — A860

1988, May 23   Perf. 13½x14
1743 A860 650 l multi 1.10 .55

Bronze Sculpture, Pergola — A861

1988, June 4   Engr.   Perf. 14
1744 A861 500 l Horse .80 .40
1745 A861 650 l Woman 1.10 .55

Bologna University, 900th Anniv. — A862

1988, June 10   Engr.   Perf. 13½x14
1746 A862 500 l violet .80 .40

Piazza Type of 1987

Designs: 400 l, Piazza del Duomo, Pistoia. 550 l, Piazza del Unita d'Italia, Trieste.

Litho. & Engr.
1988, July 2   Perf. 14x13½
1747 A844 400 l multi .70 .30
1748 A844 550 l multi .95 .40

Folk Celebration Type of 1982

Discesa Dei Candelieri, Sassari: Man wearing period costume, column and bearers.

1988, Aug. 13   Photo.   Perf. 13½x14
1749 A754 550 l multi 1.40 .40

Intl. Gastroenterology and Digestive Endoscopy Congress, Rome — A863

1988, Sept. 5
1750 A863 750 l multi 1.25 .60

Neorealistic Films — A864

Italian films amd directors: 500 l, Ossessione, 1942, by Luchino Visconti. 650 l, Ladri di Biciclette, 1948, by Vittorio DeSica. 2400 l, Roma Citta Aperta, 1945, by Roberto Rossellini. 3050 l, Riso Amaro, 1949, by Giuseppe DeSantis.

1988, Oct. 13   Litho.   Perf. 14x13½
1751 A864 500 l multi .80 .40
1752 A864 650 l multi 1.10 .55
1753 A864 2400 l multi 4.00 2.00
1754 A864 3050 l multi 5.00 2.50
  Nos. 1751-1754 (4) 10.90 5.45

Elsag — A865

Aluminia — A866

State Mint and Polygraphic Insitute — A867

Italian Industries.

1988, Oct. 19   Photo.
1755 A865 750 l multi 1.25 .65
1756 A866 750 l multi 1.25 .65

Photo. & Engr.
1757 A867 750 l multi 1.25 .65
  Nos. 1755-1757 (3) 3.75 1.95

Christmas: *Nativity*, by Pasquale Celommi, Church of the Virgin's Assumption A868

1988, Oct. 29   Photo.   Perf. 13½x14
1758 A868 650 l multi 1.40 .55

Christmas A869

Photo. & Engr.
1988, Nov. 12   Perf. 14x13½
1759 A869 500 l dark blue grn & chest brn 1.40 .40

St. Charles Borromeo (1538-1584), Ecclesiastical Reformer — A870

1988, Nov. 4   Litho. & Engr.
1760 A870 2400 l multi 4.00 2.25

Stamp Day — A871

Japan #69 & stamp designer Edoardo Chiossone.

1988, Dec. 9   Photo.   Perf. 13½x14
1761 A871 500 l multi .80 .40

Campaign Against AIDS — A872

1989, Jan. 13
1762 A872 650 l multi 1.10 .55

Paris-Peking Rally — A873

1989, Jan. 21   Perf. 14½x13½
1763 A873 3150 l Map, Itala race car 5.25 2.50

School Type of 1988
1989   Photo. & Engr.   Perf. 14x13½
1764 A852 650 l multi 1.10 .55

Piazza Type of 1987

No. 1765, Piazza Del Duomo, Catanzaro. No. 1766, Piazza Di Spagna, Rome.

Litho. & Engr.
1989, Apr. 10   Perf. 14x13½
1765 A844 400 l multi .85 .30
1766 A844 400 l multi .85 .30

Velo World Yachting Championships A875

1989, Apr. 8   Photo.   Perf. 14
1767 A875 3050 l multi 5.00 2.50

Artistic Heritage Type of 1987

Art and architecture: 500 l, King with scepter and orb, Palazzo Della Ragione, Padova, vert. 650 l, Crypt of St. Nicolas, St. Nicolas Basilica, Bari, vert.

1989, Apr. 8   Litho. & Engr., Engr.
1768 A847 500 l multi .80 .40
1769 A847 650 l indigo 1.10 .55

Europa 1989 — A876

Children's games.

Perf. 14x13½, 13½x14
1989, May 8   Photo.
1770 A876 500 l Leapfrog, horiz. 1.10 .50
1771 A876 650 l shown 1.60 .50
1772 A876 750 l Sack race, horiz. 1.60 .50
  Nos. 1770-1772 (3) 4.30 1.50

European Parliament 3rd Elections — A877

1989, June 3   *Perf. 13½x14*
1773 A877 500 l multi   1.00 .35
No. 1773 also inscribed in European Currency Units "ECU 0,31."

Pisa University — A878

1989, May 29   **Engr.**   *Perf. 14x13½*
1774 A878 500 l violet   .80 .40

Folk Celebration Type of 1982
Priest and Flower Feast street scene.

1989, May 27   **Photo.**   *Perf. 13½x14*
1775 A754 400 l multi   .60 .30

Landscape Type of 1974
1989, June 10   **Photo.**   *Perf. 14*
1776 A616 500 l Naxos Gardens   1.00 .35
1777 A616 500 l Spotorno   1.00 .35
1778 A616 500 l Pompei   1.00 .35
1779 A616 500 l Grottammare   1.00 .35
    Nos. 1776-1779 (4)   4.00 1.40

Ministry of Posts, Cent. A879

1989, June 24   *Perf. 14x13½*
1780 A879 500 l Posthorn, No. 52   .80 .40
1781 A879 2400 l Posthorn, Earth   4.00 2.00

INTER Soccer Championships — A880

1989, June 26
1782 A880 650 l multi   1.10 .55

Interparliamentary Union, Cent. — A881

1989, June 28
1783 A881 750 l multi   1.25 .60

French Revolution, Bicent. — A882

1989, July 7   **Photo.**   *Perf. 14*
1784 A882 3150 l multi   5.00 2.25

Fortified Walls of Corinaldo, by Francesco di Giorgio Martini (1439-1502) — A883

Litho. & Engr.
1989, Sept. 2   *Perf. 14*
1785 A883 500 l multi   .90 .40

Charlie Chaplin (1889-1977) — A884

1989, Sept. 23   **Engr.**   *Perf. 14x13½*
1786 A884 750 l black & sepia   1.40 .55

Naples-Portici Railway, 150th Anniv. — A885

Illustration reduced.

1989, Oct. 3   **Litho. & Engr.**
1787   550 l Denom at UL   .90 .45
1788   550 l Denom at UR   .90 .45
  a. A885 Pair, #1787-1788   2.00 1.10

Adoration of the Kings, by Correggio — A887

1989, Oct. 21   **Photo.**   *Perf. 13½x14*
1789   500 l multicolored   .80 .40
1790   500 l multicolored   .80 .40
  a. A887 Pair, #1789-1790   2.00 .90
    Christmas.

Fidardo Castle, the Stradella, Accordion — A889

Industries.

1989, Oct. 14   **Photo.**   *Perf. 14x13½*
1791 A889 450 l Music   .75 .35
1792 A889 450 l Arnoldo World Publishing   .75 .35

Stamp Day — A890

1989, Nov. 24   *Perf. 13½x14*
1793 A890 500 l Emilio Diena   1.00 .40

1990 World Soccer Championships, Italy — A891

1989, Dec. 9   **Engr.**   *Perf. 13½x14*
1794 A891 450 l multicolored   .75 .35

Columbus's First Voyage, 1474-1484 — A892

1990, Feb. 24   **Photo.**
1795   700 l Denom at UL   1.10 .55
1796   700 l Denom at UR   1.10 .55
  a. A892 Pair, #1795-1796   2.25 1.50

Souvenir Sheets

1990 World Cup Soccer Championships, Italy — A894

Soccer club emblems and stadiums in Italy.
No. 1797: a, Italy. b, US. c, Olympic Stadium, Rome. d, Municipal Stadium, Florence. e, Austria. f, Czechoslovakia.
No. 1798: a, Argentina. b, Russia. c, St. Paul Stadium, Naples. d, New Stadium, Bari. e, Cameroun. f, Romania.
No. 1799: a, Brazil. b, Costa Rica. c, Alps Stadium, Turin. d, Ferraris Stadium, Genoa. e, Sweden. f, Scotland.
No. 1800: a, UAE. b, West Germany. c, Dall'ara Stadium, Bologna. d, Meazza Stadium, Milan. e, Colombia. f, Yugoslavia.
No. 1801: a, Belgium. b, Uruguay. c, Bentegodi Stadium, Verona. d, Friuli Stadium, Udine. e, South Korea. f, Spain.
No. 1802: a, England. b, Netherlands. c, Sant'elia Stadium, Cagliari. d, La Favorita Stadium, Palermo. e, Ireland. f, Egypt.

1990, Mar. 24   *Perf. 14x13½*
1797   Sheet of 6   4.50 2.25
  a.-f. A894 450 l any single   .75 .35

1798   Sheet of 6   6.00 3.00
  a.-f. A894 600 l any single   1.00 .50
1799   Sheet of 6   6.50 3.25
  a.-f. A894 650 l any single   1.10 .55
1800   Sheet of 6   6.50 3.25
  a.-f. A894 700 l any single   1.10 .55
1801   Sheet of 6   7.50 3.75
  a.-f. A894 800 l any single   1.25 .60
1802   Sheet of 6   12.00 6.00
  a.-f. A894 1200 l any single   2.00 1.00
    Nos. 1797-1802 (6)   43.00 21.50
    See No. 1819.

Tourist Type of 1974
1990, Mar. 30   **Photo.**   *Perf. 14*
1803 A616 600 l Sabbioneta   1.00 .50
1804 A616 600 l Montepulciano   1.00 .50
1805 A616 600 l Castellammare del Golfo   1.00 .50
1806 A616 600 l San Felice Circeo   1.00 .50
    Nos. 1803-1806 (4)   4.00 2.00

Folk Celebration Type of 1982
Design: Horse race, Merano.

1990, Apr. 9   *Perf. 13½x14*
1807 A754 600 l multicolored   1.00 .50

Aurelio Saffi, Death Cent. A895

1990, Apr. 10   *Perf. 14*
1808 A895 700 l multicolored   1.10 .55

Giovanni Giorgi (1871-1950) — A896

1990, Apr. 23   *Perf. 14x13½*
1809 A896 600 l multicolored   1.00 .55

Metric System in Italy, 55th. anniv.

Labor Day, Cent. — A897

1990, Apr. 28   **Photo.**   *Perf. 13½x14*
1810 A897 600 l multicolored   1.00 .55

Naples Soccer Club, Italian Champions A898

1990, Apr. 30   *Perf. 13½x14*
1811 A898 700 l multicolored   1.25 .65

Europa A899

Post Offices: 700 l, San Silvestro Piazza, Rome. 800 l, Fondaco Tedeschi, Venice.

1990, May 7 **Perf. 14x13½**
1812 A899 700 l multicolored 1.50 .60
1813 A899 800 l multicolored 2.25 .75

Giovanni Paisiello (1740-1816), Composer A900

1990, May 9 **Perf. 14x13½**
1814 A900 450 l multicolored .75 .40

Dante Alighieri (1265-1321), Poet — A901

1990, May 12 **Perf. 14x13½**
1815 A901 700 l multicolored 1.10 .60
Dante Alighieri Soc., cent.

Mosaic (Detail) — A902

Sculpture — A903

Photo. (#1816), Litho. & Engr. (#1817)
1990, May 19 **Perf. 13½x14**
1816 A902 450 l multicolored .75 .40
1817 A903 700 l multicolored 1.10 .60

Malatestiana Music Festival, Rimini, 40th Anniv. — A904

1990, June 15 **Photo.** **Perf. 14**
1818 A904 600 l multicolored 1.00 .60

World Cup Soccer Type of 1990 Inscribed "Campione Del Mondo"
1990, July 9 **Litho.** **Perf. 14x13½**
1819 A894 600 l like No. 1800b 1.50 .60

Still Life, by Giorgio Morandi (1890-1964) — A905

1990, July 20 **Engr.** **Perf. 14**
1820 A905 750 l black 1.25 .60

Greco-Roman Wrestling, World Championships — A906

1990, Oct. 11 **Litho.** **Perf. 14x13½**
1821 A906 3200 l multicolored 5.25 2.50

Christmas — A907

Paintings of the Nativity by: 600 l, Emidio Vangelli. 750 l, Pellegrino.

1990, Oct. 26 **Perf. 14**
1822 A907 600 l multicolored 1.00 .50
1823 A907 750 l multicolored 1.25 .60

School Type of 1988 and

Italian Schools — A908

Designs: 600 l, Bernardino Telesio gymnasium, Cosenza. 750 l, University of Catania.

Litho. & Engr.
1990, Nov. 5 **Perf. 14x13½**
1824 A852 600 l multicolored 1.00 .50
Engr.
1825 A908 750 l multicolored 1.25 .60

Stamp Day — A909

Self-portrait, Corrado Mezzana (1890-1952).

1990, Nov. 16 **Litho.** **Perf. 13½x14**
1826 A909 600 l multicolored 1.10 .55

A910

1991, Jan. 5 **Litho.** **Perf. 13½x14**
1827 A910 600 l The Nativity 1.00 .50

Genoa Flower Show — A911

1991, Jan. 10 **Perf. 14**
1828 A911 750 l multicolored 1.25 .60

Seal of the Univ. of Siena — A912

1991, Jan. 15 **Photo.** **Perf. 13½x14**
1829 A912 750 l multicolored 1.25 .60

Tourist Type of 1974
1991 **Photo.**
1830 A616 600 l San Remo 1.00 .50
1831 A616 600 l Roccaraso 1.00 .50
1832 A616 600 l La Maddalena 1.00 .50
1833 A616 600 l Calgi 1.00 .50
Nos. 1830-1833 (4) 4.00 2.00

United Europe — A913

Perf. 14x13½
1991, Mar. 12 **Photo.** **Unwmk.**
1834 A913 750 l multi 1.25 .60
#1834 also carries .48 ECU denomination.

Discovery of America, 500th Anniv. (in 1992) — A914

1991, Mar. 22 **Litho.**
1835 750 l Ships leaving port 1.25 .60
1836 750 l Columbus, Queen's court 1.25 .60
a. A914 Pair, #1835-1836 2.50 1.25

Giuseppe Gioachino Belli (1791-1863), Poet — A916

1991, Apr. 15 **Litho.** **Perf. 14x13½**
1837 A916 600 l bl & gray blk 1.00 .50

Church of St. Gregory, Rome — A917

1991, Apr. 20 **Photo.** **Perf. 14x13½**
1838 A917 3200 l multicolored 5.25 2.50

Europa A918

1991, Apr. 29 **Photo.** **Perf. 14x13½**
1839 A918 750 l DRS satellite 1.60 .70
1840 A918 800 l Hermes space shuttle 1.60 .70

Santa Maria Maggiore Church, Lanciano — A919

1991, May 2 **Engr.** **Perf. 13½x14**
1841 A919 600 l brown 1.00 .50

Schools Type of 1988
Design: D. A. Azuni school, Sassari.

Litho. & Engr.
1991, May 3 **Perf. 14x13½**
1842 A852 600 l multicolored 1.00 .50

Team Genoa, Italian Soccer Champions, 1990-91 — A920

1991, May 27 **Photo.** **Perf. 13½x14**
1843 A920 3000 l multicolored 5.00 3.25

Basketball, Cent. — A921

1991, June 5
1844 A921 500 l multicolored .80 .40

Children's Rights — A922

1991, June 14
1845	A922	600 l	shown	1.00	.50
1846	A922	750 l	Man, child with balloon	1.25	.60

Art and Culture A923

Designs: 600 l, Sculpture by Pericle Fazzini (b. 1913). 3200 l, Exhibition Hall, Turin, designed by Pier Luigi Nervi (1891-1979).

Litho. & Engr.
1991, June 21   **Perf. 14**
1847	A923	600 l	multicolored	1.00	.50
1848	A923	3200 l	multicolored	5.25	2.50

Egyptian Museum, Turin — A924

1991, Aug. 31   **Litho.**   **Perf. 13½x14**
1849	A924	750 l	grn, yel & gold	1.25	.60

Luigi Galvani (1737-1798), Electrophysicist — A925

1991, Sept. 24   **Perf. 14x13½**
1850	A925	750 l	multicolored	1.25	.60

Radio, cent. (in 1995). See Nos. 1873, 1928, 1964.

Nature Protection A926

1991, Oct. 10   **Photo.**   **Perf. 14x13½**
1851	A926	500 l	Marevivo posidonia	1.25	.75
1852	A926	500 l	Falco pellegrino	1.25	.75
1853	A926	500 l	Cervo sardo	1.25	.75
1854	A926	500 l	Orso marsicano	1.25	.75
		Nos. 1851-1854 (4)		5.00	3.00

World Wildlife Fund.

Wolfgang Amadeus Mozart, Death Bicent. — A927

1991, Oct. 7   **Perf. 13½x14**
1855	A927	800 l	multicolored	1.25	.60

Christmas A928

1991, Oct. 18
1856	A928	600 l	multicolored	1.00	.50

Giulio and Alberto Bolaffi, Philatelists — A929

1991, Oct. 25   **Perf. 14**
1857	A929	750 l	multicolored	1.25	.60

Stamp Day.

Pietro Nenni (1891-1980), Politician — A930

1991, Oct. 30
1858	A930	750 l	multicolored	1.25	.60

Fountain of Neptune, Florence, by Bartolomeo Ammannati (1511-1592) — A931

1992, Feb. 6   **Photo.**   **Perf. 13½x14**
1859	A931	750 l	multicolored	1.25	.60

22nd European Indoor Track Championships — A932

1992, Jan. 30   **Perf. 14x13½**
1860	A932	600 l	multicolored	1.00	.50

University of Ferrara, 600th Anniv. — A933

1992, Mar. 4   **Photo.**   **Perf. 13½x14**
1861	A933	750 l	multicolored	1.25	.60

Castle Type of 1980
Perf. 14x13½
1992-94   **Photo.**   **Wmk. 303**
1862	A717	200 l	Cerro al Volturno	.30	.20
1863	A717	250 l	Mondavio	.40	.20
1864	A717	300 l	Bari	.50	.20
1865	A717	450 l	Bosa	.75	.35
1866	A717	850 l	Arechi, Salerno	1.50	.75
		Nos. 1862-1866 (5)		3.45	1.70

Issued: 200 l, 250 l, 300 l, 450 l, 2/24/94; 850 l, 3/7/92.
This is an expanding set. Numbers will change if necessary.

University of Naples — A934

1992, Mar. 9   **Unwmk.**   **Perf. 14x13½**
1872	A934	750 l	multicolored	1.25	.60

Radio Cent. Type of 1991

Alessandro Volta (1745-1827), Italian physicist.

1992, Mar. 26
1873	A925	750 l	multicolored	1.25	.60

Radio, cent. (in 1995).

Genoa '92 Intl. Philatelic Exhibition — A935

1992, Mar. 27   **Perf. 13½x14**
1874	A935	750 l	multicolored	1.25	.60

Lorenzo de Medici (1449-1492) A936

1992, Apr. 8   **Perf. 14**
1875	A936	750 l	bl & org brn	1.25	.60

Filippini Institute, 300th Anniv. — A937

1992, May 2   **Photo.**   **Perf. 13½x14**
1876	A937	750 l	multicolored	1.25	.60

Discovery of America, 500th Anniv. A938

#1877, Columbus seeking Queen Isabella's support. #1878, Columbus' fleet. #1879, Sighting land. #1880, Landing in New World.

1992, Apr. 24   **Photo.**   **Perf. 14x13½**
1877	A938	500 l	multicolored	.90	.45
1878	A938	500 l	multicolored	.90	.45
1879	A938	500 l	multicolored	.90	.45
1880	A938	500 l	multicolored	.90	.45
a.		Block of 4, #1877-1880		3.75	1.90

See US Nos. 2620-2623.

Discovery of America, 500th Anniv. — A939

Designs: 750 l, Monument to Columbus, Genoa. 850 l, Globe, Genoa '92 Exhibition emblem.

1992, May 2   **Perf. 13½x14**
1881	A939	750 l	multicolored	1.40	.65
1882	A939	850 l	multicolored	1.75	.75

Europa.

Miniature Sheets

Voyages of Columbus — A940

Columbus: #1883: a, Presenting natives. b, Announcing his discovery. c, In chains.
#1884: a, Welcomed at Barcelona. b, Restored to favor. c, Describing his 3rd voyage.
#1885: a, In sight of land. b, Fleet. c, Queen Isabella pledging her jewels.
#1886: a, Soliciting aid from Isabella. b, At La Rabida. c, Recall.
#1887: a, Landing. b, Santa Maria. c, Queen Isabella and Columbus. #1888, Columbus.
#1883-1888 are similar in design to US #230-245.

1992, May 22   **Engr.**   **Perf. 10½**
1883	A940	Sheet of 3		7.25	3.75
a.		50 l olive black		.20	.20
b.		300 l dark blue green		.50	.25
c.		4000 l red violet		6.50	3.00
1884	A940	Sheet of 3		6.25	3.00
a.		100 l brown violet		.20	.20
b.		800 l magenta		1.25	.60
c.		3000 l green		5.00	2.40

1885	A940	Sheet of 3	4.25	2.00
a.		200 l dark blue	.30	.20
b.		900 l ultra	1.50	.75
c.		1500 l orange	2.50	1.25
1886	A940	Sheet of 3	3.50	1.75
a.		400 l chocolate	.65	.30
b.		700 l vermillion	1.10	.55
c.		1000 l slate blue	1.60	.80
1887	A940	Sheet of 3	5.00	2.40
a.		500 l brown violet	.80	.40
b.		600 l dark green	1.00	.50
c.		2000 l crimson lake	3.25	1.50
1888	A940	5000 l Sheet of 1	8.25	4.00
		Nos. 1883-1888 (6)	34.50	16.90

See US Nos. 2624-2629, Portugal Nos. 1918-1923 and Spain Nos. 2677-2682.

Tour of Italy Bicycle Race A941

1992, May 23   Photo.   Perf. 14x13½

1889	A941	750 l Ocean	1.50	.75
1890	A941	750 l Mountains	1.50	.75
a.		Pair, #1889-1890	3.00	1.50

No. 1890a printed in continuous design.

Milan, Italian Soccer Champions A942

1992, May 25   Perf. 13½x14

1891	A942	750 l black, red & grn	1.50	.75

Beach Resorts A943

1992   Perf. 14x13½

1892	A943	750 l Viareggio	1.25	.60
1893	A943	750 l Rimini	1.25	.60

Issued: #1892, May 30; #1893, June 13.

Tazio Nuvolari (1892-1953), Race Car Driver — A944

1992, June 5   Perf. 14x13½

1900	A944	3200 l multicolored	5.25	2.75

Tourism Type of 1974

1992, June 30   Perf. 14

1901	A616	600 l Arcevia	1.00	.50
1902	A616	600 l Maratea	1.00	.50
1903	A616	600 l Braies	1.00	.50
1904	A616	600 l Pantelleria	1.00	.50
		Nos. 1901-1904 (4)	4.00	2.00

The Shepherds, by Jacopo da Ponte — A945

Litho. & Engr.

1992, Sept. 5   Perf. 14

1905	A945	750 l multicolored	1.25	.60

Discovery of America, 500th Anniv. — A946

500 l, Columbus' house, Genoa. 600 l, Columbus' fleet. 750 l, Map. 850 l, Columbus pointing to land. 1200 l, Coming ashore. 3200 l, Columbus, art by Michelangelo.

1992, Sept. 18   Photo.   Perf. 13½x14

1906	A946	500 l multicolored	.80	.40
1907	A946	600 l multicolored	1.00	.50
1908	A946	750 l multicolored	1.25	.60
1909	A946	850 l multicolored	1.40	.70
1910	A946	1200 l multicolored	2.00	1.00
1911	A946	3200 l multicolored	5.25	2.50
		Nos. 1906-1911 (6)	11.70	5.70

Genoa '92.

Stamp Day — A947

1992, Sept. 22   Perf. 14

1912	A947	750 l multicolored	1.25	.70

Self-Adhesive
Perf. 13½

1913	A947	750 l multicolored	2.25	.70

Lions Intl., 75th Anniv. A948

1992, Sept. 24   Perf. 14x13½

1914	A948	3000 l multicolored	5.00	2.50

Single European Market A949

1992, Oct. 5   Photo.   Perf. 14x13½

1915	A949	600 l multicolored	1.00	.50

Intl. Conference on Nutrition, Rome A950

1992, Oct. 16   Photo.   Perf. 14x13½

1916	A950	500 l multicolored	.80	.40

Christmas A951

1992, Oct. 31

1917	A951	600 l multicolored	1.00	.50

Miniature Sheet

United Europe — A952

Buildings on natl. flags, inscriptions in native language: a, Italy (Benvenuta). b, Belgium (Vienvenue, Welkom). c, Denmark (Velkommen). d, France (Bienvenue L'Europe). e, Germany (Willkommen). f, Greece. g, Ireland (Failte). h, Luxembourg (Bienvenue Europe). i, Netherlands (Welkom). j, Portugal (Bem-Vinda). k, United Kingdom (Welcome). l, Spain (Bienvenida).

1993, Jan. 20   Photo.   Perf. 13½x14
Sheet of 12

1918	A952	750 l #a.-l.	15.00	15.00

Meeting of Veterans of 1943 Battle of Nikolajewka, Russia — A953

1993, Jan. 23   Litho.   Perf. 14x13½

1919	A953	600 l multicolored	1.00	.50

Carlo Goldoni (1707-93), Playwright A954

Paintings depicting scenes from plays: No. 1920, Man in harlequin costume leaning on picture. No. 1921, Woman seated in front of harlequins.

1993, Feb. 6   Photo.   Perf. 13½x14

1920	A954	500 l multicolored	.80	.40
1921	A954	500 l multicolored	.80	.40

Mosaic from the Piazza Armerina A955

Photo. & Engr.

1993, Feb. 20   Perf. 14

1922	A955	750 l multicolored	1.25	.60

Natl. Health Day Promoting a Healthy Heart A956

1993, Mar. 5   Photo.   Perf. 14x13½

1923	A956	750 l multicolored	1.25	.60

Cats A957

1993, Mar. 6   Perf. 14x13½, 13½x14

1924	A957	600 l European	1.00	.50
1925	A957	600 l Maine coon, vert.	1.00	.50
1926	A957	600 l Devon Rex, vert.	1.00	.50
1927	A957	600 l White Persian	1.00	.50
		Nos. 1924-1927 (4)	4.00	2.00

Radio Cent. Type of 1991

Design: 750 l, Temistocle Calzecchi Onesti.

1993, Mar. 26   Litho.   Perf. 14x13½

1928	A925	750 l multicolored	1.25	.60

Radio cent. (in 1995).

City Scene, by Francesco Guardi (1712-1793) — A958

Photo. & Engr.

1993, Apr. 6   Perf. 14

1929	A958	3200 l multicolored	5.25	2.50

Horace (Quintus Horatius Flaccus), Poet and Satirist, 2000th Anniv. of Death — A959

1993, Apr. 19   Photo.   Perf. 13½x14

1930	A959	600 l multicolored	1.00	.50

Contemporary Paintings — A960

Europa: 750 l, Carousel Animals, by Lino Bianchi Barriviera. 850 l, Abstract, by Gino Severini.

1993, May 3

1931	A960	750 l multicolored	1.25	.60
1932	A960	850 l multicolored	1.40	.70

Natl. Soccer Champions, Milan — A961

1993, May 24
1933 A961 750 l multicolored   1.25 .60

Natl. Academy of St. Luke, 400th Anniv. — A962

1993, May 31   **Photo.**
1934 A962 750 l multicolored   1.25 .60

St. Giuseppe Benedetto Cottolengo (1786-1842) A963

1993, May   **Photo. & Engr.**
1935 A963 750 l multicolored   1.25 .60

Family Fest '93 — A964

1993, June 5   **Photo.**   **Perf. 14x13½**
1936 A964 750 l multicolored   1.25 .60

Tourism A965

1993, June 28   **Photo.**   **Perf. 14x13½**
1937 A965 600 l Palmanova   1.00 .50
1938 A965 600 l Senigallia   1.00 .50
1939 A965 600 l Carloforte   1.00 .50
1940 A965 600 l Sorrento   1.00 .50
    Nos. 1937-1940 (4)   4.00 2.00
    See Nos. 1972-1975, 2032-2035.

1993 World Kayaking Championships, Trentino — A966

1993, July 1   **Perf. 13½x14**
1941 A966 750 l multicolored   1.25 .60

Regina Margherita Observatory, Cent. — A967

1993, Sept. 4   **Photo.**   **Perf. 14x13½**
1942 A967 500 l multicolored   1.00 .50

Museum Treasures A968

Designs: No. 1943, Concert, by Bartolomeo Manfredi. No. 1944, Ancient map of Foggia. 750 l, Illuminated page with "S," vert. 850 l, The Death of Adonis, by Sebastiano Del Piombo.

Perf. 14x13½, 13½x14
1993, Nov. 27   **Litho.**
1943 A968 600 l multicolored   1.00 .50
1944 A968 600 l multicolored   1.00 .50
1945 A968 750 l multicolored   1.25 .60
1946 A968 850 l multicolored   1.40 .70
    Nos. 1943-1946 (4)   4.65 2.30

Holy Stairway, Veroli — A969

1993, Sept. 25   **Photo.**   **Perf. 13½x14**
1947 A969 750 l multicolored   1.25 .60

World War II — A970

Events of 1943: No. 1948, Deportation of Jews from Italy, Oct. 16, 1943. No. 1949, Soldiers, helmet (Battle of Naples). No. 1950, Execution of the Cervi Brothers.

1993, Sept. 25
1948 A970 750 l multicolored   1.25 .60
1949 A970 750 l multicolored   1.25 .60
1950 A970 750 l multicolored   1.25 .60
    Nos. 1948-1950 (3)   3.75 1.80
    See Nos. 1984-1986.

Thurn and Taxis Postal History A971

#1951, Coach. #1952, Coat of arms. #1953, Cart. #1954, Post rider on galloping horse. #1955, Post rider on walking horse.

1993, Oct. 2   **Perf. 14x13½**
1951 A971 750 l multicolored   1.25 .60
1952 A971 750 l multicolored   1.25 .60
1953 A971 750 l multicolored   1.25 .60
1954 A971 750 l multicolored   1.25 .60
1955 A971 750 l multicolored   1.25 .60
    Nos. 1951-1955 (5)   6.25 3.00

Perf. 14 Horiz.
1951a A971 750 l   1.25 .60
1952a A971 750 l   1.25 .60
1953a A971 750 l   1.25 .60
1954a A971 750 l   1.25 .60
1955a A971 750 l   1.25 .60
   b.   Booklet pane of 5, #1951a-1955a   5.00

Bank of Italy, Cent. A972

1993, Oct. 15   **Perf. 14x13½**
1956 A972 750 l Bank exterior   1.25 .60
1957 A972 1000 l 1000 Lire note   1.60 .80

Christmas A973

Designs: 600 l, Living Creche in the town of Corchiano. 750 l, Detail of The Annunciation, by Piero Della Francesca.

1993, Oct. 26   **Litho.**   **Perf. 13½x14**
1958 A973 600 l multicolored   1.00 .50
1959 A973 750 l multicolored   1.25 .60

Stamp Day A974

1993, Nov. 12   **Photo.**   **Perf. 14**
1960 A974 600 l blue & red   1.00 .50
First Italian colonial postage stamps, cent.

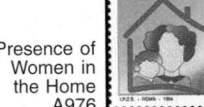

Circus — A975

1994, Jan. 8   **Litho.**   **Perf. 13½x14**
1961 A975 600 l Acrobat, horses   1.00 .50
1962 A975 750 l Clown performing   1.25 .60

Presence of Women in the Home A976

1994, Feb. 14   **Photo.**   **Perf. 14**
1963 A976 750 l multicolored   1.25 .60

Radio Cent. Type of 1991
750 l, Augusto Righi (1850-1920), physicist.

Perf. 14x13½
1994, Mar. 11   **Photo.**   **Unwmk.**
1964 A925 750 l multicolored   1.25 .60
Radio cent. (in 1995).

Dogs A977

1994, Mar. 12   **Perf. 14x13**
1965 A977 600 l German shepherd   1.00 .50
1966 A977 600 l Abruzzi sheepdog   1.00 .50
1967 A977 600 l Boxer   1.00 .50
1968 A977 600 l Dalmatian   1.00 .50
    Nos. 1965-1968 (4)   4.00 2.00

Italian Cuisine — A978

1994, Mar. 24   **Perf. 13x14**
1969 A978 500 l Breads   .80 .40
1970 A978 600 l Pasta   1.00 .50

Procession Honoring Apparition of Christ, Tarquinia — A979

1994, Apr. 2   **Perf. 13½**
1971 A979 750 l multicolored   1.25 .60

Tourism Type of 1993
1994, Apr. 23   **Photo.**   **Perf. 14x13½**
1972 A965 600 l Orta San Giulio   1.00 .50
1973 A965 600 l Santa Marinella   1.00 .50
1974 A965 600 l Messina   1.00 .50
1975 A965 600 l Monticchio, Potenza   1.00 .50
    Nos. 1972-1975 (4)   4.00 2.00

A981

Nobel Prize Winners: 750 l, Camillo Golgi (1844-1926), Physician, Medicine, 1906. 850 l, Guilio Natta (1903-), Chemistry, 1963.

1994, May 2   **Photo.**   **Perf. 13½x14**
1976 A981 750 l multicolored   *1.25 .60*
1977 A981 850 l multicolored   *1.40 .70*

Publication of "Summa de Arithemtica, Geometria, Proportioni et Proportionalita," 500th Anniv. — A982

Fra Luca Pacioli (c. 1445-1514), mathematician.

1994, May 2   **Photo.**   **Perf. 14x13**
1978 A982 750 l multicolored   1.25 .60

Lajos Kossuth (1802-94) — A983

1994, Apr. 30   Photo.   Perf. 13½x14
1979 A983 3750 l multicolored   6.00 3.00

Milan, Winners of 1993-94 Italian Soccer Championships — A984

1994, May 2   Perf. 14x13½
1980 A984 750 l multicolored   1.25   .60

World Swimming Championships A985

1994, May 2   Photo.   Perf. 13½x14
1981 A985 600 l Diving   1.00   .50
1982 A985 750 l Water polo   1.25   .60

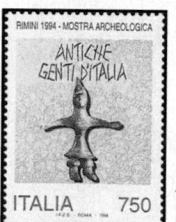

Archaeology Exhibition, Rimini — A986

1994, May 6
1983 A986 750 l multicolored   1.25   .60

World War II Type of 1993

Events of 1944: No. 1984, Destruction of Monte Cassino. No. 1985, Massacre of the Ardeatine Caves. No. 1986, Massacre at Marzabotto.

1994, May 18
1984 A970 750 l multicolored   1.25   .60
1985 A970 750 l multicolored   1.25   .60
1986 A970 750 l multicolored   1.25   .60
    Nos. 1984-1986 (3)   3.75 1.80

22nd Natl. Eucharistic Congress, Siena — A987

1994, May 28   Photo.   Perf. 13½x14
1987 A987 600 l multicolored   1.00   .50

Ariadne, Venus and Bacchus, by Tintoretto (1518-94) — A988

1994, May 31   Perf. 14
1988 A988 750 l multicolored   1.25   .60

Brotherhood of Mercy, Florence, 700th Anniv. — A989

1994, June 4   Perf. 14x13½
1989 A989 750 l multicolored   1.25   .60

European Parliamentary Elections — A990

1994, June 11   Photo.   Perf. 13½x14
1990 A990 600 l multicolored   1.00   .50

Natl. Museums — A991

#1991, Attic Krater, Natl. Archaeological Museum. #1992, Ancient drawing, Natl. Archives. 750 l, Statue, Natl. Roman Museum. 850 l, Medallion, Natl. Archives.

1994, June 16
1991 A991 600 l multicolored   1.00   .50
1992 A991 600 l multicolored   1.00   .50
1993 A991 750 l multicolored   1.25   .60
1994 A991 850 l multicolored   1.40   .70
    Nos. 1991-1994 (4)   4.65 2.30

Intl. Olympic Committee, Cent. — A992

1994, June 23
1995 A992 850 l multicolored   1.40   .70

G-7 Summit, Naples — A993

1994, July 8
1996 A993 600 l multicolored   1.00   .50
    A 750 l in this this design was printed but not issued.

A995   A996

1994, Sept. 8   Photo.   Perf. 14
1998 A995 500 l multicolored   .80   .40
    Basilica of Loreto, 500th anniv.

1994, Sept. 19
1999 A996 750 l multicolored   1.25   .60
    Frederick II (1194-1250), Holy Roman Emperor.

Stamp Day — A998

Designs: 600 l, Pietro Miliani (1744-1817), paper manufacturer. 750 l, Convent of San Domenico.

1994, Sept. 16   Photo.   Perf. 13½x14
2001 A998 600 l multicolored   1.00   .50
2002 A998 750 l multicolored   1.25   .60

Basilica of St. Mark, 900th Anniv. A999

1994, Oct. 8   Photo.   Perf. 13½x13
2003 A999 750 l multicolored   1.25   .60
 a.   Souvenir sheet of 2, tete beche   2.50 2.50

No. 2003 printed with se-tenant label. No. 2003a contains one each No. 2003 and San Marino No. 1314. Only No. 2003 was valid for postage in Italy. See San Marino No. 1314.

Christmas A1000

600 l, The Annunciation, by Melozzo da Forli. 750 l, Madonna and Child, by Lattanzio da Rimini.

1994, Nov. 5   Photo.   Perf. 13½x14
2004 A1000 600 l multicolored   1.00   .50
2005 A1000 750 l multicolored   1.25   .60

Italian Touring Club, Cent. — A1001

1994, Nov. 8
2006 A1001 600 l multicolored   1.00   .50

CREDIOP, 75th Anniv. — A1002

1994, Nov. 11
2007 A1002 750 l multicolored   1.25   .60

Giovanni Gentile (1875-1944), Philosopher A1003

1994, Nov. 21
2008 A1003 750 l multicolored   1.25   .60

Querini Dubois Palace, Venice — A1004

1994   Perf. 13½x14
2009 A1004 600 l red & silver   1.00   .50

New Italian Postal Emblem A1005

1994   Perf. 14x13½
2010 A1005 750 l red, black & green   1.25   .60
2011 A1005 750 l red brown   1.25   .60
 a.   Pair, #2010-2011   2.50 1.25
    See Nos. 2059-2060.

World Speed Skating Championships — A1006

1995, Feb. 6   Photo.   Perf. 14x13½
2012 A1006 750 l multicolored   1.25   .60

Achille Beltrame (1871-1945)
A1007

Design: 500 l, Cover of first issue of LA DOMENICA DEL CORRIERE.

1995, Feb. 18   Photo.   Perf. 13½x14
2013 A1007 500 l multicolored   .80 .40

Italian Food — A1008

1995, Mar. 4
2014 A1008 500 l Rice   .80 .40
2015 A1008 750 l Olives, olive oil 1.25 .60
    See Nos. 2068-2069.

Birds A1009

1995, Mar. 11   Photo.   Perf. 14x13½
2016 A1009 600 l Heron   1.00 .50
2017 A1009 600 l Vulture   1.00 .50
2018 A1009 600 l Royal eagle   1.00 .50
2019 A1009 600 l Alpine chaffinch   1.00 .50
    Nos. 2016-2019 (4)   4.00 2.00

UN, 50th Anniv. A1010

1995, Mar. 24   Photo.   Perf. 14x13½
2020 A1010 850 l multicolored 1.40 .70

Fifth Day of Milan War Memorial, by Giuseppe Grandi, Cent. A1011

1995, Mar. 25   Photo.   Perf. 14x13½
2021 A1011 750 l gold, black & blue 1.25 .60

Miniature Sheet

End of World War II, 50th Anniv. — A1012

Designs: a, Mafalda de Savoy, concentration camp, barbed wire. b, Allied DUKW, Battles of Anzio and Nettuno. c, Women in World War II, Teresa Gullace. d, Gold Medal of Valor, Palazzo Vecchio, Florence. e, Gold Medal of Valor, building, Vittorio Veneto. f, Gold Medal of Valor, Cathedral, Cagliari. g, Mountain Battalion. h, Air dropping supplies, Balkans. i, Atlantic fleet.

1995, Mar. 31   Photo.   Perf. 14x13½
2022 A1012 750 l Sheet of 9,
    #a.-i.   11.00 5.50

Natl. Treasures A1013

Designs: No. 2023, Illuminated manuscript with "P," State Archives, Rome. No. 2024, Painting of Port of Naples, by Tavola Strozzi, Natl. Museum of San Martino, horiz. No. 2025, Illuminated manuscript with "I," Christ, State Archives, Mantua. No. 2026, Painting, Sacred and Profane Love, by Titian, Borghese Gallery and Museum, Rome, horiz.

Perf. 13½x14, 14x13½
1995, Apr. 28   Photo.
2023 A1013 500 l multicolored   .80 .40
2024 A1013 500 l multicolored   .80 .40
2025 A1013 750 l multicolored   1.25 .60
2026 A1013 850 l multicolored   1.40 .70
    Nos. 2023-2026 (4)   4.25 2.10

Venice Biennial, Cent. — A1014

1995, Apr. 29   Perf. 13½x14
2027 A1014 750 l multicolored   1.25 .60

Basilica of Santa Croce, Florence A1015

1995, May 3   Engr.
2028 A1015 750 l deep brn blk   1.25 .60

Peace & Freedom A1016

Europa: 750 l, Family, liberating soldiers, Italian flag. 850 l, Stars of European flag, church, mosque.

1995, May 5   Photo.   Perf. 13½x14
2029 A1016 750 l multicolored   1.25 .60
2030 A1016 850 l multicolored   1.40 .70

Volleyball, Cent. — A1017

1995, May 8
2031 A1017 750 l multicolored   1.25 .60

Tourism Type of 1993
1995, May 12   Photo.   Perf. 14x13½
2032 A965 750 l Nuoro   1.25 .60
2033 A965 750 l Susa   1.25 .60
2034 A965 750 l Alatri   1.25 .60
2035 A965 750 l Venosa   1.25 .60
    Nos. 2032-2035 (4)   5.00 2.40

Discovery of the X-Ray, Cent. A1018

1995, June 2
2036 A1018 750 l multicolored   1.25 .60

1994-95 Natl. Soccer Championship Team, Juventus A1019

1995, June 5   Perf. 13½x14
2037 A1019 750 l multicolored   1.25 .60

Radio, Cent. A1020

Designs: 750 l, Griffone House. 850 l, Guglielmo Marconi, transmitting equipment.

1995, June 8   Perf. 14x13½
2038 A1020 750 l multicolored   1.25 .60
**   Perf. 14**
2039 A1020 850 l multicolored   1.40 .70

No. 2039 is 36x21mm. See Germany No. 1900, Ireland No. 974a, San Marino Nos. 1336-1337, Vatican City Nos. 978-979.

A1021

St. Anthony of Padua (1195-1231) — A1022

Perf. 13½x14, 14x13½
1995, June 13
2040 A1021 750 l multicolored   1.25 .60
2041 A1022 850 l multicolored   1.40 .70

    See Brazil No. 2539 and Portugal Nos. 2054-2057.

Historical Public Gardens A1023

Designs: No. 2042, Durazzo Pallavicini, Pegli. No. 2043, Boboli, Firenze. No. 2044, Ninfa, Cisterna di Latina. No. 2045, Royal Park, Caserta.

Litho. & Engr.
1995, June 24   Perf. 14x13½
2042 A1023 750 l multicolored   1.25 .60
2043 A1023 750 l multicolored   1.25 .60
2044 A1023 750 l multicolored   1.25 .60
2045 A1023 750 l multicolored   1.25 .60
    Nos. 2042-2045 (4)   5.00 2.40

Congress of European Society of Ophthalmology A1024

1995, June 24   Litho.   Perf. 13½x14
2046 A1024 750 l multicolored   1.25 .60

The Sailors' Wives, by Massimo Campigli (1895-1971) — A1025

1995, July 4   Photo.   Perf. 14
2047 A1025 750 l multicolored   1.25 .60

14th World Conference on Relativity, Florence A1026

1995, Aug. 7   Litho.   Perf. 14x13
2048 A1026 750 l Galileo, Einstein   1.25 .60

Motion Pictures, Cent. — A1027

#2049, Son of the Shiek, Rudolph Valentino. #2050, L'oro Di Napoli, Toto. #2051, Le Notti Di Cabiria, F. Fellini. #2052, Cinecitta '95.

Litho. & Engr.

1995, Aug. 29			Perf. 13½x14	
2049	A1027	750 l multicolored	1.25	.60
2050	A1027	750 l multicolored	1.25	.60
2051	A1027	750 l multicolored	1.25	.60
2052	A1027	750 l multicolored	1.25	.60
		Nos. 2049-2052 (4)	5.00	2.40

See #2099-2101, 2170-2172, 2269-2271.

FAO, 50th Anniv. A1028

1995, Sept. 1		Photo.	Perf. 14x13½	
2053	A1028	850 l multicolored	1.25	.60

Basilica of Pontida & Death of St. Albert of Prezzate, 900th Anniv. A1029

1995, Sept. 2			Engr.	
2054	A1029	1000 l blue & brown	1.60	.80

ROMA '95, First World Military Games — A1030

1995, Sept. 6		Photo.	Perf. 13½x14	
2055	A1030	850 l multicolored	1.40	.70

Italian News Agency (ANSA), 50th Anniv. A1031

1995, Oct. 27		Photo.	Perf. 14x13½	
2056	A1031	750 l multicolored	1.25	.60

Christmas A1032

Designs: 750 l, Nativity figurines, Cathedral of Polignano a Mare, by Stefano da Putignano. 850 l, Adoration of the Magi, by Fra Angelico.

1995, Nov. 18				
2057	A1032	750 l multicolored	1.25	.60
2058	A1032	850 l multicolored	1.40	.70

New Italian Postal Emblem Type of 1994

1995, Dec. 9		Photo.	Perf. 13½x14	
		Size: 26x18mm		
2059	A1005	750 l like No. 2011	1.25	.60
a.		Booklet pane of 8	10.00	
		Complete booklet, #2059a	10.00	
2060	A1005	850 l like No. 2010	1.40	.70
a.		Booklet pane of 8	11.50	
		Complete booklet, #2060a	11.50	

Renato Mondolfo A1033

1995, Dec. 9		Photo.	Perf. 14x13½	
2061	A1033	750 l multicolored	1.25	.60

Philately Day.

F.T. Marinetti (1876-1944), Poet and Ideologue — A1034

1996, Jan. 19		Photo.	Perf. 14	
2062	A1034	750 l multicolored	1.25	.60

Collections from Natl. Museum and Archives A1035

#2063, Arms of the Academy of Georgofili, Florence. #2064, Illuminated manuscript from Lucca (1372), vert. #2065, Manuscript of Gabriele D'Annunzio (1863-1938), author, soldier, political leader. #2066, French miniature, c. 1486.

1996, Feb. 26		Perf. 14x13½, 13½x14		
2063	A1035	750 l multicolored	1.25	.60
2064	A1035	750 l multicolored	1.25	.60
2065	A1035	850 l multicolored	1.40	.70
2066	A1035	850 l multicolored	1.40	.70
		Nos. 2063-2066 (4)	5.30	2.60

Sarah and the Angel, by Tiepolo (1696-1770) — A1036

1996, Mar. 5			Perf. 14	
2067	A1036	1000 l multicolored	1.60	.80

Italian Food Type of 1995

1996, Mar. 20			Perf. 13½x14	
2068	A1008	500 l White wine, grapes	.80	.40
2069	A1008	750 l Red wine, grapes	1.25	.60

CHINA '96, 9th Asian Intl. Philatelic Exhibition A1037

1996, Mar. 22			Perf. 14x13½	
2070	A1037	1250 l multicolored	2.00	1.00

Marco Polo's return from China, 700th anniv. (in 1995).
See San Marino No. 1350.

Cathedral of Milan — A1038

No. 2071, Front entrance. No. 2072, Corner, side view.

1996, Mar. 23			Perf. 13½x14	
2071	A1038	750 l multicolored	1.25	.60
2072	A1038	750 l multicolored	1.25	.60
a.		Pair, #2071-2072	2.50	1.25
b.		Booklet pane, 4 #2072a	11.50	
		Complete booklet, #2072b	11.50	

No. 2072a is a continuous design.
ITALIA '98, Intl. Philatelic Exhibition, Milan.

A1039

1996, Apr. 3		Perf. 13½x14, 14x13½		
2073	A1039	750 l shown	1.25	.60
2074	A1039	750 l Globe, "100"	1.25	.60

Natl. Press Federation, 50th anniv. (#2073). "La Gazzetta dello Sport," cent. (#2074), horiz.

Intl. Museum of Postal Images, Belvedere Ostrense A1040

1996, Apr. 13		Photo.	Perf. 13½x14	
2075	A1040	500 l multicolored	.80	.40

Academy of Finance Police, Cent. — A1040a

1996, Apr. 13				
2076	A1040a	750 l multicolored	1.25	.60

RAMOGE Agreement Between France, Italy, Monaco, 20th Anniv. A1041

Photo. & Engr.

1996, May 14			Perf. 14x13½	
2077	A1041	750 l multicolored	1.25	.60

See France No. 2524, Monaco No. 1998.

Rome-New York Trans-Continental Drive — A1042

1996, Apr. 13		Photo.	Perf. 13½x14	
2078	A1042	4650 l multicolored	7.50	3.75

Europa (Famous Women) A1043

750 l, Carina Negrone, pilot. 850 l, Adelaide Ristori, actress.

1996, Apr. 29		Photo.	Perf. 13½x14	
2079	A1043	750 l multicolored	1.25	.60
2080	A1043	850 l multicolored	1.40	.70

St. Celestine V (1215-96) A1044

Litho. & Engr.

1996, May 18			Perf. 14x13½	
2081	A1044	750 l multicolored	1.25	.60

Tourism A1045

#2082, Pienza Cathedral. #2083, St. Anthony's Church, Diano Marina. #2084, Belltower of Church of St. Michael the Archangel, Monte Sant'Angelo. #2085, Prehistoric stone dwelling, Lampedusa.

1996, May 18		Photo.	Perf. 14x13½	
2082	A1045	750 l multicolored	1.25	.60
2083	A1045	750 l multicolored	1.25	.60
2084	A1045	750 l multicolored	1.25	.60
2085	A1045	750 l multicolored	1.25	.60
		Nos. 2082-2085 (4)	5.00	2.40

Consecration of Reconstructed Farfa Abbey, 500th Anniv. — A1046

1996, May 18		Photo.	Perf. 13½x14	
2086	A1046	1000 l multicolored	1.60	.80

Mediterranean Fair, Palermo — A1047

1996, May 25 *Perf. 14x13½*
2087 A1047 750 l multicolored 1.25 .60

Italian Republic, 50th Anniv. — A1048

1996, June 1 *Perf. 13½x14*
2088 A1048 750 l multicolored 1.25 .60

Production of Vespa Motor Scooters, 50th Anniv. — A1049

1996, June 20
2089 A1049 750 l multicolored 1.25 .60

First Meeting of European Economic Community, Messina and Venice, 40th Anniv. — A1050

1996, June 21 *Perf. 14*
2090 A1050 750 l multicolored 1.25 .60

Modern Olympic Games, Cent. A1051

Designs: 500 l, Runners, 1896. 750 l, Discus, Atlanta skyline, vert. 850 l, Gymnast on rings, basketball, Atlanta stadium. 1250 l, 1896 stadium, Athens, 1996 stadium, Atlanta, vert.

Perf. 14x13½, 13½x14
1996, July 1 *Photo.*
2091 A1051 500 l multicolored .80 .40
2092 A1051 750 l multicolored 1.25 .60
2093 A1051 850 l multicolored 1.40 .70
2094 A1051 1250 l multicolored 2.00 1.00
  Nos. 2091-2094 (4) 5.45 2.70

Butterflies A1052

#2095, Melanargia arge. #2096, Papilio hospiton. #2097, Zygaena rubicundus. #2098, Acanthobrahmaea europaea.

1996, Aug. 26 *Perf. 14x13½*
2095 A1052 750 l multicolored 1.25 .60
2096 A1052 750 l multicolored 1.25 .60
2097 A1052 750 l multicolored 1.25 .60
2098 A1052 750 l multicolored 1.25 .60
  Nos. 2095-2098 (4) 5.00 2.40

Motion Picture Type of 1995
#2099, Massimo Troisi in "Scusate Il Ritardo." #2100, Aldo Fabrizi in "Prima Comunione." #2101, Bartolomeo Pagano as Maciste in "Cabiria."

Photo. & Engr.
1996, Aug. 30 *Perf. 13½x14*
2099 A1027 750 l multicolored 1.25 .60
2100 A1027 750 l multicolored 1.25 .60
2101 A1027 750 l multicolored 1.25 .60
  Nos. 2099-2101 (3) 3.75 1.80

A1054

1996, Sept. 7 Photo. *Perf. 13½x14*
2102 A1054 750 l multicolored 1.25 .60
Milan, 1995-96 national soccer champions.

The Duomo, Cathedral of Santa Maria del Fiore, Florence, 700th Anniv. A1055

1996, Sept. 7 Engr. *Perf. 14x13½*
2103 A1055 750 l dark blue 1.25 .60

13th Intl. Congress of Prehistoric Science — A1056

1996, Sept. 9 Photo. *Perf. 13½x14*
2104 A1056 850 l multicolored 1.40 .70

Levant Fair, Bari A1057

1996, Sept. 13 Photo. *Perf. 14x13½*
2105 A1057 750 l multicolored 1.25 .60

1997 Mediterranean Games, Bari — A1058

1996, Sept. 13 *Perf. 13½x14*
2106 A1058 750 l multicolored 1.25 .60

Juventus, 1995-96 European Soccer Champions A1059

1996, Sept. 14
2107 A1059 750 l multicolored 1.25 .60

Alessandro Pertini (1896-1990), Former President A1060

1996, Sept. 25 Photo. *Perf. 13½x14*
2108 A1060 750 l multicolored 1.25 .60

Eugenio Montale (1896-1981), Poet — A1061

1996, Oct. 12 *Litho. & Engr.*
2109 A1061 750 l blue & brown 1.25 .60

Annunciation, by Pietro da Cortona (1596-1669) A1062

1996, Oct. 31 *Photo.*
2110 A1062 500 l multicolored .80 .40

Invitation to Philately A1063

Designs: 750 l, Tex Willer, western scene. 850 l, Seagulls, gondola, city, Corto Maltese.

Litho. & Engr.
1996, Oct. 31 *Perf. 14x13½*
2111 A1063 750 l multicolored 1.25 .60
2112 A1063 850 l multicolored 1.40 .70

Stamp Day — A1064

1996, Nov. 8 Photo. *Perf. 13½x14*
2113 A1064 750 l multicolored 1.25 .60

Universities of Italy — A1065

Perf. 13½x14, 14x13½
1996, Nov. 9 *Engr.*
Designs: No. 2114, Agrarian School, cent., University of Perugia. No. 2115, University of Sassari (1562-1996), horiz. No. 2116, University of Salerno

2114 A1065 750 l brown 1.25 .60
2115 A1065 750 l green 1.25 .60
2116 A1065 750 l blue 1.25 .60
  Nos. 2114-2116 (3) 3.75 1.80

World Food Day — A1066

1996, Nov. 13 Photo. *Perf. 14x13½*
2117 A1066 850 l green & black 1.40 .70

Christmas A1067

Designs: 750 l, Madonna and Child, by Pisanello. 850 l, Santa, toys, horiz.

Perf. 13½x14, 14x13½
1996, Nov. 15
2118 A1067 750 l multicolored 1.25 .60
2119 A1067 850 l multicolored 1.40 .70

UNESCO, 50th Anniv. — A1068

850 l, UNICEF 50th Anniv., baby, globe, emblem.

1996, Nov. 20 *Perf. 13½x14*
2120 A1068 750 l multicolored 1.25 .60
2121 A1068 850 l multicolored 1.40 .70

Natl. Institute of Statistics, 70th Anniv. — A1069

1996, Nov. 26
2122 A1069 750 l multicolored 1.25 .60

"Strega" Literary Award 50th Anniv. — A1070

1996, Nov. 29
2123 A1070 3400 l multicolored   5.50 2.75

First Natl. Flag, Bicent. — A1071

1997, Jan. 7   Photo.   Perf. 13½x14
2124 A1071 750 l multicolored   1.25 .60

Sestrieres '97, World Alpine Skiing Championships A1072

1997, Feb. 1   Photo.   Perf. 13½x14
2125 A1072 750 l shown   1.25 .60
2126 A1072 850 l Ski of colors   1.40 .70

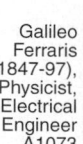 Galileo Ferraris (1847-97), Physicist, Electrical Engineer A1073

1997, Feb. 7   Perf. 14x13½
2127 A1073 750 l multicolored   1.25 .60

Emanuela Loi (1967-92), Police Woman Killed by Mafia — A1074

1997, Mar. 8
2128 A1074 750 l multicolored   1.25 .60

Italia '98, World Philatelic Exhibition, Milan — A1075

Designs: a, Airmail philately. b, Topical philately. c, Postal history. d, Philatelic literature.

1997, Mar. 21   Litho.   Perf. 13½x14
2129   Sheet of 4   5.00 2.50
  a.-d.   A1075 750 l any single   1.25 .60

Statue of Marcus Aurelius (121-180), Roman Emperor A1076

1997, Mar. 25   Photo.
2130 A1076 750 l multicolored   1.25 .60
Treaty of Rome, 40th anniv.

St. Ambrose (339-397), Bishop of Milan — A1077

Litho. & Engr.
1997, Apr. 4   Perf. 14
2131 A1077 1000 l multicolored   1.60 .80

St. Geminian, 1600th Death Anniv. — A1078

1997, Apr. 4   Photo.   Perf. 13½x14
2132 A1078 750 l multicolored   1.25 .60

University of Rome A1079

Design: No. 2134, University of Padua.

1997, Apr. 14   Engr.   Perf. 14x13½
2133 A1079 750 l claret   1.25 .60
2134 A1079 750 l blue   1.25 .60

Founding of Rome, 2750th Anniv. A1080

1997, Apr. 21   Photo.   Perf. 14x13½
2135 A1080 850 l multicolored   1.40 .70

Timoleontee Wall, Gela — A1081

1997, Apr. 24
2136 A1081 750 l multicolored   1.25 .60

Antonio Gramsci (1891-1937), Politician — A1082

1997, Apr. 26   Photo.   Perf. 14
2137 A1082 850 l multicolored   1.40 .70

Monastery Church, Pavia, 500th Anniv. — A1083

1997, May 3   Perf. 13½x14
2138 A1083 1000 l multicolored   1.60 .80

Stories and Legends A1084

Europa: 800 l, Cobbler's workshop. 900 l, Street singer, vert.

Perf. 14x13, 13x14
1997, May 5   Photo.
2139 A1084 800 l multicolored   1.25 .60
2140 A1084 900 l multicolored   1.50 .75

Massimo Theatre, Palermo, Cent. — A1085

1997, May 16   Photo.   Perf. 13½x14
2141 A1085 800 l multicolored   1.25 .60

Tourism A1086

Designs: No. 2142, St. Vitalian Basilica, Ravenna. No. 2143, Tomb of Marcus Tullius Cicero (106-43BC), Formia. No. 2144, College of Assumption of the Holy Mary, Positano. No. 2145, St. Sebastian Church, Acireale.

1997, May 17   Photo.   Perf. 14x13
2142 A1086 800 l multicolored   1.25 .60
2143 A1086 800 l multicolored   1.25 .60
2144 A1086 800 l multicolored   1.25 .60
2145 A1086 800 l multicolored   1.25 .60
    Nos. 2142-2145 (4)   5.00 2.40

Book Fair, Turin — A1087

1997, May 22   Perf. 13½x14
2146 A1087 800 l multicolored   1.25 .60

Queen Paola of Belgium, 60th Birthday A1088

1997, May 23   Photo.   Perf. 14x13½
2147 A1088 750 l San Angelo Castle   1.25 .60
See Belgium No. 1652.

Rome Fair A1089

1997, May 24   Photo.   Perf. 14x13½
2148 A1089 800 l multicolored   1.25 .60

Cathedral of Orvieto — A1090

1997, May 31   Engr.   Perf. 13x14
2149 A1090 450 l deep violet   .75 .35

Fr. Giuseppe Morosini (1913-44) A1091

1997, June 4   Photo.
2150 A1091 800 l multicolored   1.25 .60

Bologna Fair A1092

1997, June 7   Perf. 14x13
2151 A1092 800 l multicolored   1.25 .60

Juventus, 1996-97 Italian Soccer Champions
A1093

1997, June 7   Perf. 13½x14
2152 A1093 800 l multicolored   1.25   .60

Abruzzo Natl. Park, 75th Anniv. — A1094

1997, June 7   Photo. Perf. 13½x14
2153 A1094 800 l multicolored   1.25   .60

Italian Naval League, Cent. — A1095

1997, June 10   Photo. Perf. 13½x14
2154 A1095 800 l multicolored   1.25   .60

13th Mediterranean Games, Bari — A1096

1997, June 13   Perf. 14x13½
2155 A1096 900 l multicolored   1.50   .75

Public Gardens
A1097

Designs: No. 2156, Miramare-Trieste Park. No. 2157, Cavour-Santena. No. 2158, Villa Sciarra, Rome. No. 2159, Orto Botanical Gardens, Palermo.

Photo. & Engr.
1997, June 14   Perf. 14x13½
2156 A1097 800 l multicolored   1.25   .60
2157 A1097 800 l multicolored   1.25   .60
2158 A1097 800 l multicolored   1.25   .60
2159 A1097 800 l multicolored   1.25   .60
       Nos. 2156-2159 (4)   5.00 2.40

Italian Labor Force — A1098

Perf. 13½x14, 14x13½
1997, June 20
2160 A1098 800 l Industry   1.25   .60
2161 A1098 900 l Agriculture,
              horiz.   1.50   .75

John Cabot's Voyage to Canada, 500th Anniv.
A1099

1997, June 24   Litho.   Perf. 14
2162 A1099 1300 l multicolored   2.10 1.00
       See Canada No. 1649.

Pietro Verri (1728-97), Economist, Journalist
A1100

1997, June 28   Perf. 13½x14
2163 A1100 3600 l multicolored   6.00 3.00

Madonna of the Rosary by Pomarancio il Vecchio (Niccolo Cercignani)(d. 1597) — A1101

650 l, The Miracle of Ostia, by Paolo de Dono Uccello (1397-1475).

1997, July 19   Photo. Perf. 13½x14
2164 A1101 450 l multicolored   .75   .35
       Size: 26x37mm
2165 A1101 650 l multicolored   1.00   .50

Varia di Palmi Festival — A1102

1997, Aug. 2   Perf. 13½x14
2166 A1102 800 l multicolored   1.25   .60

Universiade 97, Sicily
A1103

1997, Aug. 19   Photo. Perf. 14x13½
2167 A1103 450 l Basketball   .75   .35
2168 A1103 800 l High jump   1.25   .60

Antonio Rosmini (1797-1855), Priest, Philosopher — A1104

1997, Aug. 26
2169 A1104 800 l multicolored   1.25   .60

Motion Picture Type of 1995
#2170, Pietro Germi in "The Railway Man."
#2171, Anna Magnani in "Mamma Roma."
#2172, Ugo Tognazzi in "My Dear Friends."

Photo. & Engr.
1997, Aug. 27   Perf. 13½x14
2170 A1027 800 l multicolored   1.25   .60
2171 A1027 800 l multicolored   1.25   .60
2172 A1027 800 l multicolored   1.25   .60
       Nos. 2170-2172 (3)   3.75 1.80

Viareggio Literary Prize
A1106

1997, Aug. 30   Photo. Perf. 14x13½
2173 A1106 4000 l multicolored   6.50 3.25

Intl. Fair, Bolzano
A1107

1997, Sept. 1
2174 A1107 800 l multicolored   1.25   .60

A1108

Artifacts and Paintings from Natl. Museums and Galleries: 450 l, Bronze head, 500BC, National Museum, Reggio Calabria. 650 l, Madonna and Child with Two Vases of Roses, by Ercole di Roberti, Natl. Picture Gallery, Ferrara. 800 l, Miniature of troubadour, Sordello da Goito, Arco Palace Museum, Manta. 900 l, St. George and the Dragon, Vitale da Bologna, Natl. Picture Gallery, Bologna.

1997, Sept. 13   Photo. Perf. 13½x14
2175 A1108 450 l multicolored   .75   .35
2176 A1108 650 l multicolored   1.00   .50
2177 A1108 800 l multicolored   1.25   .60
2178 A1108 900 l multicolored   1.50   .75
       Nos. 2175-2178 (4)   4.50 2.20

Pope Paul VI (1897-1978)
A1109

1997, Sept. 26   Engr. Perf. 13x14
2179 A1109 4000 l dark blue   6.50 3.25

Milan Fair
A1110

1997, Sept. 30   Photo. Perf. 14x13
2180 A1110 800 l multicolored   1.25   .60

Marshall Plan, 50th Anniv. — A1111

1997, Oct. 17
2181 A1111 800 l multicolored   1.25   .60

Christmas
A1112

Nativity scenes: 800 l, Molded polychrome, from Church of St. Francis, Leonessa. 900 l, Fresco, from Baglioni Chapel, St. Mother Mary Church, Spello.

1997, Oct. 18
2183 A1112 800 l multicolored   1.25   .60
2184 A1112 900 l multicolored   1.50   .25

Aristide Merloni (1897-1970)
A1113

1997, Oct. 24   Perf. 13x14
2185 A1113 800 l multicolored   1.25   .60

Giovanni Battista Cavalcaselle (1819-97), Art Historian
A1114

Litho. & Engr.
1997, Oct. 31   Perf. 13½x14
2186 A1114 800 l multicolored   1.25   .60

Philately Day — A1115

1997, Dec. 5   Photo.
2187 A1115 800 l multicolored   1.25   .60

Emigration of Italian Population of
Dalmatia, Istria & Fiume, 50th Anniv.
A1116

1997, Dec. 6   *Perf. 14x13½*
2188 A1116 800 l multicolored   1.25   .60

State
Highway
Police,
50th Anniv.
A1117

1997, Dec. 12
2189 A1117 800 l multicolored   1.25   .60

Constitution, 50th
Anniv. — A1118

1998, Jan. 2   Photo.   *Perf. 13½x14*
2190 A1118 800 l multicolored   1.25   .60

Hercules
and the
Hydra, by
Antonio Del
Pollaiolo
(1429-98)
A1119

1998, Jan. 3   *Perf. 14*
2191 A1119 800 l multicolored   1.25   .60
See Nos. 2278, 2319.

Famous
Writers
A1120

450 l, Bertolt Brecht (1898-1956), playwright. 650 l, Federico Garcia Lorca (1898-
1936), poet, dramatist. 800 l, Curzio Malaparte
(Kurt Suckert) (1898-1957), journalist, writer.
900 l, Leonida Repaci (1898-1985), writer.

1998, Feb. 2   *Perf. 14x13½*
2192 A1120 450 l multi   .75   .35
2193 A1120 650 l multi   1.00   .50
2194 A1120 800 l multi   1.25   .60
2195 A1120 900 l multi, vert.   1.50   .75
   Nos. 2192-2195 (4)   4.50 2.20

Verona
Fair, Cent.
A1121

1998, Feb. 11   Photo.   *Perf. 14x13½*
2196 A1121 800 l multicolored   1.25   .60

Jewish Emancipation, 150th
Anniv. — A1122

1998, Mar. 28   *Perf. 14*
2197 A1122 800 l multicolored   1.25   .60

National Festivals
A1123

1998, Apr. 3   Litho.   *Perf. 13½x14*
2198 A1123 800 l Umbria Jazz   1.25   .60
2199 A1123 900 l Giffoni Film   1.50   .75
     Europa.

Completion of "The Last Supper," by
Leonardo da Vinci (1452-1519), 500th
Anniv. — A1124

1998, Apr. 4   Engr.   *Perf. 14x13½*
2200 A1124 800 l red brown   1.25   .60

Gaetano Donizetti (1797-1848),
Composer — A1125

1998, Apr. 8   Photo.
2201 A1125 800 l multicolored   1.25   .60

Italian Opera,
400th
Anniv. — A1126

1998, Apr. 8   *Perf. 13½x14*
2202 A1126 800 l multicolored   1.25   .60

Cathedral of
Turin, 500th
anniv., and
Shroud of
Turin — A1127

1998, Apr. 18   Photo.   *Perf. 13½x14*
2203 A1127 800 l multicolored   1.25   .60

Tourism
A1128

#2204, Castle, Otranto. #2205, Mori Foun-
tain and Castle, Marino. #2206, Village and
chapel, Livigno. #2207, Marciana Marina, Elba
Island.

1998, Apr. 18   Litho.   *Perf. 14x13½*
2204 A1128 800 l multicolored   1.25   .60
2205 A1128 800 l multicolored   1.25   .60
2206 A1128 800 l multicolored   1.25   .60
2207 A1128 800 l multicolored   1.25   .60
   Nos. 2204-2207 (4)   5.00 2.40
     See Nos. 2283-2286.

Sardinia
Intl. Fair
A1129

1998, Apr. 23   Photo.   *Perf. 14x13½*
2208 A1129 800 l multicolored   1.25   .60

The Charge of
Carabinieri at
Pastrengo, by
Sebastiano de
Albertis (1828-97)
A1130

1998, Apr. 30   *Perf. 13½x14*
2209 A1130 800 l multicolored   1.25   .60

A1131

1998, May 11   Photo.   *Perf. 13½x14*
2210 A1131 800 l Padua Fair   1.25   .60

Juventus, 1997-
98 Italian Soccer
Champions
A1132

1998, May 18
2211 A1132 800 l multicolored   1.25   .60

Polytechnical School, Turin — A1133

1998, May 18   Engr.   *Perf. 14x13½*
2212 A1133 800 l dark blue   1.25   .60

World Food
Program — A1134

1998, May 22   Photo.
2213 A1134 900 l multicolored   1.50   .75

4th Intl. Convention on Fossils,
Evolution, and Environment,
Pergola — A1135

1998, May 30   Photo.   *Perf. 14x13½*
2214 A1135 800 l multicolored   1.25   .60

Carthusian
Monastery
of Santa
Maria di
Pesio,
825th
Anniv.
A1136

1998, May 30
2215 A1136 800 l multicolored   1.25   .60

A1137

1998, June 2   *Perf. 13½x14*
2216 A1137 800 l multicolored   1.25   .60
Honoring the fallen of the Italian police
corps.

6th World
Congress of
Endoscopic
Surgery — A1138

1998, June 3
2217 A1138 900 l multicolored   1.50   .75

Italian Museums
A1139

#2218, Regional Archeological Museum, Agrigento. #2219, Natl. Museum of the Risorgimento, Turin. #2220, Peggy Guggenheim Collection, Venier Dei Leoni Palace, Venice.

1998, June 6   Perf. 13½x14, 14x13½
2218 A1139 800 l multi   1.25 .60
2219 A1139 800 l multi, horiz. 1.25 .60
2220 A1139 800 l multi, horiz. 1.25 .60
      Nos. 2218-2220 (3)   3.75 1.80

A1140

1998, June 13   Perf. 13½x14
2221 A1140 800 l Vicenza Fair 1.25 .60

Giacomo Leopardi (1798-1837),
Poet — A1141

1998, June 29 Photo. Perf. 14x13½
2222 A1141 800 l dark brn & sep 1.25 .60

Women in
Art — A1142

Paintings: 100 l, "Young Velca," Etruscan tomb. 450 l, Detail from, "Herod's Feast," by Filippo Lippi. 650 l, Woman in profile, by Fra Benci. 800 l, "Lady with the Unicorn," by Raphael. 1000 l, sculpture of Constanza Buonarelli, by Gian Lorenzo Bernini.

1998, July 8   Photo.   Perf. 14x13½
2223 A1142 100 l blk & multi   .20   .20
2224 A1142 450 l vio & multi   .75   .35
2225 A1142 650 l gray grn &
                     multi   1.00 .50
Engr.
Wmk. 303
2226 A1142 800 l red brn &
                     multi   1.25 .60
2227 A1142 1000 l grn bl & multi 1.60 .80
      Nos. 2223-2227 (5)   4.80 2.45

Denominated in Lira and Euros
1999, Jan. 28 Photo. Perf. 14x13½
2228 A1142 100 l blk & multi   .20   .20
2229 A1142 450 l vio & multi   .70   .35
2230 A1142 650 l gray grn &
                     multi   .95   .45
Engr.
Wmk. 303
2231 A1142 800 l red brn &
                     multi   1.10 .55
2232 A1142 1000 l grn bl & multi 1.50 .75
      Nos. 2228-2232 (5)   4.45 2.30
      See Nos. 2436-2453.

33rd World
Baseball
Cup
A1143

1998, July 21   Photo.   Unwmk.
2251 A1143 900 l multicolored 1.50 .75

Columbus' Landing in Venezuela and
Exploration of Amerigo Vespucci,
500th Anniv.
A1144

1998, Aug. 12
2252 A1144 1300 l multicolored 2.10 1.00
      See Venezuela No. 1595.

Riccione Intl.
Stamp Fair, 50th
Anniv. — A1145

1998, Aug. 28   Perf. 13½x14
2253 A1145 800 l multicolored 1.25 .60

Mother
Teresa
(1910-97)
A1146

1998, Sept. 5   Perf. 14x13½, 13½x14
2254 A1146 800 l shown   1.25 .60
2255 A1146 900 l Portrait, vert. 1.50 .75
      See Albania Nos. 2578-2579.

Father Pio da Pietrelcina (1887-
1968) — A1147

1998, Sept. 23 Engr.   Perf. 14x13½
2256 A1147 800 l deep blue   1.25 .60

1998 World Equestrian
Championships, Rome — A1148

1998, Oct. 2   Photo.   Perf. 14x13½
2257 A1148 4000 l multicolored 6.50 3.25

School of Higher Education in
Telecommunications, Rome — A1149

1998, Oct. 9   Engr.   Perf. 14x13½
2258 A1149 800 l deep blue   1.25 .60

Italia '98, Intl. Philatelic
Exhibition — A1150

1998, Oct. 23   Photo.   Perf. 14
2259 A1150 800 l Pope John
                    Paul II   1.25 .60
      See San Marino No. 1430 and Vatican City
No. 1085.

Armed
Forces Day
A1151

Emblem from branch of the military and: No. 2260, Aircraft carrier "Giuseppe Garibaldi," Navy. No. 2261, Eurofighter 2000, Air Force. No. 2262, Officer, Carabinieri (police force), vert. No. 2263, Italian monument, El Alamein battlefield, vert.

Perf. 14x13½, 13½x14
1998, Oct. 24   Photo.
2260 A1151 800 l multicolored 1.25 .60
2261 A1151 800 l multicolored 1.25 .60
2262 A1151 800 l multicolored 1.25 .60
2263 A1151 800 l multicolored 1.25 .60
      Nos. 2260-2263 (4)   5.00 2.40

Nos. 2260-2263 were printed se-tenant with Italia '98 label. Air Force, 75th anniv. (#2261).

Art Day — A1152

1998, Oct. 25   Perf. 13½x14
2264 A1152 800 l Dionysus   1.25 .60
      Italia '98.

Enzo Ferrari (1898-1988) Automobile
Manufacturer — A1153

a, 1931 Bobbio-Passo del Penice. b, 1952 Ferrari F1. c, 1963 Ferrari GTO. d, 1998 Ferrari F1.

1998, Oct. 26   Litho.   Perf. 13½
2265 A1153 800 l Sheet of 4,
                    #a.-d.   5.25 2.50
      Italia '98.

Universal Declaration of Human
Rights, 50th Anniv. — A1154

1998, Oct. 27 Photo. Perf. 14x13½
2266 A1154 1400 l multicolored 2.25 1.10
      Printed se-tenant with a label. Italia '98.

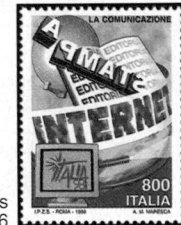

Europe
Day — A1155

1998, Oct. 28   Perf. 13½x14
2267 A1155 800 l multicolored 1.25 .60
Die Cut Perf. 11
Self-Adhesive
Booklet Stamp
2268 A1155 800 l multicolored 1.25 .60
  a.   Booklet pane of 6   7.50
        Complete booklet, #2268a 7.50

Motion Picture Type of 1995

Motion pictures, stars: 450 l, "Ti Conosco Mascherina," Eduardo de Filippo. 800 l, "Fantasmi a Roma," Antonio Pietrangeli. 900 l, "Il Signor Max," Mario Camerini.

1998, Oct. 29   Litho. & Engr.
2269 A1027 450 l multicolored   .75 .35
2270 A1027 800 l multicolored 1.25 .60
2271 A1027 900 l multicolored 1.50 .75
      Nos. 2269-2271 (3)   3.50 1.70

Nos. 2269-2271 each printed se-tenant with label. Italia '98.

Communications
Day — A1156

1998, Oct. 31   Photo.
2272 A1156 800 l multicolored 1.25 .60

Souvenir Sheet

Stamp Day — A1157

Illustration reduced.

1998, Nov. 1   Litho.
2273 A1157 4000 l multicolored 6.50 3.25
      Italia '98.

Christmas
A1158

800 l, Sculpture, "The Epiphany," Church of St. Mark, Seminara, vert. 900 l, Adoration of the shepherds, drawing by Giulio Romano.

Perf. 13½x14, 14x13½

1998, Nov. 28			Engr.
2274	A1158	800 l deep blue	1.25	.60
2275	A1158	900 l brown	1.50	.75

The Ecstasy of St. Teresa, Sculpture by Gian Lorenzo Bernini — A1159

1998, Dec. 1	Photo.	Perf. 13½x14
2276	A1159	900 l multicolored	1.50	.75

Emancipation of Valdesi, 150th Anniv. — A1160

1998, Dec. 4		Perf. 14
2277	A1160	800 l multicolored	1.25	.60

Art Type of 1998

Conception of Space, by Lucio Fontana (1899-1968).

1999, Feb. 19	Photo.	Perf. 14
2278	A1119	450 l multicolored	.75	.35

National Parks
A1162

Europa: 800 l, Wolf, Calabria, vert. 900 l, Birds, Tuscan Archipelago.

Perf. 13¼x14, 14x13¼

1999, Mar. 12		Photo.
2279	A1162	800 l multicolored	1.25	.60
2280	A1162	900 l multicolored	1.50	.75

Holy Year 2000 — A1163

1999, Mar. 13		Perf. 13¼x13¾
2281	A1163	1400 l Holy Door	2.25	1.10

St. Egidio Church, Cellere
A1164

1999, Apr. 10	Engr.	Perf. 13¾x13½
2282	A1164	800 l brown lake	1.25	.60

Tourism Type of 1998

#2283, Earthen pyramids, Segonzano. #2284, Waterfalls, river, Terni. #2285, Buildings, Lecce. #2286, Walls around Lipari.

1999, Apr. 17	Photo.	Perf. 14x13¼
2283	A1128	800 l multicolored	1.25	.60
2284	A1128	800 l multicolored	1.25	.60
2285	A1128	800 l multicolored	1.25	.60
2286	A1128	800 l multicolored	1.25	.60
	Nos. 2283-2286 (4)		5.00	2.40

Museums
A1165

#2287, Swan on Lake, Casina della Civette, Rome. #2288, "Iulia Bela," International Ceramics Museaum, Faenza, vert. #2289, Bells, Marinelli Historic Bell Museum, Agnone.

Perf. 14x13¼, 13¼x14

1999, Apr. 17		Photo.
2287	A1165	800 l multicolored	1.25	.60
2288	A1165	800 l multicolored	1.25	.60
2289	A1165	800 l multicolored	1.25	.60
	Nos. 2287-2289 (3)		3.75	1.80

Constitutional Court — A1166

Perf. 13¾x13¼

1999, Apr. 23		Photo.
2290	A1166	800 l multicolored	1.25	.60

Natl. Firefighting Service
A1167

1999, Apr. 29		
2291	A1167	800 l multicolored	1.25	.60

Military Academy of Modena — A1168

1999, May 3	Photo.	Perf. 13¼x14
2292	A1168	800 l multicolored	1.25	.60

50th Anniv. of Death of Grande Torino Soccer Team in Airplane Crash
A1169

1999, May 4	Photo.	Perf. 14x13¼
2293	A1169	800 l Plane, team members	1.25	.60
2294	A1169	900 l Superga Basilica, names	1.50	.75

Council of Europe, 50th Anniv.
A1170

1999, May 5	Photo.	Perf. 14x13¼
2295	A1170	800 l multicolored	1.25	.60

Milan, 1998-99 Italian Soccer Champions
A1171

1999, June 7	Photo.	Perf. 13¼x14
2296	A1171	800 l multicolored	1.25	.60

Elections for European Parliament, 20th Anniv.
A1172

1999, June 10	Photo.	Perf. 14x13¼
2297	A1172	800 l multicolored	1.25	.60

Priority Mail
A1173

Typo. & Silk-screened
1999, June 14		Die Cut 11¼

Self-Adhesive

2298	A1173	1200 l multicolored	2.00	1.00
a.		Bklt. pane of 4 + 4 etiquettes	8.00	
		Complete booklet, #2298a	8.00	
b.		Bklt. pane of 8, no etiquettes	16.00	
		Complete booklet, #2298b	16.00	

No. 2298 was intended for Priority Mail service. Self-adhesive blue etiquettes to be used with each stamp on mail were provided on the sheets and in booklets of 4 stamps.
The backing paper from the sheet stamps is rouletted, while the backing paper in the booklets is not.
See No. 2324.

Fausto Coppi (1919-60), Cyclist
A1174

1999, June 12	Photo.	Perf. 14x13¼
2299	A1174	800 l multi	1.25	.60

Fiat Automobile Co., Cent. — A1175

1999, July 10	Photo.	Perf. 13¼x14
2300	A1175	4800 l multi	7.75	3.75

Statue of Our Lady of the Snows, Mt. Rocciamelone, Cent. — A1176

1999, July 19		
2301	A1176	800 l multi	1.25	.60

Eleonora de Fonseca Pimentel (1752-1799), Writer — A1177

1999, Aug. 20		Perf. 14x13¼
2302	A1177	800 l multi	1.25	.60

30th World Canoe Championships — A1178

1999, Aug. 26		
2303	A1178	900 l multi	1.50	.75

Johann Wolfgang von Goethe (1749-1832), German Poet — A1179

1999, Aug. 28		
2304	A1179	4000 l multi	6.50	3.00

World Cycling Championships
A1180

1999, Sept. 15	Photo.	Perf. 13¼x14
2305	A1180	1400 l multi	2.25	1.10

Stamp
Day — A1181

1999, Sept. 25 Photo. Perf. 13¼x14
2306 A1181 800 l multi   1.25 .60

Basilica of St. Francis, Assisi — A1182

Litho. & Engr.
1999, Sept. 25 Perf. 14x13¼
2307 A1182 800 l multi   1.25 .60

Giuseppe Parini
(1729-99),
Poet — A1183

1999, Oct. 2 Engr. Perf. 13¼x14
2308 A1183 800 l blue gray   1.25 .60

Alessandro
Volta's Pile,
Bicent. — A1184

1999, Oct. 11 Photo.
2309 A1184 3000 l multi   5.00 2.25

UPU,
125th
Anniv.
A1185

1999, Oct. 18 Perf. 14x13¼
2310 A1185 900 l multi   1.50 .70

Goffredo Mameli (1827-49), Lyricist of
Natl. Anthem, Nos. 506, 518 — A1186

1999, Oct. 22 Perf. 14
2311 A1186 1500 l multi   2.40 1.10

"Stamps, Our Friends" — A1187

Various abstract designs: a, 450 l. b, 650 l.
c, 800 l. d, 1000 l.

1999, Oct. 23 Perf. 13¼x14
2312 A1187 Sheet of 4, #a.-d.   4.75 2.25

A1188

1999, Nov. 4
2313 A1188 900 l 1899 Military
     Conscript   1.50 .70

Christmas
A1189

Designs: 800 l, Santa Claus, reindeer and
sleigh. 1000 l, Nativity, By Dosso Dossi.

1999, Nov. 5 Photo.
2314 A1189 800 l multi   1.25 .60
2315 A1189 1000 l multi   1.60 .75
   See Finland Nos. 1117-1119.

Holy Year
2000
A1190

#2316, Map by Conrad Peutinger, 1507.
#2317, 18th cent. print of pilgrims in Rome.
#2318, Bas-relief, facade of Fidenza Duomo.

1999, Nov. 24 Photo. Perf. 14x13¼
2316 A1190 1000 l multi   1.60 .75
2317 A1190 1000 l multi   1.60 .75
2318 A1190 1000 l multi   1.60 .75
     Nos. 2316-2318 (3)   4.80 2.25

Art Type of 1998
Design: Restless Leopard, by Antonio
Ligabue (1899-1965), horiz.

1999, Nov. 27 Photo. Perf. 14
2319 A1119 1000 l multi   1.60 .75

Schools
A1191

Designs: 450 l, State Institute of Art, Urbino.
650 l, Normal Superior School, Pisa.

1999, Nov. 27 Engr. Perf. 14x13¼
2320 A1191 450 l black   .75 .35
2321 A1191 650 l brown   1.00 .45

Year 2000
A1192

1999, Nov. 27 Photo.
2322 A1192 4800 l multi   7.75 3.50

Souvenir Sheet

Millennium — A1193

Designs: a, The past. b, The future.

2000, Jan. 1 Litho. Perf. 14x13¼
2323 A1193 Sheet of 2   6.50 6.50
a.-b.   A1193 2000 l Any single   3.25 1.50
   See #2330-2332, 2365-2366.

**Priority Mail Type of 1999 Redrawn
With Yellow Rectangle at Center
Typo. & Silk-Screened**
2000, Jan. 10 Die Cut 11¼
Self-Adhesive
2324 A1173 1200 l multi   2.00 .90
   No. 2324 was intended for Priority Mail service. A self-adhesive blue etiquette is adjacent
to the stamp. See No. 2393 for similar stamp
with Posta Prioritaria in lower case letters.

First Performance of Opera "Tosca,"
Cent. — A1194

Litho. & Engr.
2000, Jan. 14 Perf. 14x13¼
2325 A1194 800 l multi   1.25 .50

Basilica of St.
Paul — A1195

2000, Jan. 18 Photo. Perf. 13¼x14
2326 A1195 1000 l multi   1.60 .70
   Holy Year 2000.

Six Nation Rugby
Tournament — A1196

2000, Feb. 5 Perf. 14x13¼
2327 A1196 800 l multi   1.25 .50

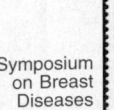

5th Symposium
on Breast
Diseases
A1197

2000, Feb. 12 Perf. 13¼x14
2328 A1197 800 l shown   1.25 .50
2329 A1197 1000 l Woman hold-
     ing rose   1.60 .70

Millennium Type of 2000
Souvenir Sheet
No. 2330: a, Art. b, Science.
No. 2331: a, Nature. b, The city.
No. 2332: a, Generations. b, Space.

2000 Litho. Perf. 14x13¼
2330 Sheet of 2   2.50 2.50
a.-b. A1193 800 l Any single   1.25 .50
2331 Sheet of 2   2.50 2.50
a.-b. A1193 800 l Any single   1.25 .50
2332 Sheet of 2   2.50 2.50
a.-b. A1193 800 l Any single   1.25 .50
   Issued: #2330, 3/4; #2331, 5/4; #2332, 7/4.

Skiing World
Cup — A1198

2000, Mar. 7 Photo. Perf. 13¼x14
2333 A1198 4800 l multi   7.75 3.50

Souvenir Sheet

Italian Design — A1199

Household furnishings designed by:
a, Achille & Pier Giacomo Castiglioni, Ettore
Sottsass, Jr. Carlo Bartoli, Aldo Rossi. b,
Mario Bellini, Alessandro Mendini, Vico Magis-
tretti, Alberto Meda & Paolo Rizzatto. c, Gio
Ponti, Gatti Paolini Teodoro, Massimo Morozzi,
Tobia Scarpa. d, Pietro Chiesa, Joe Colombo,
Cini Boeri & Tomu Katayanagi, Lodovico
Acerbis & Giotto Stoppino. e, Gaetano Pesce,
Antonio Citterio & Oliver Loew, Enzo Mari, De
Pas D'Urbino Lomazzi. f, Marco Zanuso, Anna
Castelli Ferrieri, Michele de Lucchi & Gian-
carlo Fassina, Bruno Munari.

2000, Mar. 9 Litho. Perf. 13¼
2334 Sheet of 6   7.50 7.50
a.-f. A1199 800 l Any single   1.25 .50

Holy Year
2000
A1200

Paintings depicting the life of Jesus:
450 l, The Adoration of the Shepherds, by
Ghirlandaio. 650 l, The Baptism and Temptation of Christ, by Veronese, vert. 800 l, The
Last Supper, by Ghirlandaio, vert. 1000 l,
Fresco from Episodes of the Life of the Virgin
Mary and Christ, by Giotto. 1200 l, The Resurrection of Christ, by Piero della Francesca,
vert.

Perf. 14x13¼, 13¼x14

2000, Mar. 10   Litho.
2335	A1200	450 l multi	.75	.35
2336	A1200	650 l multi	1.00	.40
2337	A1200	800 l multi	1.25	.50
2338	A1200	1000 l multi	1.60	.70
2339	A1200	1200 l multi	2.00	.90

Nos. 2335-2339 (5)   6.60 2.85

La Civiltá Cattolica, 150th Anniv. A1201

2000, Apr. 6   Photo.   *Perf. 14x13¼*
2340   A1201   800 l multi   1.25   .55

San Giuseppe de Merode College, Rome, 150th Anniv. A1202

2000, Apr. 8
2341   A1202   800 l multi   1.25   .55

Intl. Cycling Union, Cent. — A1203

2000, Apr. 14   Photo.   *Perf. 13¼x14*
2342   A1203   1500 l multi   2.40 1.00

Tourism — A1204

Designs: No. 2343, Terre di Franciacorta, Brescia. No. 2344, Dunarobba Petrified Forest, Avigliano Umbro. No. 2345, Ercolano. No. 2346, Bella di Taormina Island.

2000, Apr. 14   *Perf. 14x13¼*
2343	A1204	800 l multi	1.25	.50
2344	A1204	800 l multi	1.25	.50
2345	A1204	800 l multi	1.25	.50
2346	A1204	800 l multi	1.25	.50

Nos. 2343-2346 (4)   5.00 2.00

Little Holy Society, Caltanissetta — A1205

2000, Apr. 19
2347   A1205   800 l multi   1.25   .50

Niccolò Piccinni (1728-1800), Opera Composer A1206

2000, May 6   *Perf. 13¼x14*
2348   A1206   4000 l multi   6.50 2.75

Europa, 2000
Common Design Type

2000, May 9
2349   CD17   800 l multi   1.25   .50

Post and Telecommunications Historical Museum — A1207

No. 2350, Ship, telecommunications equipment. No. 2351, #19, 20.

2000, May 9   Litho.   *Perf. 14x13¼*
2350	A1207	800 l multi	1.25	.50
2351	A1207	800 l multi	1.25	.50

Lazio, 1999-2000 Soccer Champions A1208

2000, May 20   Photo.   *Perf. 13¼x14*
2352   A1208   800 l multi   1.25   .50

Monza Cathedral A1209

2000, May 31
2353   A1209   800 l multi   1.25   .50

Rome, Headquarters of UN Food and Agriculture Agencies A1210

2000, June 17   Photo.   *Perf. 13¼x14*
2354   A1210   1000 l multi   1.60   .70

Jesus the Redeemer Monument, Nuoro, Cent. — A1211

2000, June 24
2355   A1211   800 l multi   1.25   .50

Società Italiana per Condotte d'Acqua, Construction Company, 120th Anniv. — A1212

2000, June 28   *Perf. 14x13¼*
2356   A1212   800 l multi   1.25   .50

Stampin' the Future Children's Stamp Design Contest Winner — A1213

2000, July 7   *Perf. 13¼x14*
2357   A1213   1000 l multi   1.60   .70

Archery World Championships, Campagna A1214

2000, July 8
2358   A1214   1500 l multi   2.40 1.00

World Cycling Championships A1215

2000, July 31   Photo.   *Perf. 13¼x14*
2359   A1215   800 l multi   1.25   .50

Madonna and Child, by Carlo Crivelli A1216

Sant'Orso Fair, 1000th Anniv. A1217

Litho. & Engr.

2000, Aug. 8   *Perf. 14*
2360   A1216   800 l multi   1.25   .50

2000, Aug. 8   Photo.   *Perf. 14x13¼*
2361   A1217   1000 l multi   1.60   .70

18th World Congress of Transplantation Society A1218

2000, Aug. 26   Photo.   *Perf. 13¼x14*
2362   A1218   1000 l multi   1.60   .70

2000 Summer Olympics, Sydney — A1219

Designs: 800 l, Celebrating athlete, Olympic stadium, Sydney. 1000 l, Myron's Discobolus, Sydney skyline.

2000, Sept. 1
2363	A1219	800 l multi	1.25	.50
2364	A1219	1000 l multi	1.60	.70

Millennium Type of 2000
Souvenir Sheet

No. 2365, vert.: a, War. b, Peace.

2000   Litho.   *Perf. 13¼x14*
2365		Sheet of 2	2.50	2.50
a.-b.	A1193	800 l Any single	1.25	.50

Issued: No. 2365, 9/4.

Millennium Type of 2000

No. 2366: a, Meditation. b, Expression.

2000, Nov. 4   Litho.   *Perf. 14x13¼*
2366		Sheet of 2	2.50	2.50
a.-b.	A1193	800 l Any single	1.25	.50

Issued: No. 2366, 11/4.

Battle of Marengo, Bicent. — A1220

2000, Sept. 8   Photo.   *Perf. 13¼x14*
2367   A1220   800 l multi   1.25   .50

Fellini Film
Year — A1221

2000, Sept. 20 Photo. Perf. 13¼x14
2368 A1221 800 l multi   1.25 .50

Philately
Day
A1222

2000, Sept. 23 Photo. Perf. 14x13¼
2369 A1222 800 l multi   1.25 .50

Father Luigi Maria Monti (1825-
1900) — A1223

2000, Sept. 30 Photo. Perf. 14x13¼
2370 A1223 800 l multi   1.25 .50

Antonio Salieri
(1750-1825),
Composer
A1224

2000, Sept. 30   Perf. 13¼x14
2371 A1224 4800 l multi   7.75 3.25

2000
Paralympics,
Sydney — A1225

2000, Oct. 2 Photo. Perf. 13¼x14
2372 A1225 1500 l multi   2.40 1.10

World Mathematics Year — A1226

2000, Oct. 14 Photo. Perf. 14x13¼
2373 A1226 800 l multi   1.25 .50

Voluntarism
A1227

2000, Oct. 18   Perf. 13¼x14
2374 A1227 800 l multi   1.25 .50

Giordano Bruno (1548-1600),
Philosopher — A1228

2000, Oct. 20   Perf. 14x13¼
2375 A1228 800 l multi   1.25 .50

Madonna
and Child,
by Luca
Della
Robbia
A1229

Litho. & Engr.
2000, Oct. 25   Perf. 14
2376 A1229 800 l multi   1.25 .50

Accademia
Roveretana Degli
Agiati, 250th
Anniv. — A1230

2000, Oct. 26 Photo. Perf. 13¼x14
2377 A1230 800 l multi   1.25 .50

Gaetano Martino (1900-67),
Statesman — A1231

2000, Nov. 3   Photo.   Perf. 14
2378 A1231 800 l multi   1.25 .50

Perseus, by Benvenuto Cellini (1500-
71), Sculptor — A1232

Litho. & Engr.
2000, Nov. 3   Perf. 14
2379 A1232 1200 l multi   2.00 .85

Schools
A1233

Designs: 800 l, Camerino University. 1000 l,
Calabria University, Cosenza.

2000, Nov. 6 Engr. Perf. 14x13¼
2380 A1233 800 l blue   1.25 .50
2381 A1233 1000 l blue   1.60 .70

Christmas
A1234

Designs: 800 l, Snowflakes. 1000 l, Creche,
Matera Cathedral, horiz.

Perf. 13¼x14, 14x13¼
2000, Nov. 6   Photo.
2382 A1234 800 l multi   1.25 .50
2383 A1234 1000 l multi   1.60 .70

World
Snowboarding
Championships
A1235

2001, Jan. 15 Photo. Perf. 13¼x14
2384 A1235 1000 l multi   1.60 .70

The Annunciation, by
Botticelli — A1236

2001, Jan. 18   Perf. 14
2385 A1236 1000 l multi   1.60 .70
Exhibit of Italian art at Natl. Museum of
Western Art, Tokyo.

Souvenir Sheet

Opera Composers — A1237

No. 2386: a, Vincenzo Bellini (1801-35). b,
Domenico Cimarosa (1749-1801). c, Gaspare
Luigi Pacifico Spontini (1774-1851). d, Giu-
seppe Verdi (1813-1901).

2001, Jan. 27 Litho. Perf. 13¼x14
2386 A1237 Sheet of 4   5.00 5.00
a.-d.   800 l Any single   1.25 .50

St. Rose of Viterbo
(1235-1252)
A1238

2001, Mar. 6 Photo. Perf. 13¼x14
2387 A1238 800 l multi   1.25 .50

Souvenir Sheet

Ferrari, 2000 Formula 1 World
Champions — A1239

2001, Mar. 9 Litho. Perf. 14x13¼
2388 A1239 5000 l multi   8.25 8.25

Santa Maria Abbey, Sylvis — A1240

2001, Mar. 10 Engr. Perf. 14
2389 A1240 800 l blue   1.25 .50

Postage Stamp
Sesquicentennials — A1241

Designs: No. 2390, Tuscany #1. No. 2391, Sardinia #1. No. 2392, Lombardy-Venetia #1.

2001, Mar. 31 Photo. Perf. 13¼x14
2390 A1241 800 l multi   1.25   .50
2391 A1241 800 l multi   1.25   .50
2392 A1241 800 l multi   1.25   .50
    Nos. 2390-2392 (3)   3.75 1.50

Priority Mail
A1242

**Serpentine Die Cut 11
Typo & Silk Screened
2001, Apr. 10
Self-Adhesive**
2393 A1242 1200 l multi   2.00   .85
  a.   Booklet pane of 4 + 4 eti-
       quettes   8.00
       Booklet. #2393a   8.00

Compare with No. 2324. No. 2393 was intended for Priority Mail service. A self-adhesive blue etiquette is adjacent to the stamp.
    See Nos. 2466-2471, 2582-2585B, 2613A-2615, 2691A-2691B.

Tourism
A1243

2001, Apr. 14 Photo. Perf. 14x13¼
2394 A1243 800 l Stintino   1.25   .50
2395 A1243 800 l Comacchio   1.25   .50
2396 A1243 800 l Diamante   1.25   .50
2397 A1243 800 l Pioraco   1.25   .50
    Nos. 2394-2397 (4)   5.00 2.00

Nature and the
Environment
A1244

Designs: 450 l, Campanula. 650 l, Marmots. 800 l, Storks. 1000 l, World Day Against Desertification.

2001, Apr. 21 Perf. 13¼x14
2398 A1244 450 l multi   .75   .35
2399 A1244 650 l multi   1.00   .40
2400 A1244 800 l multi   1.25   .50
2401 A1244 1000 l multi   1.60   .70
    Nos. 2398-2401 (4)   4.60 1.95

General
Agricultural
Confederation
A1245

2001, Apr. 24 Photo. Perf. 13¼x14
2402 A1245 800 l multi   1.25   .50

Gorizia,
1000th
Anniv.
A1246

2001, Apr. 28 Perf. 14x13¼
2403 A1246 800 l multi   1.25   .50

Europa
A1247

2001, May 4 Photo. Perf. 14x13¼
2404 A1247 800 l multi   1.25   .50

European Union's Charter of
Fundamental Rights — A1248

2001, May 9 Photo. Perf. 14x13¼
2405 A1248 800 l multi   1.25   .50

2001, May 9 Photo. Perf. 13¼x14
2406 A1249 800 l multi   1.25   .50

Order of the
Knights of Labor,
Cent. — A1249

Workplace Injury
Memorial
Day — A1250

2001, May 19
2407 A1250 800 l multi   1.25   .50

Art and
Student
Creativity
Day
A1251

Children's art by: No. 2408, Lucia Catena. No. 2409, Luigi Di Cristo. No. 2410, Barbara Grilli. No. 2411, Rita Vergari, vert.

2001, May 26 Perf. 13¼x14, 14x13¼
2408 A1251 800 l multi   1.25   .50
2409 A1251 800 l multi   1.25   .50
2410 A1251 800 l multi   1.25   .50
2411 A1251 800 l multi   1.25   .50
    Nos. 2408-2411 (4)   5.00 2.00

Masaccio (1401-28), Painter — A1252

2001, June 1 Perf. 13¼x14
2412 A1252 800 l multi   1.25   .50

Madonna of
Senigallia,
by Piero
della
Francesca
A1253

Litho. & Engr.
2001, June 9 Perf. 14
2413 A1253 800 l multi   1.25   .50

Panathlon
International, 50th
Anniv. — A1254

2001, June 12 Photo. Perf. 13¼x14
2414 A1254 800 l multi   1.25   .50

Republic of San
Marino, 1700th
Anniv. — A1255

2001, June 23
2415 A1255 800 l multi   1.25   .50

Rome, 2000-2001
Soccer
Champions
A1256

2001, June 23 Photo. Perf. 13¼x14
2416 A1256 800 l multi   1.25   .50

Harbormaster's Corps and Coast
Guard — A1257

2001, July 20 Photo. Perf. 14x13¼
2417 A1257 800 l multi   1.25   .50

Salvatore
Quasimodo (1901-68),
Writer — A1258

2001, Aug. 20 Perf. 13¼x14
2418 A1258 1500 l multi   2.40 1.00

Octagonal Room, Domus Aurea
(Golden House of Nero),
Rome — A1259

2001, Aug. 31 Engr. Perf. 14
2419 A1259 1000 l multi   1.60   .70

Italian
Design
A1260

Household furnishings designed by: a, Piero Lissoni, Patricia Urquiola and Anna Bartoli. b, Monica Graffeo and Rodolfo Dordoni. c, Ferruccio Laviani and Massimo Iosa Ghini. d, Anna Gili and Miki Astori. e, Marco Ferreri, M. Cananzi and R. Semprini. f, Stefano Giovannoni and Massimiliano Datti.

2001, Sept. 1 Litho. Perf. 13¼
2420   Sheet of 6   7.50 7.50
  a.-f. A1260 800 l Any single 1.25   .50

Cent. of II Quarto Stato, Painting by
Giuseppe Pellizza da
Volpedo — A1261

2001, Sept. 15 Engr. Perf. 14x13¼
2421 A1261 1000 l brown   1.60   .70

Discovery of
Mummified Man
"Otzi" in Melting
Glacier, 10th
Anniv. — A1262

2001, Sept. 19 Photo. Perf. 13¼x14
2422 A1262 800 l multi   1.25   .50

Stamp Day
A1263

2001, Sept. 22   Perf. 14x13¼
2423 A1263 800 l multi   1.25   .50

Enrico Fermi
(1901-54),
Physicist — A1264

2001, Sept. 29   Perf. 13¼x14
2424 A1264 800 l multi   1.25   .50

Schools
A1265

Designs: No. 2425, Pavia University. No. 2426, Bari University, vert. No. 2427, Camilo Cavour State Science High School, Rome.

Perf. 14x13¼, 13¼x14
2001, Sept. 29   Engr.
2425 A1265 800 l blue   1.25   .50
2426 A1265 800 l red brown   1.25   .50
2427 A1265 800 l Prus blue   1.25   .50
   Nos. 2425-2427 (3)   3.75 1.50

Latin Union
A1266

2001, Oct. 12 Photo.   Perf. 14x13¼
2428 A1266 800 l multi   1.25   .50

Natl. Archaeological Museum,
Taranto — A1267

2001, Oct. 12 Photo.   Perf. 14x13¼
2429 A1267 1000 l multi   1.60   .70

Intl. Food and
Agriculture
Organizations
A1268

Wheat and emblem of: a, Intl. Fund for Agricultural Development. b, Food and Agriculture Organization and farmer (49x27mm). c, World Food Program.

2001, Oct. 16 Photo.   Perf. 14x13¼
2430   Horiz. strip of 3   3.75 3.75
a.-c. A1268 800 l Any single   1.25   .50

Enthroned
Christ and
Angels,
Sancta
Sanctorum,
St. John
Lateran
Basilica
A1269

Litho. & Engr.
2001, Oct. 19   Perf. 14
2431 A1269 800 l multi   1.25   .50

Madonna
and Child,
by Macrino
d'Alba
A1270

2001, Oct. 20
2432 A1270 800 l multi   1.25   .50

A1271

Christmas
A1272

2001, Oct. 30 Photo.   Perf. 14x13¼
2433 A1271 800 l multi   1.25   .50
2434 A1272 1000 l multi   1.60   .70

Souvenir Sheet

Italian Silk Industry — A1273

Silk-screened on Silk
2001, Nov. 29   Imperf.
2435 A1273 5000 l multi   8.25 8.25

100 Cents = 1 Euro (€)
Women in Art Type of 1998 With
Denominations in Euros Only

Designs: 1c, Hebe, sculpture by Antonio Canova. 2c, Profile of woman from Syracuse tetradrachm. 3c, Queen of Sheba from "The Meeting of King Solomon and the Queen of Sheba," painting by Piero della Francesca. 5c, "Young Velca," Etruscan tomb. 10c, Head of terra cotta statue, 3rd cent. BC. 20c, Detail from "Herod's Feast," by Fra Filippo Lippi. 41c, "Lady with the Unicorn," by Raphael. 45c, "Venus of Urbina," by Titian. 50c, "Antea," by Parmigianino. 65c, "Princess of Trebizonde," by Antonio Pisano. 77c, "Primavera," by Botticelli. 85c, "Courtesan," by Vittore Carpaccio.

Perf. 14x13¼, 13¼x13½ (#2447,
2449, 2450, 2452, 2453)
2002-04   Photo.
2436 A1142 1c multi   .20   .20
a.   Perf. 13¼x13½   .20   .20

2437 A1142 2c multi   .20   .20
a.   Perf. 13¼x13½   .20   .20
2438 A1142 3c multi   .20   .20
a.   Perf. 13¼x13½   .20   .20
2440 A1142 5c multi   .20   .20
a.   Perf. 13¼x13½   .20   .20
2441 A1142 10c multi   .25   .20
a.   Perf. 13¼x13½ ('04)   .30   .20
2443 A1142 20c multi   .60   .20
a.   Perf. 13¼x13½   .60   .20
2444 A1142 23c multi   .70   .20

Engr.
Wmk. 303
2446 A1142 41c multi   1.25   .45
a.   Perf. 13¼x13½   1.00   .35
2447 A1142 45c multi   1.40   .55
2448 A1142 50c multi   1.50   .55
a.   Perf. 13¼x13½   1.50   .55
2449 A1142 65c multi   1.90   .70
2450 A1142 70c multi   2.10   .75
2451 A1142 77c multi   2.25   .80
a.   Perf. 13¼x13½   2.25   .80
2452 A1142 85c multi   2.50   .90
2453 A1142 90c multi   2.75 1.00
   Nos. 2436-2453 (15)   18.00 7.05

Issued: 2c, 5c, 10c, 23c, 41c, 50c, No. 2451, 1/1. 1c, 3c, 20c, 3/1; Nos. 2437a, 2438a, 2004; No. 2446a, 2003. No. 2451a, 2004 (?); Nos. 2436a, 2440a, 2448a, 2004; 45c, 1/27/04; 65c, 3/20/04; 85c, 2/17/04; No. 2443a, 2004; 70c, 7/31/04; 90c, 6/26/04; No. 2441a, 2004. This is an expanding set.
No. 2446 was reprinted in 2003 with imprint "I.P.Z.S. S.p.A.-Roma."

Italia — A1274

Perf. 14x13¼, 13¼x13½ (#2460,
2461A, 2462)
2002   Engr.   Unwmk.
2454 A1274 €1 multi   3.00 1.50
2455 A1274 €1.24 multi   3.75 1.75
2457 A1274 €1.55 multi   4.50 2.25
2459 A1274 €2.17 multi   6.50 3.25
2460 A1274 €2.35 multi   7.00 3.50
2461 A1274 €2.58 multi   7.75 3.75
2461A A1274 €2.80 multi   8.50 4.25
2462 A1274 €3 multi   9.00 4.50
2463 A1274 €3.62 multi   10.50 5.25
2465 A1274 €6.20 multi   18.00 10.00
   Nos. 2454-2465 (10)   78.50 39.00

Issued: €1, €1.24, €1.55, €2.17, €2.58, €3.62, 1/2. €6.20, 3/1. Nos. 2436a, 2440a, 2448a, 2004; 45c, 1/27/04; 65c, 3/20/04; 85c, 2/17/04.
Compare Type A1274 with Type A1407.

Priority Mail Type of 2001 with Euro
Denominations Only
Typo. & Silk Screened
2002, Jan. 2   Serpentine Die Cut 11
Self-Adhesive
Background Color
2466 A1242 62c yellow   1.90   .95
   Booklet, 4 #2466   7.50
2467 A1242 77c blue green 2.25 1.10
2468 A1242 €1 blue   3.00 1.50
2469 A1242 €1.24 yel green 3.75 1.75
2470 A1242 €1.86 rose   5.50 2.75
2471 A1242 €4.13 lilac   12.00 6.00
   Nos. 2466-2471 (6)   28.40 14.05

A self-adhesive etiquette is adjacent to each stamp.
No. 2466-2471 were reprinted in 2003 with imprint "I.P.Z.S. S.p.A.-Roma-2003." No. 2468 was reprinted in 2004 with imprint "I.P.Z.S. S.p.A. - Roma - 2004."

Introduction of the Euro — A1275

No. 2472: a, 1285 Venetian ducat. b, 1252 Genoan genovino and Florentine florin.
No. 2473: a, Euro symbol and flags. b, 1946 Italian 1-lira coin and new 1-euro coin. Illustration reduced.

2002, Jan. 2 Photo.   Perf. 14x13¼
2472 A1275 Horiz. pair   2.50   .90
a.-b.   41c Either single 1.25   .45
2473 A1275 Horiz. pair   2.50   .90
a.-b.   41c Either single 1.25   .45

Blessed
Josemaría
Escrivá
(1902-75),
Founder of
Opus Dei
A1276

2002, Jan. 9
2474 A1276 41c multi   1.25   .45

Luigi
Bocconi and
Luigi
Bocconi
Commercial
University,
Milan
A1277

2002, Jan. 24
2475 A1277 41c multi   1.25   .45

Parma Stamps,
150th
Anniv. — A1278

2002, Jan. 26   Perf. 13¼x14
2476 A1278 41c No. 1   1.25   .45

Intl. Year of
Mountains
A1279

2001, Feb. 1
2477 A1279 41c multi   1.25   .45

2006 Winter
Olympics,
Turin — A1280

2002, Feb. 23
2478 A1280 41c multi   1.25   .45

Malato Alla Fonte, Sculpture by
Arnolfo de Cambio — A1281

2002, Mar. 8   Engr.   Perf. 14
2479 A1281 41c red lilac 1.25   .45

Tourism
A1282

Designs: No. 2480, Venaria Reale. No. 2481, San Gimignano. No. 2482, Sannicandro di Bari. No. 2483, Capo d'Orlando.

2002, Mar. 23	Photo.	Perf. 14x13¼		
2480	A1282	41c multi	1.25	.45
2481	A1282	41c multi	1.25	.45
2482	A1282	41c multi	1.25	.45
2483	A1282	41c multi	1.25	.45
	Nos. 2480-2483 (4)		5.00	1.80

See Nos. 2598-2600.

Santa Maria Della Grazie Sanctuary, Spezzano Albanese — A1283

2002, Apr. 3	Engr.	Perf. 14		
2484	A1283	41c red brown	1.25	.45

State Police, 150th Anniv. A1284

2002, Apr. 12	Photo.	Perf. 14x13¼		
2485	A1284	41c multi	1.25	.45

Fr. Matteo Ricci (1552-1610), Missionary in China, Geographer — A1285

2002, Apr. 20

2486	A1285	41c multi	1.25	.45

Europa A1286

2002, May 4	Photo.	Perf. 14x13¼		
2487	A1286	41c multi	1.25	.45

Francesco Morosini Naval School, Venice A1287

2002, May 4

2488	A1287	41c multi	1.25	.45

Italian Cinema — A1288

Designs: No. 2489, Umberto D., directed by Vittorio De Sica. No. 2490, Miracle in Milan, written by Cesare Zavattini.

Litho. & Engr.

2002, May 10		Perf. 13¼x14		
2489	A1288	41c multi	1.25	.45
2490	A1288	41c multi	1.25	.45

Juventus, 2001-02 Italian Soccer Champions A1289

2002, May 18		Photo.		
2491	A1289	41c multi	1.25	.45

Giovanni Falcone (1939-92) and Paolo Borsellino (1940-92), Judges Assassinated by Mafia — A1290

2002, May 23		Perf. 14x13¼		
2492	A1290	62c multi	1.90	.75

NATO-Russia Summit Meeting, Rome — A1291

2002, May 28	Photo.	Perf. 14x13¼		
2493	A1291	41c multi	1.25	.45

World Kayak Championships, Valsesia — A1292

2002, May 30		Perf. 13¼x14		
2494	A1292	52c multi	1.50	.60

Italian Military Forces in Peace Missions — A1293

2002, June 1

2495	A1293	41c multi	1.25	.45

Modena Stamps, 150th Anniv. — A1294

2002, June 1	Photo.	Perf. 13¼x14		
2496	A1294	41c multi	1.25	.45

Alfredo Binda (1902-86), Cyclist — A1295

2002, June 14	Photo.	Perf. 13¼x14		
2497	A1295	41c multi	1.25	.45

St. Pio of Pietrelcina (1887-1968) — A1296

2002, June 16		Perf. 14		
2498	A1296	41c multi	1.25	.45

Monument to the Massacre of the Acqui Division — A1297

2002, June 21		Perf. 13¼x14		
2499	A1297	41c multi	1.25	.45

The Crucifixion, by Cimabue A1298

Litho. & Engr.

2002, June 22		Perf. 14		
2500	A1298	€2.58 multi	7.75	3.00

Prefectural Institute, Bicent. A1299

2002, June 24	Photo.	Perf. 14x13¼		
2501	A1299	41c multi	1.25	.45

St. Maria Goretti (1890-1902) A1300

2002, July 6		Perf. 13¼x14		
2502	A1300	41c multi	1.25	.45

Jules Cardinal Mazarin (1602-61), and Birthplace A1301

2002, July 13	Photo.	Perf. 14x13¼		
2503	A1301	41c multi	1.25	.45

Italians Around the World — A1302

2002, Aug. 8		Perf. 13¼x14		
2504	A1302	52c multi	1.50	.60

Monument to Sant'Anna di Stazzema Massacre A1303

2002, Aug. 17

2505	A1303	41c multi	1.25	.45

UNESCO World Heritage Sites — A1304

Designs: 41c, Pisa. 52c, Aeolian Islands. Illustration reduced.

2002, Aug. 30		Perf. 14		
2506	A1304	41c multi + label	1.25	.45
2507	A1304	52c multi + label	1.50	.60

Italian Design A1305

Apparel by: a, Krizia. b, Dolce e Gabbana. c, Gianfranco Ferre. d, Giorgio Armani. e, Laura Biagiotti. f, Prada.

2002, Aug. 30		Litho.		
2508		Sheet of 6	7.50	7.50
a.-f.	A1305	41c Any single	1.25	.45

Carlo Alberto Dalla Chiesa (1920-82), Prefect of Palermo Assassinated by Mafia — A1306

2002, Sept. 3	Photo.	Perf. 13¼x14		
2509	A1306	41c multi	1.25	.45

Concordia Theater, Monte Castello de Vibio — A1307

Litho. & Engr.

2002, Sept. 7   **Perf. 14**
2510 A1307 41c multi   1.25   .45

Sailboat Gathering, Imperia A1308

2002, Sept. 11   **Photo.**   **Perf. 14x13¼**
2511 A1308 41c multi   1.25   .45

Santa Giulia Museum, Brescia — A1309

Palazzo Altemps, Roman Natl. Museum A1310

Perf. 13¼x14, 14x13¼

2002, Oct. 4   **Photo.**
2512 A1309 41c multi   1.25   .45
2513 A1310 41c multi   1.25   .45

Roman States Postage Stamps, 150th Anniv. — A1311

2002, Oct. 4   **Photo.**   **Perf. 13¼x14**
2514 A1311 41c Roman States
         #6   1.25   .45

Flora and Fauna — A1312

2002, Oct. 11
2515 A1312 23c Orchid   .70   .30
2516 A1312 52c Lynx   1.50   .60
2517 A1312 77c Stag beetle   2.25   .90
     Nos. 2515-2517 (3)   4.45 1.80

World Food Day — A1313

2002, Oct. 16   **Photo.**   **Perf. 13¼x14**
2518 A1313 41c multi   1.25   .45

Forestry Corps — A1314

2002, Oct. 22
2519 A1314 41c multi   1.25   .45

Father Carlo Gnocchi (1902-56), Founder of Fondazione Pro Juventute A1315

2002, Oct. 25
2520 A1315 41c multi   1.25   .45

2002 Muscular Dystrophy Telethon A1316

2002, Oct. 31   **Perf. 14x13¼**
2521 A1316 41c multi   1.25   .45

Christmas A1317

Designs: 41c, Nativity. 62c, Child with candle, Christmas tree, vert.

Perf. 14x13¼, 13¼x14

2002, Oct. 31   **Photo.**
2522 A1317 41c multi   1.25   .45
2523 A1317 62c multi   1.90   .75

Women's Sports — A1318

2002, Nov. 20   **Photo.**   **Perf. 13¼x14**
2524 A1318 41c multi   1.25   .45

Stamp Day A1319

2002, Nov. 29
2525 A1319 62c multi   1.90   .75

2002 World Cup Soccer Championships, Japan and Korea — A1320

No. 2526: a, Flags, soccer ball and field (33mm diameter). b, Soccer player, years of Italian championships. Illustration reduced.

2002, Nov. 29   **Litho.**   **Perf. 14**
2526 A1320   Horiz. pair   3.00 1.50
   a.-b.   52c Either single   1.50   .60
   See Argentina No. 2184, Brazil No. 2840, France No. 2891, Germany No. 2163 and Uruguay No. 1946.

Vittorio Emanuele Orlando (1860-1952), Politician — A1321

2002, Dec. 4   **Photo.**   **Perf. 13¼x14**
2527 A1321 41c multi   1.25   .45

2003 Winter Universiade Games, Tarvisio — A1322

2003, Jan. 16   **Photo.**   **Perf. 13½x14**
2528 A1322 52c multi   1.50   .60

"La Repubblica Italiana" Philatelic Exhibition, Rome A1323

2003, Jan. 16   **Perf. 14**
2529 A1323 62c multi   1.90   .75
   a.   Booklet pane of 5   9.50   —
      Complete booklet, #2529a   9.50

World Cyclocross Championships, Monopoli — A1324

2003, Feb. 1   **Photo.**   **Perf. 13¼x14**
2530 A1324 41c multi   1.25   .60

Alinari Brothers Photographic Studio, 150th Anniv. — A1325

Illustration reduced.

2003, Feb. 1   **Perf. 14x13¼**
2531 A1325 77c multi + label   2.25 1.10

European Year of the Disabled A1326

2003, Feb. 14
2532 A1326 41c multi   1.25   .60

World Nordic Skiing Championships, Val di Fiemme — A1327

2003, Feb. 18   **Photo.**   **Perf. 14x13¼**
2533 A1327 41c multi   1.25   .60

National Civil Service — A1328

2003, Feb. 25   **Photo.**   **Perf. 14x13¼**
2534 A1328 62c multi + label   1.90   .75

Duel of Barletta, 500th Anniv. A1329

2003, Mar. 6
2535 A1329 41c multi   1.25   .60

Torquato Tasso High School, Rome — A1330

2003, Mar. 11   **Photo.**   **Perf. 14**
2536 A1330 41c multi   1.25   .60

Encounter at the Golden Door, by Giotto A1331

2003, Mar. 20   **Litho. & Engr.**
2537 A1331 41c multi   1.25 .60

Gian Rinaldo Carli High School, Pisino d'Istria — A1332

2003, Mar. 24   **Photo.**
2538 A1332 41c multi   1.25 .60

Lincei Academy, 400th Anniv. — A1333

    Litho. & Engr.
2003, Mar. 26   **Perf. 13¼x14**
2539 A1333 41c multi   1.25 .60

World Junior Fencing Championships, Trapani — A1334

2003, Apr. 4   **Photo.**   **Perf. 14x13¼**
2540 A1334 41c multi   1.25 .60

Acquasanta Golf Club, Rome, Cent. A1335

2003, Apr. 5
2541 A1335 77c multi   2.25 1.10

Tourism Type of 2002

2003, Apr. 5
2542 A1282 41c Sestri Levante   1.25 .60
2543 A1282 41c Lanciano   1.25 .60
2544 A1282 41c Procida   1.25 .60
    Nos. 2542-2544 (3)   3.75 1.80

La Sapienza University, Rome, 700th Anniv. — A1336

2003, Apr. 10   **Photo.**   **Perf. 14**
2545 A1336 41c multi   1.25 .60

Natl. Pasta Museum, Rome — A1337

2003, Apr. 17   **Perf. 13¼x14**
2546 A1337 41c multi   1.25 .60

Guido Carli Free Intl. University for Social Studies — A1338

2003, Apr. 23   **Photo.**   **Perf. 14**
2547 A1338 €2.58 multi   7.75 3.75

Europa — A1339

Poster art by Marcello Dudovich: 41c, Woman in blue dress. 52c, Women in white dresses.

2003, May 5   **Photo.**   **Perf. 13¼x14**
2548 A1339 41c multi   1.25 .60
2549 A1339 52c multi   1.50 .75

Central State Archives, 50th Anniv. A1340

2003, May 8   **Perf. 14x13¼**
2550 A1340 41c multi   1.25 .60

Veronafil Philatelic Exhibition, Verona A1341

2003, May 9
2551 A1341 41c multi   1.25 .60

Aldo Moro (1916-78), Premier — A1342

2003, May 9   **Perf. 13¼x14**
2552 A1342 62c multi   1.90 .95

Souvenir Sheet

Antonio Meucci (1808-96), Telephone Pioneer — A1343

2003, May 28   **Litho.**
2553 A1343 52c multi   1.50 .75

Father Eugenio Barsanti and Felice Matteucci, Internal Combustion Engine Pioneers A1344

2003, May 31   **Photo.**   **Perf. 14x13¼**
2554 A1344 52c multi   1.50 .75

Post Office, Latina A1345

2003, June 30   **Engr.**   **Perf. 14**
2555 A1345 41c blue   1.25 .60
    City of Latina, 70th anniv.

Italian Presidency of the Council of the European Union A1346

2003, July 1   **Photo.**   **Perf. 14x13¼**
2556 A1346 41c multi   1.25 .60

Ezio Vanoni (1903-56), Economist A1347

2003, July 1   **Perf. 13¼x14**
2557 A1347 €2.58 multi   7.75 3.75

The Assumption, by Corrado Giaquinto (c. 1694-1765) A1348

2003, July 2   **Perf. 14**
2558 A1348 77c multi   2.25 1.10

Eugenio Balzan (1874-1953), Journalist — A1349

2003, July 15   **Photo.**   **Perf. 14x13¼**
2559 A1349 41c multi   1.25 .60

Francesco Mazzola "Il Parmigianino," (1503-40), Painter — A1350

2003, Aug. 23   **Photo.**   **Perf. 14x14¼**
2560 A1350 41c multi   1.25 .60

Juventus, 2002-03 Italian Soccer Champions A1351

2003, Aug. 30   **Perf. 13¼x14**
2561 A1351 41c multi   1.25 .60

Abbey of St. Sylvester I, Nonantola — A1352

    Litho. & Engr.
2003, Sept. 6   **Perf. 14**
2562 A1352 41c multi   1.25 .60

Italian Aviation Pioneers A1353

2003, Sept. 12 Photo. *Perf. 13x13¼*
2563	A1353	52c	Mario Calderara	1.50	.75
2564	A1353	52c	Mario Cobianchi	1.50	.75
2565	A1353	52c	Gianni Caproni	1.50	.75
2566	A1353	52c	Alessandro Marchetti	1.50	.75
a.			Souvenir sheet, #2563-2566	6.00	6.00

Giovanni Giolitti (1842-1928), Premier — A1354

2003, Sept. 13 Photo. *Perf. 14x13¼*
2567 A1354 41c multi   1.25 .60

Europalia Italia Festival, Belgium A1355

Designs: 41c, Still Life, by Giorgio Morandi. 52c, 1947 Cisitalia 202, designed by Battista Pininfarina.

2003, Sept. 13
2568 A1355 41c multi   1.25 .60
2569 A1355 52c multi   1.50 .75

See Belgium Nos. 1980-1981.

Cent. of First Publication of Leonardo Magazine, by Attilio Vallecchi (1880-1946) A1356

2003, Sept. 27 Photo. *Perf. 13x13¼*
2570 A1356 41c multi   1.25 .60

The Family — A1357

2003, Oct. 3 *Perf. 13¼x13*
2571 A1357 77c multi   2.25 1.10

Maestà, by Duccio di Buoninsegna A1358

2003, Oct. 4
2572 A1358 41c multi   1.25 .60

Exhibition of paintings by Duccio di Buoninsegna, Siena.

Vittorio Alfieri (1749-1803), Poet — A1359

2003, Oct. 8 *Perf. 13x13¼*
2573 A1359 41c multi   1.25 .60

Ugo La Malfa (1903-79), Government Minister — A1360

2003, Oct. 13 *Perf. 13¼x13*
2574 A1360 62c multi   1.90 .95

Bernardino Ramazzini (1633-1714), Physician — A1361

2003, Oct. 15 *Perf. 13x13¼*
2575 A1361 41c multi   1.25 .60

Confedilizia Property Owner's Organization, 120th Anniv. — A1362

2003, Oct. 15 *Perf. 13¼x13*
2576 A1362 €2.58 multi   7.75 3.75

Nativity, by Gian Paolo Cavagna — A1363

Poinsettia A1364

2003, Oct. 24
2577 A1363 41c multi   1.25 .60
2578 A1364 62c multi   1.90 .95

Christmas.

Futurist Art by Giacomo Balla A1365

Designs: 41c, Forme Grido Viva L'Italia. 52c, Linee-Forza del Pugno di Boccioni.

2003, Nov. 26 Photo. *Perf. 13x13¼*
2579 A1365 41c multi   1.25 .60
2580 A1365 52c multi   1.50 .75

Philately Day A1366

2003, Nov. 28 Photo. *Perf. 13x13¼*
2581 A1366 41c multi   1.25 .60

Priority Mail Type of 2001 With Euro Denominations Only
Typo. & Silk Screened

2004		**Serpentine Die Cut 11**		
		Self-Adhesive		
		Background Color		
2582	A1242	60c	orange (gold frame)	1.75	.85
2583	A1242	80c	yellow brown	2.40	1.25
2584	A1242	€1.40	green	4.25	2.00
2585	A1242	€1.50	gray	4.50	2.25

Photo.
2585A	A1242	60c	dull orange (bronze frame)	1.75	.85
2585B	A1242	80c	dull brn (bronze frame)	2.40	1.25
		Nos. 2582-2585B (6)		17.05	8.45

Issued: 60c, 1/2; €1.40, 1/10; 80c, €1.50, No. 2585A, 3/19/04. A self-adhesive etiquette is adjacent to each stamp.
The frame has a splotchy appearance on Nos. 2585A and 2585B.
No. 2585A exists dated 2005. Undated examples of No. 2585B were issued in 2008. See No. 2613A.

A1367

Television Transmissions in Italy, 50th Anniv. — A1368

2004, Jan. 3 Photo. *Perf. 13x13¼*
2586 A1367 41c multi   1.25 .60
2587 A1368 62c multi   1.90 .95

Giorgio La Pira (1904-77), Judge A1369

2004, Jan. 9 Photo. *Perf. 13x13¼*
2588 A1369 41c multi   1.25 .60

Genoa, 2004 European Cultural Capital — A1370

2004, Feb. 12 Photo. *Perf. 13¼x13*
2589 A1370 45c multi   1.25 .60

2006 Winter Olympics, Turin — A1371

Designs: 23c, Santa Maria Assunta Church, Pragelato. 45c, San Pietro Apostolo Church, Bardonecchia. 62c, Mole Antonelliana, Turin. 65c, Fountain, Sauze d'Oulx.

2004, Mar. 9
2590 A1371 23c multi   .70 .35
2591 A1371 45c multi   1.25 .60
2592 A1371 62c multi   1.90 .95
2593 A1371 65c multi   1.90 .95
   Nos. 2590-2593 (4)   5.75 2.85

Petrarch (1304-74), Poet — A1372

2004, Mar. 18
2594 A1372 45c multi   1.25 .60

Giorgio Amarelli Licorice Museum, Rossano — A1373

2004, Apr. 3 *Perf. 14*
2595 A1373 45c multi   1.25 .60

Road Safety A1374

Designs: 60c, Car dashboard, traffic signs. 62c, Seat belt, map of Italy, vert.

2004, Apr. 7 *Perf. 13x13¼, 13¼x13*
2596 A1374 60c multi   1.75 .85
2597 A1374 62c multi   1.90 .95

Tourism Type of 2002
2004, Apr. 10 Photo. *Perf. 13x13¼*
2598 A1282 45c Vignola   1.25 .60
2599 A1282 45c Viterbo   1.25 .60
2600 A1282 45c Isole Egadi   1.25 .60
   Nos. 2598-2600 (3)   3.75 1.80

Casa del Fascio, Como, Designed by Giuseppe Terragni (1904-43), Architect A1375

2004, Apr. 17   *Perf. 13x13¼*
2601 A1375 85c multi   2.50 1.25

Souvenir Sheet

Rome-Bangkok Foundation — A1376

No. 2602: a, Wat Saket, Bangkok. b, Colosseum, Rome.

2004, Apr. 21 Litho.   *Perf. 14x13¼*
2602 A1376   Sheet of 2   3.75 3.75
a.-b.   65c Either single   1.90 .95

See Thailand No. 2125.

Martyrdom of St. George, 1700th Anniv. — A1377

2004, Apr. 23 Photo.   *Perf. 14*
2603 A1377 €2.80 multi   8.50 4.25

Europa A1378

Map of Europe and: 45c, Closed suitcase. 62c, Open suitcase.

2004, May 7   *Perf. 13x13¼*
2604 A1378 45c multi   1.25 .60
2605 A1378 62c multi   1.90 .95

Souvenir Sheet

L'Aquila - Foggia Livestock Trail — A1379

2004, May 8 Litho.   *Perf. 14x13¼*
2606 A1379 45c multi   1.25 .60

Great Synagogue, Rome — A1380

2004, May 20 Photo.   *Perf. 13¼x14*
2607 A1380 60c shown   1.75 .85
2608 A1380 62c Synagogue, diff.   1.90 .95

See Israel Nos. 1564-1565.

Milan, 2003-04 Italian Soccer Champions A1381

2004, May 22   *Perf. 13x13¼*
2609 A1381 45c multi   1.25 .60

50th Puccini Festival — A1382

2004, May 28 Photo.   *Perf. 13¼x13*
2610 A1382 60c multi   1.75 .85

University of Turin, 600th Anniv. — A1383

2004, June 3 Engr.   *Perf. 14*
2611 A1383 45c brown   1.25 .60

Achille Varzi (1904-48), Automobile and Motorcycle Racer A1384

2004, June 5 Photo.   *Perf. 13x13¼*
2612 A1384 45c multi   1.25 .60

Penitentiary Police Corps — A1385

2004, June 16 Photo.   *Perf. 13x13¼*
2613 A1385 45c multi   1.25 .60

Priority Mail Type of 2001 With Euro Denominations Only
Serpentine Die Cut 11
2004, June 16   **Photo.**
Self-Adhesive
Background Color
2613A A1242 €1.40 blue green   4.25 2.00
2614   A1242   €2 slate grn (bronze frame)   6.00 3.00
2615   A1242 €2.20 rose   6.50 3.25
   Nos. 2613A-2615 (3)   16.75 8.25

Issued: €2, 6/16; €1.40, July; €2.20, 6/26.
A self-adhesive etiquette is adjacent to each stamp.
No. 2613A has a less obvious coating over the circled "P" that shines most when viewed from an oblique angle. No. 2613A exists dated 2006. Undated examples of No. 2613A were issued in 2007. Undated examples of Nos. 2614 and 2615 were issued in 2008.

Ascent of K2 By Italian Mountaineers, 50th Anniv. — A1386

2004, July 31 Photo.   *Perf. 13¼x13*
2616 A1386 65c multi   1.90 .95

Italian Regions A1387

2004, Aug. 27   *Perf. 14x13¼*
2617 A1387 45c Liguria   1.25 .60
2618 A1387 45c Emilia Romagna   1.25 .60
2619 A1387 45c Abruzzo   1.25 .60
2620 A1387 45c Basilicata   1.25 .60
   Nos. 2617-2620 (4)   5.00 2.40

See Nos. 2654-2657, 2746-2749, 2796-2799, 2876-2879.

Apparition of Madonna of Tirano, 500th Anniv. — A1388

2004, Sept. 4   *Perf. 13¼x13*
2621 A1388 45c multi   1.25 .60

St. Nilus of Rossano (c. 905-1005), Abbot — A1389

2004, Sept. 25 Photo.   *Perf. 14¼x14*
2622 A1389 45c multi   1.25 .60

State Archives, Florence — A1390

2004, Sept. 30 Photo.   *Perf. 14¼x14*
2623 A1390 45c multi   1.25 .60

Lacemaking — A1391

2004, Oct. 8 Embroidered   *Imperf.*
Self-Adhesive
2624 A1391 €2.80 blue & gray   8.50 4.25

Filo d'Oro Society — A1392

2004, Oct. 9 Photo.   *Perf. 13¼x13*
2625 A1392 45c multi   1.25 .60

Victor Emmanuel III State Technical Institute, Lucera A1393

2004, Oct. 16   *Perf. 14x14¼*
2626 A1393 45c multi   1.25 .60

Father Luigi Guanella (1842-1915) A1394

2004, Oct. 19 Photo.   *Perf. 13¼x13*
2627 A1394 45c multi   1.25 .60

Return of Trieste to Italy, 50th Anniv. A1395

2004, Oct. 26   *Perf. 13x13¼*
2628 A1395 45c multi   1.25 .60
a.   Booklet pane of 4   5.00 —
    Complete booklet, #2628a   5.00

Military Information and Security Service A1396

2004, Oct. 27 Photo. Perf. 13x13¼
2629 A1396 60c multi 1.75 .85

European Constitution — A1397

2004, Oct. 29
2630 A1397 62c multi 1.90 .95

Venice Dockyards, 900th Anniv. A1398

2004, Oct. 30 Photo. Perf. 13x13¼
2631 A1398 €2.80 multi 8.50 4.25

Live Nativity Scene, Tricase A1399

2004, Oct. 30 Photo. Perf. 13x13¼
2632 A1399 45c multi 1.25 .60

Photo. & Embossed
Perf. 13¼x13
2633 A1400 62c multi 1.90 .95

Christmas Tree — A1400

Hands and Braille Book — A1401

Photo. & Embossed
2004, Nov. 6 Perf. 14
2634 A1401 45c multi 1.25 .60

Martyrdom of St. Lucy, 1700th Anniv. — A1402

2004, Nov. 6 Photo. Perf. 13¼x13
2635 A1402 45c multi 1.25 .60

Philately Day — A1403

2004, Nov. 12 Perf. 13¼x14
2636 A1403 45c multi 1.25 .60

Tenth "Sport For All" World Congress A1404

2004, Nov. 12 Photo. Perf. 13¼x13
2637 A1404 65c multi 1.90 .95

Maria Santissima Assunta Free University, Rome — A1405

2004, Nov. 15 Perf. 14
2638 A1405 45c multi 1.25 .60

Souvenir Sheet

Italian-made Footwear — A1406

No. 2639: a, Woman's shoe by Casadei. b, Men's shoes by Moreschi. c, Men's shoe by Fratelli Rosetti. d, Athletic shoe by Superga.

2004, Nov. 27 Photo. Perf. 13¼x13
2639 A1406 Sheet of 4 5.00 5.00
　a.-d. 45c Any single 1.25 .60

Italia With Large Numerals — A1407

Perf. 13¼x13½
2005, Jan. 21 Engr. Unwmk.
2640 A1407 €1 multi 3.00 1.50

Compare type A1407 with type A1274.

Italian Auto Club, Cent. — A1408

2005, Jan. 21 Photo. Perf. 13¼x13
2648 A1408 45c multi 1.25 .60

Luigi Calabresi (1937-72), Assassinated Police Commissioner A1409

2005, Jan. 26
2649 A1409 45c multi 1.25 .60

Exodus of Italians From Istria, Fiume and Dalmatia, 60th Anniv. A1410

2005, Feb. 10 Photo. Perf. 14x13¼
2650 A1410 45c multi 1.25 .60

Rotary International, Cent. — A1411

2005, Feb. 23 Perf. 13¼x14
2651 A1411 65c multi 1.90 .95

Sassari Brigade A1412

2005, Mar. 1 Perf. 14x13¼
2652 A1412 45c multi 1.25 .60

14th Art Quadrennial, Rome — A1413

2005, Mar. 4
2653 A1413 45c multi 1.25 .60

Italian Regions Type of 2004
2005, Mar. 18 Perf. 13x13¼
2654 A1387 45c Lombardy 1.25 .60
2655 A1387 45c Friuli-Venezia
　　　　　Giulia 1.25 .60
2656 A1387 45c Campania 1.25 .60
2657 A1387 45c Calabria 1.25 .60
　Nos. 2654-2657 (4) 5.00 2.40

2006 Winter Olympics, Turin — A1414

Turin Olympics emblem and: 23c, Pinerolo. 45c, Cesana Torinese. 60c, Mascots Neve and Gliz. 62c, Sestriere.

2005, Mar. 21 Perf. 13¼x13
2658 A1414 23c multi .70 .35
2659 A1414 45c multi 1.25 .60
2660 A1414 60c multi 1.75 .85
2661 A1414 62c multi 1.90 .95
　Nos. 2658-2661 (4) 5.60 2.75

Intl. Year of Physics A1415

2005, Mar. 29 Perf. 14x13¼
2662 A1415 85c multi 2.50 1.25

Opening of New Milan Fair Complex A1416

2005, Mar. 31
2663 A1416 45c multi 1.25 .60

State Railways, Cent. A1417

2005, Apr. 22 Photo. Perf. 13x13¼
2664 A1417 45c multi 1.25 .60

Italian Army — A1418

2005, Apr. 29 *Perf. 13¼x13*
2665 A1418 45c multi 1.25 .60

Europa — A1419

2005, May 9 **Photo.** *Perf. 13¼x13*
2666 A1419 45c Wheat 1.10 .55
2667 A1419 62c Grapes 1.90 .95

St. Ignatius of Làconi (1701-81) A1420

2005, May 11 **Photo.** *Perf. 13¼x13*
2668 A1420 45c multi 1.25 .60

Commercial Confederation, 60th Anniv. — A1421

2005, May 18
2669 A1421 60c multi 1.75 .85

Tommaso Campanella High School, Reggio Calabria — A1422

2005, May 20 **Photo.** *Perf. 13x13¼*
2670 A1422 45c multi 1.25 .60

San Giuseppe da Copertino Basilica A1423

2005, May 21 **Engr.** *Perf. 14*
2671 A1423 45c blue gray 1.25 .60

Tourism — A1424

2005, May 26 **Photo.**
2672 A1424 45c Asolo 1.25 .60
2673 A1424 45c Rocchetta a Volturno 1.25 .60
2674 A1424 45c Amalfi 1.25 .60
 Nos. 2672-2674 (3) 3.75 1.80
 See Nos. 2734-2736, 2803-2806, 2887-2890, 2948-2951.

St. Gerardo Maiella (1726-55) A1425

2005, May 28 *Perf. 13x13¼*
2675 A1425 45c multi 1.25 .60

Juventus, 2004-05 Italian Soccer Champions A1426

2005, June 6 *Perf. 13¼x13*
2676 A1426 45c multi 1.25 .60

Ratification of Modifications to Italy-Vatican Concordat, 20th Anniv. — A1427

Arms of Vatican City and Italy and: 45c, Map. €2.80, Pen.

2005, June 9 *Perf. 13x13¼*
2677 A1427 45c multi 1.25 .60
2678 A1427 €2.80 multi 8.50 4.25
 See Vatican City Nos. 1301-1302.

First Italian Dirigible Flight by Almerico da Schio, Cent. A1428

2005, June 17 **Photo.** *Perf. 13x13¼*
2679 A1428 €3 multi 9.00 4.75

European Youth Olympic Festival, Lignano Sabbiadoro — A1429

2005, June 20 **Photo.** *Perf. 13¼x13*
2680 A1429 62c multi 1.90 .95

Intl. Day Against Illegal Drugs A1430

2005, June 25 **Photo.** *Perf. 13x13¼*
2681 A1430 45c multi 1.25 .60

Institute for Maritime Trades Social Insurance A1431

2005, June 28
2682 A1431 45c multi 1.25 .60

Leo Longanesi (1905-57), Writer — A1432

2005, Aug. 26 **Engr.** *Perf. 13¼x14*
2683 A1432 45c dark blue 1.25 .60

Alberto Ascari (1918-55), Race Car Driver A1433

2005, Sept. 2 **Photo.** *Perf. 13x13¼*
2684 A1433 €2.80 multi 8.50 4.25

A1434

National Military Aerobatic Team A1435

2005, Sept. 3 **Photo.** *Perf. 13x13¼*
2685 A1434 45c multi 1.25 .60
2686 A1435 60c multi 1.75 .85

Pietro Savorgnan di Brazzà (1852-1905), Explorer of Africa — A1436

2005, Sept. 14 **Photo.** *Perf. 13¼x13*
2687 A1436 45c multi 1.25 .60

Guido Gonella (1905-82), Politician, Journalist A1437

2005, Sept. 17
2688 A1437 45c multi 1.25 .60

Italian Participation in Exploration of Mars — A1438

Photo. With Hologram Applied
2005, Sept. 21 *Die Cut*
 Self-Adhesive
2689 A1438 80c multi 2.40 1.25
 Printed in sheets of 4.

Intercultura, 50th Anniv. — A1439

2005, Sept. 23 **Photo.** *Perf. 13x13¼*
2690 A1439 60c multi 1.75 .85

Souvenir Sheet

Louis Vuitton Cup Acts 8 & 9 (Races to Determine America's Cup Challenger), Trapani — A1440

2005, Sept. 28 Photo.   Perf. 13¼x13
2691 A1440 €2.80 multi   8.50 4.25

Priority Mail Type of 2001 With Euro Denominations Only
**2005 Photo.   Serpentine Die Cut 11
Self-Adhesive**
Inscribed "I. P. Z. S. S. p. A. - ROMA 2005" at Bottom
Background Color
2691A A1242 62c yellow   1.90 .95
2691B A1242 €1.50 gray   4.50 2.25

Issued: 62c, Oct.; €1.50, Dec.
Nos. 2466 and 2585 have different printer's inscriptions and have a more easily seen coating over the circled "P" than on Nos. 2691A and 2691B. The coating over the circled "P" on Nos. 2691A and 2691B shines most when viewed from an oblique angle. A self-adhesive etiquette is adjacent to each stamp. Nos. 2691A and 2691B have self-adhesive selvage surrounding the stamp and etiquette. This selvage is not found on Nos. 2466 and 2585.
Mo. 2691B exists without year date and without etiquette, issued in 2007.

Stamp Day — A1441

2005, Oct. 7 Photo.   Perf. 13¼x13
2692 A1441 45c multi   1.25 .60

Italian Organ Donation Association A1442

2005, Oct. 7 Photo.   Perf. 13¼x13
2693 A1442 60c multi   1.75 .85

National Association of Communities A1443

2005, Oct. 19
2694 A1443 45c multi   1.25 .60

Story of Sts. Stephan and John The Baptist, by Fra Filippo Lippi A1444

2005, Oct. 25   Perf. 13x13¼
2695 A1444 45c shown   1.25 .60
2696 A1444 €1.50 Four men   4.50 2.25

A1445

Christmas A1446

2005, Oct. 31 Photo.   Perf. 13x13¼
2697 A1445 45c multi   1.25 .60

Perf. 13¼x13
2698 A1446 62c multi   1.90 .95

Alcide De Gasperi (1881-1954), Prime Minister — A1447

2005, Nov. 9 Photo.   Perf. 13¼x13
2699 A1447 62c multi   1.90 .95

Giuseppe Mazzini (1805-72), Revolution Leader A1448

2005, Nov. 10 Photo.   Perf. 13¼x13
2700 A1448 45c multi   1.25 .60

National Civil Protection A1449

2005, Nov. 16 Photo.   Perf. 13¼x13
2701 A1449 45c multi   1.25 .60

Italian Red Cross — A1450

2005, Nov. 16
2702 A1450 45c multi   1.25 .60

Admission to United Nations, 50th Anniv. A1451

2005, Nov. 23   Perf. 13x13¼
2703 A1451 70c multi   2.10 1.00

Popes Reigning in 2005 A1452

Designs: 45c, Pope John Paul II (1920-2005). 65c, Pope Benedict XVI.

2005, Nov. 26 Photo.   Perf. 13x13¼
2704 A1452 45c multi   1.25 .60
2705 A1452 65c multi   1.90 .95

Reconstitution of Caserta Province, 60th Anniv. — A1453

2005, Dec. 5 Photo.   Perf. 13x13¼
2706 A1453 45c multi   1.25 .60

Opening of Enrico Toti Submarine Exhibit at Natl. Museum of Science and Technology, Milan A1454

2005, Dec. 7
2707 A1454 82c multi   2.40 1.25

Eighteenth Birthday Greetings A1455

2006, Jan. 1 Photo.   Perf. 13½x13
2708 A1455 45c blue & multi   1.25 .60
2709 A1455 45c pink & multi   1.25 .60

Souvenir sheets of 1 of redrawn stamps similar to Nos. 2708-2709 exist from a limited printing.

Panini, Soccer Card and Sticker Creators A1456

2006, Jan. 30 Photo.   Perf. 13x13¼
2710 A1456 €2.80 multi   8.50 4.25

Quattroruote Magazine, 50th Anniv. — A1457

2006, Feb. 1   Perf. 13¼x13
2711 A1457 62c multi   1.90 .95

Carlo Bo University, Urbino, 500th Anniv. — A1458

Ernesto Cairoli State High School, Varese — A1459

Alessandron Tassoni State Science High School, Modena — A1460

Agostino Nifo State High School, Sessa Aurunca — A1461

2006, Feb. 6
2712	A1458	45c multi	1.25	.60
2713	A1459	45c multi	1.25	.60
2714	A1460	45c multi	1.25	.60
2715	A1461	45c multi	1.25	.60
	Nos. 2712-2715 (4)		5.00	2.40

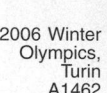

2006 Winter Olympics, Turin — A1462

2006, Feb. 8   *Perf. 13x13¼*
2716	A1462	23c Biathlon	.70	.35
2717	A1462	45c Figure skating	1.25	.60
2718	A1462	65c Ice hockey	1.90	.95
2719	A1462	70c Curling	2.10	1.00
2720	A1462	85c Bobsled	2.50	1.25
2721	A1462	90c Alpine skiing	2.75	1.90
2722	A1462	€1 Torch	3.00	1.50
2723	A1462	€1.30 Luge	4.00	2.00
2724	A1462	€1.70 Medals	5.00	2.50
a.		Souvenir sheet, #2716-2724	24.00	12.00
	Nos. 2716-2724 (9)		23.20	12.05

Nos. 23, 45, 79 and 239 — A1463

2006, Feb. 9   Photo.   *Perf. 13¼x13*
2725	A1463	60c multi	1.75	.85
a.		Booklet pane of 4	7.00	—
		Complete booklet, #2725a	7.00	

Kingdom of Italy Stamp Show, Rome.

Dalmatian Historical Society, 80th Anniv. A1464

2006, Feb. 10   Engr.   *Perf. 13x13¼*
2726	A1464	45c red vio & dk bl	1.25	.60

Detail of Fresco From Mantua Castle Bridal Chamber, by Andrea Mantegna (1431-1506) — A1465

2006, Feb. 25   Photo.   *Perf. 13x13¼*
2727	A1465	45c multi	1.25	.60

2006 Winter Paralympics, Turin — A1466

2006, Mar. 9   *Perf. 13¼x13*
2728	A1466	60c multi	1.75	.85

Items Made in Italy A1467

2006, Mar. 11   *Perf. 13x13¼*
2729	A1467	60c Gelato	1.75	.85
2730	A1467	€2.80 Carrara marble	8.50	4.25

National Singers Association, 25th Anniv. — A1468

2006, Mar. 17
2731	A1468	45c multi	1.25	.60

Aircraft Carrier "Cavour" A1469

2006, Mar. 17
2732	A1469	60c multi	1.75	.85

Opening of Sempione Tunnel — A1470

2006, Mar. 18   *Perf. 13¼x13*
2733	A1470	62c multi	1.90	.95

Tourism Type of 2005

2006, Mar. 24
2734	A1424	45c Lago di Como	1.25	.60
2735	A1424	45c Marina di Pietrasanta	1.25	.60
2736	A1424	45c Pozzuoli	1.25	.60
	Nos. 2734-2736 (3)		3.75	1.80

Intl. Day of Mountains A1471

2006, Mar. 30   *Perf. 13x13¼*
2737	A1471	60c multi	1.75	.85

Madonna and Child Icon, Mondragone Basilica — A1472

2006, Apr. 1
2738	A1472	45c multi	1.25	.60

First Vote for Italian Citizens Abroad — A1473

2006, Apr. 3   *Perf. 13¼x13*
2739	A1473	62c multi	1.90	.95

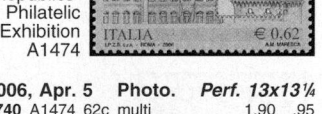

"Two Republics" Philatelic Exhibition A1474

2006, Apr. 5   Photo.   *Perf. 13x13¼*
2740	A1474	62c multi	1.90	.95
a.		Souvenir sheet, #2740, San Marino #1676a	4.00	4.00

See San Marino No. 1676. On No. 2740a, the Italian stamp is on the left. On San Marino No. 1676, the Italian stamp is on the right. Both stamps in No. 2740a have text printed on reverse.

Matterhorn Ski School, 70th Anniv. — A1475

2006, Apr. 13   Photo.   *Perf. 13¼x13*
2741	A1475	45c multi	1.25	.60

Madonna of Humility, by Gentile da Fabriano A1476

2006, Apr. 20   Photo.   *Perf. 13¼x13*
2742	A1476	€2.80 multi	8.50	4.50

Il Giorno Newspaper, 50th Anniv. — A1477

2006, Apr. 21   *Perf. 13¼x13*
2743	A1477	45c multi	1.25	.60

Constitutional Court, 50th Anniv. — A1478

2006, Apr. 22   Engr.
2744	A1478	45c blue	1.25	.60

Enrico Mattei (1906-62), Public Administrator A1479

2006, Apr. 29   Photo.   *Perf. 13¼x13*
2745	A1479	45c multi	1.25	.60

Italian Regions Type of 2004

2006, Apr. 29   *Perf. 13¼x13*
2746	A1387	45c Piedmont	1.25	.60
2747	A1387	45c Tuscany	1.25	.60
2748	A1387	45c Lazio	1.25	.60
2749	A1387	45c Puglia	1.25	.60
	Nos. 2746-2749 (4)		5.00	2.40

Targa Floria Automobile Race Track, Cent. — A1480

2006, May 6   Photo.   *Perf. 13¼x13*
2750	A1480	60c multi	1.75	.85

Christopher Columbus (1451-1506),
Explorer — A1481

2006, May 6   Photo.   Perf. 13x13¼
2751 A1481 62c multi   1.90   .95

Europa
A1482

People sitting on wall: 45c, View of faces.
62c, View of backs.

2006, May 8
2752 A1482 45c multi   1.25   .60
2753 A1482 62c multi   1.90   .95

General
Assembly
of Intl.
Military
Sport
Council,
Rome
A1483

2006, May 9
2754 A1483 45c multi   1.25   .60

2006 World
Team Chess
Championships,
Turin — A1484

2006, May 20   Photo.   Perf. 13¼x13
2755 A1484 62c multi   1.90   .95

Constituent
Assembly,
60th Anniv.
A1485

2006, June 1   Perf. 13x13¼
2756 A1485 60c multi   1.75   .85

Woman Suffrage,
60th
Anniv. — A1486

2006, June 1   Perf. 13¼x13
2757 A1486 60c multi   1.75   .85

2006 World Bridge Championships,
Verona — A1487

2006, June 9   Perf. 13x13¼
2758 A1487 65c multi   1.90   .95

Salto di Quirra
Proving Grounds,
50th
Anniv. — A1488

2006, June 13   Perf. 13¼x13
2759 A1488 60c multi   1.75   .85

Customs
Department
General
Headquarters,
Cent. — A1489

Customs
Cadet
Legion,
Cent.
A1490

2006, June 21   Perf. 13¼x13
2760 A1489 60c multi   1.75   .85
       Perf. 13x13¼
2761 A1490 60c multi   1.75   .85

Reopening of
Greek Theater,
Tindari, 50th
Anniv. — A1491

2006, July 6   Perf. 13¼x13
2762 A1491 €1.50 multi   4.50 2.25

Autostrada
del Sole,
50th Anniv.
A1492

2006, July 10   Perf. 13x13¼
2763 A1492 60c multi   1.75   .85

Terrorist Bombing
in Bologna, 26th
Anniv. — A1493

2006, Aug. 2   Perf. 13¼x13
2764 A1493 60c multi   1.75   .85

Italian Philatelic Union, 40th
Anniv. — A1494

Illustration reduced.

2006, Sept. 1   Perf. 13x13¼
2765 A1494 60c multi + label 1.75   .85

St. Gregory the
Great (540-604)
A1495

2006, Sept. 2   Perf. 13¼x13
2766 A1495 60c multi   1.75   .85

Victory of
Italian 2006
World Cup
Soccer
Team
A1496

2006, Sept. 9   Photo.   Perf. 13x13¼
2767 A1496 €1 multi   3.00 1.50

Victims of
Terrorism
A1497

2006, Sept. 16
2768 A1497 60c multi   1.75   .85

Ettore Majorana
(1906-38?),
Physicist
A1498

2006, Sept. 18   Perf. 13¼x13
2769 A1498 60c multi   1.75   .85

Saints
A1499

Designs: No. 2770, St. Ignatius of Loyola
(1491-1556). No. 2771, St. Francis Xavier
(1506-52).

2006, Sept. 27   Perf. 13x13¼
2770 A1499 60c multi   1.75   .85
2771 A1499 60c multi   1.75   .85

World Fencing Championships,
Turin — A1500

2006, Sept. 29
2772 A1500 65c multi   1.90   .95

Lottery,
500th
Anniv.
A1501

2006, Oct. 6   Photo.   Perf. 13x13¼
2773 A1501 60c multi   1.75   .85

Philately
Day
A1502

2006, Oct. 6
2774 A1502 60c multi   1.75   .85

Land and
Marine
Area
Protection
System
A1503

2006, Oct. 6
2775 A1503 65c multi   1.90   .95

Luchino Visconti
(1906-76), Film
Director — A1504

2006, Oct. 13   Perf. 13¼x13
2776 A1504 60c multi   1.75   .85

Dino Buzzati (1906-72), Writer A1505

2006, Oct. 16 *Perf. 13x13¼*
2777 A1505 60c multi   1.50 .75

Adoration of the Magi, by Jacopo Bassano A1506

Christmas Tree — A1507

2006, Oct. 28 **Engr.** *Perf. 13x13¼*
2778 A1506 60c rose   1.60 .80
Photo.
Perf. 13¼x13
2779 A1507 65c multi   1.75 .85

Vittoriano Building, Tomb of the Unknown Soldier, Rome A1508

2006, Nov. 11 **Photo.** *Perf. 13x13¼*
2780 A1508 60c multi   1.60 .80

Cathedral of St. Evasius, Casale Monteferrato — A1509

2007, Jan. 4 **Engr.** *Perf. 13x13¼*
2781 A1509 60c rose   1.60 .80

First Montessori School, Cent. — A1510

2007, Jan. 5 **Photo.** *Perf. 13¼x13*
2782 A1510 60c multi   1.60 .80

School for Public Administration, 50th Anniv. — A1511

2007, Jan. 10 **Photo.** *Perf. 13x13¼*
2783 A1511 65c multi   1.75 .85

Parma Cathedral — A1512

2007, Jan. 13 **Engr.** *Perf. 13¼x13*
2784 A1512 60c green   1.60 .80

Arturo Toscanini (1867-1957), Conductor A1513

2007, Jan. 16 **Photo.**
2785 A1513 60c multi   1.60 .80

St. Francis of Paola (1416-1507) — A1514

2007, Jan. 27 *Perf. 13x13¼*
2786 A1514 60c multi   1.60 .80

Ferrante Gonzaga (1507-57), Soldier A1515

2007, Jan. 27
2787 A1515 €1 multi   2.60 1.40

Antonio Genovesi Salerno Foundation, 20th Anniv. — A1516

2007, Jan. 29 **Photo.** *Perf. 13x13¼*
2788 A1516 60c multi   1.60 .80

Relocation of Istrian Area Refugees to Giuliana di Fertilia District, Sardinia, 60th Anniv. A1517

2007, Feb. 10 **Photo.** *Perf. 13x13¼*
2789 A1517 60c multi   1.60 .80

Father Lodovico Acernese (1835-1916) A1518

2007, Feb. 16 **Photo.** *Perf. 13¼x13*
2790 A1518 23c multi   .60 .30

Giosuè Carducci (1835-1907), 1906 Nobel Laureate in Literature — A1519

2007, Feb. 16 **Photo.** *Perf. 13x13¼*
2791 A1519 60c multi   1.60 .80

University of Brescia — A1520

2007, Feb. 26 *Perf. 13¼x13*
2792 A1520 60c multi   1.60 .80

European Equal Opportunity Year — A1521

2007, Mar. 1 **Photo.** *Perf. 13¼x13*
2793 A1521 60c multi   1.60 .80

Scipione Maffei State High School, Verona — A1522

2007, Mar. 14 **Photo.** *Perf. 13¼x13*
2794 A1522 60c multi   1.60 .80

Nicolò Carosio (1907-84), Radio Sportscaster — A1523

2007, Mar. 15 *Perf. 13x13¼*
2795 A1523 65c multi   1.75 .85

Italian Regions Type of 2004
2007, Mar. 16 **Photo.** *Perf. 13x13¼*
2796 A1387 60c Trentino-Alto Adige   1.60 .80
2797 A1387 60c Marche   1.60 .80
2798 A1387 60c Umbria   1.60 .80
2799 A1387 60c Sardinia   1.60 .80
  Nos. 2796-2799 (4)   6.40 3.20

Venice, UNESCO World Heritage Site — A1524

2007, Mar. 16 **Engr.** *Perf. 13¼x13*
2800 A1524 60c black   1.60 .80

Intl. Electrotechnical Commission A1525

2007, Mar. 16 **Photo.** *Perf. 13x13¼*
2801 A1525 €1.50 multi   4.00 2.00

Souvenir Sheet

Treaty of Rome, 50th Anniv. — A1526

2007, Mar. 25 **Photo.** *Perf. 13x13¼*
2802 A1526   Sheet of 2   3.50 3.50
  a.   60c Stars and "50"   1.60 .80
  b.   65c "Insieme dal 1957"   1.75 .85

Tourism Type of 2005
2005, Apr. 13 *Perf. 13¼x13*
2803 A1424 60c Brunico-Bruneck 1.75 .85
2804 A1424 60c Gaeta   1.75 .85
2805 A1424 60c Massafra   1.75 .85
2806 A1424 60c Cattolica Er- aclea   1.75 .85
  Nos. 2803-2806 (4)   7.00 3.40

Giuseppe Tomasi di Lampedusa (1896-1957), Writer — A1527

2007, Apr. 14 Photo. Perf. 13¼x13
2807 A1527 60c multi   1.75 .85

Forum, Rome A1528

2007, Apr. 21   Perf. 13x13¼
2808 A1528 60c multi   1.75 .85

Europa — A1529

Scouts: 60c, In canoe. 65c, At campfire.

2007, Apr. 23   Perf. 13¼x13
2809 A1529 60c multi   1.75 .85
2810 A1529 65c multi   1.90 .95
  a. Souvenir sheet, #2809-2810   3.75 1.90

Duccio Galamberti (1906-44), World War II Resistance Leader — A1530

2007, Apr. 24
2811 A1530 60c multi   1.75 .85

School of Economics and Finance, Rome, 50th Anniv. A1531

2007, Apr. 27   Perf. 13x13¼
2812 A1531 €2.80 multi   7.75 3.75

Cinecittà Film Studios, Rome, 70th Anniv. A1532

2007, Apr. 28
2813 A1532 65c multi   1.75 .85

Polirone Monastery, San Benedetto Po, 1000th Anniv. — A1533

2007, May 5 Engr. Perf. 13¼x13
2814 A1533 60c blue & blk   1.60 .80

Malatesta Castle, Montefiore Conca — A1534

2007, May 12
2815 A1534 60c brown   1.60 .80

Bancarella Musica Folk Music Project — A1535

2007, May 23   Photo.
2816 A1535 60c multi   1.60 .80

Emblem of Lamborghini Automobiles A1536

2007, May 23
2817 A1536 85c multi   2.40 1.25

F. C. Internazionale, 2006-07 Italian Soccer Champions A1537

2007, June 4 Photo. Perf. 13¼
2818 A1537 60c multi   1.60 .80

Chianca Dolmen — A1538

2007, June 9 Engr. Perf. 13¼x13
2819 A1538 60c brown   1.75 .85

Luigi Ganna, (1883-1957), Cyclist — A1539

2007, June 9 Photo. Perf. 13¼x13
2820 A1539 60c multi   1.60 .80

Altiero Spinelli (1907-86), Writer and Politician A1540

2007, June 21   Perf. 13x13¼
2821 A1540 60c multi   1.60 .80

Two Worlds Festival, 50th Anniv. A1541

2007, June 29 Photo. Perf. 13x13¼
2822 A1541 60c multi   1.75 .85

San Vincenzo Basilica, Galliano — A1542

**2007, July 2 Litho. Rouleted 7
On Wood Veneer
Self-Adhesive**
2823 A1542 €2.80 black   7.75 3.75

Fiat 500 Automobile A1543

2007, July 4 Photo. Perf. 13x13¼
2824 A1543 60c multi   1.75 .85

Giuseppe Garibaldi (1807 82), Patriot A1544

2007, July 4
2825 A1544 65c multi   1.90 .95

Capt. Maurizio Poggiali (1965-97), Pilot A1545

2007, July 6
2826 A1545 60c multi   1.75 .85

Roman Speleology Club A1546

2007, July 9
2827 A1546 €1.40 multi   4.00 2.00

Primo Carnera (1906-67), Boxer A1547

2007, July 13
2828 A1547 60c multi   1.75 .85

Marco Foscarini School, Venice — A1548

St. Pius V Institute for Political Studies, Rome — A1549

Salerno Medical College — A1550

2007, Sept. 17 Photo. Perf. 13¼x13
2829 A1548 60c multi 1.75 .85
2830 A1549 60c multi 1.75 .85
2831 A1550 60c multi 1.75 .85
Nos. 2829-2831 (3) 5.25 2.55

Protected Donkey Breeds A1551

2007, Sept. 22 Perf. 13x13¼
2832 A1551 60c multi 1.75 .85

31st European Women's Basketball Championships A1552

2007, Sept. 22 Perf. 13¼x13
2833 A1552 65c multi 1.90 .95

Sacra di San Michele Abbey, Sant'Ambroglio di Torino — A1553

2007, Sept. 29 Engr.
2834 A1553 60c red brown 1.75 .85

Concetto Marchesi (1878-1957), Historian A1554

2007, Oct. 1 Photo.
2835 A1554 60c multi 1.75 .85

Jacopo Barozzi (Il Vignola) (1507-73), Architect A1555

2007, Oct. 1 Perf. 13x13¼
2836 A1555 €2.80 multi 8.00 4.00

Grandparent's Day — A1556

2007, Oct. 2
2837 A1556 60c multi 1.75 .85

Philately Day — A1557

2007, Oct. 12 Perf. 13¼x13
2838 A1557 60c multi 1.75 .85

Cupid and Psyche, Sculpture by Antonio Canova (1757-1822) — A1558

2007, Oct. 12 Engr. Perf. 13x13¼
2839 A1558 €1.50 black 4.25 2.10

Miniature Sheet

Entertainers — A1559

No. 2840: a, Beniamino Gigli (1890-1957), opera singer. b, Maria Callas (1923-77), opera singer. c, Amedeo Nazzari (1907-79), actor.

2007, Oct. 18 Photo. Perf. 13¼x13
2840 A1559 Sheet of 3 5.25 2.60
a.-c. 60c Any single 1.75 .85

Giuseppe Di Vittorio (1892-1957), Union Leader — A1560

2007, Nov. 3 Perf. 13x13¼
2841 A1560 60c multi 1.75 .85

Mondadori Publishing House, Cent. A1561

2007, Nov. 12
2842 A1561 60c multi 1.75 .85

Madonna and Child, by Giovan Battista Cima da Conegliano A1562

Snow-covered House and Trees — A1563

2007, Nov. 20 Engr. Perf. 13¼x13
2843 A1562 60c green 1.75 .85
Photo.
2844 A1563 65c multi 1.90 .95
Christmas.

Italian 2007-08 Term on UN Security Council A1564

2007, Dec. 1 Photo. Perf. 13x13¼
2845 A1564 85c multi 2.50 1.25

Governor's Palace, Fiume (Rijeka, Croatia) A1565

2007, Dec. 10
2846 A1565 65c multi 1.90 .95

Italian Constitution, 60th Anniv. — A1566

2008, Jan. 2 Perf. 13¼x13
2847 A1566 60c multi 1.75 .90

Italian Red Cross Volunteer Nursing Corps, Cent. — A1567

2008, Jan. 29
2848 A1567 60c multi 1.75 .90

Amintore Fanfani (1908-99), Politician A1568

2008, Feb. 6 Perf. 13x13¼
2849 A1568 €1 multi 3.00 1.50

Italian Stock Exchange, Bicent. — A1569

2008, Feb. 8 Perf. 13¼x13
2850 A1569 65c multi 2.00 1.00

Olivetti Typewriter and First Olivetti Factory A1570

2008, Feb. 12 Perf. 13¼x13
2851 A1570 60c multi 1.90 .95
Olivetti Corporation, Cent.

Villa Reale, Monza, Designed by Giuseppe Piermarini A1571

2008, Feb. 18 Engr. Perf. 13x13¼
2852 A1571 €1.40 black & blue 4.25 2.10

Natl. Council of Economics and Labor, 50th Anniv. A1572

2008, Feb. 20 Photo.
2853 A1572 €1.50 multi 4.75 2.40

Dorando Pietri (1885-1942), Marathon Runner — A1573

2008, Feb. 23
2854 A1573 60c multi 1.90 .95

Souvenir Sheet

Song, "Nel Blu, Dipinto di Blu," 50th Anniv. — A1574

2008, Feb. 25 *Perf. 13¼x13*
2855 A1574 60c multi 1.90 .95

Anna Magnani (1908-73), Actress — A1575

2008, Mar. 7
2856 A1575 60c multi 1.90 .95

Emblem of Ricordi Publishing House and La Scala Theater, Milan A1576

2008, Mar. 7 Photo. *Perf. 13¼x13*
2857 A1576 60c indigo & gray 1.90 .95
Ricordi Music Publishing House, bicent.

Italia 2009 Intl. Philatelic Exhibition, Rome — A1577

Exhibition emblem and: 60c, Congress Center. 65c, Colosseum.

2008, Mar. 7 Photo. *Perf. 13¼x13*
2858 A1577 60c multi 1.90 .95
2859 A1577 65c multi 2.00 1.00

Carlo Combi High School, Capodistria — A1578

2008, Mar. 8
2860 A1578 60c multi 1.90 .95

Edmondo de Amicis (1846-1908), Writer — A1579

2008, Mar. 11 Photo. *Perf. 13¼x13*
2861 A1579 60c multi 1.90 .95

Self-portrait, by Bernardino di Betto (Pintoricchio, c. 1454-1513) — A1580

2008, Mar. 14 *Perf. 13x13¼*
2862 A1580 60c multi 1.90 .95

Running of the Madonna, Sulmona — A1581

2008, Mar. 15 *Perf. 13¼x13*
2863 A1581 60c multi 1.90 .95

Italian Rowing Federation, 120th Anniv. A1582

2008, Mar. 31 Photo. *Perf. 13¼x13*
2864 A1582 65c multi 2.10 1.10

Confirmation of the Rule, by Giotto — A1583

2008, Apr. 16 Photo. *Perf. 13x13¼*
2865 A1583 60c multi 1.90 .95
Rule of life of St. Francis of Assisi, 700th anniv.

Imperial Forum, Rome A1584

2008, Apr. 21
2866 A1584 60c multi 1.90 .95

Italian National Press Federation, Cent. — A1585

2008, Apr. 23 *Perf. 13¼x13*
2867 A1585 60c multi 1.90 .95

Flight, Sculpture by Pasquale Basile A1586

2008, Apr. 23 *Perf. 13x13¼*
2868 A1586 €1.40 multi 4.50 2.25
Intl. Decade of Education for Sustainable Development.

Giovannino Guareschi (1908-68), Journalist A1587

2008, May 1 Photo. *Perf. 13¼x13*
2869 A1587 60c multi 1.90 .95

Ludovico Geymonat (1908-91), Philosopher — A1588

2008, May 8 *Perf. 13¼x13*
2870 A1588 60c multi 1.90 .95

Europa — A1589

Designs: 60c, Red mailbox. 65c, Brown mailbox.

2008, May 9 Photo. *Perf. 13¼x13*
2871 A1589 60c multi 1.90 .95
2872 A1589 65c multi 2.00 1.00

Works of Andrea Palladio (1508-80), Architect A1590

Designs: 60c, Alpini Bridge, Bassano. 65c, Palladian Basilica, Vicenza.

2008, May 10 Engr. *Perf. 13x13¼*
2873 A1590 60c multi 1.90 .95
2874 A1590 65c multi 2.10 1.10

St. Francis Caracciolo (1563-1608) — A1591

2008, May 23 Photo. *Perf. 13¼x13*
2875 A1591 60c multi 1.90 .95

Italian Regions Type of 2004
2008, May 23 Photo. *Perf. 13¼x13*
2876 A1387 60c Valle d'Aosta 1.90 .95
2877 A1387 60c Veneto 1.90 .95
2878 A1387 60c Molise 1.90 .95
2879 A1387 60c Sicily 1.90 .95
Nos. 2876-2879 (4) 7.60 3.80

Guastalla School, Monza — A1592

2008, May 24 Photo. *Perf. 13¼x13*
2880 A1592 60c dk & lt blue 1.90 .95

Ducati Desmosedici GP7 Motorcycle — A1593

2008, May 31 *Perf. 13¼x13*
2881 A1593 60c multi 1.90 .95

Giacomo Puccini (1858-1924), Composer A1594

2008, June 21 Photo. Perf. 13¼x13
2882 A1594 €1.50 multi 4.75 2.40

F. C. Internazionale, 2007-08 Italian Soccer Champions — A1595

2008, July 4 Photo. Perf. 13x13¼
2883 A1595 60c multi 1.90 .95

2008 Summer Olympics, Beijing A1596

Olympic rings and: 60c, Torch bearer and map. 85c, Greek and Chinese athletes.

2008, July 7 Photo. Perf. 13x13¼
2884 A1596 60c multi 1.90 .95
2885 A1596 85c multi 2.75 1.40

Tommaso Landolfi (1908-79), Writer A1597

2008, July 19 Photo. Perf. 13x13¼
2886 A1597 60c multi 1.90 .95

Tourism Type of 2005
2008, July 24 Photo. Perf. 13¼x13
2887 A1424 60c Tre Cime di Lavaredo 1.90 .95
2888 A1424 60c Introdacqua 1.90 .95
2889 A1424 60c Casamicciola Terme 1.90 .95
2890 A1424 60c Mamoiada 1.90 .95
Nos. 2887-2890 (4) 7.60 3.80

Bowl of Saffron and Crocuses — A1598

Ingredients for Spaghetti all'Amatriciana — A1599

2008 Photo. Perf. 13¼x13
2891 A1598 60c multi 1.90 .95
Perf. 13x13¼
2892 A1599 60c multi 1.90 .95
Issued: No. 2891, 7/26; No. 2892, 8/29.

Bell Tower, Treviglio A1600

2008, Aug. 30 Engr. Perf. 13x13¼
2893 A1600 60c multi 1.75 .85

Dante Alighieri High School, Gorizia — A1601

Seal of the University of Perugia — A1602

2008, Sept. 8 Photo. Perf. 13¼x13
2894 A1601 60c multi 1.75 .85
2895 A1602 60c multi 1.75 .85

Cesare Pavese (1908-50), Writer — A1603

2008, Sept. 9
2896 A1603 65c multi 1.90 .95

Alberico Gentili (1552-1608), Jurist — A1604

2008, Sept. 13 Perf. 13x13¼
2897 A1604 65c multi 1.90 .95

Malatestiana Library, Cesena — A1605

2008, Sept. 19 Engr. Perf. 13¼x13
2898 A1605 60c black 1.75 .85

World Road Cycling Championships, Varese — A1606

2008, Sept. 22 Photo. Perf. 13¼x13
2899 A1606 60c multi 1.75 .85

Philately Day — A1607

2008, Oct. 10 Perf. 13¼x13
2900 A1607 60c multi 1.60 .80

Italia 2009 Intl. Philatelic Exhibition, Rome A1608

2008, Oct. 10 Photo. Perf. 13x13¼
2901 A1608 85c multi 2.40 1.25
Litho. on Gold Foil
Self-Adhesive
Rouletted 8
2902 A1608 €2.80 multi 7.50 3.75

Local Police — A1609

2008, Oct. 23 Photo. Perf. 13¼x13
2903 A1609 60c multi 1.60 .80

Oath of the Plebian Tribune, 2500th Anniv. A1610

2008, Oct. 24 Perf. 13x13¼
2904 A1610 60c multi 1.60 .80

Madonna and Child Enthroned with Two Angels, by Lorenzo di Credi — A1611

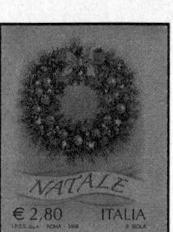

Wreath — A1612

2008, Oct. 30 Photo. Perf. 13¼x13
2905 A1611 60c multi 1.60 .80
Litho. on Gold Foil
Self-Adhesive
Rouletted 8
2906 A1612 €2.80 multi 7.25 3.75
Christmas.

UNESCO World Heritage Sites — A1613

Designs: 60c, Val d'Orcia. €2.80, Historic Center of Urbino.

2008, Oct. 31 Engr. Perf. 13¼x13
2907 A1613 60c multi 1.60 .80
2908 A1613 €2.80 blue & black 7.25 3.75

Messina Earthquake, Cent. — A1614

2008, Nov. 3 Photo. Perf. 13x13¼
2909 A1614 60c multi 1.60 .80

Corriere dei Piccoli Comic Strips, Cent. A1615

2008, Nov. 8
2910 A1615 60c multi 1.60 .80

Charles Darwin (1809-82), Naturalist A1616

2009, Feb. 12
2911 A1616 65c multi   1.75 .85

Souvenir Sheet

Song, "Tintarella di Luna," 50th Anniv. — A1617

2009, Feb. 17   *Perf. 13¼x13*
2912 A1617 60c multi   1.60 .80

5th Natl. Conference on Drugs, Trieste — A1618

2009, Mar. 12
2913 A1618 60c multi   1.60 .80

Valle Camonica Rock Drawing UNESCO World Heritage Site — A1619

2009, Mar. 27   Engr.
2914 A1619 €2.80 brown   7.75 3.75

Italia 2009 Intl. Philatelic Exhibition, Rome — A1620

People and: 60c, Italian stamps. €1, Map of Europe.

2009, Mar. 27   Photo.
2915 A1620 60c multi   1.60 .80
2916 A1620 €1 multi   2.75 1.40

Father Primo Mazzolari (1890-1959), Writer on Social and Religious Issues — A1621

2009, Apr. 14   *Perf. 13x13¼*
2917 A1621 60c multi   1.60 .80

Sardinia Grenadier Corps, 350th Anniv. A1622

2009, Apr. 16
2918 A1622 60c multi   1.60 .80

Piazza di Spagna, Spanish Steps, Fontana della Barcaccia, Rome A1623

2009, Apr. 21
2919 A1623 60c multi   1.60 .80

Indro Montanelli (1909-2001), Journalist A1624

2009, Apr. 22   *Perf. 13¼x13*
2920 A1624 60c multi   1.60 .80

Bulgari Jewelers, 125th Anniv. — A1625

2009, Apr. 24
2921 A1625 60c multi   1.60 .80

Italy-Switzerland Chamber of Commerce, Cent. — A1626

2009, May 2   *Perf. 13x13¼*
2922 A1626 60c multi   1.75 .85

Carabinieri Command for Cultural Heritage Protection A1627

2009, May 4
2923 A1627 60c multi   1.75 .85

16th Mediterranean Games, Pescara — A1628

2009, May 5
2924 A1628 60c multi   1.75 .85

European Parliament Elections A1629

2009, May 7
2925 A1629 60c multi   1.75 .85

Europa A1630

Designs: 60c, Galileo National Telescope, La Palma, Canary Islands. 65c, AGILE astronomical satellite.

2009, May 7
2926 A1630 60c multi   1.75 .85
2927 A1630 65c multi   1.90 .95

Intl. Year of Astronomy.

Giro d'Italia Bicycle Race, Cent. — A1631

2009, May 9   *Perf. 13¼x13*
2928 A1631 60c multi   1.75 .85

Academy of Italian-German Studies, Merano, 50th Anniv. — A1632

2009, May 9   *Perf. 13x13¼*
2929 A1632 60c multi   1.75 .85

Mille Miglia Auto Race A1633

2009, May 14   *Perf. 13x13¼*
2930 A1633 60c multi   1.75 .85

Festival of Mysteries, Campobasso A1634

2009, May 22   *Perf. 13¼*
2931 A1634 60c multi   1.75 .85

Cathedral of Santa Maria Madre di Dio, Rieti — A1635

2009, May 27 Engr. *Perf. 13¼x13*
2932 A1635 60c black   1.75 .85

Giovanni Palatucci (1909-45), Police Official Who Saved Jews From Deportation A1636

2009, May 29   Photo.
2933 A1636 60c multi   1.75 .85

Gilera Motorbikes, Cent. — A1637

2009, June 6   *Perf. 13x13¼*
2934 A1637 60c multi   1.75 .85

Postage Stamps of Sicily, 150th Anniv. A1638

**2009, June 18 Photo. *Perf. 13x13¼*
2935 A1638 60c multi   1.75 .85

Souvenir Sheet

2009 Baseball World Cup
Tournament — A1639

2009, June 20 Photo. Perf. 13x13¼
2936 A1639 60c multi   1.75 .85

St. Giovanni
Leonardi (1541-
1609)
A1640

2009, June 23   Perf. 13¼x13
2937 A1640 60c multi   1.75 .85

F. C.
Internazionale,
2008-09 Italian
Soccer
Champions
A1641

2009, June 25
2938 A1641 60c multi   1.75 .85

San Daniele Prosciutto, 500th Anniv.
of Historical Documentation of
Production — A1642

2009, June 26   Perf. 13x13¼
2939 A1642 60c multi   1.75 .85

St. Mark's
Square,
Venice
A1643

2009, July 2
2940 A1643 60c multi   1.75 .85

Envelope
A1644

2009 Engr.   Serpentine Die Cut 11
Self-Adhesive
Denomination Color
2941 A1644   60c blue   1.75   .85
2942 A1644 €1.40 red   4.00 2.00
2943 A1644 €1.50 green   4.25 2.75
2944 A1644 €2 brown   5.75 2.75
2945 A1644 €3.30 black   9.75 5.00
   Nos. 2941-2945 (5)   25.50 12.70
   Issued: Nos. 2941-2944, 7/7. No. 2945,
10/31.

Insurrection of the Women of Carrara,
65th Anniv. — A1645

2009, July 7 Photo. Perf. 13x13¼
2946 A1645 €1.50 multi   4.25 2.10

G8 Summit,
L'Aquila — A1646

2009, July 8 Photo. Perf. 13¼x13
2947 A1646 65c multi   1.90 .95

Tourism Type of 2005
2009, July 10 Photo. Perf. 13¼x13
2948 A1424 60c Verezzi   1.75   .85
2949 A1424 60c Isola del Giglio 1.75 .85
2950 A1424 60c Costa degli Dei,
                  Capo Vaticano   1.75 .85
2951 A1424 60c Gole
                  dell'Alcantara 1.75 .85
   Nos. 2948-2951 (4)   7.00 3.40

La Nazione
Newspaper,
Florence, 150th
Anniv. — A1647

2009, July 14
2952 A1647 60c multi   1.75 .85

13th World Aquatics Championships,
Rome — A1648

2009, July 18   Engr. & Embossed
2953 A1648 €1.50 blue   4.25 2.10

Forest Fire
Prevention
A1649

2009, Aug. 1   Photo.
2954 A1649 60c multi   1.75 .85

30th Rimini
Meeting
A1650

2009, Aug. 25
2955 A1650 60c green & black   1.75 .85

Montebello
Lancers Cavalry
Regiment, 150th
Anniv. — A1651

2009, Sept. 4
2956 A1651 60c multi   1.75 .85

Painting by
Francesco
Solimena
A1652

2009, Sept. 17 Photo. Perf. 13x13¼
2957 A1652 60c multi   1.75 .90

Portrait of a Woman, by Giovanni
Ambrogio de Predis, and Ambrosian
Academy Library and Gallery,
Milan — A1653

2009, Sept. 21 Engr. Perf. 13¼x13
2958 A1653 €1.40 black   4.25 2.10

Emilio
Alessandrini
(1942-79),
Magistrate Killed
by Terrorists
A1654

2009, Sept. 26 Photo. Perf. 13¼x13
2959 A1654 60c multi   1.75 .85

Souvenir Sheet

Christian Roots of Europe — A1655

No. 2960: a, Green cross, yellow brown
map. b, Yellow brown cross, green map.

2009, Oct. 7   Perf. 13x13¼
2960 A1655 Sheet of 2   3.75 1.90
  a.   60c multi   1.75   .90
  b.   65c multi   2.00 1.00

L'Unione Sarda
Newspaper, 120th
Anniv. — A1656

2009, Oct. 13   Perf. 13¼x13
2961 A1656 60c multi   1.75 .90

Father Luigi
Sturzo (1871-
1959), Politician
A1657

2009, Oct. 14
2962 A1657 €1.50 multi   4.50 2.25

Norberto Bobbio
(1909-2004),
Historian
A1658

2009, Oct. 16
2963 A1658 65c multi   2.00 1.00

Fathers Giovanni Minozzi (1884-1959) and Giovanni Semeria (1867-1931), Founders of Natl. Institute of Southern Italy — A1659

2009, Oct. 19
2964 A1659 60c multi 1.75 .90

Philately Day A1660

2009, Oct. 21 Perf. 13x13¼
2965 A1660 60c multi 1.75 .90

Italian Language Day — A1661

2009, Oct. 21 Photo. Perf. 13¼x13
2966 A1661 60c multi + label 1.75 .90
Printed in sheets of 5 + 5 labels. See San Marino No. 1801; Vatican City No. 1426.

Sports Day at Italia 2009 Intl. Philatelic Exhibition, Rome — A1662

Sports figures: 60c, Gino Bartali (1914-2000), cyclist. 65c, Valentino Mazzola (1919-49), soccer player. €1.40, Michele Alboreto (1956-2001), race car driver.

2009, Oct. 22 Photo. Perf. 13¼x13
2967 A1662 60c multi 1.75 .90
2968 A1662 65c multi 2.00 1.00
2969 A1662 €1.40 multi 4.25 2.10
Nos. 2967-2969 (3) 8.00 4.00

Souvenir Sheet

Diplomatic Relations Between Italy and Bulgaria, 130th Anniv. — A1663

2009, Oct. 22 Perf. 13¼
2970 A1663 65c multi 2.00 1.00
See Bulgaria No.

Adoration of the Shepherds, by Domenico Piola (1627-1703) — A1664

Ornaments — A1665

2009, Oct. 23 Perf. 13¼x13
2971 A1664 60c multi 1.75 .90
Self-Adhesive
Serpentine Die Cut 11
2972 A1665 60c multi 1.75 .90
Christmas.

Souvenir Sheet

Comic Strips — A1666

No. 2973: a, Cocco Bill, by Benito Jacovitti. b, Diabolik, by Angela and Luciana Giussani. c, Lupo Alberto, by Silver.

2009, Oct. 23 Perf. 13x13¼
2973 A1666 Sheet of 3 9.00 4.50
a.-c. €1 Any single 3.00 1.50
Collector's Day at Italia 2009 Intl. Philatelic Exhibition, Rome.

Music Day at Italia 2009 Intl. Philatelic Exhibition, Rome — A1667

Designs: 65c, Luciano Pavarotti (1935-2007), singer. €1, Mino Reitano (1944-2009), singer. €1.50, Nino Rota (1911-79), composer.

2009, Oct. 24 Perf. 13¼
2974 A1667 65c multi 2.00 1.00
2975 A1667 €1 multi 3.00 1.50
2976 A1667 €1.50 multi 4.50 2.25
Nos. 2974-2976 (3) 9.50 4.75

Europe Day at Italia 2009 Intl. Philatelic Exhibition, Rome A1668

No. 2977 — Roman architectural works: a, Pont du Gard, France. b, Hadrian's Wall, Great Britain. c, Odeon of Patras, Greece. d, Porta Nigra, Trier, Germany. e, Segovia Aqueduct, Spain.

2009, Oct. 25 Serpentine Die Cut 11
Self-Adhesive
2977 Booklet pane of 5 + label 10.00
a.-e. A1668 65c Any single 2.00 1.00
Complete booklet, #2977 10.00

Art of the 20th Century — A1669

Designs: 60c, Guantanamera, sculpture by Giacomo Manzù (1908-91). 65c, Danza dell'Orzo (The Bear Dance), by Gino Severini (1883-1966). 85c, Donna e Ambiente, by Federico de Pistoris (1898-1975).

2009, Oct. 30 Perf. 13¼x13
2978 A1669 60c multi 1.75 .90
2979 A1669 65c multi 2.00 1.00
2980 A1669 85c multi 2.60 1.25
Nos. 2978-2980 (3) 6.35 3.15

Giorgio Perlasca (1910-92), Rescuer of Jews in World War II — A1670

2010, Jan. 31 Photo. Perf. 13x13¼
2981 A1670 60c multi 1.75 .85

Souvenir Sheet

Santa Maria de Collemaggio Basilica, L'Aquila — A1671

2010, Feb. 10 Photo. Perf. 13¼x13
2982 A1671 60c multi 1.75 .85

Folk Festivals Type of 2009

Designs: No. 2983, Acireale Carnival. No. 2984, Jousting tournament, Sa Sartiglia, Oristano.

2010, Feb. 12 Photo. Perf. 13½
2983 A1634 60c multi 1.75 .85
2984 A1634 60c multi 1.75 .85

2010 Winter Olympics, Vancouver A1672

Serpentine Die Cut 11
2010, Feb. 12
Self-Adhesive
2985 A1672 85c multi 2.40 1.25

2010 Youth Olympics, Singapore — A1673

2010, Feb. 12 Photo.
Self-Adhesive
2986 A1673 85c multi 2.40 1.25

Mario Pannunzio (1910-68), Journalist A1674

2010, Mar. 5 Perf. 13x13¼
2987 A1674 60c multi 1.75 .85

Ennio Flaiano (1910-72), Screenwriter A1675

2010, Mar. 5 Photo. Perf. 13¼x13
2988 A1675 60c multi 1.75 .85

Madonna dei Miracoli Basilica, Motta di Livenza — A1676

2010, Mar. 9
2989 A1676 60c black 1.60 .80

Massimo D'Azeglio, First President of Province of Milan, and Isimbardi Palace A1677

2010, Mar. 19 Perf. 13x13¼
2990 A1677 60c multi 1.60 .80
Province of Milan, 150th anniv.

Alfa Romeo Automobiles, Cent. — A1678

No. 2991: a, 1910 24HP. b, 2010 Giulietta.

2010, Mar. 20
2991   Horiz. pair + central la-   3.25 1.60
    bel
 a.-b. A1678 60c Either single   1.60   .80

Burial of Christ with Three Angels Holding the Shroud, by Gerolamo della Rovere — A1679

2010, Mar. 22   **Perf. 13¼x13**
2992 A1679 60c multi   1.60   .80

Confindustria (Federation of Employers), Cent. — A1680

2010, May 5   **Perf. 13x13¼**
2993 A1680 €1.40 multi   3.75 1.90

Miniature Sheet

Expedition of the Thousand, 150th Anniv. — A1681

No. 2994 — Paintings: a, Garibaldi Sets Sail From Quarto, by V. Azzola. b, Landing at Marsala, by unknown artist. c, Battle of Calatafimi, by Remigio Legat. d, Encounter in Teano of Garibaldi and Victor Emmanuel II, by Pietro Aldi.

2010, May 5
2994 A1681   Sheet of 4   8.00 4.00
 a.   60c multi   1.50   .75
 b.   65c multi   1.75   .85
 c.   85c multi   2.25 1.10
 d.   €1 multi   2.50 1.25

Rhaetian Railway in the Albula - Bernina Landscapes UNESCO World Heritage Site — A1682

2010, May 6   **Perf. 13¼x13**
2995 A1682 65c multi   1.75   .85

Pinocchio, by Carlo Collodi — A1683

Geronimo Stilton, by Elisabetta Dami — A1684

2010, May 7
2996 A1683 60c multi   1.50   .75
2997 A1684 65c multi   1.75   .85

Europa.

Sister Maria Domenica Brun Barbentini (1789-1868), Founder of the Congregation of the Sister Servants of the Sick of St. Camillus — A1685

2010, May 22   **Perf. 13x13¼**
2998 A1685 60c multi   1.50   .75

Hanbury Botanic Gardens, Ventimiglia A1686

2010, May 29
2999 A1686 60c multi   1.50   .75

Tourism Type of 2005 and

1955 Tourism Poster — A1687

2010, June 4   **Perf. 13¼x13**
3000 A1424 60c Courmayeur   1.50   .75
3001 A1424 60c Todi   1.50   .75
3002 A1424 60c Viggiano   1.50   .75
3003 A1424 60c Isole Tremiti   1.50   .75
    Nos. 3000-3003 (4)   6.00 3.00

Self-Adhesive
Serpentine Die Cut 11
3004 A1687 60c multi   1.50   .75

Camilo Benso, Count of Cavour (1810-61), Statesman A1688

2010, June 6   **Perf. 13¼x13**
3005 A1688 60c multi   1.50   .75

Association of Italian Joint Stock Companies, Cent. A1689

2010, June 17 Photo.   Perf. 13x13¼
3006 A1689 60c multi   1.50   .75

F.C. Internazionale, 2009-10 Italian Soccer Champions A1690

2010, June 24   **Perf. 13¼x13**
3007 A1690 60c multi   1.50   .75

Federacciai Iron and Steel Plant, Bagnoli, Cent. — A1691

Litho. & Silk-Screened
2010, June 28   **Perf. 13¼x14**
3008 A1691 €3.30 black   8.25 4.25

No. 3008 is coated with a varnish producing a rough surface, and is printed with a special ink that allows the stamp to be lifted by a magnet.

Envelope A1692

Serpentine Die Cut 11x11¼
2010, July 1   **Photo.**
Self-Adhesive
Color of Denomination
3009 A1692 5c dark blue   .20   .20
3010 A1692 10c black   .25   .20
3011 A1692 20c blue green   .50   .25
    Nos. 3009-3011 (3)   .95   .65

Giovanni Virginio Schiaparelli (1835-1910), Astronomer — A1693

2010, July 2   **Perf. 13x13¼**
3012 A1693 65c multi   1.75   .85

Pope Benedict XVI, Statue of Pope Celestine V — A1694

2010, July 4   **Perf. 13¼x13**
3013 A1694 60c multi   1.50   .75

Celestinian Jubliee Year.

David with the Head of Goliath, by Caravaggio (1571-1610) — A1695

2010, July 16   **Perf. 13x13¼**
3014 A1695 60c multi   1.60   .80

Ettore Paratore (1907-2000), Latin Scholar, Mosaic and Theater Mask — A1696

2010, July 17   **Perf. 13¼x13**
3015 A1696 65c multi   1.75   .85

50th Plautus Festival, Sarsina.

Samnite Theater, Pietrabbondante — A1697

2010, July 31   **Engr.**
3016 A1697 60c brown   1.60   .80

Joe Petrosino (1860-1909), New York City Policeman, Statue of Liberty, Brooklyn Bridge — A1698

2010, Aug. 30 Photo. Perf. 13x13¼
3017 A1698 85c multi   2.25 1.10

1960 Summer Olympics, Rome, 50th Anniv. A1699

2010, Sept. 7
3018 A1699 60c multi　　　　1.60 .80

First National Gathering of Fire Brigades, Cortina d'Ampezzo A1700

2010, Sept. 10　　*Perf. 13x13¼*
3019 A1700 60c multi　　　　1.60 .80

National Aerobatic Team, 50th Anniv. A1701

2010, Sept. 11
3020 A1701 60c multi　　　　1.75 .85

Piazzale di Porta Pia, Rome A1702

2010, Sept. 20
3021 A1702 60c multi　　　　1.75 .85

Men's Volleyball World Championships, Italy — A1703

Engr. & Embossed
2010, Sept. 24　　*Perf. 13x13¼*
3022 A1703 85c blue　　　　2.40 1.25

Souvenir Sheet

Turin-Salerno High Speed Rail Line — A1705

2010, Oct. 2　Photo.　*Perf. 13x13¼*
3024 A1705 60c multi　　　　1.75 .85

Corriere Adriatico Newspaper, Ancona, 150th Anniv. — A1706

2010, Oct. 5　　*Perf. 13¼x13*
3025 A1706 60c multi　　　　1.75 .85

National Anti-trust Authority, 20th Anniv. A1707

2010, Oct. 10　　*Perf. 13x13¼*
3026 A1707 €1.40 multi　　　4.00 2.00

School of Oenology, Conegliano A1708

2010, Oct. 21　　*Perf. 13x13¼*
3027 A1708 60c multi　　　　1.75 .85

Leonardo Sciascia (1921-89), Writer A1709

2010, Oct. 23　　　　**Engr.**
3028 A1709 60c black　　　　1.75 .85

Italian Tennis Federation, Cent. A1710

2010, Oct. 25　　　　**Photo.**
3029 A1710 60c multi　　　　1.75 .85

Souvenir Sheet

Italian Film Personalities — A1712

No. 3031: a, Federico Fellini (1920-93), director. b, Vittorio Gassman (1922-2000), actor, director. c, Alberto Sordi (1920-2003), actor, director.

2010, Oct. 28　Photo.　*Perf. 13¼x13*
3031 A1712　Sheet of 3　　5.25 2.60
a.-c.　　60c Any single　　1.75 .85

Philately Day — A1713

2010, Oct. 29
3032 A1713 60c multi　　　　1.75 .85

Frette Textiles, 150th Anniv. — A1714

2010, Oct. 29
3033 A1714 60c multi　　　　1.75 .85

Adoration of the Magi, by Sandro Botticelli — A1715

Toy Train A1716

2010, Oct. 29　　*Perf. 13¼x13*
3034 A1715 60c multi　　　　1.75 .85
　　　　　　　Perf. 13x13¼
3035 A1716 65c multi　　　　1.90 .95
Christmas.

Mario Mazzuca (1910-83), Rugby Player A1717

2010, Oct. 30　　*Perf. 13x13¼*
3036 A1717 60c multi　　　　1.75 .85

Gentilini Cookies, 120th Anniv. — A1718

2010, Oct. 31　　*Perf. 13¼x13*
3037 A1718 60c multi　　　　1.75 .85

SEMI-POSTAL STAMPS

Many issues of Italy and Italian Colonies include one or more semi-postal denominations. To avoid splitting sets, these issues are generally listed as regular postage, airmail, etc., unless all values carry a surtax.

Italian Flag — SP1

Italian Eagle Bearing Arms of Savoy — SP2

1915-16　Typo.　Wmk. 140　Perf. 14
B1　SP1 10c + 5c rose　　8.50 10.00
B2　SP2 15c + 5c slate　　6.75 8.50
B3　SP2 20c + 5c orange　32.50 60.00
　　Nos. B1-B3 (3)　　47.75 78.50
　　Set, never hinged　　125.00

No. B2 Surcharged

1916
B4　SP2 20c on 15c + 5c　21.00 50.00
　　　Never hinged　　52.50
a.　Double overprint　　600.00 —
　　　Never hinged
b.　Inverted overprint　600.00 1,000.
　　　Never hinged
c.　Pair, one without
　　　surcharge　　　1,350.
　　　Never hinged　　2,000.

Regular Issues of 1906-16 Overprinted in Blue or Red

1921

B5	A48 10c claret (Bl)	1,275.	1,350.
a.	Double overprint	1,500.	
B6	A50 20c brn org (Bl)	1,875.	425.00
B7	A49 25c blue (R)	250.00	150.00
a.	Double overprint	425.00	
B8	A49 40c brn (Bl)	100.00	21.00
a.	Inverted overprint	170.00	150.00
	Nos. B5-B8 (4)	3,500.	1,946.
	Set, never hinged	5,500.	

Regular Issues of 1901-22 Overprinted in Black, Blue, Brown or Red

1922-23

B9	A48 10c cl ('23) (Bk)	105.00	75.00
a.	Blue ovpt.	105.00	75.00
	Never hinged	210.00	
b.	Brown ovpt.	105.00	75.00
	Never hinged	210.00	
d.	Blk ovpt. double	170.00	
e.	As "b," ovpt. double	185.00	
B10	A48 15c slate (Org)	375.00	450.00
a.	Blue ovpt.	1,000.	925.00
	Never hinged	2,000.	
b.	Red overprint	450.00	500.00
	Never hinged	925.00	
B11	A50 20c brn org (Bk)	425.00	450.00
a.	Blue ovpt.	850.00	450.00
	Never hinged	1,700.	
b.	Blk ovpt.	850.00	725.00
	Never hinged	1,700.	
B12	A49 25c blue (BK; '23)	140.00	110.00
b.	Red Overprint	375.00	450.00
	Never hinged	750.00	
c.	Orange ovpt.	375.00	450.00
	Never hinged	750.00	
B12A	A49 30c org brn (Bk)	275.00	190.00
B13	A49 40c brn (Bl)	210.00	110.00
a.	Black ovpt.	210.00	110.00
	Never hinged	425.00	
b.	As "a," invtd. ovpt.	—	—
B14	A49 50c vio ('23) (Bk)	750.00	675.00
a.	Blue overprint		
B15	A49 60c car (Bk)	2,700.	2,375.
B15A	A49 85c choc (Bk)	375.00	450.00
B16	A46 1 l brn & grn ('23) (Bk)	4,650.	2,750.
a.	Inverted overprint	5,250.	
	Never hinged	6,000.	
	Nos. B9-B16 (10)	10,005.	7,635.
	Set, never hinged	14,250.	

The stamps overprinted "B. L. P." were sold by the Government below face value to the National Federation for Assisting War Invalids. Most of them were affixed to special envelopes (Buste Lettere Postali) which bore advertisements. The Federation was permitted to sell these envelopes at a reduction of 5c from the face value of each stamp. The profits for the war invalids were derived from the advertisements.

Values of Nos. B5-B16 unused are for stamps with original gum. Most copies without gum or with part gum sell for about a quarter of values quoted. Uncanceled stamps affixed to the special envelopes usually sell for about half value.

The overprint on Nos. B9-B16 is wider (13½mm) than that on Nos. B5-B8 (11mm). The 1922-23 overprint exists both typo. and litho. on 10c, 15c, 20c and 25c; only litho. on 40c, 50c, 60c and 1 l; and only typo. on 30c and 85c.

Counterfeits of the B.L.P. overprints exist.

Administering Fascist Oath — SP3

1923, Oct. 29   *Perf. 14x14½*

B17	SP3 30c + 30c brown	32.50	115.00
B18	SP3 50c + 50c violet	32.50	115.00
a.	Horiz. pair, imperf between	1,100.	
B19	SP3 1 l + 1 l gray	32.50	115.00
	Nos. B17-B19 (3)	97.50	345.00
	Set, never hinged	250.00	

The surtax was given to the Benevolent Fund of the Black Shirts (the Italian National Militia).

Anniv. of the March of the Fascisti on Rome.

St. Maria Maggiore SP4

Pope Opening Holy Door SP8

Designs: 30c+15c, St. John Lateran. 50c+25c, St. Paul's Church. 60c+30c, St. Peter's Basilica. 5 l+2.50 l, Pope closing Holy Door.

1924, Dec. 24   *Perf. 12*

B20	SP4 20c + 10c dk grn & brn	4.25	12.50
B21	SP4 30c + 15c dk brn & brn	4.25	12.50
B22	SP4 50c + 25c vio & brn	4.25	12.50
B23	SP4 60c + 30c dp rose & brn	4.25	37.50
B24	SP8 1 l + 50c dp bl & vio	6.75	37.50
B25	SP8 5 l + 2.50 l org brn & vio	8.50	75.00
	Nos. B20-B25 (6)	32.25	187.50
	Set, never hinged	80.00	

The surtax was contributed toward the Holy Year expenses.

Castle of St. Angelo SP10

Victor Emmanuel II — SP14

Designs: 50c+20c, 60c+30c, Aqueduct of Claudius. 1.25 l+50c, 1.25 l+60c, Capitol, Roman Forum. 5 l+2 l, 5 l+2.50 l, People's Gate.

Unwmk.

1926, Oct. 26   Engr.   *Perf. 11*

B26	SP10 40c + 20c dk brn & blk	3.50	18.00
B27	SP10 60c + 30c brn red & ol brn	3.50	18.00
B28	SP10 1.25 l + 60c bl grn & blk	3.50	55.00
B29	SP10 5 l + 2.50 l dk bl & blk	5.00	160.00
	Nos. B26-B29 (4)	15.50	251.00
	Set, never hinged	37.50	

Stamps inscribed "Poste Italiane" and "Fiere Campionaria di Tripoli" are listed in Libya.

1928, Mar. 1

B30	SP10 30c + 10c dl vio & blk	11.50	37.50
B31	SP10 50c + 20c ol grn & sl	20.00	37.50
B32	SP10 1.25 l + 50c dp bl & blk	25.00	75.00
B33	SP10 5 l + 2 l brn red & blk	55.00	300.00
	Nos. B30-B33 (4)	111.50	450.00
	Set, never hinged	275.00	

The tax on Nos. B26 to B33 was devoted to the charitable work of the Voluntary Militia for National Defense.

See Nos. B35-B38.

1929, Jan. 4   Photo.   *Perf. 14*

B34	SP14 50c + 10c ol grn	4.25	9.25
	Never hinged	10.50	

50th anniv. of the death of King Victor Emmanuel II. The surtax was for veterans.

Type of 1926 Issue

Designs in same order.

1930, July 1   Engr.

B35	SP10 30c + 10c dk grn & vio	2.50	27.50
B36	SP10 50c + 10c dk grn & bl grn	3.50	22.50
B37	SP10 1.25 l + 30c ind & grn	8.50	60.00
B38	SP10 5 l + 1.50 l blk brn & ol brn	17.00	225.00
	Nos. B35-B38 (4)	31.50	335.00
	Set, never hinged	77.50	

The surtax was for the charitable work of the Voluntary Militia for National Defense.

Militiamen at Ceremonial Fire with Quotation from Leonardo da Vinci — SP15

Symbolical of Pride for Militia — SP16

Symbolical of Militia Guarding Immortality of Italy SP17

Militia Passing Through Arch of Constantine SP18

1935, July 1   Photo.   Wmk. 140

B39	SP15 20c + 10c rose red	10.00	12.00
B40	SP16 25c + 15c green	10.00	18.00
B41	SP17 50c + 30c purple	10.00	22.50
B42	SP18 1.25 l + 75c blue	10.00	35.00
	Nos. B39-B42 (4)	40.00	87.50
	Set, never hinged	100.00	
	Nos. B39-B42,CB3 (5)	50.00	125.00
	Set, never hinged	117.50	

The surtax was for the Militia.

Roman Battle SP19

Roman Warriors SP20

1941, Dec. 13

B43	SP19 20c + 10c rose red	.20	.55
B44	SP19 30c + 15c brown	.20	.70
B45	SP20 50c + 25c violet	.25	.85
B46	SP20 1.25 l + 1 l blue	.30	.90
	Nos. B43-B46 (4)	.95	3.00
	Set, never hinged	4.50	

2,000th anniv. of the birth of Livy (59 B.C.-17 A.D.), Roman historian.

Catalogue values for unused stamps in this section, from this point to the end of the section, are for Never Hinged items.

Aid for Flood Victims — SP21

1995, Jan. 2   Photo.   *Perf. 13½x14*

B47	SP21 750 l +2250 l multi	4.00	3.50

Queen Helen (1873-1952) SP22

2002, Mar. 2   Photo.   *Perf. 13¼x14*

B48	SP22 41c + 21c multi	1.10	1.10

Surtax for breast cancer research and prevention.

Intl. Commission on Occupational Health, 28th Congress — SP23

2006, Mar. 8   Photo.   *Perf. 13x13¼*

B49	SP23 60c +30c multi	2.25	2.25

Surtax for breast cancer research.

Nursing — SP24

Serpentine Die Cut 11
2010, May 16   Photo.
Self-Adhesive

B50	SP24 60c +30c multi	2.25	2.25

Surtax for breast cancer research.

AIR POST STAMPS

Used values for Nos. C1-C105 are for postally used stamps with legible cancellations. Forged cancels on these issues abound, and expertization is srongly recommended.

Special Delivery Stamp No. E1 Overprinted

			1917, May	Wmk. 140	Perf. 14
C1	SD1	25c rose red	18.00	42.50
		Never hinged	45.00	

Type of SD3 Surcharged in Black

1917, June 27

C2	SD3	25c on 40c violet	21.00	50.00
		Never hinged	55.00	

Type SD3 was not issued without surcharge.

AP2

1926-28 — **Typo.**

C3	AP2	50c rose red ('28)	18.00	12.50
C4	AP2	60c gray	5.00	12.50
C5	AP2	80c brn vio & brn ('28)	32.50	125.00
C6	AP2	1 l blue	12.00	12.50
C7	AP2	1.20 l brn ('27)	29.00	125.00

C8	AP2	1.50 l buff	18.00	32.50
C9	AP2	5 l gray grn	42.50	115.00
		Nos. C3-C9 (7)	157.00	435.00
		Set, never hinged		375.00

Nos. C4 and C6 Surcharged

1927, Sept. 16

C10	AP2	50c on 60c gray	20.00	80.00
a.		Pair, one without surcharge	1,600.	
C11	AP2	80c on 1 l blue	57.50	250.00
		Set, never hinged		190.00

Pegasus AP3

Wings AP4

Spirit of Flight — AP5

Arrows AP6

1930-32 — **Photo.** — **Wmk. 140**

C12	AP4	25c dk grn ('32)	.20	.20
C13	AP3	50c olive brn	.20	.20
C14	AP5	75c org brn ('32)	.40	.20
C15	AP4	80c org red	.20	.70
C16	AP5	1 l purple	.20	.20
C17	AP6	2 l deep blue	.40	.20
C18	AP3	5 l dk green	.80	1.60
C19	AP3	10 l dp car	1.60	6.50
		Nos. C12-C19 (8)	4.00	9.80
		Set, never hinged		10.00

The 50c, 1 l and 2 l were reprinted in 1942 with labels similar to those of Nos. 427-438, but were not issued. Value, set of 3: unused $550; never hinged $1,100.

For overprints see Nos. MC1-MC5. For overprints and surcharges on design AP6 see Nos. C52-C55; Yugoslavia-Ljubljana NB9-NB20, NC11-NC17.

Ferrucci Type of Postage

Statue of Ferrucci.

1930, July 10

C20	A104	50c purple	4.00	18.00
C21	A104	1 l orange brn	4.00	20.00
C22	A104	5 l + 2 l brn vio	16.00	130.00
		Nos. C20-C22 (3)	24.00	168.00
		Set, never hinged		60.00

For overprinted types see Aegean Islands Nos. C1-C3.

Virgil Type of Postage

Jupiter sending forth his eagle.

1930, Oct. 21 — **Photo.** — **Wmk. 140**

C23	A106	50c lt brown	24.00	40.00
C24	A106	1 l orange	24.00	45.00

Engr.
Unwmk.

C25	A106	7.70 l + 1.30 l vio brn	57.50	450.00
C26	A106	9 l + 2 l indigo	65.00	500.00
		Nos. C23-C26 (4)	170.50	1,035.
		Set, never hinged		430.00

The surtax on Nos. C25-C26 was for the National Institute Figli del Littorio.

For overprinted types see Aegean Islands Nos. C4-C7.

Trans-Atlantic Squadron — AP9

1930, Dec. 15 — **Photo.** — **Wmk. 140**

C27	AP9	7.70 l Prus bl & gray	450.00	1,350.
		Never hinged	900.00	
a.		Seven stars instead of six	1,500.	—
		Never hinged	3,000.	

Flight by Italian aviators from Rome to Rio de Janeiro, Dec. 1930-Jan. 12, 1931.

Leonardo da Vinci's Flying Machine AP10

Leonardo da Vinci AP11

Leonardo da Vinci — AP12

1932

C28	AP10	50c olive brn	5.00	14.50
C29	AP11	1 l violet	6.50	16.00
C30	AP11	3 l brown red	8.00	40.00
C31	AP11	5 l dp green	13.00	47.50
C32	AP10	7.70 l + 2 l dk bl	10.00	140.00
C33	AP11	10 l + 2.50 l blk brn	11.50	250.00
		Nos. C28-C33 (6)	54.00	508.00
		Set, never hinged		135.00

Engr.
Unwmk.

C34	AP12	100 l brt bl & grnsh blk	45.00	800.00
		Never hinged	110.00	
a.		Thin paper	200.00	1,450.

Dante Alighieri Soc. and especially Leonardo da Vinci, to whom the invention of a flying machine has been attributed. Surtax was for the benefit of the Society.

Inscription on No. C34: "Man with his large wings by beating against the air will be able to dominate it and lift himself above it".

Issued: #C28-C33, Mar. 14; #C34, Aug. 6.

For overprinted types see Aegean Islands Nos. C8-C13.

Garibaldi's Home at Caprera AP13

Farmhouse where Anita Garibaldi Died AP14

50c, 1 l+25c, Garibaldi's home, Caprera. 2 l+50c, Anita Garibaldi. 5 l+1 l, Giuseppe Garibaldi.

1932, Apr. 6 — **Photo.** — **Wmk. 140**

C35	AP13	50c copper red	5.00	8.00
C36	AP14	80c deep green	5.00	13.00
C37	AP13	1 l + 25c red brn	8.00	32.50
C38	AP13	2 l + 50c dp bl	13.00	45.00
C39	AP14	5 l + 1 l dp grn	13.00	52.50
		Nos. C35-C39 (5)	44.00	151.00
		Set, never hinged		110.00

50th anniv. of the death of Giuseppe Garibaldi, patriot. The surtax was for the benefit of the Garibaldi Volunteers.

For overprinted types see Aegean Islands Nos. C15-C19.

March on Rome Type of Postage

50c, Eagle sculpture and airplane. 75c, Italian buildings from the air.

1932, Oct. 27 — **Perf. 14**

C40	A146	50c dark brown	3.25	10.00
C41	A146	75c orange brn	10.00	32.50
		Set, never hinged		32.50

Graf Zeppelin Issue

Zeppelin over Pyramid of Caius Cestius AP19

5 l, Tomb of Cecilia Metella. 10 l, Stadium of Mussolini. 12 l, St. Angelo Castle and Bridge. 15 l, Roman Forum. 20 l, Imperial Avenue.

1933, Apr. 24

C42	AP19	3 l black & grn	23.00	100.00
C43	AP19	5 l green & brn	23.00	110.00
C44	AP19	10 l car & dl bl	23.00	260.00
C45	AP19	12 l dk bl & red org	23.00	450.00
C46	AP19	15 l dk brn & gray	23.00	525.00
C47	AP19	20 l org brn & bl	23.00	575.00
a.		Vertical pair, imperf. between	9,000.	
		Never hinged	14,000.	
		Nos. C42-C47 (6)	138.00	2,020.
		Set, never hinged		325.00

Balbo's Trans-Atlantic Flight Issue

Italian Flag

King Victor Emmanuel III

Allegory "Flight" — AP25

#C49, Colosseum at Rome, Chicago skyline. #C48-C49 consist of 3 parts; Italian flag, Victor Emmanuel III, & scene arranged horizontally.

1933, May 20

C48	AP25	5.25 l + 19.75 l red, grn & ultra	125.00	1,800.
		Never hinged	250.00	
a.		Left stamp without ovpt.	25,000.	
		Never hinged	37,500.	
C49	AP25	5.25 l + 44.75 l grn, red & ultra	160.00	1,800.
		Never hinged	325.00	

Transatlantic Flight, Rome-Chicago, of 24-seaplane squadron led by Gen. Italo Balbo. Center and right sections paid postage. At left is registered air express label overprinted "APPARECCHIO" and abbreviated pilot's name. Twenty triptychs of each value differ in name overprint.

No. C49 overprinted "VOLO DI RITORNO/NEW YORK-ROMA" was not issued; flight canceled. Value: unused $29,000; never hinged $43,000.

For overprints see Nos. CO1, Aegean Islands C26-C27.

Type of Air Post Stamp of 1930 Surcharged in Black

1934, Jan. 18

C52	AP6	2 l on 2 l yel	7.25	75.00
C53	AP6	3 l on 2 l yel grn	7.25	105.00
C54	AP6	5 l on 2 l rose	7.25	210.00
C55	AP6	10 l on 2 l vio	7.25	300.00
		Nos. C52-C55 (4)	29.00	690.00
		Set, never hinged	72.50	

For use on mail carried on a special flight from Rome to Buenos Aires.

Annexation of Fiume Type

25c, 75c, View of Fiume Harbor. 50c, 1 l+50c, Monument to the Dead. 2 l+1.50 l, Venetian Lions. 3 l+2 l, Julian wall.

1934, Mar. 12

C56	A166	25c green	.95	4.00
C57	A166	50c brown	.95	2.40
C58	A166	75c org brn	.95	10.00
C59	A166	1 l	.95	16.00
C60	A166	2 l + 1.50 l dl bl	.95	21.00
C61	A166	3 l + 2 l blk brn	.95	23.00
		Nos. C56-C61 (6)	4.80	76.40
		Set, never hinged	14.40	

Airplane and View of Stadium AP32

Soccer Player and Plane AP33

Airplane and Stadium Entrance AP35

Airplane over Stadium AP34

1934, May 24

C62	AP32	50c car rose	11.00	40.00
C63	AP33	75c gray blue	17.50	47.50
C64	AP34	5 l + 2.50 l ol grn	52.50	325.00
C65	AP35	10 l + 5 l brn blk	52.50	475.00
		Nos. C62-C65 (4)	133.50	887.50
		Set, never hinged	332.50	

2nd World Soccer Championships.
For overprinted types see Aegean Islands Nos. C28-C31.

Zeppelin under Fire AP36

Air Force Memorial — AP40

Designs: 25c, 80c, Zeppelin under fire. 50c, 75c, Motorboat patrol. 1 l+50c, Desert infantry. 2 l+1 l, Plane attacking troops.

1934, Apr. 24

C66	AP36	25c dk green	3.25	6.50
C67	AP36	50c gray	3.25	8.00
C68	AP36	75c dk brown	3.25	10.00
C69	AP36	80c slate blue	3.25	12.00
C70	AP36	1 l + 50c red brn	8.00	30.00
C71	AP36	2 l + 1 l brt bl	11.50	37.50
C72	AP40	3 l + 2 l brn blk	16.00	45.00
		Nos. C66-C72 (7)	48.50	149.00
		Set, never hinged	120.00	

Cent. of the institution of the Military Medal of Valor.
For overprinted types see Aegean Islands Nos. C32-C38.

King Victor Emmanuel III — AP41

1934, Nov. 5

C73	AP41	1 l purple	3.25	60.00
C74	AP41	2 l brt blue	3.25	70.00
C75	AP41	4 l red brown	7.50	225.00
C76	AP41	5 l dull green	7.50	300.00
C77	AP41	8 l rose red	23.00	400.00
C78	AP41	10 l brown	25.00	550.00
		Nos. C73-C78 (6)	69.50	1,605.
		Set, never hinged	160.00	

65th birthday of King Victor Emmanuel III and the nonstop flight from Rome to Mogadiscio.
For overprint see No. CO2.

Muse Playing Harp AP42

Angelic Dirge for Bellini AP43

Scene from Bellini Opera, La Sonnambula — AP44

1935, Sept. 24

C79	AP42	25c dull yellow	4.75	13.00
C80	AP42	50c brown	4.75	11.00
C81	AP42	60c rose carmine	16.00	29.00
C82	AP43	1 l + 1 l purple	25.00	175.00
C83	AP44	5 l + 2 l green	32.50	260.00
		Nos. C79-C83 (5)	83.00	488.00
		Set, never hinged	200.00	

Vincenzo Bellini, (1801-35), operatic composer.

Quintus Horatius Flaccus Type

25c, Seaplane in Flight. 50c, 1 l+1 l, Monoplane over valley. 60c, Oak and eagle. 5 l+2 l, Ruins of ancient Rome.

1936, July 1

C84	A197	25c dp green	3.25	12.00
C85	A197	50c dk brown	5.00	20.00
C86	A197	60c scarlet	8.50	20.00
C87	A197	1 l + 1 l vio	20.00	175.00
C88	A197	5 l + 2 l slate bl	25.00	275.00
		Nos. C84-C88 (5)	61.75	494.00
		Set, never hinged	150.00	

Child of the Balilla AP49

Heads of Children AP50

1937, June 28

C89	AP49	25c dk bl grn	8.00	20.00
C90	AP50	50c brown	16.00	14.50
C91	AP49	1 l purple	12.00	24.00
C92	AP50	2 l + 1 l dk bl	16.00	140.00
C93	AP49	3 l + 2 l org	20.00	225.00
C94	AP50	5 l + 3 l rose lake	24.00	260.00
		Nos. C89-C94 (6)	96.00	683.50
		Set, never hinged	240.00	

Summer Exhibition for Child Welfare. The surtax on Nos. C92-C94 was used to support summer camps for poor children.

Prosperous Italy AP51

50c, Prolific Italy. 80c, Apollo's steeds. 1 l+1 l, Map & Roman Standard. 5 l+1 l, Augustus Caesar.

1937, Sept. 23

C95	AP51	25c red vio	8.00	12.00
C96	AP51	50c olive brn	8.00	10.00
C97	AP51	80c orange brn	24.00	16.00
C98	AP51	1 l + 1 l dk bl	30.00	125.00
C99	AP51	5 l + 1 l dl vio	65.00	250.00
		Nos. C95-C99 (5)	135.00	413.00
		Set, never hinged	325.00	

Bimillenary of the birth of Augustus Caesar (Octavianus) on the occasion of the exhibition opened in Rome by Mussolini on Sept. 22nd, 1937.
For overprinted types see Aegean Islands Nos. C39-C43.

King Victor Emmanuel III — AP56

25c, 3 l, King Victor Emmanuel III. 50c, 1 l, Dante Alighieri. 2 l, 5 l, Leonardo da Vinci.

1938, Oct. 28

C100	AP56	25c dull green	5.00	6.50
C101	AP56	50c dk yel brn	5.00	6.50
C102	AP56	1 l violet	8.00	10.00
C103	AP56	2 l royal blue	8.00	37.50
C104	AP56	3 l brown car	13.00	45.00
C105	AP56	5 l dp green	15.00	65.00
		Nos. C100-C105 (6)	54.00	170.50
		Set, never hinged	135.00	

Proclamation of the Empire.

Plane and Clasped Hands AP59

Swallows in Flight AP60

1945-47 Wmk. 277 Photo. Perf. 14

C106	AP59	1 l slate bl	.20	.20
C107	AP59	2 l dk blue	.20	.20
C108	AP59	3.20 l red org	.20	.20
C109	AP60	5 l dk green	.20	.20
C110	AP60	10 l car rose	.20	.20
C111	AP60	25 l dk bl ('46)	6.50	13.00
C112	AP60	25 l brown ('47)	.20	.20

C113	AP59	50 l dk grn ('46)	14.00	20.00
C114	AP59	50 l violet ('47)	.20	.20
		Nos. C106-C114 (9)	21.90	34.40
		Set, never hinged	40.00	

Issued: #C111, C113, 7/13/46; #C112, C114, 4/21/47.
See Nos. C130-C131. For surcharges and overprints see Nos. C115, C136, 1LNC1-1LNC7, Trieste C1-C6, C17-C22.

No. C108 Surcharged in Black

1947, July 1

C115	AP59	6 l on 3.20 l	.20	.20
a.		Never hinged	.20	
		Pair, one without surcharge	1,200.	
b.		Inverted surcharge		22,500.

Radio on Land — AP61

Plane over Capitol Bell Tower — AP65

Designs: 6 l, 25 l, Radio on land. 10 l, 35 l, Radio at sea. 20 l, 50 l, Radio in the skies.

1947, Aug. 1 Photo. Perf. 14

C116	AP61	6 l dp violet	.20	.20
C117	AP61	10 l dk car rose	.20	.20
C118	AP61	20 l dp orange	.75	.75
C119	AP61	25 l aqua	1.10	1.60
C120	AP61	35 l brt blue	1.10	2.40
C121	AP61	50 l lilac rose	3.00	5.00
		Nos. C116-C121 (6)	6.35	10.15
		Set, never hinged	10.00	

50th anniv. of radio.
For overprints see Trieste Nos. C7-C12.

1948

C123	AP65	100 l green	1.10	.20
C124	AP65	300 l lilac rose	.20	.60
C125	AP65	500 l ultra	.40	1.20

Engr.

C126	AP65	1000 l dk brown	.65	2.40
a.		Vert. pair, imperf. btwn.	275.00	275.00
b.		Perf. 14x13	.75	2.40
		Nos. C123-C126 (4)	2.35	4.40
		Set, never hinged	11.00	

See No. C132-C135. For overprints see Trieste Nos. C13-C16, C23-C26.

St. Catherine Carrying Cross AP66

200 l, St. Catherine with outstretched arms.

1948, Mar. 1 Photo.

C127	AP66	100 l bl vio & brn org	47.50	40.00
C128	AP66	200 l dp blue & bis	26.00	25.00
		Set, never hinged	150.00	

600th anniversary of the birth of St. Catherine of Siena, patroness of Italy.

Giuseppe Mazzini (1805-1872), Patriot — AP67

1955, Dec. 31   Wmk. 303   Perf. 14
C129 AP67 100 l Prus green   1.60 1.40

Types of 1945-46, 1948
1955-62   Wmk. 303   Perf. 14
C130 AP60   5 l green ('62)   .20   .20
C131 AP59 50 l vio ('57)   .20   .20
C132 AP65 100 l green   .75   .20
C133 AP65 300 l lil rose   .85   .55
C134 AP65 500 l ultra ('56)   1.00   .90

Engr.
Perf. 13½
C135 AP65 1000 l maroon ('59) 2.00 2.00
Nos. C130-C135 (6)   5.00 4.05

Fluorescent Paper
See note below No. 998.
No. C132 was issued on both ordinary and fluorescent paper. The design of the fluorescent stamp is smaller.
Airmail stamps issued only on fluorescent paper are Nos. C139-C140.

Type of 1945-46 Surcharged in Ultramarine

1956, Feb. 24
C136 AP59 120 l on 50 l mag   1.25 1.60
Visit of Pres. Giovanni Gronchi to the US and Canada.

Madonna of Bruges, by Michelangelo AP68

Wmk. 303
1964, Feb. 18   Photo.   Perf. 14
C137 AP68 185 l black   .30   .30
Michelangelo Buonarroti (1475-1564), artist.

Verrazano Type of Regular Issue
1964, Nov. 21   Wmk. 303   Perf. 14
C138 A481 130 l blk & dull grn .20   .20
See note after No. 901.

Adoration of the Kings, by Gentile da Fabriano — AP69

1970, Dec. 12   Photo.   Unwmk.
C139 AP69 150 l multicolored   .30   .20
Christmas 1970.

Aviation Type of Regular Issue
Design: F-140S Starfighter over Aeronautical Academy, Pozzuoli.

1973, Mar. 28   Photo.   Perf. 14x13½
C140 A590 150 l multicolored   .30   .20

AIR POST SEMI-POSTAL STAMPS

Holy Year Type of Postage
Dome of St. Peter's, dove with olive branch, Church of the Holy Sepulcher.

Wmk. 140
1933, Oct. 23   Photo.   Perf. 14
CB1 A163 50c + 25c org
            brn   2.40 16.00
CB2 A163 75c + 50c brn vio   4.00 45.00
Set, never hinged   16.00

Symbolical of Military Air Force — SPAP2

1935, July 1
CB3 SPAP2 50c + 50c brown   10.00 37.50
The surtax was for the Militia.

AIR POST SPECIAL DELIVERY STAMPS

Garibaldi, Anita Garibaldi, Plane APSD1

Wmk. 140
1932, June 2   Photo.   Perf. 14
CE1 APSD1 2.25 l + 1 l   16.00 52.50
CE2 APSD1 4.50 l + 1.50 l   16.00 52.50
Set, never hinged   80.00

Death of Giuseppe Garibaldi, 50th anniv.
For overprinted types see Aegean Islands Nos. CE1-CE2.

Airplane and Sunburst APSD2

1933-34
CE3 APSD2 2 l gray blk
              ('34)   .20 2.40
CE4 APSD2 2.25 l gray blk   6.50 180.00
Set, never hinged   17.00

For overprint and surcharge see Nos. MCE1, Yugoslavia-Ljubljana NCE1.

Annexation of Fiume Type
Flag raising before Fascist headquarters.

1934, Mar. 12
CE5 A166 2 l + 1.25 l   4.75 29.00
CE6 A166 2.25 l + 1.25 l   .95 23.00
CE7 A166 4.50 l + 2 l   .95 25.00
Nos. CE5-CE7 (3)   5.60 77.00
Set, never hinged   17.00

Triumphal Arch in Rome APSD4

1934, Aug. 31
CE8 APSD4 2 l + 1.25 l
              brown   16.00 40.00
CE9 APSD4 4.50 l + 2 l cop
              red   20.00 40.00
Set, never hinged   90.00

Centenary of the institution of the Military Medal of Valor.
For overprinted types see Aegean Islands Nos. CE3-CE4.

AIR POST OFFICIAL STAMPS

Balbo Flight Type of Air Post Stamp of 1933 Overprinted

1933   Wmk. 140   Perf. 14
CO1 AP25 5.25 l + 44.75 l
            red, grn
            & red
            vio   3,100. 12,500.
Never hinged   4,750.

Type of Air Post Stamp of 1934 Overprinted in Gold

1934
CO2 AP41 10 l blue blk   825.00 12,500.
Never hinged   1,600.

65th birthday of King Victor Emmanuel III and the non-stop flight from Rome to Mogadiscio.

PNEUMATIC POST STAMPS

PN1

1913-28   Wmk. 140   Typo.   Perf. 14
D1 PN1 10c brown   2.75 22.50
D2 PN1 15c brn vio ('28)   2.40 12.50
 a.   15c dull violet ('21) 3.25 22.50
D3 PN1 15c rose red ('28)   8.00 20.00
D4 PN1 15c claret ('28)   2.40 12.50
D5 PN1 20c brn vio ('25)   18.00 40.00
D6 PN1 30c blue ('23)   8.00 125.00
D7 PN1 35c rose red ('27) 20.00 200.00
D8 PN1 40c dp red ('26)   24.00 290.00
Nos. D1-D8 (8)   85.55 722.50

Nos. D1, D2a, D5-D6, D8 Surcharged Like Nos. C10-C11

1924-27
D9   PN1 15c on 10c   4.00 27.00
D10 PN1 15c on 20c ('27)   8.00 50.00
D11 PN1 20c on 10c ('25)   8.00 52.50
D12 PN1 20c on 15c ('25)   10.00 32.50
D13 PN1 35c on 40c ('27)   21.00 225.00
D14 PN1 40c on 30c ('25)   10.00 250.00
Nos. D9-D14 (6)   61.00 637.00

Dante Alighieri PN2

Galileo Galilei PN3

1933, Mar. 29   Photo.
D15 PN2 15c dark violet   .30 1.60
D16 PN3 35c rose red   .30 5.00

Similar to Types of 1933, Without "REGNO"
1945, Oct. 22   Wmk. 277
D17 PN2 60c dull brown   .20 3.25
D18 PN3 1.40 l dull blue   .20 3.25

Minerva — PN6

1947, Nov. 15
D19 PN6 3 l rose lilac   6.50 10.50
D20 PN6 5 l aqua   .20   .20
Set, never hinged   8.50

Catalogue values for unused stamps in this section, from this point to the end of the section, are for Never Hinged items.

1958-66   Wmk. 303
D21 PN6 10 l rose red   .20   .20
D22 PN6 20 l sapphire ('66) .20   .20

SPECIAL DELIVERY STAMPS

Victor Emmanuel III — SD1

1903-26   Typo.   Wmk. 140   Perf. 14
E1 SD1 25c rose red   50.00 1.20
 a.   Imperf., pair   500.00 625.00
E2 SD1 50c dl red ('20)   5.00 1.75
E3 SD1 60c dl red ('22)   8.00 1.20
E4 SD1 70c dl red ('25)   .80   .35
E5 SD1 1.25 l dp bl ('26)   .25   .20
Nos. E1-E5 (5)   64.05 4.70

No. E1 is almost always found poorly centered, and it is valued thus.
For overprints and surcharges see Nos. C1, E11, E13, Austria NE1-NE2, Dalmatia E1, Offices in Crete, Offices in Africa, Offices in Turkish Empire.

Victor Emmanuel III — SD2

1908-26
E6 SD2 30c blue & rose   1.60 4.00
E7 SD2 2 l bl & red ('25)   8.00 90.00
E8 SD2 2.50 l bl & red ('26) 2.75 8.00
Nos. E6-E8 (3)   12.35 102.00

The 1.20 lire blue and red (see No. E12) was prepared in 1922, but not issued. Value: unused $200; never hinged $400.
For surcharges and overprints see Nos. E10, E12, Austria NE3, Dalmatia E2, Offices in China, Offices in Africa, Offices in Turkish Empire.

SD3

1917, Nov.
E9 SD3 25c on 40c violet   32.50 100.00
Type SD3 not issued without surcharge.
For surcharge see No. C2.

No. E6 Surcharged

1921, Oct.
E10	SD2	1.20 l on 30c	2.00	16.00
a.		Comma in value omitted	12.50	50.00
b.		Double surcharge	325.00	

No. E2 Surcharged

1922, Jan. 9
E11	SD1	60c on 50c dull red	40.00	2.00
a.		Inverted surcharge	290.00	290.00
b.		Double surcharge		1,300.
c.		Imperf., pair	500.00	625.00

Type of 1908 Surcharged

1924, May
E12	SD2	1.60 l on 1.20 l bl & red	1.60	80.00
a.		Double surch., one inverted		310.00

No. E3 Surcharged like No. E11
1925, Apr. 11
E13	SD1	70c on 60c dull red	.90	1.20
a.		Inverted surcharge	325.00	400.00

Victor Emmanuel III — SD4

1932-33 Photo.
E14	SD4	1.25 l green	.20	.20
E15	SD4	2.50 l dp org ('33)	.25	5.75

For overprints and surcharges see Italian Social Republic Nos. E1-E2; Yugoslavia-Ljubljana NB5-NB8, NE1.

March on Rome Type of Postage

1.25 l Ancient Pillars and Entrenchments.
2.50 l, Head of Mussolini, trophies of flags, etc.

1932, Oct. 27
E16	A146	1.25 l deep green	2.40	1.75
E17	A146	2.50 l deep orange	8.00	160.00
		Set, never hinged	34.00	

"Italia" SD7

1945, Aug. Wmk. 277 Perf. 14
E18	SD7	5 l rose carmine	.20	1.00

Winged Foot SD8

Rearing Horse and Torch-Bearer — SD9

1945-51
E19	SD8	5 l henna brn	.20	.20
E20	SD9	10 l deep blue	.20	.20
E21	SD9	15 l dk car rose ('47)	1.60	.20
E22	SD8	25 l brt red org ('47)	22.50	.20
E23	SD8	30 l dp vio ('46)	3.00	3.25
E24	SD8	50 l lil rose ('51)	22.50	.20
E25	SD9	60 l car rose ('48)	35.00	.20
		Nos. E19-E25 (7)	85.00	4.45
		Set, never hinged	160.00	

See No. E32. For overprints see Nos. 1LNE1-1LNE2, Trieste E1-E4, E6-E7.

Type of Regular Issue of 1948
Inscribed: "Espresso"
1948, Sept. 18 Photo. Perf. 14
E26	A272	35 l violet (Naples)	75.00	20.00
		Never hinged	150.00	

> Catalogue values for unused stamps in this section, from this point to the end of the section, are for Never Hinged items.

Type of 1945-51
1955, July 7 Wmk. 303 Perf. 14
E32	SD8	50 l lilac rose	5.75	.20

Etruscan Winged Horses SD10

1958-76 Photo.
Size: 36½x20¼mm
E33	SD10	75 l magenta	.20	.20

Size: 36x20mm
E34	SD10	150 l dl bl grn ('68)	.25	.20
a.		Size: 36½x20¼mm ('66)	.40	.20
E35	SD10	250 l blue ('74)	.30	.20
E36	SD10	300 l brown ('76)	.40	.20
		Nos. E33-E36 (4)	1.15	.80

Nos. E34-E36 are fluorescent.

AUTHORIZED DELIVERY STAMPS

For the payment of a special tax for the authorized delivery of correspondence privately instead of through the post office.

AD1   Coat of Arms — AD2

1928 Wmk. 140 Typo. Perf. 14
EY1	AD1	10c dull blue	6.50	.60
a.		Perf. 11	32.50	4.00

1930 Photo. Perf. 14
EY2	AD2	10c dark brown	.20	.20

For surcharge and overprint see Nos. EY3, Italian Social Republic EY1.

No. EY2 Surcharged in Black

1945
EY3	AD2	40c on 10c dark brown	.50	1.20

Coat of Arms — AD3   "Italia" — AD4

1945-46 Photo. Wmk. 277
EY4	AD3	40c dark brown	.25	1.00
EY5	AD3	1 l dk brown ('46)	3.25	5.00

For overprint see Trieste No. EY1.

1947-52
Size: 27½x22½mm
EY6	AD4	1 l brt grnsh bl	.20	.20
EY7	AD4	8 l brt red ('48)	10.00	.20

Size: 20½x16½mm
EY8	AD4	15 l violet ('49)	27.50	.20
EY9	AD4	20 l rose vio ('52)	2.00	.20
		Nos. EY6-EY9 (4)	39.70	.80
		Set, never hinged	125.00	

For overprints see Trieste Nos. EY2-EY5.

> Catalogue values for unused stamps in this section, from this point to the end of the section, are for Never Hinged items.

Italia Type of 1947
1955-90 Wmk. 303 Photo. Perf. 14
Size: 20½x16½mm
EY11	AD4	20 l rose vio	.20	.20
EY12	AD4	30 l Prus grn ('65)	.20	.20
EY13	AD4	35 l ocher ('74)	.20	.20
EY14	AD4	110 l lt ultra ('77)	.20	.20
EY15	AD4	270 l brt pink ('84)	.75	.25

Size: 19½x16½mm
EY16	AD4	300 l rose & grn ('87)	.60	.40
EY17	AD4	370 l tan & brn vio	.65	.40
		Nos. EY11-EY17 (7)	2.80	1.85

Issue date: 370 l, Sept. 24, 1990.

POSTAGE DUE STAMPS

Unused values for Postage Due stamps are for examples with full original gum. Stamps with part gum or privately gummed sell for much less.

D1   D2

1863 Unwmk. Litho. Imperf.
J1	D1	10c yellow	2,000.	225.00
		No gum	85.00	
a.		10c yellow orange	2,100.	250.00
		No gum	90.00	

1869 Wmk. 140 Typo. Perf. 14
J2	D2	10c buff	5,000.	65.00

D3   D4

1870-1925
J3	D3	1c buff & mag	4.00	12.50
J4	D3	2c buff & mag	13.00	25.00
J5	D3	5c buff & mag	1.60	.80
J6	D3	10c buff & mag		
		('71)	1.60	.80
b.		Imperf., single		2,100.
J7	D3	20c buff & mag		
		('94)	16.00	.80
a.		Imperf., pair	250.00	250.00
J8	D3	30c buff & mag	5.00	1.25
b.		Imperf., pair	2,900.	1,600.
J9	D3	40c buff & mag	5.00	2.40
J10	D3	50c buff & mag	5.00	1.25
b.		Imperf., single		1,800.
J11	D3	60c buff & mag	950.00	4.00
J12	D3	60c buff & brn		
		('25)	40.00	15.00

J13	D3	1 l lt bl & brn	5,300.	20.00
J14	D3	1 l bl & mag		
		('94)	40.00	1.25
a.		Imperf., pair	160.00	180.00
J15	D3	2 l lt bl & brn	5,300.	32.50
J16	D3	2 l bl & mag		
		('03)	57.50	6.50
J17	D3	5 l bl & brn		
		('74)	540.00	37.50
J18	D3	5 l bl & mag		
		('03)	200.00	32.50
J19	D3	10 l bl & brn		
		('74)	6,500.	37.50
J20	D3	10 l bl & mag		
		('94)	200.00	6.50

Early printings of 5c, 10c, 30c, 40c, 50c and 60c were in buff and magenta, later ones (1890-94) in stronger shades. The earlier, paler shades and their inverted-numeral varieties sell for considerably more than those of the later shades. Values are for the later shades.

For surcharges and overprints see Nos. J25-J27, Offices in China, Offices in Turkish Empire.

Numeral Inverted
J3a	D3	1c	4,500.	2,900.
J4a	D3	2c	11,500.	4,000.
J5a	D3	5c	6.50	12.50
J6a	D3	10c	8.00	16.00
J7b	D3	20c	65.00	60.00
J8a	D3	30c	12.50	25.00
J9a	D3	40c	540.00	650.00
J10a	D3	50c	60.00	80.00
J11a	D3	60c	540.00	400.00
J13a	D3	1 l		
J14b	D3	1 l	4,500.	3,250.
J15a	D3	2 l		2,900.
J16a	D3	2 l	3,750.	3,750.
J17a	D3	5 l		1,450.
J19a	D3	10 l	17,500.	325.00

1884-1903
J21	D4	50 l green	90.00	80.00
J22	D4	50 l yellow ('03)	100.00	50.00
J23	D4	100 l claret	90.00	40.00
J24	D4	100 l blue ('03)	80.00	20.00
		Nos. J21-J24 (4)	360.00	190.00

Nos. J3 & J4 Surcharged in Black

1890-91
J25	D3	10c on 2c	130.00	37.50
J26	D3	20c on 1c	540.00	29.00
a.		Inverted surcharge		10,000.
J27	D3	30c on 2c	1,800.	12.50
a.		Inverted surcharge		2,700.
		Nos. J25-J27 (3)	2,470.	79.00

Coat of Arms
D6   D7

1934 Photo.
J28	D6	5c brown	.80	.40
J29	D6	10c blue	.80	.40
J30	D6	20c rose red	.80	.40
J31	D6	25c green	.80	.40
J32	D6	30c red org	.80	.40
J33	D6	40c blk brn	.80	3.25
J34	D6	50c violet	.80	.40
J35	D6	60c slate blk	.80	8.00
J36	D7	1 l red org	.80	.40
J37	D7	2 l green	.80	.40
J38	D7	5 l violet	1.60	.80
J39	D7	10 l blue	6.50	5.75
J40	D7	20 l car rose	12.50	21.00
		Nos. J28-J40 (13)	28.60	42.00

For overprints and surcharges see Italian Social Republic #J1-J13, Yugoslavia-Ljubljana NJ14-NJ22.

D8   D9

1945-46 Unwmk. Perf. 14
J41	D8	5c brn, grayish ('46)	2.40	5.00
J42	D8	10c blue	.45	1.00
J43	D8	20c rose red, grayish		
		('46)	2.00	1.00
J44	D8	25c dk grn	.45	1.00
J45	D8	30c red org	.45	1.00
J46	D8	40c blk brn	.45	1.00
J47	D8	50c violet	.45	5.00
J48	D8	60c black	.45	5.00
J49	D9	1 l red org	.45	1.00

J50	D9	2 l green	.45	1.00
J51	D9	5 l violet	.45	1.00
J52	D9	10 l blue	.45	1.00
J53	D9	20 l car rose	.45	1.00
		Nos. J41-J53 (13)	9.35	25.00

Nos. J41 and J43 have yellow gum.

Wmk. 277

J54	D8	10c dark blue	.20	5.00
J55	D8	25c dk grn	1.25	5.75
J56	D8	30c red org	1.25	10.00
J57	D8	40c blk brn	.20	.20
J58	D8	50c vio ('46)	5.75	5.75
J59	D8	60c bl blk ('46)	7.50	20.00
J60	D8	1 l red org	.20	.20
J61	D9	2 l dk grn	.20	.20
J62	D9	5 l violet	12.00	7.50
J63	D9	10 l dark blue	18.00	10.00
J64	D9	20 l car rose	29.00	25.00
		Nos. J54-J64 (11)	75.55	89.60
		Set, never hinged	190.00	

For overprints see Trieste Nos. J1, J3-J5.

D10

1947-54 Photo.   *Perf. 14*

J65	D10	1 l red orange	.20	.20
J66	D10	2 l dk green	.20	.20
J67	D10	3 l carmine	.50	2.40
J68	D10	4 l brown	.30	1.25
J69	D10	5 l violet	.65	.20
J70	D10	6 l vio blue	2.00	3.00
J71	D10	8 l rose vio	8.50	4.00
J72	D10	10 l deep blue	.75	.20
J73	D10	12 l golden brn	3.25	3.25
J74	D10	20 l lil rose	35.00	.20
J75	D10	25 l dk red ('54)	35.00	.80
J76	D10	50 l aqua	25.00	.20
J77	D10	100 l org yel ('52)	8.00	.20

Engr.
Perf. 13½x14

J78	D10	500 l dp bl & dk car ('52)	8.50	.40
a.		Perf. 11x13	10.00	.40
b.		Perf. 13	10.00	.40
		Nos. J65-J78 (14)	127.85	16.75
		Set, never hinged	325.00	

For overprints see Trieste Nos. J2, J6-J29.

> **Catalogue values for unused stamps in this section, from this point to the end of the section, are for Never Hinged items.**

1955-91 Wmk. 303 Photo. *Perf. 14*

J83	D10	5 l violet	.20	.20
J85	D10	8 l rose vio	200.00	225.00
J86	D10	10 l deep blue	.20	.20
J87	D10	20 l lil rose	.20	.20
J88	D10	25 l dk red	.20	.20
J89	D10	30 l gray brn ('61)	.30	.20
J90	D10	40 l dl brn ('66)	.20	.20
J91	D10	50 l aqua	.30	.20
a.		Type II	.30	.20
J92	D10	100 l org yel ('58)	.25	.20

Engr.

J93	D10	500 l dp bl & dk car ('61)	3.25	.20
J94	D10	900 l dp car & gray grn ('84)	1.20	.25
J95	D10	1500 l brown & orange	3.00	1.60
		Nos. J83,J86-J95 (11)	9.30	3.65

Type I imprint on No. J91 reads: "1ST POL. STATO OFF. CARET VALORI". Type II imprint reads: "I.P.Z.S. OFF. CARTE VALORI" (1992). No. J91 has lighter background with more distinguishable lettering and design.
No. J92 exists with both Type I & Type II imprints.
Nos. J92 and J93 exist with "I. P. Z. S. ROMA" imprint.
Issue date: 1500 l, Feb. 20, 1991.

MILITARY STAMPS

Regular Stamps, 1929-42, Overprinted

1943   **Wmk. 140**   *Perf. 14*

M1	A90	5c ol brn	.60	.80
M2	A92	10c dk brn	.60	.80
M3	A93	15c slate grn	.60	.80
M4	A91	20c rose red	.60	.80
M5	A94	25c dp grn	.60	.80
M6	A95	30c ol brn	.60	.80
M7	A95	50c purple	.60	.40
M8	A91	1 l dk pur	4.25	20.00
M9	A94	1.25 l deep blue	.60	1.00
M10	A92	1.75 l red org	.60	.80
M11	A93	2 l car lake	.60	1.00
M12	A95a	5 l rose red	.60	3.25
M13	A93	10 l purple	4.25	29.00
		Nos. M1-M13 (13)	15.10	60.25

Due to a shortage of regular postage stamps during 1944-45, this issue was used for ordinary mail. "P. M." stands for "Posta Militare."

MILITARY AIR POST STAMPS

Air Post Stamps, 1930 Overprinted Like Nos. M1-M13 in Black

1943   **Wmk. 140**   *Perf. 14*

MC1	AP3	50c olive brown	.50	.80
MC2	AP5	1 l purple	.50	.80
MC3	AP6	2 l deep blue	.50	15.00
MC4	AP3	5 l dark green	4.25	5.00
MC5	AP3	10 l deep carmine	4.25	32.50
		Nos. MC1-MC5 (5)	10.00	74.10

MILITARY AIR POST SPECIAL DELIVERY STAMPS

#CE3 Overprinted Like #M1-M13

1943   **Wmk. 140**   *Perf. 14*

MCE1	APSD2	2 l gray black	4.00	29.00

MILITARY SPECIAL DELIVERY STAMPS

#E14 Overprinted Like #M1-M13

1943   **Wmk. 140**   *Perf. 14*

ME1	SD4	1.25 l green	1.00	1.60

OFFICIAL STAMPS

O1

1875   **Wmk. 140**   **Typo.**   *Perf. 14*

O1	O1	2c lake	4.00	5.00
O2	O1	5c lake	4.00	5.00
O3	O1	20c lake	3.25	1.60
O4	O1	30c lake	3.25	3.25
O5	O1	1 l lake	6.50	16.00
O6	O1	2 l lake	20.00	50.00
O7	O1	5 l lake	80.00	160.00
O8	O1	10 l lake	150.00	135.00
		Nos. O1-O8 (8)	271.00	375.85

For surcharges see Nos. 37-44.
Stamps inscribed "Servizio Commissioni" were used in connection with the postal service but not for the payment of postage.

NEWSPAPER STAMP

N1

Typographed, Numeral Embossed
1862   **Unwmk.**   *Imperf.*

P1	N1	2c buff	52.50	110.00
a.		Numeral double	475.00	1,600.
b.		Printed on gummed side	500.00	

Black 1c and 2c stamps of similar type are listed under Sardinia.

PARCEL POST STAMPS

King Humbert
I — PP1

1884-86 Wmk. 140 Typo.   *Perf. 14*
Various Frames

Q1	PP1	10c olive gray	125.00	100.00
Q2	PP1	20c blue	250.00	160.00
Q3	PP1	50c claret	10.00	15.00
Q4	PP1	75c blue grn	10.00	15.00
Q5	PP1	1 l orange	20.00	32.50
Q6	PP1	1.75 l brown	25.00	125.00
		Nos. Q1-Q6 (6)	440.00	447.50

For surcharges see Nos. 58-63.

Parcel Post stamps from No. Q7 onward were used by affixing them to the waybill so that one half remained on it following the parcel, the other half staying on the receipt given the sender. Most used halves are right halves. Complete stamps were and are obtainable canceled, probably to order.
Both unused and used values are for complete stamps.

PP2

1914-22   **Wmk. 140**   *Perf. 13*

Q7	PP2	5c brown	5.00	11.50
Q8	PP2	10c deep blue	5.00	11.50
Q9	PP2	20c black ('17)	20.00	11.50
Q10	PP2	25c red	25.00	11.50
Q11	PP2	50c orange	32.50	25.00
Q12	PP2	1 l violet	37.50	10.00
Q13	PP2	2 l green	40.00	10.00
Q14	PP2	3 l bister	50.00	32.50
Q15	PP2	4 l slate	57.50	50.00
Q16	PP2	10 l rose lil ('22)	100.00	50.00
Q17	PP2	12 l red brn ('22)	160.00	310.00
Q18	PP2	15 l ol grn ('22)	150.00	310.00
Q19	PP2	20 l brn vio ('22)	125.00	310.00
		Nos. Q7-Q19 (13)	807.50	1,153.

Halves Used

Q7-Q14, each	.40
Q15	.80
Q16	1.60
Q17	4.00
Q18	4.00
Q19	6.50

Imperfs exist. Value per pair: 20c, 25c, 50c, 2 l, 3l, 4 l: $50 each; 10l $225.

No. Q7 Surcharged

Q20	PP2	30c on 5c brown	1.60	16.00
		Half stamp		3.25
Q21	PP2	60c on 5c brown	1.60	16.00
		Half stamp		3.25
Q22	PP2	1.50 l on 5c brown	5.50	140.00
		Half stamp		6.50
a.		Double surcharge	250.00	

No. Q16 Surcharged

Q23	PP2	3 l on 10 l rose lilac	5.50	55.00
		Half stamp		3.25
		Nos. Q20-Q23 (4)	14.20	227.00

PP3

1927-39   **Wmk. 140**

Q24	PP3	5c brn ('38)	.80	2.00
Q25	PP3	10c dp bl ('39)	.80	2.00
Q26	PP3	25c red ('32)	.80	2.00
Q27	PP3	30c ultra	.80	2.90
Q28	PP3	50c org ('32)	.80	2.00
Q29	PP3	60c red	.80	2.90
Q30	PP3	1 l lilac ('31)	.80	2.90
Q31	PP3	1 l brn vio ('36)	24.00	72.50
Q32	PP3	2 l grn ('32)	.80	2.90
Q33	PP3	3 l yel bister	.80	6.50
a.		Printed on both sides	65.00	
Q34	PP3	4 l gray	.80	6.50
Q35	PP3	10 l rose lil ('34)	2.40	40.00
Q36	PP3	20 l lil brn ('33)	3.25	57.50
		Nos. Q24-Q36 (13)	37.65	202.60

Value of used halves: Nos. Q24-Q34, each 40c; Q35 80c; Q36 $4.
For overprints see Italian Social Republic Nos. Q1-Q12.

Nos. Q24-Q30, Q32-Q36 Overprinted Between Halves in Black

1945   **Wmk. 140**   *Perf. 13*

Q37	PP3	5c brown	1.30	8.00
Q38	PP3	10c dp blue	1.30	8.00
Q39	PP3	25c red	.90	8.00
Q40	PP3	30c ultra	15.00	32.50
Q41	PP3	50c orange	1.30	8.00
Q42	PP3	60c red	1.30	8.00
Q43	PP3	1 l lilac	1.30	8.00
Q44	PP3	2 l green	1.30	8.00
Q45	PP3	3 l yel bister	1.30	8.00
Q46	PP3	4 l gray	1.30	8.00
Q47	PP3	10 l rose lilac	16.00	65.00
Q48	PP3	20 l lilac brn	24.00	140.00
		Nos. Q37-Q48 (12)	66.30	309.50
		Set, never hinged	160.00	

Halves Used

Q37-48, each	.20

Type of 1927
With Fasces Removed
1946   **Typo.**

Q55	PP3	1 l lilac	1.90	5.00
Q56	PP3	2 l green	1.40	5.00
Q57	PP3	3 l yellow org	1.90	8.00
Q58	PP3	4 l gray	4.00	8.00
Q59	PP3	10 l rose lilac	42.50	75.00
Q60	PP3	20 l lilac brn	57.50	250.00
		Nos. Q55-Q60 (6)	109.20	351.00
		Set, never hinged	260.00	

Halves Used

Q55-Q58	.20
Q59	.80
Q60	1.25

PP4

PP5

Perf. 13¼, 13¼x14, 12¼x13x13¼
1946-54   **Photo.**   **Wmk. 277**

Q61	PP4	25c dl vio bl ('48)	.20	.20
Q62	PP4	50c brown ('47)	.40	.20
Q63	PP4	1 l golden brn ('47)	.40	.20
Q64	PP4	2 l lt bl grn ('47)	.80	.20
Q65	PP4	3 l red org ('47)	.40	.20
Q66	PP4	4 l gray blk ('47)	6.50	10.00
Q67	PP4	5 l lil rose ('47)	.40	.20
a.		Perf. 13¼	.40	.20
Q68	PP4	10 l violet	8.00	.40
a.		Perf. 13¼	8.00	2.00
Q69	PP4	20 l lilac brn	3.25	.60
a.		Perf. 13¼	5.00	1.00
Q70	PP4	30 l plum ('52)	4.00	5.00
a.		Perf. 13¼	4.00	5.00
Q71	PP4	50 l rose red	16.00	2.40
a.		Perf. 13¼	16.00	2.40
Q72	PP4	100 l sapphire	40.00	45.00
a.		Perf. 13¼	140.00	45.00
Q73	PP4	200 l green ('48)	55.00	80.00
a.		Perf. 13¼	55.00	80.00
Q74	PP4	300 l brn car ('48), perf 13¼	725.00	1,050.
Q75	PP4	500 l brown ('48)	40.00	35.00
a.		Perf. 12¼x13¼	100.00	100.00

Engr.
Perf. 13

Q76	PP5	1000 l ultra ('54)	2,800.	3,100.
	Nos. Q61-Q76 (16)		3,700.	4,329.
	Set, never hinged		5,500.	

Halves Used

Q61-Q73	.20
Q74	8.00
Q75	3.25
Q76	20.00

For overprints see Trieste Nos. Q1-Q26.

> Catalogue values for unused stamps in this section, from this point to the end of the section, are for Never Hinged items.

Perf. 12½x13
1955-59   Wmk. 303   Photo.
Without Imprint

Q77	PP4	25c vio bl	.20	.20
Q77A	PP4	50c brn ('56)	3.00	3.00
Q78	PP4	5 l lil rose ('59)	.20	.20
Q79	PP4	10 l violet	.20	.20
Q80	PP4	20 l lil brn	.20	.20
Q81	PP4	30 l plum ('56)	.20	.20
Q82	PP4	40 l dl vio ('57)	.20	.20
Q83	PP4	50 l rose red	.20	.20
Q84	PP4	100 l sapphire	.20	.20
Q85	PP4	150 l org brn ('57)	.20	.20
Q86	PP4	200 l grn ('56)	.30	.20
Q87	PP4	300 l brn car ('58)	.45	.40
Q88	PP4	400 l gray blk ('57)	.55	.45
Q89	PP4	500 l brn ('57)	1.00	.60

Engr.
Perf. 13

Q90	PP5	1000 l ultra ('57)	1.25	.95
Q91	PP5	2000 l red brn & car ('57)	4 50	4.50
	Nos. Q77-Q91 (16)		12.85	11.90

Halves Used

Q77-Q89	.20
Q90-Q91	.40

1960-66   Photo.   Perf. 12½x13

Q92	PP4	60 l bright lilac	.20	.20
Q93	PP4	140 l dull red	.25	.30
Q94	PP4	280 l yellow	.60	.45
Q95	PP4	600 l olive bister	.70	.75
Q96	PP4	700 l blue ('66)	1.75	.75
Q97	PP4	800 l dp org ('66)	2.10	.95
	Nos. Q92-Q97 (6)		5.60	3.40

Halves Used

Q92-Q93	.20
Q94	.20
Q95	.40
Q96-Q97	.25

Imprint: "I.P.S.-Off. Carte Valori-Roma"

1973, Mar.   Photo.   Wmk. 303

Q98	PP4	20 l lilac brown	.20	.20
Q99	PP4	30 l plum	.20	.20

PARCEL POST AUTHORIZED DELIVERY STAMPS

For the payment of a special tax for the authorized delivery of parcels privately instead of through the post office.

PAD1

1953   Wmk. 277   Photo.   Perf. 13

QY1	PAD1	40 l orange red	12.50	12.50
QY2	PAD1	50 l ultra	160.00	160.00
QY3	PAD1	75 l brown	80.00	80.00
QY4	PAD1	110 l lil rose	80.00	80.00
	Nos. QY1-QY4 (4)		332.50	332.50
	Set, never hinged		450.00	

Halves Used

QY1	.35
QY2	1.25
QY3	3.25
QY4	3.25

For overprints see Trieste Nos. QY1-QY4.

> Catalogue values for unused stamps in this section, from this point to the end of the section, are for Never Hinged items.

1956-58   Wmk. 303   Perf. 12½x13

QY5	PAD1	40 l orange red	1.60	.90
QY6	PAD1	50 l ultra	3.25	2.25
QY7	PAD1	60 l brt vio bl ('58)	9.00	5.25
QY8	PAD1	75 l brown	375.00	160.00
QY9	PAD1	90 l lil ('58)	.35	.75
QY10	PAD1	110 l lil rose	375.00	140.00
QY11	PAD1	120 l grnsh bl ('58)	.35	.75
	Nos. QY5-QY11 (7)		764.55	309.90

Halves Used

QY5-QY6	.20
QY7	.90
QY8,QY10	8.00
QY9	.30
QY11	.25

1960-81

QY12	PAD1	70 l green ('66)	45.00	9.00
QY13	PAD1	80 l brown	.40	.40
QY14	PAD1	110 l org yel	.40	.40
QY15	PAD1	140 l black	.45	.50
QY16	PAD1	150 l car rose ('68)	.30	.50
QY17	PAD1	180 l red ('66)	.40	.60
QY18	PAD1	240 l dk bl ('66)	.45	.70

Engr.   Perf. 13½

QY19	PAD1	500 l ocher ('76)	1.40	1.40
QY20	PAD1	600 l bl grn ('79)	1.40	1.40
QY21	PAD1	900 l ultra ('81)	1.10	1.40
	Nos. QY12-QY21 (10)		51.30	16.30

Halves Used

QY12	4.00
QY13-QY15, QY18, QY21	.20
QY16, QY17, QY19	.25
QY20	.35

PAD2

Perf. 14x13½

1984   Photo.   Wmk. 303

QY22	PAD2	3000 l multi	3.50 2.50

OCCUPATION STAMPS

Issued under Austrian Occupation

Emperor Karl of Austria
OS1   OS2

Austria #M49-M67 Surcharged in Black

1918   Unwmk.   Perf. 12½

N1	OS1	2c on 1h grnsh bl	.20	.40
N2	OS1	3c on 2h red org	.20	.40
N3	OS1	4c on 3h ol gray	.20	.40
N4	OS1	6c on 5h ol grn	.20	.40
N5	OS1	7c on 6h vio	.20	.40
a.		Perf. 12½x11½	16.00	45.00
N6	OS1	11c on 10h org brn	.20	.40
N7	OS1	13c on 12h blue	.20	.40
N8	OS1	16c on 15h brt rose	.20	.40
N9	OS1	22c on 20h red brn	.20	.40
a.		Perf. 11½	8.00	24.00
N10	OS1	27c on 25h ultra	.30	1.20
N11	OS1	32c on 30h slate	.20	1.10
N12	OS1	43c on 40h ol bis	.20	.85
a.		Perf. 11½	9.50	27.50
N13	OS1	53c on 50h dp grn	.20	.80
N14	OS1	64c on 60h rose	.25	1.20
N15	OS1	85c on 80h dl bl	.20	.80
N16	OS1	95c on 90h dk vio	.20	.80
N17	OS2	2 l 11c on 2k rose, straw	.25	1.60
N18	OS2	3 l 16c on 3k grn, bl	.55	2.40
N19	OS2	4 l 22c on 4k rose, grn	.65	3.25
	Nos. N1-N19 (19)		4.80	17.60

Emperor Karl — OS3

Austria #M69-M81 Surcharged in Black

1918

N20	OS3	2c on 1h grnsh bl	5.50
N21	OS3	3c on 2h orange	5.50
N22	OS3	4c on 3h ol gray	5.50
N23	OS3	6c on 5h yel grn	5.50
N24	OS3	11c on 10h dk brn	5.50
N25	OS3	22c on 20h red	5.50
N26	OS3	27c on 25h blue	5.50
N27	OS3	32c on 30h bister	5.50
N28	OS3	48c on 45h dk sl	5.50
N29	OS3	53c on 50h dp grn	5.50
N30	OS3	64c on 60h violet	5.50
N31	OS3	85c on 80h rose	5.50
N32	OS3	95c on 90h brn vio	5.50
N33	OS2	2 l 6c on 1k ol grn, grnish	5.50
	Nos. N20-N33 (14)		77.00

Nos. N20 to N33 inclusive were never placed in use in the occupied territory. They were, however, on sale at the Post Office in Vienna for a few days before the Armistice.

OCCUPATION SPECIAL DELIVERY STAMPS

Bosnia #QE1-QE2 Surcharged

1918   Unwmk.   Perf. 12½

NE1	SH1	3c on 2h ver	5.50	16.00
NE2	SH1	6c on 5h dp grn	5.50	16.00

Nos. NE1-NE2 are on yellowish paper. Reprints on white paper sell for about 70 cents a set.

OCCUPATION POSTAGE DUE STAMPS

Bosnia #J16, J18-J19, J21-J24 Surcharged Like Nos. NE1-NE2

1918   Unwmk.   Perf. 12½

NJ1	D2	6c on 5h red	3.25	7.25
a.		Perf. 11½	5.50	12.00
NJ2	D2	11c on 10h red	2.40	3.25
a.		Perf. 11½	5.50	12.00
NJ3	D2	16c on 15h red	.80	4.00
NJ4	D2	27c on 25h red	.80	4.00
NJ5	D2	32c on 30h red	.80	4.00
NJ6	D2	43c on 40h red	.80	4.00
NJ7	D2	53c on 50h red	.80	4.00
	Nos. NJ1-NJ7 (7)		9.65	30.50

OCCUPATION NEWSPAPER STAMPS

Austrian #MP1-MP4 Surcharged

1918   Unwmk.   Perf. 12½

NP1	MN1	3c on 2h blue	.20	.40
a.		Perf. 11½	4.75	16.00
NP2	MN1	7c on 6h org	.25	1.20
NP3	MN1	11c on 10h car	.25	1.20
NP4	MN1	22c on 20h brn	.25	1.20
a.		Perf. 11½	80.00	160.00
	Nos. NP1-NP4 (4)		.95	4.00

A.M.G.

Issued jointly by the Allied Military Government of the United States and

Great Britain, for civilian use in areas under Allied occupation.

> Catalogue values for unused stamps in this section are for Never Hinged items.

OS4

Offset Printing
"Italy Centesimi" (or "Lira") in Black

1943   Unwmk.   Perf. 11

1N1	OS4	15c pale orange	1.60	1.00
1N2	OS4	25c pale citron	1.60	1.00
1N3	OS4	30c light gray	1.60	1.00
1N4	OS4	50c light violet	1.60	1.00
1N5	OS4	60c orange yellow	1.60	2.00
1N6	OS4	1 l lt yel green	1.60	1.00
1N7	OS4	2 l deep rose	2.50	2.00
1N8	OS4	5 l light blue	3.50	3.25
1N9	OS4	10 l buff	3.50	5.00
	Nos. 1N1-1N9 (9)		19.10	17.25

Italy Nos. 217, 220 and 221 Overprinted in Blue, Vermilion, Carmine or Orange

1943, Dec. 10   Wmk. 140   Perf. 14

1N10	A91	20c rose red (Bl)	1.50	3.00
1N11	A93	35c dp blue (C)	17.50	19.00
a.		35c deep blue (V)	35.00	60.00
1N13	A95	50c purple (C)	.75	1.10
a.		50c purple (O)	.90	2.00
	Nos. 1N10-1N13 (3)		19.75	23.10

Nos. 1N1-1N9 were for use in Sicily, Nos. 1N10-1N13 for use in Naples.

VENEZA GIULIA

> Catalogue values for unused stamps in this section are for Never Hinged items.

Stamps of Italy, 1929 to 1945 Overprinted in Black:

a   b

On Stamps of 1929

1945-47   Wmk. 140   Perf. 14

1LN1	A92	10c dk brown (a)	.30	.35
1LN1A	A91	20c rose red ('47) (a)	.40	.50

On Stamps of 1945

1945   Wmk. 277   Perf. 14

1LN2	A249 (a)	20c rose red	.35	.50
1LN3	A248 (a)	60c sl grn	.45	.35
1LN4	A249 (a)	1 l dp vio	.30	.35
1LN5	A251 (a)	2 l dk red	.35	.35
1LN6	A252 (b)	5 l dk red	.65	.50
1LN7	A251 (a)	10 l purple	.90	1.25
	Nos. 1LN2-1LN7 (6)		3.00	3.30

On Stamps of 1945

1945-46   Unwmk.

1LN7A	A250(a)	10c dk brn ('46)	.30	.25
1LN7B	A249(a)	20c rose red ('46)	.25	.50
1LN8	A251(a)	60c red org	.25	.25
	Nos. 1LN7A-1LN8 (3)		.80	1.00

On Air Post Stamp of 1930

1945   Wmk. 140   Perf. 14

1LN9	AP3 (a)	50c olive brn	.25	.50

On Stamp of 1929

1946

1LN10	A91 (a)	20 l lt green	2.25	6.50

On Stamps of 1945
Wmk. 277

1LN11	A260 (a)	25 l dk green	8.00	8.00
1LN12	A260 (a)	50 l dk vio brn	8.00	15.00

Italy No. 477 Overprinted in Black

1LN13	A261	100 l car lake	29.00	65.00
	Nos. 1LN10-1LN13 (4)		47.25	94.50

Stamps of Italy, 1945-47 Overprinted Type "a" in Black

1947

1LN14	A259	25c brt bl grn	.25	1.00
1LN15	A258	1 l claret brn	.60	.35
1LN16	A259	3 l red	.45	.25
1LN17	A259	4 l red org	.70	.25
1LN18	A257	6 l deep violet	2.00	1.90
1LN19	A259	20 l dk red vio	55.00	4.00
	Nos. 1LN14-1LN19 (6)		59.00	7.75

Some denominations of the Venezia Giulia A.M.G. issues exist with inverted overprint; several values exist in horizontal and vertical pairs, one stamp without overprint.

OCCUPATION AIR POST STAMPS

> Catalogue values for unused stamps in this section are for Never Hinged items.

Italy Nos. C106-C107 and C109-C113 Overprinted Like 1LN13 in Black

			Wmk. 277	Perf. 14
1946-47				
1LNC1	AP59	1 l sl blue ('47)	.40	5.00
1LNC2	AP60	2 l dk blue ('47)	.40	2.50
1LNC3	AP60	5 l dk green ('47)	3.00	1.50
1LNC4	AP59	10 l car rose ('47)	3.00	1.50
1LNC5	AP60	25 l dk blue	3.00	1.50
1LNC6	AP60	25 l brown ('47)	35.00	35.00
1LNC7	AP59	50 l dk green	6.50	10.00
	Nos. 1LNC1-1LNC7 (7)		51.30	57.00

Nos. 1LNC5 and 1LNC7 exist with inverted overprint; No. 1LNC5 with double overprint, one inverted.

OCCUPATION SPECIAL DELIVERY STAMPS

> Catalogue values for unused stamps in this section are for Never Hinged items.

Italy Nos. E20 and E23 Overprinted Like 1LN13 in Black

			Wmk. 277	Perf. 14
1946				
1LNE1	SD9	10 l deep blue	4.00	1.60
1LNE2	SD8	30 l deep violet	8.75	19.00

ITALIAN SOCIAL REPUBLIC

On Sept. 15, 1943, Mussolini proclaimed the establishment of a Republican fascist party and a new fascist government. This government's authority covered only the Northern Italy area occupied by the Germans.

> Catalogue values for unused stamps in this section are for hinged stamps. Never hinged examples are valued at 2-2.5 times the values shown.

Italy Nos. 218, 219, 221 to 223 and 231 Overprinted in Black or Red:

a

b

c

			Wmk. 140	Perf. 14
1944				
1	A94(a)	25c deep grn	.30	2.00
2	A95(b)	30c ol brn (R)	.30	2.00
3	A95(c)	50c pur (R)	.30	2.00
4	A94(a)	75c rose red	.30	2.00
5	A94(b)	1.25 l dp bl (R)	.30	2.00
5A	A94(b)	50 l dp vio (R)	250.00	3,100.
	Nos. 1-5 (5)		1.50	10.00

Nos. 1 to 5 exist with overprint inverted. Value, each: unused $40; used $25.
No. 1 exists with overprint "b." Value: unused, $55; used $550.
Counterfeits of No. 5A exist.

Italy Nos. 427 to 438 Overprinted Same in Black or Red

6	A243(a)	25c deep green	.45	3.25
7	A244(a)	25c deep green	.45	3.25
8	A245(a)	25c deep green	.45	3.25
9	A246(a)	25c deep green	.45	3.25
10	A243(b)	30c olive brown (R)	.45	—
11	A244(b)	30c olive brown (R)	.45	—
12	A245(b)	30c olive brown (R)	.45	—
13	A246(b)	30c olive brown (R)	.45	—
14	A243(c)	50c purple (R)	.45	3.25
15	A244(c)	50c purple (R)	.45	3.25
16	A245(c)	50c purple (R)	.45	3.25
17	A246(c)	50c purple (R)	.45	3.25
	Nos. 6-17 (12)		5.40	26.00

Loggia dei Mercanti, Bologna — A1

Basilica of San Lorenzo, Rome — A2

Drummer Boy — A3

			Photo.	Perf. 14
1944				
18	A1	20c crimson	.20	.60
19	A2	25c green	.20	.60
20	A3	30c brown	.20	.60
21	A3	75c dark red	.20	1.60
	Nos. 18-21 (4)		.80	3.40

For surcharges see Italy Nos. 461-462.

Church of St. Ciriaco, Ancona A4

Monte Cassino Abbey A5

Loggia dei Mercanti, Bologna A6

Basilica of San Lorenzo, Rome A7

Statue of "Rome" A8

Basilica of St. Maria delle Grazie, Milan A9

				Unwmk.
1944				
22	A4	5c brown	.20	.35
23	A5	10c brown	.20	.20
24	A6	20c rose red	.20	.20
25	A7	25c deep green	.20	.20
26	A3	30c brown	.20	.20
27	A8	50c purple	.20	.20
28	A5	75c dark red	1.25	25.00
29	A3	1 l purple	.20	.20
30	A9	1.25 l blue	.80	16.00
31	A9	3 l deep green	.80	50.00
	Nos. 22-31 (10)		4.25	92.55

Bandiera Brothers — A10

1944, Dec. 6

32	A10	25c deep green	.35	.55
33	A10	1 l purple	.35	.55
34	A102.50 l rose red		.35	7.50
	Nos. 32-34 (3)		1.05	8.60

Cent. of the execution of Attilio (1811-44) and Emilio Bandiera (1819-44), revolutionary patriots who were shot at Cosenza, July 23, 1844, by Neapolitan authorities after an unsuccessful raid.

This set was overprinted in 1945 by the committee of the National Philatelic Convention to publicize that gathering at Venice.

SPECIAL DELIVERY STAMPS

Italy Nos. E14 and E15 Overprinted in Red or Black

			Wmk. 140	Perf. 14
1944				
E1	SD4	1.25 l green (R)	.25	.60
E2	SD4	2.50 l deep orange	.25	25.00

Cathedral, Palermo SD1

				Photo.
1944				
E3	SD1	1.25 l green	.25	1.00

AUTHORIZED DELIVERY STAMP

> Catalogue values for unused stamps in this section are for Never Hinged items.

Italy No. EY2 Overprinted

			Wmk. 140	Perf. 14
1944				
EY1	AD2	10c dark brown	.25	.80

Italy No. EY2 with overprint type a and type b were prepared but not issued. Values: type a, unused $130, never hinged $325; type b, unused $240, never hinged $600.

POSTAGE DUE STAMPS

Italy #28-J40 Overprinted Like #EY1

			Wmk. 140	Perf. 14
1944				
J1	D6	5c brown	5.00	8.00
J2	D6	10c blue	5.00	6.50
J3	D6	20c rose red	5.00	6.50
J4	D6	25c green	5.00	6.50
J5	D6	30c red org	5.00	12.50
J6	D6	40c blk brn	5.00	16.00
J7	D6	50c violet	5.00	5.75
J8	D6	60c slate blk	25.00	50.00
J9	D7	1 l red org	5.00	5.75
J10	D7	2 l green	16.00	29.00
J11	D7	5 l violet	45.00	250.00
J12	D7	10 l blue	80.00	400.00
J13	D7	20 l car rose	80.00	450.00
	Nos. J1-J13 (13)		286.00	1,246.

PARCEL POST STAMPS

Both unused and used values are for complete stamps.

Italian Parcel Post Stamps and Types of 1927-39 Overprinted

			Wmk. 140	Perf. 13
1944				
Q1	PP3	5c brown	6.50	75.00
Q2	PP3	10c deep blue	6.50	75.00
Q3	PP3	25c carmine	6.50	80.00
Q4	PP3	30c ultra	6.50	80.00
Q5	PP3	50c orange	6.50	75.00
Q6	PP3	60c red	6.50	290.00
Q7	PP3	1 l lilac	6.50	75.00
Q8	PP3	2 l green	375.00	1,800.
Q9	PP3	3 l yel bister	50.00	550.00
Q10	PP3	4 l gray	90.00	650.00
Q11	PP3	10 l rose lilac	190.00	250.00
Q12	PP3	20 l lilac brn	500.00	3,750.
	Nos. Q1-Q12 (12)		1,250.	7,750.

No parcel post service existed in 1944. Nos. Q1-Q12 were used undivided, for regular postage.

ITALIAN OFFICES ABROAD

Stamps listed under this heading were issued for use in the Italian Post Offices which, for various reasons, were maintained from time to time in foreign countries.

100 Centesimi = 1 Lira

GENERAL ISSUE

Values of Italian Offices Abroad stamps vary tremendously according to condition. Quotations are for very fine examples, and values for unused stamps are for examples with original gum as defined in the catalogue introduction. Extremely fine or superb examples sell at much higher prices, and fine or poor examples sell at greatly reduced prices. In addition, unused examples without gum are discounted severely.

Very fine examples of Nos. 1-17 will have perforations barely clear of the frameline or design due to the narrow spacing of the stamps on the plates.

Italian Stamps with Corner Designs Slightly Altered and Overprinted

		1874-78	Wmk. 140	Perf. 14	
1	A6	1c ol grn		26.00	40.00
a.		Inverted overprint		30,000.	
c.		2 dots in lower right corner		70.00	225.00
d.		Three dots in upper right corner		320.00	1,450.
e.		Without overprint		60,000.	
2	A7	2c org brn		27.50	42.50
a.		Without overprint		60,000.	
3	A8	5c slate grn		875.00	45.00
a.		Lower right corner not altered		17,500.	2,000.
4	A8	10c buff		850.00	85.00
a.		Upper left corner not altered		22,500.	1,250.
b.		None of the corners altered		—	55,000.
c.		Lower corners not altered		—	9,250.
5	A8	10c blue ('78)		500.00	28.00
6	A15	20c blue		2,150.	46.00
7	A15	20c org ('78)		8,500.	25.00
8	A8	30c brown		7.00	25.00
a.		None of the corners altered		40,000.	
b.		Right lower corner not altered		—	—
c.		Double overprint		—	—
9	A8	40c rose		7.00	25.00
10	A8	60c lilac		17.00	250.00
11	A13	2 l vermilion		215.00	800.00

		1881			
12	A17	5c green		21.00	17.50
13	A17	10c claret		7.00	14.25
14	A17	20c orange		7.00	8.50
a.		Double overprint, on piece		—	—
15	A17	25c blue		7.00	21.50
16	A17	50c violet		17.50	70.00
17	A17	2 l vermilion		21.50	—
		Nos. 12-17 (6)		81.00	
		Nos. 12-16 (5)		149.50	

The "Estero" stamps were used in various parts of the world, South America, Africa, Turkey, etc.

Forged cancellations exist on Nos. 1-2, 9-11, 16.

OFFICES IN CHINA

100 Cents = 1 Dollar

PEKING

Italian Stamps of 1901-16 Handstamped

		Wmk. 140, Unwmk.			
		1917	Perf. 12, 13½, 14		
1	A48	2c on 5c green		215.00	215.00
a.		Inverted surcharge		250.00	200.00
b.		Double surcharge, one inverted		775.00	575.00
c.		4c on 5c green		6,000.	
3	A48	4c on 10c claret (No. 95)		525.00	325.00
a.		Inverted surcharge		150.00	75.00
b.		Double surcharge, one inverted		325.00	190.00
c.		4c on 10c claret (No. 79)		—	
5	A58	8c on 15c slate		1,050.	775.00
a.		8c on 15c slate		4,250.	3,500.
c.		Pair, one without surcharge		—	
7	A58	8c on 20c on 15c slate		4,250.	3,000.
a.		Inverted surcharge		4,000.	2,650.
8	A50	8c on 20c brn org (No. 112)		8,500.	3,250.
a.		Inverted surcharge		8,000.	2,850.
9	A49	20c on 50c vio		50,000.	27,500.
a.		Inverted surcharge		40,000.	25,000.
b.		40c on 50c violet		17,500.	17,500.
c.		As "b," inverted surcharge		16,000.	16,000.
11	A46	40c on 1 l brn & grn		300,000.	45,000.
a.		Inverted surcharge		250,000.	37,500.

Excellent forgeries exist of the higher valued stamps of Offices in China.

Italian Stamps of 1901-16 Overprinted

		1917-18			
12	A42	1c brown		28.00	40.00
13	A43	2c orange brown		28.00	40.00
a.		Double overprint		285.00	
14	A48	5c green		7.00	14.00
a.		Double overprint		200.00	
15	A48	10c claret		7.00	14.00
16	A50	20c brn org (No. 112)		200.00	215.00
17	A49	25c blue		7.00	21.00
18	A49	50c violet		7.00	21.00
19	A46	1 l brown & grn		17.50	35.00
20	A46	5 l blue & rose		28.00	62.50
21	A51	10 l gray grn & red		250.00	450.00
		Nos. 12-21 (10)		579.50	912.50

Italy No. 113, the watermarked 20c brown orange, was also overprinted "Pechino," but not issued. Value: hinged $20; never hinged $50.

Italian Stamps of 1901-16 Surcharged:

1 CENT Pechino	2 dollari	Pechinc
a		b

TWO DOLLARS:
Type I — Surcharged "2 dollari" as illustration "b."
Type II — Surcharged "2 DOLLARI."
Type III — Surcharged "2 dollari." "Pechino" measures 11½mm wide, instead of 13mm.

		1918-19	Perf. 14		
22	A42	½c on 1c brown		200.00	200.00
a.		Surcharged "1 cents"		800.00	800.00
23	A43	1c on 2c org brn		7.00	14.00
a.		Surcharged "1 cents"		400.00	400.00
24	A48	2c on 5c green		7.00	14.00
25	A48	4c on 10c claret		7.00	14.00
26	A50	8c on 20c brn org (No. 112)		35.00	28.00
a.		"8 CENTS" doubled		425.00	425.00
27	A49	10c on 25c blue		15.50	28.00
a.		"10 CENTS" doubled		425.00	425.00
28	A49	20c on 50c violet		21.50	28.00
29	A46	40c on 1 l brown & green		250.00	300.00
30	A46	$2 on 5 l bl & rose (type I)		400.00	700.00
a.		Type II		100,000.	80,000.
b.		Type III		16,000.	16,000.
		Nos. 22-30 (9)		943.00	1,326.

Italy No. 100 Surcharged

		1919			
32	A49	10c on 25c blue		5.25	14.00

Imperf. examples of No. 32 are proofs.

PEKING SPECIAL DELIVERY STAMPS

Italian Special Delivery Stamp 1908 Overprinted Like Nos. 12-21

		1917	Wmk. 140	Perf. 14	
E1	SD2	30c blue & rose		11.00	35.00

No. E1 Surcharged

		1918			
E2	SD2	12c on 30c bl & rose		85.00	300.00

PEKING POSTAGE DUE STAMPS

Italian Postage Due Stamps Overprinted Like Nos. 12-21

		1917	Wmk. 140	Perf. 14	
J1	D3	10c buff & magenta		4.25	11.00
a.		Double overprint		280.00	
J2	D3	20c buff & magenta		4.25	11.00
J3	D3	30c buff & magenta		4.25	11.00
J4	D3	40c buff & magenta		8.50	11.00
		Nos. J1-J4 (4)		21.25	44.00

Nos. J1-J4 Surcharged Like No. E2

		1918			
J5	D3	4c on 10c		110,000.	80,000.
J6	D3	8c on 20c		28.50	70.00
a.		Pair, one without surcharge		1,450.	
J7	D3	12c on 30c		85.00	175.00
J8	D3	16c on 40c		350.00	650.00

In 1919, the same new values were surcharged on Italy Nos. J6-J9 in a different style: four lines to cancel the denomination, and "-PECHINO- 4 CENTS." These were not issued. Value $10 each, never hinged $25 each.

TIENTSIN

Italian Stamps of 1906 Handstamped

		Wmk. 140, Unwmk.			
		1917	Perf. 12, 13½, 14		
1	A48	2c on 5c green		460.00	460.00
a.		Surcharge inverted		425.00	425.00
b.		Double surcharge		850.00	550.00
c.		4c on 5c green		12,500.	
d.		Double surcharge, one inverted		925.00	120.00
2	A48	4c on 10c claret		850.00	700.00
a.		Surcharge inverted		800.00	650.00
b.		Double surcharge		1,275.	775.00
c.		Double surcharge, one inverted		1,400.	850.00
4	A58	6c on 15c slate		1,750.	1,400.
a.		Surcharge inverted		1,700.	1,250.
b.		4c on 15c slate		5,250.	5,000.
		Nos. 1-4 (3)		3,060.	2,560.

Italian Stamps of 1901-16 Overprinted

		1917-18			
5	A42	1c brown		28.00	40.00
a.		Inverted overprint		400.00	400.00
6	A43	2c orange brn		28.00	40.00
7	A48	5c green		7.00	14.00

8	A48	10c claret		7.00	14.00
a.		Double overprint		425.00	
9	A50	20c brn org (#112)		200.00	215.00
10	A49	25c blue		7.00	21.00
11	A49	50c violet		7.00	21.00
12	A46	1 l brown & grn		17.50	35.00
13	A46	5 l blue & rose		28.00	62.50
14	A51	10 l gray grn & red		250.00	450.00
		Nos. 5-14 (10)		579.50	912.50

Italy No. 113, the watermarked 20c brown orange was also overprinted "Tientsin," but not issued. Value: hinged $20; never hinged $50.

Italian Stamps of 1901-16 Surcharged:

1 CENT Tientsin	2 Dollari Tientsin
a	b

TWO DOLLARS:
Type I — Surcharged "2 Dollari" as illustration "b."
Type II — Surcharged "2 dollari."
Type III — Surcharged "2 Dollari." "Tientsin" measures 10mm wide instead of 13mm.

		1918-21	Perf. 14		
15	A42	½c on 1c brown		200.00	200.00
a.		Inverted surcharge		425.00	425.00
b.		Surcharged "1 cents"		650.00	625.00
16	A43	1c on 2c org brn		7.00	14.00
a.		Surcharged "1 cents"		425.00	425.00
b.		Inverted surcharge		350.00	350.00
17	A48	2c on 5c green		7.00	14.00
18	A48	4c on 10c claret		7.00	14.00
19	A50	8c on 20c brn org (#112)		35.00	28.00
20	A49	10c on 25c blue		15.50	28.00
21	A49	20c on 50c violet		21.00	28.00
22	A46	40c on 1 l brn & grn		250.00	300.00

23   A46 $2 on 5 l bl & rose (type I)   400.00   700.00
a.   Type II   17,000.   13,500.
b.   Type III ('21)   16,000.   13,500.
Nos. 15-23 (9)   942.50   1,326.

SPECIAL DELIVERY STAMPS

Italian Special Delivery Stamp of 1908 Overprinted

1917   **Wmk. 140**   *Perf. 14*
E1   SD2   30c blue & rose   11.00   35.00

No. E1 Surcharged

1918
E2   SD2   12c on 30c bl & rose   85.00   300.00

POSTAGE DUE STAMPS

Italian Postage Due Stamps Overprinted

1917   **Wmk. 140**   *Perf. 14*
J1   D3   10c buff & magenta   4.25   11.00
a.   Double overprint   325.00
J2   D3   20c buff & magenta   4.25   11.00
J3   D3   30c buff & magenta   4.25   11.00
a.   Double overprint   325.00
J4   D3   40c buff & magenta   8.50   11.00
Nos. J1-J4 (4)   21.25   44.00

Nos. J1-J4 Surcharged

1918
J5   D3   4c on 10c   7,500.   7,500.
J6   D3   8c on 20c   28.00   70.00
a.   "8 CENTS" double   2,100.
J7   D3   12c on 30c   85.00   180.00
J8   D3   16c on 40c   350.00   650.00

In 1919, the same new values were surcharged on Italy Nos. J6-J9 in a different style: four lines to cancel the denomination, and "-TIENTSIN- 4 CENTS." These were not issued. Value $8 each, never hinged $20 each.

OFFICES IN CRETE

40 Paras = 1 Piaster
100 Centesimi = 1 Lira (1906)
Italy Nos. 70 and 81 Surcharged in Red or Black

a   b

1900-01   **Wmk. 140**   *Perf. 14*
1   A36(a)   1pi on 25c blue   6.00   70.00
2   A45(b)   1pi on 25c dp bl (Bk) ('01)   4.25   8.75

Italian Stamps Overprinted

1906
On Nos. 76-79, 92, 81, 83-85, 87, 91
3   A42   1c brown   2.00   2.00
a.   Pair, one without ovpt.   1,125.
b.   Double overprint   325.00
4   A43   2c org brn   2.00   2.00
a.   Imperf., pair   2,250.
b.   Double overprint   325.00
5   A44   5c bl grn   3.50   3.00
6   A45   10c claret   325.00   210.00
7   A45   15c on 20c org   3.50   2.75
8   A45   25c blue   12.50   15.50
9   A45   40c brown   12.50   15.50
10   A45   45c ol grn   10.50   15.50
11   A45   50c violet   12.50   21.50
12   A46   1 l brn & grn   70.00   85.00
13   A46   5 l bl & rose   425.00   425.00
Nos. 3-13 (11)   879.00   797.75

On Nos. 94-95, 100, 104-105
1907-10
14   A48   5c green   2.00   1.40
a.   Inverted overprint   325.00
15   A48   10c claret   2.00   1.40
a.   Double overprint   325.00
16   A49   25c blue   3.50   10.50
17   A49   40c brown   32.50   32.50
18   A49   50c violet   3.50   10.50
Nos. 14-18 (5)   43.50   56.30

On No. 111 in Violet
1912   **Unwmk.**   *Perf. 13x13½*
19   A50   15c slate black   3.50   3.50

SPECIAL DELIVERY STAMPS

Special Delivery Stamp of Italy Overprinted

1906   **Wmk. 140**   *Perf. 14*
E1   SD1   25c rose red   8.50   17.50

OFFICES IN AFRICA

40 Paras = 1 Piaster
100 Centesimi = 1 Lira (1910)
BENGASI

Italy No. 81 Surcharged in Black

1901   **Wmk. 140**   *Perf. 14*
1   A45   1pi on 25c dp bl   52.50   140.00

Same Surcharge on Italy No. 100

1911
1A   A49   1pi on 25c blue   52.50   140.00

TRIPOLI

Italian Stamps of 1901-09 Overprinted in Black or Violet

1909   **Wmk. 140**
2   A42   1c brown   4.25   2.75
a.   Inverted overprint   250.00
3   A43   2c orange brn   2.00   2.75
4   A48   5c green   140.00   8.50
a.   Double overprint   275.00
5   A48   10c claret   2.75   2.75
a.   Double overprint   200.00   200.00
6   A49   25c blue   2.00   2.75
7   A49   40c brown   7.00   7.00
8   A49   50c violet   8.50   8.50
  Perf. 13½x14
  Unwmk.
9   A50   15c slate blk (V)   4.25   4.25
Nos. 2-9 (8)   170.75   39.25

Italian Stamps of 1901 Overprinted

1909   **Wmk. 140**   *Perf. 14*
10   A46   1 l brown & grn   125.00   85.00
11   A46   5 l blue & rose   42.50   250.00

Same Overprint on Italy Nos. 76-77
1915
12   A42   1c brown   2.75
13   A43   2c orange brown   2.75

Nos. 12-13 were prepared but not issued. No. 12 exists as a pair, one without overprint, value $2,000 hinged, $3,250 never hinged. No. 12 also exists with inverted overprint.

SPECIAL DELIVERY STAMPS

Italy Nos. E1, E6 Overprinted Like Nos. 10-11

1909   **Wmk. 140**   *Perf. 14*
E1   SD1   25c rose red   17.00   10.50
E2   SD2   30c blue & rose   5.75   14.00

Tripoli was ceded by Turkey to Italy in Oct., 1912, and became known as the Colony of Libia. Later issues will be found under Libya.

OFFICES IN TURKISH EMPIRE

40 Paras = 1 Piaster

Various powers maintained post offices in the Turkish Empire before World War I by authority of treaties which ended with the signing of the Treaty of Lausanne in 1923. The foreign post offices were closed Oct. 27, 1923.

GENERAL ISSUE

Italian Stamps of 1906-08 Surcharged

Printed at Turin
1908   **Wmk. 140**
1   A48   10pa on 5c green   7.00   3.50
2   A48   20pa on 10c claret   7.00   3.50
3   A49   40pa on 25c blue   2.00   2.00
4   A49   80pa on 50c violet   4.25   3.50
See Janina Nos. 1-4.

Surcharged in Violet

Unwmk.
5   A47   30pa on 15c slate   2.00   2.00
Nos. 1-5 (5)   22.25   14.50

Nos. 1, 2, 3 and 5 were first issued in Janina, Albania, and subsequently for general use. They can only be distinguished by the cancellations.

Italian Stamps of 1901-08 Surcharged:

Nos. 6-8   No. 9

Nos. 10-12

Printed at Constantinople
1908   **First Printing**
6   A48   10pa on 5c green   265.   300.
a.   Vert. pair, one without surcharge   2,750.
7   A48   20pa on 10c claret   265.   300.
8   A47   30pa on 15c slate   925.   1,000.
9   A49   1pi on 25c blue   925.   1,000.
a.   "PIASTRE"   1,550.   1,550.
10   A49   2pi on 50c violet   2,300.   2,650.
11   A46   4pi on 1 l brn & grn   12,750.   8,500.
12   A46   20pi on 5 l bl & rose   32,500.   25,000.

On Nos. 8, 9 and 10 the surcharge is at the top of the stamp. No. 11 has the "4" closed at the top. No. 12 has the "20" wide.

Second Printing
Surcharged:

Nos. 13-15   No. 16

Nos. 17-19

13   A48   10pa on 5c green   25.00   27.50
14   A48   20pa on 10c claret   25.00   27.50
15   A47   30pa on 15c slate   85.00   65.00
a.   Double surcharge   210.00   210.00
b.   Triple surcharge   525.00   525.00
16   A49   1pi on 25c blue   25.00   27.50
a.   "PIPSTRA"   175.00   175.00
b.   "1" omitted   175.00   175.00
17   A49   2pi on 50c violet   155.00   155.00
a.   Surcharged "20 PIASTRE"   1,800.   1,825.
b.   "20" with "0" scratched out   600.00   600.00
c.   "2" 5mm from "PIASTRE"   450.00   450.00
18   A46   4pi on 1 l brn & grn   1,125.   1,125.
19   A46   20pi on 5 l bl & rose   7,750.   3,400.
Nos. 13-19 (7)   9,190.   4,827.

On No. 18 the "4" is open at the top.

Third Printing

Surcharged in Red

20   A47   30pa on 15c slate   7.00   7.00
a.   Double surcharge   225.00   225.00

Fourth Printing
Surcharged:

20B	A46	4pi on 1 l brn & grn	50.00	70.00
c.		Inverted "S"	155.00	155.00
20D	A46	20pi on 5 l bl & rose	155.00	200.00
i.		Inverted "S"	425.00	425.00

Fifth Printing
Surcharged

20E	A46	4pi on 1 l brn & grn	42.50	55.00
f.		Surch. "20 PIASTRE"	2,000.	
20G	A46	20pi on 5 l bl & rose	425.50	55.00
h.		Double surcharge	1,250.	1,250.

Italian Stamps of 1906-19 Surcharged

1921

21	A48	1pi on 5c green	240.00	350.00
22	A48	2pi on 15c slate	5.50	8.50
23	A50	4pi on 20c brn org (No. 113)	60.00	70.00
24	A49	5pi on 25c blue	60.00	70.00
a.		Double surcharge	275.00	
25	A49	10pi on 60c carmine	3.50	5.75
		Nos. 21-25 (5)	369.00	504.25

No. 21 is almost always found poorly centered, and it is valued thus.
On No. 25 the "10" is placed above "PIASTRE."

Italian Stamps of 1901-19 Surcharged

n   o

1922

26	A42(n)	10pa on 1c brown	2.10	2.50
27	A43(n)	20pa on 2c org brn	2.10	2.50
28	A48(n)	30pa on 5c green	5.50	5.50
29	A48(o)	1pi20pa on 15c slate	6.25	2.50
30	A50(o)	3pi on 20c brn org (#113)	8.50	15.50
31	A49(o)	3pi30pa on 25c blue	4.25	2.50
32	A49(o)	7pi20pa on 60c carmine	8.50	5.50
33	A46(n)	15pi on 1 l brn & grn	25.00	42.50
		Nos. 26-33 (8)	62.20	79.00

On No. 32, the distance between the two lines is 2mm. See note after No. 58A.

Italy No. 100 Surcharged

34	A49	3.75pi on 25c blue	2.10	2.50

Italian Stamps of 1901-20 Surcharged:

q   r

1922

35	A48	30pi on 5c green	3.50	15.50
36	A49	1.50pi on 25c blue	2.10	8.50
37	A49	3.75pi on 40c brown	2.75	10.00
a.		Double surcharge	275.00	
38	A49	4.50pi on 50c violet	7.00	21.00
39	A49	7.50pi on 60c carmine	5.50	15.50
a.		Double surcharge	325.00	
b.		Pair, one without surcharge	1,400.	
40	A49	15pi on 85c red brn	10.50	35.00
41	A46	18.75pi on 1 l brn & grn	5.00	28.00

On No. 40 the numerals of the surcharge are above "PIASTRE."
On No. 42 the figure "4" is open at top. See note after No. 61.
On No. 43 the figure "9" has a curved or arched bottom. See note after No. 62.

Surcharged

42	A46	45pa on 5 l bl & rose	350.00	550.00
43	A51	90pa on 10 l gray grn & red	375.00	700.00

Italian Stamps of 1901-17 Surcharged Type "q" or:

44	A43	30pa on 2c org brn	2.10	5.50
45	A50	1.50pi on 20c brn org (#113)	2.10	5.50
		Nos. 35-45 (11)	765.55	1,394.

Italian Stamps of 1901-20 Surcharged in Black or Red

46	A48	30pa on 5c green	1.40	2.10
47	A48	1½pi on 10c claret	1.40	2.10
48	A49	3pi on 25c blue	14.00	5.25
49	A49	3¾pi on 40c brown	2.10	2.10
50	A49	4½pi on 50c violet	35.00	30.00
51	A49	7½pi on 85c red brn	5.50	7.00
a.		"PIASIRE"	35.00	35.00
52	A46	7½pi on 1 l brn & grn (R)	7.00	9.00
a.		Double surcharge	140.00	160.00
b.		"PIASIRE"	42.50	42.50
53	A46	15pi on 1 l brn & grn	52.50	125.00
54	A46	45pi on 5 l blue & rose	90.00	87.50
55	A51	90pi on 10 l gray grn & red	70.00	160.00
		Nos. 46-55 (10)	278.90	430.05

Italian Stamps of 1901-20 Surcharged Type "o" or:

No. 58   No. 59

Nos. 61-62

1923

56	A49	1pi20pa on 25c blue	10.50	
57	A49	3pi30pa on 40c brown	10.50	
58	A49	4pi20pa on 50c violet	10.50	
58A	A49	7pi20pa on 60c car	31.50	
59	A49	15pi on 85c red brn	10.50	
60	A46	18pi30pa on 1 l brn & grn	10.50	
a.		Double surcharge	275.00	
61	A46	45pi on 5 l bl & rose	31.50	
62	A51	90pi on 10 l gray grn & red	28.00	
		Nos. 56-62 (8)	143.50	

On No. 58A the distance between the lines is 1.5mm. On No. 61 the figure "4" is closed at top. On No. 62 the figure "9" is nearly rectilinear at bottom.
Nos. 56-62 were not issued.

SPECIAL DELIVERY STAMPS

Italian Special Delivery Stamps Surcharged

Surcharged

1908   **Wmk. 140**   *Perf. 14*

E1	SD1	1pi on 25c rose red	2.10	3.50

Surcharged

1910

E2	SD2	60pa on 30c blue & rose	4.25	5.00

Surcharged

1922

E3	SD2	15pi on 1.20 l on 30c bl & rose	28.00	70.00

On No. E3, lines obliterate the first two denominations.

Surcharged

15 PIASTRE

1922

E4	SD2	15pi on 30c bl & rose	425.00	850.00

Surcharged

1923

E5	SD2	15pi on 1.20 l blue & red	14.00	

No. E5 was not regularly issued.

ALBANIA

Stamps of Italy Surcharged in Black

1902   **Wmk. 140**   *Perf. 14*

1	A44	10pa on 5c green	4.25	2.10
2	A45	35pa on 20c orange	6.25	5.50
3	A45	40pa on 25c blue	12.50	5.50
		Nos. 1-3 (3)	23.00	13.10

Nos. 1-3 with red surcharges are proofs.

1907

4	A48	10pa on 5c green	42.50	50.00
5	A48	20pa on 10c claret	28.00	21.00
6	A45	80pa on 50c violet	28.00	21.00
		Nos. 4-6 (3)	98.50	92.00

No. 5 is almost always found poorly centered, and it is valued thus.

CONSTANTINOPLE

Stamps of Italy Surcharged in Black or Violet

Wmk. 140, Unwmk. (#3)

1909-11   *Perf. 14, 12*

1	A48	10pa on 5c green	2.10	2.10
2	A48	20pa on 10c claret	2.10	2.10
3	A47	30pa on 15c slate (V)	2.10	2.10
4	A49	1pi on 25c blue	2.10	2.10
a.		Double surcharge	185.00	185.00
5	A49	2pi on 50c violet	4.25	2.75

Surcharged

6	A46	4pi on 1 l brn & grn	4.25	3.50
7	A46	20pi on 5 l bl & rose	52.50	52.50
8	A51	40pi on 10 l gray grn & red	6.50	25.00
		Nos. 1-8 (8)	75.90	92.15

Italian Stamps of 1901-19 Surcharged:

Nos. 10, 12-13   Nos. 9, 11

1922

9	A48	20pa on 5c green	17.50	28.00
10	A48	1pi20pa on 15c slate	2.10	2.10
11	A49	3pi on 30c org brn	2.10	
12	A49	3pi30pa on 40c brown	2.10	2.10
13	A46	7pi20pa on 1 l brn & grn	2.10	2.10
		Nos. 9-13 (5)	25.90	36.40

Italian Stamps of 1901-20 Surcharged

[stamp image: COSTANTINOPOLI PIASTRE 1 PARÀ 20]

1923

14	A48	30pa on 5c green	2.75	2.10
15	A49	1pi20pa on 25c blue	2.75	2.10
16	A49	3pi30pa on 40c brown	2.75	1.75
17	A49	4pi20pa on 50c violet	2.75	1.75
18	A49	7pi20pa on 60c car	2.75	1.75

[middle-left column stamp images and surcharge examples]

Italian Stamps of 1901-17 Surcharged Type "q" or:

[surcharge type images: 30 PARÀ / PIASTRE 3,75 — q, r]

[Italy No. 100 surcharged: Piastre 3,75]

[stamp: 45 PIASTRE; 1,50 PIASTRE; 1½ PIASTRE]

19	A49	15pi on 85c red brn	2.75	2.75
20	A46	18pi30pa on 1 l brn & grn	2.75	2.75
21	A46	45pi on 5 l bl & rose	2.75	6.50
22	A51	90pi on 10 l gray grn & red	2.75	7.00
		Nos. 14-22 (9)	24.75	28.45

CONSTANTINOPLE SPECIAL DELIVERY STAMP

Unissued Italian Special Delivery Stamp of 1922 Surcharged in Black

1923   **Wmk. 140**   **Perf. 14**

E1	SD2	15pi on 1.20 l bl & red	6.50	35.00

CONSTANTINOPLE POSTAGE DUE STAMPS

Italian Postage Due Stamps of 1870-1903 Overprinted

1922   **Wmk. 140**   **Perf. 14**

J1	D3	10c buff & mag	70.00	100.00
J2	D3	30c buff & mag	70.00	100.00
J3	D3	60c buff & mag	70.00	100.00
J4	D3	1 l blue & mag	70.00	100.00
J5	D3	2 l blue & mag	1,400.	1,650.
J6	D3	5 l blue & mag	650.00	900.00
		Nos. J1-J6 (6)	2,330.	2,950.

A circular control mark with the inscription "Poste Italiane Constantinopoli" and with the arms of the Kingdom of Italy (Savoy Cross) in the center was applied to each block of four of these stamps in black. Value, set of 6 blocks of four with control marks, $12,500.

DURAZZO

Stamps of Italy Surcharged in Black or Violet

Wmk. 140, Unwmk. (#3)

1909-11   **Perf. 14, 12**

1	A48	10pa on 5c green	1.40	2.75
2	A48	20pa on 10c claret	1.40	2.75
3	A47	30pa on 15c slate (V)	62.50	3.50
4	A49	1pi on 25c blue	2.10	3.50
5	A49	2pi on 50c violet	2.10	3.50

Surcharged

6	A46	4pi on 1 l brn & grn	3.50	4.25
7	A46	20pi on 5 l bl & rose	265.00	225.00
8	A51	40pi on 10 l gray grn & red	17.50	105.00
		Nos. 1-8 (8)	355.50	350.25

No. 3 Surcharged

1916   **Unwmk.**   **Perf. 12**

9	A47	20c on 30pa on 15c slate	4.25	17.50

JANINA

Stamps of Italy Surcharged

1902-07   **Wmk. 140**   **Perf. 14**

1	A44	10pa on 5c green	8.50	2.75
2	A45	35pa on 20c orange	5.50	3.50
3	A45	40pa on 25c blue	31.50	8.50
4	A45	80pa on 50c vio ('07)	52.50	37.50
		Nos. 1-4 (4)	98.00	52.25

Surcharged in Black or Violet

Wmk. 140, Unwmk. (#7)

1909-11   **Perf. 14, 12**

5	A48	10pa on 5c green	1.40	2.75
6	A48	20pa on 10c claret	1.40	2.75
7	A47	30pa on 15c slate (V)	1.40	2.75
8	A49	1pi on 25c blue	1.40	2.75
9	A49	2pi on 50c violet	1.40	3.50

Surcharged

10	A46	4pi on 1 l brn & grn	3.50	4.25
11	A46	20pi on 5 l bl & rose	300.00	325.00
12	A51	40pi on 10 l gray grn & red	17.50	105.00
		Nos. 5-12 (8)	328.00	448.75

JERUSALEM

Stamps of Italy Surcharged in Black or Violet

Wmk. 140, Unwmk. (#3)

1909-11   **Perf. 14, 12**

1	A48	10pa on 5c green	5.50	15.50
2	A48	20pa on 10c claret	5.50	15.50
3	A47	30pa on 15c slate (V)	5.50	21.00
4	A49	1pi on 25c blue	5.50	15.50
5	A49	2pi on 50c violet	21.00	50.00

Surcharged

6	A46	4pi on 1 l brn & grn	28.00	70.00
7	A46	20pi on 5 l bl & rose	1,000.	1,125.
8	A51	40pi on 10 l gray grn & red	42.50	500.00
		Nos. 1-8 (8)	1,113.	1,812.

Forged cancellations exist on Nos. 1-8.

SALONIKA

Stamps of Italy Surcharged in Black or Violet

Wmk. 140, Unwmk. (#3)

1909-11   **Perf. 14, 12**

1	A48	10pa on 5c green	1.40	2.75
2	A48	20pa on 10c claret	1.40	2.75
3	A47	30pa on 15c slate (V)	2.10	2.75
4	A49	1pi on 25c blue	2.10	2.75
5	A49	2pi on 50c violet	2.10	3.50

Surcharged

6	A46	4pi on 1 l brn & grn	3.50	4.25
7	A46	20pi on 5 l bl & rose	450.00	575.00
8	A51	40pi on 10 l gray grn & red	17.50	115.00
		Nos. 1-8 (8)	480.10	708.75

SCUTARI

Stamps of Italy Surcharged in Black or Violet

Wmk. 140, Unwmk. (#3)

1909-11   **Perf. 14, 12**

1	A48	10pa on 5c green	1.40	2.75
2	A48	20pa on 10c claret	1.40	2.75
3	A47	30pa on 15c slate (V)	21.00	5.50
4	A49	1pi on 25c blue	1.40	2.75
5	A49	2pi on 50c violet	1.40	4.25

Surcharged

6	A46	4pi on 1 l brn & grn	2.75	4.25
7	A46	20pi on 5 l bl & rose	28.00	42.50
8	A51	40pi on 10 l gray grn & red	60.00	140.00
		Nos. 1-8 (8)	117.35	204.75

Surcharged like Nos. 1-5

1915

9	A43	4pa on 2c orange brn	2.10	5.00

No. 3 Surcharged

10	A47	20c on 30pa on 15c slate	5.25	22.50

1916   **Unwmk.**   **Perf. 12**

SMYRNA

Stamps of Italy Surcharged in Black or Violet

Wmk. 140, Unwmk. (#3)

1909-11   **Perf. 14, 12**

1	A48	10pa on 5c green	1.40	1.40
2	A48	20pa on 10c claret	1.40	1.40
3	A47	30pa on 15c slate (V)	2.75	4.25
4	A49	1pi on 25c blue	2.75	4.25
5	A49	2pi on 50c violet	3.50	5.50

Surcharged

6	A46	4pi on 1 l brn & grn	4.25	7.00
7	A46	20pi on 5 l bl & rose	155.00	200.00
8	A51	40pi on 10 l gray grn & red	17.50	105.00
		Nos. 1-8 (8)	188.55	328.80

Italian Stamps of 1901-22 Surcharged:

Nos. 10, 12-13   Nos. 9, 11

1922

9	A48	20pa on 5c green	28.00	
10	A48	1pi20pa on 15c slate	1.40	
11	A49	3pi on 30c org brn	1.40	
12	A49	3pi30pa on 40c brown	2.75	
13	A46	7pi20pa on 1 l brn & grn	2.75	
		Nos. 9-13 (5)	36.30	

Nos. 9-13 were not issued.

VALONA

Stamps of Italy Surcharged in Black or Violet

Wmk. 140, Unwmk. (#3)

1909-11   **Perf. 14, 12**

1	A48	10pa on 5c green	1.40	3.50
2	A48	20pa on 10c claret	1.40	2.75
3	A47	30pa on 15c slate (V)	14.00	5.50
4	A49	1pi on 25c blue	2.10	2.75
5	A49	2pi on 50c violet	2.10	3.50

Surcharged

6	A46	4pi on 1 l brn & grn	2.10	3.50
7	A46	20pi on 5 l bl & rose	45.00	52.50
8	A51	40pi on 10 l gray grn & red	50.00	140.00
		Nos. 1-8 (8)	118.10	214.00

Italy No. 123 Surcharged in Violet or Red Violet

1916

9	A58	30pa on 15c slate (V)	4.25	12.50
a.		Red violet surcharge	8.50	25.00

No. 9 Surcharged

10 A58 20c on 30pa on 15c
slate   2.10   *17.50*

AEGEAN ISLANDS
(Dodecanese)

A group of islands in the Aegean Sea off the coast of Turkey. They were occupied by Italy during the Tripoli War and were ceded to Italy by Turkey in 1924 by the Treaty of Lausanne. Stamps of Italy overprinted with the name of the island were in use at the post offices maintained in the various islands.

Rhodes, on the island of the same name, was capital of the entire group.

100 Centesimi = 1 Lira

GENERAL ISSUE

Italian Stamps of 1907-08 Overprinted

		1912	Wmk. 140	Perf. 14
1	A49	25c blue	42.50	28.00
a.		Inverted overprint	225.00	225.00
2	A49	50c violet	42.50	28.00
a.		Inverted overprint	225.00	225.00

Virgil Issue
Types of Italian Stamps of 1930 Overprinted in Red or Blue

		1930 Photo.	Wmk. 140	Perf. 14
3	A106	15c vio blk	1.10	14.00
4	A106	20c org brn	1.10	14.00
5	A106	25c dk green	1.10	6.00
6	A106	30c lt brown	1.10	6.00
7	A106	50c dull vio	1.10	6.00
8	A106	75c rose red	1.10	14.00
9	A106	1.25 l gray bl	1.25	17.50

Engr.
Unwmk.

10	A106	5 l + 1.50 l dk vio	3.50	35.00
11	A106	10 l + 2.50 l ol brn	3.50	35.00
		Nos. 3-11,C4-C7 (13)	*28.35*	*322.50*

St. Anthony of Padua Issue

Types of Italian Stamps of 1931 Overprinted in Blue or Red

		1932 Photo.	Wmk. 140	Perf. 14
12	A116	20c black brn	28.00	21.00
13	A116	25c dull grn	28.00	21.00
14	A118	30c brown org	28.00	25.00
15	A118	50c dull vio	28.00	17.50
16	A120	1.25 l gray bl	28.00	28.00

Engr.
Unwmk.

17	A121	75c lt red	28.00	40.00
18	A122	5 l + 2.50 l dp org	28.00	140.00
		Nos. 12-18 (7)	*196.00*	*292.50*

Dante Alighieri Society Issue

Types of Italian Stamps of 1932 Overprinted

		1932 Photo.	Wmk. 140
19	A126	10c grnsh gray	1.35	5.50
20	A126	15c black vio	1.35	5.50
21	A126	20c brown org	1.35	5.50
22	A126	25c dp green	1.35	5.50
23	A126	30c dp org	1.35	5.50
24	A126	50c dull vio	1.35	2.75
25	A126	75c rose red	1.35	8.50
26	A126	1.25 l blue	1.35	7.00
27	A126	1.75 l ol brn	2.10	8.50
28	A126	2.75 l car rose	2.10	8.50
29	A126	5 l + 2 l dp vio	2.75	21.00
30	A126	10 l + 2.50 l dk brn	2.75	35.00
		Nos. 19-30 (12)	*20.50*	*118.75*

See Nos. C8-C14.

Soccer Issue
Types of Italy, "Soccer" Issue, Overprinted in Black or Red

		1934		
31	A173	20c brn rose (Bk)	70.00	85.00
32	A174	25c green (R)	70.00	85.00
33	A174	50c violet (R)	250.00	55.00
34	A174	1.25 l gray bl (R)	70.00	155.00
35	A175	5 l +2.50 l bl (R)	170.00	335.00
		Nos. 31-35 (5)	*530.00*	*715.00*

See Nos. C28-C31.

Same Overprint on Types of Medal of Valor Issue of Italy, in Red or Black

		1935		
36	A177	10c sl gray (R)	42.50	85.00
37	A178	15c brn (Bk)	42.50	85.00
38	A178	20c red org (Bk)	42.50	85.00
39	A177	25c dp grn (R)	42.50	85.00
40	A178	30c lake (Bk)	42.50	85.00
41	A178	50c ol grn (Bk)	42.50	85.00
42	A178	75c rose red (Bk)	42.50	85.00
43	A178	1.25 l dp bl (R)	42.50	85.00
44	A177	1.75 l + 1 l pur (R)	42.50	85.00
45	A178	2.55 l + 2 l dk car (Bk)	42.50	85.00
46	A178	2.75 l + 2 l org brn (Bk)	42.50	85.00
		Nos. 36-46 (11)	*467.50*	*935.00*

See Nos. C32-C38, CE3-CE4.

Types of Italy, 1937, Overprinted in Blue or Red

		1938	Wmk. 140	Perf. 14
47	A208	10c dk brn (Bl)	3.25	7.00
48	A208	15c pur (R)	3.25	7.00
49	A208	20c yel bis (R)	3.25	7.00
50	A208	25c myr grn (R)	3.25	7.00
51	A208	30c dp cl (R)	3.25	7.00
52	A208	50c sl grn (R)	3.25	12.50
53	A208	75c rose red (Bl)	3.25	12.50
54	A208	1.25 l dk bl (R)	3.25	12.50
55	A208	1.75 l + 1 l dp org (Bl)	5.25	24.50
56	A208	2.55 l + 2 l ol brn (R)	5.25	24.50
		Nos. 47-56 (10)	*36.50*	*121.50*

Bimillenary of birth of Augustus Caesar (Octavianus), first Roman emperor.

See Nos. C39-C43.

Same Overprint of Type of Italy, 1937, in Red

		1938		
57	A222	1.25 l deep blue	1.40	2.10
58	A222	2.75 l + 2 l brown	1.60	8.50

600th anniversary of the death of Giotto di Bondone, Italian painter.

Statue of Roman Wolf — A1   Arms of Rhodes — A2

Dante's House, Rhodes A3

		1940	Photo.
59	A1	5c lt brown	.70	1.10
60	A2	10c pale org	.70	1.10
61	A3	25c blue grn	1.00	1.75
62	A1	50c rose vlo	1.00	1.75
63	A2	75c dull ver	1.00	3.50
64	A3	1.25 l dull blue	1.00	3.50
65	A2	2 l + 75c rose	1.00	21.00
		Nos. 59-65,C44-C47 (11)	*11.40*	*64.70*

Triennial Overseas Exposition, Naples.

AIR POST STAMPS

Ferrucci Issue
Types of Italian Air Post Stamps of 1930 Overprinted in Blue or Red Like Nos. 12-18

		1930	Wmk. 140	Perf. 14
C1	A104	50c brn vio (Bl)	8.50	20.00
C2	A104	1 l dk bl (R)	8.50	20.00
C3	A104	5 l + 2 l dp car (Bl)	17.50	55.00
		Nos. C1-C3 (3)	*34.00*	*97.00*

Nos. C1-C3 were sold at Rhodes only.

Virgil Issue
Types of Italian Air Post Stamps of 1930 Overprinted in Red or Blue Like Nos. 3-11

		1930	Photo.	
C4	A106	50c dp grn (R)	2.10	28.00
C5	A106	1 l rose red (Bl)	2.10	28.00

Engr.
Unwmk.

C6	A106	7.70 l + 1.30 l dk brn (R)	3.50	35.00
C7	A106	9 l + 2 l gray (R)	3.50	57.50
		Nos. C4-C7 (4)	*11.20*	*148.50*

Dante Alighieri Society Issue
Types of Italian Air Post Stamps of 1932 Overprinted Like Nos. 19-30

		1932	Wmk. 140	
C8	AP10	50c car rose	1.40	5.50
C9	AP11	1 l dp grn	1.40	5.50
C10	AP11	3 l dl vio	1.40	7.00
C11	AP11	5 l dp org	1.40	7.00
C12	AP11	7.70 l + 2 l ol brn	3.50	17.50
C13	AP11	10 l + 2.50 l dk bl	3.50	17.50
		Nos. C8-C13 (6)	*12.60*	*60.00*

Leonardo da Vinci — AP12

		1932 Photo.	Perf. 14½
C14	AP12	100 l dp bl & grnsh gray	17.00	120.00

Garibaldi Types of Italian Air Post Stamps of 1932 Overprinted in Red or Blue Like Nos. 12-18

		1932		
C15	AP13	50c deep green	45.00	115.00
C16	AP14	80c copper red	45.00	115.00
C17	AP13	1 l + 25c dl bl	45.00	115.00
C18	AP13	2 l + 50c red brn	45.00	115.00
C19	AP14	5 l + 1 l bluish sl	45.00	115.00
		Nos. C15-C19 (5)	*225.00*	*575.00*

See Nos. CE1-CE2.

Graf Zeppelin over Rhodes AP17

		1933		Perf. 14
C20	AP17	3 l olive brn	60.00	200.00
C21	AP17	5 l dp vio	60.00	225.00
C22	AP17	10 l dk green	60.00	350.00
C23	AP17	12 l dk blue	60.00	400.00
C24	AP17	15 l car rose	60.00	400.00
C25	AP17	20 l gray blk	60.00	400.00
		Nos. C20-C25 (6)	*360.00*	*1,975.*

Balbo Flight Issue
Types of Italian Air Post Stamps of 1933 Overprinted

		1933	Wmk. 140	Perf. 14
C26	AP25	5.25 l + 19.75 l grn, red & bl gray	52.50	150.00
C27	AP25	5.25 l + 44.75 l red, grn & bl gray	52.50	150.00

Soccer Issue
Types of Italian Air Post Stamps of 1934 Overprinted in Black or Red Like #31-35

		1934		
C28	AP32	50c brown (R)	14.00	62.50
C29	AP33	75c rose red)	14.00	62.50
C30	AP34	5 l + 2.50 l red org	24.50	125.00
C31	AP34	10 l + 5 l grn (R)	24.50	155.00
		Nos. C28-C31 (4)	*77.00*	*405.00*

Types of Medal of Valor Issue of Italy Overprinted in Red or Black Like #31-35

		1935		
C32	AP36	25c dp grn	60.00	100.00
C33	AP36	50c blk brn (R)	60.00	100.00
C34	AP36	75c rose	60.00	100.00
C35	AP36	80c dk brn	60.00	100.00
C36	AP36	1 l + 50c ol grn	42.50	100.00
C37	AP36	2 l + 1 l dp bl	42.50	100.00
C38	AP40	3 l + 2 l vio (R)	42.50	100.00
		Nos. C32-C38 (7)	*367.50*	*700.00*

Types of Italy Air Post Stamps, 1937, Overprinted in Blue or Red Like #47-56

		1938	Wmk. 140	Perf. 14
C39	AP51	25c dl gray vio (R)	3.75	7.00
C40	AP51	50c grn (R)	3.75	7.00
C41	AP51	80c brt bl (R)	3.75	21.00

C42 AP51 1 l + 1 l rose lake 6.25 25.00
C43 AP51 5 l + 1 l rose red 10.00 50.00
    Nos. C39-C43 (5) 27.50 110.00

Bimillenary of the birth of Augustus Caesar (Octavianus).

Statues of Stag and Roman Wolf AP18

Plane over Government Palace, Rhodes — AP19

1940				Photo.
C44	AP18	50c olive blk	1.60	3.50
C45	AP19	1 l dk vio	1.60	3.50
C46	AP18	2 l + 75c dk bl	1.60	8.50
C47	AP19	5 l + 2.50 l cop brn	1.60	15.50
		Nos. C44-C47 (4)	6.40	31.00

Triennial Overseas Exposition, Naples.

AIR POST SPECIAL DELIVERY STAMPS

Type of Italian Garibaldi Air Post Special Delivery Stamps Overprinted in Blue or Ocher Like Nos. 12-18

1932		Wmk. 140		Perf. 14
CE1	APSD1	2.25 l + 1 l bl & rose & (Bl)	70.00	200.00
CE2	APSD1	4.50 l + 1.50 l ocher & gray (O)	70.00	200.00

Type of Medal of Valor Issue of Italy, Overprinted in Black Like Nos. 31-35

1935				
CE3	APSD4	2 l + 1.25 l dp bl	42.50	100.00
CE4	APSD4	4.50 l + 2 l grn	42.50	100.00

ISSUES FOR THE INDIVIDUAL ISLANDS

Italian Stamps of 1901-20 Overprinted with Names of Various Islands as

a   b

c

The 1912-22 issues of each island have type "a" overprint in black on all values except 15c (type A58) and 20c on 15c, which have type "b" overprint in violet.
The 1930-32 Ferruci and Garibaldi issues are types of the Italian issues overprinted type "c."

CALCHI

Overprinted "Karki" in Black or Violet

1912-22		Wmk. 140	Perf. 13½, 14	
1	A43	2c orange brn	5.75	5.50
a.		Double overprint	300.00	500.00
2	A48	5c green	3.50	3.50
3	A48	10c claret	1.00	5.50

4	A48	15c slate ('22)	3.25	35.00
a.		Double overprint	300.00	
5	A50	20c brn org ('21)	3.25	31.50
6	A49	25c blue	1.00	5.50
7	A49	40c brown	1.00	5.50
8	A49	50c violet	1.00	12.50
		Unwmk.		
9	A58	15c slate (V)	32.50	12.75
10	A50	20c brn org ('17)	105.00	125.00
		Nos. 1-10 (10)	157.25	242.25

No. 9 Surcharged

1916			Perf. 13½	
11	A58	20c on 15c slate	2.10	21.00

Ferrucci Issue
Types of Italy
Overprinted in Red or Blue

1930		Wmk. 140		Perf. 14
12	A102	20c vio (R)	3.50	7.00
13	A103	25c dk grn (R)	3.50	7.00
14	A103	50c blk (R)	3.50	12.50
15	A103	1.25 l dp bl (R)	3.50	12.50
16	A104	5 l + 2 l dp car (Bl)	8.50	22.50
		Nos. 12-16 (5)	22.50	61.50

Garibaldi Issue
Types of Italy
Overprinted "CARCHI" in Red or Blue

1932				
17	A138	10c brown	17.00	28.00
18	A138	20c red brn (Bl)	17.00	28.00
19	A138	25c dp grn	17.00	28.00
20	A138	30c bluish sl	17.00	28.00
21	A138	50c red vio (Bl)	17.00	28.00
22	A141	75c cop red (Bl)	17.00	28.00
23	A141	1.25 l dl bl	17.00	28.00
24	A141	1.75 l + 25c brn	17.00	28.00
25	A144	2.55 l + 50c org (Bl)	17.00	30.00
26	A145	5 l + 1 l dl vio	17.00	30.00
		Nos. 17-26 (10)	170.00	284.00

CALINO

Overprinted "Calimno" in Black or Violet

1912-21		Wmk. 140	Perf. 13½, 14	
1	A43	2c orange brn	5.75	5.75
2	A48	5c green	2.10	5.75
3	A48	10c claret	1.00	5.75
4	A48	15c slate ('21)	3.25	38.50
5	A50	20c brn org ('21)	3.25	38.50
6	A49	25c blue	5.75	5.75
7	A49	40c brown	1.00	5.75
8	A49	50c violet	1.00	12.75
		Unwmk.		
9	A58	15c slate (V)	20.00	12.00
10	A50	20c brn org ('17)	57.50	115.00
		Nos. 1-10 (10)	100.60	245.50

No. 9 Surcharged Like Calchi No. 11

1916			Perf. 13½	
11	A58	20c on 15c slate	12.75	25.00

Ferrucci Issue
Types of Italy
Overprinted in Red or Blue

1930		Wmk. 140		Perf. 14
12	A102	20c violet (R)	3.50	7.00
13	A103	25c dk green (R)	3.50	7.00
14	A103	50c black (R)	3.50	12.50
15	A103	1.25 l dp bl (R)	3.50	12.50
16	A104	5 l + 2 l dp car (Bl)	8.50	22.50
		Nos. 12-16 (5)	22.50	61.50

Garibaldi Issue
Types of Italy
Overprinted in Red or Blue

1932				
17	A138	10c brown	17.00	30.00
18	A138	20c red brn (Bl)	17.00	30.00
19	A138	25c dp grn	17.00	30.00
20	A138	30c bluish sl	17.00	30.00
21	A138	50c red vio (Bl)	17.00	30.00
22	A141	75c cop red (Bl)	17.00	30.00
23	A141	1.25 l dull blue	17.00	30.00
24	A141	1.75 l + 25c brn	17.00	30.00

25	A144	2.55 l + 50c org (Bl)	17.00	30.00
26	A145	5 l + 1 l dl vio	17.00	30.00
		Nos. 17-26 (10)	170.00	300.00

CASO

Overprinted "Caso" in Black or Violet

1912-21		Wmk. 140	Perf. 13½, 14	
1	A43	2c orange brn	5.75	5.75
2	A48	5c green	3.50	5.75
3	A48	10c claret	1.00	5.75
4	A48	15c slate ('21)	3.25	35.00
5	A50	20c brn org ('20)	2.10	24.50
6	A49	25c blue	1.00	5.75
7	A49	40c brown	1.00	5.75
8	A49	50c violet	1.00	11.50
		Unwmk.		
9	A58	15c slate (V)	32.50	12.75
10	A50	20c brn org ('17)	100.00	155.00
		Nos. 1-10 (10)	151.10	267.50

No. 9 Surcharged Like Calchi No. 11

1916			Perf. 13½	
11	A58	20c on 15c slate	1.00	17.50

Ferrucci Issue
Types of Italy
Overprinted in Red or Blue

1930		Wmk. 140		Perf. 14
12	A102	20c violet (R)	3.50	7.00
13	A103	25c dk green (R)	3.50	7.00
14	A103	50c black (R)	3.50	12.50
15	A103	1.25 l dp bl (R)	3.50	12.50
16	A104	5 l + 2 l dp car (Bl)	8.50	22.50
		Nos. 12-16 (5)	22.50	61.50

Garibaldi Issue
Types of Italy
Overprinted in Red or Blue

1932				
17	A138	10c brown	17.00	30.00
18	A138	20c red brn (Bl)	17.00	30.00
19	A138	25c dp grn	17.00	30.00
20	A138	30c bluish sl	17.00	30.00
21	A138	50c red vio (Bl)	17.00	30.00
22	A141	75c cop red (Bl)	17.00	30.00
23	A141	1.25 l dull blue	17.00	30.00
24	A141	1.75 l + 25c brn	17.00	30.00
25	A144	2.55 l + 50c org (Bl)	17.00	30.00
26	A145	5 l + 1 l dl vio	17.00	30.00
		Nos. 17-26 (10)	170.00	300.00

COO
(Cos, Kos)

Overprinted "Cos" in Black or Violet

1912-22		Wmk. 140	Perf. 13½, 14	
1	A43	2c orange brn	5.75	5.75
2	A48	5c green	70.00	5.75
3	A48	10c claret	3.50	5.75
4	A48	15c slate ('22)	3.25	42.50
5	A50	20c brn org ('21)	2.10	24.50
6	A49	25c blue	27.50	5.75
7	A49	40c brown	1.00	5.75
8	A49	50c violet	1.00	11.00
		Unwmk.		
9	A58	15c slate (V)	42.00	12.75
10	A50	20c brn org ('17)	42.00	155.00
		Nos. 1-10 (10)	198.10	274.50

No. 9 Surcharged Like Calchi No. 11

1916			Perf. 13½	
11	A58	20c on 15c slate	12.75	28.00

Ferrucci Issue
Types of Italy
Overprinted in Red or Blue

1930		Wmk. 140		Perf. 14
12	A102	20c violet (R)	3.50	7.00
13	A103	25c dk green (R)	3.50	7.00
14	A103	50c black (R)	3.50	12.50
15	A103	1.25 l dp bl (R)	3.50	12.50
16	A104	5 l + 2 l dp car (Bl)	8.50	22.50
		Nos. 12-16 (5)	22.50	61.50

Garibaldi Issue
Types of Italy
Overprinted in Red or Blue

1932				
17	A138	10c brown	17.00	30.00
18	A138	20c red brn (Bl)	17.00	30.00
19	A138	25c dp grn	17.00	30.00
20	A138	30c bluish sl	17.00	30.00
21	A138	50c red vio (Bl)	17.00	30.00
22	A141	75c cop red (Bl)	17.00	30.00

23	A141	1.25 l dull blue	17.00	30.00
24	A141	1.75 l + 25c brn	17.00	30.00
25	A144	2.55 l + 50c org (Bl)	17.00	30.00
26	A145	5 l + 1 l dl vio	17.00	30.00
		Nos. 17-26 (10)	170.00	300.00

LERO

Overprinted "Leros" in Black or Violet

1912-22		Wmk. 140	Perf. 13½, 14	
1	A43	2c orange brn	6.50	5.75
2	A48	5c green	5.75	5.75
3	A48	10c claret	2.10	5.75
4	A48	15c slate ('22)	3.25	28.00
5	A50	20c brn org ('21)	125.00	87.50
6	A49	25c blue	52.50	5.75
7	A49	40c brown	3.50	5.75
8	A49	50c violet	1.00	12.75
		Unwmk.		
9	A58	15c slate (V)	62.00	12.75
10	A50	20c brn org ('17)	42.50	155.00
		Nos. 1-10 (10)	304.10	324.75

No. 9 Surcharged Like Calchi No. 11

1916			Perf. 13½	
11	A58	20c on 15c slate	12.75	28.00

Ferrucci Issue
Types of Italy
Overprinted in Red or Blue

1930		Wmk. 140		Perf. 14
12	A102	20c violet (R)	3.50	7.00
13	A103	25c dk green (R)	3.50	7.00
14	A103	50c black (R)	3.50	12.50
15	A103	1.25 l dp bl (R)	3.50	12.50
16	A104	5 l + 2 l dp car (Bl)	8.50	22.50
		Nos. 12-16 (5)	22.50	61.50

Garibaldi Issue
Types of Italy
Overprinted in Red or Blue

1932				
17	A138	10c brown	17.00	30.00
18	A138	20c red brn (Bl)	17.00	30.00
19	A138	25c dp grn	17.00	30.00
20	A138	30c bluish sl	17.00	30.00
21	A138	50c red vio (Bl)	17.00	30.00
22	A141	75c cop red (Bl)	17.00	30.00
23	A141	1.25 l dull blue	17.00	30.00
24	A141	1.75 l + 25c brn	17.00	30.00
25	A144	2.55 l + 50c org (Bl)	17.00	30.00
26	A145	5 l + 1 l dl vio	17.00	30.00
		Nos. 17-26 (10)	170.00	300.00

LISSO

Overprinted "Lipso" in Black or Violet

1912-22		Wmk. 140	Perf. 13½, 14	
1	A43	2c orange brn	5.75	5.75
2	A48	5c green	3.50	5.75
3	A48	10c claret	2.10	5.75
4	A48	15c slate ('22)	3.25	35.00
5	A50	20c brn org ('21)	3.25	35.00
6	A49	25c blue	1.00	5.75
7	A49	40c brown	2.10	5.75
8	A49	50c violet	1.00	12.50
		Unwmk.		
9	A58	15c slate (V)	31.00	12.75
10	A50	20c brn org ('17)	70.00	155.00
		Nos. 1-10 (10)	122.95	272.00

No. 9 Surcharged Like Calchi No. 11

1916			Perf. 13½	
11	A58	20c on 15c slate	1.00	21.00

Ferrucci Issue
Types of Italy
Overprinted in Red or Blue

1930		Wmk. 140		Perf. 14
12	A102	20c violet (R)	3.50	7.00
13	A103	25c dk green (R)	3.50	7.00
14	A103	50c black (R)	3.50	12.50
15	A103	1.25 l dp bl (R)	3.50	12.50
16	A104	5 l + 2 l dp car (Bl)	8.50	22.50
		Nos. 12-16 (5)	22.50	61.50

Garibaldi Issue
Types of Italy
Overprinted "LIPSO" in Red or Blue

1932				
17	A138	10c brown	17.00	30.00
18	A138	20c red brn (Bl)	17.00	30.00
19	A138	25c dp grn	17.00	30.00
20	A138	30c bluish sl	17.00	30.00
21	A138	50c red vio (Bl)	17.00	30.00
22	A141	75c cop red (Bl)	17.00	30.00

23	A141	1.25 l dull blue	17.00	30.00
24	A141	1.75 l + 25c brn	17.00	30.00
25	A144	2.55 l + 50c org (BI)	17.00	30.00
26	A145	5 l + 1 l dl vio	17.00	30.00
		Nos. 17-26 (10)	170.00	300.00

NISIRO

Overprinted "Nisiros" in Black or Violet

1912-22   Wmk. 140   Perf. 13½, 14

1	A43	2c orange brn	5.60	5.75
2	A48	5c green	3.50	5.75
3	A48	10c claret	1.00	5.75
4	A48	15c slate ('22)	21.00	42.50
5	A50	20c brn org ('21)	85.00	100.00
6	A49	25c blue	2.10	5.75
7	A49	40c brown	1.00	5.75
8	A49	50c violet	3.50	10.50

Unwmk.

9	A58	15c slate (V)	27.50	12.75
10	A50	20c brn org ('17)	105.00	155.00
		Nos. 1-10 (10)	255.20	349.50

No. 9 Surcharged Like Calchi No. 11

1916   Perf. 13½

11	A58	20c on 15c slate	1.00	24.50

Ferrucci Issue
Types of Italy
Overprinted in Red or Blue

1930   Wmk. 140   Perf. 14

12	A102	20c violet (R)	3.50	7.00
13	A103	25c dk green (R)	3.50	7.00
14	A103	50c black (R)	3.50	12.50
15	A103	1.25 l dp bl (R)	3.50	12.50
16	A104	5 l + 2 l dp car (BI)	8.50	22.50
		Nos. 12-16 (5)	22.50	61.50

Garibaldi Issue
Types of Italy
Overprinted in Red or Blue

1932

17	A138	10c brown	17.00	30.00
18	A138	20c red brn (BI)	17.00	30.00
19	A138	25c dp grn	17.00	30.00
20	A138	30c bluish sl	17.00	30.00
21	A138	50c red vio (BI)	17.00	30.00
22	A141	75c cop red (BI)	17.00	30.00
23	A141	1.25 l dull blue	17.00	30.00
24	A141	1.75 l + 25c brn	17.00	30.00
25	A144	2.55 l + 50c org (BI)	17.00	30.00
26	A145	5 l + 1 l dl vio	17.00	30.00
		Nos. 17-26 (10)	170.00	300.00

PATMO

Overprinted "Patmos" in Black or Violet

1912-22   Wmk. 140   Perf. 13½, 14

1	A43	2c orange brn	5.75	5.75
2	A48	5c green	3.50	5.75
3	A48	10c claret	2.10	5.75
4	A48	15c slate ('22)	3.25	37.50
5	A50	20c brn org ('21)	125.00	155.00
6	A49	25c blue	1.00	5.75
7	A49	40c brown	3.50	5.75
8	A49	50c violet	1.00	10.50

Unwmk.

9	A58	15c slate (V)	28.00	12.75
10	A50	20c brn org ('17)	70.00	155.00
		Nos. 1-10 (10)	243.10	399.50

No. 9 Surcharged Like Calchi No. 11

1916   Perf. 13½

11	A58	20c on 15c slate	12.50	28.00

Ferrucci Issue
Types of Italy
Overprinted in Red or Blue

1930   Wmk. 140   Perf. 14

12	A102	20c violet (R)	3.50	7.00
13	A103	25c dk green (R)	3.50	7.00
14	A103	50c black (R)	3.50	12.50
15	A103	1.25 l dp bl (R)	3.50	12.50
16	A104	5 l + 2 l dp car (BI)	8.50	22.50
		Nos. 12-16 (5)	22.50	61.50

Garibaldi Issue
Types of Italy
Overprinted in Red or Blue

1932

17	A138	10c brown	17.00	30.00
18	A138	20c red brn (BI)	17.00	30.00
19	A138	25c dp grn	17.00	30.00
20	A138	30c bluish sl	17.00	30.00
21	A138	50c red vio (BI)	17.00	30.00
22	A141	75c cop red (BI)	17.00	30.00
23	A141	1.25 l dull blue	17.00	30.00
24	A141	1.75 l + 25c brn	17.00	30.00
25	A144	2.55 l + 50c org (BI)	17.00	30.00
26	A145	5 l + 1 l dl vio	17.00	30.00
		Nos. 17-26 (10)	170.00	300.00

PISCOPI

Overprinted "Piscopi" in Black or Violet

1912-21   Wmk. 140   Perf. 13½, 14

1	A43	2c orange brn	5.75	5.75
2	A48	5c green	3.50	5.75
3	A48	10c claret	1.00	5.75
4	A48	15c slate ('21)	12.75	28.00
5	A50	20c brn org ('21)	42.50	45.00
6	A49	25c blue	1.00	5.75
7	A49	40c brown	1.00	5.75
8	A49	50c violet	1.00	12.50

Unwmk.

9	A58	15c slate (V)	31.50	12.75
10	A50	20c brn org ('17)	70.00	155.00
		Nos. 1-10 (10)	170.00	282.00

No. 9 Surcharged Like Calchi No. 11

1916   Perf. 13½

11	A58	20c on 15c slate	1.00	24.50

Ferrucci Issue
Types of Italy
Overprinted in Red or Blue

1930   Wmk. 140   Perf. 14

12	A102	20c violet (R)	3.50	7.00
13	A103	25c dk green (R)	3.50	7.00
14	A103	50c black (R)	3.50	12.50
15	A103	1.25 l dp bl (R)	3.50	12.50
16	A104	5 l + 2 l dp car (BI)	8.50	22.50
		Nos. 12-16 (5)	22.50	61.50

Garibaldi Issue
Types of Italy
Overprinted in Red or Blue

1932

17	A138	10c brown	17.00	30.00
18	A138	20c red brn (BI)	17.00	30.00
19	A138	25c dp grn	17.00	30.00
20	A138	30c bluish sl	17.00	30.00
21	A138	50c red vio (BI)	17.00	30.00
22	A141	75c cop red (BI)	17.00	30.00
23	A141	1.25 l dull blue	17.00	30.00
24	A141	1.75 l + 25c brn	17.00	30.00
25	A144	2.55 l + 50c org (BI)	17.00	30.00
26	A145	5 l + 1 l dl vio	17.00	30.00
		Nos. 17-26 (10)	170.00	300.00

RHODES

(Rodi)
Overprinted "Rodi" in Black or Violet

1912-24   Wmk. 140   Perf. 13½, 14

1	A43	2c org brn	1.00	5.75
2	A48	5c green	3.50	5.75
a.		Double overprint	300.00	500.00
3	A48	10c claret	1.00	5.75
4	A48	15c slate ('21)	125.00	50.00
5	A45	20c org ('16)	2.10	5.75
6	A50	20c brn org ('19)	5.25	12.50
a.		Double overprint	70.00	
7	A49	25c blue	3.50	5.75
8	A49	40c brown	4.25	5.75
9	A49	50c violet	1.00	12.50
10	A49	85c red brn ('22)	70.00	110.00
11	A46	1 l brn & grn ('24)	2.10	

No. 11 was not regularly issued.

Unwmk.

12	A58	15c slate (V)	32.50	12.50
13	A50	20c brn org ('17)	155.00	155.00
		Nos. 1-13 (13)	406.20	387.00

No. 12 Surcharged Like Calchi No. 11

1916   Perf. 13½

14	A58	20c on 15c slate	105.00	125.00

Windmill, Rhodes — A1   Medieval Galley — A2

Christian Knight — A3

Crusader Kneeling in Prayer — A4

Crusader's Tomb — A5

No Imprint

1929   Unwmk.   Litho.   Perf. 11

15	A1	5c magenta	10.00	2.10
16	A2	10c olive brn	10.00	1.40
17	A3	20c rose red	10.00	.70
18	A3	25c green	10.00	.70
19	A4	30c dk blue	55.00	2.10
20	A5	50c dk brown	10.00	.70
21	A5	1.25 l dk blue	10.00	2.10
22	A4	5 l magenta	70.00	100.00
23	A4	10 l olive brn	210.00	1,050.
		Nos. 15-23 (9)	395.00	1,159.

Visit of the King and Queen of Italy to the Aegean Islands. The stamps are inscribed "Rodi" but were available for use in all the Aegean Islands.

Nos. 15-23 and C1-C4 were used in eastern Crete in 1941-42 with Greek postmarks.

See Nos. 55-63.

Ferrucci Issue
Overprinted in Red or Blue

1930   Wmk. 140   Perf. 14

24	A102	20c violet (R)	3.50	7.00
25	A103	25c dk green (R)	3.50	7.00
26	A103	50c black (R)	3.50	12.50
27	A103	1.25 l dp blue (R)	3.50	12.50
28	A104	5 l + 2 l dp car (BI)	8.50	22.50
		Nos. 24-28 (5)	22.50	61.50

Hydrological Congress Issue

Rhodes Issue of 1929 Overprinted

1930   Unwmk.   Perf. 11

29	A1	5c magenta	55.00	50.00
30	A2	10c olive brn	55.00	50.00
31	A3	20c rose red	62.50	50.00
32	A3	25c green	70.00	50.00
33	A4	30c dk blue	55.00	50.00
34	A5	50c dk brown	525.00	85.00
35	A5	1.25 l dk blue	385.00	125.00
36	A4	5 l magenta	350.00	525.00
37	A4	10 l olive grn	350.00	550.00
		Nos. 29-37 (9)	1,907.	1,535.

Rhodes Issue of 1929 Overprinted in Blue or Red

1931

38	A1	5c mag (BI)	7.00	16.75
39	A2	10c ol brn (R)	7.00	16.75
40	A3	20c rose red (BI)	7.00	28.00
41	A3	25c green (R)	7.00	28.00
42	A4	30c dk blue (R)	7.00	28.00
43	A5	50c dk brown	52.50	62.50
44	A5	1.25 l dk bl (R)	45.00	100.00
		Nos. 38-44 (7)	132.50	280.00

Italian Eucharistic Congress, 1931.

Garibaldi Issue
Types of Italy
Overprinted in Red or Blue

1932   Wmk. 140   Perf. 14

45	A138	10c brown	17.00	28.00
46	A138	20c red brn (BI)	17.00	28.00
47	A138	25c dp grn	17.00	28.00
48	A138	30c bluish sl	17.00	28.00
49	A138	50c red vio (BI)	17.00	28.00
50	A141	75c cop red (BI)	17.00	28.00
51	A141	1.25 l dl bl	17.00	28.00
52	A141	1.75 l + 25c brn	17.00	28.00
53	A144	2.55 l + 50c org (BI)	17.00	28.00
54	A145	5 l + 1 l dl vio	17.00	28.00
		Nos. 45-54 (10)	170.00	280.00

Types of Rhodes Issue of 1929
Imprint: "Officina Carte-Valori Roma"

1932

55	A1	5c rose lake	1.40	.20
56	A2	10c dk brn	1.40	.20
57	A3	20c red	1.40	.20
58	A3	25c dl grn	1.40	.20
59	A4	30c dl bl	1.40	.20
60	A5	50c blk brn	1.40	.20
61	A5	1.25 l dp bl	1.40	.20
62	A4	5 l rose lake	1.40	2.00
63	A4	10 l ol brn	2.15	4.20
		Nos. 55-63 (9)	13.35	7.60

Aerial View of Rhodes A6

Map of Rhodes — A7   Deer and Palm — A8

1932   Wmk. 140   Litho.   Perf. 11

Shield in Red

64	A6	5c blk & red	8.50	21.00
65	A6	10c blk & vio bl	8.50	17.50
66	A6	20c blk & dl yel	8.50	17.50
67	A6	25c lil & blk	8.50	17.50
68	A6	30c blk & pink	8.50	17.50

Shield and Map Dots in Red

69	A7	50c blk & gray	8.50	17.50
70	A7	1.25 l red brn & gray	8.50	35.00
71	A7	5 l dk bl & gray	21.00	87.50
72	A7	10 l dk grn & gray	60.00	160.00
73	A7	25 l choc & gray	250.00	1,050.
		Nos. 64-73 (10)	390.50	1,441.

20th anniv. of the Italian occupation and 10th anniv. of Fascist rule.

1935, Apr.   Photo.   Wmk. 140

74	A8	5c orange	21.00	27.50
75	A8	10c brown	21.00	27.50
76	A8	20c car rose	21.00	35.00
77	A8	25c green	21.00	35.00
78	A8	30c purple	21.00	42.50
79	A8	50c red brn	21.00	42.50
80	A8	1.25 l blue	21.00	100.00
81	A8	5 l yellow	175.00	325.00
		Nos. 74-81 (8)	322.00	635.00

Holy Year.

The above overprints on No. 55 are stated to have been prepared locally for use on German military correspondence, but banned by postal authorities in Berlin.

RHODES SEMI-POSTAL STAMPS

Rhodes Nos. 55-62 Surcharged in Black or Red

1943 **Wmk. 140** **Perf. 14**

B1	A1	4c + 5c rose lake	2.50	2.50
B2	A2	10c + 10c dk brn	2.50	2.50
B3	A3	20c + 20c red	2.50	2.50
B4	A3	25c + 25c dl grn	2.50	2.50
B5	A4	30c + 30c dl bl (R)	4.25	3.25
B6	A5	50c + 50c blk brn	4.25	3.25
B7	A5	1.25 l + 1.25 l dp bl (R)	5.00	5.00
B8	A4	5 l + 5 l rose lake	100.00	150.00
		Nos. B1-B8 (8)	123.50	171.50

The surtax was for general relief.

Rhodes Nos. 55-58, 60 and 61 Surcharged in Black or Red

1944

B9	A1	5c + 3 l rose lake	2.50	5.75
B10	A2	10c + 3 l dk brn (R)	2.50	5.75
B11	A3	20c + 3 l red	2.50	5.75
B12	A3	25c +3 l dl grn (R)	2.50	5.75
B13	A5	50c + 5 l blk brn (R)	2.50	5.75
B14	A5	1.25 l + 5 l dp bl (R)	30.00	45.00
		Nos. B9-B14 (6)	42.50	73.75

The surtax was for war victims.

Rhodes Nos. 62 and 63 Surcharged in Red

1945

B17	A4	5 l + 10 l rose lake	10.00	21.00
B18	A4	10 l + 10 l ol brn	10.00	21.00

The surtax was for the Red Cross.

RHODES AIR POST STAMPS

Symbolical of Flight — AP18

Wmk. 140 Upright (No. C1), Sideways (No. C2a-C4a)

1935-38 **Typo.** **Perf. 14**

C1	AP18	50c black & yellow	.75	.40
C2a	AP18	80c black & mag	.75	2.10
C3a	AP18	1 l black & green	.75	.40
C4a	AP18	5 l black & red vio	1.50	4.50
		Nos. C1-C4a (4)	4.25	8.30

Nos. C2a-C4a were issued in 1937-38, on paper with sideways watermark. The 1935 first printing, which includes C1, is on paper within which the watermark is upright. For detailed listings, see the *Scott Classic Specialized Catalogue.*

RHODES AIR POST SEMI-POSTAL STAMPS

Rhodes Nos. C1-C4 Surcharged in Silver

1944 **Wmk. 140** **Perf. 14**

CB1	AP18	50c + 2 l	10.00	3.25
CB2	AP18	80c + 2 l	10.00	6.75
CB3	AP18	1 l + 2 l	15.00	8.50
CB4	AP18	5 l + 2 l	100.00	110.00
		Nos. CB1-CB4 (4)	135.00	128.50

The surtax was for war victims.

RHODES SPECIAL DELIVERY STAMPS

Stag — SD1

1936 **Photo.** **Wmk. 140** **Perf. 14**

E1	SD1	1.25 l green	3.50	3.50
E2	SD1	2.50 l vermilion	5.00	5.00

Nos. 58 and 57 Surcharged in Black

1943

E3	A3	1.25 l on 25c dl grn	.35	1.10
E4	A3	2.50 l on 20c red	.35	1.10

RHODES SEMI-POSTAL SPECIAL DELIVERY STAMPS

Rhodes Nos. E1 and E2 Surcharged in Red or Black

1943 **Wmk. 140** **Perf. 14**

EB1	SD1	1.25 l + 1.25 l (R)	26.00	17.50
EB2	SD1	2.50 l + 2.50 l	32.50	22.50

The surtax was for general relief.

RHODES POSTAGE DUE STAMPS

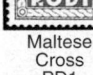

Maltese Cross PD1

Immortelle PD2

1934 **Photo.** **Wmk. 140** **Perf. 13**

J1	PD1	5c vermilion	3.50	5.50
J2	PD1	10c carmine	3.50	5.50
J3	PD1	20c dk grn	3.50	4.25
J4	PD1	30c purple	3.50	5.00
J5	PD1	40c dk bl	3.50	10.00
J6	PD2	50c vermilion	3.50	4.25
J7	PD2	60c carmine	3.50	20.00
J8	PD2	1 l dk grn	3.50	20.00
J9	PD2	2 l purple	3.50	10.00
		Nos. J1-J9 (9)	31.50	83.75

RHODES PARCEL POST STAMPS

Both unused and used values are for complete stamps.

PP1

PP2

1934 **Photo.** **Wmk. 140** **Perf. 13**

Q1	PP1	5c vermilion	5.00	8.50
Q2	PP1	10c carmine	5.00	8.50
Q3	PP1	20c dk green	5.00	8.50
Q4	PP1	25c purple	5.00	8.50
Q5	PP1	50c dk blue	5.00	8.50
Q6	PP1	60c black	5.00	8.50
Q7	PP2	1 l vermilion	5.00	8.50
Q8	PP2	2 l carmine	5.00	8.50
Q9	PP2	3 l dk green	5.00	8.50
Q10	PP2	4 l purple	5.00	8.50
Q11	PP2	10 l dk blue	5.00	8.50
		Nos. Q1-Q11 (11)	55.00	93.50

Value of used halves, Nos. Q1-Q11, each 80 cents.
See note preceding No. Q7 of Italy.

SCARPANTO

Overprinted "Scarpanto" in Black or Violet

1912-22 **Wmk. 140** **Perf. 13½, 14**

1	A43	2c org brn	6.50	5.75
2	A48	5c green	2.10	5.75
3	A48	10c claret	1.00	5.75
4	A48	15c slate ('22)	12.50	28.00
5	A50	20c brn org ('21)	42.50	45.00
6	A49	25c blue	6.25	5.75
7	A49	40c brown	1.00	5.75
8	A49	50c violet	2.10	12.75
		Unwmk.		
9	A58	15c slate (V)	24.50	12.75
10	A50	20c brn org ('17)	105.00	155.00
		Nos. 1-10 (10)	203.45	282.25

No 9 Surcharged Like Calchi No. 11

1916 **Perf. 13½**

11	A58	20c on 15c slate	1.00	25.00

Ferrucci Issue
Types of Italy
Overprinted in Red or Blue

1930 **Wmk. 140** **Perf. 14**

12	A102	20c violet (R)	3.50	7.00
13	A103	25c dk green (R)	3.50	7.00
14	A103	50c black (R)	3.50	12.50
15	A103	1.25 l dp bl (R)	3.50	12.50
16	A104	5 l + 2 l dp car (Bl)	8.50	22.50
		Nos. 12-16 (5)	22.50	61.50

Garibaldi Issue
Types of Italy
Overprinted in Red or Blue

1932

17	A138	10c brown	17.00	28.00
18	A138	20c red brn (Bl)	17.00	28.00
19	A138	25c dp grn	17.00	28.00
20	A138	30c bluish sl	17.00	28.00
21	A138	50c red vio (Bl)	17.00	28.00
22	A141	75c cop red (Bl)	17.00	28.00
23	A141	1.25 l dull blue	17.00	28.00
24	A141	1.75 l + 25c brn	17.00	28.00
25	A144	2.55 l + 50c org (Bl)	17.00	28.00
26	A145	5 l + 1 l dl vio	17.00	28.00
		Nos. 17-26 (10)	170.00	280.00

SIMI

Overprinted "Simi" in Black or Violet

1912-21 **Wmk. 140** **Perf. 13½, 14**

1	A43	2c org brn	12.50	5.75
2	A48	5c green	24.50	5.75
3	A48	10c claret	1.00	5.75
4	A48	15c slate ('21)	105.00	50.00
5	A50	20c brn org ('21)	52.50	28.00
6	A49	25c blue	6.25	5.75
7	A49	40c brown	1.00	5.75
8	A49	50c violet	1.00	12.75
		Unwmk.		
9	A58	15c slate	52.50	12.75
10	A50	20c brn org ('17)	52.50	87.50
		Nos. 1-10 (10)	308.75	219.75

No. 9 Surcharged Like Calchi No. 11

1916 **Perf. 13½**

11	A58	20c on 15c slate	6.25	21.00

Ferrucci Issue
Types of Italy
Overprinted in Red or Blue

1930 **Wmk. 140** **Perf. 14**

12	A102	20c violet (R)	3.50	7.00
13	A103	25c dk green (R)	3.50	7.00
14	A103	50c black (R)	3.50	12.50
15	A103	1.25 l dp bl (R)	3.50	12.50
16	A104	5 l + 2 l dp car (Bl)	8.50	22.50
		Nos. 12-16 (5)	22.50	61.50

Garibaldi Issue
Types of Italy
Overprinted in Red or Blue

1932

17	A138	10c brown	17.00	28.00
18	A138	20c red brn (Bl)	17.00	28.00
19	A138	25c dp grn	17.00	28.00
20	A138	30c bluish sl	17.00	28.00
21	A138	50c red vio (Bl)	17.00	28.00
22	A141	75c cop red (Bl)	17.00	28.00
23	A141	1.25 l dull blue	17.00	28.00
24	A141	1.75 l + 25c brn	17.00	28.00
25	A144	2.55 l + 50c org (Bl)	17.00	28.00
26	A145	5 l + 1 l dl vio	17.00	28.00
		Nos. 17-26 (10)	170.00	280.00

STAMPALIA

Overprinted "Stampalia" in Black or Violet

1912-21 **Wmk. 140** **Perf. 13½, 14**

1	A43	2c org brn	5.75	5.75
2	A48	5c green	1.00	5.75
3	A48	10c claret	1.00	5.75
4	A48	15c slate ('21)	8.50	27.50
5	A50	20c brn org ('21)	34.00	50.00
6	A49	25c blue	1.00	5.75
7	A49	40c brown	3.50	5.75
8	A49	50c violet	1.00	12.75
		Unwmk.		
9	A58	15c slate (V)	31.50	12.75
10	A50	20c brn org ('17)	70.00	87.50
		Nos. 1-10 (10)	157.25	219.25

No. 9 Surcharged Like Calchi No. 11

1916 **Perf. 13½**

11	A58	20c on 15c slate	1.00	21.00

Ferrucci Issue
Types of Italy
Overprinted in Red or Blue

1930 **Wmk. 140** **Perf. 14**

12	A102	20c violet (R)	3.50	7.00
13	A103	25c dk green (R)	3.50	7.00
14	A103	50c black (R)	3.50	12.50
15	A103	1.25 l dp bl (R)	3.50	12.50
16	A104	5 l + 2 l dp car (Bl)	8.50	22.50
		Nos. 12-16 (5)	22.50	61.50

Garibaldi Issue
Types of Italy
Overprinted in Red or Blue

1932

17	A138	10c brown	17.00	28.00
18	A138	20c red brn (Bl)	17.00	28.00
19	A138	25c dp grn	17.00	28.00
20	A138	30c bluish sl	17.00	28.00
21	A138	50c red vio (Bl)	17.00	28.00
22	A141	75c cop red (Bl)	17.00	28.00
23	A141	1.25 l dull blue	17.00	28.00
24	A141	1.75 l + 25c brn	17.00	28.00
25	A144	2.55 l + 50c org (Bl)	17.00	28.00
26	A145	5 l + 1 l dl vio	17.00	28.00
		Nos. 17-26 (10)	170.00	280.00

TRIESTE

A free territory (1947-1954) on the Adriatic Sea between Italy and Yugoslavia. In 1954 the territory was divided, Italy acquiring the northern section and seaport, Yugoslavia the southern section (Zone B).

> Catalogue values for all unused stamps in this country are for Never Hinged items.

ZONE A

Issued jointly by the Allied Military Government of the United States and Great Britain
Stamps of Italy 1945-47 Overprinted:

a b

c

1947, Oct. 1   Wmk. 277   Perf. 14

1	A259(a)	25c brt bl grn	.20	1.60
2	A255(a)	50c dp vio	.20	1.60
3	A257(a)	1 l dk grn	.20	.20
4	A258(a)	2 l dk cl brn	.20	.20
5	A259(a)	3 l red	.20	.20
6	A259(a)	4 l red org	.20	.20
7	A256(a)	5 l deep blue	.20	.20
8	A257(a)	6 l dp vio	.20	.20
9	A255(a)	10 l slate	.20	.20
10	A257(a)	15 l deep blue	2.40	.20
11	A259(a)	20 l dk red vio	4.00	.20
12	A260(b)	25 l dk blue	5.50	11.00
13	A260(b)	50 l dk vio brn	6.50	5.50

Perf. 14x13½

14	A261(c)	100 l car lake	45.00	35.00
		Nos. 1-14 (14)	65.20	56.50

The letters "F. T. T." are the initials of "Free Territory of Trieste."

Italy Nos. 486-488 Ovptd. Type "a"
1948, Mar. 1   Perf. 14

15	A255	8 l dk green	4.00	6.50
16	A256	10 l red org	14.50	4.50
17	A259	30 l dk blue	250.00	14.50
		Nos. 15-17 (3)	268.50	21.25

Italy Nos. 495 to 506 Overprinted

d

1948, July 1

18	A272	3 l dk brn	.40	.40
19	A272	4 l red vio	.40	.40
20	A272	5 l deep blue	.40	.40
21	A272	6 l dp yel grn	.80	.40
22	A272	8 l brown	.40	.40
23	A272	10 l org red	.80	.40
24	A272	12 l dk gray grn	.80	1.25
25	A272	15 l gray blk	17.50	16.00
26	A272	20 l car rose	32.50	16.00
27	A272	30 l brt ultra	2.50	2.50
28	A272	50 l violet	19.00	30.00
29	A272	100 l bl blk	47.50	72.50
		Nos. 18-29 (12)	123.00	140.65

Italy, Nos. 486 to 488, Overprinted in Carmine

1948, Sept. 8

30	A255	8 l dk green	.30	.25
31	A256	10 l red org	.30	.25
32	A259	30 l dk blue	2.00	2.00
		Nos. 30-32,C17-C19 (3)	2.60	2.50

The overprint is embossed.

Italy, No. 507, Overprinted Type "d" in Carmine
1948, Oct. 15

33	A273	15 l dk green	4.75	4.75

Italy, No. 508, Overprinted in Green

e

1948, Nov. 15

34	A274	15 l dk brown	16.00	4.00

Italy, No. 509, Overprinted Type "d" in Red
1949, May 2   Wmk. 277   Perf. 14

35	A275	20 l dk brown	16.00	8.00

Italy, Nos. 510 to 513, Overprinted

f

1949, May 2   Buff Background

36	A276	5 l red brown	.80	1.60
37	A276	15 l dk green	13.00	24.00
38	A276	20 l dp red brn	7.25	1.60
39	A276	50 l dk blue	16.00	12.00
		Nos. 36-39 (4)	37.05	39.20

Italy, No. 514, Overprinted Type "d" in Red
1949, May 2

40	A277	50 l brt ultra	5.50	5.50

Italy, No. 518, Overprinted Type "d" in Red
1949, May 30

41	A279	100 l brown	72.50	120.00

Italy, Nos. 515-517, Ovptd. Type "f"
1949, June 15

42	A278	5 l dk green	14.50	9.50
43	A278	15 l violet	14.50	17.50
44	A278	20 l brown	14.50	14.50
		Nos. 42-44 (3)	43.50	41.50

Italy, Nos. 519 and 520, Overprinted Type "e" in Carmine
1949, July 16

45	A280	20 l gray	14.50	8.00
46	A281	20 l brown	14.50	8.00

Italy, No. 521 Overprinted in Green

g

1949, June 8

47	A282	20 l brown red	8.00	8.00

Italy, No. 522, Overprinted Type "f" in Carmine
1949, July 8

49	A283	20 l violet	22.50	16.00

Italy, No. 523 Overprinted Type "e", without Periods, in Black
1949, Aug. 27

50	A284	20 l violet blue	16.00	8.00

Italy, No. 524 Ovptd. Type "f"
1949, Aug. 27

51	A285	20 l violet	24.00	24.00

Italy, No. 525, Overprinted Type "d" in Green
1949, Sept. 10

52	A286	20 l red	14.50	8.00

Italy Nos. 526 and 527 Overprinted

h

Wmk. 277

1949, Nov. 7   Photo.   Perf. 14

53	A287	20 l rose car	6.50	6.50
54	A288	50 l deep blue	24.00	26.00

Same Overprint on No. 528
1949, Nov. 7

55	A289	20 l dp grn	8.75	6.50

Same Overprint on No. 529
1949, Nov. 7

56	A290	20 l brt blue	5.50	4.75

Same Overprint in Red on No. 530
1949, Dec. 28

57	A291	20 l violet blk	7.25	4.00

Same Overprint in Black on Italian Stamps of 1945-48
1949-50   Photo.

58	A257	1 l dk green	.20	1.00
59	A258	2 l dk cl brn	.20	.20
60	A259	3 l red	.20	.20
61	A256	5 l deep blue	.20	.20
62	A257	6 l dp violet	.20	.20
63	A255	8 l dk green	55.00	35.00
64	A256	10 l red org	.20	.20
65	A257	15 l deep blue	4.00	.80
66	A259	20 l dk red vio	2.40	.20
67	A260	25 l dk grn ('50)	40.00	4.75
68	A260	50 l dk vio brn ('50)	60.00	4.00

Engr.

69	A261	100 l car lake	120.00	24.00
		Nos. 58-69 (12)	282.60	70.75

Issued: 3 l, 20 l, 10/21; 5 l, 11/5; 10 l, 11/7; 100 l, 11/23; 15 l, 11/28; 1 l, 2 l, 6 l, 8 l, 12/28; 50 l, 1/19; 25 l, 2/25.

Italy, No. 531, Overprinted Type "g" in Carmine
1950, Apr. 12

70	A292	20 l brown	7.25	4.00

Same Overprint in Carmine on Italy, No. 532
1950, Apr. 29

71	A293	20 l vio gray	4.00	4.00

Same Overprint in Carmine on Italy, Nos. 533 and 534
1950, May 22

72	A294	20 l olive green	4.75	4.75
73	A295	55 l blue	17.50	17.50

Italy, Nos. 535 and 536, Overprinted Type "h" in Black
1950, May 29

74	A296	20 l violet	4.75	4.75
75	A296	55 l blue	17.50	17.50

Italy, No. 537, Overprinted Type "g" in Carmine
1950, July 10

76	A297	20 l gray grn	4.75	4.00

Same Overprint in Carmine on Italy, Nos. 538-539
1950, July 15

77	A298	20 l purple	8.00	4.75
78	A298	55 l blue	27.50	32.50

Italy, No. 540, Overprinted Type "h"
1950, July 22

79	A299	20 l brown	8.75	5.50

Italy, No. 541 Overprinted in Carmine

i

1950, July 29

80	A300	20 l dk grn	7.25	5.50

Italy, No. 542, Overprinted Type "g"
1950, Aug. 21

81	A301	20 l chnt brn	4.00	4.00

Italy, Nos. 473A and 474, Overprinted

1950, Aug. 27

82	A257	15 l deep blue	6.50	4.75
83	A259	20 l dk red vio	6.50	2.40

Trieste Fair.

Italy, No. 543, Overprinted Type "i" in Carmine
1950, Sept. 11

84	A302	20 l indigo	4.00	3.25

Italy Nos. 544-546, Ovptd. Type "h"
1950, Sept. 16   Wmk. 277   Perf. 14

85	A303	5 l dp cl & grn	1.60	4.00
86	A303	20 l brn & grn	4.00	4.00
87	A303	55 l dp ultra & brn	30.00	35.00
		Nos. 85-87 (3)	35.60	43.00

Same, in Black, on Italy No. 547
1950, Sept. 16

88	A304	20 l ol brn & red brn	4.50	4.00

Same, in Black, on Italy No. 548
1950, Sept. 16

89	A305	20 l cr & gray blk	7.25	4.75

Italy, Nos. 549 to 565, Overprinted Type "g" in Black
1950, Oct. 20

90	A306	50c violet blue	.20	.20
91	A306	1 l dk blue vio	.20	.20
92	A306	2 l sepia	.20	.20
93	A306	5 l dk gray	.20	.20
94	A306	6 l chocolate	.25	.20
95	A306	10 l deep green	.80	.20
96	A306	12 l dp blue grn	2.40	.80
97	A306	15 l dk gray bl	2.40	.20
98	A306	20 l blue vio	2.40	.20
99	A306	25 l brown org	3.25	.20
100	A306	30 l magenta	1.60	.20
101	A306	35 l crimson	2.75	1.60
102	A306	40 l brown	1.75	1.60
103	A306	50 l violet	.80	.80
104	A306	55 l deep blue	.80	.80
105	A306	60 l red	9.50	11.00
106	A306	65 l dk green	.80	.80

Italy Nos. 566 and 567 Overprinted

k

Perf. 14, 14x13½
Engr.

107	A306	100 l brown org	7.25	.20
108	A306	200 l olive brn	5.50	8.00
		Nos. 90-108 (19)	43.05	28.20

Italy Nos. 568 and 569 Overprinted Type "k" in Black

1951, Mar. 27   Photo.   *Perf. 14*
109   A307   20 l red vio & red   4.75   4.75
110   A307   55 l ultra & bl   55.00   55.00

Italy No. 570 Overprinted Type "g"

1951, Apr. 2
111   A308   20 l dk grn   3.25   3.25

Same, on Italy No. 571

1951, Apr. 11
112   A309   20 l bl vio   4.00   3.25

Italy Nos. 572 and 573 Overprinted

1951, Apr. 12
113   A310(h)   20 l brown   4.00   4.00
114   A311(g)   55 l deep blue   5.50   5.50

Italy Nos. 574 to 576 Overprinted Type "h" in Black

1951, May 18   Fleur-de-Lis in Red
115   A312   5 l dk brown   8.75   50.00
116   A312   10 l Prus grn   8.75   50.00
117   A312   15 l vio bl   8.75   50.00
   Nos. 115-117 (3)   26.25   150.00

Italy No. 577 Overprinted

m

1951, Apr. 26
118   A313   20 l purple   4.00   4.00

Italy No. 578 Overprinted Type "h"

1951, May 5
119   A314   20 l Prus green   4.00   4.00

Italy Nos. 579-580 Ovptd. Type "g"

1951, June 18
120   A315   20 l violet   1.60   1.60
121   A315   55 l brt blue   4.00   4.00

Nos. 94, 98 and 104 Overprinted

1951, June 24
122   A306   6 l chocolate   .80   *1.75*
123   A306   20 l blue violet   1.75   .80
124   A306   55 l deep blue   1.75   1.75
   Nos. 122-124 (3)   4.30   4.30

Issued to publicize the Trieste Fair, 1951.

Italy No. 581 Overprinted

1951, July 23
125   A316   20 l brn & red brn   3.25   3.25

Italy Nos. 582 and 583 Overprinted Types "n" and "h" in Red

1951, July 23
126   A317(n)   20 l grnsh gray & blk   2.40   2.40
127   A318(h)   55 l vio bl & pale sal   4.00   4.00

Italy No. 584 Overprinted Type "g" in Carmine

1951, Aug. 23
128   A319   25 l gray blk   14.50   5.50

Overprint "g" on Italy No. 585

1951, Sept. 8
129   A320   25 l deep blue   3.25   3.25

Italy No. 586 Overprinted Type "h" in Red

1951, Sept. 15
130   A321   25 l dk brn   3.25   3.25

Italy Nos. 587-589 Overprinted in Blue

o

1951, Oct. 11
131   A322   10 l dk brn & gray   1.60   1.60
132   A322   25 l rose red & bl grn   1.60   1.60
133   A322   60 l vio bl & red org   3.25   3.25
   Nos. 131-133 (3)   6.45   6.45

Italy Nos. 590-591 Overprinted

p

1951, Oct. 31   Photo.
Overprint Spaced to Fit Design
134   A323   10 l green   2.00   2.00
135   A324   25 l vio gray   2.00   2.00

Italy Nos. 592-593 Ovptd. Type "k"

1951, Nov. 21
136   A325   10 l ol & dull grn   2.00   2.00
137   A326   25 l dull green   2.00   2.00

Italy Nos. 594-596 Overprinted Types "k" or "p" in Black

1951, Nov. 23
Overprint "p" Spaced to Fit Design
138   A327(p)   10 l vio brn & dk grn   1.60   1.60
139   A327(k)   25 l red brn & dk brn   1.60   .80
140   A327(p)   60 l dp grn & ind   3.25   3.25
   Nos. 138-140 (3)   6.45   5.65

Italy No. 597 Overprinted Type "p"

1952, Jan. 28   Wmk. 277   *Perf. 14*
Overprint Spaced to Fit Design
141   A328   25 l gray & gray blk   3.25   2.40

Italy No. 598 Overprinted Type "k"

1952, Feb. 2
142   A329   25 l dl grn & ol bis   3.25   2.40

Same on Italy No. 599

1952, Mar. 26
143   A330   25 l brn & sl blk   3.25   2.40

Same on Italy No. 600

1952, Apr. 12
144   A331   60 l ultra   3.25   *4.00*

Same on Italy No. 601

1952, Apr. 16
145   A332   25 l dp orange   .80   .40

Stamps of Italy Overprinted "AMG FTT" in Various Sizes and Arrangements
On Nos. 602-603

1952, June 14   Wmk. 277   *Perf. 14*
146   A333   25 l blk & red brn   1.60   1.60
147   A333   60 l blk & ultra   2.40   2.40

On No. 604

1952, June 7
148   A334   25 l bright blue   3.25   2.40

On No. 605

1952, June 14
149   A335   25 l black & yellow   3.25   2.40

On No. 606

1952, June 19
150   A336   25 l bl gray, red & dk bl (R)   3.25   2.40

On No. 607

1952, June 28
151   A337   25 l dp grn, dk brn & red   3.25   2.40

On No. 608

1952, Sept. 6
152   A338   25 l dark green   3.25   2.40

On No. 609 in Bronze

1952, Sept. 20
153   A339   25 l purple   3.25   2.40

On No. 610

1952, Oct. 4
154   A340   25 l gray   3.25   2.40

On No. 611

1952, Oct. 1
155   A341   60 l vio bl & dk bl   4.00   4.00

On No. 612

1952, Nov. 21   *Perf. 13*
156   A342   25 l brn & dk brn   3.25   2.40

On Nos. 613-615

1952, Nov. 3   *Perf. 14*
157   A343   10 l dk green   .80   .40
158   A344   25 l blk & dk brn   1.60   .30
159   A344   60 l blk & blue   1.60   2.00
   Nos. 157-159 (3)   4.00   2.70

On Nos. 616-617

1952, Dec. 6
160   A345   25 l dk green   3.25   2.40
161   A346   25 l brown   3.25   2.40

On No. 618

1953, Jan. 5
162   A347   25 l gray blk & dk bl (Bl)   3.25   2.40

On Nos. 601A-601B

1952, Dec. 31
163   A332a   60 l ultra (G)   2.40   *3.25*
164   A332   80 l brown car   3.25   2.40

On No. 621

1953, Feb. 21
165   A349   25 l car lake   3.25   2.40

On No. 622

1953, Apr. 24
166   A350   25 l violet   3.25   2.40

On No. 623

1953, Apr. 30
167   A351   25 l violet   3.25   2.40

On No. 624

1953, May 30
168   A352   25 l dark brown   3.25   2.40

On No. 625

1953, June 27
169   A353   25 l brn & dull red   3.25   2.40

On Nos. 626-633

1953-54
170   A354   5 l gray   .20   *.30*
171   A354   10 l org ver   .25   .20
172   A354   12 l dull grn   .25   .20
172A   A354   13 l brt lil rose ('54)   .25   .20
173   A354   20 l brown   .80   .80
174   A354   25 l purple   .80   .90
175   A354   35 l rose car   3.25   2.40
176   A354   60 l blue   4.00   3.25
177   A354   80 l org brn   11.00   8.00
   Nos. 170-177 (9)   20.80   16.25

Issue dates: 13 l, Feb. 1. Others, June 16.

Italy, Nos. 554, 558 and 564 Overprinted in Red or Green

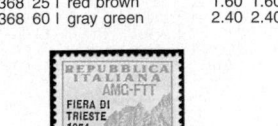

1953, June 27
178   A306   10 l dp green (R)   .80   .80
179   A306   25 l brown org   .80   .40
180   A306   60 l red   2.40   2.00
   Nos. 178-180 (3)   4.00   3.20

5th International Sample Fair of Trieste.

On No. 634

1953, July 11
181   A355   25 l blue green   3.25   2.40

On Nos. 635-636

1953, July 16
182   A356   25 l dark brown   1.60   *.80*
183   A356   60 l deep blue   2.40   *3.25*

On Nos. 637-638

1953, Aug. 6
184   A357   25 l org & Prus bl   1.60   1.60
185   A357   60 l lil rose & dk vio bl   3.25   3.25

On No. 639

1953, Aug. 13
186   A358   25 l dk brn & dl grn   3.25   2.40

On No. 640

1953, Sept. 5
187   A359   25 l dk gray & brn   3.25   2.40

On Nos. 641-646

1954, Jan. 26
188   A360   10 l dk brn & red brn   .40   .40
189   A361   12 l lt bl & gray   .40   .40
190   A361   20 l brn org & dk brn   .40   .40
191   A360   25 l dk grn & pale bl   .40   .40
192   A361   35 l cream & brn   2.40   2.40
193   A361   60 l bl grn & ind   2.40   2.40
   Nos. 188-193 (6)   6.40   6.40

On Nos. 647-648

1954, Feb. 11
194   A362   25 l dk brn & choc   1.60   *.80*
195   A362   60 l bl & ultra   2.40   *3.25*

On Nos. 649-650

1954, Feb. 25
196   A363   25 l purple   1.60   *.80*
197   A363   60 l dp bl grn   2.40   *3.25*

On No. 651

1954, Mar. 20
198   A364   25 l purple   3.25   2.40

On No. 652

1954, Apr. 24
199   A365   25 l gray blk   3.25   2.40

On No. 653

1954, June 1
200   A366   25 l gray, org brn & blk   3.25   2.40

On No. 654

1954, June 19
201   A367   25 l dk grnsh gray   3.25   2.40

On Nos. 655-656

1954, July 8
202   A368   25 l red brown   1.60   1.60
203   A368   60 l gray green   2.40   2.40

Nos. 644, 646 With Additional Overprint

1954, June 17

204	A360	25 l dk grn & pale bl	1.60	1.60
205	A361	60 l bl grn & indigo	2.40	2.40

International Sample Fair of Trieste.

On No. 657

1954, Sept. 6

206	A369	25 l dp grn & red	3.25	2.40

On Nos. 658-659

1954, Oct. 30

207	A370	25 l rose red	1.60	1.60
208	A370	60 l blue	2.40	2.40

OCCUPATION AIR POST STAMPS

Air Post Stamps of Italy, 1945-47, Overprinted Type "c" in Black

1947, Oct. 1   Wmk. 277   Perf. 14

C1	AP59	1 l slate bl	.20	.20
C2	AP60	2 l dk blue	.20	.20
C3	AP60	5 l dk green	8.00	6.50
C4	AP59	10 l car rose	8.00	6.50
C5	AP59	25 l brown	20.00	12.00
C6	AP59	50 l violet	100.00	20.00
		Nos. C1-C6 (6)	136.40	45.40

Italy, Nos. C116 to C121, Overprinted Type "b" in Black

1947, Nov. 19

C7	AP61	6 l dp violet	2.40	4.00
C8	AP61	10 l dk car rose	2.40	4.00
C9	AP61	20 l dp org	19.00	14.50
C10	AP61	25 l aqua	3.25	4.75
C11	AP61	35 l brt blue	3.25	6.50
C12	AP61	50 l lilac rose	19.00	11.00
		Nos. C7-C12 (6)	49.30	44.75

Italy, Nos. C123 to C126, Overprinted Type "f" in Black

1948

C13	AP65	100 l green	120.00	8.00
C14	AP65	300 l lil rose	25.00	35.00
C15	AP65	500 l ultra	45.00	47.50
C16	AP65	1000 l dk brown	250.00	340.00
		Nos. C13-C16 (4)	440.00	430.50

Issue date: Nos. C13-C15, Mar. 1.

Italy, No. C110, C113 and C114, Overprinted in Black

(Reduced Illustration)

1948, Sept. 8

C17	AP59	10 l carmine rose	.40	.40
C18	AP60	25 l brown	.80	.80
C19	AP59	50 l violet	1.20	1.20
		Nos. C17-C19 (3)	2.40	2.40

The overprint is embossed.

Italy Air Post Stamps of 1945-48 Overprinted Type "h" in Black

1949-52

C20	AP59	10 l car rose	.20	.20
C21	AP60	25 l brown ('50)	.20	.20
C22	AP59	50 l violet	.20	.20
C23	AP65	100 l green	.80	.20
C24	AP65	300 l lil rose ('50)	17.50	27.50
C25	AP65	500 l ultra ('50)	45.00	32.50
C26	AP65	1000 l dk brn ('52)	67.50	87.50
		Nos. C20-C26 (7)	131.40	148.30

No. C26 is found in two perforations: 14 and 14x13.
Issued: 100 l, 11/7; 50 l, 12/5; 10 l, 12/28; 25 l, 1/23; 300 l, 500 l, 11/25; 1000 l, 2/18.

OCCUPATION SPECIAL DELIVERY STAMPS

Special Delivery Stamps of Italy 1946-48 Overprinted Type "c"

1947-48   Wmk. 277   Perf. 14

E1	SD9	15 l dk car rose	.20	.30
E2	SD8	25 l brt red org ('48)	80.00	24.00
E3	SD8	30 l dp vio	.60	.60
E4	SD9	60 l car rose ('48)	80.00	32.50
		Nos. E1-E4 (4)	160.80	57.40

Issue dates: Oct. 1, 1947. Mar. 1, 1948.

Italy No. E26, Overprinted Type "d"

1948, Sept. 24

E5	A272	35 l violet	4.00	4.00

Italy No. E25, Overprinted Type "h"

1950, Sept. 27

E6	SD9	60 l car rose	8.75	3.25

Italy No. E32 Overprinted Type "k"

1952, Feb. 4

E7	SD8	50 l lilac rose	8.75	3.25

OCCUPATION AUTHORIZED DELIVERY STAMPS

Authorized Delivery Stamp of Italy, 1946 Overprinted Type "a" in Black

1947, Oct. 1   Wmk. 277   Perf. 14

EY1	AD3	1 l dark brown	.80	1.60

Italy, No. EY7 Overprinted in Black

1947, Oct. 29

EY2	AD4	8 l bright red	14.50	4.75

Italy, No. EY8, Overprinted Type "a" in Black

1949, July 30

EY3	AD4	15 l violet	80.00	40.00

Same, Overprinted Type "h" in Black

1949, Nov. 7

EY4	AD4	15 l violet	1.60	2.00

Italy No. EY9 Overprinted Type "h" in Black

1952, Feb. 4

EY5	AD4	20 l rose violet	14.50	2.40

OCCUPATION POSTAGE DUE STAMPS

Postage Due Stamps of Italy 1945-47, Overprinted Type "a"

1947, Oct. 1   Wmk. 277   Perf. 14

J1	D9	1 l red orange	.80	.80
J2	D10	2 l dk green	.40	.80
J3	D9	5 l violet	8.00	1.60
J4	D9	10 l dk blue	12.50	6.50
J5	D9	20 l car rose	27.50	8.00
J6	D10	50 l aqua	2.40	1.60
		Nos. J1-J6 (6)	51.60	19.30

Same Overprint on Postage Due Stamps of Italy, 1947

1949

J7	D10	1 l red orange	.40	.80
J8	D10	3 l carmine	.80	3.25
J9	D10	4 l brown	17.50	32.50
J10	D10	5 l violet	140.00	45.00
J11	D10	6 l vio blue	47.50	65.00
J12	D10	8 l rose vio	95.00	160.00
J13	D10	10 l deep blue	210.00	45.00
J14	D10	12 l golden brn	32.50	47.50
J15	D10	20 l lilac rose	32.50	14.50
		Nos. J7-J15 (9)	576.20	413.55

Issued: 3 l, 4 l, 6 l, 8 l, 12 l, 1/24; others, 4/15.

Postage Due Stamps of Italy, 1947-54, Overprinted Type "h"

1949-54

J16	D10	1 l red orange	.25	.20
J17	D10	2 l dk green	.25	.20
J18	D10	3 l car ('54)	.25	.50
J20	D10	5 l violet	1.25	.20
J21	D10	6 l vio bl ('50)	.25	.20
J22	D10	8 l rose vio ('50)	.25	1.00
J23	D10	10 l deep blue	.35	1.00
J24	D10	12 l gldn brn ('50)	1.60	1.00
J25	D10	20 l lilac rose	4.00	.20
J26	D10	25 l dk red ('54)	5.50	3.25
J27	D10	50 l aqua ('50)	6.50	.25
J28	D10	100 l org yel ('52)	9.50	1.60
J29	D10	500 l dp bl & dk car ('52)	100.00	80.00
		Nos. J16-J29 (13)	129.95	89.60

Issued: 5 l, 10 l, 11/7; 1 l, 11/22; 2 l, 20 l, 12/28; 6 l, 8 l, 12 l, 5/16; 50 l, 11/25; 100 l, 11/11; 500 l, 6/19; 3 l, 1/24; 25 l, 2/1.

OCCUPATION PARCEL POST STAMPS

See note preceding Italy No. Q7.

Parcel Post Stamps of Italy, 1946-48, Overprinted:

1947-48   Wmk. 277   Perf. 13½

Q1	PP4	1 l golden brn	.80	2.40
Q2	PP4	2 l lt bl grn	1.00	4.00
Q3	PP4	3 l red org	.80	4.00
Q4	PP4	4 l gray blk	1.25	4.75
Q5	PP4	5 l lil rose ('48)	24.00	32.50
Q6	PP4	10 l violet	8.00	20.00
Q7	PP4	20 l lilac brn	8.00	20.00
Q8	PP4	50 l rose red	11.00	35.00
Q9	PP4	100 l sapphire	16.00	45.00
Q10	PP4	200 l grn ('48)	575.00	1,000.
Q11	PP4	300 l brn car ('48)	350.00	525.00
Q12	PP4	500 l brn ('48)	200.00	300.00
		Nos. Q1-Q12 (12)	1,195.	1,992.

Halves Used

Q1-Q4	.40
Q5	.40
Q6-Q7	.40
Q8	.40
Q9	.40
Q10	.80
Q11	.60
Q12	.60

Issued: #Q1-Q4, Q6-Q9, Oct. 1; others, Mar. 1.

Parcel Post Stamps of Italy, 1946-54, Overprinted:

1949-54

Q13	PP4	1 l gldn brn ('50)	1.60	1.60
Q14	PP4	2 l lt bl grn ('51)	.80	1.00
Q15	PP4	3 l red org ('51)	.80	1.00
Q16	PP4	4 l gray blk ('51)	.80	1.00
Q17	PP4	5 l lilac rose	.80	1.00
Q18	PP4	10 l violet	2.00	2.00
Q19	PP4	20 l lil brn	2.00	2.00
Q20	PP4	30 l plum ('52)	.80	1.00
Q21	PP4	50 l rose red ('50)	1.60	1.60
Q22	PP4	100 l saph ('50)	3.50	6.50
Q23	PP4	200 l green	25.00	65.00
Q24	PP4	300 l brn car ('50)	125.00	190.00
Q25	PP4	500 l brn ('51)	72.50	110.00

Perf. 13x13½

Q26	PP5	1000 l ultra ('54)	325.00	475.00
		Nos. Q13-Q26 (14)	562.20	858.70

Halves Used

Q13-Q18, Q20	.40
Q19, Q22	.40
Q21	.40
Q23	.80
Q24	.80
Q25	.80
Q26	2.00

Pairs of Q18 exist with 5mm between overprints instead of 11mm. Value $2,000.
Issued: 20 l, 200 l, 11/22; 5 l, 10 l, 11/28; 300 l, 1/19; 50 l, 3/10; 1 l, 10/7; 100 l, 11/9; 500 l, 11/25; 2 l, 3 l, 4 l, 8/1; 30 l, 3/6; 1000 l, 8/12.

PARCEL POST AUTHORIZED DELIVERY STAMPS

For the payment of a special tax for the authorized delivery of parcels privately instead of through the post office. Both unused and used values are for complete stamps.

Parcel Post Authorized Delivery Stamps of Italy 1953 Overprinted in Black like Nos. Q13-Q26

1953, July 8   Wmk. 277

QY1	PAD1	40 l org red	19.00	6.50
QY2	PAD1	50 l ultra	19.00	6.50
QY3	PAD1	75 l brown	19.00	12.00
QY4	PAD1	110 l lilac rose	19.00	12.00
		Nos. QY1-QY4 (4)	76.00	37.00

Halves Used

QY1	.20
QY2	.20
QY3-QY4	.35

IVORY COAST

ˈiv-rē ˈkōst

LOCATION — West coast of Africa, bordering on Gulf of Guinea
GOVT. — Republic
AREA — 127,520 sq. mi.
POP. — 15,818,068 (1999 est.)
CAPITAL — Yamoussoukro

The former French colony of Ivory Coast became part of French West Africa and used its stamps, starting in 1945. On December 4, 1958, Ivory Coast became a republic, with full independence on August 7, 1960.

100 Centimes = 1 Franc

Catalogue values for unused stamps in this country are for Never Hinged items, beginning with Scott 167 in the regular postage section, Scott B15 in the semipostal section, Scott C14 in the airpost section, Scott J19 in the postage due section, Scott M1 in the military section, and Scott O1 in the official section.

Navigation and
Commerce — A1

Perf. 14x13½

1892-1900 Typo. Unwmk.
Colony Name in Blue or Carmine

1	A1	1c black, *lil bl*	2.00	2.40
2	A1	2c brown, *buff*	2.75	3.25
3	A1	4c claret, *lav*	4.75	4.75
4	A1	5c green, *grnsh*	13.50	9.00
5	A1	10c black, *lavender*	20.00	12.50
6	A1	10c red ('00)	130.00	110.00
7	A1	15c blue, quadrille paper	32.50	13.50
8	A1	15c gray ('00)	20.00	5.75
9	A1	20c red, *green*	21.00	16.00
10	A1	25c black, *rose*	24.00	6.50
11	A1	25c blue ('00)	40.00	37.50
12	A1	30c brown, *bister*	35.00	27.50
13	A1	40c red, *straw*	27.50	16.00
14	A1	50c car, *rose*	80.00	65.00
15	A1	50c brn, *azure* ('00)	37.50	32.50
16	A1	75c deep vio, *org*	32.50	32.50
17	A1	1fr brnz grn, *straw*	52.50	45.00
		Nos. 1-17 (17)	575.50	439.65

Perf. 13½x14 stamps are counterfeits.
For surcharges see Nos. 18-20, 37-41.

Nos. 12, 16-17
Surcharged in Black

1904

18	A1	0.05c on 30c brn, *bis*	87.50	87.50
19	A1	0.10c on 75c vio, *org*	18.00	18.00
20	A1	0.15c on 1fr brnz grn, *straw*	26.00	26.00
		Nos. 18-20 (3)	131.50	131.50

Gen. Louis
Faidherbe
A2

Oil Palm — A3

Dr. N.
Eugène
Ballay
A4

1906-07
Name of Colony in Red or Blue

21	A2	1c slate	2.00	2.00
a.		"CÔTE D'IVOIRE" omitted	160.00	160.00
22	A2	2c chocolate	2.00	2.00
23	A2	4c choc, *gray bl*	2.40	2.40
a.		"CÔTE D'IVOIRE" double	225.00	
b.		"CÔTE D'IVOIRE" omitted	190.00	
24	A2	5c green	4.00	2.75
a.		"CÔTE D'IVOIRE" omitted	110.00	92.50
b.		"CÔTE D'IVOIRE" omitted		400.00
25	A2	10c carmine (B)	9.50	6.50
a.		"CÔTE D'IVOIRE" double	210.00	400.00
26	A3	20c black, *azure*	10.00	9.50
27	A3	25c bl, *pinkish*	9.50	6.00
28	A3	30c choc, *pnksh*	12.50	8.75
30	A3	35c black, *yel*	12.50	5.75
a.		"CÔTE D'IVOIRE" omitted	225.00	
31	A3	45c choc, *grnsh*	18.00	12.50
32	A3	50c deep violet	16.00	12.50
33	A3	75c blue, *org*	16.00	12.50
34	A4	1fr black, *azure*	40.00	35.00
35	A4	2fr blue, *pink*	52.50	50.00
36	A4	5fr car, *straw* (B)	100.00	95.00
		Nos. 21-36 (16)	306.90	263.15

Stamps of 1892-1900 Surcharged in Carmine or Black

1912

37	A1	5c on 15c gray (C)	1.60	1.60
38	A1	5c on 30c brn, *bis* (C)	2.40	2.75
39	A1	10c on 40c red, *straw*	2.40	2.75
a.		Pair, one without surcharge	75.00	75.00
40	A1	10c on 50c brn, *az* (C)	4.00	4.75
41	A1	10c on 75c dp vio, *org*	9.00	10.00
		Nos. 37-41 (5)	19.40	21.85

Two spacings between the surcharged numerals are found on Nos. 37 to 41. For detailed listings, see the *Scott Classic Specialized Catalogue of Stamps and Covers.*

River
Scene
A5

1913-35

42	A5	1c vio brn & vio	.25	.25
43	A5	2c brown & blk	.25	.25
44	A5	4c vio & vio brn	.30	.30
45	A5	5c yel grn & bl grn	1.10	.50
46	A5	5c choc & ol brn ('22)	.30	.30
47	A5	10c red org & rose	2.00	.95
48	A5	10c yel grn & bl grn ('22)	.70	.70
49	A5	10c car rose, *bluish* ('26)	.30	.30
50	A5	15c org & rose ('17)	1.75	.80
51	A5	20c black & gray	.80	.55
52	A5	25c ultra & bl	11.00	6.50
53	A5	25c blk & vio ('22)	.55	.55
54	A5	30c choc & brn	2.40	2.00
55	A5	30c red org & rose ('22)	2.75	2.75
56	A5	30c lt bl & rose red ('26)	.50	.50
57	A5	30c dl grn & grn ('27)	.80	.80
58	A5	35c vio & org	.95	.80
59	A5	40c gray & bl grn	1.60	.80
60	A5	45c red org & choc	1.00	.80
61	A5	45c dp rose & mar ('34)	6.25	5.00
62	A5	50c black & vio	5.00	3.50
63	A5	50c ultra & bl ('22)	2.00	2.00
64	A5	50c ol grn & bl ('25)	.80	.80
65	A5	60c vio, *pnksh* ('25)	.80	.80
66	A5	65c car rose & ol grn ('26)	1.60	1.60
67	A5	75c brn & rose	1.00	.80
68	A5	75c ind & ultra ('34)	4.50	4.00
69	A5	85c red vio & blk ('26)	1.60	1.60
70	A5	90c brn red & rose ('30)	17.50	13.50
71	A5	1fr org & black	1.10	1.00
72	A5	1.10fr dl grn & dk brn ('28)	7.75	7.00
73	A5	1.50fr lt bl & dp bl ('30)	10.00	7.50
74	A5	1.75fr lt ultra & mag ('35)	17.50	9.50
75	A5	2fr brn & blue	6.00	2.90
76	A5	3fr red vio ('30)	11.00	7.50
77	A5	5fr dk bl & choc	10.00	5.75
		Nos. 42-77 (36)	133.70	95.15

Nos. 45, 47, 50, 52, 56 and 58 exist on both ordinary and chalky paper. See the *Scott Classic Specialized Catalogue of Stamps & Covers 1840-1940* for listings.

For surcharges see Nos. 78-91, B1.

Nos. 45, 47 and 52, pasted on cardboard and overprinted "Valeur d'echange" and value of basic stamp, were used as emergency currency in 1920.

Stamps and Type of 1913-34 Surcharged

1922-34

78	A5	50c on 45c dp rose & maroon ('34)	4.00	2.75
79	A5	50c on 75c indigo & ultra ('34)	2.40	2.00
80	A5	50c on 90c brn red & rose ('34)	2.40	2.40
81	A5	60c on 75c vio, *pnksh* ('35)	.65	.65
a.		Surcharge omitted	160.00	175.00
82	A5	65c on 15c orange & rose ('25)	1.25	1.25
83	A5	85c on 75c brown & rose ('25)	1.60	1.25
		Nos. 78-83 (6)	12.30	10.30

Stamps and Type of 1913 Surcharged with New Value and Bars

1924-27

84	A5	25c on 2fr (R)	1.10	1.10
85	A5	25c on 5fr	1.10	1.10
86	A5	90c on 75c brn red & cer ('27)	2.00	1.60
a.		Surcharge omitted	240.00	
87	A5	1.25fr on 1fr dk bl & ultra (R) ('26)	1.25	1.25
88	A5	1.50fr on 1fr lt bl & dk blue ('27)	2.00	2.00
89	A5	3fr on 5fr brn red & bl grn ('27)	6.00	6.00
a.		Double surcharge	160.00	
90	A5	10fr on 5fr dl red & rose lil ('27)	17.50	16.00
91	A5	20fr on 5fr bl grn & ver ('27)	21.00	19.00
		Nos. 84-91 (8)	51.95	48.05

Common Design Types pictured following the introduction.

Colonial Exposition Issue
Common Design Types
Name of Country in Black

		1931 Engr.	**Perf. 12½**	
92	CD70	40c deep green	4.00	4.00
93	CD71	50c violet	6.50	6.50
94	CD72	90c red orange	5.50	5.50
95	CD73	1.50fr dull blue	6.50	6.50
		Nos. 92-95 (4)	22.50	22.50

Stamps of Upper
Volta 1928,
Overprinted

1933 **Perf. 13½x14**

96	A5	2c brown & lilac	.25	.25
a.		Inverted overprint	27.50	
b.		Double overprint	40.00	47.50
97	A5	4c blk & yellow	.35	.35
a.		Inverted overprint	100.00	
b.		Double overprint	65.00	72.50
98	A5	5c ind & gray bl	.65	.65
a.		Inverted overprint	47.50	
b.		Double overprint	65.00	
99	A5	10c indigo & pink	.50	.50
100	A5	15c brown & blue	1.25	1.00
101	A5	20c brown & green	1.25	1.00
102	A5	25c brn & yellow	2.25	1.90
103	A6	30c dp grn & brn	2.75	2.00
a.		Double overprint	75.00	
104	A6	45c brown & blue	10.00	6.50
a.		Inverted overprint	80.00	
b.		Double overprint	120.00	
105	A6	65c indigo & bl	4.00	2.90
a.		Double overprint	95.00	
106	A6	75c black & lilac	4.75	2.50
a.		Double overprint	95.00	
107	A6	90c brn red & lil	4.00	2.90

Overprinted

108	A7	1fr brown & green	4.75	3.25
a.		Inverted overprint	150.00	160.00
109	A7	1.50fr ultra & grysh	4.50	2.90
a.		Inverted overprint	150.00	
b.		Double overprint	95.00	

Surcharged

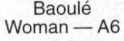

110	A6	1.25fr on 40c blk & pink	3.00	2.25
a.		Double overprint	100.00	
111	A6	1.75fr on 50c blk & green	5.25	3.25
a.		Double overprint	100.00	
		Nos. 96-111 (16)	49.50	33.95

Baoulé
Woman — A6

Rapids on
Comoe
River — A9

Mosque at Bobo-Dioulasso — A7

Coastal
Scene
A8

1936-44 — Perf. 13

112	A6	1c carmine rose	.25	.25
113	A6	2c ultramarine	.25	.25
114	A6	3c dp grn ('40)	.25	.25
115	A6	4c chocolate	.25	.25
116	A6	5c violet	.25	.25
117	A6	10c Prussian bl	.25	.25
118	A6	15c copper red	.25	.25
119	A7	20c ultramarine	.35	.25
120	A7	25c copper red	.50	.25
121	A7	30c blue green	.35	.35
122	A7	30c brown ('40)	.25	.25
123	A7	35c dp grn ('38)	.85	.65
124	A7	40c carmine rose	.50	.35
125	A7	45c brown	.65	.65
126	A7	45c blue grn ('40)	.35	.35
127	A7	50c plum	.50	.50
128	A7	55c dark vio ('38)	.60	.60
129	A8	60c car rose ('40)	.40	.40
130	A8	65c red brown	.65	.50
131	A8	70c red brn ('40)	.65	.65
132	A8	75c dark violet	1.25	.75
133	A8	80c blk brn ('38)	1.50	.95
134	A8	90c carmine rose	10.00	5.50
135	A8	90c dk grn ('39)	.85	.80
136	A8	1fr dark green	5.00	2.75
137	A8	1fr car rose ('38)	1.75	.95
138	A8	1fr dk vio ('40)	.65	.65
139	A8	1.25fr copper red	.50	.40
140	A8	1.40fr ultra ('40)	.65	.65
141	A8	1.50fr ultramarine	.60	.40
141A	A8	1.50fr grnsh blk ('42)	2.25	2.00
142	A8	1.60fr blk brn ('40)	1.25	1.00
143	A8	1.75fr carmine rose	.65	.40
144	A9	1.75fr dull ('38)	1.25	.85
145	A9	2fr ultramarine	.85	.60
146	A9	2.25fr dark bl ('39)	1.25	1.25
147	A9	2.50fr rose red ('40)	1.75	1.40
148	A9	3fr green	.95	.60
149	A9	5fr chocolate	1.00	.65
150	A9	10fr violet	1.50	1.00
151	A9	20fr copper red	2.75	1.00
		Nos. 112-151 (41)	46.55	32.85

For types A7, A8 and A9 without "RF," see Nos. 166A-166D.
For surcharges see Nos. B8-B11.

Paris International Exposition Issue
Common Design Types

1937 — Perf. 13

152	CD74	20c deep violet	2.00	2.00
153	CD75	30c dark green	2.00	2.00
154	CD76	40c carmine rose	2.00	2.00
155	CD77	50c dk brn & bl	1.60	1.60
156	CD78	90c red	1.60	1.60
157	CD79	1.50fr ultra	2.00	2.00
		Nos. 152-157 (6)	11.20	11.20

Colonial Arts Exhibition Issue
Souvenir Sheet
Common Design Type

1937 — Imperf.

158	CD76	3fr sepia	8.75	10.00

Louis Gustave Binger A10

1937 — Perf. 13

159	A10	65c red brown	.65	.65

Death of Governor General Binger; 50th anniv. of his exploration of the Niger.

Caillie Issue
Common Design Type

1939 — Engr. — Perf. 12½x12

160	CD81	90c org brn & org	.80	.80
161	CD81	2fr bright violet	1.20	1.20
162	CD81	2.25fr ultra & dk bl	1.20	1.20
		Nos. 160-162 (3)	3.20	3.20

New York World's Fair Issue
Common Design Type

1939

163	CD82	1.25fr carmine lake	1.50	1.50
164	CD82	2.25fr ultramarine	1.50	1.50

Ebrié Lagoon and Marshal Pétain A11

1941

165	A11	1fr green	.80	—
166	A11	2.50fr deep blue	.85	—

For surcharges, see Nos. B14A-B14B.

Types of 1936-40 Without "RF"

1944 — Perf. 13

166A	A7	30c brown		1.60
166B	A8	60c car rose		1.75
166C	A8	1fr dark violet		1.75
166D	A9	20fr copper red		3.75
		Nos. 166A-166D (4)		8.85

Nos. 166A-166D were issued by the Vichy government in France, but were not placed on sale in Ivory Coast.

For other stamps inscribed Cote d'Ivoire and Afrique Occidentale Francaise see French West Africa Nos. 58, 72, 77.

> Catalogue values for unused stamps in this section, from this point to the end of the section, are for Never Hinged items.

Republic

Elephant A12

President Felix Houphouet-Boigny A13

1959, Oct. 1 — Engr. — Perf. 13

167	A12	10fr black & emerald	1.00	.35
168	A12	25fr vio brn & olive	1.50	.55
169	A12	30fr ol blk & grnsh bl	1.75	1.10
		Nos. 167-169 (3)	4.25	2.00

Imperforates
Most Ivory Coast stamps from 1959 onward exist imperforate in issued and trial colors, and also in small presentation sheets in issued colors.

1959, Dec. 4 — Unwmk.

170	A13	25fr violet brown	1.00	.60

Proclamation of the Republic, 1st anniv.

Bété Mask — A14

Designs: Masks of 5 tribes: Bété, Guéré, Baoulé, Senufo and Guro. #174-176 horiz.

1960 — Perf. 13

171	A14	50c pale brn & vio brn	.20	.20
172	A14	1fr violet & mag	.20	.20
173	A14	2fr ultra & bl grn	.25	.20
174	A14	4fr dk grn & org	.25	.20
175	A14	5fr ver & brown	.40	.30
176	A14	6fr dark brn & vio	.50	.40
177	A14	45fr dk grn & brn vio	1.80	1.00
178	A14	50fr dk brn & grnsh bl	2.75	1.20
179	A14	85fr car & slate grn	5.00	2.25
		Nos. 171-179 (9)	11.35	5.95

C.C.T.A. Issue
Common Design Type

1960, May 16 — Engr. — Perf. 13

180	CD106	25fr grnsh bl & vio	1.10	.50

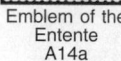

Emblem of the Entente A14a

Blood Lilies A16

Young Couple with Olive Branch and Globe — A15

1960, May 29 — Photo. — Perf. 13x13½

181	A14a	25fr multicolored	1.40	1.00

1st anniv. of the Entente (Dahomey, Ivory Coast, Niger and Upper Volta).

1961, Aug. 7 — Engr. — Perf. 13

182	A15	25fr emer, bister & blk	1.00	.50

First anniversary of Independence.

1961-62

Designs: Various Local Plants & Orchids.

183	A16	5fr dk grn, red & orange ('62)	1.10	.35
184	A16	10fr ultra, claret & yel	.65	.35
185	A16	15fr org, rose lil & green ('62)	2.10	.50
186	A16	20fr brn, dk red & yel	1.25	.50
187	A16	25fr grn, red brn & yel	1.10	.50
188	A16	30fr blk, car & green	1.50	.75
189	A16	70fr green, ver & yel	4.00	1.60
190	A16	85fr brn, lil, yel & grn	6.00	2.00
		Nos. 183-190 (8)	17.70	6.55

Early Letter Carrier and Modern Mailman — A17

1961, Oct. 14 — Unwmk. — Perf. 13

191	A17	25fr choc, emer & bl	1.00	.70

Issued for Stamp Day.

Ayamé Dam — A18

1961, Nov. 18 — Engr.

192	A18	25fr grnsh bl, blk & grn	1.25	.50

Swimming Race A19

1961, Dec. 23 — Unwmk. — Perf. 13

193	A19	5fr shown	.45	.20
194	A19	20fr Basketball	.65	.30
195	A19	25fr Soccer	1.10	.45
		Nos. 193-195 (3)	2.20	.95

Abidjan Games, Dec. 24-31. See No. C17.

Palms — A20

1962, Feb. 5 — Photo. — Perf. 12x12½

196	A20	25fr brn, blue & org	1.10	.45

Commission for Technical Co-operation in Africa South of the Sahara, 17th session, Abidjan, 2/5-16.

Fort Assinie and Assinie River — A21

1962, May 26 — Engr. — Perf. 13

197	A21	85fr Prus grn, grn & dl red brn	3.25	1.50

Centenary of the Ivory Coast post.

African and Malagasy Union Issue
Common Design Type

1962, Sept. 8 — Photo. — Perf. 12½x12

198	CD110	30fr multicolored	2.10	.75

African and Malagasy Union, 1st anniv.

Fair Emblem, Cotton and Spindles — A22

1963, Jan. 26 — Engr. — Perf. 13

199	A22	50fr grn, brn org & sepia	3.00	1.10

Bouake Fair, Jan. 26-Feb. 4.

Stylized Map of Africa A23

1963, May 25 — Photo. — Perf. 12½x12

200	A23	30fr ultra & emerald	1.40	1.00

Conference of African heads of state for African unity, Addis Ababa.

Hartebeest A24

UNESCO Emblem, Scales and Globe A25

Designs: 1fr, Yellow-backed duiker, horiz. 2fr, Potto. 4fr, Beecroft's hyrax, horiz. 5fr, Water chevrotain. 15fr, Forest hog, horiz. 20fr, Wart hog, horiz. 25fr, Bongo (antelope). 45fr, Cape hunting dogs, or hyenas, horiz. 50fr, Black-and-white colobus (monkey).

1963-64   Engr.   Perf. 13

201 A24	1fr choc, grn & yellow ('64)	.75	.20
202 A24	2fr blk, dk bl, gray ol & brown ('64)	.75	.20
203 A24	4fr red brn, dk bl, brn & black ('64)	.65	.30
204 A24	5fr sl grn, brn & citron ('64)	.65	.30
205 A24	10fr ol grn & ocher	.85	.30
206 A24	15fr red brn, grn & black ('64)	1.40	.45
207 A24	20fr red org grn & blk	1.75	.45
208 A24	25fr red brn & green	2.40	.60
209 A24	45fr choc, bl grn & yel green	5.00	1.50
210 A24	50fr red brn, grn & blk	7.00	.85
a.	Min. sheet of 4, #205, 207, 209-210	35.00	35.00
	Nos. 201-210 (10)	21.20	6.30

See Nos. 218-220.

1963, Dec. 10   Unwmk.

211 A25	85fr dk bl, blk & org	2.25	.80

Universal Declaration of Human Rights, 15th anniv.

Sun Radiating from Ivory Coast over Africa A26

Weather Station and Balloon A27

1964, Mar. 17   Photo.   Perf. 12x12½

212 A26	30fr grn, dl vio & red	1.10	.45

Inter-African Conference of Natl. Education Ministers.

1964, Mar. 23   Perf. 13x12½

213 A27	25fr multicolored	1.25	.60

World Meteorological Day, Mar. 23.

Physician Vaccinating Child — A28

1964, May 8   Engr.   Perf. 13

214 A28	50fr dk brn, bl & red	1.90	.70

Issued to honor the National Red Cross.

Wrestlers, Globe and Torch — A29

1964, June 27   Unwmk.   Perf. 13

215 A29	35fr Globe, torch, athletes, vert.	1.75	.60
216 A29	65fr shown	3.25	1.20

18th Olympic Games, Tokyo, Oct. 10-25.

Europafrica Issue, 1964
Common Design Type

Design: 30fr, White man and black man beneath tree of industrial symbols.

1964, July 20   Photo.   Perf. 12x13

217 CD116	30fr multicolored	1.30	.35

Animal Type of 1963-64

Designs: 5fr, Manatee, horiz. 10fr, Pygmy hippopotamus, horiz. 15fr, Royal antelope.

1964, Oct. 17   Engr.   Perf. 13

218 A24	5fr yel grn, sl grn & brn	1.00	.30
219 A24	10fr sep, Prus grn & dp cl	2.40	.45
220 A24	15fr lil rose, grn & org brn	3.50	.45
	Nos. 218-220 (3)	6.90	1.20

Co-operation Issue
Common Design Type

1964, Nov. 7   Unwmk.   Perf. 13

221 CD119	25fr grn, dk brn & red	1.10	.35

Korhogo Mail Carriers with Guard, 1914 — A30

1964, Nov. 28   Engr.

222 A30	85fr blk, brn, bl & brn red	3.25	1.40

Issued for Stamp Day.

Potter A31

Artisans: 10fr, Wood carvers. 20fr, Ivory carver. 25fr, Weaver.

1965, Mar. 27   Engr.   Perf. 13

223 A31	5fr mag, green & blk	.45	.25
224 A31	10fr red lil, grn & blk	.55	.25
225 A31	20fr bis, dp bl & dk brn	1.00	.30
226 A31	25fr brn, olive & car	1.25	.45
	Nos. 223-226 (4)	3.25	1.25

Unloading Mail, 1900 A32

1965, Apr. 24   Unwmk.   Perf. 13

227 A32	30fr multicolored	1.40	.70

Issued for Stamp Day.

A32a

ITU emblem, old and new telecommunication equipment.

1965, May 17

228 A32a	85fr mar, brt grn & dk bl	2.75	.70

ITU, centenary.

Abidjan Railroad Station A33

1965, June 12   Engr.   Perf. 13

229 A33	30fr magenta, bl & brn ol	1.75	.80

Pres. Felix Houphouet-Boigny and Map of Ivory Coast — A34

1965, Aug. 7   Photo.   Perf. 12½x13

230 A34	30fr multicolored	1.10	.45

Fifth anniversary of Independence.

Hammerhead Stork — A35

Baoulé Mother and Child, Carved in Wood — A37

Mail Train, 1906 — A36

Birds: 1fr, Bruce's green pigeon, horiz. 2fr, Spur-winged goose, horiz. 5fr, Stone partridge. 15fr, White-breasted guinea fowl. 30fr, Namaqua dove, horiz. 50fr, Lizard buzzard, horiz. 75fr, Yellow-billed stork. 90fr, Forest (or Latham's) francolin.

1965-66   Engr.   Perf. 13

231 A35	1fr yel grn, pur & yellow ('66)	1.00	.30
232 A35	2fr slate grn, blk & red ('66)	1.00	.40
233 A35	5fr dk ol, dk brn & brn red ('66)	1.25	.45
234 A35	10fr red lil, blk & red brown	1.40	.30
235 A35	15fr sl grn, gray & ver	1.50	.40
236 A35	30fr sl grn, mar & red brown	2.10	.65
237 A35	50fr brn, blk & chlky bl	3.75	1.40
238 A35	75fr org, mar & sl grn	6.50	1.60
239 A35	90fr emerald, blk & brown ('66)	7.50	3.25
	Nos. 231-239 (9)	26.00	8.35

1966, Mar. 26   Engr.   Perf. 13

240 A36	30fr grn, blk & mar	2.75	1.00

Issued for Stamp Day.

1966, Apr. 9   Unwmk.

Designs: 10fr, Unguent vessel, Wamougo mask lid. 20fr, Atié carved drums. 30fr, Bété female ancestral figure.

241 A37	5fr blk & emerald	.50	.25
242 A37	10fr purple & blk	.80	.30
243 A37	20fr orange & blk	2.25	.80
244 A37	30fr red & black	2.60	1.10
	Nos. 241-244 (4)	6.15	2.45

Intl. Negro Arts Festival, Dakar, Senegal, 4/1-24.

Hotel Ivoire A38

1966, Apr. 30   Engr.   Perf. 13

245 A38	15fr bl, grn, red & olive	.90	.40

Farm Tractor A39

1966, Aug. 7   Photo.   Perf. 12½x12

246 A39	30fr multicolored	1.10	.55

6th anniversary of independence.

Uniformed Teacher and Villagers A40

1966, Sept. 1   Engr.   Perf. 13

247 A40	30fr dk red, indigo & dk brn	1.10	.50

National School of Administration.

Veterinarian Treating Cattle A41

1966, Oct. 22   Engr.   Perf. 13

248 A41	30fr ol, bl & dp brn	1.10	.50

Campaign against cattle plague.

Man, Waves, UNESCO Emblem — A42

Delivery of Gift Parcels — A43

1966, Nov. 14   Engr.   Perf. 13

249 A42	30fr dp bl & vio brn	1.10	.55

UNESCO, 20th anniv.

1966, Dec. 11   Engr.   Perf. 13

250 A43	30fr dk bl, brn & blk	1.10	.55

UNICEF, 20th anniv.

Bouaké Hospital and Red Cross A44

1966, Dec. 20

251 A44	30fr red brn, red & lilac	1.10	.55

Sikorsky S-43 Seaplane and Boats — A45

1967, Mar. 25   Engr.   Perf. 13

252 A45	30fr indigo, bl grn & brn	3.50	1.20

Stamp Day. 30th anniv. of the Sikorsky S-43 flying boat route.

Pineapple
Harvest
A46

1967 **Engr.** **Perf. 13**
253 A46 20fr shown .65 .40
254 A46 30fr Cabbage tree .90 .50
255 A46 100fr Bananas 3.75 1.20
Nos. 253-255 (3) 5.30 2.10
Issue dates: 30fr, June 24; others, Mar. 25.

Genie, Protector of
Assamlangangan
A47

1967, July 31 **Engr.** **Perf. 13**
256 A47 30fr grn, blk & maroon 1.10 .55
Intl. PEN Club (writers' organization), 25th
Congress, Abidjan, July 31-Aug. 5.

Old and
New
Houses
A48

1967, Aug. 7 **Photo.** **Perf. 12½x12**
257 A48 30fr multicolored 1.10 .55
7th anniversary of independence.

Lions
Emblem
and
Elephant's
Head
A49

1967, Sept. 2 **Photo.** **Perf. 12½x13**
258 A49 30fr lt bl & multi 1.50 .60
50th anniversary of Lions International.

Monetary Union Issue
Common Design Type
1967, Nov. 4 **Engr.** **Perf. 13**
259 CD125 30fr car, slate grn &
blk .90 .40

Allegory of
French
Recognition of
Ivory
Coast — A50

Tabou Radio
Station — A51

1967, Nov. 17 **Photo.** **Perf. 13x12½**
260 A50 90fr multicolored 3.00 .95
Days of Recognition, 20th anniv. See No.
298.

1968, Mar. 9 **Engr.** **Perf. 13**
261 A51 30fr dk grn, brn & brt
grn 1.25 .55
Issued for Stamp Day.

Cotton
Mill — A52

Designs: 5fr, Palm oil extraction plant. 15fr,
Abidjan oil refinery. 20fr, Unloading raw cotton and spinning machine, vert. 30fr, Flour
mill. 50fr, Cacao butter extractor. 70fr, Instant
coffee factory, vert. 90fr, Saw mill and timber.

1968 **Engr.** **Perf. 13**
262 A52 5fr ver, slate grn & blk .45 .20
263 A52 10fr dk grn, gray & ol
bis .75 .20
264 A52 15fr ver, lt ultra & blk 1.60 .65
265 A52 20fr Prus blue & choc 1.25 .65
266 A52 30fr dk grn, brt bl &
brown 1.25 .65
267 A52 50fr red, brt grn & blk 2.00 .90
268 A52 70fr dk brn, bl & brn 2.75 1.00
269 A52 90fr dp bl, blk & brn 3.50 1.60
Nos. 262-269 (8) 13.55 5.75
Issued: 5fr, 15fr, June 8; 10fr, 20fr, 90fr,
Mar. 23; others, Oct. 5.

Canoe
Race
A53

1968, Apr. 6 **Engr.** **Perf. 13**
270 A53 30fr shown 1.10 .50
271 A53 100fr Runners 3.00 .90
19th Olympic Games, Mexico City, 10/12-27.

Queen
Pokou
Sacrificing
her
Son — A54

1968, Aug. 7 **Photo.** **Perf. 12½x12**
272 A54 30fr multicolored 1.10 .50
8th anniversary of independence.

Vaccination,
WHO
Emblem
and
Elephant's
Head
A55

1968, Sept. 28 **Engr.** **Perf. 13**
273 A55 30fr choc, brt bl & maroon 1.10 .50
WHO, 20th anniversary.

Antelope in
Forest — A56

1968, Oct. 26 **Engr.** **Perf. 13**
274 A56 30fr ultra, brn & olive 6.00 1.25
Protection of fauna and flora.

Abidjan Anthropological Museum and
Carved Screen — A57

1968, Nov. 2
275 A57 30fr vio bl, ol & rose
mag 1.10 .50

Human
Rights
Flame and
Statues of
"Justitia"
A58

1968, Nov. 9 **Engr.** **Perf. 13**
276 A58 30fr slate, org & dk brn 1.10 .50
International Human Rights Year.

"Ville de
Maranhao"
at Grand
Bassam
A59

1969, Mar. 8 **Engr.** **Perf. 13**
277 A59 30fr brn, brt bl & grn 1.75 .55
Issued for Stamp Day.

Opening of Hotel Ivoire,
Abidjan — A60

1969, Mar. 29
278 A60 30fr ver, bl & grn 1.25 .50

Carved
Figure — A61

Mountains and
Radio Tower,
Man — A62

1969, July 5 **Engr.** **Perf. 13**
279 A61 30fr red lil, blk & red org 1.20 .60
Ivory Coast art exhibition, Fine Arts
Museum, Vevey, Switzerland, 7/12-9/22.

1969, Aug. 7 **Engr.** **Perf. 13**
280 A62 30fr dl brn, sl & grn 1.40 .50
9th anniversary of independence.

Development Bank Issue
Common Design Type
Design: Development Bank emblem and
Ivory Coast coat of arms.

1969, Sept. 6
281 CD130 30fr ocher, grn & mar .85 .40

Arms of Bouake — A63

Sport
Fishing and
SKAL
Emblem
A64

Coats of Arms: 15fr, Abidjan. 30fr, Ivory
Coast.

1969 **Photo.** **Perf. 13**
282 A63 10fr multicolored .45 .20
283 A63 15fr multicolored .55 .25
284 A63 30fr multicolored .90 .25
Nos. 282-284 (3) 1.90 .70
Issued: 10fr, 10/25; 15fr, 12/27; 30fr, 12/20.
See Nos. 335-336, 378-382, design A297.

1969, Nov. 22 **Engr.** **Perf. 13**
285 A64 30fr shown 4.00 .55
286 A64 100fr Vacation village,
SKAL emblem 5.00 1.40
1st Intl. Congress in Africa of the SKAL
Tourist Assoc., Abidjan, Nov. 23-28.

ASECNA Issue
Common Design Type
1969, Dec. 13 **Engr.** **Perf. 13**
287 CD132 30fr vermilion 1.00 .40

University Center, Abidjan — A65

1970, Feb. 26 **Engr.** **Perf. 13**
288 A65 30fr indigo & yel grn 1.00 .50
Higher education in Ivory Coast, 10th anniv.

Gabriel
Dadié and
Telegraph
Operator
A66

1970, Mar. 7 **Engr.** **Perf. 13**
289 A66 30fr dk red, sl grn & blk .80 .40
Stamp Day; Gabriel Dadié (1891-1953) 1st
native-born postal administrator.

University of Abidjan — A67

1970, Mar. 21 **Photo.**
290 A67 30fr Prus bl, dk pur & dk
yel grn 1.00 .50
3rd General Assembly of the Assoc. of
French-language Universities (A.U.P.E.L.F.).

Safety Match
Production — A68

1970, May 9 **Engr.** **Perf. 13**
291 A68 5fr shown .45 .45
292 A68 20fr Textile industry .65 .40
293 A68 50fr Shipbuilding 1.75 .50
Nos. 291-293 (3) 2.85 1.35

Radar, Classroom with
Television — A69

1970, May 17
294 A69 40fr red, grn & gray olive   1.20   .55
Issued for World Telecommunications Day.

UPU Headquarters Issue
Common Design Type
1970, May 20
295 CD133 30fr lil, brt grn & olive 1.20 .50

UN
Emblem,
Lion,
Antelopes
and Plane
A70

1970, June 27   Engr.   Perf. 13
296 A70 30fr dk red brn, ultra &
dk green   3.50 1.25
25th anniversary of the United Nations.

Coffee Branch
and Bags
Showing
Increased
Production
A71

1970, Aug. 7   Engr.   Perf. 13
297 A71 30fr org, bluish grn &
gray   1.50 .50
Tenth anniversary of independence.

Type of 1967
1970, Oct. 29   Photo.   Perf. 12x12½
298 A50 40fr multicolored   1.20 .50
Ivory Coast Democratic Party, 5th Congress.

Power Plant
at
Uridi — A73

1970, Nov. 21   Engr.   Perf. 13
299 A73 40fr multicolored   2.25 .40

Independence, 10th Anniv. — A73a

Designs: Nos. 299A, 299D, Pres.
Houphouet-Boigny, Gen. Charles DeGaulle.
Nos. 299B, 299F, Pres. Houphouet-Boigny,
elephants. Nos. 299C, 299E, Coat of arms.

1970, Nov. 27   Embossed   Perf. 10½
Die Cut
299A	A73a	300fr Silver	15.00	15.00
299B	A73a	300fr Silver	15.00	15.00
299C	A73a	300fr Silver	15.00	15.00
g.		Pair, #299B-299C	35.00	35.00
299D	A73a	1000fr Gold	45.00	45.00
299E	A73a	1000fr Gold	45.00	45.00

Litho. & Embossed
299F	A73a	1200fr Gold & multi	45.00	45.00
h.		Pair, #299E-299F	100.00	100.00

Nos. 299B, 299F are airmail.

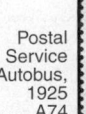

Postal
Service
Autobus,
1925
A74

1971, Mar. 6   Engr.   Perf. 13
300 A74 40fr dp grn, dk brn &
gldn brn   2.75 .50
Stamp Day.

Marginella
Desjardini
A75

Marine Life: 1fr, Aporrhaispes gallinae. 5fr,
Neptunus validus. 10fr, Hermodice caruncu-
lata, vert. No. 305, Natica fanel, vert. No.
306, Goniaster cuspidatus, vert. No. 307,
Xenorhora digitata. 25fr, Conus prometheus.
35fr, Polycheles typhlops, vert. No. 310,
Conus genuanus. No. 311, Chlamys flabellum.
45fr, Strombus bubonius. 50fr,
Enoplometopus callistus, vert. 65fr, Cypraea
stercoraria.

1971-72   Engr.   Perf. 13
301	A75	1fr olive & multi	.50	.20
302	A75	5fr red & multi	.50	.30
303	A75	10fr emer & multi	1.00	.30
304	A75	15fr brt bl & multi	1.00	.35
305	A75	15fr dp car & multi	1.50	.40
306	A75	20fr ocher & car	1.90	.50
307	A75	20fr ver & multi	2.25	.65
308	A75	25fr dk car, rose brn & black	1.25	.35
309	A75	35fr yel & multi	2.50	.75
310	A75	40fr emer & multi	4.00	1.25
311	A75	40fr brown & multi	3.25	1.10
312	A75	45fr multi	4.50	1.50
313	A75	50fr green & multi	5.00	1.60
314	A75	65fr bl, rose brn & sl grn	3.50	1.50
		Nos. 301-314 (14)	32.65	10.75

Issued: #304, 306, 310, 4/24/71; 5fr, 35fr,
50fr, 6/5/71; 1fr, 10fr, #311, 10/23/71; 25fr,
65fr, 1/29/72; #305, 307, 45fr, 4/3/72.

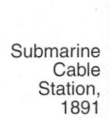

Submarine
Cable
Station,
1891
A76

1971, May 17
315 A76 100fr bl, ocher & olive   2.50 .85
3rd World Telecommunications Day.

Apprentice and
Lathe — A77

1971, June 19   Engr.   Perf. 13
316 A77 35fr grn, slate & org brn 1.00 .40
Technical instruction and professional
training.

Map of Africa and Telcommunications
System — A78

1971, June 26   Perf. 13x12½
317 A78 45fr magenta & multi   1.00 .40
Pan-African Telecommunications system.

Bondoukou Market — A79

1971, Aug. 7   Engr.   Perf. 13
Size: 48x27mm
318 A79 35fr ultra, brn & slate   1.00 .45
11th anniv. of independence. See No. C46.

White,
Black and
Yellow
Girls — A80

1971, Oct. 10   Photo.   Perf. 13
319 A80 40fr shown   .80 .25
320 A80 45fr Boys around globe   .80 .25
Intl. Year Against Racial Discrimination.

Gaming
Table and
Lottery
Tickets
A81

1971, Nov. 13   Perf. 12½
321 A81 35fr green & multi   1.25 .50
National lottery.

Electric Power
Installations — A82

1971, Dec. 18   Perf. 13
322 A82 35fr red brn & multi   2.25 .50

Cogwheel
and
Workers
A83

1972, Mar. 18   Engr.   Perf. 13
323 A83 35fr org, bl & dk brn   .75 .40
Technical Cooperation Week.

"Your Heart is
Your
Health" — A84

Girls Reading,
Book Year
Emblem — A85

1972, Apr. 7   Photo.   Perf. 12½x13
324 A84 40fr blue, olive & red   1.00 .50
World Health Day.

Perf. 12½x13, 13x12½
1972, Apr. 22   Engr.
325 A85 35fr Boys reading, horiz. .75 .25
326 A85 40fr shown   1.00 .40
International Book Year.

Postal
Sorting
Center,
Abidjan
A86

1972, May 13   Perf. 13
327 A86 40fr dk grn, rose lil & bis 1.25 .40
Stamp Day.

Radio Tower,
Abobo, and ITU
Emblem — A87

1972, May 17   Engr.   Perf. 13
328 A87 40fr blue, red & grn   2.25 .75
4th World Telecommunications Day.

Computer
Operator,
Punch Card
A88

1972, June 24
329 A88 40fr brt grn, bl & red   2.25 .60
Development of computerized information.

View of Odienné — A89

1972, Aug. 7   Engr.   Perf. 13
330 A89 35fr bl, grn & brn   1.00 .60
12th anniversary of independence.

West African Monetary Union Issue
Common Design Type

1972, Nov. 2   Engr.   Perf. 13
331 CD136 40fr brn, gray & red lilac   1.00   .50

Diamond and Diamond Mine — A90

1972, Nov. 4
332 A90 40fr Prus bl, slate & org brn   3.50 1.75

Pasteur Institute, Louis Pasteur A91

1972, Nov. 21
333 A91 35fr vio bl, grn & brn   1.25   .50

Pasteur (1822-1895), chemist and bacteriologist.

Children at Village Pump A92

1972, Dec. 9   Engr.   Perf. 13
334 A92 35fr dk red, grn & blk   1.25   .40

Water campaign. See No. 360.

Arms Type of 1969

1973   Photo.   Perf. 12
335 A63 5fr Daloa   .50   .25
336 A63 10fr Gagnoa   .50   .25

Nos. 335-336 are 16½-17x22mm and have "DELRIEU" below design at right. Nos. 282-284 are 17x23mm and have no name at lower right.

Dr. Armauer G. Hansen — A93

1973, Feb. 3   Engr.   Perf. 13
342 A93 35fr lil, dp bl & brn   1.25   .40

Centenary of the discovery of the Hansen bacillus, the cause of leprosy.

Lake Village Bletankoro — A94

1973, Mar. 10   Engr.   Perf. 13
343 A94 200fr choc, bl & grn   5.00 2.00

Balistes Capriscus A95

Fish: 20fr, Pseudupeneus prayensis. 25fr, Cephalopholis taeniops. 35fr, Priacanthus arenatus. 50fr, Xyrichthys novacula.

1973-74   Engr.   Perf. 13
344 A95 15fr ind & slate grn   1.75   .60
345 A95 20fr lilac & multi   3.00   .75
346 A95 25fr slate grn & rose ('74)   4.50   .75
347 A95 35fr rose red & slate grn   3.25   .90
348 A95 50fr blk, ultra & rose red   4.50 1.10
   Nos. 344-348 (5)   17.00 4.10

Issued: 50fr, 3/24; 15fr, 20fr, 7/7; 35fr, 12/1; 25fr, 3/2.

Children A96

1973, Apr. 7   Engr.   Perf. 13
354 A96 40fr grn, blk & dl red   1.25   .45

Establishment of first children's village in Africa (SOS villages for homeless children).

Parliament, Abidjan — A97

1973, Apr. 24   Photo.   Perf. 13x12½
355 A97 100fr multicolored   1.40   .45

112th session of the Inter-parliamentary Council.

Teacher and PAC Store A98

1973, May 12   Photo.   Perf. 13x12½
356 A98 40fr multicolored   .75   .25

Commercial Action Program (PAC).

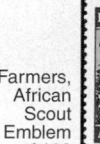

Mother, Typist, Dress Form and Pot — A99

1973, May 26
357 A99 35fr multicolored   1.00   .40

Technical instruction for women.

Farmers, African Scout Emblem A100

1973, July 16   Photo.   Perf. 13x12½
358 A100 40fr multicolored   1.00   .60

24th Boy Scout World Conference, Nairobi, Kenya, July 16-21.

Party Headquarters, Yamoussokro — A101

1973, Aug. 7   Photo.   Perf. 13
359 A101 35fr multicolored   1.00   .50

Children at Dry Pump A102

1973, Aug. 16   Engr.
360 A102 40fr multicolored   1.25   .45

African solidarity in drought emergency.

African Postal Union Issue
Common Design Type

1973, Sept. 12   Engr.   Perf. 13
361 CD137 100fr pur, blk & red   2.50 1.00

Decorated Arrow Heads, Abidjan Museum — A103

1973, Sept. 15   Photo.   Perf. 12½x13
362 A103 5fr blk, brn red & brn   .60   .25

Ivory Coast No. 1 — A104

1973, Oct. 9   Engr.   Perf. 13
363 A104 40fr emer, blk & org   1.30   .60

Stamp Day.

Highway Intersection A105

1973, Oct. 13
364 A105 35fr blue, blk & grn   1.00   .45

Indenie-Abidjan intersection.

Map of Africa, Federation Emblem — A106

Elephant Emblem — A107

1973, Oct. 26   Photo.   Perf. 13
365 A106 40fr ultra, red brn & vio bl   .85   .30

Intl. Social Security Federation, 18th General Assembly, Abidjan, Oct. 26-Nov. 3.

1973, Nov. 19
366 A107 40fr blk & bister   .85   .30

7th World Congress of the Universal Federation of World Travel Agents' Associations, Abidjan.

Kong Mosque — A108

1974, Mar. 9
367 A108 35fr bl, grn & brn   1.25   .60

People and Sun A109

1974, Apr. 20   Photo.   Perf. 13
368 A109 35fr multicolored   .85   .40

Permanent Mission to UN.

Grand Lahou Post Office — A110

1974, May 17   Engr.   Perf. 13
369 A110 35fr multicolored   1.00   .60

Stamp Day.

Map and Flags of Members A110a

1974, May 29   Photo.   Perf. 13x12½
370 A110a 40fr blue & multi   .75   .25

15th anniversary of the Council of Accord.

Pres. Houphouet-Boigny
A111   A112

1974-76   Engr.   Perf. 13
371 A111 25fr grn, org & brn   .65   .25
  a.   Booklet pane of 10   6.50
  b.   Booklet pane of 20   13.00
373 A112 35fr org, grn & brn   1.00   .20
  a.   Booklet pane of 10   10.00
  b.   Booklet pane of 20   20.00
374 A112 40fr grn, org & brn   1.00   .20
  a.   Booklet pane of 10   10.00
375 A112 60fr bl, car & brn ('76)   .90   .40
376 A112 65fr car, bl & brn ('76)   .90   .40
   Nos. 371-376 (5)   4.45 1.45

See Nos. 783-792.

Ivory Coast Arms Type of 1969 with
smaller "P" and "s" in "Postes"

1974, June 29		Photo.	Perf. 12	
378	A63	35fr brn, emer & gold	.70	.20
a.		Booklet pane of 10	7.50	
b.		Booklet pane of 20	15.00	
379	A63	40fr vio, bl, emer & gold	.90	.20
a.		Booklet pane of 10	10.00	
b.		Booklet pane of 20	20.00	

1976, Jan.

Inscribed: "COTE D'IVOIRE"

380	A63	60fr car, gold & emer	.90	.25
381	A63	65fr grn, gold & emer	.90	.30
382	A63	70fr bl, gold & emer	1.00	.40
		Nos. 378-382 (5)	4.40	1.35

See design A297.

WPY
Emblem — A114

1974, Aug. 19   Engr.   Perf. 13
383 A114 40fr emerald & blue   1.00   .30

World Population Year.

Cotton
Harvest — A115

1974, Sept. 21   Litho.   Perf. 12½x13
384 A115 50fr multicolored   1.25   .50

UPU
Centenary
A116

1974, Oct. 9   Engr.   Perf. 13
385 A116 40fr multicolored   .90   .30

See Nos. C59-C60.

Plowing
Farmer,
Service
Emblem
A117

1974, Dec. 7   Photo.   Perf. 13
386 A117 35fr multicolored   .75   .30

14th anniversary of independence.

National Library, First Anniv. — A118

1975, Jan. 9   Photo.   Perf. 13
387 A118 40fr multicolored   .75   .30

Raoul Follereau
and Blind
Students — A119

1975, Jan. 26   Engr.   Perf. 13
388 A119 35fr multicolored   2.00   .80

Follereau, educator of the blind and lepers.

Congress
Emblem — A120

1975, Mar. 4   Photo.   Perf. 12½x13
389 A120 40fr blk & emerald   .75   .30

52nd Congress of the Intl. Assoc. of Seed
Crushers, Abidjan, Mar. 2-7.

Coffee Cultivation
A121

1975, Mar. 15   Perf. 13½x13
390 A121 5fr Flowering branch   .40   .20
391 A121 10fr Branch with beans   .70   .20

Sassandra Wharf — A122

1975, Apr. 19   Engr.   Perf. 13
392 A122 100fr multicolored   2.50   1.50

Letter
Sorting
A123

1975, Apr. 26   Photo.   Perf. 13
393 A123 40fr multicolored   1.25   .60

Stamp Day.

Cotton
Flower — A124

Cotton
Bolls — A125

1975, May 3   Photo.   Perf. 13
394 A124 5fr multicolored   .45   .45
395 A125 10fr multicolored   .80   .45

Cotton cultivation.

Marie Kore, Women's Year
Emblem — A126

1975, May 19   Engr.   Perf. 13
396 A126 45fr lt bl, yel grn & brn   1.00   .50

International Women's Year.

Fort Dabou — A127

1975, June 7   Engr.   Perf. 13
397 A127 50fr multicolored   1.00   .65

Abidjan Harbor — A128

40fr, Grand Bassam wharf, 1906. 100fr,
Planned harbor expansion on Locodjro.

1975, July 1   Photo.   Perf. 13
398 A128 35fr multicolored   1.25   .60

Miniature Sheet

399		Sheet of 3	10.00	10.00
a.		A128 40fr multi, vert.	4.00	4.00
b.		A128 100fr multi	4.00	4.00

25th anniversary of Abidjan Harbor. No. 399
contains Nos. 398, 399a, 399b.

Cacao Pods on
Tree — A129

1975, Aug. 2
400 A129 35fr multicolored   2.25   .65

Farm
Workers
A130

1975, Oct. 4   Photo.   Perf. 13x12½
401 A130 50fr multicolored   1.00   .60

Natl. Org. for Rural Development.

Railroad Bridge, N'zi River — A131

1975, Dec. 7   Photo.   Perf. 13
402 A131 60fr multicolored   6.00   1.50

15th anniversary of independence.

Baoulé Mother
and Child,
Carved in
Wood — A132

1976, Jan. 24   Litho.   Perf. 13
403 A132 65fr black & multi   2.25   .75

Baoulé
Mask
A133

Chief
Abron's
Chair
A133a

1976, Feb. 7   Photo.   Perf. 12½
404 A133 20fr multicolored   .65   .25
405 A133a 150fr multicolored   3.25   1.25

Senufo
Statuette — A134

1976, Feb. 21   Perf. 13x13½
406 A134 25fr ocher & multi   1.25   .60

Telephones 1876
and
1976 — A135

1976, Mar. 10   Litho.   *Perf. 12*
407 A135 70fr multicolored   1.25   .65
  Centenary of first telephone call by Alexander Graham Bell, Mar. 10, 1876.

Ivory Coast
Map,
Pigeon,
Carving
A136

1976, Apr. 10   Photo.   *Perf. 12½*
408 A136 65fr multicolored   1.00   .50
  20th Stamp Day.

Smiling Trees and
Cat — A137

1976, June 5   Litho.   *Perf. 12½*
409 A137 65fr multicolored   1.25   .60
  Nature protection.

Children with
Books — A138

1976, July 3   Photo.   *Perf. 12½x13*
410 A138 65fr multicolored   1.30   .60

Runner, Maple Leaf, Olympic
Rings — A139

1976, July 17   Litho.   *Perf. 12*
411 A139 60fr Javelin, vert.   1.25   .60
412 A139 65fr shown   1.25   .60
  21st Olympic Games, Montreal, Canada, July 17-Aug. 1.

Mohammad Ali Jinnah — A139a

1976, Aug. 14   Litho.   *Perf. 13*
412A A139a 50fr multicolored   65.00 15.00
  1st Governor-General of Pakistan.

Cashew
A140

1976, Sept. 18   *Perf. 12½*
413 A140 65fr blue & multi   2.25   .80

Highway and Conference
Emblem — A141

1976, Oct. 25   Litho.   *Perf. 12½x12*
414 A141 60fr multicolored   1.00   .50
  3rd African Highway Conference, Abidjan, July 25-30.

Pres. Houphouet-
Boigny
A142

1976-77   Photo.   *Perf. 13½x12½*
415 A142 35fr brn, red lil & blk
          ('77)   225.00   —
416 A142 40fr brt grn, ocher &
          brn blk   4.50   .75
  a.   Bklt. pane of 12 (8#416,
          4#417)   55.00
417 A142 45fr ocher, brt grn &
          brn blk   4.50 1.00
418 A142 60fr brn, mag & brn
          blk   6.00 1.00
419 A142 65fr grn, org & brn
          blk   7.00 1.50
    Nos. 416-419 (4)   22.00 4.25
  The 40fr and 45fr issued in booklet and coil; 35fr, 60fr and 65fr in coil only.
  Stamps from booklets are imperf. on one side or two adjoining sides. Coils have control number on back of every 10th stamp.

John Paul Jones, American Marine
and Ship — A143

  American Bicentennial: 125fr, Count de Rochambeau and grenadier of Touraine Regiment. 150fr, Admiral Count Jean Baptiste d'Estaing and French marine. 175fr, Lafayette and grenadier of Soissons Regiment. 200fr, Jefferson, American soldier, Declaration of Independence. 500fr, Washington, US flag, Continental officer.

1976, Nov. 27   Litho.   *Perf. 11*
421 A143 100fr multicolored   1.50   .30
422 A143 125fr multicolored   1.90   .50
423 A143 150fr multicolored   2.25   .60
424 A143 175fr multicolored   2.25   .75
425 A143 200fr multicolored   2.40   .75
    Nos. 421-425 (5)   10.30 2.90
Souvenir Sheet
426 A143 500fr multicolored   7.00 2.50

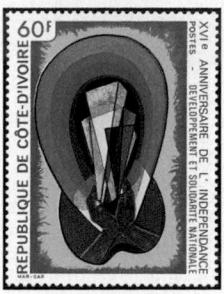

"Development and Solidarity" — A144

1976, Dec. 7   Photo.   *Perf. 13*
427 A144 60fr multicolored   1.00   .60
  16th anniversary of independence.

Benin Head,
Ivory Coast
Arms — A145

1977, Jan. 15   Photo.   *Perf. 13*
428 A145 65fr gold, dk brn & grn 1.25   .75
  2nd World Black and African Festival, Lagos, Nigeria, Jan. 15-Feb. 12.

Musical Instruments — A146

1977, Mar. 5   Engr.   *Perf. 13*
429 A146 5fr Baoule bells   .35   .25
430 A146 10fr Senufo balafon   .35   .25
431 A146 20fr Dida drum   .55   .25
    Nos. 429-431 (3)   1.25   .75

Air Afrique
Plane
Unloading
Mail
A147

1977, Apr. 9   Litho.   *Perf. 13*
432 A147 60fr multicolored   1.25   .60
  Stamp Day.

Sassenage Castle, Grenoble — A148

1977, May 21   Litho.   *Perf. 12½*
433 A148 100fr multicolored   2.25   .75
  Intl. French Language Council, 10th anniv.

Orville and Wilbur Wright, "Wright
Flyer," 1903 — A149

  History of Aviation: 75fr, Louis Bleriot crossing English Channel, 1909. 100fr, Ross Smith and Vickers-Vimy (flew England-Australia, 1919). 200fr, Charles A. Lindbergh and "Spirit of St. Louis" (flew New York-Paris, 1927). 300fr, Supersonic jet Concorde, 1976. 500fr, Lindbergh in flying suit and "Spirit of St. Louis."

1977, June 27   Litho.   *Perf. 14*
434 A149 60fr multi   1.10   .30
435 A149 75fr multi   1.25   .30
436 A149 100fr multi   1.50   .30
437 A149 200fr multi   3.25   .75
438 A149 300fr multi   5.00 1.25
    Nos. 434-438 (5)   12.10 2.90
Souvenir Sheet
439 A149 500fr multi   6.50 2.00

Santos Dumont's "Ville de Paris,"
1907 — A150

  65fr, LZ1 at takeoff. 150fr, "Schwaben" LZ10 over Germany. 200fr, "Bodensee" LZ120, 1919. 300fr, LZ127 over Sphinx & pyramids.

1977, Sept. 3   Litho.   *Perf. 11*
440 A150 60fr multi   1.00   .25
441 A150 65fr multi   1.00   .25
442 A150 150fr multi   2.25   .50
443 A150 200fr multi   3.25   .75
444 A150 300fr multi   4.00 1.00
    Nos. 440-444 (5)   11.50 2.75
  History of the Zeppelin. Exist imperf.
  See No. C63.

Congress
Emblem — A151

1977, Sept. 12   Photo.   *Perf. 12½*
445 A151 60fr lt & dk grn   .90   .50
  17th Intl. Congress of Administrative Sciences in Africa, Abidjan, Sept. 12-16.

A152

1977, Nov. 12   Photo.   Perf. 13½x14
446   A152   65fr multicolored   3.50   .75
Yamoussoukro, 1st Ivory Coast container ship.

Butterflies
A152a

Designs: 30fr, Epiphora rectifascia boolana. 60fr, Charaxes jasius epijasius. 65fr, Imbrasia arata. 100fr, Palla decius.

1977, Nov.   Photo.   Perf. 14x13
446A   A152a   30fr multi   —   2.25
446B   A152a   60fr multi   —   17.50
446C   A152a   65fr multi   —   4.00
446D   A152a   100fr multi   —   6.00
        Nos. 446A-446D (4)   29.75
        Set, unused   280.00

A153

Hand Holding Produce, Generators, Factories.

1977, Dec. 7   Photo.   Perf. 13½
447   A153   60fr multicolored   1.00   .50
17th anniversary of independence.

Flowers — A153a

1977   Photo.   Perf. 13x14
447A   A153a   5fr Strophanthus
                        hispidus   —   —
447B   A153a   20fr Anthurium
                        cultorum   —   —
447C   A153a   60fr Arachnis
                        flos-aeris   —   —
447D   A153a   65fr Renanthera
                        storiei   —   —
        Set, unused   500.00

Presidents Giscard d'Estaing and
Houphouet-Boigny — A154

1978, Jan. 11   Perf. 13
448   A154   60fr multicolored   1.25   .35
449   A154   65fr multicolored   1.40   .35
450   A154   100fr multicolored   1.75   .75
  a.   Souvenir sheet, 500fr   10.00   10.00
        Nos. 448-450 (3)   4.40   1.45

Visit of Pres. Valery Giscard d'Estaing. No. 450a contains one stamp.

St. George and the Dragon, by Rubens
A155

Paintings by Peter Paul Rubens (1577-1640). 300fr, The Birth of Louis XIII. 500fr, Virgin & Child.

1978, Mar. 4   Litho.   Perf. 13½
451   A155   65fr gold & multi   .90   .25
452   A155   150fr gold & multi   2.25   .60
453   A155   250fr gold & multi   3.25   .80
454   A155   300fr gold & multi   4.50   1.00
        Nos. 451-454 (4)   10.90   2.65

Souvenir Sheet
455   A155   500fr gold & multi   6.00   2.25

Royal Guards — A156

1978, Apr. 1   Litho.   Perf. 12½
456   A156   60fr shown   1.25   .35
457   A156   65fr Cosmological
                        figures   1.25   .35

Rural Postal Center — A157

1978, Apr. 8
458   A157   60fr multicolored   1.00   .50
Stamp Day.

Antenna,
ITU Emblem
A158

1978, May 17   Perf. 13
459   A158   60fr multicolored   1.00   .50
10th World Telecommunications Day.

Svante August Arrhenius, Electrolytic
Apparatus — A159

Nobel Prize Winners: 75fr, Jules Bordet, child, mountains, eagle and Petri dish. 100fr, André Gide, and St. Peter's, Rome. 200fr, John Steinbeck and horse farm. 300fr, Children with flowers and UNICEF emblem. 500fr, Max Planck, rockets and earth.

1978, May 27   Litho.   Perf. 13½
460   A159   60fr multi   .75   .20
461   A159   75fr multi   1.00   .25
462   A159   100fr multi   1.25   .30
463   A159   200fr multi   2.50   .60
464   A159   300fr multi   4.25   .90
        Nos. 460-464 (5)   9.75   2.25

Souvenir Sheet
465   A159   500fr multi   5.50   1.50

Soccer Ball, Player and Argentina '78
Emblem — A160

Soccer Ball, Argentina '78 Emblem and: 65fr, Player, vert. 100fr, Player, diff. 150fr, Goalkeeper. 300fr, Ball as sun, and player, vert. 500fr, Ball as globe with Argentina on map of South America.

1978, June 17
466   A160   60fr multi   .75   .20
467   A160   65fr multi   1.00   .25
468   A160   100fr multi   1.25   .50
469   A160   150fr multi   1.75   .50
470   A160   300fr multi   3.50   .90
        Nos. 466-470 (5)   8.25   2.35

Souvenir Sheet
471   A160   500fr multi   5.00   1.50
11th World Cup Soccer Championship, Argentina, June 1-25.

Miniodes
Discolor
A161

Butterflies: 65fr, Charaxes lactetinctus. 100fr, Papilio zalmoxis. 200fr, Papilio antimachus.

1978, July 8   Photo.   Perf. 14x13
472   A161   60fr multicolored   3.75   1.00
473   A161   65fr multicolored   3.75   1.00
474   A161   100fr multicolored   5.50   1.75
475   A161   200fr multicolored   10.00   4.00
        Nos. 472-475 (4)   23.00   7.75

Cricket
A162

Insects: 20fr, 60fr, Various hemiptera. 65fr, Goliath beetle.

1978, Aug. 26   Litho.   Perf. 12½
476   A162   10fr multicolored   1.10   .40
477   A162   20fr multicolored   1.75   .40
478   A162   60fr multicolored   3.50   1.00
479   A162   65fr multicolored   5.00   1.25
        Nos. 476-479 (4)   11.35   3.05

Stylized
Figures
Emerging
from TV
Screen
A163

65fr, Passengers on train made up of TV sets.

1978, Sept. 18   Perf. 13
480   A163   60fr multicolored   1.10   .30
481   A163   65fr multicolored   1.10   .30
Educational television programs.

Map of
Ivory
Coast,
Mobile Drill
Platform
Ship
A164

Map of Ivory Coast, Ram at Discovery Site and: 65fr, Gold goblets. 500fr, Pres. Houphouet-Boigny holding gold goblets.

1978, Oct. 18   Litho.   Perf. 12½x12
482   A164   60fr multicolored   1.50   .50
483   A164   65fr multicolored   1.50   .50

Souvenir Sheet
484   A164   500fr multicolored   12.00   12.00
Announcement of oil discovery off the coast of Ivory Coast, 1st anniv.

National
Assembly,
Paris, UPU
Emblem
A165

1978, Dec. 2   Litho.   Perf. 13½
485   A165   200fr multicolored   2.25   1.00
Congress of Paris, centenary.

Drummer
A166

1978, Dec. 7   Photo.   Perf. 12½x13
486   A166   60fr multicolored   1.25   .50
18th anniversary of independence.

Poster — A167

Design: 65fr, Arrows made of flags, and television screen.

1978, Dec. 12
487 A167 60fr multicolored 1.00 .40
488 A167 65fr multicolored 1.00 .40

Technical cooperation among developing countries with the help of educational television.

Plowing — A168

1979, Jan. 27 Photo. Perf. 13
489 A168 100fr multicolored 2.25 .50

King Hassan II, Pres. Houphouet-Boigny, Flags and Map of Morocco and Ivory Coast — A169

1979, Jan. 27 Photo. Perf. 13
490 A169 60fr multicolored *3.00* 1.00
491 A169 65fr multicolored *4.00* 1.25
492 A169 500fr multicolored *20.00* 8.50
Nos. 490-492 (3) 27.00

Visit of King Hassan of Morocco to Ivory Coast. The visit never took place and the stamps were not issued. To recover the printing costs the stamps were sold in Paris for one day.

Horus — A170

1979, Feb. 17 Litho. Perf. 12½
493 A170 200fr multi 3.00 1.50
494 A170 500fr Vulture with ankh, cartouches 6.50 3.50

UNESCO drive to save Temples of Philae.

Flowers — A171

1979, Feb. 24
495 A171 30fr Locranthus 1.25 .50
496 A171 60fr Vanda Josephine 1.75 .60
497 A171 65fr Renanthera storiei 2.00 .90
Nos. 495-497 (3) 5.00 2.00

Wildlife Protection A172

1979, Mar. 24 Photo. Perf. 13x13½
498 A172 50fr Hippopotamus 2.50 .80

Globe and Emblem — A173   Child Riding Dove — A174

1979, Apr. 1 Litho. Perf. 12x12½
499 A173 60fr multicolored .75 .50
500 A174 65fr multicolored .85 .50
501 A173 100fr multicolored 1.60 1.00
502 A174 500fr multicolored 6.25 3.50
Nos. 499-502 (4) 9.45 5.50

International Year of the Child.

Rural Mail Delivery — A175

1979, Apr. 7 Perf. 12½
503 A175 60fr multicolored 1.25 .35

Stamp Day.

Korhogo Cathedral — A176

1979, Apr. 9 Perf. 13
504 A176 60fr multicolored 1.00 .45

Arrival of Catholic missionaries, 75th anniv.

Crying Child — A177

1979, May 17 Litho. Perf. 12½
505 A177 65fr multicolored 1.00 .50

10th anniv. of SOS Village (for homeless children).

Euphaedra Xypete A178

Butterflies: 65fr, Pseudacraea bois duvali. 70fr, Auchenisa schausi.

1979, May 26 Perf. 13x13½
506 A178 60fr multicolored 2.50 1.00
507 A178 65fr multicolored 3.00 1.00
508 A178 70fr multicolored 4.50 1.50
Nos. 506-508 (3) 10.00 3.50

Endangered Animals — A179

1979, June 2
509 A179 5fr Antelopes 1.00 .40
510 A179 20fr Duikerbok 1.50 .50
511 A179 60fr Aardvark 4.50 1.50
Nos. 509-511 (3) 7.00 2.40

UPU Emblem, Radar, Truck and Ship — A180

#513, Ancestral figure & antelope, vert.

1979, June 8 Engr. Perf. 13
512 A180 70fr multi 3.50 2.50

Photo.
513 A180 70fr multi 3.50 2.50

Philexafrique II, Libreville, Gabon, June 8-17. Nos. 512, 513 each printed in sheets of 10 with 5 labels showing exhibition emblem.

Rowland Hill, Steam Locomotive, Great Britain No. 75 — A181

Rowland Hill, Locomotives and: 75fr, Ivory Coast #125. 100fr, Hawaii #4. 150fr, Japan #30, syll. 3. 300fr, France #2. 500fr, Ivory Coast #123.

1979, July 7 Litho. Perf. 13½
514 A181 60fr multi .75 .25
515 A181 75fr multi .90 .25
516 A181 100fr multi 1.50 .40
517 A181 150fr multi 1.75 .50
518 A181 300fr multi 3.75 .75
Nos. 514-518 (5) 8.65 2.15

Souvenir Sheet
519 A181 500fr multi 7.00 2.00

Sir Rowland Hill (1795-1879), originator of penny postage.

Insects — A181a

A181b

1979 Photo. Perf. 14x13, 13x14
519A A181a 30fr Wasp 15.00 2.50
519B A181a 60fr Praying mantis, vert. 30.00 4.00
519C A181a 65fr Cricket 40.00 4.00
Nos. 519A-519C (3) 85.00 10.50

1979 Photo. Perf. 13x14
Musical instruments.
519D A181b 100fr Harp 35.00 14.00
519E A181b 150fr Whistles 50.00 20.00

"TELECOM 79" — A182   Culture Day — A183

1979, Sept. 20 Litho. Perf. 13x12½
520 A182 60fr multicolored 1.00 .40

3rd World Telecommunications Exhibition, Geneva, Sept. 20-26.

1979, Oct. 13 Perf. 12½
521 A183 65fr multicolored 1.00 .40

Fish — A183a

1979 Photo. Perf. 14x13
521A A183a 60fr Pterois volitans 150.00 —
521B A183a 65fr Coelacanth 150.00 —

Boxing — A184

1979, Oct. 27   Litho.   Perf. 14x13½

522	A184	60fr shown	.75	.25
523	A184	65fr Running	.75	.25
524	A184	100fr Soccer	1.25	.30
525	A184	150fr Bicycling	1.75	.50
526	A184	300fr Wrestling	3.50	1.25
		Nos. 522-526 (5)	8.00	2.55

Souvenir Sheet

527	A184	500fr Gymnastics	6.00	2.00

Pre-Olympic Year.

Wildlife Fund Emblem and Jentink's Duiker — A185

Wildlife Protection: 60fr, Colobus Monkey. 75fr, Manatees. 100fr, Epixerus ebii. 150fr, Hippopotamus. 300fr, Chimpanzee.

1979, Nov. 3   Litho.   Perf. 14½

528	A185	40fr multi	3.25	.30
529	A185	60fr multi	3.50	.50
530	A185	75fr multi	5.00	.50
531	A185	100fr multi	7.00	.50
532	A185	150fr multi	10.50	1.00
533	A185	300fr multi	21.00	2.00
		Nos. 528-533 (6)	50.25	5.05

Raoul Follerau Institute, Adzope — A186

1979, Dec. 6   Litho.   Perf. 12½

534	A186	60fr multi	1.50	.50

Independence, 19th Anniversary A187

1979, Dec. 7   Litho.   Perf. 14x13½

535	A187	60fr multicolored	1.25	.25

Fireball A188

Local Flora: 5fr, Clerodendron thomsonae, vert. 50fr, Costus incanusiamus, vert. 60fr, Ficus elastica abidjan, vert.

1980   Litho.   Perf. 12½

536	A188	5fr multicolored	.30	.20
537	A188	10fr multicolored	.40	.20
538	A188	50fr multicolored	1.25	.30
539	A188	60fr multicolored	1.40	.30
		Nos. 536-539 (4)	3.35	1.00

Issued: 5fr, 10fr, Jan. 26; 50fr, 60fr, Feb. 16.

Rotary Intl., 75th Anniv. — A189

1980, Feb. 23   Photo.   Perf. 13½

540	A189	65fr multicolored	1.00	.40

International Archives Day — A190

1980, Feb. 26   Litho.

541	A190	65fr multicolored	1.00	.45

Astronaut Shaking Hands with Boy — A191

Path of Apollo 11 — A192

1980, July 6   Photo.

542	A191	60fr multicolored	.90	.50
543	A192	65fr multicolored	.90	.50
544	A191	70fr multicolored	1.75	.75
545	A192	150fr multicolored	3.00	1.75
		Nos. 542-545 (4)	6.55	3.50

Apollo 11 moon landing, 10th anniv. (1979).

Jet and Map of Africa A193

1980, Mar. 22   Perf. 12½

546	A193	60fr multicolored	1.00	.35

ASECNA (Air Safety Board), 20th anniv.

Boys and Stamp Album, Globe — A194

1980, Apr. 12   Litho.   Perf. 12½

547	A194	65fr bl grn & red brn	1.25	.30

Stamp Day; Youth philately.

Missionary and Church, Aboisso A195

1980, Apr. 26   Photo.   Perf. 13x13½

548	A195	60fr multicolored	1.25	.50

Settlement of the Holy Fathers at Aboisso, 75th anniversary.

Fight Against Cigarette Smoking A196

1980, May 3   Perf. 12½

549	A196	60fr multicolored	1.25	.30

Pope John Paul II, Pres. Houphouet-Boigny — A197

1980, May 10   Photo.   Perf. 13

550	A197	65fr multicolored	3.50	1.25

Visit of Pope John Paul II to Ivory Coast.

Le Belier Locomotive A198

1980, May 17   Litho.   Perf. 13

551	A198	60fr shown	.75	.35
552	A198	65fr Abidjan Railroad Station, 1904	.85	.35
553	A198	100fr Passenger car, 1908	1.75	.70
554	A198	150fr Steam locomotive, 1940	2.25	1.00
		Nos. 551-554 (4)	5.60	2.40

Central Bank of West African States, 1st Anniversary A199

1980, May 26   Litho.   Perf. 12x12½

555	A199	60fr multicolored	1.00	.40

Lujtanus Sebae A200

1980, Apr. 19   Photo.   Perf. 14

556	A200	60fr shown	3.50	.75
557	A200	65fr Monodactylus sebae, vert.	3.75	1.25
558	A200	100fr Colisa fasciata	4.50	1.50
		Nos. 556-558 (3)	11.75	3.50

Snake — A201

1980, July 12   Litho.   Perf. 12½

559	A201	60fr shown	2.25	.75
560	A201	150fr Toad	5.00	1.75

Tourists in Village, by K. Ehouman Pierre A202

Conference Emblem — A203

1980, Aug. 9

561	A202	60fr multicolored	.75	.30
562	A203	65fr multicolored	.75	.30

National Tourist Office, Abidjan; World Tourism Conference, Manila.

Forticula Auricularia A204

Perf. 14x13, 13x14

1980, Sept. 6   Photo.

563	A204	60fr shown	5.00	2.25
564	A204	65fr Praying mantis, vert.	5.00	2.25

Perf. 13½x13, 13x13½

1980, Oct. 11   Photo.

Designs: 60fr, 200fr, Various grasshoppers.

565	A204	60fr multi, vert.	2.50	1.50
566	A204	200fr multi	7.50	3.50

Hands Free from Chain, Map of Ivory Coast, Pres. Houphouet-Boigny — A205

Pres. Houphouet-Boigny, Symbols of Development — A206

Perf. 12½x13, 14x14½ (A206)
1980, Oct. 18
567	A205	60fr shown	1.40	.75
568	A206	65fr shown	1.40	.75
569	A205	70fr Map, colors, document	2.00	1.00
570	A205	150fr like #567	4.50	2.75
571	A206	300fr like #568	8.00	4.50
		Nos. 567-571 (5)	17.30	9.75

Pres. Houphouet-Boigny, 75th birthday.

7th PDCI and RDA Congress A207

1980, Oct. 25   *Perf. 12½*
572	A207	60fr multicolored	1.00	.30
573	A207	65fr multicolored	1.00	.30

River Cruise Boat Sotra A208

1980, Dec. 6   **Litho.**   *Perf. 13x13½*
574	A208	60fr multicolored	1.25	.50

View of Abidjan — A209

1980, Dec. 7   *Perf. 13x12½*
575	A209	60fr multicolored	1.00	.30

20th anniversary of independence.

Universities Association Emblem — A210

African Postal Union, 5th Anniversary A211

1980, Dec. 16   *Perf. 12½*
576	A210	60fr multicolored	1.00	.50

African Universities Assoc., 5th General Conf.

1980, Dec. 24   **Photo.**   *Perf. 13½*
577	A211	150fr multi	1.75	.50

Herichtys Cyanoguttatum — A212

1981, Mar. 14   **Litho.**   *Perf. 12½*
578	A212	60fr shown	1.25	.75
579	A212	65fr Labeo bicolor	1.25	.75
580	A212	200fr Tetraodon fluviatilis	3.50	2.00
		Nos. 578-580 (3)	6.00	3.50

Birds — A212a

1980, Dec. 30   **Photo.**   *Perf. 14½x14*
580A	A212a	60fr Spreo superbus	65.00	15.00
580B	A212a	65fr Tockus camurus	65.00	15.00
580C	A212a	65fr Balearica pavonina	70.00	16.00
580D	A212a	100fr Ephippiorhynchus	200.00	175.00
		Nos. 580A-580D (4)	400.00	221.00

Post Office, Grand Lahou A213

25th Anniv. of Ivory Coast Philatelic Club A214

1981, May 2   **Litho.**   *Perf. 12½*
581	A213	60fr multicolored	1.00	.30
582	A214	65fr multicolored	1.00	.30

Stamp Day.

13th World Telecommunications Day — A215

1981, May 17
583	A215	30fr multicolored	.50	.20
584	A215	60fr multicolored	1.00	.35

Viking Satellite Landing, 1976 — A216

Space Conquest: Columbia space shuttle.

1981, June 13   **Litho.**   *Perf. 13½*
585	A216	60fr multi	.75	.25
586	A216	75fr multi	.90	.30
587	A216	125fr multi	1.40	.60
588	A216	300fr multi	3.50	1.25
		Nos. 585-588 (4)	6.55	2.40

Souvenir Sheet
589	A216	500fr multi	5.25	1.25

Local Flowers — A217

Prince Charles and Lady Diana, Coach — A218

1981, July 4   **Photo.**   *Perf. 14½x14*
590	A217	50fr Amorphophallus	1.75	.60
591	A217	60fr Sugar Cane	2.25	1.25
592	A217	100fr Heliconia ivoirea	4.00	1.75
		Nos. 590-592 (3)	8.00	3.60

1981, Aug. 8   **Litho.**   *Perf. 12½*
Royal Wedding: Couple and coaches.
593	A218	80fr multi	.90	.25
594	A218	100fr multi	1.25	.50
595	A218	125fr multi	1.75	.85
		Nos. 593-595 (3)	3.90	1.60

Souvenir Sheet
596	A218	500fr multi	6.00	2.00

For overprints see Nos. 642-645.

Elephant on Flag and Map — A219

1981, Sept.   **Litho.**   *Perf. 12½*
597	A219	80fr multicolored	.75	.25
598	A219	100fr multicolored	1.00	.50
599	A219	125fr multicolored	1.50	.60
		Nos. 597-599 (3)	3.25	1.35

See Nos. 662-666, 833.

Soccer Players A220

Soccer players.

1981, Sept. 19   *Perf. 14*
600	A220	70fr multi, horiz.	.75	.40
601	A220	80fr multi, horiz.	.80	.50
602	A220	100fr multi	1.00	.60

603	A220	150fr multi	1.50	.90
604	A220	350fr multi	3.75	1.75
		Nos. 600-604 (5)	7.80	4.15

Souvenir Sheet
605	A220	500fr multi, horz.	5.00	2.00

ESPANA '82 World Cup Soccer Championship.
For overprints see Nos. 651-656.

West African Rice Development Assoc., 10th Anniv. — A221

1981, Oct. 3   *Perf. 12½*
606	A221	80fr multicolored	1.25	.50

World Food Day A222

1981, Oct. 18
607	A222	100fr multicolored	1.25	.60

Post Day — A223

1981, Oct. 9   **Litho.**   *Perf. 12½*
608	A223	70fr multicolored	.75	.30
609	A223	80fr multicolored	.85	.50
610	A223	100fr multicolored	1.25	.60
		Nos. 608-610 (3)	2.85	1.40

75th Anniv. of Grand Prix — A224

Designs: Winners and their cars.

1981, Nov. 21   *Perf. 14*
611	A224	15fr Felice Nazarro, 1907	.25	.20
612	A224	40fr Jim Clark, 1962	.50	.20
613	A224	80fr Fiat, 1907	1.00	.45
614	A224	100fr Auto Union, 1936	1.25	.50
615	A224	125fr Ferrari, 1961	1.75	.60
		Nos. 611-615 (5)	4.75	1.95

Souvenir Sheet
616	A224	500fr 1933 car	6.00	2.25

21st Anniv. of Independence — A225

1981, Dec. 7 — **Perf. 13x12½**
617 A225 50fr multicolored .60 .30
618 A225 80fr multicolored 1.10 .50

Traditional
Hairstyle — A226

Rotary Emblem
on Map
of — A228

Stamp Day Africa — A227

Designs: Various hairstyles.

1981, Dec. 19　Photo.　Perf. 14½x14
619 A226 80fr multicolored 1.75 .85
620 A226 100fr multicolored 2.75 1.25
621 A226 125fr multicolored 3.50 1.75
　　Nos. 619-621 (3) 8.00 3.85

1982, Apr. 3　Litho.　Perf. 12½x12
622 A227 100fr Bingerville P.O.,
　　　1902 1.25 .60

1982, Apr. 13　　　Perf. 12½
623 A228 100fr ultra & gold 1.25 .60

Pres. Houphouet-Boigny's Rotary Goodwill
Conference, Abidjan, Apr. 13-15.

250th Birth Anniv. of George
Washington — A229

Anniversaries: 100fr, Auguste Piccard
(1884-1962), Swiss physicist. 350fr, Goethe
(1749-1832). 450fr, 500fr, Princess Diana,
21st birthday (portraits).

1982, May 15　Litho.　Perf. 13
624 A229 80fr multi .75 .35
625 A229 100fr multi 1.00 .50
626 A229 350fr multi 4.00 1.25
627 A229 450fr multi 5.00 1.50
　　Nos. 624-627 (4) 10.75 3.60
Souvenir Sheet
628 A229 500fr multi 4.50 1.25

Visit of French Pres. Mitterand, May
21-24 — A230

1982, May 21　Photo.　Perf. 13½
629 A230 100fr multicolored 1.00 .40

14th World Telecommunications
Day — A231

1982, May 29　Litho.　Perf. 13
630 A231 80fr multicolored .90 .25

Scouting
Year — A232

Scouts sailing, diff. 80fr, 150fr, 350fr, 500fr
vert.

1982, May 29　　　Perf. 12½
631 A232 80fr multi .90 .30
632 A232 100fr multi 1.50 .35
633 A232 150fr multi 1.90 .60
634 A232 350fr multi 4.00 1.25
　　Nos. 631-634 (4) 8.30 2.50
Souvenir Sheet
635 A232 500fr multi 7.00 2.50

TB Bacillus
Centenary
A233

1982, June 5　Photo.　Perf. 13x13½
636 A233 30fr brown & multi .75 .35
637 A233 80fr lt grn & multi 1.25 .65

UN Conference
on Human
Environment, 10th
Anniv. — A234

1982, July　Photo.　Perf. 13½x13
638 A234 40fr multicolored .70 .30
639 A234 80fr multicolored 1.25 .50

League of Ivory
Coast
Secretaries, First
Congress — A235

1982, Aug. 9　Litho.　Perf. 12½x13
640 A235 80fr tan & multi 1.00 .40
641 A235 100fr silver & multi 1.25 .50

593-596 Overprinted in Blue:
"NAISSANCE / ROYALE 1982"

1982, Aug. 21　　　Perf. 12½
642 A218 80fr multi 1.20 .50
643 A218 100fr multi 1.25 .60
644 A218 125fr multi 1.50 .75
　　Nos. 642-644 (3) 3.95 1.85
Souvenir Sheet
645 A218 500fr multi 5.00 5.00

Birth of Prince William of Wales, June 21.

La Colombe de l'Avenir, 1962, by
Pablo Picasso (1881-1973) — A236

Picasso Paintings: 80fr, Child with Dove,
1901. 100fr, Self-portrait, 1901. 185fr, Les
Demoiselles d'Avignon, 1907. 350fr, The
Dream, 1932. Nos. 646-649 vert.

1982, Sept. 4　Litho.　Perf. 13
646 A236 80fr multi 1.00 .40
647 A236 100fr multi 1.25 .40
648 A236 185fr multi 3.00 .75
649 A236 350fr multi 4.50 1.75
650 A236 500fr multi 6.50 2.00
　　Nos. 646-650 (5) 16.25 5.30

Nos. 600-605 Overprinted with World
Cup Winners 1966-1982 in Black on
Silver

1982, Oct. 9　Litho.　Perf. 14
651 A220 70fr multi .75 .30
652 A220 80fr multi .90 .60
653 A220 100fr multi 1.20 .60
654 A220 150fr multi 1.75 1.00
655 A220 350fr multi 4.00 2.00
　　Nos. 651-655 (5) 8.60 4.50
Souvenir Sheet
656 A220 500fr multi 6.50 6.50

Italy's victory in 1982 World Cup.

13th World UPU Day — A237

Designs: 80fr, P.O. counter. 100fr, Postel-
2001 building, Abidjan, vert. 350fr, Postal
workers. 500fr, Postel-2001 interior.

1982, Oct. 23　　　Perf. 12½
657 A237 80fr multi .80 .50
658 A237 100fr multi 1.40 .50
659 A237 350fr multi 4.00 1.75
Size: 48x37mm
Perf. 13
660 A237 500fr multi 4.75 2.25
　　Nos. 657-660 (4) 10.95 5.00

22nd Anniv. of Independence — A238

1982, Dec. 7　　　Perf. 13
661 A238 100fr multicolored 1.25 .60

Elephant Type of 1981

1982-84
662 A219 5fr multicolored .20 .20
662A A219 10fr multi ('84) .45 .20
662B A219 20fr multicolored .45 .20
663 A219 25fr multicolored .40 .20
664 A219 30fr multicolored .40 .20
665 A219 40fr multicolored .60 .20
666 A219 50fr multicolored .60 .20
　　Nos. 662-666 (7) 3.10 1.40

Man
Waterfall
A238a

1982　　Photo.　Perf. 15x14
666A A238a 80fr shown 20.00 2.00
666B A238a 80fr Boisee Sa-
　　　vanna 30.00 1.75
666C A238a 500fr like #666A 65.00 7.00
　　Nos. 666A-666C (3) 115.00 10.75
Issued: #666B, Dec. 18; others, Nov. 27.

20th Anniv.
of West
African
Monetary
Union
A239

1982, Dec. 21　Litho.　Perf. 12½
667 A239 100fr Emblem 1.25 .50

Abouissa
Children's
Village
A240

1983, Mar. 5　Photo.　Perf. 13½x13
668 A240 125fr multicolored 1.75 .75

Anteater
A241

1983, Mar. 12　Litho.　Perf. 12½x13
669 A241 35fr Pangolin, vert. .60 .20
670 A241 90fr shown 1.20 .50
671 A241 100fr Colobus monkey,
　　　vert. 1.50 .60
672 A241 125fr Buffalo 1.75 .75
　　Nos. 669-672 (4) 5.05 2.05

Stamp Day — A242

1983, Mar. 19　Litho.　Perf. 12½
673 A242 100fr Grand Bassam
　　　P.O., 1903 1.25 .60

Easter
1983
A243

Paintings by Rubens (1577-1640). 100fr, 400fr, 500fr vert.

1983, Apr. 9   *Perf. 13*
674 A243 100fr Descent from
      the Cross   1.10   .30
675 A243 125fr Resurrection   1.30   .50
676 A243 350fr Crucifixion   3.50   1.25
677 A243 400fr Piercing of the
      Sword   4.50   1.50
678 A243 500fr Descent, diff.   5.00   2.00
    Nos. 674-678 (5)   15.40   5.55

25th Anniv. of UN Economic
Commission for Africa — A244

1983, Apr. 29   *Litho.*   *Perf. 13x12½*
679 A244 100fr multicolored   1.25   .60

Gray
Parakeet
A245

1983, June 11
680 A245 100fr Fish eagle, vert.   2.00   1.00
681 A245 125fr shown   2.75   .75
682 A245 150fr Touracoes   4.25   1.00
    Nos. 680-682 (3)   9.00   2.75

World Communications Year — A245a

Designs: 100fr, Tower, telephone, operators. 125fr, Buildings, satellite dish.

1983, July 16   *Perf. 12½x13*
682A A245a 100fr multi   125.00   —
682B A245a 125fr multi   125.00   —

A246

1983, Sept. 3   *Litho.*   *Perf. 12½*
683 A246 50fr Flali, Gouro   .50   .30
684 A246 100fr Masked dancer,
      Guere   1.10   .50

---

685 A246 125fr Stilt dancer,
      Yacouba   1.50   .60
    Nos. 683-685 (3)   3.10   1.40

20th Anniv. of the Ivory Hotel,
Abidjan — A249

1983, Sept. 7   *Perf. 13*
693 A249 100fr multicolored   1.25   .60

Ecology in
Action
A250

1983, Oct. 24   *Litho.*
694 A250 25fr Forest after fire   .75   .40
695 A250 100fr Animals fleeing   2.00   .80
696 A250 125fr Animals grazing   2.75   2.10
    Nos. 694-696 (3)   5.50   3.30

Raphael (1483-1520), 500th Birth
Anniv. — A252

Paintings: 100fr, Christ and St. Peter. 125fr, Study for St. Joseph, vert. 350fr, Virgin of the House of Orleans, vert. 500fr, Virgin with the Blue Diadem, vert.

1983, Nov. 5   *Litho.*   *Perf. 13*
698 A252 100fr multi   1.20   .35
699 A252 125fr multi   1.50   .50
700 A252 350fr multi   3.75   1.50
701 A252 500fr multi   5.00   2.00
    Nos. 698-701 (4)   11.45   4.35

Auto Race
A253

1983, Oct. 24   *Litho.*   *Perf. 12½*
702 A253 100fr Car, map   1.50   .60

Flowers — A254

1983, Nov. 26   *Photo.*   *Perf. 14x15*
703 A254 100fr Fleurs
      d'Ananas   150.00   —
704 A254 125fr Heliconia
      Rostrata   10.00   2.50
705 A254 150fr Rose de
      Porcelaine   10.00   2.50
    Nos. 703-705 (3)   170.00

23rd Anniv. of Independence — A255

1983, Dec. 7
706 A255 100fr multicolored   1.25   .50

First Audio-visual Forum,
Abidjan — A256

1984, Jan. 25   *Litho.*   *Perf. 13x12½*
707 A256 100fr Screen, arrow   1.25   .50

14th African
Soccer
Cup — A257

1984, Mar. 4   *Photo.*   *Perf. 12½*
708 A257 100fr Emblem   1.00   .40
709 A257 200fr Maps shaking
      hands   2.00   1.00

Local Insects
A258

1984, Mar. 24   *Litho.*   *Perf. 13*
710 A258 100fr Argiope, vert.   2.00   .75
711 A258 125fr Polistes gallicus   2.25   1.00

Stamp Day — A259

1984, Apr. 7   *Litho.*   *Perf. 12½*
712 A259 100fr Abidjan P.O.,
      1934   1.25   .50

Lions
Emblem
A260

1984, Apr. 27   *Perf. 13½x13*
713 A260 100fr multicolored   1.00   .50
714 A260 125fr multicolored   1.75   .75

3rd Convention of Multi-district 403, Abidjan,
Apr. 27-29.

16th World Telecommunications
Day — A261

1984, May 17   *Perf. 12½*
715 A261 100fr multi   1.25   .50

Council of Unity,
25th
Anniv. — A262

1984, May 29
716 A262 100fr multicolored   1.25   .40
717 A262 125fr multicolored   1.50   .50

First Governmental Palace, Grand-
Bassam — A263

1984, July 14   *Litho.*   *Perf. 12½*
718 A263 100fr shown   1.25   .40
719 A263 125fr Palace of Justice,
      Grand-Bassam   1.50   .60

Men Playing Eklan — A264

1984, Aug. 11   *Perf. 13*
720 A264 100fr Board   1.40   .40
721 A264 125fr shown   1.50   .60

Locomotive "Gazelle" — A265

1984   *Perf. 12½*
722 A265 100fr shown   1.25   .50
723 A265 100fr Cargo ship   1.25   .50
724 A265 125fr Superpacific   2.00   .60
725 A265 125fr Cargo ship, diff.   1.50   .60
726 A265 350fr Pacific type 10   4.50   1.50
727 A265 350fr Ocean liner   4.00   1.50
728 A265 500fr Mallet class
      GT2   6.50   2.25
729 A265 500fr Ocean liner, diff.   6.50   2.25
    Nos. 722-729 (8)   27.50   9.70

Issue dates: trains, Aug. 25; ships, Sept. 1.

Stamp Day
A266

1984, Oct. 20 Litho. Perf. 12½
730 A266 100fr Map, post offices 1.50 .50

10th Anniv.,
West
African
Union
A267

1984, Oct. 27 Litho. Perf. 13½
731 A267 100fr Map, member
nations 1.00 .50

Wildlife — A267a

1984, Nov. 3 Photo. Perf. 14½x15
731A A267a 100fr Tragelaphus
scriptus 75.00 12.00
731B A267a 150fr Felis serval 75.00 12.00

Tourism
A267b

1984, Nov. 10 Photo. Perf. 15x14½
731C A267b 50fr Le Club Val-
tur 65.00 11.00
731D A267b 100fr Grand
Lahou 65.00 11.00

Flowers — A267c

1984, Nov. 17 Photo. Perf. 14½x15
731E A267c 100fr Allamanda
carthartica 75.00 12.00
731F A267c 125fr Baobob 75.00 12.00

90th Anniv.,
Ivory Coast
Postage
Stamps
A268

1984, Nov. 23 Litho. Perf. 12½
732 A268 125fr Book cover 1.50 .75

24th Anniv. of Independence — A269

1984, Dec. 7 Litho. Perf. 12½
733 A269 100fr Citizens, outline
map 1.00 .50

Rotary Intl.
Conf. — A270

1985, Jan. 16 Litho. Perf. 12½x13
734 A270 100fr multicolored 1.00 .50
735 A270 125fr multicolored 1.25 .60

Traditional
Costumes
A271

1985, Feb. 16 Litho. Perf. 13½
736 A271 90fr Dan le Babou 1.50 .50
737 A271 100fr Post-natal gown 1.50 .60

Birds — A271a

1985 Photo. Perf. 14½x15
737A A271a 25fr Marabout 150.00 17.50
737B A271a 100fr Jacana 150.00 17.50
737C A271a 350fr Ibis 150.00 17.50
Nos. 737A-737C (3) 450.00

Issued: Nos. 737A, 737B, Mar. No. 737C,
8/17.

Stamp Day — A272

1985, Apr. 13 Litho. Perf. 12½
738 A272 100fr Riverboat Adjame 2.25 1.00

18th District of Zonta Intl., 7th
Conference, Abidjan, Apr. 25-
27 — A273

1985, Apr. 25 Litho. Perf. 13½
739 A273 125fr Zonta Intl. emblem 1.40 .75

Bondoukou — A273a

100fr, Marche de Bondoukou. 125fr,
Mosque, Samatiguila.

1985 Litho. Perf. 14½x13½
739A A273a 100fr mul-
ticolored 140.00 9.00
739B A273a 125fr mul-
ticolored 140.00 9.00
739C A273a 200fr mul-
ticolored 140.00 9.00
Nos. 739A-739C (3) 420.00 27.00

PHILEXAFRICA '85, Lome — A274

1985, May 15 Perf. 13
740 A274 200fr Factory, jet, van 2.25 1.10
741 A274 200fr Youth sports,
farming 2.25 1.10
a. Pair, Nos. 740-741 + label 6.00 6.00

African Development Bank, 20th
Anniv. — A275

1985, June 18
742 A275 100fr Senegal chemical
industry 1.00 .50
743 A275 125fr Gambian tree
nursery 1.25 .75

Intl. Youth Year — A276

1985, July 20 Perf. 12½
744 A276 125fr Map, profiles,
dove 1.40 .60

Natl. Armed
Forces, 25th
Anniv. — A277

Emblems: No. 745, Presidential Guard.
No. 746, F.A.N.C.I. 125fr, Air Transport & Liai-
son Group, G.A.T.L. 200fr, National Marines.
350fr, National Gendarmerie.

1985, July 27 Perf. 12½x13
745 A277 100fr dp rose lil &
gold 1.00 .50
746 A277 100fr dark bl & gold 1.00 .50
747 A277 125fr blk brn & gold 1.50 .60
748 A277 200fr blk brn & gold 2.25 1.00
749 A277 350fr brt ultra & sil 3.50 2.00
Nos. 745-749 (5) 9.25 4.60

1986 World Cup Soccer Preliminaries,
Mexico — A279

1985, Aug. Perf. 13
751 A279 100fr Heading the ball 1.00 .50
752 A279 150fr Tackle 1.50 .90
753 A279 200fr Dribbling 1.75 1.20
754 A279 350fr Passing 3.75 2.00
Nos. 751-754 (4) 8.00 4.60

Souvenir Sheet

755 A279 500fr Power shot 5.00 2.00

Ivory Coast —
Sovereign Military
Order of Malta
Postal
Convention, Dec.
19, 1984 — A280

1985, Aug. 31 Perf. 13x12½
756 A280 125fr Natl. arms 1.25 .75
757 A280 350fr S.M.O.M. arms 3.50 2.00

Visit of Pope John Paul II — A281

1985, Sept. 24 Perf. 13
Overprint in Black
758 A281 100fr Portrait, St.
Paul's Cathe-
dral, Abidjan 2.25 1.00

The overprint, "Consecration de la
Cathedrale Saint Paul d'Abidjon," was added
to explain the reason for the visit of the Pope.
Copies without overprint exist but were not
issued.

UN Child
Survival
Campaign
A282

1985, Oct. 5 Litho. Perf. 13½x14
759 A282 100fr Breast-feeding 1.00 .50
760 A282 100fr Oral rehydration
therapy 1.00 .50
761 A282 100fr Mother and child 1.00 .50
762 A282 100fr Vaccination 1.00 .50
Nos. 759-762 (4) 4.00 2.00

UN 40th Anniv. — A283

1985, Oct. 31 *Perf. 13*
763 A283 100fr multicolored 1.25 .50
Admission to UN, 25th anniv.

World Wildlife Fund — A284

Striped antelopes.

1985, Nov. 30
764 A284 50fr multicolored 7.00 1.00
765 A284 60fr multicolored 9.00 2.00
766 A284 75fr multicolored 18.00 3.00
767 A284 100fr multicolored 27.50 5.00
Nos. 764-767 (4) 61.50 11.00

City Skyline — A285

1985, Nov. 21 *Litho.* *Perf. 13*
768 A285 125fr multicolored 1.50 .75
Expo '85 national industrial exhibition.

Return to the
Land Campaign
A286

Handicrafts
A287

1985, Dec. 7 *Perf. 12½*
769 A286 125fr multicolored 1.50 .75
Natl. independence, 25th anniv.

Flowers — A286a

100fr, L'Amorphophallus staudtii. 125fr, Crinum scillifolium. 200fr, Triphyophyllum peltatum.

1985, Dec. 28 *Litho.* *Perf. 14x15*
769A A286a 100fr multi 140.00 10.00
769B A286a 125fr multi 140.00 10.00
769C A286a 200fr multi 140.00 10.00
Nos. 769A-769C (3) 420.00 30.00

1986, Jan. *Perf. 13½*
770 A287 125fr Spinning thread 1.50 .75
771 A287 155fr Painting 2.00 1.00

Flora — A288

Cooking Utensils,
Natl. Museum,
Abidjan — A289

1986, Feb. 22 *Litho.* *Perf. 13½*
772 A288 40fr Omphalocarpum
elatum .50 .20
773 A288 50fr Momordica
charantia .60 .25
774 A288 125fr Milletia takou 1.50 1.00
775 A288 200fr Costus afer 2.25 1.25
Nos. 772-775 (4) 4.85 2.70

1986, Mar. 6 *Perf. 13x12½, 12½x13*
776 A289 20fr We bowl .20 .20
777 A289 30fr Baoule bowl .30 .20
778 A289 90fr Baoule platter 1.25 .50
779 A289 125fr Dan scoop 1.40 .75
780 A289 440fr Baoule lidded pot 5.00 2.50
Nos. 776-780 (5) 8.15 4.15

Nos. 776-778 horiz.

Natl. Pedagogic and Vocational
School, 10th Anniv. — A290

1986, Mar. 20 *Perf. 13½*
781 A290 125fr multicolored 1.50 .60

Cable Ship Stephan, 1910 — A291

1986, Apr. 12 *Litho.* *Perf. 12½*
782 A291 125fr multicolored 2.25 .60
Stamp Day.

Houphouet-Boigny Type of 1974-76
1986, Apr. *Engr.* *Perf. 13*
783 A112 5fr dk red, dp rose lil
& brn .20 .20
784 A112 10fr gray grn, brt bl &
brn .20 .20
785 A112 20fr brt ver, blk brn &
brn .20 .20
786 A112 25fr bl, dp rose lil &
brn .25 .20
787 A112 30fr brt ver, blk brn &
brn .25 .20
789 A112 50fr lake, dk vio & brn .50 .25
790 A112 90fr dk brn vio, rose
lake & brn .90 .40
791 A112 125fr brt lil rose, brt
ver & brn 1.50 .50
792 A112 155fr dk brn vio, Prus
bl & brn 1.50 .60
Nos. 783-792 (9) 5.50 2.75

The 1986 printing of the 40fr is in slightly darker colors than No. 374.

Natl. Youth and
Sports Institute,
25th
Anniv. — A293

1986, May 9 *Litho.* *Perf. 12½*
793 A293 125fr brt org & dk yel
grn 1.50 .60

Fish
A294

5fr, Polypterus endlicheri. 125fr, Synodontis punctifer. 150fr, Protopterus annectens. 155fr, Synodontis koensis. 440fr, Malapterurus electricus.

1986, July 5 *Litho.* *Perf. 14½x13½*
794 A294 5fr multi .20 .20
795 A294 125fr multi 1.50 .60
796 A294 150fr multi 2.00 .75
797 A294 155fr multi 2.10 .75
798 A294 440fr multi 6.00 2.25
Nos. 794-798 (5) 11.80 4.55

Enthronement of a Chief, Agni
District — A295

1986, July 19 *Perf. 13½x14½*
799 A295 50fr Drummer, vert. .50 .40
800 A295 350fr Chief in litter 4.00 2.00
801 A295 440fr Royal entourage 5.00 3.00
Nos. 799-801 (3) 9.50 5.40

Rural Houses — A296

1986, Aug. 2 *Litho.* *Perf. 14x15*
802 A296 125fr Baoule aoulo 1.40 .60
803 A296 155fr Upper Antiam
eva 1.75 1.00
804 A296 350fr Lobi soukala 3.75 1.75
Nos. 802-804 (3) 6.90 3.35

Coat of
Arms
A297

Coastal
Landscapes
A298

1986-87 *Engr.* *Perf. 13*
807 A297 50fr bright org .50 .25
808 A297 125fr dark green 1.50 .40
809 A297 155fr crimson 1.75 .40
810 A297 195fr blue ('87) 2.00 .40
Nos. 807-810 (4) 5.75 1.45

Issue dates: 50fr, 125fr, 155fr, Aug. 23.

Perf. 14x15, 15x14
1986, Aug. 30 *Litho.*
820 A298 125fr Grand Bereby 1.75 .75
821 A298 155fr Sableux Boubele,
horiz. 2.25 1.25

Oceanographic Research
Center — A299

Perf. 14½x13½
1986, Sept. 13 *Litho.*
822 A299 125fr Fishing grounds 1.40 .60
823 A299 155fr Net fishing 1.75 1.00

Intl. Peace
Year — A300

1986, Oct. 16 *Litho.* *Perf. 14x13½*
824 A300 155fr multicolored 1.75 .75

Research and Development — A301

1986, Nov. 15 *Perf. 13½x14*
825 A301 125fr Bull 1.75 1.00
826 A301 155fr Wheat 1.75 1.00

Natl. Independence, 26th
Anniv. — A302

1986, Dec. 6 *Litho.* *Perf. 13½x14*
827 A302 155fr multicolored 1.75 .75

Rural Housing A303

1987, Mar. 14   Litho.   Perf. 13½x14
828 A303 190fr Guesseple Dan   2.25 1.25
829 A303 550fr M'Bagui Senoufo   6.50 3.50

Stamp Day — A304

Jean Mermoz College, 25th Anniv. — A305

1987, Apr. 4   Perf. 13x13½
830 A304 155fr Mailman, 1918   1.75 1.00

1987, Apr. 9   Perf. 13
831 A305 40fr Cock, elephant   .50 .25
832 A305 155fr Dove, children   1.75 .75

Elephant Type of 1981

1987, Apr. 9
833 A219 35fr multicolored   .50 .20

Fouilles, by Krah N'Guessan A306

Paintings by local artists: 500fr, Cortege Ceremonial, by Santoni Gerard.

1987, Aug. 14   Litho.   Perf. 14½x15
841 A306 195fr multi   2.25 1.25
842 A306 500fr multi   5.50 3.50

World Post Day, Express Mail Service A307

1987, Oct. 9   Perf. 13½
843 A307 155fr multi   1.75 1.00
844 A307 195fr multi   2.25 1.25

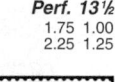

Intl. Trade Cent. A308

1987, Oct. 24
845 A308 155fr multi   1.75 1.00

A309

1987, Dec. 5   Litho.   Perf. 14x13½
846 A309 155fr multicolored   1.75 1.00

Natl. Independence, 27th anniv.

A310

1988, Feb. 20   Litho.   Perf. 14x13½
847 A310 155fr multicolored   1.75 1.00

Lions Club for child survival.

The Modest Canary, by Monne Bou A311

Paintings by local artists: 20fr, The Couple, by K.J. Houra, vert. 150fr, The Eternal Dance, by Bou, vert. 155fr, La Termitiere, by Mathilde Moro, vert. 195fr, The Sun of Independence, by Michel Kodjo, vert.

1988, Jan. 30   Perf. 12½x13, 13x12½
848 A311 20fr multi   .30 .20
849 A311 30fr shown   .30 .20
850 A311 150fr multi   1.75 .75
851 A311 155fr multi   1.75 .75
852 A311 195fr multi   2.50 1.00
    Nos. 848-852 (5)   6.60 2.90

Stamp Day A312

1988, Apr. 4   Litho.   Perf. 13
853 A312 155fr Bereby P.O., c. 1900   1.75 1.00

A313

1988, Apr. 18   Litho.   Perf. 15x14
854 A313 195fr blk & dark red   2.75 1.75

15th French-Language Nations Cardiology Congress, Abidjan, Apr. 18-20.

A314

1988, May 21   Litho.   Perf. 12x13
855 A314 195fr multicolored   2.25 1.25

Intl. Fund for Agricultural Development (IFAD), 10th anniv.

1st Intl. Day for the Campaign Against Drug Abuse and Drug Trafficking A315

1988, Aug. 27   Litho.   Perf. 13½
856 A315 155fr multi   2.00 1.25

Stone Heads — A316

Natl. Independence 28th Anniv. — A318

World Post Day — A317

Various stone heads from the Niangoran-Bouah Archaeological Collection.

Litho. & Engr.
1988, July 9   Perf. 13x14½
857 A316 5fr beige & sep   .25 .20
858 A316 10fr buff & sep   .25 .20
859 A316 30fr pale grn & sep   .30 .20
860 A316 155fr pale yel & sep   2.00 1.00
861 A316 195fr pale yel grn & sep 2.75 1.25
    Nos. 857-861 (5)   5.55 2.85

1988, Oct. 15   Litho.   Perf. 14
862 A317 155fr multi   1.75 1.00

1988, Dec. 6   Perf. 11½x12
Year of the Forest: 40fr, Healthy trees. No. 864, Stop forest fires. No. 865, Planting trees.
863 A318 40fr multi   .60 .25
864 A318 155fr multi   2.25 .90
865 A318 155fr multi   2.25 .90
    Nos. 863-865 (3)   5.10 2.05

History of Money A319

1989, Feb. 25   Litho.   Perf. 12x11½
Granite Paper
866 A319 50fr shown   1.00 .25
867 A319 195fr Senegal bank notes, 1854, 1901   2.75 1.25

See Nos. 885-886, 896-898, 915. For surcharges see Nos. 904-905.

"Valeur d'echange 0fr.25" on 25c Type A5, 1920 A320

1989, Apr.   Perf. 12½
868 A320 155fr multi   2.00 1.00

Stamp Day.

Jewelry from the National Museum Collection A321

1989, Mar. 25   Litho.   Perf. 14
869 A321 90fr Voltaic bracelets   1.25 .60
870 A321 155fr Anklets   2.25 1.25

Sculptures by Christian Lattier A322

Perf. 11½x12, 12x11½
1989, May 13   Granite Paper
871 A322 40fr The Old Man and the Infant, vert.   .50 .25
872 A322 155fr The Saxophone Player, vert.   2.00 1.00
873 A322 550fr The Panther   6.00 3.25
    Nos. 871-873 (3)   8.50 4.50

For surcharge see No. 903.

Council for Rural Development, 30th Anniv. — A323

1989, May 29   Perf. 15x14
874 A323 75fr Flags, well, tractor, field   1.25 .40

See Togo No. 1526.

Intl. Peace Congress — A324

1989, June   Litho.   Perf. 13
875 A324 195fr multi   2.25 1.00

Rural Habitat A325

1989, June 10   Litho.   Perf. 14
876 A325 155fr Hut, Sirikukube
            Dida   1.75 1.00
For surcharge see No. 902.

Sekou Watara, King of Kong (1710-1745) — A326

Designs: No. 878, Bastille, Declaration of Human Rights and Citizenship.

1989, July 7   Litho.   Perf. 13
877 A326 200fr shown   3.50 1.75
878 A326 200fr multi   3.50 1.75
  a.   Pair, Nos. 877-878 + label 8.50 7.50

PHILEXFRANCE '89, French revolution bicent.

Endangered Species — A327

1989, Sept. 16   Perf. 12x11½
Granite Paper
879 A327 25fr Varanus niloticus .50 .30
880 A327 100fr Crocodylus
            niloticus   2.00 1.25

World Post
Day
A328

1989, Oct. 9   Litho.   Perf. 12½x13
881 A328 195fr multi   2.25 1.00

CAPTEAO,
30th Anniv.
A329

1989, Oct. 28   Litho.   Perf. 12½
882 A329 155fr multicolored   2.00 1.00
Conference of Postal and Telecommunication Administrations of West African Nations.

A330

A331

1989, Dec. 7   Perf. 13
883 A330 155fr multicolored   1.75 1.00
Natl. independence, 29th anniv.

1990, Jan. 18   Litho.   Perf. 13
884 A331 155fr multicolored   1.75 1.00
Pan-African Union, 10th anniv.

History of Money Type of 1989
1990, Mar. 17   Litho.   Perf. 12x11½
Granite Paper
885 A319 155fr 1923 25fr note   1.75 1.00
886 A319 195fr 1, 2, 5fr notes 3.00 1.50

Stamp Day
A332

1990, Apr. 21   Litho.   Perf. 13x12½
887 A332 155fr Packet Africa   2.25 1.00

Multinational
Postal School,
20th
Anniv. — A333

1990, May 31   Perf. 12½
888 A333 155fr multicolored   1.75 .90

Rural
Village
A334

1990, June 30   Perf. 14
889 A334 155fr multicolored   1.75 .60

Intl.
Literacy
Year
A335

1990, July 28   Perf. 15x14
890 A335 195fr multicolored   2.25 1.00

Dedication of Basilica of Notre Dame
of Peace, Yamoussoukro — A336

1990, Sept. 8   Perf. 14½x13½
891 A336 155fr shown   1.75 .80
892 A336 195fr Basilica, diff. 2.75 1.25

Visit of Pope John Paul II — A337

1990, Sept. 9   Perf. 13
893 A337 500fr multicolored   6.00 3.00

World Post
Day — A338

1990, Oct. 9   Litho.   Perf. 14x15
894 A338 195fr multicolored   4.00 1.50

Independence, 30th Anniv. — A339

1990, Dec. 6   Litho.   Perf. 13½x14½
895 A339 155fr multicolored   2.25 .90

History of Money Type of 1989
1991, Mar. 1   Litho.   Perf. 11½
Granite Paper
896 A319 40fr French West Afri-
            ca 1942 5fr,
            100fr notes   .55   .25
897 A319 155fr like #896   1.75 .85
898 A319 195fr French West Afri-
            ca & Togo 50fr,
            500fr notes   2.40 1.25
  Nos. 896-898 (3)   4.70 2.35
For surcharges see Nos. 904-905.

Stamp Day
A340

1991, May 18   Litho.   Perf. 13½
899 A340 150fr multicolored   1.75 .55

Miniature Sheets of 9

French Open Tennis Championships,
Cent. — A341

Tennis Players: No. 900a, Henri Cochet. b, Rene Lacoste. c, Jean Borotra. d, Don Budge. e, Marcel Bernard. f, Ken Rosewall. g, Rod Laver. h, Bjorn Borg. i, Yannick Noah.
No. 901a, Suzanne Lenglen. b, Helen Wills Moody. c, Simone Mathieu. d, Maureen Connolly. e, Francoise Durr. f, Margaret Court. g, Chris Evert. h, Martina Navratilova. i, Steffi Graf.

1991, May 24   Litho.   Perf. 13½
900 A341 200fr #a.-i.   22.50 22.50
901 A341 200fr #a.-i.   22.50 22.50

Nos. 872, 876, 897-898 Surcharged

Perfs. as Before
1991, July 15   Litho.
902 A325 150fr on 155fr #876   1.75 .55
Granite Paper
903 A322 150fr on 155fr #872   1.75 .55
904 A319 150fr on 155fr #897   1.75 .65
905 A319 200fr on 195fr #898   2.25 .80
  Nos. 902-905 (4)   7.50 2.55
Location of obliterator and surcharge varies.

Packet Boats
A342

1991, June 28   Litho.   Perf. 12x11½
Granite Paper
906 A342 50fr Europe   .65   .25
907 A342 550fr Asia   6.00 3.00

World Post
Day
A343

1991, Oct. 9   Perf. 13
908 A343 50fr shown   .65   .25
909 A343 100fr SIPE, globe   1.25 .50

Tribal
Drums — A344

1991   Litho.   Perf. 14x15
910 A344 5fr We   .20   .20
911 A344 25fr Krou, Soubre re-
            gion   .20   .20
912 A344 150fr Sinematiali   2.00 1.10
913 A344 200fr Akye, Alepe re-
            gion   2.50 1.25
  Nos. 910-913 (4)   4.90 2.75

Independence, 31st Anniv. — A345

1991, Dec. 7   Litho.   Perf. 13½x14½
914 A345 150fr multicolored   2.25   .80

History of Money Type of 1989
1991, Dec. 8   Perf. 12x11½
Granite Paper
915 A319 100fr like #898   1.25   .70

Flowers
A346

Various flowers.

1991, Dec. 20   Engr.   Perf. 13
916 A346 150fr grn, blk & mag,
           vert.   1.75   .65
917 A346 200fr grn, olive & rose
           car   2.25   .85

African Soccer
Championships — A347

Designs: 150fr, Elephants holding trophy,
map, soccer ball, vert.

1992, Apr. 22   Litho.   Perf. 13
918 A347 20fr multicolored   .35   .25
919 A347 150fr multicolored   2.00 1.25

Animals
A348

1992, May 5   Engr.   Perf. 13x12½
920 A348 5fr Viverra civetta   .20   .20
921 A348 40fr Nandinia binotata   .55   .20
922 A348 150fr Tragelaphus
           euryceros   2.25   .80
923 A348 500fr Panthera pardus   5.50 3.25
       Nos. 920-923 (4)   8.50 4.45

World Post Day — A349

1992, Oct. 7   Litho.   Perf. 13
924 A349 150fr black & blue   1.75   .80

First Ivory Coast Postage Stamp,
Cent. — A350

Designs: a, #3, #197. b, #182, #909 with
mail trucks, post office boxes.

1992, Oct. 7
925 A350 150fr Pair, #a.-b. + la-
           bel   5.00 3.50

Funeral
Monuments
A351

Various grave site monuments.

1992, Dec. 30   Engr.   Perf. 13
926 A351 5fr multicolored   .20   .20
927 A351 50fr multicolored   .75   .25
928 A351 150fr multicolored   1.75   .80
929 A351 400fr multicolored   4.25 1.75
       Nos. 926-929 (4)   6.95 3.00

Intl.
Abidjan
Marathon
A351a

1992, Nov. 20   Litho.   Perf. 11½
Granite Paper
929A A351a 150fr Flags, run-
             ners   1.25   .50
929B A351a 200fr Runners   2.50   .75
       Nos. 929A-929B were not available in the
philatelic market until Apr. 1994.

Gold Mine of Ity,
1st
Anniv. — A351b

1992, Nov. 8   Litho.   Perf. 14x15
929C A351b 200fr multicolored   3.00 1.20
       No. 929C was not available in the philatelic
market until Apr. 1994.

32nd Anniv. of
Independence
A351c

1992, Nov. 8   Litho.   Perf. 14x15
929C A351b 200fr multicolored   3.00 1.20

1992, Dec. 4
150fr, People, flag, Statue of Liberty, map.
929D A351c 30fr shown   .50   .35
929E A351c 150fr multicolored   2.25   .75
       Nos. 929D-929E were not available in the
philatelic market until Apr. 1994.

Tourist
Attractions
— A351d

Environmental
Summit — A351e

Perf. 14x15, 15x14
1992, Sept. 4   Litho.
929F A351d 10fr Modern ho-
             tel, horiz.   —   —
929G A351d 25fr Dent de
             Man   35.00 —
929H A351d 100fr Resort,
             horiz.   45.00 —
929I A351d 200fr Map of tour-
             ist sites   65.00 —

Perf. 11½x12, 12x11½
1992, June 5   Litho.
200fr, Prevent water pollution, horiz.
Granite Paper
929J A351e 150fr multicolored   70.00
929K A351e 200fr multicolored   70.00

Stamp Day
A352

Designs showing children interested in philately: No. 930, Girl, stamp collection, #169.
No. 931, Girl, #431, #446B, #186, and #920.
150fr, Boy sitting under tree, stamp exhibition.

1993, Apr. 17   Litho.   Perf. 13½
930 A352 50fr multicolored   .55   .25
931 A352 50fr multicolored   .55   .25
932 A352 150fr multicolored   2.00   .75
       Nos. 930-932 (3)   3.10 1.25

A353   A354

Medicinal plants.

1993, May 14   Litho.   Perf. 11½x12
Granite Paper
933 A353 5fr Argemone mexi-
           cana   .35   .20
934 A353 20fr Hibiscus esculen-
           tus   .45   .20
935 A353 200fr Cassia alata   2.50 1.25
       Nos. 933-935 (3)   3.30 1.65

1993, Aug. 27   Photo.   Perf. 12x11½
Orchids: 10fr, Calyptrochilum emarginatum.
50fr, Plectrelminthus caudathus. 150fr,
Eulophia guineensis.
Granite Paper
936 A354 10fr multicolored   .20   .20
937 A354 50fr multicolored   .40   .25
938 A354 150fr multicolored   1.75   .90
       Nos. 936-938 (3)   2.35 1.35

Ivory Coast
Colony,
Cent.
A355

25fr, Organization charter. 100fr, Colonial
Governor Louis Gustave Binger, Pres. F.
Houphouet-Boigny. 500fr, Natives selecting
goods for trade.

1993, Sept. 17   Perf. 13x12½
939 A355 25fr green & black   .35   .20
940 A355 100fr blue & black   1.25   .75
941 A355 500fr brown & black   6.00 3.50
       Nos. 939-941 (3)   7.60 4.45

Elimination Round
of 1994 World
Cup Soccer
Championships,
US — A356

Designs: 150fr, Cartoon soccer players.
200fr, Three players. 300fr, Two players. 400fr,
Cartoon players, diff.

1993, Sept. 24   Litho.   Perf. 14x15
942 A356 150fr multicolored   1.25   .55
943 A356 200fr multicolored   2.25   .85
944 A356 300fr multicolored   3.50 1.75
945 A356 400fr multicolored   4.50 2.50
       Nos. 942-945 (4)   11.50 5.65

World Post
Day
A357

Designs: 30fr, Map of Ivory Coast. 200fr,
Post office, Bouake.

1993, Oct. 9   Perf. 13x13½
946 A357 30fr multicolored   .35   .20
947 A357 200fr multicolored   2.40 1.25

African
Biennial
of Plastic Arts,
Abidjan
A358

Perf. 14½x13½
1993, Nov. 24   Litho.
948 A358 200fr multicolored   2.00 1.00

Independence,
33rd
Anniv. — A359

1993, Dec. 7   Litho.   Perf. 13½x13
950 A359 200fr multicolored   2.50 1.00

Pres. Felix Houphouet-Boigny (1905-93) — A360

Pres. Houphouet-Boigny and: Nos. 951a, 952a, 953a, Modern buildings, technology. Nos. 951b, 952b, 953b, Agriculture, shipping. Nos. 951c, 952c, 953c, Dove, rainbow, Presidential palace.

1994, Feb. 5   Litho.   Perf. 13
951 A360 150fr Strip of 3, #a.-
        c.   3.00   2.00
952 A360 200fr Strip of 3, #a.-
        c.   4.00   3.00

Souvenir Sheet
Perf. 12
953 A360 500fr Sheet of 3,
        #a.-c.   12.00 12.00

Raoul Follereau, Campaign Against Leprosy A361

1994, Feb. 20   Litho.   Perf. 13
954 A361 150fr multicolored   1.25   .50

RASCOM (Regional African Satellite Communications Organization), 1st Meeting, Abidjan — A362

1994, Jan. 19   Litho.   Perf. 14x13
955 A362 150fr multicolored   1.25   .40

Woman Carrying Basket — A363

Litho. & Engr.
1994-95   Perf. 13½x13
Color of Border
956   A363   5fr orange   .20   .20
956A   A363 10fr green   .20   .20
956B   A363 20fr red   .20   .20
957   A363 25fr blue   .20   .20
957A   A363 30fr olive bister   .20   .20
958   A363 40fr yellow green   .20   .20
959   A363 50fr brown   .25   .20
960   A363 75fr lilac rose   .30   .20
961   A363 150fr bright green   .70   .35
961A   A363 180fr pale lake   .95   .50
961B   A363 280fr gray   1.40   .70
962   A363 300fr violet   1.40   .70
        Nos. 956-962 (12)   6.20 3.85

Issued: 30fr, 180fr, 280fr, 5/16/95, dated 1994; others, 11/4/94.

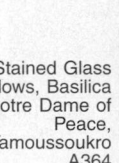

Stained Glass Windows, Basilica of Notre Dame of Peace, Yamoussoukro A364

Designs: 25fr, Christ, world map. 150fr, Christ, fishermen. 200fr, Madonna and Child. 600fr, Aerial view of Cathedral, Yamoussoukro.

1994, Nov. 18   Litho.   Perf. 14
963 A364 25fr lilac rose & multi   .35   .20
964 A364 150fr pale orange &
               multi   1.25   .60
965 A364 200fr yellow & mulit   1.40   .80
        Nos. 963-965 (3)   3.00 1.60

Souvenir Sheet
966 A364 600fr multicolored   5.00 5.00

Natl. Independence, 34th Anniv. — A365

1994, Dec. 6   Litho.   Perf. 12
967 A365 150fr multicolored   1.00   .40

Snakes A366

Designs: 10fr, Python regius. 20fr, Philothamnus semivariegatus. 100fr, Dendroaspis veridis. 180fr, Bitis arietans. 500fr, Bitis nasicornis.

1995, June 23   Litho.   Perf. 13
968 A366 10fr multicolored   .20   .20
969 A366 20fr multicolored   .20   .20
970 A366 100fr multicolored   .65   .25
971 A366 180fr multicolored   1.40   .75
972 A366 500fr multicolored   3.00 1.50
        Nos. 968-972 (5)   5.45 2.90

FAO, 50th Anniv. — A367

UN, 50th Anniv. — A368

1995, Aug. 4   Litho.   Perf. 11½
973 A367 100fr multicolored   1.00   .35
974 A368 280fr multicolored   2.75   .75

Mushrooms A369

Designs: 30fr, Lentinus tuber-regium. 50fr, Volvariella volvacea. 180fr, Dictyophora indusiata. 250fr, Termitomyces schimperi.

1995, Sept. 8   Perf. 14x13½
975 A369 30fr multicolored   .50   .35
976 A369 50fr multicolored   .90   .70
977 A369 180fr multicolored   2.75 1.00
978 A369 250fr multicolored   3.00 2.00
    a.   Block of 4, #975-978   8.50 6.00
#978a was issued in sheets of 16 stamps.

Louis Pasteur (1822-95) A370

1995, Sept. 28   Perf. 11½
979 A370 280fr   1.75   .75

School Philatelic Clubs A371

1995, Oct. 6   Perf. 13½
980 A371 50fr GSR   .65   .20
981 A371 180fr LBP   2.00   .80

Butterflies

Designs: 180fr, Pala decius. 280fr, Papilio dardanus. 550fr, Papilio menestheus.

1995   Litho.   Perf. 15x14
981A A371a 180fr multicolored   12.00 1.00
981B A371a 280fr multicolored   17.50 1.50
981C A371a 550fr multicolored   22.50 2.50
        Nos. 981A-981C (3)   52.00 5.00

Transportation in Abidjan — A372

Designs: 180fr, People pushing, pulling cart of grain, automobiles, bus on street. 280fr, People getting into bus in middle of traffic.

1996, May 24   Perf. 13½
982 A372 180fr multicolored   1.25   .60
983 A372 280fr multicolored   2.00 1.00

Fish A373

Designs: 50fr, Heterotis niloticus. 180fr, Auchenoglanis occidentalis. 700fr, Schilbe mandibularis.

1996, June
984 A373 50fr multicolored   .40   .30
985 A373 180fr multicolored   1.25   .75
986 A373 700fr multicolored   5.00 2.50
        Nos. 984-986 (3)   6.65 3.55

A374

A375

Orchids: 40fr, Cyrtorchis arcuata. 100fr, Eulophia horsfalii. 180fr, Eulophidium maculatum. 200fr, Ansellia africana.

1996, July 12   Litho.   Perf. 13½x13
987 A374 40fr multicolored   .40   .30
988 A374 100fr multicolored   1.00   .75
989 A374 180fr multicolored   2.00 1.25
990 A374 200fr multicolored   2.00 1.25
        Nos. 987-990 (4)   5.40 3.55

1996, Nov. 19
991 A375 200fr Boxing   1.25   .60
992 A375 280fr Running   2.00 1.00
993 A375 400fr Long jump   2.50 1.25
994 A375 500fr Natl. Olympic
               Committee em-
               blem   3.25 1.75
        Nos. 991-994 (4)   9.00 4.60

1996 Summer Olympic Games, Atlanta.

Carved Canes A376

180fr, Cane of Birifor hunter. 200fr, Cane of Chief Lobi. 280fr, Cane of Chief Lobi (Gbobéri).

1996, Sept. 20   Litho.   Perf. 11½
995 A376 180fr black & green   1.25   .60
996 A376 200fr black & org yel   1.25   .70
997 A376 280fr black & lilac   2.00 1.00
        Nos. 995-997 (3)   4.50 2.30

Water Flowers A377

Designs: 50fr, Nelumbo nucifera. 180fr, Nymphea lotus. 280fr, Nymphea capensis. 700fr, Nymphea alba.

1997, June 20   Litho.   Perf. 13½x14
998   A377 50fr multicolored   .30   .25
999   A377 180fr multicolored   1.25   .60
1000 A377 280fr multicolored   2.00 1.00
1001 A377 700fr multicolored   4.50 2.50
        Nos. 998-1001 (4)   8.05 4.35

Basilica of Our Lady of Peace, Yamoussoukro — A378

a, 180fr, Pres. Felix Houphouet-Boigny, exterior view of basilica. b, 200fr, Interior view. c, 280fr, Aerial view, Pope John Paul II.

1997, July 8   Litho.   Perf. 13
1002 A378   Strip of 3, #a.-c. 5.00 4.00

Traditional Jewelry — A379

Various beaded necklaces.

1997, Aug. 22			Perf. 11½	
1003	A379	50fr plum & black	.35	.25
1004	A379	100fr plum & black	.75	.50
1005	A379	180fr plum & black	1.25	.75
	Nos. 1003-1005 (3)		2.35	1.50

A379a

A380

Various stone heads of Gohitafla.

1997, Oct. 10	Litho.		Perf. 11½	
Granite Paper				
1006	A379a	100fr red & multi	.65	.25
1007	A379a	180fr blue & multi	1.25	.75
1008	A379a	500fr green & multi	3.00	1.50
	Nos. 1006-1008 (3)		4.90	2.50

1997, Nov. 28			Perf. 13½	
Work tools: 180fr, Pulley. 280fr, Comb. 300fr, Navette, horiz.				
1009	A380	180fr orange & multi	1.25	.50
1010	A380	280fr green & multi	1.75	.75
1011	A380	300fr blue & multi	1.75	.75
	Nos. 1009-1011 (3)		4.75	2.00

Endangered Species A381

Designs: 180fr, African manatee. 280fr, Jentink's duiker. 400fr, Kob antelope.

1997, Dec. 19	Photo.		Perf. 11½	
1012	A381	180fr multicolored	1.75	1.00
1013	A381	280fr multicolored	1.75	1.00
1014	A381	400fr multicolored	2.50	1.25
	Nos. 1012-1014 (3)		6.00	3.25

1998 World Cup Soccer Championships, France — A382

Paris landmarks in background and: 180fr, Player, ball depicted with angry face. 280fr, Flags of nations inside outline of player. 400fr, Player taking shot on goal. 500fr, Two players, mascot, vert.

	Perf. 13x13½, 13½x13			
1998, June 5			Litho.	
1015	A382	180fr multicolored	1.25	.60
1016	A382	280fr multicolored	1.75	1.00
1017	A382	400fr multicolored	2.50	1.75
1018	A382	500fr multicolored	3.00	1.25
	Nos. 1015-1018 (4)		8.50	4.10

Mushrooms A383

Endemic Plants — A384

50fr, Agaricus bingensis. 180fr, Lactarius gymnocarpus. 280fr, Termitomyces le testui.

1998, June 26	Litho.		Perf. 13½x13	
1019	A383	50fr multicolored	.65	.40
1020	A383	180fr multicolored	1.50	1.00
1021	A383	280fr multicolored	2.25	1.25
	Nos. 1019-1021 (3)		4.40	2.65

See No. B20A.

1998, July 10			Perf. 12	
Designs: 40fr, Hutchinsonia barbata. 100fr, Synsepalum aubrevillei. 180fr, Cola lorougnonis.				
	Granite Paper			
1022	A384	40fr multicolored	.45	.20
1023	A384	100fr multicolored	.90	.50
1024	A384	180fr multicolored	1.25	.75
	Nos. 1022-1024 (3)		2.60	1.45

Traditional Costumes from Grand-Bassam Museum — A385

1998, Nov. 13	Litho.		Perf. 13½x13	
1025	A385	180fr Tapa	1.25	.75
1026	A385	280fr Raffia	1.75	1.25

Trains of Africa A386

180fr, South African Railway, 1918. 280fr, Garret 2-8-2+2-8-2 Beyer Peacock, 1925. 500fr, Cecil Rhodes.

1999, Feb. 26	Litho.		Perf. 13½	
1027	A386	180fr multicolored	1.25	.75
1028	A386	280fr multicolored	2.00	1.25
	Souvenir Sheet			
1029	A386	500fr multicolored	2.50	2.50

See No. B20B.

PhilexFrance '99, World Philatelic Exhibition — A387

Animals: 180fr+20fr, Loxodonta africana. 250fr, Syncerus caffer. 280fr, Pan troglodytes. 400fr, Cercopithecus aethiops.

1999, July 2	Litho.		Perf. 13x13¼	
1030	A387	180fr +20fr multi	1.75	1.25
1031	A387	250fr multicolored	1.75	1.25
1032	A387	280fr multicolored	1.90	1.25
1033	A387	400fr multicolored	2.50	1.75
	Nos. 1030-1033 (4)		7.90	5.50

UPU, 125th Anniv. A388

UPU emblem and: 180fr+20fr, Carved heads. 280fr, Methods of delivering mail.

1999, June 25			Perf. 11¾x11½	
1034	A388	180fr +20fr multi	1.25	.75
1035	A388	280fr multicolored	1.75	1.25

Flowers A389

Ahouakro Rock Formations A390

Designs: 100fr, Ancistrochilus rothschilianus. 180fr+20fr, Brachycorythis pubescens. 200fr, Bulbophyllum barbigerum. 280fr, Habenaria macrandra.

1999, July 27	Litho.		Perf. 13¼x13	
1036	A389	100fr multicolored	.60	.35
1037	A389	180fr +20fr multi	1.60	1.25
1038	A389	200fr multicolored	1.60	1.25
1039	A389	280fr multicolored	2.00	1.25
	Nos. 1036-1039 (4)		5.80	4.10

	Perf. 13¼x14, 14x13¼			
1999, Aug. 6			Litho.	
Various rock formations.				
1040	A390	180fr +20fr multi, horiz.	1.75	.75
1041	A390	280fr multi, horiz.	1.75	1.00
1042	A390	400fr multi	2.50	1.75
	Nos. 1040-1042 (3)		6.00	3.50

PhilexFrance 99 — A391

1999, July 2	Litho.		Perf. 13	
1043	A391	280fr multicolored	4.00	4.00

No. 1043 has a holographic image. Soaking in water may affect hologram.

Birds — A392

Designs: 50fr, Oriolus auratus. 180fr + 20fr, Nectarinia cinnyris venusta. 280fr, Trenon vinago australis. 300fr, Psittacus eithacus.

1999, Oct. 29	Litho.		Perf. 13¼x13	
1044	A392	50fr multi	.45	.25
1045	A392	180fr + 20fr multi	1.50	1.00
1046	A392	280fr multi	2.25	1.25
1047	A392	300fr multi	2.25	1.25
	Nos. 1044-1047 (4)		6.45	3.75

Fish A393

Designs: 100fr, Synodontis schall. 180fr + 20fr, Chromidotilapia guntheri. 280fr, Distichodus rostratus.

1999, Nov. 19			Perf. 13½x13¼	
1048	A393	100fr multi	.75	.35
1049	A393	180fr +20fr multi	1.50	1.00
1050	A393	280fr multi	2.25	1.50
	Nos. 1048-1050 (3)		4.50	2.85

Challenges for Ivory Coast in Third Millennium — A394

Designs: 100fr, Education. 180fr +20fr, Agriculture. 200fr, Industry. 250fr, Information. 280fr, Peace. 400fr, Culture.

1999, Dec. 10			Perf. 13½x13¾	
1051	A394	100fr multi	.65	.35
1052	A394	180fr +20fr multi	1.25	.75
1053	A394	200fr multi	1.25	.75
1054	A394	250fr multi	1.50	1.00
1055	A394	280fr multi	1.50	1.00
1056	A394	400fr multi	1.75	1.75
	Nos. 1051-1056 (6)		7.90	5.60

Native Masks A395

	Perf. 13½x13¼, 13¼x13½			
2000, June 30			Litho.	
1057	A395	30fr Wambélé	.35	.20
1058	A395	180fr +20fr Djè	1.25	.80
1059	A395	400fr Korobla, vert.	2.25	1.75
	Nos. 1057-1059 (3)		3.85	2.75

Edible Plants — A396

Designs: 30fr, Blighia sapida. 180fr+20fr, Ricinodendron heudelotii. 300fr, Telfaira occidentalis. 400fr, Napoleonaea vogelii.

2000, July 14 **Perf. 13¼x13½**
1060 A396 30fr multi .35 .20
1061 A396 180fr +20fr multi 1.40 .80
1062 A396 300fr multi 1.75 1.25
1063 A396 400fr multi 2.25 2.00
Nos. 1060-1063 (4) 5.75 4.25

Pres. Robert
Guei,
Elephant,
Map and
Dove — A397

2000, Aug. 4 **Perf. 13¾x13¼**
1064 A397 180fr +20fr red & mul- ti 1.25 .80
1065 A397 400fr yel & multi 2.50 1.75
Independence, 40th anniv., coup d'etat of Robert Guei.

Cacao — A398

Frame colors: 5fr, Dark blue green. 10fr, Light brown. 20fr, Claret. 25fr, Blue. 30fr, Greenish black. 40fr, Cerise. 50fr, Golden brown. 100fr, Brown. 180fr+20fr, Orange. 300fr, Blue violet. 350fr, Prussian blue. 400fr, Emerald. 600fr, Olive green.

Perf. 11½x11¾
2000, Aug. 25 **Photo.**
Granite Paper
1066-1078 A398 Set of 13 10.00 7.00

National Lottery,
30th
Anniv. — A399

Denominations: 180fr+20fr, 400fr.

2000, Aug. 30 Litho. **Perf. 13¼x13**
1079-1080 A399 Set of 2 3.50 2.50

2000
Summer
Olympics,
Sydney
A400

Designs: 180fr+20fr, Soccer. 400fr, Kangaroo. 600fr, Runners. 750fr, Bird over stadium.

2000, Sept. 8 **Perf. 13½x13¼**
1081-1084 A400 Set of 4 12.00 9.00

Hairstyles — A401

Various hairstyles: 180fr+20fr, 300fr, 400fr, 500fr.

2000, Sept. 22 **Perf. 13¾x13¼**
1085-1088 A401 Set of 4 8.50 6.50

Release of
Nelson Mandela,
10th
Anniv. — A402

2000, Oct. 6 Photo. **Perf. 12x11¾**
1089 A402 300fr multi 1.75 1.25

Historic
Monuments
A403

Designs: 180fr+20fr, Queen Pokou. 400fr, Akwaba. 600fr, Invocation of the Spirits.

2000, Nov. 10 Litho. **Perf. 13½x13**
1090-1092 A403 Set of 3 7.00 6.00

UN High Commisioner for Refugees,
50th Anniv. — A404

2000, Dec. 8 Photo. **Perf. 11¾x12**
1093 A404 400fr multi 2.50 1.75

Abokouamekro Animal Park — A405

Designs: 50fr, Cattle. 100fr, Rhinoceroses. 180fr+20fr, Rhinoceros. 400fr+20fr, Cattle.

2001, May 14 Litho. **Perf. 13½x13¼**
1094-1097 A405 Set of 4 5.00 3.00

Sculpted
Columns in
National
Museum — A406

Designs: 100fr, Alingué, Wouo Anouman. 180fr+20fr, Blolo Bian, Blolo B1a. 300fr+20fr, Botoumo. 400fr+20fr, Odi Oka.

2001, June 18 **Perf. 13¼x13**
1098-1101 A406 Set of 4 5.00 5.00

Elimination Rounds for World Cup
Soccer Championships — A407

Various soccer plays: 180fr + 20fr, 400fr + 20fr, 600fr + 20fr, 700fr.

2001, Aug. 21 Litho. **Perf. 13x13¼**
1102-1105 A407 Set of 4 10.00 10.00

The following items inscribed "Republique de Cote d'Ivoire" have been declared "illegal" by Ivory Coast postal authorities:

Sheets of nine 100fr stamps: Marilyn Monroe (2 different).

Sheets of six 100fr stamps: Shells and Rotary emblem (2 different), Dogs and Scouting emblem (2 different), Butterflies and Scouting emblem (2 different), Orchids (2 different), Motorbike races and Rotary emblem (2 different), Table tennis players (2 different), Old fire engines (2 different), Elvis Presley (2 different), Marilyn Monroe, Pope John Paul II.

Sheets of six stamps: Trains (4 different).

Souvenir sheets of one stamp: Trains (4 different).

Sheet of ten 200fr Stamps: Birds.

Sheets of nine stamps of various denominations: Japanese Women, Earle K. Bergey, Julie Bell, Michael Möbius, Nudes.

Sheet of eight stamps of various denominations: Nature Conservancy.

Sheets of eight 300fr stamps: Owls and Mushrooms, Lighthouses and Penguins.

Sheets of eight 100fr stamps: Anthony Hopkins, Ben Affleck, Eminem.

Sheets of six stamps of various denominations: Spirited Away, Nature Conservancy, Nudes

Sheets of six 500fr stamps: History of World Aircraft (5 different), Red Cross and Rotary emblem, Japanese Women, Actresses, Women Tennis Players, Marilyn Monroe.

Sheet of six 450fr stamps: The Lord of the Rings.

Sheets of six 400fr stamps: Beatles (2 different).

Sheets of six 350fr stamps: Uniforms of World War II (5 different).

Sheets of Six 300fr stamps: Harry Potter (3 different), Fire Engines (2 different), Owls and Mushrooms.

Sheets of six 200fr stamps: Dogs and Scouting emblem, Lighthouses and Rotary emblem.

Sheets of six 100fr stamps: Pope John Paul II, Celine Dion, Pierce Brosnan, Classic Automobiles.

Sheets of four 100fr stamps: AC/DC, Backstreet Boys, Bee Gees, Beatles, Doors, Freddie Mercury, KISS, Madonna, Metallica, Queen, Rolling Stones.

Sheets of three stamps of various denominations: Nature Conservancy (2 different), Fairy Tales, Fantasy Tales, Dinosaurs, Steam Railways.

Sheet of two 1000fr stamps: Pope John Paul II.

Sheets of Two 500fr stamps: Nature Conservancy, Mother Teresa and Pope John Paul II.

Sheets of two 250fr stamps: Pope John Paul II (3 different).

Souvenir sheets of one 1000fr stamp: Dinosaurs, Fish, Owl and Scouting emblem.

Souvenir sheets of one 500fr stamp: Snow White, Nature Conservancy, Pope John Paul II.

Souvenir sheets of one 300fr stamp: Harry Potter (2 different).

Souvenir sheets of one 250fr stamp: Disney Cartoons and Scouting emblem (10 different).

Souvenir sheets of one 150fr stamp: Fire Engines and Scouting emblem (5 different).

Souvenir sheets of one 100fr stamp: Sorayama (5 different), Locomotives (2 different).

Korhogo
Art
A408

Designs: 100fr, Shown. 180fr+20fr, Hunters and wildlife. 400fr+20fr, Painter, vert.

2001, Nov. 27   **Litho.**   **Perf. 14**
1106-1108   A408   Set of 3   4.00   4.00

A409

2002 World Cup Soccer Championships, Japan and Korea — A410

Design: 300fr+20fr, Caricatures of soccer players in action, horiz.

Perf. 13¾, 13x13¼ (#1110), 13¼x13 (#1112)
2002, June 6   **Litho.**
1109   A409   180fr +20fr grn & multi   1.25   1.25
1110   A410   300fr +20fr multi   2.25   2.25
1111   A409   400fr + 20fr red & multi   2.75   2.75
    Complete booklet, 10 #1111   30.00   30.00
1112   A410   600fr +20fr shown   4.00   4.00
    Souvenir Sheet
1113   A409   500fr red & multi   3.50   3.50

Ivory Coast — People's Republic of China Diplomatic Relations, 20th Anniv.
A411

2003, July 9   **Litho.**   **Perf. 12**
1114   A411   180fr grn & multi   1.00   1.00
1115   A411   400fr org & multi   2.00   2.00
1116   A411   650fr red & multi   3.50   3.50
    Nos. 1114-1116 (3)   6.50   6.50

Sculpted Columns in Museum of Civilizations
A412

Designs: 20fr, Alinguè Bia column. 100fr, Laliè column. 180fr+20fr, Tre Ni Tre column. 300fr+20fr, Golikplé-Kplé column.

2003, Nov. 27   **Litho.**   **Perf. 13½x13**
1117   A412   20fr multi   .20   .20
1118   A412   100fr multi   .50   .50
1119   A412   180fr +20fr shown   1.00   1.00
1120   A412   300fr +20fr multi   1.50   1.50
    Nos. 1117-1120 (4)   3.20   3.20

Paintings by Unknown Artists — A413

Designs: 50fr, Au Revoir. 100fr, Ballet. 250fr, Le Chef, horiz. 500fr, Ligne de Main, horiz. 825fr, Appel, horiz.

Perf. 13¼x13, 13x13¼
2004, June 15   **Litho.**
1121-1125   A413   Set of 5   —

Independence, 44th Anniv. — A414

Denominations: 100fr, 250fr.

2004, Aug. 7   **Perf. 13¼x13**
1126-1127   A414   Set of 2   —

2004 Summer Olympics, Athens A415

Designs: 50fr, Sprint race. 100fr, Greco-Roman wrestling, vert. 250fr, Torch bearer, vert. 825fr, Discus throw, vert. 1000fr, Sprint race.

Perf. 13x13¼, 13¼x13
2004, Aug. 13
1128-1131   A415   Set of 4   —
    Souvenir Sheet
1131A   A415   1000fr multi   8.25   8.25

National Reconciliation A416

2004, Sept. 28   **Litho.**   **Perf. 13¼x13**
1132   A416   50fr shown   —
1133   A416   250fr multi   —

Promotion of Women A417

2004, Nov. 26   **Litho.**   **Perf. 14x13½**
1134   A417   250fr multi   —

Molothrus Bonariensis A418

Perf. 14¼x13½
2004, Dec. 22   **Litho.**
1135   A418   50fr multi   —

Trichosurus Vulpecula A419

2004, Dec. 22   **Perf. 14x13¼**
1136   A419   100fr multi   2.25   2.25

Flora — A420

Design: 250fr, Cassia tuhovaliana.

2004, Dec. 22   **Perf. 13½x14¼**
1137   A420   250fr multi   —
    An additional stamp was issued in this set. The editors would like to examine any example.

Tenth General Assembly of African Organization of Supreme Audit Institutions A421

Frame color: 250fr, Blue. 350fr, Purple.

2005, July 18   **Litho.**   **Perf. 13¼**
1139-1140   A421   Set of 2   —

"Culture and Excellence" — A422

Designs: 100fr, Dan spoon. 250fr, Sénoufo cane, vert.

2005, July 25   **Perf. 13x13½, 13½x13**
1141-1142   A422   Set of 2   —

World Summit on the Information Society, Tunis — A423

Frame color: 30fr, Red. 220fr, Green.

2005, Sept. 28   **Perf. 13¼**
1143-1144   A423   Set of 2   —

Women's Hairstyles A424

Various hairstyles: 70fr, 100fr, 250fr, 350fr.

2005, Nov. 3
1145-1148   A424   Set of 4   —

Kings and Chiefs — A425

Designs: 30fr, Tchaman chief standing. 70fr, Tchaman chief, diff. 80fr, Yacouba, Baoulé and Abron chiefs, horiz. 250fr, Akan king and staff-bearer, horiz. 1000fr, Yacouba, Baoulé, and Abron chiefs, horiz.

2005, Nov. 22   A425   Set of 4   —
1149-1152
    Souvenir Sheet
1152A   A425   1000fr multi   8.25   8.25

Masks — A426

Designs: 70fr, Dan. 220fr, Gu. 250fr, Zamblé.

2005, Dec. 22
1153-1155   A426   Set of 3   —

Europa Stamps, 50th Anniv. (in 2006) — A427

Map of Ivory Coast and: 30fr, Corn and map of Ireland. 70fr, Rubber tree and map of Germany. 80fr, Cotton plant and map of Poland. 220fr, Bananas and map of Netherlands. 250fr, Pineapple and map of Czech Republic. 350fr, Cacao and map of Belgium. 400fr, Sweet potatoes and map of Great Britain. 650fr, Coffee beans and map of Italy. 1000fr, Peanuts and map of Portugal. 2775fr, Palm nut and map of Spain.

2005, Dec. 23   **Litho.**   **Perf. 13¼**
1156-1165   A427   Set of 10   22.00   22.00
1160a   Miniature sheet, #1156-1160   2.40   2.40
1165a   Miniature sheet, #1161-1165   19.50   19.50
1165b   Miniature sheet, #1156-1165   22.00   22.00

Coffee Branches, Flowers and Cherries — A428

Designs: 220fr, Coffea arabusta. 250fr, Coffea liberica.

2005, Dec. 28   **Litho.**   **Perf. 13¼**
1166-1167   A428   Set of 2   —

Mushrooms
A429

Designs: 220fr, Marasmius zenkeri. 250fr, Cantharellus rufopunctatus.

2005, Dec. 28
1168-1169 A429 Set of 2   4.75 4.75

Endangered
Plants — A430

Designs: 30fr, Dorstenia astyanactis. 70fr, Monosalpinx guillaumetii. 80fr, Monanthotaxis capea. 100fr, Okoubaka aubrevillei.

2005, Dec. 28   Litho.   Perf. 13¼
1170 A430 30fr multi   — —
1171 A430 70fr multi   — —
1172 A430 80fr multi   — —
1173 A430 100fr multi   — —

Urban Transportation — A431

Designs: 30fr, Buses, automobiles, ferry. 80fr, Buses, automobiles, ferry, diff.

2005, Dec. 29   Litho.   Perf. 13¼
1174-1175 A431 Set of 2   — —

Léopold Sédar Senghor (1906-2001),
First President of Senegal — A432

Denominations: 50fr, 250fr.

2006, Mar. 20   Litho.   Perf. 13½
1176-1177 A432 Set of 2   2.40 2.40

A433

2006 World Cup Soccer
Championships, Germany — A434

Designs: 50fr, Emblem. 100fr, Goalie making save. 200fr, World Cup. 250fr, Mascot. 1000fr, Mascot.

2006, June 9   Litho.   Perf. 13x13¼
1178 A433 50fr multi   — —
1179 A434 100fr multi   — —
1180 A433 200fr multi   — —
1181 A433 250fr multi   — —

Souvenir Sheet
Perf. 13¾
1182 A433 1000fr multi   — —

China-Africa
Forum, Beijing
A435

Designs: 250fr, Map of Africa and China. 650fr, Forum venue.

2006, Nov. 28   Perf. 12x12¼
1183-1184 A435 Set of 2   7.50 7.50

Pardon
A436

Denominations: 50fr, 250fr.

2008, June 25   Perf. 13x13¼
1185-1186 A436 Set of 2   3.00 3.00

SEMI-POSTAL STAMPS

No. 47
Surcharged
in Red

1915   Unwmk.   Perf. 14x13½
B1   A5 10c + 5c   1.60 1.60
   a.   Double surcharge   80.00 80.00
Issued on ordinary and chalky paper.

Curie Issue
Common Design Type
1938   Perf. 13
B2   CD80 1.75fr + 50c brt ultra   11.00 9.50

French Revolution Issue
Common Design Type
1939   Photo.
Name and Value Typo. in Black
B3   CD83   45c + 25c grn   8.75 8.75
B4   CD83   70c + 30c brn   8.75 8.75
B5   CD83   90c + 35c red org   8.75 8.75
B6   CD83   1.25fr + 1fr rose pink   8.75 8.75
B7   CD83   2.25fr + 2fr blue   8.75 8.75
   Nos. B3-B7 (5)   43.75 43.75

Stamps of
1936-38
Surcharged
in Red or
Black

1941
B8   A7   50c + 1fr plum (Bk)   2.50 2.50
B9   A8   80c + 2fr blk brn (R)   10.50 10.50
B10 A8   1.50fr + 2fr ultra (R)   11.50 11.50
B11 A9   2fr + 3fr ultra (Bk)   12.50 12.50
   Nos. B8-B11 (4)   37.00 37.00

Common Design Type and

Native
Engineer
SP1

Senegalese
Light
Artillery
SP2

1941   Photo.   Perf. 13½
B12 SP1   1fr + 1fr red   1.25
B13 CD86 1.50fr + 3fr claret   1.25
B14 SP2   2.50fr + 1fr blue   1.25
   Nos. B12-B14 (3)   3.75
Nos. B12-B14 were issued by the Vichy government in France, but were not placed on sale in Ivory Coast.

Nos. 165-166
Surcharged in Black or Red

1944   Engr.   Perf. 12½x12
B14A   50c + 1.50fr on 2.50fr deep blue (R)   .80
B14B   + 2.50fr on 1fr green   .80
Colonial Development Fund.
Nos. B14A-B14B were issued by the Vichy government in France, but were not placed on sale in Ivory Coast.

> **Catalogue values for unused stamps in this section, from this point to the end of the section, are for Never Hinged items.**

Republic
Anti-Malaria Issue
Common Design Type
1962, Apr. 7   Engr.   Perf. 12½x12
B15 CD108 25fr + 5fr ol grn   1.25 1.25

Freedom from Hunger Issue
Common Design Type
1963, Mar. 21   Perf. 13
B16 CD112 25fr + 5fr red lil, dk vio & brn   1.50 1.50

Red Cross - Red
Crescent Soc.,
Child Survival
Campaign — SP3

1987, May 8   Litho.   Perf. 13½
B17 SP3 195fr +5fr multi   2.50 2.50
No. B17 surcharged "+5fr" in red. Not issued without surcharge. Surtax for the Red Cross - Red Crescent Soc.

Organization of African Unity, 25th
Anniv. — SP4

1988, Nov. 19   Litho.   Perf. 12½x13
B18 SP4 195fr +5fr multi   2.25 2.25

Marie Therese Houphouet-Boigny and
N'Daya Intl. Emblem — SP5

1988, Dec. 9   Litho.   Perf. 13
B19 SP5 195fr +5fr multi   2.50 2.25
N'Daya Intl., 1st anniv.

See postage issues, beginning with #1030, for semi-postal stamps that are part of sets with regular postage stamps.

Council of Understanding, Solidarity &
Rural Development, 40th
Anniv. — SP6

1999, May 29   Litho.   Perf. 13x13½
B20 SP6 180fr +20fr multi   1.20 1.20

Postage Types of 1998-99 With
Added Surtax
1999 ?   Litho.   Perf. 12
Granite Paper (#B20A)
B20A A383 180fr +20fr Like #1024   —
Perf. 13½
B20B A386 180fr +20fr Like #1027   —
Nos. B20A-B20B apparently were not issued with Nos. 1022-1024 and 1027-1029.

Independence,
41st Anniv. — SP7

2001, Aug. 7   Litho.   Perf. 13¼x13½
B21 SP7 180fr +20fr multi   1.10 1.10

Year of
Dialogue
Among
Civilizations
SP8

2001, Oct. 9   Perf. 13x13¼
B22 SP8 400fr +20fr multi   2.25 2.25

Second Republic, 1st Anniv. SP9

2001, Oct. 26
B23 SP9 180fr +20fr multi   1.10 1.10

Planned 2004 Universal Postal Union Congress, Abidjan — SP10

Vignette size: 180fr+20fr, 23x37mm. 400fr+20fr, 26x37mm. 600fr+20fr, 36x49mm.

Perf. 13, 13¼x13 (#B25)
2001, Dec. 21   **Litho.**
B24 SP10 180fr +20fr multi   1.00 1.00
   a.   Souvenir sheet of 1   5.00 5.00
B25 SP10 400fr +20fr multi   2.25 2.25
B26 SP10 600fr +20fr multi   3.25 3.25

On Nos. B24-B26 and B24a portions of the design were applied by a thermographic process producing a shiny raised effect. No. B24a sold for 1000fr and contains imperforate examples of Nos. B25 and B26 in the margin, which are surmised to be invalid for postage as the face value of these two stamps exceeds the selling price of the sheet. The 2004 UPU Congress was moved from Abidjan to Bucharest, Romania due to political unrest in the Ivory Coast.

St. Valentine's Day — SP11

Serpentine Die Cut
2002, Feb. 14   **Litho.**
Booklet Stamp
Self-Adhesive
B27 SP11 180fr +20fr multi   1.10 1.10
   a.   Booklet pane of 8   9.00

Jean Mermoz Intl. College, Abidjan, 40th Anniv. SP12

Panel color: 180fr+20fr, Tan. 400fr+20fr, Red.

2002, Apr. 19   **Perf. 13½x13¼**
B28-B29 SP12   Set of 2   3.00 3.00

Decentralization SP14

Denomination color: 180fr+20fr, Green. 400fr+20fr, Blue.

2002, Dec. 4   **Litho.**   **Perf. 13¼x13**
B34-B35 SP14   Set of 2   3.00 3.00

SP15

Campaign Against AIDS — SP16

Illustration SP15 reduced.

2003, Dec. 22   **Litho.**   **Perf. 13¼**
B36 SP15 180fr +20fr multi   1.00 1.00
         Perf. 13¾
B37 SP16 400fr +20fr multi   2.00 2.00
Values for No. B37 are for stamps with surrounding selvage.

AIR POST STAMPS

Common Design Type
1940   Unwmk.   Engr.   Perf. 12½x12
C1 CD85 1.90fr ultramarine   .40 .40
C2 CD85 2.90fr dark red   .40 .40
C3 CD85 4.50fr dk gray grn   .75 .75
C4 CD85 4.90fr yel bister   1.00 1.00
C5 CD85 6.90fr deep orange   1.50 1.50
     Nos. C1-C5 (5)   4.05 4.05

Common Design Types
1942
C6 CD88 50c car & blue   .25
C7 CD88 1fr brn & black   .50
C8 CD88 2fr dk grn & red brn   .80
C9 CD88 3fr dk blue & scar   .85
C10 CD88 5fr vio & dk red   .85

Frame Engraved, Center Typographed
C11 CD89 10fr multicolored   1.10
C12 CD89 20fr multicolored   1.50
C13 CD89 50fr multicolored   2.10
     Nos. C6-C13 (8)   7.95

There is doubt whether Nos. C6-C12 were officially placed in use.

> **Catalogue values for unused stamps in this section, from this point to the end of the section, are for Never Hinged items.**

Republic

Lapalud Place and Post Office, Abidjan — AP1

Designs: 200fr, Houphouet-Boigny Bridge. 500fr, Ayamê dam.

1959, Oct. 1   **Engr.**   **Perf. 13**
C14 AP1 100fr multicolored   4.00 .80
C15 AP1 200fr multicolored   6.00 2.50
C16 AP1 500fr multicolored   13.00 5.00
     Nos. C14-C16 (3)   23.00 8.30

Sports Type of 1961
1961, Dec. 23
C17 A19 100fr High jump   4.50 2.25

Air Afrique Issue
Common Design Type
1962, Feb. 17   Unwmk.   Perf. 13
C18 CD107 50fr Prus bl, choc & org brn   2.00 1.25

Village in Man Region — AP2

1962, June 23   **Engr.**   **Perf. 13**
C19 AP2 200fr Street in Odienne, vert.   7.50 3.00
C20 AP2 500fr shown   13.00 5.00

UN Headquarters, New York — AP3

1962, Sept. 20   **Perf. 13**
C21 AP3 100fr multi   3.00 1.25
Admission to the UN, 2nd anniv.

Sassandra Bay — AP4

1963   **Unwmk.**   **Perf. 13**
C22 AP4 50fr Moossou bridge   2.25 .75
C23 AP4 100fr shown   3.25 1.75
C24 AP4 200fr Comoe River   6.00 2.75
     Nos. C22-C24 (3)   11.50 5.25

African Postal Union Issue
Common Design Type
1963, Sept. 8   **Photo.**   **Perf. 12½**
C25 CD114 85fr org brn, ocher & red   2.50 1.50

1963 Air Afrique Issue
Common Design Type
1963, Nov. 19   Unwmk.   Perf. 13x12
C26 CD115 25fr crim, gray, blk & grn   1.00 .50

Ramses II and Queen Nefertari — AP5

President John F. Kennedy (1917-63) — AP7

Arms of Republic — AP6

1964, Mar. 7   **Engr.**   **Perf. 13**
C27 AP5 60fr car, blk & red brn   3.00 1.50
UNESCO campaign to save historic monuments in Nubia.

1964, June 13   **Photo.**
C28 AP6 200fr ultra, yel grn & gold   5.00 2.25

1964, Nov. 14   Unwmk.   Perf. 12½
C29 AP7 100fr gray, cl brn & blk   3.00 1.50
   a.   Souvenir sheet of 4   15.00 15.00

Liana Bridge, Lieupleu — AP8

1965, Dec. 4   **Engr.**   **Perf. 13**
C30 AP8 100fr ol grn, dk grn & dk red brn   3.50 1.75

Street in Kong — AP9

1966, Mar. 5   **Engr.**   **Perf. 13**
C31 AP9 300fr brt bl, bis brn & vio brn   9.00 5.00

Air Afrique Issue, 1966
Common Design Type
1966, Aug. 20   **Photo.**   **Perf. 13**
C32 CD123 30fr dk grn, blk & gray   1.00 .60

Air Afrique Headquarters AP10

1967, Feb. 4   **Engr.**   **Perf. 13**
C33 AP10 500fr emer, ind & ocher   12.50 6.00
Opening of Air Afrique headquarters in Abidjan.

African Postal Union Issue, 1967
Common Design Type
1967, Sept. 9   **Engr.**   **Perf. 13**
C34 CD124 100fr blk, vio & car lake   3.50 1.50

Senufo Village — AP11

1968   **Engr.**   *Perf. 13*
C35 AP11 100fr shown   3.50 1.25
C36 AP11 500fr Tiegba village   12.50 4.50
Issue dates: 100fr, Feb. 17; 500fr, Apr. 27.

PHILEXAFRIQUE Issue

Street in Grand Bassam, by
Achalme — AP12

1969, Jan. 11   **Photo.**   *Perf. 12x12½*
C37 AP12 100fr grn & multi   5.00 5.00
PHILEXAFRIQUE Phil. Exhib., Abidjan,
Feb. 14-23. Printed with alternating green
label. Value, single with attached label, $6.

2nd PHILEXAFRIQUE Issue
Common Design Type

50fr, Ivory Coast #130 & view of San Pedro.
100fr, Ivory Coast #149 & man wearing chief's
garments, vert. 200fr, Ivory Coast #77 # Exhibition Hall, Abidjan.

1969, Feb. 14   **Engr.**   *Perf. 13*
C38 CD128 50fr grn, brn red
       & deep bl   3.25 3.25
C39 CD128 100fr brn, org &
       dp blue   5.00 5.00
C40 CD128 200fr brn, gray &
       dp blue   7.50 7.50
   a.   Min. sheet of 3, #C38-C40   20.00 20.00
   Nos. C38-C40 (3)   15.75 15.75
Opening of PHILEXAFRIQUE.

Man Waterfall — AP13

Mount Niangbo — AP14

1970   **Engr.**   *Perf. 13*
C41 AP13 100fr multicolored   3.50 1.50
C42 AP14 200fr multicolored   4.50 2.00
Issue dates: 100fr, Jan. 6; 200fr, July 18.

San Pedro Harbor — AP15

1971, Mar. 21   **Engr.**   *Perf. 13*
C43 AP15 100fr multicolored   2.25 1.00

Treichville Swimming Pool — AP16

1971, May 29   **Photo.**   *Perf. 12½*
C44 AP16 100fr multicolored   3.00 1.50

Aerial View of Coast Line — AP17

1971, July 3   **Engr.**   *Perf. 13*
C45 AP17 500fr multi   12.00 6.00
Tourist publicity for the African Riviera.

**Bondoukou Market Type of Regular
Issue**

Design: 200fr, Similar to No. 318, but without people at left and in center.

Embossed on Gold Paper
1971, Aug. 7   *Perf. 12½*
Size: 36x26mm
C46 A79 200fr gold, ultra & blk   5.00 2.50

African Postal Union Issue, 1971
Common Design Type

Design: 100fr, Ivory Coast coat of arms and
UAMPT building, Brazzaville, Congo.

1971, Nov. 13   **Photo.**   *Perf. 13x13½*
C47 CD135 100fr bl & multi   2.00 1.00

Lion
of St.
Mark
AP18

1972, Feb. 5   **Photo.**   *Perf. 12½*
C48 AP18 100fr shown   3.50 1.75
C49 AP18 200fr Waves, St.
     Mark's Basilica,
     Venice   6.00 3.25
UNESCO campaign to save Venice.

Kawara Mosque — AP19

1972, Apr. 29   **Engr.**   *Perf. 13*
C50 AP19 500fr bl, brn & ocher   12.50 6.50

View of Gouessesso — AP20

1972   **Engr.**   *Perf. 13*
C51 AP20 100fr shown   3.25 1.25
C52 AP20 200fr Jacqueville
     Lake   4.75 1.75
C53 AP20 500fr Kossou Dam   10.00 6.00
   Nos. C51-C53 (3)   18.00 9.00
Issued: 100fr, 6/10; 200fr, 1/8; 500fr, 11/17.

Akakro Radar Earth Station — AP21

1972, Nov. 27   **Engr.**   *Perf. 13*
C54 AP21 200fr brt bl, sl grn &
       choc   4.50 1.75

The Judgment of Solomon, by Nandjui
Legue — AP22

1973, Aug. 26   **Photo.**   *Perf. 13*
C55 AP22 500fr multi   12.50 6.00
6th World Peace Conference for Justice.

Sassandra River Bridge — AP23

1974, May 4   **Engr.**   *Perf. 13*
C56 AP23 100fr blk & yel grn   2.25 .75
C57 AP23 500fr slate grn & brn   12.00 4.25

Vridi Soap Factory, Abidjan — AP24

1974, July 6   **Photo.**   *Perf. 13*
C58 AP24 200fr multi   3.50 1.75

UPU Emblem,
Ivory Coast Flag,
Post Runner and
Jet — AP25

1974, Oct. 9   **Photo.**   *Perf. 13*
C59 AP25 200fr multi   5.00 3.00
C60 AP25 300fr multi   6.00 4.00
Centenary of Universal Postal Union.

Fly Whisk and
Panga Knife,
Symbols of
Akans Royal
Family — AP26

1976, Apr. 3   **Photo.**   *Perf. 12½x13*
C61 AP26 200fr brt bl & multi   5.00 2.00

Tingrela Mosque — AP27

1977, May 7   **Engr.**   *Perf. 13*
C62 AP27 500fr multi   7.50 4.50

Zeppelin Type of 1977
Souvenir Sheet

"Graf Zeppelin" LZ 127 over New York.

1977, Sept. 3   **Litho.**   *Perf. 11*
C63 A150 500fr multi   6.25 1.90
     Exists imperf.

Philexafrique II - Essen Issue
Common Design Types

#C64, Elephant and Ivory Coast No. 239.
#C65, Pheasant and Bavaria No. 1.

1978, Nov. 1   **Litho.**   *Perf. 13x12½*
C64 CD138 100fr multi   3.50 2.50
C65 CD139 100fr multi   3.50 2.50
   a.   Pair, #C64-C65 + label   8.00 8.00

Gymnast, Olympic Rings — AP28

Various gymnasts. 75fr, 150fr, 350fr, vert.

1980, July 24   **Litho.**   *Perf. 14½*
C66 AP28 75fr multi   1.25 .25
C67 AP28 150fr multi   1.75 .45
C68 AP28 250fr multi   3.25 1.00
C69 AP28 350fr multi   3.75 1.25
   Nos. C66-C69 (4)   10.00 2.95
Souvenir Sheet
C70 AP28 500fr multi   6.00 2.00
22nd Summer Olympic Games, Moscow,
July 19-Aug. 3.

President Houphouet-Boigny, 75th
Birthday AP28a

Embossed Die Cut
1980, Oct. 18   *Perf. 10½*
C70A AP28a 2000fr Silver   22.50 22.50
C70B AP28a 3000fr Gold   37.50 37.50

Manned Flight Bicentenary — AP29

Various balloons. 100fr, 125fr, 350fr vert.

1983, Apr. 2   **Litho.**   **Perf. 13**
C71 AP29 100fr Montgolfier, 1783   1.00   .35
C72 AP29 125fr Hydrogen, 1783   1.50   .45
C73 AP29 150fr Mail transport, 1870   1.75   .50
C74 AP29 350fr Double Eagle II, 1978   4.50   1.00
C75 AP29 500fr Dirigible   6.50   1.75
Nos. C71-C75 (5)   15.25   4.05

Pre-Olympic Year — AP30

Various swimming events.

1983, July 9   **Litho.**   **Perf. 14**
C76 AP30 100fr Crawl   1.00   .35
C77 AP30 125fr Diving   1.25   .50
C78 AP30 350fr Backstroke   3.50   1.25
C79 AP30 400fr Butterfly   4.25   1.50
Nos. C76-C79 (4)   10.00   3.60

Souvenir Sheet

C80 AP30 500fr Water polo   6.50   2.00

1984 Summer Olympics — AP31

Pentathlon.

1984, Mar.   **Perf. 12½**
C81 AP31 100fr Swimming   1.00   .30
C82 AP31 125fr Running   1.25   .40
C83 AP31 185fr Shooting   1.75   .60
C84 AP31 350fr Fencing   3.75   1.25
Nos. C81-C84 (4)   7.75   2.55

Souvenir Sheet

C85 AP31 500fr Equestrian   6.00   1.50

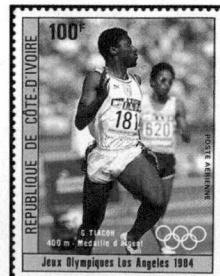

Los Angeles Olympics Winners AP32

1984, Dec. 15   **Litho.**   **Perf. 13**
C86 AP32 100fr Tiacoh, silver   1.25   .25
C87 AP32 150fr Lewis, gold   1.75   .40
C88 AP32 200fr Babers, gold   2.50   .75
C89 AP32 500fr Cruz, gold   5.00   1.50
Nos. C86-C89 (4)   10.50   2.90

Christmas AP33

Paintings: 100fr, Virgin and Child, by Correggio. 200fr, Holy Family with Angels, by Andrea del Sarto. 400fr, Virgin and Child, by Bellini.

1985, Jan. 12   **Perf. 13**
C90 AP33 100fr multi   1.20   .40
C91 AP33 200fr multi   2.25   .90
C92 AP33 400fr multi   4.00   2.00
Nos. C90-C92 (3)   7.45   3.30

Nos. C91-C92 have incorrect frame inscriptions.

Audubon Birth Bicentenary — AP34

Birds: 100fr, Mergus serrator. 150fr, Pelecanus erythrorhynchos. 200fr, Mycteria americana. 350fr, Melanitta deglandi.

1985, June 8   **Litho.**   **Perf. 13**
C93 AP34 100fr multi   1.20   .45
C94 AP34 150fr multi, vert.   1.75   .70
C95 AP34 200fr multi, vert.   3.00   1.00
C96 AP34 350fr multi   4.25   2.00
Nos. C93-C96 (4)   10.20   4.15

PHILEXAFRICA '85, Lome, Togo — AP35

1985, Nov. 16   **Litho.**   **Perf. 13**
C97 AP35 250fr shown   3.75   2.00
C98 AP35 250fr Soccer, boys and deer   3.75   2.00
a.   Pair, #C97-C98 + label   9.00   6.00

Edmond Halley, Computer Drawing of Comet — AP36

Return of Halley's Comet: 155fr, Sir William Herschel, Uranus. 190fr, Space probe, comet. 350fr, MS T-5 probe, comet. 440fr, Skylab, Kohoutek comet.

1986, Jan.   **Litho.**   **Perf. 13**
C99 AP36 125fr shown   1.25   .50
C100 AP36 155fr multi   1.50   .75
C101 AP36 190fr multi   1.90   .90
C102 AP36 350fr multi   3.50   1.75
C103 AP36 440fr multi   4.25   2.25
Nos. C99-C103 (5)   12.40   6.15

1986 World Cup Soccer Championships, Mexico — AP37

Various soccer plays.

1986, Apr. 26   **Litho.**   **Perf. 13**
C104 AP37 90fr multi   .90   .35
C105 AP37 125fr multi   1.25   .60
C106 AP37 155fr multi   1.75   .75
C107 AP37 440fr multi   4.50   2.25
C108 AP37 500fr multi   5.00   2.50
Nos. C104-C108 (5)   13.40   6.45

Souvenir Sheet

Perf. 13½x13

C109 AP37 600fr multi   6.50   2.00

AP38

1988 Summer Olympics, Seoul — AP39

Sailing sports.

1987, May 23   **Litho.**   **Perf. 12½**
C110 AP38 155fr Soling Class   1.50   .60
C111 AP38 195fr Windsurfing   2.25   .75
C112 AP38 250fr 470 Class   3.00   1.00
C113 AP38 550fr Windsurfing, diff.   6.00   2.50
Nos. C110-C113 (4)   12.75   4.85

Souvenir Sheet

C114 AP39 650fr 470 Class, diff.   7.00   2.25

1988 Summer Olympics, Seoul — AP40

1988, June 18   **Litho.**   **Perf. 13**
C115 AP40 100fr Gymnastic rings   .90   .40
C116 AP40 155fr Women's handball   1.25   .60
C117 AP40 195fr Boxing   2.00   .75
C118 AP40 500fr Parallel bars   5.00   2.00
Nos. C115-C118 (4)   9.15   3.75

Souvenir Sheet

C119 AP40 500fr Horizontal bar   *14.00*   1.60

1990 World Cup Soccer Championships, Italy — AP41

Italian monuments and various athletes.

1989, Nov. 25   **Litho.**   **Perf. 13**
C120 AP41 195fr Milan Cathedral   2.00   .75
C121 AP41 300fr Columbus Monument, Genoa   3.00   1.25
C122 AP41 450fr Turin   4.25   1.75
C123 AP41 550fr Bologna   6.00   2.00
Nos. C120-C123 (4)   15.25   5.75

World Cup Soccer Championships, Italy — AP42

Various plays.

1990, May 31   **Litho.**   **Perf. 13**
C124 AP42 155fr multicolored   1.60   .60
C125 AP42 195fr multicolored   2.00   .75
C126 AP42 500fr multicolored   5.00   2.00
C127 AP42 600fr multicolored   7.00   2.50
Nos. C124-C127 (4)   15.60   5.85

AIR POST SEMI-POSTAL STAMPS

Types of Dahomey Air Post Semi-Postal Issue
Perf. 13½x12½, 13 (#CB3)
Photo, Engr. (#CB3)
1942, June 22
CB1 SPAP1 1.50fr + 3.50fr green   1.00   *5.50*
CB2 SPAP2 2fr + 6fr brown   1.00   *5.50*
CB3 SPAP2 3fr + 9fr car red   1.00   *5.50*
Nos. CB1-CB3 (3)   3.00   *16.50*

Native children's welfare fund.

Colonial Education Fund
Common Design Type
Perf. 12½x13½
1942, June 22   **Engr.**
CB4 CD86a 1.20fr + 1.80fr blue & red   1.00   *5.50*

POSTAGE DUE STAMPS

Natives — D1   D2

Perf. 14x13½
1906-07   **Unwmk.**   **Typo.**
J1 D1 5c grn, *greenish*   4.00   4.00
J2 D1 10c red brown   4.00   4.00
J3 D1 15c dark blue   6.50   6.50
J4 D1 20c blk, *yellow*   9.50   9.50
J5 D1 30c red, *straw*   9.50   9.50
J6 D1 50c violet   7.25   7.25
J7 D1 60c black, *buff*   32.50   32.50
J8 D1 1fr blk, *pinkish*   35.00   35.00
Nos. J1-J8 (8)   108.25   108.25

1914

J9	D2	5c green	.25	.25
J10	D2	10c rose	.30	.30
J11	D2	15c gray	.30	.30
J12	D2	20c brown	.55	.55
J13	D2	30c blue	.55	.55
J14	D2	50c black	.90	.90
J15	D2	60c orange	1.25	1.25
J16	D2	1fr violet	1.50	1.50
		Nos. J9-J16 (8)	5.60	5.60

Type of 1914 Issue
Surcharged

1927

J17	D2	2fr on 1fr lilac rose	2.75	2.75
J18	D2	3fr on 1fr org brown	2.75	2.75

Catalogue values for unused stamps in this section, from this point to the end of the section, are for Never Hinged items.

Republic

Guéré
Mask — D3

Mask — D4

1960   Engr.   Perf. 14x13
Denomination Typographed in Black

J19	D3	1fr purple	.20	.20
J20	D3	2fr bright green	.20	.20
J21	D3	5fr orange yellow	.50	.50
J22	D3	10fr ultramarine	.90	.90
J23	D3	20fr lilac rose	1.60	1.60
		Nos. J19-J23 (5)	3.40	3.40

1962, Nov. 3   Typo.   Perf. 13½x14

Designs: Various masks and heads, Bingerville school of art.

J24	D4	1fr org & brt blue	.20	.20
J25	D4	2fr black & red	.30	.30
J26	D4	5fr red & dark grn	.40	.40
J27	D4	10fr green & lilac	.90	.90
J28	D4	20fr dark pur & blk	1.60	1.60
		Nos. J24-J28 (5)	3.40	3.40

Baoulé
Weight — D5

Gold
Weight — D6

Designs: Various Baoulé weights.

1968, May 18   Photo.   Perf. 13

J29	D5	5fr cit, brn & bl grn	.20	.20
J30	D5	10fr lt bl, brn & bl grn	.30	.30
J31	D5	15fr sal, brn & bl grn	.80	.80
J32	D5	20fr gray, car & bl grn	1.10	1.10
J33	D5	30fr bis, brn & bl grn	1.50	1.50
		Nos. J29-J33 (5)	3.90	3.90

1972, May 27   Engr.

Designs: Various gold weights.

J34	D6	20fr vio bl & org red	.90	.90
J35	D6	40fr ver & ocher	1.50	1.50
J36	D6	50fr orange & chocolate	2.00	2.00
J37	D6	100fr slate grn & ocher	4.00	4.00
		Nos. J34-J37 (4)	8.40	8.40

It has been reported that Nos. J34-J37 were used briefly as regular postage for domestic use. Examples of use as postage to foreign addresses exists.

MILITARY STAMP

The catalogue value for the unused stamp in this section is for Never Hinged.

Coat of Arms — M1

Perf. 13x14

1967, Jan. 1   Unwmk.   Typo.

M1	M1	multi	3.50	3.50

OFFICIAL STAMPS

Catalogue values for unused stamps in this section are for Never Hinged items.

Ivory Coast Coat of Arms — O1

1974, Jan. 1   Photo.   Perf. 12

O1	O1	(35fr) green & multi	.75	.25
O2	O1	(75fr) orange & multi	1.20	.45
O3	O1	(100fr) lil rose & multi	1.50	.80
O4	O1	(250fr) violet & multi	4.00	1.50
		Nos. O1-O4 (4)	7.45	3.00

PARCEL POST STAMPS

Postage Due Stamps of French Colonies Overprinted

Overprinted in Black

1903   Unwmk.   Imperf.

Q1	D1	50c lilac	42.50	40.00
Q2	D1	1fr rose, *buff*	42.50	40.00

Overprinted in Black

Q3	D1	50c lilac	3,300.	3,400.
Q4	D1	1fr rose, *buff*	3,300.	3,400.

Accents on "O" of "COTE"

Nos. Q7-Q8, Q11-Q12, Q15, Q17-Q18, Q21-Q22, Q24-Q25 exist with or without accent.

Overprinted

Red Overprint

Q5	D1	50c lilac	120.00	120.00
a.		Inverted overprint	425.00	425.00

Blue Black Overprint

Q6	D1	1fr rose, *buff*	87.50	87.50
a.		Inverted overprint	350.00	350.00

Surcharged in Black

a

b

c

d

e

f

g

h

1903

Q7	D1	50c on 15c pale grn	16.00	16.00
a.		Inverted surcharge	225.00	225.00
Q8	D1	50c on 60c brn, *buff*	35.00	35.00
a.		Inverted surcharge	225.00	225.00
Q9		(a)1fr on 5c blue	4,400.	3,600.
Q10		(b)1fr on 5c blue	4,400.	2,800.
Q11		(c)1fr on 5c blue	18.00	16.00
a.		Inverted surcharge	950.00	950.00
Q12		(d)1fr on 5c blue	27.50	24.00
Q13		(e)1fr on 5c blue	4,800.	4,000.
Q14		(f)1fr on 5c blue	12,000.	9,500.
Q15		(g)1fr on 5c blue	110.00	110.00
Q16		(h)1fr on 5c blue	3,750.	3,850.
Q17		(c)1fr on 10c gray brn	27.50	24.00
a.		Inverted surcharge	325.00	325.00
Q18		(d)1fr on 10c gray brn	47.50	45.00
a.		Inverted surcharge	475.00	475.00
Q19		(g)1fr on 10c gray brn	4,000.	3,850.
Q20		(h)1fr on 10c gray brn	46,000.	

Some authorities regard Nos. Q9 and Q10 as essays. A sub-type of type "a" has smaller, bold "XX" without serifs.

Surcharged in Black:

j

k

Colis Postaux

Q21	(j)	4fr on 60c brn, *buff*	140.00	140.00
a.		Double surcharge		5,600.
Q22	(k)	4fr on 60c brn, *buff*	375.00	375.00
Q23	(l)	4fr on 60c brn, *buff*	1,200.	1,000.

Surcharged in Black

Q24	D1	4fr on 15c green	130.00	130.00
a.		One large star	525.00	525.00
b.		Two large stars	300.00	300.00
Q25	D1	4fr on 30c rose	130.00	130.00
a.		One large star	525.00	525.00
b.		Two large stars	300.00	300.00

Overprinted in Black

1904

Q26	D1	50c lilac	45.00	45.00
a.		Inverted overprint		
Q27	D1	1fr rose, *buff*	45.00	45.00
a.		Inverted overprint		

Overprinted in Black

Q28	D1	50c lilac	42.50	42.50
a.		Inverted overprint	225.00	225.00
Q29	D1	1fr rose, *buff*	42.50	42.50
a.		Inverted overprint	225.00	225.00

Surcharged in Black

Q30	D1	4fr on 5c blue	240.00	240.00
Q31	D1	8fr on 15c green	240.00	240.00

Overprinted in Black

1905

Q32	D1	50c lilac	92.50	92.50
Q33	D1	1fr rose, *buff*	92.50	92.50

Surcharged in Black

Q34	D1	2fr on 1fr rose, *buff*	240.00	240.00
Q35	D1	4fr on 1fr rose, *buff*	240.00	240.00
a.		Italic "4"	2,200.	2,200.
Q36	D1	8fr on 1fr rose, *buff*	700.00	700.00

Illustrated Identifier

This section pictures stamps or parts of stamp designs that will help identify postage stamps that do not have English words on them.

Many of the symbols that identify stamps of countries are shown here as well as typical examples of their stamps.

See the Index and Identifier on the previous pages for stamps with inscriptions such as "sen," "posta," "Baja Porto," "Helvetia," "K.S.A.", etc.

Linn's Stamp Identifier is now available. The 144 pages include more 2,000 inscriptions and over 500 large stamp illustrations. Available from Linn's Stamp News, P.O. Box 29, Sidney, OH 45365-0029.

1. HEADS, PICTURES AND NUMERALS

GREAT BRITAIN

Great Britain stamps never show the country name, but, except for postage dues, show a picture of the reigning monarch.

Victoria

Edward VII   George V   Edward VIII

George VI

Elizabeth II

Some George VI and Elizabeth II stamps are surcharged in annas, new paisa or rupees. These are listed under Oman.

Silhouette (sometimes facing right, generally at the top of stamp)

The silhouette indicates this is a British stamp. It is not a U.S. stamp.

VICTORIA

Queen Victoria

INDIA

Other stamps of India show this portrait of Queen Victoria and the words "Service" (or "Postage") and "Annas."

AUSTRIA

YUGOSLAVIA

(Also BOSNIA & HERZEGOVINA if imperf.)

BOSNIA & HERZEGOVINA

Denominations also appear in top corners instead of bottom corners.

HUNGARY

Another stamp has posthorn facing left

BRAZIL

AUSTRALIA

Kangaroo and Emu

GERMANY

Mecklenburg-Vorpommern

SWITZERLAND

PALAU

2. ORIENTAL INSCRIPTIONS

CHINA

Any stamp with this one character is from China (Imperial, Republic or People's Republic). This character appears in a four-character overprint on stamps of Manchukuo. These stamps are local provisionals, which are unlisted. Other overprinted Manchukuo stamps show this character, but have more than four characters in the overprints. These are listed in People's Republic of China.

  Some Chinese stamps show the Sun.

Most stamps of Republic of China show this series of characters.

Stamps with the China character and this character are from People's Republic of China.

Calligraphic form of People's Republic of China

（一）	（二）	（三）	（四）	（五）	（六）
1	2	3	4	5	6
（七）	（八）	（九）	（十）	（一十）	（二十）
7	8	9	10	11	12

Chinese stamps without China character

REPUBLIC OF CHINA

PEOPLE'S REPUBLIC OF CHINA

Mao Tse-tung

MANCHUKUO

Temple   Emperor Pu-Yi

The first 3 characters are common to
many Manchukuo stamps.

The last 3 characters are common
to other Manchukuo stamps.

Orchid Crest

Manchukuo
stamp with-
out these
elements

JAPAN

Chrysanthemum Crest   Country Name

Japanese stamps without these elements

The number of characters in the center and the
design of dragons on the sides will vary.

RYUKYU ISLANDS

Country Name

PHILIPPINES
(Japanese Occupation)

Country Name

NETHERLANDS INDIES
(Japanese Occupation)

JAVA   **SUMATRA**

Java   Sumatra

MOLUCCAS, CELEBES AND
SOUTH BORNEO

NORTH BORNEO
(Japanese Occupation)

Indicates Japanese   Country
Occupation   Name

MALAYA
(Japanese Occupation)

Indicates Japanese Occupation   Country Name

BURMA
Union of Myanmar

ပြည်ထောင်စုမြန်မာနိုင်ငံတော်
Union of Myanmar
(Japanese Occupation)

Indicates Japanese Occupation   Country Name

Other Burma Japanese Occupation stamps without these elements

Burmese Script

KOREA

These two characters, in any order, are common to stamps from the Republic of Korea (South Korea) or of the People's Democratic Republic of Korea (North Korea).

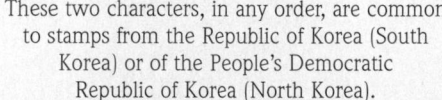

This series of four characters can be found on the stamps of both Koreas. Most stamps of the Democratic People's Republic of Korea (North Korea) have just this inscription.

대한민국 우표

Indicates Republic of Korea (South Korea)

South Korean postage stamps issed after 1952 do not show currency expressed in Latin letters. Stamps wiith "HW," "HWAN," "WON," "WN," "W" or "W" with two lines through it, if not illustrated in listings of stamps before this date, are revenues. North Korean postage stamps do not have currency expressed in Latin letters.

Yin Yang appears on some stamps.

South Korean stamps show Yin Yang and starting in 1966, 'KOREA' in Latin letters

Example of South Korean stamps lacking Latin text, Yin Yang and standard Korean text of country name. North Korean stamps never show Yin Yang and starting in 1976 are inscribed "DPRK" or "DPR KOREA" in Latin letters.

THAILAND

Country Name

King Chulalongkorn

King Prajadhipok and Chao P'ya Chakri

3. CENTRAL AND EASTERN ASIAN INSCRIPTIONS

INDIA - FEUDATORY STATES

Alwar

Bhor

Bundi

Similar stamps come with different designs in corners and differently drawn daggers (at center of circle).

Dhar   Duttia

Faridkot

Hyderabad

Similar stamps exist with different central design which is inscribed "Postage" or "Post & Receipt."

Indore

Jammu & Kashmir

Text varies.

Jasdan

Jhalawar

Kotah

Size and text varies

Nandgaon

Nowanuggur

Poonch

Similar stamps exist
in various sizes with different text

Rajasthan

Rajpeepla

Soruth

Tonk

BANGLADESH

Country Name

NEPAL

Similar stamps are smaller, have squares in
upper corners and have five or nine
characters in central bottom panel.

TANNU TUVA   ISRAEL

GEORGIA

This inscription is found on
other pictorial stamps.

Country Name

ARMENIA

The four characters are found somewhere
on pictorial stamps. On some stamps only
the middle two are found.

4. AFRICAN INSCRIPTIONS

ETHIOPIA

5. ARABIC INSCRIPTIONS

AFGHANISTAN

Many early Afghanistan stamps show Tiger's head, many of these have ornaments protruding from outer ring, others show inscriptions in black.

Arabic Script

Crest of King Amanullah

Mosque Gate & Crossed Cannons

The four characters are found somewhere on pictorial stamps. On some stamps only the middle two are found.

BAHRAIN

EGYPT

Postage

IRAN

Country Name

Royal Crown

Lion with Sword

Symbol

IRAQ

JORDAN

LEBANON

Similar types have
denominations at top and
slightly different design.

LIBYA

Country Name in various styles

Other Libya stamps show Eagle and Shield (head
facing either direction) or Red, White and Black
Shield (with or without eagle in center).

Without Country Name

SAUDI ARABIA

Tughra (Central design)

← Palm Tree and Swords

SYRIA

Arab Government Issues

THRACE   YEMEN

PAKISTAN

PAKISTAN - BAHAWALPUR

Country Name in top panel, star and crescent

TURKEY

Star & Crescent is a device found on many Turkish stamps, but is also found on stamps from other Arabic areas (see Pakistan-Bahawalpur)

Tughra (similar tughras can be found on stamps of Turkey in Asia, Afghanistan and Saudi Arabia)

Mohammed V

Mustafa Kemal

Plane, Star and Crescent

TURKEY IN ASIA

Other Turkey in Asia pictorials show star & crescent.
Other stamps show tughra shown under Turkey.

6. GREEK INSCRIPTIONS

GREECE

Country Name in various styles
(Some Crete stamps overprinted with the Greece country name are listed in Crete.)

Lepta

Drachma   Drachmas   Lepton

Abbreviated Country Name

Other forms of Country Name

No country name

CRETE

Country Name

Crete stamps with a surcharge that have the year "1922" are listed under Greeece.

EPIRUS

Similar stamps have text above the eagle.

IONIAN IS.

---

7. CYRILLIC INSCRIPTIONS

RUSSIA

Postage Stamp

Imperial Eagle

Postage in various styles

Abbreviation for Kopeck   Abbreviation for Ruble   Russia

Abbreviation for Russian Soviet Federated Socialist Republic
RSFSR stamps were overprinted (see below)

Abbreviation for Union of Soviet Socialist Republics

This item is footnoted in Latvia

RUSSIA - Army of the North

"OKCA"

RUSSIA - Wenden

RUSSIAN OFFICES IN THE TURKISH EMPIRE

 These letters appear on other stamps of the Russian offices.

The unoverprinted version of this stamp and a similar stamp were overprinted by various countries (see below).

ARMENIA

BELARUS

FAR EASTERN REPUBLIC

Country Name

SOUTH RUSSIA

Country Name

FINLAND

Circles and Dots
on stamps similar
to Imperial
Russia issues

BATUM

Forms of Country Name

TRANSCAUCASIAN
FEDERATED REPUBLICS

 Abbreviation for
Country Name

KAZAKHSTAN

Country Name

KYRGYZSTAN

Country
Name

ROMANIA

TADJIKISTAN

Country Name & Abbreviation

UKRAINE

Country Name in various forms

The trident appears   Abbreviation for
on many stamps,   Ukrainian Soviet
usually as an overprint.   Socialist Republic

WESTERN UKRAINE

Abbreviation for
Country Name

AZERBAIJAN

Country Name

Abbreviation for Azerbaijan
Soviet Socialist Republic

MONTENEGRO

ЦРНА ГОРА

Country Name in various forms

Abbreviation for country name

No country name (A similar Montenegro stamp without country name has same vignette.)

SERBIA

Country Name in various forms

Abbreviation for country name

No country name

SERBIA & MONTENEGRO

YUGOSLAVIA

Showing country name

No Country Name

MACEDONIA

МАКЕДОНИЈА

Country Name

МАКЕДОНСКИ

Different form of Country Name

BOSNIA & HERZEGOVINA
(Serb Administration)

РЕПУБЛИКА СРПСКА

Country Name

Different form of Country Name

No Country Name

BULGARIA

Country Name   Postage

Stotinka

Stotinki (plural)   Abbreviation for Stotinki

Country Name in various forms and styles

No country name

Abbreviation for Lev, leva

MONGOLIA

ШУУДАН   ТВГРВГ

Country name in   Tugrik in Cyrillic
one word

МОНГОЛ ШУУДАН

Country name in   Mung in Cyrillic
two words

Mung
in Mongolian

Tugrik
in Mongolian

Arms

No Country Name

1 cent 1

INDEX AND IDENTIFIER

All page numbers shown are those in this Volume 3.

Postage stamps that do not have English words on them are shown in the Illustrated Identifier.

Vol. 3 Number Additions, Deletions & Changes

Number in 2011 Catalogue	Number in 2012 Catalogue	Number in 2011 Catalogue	Number in 2012 Catalogue

Gabon

new	78a
new	90b
new	93c
new	96a

German East Africa

N109a	deleted

Gold Coast

new	J5b
new	J6b
new	J7b

Great Britain

new	50b

Machins

MH275A	MH236
MH275Aa	MH236a
new	MH292b
MH293c	deleted
MH298c	deleted

Guernsey

new	486c
new	1045a-1050a

Jersey

new	778a-785a
new	778b-785b
new	786a-789a
new	786d-789d
789a	789b
new	789c
new	789e
786a	786f
787a	787f
788a	788f
789b	789f
789c	789g
new	981f
new	981g
new	981h
new	1011f-1011k
new	1012g-1012l
new	1011l-1011q
new	1012m-1012r
new	1092l-1092q
new	1217a
new	1218a
new	1219a
new	1220a
1220a	1220b
new	1220c

Isle of Man

new	147a
new	352a
new	354a
new	355a
355a	355b
355b	355c
new	356d
new	358e
358e	358f
358f	358g

Haiti

32a	deleted
new	49a

Hong Kong

new	67b
new	68b
new	68c
new	162b
162B	162C
new	163a
new	163Bc
new	164Ab
new	165Ab
new	166Ab
J19a	J22

Hong Kong

new	J22f
J20a	J22A
new	J22Ag
new	J22Bh
J22	J22C
new	J22Ci
new	J22D
new	J22E
J21b	deleted
J22a	deleted

India, Convention States
Faridkot

new	4b
new	O1b
new	O1c

India, Feudatory States
Cochin

new	97a
new	O23a

Travancore

new	4a
new	6b

Travancore-Cochin

new	O13a

Iran

new	35a
new	653a
new	668a
new	911a
new	913a
new	914a
2958-2961	2957-2960
2962	2961

Ireland

new	1113Gk

Italy

new	955
137a	137c

Italian Offices Abroad
Crete

new	3b
new	15a

Ivory Coast

new	25b
new	89a
101a	100a

INDEX TO ADVERTISERS
2012 VOLUME 3

2012
VOLUME 3
DEALER DIRECTORY
YELLOW PAGE LISTINGS

This section of your Scott Catalogue contains advertisements to help you conveniently find what you need, when you need it...!

Accessories

BROOKLYN GALLERY COIN & STAMP, INC.
8725 4th Ave.
Brooklyn, NY 11209
PH: 718-745-5701
FAX: 718-745-2775
info@brooklyngallery.com
www.brooklyngallery.com

Appraisals

PHILIP WEISS AUCTIONS
1 Neil Ct.
Oceanside, NY 11572
PH: 516-594-0731
FAX: 516-594-9414
phil@prwauctions.com
www.prwauctions.com

Asia

MICHAEL ROGERS, INC.
Suite 4-1
415 S. Orlando Ave.
Winter Park, FL 32789-3683
PH: 407-644-2290
PH: 800-843-3751
FAX: 407-645-4434
Stamps@michaelrogersinc.com
www.michaelrogersinc.com

THE STAMP ACT
PO Box 1136
Belmont, CA 94002
PH: 650-703-2342
PH: 650-592-3315
FAX: 650-508-8104
thestampact@sbcglobal.net
www.thestampact.com

Auctions

DANIEL F. KELLEHER AUCTIONS LLC
PMB 44
60 Newtown Rd
Danbury, CT 06810
PH: 203-297-6056
FAX: 203-297-6059
info@kelleherauctions.com
www.kelleherauctions.com

JACQUES C. SCHIFF, JR., INC.
195 Main St.
Ridgefield Park, NJ 07660
PH: 201-641-5566
FAX: 201-641-5705

MICHAEL ROGERS, INC.
Suite 4-1
415 S. Orlando Ave.
Winter Park, FL 32789-3683
PH: 407-644-2290
PH: 800-843-3751
FAX: 407-645-4434
Stamps@michaelrogersinc.com
www.michaelrogersinc.com

PHILIP WEISS AUCTIONS
1 Neil Ct.
Oceanside, NY 11572
PH: 516-594-0731
FAX: 516-594-9414
phil@prwauctions.com
www.prwauctions.com

R. MARESCH & SON LTD.
5th Floor - 6075 Yonge St.
Toronto, ON M2M 3W2
CANADA
PH: 416-363-7777
FAX: 416-363-6511
www.maresch.com

Auctions

THE STAMP CENTER DUTCH COUNTRY AUCTIONS
4115 Concord Pike
Wilmington, DE 19803
PH: 302-478-8740
FAX: 302-478-8779
auctions@thestampcenter.com
www.thestampcenter.com

Auctions - Public

ALAN BLAIR AUCTIONS, L.L.C.
Suite 1
5405 Lakeside Ave.
Richmond, VA 23228-6060
PH: 800-689-5602
FAX: 804-262-9307
alanblair@verizon.net
www.alanblairstamps.com

British Commonwealth

ARON R. HALBERSTAM PHILATELISTS, LTD.
PO Box 150168
Van Brunt Station
Brooklyn, NY 11215-0168
PH: 718-788-3978
FAX: 718-965-3099
arh@arhstamps.com
www.arhstamps.com

British Commonwealth

WWW.WORLDSTAMPS.COM
PO Box 4743
Pinehurst, NC 28374
PH: 910-295-2048
FAX: 910-295-2049
by mail:
Frank Geiger Philatelists
info@WorldStamps.com
www.WorldStamps.com

Central America

GUY SHAW
PO Box 27138
San Diego, CA 92198
PH/FAX: 858-485-8269
guyshaw@guyshaw.com
www.guyshaw.com

China

MICHAEL ROGERS, INC.
Suite 4-1
415 S. Orlando Ave.
Winter Park, FL 32789-3683
PH: 407-644-2290
PH: 800-843-3751
FAX: 407-645-4434
Stamps@michaelrogersinc.com
www.michaelrogersinc.com

THE STAMP ACT
PO Box 1136
Belmont, CA 94002
PH: 650-703-2342
PH: 650-592-3315
FAX: 650-508-8104
thestampact@sbcglobal.net
www.thestampact.com

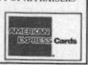

Ducks

MICHAEL JAFFE
PO Box 61484
Vancouver, WA 98666
PH: 360-695-6161
PH: 800-782-6770
FAX: 360-695-1616
mjaffe@brookmanstamps.com
www.brookmanstamps.com

German Colonies

COLONIAL STAMP COMPANY
5757 Wilshire Blvd. PH #8
Los Angeles, CA 90036
PH: 323-933-9435
FAX: 323-939-9930
Toll Free in North America
PH: 877-272-6693
FAX: 877-272-6694
info@colonialstampcompany.com
www.colonialstampcompany.com

German E. Africa (B & G)

COLONIAL STAMP COMPANY
5757 Wilshire Blvd. PH #8
Los Angeles, CA 90036
PH: 323-933-9435
FAX: 323-939-9930
Toll Free in North America
PH: 877-272-6693
FAX: 877-272-6694
info@colonialstampcompany.com
www.colonialstampcompany.com

German New Guinea (B & G)

COLONIAL STAMP COMPANY
5757 Wilshire Blvd. PH #8
Los Angeles, CA 90036
PH: 323-933-9435
FAX: 323-939-9930
Toll Free in North America
PH: 877-272-6693
FAX: 877-272-6694
info@colonialstampcompany.com
www.colonialstampcompany.com

German So. West Africa

COLONIAL STAMP COMPANY
5757 Wilshire Blvd. PH #8
Los Angeles, CA 90036
PH: 323-933-9435
FAX: 323-939-9930
Toll Free in North America
PH: 877-272-6693
FAX: 877-272-6694
info@colonialstampcompany.com
www.colonialstampcompany.com

German States

COLONIAL STAMP COMPANY
5757 Wilshire Blvd. PH #8
Los Angeles, CA 90036
PH: 323-933-9435
FAX: 323-939-9930
Toll Free in North America
PH: 877-272-6693
FAX: 877-272-6694
info@colonialstampcompany.com
www.colonialstampcompany.com

Germany

HENRY GITNER PHILATELISTS, INC.
PO Box 3077-S
Middletown, NY 10940
PH: 845-343-5151
PH: 800-947-8267
FAX: 845-343-0068
hgitner@hgitner.com
www.hgitner.com

Gold Coast

COLONIAL STAMP COMPANY
5757 Wilshire Blvd. PH #8
Los Angeles, CA 90036
PH: 323-933-9435
FAX: 323-939-9930
Toll Free in North America
PH: 877-272-6693
FAX: 877-272-6694
info@colonialstampcompany.com
www.colonialstampcompany.com

Great Britain

ARON R. HALBERSTAM PHILATELISTS, LTD.
PO Box 150168
Van Brunt Station
Brooklyn, NY 11215-0168
PH: 718-788-3978
FAX: 718-965-3099
arh@arhstamps.com
www.arhstamps.com

Great Britain

COLONIAL STAMP COMPANY
5757 Wilshire Blvd. PH #8
Los Angeles, CA 90036
PH: 323-933-9435
FAX: 323-939-9930
Toll Free in North America
PH: 877-272-6693
FAX: 877-272-6694
info@colonialstampcompany.com
www.colonialstampcompany.com

WWW.WORLDSTAMPS.COM
PO Box 4743
Pinehurst, NC 28374
PH: 910-295-2048
FAX: 910-295-2049
by mail:
Frank Geiger Philatelists
info@WorldStamps.com
www.WorldStamps.com

Hong Kong

ARON R. HALBERSTAM PHILATELISTS, LTD.
PO Box 150168
Van Brunt Station
Brooklyn, NY 11215-0168
PH: 718-788-3978
FAX: 718-965-3099
arh@arhstamps.com
www.arhstamps.com

COLONIAL STAMP COMPANY
5757 Wilshire Blvd. PH #8
Los Angeles, CA 90036
PH: 323-933-9435
FAX: 323-939-9930
Toll Free in North America
PH: 877-272-6693
FAX: 877-272-6694
info@colonialstampcompany.com
www.colonialstampcompany.com

THE STAMP ACT
PO Box 1136
Belmont, CA 94002
PH: 650-703-2342
PH: 650-592-3315
FAX: 650-508-8104
thestampact@sbcglobal.net
www.thestampact.com

Hungary

WWW.WORLDSTAMPS.COM
PO Box 4743
Pinehurst, NC 28374
PH: 910-295-2048
FAX: 910-295-2049
by mail:
Frank Geiger Philatelists
info@WorldStamps.com
www.WorldStamps.com

India

WWW.WORLDSTAMPS.COM
PO Box 4743
Pinehurst, NC 28374
PH: 910-295-2048
FAX: 910-295-2049
by mail:
Frank Geiger Philatelists
info@WorldStamps.com
www.WorldStamps.com

India & States

COLONIAL STAMP COMPANY
5757 Wilshire Blvd. PH #8
Los Angeles, CA 90036
PH: 323-933-9435
FAX: 323-939-9930
Toll Free in North America
PH: 877-272-6693
FAX: 877-272-6694
info@colonialstampcompany.com
www.colonialstampcompany.com

Iraq

COLONIAL STAMP COMPANY
5757 Wilshire Blvd. PH #8
Los Angeles, CA 90036
PH: 323-933-9435
FAX: 323-939-9930
Toll Free in North America
PH: 877-272-6693
FAX: 877-272-6694
info@colonialstampcompany.com
www.colonialstampcompany.com

Israel

HENRY GITNER PHILATELISTS, INC.
PO Box 3077-S
Middletown, NY 10940
PH: 845-343-5151
PH: 800-947-8267
FAX: 845-343-0068
hgitner@hgitner.com
www.hgitner.com

Italy

HENRY GITNER PHILATELISTS, INC.
PO Box 3077-S
Middletown, NY 10940
PH: 845-343-5151
PH: 800-947-8267
FAX: 845-343-0068
hgitner@hgitner.com
www.hgitner.com

Japan

MICHAEL ROGERS, INC.
Suite 4-1
415 S. Orlando Ave.
Winter Park, FL 32789-3683
PH: 407-644-2290
PH: 800-843-3751
FAX: 407-645-4434
Stamps@michaelrogersinc.com
www.michaelrogersinc.com

Korea

MICHAEL ROGERS, INC.
Suite 4-1
415 S. Orlando Ave.
Winter Park, FL 32789-3683
PH: 407-644-2290
PH: 800-843-3751
FAX: 407-645-4434
Stamps@michaelrogersinc.com
www.michaelrogersinc.com

Latin America

GUY SHAW
PO Box 27138
San Diego, CA 92198
PH/FAX: 858-485-8269
guyshaw@guyshaw.com
www.guyshaw.com

Manchukuo

MICHAEL ROGERS, INC.
Suite 4-1
415 S. Orlando Ave.
Winter Park, FL 32789-3683
PH: 407-644-2290
PH: 800-843-3751
FAX: 407-645-4434
Stamps@michaelrogersinc.com
www.michaelrogersinc.com

Middle East-Arab

MICHAEL ROGERS, INC.
Suite 4-1
415 S. Orlando Ave.
Winter Park, FL 32789-3683
PH: 407-644-2290
PH: 800-843-3751
FAX: 407-645-4434
Stamps@michaelrogersinc.com
www.michaelrogersinc.com

New Issues

DAVIDSON'S STAMP SERVICE
PO Box 36355
Indianapolis, IN 46236-0355
PH: 317-826-2620
ed-davidson@earthlink.net
www.newstampissues.com

New Issues - Retail

BOMBAY PHILATELIC INC.
PO Box 301
Wake Forest, NC 27588
PH: 561-499-7990
FAX: 561-499-7553
sales@bombaystamps.com
www.bombaystamps.com

South America

GUY SHAW
PO Box 27138
San Diego, CA 92198
PH/FAX: 858-485-8269
guyshaw@guyshaw.com
www.guyshaw.com

Stamp Stores

Arizona

A TO Z STAMPS & COINS
4950 E. Thomas Rd.
Phoenix, AZ 85018
OFFICE: 480-844-9878
CELL: 248-709-8939
michael@azstampcoin.com
www.WorldwideStamps.com

California

BROSIUS STAMP, COIN & SUPPLIES
2105 Main St.
Santa Monica, CA 90405
PH: 310-396-7480
FAX: 310-396-7455
brosius.stamp.coin@hotmail
.com

COLONIAL STAMP CO./ BRITISH EMPIRE SPECIALIST
5757 Wilshire Blvd. PH #8
(by appt.)
Los Angeles, CA 90036
PH: 323-933-9435
FAX: 323-939-9930
Toll Free in North America
PH: 877-272-6693
FAX: 877-272-6694
info@colonialstampcompany.com
www.colonialstampcompany.com

FISCHER-WOLK PHILATELICS
Suite 211
22762 Aspan St.
Lake Forest, CA 92630
PH: 949-837-2932
fischerwolk@fw.occoxmail.com

NATICK STAMPS & HOBBIES
PO Box 80613
San Marino, CA 91118
PH: 626-285-1384
natickco@att.net
Ebay ID: attickmwj

Connecticut

SILVER CITY COIN & STAMP
41 Colony St.
Meriden, CT 06451
PH: 203-235-7634
FAX: 203-237-4915

Georgia

STAMPS UNLIMITED OF GEORGIA, INC.
Suite 1460
100 Peachtree St.
Atlanta, GA 30303
PH: 404-688-9161
tonyroozen@yahoo.com

Illinois

DR. ROBERT FRIEDMAN & SONS
2029 W. 75th St.
Woodridge, IL 60517
PH: 800-588-8100
FAX: 630-985-1588
drbobstamps@yahoo.com
www.drbobfriedmanstamps.com

Indiana

KNIGHT STAMP & COIN CO.
237 Main St.
Hobart, IN 46342
PH: 219-942-4341
PH: 800-634-2646
knight@knightcoin.com
www.knightcoin.com

Missouri

DAVID SEMSROTT STAMPS
11235 Manchester Rd.
St. Louis (Kirkwood), MO 63122
PH: 314-984-8361
fixodine@sbcglobal.net
www.DavidSemsrott.com

New Jersey

BERGEN STAMPS & COLLECTIBLES
306 Queen Anne Rd.
Teaneck, NJ 07666
PH: 201-836-8987

MILLBURN PHILATELY LLC
45 Essex Street
Millburn, NJ 07041
PH: 973-921-0202
millburnstampsandbooks@gmail
.com
www.stampsandbooks.com

TRENTON STAMP & COIN CO.
Thomas DeLuca
Store: Forest Glen Plaza
1804 Route 33
Hamilton Square, NJ 08690
Mail: PO Box 8574
Trenton, NJ 08650
PH: 800-446-8664
PH: 609-584-8100
FAX: 609-587-8664
TOMD4TSC@aol.com

New York

CHAMPION STAMP CO., INC.
432 W. 54th St.
New York, NY 10019
PH: 212-489-8130
FAX: 212-581-8130
championstamp@aol.com
www.championstamp.com

Ohio

HILLTOP STAMP SERVICE
Richard A. Peterson
PO Box 626
Wooster, OH 44691
PH: 330-262-8907 (0)
PH: 330-262-5378
hilltop@bright.net

THE LINK STAMP CO.
3461 E. Livingston Ave.
Columbus, OH 43227
PH/FAX: 614-237-4125
PH/FAX: 800-546-5726

Virginia

KENNEDY'S STAMPS & COINS, INC.
7059 Brookfield Plaza
Springfield, VA 22150
PH: 703-569-7300
FAX: 703-569-7644
j.w.kennedy@verizon.net

LATHEROW & CO., INC.
5054 Lee Hwy.
Arlington, VA 22207
PH: 703-538-2727
PH: 800-647-4624
FAX: 703-538-5210
latherow@filatco.com

Topicals

E. JOSEPH McCONNELL, INC.
PO Box 683
Monroe, NY 10949
PH: 845-783-9791
FAX: 845-782-0347
ejstamps@gmail.com
www.EJMcConnell.com

Topicals-Columbus

MR. COLUMBUS
PO Box 1492
Fennville, MI 49408
PH: 269-543-4755
Mr.Columbus1492@gmail.com

United States

ACS STAMP COMPANY
10831 Chambers Way
Commerce City, CO 80022
PH: 303-841-8666
ACS@ACSStamp.com
www.acsstamp.com

A TO Z STAMPS & COINS
4950 E. Thomas Rd.
Phoenix, AZ 85018
OFFICE: 480-844-9878
CELL: 248-709-8939
michael@azstampcoin.com
www.WorldwideStamps.com

BROOKMAN STAMP CO.
PO Box 90
Vancouver, WA 98666
PH: 360-695-1391
PH: 800-545-4871
FAX: 360-695-1616
larry@brookmanstamps.com
www.brookmanstamps.com

Stamp Shows

U.S.-Collections Wanted

DR. ROBERT FRIEDMAN & SONS
2029 W. 75th St.
Woodridge, IL 60517
PH: 800-588-8100
FAX: 630-985-1588
drbobstamps@yahoo.com
www.drbobfriedmanstamps.com

Want Lists

CHARLES P. SCHWARTZ
PO Box 165
Mora, MN 55051
PH: 320-679-4705
cpschw@yahoo.com

Want Lists-British Empire 1840-1935 German Cols./Offices

COLONIAL STAMP COMPANY
5757 Wilshire Blvd. PH #8
Los Angeles, CA 90036
PH: 323-933-9435
FAX: 323-939-9930
Toll Free in North America
PH: 877-272-6693
FAX: 877-272-6694
info@colonialstampcompany.com
www.colonialstampcompany.com

Wanted-Worldwide Collections

A TO Z STAMPS & COINS
4950 E. Thomas Rd.
Phoenix, AZ 85018
OFFICE: 480-844-9878
CELL: 248-709-8939
michael@azstampcoin.com
www.WorldwideStamps.com

DANIEL F. KELLEHER AUCTIONS LLC
PMB 44
60 Newtown Rd
Danbury, CT 06810
PH: 203-297-6056
FAX: 203-297-6059
info@kelleherauctions.com
www.kelleherauctions.com

DR. ROBERT FRIEDMAN & SONS
2029 W. 75th St.
Woodridge, IL 60517
PH: 800-588-8100
FAX: 630-985-1588
drbobstamps@yahoo.com
www.drbobfriedmanstamps.com

Wanted-Worldwide Collections

THE STAMP CENTER DUTCH COUNTRY AUCTIONS
4115 Concord Pike
Wilmington, DE 19803
PH: 302-478-8740
FAX: 302-478-8779
auctions@thestampcenter.com
www.thestampcenter.com

Websites

ACS STAMP COMPANY
10831 Chambers Way
Commerce City, CO 80022
PH: 303-841-8666
ACS@ACSStamp.com
www.acsstamp.com

MILLBURN PHILATELY LLC
45 Essex Street
Millburn, NJ 07041
PH: 973-921-0202
millburnstampsandbooks@gmail.com
www.stampsandbooks.com

Worldwide

A TO Z STAMPS & COINS
4950 E. Thomas Rd.
Phoenix, AZ 85018
OFFICE: 480-844-9878
CELL: 248-709-8939
michael@azstampcoin.com
www.WorldwideStamps.com